Sporting News BOOKS

# BASEBALL GUIDE

2005 EDITION

## EXPLANATION OF STATISTICAL ABBREVIATIONS

**A:** assists. **AB:** at-bats. **Avg.:** batting average (hits divided by at-bats). **BB:** bases on balls. **Bk.:** balks. **CG:** complete games. **CS:** caught stealing. **E:** errors. **ER:** earned runs. **ERA:** earned-run average (earned runs times nine divided by innings pitched). **G:** games. **GB:** games behind. **GF:** games finished. **GDP:** grounding into double plays. **GS:** games started. **H:** hits. **HB:** hit batsmen. **HP:** hit by pitches. **HR:** home runs. **IBB:** intentional bases on balls. **IP:** innings pitched. **L:** losses. **LOB:** runners left on base. **OBP:** on-base percentage (hits plus bases on balls plus hit by pitches divided by at-bats plus bases on balls plus hit by pitches plus sacrifice flies). **Pct.:** winning percentage. **PO:** putouts. **Pos.:** position. **R:** runs. **RBI:** runs batted in. **Rel.:** relief appearances. **SB:** stolen bases. **SF:** sacrifice flies (run-scoring flyouts). **SH:** sacrifice hits (bunts that advance one or more runners but result in the batter being retired at first base or reaching first on an error). **ShO:** shutouts. **Slg.:** slugging percentage (total bases divided by at-bats). **SO:** strikeouts. **Sv.:** saves. **Sv. Op.:** save opportunities. **TB:** total bases (hits plus doubles plus two times the number of triples plus three times the number of home runs). **TBF:** total batters faced. **TC:** total chances (putouts plus assists plus errors). **TPA:** total plate appearances (at-bats plus bases on balls plus sacrifice hits plus sacrifice flies plus hit by pitches plus times reaching base on catcher's interference). **W:** wins. **WP:** wild pitches. **2B:** doubles. **3B:** triples.

**Editors:** Joe Hoppel, Corrie Anderson, Katie Koss, Kathy Sheldon
**Stats Inc. Editor:** Tony Nistler.

**ON THE COVER:** Manny Ramirez by Albert Dickson / TSN; Johan Santana by John Dunn for TSN; Scott Rolen by Albert Dickson / TSN; Roy Oswalt by Albert Dickson for TSN.

Major league statistics compiled by STATS Inc., a News Corporation company, 8130 Lehigh Avenue, Morton Grove, IL 60053. STATS is a trademark of Sports Team Analysis and Tracking Systems, Inc.

Minor league statistics provided by SportsTicker.



ISBN: 0-89204-770-4

10 9 8 7 6 5 4 3 2 1

# CONTENTS

# 2005 SEASON

## Major League Baseball directories

### Team by team

# MAJOR LEAGUE BASEBALL

**Address**
245 Park Avenue
New York, NY 10167
**Telephone**
212-931-7800
**FAX**
212-949-5654
**Website**
www.mlb.com
**Commissioner of baseball**
Allan H. "Bud" Selig
**President and chief operating officer**
Robert DuPuy
**Executive v.p., baseball operations**
Richard "Sandy" Alderson
**Executive vice president, business**
Timothy J. Brosnan
**Executive v.p,, labor relations and human resources**
Robert D. Manfred
**Executive v.p., administration**
John McHale
**Executive v.p., finance**
Jonathan Mariner
**Senior v.p., international business operations**
Paul Archey
**Senior v.p. and general counsel, labor relations**
Frank Coonelly
**Senior v.p., club relations and scheduling**
Katy Feeney
**Senior v.p., security and facilities**
Kevin Hallinan
**Senior v.p., public relations**
Richard Levin
**Senior v.p., club relations**
Phyllis Merhige
**Senior v.p., special events**
Marla Miller
**Senior v.p. and general counsel**
Ethan Orlinsky
**Senior v.p. and general counsel**
Tom Ostertag
**Senioe v.p., marketing and advertising**
Jacqueline Parkes
**Senior v.p., licensing**
Howard Smith
**Senior v.p., baseball operations**
Jimmie Lee Solomon
**Senior v.p., broadcasting**
Chris Tully
**V.p., domestic licensing**
Steve Armus
**V.p., community affairs**
Tom Brasuell
**V.p., baseball operations and admin.**
Ed Burns
**V.p., management information systems**
Julio Carbonell
**V.p., accounting and treasurer**
Bob Clark
**V.p., public relations operations**
Patrick Courtney
**V.p., MLB Productions**
David Gavant
**V.p., domestic licensing-Cooperstown**
Colin Hagen
**V.p., publishing and photographs**
Don Hintze
**V.p., international licensing**
Shawn Lawson-Cummings
**V.p., strategic planning, recruiting and diversity**
Wendy Lewis
**V.p., broadcast operations**
Bernadette McDonald
**V.p., international baseball operations**
Lou Melendez
**V.p., design services**
Anne Occi
**V.p., human resources**
Ray Scott
**V.p., programming and business affairs**
Elizabeth Scott
**V.p., finance**
Kathleen Torres
**V.p., on-field operations**
Bob Watson
**Executive director, Baseball Tomorrow fund**
Cathy Bradley
**Executive producer, international TV and broadcast**
Russell Gabay

## OTHER ORGANIZATIONS

### LABOR RELATIONS COMMITTEE

**Address**
245 Park Avenue
New York, NY 10167
**Telephone**
212-931-7401
212-949-5690 (FAX)
**Exec. vice president, labor relations and human resources**
Robert D. Manfred Jr.
**Sr. v.p. & gen. counsel, labor relations**
Francis Coonelly
**Deputy general counsel**
Jennifer Gefsky
**Counsel**
Paul Mifsud
**Director, salary and contract admin.**
John Abbamondi

### BASEBALL ASSISTANCE TEAM INC.

**Address**
245 Park Avenue
New York, NY 10167
**Telephone**
212-931-7821
**Chairman**
Bobby Murcer
**President**
Ted Sizmore
**Vice presidents**
Frank Torre
Greg Wilcox
Earl Wilson
**Executive director**
James J. Martin
**Secretary**
Thomas J. Ostertag
**Treasurer**
Jonathan Mariner

### ASSOCIATION OF PROFESSIONAL BASEBALL PLAYERS OF AMERICA

**Address**
1820 W. Orangewood Ave., Suite 206
Orange, CA 92868
**Telephone**
714-935-9993
714-935-0431 (FAX)
**President**
Roland Hemond
**Vice presidents**
Tal Smith
Dick Wagner
Bob Kennedy
**Secretary/treasurer**
Dick Beverage

### NATIONAL BASEBALL HALL OF FAME AND MUSEUM

**Address**
25 Main Street
Cooperstown, NY 13326
**Telephone**
607-547-7200
607-547-2044 (FAX)
**Hall of Fame board of directors chairman**
Jane Forbes Clark
**President**
Dale Petroskey
**V.p. of business and administration**
Bill Haase
**V.p. and chief curator**
William T. Spencer Jr.
**Curator of collections**
Peter P. Clark
**Controller**
Frances L. Althiser
**Librarian**
James L. Gates

**V.p. of communications and education**
Jeff Idelson

## MAJOR LEAGUE SCOUTING BUREAU

**Address**
3500 Porsche Way, Suite 100
Ontario, CA 91764

**Telephone**
909-980-1881
909-980-7794 (FAX)

**Director**
Frank Marcos

## MAJOR LEAGUE BASEBALL PLAYERS ASSOCIATION

**Address**
12 E. 49th St., 24th Floor
New York, NY 10017

**Telephone**
212-826-0808
212-752-3649 (FAX)

**Executive director and general counsel**
Donald M. Fehr

**Special assistants**
Bobby Bonilla
Phil Bradley
Steve Rogers

**C.O.O.**
Eugene D. Orza

**General counsel**
Michael Weiner

**Assistant general counsel**
Jeff Fannell
Doyle R. Pryor

**Counsel**
Robert Leneghan

**Director of licensing**
Judy Heeter

**Director of communications**
Chris Dahl

## MINOR LEAGUE BASEBALL NATIONAL ASSOCIATION OF PROFESSIONAL BASEBALL LEAGUES

**Address**
P.O. Box A
St. Petersburg, FL 33731

**Telephone**
727-822-6937
727-821-5819 (FAX)

**President/CEO**
Mike Moore

**Vice president**
Stan Brand

**Vice president, administration/COO**
Pat O'Connor

**General counsel**
Scott Poley

**Special counsel**
George Yund

**Exec. director/business operations**
Misann Ellmaker

**Executive director/Professional Baseball Umpire Corporation**
Mike Fitzpatrick

**Director/media relations**
Jim Ferguson

**Director/baseball operations**
Tim Brunswick

**Director of Professional Baseball Employment Opportunities**
Ann Perkins

## MAJOR LEAGUE BASEBALL PLAYERS ALUMNI ASSOC.

**Address**
1631 Mesa Ave., Suite B
Colorado Springs, CO 80906

**Telephone**
719-477-1870
719-477-1875 (FAX)

**President**
Brooks Robinson

**Vice presidents**
Bob Boone
George Brett
Mike Hegan
Chuck Hinton
Al Kaline
Carl Erskine
Rusty Staub
Robin Yount

**Vice chairman**
Fred Valentine

## WORLD UMPIRES ASSOCIATION

**Address**
P.O. Box 760
Cocoa, FL 32923-0760

**Telephone**
321-637-3471
321-633-7018 (FAX)

**President**
John Hirschbeck

**Vice president**
Joe Brinkman

**Secretary/treasurer**
Tim Welke

**Labor counsel**
Joel Smith

## BASEBALL WRITERS' ASSOCIATION OF AMERICA

**President**
T.R. Sullivan, Fort Worth Star-Telegram

**Vice president**
Peter Schmuck, Baltimore Sun

**Secretary/treasurer**
Jack O'Connell, Hartford Courant

## ELIAS SPORTS BUREAU

**Address**
500 Fifth Ave.
New York, NY 10110

**Telephone**
212-869-1530
212-354-0980 (FAX)

**President**
Seymour Siwoff

## SPORTSTICKER ENTERPRISES, L.P.

**Address**
Building B
ESPN Plaza
Bristol, CT 06010

**Telephone**
860-766-1899
800-367-8935
800-336-0383 (FAX)

**General manager**
Jim Morganthaler

**Director, minor league operations**
Jim Keller

**Assistant dir., minor league operations**
Michael Walczak

# ANAHEIM ANGELS

## AMERICAN LEAGUE WEST DIVISION

## 2005 SEASON

### Angels Schedule

Home games shaded.
All-Star Game July 12 at Detroit. Schedule subject to change.

**April**

| SUN | MON | TUE | WED | THU | FRI | SAT |
|---|---|---|---|---|---|---|
| 3 | 4 | 5 TEX | 6 TEX | 7 TEX | 8 KC | 9 KC |
| 10 KC | 11 TEX | 12 TEX | 13 TEX | 14 | 15 OAK | 16 OAK |
| 17 OAK | 18 SEA | 19 SEA | 20 CLE | 21 CLE | 22 OAK | 23 OAK |
| 24 OAK | 25 | 26 NYY | 27 NYY | 28 NYY | 29 MIN | 30 MIN |

**May**

| SUN | MON | TUE | WED | THU | FRI | SAT |
|---|---|---|---|---|---|---|
| 1 MIN | 2 SEA | 3 SEA | 4 SEA | 5 | 6 DET | 7 DET |
| 8 DET | 9 CLE | 10 CLE | 11 CLE | 12 | 13 DET | 14 DET |
| 15 DET | 16 CLE | 17 CLE | 18 CLE | 19 | 20 LA | 21 LA |
| 22 LA | 23 CHW | 24 CHW | 25 CHW | 26 CHW | 27 KC | 28 KC |
| 29 KC | 30 CHW | 31 CHW | | | | |

**June**

| SUN | MON | TUE | WED | THU | FRI | SAT |
|---|---|---|---|---|---|---|
| | | | 1 CHW | 2 | 3 BOS | 4 BOS |
| 5 BOS | 6 ATL | 7 ATL | 8 ATL | 9 | 10 NYM | 11 NYM |
| 12 NYM | 13 WAS | 14 WAS | 15 WAS | 16 | 17 FLA | 18 FLA |
| 19 FLA | 20 TEX | 21 TEX | 22 TEX | 23 | 24 LA | 25 LA |
| 26 LA | 27 TEX | 28 TEX | 29 TEX | 30 TEX | | |

**July**

| SUN | MON | TUE | WED | THU | FRI | SAT |
|---|---|---|---|---|---|---|
| | | | | | 1 KC | 2 KC |
| 3 KC | 4 MIN | 5 MIN | 6 MIN | 7 SEA | 8 SEA | 9 SEA |
| 10 SEA | 11 | 12 All-Star | 13 | 14 MIN | 15 MIN | 16 MIN |
| 17 MIN | 18 OAK | 19 OAK | 20 OAK | 21 NYY | 22 NYY | 23 NYY |
| 24 NYY | 25 | 26 TOR | 27 TOR | 28 TOR | 29 NYY | 30 NYY |
| 31 NYY | | | | | | |

**August**

| SUN | MON | TUE | WED | THU | FRI | SAT |
|---|---|---|---|---|---|---|
| | 1 | 2 BAL | 3 BAL | 4 BAL | 5 TB | 6 TB |
| 7 TB | 8 | 9 OAK | 10 OAK | 11 OAK | 12 SEA | 13 SEA |
| 14 SEA | 15 TOR | 16 TOR | 17 TOR | 18 BOS | 19 BOS | 20 BOS |
| 21 BOS | 22 | 23 BAL | 24 BAL | 25 BAL | 26 TB | 27 TB |
| 28 TB | 29 | 30 OAK | 31 OAK | | | |

**September**

| SUN | MON | TUE | WED | THU | FRI | SAT |
|---|---|---|---|---|---|---|
| | | | | 1 OAK | 2 SEA | 3 SEA |
| 4 SEA | 5 | 6 BOS | 7 BOS | 8 BOS | 9 CHW | 10 CHW |
| 11 CHW | 12 SEA | 13 SEA | 14 SEA | 15 DET | 16 DET | 17 DET |
| 18 DET | 19 | 20 TEX | 21 TEX | 22 TEX | 23 TB | 24 TB |
| 25 TB | 26 OAK | 27 OAK | 28 OAK | 29 OAK | 30 TEX | |

**October**

| SUN | MON | TUE | WED | THU | FRI | SAT |
|---|---|---|---|---|---|---|
| | | | | | | 1 TEX |
| 2 TEX | 3 | 4 | 5 | 6 | 7 | 8 |

Home games shaded. All-Star Game July 12 at Detroit. Schedule subject to change.

### CLUB DIRECTORY

**Owner**
Arturo Moreno
**President**
Dennis Kuhl
**Vice president and general manager**
Bill Stoneman
**Vice president, communications**
Tim Mead
**Assistant general manager**
Ken Forsch
**Special assistants to the g.m.**
Preston Gomez
Gary Sutherland
**Director, scouting**
Eddie Bane
**Director, player development**
Tony Reagins
**Manager, baseball operations**
Abe Flores
**Manager, baseball information**
Larry Babcock
**Manager, media services**
Nancy Mazmanian
**Manager, community development**
Matt Bennett

### MINOR LEAGUE AFFILIATES

| Class | Team | League | Manager |
|---|---|---|---|
| AAA | Salt Lake | Pacific Coast | Dino Ebel |
| AA | Arkansas | Texas | Tyrone Boykin |
| Advanced A | Rancho Cucamonga | California | Bobby Meacham |
| A | Cedar Rapids | Midwest | Bobby Magallanes |
| Advanced Rookie | Orem Owlz | Pioneer | Tom Kotchman |
| Rookie | Mesa | Arizona | Brian Harper |

### BROADCAST INFORMATION

**Radio:** ESPN-AM (710).
**TV:** KCAL-TV (Channel 9).
**Cable TV:** Fox Sports West.

### SPRING TRAINING

**Ballpark (city):** Tempe Diablo Stadium (Tempe, Ariz.).
**Ticket information:** 714-940-2000.

**For more on the Angels, go to msn.foxsports.com/mlb/teams.**

Guerrero

## SPRING TRAINING ROSTER

**Manager**—Mike Scioscia (14).
**Coaches**—Bud Black (24), Alfredo Griffin (4), Mickey Hatcher (7), Joe Maddon (70), Orlando Mercado (48), Ron Roenicke (61).

| No. | PITCHERS | B/T | Ht./Wt. | Age* | 2004 Clubs |
|---|---|---|---|---|---|
| 43 | Bittner, Tim | L/L | 6-2/200 | 24 | Arkansas |
| 51 | Bootcheck, Chris | R/R | 6-5/200 | 26 | Salt Lake |
| | Byrd, Paul | R/R | 6-1/190 | 34 | Greenville, Richmond, Atlanta |
| 40 | Colon, Bartolo | R/R | 5-11/250 | 31 | Anaheim |
| 53 | Donnelly, Brendan | R/R | 6-3/240 | 33 | Rancho Cucamonga, Salt Lake, Anaheim |
| 60 | Dunn, Scott | R/R | 6-3/200 | 26 | Salt Lake, Anaheim |
| 45 | Escobar, Kelvim | R/R | 6-1/210 | 28 | Anaheim |
| 63 | Gregg, Kevin | R/R | 6-6/220 | 26 | Anaheim |
| 52 | Hensley, Matt | R/R | 6-2/220 | 26 | Salt Lake, Anaheim |
| 41 | Lackey, John | R/R | 6-6/235 | 26 | Anaheim |
| | Moseley, Dustin | R/R | 6-4/190 | 23 | Chattanooga, Louisville |
| 57 | Rodriguez, Francisco | R/R | 6-0/185 | 23 | Anaheim |
| | Santana, Ervin | R/R | 6-2/160 | 22 | Arkansas |
| | Saunders, Joe | L/L | 6-3/210 | 23 | Rancho Cucamonga, Arkansas |
| | Shell, Steven | R/R | 6-5/200 | 22 | Rancho Cucamonga |
| 62 | Shields, Scot | R/R | 6-1/170 | 29 | Anaheim |
| 56 | Washburn, Jarrod | L/L | 6-1/195 | 30 | Rancho Cucamonga, Anaheim |
| | Woods, Jake | L/L | 6-1/190 | 23 | Arkansas, Salt Lake |
| | Yan, Esteban | R/R | 6-4/255 | 29 | Detroit |
| **No.** | **CATCHERS** | **B/T** | **Ht./Wt.** | **Age*** | **2004 Clubs** |
| | Mathis, Jeff | R/R | 6-1/185 | 22 | Arkansas |
| 1 | Molina, Bengie | R/R | 5-11/220 | 30 | Anaheim |
| 28 | Molina, Jose | R/R | 6-2/220 | 29 | Anaheim |
| 43 | Nieves, Wil | R/R | 5-11/190 | 27 | Salt Lake |
| 8 | Paul, Josh | R/R | 6-1/200 | 29 | Anaheim |
| **No.** | **INFIELDERS** | **B/T** | **Ht./Wt.** | **Age*** | **2004 Clubs** |
| | Cabrera, Orlando | R/R | 5-10/190 | 30 | Montreal, Boston |
| | Callaspo, Alberto | B/R | 5-10/175 | 21 | Arkansas |
| 17 | Erstad, Darin | L/L | 6-2/210 | 30 | Salt Lake, Anaheim |
| 9 | Figgins, Chone | B/R | 5-8/160 | 27 | Anaheim |
| 6 | Izturis, Maicer | B/R | 5-8/155 | 24 | Edmonton, Montreal |
| 2 | Kennedy, Adam | L/R | 6-1/185 | 29 | Anaheim |
| 35 | Kotchman, Casey | L/L | 6-3/210 | 22 | Arkansas, Salt Lake, Anaheim |
| 23 | McPherson, Dallas | L/R | 6-4/230 | 24 | Arkansas, Salt Lake, Anaheim |
| | Morales, Kendry | B/R | 6-1/220 | 21 | Did Not Play |
| | Quinlan, Robb | R/R | 6-1/200 | 28 | Salt Lake, Anaheim |
| **No.** | **OUTFIELDERS** | **B/T** | **Ht./Wt.** | **Age*** | **2004 Clubs** |
| 16 | Anderson, Garret | L/L | 6-3/225 | 32 | Rancho Cuca., Anaheim |
| 55 | DaVanon, Jeff | B/R | 6-0/200 | 31 | Salt Lake, Anaheim |
| 12 | Finley, Steve | L/L | 6-2/194 | 40 | Arizona, Los Angeles |
| 27 | Guerrero, Vladimir | R/R | 6-3/220 | 29 | Anaheim |
| 59 | Rivera, Juan | R/R | 6-2/205 | 26 | Montreal |
| 15 | Salmon, Tim | R/R | 6-3/235 | 37 | Rancho Cuca., Anaheim |

*Age as of April 1, 2005.

## BALLPARK INFORMATION

**Ballpark (capacity, surface)**
Angel Stadium of Anaheim
(45,050, grass)

**Address**
2000 Gene Autry Way
Anaheim, CA 92806

**Official website**
www.angelsbaseball.com

**Business phone**
714-940-2000

**Ticket information**
714-634-2000

**Field dimensions (from home plate)**
To left field at foul line, 330 feet
To center field, 400 feet
To right field at foul line, 330

**First game played**
April 19, 1966 (White Sox 3, Angels 1)

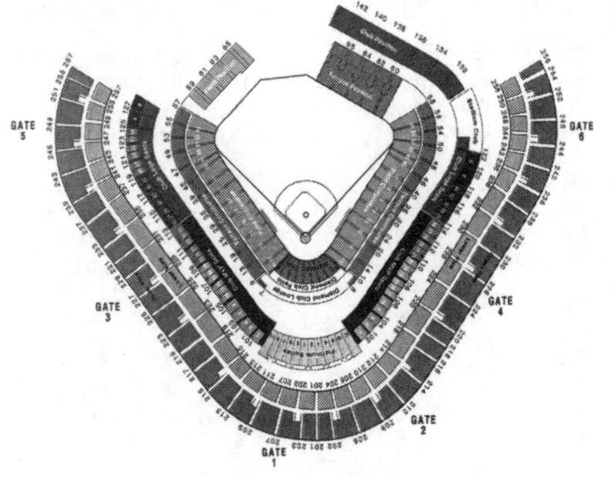

# 2004REVIEW

## DAY BY DAY

| Date | Opp. | Res. | Score | (inn.*) | Hits | Opp. hits | Winning pitcher | Losing pitcher | Save | Record | Pos. | GB |
|---|---|---|---|---|---|---|---|---|---|---|---|---|
| 4-6 | At Sea. | W | 10-5 | | 12 | 7 | Colon | Moyer | | 1-0 | 2nd | 0.5 |
| 4-7 | At Sea. | W | 10-7 | | 16 | 13 | Washburn | Pineiro | Percival | 2-0 | 1st | +0.5 |
| 4-8 | At Sea. | W | 5-1 | | 9 | 7 | Shields | Hasegawa | | 3-0 | 1st | +1.0 |
| 4-9 | At Tex. | L | 4-12 | | 9 | 18 | Dickey | Ortiz | | 3-1 | T1st | ... |
| 4-10 | At Tex. | L | 6-12 | | 8 | 18 | Rogers | Lackey | | 3-2 | T2nd | 1.0 |
| 4-11 | At Tex. | W | 7-2 | | 13 | 8 | Colon | Park | | 4-2 | T1st | ... |
| 4-12 | At Tex. | L | 6-7 | | 8 | 11 | Almanzar | Washburn | Cordero | 4-3 | T2nd | 0.5 |
| 4-13 | Sea. | W | 7-5 | | 11 | 11 | Shields | Soriano | Percival | 5-3 | 2nd | 0.5 |
| 4-14 | Sea. | W | 6-5 | | 14 | 12 | Percival | Hasegawa | | 6-3 | 2nd | 0.5 |
| 4-15 | Sea. | L | 2-6 | | 5 | 8 | Franklin | Lackey | | 6-4 | 2nd | 0.5 |
| 4-16 | Oak. | L | 0-3 | | 6 | 9 | Hudson | Colon | Rhodes | 6-5 | T2nd | 1.5 |
| 4-17 | Oak. | W | 6-3 | | 7 | 7 | Washburn | Mulder | | 7-5 | 2nd | 0.5 |
| 4-18 | Oak. | L | 1-7 | | 5 | 13 | Zito | Escobar | Hammond | 7-6 | 2nd | 1.5 |
| 4-20 | Tex. | L | 3-6 | | 9 | 11 | Rogers | Ortiz | Cordero | 7-7 | T2nd | 1.0 |
| 4-21 | Tex. | L | 1-4 | | 6 | 9 | Dickey | Lackey | Cordero | 7-8 | 3rd | 2.0 |
| 4-22 | Tex. | W | 7-5 | | 8 | 8 | Colon | Park | Percival | 8-8 | T2nd | 2.0 |
| 4-23 | At Oak. | W | 12-2 | | 14 | 8 | Washburn | Zito | Gregg | 9-8 | T2nd | 1.0 |
| 4-24 | At Oak. | W | 6-3 | | 13 | 7 | Escobar | Redman | Percival | 10-8 | T1st | ... |
| 4-25 | At Oak. | W | 4-3 | | 7 | 6 | Ortiz | Harden | Percival | 11-8 | T1st | ... |
| 4-27 | At Det. | W | 10-4 | | 15 | 6 | Lackey | Cornejo | Shields | 12-8 | T1st | ... |
| 4-28 | At Det. | L | 2-10 | | 8 | 15 | Maroth | Colon | | 12-9 | T1st | ... |
| 4-29 | At Det. | W | 12-3 | | 14 | 10 | Washburn | Robertson | | 13-9 | T1st | ... |
| 4-30 | At Min. | L | 3-6 | | 9 | 15 | Silva | Ortiz | Nathan | 13-10 | 2nd | 0.5 |
| 5-1 | At Min. | W | 1-0 | | 10 | 4 | Rodriguez | Rincon | Percival | 14-10 | 2nd | 1.0 |
| 5-2 | At Min. | W | 3-1 | | 7 | 7 | Lackey | Romero | Percival | 15-10 | 2nd | 1.0 |
| 5-3 | Det. | W | 11-9 | | 14 | 15 | Gregg | Levine | Percival | 16-10 | 2nd | 1.0 |
| 5-4 | Det. | W | 11-4 | | 13 | 8 | Washburn | Robertson | | 17-10 | T1st | ... |
| 5-5 | Det. | W | 6-3 | | 7 | 5 | Escobar | Johnson | Percival | 18-10 | T1st | ... |
| 5-6 | T.B. | W | 7-3 | | 11 | 8 | Sele | Gonzalez | Shields | 19-10 | 1st | +0.5 |
| 5-7 | T.B. | W | 1-0 | | 8 | 3 | Lackey | Hendrickson | | 20-10 | 1st | +1.5 |
| 5-8 | T.B. | W | 7-2 | | 9 | 3 | Colon | Abbott | | 21-10 | 1st | +1.5 |
| 5-9 | T.B. | W | 8-4 | | 11 | 11 | Washburn | Zambrano | Rodriguez | 22-10 | 1st | +2.5 |
| 5-11 | At N.Y. | L | 7-8 | (10) | 12 | 13 | Gordon | Weber | | 22-11 | 1st | +1.5 |
| 5-12 | At N.Y. | W | 11-2 | | 11 | 7 | Sele | Vazquez | | 23-11 | 1st | +1.5 |
| 5-13 | At N.Y. | L | 4-7 | | 7 | 11 | Lieber | Lackey | Rivera | 23-12 | 1st | +1.5 |
| 5-14 | At Bal. | W | 10-9 | (10) | 15 | 11 | Percival | Julio | Shields | 24-12 | 1st | +2.5 |
| 5-15 | At Bal. | W | 7-4 | | 11 | 6 | Washburn | DuBose | Percival | 25-12 | 1st | +2.5 |
| 5-16 | At Bal. | L | 0-4 | | 5 | 9 | Ponson | Escobar | | 25-13 | 1st | +2.5 |
| 5-18 | N.Y. | W | 1-0 | (11) | 11 | 3 | Shields | Quantrill | | 26-13 | 1st | +3.5 |
| 5-19 | N.Y. | L | 2-4 | | 7 | 7 | Lieber | Lackey | Rivera | 26-14 | 1st | +3.5 |
| 5-20 | N.Y. | L | 2-6 | | 9 | 11 | Mussina | Colon | | 26-15 | 1st | +2.5 |
| 5-21 | Bal. | W | 5-3 | | 12 | 11 | Shields | DeJean | Percival | 27-15 | 1st | +2.5 |
| 5-22 | Bal. | W | 3-2 | | 9 | 6 | Escobar | Ponson | Percival | 28-15 | 1st | +2.5 |
| 5-23 | Bal. | W | 8-3 | | 12 | 11 | Sele | Cabrera | | 29-15 | 1st | +3.5 |
| 5-24 | At Tor. | L | 5-6 | (10) | 12 | 10 | Frasor | Weber | | 29-16 | 1st | +3.0 |
| 5-26 | At Tor. | L | 5-6 | | 8 | 12 | Adams | Percival | | 29-17 | 1st | +2.5 |
| 5-27 | At Tor. | L | 2-3 | | 4 | 8 | Halladay | Washburn | Frasor | 29-18 | 1st | +2.5 |
| 5-28 | At Chi. | L | 3-4 | | 10 | 12 | Takatsu | Ortiz | | 29-19 | 1st | +2.5 |
| 5-29 | At Chi. | W | 5-1 | | 13 | 5 | Sele | Rauch | | 30-19 | 1st | +3.5 |
| 5-30 | At Chi. | L | 2-11 | | 5 | 14 | Schoeneweis | Lackey | | 30-20 | 1st | +2.5 |
| 6-1 | Bos. | W | 7-6 | | 9 | 13 | Gregg | Arroyo | Percival | 31-20 | 1st | +2.5 |
| 6-2 | Bos. | W | 10-7 | | 17 | 10 | Ortiz | Timlin | Rodriguez | 32-20 | 1st | +2.5 |
| 6-3 | Cle. | W | 5-2 | | 11 | 9 | Escobar | Lee | | 33-20 | 1st | +3.0 |
| 6-4 | Cle. | L | 6-9 | | 9 | 14 | Riske | Rodriguez | Jimenez | 33-21 | 1st | +3.0 |
| 6-5 | Cle. | L | 2-3 | | 7 | 9 | White | Lackey | Jimenez | 33-22 | 1st | +2.0 |
| 6-6 | Cle. | L | 0-7 | | 5 | 9 | Sabathia | Colon | | 33-23 | 1st | +1.5 |
| 6-8 | Mil. | L | 0-1 | (17) | 4 | 9 | Kinney | Ortiz | Kolb | 33-24 | T1st | ... |
| 6-9 | Mil. | L | 2-12 | | 14 | 17 | Santos | Washburn | Burba | 33-25 | 2nd | 1.0 |
| 6-10 | Mil. | W | 5-4 | | 8 | 8 | Gregg | Bennett | Rodriguez | 34-25 | 3rd | 0.5 |
| 6-11 | Chi. | W | 3-2 | | 8 | 7 | Lackey | Maddux | Rodriguez | 35-25 | 2nd | 0.5 |
| 6-12 | Chi. | L | 5-10 | | 13 | 13 | Rusch | Colon | Hawkins | 35-26 | 3rd | 1.5 |
| 6-13 | Chi. | L | 5-6 | (15) | 13 | 14 | Leicester | Hensley | | 35-27 | 3rd | 2.5 |
| 6-15 | At Pit. | W | 4-2 | | 11 | 6 | Shields | Torres | Rodriguez | 36-27 | 2nd | 1.5 |
| 6-16 | At Pit. | L | 3-5 | | 10 | 9 | Fogg | Lackey | Mesa | 36-28 | 2nd | 1.5 |
| 6-17 | At Pit. | L | 2-5 | | 7 | 11 | Benson | Colon | Mesa | 36-29 | 2nd | 1.5 |
| 6-18 | At Hou. | L | 0-5 | | 5 | 10 | Munro | Escobar | | 36-30 | 3rd | 2.5 |

| Date | Opp. | Res. | Score | (inn.*) | Hits | Opp. hits | Winning pitcher | Losing pitcher | Save | Record | Pos. | GB |
|---|---|---|---|---|---|---|---|---|---|---|---|---|
| 6-19 | At Hou. | W | 6-4 | | 13 | 8 | Ortiz | Clemens | Rodriguez | 37-30 | 3rd | 1.5 |
| 6-20 | At Hou. | L | 1-3 | | 8 | 7 | Miller | Hensley | Dotel | 37-31 | 3rd | 1.5 |
| 6-21 | Oak. | W | 10-3 | | 13 | 9 | Lackey | Harden | | 38-31 | 3rd | 0.5 |
| 6-22 | Oak. | W | 6-1 | | 9 | 5 | Colon | Hudson | | 39-31 | 2nd | 0.5 |
| 6-23 | Oak. | L | 1-7 | | 8 | 11 | Redman | Escobar | | 39-32 | 3rd | 1.5 |
| 6-24 | Oak. | L | 1-2 | | 4 | 5 | Mulder | Shields | | 39-33 | 3rd | 2.5 |
| 6-25 | At L.A. | W | 13-0 | | 22 | 4 | Washburn | Lima | | 40-33 | 3rd | 2.5 |
| 6-26 | At L.A. | W | 7-5 | | 8 | 6 | Donnelly | Mota | Rodriguez | 41-33 | 3rd | 2.5 |
| 6-27 | At L.A. | L | 5-10 | | 7 | 13 | Ishii | Colon | | 41-34 | 3rd | 2.5 |
| 6-29 | At Oak. | L | 4-5 | | 9 | 10 | Mulder | Donnelly | Dotel | 41-35 | 3rd | 3.0 |
| 6-30 | At Oak. | L | 2-4 | | 5 | 10 | Bradford | Shields | Dotel | 41-36 | 3rd | 4.0 |
| 7-1 | At Oak. | L | 3-7 | | 12 | 12 | Saarloos | Washburn | | 41-37 | 3rd | 4.0 |
| 7-2 | L.A. | W | 7-3 | | 9 | 4 | Sele | Ishii | | 42-37 | 3rd | 3.0 |
| 7-3 | L.A. | L | 5-8 | | 6 | 9 | Mota | Colon | Gagne | 42-38 | 3rd | 3.5 |
| 7-4 | L.A. | L | 2-6 | | 9 | 5 | Weaver | Escobar | | 42-39 | 3rd | 4.5 |
| 7-6 | At Chi. | W | 6-2 | | 10 | 4 | Lackey | Garcia | | 43-39 | 3rd | 3.5 |
| 7-7 | At Chi. | W | 12-0 | | 13 | 4 | Washburn | Schoeneweis | | 44-39 | 3rd | 3.5 |
| 7-8 | At Chi. | L | 8-9 | | 14 | 15 | Marte | Donnelly | | 44-40 | 3rd | 4.5 |
| 7-9 | At Tor. | W | 5-4 | | 16 | 5 | Colon | Halladay | Percival | 45-40 | 3rd | 3.5 |
| 7-10 | At Tor. | W | 11-2 | | 12 | 7 | Escobar | Lilly | | 46-40 | 3rd | 2.5 |
| 7-11 | At Tor. | W | 5-2 | | 12 | 7 | Lackey | Batista | Percival | 47-40 | 3rd | 2.5 |
| 7-15 | Bos. | W | 8-1 | | 16 | 4 | Washburn | Lowe | | 48-40 | 3rd | 2.0 |
| 7-16 | Bos. | L | 2-4 | | 7 | 10 | Martinez | Escobar | Foulke | 48-41 | 3rd | 3.0 |
| 7-17 | Bos. | W | 8-3 | | 13 | 5 | Colon | Wakefield | | 49-41 | 3rd | 3.0 |
| 7-18 | Bos. | L | 2-6 | | 5 | 11 | Schilling | Lackey | | 49-42 | 3rd | 4.0 |
| 7-19 | Cle. | L | 5-8 | (10) | 10 | 12 | Riske | Percival | Miller | 49-43 | 3rd | 4.0 |
| 7-20 | Cle. | L | 5-14 | | 12 | 19 | Westbrook | Washburn | | 49-44 | 3rd | 5.0 |
| 7-21 | At Tex. | L | 2-3 | | 5 | 6 | Drese | Escobar | Cordero | 49-45 | 3rd | 6.0 |
| 7-22 | At Tex. | W | 11-1 | | 17 | 4 | Colon | Rodriguez | | 50-45 | 3rd | 5.0 |
| 7-23 | At Sea. | W | 8-2 | | 13 | 9 | Lackey | Moyer | | 51-45 | 3rd | 5.0 |
| 7-24 | At Sea. | W | 8-4 | | 14 | 9 | Sele | Mateo | | 52-45 | 3rd | 4.0 |
| 7-25 | At Sea. | L | 2-6 | | 6 | 8 | Pineiro | Ortiz | | 52-46 | 3rd | 4.0 |
| 7-26 | Tex. | L | 1-6 | | 13 | 8 | Drese | Escobar | | 52-47 | 3rd | 5.0 |
| 7-27 | Tex. | W | 2-0 | | 8 | 1 | Colon | Regilio | Percival | 53-47 | 3rd | 4.0 |
| 7-28 | Tex. | W | 2-0 | | 10 | 3 | Lackey | Rogers | Percival | 54-47 | 3rd | 3.0 |
| 7-29 | Sea. | L | 5-6 | (13) | 12 | 18 | Madritsch | Gregg | | 54-48 | 3rd | 3.5 |
| 7-30 | Sea. | W | 6-5 | | 11 | 7 | Donnelly | Putz | Percival | 55-48 | 3rd | 3.0 |
| 7-31 | Sea. | W | 9-8 | (11) | 16 | 14 | Donnelly | Guardado | | 56-48 | 3rd | 2.5 |
| 8-1 | Sea. | W | 3-2 | | 7 | 10 | Colon | Franklin | Shields | 57-48 | 3rd | 2.5 |
| 8-3 | At Min. | L | 0-10 | | 11 | 11 | Silva | Lackey | | 57-49 | 3rd | 3.5 |
| 8-4 | At Min. | L | 3-6 | | 10 | 11 | Lohse | Ortiz | Nathan | 57-50 | 3rd | 3.5 |
| 8-5 | At Min. | W | 8-3 | | 15 | 6 | Sele | Mulholland | | 58-50 | 3rd | 3.0 |
| 8-6 | At K.C. | W | 3-0 | | 7 | 7 | Escobar | May | Percival | 59-50 | 3rd | 2.5 |
| 8-7 | At K.C. | W | 7-5 | | 10 | 12 | Colon | Reyes | Percival | 60-50 | 3rd | 1.5 |
| 8-8 | At K.C. | W | 6-4 | | 8 | 11 | Donnelly | Field | Rodriguez | 61-50 | 3rd | 1.5 |
| 8-9 | At K.C. | W | 5-3 | | 11 | 7 | Gregg | Cerda | Percival | 62-50 | 2nd | 1.5 |
| 8-10 | Bal. | L | 3-11 | | 6 | 20 | Cabrera | Sele | | 62-51 | 3rd | 2.5 |
| 8-11 | Bal. | W | 4-2 | | 6 | 9 | Escobar | Grimsley | Percival | 63-51 | 2nd | 1.5 |
| 8-12 | Bal. | L | 1-6 | | 6 | 14 | Lopez | Colon | | 63-52 | 2nd | 1.5 |
| 8-13 | Det. | L | 3-5 | | 9 | 14 | Yan | Percival | Urbina | 63-53 | 3rd | 1.5 |
| 8-14 | Det. | W | 11-8 | | 17 | 11 | Gregg | Novoa | Rodriguez | 64-53 | 3rd | 1.5 |
| 8-15 | Det. | W | 3-2 | | 6 | 7 | Shields | Johnson | Percival | 65-53 | 3rd | 0.5 |
| 8-17 | At T.B. | L | 3-8 | | 9 | 9 | Brazelton | Escobar | | 65-54 | 3rd | 2.0 |
| 8-18 | At T.B. | W | 6-4 | | 8 | 5 | Colon | Hendrickson | | 66-54 | 3rd | 2.0 |
| 8-19 | At T.B. | W | 10-7 | | 12 | 13 | Lackey | Bell | Rodriguez | 67-54 | 3rd | 1.5 |
| 8-20 | At N.Y. | W | 5-0 | | 13 | 5 | Ortiz | Lieber | | 68-54 | 3rd | 1.5 |
| 8-21 | At N.Y. | W | 6-1 | | 13 | 8 | Shields | Loaiza | | 69-54 | 3rd | 1.5 |
| 8-22 | At N.Y. | W | 4-3 | | 10 | 4 | Escobar | Brown | Percival | 70-54 | 3rd | 0.5 |
| 8-23 | K.C. | W | 9-4 | | 13 | 7 | Colon | May | | 71-54 | 2nd | 0.5 |
| 8-24 | K.C. | W | 7-5 | | 15 | 9 | Lackey | Reyes | Percival | 72-54 | 2nd | 0.5 |
| 8-25 | K.C. | W | 21-6 | | 22 | 15 | Ortiz | Wood | | 73-54 | 2nd | 0.5 |
| 8-27 | Min. | W | 9-6 | | 16 | 11 | Sele | Radke | Percival | 74-54 | 2nd | 1.0 |
| 8-28 | Min. | L | 1-7 | | 6 | 12 | Santana | Colon | | 74-55 | 2nd | 2.0 |
| 8-29 | Min. | W | 4-2 | | 7 | 5 | Rodriguez | Rincon | | 75-55 | 2nd | 2.0 |
| 8-31 | At Bos. | L | 7-10 | | 15 | 16 | Schilling | Lackey | Foulke | 75-56 | 2nd | 3.0 |
| 9-1 | At Bos. | L | 7-12 | | 11 | 16 | Adams | Sele | | 75-57 | 2nd | 3.0 |
| 9-2 | At Bos. | L | 3-4 | | 8 | 12 | Lowe | Colon | Foulke | 75-58 | 2nd | 4.0 |
| 9-3 | At Cle. | W | 10-5 | | 13 | 10 | Escobar | Elarton | | 76-58 | 2nd | 4.0 |
| 9-4 | At Cle. | W | 6-1 | | 9 | 6 | Washburn | Davis | | 77-58 | 2nd | 4.0 |

| Date | Opp. | Res. | Score | (inn.*) | Hits | Opp. hits | Winning pitcher | Losing pitcher | Save | Record | Pos. | GB |
|---|---|---|---|---|---|---|---|---|---|---|---|---|
| 9-5 | At Cle. | W | 2-1 | | 7 | 2 | Lackey | Westbrook | Rodriguez | 78-58 | 2nd | 3.0 |
| 9-7 | Tor. | W | 5-2 | | 11 | 6 | Colon | Bush | Percival | 79-58 | 2nd | 1.5 |
| 9-8 | Tor. | L | 0-1 | | 2 | 5 | Miller | Escobar | Speier | 79-59 | 2nd | 1.5 |
| 9-9 | Tor. | L | 4-5 | | 7 | 6 | Lilly | Washburn | Speier | 79-60 | 2nd | 2.0 |
| 9-10 | Chi. | W | 7-5 | | 11 | 12 | Rodriguez | Bajenaru | Percival | 80-60 | 2nd | 1.0 |
| 9-11 | Chi. | L | 6-13 | | 10 | 16 | Grilli | Sele | | 80-61 | 2nd | 2.0 |
| 9-12 | Chi. | W | 11-0 | | 15 | 6 | Colon | Contreras | | 81-61 | 2nd | 2.0 |
| 9-13 | At Sea. | W | 5-1 | | 8 | 7 | Escobar | Baek | Rodriguez | 82-61 | 2nd | 2.0 |
| 9-14 | At Sea. | L | 2-3 | | 8 | 7 | Madritsch | Washburn | Putz | 82-62 | 2nd | 2.0 |
| 9-15 | At Sea. | L | 0-1 | | 2 | 6 | Franklin | Lackey | | 82-63 | 2nd | 2.0 |
| 9-16 | At Sea. | W | 6-1 | | 5 | 6 | Sele | Moyer | | 83-63 | 2nd | 2.0 |
| 9-17 | Tex. | W | 9-5 | | 15 | 6 | Colon | Park | | 84-63 | 2nd | 1.0 |
| 9-18 | Tex. | L | 0-2 | | 6 | 5 | Ramirez | Escobar | Cordero | 84-64 | 2nd | 2.0 |
| 9-19 | Tex. | L | 0-1 | | 6 | 7 | Young | Washburn | Cordero | 84-65 | 2nd | 3.0 |
| 9-20 | Sea. | W | 5-2 | | 12 | 12 | Lackey | Franklin | Percival | 85-65 | 2nd | 2.5 |
| 9-21 | Sea. | L | 3-7 | | 7 | 18 | Moyer | Sele | | 85-66 | 2nd | 2.5 |
| 9-22 | Sea. | L | 6-16 | | 7 | 24 | Meche | Colon | | 85-67 | 2nd | 2.5 |
| 9-24 | Oak. | L | 3-6 | | 7 | 12 | Harden | Escobar | | 85-68 | T2nd | 3.0 |
| 9-25 | Oak. | W | 5-3 | | 8 | 5 | Rodriguez | Bradford | Percival | 86-68 | T2nd | 2.0 |
| 9-26 | Oak. | W | 6-2 | | 9 | 6 | Lackey | Mulder | | 87-68 | 2nd | 1.0 |
| 9-27 | At Tex. | W | 5-3 | | 7 | 5 | Colon | Rogers | Percival | 88-68 | 2nd | 1.0 |
| 9-28 | At Tex. | W | 8-2 | | 11 | 3 | Escobar | Park | | 89-68 | T1st | ... |
| 9-29 | At Tex. | W | 8-7 | (11) | 11 | 11 | Shields | Cordero | Percival | 90-68 | 1st | +1.0 |
| 9-30 | At Tex. | L | 3-6 | | 8 | 8 | Young | Lackey | Dickey | 90-69 | T1st | ... |
| 10-1 | At Oak. | W | 10-0 | | 14 | 4 | Colon | Mulder | | 91-69 | 1st | +1.0 |
| 10-2 | At Oak. | W | 5-4 | | 7 | 7 | Donnelly | Rincon | Percival | 92-69 | 1st | +2.0 |
| 10-3 | At Oak. | L | 2-3 | | 6 | 7 | Duchscherer | Gregg | | 92-70 | 1st | +1.0 |

Monthly records: April (13-10), May (17-10), June (11-16), July (15-12), August (19-8), September (15-13), October (2-1).
*Innings, if other than nine.

## RECORDS

**2004 regular-season record:** 92-70
**Position:** 1st in A.L. West
**Home:** 45-36 **Road:** 47-34
**A.L. East:** 25-18 **A.L. Central:** 28-15
**A.L. West:** 32-26 **N.L.** 7-11
**Vs. LH starters:** 34-17
**Vs. RH starters:** 58-53
**Grass:** 84-63 **Artificial:** 8-7
**Day:** 26-19 **Night:** 66-51
**1-Run:** 19-21 **X-inn.:** 4-6
**Doubleheaders:** 0-0-0
**Team record past five years:** 425-385 (.525, ranks 7th in league in that span)

## TEAM LEADERS

**Batting average:** Vladimir Guerrero (.337).
**At-bats:** Vladimir Guerrero (612).
**Runs:** Vladimir Guerrero (124).
**Hits:** Vladimir Guerrero (206).
**Total Bases:** Vladimir Guerrero (366).
**Doubles:** Vladimir Guerrero (39).
**Triples:** Chone Figgins (17).
**Home runs:** Vladimir Guerrero (39).
**Runs batted in:** Vladimir Guerrero (126).
**Stolen bases:** Chone Figgins (34).
**Slugging percentage:** Vladimir Guerrero (.598).
**On-base percentage:** Vladimir Guerrero (.391).
**Wins:** Bartolo Colon (18).
**Earned-run average:** Scot Shields (3.33).
**Complete games:** John Lackey, Jarrod Washburn (1).
**Shutouts:** John Lackey, Jarrod Washburn (1).
**Saves:** Troy Percival (33).
**Innings pitched:** Bartolo Colon, Kelvim Escobar (208.1).
**Strikeouts:** Kelvim Escobar (191).

## GAMES BY POSITION

**Catcher:** Bengie Molina 89, Jose Molina 70, Josh Paul 37.
**First base:** Darin Erstad 124, Casey Kotchman 34, Robb Quinlan 13, Shane Halter 4, Jose Molina 2, Andres Galarraga 1, Adam Riggs 1.
**Second base:** Adam Kennedy 144, Chone Figgins 20, Alfredo Amezaga 16, Shane Halter 6, Adam Riggs 1.
**Third base:** Chone Figgins 92, Shane Halter 33, Robb Quinlan 32, Alfredo Amezaga 26, Troy Glaus 19, Dallas McPherson 14.
**Shortstop:** David Eckstein 138, Alfredo Amezaga 32, Chone Figgins 13, Shane Halter 3.
**Outfield:** Vladimir Guerrero 143, Jose Guillen 136, Garret Anderson 94, Jeff DaVanon 81, Chone Figgins 57, Curtis Pride 24, Robb Quinlan 9, Adam Riggs 8, Tim Salmon 8, Raul Mondesi 7, Josh Paul 4.
**Designated hitter:** Troy Glaus 39, Tim Salmon 39, Jeff DaVanon 19, Garret Anderson 18, Vladimir Guerrero 13, Jose Guillen 10, Bengie Molina 5, Andres Galarraga 4, Robb Quinlan 4, Adam Riggs 4, Shane Halter 3, Casey Kotchman 2, Josh Paul 2, Curtis Pride 2, Alfredo Amezaga 1, David Eckstein 1, Chone Figgins 1, Jose Molina 1, Raul Mondesi 1

## TOP DRAFT CHOICES

1. **Jered Weaver,** RHP, Long Beach State.
4. **Patrick White,** OF, Daphne (Ala.) H.S.
5. **Luis Rivera,** OF, Ramon Vila Mayo H.S., Rio Piedras, Puerto Rico.
6. **Josh LeBlanc,** 2B, Southern University.
7. **Bill Layman,** RHP, North Florida.
8. **Freddy Sandoval,** 3B, University of San Diego.
9. **Hainley Statia,** SS, Trinity Christian Academy, Boynton Beach, Fla.
10. **Doug Reinhardt,** 3B, Santa Margarita Catholic H.S., Laguna Beach, Calif.

# BALTIMORE ORIOLES
## AMERICAN LEAGUE EAST DIVISION

## 2005 SEASON

**Orioles Schedule**
Home games shaded.
All-Star Game July 12 at Detroit. Schedule subject to change.

**April**

| SUN | MON | TUE | WED | THU | FRI | SAT |
|---|---|---|---|---|---|---|
| 3 | 4 OAK | 5 | 6 OAK | 7 OAK | 8 NYY | 9 NYY |
| 10 NYY | 11 | 12 TB | 13 TB | 14 TB | 15 NYY | 16 NYY |
| 17 NYY | 18 DET | 19 DET | 20 BOS | 21 BOS | 22 TOR | 23 TOR |
| 24 TOR | 25 BOS | 26 BOS | 27 BOS | 28 | 29 TB | 30 TB |

**May**

| SUN | MON | TUE | WED | THU | FRI | SAT |
|---|---|---|---|---|---|---|
| 1 TB | 2 TOR | 3 TOR | 4 TOR | 5 | 6 KC | 7 KC |
| 8 KC | 9 MIN | 10 MIN | 11 MIN | 12 CHW | 13 CHW | 14 CHW |
| 15 CHW | 16 | 17 KC | 18 KC | 19 KC | 20 PHI | 21 PHI |
| 22 PHI | 23 | 24 SEA | 25 SEA | 26 SEA | 27 DET | 28 DET |
| 29 DET | 30 BOS | 31 BOS | | | | |

**June**

| SUN | MON | TUE | WED | THU | FRI | SAT |
|---|---|---|---|---|---|---|
| | | | 1 BOS | 2 | 3 DET | 4 DET |
| 5 DET | 6 PIT | 7 PIT | 8 PIT | 9 | 10 CIN | 11 CIN |
| 12 CIN | 13 HOU | 14 HOU | 15 HOU | 16 | 17 COL | 18 COL |
| 19 COL | 20 TOR | 21 TOR | 22 TOR | 23 TOR | 24 ATL | 25 ATL |
| 26 ATL | 27 NYY | 28 NYY | 29 NYY | 30 CLE | | |

**July**

| SUN | MON | TUE | WED | THU | FRI | SAT |
|---|---|---|---|---|---|---|
| | | | | | 1 CLE | 2 CLE |
| 3 CLE | 4 NYY | 5 NYY | 6 | 7 BOS | 8 BOS | 9 BOS |
| 10 BOS | 11 | 12 All-Star | 13 | 14 SEA | 15 SEA | 16 SEA |
| 17 SEA | 18 MIN | 19 MIN | 20 MIN | 21 | 22 TB | 23 TB |
| 24 TB | 25 TEX | 26 TEX | 27 TEX | 28 TEX | 29 CHW | 30 CHW |
| 31 CHW | | | | | | |

**August**

| SUN | MON | TUE | WED | THU | FRI | SAT |
|---|---|---|---|---|---|---|
| | 1 CHW | 2 ANA | 3 ANA | 4 ANA | 5 TEX | 6 TEX |
| 7 TEX | 8 | 9 TB | 10 TB | 11 TB | 12 TOR | 13 TOR |
| 14 TOR | 15 OAK | 16 OAK | 17 OAK | 18 | 19 CLE | 20 CLE |
| 21 CLE | 22 | 23 ANA | 24 ANA | 25 ANA | 26 OAK | 27 OAK |
| 28 OAK | 29 OAK | 30 TOR | 31 TOR | | | |

**September**

| SUN | MON | TUE | WED | THU | FRI | SAT |
|---|---|---|---|---|---|---|
| | | | | 1 TOR | 2 BOS | 3 BOS |
| 4 BOS | 5 TOR | 6 TOR | 7 TOR | 8 | 9 SEA | 10 SEA |
| 11 SEA | 12 TEX | 13 TEX | 14 TEX | 15 | 16 TB | 17 TB |
| 18 TB | 19 NYY | 20 NYY | 21 NYY | 22 NYY | 23 BOS | 24 BOS |
| 25 BOS | 26 | 27 NYY | 28 NYY | 29 NYY | 30 TB | |

**October**

| SUN | MON | TUE | WED | THU | FRI | SAT |
|---|---|---|---|---|---|---|
| | | | | | | 1 TB |
| 2 TB | 3 | 4 | 5 | 6 | 7 | 8 |

Home games shaded. All-Star Game July 12 at Detroit. Schedule subject to change.

### CLUB DIRECTORY

**Chairman of the board/CEO**
Peter G. Angelos
**Vice chairman/COO**
Joseph E. Foss
**Executive vice president**
John P. Angelos
**Vice president/CFO**
Robert A. Ames, CPA
**Exec. vice president /baseball operations**
Jim Beattie
**Vice president/baseball operations**
Mike Flanagan
**Director/baseball administration**
Ed Kenney Jr.
**Asst. to the v.p./baseball operations**
Dave Ritterpusch
**Director/scouting**
Joe Jordan
**Director/minor league operations**
David Stockstill
**Asst. director/minor league operations**
Tripp Norton
**Traveling secretary**
Philip E. Itzoe
**V.p./corporate sponsorship and sales**
T.J. Brightman
**Executive director/communications**
Spiro Alafassos
**Sr. director/public affairs and advertising**
Matthew P. Dryer

### MINOR LEAGUE AFFILIATES

| Class | Team | League | Manager |
|---|---|---|---|
| AAA | Ottawa | International | Dave Trembley |
| AA | Bowie | Eastern | Don Werner |
| Advanced A | Frederick | Carolina | Bien Figueroa |
| A | Delmarva | South Atlantic | Gary Kendall |
| Short-Season A | Aberdeen | New York-Pennsylvania | Andy Etchebarren |
| Advanced Rookie | Bluefield | Appalachian | Jesus Alfaro |

### BROADCAST INFORMATION

**Radio:** TBA.
**Cable TV:** Comcast SportsNet.

### SPRING TRAINING

**Ballpark (city):** Fort Lauderdale Stadium (Fort Lauderdale, Fla.).
**Ticket information:** 954-776-1921.

**For more on the Orioles, go to msn.foxsports.com/mlb/teams.**

Tejada

## SPRING TRAINING ROSTER

**Manager**—Lee Mazzilli (13).
**Coaches**—Terry Crowley (48), Rick Dempsey (24), Elrod Hendricks (44), Ray Miller, Sam Perlozzo (2), Tom Trebelhorn (49).

| No. | PITCHERS | B/T | Ht./Wt. | Age* | 2004 Clubs |
|---|---|---|---|---|---|
| 29 | Ainsworth, Kurt | R/R | 6-3/208 | 26 | Baltimore, Ottawa, Aberdeen |
| 30 | Bauer, Rick | R/R | 6-6/223 | 28 | Bowie, Ottawa, Baltimore |
| 45 | Bedard, Erik | L/L | 6-1/189 | 26 | Ottawa, Baltimore |
| 61 | Borkowski, Dave | R/R | 6-1/200 | 28 | Ottawa, Baltimore |
| 35 | Cabrera, Daniel | R/R | 6-7/230 | 23 | Bowie, Baltimore |
| 64 | Chen, Bruce | L/L | 6-1/210 | 27 | Syracuse, Ottawa, Baltimore |
| | Crouthers, Dave | R/.R | 6-3/202 | 25 | Bowie |
| 28 | DuBose, Eric | L/L | 6-3/216 | 28 | Baltimore |
| | Forystek, Brian | L/L | 6-1/182 | 26 | Bowie, Ottawa |
| 38 | Grimsley, Jason | R/R | 6-3/205 | 37 | Kansas City, Baltimore |
| 50 | Julio, Jorge | R/R | 6-1/232 | 26 | Baltimore |
| | Kline, Steve | B/L | 6-1/215 | 32 | St. Louis |
| | Loewen, Adam | L/L | 6-5/219 | 20 | Delmarva, Frederick |
| 19 | Lopez, Rodrigo | R/R | 6-1/190 | 29 | Baltimore |
| 49 | Maine, John | R/R | 6-4/193 | 23 | Bowie, Baltimore, Ottawa |
| 36 | Parrish, John | L/L | 5-11/192 | 27 | Baltimore |
| 43 | Ponson, Sidney | R/R | 6-1/266 | 28 | Baltimore |
| 47 | Rakers, Aaron | R/R | 6-3/205 | 28 | Ottawa, Baltimore |
| 12 | Riley, Matt | L/L | 6-1/221 | 25 | Ottawa, Baltimore |
| 40 | Rodriguez, Eddy | R/R | 6-1/194 | 23 | Ottawa, Baltimore |
| 52 | Ryan, B.J. | L/L | 6-6/249 | 29 | Baltimore |
| | Sequea, Jacobo | R/R | 6-1/195 | 23 | Bowie |
| 53 | Williams, Todd | R/R | 6-3/210 | 34 | Oklahoma, Ottawa, Baltimore |

| No. | CATCHERS | B/T | Ht./Wt. | Age* | 2004 Clubs |
|---|---|---|---|---|---|
| 9 | Gil, Geronimo | R/R | 6-2/234 | 29 | Ottawa, Baltimore |
| 18 | Lopez, Javy | R/R | 6-3/224 | 34 | Baltimore |
| | Whiteside, Eli | R/R | 6-2/215 | 25 | Bowie |

| No. | INFIELDERS | B/T | Ht./Wt. | Age* | 2004 Clubs |
|---|---|---|---|---|---|
| | Fontenot, Mike | L/L | 5-8/167 | 24 | Ottawa |
| 15 | Hairston Jr., Jerry | R/R | 5-10/183 | 28 | Bowie, Baltimore |
| 6 | Mora, Melvin | R/R | 5-11/200 | 33 | Baltimore |
| 11 | Newhan, David | L/R | 5-10/180 | 31 | Oklahoma, Baltimore |
| 25 | Palmeiro, Rafael | L/L | 6-0/214 | 40 | Baltimore |
| 1 | Roberts, Brian | B/R | 5-9/176 | 27 | Baltimore |
| 10 | Tejada, Miguel | R/R | 5-9/209 | 28 | Baltimore |
| | Young, Walter | L/R | 6-5/305 | 25 | Bowie |

| No. | OUTFIELDERS | B/T | Ht./Wt. | Age* | 2004 Clubs |
|---|---|---|---|---|---|
| 3 | Bigbie, Larry | L/R | 6-4/207 | 27 | Frederick, Baltimore |
| 31 | Gibbons, Jay | L/L | 6-0/197 | 28 | Frederick, Bowie, Baltimore |
| 63 | Majewski, Val | L/L | 6-2/200 | 23 | Bowie, Baltimore |
| 32 | Matos, Luis | R/R | 6-0/208 | 26 | Baltimore |
| 16 | Raines Jr., Tim | R/R | 5-10/190 | 25 | Ottawa, Baltimore |
| 17 | Surhoff, B.J. | L/R | 6-1/210 | 40 | Baltimore |

*Age as of April 1, 2005.

## BALLPARK INFORMATION

**Ballpark (capacity, surface)**
Oriole Park at Camden Yards (48,190, grass)

**Address**
333 W. Camden St.
Baltimore, MD 21201

**Official website**
www.theorioles.com

**Business phone**
410-685-9800

**Ticket information**
410-481-SEAT

**Field dimensions (from home plate)**
To left field at foul line, 333 feet
To center field, 400 feet
To right field at foul line, 318

**First game played**
April 6, 1992 (Orioles 2, Indians 0)

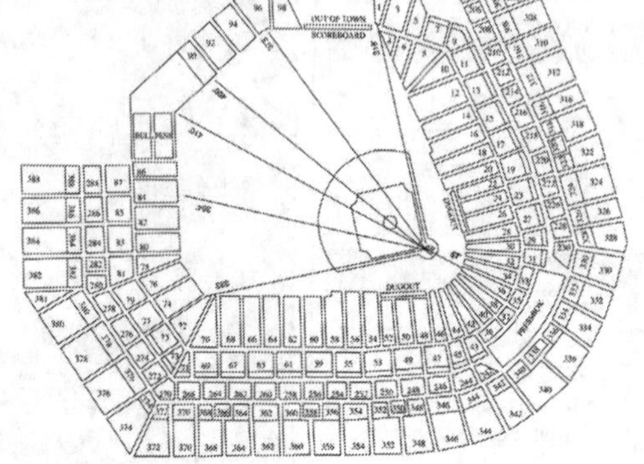

# 2004 REVIEW

## DAY BY DAY

| Date | Opp. | Res. | Score | (inn.*) | Hits | Opp. hits | Winning pitcher | Losing pitcher | Save | Record | Pos. | GB |
|---|---|---|---|---|---|---|---|---|---|---|---|---|
| 4-4 | Bos. | W | 7-2 | | 11 | 11 | Ponson | Martinez | Ryan | 1-0 | 1st | +0.5 |
| 4-6 | Bos. | L | 1-4 | | 6 | 5 | Schilling | DuBose | Foulke | 1-1 | T2nd | 0.5 |
| 4-7 | Bos. | L | 3-10 | | 10 | 14 | Lowe | Ainsworth | | 1-2 | 4th | 1.0 |
| 4-8 | Bos. | W | 3-2 | (13) | 7 | 6 | Lopez | Jones | | 2-2 | T2nd | 0.5 |
| 4-9 | At T.B. | L | 3-4 | (10) | 9 | 7 | Baez | Parrish | | 2-3 | T3rd | 1.0 |
| 4-10 | At T.B. | W | 11-3 | | 16 | 7 | Bauer | Gonzalez | | 3-3 | T1st | ... |
| 4-11 | At T.B. | L | 1-10 | | 8 | 11 | Zambrano | DuBose | | 3-4 | 4th | 1.0 |
| 4-15 | At Bos. | W | 12-7 | (11) | 14 | 11 | Groom | Arroyo | | 4-4 | T2nd | 0.5 |
| 4-16 | At Tor. | W | 11-2 | | 12 | 2 | Riley | Batista | | 5-4 | T1st | ... |
| 4-17 | At Tor. | W | 5-3 | | 12 | 6 | Ryan | Speier | Julio | 6-4 | T1st | ... |
| 4-18 | At Tor. | W | 7-0 | | 12 | 4 | DuBose | Hentgen | | 7-4 | 1st | +1.0 |
| 4-20 | T.B. | W | 9-1 | | 14 | 4 | Ponson | Hendrickson | | 8-4 | 1st | +0.5 |
| 4-21 | T.B. | L | 3-7 | | 4 | 12 | Abbott | Riley | | 8-5 | 2nd | 0.5 |
| 4-22 | T.B. | W | 7-6 | | 9 | 7 | Parrish | Gaudin | Julio | 9-5 | 1st | +0.5 |
| 4-23 | Tor. | W | 11-3 | | 15 | 8 | DuBose | Towers | | 10-5 | 1st | +0.5 |
| 4-24 | Tor. | L | 4-5 | (12) | 11 | 14 | Ligtenberg | DeJean | | 10-6 | 2nd | 0.5 |
| 4-25 | Tor. | L | 3-15 | | 7 | 17 | Halladay | Ponson | | 10-7 | 2nd | 1.5 |
| 4-27 | Sea. | L | 5-7 | | 12 | 13 | Villone | Lopez | Guardado | 10-8 | 2nd | 2.0 |
| 4-28 | Sea. | W | 3-1 | | 7 | 4 | Parrish | Hasegawa | Julio | 11-8 | 2nd | 2.0 |
| 4-29 | Sea. | W | 9-5 | | 15 | 5 | DuBose | Pineiro | | 12-8 | 2nd | 2.5 |
| 4-30 | At Cle. | L | 2-11 | | 7 | 15 | Lee | Ponson | | 12-9 | 2nd | 3.0 |
| 5-1 | At Cle. | L | 2-3 | (13) | 10 | 10 | Durbin | DeJean | | 12-10 | 2nd | 2.5 |
| 5-3 | Chi. | L | 4-5 | | 6 | 8 | Schoeneweis | DeJean | Koch | 12-11 | 3rd | 2.0 |
| 5-4 | Chi. | W | 10-3 | | 13 | 5 | Lopez | Loaiza | | 13-11 | 3rd | 1.0 |
| 5-5 | Chi. | L | 5-6 | | 12 | 11 | Takatsu | Ryan | Koch | 13-12 | 3rd | 2.0 |
| 5-7 | Cle. | W | 3-2 | (10) | 7 | 10 | Julio | Durbin | | 14-12 | 3rd | 2.5 |
| 5-8 | Cle. | W | 10-7 | | 14 | 7 | Parrish | Stewart | Julio | 15-12 | 3rd | 2.5 |
| 5-9 | Cle. | W | 12-11 | | 16 | 15 | Lopez | Riske | Julio | 16-12 | 3rd | 1.5 |
| 5-11 | At Chi. | L | 0-15 | | 4 | 19 | Buehrle | Ponson | | 16-13 | 3rd | 2.0 |
| 5-13! | At Chi. | W | 1-0 | | 6 | 3 | Cabrera | Garland | Julio | 17-13 | | |
| 5-13& | At Chi. | L | 5-6 | | 8 | 7 | Jackson | Bedard | Koch | 17-14 | 3rd | 1.5 |
| 5-14 | Ana. | L | 9-10 | (10) | 11 | 15 | Percival | Julio | Shields | 17-15 | 3rd | 2.5 |
| 5-15 | Ana. | L | 4-7 | | 6 | 11 | Washburn | DuBose | Percival | 17-16 | 3rd | 3.0 |
| 5-16 | Ana. | W | 4-0 | | 9 | 5 | Ponson | Escobar | | 18-16 | 3rd | 2.5 |
| 5-18 | At Sea. | W | 7-2 | | 10 | 6 | Cabrera | Garcia | | 19-16 | 3rd | 2.0 |
| 5-19 | At Sea. | W | 5-2 | | 10 | 7 | Bedard | Franklin | Julio | 20-16 | 3rd | 2.0 |
| 5-20 | At Sea. | L | 0-11 | | 8 | 13 | Moyer | Lopez | | 20-17 | 3rd | 2.5 |
| 5-21 | At Ana. | L | 3-5 | | 11 | 12 | Shields | DeJean | Percival | 20-18 | 3rd | 3.0 |
| 5-22 | At Ana. | L | 2-3 | | 6 | 9 | Escobar | Ponson | Percival | 20-19 | 3rd | 4.0 |
| 5-23 | At Ana. | L | 3-8 | | 11 | 12 | Sele | Cabrera | | 20-20 | 3rd | 5.0 |
| 5-25 | N.Y. | L | 3-11 | | 7 | 14 | Lieber | Bedard | | 20-21 | 3rd | 6.0 |
| 5-26 | N.Y. | L | 9-12 | | 14 | 16 | Sturtze | Ryan | Rivera | 20-22 | 3rd | 7.0 |
| 5-27 | N.Y. | L | 5-18 | | 14 | 21 | Contreras | Ponson | | 20-23 | 3rd | 7.0 |
| 5-28 | At Det. | W | 7-5 | | 13 | 10 | DuBose | Johnson | Julio | 21-23 | 3rd | 7.0 |
| 5-29 | At Det. | W | 8-4 | | 13 | 9 | Cabrera | Bonderman | Parrish | 22-23 | 3rd | 6.5 |
| 5-30 | At Det. | W | 7-3 | | 13 | 9 | Groom | Urbina | | 23-23 | 3rd | 6.0 |
| 5-31 | At Bos. | W | 13-4 | | 16 | 9 | Lopez | Lowe | | 24-23 | 3rd | 5.0 |
| 6-1 | At N.Y. | L | 7-8 | | 14 | 13 | Mussina | Ponson | Rivera | 24-24 | 3rd | 6.0 |
| 6-2 | At N.Y. | L | 5-6 | | 9 | 3 | Prinz | DuBose | Rivera | 24-25 | 3rd | 7.0 |
| 6-3 | At N.Y. | L | 2-5 | | 5 | 10 | Vazquez | Parrish | Rivera | 24-26 | 3rd | 8.0 |
| 6-4 | T.B. | L | 7-8 | (11) | 6 | 14 | Carter | DeJean | Baez | 24-27 | 3rd | 9.0 |
| 6-6 | T.B. | W | 5-4 | | 11 | 12 | Lopez | Bell | Julio | 25-27 | 3rd | 8.5 |
| 6-8 | Ari. | L | 1-8 | | 5 | 14 | Johnson | Ponson | | 25-28 | 3rd | 9.5 |
| 6-9 | Ari. | W | 8-2 | | 10 | 7 | Parrish | Randolph | | 26-28 | 3rd | 9.5 |
| 6-10 | Ari. | L | 0-3 | | 7 | 4 | Fossum | Cabrera | Valverde | 26-29 | 3rd | 10.5 |
| 6-12# | S.F | L | 6-9 | (11) | 10 | 12 | Herges | Julio | | 26-30 | | |
| 6-12$ | S.F | W | 5-4 | (12) | 14 | 5 | Parrish | Eyre | | 27-30 | 3rd | 10.5 |
| 6-13 | S.F | L | 3-7 | | 6 | 15 | Williams | Ponson | Walker | 27-31 | 3rd | 11.5 |
| 6-14 | At Cle. | L | 0-14 | | 4 | 15 | Westbrook | DuBose | | 27-32 | 3rd | 12.0 |
| 6-15 | At L.A. | L | 1-5 | | 5 | 10 | Lima | Cabrera | Gagne | 27-33 | 3rd | 13.0 |
| 6-16 | At L.A. | L | 3-6 | | 8 | 10 | Perez | Riley | Gagne | 27-34 | 4th | 14.0 |
| 6-17 | At L.A. | L | 3-4 | | 10 | 9 | Mota | Lopez | Gagne | 27-35 | 4th | 14.0 |
| 6-18 | At Col. | L | 3-5 | | 9 | 9 | Estes | Ponson | Chacon | 27-36 | 5th | 14.0 |
| 6-19 | At Col. | L | 6-11 | | 14 | 13 | Fassero | DuBose | | 27-37 | 5th | 15.0 |
| 6-20 | At Col. | W | 4-2 | | 6 | 6 | Ryan | Chacon | Julio | 28-37 | 5th | 14.0 |
| 6-22 | N.Y. | L | 4-10 | | 5 | 8 | Mussina | Riley | | 28-38 | 5th | 15.0 |
| 6-23 | N.Y. | W | 13-2 | | 17 | 7 | Bedard | Lieber | | 29-38 | 5th | 14.0 |

| Date | Opp. | Res. | Score | (inn.*) | Hits | Opp. hits | Winning pitcher | Losing pitcher | Save | Record | Pos. | GB |
|---|---|---|---|---|---|---|---|---|---|---|---|---|
| 6-24 | N.Y. | L | 2-5 | | 9 | 10 | Vazquez | Ponson | Rivera | 29-39 | 5th | 15.0 |
| 6-25 | Atl. | W | 5-0 | | 10 | 4 | Cabrera | Byrd | | 30-39 | 5th | 14.5 |
| 6-26 | Atl. | L | 0-5 | | 10 | 9 | Ortiz | Lopez | Smoltz | 30-40 | 5th | 14.5 |
| 6-27 | Atl. | L | 7-8 | | 13 | 14 | Cruz | Grimsley | Smoltz | 30-41 | 5th | 16.0 |
| 6-28 | At K.C. | W | 10-1 | | 13 | 7 | Bedard | May | | 31-41 | 5th | 15.5 |
| 6-29 | At K.C. | L | 3-4 | | 8 | 10 | Wood | Ponson | Camp | 31-42 | 5th | 16.5 |
| 6-30 | At K.C. | W | 13-4 | | 15 | 5 | Cabrera | Anderson | | 32-42 | 5th | 16.5 |
| 7-1 | At K.C. | W | 3-2 | | 10 | 4 | Lopez | Greinke | Julio | 33-42 | 5th | 16.5 |
| 7-2 | At Phi. | W | 7-6 | (16) | 15 | 10 | Rodriguez | Powell | Cabrera | 34-42 | 4th | 15.5 |
| 7-3 | At Phi. | L | 6-7 | | 9 | 10 | Cormier | Grimsley | Wagner | 34-43 | 5th | 15.5 |
| 7-4 | At Phi. | L | 2-5 | | 8 | 10 | Milton | Ponson | Worrell | 34-44 | 5th | 15.5 |
| 7-5# | T.B. | W | 4-2 | | 11 | 4 | Ryan | Brazelton | Julio | 35-44 | | |
| 7-5$ | T.B. | W | 8-2 | | 15 | 6 | Borkowski | Gonzalez | | 36-44 | 4th | 15.0 |
| 7-6 | T.B. | L | 1-3 | | 8 | 12 | Hendrickson | Lopez | Baez | 36-45 | 5th | 15.0 |
| 7-7 | T.B. | L | 3-13 | | 6 | 14 | Bell | Parrish | | 36-46 | 5th | 15.0 |
| 7-9 | K.C. | L | 0-7 | | 5 | 11 | May | Bedard | | 36-47 | 5th | 16.5 |
| 7-10 | K.C. | W | 7-2 | | 13 | 5 | Cabrera | Wood | | 37-47 | 5th | 16.5 |
| 7-11 | K.C. | L | 7-11 | | 12 | 17 | Gobble | Lopez | | 37-48 | 5th | 17.5 |
| 7-15 | At T.B. | W | 5-4 | | 9 | 10 | Cabrera | Harper | Julio | 38-48 | 5th | 17.5 |
| 7-16 | At T.B. | L | 0-2 | | 3 | 9 | Halama | Bedard | Baez | 38-49 | 5th | 17.5 |
| 7-17 | At T.B. | W | 3-2 | | 7 | 7 | Lopez | Brazelton | Julio | 39-49 | 4th | 17.5 |
| 7-18 | At T.B. | L | 2-7 | | 4 | 11 | Hendrickson | Borkowski | | 39-50 | 4th | 17.5 |
| 7-19 | At K.C. | W | 7-4 | | 12 | 10 | Ponson | Anderson | | 40-50 | 4th | 16.5 |
| 7-20 | At K.C. | W | 12-3 | | 16 | 12 | Cabrera | Greinke | | 41-50 | 4th | 16.5 |
| 7-21 | At Bos. | W | 10-5 | | 15 | 8 | Bedard | Martinez | | 42-50 | 4th | 16.5 |
| 7-22# | At Bos. | W | 8-3 | | 11 | 11 | Lopez | Alvarez | | 43-50 | | |
| 7-22$ | At Bos. | L | 0-4 | | 10 | 7 | Wakefield | Borkowski | | 43-51 | 4th | 17.0 |
| 7-23 | Min. | L | 3-7 | | 10 | 12 | Silva | Maine | | 43-52 | 4th | 18.0 |
| 7-24 | Min. | W | 4-2 | | 5 | 4 | Ponson | Roa | Julio | 44-52 | 4th | 17.0 |
| 7-25 | Min. | L | 4-8 | | 9 | 15 | Lohse | Cabrera | | 44-53 | 4th | 17.0 |
| 7-26 | Bos. | L | 5-12 | | 9 | 13 | Martinez | Bedard | | 44-54 | 4th | 18.0 |
| 7-28 | Bos. | W | 4-1 | | 7 | 4 | Borkowski | Schilling | | 45-54 | 4th | 17.5 |
| 7-29 | At N.Y. | W | 9-1 | | 12 | 4 | Ponson | Contreras | | 46-54 | 4th | 16.5 |
| 7-30 | At N.Y. | L | 1-2 | | 7 | 8 | Brown | Cabrera | Rivera | 46-55 | 4th | 17.5 |
| 7-31 | At N.Y. | L | 4-6 | | 7 | 10 | Vazquez | Bedard | Rivera | 46-56 | 4th | 18.5 |
| 8-1 | At N.Y. | L | 7-9 | | 14 | 9 | Hernandez | Lopez | Rivera | 46-57 | 4th | 19.5 |
| 8-3# | Sea. | W | 9-7 | | 10 | 16 | Grimsley | Nageotte | Julio | 47-57 | | |
| 8-3$ | Sea. | W | 5-4 | | 11 | 15 | Julio | Sherrill | | 48-57 | 4th | 18.0 |
| 8-4 | Sea. | W | 6-3 | | 10 | 9 | Williams | Hasegawa | Julio | 49-57 | 4th | 18.0 |
| 8-6 | Tex. | W | 9-1 | | 8 | 7 | Bedard | Regilio | | 50-57 | 4th | 18.5 |
| 8-7 | Tex. | W | 3-1 | | 10 | 4 | Lopez | Erickson | Julio | 51-57 | 4th | 18.5 |
| 8-8 | Tex. | W | 11-5 | | 13 | 9 | Ponson | Rogers | | 52-57 | 4th | 18.5 |
| 8-9 | Tex. | W | 7-3 | | 9 | 8 | Borkowski | Bacsik | | 53-57 | 4th | 17.5 |
| 8-10 | At Ana. | W | 11-3 | | 20 | 6 | Cabrera | Sele | | 54-57 | 3rd | 16.5 |
| 8-11 | At Ana. | L | 2-4 | | 9 | 6 | Escobar | Grimsley | Percival | 54-58 | 3rd | 17.5 |
| 8-12 | At Ana. | W | 6-1 | | 14 | 6 | Lopez | Colon | | 55-58 | 3rd | 17.5 |
| 8-13 | At Tor. | W | 4-0 | | 11 | 5 | Ponson | Batista | | 56-58 | 3rd | 17.5 |
| 8-14 | At Tor. | L | 2-7 | | 6 | 14 | Towers | Borkowski | | 56-59 | 3rd | 18.5 |
| 8-15 | At Tor. | W | 11-7 | | 17 | 11 | Groom | Chulk | | 57-59 | 3rd | 17.5 |
| 8-16 | Oak. | L | 1-3 | | 7 | 9 | Redman | Bedard | Dotel | 57-60 | 3rd | 18.0 |
| 8-17 | Oak. | L | 0-11 | | 5 | 13 | Hudson | Lopez | | 57-61 | 3rd | 18.0 |
| 8-18 | Oak. | L | 4-5 | | 6 | 11 | Mulder | Ryan | Dotel | 57-62 | 3rd | 18.0 |
| 8-20 | Tor. | L | 4-14 | | 10 | 14 | Towers | Borkowski | | 57-63 | 3rd | 18.5 |
| 8-21 | Tor. | L | 4-10 | | 10 | 15 | Bush | Cabrera | | 57-64 | 3rd | 18.5 |
| 8-22 | Tor. | L | 5-8 | | 13 | 12 | Miller | Bedard | Frasor | 57-65 | 3rd | 18.5 |
| 8-23 | At Oak. | L | 3-4 | | 8 | 12 | Hudson | Groom | Dotel | 57-66 | 3rd | 19.5 |
| 8-24 | At Oak. | L | 2-6 | | 5 | 9 | Mulder | Ponson | | 57-67 | 4th | 20.5 |
| 8-25 | At Oak. | L | 0-3 | | 5 | 5 | Dotel | Ryan | | 57-68 | 4th | 20.5 |
| 8-26 | At Oak. | L | 4-9 | | 8 | 9 | Zito | Cabrera | | 57-69 | 4th | 21.5 |
| 8-27 | At Tex. | L | 4-6 | | 10 | 9 | Wasdin | Bedard | Cordero | 57-70 | 4th | 22.5 |
| 8-28 | At Tex. | L | 3-4 | | 6 | 7 | Francisco | Ryan | Cordero | 57-71 | 4th | 23.5 |
| 8-29 | At Tex. | W | 7-6 | | 10 | 15 | Ponson | Young | Julio | 58-71 | 4th | 22.5 |
| 8-31 | At T.B. | W | 10-6 | (12) | 17 | 11 | Groom | Carter | | 59-71 | 3rd | 21.5 |
| 9-1 | At T.B. | W | 8-0 | | 16 | 2 | Cabrera | Hendrickson | | 60-71 | 3rd | 21.5 |
| 9-2 | At T.B. | W | 13-2 | | 14 | 6 | Bedard | Brazelton | | 61-71 | 3rd | 21.5 |
| 9-3 | At N.Y. | W | 3-1 | | 6 | 6 | Lopez | Brown | Julio | 62-71 | 3rd | 20.5 |
| 9-4 | At N.Y. | W | 7-0 | | 14 | 2 | Ponson | Mussina | | 63-71 | 3rd | 19.5 |
| 9-5 | At N.Y. | L | 3-4 | | 9 | 7 | Rivera | Julio | | 63-72 | 3rd | 20.5 |
| 9-6 | Min. | W | 4-1 | | 10 | 4 | Cabrera | Mulholland | Julio | 64-72 | 3rd | 20.5 |
| 9-7 | Min. | L | 1-3 | | 5 | 4 | Romero | Julio | Nathan | 64-73 | 3rd | 21.5 |

| Date | Opp. | Res. | Score | (inn.*) | Hits | Opp. hits | Winning pitcher | Losing pitcher | Save | Record | Pos. | GB |
|---|---|---|---|---|---|---|---|---|---|---|---|---|
| 9-8 | Min. | L | 0-9 | | 6 | 12 | Santana | Bedard | | 64-74 | 3rd | 22.0 |
| 9-10 | N.Y. | W | 14-8 | | 14 | 13 | Lopez | Vazquez | | 65-74 | 3rd | 22.0 |
| 9-11 | N.Y. | L | 2-5 | | 7 | 10 | Hernandez | Ponson | Rivera | 65-75 | 3rd | 23.0 |
| 9-12 | N.Y. | L | 7-9 | | 13 | 11 | Gordon | Julio | Rivera | 65-76 | 3rd | 24.0 |
| 9-13 | At Tor. | W | 9-1 | | 12 | 5 | Chen | Miller | | 66-76 | 3rd | 23.0 |
| 9-15 | At Tor. | L | 0-3 | | 8 | 5 | Lilly | Riley | Speier | 66-77 | 3rd | 24.5 |
| 9-16 | At Tor. | W | 9-5 | | 12 | 13 | Lopez | Batista | | 67-77 | 3rd | 24.0 |
| 9-17 | At Min. | W | 11-2 | | 12 | 6 | Ponson | Mulholland | | 68-77 | 3rd | 23.0 |
| 9-18 | At Min. | W | 12-3 | | 18 | 6 | Cabrera | Radke | | 69-77 | 3rd | 23.0 |
| 9-19 | At Min. | L | 1-5 | | 9 | 8 | Santana | Chen | | 69-78 | 3rd | 24.0 |
| 9-20 | At Bos. | W | 9-6 | | 8 | 10 | Grimsley | Wakefield | Julio | 70-78 | 3rd | 23.0 |
| 9-21 | At Bos. | L | 2-3 | | 5 | 7 | Foulke | Ryan | | 70-79 | 3rd | 24.0 |
| 9-22 | At Bos. | L | 6-7 | (12) | 12 | 13 | Leskanic | Bauer | | 70-80 | 3rd | 24.0 |
| 9-23 | At Bos. | W | 9-7 | | 15 | 11 | Williams | Mendoza | | 71-80 | 3rd | 24.0 |
| 9-24 | Det. | W | 7-5 | | 13 | 7 | Parrish | Yan | | 72-80 | 3rd | 24.0 |
| 9-25 | Det. | W | 3-0 | | 6 | 5 | Riley | Bonderman | Ryan | 73-80 | 3rd | 23.0 |
| 9-26 | Det. | W | 5-0 | | 11 | 3 | Lopez | Maroth | | 74-80 | 3rd | 22.0 |
| 9-27 | Tor. | L | 1-4 | | 7 | 11 | League | Ponson | Batista | 74-81 | 3rd | 22.5 |
| 9-29! | Tor. | W | 7-6 | | 9 | 9 | Ryan | Speier | | 75-81 | | |
| 9-29& | Tor. | W | 4-0 | | 8 | 4 | Bauer | Chacin | | 76-81 | 3rd | 22.5 |
| 9-30 | Tor. | W | 9-3 | | 14 | 6 | Riley | Towers | | 77-81 | 3rd | 22.5 |
| 10-1 | Bos. | L | 3-8 | | 9 | 11 | Wakefield | Lopez | | 77-82 | 3rd | 22.5 |
| 10-2# | Bos. | L | 5-7 | | 10 | 8 | Adams | Cabrera | Foulke | 77-83 | | |
| 10-2$ | Bos. | L | 5-7 | | 9 | 11 | Kim | Grimsley | Leskanic | 77-84 | 3rd | 23.0 |
| 10-3 | Bos. | W | 3-2 | | 7 | 7 | Chen | Williamson | Ryan | 78-84 | 3rd | 23.0 |

Monthly records: April (12-9), May (12-14), June (8-19), July (14-14), August (13-15), September (18-10), October (1-3).
*Innings, if other than nine. ! First game of a doubleheader. & Second game of a doubleheader. # Day separate admission. $ Night separate admission.

## RECORDS

**2004 regular-season record:** 78-84
**Position:** 3rd in A.L. East
**Home:** 38-43 **Road:** 40-41
**A.L. East:** 37-39 **A.L. Central:** 21-15
**A.L. West:** 15-17 **N.L.** 5-13
**Vs. LH starters:** 22-29
**Vs. RH starters:** 56-55
**Grass:** 63-77 **Artificial:** 15-7
**Day:** 28-29 **Night:** 50-55
**1-Run:** 15-22 **X-inn.:** 6-7
**Doubleheaders:** 1-0-1
**Team record past five years:** 353-456 (.436, ranks 11th in league in that span)

## TEAM LEADERS

**Batting average:** Melvin Mora (.340).
**At-bats:** Miguel Tejada (653).
**Runs:** Melvin Mora (111).
**Hits:** Miguel Tejada (203).
**Total Bases:** Miguel Tejada (349).
**Doubles:** Brian Roberts (50).
**Triples**: David Newhan (7).
**Home runs:** Miguel Tejada (34).
**Runs batted in:** Miguel Tejada (150).
**Stolen bases:** Brian Roberts (29).
**Slugging percentage:** Melvin Mora (.562).
**On-base percentage:** Melvin Mora (.419).
**Wins:** Rodrigo Lopez (14).
**Earned-run average:** Rodrigo Lopez (3.59).
**Complete games:** Sidney Ponson (5).
**Shutouts:** Sidney Ponson (2).
**Saves:** Jorge Julio (22).
**Innings pitched:** Sidney Ponson (215.2).
**Strikeouts:** B.J. Ryan (122).

## GAMES BY POSITION

**Catcher:** Javy Lopez 132, Robert Machado 35, Geronimo Gil 11, Keith Osik 11, Ken Huckaby 8.
**First base:** Rafael Palmeiro 130, Jose Leon 16, Jay Gibbons 14, B.J. Surhoff 10, Luis Lopez 6, David Newhan 2, David Segui 2, Karim Garcia 1.
**Second base:** Brian Roberts 150, Jerry Hairston Jr. 12, Luis Lopez 6.
**Third base:** Melvin Mora 137, David Newhan 17, Luis Lopez 11, Jose Leon 6, Jose Bautista 4, Jerry Hairston Jr. 1.
**Shortstop:** Miguel Tejada 162, Luis Lopez 14, Melvin Mora 1.
**Outfield:** Larry Bigbie 134, Luis Matos 89, B.J. Surhoff 70, Jay Gibbons 66, Jerry Hairston Jr. 52, David Newhan 42, Tim Raines Jr. 38, Karim Garcia 19, Darnell McDonald 13, Jose Bautista 6, Chad Mottola 5, Val Majewski 4.
**Designated hitter:** David Newhan 32, Jerry Hairston Jr. 21, Javy Lopez 21, Rafael Palmeiro 20, B.J. Surhoff 18, Jay Gibbons 16, David Segui 15, Luis Lopez 8, Brian Roberts 6, Jose Leon 5, Tim Raines Jr. 4, Val Majewski 3, Jose Bautista 2, Larry Bigbie 2, Darnell McDonald 1, Melvin Mora 1.

## TOP DRAFT CHOICES

1. **Wade Townsend,** RHP, Rice.
3. **Jeff Fiorentino,** C/1B, Florida Atlantic.
4. **Brad Bergesen,** RHP, Foothills H.S., Pleasanton, Calif.
5. **C.J. Smith,** OF, Florida.
6. **Bryce Chamberlin,** RHP, Washington State.
7. **Seth Johnston,** 2B, Texas.
8. **David Haehnel,** LHP, Illinois-Chicago.
9. **Joey Howell,** OF, Santaluces H.S., West Palm Beach, Fla.
10. **Drew Moffitt,** OF, Wichita State.

# BOSTON RED SOX

## AMERICAN LEAGUE EAST DIVISION

## 2005 SEASON

### Red Sox Schedule

Home games shaded.
All-Star Game July 12 at Detroit. Schedule subject to change.

**April**

| SUN | MON | TUE | WED | THU | FRI | SAT |
|---|---|---|---|---|---|---|
| 3 NYY | 4 | 5 | 6 NYY | 7 NYY | 8 TOR | 9 TOR |
| 10 TOR | 11 NYY | 12 | 13 NYY | 14 NYY | 15 TB | 16 TB |
| 17 TB | 18 TOR | 19 TOR | 20 BAL | 21 BAL | 22 TB | 23 TB |
| 24 TB | 25 BAL | 26 BAL | 27 BAL | 28 | 29 TEX | 30 TEX |

**May**

| SUN | MON | TUE | WED | THU | FRI | SAT |
|---|---|---|---|---|---|---|
| 1 TEX | 2 DET | 3 DET | 4 DET | 5 DET | 6 SEA | 7 SEA |
| 8 SEA | 9 OAK | 10 OAK | 11 OAK | 12 | 13 SEA | 14 SEA |
| 15 SEA | 16 OAK | 17 OAK | 18 OAK | 19 | 20 ATL | 21 ATL |
| 22 ATL | 23 | 24 TOR | 25 TOR | 26 TOR | 27 NYY | 28 NYY |
| 29 NYY | 30 BAL | 31 BAL | | | | |

**June**

| SUN | MON | TUE | WED | THU | FRI | SAT |
|---|---|---|---|---|---|---|
| | | | 1 BAL | 2 | 3 ANA | 4 ANA |
| 5 ANA | 6 STL | 7 STL | 8 STL | 9 | 10 CHC | 11 CHC |
| 12 CHC | 13 CIN | 14 CIN | 15 CIN | 16 | 17 PIT | 18 PIT |
| 19 PIT | 20 CLE | 21 CLE | 22 CLE | 23 | 24 PHI | 25 PHI |
| 26 PHI | 27 CLE | 28 CLE | 29 CLE | 30 | | |

**July**

| SUN | MON | TUE | WED | THU | FRI | SAT |
|---|---|---|---|---|---|---|
| | | | | | 1 TOR | 2 TOR |
| 3 TOR | 4 TEX | 5 TEX | 6 TEX | 7 BAL | 8 BAL | 9 BAL |
| 10 BAL | 11 | 12 All-Star | 13 | 14 NYY | 15 NYY | 16 NYY |
| 17 NYY | 18 TB | 19 TB | 20 TB | 21 CHW | 22 CHW | 23 CHW |
| 24 CHW | 25 TB | 26 TB | 27 TB | 28 | 29 MIN | 30 MIN |
| 31 MIN | | | | | | |

**August**

| SUN | MON | TUE | WED | THU | FRI | SAT |
|---|---|---|---|---|---|---|
| | 1 | 2 KC | 3 KC | 4 KC | 5 MIN | 6 MIN |
| 7 MIN | 8 TEX | 9 TEX | 10 TEX | 11 | 12 CHW | 13 CHW |
| 14 CHW | 15 DET | 16 DET | 17 DET | 18 ANA | 19 ANA | 20 ANA |
| 21 ANA | 22 | 23 KC | 24 KC | 25 KC | 26 DET | 27 DET |
| 28 DET | 29 TB | 30 TB | 31 TB | | | |

**September**

| SUN | MON | TUE | WED | THU | FRI | SAT |
|---|---|---|---|---|---|---|
| | | | | 1 TB | 2 BAL | 3 BAL |
| 4 BAL | 5 | 6 ANA | 7 ANA | 8 ANA | 9 NYY | 10 NYY |
| 11 NYY | 12 TOR | 13 TOR | 14 TOR | 15 OAK | 16 OAK | 17 OAK |
| 18 OAK | 19 TB | 20 TB | 21 TB | 22 | 23 BAL | 24 BAL |
| 25 BAL | 26 TOR | 27 TOR | 28 TOR | 29 TOR | 30 NYY | |

**October**

| SUN | MON | TUE | WED | THU | FRI | SAT |
|---|---|---|---|---|---|---|
| | | | | | | 1 NYY |
| 2 NYY | 3 | 4 | 5 | 6 | 7 | 8 |

Home games shaded. All-Star Game July 12 at Detroit. Schedule subject to change.

### CLUB DIRECTORY

**Principal owner**
John W. Henry

**President/chief executive officer**
Larry Lucchino

**Senior vice president/General manager**
Theo Epstein

**Vice president/baseball operations**
Michael D. Port

**Assistant general manager**
Joshua H. Byrnes

**Senior Advisor/Baseball projects**
Jeremy Kapstein

**Director of player development**
Benjamin P. Cherington

**Special assistant to the G.M./scouting**
Bill Lajoie

**Special asst./player dev., int'l scouting**
Craig Shipley

**Vice president, publications and archives**
Richard L. Bresciani

**Vice president and club counsel**
Elaine W. Steward

**Director of public relations**
Glenn Geffner

**Executive VP/public affairs**
Charles Steinberg

**Senior VP/Fenway affairs**
Larry Cancro

**Senior VP/corporate relations**
Meg Vaillancourt

### MINOR LEAGUE AFFILIATES

| Class | Team | League | Manager |
|---|---|---|---|
| AAA | Pawtucket | International | Ron Johnson |
| AA | Portland | Eastern | Todd Claus |
| Advanced A | Wimington | Carolina | Dann Bilardello |
| A | Capital City | South Atlantic | Chad Epperson |
| Short-Season A | Lowell | New York-Pennsylvania | Luis Alicea |
| Rookie | Gulf Coast Red Sox | Gulf Coast | Ralph Treuel |

### BROADCAST INFORMATION

**Radio:** WEEI-AM (850).
**TV:** UPN and CBS4 (Channels 38 and 4).
**Cable TV:** New England Sports Network.

### SPRING TRAINING

**Ballpark (city):** City of Palms Park (Fort Myers, Fla.).
**Ticket information:** 239-334-4700.

**For more on the Red Sox, go to msn.foxsports.com/mlb/teams.**

Ortiz

## SPRING TRAINING ROSTER

**Manager**—Terry Francona (47).
**Coaches**—Ron Jackson (22), Lynn Jones (35), Brad Mills (2), Dale Sveum (41), Dave Wallace (37).

| No. | PITCHERS | B/T | Ht./Wt. | Age* | 2004 Clubs |
|---|---|---|---|---|---|
| 59 | Alvarez, Abe | L/L | 6-2/190 | 22 | Boston, Portland |
| 61 | Arroyo, Bronson | R/R | 6-5/190 | 28 | Boston |
| | Bausher, Tim | R/R | 6-4/200 | 25 | Huntsville, Tulsa |
| | Cedeno, Juan | L/L | 6-0/175 | 21 | Sarasota |
| | Clement, Matt | R/R | 6-3/210 | 30 | Chicago N.L. |
| | Delcarmen, Manny | R/R | 6-2/190 | 23 | Sarasota |
| | DiNardo, Lenny | L/L | 6-4/195 | 25 | Sarasota, Pawtucket, Boston, G.C. Red Sox, Portland |
| 43 | Embree, Alan | L/L | 6-2/190 | 35 | Boston |
| 29 | Foulke, Keith | R/R | 6-0/210 | 32 | Boston |
| | Halama, John | L/L | 6-5/215 | 33 | Tampa Bay |
| 51 | Kim, Byung-Hyun | R/R | 5-9/180 | 26 | Sarasota, Pawtucket, Boston |
| 46 | Malaska, Mark | L/L | 6-3/208 | 27 | Boston, Pawtucket |
| | Mantei, Matt | R/R | 6-1/198 | 31 | Arizona |
| 67 | Martinez, Anastacio | R/R | 6-2/180 | 26 | Boston, Pawtucket |
| | Mendoza, Luis | L/R | 6-3/205 | 21 | Sarasota |
| | Miller, Wade | R/R | 6-2/220 | 28 | Houston |
| | Sanchez, Anibal | R/R | 6-0/180 | 21 | Lowell |
| 38 | Schilling, Curt | R/R | 6-5/235 | 38 | Boston |
| | Smith, Chris | L/L | 6-2/200 | 23 | Aberdeen, Portland |
| 50 | Timlin, Mike | R/R | 6-4/210 | 39 | Boston |
| 49 | Wakefield, Tim | R/R | 6-2/210 | 38 | Boston |
| | Wells, David | L/L | 6-4/248 | 41 | San Diego |

| No. | CATCHERS | B/T | Ht./Wt. | Age* | 2004 Clubs |
|---|---|---|---|---|---|
| 28 | Mirabelli, Doug | R/R | 6-1/220 | 34 | Boston |
| | Shoppach, Kelly | R/R | 6-1/210 | 24 | Pawtucket |
| 33 | Varitek, Jason | B/R | 6-2/230 | 32 | Boston |

| No. | INFIELDERS | B/T | Ht./Wt. | Age* | 2004 Clubs |
|---|---|---|---|---|---|
| 12 | Bellhorn, Mark | B/R | 6-1/205 | 30 | Pawtucket, Boston |
| 13 | Mientkiewicz, D. | L/R | 6-2/206 | 30 | Minnesota, Boston |
| 15 | Millar, Kevin | R/R | 6-0/210 | 33 | Boston |
| 11 | Mueller, Bill | B/R | 5-10/180 | 34 | Pawtucket, Boston |
| 34 | Ortiz, David | L/L | 6-4/230 | 29 | Boston |
| | Ramirez, Hanley | S/R | 6-3/195 | 21 | Boston, Sarasota, Portland |
| | Renteria, Edgar | R/R | 6-1/200 | 29 | St. Louis |
| | Vazquez, Ramon | L/R | 5-11/170 | 28 | Portland, San Diego |
| 20 | Youkilis, Kevin | R/R | 6-1/220 | 26 | Pawtucket, Lowell, Boston |

| No. | OUTFIELDERS | B/T | Ht./Wt. | Age* | 2004 Clubs |
|---|---|---|---|---|---|
| 18 | Damon, Johnny | L/L | 6-2/190 | 31 | Boston |
| 37 | Hyzdu, Adam | R/R | 6-2/220 | 33 | Pawtucket, Boston |
| 7 | Nixon, Trot | L/L | 6-2/211 | 30 | Sarasota, Pawtucket, Boston |
| | Payton, Jay | R/R | 5-10/185 | 32 | San Diego |
| 24 | Ramirez, Manny | R/R | 6-0/213 | 32 | Boston |
| | Stern, Adam | L/R | 5-11/190 | 25 | Greenville |

*Age as of April 1, 2005.

## BALLPARK INFORMATION

**Ballpark (capacity, surface)**
Fenway Park (36,298; grass)

**Address**
4 Yawkey Way
Boston, MA 02215-3496

**Official website**
www.redsox.com

**Business phone**
617-226-6000

**Ticket information**
617-482-4769

**Field dimensions (from home plate)**
To left field at foul line, 301 feet
To center field triangle, 420 feet
To right field at foul line, 302 feet

**First game played**
April 20, 1912
(Red Sox 7, New York Highlanders 6)

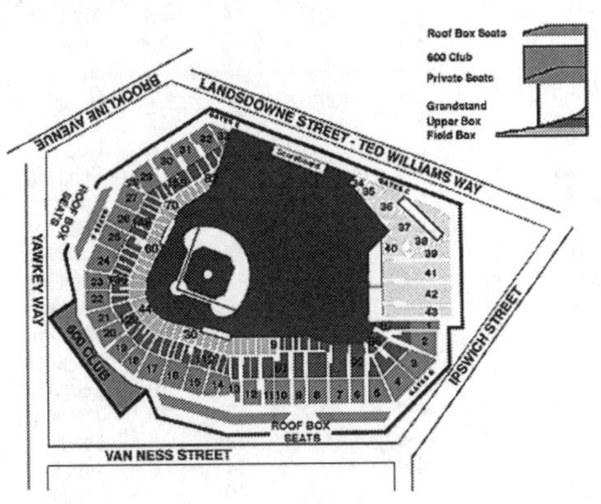

# 2004 REVIEW

## DAY BY DAY

| Date | Opp. | Res. | Score | (inn.*) | Hits | Opp. hits | Winning pitcher | Losing pitcher | Save | Record | Pos. | GB |
|---|---|---|---|---|---|---|---|---|---|---|---|---|
| 4-4 | At Bal. | L | 2-7 | | 11 | 11 | Ponson | Martinez | Ryan | 0-1 | 5th | 1.0 |
| 4-6 | At Bal. | W | 4-1 | | 5 | 6 | Schilling | DuBose | Foulke | 1-1 | T2nd | 0.5 |
| 4-7 | At Bal. | W | 10-3 | | 14 | 10 | Lowe | Ainsworth | | 2-1 | 1st | +0.5 |
| 4-8 | At Bal. | L | 2-3 | (13) | 6 | 7 | Lopez | Jones | | 2-2 | T2nd | 0.5 |
| 4-9 | Tor. | L | 5-10 | | 6 | 14 | Speier | Timlin | | 2-3 | T3rd | 1.0 |
| 4-10 | Tor. | W | 4-1 | | 9 | 5 | Martinez | Halladay | Foulke | 3-3 | T1st | ... |
| 4-11 | Tor. | W | 6-4 | (12) | 10 | 8 | Malaska | Lopez | | 4-3 | T1st | ... |
| 4-15 | Bal. | L | 7-12 | (11) | 11 | 14 | Groom | Arroyo | | 4-4 | T2nd | 0.5 |
| 4-16 | N.Y. | W | 6-2 | | 9 | 4 | Wakefield | Vazquez | | 5-4 | T1st | ... |
| 4-17 | N.Y. | W | 5-2 | | 10 | 8 | Schilling | Mussina | | 6-4 | T1st | ... |
| 4-18 | N.Y. | L | 3-7 | | 9 | 10 | Quantrill | Lowe | | 6-5 | 2nd | 1.0 |
| 4-19 | N.Y. | W | 5-4 | | 13 | 10 | Timlin | Gordon | Foulke | 7-5 | 2nd | 0.5 |
| 4-20 | At Tor. | W | 4-2 | | 11 | 5 | Martinez | Halladay | Foulke | 8-5 | 2nd | 0.5 |
| 4-21 | At Tor. | W | 4-2 | | 8 | 6 | Wakefield | Lilly | Foulke | 9-5 | 1st | +0.5 |
| 4-22 | At Tor. | L | 3-7 | | 10 | 14 | Adams | Schilling | | 9-6 | 2nd | 0.5 |
| 4-23 | At N.Y. | W | 11-2 | | 12 | 7 | Lowe | Contreras | | 10-6 | 2nd | 0.5 |
| 4-24 | At N.Y. | W | 3-2 | (12) | 6 | 4 | Foulke | Quantrill | Timlin | 11-6 | 1st | +0.5 |
| 4-25 | At N.Y. | W | 2-0 | | 4 | 4 | Martinez | Vazquez | Williamson | 12-6 | 1st | +1.5 |
| 4-28 | T.B. | W | 6-0 | | 12 | 5 | Schilling | Abbott | | 13-6 | 1st | +2.0 |
| 4-29# | T.B. | W | 4-0 | | 8 | 3 | Kim | Zambrano | | 14-6 | | |
| 4-29$ | T.B. | W | 7-3 | | 12 | 9 | Lowe | Moss | | 15-6 | 1st | +2.5 |
| 5-1! | At Tex. | L | 3-4 | | 9 | 6 | Ramirez | Malaska | Cordero | 15-7 | | |
| 5-1& | At Tex. | L | 5-8 | | 11 | 14 | Benoit | Martinez | Cordero | 15-8 | 1st | +2.5 |
| 5-2 | At Tex. | L | 1-4 | | 4 | 7 | Dickey | Wakefield | Cordero | 15-9 | 1st | +1.5 |
| 5-3 | At Cle. | L | 1-2 | | 8 | 7 | Westbrook | Schilling | Betancourt | 15-10 | 1st | +1.0 |
| 5-4 | At Cle. | L | 6-7 | | 11 | 12 | Davis | Lowe | Betancourt | 15-11 | T1st | ... |
| 5-5 | At Cle. | W | 9-5 | | 11 | 10 | Arroyo | D'Amico | | 16-11 | T1st | ... |
| 5-6 | At Cle. | W | 5-2 | | 11 | 5 | Martinez | Sabathia | Foulke | 17-11 | 1st | +1.0 |
| 5-7 | K.C. | W | 7-6 | | 13 | 9 | Timlin | MacDougal | | 18-11 | 1st | +2.0 |
| 5-8 | K.C. | W | 9-1 | | 11 | 5 | Schilling | Gobble | | 19-11 | 1st | +2.0 |
| 5-9 | K.C. | L | 4-8 | | 9 | 9 | May | Lowe | | 19-12 | 1st | +1.0 |
| 5-10 | Cle. | L | 6-10 | | 11 | 13 | Durbin | Kim | | 19-13 | 1st | +0.5 |
| 5-11 | Cle. | W | 5-3 | | 10 | 6 | Embree | Jimenez | Foulke | 20-13 | 1st | +0.5 |
| 5-12 | Cle. | L | 4-6 | | 9 | 9 | Lee | Wakefield | | 20-14 | 1st | +0.5 |
| 5-13 | At Tor. | L | 6-12 | | 13 | 17 | Batista | Schilling | | 20-15 | 2nd | 0.5 |
| 5-14 | At Tor. | W | 9-3 | | 10 | 4 | Embree | Ligtenberg | | 21-15 | 2nd | 0.5 |
| 5-15 | At Tor. | W | 4-0 | | 6 | 4 | Arroyo | Hentgen | | 22-15 | 1st | +0.5 |
| 5-16 | At Tor. | L | 1-3 | | 8 | 8 | Halladay | Martinez | Adams | 22-16 | 2nd | 0.5 |
| 5-18 | At T.B. | W | 7-3 | | 11 | 4 | Wakefield | Hendrickson | | 23-16 | 1st | +0.5 |
| 5-19 | At T.B. | W | 4-1 | | 6 | 6 | Schilling | Bell | Foulke | 24-16 | 1st | +0.5 |
| 5-20 | At T.B. | L | 6-9 | | 6 | 16 | Sosa | Lowe | Baez | 24-17 | 2nd | 0.5 |
| 5-21 | Tor. | W | 11-5 | | 11 | 7 | Timlin | Nakamura | | 25-17 | 1st | +0.5 |
| 5-22 | Tor. | W | 5-2 | | 11 | 6 | Martinez | Ligtenberg | Foulke | 26-17 | 1st | +1.5 |
| 5-23 | Tor. | W | 7-2 | | 7 | 7 | Wakefield | Batista | | 27-17 | 1st | +1.5 |
| 5-25 | Oak. | W | 12-2 | | 19 | 10 | Schilling | Hudson | | 28-17 | 1st | +1.5 |
| 5-26 | Oak. | W | 9-6 | | 9 | 14 | Lowe | Redman | Foulke | 29-17 | 1st | +1.5 |
| 5-27 | Oak. | L | 2-15 | | 6 | 17 | Mulder | Arroyo | | 29-18 | 1st | +0.5 |
| 5-28 | Sea. | W | 8-4 | | 9 | 11 | Martinez | Pineiro | | 30-18 | 1st | +0.5 |
| 5-29 | Sea. | L | 4-5 | | 10 | 11 | Garcia | Wakefield | Guardado | 30-19 | 2nd | 0.5 |
| 5-30 | Sea. | W | 9-7 | (12) | 14 | 8 | Martinez | Putz | | 31-19 | 1st | +0.5 |
| 5-31 | Bal. | L | 4-13 | | 9 | 16 | Lopez | Lowe | | 31-20 | 2nd | ... |
| 6-1 | At Ana. | L | 6-7 | | 13 | 9 | Gregg | Arroyo | Percival | 31-21 | 2nd | 1.0 |
| 6-2 | At Ana. | L | 7-10 | | 10 | 17 | Ortiz | Timlin | Rodriguez | 31-22 | 2nd | 2.0 |
| 6-4 | At K.C. | L | 2-5 | | 6 | 9 | Gobble | Wakefield | Affeldt | 31-23 | 2nd | 3.5 |
| 6-5 | At K.C. | W | 8-4 | | 13 | 7 | Schilling | May | | 32-23 | 2nd | 2.5 |
| 6-6 | At K.C. | W | 5-3 | | 7 | 4 | Lowe | Grimsley | Foulke | 33-23 | 2nd | 2.5 |
| 6-8 | S.D. | W | 1-0 | | 9 | 2 | Martinez | Osuna | Foulke | 34-23 | 2nd | 2.5 |
| 6-9 | S.D. | L | 1-8 | | 7 | 12 | Lawrence | Arroyo | | 34-24 | 2nd | 3.5 |
| 6-10 | S.D. | W | 9-3 | | 13 | 11 | Schilling | Valdez | | 35-24 | 2nd | 3.5 |
| 6-11 | L.A. | W | 2-1 | | 7 | 7 | Foulke | Martin | | 36-24 | 2nd | 2.5 |
| 6-12 | L.A. | L | 5-14 | | 5 | 15 | Weaver | Wakefield | | 36-25 | 2nd | 3.5 |
| 6-13 | L.A. | W | 4-1 | | 6 | 8 | Martinez | Nomo | Foulke | 37-25 | 2nd | 3.5 |
| 6-15 | At Col. | L | 3-6 | | 9 | 10 | Kennedy | Arroyo | Chacon | 37-26 | 2nd | 4.5 |
| 6-16 | At Col. | L | 6-7 | | 13 | 10 | Jennings | Schilling | Chacon | 37-27 | 2nd | 5.5 |
| 6-17 | At Col. | W | 11-0 | | 14 | 6 | Lowe | Cook | | 38-27 | 2nd | 4.5 |
| 6-18 | At S.F | W | 14-9 | | 14 | 8 | Timlin | Williams | | 39-27 | 2nd | 3.5 |
| 6-19 | At S.F | L | 4-6 | | 10 | 8 | Herges | Embree | | 39-28 | 2nd | 4.5 |

| Date | Opp. | Res. | Score | (inn.*) | Hits | Opp. hits | Winning pitcher | Losing pitcher | Save | Record | Pos. | GB |
|---|---|---|---|---|---|---|---|---|---|---|---|---|
| 6-20 | At S.F | L | 0-4 | | 1 | 6 | Schmidt | Arroyo | | 39-29 | 2nd | 4.5 |
| 6-22 | Min. | W | 9-2 | | 13 | 7 | Schilling | Lohse | | 40-29 | 2nd | 4.5 |
| 6-23 | Min. | L | 2-4 | | 8 | 9 | Silva | Lowe | Nathan | 40-30 | 2nd | 4.5 |
| 6-24 | Min. | L | 3-4 | (10) | 10 | 8 | Balfour | Foulke | Nathan | 40-31 | 2nd | 5.5 |
| 6-25 | Phi. | W | 12-1 | (8) | 13 | 2 | Martinez | Abbott | | 41-31 | 2nd | 5.0 |
| 6-26 | Phi. | L | 2-9 | | 14 | 13 | Madson | Arroyo | | 41-32 | 2nd | 5.0 |
| 6-27 | Phi. | W | 12-3 | | 12 | 12 | Schilling | Myers | | 42-32 | 2nd | 5.5 |
| 6-29 | At N.Y. | L | 3-11 | | 9 | 12 | Vazquez | Lowe | | 42-33 | 2nd | 6.5 |
| 6-30 | At N.Y. | L | 2-4 | | 8 | 6 | Gordon | Timlin | Rivera | 42-34 | 2nd | 7.5 |
| 7-1 | At N.Y. | L | 4-5 | (13) | 10 | 11 | Sturtze | Leskanic | | 42-35 | 2nd | 8.5 |
| 7-2 | At Atl. | L | 3-6 | (12) | 10 | 11 | Cruz | Martinez | | 42-36 | 2nd | 8.5 |
| 7-3 | At Atl. | W | 6-1 | | 11 | 6 | Schilling | Thomson | | 43-36 | 2nd | 7.5 |
| 7-4 | At Atl. | L | 4-10 | | 11 | 11 | Hampton | Lowe | | 43-37 | 2nd | 7.5 |
| 7-6 | Oak. | W | 11-0 | | 17 | 4 | Wakefield | Zito | | 44-37 | 2nd | 7.0 |
| 7-7 | Oak. | W | 11-3 | | 15 | 6 | Martinez | Redman | | 45-37 | 2nd | 6.0 |
| 7-8 | Oak. | W | 8-7 | (10) | 14 | 17 | Leskanic | Lehr | | 46-37 | 2nd | 6.0 |
| 7-9 | Tex. | W | 7-0 | | 13 | 3 | Arroyo | Benoit | | 47-37 | 2nd | 6.0 |
| 7-10 | Tex. | W | 14-6 | | 21 | 5 | Lowe | Rogers | | 48-37 | 2nd | 6.0 |
| 7-11 | Tex. | L | 5-6 | | 7 | 17 | Shouse | Foulke | Cordero | 48-38 | 2nd | 7.0 |
| 7-15 | At Ana. | L | 1-8 | | 4 | 16 | Washburn | Lowe | | 48-39 | 2nd | 8.0 |
| 7-16 | At Ana. | W | 4-2 | | 10 | 7 | Martinez | Escobar | Foulke | 49-39 | 2nd | 7.0 |
| 7-17 | At Ana. | L | 3-8 | | 5 | 13 | Colon | Wakefield | | 49-40 | 2nd | 8.0 |
| 7-18 | At Ana. | W | 6-2 | | 11 | 5 | Schilling | Lackey | | 50-40 | 2nd | 7.0 |
| 7-19 | At Sea. | L | 4-8 | (11) | 9 | 10 | Myers | Leskanic | | 50-41 | 2nd | 7.0 |
| 7-20 | At Sea. | W | 9-7 | | 10 | 18 | Lowe | Pineiro | Foulke | 51-41 | 2nd | 7.0 |
| 7-21 | Bal. | L | 5-10 | | 8 | 15 | Bedard | Martinez | | 51-42 | 2nd | 8.0 |
| 7-22# | Bal. | L | 3-8 | | 11 | 11 | Lopez | Alvarez | | 51-43 | | |
| 7-22$ | Bal. | W | 4-0 | | 7 | 10 | Wakefield | Borkowski | | 52-43 | 2nd | 8.5 |
| 7-23 | N.Y. | L | 7-8 | | 11 | 14 | Gordon | Foulke | Rivera | 52-44 | 2nd | 9.5 |
| 7-24 | N.Y. | W | 11-10 | | 15 | 12 | Mendoza | Rivera | | 53-44 | 2nd | 8.5 |
| 7-25 | N.Y. | W | 9-6 | | 13 | 9 | Lowe | Contreras | Foulke | 54-44 | 2nd | 7.5 |
| 7-26 | At Bal. | W | 12-5 | | 13 | 9 | Martinez | Bedard | | 55-44 | 2nd | 7.5 |
| 7-28 | At Bal. | L | 1-4 | | 4 | 7 | Borkowski | Schilling | | 55-45 | 2nd | 8.0 |
| 7-30 | At Min. | W | 8-2 | | 16 | 9 | Arroyo | Lohse | | 56-45 | 2nd | 7.5 |
| 7-31 | At Min. | L | 4-5 | | 10 | 9 | Rincon | Embree | Nathan | 56-46 | 2nd | 8.5 |
| 8-1 | At Min. | L | 3-4 | | 2 | 9 | Santana | Timlin | Nathan | 56-47 | 2nd | 9.5 |
| 8-2 | At T.B. | W | 6-3 | | 8 | 4 | Wakefield | Hendrickson | Foulke | 57-47 | 2nd | 9.0 |
| 8-3 | At T.B. | W | 5-2 | | 9 | 6 | Schilling | Bell | | 58-47 | 2nd | 8.0 |
| 8-4 | At T.B. | L | 4-5 | | 8 | 6 | Harper | Arroyo | Baez | 58-48 | 2nd | 9.0 |
| 8-6 | At Det. | L | 3-4 | | 10 | 10 | Novoa | Lowe | Urbina | 58-49 | 2nd | 10.5 |
| 8-7 | At Det. | W | 7-4 | | 8 | 7 | Martinez | Bonderman | | 59-49 | 2nd | 10.5 |
| 8-8 | At Det. | W | 11-9 | | 14 | 11 | Wakefield | Robertson | Foulke | 60-49 | 2nd | 10.5 |
| 8-9 | T.B. | L | 3-8 | | 11 | 13 | Halama | Schilling | | 60-50 | 2nd | 10.5 |
| 8-10 | T.B. | W | 8-4 | | 9 | 9 | Arroyo | Sosa | | 61-50 | 2nd | 9.5 |
| 8-11 | T.B. | W | 14-4 | | 15 | 11 | Lowe | Brazelton | | 62-50 | 2nd | 9.5 |
| 8-12 | T.B. | W | 6-0 | | 15 | 6 | Martinez | Hendrickson | | 63-50 | 2nd | 9.5 |
| 8-13 | Chi. | L | 7-8 | | 9 | 11 | Contreras | Wakefield | Takatsu | 63-51 | 2nd | 10.5 |
| 8-14 | Chi. | W | 4-3 | | 9 | 5 | Schilling | Adkins | Foulke | 64-51 | 2nd | 10.5 |
| 8-15 | Chi. | L | 4-5 | | 12 | 10 | Buehrle | Arroyo | Takatsu | 64-52 | 2nd | 10.5 |
| 8-16 | Tor. | W | 8-4 | | 10 | 6 | Lowe | Miller | Foulke | 65-52 | 2nd | 10.0 |
| 8-17 | Tor. | W | 5-4 | | 7 | 8 | Foulke | Frederick | | 66-52 | 2nd | 9.0 |
| 8-18 | Tor. | W | 6-4 | | 8 | 9 | Wakefield | Batista | | 67-52 | 2nd | 8.0 |
| 8-20 | At Chi. | W | 10-1 | | 13 | 5 | Schilling | Buehrle | | 68-52 | 2nd | 7.5 |
| 8-21 | At Chi. | W | 10-7 | | 15 | 11 | Arroyo | Stewart | Foulke | 69-52 | 2nd | 6.5 |
| 8-22 | At Chi. | W | 6-5 | | 11 | 8 | Leskanic | Marte | Foulke | 70-52 | 2nd | 5.5 |
| 8-23 | At Tor. | L | 0-3 | | 3 | 4 | Lilly | Martinez | | 70-53 | 2nd | 6.5 |
| 8-24 | At Tor. | W | 5-4 | | 8 | 12 | Wakefield | Batista | Foulke | 71-53 | 2nd | 6.5 |
| 8-25 | At Tor. | W | 11-5 | | 17 | 12 | Schilling | Towers | | 72-53 | 2nd | 5.5 |
| 8-26 | Det. | W | 4-1 | | 12 | 6 | Arroyo | Johnson | Foulke | 73-53 | 2nd | 5.5 |
| 8-27 | Det. | W | 5-3 | | 11 | 9 | Lowe | Maroth | Leskanic | 74-53 | 2nd | 5.5 |
| 8-28 | Det. | W | 5-1 | | 9 | 4 | Martinez | Bonderman | | 75-53 | 2nd | 5.5 |
| 8-29 | Det. | W | 6-1 | | 10 | 3 | Wakefield | Ledezma | | 76-53 | 2nd | 4.5 |
| 8-31 | Ana. | W | 10-7 | | 16 | 15 | Schilling | Lackey | Foulke | 77-53 | 2nd | 3.5 |
| 9-1 | Ana. | W | 12-7 | | 16 | 11 | Adams | Sele | | 78-53 | 2nd | 3.5 |
| 9-2 | Ana. | W | 4-3 | | 12 | 8 | Lowe | Colon | Foulke | 79-53 | 2nd | 3.5 |
| 9-3 | Tex. | W | 2-0 | | 5 | 6 | Martinez | Wasdin | Foulke | 80-53 | 2nd | 2.5 |
| 9-4 | Tex. | L | 6-8 | | 5 | 10 | Young | Wakefield | Cordero | 80-54 | 2nd | 2.5 |
| 9-5 | Tex. | W | 6-5 | | 11 | 8 | Schilling | Drese | | 81-54 | 2nd | 2.5 |
| 9-6 | At Oak. | W | 8-3 | | 13 | 7 | Arroyo | Zito | | 82-54 | 2nd | 2.5 |
| 9-7 | At Oak. | W | 7-1 | | 11 | 5 | Lowe | Redman | | 83-54 | 2nd | 2.5 |

| Date | Opp. | Res. | Score | (inn.*) | Hits | Opp. hits | Winning pitcher | Losing pitcher | Save | Record | Pos. | GB |
|---|---|---|---|---|---|---|---|---|---|---|---|---|
| 9-8 | At Oak. | W | 8-3 | | 8 | 7 | Martinez | Hudson | Foulke | 84-54 | 2nd | 2.0 |
| 9-9 | At Sea. | L | 1-7 | | 8 | 9 | Madritsch | Wakefield | | 84-55 | 2nd | 3.5 |
| 9-10 | At Sea. | W | 13-2 | | 11 | 6 | Schilling | Franklin | | 85-55 | 2nd | 2.5 |
| 9-11 | At Sea. | W | 9-0 | | 7 | 5 | Arroyo | Moyer | | 86-55 | 2nd | 2.5 |
| 9-12 | At Sea. | L | 0-2 | | 5 | 6 | Meche | Lowe | | 86-56 | 2nd | 3.5 |
| 9-14 | T.B. | L | 2-5 | | 5 | 10 | Kazmir | Martinez | Baez | 86-57 | 2nd | 4.0 |
| 9-15 | T.B. | W | 8-6 | | 12 | 8 | Myers | Nunez | Foulke | 87-57 | 2nd | 4.0 |
| 9-16 | T.B. | W | 11-4 | | 13 | 10 | Schilling | Hendrickson | | 88-57 | 2nd | 3.5 |
| 9-17 | At N.Y. | W | 3-2 | | 6 | 4 | Timlin | Rivera | Foulke | 89-57 | 2nd | 2.5 |
| 9-18 | At N.Y. | L | 4-14 | | 6 | 15 | Lieber | Lowe | | 89-58 | 2nd | 3.5 |
| 9-19 | At N.Y. | L | 1-11 | | 8 | 13 | Mussina | Martinez | | 89-59 | 2nd | 4.5 |
| 9-20 | Bal. | L | 6-9 | | 10 | 8 | Grimsley | Wakefield | Julio | 89-60 | 2nd | 4.5 |
| 9-21 | Bal. | W | 3-2 | | 7 | 5 | Foulke | Ryan | | 90-60 | 2nd | 4.5 |
| 9-22 | Bal. | W | 7-6 | (12) | 13 | 12 | Leskanic | Bauer | | 91-60 | 2nd | 3.5 |
| 9-23 | Bal. | L | 7-9 | | 11 | 15 | Williams | Mendoza | | 91-61 | 2nd | 4.5 |
| 9-24 | N.Y. | L | 4-6 | | 7 | 11 | Gordon | Martinez | Rivera | 91-62 | 2nd | 5.5 |
| 9-25 | N.Y. | W | 12-5 | | 13 | 5 | Foulke | Quantrill | | 92-62 | 2nd | 4.5 |
| 9-26 | N.Y. | W | 11-4 | | 13 | 3 | Schilling | Brown | | 93-62 | 2nd | 3.5 |
| 9-27 | At T.B. | W | 7-3 | | 12 | 7 | Arroyo | Sosa | | 94-62 | 2nd | 3.0 |
| 9-28 | At T.B. | W | 10-8 | (11) | 13 | 12 | Mendoza | Baez | Foulke | 95-62 | 2nd | 2.5 |
| 9-29 | At T.B. | L | 4-9 | | 7 | 14 | Waechter | Martinez | Miller | 95-63 | 2nd | 4.0 |
| 10-1 | At Bal. | W | 8-3 | | 11 | 9 | Wakefield | Lopez | | 96-63 | 2nd | 3.5 |
| 10-2# | At Bal. | W | 7-5 | | 8 | 10 | Adams | Cabrera | Foulke | 97-63 | | |
| 10-2$ | At Bal. | W | 7-5 | | 11 | 9 | Kim | Grimsley | Leskanic | 98-63 | 2nd | 2.0 |
| 10-3 | At Bal. | L | 2-3 | | 7 | 7 | Chen | Williamson | Ryan | 98-64 | 2nd | 3.0 |

Monthly records: April (15-6), May (16-14), June (11-14), July (14-12), August (21-7), September (18-10), October (3-1).
*Innings, if other than nine. ! First game of a doubleheader. & Second game of a doubleheader. # Day separate admission. $ Night separate admission.

## RECORDS

**2004 regular-season record:** 98-64
**Position:** 2nd in A.L. East
**Home:** 55-26 **Road:** 43-38
**A.L. East:** 48-28 **A.L. Central:** 19-13
**A.L. West:** 22-14 **N.L.** 9-9
**Vs. LH starters:** 32-24
**Vs. RH starters:** 66-40
**Grass:** 85-55 **Artificial:** 13-9
**Day:** 24-21 **Night:** 74-43
**1-Run:** 16-18 **X-inn.:** 6-6
**Doubleheaders:** 0-1-0
**Team record past five years:** 453-356 (.560, ranks 4th in league in that span)

## TEAM LEADERS

**Batting average:** Manny Ramirez (.308).
**At-bats:** Johnny Damon (621).
**Runs:** Johnny Damon (123).
**Hits:** Johnny Damon (189).
**Total Bases:** David Ortiz (351).
**Doubles:** David Ortiz (47).
**Triples:** Johnny Damon (6).
**Home runs:** Manny Ramirez (43).
**Runs batted in:** David Ortiz (139).
**Stolen bases:** Johnny Damon (19).
**Slugging percentage:** Manny Ramirez (.613).
**On-base percentage:** Manny Ramirez (.397).
**Wins:** Curt Schilling (21).
**Earned-run average:** Curt Schilling (3.26).
**Complete games:** Curt Schilling (3).
**Shutouts:** Pedro Martinez (1).
**Saves:** Keith Foulke (32).
**Innings pitched:** Curt Schilling (226.2).
**Strikeouts:** Pedro Martinez (227).

## GAMES BY POSITION

**Catcher:** Jason Varitek 130, Doug Mirabelli 53, Sandy Martinez 3, Andy Dominique 1.
**First base:** Kevin Millar 69, Dave McCarty 67, Doug Mientkiewicz 47, David Ortiz 34, Brian Daubach 14, Andy Dominique 5.
**Second base:** Mark Bellhorn 124, Pokey Reese 30, Ricky Gutierrez 14, Bill Mueller 14, Cesar Crespo 11, Doug Mientkiewicz 1.
**Third base:** Bill Mueller 96, Kevin Youkilis 65, Mark Bellhorn 16, Earl Snyder 1.
**Shortstop:** Pokey Reese 71, Orlando Cabrera 57, Nomar Garciaparra 37, Cesar Crespo 27, Ricky Gutierrez 6, Mark Bellhorn 1.
**Outfield:** Johnny Damon 148, Manny Ramirez 132, Gabe Kapler 127, Kevin Millar 74, Trot Nixon 40, Dave Roberts 38, Cesar Crespo 19, Dave McCarty 17, Adam Hyzdu 14, Brian Daubach 7.
**Designated hitter:** David Ortiz 115, Manny Ramirez 19, Ellis Burks 9, Kevin Millar 8, Doug Mirabelli 4, Dave McCarty 3, Trot Nixon 3, Adam Hyzdu 2, Gabe Kapler 2, Kevin Youkilis 2, Mark Bellhorn 1, Johnny Damon1, Nomar Garciaparra 1, Dave Roberts 1, Jason Varitek 1.

## TOP DRAFT CHOICES

2. **Dustin Pedroia,** SS, Arizona State.
3. **Andrew Dobies,** LHP, Virginia.
4. **Tommy Hottovy,** LHP, Wichita State.
5. **Ryan Schroyer,** RHP, San Diego State.
6. **Cla Meredith,** RHP, Virginia Commonwealth.
7. **Pat Perry,** C, Northern Colorado.
8. **Kyle Bono,** RHP, Central Florida.
9. **Matt Vanderbosch,** OF, Oral Roberts.
10. **Steve Pearce,** 1B, South Carolina.

# CHICAGO WHITE SOX
## AMERICAN LEAGUE CENTRAL DIVISION

## 2005 SEASON

### White Sox Schedule
Home games shaded.
All-Star Game July 12 at Detroit. Schedule subject to change.

**April**

| SUN | MON | TUE | WED | THU | FRI | SAT |
|---|---|---|---|---|---|---|
| 3 | 4 CLE | 5 | 6 CLE | 7 CLE | 8 MIN | 9 MIN |
| 10 MIN | 11 CLE | 12 | 13 CLE | 14 CLE | 15 SEA | 16 SEA |
| 17 SEA | 18 MIN | 19 MIN | 20 DET | 21 DET | 22 KC | 23 KC |
| 24 KC | 25 OAK | 26 OAK | 27 OAK | 28 | 29 DET | 30 DET |

**May**

| SUN | MON | TUE | WED | THU | FRI | SAT |
|---|---|---|---|---|---|---|
| 1 DET | 2 | 3 KC | 4 KC | 5 KC | 6 TOR | 7 TOR |
| 8 TOR | 9 TB | 10 TB | 11 TB | 12 BAL | 13 BAL | 14 BAL |
| 15 BAL | 16 TEX | 17 TEX | 18 TEX | 19 | 20 CHC | 21 CHC |
| 22 CHC | 23 ANA | 24 ANA | 25 ANA | 26 ANA | 27 TEX | 28 TEX |
| 29 TEX | 30 ANA | 31 ANA | | | | |

**June**

| SUN | MON | TUE | WED | THU | FRI | SAT |
|---|---|---|---|---|---|---|
| | | | 1 ANA | 2 | 3 CLE | 4 CLE |
| 5 CLE | 6 COL | 7 COL | 8 COL | 9 | 10 SD | 11 SD |
| 12 SD | 13 ARI | 14 ARI | 15 ARI | 16 | 17 LA | 18 LA |
| 19 LA | 20 KC | 21 KC | 22 KC | 23 | 24 CHC | 25 CHC |
| 26 CHC | 27 | 28 DET | 29 DET | 30 DET | | |

**July**

| SUN | MON | TUE | WED | THU | FRI | SAT |
|---|---|---|---|---|---|---|
| | | | | | 1 OAK | 2 OAK |
| 3 OAK | 4 TB | 5 TB | 6 TB | 7 | 8 OAK | 9 OAK |
| 10 OAK | 11 | 12 All-Star | 13 | 14 CLE | 15 CLE | 16 CLE |
| 17 CLE | 18 DET | 19 DET | 20 DET | 21 BOS | 22 BOS | 23 BOS |
| 24 BOS | 25 KC | 26 KC | 27 KC | 28 | 29 BAL | 30 BAL |
| 31 BAL | | | | | | |

**August**

| SUN | MON | TUE | WED | THU | FRI | SAT |
|---|---|---|---|---|---|---|
| | 1 BAL | 2 TOR | 3 TOR | 4 TOR | 5 SEA | 6 SEA |
| 7 SEA | 8 NYY | 9 NYY | 10 NYY | 11 | 12 BOS | 13 BOS |
| 14 BOS | 15 MIN | 16 MIN | 17 MIN | 18 | 19 NYY | 20 NYY |
| 21 NYY | 22 | 23 MIN | 24 MIN | 25 MIN | 26 SEA | 27 SEA |
| 28 SEA | 29 TEX | 30 TEX | 31 TEX | | | |

**September**

| SUN | MON | TUE | WED | THU | FRI | SAT |
|---|---|---|---|---|---|---|
| | | | | 1 DET | 2 DET | 3 DET |
| 4 DET | 5 | 6 KC | 7 KC | 8 KC | 9 ANA | 10 ANA |
| 11 ANA | 12 | 13 KC | 14 KC | 15 KC | 16 MIN | 17 MIN |
| 18 MIN | 19 CLE | 20 CLE | 21 CLE | 22 MIN | 23 MIN | 24 MIN |
| 25 MIN | 26 DET | 27 DET | 28 DET | 29 DET | 30 CLE | |

**October**

| SUN | MON | TUE | WED | THU | FRI | SAT |
|---|---|---|---|---|---|---|
| | | | | | | 1 CLE |
| 2 CLE | 3 | 4 | 5 | 6 | 7 | 8 |

Home games shaded. All-Star Game July 12 at Detroit. Schedule subject to change.

### CLUB DIRECTORY

**Chairman**
Jerry Reinsdorf
**Vice chairman**
Eddie Einhorn
**Executive vice president**
Howard Pizer
**Senior vice president, general manager**
Ken Williams
**Vice president, free agent and major league scouting**
Larry Monroe
**Executive advisor to Ken Williams**
Roland Hemond
**Assistant general manager**
Rick Hahn
**Senior director of scouting**
Duane Shaffer
**Director of scouting, special assignments**
Doug Laumann
**Director of player development**
Dave Wilder
**Director of community relations**
Christine O'Reilly
**Director of public relations**
Scott Reifert

### MINOR LEAGUE AFFILIATES

| Class | Team | League | Manager |
|---|---|---|---|
| AAA | Charlotte | International | Nick Leyva |
| AA | Birmingham | Southern | Razor Shines |
| Advanced A | Winston-Salem | Carolina | Chris Cron |
| A | Kannapolis | South Atlantic | Nick Capra |
| Advanced Rookie | Bristol | Appalachian | Jerry Hairston |
| Advanced Rookie | Great Falls | Pioneer | John Orton |

### BROADCAST INFORMATION

**Radio:** ESPN-AM (1000).
**TV:** WGN-TV (Channel 9).
**Cable TV:** Comcast SportsNet.

### SPRING TRAINING

**Ballpark (city):** Tucson Electric Park (Tucson, Ariz.).
**Ticket information:** 520-434-1111.

**For more on the White Sox, go to msn.foxsports.com/mlb/teams.**

Thomas

## SPRING TRAINING ROSTER

**Manager**—Ozzie Guillen (13).
**Coaches**—Harold Baines (3), Don Cooper (21), Joey Cora (28), Art Kusnyer (53), Tim Raines, Greg Walker (29).

| No. | PITCHERS | B/T | Ht./Wt. | Age* | 2004 Clubs |
|---|---|---|---|---|---|
| 37 | Adkins, Jon | L/R | 5-11/210 | 27 | Chicago A.L. |
| 57 | Bajenaru, Jeff | R/R | 6-1/190 | 27 | Birmingham, Charlotte, Chicago A.L. |
| 56 | Buehrle, Mark | L/L | 6-2/220 | 26 | Chicago A.L. |
| 52 | Contreras, Jose | R/R | 6-4/224 | 33 | Columbus, New York A.L., Chicago A.L. |
| 46 | Cotts, Neal | L/L | 6-2/200 | 25 | Chicago A.L. |
| 54 | Diaz, Felix | R/R | 6-1/180 | 24 | Charlotte, Chicago A.L. |
| 34 | Garcia, Freddy | R/R | 6-4/240 | 29 | Seattle, Chicago A.L. |
| 52 | Garland, Jon | R/R | 6-6/210 | 25 | Chicago A.L. |
| 41 | Grilli, Jason | R/R | 6-4/185 | 28 | Charlotte, Chicago A.L. |
| | Hermanson, D. | R/R | 6-2/200 | 32 | San Francisco |
| | Hernandez, O. | R/R | 6-2/220 | 35 | Tampa, Columbus, New York A.L. |
| | Honel, Kris | R/R | 6-5/190 | 22 | Bristol, Birmingham |
| | Jenks, Bobby | R/R | 6-3/270 | 24 | Arizona Angels, Ranco Cucamonga, Salt Lake |
| 43 | Marte, Damaso | L/L | 6-2/200 | 30 | Chicago A.L. |
| 49 | Munoz, Arnie | L/L | 5-9/170 | 22 | Birmingham, Charlotte, Chicago A.L. |
| 18 | Politte, Cliff | R/R | 5-11/200 | 31 | Chicago A.L. |
| | Reynoso, Paulino | L/L | 6-3/190 | 24 | Winston-Salem |
| | Smith, Matt | R/R | 6-5/240 | 26 | Birmingham |
| 10 | Takatsu, Shingo | R/R | 6-0/180 | 36 | Chicago A.L. |
| | Tracey, Sean | L/R | 6-3/210 | 24 | Winston-Salem |
| | Vizcaino, Luis | R/R | 5-11/184 | 30 | Milwaukee |
| | Walker, Kevin | L/L | 6-4/190 | 28 | San Francisco, Fresno |
| **No.** | **CATCHERS** | **B/T** | **Ht./Wt.** | **Age*** | **2004 Clubs** |
| 27 | Burke, Jamie | R/R | 6-0/220 | 33 | Charlotte, Chicago A.L. |
| 31 | Davis, Ben | B/R | 6-4/225 | 28 | Seattle, Tacoma, Chicago A.L. |
| | Pierzynski, A.J. | L/R | 6-3/245 | 28 | San Francisco |
| **No.** | **INFIELDERS** | **B/T** | **Ht./Wt.** | **Age*** | **2004 Clubs** |
| 24 | Crede, Joe | R/R | 6-1/200 | 26 | Chicago A.L. |
| 26 | Gload, Ross | L/L | 6-0/185 | 28 | Chicago A.L. |
| 1 | Harris, Willie | L/R | 5-9/170 | 26 | Chicago A.L. |
| 14 | Konerko, Paul | R/R | 6-2/215 | 29 | Chicago A.L. |
| | Lopez, Pedro | R/R | 6-1/160 | 20 | Winston-Salem, Birmingham |
| | Rogowski, Casey | L/L | 6-3/230 | 23 | Winston-Salem |
| 4 | Uribe, Juan | R/R | 5-11/175 | 25 | Chicago A.L. |
| 35 | Thomas, Frank | R/R | 6-5/275 | 36 | Chicago A.L. |
| 39 | Valdez, Wilson | R/R | 5-11/160 | 26 | Albuquerque, Charlotte, Chicago A.L. |
| **No.** | **OUTFIELDERS** | **B/T** | **Ht./Wt.** | **Age*** | **2004 Clubs** |
| 25 | Borchard, Joe | B/R | 6-5/220 | 26 | Charlotte, Chicago A.L. |
| | Dye, Jermaine | R/R | 6-5/220 | 31 | Oakland |
| | Escobar, Alex | R/R | 6-1/190 | 26 | Cleveland, Buffalo |
| 8 | Everett, Carl | B/R | 6-0/215 | 33 | Brevard County, Montreal, Chicago A.L. |
| 7 | Perez, Timo | L/L | 5-9/167 | 29 | Chicago A.L. |
| | Podsednik, Scott | L/L | 6-0/188 | 29 | Milwaukee |
| 33 | Rowand, Aaron | R/R | 6-0/205 | 27 | Chicago A.L. |

*Age as of April 1, 2005.

## BALLPARK INFORMATION

**Ballpark (capacity, surface)**
U.S. Cellular Field (47098, grass)

**Address**
333 W. 35th St.
Chicago, IL 60616

**Official website**
www.whitesox.com

**Business phone**
312-674-1000

**Ticket information**
312-674-1000

**Field dimensions (from home plate)**
To left field at foul line, 330 feet
To center field, 400 feet
To right field at foul line, 335 feet

**First game played**
April 18, 1991 (Tigers 16, White Sox 0)

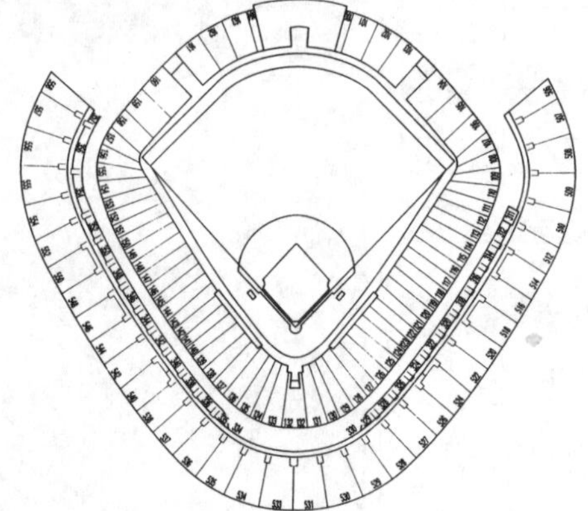

# 2004 REVIEW

## DAY BY DAY

| Date | Opp. | Res. | Score | (inn.*) | Hits | Opp. hits | Winning pitcher | Losing pitcher | Save | Record | Pos. | GB |
|---|---|---|---|---|---|---|---|---|---|---|---|---|
| 4-5 | At K.C. | L | 7-9 | | 12 | 13 | Carrasco | Marte | | 0-1 | T4th | 1.0 |
| 4-7 | At K.C. | W | 4-3 | | 8 | 8 | Loaiza | May | Koch | 1-1 | T3rd | 1.5 |
| 4-8 | At N.Y. | L | 1-3 | | 4 | 7 | Vazquez | Schoeneweis | Rivera | 1-2 | T4th | 2.5 |
| 4-9 | At N.Y. | W | 9-3 | | 10 | 6 | Garland | Contreras | | 2-2 | T2nd | 2.0 |
| 4-10 | At N.Y. | W | 7-3 | | 13 | 4 | Buehrle | DePaula | | 3-2 | T2nd | 1.0 |
| 4-11 | At N.Y. | L | 4-5 | | 9 | 7 | Mussina | Wright | Rivera | 3-3 | T3rd | 2.0 |
| 4-13 | K.C. | W | 12-5 | | 14 | 8 | Loaiza | May | | 4-3 | T2nd | 1.0 |
| 4-14 | K.C. | W | 10-9 | | 14 | 12 | Adkins | Leskanic | | 5-3 | 2nd | 1.0 |
| 4-15 | K.C. | W | 6-5 | (10) | 8 | 9 | Marte | Carrasco | | 6-3 | T1st | ... |
| 4-16 | At T.B. | L | 0-3 | | 4 | 6 | Abbott | Wright | Baez | 6-4 | T1st | ... |
| 4-17 | At T.B. | W | 4-1 | | 10 | 6 | Schoeneweis | Zambrano | Marte | 7-4 | T1st | ... |
| 4-18 | At T.B. | W | 5-0 | | 10 | 2 | Loaiza | Gonzalez | | 8-4 | T1st | ... |
| 4-20 | N.Y. | L | 8-11 | | 13 | 16 | Quantrill | Buehrle | Rivera | 8-5 | 2nd | 1.0 |
| 4-21 | N.Y. | L | 1-3 | | 5 | 5 | Vazquez | Garland | Rivera | 8-6 | 3rd | 1.0 |
| 4-22 | N.Y. | W | 4-3 | | 9 | 7 | Schoeneweis | Mussina | Marte | 9-6 | 2nd | 1.0 |
| 4-23 | T.B. | W | 3-2 | (10) | 5 | 9 | Koch | Baez | | 10-6 | 2nd | 1.0 |
| 4-24 | T.B. | L | 1-4 | | 6 | 9 | Waechter | Wright | Baez | 10-7 | 3rd | 1.0 |
| 4-25 | T.B. | W | 6-5 | | 9 | 13 | Adkins | Miller | | 11-7 | 2nd | 1.0 |
| 4-27 | Cle. | L | 7-11 | (10) | 16 | 16 | Betancourt | Adkins | | 11-8 | 2nd | 1.5 |
| 4-28 | Cle. | W | 9-8 | | 15 | 11 | Jackson | Betancourt | | 12-8 | 2nd | 1.5 |
| 4-29 | Tor. | W | 6-4 | | 11 | 8 | Loaiza | Nakamura | Koch | 13-8 | 2nd | 1.0 |
| 5-1# | Tor. | W | 4-3 | (10) | 7 | 8 | Takatsu | Speier | | 14-8 | | |
| 5-1$ | Tor. | L | 6-10 | | 11 | 18 | Lilly | Wright | | 14-9 | 2nd | 1.0 |
| 5-2 | Tor. | W | 3-2 | | 6 | 11 | Garland | Batista | Koch | 15-9 | T1st | ... |
| 5-3 | At Bal. | W | 5-4 | | 8 | 6 | Schoeneweis | DeJean | Koch | 16-9 | 1st | +0.5 |
| 5-4 | At Bal. | L | 3-10 | | 5 | 13 | Lopez | Loaiza | | 16-10 | 1st | +0.5 |
| 5-5 | At Bal. | W | 6-5 | | 11 | 12 | Takatsu | Ryan | Koch | 17-10 | 1st | +0.5 |
| 5-7 | At Tor. | L | 4-5 | | 9 | 8 | Adams | Politte | | 17-11 | 1st | +1.0 |
| 5-8 | At Tor. | L | 2-4 | | 8 | 7 | Frasor | Cotts | Adams | 17-12 | T1st | ... |
| 5-9 | At Tor. | L | 2-5 | | 8 | 9 | Miller | Loaiza | Ligtenberg | 17-13 | T1st | ... |
| 5-11 | Bal. | W | 15-0 | | 19 | 4 | Buehrle | Ponson | | 18-13 | T1st | ... |
| 5-13! | Bal. | L | 0-1 | | 3 | 6 | Cabrera | Garland | Julio | 18-14 | | |
| 5-13& | Bal. | W | 6-5 | | 7 | 8 | Jackson | Bedard | Koch | 19-14 | 2nd | 1.0 |
| 5-14 | Min. | L | 2-3 | | 5 | 11 | Rincon | Marte | Nathan | 19-15 | 2nd | 2.0 |
| 5-15 | Min. | L | 1-4 | | 4 | 7 | Greisinger | Loaiza | Nathan | 19-16 | 2nd | 3.0 |
| 5-16 | Min. | W | 11-0 | | 15 | 8 | Buehrle | Silva | | 20-16 | 2nd | 2.0 |
| 5-17 | At Cle. | L | 2-7 | | 5 | 16 | Lee | Diaz | | 20-17 | 2nd | 3.0 |
| 5-18 | At Cle. | W | 4-2 | | 7 | 7 | Garland | Durbin | Koch | 21-17 | 2nd | 2.0 |
| 5-19 | At Cle. | W | 15-3 | | 18 | 6 | Schoeneweis | Davis | | 22-17 | 2nd | 2.0 |
| 5-20 | At Min. | W | 10-3 | | 16 | 10 | Loaiza | Greisinger | | 23-17 | 2nd | 1.0 |
| 5-21 | At Min. | W | 8-2 | | 12 | 8 | Buehrle | Silva | | 24-17 | T1st | ... |
| 5-22 | At Min. | L | 1-9 | | 7 | 14 | Radke | Cotts | | 24-18 | 2nd | 1.0 |
| 5-23 | At Min. | W | 17-7 | | 23 | 11 | Garland | Santana | | 25-18 | T1st | ... |
| 5-25 | Tex. | L | 4-7 | | 12 | 12 | Rogers | Schoeneweis | Cordero | 25-19 | T1st | ... |
| 5-26 | Tex. | W | 4-0 | | 7 | 3 | Loaiza | Benoit | | 26-19 | T1st | ... |
| 5-27 | Tex. | W | 9-0 | | 13 | 10 | Buehrle | Drese | | 27-19 | 1st | +1.0 |
| 5-28 | Ana. | W | 4-3 | | 12 | 10 | Takatsu | Ortiz | | 28-19 | 1st | +2.0 |
| 5-29 | Ana. | L | 1-5 | | 5 | 13 | Sele | Rauch | | 28-20 | 1st | +2.0 |
| 5-30 | Ana. | W | 11-2 | | 14 | 5 | Schoeneweis | Lackey | | 29-20 | 1st | +2.0 |
| 6-1 | At Oak. | L | 4-6 | (12) | 10 | 11 | Duchscherer | Cotts | | 29-21 | 1st | +1.5 |
| 6-2 | At Oak. | L | 2-3 | (10) | 11 | 8 | Rhodes | Adkins | | 29-22 | 1st | +1.5 |
| 6-4 | At Sea. | W | 4-2 | | 9 | 5 | Garland | Garcia | Koch | 30-22 | 1st | +2.0 |
| 6-5 | At Sea. | L | 2-4 | | 6 | 7 | Franklin | Schoeneweis | Guardado | 30-23 | 1st | +2.0 |
| 6-6 | At Sea. | L | 4-5 | | 9 | 11 | Hasegawa | Koch | | 30-24 | 1st | +1.0 |
| 6-8 | Phi. | W | 14-11 | | 15 | 15 | Buehrle | Telemaco | Politte | 31-24 | 1st | +1.0 |
| 6-9 | Phi. | L | 10-13 | | 14 | 14 | Milton | Garland | | 31-25 | 1st | ... |
| 6-11 | Atl. | L | 4-6 | | 6 | 10 | Wright | Schoeneweis | | 31-26 | 2nd | 0.5 |
| 6-12 | Atl. | W | 10-8 | | 14 | 12 | Loaiza | Thomson | Takatsu | 32-26 | 2nd | 0.5 |
| 6-13 | Atl. | W | 10-3 | | 13 | 8 | Buehrle | Smith | | 33-26 | 1st | +0.5 |
| 6-15 | At Fla. | W | 7-5 | (10) | 8 | 7 | Marte | Borland | Takatsu | 34-26 | 1st | +0.5 |
| 6-16 | At Fla. | L | 0-4 | | 3 | 13 | Pavano | Schoeneweis | | 34-27 | 2nd | 0.5 |
| 6-17 | At Fla. | L | 1-2 | (11) | 7 | 6 | Benitez | Politte | | 34-28 | 2nd | 1.5 |
| 6-18 | At Mon. | W | 11-7 | | 18 | 12 | Cotts | Ayala | Marte | 35-28 | 2nd | 0.5 |
| 6-19 | At Mon. | L | 14-17 | | 15 | 18 | Fikac | Munoz | Cordero | 35-29 | 2nd | 0.5 |
| 6-20 | At Mon. | L | 2-4 | | 8 | 3 | Cordero | Garland | | 35-30 | 2nd | 1.5 |
| 6-21 | Cle. | L | 1-5 | | 4 | 10 | Sabathia | Schoeneweis | | 35-31 | 2nd | 2.0 |
| 6-22 | Cle. | W | 11-9 | (10) | 15 | 13 | Takatsu | Jimenez | | 36-31 | 2nd | 1.0 |

| Date | Opp. | Res. | Score | (inn.*) | Hits | Opp. hits | Winning pitcher | Losing pitcher | Save | Record | Pos. | GB |
|---|---|---|---|---|---|---|---|---|---|---|---|---|
| 6-23 | Cle. | L | 5-9 | | 8 | 11 | Lee | Buehrle | | 36-32 | 2nd | 2.0 |
| 6-24 | Cle. | W | 7-1 | | 9 | 6 | Rauch | Westbrook | | 37-32 | 2nd | 2.0 |
| 6-25 | Chi. | L | 4-7 | | 6 | 8 | Prior | Garland | Hawkins | 37-33 | 2nd | 3.0 |
| 6-26 | Chi. | W | 6-3 | | 11 | 7 | Diaz | Zambrano | Takatsu | 38-33 | 2nd | 2.0 |
| 6-27 | Chi. | W | 9-4 | | 11 | 10 | Loaiza | Maddux | | 39-33 | 2nd | 1.0 |
| 6-29 | At Min. | W | 6-2 | | 11 | 9 | Buehrle | Silva | | 40-33 | 1st | ... |
| 6-30 | At Min. | W | 9-6 | | 13 | 9 | Garcia | Radke | | 41-33 | 1st | +1.0 |
| 7-1 | At Min. | W | 2-1 | | 4 | 8 | Garland | Santana | Marte | 42-33 | 1st | +2.0 |
| 7-2 | At Chi. | L | 2-6 | | 3 | 12 | Zambrano | Loaiza | | 42-34 | 1st | +1.0 |
| 7-3 | At Chi. | L | 2-4 | (6) | 6 | 7 | Maddux | Diaz | Wuertz | 42-35 | 1st | ... |
| 7-4 | At Chi. | L | 1-2 | | 6 | 6 | Hawkins | Takatsu | | 42-36 | 1st | ... |
| 7-6 | Ana. | L | 2-6 | | 4 | 10 | Lackey | Garcia | | 42-37 | 2nd | 1.5 |
| 7-7 | Ana. | L | 0-12 | | 4 | 13 | Washburn | Schoeneweis | | 42-38 | 2nd | 2.5 |
| 7-8 | Ana. | W | 9-8 | | 15 | 14 | Marte | Donnelly | | 43-38 | 2nd | 2.5 |
| 7-9 | Sea. | W | 6-2 | | 9 | 7 | Garland | Pineiro | | 44-38 | 2nd | 1.5 |
| 7-10 | Sea. | W | 3-2 | | 3 | 9 | Buehrle | Thornton | Takatsu | 45-38 | 2nd | 0.5 |
| 7-11 | Sea. | W | 4-3 | | 5 | 7 | Garcia | Moyer | Takatsu | 46-38 | 1st | +0.5 |
| 7-15 | At Oak. | L | 2-4 | | 4 | 6 | Harden | Garland | Dotel | 46-39 | 1st | +0.5 |
| 7-16 | At Oak. | L | 1-5 | | 7 | 13 | Zito | Buehrle | Dotel | 46-40 | 1st | +0.5 |
| 7-17 | At Oak. | W | 5-2 | | 6 | 4 | Garcia | Redman | Takatsu | 47-40 | 1st | +0.5 |
| 7-18 | At Oak. | L | 3-5 | | 3 | 9 | Mulder | Loaiza | Dotel | 47-41 | 1st | +0.5 |
| 7-19 | At Tex. | W | 12-6 | | 17 | 8 | Schoeneweis | Benoit | | 48-41 | 1st | +0.5 |
| 7-20 | At Tex. | L | 4-6 | | 7 | 10 | Almanzar | Marte | Cordero | 48-42 | 2nd | 0.5 |
| 7-21 | At Cle. | W | 14-0 | | 19 | 2 | Buehrle | Lee | | 49-42 | 2nd | 0.5 |
| 7-22 | At Cle. | W | 3-0 | | 8 | 6 | Garcia | Sabathia | Takatsu | 50-42 | 2nd | 0.5 |
| 7-23 | Det. | W | 6-4 | | 9 | 7 | Loaiza | Robertson | Takatsu | 51-42 | 2nd | 0.5 |
| 7-24 | Det. | W | 7-6 | | 7 | 10 | Marte | Urbina | | 52-42 | 1st | +0.5 |
| 7-25 | Det. | L | 2-9 | | 10 | 10 | Ledezma | Garland | | 52-43 | 2nd | 0.5 |
| 7-26 | Min. | L | 2-6 | | 6 | 14 | Radke | Buehrle | | 52-44 | 2nd | 1.5 |
| 7-27 | Min. | L | 3-7 | | 4 | 10 | Santana | Garcia | | 52-45 | 2nd | 2.5 |
| 7-28 | Min. | L | 4-5 | (10) | 10 | 10 | Mulholland | Takatsu | Nathan | 52-46 | 2nd | 3.5 |
| 7-29 | At Det. | L | 2-3 | | 5 | 5 | Johnson | Schoeneweis | Urbina | 52-47 | 2nd | 4.0 |
| 7-30 | At Det. | L | 4-5 | | 9 | 7 | Yan | Marte | Urbina | 52-48 | 2nd | 4.0 |
| 7-31 | At Det. | L | 2-3 | (10) | 5 | 7 | Urbina | Politte | | 52-49 | 2nd | 5.0 |
| 8-1 | At Det. | W | 6-4 | | 14 | 5 | Garcia | Bonderman | Takatsu | 53-49 | 2nd | 5.0 |
| 8-3 | At K.C. | W | 12-4 | | 11 | 6 | Contreras | Wood | | 54-49 | 2nd | 5.0 |
| 8-4 | At K.C. | L | 0-11 | | 2 | 17 | Anderson | Schoeneweis | | 54-50 | 2nd | 6.0 |
| 8-5 | At K.C. | L | 4-6 | | 8 | 7 | Greinke | Garland | Field | 54-51 | 2nd | 6.0 |
| 8-6 | Cle. | L | 2-3 | | 6 | 9 | Sabathia | Buehrle | Wickman | 54-52 | 2nd | 6.0 |
| 8-7 | Cle. | L | 5-6 | | 8 | 13 | Miller | Takatsu | Wickman | 54-53 | 3rd | 7.0 |
| 8-8 | Cle. | W | 3-2 | | 8 | 7 | Takatsu | Betancourt | | 55-53 | 2nd | 6.0 |
| 8-9 | Cle. | L | 11-13 | | 12 | 16 | Westbrook | Diaz | | 55-54 | 3rd | 6.0 |
| 8-10 | K.C. | W | 9-3 | | 14 | 8 | Garland | Greinke | | 56-54 | 3rd | 5.0 |
| 8-11 | K.C. | L | 2-4 | | 4 | 9 | May | Buehrle | Cerda | 56-55 | 3rd | 5.0 |
| 8-12 | K.C. | W | 3-2 | | 5 | 9 | Garcia | Serrano | Takatsu | 57-55 | 3rd | 5.0 |
| 8-13 | At Bos. | W | 8-7 | | 11 | 9 | Contreras | Wakefield | Takatsu | 58-55 | 3rd | 4.0 |
| 8-14 | At Bos. | L | 3-4 | | 5 | 9 | Schilling | Adkins | Foulke | 58-56 | 3rd | 4.0 |
| 8-15 | At Bos. | W | 5-4 | | 10 | 12 | Buehrle | Arroyo | Takatsu | 59-56 | 3rd | 4.0 |
| 8-17 | Det. | L | 8-11 | | 12 | 15 | Maroth | Garcia | Urbina | 59-57 | 3rd | 5.0 |
| 8-18 | Det. | W | 9-2 | | 9 | 7 | Contreras | Bonderman | | 60-57 | 3rd | 5.0 |
| 8-19 | Det. | L | 4-8 | | 9 | 9 | Ledezma | Garland | Knotts | 60-58 | 3rd | 5.0 |
| 8-20 | Bos. | L | 1-10 | | 5 | 13 | Schilling | Buehrle | | 60-59 | 3rd | 6.0 |
| 8-21 | Bos. | L | 7-10 | | 11 | 15 | Arroyo | Stewart | Foulke | 60-60 | 3rd | 7.0 |
| 8-22 | Bos. | L | 5-6 | | 8 | 11 | Leskanic | Marte | Foulke | 60-61 | 3rd | 8.0 |
| 8-23 | At Det. | L | 0-7 | | 7 | 8 | Bonderman | Contreras | | 60-62 | 3rd | 9.0 |
| 8-24 | At Det. | W | 9-5 | | 11 | 10 | Garland | Ledezma | | 61-62 | 3rd | 8.0 |
| 8-25 | At Det. | L | 4-5 | | 10 | 12 | Robertson | Buehrle | | 61-63 | 3rd | 9.0 |
| 8-26 | At Cle. | W | 14-9 | | 16 | 14 | Cotts | Durbin | | 62-63 | 3rd | 8.0 |
| 8-27 | At Cle. | L | 3-6 | | 9 | 6 | Sabathia | Grilli | Wickman | 62-64 | 3rd | 8.0 |
| 8-28 | At Cle. | W | 5-3 | | 8 | 10 | Contreras | Lee | Takatsu | 63-64 | 3rd | 8.0 |
| 8-29 | At Cle. | L | 0-9 | | 2 | 12 | Elarton | Garland | | 63-65 | 3rd | 8.0 |
| 8-30 | Phi. | W | 9-8 | | 15 | 12 | Buehrle | Hernandez | Takatsu | 64-65 | 3rd | 7.5 |
| 8-31 | Oak. | L | 2-7 | | 6 | 10 | Harden | Diaz | | 64-66 | 3rd | 8.5 |
| 9-1 | Oak. | W | 5-4 | | 11 | 11 | Takatsu | Duchscherer | | 65-66 | 3rd | 8.5 |
| 9-2 | Oak. | L | 2-4 | | 5 | 7 | Redman | Contreras | Dotel | 65-67 | 3rd | 9.5 |
| 9-3 | Sea. | W | 7-5 | | 8 | 11 | Garland | Madritsch | Takatsu | 66-67 | 2nd | 9.5 |
| 9-4 | Sea. | W | 8-7 | | 14 | 15 | Buehrle | Franklin | Takatsu | 67-67 | 2nd | 9.5 |
| 9-5 | Sea. | W | 6-2 | | 6 | 9 | Diaz | Moyer | Marte | 68-67 | 2nd | 8.5 |
| 9-6 | At Tex. | W | 7-4 | | 9 | 11 | Grilli | Park | | 69-67 | 2nd | 7.5 |
| 9-7 | At Tex. | L | 3-10 | | 9 | 12 | Rogers | Contreras | | 69-68 | 2nd | 8.5 |

| Date | Opp. | Res. | Score | (inn.*) | Hits | Opp. hits | Winning pitcher | Losing pitcher | Save | Record | Pos. | GB |
|---|---|---|---|---|---|---|---|---|---|---|---|---|
| 9-8 | At Tex. | W | 5-2 | | 8 | 5 | Garcia | Wasdin | Takatsu | 70-68 | 2nd | 8.5 |
| 9-9 | At Tex. | W | 7-3 | | 10 | 3 | Buehrle | Young | | 71-68 | 2nd | 8.0 |
| 9-10 | At Ana. | L | 5-7 | | 12 | 11 | Rodriguez | Bajenaru | Percival | 71-69 | 2nd | 9.0 |
| 9-11 | At Ana. | W | 13-6 | | 16 | 10 | Grilli | Sele | | 72-69 | 2nd | 9.0 |
| 9-12 | At Ana. | L | 0-11 | | 6 | 15 | Colon | Contreras | | 72-70 | 2nd | 10.0 |
| 9-14 | At Min. | L | 2-10 | | 6 | 8 | Santana | Garcia | | 72-71 | 2nd | 11.5 |
| 9-15 | At Min. | L | 1-6 | | 5 | 9 | Silva | Buehrle | | 72-72 | 2nd | 12.5 |
| 9-16 | At Min. | L | 1-10 | | 4 | 14 | Lohse | Garland | | 72-73 | 2nd | 13.5 |
| 9-17 | Det. | L | 10-11 | (10) | 16 | 11 | Yan | Takatsu | Ennis | 72-74 | 2nd | 13.5 |
| 9-18 | Det. | W | 9-8 | (12) | 12 | 10 | Marte | Levine | | 73-74 | 2nd | 12.5 |
| 9-19 | Det. | W | 6-1 | | 7 | 6 | Garcia | Bonderman | | 74-74 | 2nd | 12.5 |
| 9-20 | Min. | L | 2-8 | | 8 | 12 | Silva | Buehrle | | 74-75 | 2nd | 13.5 |
| 9-21 | Min. | W | 8-6 | | 9 | 10 | Cotts | Romero | Takatsu | 75-75 | 2nd | 12.5 |
| 9-22 | Min. | W | 7-6 | | 12 | 9 | Cotts | Roa | | 76-75 | 2nd | 11.5 |
| 9-23 | K.C. | W | 7-6 | | 10 | 10 | Marte | Affeldt | | 77-75 | 2nd | 10.5 |
| 9-24 | K.C. | L | 6-8 | | 12 | 11 | Gobble | Diaz | | 77-76 | 2nd | 11.5 |
| 9-25 | K.C. | W | 5-1 | | 7 | 4 | Buehrle | Bautista | | 78-76 | 2nd | 10.5 |
| 9-26 | K.C. | W | 5-1 | | 9 | 5 | Garland | Anderson | Marte | 79-76 | 2nd | 10.5 |
| 9-27 | At Det. | L | 2-4 | | 6 | 3 | Knotts | Grilli | Yan | 79-77 | 2nd | 11.0 |
| 9-28 | At Det. | L | 4-6 | | 7 | 10 | German | Cotts | Yan | 79-78 | 2nd | 11.5 |
| 9-29 | At Det. | W | 11-2 | | 12 | 8 | Garcia | Johnson | | 80-78 | 2nd | 10.0 |
| 9-30 | At K.C. | W | 9-2 | | 12 | 4 | Buehrle | Camp | | 81-78 | 2nd | 9.0 |
| 10-1 | At K.C. | W | 4-2 | | 8 | 7 | Garland | Cerda | Takatsu | 82-78 | 2nd | 9.0 |
| 10-2 | At K.C. | L | 2-10 | | 7 | 14 | Anderson | Grilli | | 82-79 | 2nd | 9.5 |
| 10-3 | At K.C. | W | 5-0 | | 11 | 3 | Contreras | Greinke | | 83-79 | 2nd | 9.0 |

Monthly records: April (13-8), May (16-12), June (12-13), July (11-16), August (12-17), September (17-12), October (2-1).
*Innings, if other than nine. ! First game of a doubleheader. & Second game of a doubleheader. # Day separate admission. $ Night separate admission.

## RECORDS

**2004 regular-season record:** 83-79
**Position:** 2nd in A.L. Central
**Home:** 46-35 **Road:** 37-44
**A.L. East:** 16-16 **A.L. Central:** 40-36
**A.L. West:** 19-17 **N.L.** 8-10
**Vs. LH starters:** 21-35
**Vs. RH starters:** 62-44
**Grass:** 74-69 **Artificial:** 9-10
**Day:** 34-21 **Night:** 49-58
**1-Run:** 28-18 **X-inn.:** 6-7
**Doubleheaders:** 0-0-2
**Team record past five years:** 428-382 (.528, ranks 6th in league in that span)

## TEAM LEADERS

**Batting average:** Aaron Rowand (.310).
**At-bats:** Carlos Lee (591).
**Runs:** Carlos Lee (103).
**Hits:** Carlos Lee (180).
**Total Bases:** Carlos Lee (310).
**Doubles:** Aaron Rowand (38).
**Triples:** Juan Uribe (6).
**Home runs:** Paul Konerko (41).
**Runs batted in:** Paul Konerko (117).
**Stolen bases:** Willie Harris (19).
**Slugging percentage:** Frank Thomas (.563).
**On-base percentage:** Frank Thomas (.434).
**Wins:** Mark Buehrle (16).
**Earned-run average:** Mark Buehrle (3.89).
**Complete games:** Mark Buehrle (4).
**Shutouts:** Mark Buehrle, Esteban Loaiza (1).
**Saves:** Shingo Takatsu (19).
**Innings pitched:** Mark Buehrle (245.1).
**Strikeouts:** Mark Buehrle (165).

## GAMES BY POSITION

**Catcher:** Ben Davis 53, Sandy Alomar Jr. 49, Miguel Olivo 46, Jamie Burke 45.
**First base:** Paul Konerko 139, Ross Gload 42, Frank Thomas 4, Jamie Burke 2.
**Second base:** Willie Harris 92, Juan Uribe 77, Roberto Alomar 13, Wilson Valdez 5.
**Third base:** Joe Crede 144, Juan Uribe 27, Kelly Dransfeldt 3, Jamie Burke 2.
**Shortstop:** Jose Valentin 122, Juan Uribe 38, Wilson Valdez 12, Kelly Dransfeldt 8.
**Outfield:** Carlos Lee 148, Aaron Rowand 137, Timo Perez 80, Joe Borchard 56, Magglio Ordonez 43, Ross Gload 39, Willie Harris 30, Jamie Burke 2, Carl Everett 1.
**Designated hitter:** Frank Thomas 65, Carl Everett 41, Paul Konerko 16, Ross Gload 13, Magglio Ordonez 7, Timo Perez 6, Roberto Alomar 5, Carlos Lee 5, Joe Borchard 4, Jamie Burke 3, Willie Harris 2, Juan Uribe 2, Jose Valentin 2, Sandy Alomar Jr. 1, Kelly Dransfeldt 1.

## TOP DRAFT CHOICES

1a. **Josh Fields,** 3B, Oklahoma State.
1b. **Tyler Lumsden,** LHP, Clemson.
1c. **Gio Gonzalez,** LHP, Monsignor Pace H.S., Miami.
2a. **Wes Whisler,** LHP, UCLA.
2b. **Donny Lucy,** C, Stanford.
2c. **Ray Liotta,** LHP, Gulf Coast (Fla.) CC.
3. **Grant Hansen,** RHP, Oklahoma City.
4. **Lucas Harrell,** RHP, Ozark (Mo.) H.S.
5. **Brandon Allen,** OF, Montgomery (Texas) H.S.
6. **Adam Russell,** RHP, Ohio U.
7. **Tim Murphey,** LHP, Glascock County H.S., Gibson, Ga.
8. **Nick Lemon**, RHP, Brigham Young.
9. **Ryan McCarthy**, 3B, UCLA.
10. **Adam Ricks**, 2B, Miami (Fla.).

# CLEVELAND INDIANS
## AMERICAN LEAGUE CENTRAL DIVISION

## 2005 SEASON

### Indians Schedule
Home games shaded.
All-Star Game July 12 at Detroit. Schedule subject to change.

**April**

| SUN | MON | TUE | WED | THU | FRI | SAT |
|---|---|---|---|---|---|---|
| 3 | 4 CHW | 5 | 6 CHW | 7 CHW | 8 DET | 9 DET |
| 10 DET | 11 CHW | 12 | 13 CHW | 14 CHW | 15 MIN | 16 MIN |
| 17 MIN | 18 KC | 19 KC | 20 ANA | 21 ANA | 22 SEA | 23 SEA |
| 24 SEA | 25 | 26 DET | 27 DET | 28 DET | 29 KC | 30 KC |

**May**

| SUN | MON | TUE | WED | THU | FRI | SAT |
|---|---|---|---|---|---|---|
| 1 KC | 2 | 3 MIN | 4 MIN | 5 MIN | 6 TEX | 7 TEX |
| 8 TEX | 9 ANA | 10 ANA | 11 ANA | 12 | 13 TOR | 14 TOR |
| 15 TOR | 16 ANA | 17 ANA | 18 ANA | 19 | 20 CIN | 21 CIN |
| 22 CIN | 23 MIN | 24 MIN | 25 MIN | 26 MIN | 27 OAK | 28 OAK |
| 29 OAK | 30 | 31 MIN | | | | |

**June**

| SUN | MON | TUE | WED | THU | FRI | SAT |
|---|---|---|---|---|---|---|
| | | | 1 MIN | 2 MIN | 3 CHW | 4 CHW |
| 5 CHW | 6 | 7 SD | 8 SD | 9 SD | 10 SF | 11 SF |
| 12 SF | 13 | 14 COL | 15 COL | 16 COL | 17 ARI | 18 ARI |
| 19 ARI | 20 BOS | 21 BOS | 22 BOS | 23 | 24 CIN | 25 CIN |
| 26 CIN | 27 BOS | 28 BOS | 29 BOS | 30 BAL | | |

**July**

| SUN | MON | TUE | WED | THU | FRI | SAT |
|---|---|---|---|---|---|---|
| | | | | | 1 BAL | 2 BAL |
| 3 BAL | 4 DET | 5 DET | 6 DET | 7 NYY | 8 NYY | 9 NYY |
| 10 NYY | 11 | 12 All-Star | 13 | 14 CHW | 15 CHW | 16 CHW |
| 17 CHW | 18 KC | 19 KC | 20 KC | 21 KC | 22 SEA | 23 SEA |
| 24 SEA | 25 OAK | 26 OAK | 27 OAK | 28 SEA | 29 SEA | 30 SEA |
| 31 SEA | | | | | | |

**August**

| SUN | MON | TUE | WED | THU | FRI | SAT |
|---|---|---|---|---|---|---|
| | 1 | 2 NYY | 3 NYY | 4 NYY | 5 DET | 6 DET |
| 7 DET | 8 | 9 KC | 10 KC | 11 KC | 12 TB | 13 TB |
| 14 TB | 15 | 16 TEX | 17 TEX | 18 TEX | 19 BAL | 20 BAL |
| 21 BAL | 22 TB | 23 TB | 24 TB | 25 TB | 26 TOR | 27 TOR |
| 28 TOR | 29 DET | 30 DET | 31 DET | | | |

**September**

| SUN | MON | TUE | WED | THU | FRI | SAT |
|---|---|---|---|---|---|---|
| | | | | 1 | 2 MIN | 3 MIN |
| 4 MIN | 5 DET | 6 DET | 7 DET | 8 | 9 MIN | 10 MIN |
| 11 MIN | 12 OAK | 13 OAK | 14 OAK | 15 | 16 KC | 17 KC |
| 18 KC | 19 CHW | 20 CHW | 21 CHW | 22 KC | 23 KC | 24 KC |
| 25 KC | 26 | 27 TB | 28 TB | 29 TB | 30 CHW | |

**October**

| SUN | MON | TUE | WED | THU | FRI | SAT |
|---|---|---|---|---|---|---|
| | | | | | | 1 CHW |
| 2 CHW | 3 | 4 | 5 | 6 | 7 | 8 |

Home games shaded. All-Star Game July 12 at Detroit. Schedule subject to change.

### CLUB DIRECTORY

**Owner and chief executive officer**
Lawrence J. Dolan
**Executive vice president, general manager**
Mark Shapiro
**Vice president, public relations**
Bob DiBiasio
**Vice president, ballpark operations**
Jim Folk
**Assistant general manager**
John Mirabelli
**Assistant general manager**
Chris Antonetti
**Director of player development**
John Farrell
**Director of player personnel**
Steve Lubratich
**Director of media relations**
Bart Swain

### MINOR LEAGUE AFFILIATES

| Class | Team | League | Manager |
|---|---|---|---|
| AAA | Buffalo | International | Marty Brown |
| AA | Akron | Eastern | Torey Lovullo |
| Advanced A | Kinston | Carolina | Luis Rivera |
| A | Lake County | South Atlantic | Mike Sarbaugh |
| Short-Season A | Mahoning Valley | New York-Pennsylvania | Rouglas Odor |
| Advanced Rookie | Burlington | Appalachian | Sean McNally |

### BROADCAST INFORMATION

**Radio:** WTAM-AM (1100).
**Cable TV:** Fox Sports Net Ohio.

### SPRING TRAINING

**Ballpark (city):** Chain Of Lakes (Winter Haven, Fla.).
**Ticket information:** 863-293-3900.

**For more on the Indians, go to msn.foxsports.com/mlb/teams.**

Sabathia

## SPRING TRAINING ROSTER

**Manager**—Eric Wedge (22).
**Coaches**—Buddy Bell (25), Jeff Datz (29), Luis Isaac (4), Eddie Murray (33), Joel Skinner (35), Carl Willis (57).

| No. | PITCHERS | B/T | Ht./Wt. | Age* | 2004 Clubs |
|---|---|---|---|---|---|
| 56 | Bartosh, Cliff | L/L | 6-2/180 | 25 | Buffalo, Cleveland |
| 63 | Betancourt, Rafael | R/R | 6-2/200 | 29 | Akron, Cleveland |
| | Brown, Andrew | R/R | 6-6/230 | 24 | Jacksonville, Akron, Buffalo |
| 64 | Cabrera, Fernando | R/R | 6-4/170 | 23 | Buffalo, Cleveland, |
| | Carmona, Fausto | R/R | 6-4/185 | 21 | Kinston, Akron, Buffalo |
| 55 | Cruceta, Francisco | R/R | 6-2/180 | 23 | Akron, Buffalo, Cleveland |
| 50 | Davis, Jason | R/R | 6-6/210 | 24 | Buffalo, Cleveland |
| 57 | Denney, Kyle | R/R | 6-2/195 | 27 | Buffalo, Cleveland |
| | Dittler, Jake | R/R | 6-4/220 | 22 | Akron |
| 39 | Elarton, Scott | R/R | 6-8/240 | 29 | Colorado, Buffalo, Cleveland |
| 53 | Guthrie, Jeremy | R/R | 6-1/200 | 25 | Buffalo, Akron, Cleveland |
| 62 | Howry, Bob | L/R | 6-5/220 | 31 | Buffalo, Cleveland |
| 34 | Lee, Cliff | L/L | 6-3/190 | 26 | Cleveland |
| 59 | Miller, Matt | R/R | 6-3/215 | 33 | Buffalo, Cleveland |
| | Rhodes, Arthur | L/L | 6-2/212 | 35 | Sacramento, Oakland |
| 54 | Riske, David | R/R | 6-2/190 | 28 | Cleveland |
| 52 | Sabathia, C.C. | L/L | 6-7/290 | 24 | Cleveland |
| | Sauerbeck, Scott | R/L | 6-3/200 | 33 | Did Not Play |
| 61 | Stanford, Jason | L/L | 6-2/200 | 28 | Cleveland, Buffalo |
| 32 | Tadano, Kazuhito | R/R | 6-0/180 | 24 | Buffalo, Cleveland |
| 30 | Tallet, Brian | L/L | 6-7/208 | 27 | Mahoning Valley, Lake County, Akron, Buffalo |
| 37 | Westbrook, Jake | R/R | 6-3/185 | 27 | Cleveland |
| 26 | Wickman, Bob | R/R | 6-1/240 | 36 | Akron, Buffalo, Cleveland |

| No. | CATCHERS | B/T | Ht./Wt. | Age* | 2004 Clubs |
|---|---|---|---|---|---|
| 44 | Bard, Josh | B/R | 6-3/215 | 27 | Akron, Buffalo, Cleveland |
| 41 | Martinez, Victor | B/R | 6-2/190 | 26 | Cleveland |

| No. | INFIELDERS | B/T | Ht./Wt. | Age* | 2004 Clubs |
|---|---|---|---|---|---|
| 20 | Belliard, Ronnie | R/R | 5-8/197 | 29 | Cleveland |
| 1 | Blake, Casey | R/R | 6-2/210 | 31 | Cleveland |
| 17 | Boone, Aaron | R/R | 6-2/200 | 32 | Did Not Play |
| 23 | Broussard, Ben | L/L | 6-2/220 | 28 | Cleveland |
| 48 | Hafner, Travis | L/R | 6-3/240 | 27 | Cleveland |
| | Hernandez, Jose | R/R | 6-1/190 | 35 | Los Angeles |
| 16 | Peralta, Jhonny | R/R | 6-1/185 | 22 | Buffalo, Cleveland |
| 7 | Phillips, Brandon | R/R | 5-11/185 | 23 | Buffalo, Cleveland |
| | Smith, Corey | R/R | 6-1/210 | 22 | Akron, Buffalo |

| No. | OUTFIELDERS | B/T | Ht./Wt. | Age* | 2004 Clubs |
|---|---|---|---|---|---|
| 10 | Crisp, Coco | B/R | 6-0/185 | 25 | Cleveland |
| 9 | Gerut, Jody | L/L | 6-0/190 | 27 | Cleveland |
| | Gutierrez, Franklin | R/R | 6-2/175 | 22 | Akron, Buffalo |
| 38 | Ludwick, Ryan | R/L | 6-3/203 | 26 | Akron, Buffalo, Cleveland |
| 24 | Sizemore, Grady | L/L | 6-2/200 | 22 | Buffalo, Cleveland |

*Age as of April 1, 2005.

## BALLPARK INFORMATION

**Ballpark (capacity, surface)**
Jacobs Field (43,368, grass)
**Address**
2401 Ontario St.
Cleveland, OH 44115
**Official website**
www.indians.com
**Business phone**
216-420-4200
**Ticket information**
216-420-HITS, 1-866-48-TRIBE
**Field dimensions (from home plate)**
To left field at foul line, 325 feet
To center field, 405 feet
To right field at foul line, 325 feet
**First game played**
April 4, 1994
(Indians 4, Mariners 3, 11 innings)

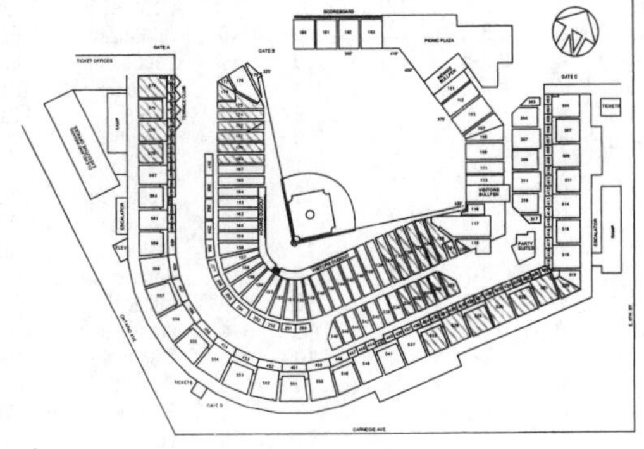

# 2004 REVIEW

## DAY BY DAY

| Date | Opp. | Res. | Score | (inn.*) | Hits | Opp. hits | Winning pitcher | Losing pitcher | Save | Record | Pos. | GB |
|---|---|---|---|---|---|---|---|---|---|---|---|---|
| 4-5 | At Min. | L | 4-7 | (11) | 17 | 10 | Rincon | Durbin | | 0-1 | T4th | 1.0 |
| 4-6 | At Min. | L | 6-7 | (15) | 12 | 15 | Roa | Westbrook | | 0-2 | 5th | 2.0 |
| 4-7 | At Min. | W | 11-4 | | 16 | 11 | Durbin | Lohse | | 1-2 | 5th | 2.0 |
| 4-8 | At K.C. | W | 6-1 | | 9 | 5 | D'Amico | Affeldt | | 2-2 | T2nd | 2.0 |
| 4-9 | At K.C. | L | 1-3 | | 7 | 11 | Grimsley | Cressend | Leskanic | 2-3 | 5th | 2.5 |
| 4-10 | At K.C. | L | 6-7 | (10) | 12 | 12 | Sullivan | Betancourt | | 2-4 | 5th | 2.5 |
| 4-11 | At K.C. | L | 3-5 | | 8 | 8 | Sullivan | Jimenez | Leskanic | 2-5 | 5th | 3.5 |
| 4-12 | Min. | W | 6-3 | | 8 | 8 | Lee | Lohse | | 3-5 | 5th | 3.0 |
| 4-14 | Min. | L | 6-10 | | 10 | 15 | Silva | D'Amico | Rincon | 3-6 | 5th | 3.5 |
| 4-15 | Min. | L | 0-3 | | 4 | 9 | Radke | Stanford | Nathan | 3-7 | 5th | 3.5 |
| 4-16 | Det. | W | 10-3 | | 19 | 8 | Sabathia | Cornejo | | 4-7 | 5th | 2.5 |
| 4-17 | Det. | L | 1-6 | | 11 | 12 | Maroth | Davis | | 4-8 | 5th | 3.5 |
| 4-18 | Det. | W | 9-7 | | 12 | 11 | Lee | Bonderman | Riske | 5-8 | 4th | 3.5 |
| 4-19 | Det. | L | 4-10 | | 8 | 8 | Levine | Betancourt | | 5-9 | 4th | 4.0 |
| 4-20 | K.C. | L | 5-15 | | 9 | 14 | Anderson | Durbin | | 5-10 | 5th | 5.0 |
| 4-22 | K.C. | W | 5-4 | | 5 | 11 | Betancourt | Grimsley | Riske | 6-10 | 4th | 4.5 |
| 4-23 | At Det. | L | 3-17 | | 6 | 16 | Bonderman | Davis | Yan | 6-11 | 4th | 5.5 |
| 4-24 | At Det. | L | 2-5 | | 6 | 9 | Urbina | Stewart | | 6-12 | 5th | 5.5 |
| 4-25 | At Det. | W | 3-2 | | 6 | 2 | Westbrook | Johnson | | 7-12 | 4th | 5.5 |
| 4-27 | At Chi. | W | 11-7 | (10) | 16 | 16 | Betancourt | Adkins | | 8-12 | 4th | 5.0 |
| 4-28 | At Chi. | L | 8-9 | | 11 | 15 | Jackson | Betancourt | | 8-13 | 4th | 6.0 |
| 4-30 | Bal. | W | 11-2 | | 15 | 7 | Lee | Ponson | | 9-13 | 4th | 6.0 |
| 5-1 | Bal. | W | 3-2 | (13) | 10 | 10 | Durbin | DeJean | | 10-13 | 4th | 5.0 |
| 5-3 | Bos. | W | 2-1 | | 7 | 8 | Westbrook | Schilling | Betancourt | 11-13 | 4th | 4.5 |
| 5-4 | Bos. | W | 7-6 | | 12 | 11 | Davis | Lowe | Betancourt | 12-13 | 4th | 3.5 |
| 5-5 | Bos. | L | 5-9 | | 10 | 11 | Arroyo | D'Amico | | 12-14 | 4th | 4.5 |
| 5-6 | Bos. | L | 2-5 | | 5 | 11 | Martinez | Sabathia | Foulke | 12-15 | 4th | 5.0 |
| 5-7 | At Bal. | L | 2-3 | (10) | 10 | 7 | Julio | Durbin | | 12-16 | 4th | 5.0 |
| 5-8 | At Bal. | L | 7-10 | | 7 | 14 | Parrish | Stewart | Julio | 12-17 | 4th | 5.0 |
| 5-9 | At Bal. | L | 11-12 | | 15 | 16 | Lopez | Riske | Julio | 12-18 | 4th | 5.0 |
| 5-10 | At Bos. | W | 10-6 | | 13 | 11 | Durbin | Kim | | 13-18 | 4th | 4.5 |
| 5-11 | At Bos. | L | 3-5 | | 6 | 10 | Embree | Jimenez | Foulke | 13-19 | 4th | 5.5 |
| 5-12 | At Bos. | W | 6-4 | | 9 | 9 | Lee | Wakefield | | 14-19 | 4th | 5.5 |
| 5-14 | T.B. | W | 8-7 | (10) | 13 | 12 | White | Carter | | 15-19 | 4th | 6.0 |
| 5-15 | T.B. | W | 9-7 | | 8 | 10 | Westbrook | Zambrano | | 16-19 | 4th | 6.0 |
| 5-16 | T.B. | W | 10-0 | | 10 | 6 | Sabathia | Waechter | | 17-19 | 4th | 5.0 |
| 5-17 | Chi. | W | 7-2 | | 16 | 5 | Lee | Diaz | | 18-19 | T3rd | 5.0 |
| 5-18 | Chi. | L | 2-4 | | 7 | 7 | Garland | Durbin | Koch | 18-20 | 4th | 5.0 |
| 5-19 | Chi. | L | 3-15 | | 6 | 18 | Schoeneweis | Davis | | 18-21 | 4th | 6.0 |
| 5-21 | At T.B. | L | 3-5 | | 8 | 10 | Miller | Sabathia | Baez | 18-22 | 4th | 5.5 |
| 5-22 | At T.B. | L | 3-6 | | 7 | 7 | Waechter | Westbrook | Sosa | 18-23 | 4th | 6.5 |
| 5-23 | At T.B. | L | 4-5 | (10) | 9 | 8 | Harper | Riske | | 18-24 | 4th | 6.5 |
| 5-25 | Sea. | L | 4-5 | (12) | 7 | 12 | Myers | Jimenez | Guardado | 18-25 | 4th | 6.5 |
| 5-26 | Sea. | L | 3-7 | | 8 | 13 | Moyer | Sabathia | Guardado | 18-26 | 4th | 7.5 |
| 5-27 | Sea. | W | 9-5 | | 13 | 8 | Westbrook | Meche | | 19-26 | 4th | 7.5 |
| 5-28 | Oak. | W | 1-0 | | 4 | 8 | Jimenez | Mecir | | 20-26 | 4th | 7.5 |
| 5-29 | Oak. | W | 8-6 | | 8 | 9 | Riske | Rhodes | Jimenez | 21-26 | 4th | 6.5 |
| 5-30 | Oak. | W | 4-3 | | 13 | 10 | White | Rhodes | | 22-26 | 3rd | 6.5 |
| 6-1 | Tex. | L | 5-6 | (12) | 9 | 9 | Ramirez | White | Cordero | 22-27 | 4th | 6.5 |
| 6-2 | Tex. | L | 3-5 | | 9 | 10 | Almanzar | Betancourt | Cordero | 22-28 | 4th | 6.5 |
| 6-3 | At Ana. | L | 2-5 | | 9 | 11 | Escobar | Lee | | 22-29 | 4th | 7.0 |
| 6-4 | At Ana. | W | 9-6 | | 14 | 9 | Riske | Rodriguez | Jimenez | 23-29 | 4th | 7.0 |
| 6-5 | At Ana. | W | 3-2 | | 9 | 7 | White | Lackey | Jimenez | 24-29 | 4th | 6.0 |
| 6-6 | At Ana. | W | 7-0 | | 9 | 5 | Sabathia | Colon | | 25-29 | 3rd | 5.0 |
| 6-8 | Fla. | L | 5-7 | | 11 | 12 | Bump | Jimenez | Benitez | 25-30 | 3rd | 6.0 |
| 6-9 | Fla. | W | 8-1 | | 13 | 6 | Westbrook | Burnett | | 26-30 | 3rd | 5.0 |
| 6-10 | Fla. | L | 1-4 | | 4 | 12 | Pavano | Davis | Benitez | 26-31 | 4th | 6.0 |
| 6-11 | Cin. | W | 6-5 | (11) | 12 | 10 | Riske | Norton | | 27-31 | 4th | 5.0 |
| 6-12 | Cin. | W | 8-7 | | 9 | 10 | Betancourt | Norton | Jimenez | 28-31 | 4th | 5.0 |
| 6-13 | Cin. | W | 10-8 | | 10 | 8 | Miller | Reith | Jimenez | 29-31 | 3rd | 4.5 |
| 6-14 | Bal. | W | 14-0 | | 15 | 4 | Westbrook | DuBose | | 30-31 | 3rd | 4.0 |
| 6-15 | At N.Y. | L | 2-7 | | 10 | 14 | Trachsel | Davis | | 30-32 | 3rd | 5.0 |
| 6-16 | At N.Y. | W | 9-1 | | 14 | 6 | Sabathia | Ginter | | 31-32 | 3rd | 4.5 |
| 6-17 | At N.Y. | L | 2-6 | | 5 | 8 | Bottalico | White | | 31-33 | 3rd | 5.5 |
| 6-18 | At Atl. | W | 4-2 | | 11 | 6 | Lee | Hampton | Jimenez | 32-33 | 3rd | 4.5 |

| Date | Opp. | Res. | Score | (inn.*) | Hits | Opp. hits | Winning pitcher | Losing pitcher | Save | Record | Pos. | GB |
|---|---|---|---|---|---|---|---|---|---|---|---|---|
| 6-19 | At Atl. | L | 0-4 | | 6 | 9 | Byrd | Westbrook | Smoltz | 32-34 | 3rd | 4.5 |
| 6-20 | At Atl. | W | 5-2 | | 11 | 4 | Davis | Ortiz | Jimenez | 33-34 | 3rd | 4.5 |
| 6-21 | At Chi. | W | 5-1 | | 10 | 4 | Sabathia | Schoeneweis | | 34-34 | 3rd | 4.0 |
| 6-22 | At Chi. | L | 9-11 | (10) | 13 | 15 | Takatsu | Jimenez | | 34-35 | 3rd | 4.0 |
| 6-23 | At Chi. | W | 9-5 | | 11 | 8 | Lee | Buehrle | | 35-35 | 3rd | 4.0 |
| 6-24 | At Chi. | L | 1-7 | | 6 | 9 | Rauch | Westbrook | | 35-36 | 3rd | 5.0 |
| 6-25 | Col. | L | 8-10 | (10) | 7 | 15 | Reed | Jimenez | Chacon | 35-37 | 3rd | 6.0 |
| 6-26 | Col. | W | 4-3 | (12) | 17 | 10 | Robertson | Reed | | 36-37 | 3rd | 5.0 |
| 6-27 | Col. | W | 5-3 | | 10 | 5 | Miller | Jennings | Jimenez | 37-37 | 3rd | 4.0 |
| 6-29 | At Det. | L | 7-9 | (11) | 11 | 15 | Dingman | Jimenez | | 37-38 | 3rd | 4.0 |
| 6-30 | At Det. | L | 5-12 | | 10 | 17 | Robertson | Davis | | 37-39 | T3rd | 5.0 |
| 7-1 | At Det. | W | 7-6 | (10) | 11 | 11 | Riske | Urbina | White | 38-39 | 3rd | 5.0 |
| 7-2 | At Cin. | W | 15-2 | | 15 | 8 | Tadano | Sanchez | | 39-39 | 3rd | 4.0 |
| 7-3 | At Cin. | L | 2-4 | | 8 | 7 | Wilson | Elarton | Graves | 39-40 | 3rd | 4.0 |
| 7-4 | At Cin. | L | 4-5 | (11) | 12 | 13 | Jones | White | | 39-41 | 3rd | 4.0 |
| 7-5 | Tex. | L | 5-8 | | 8 | 11 | Rogers | Sabathia | Cordero | 39-42 | 3rd | 5.0 |
| 7-6 | Tex. | W | 4-1 | | 7 | 6 | Lee | Bierbrodt | Riske | 40-42 | 3rd | 5.0 |
| 7-7 | Tex. | L | 8-9 | | 11 | 14 | Mahay | Robertson | Cordero | 40-43 | 3rd | 6.0 |
| 7-8 | Tex. | L | 0-10 | | 3 | 11 | Rodriguez | Elarton | | 40-44 | 3rd | 7.0 |
| 7-9 | Oak. | W | 5-4 | | 6 | 9 | Howry | Dotel | | 41-44 | 3rd | 6.0 |
| 7-10 | Oak. | L | 7-16 | | 11 | 19 | Mulder | White | | 41-45 | T3rd | 6.0 |
| 7-11 | Oak. | W | 4-1 | | 9 | 9 | Lee | Zito | Riske | 42-45 | T3rd | 5.5 |
| 7-15 | At Sea. | L | 1-2 | | 5 | 4 | Pineiro | Westbrook | Guardado | 42-46 | T3rd | 5.5 |
| 7-16 | At Sea. | W | 18-6 | | 21 | 7 | Lee | Blackley | | 43-46 | T3rd | 4.5 |
| 7-17 | At Sea. | W | 6-5 | | 9 | 13 | Sabathia | Franklin | Riske | 44-46 | 3rd | 4.5 |
| 7-18 | At Sea. | L | 5-7 | | 11 | 10 | Hasegawa | Miller | Guardado | 44-47 | T3rd | 4.5 |
| 7-19 | At Ana. | W | 8-5 | (10) | 12 | 10 | Riske | Percival | Miller | 45-47 | 3rd | 4.5 |
| 7-20 | At Ana. | W | 14-5 | | 19 | 12 | Westbrook | Washburn | | 46-47 | 3rd | 4.0 |
| 7-21 | Chi. | L | 0-14 | | 2 | 19 | Buehrle | Lee | | 46-48 | 3rd | 5.0 |
| 7-22 | Chi. | L | 0-3 | | 6 | 8 | Garcia | Sabathia | Takatsu | 46-49 | 3rd | 6.0 |
| 7-23 | K.C. | W | 3-2 | (11) | 11 | 11 | White | Field | | 47-49 | 3rd | 6.0 |
| 7-24# | K.C. | W | 10-2 | | 14 | 6 | Durbin | George | | 48-49 | | |
| 7-24$ | K.C. | W | 4-3 | | 8 | 8 | Miller | Sullivan | | 49-49 | 3rd | 5.0 |
| 7-25 | K.C. | W | 5-1 | | 8 | 6 | Westbrook | Greinke | | 50-49 | 3rd | 4.5 |
| 7-26 | Det. | L | 4-13 | | 8 | 17 | Maroth | Lee | | 50-50 | 3rd | 5.5 |
| 7-27 | Det. | W | 10-6 | | 13 | 8 | Sabathia | Knotts | | 51-50 | 3rd | 5.5 |
| 7-28 | Det. | W | 5-4 | | 11 | 6 | Elarton | Walker | Wickman | 52-50 | 3rd | 5.5 |
| 7-30 | At K.C. | W | 7-6 | (11) | 13 | 9 | Betancourt | Sullivan | | 53-50 | 3rd | 4.5 |
| 7-31 | At K.C. | L | 3-10 | | 9 | 16 | Greinke | Tadano | | 53-51 | 3rd | 5.5 |
| 8-1 | At K.C. | L | 7-8 | | 13 | 11 | May | Sabathia | Camp | 53-52 | 3rd | 6.5 |
| 8-2 | At Tor. | L | 1-6 | | 6 | 8 | Lilly | Lee | | 53-53 | 3rd | 7.0 |
| 8-3 | At Tor. | L | 6-7 | | 8 | 11 | Speier | Betancourt | Frasor | 53-54 | 3rd | 8.0 |
| 8-4 | At Tor. | W | 14-5 | | 21 | 11 | Westbrook | Towers | | 54-54 | 3rd | 8.0 |
| 8-5 | At Tor. | W | 6-3 | (10) | 10 | 9 | Betancourt | Ligtenberg | Wickman | 55-54 | 3rd | 7.0 |
| 8-6 | At Chi. | W | 3-2 | | 9 | 6 | Sabathia | Buehrle | Wickman | 56-54 | 3rd | 6.0 |
| 8-7 | At Chi. | W | 6-5 | | 13 | 8 | Miller | Takatsu | Wickman | 57-54 | 2nd | 6.0 |
| 8-8 | At Chi. | L | 2-3 | | 7 | 8 | Takatsu | Betancourt | | 57-55 | 3rd | 6.0 |
| 8-9 | At Chi. | W | 13-11 | | 16 | 12 | Westbrook | Diaz | | 58-55 | 2nd | 5.0 |
| 8-10 | Tor. | W | 2-0 | | 8 | 5 | Durbin | Bush | Wickman | 59-55 | 2nd | 4.0 |
| 8-11 | Tor. | W | 3-2 | | 7 | 7 | Sabathia | Frederick | Wickman | 60-55 | 2nd | 3.0 |
| 8-12 | Tor. | W | 6-2 | | 7 | 3 | Riske | Ligtenberg | | 61-55 | 2nd | 3.0 |
| 8-13 | Min. | W | 8-2 | | 13 | 10 | Elarton | Silva | | 62-55 | 2nd | 2.0 |
| 8-14 | Min. | W | 7-1 | | 8 | 8 | Westbrook | Lohse | | 63-55 | 2nd | 1.0 |
| 8-15 | Min. | L | 2-4 | (10) | 7 | 9 | Rincon | White | Nathan | 63-56 | 2nd | 2.0 |
| 8-16 | At Tex. | L | 2-5 | | 6 | 8 | Ramirez | Sabathia | Cordero | 63-57 | 2nd | 2.5 |
| 8-17 | At Tex. | L | 4-16 | | 9 | 17 | Erickson | Lee | Brocail | 63-58 | 2nd | 3.5 |
| 8-18 | At Tex. | L | 2-5 | | 12 | 9 | Rogers | Elarton | Cordero | 63-59 | 2nd | 4.5 |
| 8-20 | At Min. | L | 1-5 | | 3 | 9 | Lohse | Westbrook | | 63-60 | 2nd | 5.0 |
| 8-21 | At Min. | L | 1-8 | | 7 | 8 | Mulholland | Durbin | | 63-61 | 2nd | 6.0 |
| 8-22 | At Min. | L | 3-7 | | 9 | 11 | Radke | Sabathia | | 63-62 | 2nd | 7.0 |
| 8-23 | N.Y. | L | 4-6 | | 8 | 9 | Gordon | Wickman | Rivera | 63-63 | 2nd | 8.0 |
| 8-24 | N.Y. | L | 4-5 | | 7 | 12 | Gordon | Wickman | Rivera | 63-64 | 2nd | 8.0 |
| 8-25 | N.Y. | W | 4-3 | | 7 | 6 | Riske | Gordon | Betancourt | 64-64 | 2nd | 8.0 |
| 8-26 | Chi. | L | 9-14 | | 14 | 16 | Cotts | Durbin | | 64-65 | 2nd | 8.0 |
| 8-27 | Chi. | W | 6-3 | | 6 | 9 | Sabathia | Grilli | Wickman | 65-65 | 2nd | 7.0 |
| 8-28 | Chi. | L | 3-5 | | 10 | 8 | Contreras | Lee | Takatsu | 65-66 | 2nd | 8.0 |
| 8-29 | Chi. | W | 9-0 | | 12 | 2 | Elarton | Garland | | 66-66 | 2nd | 7.0 |
| 8-31 | At N.Y. | W | 22-0 | | 22 | 5 | Westbrook | Vazquez | | 67-66 | 2nd | 7.0 |
| 9-1 | At N.Y. | L | 3-5 | | 6 | 9 | Hernandez | Sabathia | Rivera | 67-67 | 2nd | 8.0 |
| 9-2 | At N.Y. | L | 1-9 | | 8 | 11 | Lieber | Lee | | 67-68 | 2nd | 9.0 |

| Date | Opp. | Res. | Score | (inn.*) | Hits | Opp. hits | Winning pitcher | Losing pitcher | Save | Record | Pos. | GB |
|---|---|---|---|---|---|---|---|---|---|---|---|---|
| 9-3 | Ana. | L | 5-10 | | 10 | 13 | Escobar | Elarton | | 67-69 | 3rd | 10.0 |
| 9-4 | Ana. | L | 1-6 | | 6 | 9 | Washburn | Davis | | 67-70 | 3rd | 11.0 |
| 9-5 | Ana. | L | 1-2 | | 2 | 7 | Lackey | Westbrook | Rodriguez | 67-71 | 3rd | 11.0 |
| 9-6 | At Sea. | W | 5-0 | | 5 | 5 | Sabathia | Meche | | 68-71 | 3rd | 10.0 |
| 9-8 | At Sea. | W | 9-5 | | 14 | 7 | Lee | Baek | | 69-71 | 3rd | 10.5 |
| 9-10 | At Oak. | W | 4-3 | (12) | 10 | 8 | White | Duchscherer | Wickman | 70-71 | 3rd | 10.5 |
| 9-11 | At Oak. | L | 4-5 | | 9 | 8 | Rincon | Howry | Dotel | 70-72 | 3rd | 11.5 |
| 9-12 | At Oak. | L | 0-1 | | 6 | 5 | Zito | Westbrook | Dotel | 70-73 | 3rd | 12.5 |
| 9-14 | Det. | L | 3-11 | | 8 | 16 | Bonderman | Denney | | 70-74 | 3rd | 14.0 |
| 9-15 | Det. | W | 5-3 | | 11 | 6 | Howry | Yan | Wickman | 71-74 | 3rd | 14.0 |
| 9-16 | Det. | L | 4-6 | | 8 | 8 | Walker | Sabathia | Yan | 71-75 | 3rd | 15.0 |
| 9-17 | K.C. | L | 4-6 | | 6 | 12 | Wood | Westbrook | Affeldt | 71-76 | 3rd | 15.0 |
| 9-18 | K.C. | L | 1-7 | | 4 | 9 | Gobble | Lee | | 71-77 | 3rd | 15.0 |
| 9-19 | K.C. | W | 8-3 | | 13 | 10 | Denney | Bautista | | 72-77 | 3rd | 15.0 |
| 9-20 | At Det. | L | 1-3 | | 8 | 8 | Maroth | Elarton | Yan | 72-78 | 3rd | 16.0 |
| 9-21 | At Det. | W | 8-7 | | 12 | 9 | Howry | Yan | Wickman | 73-78 | 3rd | 15.0 |
| 9-22 | At Det. | W | 7-6 | | 9 | 10 | Westbrook | Ledezma | | 74-78 | 3rd | 14.0 |
| 9-23 | Min. | W | 9-7 | | 13 | 14 | Lee | Durbin | Betancourt | 75-78 | 3rd | 13.0 |
| 9-24 | Min. | L | 2-8 | | 4 | 15 | Santana | Denney | | 75-79 | 3rd | 14.0 |
| 9-25 | Min. | W | 5-3 | | 5 | 6 | Howry | Romero | Wickman | 76-79 | 3rd | 13.0 |
| 9-26 | Min. | L | 2-6 | | 9 | 8 | Silva | Cruceta | | 76-80 | 3rd | 14.0 |
| 9-27 | At K.C. | W | 6-1 | | 11 | 5 | Westbrook | Cerda | | 77-80 | 3rd | 13.5 |
| 9-28 | At K.C. | W | 5-1 | | 10 | 3 | Lee | May | | 78-80 | 3rd | 13.0 |
| 9-29 | At K.C. | W | 5-2 | | 10 | 10 | Bartosh | Wood | Wickman | 79-80 | 3rd | 11.5 |
| | | | | | | | | | | | | |
| 10-1 | At Min. | L | 3-4 | | 8 | 8 | Crain | Howry | Nathan | 79-81 | 3rd | 12.0 |
| 10-2 | At Min. | L | 5-6 | (12) | 12 | 14 | Lohse | Riske | | 79-82 | 3rd | 12.0 |
| 10-3 | At Min. | W | 5-2 | | 9 | 5 | Lee | Lohse | Wickman | 80-82 | 3rd | 12.0 |

Monthly records: April (9-13), May (13-13), June (15-13), July (16-12), August (14-15), September (12-14), October (1-2).
*Innings, if other than nine. # Day separate admission. $ Night separate admission.

## RECORDS

**2004 regular-season record**: 80-82
**Position:** 3rd in A.L. Central
**Home:** 44-37 **Road:** 36-45
**A.L. East:** 17-15 **A.L. Central:** 36-40
**A.L. West:** 17-19 **N.L.** 10-8
**Vs. LH starters:** 24-34
**Vs. RH starters:** 56-48
**Grass:** 76-70 **Artificial:** 4-12
**Day:** 23-22 **Night:** 57-60
**1-Run:** 26-20 **X-inn.:** 11-13
**Doubleheaders:** 0-0-0
**Team record past five years:** 403-407 (.498, ranks 8th in league in that span)

## TEAM LEADERS

**Batting average:** Travis Hafner (.311).
**At-bats:** Ronnie Belliard (599).
**Runs:** Matt Lawton (109).
**Hits:** Ronnie Belliard (169).
**Total Bases:** Casey Blake (285).
**Doubles:** Ronnie Belliard (48).
**Triples:** Ben Broussard, Jody Gerut (5).
**Home runs:** Casey Blake, Travis Hafner (28).
**Runs batted in:** Travis Hafner (109).
**Stolen bases:** Matt Lawton (23).
**Slugging percentage:** Travis Hafner (.583).
**On-base percentage:** Travis Hafner (.410).
**Wins:** Cliff Lee, Jake Westbrook (14).
**Earned-run average:** Jake Westbrook (3.38).
**Complete games:** Jake Westbrook (5).
**Shutouts:** Scott Elarton, C.C. Sabathia, Jake Westbrook (1).
**Saves:** Bob Wickman (13).
**Innings pitched:** Jake Westbrook (215.2).
**Strikeouts:** Cliff Lee (161).

## GAMES BY POSITION

**Catcher:** Victor Martinez 132, Tim Laker 41, Josh Bard 7, Sandy Martinez 1.
**First base:** Ben Broussard 133, Lou Merloni 42, Travis Hafner 11, Casey Blake 8, Josh Phelps 8.
**Second base:** Ronnie Belliard 151, John McDonald 12, Lou Merloni 7, Brandon Phillips 6.
**Third base:** Casey Blake 152, Lou Merloni 10, John McDonald 9, Jhonny Peralta 2.
**Shortstop:** Omar Vizquel 147, John McDonald 30, Jhonny Peralta 7.
**Outfield:** Matt Lawton 142, Jody Gerut 131, Coco Crisp 128, Alex Escobar 42, Grady Sizemore 42, Ryan Ludwick 15, Mark Little 11, Raul Gonzalez 4, Lou Merloni 4.
**Designated hitter:** Travis Hafner 128, Josh Phelps 16, Victor Martinez 8, John McDonald 8, Coco Crisp 6, Alex Escobar 3, Matt Lawton 3, Lou Merloni 3, Ernie Young 2, Ronnie Belliard 1, Jody Gerut 1.

## TOP DRAFT CHOICES

1. **Jeremy Sowers,** LHP, Vanderbilt.
2. **Justin Hoyman,** RHP, Florida.
3. **Scott Lewis,** LHP, Ohio State.
4. **Chuck Lofgren,** LHP, Serra H.S., Burlingame, Calif.
5. **Mike Butia,** James Madison.
6. **Cody Bunkelman,** RHP, Itasca (Minn.) CC.
7. **Mark Jecmen,** RHP, Stanford.
8. **Justin Pekarek,** LHP, Nebraska.
9. **Chris Niesel,** RHP, Notre Dame.
10. **Reinaldo Alicano,** OF, Josefina Barcelo H.S., Guaynabo, Puerto Rico.

# DETROIT TIGERS
## AMERICAN LEAGUE CENTRAL DIVISION

## 2005 SEASON

### Tigers Schedule
Home games shaded.
All-Star Game July 12 at Detroit. Schedule subject to change.

**April**

| SUN | MON | TUE | WED | THU | FRI | SAT |
|---|---|---|---|---|---|---|
| 3 | 4 KC | 5 | 6 KC | 7 KC | 8 CLE | 9 CLE |
| 10 CLE | 11 | 12 MIN | 13 MIN | 14 MIN | 15 KC | 16 KC |
| 17 KC | 18 BAL | 19 BAL | 20 CHW | 21 CHW | 22 MIN | 23 MIN |
| 24 MIN | 25 | 26 CLE | 27 CLE | 28 CLE | 29 CHW | 30 CHW |

**May**

| SUN | MON | TUE | WED | THU | FRI | SAT |
|---|---|---|---|---|---|---|
| 1 CHW | 2 BOS | 3 BOS | 4 BOS | 5 BOS | 6 ANA | 7 ANA |
| 8 ANA | 9 TEX | 10 TEX | 11 TEX | 12 | 13 ANA | 14 ANA |
| 15 ANA | 16 | 17 TB | 18 TB | 19 TB | 20 ARI | 21 ARI |
| 22 ARI | 23 | 24 NYY | 25 NYY | 26 NYY | 27 BAL | 28 BAL |
| 29 BAL | 30 | 31 TEX | | | | |

**June**

| SUN | MON | TUE | WED | THU | FRI | SAT |
|---|---|---|---|---|---|---|
| | | | 1 TEX | 2 TEX | 3 BAL | 4 BAL |
| 5 BAL | 6 LA | 7 LA | 8 LA | 9 | 10 COL | 11 COL |
| 12 COL | 13 | 14 SD | 15 SD | 16 SD | 17 SF | 18 SF |
| 19 SF | 20 | 21 MIN | 22 MIN | 23 MIN | 24 ARI | 25 ARI |
| 26 ARI | 27 | 28 CHW | 29 CHW | 30 CHW | | |

**July**

| SUN | MON | TUE | WED | THU | FRI | SAT |
|---|---|---|---|---|---|---|
| | | | | | 1 NYY | 2 NYY |
| 3 NYY | 4 CLE | 5 CLE | 6 CLE | 7 TB | 8 TB | 9 TB |
| 10 TB | 11 | 12 All-Star | 13 | 14 KC | 15 KC | 16 KC |
| 17 KC | 18 CHW | 19 CHW | 20 CHW | 21 MIN | 22 MIN | 23 MIN |
| 24 MIN | 25 SEA | 26 SEA | 27 SEA | 28 | 29 OAK | 30 OAK |
| 31 OAK | | | | | | |

**August**

| SUN | MON | TUE | WED | THU | FRI | SAT |
|---|---|---|---|---|---|---|
| | 1 | 2 SEA | 3 SEA | 4 SEA | 5 CLE | 6 CLE |
| 7 CLE | 8 TOR | 9 TOR | 10 TOR | 11 TOR | 12 KC | 13 KC |
| 14 KC | 15 BOS | 16 BOS | 17 BOS | 18 | 19 TOR | 20 TOR |
| 21 TOR | 22 | 23 OAK | 24 OAK | 25 OAK | 26 BOS | 27 BOS |
| 28 BOS | 29 CLE | 30 CLE | 31 CLE | | | |

**September**

| SUN | MON | TUE | WED | THU | FRI | SAT |
|---|---|---|---|---|---|---|
| | | | | 1 CHW | 2 CHW | 3 CHW |
| 4 CHW | 5 CLE | 6 CLE | 7 CLE | 8 | 9 KC | 10 KC |
| 11 KC | 12 MIN | 13 MIN | 14 MIN | 15 ANA | 16 ANA | 17 ANA |
| 18 ANA | 19 KC | 20 KC | 21 KC | 22 | 23 SEA | 24 SEA |
| 25 SEA | 26 CHW | 27 CHW | 28 CHW | 29 CHW | 30 MIN | |

**October**

| SUN | MON | TUE | WED | THU | FRI | SAT |
|---|---|---|---|---|---|---|
| | | | | | | 1 MIN |
| 2 MIN | 3 | 4 | 5 | 6 | 7 | 8 |

Home games shaded. All-Star Game July 12 at Detroit. Schedule subject to change.

### CLUB DIRECTORY

**Owner/director**
Michael Ilitch
**President, CEO, general manager**
David Dombrowski
**Special assistants to the president**
Al Kaline, Willie Horton
**Senior vice president**
Jim Devellano
**Director of baseball operations**
Mike Smith
**Vice president of player personnel**
Scott Reid
**V.p., assistant general manager**
Al Avila
**V.p. of amateur scouting**
David Chadd
**Director of minor league operations**
Dan Lunetta
**Senior director of communications**
Cliff Russell
**Senior advisor, minor leagues**
Dave Miller
**Media relations coordinator**
Rick Thompson
**Broadcasting and media relations mgr.**
Molly Light
**Director, community relations**
Celia Bobrowsky

### MINOR LEAGUE AFFILIATES

| Class | Team | League | Manager |
|---|---|---|---|
| AAA | Toledo | International | Larry Parrish |
| AA | Erie | Eastern | Duffy Dyer |
| Advanced A | Lakeland | Florida State | Mike Rojas |
| A | West Michigan | Midwest | Matt Walbeck |
| Short-Seasom A | Oneonta | New York-Pennsylvania | TBA |
| Rookie | Gulf Coast Tigers | Gulf Coast | Kevin Bradshaw |

### BROADCAST INFORMATION

**Radio:** WXYT-AM (1270).
**Cable TV:** Fox Sports Net Detroit.

### SPRING TRAINING

**Ballpark (city):** Joker Marchant Stadium (Lakeland, Fla.).
**Ticket information:** 863-686-8075.

**For more on the Tigers, go to msn.foxsports.com/mlb/teams.**

Rodriguez

## SPRING TRAINING ROSTER

Manager—Alan Trammell (3).
Coaches—Bob Cluck (54), Bruce Fields (29), Kirk Gibson (22), Mick Kelleher (18), Lance Parrish (13), Juan Samuel (8).

| No. | PITCHERS | B/T | Ht./Wt. | Age* | 2004 Clubs |
|---|---|---|---|---|---|
| | Baugh, Kenny | R/R | 6-4/195 | 26 | Erie |
| 38 | Bonderman, Jeremy | R/R | 6-2/210 | 22 | Detroit |
| 51 | Colyer, Steve | L/L | 6-4/205 | 26 | Toledo, Detroit |
| 62 | German, Franklyn | R/R | 6-7/270 | 25 | Toledo, Detroit |
| 21 | Johnson, Jason | R/R | 6-6/217 | 31 | Detroit |
| 35 | Knotts, Gary | R/R | 6-4/230 | 28 | Detroit |
| | Larrison, Preston | R/R | 6-4/235 | 24 | Erie |
| 41 | Ledezma, Wilfredo | L/L | 6-4/212 | 24 | Erie, Detroit |
| | Lewis, Colby | R/R | 6-4/230 | 25 | Texas |
| 46 | Maroth, Mike | L/L | 6-0/190 | 27 | Detroit |
| 51 | Novoa, Roberto | R/R | 6-5/200 | 25 | Erie, Detroit |
| | Percival, Troy | R/R | 6-3/235 | 35 | Anaheim |
| 37 | Robertson, Nate | R/L | 6-2/215 | 27 | Detroit |
| 56 | Rodney, Fernando | R/R | 5-11/208 | 28 | Did Not Play |
| 48 | Spurling, Chris | R/R | 6-5/228 | 27 | Did Not Play |
| 74 | Urbina, Ugueth | R/R | 6-0/205 | 31 | Lakeland, Detroit |
| | Verlander, Justin | R/R | 6-4/200 | 22 | Did Not Play |
| 32 | Walker, Jamie | L/L | 6-2/195 | 33 | Detroit |
| | Woodyard, Mark | R/R | 6-2/195 | 26 | Erie |

| No. | CATCHERS | B/T | Ht./Wt. | Age* | 2004 Clubs |
|---|---|---|---|---|---|
| 15 | Inge, Brandon | R/R | 5-11/195 | 27 | Detroit |
| 7 | Rodriguez, Ivan | R/R | 5-9/218 | 33 | Detroit |
| | Shelton, Chris | R/R | 6-0/220 | 24 | Toledo |
| 3 | Wilson, Vance | R/R | 5-11/190 | 32 | Norfolk, Binghamton, New York N.L., |

| No. | INFIELDERS | B/T | Ht./Wt. | Age* | 2004 Clubs |
|---|---|---|---|---|---|
| 9 | Guillen, Carlos | B/R | 6-1/204 | 29 | Detroit |
| 20 | Infante, Omar | R/R | 6-0/176 | 23 | Detroit |
| | Martinez, Ramon | R/R | 6-1/190 | 22 | Chicago N.L. |
| 12 | Pena, Carlos | L/L | 6-2/215 | 26 | Detroit |
| 55 | Raburn, Ryan | R/R | 6-0/185 | 23 | Lakeland, Erie, Detroit |
| 44 | Smith, Jason | L/R | 6-3/199 | 27 | Toledo, Detroit |
| 10 | Vina, Fernando | L/R | 5-9/180 | 35 | Detroit |
| | Young, Dmitri | B/R | 6-2/245 | 31 | Toledo, Detroit |

| No. | OUTFIELDERS | B/T | Ht./Wt. | Age* | 2004 Clubs |
|---|---|---|---|---|---|
| | Gettis, Byron | R/R | 6-0/240 | 25 | Kansas City, Omaha, Wichita |
| 26 | Granderson, Curtis | L/R | 6-1/185 | 24 | Erie, Detroit |
| 4 | Higginson, Bobby | L/R | 5-11/195 | 34 | Detroit |
| 40 | Logan, Nook | B/R | 6-2/180 | 25 | Toledo, Detroit |
| 27 | Monroe, Craig | R/R | 6-1/220 | 28 | Toledo, Detroit |
| 19 | Sanchez, Alex | L/L | 5-10/180 | 28 | Toledo, Detroit |
| 33 | Thames, Marcus | R/R | 6-2/205 | 28 | Toledo, Detroit |
| 24 | White, Rondell | R/R | 6-1/225 | 33 | Detroit |
| | Wise, Dewayne | L/L | 6-1/180 | 27 | Myrtle Beach, Rome, Richmond, Atlanta |

*Age as of April 1, 2005.

## BALLPARK INFORMATION

**Ballpark (capacity, surface)**
Comerica Park (40,120, grass)

**Address**
2100 Woodward
Detroit, MI 48201

**Official website**
www.detroittigers.com

**Business phone**
313-471-2000

**Ticket information**
313-471-2255

**Field dimensions (from home plate)**
To left field at foul line, 345 feet
To center field, 420 feet
To right field at foul line, 330 feet

**First game played**
April 11, 2000 (Tigers 5, Mariners 2)

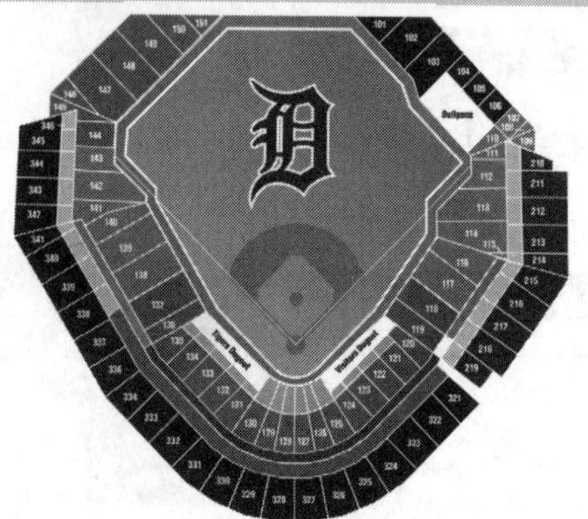

# 2004 REVIEW
## DAY BY DAY

| Date | Opp. | Res. | Score | (inn.*) | Hits | Opp. hits | Winning pitcher | Losing pitcher | Save | Record | Pos. | GB |
|---|---|---|---|---|---|---|---|---|---|---|---|---|
| 4-5 | At Tor. | W | 7-0 | | 11 | 8 | Johnson | Halladay | | 1-0 | T1st | ... |
| 4-6 | At Tor. | W | 7-3 | | 12 | 6 | Maroth | Batista | Robertson | 2-0 | T1st | ... |
| 4-7 | At Tor. | W | 6-3 | | 6 | 5 | Bonderman | Hentgen | | 3-0 | 1st | +1.0 |
| 4-8 | Min. | W | 10-6 | | 14 | 10 | Cornejo | Fultz | | 4-0 | 1st | +2.0 |
| 4-10 | Min. | L | 5-10 | | 9 | 15 | Radke | Johnson | | 4-1 | 1st | +1.0 |
| 4-11 | Min. | W | 6-5 | (10) | 10 | 14 | Colyer | Roa | | 5-1 | 1st | +1.0 |
| 4-13 | Tor. | L | 5-7 | | 10 | 10 | Adams | Patterson | Speier | 5-2 | 1st | +1.0 |
| 4-14 | Tor. | W | 5-3 | | 8 | 9 | Robertson | Lilly | Patterson | 6-2 | 1st | +1.0 |
| 4-15 | Tor. | L | 0-11 | | 8 | 12 | Halladay | Johnson | | 6-3 | T1st | ... |
| 4-16 | At Cle. | L | 3-10 | | 8 | 19 | Sabathia | Cornejo | | 6-4 | T1st | ... |
| 4-17 | At Cle. | W | 6-1 | | 12 | 11 | Maroth | Davis | | 7-4 | T1st | ... |
| 4-18 | At Cle. | L | 7-9 | | 11 | 12 | Lee | Bonderman | Riske | 7-5 | 3rd | 1.0 |
| 4-19 | At Cle. | W | 10-4 | | 8 | 8 | Levine | Betancourt | | 8-5 | 3rd | 0.5 |
| 4-20 | At Min. | L | 4-6 | | 7 | 9 | Silva | Johnson | Nathan | 8-6 | 3rd | 1.5 |
| 4-21 | At Min. | W | 11-8 | | 15 | 12 | Levine | Radke | Urbina | 9-6 | 2nd | 0.5 |
| 4-22 | At Min. | L | 3-4 | | 10 | 8 | Santana | Maroth | Nathan | 9-7 | 3rd | 1.5 |
| 4-23 | Cle. | W | 17-3 | | 16 | 6 | Bonderman | Davis | Yan | 10-7 | 3rd | 1.5 |
| 4-24 | Cle. | W | 5-2 | | 9 | 6 | Urbina | Stewart | | 11-7 | 2nd | 0.5 |
| 4-25 | Cle. | L | 2-3 | | 2 | 6 | Westbrook | Johnson | | 11-8 | 3rd | 1.5 |
| 4-27 | Ana. | L | 4-10 | | 6 | 15 | Lackey | Cornejo | Shields | 11-9 | 3rd | 2.0 |
| 4-28 | Ana. | W | 10-2 | | 15 | 8 | Maroth | Colon | | 12-9 | 3rd | 2.0 |
| 4-29 | Ana. | L | 3-12 | | 10 | 14 | Washburn | Robertson | | 12-10 | 3rd | 2.5 |
| 4-30 | Sea. | L | 1-3 | (10) | 4 | 9 | Myers | Levine | Guardado | 12-11 | 3rd | 3.5 |
| 5-1 | Sea. | W | 4-2 | | 9 | 6 | Bonderman | Franklin | Urbina | 13-11 | 3rd | 2.5 |
| 5-2 | Sea. | L | 2-12 | | 4 | 14 | Meche | Cornejo | | 13-12 | 3rd | 2.5 |
| 5-3 | At Ana. | L | 9-11 | | 15 | 14 | Gregg | Levine | Percival | 13-13 | 3rd | 3.5 |
| 5-4 | At Ana. | L | 4-11 | | 8 | 13 | Washburn | Robertson | | 13-14 | 3rd | 3.5 |
| 5-5 | At Ana. | L | 3-6 | | 5 | 7 | Escobar | Johnson | Percival | 13-15 | 3rd | 4.5 |
| 5-7 | At Tex. | W | 8-7 | | 10 | 9 | Levine | Ramirez | Urbina | 14-15 | 3rd | 3.5 |
| 5-8 | At Tex. | L | 15-16 | (10) | 16 | 16 | Cordero | Urbina | | 14-16 | 3rd | 3.5 |
| 5-9 | At Tex. | W | 5-3 | | 6 | 3 | Robertson | Rogers | Urbina | 15-16 | 3rd | 2.5 |
| 5-11 | Oak. | L | 4-5 | (15) | 14 | 16 | Duchscherer | Patterson | Mecir | 15-17 | 3rd | 3.5 |
| 5-12 | Oak. | L | 1-2 | | 7 | 4 | Harden | Bonderman | Rhodes | 15-18 | 3rd | 4.5 |
| 5-13 | Oak. | W | 3-1 | | 12 | 5 | Maroth | Redman | Urbina | 16-18 | 3rd | 4.5 |
| 5-14 | Tex. | W | 7-1 | | 9 | 2 | Knotts | Benoit | Yan | 17-18 | 3rd | 4.5 |
| 5-15 | Tex. | L | 1-6 | | 9 | 9 | Rogers | Robertson | | 17-19 | 3rd | 5.5 |
| 5-16 | Tex. | W | 3-1 | | 11 | 6 | Johnson | Drese | Urbina | 18-19 | 3rd | 4.5 |
| 5-18 | At Oak. | W | 5-1 | | 8 | 4 | Bonderman | Harden | | 19-19 | 3rd | 4.0 |
| 5-19 | At Oak. | L | 2-6 | | 9 | 13 | Redman | Maroth | | 19-20 | 3rd | 5.0 |
| 5-20 | At Oak. | L | 2-3 | | 10 | 8 | Hudson | Walker | Rhodes | 19-21 | 3rd | 5.0 |
| 5-21 | At Sea. | W | 5-0 | | 8 | 8 | Robertson | Meche | | 20-21 | 3rd | 4.0 |
| 5-22 | At Sea. | W | 8-4 | | 12 | 7 | Johnson | Putz | | 21-21 | 3rd | 4.0 |
| 5-23 | At Sea. | L | 1-3 | | 5 | 9 | Garcia | Bonderman | Guardado | 21-22 | 3rd | 4.0 |
| 5-25 | At K.C. | L | 3-4 | | 8 | 10 | Grimsley | Maroth | Affeldt | 21-23 | 3rd | 4.0 |
| 5-26 | At K.C. | L | 3-7 | | 12 | 10 | May | Knotts | Affeldt | 21-24 | 3rd | 5.0 |
| 5-27 | At K.C. | W | 17-7 | | 27 | 10 | Robertson | Anderson | | 22-24 | 3rd | 5.0 |
| 5-28 | Bal. | L | 5-7 | | 10 | 13 | DuBose | Johnson | Julio | 22-25 | 3rd | 6.0 |
| 5-29 | Bal. | L | 4-8 | | 9 | 13 | Cabrera | Bonderman | Parrish | 22-26 | 3rd | 6.0 |
| 5-30 | Bal. | L | 3-7 | | 9 | 13 | Groom | Urbina | | 22-27 | 4th | 7.0 |
| 5-31 | K.C. | W | 8-4 | | 14 | 9 | Knotts | May | | 23-27 | 3rd | 6.5 |
| 6-1 | K.C. | L | 3-5 | | 10 | 11 | Grimsley | Yan | Affeldt | 23-28 | 3rd | 6.5 |
| 6-2 | K.C. | W | 2-0 | | 6 | 9 | Johnson | Greinke | Urbina | 24-28 | 3rd | 5.5 |
| 6-3 | K.C. | L | 6-9 | | 8 | 16 | Reyes | Bonderman | Affeldt | 24-29 | 3rd | 6.0 |
| 6-4 | At Min. | L | 2-3 | | 7 | 7 | Nathan | Walker | | 24-30 | 3rd | 7.0 |
| 6-5 | At Min. | W | 6-0 | | 12 | 3 | Knotts | Greisinger | | 25-30 | 3rd | 6.0 |
| 6-6 | At Min. | L | 5-6 | | 13 | 10 | Romero | Yan | Nathan | 25-31 | 4th | 6.0 |
| 6-8 | Atl. | L | 3-4 | (10) | 10 | 8 | Reitsma | Patterson | Smoltz | 25-32 | 4th | 7.0 |
| 6-9 | Atl. | W | 4-2 | | 11 | 8 | Dingman | Thomson | Urbina | 26-32 | 4th | 6.0 |
| 6-10 | Atl. | W | 7-4 | | 8 | 9 | Maroth | Alfonseca | Urbina | 27-32 | 3rd | 6.0 |
| 6-11 | Fla. | W | 8-4 | | 11 | 5 | Knotts | Phelps | | 28-32 | 3rd | 5.0 |
| 6-12 | Fla. | W | 6-2 | | 9 | 7 | Robertson | Penny | Urbina | 29-32 | 3rd | 5.0 |
| 6-13 | Fla. | L | 2-9 | | 7 | 15 | Willis | Johnson | | 29-33 | 4th | 5.5 |
| 6-15 | At Phi. | W | 10-3 | | 11 | 2 | Bonderman | Powell | | 30-33 | 4th | 5.5 |
| 6-17# | At Phi. | L | 2-6 | | 7 | 7 | Myers | Maroth | | 30-34 | | |
| 6-17$ | At Phi. | W | 5-4 | (11) | 14 | 11 | Urbina | Madson | Patterson | 31-34 | 4th | 6.0 |

| Date | Opp. | Res. | Score | (inn.*) | Hits | Opp. hits | Winning pitcher | Losing pitcher | Save | Record | Pos. | GB |
|---|---|---|---|---|---|---|---|---|---|---|---|---|
| 6-18 | At N.Y. | L | 2-3 | | 8 | 7 | Looper | Patterson | | 31-35 | 4th | 6.0 |
| 6-19 | At N.Y. | L | 3-4 | (10) | 9 | 9 | Looper | Dingman | | 31-36 | 4th | 6.0 |
| 6-20 | At N.Y. | L | 1-6 | | 5 | 7 | Trachsel | Bonderman | | 31-37 | 4th | 7.0 |
| 6-22 | At K.C. | L | 1-8 | | 4 | 13 | Gobble | Maroth | Field | 31-38 | 4th | 7.0 |
| 6-23 | At K.C. | L | 3-7 | | 11 | 10 | May | Knotts | | 31-39 | 4th | 8.0 |
| 6-24 | At K.C. | W | 12-3 | | 17 | 4 | Robertson | George | | 32-39 | 4th | 8.0 |
| 6-25 | Ari. | W | 2-1 | | 4 | 1 | Johnson | Webb | Urbina | 33-39 | 4th | 8.0 |
| 6-26 | Ari. | W | 7-6 | | 8 | 10 | Urbina | Villafuerte | | 34-39 | 4th | 7.0 |
| 6-27 | Ari. | W | 9-5 | | 15 | 9 | Walker | Villafuerte | | 35-39 | 4th | 6.0 |
| 6-29 | Cle. | W | 9-7 | (11) | 15 | 11 | Dingman | Jimenez | | 36-39 | 4th | 5.0 |
| 6-30 | Cle. | W | 12-5 | | 17 | 10 | Robertson | Davis | | 37-39 | T3rd | 5.0 |
| 7-1 | Cle. | L | 6-7 | (10) | 11 | 11 | Riske | Urbina | White | 37-40 | 4th | 6.0 |
| 7-2 | At Col. | L | 8-9 | (10) | 16 | 15 | Chacon | Walker | | 37-41 | 4th | 6.0 |
| 7-3 | At Col. | L | 6-11 | | 12 | 16 | Jennings | Maroth | | 37-42 | 4th | 6.0 |
| 7-4 | At Col. | L | 8-10 | | 12 | 10 | Bernero | Knotts | Chacon | 37-43 | 4th | 6.0 |
| 7-5 | At N.Y. | L | 3-10 | | 7 | 11 | Lieber | Robertson | | 37-44 | 4th | 7.0 |
| 7-6 | At N.Y. | W | 9-1 | | 14 | 6 | Johnson | Mussina | | 38-44 | 4th | 7.0 |
| 7-7 | At N.Y. | W | 10-8 | | 13 | 10 | Bonderman | Halsey | Urbina | 39-44 | 4th | 7.0 |
| 7-8 | At Min. | L | 1-7 | | 8 | 9 | Balfour | Maroth | | 39-45 | 4th | 8.0 |
| 7-9 | At Min. | W | 5-3 | | 10 | 9 | Knotts | Silva | Urbina | 40-45 | 4th | 7.0 |
| 7-10 | At Min. | W | 4-2 | | 7 | 9 | Robertson | Radke | Urbina | 41-45 | T3rd | 6.0 |
| 7-11 | At Min. | W | 2-0 | | 2 | 5 | Johnson | Santana | | 42-45 | T3rd | 5.5 |
| 7-15 | N.Y. | L | 1-5 | | 4 | 5 | Contreras | Bonderman | | 42-46 | T3rd | 5.5 |
| 7-16 | N.Y. | W | 8-0 | | 12 | 1 | Maroth | Vazquez | | 43-46 | T3rd | 4.5 |
| 7-17 | N.Y. | L | 3-5 | | 9 | 13 | Hernandez | Knotts | Rivera | 43-47 | 4th | 5.5 |
| 7-18 | N.Y. | W | 4-2 | | 10 | 7 | Robertson | Lieber | Urbina | 44-47 | T3rd | 4.5 |
| 7-19 | Min. | L | 1-3 | | 5 | 7 | Mulholland | Johnson | Nathan | 44-48 | 4th | 5.5 |
| 7-20 | Min. | L | 4-5 | (10) | 10 | 6 | Balfour | Urbina | Nathan | 44-49 | 4th | 6.0 |
| 7-21 | K.C. | W | 4-2 | | 8 | 8 | Maroth | May | Walker | 45-49 | 4th | 6.0 |
| 7-22 | K.C. | L | 7-13 | | 12 | 17 | Gobble | Knotts | | 45-50 | 4th | 7.0 |
| 7-23 | At Chi. | L | 4-6 | | 7 | 9 | Loaiza | Robertson | Takatsu | 45-51 | 4th | 8.0 |
| 7-24 | At Chi. | L | 6-7 | | 10 | 7 | Marte | Urbina | | 45-52 | 4th | 8.5 |
| 7-25 | At Chi. | W | 9-2 | | 10 | 10 | Ledezma | Garland | | 46-52 | 4th | 8.0 |
| 7-26 | At Cle. | W | 13-4 | | 17 | 8 | Maroth | Lee | | 47-52 | 4th | 8.0 |
| 7-27 | At Cle. | L | 6-10 | | 8 | 13 | Sabathia | Knotts | | 47-53 | 4th | 9.0 |
| 7-28 | At Cle. | L | 4-5 | | 6 | 11 | Elarton | Walker | Wickman | 47-54 | 4th | 10.0 |
| 7-29 | Chi. | W | 3-2 | | 5 | 5 | Johnson | Schoeneweis | Urbina | 48-54 | 4th | 9.5 |
| 7-30 | Chi. | W | 5-4 | | 7 | 9 | Yan | Marte | Urbina | 49-54 | 4th | 8.5 |
| 7-31 | Chi. | W | 3-2 | (10) | 7 | 5 | Urbina | Politte | | 50-54 | 4th | 8.5 |
| 8-1 | Chi. | L | 4-6 | | 5 | 14 | Garcia | Bonderman | Takatsu | 50-55 | 4th | 9.5 |
| 8-3 | Tex. | L | 4-5 | | 8 | 9 | Francisco | Robertson | Cordero | 50-56 | 4th | 10.5 |
| 8-4 | Tex. | L | 0-8 | | 4 | 15 | Bacsik | Johnson | | 50-57 | 4th | 11.5 |
| 8-5 | Tex. | L | 1-2 | | 8 | 5 | Drese | Yan | Cordero | 50-58 | 4th | 11.5 |
| 8-6 | Bos. | W | 4-3 | | 10 | 10 | Novoa | Lowe | Urbina | 51-58 | 4th | 10.5 |
| 8-7 | Bos. | L | 4-7 | | 7 | 8 | Martinez | Bonderman | | 51-59 | 4th | 11.5 |
| 8-8 | Bos. | L | 9-11 | | 11 | 14 | Wakefield | Robertson | Foulke | 51-60 | 4th | 11.5 |
| 8-10 | At Oak. | L | 4-5 | | 7 | 7 | Zito | Johnson | Dotel | 51-61 | 4th | 11.0 |
| 8-11 | At Oak. | W | 11-3 | | 13 | 8 | Ledezma | Redman | | 52-61 | 4th | 10.0 |
| 8-12 | At Oak. | W | 5-3 | | 11 | 9 | Maroth | Duchscherer | Urbina | 53-61 | 4th | 10.0 |
| 8-13 | At Ana. | W | 5-3 | | 14 | 9 | Yan | Percival | Urbina | 54-61 | 4th | 9.0 |
| 8-14 | At Ana. | L | 8-11 | | 11 | 17 | Gregg | Novoa | Rodriguez | 54-62 | 4th | 9.0 |
| 8-15 | At Ana. | L | 2-3 | | 7 | 6 | Shields | Johnson | Percival | 54-63 | 4th | 10.0 |
| 8-17 | At Chi. | W | 11-8 | | 15 | 12 | Maroth | Garcia | Urbina | 55-63 | 4th | 10.0 |
| 8-18 | At Chi. | L | 2-9 | | 7 | 9 | Contreras | Bonderman | | 55-64 | 4th | 11.0 |
| 8-19 | At Chi. | W | 8-4 | | 9 | 9 | Ledezma | Garland | Knotts | 56-64 | 4th | 10.0 |
| 8-20 | Sea. | W | 8-3 | | 13 | 9 | Robertson | Villone | | 57-64 | 4th | 10.0 |
| 8-21 | Sea. | W | 11-10 | (11) | 15 | 21 | Walker | Atchison | | 58-64 | 4th | 10.0 |
| 8-22 | Sea. | L | 3-5 | | 10 | 11 | Meche | Maroth | Putz | 58-65 | 4th | 11.0 |
| 8-23 | Chi. | W | 7-0 | | 8 | 7 | Bonderman | Contreras | | 59-65 | 4th | 11.0 |
| 8-24 | Chi. | L | 5-9 | | 10 | 11 | Garland | Ledezma | | 59-66 | 4th | 11.0 |
| 8-25 | Chi. | W | 5-4 | | 12 | 10 | Robertson | Buehrle | | 60-66 | 4th | 11.0 |
| 8-26 | At Bos. | L | 1-4 | | 6 | 12 | Arroyo | Johnson | Foulke | 60-67 | 4th | 11.0 |
| 8-27 | At Bos. | L | 3-5 | | 9 | 11 | Lowe | Maroth | Leskanic | 60-68 | 4th | 11.0 |
| 8-28 | At Bos. | L | 1-5 | | 4 | 9 | Martinez | Bonderman | | 60-69 | 4th | 12.0 |
| 8-29 | At Bos. | L | 1-6 | | 3 | 10 | Wakefield | Ledezma | | 60-70 | 4th | 12.0 |
| 8-30 | At K.C. | W | 9-1 | | 11 | 6 | Robertson | Wood | | 61-70 | 4th | 11.5 |
| 8-31 | At K.C. | L | 8-9 | | 15 | 17 | Affeldt | Urbina | | 61-71 | 4th | 12.5 |
| 9-1 | At K.C. | L | 0-1 | | 4 | 6 | Greinke | Maroth | Affeldt | 61-72 | 4th | 13.5 |
| 9-3 | At T.B. | W | 4-2 | | 7 | 4 | Bonderman | Kazmir | Yan | 62-72 | 4th | 14.0 |
| 9-6 | K.C. | W | 7-3 | | 11 | 9 | Ledezma | Bautista | Knotts | 63-72 | 4th | 13.0 |
| 9-7 | K.C. | L | 2-6 | | 9 | 13 | Serrano | Robertson | | 63-73 | 4th | 14.0 |

| Date | Opp. | Res. | Score | (inn.*) | Hits | Opp. hits | Winning pitcher | Losing pitcher | Save | Record | Pos. | GB |
|---|---|---|---|---|---|---|---|---|---|---|---|---|
| 9-9! | K.C. | L | 5-26 | | 10 | 26 | Greinke | Johnson | | 63-74 | | |
| 9-9& | K.C. | W | 8-0 | | 10 | 7 | Bonderman | May | | 64-74 | 4th | 14.5 |
| 9-10 | Min. | L | 1-4 | | 10 | 9 | Silva | Maroth | Nathan | 64-75 | 4th | 15.5 |
| 9-11 | Min. | L | 2-3 | | 7 | 9 | Crain | Levine | Nathan | 64-76 | 4th | 16.5 |
| 9-12 | Min. | L | 5-8 | | 13 | 15 | Mulholland | Robertson | Nathan | 64-77 | 4th | 17.5 |
| 9-13 | Min. | L | 3-5 | | 8 | 11 | Radke | Johnson | Nathan | 64-78 | 4th | 18.5 |
| 9-14 | At Cle. | W | 11-3 | | 16 | 8 | Bonderman | Denney | | 65-78 | 4th | 18.5 |
| 9-15 | At Cle. | L | 3-5 | | 6 | 11 | Howry | Yan | Wickman | 65-79 | 4th | 19.5 |
| 9-16 | At Cle. | W | 6-4 | | 8 | 8 | Walker | Sabathia | Yan | 66-79 | 4th | 19.5 |
| 9-17 | At Chi. | W | 11-10 | (10) | 11 | 16 | Yan | Takatsu | Ennis | 67-79 | 4th | 18.5 |
| 9-18 | At Chi. | L | 8-9 | (12) | 10 | 12 | Marte | Levine | | 67-80 | 4th | 18.5 |
| 9-19 | At Chi. | L | 1-6 | | 6 | 7 | Garcia | Bonderman | | 67-81 | 4th | 19.5 |
| 9-20 | Cle. | W | 3-1 | | 8 | 8 | Maroth | Elarton | Yan | 68-81 | 4th | 19.5 |
| 9-21 | Cle. | L | 7-8 | | 9 | 12 | Howry | Yan | Wickman | 68-82 | 4th | 19.5 |
| 9-22 | Cle. | L | 6-7 | | 10 | 9 | Westbrook | Ledezma | | 68-83 | 4th | 19.5 |
| 9-24 | At Bal. | L | 5-7 | | 7 | 13 | Parrish | Yan | | 68-84 | 4th | 20.0 |
| 9-25 | At Bal. | L | 0-3 | | 5 | 6 | Riley | Bonderman | Ryan | 68-85 | 4th | 20.0 |
| 9-26 | At Bal. | L | 0-5 | | 3 | 11 | Lopez | Maroth | | 68-86 | 4th | 21.0 |
| 9-27 | Chi. | W | 4-2 | | 3 | 6 | Knotts | Grilli | Yan | 69-86 | 4th | 20.5 |
| 9-28 | Chi. | W | 6-4 | | 10 | 7 | German | Cotts | Yan | 70-86 | 4th | 20.0 |
| 9-29 | Chi. | L | 2-11 | | 8 | 12 | Garcia | Johnson | | 70-87 | 4th | 19.5 |
| 9-30! | At T.B. | W | 8-0 | | 16 | 4 | Bonderman | Brazelton | | 71-87 | | |
| 9-30& | At T.B. | L | 4-6 | | 8 | 11 | Harper | Dingman | Baez | 71-88 | 4th | 19.0 |
| 10-1 | T.B. | L | 1-4 | | 4 | 8 | Bell | Maroth | | 71-89 | 4th | 20.0 |
| 10-2 | T.B. | W | 5-1 | | 6 | 4 | Knotts | Kazmir | | 72-89 | 4th | 19.5 |
| 10-3 | T.B. | L | 4-7 | | 12 | 11 | Halama | Robertson | | 72-90 | 4th | 20.0 |

Monthly records: April (12-11), May (11-16), June (14-12), July (13-15), August (11-17), September (10-17), October (1-2).
*Innings, if other than nine. ! First game of a doubleheader. & Second game of a doubleheader. # Day separate admission. $ Night separate admission.

## RECORDS

**2004 regular-season record:** 72-90
**Position:** 4th in A.L. Central
**Home:** 38-43 **Road:** 34-47
**A.L. East:** 12-20 **A.L. Central:** 36-40
**A.L. West:** 15-21 **N.L.** 9-9
**Vs. LH starters:** 24-38
**Vs. RH starters:** 48-52
**Grass:** 62-84 **Artificial:** 10-6
**Day:** 24-33 **Night:** 48-57
**1-Run:** 12-27 **X-inn.:** 6-9
**Doubleheaders:** 0-0-2
**Team record past five years:** 315-494 (.389, ranks 14th in league in that span)

## TEAM LEADERS

**Batting average:** Ivan Rodriguez (.334).
**At-bats:** Ivan Rodriguez (527).
**Runs:** Carlos Guillen (97).
**Hits:** Ivan Rodriguez (176).
**Total Bases:** Carlos Guillen (283).
**Doubles:** Carlos Guillen (37).
**Triples:** Carlos Guillen (10).
**Home runs:** Carlos Pena (27).
**Runs batted in:** Carlos Guillen (97).
**Stolen bases:** Alex Sanchez (19).
**Slugging percentage:** Carlos Guillen (.542).
**On-base percentage:** Ivan Rodriguez (.383).
**Wins:** Nate Robertson (12).
**Earned-run average:** Mike Maroth (4.31).
**Complete games:** Jeremy Bonderman, Jason Johnson, Mike Maroth (2).
**Shutouts:** Jeremy Bonderman (2).
**Saves:** Ugueth Urbina (21).
**Innings pitched:** Mike Maroth (217.0).
**Strikeouts:** Jeremy Bonderman (168).

## GAMES BY POSITION

**Catcher:** Ivan Rodriguez 124, Brandon Inge 39, Mike DiFelice 12, Chris Shelton 6, Eric Munson 1.
**First base:** Carlos Pena 135, Dmitri Young 25, Chris Shelton 8, Greg Norton 7.
**Second base:** Omar Infante 105, Jason Smith 34, Fernando Vina 29, Ryan Raburn 11.
**Third base:** Eric Munson 94, Brandon Inge 73, Greg Norton 18, Omar Infante 10, Jason Smith 5, Dmitri Young 1.
**Shortstop:** Carlos Guillen 135, Omar Infante 23, Jason Smith 20.
**Outfield:** Craig Monroe 125, Bobby Higginson 115, Alex Sanchez 78, Rondell White 74, Marcus Thames 52, Nook Logan 46, Brandon Inge 26, Curtis Granderson 8, Greg Norton 6, Omar Infante 5, Dmitri Young 2, Chris Shelton 1, Andres Torres 1.
**Designated hitter:** Dmitri Young 74, Rondell White 43, Chris Shelton 11, Bobby Higginson 10, Ivan Rodriguez 8, Eric Munson 7, Greg Norton 7, Carlos Pena 5, Marcus Thames 5, Craig Monroe 2, Jason Smith 2, Andres Torres 2, Mike DiFelice 1, Alex Sanchez 1.

## TOP DRAFT CHOICES

1. **Justin Verlander,** RHP, Old Dominion.
2. **Eric Beattie,** RHP, Tampa.
3. **Jeff Frazier,** OF, Rutgers.
4. **Collin Mahoney,** RHP, Clemson.
5. **Andrew Kown,** RHP, Georgia Tech.
6. **Brent Dlugach,** SS, Memphis.
7. **Chris Carpenter,** RHP, Bryan (Ohio) H.S.
8. **Luke French,** LHP, Heritage H.S., Littleton, Colo.
9. **Brandon Timm,** OF, Broken Arrow (Okla.) H.S.
10. **Cory Middleton,** SS, Escambia H.S., Pensacola, Fla.

# KANSAS CITY ROYALS

## AMERICAN LEAGUE CENTRAL DIVISION

## 2005 SEASON

### Royals Schedule

Home games shaded.
All-Star Game July 12 at Detroit. Schedule subject to change.

**April**

| SUN | MON | TUE | WED | THU | FRI | SAT |
|---|---|---|---|---|---|---|
| 3 | 4 DET | 5 | 6 DET | 7 DET | 8 ANA | 9 ANA |
| 10 ANA | 11 SEA | 12 | 13 SEA | 14 SEA | 15 DET | 16 DET |
| 17 DET | 18 CLE | 19 CLE | 20 MIN | 21 MIN | 22 CHW | 23 CHW |
| 24 CHW | 25 | 26 MIN | 27 MIN | 28 MIN | 29 CLE | 30 CLE |

**May**

| SUN | MON | TUE | WED | THU | FRI | SAT |
|---|---|---|---|---|---|---|
| 1 CLE | 2 | 3 CHW | 4 CHW | 5 CHW | 6 BAL | 7 BAL |
| 8 BAL | 9 TOR | 10 TOR | 11 TOR | 12 TB | 13 TB | 14 TB |
| 15 TB | 16 | 17 BAL | 18 BAL | 19 BAL | 20 STL | 21 STL |
| 22 STL | 23 | 24 TEX | 25 TEX | 26 TEX | 27 ANA | 28 ANA |
| 29 ANA | 30 | 31 NYY | | | | |

**June**

| SUN | MON | TUE | WED | THU | FRI | SAT |
|---|---|---|---|---|---|---|
| | | | 1 NYY | 2 NYY | 3 TEX | 4 TEX |
| 5 TEX | 6 | 7 SF | 8 SF | 9 SF | 10 ARI | 11 ARI |
| 12 ARI | 13 | 14 LA | 15 LA | 16 LA | 17 HOU | 18 HOU |
| 19 HOU | 20 CHW | 21 CHW | 22 CHW | 23 | 24 COL | 25 COL |
| 26 COL | 27 MIN | 28 MIN | 29 MIN | 30 | | |

**July**

| SUN | MON | TUE | WED | THU | FRI | SAT |
|---|---|---|---|---|---|---|
| | | | | | 1 ANA | 2 ANA |
| 3 ANA | 4 SEA | 5 SEA | 6 SEA | 7 MIN | 8 MIN | 9 MIN |
| 10 MIN | 11 | 12 All-Star | 13 | 14 DET | 15 DET | 16 DET |
| 17 DET | 18 CLE | 19 CLE | 20 CLE | 21 CLE | 22 TOR | 23 TOR |
| 24 TOR | 25 CHW | 26 CHW | 27 CHW | 28 TB | 29 TB | 30 TB |
| 31 TB | | | | | | |

**August**

| SUN | MON | TUE | WED | THU | FRI | SAT |
|---|---|---|---|---|---|---|
| | 1 | 2 BOS | 3 BOS | 4 BOS | 5 OAK | 6 OAK |
| 7 OAK | 8 | 9 CLE | 10 CLE | 11 CLE | 12 DET | 13 DET |
| 14 DET | 15 SEA | 16 SEA | 17 SEA | 18 | 19 OAK | 20 OAK |
| 21 OAK | 22 | 23 BOS | 24 BOS | 25 BOS | 26 NYY | 27 NYY |
| 28 NYY | 29 MIN | 30 MIN | 31 MIN | | | |

**September**

| SUN | MON | TUE | WED | THU | FRI | SAT |
|---|---|---|---|---|---|---|
| | | | | 1 TEX | 2 TEX | 3 TEX |
| 4 TEX | 5 | 6 CHW | 7 CHW | 8 CHW | 9 DET | 10 DET |
| 11 DET | 12 | 13 CHW | 14 CHW | 15 CHW | 16 CLE | 17 CLE |
| 18 CLE | 19 DET | 20 DET | 21 DET | 22 CLE | 23 CLE | 24 CLE |
| 25 CLE | 26 MIN | 27 MIN | 28 MIN | 29 MIN | 30 TOR | |

**October**

| SUN | MON | TUE | WED | THU | FRI | SAT |
|---|---|---|---|---|---|---|
| | | | | | | 1 TOR |
| 2 TOR | 3 | 4 | 5 | 6 | 7 | 8 |

Home games shaded. All-Star Game July 12 at Detroit. Schedule subject to change.

### CLUB DIRECTORY

**Chairman/owner**
David Glass

**President**
Dan Glass

**Sr. v.p. & g.m., baseball operations**
Allard Baird

**V.P. & asst. g.m., baseball operations**
Muzzy Jackson

**Vice president, baseball operations**
George Brett

**Vice president, broadcasting & p.r.**
David Witty

**Senior advisor to the general manager**
Art Stewart

**Assistant to the general manager**
Brian Murphy

**Director, baseball operations**
Jin Wong

**Sr. director, player personnel**
Donny Rowland

**Senior director, scouting**
Deric Ladnier

**Director, player development**
Shaun McGinn

**Director of public relations**
Aaron Babcock

**Manager, broadcast and media services**
Chris Stathos

**Manager, media relations**
Lora Grosshans

### MINOR LEAGUE AFFILIATES

| Class | Team | League | Manager |
|---|---|---|---|
| AAA | Omaha | Pacific Coast | Mike Jirschele |
| AA | Wichita | Texas | Frank White |
| Advanced A | High Desert | California | Billy Gardner Jr. |
| A | Burlington | Midwest | Jim Gabella |
| Advanced Rookie | Idaho Falls | Pioneer | Brian Rupp |
| Rookie | Arizona Royals | Arizona | Lloyd Simmons |

### BROADCAST INFORMATION

**Radio:** WHB-AM (810).
**Cable TV:** Royals Television Network, LLC.

### SPRING TRAINING

**Ballpark (city):** Surprise Stadium (Surprise, Ariz.).
**Ticket information:** 623-594-5600.

**For more on the Royals, go to msn.foxsports.com/mlb/teams.**

Harvey

## SPRING TRAINING ROSTER

**Manager**—Tony Pena (6).
**Coaches**—Guy Hansen, Joe Jones, Jeff Pentland (26), Brian Poldberg (25), Bob Schaefer (44), Luis Silverio (17).

| No. | PITCHERS | B/T | Ht./Wt. | Age* | 2004 Clubs |
|---|---|---|---|---|---|
| 48 | Affeldt, Jeremy | L/L | 6-4/215 | 25 | Omaha, Kansas City |
| 19 | Anderson, Brian | R/L | 6-1/185 | 32 | Kansas City |
| | Bass, Brian | R/R | 6-0/190 | 23 | Arizona Royals, Wichita |
| 27 | Bautista, Denny | R/R | 6-5/170 | 24 | Baltimore, Bowie, Wichita, Kansas City |
| | Burgos, Ambiorix | R/R | 6-0/180 | 20 | Burlington |
| 58 | Camp, Shawn | R/R | 6-1/200 | 29 | Omaha, Kansas City |
| 21 | Carrasco, D.J. | R/R | 6-1/215 | 27 | Omaha, Kansas City |
| 56 | Cerda, Jaime | L/L | 6-0/175 | 26 | Omaha, Kansas City |
| 57 | Field, Nate | R/R | 6-2/200 | 28 | Kansas City |
| 32 | George, Chris | L/L | 6-2/200 | 25 | Omaha, Kansas City |
| 41 | Gobble, Jimmy | L/L | 6-3/190 | 23 | Omaha, Kansas City |
| 23 | Greinke, Zack | R/R | 6-2/200 | 21 | Omaha, Kansas City |
| 40 | Hernandez, Ru. | R/R | 6-1/205 | 26 | Did Not Play |
| | Lima, Jose | R/R | 6-2/205 | 32 | Los Angeles |
| | Lowery, Devon | L/R | 6-1/190 | 22 | Wilmington |
| 54 | MacDougal, Mike | B/R | 6-4/195 | 28 | Omaha, Wichita, Kansas City |
| | Nunez, Leo | R/R | 6-2/150 | 21 | Hickory |
| | Sisco, Andrew | L/L | 6-9/265 | 22 | Daytona |
| 36 | Snyder, Kyle | B/R | 6-8/220 | 27 | Did Not Play |
| 47 | Sullivan, Scott | R/R | 6-3/210 | 34 | Kansas City |
| 49 | Tankersley, Dennis | R/R | 6-2/185 | 26 | Portland, San Diego |
| 46 | Wood, Mike | R/R | 6-3/210 | 24 | Sacramento, Kansas City |

| No. | CATCHERS | B/T | Ht./Wt. | Age* | 2004 Clubs |
|---|---|---|---|---|---|
| 2 | Buck, John | R/R | 6-3/210 | 24 | New Orleans, Kansas City |
| 30 | Castillo, Alberto | R/R | 6-0/216 | 34 | Omaha, Kansas City |
| | Huber, Justin | R/R | 6-5/190 | 22 | St. Lucie, Binghamton, Norfolk |
| | Phillips, Paul | R/R | 5-11/185 | 26 | Omaha, Kansas City |

| No. | INFIELDERS | B/T | Ht./Wt. | Age* | 2004 Clubs |
|---|---|---|---|---|---|
| 4 | Berroa, Angel | R/R | 6-0/175 | 26 | Wichita, Kansas City |
| 3 | Blanco, Andres | B/R | 5-10/155 | 20 | Kansas City, Wichita |
| 30 | Gotay, Ruben | B/R | 5-11/160 | 22 | Wichita, Kansas City |
| 14 | Graffanino, Tony | R/R | 6-1/190 | 32 | Omaha, Kansas City |
| 28 | Harvey, Ken | R/R | 6-2/240 | 27 | Kansas City |
| 31 | Murphy, Donnie | R/R | 5-10/180 | 22 | Wilmington, Kansas City |
| | Pickering, Calvin | L/L | 6-5/260 | 28 | Omaha |
| 29 | Sweeney, Mike | R/R | 6-3/225 | 31 | Kansas City |
| | Teahen, Mark | L/R | 6-3/210 | 23 | Midland, Sacramento, Omaha |
| | Truby, Chris | R/R | 6-2/210 | 31 | Nashville |

| No. | OUTFIELDERS | B/T | Ht./Wt. | Age* | 2004 Clubs |
|---|---|---|---|---|---|
| | DeJesus, David | L/L | 6-0/175 | 25 | Omaha, Kansas City |
| | Long, Terrence | L/L | 6-1/200 | 29 | San Diego |
| | Marrero, Eli | R/R | 6-1/180 | 31 | Greenville, Richmond, Atlanta |
| 38 | Nunez, Abraham | B/R | 6-3/210 | 28 | Florida, Kansas City |
| 12 | Stairs, Matt | L/R | 5-9/210 | 37 | Kansas City |

*Age as of April 1, 2005.

## BALLPARK INFORMATION

**Ballpark (capacity, surface)**
Kauffman Stadium (40,793, grass)

**Address**
P.O. Box 419969
Kansas City, MO 64141-6969

**Official website**
www.kcroyals.com

**Business phone**
816-921-8000

**Ticket information**
816-504-4040, 800-6ROYALS

**Field dimensions (from home plate)**
To left field at foul line, 330 feet
To center field, 410 feet
To right field at foul line, 330 feet

**First game played**
April 10, 1973 (Royals 12, Rangers 1)

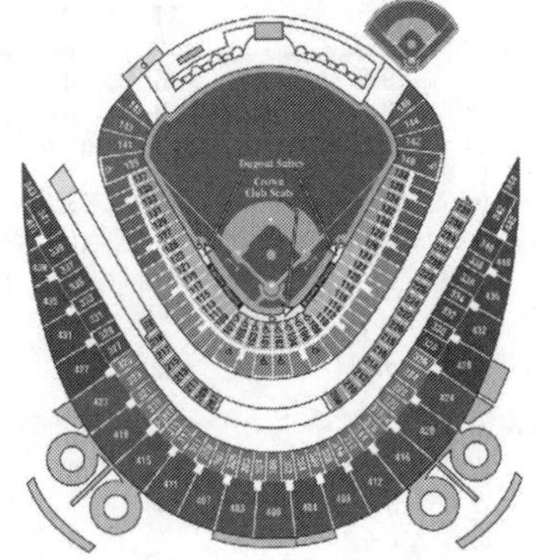

# 2004 REVIEW
## DAY BY DAY

| Date | Opp. | Res. | Score | (inn.*) | Hits | Opp. hits | Winning pitcher | Losing pitcher | Save | Record | Pos. | GB |
|---|---|---|---|---|---|---|---|---|---|---|---|---|
| 4-5 | Chi. | W | 9-7 | | 13 | 12 | Carrasco | Marte | | 1-0 | T1st | ... |
| 4-7 | Chi. | L | 3-4 | | 8 | 8 | Loaiza | May | Koch | 1-1 | T3rd | 1.5 |
| 4-8 | Cle. | L | 1-6 | | 5 | 9 | D'Amico | Affeldt | | 1-2 | T4th | 2.5 |
| 4-9 | Cle. | W | 3-1 | | 11 | 7 | Grimsley | Cressend | Leskanic | 2-2 | T2nd | 2.0 |
| 4-10 | Cle. | W | 7-6 | (10) | 12 | 12 | Sullivan | Betancourt | | 3-2 | T2nd | 1.0 |
| 4-11 | Cle. | W | 5-3 | | 8 | 8 | Sullivan | Jimenez | Leskanic | 4-2 | 2nd | 1.0 |
| 4-13 | At Chi. | L | 5-12 | | 8 | 14 | Loaiza | May | | 4-3 | T2nd | 1.0 |
| 4-14 | At Chi. | L | 9-10 | | 12 | 14 | Adkins | Leskanic | | 4-4 | T3rd | 2.0 |
| 4-15 | At Chi. | L | 5-6 | (10) | 9 | 8 | Marte | Carrasco | | 4-5 | 4th | 2.0 |
| 4-16 | At Min. | L | 7-9 | | 9 | 11 | Rincon | Cerda | Nathan | 4-6 | 4th | 2.0 |
| 4-17 | At Min. | L | 4-8 | | 11 | 7 | Lohse | Appier | Romero | 4-7 | 4th | 3.0 |
| 4-18 | At Min. | L | 3-8 | | 7 | 12 | Roa | May | | 4-8 | 5th | 4.0 |
| 4-20 | At Cle. | W | 15-5 | | 14 | 9 | Anderson | Durbin | | 5-8 | 4th | 4.0 |
| 4-22 | At Cle. | L | 4-5 | | 11 | 5 | Betancourt | Grimsley | Riske | 5-9 | 5th | 4.5 |
| 4-23 | Min. | L | 5-7 | | 12 | 10 | Romero | Leskanic | Nathan | 5-10 | 5th | 5.5 |
| 4-24 | Min. | W | 10-1 | | 15 | 6 | Camp | Greisinger | | 6-10 | 4th | 4.5 |
| 4-25 | Min. | L | 2-4 | | 10 | 10 | Silva | Anderson | Nathan | 6-11 | 5th | 5.5 |
| 4-27 | Tex. | L | 2-3 | | 7 | 10 | Dickey | Affeldt | Cordero | 6-12 | 5th | 6.0 |
| 4-28 | Tex. | W | 5-3 | | 9 | 13 | Gobble | Rogers | MacDougal | 7-12 | 5th | 6.0 |
| 4-29 | Tex. | L | 7-9 | | 11 | 13 | Almanzar | Leskanic | Cordero | 7-13 | 5th | 6.5 |
| 4-30 | At N.Y. | L | 2-5 | | 3 | 9 | Vazquez | Anderson | Rivera | 7-14 | 5th | 7.5 |
| 5-1 | At N.Y. | L | 4-12 | | 7 | 14 | Lieber | Villacis | | 7-15 | 5th | 7.5 |
| 5-2 | At N.Y. | L | 2-4 | | 9 | 8 | Mussina | Affeldt | Rivera | 7-16 | 5th | 7.5 |
| 5-3 | At Tor. | W | 3-2 | (10) | 8 | 7 | Field | Adams | Cerda | 8-16 | 5th | 7.5 |
| 5-4 | At Tor. | L | 4-5 | | 7 | 9 | Hentgen | May | Frasor | 8-17 | 5th | 7.5 |
| 5-5 | At Tor. | L | 3-10 | | 12 | 14 | Halladay | Anderson | | 8-18 | 5th | 8.5 |
| 5-7 | At Bos. | L | 6-7 | | 9 | 13 | Timlin | MacDougal | | 8-19 | 5th | 8.5 |
| 5-8 | At Bos. | L | 1-9 | | 5 | 11 | Schilling | Gobble | | 8-20 | 5th | 8.5 |
| 5-9 | At Bos. | W | 8-4 | | 9 | 9 | May | Lowe | | 9-20 | 5th | 7.5 |
| 5-10 | Tor. | L | 3-9 | | 8 | 16 | Hentgen | Anderson | | 9-21 | 5th | 8.0 |
| 5-11 | Tor. | W | 5-1 | | 8 | 6 | Camp | Halladay | | 10-21 | 5th | 8.0 |
| 5-12 | Tor. | W | 4-3 | | 9 | 11 | Field | Adams | | 11-21 | 5th | 8.0 |
| 5-14 | Oak. | L | 2-6 | | 6 | 11 | Hudson | Gobble | | 11-22 | 5th | 9.5 |
| 5-15 | Oak. | L | 1-3 | | 4 | 5 | Mulder | May | | 11-23 | 5th | 10.5 |
| 5-16 | Oak. | L | 2-6 | | 5 | 10 | Zito | Anderson | | 11-24 | 5th | 10.5 |
| 5-18 | At Tex. | W | 7-6 | | 16 | 9 | Sullivan | Dickey | Field | 12-24 | 5th | 10.0 |
| 5-19 | At Tex. | W | 5-3 | | 4 | 7 | Gobble | Park | Huisman | 13-24 | 5th | 10.0 |
| 5-20 | At Tex. | L | 3-6 | | 11 | 12 | Rogers | May | Cordero | 13-25 | 5th | 10.0 |
| 5-21 | At Oak. | L | 0-7 | | 3 | 12 | Mulder | Anderson | | 13-26 | 5th | 10.0 |
| 5-22 | At Oak. | L | 4-5 | (11) | 10 | 12 | Duchscherer | Sullivan | | 13-27 | 5th | 11.0 |
| 5-23 | At Oak. | L | 2-3 | (10) | 10 | 7 | Rhodes | Field | | 13-28 | 5th | 11.0 |
| 5-25 | Det. | W | 4-3 | | 10 | 8 | Grimsley | Maroth | Affeldt | 14-28 | 5th | 10.0 |
| 5-26 | Det. | W | 7-3 | | 10 | 12 | May | Knotts | Affeldt | 15-28 | 5th | 10.0 |
| 5-27 | Det. | L | 7-17 | | 10 | 27 | Robertson | Anderson | | 15-29 | 5th | 11.0 |
| 5-28 | Min. | W | 2-1 | | 8 | 7 | Affeldt | Rincon | | 16-29 | 5th | 11.0 |
| 5-29 | Min. | W | 5-2 | | 7 | 8 | Reyes | Santana | Affeldt | 17-29 | 5th | 10.0 |
| 5-30 | Min. | L | 3-8 | | 12 | 12 | Lohse | Gobble | | 17-30 | 5th | 11.0 |
| 5-31 | At Det. | L | 4-8 | | 9 | 14 | Knotts | May | | 17-31 | 5th | 11.5 |
| 6-1 | At Det. | W | 5-3 | | 11 | 10 | Grimsley | Yan | Affeldt | 18-31 | 5th | 10.5 |
| 6-2 | At Det. | L | 0-2 | | 9 | 6 | Johnson | Greinke | Urbina | 18-32 | 5th | 10.5 |
| 6-3 | At Det. | W | 9-6 | | 16 | 8 | Reyes | Bonderman | Affeldt | 19-32 | 5th | 10.0 |
| 6-4 | Bos. | W | 5-2 | | 9 | 6 | Gobble | Wakefield | Affeldt | 20-32 | 5th | 10.0 |
| 6-5 | Bos. | L | 4-8 | | 7 | 13 | Schilling | May | | 20-33 | 5th | 10.0 |
| 6-6 | Bos. | L | 3-5 | | 4 | 7 | Lowe | Grimsley | Foulke | 20-34 | 5th | 10.0 |
| 6-8 | Mon. | W | 4-2 | | 5 | 7 | Greinke | Armas | Affeldt | 21-34 | 5th | 10.0 |
| 6-10! | Mon. | L | 0-8 | | 6 | 16 | Day | Reyes | | 21-35 | | |
| 6-10& | Mon. | L | 2-7 | | 6 | 8 | Kim | Gobble | | 21-36 | 5th | 11.0 |
| 6-11 | N.Y. | W | 7-5 | | 9 | 17 | May | Seo | Affeldt | 22-36 | 5th | 10.0 |
| 6-12 | N.Y. | W | 4-3 | | 6 | 8 | Affeldt | Weathers | | 23-36 | 5th | 10.0 |
| 6-13 | N.Y. | L | 2-5 | | 4 | 5 | Glavine | Greinke | Looper | 23-37 | 5th | 10.5 |
| 6-15 | At Atl. | L | 2-3 | | 8 | 8 | Reitsma | Grimsley | Smoltz | 23-38 | 5th | 11.5 |
| 6-16 | At Atl. | W | 10-4 | | 20 | 8 | Cerda | Reitsma | | 24-38 | 5th | 11.0 |
| 6-17 | At Atl. | W | 10-4 | | 13 | 10 | May | Thomson | | 25-38 | 5th | 11.0 |
| 6-18 | At Phi. | W | 10-4 | | 14 | 10 | George | Abbott | | 26-38 | 5th | 10.0 |
| 6-19 | At Phi. | L | 2-4 | | 7 | 6 | Milton | Greinke | Wagner | 26-39 | 5th | 10.0 |

| Date | Opp. | Res. | Score | (inn.*) | Hits | Opp. hits | Winning pitcher | Losing pitcher | Save | Record | Pos. | GB |
|---|---|---|---|---|---|---|---|---|---|---|---|---|
| 6-20 | At Phi. | L | 2-8 | | 7 | 10 | Powell | Reyes | | 26-40 | 5th | 11.0 |
| 6-22 | Det. | W | 8-1 | | 13 | 4 | Gobble | Maroth | Field | 27-40 | 5th | 10.0 |
| 6-23 | Det. | W | 7-3 | | 10 | 11 | May | Knotts | | 28-40 | 5th | 10.0 |
| 6-24 | Det. | L | 3-12 | | 4 | 17 | Robertson | George | | 28-41 | 5th | 11.0 |
| 6-25 | StL. | L | 2-5 | | 6 | 10 | Morris | Greinke | Isringhausen | 28-42 | 5th | 12.0 |
| 6-26 | StL. | L | 1-3 | (10) | 11 | 9 | Tavarez | Seanez | Isringhausen | 28-43 | 5th | 12.0 |
| 6-27 | StL. | L | 3-10 | | 8 | 15 | Marquis | Gobble | | 28-44 | 5th | 12.0 |
| 6-28 | Bal. | L | 1-10 | | 7 | 13 | Bedard | May | | 28-45 | 5th | 12.5 |
| 6-29 | Bal. | W | 4-3 | | 10 | 8 | Wood | Ponson | Camp | 29-45 | 5th | 11.5 |
| 6-30 | Bal. | L | 4-13 | | 5 | 15 | Cabrera | Anderson | | 29-46 | 5th | 12.5 |
| 7-1 | Bal. | L | 2-3 | | 4 | 10 | Lopez | Greinke | Julio | 29-47 | 5th | 13.5 |
| 7-2 | At S.D. | L | 5-7 | | 7 | 12 | Peavy | Reyes | Hoffman | 29-48 | 5th | 13.5 |
| 7-3 | At S.D. | L | 4-5 | | 3 | 8 | Linebrink | Sullivan | Hoffman | 29-49 | 5th | 13.5 |
| 7-4 | At S.D. | L | 1-7 | | 6 | 13 | Wells | Wood | | 29-50 | 5th | 13.5 |
| 7-5 | At Min. | L | 0-9 | | 4 | 13 | Radke | Gobble | | 29-51 | 5th | 14.5 |
| 7-6 | At Min. | L | 0-4 | | 3 | 6 | Santana | Greinke | | 29-52 | 5th | 15.5 |
| 7-7 | At Min. | L | 0-12 | | 6 | 15 | Lohse | Reyes | | 29-53 | 5th | 16.5 |
| 7-9 | At Bal. | W | 7-0 | | 11 | 5 | May | Bedard | | 30-53 | 5th | 16.0 |
| 7-10 | At Bal. | L | 2-7 | | 5 | 13 | Cabrera | Wood | | 30-54 | 5th | 16.0 |
| 7-11 | At Bal. | W | 11-7 | | 17 | 12 | Gobble | Lopez | | 31-54 | 5th | 15.5 |
| 7-15 | Min. | W | 3-1 | | 11 | 5 | Greinke | Lohse | Bukvich | 32-54 | 5th | 14.5 |
| 7-16 | Min. | W | 12-3 | | 17 | 7 | May | Radke | | 33-54 | 5th | 13.5 |
| 7-17 | Min. | L | 1-4 | | 1 | 7 | Santana | Gobble | Nathan | 33-55 | 5th | 14.5 |
| 7-18 | Min. | W | 4-3 | (10) | 8 | 10 | Reyes | Balfour | | 34-55 | 5th | 13.5 |
| 7-19 | Bal. | L | 4-7 | | 10 | 12 | Ponson | Anderson | | 34-56 | 5th | 14.5 |
| 7-20 | Bal. | L | 3-12 | | 12 | 16 | Cabrera | Greinke | | 34-57 | 5th | 15.0 |
| 7-21 | At Det. | L | 2-4 | | 8 | 8 | Maroth | May | Walker | 34-58 | 5th | 16.0 |
| 7-22 | At Det. | W | 13-7 | | 17 | 12 | Gobble | Knotts | | 35-58 | 5th | 16.0 |
| 7-23 | At Cle. | L | 2-3 | (11) | 11 | 11 | White | Field | | 35-59 | 5th | 17.0 |
| 7-24# | At Cle. | L | 2-10 | | 6 | 14 | Durbin | George | | 35-60 | | |
| 7-24$ | At Cle. | L | 3-4 | | 8 | 8 | Miller | Sullivan | | 35-61 | 5th | 18.0 |
| 7-25 | At Cle. | L | 1-5 | | 6 | 8 | Westbrook | Greinke | | 35-62 | 5th | 18.5 |
| 7-27 | At T.B. | L | 2-6 | | 7 | 10 | Brazelton | May | | 35-63 | 5th | 20.0 |
| 7-28 | At T.B. | L | 1-10 | | 4 | 15 | Hendrickson | Gobble | | 35-64 | 5th | 21.0 |
| 7-29 | At T.B. | L | 0-2 | | 4 | 7 | Bell | Wood | Baez | 35-65 | 5th | 21.5 |
| 7-30 | Cle. | L | 6-7 | (11) | 9 | 13 | Betancourt | Sullivan | | 35-66 | 5th | 21.5 |
| 7-31 | Cle. | W | 10-3 | | 16 | 9 | Greinke | Tadano | | 36-66 | 5th | 21.5 |
| 8-1 | Cle. | W | 8-7 | | 11 | 13 | May | Sabathia | Camp | 37-66 | 5th | 21.5 |
| 8-3 | Chi. | L | 4-12 | | 6 | 11 | Contreras | Wood | | 37-67 | 5th | 22.5 |
| 8-4 | Chi. | W | 11-0 | | 17 | 2 | Anderson | Schoeneweis | | 38-67 | 5th | 22.5 |
| 8-5 | Chi. | W | 6-4 | | 7 | 8 | Greinke | Garland | Field | 39-67 | 5th | 21.5 |
| 8-6 | Ana. | L | 0-3 | | 7 | 7 | Escobar | May | Percival | 39-68 | 5th | 21.5 |
| 8-7 | Ana. | L | 5-7 | | 12 | 10 | Colon | Reyes | Percival | 39-69 | 5th | 22.5 |
| 8-8 | Ana. | L | 4-6 | | 11 | 8 | Donnelly | Field | Rodriguez | 39-70 | 5th | 22.5 |
| 8-9 | Ana. | L | 3-5 | | 7 | 11 | Gregg | Cerda | Percival | 39-71 | 5th | 22.5 |
| 8-10 | At Chi. | L | 3-9 | | 8 | 14 | Garland | Greinke | | 39-72 | 5th | 22.5 |
| 8-11 | At Chi. | W | 4-2 | | 9 | 4 | May | Buehrle | Cerda | 40-72 | 5th | 21.5 |
| 8-12 | At Chi. | L | 2-3 | | 9 | 5 | Garcia | Serrano | Takatsu | 40-73 | 5th | 22.5 |
| 8-13 | At Oak. | W | 10-3 | | 9 | 10 | Wood | Mulder | | 41-73 | 5th | 21.5 |
| 8-14 | At Oak. | L | 1-6 | | 5 | 10 | Harden | Anderson | | 41-74 | 5th | 21.5 |
| 8-15 | At Oak. | W | 6-1 | | 10 | 7 | Greinke | Zito | | 42-74 | 5th | 21.5 |
| 8-17 | Sea. | L | 3-16 | | 8 | 20 | Madritsch | May | | 42-75 | 5th | 22.5 |
| 8-18 | Sea. | W | 3-2 | | 5 | 5 | Carrasco | Franklin | | 43-75 | 5th | 22.5 |
| 8-20 | Tex. | L | 3-5 | | 7 | 4 | Drese | Wood | Cordero | 43-76 | 5th | 23.0 |
| 8-21 | Tex. | L | 3-5 | | 10 | 10 | Francisco | Anderson | Cordero | 43-77 | 5th | 24.0 |
| 8-22 | Tex. | W | 10-2 | | 10 | 8 | Greinke | Erickson | | 44-77 | 5th | 24.0 |
| 8-23 | At Ana. | L | 4-9 | | 7 | 13 | Colon | May | | 44-78 | 5th | 25.0 |
| 8-24 | At Ana. | L | 5-7 | | 9 | 15 | Lackey | Reyes | Percival | 44-79 | 5th | 25.0 |
| 8-25 | At Ana. | L | 6-21 | | 15 | 22 | Ortiz | Wood | | 44-80 | 5th | 26.0 |
| 8-26 | At Sea. | W | 7-3 | | 11 | 8 | Anderson | Moyer | | 45-80 | 5th | 25.0 |
| 8-27 | At Sea. | L | 5-7 | | 9 | 14 | Sherrill | Carrasco | Putz | 45-81 | 5th | 25.0 |
| 8-28! | At Sea. | L | 7-9 | | 9 | 12 | Thornton | May | Putz | 45-82 | | |
| 8-28& | At Sea. | L | 3-5 | (12) | 10 | 12 | Baek | Kinney | | 45-83 | 5th | 26.5 |
| 8-29 | At Sea. | L | 4-5 | | 11 | 8 | Villone | Reyes | | 45-84 | 5th | 26.5 |
| 8-30 | Det. | L | 1-9 | | 6 | 11 | Robertson | Wood | | 45-85 | 5th | 27.0 |
| 8-31 | Det. | W | 9-8 | | 17 | 15 | Affeldt | Urbina | | 46-85 | 5th | 27.0 |
| 9-1 | Det. | W | 1-0 | | 6 | 4 | Greinke | Maroth | Affeldt | 47-85 | 5th | 27.0 |
| 9-3 | At Min. | L | 0-2 | | 2 | 9 | Santana | May | Nathan | 47-86 | 5th | 28.5 |
| 9-4 | At Min. | L | 3-4 | | 8 | 7 | Romero | Reyes | | 47-87 | 5th | 29.5 |

| Date | Opp. | Res. | Score | (inn.*) | Hits | Opp. hits | Winning pitcher | Losing pitcher | Save | Record | Pos. | GB |
|---|---|---|---|---|---|---|---|---|---|---|---|---|
| 9-5 | At Min. | W | 12-3 | | 13 | 6 | Gobble | Lohse | | 48-87 | 5th | 28.5 |
| 9-6 | At Det. | L | 3-7 | | 9 | 11 | Ledezma | Bautista | Knotts | 48-88 | 5th | 28.5 |
| 9-7 | At Det. | W | 6-2 | | 13 | 9 | Serrano | Robertson | | 49-88 | 5th | 28.5 |
| 9-9! | At Det. | W | 26-5 | | 26 | 10 | Greinke | Johnson | | 50-88 | | |
| 9-9& | At Det. | L | 0-8 | | 7 | 10 | Bonderman | May | | 50-89 | 5th | 29.0 |
| 9-10 | T.B. | W | 8-5 | | 10 | 11 | Reyes | Nunez | Affeldt | 51-89 | 5th | 29.0 |
| 9-11 | T.B. | L | 6-8 | | 11 | 13 | Bell | Serrano | Baez | 51-90 | 5th | 30.0 |
| 9-12 | T.B. | L | 2-7 | | 10 | 15 | Sosa | Bautista | | 51-91 | 5th | 31.0 |
| 9-13 | N.Y. | W | 17-8 | | 18 | 16 | Anderson | Halsey | | 52-91 | 5th | 31.0 |
| 9-14 | N.Y. | L | 0-4 | | 3 | 6 | Mussina | Greinke | | 52-92 | 5th | 32.0 |
| 9-15 | N.Y. | L | 0-3 | | 4 | 6 | Vazquez | May | Rivera | 52-93 | 5th | 33.0 |
| 9-17 | At Cle. | W | 6-4 | | 12 | 6 | Wood | Westbrook | Affeldt | 53-93 | 5th | 32.5 |
| 9-18 | At Cle. | W | 7-1 | | 9 | 4 | Gobble | Lee | | 54-93 | 5th | 31.5 |
| 9-19 | At Cle. | L | 3-8 | | 10 | 13 | Denney | Bautista | | 54-94 | 5th | 32.5 |
| 9-20 | At T.B. | W | 6-3 | | 9 | 8 | Anderson | Sosa | Affeldt | 55-94 | 5th | 32.5 |
| 9-21 | At T.B. | L | 4-7 | | 8 | 14 | Hendrickson | Camp | Baez | 55-95 | 5th | 32.5 |
| 9-22 | At T.B. | W | 7-6 | (10) | 9 | 14 | MacDougal | Sosa | Affeldt | 56-95 | 5th | 31.5 |
| 9-23 | At Chi. | L | 6-7 | | 10 | 10 | Marte | Affeldt | | 56-96 | 5th | 31.5 |
| 9-24 | At Chi. | W | 8-6 | | 11 | 12 | Gobble | Diaz | | 57-96 | 5th | 31.5 |
| 9-25 | At Chi. | L | 1-5 | | 4 | 7 | Buehrle | Bautista | | 57-97 | 5th | 31.5 |
| 9-26 | At Chi. | L | 1-5 | | 5 | 9 | Garland | Anderson | Marte | 57-98 | 5th | 32.5 |
| 9-27 | Cle. | L | 1-6 | | 5 | 11 | Westbrook | Cerda | | 57-99 | 5th | 33.0 |
| 9-28 | Cle. | L | 1-5 | | 3 | 10 | Lee | May | | 57-100 | 5th | 33.5 |
| 9-29 | Cle. | L | 2-5 | | 10 | 10 | Bartosh | Wood | Wickman | 57-101 | 5th | 33.0 |
| 9-30 | Chi. | L | 2-9 | | 4 | 12 | Buehrle | Camp | | 57-102 | 5th | 33.0 |
| 10-1 | Chi. | L | 2-4 | | 7 | 8 | Garland | Cerda | Takatsu | 57-103 | 5th | 34.0 |
| 10-2 | Chi. | W | 10-2 | | 14 | 7 | Anderson | Grilli | | 58-103 | 5th | 33.5 |
| 10-3 | Chi. | L | 0-5 | | 3 | 11 | Contreras | Greinke | | 58-104 | 5th | 34.0 |

Monthly records: April (7-14), May (10-17), June (12-15), July (7-20), August (10-19), September (11-17), October (1-2).
*Innings, if other than nine. ! First game of a doubleheader. & Second game of a doubleheader. # Day separate admission. $ Night separate admission.

## RECORDS

**2004 regular-season record:** 58-104
**Position:** 5th in A.L. Central
**Home:** 33-47 **Road:** 25-57
**A.L. East:** 12-24 **A.L. Central:** 32-44
**A.L. West:** 8-24 **N.L.** 6-12
**Vs. LH starters:** 22-25
**Vs. RH starters:** 36-79
**Grass:** 54-90 **Artificial:** 4-14
**Day:** 17-44 **Night:** 41-60
**1-Run:** 14-19 **X-inn.:** 4-7
**Doubleheaders:** 0-2-1
**Team record past five years:** 345-465 (.426, ranks 12th in league in that span)

## TEAM LEADERS

**Batting average:** Ken Harvey (.287).
**At-bats:** Angel Berroa (512).
**Runs:** Angel Berroa (72).
**Hits:** Joe Randa (139).
**Total Bases:** Mike Sweeney (207).
**Doubles:** Joe Randa (31).
**Triples:** Angel Berroa (6).
**Home runs:** Mike Sweeney (22).
**Runs batted in:** Mike Sweeney (79).
**Stolen bases:** Carlos Beltran, Angel Berroa (14).
**Slugging percentage:** Carlos Beltran (.534).
**On-base percentage:** Carlos Beltran (.367).
**Wins:** Jimmy Gobble, Darrell May (9).
Earned-run average: Zack Greinke (3.97).
**Complete games:** Darrell May (3).
**Shutouts:** Brian Anderson, Darrell May (1).
**Saves:** Jeremy Affeldt (13).
Innings pitched: Darrell May (186.0).
Strikeouts: Darrell May (120).

## GAMES BY POSITION

**Catcher:** John Buck 68, Benito Santiago 49, Alberto Castillo 29, Kelly Stinnett 20, Paul Phillips 4, Mike Tonis 2.
**First base:** Ken Harvey 73, Mike Sweeney 55, Matt Stairs 30, Calvin Pickering 8, Joe Randa 3, Wilton Guerrero 2, Mendy Lopez 2.
**Second base:** Tony Graffanino 75, Ruben Gotay 42, Desi Relaford 36, Wilton Guerrero 8, Donnie Murphy 7, Mendy Lopez 6, Damian Jackson 1.
Third base: Joe Randa 119, Desi Relaford 42, Jose Bautista 11, Mendy Lopez 4, Wilton Guerrero 2.
**Shortstop:** Angel Berroa 133, Andres Blanco 19, Desi Relaford 12, Mendy Lopez 4, Wilton Guerrero 3, Damian Jackson 1.
**Outfield:** David DeJesus 94, Matt Stairs 71, Carlos Beltran 69, Abraham Nunez 57, Dee Brown 53, Aaron Guiel 39, Desi Relaford 32, Ruben Mateo 30, Juan Gonzalez 29, Byron Gettis 21, Alexis Gomez 12, Brandon Berger 11, Adrian Brown 5, Damian Jackson 5, Ken Harvey 4, Mendy Lopez 4, Wilton Guerrero 3, Rich Thompson 3, Jose Bautista 1.
**Designated hitter:** Mike Sweeney 48, Ken Harvey 41, Calvin Pickering 27, Matt Stairs 22, Joe Randa 6, Juan Gonzalez 4, John Buck 3, Wilton Guerrero 2, Aaron Guiel 2, Damian Jackson 2, Abraham Nunez 2, Dee Brown 1, Alexis Gomez 1, Rich Thompson 1.

## TOP DRAFT CHOICES

1a. **Billy Butler,** 1B-3B, Wolfson H.S., Jacksonville.
1b. **Matt Campbell,** LHP, South Carolina.
1c. **J.P. Howell,** LHP, Texas.
2a. **Billy Buckner,** RHP, South Carolina.
2b. **Erik Cordier,** RHP, Southern Door H.S., Brussels, Wis.
3. **Josh Johnson,** SS, Middleton H.S., Tampa.
4. **Nate Moore,** RHP, Troy.
5. **Henry Barrera,** RHP, Rosemead (Calif.) H.S.
6. **Chad Blackwell,** RHP, South Carolina.
7. **Matt Green,** RHP, Louisiana-Monroe.
8. **Ed Lucas,** SS, Dartmouth.
9. **Chris McConnell**, SS, Delsea H.S., Franklinville, N.J.
10. **Bobby Beeson**, LHP, Southern Arkansas.

# MINNESOTA TWINS
## AMERICAN LEAGUE CENTRAL DIVISION



## 2005 SEASON

### Twins Schedule

Home games shaded.
All-Star Game July 12 at Detroit. Schedule subject to change.

**April**

| SUN | MON | TUE | WED | THU | FRI | SAT |
|---|---|---|---|---|---|---|
| 3 | 4 SEA | 5 SEA | 6 SEA | 7 | 8 CHW | 9 CHW |
| 10 CHW | 11 | 12 DET | 13 DET | 14 DET | 15 CLE | 16 CLE |
| 17 CLE | 18 CHW | 19 CHW | 20 KC | 21 KC | 22 DET | 23 DET |
| 24 DET | 25 | 26 KC | 27 KC | 28 KC | 29 ANA | 30 ANA |

**May**

| SUN | MON | TUE | WED | THU | FRI | SAT |
|---|---|---|---|---|---|---|
| 1 ANA | 2 | 3 CLE | 4 CLE | 5 CLE | 6 TB | 7 TB |
| 8 TB | 9 BAL | 10 BAL | 11 BAL | 12 | 13 TEX | 14 TEX |
| 15 TEX | 16 | 17 TOR | 18 TOR | 19 TOR | 20 MIL | 21 MIL |
| 22 MIL | 23 CLE | 24 CLE | 25 CLE | 26 CLE | 27 TOR | 28 TOR |
| 29 TOR | 30 | 31 CLE | | | | |

**June**

| SUN | MON | TUE | WED | THU | FRI | SAT |
|---|---|---|---|---|---|---|
| | | | 1 CLE | 2 CLE | 3 NYY | 4 NYY |
| 5 NYY | 6 | 7 ARI | 8 ARI | 9 ARI | 10 LA | 11 LA |
| 12 LA | 13 | 14 SF | 15 SF | 16 SF | 17 SD | 18 SD |
| 19 SD | 20 | 21 DET | 22 DET | 23 DET | 24 MIL | 25 MIL |
| 26 MIL | 27 KC | 28 KC | 29 KC | 30 | | |

**July**

| SUN | MON | TUE | WED | THU | FRI | SAT |
|---|---|---|---|---|---|---|
| | | | | | 1 TB | 2 TB |
| 3 TB | 4 ANA | 5 ANA | 6 ANA | 7 KC | 8 KC | 9 KC |
| 10 KC | 11 | 12 All-Star | 13 | 14 ANA | 15 ANA | 16 ANA |
| 17 ANA | 18 BAL | 19 BAL | 20 BAL | 21 DET | 22 DET | 23 DET |
| 24 DET | 25 | 26 NYY | 27 NYY | 28 NYY | 29 BOS | 30 BOS |
| 31 BOS | | | | | | |

**August**

| SUN | MON | TUE | WED | THU | FRI | SAT |
|---|---|---|---|---|---|---|
| | 1 OAK | 2 OAK | 3 OAK | 4 OAK | 5 BOS | 6 BOS |
| 7 BOS | 8 SEA | 9 SEA | 10 SEA | 11 | 12 OAK | 13 OAK |
| 14 OAK | 15 CHW | 16 CHW | 17 CHW | 18 SEA | 19 SEA | 20 SEA |
| 21 SEA | 22 | 23 CHW | 24 CHW | 25 CHW | 26 TEX | 27 TEX |
| 28 TEX | 29 KC | 30 KC | 31 KC | | | |

**September**

| SUN | MON | TUE | WED | THU | FRI | SAT |
|---|---|---|---|---|---|---|
| | | | | 1 | 2 CLE | 3 CLE |
| 4 CLE | 5 TEX | 6 TEX | 7 TEX | 8 | 9 CLE | 10 CLE |
| 11 CLE | 12 DET | 13 DET | 14 DET | 15 | 16 CHW | 17 CHW |
| 18 CHW | 19 OAK | 20 OAK | 21 OAK | 22 CHW | 23 CHW | 24 CHW |
| 25 CHW | 26 KC | 27 KC | 28 KC | 29 KC | 30 DET | |

**October**

| SUN | MON | TUE | WED | THU | FRI | SAT |
|---|---|---|---|---|---|---|
| | | | | | | 1 DET |
| 2 DET | 3 | 4 | 5 | 6 | 7 | 8 |

Home games shaded. All-Star Game July 12 at Detroit. Schedule subject to change.

## CLUB DIRECTORY

**Owner**
Carl R. Pohlad

**President, Twins Sports Inc.**
T. Geron Bell

**President, Minnesota Twins**
Dave St. Peter

**Vice president, general manager**
Terry Ryan

**Vice president, asst. general manager**
Bill Smith

**Vice president, operations**
Matt Hoy

**Assistant general manager**
Wayne Krivsky

**Director of minor leagues**
Jim Rantz

**Director of baseball operations**
Rob Antony

**Director of scouting**
Mike Radcliff

**Director of communications**
Brad Ruiter

**Media relations manager**
Sean Harlin

## MINOR LEAGUE AFFILIATES

| Class | Team | League | Manager |
|---|---|---|---|
| AAA | Rochester | International | Phil Roof |
| AA | New Britain | Eastern | Stan Cliburn |
| Advanced A | Fort Myers | Florida State | Jose Marzan |
| A | Beloit | Midwest | Kevin Bolles |
| Advanced Rookie | Elizabethton | Appalachian | Ray Smith |
| Rookie | Gulf Coast Twins | Gulf Coast | Riccardo Ingram |

## BROADCAST INFORMATION

**Radio:** WCCO-AM (830).
**TV:** KSTC-TV (Channel 45).
**Cable TV:** Fox Sport Net North.

## SPRING TRAINING

**Ballpark (city):** Lee County Sports Complex (Fort Myers, Fla.).
**Ticket information:** 800-33-TWINS.

**For more on the Twins, go to msn.foxsports.com/mlb/teams.**

Santana

## SPRING TRAINING ROSTER

Manager—Ron Gardenhire (35).
Coaches—Rick Anderson (40), Steve Liddle (9), Al Newman (62), Rick Stelmaszek (43), Scott Ullger (46), Jerry White (13).

| No. | PITCHERS | B/T | Ht./Wt. | Age* | 2004 Clubs |
|---|---|---|---|---|---|
| 19 | Balfour, Grant | R/R | 6-2/188 | 27 | Minnesota |
| | Bonser, Boof | R/R | 6-4/230 | 23 | New Britain, Rochester |
| | Bowyer, Travis | R/R | 6-3/215 | 23 | Fort Myers, New Britain |
| 28 | Crain, Jesse | R/R | 6-1/205 | 23 | Rochester, Minnesota |
| 31 | Durbin, J.D. | R/R | 6-0/200 | 23 | New Britain, Rochester, Minnesota |
| | Gassner, Dave | R/L | 6-2/190 | 26 | Rochester |
| 54 | Guerrier, Matt | R/R | 6-3/185 | 26 | Rochester, Minnesota |
| | Liriano, Francisco | L/L | 6-2/185 | 21 | Fort Myers, New Britain |
| 49 | Lohse, Kyle | R/R | 6-2/201 | 26 | Minnesota |
| 25 | Mays, Joe | B/R | 6-1/192 | 29 | Did Not Play |
| 36 | Nathan, Joe | R/R | 6-4/205 | 30 | Minnesota |
| 22 | Radke, Brad | R/R | 6-2/184 | 32 | Minnesota |
| 39 | Rincon, Juan | R/R | 5-11/201 | 26 | Minnesota |
| 33 | Romero, J.C. | B/L | 5-11/198 | 28 | Rochester, Minnesota |
| | Rowland-Smith, R. | L/L | 6-3/205 | 22 | Inland Empire |
| 57 | Santana, Johan | L/L | 6-0/206 | 26 | Minnesota |
| 52 | Silva, Carlos | R/R | 6-4/240 | 25 | Minnesota |
| | Tyler, Scott | R/R | 6-5/240 | 22 | Quad Cities |

| No. | CATCHERS | B/T | Ht./Wt. | Age* | 2004 Clubs |
|---|---|---|---|---|---|
| 44 | Bowen, Rob | B/R | 6-3/216 | 24 | Minnesota, New Britain |
| | LeCroy, Matt | R/R | 6-2/225 | 29 | Minnesota |
| 7 | Mauer, Joe | L/R | 6-4/220 | 21 | Fort Myers, Rochester, Minnesota |
| | Miller, Corky | R/R | 6-1/225 | 29 | Louisville, Cincinnati |
| | Redmond, Mike | R/R | 5-11/200 | 33 | Florida |

| No. | INFIELDERS | B/T | Ht./Wt. | Age* | 2004 Clubs |
|---|---|---|---|---|---|
| 18 | Bartlett, Jason | R/R | 6-0/180 | 25 | G.C. Twins, Rochester, Minnesota |
| | Castro, Juan | R/R | 5-11/195 | 32 | Louisville, Cincinnati |
| 5 | Cuddyer, Michael | R/R | 6-2/222 | 26 | Minnesota |
| 27 | Morneau, Justin | L/R | 6-4/228 | 23 | Rochester, Minnesota |
| 4 | Ojeda, Augie | B/R | 5-8/175 | 30 | Rochester, Minnesota |
| 8 | Punto, Nick | B/R | 5-9/176 | 27 | Quad Cities, Minnesota |
| 2 | Rivas, Luis | R/R | 5-11/186 | 25 | Rochester, Minnesota |
| | Rodriguez, Luis | B/R | 5-9/180 | 24 | Rochester |
| 32 | Tiffee, Terry | B/R | 6-3/210 | 25 | Rochester, Minnesota |

| No. | OUTFIELDERS | B/T | Ht./Wt. | Age* | 2004 Clubs |
|---|---|---|---|---|---|
| 20 | Ford, Lew | R/R | 6-0/195 | 28 | Rochester, Minnesota |
| 48 | Hunter, Torii | R/R | 6-2/211 | 29 | Minnesota |
| 11 | Jones, Jacque | L/L | 5-10/195 | 29 | Minnesota |
| | Jones, Garrett | L/L | 6-4/220 | 23 | Fort Myers, New Britain |
| 1 | Kubel, Jason | L/R | 5-11/200 | 22 | New Britain, Rochester, Minnesota |
| 41 | Restovich, Michael | R/R | 6-4/257 | 26 | Rochester, Minnesota |
| 12 | Ryan, Michael | L/R | 6-0/193 | 27 | Minnesota, Rochester |
| 23 | Stewart, Shannon | R/R | 5-11/200 | 31 | Rochester, Minnesota |

*Age as of April 1, 2005.

## BALLPARK INFORMATION

**Ballpark (capacity, surface)**
Hubert H. Humphrey Metrodome (45,423, artificial)

**Address**
34 Kirby Puckett Place
Minneapolis, MN 55415

**Official website**
www.twinsbaseball.com

**Business phone**
612-375-1366

**Ticket information**
1-800-338-9467

**Field dimensions (from home plate)**
To left field at foul line, 343 feet
To center field, 408 feet
To right field at foul line, 327 feet

**First game played**
April 6, 1982 (Mariners 11, Twins 7)

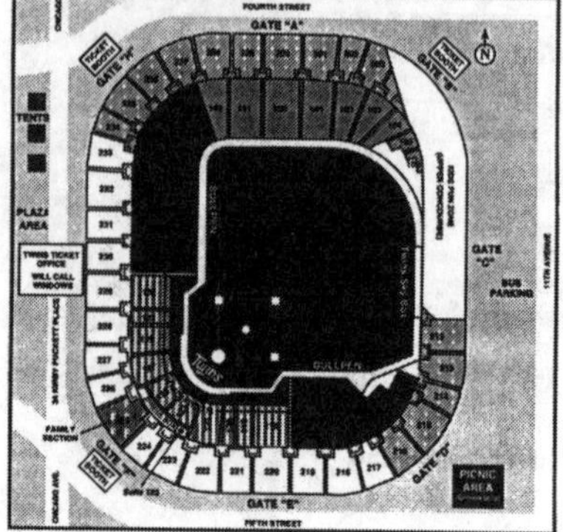

# 2004 REVIEW
## DAY BY DAY

| Date | Opp. | Res. | Score | (inn.*) | Hits | Opp. hits | Winning pitcher | Losing pitcher | Save | Record | Pos. | GB |
|---|---|---|---|---|---|---|---|---|---|---|---|---|
| 4-5 | Cle. | W | 7-4 | (11) | 10 | 17 | Rincon | Durbin | | 1-0 | T1st | ... |
| 4-6 | Cle. | W | 7-6 | (15) | 15 | 12 | Roa | Westbrook | | 2-0 | T1st | ... |
| 4-7 | Cle. | L | 4-11 | | 11 | 16 | Durbin | Lohse | | 2-1 | 2nd | 1.0 |
| 4-8 | At Det. | L | 6-10 | | 10 | 14 | Cornejo | Fultz | | 2-2 | T2nd | 2.0 |
| 4-10 | At Det. | W | 10-5 | | 15 | 9 | Radke | Johnson | | 3-2 | T2nd | 1.0 |
| 4-11 | At Det. | L | 5-6 | (10) | 14 | 10 | Colyer | Roa | | 3-3 | T3rd | 2.0 |
| 4-12 | At Cle. | L | 3-6 | | 8 | 8 | Lee | Lohse | | 3-4 | 4th | 2.5 |
| 4-14 | At Cle. | W | 10-6 | | 15 | 10 | Silva | D'Amico | Rincon | 4-4 | T3rd | 2.0 |
| 4-15 | At Cle. | W | 3-0 | | 9 | 4 | Radke | Stanford | Nathan | 5-4 | 3rd | 1.0 |
| 4-16 | K.C. | W | 9-7 | | 11 | 9 | Rincon | Cerda | Nathan | 6-4 | T1st | ... |
| 4-17 | K.C. | W | 8-4 | | 7 | 11 | Lohse | Appier | Romero | 7-4 | T1st | ... |
| 4-18 | K.C. | W | 8-3 | | 12 | 7 | Roa | May | | 8-4 | T1st | ... |
| 4-20 | Det. | W | 6-4 | | 9 | 7 | Silva | Johnson | Nathan | 9-4 | 1st | +1.0 |
| 4-21 | Det. | L | 8-11 | | 12 | 15 | Levine | Radke | Urbina | 9-5 | 1st | +0.5 |
| 4-22 | Det. | W | 4-3 | | 8 | 10 | Santana | Maroth | Nathan | 10-5 | 1st | +1.0 |
| 4-23 | At K.C. | W | 7-5 | | 10 | 12 | Romero | Leskanic | Nathan | 11-5 | 1st | +1.0 |
| 4-24 | At K.C. | L | 1-10 | | 6 | 15 | Camp | Greisinger | | 11-6 | 1st | +0.5 |
| 4-25 | At K.C. | W | 4-2 | | 10 | 10 | Silva | Anderson | Nathan | 12-6 | 1st | +1.0 |
| 4-26 | Tor. | L | 1-6 | | 2 | 14 | Lilly | Radke | | 12-7 | 1st | +0.5 |
| 4-27 | Tor. | W | 7-4 | | 11 | 9 | Rincon | Speier | | 13-7 | 1st | +1.5 |
| 4-28 | Tor. | W | 9-5 | | 12 | 13 | Rincon | Frasor | | 14-7 | 1st | +1.5 |
| 4-30 | Ana. | W | 6-3 | | 15 | 9 | Silva | Ortiz | Nathan | 15-7 | 1st | +1.5 |
| 5-1 | Ana. | L | 0-1 | | 4 | 10 | Rodriguez | Rincon | Percival | 15-8 | 1st | +1.0 |
| 5-2 | Ana. | L | 1-3 | | 7 | 7 | Lackey | Romero | Percival | 15-9 | T1st | ... |
| 5-4 | At Sea. | L | 3-4 | (16) | 9 | 13 | Villone | Greisinger | | 15-10 | 2nd | 0.5 |
| 5-5 | At Sea. | W | 5-1 | | 11 | 5 | Silva | Pineiro | | 16-10 | 2nd | 0.5 |
| 5-6 | At Sea. | L | 1-2 | | 7 | 5 | Garcia | Rincon | Guardado | 16-11 | 2nd | 1.0 |
| 5-7 | At Oak. | L | 9-11 | (13) | 16 | 15 | Bradford | Mulholland | | 16-12 | 2nd | 1.0 |
| 5-8 | At Oak. | W | 3-2 | (10) | 10 | 10 | Romero | Mecir | Nathan | 17-12 | T1st | ... |
| 5-9 | At Oak. | L | 4-8 | | 6 | 11 | Mulder | Lohse | | 17-13 | T1st | ... |
| 5-11 | Sea. | W | 7-6 | (11) | 10 | 18 | Fultz | Villone | | 18-13 | T1st | ... |
| 5-12 | Sea. | W | 4-3 | | 7 | 10 | Radke | Garcia | Nathan | 19-13 | 1st | +0.5 |
| 5-13 | Sea. | W | 1-0 | | 8 | 8 | Santana | Franklin | Nathan | 20-13 | 1st | +1.0 |
| 5-14 | At Chi. | W | 3-2 | | 11 | 5 | Rincon | Marte | Nathan | 21-13 | 1st | +2.0 |
| 5-15 | At Chi. | W | 4-1 | | 7 | 4 | Greisinger | Loaiza | Nathan | 22-13 | 1st | +3.0 |
| 5-16 | At Chi. | L | 0-11 | | 8 | 15 | Buehrle | Silva | | 22-14 | 1st | +2.0 |
| 5-17 | At Tor. | W | 9-5 | | 13 | 9 | Rincon | Nakamura | Fultz | 23-14 | 1st | +3.0 |
| 5-18 | At Tor. | L | 3-5 | | 5 | 11 | Batista | Santana | Adams | 23-15 | 1st | +2.0 |
| 5-19 | At Tor. | W | 6-5 | | 9 | 8 | Fultz | Adams | Nathan | 24-15 | 1st | +2.0 |
| 5-20 | Chi. | L | 3-10 | | 10 | 16 | Loaiza | Greisinger | | 24-16 | 1st | +1.0 |
| 5-21 | Chi. | L | 2-8 | | 8 | 12 | Buehrle | Silva | | 24-17 | T1st | ... |
| 5-22 | Chi. | W | 9-1 | | 14 | 7 | Radke | Cotts | | 25-17 | 1st | +1.0 |
| 5-23 | Chi. | L | 7-17 | | 11 | 23 | Garland | Santana | | 25-18 | T1st | ... |
| 5-25 | At T.B. | L | 1-6 | | 5 | 9 | Zambrano | Lohse | | 25-19 | T1st | ... |
| 5-26 | At T.B. | W | 4-2 | | 8 | 7 | Greisinger | Bell | Nathan | 26-19 | T1st | ... |
| 5-27 | At T.B. | L | 4-5 | | 7 | 12 | Halama | Silva | Baez | 26-20 | 2nd | 1.0 |
| 5-28 | At K.C. | L | 1-2 | | 7 | 8 | Affeldt | Rincon | | 26-21 | 2nd | 2.0 |
| 5-29 | At K.C. | L | 2-5 | | 8 | 7 | Reyes | Santana | Affeldt | 26-22 | 2nd | 2.0 |
| 5-30 | At K.C. | W | 8-3 | | 12 | 12 | Lohse | Gobble | | 27-22 | 2nd | 2.0 |
| 5-31 | T.B. | L | 3-7 | | 4 | 8 | Bell | Greisinger | | 27-23 | 2nd | 2.5 |
| 6-1 | T.B. | W | 16-4 | | 14 | 9 | Silva | Abbott | | 28-23 | 2nd | 1.5 |
| 6-2 | T.B. | L | 2-4 | | 4 | 11 | Waechter | Radke | Baez | 28-24 | 2nd | 1.5 |
| 6-3 | T.B. | L | 2-5 | | 6 | 6 | Hendrickson | Santana | Baez | 28-25 | 2nd | 2.0 |
| 6-4 | Det. | W | 3-2 | | 7 | 7 | Nathan | Walker | | 29-25 | 2nd | 2.0 |
| 6-5 | Det. | L | 0-6 | | 3 | 12 | Knotts | Greisinger | | 29-26 | 2nd | 2.0 |
| 6-6 | Det. | W | 6-5 | | 10 | 13 | Romero | Yan | Nathan | 30-26 | 2nd | 1.0 |
| 6-8 | N.Y. | W | 2-1 | | 7 | 5 | Rincon | Stanton | | 31-26 | 2nd | 1.0 |
| 6-9 | N.Y. | W | 5-3 | | 8 | 9 | Santana | Trachsel | Nathan | 32-26 | 2nd | ... |
| 6-10 | N.Y. | W | 3-2 | (15) | 12 | 8 | Balfour | Bottalico | | 33-26 | 1st | +0.5 |
| 6-11 | Phi. | L | 6-11 | | 12 | 14 | Worrell | Mulholland | | 33-27 | 1st | +0.5 |
| 6-12 | Phi. | W | 6-1 | | 11 | 9 | Silva | Millwood | | 34-27 | 1st | +0.5 |
| 6-13 | Phi. | L | 1-2 | | 7 | 7 | Cormier | Fultz | Wagner | 34-28 | 2nd | 0.5 |
| 6-15 | At Mon. | W | 8-2 | | 9 | 4 | Santana | Day | | 35-28 | 2nd | 0.5 |
| 6-16 | At Mon. | W | 5-4 | (11) | 9 | 8 | Rincon | Fikac | Nathan | 36-28 | 1st | +0.5 |
| 6-17 | At Mon. | W | 6-4 | | 10 | 11 | Fultz | Hernandez | Nathan | 37-28 | 1st | +1.5 |

| Date | Opp. | Res. | Score | (inn.*) | Hits | Opp. hits | Winning pitcher | Losing pitcher | Save | Record | Pos. | GB |
|---|---|---|---|---|---|---|---|---|---|---|---|---|
| 6-18 | At Mil. | L | 1-4 | | 5 | 11 | Sheets | Silva | Kolb | 37-29 | 1st | +0.5 |
| 6-19 | At Mil. | L | 6-7 | | 12 | 12 | Vizcaino | Mulholland | Kolb | 37-30 | 1st | +0.5 |
| 6-20 | At Mil. | W | 4-2 | | 8 | 6 | Santana | Santos | Nathan | 38-30 | 1st | +1.5 |
| 6-22 | At Bos. | L | 2-9 | | 7 | 13 | Schilling | Lohse | | 38-31 | 1st | +1.0 |
| 6-23 | At Bos. | W | 4-2 | | 9 | 8 | Silva | Lowe | Nathan | 39-31 | 1st | +2.0 |
| 6-24 | At Bos. | W | 4-3 | (10) | 8 | 10 | Balfour | Foulke | Nathan | 40-31 | 1st | +2.0 |
| 6-25 | Mil. | W | 6-3 | | 11 | 7 | Santana | Obermueller | Nathan | 41-31 | 1st | +3.0 |
| 6-26 | Mil. | L | 2-7 | | 5 | 14 | Santos | Guerrier | | 41-32 | 1st | +2.0 |
| 6-27 | Mil. | L | 3-7 | | 9 | 10 | Davis | Lohse | | 41-33 | 1st | +1.0 |
| 6-29 | Chi. | L | 2-6 | | 9 | 11 | Buehrle | Silva | | 41-34 | 2nd | ... |
| 6-30 | Chi. | L | 6-9 | | 9 | 13 | Garcia | Radke | | 41-35 | 2nd | 1.0 |
| 7-1 | Chi. | L | 1-2 | | 8 | 4 | Garland | Santana | Marte | 41-36 | 2nd | 2.0 |
| 7-2 | At Ari. | W | 6-5 | | 9 | 12 | Romero | Randolph | Nathan | 42-36 | 2nd | 1.0 |
| 7-3 | At Ari. | W | 8-4 | | 14 | 7 | Mulholland | Good | Rincon | 43-36 | 2nd | ... |
| 7-4 | At Ari. | L | 2-6 | | 5 | 12 | Johnson | Silva | | 43-37 | 2nd | ... |
| 7-5 | K.C. | W | 9-0 | | 13 | 4 | Radke | Gobble | | 44-37 | 1st | +0.5 |
| 7-6 | K.C. | W | 4-0 | | 6 | 3 | Santana | Greinke | | 45-37 | 1st | +1.5 |
| 7-7 | K.C. | W | 12-0 | | 15 | 6 | Lohse | Reyes | | 46-37 | 1st | +2.5 |
| 7-8 | Det. | W | 7-1 | | 9 | 8 | Balfour | Maroth | | 47-37 | 1st | +2.5 |
| 7-9 | Det. | L | 3-5 | | 9 | 10 | Knotts | Silva | Urbina | 47-38 | 1st | +1.5 |
| 7-10 | Det. | L | 2-4 | | 9 | 7 | Robertson | Radke | Urbina | 47-39 | 1st | +0.5 |
| 7-11 | Det. | L | 0-2 | | 5 | 2 | Johnson | Santana | | 47-40 | 2nd | 0.5 |
| 7-15 | At K.C. | L | 1-3 | | 5 | 11 | Greinke | Lohse | Bukvich | 47-41 | 2nd | 0.5 |
| 7-16 | At K.C. | L | 3-12 | | 7 | 17 | May | Radke | | 47-42 | 2nd | 0.5 |
| 7-17 | At K.C. | W | 4-1 | | 7 | 1 | Santana | Gobble | Nathan | 48-42 | 2nd | 0.5 |
| 7-18 | At K.C. | L | 3-4 | (10) | 10 | 8 | Reyes | Balfour | | 48-43 | 2nd | 0.5 |
| 7-19 | At Det. | W | 3-1 | | 7 | 5 | Mulholland | Johnson | Nathan | 49-43 | 2nd | 0.5 |
| 7-20 | At Det. | W | 5-4 | (10) | 6 | 10 | Balfour | Urbina | Nathan | 50-43 | 1st | +0.5 |
| 7-21 | T.B. | W | 12-2 | | 17 | 8 | Radke | Halama | | 51-43 | 1st | +0.5 |
| 7-22 | T.B. | W | 7-5 | | 6 | 6 | Romero | Harper | Nathan | 52-43 | 1st | +0.5 |
| 7-23 | At Bal. | W | 7-3 | | 12 | 10 | Silva | Maine | | 53-43 | 1st | +0.5 |
| 7-24 | At Bal. | L | 2-4 | | 4 | 5 | Ponson | Roa | Julio | 53-44 | 2nd | 0.5 |
| 7-25 | At Bal. | W | 8-4 | | 15 | 9 | Lohse | Cabrera | | 54-44 | 1st | +0.5 |
| 7-26 | At Chi. | W | 6-2 | | 14 | 6 | Radke | Buehrle | | 55-44 | 1st | +1.5 |
| 7-27 | At Chi. | W | 7-3 | | 10 | 4 | Santana | Garcia | | 56-44 | 1st | +2.5 |
| 7-28 | At Chi. | W | 5-4 | (10) | 10 | 10 | Mulholland | Takatsu | Nathan | 57-44 | 1st | +3.5 |
| 7-30 | Bos. | L | 2-8 | | 9 | 16 | Arroyo | Lohse | | 57-45 | 1st | +4.0 |
| 7-31 | Bos. | W | 5-4 | | 9 | 10 | Rincon | Embree | Nathan | 58-45 | 1st | +5.0 |
| 8-1 | Bos. | W | 4-3 | | 9 | 2 | Santana | Timlin | Nathan | 59-45 | 1st | +5.0 |
| 8-3 | Ana. | W | 10-0 | | 11 | 11 | Silva | Lackey | | 60-45 | 1st | +5.0 |
| 8-4 | Ana. | W | 6-3 | | 11 | 10 | Lohse | Ortiz | Nathan | 61-45 | 1st | +6.0 |
| 8-5 | Ana. | L | 3-8 | | 6 | 15 | Sele | Mulholland | | 61-46 | 1st | +6.0 |
| 8-6 | Oak. | L | 1-3 | (11) | 4 | 8 | Dotel | Rincon | | 61-47 | 1st | +6.0 |
| 8-7 | Oak. | W | 4-3 | | 12 | 9 | Santana | Hudson | Nathan | 62-47 | 1st | +6.0 |
| 8-8 | Oak. | L | 5-6 | (18) | 11 | 16 | Hammond | Mulholland | Dotel | 62-48 | 1st | +6.0 |
| 8-9 | Oak. | L | 2-8 | | 7 | 12 | Harden | Lohse | | 62-49 | 1st | +5.0 |
| 8-10 | At Sea. | L | 3-4 | | 4 | 10 | Meche | Mulholland | Putz | 62-50 | 1st | +4.0 |
| 8-11 | At Sea. | L | 3-4 | | 6 | 7 | Sherrill | Rincon | | 62-51 | 1st | +3.0 |
| 8-12 | At Sea. | W | 6-3 | | 10 | 9 | Santana | Franklin | Nathan | 63-51 | 1st | +3.0 |
| 8-13 | At Cle. | L | 2-8 | | 10 | 13 | Elarton | Silva | | 63-52 | 1st | +2.0 |
| 8-14 | At Cle. | L | 1-7 | | 8 | 8 | Westbrook | Lohse | | 63-53 | 1st | +1.0 |
| 8-15 | At Cle. | W | 4-2 | (10) | 9 | 7 | Rincon | White | Nathan | 64-53 | 1st | +2.0 |
| 8-17 | N.Y. | W | 8-2 | | 13 | 9 | Radke | Vazquez | | 65-53 | 1st | +3.5 |
| 8-18 | N.Y. | W | 7-2 | | 10 | 6 | Santana | Mussina | | 66-53 | 1st | +4.5 |
| 8-19 | N.Y. | L | 10-13 | | 13 | 16 | Gordon | Nathan | Rivera | 66-54 | 1st | +4.0 |
| 8-20 | Cle. | W | 5-1 | | 9 | 3 | Lohse | Westbrook | | 67-54 | 1st | +5.0 |
| 8-21 | Cle. | W | 8-1 | | 8 | 7 | Mulholland | Durbin | | 68-54 | 1st | +6.0 |
| 8-22 | Cle. | W | 7-3 | | 11 | 9 | Radke | Sabathia | | 69-54 | 1st | +7.0 |
| 8-23 | At Tex. | W | 7-4 | | 11 | 7 | Santana | Rogers | | 70-54 | 1st | +8.0 |
| 8-24 | At Tex. | L | 4-5 | | 7 | 11 | Cordero | Nathan | | 70-55 | 1st | +8.0 |
| 8-25 | At Tex. | W | 8-5 | | 17 | 13 | Lohse | Drese | Nathan | 71-55 | 1st | +8.0 |
| 8-26 | At Tex. | L | 3-8 | | 6 | 15 | Park | Mulholland | | 71-56 | 1st | +8.0 |
| 8-27 | At Ana. | L | 6-9 | | 11 | 16 | Sele | Radke | Percival | 71-57 | 1st | +7.0 |
| 8-28 | At Ana. | W | 7-1 | | 12 | 6 | Santana | Colon | | 72-57 | 1st | +8.0 |
| 8-29 | At Ana. | L | 2-4 | | 5 | 7 | Rodriguez | Rincon | | 72-58 | 1st | +7.0 |
| 8-31 | Tex. | W | 8-5 | (11) | 13 | 10 | Rincon | Almanzar | | 73-58 | 1st | +7.0 |
| 9-1 | Tex. | W | 4-2 | | 11 | 8 | Crain | Cordero | Nathan | 74-58 | 1st | +8.0 |
| 9-2 | Tex. | W | 2-0 | | 6 | 5 | Radke | Rogers | Nathan | 75-58 | 1st | +9.0 |
| 9-3 | K.C. | W | 2-0 | | 9 | 2 | Santana | May | Nathan | 76-58 | 1st | +9.5 |
| 9-4 | K.C. | W | 4-3 | | 7 | 8 | Romero | Reyes | | 77-58 | 1st | +9.5 |

| Date | Opp. | Res. | Score | (inn.*) | Hits | Opp. hits | Winning pitcher | Losing pitcher | Save | Record | Pos. | GB |
|---|---|---|---|---|---|---|---|---|---|---|---|---|
| 9-5 | K.C. | L | 3-12 | | 6 | 13 | Gobble | Lohse | | 77-59 | 1st | +8.5 |
| 9-6 | At Bal. | L | 1-4 | | 4 | 10 | Cabrera | Mulholland | Julio | 77-60 | 1st | +7.5 |
| 9-7 | At Bal. | W | 3-1 | | 4 | 5 | Romero | Julio | Nathan | 78-60 | 1st | +8.5 |
| 9-8 | At Bal. | W | 9-0 | | 12 | 6 | Santana | Bedard | | 79-60 | 1st | +8.5 |
| 9-10 | At Det. | W | 4-1 | | 9 | 10 | Silva | Maroth | Nathan | 80-60 | 1st | +9.0 |
| 9-11 | At Det. | W | 3-2 | | 9 | 7 | Crain | Levine | Nathan | 81-60 | 1st | +9.0 |
| 9-12 | At Det. | W | 8-5 | | 15 | 13 | Mulholland | Robertson | Nathan | 82-60 | 1st | +10.0 |
| 9-13 | At Det. | W | 5-3 | | 11 | 8 | Radke | Johnson | Nathan | 83-60 | 1st | +10.5 |
| 9-14 | Chi. | W | 10-2 | | 8 | 6 | Santana | Garcia | | 84-60 | 1st | +11.5 |
| 9-15 | Chi. | W | 6-1 | | 9 | 5 | Silva | Buehrle | | 85-60 | 1st | +12.5 |
| 9-16 | Chi. | W | 10-1 | | 14 | 4 | Lohse | Garland | | 86-60 | 1st | +13.5 |
| 9-17 | Bal. | L | 2-11 | | 6 | 12 | Ponson | Mulholland | | 86-61 | 1st | +13.5 |
| 9-18 | Bal. | L | 3-12 | | 6 | 18 | Cabrera | Radke | | 86-62 | 1st | +12.5 |
| 9-19 | Bal. | W | 5-1 | | 8 | 9 | Santana | Chen | | 87-62 | 1st | +12.5 |
| 9-20 | At Chi. | W | 8-2 | | 12 | 8 | Silva | Buehrle | | 88-62 | 1st | +13.5 |
| 9-21 | At Chi. | L | 6-8 | | 10 | 9 | Cotts | Romero | Takatsu | 88-63 | 1st | +12.5 |
| 9-22 | At Chi. | L | 6-7 | | 9 | 12 | Cotts | Roa | | 88-64 | 1st | +11.5 |
| 9-23 | At Cle. | L | 7-9 | | 14 | 13 | Lee | Durbin | Betancourt | 88-65 | 1st | +10.5 |
| 9-24 | At Cle. | W | 8-2 | | 15 | 4 | Santana | Denney | | 89-65 | 1st | +11.5 |
| 9-25 | At Cle. | L | 3-5 | | 6 | 5 | Howry | Romero | Wickman | 89-66 | 1st | +10.5 |
| 9-26 | At Cle. | W | 6-2 | | 8 | 9 | Silva | Cruceta | | 90-66 | 1st | +10.5 |
| 9-29! | At N.Y. | L | 3-5 | | 10 | 8 | Quantrill | Romero | Rivera | 90-67 | | |
| 9-29& | At N.Y. | L | 4-5 | | 12 | 8 | Lieber | Lohse | Rivera | 90-68 | 1st | +10.0 |
| 9-30 | At N.Y. | L | 4-6 | | 8 | 12 | Gordon | Fultz | | 90-69 | 1st | +9.0 |
| 10-1 | Cle. | W | 4-3 | | 8 | 8 | Crain | Howry | Nathan | 91-69 | 1st | +9.0 |
| 10-2 | Cle. | W | 6-5 | (12) | 14 | 12 | Lohse | Riske | | 92-69 | 1st | +9.5 |
| 10-3 | Cle. | L | 2-5 | | 5 | 9 | Lee | Lohse | Wickman | 92-70 | 1st | +9.0 |

Monthly records: April (15-7), May (12-16), June (14-12), July (17-10), August (15-13), September (17-11), October (2-1).
*Innings, if other than nine. ! First game of a doubleheader. & Second game of a doubleheader.

## RECORDS

**2004 regular-season record:** 92-70
**Position:** 1st in A.L. Central
**Home:** 49-32 **Road:** 43-38
**A.L. East:** 19-17 **A.L. Central:** 46-30
**A.L. West:** 16-16 **N.L.** 11-7
**Vs. LH starters:** 30-23
**Vs. RH starters:** 62-47
**Grass:** 37-35 **Artificial:** 55-35
**Day:** 27-25 **Night:** 65-45
**1-Run:** 24-16 **X-inn.:** 12-6
**Doubleheaders:** 0-1-0
**Team record past five years:** 430-379 (.532, ranks 5th in league in that span)

## TEAM LEADERS

**Batting average:** Shannon Stewart (.304).
**At-bats:** Cristian Guzman (576).
**Runs:** Lew Ford (89).
**Hits:** Lew Ford (170).
**Total Bases:** Lew Ford (254).
**Doubles:** Torii Hunter (37).
**Triples:** Luis Rivas (5).
**Home runs:** Corey Koskie (25).
**Runs batted in:** Torii Hunter (81).
**Stolen bases:** Torii Hunter (21).
**Slugging percentage:** Justin Morneau (.536).
**On-base percentage:** Lew Ford (.381).
**Wins:** Johan Santana (20).
**Earned-run average:** Johan Santana (2.61).
**Complete games:** Kyle Lohse, Brad Radke, Johan Santana, Carlos Silva (1).
**Shutouts:** Kyle Lohse, Brad Radke, Johan Santana, Carlos Silva (1).
**Saves:** Joe Nathan (44).
**Innings pitched:** Johan Santana (228.0).
**Strikeouts:** Johan Santana (265).

## GAMES BY POSITION

**Catcher:** Henry Blanco 114, Joe Mauer 32, Matthew LeCroy 26, Pat Borders 19, Rob Bowen 15.
**First base:** Doug Mientkiewicz 77, Justin Morneau 61, Matthew LeCroy 23, Michael Cuddyer 10, Jose Offerman 7, Terry Tiffee 1.
**Second base:** Luis Rivas 109, Michael Cuddyer 48, Augie Ojeda 20, Nick Punto 19, Alex Prieto 8, Jose Offerman 3, Jason Bartlett 1.
**Third base:** Corey Koskie 115, Michael Cuddyer 43, Terry Tiffee 12, Alex Prieto 5, Augie Ojeda 4, Nick Punto 2.
**Shortstop:** Cristian Guzman 145, Nick Punto 11, Augie Ojeda 7, Jason Bartlett 5, Alex Prieto 3.
**Outfield:** Jacque Jones 142, Lew Ford 126, Torii Hunter 126, Shannon Stewart 71, Michael Restovich 19, Michael Cuddyer 15, Michael Ryan 15, Jason Kubel 10, Nick Punto 2.
**Designated hitter:** Jose Offerman 39, Matthew LeCroy 30, Lew Ford 26, Shannon Stewart 21, Justin Morneau 11, Michael Ryan 11, Torii Hunter 10, Jason Kubel 9, Michael Cuddyer 5, Michael Restovich 5, Jacque Jones 3, Nick Punto 3, Jason Bartlett 1, Rob Bowen 1, Corey Koskie 1, Joe Mauer 1, Alex Prieto 1, Terry Tiffee 1.

## TOP DRAFT CHOICES

1a. **Trevor Plouffe,** SS, Crespi H.S., Northridge, Calif.
1b. **Glen Perkins,** LHP, Minnesota.
1c. **Kyle Waldrop,** RHP, Farragut H.S., Knoxville, Tenn.
1d. **Matt Foxx,** RHP, Central Florida.
1e. **Jay Rainville,** RHP, Bishop Hendricken H.S., Pawtucket, R.I.
2. **Anthony Swarzak,** RHP, Nova H.S., Fort Lauderdale, Fla.
3. **Eduardo Morlan,** RHP, Coral Park H.S., Miami.
4. **Mark Robinson,** OF, Mountain View H.S., El Monte, Calif.
5. **Jeff Schoenbachler,** LHP, Reno (Nev.) H.S.
6. **Patrick Bryant,** RHP, Pensacola Catholic H.S., Gulf Breeze, Fla.
7. **John Williams,** LHP, Middle Tennessee State.
8. **Jay Sawatski,** LHP, Arkansas.
9. **J.P. Martinez,** RHP, New Orleans.
10. **Jeremy Pickrel,** OF, Illinois State

# NEW YORK YANKEES

## *AMERICAN LEAGUE EAST DIVISION*

## 2005 SEASON

### Yankees Schedule

Home games shaded.
All-Star Game July 12 at Detroit. Schedule subject to change.

**April**

| SUN | MON | TUE | WED | THU | FRI | SAT |
|---|---|---|---|---|---|---|
| 3 BOS | 4 | 5 | 6 BOS | 7 BOS | 8 BAL | 9 BAL |
| 10 BAL | 11 BOS | 12 | 13 BOS | 14 BOS | 15 BAL | 16 BAL |
| 17 BAL | 18 TB | 19 TB | 20 TOR | 21 TOR | 22 TEX | 23 TEX |
| 24 TEX | 25 | 26 ANA | 27 ANA | 28 ANA | 29 TOR | 30 TOR |

**May**

| SUN | MON | TUE | WED | THU | FRI | SAT |
|---|---|---|---|---|---|---|
| 1 TOR | 2 TB | 3 TB | 4 TB | 5 TB | 6 OAK | 7 OAK |
| 8 OAK | 9 SEA | 10 SEA | 11 SEA | 12 | 13 OAK | 14 OAK |
| 15 OAK | 16 SEA | 17 SEA | 18 SEA | 19 | 20 NYM | 21 NYM |
| 22 NYM | 23 | 24 DET | 25 DET | 26 DET | 27 BOS | 28 BOS |
| 29 BOS | 30 | 31 KC | | | | |

**June**

| SUN | MON | TUE | WED | THU | FRI | SAT |
|---|---|---|---|---|---|---|
| | | | 1 KC | 2 KC | 3 MIN | 4 MIN |
| 5 MIN | 6 MIL | 7 MIL | 8 MIL | 9 | 10 STL | 11 STL |
| 12 STL | 13 | 14 PIT | 15 PIT | 16 PIT | 17 CHC | 18 CHC |
| 19 CHC | 20 TB | 21 TB | 22 TB | 23 TB | 24 NYM | 25 NYM |
| 26 NYM | 27 BAL | 28 BAL | 29 BAL | 30 | | |

**July**

| SUN | MON | TUE | WED | THU | FRI | SAT |
|---|---|---|---|---|---|---|
| | | | | | 1 DET | 2 DET |
| 3 DET | 4 BAL | 5 BAL | 6 | 7 CLE | 8 CLE | 9 CLE |
| 10 CLE | 11 | 12 All-Star | 13 | 14 BOS | 15 BOS | 16 BOS |
| 17 BOS | 18 TEX | 19 TEX | 20 TEX | 21 ANA | 22 ANA | 23 ANA |
| 24 ANA | 25 | 26 MIN | 27 MIN | 28 MIN | 29 ANA | 30 ANA |
| 31 ANA | | | | | | |

**August**

| SUN | MON | TUE | WED | THU | FRI | SAT |
|---|---|---|---|---|---|---|
| | 1 | 2 CLE | 3 CLE | 4 CLE | 5 TOR | 6 TOR |
| 7 TOR | 8 CHW | 9 CHW | 10 CHW | 11 TEX | 12 TEX | 13 TEX |
| 14 TEX | 15 TB | 16 TB | 17 TB | 18 | 19 CHW | 20 CHW |
| 21 CHW | 22 TOR | 23 TOR | 24 TOR | 25 TOR | 26 KC | 27 KC |
| 28 KC | 29 SEA | 30 SEA | 31 SEA | | | |

**September**

| SUN | MON | TUE | WED | THU | FRI | SAT |
|---|---|---|---|---|---|---|
| | | | | 1 SEA | 2 OAK | 3 OAK |
| 4 OAK | 5 | 6 TB | 7 TB | 8 TB | 9 BOS | 10 BOS |
| 11 BOS | 12 | 13 TB | 14 TB | 15 TB | 16 TOR | 17 TOR |
| 18 TOR | 19 BAL | 20 BAL | 21 BAL | 22 BAL | 23 TOR | 24 TOR |
| 25 TOR | 26 | 27 BAL | 28 BAL | 29 BAL | 30 BOS | |

**October**

| SUN | MON | TUE | WED | THU | FRI | SAT |
|---|---|---|---|---|---|---|
| | | | | | | 1 BOS |
| 2 BOS | 3 | 4 | 5 | 6 | 7 | 8 |

Home games shaded. All-Star Game July 12 at Detroit. Schedule subject to change.

### CLUB DIRECTORY

**Principal owner**
George M. Steinbrenner III

**President**
Randy Levine

**Special advisers**
Yogi Berra, Reggie Jackson, Clyde King

**Senior vice president, general manager**
Brian Cashman

**Sr. vice president, baseball operations**
Mark Newman

**Sr. vice president, player personnel**
Gordon Blakeley

**Vice president, assistant g.m.**
Jean Afterman

**Vice president and senior adviser**
Gene Michael

**Vice president, scouting**
Lin Garrett

**Vice president, player personnel**
Billy Connors

**V.p., corp. and community relations**
Brian Smith

**Vice president, major league scouting**
Damon Oppenheimer

**Director of media relations and publicity**
Rick Cerrone

### MINOR LEAGUE AFFILIATES

| Class | Team | League | Manager |
|---|---|---|---|
| AAA | Columbus | International | Bucky Dent |
| AA | Trenton | Eastern | Bill Masse |
| Advanced A | Tampa | Florida State | Sam Arena |
| A | Charleston (S.C.) | South Atlantic | Dave Echols |
| Short-Season A | Staten Island | New York-Pennsylvania | Tommy John |
| Rookie | Gulf Coast Yankees | Gulf Coast | Oscar Acosta |

### BROADCAST INFORMATION

**Radio:** WCBS-AM (880).
**TV:** WCBS-TV (Channel 2).
**Cable TV:** Yankee Entertainment and Sports Network.

### SPRING TRAINING

**Ballpark (city):** Legends Field (Tampa, Fla.).
**Ticket information:** 813-879-2244, 813-287-8844.

**For more on the Yankees, go to msn.foxsports.com/mlb/teams.**

Rodriguez

Jeter

## SPRING TRAINING ROSTER

**Manager**—Joe Torre (6).
**Coaches**—Neil Allen, Joe Girardi, Don Mattingly (23), Luis Sojo (53), Mel Stottlemyre (34), Roy White (54).

| No. | PITCHERS | B/T | Ht./Wt. | Age* | 2004 Clubs |
|---|---|---|---|---|---|
| | Anderson, Jason | L/R | 6-0/188 | 25 | Cleveland, Buffalo, Columbus |
| | Bean, Colter | R/R | 6-6/255 | 28 | Columbus |
| 27 | Brown, Kevin | R/R | 6-4/220 | 40 | Trenton, Columbus, Staten Island, New York A.L. |
| 43 | DePaula, Jorge | R/R | 6-1/160 | 26 | New York A.L |
| 36 | Gordon, Tom | R/R | 5-10/190 | 37 | New York A.L. |
| 57 | Graman, Alex | L/L | 6-4/210 | 27 | New York A.L., Columbus |
| | Henn, Sean | R/L | 6-5/200 | 23 | Trenton |
| | Johnson, Randy | R/L | 6-10/231 | 41 | Arizona |
| 31 | Karsay, Steve | R/R | 6-3/210 | 33 | Trenton, Staten Island, Columbus, New York A.L. |
| | Marsonek, Sam | R/R | 6-6/225 | 26 | Columbus, New York A.L., G.C. Yankees, Tampa |
| 35 | Mussina, Mike | L/R | 6-2/185 | 36 | Columbus, New York A.L. |
| | Pavano, Carl | R/R | 6-5/241 | 29 | Florida |
| 47 | Prinz, Bret | R/R | 6-2/216 | 27 | Columbus, New York A.L. |
| 57 | Proctor, Scott | R/R | 6-1/198 | 28 | Columbus, New York A.L. |
| 48 | Quantrill, Paul | L/R | 6-1/198 | 36 | New York A.L. |
| | Ramirez, Ramon | R/R | 5-11/190 | 23 | Trenton, Columbus |
| 42 | Rivera, Mariano | R/R | 6-2/170 | 35 | New York A.L. |
| | Rodriguez, Felix | R/R | 6-1/198 | 32 | San Francisco, Philadelphia |
| | Sierra, Edwardo | R/R | 6-3/185 | 22 | Tampa |
| 29 | Stanton, Mike | L/L | 6-1/215 | 37 | New York N.L. |
| 56 | Sturtze, Tanyon | R/R | 6-5/200 | 34 | Las Vegas, New York A.L. |
| | Wang, Chien-Ming | R/R | 6-3/200 | 25 | Trenton, Columbus |
| | Wright, Jaret | R/R | 6-2/230 | 29 | Atlanta |

| No. | CATCHERS | B/T | Ht./Wt. | Age* | 2004 Clubs |
|---|---|---|---|---|---|
| 17 | Flaherty, John | R/R | 6-1/200 | 37 | New York A.L. |
| 20 | Posada, Jorge | B/R | 6-2/205 | 33 | New York A.L. |

| No. | INFIELDERS | B/T | Ht./Wt. | Age* | 2004 Clubs |
|---|---|---|---|---|---|
| | Cano, Robinson | L/R | 6-0/175 | 22 | Trenton, Columbus |
| | Escalona, Felix | R/R | 6-0/190 | 26 | Columbus, New York A.L. |
| 25 | Giambi, Jason | L/R | 6-3/230 | 34 | Tampa, New York A.L. |
| 2 | Jeter, Derek | R/R | 6-3/195 | 30 | New York A.L. |
| | Martinez, Tino | L/R | 6-2/230 | 37 | Tampa Bay |
| 39 | Phillips, Andy | R/R | 6-0/205 | 27 | Trenton, Columbus, New York A.L. |
| 13 | Rodriguez, Alex | R/R | 6-3/210 | 29 | New York A.L. |
| | Tejeda, Ferdin | R/R | 5-11/170 | 22 | Tampa, Lake Elsinore, Trenton |
| | Womack, Tony | L/R | 5-9/170 | 35 | St. Louis |

| No. | OUTFIELDERS | B/T | Ht./Wt. | Age* | 2004 Clubs |
|---|---|---|---|---|---|
| 19 | Crosby, Bubba | L/L | 5-11/185 | 28 | Columbus, New York A.L. |
| 55 | Matsui, Hideki | L/R | 6-2/230 | 30 | New York A.L. |
| 11 | Sheffield, Gary | R/R | 6-0/205 | 36 | New York A.L. |
| 51 | Williams, Bernie | B/R | 6-2/205 | 36 | New York A.L. |

*Age as of April 1, 2005.

## BALLPARK INFORMATION

**Ballpark (capacity, surface)**
Yankee Stadium (57,478, grass)

**Address**
Yankee Stadium
E. 161 St. and River Ave.
Bronx, NY 10451

**Official website**
www.yankees.com

**Business phone**
718-293-4300

**Ticket information**
212-307-1212, 718-293-6013

**Field dimensions (from home plate)**
To left field at foul line, 318 feet
To center field, 408 feet
To right field at foul line, 314 feet

**First game played**
April 18, 1923 (Yankees 4, Red Sox 1)

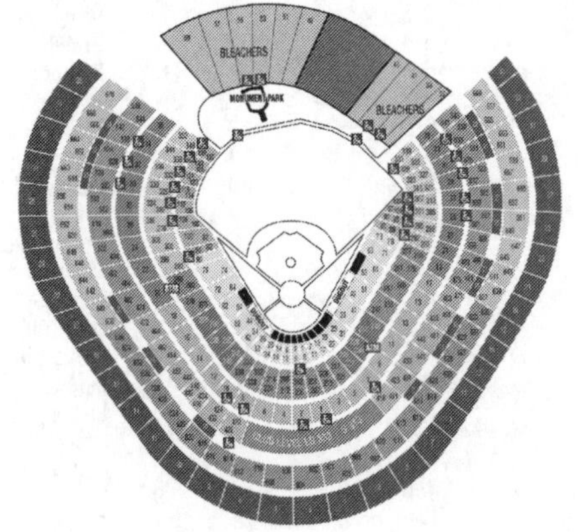

# 2004 REVIEW
## DAY BY DAY

| Date | Opp. | Res. | Score | (inn.*) | Hits | Opp. hits | Winning pitcher | Losing pitcher | Save | Record | Pos. | GB |
|---|---|---|---|---|---|---|---|---|---|---|---|---|
| 3-30^ | At T.B. | L | 3-8 | | 7 | 15 | Zambrano | Mussina | | 0-1 | T1st | ... |
| 3-31^ | At T.B. | W | 12-1 | | 11 | 6 | Brown | Gonzalez | | 1-1 | T1st | ... |
| 4-6 | At T.B. | L | 4-9 | | 4 | 14 | Zambrano | Mussina | | 1-2 | 4th | 1.0 |
| 4-7 | At T.B. | W | 3-2 | | 7 | 8 | Brown | Abbott | Rivera | 2-2 | T2nd | 0.5 |
| 4-8 | Chi. | W | 3-1 | | 7 | 4 | Vazquez | Schoeneweis | Rivera | 3-2 | 1st | +0.5 |
| 4-9 | Chi. | L | 3-9 | | 6 | 10 | Garland | Contreras | | 3-3 | 2nd | 0.5 |
| 4-10 | Chi. | L | 3-7 | | 4 | 13 | Buehrle | DePaula | | 3-4 | 4th | 0.5 |
| 4-11 | Chi. | W | 5-4 | | 7 | 9 | Mussina | Wright | Rivera | 4-4 | 3rd | 0.5 |
| 4-14 | T.B. | W | 5-1 | | 7 | 7 | Brown | Hendrickson | | 5-4 | 2nd | ... |
| 4-16 | At Bos. | L | 2-6 | | 4 | 9 | Wakefield | Vazquez | | 5-5 | 4th | 0.5 |
| 4-17 | At Bos. | L | 2-5 | | 8 | 10 | Schilling | Mussina | | 5-6 | 4th | 1.5 |
| 4-18 | At Bos. | W | 7-3 | | 10 | 9 | Quantrill | Lowe | | 6-6 | 3rd | 1.5 |
| 4-19 | At Bos. | L | 4-5 | | 10 | 13 | Timlin | Gordon | Foulke | 6-7 | 3rd | 2.0 |
| 4-20 | At Chi. | W | 11-8 | | 16 | 13 | Quantrill | Buehrle | Rivera | 7-7 | 3rd | 2.0 |
| 4-21 | At Chi. | W | 3-1 | | 5 | 5 | Vazquez | Garland | Rivera | 8-7 | 3rd | 1.5 |
| 4-22 | At Chi. | L | 3-4 | | 7 | 9 | Schoeneweis | Mussina | Marte | 8-8 | 3rd | 2.0 |
| 4-23 | Bos. | L | 2-11 | | 7 | 12 | Lowe | Contreras | | 8-9 | 3rd | 3.0 |
| 4-24 | Bos. | L | 2-3 | (12) | 4 | 6 | Foulke | Quantrill | Timlin | 8-10 | 3rd | 3.5 |
| 4-25 | Bos. | L | 0-2 | | 4 | 4 | Martinez | Vazquez | Williamson | 8-11 | 3rd | 4.5 |
| 4-27 | Oak. | W | 10-8 | | 10 | 16 | Osborne | Mecir | Rivera | 9-11 | 3rd | 4.0 |
| 4-28 | Oak. | W | 5-1 | | 9 | 5 | Contreras | Mulder | Gordon | 10-11 | 3rd | 4.0 |
| 4-29 | Oak. | W | 7-5 | | 10 | 10 | Brown | Zito | Rivera | 11-11 | 3rd | 4.5 |
| 4-30 | K.C. | W | 5-2 | | 9 | 3 | Vazquez | Anderson | Rivera | 12-11 | 3rd | 4.0 |
| 5-1 | K.C. | W | 12-4 | | 14 | 7 | Lieber | Villacis | | 13-11 | 3rd | 2.5 |
| 5-2 | K.C. | W | 4-2 | | 8 | 9 | Mussina | Affeldt | Rivera | 14-11 | 2nd | 1.5 |
| 5-4 | At Oak. | W | 10-8 | | 17 | 7 | Osborne | Bradford | Rivera | 15-11 | T1st | ... |
| 5-5 | At Oak. | W | 4-3 | | 11 | 10 | Quantrill | Rhodes | Rivera | 16-11 | T1st | ... |
| 5-6 | At Oak. | L | 4-7 | | 6 | 10 | Harden | Vazquez | Mecir | 16-12 | 2nd | 1.0 |
| 5-7 | At Sea. | L | 2-6 | | 7 | 12 | Franklin | Lieber | | 16-13 | 2nd | 2.0 |
| 5-8 | At Sea. | W | 6-0 | | 11 | 4 | Mussina | Meche | | 17-13 | 2nd | 2.0 |
| 5-9 | At Sea. | W | 7-6 | | 9 | 8 | Quantrill | Soriano | Rivera | 18-13 | 2nd | 1.0 |
| 5-11 | Ana. | W | 8-7 | (10) | 13 | 12 | Gordon | Weber | | 19-13 | 2nd | 0.5 |
| 5-12 | Ana. | L | 2-11 | | 7 | 11 | Sele | Vazquez | | 19-14 | 2nd | 0.5 |
| 5-13 | Ana. | W | 7-4 | | 11 | 7 | Lieber | Lackey | Rivera | 20-14 | 1st | +0.5 |
| 5-14 | Sea. | W | 9-5 | | 8 | 12 | Mussina | Villone | | 21-14 | 1st | +0.5 |
| 5-15 | Sea. | L | 7-13 | (13) | 14 | 15 | Guardado | White | | 21-15 | 2nd | 0.5 |
| 5-16 | Sea. | W | 2-1 | | 5 | 9 | Brown | Pineiro | Rivera | 22-15 | 1st | +0.5 |
| 5-18 | At Ana. | L | 0-1 | (11) | 3 | 11 | Shields | Quantrill | | 22-16 | 2nd | 0.5 |
| 5-19 | At Ana. | W | 4-2 | | 7 | 7 | Lieber | Lackey | Rivera | 23-16 | 2nd | 0.5 |
| 5-20 | At Ana. | W | 6-2 | | 11 | 9 | Mussina | Colon | | 24-16 | 1st | +0.5 |
| 5-21 | At Tex. | L | 7-9 | | 15 | 14 | Benoit | Brown | Cordero | 24-17 | 2nd | 0.5 |
| 5-22 | At Tex. | L | 3-4 | | 7 | 6 | Almanzar | Gordon | | 24-18 | 2nd | 1.5 |
| 5-23 | At Tex. | W | 8-3 | | 13 | 7 | Vazquez | Dickey | | 25-18 | 2nd | 1.5 |
| 5-25 | At Bal. | W | 11-3 | | 14 | 7 | Lieber | Bedard | | 26-18 | 2nd | 1.5 |
| 5-26 | At Bal. | W | 12-9 | | 16 | 14 | Sturtze | Ryan | Rivera | 27-18 | 2nd | 1.5 |
| 5-27 | At Bal. | W | 18-5 | | 21 | 14 | Contreras | Ponson | | 28-18 | 2nd | 0.5 |
| 5-28 | At T.B. | W | 7-5 | | 9 | 12 | Vazquez | Waechter | Rivera | 29-18 | 2nd | 0.5 |
| 5-29 | At T.B. | W | 5-3 | | 10 | 4 | Brown | Hendrickson | Rivera | 30-18 | 1st | +0.5 |
| 5-30 | At T.B. | L | 6-7 | | 11 | 13 | Zambrano | Lieber | Baez | 30-19 | 2nd | 0.5 |
| 6-1 | Bal. | W | 8-7 | | 13 | 14 | Mussina | Ponson | Rivera | 31-19 | 1st | +1.0 |
| 6-2 | Bal. | W | 6-5 | | 3 | 9 | Prinz | DuBose | Rivera | 32-19 | 1st | +2.0 |
| 6-3 | Bal. | W | 5-2 | | 10 | 5 | Vazquez | Parrish | Rivera | 33-19 | 1st | +2.5 |
| 6-4 | Tex. | W | 7-6 | | 9 | 9 | Brown | Powell | Rivera | 34-19 | 1st | +3.5 |
| 6-5 | Tex. | L | 1-8 | | 6 | 12 | Dominguez | Lieber | | 34-20 | 1st | +2.5 |
| 6-6 | Tex. | W | 2-1 | | 7 | 6 | Mussina | Drese | Rivera | 35-20 | 1st | +2.5 |
| 6-8 | Col. | W | 2-1 | | 6 | 6 | Vazquez | Fassero | Rivera | 36-20 | 1st | +2.5 |
| 6-9 | Col. | W | 7-5 | | 11 | 8 | Quantrill | Kennedy | Rivera | 37-20 | 1st | +3.5 |
| 6-10 | Col. | W | 10-4 | | 12 | 7 | Contreras | Jennings | | 38-20 | 1st | +3.5 |
| 6-11 | S.D. | L | 2-10 | | 4 | 12 | Eaton | Heredia | Otsuka | 38-21 | 1st | +2.5 |
| 6-12 | S.D. | W | 3-2 | | 8 | 13 | Lieber | Tankersley | Rivera | 39-21 | 1st | +3.5 |
| 6-13 | S.D. | W | 6-5 | (12) | 12 | 12 | Heredia | Beck | | 40-21 | 1st | +3.5 |
| 6-15 | At Ari. | W | 4-2 | | 12 | 6 | Contreras | Webb | Rivera | 41-21 | 1st | +4.5 |
| 6-16 | At Ari. | W | 9-4 | | 11 | 9 | Sturtze | Fossum | | 42-21 | 1st | +5.5 |
| 6-17 | At Ari. | L | 1-6 | | 4 | 11 | Sparks | Lieber | Dessens | 42-22 | 1st | +4.5 |

| Date | Opp. | Res. | Score | (inn.*) | Hits | Opp. hits | Winning pitcher | Losing pitcher | Save | Record | Pos. | GB |
|---|---|---|---|---|---|---|---|---|---|---|---|---|
| 6-18 | At L.A. | L | 3-6 | | 8 | 11 | Weaver | Vazquez | Gagne | 42-23 | 1st | +3.5 |
| 6-19 | At L.A. | W | 6-2 | | 7 | 8 | Halsey | Nomo | | 43-23 | 1st | +4.5 |
| 6-20 | At L.A. | L | 4-5 | | 9 | 9 | Lima | Contreras | Gagne | 43-24 | 1st | +4.5 |
| 6-22 | At Bal. | W | 10-4 | | 8 | 5 | Mussina | Riley | | 44-24 | 1st | +4.5 |
| 6-23 | At Bal. | L | 2-13 | | 7 | 17 | Bedard | Lieber | | 44-25 | 1st | +4.5 |
| 6-24 | At Bal. | W | 5-2 | | 10 | 9 | Vazquez | Ponson | Rivera | 45-25 | 1st | +5.5 |
| 6-26 | N.Y. | L | 3-9 | | 6 | 12 | Leiter | Halsey | | 45-26 | 1st | +5.0 |
| 6-27# | N.Y. | W | 8-1 | | 8 | 3 | Contreras | Trachsel | Gordon | 46-26 | | |
| 6-27$ | N.Y. | W | 11-6 | | 12 | 10 | Mussina | Ginter | | 47-26 | 1st | +5.5 |
| 6-29 | Bos. | W | 11-3 | | 12 | 9 | Vazquez | Lowe | | 48-26 | 1st | +6.5 |
| 6-30 | Bos. | W | 4-2 | | 6 | 8 | Gordon | Timlin | Rivera | 49-26 | 1st | +7.5 |
| 7-1 | Bos. | W | 5-4 | (13) | 11 | 10 | Sturtze | Leskanic | | 50-26 | 1st | +8.5 |
| 7-2 | At N.Y. | L | 2-11 | | 4 | 14 | Trachsel | Mussina | | 50-27 | 1st | +8.5 |
| 7-3 | At N.Y. | L | 9-10 | | 12 | 11 | Franco | Sturtze | | 50-28 | 1st | +7.5 |
| 7-4 | At N.Y. | L | 5-6 | | 16 | 8 | Moreno | Gordon | Looper | 50-29 | 1st | +7.5 |
| 7-5 | Det. | W | 10-3 | | 11 | 7 | Lieber | Robertson | | 51-29 | 1st | +8.0 |
| 7-6 | Det. | L | 1-9 | | 6 | 14 | Johnson | Mussina | | 51-30 | 1st | +7.0 |
| 7-7 | Det. | L | 8-10 | | 10 | 13 | Bonderman | Halsey | Urbina | 51-31 | 1st | +6.0 |
| 7-8 | T.B. | W | 7-1 | | 9 | 6 | Contreras | Zambrano | Rivera | 52-31 | 1st | +6.0 |
| 7-9 | T.B. | W | 5-4 | | 12 | 7 | Vazquez | Colome | Rivera | 53-31 | 1st | +6.0 |
| 7-10 | T.B. | W | 6-3 | | 5 | 10 | Lieber | Brazelton | Rivera | 54-31 | 1st | +6.0 |
| 7-11 | T.B. | W | 10-3 | | 15 | 9 | Hernandez | Hendrickson | | 55-31 | 1st | +7.0 |
| 7-15 | At Det. | W | 5-1 | | 5 | 4 | Contreras | Bonderman | | 56-31 | 1st | +8.0 |
| 7-16 | At Det. | L | 0-8 | | 1 | 12 | Maroth | Vazquez | | 56-32 | 1st | +7.0 |
| 7-17 | At Det. | W | 5-3 | | 13 | 9 | Hernandez | Knotts | Rivera | 57-32 | 1st | +8.0 |
| 7-18 | At Det. | L | 2-4 | | 7 | 10 | Robertson | Lieber | Urbina | 57-33 | 1st | +7.0 |
| 7-19 | At T.B. | L | 7-9 | | 8 | 13 | Carter | Sturtze | Baez | 57-34 | 1st | +7.0 |
| 7-20 | At T.B. | W | 4-2 | | 6 | 6 | Contreras | Zambrano | Rivera | 58-34 | 1st | +7.0 |
| 7-21 | Tor. | W | 10-3 | | 15 | 11 | Vazquez | Hentgen | | 59-34 | 1st | +8.0 |
| 7-22 | Tor. | W | 1-0 | | 4 | 5 | Rivera | Chulk | | 60-34 | 1st | +8.5 |
| 7-23 | At Bos. | W | 8-7 | | 14 | 11 | Gordon | Foulke | Rivera | 61-34 | 1st | +9.5 |
| 7-24 | At Bos. | L | 10-11 | | 12 | 15 | Mendoza | Rivera | | 61-35 | 1st | +8.5 |
| 7-25 | At Bos. | L | 6-9 | | 9 | 13 | Lowe | Contreras | Foulke | 61-36 | 1st | +7.5 |
| 7-26 | At Tor. | W | 6-5 | (10) | 11 | 9 | Rivera | Frasor | | 62-36 | 1st | +7.5 |
| 7-27 | At Tor. | W | 7-4 | | 7 | 13 | Proctor | Ligtenberg | Gordon | 63-36 | 1st | +8.0 |
| 7-28 | At Tor. | L | 2-3 | (10) | 9 | 10 | Frasor | Proctor | | 63-37 | 1st | +8.0 |
| 7-29 | Bal. | L | 1-9 | | 4 | 12 | Ponson | Contreras | | 63-38 | 1st | +7.5 |
| 7-30 | Bal. | W | 2-1 | | 8 | 7 | Brown | Cabrera | Rivera | 64-38 | 1st | +7.5 |
| 7-31 | Bal. | W | 6-4 | | 10 | 7 | Vazquez | Bedard | Rivera | 65-38 | 1st | +8.5 |
| 8-1 | Bal. | W | 9-7 | | 9 | 14 | Hernandez | Lopez | Rivera | 66-38 | 1st | +9.5 |
| 8-3 | Oak. | L | 4-13 | | 8 | 15 | Mulder | Lieber | | 66-39 | 1st | +8.0 |
| 8-4 | Oak. | W | 8-6 | (11) | 15 | 12 | Rivera | Duchscherer | | 67-39 | 1st | +9.0 |
| 8-5 | Oak. | W | 5-1 | | 12 | 4 | Brown | Zito | | 68-39 | 1st | +9.5 |
| 8-6 | Tor. | W | 11-4 | | 13 | 8 | Vazquez | Douglass | | 69-39 | 1st | +10.5 |
| 8-7 | Tor. | W | 6-0 | | 11 | 6 | Hernandez | Lilly | | 70-39 | 1st | +10.5 |
| 8-8 | Tor. | W | 8-2 | | 13 | 4 | Lieber | Batista | | 71-39 | 1st | +10.5 |
| 8-9 | Tor. | L | 4-5 | | 7 | 12 | Towers | Loaiza | Frasor | 71-40 | 1st | +10.5 |
| 8-10 | At Tex. | L | 1-7 | | 6 | 9 | Drese | Brown | | 71-41 | 1st | +9.5 |
| 8-11 | At Tex. | W | 4-2 | | 6 | 5 | Sturtze | Regilio | Rivera | 72-41 | 1st | +9.5 |
| 8-12 | At Tex. | W | 5-1 | | 10 | 5 | Hernandez | Erickson | | 73-41 | 1st | +9.5 |
| 8-13 | At Sea. | W | 11-3 | | 14 | 7 | Lieber | Villone | | 74-41 | 1st | +10.5 |
| 8-14 | At Sea. | W | 6-4 | | 9 | 11 | Quantrill | Hasegawa | Rivera | 75-41 | 1st | +10.5 |
| 8-15 | At Sea. | L | 3-7 | | 8 | 12 | Meche | Nitkowski | | 75-42 | 1st | +10.5 |
| 8-17 | At Min. | L | 2-8 | | 9 | 13 | Radke | Vazquez | | 75-43 | 1st | +9.0 |
| 8-18 | At Min. | L | 2-7 | | 6 | 10 | Santana | Mussina | | 75-44 | 1st | +8.0 |
| 8-19 | At Min. | W | 13-10 | | 16 | 13 | Gordon | Nathan | Rivera | 76-44 | 1st | +8.5 |
| 8-20 | Ana. | L | 0-5 | | 5 | 13 | Ortiz | Lieber | | 76-45 | 1st | +7.5 |
| 8-21 | Ana. | L | 1-6 | | 8 | 13 | Shields | Loaiza | | 76-46 | 1st | +6.5 |
| 8-22 | Ana. | L | 3-4 | | 4 | 10 | Escobar | Brown | Percival | 76-47 | 1st | +5.5 |
| 8-23 | At Cle. | W | 6-4 | | 9 | 8 | Gordon | Wickman | Rivera | 77-47 | 1st | +6.5 |
| 8-24 | At Cle. | W | 5-4 | | 12 | 7 | Gordon | Wickman | Rivera | 78-47 | 1st | +6.5 |
| 8-25 | At Cle. | L | 3-4 | | 6 | 7 | Riske | Gordon | Betancourt | 78-48 | 1st | +5.5 |
| 8-26 | At Tor. | W | 7-4 | | 11 | 6 | Nitkowski | Frasor | Rivera | 79-48 | 1st | +5.5 |
| 8-27 | At Tor. | W | 8-7 | | 9 | 12 | Sturtze | Miller | Gordon | 80-48 | 1st | +5.5 |
| 8-28 | At Tor. | W | 18-6 | | 19 | 9 | Brown | Lilly | Rivera | 81-48 | 1st | +5.5 |
| 8-29 | At Tor. | L | 4-6 | | 12 | 7 | Batista | Mussina | Frasor | 81-49 | 1st | +4.5 |
| 8-31 | Cle. | L | 0-22 | | 5 | 22 | Westbrook | Vazquez | | 81-50 | 1st | +3.5 |
| 9-1 | Cle. | W | 5-3 | | 9 | 6 | Hernandez | Sabathia | Rivera | 82-50 | 1st | +3.5 |
| 9-2 | Cle. | W | 9-1 | | 11 | 8 | Lieber | Lee | | 83-50 | 1st | +3.5 |
| 9-3 | Bal. | L | 1-3 | | 6 | 6 | Lopez | Brown | Julio | 83-51 | 1st | +2.5 |
| 9-4 | Bal. | L | 0-7 | | 2 | 14 | Ponson | Mussina | | 83-52 | 1st | +2.5 |

| Date | Opp. | Res. | Score | (inn.*) | Hits | Opp. hits | Winning pitcher | Losing pitcher | Save | Record | Pos. | GB |
|---|---|---|---|---|---|---|---|---|---|---|---|---|
| 9-5 | Bal. | W | 4-3 | | 7 | 9 | Rivera | Julio | | 84-52 | 1st | +2.5 |
| 9-6! | T.B. | W | 7-4 | | 12 | 8 | Hernandez | Waechter | Quantrill | 85-52 | | |
| 9-7 | T.B. | W | 11-2 | | 16 | 10 | Lieber | Sosa | | 86-52 | 1st | +2.5 |
| 9-9! | T.B. | W | 9-1 | | 12 | 5 | Mussina | Brazelton | | 87-52 | | |
| 9-9& | T.B. | W | 10-5 | | 14 | 13 | Sturtze | Bell | | 88-52 | 1st | +3.5 |
| 9-10 | At Bal. | L | 8-14 | | 13 | 14 | Lopez | Vazquez | | 88-53 | 1st | +2.5 |
| 9-11 | At Bal. | W | 5-2 | | 10 | 7 | Hernandez | Ponson | Rivera | 89-53 | 1st | +2.5 |
| 9-12 | At Bal. | W | 9-7 | | 11 | 13 | Gordon | Julio | Rivera | 90-53 | 1st | +3.5 |
| 9-13 | At K.C. | L | 8-17 | | 16 | 18 | Anderson | Halsey | | 90-54 | 1st | +3.0 |
| 9-14 | At K.C. | W | 4-0 | | 6 | 3 | Mussina | Greinke | | 91-54 | 1st | +4.0 |
| 9-15 | At K.C. | W | 3-0 | | 6 | 4 | Vazquez | May | Rivera | 92-54 | 1st | +4.0 |
| 9-17 | Bos. | L | 2-3 | | 4 | 6 | Timlin | Rivera | Foulke | 92-55 | 1st | +2.5 |
| 9-18 | Bos. | W | 14-4 | | 15 | 6 | Lieber | Lowe | | 93-55 | 1st | +3.5 |
| 9-19 | Bos. | W | 11-1 | | 13 | 8 | Mussina | Martinez | | 94-55 | 1st | +4.5 |
| 9-20 | Tor. | L | 3-6 | | 7 | 13 | Chacin | Vazquez | Batista | 94-56 | 1st | +4.5 |
| 9-21 | Tor. | W | 5-3 | | 11 | 5 | Loaiza | Halladay | Rivera | 95-56 | 1st | +4.5 |
| 9-22 | Tor. | L | 4-5 | | 8 | 10 | Lilly | Hernandez | Batista | 95-57 | 1st | +3.5 |
| 9-23 | T.B. | W | 7-3 | | 12 | 11 | Lieber | Ritchie | | 96-57 | 1st | +4.5 |
| 9-24 | At Bos. | W | 6-4 | | 11 | 7 | Gordon | Martinez | Rivera | 97-57 | 1st | +5.5 |
| 9-25 | At Bos. | L | 5-12 | | 5 | 13 | Foulke | Quantrill | | 97-58 | 1st | +4.5 |
| 9-26 | At Bos. | L | 4-11 | | 3 | 13 | Schilling | Brown | | 97-59 | 1st | +3.5 |
| 9-29! | Min. | W | 5-3 | | 8 | 10 | Quantrill | Romero | Rivera | 98-59 | | |
| 9-29& | Min. | W | 5-4 | | 8 | 12 | Lieber | Lohse | Rivera | 99-59 | 1st | +4.0 |
| 9-30 | Min. | W | 6-4 | | 12 | 8 | Gordon | Fultz | | 100-59 | 1st | +4.5 |
| 10-1 | At Tor. | L | 0-7 | | 2 | 7 | Bush | Hernandez | | 100-60 | 1st | +3.5 |
| 10-2 | At Tor. | L | 2-4 | | 8 | 6 | Halladay | Brown | Batista | 100-61 | 1st | +2.0 |
| 10-3 | At Tor. | W | 3-2 | | 7 | 8 | Proctor | Towers | Sturtze | 101-61 | 1st | +3.0 |

Monthly records: March (1-1), April (11-10), May (18-8), June (19-7), July (16-12), August (16-12), September (19-9), October (1-2).
*Innings, if other than nine. ^ At Tokyo, Japan. ! First game of a doubleheader. & Second game of a doubleheader. # Day separate admission. $ Night separate admission.

## RECORDS

**2004 regular-season record:** 101-61
**Position:** 1st in A.L. East
**Home:** 57-24 **Road:** 44-37
**A.L. East:** 49-27 **A.L. Central:** 20-12
**A.L. West:** 22-14 **N.L.** 10-8
**Vs. LH starters:** 36-12
**Vs. RH starters:** 65-49
**Grass:** 89-51 **Artificial:** 12-10
**Day:** 37-24 **Night:** 64-37
**1-Run:** 24-16 **X-inn.:** 5-4
**Doubleheaders:** 2-0-0
**Team record past five years:** 487-319 (.604, ranks 1st in league in that span)

## TEAM LEADERS

**Batting average:** Hideki Matsui (.298).
**At-bats:** Derek Jeter (643).
**Runs:** Gary Sheffield (117).
**Hits:** Derek Jeter (188).
**Total Bases:** Alex Rodriguez (308).
**Doubles:** Derek Jeter (44).
**Triples:** Kenny Lofton (7).
**Home runs:** Alex Rodriguez, Gary Sheffield (36).
**Runs batted in:** Gary Sheffield (121).
**Stolen bases:** Alex Rodriguez (28).
**Slugging percentage:** Gary Sheffield (.534).
**On-base percentage:** Jorge Posada (.400).
**Wins:** Jon Lieber, Javier Vazquez (14).
**Earned-run average:** Kevin Brown (4.09).
**Complete games:** Mike Mussina (1).
**Shutouts:** None.
**Saves:** Mariano Rivera (53).
**Innings pitched:** Javier Vazquez (198.0).
**Strikeouts:** Javier Vazquez (150).

## GAMES BY POSITION

**Catcher:** Jorge Posada 134, John Flaherty 46, Dioner Navarro 4.
**First base:** Tony Clark 99, Jason Giambi 47, John Olerud 47, Travis Lee 6, Miguel Cairo 1.
**Second base:** Miguel Cairo 113, Enrique Wilson 80, Homer Bush 4.
**Third base:** Alex Rodriguez 155, Miguel Cairo 8, Andy Phillips 4, Gary Sheffield 2, Felix Escalona 1.
**Shortstop:** Derek Jeter 154, Enrique Wilson 16, Felix Escalona 4, Miguel Cairo 3, Alex Rodriguez 2.
**Outfield:** Hideki Matsui 160, Gary Sheffield 136, Bernie Williams 97, Kenny Lofton 74, Bubba Crosby 45, Ruben Sierra 29.
**Designated hitter:** Ruben Sierra 56, Bernie Williams 50, Jason Giambi 28, Gary Sheffield 18, Kenny Lofton 4, Homer Bush 2, Bubba Crosby 2, Tony Clark 1, Andy Phillips 1.

## TOP DRAFT CHOICES

1a. **Philip Hughes,** RHP, Foothill H.S., Santa Ana, Calif.
1b. **Jon Poterson,** C, Chandler (Ariz.) H.S.
1c. **Jeff Marquez,** RHP, Sacramento CC.
2. **Brett Smith,** RHP, UC Irvine.
3. **Christian Garcia,** RHP, Gulliver Prep, Miami.
4. **Jason Jones,** RHP, Liberty.
5. **Jesse Hoover,** RHP, Indiana Tech.
6. **Nate Phillips,** SS, Grace Prep Academy, Roanoke, Texas.
7. **Alex Garabedian,** C, Columbus H.S., Miami.
8. **Mike Martinez,** RHP, Cal State Fullerton.
9. **Grant Plumley,** SS, Oral Roberts.
10. **Ben Scheinbaum,** LHP, UNLV.

# OAKLAND ATHLETICS

## AMERICAN LEAGUE WEST DIVISION



## 2005 SEASON

### Athletics Schedule

Home games shaded.
All-Star Game July 12 at Detroit. Schedule subject to change.

**April**

| SUN | MON | TUE | WED | THU | FRI | SAT |
|---|---|---|---|---|---|---|
| 3 | 4 BAL | 5 | 6 BAL | 7 BAL | 8 TB | 9 TB |
| 10 TB | 11 TOR | 12 TOR | 13 TOR | 14 | 15 ANA | 16 ANA |
| 17 ANA | 18 TEX | 19 TEX | 20 SEA | 21 SEA | 22 ANA | 23 ANA |
| 24 ANA | 25 CHW | 26 CHW | 27 CHW | 28 | 29 SEA | 30 SEA |

**May**

| SUN | MON | TUE | WED | THU | FRI | SAT |
|---|---|---|---|---|---|---|
| 1 SEA | 2 TEX | 3 TEX | 4 TEX | 5 | 6 NYY | 7 NYY |
| 8 NYY | 9 BOS | 10 BOS | 11 BOS | 12 | 13 NYY | 14 NYY |
| 15 NYY | 16 BOS | 17 BOS | 18 BOS | 19 | 20 SF | 21 SF |
| 22 SF | 23 | 24 TB | 25 TB | 26 TB | 27 CLE | 28 CLE |
| 29 CLE | 30 TB | 31 TB | | | | |

**June**

| SUN | MON | TUE | WED | THU | FRI | SAT |
|---|---|---|---|---|---|---|
| | | | 1 TB | 2 TOR | 3 TOR | 4 TOR |
| 5 TOR | 6 | 7 WAS | 8 WAS | 9 WAS | 10 ATL | 11 ATL |
| 12 ATL | 13 | 14 NYM | 15 NYM | 16 NYM | 17 PHI | 18 PHI |
| 19 PHI | 20 SEA | 21 SEA | 22 SEA | 23 SEA | 24 SF | 25 SF |
| 26 SF | 27 | 28 SEA | 29 SEA | 30 SEA | | |

**July**

| SUN | MON | TUE | WED | THU | FRI | SAT |
|---|---|---|---|---|---|---|
| | | | | | 1 CHW | 2 CHW |
| 3 CHW | 4 | 5 TOR | 6 TOR | 7 TOR | 8 CHW | 9 CHW |
| 10 CHW | 11 | 12 All-Star | 13 | 14 TEX | 15 TEX | 16 TEX |
| 17 TEX | 18 ANA | 19 ANA | 20 ANA | 21 TEX | 22 TEX | 23 TEX |
| 24 TEX | 25 CLE | 26 CLE | 27 CLE | 28 | 29 DET | 30 DET |
| 31 DET | | | | | | |

**August**

| SUN | MON | TUE | WED | THU | FRI | SAT |
|---|---|---|---|---|---|---|
| | 1 MIN | 2 MIN | 3 MIN | 4 MIN | 5 KC | 6 KC |
| 7 KC | 8 | 9 ANA | 10 ANA | 11 ANA | 12 MIN | 13 MIN |
| 14 MIN | 15 BAL | 16 BAL | 17 BAL | 18 | 19 KC | 20 KC |
| 21 KC | 22 | 23 DET | 24 DET | 25 DET | 26 BAL | 27 BAL |
| 28 BAL | 29 BAL | 30 ANA | 31 ANA | | | |

**September**

| SUN | MON | TUE | WED | THU | FRI | SAT |
|---|---|---|---|---|---|---|
| | | | | 1 ANA | 2 NYY | 3 NYY |
| 4 NYY | 5 SEA | 6 SEA | 7 SEA | 8 | 9 TEX | 10 TEX |
| 11 TEX | 12 CLE | 13 CLE | 14 CLE | 15 BOS | 16 BOS | 17 BOS |
| 18 BOS | 19 MIN | 20 MIN | 21 MIN | 22 | 23 TEX | 24 TEX |
| 25 TEX | 26 ANA | 27 ANA | 28 ANA | 29 ANA | 30 SEA | |

**October**

| SUN | MON | TUE | WED | THU | FRI | SAT |
|---|---|---|---|---|---|---|
| | | | | | | 1 SEA |
| 2 SEA | 3 | 4 | 5 | 6 | 7 | 8 |

Home games shaded. All-Star Game July 12 at Detroit. Schedule subject to change.

### CLUB DIRECTORY

**Owners**
Stephen C. Schott
Ken Hofmann

**President**
Michael P. Crowley

**Vice president and general manager**
Billy Beane

**Assistant general manager**
David Forst

**Special assistants to general manager**
Randy Johnson
Matt Keough

**Director of player development**
Keith Lieppman

**Coordinator of scouting**
Bryn Alderson

**Director of minor league operations**
Ted Polakowski

**V.p., broadcasting and communications**
Ken Pries

**Director of public relations**
Jim Young

**Baseball information manager**
Mike Selleck

### MINOR LEAGUE AFFILIATES

| Class | Team | League | Manager |
|---|---|---|---|
| AAA | Sacramento | Pacific Coast | Tony DeFrancesco |
| AA | Midland | Texas | Von Hayes |
| Advanced A | Stockton | California | Todd Stevenson |
| A | Kane County | Midwest | Dave Joppie |
| Short-Season A | Vancouver | Northwest | Dennis Rogers |
| Rookie | Scottsdale A's | Arizona | Ruben Escalera |

### BROADCAST INFORMATION

**Radio:** KFRC-AM (610).
**TV:** KICU-TV (Channel 36).
**Cable TV:** Fox Sports Bay Area.

### SPRING TRAINING

**Ballpark (city):** Phoenix Stadium (Phoenix, Ariz.).
**Ticket information:** 602-392-0074.

**For more on the Athletics, go to msn.foxsports.com/mlb/teams.**

Chavez

## SPRING TRAINING ROSTER

**Manager**—Ken Macha (39).
**Coaches**—Brad Fischer (35), Bob Geren (52), Dave Hudgens (48), Rene Lachemann, Ron Washington (38), Curt Young (41).

| No. | PITCHERS | B/T | Ht./Wt. | Age* | 2004 Clubs |
|---|---|---|---|---|---|
| 64 | Blanton, Joe | R/R | 6-3/225 | 24 | Sacramento, Oakland |
| 54 | Bradford, Chad | R/R | 6-5/203 | 30 | Sacramento, Oakland |
| | Calero, Kiko | R/R | 6-1/180 | 30 | Memphis, St. Louis |
| | Cruz, Juan | R/R | 6-2/165 | 26 | Atlanta |
| 28 | Dotel, Octavio | R/R | 6-0/210 | 31 | Houston, Oakland |
| 58 | Duchscherer, Justin | R/R | 6-3/190 | 27 | Oakland |
| | Etherton, Seth | R/R | 6-1/200 | 28 | Chattanooga, Louisville |
| | Garcia, Jairo | R/R | 6-0/164 | 22 | Kane County, Midland, Sacramento, Oakland |
| 40 | Harden, Rich | L/R | 6-1/180 | 23 | Sacramento, Oakland |
| | Haren, Danny | R/R | 6-5/220 | 24 | Memphis, St. Louis |
| | Harikkala, Tim | R/R | 6-2/185 | 33 | Colorado Springs, Colorado |
| | Johnson, Tyler | B/L | 6-2/180 | 23 | Tennessee |
| | Mabeus, Chris | R/R | 6-3/210 | 26 | Midland, Sacramento |
| | Meyer, Dan | R/L | 6-3/210 | 23 | Greenville, Richmond, Atlanta |
| | Rheinecker, John | L/L | 6-2/215 | 25 | Sacramento |
| 73 | Rincon, Ricardo | L/L | 5-9/190 | 34 | Oakland |
| 75 | Zito, Barry | L/L | 6-4/215 | 26 | Oakland |

| No. | CATCHERS | B/T | Ht./Wt. | Age* | 2004 Clubs |
|---|---|---|---|---|---|
| | Baker, John | L/R | 6-1/215 | 24 | Midland, Sacramento |
| | Brown, Jeremy | R/R | 5-10/210 | 25 | Midland |
| | Kendall, Jason | R/R | 6-0/195 | 30 | Pittsburgh |
| 17 | Melhuse, Adam | B/R | 6-2/200 | 33 | Oakland |

| No. | INFIELDERS | B/T | Ht./Wt. | Age* | 2004 Clubs |
|---|---|---|---|---|---|
| | Bynum, Freddie | L/R | 6-1/180 | 25 | Midland, Sacramento |
| 3 | Chavez, Eric | L/R | 6-1/206 | 27 | Sacramento, Oakland |
| 7 | Crosby, Bobby | R/R | 6-3/195 | 25 | Oakland |
| 44 | Durazo, Erubiel | L/L | 6-3/240 | 30 | Oakland |
| 14 | Ellis, Mark | R/R | 5-11/180 | 27 | Did Not Play |
| | Ginter, Keith | R/R | 5-10/195 | 28 | Indianapolis, Milwaukee |
| 10 | Hatteberg, Scott | L/R | 6-1/210 | 35 | Oakland |
| | Johnson, Dan | L/R | 6-2/220 | 25 | Sacramento |
| | Morrissey, Adam | R/R | 5-11/170 | 23 | Sacramento |
| | Rouse, Mike | L/R | 5-11/185 | 24 | Sacramento |
| 26 | Scutaro, Marco | R/R | 5-10/170 | 29 | Oakland |

| No. | OUTFIELDERS | B/T | Ht./Wt. | Age* | 2004 Clubs |
|---|---|---|---|---|---|
| 22 | Byrnes, Eric | R/R | 6-2/210 | 29 | Oakland |
| 23 | Kielty, Bobby | B/R | 6-1/225 | 28 | Oakland |
| 21 | Kotsay, Mark | L/L | 6-0/201 | 29 | Oakland |
| | Perry, Jason | L/R | 6-0/200 | 24 | Modesto, Midland |
| 33 | Swisher, Nick | B/L | 6-0/194 | 24 | Sacramento, Oakland |
| | Thomas, Charles | L/L | 6-0/190 | 26 | Richmond, Atlanta |
| 12 | Watson, Matt | L/R | 5-11/200 | 26 | Sacramento |

*Age as of April 1, 2005.

## BALLPARK INFORMATION

**Ballpark (capacity, surface)**
The Network Associates Coliseum (43,662, grass)

**Address**
Oakland Athletics
7000 Coliseum Way
Oakland, CA 94621

**Official website**
www.oaklandathletics.com

**Business phone**
510-638-4900

**Ticket information**
510-638-4627

**Field dimensions (from home plate)**
To left field at foul line, 330 feet
To center field, 400 feet
To right field at foul line, 330 feet

**First game played**
April 17, 1968 (Orioles 4, Athletics 1)

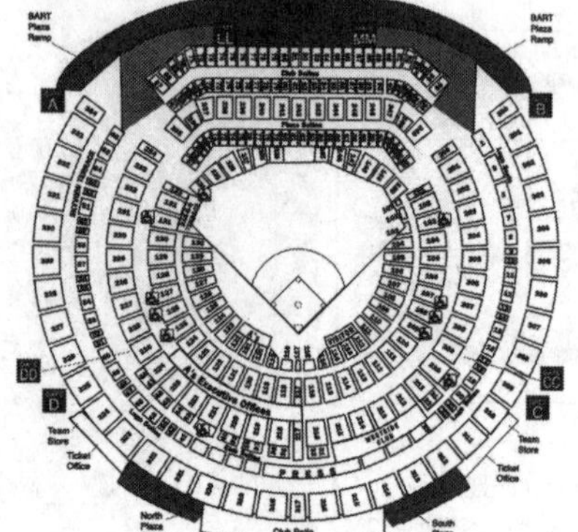

# 2004 REVIEW

## DAY BY DAY

| Date | Opp. | Res. | Score | (inn.*) | Hits | Opp. hits | Winning pitcher | Losing pitcher | Save | Record | Pos. | GB |
|---|---|---|---|---|---|---|---|---|---|---|---|---|
| 4-5 | Tex. | W | 5-4 | | 9 | 11 | Bradford | Nelson | Rhodes | 1-0 | 1st | +0.5 |
| 4-6 | Tex. | W | 3-1 | | 7 | 5 | Mulder | Park | Rhodes | 2-0 | 1st | +0.5 |
| 4-7 | Tex. | L | 1-2 | | 5 | 7 | Lewis | Zito | Cordero | 2-1 | 2nd | 0.5 |
| 4-9 | Sea. | W | 8-6 | | 12 | 13 | Hammond | Soriano | Rhodes | 3-1 | T1st | ... |
| 4-10 | Sea. | W | 2-1 | | 8 | 4 | Hudson | Meche | | 4-1 | 1st | +1.0 |
| 4-11 | Sea. | L | 4-9 | (10) | 11 | 14 | Hasegawa | Hammond | | 4-2 | T1st | ... |
| 4-13 | At Tex. | W | 10-9 | | 16 | 16 | Zito | Callaway | Rhodes | 5-2 | 1st | +0.5 |
| 4-14 | At Tex. | W | 9-4 | | 11 | 12 | Redman | Dickey | | 6-2 | 1st | +0.5 |
| 4-15 | At Tex. | L | 2-7 | | 8 | 16 | Rogers | Harden | | 6-3 | 1st | +0.5 |
| 4-16 | At Ana. | W | 3-0 | | 9 | 6 | Hudson | Colon | Rhodes | 7-3 | 1st | +1.5 |
| 4-17 | At Ana. | L | 3-6 | | 7 | 7 | Washburn | Mulder | | 7-4 | 1st | +0.5 |
| 4-18 | At Ana. | W | 7-1 | | 13 | 5 | Zito | Escobar | Hammond | 8-4 | 1st | +1.5 |
| 4-19 | At Sea. | L | 1-2 | (14) | 10 | 10 | Jarvis | Duchscherer | | 8-5 | 1st | +1.0 |
| 4-20 | At Sea. | L | 1-2 | | 3 | 4 | Villone | Mecir | | 8-6 | 1st | +1.0 |
| 4-21 | At Sea. | W | 7-4 | | 10 | 9 | Hudson | Myers | Rhodes | 9-6 | 1st | +1.0 |
| 4-22 | At Sea. | W | 8-2 | | 13 | 7 | Mulder | Moyer | | 10-6 | 1st | +2.0 |
| 4-23 | Ana. | L | 2-12 | | 8 | 14 | Washburn | Zito | Gregg | 10-7 | 1st | +1.0 |
| 4-24 | Ana. | L | 3-6 | | 7 | 13 | Escobar | Redman | Percival | 10-8 | T1st | ... |
| 4-25 | Ana. | L | 3-4 | | 6 | 7 | Ortiz | Harden | Percival | 10-9 | 3rd | 1.0 |
| 4-27 | At N.Y. | L | 8-10 | | 16 | 10 | Osborne | Mecir | Rivera | 10-10 | 3rd | 2.0 |
| 4-28 | At N.Y. | L | 1-5 | | 5 | 9 | Contreras | Mulder | Gordon | 10-11 | 3rd | 2.0 |
| 4-29 | At N.Y. | L | 5-7 | | 10 | 10 | Brown | Zito | Rivera | 10-12 | 3rd | 3.0 |
| 4-30 | At T.B. | W | 4-2 | | 4 | 8 | Redman | Waechter | | 11-12 | 3rd | 2.5 |
| 5-1 | At T.B. | W | 6-5 | | 11 | 11 | Hammond | Carter | | 12-12 | 3rd | 3.0 |
| 5-2 | At T.B. | L | 2-8 | | 7 | 9 | Hendrickson | Hudson | | 12-13 | 3rd | 4.0 |
| 5-4 | N.Y. | L | 8-10 | | 7 | 17 | Osborne | Bradford | Rivera | 12-14 | 3rd | 4.5 |
| 5-5 | N.Y. | L | 3-4 | | 10 | 11 | Quantrill | Rhodes | Rivera | 12-15 | 3rd | 5.5 |
| 5-6 | N.Y. | W | 7-4 | | 10 | 6 | Harden | Vazquez | Mecir | 13-15 | 3rd | 5.5 |
| 5-7 | Min. | W | 11-9 | (13) | 15 | 16 | Bradford | Mulholland | | 14-15 | 3rd | 5.5 |
| 5-8 | Min. | L | 2-3 | (10) | 10 | 10 | Romero | Mecir | Nathan | 14-16 | 3rd | 6.5 |
| 5-9 | Min. | W | 8-4 | | 11 | 6 | Mulder | Lohse | | 15-16 | 3rd | 6.5 |
| 5-11 | At Det. | W | 5-4 | (15) | 16 | 14 | Duchscherer | Patterson | Mecir | 16-16 | 3rd | 5.5 |
| 5-12 | At Det. | W | 2-1 | | 4 | 7 | Harden | Bonderman | Rhodes | 17-16 | 3rd | 5.5 |
| 5-13 | At Det. | L | 1-3 | | 5 | 12 | Maroth | Redman | Urbina | 17-17 | 3rd | 5.5 |
| 5-14 | At K.C. | W | 6-2 | | 11 | 6 | Hudson | Gobble | | 18-17 | 3rd | 5.5 |
| 5-15 | At K.C. | W | 3-1 | | 5 | 4 | Mulder | May | | 19-17 | 3rd | 5.5 |
| 5-16 | At K.C. | W | 6-2 | | 10 | 5 | Zito | Anderson | | 20-17 | 3rd | 4.5 |
| 5-18 | Det. | L | 1-5 | | 4 | 8 | Bonderman | Harden | | 20-18 | 3rd | 5.5 |
| 5-19 | Det. | W | 6-2 | | 13 | 9 | Redman | Maroth | | 21-18 | 3rd | 4.5 |
| 5-20 | Det. | W | 3-2 | | 8 | 10 | Hudson | Walker | Rhodes | 22-18 | 3rd | 3.5 |
| 5-21 | K.C. | W | 7-0 | | 12 | 3 | Mulder | Anderson | | 23-18 | 3rd | 3.5 |
| 5-22 | K.C. | W | 5-4 | (11) | 12 | 10 | Duchscherer | Sullivan | | 24-18 | 3rd | 3.5 |
| 5-23 | K.C. | W | 3-2 | (10) | 7 | 10 | Rhodes | Field | | 25-18 | T2nd | 3.5 |
| 5-25 | At Bos. | L | 2-12 | | 10 | 19 | Schilling | Hudson | | 25-19 | 3rd | 3.5 |
| 5-26 | At Bos. | L | 6-9 | | 14 | 9 | Lowe | Redman | Foulke | 25-20 | 3rd | 3.5 |
| 5-27 | At Bos. | W | 15-2 | | 17 | 6 | Mulder | Arroyo | | 26-20 | T2nd | 2.5 |
| 5-28 | At Cle. | L | 0-1 | | 8 | 4 | Jimenez | Mecir | | 26-21 | T2nd | 2.5 |
| 5-29 | At Cle. | L | 6-8 | | 9 | 8 | Riske | Rhodes | Jimenez | 26-22 | T2nd | 3.5 |
| 5-30 | At Cle. | L | 3-4 | | 10 | 13 | White | Rhodes | | 26-23 | 3rd | 3.5 |
| 6-1 | Chi. | W | 6-4 | (12) | 11 | 10 | Duchscherer | Cotts | | 27-23 | 3rd | 3.5 |
| 6-2 | Chi. | W | 3-2 | (10) | 8 | 11 | Rhodes | Adkins | | 28-23 | 3rd | 3.5 |
| 6-3 | Tor. | W | 2-1 | (11) | 7 | 6 | Bradford | Adams | | 29-23 | 3rd | 3.5 |
| 6-4 | Tor. | L | 1-6 | | 8 | 10 | Towers | Bradford | Chulk | 29-24 | 3rd | 3.5 |
| 6-5 | Tor. | W | 4-0 | | 4 | 8 | Hudson | Hentgen | | 30-24 | 3rd | 2.5 |
| 6-6 | Tor. | W | 8-3 | | 10 | 5 | Redman | Kershner | | 31-24 | 2nd | 1.5 |
| 6-7 | Cin. | W | 13-2 | | 15 | 6 | Mulder | Lidle | | 32-24 | 2nd | 1.0 |
| 6-8 | Cin. | W | 10-6 | | 14 | 13 | Zito | Bong | Rhodes | 33-24 | T1st | ... |
| 6-9 | Cin. | W | 17-8 | | 22 | 10 | Harden | Acevedo | | 34-24 | 1st | +1.0 |
| 6-11 | Pit. | W | 6-1 | | 7 | 7 | Hudson | Benson | | 35-24 | 1st | +0.5 |
| 6-12 | Pit. | W | 12-11 | | 18 | 16 | Rhodes | Corey | | 36-24 | 1st | +1.5 |
| 6-13 | Pit. | W | 13-3 | | 18 | 4 | Mulder | Wells | | 37-24 | 1st | +2.5 |
| 6-15 | At StL. | L | 4-8 | | 8 | 12 | Morris | Bradford | Isringhausen | 37-25 | 1st | +1.5 |
| 6-16 | At StL. | L | 2-6 | | 6 | 10 | Marquis | Harden | Calero | 37-26 | 1st | +1.5 |
| 6-17 | At StL. | L | 4-5 | | 9 | 11 | King | Mecir | | 37-27 | 1st | +1.5 |
| 6-18 | At Chi. | W | 2-1 | | 8 | 4 | Redman | Clement | Bradford | 38-27 | 1st | +2.5 |
| 6-19 | At Chi. | L | 3-4 | | 9 | 13 | Farnsworth | Bradford | | 38-28 | 1st | +1.5 |

| Date | Opp. | Res. | Score | (inn.*) | Hits | Opp. hits | Winning pitcher | Losing pitcher | Save | Record | Pos. | GB |
|---|---|---|---|---|---|---|---|---|---|---|---|---|
| 6-20 | At Chi. | L | 3-5 | | 8 | 10 | Zambrano | Zito | | 38-29 | 1st | +0.5 |
| 6-21 | At Ana. | L | 3-10 | | 9 | 13 | Lackey | Harden | | 38-30 | 2nd | ... |
| 6-22 | At Ana. | L | 1-6 | | 5 | 9 | Colon | Hudson | | 38-31 | 3rd | 1.0 |
| 6-23 | At Ana. | W | 7-1 | | 11 | 8 | Redman | Escobar | | 39-31 | 2nd | 1.0 |
| 6-24 | At Ana. | W | 2-1 | | 5 | 4 | Mulder | Shields | | 40-31 | 2nd | 1.0 |
| 6-25 | S.F | L | 4-6 | | 8 | 8 | Schmidt | Zito | Herges | 40-32 | 2nd | 2.0 |
| 6-26 | S.F | W | 8-7 | (10) | 15 | 12 | Dotel | Brower | | 41-32 | 2nd | 2.0 |
| 6-27 | S.F | L | 2-5 | | 7 | 9 | Hermanson | Redman | Herges | 41-33 | 2nd | 2.0 |
| 6-29 | Ana. | W | 5-4 | | 10 | 9 | Mulder | Donnelly | Dotel | 42-33 | 2nd | 1.5 |
| 6-30 | Ana. | W | 4-2 | | 10 | 5 | Bradford | Shields | Dotel | 43-33 | 2nd | 1.5 |
| 7-1 | Ana. | W | 7-3 | | 12 | 12 | Saarloos | Washburn | | 44-33 | 2nd | 0.5 |
| 7-2 | At S.F | L | 3-7 | | 8 | 7 | Rueter | Redman | | 44-34 | 2nd | 0.5 |
| 7-3 | At S.F | W | 6-2 | | 13 | 4 | Duchscherer | Herges | | 45-34 | 1st | +0.5 |
| 7-4 | At S.F | W | 9-6 | | 13 | 12 | Mulder | Williams | | 46-34 | 1st | +0.5 |
| 7-6 | At Bos. | L | 0-11 | | 4 | 17 | Wakefield | Zito | | 46-35 | T1st | ... |
| 7-7 | At Bos. | L | 3-11 | | 6 | 15 | Martinez | Redman | | 46-36 | 2nd | 1.0 |
| 7-8 | At Bos. | L | 7-8 | (10) | 17 | 14 | Leskanic | Lehr | | 46-37 | 2nd | 2.0 |
| 7-9 | At Cle. | L | 4-5 | | 9 | 6 | Howry | Dotel | | 46-38 | 2nd | 2.0 |
| 7-10 | At Cle. | W | 16-7 | | 19 | 11 | Mulder | White | | 47-38 | 2nd | 1.0 |
| 7-11 | At Cle. | L | 1-4 | | 9 | 9 | Lee | Zito | Riske | 47-39 | 2nd | 2.0 |
| 7-15 | Chi. | W | 4-2 | | 6 | 4 | Harden | Garland | Dotel | 48-39 | 2nd | 1.5 |
| 7-16 | Chi. | W | 5-1 | | 13 | 7 | Zito | Buehrle | Dotel | 49-39 | 2nd | 1.5 |
| 7-17 | Chi. | L | 2-5 | | 4 | 6 | Garcia | Redman | Takatsu | 49-40 | 2nd | 2.5 |
| 7-18 | Chi. | W | 5-3 | | 9 | 3 | Mulder | Loaiza | Dotel | 50-40 | 2nd | 2.5 |
| 7-19 | Tor. | L | 3-5 | | 9 | 12 | Towers | Saarloos | Frasor | 50-41 | 2nd | 2.5 |
| 7-20 | Tor. | W | 1-0 | (14) | 8 | 3 | Lehr | Speier | | 51-41 | 2nd | 2.5 |
| 7-21 | At Sea. | L | 5-6 | (10) | 10 | 12 | Madritsch | Duchscherer | | 51-42 | 2nd | 3.5 |
| 7-22 | At Sea. | L | 2-4 | | 9 | 7 | Hasegawa | Redman | Guardado | 51-43 | 2nd | 3.5 |
| 7-23 | Tex. | L | 3-8 | | 8 | 12 | Rogers | Mulder | | 51-44 | 2nd | 4.5 |
| 7-24 | Tex. | W | 6-2 | | 11 | 4 | Saarloos | Dickey | | 52-44 | 2nd | 3.5 |
| 7-25 | Tex. | W | 9-2 | | 14 | 2 | Harden | Wasdin | | 53-44 | 2nd | 2.5 |
| 7-26 | Sea. | W | 14-5 | | 13 | 12 | Zito | Blackley | | 54-44 | 2nd | 2.5 |
| 7-27 | Sea. | W | 5-3 | | 7 | 9 | Redman | Franklin | Dotel | 55-44 | 2nd | 1.5 |
| 7-28 | Sea. | W | 3-2 | | 7 | 8 | Mulder | Mateo | | 56-44 | 2nd | 0.5 |
| 7-29 | At Tex. | W | 7-6 | | 11 | 11 | Bradford | Almanzar | Dotel | 57-44 | 1st | +0.5 |
| 7-30 | At Tex. | L | 5-7 | | 9 | 9 | Francisco | Bradford | Cordero | 57-45 | 2nd | 0.5 |
| 7-31 | At Tex. | W | 9-4 | | 11 | 6 | Zito | Drese | | 58-45 | 1st | +0.5 |
| 8-1 | At Tex. | W | 4-1 | | 9 | 6 | Redman | Regilio | Dotel | 59-45 | 1st | +1.5 |
| 8-3 | At N.Y. | W | 13-4 | | 15 | 8 | Mulder | Lieber | | 60-45 | 1st | +1.5 |
| 8-4 | At N.Y. | L | 6-8 | (11) | 12 | 15 | Rivera | Duchscherer | | 60-46 | 1st | +0.5 |
| 8-5 | At N.Y. | L | 1-5 | | 4 | 12 | Brown | Zito | | 60-47 | 2nd | 0.5 |
| 8-6 | At Min. | W | 3-1 | (11) | 8 | 4 | Dotel | Rincon | | 61-47 | 1st | +0.5 |
| 8-7 | At Min. | L | 3-4 | | 9 | 12 | Santana | Hudson | Nathan | 61-48 | 1st | +0.5 |
| 8-8 | At Min. | W | 6-5 | (18) | 16 | 11 | Hammond | Mulholland | Dotel | 62-48 | 1st | +1.5 |
| 8-9 | At Min. | W | 8-2 | | 12 | 7 | Harden | Lohse | | 63-48 | 1st | +1.5 |
| 8-10 | Det. | W | 5-4 | | 7 | 7 | Zito | Johnson | Dotel | 64-48 | 1st | +2.5 |
| 8-11 | Det. | L | 3-11 | | 8 | 13 | Ledezma | Redman | | 64-49 | 1st | +1.5 |
| 8-12 | Det. | L | 3-5 | | 9 | 11 | Maroth | Duchscherer | Urbina | 64-50 | 1st | +1.5 |
| 8-13 | K.C. | L | 3-10 | | 10 | 9 | Wood | Mulder | | 64-51 | 1st | +1.5 |
| 8-14 | K.C. | W | 6-1 | | 10 | 5 | Harden | Anderson | | 65-51 | 1st | +1.5 |
| 8-15 | K.C. | L | 1-6 | | 7 | 10 | Greinke | Zito | | 65-52 | 1st | +0.5 |
| 8-16 | At Bal. | W | 3-1 | | 9 | 7 | Redman | Bedard | Dotel | 66-52 | 1st | +0.5 |
| 8-17 | At Bal. | W | 11-0 | | 13 | 5 | Hudson | Lopez | | 67-52 | 1st | +0.5 |
| 8-18 | At Bal. | W | 5-4 | | 11 | 6 | Mulder | Ryan | Dotel | 68-52 | 1st | +0.5 |
| 8-20 | At T.B. | W | 9-5 | | 14 | 8 | Harden | Sosa | Dotel | 69-52 | 1st | +0.5 |
| 8-21 | At T.B. | W | 5-0 | | 9 | 5 | Zito | Halama | | 70-52 | 1st | +0.5 |
| 8-22 | At T.B. | L | 1-2 | | 5 | 6 | Brazelton | Redman | Colome | 70-53 | 1st | +0.5 |
| 8-23 | Bal. | W | 4-3 | | 12 | 8 | Hudson | Groom | Dotel | 71-53 | 1st | +0.5 |
| 8-24 | Bal. | W | 6-2 | | 9 | 5 | Mulder | Ponson | | 72-53 | 1st | +0.5 |
| 8-25 | Bal. | W | 3-0 | | 5 | 5 | Dotel | Ryan | | 73-53 | 1st | +0.5 |
| 8-26 | Bal. | W | 9-4 | | 9 | 8 | Zito | Cabrera | | 74-53 | 1st | +1.0 |
| 8-27 | T.B. | W | 8-7 | | 13 | 15 | Duchscherer | Hendrickson | Dotel | 75-53 | 1st | +1.0 |
| 8-28 | T.B. | W | 5-4 | | 8 | 5 | Hudson | Brazelton | Dotel | 76-53 | 1st | +2.0 |
| 8-29 | T.B. | W | 9-6 | | 12 | 12 | Dotel | Baez | | 77-53 | 1st | +2.0 |
| 8-31 | At Chi. | W | 7-2 | | 10 | 6 | Harden | Diaz | | 78-53 | 1st | +3.0 |
| 9-1 | At Chi. | L | 4-5 | | 11 | 11 | Takatsu | Duchscherer | | 78-54 | 1st | +3.0 |
| 9-2 | At Chi. | W | 4-2 | | 7 | 5 | Redman | Contreras | Dotel | 79-54 | 1st | +4.0 |
| 9-3 | At Tor. | W | 7-4 | | 13 | 9 | Hudson | Lilly | Dotel | 80-54 | 1st | +4.0 |
| 9-4 | At Tor. | W | 9-5 | | 10 | 11 | Hammond | Frasor | | 81-54 | 1st | +4.0 |
| 9-5 | At Tor. | L | 5-13 | | 10 | 10 | Glynn | Harden | | 81-55 | 1st | +3.0 |
| 9-6 | Bos. | L | 3-8 | | 7 | 13 | Arroyo | Zito | | 81-56 | 1st | +2.5 |

| Date | Opp. | Res. | Score | (inn.*) | Hits | Opp. hits | Winning pitcher | Losing pitcher | Save | Record | Pos. | GB |
|---|---|---|---|---|---|---|---|---|---|---|---|---|
| 9-7 | Bos. | L | 1-7 | | 5 | 11 | Lowe | Redman | | 81-57 | 1st | +1.5 |
| 9-8 | Bos. | L | 3-8 | | 7 | 8 | Martinez | Hudson | Foulke | 81-58 | 1st | +1.5 |
| 9-10 | Cle. | L | 3-4 | (12) | 8 | 10 | White | Duchscherer | Wickman | 81-59 | 1st | +1.0 |
| 9-11 | Cle. | W | 5-4 | | 8 | 9 | Rincon | Howry | Dotel | 82-59 | 1st | +2.0 |
| 9-12 | Cle. | W | 1-0 | | 5 | 6 | Zito | Westbrook | Dotel | 83-59 | 1st | +2.0 |
| 9-13 | Tex. | W | 7-6 | (10) | 8 | 12 | Duchscherer | Cordero | | 84-59 | 1st | +2.0 |
| 9-14 | Tex. | L | 9-12 | | 13 | 15 | Brocail | Redman | | 84-60 | 1st | +2.0 |
| 9-15 | Tex. | L | 3-10 | | 10 | 14 | Drese | Mulder | | 84-61 | 1st | +2.0 |
| 9-16 | Tex. | W | 5-4 | | 12 | 7 | Harden | Rogers | Dotel | 85-61 | 1st | +2.0 |
| 9-17 | At Sea. | L | 3-6 | | 9 | 10 | Villone | Bradford | Putz | 85-62 | 1st | +1.0 |
| 9-18 | At Sea. | W | 7-4 | | 12 | 9 | Hudson | Baek | | 86-62 | 1st | +2.0 |
| 9-19 | At Sea. | W | 2-1 | | 9 | 8 | Redman | Madritsch | Dotel | 87-62 | 1st | +3.0 |
| 9-21 | At Tex. | L | 4-9 | | 11 | 10 | Drese | Mulder | | 87-63 | 1st | +2.5 |
| 9-22 | At Tex. | L | 3-5 | | 11 | 9 | Rogers | Zito | Cordero | 87-64 | 1st | +2.5 |
| 9-23 | At Tex. | L | 4-5 | | 10 | 10 | Nelson | Dotel | | 87-65 | 1st | +2.0 |
| 9-24 | At Ana. | W | 6-3 | | 12 | 7 | Harden | Escobar | | 88-65 | 1st | +3.0 |
| 9-25 | At Ana. | L | 3-5 | | 5 | 8 | Rodriguez | Bradford | Percival | 88-66 | 1st | +2.0 |
| 9-26 | At Ana. | L | 2-6 | | 6 | 9 | Lackey | Mulder | | 88-67 | 1st | +1.0 |
| 9-27 | Sea. | W | 6-5 | | 13 | 8 | Dotel | Villone | | 89-67 | 1st | +1.0 |
| 9-28 | Sea. | L | 2-7 | | 9 | 13 | Meche | Hudson | | 89-68 | T1st | ... |
| 9-29 | Sea. | L | 2-4 | | 3 | 10 | Madritsch | Harden | | 89-69 | 2nd | 1.0 |
| 9-30 | Sea. | W | 3-2 | | 5 | 9 | Dotel | Atchison | | 90-69 | T1st | ... |
| 10-1 | Ana. | L | 0-10 | | 4 | 14 | Colon | Mulder | | 90-70 | 2nd | 1.0 |
| 10-2 | Ana. | L | 4-5 | | 7 | 7 | Donnelly | Rincon | Percival | 90-71 | 2nd | 2.0 |
| 10-3 | Ana. | W | 3-2 | | 7 | 6 | Duchscherer | Gregg | | 91-71 | 2nd | 1.0 |

Monthly records: April (11-12), May (15-11), June (17-10), July (15-12), August (20-8), September (12-16), October (1-2).
*Innings, if other than nine.



## RECORDS

**2004 regular-season record:** 91-71
**Position:** 2nd in A.L. West
**Home:** 52-29 **Road:** 39-42
**A.L. East:** 23-20 **A.L. Central:** 27-16
**A.L. West:** 31-27 **N.L.** 10-8
**Vs. LH starters:** 29-18
**Vs. RH starters:** 62-53
**Grass:** 82-67 **Artificial:** 9-4
**Day:** 36-24 **Night:** 55-47
1-Run: 33-19 **X-inn.:** 12-7
**Doubleheaders:** 0-0-0
**Team record past five years:** 483-326 (.597, ranks 2nd in league in that span)

## TEAM LEADERS

**Batting average:** Erubiel Durazo (.321).
**At-bats:** Mark Kotsay (606).
**Runs:** Eric Byrnes (91).
**Hits:** Mark Kotsay (190).
**Total Bases:** Mark Kotsay (278).
**Doubles:** Eric Byrnes (39).
**Triples:** Jermaine Dye (4).
**Home runs:** Eric Chavez (29).
**Runs batted in:** Erubiel Durazo (88).
**Stolen bases:** Eric Byrnes (17).
**Slugging percentage:** Erubiel Durazo (.523).
**On-base percentage:** Eric Chavez (.397).
**Wins:** Mark Mulder (17).
**Earned-run average:** Tim Hudson (3.53).
**Complete games:** Mark Mulder (5).
**Shutouts:** Tim Hudson (2).
**Saves:** Octavio Dotel (22).
**Innings pitched:** Mark Mulder (225.2).
**Strikeouts:** Rich Harden (167).

## GAMES BY POSITION

**Catcher:** Damian Miller 109, Adam Melhuse 64, Mike Rose 2.
**First base:** Scott Hatteberg 148, Eric Karros 22, Erubiel Durazo 4, Billy McMillon 3, Nick Swisher 3, Adam Melhuse 1.
**Second base:** Marco Scutaro 123, Mark McLemore 47, Frank Menechino 12, Esteban German 10.
**Third base:** Eric Chavez 125, Mark McLemore 27, Esteban German 15, Ramon A. Castro 6, Adam Melhuse 3, Marco Scutaro 1.
**Shortstop:** Bobby Crosby 151, Marco Scutaro 16, Ramon A. Castro 1.
**Outfield:** Mark Kotsay 145, Eric Byrnes 141, Jermaine Dye 134, Bobby Kielty 67, Billy McMillon 21, Nick Swisher 16, Eric Chavez 1, Mark McLemore 1.
**Designated hitter:** Erubiel Durazo 132, Bobby Kielty 11, Eric Karros 10, Billy McMillon 6, Jermaine Dye 2, Esteban German 2, Scott Hatteberg 2, Nick Swisher 2, Eric Byrnes 1, Ramon A. Castro 1, Mark Kotsay 1.

## TOP DRAFT CHOICES

1a. **Landon Powell,** C, South Carolina.
1b. **Richie Robnett,** OF, Fresno State.
1c. **Danny Putnam,** OF, Stanford.
1d. **Huston Street,** RHP, Texas.
2a. **Michael Rogers,** RHP, North Carolina St.
2b. **Kurt Suzuki,** C, Cal State Fullerton.
3. **Jason Windsor,** RHP, Cal State Fullerton.
4. **Ryan Webb,** RHP, Clearwater Central Catholic H.S., Palm Harbor, Fla.
5. **Kevin Melillo,** 2B, South Carolina.
6. **Derek Tharpe,** LHP, Tennessee.
7. **Jarod McAuliff,** RHP, Oklahoma.
8. **Myron Leslie**, 3B, South Florida
9. **Chad Boyd**, OF, El Camino Real H.S., West Hills, Calif.
10. **Tom Everidge**, 1B, Sonoma State.

# SEATTLE MARINERS
## AMERICAN LEAGUE WEST DIVISION

## 2005 SEASON

### Mariners Schedule
Home games shaded.
All-Star Game July 12 at Detroit. Schedule subject to change.

**April**

| SUN | MON | TUE | WED | THU | FRI | SAT |
|---|---|---|---|---|---|---|
| 3 | 4 MIN | 5 MIN | 6 MIN | 7 | 8 TEX | 9 TEX |
| 10 TEX | 11 KC | 12 | 13 KC | 14 KC | 15 CHW | 16 CHW |
| 17 CHW | 18 ANA | 19 ANA | 20 OAK | 21 OAK | 22 CLE | 23 CLE |
| 24 CLE | 25 | 26 TEX | 27 TEX | 28 TEX | 29 OAK | 30 OAK |

**May**

| SUN | MON | TUE | WED | THU | FRI | SAT |
|---|---|---|---|---|---|---|
| 1 OAK | 2 ANA | 3 ANA | 4 ANA | 5 | 6 BOS | 7 BOS |
| 8 BOS | 9 NYY | 10 NYY | 11 NYY | 12 | 13 BOS | 14 BOS |
| 15 BOS | 16 NYY | 17 NYY | 18 NYY | 19 | 20 SD | 21 SD |
| 22 SD | 23 | 24 BAL | 25 BAL | 26 BAL | 27 TB | 28 TB |
| 29 TB | 30 TOR | 31 TOR | | | | |

**June**

| SUN | MON | TUE | WED | THU | FRI | SAT |
|---|---|---|---|---|---|---|
| | | | 1 TOR | 2 | 3 TB | 4 TB |
| 5 TB | 6 | 7 FLA | 8 FLA | 9 FLA | 10 WAS | 11 WAS |
| 12 WAS | 13 | 14 PHI | 15 PHI | 16 PHI | 17 NYM | 18 NYM |
| 19 NYM | 20 OAK | 21 OAK | 22 OAK | 23 OAK | 24 SD | 25 SD |
| 26 SD | 27 | 28 OAK | 29 OAK | 30 OAK | | |

**July**

| SUN | MON | TUE | WED | THU | FRI | SAT |
|---|---|---|---|---|---|---|
| | | | | | 1 TEX | 2 TEX |
| 3 TEX | 4 KC | 5 KC | 6 KC | 7 ANA | 8 ANA | 9 ANA |
| 10 ANA | 11 | 12 All-Star | 13 | 14 BAL | 15 BAL | 16 BAL |
| 17 BAL | 18 | 19 TOR | 20 TOR | 21 TOR | 22 CLE | 23 CLE |
| 24 CLE | 25 DET | 26 DET | 27 DET | 28 CLE | 29 CLE | 30 CLE |
| 31 CLE | | | | | | |

**August**

| SUN | MON | TUE | WED | THU | FRI | SAT |
|---|---|---|---|---|---|---|
| | 1 | 2 DET | 3 DET | 4 DET | 5 CHW | 6 CHW |
| 7 CHW | 8 MIN | 9 MIN | 10 MIN | 11 | 12 ANA | 13 ANA |
| 14 ANA | 15 KC | 16 KC | 17 KC | 18 MIN | 19 MIN | 20 MIN |
| 21 MIN | 22 | 23 TEX | 24 TEX | 25 TEX | 26 CHW | 27 CHW |
| 28 CHW | 29 NYY | 30 NYY | 31 NYY | | | |

**September**

| SUN | MON | TUE | WED | THU | FRI | SAT |
|---|---|---|---|---|---|---|
| | | | | 1 NYY | 2 ANA | 3 ANA |
| 4 ANA | 5 OAK | 6 OAK | 7 OAK | 8 | 9 BAL | 10 BAL |
| 11 BAL | 12 ANA | 13 ANA | 14 ANA | 15 TEX | 16 TEX | 17 TEX |
| 18 TEX | 19 TOR | 20 TOR | 21 TOR | 22 TOR | 23 DET | 24 DET |
| 25 DET | 26 | 27 TEX | 28 TEX | 29 TEX | 30 OAK | |

**October**

| SUN | MON | TUE | WED | THU | FRI | SAT |
|---|---|---|---|---|---|---|
| | | | | | | 1 OAK |
| 2 OAK | 3 | 4 | 5 | 6 | 7 | 8 |

Home games shaded. All-Star Game July 12 at Detroit. Schedule subject to change.

### CLUB DIRECTORY

**Chairman & chief executive officer**
Howard Lincoln

**President and chief operating officer**
Chuck Armstrong

**Executive v.p., baseball operations**
Bill Bavasi

**Special consultant**
Pat Gillick

**Special assistants**
John Boles, Dan Evans

**Vice president, baseball administration**
Lee Pelekoudas

**Vice president, player development and scouting**
Benny Looper

**Director, player development**
Frank Mattox

**Vice president,scouting**
Bob Fontaine

**Director, professional scouting**
Ken Compton

**Director, baseball information**
Tim Hevly

**Vice president, communications**
Randy Adamack

### MINOR LEAGUE AFFILIATES

| Class | Team | League | Manager |
|---|---|---|---|
| AAA | Tacoma | Pacific Coast | Dan Rohn |
| AA | San Antonio | Texas | Dave Brundage |
| Advanced A | Inland Empire | California | Daren Brown |
| A | Wisconsin | Midwest | Steve Roadcap |
| Short-Season A | Everett | Northwest | Pedro Grifol |
| Rookie | Peoria Mariners | Arizona | Scott Steinmann |

### BROADCAST INFORMATION

**Radio:** KOMO-AM (1000).
**TV:** KSTW (Channel 11).
**Cable TV:** Fox Sports Net Northwest.

### SPRING TRAINING

**Ballpark:** Peoria Stadium (Peoria, Ariz.).
**Ticket information:** 480-784-4444.

**For more on the Mariners, go to msn.foxsports.com/mlb/teams.**

Suzuki

## SPRING TRAINING ROSTER

**Manager**—Mike Hargrove (21).
**Coaches**—Don Baylor (25), Carlos Garcia, Ron Hassey, Jeff Newman (5), Bryan Price (34), Jim Slaton.

| No. | PITCHERS | B/T | Ht./Wt. | Age* | 2004 Clubs |
|---|---|---|---|---|---|
| 27 | Atchison, Scott | R/R | 6-2/180 | 29 | Tacoma, Seattle |
| 57 | Baek, Cha Seung | R/R | 6-4/190 | 24 | Arizona Mariners, San Antonio, Tacoma, Seattle |
| 48 | Blackley, Travis | L/L | 6-3/190 | 22 | Seattle, Tacoma |
| 45 | Franklin, Ryan | R/R | 6-3/180 | 32 | Seattle |
| 18 | Guardado, Eddie | R/L | 6-0/205 | 34 | Seattle |
| 17 | Hasegawa, S. | R/R | 5-11/180 | 36 | Seattle |
| 46 | Looper, Aaron | R/R | 6-2/185 | 28 | Tacoma |
| 56 | Madritsch, Bobby | L/L | 6-2/190 | 29 | Tacoma, Seattle |
| 40 | Mateo, Julio | R/R | 6-0/177 | 27 | Seattle |
| 55 | Meche, Gil | R/R | 6-3/200 | 26 | Tacoma, Seattle |
| 50 | Moyer, Jamie | L/L | 6-0/175 | 42 | Seattle |
| 37 | Nageotte, Clint | R/R | 6-3/200 | 24 | Tacoma, Seattle |
| 38 | Pineiro, Joel | R/R | 6-1/200 | 26 | Seattle |
| 20 | Putz, J.J. | R/R | 6-5/220 | 28 | Tacoma, Seattle |
| 52 | Sherrill, George | L/L | 6-0/210 | 27 | Tacoma, Seattle |
| 39 | Soriano, Rafael | R/R | 6-1/175 | 25 | Inland Empire, San Antonio, Seattle, Tacoma |
| 53 | Thornton, Matt | L/L | 6-6/220 | 28 | Tacoma, Seattle |
| 47 | Villone, Ron | L/L | 6-3/230 | 35 | Seattle |

| No. | CATCHERS | B/T | Ht./Wt. | Age* | 2004 Clubs |
|---|---|---|---|---|---|
| 8 | Olivo, Miguel | R/R | 6-0/215 | 26 | Chicago A.L., Everett, Seattle |
| 59 | Rivera, Rene | R/R | 5-10/190 | 21 | Tacoma, Inland Empire, Seattle |
| 6 | Wilson, Dan | R/R | 6-3/215 | 36 | Seattle |

| No. | INFIELDERS | B/T | Ht./Wt. | Age* | 2004 Clubs |
|---|---|---|---|---|---|
| | Beltre, Adrian | R/R | 5-11/220 | 25 | Los Angeles |
| 16 | Bloomquist, Willie | R/R | 5-11/185 | 27 | Tacoma, Seattle |
| 29 | Boone, Bret | R/R | 5-10/190 | 35 | Seattle |
| 53 | Dobbs, Greg | L/R | 6-1/205 | 26 | San Antonio, Tacoma, Seattle |
| 33 | Jacobsen, Bucky | R/R | 6-4/220 | 29 | Tacoma, Seattle |
| 26 | Leone, Justin | R/R | 6-1/190 | 27 | Tacoma, Seattle |
| 22 | Lopez, Jose | R/R | 6-2/170 | 21 | Arizona Mariners, Tacoma, Seattle |
| | Morse, Mike | R/R | 6-4/220 | 23 | Birmingham, San Antonio |
| | Reese, Pokey | R/R | 5-11/180 | 31 | Boston |
| | Sexson, Richie | R/R | 6-8/237 | 30 | Arizona |
| 23 | Spiezio, Scott | B/R | 6-2/220 | 32 | Inland Empire, Seattle |

| No. | OUTFIELDERS | B/T | Ht./Wt. | Age* | 2004 Clubs |
|---|---|---|---|---|---|
| | Balentien, Wladimir | R/R | 6-2/165 | 20 | Wisconsin, Inland Empire |
| | Choo, Shin-Soo | L/L | 5-11/180 | 22 | San Antonio |
| 28 | Ibanez, Raul | L/R | 6-2/200 | 32 | Tacoma, Seattle |
| 58 | Reed, Jeremy | L/L | 6-0/185 | 23 | Charlotte, Tacoma, Seattle |
| 41 | Snelling, Chris | L/L | 5-10/165 | 23 | Arizona Mariners |
| | Strong, Jamal | R/R | 5-1/180 | 26 | Peoria, Tacoma |
| 51 | Suzuki, Ichiro | L/R | 5-9/172 | 31 | Seattle |
| 2 | Winn, Randy | B/R | 6-2/197 | 30 | Seattle |

*Age as of April 1, 2005.

## BALLPARK INFORMATION

**Ballpark (capacity, surface)**
Safeco Field (47,447, grass).

**Address**
1250 First Avenue South
Seattle, WA 98134

**Official website**
www.seattlemariners.com

**Business phone**
206-346-4000

**Ticket information**
206-346-4001

**Field dimensions (from home plate)**
To left field at foul line, 331 feet
To center field, 405 feet
To right field at foul line, 326 feet

**First game played**
July 15, 1999 (Padres 3, Mariners 2)

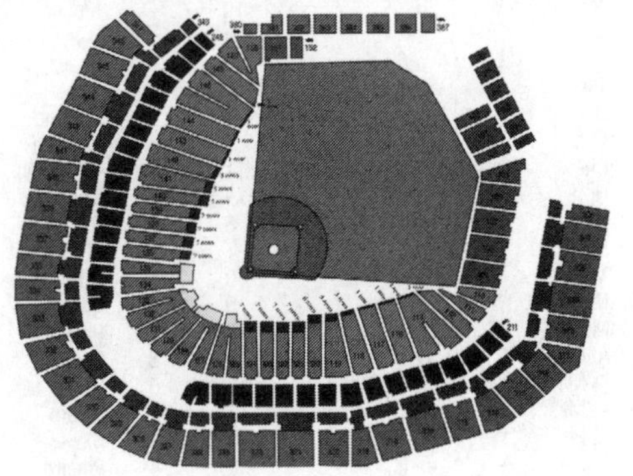

# 2004 REVIEW

## DAY BY DAY

| Date | Opp. | Res. | Score | (inn.*) | Hits | Opp. hits | Winning pitcher | Losing pitcher | Save | Record | Pos. | GB |
|---|---|---|---|---|---|---|---|---|---|---|---|---|
| 4-6 | Ana. | L | 5-10 | | 7 | 12 | Colon | Moyer | | 0-1 | 3rd | 1.5 |
| 4-7 | Ana. | L | 7-10 | | 13 | 16 | Washburn | Pineiro | Percival | 0-2 | 4th | 2.0 |
| 4-8 | Ana. | L | 1-5 | | 7 | 9 | Shields | Hasegawa | | 0-3 | 4th | 3.0 |
| 4-9 | At Oak. | L | 6-8 | | 13 | 12 | Hammond | Soriano | Rhodes | 0-4 | 4th | 3.0 |
| 4-10 | At Oak. | L | 1-2 | | 4 | 8 | Hudson | Meche | | 0-5 | 4th | 4.0 |
| 4-11 | At Oak. | W | 9-4 | (10) | 14 | 11 | Hasegawa | Hammond | | 1-5 | 4th | 3.0 |
| 4-13 | At Ana. | L | 5-7 | | 11 | 11 | Shields | Soriano | Percival | 1-6 | 4th | 4.0 |
| 4-14 | At Ana. | L | 5-6 | | 12 | 14 | Percival | Hasegawa | | 1-7 | 4th | 5.0 |
| 4-15 | At Ana. | W | 6-2 | | 8 | 5 | Franklin | Lackey | | 2-7 | 4th | 4.0 |
| 4-16 | Tex. | L | 0-5 | | 8 | 11 | Park | Meche | | 2-8 | 4th | 5.0 |
| 4-17 | Tex. | W | 4-1 | | 5 | 4 | Moyer | Lewis | Guardado | 3-8 | 4th | 4.0 |
| 4-18 | Tex. | W | 4-2 | | 10 | 6 | Pineiro | Ramirez | Guardado | 4-8 | 4th | 4.0 |
| 4-19 | Oak. | W | 2-1 | (14) | 10 | 10 | Jarvis | Duchscherer | | 5-8 | 4th | 3.0 |
| 4-20 | Oak. | W | 2-1 | | 4 | 3 | Villone | Mecir | | 6-8 | 4th | 2.0 |
| 4-21 | Oak. | L | 4-7 | | 9 | 10 | Hudson | Myers | Rhodes | 6-9 | 4th | 3.0 |
| 4-22 | Oak. | L | 2-8 | | 7 | 13 | Mulder | Moyer | | 6-10 | 4th | 4.0 |
| 4-23 | At Tex. | L | 8-10 | | 12 | 15 | Drese | Pineiro | Cordero | 6-11 | 4th | 4.0 |
| 4-24 | At Tex. | L | 0-3 | | 7 | 9 | Powell | Garcia | Nelson | 6-12 | 4th | 4.0 |
| 4-25 | At Tex. | L | 6-14 | | 15 | 17 | Almanzar | Franklin | | 6-13 | 4th | 5.0 |
| 4-27 | At Bal. | W | 7-5 | | 13 | 12 | Villone | Lopez | Guardado | 7-13 | 4th | 5.0 |
| 4-28 | At Bal. | L | 1-3 | | 4 | 7 | Parrish | Hasegawa | Julio | 7-14 | 4th | 5.0 |
| 4-29 | At Bal. | L | 5-9 | | 5 | 15 | DuBose | Pineiro | | 7-15 | 4th | 6.0 |
| 4-30 | At Det. | W | 3-1 | (10) | 9 | 4 | Myers | Levine | Guardado | 8-15 | 4th | 5.5 |
| 5-1 | At Det. | L | 2-4 | | 6 | 9 | Bonderman | Franklin | Urbina | 8-16 | 4th | 7.0 |
| 5-2 | At Det. | W | 12-2 | | 14 | 4 | Meche | Cornejo | | 9-16 | 4th | 7.0 |
| 5-4 | Min. | W | 4-3 | (16) | 13 | 9 | Villone | Greisinger | | 10-16 | 4th | 6.5 |
| 5-5 | Min. | L | 1-5 | | 5 | 11 | Silva | Pineiro | | 10-17 | 4th | 7.5 |
| 5-6 | Min. | W | 2-1 | | 5 | 7 | Garcia | Rincon | Guardado | 11-17 | 4th | 7.5 |
| 5-7 | N.Y. | W | 6-2 | | 12 | 7 | Franklin | Lieber | | 12-17 | 4th | 7.5 |
| 5-8 | N.Y. | L | 0-6 | | 4 | 11 | Mussina | Meche | | 12-18 | 4th | 8.5 |
| 5-9 | N.Y. | L | 6-7 | | 8 | 9 | Quantrill | Soriano | Rivera | 12-19 | 4th | 9.5 |
| 5-11 | At Min. | L | 6-7 | (11) | 18 | 10 | Fultz | Villone | | 12-20 | 4th | 9.5 |
| 5-12 | At Min. | L | 3-4 | | 10 | 7 | Radke | Garcia | Nathan | 12-21 | 4th | 10.5 |
| 5-13 | At Min. | L | 0-1 | | 8 | 8 | Santana | Franklin | Nathan | 12-22 | 4th | 10.5 |
| 5-14 | At N.Y. | L | 5-9 | | 12 | 8 | Mussina | Villone | | 12-23 | 4th | 11.5 |
| 5-15 | At N.Y. | W | 13-7 | (13) | 15 | 14 | Guardado | White | | 13-23 | 4th | 11.5 |
| 5-16 | At N.Y. | L | 1-2 | | 9 | 5 | Brown | Pineiro | Rivera | 13-24 | 4th | 11.5 |
| 5-18 | Bal. | L | 2-7 | | 6 | 10 | Cabrera | Garcia | | 13-25 | 4th | 12.5 |
| 5-19 | Bal. | L | 2-5 | | 7 | 10 | Bedard | Franklin | Julio | 13-26 | 4th | 12.5 |
| 5-20 | Bal. | W | 11-0 | | 13 | 8 | Moyer | Lopez | | 14-26 | 4th | 11.5 |
| 5-21 | Det. | L | 0-5 | | 8 | 8 | Robertson | Meche | | 14-27 | 4th | 12.5 |
| 5-22 | Det. | L | 4-8 | | 7 | 12 | Johnson | Putz | | 14-28 | 4th | 13.5 |
| 5-23 | Det. | W | 3-1 | | 9 | 5 | Garcia | Bonderman | Guardado | 15-28 | 4th | 13.5 |
| 5-25 | At Cle. | W | 5-4 | (12) | 12 | 7 | Myers | Jimenez | Guardado | 16-28 | 4th | 12.5 |
| 5-26 | At Cle. | W | 7-3 | | 13 | 8 | Moyer | Sabathia | Guardado | 17-28 | 4th | 11.5 |
| 5-27 | At Cle. | L | 5-9 | | 8 | 13 | Westbrook | Meche | | 17-29 | 4th | 11.5 |
| 5-28 | At Bos. | L | 4-8 | | 11 | 9 | Martinez | Pineiro | | 17-30 | 4th | 11.5 |
| 5-29 | At Bos. | W | 5-4 | | 11 | 10 | Garcia | Wakefield | Guardado | 18-30 | 4th | 11.5 |
| 5-30 | At Bos. | L | 7-9 | (12) | 8 | 14 | Martinez | Putz | | 18-31 | 4th | 11.5 |
| 5-31 | Tor. | W | 6-2 | | 10 | 7 | Moyer | Hentgen | | 19-31 | 4th | 11.0 |
| 6-1 | Tor. | L | 5-6 | | 9 | 8 | Lopez | Nageotte | Frasor | 19-32 | 4th | 12.0 |
| 6-2 | Tor. | L | 3-5 | | 10 | 7 | Lilly | Pineiro | Ligtenberg | 19-33 | 4th | 13.0 |
| 6-4 | Chi. | L | 2-4 | | 5 | 9 | Garland | Garcia | Koch | 19-34 | 4th | 13.5 |
| 6-5 | Chi. | W | 4-2 | | 7 | 6 | Franklin | Schoeneweis | Guardado | 20-34 | 4th | 12.5 |
| 6-6 | Chi. | W | 5-4 | | 11 | 9 | Hasegawa | Koch | | 21-34 | 4th | 11.5 |
| 6-7 | Hou. | W | 5-0 | | 11 | 8 | Nageotte | Duckworth | Mateo | 22-34 | 4th | 11.0 |
| 6-8 | Hou. | L | 0-1 | | 6 | 3 | Clemens | Pineiro | Dotel | 22-35 | 4th | 11.0 |
| 6-9 | Hou. | L | 0-3 | | 7 | 7 | Miller | Garcia | Dotel | 22-36 | 4th | 12.0 |
| 6-11 | Mon. | W | 1-0 | | 10 | 5 | Guardado | Hernandez | | 23-36 | 4th | 12.0 |
| 6-12 | Mon. | W | 3-0 | | 5 | 8 | Moyer | Vargas | Guardado | 24-36 | 4th | 12.0 |
| 6-13 | Mon. | W | 8-1 | | 14 | 6 | Pineiro | Armas | | 25-36 | 4th | 12.0 |
| 6-15 | At Mil. | L | 0-3 | | 2 | 8 | Santos | Garcia | Kolb | 25-37 | 4th | 12.0 |
| 6-16 | At Mil. | L | 1-4 | | 6 | 5 | Davis | Nageotte | Kolb | 25-38 | 4th | 12.0 |
| 6-17 | At Mil. | W | 6-3 | | 11 | 10 | Myers | Kinney | Guardado | 26-38 | 4th | 11.0 |
| 6-18 | At Pit. | W | 5-4 | | 9 | 7 | Moyer | Vogelsong | Guardado | 27-38 | 4th | 11.0 |
| 6-19 | At Pit. | W | 5-1 | | 8 | 4 | Pineiro | Burnett | | 28-38 | 4th | 10.0 |
| 6-20 | At Pit. | W | 5-4 | | 6 | 9 | Garcia | Perez | Guardado | 29-38 | 4th | 9.0 |

| Date | Opp. | Res. | Score | (inn.*) | Hits | Opp. hits | Winning pitcher | Losing pitcher | Save | Record | Pos. | GB |
|---|---|---|---|---|---|---|---|---|---|---|---|---|
| 6-22 | At Tex. | L | 2-10 | | 5 | 13 | Drese | Nageotte | | 29-39 | 4th | 9.5 |
| 6-23 | At Tex. | L | 3-6 | | 8 | 12 | Bierbrodt | Franklin | Cordero | 29-40 | 4th | 10.5 |
| 6-24 | At Tex. | L | 7-9 | (18) | 12 | 23 | Shouse | Moyer | | 29-41 | 4th | 11.5 |
| 6-25 | S.D. | L | 2-3 | | 8 | 4 | Lawrence | Garcia | Hoffman | 29-42 | 4th | 12.5 |
| 6-26 | S.D. | W | 7-3 | | 13 | 8 | Mateo | Valdez | | 30-42 | 4th | 12.5 |
| 6-27 | S.D. | L | 1-5 | | 3 | 7 | Eaton | Moyer | | 30-43 | 4th | 12.5 |
| 6-28 | Tex. | L | 5-8 | | 9 | 16 | Rodriguez | Franklin | Cordero | 30-44 | 4th | 13.5 |
| 6-29 | Tex. | W | 4-3 | | 8 | 6 | Pineiro | Benoit | Guardado | 31-44 | 4th | 12.5 |
| 6-30 | Tex. | L | 6-9 | | 9 | 16 | Rogers | Nageotte | Cordero | 31-45 | 4th | 13.5 |
| 7-1 | Tex. | W | 8-4 | | 12 | 6 | Blackley | Wasdin | | 32-45 | 4th | 12.5 |
| 7-2 | At StL. | L | 2-11 | | 6 | 11 | Williams | Thornton | | 32-46 | 4th | 12.5 |
| 7-3 | At StL. | L | 1-8 | | 6 | 13 | Marquis | Franklin | | 32-47 | 4th | 13.0 |
| 7-4 | At StL. | L | 1-2 | | 6 | 6 | Suppan | Pineiro | Isringhausen | 32-48 | 4th | 14.0 |
| 7-6 | At Tor. | L | 6-7 | | 10 | 12 | Batista | Moyer | Frasor | 32-49 | 4th | 14.0 |
| 7-7 | At Tor. | L | 4-12 | | 13 | 11 | Towers | Blackley | | 32-50 | 4th | 15.0 |
| 7-8 | At Tor. | L | 8-10 | | 14 | 17 | Speier | Guardado | | 32-51 | 4th | 16.0 |
| 7-9 | At Chi. | L | 2-6 | | 7 | 9 | Garland | Pineiro | | 32-52 | 4th | 16.0 |
| 7-10 | At Chi. | L | 2-3 | | 9 | 3 | Buehrle | Thornton | Takatsu | 32-53 | 4th | 16.0 |
| 7-11 | At Chi. | L | 3-4 | | 7 | 5 | Garcia | Moyer | Takatsu | 32-54 | 4th | 17.0 |
| 7-15 | Cle. | W | 2-1 | | 4 | 5 | Pineiro | Westbrook | Guardado | 33-54 | 4th | 16.5 |
| 7-16 | Cle. | L | 6-18 | | 7 | 21 | Lee | Blackley | | 33-55 | 4th | 17.5 |
| 7-17 | Cle. | L | 5-6 | | 13 | 9 | Sabathia | Franklin | Riske | 33-56 | 4th | 18.5 |
| 7-18 | Cle. | W | 7-5 | | 10 | 11 | Hasegawa | Miller | Guardado | 34-56 | 4th | 18.5 |
| 7-19 | Bos. | W | 8-4 | (11) | 10 | 9 | Myers | Leskanic | | 35-56 | 4th | 17.5 |
| 7-20 | Bos. | L | 7-9 | | 18 | 10 | Lowe | Pineiro | Foulke | 35-57 | 4th | 18.5 |
| 7-21 | Oak. | W | 6-5 | (10) | 12 | 10 | Madritsch | Duchscherer | | 36-57 | 4th | 18.5 |
| 7-22 | Oak. | W | 4-2 | | 7 | 9 | Hasegawa | Redman | Guardado | 37-57 | 4th | 17.5 |
| 7-23 | Ana. | L | 2-8 | | 9 | 13 | Lackey | Moyer | | 37-58 | 4th | 18.5 |
| 7-24 | Ana. | L | 4-8 | | 9 | 14 | Sele | Mateo | | 37-59 | 4th | 18.5 |
| 7-25 | Ana. | W | 6-2 | | 8 | 6 | Pineiro | Ortiz | | 38-59 | 4th | 17.5 |
| 7-26 | At Oak. | L | 5-14 | | 12 | 13 | Zito | Blackley | | 38-60 | 4th | 18.5 |
| 7-27 | At Oak. | L | 3-5 | | 9 | 7 | Redman | Franklin | Dotel | 38-61 | 4th | 18.5 |
| 7-28 | At Oak. | L | 2-3 | | 8 | 7 | Mulder | Mateo | | 38-62 | 4th | 18.5 |
| 7-29 | At Ana. | W | 6-5 | (13) | 18 | 12 | Madritsch | Gregg | | 39-62 | 4th | 18.0 |
| 7-30 | At Ana. | L | 5-6 | | 7 | 11 | Donnelly | Putz | Percival | 39-63 | 4th | 18.5 |
| 7-31 | At Ana. | L | 8-9 | (11) | 14 | 16 | Donnelly | Guardado | | 39-64 | 4th | 19.0 |
| 8-1 | At Ana. | L | 2-3 | | 10 | 7 | Colon | Franklin | Shields | 39-65 | 4th | 20.0 |
| 8-3# | At Bal. | L | 7-9 | | 16 | 10 | Grimsley | Nageotte | Julio | 39-66 | | |
| 8-3$ | At Bal. | L | 4-5 | | 15 | 11 | Julio | Sherrill | | 39-67 | 4th | 21.5 |
| 8-4 | At Bal. | L | 3-6 | | 9 | 10 | Williams | Hasegawa | Julio | 39-68 | 4th | 21.5 |
| 8-5 | At T.B. | W | 4-2 | (11) | 10 | 6 | Atchison | Baez | | 40-68 | 4th | 21.0 |
| 8-6 | At T.B. | L | 1-2 | (10) | 2 | 9 | Harper | Nageotte | | 40-69 | 4th | 21.5 |
| 8-7 | At T.B. | W | 5-2 | | 12 | 4 | Villone | Hendrickson | Putz | 41-69 | 4th | 20.5 |
| 8-8 | At T.B. | L | 1-5 | | 9 | 15 | Bell | Moyer | Baez | 41-70 | 4th | 21.5 |
| 8-10 | Min. | W | 4-3 | | 10 | 4 | Meche | Mulholland | Putz | 42-70 | 4th | 22.0 |
| 8-11 | Min. | W | 4-3 | | 7 | 6 | Sherrill | Rincon | | 43-70 | 4th | 21.0 |
| 8-12 | Min. | L | 3-6 | | 9 | 10 | Santana | Franklin | Nathan | 43-71 | 4th | 21.0 |
| 8-13 | N.Y. | L | 3-11 | | 7 | 14 | Lieber | Villone | | 43-72 | 4th | 21.0 |
| 8-14 | N.Y. | L | 4-6 | | 11 | 9 | Quantrill | Hasegawa | Rivera | 43-73 | 4th | 22.0 |
| 8-15 | N.Y. | W | 7-3 | | 12 | 8 | Meche | Nitkowski | | 44-73 | 4th | 21.0 |
| 8-17 | At K.C. | W | 16-3 | | 20 | 8 | Madritsch | May | | 45-73 | 4th | 21.5 |
| 8-18 | At K.C. | L | 2-3 | | 5 | 5 | Carrasco | Franklin | | 45-74 | 4th | 22.5 |
| 8-20 | At Det. | L | 3-8 | | 9 | 13 | Robertson | Villone | | 45-75 | 4th | 23.5 |
| 8-21 | At Det. | L | 10-11 | (11) | 21 | 15 | Walker | Atchison | | 45-76 | 4th | 24.5 |
| 8-22 | At Det. | W | 5-3 | | 11 | 10 | Meche | Maroth | Putz | 46-76 | 4th | 23.5 |
| 8-23 | T.B. | L | 0-9 | | 5 | 10 | Kazmir | Madritsch | | 46-77 | 4th | 24.5 |
| 8-24 | T.B. | L | 5-6 | | 7 | 11 | Bell | Franklin | | 46-78 | 4th | 25.5 |
| 8-25 | T.B. | L | 5-6 | | 7 | 9 | Harper | Atchison | Baez | 46-79 | 4th | 26.5 |
| 8-26 | K.C. | L | 3-7 | | 8 | 11 | Anderson | Moyer | | 46-80 | 4th | 27.5 |
| 8-27 | K.C. | W | 7-5 | | 14 | 9 | Sherrill | Carrasco | Putz | 47-80 | 4th | 27.5 |
| 8-28! | K.C. | W | 9-7 | | 12 | 9 | Thornton | May | Putz | 48-80 | | |
| 8-28& | K.C. | W | 5-3 | (12) | 12 | 10 | Baek | Kinney | | 49-80 | 4th | 27.0 |
| 8-29 | K.C. | W | 5-4 | | 8 | 11 | Villone | Reyes | | 50-80 | 4th | 27.0 |
| 8-31 | At Tor. | W | 7-5 | | 16 | 10 | Atchison | Ligtenberg | Putz | 51-80 | 4th | 27.0 |
| 9-1 | At Tor. | L | 2-4 | | 6 | 8 | Bush | Villone | Speier | 51-81 | 4th | 27.0 |
| 9-2 | At Tor. | L | 6-8 | | 11 | 13 | File | Baek | Speier | 51-82 | 4th | 28.0 |
| 9-3 | At Chi. | L | 5-7 | | 11 | 8 | Garland | Madritsch | Takatsu | 51-83 | 4th | 29.0 |
| 9-4 | At Chi. | L | 7-8 | | 15 | 14 | Buehrle | Franklin | Takatsu | 51-84 | 4th | 30.0 |
| 9-5 | At Chi. | L | 2-6 | | 9 | 6 | Diaz | Moyer | Marte | 51-85 | 4th | 30.0 |
| 9-6 | Cle. | L | 0-5 | | 5 | 5 | Sabathia | Meche | | 51-86 | 4th | 30.0 |

| Date | Opp. | Res. | Score | (inn.*) | Hits | Opp. hits | Winning pitcher | Losing pitcher | Save | Record | Pos. | GB |
|---|---|---|---|---|---|---|---|---|---|---|---|---|
| 9-8 | Cle. | L | 5-9 | | 7 | 14 | Lee | Baek | | 51-87 | 4th | 29.5 |
| 9-9 | Bos. | W | 7-1 | | 9 | 8 | Madritsch | Wakefield | | 52-87 | 4th | 29.0 |
| 9-10 | Bos. | L | 2-13 | | 6 | 11 | Schilling | Franklin | | 52-88 | 4th | 29.0 |
| 9-11 | Bos. | L | 0-9 | | 5 | 7 | Arroyo | Moyer | | 52-89 | 4th | 30.0 |
| 9-12 | Bos. | W | 2-0 | | 6 | 5 | Meche | Lowe | | 53-89 | 4th | 30.0 |
| 9-13 | Ana. | L | 1-5 | | 7 | 8 | Escobar | Baek | Rodriguez | 53-90 | 4th | 31.0 |
| 9-14 | Ana. | W | 3-2 | | 7 | 8 | Madritsch | Washburn | Putz | 54-90 | 4th | 30.0 |
| 9-15 | Ana. | W | 1-0 | | 6 | 2 | Franklin | Lackey | | 55-90 | 4th | 29.0 |
| 9-16 | Ana. | L | 1-6 | | 6 | 5 | Sele | Moyer | | 55-91 | 4th | 30.0 |
| 9-17 | Oak. | W | 6-3 | | 10 | 9 | Villone | Bradford | Putz | 56-91 | 4th | 29.0 |
| 9-18 | Oak. | L | 4-7 | | 9 | 12 | Hudson | Baek | | 56-92 | 4th | 30.0 |
| 9-19 | Oak. | L | 1-2 | | 8 | 9 | Redman | Madritsch | Dotel | 56-93 | 4th | 31.0 |
| 9-20 | At Ana. | L | 2-5 | | 12 | 12 | Lackey | Franklin | Percival | 56-94 | 4th | 31.5 |
| 9-21 | At Ana. | W | 7-3 | | 18 | 7 | Moyer | Sele | | 57-94 | 4th | 30.5 |
| 9-22 | At Ana. | W | 16-6 | | 24 | 7 | Meche | Colon | | 58-94 | 4th | 29.5 |
| 9-24 | At Tex. | W | 8-7 | | 14 | 11 | Villone | Cordero | Putz | 59-94 | 4th | 29.0 |
| 9-25 | At Tex. | L | 4-5 | | 8 | 8 | Dickey | Hasegawa | Cordero | 59-95 | 4th | 29.0 |
| 9-26 | At Tex. | W | 9-0 | | 13 | 3 | Baek | Drese | | 60-95 | 4th | 28.0 |
| 9-27 | At Oak. | L | 5-6 | | 8 | 13 | Dotel | Villone | | 60-96 | 4th | 29.0 |
| 9-28 | At Oak. | W | 7-2 | | 13 | 9 | Meche | Hudson | | 61-96 | 4th | 28.0 |
| 9-29 | At Oak. | W | 4-2 | | 10 | 3 | Madritsch | Harden | | 62-96 | 4th | 28.0 |
| 9-30 | At Oak. | L | 2-3 | | 9 | 5 | Dotel | Atchison | | 62-97 | 4th | 28.0 |
| 10-1 | Tex. | W | 8-3 | | 18 | 5 | Villone | Drese | | 63-97 | 4th | 28.0 |
| 10-2 | Tex. | L | 4-10 | | 10 | 16 | Rogers | Moyer | | 63-98 | 4th | 29.0 |
| 10-3 | Tex. | L | 0-3 | | 4 | 9 | Park | Meche | Cordero | 63-99 | 4th | 29.0 |

Monthly records: April (8-15), May (11-16), June (12-14), July (8-19), August (12-16), September (11-17), October (1-2).
*Innings, if other than nine. ! First game of a doubleheader. & Second game of a doubleheader. # Day separate admission. $ Night separate admission.

## RECORDS

**2004 regular-season record:** 63-99
**Position:** 4th in A.L. West
**Home:** 38-44 **Road:** 25-55
**A.L. East:** 13-30 **A.L. Central:** 19-24
**A.L. West:** 22-36 **N.L.** 9-9
**Vs. LH starters:** 19-31
**Vs. RH starters:** 44-68
**Grass:** 60-89 **Artificial:** 3-10
**Day:** 20-29 **Night:** 43-70
**1-Run:** 20-30 **X-inn.:** 11-6
**Doubleheaders:** 1-0-0
**Team record past five years:** 456-354 (.563, ranks 3rd in league in that span)

## TEAM LEADERS

**Batting average:** Ichiro Suzuki (.372).
**At-bats:** Ichiro Suzuki (704).
**Runs:** Ichiro Suzuki (101).
**Hits:** Ichiro Suzuki (262).
**Total Bases:** Ichiro Suzuki (320).
**Doubles:** Randy Winn (34).
**Triples:** Randy Winn (6).
**Home runs:** Bret Boone (24).
**Runs batted in:** Bret Boone (83).
**Stolen bases:** Ichiro Suzuki (36).
**Slugging percentage:** Raul Ibanez (.472).
**On-base percentage:** Ichiro Suzuki (.414).
**Wins:** Ron Villone (8).
**Earned-run average:** Freddy Garcia (3.20).
**Complete games:** Ryan Franklin (2).
**Shutouts:** Ryan Franklin, Gil Meche (1).
**Saves:** Eddie Guardado (18).
**Innings pitched:** Jamie Moyer (202.0).
**Strikeouts:** Jamie Moyer (125).

## GAMES BY POSITION

**Catcher**: Dan Wilson 103, Miguel Olivo 49, Pat Borders 19, Ben Davis 14, Rene Rivera 2.
**First base:** John Olerud 77, Scott Spiezio 42, Jolbert Cabrera 23, Bucky Jacobsen 21, Willie Bloomquist 19, Raul Ibanez 10, Dave Hansen 7.
**Second base:** Bret Boone 148, Jolbert Cabrera 18, Mickey Lopez 3, Willie Bloomquist 1.
**Third base:** Scott Spiezio 66, Jolbert Cabrera 36, Willie Bloomquist 31, Justin Leone 28, Greg Dobbs 14, Dave Hansen 6, Jose Lopez 1, Edgar Martinez 0.
**Shortstop:** Rich Aurilia 73, Jose Lopez 57, Willie Bloomquist 20, Ramon Santiago 16, Jolbert Cabrera 14, Justin Leone 2.
**Outfield:** Ichiro Suzuki 158, Randy Winn 154, Raul Ibanez 112, Hiram Bocachica 44, Jolbert Cabrera 23, Jeremy Reed 16, Willie Bloomquist 9, Quinton McCracken 8.
**Designated hitter:** Edgar Martinez 122, Bucky Jacobsen 20, Dave Hansen 8, Willie Bloomquist 6, Quinton McCracken 6, Jolbert Cabrera 5, Hiram Bocachica 3, Mickey Lopez 3, Ichiro Suzuki 3, Raul Ibanez 2, Ramon Santiago 2, Scott Spiezio 2, Randy Winn 2, Greg Dobbs 1, Justin Leone 1.

## TOP DRAFT CHOICES

3. **Matt Tuiasosopo,** SS, Woodinville (Wash.) H.S.
4. **Rob Johnson,** C, Houston.
5. **Mark Lowe,** RHP, Texas-Arlington.
6. **Jermaine Brock,** OF, Ottawa Hills H.S., Grand Rapids, Mich.
7. **Sebastien Boucher,** OF, Bethune-Cookman.
8. **Marshall Hubbard,** OF, North Carolina.
9. **Jeff Dominguez,** SS, Puerto Rico Baseball Academy, Carolina, P.R.
10. **Eric Carter,** RHP, Delaware State.

# TAMPA BAY DEVIL RAYS

## AMERICAN LEAGUE EAST DIVISION



## 2005 SEASON

### Devil Rays Schedule

Home games shaded.
All-Star Game July 12 at Detroit. Schedule subject to change.

**April**

| SUN | MON | TUE | WED | THU | FRI | SAT |
|---|---|---|---|---|---|---|
| 3 | 4 TOR | 5 TOR | 6 TOR | 7 | 8 OAK | 9 OAK |
| 10 OAK | 11 | 12 BAL | 13 BAL | 14 BAL | 15 BOS | 16 BOS |
| 17 BOS | 18 NYY | 19 NYY | 20 TEX | 21 TEX | 22 BOS | 23 BOS |
| 24 BOS | 25 | 26 TOR | 27 TOR | 28 TOR | 29 BAL | 30 BAL |

**May**

| SUN | MON | TUE | WED | THU | FRI | SAT |
|---|---|---|---|---|---|---|
| 1 BAL | 2 NYY | 3 NYY | 4 NYY | 5 NYY | 6 MIN | 7 MIN |
| 8 MIN | 9 CHW | 10 CHW | 11 CHW | 12 KC | 13 KC | 14 KC |
| 15 KC | 16 | 17 DET | 18 DET | 19 DET | 20 FLA | 21 FLA |
| 22 FLA | 23 | 24 OAK | 25 OAK | 26 OAK | 27 SEA | 28 SEA |
| 29 SEA | 30 OAK | 31 OAK | | | | |

**June**

| SUN | MON | TUE | WED | THU | FRI | SAT |
|---|---|---|---|---|---|---|
| | | | 1 OAK | 2 | 3 SEA | 4 SEA |
| 5 SEA | 6 | 7 CIN | 8 CIN | 9 CIN | 10 PIT | 11 PIT |
| 12 PIT | 13 MIL | 14 MIL | 15 MIL | 16 | 17 STL | 18 STL |
| 19 STL | 20 NYY | 21 NYY | 22 NYY | 23 NYY | 24 FLA | 25 FLA |
| 26 FLA | 27 TOR | 28 TOR | 29 TOR | 30 | | |

**July**

| SUN | MON | TUE | WED | THU | FRI | SAT |
|---|---|---|---|---|---|---|
| | | | | | 1 MIN | 2 MIN |
| 3 MIN | 4 CHW | 5 CHW | 6 CHW | 7 DET | 8 DET | 9 DET |
| 10 DET | 11 | 12 All-Star | 13 | 14 TOR | 15 TOR | 16 TOR |
| 17 TOR | 18 BOS | 19 BOS | 20 BOS | 21 | 22 BAL | 23 BAL |
| 24 BAL | 25 BOS | 26 BOS | 27 BOS | 28 KC | 29 KC | 30 KC |
| 31 KC | | | | | | |

**August**

| SUN | MON | TUE | WED | THU | FRI | SAT |
|---|---|---|---|---|---|---|
| | 1 | 2 TEX | 3 TEX | 4 TEX | 5 ANA | 6 ANA |
| 7 ANA | 8 | 9 BAL | 10 BAL | 11 BAL | 12 CLE | 13 CLE |
| 14 CLE | 15 NYY | 16 NYY | 17 NYY | 18 | 19 TEX | 20 TEX |
| 21 TEX | 22 CLE | 23 CLE | 24 CLE | 25 CLE | 26 ANA | 27 ANA |
| 28 ANA | 29 BOS | 30 BOS | 31 BOS | | | |

**September**

| SUN | MON | TUE | WED | THU | FRI | SAT |
|---|---|---|---|---|---|---|
| | | | | 1 BOS | 2 TOR | 3 TOR |
| 4 TOR | 5 | 6 NYY | 7 NYY | 8 NYY | 9 TOR | 10 TOR |
| 11 TOR | 12 | 13 NYY | 14 NYY | 15 NYY | 16 BAL | 17 BAL |
| 18 BAL | 19 BOS | 20 BOS | 21 BOS | 22 | 23 ANA | 24 ANA |
| 25 ANA | 26 | 27 CLE | 28 CLE | 29 CLE | 30 BAL | |

**October**

| SUN | MON | TUE | WED | THU | FRI | SAT |
|---|---|---|---|---|---|---|
| | | | | | | 1 BAL |
| 2 BAL | 3 | 4 | 5 | 6 | 7 | 8 |

Home games shaded. All-Star Game July 12 at Detroit. Schedule subject to change.

### CLUB DIRECTORY

**Managing general partner/CEO**
Vincent J. Naimoli

**Sr. v.p. baseball operations/g.m.**
Chuck LaMar

**Assistant general managers**
Bart Braun, Scott Proefrock

**Senior baseball advisor**
Don Zimmer

**Special assistant to the g.m.**
Rick Williams, Tim Wilken

**Vice president of public relations**
Rick Vaughn

**Vice president of community relations**
Roni Costello

**Director of scouting and player personnel**
Cam Bonifay

**Director of media relations**
Chris Costello

### MINOR LEAGUE AFFILIATES

| Class | Team | League | Manager |
|---|---|---|---|
| AAA | Durham | International | Bill Evers |
| AA | Montgomery | Southern | Charlie Montoyo |
| Advanced A | Visalia | California | Mako Oliveras |
| A | Southwest Michigan | Midwest | Steve Livesey |
| Short-Season A | Hudson Valley | New York-Penn | Dave Howard |
| Advanced Rookie | Princeton | Appalachian | Jamie Nelson |

### BROADCAST INFORMATION

**Radio:** WHNZ-AM (1250).
**Television:** PAX TV.
**Cable TV:** Fox Sports Net Florida

### SPRING TRAINING

**Ballpark (city):** Progress Energy Park Home of Al Lang Field (St. Petersburg, Fla.).
**Ticket information:** 727-825-3250.

**For more on the Devil Rays, go to msn.foxsports.com/mlb/teams.**

Baldelli

## SPRING TRAINING ROSTER

**Manager**—Lou Piniella (14).
**Coaches**—Lee Elia (4), Tom Foley (6), Billy Hatcher (2), Chuck Hernandez (55), John McLaren (7), Matt Sinatro (15).

| No. | PITCHERS | B/T | Ht./Wt. | Age* | 2004 Clubs |
|---|---|---|---|---|---|
| 28 | Baez, Danys | R/R | 6-3/225 | 27 | Tampa Bay |
| 41 | Bell, Rob | R/R | 6-5/225 | 28 | Durham, Tampa Bay |
| 45 | Brazelton, Dewon | R/R | 6-4/214 | 24 | Durham, Tampa Bay |
| 38 | Carter, Lance | R/R | 6-1/190 | 30 | Tampa Bay |
| 49 | Colome, Jesus | R/R | 6-4/205 | 27 | Durham, Tampa Bay |
| | Diaz, Jose | R/R | 6-0/225 | 24 | Binghamton, Montgomery |
| | Garcia, Angel | R/R | 6-7/220 | 21 | G.C. Twins, Quad City |
| | Hammel, Jason | R/R | 6-6/200 | 22 | Charleston-SC, Bakersfield |
| 58 | Harper, Travis | L/R | 6-4/192 | 28 | Durham, Tampa Bay |
| 30 | Hendrickson, Mark | L/L | 6-9/230 | 30 | Tampa Bay |
| | Hines, Carlos | R/R | 6-3/190 | 24 | Montgomery |
| 57 | Kazmir, Scott | L/L | 6-0/170 | 21 | St. Lucie, Binghamton, Montgomery, Tampa Bay |
| 37 | McClung, Seth | L/R | 6-6/235 | 24 | Montgomery, Charleston-SC, Durham |
| 51 | Miller, Trever | R/L | 6-3/200 | 31 | Tampa Bay |
| 47 | Nunez, Franklin | R/R | 6-0/175 | 28 | Montgomery, Durham, Tampa Bay |
| 46 | Seay, Bobby | L/L | 6-2/235 | 26 | Durham, Tampa Bay |
| | Seddon, Chris | L/L | 6-3/190 | 21 | Bakersfield, Montgomery |
| 36 | Sosa, Jorge | B/R | 6-2/170 | 27 | Durham, Tampa Bay |
| | Stokes, Brian | R/R | 6-1/203 | 25 | Did Not Play |
| 48 | Switzer, Jon | L/L | 6-3/191 | 25 | Did Not Play |
| 40 | Waechter, Doug | R/R | 6-4/209 | 24 | Durham, Tampa Bay |
| 53 | Webb, John | R/R | 6-3/220 | 225 | Montgomery, Durham, Tampa Bay |

| No. | CATCHERS | B/T | Ht./Wt. | Age* | 2004 Clubs |
|---|---|---|---|---|---|
| | Cash, Kevin | R/R | 6-0/185 | 27 | Toronto |
| 44 | Hall, Toby | R/R | 6-3/240 | 29 | Tampa Bay |
| | LaForest, Pete | L/R | 6-2/208 | 27 | Durham |

| No. | INFIELDERS | B/T | Ht./Wt. | Age* | 2004 Clubs |
|---|---|---|---|---|---|
| 59 | Cantu, Jorge | R/R | 6-1/184 | 23 | Durham, Tampa Bay |
| | Gonzalez, Alex S. | R/R | 6-0/200 | 31 | Iowa, Chicago N.L., Montreal, San Diego |
| 19 | Huff, Aubrey | L/R | 6-4/231 | 28 | Tampa Bay |
| 23 | Lugo, Julio | R/R | 6-1/170 | 29 | Tampa Bay |
| 33 | Perez, Eduardo | R/R | 6-4/240 | 35 | Tampa Bay |
| | Phelps, Josh | R/R | 6-3/220 | 26 | Toronto, Cleveland |
| 9 | Upton, B.J. | R/R | 6-3/180 | 20 | Montgomery, Durham, Tampa Bay |

| No. | OUTFIELDERS | B/T | Ht./Wt. | Age* | 2004 Clubs |
|---|---|---|---|---|---|
| 5 | Baldelli, Rocco | R/R | 6-4/187 | 23 | Tampa Bay |
| 13 | Crawford, Carl | L/L | 6-2/219 | 23 | Tampa Bay |
| 22 | Cruz Jr., Jose | B/R | 6-0/210 | 30 | Tampa Bay |
| 25 | Diaz, Matt | R/R | 6-1/206 | 27 | Durham, Tampa Bay |
| 43 | Gathright, Joey | L/R | 5-10/170 | 23 | Montgomery, Tampa Bay, Durham |
| | Gomes, Jonny | R/R | 6-1/205 | 24 | Tampa Bay, Durham |
| | Young, Delmon | R/R | 6-3/205 | 19 | Charleston-SC |

*Age as of April 1, 2005.

## BALLPARK INFORMATION

**Ballpark (capacity, surface)**
Tropicana Field (44,445, artificial)
**Address**
One Tropicana Drive
St. Petersburg, FL 33705
**Official website**
www.devilrays.com
**Business phone**
727-825-3137
**Ticket information**
727-825-3250
**Field dimensions (from home plate)**
To left field at foul line, 315 feet
To center field, 404 feet
To right field at foul line, 322 feet
**First game played**
March 31, 1998 (Tigers 11, Devil Rays 6)

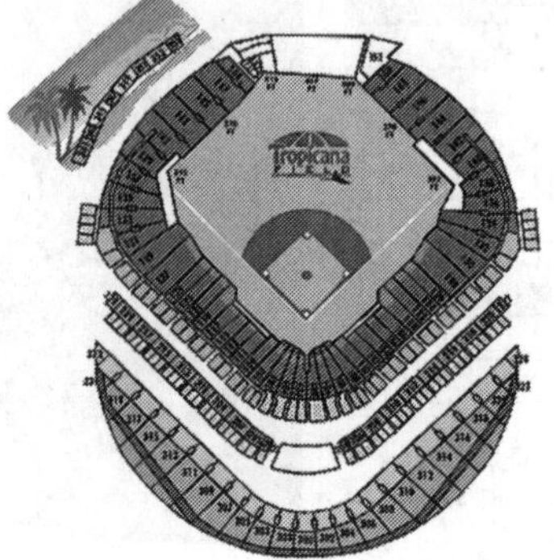

# 2004 REVIEW

## DAY BY DAY



| Date | Opp. | Res. | Score | (inn.*) | Hits | Opp. hits | Winning pitcher | Losing pitcher | Save | Record | Pos. | GB |
|---|---|---|---|---|---|---|---|---|---|---|---|---|
| 3-30^ | N.Y. | W | 8-3 | | 15 | 7 | Zambrano | Mussina | | 1-0 | T1st | ... |
| 3-31^ | N.Y. | L | 1-12 | | 6 | 11 | Brown | Gonzalez | | 1-1 | T1st | ... |
| 4-6 | N.Y. | W | 9-4 | | 14 | 4 | Zambrano | Mussina | | 2-1 | 1st | +0.5 |
| 4-7 | N.Y. | L | 2-3 | | 8 | 7 | Brown | Abbott | Rivera | 2-2 | T2nd | 0.5 |
| 4-9 | Bal. | W | 4-3 | (10) | 7 | 9 | Baez | Parrish | | 3-2 | 1st | +0.5 |
| 4-10 | Bal. | L | 3-11 | | 7 | 16 | Bauer | Gonzalez | | 3-3 | T1st | ... |
| 4-11 | Bal. | W | 10-1 | | 11 | 8 | Zambrano | DuBose | | 4-3 | T1st | ... |
| 4-14 | At N.Y. | L | 1-5 | | 7 | 7 | Brown | Hendrickson | | 4-4 | 3rd | 0.5 |
| 4-16 | Chi. | W | 3-0 | | 6 | 4 | Abbott | Wright | Baez | 5-4 | T1st | ... |
| 4-17 | Chi. | L | 1-4 | | 6 | 10 | Schoeneweis | Zambrano | Marte | 5-5 | 3rd | 1.0 |
| 4-18 | Chi. | L | 0-5 | | 2 | 10 | Loaiza | Gonzalez | | 5-6 | 4th | 2.0 |
| 4-20 | At Bal. | L | 1-9 | | 4 | 14 | Ponson | Hendrickson | | 5-7 | 4th | 3.0 |
| 4-21 | At Bal. | W | 7-3 | | 12 | 4 | Abbott | Riley | | 6-7 | 4th | 2.5 |
| 4-22 | At Bal. | L | 6-7 | | 7 | 9 | Parrish | Gaudin | Julio | 6-8 | 4th | 3.0 |
| 4-23 | At Chi. | L | 2-3 | (10) | 9 | 5 | Koch | Baez | | 6-9 | 4th | 4.0 |
| 4-24 | At Chi. | W | 4-1 | | 9 | 6 | Waechter | Wright | Baez | 7-9 | 4th | 3.5 |
| 4-25 | At Chi. | L | 5-6 | | 13 | 9 | Adkins | Miller | | 7-10 | 4th | 4.5 |
| 4-28 | At Bos. | L | 0-6 | | 5 | 12 | Schilling | Abbott | | 7-11 | 4th | 5.5 |
| 4-29# | At Bos. | L | 0-4 | | 3 | 8 | Kim | Zambrano | | 7-12 | | |
| 4-29$ | At Bos. | L | 3-7 | | 9 | 12 | Lowe | Moss | | 7-13 | 4th | 7.5 |
| 4-30 | Oak. | L | 2-4 | | 8 | 4 | Redman | Waechter | | 7-14 | 4th | 8.0 |
| 5-1 | Oak. | L | 5-6 | | 11 | 11 | Hammond | Carter | | 7-15 | 5th | 7.5 |
| 5-2 | Oak. | W | 8-2 | | 9 | 7 | Hendrickson | Hudson | | 8-15 | 4th | 6.5 |
| 5-3 | At Tex. | L | 0-9 | | 4 | 10 | Rogers | Abbott | | 8-16 | 4th | 6.5 |
| 5-4 | At Tex. | W | 5-4 | | 10 | 6 | Carter | Nelson | Baez | 9-16 | 4th | 5.5 |
| 5-5 | At Tex. | L | 1-6 | | 7 | 11 | Drese | Waechter | | 9-17 | 5th | 6.5 |
| 5-6 | At Ana. | L | 3-7 | | 8 | 11 | Sele | Gonzalez | Shields | 9-18 | 5th | 7.5 |
| 5-7 | At Ana. | L | 0-1 | | 3 | 8 | Lackey | Hendrickson | | 9-19 | 5th | 8.5 |
| 5-8 | At Ana. | L | 2-7 | | 3 | 9 | Colon | Abbott | | 9-20 | 5th | 9.5 |
| 5-9 | At Ana. | L | 4-8 | | 11 | 11 | Washburn | Zambrano | Rodriguez | 9-21 | 5th | 9.5 |
| 5-11 | Tex. | L | 4-5 | | 5 | 7 | Ramirez | Waechter | Cordero | 9-22 | 5th | 10.0 |
| 5-12 | Tex. | L | 8-9 | | 9 | 11 | Park | Halama | Cordero | 9-23 | 5th | 10.0 |
| 5-13 | Tex. | W | 6-3 | | 13 | 8 | Hendrickson | Dickey | Baez | 10-23 | 5th | 9.5 |
| 5-14 | At Cle. | L | 7-8 | (10) | 12 | 13 | White | Carter | | 10-24 | 5th | 10.5 |
| 5-15 | At Cle. | L | 7-9 | | 10 | 8 | Westbrook | Zambrano | | 10-25 | 5th | 11.0 |
| 5-16 | At Cle. | L | 0-10 | | 6 | 10 | Sabathia | Waechter | | 10-26 | 5th | 11.5 |
| 5-18 | Bos. | L | 3-7 | | 4 | 11 | Wakefield | Hendrickson | | 10-27 | 5th | 12.0 |
| 5-19 | Bos. | L | 1-4 | | 6 | 6 | Schilling | Bell | Foulke | 10-28 | 5th | 13.0 |
| 5-20 | Bos. | W | 9-6 | | 16 | 6 | Sosa | Lowe | Baez | 11-28 | 5th | 12.5 |
| 5-21 | Cle. | W | 5-3 | | 10 | 8 | Miller | Sabathia | Baez | 12-28 | 5th | 12.0 |
| 5-22 | Cle. | W | 6-3 | | 7 | 7 | Waechter | Westbrook | Sosa | 13-28 | 5th | 12.0 |
| 5-23 | Cle. | W | 5-4 | (10) | 8 | 9 | Harper | Riske | | 14-28 | 5th | 12.0 |
| 5-25 | Min. | W | 6-1 | | 9 | 5 | Zambrano | Lohse | | 15-28 | 5th | 12.0 |
| 5-26 | Min. | L | 2-4 | | 7 | 8 | Greisinger | Bell | Nathan | 15-29 | 5th | 13.0 |
| 5-27 | Min. | W | 5-4 | | 12 | 7 | Halama | Silva | Baez | 16-29 | 5th | 12.0 |
| 5-28 | N.Y. | L | 5-7 | | 12 | 9 | Vazquez | Waechter | Rivera | 16-30 | 5th | 13.0 |
| 5-29 | N.Y. | L | 3-5 | | 4 | 10 | Brown | Hendrickson | Rivera | 16-31 | 5th | 13.5 |
| 5-30 | N.Y. | W | 7-6 | | 13 | 11 | Zambrano | Lieber | Baez | 17-31 | 5th | 13.0 |
| 5-31 | At Min. | W | 7-3 | | 8 | 4 | Bell | Greisinger | | 18-31 | 5th | 12.0 |
| 6-1 | At Min. | L | 4-16 | | 9 | 14 | Silva | Abbott | | 18-32 | 5th | 13.0 |
| 6-2 | At Min. | W | 4-2 | | 11 | 4 | Waechter | Radke | Baez | 19-32 | 5th | 13.0 |
| 6-3 | At Min. | W | 5-2 | | 6 | 6 | Hendrickson | Santana | Baez | 20-32 | 5th | 13.0 |
| 6-4 | At Bal. | W | 8-7 | (11) | 14 | 6 | Carter | DeJean | Baez | 21-32 | 5th | 13.0 |
| 6-6 | At Bal. | L | 4-5 | | 12 | 11 | Lopez | Bell | Julio | 21-33 | 5th | 13.5 |
| 6-8 | S.F | L | 3-7 | | 6 | 10 | Williams | Waechter | | 21-34 | 5th | 14.5 |
| 6-9 | S.F | W | 4-3 | (10) | 8 | 11 | Baez | Walker | | 22-34 | 5th | 14.5 |
| 6-10 | S.F | W | 5-2 | | 9 | 5 | Zambrano | Rueter | Colome | 23-34 | 5th | 14.5 |
| 6-11 | Col. | W | 8-7 | (10) | 13 | 13 | Baez | Chacon | | 24-34 | 5th | 13.5 |
| 6-12 | Col. | W | 10-7 | | 8 | 10 | Halama | Harikkala | | 25-34 | 5th | 13.5 |
| 6-13 | Col. | W | 3-2 | | 11 | 9 | Colome | Chacon | | 26-34 | 5th | 13.5 |
| 6-15 | At S.D. | W | 5-2 | | 12 | 7 | Hendrickson | Lawrence | | 27-34 | 4th | 13.5 |
| 6-16 | At S.D. | W | 9-6 | | 15 | 11 | Zambrano | Linebrink | Baez | 28-34 | 3rd | 13.5 |
| 6-17 | At S.D. | W | 4-1 | | 5 | 10 | Gaudin | Eaton | Baez | 29-34 | 3rd | 12.5 |
| 6-18 | At Ari. | W | 6-2 | | 10 | 9 | Halama | Johnson | | 30-34 | 3rd | 11.5 |
| 6-19 | At Ari. | W | 11-4 | | 11 | 11 | Bell | Cormier | | 31-34 | 3rd | 11.5 |

| Date | Opp. | Res. | Score | (inn.*) | Hits | Opp. hits | Winning pitcher | Losing pitcher | Save | Record | Pos. | GB |
|---|---|---|---|---|---|---|---|---|---|---|---|---|
| 6-20 | At Ari. | W | 2-1 | | 8 | 7 | Hendrickson | Webb | Colome | 32-34 | 3rd | 10.5 |
| 6-22 | At Tor. | W | 5-1 | | 9 | 3 | Harper | Hentgen | | 33-34 | 3rd | 10.5 |
| 6-23 | At Tor. | L | 1-2 | (10) | 6 | 7 | Frasor | Colome | | 33-35 | 3rd | 10.5 |
| 6-24 | At Tor. | W | 19-13 | | 24 | 15 | Halama | Lilly | | 34-35 | 3rd | 10.5 |
| 6-25 | Fla. | W | 2-0 | | 3 | 2 | Brazelton | Burnett | Baez | 35-35 | 3rd | 10.0 |
| 6-26 | Fla. | W | 6-4 | | 7 | 7 | Sosa | Manzanillo | Baez | 36-35 | 3rd | 9.0 |
| 6-27 | Fla. | L | 4-11 | | 10 | 17 | Pavano | Gaudin | | 36-36 | 3rd | 10.5 |
| 6-28 | Tor. | W | 10-2 | | 14 | 7 | Zambrano | Halladay | | 37-36 | 3rd | 10.0 |
| 6-29 | Tor. | L | 0-4 | | 3 | 13 | Lilly | Halama | | 37-37 | 3rd | 11.0 |
| 6-30 | Tor. | W | 6-2 | | 11 | 10 | Brazelton | Towers | | 38-37 | 3rd | 11.0 |
| 7-1 | Tor. | L | 0-14 | | 5 | 20 | Batista | Hendrickson | | 38-38 | 3rd | 12.0 |
| 7-2 | At Fla. | W | 4-2 | | 14 | 8 | Colome | Pavano | Baez | 39-38 | 3rd | 11.0 |
| 7-3 | At Fla. | W | 6-1 | | 9 | 5 | Zambrano | Penny | | 40-38 | 3rd | 10.0 |
| 7-4 | At Fla. | L | 3-4 | | 7 | 9 | Burnett | Halama | Benitez | 40-39 | 3rd | 10.0 |
| 7-5# | At Bal. | L | 2-4 | | 4 | 11 | Ryan | Brazelton | Julio | 40-40 | | |
| 7-5$ | At Bal. | L | 2-8 | | 6 | 15 | Borkowski | Gonzalez | | 40-41 | 3rd | 11.5 |
| 7-6 | At Bal. | W | 3-1 | | 12 | 8 | Hendrickson | Lopez | Baez | 41-41 | 3rd | 10.5 |
| 7-7 | At Bal. | W | 13-3 | | 14 | 6 | Bell | Parrish | | 42-41 | 3rd | 9.5 |
| 7-8 | At N.Y. | L | 1-7 | | 6 | 9 | Contreras | Zambrano | Rivera | 42-42 | 3rd | 10.5 |
| 7-9 | At N.Y. | L | 4-5 | | 7 | 12 | Vazquez | Colome | Rivera | 42-43 | 3rd | 11.5 |
| 7-10 | At N.Y. | L | 3-6 | | 10 | 5 | Lieber | Brazelton | Rivera | 42-44 | 3rd | 12.5 |
| 7-11 | At N.Y. | L | 3-10 | | 9 | 15 | Hernandez | Hendrickson | | 42-45 | 3rd | 13.5 |
| 7-15 | Bal. | L | 4-5 | | 10 | 9 | Cabrera | Harper | Julio | 42-46 | 3rd | 14.5 |
| 7-16 | Bal. | W | 2-0 | | 9 | 3 | Halama | Bedard | Baez | 43-46 | 3rd | 13.5 |
| 7-17 | Bal. | L | 2-3 | | 7 | 7 | Lopez | Brazelton | Julio | 43-47 | 3rd | 14.5 |
| 7-18 | Bal. | W | 7-2 | | 11 | 4 | Hendrickson | Borkowski | | 44-47 | 3rd | 13.5 |
| 7-19 | N.Y. | W | 9-7 | | 13 | 8 | Carter | Sturtze | Baez | 45-47 | 3rd | 12.5 |
| 7-20 | N.Y. | L | 2-4 | | 6 | 6 | Contreras | Zambrano | Rivera | 45-48 | 3rd | 13.5 |
| 7-21 | At Min. | L | 2-12 | | 8 | 17 | Radke | Halama | | 45-49 | 3rd | 14.5 |
| 7-22 | At Min. | L | 5-7 | | 6 | 6 | Romero | Harper | Nathan | 45-50 | 3rd | 15.5 |
| 7-23 | At Tor. | L | 4-7 | | 8 | 12 | Batista | Hendrickson | Frasor | 45-51 | 3rd | 16.5 |
| 7-24 | At Tor. | L | 2-4 | | 8 | 7 | Towers | Bell | Frasor | 45-52 | 3rd | 16.5 |
| 7-25 | At Tor. | L | 3-5 | | 9 | 7 | Bush | Zambrano | Ligtenberg | 45-53 | 3rd | 16.5 |
| 7-27 | K.C. | W | 6-2 | | 10 | 7 | Brazelton | May | | 46-53 | 3rd | 17.0 |
| 7-28 | K.C. | W | 10-1 | | 15 | 4 | Hendrickson | Gobble | | 47-53 | 3rd | 16.0 |
| 7-29 | K.C. | W | 2-0 | | 7 | 4 | Bell | Wood | Baez | 48-53 | 3rd | 15.0 |
| 7-30 | Tor. | L | 0-3 | | 2 | 8 | Towers | Halama | Frasor | 48-54 | 3rd | 16.0 |
| 7-31 | Tor. | W | 6-5 | | 8 | 10 | Sosa | Bush | Baez | 49-54 | 3rd | 16.0 |
| 8-1 | Tor. | W | 5-3 | | 9 | 6 | Brazelton | Douglass | Baez | 50-54 | 3rd | 16.0 |
| 8-2 | Bos. | L | 3-6 | | 4 | 8 | Wakefield | Hendrickson | Foulke | 50-55 | 3rd | 16.5 |
| 8-3 | Bos. | L | 2-5 | | 6 | 9 | Schilling | Bell | | 50-56 | 3rd | 16.5 |
| 8-4 | Bos. | W | 5-4 | | 6 | 8 | Harper | Arroyo | Baez | 51-56 | 3rd | 16.5 |
| 8-5 | Sea. | L | 2-4 | (11) | 6 | 10 | Atchison | Baez | | 51-57 | 3rd | 17.5 |
| 8-6 | Sea. | W | 2-1 | (10) | 9 | 2 | Harper | Nageotte | | 52-57 | 3rd | 17.5 |
| 8-7 | Sea. | L | 2-5 | | 4 | 12 | Villone | Hendrickson | Putz | 52-58 | 3rd | 18.5 |
| 8-8 | Sea. | W | 5-1 | | 15 | 9 | Bell | Moyer | Baez | 53-58 | 3rd | 18.5 |
| 8-9 | At Bos. | W | 8-3 | | 13 | 11 | Halama | Schilling | | 54-58 | 3rd | 17.5 |
| 8-10 | At Bos. | L | 4-8 | | 9 | 9 | Arroyo | Sosa | | 54-59 | 4th | 17.5 |
| 8-11 | At Bos. | L | 4-14 | | 11 | 15 | Lowe | Brazelton | | 54-60 | 4th | 18.5 |
| 8-12 | At Bos. | L | 0-6 | | 6 | 15 | Martinez | Hendrickson | | 54-61 | 4th | 19.5 |
| 8-13 | At Tex. | L | 3-5 | | 10 | 6 | Rogers | Bell | Cordero | 54-62 | 4th | 20.5 |
| 8-14 | At Tex. | L | 5-6 | | 10 | 8 | Brocail | Nunez | Cordero | 54-63 | 4th | 21.5 |
| 8-15 | At Tex. | L | 2-6 | | 7 | 7 | Drese | Sosa | | 54-64 | 4th | 21.5 |
| 8-17 | Ana. | W | 8-3 | | 9 | 9 | Brazelton | Escobar | | 55-64 | 4th | 20.5 |
| 8-18 | Ana. | L | 4-6 | | 5 | 8 | Colon | Hendrickson | | 55-65 | 4th | 20.5 |
| 8-19 | Ana. | L | 7-10 | | 13 | 12 | Lackey | Bell | Rodriguez | 55-66 | 4th | 21.5 |
| 8-20 | Oak. | L | 5-9 | | 8 | 14 | Harden | Sosa | Dotel | 55-67 | 4th | 21.5 |
| 8-21 | Oak. | L | 0-5 | | 5 | 9 | Zito | Halama | | 55-68 | 4th | 21.5 |
| 8-22 | Oak. | W | 2-1 | | 6 | 5 | Brazelton | Redman | Colome | 56-68 | 4th | 20.5 |
| 8-23 | At Sea. | W | 9-0 | | 10 | 5 | Kazmir | Madritsch | | 57-68 | 4th | 20.5 |
| 8-24 | At Sea. | W | 6-5 | | 11 | 7 | Bell | Franklin | | 58-68 | 3rd | 20.5 |
| 8-25 | At Sea. | W | 6-5 | | 9 | 7 | Harper | Atchison | Baez | 59-68 | 3rd | 19.5 |
| 8-27 | At Oak. | L | 7-8 | | 15 | 13 | Duchscherer | Hendrickson | Dotel | 59-69 | 3rd | 21.0 |
| 8-28 | At Oak. | L | 4-5 | | 5 | 8 | Hudson | Brazelton | Dotel | 59-70 | 3rd | 22.0 |
| 8-29 | At Oak. | L | 6-9 | | 12 | 12 | Dotel | Baez | | 59-71 | 3rd | 22.0 |
| 8-31 | Bal. | L | 6-10 | (12) | 11 | 17 | Groom | Carter | | 59-72 | 4th | 22.0 |
| 9-1 | Bal. | L | 0-8 | | 2 | 16 | Cabrera | Hendrickson | | 59-73 | 4th | 23.0 |
| 9-2 | Bal. | L | 2-13 | | 6 | 14 | Bedard | Brazelton | | 59-74 | 4th | 24.0 |
| 9-3 | Det. | L | 2-4 | | 4 | 7 | Bonderman | Kazmir | Yan | 59-75 | 4th | 24.0 |

| Date | Opp. | Res. | Score | (inn.*) | Hits | Opp. hits | Winning pitcher | Losing pitcher | Save | Record | Pos. | GB |
|---|---|---|---|---|---|---|---|---|---|---|---|---|
| 9-6! | At N.Y. | L | 4-7 | | 8 | 12 | Hernandez | Waechter | Quantrill | 59-76 | | |
| 9-7 | At N.Y. | L | 2-11 | | 10 | 16 | Lieber | Sosa | | 59-77 | 4th | 26.0 |
| 9-9! | At N.Y. | L | 1-9 | | 5 | 12 | Mussina | Brazelton | | 59-78 | | |
| 9-9& | At N.Y. | L | 5-10 | | 13 | 14 | Sturtze | Bell | | 59-79 | 4th | 28.0 |
| 9-10 | At K.C. | L | 5-8 | | 11 | 10 | Reyes | Nunez | Affeldt | 59-80 | 4th | 28.0 |
| 9-11 | At K.C. | W | 8-6 | | 13 | 11 | Bell | Serrano | Baez | 60-80 | 4th | 28.0 |
| 9-12 | At K.C. | W | 7-2 | | 15 | 10 | Sosa | Bautista | | 61-80 | 4th | 28.0 |
| 9-14 | At Bos. | W | 5-2 | | 10 | 5 | Kazmir | Martinez | Baez | 62-80 | 4th | 27.5 |
| 9-15 | At Bos. | L | 6-8 | | 8 | 12 | Myers | Nunez | Foulke | 62-81 | 4th | 28.5 |
| 9-16 | At Bos. | L | 4-11 | | 10 | 13 | Schilling | Hendrickson | | 62-82 | 4th | 29.0 |
| 9-17 | At Tor. | W | 11-4 | | 12 | 5 | Waechter | Towers | | 63-82 | 4th | 28.0 |
| 9-18 | At Tor. | L | 2-4 | | 3 | 7 | Bush | Ritchie | Batista | 63-83 | 4th | 29.0 |
| 9-19 | At Tor. | L | 7-9 | | 10 | 11 | Chulk | Kazmir | Speier | 63-84 | 4th | 30.0 |
| 9-20 | K.C. | L | 3-6 | | 8 | 9 | Anderson | Sosa | Affeldt | 63-85 | 4th | 30.0 |
| 9-21 | K.C. | W | 7-4 | | 14 | 8 | Hendrickson | Camp | Baez | 64-85 | 4th | 30.0 |
| 9-22 | K.C. | L | 6-7 | (10) | 14 | 9 | MacDougal | Sosa | Affeldt | 64-86 | 4th | 30.0 |
| 9-23 | At N.Y. | L | 3-7 | | 11 | 12 | Lieber | Ritchie | | 64-87 | 4th | 31.0 |
| 9-24 | Tor. | W | 4-2 | | 8 | 7 | Hendrickson | Towers | Baez | 65-87 | 4th | 31.0 |
| 9-25 | Tor. | W | 6-5 | | 6 | 5 | Baez | Batista | | 66-87 | 4th | 30.0 |
| 9-27 | Bos. | L | 3-7 | | 7 | 12 | Arroyo | Sosa | | 66-88 | 4th | 30.0 |
| 9-28 | Bos. | L | 8-10 | (11) | 12 | 13 | Mendoza | Baez | Foulke | 66-89 | 4th | 30.5 |
| 9-29 | Bos. | W | 9-4 | | 14 | 7 | Waechter | Martinez | Miller | 67-89 | 4th | 31.0 |
| 9-30! | Det. | L | 0-8 | | 4 | 16 | Bonderman | Brazelton | | 67-90 | | |
| 9-30& | Det. | W | 6-4 | | 11 | 8 | Harper | Dingman | Baez | 68-90 | 4th | 31.5 |
| 10-1 | At Det. | W | 4-1 | | 8 | 4 | Bell | Maroth | | 69-90 | 4th | 30.5 |
| 10-2 | At Det. | L | 1-5 | | 4 | 6 | Knotts | Kazmir | | 69-91 | 4th | 30.5 |
| 10-3 | At Det. | W | 7-4 | | 11 | 12 | Halama | Robertson | | 70-91 | 4th | 30.5 |

Monthly records: March (1-1), April (6-13), May (11-17), June (20-6), July (11-17), August (10-18), September (9-18), October (2-1).
*Innings, if other than nine. ^ At Tokyo, Japan. ! First game of a doubleheader. & Second game of a doubleheader. # Day separate admission. $ Night separate admission.

## RECORDS

**2004 regular-season record:** 70-91
**Position:** 4th in A.L. East
**Home:** 41-39 **Road:** 29-52
**A.L. East:** 26-49 **A.L. Central:** 19-17
**A.L. West:** 10-22 **N.L.** 15-3
**Vs. LH starters:** 25-21
**Vs. RH starters:** 45-70
**Grass:** 23-43 **Artificial:** 47-48
**Day:** 20-29 **Night:** 50-62
**1-Run:** 17-19 **X-inn.:** 6-7
**Doubleheaders:** 0-1-1
**Team record past five years:** 319-488 (.395, ranks 13th in league in that span)

## TEAM LEADERS

**Batting average:** Aubrey Huff (.297).
**At-bats:** Carl Crawford (626).
**Runs:** Carl Crawford (104).
**Hits:** Carl Crawford (185).
**Total Bases:** Aubrey Huff (296).
**Doubles:** Julio Lugo (41).
**Triples:** Carl Crawford (19).
**Home runs:** Aubrey Huff (29).
**Runs batted in:** Aubrey Huff (104).
**Stolen bases:** Carl Crawford (59).
**Slugging percentage:** Aubrey Huff (.493).
**On-base percentage:** Tino Martinez (.362).
**Wins:** Mark Hendrickson (10).
**Earned-run average:** Victor Zambrano (4.43).
**Complete games:** Mark Hendrickson (2).
**Shutouts:** None.
**Saves:** Danys Baez (30).
**Innings pitched:** Mark Hendrickson (183.1).
**Strikeouts:** Victor Zambrano (109).

## GAMES BY POSITION

**Catcher:** Toby Hall 119, Brook Fordyce 51, Robert Fick 3.
**First base:** Tino Martinez 114, Aubrey Huff 38, Robert Fick 10, Fred McGriff 6, Eduardo Perez 5, Geoff Blum 2, Damian Rolls 1, Randall Simon 1.
**Second base:** Rey Sanchez 87, Geoff Blum 52, Jorge Cantu 33, Julio Lugo 8, Damian Rolls 2, Jason Romano 1.
**Third base:** Aubrey Huff 87, Geoff Blum 59, Damian Rolls 19, B.J. Upton 13, Jorge Cantu 11, Jose Bautista 2, Eduardo Perez 1.
**Shortstop:** Julio Lugo 143, B.J. Upton 16, Rey Sanchez 4, Charles Gipson 2, Geoff Blum 1, Jorge Cantu 1.
**Outfield:** Jose Cruz Jr. 152, Carl Crawford 145, Rocco Baldelli 124, Damian Rolls 24, Robert Fick 21, Joey Gathright 16, Aubrey Huff 9, Jose Bautista 8, Geoff Blum 7, Matt Diaz 4, Eduardo Perez 3, Midre Cummings 2, Charles Gipson 2, Jason Romano 1, B.J. Upton 1.
**Designated hitter:** Robert Fick 34, Aubrey Huff 34, Tino Martinez 19, Fred McGriff 14, B.J. Upton 14, Rocco Baldelli 13, Midre Cummings 12, Randall Simon 6, Carl Crawford 5, Julio Lugo 5, Damian Rolls 5, Jorge Cantu 4, Matt Diaz 4, Jonny Gomes 4, Eduardo Perez 3, Geoff Blum 2, Jose Bautista 1, Brook Fordyce 1, Joey Gathright 1, Charles Gipson 1.

## TOP DRAFT CHOICES

1. **Jeff Niemann,** RHP, Rice.
2. **Reid Brignac,** SS, St. Amant (La.) H.S.
3. **Wade Davis,** RHP, Lake Wales (Fla.) H.S.
4. **Matt Spring,** C, Dixie State (Utah).
5. **Jacob McGee,** LHP, Edward Reed H.S., Sparks, Nev.
6. **Ryan Royster,** OF, Churchill H.S., Eugene, Ore.
7. **Fernando Perez,** OF, Columbia.
8. **Rhyne Hughes,** 1B Pearl River CC (Miss.).
9. **Joseph Muro,** RHP, Mt. San Antonio (Calif.).
10. **Matt Walker,** RHP, Central High School, Baton Rouge, La.

# TEXAS RANGERS

## *AMERICAN LEAGUE WEST DIVISION*

## 2005 SEASON

### Rangers Schedule

Home games shaded.
All-Star Game July 12 at Detroit. Schedule subject to change.

**April**

| SUN | MON | TUE | WED | THU | FRI | SAT |
|---|---|---|---|---|---|---|
| 3 | 4 | 5 ANA | 6 ANA | 7 ANA | 8 SEA | 9 SEA |
| 10 SEA | 11 ANA | 12 ANA | 13 ANA | 14 TOR | 15 TOR | 16 TOR |
| 17 TOR | 18 OAK | 19 OAK | 20 TB | 21 TB | 22 NYY | 23 NYY |
| 24 NYY | 25 | 26 SEA | 27 SEA | 28 SEA | 29 BOS | 30 BOS |

**May**

| SUN | MON | TUE | WED | THU | FRI | SAT |
|---|---|---|---|---|---|---|
| 1 BOS | 2 OAK | 3 OAK | 4 OAK | 5 | 6 CLE | 7 CLE |
| 8 CLE | 9 DET | 10 DET | 11 DET | 12 | 13 MIN | 14 MIN |
| 15 MIN | 16 CHW | 17 CHW | 18 CHW | 19 | 20 HOU | 21 HOU |
| 22 HOU | 23 | 24 KC | 25 KC | 26 KC | 27 CHW | 28 CHW |
| 29 CHW | 30 | 31 DET | | | | |

**June**

| SUN | MON | TUE | WED | THU | FRI | SAT |
|---|---|---|---|---|---|---|
| | | | 1 DET | 2 DET | 3 KC | 4 KC |
| 5 KC | 6 | 7 PHI | 8 PHI | 9 PHI | 10 FLA | 11 FLA |
| 12 FLA | 13 ATL | 14 ATL | 15 ATL | 16 | 17 WAS | 18 WAS |
| 19 WAS | 20 ANA | 21 ANA | 22 ANA | 23 | 24 HOU | 25 HOU |
| 26 HOU | 27 ANA | 28 ANA | 29 ANA | 30 ANA | | |

**July**

| SUN | MON | TUE | WED | THU | FRI | SAT |
|---|---|---|---|---|---|---|
| | | | | | 1 SEA | 2 SEA |
| 3 SEA | 4 BOS | 5 BOS | 6 BOS | 7 | 8 TOR | 9 TOR |
| 10 TOR | 11 | 12 All-Star | 13 | 14 OAK | 15 OAK | 16 OAK |
| 17 OAK | 18 NYY | 19 NYY | 20 NYY | 21 OAK | 22 OAK | 23 OAK |
| 24 OAK | 25 BAL | 26 BAL | 27 BAL | 28 BAL | 29 TOR | 30 TOR |
| 31 TOR | | | | | | |

**August**

| SUN | MON | TUE | WED | THU | FRI | SAT |
|---|---|---|---|---|---|---|
| | 1 | 2 TB | 3 TB | 4 TB | 5 BAL | 6 BAL |
| 7 BAL | 8 BOS | 9 BOS | 10 BOS | 11 NYY | 12 NYY | 13 NYY |
| 14 NYY | 15 | 16 CLE | 17 CLE | 18 CLE | 19 TB | 20 TB |
| 21 TB | 22 | 23 SEA | 24 SEA | 25 SEA | 26 MIN | 27 MIN |
| 28 MIN | 29 CHW | 30 CHW | 31 CHW | | | |

**September**

| SUN | MON | TUE | WED | THU | FRI | SAT |
|---|---|---|---|---|---|---|
| | | | | 1 KC | 2 KC | 3 KC |
| 4 KC | 5 MIN | 6 MIN | 7 MIN | 8 | 9 OAK | 10 OAK |
| 11 OAK | 12 BAL | 13 BAL | 14 BAL | 15 SEA | 16 SEA | 17 SEA |
| 18 SEA | 19 | 20 ANA | 21 ANA | 22 ANA | 23 OAK | 24 OAK |
| 25 OAK | 26 | 27 SEA | 28 SEA | 29 SEA | 30 ANA | |

**October**

| SUN | MON | TUE | WED | THU | FRI | SAT |
|---|---|---|---|---|---|---|
| | | | | | | 1 ANA |
| 2 ANA | 3 | 4 | 5 | 6 | 7 | 8 |

Home games shaded. All-Star Game July 12 at Detroit. Schedule subject to change.

### CLUB DIRECTORY

**Chairman of the board and owner**
Thomas O. Hicks

**President**
Jeff Cogen

**Exec. vice president, general manager**
John Hart

**Vice president, community dev./relations**
Norm Lyons

**Assistant general manager**
Jon Daniels

**Director of scouting**
Ron Hopkins

**Director of minor league operations**
John Lombardo

**Director, community relations**
Taunee Paur Taylor

**Senior Director, baseball media relations**
Gregg Elkin

### MINOR LEAGUE AFFILIATES

| Class | Team | League | Manager |
|---|---|---|---|
| AAA | Oklahoma | Pacific Coast | Bobby Jones |
| AA | Frisco | Texas | Darryl Kennedy |
| Advanced A | Bakersfield | California | Arnie Beyeler |
| A | Clinton | Midwest | Carlos Subero |
| Short-Season A | Spokane | Northwest | Greg Riddoch |
| Rookie | Arizona Rangers | Arizona | Pedro Lopez |

### BROADCAST INFORMATION

**Radio:** KRLD-AM (1080); KESS (1270), Spanish.
**TV:** KDFW (Channel 4); KDFI (Channel 27).
**Cable TV:** Fox Sports Southwest.

### SPRING TRAINING

**Ballpark (city):** Surprise Stadium (Surprise, Ariz.).
**Ticket information:** 623-594-5600.

**For more on the Rangers, go to msn.foxsports.com/mlb/teams.**

Cordero

## SPRING TRAINING ROSTER

**Manager**—Buck Showalter (11).
**Coaches**—Mark Connor (52), DeMarlo Hale (16), Orel Hershiser (55), Rudy Jaramillo (8), Steve Smith (1), Don Wakamatsu (18).

| No. | PITCHERS | B/T | Ht./Wt. | Age* | 2004 Clubs |
|---|---|---|---|---|---|
| 40 | Almanzar, Carlos | R/R | 6-2/200 | 31 | Texas |
| 53 | Benoit, Joaquin | R/R | 6-3/220 | 27 | Frisco, Texas |
| 46 | Brocail, Doug | L/R | 6-5/235 | 37 | Oklahoma, Frisco, Texas |
| 31 | Cordero, Francisco | R/R | 6-2/235 | 29 | Texas |
| 45 | Dickey, R.A. | R/R | 6-3/220 | 30 | Frisco, Texas |
| 41 | Dominguez, Juan | R/R | 6-2/195 | 24 | Oklahoma, Frisco, Texas |
| 38 | Drese, Ryan | R/R | 6-3/235 | 28 | Oklahoma, Texas |
| 50 | Francisco, Frank | R/R | 6-2/180 | 25 | Frisco, Texas |
| 57 | Hughes, Travis | R/R | 6-5/240 | 26 | Frisco, Oklahoma, Texas |
| 44 | Loe, Kameron | R/R | 6-8/225 | 23 | Frisco, Oklahoma, Texas |
| 32 | Mahay, Ron | L/L | 6-2/185 | 33 | Texas |
| | Masset, Nick | R/R | 6-4/230 | 22 | Stockton, Frisco |
| | Montero, Agustin | R/R | 6-3/210 | 27 | Jacksonville, Las Vegas |
| | Moreno, Edwin | R/R | 6-1/200 | 24 | Frisco |
| 61 | Park, Chan Ho | R/R | 6-2/210 | 31 | Rangers, Frisco, Oklahoma, Texas |
| 54 | Ramirez, Erasmo | L/L | 6-0/190 | 28 | Oklahoma, Texas |
| 57 | Regilio, Nick | R/R | 6-2/205 | 26 | Texas, Oklahoma |
| 30 | Rodriguez, Ricardo | R/R | 6-3/190 | 26 | Oklahoma, Texas |
| 37 | Rogers, Kenny | L/L | 6-1/211 | 40 | Texas |
| | Rupe, Josh | R/R | 6-2/195 | 22 | Spokane, Stockton, Frisco |
| 58 | Shouse, Brian | L/L | 5-11/190 | 36 | Oklahoma, Texas |
| | Wing, Ryan | L/L | 6-2/170 | 23 | Did Not Play |
| | Young, Chris | R/R | 6-10/250 | 25 | Frisco, Oklahoma, Texas |

| No. | CATCHERS | B/T | Ht./Wt. | Age* | 2004 Clubs |
|---|---|---|---|---|---|
| | Alomar Jr., Sandy | R/R | 6-5/235 | 38 | Chicago A.L. |
| 27 | Barajas, Rod | R/R | 6-2/220 | 29 | Texas |
| 6 | Laird, Gerald | R/R | 6-2/220 | 25 | Oklahoma, Texas |

| No. | INFIELDERS | B/T | Ht./Wt. | Age* | 2004 Clubs |
|---|---|---|---|---|---|
| 9 | Blalock, Hank | L/R | 6-1/200 | 24 | Texas |
| | Botts, Jason | R/R | 6-6/250 | 24 | Frisco |
| | Bourgeois, Jason | B/R | 5-9/185 | 23 | Frisco |
| 24 | Gonzalez, Adrian | L/L | 6-2/220 | 22 | Oklahoma, Texas |
| 12 | Soriano, Alfonso | R/R | 6-1/180 | 29 | Texas |
| 23 | Teixeira, Mark | B/R | 6-3/220 | 24 | Frisco, Texas |
| | Yan, Ruddy | B/R | 6-0/165 | 23 | Birmingham |
| 10 | Young, Michael | R/R | 6-1/190 | 28 | Texas |

| No. | OUTFIELDERS | B/T | Ht./Wt. | Age* | 2004 Clubs |
|---|---|---|---|---|---|
| 22 | Dellucci, David | L/L | 5-11/190 | 31 | Texas |
| | Hidalgo, Richard | R/R | 6-3/220 | 29 | Houston, New York N.L. |
| 14 | Matthews Gary | B/R | 6-3/225 | 30 | Oklahoma, Texas |
| 28 | Mench, Kevin | R/R | 6-0/225 | 27 | Frisco, Texas |
| 2 | Nivar, Ramon | R/R | 5-10/185 | 25 | Texas, Oklahoma |
| 17 | Nix, Laynce | L/L | 6-0/200 | 24 | Frisco |

*Age as of April 1, 2005.

## BALLPARK INFORMATION

**Ballpark (capacity, surface)**
Ameriquest Field in Arlington (48,915, grass)
**Address**
1000 Ballpark Way
Arlington, TX 76011
**Official website**
www.texasrangers.com
**Business phone**
817-273-5222
**Ticket information**
817-273-5100
**Field dimensions (from home plate)**
To left field at foul line, 332 feet
To center field, 400 feet
To right field at foul line, 325 feet
**First game played**
April 11, 1994 (Brewers 4, Rangers 3)

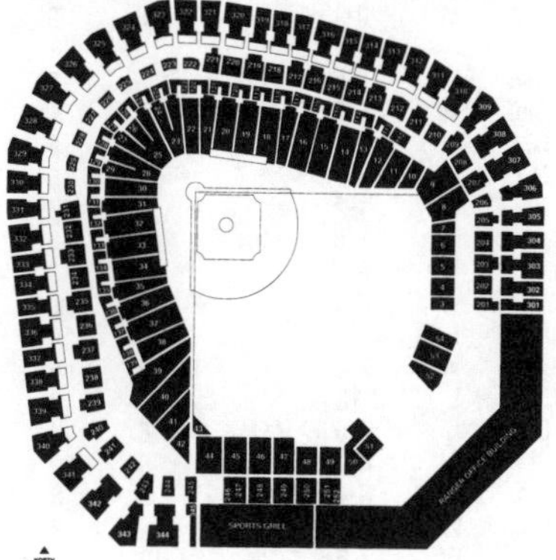

# 2004 REVIEW

## DAY BY DAY

| Date | Opp. | Res. | Score | (inn.*) | Hits | Opp. hits | Winning pitcher | Losing pitcher | Save | Record | Pos. | GB |
|---|---|---|---|---|---|---|---|---|---|---|---|---|
| 4-5 | At Oak. | L | 4-5 | | 11 | 9 | Bradford | Nelson | Rhodes | 0-1 | 4th | 1.0 |
| 4-6 | At Oak. | L | 1-3 | | 5 | 7 | Mulder | Park | Rhodes | 0-2 | 4th | 2.0 |
| 4-7 | At Oak. | W | 2-1 | | 7 | 5 | Lewis | Zito | Cordero | 1-2 | 3rd | 1.5 |
| 4-9 | Ana. | W | 12-4 | | 18 | 9 | Dickey | Ortiz | | 2-2 | 3rd | 1.0 |
| 4-10 | Ana. | W | 12-6 | | 18 | 8 | Rogers | Lackey | | 3-2 | T2nd | 1.0 |
| 4-11 | Ana. | L | 2-7 | | 8 | 13 | Colon | Park | | 3-3 | 3rd | 1.0 |
| 4-12 | Ana. | W | 7-6 | | 11 | 8 | Almanzar | Washburn | Cordero | 4-3 | T2nd | 0.5 |
| 4-13 | Oak. | L | 9-10 | | 16 | 16 | Zito | Callaway | Rhodes | 4-4 | 3rd | 1.5 |
| 4-14 | Oak. | L | 4-9 | | 12 | 11 | Redman | Dickey | | 4-5 | 3rd | 2.5 |
| 4-15 | Oak. | W | 7-2 | | 16 | 8 | Rogers | Harden | | 5-5 | 3rd | 1.5 |
| 4-16 | At Sea. | W | 5-0 | | 11 | 8 | Park | Meche | | 6-5 | T2nd | 1.5 |
| 4-17 | At Sea. | L | 1-4 | | 4 | 5 | Moyer | Lewis | Guardado | 6-6 | 3rd | 1.5 |
| 4-18 | At Sea. | L | 2-4 | | 6 | 10 | Pineiro | Ramirez | Guardado | 6-7 | 3rd | 2.5 |
| 4-20 | At Ana. | W | 6-3 | | 11 | 9 | Rogers | Ortiz | Cordero | 7-7 | T2nd | 1.0 |
| 4-21 | At Ana. | W | 4-1 | | 9 | 6 | Dickey | Lackey | Cordero | 8-7 | 2nd | 1.0 |
| 4-22 | At Ana. | L | 5-7 | | 8 | 8 | Colon | Park | Percival | 8-8 | T2nd | 2.0 |
| 4-23 | Sea. | W | 10-8 | | 15 | 12 | Drese | Pineiro | Cordero | 9-8 | T2nd | 1.0 |
| 4-24 | Sea. | W | 3-0 | | 9 | 7 | Powell | Garcia | Nelson | 10-8 | T1st | ... |
| 4-25 | Sea. | W | 14-6 | | 17 | 15 | Almanzar | Franklin | | 11-8 | T1st | ... |
| 4-27 | At K.C. | W | 3-2 | | 10 | 7 | Dickey | Affeldt | Cordero | 12-8 | T1st | ... |
| 4-28 | At K.C. | L | 3-5 | | 13 | 9 | Gobble | Rogers | MacDougal | 12-9 | T1st | ... |
| 4-29 | At K.C. | W | 9-7 | | 13 | 11 | Almanzar | Leskanic | Cordero | 13-9 | T1st | ... |
| 5-1! | Bos. | W | 4-3 | | 6 | 9 | Ramirez | Malaska | Cordero | 14-9 | | |
| 5-1& | Bos. | W | 8-5 | | 14 | 11 | Benoit | Martinez | Cordero | 15-9 | 1st | +1.0 |
| 5-2 | Bos. | W | 4-1 | | 7 | 4 | Dickey | Wakefield | Cordero | 16-9 | 1st | +1.0 |
| 5-3 | T.B. | W | 9-0 | | 10 | 4 | Rogers | Abbott | | 17-9 | 1st | +1.0 |
| 5-4 | T.B. | L | 4-5 | | 6 | 10 | Carter | Nelson | Baez | 17-10 | T1st | ... |
| 5-5 | T.B. | W | 6-1 | | 11 | 7 | Drese | Waechter | | 18-10 | T1st | ... |
| 5-7 | Det. | L | 7-8 | | 9 | 10 | Levine | Ramirez | Urbina | 18-11 | 2nd | 1.5 |
| 5-8 | Det. | W | 16-15 | (10) | 16 | 16 | Cordero | Urbina | | 19-11 | 2nd | 1.5 |
| 5-9 | Det. | L | 3-5 | | 3 | 6 | Robertson | Rogers | Urbina | 19-12 | 2nd | 2.5 |
| 5-11 | At T.B. | W | 5-4 | | 7 | 5 | Ramirez | Waechter | Cordero | 20-12 | 2nd | 1.5 |
| 5-12 | At T.B. | W | 9-8 | | 11 | 9 | Park | Halama | Cordero | 21-12 | 2nd | 1.5 |
| 5-13 | At T.B. | L | 3-6 | | 8 | 13 | Hendrickson | Dickey | Baez | 21-13 | 2nd | 1.5 |
| 5-14 | At Det. | L | 1-7 | | 2 | 9 | Knotts | Benoit | Yan | 21-14 | 2nd | 2.5 |
| 5-15 | At Det. | W | 6-1 | | 9 | 9 | Rogers | Robertson | | 22-14 | 2nd | 2.5 |
| 5-16 | At Det. | L | 1-3 | | 6 | 11 | Johnson | Drese | Urbina | 22-15 | 2nd | 2.5 |
| 5-18 | K.C. | L | 6-7 | | 9 | 16 | Sullivan | Dickey | Field | 22-16 | 2nd | 3.5 |
| 5-19 | K.C. | L | 3-5 | | 7 | 4 | Gobble | Park | Huisman | 22-17 | 2nd | 3.5 |
| 5-20 | K.C. | W | 6-3 | | 12 | 11 | Rogers | May | Cordero | 23-17 | 2nd | 2.5 |
| 5-21 | N.Y. | W | 9-7 | | 14 | 15 | Benoit | Brown | Cordero | 24-17 | 2nd | 2.5 |
| 5-22 | N.Y. | W | 4-3 | | 6 | 7 | Almanzar | Gordon | | 25-17 | 2nd | 2.5 |
| 5-23 | N.Y. | L | 3-8 | | 7 | 13 | Vazquez | Dickey | | 25-18 | T2nd | 3.5 |
| 5-25 | At Chi. | W | 7-4 | | 12 | 12 | Rogers | Schoeneweis | Cordero | 26-18 | 2nd | 2.5 |
| 5-26 | At Chi. | L | 0-4 | | 3 | 7 | Loaiza | Benoit | | 26-19 | 2nd | 2.5 |
| 5-27 | At Chi. | L | 0-9 | | 10 | 13 | Buehrle | Drese | | 26-20 | T2nd | 2.5 |
| 5-28 | At Tor. | L | 4-5 | | 10 | 9 | Lilly | Dickey | Frasor | 26-21 | T2nd | 2.5 |
| 5-29 | At Tor. | L | 2-6 | | 6 | 12 | Batista | Dominguez | | 26-22 | T2nd | 3.5 |
| 5-30 | At Tor. | W | 4-2 | | 9 | 9 | Rogers | Miller | Cordero | 27-22 | 2nd | 2.5 |
| 6-1 | At Cle. | W | 6-5 | (12) | 9 | 9 | Ramirez | White | Cordero | 28-22 | 2nd | 2.5 |
| 6-2 | At Cle. | W | 5-3 | | 10 | 9 | Almanzar | Betancourt | Cordero | 29-22 | 2nd | 2.5 |
| 6-4 | At N.Y. | L | 6-7 | | 9 | 9 | Brown | Powell | Rivera | 29-23 | 2nd | 3.0 |
| 6-5 | At N.Y. | W | 8-1 | | 12 | 6 | Dominguez | Lieber | | 30-23 | 2nd | 2.0 |
| 6-6 | At N.Y. | L | 1-2 | | 6 | 7 | Mussina | Drese | Rivera | 30-24 | 3rd | 2.0 |
| 6-7 | Pit. | W | 6-5 | (10) | 13 | 6 | Cordero | Johnston | | 31-24 | 3rd | 1.5 |
| 6-10! | Pit. | W | 9-7 | | 5 | 13 | Francisco | Meadows | Cordero | 32-24 | | |
| 6-10& | Pit. | W | 10-4 | | 13 | 10 | Rogers | Fogg | | 33-24 | 2nd | 0.5 |
| 6-11 | StL. | L | 7-12 | | 10 | 15 | Suppan | Dominguez | | 33-25 | 3rd | 1.5 |
| 6-12 | StL. | W | 7-2 | | 12 | 5 | Drese | Carpenter | | 34-25 | 2nd | 1.5 |
| 6-13 | StL. | L | 2-13 | | 6 | 14 | Williams | Dickey | | 34-26 | 2nd | 2.5 |
| 6-15 | At Cin. | L | 4-5 | (11) | 6 | 14 | Jones | Ramirez | | 34-27 | 3rd | 2.5 |
| 6-16 | At Cin. | L | 4-7 | | 9 | 10 | Norton | Francisco | | 34-28 | 3rd | 2.5 |
| 6-17 | At Cin. | L | 3-4 | | 7 | 8 | Van Poppel | Drese | Graves | 34-29 | 3rd | 2.5 |
| 6-18 | At Fla. | W | 8-1 | | 14 | 8 | Wasdin | Penny | | 35-29 | 2nd | 2.5 |
| 6-19 | At Fla. | W | 7-6 | | 12 | 9 | Dickey | Willis | Cordero | 36-29 | 2nd | 1.5 |

| Date | Opp. | Res. | Score | (inn.*) | Hits | Opp. hits | Winning pitcher | Losing pitcher | Save | Record | Pos. | GB |
|---|---|---|---|---|---|---|---|---|---|---|---|---|
| 6-20 | At Fla. | W | 4-2 | (11) | 6 | 7 | Mahay | Koch | | 37-29 | 2nd | 0.5 |
| 6-22 | Sea. | W | 10-2 | | 13 | 5 | Drese | Nageotte | | 38-29 | 1st | +0.5 |
| 6-23 | Sea. | W | 6-3 | | 12 | 8 | Bierbrodt | Franklin | Cordero | 39-29 | 1st | +1.0 |
| 6-24 | Sea. | W | 9-7 | (18) | 23 | 12 | Shouse | Moyer | | 40-29 | 1st | +1.0 |
| 6-25 | Hou. | W | 3-1 | | 6 | 3 | Rogers | Miller | | 41-29 | 1st | +2.0 |
| 6-26 | Hou. | W | 8-7 | | 16 | 10 | Almanzar | Miceli | Cordero | 42-29 | 1st | +2.0 |
| 6-27 | Hou. | L | 0-1 | | 4 | 6 | Oswalt | Drese | Lidge | 42-30 | 1st | +2.0 |
| 6-28 | At Sea. | W | 8-5 | | 16 | 9 | Rodriguez | Franklin | Cordero | 43-30 | 1st | +2.5 |
| 6-29 | At Sea. | L | 3-4 | | 6 | 8 | Pineiro | Benoit | Guardado | 43-31 | 1st | +1.5 |
| 6-30 | At Sea. | W | 9-6 | | 16 | 9 | Rogers | Nageotte | Cordero | 44-31 | 1st | +1.5 |
| 7-1 | At Sea. | L | 4-8 | | 6 | 12 | Blackley | Wasdin | | 44-32 | 1st | +0.5 |
| 7-2 | At Hou. | L | 5-7 | | 9 | 10 | Oswalt | Almanzar | Lidge | 44-33 | 1st | +0.5 |
| 7-3 | At Hou. | L | 8-10 | | 10 | 10 | Weathers | Brocail | Miceli | 44-34 | 2nd | 0.5 |
| 7-4 | At Hou. | W | 18-3 | | 16 | 8 | Benoit | Pettitte | | 45-34 | 2nd | 0.5 |
| 7-5 | At Cle. | W | 8-5 | | 11 | 8 | Rogers | Sabathia | Cordero | 46-34 | T1st | ... |
| 7-6 | At Cle. | L | 1-4 | | 6 | 7 | Lee | Bierbrodt | Riske | 46-35 | T1st | ... |
| 7-7 | At Cle. | W | 9-8 | | 14 | 11 | Mahay | Robertson | Cordero | 47-35 | 1st | +1.0 |
| 7-8 | At Cle. | W | 10-0 | | 11 | 3 | Rodriguez | Elarton | | 48-35 | 1st | +2.0 |
| 7-9 | At Bos. | L | 0-7 | | 3 | 13 | Arroyo | Benoit | | 48-36 | 1st | +2.0 |
| 7-10 | At Bos. | L | 6-14 | | 5 | 21 | Lowe | Rogers | | 48-37 | 1st | +1.0 |
| 7-11 | At Bos. | W | 6-5 | | 17 | 7 | Shouse | Foulke | Cordero | 49-37 | 1st | +2.0 |
| 7-16 | Tor. | W | 11-2 | | 15 | 9 | Drese | Halladay | | 50-37 | 1st | +1.5 |
| 7-17 | Tor. | W | 4-0 | | 6 | 8 | Rodriguez | Lilly | | 51-37 | 1st | +2.5 |
| 7-18 | Tor. | W | 7-5 | | 5 | 13 | Brocail | Chulk | Cordero | 52-37 | 1st | +2.5 |
| 7-19 | Chi. | L | 6-12 | | 8 | 17 | Schoeneweis | Benoit | | 52-38 | 1st | +2.5 |
| 7-20 | Chi. | W | 6-4 | | 10 | 7 | Almanzar | Marte | Cordero | 53-38 | 1st | +2.5 |
| 7-21 | Ana. | W | 3-2 | | 6 | 5 | Drese | Escobar | Cordero | 54-38 | 1st | +3.5 |
| 7-22 | Ana. | L | 1-11 | | 4 | 17 | Colon | Rodriguez | | 54-39 | 1st | +3.5 |
| 7-23 | At Oak. | W | 8-3 | | 12 | 8 | Rogers | Mulder | | 55-39 | 1st | +4.5 |
| 7-24 | At Oak. | L | 2-6 | | 4 | 11 | Saarloos | Dickey | | 55-40 | 1st | +3.5 |
| 7-25 | At Oak. | L | 2-9 | | 2 | 14 | Harden | Wasdin | | 55-41 | 1st | +2.5 |
| 7-26 | At Ana. | W | 6-1 | | 8 | 13 | Drese | Escobar | | 56-41 | 1st | +2.5 |
| 7-27 | At Ana. | L | 0-2 | | 1 | 8 | Colon | Regilio | Percival | 56-42 | 1st | +1.5 |
| 7-28 | At Ana. | L | 0-2 | | 3 | 10 | Lackey | Rogers | Percival | 56-43 | 1st | +0.5 |
| 7-29 | Oak. | L | 6-7 | | 11 | 11 | Bradford | Almanzar | Dotel | 56-44 | 2nd | 0.5 |
| 7-30 | Oak. | W | 7-5 | | 9 | 9 | Francisco | Bradford | Cordero | 57-44 | 1st | +0.5 |
| 7-31 | Oak. | L | 4-9 | | 6 | 11 | Zito | Drese | | 57-45 | 2nd | 0.5 |
| 8-1 | Oak. | L | 1-4 | | 6 | 9 | Redman | Regilio | Dotel | 57-46 | 2nd | 1.5 |
| 8-3 | At Det. | W | 5-4 | | 9 | 8 | Francisco | Robertson | Cordero | 58-46 | 2nd | 1.5 |
| 8-4 | At Det. | W | 8-0 | | 15 | 4 | Bacsik | Johnson | | 59-46 | 2nd | 0.5 |
| 8-5 | At Det. | W | 2-1 | | 5 | 8 | Drese | Yan | Cordero | 60-46 | 1st | +0.5 |
| 8-6 | At Bal. | L | 1-9 | | 7 | 8 | Bedard | Regilio | | 60-47 | 2nd | 0.5 |
| 8-7 | At Bal. | L | 1-3 | | 4 | 10 | Lopez | Erickson | Julio | 60-48 | 2nd | 0.5 |
| 8-8 | At Bal. | L | 5-11 | | 9 | 13 | Ponson | Rogers | | 60-49 | 2nd | 1.5 |
| 8-9 | At Bal. | L | 3-7 | | 8 | 9 | Borkowski | Bacsik | | 60-50 | 3rd | 2.5 |
| 8-10 | N.Y. | W | 7-1 | | 9 | 6 | Drese | Brown | | 61-50 | 2nd | 2.5 |
| 8-11 | N.Y. | L | 2-4 | | 5 | 6 | Sturtze | Regilio | Rivera | 61-51 | 3rd | 2.5 |
| 8-12 | N.Y. | L | 1-5 | | 5 | 10 | Hernandez | Erickson | | 61-52 | 3rd | 2.5 |
| 8-13 | T.B. | W | 5-3 | | 6 | 10 | Rogers | Bell | Cordero | 62-52 | 2nd | 1.5 |
| 8-14 | T.B. | W | 6-5 | | 8 | 10 | Brocail | Nunez | Cordero | 63-52 | 2nd | 1.5 |
| 8-15 | T.B. | W | 6-2 | | 7 | 7 | Drese | Sosa | | 64-52 | 2nd | 0.5 |
| 8-16 | Cle. | W | 5-2 | | 8 | 6 | Ramirez | Sabathia | Cordero | 65-52 | 2nd | 0.5 |
| 8-17 | Cle. | W | 16-4 | | 17 | 9 | Erickson | Lee | Brocail | 66-52 | 2nd | 0.5 |
| 8-18 | Cle. | W | 5-2 | | 9 | 12 | Rogers | Elarton | Cordero | 67-52 | 2nd | 0.5 |
| 8-20 | At K.C. | W | 5-3 | | 4 | 7 | Drese | Wood | Cordero | 68-52 | 2nd | 0.5 |
| 8-21 | At K.C. | W | 5-3 | | 10 | 10 | Francisco | Anderson | Cordero | 69-52 | 2nd | 0.5 |
| 8-22 | At K.C. | L | 2-10 | | 8 | 10 | Greinke | Erickson | | 69-53 | 2nd | 0.5 |
| 8-23 | Min. | L | 4-7 | | 7 | 11 | Santana | Rogers | | 69-54 | 3rd | 1.5 |
| 8-24 | Min. | W | 5-4 | | 11 | 7 | Cordero | Nathan | | 70-54 | 3rd | 1.5 |
| 8-25 | Min. | L | 5-8 | | 13 | 17 | Lohse | Drese | Nathan | 70-55 | 3rd | 2.5 |
| 8-26 | Min. | W | 8-3 | | 15 | 6 | Park | Mulholland | | 71-55 | 3rd | 2.5 |
| 8-27 | Bal. | W | 6-4 | | 9 | 10 | Wasdin | Bedard | Cordero | 72-55 | 3rd | 2.5 |
| 8-28 | Bal. | W | 4-3 | | 7 | 6 | Francisco | Ryan | Cordero | 73-55 | 3rd | 2.5 |
| 8-29 | Bal. | L | 6-7 | | 15 | 10 | Ponson | Young | Julio | 73-56 | 3rd | 3.5 |
| 8-31 | At Min. | L | 5-8 | (11) | 10 | 13 | Rincon | Almanzar | | 73-57 | 3rd | 4.5 |
| 9-1 | At Min. | L | 2-4 | | 8 | 11 | Crain | Cordero | Nathan | 73-58 | 3rd | 4.5 |
| 9-2 | At Min. | L | 0-2 | | 5 | 6 | Radke | Rogers | Nathan | 73-59 | 3rd | 5.5 |
| 9-3 | At Bos. | L | 0-2 | | 6 | 5 | Martinez | Wasdin | Foulke | 73-60 | 3rd | 6.5 |

| Date | Opp. | Res. | Score | (inn.*) | Hits | Opp. hits | Winning pitcher | Losing pitcher | Save | Record | Pos. | GB |
|---|---|---|---|---|---|---|---|---|---|---|---|---|
| 9-4 | At Bos. | W | 8-6 | | 10 | 5 | Young | Wakefield | Cordero | 74-60 | 3rd | 6.5 |
| 9-5 | At Bos. | L | 5-6 | | 8 | 11 | Schilling | Drese | | 74-61 | 3rd | 6.5 |
| 9-6 | Chi. | L | 4-7 | | 11 | 9 | Grilli | Park | | 74-62 | 3rd | 6.5 |
| 9-7 | Chi. | W | 10-3 | | 12 | 9 | Rogers | Contreras | | 75-62 | 3rd | 5.5 |
| 9-8 | Chi. | L | 2-5 | | 5 | 8 | Garcia | Wasdin | Takatsu | 75-63 | 3rd | 5.5 |
| 9-9 | Chi. | L | 3-7 | | 3 | 10 | Buehrle | Young | | 75-64 | 3rd | 6.0 |
| 9-10 | Tor. | W | 10-3 | | 17 | 8 | Drese | Batista | | 76-64 | 3rd | 5.0 |
| 9-11 | Tor. | W | 10-7 | | 12 | 12 | Mahay | Frasor | Cordero | 77-64 | 3rd | 5.0 |
| 9-12 | Tor. | W | 7-6 | | 8 | 12 | Brocail | Speier | Cordero | 78-64 | 3rd | 5.0 |
| 9-13 | At Oak. | L | 6-7 | (10) | 12 | 8 | Duchscherer | Cordero | | 78-65 | 3rd | 6.0 |
| 9-14 | At Oak. | W | 12-9 | | 15 | 13 | Brocail | Redman | | 79-65 | 3rd | 5.0 |
| 9-15 | At Oak. | W | 10-3 | | 14 | 10 | Drese | Mulder | | 80-65 | 3rd | 4.0 |
| 9-16 | At Oak. | L | 4-5 | | 7 | 12 | Harden | Rogers | Dotel | 80-66 | 3rd | 5.0 |
| 9-17 | At Ana. | L | 5-9 | | 6 | 15 | Colon | Park | | 80-67 | 3rd | 5.0 |
| 9-18 | At Ana. | W | 2-0 | | 5 | 6 | Ramirez | Escobar | Cordero | 81-67 | 3rd | 5.0 |
| 9-19 | At Ana. | W | 1-0 | | 7 | 6 | Young | Washburn | Cordero | 82-67 | 3rd | 5.0 |
| 9-21 | Oak. | W | 9-4 | | 10 | 11 | Drese | Mulder | | 83-67 | 3rd | 4.0 |
| 9-22 | Oak. | W | 5-3 | | 9 | 11 | Rogers | Zito | Cordero | 84-67 | 3rd | 3.0 |
| 9-23 | Oak. | W | 5-4 | | 10 | 10 | Nelson | Dotel | | 85-67 | T2nd | 2.0 |
| 9-24 | Sea. | L | 7-8 | | 11 | 14 | Villone | Cordero | Putz | 85-68 | T2nd | 3.0 |
| 9-25 | Sea. | W | 5-4 | | 8 | 8 | Dickey | Hasegawa | Cordero | 86-68 | T2nd | 2.0 |
| 9-26 | Sea. | L | 0-9 | | 3 | 13 | Baek | Drese | | 86-69 | 3rd | 2.0 |
| 9-27 | Ana. | L | 3-5 | | 5 | 7 | Colon | Rogers | Percival | 86-70 | 3rd | 3.0 |
| 9-28 | Ana. | L | 2-8 | | 3 | 11 | Escobar | Park | | 86-71 | 3rd | 3.0 |
| 9-29 | Ana. | L | 7-8 | (11) | 11 | 11 | Shields | Cordero | Percival | 86-72 | 3rd | 4.0 |
| 9-30 | Ana. | W | 6-3 | | 8 | 8 | Young | Lackey | Dickey | 87-72 | 3rd | 3.0 |
| 10-1 | At Sea. | L | 3-8 | | 5 | 18 | Villone | Drese | | 87-73 | 3rd | 4.0 |
| 10-2 | At Sea. | W | 10-4 | | 16 | 10 | Rogers | Moyer | | 88-73 | 3rd | 4.0 |
| 10-3 | At Sea. | W | 3-0 | | 9 | 4 | Park | Meche | Cordero | 89-73 | 3rd | 3.0 |

Monthly records: April (13-9), May (14-13), June (17-9), July (13-14), August (16-12), September (14-15), October (2-1).
*Innings, if other than nine. ! First game of a doubleheader. & Second game of a doubleheader.

## RECORDS

**2004 regular-season record:** 89-73
**Position:** 3rd in A.L. West
**Home:** 51-30 **Road:** 38-43
**A.L. East:** 25-18 **A.L. Central:** 23-20
**A.L. West:** 31-27 **N.L.** 10-8
**Vs. LH starters:** 29-24
**Vs. RH starters:** 60-49
**Grass:** 86-67 **Artificial:** 3-6
**Day:** 25-26 **Night:** 64-47
**1-Run:** 24-19 **X-inn.:** 5-4
**Doubleheaders:** 2-0-0
**Team record past five years:** 376-434 (.464, ranks 10th in league in that span)

## TEAM LEADERS

**Batting average:** Michael Young (.313).
**At-bats:** Michael Young (690).
**Runs:** Michael Young (114).
**Hits:** Michael Young (216).
**Total Bases:** Michael Young (333).
**Doubles:** Hank Blalock (38).
**Triples:** Michael Young (9).
**Home runs:** Mark Teixeira (38).
**Runs batted in:** Mark Teixeira (112).
**Stolen bases:** Alfonso Soriano (18).
**Slugging percentage:** Mark Teixeira (.560).
**On-base percentage:** Eric Young (.377).
**Wins:** Kenny Rogers (18).
**Earned-run average:** Ryan Drese (4.20).
**Complete games:** Ryan Drese, Kenny Rogers (2).
**Shutouts:** Ricardo Rodriguez, Kenny Rogers (1).
**Saves:** Francisco Cordero (49).
**Innings pitched:** Kenny Rogers (211.2).
**Strikeouts:** Kenny Rogers (126).

## GAMES BY POSITION

**Catcher:** Rod Barajas 105, Gerald Laird 49, Ken Huckaby 16, Danny Ardoin 6.
**First base:** Mark Teixeira 142, Herbert Perry 15, Adrian Gonzalez 11, Brad Fullmer 4, Rod Barajas 2.
**Second base:** Alfonso Soriano 142, Eric Young 20, Manny Alexander 11, Andy Fox 3.
**Third base:** Hank Blalock 159, Herbert Perry 6, Manny Alexander 3, Andy Fox 2, Eric Young 1.
**Shortstop:** Michael Young 158, Eric Young 8, Manny Alexander 7.
**Outfield:** Laynce Nix 114, Kevin Mench 109, David Dellucci 94, Gary Matthews Jr. 85, Eric Young 53, Brian Jordan 44, Jason Conti 21, Chad Allen 13, Mark Teixeira 7, Ramon Nivar 6, Andy Fox 2.
**Designated hitter:** Brad Fullmer 66, Eric Young 23, Herbert Perry 21, Brian Jordan 17, Kevin Mench 14, David Dellucci 9, Chad Allen 5, Alfonso Soriano 3, Mark Teixeira 2, Michael Young 2, Andy Fox 1, Adrian Gonzalez 1, Gary Matthews Jr. 1.

## TOP DRAFT CHOICES

1a. **Thomas Diamond,** RHP, New Orleans.
1b. **Eric Hurley,** RHP, Wolfson H.S., Jacksonville.
2. **K.C. Herren,** OF, Auburn (Wash.) H.S.
3. **Michael Schlact,** RHP, Wheeler H.S., Marietta, Ga.
4. **Brandon Boggs,** OF, Georgia Tech.
5. **Mike Nickeas,** C, Georgia Tech.
6. **Bill Susdorf,** OF, UCLA.
7. **Ben Harrison,** OF, Florida.
8. **Mark Roberts,** RHP, Oklahoma.
9. **Jim Fasano,** 1B, Richmond.
10. **Justin Maxwell,** OF, Maryland.

# TORONTO BLUE JAYS
## *AMERICAN LEAGUE EAST DIVISION*



## 2005 SEASON

### Blue Jays Schedule

Home games shaded.
All-Star Game July 12 at Detroit. Schedule subject to change.

**April**

| SUN | MON | TUE | WED | THU | FRI | SAT |
|---|---|---|---|---|---|---|
| 3 | 4 TB | 5 TB | 6 TB | 7 | 8 BOS | 9 BOS |
| 10 BOS | 11 OAK | 12 OAK | 13 OAK | 14 TEX | 15 TEX | 16 TEX |
| 17 TEX | 18 BOS | 19 BOS | 20 NYY | 21 NYY | 22 BAL | 23 BAL |
| 24 BAL | 25 | 26 TB | 27 TB | 28 TB | 29 NYY | 30 NYY |

**May**

| SUN | MON | TUE | WED | THU | FRI | SAT |
|---|---|---|---|---|---|---|
| 1 NYY | 2 BAL | 3 BAL | 4 BAL | 5 | 6 CHW | 7 CHW |
| 8 CHW | 9 KC | 10 KC | 11 KC | 12 | 13 CLE | 14 CLE |
| 15 CLE | 16 | 17 MIN | 18 MIN | 19 MIN | 20 WAS | 21 WAS |
| 22 WAS | 23 | 24 BOS | 25 BOS | 26 BOS | 27 MIN | 28 MIN |
| 29 MIN | 30 SEA | 31 SEA | | | | |

**June**

| SUN | MON | TUE | WED | THU | FRI | SAT |
|---|---|---|---|---|---|---|
| | | | 1 SEA | 2 OAK | 3 OAK | 4 OAK |
| 5 OAK | 6 CHC | 7 CHC | 8 CHC | 9 | 10 HOU | 11 HOU |
| 12 HOU | 13 STL | 14 STL | 15 STL | 16 | 17 MIL | 18 MIL |
| 19 MIL | 20 BAL | 21 BAL | 22 BAL | 23 BAL | 24 WAS | 25 WAS |
| 26 WAS | 27 TB | 28 TB | 29 TB | 30 | | |

**July**

| SUN | MON | TUE | WED | THU | FRI | SAT |
|---|---|---|---|---|---|---|
| | | | | | 1 BOS | 2 BOS |
| 3 BOS | 4 | 5 OAK | 6 OAK | 7 OAK | 8 TEX | 9 TEX |
| 10 TEX | 11 | 12 All-Star | 13 | 14 TB | 15 TB | 16 TB |
| 17 TB | 18 | 19 SEA | 20 SEA | 21 SEA | 22 KC | 23 KC |
| 24 KC | 25 | 26 ANA | 27 ANA | 28 ANA | 29 TEX | 30 TEX |
| 31 TEX | | | | | | |

**August**

| SUN | MON | TUE | WED | THU | FRI | SAT |
|---|---|---|---|---|---|---|
| | 1 | 2 CHW | 3 CHW | 4 CHW | 5 NYY | 6 NYY |
| 7 NYY | 8 DET | 9 DET | 10 DET | 11 DET | 12 BAL | 13 BAL |
| 14 BAL | 15 ANA | 16 ANA | 17 ANA | 18 | 19 DET | 20 DET |
| 21 DET | 22 NYY | 23 NYY | 24 NYY | 25 NYY | 26 CLE | 27 CLE |
| 28 CLE | 29 | 30 BAL | 31 BAL | | | |

**September**

| SUN | MON | TUE | WED | THU | FRI | SAT |
|---|---|---|---|---|---|---|
| | | | | 1 BAL | 2 TB | 3 TB |
| 4 TB | 5 BAL | 6 BAL | 7 BAL | 8 | 9 TB | 10 TB |
| 11 TB | 12 BOS | 13 BOS | 14 BOS | 15 | 16 NYY | 17 NYY |
| 18 NYY | 19 SEA | 20 SEA | 21 SEA | 22 SEA | 23 NYY | 24 NYY |
| 25 NYY | 26 BOS | 27 BOS | 28 BOS | 29 BOS | 30 KC | |

**October**

| SUN | MON | TUE | WED | THU | FRI | SAT |
|---|---|---|---|---|---|---|
| | | | | | | 1 KC |
| 2 KC | 3 | 4 | 5 | 6 | 7 | 8 |

Home games shaded. All-Star Game July 12 at Detroit. Schedule subject to change.

## CLUB DIRECTORY

**President and CEO**
Paul Godfrey
**Senior v.p., baseball & general manager**
J.P. Ricciardi
**Senior vice president, communications and external affairs**
Rob Godfrey
**Vice president, baseball**
Bob Mattick
**V.p., baseball operations & asst. g.m.**
Tim McCleary
**Assistants to the general manager**
Chris Buckley, Keith Law, Bart Given
**Special assistant to general manager**
Bill Livesey
**Director of player personnel**
Tony LaCava
**Manager of minor league operations**
Charlie Wilson
**Vice president, special projects**
Howard Starkman
**Director, player development**
Dick Scott
**Director, scouting**
Jon Lalonde
**Director, communications**
Jay Stenhouse
**Director of public relations**
Will Hill

## MINOR LEAGUE AFFILIATES

| Class | Team | League | Manager |
|---|---|---|---|
| AAA | Syracuse | International | Marty Pevey |
| AA | New Hampshire | Eastern | Mike Basso |
| Advanced A | Dunedin | Florida State | Omar Malave |
| A | Lansing | Midwest | Ken Joyce |
| Short-Season A | Auburn | New York-Penn | Dennis Holmberg |
| Advanced Rookie | Pulaski | Appalachian | Gary Cathcart |

## BROADCAST INFORMATION

**Radio:** The Fan (590).
**Cable TV:** Rogers SportsNet (RSN), TSN.

## SPRING TRAINING

**Ballpark (city):** Knology Park (Dunedin, Fla.).
**Ticket information:** 800-707-8269; 727-733-0429.

**For more on the Blue Jays, go to msn.foxsports.com/mlb/teams.**

Wells

## SPRING TRAINING ROSTER

**Manager**—John Gibbons (58).

**Coaches**—Brad Arnsberg, Mike Barnett (56), Brian Butterfield (55), Bruce Walton (52), Ernie Whitt.

| No. | PITCHERS | B/T | Ht./Wt. | Age* | 2004 Clubs |
|---|---|---|---|---|---|
| | Arnold, Jason | | 6-3/210 | 25 | Syracuse, Dunedin, New Hampshire |
| 43 | Batista, Miguel | R/R | 6-1/197 | 34 | Toronto |
| 49 | Bush, David | R/R | 6-2/212 | 25 | Syracuse, Toronto |
| 39 | Chacin, Gustavo | L/L | 5-11/193 | 24 | Syracuse, New Hampshire, Toronto |
| 50 | Chulk, Vinnie | R/R | 6-2/195 | 26 | Syracuse, Toronto |
| 54 | Frasor, Jason | R/R | 5-10/170 | 27 | Syracuse, Toronto |
| | Gaudin, Chad | R/R | 5-11/165 | 22 | Durham, Tampa Bay |
| 51 | Glynn, Ryan | R/R | 6-3/200 | 30 | Richmond, Syracuse, Toronto |
| 32 | Halladay, Roy | R/R | 6-6/230 | 27 | Toronto |
| 35 | League, Brandon | R/R | 6-3/192 | 22 | New Hampshire, Toronto |
| 46 | Ligtenberg, Kerry | R/R | 6-2/222 | 33 | Toronto |
| 31 | Lilly, Ted | L/L | 6-1/190 | 29 | Toronto |
| | McGowan, Dustin | R/R | 6-3/220 | 23 | New Hampshire |
| 34 | Miller, Justin | R/R | 6-2/209 | 27 | Syracuse, Toronto |
| | Perkins, Vince | L/R | 6-5/220 | 23 | Dunedin |
| | Peterson, Adam | R/R | 6-3/220 | 25 | New Hampshire, Toronto, Syracuse |
| | Ramirez, Ismael | R/R | 6-3/210 | 24 | Dunedin |
| | Rosario, Francisco | R/R | 6-0/195 | 24 | Dunedin, New Hampshire |
| 30 | Speier, Justin | R/R | 6-4/205 | 31 | Dunedin, Toronto |
| 7 | Towers, Josh | R/R | 6-1/188 | 28 | Syracuse, Toronto |
| **No.** | **CATCHERS** | **B/T** | **Ht./Wt.** | **Age*** | **2004 Clubs** |
| 16 | Quiroz, Guillermo | R/R | 6-1/202 | 23 | Syracuse, Toronto |
| 28 | Myers, Greg | L/R | 6-2/225 | 38 | Toronto |
| | Zaun, Gregg | B/R | 5-10/190 | 33 | Syracuse, Toronto |
| **No.** | **INFIELDERS** | **B/T** | **Ht./Wt.** | **Age*** | **2004 Clubs** |
| 8 | Adams, Russ | L/R | 6-1/180 | 24 | Syracuse, Toronto |
| | Crozier, Eric | L/L | 6-4/200 | 26 | Buffalo, Syracuse |
| | Hattig, John | S/R | 6-2/215 | 25 | New Hampshire, Portland |
| 11 | Hinske, Eric | L/R | 6-2/235 | 27 | Toronto |
| 1 | Hudson, Orlando | B/R | 6-0/185 | 27 | Toronto |
| | Koskie, Corey | L/R | 6-3/219 | 31 | Minnesota |
| 8 | McDonald, John | R/R | 5-11/175 | 30 | Cleveland |
| 41 | Menechino, Frank | R/R | 5-8/198 | 34 | Midland, Sacramento, Oakland, Toronto |
| | Tablado, Raul | R/R | 6-2/195 | 23 | Dunedin |
| **No.** | **OUTFIELDERS** | **B/T** | **Ht./Wt.** | **Age*** | **2004 Clubs** |
| 27 | Catalanotto, Frank | L/R | 5-11/195 | 30 | Toronto |
| | Griffin, John-Ford | L/L | 6-2/215 | 25 | New Hampshire |
| 21 | Gross, Gabe | L/R | 6-3/209 | 25 | Syracuse, Toronto |
| 37 | Johnson, Reed | R/R | 5-10/180 | 28 | Toronto |
| | Negron, Miguel | L/L | 6-2/170 | 22 | Dunedin |
| 15 | Rios, Alexis | R/R | 6-5/194 | 24 | Syracuse, Toronto |
| 10 | Wells, Vernon | R/R | 6-1/225 | 26 | Toronto |

*Age as of April 1, 2005.

## BALLPARK INFORMATION

**Ballpark (capacity, surface)**
SkyDome (50,516, artificial)

**Address**
One Blue Jays Way
Suite 3200
Toronto, Ontario M5V 1J1

**Official website**
www.bluejays.com

**Business phone**
416-341-1000

**Ticket information**
416-341-1234 and 1-888-OK GO JAY

**Field dimensions (from home plate)**
To left field at foul line, 330 feet
To center field, 400 feet
To right field at foul line, 330 feet

**First game played**
June 5, 1989 (Brewers 5, Blue Jays 3)

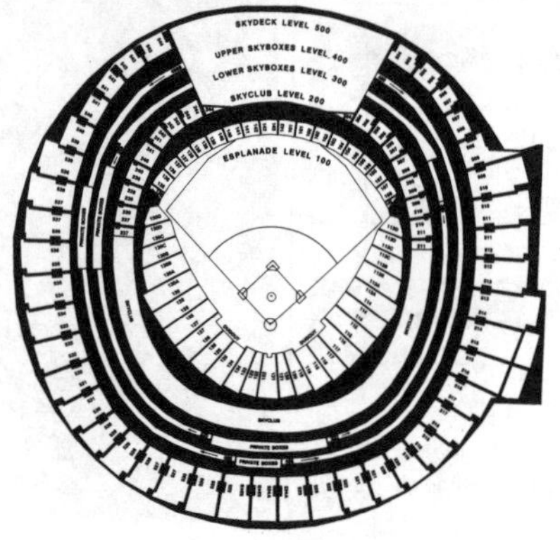

# 2004 REVIEW
## DAY BY DAY

| Date | Opp. | Res. | Score | (inn.*) | Hits | Opp. hits | Winning pitcher | Losing pitcher | Save | Record | Pos. | GB |
|---|---|---|---|---|---|---|---|---|---|---|---|---|
| 4-5 | Det. | L | 0-7 | | 8 | 11 | Johnson | Halladay | | 0-1 | T4th | 1.0 |
| 4-6 | Det. | L | 3-7 | | 6 | 12 | Maroth | Batista | Robertson | 0-2 | 5th | 1.5 |
| 4-7 | Det. | L | 3-6 | | 5 | 6 | Bonderman | Hentgen | | 0-3 | 5th | 2.0 |
| 4-9 | At Bos. | W | 10-5 | | 14 | 6 | Speier | Timlin | | 1-3 | 5th | 1.5 |
| 4-10 | At Bos. | L | 1-4 | | 5 | 9 | Martinez | Halladay | Foulke | 1-4 | 5th | 1.5 |
| 4-11 | At Bos. | L | 4-6 | (12) | 8 | 10 | Malaska | Lopez | | 1-5 | 5th | 2.5 |
| 4-13 | At Det. | W | 7-5 | | 10 | 10 | Adams | Patterson | Speier | 2-5 | 5th | 2.0 |
| 4-14 | At Det. | L | 3-5 | | 9 | 8 | Robertson | Lilly | Patterson | 2-6 | 5th | 2.5 |
| 4-15 | At Det. | W | 11-0 | | 12 | 8 | Halladay | Johnson | | 3-6 | 5th | 2.0 |
| 4-16 | Bal. | L | 2-11 | | 2 | 12 | Riley | Batista | | 3-7 | 5th | 2.5 |
| 4-17 | Bal. | L | 3-5 | | 6 | 12 | Ryan | Speier | Julio | 3-8 | 5th | 3.5 |
| 4-18 | Bal. | L | 0-7 | | 4 | 12 | DuBose | Hentgen | | 3-9 | 5th | 4.5 |
| 4-20 | Bos. | L | 2-4 | | 5 | 11 | Martinez | Halladay | Foulke | 3-10 | 5th | 5.5 |
| 4-21 | Bos. | L | 2-4 | | 6 | 8 | Wakefield | Lilly | Foulke | 3-11 | 5th | 6.0 |
| 4-22 | Bos. | W | 7-3 | | 14 | 10 | Adams | Schilling | | 4-11 | 5th | 5.5 |
| 4-23 | At Bal. | L | 3-11 | | 8 | 15 | DuBose | Towers | | 4-12 | 5th | 6.5 |
| 4-24 | At Bal. | W | 5-4 | (12) | 14 | 11 | Ligtenberg | DeJean | | 5-12 | 5th | 6.0 |
| 4-25 | At Bal. | W | 15-3 | | 17 | 7 | Halladay | Ponson | | 6-12 | 5th | 6.0 |
| 4-26 | At Min. | W | 6-1 | | 14 | 2 | Lilly | Radke | | 7-12 | 5th | 5.5 |
| 4-27 | At Min. | L | 4-7 | | 9 | 11 | Rincon | Speier | | 7-13 | 5th | 6.0 |
| 4-28 | At Min. | L | 5-9 | | 13 | 12 | Rincon | Frasor | | 7-14 | 5th | 7.0 |
| 4-29 | At Chi. | L | 4-6 | | 8 | 11 | Loaiza | Nakamura | Koch | 7-15 | 5th | 8.5 |
| 5-1! | At Chi. | L | 3-4 | (10) | 8 | 7 | Takatsu | Speier | | 7-16 | | |
| 5-1& | At Chi. | W | 10-6 | | 18 | 11 | Lilly | Wright | | 8-16 | 4th | 7.5 |
| 5-2 | At Chi. | L | 2-3 | | 11 | 6 | Garland | Batista | Koch | 8-17 | 5th | 7.5 |
| 5-3 | K.C. | L | 2-3 | (10) | 7 | 8 | Field | Adams | Cerda | 8-18 | 5th | 7.5 |
| 5-4 | K.C. | W | 5-4 | | 9 | 7 | Hentgen | May | Frasor | 9-18 | 5th | 6.5 |
| 5-5 | K.C. | W | 10-3 | | 14 | 12 | Halladay | Anderson | | 10-18 | 4th | 6.5 |
| 5-7 | Chi. | W | 5-4 | | 8 | 9 | Adams | Politte | | 11-18 | 4th | 7.0 |
| 5-8 | Chi. | W | 4-2 | | 7 | 8 | Frasor | Cotts | Adams | 12-18 | 4th | 7.0 |
| 5-9 | Chi. | W | 5-2 | | 9 | 8 | Miller | Loaiza | Ligtenberg | 13-18 | 4th | 6.0 |
| 5-10 | At K.C. | W | 9-3 | | 16 | 8 | Hentgen | Anderson | | 14-18 | 4th | 5.0 |
| 5-11 | At K.C. | L | 1-5 | | 6 | 8 | Camp | Halladay | | 14-19 | 4th | 6.0 |
| 5-12 | At K.C. | L | 3-4 | | 11 | 9 | Field | Adams | | 14-20 | 4th | 6.0 |
| 5-13 | Bos. | W | 12-6 | | 17 | 13 | Batista | Schilling | | 15-20 | 4th | 5.5 |
| 5-14 | Bos. | L | 3-9 | | 4 | 10 | Embree | Ligtenberg | | 15-21 | 4th | 6.5 |
| 5-15 | Bos. | L | 0-4 | | 4 | 6 | Arroyo | Hentgen | | 15-22 | 4th | 7.0 |
| 5-16 | Bos. | W | 3-1 | | 8 | 8 | Halladay | Martinez | Adams | 16-22 | 4th | 6.5 |
| 5-17 | Min. | L | 5-9 | | 9 | 13 | Rincon | Nakamura | Fultz | 16-23 | 4th | 7.0 |
| 5-18 | Min. | W | 5-3 | | 11 | 5 | Batista | Santana | Adams | 17-23 | 4th | 6.5 |
| 5-19 | Min. | L | 5-6 | | 8 | 9 | Fultz | Adams | Nathan | 17-24 | 4th | 7.5 |
| 5-21 | At Bos. | L | 5-11 | | 7 | 11 | Timlin | Nakamura | | 17-25 | 4th | 8.0 |
| 5-22 | At Bos. | L | 2-5 | | 6 | 11 | Martinez | Ligtenberg | Foulke | 17-26 | 4th | 9.0 |
| 5-23 | At Bos. | L | 2-7 | | 7 | 7 | Wakefield | Batista | | 17-27 | 4th | 10.0 |
| 5-24 | Ana. | W | 6-5 | (10) | 10 | 12 | Frasor | Weber | | 18-27 | 4th | 9.5 |
| 5-26 | Ana. | W | 6-5 | | 12 | 8 | Adams | Percival | | 19-27 | 4th | 10.0 |
| 5-27 | Ana. | W | 3-2 | | 8 | 4 | Halladay | Washburn | Frasor | 20-27 | 4th | 9.0 |
| 5-28 | Tex. | W | 5-4 | | 9 | 10 | Lilly | Dickey | Frasor | 21-27 | 4th | 9.0 |
| 5-29 | Tex. | W | 6-2 | | 12 | 6 | Batista | Dominguez | | 22-27 | 4th | 8.5 |
| 5-30 | Tex. | L | 2-4 | | 9 | 9 | Rogers | Miller | Cordero | 22-28 | 4th | 9.0 |
| 5-31 | At Sea. | L | 2-6 | | 7 | 10 | Moyer | Hentgen | | 22-29 | 4th | 9.0 |
| 6-1 | At Sea. | W | 6-5 | | 8 | 9 | Lopez | Nageotte | Frasor | 23-29 | 4th | 9.0 |
| 6-2 | At Sea. | W | 5-3 | | 7 | 10 | Lilly | Pineiro | Ligtenberg | 24-29 | 4th | 9.0 |
| 6-3 | At Oak. | L | 1-2 | (11) | 6 | 7 | Bradford | Adams | | 24-30 | 4th | 10.0 |
| 6-4 | At Oak. | W | 6-1 | | 10 | 8 | Towers | Bradford | Chulk | 25-30 | 4th | 10.0 |
| 6-5 | At Oak. | L | 0-4 | | 8 | 4 | Hudson | Hentgen | | 25-31 | 4th | 10.0 |
| 6-6 | At Oak. | L | 3-8 | | 5 | 10 | Redman | Kershner | | 25-32 | 4th | 11.0 |
| 6-8 | L.A. | W | 7-1 | | 10 | 8 | Lilly | Nomo | | 26-32 | 4th | 11.0 |
| 6-9 | L.A. | W | 4-0 | | 7 | 4 | Batista | Lima | | 27-32 | 4th | 11.0 |
| 6-10 | L.A. | L | 1-6 | | 6 | 14 | Ishii | Towers | | 27-33 | 4th | 12.0 |
| 6-11 | Ari. | L | 2-3 | | 8 | 10 | Choate | Frasor | Valverde | 27-34 | 4th | 12.0 |
| 6-12 | Ari. | W | 15-4 | | 15 | 8 | Halladay | Good | Chulk | 28-34 | 4th | 12.0 |
| 6-13 | Ari. | L | 3-5 | | 8 | 8 | Johnson | Lilly | Valverde | 28-35 | 4th | 13.0 |
| 6-15 | At S.F | L | 3-4 | | 12 | 7 | Schmidt | Batista | Herges | 28-36 | 5th | 14.0 |
| 6-16 | At S.F | L | 2-10 | | 9 | 13 | Rueter | Hentgen | | 28-37 | 5th | 15.0 |
| 6-17 | At S.F | L | 5-8 | | 10 | 10 | Brower | Speier | Herges | 28-38 | 5th | 15.0 |

| Date | Opp. | Res. | Score | (inn.*) | Hits | Opp. hits | Winning pitcher | Losing pitcher | Save | Record | Pos. | GB |
|---|---|---|---|---|---|---|---|---|---|---|---|---|
| 6-18 | At S.D. | W | 3-2 | | 7 | 6 | Lilly | Wells | Frasor | 29-38 | 4th | 14.0 |
| 6-19 | At S.D. | L | 2-3 | | 7 | 8 | Linebrink | Speier | Hoffman | 29-39 | 4th | 15.0 |
| 6-20 | At S.D. | W | 3-0 | | 10 | 7 | Batista | Lawrence | Frasor | 30-39 | 4th | 14.0 |
| 6-22 | T.B. | L | 1-5 | | 3 | 9 | Harper | Hentgen | | 30-40 | 4th | 15.0 |
| 6-23 | T.B. | W | 2-1 | (10) | 7 | 6 | Frasor | Colome | | 31-40 | 4th | 14.0 |
| 6-24 | T.B. | L | 13-19 | | 15 | 24 | Halama | Lilly | | 31-41 | 4th | 15.0 |
| 6-25 | Mon. | W | 3-1 | | 9 | 8 | Towers | Day | Frasor | 32-41 | 4th | 14.5 |
| 6-26 | Mon. | W | 10-5 | | 13 | 9 | Batista | Downs | | 33-41 | 4th | 13.5 |
| 6-27 | Mon. | L | 4-9 | | 9 | 8 | Hernandez | Hentgen | | 33-42 | 4th | 15.0 |
| 6-28 | At T.B. | L | 2-10 | | 7 | 14 | Zambrano | Halladay | | 33-43 | 4th | 15.5 |
| 6-29 | At T.B. | W | 4-0 | | 13 | 3 | Lilly | Halama | | 34-43 | 4th | 15.5 |
| 6-30 | At T.B. | L | 2-6 | | 10 | 11 | Brazelton | Towers | | 34-44 | 4th | 16.5 |
| 7-1 | At T.B. | W | 14-0 | | 20 | 5 | Batista | Hendrickson | | 35-44 | 4th | 16.5 |
| 7-2@ | At Mon. | L | 0-2 | | 4 | 7 | Hernandez | Bush | | 35-45 | 5th | 16.5 |
| 7-3@ | At Mon. | W | 2-0 | | 8 | 6 | Halladay | Armas | Frasor | 36-45 | 4th | 15.5 |
| 7-4@ | At Mon. | L | 4-6 | | 9 | 10 | Hill | Lilly | Horgan | 36-46 | 4th | 15.5 |
| 7-6 | Sea. | W | 7-6 | | 12 | 10 | Batista | Moyer | Frasor | 37-46 | 4th | 15.0 |
| 7-7 | Sea. | W | 12-4 | | 11 | 13 | Towers | Blackley | | 38-46 | 4th | 14.0 |
| 7-8 | Sea. | W | 10-8 | | 17 | 14 | Speier | Guardado | | 39-46 | 4th | 14.0 |
| 7-9 | Ana. | L | 4-5 | | 5 | 16 | Colon | Halladay | Percival | 39-47 | 4th | 15.0 |
| 7-10 | Ana. | L | 2-11 | | 7 | 12 | Escobar | Lilly | | 39-48 | 4th | 16.0 |
| 7-11 | Ana. | L | 2-5 | | 7 | 12 | Lackey | Batista | Percival | 39-49 | 4th | 17.0 |
| 7-16 | At Tex. | L | 2-11 | | 9 | 15 | Drese | Halladay | | 39-50 | 4th | 17.5 |
| 7-17 | At Tex. | L | 0-4 | | 8 | 6 | Rodriguez | Lilly | | 39-51 | 5th | 18.5 |
| 7-18 | At Tex. | L | 5-7 | | 13 | 5 | Brocail | Chulk | Cordero | 39-52 | 5th | 18.5 |
| 7-19 | At Oak. | W | 5-3 | | 12 | 9 | Towers | Saarloos | Frasor | 40-52 | 5th | 17.5 |
| 7-20 | At Oak. | L | 0-1 | (14) | 3 | 8 | Lehr | Speier | | 40-53 | 5th | 18.5 |
| 7-21 | At N.Y. | L | 3-10 | | 11 | 15 | Vazquez | Hentgen | | 40-54 | 5th | 19.5 |
| 7-22 | At N.Y. | L | 0-1 | | 5 | 4 | Rivera | Chulk | | 40-55 | 5th | 20.5 |
| 7-23 | T.B. | W | 7-4 | | 12 | 8 | Batista | Hendrickson | Frasor | 41-55 | 5th | 20.5 |
| 7-24 | T.B. | W | 4-2 | | 7 | 8 | Towers | Bell | Frasor | 42-55 | 5th | 19.5 |
| 7-25 | T.B. | W | 5-3 | | 7 | 9 | Bush | Zambrano | Ligtenberg | 43-55 | 5th | 18.5 |
| 7-26 | N.Y. | L | 5-6 | (10) | 9 | 11 | Rivera | Frasor | | 43-56 | 5th | 19.5 |
| 7-27 | N.Y. | L | 4-7 | | 13 | 7 | Proctor | Ligtenberg | Gordon | 43-57 | 5th | 20.5 |
| 7-28 | N.Y. | W | 3-2 | (10) | 10 | 9 | Frasor | Proctor | | 44-57 | 5th | 19.5 |
| 7-30 | At T.B. | W | 3-0 | | 8 | 2 | Towers | Halama | Frasor | 45-57 | 5th | 19.0 |
| 7-31 | At T.B. | L | 5-6 | | 10 | 8 | Sosa | Bush | Baez | 45-58 | 5th | 20.0 |
| 8-1 | At T.B. | L | 3-5 | | 6 | 9 | Brazelton | Douglass | Baez | 45-59 | 5th | 21.0 |
| 8-2 | Cle. | W | 6-1 | | 8 | 6 | Lilly | Lee | | 46-59 | 5th | 20.5 |
| 8-3 | Cle. | W | 7-6 | | 11 | 8 | Speier | Betancourt | Frasor | 47-59 | 5th | 19.5 |
| 8-4 | Cle. | L | 5-14 | | 11 | 21 | Westbrook | Towers | | 47-60 | 5th | 20.5 |
| 8-5 | Cle. | L | 3-6 | (10) | 9 | 10 | Betancourt | Ligtenberg | Wickman | 47-61 | 5th | 21.5 |
| 8-6 | At N.Y. | L | 4-11 | | 8 | 13 | Vazquez | Douglass | | 47-62 | 5th | 22.5 |
| 8-7 | At N.Y. | L | 0-6 | | 6 | 11 | Hernandez | Lilly | | 47-63 | 5th | 23.5 |
| 8-8 | At N.Y. | L | 2-8 | | 4 | 13 | Lieber | Batista | | 47-64 | 5th | 24.5 |
| 8-9 | At N.Y. | W | 5-4 | | 12 | 7 | Towers | Loaiza | Frasor | 48-64 | 5th | 23.5 |
| 8-10 | At Cle. | L | 0-2 | | 5 | 8 | Durbin | Bush | Wickman | 48-65 | 5th | 23.5 |
| 8-11 | At Cle. | L | 2-3 | | 7 | 7 | Sabathia | Frederick | Wickman | 48-66 | 5th | 24.5 |
| 8-12 | At Cle. | L | 2-6 | | 3 | 7 | Riske | Ligtenberg | | 48-67 | 5th | 25.5 |
| 8-13 | Bal. | L | 0-4 | | 5 | 11 | Ponson | Batista | | 48-68 | 5th | 26.5 |
| 8-14 | Bal. | W | 7-2 | | 14 | 6 | Towers | Borkowski | | 49-68 | 5th | 26.5 |
| 8-15 | Bal. | L | 7-11 | | 11 | 17 | Groom | Chulk | | 49-69 | 5th | 26.5 |
| 8-16 | At Bos. | L | 4-8 | | 6 | 10 | Lowe | Miller | Foulke | 49-70 | 5th | 27.0 |
| 8-17 | At Bos. | L | 4-5 | | 8 | 7 | Foulke | Frederick | | 49-71 | 5th | 27.0 |
| 8-18 | At Bos. | L | 4-6 | | 9 | 8 | Wakefield | Batista | | 49-72 | 5th | 27.0 |
| 8-20 | At Bal. | W | 14-4 | | 14 | 10 | Towers | Borkowski | | 50-72 | 5th | 26.5 |
| 8-21 | At Bal. | W | 10-4 | | 15 | 10 | Bush | Cabrera | | 51-72 | 5th | 25.5 |
| 8-22 | At Bal. | W | 8-5 | | 12 | 13 | Miller | Bedard | Frasor | 52-72 | 5th | 24.5 |
| 8-23 | Bos. | W | 3-0 | | 4 | 3 | Lilly | Martinez | | 53-72 | 5th | 24.5 |
| 8-24 | Bos. | L | 4-5 | | 12 | 8 | Wakefield | Batista | Foulke | 53-73 | 5th | 25.5 |
| 8-25 | Bos. | L | 5-11 | | 12 | 17 | Schilling | Towers | | 53-74 | 5th | 25.5 |
| 8-26 | N.Y. | L | 4-7 | | 6 | 11 | Nitkowski | Frasor | Rivera | 53-75 | 5th | 26.5 |
| 8-27 | N.Y. | L | 7-8 | | 12 | 9 | Sturtze | Miller | Gordon | 53-76 | 5th | 27.5 |
| 8-28 | N.Y. | L | 6-18 | | 9 | 19 | Brown | Lilly | Rivera | 53-77 | 5th | 28.5 |
| 8-29 | N.Y. | W | 6-4 | | 7 | 12 | Batista | Mussina | Frasor | 54-77 | 5th | 27.5 |
| 8-31 | Sea. | L | 5-7 | | 10 | 16 | Atchison | Ligtenberg | Putz | 54-78 | 5th | 27.5 |
| 9-1 | Sea. | W | 4-2 | | 8 | 6 | Bush | Villone | Speier | 55-78 | 5th | 27.5 |
| 9-2 | Sea. | W | 8-6 | | 13 | 11 | File | Baek | Speier | 56-78 | 5th | 27.5 |
| 9-3 | Oak. | L | 4-7 | | 9 | 13 | Hudson | Lilly | Dotel | 56-79 | 5th | 27.5 |

| Date | Opp. | Res. | Score | (inn.*) | Hits | Opp. hits | Winning pitcher | Losing pitcher | Save | Record | Pos. | GB |
|---|---|---|---|---|---|---|---|---|---|---|---|---|
| 9-4 | Oak. | L | 5-9 | | 11 | 10 | Hammond | Frasor | | 56-80 | 5th | 27.5 |
| 9-5 | Oak. | W | 13-5 | | 10 | 10 | Glynn | Harden | | 57-80 | 5th | 27.5 |
| 9-7 | At Ana. | L | 2-5 | | 6 | 11 | Colon | Bush | Percival | 57-81 | 5th | 29.0 |
| 9-8 | At Ana. | W | 1-0 | | 5 | 2 | Miller | Escobar | Speier | 58-81 | 5th | 28.5 |
| 9-9 | At Ana. | W | 5-4 | | 6 | 7 | Lilly | Washburn | Speier | 59-81 | 5th | 29.0 |
| 9-10 | At Tex. | L | 3-10 | | 8 | 17 | Drese | Batista | | 59-82 | 5th | 29.0 |
| 9-11 | At Tex. | L | 7-10 | | 12 | 12 | Mahay | Frasor | Cordero | 59-83 | 5th | 30.0 |
| 9-12 | At Tex. | L | 6-7 | | 12 | 8 | Brocail | Speier | Cordero | 59-84 | 5th | 31.0 |
| 9-13 | Bal. | L | 1-9 | | 5 | 12 | Chen | Miller | | 59-85 | 5th | 31.0 |
| 9-15 | Bal. | W | 3-0 | | 5 | 8 | Lilly | Riley | Speier | 60-85 | 5th | 31.5 |
| 9-16 | Bal. | L | 5-9 | | 13 | 12 | Lopez | Batista | | 60-86 | 5th | 32.0 |
| 9-17 | T.B. | L | 4-11 | | 5 | 12 | Waechter | Towers | | 60-87 | 5th | 32.0 |
| 9-18 | T.B. | W | 4-2 | | 7 | 3 | Bush | Ritchie | Batista | 61-87 | 5th | 32.0 |
| 9-19 | T.B. | W | 9-7 | | 11 | 10 | Chulk | Kazmir | Speier | 62-87 | 5th | 32.0 |
| 9-20 | At N.Y. | W | 6-3 | | 13 | 7 | Chacin | Vazquez | Batista | 63-87 | 5th | 31.0 |
| 9-21 | At N.Y. | L | 3-5 | | 5 | 11 | Loaiza | Halladay | Rivera | 63-88 | 5th | 32.0 |
| 9-22 | At N.Y. | W | 5-4 | | 10 | 8 | Lilly | Hernandez | Batista | 64-88 | 5th | 31.0 |
| 9-24 | At T.B. | L | 2-4 | | 7 | 8 | Hendrickson | Towers | Baez | 64-89 | 5th | 32.5 |
| 9-25 | At T.B. | L | 5-6 | | 5 | 6 | Baez | Batista | | 64-90 | 5th | 32.5 |
| 9-27 | At Bal. | W | 4-1 | | 11 | 7 | League | Ponson | Batista | 65-90 | 5th | 31.5 |
| 9-29! | At Bal. | L | 6-7 | | 9 | 9 | Ryan | Speier | | 65-91 | | |
| 9-29& | At Bal. | L | 0-4 | | 4 | 8 | Bauer | Chacin | | 65-92 | 5th | 33.5 |
| 9-30 | At Bal. | L | 3-9 | | 6 | 14 | Riley | Towers | | 65-93 | 5th | 34.5 |
| 10-1 | N.Y. | W | 7-0 | | 7 | 2 | Bush | Hernandez | | 66-93 | 5th | 33.5 |
| 10-2 | N.Y. | W | 4-2 | | 6 | 8 | Halladay | Brown | Batista | 67-93 | 5th | 32.5 |
| 10-3 | N.Y. | L | 2-3 | | 8 | 7 | Proctor | Towers | Sturtze | 67-94 | 5th | 33.5 |

Monthly records: April (7-15), May (15-14), June (12-15), July (11-14), August (9-20), September (11-15), October (2-1). *Innings, if other than nine. @ At Hiram Bithorn Stadium, San Juan, Puerto Rico. ! First game of a doubleheader. & Second game of a doubleheader.

## RECORDS

**2004 regular-season record:** 67-94
**Position:** 5th in A.L. East
**Home:** 40-41 **Road:** 27-53
**A.L. East:** 29-46 **A.L. Central:** 13-19
**A.L. West:** 17-19 **N.L.** 8-10
**Vs. LH starters:** 20-29
**Vs. RH starters:** 47-65
**Grass:** 22-43 **Artificial:** 45-51
**Day:** 24-31 **Night:** 43-63
**1-Run:** 17-22 **X-inn.:** 4-7
**Doubleheaders:** 0-1-1
**Team record past five years:** 394-415 (.487, ranks 9th in league in that span)

## TEAM LEADERS

**Batting average:** Alexis Rios (.286).
**At-bats:** Eric Hinske (570).
**Runs:** Vernon Wells (82).
**Hits:** Vernon Wells (146).
**Total Bases:** Vernon Wells (253).
**Doubles:** Vernon Wells (34).
**Triples:** Orlando Hudson, Alexis Rios (7).
**Home runs:** Carlos Delgado (32).
**Runs batted in:** Carlos Delgado (99).
**Stolen bases:** Alexis Rios (15).
**Slugging percentage:** Carlos Delgado (.535).
**On-base percentage:** Carlos Delgado (.372).
**Wins:** Ted Lilly (12).
**Earned-run average:** David Bush (3.69).
**Complete games:** Miguel Batista, Ted Lilly (2).
**Shutouts:** Miguel Batista, David Bush, Roy Halladay, Ted Lilly (1).
**Saves:** Jason Frasor (17).
**Innings pitched:** Miguel Batista (198.2).
**Strikeouts:** Ted Lilly (168).

## GAMES BY POSITION

**Catcher:** Gregg Zaun 97, Kevin Cash 60, Guillermo Quiroz 15, Greg Myers 4, Bobby Estalella 3.
**First base:** Carlos Delgado 120, Chris Gomez 19, Josh Phelps 12, Howie Clark 11, Dave Berg 7, Eric Crozier 5.
**Second base:** Orlando Hudson 133, Frank Menechino 30, Dave Berg 4, Chris Gomez 3, Howie Clark 1.
**Third base:** Eric Hinske 153, Frank Menechino 7, Chris Gomez 5, Dave Berg 3, Howie Clark 1.
**Shortstop:** Chris Gomez 77, Chris Woodward 64, Russ Adams 21, Frank Menechino 14.
**Outfield:** Reed Johnson 137, Vernon Wells 131, Alexis Rios 111, Frank Catalanotto 41, Gabe Gross 38, Dave Berg 31, Howie Clark 19, Simon Pond 9, Chad Hermansen 4.
**Designated hitter:** Josh Phelps 65, Frank Catalanotto 29, Frank Menechino 19, Eric Crozier 8, Carlos Delgado 8, Dave Berg 7, Gabe Gross 7, Simon Pond 6, Gregg Zaun 6, Chris Gomez 5, Howie Clark 4, Reed Johnson 4, Vernon Wells 3, Bobby Estalella 2, Guillermo Quiroz 2, Chris Woodward 2, Eric Hinske 1, Greg Myers 1.

## TOP DRAFT CHOICES

1a. **David Purcey,** LHP, Oklahoma.
1b. **Zach Jackson,** LHP, Texas A&M.
2. **Curtis Thigpen,** C, Texas.
3a. **Adam Lind,** 1B, South Alabama.
3b. **Danny Hill,** RHP, Missouri.
4. **Casey Janssen,** RHP, UCLA.
5. **Ryan Klosterman,** SS, Vanderbilt.
6. **Cory Patton,** OF, Texas A&M.
7. **Randy Dicken,** RHP, Shippensburg.
8. **Chip Cannon,** 1B, The Citadel.
9. **Joey Metropoulos,** 1B, USC.
10. **Brian Hill,** 2B, Stanford.

# ARIZONA DIAMONDBACKS

## NATIONAL LEAGUE WEST DIVISION

## 2005 SEASON

**Diamondbacks Schedule**
Home games shaded.
All-Star Game July 12 at Detroit. Schedule subject to change.

**April**

| SUN | MON | TUE | WED | THU | FRI | SAT |
|---|---|---|---|---|---|---|
| 3 | 4 CHC | 5 CHC | 6 CHC | 7 CHC | 8 LA | 9 LA |
| 10 LA | 11 COL | 12 COL | 13 COL | 14 WAS | 15 | 16 WAS |
| 17 WAS | 18 COL | 19 COL | 20 SF | 21 SF | 22 SD | 23 SD |
| 24 SD | 25 LA | 26 LA | 27 LA | 28 | 29 SD | 30 SD |

**May**

| SUN | MON | TUE | WED | THU | FRI | SAT |
|---|---|---|---|---|---|---|
| 1 SD | 2 SF | 3 SF | 4 SF | 5 PIT | 6 PIT | 7 PIT |
| 8 PIT | 9 WAS | 10 WAS | 11 WAS | 12 COL | 13 COL | 14 COL |
| 15 COL | 16 | 17 HOU | 18 HOU | 19 HOU | 20 DET | 21 DET |
| 22 DET | 23 | 24 SD | 25 SD | 26 SD | 27 LA | 28 LA |
| 29 LA | 30 | 31 NYM | | | | |

**June**

| SUN | MON | TUE | WED | THU | FRI | SAT |
|---|---|---|---|---|---|---|
| | | | 1 NYM | 2 NYM | 3 PHI | 4 PHI |
| 5 PHI | 6 PHI | 7 MIN | 8 MIN | 9 MIN | 10 KC | 11 KC |
| 12 KC | 13 CHW | 14 CHW | 15 CHW | 16 | 17 CLE | 18 CLE |
| 19 CLE | 20 SF | 21 SF | 22 SF | 23 SF | 24 DET | 25 DET |
| 26 DET | 27 | 28 SF | 29 SF | 30 SF | | |

**July**

| SUN | MON | TUE | WED | THU | FRI | SAT |
|---|---|---|---|---|---|---|
| | | | | | 1 LA | 2 LA |
| 3 LA | 4 STL | 5 STL | 6 STL | 7 STL | 8 CIN | 9 CIN |
| 10 CIN | 11 | 12 All-Star | 13 | 14 SD | 15 SD | 16 SD |
| 17 SD | 18 FLA | 19 FLA | 20 FLA | 21 | 22 ATL | 23 ATL |
| 24 ATL | 25 MIL | 26 MIL | 27 MIL | 28 CHC | 29 CHC | 30 CHC |
| 31 CHC | | | | | | |

**August**

| SUN | MON | TUE | WED | THU | FRI | SAT |
|---|---|---|---|---|---|---|
| | 1 | 2 HOU | 3 HOU | 4 HOU | 5 COL | 6 COL |
| 7 COL | 8 | 9 FLA | 10 FLA | 11 FLA | 12 ATL | 13 ATL |
| 14 ATL | 15 | 16 STL | 17 STL | 18 STL | 19 CIN | 20 CIN |
| 21 CIN | 22 NYM | 23 NYM | 24 NYM | 25 NYM | 26 PHI | 27 PHI |
| 28 PHI | 29 SD | 30 SD | 31 SD | | | |

**September**

| SUN | MON | TUE | WED | THU | FRI | SAT |
|---|---|---|---|---|---|---|
| | | | | 1 | 2 SF | 3 SF |
| 4 SF | 5 | 6 PIT | 7 PIT | 8 PIT | 9 COL | 10 COL |
| 11 COL | 12 | 13 MIL | 14 MIL | 15 MIL | 16 COL | 17 COL |
| 18 COL | 19 | 20 LA | 21 LA | 22 LA | 23 SD | 24 SD |
| 25 SD | 26 | 27 LA | 28 LA | 29 LA | 30 SF | |

**October**

| SUN | MON | TUE | WED | THU | FRI | SAT |
|---|---|---|---|---|---|---|
| | | | | | | 1 SF |
| 2 SF | 3 | 4 | 5 | 6 | 7 | 8 |

Home games shaded. All-Star Game July 12 at Detroit. Schedule subject to change.

### CLUB DIRECTORY

**President**
Richard Dozer

**Sr. vice president and general manager**
Joe Garagiola Jr.

**Sr. vice president, finance**
Thomas Harris

**Vice president, sales & marketing**
Mark Fernandez

**Vice president, tickets & special services**
Dianne Aguilar

**Vice president, event services**
Russ Amaral

**Vice president, special assistant to g.m.**
Bob Gebhard

**Assistant general manager**
Bob Miller

**Assistant director of player development**
Fred Seymour

**Director of public relations**
Mike Swanson

### MINOR LEAGUE AFFILIATES

| Class | Team | League | Manager |
|---|---|---|---|
| AAA | Tucson | Pacific Coast | Chip Hale |
| AA | Tennessee | Southern | Tony Perezchica |
| Advanced A | Lancaster | California | Bill Plummer |
| A | South Bend | Midwest | Tim Arseneau |
| Short-Season A | Yakima | Northwest | Jay Gainer |
| Advanced Rookie | Missoula | Pioneer | Jim Presley |

### BROADCAST INFORMATION

**Radio:** KTAR-AM (620).
**TV:** KTVK (Channel 3)
**Cable TV:** Fox Sports Net Arizona.

### SPRING TRAINING

**Ballpark (city):** Tucson Electric Park (Tucson, Ariz.).
**Ticket information:** 866-672-1343.

**For more on the Diamondbacks, go to msn.foxsports.com/mlb/teams.**

Cintron

## SPRING TRAINING ROSTER

**Manager**—Bob Melvin.
**Coaches**—Mike Aldrete, Jay Bell, Brett Butler, Mark Davis, Glenn Sherlock, Carlos Tosca.

| No. | PITCHERS | B/T | Ht./Wt. | Age* | 2004 Clubs |
|---|---|---|---|---|---|
| 41 | Aquino, Greg | R/R | 6-1/188 | 27 | Tucson, Arizona |
| 30 | Bruney, Brian | R/R | 6-3/226 | 23 | Tucson, Arizona |
| | Bulger, Jason | R/R | 6-4/215 | 26 | Lancaster, El Paso |
| 33 | Choate, Randy | L/L | 6-2/195 | 29 | Tucson, Arizona |
| 32 | Cormier, Lance | R/R | 6-1/192 | 24 | El Paso, Tucson, Arizona |
| 54 | Daigle, Casey | R/R | 6-5/217 | 23 | Arizona, Tucson |
| | Estes, Shawn | R/L | 6-2/200 | 32 | Colorado |
| 16 | Fossum, Casey | L/L | 6-1/160 | 27 | El Paso, Tucson, Arizona |
| 49 | Gonzalez, Edgar | R/R | 6-0/215 | 22 | Tucson, Arizona |
| | Gonzalez, Enrique | R/R | 5-10/195 | 22 | Lancaster |
| 44 | Gosling, Mike | L/L | 6-0/210 | 24 | Tucson, Arizona |
| | Halsey, Brad | L/L | 6-1/180 | 24 | Columbus, New York A.L. |
| 22 | Koplove, Mike | R/R | 5-10/178 | 28 | Arizona |
| 38 | Lyon, Brandon | R/R | 6-1/185 | 25 | Tucson |
| | Murphy, Bill | L/L | 6-0/190 | 23 | Carolina, El Paso |
| | Nippert, Dustin | R/R | 6-7/200 | 23 | El Paso |
| 48 | Ortiz, Russ | R/R | 6-1/208 | 30 | Atlanta |
| | Pena, Ramon | R/R | 6-2/190 | 23 | El Paso |
| | Peterson, Adam | R/R | 6-3/220 | 25 | New Hampshire, Toronto, Syracuse |
| | Stockman, Phil | R/R | 6-6/200 | 25 | El Paso, Tucson |
| 47 | Valverde, Jose | R/R | 6-4/254 | 25 | Arizona, Tucson |
| | Vazquez, Javier | R/R | 6-2/205 | 28 | New York A.L. |
| 56 | Villarreal, Oscar | L/R | 6-0/205 | 23 | Arizona, Tucson |
| 55 | Webb, Brandon | R/R | 6-2/228 | 25 | Arizona |
| | Wechsler, Justin | R/R | 6-2/240 | 24 | Lancaster |

| No. | CATCHERS | B/T | Ht./Wt. | Age* | 2004 Clubs |
|---|---|---|---|---|---|
| 7 | Hammock, Robby | R/R | 5-10/187 | 27 | Tucson, Lancaster, Arizona |
| 15 | Hill, Koyie | B/R | 6-0/190 | 26 | Las Vegas, Arizona |
| 19 | Snyder, Chris | R/R | 6-3/220 | 24 | El Paso, Arizona |

| No. | INFIELDERS | B/T | Ht./Wt. | Age* | 2004 Clubs |
|---|---|---|---|---|---|
| 10 | Cintron, Alex | B/R | 6-2/199 | 26 | Arizona |
| | Clayton, Royce | R/R | 6-0/185 | 35 | Colorado |
| | Counsell, Craig | L/R | 6-0/184 | 34 | Milwaukee |
| 2 | Gil, Jerry | R/R | 6-3/183 | 22 | Tucson, Arizona |
| | Glaus, Troy | R/R | 6-5/240 | 28 | Rancho Cuca., Anaheim |
| 15 | Green, Shawn | L/L | 6-4/200 | 32 | Los Angeles |
| 5 | Hairston, Scott | R/R | 6-0/188 | 24 | Tucson, Arizona |
| 8 | Kata, Matt | B/R | 6-1/185 | 27 | Arizona |
| 18 | Tracy, Chad | L/R | 6-2/200 | 24 | Tucson, Arizona |

| No. | OUTFIELDERS | B/T | Ht./Wt. | Age* | 2004 Clubs |
|---|---|---|---|---|---|
| | Abercrombie, R. | R/R | 6-3/210 | 24 | Vero Beach, Jacksonville, Lancaster |
| 20 | Gonzalez, Luis | L/R | 6-2/200 | 37 | Arizona |
| 43 | Kroeger, Josh | L/L | 6-2/200 | 22 | El Paso, Tucson, Arizona |
| 65 | Terrero, Luis | R/R | 6-2/206 | 24 | Tucson, Arizona |
| | Williams, Marland | R/R | 5-9/175 | 23 | El Paso |

*Age as of April 1, 2005.

## BALLPARK INFORMATION

**Ballpark (capacity, surface)**
Bank One Ballpark (49,033, grass)

**Address**
401 East Jefferson
Phoenix, AZ 85004

**Official website**
www.diamondbacks.com

**Business phone**
602-462-6500

**Ticket information**
602-514-8400

**Field dimensions (from home plate)**
To left field at foul line, 330 feet
To center field, 407 feet
To right field at foul line, 334 feet

**First game played**
March 31, 1998 (Rockies 9, Diamondbacks 2)

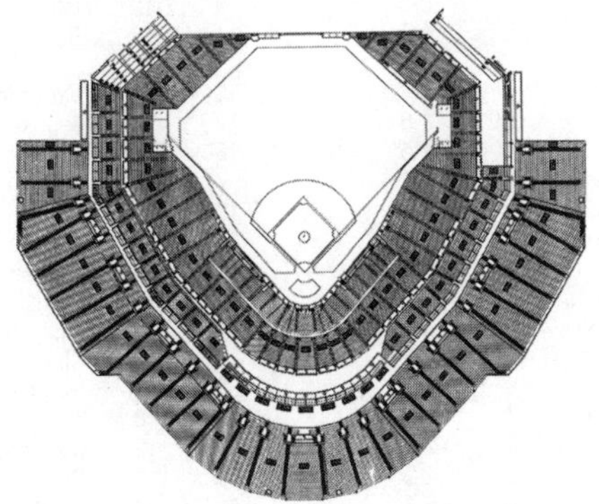

# 2004 REVIEW

## DAY BY DAY

| Date | Opp. | Res. | Score | (inn.*) | Hits | Opp. hits | Winning pitcher | Losing pitcher | Save | Record | Pos. | GB |
|---|---|---|---|---|---|---|---|---|---|---|---|---|
| 4-6 | Col. | L | 2-6 | | 3 | 11 | Estes | Johnson | | 0-1 | 5th | 1.5 |
| 4-7 | Col. | W | 9-5 | | 12 | 9 | Webb | Jennings | Mantei | 1-1 | T3rd | 0.5 |
| 4-8 | Col. | W | 6-5 | (11) | 8 | 11 | Randolph | Chacon | | 2-1 | T1st | ... |
| 4-9 | StL. | L | 6-13 | | 11 | 17 | Carpenter | Daigle | | 2-2 | T2nd | 1.0 |
| 4-10 | StL. | L | 2-10 | | 5 | 13 | Morris | Sparks | | 2-3 | T3rd | 2.0 |
| 4-11 | StL. | L | 5-6 | | 8 | 11 | Lincoln | Mantei | Isringhausen | 2-4 | T4th | 2.0 |
| 4-12 | At Col. | L | 4-7 | | 9 | 8 | Nunez | Koplove | Chacon | 2-5 | 5th | 2.5 |
| 4-14 | At Col. | L | 4-14 | | 9 | 15 | Kennedy | Dessens | | 2-6 | 5th | 3.0 |
| 4-15 | At Col. | W | 11-10 | | 9 | 10 | Koplove | Elarton | Mantei | 3-6 | 5th | 3.0 |
| 4-16 | At S.D. | W | 5-0 | | 7 | 2 | Johnson | Peavy | | 4-6 | T3rd | 3.0 |
| 4-17 | At S.D. | L | 2-3 | | 6 | 3 | Valdez | Webb | Hoffman | 4-7 | T4th | 4.0 |
| 4-18 | At S.D. | L | 5-6 | | 8 | 13 | Oropesa | Mantei | | 4-8 | 5th | 5.0 |
| 4-20 | At Mil. | L | 2-4 | | 9 | 10 | Sheets | Dessens | Kolb | 4-9 | 5th | 5.0 |
| 4-21 | At Mil. | L | 6-10 | | 8 | 10 | Ford | Johnson | | 4-10 | 5th | 6.0 |
| 4-22 | At Mil. | W | 11-9 | (15) | 20 | 8 | Sparks | Hernandez | | 5-10 | 5th | 5.0 |
| 4-23 | S.D. | W | 5-2 | | 9 | 4 | Koplove | Eaton | Mantei | 6-10 | 4th | 5.0 |
| 4-24 | S.D. | L | 2-4 | | 6 | 7 | Otsuka | Villarreal | Hoffman | 6-11 | 5th | 5.0 |
| 4-25 | S.D. | W | 12-7 | | 14 | 12 | Dessens | Lawrence | | 7-11 | 4th | 5.0 |
| 4-26 | Chi. | W | 9-0 | | 12 | 5 | Johnson | Zambrano | | 8-11 | T3rd | 4.5 |
| 4-27 | Chi. | W | 10-1 | | 13 | 5 | Webb | Mitre | | 9-11 | T3rd | 3.5 |
| 4-28 | Chi. | L | 3-4 | | 9 | 6 | Hawkins | Mantei | Borowski | 9-12 | T3rd | 4.5 |
| 4-30 | At Phi. | L | 0-4 | | 5 | 6 | Wolf | Dessens | | 9-13 | 5th | 5.0 |
| 5-1 | At Phi. | W | 6-4 | | 12 | 9 | Johnson | Padilla | Mantei | 10-13 | T4th | 5.0 |
| 5-2 | At Phi. | L | 5-6 | (14) | 11 | 8 | Madson | Villarreal | | 10-14 | 5th | 5.0 |
| 5-4 | At Chi. | W | 6-3 | | 10 | 5 | Sparks | Mitre | Valverde | 11-14 | T4th | 5.0 |
| 5-5 | At Chi. | W | 2-0 | | 4 | 6 | Daigle | Wood | Valverde | 12-14 | T3rd | 4.0 |
| 5-6 | At Chi. | L | 3-11 | | 8 | 15 | Clement | Dessens | | 12-15 | T3rd | 5.0 |
| 5-7 | Phi. | L | 1-4 | | 6 | 8 | Padilla | Johnson | Wagner | 12-16 | T4th | 6.0 |
| 5-8 | Phi. | L | 7-8 | | 13 | 10 | Milton | Webb | Worrell | 12-17 | 5th | 7.0 |
| 5-9 | Phi. | L | 1-7 | | 9 | 10 | Myers | Sparks | | 12-18 | 5th | 8.0 |
| 5-10 | N.Y. | W | 12-8 | | 14 | 17 | Daigle | Baldwin | | 13-18 | 5th | 7.5 |
| 5-11 | N.Y. | W | 9-5 | | 10 | 7 | Bruney | Leiter | | 14-18 | 3rd | 7.5 |
| 5-12 | N.Y. | L | 0-1 | | 3 | 3 | Glavine | Johnson | Looper | 14-19 | 4th | 8.5 |
| 5-13 | N.Y. | L | 4-7 | | 8 | 8 | Seo | Webb | Looper | 14-20 | 5th | 8.5 |
| 5-14 | Mon. | L | 3-4 | | 6 | 7 | Cordero | Valverde | Biddle | 14-21 | 5th | 8.5 |
| 5-15 | Mon. | L | 0-5 | | 7 | 9 | Vargas | Daigle | | 14-22 | 5th | 8.5 |
| 5-16 | Mon. | L | 1-6 | | 6 | 11 | Hernandez | Sparks | | 14-23 | 5th | 8.5 |
| 5-18 | At Atl. | W | 2-0 | | 8 | 0 | Johnson | Hampton | | 15-23 | 5th | 7.5 |
| 5-19 | At Atl. | W | 6-4 | (11) | 9 | 10 | Bruney | Almanza | | 16-23 | 4th | 6.5 |
| 5-20 | At Atl. | L | 1-5 | | 3 | 9 | Ramirez | Fossum | | 16-24 | 5th | 6.5 |
| 5-21 | At Fla. | L | 5-6 | (10) | 8 | 9 | Benitez | Bruney | | 16-25 | 5th | 6.5 |
| 5-22 | At Fla. | L | 2-11 | | 6 | 11 | Penny | Sparks | | 16-26 | 5th | 7.5 |
| 5-23 | At Fla. | W | 4-3 | | 11 | 5 | Johnson | Willis | Valverde | 17-26 | T4th | 6.5 |
| 5-24 | At Fla. | L | 5-13 | | 11 | 12 | Pavano | Webb | | 17-27 | 5th | 7.0 |
| 5-25 | At S.F | L | 1-4 | | 5 | 11 | Schmidt | Fossum | Herges | 17-28 | 5th | 8.0 |
| 5-26 | At S.F | L | 3-4 | | 10 | 6 | Rodriguez | Bruney | Herges | 17-29 | 5th | 8.0 |
| 5-27 | At S.F | L | 4-5 | (10) | 10 | 7 | Walker | Valverde | | 17-30 | 5th | 9.0 |
| 5-28 | At L.A. | W | 6-3 | | 8 | 9 | Johnson | Alvarez | Dessens | 18-30 | 5th | 9.0 |
| 5-29 | At L.A. | L | 0-10 | | 3 | 13 | Lima | Webb | | 18-31 | 5th | 9.0 |
| 5-30 | At L.A. | L | 0-3 | | 4 | 12 | Ishii | Fossum | Gagne | 18-32 | 5th | 10.0 |
| 5-31 | S.F | L | 4-8 | | 11 | 9 | Rueter | Daigle | | 18-33 | 5th | 10.0 |
| 6-1 | S.F | W | 6-5 | | 8 | 8 | Valverde | Christiansen | | 19-33 | 5th | 9.0 |
| 6-2 | S.F | W | 8-6 | | 12 | 13 | Johnson | Tomko | Valverde | 20-33 | 5th | 9.0 |
| 6-3 | S.F | W | 11-5 | | 16 | 7 | Webb | Williams | | 21-33 | 4th | 8.5 |
| 6-4 | L.A. | L | 3-7 | | 7 | 12 | Ishii | Fossum | Mota | 21-34 | 4th | 9.5 |
| 6-5 | L.A. | L | 3-10 | | 10 | 15 | Perez | Gonzalez | | 21-35 | 5th | 10.5 |
| 6-6 | L.A. | W | 6-5 | | 13 | 14 | Service | Dreifort | Valverde | 22-35 | 4th | 9.5 |
| 6-8 | At Bal. | W | 8-1 | | 14 | 5 | Johnson | Ponson | | 23-35 | 4th | 8.5 |
| 6-9 | At Bal. | L | 2-8 | | 7 | 10 | Parrish | Randolph | | 23-36 | 4th | 9.5 |
| 6-10 | At Bal. | W | 3-0 | | 4 | 7 | Fossum | Cabrera | Valverde | 24-36 | 4th | 8.5 |
| 6-11 | At Tor. | W | 3-2 | | 10 | 8 | Choate | Frasor | Valverde | 25-36 | 4th | 8.5 |
| 6-12 | At Tor. | L | 4-15 | | 8 | 15 | Halladay | Good | Chulk | 25-37 | 4th | 8.5 |
| 6-13 | At Tor. | W | 5-3 | | 8 | 8 | Johnson | Lilly | Valverde | 26-37 | 4th | 7.5 |
| 6-15 | N.Y. | L | 2-4 | | 6 | 12 | Contreras | Webb | Rivera | 26-38 | 4th | 8.5 |
| 6-16 | N.Y. | L | 4-9 | | 9 | 11 | Sturtze | Fossum | | 26-39 | 4th | 9.5 |
| 6-17 | N.Y. | W | 6-1 | | 11 | 4 | Sparks | Lieber | Dessens | 27-39 | 4th | 9.5 |

| Date | Opp. | Res. | Score | (inn.*) | Hits | Opp. hits | Winning pitcher | Losing pitcher | Save | Record | Pos. | GB |
|---|---|---|---|---|---|---|---|---|---|---|---|---|
| 6-18 | T.B. | L | 2-6 | | 9 | 10 | Halama | Johnson | | 27-40 | 4th | 10.5 |
| 6-19 | T.B. | L | 4-11 | | 11 | 11 | Bell | Cormier | | 27-41 | 4th | 10.5 |
| 6-20 | T.B. | L | 1-2 | | 7 | 8 | Hendrickson | Webb | Colome | 27-42 | 4th | 11.5 |
| 6-21 | At S.D. | L | 1-3 | | 7 | 9 | Valdez | Fossum | Hoffman | 27-43 | 4th | 11.5 |
| 6-22 | At S.D. | L | 1-2 | (10) | 7 | 5 | Hoffman | Koplove | | 27-44 | 4th | 12.0 |
| 6-23 | At S.D. | L | 3-4 | | 13 | 8 | Otsuka | Dessens | | 27-45 | 4th | 13.0 |
| 6-25 | At Det. | L | 1-2 | | 1 | 4 | Johnson | Webb | Urbina | 27-46 | 5th | 14.5 |
| 6-26 | At Det. | L | 6-7 | | 10 | 8 | Urbina | Villafuerte | | 27-47 | 5th | 14.5 |
| 6-27 | At Det. | L | 5-9 | | 9 | 15 | Walker | Villafuerte | | 27-48 | 5th | 15.5 |
| 6-28 | S.D. | L | 5-10 | | 13 | 17 | Wells | Reynolds | | 27-49 | 5th | 16.0 |
| 6-29 | S.D. | L | 2-3 | | 9 | 6 | Sweeney | Johnson | Hoffman | 27-50 | 5th | 16.0 |
| 6-30 | S.D. | W | 8-5 | | 10 | 11 | Randolph | Neal | Koplove | 28-50 | 5th | 16.0 |
| 7-1 | S.D. | W | 7-5 | | 9 | 7 | Fossum | Valdez | Koplove | 29-50 | 4th | 15.0 |
| 7-2 | Min. | L | 5-6 | | 12 | 9 | Romero | Randolph | Nathan | 29-51 | 5th | 16.0 |
| 7-3 | Min. | L | 4-8 | | 7 | 14 | Mulholland | Good | Rincon | 29-52 | 5th | 16.0 |
| 7-4 | Min. | W | 6-2 | | 12 | 5 | Johnson | Silva | | 30-52 | 5th | 15.0 |
| 7-5 | At L.A. | L | 5-6 | (10) | 10 | 6 | Carrara | Villafuerte | | 30-53 | 5th | 15.5 |
| 7-6 | At L.A. | L | 1-4 | | 8 | 9 | Lima | Fossum | Gagne | 30-54 | 5th | 16.5 |
| 7-7 | At L.A. | L | 0-11 | | 1 | 11 | Ishii | Sparks | | 30-55 | 5th | 16.5 |
| 7-8 | At S.F | W | 8-4 | | 13 | 12 | Good | Hermanson | | 31-55 | 5th | 16.5 |
| 7-9 | At S.F | L | 3-8 | | 5 | 10 | Williams | Johnson | | 31-56 | 5th | 16.5 |
| 7-10 | At S.F | L | 1-3 | | 5 | 8 | Tomko | Webb | Herges | 31-57 | 5th | 17.5 |
| 7-11 | At S.F | L | 2-9 | | 5 | 12 | Schmidt | Fossum | | 31-58 | 5th | 18.5 |
| 7-15 | L.A. | L | 3-4 | | 8 | 7 | Alvarez | Choate | Gagne | 31-59 | 5th | 19.5 |
| 7-16 | L.A. | L | 2-6 | | 6 | 8 | Ishii | Webb | | 31-60 | 5th | 20.5 |
| 7-17 | L.A. | L | 6-7 | | 14 | 9 | Mota | Bruney | Gagne | 31-61 | 5th | 21.5 |
| 7-18 | L.A. | L | 3-10 | | 12 | 15 | Lima | Dessens | | 31-62 | 5th | 22.5 |
| 7-19 | S.F | L | 1-6 | | 10 | 8 | Tomko | Sparks | | 31-63 | 5th | 23.5 |
| 7-20 | S.F | L | 1-3 | | 7 | 9 | Williams | Johnson | Christiansen | 31-64 | 5th | 24.5 |
| 7-21 | Hou. | L | 2-5 | | 7 | 10 | Pettitte | Webb | Lidge | 31-65 | 5th | 24.5 |
| 7-22 | Hou. | L | 3-10 | | 7 | 13 | Oswalt | Gonzalez | | 31-66 | 5th | 25.5 |
| 7-23 | Col. | L | 2-8 | | 7 | 6 | Fassero | Fossum | | 31-67 | 5th | 26.5 |
| 7-24 | Col. | L | 2-8 | | 9 | 10 | Wright | Cormier | | 31-68 | 5th | 27.5 |
| 7-25 | Col. | L | 2-3 | | 6 | 8 | Jennings | Choate | Chacon | 31-69 | 5th | 27.5 |
| 7-26 | At Hou. | W | 4-1 | | 8 | 6 | Webb | Pettitte | Aquino | 32-69 | 5th | 27.5 |
| 7-27 | At Hou. | L | 3-10 | | 6 | 12 | Oswalt | Gonzalez | | 32-70 | 5th | 27.5 |
| 7-28 | At Hou. | L | 1-6 | | 6 | 12 | Clemens | Fossum | | 32-71 | 5th | 27.5 |
| 7-29 | At Hou. | W | 6-4 | | 13 | 9 | Cormier | Redding | Aquino | 33-71 | 5th | 27.5 |
| 7-30 | At Col. | L | 1-4 | | 9 | 6 | Jennings | Johnson | Chacon | 33-72 | 5th | 28.5 |
| 7-31 | At Col. | L | 4-8 | | 8 | 10 | Estes | Webb | Chacon | 33-73 | 5th | 28.5 |
| 8-1 | At Col. | L | 2-10 | | 7 | 15 | Cook | Gonzalez | | 33-74 | 5th | 29.5 |
| 8-3 | Fla. | W | 5-3 | | 10 | 9 | Koplove | Willis | Aquino | 34-74 | 5th | 29.5 |
| 8-4 | Fla. | W | 11-6 | | 14 | 10 | Johnson | Beckett | | 35-74 | 5th | 29.5 |
| 8-5 | Fla. | L | 5-11 | | 9 | 14 | Pavano | Cormier | Mota | 35-75 | 5th | 30.5 |
| 8-6 | Atl. | L | 2-4 | | 9 | 10 | Wright | Webb | Reitsma | 35-76 | 5th | 30.5 |
| 8-7 | Atl. | L | 2-6 | | 7 | 10 | Byrd | Gonzalez | | 35-77 | 5th | 31.5 |
| 8-8 | Atl. | L | 4-11 | | 9 | 15 | Ortiz | Fossum | | 35-78 | 5th | 31.5 |
| 8-10 | At Mon. | L | 0-4 | | 8 | 8 | Hernandez | Johnson | | 35-79 | 5th | 32.5 |
| 8-11 | At Mon. | L | 3-7 | | 8 | 8 | Patterson | Webb | | 35-80 | 5th | 33.5 |
| 8-12 | At Mon. | L | 5-7 | | 11 | 13 | Ayala | Cormier | Cordero | 35-81 | 5th | 33.5 |
| 8-13 | At N.Y. | L | 6-10 | | 8 | 11 | Benson | Fossum | | 35-82 | 5th | 34.5 |
| 8-14 | At N.Y. | L | 3-4 | | 10 | 8 | Leiter | Gonzalez | Looper | 35-83 | 5th | 34.5 |
| 8-15 | At N.Y. | W | 2-0 | | 10 | 5 | Johnson | Trachsel | Aquino | 36-83 | 5th | 34.5 |
| 8-16 | Pit. | L | 7-8 | (10) | 13 | 12 | Mesa | Aquino | Gonzalez | 36-84 | 5th | 34.5 |
| 8-17 | Pit. | L | 1-7 | | 7 | 12 | Vogelsong | Randolph | | 36-85 | 5th | 35.5 |
| 8-18 | Pit. | W | 6-3 | | 8 | 7 | Fossum | VanBenschoten | Aquino | 37-85 | 5th | 34.5 |
| 8-20 | Cin. | L | 0-2 | | 6 | 5 | Hudson | Johnson | Valentine | 37-86 | 5th | 35.0 |
| 8-21 | Cin. | W | 2-1 | | 6 | 4 | Webb | Harang | Aquino | 38-86 | 5th | 35.0 |
| 8-22 | Cin. | L | 1-11 | | 6 | 10 | Claussen | Randolph | | 38-87 | 5th | 35.0 |
| 8-23 | At Pit. | W | 5-4 | | 10 | 11 | Nance | Grabow | Aquino | 39-87 | 5th | 34.0 |
| 8-24 | At Pit. | L | 1-3 | | 5 | 8 | Perez | Gonzalez | Mesa | 39-88 | 5th | 35.0 |
| 8-25 | At Pit. | L | 1-2 | | 9 | 3 | Fogg | Johnson | Mesa | 39-89 | 5th | 35.0 |
| 8-27 | At Cin. | W | 4-3 | (11) | 13 | 7 | Bruney | Valentine | Aquino | 40-89 | 5th | 34.5 |
| 8-28 | At Cin. | W | 6-3 | | 13 | 4 | Fossum | Norton | Aquino | 41-89 | 5th | 34.5 |
| 8-29 | At Cin. | L | 2-6 | | 8 | 6 | Van Poppel | Fetters | | 41-90 | 5th | 35.5 |
| 8-31 | L.A. | L | 1-4 | (13) | 8 | 7 | Gagne | Bruney | Carrara | 41-91 | 5th | 36.5 |
| 9-1 | L.A. | W | 3-1 | | 6 | 4 | Webb | Nomo | Aquino | 42-91 | 5th | 35.5 |
| 9-2 | L.A. | L | 4-8 | | 11 | 8 | Brazoban | Nance | Gagne | 42-92 | 5th | 36.5 |

| Date | Opp. | Res. | Score | (inn.*) | Hits | Opp. hits | Winning pitcher | Losing pitcher | Save | Record | Pos. | GB |
|---|---|---|---|---|---|---|---|---|---|---|---|---|
| 9-3 | At S.F | L | 7-18 | | 15 | 18 | Burba | Gonzalez | | 42-93 | 5th | 36.5 |
| 9-4 | At S.F | L | 7-9 | | 13 | 11 | Eyre | Koplove | Hermanson | 42-94 | 5th | 36.5 |
| 9-5 | At S.F | L | 1-4 | | 6 | 8 | Tomko | Johnson | Hermanson | 42-95 | 5th | 36.5 |
| 9-7 | At L.A. | L | 2-8 | | 7 | 10 | Nomo | Webb | | 42-96 | 5th | 37.5 |
| 9-8 | At L.A. | L | 5-6 | | 7 | 12 | Gagne | Koplove | | 42-97 | 5th | 38.5 |
| 9-9 | At L.A. | L | 3-5 | | 6 | 10 | Lima | Gonzalez | Gagne | 42-98 | 5th | 39.5 |
| 9-10 | S.F | W | 2-1 | | 4 | 5 | Johnson | Brower | Aquino | 43-98 | 5th | 39.5 |
| 9-11 | S.F | L | 3-5 | | 7 | 9 | Lowry | Randolph | Hermanson | 43-99 | 5th | 40.5 |
| 9-12 | S.F | L | 2-5 | | 4 | 8 | Schmidt | Choate | | 43-100 | 5th | 40.5 |
| 9-13 | Col. | L | 2-9 | | 8 | 13 | Kennedy | Fossum | | 43-101 | 5th | 40.5 |
| 9-14 | Col. | W | 4-3 | (13) | 13 | 6 | Choate | Reed | | 44-101 | 5th | 40.5 |
| 9-15 | Col. | W | 3-2 | | 10 | 5 | Johnson | Estes | Aquino | 45-101 | 5th | 39.5 |
| 9-16 | Col. | W | 8-5 | | 14 | 8 | Durbin | Dohmann | Fetters | 46-101 | 5th | 38.5 |
| 9-17 | At StL. | L | 3-4 | | 8 | 8 | Isringhausen | Service | | 46-102 | 5th | 39.5 |
| 9-18 | At StL. | L | 0-7 | | 6 | 9 | Haren | Fossum | | 46-103 | 5th | 39.5 |
| 9-19 | At StL. | W | 3-2 | | 3 | 8 | Gosling | Suppan | Aquino | 47-103 | 5th | 39.5 |
| 9-22 | At Col. | L | 2-4 | | 8 | 10 | Estes | Johnson | Chacon | 47-104 | 5th | 39.0 |
| 9-23! | At Col. | L | 1-7 | | 9 | 13 | Francis | Webb | | 47-105 | | |
| 9-23& | At Col. | L | 1-2 | (10) | 9 | 12 | Simpson | Choate | | 47-106 | 5th | 40.5 |
| 9-24 | At S.D. | L | 5-6 | | 13 | 10 | Otsuka | Aquino | | 47-107 | 5th | 41.5 |
| 9-25 | At S.D. | L | 5-6 | | 10 | 8 | Osuna | Durbin | Hoffman | 47-108 | 5th | 41.5 |
| 9-26 | At S.D. | L | 1-7 | | 6 | 12 | Peavy | Sparks | | 47-109 | 5th | 42.5 |
| 9-27 | Mil. | W | 3-1 | | 10 | 6 | Johnson | Sheets | Aquino | 48-109 | 5th | 42.5 |
| 9-28 | Mil. | W | 9-8 | (11) | 10 | 12 | Koplove | Kieschnick | | 49-109 | 5th | 42.5 |
| 9-29 | Mil. | L | 1-4 | | 7 | 8 | Glover | Fossum | Vizcaino | 49-110 | 5th | 42.5 |
| 10-1 | S.D. | L | 2-3 | | 5 | 7 | Peavy | Gosling | Hoffman | 49-111 | 5th | 43.0 |
| 10-2 | S.D. | W | 7-6 | | 11 | 10 | Johnson | Bynum | Aquino | 50-111 | 5th | 43.0 |
| 10-3 | S.D. | W | 4-1 | | 10 | 6 | Webb | Wells | Aquino | 51-111 | 5th | 42.0 |

Monthly records: April (9-13), May (9-20), June (10-17), July (5-23), August (8-18), September (8-19), October (2-1).
*Innings, if other than nine. ! First game of a doubleheader. & Second game of a doubleheader.

## RECORDS

**2004 regular-season record:** 51-111
**Position:** 5th in N.L. West
**Home:** 29-52 **Road:** 22-59
**N.L. East:** 9-23 **N.L. Central:** 15-21
**N.L. West:** 21-55 **A.L.** 6-12
**Vs. LH starters:** 13-41
**Vs. RH starters:** 38-70
**Grass:** 49-107 **Artificial:** 2-4
**Day:** 12-30 **Night:** 39-81
**1-Run:** 15-31 **X-inn.:** 6-8
**Doubleheaders:** 0-1-0
**Team record past five years:** 410-400 (.506, ranks 6th in league in that span)

## TEAM LEADERS

**Batting average:** Shea Hillenbrand (.310).
**At-bats:** Alex Cintron (564).
**Runs:** Luis Gonzalez (69).
**Hits:** Shea Hillenbrand (174).
**Total Bases:** Shea Hillenbrand (261).
**Doubles:** Shea Hillenbrand (36).
**Triples:** Alex Cintron (7).
**Home runs:** Steve Finley (23).
**Runs batted in:** Shea Hillenbrand (80).
**Stolen bases:** Luis Terrero (10).
**Slugging percentage:** Luis Gonzalez (.493).
**On-base percentage:** Luis Gonzalez (.373).
**Wins:** Randy Johnson (16).
**Earned-run average:** Randy Johnson (2.60).
**Complete games:** Randy Johnson (4).
**Shutouts:** Randy Johnson (2).
**Saves:** Greg Aquino (16).
**Innings pitched:** Randy Johnson (245.2).
**Strikeouts:** Randy Johnson (290).

## GAMES BY POSITION

**Catcher:** Juan Brito 54, Robby Hammock 46, Brent Mayne 30, Chris Snyder 29, Koyie Hill 11, Bobby Estalella 6.
**First base:** Shea Hillenbrand 131, Richie Sexson 23, Chad Tracy 11, Alan Zinter 8, Carlos Baerga 6, Greg Colbrunn 2, Brent Mayne 1.
**Second base:** Scott Hairston 85, Matt Kata 38, Roberto Alomar 28, Alex Cintron 19, Andy Green 14, Donnie Sadler 2.
**Third base:** Chad Tracy 135, Tim Olson 19, Andy Green 18, Shea Hillenbrand 17, Matt Kata 3, Donnie Sadler 2, Alex Cintron 1, Robby Hammock 1.
**Shortstop:** Alex Cintron 133, Jerry Gil 28, Tim Olson 17, Donnie Sadler 3, Matt Kata 1.
**Outfield:** Danny Bautista 137, Luis Gonzalez 104, Steve Finley 103, Luis Terrero 61, Quinton McCracken 37, Doug DeVore 31, Josh Kroeger 19, Robby Hammock 12, Andy Green 9, Donnie Sadler 6, Tim Olson 4, Scott Hairston 3, Chad Tracy 1.
**Designated hitter:** Carlos Baerga 2, Greg Colbrunn 2, Alan Zinter 2, Roberto Alomar 1, Danny Bautista 1, Steve Finley 1, Luis Gonzalez 1.

## TOP DRAFT CHOICES

1. **Stephen Drew,** SS, Florida State.
2. **Jon Zeringue,** OF, Louisiana State.
3. **Garrett Mock,** RHP, Houston.
4. **Ross Ohlendorf,** RHP, Princeton.
5. **Cesar Nicolas,** 1B, Vanderbilt.
6. **Brandon Burgess,** OF, Sonoma State.
7. **Koley Kolberg,** RHP, Arizona.
8. **Jimmy Shull,** RHP, Cal Poly-San Luis Obispo.
9. **A.J. Shappi,** RHP, UC Riverside.
10. **Steven Jackson,** RHP, Clemson.

# ATLANTA BRAVES
## *NATIONAL LEAGUE EAST DIVISION*

## 2005 SEASON

### Brewers Schedule
Home games shaded.
All-Star Game July 12 at Detroit. Schedule subject to change.

**April**

| SUN | MON | TUE | WED | THU | FRI | SAT |
|---|---|---|---|---|---|---|
| 3 | 4 PIT | 5 | 6 PIT | 7 | 8 CHC | 9 CHC |
| 10 CHC | 11 PIT | 12 PIT | 13 PIT | 14 | 15 STL | 16 STL |
| 17 STL | 18 LA | 19 LA | 20 HOU | 21 HOU | 22 SF | 23 SF |
| 24 SF | 25 STL | 26 STL | 27 STL | 28 | 29 CIN | 30 CIN |

**May**

| SUN | MON | TUE | WED | THU | FRI | SAT |
|---|---|---|---|---|---|---|
| 1 CIN | 2 | 3 CHC | 4 CHC | 5 CHC | 6 NYM | 7 NYM |
| 8 NYM | 9 PHI | 10 PHI | 11 PHI | 12 | 13 PIT | 14 PIT |
| 15 PIT | 16 WAS | 17 WAS | 18 WAS | 19 WAS | 20 MIN | 21 MIN |
| 22 MIN | 23 COL | 24 COL | 25 COL | 26 | 27 HOU | 28 HOU |
| 29 HOU | 30 SD | 31 SD | | | | |

**June**

| SUN | MON | TUE | WED | THU | FRI | SAT |
|---|---|---|---|---|---|---|
| | | | 1 SD | 2 LA | 3 LA | 4 LA |
| 5 LA | 6 NYY | 7 NYY | 8 NYY | 9 | 10 PHI | 11 PHI |
| 12 PHI | 13 TB | 14 TB | 15 TB | 16 | 17 TOR | 18 TOR |
| 19 TOR | 20 CHC | 21 CHC | 22 CHC | 23 CHC | 24 MIN | 25 MIN |
| 26 MIN | 27 | 28 CHC | 29 CHC | 30 CHC | | |

**July**

| SUN | MON | TUE | WED | THU | FRI | SAT |
|---|---|---|---|---|---|---|
| | | | | | 1 PIT | 2 PIT |
| 3 PIT | 4 FLA | 5 FLA | 6 FLA | 7 FLA | 8 ATL | 9 ATL |
| 10 ATL | 11 | 12 All-Star | 13 | 14 WAS | 15 WAS | 16 WAS |
| 17 WAS | 18 STL | 19 STL | 20 STL | 21 STL | 22 CIN | 23 CIN |
| 24 CIN | 25 ARI | 26 ARI | 27 ARI | 28 SF | 29 SF | 30 SF |
| 31 SF | | | | | | |

**August**

| SUN | MON | TUE | WED | THU | FRI | SAT |
|---|---|---|---|---|---|---|
| | 1 | 2 NYM | 3 NYM | 4 NYM | 5 PHI | 6 PHI |
| 7 PHI | 8 STL | 9 STL | 10 STL | 11 | 12 CIN | 13 CIN |
| 14 CIN | 15 COL | 16 COL | 17 COL | 18 HOU | 19 HOU | 20 HOU |
| 21 HOU | 22 | 23 FLA | 24 FLA | 25 FLA | 26 ATL | 27 ATL |
| 28 ATL | 29 | 30 PIT | 31 PIT | | | |

**September**

| SUN | MON | TUE | WED | THU | FRI | SAT |
|---|---|---|---|---|---|---|
| | | | | 1 SD | 2 SD | 3 SD |
| 4 SD | 5 CIN | 6 CIN | 7 CIN | 8 | 9 HOU | 10 HOU |
| 11 HOU | 12 | 13 ARI | 14 ARI | 15 ARI | 16 HOU | 17 HOU |
| 18 HOU | 19 | 20 CHC | 21 CHC | 22 CHC | 23 STL | 24 STL |
| 25 STL | 26 CIN | 27 CIN | 28 CIN | 29 CIN | 30 PIT | |

**October**

| SUN | MON | TUE | WED | THU | FRI | SAT |
|---|---|---|---|---|---|---|
| | | | | | | 1 PIT |
| 2 PIT | 3 | 4 | 5 | 6 | 7 | 8 |

Home games shaded. All-Star Game July 12 at Detroit. Schedule subject to change.

### CLUB DIRECTORY

**Chairman and president**
Terry McGuirk
**Chairman emeritus**
William C. Bartholomay
**Senior v.p. and asst. to the president**
Henry L. Aaron
**Executive v.p. and general manager**
John Schuerholz
**Vice president, assistant g.m.**
Frank Wren
**Executive v.p., business operations**
Mike Plant
**Senior v.p., sales & marketing**
Derek Schiller
**Sr. v.p., public relations/communications**
Greg Hughes
**Sr. v.p., entertainment & sports human resources**
Loretta Walker
**Vice president, team counsel**
John Cooper
**Vice president, controller**
Chip Moore

### MINOR LEAGUE AFFILIATES

| Class | Team | League | Manager |
|---|---|---|---|
| AAA | Richmond | International | Pat Kelly |
| AA | Mississippi | Southern | Brian Snitker |
| Advanced A | Myrtle Beach | Carolina | Randy Ingle |
| A | Rome | South Atlantic | Rocket Wheeler |
| Advanced Rookie | Danville | Appalachian | Paul Runge |
| Rookie | Gulf Coast Braves | Gulf Coast | Luis Ortiz |

### BROADCAST INFORMATION

**Radio:** WGST-AM (640).
**TV:** TBS-TV (Channel 17).
**Cable TV:** Fox Sports Net South, Turner South.

### SPRING TRAINING

**Ballpark (city):** Cracker Jack Stadium - Walt Disney's Wide World of Sports (Kissimmee, Fla.).
**Ticket information:** 407-839-3900, 407-939-4263.

**For more on the Braves, go to msn.foxsports.com/mlb/teams.**

Smoltz

## SPRING TRAINING ROSTER

**Manager**—Bobby Cox (6).
**Coaches**—Pat Corrales (39), Bobby Dews (53), Fredi Gonzalez (33), Glenn Hubbard (17), Leo Mazzone (54), Terry Pendleton (9).

| No. | PITCHERS | B/T | Ht./Wt. | Age* | 2004 Clubs |
|---|---|---|---|---|---|
| | Boyer, Blaine | R/R | 6-3/215 | 23 | Myrtle Beach |
| 40 | Colon, Roman | R/R | 6-6/225 | 25 | Richmond, Greenville, Atlanta |
| | Davies, Kyle | R/R | 6-2/190 | 21 | Myrtle Beach, Greenville, Richmond |
| 49 | Gryboski, Kevin | R/R | 6-5/225 | 31 | Atlanta |
| 32 | Hampton, Mike | R/L | 5-10/195 | 32 | Atlanta |
| 15 | Hudson, Tim | R/R | 6-1/164 | 29 | Sacramento, Oakland |
| | Kolb, Dan | R/R | 6-4/240 | 30 | Milwaukee |
| | Lerew, Anthony | L/R | 6-3/220 | 22 | Myrtle Beach |
| | McBride, Macay | L/L | 5-11/210 | 22 | Greenville |
| 38 | Martin, Tom | L/L | 6-1/206 | 34 | Los Angeles, Atlanta |
| 30 | Ramirez, Horacio | L/L | 6-1/219 | 25 | Greenville, Richmond, Atlanta |
| 37 | Reitsma, Chris | R/R | 6-5/235 | 27 | Atlanta |
| 29 | Smoltz, John | R/R | 6-3/220 | 37 | Atlanta |
| 50 | Thomson, John | R/R | 6-3/220 | 31 | Atlanta |
| | Vasquez, Jorge | R/R | 6-1/165 | 26 | Kansas City, Wichita |

| No. | CATCHERS | B/T | Ht./Wt. | Age* | 2004 Clubs |
|---|---|---|---|---|---|
| 23 | Estrada, Johnny | B/R | 5-11/209 | 28 | Atlanta |
| 12 | Perez, Eddie | R/R | 6-1/220 | 36 | Atlanta |

| No. | INFIELDERS | B/T | Ht./Wt. | Age* | 2004 Clubs |
|---|---|---|---|---|---|
| 24 | Betemit, Wilson | B/R | 6-3/190 | 24 | Richmond, Atlanta |
| 14 | Franco, Julio | R/R | 6-1/188 | 46 | Atlanta |
| 1 | Furcal, Rafael | B/R | 5-10/165 | 26 | Atlanta |
| 22 | Giles, Marcus | R/R | 5-8/180 | 26 | Rome, Myrtle Beach, Atlanta |
| | Marte, Andy | R/R | 61/185 | 21 | Greenville, G.C. Braves |
| 20 | Green, Nick | R/R | 6-0/178 | 26 | Richmond, Atlanta |
| | Hernandez, Luis | S/R | 5-10/140 | 20 | Myrtle Beach |
| | Johnson, Kelly | L/R | 6-1/205 | 23 | Greenville |
| 10 | Jones, Chipper | B/R | 6-4/210 | 32 | Rome, Atlanta |
| 19 | LaRoche, Adam | L/L | 6-3/180 | 25 | Richmond, Atlanta |
| | Orr, Pete | L/R | 6-1/175 | 25 | Richmond |
| | Pena, Tony | R/R | 6-1/180 | 24 | Greenville |
| | Thorman, Scott | L/R | 6-3/235 | 23 | Myrtle Beach, Greenville |

| No. | OUTFIELDERS | B/T | Ht./Wt. | Age* | 2004 Clubs |
|---|---|---|---|---|---|
| 25 | Jones, Andruw | R/R | 6-1/210 | 27 | Atlanta |
| 18 | Langerhans, Ryan | L/L | 6-3/195 | 25 | Richmond |
| | Joseph, Onil | R/R | 6-2/165 | 23 | Myrtle Beach |
| | McCarthy, Bill | R/R | 6-1/205 | 25 | Greenville, Richmond |

*Age as of April 1, 2005.

## BALLPARK INFORMATION

**Ballpark (capacity, surface)**
Turner Field (50,091, grass)

**Address**
P.O. Box 4064
Atlanta, GA 30302

**Official website**
www.atlantabraves.com

**Business phone**
404-522-7630

**Ticket information**
404-249-6400 or 800-326-4000

**Field dimensions (from home plate)**
To left field at foul line, 335 feet
To center field, 401 feet
To right field at foul line, 330 feet

**First game played**
April 4, 1997 (Braves 5, Cubs 4)

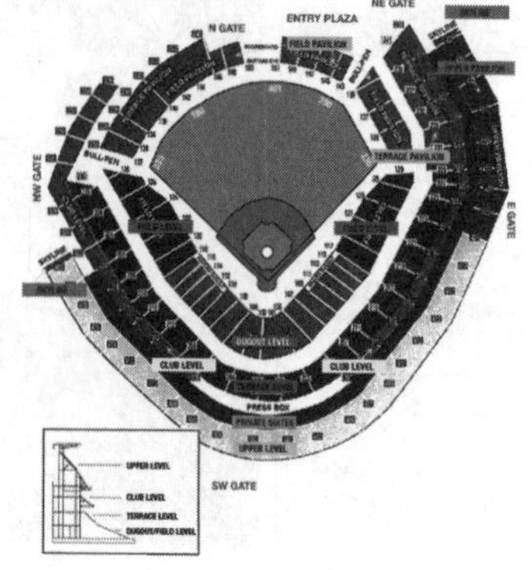

# 2004 REVIEW

## DAY BY DAY

| Date | Opp. | Res. | Score | (inn.*) | Hits | Opp. hits | Winning pitcher | Losing pitcher | Save | Record | Pos. | GB |
|---|---|---|---|---|---|---|---|---|---|---|---|---|
| 4-6 | N.Y. | L | 2-7 | | 6 | 10 | Glavine | Ortiz | | 0-1 | T3rd | 1.0 |
| 4-7 | N.Y. | W | 18-10 | | 19 | 15 | Gryboski | Trachsel | | 1-1 | T1st | ... |
| 4-8 | N.Y. | W | 10-8 | | 15 | 13 | Cunnane | Franco | Smoltz | 2-1 | T1st | ... |
| 4-9 | Chi. | L | 1-2 | (15) | 6 | 12 | Mercker | Cunnane | Borowski | 2-2 | T2nd | 1.0 |
| 4-10 | Chi. | W | 5-2 | | 6 | 4 | Alfonseca | Pratt | Gryboski | 3-2 | 2nd | 1.0 |
| 4-11 | Chi. | L | 2-10 | | 7 | 14 | Wood | Ortiz | | 3-3 | T2nd | 2.0 |
| 4-12 | At N.Y. | L | 6-10 | | 10 | 13 | Trachsel | Hampton | Looper | 3-4 | 3rd | 2.5 |
| 4-14 | At N.Y. | W | 6-1 | | 9 | 8 | Thomson | Yates | | 4-4 | T2nd | 3.0 |
| 4-15 | At N.Y. | L | 0-4 | | 4 | 9 | Leiter | Ramirez | | 4-5 | 3rd | 4.0 |
| 4-16 | Fla. | W | 5-4 | | 8 | 7 | Wright | Oliver | Smoltz | 5-5 | T2nd | 3.0 |
| 4-17 | Fla. | W | 4-1 | | 8 | 6 | Ortiz | Beckett | Smoltz | 6-5 | 2nd | 2.0 |
| 4-18 | Fla. | W | 3-2 | (10) | 6 | 7 | Alfonseca | Perisho | | 7-5 | 2nd | 1.0 |
| 4-20 | At Cin. | L | 2-3 | | 4 | 7 | Acevedo | Thomson | Graves | 7-6 | 2nd | 2.0 |
| 4-21 | At Cin. | W | 9-5 | (10) | 10 | 9 | Reitsma | Reith | | 8-6 | 2nd | 2.0 |
| 4-22 | At Cin. | L | 3-5 | (5) | 5 | 5 | Lidle | Wright | | 8-7 | 2nd | 3.0 |
| 4-23 | At Fla. | W | 6-1 | | 9 | 4 | Ortiz | Beckett | | 9-7 | 2nd | 2.0 |
| 4-24 | At Fla. | L | 4-7 | | 14 | 13 | Penny | Hampton | Benitez | 9-8 | 2nd | 3.0 |
| 4-25 | At Fla. | W | 7-2 | | 11 | 9 | Thomson | Bump | | 10-8 | 2nd | 2.0 |
| 4-26 | At S.F | L | 2-3 | | 6 | 6 | Schmidt | Ramirez | Herges | 10-9 | 2nd | 3.0 |
| 4-27 | At S.F | W | 12-3 | | 18 | 10 | Wright | Rueter | | 11-9 | 2nd | 2.0 |
| 4-28 | At S.F | L | 7-10 | | 12 | 14 | Tomko | Ortiz | | 11-10 | 2nd | 3.0 |
| 5-1# | At Col. | L | 2-3 | | 8 | 10 | Nunez | Reitsma | Chacon | 11-11 | | |
| 5-1$ | At Col. | W | 11-7 | | 12 | 14 | Nitkowski | Nunez | | 12-11 | 2nd | 2.5 |
| 5-2 | At Col. | L | 4-13 | | 11 | 14 | Estes | Ramirez | | 12-12 | 2nd | 2.5 |
| 5-4 | S.D. | W | 4-2 | | 7 | 7 | Ortiz | Eaton | Smoltz | 13-12 | 2nd | 1.5 |
| 5-5 | S.D. | L | 0-2 | | 5 | 11 | Wells | Wright | Hoffman | 13-13 | 2nd | 2.5 |
| 5-6 | S.D. | L | 3-7 | | 6 | 13 | Lawrence | Hampton | | 13-14 | 2nd | 2.5 |
| 5-7 | Hou. | L | 3-5 | | 9 | 12 | Redding | Thomson | Dotel | 13-15 | 3rd | 3.5 |
| 5-8 | Hou. | W | 5-4 | (10) | 9 | 12 | Alfonseca | Stone | | 14-15 | 3rd | 2.5 |
| 5-9 | Hou. | L | 1-2 | | 3 | 3 | Pettitte | Ortiz | Dotel | 14-16 | 3rd | 3.5 |
| 5-11 | At StL. | L | 1-5 | | 4 | 8 | Williams | Wright | | 14-17 | 3rd | 3.5 |
| 5-12 | At StL. | L | 2-5 | | 7 | 12 | Morris | Hampton | Isringhausen | 14-18 | 4th | 4.5 |
| 5-13 | At StL. | W | 6-5 | | 13 | 11 | Alfonseca | Suppan | Smoltz | 15-18 | 4th | 4.5 |
| 5-14 | At Mil. | W | 2-0 | | 8 | 5 | Ramirez | Vizcaino | Smoltz | 16-18 | 4th | 3.5 |
| 5-15 | At Mil. | W | 11-6 | | 15 | 6 | Alfonseca | Kinney | | 17-18 | 3rd | 2.5 |
| 5-16 | At Mil. | L | 1-4 | | 3 | 8 | Sheets | Wright | | 17-19 | 4th | 3.5 |
| 5-18 | Ari. | L | 0-2 | | 0 | 8 | Johnson | Hampton | | 17-20 | 4th | 3.5 |
| 5-19 | Ari. | L | 4-6 | (11) | 10 | 9 | Bruney | Almanza | | 17-21 | 4th | 4.0 |
| 5-20 | Ari. | W | 5-1 | | 9 | 3 | Ramirez | Fossum | | 18-21 | 4th | 4.0 |
| 5-21 | L.A. | W | 2-0 | | 6 | 6 | Ortiz | Perez | Smoltz | 19-21 | 4th | 4.0 |
| 5-22 | L.A. | L | 4-7 | | 8 | 13 | Weaver | Wright | | 19-22 | 4th | 4.5 |
| 5-23 | L.A. | W | 5-1 | | 10 | 13 | Hampton | Alvarez | | 20-22 | 4th | 4.0 |
| 5-24 | At Mon. | W | 5-0 | | 9 | 11 | Thomson | Day | | 21-22 | 4th | 3.5 |
| 5-25 | At Mon. | L | 1-3 | | 7 | 9 | Ohka | Ramirez | Biddle | 21-23 | 4th | 3.5 |
| 5-26 | At Mon. | W | 6-1 | | 13 | 5 | Ortiz | Hernandez | | 22-23 | 4th | 3.5 |
| 5-27 | At Phi. | W | 6-1 | | 9 | 6 | Wright | Millwood | | 23-23 | T3rd | 3.5 |
| 5-28 | At Phi. | L | 2-3 | (10) | 9 | 12 | Worrell | Alfonseca | | 23-24 | T3rd | 4.5 |
| 5-29 | At Phi. | W | 9-3 | | 13 | 9 | Thomson | Padilla | | 24-24 | 3rd | 4.5 |
| 5-30 | At Phi. | L | 1-4 | | 4 | 4 | Milton | Smith | Worrell | 24-25 | 3rd | 5.5 |
| 5-31 | Mon. | W | 8-2 | | 8 | 6 | Ortiz | Hernandez | | 25-25 | 3rd | 4.5 |
| 6-1 | Mon. | W | 7-6 | | 9 | 9 | Almanza | Biddle | | 26-25 | 3rd | 3.5 |
| 6-2 | Mon. | L | 4-8 | | 7 | 17 | Vargas | Hampton | | 26-26 | T3rd | 3.5 |
| 6-3 | Phi. | W | 8-4 | | 13 | 11 | Thomson | Hancock | | 27-26 | T3rd | 2.5 |
| 6-4 | Phi. | L | 1-9 | | 6 | 11 | Milton | Smith | | 27-27 | T3rd | 3.5 |
| 6-5 | Phi. | L | 3-5 | | 8 | 10 | Myers | Ortiz | Worrell | 27-28 | T3rd | 4.5 |
| 6-6 | Phi. | W | 6-4 | | 9 | 9 | Wright | Millwood | Smoltz | 28-28 | T3rd | 3.5 |
| 6-8 | At Det. | W | 4-3 | (10) | 8 | 10 | Reitsma | Patterson | Smoltz | 29-28 | 3rd | 3.5 |
| 6-9 | At Det. | L | 2-4 | | 8 | 11 | Dingman | Thomson | Urbina | 29-29 | 3rd | 3.5 |
| 6-10 | At Det. | L | 4-7 | | 9 | 8 | Maroth | Alfonseca | Urbina | 29-30 | 3rd | 4.5 |
| 6-11 | At Chi. | W | 6-4 | | 10 | 6 | Wright | Schoeneweis | | 30-30 | 3rd | 3.5 |
| 6-12 | At Chi. | L | 8-10 | | 12 | 14 | Loaiza | Thomson | Takatsu | 30-31 | 3rd | 3.5 |
| 6-13 | At Chi. | L | 3-10 | | 8 | 13 | Buehrle | Smith | | 30-32 | 3rd | 4.5 |
| 6-15 | K.C. | W | 3-2 | | 8 | 8 | Reitsma | Grimsley | Smoltz | 31-32 | 3rd | 3.5 |
| 6-16 | K.C. | L | 4-10 | | 8 | 20 | Cerda | Reitsma | | 31-33 | 3rd | 4.5 |
| 6-17 | K.C. | L | 4-10 | | 10 | 13 | May | Thomson | | 31-34 | T3rd | 5.5 |
| 6-18 | Cle. | L | 2-4 | | 6 | 11 | Lee | Hampton | Jimenez | 31-35 | 4th | 5.5 |

| Date | Opp. | Res. | Score | (inn.*) | Hits | Opp. hits | Winning pitcher | Losing pitcher | Save | Record | Pos. | GB |
|---|---|---|---|---|---|---|---|---|---|---|---|---|
| 6-19 | Cle. | W | 4-0 | | 9 | 6 | Byrd | Westbrook | Smoltz | 32-35 | 4th | 4.5 |
| 6-20 | Cle. | L | 2-5 | | 4 | 11 | Davis | Ortiz | Jimenez | 32-36 | 4th | 4.5 |
| 6-22 | At Fla. | L | 3-4 | | 11 | 6 | Pavano | Gryboski | Benitez | 32-37 | 4th | 5.5 |
| 6-23 | At Fla. | L | 0-6 | | 4 | 10 | Penny | Thomson | | 32-38 | 4th | 6.5 |
| 6-24 | At Fla. | W | 9-4 | | 13 | 10 | Hampton | Willis | | 33-38 | 4th | 5.5 |
| 6-25 | At Bal. | L | 0-5 | | 4 | 10 | Cabrera | Byrd | | 33-39 | 4th | 5.5 |
| 6-26 | At Bal. | W | 5-0 | | 9 | 10 | Ortiz | Lopez | Smoltz | 34-39 | 4th | 4.5 |
| 6-27 | At Bal. | W | 8-7 | | 14 | 13 | Cruz | Grimsley | Smoltz | 35-39 | 4th | 4.5 |
| 6-28 | Fla. | W | 6-1 | | 11 | 3 | Thomson | Penny | | 36-39 | 4th | 3.5 |
| 6-29 | Fla. | L | 4-5 | | 11 | 8 | Manzanillo | Hampton | Benitez | 36-40 | 4th | 4.5 |
| 6-30 | Fla. | W | 9-6 | | 17 | 12 | McConnell | Oliver | Smoltz | 37-40 | 4th | 3.5 |
| 7-1 | Fla. | W | 9-1 | | 9 | 7 | Ortiz | Tejera | | 38-40 | 4th | 3.5 |
| 7-2 | Bos. | W | 6-3 | (12) | 11 | 10 | Cruz | Martinez | | 39-40 | 4th | 2.5 |
| 7-3 | Bos. | L | 1-6 | | 6 | 11 | Schilling | Thomson | | 39-41 | 4th | 3.5 |
| 7-4 | Bos. | W | 10-4 | | 11 | 11 | Hampton | Lowe | | 40-41 | 4th | 3.5 |
| 7-5@ | At Mon. | W | 11-4 | | 13 | 11 | Byrd | Day | | 41-41 | 4th | 3.5 |
| 7-6@ | At Mon. | W | 1-0 | | 7 | 5 | Ortiz | Downs | Smoltz | 42-41 | 4th | 2.5 |
| 7-7@ | At Mon. | W | 14-2 | | 17 | 9 | Wright | Hernandez | | 43-41 | 3rd | 1.5 |
| 7-9 | At Phi. | L | 6-7 | (10) | 11 | 12 | Wagner | Alfonseca | | 43-42 | 3rd | 3.0 |
| 7-10 | At Phi. | W | 4-0 | | 7 | 5 | Hampton | Abbott | | 44-42 | T2nd | 2.0 |
| 7-11 | At Phi. | W | 6-4 | | 16 | 8 | Ortiz | Wolf | Smoltz | 45-42 | 2nd | 1.0 |
| 7-15 | Mon. | W | 8-0 | | 11 | 5 | Wright | Hernandez | | 46-42 | T1st | ... |
| 7-16 | Mon. | L | 1-5 | | 6 | 8 | Horgan | Byrd | | 46-43 | 2nd | 1.0 |
| 7-17 | Mon. | W | 6-2 | | 9 | 2 | Ortiz | Bentz | Smoltz | 47-43 | 2nd | 1.0 |
| 7-18 | Mon. | W | 16-5 | | 15 | 13 | Thomson | Downs | | 48-43 | T1st | ... |
| 7-19 | Phi. | W | 4-2 | | 9 | 6 | Hampton | Abbott | Smoltz | 49-43 | 1st | +1.0 |
| 7-20 | Phi. | L | 3-4 | (10) | 8 | 8 | Worrell | Alfonseca | Wagner | 49-44 | T1st | ... |
| 7-21 | Pit. | L | 3-4 | | 6 | 8 | Benson | Byrd | Mesa | 49-45 | 2nd | 1.0 |
| 7-22 | Pit. | W | 2-1 | (10) | 6 | 8 | Reitsma | Torres | | 50-45 | T1st | ... |
| 7-24 | At N.Y. | W | 5-2 | | 11 | 7 | Thomson | Stanton | Smoltz | 51-45 | 1st | +0.5 |
| 7-25 | At N.Y. | W | 4-3 | | 7 | 7 | Hampton | Trachsel | Smoltz | 52-45 | 1st | +0.5 |
| 7-26 | At Pit. | W | 4-2 | | 8 | 6 | Wright | Benson | Smoltz | 53-45 | 1st | +1.5 |
| 7-27 | At Pit. | L | 4-8 | | 12 | 11 | Gonzalez | Gryboski | | 53-46 | 1st | +1.5 |
| 7-28 | At Pit. | W | 1-0 | | 5 | 11 | Ortiz | Perez | Smoltz | 54-46 | 1st | +2.5 |
| 7-29 | At Pit. | W | 3-2 | | 10 | 6 | Cruz | Mesa | Smoltz | 55-46 | 1st | +3.5 |
| 7-30 | N.Y. | W | 3-1 | | 9 | 7 | Hampton | Trachsel | Smoltz | 56-46 | 1st | +4.5 |
| 7-31 | N.Y. | W | 8-0 | | 11 | 5 | Wright | Benson | | 57-46 | 1st | +4.5 |
| 8-1 | N.Y. | W | 6-5 | | 14 | 6 | Byrd | Glavine | Smoltz | 58-46 | 1st | +5.5 |
| 8-3 | At Hou. | L | 2-3 | | 4 | 9 | Miceli | Reitsma | Lidge | 58-47 | 1st | +4.5 |
| 8-4 | At Hou. | W | 5-4 | | 12 | 6 | Thomson | Munro | Smoltz | 59-47 | 1st | +4.5 |
| 8-5 | At Hou. | W | 6-5 | | 11 | 9 | Cruz | Miceli | Smoltz | 60-47 | 1st | +4.5 |
| 8-6 | At Ari. | W | 4-2 | | 10 | 9 | Wright | Webb | Reitsma | 61-47 | 1st | +4.5 |
| 8-7 | At Ari. | W | 6-2 | | 10 | 7 | Byrd | Gonzalez | | 62-47 | 1st | +5.5 |
| 8-8 | At Ari. | W | 11-4 | | 15 | 9 | Ortiz | Fossum | | 63-47 | 1st | +5.5 |
| 8-10 | Mil. | L | 2-3 | (10) | 8 | 8 | Adams | Martin | Kolb | 63-48 | 1st | +6.0 |
| 8-11 | Mil. | W | 10-3 | | 15 | 12 | Hampton | Santos | | 64-48 | 1st | +6.0 |
| 8-12 | Mil. | W | 4-2 | | 7 | 5 | Wright | Sheets | Smoltz | 65-48 | 1st | +7.0 |
| 8-13 | StL. | L | 1-4 | | 3 | 8 | Williams | Byrd | Isringhausen | 65-49 | 1st | +7.0 |
| 8-14 | StL. | W | 9-7 | | 15 | 10 | Alfonseca | King | Smoltz | 66-49 | 1st | +8.0 |
| 8-15 | StL. | L | 4-10 | | 10 | 11 | Haren | Thomson | | 66-50 | 1st | +8.0 |
| 8-16 | At S.D. | W | 5-4 | | 7 | 11 | Hampton | Hitchcock | Smoltz | 67-50 | 1st | +8.0 |
| 8-17 | At S.D. | L | 6-11 | | 8 | 17 | Peavy | Wright | | 67-51 | 1st | +8.0 |
| 8-18 | At S.D. | W | 6-5 | | 15 | 9 | Reitsma | Hoffman | Smoltz | 68-51 | 1st | +8.0 |
| 8-19 | At L.A. | W | 6-5 | | 8 | 8 | Reitsma | Gagne | Smoltz | 69-51 | 1st | +8.5 |
| 8-20 | At L.A. | L | 2-3 | (11) | 10 | 7 | Carrara | Cruz | | 69-52 | 1st | +8.5 |
| 8-21 | At L.A. | L | 4-7 | | 13 | 10 | Weaver | Hampton | Carrara | 69-53 | 1st | +7.5 |
| 8-22 | At L.A. | W | 10-1 | | 19 | 5 | Wright | Alvarez | | 70-53 | 1st | +7.5 |
| 8-24 | Col. | W | 6-5 | | 14 | 11 | Gryboski | Harikkala | Smoltz | 71-53 | 1st | +7.5 |
| 8-25 | Col. | W | 8-1 | | 13 | 6 | Thomson | Francis | | 72-53 | 1st | +8.5 |
| 8-26 | Col. | W | 6-4 | | 11 | 10 | Hampton | Wright | Smoltz | 73-53 | 1st | +9.5 |
| 8-27 | S.F | W | 5-3 | | 10 | 7 | Wright | Rueter | Smoltz | 74-53 | 1st | +9.5 |
| 8-28 | S.F | W | 9-3 | | 15 | 6 | Byrd | Schmidt | | 75-53 | 1st | +9.5 |
| 8-29 | S.F | L | 5-9 | | 12 | 14 | Christiansen | Ortiz | Hermanson | 75-54 | 1st | +8.5 |
| 8-30 | S.F | W | 7-6 | | 13 | 9 | Colon | Hermanson | | 76-54 | 1st | +8.5 |
| 8-31 | At Phi. | W | 5-3 | | 10 | 6 | Hampton | Milton | | 77-54 | 1st | +8.5 |
| 9-1 | At Phi. | W | 7-2 | | 13 | 9 | Wright | Padilla | | 78-54 | 1st | +8.5 |
| 9-3 | At Mon. | W | 7-1 | | 9 | 4 | Byrd | Downs | | 79-54 | 1st | +8.5 |
| 9-4 | At Mon. | W | 9-0 | | 13 | 3 | Ortiz | Patterson | | 80-54 | 1st | +9.0 |
| 9-5 | At Mon. | L | 3-4 | (12) | 6 | 12 | Tucker | Cruz | | 80-55 | 1st | +8.5 |

| Date | Opp. | Res. | Score | (inn.*) | Hits | Opp. hits | Winning pitcher | Losing pitcher | Save | Record | Pos. | GB |
|---|---|---|---|---|---|---|---|---|---|---|---|---|
| 9-6 | Phi. | W | 3-1 | | 12 | 7 | Smith | Milton | Smoltz | 81-55 | 1st | +9.0 |
| 9-8! | Phi. | L | 3-5 | | 4 | 11 | Madson | Reitsma | Wagner | 81-56 | | |
| 9-8& | Phi. | L | 1-4 | | 3 | 10 | Jones | Byrd | Worrell | 81-57 | 1st | +7.0 |
| 9-9 | Phi. | L | 4-9 | | 9 | 14 | Madson | Colon | | 81-58 | 1st | +7.0 |
| 9-10 | Mon. | W | 4-3 | | 6 | 13 | Thomson | Patterson | Smoltz | 82-58 | 1st | +7.5 |
| 9-11 | Mon. | W | 8-1 | | 11 | 6 | Cruz | Hernandez | | 83-58 | 1st | +8.5 |
| 9-12 | Mon. | W | 9-8 | (12) | 15 | 14 | Cruz | Ayala | | 84-58 | 1st | +8.5 |
| 9-13! | At N.Y. | L | 7-9 | | 11 | 11 | Heilman | Wright | | 84-59 | | |
| 9-13& | At N.Y. | W | 7-1 | | 13 | 7 | Byrd | Seo | | 85-59 | 1st | +8.0 |
| 9-14 | At N.Y. | L | 0-7 | | 4 | 12 | Benson | Ortiz | | 85-60 | 1st | +7.0 |
| 9-15 | At N.Y. | W | 2-0 | | 4 | 6 | Thomson | Leiter | Smoltz | 86-60 | 1st | +8.5 |
| 9-16 | At N.Y. | L | 4-9 | | 9 | 12 | Trachsel | Capellan | | 86-61 | 1st | +7.5 |
| 9-17 | At Fla. | W | 8-1 | | 11 | 14 | Byrd | Kensing | | 87-61 | 1st | +8.5 |
| 9-18 | At Fla. | W | 4-2 | | 8 | 4 | Wright | Beckett | Smoltz | 88-61 | 1st | +9.5 |
| 9-19 | At Fla. | L | 0-3 | | 3 | 9 | Valdez | Ortiz | Benitez | 88-62 | 1st | +8.5 |
| 9-21 | Cin. | W | 5-4 | | 12 | 9 | Thomson | Claussen | Smoltz | 89-62 | 1st | +9.5 |
| 9-22 | Cin. | L | 8-11 | | 6 | 17 | Norton | Smoltz | Valentine | 89-63 | 1st | +9.5 |
| 9-23 | Cin. | L | 2-3 | | 6 | 5 | Hudson | Wright | White | 89-64 | 1st | +9.5 |
| 9-24 | Fla. | W | 8-7 | | 11 | 9 | Smith | Mota | Smoltz | 90-64 | 1st | +10.5 |
| 9-25 | Fla. | W | 1-0 | | 2 | 4 | Hampton | Pavano | Reitsma | 91-64 | 1st | +10.5 |
| 9-26 | Fla. | W | 6-3 | | 9 | 8 | Thomson | Willis | | 92-64 | 1st | +10.5 |
| 9-28! | N.Y. | L | 1-2 | | 4 | 8 | Trachsel | Byrd | Looper | 92-65 | | |
| 9-28& | N.Y. | W | 5-2 | | 7 | 11 | Colon | Glavine | Smoltz | 93-65 | 1st | +11.0 |
| 9-29 | N.Y. | W | 6-3 | | 10 | 7 | Ortiz | Heilman | Smoltz | 94-65 | 1st | +10.5 |
| 10-1 | At Chi. | W | 5-4 | | 10 | 8 | Hampton | Wood | Gryboski | 95-65 | 1st | +10.0 |
| 10-2 | At Chi. | W | 8-6 | | 14 | 9 | Gryboski | Farnsworth | Smoltz | 96-65 | 1st | +11.0 |
| 10-3 | At Chi. | L | 8-10 | | 11 | 15 | Maddux | Byrd | Hawkins | 96-66 | 1st | +10.0 |

Monthly records: April (11-10), May (14-15), June (12-15), July (20-6), August (20-8), September (17-11), October (2-1).
*Innings, if other than nine. @ At Hiram Bithorn Stadium, San Juan, Puerto Rico. ! First game of a doubleheader. & Second game of a doubleheader. # Day separate admission. $ Night separate admission.

## RECORDS

**2004 regular-season record:** 96-66
**Position:** 1st in N.L. East
**Home:** 49-32 **Road:** 47-34
**N.L. East:** 51-25 **N.L. Central:** 18-18
**N.L. West:** 19-13 **A.L.** 8-10
**Vs. LH starters:** 34-19
**Vs. RH starters:** 62-47
**Grass:** 89-64 **Artificial:** 7-2
**Day:** 28-19 **Night:** 68-47
**1-Run:** 27-17 **X-inn.:** 7-8
**Doubleheaders:** 0-1-2
**Team record past five years:** 481-327 (.595, ranks 1st in league in that span)

## TEAM LEADERS

**Batting average:** Johnny Estrada (.314).
**At-bats:** Andruw Jones (570).
**Runs:** J.D. Drew (118).
**Hits:** J.D. Drew (158).
**Total Bases:** J.D. Drew (295).
**Doubles:** Johnny Estrada (36).
**Triples:** J.D. Drew (8).
**Home runs:** J.D. Drew (31).
**Runs batted in:** Chipper Jones (96).
**Stolen bases:** Rafael Furcal (29).
**Slugging percentage:** J.D. Drew (.569).
**On-base percentage:** J.D. Drew (.436).
**Wins:** Russ Ortiz, Jaret Wright (15).
**Earned-run average:** Jaret Wright (3.28).
**Complete games:** Russ Ortiz (2).
**Shutouts:** Russ Ortiz (1).
**Saves:** John Smoltz (44).
**Innings pitched:** Russ Ortiz (204.2).
**Strikeouts:** Jaret Wright (159).

## GAMES BY POSITION

**Catcher:** Johnny Estrada 133, Eddie Perez 66.
**First base:** Adam LaRoche 98, Julio Franco 84, Mike Hessman 16, Eddie Perez 1.
**Second base:** Marcus Giles 97, Nick Green 75, Jesse Garcia 11, Mark DeRosa 5, Rafael Furcal 1.
**Third base:** Chipper Jones 96, Mark DeRosa 72, Wilson Betemit 7, Mike Hessman 7, Nick Green 5, Jesse Garcia 3.
**Shortstop:** Rafael Furcal 131, Jesse Garcia 25, Wilson Betemit 11, Mark DeRosa 11.
**Outfield:** Andruw Jones 154, J.D. Drew 142, Eli Marrero 73, Charles Thomas 71, Dewayne Wise 56, Chipper Jones 29, Damon Hollins 6, Mark DeRosa 3, Mike Hessman 3, Nick Green 1.
**Designated hitter:** Chipper Jones 7, J.D. Drew 1, Julio Franco 1.

## TOP DRAFT CHOICES

2. **Eric Campbell,** 3B, Gibson Southern H.S., Owensville, Ind.
3. **J.C. Holt,** 2B, Louisiana State.
4. **James Parr,** RHP, La Cueva H.S., Albuquerque, N.M.
5. **Van Pope,** 3B, Meridian (Miss.) CC.
6. **Clint Sammons,** C, Georgia.
7. **Trae Wiggins,** LHP, Brewton-Parker College.
8. **Derrick Arnold,** SS, Tallahassee (Fla.) CC.
9. **Jeff Katz,** RHP, Cheshire (Conn.) H.S.
10. **Brady Endi,** LHP, Wisconsin-Whitewater.

# CHICAGO CUBS
## NATIONAL LEAGUE CENTRAL DIVISION

## 2005 SEASON

### Cubs Schedule
Home games shaded.
All-Star Game July 12 at Detroit. Schedule subject to change.

**April**

| SUN | MON | TUE | WED | THU | FRI | SAT |
|---|---|---|---|---|---|---|
| 3 | 4 ARI | 5 ARI | 6 ARI | 7 ARI | 8 MIL | 9 MIL |
| 10 MIL | 11 SD | 12 SD | 13 SD | 14 | 15 PIT | 16 PIT |
| 17 PIT | 18 CIN | 19 CIN | 20 STL | 21 STL | 22 PIT | 23 PIT |
| 24 PIT | 25 CIN | 26 CIN | 27 CIN | 28 | 29 HOU | 30 HOU |

**May**

| SUN | MON | TUE | WED | THU | FRI | SAT |
|---|---|---|---|---|---|---|
| 1 HOU | 2 | 3 MIL | 4 MIL | 5 MIL | 6 PHI | 7 PHI |
| 8 PHI | 9 NYM | 10 NYM | 11 NYM | 12 | 13 WAS | 14 WAS |
| 15 WAS | 16 | 17 PIT | 18 PIT | 19 | 20 CHW | 21 CHW |
| 22 CHW | 23 HOU | 24 HOU | 25 HOU | 26 COL | 27 COL | 28 COL |
| 29 COL | 30 LA | 31 LA | | | | |

**June**

| SUN | MON | TUE | WED | THU | FRI | SAT |
|---|---|---|---|---|---|---|
| | | | 1 LA | 2 SD | 3 SD | 4 SD |
| 5 SD | 6 TOR | 7 TOR | 8 TOR | 9 | 10 BOS | 11 BOS |
| 12 BOS | 13 FLA | 14 FLA | 15 FLA | 16 | 17 NYY | 18 NYY |
| 19 NYY | 20 MIL | 21 MIL | 22 MIL | 23 MIL | 24 CHW | 25 CHW |
| 26 CHW | 27 | 28 MIL | 29 MIL | 30 MIL | | |

**July**

| SUN | MON | TUE | WED | THU | FRI | SAT |
|---|---|---|---|---|---|---|
| | | | | | 1 WAS | 2 WAS |
| 3 WAS | 4 ATL | 5 ATL | 6 ATL | 7 ATL | 8 FLA | 9 FLA |
| 10 FLA | 11 | 12 All-Star | 13 | 14 | 15 PIT | 16 PIT |
| 17 PIT | 18 CIN | 19 CIN | 20 CIN | 21 CIN | 22 STL | 23 STL |
| 24 STL | 25 SF | 26 SF | 27 SF | 28 ARI | 29 ARI | 30 ARI |
| 31 ARI | | | | | | |

**August**

| SUN | MON | TUE | WED | THU | FRI | SAT |
|---|---|---|---|---|---|---|
| | 1 | 2 PHI | 3 PHI | 4 PHI | 5 NYM | 6 NYM |
| 7 NYM | 8 CIN | 9 CIN | 10 CIN | 11 STL | 12 STL | 13 STL |
| 14 STL | 15 HOU | 16 HOU | 17 HOU | 18 | 19 COL | 20 COL |
| 21 COL | 22 ATL | 23 ATL | 24 ATL | 25 | 26 FLA | 27 FLA |
| 28 FLA | 29 LA | 30 LA | 31 LA | | | |

**September**

| SUN | MON | TUE | WED | THU | FRI | SAT |
|---|---|---|---|---|---|---|
| | | | | 1 | 2 PIT | 3 PIT |
| 4 PIT | 5 STL | 6 STL | 7 STL | 8 SF | 9 SF | 10 SF |
| 11 SF | 12 CIN | 13 CIN | 14 CIN | 15 STL | 16 STL | 17 STL |
| 18 STL | 19 | 20 MIL | 21 MIL | 22 MIL | 23 HOU | 24 HOU |
| 25 HOU | 26 | 27 PIT | 28 PIT | 29 HOU | 30 HOU | |

**October**

| SUN | MON | TUE | WED | THU | FRI | SAT |
|---|---|---|---|---|---|---|
| | | | | | | 1 HOU |
| 2 HOU | 3 | 4 | 5 | 6 | 7 | 8 |

Home games shaded. All-Star Game July 12 at Detroit. Schedule subject to change.

### CLUB DIRECTORY

**President and chief executive officer**
Andrew B. MacPhail

**Vice president, general manager**
Jim Hendry

**Director, baseball operations**
Scott Nelson

**Special assistants to the g.m.**
Keith Champion, Ken Kravec, Ed Lynch, Billy Williams

**Special assistant, player development**
Grady Little

**Special assistant, scouting consultant**
Randy Bush

**Director of scouting**
John Stockstill

**Dir. of player dev./Latin American ops.**
Oneri Fleita

**Director of media relations**
Sharon Pannozzo

### MINOR LEAGUE AFFILIATES

| Class | Team | League | Manager |
|---|---|---|---|
| AAA | Iowa | Pacific Coast | Mike Quade |
| AA | West Tenn | Southern | Bobby Dickerson |
| Advanced A | Daytona | Florida State | Steve McFarland |
| A | Peoria | Midwest | Julio Garcia |
| Short-Season A | Boise | Northwest | Tom Beyers |
| Rookie | Mesa Cubs | Arizona | Trey Forkerway |

### BROADCAST INFORMATION

**Radio:** WGN-AM (720).
**TV:** WGN-TV (Channel 9); WCIU-TV (Channel 26).
**Cable TV:** Comcast Sports Net Chicago.

### SPRING TRAINING

**Ballpark (city):** HoHoKam Park (Mesa, Ariz.).
**Ticket information:** 800-638-4253.

**For more on the Cubs, go to msn.foxsports.com/mlb/teams.**

Prior

## SPRING TRAINING ROSTER

**Manager**—Dusty Baker (12).
**Coaches**—Gene Clines (2), Sonny Jackson (15), Juan Lopez (59), Gary Matthews (36), Dick Pole (46), Larry Rothschild (47), Chris Speier.

| No. | PITCHERS | B/T | Ht./Wt. | Age* | 2004 Clubs |
|---|---|---|---|---|---|
| 48 | Borowski, Joe | R/R | 6-2/225 | 33 | Chicago N.L, Iowa |
| 46 | Dempster, Ryan | R/R | 6-2/215 | 27 | Lansing, Iowa, Chicago N.L. |
| 44 | Farnsworth, Kyle | R/R | 6-4/240 | 28 | Chicago N.L. |
|  | Guzman, Angel | R/R | 6-3/190 | 23 | Daytona, West Tenn |
| 32 | Hawkins, LaTroy | R/R | 6-5/215 | 32 | Chicago N.L. |
|  | Koronka, John | L/L | 6-1/180 | 24 | Iowa |
| 51 | Leicester, Jon | R/R | 6-2/220 | 26 | Iowa, Chicago N.L. |
| 31 | Maddux, Greg | R/R | 6-0/185 | 38 | Chicago N.L. |
| 52 | Mitre, Sergio | R/R | 6-4/210 | 24 | Iowa, Chicago N.L. |
|  | Ohman, Will | L/L | 6-2/205 | 27 | Iowa |
|  | Pinto, Renyel | L/L | 6-4/195 | 22 | West Tenn, Iowa |
| 22 | Prior, Mark | R/R | 6-5/230 | 24 | Lansing, Iowa, Chicago N.L. |
|  | Randolph, Stephen | L/L | 6-3/202 | 30 | Arizona |
| 37 | Remlinger, Mike | L/L | 6-1/215 | 39 | Iowa, Chicago N.L. |
|  | Rohlicek, Russ | R/L | 6-6/245 | 25 | West Tenn |
| 33 | Rusch, Glendon | L/L | 6-1/220 | 30 | Iowa, Chicago N.L. |
|  | Vasquez, Carlos | L/L |  |  | Daytona |
| 40 | Wellemeyer, Todd | R/R | 6-3/205 | 26 | Iowa, Chicago N.L. |
| 34 | Wood, Kerry | R/R | 6-5/225 | 27 | Iowa, Chicago N.L. |
| 43 | Wuertz, Michael | R/R | 6-3/205 | 26 | Iowa, Chicago N.L. |
| 38 | Zambrano, Carlos | B/R | 6-5/255 | 23 | Chicago N.L. |

| No. | CATCHERS | B/T | Ht./Wt. | Age* | 2004 Clubs |
|---|---|---|---|---|---|
| 8 | Barrett, Michael | R/R | 6-3/210 | 28 | Chicago N.L. |
|  | Blanco, Henry | R/R | 5-11/224 | 33 | Minnesota |
|  | Soto, Geovany | R/R |  |  | West Tenn |

| No. | INFIELDERS | B/T | Ht./Wt. | Age* | 2004 Clubs |
|---|---|---|---|---|---|
|  | Cedeno, Ronny | R/R | 6-0/180 | 22 | West Tenn |
| 5 | Garciaparra, N. | R/R | 6-0/190 | 31 | Pawtucket, Boston, Chicago N.L. |
| 25 | Lee, Derrek | R/R | 6-5/245 | 29 | Chicago N.L. |
|  | Lewis, Richard | R/R | 6-1/195 | 24 | West Tenn, Iowa |
|  | Macias, Jose | B/R | 5-8/190 | 23 | Chicago N.L. |
| 13 | Perez, Neifi | B/R | 6-0/197 | 31 | San Francisco, Iowa, Chicago N.L. |
| 16 | Ramirez, Aramis | R/R | 6-1/215 | 26 | Chicago N.L. |
| 7 | Walker, Todd | L/R | 6-0/185 | 31 | Chicago N.L. |

| No. | OUTFIELDERS | B/T | Ht./Wt. | Age* | 2004 Clubs |
|---|---|---|---|---|---|
| 4 | Dubois, Jason | R/R | 6-5/220 | 26 | Iowa, Chicago N.L. |
|  | Hollandsworth, T. | L/L | 6-2/215 | 31 | Chicago N.L. |
| 27 | Kelton, David | R/R | 6-3/205 | 25 | Chicago N.L., Iowa |
| 20 | Patterson, Corey | L/R | 5-9/180 | 25 | Chicago N.L. |
| 21 | Sosa, Sammy | R/R | 6-0/220 | 36 | West Tenn, Chicago N.L. |

*Age as of April 1, 2005.

## BALLPARK INFORMATION

**Ballpark (capacity, surface)**
Wrigley Field (39,558, grass)

**Address**
1060 W. Addison St.
Chicago, IL 60613-4397

**Official website**
www.cubs.com

**Business phone**
773-404-2827

**Ticket information**
773-404-2827

**Field dimensions (from home plate)**
To left field at foul line, 355 feet
To center field, 400 feet
To right field at foul line, 353 feet

**First game played**
April 20, 1916 (Cubs 7, Reds 6)

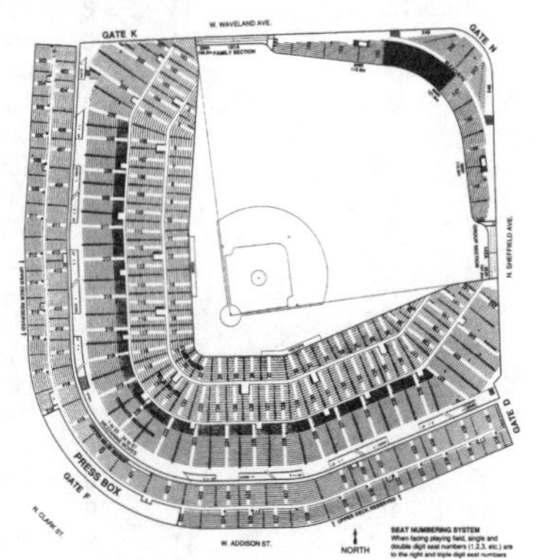

# 2004 REVIEW

## DAY BY DAY

| Date | Opp. | Res. | Score | (inn.*) | Hits | Opp. hits | Winning pitcher | Losing pitcher | Save | Record | Pos. | GB |
|---|---|---|---|---|---|---|---|---|---|---|---|---|
| 4-5 | At Cin. | W | 7-4 | | 10 | 6 | Wood | Lidle | Borowski | 1-0 | T1st | ... |
| 4-7 | At Cin. | L | 1-3 | | 7 | 4 | Wilson | Maddux | Graves | 1-1 | T2nd | 0.5 |
| 4-8 | At Cin. | L | 3-5 | | 8 | 9 | Acevedo | Clement | Graves | 1-2 | T4th | 1.5 |
| 4-9 | At Atl. | W | 2-1 | (15) | 12 | 6 | Mercker | Cunnane | Borowski | 2-2 | T3rd | 1.0 |
| 4-10 | At Atl. | L | 2-5 | | 4 | 6 | Alfonseca | Pratt | Gryboski | 2-3 | T4th | 2.0 |
| 4-11 | At Atl. | W | 10-2 | | 14 | 7 | Wood | Ortiz | | 3-3 | T4th | 1.0 |
| 4-12 | Pit. | L | 2-13 | | 3 | 17 | Benson | Maddux | Meadows | 3-4 | 6th | 2.0 |
| 4-14 | Pit. | W | 8-3 | | 12 | 6 | Clement | Vogelsong | | 4-4 | T3rd | 1.5 |
| 4-15 | Pit. | W | 10-5 | | 13 | 13 | Zambrano | Fogg | | 5-4 | 3rd | 0.5 |
| 4-16 | Cin. | W | 11-10 | | 16 | 15 | Borowski | Graves | | 6-4 | 2nd | 0.5 |
| 4-17 | Cin. | L | 2-3 | | 8 | 6 | Wagner | Wood | Graves | 6-5 | T3rd | 1.5 |
| 4-18 | Cin. | L | 10-11 | (10) | 17 | 13 | Jones | Borowski | Graves | 6-6 | 4th | 2.5 |
| 4-19 | Cin. | W | 8-1 | | 14 | 4 | Clement | Haynes | | 7-6 | 4th | 2.0 |
| 4-20 | At Pit. | W | 9-1 | | 11 | 7 | Zambrano | Vogelsong | | 8-6 | 3rd | 1.0 |
| 4-21 | At Pit. | W | 12-1 | | 15 | 7 | Mitre | Fogg | | 9-6 | T1st | ... |
| 4-23 | N.Y. | W | 3-1 | | 4 | 8 | Maddux | Seo | Borowski | 10-6 | T1st | ... |
| 4-24 | N.Y. | W | 3-0 | | 8 | 4 | Wood | Yates | Hawkins | 11-6 | T1st | ... |
| 4-25 | N.Y. | W | 4-1 | | 10 | 2 | Clement | Leiter | Borowski | 12-6 | 1st | +1.0 |
| 4-26 | At Ari. | L | 0-9 | | 5 | 12 | Johnson | Zambrano | | 12-7 | T1st | ... |
| 4-27 | At Ari. | L | 1-10 | | 5 | 13 | Webb | Mitre | | 12-8 | T1st | ... |
| 4-28 | At Ari. | W | 4-3 | | 6 | 9 | Hawkins | Mantei | Borowski | 13-8 | 1st | +1.0 |
| 4-30 | At StL. | L | 3-4 | | 10 | 5 | Kline | Farnsworth | | 13-9 | T1st | ... |
| 5-1 | At StL. | W | 4-2 | | 9 | 7 | Clement | Suppan | Borowski | 14-9 | T1st | ... |
| 5-2 | At StL. | L | 0-1 | (10) | 5 | 6 | Isringhausen | Farnsworth | | 14-10 | 2nd | 1.0 |
| 5-3 | At StL. | W | 7-3 | | 11 | 8 | Maddux | Marquis | | 15-10 | T1st | ... |
| 5-4 | Ari. | L | 3-6 | | 5 | 10 | Sparks | Mitre | Valverde | 15-11 | 2nd | 1.0 |
| 5-5 | Ari. | L | 0-2 | | 6 | 4 | Daigle | Wood | Valverde | 15-12 | 2nd | 2.0 |
| 5-6 | Ari. | W | 11-3 | | 15 | 8 | Clement | Dessens | | 16-12 | 2nd | 2.0 |
| 5-7 | Col. | W | 11-0 | | 12 | 2 | Zambrano | Estes | | 17-12 | 2nd | 2.0 |
| 5-8 | Col. | L | 3-4 | | 5 | 7 | Jennings | Maddux | Chacon | 17-13 | 2nd | 2.0 |
| 5-9 | Col. | W | 5-4 | (13) | 11 | 16 | Rusch | Fassero | | 18-13 | 2nd | 2.0 |
| 5-11 | At L.A. | L | 3-7 | | 8 | 15 | Weaver | Wood | | 18-14 | 2nd | 3.0 |
| 5-12 | At L.A. | L | 0-4 | | 5 | 7 | Alvarez | Clement | | 18-15 | 2nd | 3.0 |
| 5-13 | At L.A. | W | 7-3 | | 14 | 5 | Zambrano | Nomo | Hawkins | 19-15 | 2nd | 2.0 |
| 5-14 | At S.D. | W | 6-1 | | 12 | 5 | Maddux | Valdez | | 20-15 | 2nd | 1.0 |
| 5-15 | At S.D. | W | 7-5 | | 14 | 9 | Mitre | Eaton | Hawkins | 21-15 | 2nd | 1.0 |
| 5-16 | At S.D. | W | 4-2 | | 12 | 5 | Beltran | Wells | Borowski | 22-15 | T1st | ... |
| 5-18 | S.F | L | 0-1 | | 1 | 6 | Schmidt | Clement | | 22-16 | 2nd | 1.0 |
| 5-19 | S.F | W | 4-3 | (10) | 7 | 8 | Borowski | Brower | | 23-16 | 2nd | 1.0 |
| 5-20 | S.F | L | 3-5 | (10) | 8 | 10 | Herges | Borowski | | 23-17 | 2nd | 1.0 |
| 5-21 | StL. | L | 6-7 | | 11 | 10 | Carpenter | Mitre | Isringhausen | 23-18 | T2nd | 1.0 |
| 5-22 | StL. | W | 7-1 | | 8 | 6 | Rusch | Williams | | 24-18 | T1st | ... |
| 5-23 | StL. | W | 4-3 | | 10 | 3 | Clement | Morris | Borowski | 25-18 | T1st | ... |
| 5-25 | At Hou. | L | 0-5 | | 3 | 9 | Oswalt | Zambrano | | 25-19 | 2nd | 1.5 |
| 5-26 | At Hou. | L | 3-7 | | 8 | 13 | Lidge | Maddux | | 25-20 | 3rd | 1.5 |
| 5-28! | At Pit. | L | 5-9 | | 10 | 11 | Torres | Borowski | | 25-21 | | |
| 5-28& | At Pit. | L | 4-5 | (10) | 11 | 9 | Gonzalez | Beltran | | 25-22 | T3rd | 2.5 |
| 5-29 | At Pit. | L | 7-10 | | 12 | 16 | Fogg | Mitre | | 25-23 | 5th | 3.5 |
| 5-30 | At Pit. | W | 12-1 | | 17 | 8 | Zambrano | Grabow | | 26-23 | T3rd | 2.5 |
| 5-31 | Hou. | W | 3-1 | | 11 | 10 | Maddux | Oswalt | Borowski | 27-23 | T2nd | 2.5 |
| 6-1 | Hou. | L | 3-5 | | 6 | 9 | Miceli | Farnsworth | Dotel | 27-24 | 4th | 3.5 |
| 6-2 | Hou. | L | 1-5 | | 6 | 13 | Clemens | Clement | | 27-25 | 4th | 4.5 |
| 6-4 | Pit. | L | 1-2 | | 7 | 6 | Torres | Borowski | Mesa | 27-26 | 5th | 4.5 |
| 6-5 | Pit. | W | 6-1 | | 8 | 4 | Zambrano | Benson | | 28-26 | 4th | 4.5 |
| 6-6 | Pit. | W | 4-1 | | 8 | 6 | Maddux | Vogelsong | Hawkins | 29-26 | 4th | 4.5 |
| 6-7 | StL. | L | 3-4 | | 9 | 6 | Carpenter | Rusch | Isringhausen | 29-27 | 4th | 4.5 |
| 6-8 | StL. | W | 7-3 | | 13 | 6 | Clement | Williams | | 30-27 | 4th | 3.5 |
| 6-9 | StL. | L | 4-12 | | 11 | 13 | Morris | Prior | | 30-28 | 5th | 3.5 |
| 6-10 | StL. | W | 12-3 | | 15 | 6 | Zambrano | Haren | | 31-28 | 4th | 3.0 |
| 6-11 | At Ana. | L | 2-3 | | 7 | 8 | Lackey | Maddux | Rodriguez | 31-29 | 5th | 3.5 |
| 6-12 | At Ana. | W | 10-5 | | 13 | 13 | Rusch | Colon | Hawkins | 32-29 | 5th | 2.5 |
| 6-13 | At Ana. | W | 6-5 | (15) | 14 | 13 | Leicester | Hensley | | 33-29 | 4th | 2.5 |
| 6-14 | At Hou. | W | 7-2 | | 12 | 10 | Prior | Clemens | Anderson | 34-29 | T2nd | 2.0 |
| 6-15 | At Hou. | W | 4-2 | | 7 | 9 | Farnsworth | Dotel | Hawkins | 35-29 | T2nd | 2.0 |
| 6-16 | At Hou. | W | 4-1 | | 11 | 8 | Maddux | Redding | Hawkins | 36-29 | T2nd | 2.0 |

| Date | Opp. | Res. | Score | (inn.*) | Hits | Opp. hits | Winning pitcher | Losing pitcher | Save | Record | Pos. | GB |
|---|---|---|---|---|---|---|---|---|---|---|---|---|
| 6-17 | At Hou. | W | 5-4 | | 13 | 6 | Rusch | Oswalt | Hawkins | 37-29 | T2nd | 2.0 |
| 6-18 | Oak. | L | 1-2 | | 4 | 8 | Redman | Clement | Bradford | 37-30 | T2nd | 3.0 |
| 6-19 | Oak. | W | 4-3 | | 13 | 9 | Farnsworth | Bradford | | 38-30 | 2nd | 3.0 |
| 6-20 | Oak. | W | 5-3 | | 10 | 8 | Zambrano | Zito | | 39-30 | 2nd | 2.0 |
| 6-22 | At StL. | W | 5-4 | | 8 | 10 | Farnsworth | Isringhausen | Hawkins | 40-30 | 2nd | 1.0 |
| 6-23 | At StL. | L | 9-10 | | 14 | 9 | Kline | Remlinger | | 40-31 | 2nd | 2.0 |
| 6-24 | At StL. | L | 0-4 | | 8 | 7 | Carpenter | Clement | | 40-32 | T2nd | 3.0 |
| 6-25 | At Chi. | W | 7-4 | | 8 | 6 | Prior | Garland | Hawkins | 41-32 | T2nd | 3.0 |
| 6-26 | At Chi. | L | 3-6 | | 7 | 11 | Diaz | Zambrano | Takatsu | 41-33 | T2nd | 4.0 |
| 6-27 | At Chi. | L | 4-9 | | 10 | 11 | Loaiza | Maddux | | 41-34 | T2nd | 5.0 |
| 6-29 | Hou. | W | 7-5 | | 8 | 11 | Beltran | Weathers | Hawkins | 42-34 | 2nd | 3.5 |
| 6-30 | Hou. | L | 2-3 | | 6 | 7 | Lidge | Hawkins | | 42-35 | T2nd | 3.5 |
| 7-1 | Hou. | W | 5-4 | (10) | 9 | 7 | Leicester | Lidge | | 43-35 | 2nd | 3.0 |
| 7-2 | Chi. | W | 6-2 | | 12 | 3 | Zambrano | Loaiza | | 44-35 | 2nd | 3.0 |
| 7-3 | Chi. | W | 4-2 | (6) | 7 | 6 | Maddux | Diaz | Wuertz | 45-35 | 2nd | 3.0 |
| 7-4 | Chi. | W | 2-1 | | 6 | 6 | Hawkins | Takatsu | | 46-35 | 2nd | 3.0 |
| 7-5 | At Mil. | L | 0-1 | | 6 | 3 | Sheets | Clement | Kolb | 46-36 | 2nd | 4.0 |
| 7-6 | At Mil. | L | 2-4 | | 6 | 5 | Santos | Prior | Kolb | 46-37 | 2nd | 5.0 |
| 7-7 | At Mil. | L | 0-4 | | 4 | 9 | Davis | Zambrano | | 46-38 | 2nd | 6.0 |
| 7-9 | At StL. | L | 1-6 | | 9 | 12 | Marquis | Maddux | | 46-39 | 2nd | 7.0 |
| 7-10 | At StL. | L | 2-5 | | 7 | 10 | Suppan | Clement | Isringhausen | 46-40 | 2nd | 8.0 |
| 7-11 | At StL. | W | 8-4 | | 16 | 7 | Wood | Carpenter | | 47-40 | 2nd | 7.0 |
| 7-15 | Mil. | W | 4-1 | | 9 | 5 | Rusch | Davis | Hawkins | 48-40 | 2nd | 7.0 |
| 7-16 | Mil. | L | 2-3 | | 4 | 9 | Santos | Clement | Kolb | 48-41 | 2nd | 8.0 |
| 7-17 | Mil. | W | 5-0 | | 8 | 6 | Maddux | Sheets | | 49-41 | 2nd | 7.0 |
| 7-18 | Mil. | L | 2-4 | | 6 | 9 | Capuano | Beltran | Kolb | 49-42 | 2nd | 8.0 |
| 7-19 | StL. | L | 4-5 | | 12 | 6 | Carpenter | Zambrano | Isringhausen | 49-43 | 2nd | 9.0 |
| 7-20 | StL. | L | 8-11 | | 10 | 14 | King | Hawkins | Isringhausen | 49-44 | 3rd | 10.0 |
| 7-21 | Cin. | W | 5-4 | | 6 | 10 | Wellemeyer | Van Poppel | Hawkins | 50-44 | 2nd | 10.0 |
| 7-22 | Cin. | W | 13-2 | | 14 | 4 | Maddux | Lidle | | 51-44 | 2nd | 10.0 |
| 7-23 | At Phi. | W | 5-1 | | 8 | 7 | Wood | Myers | | 52-44 | 2nd | 9.0 |
| 7-24 | At Phi. | L | 3-4 | | 10 | 9 | Abbott | Zambrano | Worrell | 52-45 | 2nd | 9.0 |
| 7-25 | At Phi. | L | 2-3 | | 3 | 7 | Madson | Hawkins | | 52-46 | 2nd | 10.0 |
| 7-26 | At Mil. | W | 3-1 | | 8 | 5 | Clement | Santos | Hawkins | 53-46 | 2nd | 10.0 |
| 7-27 | At Mil. | W | 7-1 | | 8 | 6 | Maddux | Sheets | | 54-46 | 2nd | 10.0 |
| 7-28 | At Mil. | L | 3-6 | | 5 | 10 | Capuano | Wood | Kolb | 54-47 | 2nd | 11.0 |
| 7-29 | At Mil. | W | 4-0 | | 10 | 5 | Zambrano | Hendrickson | | 55-47 | 2nd | 10.5 |
| 7-30 | Phi. | W | 10-7 | | 14 | 11 | Leicester | Cormier | Hawkins | 56-47 | 2nd | 10.5 |
| 7-31 | Phi. | L | 3-4 | | 3 | 5 | Millwood | Clement | Worrell | 56-48 | 2nd | 10.5 |
| 8-1 | Phi. | W | 6-3 | | 8 | 11 | Mercker | Wolf | Hawkins | 57-48 | 2nd | 10.5 |
| 8-3 | At Col. | W | 5-3 | | 9 | 6 | Wood | Fassero | Hawkins | 58-48 | 2nd | 9.5 |
| 8-4 | At Col. | W | 11-8 | | 15 | 11 | Farnsworth | Chacon | | 59-48 | 2nd | 9.5 |
| 8-5 | At Col. | W | 5-1 | | 9 | 9 | Prior | Jennings | Rusch | 60-48 | 2nd | 9.5 |
| 8-6 | At S.F | L | 2-6 | | 9 | 8 | Schmidt | Clement | | 60-49 | 2nd | 10.5 |
| 8-7 | At S.F | W | 8-4 | | 12 | 11 | Maddux | Hennessey | | 61-49 | 2nd | 10.5 |
| 8-8 | At S.F | L | 3-6 | | 8 | 11 | Lowry | Wood | Hermanson | 61-50 | 2nd | 11.5 |
| 8-10 | S.D. | L | 6-8 | | 8 | 12 | Eaton | Prior | Hoffman | 61-51 | 2nd | 12.5 |
| 8-11 | S.D. | W | 5-1 | | 8 | 6 | Zambrano | Hitchcock | | 62-51 | 2nd | 12.5 |
| 8-12 | S.D. | L | 4-5 | (11) | 12 | 15 | Stone | Dempster | Hoffman | 62-52 | 2nd | 12.5 |
| 8-13 | L.A. | L | 1-8 | | 6 | 14 | Perez | Maddux | | 62-53 | 2nd | 13.5 |
| 8-14 | L.A. | W | 2-0 | | 7 | 5 | Wood | Ishii | Remlinger | 63-53 | 2nd | 12.5 |
| 8-15 | L.A. | L | 5-8 | | 10 | 12 | Sanchez | Farnsworth | Gagne | 63-54 | 2nd | 13.5 |
| 8-17 | At Mil. | L | 1-3 | | 7 | 7 | Santos | Zambrano | Kolb | 63-55 | 2nd | 15.0 |
| 8-18 | At Mil. | W | 7-5 | (11) | 12 | 9 | Mercker | Phelps | Hawkins | 64-55 | 2nd | 14.0 |
| 8-19 | At Mil. | W | 9-6 | | 11 | 7 | Maddux | Capuano | Hawkins | 65-55 | 2nd | 13.0 |
| 8-20 | At Hou. | W | 9-2 | | 13 | 6 | Rusch | Munro | | 66-55 | 2nd | 13.5 |
| 8-21 | At Hou. | L | 3-4 | | 8 | 7 | Lidge | Hawkins | | 66-56 | 2nd | 14.5 |
| 8-22 | At Hou. | W | 11-6 | | 14 | 11 | Leicester | Oswalt | | 67-56 | 2nd | 14.5 |
| 8-23 | Mil. | W | 8-3 | | 13 | 6 | Zambrano | Sheets | | 68-56 | 2nd | 14.0 |
| 8-24 | Mil. | W | 13-4 | | 13 | 10 | Clement | Capuano | Rusch | 69-56 | 2nd | 13.0 |
| 8-25 | Mil. | W | 4-2 | | 10 | 6 | Hawkins | Vizcaino | | 70-56 | 2nd | 13.0 |
| 8-26 | Hou. | W | 8-3 | | 13 | 10 | Prior | Backe | | 71-56 | 2nd | 12.0 |
| 8-27 | Hou. | L | 7-15 | | 9 | 17 | Oswalt | Wood | | 71-57 | 2nd | 13.0 |
| 8-28 | Hou. | L | 6-7 | | 11 | 10 | Clemens | Zambrano | Lidge | 71-58 | 2nd | 14.0 |
| 8-29 | Hou. | L | 3-10 | | 8 | 16 | Hernandez | Clement | | 71-59 | 2nd | 15.0 |
| 8-30 | At Mon. | W | 5-2 | | 9 | 7 | Maddux | Biddle | Hawkins | 72-59 | 2nd | 14.5 |
| 8-31 | At Mon. | L | 0-8 | | 4 | 12 | Hernandez | Prior | | 72-60 | 2nd | 15.5 |
| 9-1 | At Mon. | W | 2-1 | (11) | 11 | 7 | Hawkins | Vargas | | 73-60 | 2nd | 15.5 |
| 9-6 | Mon. | W | 9-1 | | 9 | 4 | Zambrano | Armas | | 74-60 | 2nd | 16.5 |

| Date | Opp. | Res. | Score | (inn.*) | Hits | Opp. hits | Winning pitcher | Losing pitcher | Save | Record | Pos. | GB |
|---|---|---|---|---|---|---|---|---|---|---|---|---|
| 9-7 | Mon. | L | 6-7 | (12) | 16 | 13 | Cordero | Wellemeyer | Horgan | 74-61 | 2nd | 17.5 |
| 9-8 | Mon. | L | 0-6 | | 5 | 6 | Downs | Maddux | | 74-62 | 3rd | 17.5 |
| 9-10! | Fla. | L | 0-7 | | 7 | 13 | Pavano | Wood | | 74-63 | | |
| 9-10& | Fla. | W | 11-2 | | 18 | 9 | Prior | Kensing | | 75-63 | 2nd | 17.0 |
| 9-11 | Fla. | W | 5-2 | | 11 | 6 | Dempster | Mota | Hawkins | 76-63 | 2nd | 16.0 |
| 9-12 | Fla. | L | 1-11 | | 6 | 15 | Burnett | Rusch | | 76-64 | 2nd | 17.0 |
| 9-13 | Pit. | W | 7-2 | | 7 | 8 | Maddux | Brooks | | 77-64 | 2nd | 16.5 |
| 9-14 | Pit. | W | 3-2 | (12) | 9 | 6 | Wellemeyer | Meadows | | 78-64 | 2nd | 15.5 |
| 9-15 | Pit. | W | 13-5 | | 18 | 11 | Wuertz | Perez | Dempster | 79-64 | 2nd | 15.5 |
| 9-16 | At Cin. | W | 5-4 | | 6 | 5 | Wood | Wagner | Hawkins | 80-64 | 2nd | 14.5 |
| 9-17 | At Cin. | W | 12-4 | | 13 | 10 | Zambrano | Hudson | | 81-64 | 2nd | 14.5 |
| 9-18 | At Cin. | L | 5-6 | | 12 | 10 | Harang | Maddux | Graves | 81-65 | 2nd | 15.5 |
| 9-19 | At Cin. | W | 5-1 | | 8 | 3 | Leicester | Graves | | 82-65 | 2nd | 14.5 |
| 9-20! | At Fla. | W | 5-1 | | 16 | 7 | Prior | Pavano | | 83-65 | | |
| 9-20& | At Fla. | L | 2-5 | | 5 | 4 | Weathers | Clement | Benitez | 83-66 | 2nd | 15.0 |
| 9-21 | At Pit. | W | 5-4 | (10) | 10 | 9 | Hawkins | Torres | Dempster | 84-66 | 2nd | 14.0 |
| 9-22 | At Pit. | W | 1-0 | | 5 | 6 | Zambrano | Perez | Remlinger | 85-66 | 2nd | 14.0 |
| 9-23 | At Pit. | W | 6-3 | | 8 | 9 | Maddux | Figueroa | Hawkins | 86-66 | 2nd | 14.0 |
| 9-24 | At N.Y. | W | 2-1 | (10) | 7 | 9 | Remlinger | Looper | Hawkins | 87-66 | 2nd | 14.0 |
| 9-25 | At N.Y. | L | 3-4 | (11) | 7 | 6 | Seo | Mercker | | 87-67 | 2nd | 15.0 |
| 9-26 | At N.Y. | L | 2-3 | | 3 | 8 | Leiter | Wood | Looper | 87-68 | 2nd | 16.0 |
| 9-27 | Cin. | W | 12-5 | | 12 | 8 | Zambrano | Claussen | | 88-68 | 2nd | 15.0 |
| 9-28 | Cin. | L | 3-8 | | 7 | 8 | Hancock | Maddux | | 88-69 | 2nd | 15.0 |
| 9-29 | Cin. | L | 3-4 | (12) | 8 | 9 | Riedling | Leicester | Valentine | 88-70 | 3rd | 15.0 |
| 9-30 | Cin. | L | 1-2 | (12) | 7 | 6 | Padilla | Remlinger | | 88-71 | 3rd | 15.0 |
| 10-1 | Atl. | L | 4-5 | | 8 | 10 | Hampton | Wood | Gryboski | 88-72 | 3rd | 16.0 |
| 10-2 | Atl. | L | 6-8 | | 9 | 14 | Gryboski | Farnsworth | Smoltz | 88-73 | 3rd | 16.0 |
| 10-3 | Atl. | W | 10-8 | | 15 | 11 | Maddux | Byrd | Hawkins | 89-73 | 3rd | 16.0 |

Monthly records: April (13-9), May (14-14), June (15-12), July (14-13), August (16-12), September (16-11), October (1-2).
*Innings, if other than nine. ! First game of a doubleheader. & Second game of a doubleheader.

## RECORDS

**2004 regular-season record:** 89-73
**Position:** 3rd in N.L. Central
**Home:** 45-37 **Road:** 44-36
**N.L. East:** 16-14 **N.L. Central:** 50-40
**N.L. West:** 15-15 **A.L.** 8-4
**Vs. LH starters:** 25-15
**Vs. RH starters:** 64-58
**Grass:** 87-72 **Artificial:** 2-1
**Day:** 49-38 **Night:** 40-35
**1-Run:** 19-30 **X-inn.:** 10-9
**Doubleheaders:** 0-1-2
**Team record past five years:** 397-413 (.490, ranks 9th in league in that span)

## TEAM LEADERS

**Batting average:** Aramis Ramirez (.318).
**At-bats:** Corey Patterson (631).
**Runs:** Moises Alou (106).
**Hits:** Moises Alou (176).
**Total Bases:** Moises Alou (335).
**Doubles:** Derrek Lee (39).
**Triples:** Michael Barrett, Corey Patterson (6).
**Home runs:** Moises Alou (39).
**Runs batted in:** Moises Alou (106).
**Stolen bases:** Corey Patterson (32).
**Slugging percentage:** Aramis Ramirez (.578).
**On-base percentage:** Aramis Ramirez (.373).
**Wins:** Greg Maddux, Carlos Zambrano (16).
**Earned-run average:** Carlos Zambrano (2.75).
**Complete games:** Greg Maddux (2).
**Shutouts:** Greg Maddux, Carlos Zambrano (1).
**Saves:** LaTroy Hawkins (25).
**Innings pitched:** Greg Maddux (212.2).
**Strikeouts:** Matt Clement (190).

## GAMES BY POSITION

**Catcher:** Michael Barrett 130, Paul Bako 47, Mike DiFelice 4.
**First base:** Derrek Lee 161, Todd Walker 5, Todd Hollandsworth 3, Jason Dubois 1.
**Second base:** Todd Walker 89, Mark Grudzielanek 76, Jose Macias 16, Ramon Martinez 6, Damian Jackson 5, Neifi Perez 2.
**Third base:** Aramis Ramirez 144, Ramon Martinez 24, Jose Macias 18, Brendan Harris 3.
**Shortstop:** Ramon Martinez 73, Nomar Garciaparra 42, Alex S. Gonzalez 37, Rey Ordonez 22, Neifi Perez 19.
**Outfield:** Corey Patterson 157, Moises Alou 154, Sammy Sosa 124, Todd Hollandsworth 36, Tom Goodwin 28, Jose Macias 28, Calvin Murray 8, Jason Dubois 5, Ben Grieve 4, David Kelton 3, Todd Walker 1.
**Designated hitter:** Todd Hollandsworth 3, Sammy Sosa 2, Moises Alou 1.

## TOP DRAFT CHOICES

2. **Grant Johnson,** RHP, Notre Dame.
3. **Mark Reed,** C, Bonita H.S., La Verne Calif.
4. **Chris Shaver,** LHP, William & Mary.
5. **Adrian Ortiz,** OF, Puerto Rico Baseball Academy, Caguas, P.R.
6. **Tim Layden,** LHP, Duke.
7. **Mitch Atkins,** RHP, Northeast Guilford H.S., Browns Summit, N.C.
8. **Eric Patterson,** 2B, Georgia Tech.
9. **Ryan Norwood,** 1B, East Carolina.
10. **Sam Fuld,** OF, Stanford.

# CINCINNATI REDS

## *NATIONAL LEAGUE CENTRAL DIVISION*

## 2005 SEASON

### Reds Schedule

Home games shaded.
All-Star Game July 12 at Detroit. Schedule subject to change.

**April**

| SUN | MON | TUE | WED | THU | FRI | SAT |
|---|---|---|---|---|---|---|
| 3 | 4 NYM | 5 | 6 NYM | 7 NYM | 8 HOU | 9 HOU |
| 10 HOU | 11 | 12 STL | 13 STL | 14 | 15 HOU | 16 HOU |
| 17 HOU | 18 CHC | 19 CHC | 20 PIT | 21 PIT | 22 FLA | 23 FLA |
| 24 FLA | 25 CHC | 26 CHC | 27 CHC | 28 | 29 MIL | 30 MIL |

**May**

| SUN | MON | TUE | WED | THU | FRI | SAT |
|---|---|---|---|---|---|---|
| 1 MIL | 2 STL | 3 STL | 4 STL | 5 | 6 LA | 7 LA |
| 8 LA | 9 SD | 10 SD | 11 SD | 12 PHI | 13 PHI | 14 PHI |
| 15 PHI | 16 NYM | 17 NYM | 18 NYM | 19 | 20 CLE | 21 CLE |
| 22 CLE | 23 WAS | 24 WAS | 25 WAS | 26 PIT | 27 PIT | 28 PIT |
| 29 PIT | 30 HOU | 31 HOU | | | | |

**June**

| SUN | MON | TUE | WED | THU | FRI | SAT |
|---|---|---|---|---|---|---|
| | | | 1 HOU | 2 | 3 COL | 4 COL |
| 5 COL | 6 | 7 TB | 8 TB | 9 TB | 10 BAL | 11 BAL |
| 12 BAL | 13 BOS | 14 BOS | 15 BOS | 16 ATL | 17 ATL | 18 ATL |
| 19 ATL | 20 STL | 21 STL | 22 STL | 23 | 24 CLE | 25 CLE |
| 26 CLE | 27 | 28 STL | 29 STL | 30 HOU | | |

**July**

| SUN | MON | TUE | WED | THU | FRI | SAT |
|---|---|---|---|---|---|---|
| | | | | | 1 HOU | 2 HOU |
| 3 HOU | 4 SF | 5 SF | 6 SF | 7 SF | 8 ARI | 9 ARI |
| 10 ARI | 11 | 12 All-Star | 13 | 14 | 15 COL | 16 COL |
| 17 COL | 18 CHC | 19 CHC | 20 CHC | 21 CHC | 22 MIL | 23 MIL |
| 24 MIL | 25 LA | 26 LA | 27 LA | 28 LA | 29 SD | 30 SD |
| 31 SD | | | | | | |

**August**

| SUN | MON | TUE | WED | THU | FRI | SAT |
|---|---|---|---|---|---|---|
| | 1 | 2 ATL | 3 ATL | 4 ATL | 5 FLA | 6 FLA |
| 7 FLA | 8 CHC | 9 CHC | 10 CHC | 11 | 12 MIL | 13 MIL |
| 14 MIL | 15 SF | 16 SF | 17 SF | 18 SF | 19 ARI | 20 ARI |
| 21 ARI | 22 WAS | 23 WAS | 24 WAS | 25 | 26 PIT | 27 PIT |
| 28 PIT | 29 PIT | 30 HOU | 31 HOU | | | |

**September**

| SUN | MON | TUE | WED | THU | FRI | SAT |
|---|---|---|---|---|---|---|
| | | | | 1 HOU | 2 ATL | 3 ATL |
| 4 ATL | 5 MIL | 6 MIL | 7 MIL | 8 | 9 PIT | 10 PIT |
| 11 PIT | 12 CHC | 13 CHC | 14 CHC | 15 | 16 PIT | 17 PIT |
| 18 PIT | 19 | 20 STL | 21 STL | 22 STL | 23 PHI | 24 PHI |
| 25 PHI | 26 MIL | 27 MIL | 28 MIL | 29 MIL | 30 STL | |

**October**

| SUN | MON | TUE | WED | THU | FRI | SAT |
|---|---|---|---|---|---|---|
| | | | | | | 1 STL |
| 2 STL | 3 STL | 4 | 5 | 6 | 7 | 8 |

Home games shaded. All-Star Game July 12 at Detroit. Schedule subject to change.

### CLUB DIRECTORY

**Chief operating officer**
John Allen
**General manager**
Dan O'Brien
**Assistant general manager**
Dean Taylor
**Director of major league operations**
Brad Kullman
**Director of player development**
Tim Naehring
**Director of amateur scouting**
Terry Reynolds
**Director of international scouting**
Johnny Almaraz
**Manager of Florida operations**
Jeff Maultsby
**Director of media relations**
Rob Butcher
**Travelling secretary**
Gary Wahoff
**Medical director**
Dr. Timothy Kremchek

### MINOR LEAGUE AFFILIATES

| Class | Team | League | Manager |
|---|---|---|---|
| AAA | Louisville | International | Rick Sweet |
| AA | Chattanooga | Southern | Jayhawk Owens |
| Advanced A | Sarasota | Florida State | TBA |
| A | Dayton | Midwest | Alonzo Powell |
| Advanced Rookie | Billings | Pioneer | Rick Burleson |
| Rookie | Gulf Coast Reds | Gulf Coast | Luis Aguayo |

### BROADCAST INFORMATION

**Radio:** WLW-AM (700).
**Cable TV:** Fox Sports Net.

### SPRING TRAINING

**Ballpark (city):** Ed Smith Stadium (Sarasota, Fla.).
**Ticket information:** 941-954-4101.

**For more on the Reds, go to msn.foxsports.com/mlb/teams.**

Casey

## SPRING TRAINING ROSTER

**Manager**—Dave Miley (12).
**Coaches**—Mark Berry (55), Chris Chambliss (49), Don Gullett (35), Tom Hume (47), Jerry Narron (50), Randy Whisler (53).

| No. | PITCHERS | B/T | Ht./Wt. | Age* | 2004 Clubs |
|---|---|---|---|---|---|
| 29 | Acevedo, Jose | R/R | 6-0/185 | 27 | Cincinnati |
| | Belisle, Matt | B/R | 6-3/195 | 24 | Louisville |
| 31 | Bong, Jung Keun | L/L | 6-3/215 | 24 | Cincinnati, G.C. Reds, Louisville |
| | Childress, Daylan | R/R | 6-1/200 | 26 | Chattanooga |
| 34 | Claussen, Brandon | R/L | 6-1/200 | 25 | Louisville, Cincinnati |
| | Coffey, Todd | R/R | 6-5/230 | 24 | Chattanooga, Louisville |
| | Dumatrait, Phil | R/L | 6-2/170 | 23 | Did Not Play |
| 32 | Graves, Danny | R/R | 6-0/185 | 31 | Cincinnati |
| 43 | Hancock, Josh | R/R | 6-3/205 | 26 | Scranton/W.B., Philadelphia, Cincinnati |
| 39 | Harang, Aaron | R/R | 6-7/240 | 26 | Louisville, Cincinnati |
| 54 | Hudson, Luke | R/R | 6-3/195 | 27 | Chattanooga, Louisville, Cincinnati |
| | Kozlowski, Ben | L/L | 6-6/230 | 24 | Frisco, Stockton |
| | Mercker, Kent | L/L | 6-2/205 | 37 | Chicago N.L. |
| | Milton, Eric | L/L | 6-3/208 | 29 | Philadelphia |
| | Nelson, Bubba | R/R | 6-2/195 | 23 | Chattanooga, Louisville |
| | Ortiz, Ramon | R/R | 6-0/175 | 31 | Anaheim |
| | Ramirez, Elizardo | B/R | 6-0/180 | 22 | Clearwater, Philadelphia, Reading, Chattanooga |
| | Shackelford, Brian | L/L | 6-1/190 | 28 | Louisville |
| 48 | Valentine, Joe | R/R | 6-2/210 | 25 | Louisville, Cincinnati |
| 38 | Wagner, Ryan | R/R | 6-4/210 | 22 | Louisville, Cincinnati |
| | Weathers, David | R/R | 6-3/230 | 35 | New York N.L, Houston, Florida |
| | Weber, Ben | R/R | 6-4/205 | 35 | Anaheim, Arizona Angels, Salt Lake |
| 41 | Wilson, Paul | R/R | 6-5/215 | 32 | Cincinnati |

| No. | CATCHERS | B/T | Ht./Wt. | Age* | 2004 Clubs |
|---|---|---|---|---|---|
| 23 | LaRue, Jason | R/R | 5-11/200 | 31 | Louisville, Cincinnati |
| | Perez, Miguel | R/R | 6-3/190 | 21 | Dayton, Potomac |
| | Sardinha, Dane | R/R | 6-0/215 | 25 | Louisville |
| 17 | Valentin, Javier | B/R | 5-10/192 | 29 | Cincinnati |

| No. | INFIELDERS | B/T | Ht./Wt. | Age* | 2004 Clubs |
|---|---|---|---|---|---|
| | Bergolla, William | R/R | 6-0/175 | 22 | Chattanooga |
| 21 | Casey, Sean | L/R | 6-4/225 | 30 | Cincinnati |
| | Encarnacion, Edwin | R/R | 6-1/195 | 22 | Chattanooga |
| 3 | Jimenez, D'Angelo | B/R | 6-0/195 | 27 | Cincinnati |
| 2 | Lopez, Felipe | B/R | 6-1/185 | 24 | Louisville, Cincinnati |
| 19 | Machado, Anderson | B/R | 5-11/170 | 24 | Clearwater, Scranton/W.B., Louisville, Cincinnati |
| 4 | Olmedo, Ray | B/R | 5-11/155 | 23 | Cincinnati, Louisville |
| | Randa, Joe | R/R | 5-11/190 | 35 | Kansas City |

| No. | OUTFIELDERS | B/T | Ht./Wt. | Age* | 2004 Clubs |
|---|---|---|---|---|---|
| 44 | Dunn, Adam | L/R | 6-6/240 | 25 | Cincinnati |
| 6 | Freel, Ryan | R/R | 5-10/180 | 29 | Cincinnati |
| 30 | Griffey Ken | L/L | 6-3/205 | 35 | Cincinnati |
| 28 | Kearns, Austin | R/R | 6-3/220 | 24 | Louisville, Cincinnati |
| 26 | Pena, Wily Mo | R/R | 6-3/215 | 23 | Cincinnati |

*Age as of April 1, 2005.

## BALLPARK INFORMATION

**Ballpark (capacity, surface)**
Great American Ball Park (42,271, grass)
**Address**
100 Main St.
Cincinnati, OH 45202
**Official website**
www.cincinnatireds.com
**Business phone**
513-765-7000
**Ticket information**
513-765-7400
**Field dimensions (from home plate)**
To left field at foul line, 328 feet
To center field, 404 feet
To right field at foul line, 325 feet
**First game played**
March 31, 2003 (Pirates 10, Reds 1)

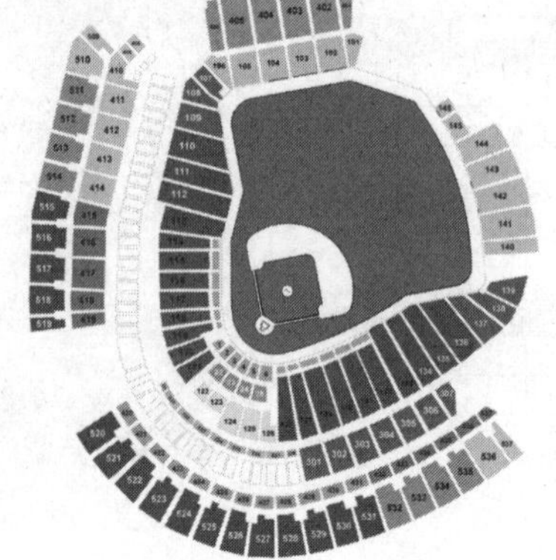

# 2004 REVIEW
## DAY BY DAY

| Date | Opp. | Res. | Score | (inn.*) | Hits | Opp. hits | Winning pitcher | Losing pitcher | Save | Record | Pos. | GB |
|---|---|---|---|---|---|---|---|---|---|---|---|---|
| 4-5 | Chi. | L | 4-7 | | 6 | 10 | Wood | Lidle | Borowski | 0-1 | T4th | 1.0 |
| 4-7 | Chi. | W | 3-1 | | 4 | 7 | Wilson | Maddux | Graves | 1-1 | T2nd | 0.5 |
| 4-8 | Chi. | W | 5-3 | | 9 | 8 | Acevedo | Clement | Graves | 2-1 | T2nd | 0.5 |
| 4-9 | Pit. | W | 5-1 | | 6 | 8 | Harang | Fogg | | 3-1 | 1st | +0.5 |
| 4-10 | Pit. | W | 3-1 | | 9 | 7 | Lidle | Wells | Graves | 4-1 | 1st | +0.5 |
| 4-11 | Pit. | L | 3-4 | | 8 | 8 | Perez | Haynes | Mesa | 4-2 | 1st | +0.5 |
| 4-12 | At Phi. | W | 4-1 | | 11 | 6 | Wilson | Wolf | Graves | 5-2 | 1st | +1.0 |
| 4-15 | At Phi. | L | 4-6 | | 7 | 8 | Cormier | Wagner | Wagner | 5-3 | 1st | ... |
| 4-16 | At Chi. | L | 10-11 | | 15 | 16 | Borowski | Graves | | 5-4 | 3rd | 1.0 |
| 4-17 | At Chi. | W | 3-2 | | 6 | 8 | Wagner | Wood | Graves | 6-4 | 2nd | 1.0 |
| 4-18 | At Chi. | W | 11-10 | (10) | 13 | 17 | Jones | Borowski | Graves | 7-4 | 2nd | 1.0 |
| 4-19 | At Chi. | L | 1-8 | | 4 | 14 | Clement | Haynes | | 7-5 | T2nd | 1.5 |
| 4-20 | Atl. | W | 3-2 | | 7 | 4 | Acevedo | Thomson | Graves | 8-5 | 2nd | 0.5 |
| 4-21 | Atl. | L | 5-9 | (10) | 9 | 10 | Reitsma | Reith | | 8-6 | 3rd | 0.5 |
| 4-22 | Atl. | W | 5-3 | (5) | 5 | 5 | Lidle | Wright | | 9-6 | T1st | ... |
| 4-23 | At Pit. | W | 6-4 | | 8 | 10 | Wilson | Wells | Graves | 10-6 | T1st | ... |
| 4-24 | At Pit. | W | 9-7 | | 15 | 16 | Van Poppel | Benson | Graves | 11-6 | T1st | ... |
| 4-25 | At Pit. | L | 0-6 | | 6 | 10 | Perez | Acevedo | | 11-7 | 2nd | 1.0 |
| 4-26 | At Pit. | W | 5-2 | | 7 | 10 | Harang | Vogelsong | Graves | 12-7 | T1st | ... |
| 4-27 | At Mil. | L | 8-9 | | 9 | 11 | Bennett | Graves | | 12-8 | T1st | ... |
| 4-28 | At Mil. | L | 9-10 | (10) | 12 | 16 | Burba | Van Poppel | | 12-9 | 2nd | 1.0 |
| 4-30 | At Hou. | L | 1-6 | | 5 | 12 | Clemens | Acevedo | | 12-10 | 3rd | 1.0 |
| 5-1 | At Hou. | L | 4-10 | | 6 | 16 | Miller | Harang | | 12-11 | 3rd | 2.0 |
| 5-2 | At Hou. | L | 5-6 | | 8 | 9 | Miceli | Jones | Dotel | 12-12 | 5th | 3.0 |
| 5-3 | At Hou. | W | 7-5 | | 9 | 10 | Riedling | Lidge | Graves | 13-12 | 4th | 2.0 |
| 5-4 | Mil. | L | 2-6 | | 6 | 9 | Santos | Haynes | | 13-13 | T4th | 3.0 |
| 5-5 | Mil. | W | 5-4 | (10) | 9 | 9 | Graves | Bennett | | 14-13 | 3rd | 3.0 |
| 5-6 | Mil. | W | 9-6 | | 10 | 10 | Jones | Bennett | Graves | 15-13 | 3rd | 3.0 |
| 5-7 | S.F | L | 1-6 | | 6 | 8 | Rueter | Lidle | Herges | 15-14 | 3rd | 4.0 |
| 5-8 | S.F | W | 5-3 | | 9 | 8 | Wilson | Hermanson | Graves | 16-14 | 3rd | 3.0 |
| 5-9 | S.F | L | 6-7 | (10) | 9 | 9 | Brower | Graves | | 16-15 | 3rd | 4.0 |
| 5-11 | At S.D. | W | 6-3 | | 8 | 8 | Harang | Wells | Graves | 17-15 | 3rd | 4.0 |
| 5-12 | At S.D. | L | 1-2 | | 9 | 6 | Lawrence | Lidle | Hoffman | 17-16 | T4th | 4.0 |
| 5-13 | At S.D. | L | 2-8 | | 10 | 6 | Peavy | Acevedo | | 17-17 | 5th | 4.0 |
| 5-14 | At L.A. | W | 2-1 | | 3 | 6 | Wilson | Ishii | Graves | 18-17 | T4th | 3.0 |
| 5-15 | At L.A. | W | 4-0 | | 6 | 6 | Van Poppel | Perez | Graves | 19-17 | 4th | 3.0 |
| 5-16 | At L.A. | W | 6-3 | | 12 | 9 | Harang | Weaver | Graves | 20-17 | 3rd | 2.0 |
| 5-18 | Col. | L | 3-8 | | 4 | 14 | Estes | Lidle | | 20-18 | 3rd | 3.0 |
| 5-19 | Col. | W | 4-3 | (10) | 9 | 7 | Riedling | Fuentes | | 21-18 | 3rd | 3.0 |
| 5-20 | Col. | W | 3-1 | | 5 | 3 | Wilson | Kennedy | Graves | 22-18 | 3rd | 2.0 |
| 5-21 | Hou. | W | 7-4 | | 10 | 8 | Wagner | Miceli | Graves | 23-18 | T2nd | 1.0 |
| 5-22 | Hou. | W | 8-7 | | 12 | 15 | Jones | Lidge | Graves | 24-18 | T1st | ... |
| 5-23 | Hou. | W | 7-0 | | 12 | 6 | Lidle | Miller | | 25-18 | T1st | ... |
| 5-24 | Hou. | W | 7-5 | | 10 | 12 | Riedling | Lidge | Graves | 26-18 | 1st | +0.5 |
| 5-25 | Fla. | W | 5-2 | | 7 | 9 | Wilson | Beckett | Jones | 27-18 | 1st | +1.5 |
| 5-26 | Fla. | L | 0-3 | | 1 | 8 | Phelps | Van Poppel | Benitez | 27-19 | 1st | +1.0 |
| 5-27 | Fla. | L | 2-5 | | 6 | 11 | Penny | Harang | Benitez | 27-20 | 1st | +0.5 |
| 5-28 | At Mon. | W | 7-6 | | 14 | 7 | Lidle | Vargas | Graves | 28-20 | 1st | +1.5 |
| 5-29 | At Mon. | W | 4-1 | | 6 | 5 | Acevedo | Day | Graves | 29-20 | 1st | +2.5 |
| 5-30 | At Mon. | L | 2-6 | | 10 | 7 | Ohka | Valentine | Cordero | 29-21 | 1st | +1.5 |
| 5-31 | At Fla. | W | 9-7 | | 10 | 14 | Riedling | Wayne | Graves | 30-21 | 1st | +2.5 |
| 6-1 | At Fla. | W | 7-6 | (10) | 12 | 12 | Reith | Bump | Graves | 31-21 | 1st | +2.5 |
| 6-2 | At Fla. | W | 3-1 | | 5 | 7 | Reith | Howard | Graves | 32-21 | 1st | +2.5 |
| 6-4 | Mon. | L | 2-4 | | 6 | 10 | Day | Acevedo | Biddle | 32-22 | 1st | +1.0 |
| 6-5 | Mon. | W | 6-3 | (10) | 10 | 5 | Jones | Cordero | | 33-22 | 1st | +1.0 |
| 6-6 | Mon. | W | 6-5 | | 10 | 9 | Matthews | Biddle | | 34-22 | 1st | +2.0 |
| 6-7 | At Oak. | L | 2-13 | | 6 | 15 | Mulder | Lidle | | 34-23 | 1st | +1.0 |
| 6-8 | At Oak. | L | 6-10 | | 13 | 14 | Zito | Bong | Rhodes | 34-24 | 1st | +1.0 |
| 6-9 | At Oak. | L | 8-17 | | 10 | 22 | Harden | Acevedo | | 34-25 | T1st | ... |
| 6-11 | At Cle. | L | 5-6 | (11) | 10 | 12 | Riske | Norton | | 34-26 | 2nd | 0.5 |
| 6-12 | At Cle. | L | 7-8 | | 10 | 9 | Betancourt | Norton | Jimenez | 34-27 | 2nd | 0.5 |
| 6-13 | At Cle. | L | 8-10 | | 8 | 10 | Miller | Reith | Jimenez | 34-28 | 2nd | 1.5 |
| 6-14 | At Phi. | L | 7-10 | | 13 | 13 | Madson | Riedling | | 34-29 | T2nd | 2.0 |
| 6-15 | Tex. | W | 5-4 | (11) | 14 | 6 | Jones | Ramirez | | 35-29 | T2nd | 2.0 |
| 6-16 | Tex. | W | 7-4 | | 10 | 9 | Norton | Francisco | | 36-29 | T2nd | 2.0 |
| 6-17 | Tex. | W | 4-3 | | 8 | 7 | Van Poppel | Drese | Graves | 37-29 | T2nd | 2.0 |

| Date | Opp. | Res. | Score | (inn.*) | Hits | Opp. hits | Winning pitcher | Losing pitcher | Save | Record | Pos. | GB |
|---|---|---|---|---|---|---|---|---|---|---|---|---|
| 6-18 | At StL. | L | 3-4 | (10) | 7 | 11 | Tavarez | Matthews | | 37-30 | T2nd | 3.0 |
| 6-19 | At StL. | L | 2-9 | | 5 | 14 | Williams | Acevedo | Isringhausen | 37-31 | 3rd | 4.0 |
| 6-20 | At StL. | W | 6-0 | | 7 | 4 | Bong | Morris | | 38-31 | 3rd | 3.0 |
| 6-22 | At N.Y. | L | 4-7 | | 10 | 11 | Franco | Wilson | Looper | 38-32 | 3rd | 3.0 |
| 6-23 | At N.Y. | W | 6-4 | (12) | 14 | 13 | Matthews | Franco | Graves | 39-32 | 3rd | 3.0 |
| 6-24 | At N.Y. | W | 6-2 | | 11 | 9 | Lidle | Glavine | | 40-32 | T2nd | 3.0 |
| 6-25 | Pit. | W | 6-4 | | 7 | 6 | Acevedo | Torres | Graves | 41-32 | T2nd | 3.0 |
| 6-26 | Pit. | L | 0-1 | | 4 | 8 | Corey | Jones | Mesa | 41-33 | T2nd | 4.0 |
| 6-27 | Pit. | L | 4-14 | | 7 | 18 | Fogg | Wilson | | 41-34 | T2nd | 5.0 |
| 6-29 | N.Y. | L | 5-7 | | 12 | 7 | Seo | Van Poppel | Looper | 41-35 | 3rd | 4.5 |
| 6-30 | N.Y. | W | 2-0 | | 9 | 4 | Lidle | Glavine | Graves | 42-35 | T2nd | 3.5 |
| 7-1 | N.Y. | L | 6-7 | | 9 | 12 | Leiter | Acevedo | Looper | 42-36 | 4th | 4.0 |
| 7-2 | Cle. | L | 2-15 | | 8 | 15 | Tadano | Sanchez | | 42-37 | 4th | 5.0 |
| 7-3 | Cle. | W | 4-2 | | 7 | 8 | Wilson | Elarton | Graves | 43-37 | 3rd | 5.0 |
| 7-4 | Cle. | W | 5-4 | (11) | 13 | 12 | Jones | White | | 44-37 | 3rd | 5.0 |
| 7-5 | At StL. | L | 1-4 | | 5 | 11 | Carpenter | Lidle | Isringhausen | 44-38 | 3rd | 6.0 |
| 7-6 | At StL. | L | 3-5 | | 8 | 7 | Morris | White | Kline | 44-39 | 4th | 7.0 |
| 7-7 | At StL. | L | 2-4 | | 4 | 10 | King | Riedling | Isringhausen | 44-40 | 4th | 8.0 |
| 7-8 | At Mil. | W | 9-3 | | 10 | 8 | Wilson | Obermueller | | 45-40 | 4th | 7.5 |
| 7-9 | At Mil. | W | 3-0 | | 7 | 7 | Harang | Capuano | Graves | 46-40 | 3rd | 7.5 |
| 7-10 | At Mil. | L | 0-5 | | 5 | 7 | Sheets | Lidle | | 46-41 | 4th | 8.5 |
| 7-11 | At Mil. | W | 9-6 | | 15 | 8 | Jones | Kolb | Graves | 47-41 | 3rd | 7.5 |
| 7-15 | StL. | L | 2-7 | | 11 | 11 | Morris | Sanchez | | 47-42 | 3rd | 8.5 |
| 7-16 | StL. | L | 5-7 | | 8 | 12 | Calero | Graves | Isringhausen | 47-43 | 4th | 9.5 |
| 7-17 | StL. | W | 7-5 | | 13 | 11 | Jones | Tavarez | Graves | 48-43 | 3rd | 8.5 |
| 7-18 | StL. | L | 4-10 | | 9 | 13 | Suppan | Acevedo | | 48-44 | 4th | 9.5 |
| 7-19 | Mil. | W | 8-4 | | 12 | 11 | Harang | Hendrickson | | 49-44 | 3rd | 9.5 |
| 7-20 | Mil. | W | 6-2 | | 10 | 6 | Claussen | Davis | | 50-44 | 2nd | 9.5 |
| 7-21 | At Chi. | L | 4-5 | | 10 | 6 | Wellemeyer | Van Poppel | Hawkins | 50-45 | 3rd | 10.5 |
| 7-22 | At Chi. | L | 2-13 | | 4 | 14 | Maddux | Lidle | | 50-46 | 3rd | 11.5 |
| 7-23 | At Pit. | L | 3-6 | | 5 | 11 | Perez | Acevedo | Mesa | 50-47 | 3rd | 11.5 |
| 7-24 | At Pit. | L | 4-14 | | 10 | 15 | Grabow | Harang | | 50-48 | 3rd | 11.5 |
| 7-25 | At Pit. | L | 5-6 | | 12 | 11 | Burnett | Van Poppel | Mesa | 50-49 | 3rd | 12.5 |
| 7-26 | StL. | L | 6-9 | (11) | 7 | 12 | King | Norton | | 50-50 | 3rd | 13.5 |
| 7-27 | StL. | L | 0-6 | | 3 | 13 | Marquis | Lidle | | 50-51 | 4th | 14.5 |
| 7-28 | StL. | L | 10-11 | | 9 | 19 | Eldred | Acevedo | Isringhausen | 50-52 | 4th | 15.5 |
| 7-30 | Hou. | W | 3-2 | (13) | 8 | 4 | Hancock | Harville | | 51-52 | T4th | 16.0 |
| 7-31 | Hou. | L | 0-8 | | 4 | 9 | Oliver | Claussen | | 51-53 | 4th | 15.5 |
| 8-1 | Hou. | L | 5-7 | | 11 | 12 | Oswalt | Riedling | Lidge | 51-54 | 5th | 16.5 |
| 8-3 | At S.F | L | 0-11 | | 3 | 15 | Lowry | Lidle | | 51-55 | 5th | 16.5 |
| 8-4 | At S.F | W | 8-7 | | 14 | 14 | Hancock | Eyre | Graves | 52-55 | 4th | 16.5 |
| 8-5 | At S.F | W | 12-3 | | 13 | 6 | Harang | Rueter | | 53-55 | 4th | 16.5 |
| 8-6 | At Col. | L | 5-8 | | 12 | 9 | Estes | Claussen | Chacon | 53-56 | 4th | 17.5 |
| 8-7 | At Col. | L | 5-9 | | 13 | 14 | Simpson | Wilson | | 53-57 | 4th | 18.5 |
| 8-8 | At Col. | W | 14-7 | | 16 | 14 | Lidle | Fassero | | 54-57 | 4th | 18.5 |
| 8-10 | L.A. | L | 2-5 | | 5 | 7 | Lima | Harang | Gagne | 54-58 | 4th | 19.5 |
| 8-11 | L.A. | L | 1-11 | | 5 | 11 | Weaver | Claussen | | 54-59 | 4th | 20.5 |
| 8-12 | L.A. | W | 6-5 | | 11 | 7 | White | Dreifort | Graves | 55-59 | 4th | 19.5 |
| 8-13 | S.D. | L | 5-14 | | 8 | 17 | Wells | Wilson | Witasick | 55-60 | 4th | 20.5 |
| 8-14 | S.D. | W | 11-5 | | 16 | 9 | Acevedo | Lawrence | | 56-60 | T3rd | 19.5 |
| 8-15 | S.D. | L | 2-7 | | 11 | 10 | Eaton | Hudson | | 56-61 | 4th | 20.5 |
| 8-16 | At StL. | L | 5-10 | | 8 | 12 | Suppan | Harang | Isringhausen | 56-62 | 5th | 21.5 |
| 8-17 | At StL. | L | 2-7 | | 8 | 10 | Eldred | Graves | | 56-63 | 5th | 22.5 |
| 8-18 | At StL. | W | 5-4 | | 9 | 9 | Hancock | Williams | Graves | 57-63 | 5th | 21.5 |
| 8-20 | At Ari. | W | 2-0 | | 5 | 6 | Hudson | Johnson | Valentine | 58-63 | T4th | 21.5 |
| 8-21 | At Ari. | L | 1-2 | | 4 | 6 | Webb | Harang | Aquino | 58-64 | T4th | 22.5 |
| 8-22 | At Ari. | W | 11-1 | | 10 | 6 | Claussen | Randolph | | 59-64 | 4th | 22.5 |
| 8-24 | StL. | W | 4-3 | (10) | 7 | 9 | Valentine | Tavarez | | 60-64 | 4th | 21.5 |
| 8-25 | StL. | L | 5-6 | | 10 | 8 | Tavarez | Valentine | Isringhausen | 60-65 | 4th | 22.5 |
| 8-26 | StL. | W | 1-0 | | 3 | 3 | Harang | Carpenter | | 61-65 | 4th | 21.5 |
| 8-27 | Ari. | L | 3-4 | (11) | 7 | 13 | Bruney | Valentine | Aquino | 61-66 | 4th | 22.5 |
| 8-28 | Ari. | L | 3-6 | | 4 | 13 | Fossum | Norton | Aquino | 61-67 | 4th | 23.5 |
| 8-29 | Ari. | W | 6-2 | | 6 | 8 | Van Poppel | Fetters | | 62-67 | 4th | 23.5 |
| 8-30 | Hou. | L | 3-11 | | 10 | 11 | Munro | Norton | | 62-68 | 4th | 24.0 |
| 8-31 | Hou. | L | 0-8 | | 6 | 11 | Backe | Harang | | 62-69 | 4th | 25.0 |
| 9-1 | Hou. | L | 3-9 | | 7 | 12 | Oswalt | Wilson | | 62-70 | T4th | 26.0 |
| 9-3 | At Mil. | L | 4-11 | | 8 | 17 | Obermueller | Claussen | | 62-71 | 4th | 27.5 |
| 9-4 | At Mil. | L | 3-7 | | 10 | 11 | Hendrickson | Hancock | Kolb | 62-72 | 4th | 28.5 |
| 9-5 | At Mil. | W | 9-2 | | 14 | 5 | Hudson | de la Rosa | | 63-72 | 4th | 28.5 |

| Date | Opp. | Res. | Score | (inn.*) | Hits | Opp. hits | Winning pitcher | Losing pitcher | Save | Record | Pos. | GB |
|---|---|---|---|---|---|---|---|---|---|---|---|---|
| 9-6 | At Hou. | L | 5-11 | | 10 | 12 | Backe | Harang | | 63-73 | 4th | 28.5 |
| 9-7 | At Hou. | L | 7-9 | | 8 | 11 | Oswalt | Wilson | | 63-74 | 4th | 29.5 |
| 9-8 | At Hou. | L | 2-5 | | 7 | 11 | Clemens | Acevedo | Lidge | 63-75 | T4th | 29.5 |
| 9-9 | Mil. | L | 2-7 | | 8 | 12 | Davis | White | | 63-76 | 5th | 30.0 |
| 9-10 | Mil. | W | 6-4 | | 8 | 9 | Hancock | Hendrickson | Graves | 64-76 | 5th | 29.0 |
| 9-11 | Mil. | W | 9-0 | | 11 | 4 | Hudson | Santos | | 65-76 | 5th | 28.0 |
| 9-12 | Mil. | L | 0-11 | | 4 | 13 | Sheets | Harang | | 65-77 | 5th | 29.0 |
| 9-13 | Phi. | W | 4-3 | | 10 | 6 | Valentine | Rodriguez | Graves | 66-77 | 4th | 28.5 |
| 9-14 | Phi. | W | 7-6 | | 8 | 11 | Wagner | Madson | Graves | 67-77 | 4th | 27.5 |
| 9-15 | Phi. | L | 1-9 | | 4 | 14 | Myers | Claussen | | 67-78 | 4th | 28.5 |
| 9-16 | Chi. | L | 4-5 | | 5 | 6 | Wood | Wagner | Hawkins | 67-79 | 4th | 28.5 |
| 9-17 | Chi. | L | 4-12 | | 10 | 13 | Zambrano | Hudson | | 67-80 | 4th | 29.5 |
| 9-18 | Chi. | W | 6-5 | | 10 | 12 | Harang | Maddux | Graves | 68-80 | 4th | 29.5 |
| 9-19 | Chi. | L | 1-5 | | 3 | 8 | Leicester | Graves | | 68-81 | T4th | 29.5 |
| 9-21 | At Atl. | L | 4-5 | | 9 | 12 | Thomson | Claussen | Smoltz | 68-82 | T4th | 30.0 |
| 9-22 | At Atl. | W | 11-8 | | 17 | 6 | Norton | Smoltz | Valentine | 69-82 | 4th | 30.0 |
| 9-23 | At Atl. | W | 3-2 | | 5 | 6 | Hudson | Wright | White | 70-82 | 4th | 30.0 |
| 9-24 | At Pit. | W | 14-8 | | 17 | 11 | Harang | Vogelsong | | 71-82 | 4th | 30.0 |
| 9-25 | At Pit. | W | 7-4 | | 11 | 11 | Wilson | Williams | Valentine | 72-82 | 4th | 30.0 |
| 9-26 | At Pit. | L | 2-4 | | 11 | 14 | Fogg | Acevedo | Mesa | 72-83 | 4th | 31.0 |
| 9-27 | At Chi. | L | 5-12 | | 8 | 12 | Zambrano | Claussen | | 72-84 | 4th | 31.0 |
| 9-28 | At Chi. | W | 8-3 | | 8 | 7 | Hancock | Maddux | | 73-84 | 4th | 30.0 |
| 9-29 | At Chi. | W | 4-3 | (12) | 9 | 8 | Riedling | Leicester | Valentine | 74-84 | 4th | 29.0 |
| 9-30 | At Chi. | W | 2-1 | (12) | 6 | 7 | Padilla | Remlinger | | 75-84 | 4th | 28.0 |
| 10-1 | Pit. | W | 5-1 | | 8 | 5 | Wilson | Williams | | 76-84 | 4th | 28.0 |
| 10-2 | Pit. | L | 1-3 | | 5 | 8 | Fogg | Van Poppel | Mesa | 76-85 | 4th | 28.0 |
| 10-3 | Pit. | L | 0-2 | | 5 | 7 | Perez | Claussen | Mesa | 76-86 | 4th | 29.0 |

Monthly records: April (12-10), May (18-11), June (12-14), July (9-18), August (11-16), September (13-15), October (1-2).
*Innings, if other than nine.

## RECORDS

**2004 regular-season record:** 76-86
**Position:** 4th in N.L. Central
**Home:** 40-41 **Road:** 36-45
**N.L. East:** 18-12 **N.L. Central:** 38-52
**N.L. West:** 15-15 **A.L.** 5-7
**Vs. LH starters:** 23-24
**Vs. RH starters:** 53-62
**Grass:** 74-85 **Artificial:** 2-1
**Day:** 27-30 **Night:** 49-56
**1-Run:** 25-20 **X-inn.:** 12-7
**Doubleheaders:** 0-0-0
**Team record past five years:** 374-436 (.462, ranks 11th in league in that span)

## TEAM LEADERS

**Batting average:** Sean Casey (.324).
**At-bats:** Sean Casey (571).
**Runs:** Adam Dunn (105).
**Hits:** Sean Casey (185).
**Total Bases:** Adam Dunn (323).
**Doubles:** Sean Casey (44).
**Triples:** Ryan Freel (8).
**Home runs:** Adam Dunn (46).
**Runs batted in:** Adam Dunn (102).
**Stolen bases:** Ryan Freel (37).
**Slugging percentage:** Adam Dunn (.569).
**On-base percentage:** Adam Dunn (.388).
**Wins:** Paul Wilson (11).
**Earned-run average:** Paul Wilson (4.36).
**Complete games:** Cory Lidle (3).
**Shutouts:** Aaron Harang, Cory Lidle (1).
**Saves:** Danny Graves (41).
**Innings pitched:** Paul Wilson (183.2).
**Strikeouts:** Aaron Harang (125).

## GAMES BY POSITION

**Catcher:** Jason LaRue 111, Javier Valentin 55, Corky Miller 12.
**First base:** Sean Casey 145, Tim Hummel 13, Adam Dunn 10, Javier Valentin 7, Jacob Cruz 6, Juan Castro 4, John Vander Wal 4.
**Second base:** D'Angelo Jimenez 146, Ryan Freel 15, Juan Castro 12, Jermaine Clark 2, Felipe Lopez 2, Tim Hummel 1.
**Third base:** Juan Castro 78, Ryan Freel 56, Brandon Larson 35, Tim Hummel 32, Felipe Lopez 24.
**Shortstop:** Barry Larkin 85, Felipe Lopez 51, Juan Castro 31, Anderson Machado 17, Ray Olmedo 7, D'Angelo Jimenez 5, Tim Hummel 1.
**Outfield:** Adam Dunn 156, Wily Mo Pena 91, Ryan Freel 89, Ken Griffey Jr. 77, Austin Kearns 60, Jacob Cruz 29, Darren Bragg 26, Jason Romano 11, Jermaine Clark 8, John Vander Wal 7, Jason LaRue 1.
**Designated hitter:** Jacob Cruz 2, Sean Casey 1, Adam Dunn 1, Ken Griffey Jr. 1, Tim Hummel 1, Jason LaRue 1.

## TOP DRAFT CHOICES

1. **Homer Bailey,** RHP, La Grange (Texas) H.S.
2. **B.J. Szymanski,** OF, Princeton.
3. **Craig Tatum,** C, Mississippi State.
4. **Rafael Gonzalez,** RHP, George Washington H.S., New York.
5. **Paul Janish,** SS, Rice.
6. **Lonny Roa,** C, Puerto Rico Baseball Academy, San Juan, P.R.
7. **Philippe Valiquette,** LHP, Edouard Montpetit H.S., St. Laurent, Quebec.
8. **Greg Goetz,** LHP, Bellevue (Wash.) CC.
9. **Tevor Lawhorn,** 2B, East Carolina.
10. **Terrell Young,** RHP, Grenada (Miss.) H.S.

# COLORADO ROCKIES

## *NATIONAL LEAGUE WEST DIVISION*

## 2005 SEASON

### Rockies Schedule

Home games shaded.
All-Star Game July 12 at Detroit. Schedule subject to change.

**April**

| SUN | MON | TUE | WED | THU | FRI | SAT |
|---|---|---|---|---|---|---|
| 3 | 4 SD | 5 | 6 SD | 7 | 8 SF | 9 SF |
| 10 SF | 11 ARI | 12 ARI | 13 ARI | 14 | 15 SF | 16 SF |
| 17 SF | 18 ARI | 19 ARI | 20 PHI | 21 PHI | 22 LA | 23 LA |
| 24 LA | 25 | 26 FLA | 27 FLA | 28 FLA | 29 LA | 30 LA |

**May**

| SUN | MON | TUE | WED | THU | FRI | SAT |
|---|---|---|---|---|---|---|
| 1 LA | 2 SD | 3 SD | 4 SD | 5 | 6 FLA | 7 FLA |
| 8 FLA | 9 ATL | 10 ATL | 11 ATL | 12 ARI | 13 ARI | 14 ARI |
| 15 ARI | 16 | 17 SF | 18 SF | 19 SF | 20 PIT | 21 PIT |
| 22 PIT | 23 MIL | 24 MIL | 25 MIL | 26 CHC | 27 CHC | 28 CHC |
| 29 CHC | 30 STL | 31 STL | | | | |

**June**

| SUN | MON | TUE | WED | THU | FRI | SAT |
|---|---|---|---|---|---|---|
| | | | 1 STL | 2 STL | 3 CIN | 4 CIN |
| 5 CIN | 6 CHW | 7 CHW | 8 CHW | 9 | 10 DET | 11 DET |
| 12 DET | 13 | 14 CLE | 15 CLE | 16 CLE | 17 BAL | 18 BAL |
| 19 BAL | 20 HOU | 21 HOU | 22 HOU | 23 | 24 KC | 25 KC |
| 26 KC | 27 HOU | 28 HOU | 29 HOU | 30 STL | | |

**July**

| SUN | MON | TUE | WED | THU | FRI | SAT |
|---|---|---|---|---|---|---|
| | | | | | 1 STL | 2 STL |
| 3 STL | 4 LA | 5 LA | 6 LA | 7 LA | 8 SD | 9 SD |
| 10 SD | 11 | 12 All-Star | 13 | 14 | 15 CIN | 16 CIN |
| 17 CIN | 18 WAS | 19 WAS | 20 WAS | 21 PIT | 22 PIT | 23 PIT |
| 24 PIT | 25 NYM | 26 NYM | 27 NYM | 28 PHI | 29 PHI | 30 PHI |
| 31 PHI | | | | | | |

**August**

| SUN | MON | TUE | WED | THU | FRI | SAT |
|---|---|---|---|---|---|---|
| | 1 | 2 SF | 3 SF | 4 SF | 5 ARI | 6 ARI |
| 7 ARI | 8 | 9 PIT | 10 PIT | 11 PIT | 12 WAS | 13 WAS |
| 14 WAS | 15 MIL | 16 MIL | 17 MIL | 18 | 19 CHC | 20 CHC |
| 21 CHC | 22 | 23 LA | 24 LA | 25 LA | 26 SD | 27 SD |
| 28 SD | 29 SF | 30 SF | 31 SF | | | |

**September**

| SUN | MON | TUE | WED | THU | FRI | SAT |
|---|---|---|---|---|---|---|
| | | | | 1 | 2 LA | 3 LA |
| 4 LA | 5 | 6 SD | 7 SD | 8 SD | 9 ARI | 10 ARI |
| 11 ARI | 12 LA | 13 LA | 14 LA | 15 | 16 ARI | 17 ARI |
| 18 ARI | 19 SD | 20 SD | 21 SD | 22 SD | 23 SF | 24 SF |
| 25 SF | 26 ATL | 27 ATL | 28 ATL | 29 NYM | 30 NYM | |

**October**

| SUN | MON | TUE | WED | THU | FRI | SAT |
|---|---|---|---|---|---|---|
| | | | | | | 1 NYM |
| 2 NYM | 3 | 4 | 5 | 6 | 7 | 8 |

Home games shaded. All-Star Game July 12 at Detroit. Schedule subject to change.

### CLUB DIRECTORY

**Chairman & chief executive officer**
Charles K. Monfort
**Vice chairman**
Richard L. Monfort
**President**
Keli S. McGregor
**Executive vice president, g.m.**
Daniel J. O'Dowd
**Sr. v.p., business operations**
Gregory D. Feasel
**Sr. v.p., chief financial officer**
Harold R. Roth
**Vice president, ballpark operations**
Kevin Kahn
**Vice president, finance**
Michael J. Kent
**Vice president, ticket ops. & sales**
Sue Ann McClaren

### MINOR LEAGUE AFFILIATES

| Class | Team | League | Manager |
|---|---|---|---|
| AAA | Colorado Springs | Pacific Coast | Marv Foley |
| AA | Tulsa | Texas | Tom Runnells |
| Advanced A | Modesto | California | Stu Cole |
| A | Asheville | South Atlantic | Joe Mikulik |
| Short-Season A | Tri-City | Northwest | TBA |
| Advanced Rookie | Casper | Pioneer | P.J. Carey |

### BROADCAST INFORMATION

**Radio:** KOA-AM (850).
**TV:** UPN (Channel 20).
**Cable TV:** Fox Sports Rocky Mountain.

### SPRING TRAINING

**Ballpark (city):** Hi Corbett Field (Tucson, Ariz.).
**Ticket information:** 1-800-388-ROCK.

**For more on the Rockies, go to msn.foxsports.com/mlb/teams.**

## SPRING TRAINING ROSTER

**Manager**—Clint Hurdle (31).
**Coaches**—Bob Apodaca (36), Dave Collins (29), Duane Espy (52), Mike Gallego, Rick Mathews (53), Jamie Quirk (8).

| No. | PITCHERS | B/T | Ht./Wt. | Age* | 2004 Clubs |
|---|---|---|---|---|---|
| | Carvajal, Marcos | R/R | 6-4/175 | 21 | Columbus, Jacksonville |
| 34 | Chacon, Shawn | R/R | 6-3/212 | 27 | Colorado |
| 28 | Cook, Aaron | R/R | 6-3/205 | 26 | Colorado Springs, Colorado |
| 47 | Dohmann, Scott | R/R | 6-1/181 | 27 | Colorado Springs, Colorado |
| 26 | Francis, Jeff | L/L | 6-5/200 | 24 | Tulsa, Colorado Springs, Colorado |
| 40 | Fuentes, Brian | L/L | 6-4/220 | 29 | Colorado Springs, Colorado |
| 32 | Jennings, Jason | L/R | 6-2/245 | 26 | Colorado |
| | Jimenez, Ubaldo | R/R | 6-4/200 | 21 | Visalia |
| 37 | Kennedy, Joe | R/L | 6-4/237 | 25 | Colorado Springs, Colorado |
| 45 | Lopez, Javier | L/L | 6-4/200 | 27 | Colorado Springs, Colorado, Greenville, Vero Beach |
| | Morillo, Juan | R/R | 6-3/190 | 21 | Tri City |
| | Narveson, Chris | L/L | 6-3/180 | 23 | Tennessee, Tulsa |
| 51 | Simpson, Allan | R/R | 6-4/185 | 27 | Colorado Springs, Colorado |
| | Speier, Ryan | R/R | 6-7/200 | 25 | Tulsa |
| | Taylor, Aaron | R/R | 6-8/245 | 27 | Inland Empire, San Antonio, Seattle |
| 71 | Tsao, Chin-hui | R/R | 6-2/177 | 23 | Asheville, Tulsa, Colorado Springs, Colorado |
| 16 | Wright, Jamey | R/R | 6-6/235 | 30 | Omaha, Colorado |
| 49 | Young, Jason | R/R | 6-5/214 | 25 | Colorado Springs, Colorado |

| No. | CATCHERS | B/T | Ht./Wt. | Age* | 2004 Clubs |
|---|---|---|---|---|---|
| 30 | Closser, J.D. | B/R | 5-10/176 | 25 | Colorado Springs, Colorado |
| 20 | Greene, Todd | R/R | 5-10/208 | 33 | Colorado Springs, Colorado |
| 23 | Johnson, Charles | R/R | 6-3/225 | 33 | Colorado |

| No. | INFIELDERS | B/T | Ht./Wt. | Age* | 2004 Clubs |
|---|---|---|---|---|---|
| | Amezaga, Alfredo | B/R | 5-10/165 | 27 | Salt Lake, Anaheim |
| 27 | Atkins, Garrett | R/R | 6-3/210 | 25 | Colorado Springs, Colorado |
| | Baker, Jeff | R/R | 6-2/210 | 25 | Visalia, Tulsa |
| 12 | Barmes, Clint | R/R | 6-0/175 | 26 | Colorado Springs, Colorado |
| 4 | Gonzalez, Luis A. | R/R | 5-11/170 | 25 | Colorado |
| 17 | Helton, Todd | L/L | 6-2/204 | 30 | Colorado |
| 6 | Miles, Aaron | B/R | 5-7/180 | 28 | Colorado Springs, Colorado |
| | Nix, Jayson | R/R | 5-11/180 | 22 | Tulsa |
| | Norton, Greg | B/R | 6-1/200 | 32 | Detroit, Toledo |
| | Relaford, Desi | B/R | 5-9/180 | 31 | Omaha, Kansas City |
| | Shealy, Ryan | R/R | 6-5/240 | 25 | Tulsa |

| No. | OUTFIELDERS | B/T | Ht./Wt. | Age* | 2004 Clubs |
|---|---|---|---|---|---|
| 21 | Freeman, Choo | R/R | 6-2/200 | 25 | Colorado Springs, Colorado |
| 11 | Hawpe, Brad | L/L | 6-3/200 | 25 | Colorado Springs, Colorado |
| 5 | Holliday, Matt | R/R | 6-4/235 | 25 | Colorado Springs, Colorado |
| | Miller, Tony | R/R | 5-9/180 | 24 | Tulsa |
| 17 | Mohr, Dustan | R/R | 6-1/214 | 28 | San Francisco |
| 3 | Piedra, Jorge | L/L | 6-0/190 | 25 | Colorado Springs, Colorado |
| | Salazar, Jeff | L/L | 6-0/180 | 24 | Visalia, Tulsa |
| | Sullivan, Cory | L/L | 6-0/180 | 24 | Did Not Play |
| 44 | Wilson, Preston | R/R | 6-2/213 | 30 | Tulsa,Colorado |

*Age as of April 1, 2005.

## BALLPARK INFORMATION

**Ballpark (capacity, surface)**
Coors Field (50,449, grass)

**Address**
2001 Blake St.
Denver, CO 80205-2000

**Official website**
www.coloradorockies.com

**Business phone**
303-292-0200

**Ticket information**
800-388-7625

**Field dimensions (from home plate)**
To left field at foul line, 347 feet
To center field, 415 feet
To right field at foul line, 350

**First game played**
April 26, 1995 (Rockies 11, Mets 9, 14 innings)

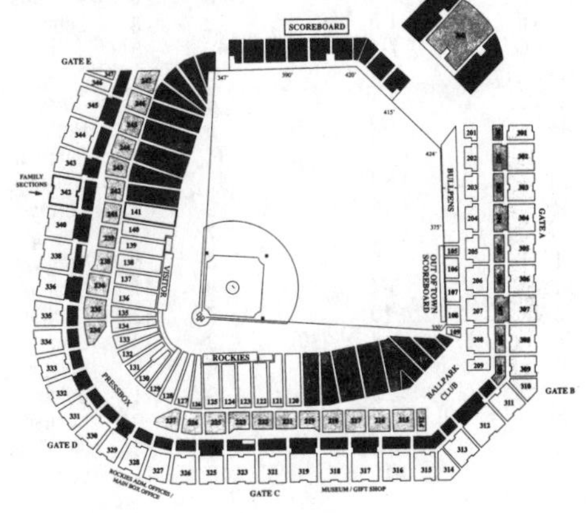

# 2004 REVIEW

## DAY BY DAY

| Date | Opp. | Res. | Score | (inn.*) | Hits | Opp. hits | Winning pitcher | Losing pitcher | Save | Record | Pos. | GB |
|---|---|---|---|---|---|---|---|---|---|---|---|---|
| 4-6 | At Ari. | W | 6-2 | | 11 | 3 | Estes | Johnson | | 1-0 | 2nd | 0.5 |
| 4-7 | At Ari. | L | 5-9 | | 9 | 12 | Webb | Jennings | Mantei | 1-1 | T3rd | 0.5 |
| 4-8 | At Ari. | L | 5-6 | (11) | 11 | 8 | Randolph | Chacon | | 1-2 | 5th | 1.0 |
| 4-9 | At L.A. | L | 1-5 | | 5 | 7 | Ishii | Elarton | Alvarez | 1-3 | 5th | 2.0 |
| 4-10 | At L.A. | L | 4-7 | | 9 | 10 | Nomo | Stark | Gagne | 1-4 | 5th | 3.0 |
| 4-11 | At L.A. | W | 4-2 | | 9 | 6 | Estes | Perez | Chacon | 2-4 | T4th | 2.0 |
| 4-12 | Ari. | W | 7-4 | | 8 | 9 | Nunez | Koplove | Chacon | 3-4 | 4th | 1.5 |
| 4-14 | Ari. | W | 14-4 | | 15 | 9 | Kennedy | Dessens | | 4-4 | T3rd | 1.0 |
| 4-15 | Ari. | L | 10-11 | | 10 | 9 | Koplove | Elarton | Mantei | 4-5 | T3rd | 2.0 |
| 4-16 | At StL. | L | 5-13 | | 8 | 16 | Morris | Stark | | 4-6 | T3rd | 3.0 |
| 4-17 | At StL. | L | 4-8 | | 11 | 13 | Marquis | Estes | | 4-7 | T4th | 4.0 |
| 4-18 | At StL. | W | 8-5 | | 10 | 11 | Jennings | Williams | Chacon | 5-7 | T3rd | 4.0 |
| 4-20 | L.A. | W | 7-1 | | 8 | 8 | Kennedy | Ishii | | 6-7 | 3rd | 3.0 |
| 4-21 | L.A. | L | 4-9 | | 10 | 13 | Nomo | Elarton | | 6-8 | 3rd | 4.0 |
| 4-22 | L.A. | W | 7-1 | (6) | 9 | 2 | Estes | Lima | | 7-8 | 3rd | 3.0 |
| 4-23 | Hou. | L | 7-13 | | 10 | 11 | Duckworth | Jennings | | 7-9 | 3rd | 4.0 |
| 4-24 | Hou. | L | 5-8 | | 11 | 10 | Clemens | Fassero | Dotel | 7-10 | 3rd | 4.0 |
| 4-25 | Hou. | W | 4-1 | | 9 | 5 | Kennedy | Miller | Chacon | 8-10 | 3rd | 4.0 |
| 4-26 | Fla. | L | 3-6 | | 7 | 10 | Pavano | Elarton | Benitez | 8-11 | T3rd | 4.5 |
| 4-27 | Fla. | W | 13-10 | | 12 | 16 | Nunez | Fox | Chacon | 9-11 | T3rd | 3.5 |
| 4-28 | Fla. | L | 4-9 | | 9 | 9 | Beckett | Jennings | | 9-12 | T3rd | 4.5 |
| 5-1# | Atl. | W | 3-2 | | 10 | 8 | Nunez | Reitsma | Chacon | 10-12 | | |
| 5-1$ | Atl. | L | 7-11 | | 14 | 12 | Nitkowski | Nunez | | 10-13 | T4th | 5.0 |
| 5-2 | Atl. | W | 13-4 | | 14 | 11 | Estes | Ramirez | | 11-13 | 4th | 4.0 |
| 5-4 | At Mon. | L | 4-10 | | 8 | 14 | Vargas | Jennings | | 11-14 | T4th | 5.0 |
| 5-5 | At Mon. | W | 2-0 | | 9 | 5 | Kennedy | Day | Chacon | 12-14 | T3rd | 4.0 |
| 5-6 | At Mon. | L | 1-3 | | 5 | 8 | Hernandez | Elarton | | 12-15 | T3rd | 5.0 |
| 5-7 | At Chi. | L | 0-11 | | 2 | 12 | Zambrano | Estes | | 12-16 | T4th | 6.0 |
| 5-8 | At Chi. | W | 4-3 | | 7 | 5 | Jennings | Maddux | Chacon | 13-16 | 3rd | 6.0 |
| 5-9 | At Chi. | L | 4-5 | (13) | 16 | 11 | Rusch | Fassero | | 13-17 | 4th | 7.0 |
| 5-11 | Pit. | L | 10-15 | (12) | 19 | 19 | Torres | Lopez | | 13-18 | 5th | 8.0 |
| 5-13! | Pit. | W | 7-5 | | 9 | 8 | Estes | Benson | Chacon | 14-18 | | |
| 5-13& | Pit. | L | 2-11 | | 7 | 21 | Perez | Jennings | | 14-19 | 4th | 8.0 |
| 5-14 | Phi. | L | 4-6 | | 9 | 10 | Milton | Kennedy | Worrell | 14-20 | 4th | 8.0 |
| 5-15 | Phi. | L | 5-16 | | 7 | 18 | Myers | Elarton | | 14-21 | 4th | 8.0 |
| 5-16 | Phi. | W | 7-6 | | 12 | 11 | Harikkala | Cormier | Chacon | 15-21 | 3rd | 7.0 |
| 5-17 | Phi. | W | 7-6 | | 14 | 12 | Fuentes | Worrell | | 16-21 | 3rd | 6.5 |
| 5-18 | At Cin. | W | 8-3 | | 14 | 4 | Estes | Lidle | | 17-21 | 3rd | 5.5 |
| 5-19 | At Cin. | L | 3-4 | (10) | 7 | 9 | Riedling | Fuentes | | 17-22 | 3rd | 5.5 |
| 5-20 | At Cin. | L | 1-3 | | 3 | 5 | Wilson | Kennedy | Graves | 17-23 | 3rd | 5.5 |
| 5-21 | At N.Y. | L | 7-9 | | 11 | 14 | Ginter | Young | | 17-24 | 4th | 5.5 |
| 5-22 | At N.Y. | L | 4-5 | | 10 | 7 | Weathers | Nunez | Looper | 17-25 | 4th | 6.5 |
| 5-23 | At N.Y. | L | 0-4 | | 1 | 9 | Glavine | Estes | | 17-26 | T4th | 6.5 |
| 5-25 | S.D. | L | 6-11 | | 13 | 16 | Linebrink | Fassero | | 17-27 | 4th | 7.5 |
| 5-26 | S.D. | W | 13-6 | | 14 | 13 | Jennings | Eaton | | 18-27 | 4th | 6.5 |
| 5-27 | S.D. | L | 3-4 | (10) | 4 | 13 | Otsuka | Nunez | Hoffman | 18-28 | 4th | 7.5 |
| 5-28 | At S.F | L | 2-4 | | 8 | 9 | Brower | Chacon | | 18-29 | 4th | 8.5 |
| 5-29 | At S.F | L | 3-5 | | 10 | 8 | Williams | Fassero | Herges | 18-30 | 4th | 8.5 |
| 5-30 | At S.F | L | 1-3 | | 3 | 8 | Schmidt | Kennedy | Herges | 18-31 | 4th | 9.5 |
| 5-31 | At S.D. | W | 7-1 | | 10 | 5 | Jennings | Eaton | | 19-31 | 4th | 8.5 |
| 6-1 | At S.D. | W | 7-1 | | 8 | 7 | Cook | Germano | | 20-31 | 4th | 7.5 |
| 6-2 | At S.D. | L | 1-2 | (10) | 6 | 7 | Hoffman | Fuentes | | 20-32 | 4th | 8.5 |
| 6-4 | S.F | L | 7-13 | | 11 | 14 | Schmidt | Fassero | | 20-33 | 5th | 9.5 |
| 6-5 | S.F | W | 11-2 | | 16 | 8 | Jennings | Rueter | | 21-33 | 4th | 9.5 |
| 6-6 | S.F | L | 4-16 | | 9 | 16 | Hermanson | Cook | | 21-34 | 5th | 9.5 |
| 6-7 | S.F | L | 5-10 | | 7 | 15 | Brower | Reed | | 21-35 | 5th | 10.0 |
| 6-8 | At N.Y. | L | 1-2 | | 6 | 6 | Vazquez | Fassero | Rivera | 21-36 | 5th | 10.0 |
| 6-9 | At N.Y. | L | 5-7 | | 8 | 11 | Quantrill | Kennedy | Rivera | 21-37 | 5th | 11.0 |
| 6-10 | At N.Y. | L | 4-10 | | 7 | 12 | Contreras | Jennings | | 21-38 | 5th | 11.0 |
| 6-11 | At T.B. | L | 7-8 | (10) | 13 | 13 | Baez | Chacon | | 21-39 | 5th | 12.0 |
| 6-12 | At T.B. | L | 7-10 | | 10 | 8 | Halama | Harikkala | | 21-40 | 5th | 12.0 |
| 6-13 | At T.B. | L | 2-3 | | 9 | 11 | Colome | Chacon | | 21-41 | 5th | 12.0 |
| 6-15 | Bos. | W | 6-3 | | 10 | 9 | Kennedy | Arroyo | Chacon | 22-41 | 5th | 12.0 |
| 6-16 | Bos. | W | 7-6 | | 10 | 13 | Jennings | Schilling | Chacon | 23-41 | 5th | 12.0 |
| 6-17 | Bos. | L | 0-11 | | 6 | 14 | Lowe | Cook | | 23-42 | 5th | 13.0 |

| Date | Opp. | Res. | Score | (inn.*) | Hits | Opp. hits | Winning pitcher | Losing pitcher | Save | Record | Pos. | GB |
|---|---|---|---|---|---|---|---|---|---|---|---|---|
| 6-18 | Bal. | W | 5-3 | | 9 | 9 | Estes | Ponson | Chacon | 24-42 | 5th | 13.0 |
| 6-19 | Bal. | W | 11-6 | | 13 | 14 | Fassero | DuBose | | 25-42 | 5th | 12.0 |
| 6-20 | Bal. | L | 2-4 | | 6 | 6 | Ryan | Chacon | Julio | 25-43 | 5th | 13.0 |
| 6-22 | At Mil. | L | 2-6 | | 9 | 10 | Davis | Lopez | | 25-44 | 5th | 13.0 |
| 6-23 | At Mil. | W | 3-2 | | 7 | 6 | Estes | Capuano | Chacon | 26-44 | 5th | 13.0 |
| 6-24 | At Mil. | W | 3-0 | | 7 | 10 | Cook | Sheets | Chacon | 27-44 | 4th | 13.0 |
| 6-25 | At Cle. | W | 10-8 | (10) | 15 | 7 | Reed | Jimenez | Chacon | 28-44 | 4th | 13.0 |
| 6-26 | At Cle. | L | 3-4 | (12) | 10 | 17 | Robertson | Reed | | 28-45 | 4th | 13.0 |
| 6-27 | At Cle. | L | 3-5 | | 5 | 10 | Miller | Jennings | Jimenez | 28-46 | 4th | 14.0 |
| 6-29 | Mil. | L | 3-6 | | 9 | 9 | Capuano | Estes | Kolb | 28-47 | 4th | 14.0 |
| 6-30 | Mil. | L | 4-5 | | 10 | 10 | Sheets | Cook | Kolb | 28-48 | 4th | 15.0 |
| 7-1 | Mil. | L | 9-10 | | 14 | 14 | Santos | Stark | Kolb | 28-49 | 5th | 15.0 |
| 7-2 | Det. | W | 9-8 | (10) | 15 | 16 | Chacon | Walker | | 29-49 | 4th | 15.0 |
| 7-3 | Det. | W | 11-6 | | 16 | 12 | Jennings | Maroth | | 30-49 | 4th | 14.0 |
| 7-4 | Det. | W | 10-8 | | 10 | 12 | Bernero | Knotts | Chacon | 31-49 | 4th | 13.0 |
| 7-5 | At S.F | W | 7-4 | | 13 | 8 | Cook | Tomko | Chacon | 32-49 | 4th | 12.5 |
| 7-6 | At S.F | W | 8-6 | | 6 | 9 | Harikkala | Christiansen | Chacon | 33-49 | 4th | 12.5 |
| 7-7 | At S.F | L | 4-8 | | 7 | 13 | Rueter | Bernero | | 33-50 | 4th | 12.5 |
| 7-8 | At S.D. | W | 5-1 | | 10 | 5 | Jennings | Eaton | | 34-50 | 4th | 12.5 |
| 7-9 | At S.D. | W | 6-5 | | 9 | 10 | Harikkala | Hoffman | Chacon | 35-50 | 4th | 11.5 |
| 7-10 | At S.D. | W | 6-2 | | 11 | 11 | Cook | Lawrence | | 36-50 | 4th | 11.5 |
| 7-11 | At S.D. | L | 2-4 | | 8 | 7 | Valdez | Stark | Hoffman | 36-51 | 4th | 12.5 |
| 7-15 | S.F | L | 5-7 | | 11 | 12 | Brower | Chacon | Eyre | 36-52 | 4th | 13.5 |
| 7-16 | S.F | W | 7-1 | | 11 | 8 | Estes | Rueter | | 37-52 | 4th | 13.5 |
| 7-17 | S.F | L | 0-4 | | 4 | 3 | Schmidt | Cook | | 37-53 | 4th | 14.5 |
| 7-18 | S.F | W | 10-9 | | 15 | 11 | Harikkala | Herges | | 38-53 | 4th | 14.5 |
| 7-19 | S.D. | L | 6-13 | | 12 | 18 | Valdez | Stark | | 38-54 | 4th | 15.5 |
| 7-20 | S.D. | L | 7-9 | | 14 | 16 | Eaton | Jennings | Hoffman | 38-55 | 4th | 16.5 |
| 7-21 | At L.A. | W | 6-5 | | 8 | 6 | Estes | Ishii | Chacon | 39-55 | 4th | 15.5 |
| 7-22 | At L.A. | L | 2-4 | | 6 | 11 | Mota | Harikkala | Gagne | 39-56 | 4th | 16.5 |
| 7-23 | At Ari. | W | 8-2 | | 6 | 7 | Fassero | Fossum | | 40-56 | 4th | 16.5 |
| 7-24 | At Ari. | W | 8-2 | | 10 | 9 | Wright | Cormier | | 41-56 | 4th | 16.5 |
| 7-25 | At Ari. | W | 3-2 | | 8 | 6 | Jennings | Choate | Chacon | 42-56 | 4th | 15.5 |
| 7-26 | L.A. | L | 7-9 | | 11 | 12 | Sanchez | Simpson | Gagne | 42-57 | 4th | 16.5 |
| 7-27 | L.A. | W | 7-2 | | 15 | 9 | Cook | Perez | | 43-57 | 4th | 15.5 |
| 7-28 | L.A. | W | 5-4 | | 11 | 11 | Reed | Mota | Chacon | 44-57 | 4th | 14.5 |
| 7-29 | L.A. | L | 2-3 | | 4 | 10 | Alvarez | Dohmann | Gagne | 44-58 | 4th | 15.5 |
| 7-30 | Ari. | W | 4-1 | | 6 | 9 | Jennings | Johnson | Chacon | 45-58 | 4th | 15.5 |
| 7-31 | Ari. | W | 8-4 | | 10 | 8 | Estes | Webb | Chacon | 46-58 | 4th | 14.5 |
| 8-1 | Ari. | W | 10-2 | | 15 | 7 | Cook | Gonzalez | | 47-58 | 4th | 14.5 |
| 8-3 | Chi. | L | 3-5 | | 6 | 9 | Wood | Fassero | Hawkins | 47-59 | 4th | 15.5 |
| 8-4 | Chi. | L | 8-11 | | 11 | 15 | Farnsworth | Chacon | | 47-60 | 4th | 16.5 |
| 8-5 | Chi. | L | 1-5 | | 9 | 9 | Prior | Jennings | Rusch | 47-61 | 4th | 17.5 |
| 8-6 | Cin. | W | 8-5 | | 9 | 12 | Estes | Claussen | Chacon | 48-61 | 4th | 16.5 |
| 8-7 | Cin. | W | 9-5 | | 14 | 13 | Simpson | Wilson | | 49-61 | 4th | 16.5 |
| 8-8 | Cin. | L | 7-14 | | 14 | 16 | Lidle | Fassero | | 49-62 | 4th | 16.5 |
| 8-9 | At Phi. | W | 4-2 | | 6 | 6 | Harikkala | Jones | Chacon | 50-62 | 4th | 16.0 |
| 8-10 | At Phi. | W | 5-4 | | 7 | 9 | Reed | Worrell | Chacon | 51-62 | 4th | 16.0 |
| 8-11 | At Phi. | L | 4-15 | | 10 | 14 | Wolf | Jennings | | 51-63 | 4th | 17.0 |
| 8-12 | At Phi. | W | 3-1 | | 8 | 5 | Estes | Lidle | Chacon | 52-63 | 4th | 16.0 |
| 8-13 | At Pit. | W | 9-3 | | 15 | 4 | Fassero | Wells | | 53-63 | 4th | 16.0 |
| 8-14 | At Pit. | L | 1-6 | | 5 | 10 | Perez | Wright | | 53-64 | 4th | 16.0 |
| 8-15 | At Pit. | L | 0-3 | | 5 | 10 | Fogg | Kennedy | Mesa | 53-65 | 4th | 17.0 |
| 8-17 | N.Y. | W | 6-4 | | 12 | 7 | Jennings | Wheeler | Chacon | 54-65 | 4th | 16.5 |
| 8-19# | N.Y. | L | 3-10 | | 12 | 15 | Benson | Estes | | 54-66 | | |
| 8-19$ | N.Y. | L | 2-4 | | 6 | 6 | Stanton | Reed | | 54-67 | 4th | 16.5 |
| 8-20 | Mon. | L | 3-4 | | 8 | 8 | Ayala | Fuentes | Cordero | 54-68 | 4th | 17.5 |
| 8-21 | Mon. | W | 5-2 | | 8 | 6 | Kennedy | Hernandez | | 55-68 | 4th | 17.5 |
| 8-22 | Mon. | L | 2-8 | | 8 | 14 | Patterson | Jennings | | 55-69 | 4th | 17.5 |
| 8-24 | At Atl. | L | 5-6 | | 11 | 14 | Gryboski | Harikkala | Smoltz | 55-70 | 4th | 18.0 |
| 8-25 | At Atl. | L | 1-8 | | 6 | 13 | Thomson | Francis | | 55-71 | 4th | 18.0 |
| 8-26 | At Atl. | L | 4-6 | | 10 | 11 | Hampton | Wright | Smoltz | 55-72 | 4th | 19.0 |
| 8-27 | At Fla. | L | 0-3 | | 4 | 9 | Valdez | Kennedy | Benitez | 55-73 | 4th | 19.0 |
| 8-28 | At Fla. | L | 3-4 | | 7 | 9 | Pavano | Reed | Benitez | 55-74 | 4th | 20.0 |
| 8-29 | At Fla. | L | 4-8 | | 9 | 13 | Burnett | Estes | | 55-75 | 4th | 21.0 |
| 8-31 | At S.F | L | 5-9 | | 7 | 10 | Tomko | Francis | Hermanson | 55-76 | 4th | 22.0 |
| 9-1 | At S.F | W | 4-1 | | 13 | 4 | Wright | Rueter | Chacon | 56-76 | 4th | 21.0 |
| 9-2 | At S.F | W | 6-5 | | 9 | 9 | Kennedy | Schmidt | Chacon | 57-76 | 4th | 21.0 |

| Date | Opp. | Res. | Score | (inn.*) | Hits | Opp. hits | Winning pitcher | Losing pitcher | Save | Record | Pos. | GB |
|---|---|---|---|---|---|---|---|---|---|---|---|---|
| 9-3 | At S.D. | L | 6-7 | | 12 | 8 | Linebrink | Dohmann | Hoffman | 57-77 | 4th | 21.0 |
| 9-4 | At S.D. | W | 8-2 | | 10 | 4 | Estes | Tankersley | | 58-77 | 4th | 20.0 |
| 9-5 | At S.D. | W | 5-2 | | 9 | 10 | Francis | Lawrence | | 59-77 | 4th | 19.0 |
| 9-7 | S.F | W | 8-7 | | 7 | 13 | Harikkala | Christiansen | Chacon | 60-77 | 4th | 19.0 |
| 9-8 | S.F | L | 3-5 | | 5 | 16 | Walker | Reed | Hermanson | 60-78 | 4th | 20.0 |
| 9-9 | S.D. | W | 9-7 | | 12 | 14 | Lopez | Linebrink | Chacon | 61-78 | 4th | 20.0 |
| 9-10 | S.D. | L | 4-10 | | 8 | 13 | Lawrence | Harikkala | | 61-79 | 4th | 21.0 |
| 9-11 | S.D. | W | 13-2 | | 18 | 8 | Francis | Eaton | | 62-79 | 4th | 21.0 |
| 9-12 | S.D. | L | 2-15 | | 7 | 18 | Peavy | Reed | | 62-80 | 4th | 21.0 |
| 9-13 | At Ari. | W | 9-2 | | 13 | 8 | Kennedy | Fossum | | 63-80 | 4th | 20.0 |
| 9-14 | At Ari. | L | 3-4 | (13) | 6 | 13 | Choate | Reed | | 63-81 | 4th | 21.0 |
| 9-15 | At Ari. | L | 2-3 | | 5 | 10 | Johnson | Estes | Aquino | 63-82 | 4th | 21.0 |
| 9-16 | At Ari. | L | 5-8 | | 8 | 14 | Durbin | Dohmann | Fetters | 63-83 | 4th | 21.0 |
| 9-17 | L.A. | L | 6-8 | (10) | 12 | 10 | Gagne | Chacon | | 63-84 | 4th | 22.0 |
| 9-18 | L.A. | W | 8-1 | | 16 | 5 | Kennedy | Perez | | 64-84 | 4th | 21.0 |
| 9-19 | L.A. | L | 6-7 | | 9 | 8 | Brazoban | Chacon | Gagne | 64-85 | 4th | 22.0 |
| 9-22 | Ari. | W | 4-2 | | 10 | 8 | Estes | Johnson | Chacon | 65-85 | 4th | 20.5 |
| 9-23! | Ari. | W | 7-1 | | 13 | 9 | Francis | Webb | | 66-85 | | |
| 9-23& | Ari. | W | 2-1 | (10) | 12 | 9 | Simpson | Choate | | 67-85 | 4th | 20.0 |
| 9-24 | StL. | L | 4-5 | | 8 | 10 | Suppan | Jennings | Calero | 67-86 | 4th | 21.0 |
| 9-25 | StL. | L | 6-10 | | 10 | 11 | Flores | Harikkala | Isringhausen | 67-87 | 4th | 21.0 |
| 9-26 | StL. | L | 3-9 | | 8 | 16 | Marquis | Gissell | Eldred | 67-88 | 4th | 22.0 |
| 9-27 | At L.A. | L | 7-8 | | 11 | 12 | Brazoban | Reed | | 67-89 | 4th | 23.0 |
| 9-28 | At L.A. | L | 4-5 | | 5 | 5 | Dessens | Harikkala | | 67-90 | 4th | 24.0 |
| 9-29 | At L.A. | W | 4-1 | | 7 | 3 | Fuentes | Brazoban | Tsao | 68-90 | 4th | 23.0 |
| 9-30 | At L.A. | L | 2-4 | (11) | 11 | 9 | Brazoban | Fuentes | | 68-91 | 4th | 24.0 |
| 10-1 | At Hou. | L | 2-4 | | 12 | 8 | Gallo | Kennedy | Lidge | 68-92 | 4th | 24.0 |
| 10-2 | At Hou. | L | 3-9 | | 7 | 10 | Oswalt | Estes | | 68-93 | 4th | 25.0 |
| 10-3 | At Hou. | L | 3-5 | | 8 | 8 | Backe | Wright | Lidge | 68-94 | 4th | 25.0 |

Monthly records: April (9-12), May (10-19), June (9-17), July (18-10), August (9-18), September (13-15), October (0-3).
*Innings, if other than nine. ! First game of a doubleheader. & Second game of a doubleheader. # Day separate admission. $ Night separate admission.

## RECORDS

**2004 regular-season record:** 68-94
**Position:** 4th in N.L. West
**Home:** 38-43 **Road:** 30-51
**N.L. East:** 11-21 **N.L. Central:** 10-26
**N.L. West:** 39-37 **A.L.** 8-10
**Vs. LH starters:** 26-21
**Vs. RH starters:** 42-73
**Grass:** 67-89 **Artificial:** 1-5
**Day:** 24-35 **Night:** 44-59
**1-Run:** 16-24 **X-inn.:** 3-11
**Doubleheaders:** 1-0-1
**Team record past five years:** 370-440 (.457, ranks 13th in league in that span)

## TEAM LEADERS

**Batting average:** Todd Helton (.347).
**At-bats:** Vinny Castilla (583).
**Runs:** Todd Helton (115).
**Hits:** Todd Helton (190).
**Total Bases:** Todd Helton (339).
**Doubles:** Todd Helton (49).
**Triples:** Jeromy Burnitz, Royce Clayton (4).
**Home runs:** Jeromy Burnitz (37).
**Runs batted in:** Vinny Castilla (131).
**Stolen bases:** Aaron Miles (12).
**Slugging percentage:** Todd Helton (.620).
**On-base percentage:** Todd Helton (.469).
**Wins:** Shawn Estes (15).
**Earned-run average:** Joe Kennedy (3.66).
**Complete games:** Aaron Cook, Shawn Estes, Joe Kennedy (1).
**Shutouts:** None.
**Saves:** Shawn Chacon (35).
**Innings pitched:** Shawn Estes (202.0).
**Strikeouts:** Jason Jennings (133).

## GAMES BY POSITION

**Catcher:** Charles Johnson 91, Todd Greene 53, J.D. Closser 32, Kit Pellow 4.
**First base:** Todd Helton 153, Mark Sweeney 15, Kit Pellow 5, Garrett Atkins 3.
**Second base:** Aaron Miles 128, Luis A. Gonzalez 40, Clint Barmes 9, Denny Hocking 8.
**Third base:** Vinny Castilla 148, Luis A. Gonzalez 18, Garrett Atkins 4, Kit Pellow 4, Denny Hocking 2, Andy Tracy 1.
**Shortstop:** Royce Clayton 144, Denny Hocking 13, Luis A. Gonzalez 10, Clint Barmes 9.
**Outfield:** Jeromy Burnitz 143, Matt Holliday 115, Preston Wilson 52, Choo Freeman 41, Kit Pellow 36, Brad Hawpe 34, Jorge Piedra 34, Larry Walker 34, Denny Hocking 30, Luis A. Gonzalez 29, Mark Sweeney 28, Rene Reyes 21, Garrett Atkins 3.
**Designated hitter:** Mark Sweeney 4, Jeromy Burnitz 3, Luis A. Gonzalez 1, Larry Walker 1.

## TOP DRAFT CHOICES

1. **Chris Nelson,** SS, Redan H.S., Decatur, Ga.
2. **Seth Smith,** OF, Mississippi.
3. **Steve Register,** RHP, Auburn.
4. **Chris Iannetta,** C, North Carolina.
5. **Matt Macri,** 3B, Notre Dame.
6. **Joe Koshansky,** 1B, Virginia.
7. **Jake Postlewait,** LHP, Oregon State.
8. **Jim Miller,** RHP, Louisiana-Monroe.
9. **Dustin Hahn,** 3B, Sacramento CC.
10. **Jarrett Grube,** RHP, Memphis.

# FLORIDA MARLINS

## NATIONAL LEAGUE EAST DIVISION

## 2005 SEASON

### Marlins Schedule

Home games shaded.
All-Star Game July 12 at Detroit. Schedule subject to change.

**April**

| SUN | MON | TUE | WED | THU | FRI | SAT |
|---|---|---|---|---|---|---|
| 3 | 4 | 5 ATL | 6 ATL | 7 ATL | 8 WAS | 9 WAS |
| 10 WAS | 11 PHI | 12 PHI | 13 PHI | 14 | 15 NYM | 16 NYM |
| 17 NYM | 18 WAS | 19 WAS | 20 NYM | 21 NYM | 22 CIN | 23 CIN |
| 24 CIN | 25 | 26 COL | 27 COL | 28 COL | 29 PHI | 30 PHI |

**May**

| SUN | MON | TUE | WED | THU | FRI | SAT |
|---|---|---|---|---|---|---|
| 1 PHI | 2 | 3 ATL | 4 ATL | 5 | 6 COL | 7 COL |
| 8 COL | 9 HOU | 10 HOU | 11 HOU | 12 | 13 SD | 14 SD |
| 15 SD | 16 LA | 17 LA | 18 LA | 19 | 20 TB | 21 TB |
| 22 TB | 23 PHI | 24 PHI | 25 PHI | 26 NYM | 27 NYM | 28 NYM |
| 29 NYM | 30 PIT | 31 PIT | | | | |

**June**

| SUN | MON | TUE | WED | THU | FRI | SAT |
|---|---|---|---|---|---|---|
| | | | 1 PIT | 2 PIT | 3 WAS | 4 WAS |
| 5 WAS | 6 | 7 SEA | 8 SEA | 9 SEA | 10 TEX | 11 TEX |
| 12 TEX | 13 CHC | 14 CHC | 15 CHC | 16 | 17 ANA | 18 ANA |
| 19 ANA | 20 | 21 ATL | 22 ATL | 23 ATL | 24 TB | 25 TB |
| 26 TB | 27 ATL | 28 ATL | 29 ATL | 30 ATL | | |

**July**

| SUN | MON | TUE | WED | THU | FRI | SAT |
|---|---|---|---|---|---|---|
| | | | | | 1 NYM | 2 NYM |
| 3 NYM | 4 MIL | 5 MIL | 6 MIL | 7 MIL | 8 CHC | 9 CHC |
| 10 CHC | 11 | 12 All-Star | 13 | 14 PHI | 15 PHI | 16 PHI |
| 17 PHI | 18 ARI | 19 ARI | 20 ARI | 21 | 22 SF | 23 SF |
| 24 SF | 25 | 26 PIT | 27 PIT | 28 PIT | 29 WAS | 30 WAS |
| 31 WAS | | | | | | |

**August**

| SUN | MON | TUE | WED | THU | FRI | SAT |
|---|---|---|---|---|---|---|
| | 1 STL | 2 STL | 3 STL | 4 STL | 5 CIN | 6 CIN |
| 7 CIN | 8 | 9 ARI | 10 ARI | 11 ARI | 12 SF | 13 SF |
| 14 SF | 15 | 16 SD | 17 SD | 18 SD | 19 LA | 20 LA |
| 21 LA | 22 LA | 23 MIL | 24 MIL | 25 MIL | 26 CHC | 27 CHC |
| 28 CHC | 29 STL | 30 STL | 31 STL | | | |

**September**

| SUN | MON | TUE | WED | THU | FRI | SAT |
|---|---|---|---|---|---|---|
| | | | | 1 | 2 NYM | 3 NYM |
| 4 NYM | 5 WAS | 6 WAS | 7 WAS | 8 WAS | 9 PHI | 10 PHI |
| 11 PHI | 12 HOU | 13 HOU | 14 HOU | 15 HOU | 16 PHI | 17 PHI |
| 18 PHI | 19 | 20 NYM | 21 NYM | 22 NYM | 23 ATL | 24 ATL |
| 25 ATL | 26 WAS | 27 WAS | 28 WAS | 29 | 30 ATL | |

**October**

| SUN | MON | TUE | WED | THU | FRI | SAT |
|---|---|---|---|---|---|---|
| | | | | | | 1 ATL |
| 2 ATL | 3 | 4 | 5 | 6 | 7 | 8 |

Home games shaded. All-Star Game July 12 at Detroit. Schedule subject to change.

### CLUB DIRECTORY

**Owner**
Jeffrey H. Loria
**President**
David P. Samson
**Vice chairman**
Joel A. Mael
**Senior v.p., chief financial officer**
Michel Bussiere
**Special assistants to president**
Andre Dawson, Tony Perez
**Senior v.p. and general manager**
Larry Beinfest
**Vice president, player personnel**
Dan Jennings
**Assistant general manager**
Michael Hill
**Director, team travel**
Bill Beck
**Special assistant to the g.m./pro scout**
Orrin Freeman
**Manager, baseball information systems**
David Kuan
**Video coordinator**
Cullen McRae
**Sr. v.p./dir. of international operations**
Fred Ferreira
**V.p., player development and scouting**
Jim Fleming
**Director of player development**
Brian Chattin
**Director of minor league operations**
Cheryl Evans
**Director, media relations**
Steve Copses

### MINOR LEAGUE AFFILIATES

| Class | Team | League | Manager |
|---|---|---|---|
| AAA | Albuquerque | Pacific Coast | Dean Treanor |
| AA | Carolina | Southern | Gary Allenson |
| Advanced A | Jupiter | Florida State | TBA |
| A | Greensboro | South Atlantic | Brandon Hyde |
| Short-Season A | Jamestown | New York-Pennsylvania | Mike Mordecai |
| Rookie | Gulf Coast Marlins | Gulf Coast | Edwin Rodriguez |

### BROADCAST INFORMATION

**Radio:** TBA
**TV:** PAX-TV
**Cable TV:** Fox Sports Net Florida

### SPRING TRAINING

**Ballpark (city):** Roger Dean Stadium (Jupiter, Fla.).
**Ticket information:** 561-775-1818.

**For more on the Marlins, go to msn.foxsports.com/mlb/teams.**

Willis

## SPRING TRAINING ROSTER

**Manager**—Jack McKeon (15).
**Coaches**—Pierre Arsenault (67), Jeff Cox (47), Luis Dorante, Harry Dunlop, Perry Hill (7), Bill Robinson (28), Mark Wiley.

| No. | PITCHERS | B/T | Ht./Wt. | Age* | 2004 Clubs |
|---|---|---|---|---|---|
| | Alfonseca, Antonio | R/R | 6-5/250 | 32 | Atlanta |
| | Bazardo, Yorman | R/R | 6-2/170 | 20 | Jupiter |
| 61 | Beckett, Josh | R/R | 6-5/222 | 24 | Florida |
| | Belisario, Ronald | R/R | 6-2/150 | 22 | G.C. Marlins, Jupiter, Carolina |
| 40 | Bump, Nate | L/R | 6-2/196 | 28 | Albuquerque, Florida |
| 34 | Burnett, A.J. | R/R | 6-4/230 | 28 | Jupiter, Albuquerque, Florida |
| | Cave, Kevin | R/R | 6-2/220 | 24 | Jupiter, Carolina |
| | Flannery, Mike | R/R | 6-1/195 | 25 | Carolina, Albuquerque |
| | Hagerty, Luke | R/L | 6-7/245 | 24 | Arizona Cubs, Boise |
| 39 | Howard, Ben | R/R | 6-0/221 | 26 | Albuquerque, Florida |
| | Jones, Todd | L/R | 6-3/230 | 36 | Cincinnati, Philadelphia |
| 54 | Kensing, Logan | R/R | 6-1/185 | 22 | Jupiter, Florida |
| | Leiter, Al | L/L | 6-3/220 | 39 | New York N.L. |
| | Messenger, Randy | R/R | 6-0/220 | 24 | Carolina |
| 59 | Mota, Guillermo | R/R | 6-4/205 | 31 | Los Angeles, Florida |
| | Resop, Chris | R/R | 6-3/200 | 22 | Greensboro |
| 46 | Riedling, John | R/R | 5-11/190 | 29 | Cincinnati |
| 91 | Spooneybarger, T. | R/R | 6-3/190 | 25 | Did Not Play |
| | Valdez, Ismael | R/R | 6-4/230 | 31 | San Diego, Florida |
| 48 | Wayne, Justin | R/R | 6-3/205 | 25 | Jupiter, Florida, Albuquerque |
| 35 | Willis, Dontrelle | L/L | 6-4/239 | 23 | Florida |

| No. | CATCHERS | B/T | Ht./Wt. | Age* | 2004 Clubs |
|---|---|---|---|---|---|
| 14 | Lo Duca, Paul | R/R | 5-10/185 | 32 | Los Angeles, Florida |
| 6 | Treanor, Matt | R/R | 6-2/220 | 29 | Albuquerque, Florida |
| | Willingham, Josh | R/R | 6-1/200 | 26 | Florida, Carolina |

| No. | INFIELDERS | B/T | Ht./Wt. | Age* | 2004 Clubs |
|---|---|---|---|---|---|
| 1 | Castillo, Luis | B/R | 5-11/190 | 29 | Florida |
| 18 | Conine, Jeff | R/R | 6-1/220 | 38 | Florida |
| | Dillon, Joe | R/R | 6-2/200 | 29 | Carolina, Albuquerque |
| 2 | Easley, Damion | R/R | 5-11/190 | 35 | Florida |
| 11 | Gonzalez, Alex | R/R | 6-0/202 | 28 | Florida |
| 19 | Lowell, Mike | R/R | 6-3/210 | 31 | Florida |
| | Stokes, Jason | R/R | 6-4/225 | 23 | Marlins, Carolina |
| | Wathan, Derek | S/R | 6-3/190 | 28 | Albuquerque |
| | Wilson, Josh | R/R | 6-1/160 | 24 | Albuquerque, Carolina |

| No. | OUTFIELDERS | B/T | Ht./Wt. | Age* | 2004 Clubs |
|---|---|---|---|---|---|
| 3 | Aguila, Chris | R/R | 5-11/180 | 26 | Albuquerque, Florida |
| 20 | Cabrera, Miguel | R/R | 6-2/210 | 21 | Florida |
| 43 | Encarnacion, Juan | R/R | 6-3/215 | 29 | Los Angeles, Florida |
| 9 | Pierre, Juan | L/L | 6-0/180 | 27 | Florida |
| | Reed, Eric | L/L | 5-11/170 | 24 | Carolina |

*Age as of April 1, 2005.

## BALLPARK INFORMATION

**Ballpark (capacity, surface)**
Pro Player Stadium (36,331, grass)
**Address**
2267 Dan Marino Blvd.
Miami, Fla. 33056
**Official website**
www.floridamarlins.com
**Business phone**
305-626-7400
**Ticket information**
1-877-MARLINS
**Field dimensions (from home plate)**
To left field at foul line, 330 feet
To center field, 434 feet
To right field at foul line, 345 feet
**First game played**
April 5, 1993 (Marlins 6, Dodgers 3)

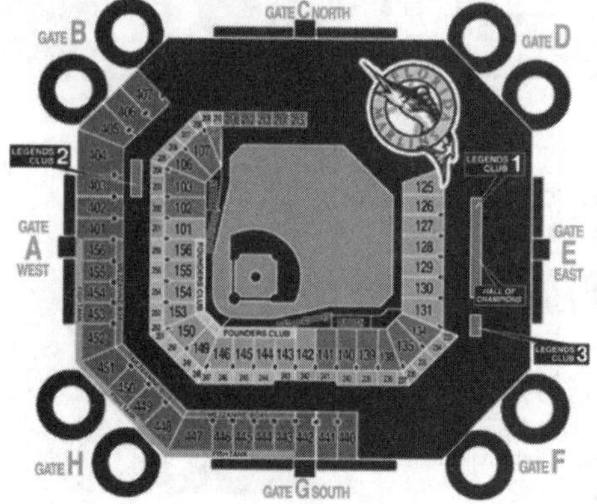

# 2004 REVIEW

## DAY BY DAY

| Date | Opp. | Res. | Score | (inn.*) | Hits | Opp. hits | Winning pitcher | Losing pitcher | Save | Record | Pos. | GB |
|---|---|---|---|---|---|---|---|---|---|---|---|---|
| 4-6 | Mon. | W | 4-3 | | 10 | 8 | Perisho | Ayala | Benitez | 1-0 | T1st | ... |
| 4-7 | Mon. | L | 2-3 | | 6 | 5 | Vargas | Penny | Biddle | 1-1 | T1st | ... |
| 4-8 | Mon. | W | 3-0 | | 11 | 5 | Willis | Ohka | Benitez | 2-1 | T1st | ... |
| 4-9 | Phi. | W | 4-3 | | 11 | 8 | Perisho | Cormier | Benitez | 3-1 | 1st | +1.0 |
| 4-10 | Phi. | W | 5-3 | | 11 | 9 | Oliver | Cormier | Benitez | 4-1 | 1st | +1.0 |
| 4-11 | Phi. | W | 3-1 | | 5 | 3 | Beckett | Millwood | Benitez | 5-1 | 1st | +2.0 |
| 4-13@ | At Mon. | W | 5-0 | | 8 | 4 | Penny | Vargas | | 6-1 | 1st | +2.0 |
| 4-14@ | At Mon. | W | 9-0 | | 15 | 8 | Willis | Ohka | | 7-1 | 1st | +3.0 |
| 4-15@ | At Mon. | W | 3-0 | | 6 | 3 | Pavano | Day | Benitez | 8-1 | 1st | +3.0 |
| 4-16 | At Atl. | L | 4-5 | | 7 | 8 | Wright | Oliver | Smoltz | 8-2 | 1st | +3.0 |
| 4-17 | At Atl. | L | 1-4 | | 6 | 8 | Ortiz | Beckett | Smoltz | 8-3 | 1st | +2.0 |
| 4-18 | At Atl. | L | 2-3 | (10) | 7 | 6 | Alfonseca | Perisho | | 8-4 | 1st | +1.0 |
| 4-20 | At Phi. | W | 3-1 | | 7 | 4 | Willis | Padilla | Benitez | 9-4 | 1st | +2.0 |
| 4-21 | At Phi. | W | 8-7 | (12) | 15 | 13 | Wayne | Madson | | 10-4 | 1st | +2.0 |
| 4-22 | At Phi. | W | 9-7 | | 13 | 11 | Oliver | Myers | Benitez | 11-4 | 1st | +3.0 |
| 4-23 | Atl. | L | 1-6 | | 4 | 9 | Ortiz | Beckett | | 11-5 | 1st | +2.0 |
| 4-24 | Atl. | W | 7-4 | | 13 | 14 | Penny | Hampton | Benitez | 12-5 | 1st | +3.0 |
| 4-25 | Atl. | L | 2-7 | | 9 | 11 | Thomson | Bump | | 12-6 | 1st | +2.0 |
| 4-26 | At Col. | W | 6-3 | | 10 | 7 | Pavano | Elarton | Benitez | 13-6 | 1st | +3.0 |
| 4-27 | At Col. | L | 10-13 | | 16 | 12 | Nunez | Fox | Chacon | 13-7 | 1st | +2.0 |
| 4-28 | At Col. | W | 9-4 | | 9 | 9 | Beckett | Jennings | | 14-7 | 1st | +3.0 |
| 4-29 | At S.F | W | 4-3 | | 6 | 9 | Wayne | Rodriguez | Gracesqui | 15-7 | 1st | +3.5 |
| 4-30 | At S.F | L | 9-12 | | 9 | 16 | Walker | Bump | Herges | 15-8 | 1st | +3.0 |
| 5-1 | At S.F | L | 3-6 | | 8 | 7 | Schmidt | Pavano | Herges | 15-9 | 1st | +2.5 |
| 5-2 | At S.F | L | 8-9 | (11) | 11 | 16 | Walker | Perisho | | 15-10 | 1st | +2.5 |
| 5-4 | L.A. | L | 3-4 | (11) | 12 | 7 | Sanchez | Wayne | Gagne | 15-11 | 1st | +1.5 |
| 5-5 | L.A. | W | 2-0 | | 6 | 5 | Penny | Weaver | Benitez | 16-11 | 1st | +2.5 |
| 5-6 | L.A. | L | 4-9 | | 7 | 14 | Ishii | Willis | Gagne | 16-12 | 1st | +2.5 |
| 5-7 | S.D. | W | 3-1 | | 10 | 4 | Pavano | Peavy | Benitez | 17-12 | 1st | +3.0 |
| 5-8 | S.D. | L | 3-6 | (10) | 7 | 17 | Otsuka | Gracesqui | Hoffman | 17-13 | 1st | +2.0 |
| 5-9 | S.D. | W | 7-4 | | 12 | 9 | Beckett | Eaton | Benitez | 18-13 | 1st | +2.0 |
| 5-11 | At Hou. | L | 1-6 | | 4 | 9 | Clemens | Penny | | 18-14 | 1st | +1.0 |
| 5-12 | At Hou. | W | 5-2 | | 10 | 6 | Willis | Miller | | 19-14 | 1st | +2.0 |
| 5-13 | At Hou. | W | 3-2 | | 9 | 8 | Perisho | Dotel | Benitez | 20-14 | 1st | +2.0 |
| 5-14 | At StL. | L | 3-6 | | 8 | 9 | Marquis | Beckett | Isringhausen | 20-15 | 1st | +1.0 |
| 5-15 | At StL. | L | 0-4 | | 5 | 6 | Carpenter | Oliver | Tavarez | 20-16 | 2nd | ... |
| 5-16 | At StL. | W | 3-2 | | 10 | 6 | Penny | Williams | Benitez | 21-16 | 1st | +1.0 |
| 5-18 | Hou. | L | 2-9 | | 7 | 15 | Miller | Willis | | 21-17 | 1st | +0.5 |
| 5-19 | Hou. | L | 2-10 | | 5 | 15 | Redding | Pavano | | 21-18 | 2nd | 0.5 |
| 5-20 | Hou. | W | 6-2 | | 12 | 5 | Beckett | Oswalt | Benitez | 22-18 | 2nd | 0.5 |
| 5-21 | Ari. | W | 6-5 | (10) | 9 | 8 | Benitez | Bruney | | 23-18 | 2nd | 0.5 |
| 5-22 | Ari. | W | 11-2 | | 11 | 6 | Penny | Sparks | | 24-18 | 1st | +0.5 |
| 5-23 | Ari. | L | 3-4 | | 5 | 11 | Johnson | Willis | Valverde | 24-19 | 2nd | 0.5 |
| 5-24 | Ari. | W | 13-5 | | 12 | 11 | Pavano | Webb | | 25-19 | 2nd | ... |
| 5-25 | At Cin. | L | 2-5 | | 9 | 7 | Wilson | Beckett | Jones | 25-20 | 2nd | ... |
| 5-26 | At Cin. | W | 3-0 | | 8 | 1 | Phelps | Van Poppel | Benitez | 26-20 | 2nd | ... |
| 5-27 | At Cin. | W | 5-2 | | 11 | 6 | Penny | Harang | Benitez | 27-20 | 1st | +1.0 |
| 5-28 | N.Y. | W | 2-1 | | 6 | 5 | Willis | Glavine | Benitez | 28-20 | 1st | +1.0 |
| 5-29 | N.Y. | W | 3-2 | (10) | 8 | 7 | Wayne | Looper | | 29-20 | 1st | +2.0 |
| 5-30 | N.Y. | W | 8-6 | | 9 | 11 | Borland | Stanton | Benitez | 30-20 | 1st | +2.0 |
| 5-31 | Cin. | L | 7-9 | | 14 | 10 | Riedling | Wayne | Graves | 30-21 | 1st | +2.0 |
| 6-1 | Cin. | L | 6-7 | (10) | 12 | 12 | Reith | Bump | Graves | 30-22 | 1st | +2.0 |
| 6-2 | Cin. | L | 1-3 | | 7 | 5 | Reith | Howard | Graves | 30-23 | 1st | +2.0 |
| 6-3 | At N.Y. | L | 1-4 | | 3 | 8 | Seo | Burnett | Looper | 30-24 | 1st | +2.0 |
| 6-4 | At N.Y. | W | 5-1 | | 9 | 6 | Pavano | Trachsel | Benitez | 31-24 | 1st | +2.0 |
| 6-5 | At N.Y. | W | 7-6 | | 14 | 12 | Perisho | Weathers | Benitez | 32-24 | 1st | +2.0 |
| 6-6 | At N.Y. | L | 2-5 | | 10 | 10 | Leiter | Penny | | 32-25 | 1st | +2.0 |
| 6-8 | At Cle. | W | 7-5 | | 12 | 11 | Bump | Jimenez | Benitez | 33-25 | 1st | +3.0 |
| 6-9 | At Cle. | L | 1-8 | | 6 | 13 | Westbrook | Burnett | | 33-26 | 1st | +2.0 |
| 6-10 | At Cle. | W | 4-1 | | 12 | 4 | Pavano | Davis | Benitez | 34-26 | 1st | +2.5 |
| 6-11 | At Det. | L | 4-8 | | 5 | 11 | Knotts | Phelps | | 34-27 | 1st | +1.5 |
| 6-12 | At Det. | L | 2-6 | | 7 | 9 | Robertson | Penny | Urbina | 34-28 | 1st | +1.5 |
| 6-13 | At Det. | W | 9-2 | | 15 | 7 | Willis | Johnson | | 35-28 | 1st | +1.5 |
| 6-15 | Chi. | L | 5-7 | (10) | 7 | 8 | Marte | Borland | Takatsu | 35-29 | 1st | +1.0 |
| 6-16 | Chi. | W | 4-0 | | 13 | 3 | Pavano | Schoeneweis | | 36-29 | 1st | +1.5 |
| 6-17 | Chi. | W | 2-1 | (11) | 6 | 7 | Benitez | Politte | | 37-29 | 1st | +2.0 |

| Date | Opp. | Res. | Score | (inn.*) | Hits | Opp. hits | Winning pitcher | Losing pitcher | Save | Record | Pos. | GB |
|---|---|---|---|---|---|---|---|---|---|---|---|---|
| 6-18 | Tex. | L | 1-8 | | 8 | 14 | Wasdin | Penny | | 37-30 | 1st | +2.0 |
| 6-19 | Tex. | L | 6-7 | | 9 | 12 | Dickey | Willis | Cordero | 37-31 | 1st | +1.0 |
| 6-20 | Tex. | L | 2-4 | (11) | 7 | 6 | Mahay | Koch | | 37-32 | 2nd | ... |
| 6-22 | Atl. | W | 4-3 | | 6 | 11 | Pavano | Gryboski | Benitez | 38-32 | 1st | +1.0 |
| 6-23 | Atl. | W | 6-0 | | 10 | 4 | Penny | Thomson | | 39-32 | 1st | +1.0 |
| 6-24 | Atl. | L | 4-9 | | 10 | 13 | Hampton | Willis | | 39-33 | 1st | +1.0 |
| 6-25 | At T.B. | L | 0-2 | | 2 | 3 | Brazelton | Burnett | Baez | 39-34 | 1st | +1.0 |
| 6-26 | At T.B. | L | 4-6 | | 7 | 7 | Sosa | Manzanillo | Baez | 39-35 | 2nd | ... |
| 6-27 | At T.B. | W | 11-4 | | 17 | 10 | Pavano | Gaudin | | 40-35 | 1st | +1.0 |
| 6-28 | At Atl. | L | 1-6 | | 3 | 11 | Thomson | Penny | | 40-36 | 2nd | ... |
| 6-29 | At Atl. | W | 5-4 | | 8 | 11 | Manzanillo | Hampton | Benitez | 41-36 | 2nd | ... |
| 6-30 | At Atl. | L | 6-9 | | 12 | 17 | McConnell | Oliver | Smoltz | 41-37 | 2nd | ... |
| 7-1 | At Atl. | L | 1-9 | | 7 | 9 | Ortiz | Tejera | | 41-38 | 2nd | 1.0 |
| 7-2 | T.B. | L | 2-4 | | 8 | 14 | Colome | Pavano | Baez | 41-39 | 2nd | 1.0 |
| 7-3 | T.B. | L | 1-6 | | 5 | 9 | Zambrano | Penny | | 41-40 | 3rd | 2.0 |
| 7-4 | T.B. | W | 4-3 | | 9 | 7 | Burnett | Halama | Benitez | 42-40 | 3rd | 2.0 |
| 7-5 | Pit. | L | 1-3 | | 6 | 7 | Wells | Beckett | Mesa | 42-41 | 3rd | 3.0 |
| 7-6 | Pit. | W | 6-3 | | 11 | 9 | Bump | Corey | Benitez | 43-41 | 3rd | 2.0 |
| 7-7 | Pit. | L | 3-4 | | 10 | 8 | Perez | Pavano | Mesa | 43-42 | 4th | 2.0 |
| 7-9 | N.Y. | L | 3-6 | | 8 | 9 | Wheeler | Manzanillo | Looper | 43-43 | 4th | 3.5 |
| 7-10 | N.Y. | W | 5-2 | | 11 | 9 | Penny | Glavine | Benitez | 44-43 | 4th | 2.5 |
| 7-11 | N.Y. | W | 5-2 | | 5 | 6 | Willis | Leiter | Benitez | 45-43 | 3rd | 1.5 |
| 7-16 | At Pit. | L | 2-6 | | 8 | 11 | Benson | Burnett | Mesa | 45-44 | T3rd | 2.0 |
| 7-17 | At Pit. | L | 2-4 | | 8 | 10 | Torres | Benitez | Mesa | 45-45 | T3rd | 3.0 |
| 7-18 | At Pit. | L | 2-4 | | 6 | 11 | Torres | Koch | Mesa | 45-46 | 4th | 3.0 |
| 7-19 | At N.Y. | W | 6-5 | | 13 | 9 | Manzanillo | Looper | Benitez | 46-46 | T3rd | 3.0 |
| 7-20 | At N.Y. | W | 9-7 | | 13 | 10 | Howard | Franco | Benitez | 47-46 | 3rd | 2.0 |
| 7-21 | At Phi. | L | 1-2 | | 7 | 8 | Millwood | Burnett | Wagner | 47-47 | T3rd | 3.0 |
| 7-22 | At Phi. | W | 10-8 | | 15 | 13 | Pavano | Wolf | Benitez | 48-47 | 3rd | 2.0 |
| 7-23 | At Mon. | L | 1-2 | | 6 | 5 | Armas | Penny | Cordero | 48-48 | 3rd | 2.5 |
| 7-24 | At Mon. | L | 2-6 | | 10 | 6 | Biddle | Willis | | 48-49 | 3rd | 3.5 |
| 7-25 | At Mon. | L | 4-6 | | 8 | 9 | Hernandez | Wayne | Ayala | 48-50 | 3rd | 4.5 |
| 7-26 | Phi. | W | 11-3 | | 12 | 12 | Burnett | Millwood | Bump | 49-50 | 3rd | 4.5 |
| 7-27 | Phi. | W | 5-2 | | 8 | 7 | Pavano | Cormier | Manzanillo | 50-50 | 3rd | 3.5 |
| 7-28 | Phi. | W | 6-3 | | 7 | 9 | Manzanillo | Worrell | | 51-50 | 3rd | 3.5 |
| 7-29 | Phi. | W | 10-1 | | 15 | 5 | Willis | Abbott | | 52-50 | T2nd | 3.5 |
| 7-30 | Mon. | L | 0-9 | | 3 | 16 | Hernandez | Beckett | | 52-51 | T2nd | 4.5 |
| 7-31 | Mon. | L | 5-8 | | 11 | 10 | Biddle | Manzanillo | Cordero | 52-52 | 3rd | 5.5 |
| 8-3 | At Ari. | L | 3-5 | | 9 | 10 | Koplove | Willis | Aquino | 52-53 | 3rd | 6.0 |
| 8-4 | At Ari. | L | 6-11 | | 10 | 14 | Johnson | Beckett | | 52-54 | 3rd | 7.0 |
| 8-5 | At Ari. | W | 11-5 | | 14 | 9 | Pavano | Cormier | Mota | 53-54 | 3rd | 7.0 |
| 8-6 | Mil. | W | 7-6 | | 10 | 8 | Koch | Kolb | | 54-54 | 3rd | 7.0 |
| 8-7 | Mil. | W | 5-0 | | 9 | 3 | Valdez | Obermueller | | 55-54 | 3rd | 7.0 |
| 8-8 | Mil. | L | 0-2 | | 7 | 8 | Capuano | Willis | Kolb | 55-55 | 3rd | 8.0 |
| 8-10 | StL. | L | 1-2 | (10) | 7 | 2 | Tavarez | Mota | Isringhausen | 55-56 | 3rd | 8.0 |
| 8-11 | StL. | L | 0-1 | | 2 | 6 | Suppan | Pavano | Isringhausen | 55-57 | 3rd | 9.0 |
| 8-12 | StL. | W | 8-2 | | 11 | 7 | Burnett | Morris | | 56-57 | 3rd | 9.0 |
| 8-13 | At Mil. | L | 4-6 | | 8 | 10 | Obermueller | Valdez | Kolb | 56-58 | 3rd | 9.0 |
| 8-14 | At Mil. | W | 11-1 | | 12 | 8 | Willis | de la Rosa | | 57-58 | 3rd | 9.0 |
| 8-15 | At Mil. | W | 5-3 | (10) | 11 | 7 | Seanez | Hendrickson | Benitez | 58-58 | T2nd | 8.0 |
| 8-16 | At L.A. | W | 4-2 | | 7 | 6 | Pavano | Dreifort | Benitez | 59-58 | 2nd | 8.0 |
| 8-17 | At L.A. | L | 1-6 | | 7 | 8 | Alvarez | Burnett | | 59-59 | 2nd | 8.0 |
| 8-18 | At L.A. | W | 6-4 | | 10 | 11 | Mota | Gagne | Benitez | 60-59 | 2nd | 8.0 |
| 8-20 | At S.D. | L | 1-6 | | 5 | 10 | Lawrence | Willis | | 60-60 | 2nd | 8.5 |
| 8-21 | At S.D. | W | 8-2 | | 15 | 6 | Beckett | Eaton | | 61-60 | 2nd | 7.5 |
| 8-22 | At S.D. | W | 8-3 | | 14 | 7 | Pavano | Hitchcock | Mota | 62-60 | 2nd | 7.5 |
| 8-24 | S.F | W | 9-1 | | 10 | 3 | Burnett | Franklin | | 63-60 | 2nd | 7.5 |
| 8-25 | S.F | L | 5-6 | (10) | 8 | 7 | Brower | Seanez | Hermanson | 63-61 | 2nd | 8.5 |
| 8-26 | S.F | L | 0-5 | | 4 | 8 | Tomko | Beckett | | 63-62 | 2nd | 9.5 |
| 8-27 | Col. | W | 3-0 | | 9 | 4 | Valdez | Kennedy | Benitez | 64-62 | 2nd | 9.5 |
| 8-28 | Col. | W | 4-3 | | 9 | 7 | Pavano | Reed | Benitez | 65-62 | 2nd | 9.5 |
| 8-29 | Col. | W | 8-4 | | 13 | 9 | Burnett | Estes | | 66-62 | 2nd | 8.5 |
| 8-30 | At N.Y. | W | 6-4 | | 12 | 10 | Seanez | Bell | Benitez | 67-62 | 2nd | 8.5 |
| 8-31 | At N.Y. | W | 5-0 | | 5 | 6 | Beckett | Trachsel | | 68-62 | 2nd | 8.5 |
| 9-1 | At N.Y. | W | 5-4 | | 8 | 9 | Valdez | Glavine | Benitez | 69-62 | 2nd | 8.5 |
| 9-2 | At N.Y. | W | 9-6 | | 12 | 10 | Pavano | Seo | | 70-62 | 2nd | 8.0 |
| 9-7 | N.Y. | W | 7-3 | | 11 | 3 | Burnett | Glavine | | 71-62 | 2nd | 8.5 |
| 9-8 | N.Y. | W | 3-0 | | 8 | 4 | Beckett | Seo | Benitez | 72-62 | 2nd | 7.0 |
| 9-9 | N.Y. | L | 0-4 | | 7 | 11 | Benson | Valdez | | 72-63 | 2nd | 7.0 |

| Date | Opp. | Res. | Score | (inn.*) | Hits | Opp. hits | Winning pitcher | Losing pitcher | Save | Record | Pos. | GB |
|---|---|---|---|---|---|---|---|---|---|---|---|---|
| 9-10! | At Chi. | W | 7-0 | | 13 | 7 | Pavano | Wood | | 73-63 | | |
| 9-10& | At Chi. | L | 2-11 | | 9 | 18 | Prior | Kensing | | 73-64 | 2nd | 7.5 |
| 9-11 | At Chi. | L | 2-5 | | 6 | 11 | Dempster | Mota | Hawkins | 73-65 | 2nd | 8.5 |
| 9-12 | At Chi. | W | 11-1 | | 15 | 6 | Burnett | Rusch | | 74-65 | 2nd | 8.5 |
| 9-13 | Mon. | W | 6-3 | | 11 | 5 | Perisho | Majewski | | 75-65 | 2nd | 8.0 |
| 9-14 | Mon. | W | 8-6 | | 13 | 11 | Seanez | Ayala | Mota | 76-65 | 2nd | 7.0 |
| 9-15! | Mon. | L | 2-6 | | 8 | 12 | Patterson | Pavano | | 76-66 | | |
| 9-15& | Mon. | L | 4-10 | | 9 | 15 | Rauch | Bump | | 76-67 | 2nd | 8.5 |
| 9-16 | Mon. | W | 4-3 | | 8 | 7 | Willis | Hernandez | Benitez | 77-67 | 2nd | 7.5 |
| 9-17 | Atl. | L | 1-8 | | 14 | 11 | Byrd | Kensing | | 77-68 | 2nd | 8.5 |
| 9-18 | Atl. | L | 2-4 | | 4 | 8 | Wright | Beckett | Smoltz | 77-69 | 2nd | 9.5 |
| 9-19 | Atl. | W | 3-0 | | 9 | 3 | Valdez | Ortiz | Benitez | 78-69 | 2nd | 8.5 |
| 9-20! | Chi. | L | 1-5 | | 7 | 16 | Prior | Pavano | | 78-70 | | |
| 9-20& | Chi. | W | 5-2 | | 4 | 5 | Weathers | Clement | Benitez | 79-70 | 2nd | 8.5 |
| 9-21 | Phi. | L | 2-4 | | 3 | 6 | Lidle | Willis | Wagner | 79-71 | 2nd | 9.5 |
| 9-22 | Phi. | L | 4-12 | | 9 | 13 | Milton | Kensing | | 79-72 | 2nd | 9.5 |
| 9-23 | Phi. | L | 8-9 | (10) | 10 | 12 | Wagner | Benitez | Jones | 79-73 | T2nd | 9.5 |
| 9-24 | At Atl. | L | 7-8 | | 9 | 11 | Smith | Mota | Smoltz | 79-74 | T2nd | 10.5 |
| 9-25 | At Atl. | L | 0-1 | | 4 | 2 | Hampton | Pavano | Reitsma | 79-75 | 3rd | 11.5 |
| 9-26 | At Atl. | L | 3-6 | | 8 | 9 | Thomson | Willis | | 79-76 | 3rd | 12.5 |
| 9-27 | At Mon. | W | 4-1 | | 10 | 4 | Beckett | Patterson | Benitez | 80-76 | 3rd | 12.0 |
| 9-28 | At Mon. | W | 5-2 | | 8 | 3 | Valdez | Ohka | Benitez | 81-76 | 3rd | 11.5 |
| 9-29 | At Mon. | W | 9-1 | | 15 | 7 | Pavano | Kim | | 82-76 | 3rd | 11.5 |
| 9-30 | At Phi. | L | 4-7 | | 8 | 13 | Jones | Mota | Wagner | 82-77 | 3rd | 12.0 |
| 10-1 | At Phi. | L | 2-6 | | 12 | 11 | Lidle | Perisho | | 82-78 | 3rd | 13.0 |
| 10-2 | At Phi. | W | 4-3 | | 5 | 9 | Beckett | Milton | Benitez | 83-78 | 3rd | 13.0 |
| 10-3 | At Phi. | L | 4-10 | | 6 | 15 | Myers | Valdez | | 83-79 | 3rd | 13.0 |

Monthly records: April (15-8), May (15-13), June (11-16), July (11-15), August (16-10), September (14-15), October (1-2). *Innings, if other than nine. @ At Hiram Bithorn Stadium, San Juan, Puerto Rico. ! First game of a doubleheader. & Second game of a doubleheader.

## RECORDS

**2004 regular-season record:** 83-79
**Position:** 3rd in N.L. East
**Home:** 42-38 **Road:** 41-41
**N.L. East:** 43-33 **N.L. Central:** 15-21
**N.L. West:** 18-14 **A.L.** 7-11
**Vs. LH starters:** 25-20
**Vs. RH starters:** 58-59
**Grass:** 76-74 **Artificial:** 7-5
**Day:** 31-18 **Night:** 52-61
**1-Run:** 20-17 **X-inn.:** 5-10
**Doubleheaders:** 0-1-2
**Team record past five years:** 408-401 (.504, ranks 7th in league in that span)

## TEAM LEADERS

**Batting average:** Juan Pierre (.326).
**At-bats:** Juan Pierre (678).
**Runs:** Miguel Cabrera (101).
**Hits:** Juan Pierre (221).
**Total Bases:** Miguel Cabrera (309).
**Doubles:** Mike Lowell (44).
**Triples:** Juan Pierre (12).
**Home runs:** Miguel Cabrera (33).
**Runs batted in:** Miguel Cabrera (112).
**Stolen bases:** Juan Pierre (45).
**Slugging percentage:** Miguel Cabrera (.512).
**On-base percentage:** Hee Seop Choi (.388).
**Wins:** Carl Pavano (18).
**Earned-run average:** Carl Pavano (3.00).
**Complete games:** Carl Pavano, Dontrelle Willis (2).
**Shutouts:** Carl Pavano (2).
**Saves:** Armando Benitez (47).
**Innings pitched:** Carl Pavano (222.1).
**Strikeouts:** Josh Beckett (152).

## GAMES BY POSITION

**Catcher:** Mike Redmond 79, Paul Lo Duca 49, Ramon Castro 31, Matt Treanor 27, Josh Willingham 5, Mike Mordecai 1.
**First base:** Hee Seop Choi 89, Jeff Conine 57, Damion Easley 18, Wil Cordero 13, Larry Sutton 1.
**Second base:** Luis Castillo 148, Damion Easley 25, Mike Mordecai 4.
**Third base:** Mike Lowell 154, Mike Mordecai 19, Damion Easley 6, Lenny Harris 3.
**Shortstop:** Alex Gonzalez 158, Damion Easley 15, Mike Mordecai 3.
**Outfield:** Juan Pierre 162, Miguel Cabrera 158, Jeff Conine 83, Juan Encarnacion 48, Abraham Nunez 48, Chris Aguila 20, Lenny Harris 14, Damion Easley 5, Wil Cordero 3, Josh Willingham 3.
**Designated hitter:** Damion Easley 3, Mike Lowell 3, Lenny Harris 2, Miguel Cabrera 1.

## TOP DRAFT CHOICES

1. **Taylor Tankersley,** LHP, Alabama.
2. **Jason Vargas,** LHP, Long Beach State.
3. **Greg Burns,** OF, Walnut H.S., West Covina, Calif.
4. **Jamar Walton,** OF, Greensville County H.S., Emporia, Va.
5. **Brad Davis,** C, Long Beach State.
6. **Brad McCann,** 3B, Clemson.
7. **Jared Gaston,** OF, Walters State (Tenn.) CC.
8. **Craig Molldrem,** RHP, Minnesota.
9. **Joe Pietro,** OF, New Orleans.
10. **Brett Carroll,** 3B, Middle Tennessee State.

# HOUSTON ASTROS

## NATIONAL LEAGUE CENTRAL DIVISION

## 2005 SEASON

### Astros Schedule

Home games shaded.
All-Star Game July 12 at Detroit. Schedule subject to change.

**April**

| SUN | MON | TUE | WED | THU | FRI | SAT |
|---|---|---|---|---|---|---|
| 3 | 4 | 5 STL | 6 STL | 7 | 8 CIN | 9 CIN |
| 10 CIN | 11 NYM | 12 | 13 NYM | 14 NYM | 15 CIN | 16 CIN |
| 17 CIN | 18 ATL | 19 ATL | 20 MIL | 21 MIL | 22 STL | 23 STL |
| 24 STL | 25 PIT | 26 PIT | 27 PIT | 28 | 29 CHC | 30 CHC |

**May**

| SUN | MON | TUE | WED | THU | FRI | SAT |
|---|---|---|---|---|---|---|
| 1 CHC | 2 PIT | 3 PIT | 4 PIT | 5 ATL | 6 ATL | 7 ATL |
| 8 ATL | 9 FLA | 10 FLA | 11 FLA | 12 SF | 13 SF | 14 SF |
| 15 SF | 16 | 17 ARI | 18 ARI | 19 ARI | 20 TEX | 21 TEX |
| 22 TEX | 23 CHC | 24 CHC | 25 CHC | 26 | 27 MIL | 28 MIL |
| 29 MIL | 30 CIN | 31 CIN | | | | |

**June**

| SUN | MON | TUE | WED | THU | FRI | SAT |
|---|---|---|---|---|---|---|
| | | | 1 CIN | 2 | 3 STL | 4 STL |
| 5 STL | 6 | 7 NYM | 8 NYM | 9 NYM | 10 TOR | 11 TOR |
| 12 TOR | 13 BAL | 14 BAL | 15 BAL | 16 | 17 KC | 18 KC |
| 19 KC | 20 COL | 21 COL | 22 COL | 23 | 24 TEX | 25 TEX |
| 26 TEX | 27 COL | 28 COL | 29 COL | 30 CIN | | |

**July**

| SUN | MON | TUE | WED | THU | FRI | SAT |
|---|---|---|---|---|---|---|
| | | | | | 1 CIN | 2 CIN |
| 3 CIN | 4 SD | 5 SD | 6 SD | 7 SD | 8 LA | 9 LA |
| 10 LA | 11 | 12 All-Star | 13 | 14 | 15 STL | 16 STL |
| 17 STL | 18 PIT | 19 PIT | 20 PIT | 21 WAS | 22 WAS | 23 WAS |
| 24 WAS | 25 PHI | 26 PHI | 27 PHI | 28 NYM | 29 NYM | 30 NYM |
| 31 NYM | | | | | | |

**August**

| SUN | MON | TUE | WED | THU | FRI | SAT |
|---|---|---|---|---|---|---|
| | 1 | 2 ARI | 3 ARI | 4 ARI | 5 SF | 6 SF |
| 7 SF | 8 | 9 WAS | 10 WAS | 11 WAS | 12 PIT | 13 PIT |
| 14 PIT | 15 CHC | 16 CHC | 17 CHC | 18 MIL | 19 MIL | 20 MIL |
| 21 MIL | 22 SD | 23 SD | 24 SD | 25 | 26 LA | 27 LA |
| 28 LA | 29 | 30 CIN | 31 CIN | | | |

**September**

| SUN | MON | TUE | WED | THU | FRI | SAT |
|---|---|---|---|---|---|---|
| | | | | 1 CIN | 2 STL | 3 STL |
| 4 STL | 5 PHI | 6 PHI | 7 PHI | 8 | 9 MIL | 10 MIL |
| 11 MIL | 12 FLA | 13 FLA | 14 FLA | 15 FLA | 16 MIL | 17 MIL |
| 18 MIL | 19 PIT | 20 PIT | 21 PIT | 22 PIT | 23 CHC | 24 CHC |
| 25 CHC | 26 | 27 STL | 28 STL | 29 CHC | 30 CHC | |

**October**

| SUN | MON | TUE | WED | THU | FRI | SAT |
|---|---|---|---|---|---|---|
| | | | | | | 1 CHC |
| 2 CHC | 3 | 4 | 5 | 6 | 7 | 8 |

Home games shaded. All-Star Game July 12 at Detroit. Schedule subject to change.

### CLUB DIRECTORY

**Chairman and chief executive officer**
Drayton McLane Jr.

**President, baseball operations**
Tal Smith

**General manager**
Tim Purpura

**Assistant g.m./dir. of player development**
Ricky Bennett

**Special assistants to the g.m.**
Enos Cabell, Al Pedrique

**Director of scouting**
David Lakey

**Coordinator of professional scouting**
J.D. Elliby

**Senior vice president, communications**
Jay Lucas

**Senior vice president, operations**
Rob Matwick

**Director of media relations**
Jimmy Stanton

### MINOR LEAGUE AFFILIATES

| Class | Team | League | Manager |
|---|---|---|---|
| AAA | Round Rock | Pacific Coast | Jackie Moore |
| AA | Corpus Christi | Texas | Dave Clark |
| Advanced A | Salem | Carolina | Ivan DeJesus |
| A | Lexington | South Atlantic | Tim Bogar |
| Short-Season A | Tri-City | New York-Pennsylvania | Gregg Langbehn |
| Advanced Rookie | Greeneville | Appalachian | Russ Nixon |

### BROADCAST INFORMATION

**Radio:** KTRH-AM (740); KLAT-AM (1010), Spanish language.
**TV:** KNWS-TV 51.
**Cable TV:** Fox Sports Net.

### SPRING TRAINING

**Ballpark (city):** Osceola County Stadium (Kissimmee, Fla.).
**Ticket information:** 321-697-3200.

For more on the Astros, go to msn.foxsports.com/mlb/teams.

Oswalt

## SPRING TRAINING ROSTER

**Manager**—Phil Garner (3).
**Coaches**—Mark Bailey (6), Cecil Cooper, Jose Cruz (25), Gary Gaetti (8), Jim Hickey (48), Doug Mansolino.

| No. | PITCHERS | B/T | Ht./Wt. | Age* | 2004 Clubs |
|---|---|---|---|---|---|
| | Astacio, Ezequiel | R/R | 6-3/150 | 25 | Round Rock |
| 37 | Backe, Brandon | R/R | 6-0/180 | 26 | New Orleans, Houston |
| | Buchholz, Taylor | R/R | 6-4/220 | 23 | New Orleans |
| 22 | Clemens, Roger | R/R | 6-4/235 | 42 | Houston |
| 56 | Duckworth, B. | R/R | 6-2/190 | 29 | New Orleans, Houston |
| 45 | Gallo, Mike | L/L | 6-0/175 | 27 | New Orleans, Houston |
| | Gothreaux, Jared | R/R | 6-0/200 | 25 | Round Rock |
| | Gutierrez, Juan | R/R | 6-3/200 | 21 | Greeneville |
| 43 | Harville, Chad | R/R | 5-9/185 | 28 | Oakland, Round Rock, Houston |
| 55 | Hernandez, Carlos | B/L | 5-10/200 | 24 | New Orleans, Houston |
| 54 | Lidge, Brad | R/R | 6-5/210 | 28 | Houston |
| | McLemore, Mark | L/L | 6-2/220 | 24 | Salem |
| 53 | Munro, Pete | R/R | 6-3/210 | 29 | Rochester, Houston |
| | Nieve, Fernando | R/R | 6-0/195 | 22 | Salem, Round Rock |
| 44 | Oswalt, Roy | R/R | 6-0/185 | 27 | Houston |
| 46 | Pettitte, Andy | L/L | 6-5/225 | 32 | Houston, Round Rock |
| 50 | Qualls, Chad | R/R | 6-5/220 | 26 | New Orleans, Houston |
| 51 | Redding, Tim | R/R | 6-0/200 | 27 | New Orleans, Houston |
| | Rodriguez, Wandy | S/L | 5-11/160 | 26 | Round Rock |
| 35 | Wheeler, Dan | R/R | 6-3/222 | 27 | Norfolk, New York N.L., Houston |

| No. | CATCHERS | B/T | Ht./Wt. | Age* | 2004 Clubs |
|---|---|---|---|---|---|
| 11 | Ausmus, Brad | R/R | 5-11/190 | 35 | Houston |
| 46 | Chavez, Raul | R/R | 5-11/215 | 32 | Houston |
| | Gimenez, Hector | S/R | 5-10/180 | 22 | Round Rock |

| No. | INFIELDERS | B/T | Ht./Wt. | Age* | 2004 Clubs |
|---|---|---|---|---|---|
| 5 | Bagwell, Jeff | R/R | 6-0/215 | 36 | Houston |
| 4 | Bruntlett, Eric | R/R | 6-0/190 | 27 | New Orleans, Houston |
| 2 | Burke, Chris | R/R | 5-11/180 | 25 | New Orleans, Houston |
| 14 | Ensberg, Morgan | R/R | 6-2/210 | 29 | Houston |
| 28 | Everett, Adam | R/R | 6-0/170 | 28 | Houston |
| 26 | Lamb, Mike | L/R | 6-1/190 | 29 | Houston |
| 10 | Vizcaino, Jose | B/R | 6-1/190 | 37 | Houston |
| | Whiteman, Tommy | R/R | 6-3/180 | 25 | Round Rock, New Orleans |

| No. | OUTFIELDERS | B/T | Ht./Wt. | Age* | 2004 Clubs |
|---|---|---|---|---|---|
| 17 | Berkman, Lance | B/L | 6-1/220 | 29 | Houston |
| 7 | Biggio, Craig | R/R | 5-11/185 | 39 | Houston |
| | Jimerson, Charlton | R/R | 6-3/210 | 25 | Round Rock |
| 24 | Lane, Jason | R/L | 6-2/220 | 28 | Houston |
| 19 | Palmeiro, Orlando | L/L | 5-11/180 | 36 | Houston |
| | Scott, Luke | L/R | 6-0/210 | 26 | Round Rock |
| 1 | Taveras, Willy | R/R | 6-0/160 | 23 | Round Rock, Houston |

*Age as of April 1, 2005.

## BALLPARK INFORMATION

**Ballpark (capacity, surface)**
Minute Maid Park (40,950, grass)

**Address**
P.O. Box 288
Houston, TX 77001-0288

**Official website**
www.astros.com

**Business phone**
713-259-8000

**Ticket information**
713-259-8500, 1-800-ASTROS-2

**Field dimensions (from home plate)**
To left field at foul line, 315 feet
To center field, 435 feet
To right field at foul line, 326 feet

**First game played**
April 7, 2000 (Phillies 4, Astros 1)

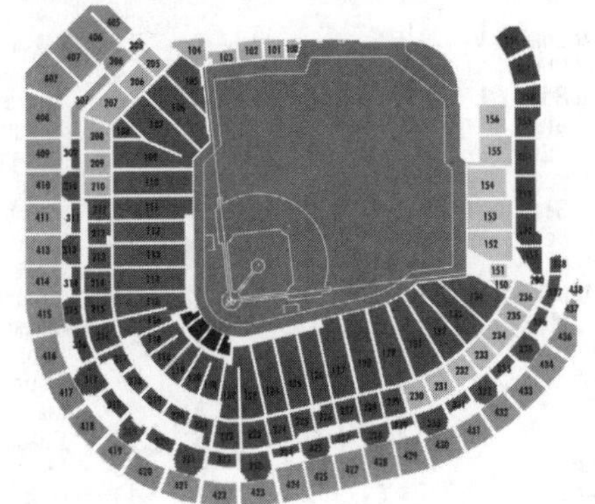

# 2004 REVIEW

## DAY BY DAY

| Date | Opp. | Res. | Score | (inn.*) | Hits | Opp. hits | Winning pitcher | Losing pitcher | Save | Record | Pos. | GB |
|---|---|---|---|---|---|---|---|---|---|---|---|---|
| 4-5 | S.F | L | 4-5 | | 9 | 10 | Rodriguez | Dotel | Herges | 0-1 | T4th | 1.0 |
| 4-6 | S.F | L | 5-7 | | 15 | 15 | Aardsma | Pettitte | Herges | 0-2 | T5th | 2.0 |
| 4-7 | S.F | W | 10-1 | | 12 | 4 | Clemens | Williams | | 1-2 | T5th | 1.0 |
| 4-9 | At Mil. | W | 13-7 | | 14 | 10 | Miller | Obermueller | | 2-2 | T3rd | 1.0 |
| 4-10 | At Mil. | L | 1-6 | | 6 | 10 | Sheets | Redding | | 2-3 | T4th | 2.0 |
| 4-11 | At Mil. | W | 7-4 | | 9 | 10 | Oswalt | Davis | | 3-3 | T4th | 1.0 |
| 4-12 | At StL. | W | 10-5 | | 11 | 9 | Stone | Lincoln | | 4-3 | T2nd | 1.0 |
| 4-13 | At StL. | W | 5-3 | | 10 | 5 | Clemens | Suppan | Dotel | 5-3 | 2nd | 0.5 |
| 4-14 | At StL. | W | 11-1 | | 14 | 5 | Miller | Carpenter | | 6-3 | 2nd | ... |
| 4-15 | Mil. | L | 2-6 | | 4 | 8 | Sheets | Redding | | 6-4 | 2nd | ... |
| 4-16 | Mil. | W | 2-0 | | 8 | 3 | Oswalt | Davis | | 7-4 | 1st | +0.5 |
| 4-17 | Mil. | W | 14-5 | | 11 | 8 | Backe | Kinney | | 8-4 | 1st | +1.0 |
| 4-18 | Mil. | W | 6-1 | | 16 | 6 | Clemens | Capuano | | 9-4 | 1st | +1.0 |
| 4-20 | StL. | L | 3-5 | | 8 | 9 | Suppan | Miller | Isringhausen | 9-5 | 1st | +0.5 |
| 4-21 | StL. | L | 6-12 | | 8 | 16 | Morris | Redding | | 9-6 | T1st | ... |
| 4-22 | StL. | L | 1-2 | (12) | 7 | 7 | Isringhausen | Miceli | Tavarez | 9-7 | T3rd | 0.5 |
| 4-23 | At Col. | W | 13-7 | | 11 | 10 | Duckworth | Jennings | | 10-7 | 3rd | 0.5 |
| 4-24 | At Col. | W | 8-5 | | 10 | 11 | Clemens | Fassero | Dotel | 11-7 | 3rd | 0.5 |
| 4-25 | At Col. | L | 1-4 | | 5 | 9 | Kennedy | Miller | Chacon | 11-8 | 3rd | 1.5 |
| 4-28 | At Pit. | L | 2-4 | | 8 | 7 | Torres | Oswalt | Mesa | 11-9 | 3rd | 1.5 |
| 4-29 | At Pit. | W | 2-0 | | 6 | 2 | Pettitte | Wells | Dotel | 12-9 | T2nd | 1.0 |
| 4-30 | Cin. | W | 6-1 | | 12 | 5 | Clemens | Acevedo | | 13-9 | T1st | ... |
| 5-1 | Cin. | W | 10-4 | | 16 | 6 | Miller | Harang | | 14-9 | T1st | ... |
| 5-2 | Cin. | W | 6-5 | | 9 | 8 | Miceli | Jones | Dotel | 15-9 | 1st | +1.0 |
| 5-3 | Cin. | L | 5-7 | | 10 | 9 | Riedling | Lidge | Graves | 15-10 | T1st | ... |
| 5-4 | Pit. | W | 4-3 | | 6 | 7 | Pettitte | Fogg | Lidge | 16-10 | 1st | +1.0 |
| 5-5 | Pit. | W | 6-2 | | 10 | 5 | Clemens | Wells | | 17-10 | 1st | +2.0 |
| 5-6 | Pit. | W | 5-2 | | 8 | 9 | Miller | Benson | | 18-10 | 1st | +2.0 |
| 5-7 | At Atl. | W | 5-3 | | 12 | 9 | Redding | Thomson | Dotel | 19-10 | 1st | +2.0 |
| 5-8 | At Atl. | L | 4-5 | (10) | 12 | 9 | Alfonseca | Stone | | 19-11 | 1st | +2.0 |
| 5-9 | At Atl. | W | 2-1 | | 3 | 3 | Pettitte | Ortiz | Dotel | 20-11 | 1st | +2.0 |
| 5-11 | Fla. | W | 6-1 | | 9 | 4 | Clemens | Penny | | 21-11 | 1st | +3.0 |
| 5-12 | Fla. | L | 2-5 | | 6 | 10 | Willis | Miller | | 21-12 | 1st | +3.0 |
| 5-13 | Fla. | L | 2-3 | | 8 | 9 | Perisho | Dotel | Benitez | 21-13 | 1st | +2.0 |
| 5-14 | N.Y. | L | 3-8 | | 6 | 11 | Trachsel | Oswalt | | 21-14 | 1st | +1.0 |
| 5-15 | N.Y. | W | 7-4 | | 12 | 6 | Pettitte | Baldwin | Dotel | 22-14 | 1st | +1.0 |
| 5-16 | N.Y. | L | 2-3 | (13) | 14 | 7 | Wheeler | Backe | | 22-15 | T1st | ... |
| 5-18 | At Fla. | W | 9-2 | | 15 | 7 | Miller | Willis | | 23-15 | 1st | +1.0 |
| 5-19 | At Fla. | W | 10-2 | | 15 | 5 | Redding | Pavano | | 24-15 | 1st | +1.0 |
| 5-20 | At Fla. | L | 2-6 | | 5 | 12 | Beckett | Oswalt | Benitez | 24-16 | 1st | +1.0 |
| 5-21 | At Cin. | L | 4-7 | | 8 | 10 | Wagner | Miceli | Graves | 24-17 | 1st | +1.0 |
| 5-22 | At Cin. | L | 7-8 | | 15 | 12 | Jones | Lidge | Graves | 24-18 | T1st | ... |
| 5-23 | At Cin. | L | 0-7 | | 6 | 12 | Lidle | Miller | | 24-19 | 3rd | 1.0 |
| 5-24 | At Cin. | L | 5-7 | | 12 | 10 | Riedling | Lidge | Graves | 24-20 | 3rd | 2.0 |
| 5-25 | Chi. | W | 5-0 | | 9 | 3 | Oswalt | Zambrano | | 25-20 | 3rd | 2.0 |
| 5-26 | Chi. | W | 7-3 | | 13 | 8 | Lidge | Maddux | | 26-20 | 2nd | 1.0 |
| 5-28 | StL. | L | 1-2 | (10) | 5 | 7 | Isringhausen | Dotel | | 26-21 | 2nd | 1.5 |
| 5-29 | StL. | L | 3-10 | | 9 | 16 | Williams | Miller | | 26-22 | T2nd | 2.5 |
| 5-30 | StL. | W | 7-1 | | 9 | 5 | Redding | Morris | | 27-22 | 2nd | 1.5 |
| 5-31 | At Chi. | L | 1-3 | | 10 | 11 | Maddux | Oswalt | Borowski | 27-23 | T2nd | 2.5 |
| 6-1 | At Chi. | W | 5-3 | | 9 | 6 | Miceli | Farnsworth | Dotel | 28-23 | T2nd | 2.5 |
| 6-2 | At Chi. | W | 5-1 | | 13 | 6 | Clemens | Clement | | 29-23 | T2nd | 2.5 |
| 6-4 | At StL. | L | 3-5 | | 10 | 6 | Morris | Miller | Isringhausen | 29-24 | 3rd | 2.5 |
| 6-5 | At StL. | L | 4-10 | | 11 | 19 | Marquis | Redding | | 29-25 | 3rd | 3.5 |
| 6-6 | At StL. | W | 3-2 | | 9 | 8 | Oswalt | Suppan | Dotel | 30-25 | 3rd | 3.5 |
| 6-7 | At Sea. | L | 0-5 | | 8 | 11 | Nageotte | Duckworth | Mateo | 30-26 | 3rd | 3.5 |
| 6-8 | At Sea. | W | 1-0 | | 3 | 6 | Clemens | Pineiro | Dotel | 31-26 | 3rd | 2.5 |
| 6-9 | At Sea. | W | 3-0 | | 7 | 7 | Miller | Garcia | Dotel | 32-26 | 3rd | 1.5 |
| 6-11 | At Mil. | L | 3-9 | | 7 | 16 | Davis | Redding | | 32-27 | 3rd | 2.0 |
| 6-12 | At Mil. | L | 4-7 | | 6 | 11 | Capuano | Oswalt | Kolb | 32-28 | 3rd | 2.0 |
| 6-13 | At Mil. | W | 5-4 | | 9 | 11 | Miceli | Sheets | Dotel | 33-28 | 3rd | 2.0 |
| 6-14 | Chi. | L | 2-7 | | 10 | 12 | Prior | Clemens | Anderson | 33-29 | 4th | 2.5 |
| 6-15 | Chi. | L | 2-4 | | 9 | 7 | Farnsworth | Dotel | Hawkins | 33-30 | 5th | 3.5 |
| 6-16 | Chi. | L | 1-4 | | 8 | 11 | Maddux | Redding | Hawkins | 33-31 | 5th | 4.5 |
| 6-17 | Chi. | L | 4-5 | | 6 | 13 | Rusch | Oswalt | Hawkins | 33-32 | 5th | 5.5 |
| 6-18 | Ana. | W | 5-0 | | 10 | 5 | Munro | Escobar | | 34-32 | 5th | 5.5 |
| 6-19 | Ana. | L | 4-6 | | 8 | 13 | Ortiz | Clemens | Rodriguez | 34-33 | 5th | 6.5 |

| Date | Opp. | Res. | Score | (inn.*) | Hits | Opp. hits | Winning pitcher | Losing pitcher | Save | Record | Pos. | GB |
|---|---|---|---|---|---|---|---|---|---|---|---|---|
| 6-20 | Ana. | W | 3-1 | | 7 | 8 | Miller | Hensley | Dotel | 35-33 | 5th | 5.5 |
| 6-21 | Pit. | W | 7-5 | | 13 | 11 | Bullinger | Fogg | Dotel | 36-33 | 5th | 5.0 |
| 6-22 | Pit. | W | 5-4 | | 8 | 10 | Oswalt | Benson | Lidge | 37-33 | 5th | 4.0 |
| 6-23 | Pit. | L | 2-7 | | 5 | 7 | Vogelsong | Munro | | 37-34 | 5th | 5.0 |
| 6-24 | Pit. | W | 3-2 | | 5 | 5 | Clemens | Burnett | Lidge | 38-34 | 4th | 5.0 |
| 6-25 | At Tex. | L | 1-3 | | 3 | 6 | Rogers | Miller | | 38-35 | 4th | 6.0 |
| 6-26 | At Tex. | L | 7-8 | | 10 | 16 | Almanzar | Miceli | Cordero | 38-36 | 5th | 7.0 |
| 6-27 | At Tex. | W | 1-0 | | 6 | 4 | Oswalt | Drese | Lidge | 39-36 | 5th | 7.0 |
| 6-29 | At Chi. | L | 5-7 | | 11 | 8 | Beltran | Weathers | Hawkins | 39-37 | 5th | 6.5 |
| 6-30 | At Chi. | W | 3-2 | | 7 | 6 | Lidge | Hawkins | | 40-37 | 5th | 5.5 |
| 7-1 | At Chi. | L | 4-5 | (10) | 7 | 9 | Leicester | Lidge | | 40-38 | 5th | 6.0 |
| 7-2 | Tex. | W | 7-5 | | 10 | 9 | Oswalt | Almanzar | Lidge | 41-38 | 5th | 6.0 |
| 7-3 | Tex. | W | 10-8 | | 10 | 10 | Weathers | Brocail | Miceli | 42-38 | 5th | 6.0 |
| 7-4 | Tex. | L | 3-18 | | 8 | 16 | Benoit | Pettitte | | 42-39 | 5th | 7.0 |
| 7-5 | At S.D. | L | 1-2 | | 5 | 5 | Lawrence | Miceli | Hoffman | 42-40 | 5th | 8.0 |
| 7-6 | At S.D. | L | 3-5 | | 5 | 9 | Valdez | Munro | Hoffman | 42-41 | 5th | 9.0 |
| 7-7 | At S.D. | W | 5-1 | | 12 | 7 | Oswalt | Peavy | Lidge | 43-41 | 5th | 9.0 |
| 7-8 | At L.A. | L | 2-7 | | 5 | 12 | Jackson | Duckworth | Martin | 43-42 | 5th | 9.5 |
| 7-9 | At L.A. | W | 3-2 | | 7 | 5 | Pettitte | Weaver | Lidge | 44-42 | 5th | 9.5 |
| 7-10 | At L.A. | L | 1-3 | | 3 | 5 | Alvarez | Clemens | Gagne | 44-43 | 5th | 10.5 |
| 7-11 | At L.A. | L | 4-7 | | 7 | 13 | Lima | Oswalt | | 44-44 | 5th | 10.5 |
| 7-16 | S.D. | L | 1-5 | | 6 | 9 | Peavy | Pettitte | | 44-45 | 5th | 12.0 |
| 7-17 | S.D. | L | 4-7 | | 10 | 8 | Wells | Oswalt | Hoffman | 44-46 | 5th | 12.0 |
| 7-18 | S.D. | W | 5-3 | | 10 | 5 | Clemens | Lawrence | Lidge | 45-46 | 5th | 12.0 |
| 7-19 | L.A. | L | 6-7 | | 6 | 11 | Carrara | Miceli | Gagne | 45-47 | 5th | 13.0 |
| 7-20 | L.A. | L | 5-7 | | 9 | 12 | Weaver | Weathers | Gagne | 45-48 | 5th | 14.0 |
| 7-21 | At Ari. | W | 5-2 | | 10 | 7 | Pettitte | Webb | Lidge | 46-48 | 5th | 14.0 |
| 7-22 | At Ari. | W | 10-3 | | 13 | 7 | Oswalt | Gonzalez | | 47-48 | 5th | 14.0 |
| 7-23 | Mil. | L | 6-7 | | 13 | 12 | Vizcaino | Lidge | Kolb | 47-49 | 5th | 14.0 |
| 7-24 | Mil. | W | 6-3 | | 11 | 6 | Redding | Hendrickson | Lidge | 48-49 | 5th | 13.0 |
| 7-25 | Mil. | W | 9-1 | | 12 | 8 | Munro | Davis | | 49-49 | 4th | 13.0 |
| 7-26 | Ari. | L | 1-4 | | 6 | 8 | Webb | Pettitte | Aquino | 49-50 | 4th | 14.0 |
| 7-27 | Ari. | W | 10-3 | | 12 | 6 | Oswalt | Gonzalez | | 50-50 | 3rd | 14.0 |
| 7-28 | Ari. | W | 6-1 | | 12 | 6 | Clemens | Fossum | | 51-50 | 3rd | 14.0 |
| 7-29 | Ari. | L | 4-6 | | 9 | 13 | Cormier | Redding | Aquino | 51-51 | 3rd | 14.5 |
| 7-30 | At Cin. | L | 2-3 | (13) | 4 | 8 | Hancock | Harville | | 51-52 | 3rd | 15.0 |
| 7-31 | At Cin. | W | 8-0 | | 9 | 4 | Oliver | Claussen | | 52-52 | 3rd | 14.5 |
| 8-1 | At Cin. | W | 7-5 | | 12 | 11 | Oswalt | Riedling | Lidge | 53-52 | 3rd | 14.5 |
| 8-3 | Atl. | W | 3-2 | | 9 | 4 | Miceli | Reitsma | Lidge | 54-52 | 3rd | 13.5 |
| 8-4 | Atl. | L | 4-5 | | 6 | 12 | Thomson | Munro | Smoltz | 54-53 | 3rd | 14.5 |
| 8-5 | Atl. | L | 5-6 | | 9 | 11 | Cruz | Miceli | Smoltz | 54-54 | 3rd | 15.5 |
| 8-6 | Mon. | W | 4-0 | | 8 | 5 | Oswalt | Biddle | | 55-54 | 3rd | 15.5 |
| 8-7 | Mon. | L | 3-8 | | 10 | 13 | Rauch | Weathers | | 55-55 | 3rd | 16.5 |
| 8-8 | Mon. | L | 2-5 | | 7 | 11 | Tucker | Clemens | | 55-56 | 3rd | 17.5 |
| 8-10 | At N.Y. | L | 3-7 | | 7 | 10 | Trachsel | Munro | | 55-57 | 3rd | 18.5 |
| 8-11 | At N.Y. | W | 5-4 | (10) | 12 | 6 | Lidge | Looper | Bullinger | 56-57 | 3rd | 18.5 |
| 8-12 | At N.Y. | L | 1-2 | | 2 | 8 | Zambrano | Weathers | Looper | 56-58 | 3rd | 18.5 |
| 8-13 | At Mon. | L | 5-6 | (12) | 7 | 11 | Vargas | Harville | | 56-59 | 3rd | 19.5 |
| 8-14 | At Mon. | L | 3-8 | | 4 | 14 | Tucker | Hernandez | | 56-60 | T3rd | 19.5 |
| 8-15 | At Mon. | W | 5-4 | | 8 | 8 | Miceli | Ayala | Lidge | 57-60 | 3rd | 19.5 |
| 8-17 | At Phi. | W | 5-0 | | 8 | 5 | Oswalt | Wolf | | 58-60 | 3rd | 20.0 |
| 8-18 | At Phi. | W | 9-8 | | 13 | 11 | Harville | Jones | Lidge | 59-60 | 3rd | 19.0 |
| 8-19 | At Phi. | W | 12-10 | | 15 | 14 | Qualls | Hernandez | Lidge | 60-60 | 3rd | 18.0 |
| 8-20 | Chi. | L | 2-9 | | 6 | 13 | Rusch | Munro | | 60-61 | 3rd | 19.5 |
| 8-21 | Chi. | W | 4-3 | | 7 | 8 | Lidge | Hawkins | | 61-61 | 3rd | 19.5 |
| 8-22 | Chi. | L | 6-11 | | 11 | 14 | Leicester | Oswalt | | 61-62 | 3rd | 20.5 |
| 8-23 | Phi. | W | 8-4 | | 10 | 10 | Clemens | Lidle | | 62-62 | 3rd | 20.0 |
| 8-24 | Phi. | W | 4-2 | | 8 | 7 | Oswalt | Jones | Lidge | 63-62 | 3rd | 19.0 |
| 8-25 | Phi. | W | 7-4 | | 7 | 5 | Qualls | Rodriguez | Lidge | 64-62 | 3rd | 19.0 |
| 8-26 | At Chi. | L | 3-8 | | 10 | 13 | Prior | Backe | | 64-63 | 3rd | 19.0 |
| 8-27 | At Chi. | W | 15-7 | | 17 | 9 | Oswalt | Wood | | 65-63 | 3rd | 19.0 |
| 8-28 | At Chi. | W | 7-6 | | 10 | 11 | Clemens | Zambrano | Lidge | 66-63 | 3rd | 19.0 |
| 8-29 | At Chi. | W | 10-3 | | 16 | 8 | Hernandez | Clement | | 67-63 | 3rd | 19.0 |
| 8-30 | At Cin. | W | 11-3 | | 11 | 10 | Munro | Norton | | 68-63 | 3rd | 18.5 |
| 8-31 | At Cin. | W | 8-0 | | 11 | 6 | Backe | Harang | | 69-63 | 3rd | 18.5 |
| 9-1 | At Cin. | W | 9-3 | | 12 | 7 | Oswalt | Wilson | | 70-63 | 3rd | 18.5 |
| 9-3 | Pit. | W | 8-6 | | 10 | 8 | Clemens | Perez | Lidge | 71-63 | 3rd | 19.0 |
| 9-4 | Pit. | W | 6-5 | | 9 | 6 | Qualls | Figueroa | Lidge | 72-63 | 3rd | 19.0 |
| 9-5 | Pit. | W | 10-5 | | 16 | 5 | Munro | Van Benschoten | | 73-63 | 3rd | 19.0 |

| Date | Opp. | Res. | Score | (inn.*) | Hits | Opp. hits | Winning pitcher | Losing pitcher | Save | Record | Pos. | GB |
|---|---|---|---|---|---|---|---|---|---|---|---|---|
| 9-6 | Cin. | W | 11-5 | | 12 | 10 | Backe | Harang | | 74-63 | 3rd | 18.0 |
| 9-7 | Cin. | W | 9-7 | | 11 | 8 | Oswalt | Wilson | | 75-63 | 3rd | 18.0 |
| 9-8 | Cin. | W | 5-2 | | 11 | 7 | Clemens | Acevedo | Lidge | 76-63 | 2nd | 17.0 |
| 9-9! | At Pit. | L | 1-3 | | 3 | 6 | Perez | Hernandez | Mesa | 76-64 | | |
| 9-9& | At Pit. | W | 9-2 | | 10 | 6 | Gallo | Fogg | | 77-64 | 2nd | 17.0 |
| 9-10 | At Pit. | L | 1-6 | | 5 | 13 | Van Benschoten | Munro | | 77-65 | 3rd | 17.0 |
| 9-11 | At Pit. | L | 2-5 | | 9 | 12 | Vogelsong | Backe | Mesa | 77-66 | 3rd | 17.0 |
| 9-12 | At Pit. | W | 5-4 | (10) | 8 | 13 | Lidge | Mesa | Qualls | 78-66 | 3rd | 17.0 |
| 9-14 | At StL. | W | 7-5 | | 15 | 9 | Clemens | Suppan | Lidge | 79-66 | 3rd | 16.0 |
| 9-15 | At StL. | L | 2-4 | | 4 | 8 | Calero | Springer | Isringhausen | 79-67 | 3rd | 17.0 |
| 9-16 | At StL. | W | 8-3 | | 8 | 10 | Harville | Marquis | | 80-67 | 3rd | 16.0 |
| 9-17 | Mil. | W | 2-1 | | 4 | 10 | Oswalt | Sheets | Lidge | 81-67 | 3rd | 16.0 |
| 9-18 | Mil. | W | 4-3 | | 6 | 11 | Harville | Glover | Lidge | 82-67 | 3rd | 16.0 |
| 9-19 | Mil. | W | 1-0 | | 4 | 2 | Clemens | Davis | Lidge | 83-67 | 3rd | 15.0 |
| 9-21 | At S.F | L | 2-9 | | 4 | 13 | Tomko | Hernandez | | 83-68 | 3rd | 15.5 |
| 9-22 | At S.F | L | 1-5 | | 5 | 11 | Lowry | Oswalt | | 83-69 | 3rd | 16.5 |
| 9-23 | At S.F | W | 7-3 | | 10 | 10 | Miceli | Hermanson | | 84-69 | 3rd | 16.5 |
| 9-24 | At Mil. | W | 1-0 | (10) | 7 | 5 | Lidge | Adams | Miceli | 85-69 | 3rd | 16.5 |
| 9-25 | At Mil. | L | 0-8 | | 6 | 11 | Obermueller | Munro | | 85-70 | 3rd | 17.5 |
| 9-26 | At Mil. | W | 11-7 | | 16 | 9 | Redding | Santos | | 86-70 | 3rd | 17.5 |
| 9-27 | StL. | W | 10-3 | | 14 | 12 | Oswalt | Williams | | 87-70 | 3rd | 16.5 |
| 9-28 | StL. | W | 2-1 | | 8 | 5 | Backe | Haren | Lidge | 88-70 | 3rd | 15.5 |
| 9-29 | StL. | W | 6-4 | | 9 | 6 | Qualls | Suppan | Lidge | 89-70 | 2nd | 14.5 |
| 10-1 | Col. | W | 4-2 | | 8 | 12 | Gallo | Kennedy | Lidge | 90-70 | 2nd | 14.0 |
| 10-2 | Col. | W | 9-3 | | 10 | 7 | Oswalt | Estes | | 91-70 | 2nd | 13.0 |
| 10-3 | Col. | W | 5-3 | | 8 | 8 | Backe | Wright | Lidge | 92-70 | 2nd | 13.0 |

Monthly records: April (13-9), May (14-14), June (13-14), July (12-15), August (17-11), September (20-7), October (3-0).
*Innings, if other than nine. ! First game of a doubleheader. & Second game of a doubleheader.

## RECORDS

**2004 regular-season record:** 92-70
**Position:** 2nd in N.L. Central
**Home:** 48-33 **Road:** 44-37
**N.L. East:** 16-14 **N.L. Central:** 55-35
**N.L. West:** 14-16 **A.L.** 7-5
**Vs. LH starters:** 19-17
**Vs. RH starters:** 73-53
**Grass:** 91-68 **Artificial:** 1-2
**Day:** 33-19 **Night:** 59-51
**1-Run:** 24-18 **X-inn.:** 3-7
**Doubleheaders:** 0-0-1
**Team record past five years:** 428-382 (.528, ranks 5th in league in that span)

## TEAM LEADERS

**Batting average:** Lance Berkman (.316).
**At-bats:** Craig Biggio (633).
**Runs:** Jeff Bagwell, Lance Berkman (104).
**Hits:** Craig Biggio (178).
**Total Bases:** Lance Berkman (308).
**Doubles:** Craig Biggio (47).
**Triples:** Jeff Kent (8).
**Home runs:** Lance Berkman (30).
**Runs batted in:** Jeff Kent (107).
**Stolen bases:** Carlos Beltran (28).
**Slugging percentage:** Lance Berkman (.566).
**On-base percentage:** Lance Berkman (.450).
**Wins:** Roy Oswalt (20).
**Earned-run average:** Roger Clemens (2.98).
**Complete games:** Roy Oswalt (2).
**Shutouts:** Roy Oswalt (2).
**Saves:** Brad Lidge (29).
**Innings pitched:** Roy Oswalt (237.0).
**Strikeouts:** Roger Clemens (218).

## GAMES BY POSITION

**Catcher:** Brad Ausmus 128, Raul Chavez 61, Chris Tremie 1.
**First base:** Jeff Bagwell 152, Mike Lamb 10, Jose Vizcaino 8, Lance Berkman 4, Jason Lane 3.
**Second base:** Jeff Kent 139, Jose Vizcaino 37, Chris Burke 7, Mike Lamb 7, Eric Bruntlett 5.
**Third base:** Morgan Ensberg 118, Mike Lamb 57, Jose Vizcaino 21.
**Shortstop:** Adam Everett 99, Jose Vizcaino 64, Eric Bruntlett 33, Jason Alfaro 3, Morgan Ensberg 1.
**Outfield:** Lance Berkman 160, Craig Biggio 149, Carlos Beltran 89, Jason Lane 76, Richard Hidalgo 56, Orlando Palmeiro 37, Willy Taveras 7, Eric Bruntlett 2.
**Designated hitter:** Jeff Bagwell 2, Jeff Kent 2, Craig Biggio 1, Mike Lamb 1.

## TOP DRAFT CHOICES

2. **Hunter Pence,** OF, Texas-Arlington.
3. **Jordan Parraz,** OF, CC of Southern Nevada.
4. **Lou Santangelo,** C, Clemson.
5. **Mitch Einertson,** 2B, Rancho Buena Vista H.S., Oceanside, Calif.
6. **Ben Zobrist,** SS, Dallas Baptist U.
7. **Andy Alvarado,** RHP, Chabot JC (Calif).
8. **Evan Englebrook,** RHP, Shippensburg.
9. **Troy Patton,** LHP, Tomball H.S., Magnolia, Texas.
10. **Eric Cavers, C,** Franklin Pierce.

# LOS ANGELES DODGERS

## NATIONAL LEAGUE WEST DIVISION



## 2005 SEASON

### Dodgers Schedule

Home games shaded.
All-Star Game July 12 at Detroit. Schedule subject to change.

**April**

| SUN | MON | TUE | WED | THU | FRI | SAT |
|---|---|---|---|---|---|---|
| 3 | 4 | 5 SF | 6 SF | 7 SF | 8 ARI | 9 ARI |
| 10 ARI | 11 | 12 SF | 13 SF | 14 | 15 SD | 16 SD |
| 17 SD | 18 MIL | 19 MIL | 20 SD | 21 SD | 22 COL | 23 COL |
| 24 COL | 25 ARI | 26 ARI | 27 ARI | 28 | 29 COL | 30 COL |

**May**

| SUN | MON | TUE | WED | THU | FRI | SAT |
|---|---|---|---|---|---|---|
| 1 COL | 2 WAS | 3 WAS | 4 WAS | 5 | 6 CIN | 7 CIN |
| 8 CIN | 9 STL | 10 STL | 11 STL | 12 STL | 13 ATL | 14 ATL |
| 15 ATL | 16 FLA | 17 FLA | 18 FLA | 19 | 20 ANA | 21 ANA |
| 22 ANA | 23 | 24 SF | 25 SF | 26 SF | 27 ARI | 28 ARI |
| 29 ARI | 30 CHC | 31 CHC | | | | |

**June**

| SUN | MON | TUE | WED | THU | FRI | SAT |
|---|---|---|---|---|---|---|
| | | | 1 CHC | 2 MIL | 3 MIL | 4 MIL |
| 5 MIL | 6 DET | 7 DET | 8 DET | 9 | 10 MIN | 11 MIN |
| 12 MIN | 13 | 14 KC | 15 KC | 16 KC | 17 CHW | 18 CHW |
| 19 CHW | 20 SD | 21 SD | 22 SD | 23 SD | 24 ANA | 25 ANA |
| 26 ANA | 27 SD | 28 SD | 29 SD | 30 | | |

**July**

| SUN | MON | TUE | WED | THU | FRI | SAT |
|---|---|---|---|---|---|---|
| | | | | | 1 ARI | 2 ARI |
| 3 ARI | 4 COL | 5 COL | 6 COL | 7 COL | 8 HOU | 9 HOU |
| 10 HOU | 11 | 12 All-Star | 13 | 14 SF | 15 SF | 16 SF |
| 17 SF | 18 | 19 PHI | 20 PHI | 21 PHI | 22 NYM | 23 NYM |
| 24 NYM | 25 CIN | 26 CIN | 27 CIN | 28 CIN | 29 STL | 30 STL |
| 31 STL | | | | | | |

**August**

| SUN | MON | TUE | WED | THU | FRI | SAT |
|---|---|---|---|---|---|---|
| | 1 | 2 WAS | 3 WAS | 4 WAS | 5 PIT | 6 PIT |
| 7 PIT | 8 | 9 PHI | 10 PHI | 11 PHI | 12 NYM | 13 NYM |
| 14 NYM | 15 | 16 ATL | 17 ATL | 18 ATL | 19 FLA | 20 FLA |
| 21 FLA | 22 FLA | 23 COL | 24 COL | 25 COL | 26 HOU | 27 HOU |
| 28 HOU | 29 CHC | 30 CHC | 31 CHC | | | |

**September**

| SUN | MON | TUE | WED | THU | FRI | SAT |
|---|---|---|---|---|---|---|
| | | | | 1 | 2 COL | 3 COL |
| 4 COL | 5 SF | 6 SF | 7 SF | 8 | 9 SD | 10 SD |
| 11 SD | 12 COL | 13 COL | 14 COL | 15 SF | 16 SF | 17 SF |
| 18 SF | 19 | 20 ARI | 21 ARI | 22 ARI | 23 PIT | 24 PIT |
| 25 PIT | 26 PIT | 27 ARI | 28 ARI | 29 ARI | 30 SD | |

**October**

| SUN | MON | TUE | WED | THU | FRI | SAT |
|---|---|---|---|---|---|---|
| | | | | | | 1 SD |
| 2 SD | 3 | 4 | 5 | 6 | 7 | 8 |

Home games shaded. All-Star Game July 12 at Detroit. Schedule subject to change.

### CLUB DIRECTORY

**Owner**
Frank H. McCourt, Jr.
**Vice chairman**
Jamie McCourt
**Executive vice president, COO**
Mary Greenspun
**Executive vice president, CMO**
Lon Rosen
**Executive vice president and G.M.**
Paul DePodesta
**Vice president, assistant G.M.**
Kim Ng
**Chief sales officer**
Greg McElroy
**Senior vice president, public affairs**
Howard Sunkin
**Senior vice president, general counsel**
Sam Fernandez
**Senior vice president**
Tommy Lasorda
**V.p., spring training & minor league facilities**
Craig Callan
**Vice president, sales**
Sergio del Prado
**Vice president, stadium operations**
Doug Duennes
**Vice president, CFO**
Cris Hurley
**Vice president, communications**
Gary Miereanu
**V.p., scouting and player development**
Roy Smith
**Director, public relations**
John Olguin
**Director, community affairs**
Erikk Aldridge

### MINOR LEAGUE AFFILIATES

| Class | Team | League | Manager |
|---|---|---|---|
| AAA | Las Vegas | Pacific Coast | Jerry Royster |
| AA | Jacksonville | Southern | John Shoemaker |
| Advanced A | Vero Beach | Florida State | Scott Little |
| A | Columbus | South Atlantic | Travis Barbary |
| Advanced Rookie | Ogden | Pioneer | Juan Bustabad |
| Rookie | Gulf Coast Dodgers | Gulf Coast | Luis Salazar |

### BROADCAST INFORMATION

**Radio:** XTRA-AM (1150); KWKW-AM (1330, Spanish language).
**TV:** KCOP-TV (Channel 13)
**Cable TV:** Fox Sports Net 2.

### SPRING TRAINING

**Ballpark (city):** Holman Stadium (Vero Beach, Fla.).
**Ticket information:** 772-569-4900.
**General number:** 772-569-4900.

**For more on the Dodgers, go to msn.foxsports.com/mlb/teams.**

Choi

## SPRING TRAINING ROSTER

**Manager**—Jim Tracy (16).
**Coaches**—Jim Colborn (48), Glenn Hoffman (35), Jim Lett (18), Manny Mota (11), John Shelby (31), Tim Wallach (25).

| No. | PITCHERS | B/T | Ht./Wt. | Age* | 2004 Clubs |
|---|---|---|---|---|---|
| 47 | Alvarez, Wilson | L/L | 6-1/255 | 35 | Los Angeles |
| 43 | Brazoban, Yhency | R/R | 6-1/170 | 24 | Jacksonville, Las Vegas, Los Angeles |
| | Brooks, Frank | L/L | 6-1/200 | 26 | Nashville, Pittsburgh |
| 55 | Carrara, Giovanni | R/R | 6-2/230 | 37 | Iowa, Las Vegas, Los Angeles |
| 46 | Dessens, Elmer | R/R | 5-10/198 | 34 | Arizona, Los Angeles |
| 37 | Dreifort, Darren | R/R | 6-2/211 | 32 | Los Angeles |
| 38 | Gagne, Eric | R/R | 6-2/234 | 29 | Los Angeles |
| | Hanrahan, Joel | R/R | 6-3/215 | 23 | Las Vegas |
| | Houlton, D.J. | R/R | 6-4/220 | 25 | Round Rock |
| 17 | Ishii, Kazuhisa | L/L | 6-0/200 | 31 | Los Angeles |
| 22 | Jackson, Edwin | R/R | 6-3/190 | 21 | Las Vegas, Los Angeles |
| | Ketchner, Ryan | L/L | 6-1/190 | 22 | Jacksonville, Las Vegas |
| | Lowe, Derek | R/R | 6-6/210 | 31 | Boston |
| | Osoria, Franquelis | R/R | 6-0/165 | 23 | Jacksonville, Las Vegas |
| 30 | Penny, Brad | R/R | 6-4/250 | 26 | Florida, Los Angeles |
| | Perez, Odalis | L/L | 6-0/150 | 27 | Los Angeles |
| | Rodriguez, Orlando | L/L | 5-10/155 | 24 | Did Not Play |
| 50 | Sanchez, Duaner | R/R | 6-0/190 | 25 | Los Angeles |
| | Thompson, Derek | L/L | 6-2/180 | 24 | Jacksonville |
| 18 | Weaver, Jeff | R/R | 6-5/200 | 28 | Los Angeles |

| No. | CATCHERS | B/T | Ht./Wt. | Age* | 2004 Clubs |
|---|---|---|---|---|---|
| | Martin, Russell | R/R | 5-11/200 | 22 | Vero Beach |
| | Navarro, Dioner | B/R | 5-10/190 | 21 | Trenton, Columbus, New York A.L. |
| 40 | Ross, David | R/R | 6-2/205 | 28 | Los Angeles |

| No. | INFIELDERS | B/T | Ht./Wt. | Age* | 2004 Clubs |
|---|---|---|---|---|---|
| | Aybar, Willy | B/R | 6-0/175 | 22 | Jacksonville |
| 5 | Choi, Hee Seop | L/L | 6-5/240 | 26 | Florida, Los Angeles |
| 3 | Izturis, Cesar | B/R | 5-9/175 | 25 | Los Angeles |
| | Kent, Jeff | R/R | 6-1/210 | 37 | Houston |
| | Myrow, Brian | L/R | 5-11/190 | 28 | Columbus, Las Vegas |
| 26 | Perez, Antonio | R/R | 5-11/170 | 25 | Las Vegas, Los Angeles |
| 8 | Saenz, Olmedo | R/R | 5-11/221 | 34 | Los Angeles |
| 49 | Thurston, Joe | L/R | 5-11/175 | 25 | Las Vegas, Los Angeles |
| | Valentin, Jose | L/R | 5-10/195 | 35 | Charlotte, Chicago A.L. |
| | Young, Delwyn | B/R | 5-10/180 | 22 | Vero Beach |

| No. | OUTFIELDERS | B/T | Ht./Wt. | Age* | 2004 Clubs |
|---|---|---|---|---|---|
| 21 | Bradley, Milton | B/R | 6-0/205 | 26 | Los Angeles |
| 52 | Chen, Chin-Feng | R/R | 6-1/189 | 27 | Las Vegas, Los Angeles |
| | Drew, J.D. | L/R | 6-1/200 | 29 | Atlanta |
| | Grabowski, Jason | L/R | 6-3/200 | 28 | Los Angeles |
| | Ledee, Ricky | L/L | 6-1/216 | 31 | Philadelphia, San Francisco |
| | Repko, Jason | R/R | 5-11/175 | 24 | Jacksonville, Las Vegas |
| | Ross, Cody | R/L | 5-11/180 | 24 | Las Vegas |
| | Stanley, Henri | L/L | 5-10/185 | 25 | Portland, Pawtucket, Las Vegas |
| 28 | Werth, Jayson | R/R | 6-5/215 | 25 | Las Vegas, Los Angeles |

*Age as of April 1, 2005.

## BALLPARK INFORMATION

**Ballpark (capacity, surface)**
Dodger Stadium (56,000, grass)

**Address**
1000 Elysian Park Ave.
Los Angeles, CA 90012

**Official website**
www.dodgers.com

**Business phone**
323-224-1500

**Ticket information**
866-DODGERS

**Field dimensions (from home plate)**
To left field at foul line, 330 feet
To center field, 395 feet
To right field at foul line, 330 feet

**First game played**
April 10, 1962 (Reds 6, Dodgers 3)

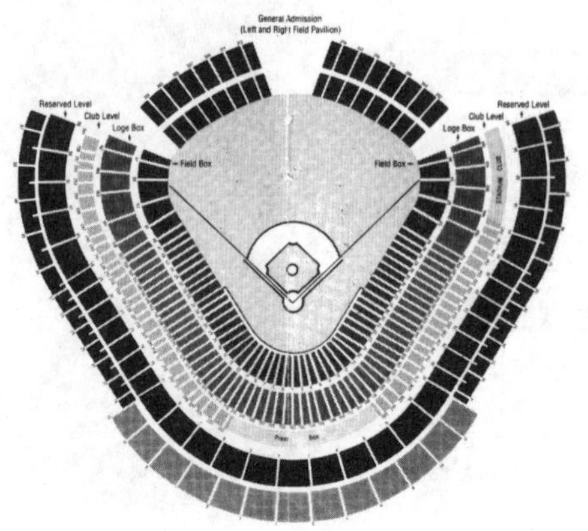

# 2004 REVIEW

## DAY BY DAY

| Date | Opp. | Res. | Score | (inn.*) | Hits | Opp. hits | Winning pitcher | Losing pitcher | Save | Record | Pos. | GB |
|---|---|---|---|---|---|---|---|---|---|---|---|---|
| 4-5 | S.D. | L | 2-8 | | 15 | 12 | Lawrence | Nomo | | 0-1 | 5th | 1.0 |
| 4-6 | S.D. | W | 5-4 | | 12 | 13 | Gagne | Otsuka | | 1-1 | T3rd | 1.0 |
| 4-7 | S.D. | W | 2-1 | (11) | 6 | 10 | Lima | Oropesa | | 2-1 | T1st | ... |
| 4-9 | Col. | W | 5-1 | | 7 | 5 | Ishii | Elarton | Alvarez | 3-1 | 1st | +1.0 |
| 4-10 | Col. | W | 7-4 | | 10 | 9 | Nomo | Stark | Gagne | 4-1 | 1st | +1.0 |
| 4-11 | Col. | L | 2-4 | | 6 | 9 | Estes | Perez | Chacon | 4-2 | 1st | +1.0 |
| 4-13 | At S.D. | L | 3-8 | | 7 | 10 | Eaton | Weaver | | 4-3 | T2nd | 0.5 |
| 4-14 | At S.D. | W | 11-4 | | 13 | 7 | Ishii | Wells | | 5-3 | 1st | +0.5 |
| 4-15 | At S.D. | W | 7-5 | | 11 | 10 | Nomo | Lawrence | Gagne | 6-3 | 1st | +1.0 |
| 4-16 | At S.F | W | 3-2 | | 4 | 3 | Perez | Schmidt | Gagne | 7-3 | 1st | +2.0 |
| 4-17 | At S.F | W | 5-4 | | 14 | 8 | Lima | Rueter | Gagne | 8-3 | 1st | +3.0 |
| 4-18 | At S.F | W | 7-6 | | 13 | 12 | Weaver | Tomko | Gagne | 9-3 | 1st | +3.0 |
| 4-20 | At Col. | L | 1-7 | | 8 | 8 | Kennedy | Ishii | | 9-4 | 1st | +2.5 |
| 4-21 | At Col. | W | 9-4 | | 13 | 10 | Nomo | Elarton | | 10-4 | 1st | +2.5 |
| 4-22 | At Col. | L | 1-7 | (6) | 2 | 9 | Estes | Lima | | 10-5 | 1st | +1.5 |
| 4-23 | S.F | W | 5-4 | (12) | 10 | 8 | Dreifort | Herges | | 11-5 | 1st | +2.5 |
| 4-24 | S.F | L | 3-5 | | 5 | 8 | Williams | Weaver | Herges | 11-6 | 1st | +1.5 |
| 4-25 | S.F | W | 9-0 | | 13 | 4 | Ishii | Cooper | | 12-6 | 1st | +2.5 |
| 4-27 | N.Y. | L | 5-9 | | 14 | 13 | Glavine | Nomo | | 12-7 | 1st | +1.0 |
| 4-28 | N.Y. | W | 3-2 | | 5 | 9 | Perez | Trachsel | Gagne | 13-7 | 1st | +1.0 |
| 4-29 | N.Y. | L | 1-6 | | 8 | 10 | Seo | Weaver | | 13-8 | 1st | ... |
| 4-30 | Mon. | W | 13-4 | | 15 | 9 | Ishii | Day | | 14-8 | 1st | ... |
| 5-1 | Mon. | W | 5-4 | | 11 | 7 | Mota | Ayala | Gagne | 15-8 | 1st | ... |
| 5-2 | Mon. | L | 4-6 | | 10 | 12 | Kim | Nomo | | 15-9 | 1st | ... |
| 5-4 | At Fla. | W | 4-3 | (11) | 7 | 12 | Sanchez | Wayne | Gagne | 16-9 | 1st | +1.0 |
| 5-5 | At Fla. | L | 0-2 | | 5 | 6 | Penny | Weaver | Benitez | 16-10 | 1st | ... |
| 5-6 | At Fla. | W | 9-4 | | 14 | 7 | Ishii | Willis | Gagne | 17-10 | 1st | ... |
| 5-7 | At Pit. | W | 4-0 | | 7 | 1 | Alvarez | Perez | | 18-10 | 1st | +1.0 |
| 5-8 | At Pit. | W | 4-3 | | 9 | 9 | Mota | Torres | Gagne | 19-10 | 1st | +1.0 |
| 5-9 | At Pit. | W | 9-7 | (14) | 16 | 10 | Falkenborg | Grabow | | 20-10 | 1st | +2.0 |
| 5-11 | Chi. | W | 7-3 | | 15 | 8 | Weaver | Wood | | 21-10 | 1st | +3.0 |
| 5-12 | Chi. | W | 4-0 | | 7 | 5 | Alvarez | Clement | | 22-10 | 1st | +3.0 |
| 5-13 | Chi. | L | 3-7 | | 5 | 14 | Zambrano | Nomo | Hawkins | 22-11 | 1st | +2.0 |
| 5-14 | Cin. | L | 1-2 | | 6 | 3 | Wilson | Ishii | Graves | 22-12 | 1st | +2.0 |
| 5-15 | Cin. | L | 0-4 | | 6 | 6 | Van Poppel | Perez | Graves | 22-13 | 1st | +2.0 |
| 5-16 | Cin. | L | 3-6 | | 9 | 12 | Harang | Weaver | Graves | 22-14 | 1st | +2.0 |
| 5-18 | At Phi. | L | 7-8 | | 10 | 11 | Padilla | Mota | Worrell | 22-15 | 1st | +1.5 |
| 5-19 | At Phi. | L | 4-9 | | 12 | 11 | Milton | Nomo | | 22-16 | 1st | ... |
| 5-20 | At Phi. | L | 0-4 | | 5 | 8 | Myers | Ishii | | 22-17 | 1st | ... |
| 5-21 | At Atl. | L | 0-2 | | 6 | 6 | Ortiz | Perez | Smoltz | 22-18 | 1st | ... |
| 5-22 | At Atl. | W | 7-4 | | 13 | 8 | Weaver | Wright | | 23-18 | 1st | ... |
| 5-23 | At Atl. | L | 1-5 | | 13 | 10 | Hampton | Alvarez | | 23-19 | 1st | ... |
| 5-25 | At Mil. | W | 5-3 | | 9 | 9 | Lima | Santos | Gagne | 24-19 | 1st | ... |
| 5-26 | At Mil. | L | 1-2 | (12) | 8 | 7 | Kinney | Sanchez | | 24-20 | 1st | ... |
| 5-27 | At Mil. | L | 1-3 | | 6 | 5 | Sheets | Weaver | Kolb | 24-21 | 2nd | 1.0 |
| 5-28 | Ari. | L | 3-6 | | 9 | 8 | Johnson | Alvarez | Dessens | 24-22 | 2nd | 2.0 |
| 5-29 | Ari. | W | 10-0 | | 13 | 3 | Lima | Webb | | 25-22 | 2nd | 1.0 |
| 5-30 | Ari. | W | 3-0 | | 12 | 4 | Ishii | Fossum | Gagne | 26-22 | 2nd | 1.0 |
| 5-31 | Mil. | W | 3-2 | (10) | 9 | 8 | Gagne | Burba | | 27-22 | 1st | ... |
| 6-1 | Mil. | L | 1-4 | | 7 | 9 | Davis | Weaver | Kolb | 27-23 | 1st | ... |
| 6-2 | Mil. | W | 5-2 | | 10 | 6 | Jackson | Hendrickson | Gagne | 28-23 | 1st | ... |
| 6-4 | At Ari. | W | 7-3 | | 12 | 7 | Ishii | Fossum | Mota | 29-23 | 1st | +1.0 |
| 6-5 | At Ari. | W | 10-3 | | 15 | 10 | Perez | Gonzalez | | 30-23 | 1st | +1.0 |
| 6-6 | At Ari. | L | 5-6 | | 14 | 13 | Service | Dreifort | Valverde | 30-24 | 1st | ... |
| 6-8 | At Tor. | L | 1-7 | | 8 | 10 | Lilly | Nomo | | 30-25 | 1st | ... |
| 6-9 | At Tor. | L | 0-4 | | 4 | 7 | Batista | Lima | | 30-26 | 2nd | 1.0 |
| 6-10 | At Tor. | W | 6-1 | | 14 | 6 | Ishii | Towers | | 31-26 | 1st | ... |
| 6-11 | At Bos. | L | 1-2 | | 7 | 7 | Foulke | Martin | | 31-27 | 2nd | 1.0 |
| 6-12 | At Bos. | W | 14-5 | | 15 | 5 | Weaver | Wakefield | | 32-27 | 1st | ... |
| 6-13 | At Bos. | L | 1-4 | | 8 | 6 | Martinez | Nomo | Foulke | 32-28 | 1st | ... |
| 6-15 | Bal. | W | 5-1 | | 10 | 5 | Lima | Cabrera | Gagne | 33-28 | 1st | +1.0 |
| 6-16 | Bal. | W | 6-3 | | 10 | 8 | Perez | Riley | Gagne | 34-28 | 1st | +1.5 |
| 6-17 | Bal. | W | 4-3 | | 9 | 10 | Mota | Lopez | Gagne | 35-28 | 1st | +1.5 |
| 6-18 | N.Y. | W | 6-3 | | 11 | 8 | Weaver | Vazquez | Gagne | 36-28 | 1st | +2.5 |
| 6-19 | N.Y. | L | 2-6 | | 8 | 7 | Halsey | Nomo | | 36-29 | 1st | +1.5 |

| Date | Opp. | Res. | Score | (inn.*) | Hits | Opp. hits | Winning pitcher | Losing pitcher | Save | Record | Pos. | GB |
|---|---|---|---|---|---|---|---|---|---|---|---|---|
| 6-20 | N.Y. | W | 5-4 | | 9 | 9 | Lima | Contreras | Gagne | 37-29 | 1st | +1.5 |
| 6-21 | At S.F | L | 2-3 | | 9 | 9 | Herges | Mota | | 37-30 | 1st | +0.5 |
| 6-22 | At S.F | L | 5-11 | | 7 | 16 | Brower | Alvarez | | 37-31 | 2nd | 0.5 |
| 6-23 | At S.F | L | 2-3 | | 8 | 7 | Williams | Weaver | Herges | 37-32 | 2nd | 1.5 |
| 6-24 | At S.F | L | 3-9 | | 8 | 12 | Tomko | Nomo | | 37-33 | 2nd | 2.5 |
| 6-25 | Ana. | L | 0-13 | | 4 | 22 | Washburn | Lima | | 37-34 | 3rd | 3.5 |
| 6-26 | Ana. | L | 5-7 | | 6 | 8 | Donnelly | Mota | Rodriguez | 37-35 | 3rd | 3.5 |
| 6-27 | Ana. | W | 10-5 | | 13 | 7 | Ishii | Colon | | 38-35 | 3rd | 3.5 |
| 6-29 | S.F | W | 2-1 | | 4 | 8 | Mota | Brower | Gagne | 39-35 | 3rd | 2.5 |
| 6-30 | S.F | L | 1-7 | | 7 | 10 | Tomko | Nomo | | 39-36 | 3rd | 3.5 |
| 7-1 | S.F | W | 5-4 | | 7 | 7 | Mota | Rodriguez | Gagne | 40-36 | 2nd | 2.5 |
| 7-2 | At Ana. | L | 3-7 | | 4 | 9 | Sele | Ishii | | 40-37 | 3rd | 3.5 |
| 7-3 | At Ana. | W | 8-5 | | 9 | 6 | Mota | Colon | Gagne | 41-37 | 3rd | 2.5 |
| 7-4 | At Ana. | W | 6-2 | | 5 | 9 | Weaver | Escobar | | 42-37 | 3rd | 1.5 |
| 7-5 | Ari. | W | 6-5 | (10) | 6 | 10 | Carrara | Villafuerte | | 43-37 | 3rd | 1.0 |
| 7-6 | Ari. | W | 4-1 | | 9 | 8 | Lima | Fossum | Gagne | 44-37 | 2nd | 1.0 |
| 7-7 | Ari. | W | 11-0 | | 11 | 1 | Ishii | Sparks | | 45-37 | 1st | ... |
| 7-8 | Hou. | W | 7-2 | | 12 | 5 | Jackson | Duckworth | Martin | 46-37 | 1st | +1.0 |
| 7-9 | Hou. | L | 2-3 | | 5 | 7 | Pettitte | Weaver | Lidge | 46-38 | 1st | +0.5 |
| 7-10 | Hou. | W | 3-1 | | 5 | 3 | Alvarez | Clemens | Gagne | 47-38 | 1st | +0.5 |
| 7-11 | Hou. | W | 7-4 | | 13 | 7 | Lima | Oswalt | | 48-38 | 1st | +0.5 |
| 7-15 | At Ari. | W | 4-3 | | 7 | 8 | Alvarez | Choate | Gagne | 49-38 | 1st | +0.5 |
| 7-16 | At Ari. | W | 6-2 | | 8 | 6 | Ishii | Webb | | 50-38 | 1st | +1.5 |
| 7-17 | At Ari. | W | 7-6 | | 9 | 14 | Mota | Bruney | Gagne | 51-38 | 1st | +1.5 |
| 7-18 | At Ari. | W | 10-3 | | 15 | 12 | Lima | Dessens | | 52-38 | 1st | +2.5 |
| 7-19 | At Hou. | W | 7-6 | | 11 | 6 | Carrara | Miceli | Gagne | 53-38 | 1st | +2.5 |
| 7-20 | At Hou. | W | 7-5 | | 12 | 9 | Weaver | Weathers | Gagne | 54-38 | 1st | +2.5 |
| 7-21 | Col. | L | 5-6 | | 6 | 8 | Estes | Ishii | Chacon | 54-39 | 1st | +2.5 |
| 7-22 | Col. | W | 4-2 | | 11 | 6 | Mota | Harikkala | Gagne | 55-39 | 1st | +2.5 |
| 7-23 | S.D. | W | 3-2 | | 5 | 6 | Gagne | Beck | | 56-39 | 1st | +3.5 |
| 7-24 | S.D. | W | 12-2 | | 14 | 7 | Alvarez | Valdez | | 57-39 | 1st | +3.5 |
| 7-25 | S.D. | L | 0-3 | | 2 | 8 | Eaton | Weaver | Hoffman | 57-40 | 1st | +3.5 |
| 7-26 | At Col. | W | 9-7 | | 12 | 11 | Sanchez | Simpson | Gagne | 58-40 | 1st | +3.5 |
| 7-27 | At Col. | L | 2-7 | | 9 | 15 | Cook | Perez | | 58-41 | 1st | +3.5 |
| 7-28 | At Col. | L | 4-5 | | 11 | 11 | Reed | Mota | Chacon | 58-42 | 1st | +2.5 |
| 7-29 | At Col. | W | 3-2 | | 10 | 4 | Alvarez | Dohmann | Gagne | 59-42 | 1st | +2.5 |
| 7-30 | At S.D. | W | 12-3 | | 15 | 8 | Weaver | Eaton | | 60-42 | 1st | +3.5 |
| 7-31 | At S.D. | L | 2-3 | | 7 | 7 | Otsuka | Dreifort | Hoffman | 60-43 | 1st | +2.5 |
| 8-1 | At S.D. | W | 2-1 | (12) | 9 | 8 | Gagne | Stone | Dreifort | 61-43 | 1st | +3.5 |
| 8-3 | Pit. | W | 3-2 | | 7 | 4 | Penny | Perez | Gagne | 62-43 | 1st | +4.5 |
| 8-4 | Pit. | W | 2-1 | | 10 | 6 | Lima | Fogg | Gagne | 63-43 | 1st | +5.5 |
| 8-5 | Pit. | W | 8-3 | | 11 | 6 | Weaver | Burnett | | 64-43 | 1st | +6.5 |
| 8-6 | Phi. | L | 5-9 | (11) | 12 | 15 | Hernandez | Gagne | | 64-44 | 1st | +5.5 |
| 8-7 | Phi. | W | 6-3 | | 7 | 9 | Perez | Abbott | Gagne | 65-44 | 1st | +6.5 |
| 8-8 | Phi. | L | 1-4 | | 4 | 8 | Myers | Penny | | 65-45 | 1st | +6.5 |
| 8-10 | At Cin. | W | 5-2 | | 7 | 5 | Lima | Harang | Gagne | 66-45 | 1st | +6.5 |
| 8-11 | At Cin. | W | 11-1 | | 11 | 5 | Weaver | Claussen | | 67-45 | 1st | +7.5 |
| 8-12 | At Cin. | L | 5-6 | | 7 | 11 | White | Dreifort | Graves | 67-46 | 1st | +6.5 |
| 8-13 | At Chi. | W | 8-1 | | 14 | 6 | Perez | Maddux | | 68-46 | 1st | +6.5 |
| 8-14 | At Chi. | L | 0-2 | | 5 | 7 | Wood | Ishii | Remlinger | 68-47 | 1st | +6.5 |
| 8-15 | At Chi. | W | 8-5 | | 12 | 10 | Sanchez | Farnsworth | Gagne | 69-47 | 1st | +6.5 |
| 8-16 | Fla. | L | 2-4 | | 6 | 7 | Pavano | Dreifort | Benitez | 69-48 | 1st | +5.5 |
| 8-17 | Fla. | W | 6-1 | | 8 | 7 | Alvarez | Burnett | | 70-48 | 1st | +5.5 |
| 8-18 | Fla. | L | 4-6 | | 11 | 10 | Mota | Gagne | Benitez | 70-49 | 1st | +5.0 |
| 8-19 | Atl. | L | 5-6 | | 8 | 8 | Reitsma | Gagne | Smoltz | 70-50 | 1st | +4.5 |
| 8-20 | Atl. | W | 3-2 | (11) | 7 | 10 | Carrara | Cruz | | 71-50 | 1st | +4.5 |
| 8-21 | Atl. | W | 7-4 | | 10 | 13 | Weaver | Hampton | Carrara | 72-50 | 1st | +5.5 |
| 8-22 | Atl. | L | 1-10 | | 5 | 19 | Wright | Alvarez | | 72-51 | 1st | +4.5 |
| 8-23 | At Mon. | L | 7-8 | | 10 | 11 | Cordero | Carrara | | 72-52 | 1st | +4.0 |
| 8-24 | At Mon. | W | 10-2 | | 10 | 8 | Ishii | Biddle | | 73-52 | 1st | +5.0 |
| 8-25 | At Mon. | L | 3-6 | | 9 | 10 | Horgan | Lima | Ayala | 73-53 | 1st | +4.0 |
| 8-26 | At Mon. | W | 10-3 | | 10 | 8 | Weaver | Hernandez | | 74-53 | 1st | +4.0 |
| 8-27 | At N.Y. | L | 2-9 | | 9 | 14 | Glavine | Alvarez | | 74-54 | 1st | +4.0 |
| 8-28 | At N.Y. | W | 4-2 | | 11 | 4 | Carrara | Stanton | Gagne | 75-54 | 1st | +5.0 |
| 8-29 | At N.Y. | W | 10-2 | | 12 | 6 | Ishii | Benson | | 76-54 | 1st | +5.0 |
| 8-31 | At Ari. | W | 4-1 | (13) | 7 | 8 | Gagne | Bruney | Carrara | 77-54 | 1st | +5.5 |
| 9-1 | At Ari. | L | 1-3 | | 4 | 6 | Webb | Nomo | Aquino | 77-55 | 1st | +5.5 |
| 9-2 | At Ari. | W | 8-4 | | 8 | 11 | Brazoban | Nance | Gagne | 78-55 | 1st | +6.5 |
| 9-3 | At StL. | L | 0-3 | | 2 | 7 | Morris | Lima | | 78-56 | 1st | +5.5 |

| Date | Opp. | Res. | Score | (inn.*) | Hits | Opp. hits | Winning pitcher | Losing pitcher | Save | Record | Pos. | GB |
|---|---|---|---|---|---|---|---|---|---|---|---|---|
| 9-4 | At StL. | L | 1-5 | | 10 | 2 | Marquis | Ishii | | 78-57 | 1st | +4.5 |
| 9-5 | At StL. | L | 5-6 | (11) | 10 | 10 | King | Carrara | | 78-58 | 1st | +3.5 |
| 9-7 | Ari. | W | 8-2 | | 10 | 7 | Nomo | Webb | | 79-58 | 1st | +4.5 |
| 9-8 | Ari. | W | 6-5 | | 12 | 7 | Gagne | Koplove | | 80-58 | 1st | +4.5 |
| 9-9 | Ari. | W | 5-3 | | 10 | 6 | Lima | Gonzalez | Gagne | 81-58 | 1st | +5.0 |
| 9-10 | StL. | W | 7-6 | | 11 | 10 | Carrara | Calero | Gagne | 82-58 | 1st | +6.0 |
| 9-11 | StL. | W | 6-5 | | 10 | 9 | Stewart | Eldred | Gagne | 83-58 | 1st | +6.0 |
| 9-12 | StL. | L | 6-7 | | 9 | 12 | Carpenter | Jackson | Isringhausen | 83-59 | 1st | +5.0 |
| 9-13 | S.D. | L | 7-9 | | 10 | 13 | Wells | Perez | Hoffman | 83-60 | 1st | +4.5 |
| 9-14 | S.D. | W | 6-3 | | 11 | 11 | Lima | Germano | Gagne | 84-60 | 1st | +4.5 |
| 9-15 | S.D. | L | 3-7 | | 8 | 13 | Lawrence | Alvarez | Hoffman | 84-61 | 1st | +3.5 |
| 9-16 | S.D. | L | 0-3 | | 7 | 9 | Eaton | Weaver | Hoffman | 84-62 | 1st | +2.5 |
| 9-17 | At Col. | W | 8-6 | (10) | 10 | 12 | Gagne | Chacon | | 85-62 | 1st | +2.5 |
| 9-18 | At Col. | L | 1-8 | | 5 | 16 | Kennedy | Perez | | 85-63 | 1st | +2.5 |
| 9-19 | At Col. | W | 7-6 | | 8 | 9 | Brazoban | Chacon | Gagne | 86-63 | 1st | +2.5 |
| 9-21 | At S.D. | L | 4-9 | | 7 | 13 | Eaton | Weaver | | 86-64 | 1st | +1.5 |
| 9-22 | At S.D. | L | 0-4 | | 3 | 6 | Peavy | Penny | | 86-65 | 1st | +0.5 |
| 9-23 | At S.D. | W | 9-6 | | 14 | 10 | Brazoban | Lawrence | Gagne | 87-65 | 1st | +1.5 |
| 9-24 | At S.F | W | 3-2 | | 12 | 3 | Perez | Rueter | Gagne | 88-65 | 1st | +2.5 |
| 9-25 | At S.F | L | 5-9 | | 9 | 11 | Eyre | Brazoban | | 88-66 | 1st | +1.5 |
| 9-26 | At S.F | W | 7-4 | | 8 | 11 | Weaver | Tomko | Gagne | 89-66 | 1st | +2.5 |
| 9-27 | Col. | W | 8-7 | | 12 | 11 | Brazoban | Reed | | 90-66 | 1st | +3.0 |
| 9-28 | Col. | W | 5-4 | | 5 | 5 | Dessens | Harikkala | | 91-66 | 1st | +3.0 |
| 9-29 | Col. | L | 1-4 | | 3 | 7 | Fuentes | Brazoban | Tsao | 91-67 | 1st | +3.0 |
| 9-30 | Col. | W | 4-2 | (11) | 9 | 11 | Brazoban | Fuentes | | 92-67 | 1st | +3.0 |
| 10-1 | S.F | L | 2-4 | | 4 | 8 | Rueter | Weaver | Hermanson | 92-68 | 1st | +2.0 |
| 10-2 | S.F | W | 7-3 | | 7 | 6 | Brazoban | Hermanson | | 93-68 | 1st | +3.0 |
| 10-3 | S.F | L | 0-10 | | 3 | 15 | Schmidt | Ishii | | 93-69 | 1st | +2.0 |

Monthly records: April (14-8), May (13-14), June (12-14), July (21-7), August (17-11), September (15-13), October (1-2).
*Innings, if other than nine.

## RECORDS

**2004 regular-season record:** 93-69
**Position:** 1st in N.L. West
**Home:** 49-32 **Road:** 44-37
**N.L. East:** 14-18 **N.L. Central:** 22-14
**N.L. West:** 47-29 **A.L.** 10-8
**Vs. LH starters:** 23-22
**Vs. RH starters:** 70-47
**Grass:** 90-65 **Artificial:** 3-4
**Day:** 23-22 **Night:** 70-47
**1-Run:** 32-16 **X-inn.:** 11-3
**Doubleheaders:** 0-0-0
**Team record past five years:** 442-368 (.546, ranks 4th in league in that span)

## TEAM LEADERS

**Batting average:** Adrian Beltre (.334).
**At-bats:** Cesar Izturis (670).
**Runs:** Adrian Beltre (104).
**Hits:** Adrian Beltre (200).
**Total Bases:** Adrian Beltre (376).
**Doubles:** Adrian Beltre, Cesar Izturis (32).
**Triples:** Cesar Izturis (9).
**Home runs:** Adrian Beltre (48).
**Runs batted in:** Adrian Beltre (121).
**Stolen bases:** Dave Roberts (33).
**Slugging percentage:** Adrian Beltre (.629).
**On-base percentage:** Adrian Beltre (.388).
**Wins:** Kazuhisa Ishii, Jose Lima, Jeff Weaver (13).
**Earned-run average:** Odalis Perez (3.25).
**Complete games:** Kazuhisa Ishii (2).
**Shutouts:** Kazuhisa Ishii (2).
**Saves:** Eric Gagne (45).
**Innings pitched:** Jeff Weaver (220.0).
**Strikeouts:** Jeff Weaver (153).

## GAMES BY POSITION

**Catcher:** Paul Lo Duca 81, David Ross 67, Brent Mayne 47, Tom Wilson 7.
**First base:** Shawn Green 111, Robin Ventura 40, Olmedo Saenz 25, Hee Seop Choi 23, Jose Hernandez 8, Jason Grabowski 3, Paul Lo Duca 3.
**Second base:** Alex Cora 138, Jose Hernandez 50, Joe Thurston 4, Antonio Perez 2, Jose Flores 1.
**Third base:** Adrian Beltre 155, Jose Hernandez 12, Robin Ventura 11, Olmedo Saenz 2, Jose Flores 1.
**Shortstop:** Cesar Izturis 159, Jose Hernandez 13, Adrian Beltre 1, Antonio Perez 1.
**Outfield:** Milton Bradley 138, Juan Encarnacion 85, Jayson Werth 79, Dave Roberts 62, Steve Finley 55, Shawn Green 52, Jason Grabowski 31, Jose Hernandez 9, Paul Lo Duca 9, Chin-Feng Chen 3.
**Designated hitter:** Olmedo Saenz 4, Jason Grabowski 3, Shawn Green 3, Jayson Werth 1.

## TOP DRAFT CHOICES

1a. **Scott Elbert,** LHP, Seneca (Mo.) H.S.
1b. **Blake DeWitt,** SS, Sikeston (Mo.) H.S.
1c. **Justin Orenduff,** RHP, Virginia Commonwealth.
2. **Blake Johnson,** RHP, Parkview Baptist H.S., Baton Rouge, La.
3. **Cory Dunlap,** 1B, Contra Costa College (Calif.).
4. **Javy Guerra,** RHP, Denton Ryan H.S., Denton, Texas.
5. **Anthony Raglani,** OF, George Washington.
6. **Daniel Batz,** 1B, Rhode Island.
7. **Barry Richmond,** OF, Spartanburg Methodist College (S.C.).
8. **Carlos Medero-Stultz,** C, Barbara Goleman H.S., Hialeah, Fla.
9. **David Nicholson,** 3B, California.
10. **Cory Wade,** RHP, Kentucky Wesleyan.

# MILWAUKEE BREWERS
## NATIONAL LEAGUE CENTRAL DIVISION

## 2005 SEASON

**Brewers Schedule**
Home games shaded.
All-Star Game July 12 at Detroit. Schedule subject to change.

**April**

| SUN | MON | TUE | WED | THU | FRI | SAT |
|---|---|---|---|---|---|---|
| 3 | 4 PIT | 5 | 6 PIT | 7 | 8 CHC | 9 CHC |
| 10 CHC | 11 PIT | 12 PIT | 13 PIT | 14 | 15 STL | 16 STL |
| 17 STL | 18 LA | 19 LA | 20 HOU | 21 HOU | 22 SF | 23 SF |
| 24 SF | 25 STL | 26 STL | 27 STL | 28 | 29 CIN | 30 CIN |

**May**

| SUN | MON | TUE | WED | THU | FRI | SAT |
|---|---|---|---|---|---|---|
| 1 CIN | 2 | 3 CHC | 4 CHC | 5 CHC | 6 NYM | 7 NYM |
| 8 NYM | 9 PHI | 10 PHI | 11 PHI | 12 | 13 PIT | 14 PIT |
| 15 PIT | 16 WAS | 17 WAS | 18 WAS | 19 WAS | 20 MIN | 21 MIN |
| 22 MIN | 23 COL | 24 COL | 25 COL | 26 | 27 HOU | 28 HOU |
| 29 HOU | 30 SD | 31 SD | | | | |

**June**

| SUN | MON | TUE | WED | THU | FRI | SAT |
|---|---|---|---|---|---|---|
| | | | 1 SD | 2 LA | 3 LA | 4 LA |
| 5 LA | 6 NYY | 7 NYY | 8 NYY | 9 | 10 PHI | 11 PHI |
| 12 PHI | 13 TB | 14 TB | 15 TB | 16 | 17 TOR | 18 TOR |
| 19 TOR | 20 CHC | 21 CHC | 22 CHC | 23 CHC | 24 MIN | 25 MIN |
| 26 MIN | 27 | 28 CHC | 29 CHC | 30 CHC | | |

**July**

| SUN | MON | TUE | WED | THU | FRI | SAT |
|---|---|---|---|---|---|---|
| | | | | | 1 PIT | 2 PIT |
| 3 PIT | 4 FLA | 5 FLA | 6 FLA | 7 FLA | 8 ATL | 9 ATL |
| 10 ATL | 11 | 12 All-Star | 13 | 14 WAS | 15 WAS | 16 WAS |
| 17 WAS | 18 STL | 19 STL | 20 STL | 21 STL | 22 CIN | 23 CIN |
| 24 CIN | 25 ARI | 26 ARI | 27 ARI | 28 SF | 29 SF | 30 SF |
| 31 SF | | | | | | |

**August**

| SUN | MON | TUE | WED | THU | FRI | SAT |
|---|---|---|---|---|---|---|
| | 1 | 2 NYM | 3 NYM | 4 NYM | 5 PHI | 6 PHI |
| 7 PHI | 8 STL | 9 STL | 10 STL | 11 | 12 CIN | 13 CIN |
| 14 CIN | 15 COL | 16 COL | 17 COL | 18 HOU | 19 HOU | 20 HOU |
| 21 HOU | 22 | 23 FLA | 24 FLA | 25 FLA | 26 ATL | 27 ATL |
| 28 ATL | 29 | 30 PIT | 31 PIT | | | |

**September**

| SUN | MON | TUE | WED | THU | FRI | SAT |
|---|---|---|---|---|---|---|
| | | | | 1 SD | 2 SD | 3 SD |
| 4 SD | 5 CIN | 6 CIN | 7 CIN | 8 | 9 HOU | 10 HOU |
| 11 HOU | 12 | 13 ARI | 14 ARI | 15 ARI | 16 HOU | 17 HOU |
| 18 HOU | 19 | 20 CHC | 21 CHC | 22 CHC | 23 STL | 24 STL |
| 25 STL | 26 CIN | 27 CIN | 28 CIN | 29 CIN | 30 PIT | |

**October**

| SUN | MON | TUE | WED | THU | FRI | SAT |
|---|---|---|---|---|---|---|
| | | | | | | 1 PIT |
| 2 PIT | 3 | 4 | 5 | 6 | 7 | 8 |

Home games shaded. All-Star Game July 12 at Detroit. Schedule subject to change.

### CLUB DIRECTORY

**Executive vice president and g.m.**
Doug Melvin
**Executive v.p., business operations**
Rick Schlesinger
**Sr. v.p., chief financial officer**
Robert J. Quinn
**Assistant general manager**
Gord Ash
**Director, community relations**
Leonard Peace
**Director, media relations**
Jon Greenberg
**Director, scouting**
Jack Zduriencik
**Special asst. to the g.m./player dev.**
Reid Nichols
**Special assistant to the g.m./scouting**
Dick Groch

### MINOR LEAGUE AFFILIATES

| Class | Team | League | Manager |
|---|---|---|---|
| AAA | Nashville | Pacific Coast | Frank Kremblas |
| AA | Huntsville | Southern | Don Money |
| Advanced A | Brevard County | Florida State | John Tamargo |
| A | West Virginia | South Atlantic | Ramon Aviles |
| Advanced Rookie | Helena | Pioneer | Ed Sedar |
| Rookie | Arizona Brewers | Arizona | Mike Guerrero |

### BROADCAST INFORMATION

**Radio:** WTMJ-AM (620).
**TV:** WCGV-TV (Channel 24).
**Cable TV:** Fox Sports North.

### SPRING TRAINING

**Ballpark (city):** Maryvale Baseball Park (Phoenix, Ariz.).
**Ticket information:** 1-800-933-7890.

For more on the Brewers, go to msn.foxsports.com/mlb/teams.

Lee

## SPRING TRAINING ROSTER

**Manager**—Ned Yost (3).
**Coaches**—Bill Castro (35), Rich Dauer (25), Rich Donnelly (45), Mike Maddux (36), Dave Nelson (14), Butch Wynegar (16).

| No. | PITCHERS | B/T | Ht./Wt. | Age* | 2004 Clubs |
|---|---|---|---|---|---|
| 46 | Adams, Mike | R/R | 6-5/190 | 26 | Indianapolis, Milwaukee |
| 57 | Bennett, Jeff | R/R | 6-3/206 | 24 | Milwaukee |
| | Capellan, Jose | R/R | 6-4/235 | 24 | Myrtle Beach, Greenville, Richmond, Atlanta |
| 39 | Capuano, Chris | L/L | 6-3/210 | 26 | Beloit, Indianapolis, High Desert, Milwaukee |
| 49 | Davis, Doug | R/L | 6-4/213 | 29 | Milwaukee |
| 47 | de la Rosa, Jorge | L/L | 6-1/190 | 23 | Indianapolis, Milwaukee |
| | Diggins, Ben | R/R | 6-7/230 | 25 | Arizona Brewers |
| 58 | Glover, Gary | R/R | 6-5/220 | 28 | Iowa, Rochester, Indianapolis, Milwaukee |
| 40 | Hendrickson, Ben | R/R | 6-4/190 | 24 | Indianapolis, Milwaukee |
| | Housman, Jeff | L/L | 6-3/180 | 23 | Huntsville, Indianapolis |
| | Jones, Mike | R/R | 6-4/200 | 21 | Huntsville |
| 55 | Kieschnick, Brooks | L/R | 6-4/251 | 32 | Indianapolis, Milwaukee |
| | Lehr, Justin | R/R | 6-1/200 | 27 | Sacramento, Oakland |
| | Narron, Sam | L/L | 6-7/200 | 23 | Frisco, Texas, Oklahoma |
| 33 | Obermueller, Wes | R/R | 6-2/209 | 28 | Indianapolis, Milwaukee |
| | Pena, Luis | R/R | 6-5/160 | 22 | Beloit |
| | Pratt, Andy | L/L | 6-0/185 | 25 | Chicago N.L., Iowa, Arizona Cubs, Lansing, West Tenn, Huntsville |
| 53 | Santos, Victor | R/R | 6-3/190 | 28 | Indianapolis, Milwaukee |
| | Sarfate, Dennis | R/R | 6-4/210 | 23 | Huntsville |
| 15 | Sheets, Ben | R/R | 6-1/218 | 26 | Milwaukee |
| | Turnbow, Derrick | R/R | 6-3/210 | 27 | Anaheim, Salt Lake |
| 26 | Wise, Matt | R/R | 6-4/200 | 29 | Indianapolis, Milwaukee |

| No. | CATCHERS | B/T | Ht./Wt. | Age* | 2004 Clubs |
|---|---|---|---|---|---|
| | Miller, Damian | R/R | 6-3/220 | 35 | Oakland |
| 21 | Moeller, Chad | R/R | 6-3/210 | 30 | Milwaukee |

| No. | INFIELDERS | B/T | Ht./Wt. | Age* | 2004 Clubs |
|---|---|---|---|---|---|
| 31 | Branyan, Russell | L/R | 6-3/195 | 29 | Richmond, Buffalo, Milwaukee |
| 2 | Hall, Bill | R/R | 6-0/195 | 25 | Milwaukee |
| | Hardy, J.J. | R/R | 6-2/181 | 22 | Indianapolis |
| 18 | Helms, Wes | R/R | 6-4/231 | 28 | Indianapolis, Milwaukee |
| 11 | Overbay, Lyle | L/L | 6-2/227 | 28 | Milwaukee |
| 37 | Spivey, Junior | R/R | 6-0/201 | 30 | Milwaukee |
| 23 | Weeks, Rickie | R/R | 6-0/195 | 22 | Huntsville |

| No. | OUTFIELDERS | B/T | Ht./Wt. | Age* | 2004 Clubs |
|---|---|---|---|---|---|
| 15 | Clark, Brady | R/R | 6-2/202 | 31 | Milwaukee |
| | Hart, Corey | R/R | 6-6/200 | 23 | Indianapolis |
| | Cruz, Nelson | R/R | 6-3/175 | 23 | Modesto, Midland, Sacramento |
| | Jenkins, Geoff | L/R | 6-1/212 | 30 | Milwaukee |
| | Krynzel, Dave | L/L | 6-1/180 | 22 | Arizona Brewers, Indianapolis, Milwaukee |
| 45 | Lee, Carlos | R/R | 6-2/240 | 28 | Chicago A.L. |
| | Nelson, Brad | L/R | 6-2/220 | 22 | Huntsville |

*Age as of April 1, 2005.

## BALLPARK INFORMATION

**Ballpark (capacity, surface)**
Miller Park (41,900, grass)
**Address**
One Brewers Way
Milwaukee, WI 53214-3652
**Official website**
www.milwaukeebrewers.com
**Business phone**
414-902-4400
**Ticket information**
414-902-4000, 800-933-7890
**Field dimensions (from home plate)**
To left field at foul line, 342 feet
To center field, 400 feet
To right field at foul line, 345 feet
**First game played**
April 6, 2001 (Brewers 5, Reds 4)

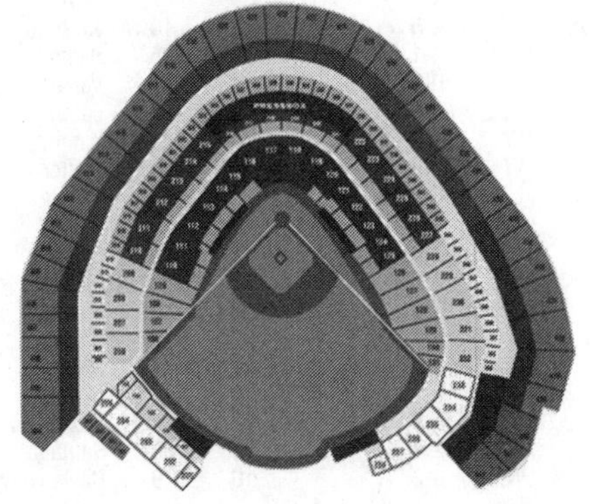

# 2004 REVIEW

## DAY BY DAY

| Date | Opp. | Res. | Score | (inn.*) | Hits | Opp. hits | Winning pitcher | Losing pitcher | Save | Record | Pos. | GB |
|---|---|---|---|---|---|---|---|---|---|---|---|---|
| 4-5 | At StL. | W | 8-6 | | 6 | 8 | Burba | Morris | Kolb | 1-0 | T1st | ... |
| 4-6 | At StL. | W | 7-5 | | 10 | 12 | Davis | Marquis | Kolb | 2-0 | 1st | +0.5 |
| 4-7 | At StL. | L | 4-9 | | 11 | 14 | Lincoln | Hernandez | | 2-1 | 1st | +0.5 |
| 4-8 | At StL. | W | 11-5 | | 15 | 5 | Capuano | Suppan | Burba | 3-1 | 1st | +0.5 |
| 4-9 | Hou. | L | 7-13 | | 10 | 14 | Miller | Obermueller | | 3-2 | 2nd | 0.5 |
| 4-10 | Hou. | W | 6-1 | | 10 | 6 | Sheets | Redding | | 4-2 | 2nd | 0.5 |
| 4-11 | Hou. | L | 4-7 | | 10 | 9 | Oswalt | Davis | | 4-3 | T2nd | 0.5 |
| 4-12 | At S.F | L | 5-7 | | 13 | 10 | Williams | Kinney | Herges | 4-4 | T4th | 1.5 |
| 4-13 | At S.F | L | 2-4 | | 7 | 8 | Hermanson | Capuano | Herges | 4-5 | T4th | 2.0 |
| 4-14 | At S.F | W | 3-0 | | 6 | 4 | Obermueller | Cooper | Kolb | 5-5 | T3rd | 1.5 |
| 4-15 | At Hou. | W | 6-2 | | 8 | 4 | Sheets | Redding | | 6-5 | 4th | 0.5 |
| 4-16 | At Hou. | L | 0-2 | | 3 | 8 | Oswalt | Davis | | 6-6 | T4th | 1.5 |
| 4-17 | At Hou. | L | 5-14 | | 8 | 11 | Backe | Kinney | | 6-7 | 6th | 2.5 |
| 4-18 | At Hou. | L | 1-6 | | 6 | 16 | Clemens | Capuano | | 6-8 | 6th | 3.5 |
| 4-20 | Ari. | W | 4-2 | | 10 | 9 | Sheets | Dessens | Kolb | 7-8 | 6th | 2.5 |
| 4-21 | Ari. | W | 10-6 | | 10 | 8 | Ford | Johnson | | 8-8 | T5th | 1.5 |
| 4-22 | Ari. | L | 9-11 | (15) | 8 | 20 | Sparks | Hernandez | | 8-9 | 6th | 2.0 |
| 4-23 | StL. | W | 2-1 | | 8 | 6 | Kieschnick | Kline | | 9-9 | 5th | 2.0 |
| 4-24 | StL. | W | 3-1 | | 6 | 5 | Saenz | Williams | Kolb | 10-9 | 4th | 2.0 |
| 4-25 | StL. | L | 2-5 | | 5 | 9 | Suppan | Sheets | | 10-10 | 5th | 3.0 |
| 4-27 | Cin. | W | 9-8 | | 11 | 9 | Bennett | Graves | | 11-10 | 4th | 1.5 |
| 4-28 | Cin. | W | 10-9 | (10) | 16 | 12 | Burba | Van Poppel | | 12-10 | 4th | 1.5 |
| 4-30 | Pit. | L | 2-4 | | 6 | 9 | Benson | Sheets | Mesa | 12-11 | T4th | 1.5 |
| 5-1 | Pit. | L | 7-8 | (10) | 13 | 9 | Boyd | Vizcaino | Mesa | 12-12 | T4th | 2.5 |
| 5-2 | Pit. | L | 3-4 | (11) | 9 | 13 | Meadows | Bennett | Mesa | 12-13 | 6th | 3.5 |
| 5-4 | At Cin. | W | 6-2 | | 9 | 6 | Santos | Haynes | | 13-13 | T4th | 3.0 |
| 5-5 | At Cin. | L | 4-5 | (10) | 9 | 9 | Graves | Bennett | | 13-14 | 5th | 4.0 |
| 5-6 | At Cin. | L | 6-9 | | 10 | 10 | Jones | Bennett | Graves | 13-15 | 5th | 5.0 |
| 5-7 | At N.Y. | W | 7-5 | | 11 | 8 | Davis | Glavine | | 14-15 | 5th | 5.0 |
| 5-8 | At N.Y. | W | 6-4 | | 12 | 2 | Kinney | Yates | Kolb | 15-15 | 4th | 4.0 |
| 5-9 | At N.Y. | L | 5-6 | (11) | 11 | 12 | Wheeler | Ford | | 15-16 | 5th | 5.0 |
| 5-11 | Mon. | W | 8-5 | (14) | 16 | 11 | Burba | Tucker | | 16-16 | 5th | 5.0 |
| 5-12 | Mon. | W | 4-3 | | 7 | 6 | Obermueller | Day | Kolb | 17-16 | T4th | 4.0 |
| 5-13 | Mon. | W | 7-4 | | 11 | 5 | Davis | Kim | Kolb | 18-16 | 3rd | 3.0 |
| 5-14 | Atl. | L | 0-2 | | 5 | 8 | Ramirez | Vizcaino | Smoltz | 18-17 | T4th | 3.0 |
| 5-15 | Atl. | L | 6-11 | | 6 | 15 | Alfonseca | Kinney | | 18-18 | 5th | 4.0 |
| 5-16 | Atl. | W | 4-1 | | 8 | 3 | Sheets | Wright | | 19-18 | 5th | 3.0 |
| 5-18@ | At Mon. | L | 2-3 | | 12 | 7 | Day | Davis | Biddle | 19-19 | 5th | 4.0 |
| 5-19@ | At Mon. | W | 6-3 | | 11 | 10 | Santos | Kim | Kolb | 20-19 | 5th | 4.0 |
| 5-20@ | At Mon. | W | 3-2 | | 6 | 8 | Adams | Biddle | Kolb | 21-19 | 5th | 3.0 |
| 5-22 | At Pit. | L | 1-3 | | 7 | 9 | Fogg | Sheets | Mesa | 21-20 | 5th | 2.5 |
| 5-23 | At Pit. | W | 2-1 | | 5 | 10 | Vizcaino | Meadows | Kolb | 22-20 | 4th | 2.5 |
| 5-25 | L.A. | L | 3-5 | | 9 | 9 | Lima | Santos | Gagne | 22-21 | 5th | 4.0 |
| 5-26 | L.A. | W | 2-1 | (12) | 7 | 8 | Kinney | Sanchez | | 23-21 | 4th | 3.0 |
| 5-27 | L.A. | W | 3-1 | | 5 | 6 | Sheets | Weaver | Kolb | 24-21 | 4th | 2.0 |
| 5-28 | S.D. | L | 3-5 | | 5 | 8 | Lawrence | Davis | Hoffman | 24-22 | 5th | 3.0 |
| 5-29 | S.D. | W | 4-3 | | 4 | 11 | Obermueller | Tankersley | Kolb | 25-22 | 4th | 3.0 |
| 5-30 | S.D. | L | 2-5 | | 10 | 8 | Valdez | Santos | Hoffman | 25-23 | 5th | 3.0 |
| 5-31 | At L.A. | L | 2-3 | (10) | 8 | 9 | Gagne | Burba | | 25-24 | 5th | 4.0 |
| 6-1 | At L.A. | W | 4-1 | | 9 | 7 | Davis | Weaver | Kolb | 26-24 | 5th | 4.0 |
| 6-2 | At L.A. | L | 2-5 | | 6 | 10 | Jackson | Hendrickson | Gagne | 26-25 | 5th | 5.0 |
| 6-4 | At S.D. | W | 3-1 | | 8 | 5 | Santos | Tankersley | Kolb | 27-25 | 4th | 4.0 |
| 6-5 | At S.D. | L | 0-4 | | 4 | 10 | Valdez | Obermueller | | 27-26 | 5th | 5.0 |
| 6-6 | At S.D. | L | 3-8 | | 5 | 12 | Eaton | Davis | | 27-27 | 5th | 6.0 |
| 6-8 | At Ana. | W | 1-0 | (17) | 9 | 4 | Kinney | Ortiz | Kolb | 28-27 | 5th | 4.5 |
| 6-9 | At Ana. | W | 12-2 | | 17 | 14 | Santos | Washburn | Burba | 29-27 | 4th | 3.5 |
| 6-10 | At Ana. | L | 4-5 | | 8 | 8 | Gregg | Bennett | Rodriguez | 29-28 | 5th | 4.0 |
| 6-11 | Hou. | W | 9-3 | | 16 | 7 | Davis | Redding | | 30-28 | 4th | 3.5 |
| 6-12 | Hou. | W | 7-4 | | 11 | 6 | Capuano | Oswalt | Kolb | 31-28 | 4th | 2.5 |
| 6-13 | Hou. | L | 4-5 | | 11 | 9 | Miceli | Sheets | Dotel | 31-29 | 5th | 3.5 |
| 6-15 | Sea. | W | 3-0 | | 8 | 2 | Santos | Garcia | Kolb | 32-29 | 4th | 3.5 |
| 6-16 | Sea. | W | 4-1 | | 5 | 6 | Davis | Nageotte | Kolb | 33-29 | 4th | 3.5 |
| 6-17 | Sea. | L | 3-6 | | 10 | 11 | Myers | Kinney | Guardado | 33-30 | 4th | 4.5 |
| 6-18 | Min. | W | 4-1 | | 11 | 5 | Sheets | Silva | Kolb | 34-30 | 4th | 4.5 |
| 6-19 | Min. | W | 7-6 | | 12 | 12 | Vizcaino | Mulholland | Kolb | 35-30 | 4th | 4.5 |
| 6-20 | Min. | L | 2-4 | | 6 | 8 | Santana | Santos | Nathan | 35-31 | 4th | 4.5 |
| 6-22 | Col. | W | 6-2 | | 10 | 9 | Davis | Lopez | | 36-31 | 4th | 3.5 |

| Date | Opp. | Res. | Score | (inn.*) | Hits | Opp. hits | Winning pitcher | Losing pitcher | Save | Record | Pos. | GB |
|---|---|---|---|---|---|---|---|---|---|---|---|---|
| 6-23 | Col. | L | 2-3 | | 6 | 7 | Estes | Capuano | Chacon | 36-32 | 4th | 4.5 |
| 6-24 | Col. | L | 0-3 | | 10 | 7 | Cook | Sheets | Chacon | 36-33 | 5th | 5.5 |
| 6-25 | At Min. | L | 3-6 | | 7 | 11 | Santana | Obermueller | Nathan | 36-34 | 5th | 6.5 |
| 6-26 | At Min. | W | 7-2 | | 14 | 5 | Santos | Guerrier | | 37-34 | 4th | 6.5 |
| 6-27 | At Min. | W | 7-3 | | 10 | 9 | Davis | Lohse | | 38-34 | 4th | 6.5 |
| 6-29 | At Col. | W | 6-3 | | 9 | 9 | Capuano | Estes | Kolb | 39-34 | 4th | 5.0 |
| 6-30 | At Col. | W | 5-4 | | 10 | 10 | Sheets | Cook | Kolb | 40-34 | 4th | 4.0 |
| 7-1 | At Col. | W | 10-9 | | 14 | 14 | Santos | Stark | Kolb | 41-34 | 3rd | 3.5 |
| 7-2! | At Pit. | L | 1-8 | | 6 | 8 | Perez | Davis | | 41-35 | | |
| 7-2& | At Pit. | L | 2-13 | | 8 | 14 | Fogg | Wise | | 41-36 | 3rd | 5.0 |
| 7-3 | At Pit. | L | 3-5 | | 13 | 11 | Benson | Obermueller | Mesa | 41-37 | 4th | 6.0 |
| 7-4 | At Pit. | L | 2-6 | | 12 | 7 | Burnett | Capuano | Mesa | 41-38 | 4th | 7.0 |
| 7-5 | Chi. | W | 1-0 | | 3 | 6 | Sheets | Clement | Kolb | 42-38 | 4th | 7.0 |
| 7-6 | Chi. | W | 4-2 | | 5 | 6 | Santos | Prior | Kolb | 43-38 | 3rd | 7.0 |
| 7-7 | Chi. | W | 4-0 | | 9 | 4 | Davis | Zambrano | | 44-38 | 3rd | 7.0 |
| 7-8 | Cin. | L | 3-9 | | 8 | 10 | Wilson | Obermueller | | 44-39 | 3rd | 7.5 |
| 7-9 | Cin. | L | 0-3 | | 7 | 7 | Harang | Capuano | Graves | 44-40 | 4th | 8.5 |
| 7-10 | Cin. | W | 5-0 | | 7 | 5 | Sheets | Lidle | | 45-40 | 3rd | 8.5 |
| 7-11 | Cin. | L | 6-9 | | 8 | 15 | Jones | Kolb | Graves | 45-41 | 4th | 8.5 |
| 7-15 | At Chi. | L | 1-4 | | 5 | 9 | Rusch | Davis | Hawkins | 45-42 | 4th | 9.5 |
| 7-16 | At Chi. | W | 3-2 | | 9 | 4 | Santos | Clement | Kolb | 46-42 | 3rd | 9.5 |
| 7-17 | At Chi. | L | 0-5 | | 6 | 8 | Maddux | Sheets | | 46-43 | 4th | 9.5 |
| 7-18 | At Chi. | W | 4-2 | | 9 | 6 | Capuano | Beltran | Kolb | 47-43 | 3rd | 9.5 |
| 7-19 | At Cin. | L | 4-8 | | 11 | 12 | Harang | Hendrickson | | 47-44 | 4th | 10.5 |
| 7-20 | At Cin. | L | 2-6 | | 6 | 10 | Claussen | Davis | | 47-45 | 4th | 11.5 |
| 7-21 | At StL. | L | 0-1 | | 5 | 3 | Williams | Santos | Isringhausen | 47-46 | 4th | 12.5 |
| 7-22 | At StL. | L | 0-4 | | 10 | 11 | Marquis | Sheets | | 47-47 | 4th | 13.5 |
| 7-23 | At Hou. | W | 7-6 | | 12 | 13 | Vizcaino | Lidge | Kolb | 48-47 | 4th | 12.5 |
| 7-24 | At Hou. | L | 3-6 | | 6 | 11 | Redding | Hendrickson | Lidge | 48-48 | 4th | 12.5 |
| 7-25 | At Hou. | L | 1-9 | | 8 | 12 | Munro | Davis | | 48-49 | 5th | 13.5 |
| 7-26 | Chi. | L | 1-3 | | 5 | 8 | Clement | Santos | Hawkins | 48-50 | 5th | 14.5 |
| 7-27 | Chi. | L | 1-7 | | 6 | 8 | Maddux | Sheets | | 48-51 | 6th | 15.5 |
| 7-28 | Chi. | W | 6-3 | | 10 | 5 | Capuano | Wood | Kolb | 49-51 | 5th | 15.5 |
| 7-29 | Chi. | L | 0-4 | | 5 | 10 | Zambrano | Hendrickson | | 49-52 | 5th | 16.0 |
| 7-30 | Pit. | W | 5-0 | | 7 | 6 | Davis | Burnett | | 50-52 | T4th | 16.0 |
| 7-31 | Pit. | L | 1-4 | | 5 | 10 | Vogelsong | Santos | Mesa | 50-53 | 5th | 16.0 |
| 8-1 | Pit. | W | 8-7 | | 17 | 13 | Vizcaino | Meadows | | 51-53 | 4th | 16.0 |
| 8-3 | N.Y. | L | 3-12 | | 8 | 16 | Leiter | Capuano | | 51-54 | 4th | 16.0 |
| 8-4 | N.Y. | L | 5-6 | | 10 | 6 | Feliciano | Adams | Looper | 51-55 | 5th | 17.0 |
| 8-5 | N.Y. | L | 6-11 | | 10 | 10 | Zambrano | Santos | | 51-56 | 5th | 18.0 |
| 8-6 | At Fla. | L | 6-7 | | 8 | 10 | Koch | Kolb | | 51-57 | 5th | 19.0 |
| 8-7 | At Fla. | L | 0-5 | | 3 | 9 | Valdez | Obermueller | | 51-58 | 5th | 20.0 |
| 8-8 | At Fla. | W | 2-0 | | 8 | 7 | Capuano | Willis | Kolb | 52-58 | 5th | 20.0 |
| 8-10 | At Atl. | W | 3-2 | (10) | 8 | 8 | Adams | Martin | Kolb | 53-58 | 5th | 20.0 |
| 8-11 | At Atl. | L | 3-10 | | 12 | 15 | Hampton | Santos | | 53-59 | 6th | 21.0 |
| 8-12 | At Atl. | L | 2-4 | | 5 | 7 | Wright | Sheets | Smoltz | 53-60 | 6th | 21.0 |
| 8-13 | Fla. | W | 6-4 | | 10 | 8 | Obermueller | Valdez | Kolb | 54-60 | 5th | 21.0 |
| 8-14 | Fla. | L | 1-11 | | 8 | 12 | Willis | de la Rosa | | 54-61 | 6th | 21.0 |
| 8-15 | Fla. | L | 3-5 | (10) | 7 | 11 | Seanez | Hendrickson | Benitez | 54-62 | 6th | 22.0 |
| 8-17 | Chi. | W | 3-1 | | 7 | 7 | Santos | Zambrano | Kolb | 55-62 | 6th | 22.5 |
| 8-18 | Chi. | L | 5-7 | (11) | 9 | 12 | Mercker | Phelps | Hawkins | 55-63 | 6th | 22.5 |
| 8-19 | Chi. | L | 6-9 | | 7 | 11 | Maddux | Capuano | Hawkins | 55-64 | 6th | 22.5 |
| 8-20 | Phi. | L | 2-4 | | 5 | 6 | Milton | Davis | Worrell | 55-65 | 6th | 24.0 |
| 8-21 | Phi. | L | 6-8 | | 8 | 12 | Geary | Vizcaino | Worrell | 55-66 | 6th | 25.0 |
| 8-22 | Phi. | L | 6-9 | (10) | 7 | 12 | Rodriguez | Kolb | Worrell | 55-67 | 6th | 26.0 |
| 8-23 | At Chi. | L | 3-8 | | 6 | 13 | Zambrano | Sheets | | 55-68 | 6th | 26.5 |
| 8-24 | At Chi. | L | 4-13 | | 10 | 13 | Clement | Capuano | Rusch | 55-69 | 6th | 26.5 |
| 8-25 | At Chi. | L | 2-4 | | 6 | 10 | Hawkins | Vizcaino | | 55-70 | 6th | 27.5 |
| 8-27 | At Phi. | L | 1-6 | | 7 | 6 | Padilla | Santos | | 55-71 | 6th | 28.0 |
| 8-28 | At Phi. | L | 3-4 | | 11 | 7 | Worrell | Adams | | 55-72 | 6th | 29.0 |
| 8-29 | At Phi. | L | 0-10 | | 4 | 16 | Lidle | Obermueller | | 55-73 | 6th | 30.0 |
| 8-30 | Pit. | L | 1-5 | | 7 | 8 | Fogg | Hendrickson | | 55-74 | 6th | 30.5 |
| 8-31 | Pit. | W | 4-2 | | 6 | 11 | Wise | V. Benschoten | Kolb | 56-74 | 6th | 30.5 |
| 9-1 | Pit. | L | 2-5 | (10) | 11 | 12 | Torres | Bennett | Mesa | 56-75 | 6th | 31.5 |
| 9-2 | Pit. | W | 7-1 | | 9 | 4 | Sheets | Williams | | 57-75 | 6th | 31.5 |
| 9-3 | Cin. | W | 11-4 | | 17 | 8 | Obermueller | Claussen | | 58-75 | 6th | 31.5 |
| 9-4 | Cin. | W | 7-3 | | 11 | 10 | Hendrickson | Hancock | Kolb | 59-75 | 6th | 31.5 |
| 9-5 | Cin. | L | 2-9 | | 5 | 14 | Hudson | de la Rosa | | 59-76 | 6th | 32.5 |
| 9-6 | At Pit. | W | 9-5 | | 8 | 10 | Glover | Vogelsong | Kolb | 60-76 | 6th | 31.5 |

| Date | Opp. | Res. | Score | (inn.*) | Hits | Opp. hits | Winning pitcher | Losing pitcher | Save | Record | Pos. | GB |
|---|---|---|---|---|---|---|---|---|---|---|---|---|
| 9-7 | At Pit. | L | 0-2 | | 3 | 7 | Williams | Sheets | Mesa | 60-77 | 6th | 32.5 |
| 9-9 | At Cin. | W | 7-2 | | 12 | 8 | Davis | White | | 61-77 | 6th | 31.5 |
| 9-10 | At Cin. | L | 4-6 | | 9 | 8 | Hancock | Hendrickson | Graves | 61-78 | 6th | 31.5 |
| 9-11 | At Cin. | L | 0-9 | | 4 | 11 | Hudson | Santos | | 61-79 | 6th | 31.5 |
| 9-12 | At Cin. | W | 11-0 | | 13 | 4 | Sheets | Harang | | 62-79 | 6th | 31.5 |
| 9-14 | S.F | L | 2-3 | | 7 | 4 | Rueter | Davis | Hermanson | 62-80 | 6th | 31.5 |
| 9-15 | S.F | L | 1-8 | | 4 | 11 | Tomko | Obermueller | | 62-81 | 6th | 32.5 |
| 9-16 | S.F | L | 0-4 | | 3 | 9 | Hennessey | Santos | | 62-82 | 6th | 32.5 |
| 9-17 | At Hou. | L | 1-2 | | 10 | 4 | Oswalt | Sheets | Lidge | 62-83 | 6th | 33.5 |
| 9-18 | At Hou. | L | 3-4 | | 11 | 6 | Harville | Glover | Lidge | 62-84 | 6th | 34.5 |
| 9-19 | At Hou. | L | 0-1 | | 2 | 4 | Clemens | Davis | Lidge | 62-85 | 6th | 34.5 |
| 9-20 | StL. | L | 4-7 | | 9 | 13 | Tavarez | Kolb | Isringhausen | 62-86 | 6th | 35.5 |
| 9-21 | StL. | W | 6-4 | | 11 | 9 | Santos | Marquis | Kolb | 63-86 | 6th | 34.5 |
| 9-22 | StL. | L | 2-3 | | 11 | 7 | Williams | Sheets | Isringhausen | 63-87 | 6th | 35.5 |
| 9-23 | StL. | L | 2-4 | | 4 | 9 | Eldred | Wise | Isringhausen | 63-88 | 6th | 36.5 |
| 9-24 | Hou. | L | 0-1 | (10) | 5 | 7 | Lidge | Adams | Miceli | 63-89 | 6th | 37.5 |
| 9-25 | Hou. | W | 8-0 | | 11 | 6 | Obermueller | Munro | | 64-89 | 6th | 37.5 |
| 9-26 | Hou. | L | 7-11 | | 9 | 16 | Redding | Santos | | 64-90 | 6th | 38.5 |
| 9-27 | At Ari. | L | 1-3 | | 6 | 10 | Johnson | Sheets | Aquino | 64-91 | 6th | 38.5 |
| 9-28 | At Ari. | L | 8-9 | (11) | 12 | 10 | Koplove | Kieschnick | | 64-92 | 6th | 38.5 |
| 9-29 | At Ari. | W | 4-1 | | 8 | 7 | Glover | Fossum | Vizcaino | 65-92 | 6th | 37.5 |
| 9-30 | At StL. | W | 7-6 | | 10 | 12 | Davis | Morris | Kolb | 66-92 | 6th | 36.5 |
| 10-1 | At StL. | L | 1-4 | | 3 | 8 | Ankiel | Hendrickson | Isringhausen | 66-93 | 6th | 37.5 |
| 10-2 | At StL. | W | 5-1 | | 8 | 8 | Sheets | Marquis | | 67-93 | 6th | 36.5 |
| 10-3 | At StL. | L | 4-9 | | 12 | 16 | Calero | de la Rosa | | 67-94 | 6th | 37.5 |

Monthly records: April (12-11), May (13-13), June (15-10), July (10-19), August (6-21), September (10-18), October (1-2). *Innings, if other than nine. @ At Hiram Bithorn Stadium, San Juan, Puerto Rico. ! First game of a doubleheader. & Second game of a doubleheader.

## RECORDS

**2004 regular-season record:** 67-94
**Position:** 6th in N.L. Central
**Home:** 36-45 **Road:** 31-49
**N.L. East:** 11-19 **N.L. Central:** 35-54
**N.L. West:** 13-17 **A.L.** 8-4
**Vs. LH starters:** 11-21
**Vs. RH starters:** 56-73
**Grass:** 63-92 **Artificial:** 4-2
**Day:** 24-32 **Night:** 43-62
**1-Run:** 18-20 **X-inn.:** 5-12
**Doubleheaders:** 0-1-0
**Team record past five years:** 332-477 (.410, ranks 16th in league in that span)

## TEAM LEADERS

**Batting average:** Lyle Overbay (.301).
**At-bats:** Scott Podsednik (640).
**Runs:** Geoff Jenkins (88).
**Hits:** Lyle Overbay (174).
**Total Bases:** Geoff Jenkins (292).
**Doubles:** Lyle Overbay (53).
**Triples:** Scott Podsednik (7).
**Home runs:** Geoff Jenkins (27).
**Runs batted in:** Geoff Jenkins (93).
**Stolen bases:** Scott Podsednik (70).
**Slugging percentage:** Keith Ginter (.479).
**On-base percentage:** Brady Clark (.385).
**Wins:** Doug Davis, Ben Sheets (12).
**Earned-run average:** Ben Sheets (2.70).
**Complete games:** Ben Sheets (5).
**Shutouts:** Wes Obermueller (1).
**Saves:** Dan Kolb (39).
**Innings pitched:** Ben Sheets (237.0).
**Strikeouts:** Ben Sheets (264).

## GAMES BY POSITION

**Catcher:** Chad Moeller 100, Gary Bennett 75, Mark Johnson 5.
**First base:** Lyle Overbay 158, Wes Helms 10, Russell Branyan 2.
**Second base:** Junior Spivey 58, Keith Ginter 54, Bill Hall 50, Trent Durrington 6, Matt Erickson 1.
**Third base:** Wes Helms 66, Keith Ginter 47, Russell Branyan 44, Trent Durrington 11, Bill Hall 11, Craig Counsell 1.
**Shortstop:** Craig Counsell 129, Bill Hall 37, Matt Erickson 1, Junior Spivey 1.
**Outfield:** Geoff Jenkins 156, Scott Podsednik 153, Brady Clark 133, Ben Grieve 65, Chris Magruder 24, Dave Krynzel 10, Jeff Liefer 3, Keith Ginter 2.
**Designated hitter:** Jeff Liefer 3, Keith Ginter 2, Trent Durrington 1, Ben Grieve 1.

## TOP DRAFT CHOICES

1. **Marc Rogers,** RHP, Mt. Ararat H.S., Orr's Island, Maine.
2. **Yovani Gallardo,** RHP, Trimble Tech, Fort Worth, Texas.
3. **Josh Wahpepah,** RHP, Cowley County (Kan.) CC.
4. **Josh Baker,** RHP, Rice.
5. **Angel Salome,** C, George Washington H.S., New York.
6. **Stephen Chapman,** OF, Marianna (Fla.) H.S.
7. **Greg Langille,** RHP, Charles Allen H.S., Bedford, Nova Scotia.
8. **Brandon Parillo,** LHP, Marina H.S., Huntington Beach, Calif.
9. **Derek DeCarlo,** RHP, Florida International.
10. **Steve Sollman,** 2B, Notre Dame.

# NEW YORK METS

## *NATIONAL LEAGUE EAST DIVISION*



## 2005 SEASON

### Mets Schedule

Home games shaded.
All-Star Game July 12 at Detroit. Schedule subject to change.

**April**

| SUN | MON | TUE | WED | THU | FRI | SAT |
|---|---|---|---|---|---|---|
| 3 | 4 CIN | 5 | 6 CIN | 7 CIN | 8 ATL | 9 ATL |
| 10 ATL | 11 HOU | 12 | 13 HOU | 14 HOU | 15 FLA | 16 FLA |
| 17 FLA | 18 PHI | 19 PHI | 20 FLA | 21 FLA | 22 WAS | 23 WAS |
| 24 WAS | 25 ATL | 26 ATL | 27 ATL | 28 | 29 WAS | 30 WAS |

**May**

| SUN | MON | TUE | WED | THU | FRI | SAT |
|---|---|---|---|---|---|---|
| 1 WAS | 2 PHI | 3 PHI | 4 PHI | 5 PHI | 6 MIL | 7 MIL |
| 8 MIL | 9 CHC | 10 CHC | 11 CHC | 12 | 13 STL | 14 STL |
| 15 STL | 16 CIN | 17 CIN | 18 CIN | 19 | 20 NYY | 21 NYY |
| 22 NYY | 23 ATL | 24 ATL | 25 ATL | 26 FLA | 27 FLA | 28 FLA |
| 29 FLA | 30 | 31 ARI | | | | |

**June**

| SUN | MON | TUE | WED | THU | FRI | SAT |
|---|---|---|---|---|---|---|
| | | | 1 ARI | 2 ARI | 3 SF | 4 SF |
| 5 SF | 6 | 7 HOU | 8 HOU | 9 HOU | 10 ANA | 11 ANA |
| 12 ANA | 13 | 14 OAK | 15 OAK | 16 OAK | 17 SEA | 18 SEA |
| 19 SEA | 20 | 21 PHI | 22 PHI | 23 PHI | 24 NYY | 25 NYY |
| 26 NYY | 27 | 28 PHI | 29 PHI | 30 PHI | | |

**July**

| SUN | MON | TUE | WED | THU | FRI | SAT |
|---|---|---|---|---|---|---|
| | | | | | 1 FLA | 2 FLA |
| 3 FLA | 4 WAS | 5 WAS | 6 WAS | 7 WAS | 8 PIT | 9 PIT |
| 10 PIT | 11 | 12 All-Star | 13 | 14 ATL | 15 ATL | 16 ATL |
| 17 ATL | 18 | 19 SD | 20 SD | 21 SD | 22 LA | 23 LA |
| 24 LA | 25 COL | 26 COL | 27 COL | 28 HOU | 29 HOU | 30 HOU |
| 31 HOU | | | | | | |

**August**

| SUN | MON | TUE | WED | THU | FRI | SAT |
|---|---|---|---|---|---|---|
| | 1 | 2 MIL | 3 MIL | 4 MIL | 5 CHC | 6 CHC |
| 7 CHC | 8 | 9 SD | 10 SD | 11 SD | 12 LA | 13 LA |
| 14 LA | 15 | 16 PIT | 17 PIT | 18 PIT | 19 WAS | 20 WAS |
| 21 WAS | 22 ARI | 23 ARI | 24 ARI | 25 ARI | 26 SF | 27 SF |
| 28 SF | 29 | 30 PHI | 31 PHI | | | |

**September**

| SUN | MON | TUE | WED | THU | FRI | SAT |
|---|---|---|---|---|---|---|
| | | | | 1 PHI | 2 FLA | 3 FLA |
| 4 FLA | 5 ATL | 6 ATL | 7 ATL | 8 STL | 9 STL | 10 STL |
| 11 STL | 12 | 13 WAS | 14 WAS | 15 WAS | 16 ATL | 17 ATL |
| 18 ATL | 19 | 20 FLA | 21 FLA | 22 FLA | 23 WAS | 24 WAS |
| 25 WAS | 26 PHI | 27 PHI | 28 PHI | 29 COL | 30 COL | |

**October**

| SUN | MON | TUE | WED | THU | FRI | SAT |
|---|---|---|---|---|---|---|
| | | | | | | 1 COL |
| 2 COL | 3 | 4 | 5 | 6 | 7 | 8 |

Home games shaded. All-Star Game July 12 at Detroit. Schedule subject to change.

## CLUB DIRECTORY

**Chairman and chief executive officer**
Fred Wilpon
**President**
Saul Katz
**Senior Executive Vice President & Chief Operating Officer**
Jeffrey S. Wilpon
**Executive Vice President and General Manager**
Omar Minaya
**Special assistants to the g.m.**
Tony Bernazard, Al Goldis, Sandy Johnson, Bill Livesey
**Senior v.p., baseball operations**
Jim Duquette
**Vice president, scouting and player development**
Gary LaRocque
**Executive v.p., business operations**
Dave Howard
**Vice president, media relations**
Jay Horwitz
**Director of minor league operations**
Kevin Morgan

## MINOR LEAGUE AFFILIATES

| Class | Team | League | Manager |
|---|---|---|---|
| AAA | Norfolk | International | Ken Oberkfell |
| AA | Binghamton | Eastern | Jack Lind |
| Advanced A | St. Lucie | Florida State | Tim Teufel |
| A | Hagerstown | South Atlantic | TBA |
| Short-Season A | Brooklyn | New York-Penn | Mookie Wilson |
| Advanced Rookie | Kingsport | Appalachian | Jesse Levis |
| Rookie | Gulf Coast Mets | Gulf Coast | Gary Carter |

## BROADCAST INFORMATION

**Radio:** WFAN-AM (660).
**TV:** WPIX-TV (Channel 11).
**Cable TV:** Fox Sports New York, MSG Network.

**For more on the Mets, go to msn.foxsports.com/mlb/teams.**

## SPRING TRAINING

**Ballpark (city):** Thomas J. White Stadium (Port St. Lucie, Fla.).
**Ticket information:** 772-871-2115.

Matsui

## SPRING TRAINING ROSTER

**Manager**—Willie Randolph.
**Coaches**—Manny Acta, Sandy Alomar Sr., Guy Conti, Rick Down, Jerry Manuel, Tom Nieto, Rick Peterson (51).

| No. | PITCHERS | B/T | Ht./Wt. | Age* | 2004 Clubs |
|---|---|---|---|---|---|
| 19 | Bell, Heath | R/R | 6-2/244 | 27 | Binghamton, Norfolk, New York N.L. |
| 34 | Benson, Kris | R/R | 6-4/195 | 30 | Pittsburgh, New York N.L. |
| | Bevis, P.J. | R/R | 6-3/175 | 24 | Norfolk, Binghamton |
| 35 | DeJean, Mike | R/R | 6-2/219 | 34 | Baltimore, New York N.L. |
| 55 | Feliciano, Pedro | L/L | 5-10/185 | 28 | Norfolk, New York N.L. |
| 43 | Fortunato, Bart. | R/R | 6-1/197 | 30 | Durham, Tampa Bay, Norfolk, New York N.L. |
| 13 | Ginter, Matt | R/R | 6-1/220 | 27 | Norfolk, New York N.L. |
| 47 | Glavine, Tom | L/L | 6-0/185 | 39 | New York N.L. |
| 48 | Heilman, Aaron | R/R | 6-5/220 | 26 | Norfolk, New York N.L. |
| | Heredia, Felix | L/L | 6-0/180 | 29 | New York A.L., Columbus, Tampa, Trenton |
| | Keppel, Bob | R/R | 6-5/205 | 22 | St. Lucie, Norfolk |
| | Lindstrom, Matt | R/R | 6-4/210 | 25 | Capital City, St. Lucie |
| 40 | Looper, Braden | R/R | 6-3/220 | 30 | New York N.L. |
| 45 | Martinez, Pedro | R/R | 5-11/180 | 33 | Boston |
| 26 | Seo, Jae Weong | R/R | 6-1/215 | 27 | Norfolk, New York N.L. |
| | Soler, Alay | R/R | 6-4/240 | 25 | Did Not Play |
| 29 | Trachsel, Steve | R/R | 6-4/205 | 34 | New York N.L. |
| 33 | Yates, Tyler | R/R | 6-4/220 | 27 | Norfolk, New York N.L. |
| 38 | Zambrano, Victor | B/R | 6-0/203 | 29 | Tampa Bay, New York N.L. |

| No. | CATCHERS | B/T | Ht./Wt. | Age* | 2004 Clubs |
|---|---|---|---|---|---|
| 10 | Hietpas, Joe | R/R | 6-3/220 | 25 | St. Lucie, Binghamton, New York N.L. |
| | Jacobs, Mike | L/R | 6-2/200 | 24 | Norfolk |
| 23 | Phillips, Jason | R/R | 6-1/210 | 28 | New York N.L. |
| 31 | Piazza, Mike | R/R | 6-3/215 | 36 | New York N.L., St. Lucie |
| 3 | Wilson, Vance | R/R | 5-11/190 | 32 | New York N.L., Binghamton, Norfolk |

| No. | INFIELDERS | B/T | Ht./Wt. | Age* | 2004 Clubs |
|---|---|---|---|---|---|
| | Baldiris, Aarom | R/R | 6-2/195 | 21 | St. Lucie, Binghamton |
| 9 | Brazell, Craig | L/R | 6-3/211 | 24 | Norfolk, New York N.L. |
| | Cairo, Miguel | R/R | 6-1/208 | 30 | New York A.L. |
| 12 | Garcia, Danny | R/R | 6-1/175 | 24 | Norfolk, New York N.L. |
| 6 | Keppinger, Jeff | R/R | 6-0/180 | 24 | Altoona, Binghamton, Norfolk, New York N.L. |
| 25 | Matsui, Kazuo | B/R | 5-10/185 | 29 | New York N.L. |
| 11 | McEwing, Joe | R/R | 5-11/210 | 32 | New York N.L. |
| 7 | Reyes, Jose | B/R | 6-0/160 | 21 | St. Lucie, Binghamton, New York N.L. |
| 5 | Wright, David | R/R | 6-0/200 | 22 | Binghamton, Norfolk, New York N.L. |

| No. | OUTFIELDERS | B/T | Ht./Wt. | Age* | 2004 Clubs |
|---|---|---|---|---|---|
| | Beltran, Carlos | B/R | 6-1/190 | 27 | Kansas City, Houston |
| | Calloway, Ron | L/L | 6-1/198 | 28 | Montreal, Edmonton |
| 44 | Cameron, Mike | R/R | 6-2/200 | 32 | New York N.L. |
| | Concepcion, A. | R/R | 6-2/180 | 21 | Brooklyn |
| 50 | Diaz, Victor | R/R | 6-0/200 | 23 | Norfolk, New York N.L. |
| 30 | Floyd, Cliff | L/R | 6-4/230 | 32 | New York N.L., St. Lucie |
| | Lydon, Wayne | R/R | 6-2/190 | 23 | Binghamton |
| | Pagan, Angel | B/R | 6-1/180 | 23 | Binghamton, Norfolk |
| 57 | Valent, Eric | L/L | 5-11/195 | 27 | New York N.L. |

*Age as of April 1, 2005.

## BALLPARK INFORMATION

**Ballpark (capacity, surface)**
Shea Stadium (57,373, grass)
**Address**
123-01 Roosevelt Ave.
Flushing, NY 11368
**Official website**
www.mets.com
**Business phone**
718-507-METS
**Ticket information**
718-507-TIXX
**Field dimensions (from home plate)**
To left field at foul line, 338 feet
To center field, 410 feet
To right field at foul line, 338 feet
**First game played**
April 17, 1964 (Pirates 4, Mets 3)

# 2004 REVIEW
## DAY BY DAY



| Date | Opp. | Res. | Score | (inn.*) | Hits | Opp. hits | Winning pitcher | Losing pitcher | Save | Record | Pos. | GB |
|---|---|---|---|---|---|---|---|---|---|---|---|---|
| 4-6 | At Atl. | W | 7-2 | | 10 | 6 | Glavine | Ortiz | | 1-0 | T1st | ... |
| 4-7 | At Atl. | L | 10-18 | | 15 | 19 | Gryboski | Trachsel | | 1-1 | T1st | ... |
| 4-8 | At Atl. | L | 8-10 | | 13 | 15 | Cunnane | Franco | Smoltz | 1-2 | T3rd | 1.0 |
| 4-9@ | At Mon. | W | 3-2 | (11) | 8 | 8 | Weathers | Ayala | Moreno | 2-2 | T2nd | 1.0 |
| 4-10@ | At Mon. | L | 0-1 | | 3 | 7 | Patterson | Seo | Biddle | 2-3 | T3rd | 2.0 |
| 4-11@ | At Mon. | W | 4-1 | | 8 | 6 | Glavine | Hernandez | Looper | 3-3 | T2nd | 2.0 |
| 4-12 | Atl. | W | 10-6 | | 13 | 10 | Trachsel | Hampton | Looper | 4-3 | 2nd | 1.5 |
| 4-14 | Atl. | L | 1-6 | | 8 | 9 | Thomson | Yates | | 4-4 | T2nd | 3.0 |
| 4-15 | Atl. | W | 4-0 | | 9 | 4 | Leiter | Ramirez | | 5-4 | 2nd | 3.0 |
| 4-16 | Pit. | L | 6-7 | | 8 | 8 | Wells | Moreno | Mesa | 5-5 | T2nd | 3.0 |
| 4-17 | Pit. | L | 1-2 | | 4 | 10 | Meadows | Trachsel | Mesa | 5-6 | 3rd | 3.0 |
| 4-18 | Pit. | L | 1-8 | | 6 | 17 | Benson | Seo | | 5-7 | 4th | 3.0 |
| 4-19 | Mon. | W | 4-1 | | 8 | 10 | Yates | Ohka | Looper | 6-7 | 3rd | 2.5 |
| 4-20 | Mon. | L | 1-2 | | 4 | 8 | Day | Weathers | Biddle | 6-8 | 3rd | 3.5 |
| 4-21 | Mon. | L | 1-2 | | 8 | 6 | Hernandez | Glavine | Biddle | 6-9 | 3rd | 4.5 |
| 4-22 | Mon. | W | 3-2 | | 6 | 5 | Trachsel | Bentz | Looper | 7-9 | 3rd | 4.5 |
| 4-23 | At Chi. | L | 1-3 | | 8 | 4 | Maddux | Seo | Borowski | 7-10 | 3rd | 4.5 |
| 4-24 | At Chi. | L | 0-3 | | 4 | 8 | Wood | Yates | Hawkins | 7-11 | 4th | 5.5 |
| 4-25 | At Chi. | L | 1-4 | | 2 | 10 | Clement | Leiter | Borowski | 7-12 | 4th | 5.5 |
| 4-27 | At L.A. | W | 9-5 | | 13 | 14 | Glavine | Nomo | | 8-12 | 4th | 5.0 |
| 4-28 | At L.A. | L | 2-3 | | 9 | 5 | Perez | Trachsel | Gagne | 8-13 | 4th | 6.0 |
| 4-29 | At L.A. | W | 6-1 | | 10 | 8 | Seo | Weaver | | 9-13 | 4th | 6.0 |
| 4-30 | At S.D. | L | 6-7 | | 12 | 12 | Lawrence | Yates | Otsuka | 9-14 | 4th | 6.0 |
| 5-1 | At S.D. | L | 1-3 | | 10 | 7 | Peavy | Franco | Hoffman | 9-15 | 4th | 6.0 |
| 5-2 | At S.D. | W | 6-2 | | 9 | 6 | Glavine | Valdez | | 10-15 | 4th | 5.0 |
| 5-4 | S.F | W | 6-2 | | 14 | 6 | Trachsel | Tomko | | 11-15 | 4th | 4.0 |
| 5-5 | S.F | W | 8-2 | | 11 | 6 | Weathers | Rodriguez | | 12-15 | 4th | 4.0 |
| 5-6 | S.F | W | 2-1 | (11) | 5 | 7 | Weathers | Brower | | 13-15 | 3rd | 3.0 |
| 5-7 | Mil. | L | 5-7 | | 8 | 11 | Davis | Glavine | | 13-16 | 4th | 4.0 |
| 5-8 | Mil. | L | 4-6 | | 2 | 12 | Kinney | Yates | Kolb | 13-17 | 4th | 4.0 |
| 5-9 | Mil. | W | 6-5 | (11) | 12 | 11 | Wheeler | Ford | | 14-17 | 4th | 4.0 |
| 5-10 | At Ari. | L | 8-12 | | 17 | 14 | Daigle | Baldwin | | 14-18 | 4th | 4.5 |
| 5-11 | At Ari. | L | 5-9 | | 7 | 10 | Bruney | Leiter | | 14-19 | 4th | 4.5 |
| 5-12 | At Ari. | W | 1-0 | | 3 | 3 | Glavine | Johnson | Looper | 15-19 | 3rd | 4.5 |
| 5-13 | At Ari. | W | 7-4 | | 8 | 8 | Seo | Webb | Looper | 16-19 | 3rd | 4.5 |
| 5-14 | At Hou. | W | 8-3 | | 11 | 6 | Trachsel | Oswalt | | 17-19 | 3rd | 3.5 |
| 5-15 | At Hou. | L | 4-7 | | 6 | 12 | Pettitte | Baldwin | Dotel | 17-20 | 4th | 3.5 |
| 5-16 | At Hou. | W | 3-2 | (13) | 7 | 14 | Wheeler | Backe | | 18-20 | 3rd | 3.5 |
| 5-18 | StL. | W | 5-4 | | 10 | 9 | Bottalico | Isringhausen | | 19-20 | 3rd | 2.5 |
| 5-19 | StL. | L | 0-1 | | 4 | 8 | Eldred | Stanton | Kline | 19-21 | 3rd | 3.0 |
| 5-20 | StL. | L | 4-11 | | 8 | 15 | Marquis | Seo | | 19-22 | 3rd | 4.0 |
| 5-21 | Col. | W | 9-7 | | 14 | 11 | Ginter | Young | | 20-22 | 3rd | 4.0 |
| 5-22 | Col. | W | 5-4 | | 7 | 10 | Weathers | Nunez | Looper | 21-22 | 3rd | 3.5 |
| 5-23 | Col. | W | 4-0 | | 9 | 1 | Glavine | Estes | | 22-22 | 3rd | 3.0 |
| 5-25 | Phi. | W | 5-0 | | 7 | 4 | Trachsel | Milton | | 23-22 | 3rd | 2.0 |
| 5-26 | Phi. | L | 4-7 | | 9 | 8 | Hernandez | Franco | Worrell | 23-23 | 3rd | 3.0 |
| 5-28 | At Fla. | L | 1-2 | | 5 | 6 | Willis | Glavine | Benitez | 23-24 | T3rd | 4.5 |
| 5-29 | At Fla. | L | 2-3 | (10) | 7 | 8 | Wayne | Looper | | 23-25 | 4th | 5.5 |
| 5-30 | At Fla. | L | 6-8 | | 11 | 9 | Borland | Stanton | Benitez | 23-26 | 4th | 6.5 |
| 5-31 | At Phi. | W | 5-3 | | 10 | 5 | Moreno | Myers | Looper | 24-26 | 4th | 5.5 |
| 6-1 | At Phi. | W | 4-1 | (10) | 9 | 9 | Bottalico | Worrell | Looper | 25-26 | 4th | 4.5 |
| 6-2 | At Phi. | W | 5-3 | (10) | 8 | 5 | Weathers | Hernandez | Looper | 26-26 | T3rd | 3.5 |
| 6-3 | Fla. | W | 4-1 | | 8 | 3 | Seo | Burnett | Looper | 27-26 | T3rd | 2.5 |
| 6-4 | Fla. | L | 1-5 | | 6 | 9 | Pavano | Trachsel | Benitez | 27-27 | T3rd | 3.5 |
| 6-5 | Fla. | L | 6-7 | | 12 | 14 | Perisho | Weathers | Benitez | 27-28 | T3rd | 4.5 |
| 6-6 | Fla. | W | 5-2 | | 10 | 10 | Leiter | Penny | | 28-28 | T3rd | 3.5 |
| 6-8 | At Min. | L | 1-2 | | 5 | 7 | Rincon | Stanton | | 28-29 | 4th | 4.5 |
| 6-9 | At Min. | L | 3-5 | | 9 | 8 | Santana | Trachsel | Nathan | 28-30 | 4th | 4.5 |
| 6-10 | At Min. | L | 2-3 | (15) | 8 | 12 | Balfour | Bottalico | | 28-31 | 4th | 5.5 |
| 6-11 | At K.C. | L | 5-7 | | 17 | 9 | May | Seo | Affeldt | 28-32 | 4th | 5.5 |
| 6-12 | At K.C. | L | 3-4 | | 8 | 6 | Affeldt | Weathers | | 28-33 | 4th | 5.5 |
| 6-13 | At K.C. | W | 5-2 | | 5 | 4 | Glavine | Greinke | Looper | 29-33 | 4th | 5.5 |
| 6-15 | Cle. | W | 7-2 | | 14 | 10 | Trachsel | Davis | | 30-33 | 4th | 4.5 |
| 6-16 | Cle. | L | 1-9 | | 6 | 14 | Sabathia | Ginter | | 30-34 | 4th | 5.5 |
| 6-17 | Cle. | W | 6-2 | | 8 | 5 | Bottalico | White | | 31-34 | T3rd | 5.5 |
| 6-18 | Det. | W | 3-2 | | 7 | 8 | Looper | Patterson | | 32-34 | 3rd | 4.5 |

| Date | Opp. | Res. | Score | (inn.*) | Hits | Opp. hits | Winning pitcher | Losing pitcher | Save | Record | Pos. | GB |
|---|---|---|---|---|---|---|---|---|---|---|---|---|
| 6-19 | Det. | W | 4-3 | (10) | 9 | 9 | Looper | Dingman | | 33-34 | 3rd | 3.5 |
| 6-20 | Det. | W | 6-1 | | 7 | 5 | Trachsel | Bonderman | | 34-34 | 3rd | 2.5 |
| 6-22 | Cin. | W | 7-4 | | 11 | 10 | Franco | Wilson | Looper | 35-34 | 3rd | 2.5 |
| 6-23 | Cin. | L | 4-6 | (12) | 13 | 14 | Matthews | Franco | Graves | 35-35 | 3rd | 3.5 |
| 6-24 | Cin. | L | 2-6 | | 9 | 11 | Lidle | Glavine | | 35-36 | 3rd | 3.5 |
| 6-26 | At N.Y. | W | 9-3 | | 12 | 6 | Leiter | Halsey | | 36-36 | 3rd | 2.0 |
| 6-27# | At N.Y. | L | 1-8 | | 3 | 8 | Contreras | Trachsel | Gordon | 36-37 | | |
| 6-27$ | At N.Y. | L | 6-11 | | 10 | 12 | Mussina | Ginter | | 36-38 | 3rd | 3.5 |
| 6-29 | At Cin. | W | 7-5 | | 7 | 12 | Seo | Van Poppel | Looper | 37-38 | 3rd | 3.0 |
| 6-30 | At Cin. | L | 0-2 | | 4 | 9 | Lidle | Glavine | Graves | 37-39 | 3rd | 3.0 |
| 7-1 | At Cin. | W | 7-6 | | 12 | 9 | Leiter | Acevedo | Looper | 38-39 | 3rd | 3.0 |
| 7-2 | N.Y. | W | 11-2 | | 14 | 4 | Trachsel | Mussina | | 39-39 | 3rd | 2.0 |
| 7-3 | N.Y. | W | 10-9 | | 11 | 12 | Franco | Sturtze | | 40-39 | 2nd | 2.0 |
| 7-4 | N.Y. | W | 6-5 | | 8 | 16 | Moreno | Gordon | Looper | 41-39 | 2nd | 2.0 |
| 7-5 | At Phi. | L | 5-6 | | 6 | 11 | Madson | Glavine | Wagner | 41-40 | 2nd | 3.0 |
| 7-6 | At Phi. | W | 4-1 | | 11 | 5 | Leiter | Wolf | Looper | 42-40 | 2nd | 2.0 |
| 7-7 | At Phi. | W | 10-1 | | 18 | 6 | Trachsel | Myers | | 43-40 | 2nd | 1.0 |
| 7-8 | At Phi. | L | 4-5 | | 11 | 8 | Wagner | Franco | | 43-41 | T2nd | 2.0 |
| 7-9 | At Fla. | W | 6-3 | | 9 | 8 | Wheeler | Manzanillo | Looper | 44-41 | 2nd | 2.0 |
| 7-10 | At Fla. | L | 2-5 | | 9 | 11 | Penny | Glavine | Benitez | 44-42 | T2nd | 2.0 |
| 7-11 | At Fla. | L | 2-5 | | 6 | 5 | Willis | Leiter | Benitez | 44-43 | 4th | 2.0 |
| 7-15 | Phi. | W | 3-2 | (11) | 8 | 7 | Parra | Hernandez | | 45-43 | T3rd | 1.0 |
| 7-16 | Phi. | L | 1-5 | | 4 | 12 | Millwood | Seo | Wagner | 45-44 | T3rd | 2.0 |
| 7-17 | Phi. | L | 2-8 | | 10 | 12 | Wolf | Glavine | | 45-45 | T3rd | 3.0 |
| 7-18 | Phi. | W | 6-1 | | 12 | 6 | Leiter | Myers | Looper | 46-45 | 3rd | 2.0 |
| 7-19 | Fla. | L | 5-6 | | 9 | 13 | Manzanillo | Looper | Benitez | 46-46 | T3rd | 3.0 |
| 7-20 | Fla. | L | 7-9 | | 10 | 13 | Howard | Franco | Benitez | 46-47 | 4th | 3.0 |
| 7-21 | Mon. | W | 5-4 | | 9 | 13 | Moreno | Horgan | Looper | 47-47 | T3rd | 3.0 |
| 7-22 | Mon. | L | 1-4 | | 9 | 8 | Ayala | Franco | Cordero | 47-48 | 4th | 3.0 |
| 7-24 | Atl. | L | 2-5 | | 7 | 11 | Thomson | Stanton | Smoltz | 47-49 | 4th | 4.0 |
| 7-25 | Atl. | L | 3-4 | | 7 | 7 | Hampton | Trachsel | Smoltz | 47-50 | 4th | 5.0 |
| 7-26 | At Mon. | L | 10-19 | | 16 | 18 | Ayala | Erickson | | 47-51 | 4th | 6.0 |
| 7-27 | At Mon. | W | 4-2 | | 9 | 10 | Glavine | Day | Looper | 48-51 | 4th | 5.0 |
| 7-28 | At Mon. | L | 4-7 | | 6 | 8 | Tucker | Seo | Cordero | 48-52 | 4th | 6.0 |
| 7-29 | At Mon. | W | 10-1 | | 14 | 6 | Leiter | Biddle | | 49-52 | 4th | 6.0 |
| 7-30 | At Atl. | L | 1-3 | | 7 | 9 | Hampton | Trachsel | Smoltz | 49-53 | 4th | 7.0 |
| 7-31 | At Atl. | L | 0-8 | | 5 | 11 | Wright | Benson | | 49-54 | 4th | 8.0 |
| 8-1 | At Atl. | L | 5-6 | | 6 | 14 | Byrd | Glavine | Smoltz | 49-55 | 4th | 9.0 |
| 8-3 | At Mil. | W | 12-3 | | 16 | 8 | Leiter | Capuano | | 50-55 | 4th | 8.0 |
| 8-4 | At Mil. | W | 6-5 | | 6 | 10 | Feliciano | Adams | Looper | 51-55 | 4th | 8.0 |
| 8-5 | At Mil. | W | 11-6 | | 10 | 10 | Zambrano | Santos | | 52-55 | 4th | 8.0 |
| 8-6 | At StL. | L | 4-6 | | 7 | 11 | Morris | Glavine | Isringhausen | 52-56 | 4th | 9.0 |
| 8-7 | At StL. | L | 1-2 | | 3 | 5 | Tavarez | Stanton | | 52-57 | 4th | 10.0 |
| 8-8 | At StL. | L | 2-6 | | 7 | 12 | Marquis | Leiter | Tavarez | 52-58 | 4th | 11.0 |
| 8-10 | Hou. | W | 7-3 | | 10 | 7 | Trachsel | Munro | | 53-58 | 4th | 10.0 |
| 8-11 | Hou. | L | 4-5 | (10) | 6 | 12 | Lidge | Looper | Bullinger | 53-59 | 4th | 11.0 |
| 8-12 | Hou. | W | 2-1 | | 8 | 2 | Zambrano | Weathers | Looper | 54-59 | 4th | 11.0 |
| 8-13 | Ari. | W | 10-6 | | 11 | 8 | Benson | Fossum | | 55-59 | 4th | 10.0 |
| 8-14 | Ari. | W | 4-3 | | 8 | 10 | Leiter | Gonzalez | Looper | 56-59 | 4th | 10.0 |
| 8-15 | Ari. | L | 0-2 | | 5 | 10 | Johnson | Trachsel | Aquino | 56-60 | 4th | 10.0 |
| 8-17 | At Col. | L | 4-6 | | 7 | 12 | Jennings | Wheeler | Chacon | 56-61 | 4th | 10.5 |
| 8-19# | At Col. | W | 10-3 | | 15 | 12 | Benson | Estes | | 57-61 | | |
| 8-19$ | At Col. | W | 4-2 | | 6 | 6 | Stanton | Reed | | 58-61 | 4th | 10.5 |
| 8-20 | At S.F | L | 3-7 | | 8 | 13 | Lowry | Trachsel | | 58-62 | 4th | 10.5 |
| 8-21 | At S.F | W | 11-9 | (12) | 17 | 15 | Stanton | Correia | Fortunato | 59-62 | 4th | 9.5 |
| 8-22 | At S.F | L | 1-3 | | 8 | 7 | Rueter | Ginter | Hermanson | 59-63 | 4th | 10.5 |
| 8-23 | S.D. | L | 4-9 | | 6 | 13 | Peavy | Heilman | | 59-64 | 4th | 11.0 |
| 8-24 | S.D. | L | 1-3 | | 4 | 9 | Wells | Benson | Hoffman | 59-65 | 4th | 12.0 |
| 8-25 | S.D. | L | 0-4 | | 6 | 10 | Lawrence | Leiter | | 59-66 | 4th | 13.0 |
| 8-26 | S.D. | L | 3-10 | | 6 | 16 | Eaton | Trachsel | | 59-67 | 4th | 14.0 |
| 8-27 | L.A. | W | 9-2 | | 14 | 9 | Glavine | Alvarez | | 60-67 | 4th | 14.0 |
| 8-28 | L.A. | L | 2-4 | | 4 | 11 | Carrara | Stanton | Gagne | 60-68 | 4th | 15.0 |
| 8-29 | L.A. | L | 2-10 | | 6 | 12 | Ishii | Benson | | 60-69 | 4th | 15.0 |
| 8-30 | Fla. | L | 4-6 | | 10 | 12 | Seanez | Bell | Benitez | 60-70 | 4th | 16.0 |
| 8-31 | Fla. | L | 0-5 | | 6 | 5 | Beckett | Trachsel | | 60-71 | 4th | 17.0 |
| 9-1 | Fla. | L | 4-5 | | 9 | 8 | Valdez | Glavine | Benitez | 60-72 | 4th | 18.0 |
| 9-2 | Fla. | L | 6-9 | | 10 | 12 | Pavano | Seo | | 60-73 | 4th | 18.5 |
| 9-3 | At Phi. | L | 1-8 | | 4 | 9 | Floyd | Bell | | 60-74 | 4th | 19.5 |
| 9-4 | At Phi. | L | 0-7 | | 3 | 7 | Lidle | Leiter | | 60-75 | 4th | 20.5 |

| Date | Opp. | Res. | Score | (inn.*) | Hits | Opp. hits | Winning pitcher | Losing pitcher | Save | Record | Pos. | GB |
|---|---|---|---|---|---|---|---|---|---|---|---|---|
| 9-5 | At Phi. | L | 2-4 | | 3 | 7 | Myers | Trachsel | Worrell | 60-76 | 4th | 20.5 |
| 9-7 | At Fla. | L | 3-7 | | 3 | 11 | Burnett | Glavine | | 60-77 | 4th | 21.5 |
| 9-8 | At Fla. | L | 0-3 | | 4 | 8 | Beckett | Seo | Benitez | 60-78 | 4th | 21.0 |
| 9-9 | At Fla. | W | 4-0 | | 11 | 7 | Benson | Valdez | | 61-78 | 4th | 20.0 |
| 9-10 | Phi. | L | 5-9 | | 10 | 13 | Jones | Bottalico | | 61-79 | 4th | 21.0 |
| 9-11 | Phi. | L | 9-11 | (13) | 15 | 13 | Hernandez | Darensbourg | Rodriguez | 61-80 | 4th | 22.0 |
| 9-12 | Phi. | L | 2-4 | | 9 | 8 | Padilla | Glavine | Worrell | 61-81 | 4th | 23.0 |
| 9-13! | Atl. | W | 9-7 | | 11 | 11 | Heilman | Wright | | 62-81 | | |
| 9-13& | Atl. | L | 1-7 | | 7 | 13 | Byrd | Seo | | 62-82 | 4th | 23.0 |
| 9-14 | Atl. | W | 7-0 | | 12 | 4 | Benson | Ortiz | | 63-82 | 4th | 22.0 |
| 9-15 | Atl. | L | 0-2 | | 6 | 4 | Thomson | Leiter | Smoltz | 63-83 | 4th | 23.0 |
| 9-16 | Atl. | W | 9-4 | | 12 | 9 | Trachsel | Capellan | | 64-83 | 4th | 22.0 |
| 9-18 | At Pit. | W | 8-7 | (10) | 11 | 7 | Yates | Torres | Looper | 65-83 | 4th | 22.5 |
| 9-19! | At Pit. | L | 0-1 | | 3 | 2 | Vogelsong | Heilman | Mesa | 65-84 | | |
| 9-19& | At Pit. | L | 1-6 | | 6 | 7 | Williams | Benson | | 65-85 | 4th | 23.0 |
| 9-21 | At Mon. | L | 1-6 | | 6 | 11 | Hernandez | Leiter | | 65-86 | 4th | 24.0 |
| 9-22 | At Mon. | W | 3-2 | | 9 | 6 | Fortunato | Ayala | Looper | 66-86 | 4th | 23.0 |
| 9-23 | At Mon. | W | 4-2 | | 9 | 7 | Glavine | Ohka | Looper | 67-86 | 4th | 22.0 |
| 9-24 | Chi. | L | 1-2 | (10) | 9 | 7 | Remlinger | Looper | Hawkins | 67-87 | 4th | 23.0 |
| 9-25 | Chi. | W | 4-3 | (11) | 6 | 7 | Seo | Mercker | | 68-87 | 4th | 23.0 |
| 9-26 | Chi. | W | 3-2 | | 8 | 3 | Leiter | Wood | Looper | 69-87 | 4th | 23.0 |
| 9-28! | At Atl. | W | 2-1 | | 8 | 4 | Trachsel | Byrd | Looper | 70-87 | | |
| 9-28& | At Atl. | L | 2-5 | | 11 | 7 | Colon | Glavine | Smoltz | 70-88 | 4th | 23.0 |
| 9-29 | At Atl. | L | 3-6 | | 7 | 10 | Ortiz | Heilman | Smoltz | 70-89 | 4th | 24.0 |
| 10-1 | Mon. | L | 2-4 | | 6 | 11 | Rauch | Feliciano | Cordero | 70-90 | 4th | 25.0 |
| 10-2 | Mon. | L | 3-6 | | 9 | 9 | Cordero | Looper | Majewski | 70-91 | 4th | 26.0 |
| 10-3 | Mon. | W | 8-1 | | 11 | 5 | Glavine | Patterson | | 71-91 | 4th | 25.0 |

Monthly records: April (9-14), May (15-12), June (13-13), July (12-15), August (11-17), September (10-18), October (1-2). *Innings, if other than nine. @ At Hiram Bithorn Stadium, San Juan, Puerto Rico. ! First game of a doubleheader. & Second game of a doubleheader. # Day separate admission. $ Night separate admission.

## RECORDS

**2004 regular-season record:** 71-91
**Position:** 4th in N.L. East
**Home:** 38-43 **Road:** 33-48
**N.L. East:** 29-47 **N.L. Central:** 15-21
**N.L. West:** 17-15 **A.L.** 10-8
**Vs. LH starters:** 17-27
**Vs. RH starters:** 54-64
**Grass:** 65-84 **Artificial:** 6-7
**Day:** 25-31 **Night:** 46-60
**1-Run:** 23-24 **X-inn.:** 11-6
**Doubleheaders:** 0-1-2
**Team record past five years:** 388-420 (.480, ranks 10th in league in that span)

## TEAM LEADERS

**Batting average:** Ty Wigginton (.285).
**At-bats:** Mike Cameron (493).
**Runs:** Mike Cameron (76).
**Hits:** Kazuo Matsui (125).
**Total Bases:** Mike Cameron (236).
**Doubles:** Kazuo Matsui (32).
**Triples:** Karim Garcia, Kazuo Matsui, Jose Reyes, Eric Valent, Ty Wigginton, Gerald Williams (2).
**Home runs:** Mike Cameron (30).
**Runs batted in:** Mike Cameron (76).
**Stolen bases:** Mike Cameron (22).
**Slugging percentage:** David Wright (.525).
**On-base percentage:** Mike Piazza (.362).
**Wins:** Steve Trachsel (12).
**Earned-run average:** Al Leiter (3.21).
**Complete games:** Kris Benson, Tom Glavine (1).
**Shutouts:** Kris Benson, Tom Glavine (1).
**Saves:** Braden Looper (29).
Innings pitched: Tom Glavine (212.1).
**Strikeouts:** Al Leiter, Steve Trachsel (117).

## GAMES BY POSITION

**Catcher:** Jason Phillips 87, Vance Wilson 69, Mike Piazza 50, Tom Wilson 3, Todd Zeile 2, Joe Hietpas 1.
**First base**: Mike Piazza 68, Todd Zeile 67, Jason Phillips 38, Eric Valent 27, Joe McEwing 11, Craig Brazell 7, Ty Wigginton 5, Brian Buchanan 1, Shane Spencer 1.
**Second base:** Danny Garcia 44, Jose Reyes 43, Joe McEwing 34, Jeff Keppinger 32, Ty Wigginton 25, Ricky Gutierrez 18, Kazuo Matsui 3.
Third base: David Wright 69, Ty Wigginton 66, Todd Zeile 46, Ricky Gutierrez 2, Joe McEwing 1.
**Shortstop:** Kazuo Matsui 110, Wilson Delgado 39, Joe McEwing 13, Jose Reyes 10.
**Outfield:** Mike Cameron 135, Cliff Floyd 106, Richard Hidalgo 86, Shane Spencer 62, Karim Garcia 51, Eric Valent 46, Gerald Williams 45, Joe McEwing 15, Victor Diaz 14, Jeff Duncan 4, Esix Snead 1.
**Designated hitter:** Mike Piazza 8, Cliff Floyd 1, Shane Spencer 1.

## TOP DRAFT CHOICES

1. **Philip Humber**, RHP, Rice.
2. **Matt Durkin**, RHP, San Jos State.
3. **Gaby Hernandez**, RHP, Belen Jesuit H.S., Miami.
4. **Aaron Hathaway,** C, Washington.
5. **Nick Evans,** 3B, St. Mary's H.S., Phoenix.
6. **Ryan Coultas,** SS, UC Davis.
7. **Scott Hyde,** RHP, George Fox University.
8. **Neil Jamison,** RHP, Long Beach State.
9. **Mike Carp,** 1B, Lakewood (Calif.) H.S.
10. **Brahiam Maldonado,** OF, St. Francis H.S., Loiza, Puerto Rico.

# PHILADELPHIA PHILLIES
## *NATIONAL LEAGUE EAST DIVISION*



## 2005 SEASON

**Phillies Schedule**
Home games shaded.
All-Star Game July 12 at Detroit. Schedule subject to change.

**April**

| SUN | MON | TUE | WED | THU | FRI | SAT |
|---|---|---|---|---|---|---|
| 3 | 4 WAS | 5 | 6 WAS | 7 WAS | 8 STL | 9 STL |
| 10 STL | 11 FLA | 12 FLA | 13 FLA | 14 | 15 ATL | 16 ATL |
| 17 ATL | 18 NYM | 19 NYM | 20 COL | 21 COL | 22 ATL | 23 ATL |
| 24 ATL | 25 WAS | 26 WAS | 27 WAS | 28 | 29 FLA | 30 FLA |

**May**

| SUN | MON | TUE | WED | THU | FRI | SAT |
|---|---|---|---|---|---|---|
| 1 FLA | 2 NYM | 3 NYM | 4 NYM | 5 NYM | 6 CHC | 7 CHC |
| 8 CHC | 9 MIL | 10 MIL | 11 MIL | 12 CIN | 13 CIN | 14 CIN |
| 15 CIN | 16 | 17 STL | 18 STL | 19 STL | 20 BAL | 21 BAL |
| 22 BAL | 23 FLA | 24 FLA | 25 FLA | 26 | 27 ATL | 28 ATL |
| 29 ATL | 30 | 31 SF | | | | |

**June**

| SUN | MON | TUE | WED | THU | FRI | SAT |
|---|---|---|---|---|---|---|
| | | | 1 SF | 2 SF | 3 ARI | 4 ARI |
| 5 ARI | 6 ARI | 7 TEX | 8 TEX | 9 TEX | 10 MIL | 11 MIL |
| 12 MIL | 13 | 14 SEA | 15 SEA | 16 SEA | 17 OAK | 18 OAK |
| 19 OAK | 20 | 21 NYM | 22 NYM | 23 NYM | 24 BOS | 25 BOS |
| 26 BOS | 27 | 28 NYM | 29 NYM | 30 NYM | | |

**July**

| SUN | MON | TUE | WED | THU | FRI | SAT |
|---|---|---|---|---|---|---|
| | | | | | 1 ATL | 2 ATL |
| 3 ATL | 4 PIT | 5 PIT | 6 PIT | 7 PIT | 8 WAS | 9 WAS |
| 10 WAS | 11 | 12 All-Star | 13 | 14 FLA | 15 FLA | 16 FLA |
| 17 FLA | 18 | 19 LA | 20 LA | 21 LA | 22 SD | 23 SD |
| 24 SD | 25 HOU | 26 HOU | 27 HOU | 28 COL | 29 COL | 30 COL |
| 31 COL | | | | | | |

**August**

| SUN | MON | TUE | WED | THU | FRI | SAT |
|---|---|---|---|---|---|---|
| | 1 | 2 CHC | 3 CHC | 4 CHC | 5 MIL | 6 MIL |
| 7 MIL | 8 | 9 LA | 10 LA | 11 LA | 12 SD | 13 SD |
| 14 SD | 15 WAS | 16 WAS | 17 WAS | 18 WAS | 19 PIT | 20 PIT |
| 21 PIT | 22 SF | 23 SF | 24 SF | 25 | 26 ARI | 27 ARI |
| 28 ARI | 29 | 30 NYM | 31 NYM | | | |

**September**

| SUN | MON | TUE | WED | THU | FRI | SAT |
|---|---|---|---|---|---|---|
| | | | | 1 NYM | 2 WAS | 3 WAS |
| 4 WAS | 5 HOU | 6 HOU | 7 HOU | 8 | 9 FLA | 10 FLA |
| 11 FLA | 12 ATL | 13 ATL | 14 ATL | 15 ATL | 16 FLA | 17 FLA |
| 18 FLA | 19 | 20 ATL | 21 ATL | 22 ATL | 23 CIN | 24 CIN |
| 25 CIN | 26 NYM | 27 NYM | 28 NYM | 29 | 30 WAS | |

**October**

| SUN | MON | TUE | WED | THU | FRI | SAT |
|---|---|---|---|---|---|---|
| | | | | | | 1 WAS |
| 2 WAS | 3 | 4 | 5 | 6 | 7 | 8 |

Home games shaded. All-Star Game July 12 at Detroit. Schedule subject to change.

### CLUB DIRECTORY

**General partner, president and CEO**
David Montgomery

**Chairman**
Bill Giles

**Vice president & general manager**
Ed Wade

**Vice president, public relations**
Larry Shenk

**Assistant general manager**
Ruben Amaro Jr.

**Asst. g.m., scouting & player dev.**
Mike Arbuckle

**Director, minor league operations**
Steve Noworyta

**Director, media relations**
Leigh Tobin

**Director, community relations**
Gene Dias

### MINOR LEAGUE AFFILIATES

| **Class** | **Team** | **League** | **Manager** |
|---|---|---|---|
| AAA | Scranton/Wilkes-Barre | International | Gene Lamont |
| AA | Reading | Eastern | Steve Swisher |
| Advanced A | Clearwater | Florida State | Greg Legg |
| A | Lakewood | South Atlantic | P.J. Forbes |
| Short-Season A | Batavia | New York-Penn | Manny Amador |
| Rookie | Gulf Coast Phillies | Gulf Coast | Jim Morrison |

### BROADCAST INFORMATION

**Radio:** WPHT-AM (950); WIP-AM (610) on Fridays.
**TV:** UPN (Channel 57).
**Cable TV:** Comcast SportsNet.

### SPRING TRAINING

**Ballpark (city):** Bright House Networks Field (Clearwater, Fla.).
**Ticket information:** 215-463-1000, 727-442-8496.

**For more on the Phillies, go to msn.foxsports.com/mlb/teams.**

Thome

## SPRING TRAINING ROSTER

**Manager**—Charlie Manuel (41)

**Coaches**—Mick Billmeyer (17), Marc Bombard (23), Bill Dancy (16), Rich Dubee (28), Ramon Henderson (31), Milt Thompson (15), Gary Varsho.

| No. | PITCHERS | B/T | Ht./Wt. | Age* | 2004 Clubs |
|---|---|---|---|---|---|
| | Adams, Terry | R/R | 6-3/220 | 32 | Toronto, Boston |
| | Brito, Eude | L/L | 5-11/160 | 26 | Reading |
| | Bucktrot, Keith | L/R | 6-2/220 | 24 | Reading |
| | Butto, Francisco | R/R | 6-1/200 | 24 | Clearwater |
| 37 | Cormier, Rheal | L/L | 5-10/195 | 37 | Philadelphia |
| 41 | Floyd, Gavin | R/R | 6-4/212 | 22 | Reading, Scranton/W.B., Philadelphia |
| 46 | Fultz, Aaron | L/L | 6-0/205 | 31 | Rochester, Minnesota |
| 56 | Geary, Geoff | R/R | 6-0/167 | 28 | Scranton/W.B., Philadelphia |
| 30 | Lidle, Cory | R/R | 5-11/192 | 33 | Cincinnati, Philadelphia |
| | Lieber, Jon | L/R | 6-2/230 | 34 | Tampa, New York A.L. |
| | Liriano, Pedro | R/R | 6-2/170 | 24 | Indianapolis, Milwaukee |
| 63 | Madson, Ryan | L/R | 6-6/190 | 24 | Reading, Philadelphia |
| 39 | Myers, Brett | R/R | 6-4/223 | 24 | Philadelphia |
| 44 | Padilla, Vicente | R/R | 6-2/219 | 27 | Clearwater, Scranton/W.B., Philadelphia |
| | Perez, Franklin | R/R | 6-2/230 | 26 | Reading, Scranton/WB |
| | Segovia, Zach | R/R | 6-2/220 | 21 | Did Not Play |
| | Tejeda, Rob | R/R | 6-3/190 | 23 | Reading |
| 47 | Telemaco, Amaury | R/R | 6-3/234 | 31 | Scranton/W.B., Philadelphia |
| 13 | Wagner, Billy | L/L | 5-11/195 | 33 | Reading, Philadelphia |
| 43 | Wolf, Randy | L/L | 6-0/200 | 28 | Reading, Philadelphia |
| 45 | Worrell, Tim | R/R | 6-4/230 | 37 | Philadelphia |

| No. | CATCHERS | B/T | Ht./Wt. | Age* | 2004 Clubs |
|---|---|---|---|---|---|
| 24 | Lieberthal, Mike | R/R | 6-0/190 | 33 | Philadelphia |
| 7 | Pratt, Todd | R/R | 6-3/236 | 38 | Philadelphia |
| | Ruiz, Carlos | R/R | 5-10/180 | 26 | Reading |

| No. | INFIELDERS | B/T | Ht./Wt. | Age* | 2004 Clubs |
|---|---|---|---|---|---|
| 4 | Bell, David | R/R | 5-10/181 | 32 | Philadelphia |
| 9 | Perez, Tomas | B/R | 5-11/192 | 31 | Philadelphia |
| 27 | Polanco, Placido | R/R | 5-10/190 | 29 | Reading, Scranton/W.B., Philadelphia |
| | Richardson, Juan | R/R | 6-1/215 | 26 | Clearwater, Reading |
| 11 | Rollins, Jimmy | B/R | 5-8/167 | 26 | Philadelphia |
| 25 | Thome, Jim | L/R | 6-4/244 | 34 | Philadelphia |
| 26 | Utley, Chase | L/R | 6-1/183 | 26 | Scranton/W.B., Philadelphia |
| 12 | Howard, Ryan | L/L | 6-4/230 | 25 | Reading, Scranton/W.B., Philadelphia |

| No. | OUTFIELDERS | B/T | Ht./Wt. | Age* | 2004 Clubs |
|---|---|---|---|---|---|
| 53 | Abreu, Bobby | L/R | 6-0/211 | 31 | Philadelphia |
| 5 | Burrell, Pat | R/R | 6-4/223 | 28 | Reading, Philadelphia |
| 29 | Byrd, Marlon | R/R | 6-0/229 | 27 | Scranton/W.B., Philadelphia |
| | Lofton, Kenny | L/L | 6-0/180 | 37 | Trenton, New York A.L. |
| 22 | Michaels, Jason | R/R | 6-0/204 | 28 | Philadelphia |
| | Roberson, Chris | R/R | 6-2/175 | 25 | Clearwater |
| | Victorino, Shane | B/R | 5-9/160 | 24 | Jacksonville, Las Vegas |

*Age as of April 1, 2005.

## BALLPARK INFORMATION

**Ballpark (capacity, surface)**
Citizens Bank Park (43,500, grass)

**Address**
One Citizens Bank Way
Philadelphia, PA 19148

**Official website**
www.phillies.com

**Business phone**
215-463-6000

**Ticket information**
215-463-1000

**Field dimensions (from home plate)**
To left field at foul line, 329 feet
To center field, 401 feet
To right field at foul line, 330 feet

**First game played**
April 12, 2004 (Reds 4, Phillies 1)

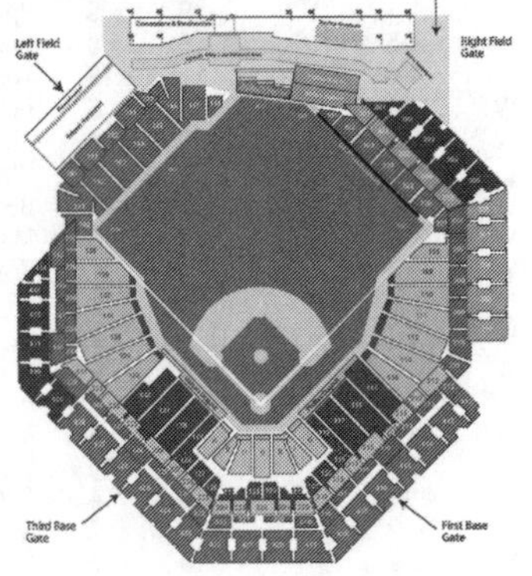

# 2004 REVIEW

## DAY BY DAY

| Date | Opp. | Res. | Score | (inn.*) | Hits | Opp. hits | Winning pitcher | Losing pitcher | Save | Record | Pos. | GB |
|---|---|---|---|---|---|---|---|---|---|---|---|---|
| 4-5 | At Pit. | L | 1-2 | | 6 | 7 | Wells | Millwood | Mesa | 0-1 | 5th | 0.5 |
| 4-7 | At Pit. | W | 5-4 | | 10 | 11 | Cormier | Boehringer | Wagner | 1-1 | T1st | ... |
| 4-8 | At Pit. | L | 2-6 | | 9 | 10 | Vogelsong | Padilla | Mesa | 1-2 | T3rd | 1.0 |
| 4-9 | At Fla. | L | 3-4 | | 8 | 11 | Perisho | Cormier | Benitez | 1-3 | T4th | 2.0 |
| 4-10 | At Fla. | L | 3-5 | | 9 | 11 | Oliver | Cormier | Benitez | 1-4 | 5th | 3.0 |
| 4-11 | At Fla. | L | 1-3 | | 3 | 5 | Beckett | Millwood | Benitez | 1-5 | 5th | 4.0 |
| 4-12 | Cin. | L | 1-4 | | 6 | 11 | Wilson | Wolf | Graves | 1-6 | 5th | 4.5 |
| 4-15 | Cin. | W | 6-4 | | 8 | 7 | Cormier | Wagner | Wagner | 2-6 | 4th | 5.5 |
| 4-16 | Mon. | W | 4-2 | | 9 | 5 | Milton | Hernandez | Wagner | 3-6 | 4th | 4.5 |
| 4-17 | Mon. | W | 6-3 | | 7 | 7 | Millwood | Patterson | Wagner | 4-6 | 4th | 3.5 |
| 4-18 | Mon. | W | 5-4 | | 8 | 9 | Wagner | Biddle | | 5-6 | 3rd | 2.5 |
| 4-20 | Fla. | L | 1-3 | | 4 | 7 | Willis | Padilla | Benitez | 5-7 | 4th | 3.5 |
| 4-21 | Fla. | L | 7-8 | (12) | 13 | 15 | Wayne | Madson | | 5-8 | 4th | 4.5 |
| 4-22 | Fla. | L | 7-9 | | 11 | 13 | Oliver | Myers | Benitez | 5-9 | 4th | 5.5 |
| 4-23 | At Mon. | W | 8-6 | | 12 | 12 | Millwood | Bentz | Wagner | 6-9 | 4th | 4.5 |
| 4-24 | At Mon. | W | 7-0 | | 17 | 4 | Wolf | Ohka | | 7-9 | 3rd | 4.5 |
| 4-25 | At Mon. | L | 0-2 | | 9 | 5 | Day | Padilla | Biddle | 7-10 | 3rd | 4.5 |
| 4-27 | At StL. | W | 7-3 | | 11 | 10 | Milton | Morris | | 8-10 | 3rd | 4.0 |
| 4-28 | At StL. | W | 6-3 | | 7 | 9 | Madson | Lincoln | Wagner | 9-10 | 3rd | 4.0 |
| 4-29 | At StL. | L | 4-5 | (13) | 8 | 14 | Lincoln | Telemaco | | 9-11 | 3rd | 5.0 |
| 4-30 | Ari. | W | 4-0 | | 6 | 5 | Wolf | Dessens | | 10-11 | 3rd | 4.0 |
| 5-1 | Ari. | L | 4-6 | | 9 | 12 | Johnson | Padilla | Mantei | 10-12 | 3rd | 4.0 |
| 5-2 | Ari. | W | 6-5 | (14) | 8 | 11 | Madson | Villarreal | | 11-12 | 3rd | 3.0 |
| 5-4 | StL. | L | 5-6 | | 8 | 10 | Carpenter | Myers | Isringhausen | 11-13 | 3rd | 3.0 |
| 5-5 | StL. | W | 5-4 | | 7 | 8 | Millwood | Williams | Wagner | 12-13 | 3rd | 3.0 |
| 5-6 | StL. | L | 4-7 | | 8 | 10 | Suppan | Wolf | Isringhausen | 12-14 | 4th | 3.0 |
| 5-7 | At Ari. | W | 4-1 | | 8 | 6 | Padilla | Johnson | Wagner | 13-14 | 2nd | 3.0 |
| 5-8 | At Ari. | W | 8-7 | | 10 | 13 | Milton | Webb | Worrell | 14-14 | 2nd | 2.0 |
| 5-9 | At Ari. | W | 7-1 | | 10 | 9 | Myers | Sparks | | 15-14 | 2nd | 2.0 |
| 5-11 | At S.F | W | 10-4 | | 15 | 9 | Millwood | Williams | | 16-14 | 2nd | 1.0 |
| 5-12 | At S.F | L | 3-4 | | 7 | 8 | Schmidt | Wolf | Herges | 16-15 | 2nd | 2.0 |
| 5-13 | At S.F | W | 4-3 | | 7 | 10 | Padilla | Rueter | Madson | 17-15 | 2nd | 2.0 |
| 5-14 | At Col. | W | 6-4 | | 10 | 9 | Milton | Kennedy | Worrell | 18-15 | 2nd | 1.0 |
| 5-15 | At Col. | W | 16-5 | | 18 | 7 | Myers | Elarton | | 19-15 | 1st | ... |
| 5-16 | At Col. | L | 6-7 | | 11 | 12 | Harikkala | Cormier | Chacon | 19-16 | 2nd | 1.0 |
| 5-17 | At Col. | L | 6-7 | | 12 | 14 | Fuentes | Worrell | | 19-17 | 2nd | 1.5 |
| 5-18 | L.A. | W | 8-7 | | 11 | 10 | Padilla | Mota | Worrell | 20-17 | 2nd | 0.5 |
| 5-19 | L.A. | W | 9-4 | | 11 | 12 | Milton | Nomo | | 21-17 | 1st | +0.5 |
| 5-20 | L.A. | W | 4-0 | | 8 | 5 | Myers | Ishii | | 22-17 | 1st | +0.5 |
| 5-21 | S.D. | W | 5-4 | | 7 | 8 | Madson | Otsuka | Worrell | 23-17 | 1st | +0.5 |
| 5-22 | S.D. | L | 6-9 | | 12 | 11 | Germano | Hernandez | | 23-18 | 2nd | 0.5 |
| 5-23 | S.D. | W | 6-4 | | 8 | 11 | Padilla | Lawrence | Worrell | 24-18 | 1st | +0.5 |
| 5-25 | At N.Y. | L | 0-5 | | 4 | 7 | Trachsel | Milton | | 24-19 | 1st | ... |
| 5-26 | At N.Y. | W | 7-4 | | 8 | 9 | Hernandez | Franco | Worrell | 25-19 | 1st | ... |
| 5-27 | Atl. | L | 1-6 | | 6 | 9 | Wright | Millwood | | 25-20 | 2nd | 1.0 |
| 5-28 | Atl. | W | 3-2 | (10) | 12 | 9 | Worrell | Alfonseca | | 26-20 | 2nd | 1.0 |
| 5-29 | Atl. | L | 3-9 | | 9 | 13 | Thomson | Padilla | | 26-21 | 2nd | 2.0 |
| 5-30 | Atl. | W | 4-1 | | 4 | 4 | Milton | Smith | Worrell | 27-21 | 2nd | 2.0 |
| 5-31 | N.Y. | L | 3-5 | | 5 | 10 | Moreno | Myers | Looper | 27-22 | 2nd | 2.0 |
| 6-1 | N.Y. | L | 1-4 | (10) | 9 | 9 | Bottalico | Worrell | Looper | 27-23 | 2nd | 2.0 |
| 6-2 | N.Y. | L | 3-5 | (10) | 5 | 8 | Weathers | Hernandez | Looper | 27-24 | 2nd | 2.0 |
| 6-3 | At Atl. | L | 4-8 | | 11 | 13 | Thomson | Hancock | | 27-25 | 2nd | 2.0 |
| 6-4 | At Atl. | W | 9-1 | | 11 | 6 | Milton | Smith | | 28-25 | 2nd | 2.0 |
| 6-5 | At Atl. | W | 5-3 | | 10 | 8 | Myers | Ortiz | Worrell | 29-25 | 2nd | 2.0 |
| 6-6 | At Atl. | L | 4-6 | | 9 | 9 | Wright | Millwood | Smoltz | 29-26 | 2nd | 2.0 |
| 6-8 | At Chi. | L | 11-14 | | 15 | 15 | Buehrle | Telemaco | Politte | 29-27 | 2nd | 3.0 |
| 6-9 | At Chi. | W | 13-10 | | 14 | 14 | Milton | Garland | | 30-27 | 2nd | 2.0 |
| 6-11 | At Min. | W | 11-6 | | 14 | 12 | Worrell | Mulholland | | 31-27 | 2nd | 1.5 |
| 6-12 | At Min. | L | 1-6 | | 9 | 11 | Silva | Millwood | | 31-28 | 2nd | 1.5 |
| 6-13 | At Min. | W | 2-1 | | 7 | 7 | Cormier | Fultz | Wagner | 32-28 | 2nd | 1.5 |
| 6-14 | Cin. | W | 10-7 | | 13 | 13 | Madson | Riedling | | 33-28 | 2nd | 1.0 |
| 6-15 | Det. | L | 3-10 | | 2 | 11 | Bonderman | Powell | | 33-29 | 2nd | 1.0 |
| 6-17# | Det. | W | 6-2 | | 7 | 7 | Myers | Maroth | | 34-29 | | |
| 6-17$ | Det. | L | 4-5 | (11) | 11 | 14 | Urbina | Madson | Patterson | 34-30 | 2nd | 2.0 |
| 6-18 | K.C. | L | 4-10 | | 10 | 14 | George | Abbott | | 34-31 | 2nd | 2.0 |
| 6-19 | K.C. | W | 4-2 | | 6 | 7 | Milton | Greinke | Wagner | 35-31 | 2nd | 1.0 |
| 6-20 | K.C. | W | 8-2 | | 10 | 7 | Powell | Reyes | | 36-31 | 1st | ... |

| Date | Opp. | Res. | Score | (inn.*) | Hits | Opp. hits | Winning pitcher | Losing pitcher | Save | Record | Pos. | GB |
|---|---|---|---|---|---|---|---|---|---|---|---|---|
| 6-22 | At Mon. | L | 2-5 | | 4 | 10 | Hernandez | Myers | Cordero | 36-32 | 2nd | 1.0 |
| 6-23 | At Mon. | W | 5-2 | | 8 | 6 | Millwood | Kim | Wagner | 37-32 | 2nd | 1.0 |
| 6-24 | At Mon. | L | 2-3 | | 5 | 7 | Armas | Milton | Cordero | 37-33 | 2nd | 1.0 |
| 6-25 | At Bos. | L | 1-12 | (8) | 2 | 13 | Martinez | Abbott | | 37-34 | 2nd | 1.0 |
| 6-26 | At Bos. | W | 9-2 | | 13 | 14 | Madson | Arroyo | | 38-34 | 1st | ... |
| 6-27 | At Bos. | L | 3-12 | | 12 | 12 | Schilling | Myers | | 38-35 | 2nd | 1.0 |
| 6-28 | Mon. | W | 14-6 | | 15 | 6 | Millwood | Kim | | 39-35 | 1st | ... |
| 6-29 | Mon. | W | 17-7 | | 17 | 8 | Milton | Hill | | 40-35 | 1st | ... |
| 6-30 | Mon. | L | 3-6 | | 8 | 9 | Horgan | Worrell | Cordero | 40-36 | 1st | ... |
| 7-1 | Mon. | W | 10-5 | | 16 | 8 | Wolf | Downs | | 41-36 | 1st | +1.0 |
| 7-2 | Bal. | L | 6-7 | (16) | 10 | 15 | Rodriguez | Powell | Cabrera | 41-37 | 1st | +1.0 |
| 7-3 | Bal. | W | 7-6 | | 10 | 9 | Cormier | Grimsley | Wagner | 42-37 | 1st | +2.0 |
| 7-4 | Bal. | W | 5-2 | | 10 | 8 | Milton | Ponson | Worrell | 43-37 | 1st | +2.0 |
| 7-5 | N.Y. | W | 6-5 | | 11 | 6 | Madson | Glavine | Wagner | 44-37 | 1st | +3.0 |
| 7-6 | N.Y. | L | 1-4 | | 5 | 11 | Leiter | Wolf | Looper | 44-38 | 1st | +2.0 |
| 7-7 | N.Y. | L | 1-10 | | 6 | 18 | Trachsel | Myers | | 44-39 | 1st | +1.0 |
| 7-8 | N.Y. | W | 5-4 | | 8 | 11 | Wagner | Franco | | 45-39 | 1st | +2.0 |
| 7-9 | Atl. | W | 7-6 | (10) | 12 | 11 | Wagner | Alfonseca | | 46-39 | 1st | +2.0 |
| 7-10 | Atl. | L | 0-4 | | 5 | 7 | Hampton | Abbott | | 46-40 | 1st | +2.0 |
| 7-11 | Atl. | L | 4-6 | | 8 | 16 | Ortiz | Wolf | Smoltz | 46-41 | 1st | +1.0 |
| 7-15 | At N.Y. | L | 2-3 | (11) | 7 | 8 | Parra | Hernandez | | 46-42 | T1st | ... |
| 7-16 | At N.Y. | W | 5-1 | | 12 | 4 | Millwood | Seo | Wagner | 47-42 | 1st | +1.0 |
| 7-17 | At N.Y. | W | 8-2 | | 12 | 10 | Wolf | Glavine | | 48-42 | 1st | +1.0 |
| 7-18 | At N.Y. | L | 1-6 | | 6 | 12 | Leiter | Myers | Looper | 48-43 | T1st | ... |
| 7-19 | At Atl. | L | 2-4 | | 6 | 9 | Hampton | Abbott | Smoltz | 48-44 | 2nd | 1.0 |
| 7-20 | At Atl. | W | 4-3 | (10) | 8 | 8 | Worrell | Alfonseca | Wagner | 49-44 | T1st | ... |
| 7-21 | Fla. | W | 2-1 | | 8 | 7 | Millwood | Burnett | Wagner | 50-44 | 1st | +1.0 |
| 7-22 | Fla. | L | 8-10 | | 13 | 15 | Pavano | Wolf | Benitez | 50-45 | T1st | ... |
| 7-23 | Chi. | L | 1-5 | | 7 | 8 | Wood | Myers | | 50-46 | 2nd | 0.5 |
| 7-24 | Chi. | W | 4-3 | | 9 | 10 | Abbott | Zambrano | Worrell | 51-46 | 2nd | 0.5 |
| 7-25 | Chi. | W | 3-2 | | 7 | 3 | Madson | Hawkins | | 52-46 | 2nd | 0.5 |
| 7-26 | At Fla. | L | 3-11 | | 12 | 12 | Burnett | Millwood | Bump | 52-47 | 2nd | 1.5 |
| 7-27 | At Fla. | L | 2-5 | | 7 | 8 | Pavano | Cormier | Manzanillo | 52-48 | 2nd | 1.5 |
| 7-28 | At Fla. | L | 3-6 | | 9 | 7 | Manzanillo | Worrell | | 52-49 | 2nd | 2.5 |
| 7-29 | At Fla. | L | 1-10 | | 5 | 15 | Willis | Abbott | | 52-50 | T2nd | 3.5 |
| 7-30 | At Chi. | L | 7-10 | | 11 | 14 | Leicester | Cormier | Hawkins | 52-51 | T2nd | 4.5 |
| 7-31 | At Chi. | W | 4-3 | | 5 | 3 | Millwood | Clement | Worrell | 53-51 | 2nd | 4.5 |
| 8-1 | At Chi. | L | 3-6 | | 11 | 8 | Mercker | Wolf | Hawkins | 53-52 | 2nd | 5.5 |
| 8-3 | At S.D. | W | 5-2 | | 8 | 9 | Myers | Lawrence | | 54-52 | 2nd | 4.5 |
| 8-4 | At S.D. | W | 7-5 | | 11 | 13 | Milton | Eaton | Worrell | 55-52 | 2nd | 4.5 |
| 8-5 | At S.D. | W | 5-3 | (10) | 9 | 9 | Rodriguez | Hoffman | Worrell | 56-52 | 2nd | 4.5 |
| 8-6 | At L.A. | W | 9-5 | (11) | 15 | 12 | Hernandez | Gagne | | 57-52 | 2nd | 4.5 |
| 8-7 | At L.A. | L | 3-6 | | 9 | 7 | Perez | Abbott | Gagne | 57-53 | 2nd | 5.5 |
| 8-8 | At L.A. | W | 4-1 | | 8 | 4 | Myers | Penny | | 58-53 | 2nd | 5.5 |
| 8-9 | Col. | L | 2-4 | | 6 | 6 | Harikkala | Jones | Chacon | 58-54 | 2nd | 6.0 |
| 8-10 | Col. | L | 4-5 | | 9 | 7 | Reed | Worrell | Chacon | 58-55 | 2nd | 6.0 |
| 8-11 | Col. | W | 15-4 | | 14 | 10 | Wolf | Jennings | | 59-55 | 2nd | 6.0 |
| 8-12 | Col. | L | 1-3 | | 5 | 8 | Estes | Lidle | Chacon | 59-56 | 2nd | 7.0 |
| 8-13 | S.F | L | 6-16 | | 9 | 18 | Hennessey | Myers | | 59-57 | 2nd | 7.0 |
| 8-14 | S.F | L | 6-7 | | 11 | 11 | Christiansen | Rodriguez | Hermanson | 59-58 | 2nd | 8.0 |
| 8-15 | S.F | L | 1-3 | | 6 | 5 | Tomko | Padilla | Hermanson | 59-59 | T2nd | 8.0 |
| 8-17 | Hou. | L | 0-5 | | 5 | 8 | Oswalt | Wolf | | 59-60 | 3rd | 8.5 |
| 8-18 | Hou. | L | 8-9 | | 11 | 13 | Harville | Jones | Lidge | 59-61 | 3rd | 9.5 |
| 8-19 | Hou. | L | 10-12 | | 14 | 15 | Qualls | Hernandez | Lidge | 59-62 | 3rd | 10.5 |
| 8-20 | At Mil. | W | 4-2 | | 6 | 5 | Milton | Davis | Worrell | 60-62 | 3rd | 9.5 |
| 8-21 | At Mil. | W | 8-6 | | 12 | 8 | Geary | Vizcaino | Worrell | 61-62 | 3rd | 8.5 |
| 8-22 | At Mil. | W | 9-6 | (10) | 12 | 7 | Rodriguez | Kolb | Worrell | 62-62 | 3rd | 8.5 |
| 8-23 | At Hou. | L | 4-8 | | 10 | 10 | Clemens | Lidle | | 62-63 | 3rd | 9.0 |
| 8-24 | At Hou. | L | 2-4 | | 7 | 8 | Oswalt | Jones | Lidge | 62-64 | 3rd | 10.0 |
| 8-25 | At Hou. | L | 4-7 | | 5 | 7 | Qualls | Rodriguez | Lidge | 62-65 | 3rd | 11.0 |
| 8-27 | Mil. | W | 6-1 | | 6 | 7 | Padilla | Santos | | 63-65 | 3rd | 11.5 |
| 8-28 | Mil. | W | 4-3 | | 7 | 11 | Worrell | Adams | | 64-65 | 3rd | 11.5 |
| 8-29 | Mil. | W | 10-0 | | 16 | 4 | Lidle | Obermueller | | 65-65 | 3rd | 10.5 |
| 8-30 | At Chi. | L | 8-9 | | 12 | 15 | Buehrle | Hernandez | Takatsu | 65-66 | 3rd | 11.5 |
| 8-31 | Atl. | L | 3-5 | | 6 | 10 | Hampton | Milton | | 65-67 | 3rd | 12.5 |
| 9-1 | Atl. | L | 2-7 | | 9 | 13 | Wright | Padilla | | 65-68 | 3rd | 13.5 |
| 9-3 | N.Y. | W | 8-1 | | 9 | 4 | Floyd | Bell | | 66-68 | 3rd | 13.5 |
| 9-4 | N.Y. | W | 7-0 | | 7 | 3 | Lidle | Leiter | | 67-68 | 3rd | 13.5 |
| 9-5 | N.Y. | W | 4-2 | | 7 | 3 | Myers | Trachsel | Worrell | 68-68 | 3rd | 12.5 |
| 9-6 | At Atl. | L | 1-3 | | 7 | 12 | Smith | Milton | Smoltz | 68-69 | 3rd | 13.5 |

| Date | Opp. | Res. | Score | (inn.*) | Hits | Opp. hits | Winning pitcher | Losing pitcher | Save | Record | Pos. | GB |
|---|---|---|---|---|---|---|---|---|---|---|---|---|
| 9-8! | At Atl. | W | 5-3 | | 11 | 4 | Madson | Reitsma | Wagner | 69-69 | | |
| 9-8& | At Atl. | W | 4-1 | | 10 | 3 | Jones | Byrd | Worrell | 70-69 | 3rd | 11.5 |
| 9-9 | At Atl. | W | 9-4 | | 14 | 9 | Madson | Colon | | 71-69 | 3rd | 10.5 |
| 9-10 | At N.Y. | W | 9-5 | | 13 | 10 | Jones | Bottalico | | 72-69 | 3rd | 10.5 |
| 9-11 | At N.Y. | W | 11-9 | (13) | 13 | 15 | Hernandez | Darensbourg | Rodriguez | 73-69 | 3rd | 10.5 |
| 9-12 | At N.Y. | W | 4-2 | | 8 | 9 | Padilla | Glavine | Worrell | 74-69 | 3rd | 10.5 |
| 9-13 | At Cin. | L | 3-4 | | 6 | 10 | Valentine | Rodriguez | Graves | 74-70 | 3rd | 11.0 |
| 9-14 | At Cin. | L | 6-7 | | 11 | 8 | Wagner | Madson | Graves | 74-71 | 3rd | 11.0 |
| 9-15 | At Cin. | W | 9-1 | | 14 | 4 | Myers | Claussen | | 75-71 | 3rd | 11.0 |
| 9-17 | Mon. | L | 8-12 | | 10 | 12 | Ayala | Worrell | | 75-72 | 3rd | 11.5 |
| 9-18 | Mon. | L | 5-6 | (14) | 11 | 11 | Cordero | Myers | Beltran | 75-73 | 3rd | 12.5 |
| 9-19 | Mon. | W | 7-2 | | 14 | 8 | Floyd | Downs | | 76-73 | 3rd | 11.5 |
| 9-21 | At Fla. | W | 4-2 | | 6 | 3 | Lidle | Willis | Wagner | 77-73 | 3rd | 11.5 |
| 9-22 | At Fla. | W | 12-4 | | 13 | 9 | Milton | Kensing | | 78-73 | 3rd | 10.5 |
| 9-23 | At Fla. | W | 9-8 | (10) | 12 | 10 | Wagner | Benitez | Jones | 79-73 | T2nd | 9.5 |
| 9-24 | At Mon. | L | 1-8 | | 7 | 11 | Kim | Myers | | 79-74 | T2nd | 10.5 |
| 9-25 | At Mon. | W | 4-3 | (10) | 10 | 6 | Worrell | Eischen | Wagner | 80-74 | 2nd | 10.5 |
| 9-26 | At Mon. | W | 2-1 | | 10 | 4 | Lidle | Hernandez | Wagner | 81-74 | 2nd | 10.5 |
| 9-27 | Pit. | L | 1-6 | | 5 | 6 | Perez | Milton | | 81-75 | 2nd | 11.0 |
| 9-29! | Pit. | W | 8-4 | | 13 | 10 | Padilla | Snell | | 82-75 | | |
| 9-29& | Pit. | W | 8-3 | | 11 | 8 | Myers | Torres | | 83-75 | 2nd | 10.5 |
| 9-30 | Fla. | W | 7-4 | | 13 | 8 | Jones | Mota | Wagner | 84-75 | 2nd | 10.0 |
| 10-1 | Fla. | W | 6-2 | | 11 | 12 | Lidle | Perisho | | 85-75 | 2nd | 10.0 |
| 10-2 | Fla. | L | 3-4 | | 9 | 5 | Beckett | Milton | Benitez | 85-76 | 2nd | 11.0 |
| 10-3 | Fla. | W | 10-4 | | 15 | 6 | Myers | Valdez | | 86-76 | 2nd | 10.0 |

Monthly records: April (10-11), May (17-11), June (13-14), July (13-15), August (12-16), September (19-8), October (2-1).
*Innings, if other than nine. ! First game of a doubleheader. & Second game of a doubleheader. # Day separate admission. $ Night separate admission.

## RECORDS

**2004 regular-season record:** 86-76
**Position:** 2nd in N.L. East
**Home:** 42-39 **Road:** 44-37
**N.L. East:** 39-37 **N.L. Central:** 18-18
**N.L. West:** 20-12 **A.L.** 9-9
**Vs. LH starters:** 23-23
**Vs. RH starters:** 63-53
**Grass:** 79-71 **Artificial:** 7-5
**Day:** 29-27 **Night:** 57-49
**1-Run:** 23-20 **X-inn.:** 10-8
**Doubleheaders:** 2-0-0
**Team record past five years:** 403-406 (.498, ranks 8th in league in that span)

## TEAM LEADERS

**Batting average:** Bobby Abreu (.301).
**At-bats:** Jimmy Rollins (657).
**Runs:** Jimmy Rollins (119).
**Hits:** Jimmy Rollins (190).
**Total Bases:** Bobby Abreu (312).
**Doubles:** Bobby Abreu (47).
**Triples:** Jimmy Rollins (12).
**Home runs:** Jim Thome (42).
**Runs batted in:** Bobby Abreu, Jim Thome (105).
**Stolen bases:** Bobby Abreu (40).
**Slugging percentage:** Jim Thome (.581).
**On-base percentage:** Bobby Abreu (.428).
**Wins:** Eric Milton (14).
**Earned-run average:** Randy Wolf (4.28).
**Complete games:** Cory Lidle (2).
**Shutouts:** Cory Lidle (2).
**Saves:** Billy Wagner (21).
**Innings pitched:** Eric Milton (201.0).
**Strikeouts:** Eric Milton (161).

## GAMES BY POSITION

**Catcher:** Mike Lieberthal 129, Todd Pratt 43, A.J. Hinch 4.
**First base:** Jim Thome 134, Chase Utley 13, Shawn Wooten 11, Tomas Perez 10, Ryan Howard 8.
**Second base:** Placido Polanco 109, Chase Utley 50, Tomas Perez 17.
**Third base:** David Bell 142, Tomas Perez 22, Placido Polanco 13, Shawn Wooten 4, Lou Collier 1.
**Shortstop:** Jimmy Rollins 154, Tomas Perez 10.
**Outfield:** Bobby Abreu 158, Pat Burrell 122, Marlon Byrd 92, Jason Michaels 78, Doug Glanville 68, Ricky Ledee 22, Lou Collier 8.
**Designated hitter:** Jim Thome 6, Ricky Ledee 2, Jason Michaels 1.

## TOP DRAFT CHOICES

1. **Greg Golson,** OF, John Connally H.S., Austin, Texas.
2. **Jason Jaramillo,** C, Oklahoma State.
3. **J.A. Happ,** LHP, Northwestern.
4. **Louis Marson,** C, Coronado H.S., Scottsdale, Ariz.
5. **Andy Baldwin,** LHP, Oregon State.
6. **Sean Gamble,** OF, Auburn.
7. **John Hardy,** 2B, Arizona.
8. **Sam Orr,** SS, Biola (Calif.).
9. **Andy Macfarlane,** OF, Treasure Valley CC (Ore.).
10. **Charles Cresswell,** C, Perryton (Texas) H.S.

# PITTSBURGH PIRATES

## *NATIONAL LEAGUE CENTRAL DIVISION*



## 2005 SEASON

### Pirates Schedule

Home games shaded.
All-Star Game July 12 at Detroit. Schedule subject to change.

**April**

| SUN | MON | TUE | WED | THU | FRI | SAT |
|---|---|---|---|---|---|---|
| 3 | 4 MIL | 5 | 6 MIL | 7 SD | 8 SD | 9 SD |
| 10 SD | 11 MIL | 12 MIL | 13 MIL | 14 | 15 CHC | 16 CHC |
| 17 CHC | 18 STL | 19 STL | 20 CIN | 21 CIN | 22 CHC | 23 CHC |
| 24 CHC | 25 HOU | 26 HOU | 27 HOU | 28 | 29 SF | 30 SF |

**May**

| SUN | MON | TUE | WED | THU | FRI | SAT |
|---|---|---|---|---|---|---|
| 1 SF | 2 HOU | 3 HOU | 4 HOU | 5 ARI | 6 ARI | 7 ARI |
| 8 ARI | 9 SF | 10 SF | 11 SF | 12 | 13 MIL | 14 MIL |
| 15 MIL | 16 | 17 CHC | 18 CHC | 19 | 20 COL | 21 COL |
| 22 COL | 23 STL | 24 STL | 25 STL | 26 CIN | 27 CIN | 28 CIN |
| 29 CIN | 30 FLA | 31 FLA | | | | |

**June**

| SUN | MON | TUE | WED | THU | FRI | SAT |
|---|---|---|---|---|---|---|
| | | | 1 FLA | 2 FLA | 3 ATL | 4 ATL |
| 5 ATL | 6 BAL | 7 BAL | 8 BAL | 9 | 10 TB | 11 TB |
| 12 TB | 13 | 14 NYY | 15 NYY | 16 NYY | 17 BOS | 18 BOS |
| 19 BOS | 20 WAS | 21 WAS | 22 WAS | 23 STL | 24 STL | 25 STL |
| 26 STL | 27 | 28 WAS | 29 WAS | 30 WAS | | |

**July**

| SUN | MON | TUE | WED | THU | FRI | SAT |
|---|---|---|---|---|---|---|
| | | | | | 1 MIL | 2 MIL |
| 3 MIL | 4 PHI | 5 PHI | 6 PHI | 7 PHI | 8 NYM | 9 NYM |
| 10 NYM | 11 | 12 All-Star | 13 | 14 | 15 CHC | 16 CHC |
| 17 CHC | 18 HOU | 19 HOU | 20 HOU | 21 COL | 22 COL | 23 COL |
| 24 COL | 25 | 26 FLA | 27 FLA | 28 FLA | 29 ATL | 30 ATL |
| 31 ATL | | | | | | |

**August**

| SUN | MON | TUE | WED | THU | FRI | SAT |
|---|---|---|---|---|---|---|
| | 1 ATL | 2 SD | 3 SD | 4 SD | 5 LA | 6 LA |
| 7 LA | 8 | 9 COL | 10 COL | 11 COL | 12 HOU | 13 HOU |
| 14 HOU | 15 | 16 NYM | 17 NYM | 18 NYM | 19 PHI | 20 PHI |
| 21 PHI | 22 STL | 23 STL | 24 STL | 25 STL | 26 CIN | 27 CIN |
| 28 CIN | 29 CIN | 30 MIL | 31 MIL | | | |

**September**

| SUN | MON | TUE | WED | THU | FRI | SAT |
|---|---|---|---|---|---|---|
| | | | | 1 | 2 CHC | 3 CHC |
| 4 CHC | 5 | 6 ARI | 7 ARI | 8 ARI | 9 CIN | 10 CIN |
| 11 CIN | 12 STL | 13 STL | 14 STL | 15 | 16 CIN | 17 CIN |
| 18 CIN | 19 HOU | 20 HOU | 21 HOU | 22 HOU | 23 LA | 24 LA |
| 25 LA | 26 LA | 27 CHC | 28 CHC | 29 | 30 MIL | |

**October**

| SUN | MON | TUE | WED | THU | FRI | SAT |
|---|---|---|---|---|---|---|
| | | | | | | 1 MIL |
| 2 MIL | 3 | 4 | 5 | 6 | 7 | 8 |

Home games shaded. All-Star Game July 12 at Detroit. Schedule subject to change.

### CLUB DIRECTORY

**General partner**
Kevin S. McClatchy
**Sr. v.p. and general manager**
Dave Littlefield
**Special assistants to the g.m.**
John Flores, Jax Robertson, Doug Strange, Pete Vuckovich, Louie Eljaua
**Vice president, sales and marketing**
Tim Schuldt
**Vice president, communications**
Patty Paytas
**Director of media relations**
Jim Trdinich
**Director of player development**
Brian Graham
**Director of promotions & advertising**
Rick Orienza

### MINOR LEAGUE AFFILIATES

| Class | Team | League | Manager |
|---|---|---|---|
| AAA | Indianapolis | International | Trent Jewett |
| AA | Altoona | Eastern | Tony Beasley |
| Advanced A | Lynchburg | Carolina | Tim Leiper |
| A | Hickory | South Atlantic | Jeff Branson |
| Short-Season A | Williamsport | New York-Penn | Tom Prince |
| Rookie | Gulf Coast Pirates | Gulf Coast | Jeff Livesey |

### BROADCAST INFORMATION

**Radio:** KDKA-AM (1020).
**Cable TV:** Fox Sports Pittsburgh.

### SPRING TRAINING

**Ballpark (city):** McKechnie Field (Bradenton, Fla.).
**Ticket information:** 941-748-4610.

**For more on the Pirates, go to msn.foxsports.com/mlb/teams.**

Perez

## SPRING TRAINING ROSTER

**Manager**— Lloyd McClendon (23).
**Coaches**—Alvaro Espinoza (10), Rusty Kuntz (48), Pete Mackanin (25), Gerald Perry (28), John Russell (13), Bruce Tanner (52), Spin Williams (54).

| No. | PITCHERS | B/T | Ht./Wt. | Age* | 2004 Clubs |
|---|---|---|---|---|---|
| | Bradley, Bobby | R/R | 6-1/180 | 24 | Altoona |
| 61 | Burnett, Sean | L/L | 5-11/190 | 22 | Nashville, Pittsburgh |
| 27 | Fogg, Josh | R/R | 6-0/203 | 28 | Pittsburgh |
| 51 | Gonzalez, Mike | R/L | 6-2/205 | 26 | Nashville, Pittsburgh |
| 39 | Grabow, John | L/L | 6-2/210 | 26 | Pittsburgh |
| 37 | Johnston, Mike | L/L | 6-2/215 | 26 | Pittsburgh, Nashville |
| 46 | Meadows, Brian | R/R | 6-4/230 | 29 | Pittsburgh |
| 49 | Mesa, Jose | R/R | 6-3/232 | 38 | Pittsburgh |
| | Miller, Jeff | R/R | 6-4/220 | 25 | Altoona |
| 48 | Perez, Oliver | L/L | 6-0/190 | 23 | Pittsburgh |
| | Peterson, Matt | R/R | 6-5/210 | 23 | Altoona, Binghamton |
| | Redman, Mark | L/L | 6-5/245 | 31 | Oakland |
| | Snell, Ian | R/R | 5-11/170 | 23 | Altoona, Pittsburgh |
| | Stewart, Cory | L/L | 6-4/180 | 25 | G.C. Pirates, Nashville |
| 16 | Torres, Salomon | R/R | 5-11/210 | 33 | Pittsburgh |
| 47 | Van Benschoten, J. | R/R | 6-4/217 | 24 | Nashville, Pittsburgh |
| 22 | Vogelsong, Ryan | R/R | 6-3/213 | 27 | Pittsburgh |
| 32 | Wells, Kip | R/R | 6-3/200 | 27 | Pittsburgh |
| 58 | Williams, Dave | L/L | 6-2/219 | 26 | Nashville, Pittsburgh |

| No. | CATCHERS | B/T | Ht./Wt. | Age* | 2004 Clubs |
|---|---|---|---|---|---|
| 11 | Cota, Humberto | R/R | 6-0/210 | 26 | Nashville, Pittsburgh |
| | Doumit, Ryan | S/R | 6-0/200 | 23 | Altoona |
| 30 | House, J.R. | R/R | 6-0/215 | 24 | Nashville, Pittsburgh |
| | Paulino, Ronny | R/R | 6-3/210 | 23 | Altoona |
| | Santiago, Benito | R/R | 6-1/200 | 40 | Kansas City |

| No. | INFIELDERS | B/T | Ht./Wt. | Age* | 2004 Clubs |
|---|---|---|---|---|---|
| | Bautista, Jose | R/R | 6-0/192 | 24 | Baltimore, Tampa Bay, Kansas City, Pittsburgh |
| 14 | Castillo, Jose | R/R | 6-1/200 | 24 | Pittsburgh |
| | Eldred, Brad | R/R | 6-5/275 | 24 | Lynchburg, Altoona |
| 17 | Hill, Bobby | B/R | 5-9/180 | 26 | Pittsburgh |
| 12 | Sanchez, Freddy | R/R | 5-10/192 | 27 | Nashville, Pittsburgh |
| 31 | Ward, Daryle | L/L | 6-2/230 | 29 | Nashville, Pittsburgh |
| 9 | Wigginton, Ty | R/R | 6-0/200 | 27 | St. Lucie, New York N.L., Pittsburgh |
| 12 | Wilson, Jack | R/R | 6-0/192 | 27 | Pittsburgh |

| No. | OUTFIELDERS | B/T | Ht./Wt. | Age* | 2004 Clubs |
|---|---|---|---|---|---|
| 38 | Bay, Jason | R/R | 6-2/200 | 26 | Nashville, Pittsburgh |
| | Clark, Howie | L/R | 5-11/180 | 31 | Toronto, Syracuse |
| | Davis, Rajai | S/R | 5-11/190 | 24 | Lynchburg |
| | Duffy, Chris | L/L | 5-10/185 | 24 | Altoona |
| | Lawton, Matt | L/R | 5-10/195 | 33 | Cleveland |
| 59 | Mackowiak, Rob | L/R | 5-10/195 | 28 | Pittsburgh |
| | McLouth, Nate | L/R | 5-11/185 | 23 | Altoona |
| 5 | Redman, Tike | L/L | 5-11/172 | 28 | Pittsburgh |
| 36 | Wilson, Craig | R/R | 6-2/220 | 28 | Pittsburgh |

*Age as of April 1, 2005.

## BALLPARK INFORMATION

**Ballpark (capacity, surface)**
PNC Park (38,496, grass)

**Address**
PNC Park at North Shore
115 Federal Street
Pittsburgh, PA 15212

**Official website**
www.pittsburghpirates.com

**Business phone**
412-323-5000

**Ticket information**
800-BUY-BUCS

**Field dimensions (from home plate)**
To left field at foul line, 325 feet
To center field, 399 feet
To right field at foul line, 320 feet

**First game played**
April 9, 2001 (Reds 8, Pirates 2)

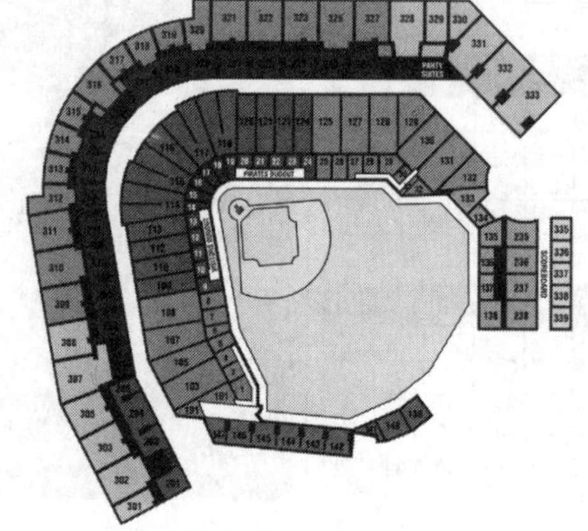

# 2004 REVIEW

## DAY BY DAY



| Date | Opp. | Res. | Score | (inn.*) | Hits | Opp. hits | Winning pitcher | Losing pitcher | Save | Record | Pos. | GB |
|---|---|---|---|---|---|---|---|---|---|---|---|---|
| 4-5 | Phi. | W | 2-1 | | 7 | 6 | Wells | Millwood | Mesa | 1-0 | T1st | ... |
| 4-7 | Phi. | L | 4-5 | | 11 | 10 | Cormier | Boehringer | Wagner | 1-1 | T2nd | 0.5 |
| 4-8 | Phi. | W | 6-2 | | 10 | 9 | Vogelsong | Padilla | Mesa | 2-1 | T2nd | 0.5 |
| 4-9 | At Cin. | L | 1-5 | | 8 | 6 | Harang | Fogg | | 2-2 | T3rd | 1.0 |
| 4-10 | At Cin. | L | 1-3 | | 7 | 9 | Lidle | Wells | Graves | 2-3 | T4th | 2.0 |
| 4-11 | At Cin. | W | 4-3 | | 8 | 8 | Perez | Haynes | Mesa | 3-3 | T4th | 1.0 |
| 4-12 | At Chi. | W | 13-2 | | 17 | 3 | Benson | Maddux | Meadows | 4-3 | T2nd | 1.0 |
| 4-14 | At Chi. | L | 3-8 | | 6 | 12 | Clement | Vogelsong | | 4-4 | T3rd | 1.5 |
| 4-15 | At Chi. | L | 5-10 | | 13 | 13 | Zambrano | Fogg | | 4-5 | 5th | 1.5 |
| 4-16 | At N.Y. | W | 7-6 | | 8 | 8 | Wells | Moreno | Mesa | 5-5 | T4th | 1.5 |
| 4-17 | At N.Y. | W | 2-1 | | 10 | 4 | Meadows | Trachsel | Mesa | 6-5 | T3rd | 1.5 |
| 4-18 | At N.Y. | W | 8-1 | | 17 | 6 | Benson | Seo | | 7-5 | 3rd | 1.5 |
| 4-20 | Chi. | L | 1-9 | | 7 | 11 | Zambrano | Vogelsong | | 7-6 | 4th | 1.5 |
| 4-21 | Chi. | L | 1-12 | | 7 | 15 | Mitre | Fogg | | 7-7 | T5th | 1.5 |
| 4-23 | Cin. | L | 4-6 | | 10 | 8 | Wilson | Wells | Graves | 7-8 | 6th | 2.5 |
| 4-24 | Cin. | L | 7-9 | | 16 | 15 | Van Poppel | Benson | Graves | 7-9 | 6th | 3.5 |
| 4-25 | Cin. | W | 6-0 | | 10 | 6 | Perez | Acevedo | | 8-9 | 6th | 3.5 |
| 4-26 | Cin. | L | 2-5 | | 10 | 7 | Harang | Vogelsong | Graves | 8-10 | 6th | 3.5 |
| 4-28 | Hou. | W | 4-2 | | 7 | 8 | Torres | Oswalt | Mesa | 9-10 | 6th | 3.0 |
| 4-29 | Hou. | L | 0-2 | | 2 | 6 | Pettitte | Wells | Dotel | 9-11 | 6th | 3.5 |
| 4-30 | At Mil. | W | 4-2 | | 9 | 6 | Benson | Sheets | Mesa | 10-11 | 6th | 2.5 |
| 5-1 | At Mil. | W | 8-7 | (10) | 9 | 13 | Boyd | Vizcaino | Mesa | 11-11 | T4th | 2.5 |
| 5-2 | At Mil. | W | 4-3 | (11) | 13 | 9 | Meadows | Bennett | Mesa | 12-11 | 3rd | 2.5 |
| 5-4 | At Hou. | L | 3-4 | | 7 | 6 | Pettitte | Fogg | Lidge | 12-12 | T4th | 3.0 |
| 5-5 | At Hou. | L | 2-6 | | 5 | 10 | Clemens | Wells | | 12-13 | 6th | 4.0 |
| 5-6 | At Hou. | L | 2-5 | | 9 | 8 | Miller | Benson | | 12-14 | 6th | 5.0 |
| 5-7 | L.A. | L | 0-4 | | 1 | 7 | Alvarez | Perez | | 12-15 | 6th | 6.0 |
| 5-8 | L.A. | L | 3-4 | | 9 | 9 | Mota | Torres | Gagne | 12-16 | 6th | 6.0 |
| 5-9 | L.A. | L | 7-9 | (14) | 10 | 16 | Falkenborg | Grabow | | 12-17 | 6th | 7.0 |
| 5-11 | At Col. | W | 15-10 | (12) | 19 | 19 | Torres | Lopez | | 13-17 | 6th | 7.0 |
| 5-13! | At Col. | L | 5-7 | | 8 | 9 | Estes | Benson | Chacon | 13-18 | | |
| 5-13& | At Col. | W | 11-2 | | 21 | 7 | Perez | Jennings | | 14-18 | 6th | 6.0 |
| 5-14 | At S.F | W | 4-2 | | 10 | 9 | Boehringer | Rodriguez | Mesa | 15-18 | 6th | 5.0 |
| 5-15 | At S.F | W | 6-4 | | 9 | 11 | Fogg | Tomko | Mesa | 16-18 | 6th | 5.0 |
| 5-16 | At S.F | W | 8-1 | | 15 | 8 | Wells | Williams | | 17-18 | 6th | 4.0 |
| 5-19! | S.D. | L | 3-6 | | 9 | 13 | Lawrence | Johnston | Hoffman | 17-19 | | |
| 5-19& | S.D. | L | 3-7 | | 7 | 9 | Peavy | Perez | | 17-20 | 6th | 6.0 |
| 5-20 | S.D. | W | 9-7 | | 14 | 7 | Gonzalez | Puffer | Mesa | 18-20 | 6th | 5.0 |
| 5-22 | Mil. | W | 3-1 | | 9 | 7 | Fogg | Sheets | Mesa | 19-20 | 6th | 3.5 |
| 5-23 | Mil. | L | 1-2 | | 10 | 5 | Vizcaino | Meadows | Kolb | 19-21 | 6th | 4.5 |
| 5-26 | At StL. | W | 11-8 | | 19 | 16 | Benson | Marquis | | 20-21 | 6th | 4.5 |
| 5-27 | At StL. | L | 3-6 | | 8 | 6 | Suppan | Vogelsong | Isringhausen | 20-22 | 6th | 4.5 |
| 5-28! | Chi. | W | 9-5 | | 11 | 10 | Torres | Borowski | | 21-22 | | |
| 5-28& | Chi. | W | 5-4 | (10) | 9 | 11 | Gonzalez | Beltran | | 22-22 | 6th | 4.0 |
| 5-29 | Chi. | W | 10-7 | | 16 | 12 | Fogg | Mitre | | 23-22 | 6th | 4.0 |
| 5-30 | Chi. | L | 1-12 | | 8 | 17 | Zambrano | Grabow | | 23-23 | 6th | 4.0 |
| 5-31 | StL. | L | 3-8 | | 10 | 13 | Marquis | Benson | | 23-24 | 6th | 5.0 |
| 6-1 | StL. | L | 1-8 | | 7 | 13 | Suppan | Vogelsong | | 23-25 | 6th | 6.0 |
| 6-2 | StL. | L | 3-5 | | 7 | 8 | Carpenter | Johnston | Isringhausen | 23-26 | 6th | 7.0 |
| 6-3 | StL. | L | 2-4 | | 9 | 7 | Williams | Perez | Isringhausen | 23-27 | 6th | 7.5 |
| 6-4 | At Chi. | W | 2-1 | | 6 | 7 | Torres | Borowski | Mesa | 24-27 | 6th | 6.5 |
| 6-5 | At Chi. | L | 1-6 | | 4 | 8 | Zambrano | Benson | | 24-28 | 6th | 7.5 |
| 6-6 | At Chi. | L | 1-4 | | 6 | 8 | Maddux | Vogelsong | Hawkins | 24-29 | 6th | 8.5 |
| 6-7 | At Tex. | L | 5-6 | (10) | 6 | 13 | Cordero | Johnston | | 24-30 | 6th | 8.5 |
| 6-10! | At Tex. | L | 7-9 | | 13 | 5 | Francisco | Meadows | Cordero | 24-31 | | |
| 6-10& | At Tex. | L | 4-10 | | 10 | 13 | Rogers | Fogg | | 24-32 | 6th | 8.5 |
| 6-11 | At Oak. | L | 1-6 | | 7 | 7 | Hudson | Benson | | 24-33 | 6th | 9.0 |
| 6-12 | At Oak. | L | 11-12 | | 16 | 18 | Rhodes | Corey | | 24-34 | 6th | 9.0 |
| 6-13 | At Oak. | L | 3-13 | | 4 | 18 | Mulder | Wells | | 24-35 | 6th | 10.0 |
| 6-15 | Ana. | L | 2-4 | | 6 | 11 | Shields | Torres | Rodriguez | 24-36 | 6th | 11.0 |
| 6-16 | Ana. | W | 5-3 | | 9 | 10 | Fogg | Lackey | Mesa | 25-36 | 6th | 11.0 |
| 6-17 | Ana. | W | 5-2 | | 11 | 7 | Benson | Colon | Mesa | 26-36 | 6th | 11.0 |
| 6-18 | Sea. | L | 4-5 | | 7 | 9 | Moyer | Vogelsong | Guardado | 26-37 | 6th | 12.0 |
| 6-19 | Sea. | L | 1-5 | | 4 | 8 | Pineiro | Burnett | | 26-38 | 6th | 13.0 |
| 6-20 | Sea. | L | 4-5 | | 9 | 6 | Garcia | Perez | Guardado | 26-39 | 6th | 13.0 |
| 6-21 | At Hou. | L | 5-7 | | 11 | 13 | Bullinger | Fogg | Dotel | 26-40 | 6th | 13.5 |
| 6-22 | At Hou. | L | 4-5 | | 10 | 8 | Oswalt | Benson | Lidge | 26-41 | 6th | 13.5 |

| Date | Opp. | Res. | Score | (inn.*) | Hits | Opp. hits | Winning pitcher | Losing pitcher | Save | Record | Pos. | GB |
|---|---|---|---|---|---|---|---|---|---|---|---|---|
| 6-23 | At Hou. | W | 7-2 | | 7 | 5 | Vogelsong | Munro | | 27-41 | 6th | 13.5 |
| 6-24 | At Hou. | L | 2-3 | | 5 | 5 | Clemens | Burnett | Lidge | 27-42 | 6th | 14.5 |
| 6-25 | At Cin. | L | 4-6 | | 6 | 7 | Acevedo | Torres | Graves | 27-43 | 6th | 15.5 |
| 6-26 | At Cin. | W | 1-0 | | 8 | 4 | Corey | Jones | Mesa | 28-43 | 6th | 15.5 |
| 6-27 | At Cin. | W | 14-4 | | 18 | 7 | Fogg | Wilson | | 29-43 | 6th | 15.5 |
| 6-28 | StL. | W | 2-1 | | 3 | 7 | Mesa | Tavarez | | 30-43 | 6th | 14.5 |
| 6-29 | StL. | W | 3-0 | | 6 | 6 | Burnett | Carpenter | Mesa | 31-43 | 6th | 13.5 |
| 6-30 | StL. | W | 6-5 | | 13 | 10 | Mesa | Tavarez | | 32-43 | 6th | 12.5 |
| 7-2! | Mil. | W | 8-1 | | 8 | 6 | Perez | Davis | | 33-43 | | |
| 7-2& | Mil. | W | 13-2 | | 14 | 8 | Fogg | Wise | | 34-43 | 6th | 12.0 |
| 7-3 | Mil. | W | 5-3 | | 11 | 13 | Benson | Obermueller | Mesa | 35-43 | 6th | 12.0 |
| 7-4 | Mil. | W | 6-2 | | 7 | 12 | Burnett | Capuano | Mesa | 36-43 | 6th | 12.0 |
| 7-5 | At Fla. | W | 3-1 | | 7 | 6 | Wells | Beckett | Mesa | 37-43 | 6th | 12.0 |
| 7-6 | At Fla. | L | 3-6 | | 9 | 11 | Bump | Corey | Benitez | 37-44 | 6th | 13.0 |
| 7-7 | At Fla. | W | 4-3 | | 8 | 10 | Perez | Pavano | Mesa | 38-44 | 6th | 13.0 |
| 7-8@ | At Mon. | L | 1-2 | | 5 | 6 | Ayala | Grabow | Cordero | 38-45 | 6th | 13.5 |
| 7-9@ | At Mon. | W | 11-0 | | 10 | 10 | Burnett | Hill | | 39-45 | 6th | 13.5 |
| 7-10@ | At Mon. | L | 0-4 | | 4 | 7 | Biddle | Wells | | 39-46 | 6th | 14.5 |
| 7-11@ | At Mon. | L | 1-2 | | 6 | 6 | Downs | Fogg | Cordero | 39-47 | 6th | 14.5 |
| 7-16 | Fla. | W | 6-2 | | 11 | 8 | Benson | Burnett | Mesa | 40-47 | 6th | 15.0 |
| 7-17 | Fla. | W | 4-2 | | 10 | 8 | Torres | Benitez | Mesa | 41-47 | 6th | 14.0 |
| 7-18 | Fla. | W | 4-2 | | 11 | 6 | Torres | Koch | Mesa | 42-47 | 6th | 14.0 |
| 7-19 | Mon. | L | 2-6 | | 6 | 11 | Horgan | Grabow | | 42-48 | 6th | 15.0 |
| 7-20 | Mon. | W | 2-1 | | 4 | 10 | Burnett | Hernandez | Mesa | 43-48 | 6th | 15.0 |
| 7-21 | At Atl. | W | 4-3 | | 8 | 6 | Benson | Byrd | Mesa | 44-48 | 6th | 15.0 |
| 7-22 | At Atl. | L | 1-2 | (10) | 8 | 6 | Reitsma | Torres | | 44-49 | 6th | 16.0 |
| 7-23 | Cin. | W | 6-3 | | 11 | 5 | Perez | Acevedo | Mesa | 45-49 | 6th | 15.0 |
| 7-24 | Cin. | W | 14-4 | | 15 | 10 | Grabow | Harang | | 46-49 | 6th | 14.0 |
| 7-25 | Cin. | W | 6-5 | | 11 | 12 | Burnett | Van Poppel | Mesa | 47-49 | 6th | 14.0 |
| 7-26 | Atl. | L | 2-4 | | 6 | 8 | Wright | Benson | Smoltz | 47-50 | 6th | 15.0 |
| 7-27 | Atl. | W | 8-4 | | 11 | 12 | Gonzalez | Gryboski | | 48-50 | 5th | 15.0 |
| 7-28 | Atl. | L | 0-1 | | 11 | 5 | Ortiz | Perez | Smoltz | 48-51 | 6th | 16.0 |
| 7-29 | Atl. | L | 2-3 | | 6 | 10 | Cruz | Mesa | Smoltz | 48-52 | 6th | 16.5 |
| 7-30 | At Mil. | L | 0-5 | | 6 | 7 | Davis | Burnett | | 48-53 | 6th | 17.5 |
| 7-31 | At Mil. | W | 4-1 | | 10 | 5 | Vogelsong | Santos | Mesa | 49-53 | 6th | 16.5 |
| 8-1 | At Mil. | L | 7-8 | | 13 | 17 | Vizcaino | Meadows | | 49-54 | 6th | 17.5 |
| 8-3 | At L.A. | L | 2-3 | | 4 | 7 | Penny | Perez | Gagne | 49-55 | 6th | 17.5 |
| 8-4 | At L.A. | L | 1-2 | | 6 | 10 | Lima | Fogg | Gagne | 49-56 | 6th | 18.5 |
| 8-5 | At L.A. | L | 3-8 | | 6 | 11 | Weaver | Burnett | | 49-57 | 6th | 19.5 |
| 8-6 | At S.D. | L | 1-13 | | 5 | 11 | Peavy | Vogelsong | | 49-58 | 6th | 20.5 |
| 8-7 | At S.D. | W | 3-1 | | 12 | 4 | Wells | Wells | Mesa | 50-58 | 6th | 20.5 |
| 8-8 | At S.D. | W | 4-2 | | 12 | 8 | Perez | Lawrence | Mesa | 51-58 | 6th | 20.5 |
| 8-10 | S.F | W | 8-7 | | 10 | 13 | Mesa | Herges | | 52-58 | 6th | 20.5 |
| 8-11 | S.F | W | 8-6 | (11) | 12 | 11 | Grabow | Hermanson | | 53-58 | 5th | 20.5 |
| 8-12 | S.F | L | 0-7 | | 4 | 10 | Schmidt | Vogelsong | | 53-59 | 5th | 20.5 |
| 8-13 | Col. | L | 3-9 | | 4 | 15 | Fassero | Wells | | 53-60 | 6th | 21.5 |
| 8-14 | Col. | W | 6-1 | | 10 | 5 | Perez | Wright | | 54-60 | 5th | 20.5 |
| 8-15 | Col. | W | 3-0 | | 10 | 5 | Fogg | Kennedy | Mesa | 55-60 | 5th | 20.5 |
| 8-16 | At Ari. | W | 8-7 | (10) | 12 | 13 | Mesa | Aquino | Gonzalez | 56-60 | 4th | 20.5 |
| 8-17 | At Ari. | W | 7-1 | | 12 | 7 | Vogelsong | Randolph | | 57-60 | 4th | 20.5 |
| 8-18 | At Ari. | L | 3-6 | | 7 | 8 | Fossum | V. Benschoten | Aquino | 57-61 | 4th | 20.5 |
| 8-19 | At StL. | W | 3-2 | (10) | 6 | 8 | Mesa | Kline | Grabow | 58-61 | 4th | 19.5 |
| 8-20# | At StL. | L | 4-5 | | 6 | 9 | Haren | Fogg | Isringhausen | 58-62 | | |
| 8-20$ | At StL. | L | 3-5 | | 8 | 11 | Carpenter | Gonzalez | Isringhausen | 58-63 | T4th | 21.5 |
| 8-21 | At StL. | L | 6-10 | | 9 | 13 | Suppan | Burnett | | 58-64 | T4th | 22.5 |
| 8-22 | At StL. | L | 4-11 | | 13 | 12 | Morris | Vogelsong | Kline | 58-65 | 5th | 23.5 |
| 8-23 | Ari. | L | 4-5 | | 11 | 10 | Nance | Grabow | Aquino | 58-66 | 5th | 24.0 |
| 8-24 | Ari. | W | 3-1 | | 8 | 5 | Perez | Gonzalez | Mesa | 59-66 | 5th | 23.0 |
| 8-25 | Ari. | W | 2-1 | | 3 | 9 | Fogg | Johnson | Mesa | 60-66 | 5th | 23.0 |
| 8-27 | StL. | L | 5-8 | | 10 | 12 | Suppan | Vogelsong | Isringhausen | 60-67 | 5th | 23.5 |
| 8-28 | StL. | L | 4-6 | | 8 | 8 | Morris | Figueroa | Isringhausen | 60-68 | 5th | 24.5 |
| 8-29 | StL. | L | 0-4 | | 4 | 7 | Marquis | Perez | Tavarez | 60-69 | 5th | 25.5 |
| 8-30 | At Mil. | W | 5-1 | | 8 | 7 | Fogg | Hendrickson | | 61-69 | 5th | 25.0 |
| 8-31 | At Mil. | L | 2-4 | | 11 | 6 | Wise | V. Benschoten | Kolb | 61-70 | 5th | 26.0 |
| 9-1 | At Mil. | W | 5-2 | (10) | 12 | 11 | Torres | Bennett | Mesa | 62-70 | T4th | 26.0 |
| 9-2 | At Mil. | L | 1-7 | | 4 | 9 | Sheets | Williams | | 62-71 | 5th | 27.0 |
| 9-3 | At Hou. | L | 6-8 | | 8 | 10 | Clemens | Perez | Lidge | 62-72 | 5th | 28.0 |
| 9-4 | At Hou. | L | 5-6 | | 6 | 9 | Qualls | Figueroa | Lidge | 62-73 | 5th | 29.0 |

| Date | Opp. | Res. | Score | (inn.*) | Hits | Opp. hits | Winning pitcher | Losing pitcher | Save | Record | Pos. | GB |
|---|---|---|---|---|---|---|---|---|---|---|---|---|
| 9-5 | At Hou. | L | 5-10 | | 5 | 16 | Munro | Van Benschoten | | 62-74 | 5th | 30.0 |
| 9-6 | Mil. | L | 5-9 | | 10 | 8 | Glover | Vogelsong | Kolb | 62-75 | 5th | 30.0 |
| 9-7 | Mil. | W | 2-0 | | 7 | 3 | Williams | Sheets | Mesa | 63-75 | 5th | 30.0 |
| 9-9! | Hou. | W | 3-1 | | 6 | 3 | Perez | Hernandez | Mesa | 64-75 | | |
| 9-9& | Hou. | L | 2-9 | | 6 | 10 | Gallo | Fogg | | 64-76 | 4th | 29.5 |
| 9-10 | Hou. | W | 6-1 | | 13 | 5 | Van Benschoten | Munro | | 65-76 | 4th | 28.5 |
| 9-11 | Hou. | W | 5-2 | | 12 | 9 | Vogelsong | Backe | Mesa | 66-76 | 4th | 27.5 |
| 9-12 | Hou. | L | 4-5 | (10) | 13 | 8 | Lidge | Mesa | Qualls | 66-77 | 4th | 28.5 |
| 9-13 | At Chi. | L | 2-7 | | 8 | 7 | Maddux | Brooks | | 66-78 | 5th | 29.0 |
| 9-14 | At Chi. | L | 2-3 | (12) | 6 | 9 | Wellemeyer | Meadows | | 66-79 | 5th | 29.0 |
| 9-15 | At Chi. | L | 5-13 | | 11 | 18 | Wuertz | Perez | Dempster | 66-80 | 5th | 30.0 |
| 9-18 | N.Y. | L | 7-8 | (10) | 7 | 11 | Yates | Torres | Looper | 66-81 | 5th | 31.0 |
| 9-19! | N.Y. | W | 1-0 | | 2 | 3 | Vogelsong | Heilman | Mesa | 67-81 | | |
| 9-19& | N.Y. | W | 6-1 | | 7 | 6 | Williams | Benson | | 68-81 | T4th | 29.5 |
| 9-21 | Chi. | L | 4-5 | (10) | 9 | 10 | Hawkins | Torres | Dempster | 68-82 | T4th | 30.0 |
| 9-22 | Chi. | L | 0-1 | | 6 | 5 | Zambrano | Perez | Remlinger | 68-83 | 5th | 31.0 |
| 9-23 | Chi. | L | 3-6 | | 9 | 8 | Maddux | Figueroa | Hawkins | 68-84 | 5th | 32.0 |
| 9-24 | Cin. | L | 8-14 | | 11 | 17 | Harang | Vogelsong | | 68-85 | 5th | 33.0 |
| 9-25 | Cin. | L | 4-7 | | 11 | 11 | Wilson | Williams | Valentine | 68-86 | 5th | 34.0 |
| 9-26 | Cin. | W | 4-2 | | 14 | 11 | Fogg | Acevedo | Mesa | 69-86 | 5th | 34.0 |
| 9-27 | At Phi. | W | 6-1 | | 6 | 5 | Perez | Milton | | 70-86 | 5th | 33.0 |
| 9-29! | At Phi. | L | 4-8 | | 10 | 13 | Padilla | Snell | | 70-87 | | |
| 9-29& | At Phi. | L | 3-8 | | 8 | 11 | Myers | Torres | | 70-88 | 5th | 33.0 |
| 10-1 | At Cin. | L | 1-5 | | 5 | 8 | Wilson | Williams | | 70-89 | 5th | 33.5 |
| 10-2 | At Cin. | W | 3-1 | | 8 | 5 | Fogg | Van Poppel | Mesa | 71-89 | 5th | 32.5 |
| 10-3 | At Cin. | W | 2-0 | | 7 | 5 | Perez | Claussen | Mesa | 72-89 | 5th | 32.5 |

Monthly records: April (10-11), May (13-13), June (9-19), July (17-10), August (12-17), September (9-18), October (2-1).
*Innings, if other than nine. @ At Hiram Bithorn Stadium, San Juan, Puerto Rico. ! First game of a doubleheader. & Second game of a doubleheader. # Day separate admission. $ Night separate admission.

## RECORDS

**2004 regular-season record:** 72-89
**Position:** 5th in N.L. Central
**Home:** 39-41 **Road:** 33-48
**N.L. East:** 17-13 **N.L. Central:** 37-52
**N.L. West:** 16-14 **A.L.** 2-10
**Vs. LH starters:** 14-21
**Vs. RH starters:** 58-68
**Grass:** 71-86 **Artificial:** 1-3
**Day:** 24-30 **Night:** 48-59
**1-Run:** 20-26 **X-inn.:** 8-7
**Doubleheaders:** 3-3-2
**Team record past five years:** 350-458 (.433, ranks 15th in league in that span)

## TEAM LEADERS

**Batting average:** Jason Kendall (.319).
**At-bats:** Jack Wilson (652).
**Runs:** Craig Wilson (97).
**Hits:** Jack Wilson (201).
**Total Bases:** Jack Wilson (299).
**Doubles:** Jack Wilson (41).
**Triples:** Jack Wilson (12).
**Home runs:** Craig Wilson (29).
**Runs batted in:** Jason Bay, Craig Wilson (82).
**Stolen bases:** Tike Redman (18).
**Slugging percentage:** Jason Bay (.550).
**On-base percentage:** Jason Kendall (.399).
**Wins:** Oliver Perez (12).
**Earned-run average:** Oliver Perez (2.98).
**Complete games:** Oliver Perez (2).
**Shutouts:** Sean Burnett, Oliver Perez (1).
**Saves:** Jose Mesa (43).
**Innings pitched:** Oliver Perez (196.0).
**Strikeouts:** Oliver Perez (239).

## GAMES BY POSITION

**Catcher:** Jason Kendall 146, Humberto Cota 24, Craig Wilson 4, J.R. House 3.
**First base:** Daryle Ward 71, Craig Wilson 65, Randall Simon 46, Carlos Rivera 7, Rob Mackowiak 1.
**Second base:** Jose Castillo 123, Bobby Hill 40, Abraham O. Nunez 32, Freddy Sanchez 3.
**Third base:** Chris Stynes 71, Ty Wigginton 56, Rob Mackowiak 55, Bobby Hill 25, Abraham O. Nunez 6, Freddy Sanchez 1.
**Shortstop:** Jack Wilson 156, Abraham O. Nunez 13, Freddy Sanchez 4, Jose Castillo 2.
**Outfield:** Tike Redman 147, Jason Bay 119, Rob Mackowiak 118, Craig Wilson 100, Raul Mondesi 26, J.J. Davis 17, Tony Alvarez 16, Jose Bautista 12, Daryle Ward 12, Ruben Mateo 10.
**Designated hitter:** Randall Simon 4, Craig Wilson 2, Ruben Mateo 1, Abraham O. Nunez 1.

## TOP DRAFT CHOICES

1. **Neil Walker,** C, Pine-Richland H.S., Gibsonia, Pa.
2. **Brian Bixler,** SS, Eastern Michigan.
3. **Eddie Prasch,** 3B, Milton H.S., Alpharetta, Ga.
4. **Joe Bauserman,** RHP, Lincoln H.S., Tallahassee, Fla.
5. **Kyle Bloom,** LHP, Illinois State.
6. **A.J. Johnson,** OF, Tallahassee (Fla.) CC.
7. **Jason Quarles,** RHP, Southern University.
8. **Eric Ridener,** RHP, Taravella H.S., Coral Springs, Fla..
9. **Christopher Covington,** OF, Brookwood H.S., Snellville, Ga.
10. **Derek Hankins,** RHP, Memphis.

# ST. LOUIS CARDINALS

## NATIONAL LEAGUE CENTRAL DIVISION

## 2005 SEASON

### CLUB DIRECTORY

**Chairman of the board/general partner**
William O. DeWitt Jr.
**Vice chairman**
Frederick O. Hanser
**President**
Mark C. Lamping
**Sr. vice president, general manager**
Walt Jocketty
**Vice president/player personnel**
Jerry Walker
**Special assistant to the general manager**
Mike Jorgensen
**Assistant general manager**
John Mozeliak
**Director, player development**
Bruce Manno
**Vice president/baseball development**
Jeff Luhnow
**Director, professional scouting**
Marteese Robinson
**Vice president, community relations**
Marty Hendin
**Director, media relations**
Brian Bartow
**Director, corp. sales/marketing & stadium entertainment**
Thane van Breusegen

### MINOR LEAGUE AFFILIATES

| Class | Team | League | Manager |
|---|---|---|---|
| AAA | Memphis | Pacific Coast | Danny Sheaffer |
| AA | Springfield | Texas | Chris Maloney |
| Advanced A | Palm Beach | Florida State | TBA |
| A | Quad Cities | Midwest | TBA |
| Short-Season A | New Jersey | New York-Pennsylvania | Mark DeJohn |
| Advanced Rookie | Johnson City | Appalachian | Tommy Kidwell |

### BROADCAST INFORMATION

**Radio:** KMOX-AM (1120).
**TV:** KPLR-TV (Channel 11).
**Cable TV:** Fox Sports Midwest.

### SPRING TRAINING

**Ballpark (city):** Roger Dean Stadium (Jupiter, Fla.).
**Ticket information:** 561-966-3309.

**For more on the Cardinals, go to msn.foxsports.com/mlb/teams.**

Pujols

### Cardinals Schedule

Home games shaded.
All-Star Game July 12 at Detroit. Schedule subject to change.

**April**

| SUN | MON | TUE | WED | THU | FRI | SAT |
|---|---|---|---|---|---|---|
| 3 | 4 | 5 HOU | 6 HOU | 7 | 8 PHI | 9 PHI |
| 10 PHI | 11 | 12 CIN | 13 CIN | 14 | 15 MIL | 16 MIL |
| 17 MIL | 18 PIT | 19 PIT | 20 CHC | 21 CHC | 22 HOU | 23 HOU |
| 24 HOU | 25 MIL | 26 MIL | 27 MIL | 28 | 29 ATL | 30 ATL |

**May**

| SUN | MON | TUE | WED | THU | FRI | SAT |
|---|---|---|---|---|---|---|
| 1 ATL | 2 CIN | 3 CIN | 4 CIN | 5 SD | 6 SD | 7 SD |
| 8 SD | 9 LA | 10 LA | 11 LA | 12 LA | 13 NYM | 14 NYM |
| 15 NYM | 16 | 17 PHI | 18 PHI | 19 PHI | 20 KC | 21 KC |
| 22 KC | 23 PIT | 24 PIT | 25 PIT | 26 | 27 WAS | 28 WAS |
| 29 WAS | 30 COL | 31 COL | | | | |

**June**

| SUN | MON | TUE | WED | THU | FRI | SAT |
|---|---|---|---|---|---|---|
| | | | 1 COL | 2 COL | 3 HOU | 4 HOU |
| 5 HOU | 6 BOS | 7 BOS | 8 BOS | 9 | 10 NYY | 11 NYY |
| 12 NYY | 13 TOR | 14 TOR | 15 TOR | 16 | 17 TB | 18 TB |
| 19 TB | 20 CIN | 21 CIN | 22 CIN | 23 PIT | 24 PIT | 25 PIT |
| 26 PIT | 27 | 28 CIN | 29 CIN | 30 COL | | |

**July**

| SUN | MON | TUE | WED | THU | FRI | SAT |
|---|---|---|---|---|---|---|
| | | | | | 1 COL | 2 COL |
| 3 COL | 4 ARI | 5 ARI | 6 ARI | 7 ARI | 8 SF | 9 SF |
| 10 SF | 11 | 12 All-Star | 13 | 14 | 15 HOU | 16 HOU |
| 17 HOU | 18 MIL | 19 MIL | 20 MIL | 21 MIL | 22 CHC | 23 CHC |
| 24 CHC | 25 | 26 SD | 27 SD | 28 SD | 29 LA | 30 LA |
| 31 LA | | | | | | |

**August**

| SUN | MON | TUE | WED | THU | FRI | SAT |
|---|---|---|---|---|---|---|
| | 1 FLA | 2 FLA | 3 FLA | 4 FLA | 5 ATL | 6 ATL |
| 7 ATL | 8 MIL | 9 MIL | 10 MIL | 11 CHC | 12 CHC | 13 CHC |
| 14 CHC | 15 | 16 ARI | 17 ARI | 18 ARI | 19 SF | 20 SF |
| 21 SF | 22 PIT | 23 PIT | 24 PIT | 25 PIT | 26 WAS | 27 WAS |
| 28 WAS | 29 FLA | 30 FLA | 31 FLA | | | |

**September**

| SUN | MON | TUE | WED | THU | FRI | SAT |
|---|---|---|---|---|---|---|
| | | | | 1 | 2 HOU | 3 HOU |
| 4 HOU | 5 CHC | 6 CHC | 7 CHC | 8 NYM | 9 NYM | 10 NYM |
| 11 NYM | 12 PIT | 13 PIT | 14 PIT | 15 CHC | 16 CHC | 17 CHC |
| 18 CHC | 19 | 20 CIN | 21 CIN | 22 CIN | 23 MIL | 24 MIL |
| 25 MIL | 26 | 27 HOU | 28 HOU | 29 | 30 CIN | |

**October**

| SUN | MON | TUE | WED | THU | FRI | SAT |
|---|---|---|---|---|---|---|
| | | | | | | 1 CIN |
| 2 CIN | 3 CIN | 4 | 5 | 6 | 7 | 8 |

Home games shaded. All-Star Game July 12 at Detroit. Schedule subject to change.

## SPRING TRAINING ROSTER

**Manager**—Tony La Russa (10).
**Coaches**—Dave Duncan (18), Marty Mason (38), Dave McKay (39), Hal McRae, Jose Oquendo (11), Joe Pettini (24).

| No. | PITCHERS | B/T | Ht./Wt. | Age* | 2004 Clubs |
|---|---|---|---|---|---|
| 49 | Ankiel, Rick | L/L | 6-1/215 | 25 | Palm Beach, Tennessee, Memphis, St. Louis |
| 68 | Cali, Carmen | L/L | 5-10/185 | 26 | Tennessee, Memphis, St. Louis |
| 29 | Carpenter, Chris | R/R | 6-6/230 | 29 | St. Louis |
| 23 | Eldred, Cal | R/R | 6-4/240 | 37 | St. Louis |
| 61 | Flores, Randy | L/L | 6-0/180 | 29 | Memphis, St. Louis |
| 44 | Isringhausen, J. | R/R | 6-3/230 | 32 | St. Louis |
| | Journell, Jimmy | R/R | 6-4/205 | 27 | Memphis |
| 56 | King, Ray | L/L | 6-1/242 | 31 | St. Louis |
| | Lincoln, Mike | R/R | 6-2/213 | 29 | St. Louis |
| 21 | Marquis, Jason | L/R | 6-1/210 | 26 | St. Louis |
| 35 | Morris, Matt | R/R | 6-5/220 | 30 | St. Louis |
| | Mulder, Mark | L/L | 6-6/208 | 27 | Oakland |
| | Myers, Mike | L/L | 6-3/219 | 35 | Seattle, Boston |
| | Parrott, Rhett | R/R | 6-2/190 | 25 | Memphis |
| 52 | Reyes, Al | R/R | 6-1/212 | 34 | Durham, Memphis, St. Louis |
| | Rust, Evan | R/R | 6-1/210 | 26 | Tennessee |
| | Rust, Evan | R/R | | | Memphis |
| 37 | Suppan, Jeff | R/R | 6-2/220 | 30 | St. Louis |
| 50 | Tavarez, Julian | L/R | 6-2/195 | 31 | St. Louis |
| | Wainwright, Adam | R/R | 6-7/205 | 23 | Memphis |

| No. | CATCHERS | B/T | Ht./Wt. | Age* | 2004 Clubs |
|---|---|---|---|---|---|
| | Diaz, Einar | R/R | 5-10/200 | 32 | Montreal |
| | Mahoney, Mike | R/R | 6-1/200 | 32 | Memphis |
| 26 | McKay, Cody | L/R | 6-0/208 | 31 | Memphis, St. Louis |
| 41 | Molina, Yadier | R/R | 5-11/225 | 22 | Memphis, St. Louis |

| No. | INFIELDERS | B/T | Ht./Wt. | Age* | 2004 Clubs |
|---|---|---|---|---|---|
| | Eckstein, David | R/R | 5-7/165 | 30 | Anaheim |
| | Gall, John | R/R | 6-0/195 | 26 | Memphis |
| | Grudzielanek, M. | R/R | 6-1/190 | 34 | Iowa, Chicago, N.L. |
| 31 | Hart, Bo | R/R | 5-11/175 | 28 | St. Louis, Memphis |
| 7 | Luna, Hector | R/R | 6-1/170 | 25 | St. Louis |
| 5 | Pujols, Albert | R/R | 6-3/225 | 25 | St. Louis |
| 27 | Rolen, Scott | R/R | 6-4/240 | 29 | St. Louis |
| | Seabol, Scott | R/R | 6-4/200 | 28 | Memphis |

| No. | OUTFIELDERS | B/T | Ht./Wt. | Age* | 2004 Clubs |
|---|---|---|---|---|---|
| 32 | Cedeno, Roger | B/R | 6-1/205 | 30 | Memphis, St. Louis |
| 15 | Edmonds, Jim | L/L | 6-1/212 | 34 | St. Louis |
| | Gorecki, Reid | R/R | 6-1/180 | 24 | Palm Beach, Tennessee |
| 47 | Mabry, John | L/R | 6-4/210 | 34 | Memphis, St. Louis |
| 16 | Sanders, Reggie | R/R | 6-1/205 | 37 | St. Louis |
| 99 | Taguchi, So | R/R | 5-10/163 | 35 | Memphis, St. Louis |
| 33 | Walker, Larry | L/R | 6-3/235 | 38 | Tulsa, Colorado, St. Louis |

*Age as of April 1, 2005.

## BALLPARK INFORMATION

**Ballpark (capacity, surface)**
Busch Stadium (50,354, grass)

**Address**
250 Stadium Plaza
St. Louis, MO 63102

**Official website**
www.stlcardinals.com

**Business phone**
314-421-3060

**Ticket information**
314-421-2400

**Field dimensions (from home plate)**
To left field at foul line, 330 feet
To center field, 402 feet
To right field at foul line, 330 feet

**First game played**
May 12, 1966 (Cardinals 4, Braves 3)

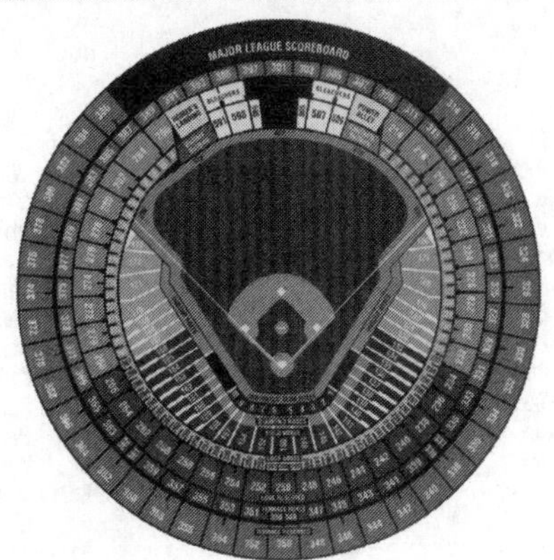

# 2004 REVIEW

## DAY BY DAY

| Date | Opp. | Res. | Score | (inn.*) | Hits | Opp. hits | Winning pitcher | Losing pitcher | Save | Record | Pos. | GB |
|---|---|---|---|---|---|---|---|---|---|---|---|---|
| 4-5 | Mil. | L | 6-8 | | 8 | 6 | Burba | Morris | Kolb | 0-1 | T4th | 1.0 |
| 4-6 | Mil. | L | 5-7 | | 12 | 10 | Davis | Marquis | Kolb | 0-2 | T5th | 2.0 |
| 4-7 | Mil. | W | 9-4 | | 14 | 11 | Lincoln | Hernandez | | 1-2 | T5th | 1.0 |
| 4-8 | Mil. | L | 5-11 | | 5 | 15 | Capuano | Suppan | Burba | 1-3 | 6th | 2.0 |
| 4-9 | At Ari. | W | 13-6 | | 17 | 11 | Carpenter | Daigle | | 2-3 | 6th | 1.5 |
| 4-10 | At Ari. | W | 10-2 | | 13 | 5 | Morris | Sparks | | 3-3 | 3rd | 1.5 |
| 4-11 | At Ari. | W | 6-5 | | 11 | 8 | Lincoln | Mantei | Isringhausen | 4-3 | T2nd | 0.5 |
| 4-12 | Hou. | L | 5-10 | | 9 | 11 | Stone | Lincoln | | 4-4 | T4th | 1.5 |
| 4-13 | Hou. | L | 3-5 | | 5 | 10 | Clemens | Suppan | Dotel | 4-5 | T4th | 2.0 |
| 4-14 | Hou. | L | 1-11 | | 5 | 14 | Miller | Carpenter | | 4-6 | 6th | 2.5 |
| 4-16 | Col. | W | 13-5 | | 16 | 8 | Morris | Stark | | 5-6 | 6th | 2.0 |
| 4-17 | Col. | W | 8-4 | | 13 | 11 | Marquis | Estes | | 6-6 | 5th | 2.0 |
| 4-18 | Col. | L | 5-8 | | 11 | 10 | Jennings | Williams | Chacon | 6-7 | 5th | 3.0 |
| 4-20 | At Hou. | W | 5-3 | | 9 | 8 | Suppan | Miller | Isringhausen | 7-7 | 5th | 2.0 |
| 4-21 | At Hou. | W | 12-6 | | 16 | 8 | Morris | Redding | | 8-7 | 4th | 1.0 |
| 4-22 | At Hou. | W | 2-1 | (12) | 7 | 7 | Isringhausen | Miceli | Tavarez | 9-7 | T3rd | 0.5 |
| 4-23 | At Mil. | L | 1-2 | | 6 | 8 | Kieschnick | Kline | | 9-8 | 4th | 1.5 |
| 4-24 | At Mil. | L | 1-3 | | 5 | 6 | Saenz | Williams | Kolb | 9-9 | 5th | 2.5 |
| 4-25 | At Mil. | W | 5-2 | | 9 | 5 | Suppan | Sheets | | 10-9 | 4th | 2.5 |
| 4-27 | Phi. | L | 3-7 | | 10 | 11 | Milton | Morris | | 10-10 | 5th | 2.0 |
| 4-28 | Phi. | L | 3-6 | | 9 | 7 | Madson | Lincoln | Wagner | 10-11 | 5th | 3.0 |
| 4-29 | Phi. | W | 5-4 | (13) | 14 | 8 | Lincoln | Telemaco | | 11-11 | 5th | 2.5 |
| 4-30 | Chi. | W | 4-3 | | 5 | 10 | Kline | Farnsworth | | 12-11 | T4th | 1.5 |
| 5-1 | Chi. | L | 2-4 | | 7 | 9 | Clement | Suppan | Borowski | 12-12 | T4th | 2.5 |
| 5-2 | Chi. | W | 1-0 | (10) | 6 | 5 | Isringhausen | Farnsworth | | 13-12 | 4th | 2.5 |
| 5-3 | Chi. | L | 3-7 | | 8 | 11 | Maddux | Marquis | | 13-13 | 5th | 2.5 |
| 5-4 | At Phi. | W | 6-5 | | 10 | 8 | Carpenter | Myers | Isringhausen | 14-13 | 3rd | 2.5 |
| 5-5 | At Phi. | L | 4-5 | | 8 | 7 | Millwood | Williams | Wagner | 14-14 | 4th | 3.5 |
| 5-6 | At Phi. | W | 7-4 | | 10 | 8 | Suppan | Wolf | Isringhausen | 15-14 | 4th | 3.5 |
| 5-7 | At Mon. | L | 2-4 | | 9 | 7 | Kim | Morris | Biddle | 15-15 | 4th | 4.5 |
| 5-8 | At Mon. | L | 0-2 | | 3 | 8 | Ohka | Marquis | Biddle | 15-16 | 5th | 4.5 |
| 5-9 | At Mon. | W | 5-2 | | 8 | 5 | Carpenter | Vargas | Isringhausen | 16-16 | 4th | 4.5 |
| 5-11 | Atl. | W | 5-1 | | 8 | 4 | Williams | Wright | | 17-16 | 4th | 4.5 |
| 5-12 | Atl. | W | 5-2 | | 12 | 7 | Morris | Hampton | Isringhausen | 18-16 | 3rd | 3.5 |
| 5-13 | Atl. | L | 5-6 | | 11 | 13 | Alfonseca | Suppan | Smoltz | 18-17 | 4th | 3.5 |
| 5-14 | Fla. | W | 6-3 | | 9 | 8 | Marquis | Beckett | Isringhausen | 19-17 | 3rd | 2.5 |
| 5-15 | Fla. | W | 4-0 | | 6 | 5 | Carpenter | Oliver | Tavarez | 20-17 | 3rd | 2.5 |
| 5-16 | Fla. | L | 2-3 | | 6 | 10 | Penny | Williams | Benitez | 20-18 | 4th | 2.5 |
| 5-18 | At N.Y. | L | 4-5 | | 9 | 10 | Bottalico | Isringhausen | | 20-19 | 4th | 3.5 |
| 5-19 | At N.Y. | W | 1-0 | | 8 | 4 | Eldred | Stanton | Kline | 21-19 | 4th | 3.5 |
| 5-20 | At N.Y. | W | 11-4 | | 15 | 8 | Marquis | Seo | | 22-19 | 4th | 2.5 |
| 5-21 | At Chi. | W | 7-6 | | 10 | 11 | Carpenter | Mitre | Isringhausen | 23-19 | 4th | 1.5 |
| 5-22 | At Chi. | L | 1-7 | | 6 | 8 | Rusch | Williams | | 23-20 | 4th | 1.5 |
| 5-23 | At Chi. | L | 3-4 | | 3 | 10 | Clement | Morris | Borowski | 23-21 | 5th | 2.5 |
| 5-26 | Pit. | L | 8-11 | | 16 | 19 | Benson | Marquis | | 23-22 | 5th | 3.5 |
| 5-27 | Pit. | W | 6-3 | | 6 | 8 | Suppan | Vogelsong | Isringhausen | 24-22 | 5th | 2.5 |
| 5-28 | At Hou. | W | 2-1 | (10) | 7 | 5 | Isringhausen | Dotel | | 25-22 | T3rd | 2.5 |
| 5-29 | At Hou. | W | 10-3 | | 16 | 9 | Williams | Miller | | 26-22 | T2nd | 2.5 |
| 5-30 | At Hou. | L | 1-7 | | 5 | 9 | Redding | Morris | | 26-23 | T3rd | 2.5 |
| 5-31 | At Pit. | W | 8-3 | | 13 | 10 | Marquis | Benson | | 27-23 | T2nd | 2.5 |
| 6-1 | At Pit. | W | 8-1 | | 13 | 7 | Suppan | Vogelsong | | 28-23 | T2nd | 2.5 |
| 6-2 | At Pit. | W | 5-3 | | 8 | 7 | Carpenter | Johnston | Isringhausen | 29-23 | T2nd | 2.5 |
| 6-3 | At Pit. | W | 4-2 | | 7 | 9 | Williams | Perez | Isringhausen | 30-23 | 2nd | 2.0 |
| 6-4 | Hou. | W | 5-3 | | 6 | 10 | Morris | Miller | Isringhausen | 31-23 | 2nd | 1.0 |
| 6-5 | Hou. | W | 10-4 | | 19 | 11 | Marquis | Redding | | 32-23 | 2nd | 1.0 |
| 6-6 | Hou. | L | 2-3 | | 8 | 9 | Oswalt | Suppan | Dotel | 32-24 | 2nd | 2.0 |
| 6-7 | At Chi. | W | 4-3 | | 6 | 9 | Carpenter | Rusch | Isringhausen | 33-24 | 2nd | 1.0 |
| 6-8 | At Chi. | L | 3-7 | | 6 | 13 | Clement | Williams | | 33-25 | 2nd | 1.0 |
| 6-9 | At Chi. | W | 12-4 | | 13 | 11 | Morris | Prior | | 34-25 | T1st | ... |
| 6-10 | At Chi. | L | 3-12 | | 6 | 15 | Zambrano | Haren | | 34-26 | 2nd | 0.5 |
| 6-11 | At Tex. | W | 12-7 | | 15 | 10 | Suppan | Dominguez | | 35-26 | 1st | +0.5 |
| 6-12 | At Tex. | L | 2-7 | | 5 | 12 | Drese | Carpenter | | 35-27 | 1st | +0.5 |
| 6-13 | At Tex. | W | 13-2 | | 14 | 6 | Williams | Dickey | | 36-27 | 1st | +1.5 |
| 6-15 | Oak. | W | 8-4 | | 12 | 8 | Morris | Bradford | Isringhausen | 37-27 | 1st | +2.0 |
| 6-16 | Oak. | W | 6-2 | | 10 | 6 | Marquis | Harden | Calero | 38-27 | 1st | +2.0 |
| 6-17 | Oak. | W | 5-4 | | 11 | 9 | King | Mecir | | 39-27 | 1st | +2.0 |

| Date | Opp. | Res. | Score | (inn.*) | Hits | Opp. hits | Winning pitcher | Losing pitcher | Save | Record | Pos. | GB |
|---|---|---|---|---|---|---|---|---|---|---|---|---|
| 6-18 | Cin. | W | 4-3 | (10) | 11 | 7 | Tavarez | Matthews | | 40-27 | 1st | +3.0 |
| 6-19 | Cin. | W | 9-2 | | 14 | 5 | Williams | Acevedo | Isringhausen | 41-27 | 1st | +3.0 |
| 6-20 | Cin. | L | 0-6 | | 4 | 7 | Bong | Morris | | 41-28 | 1st | +2.0 |
| 6-22 | Chi. | L | 4-5 | | 10 | 8 | Farnsworth | Isringhausen | Hawkins | 41-29 | 1st | +1.0 |
| 6-23 | Chi. | W | 10-9 | | 9 | 14 | Kline | Remlinger | | 42-29 | 1st | +2.0 |
| 6-24 | Chi. | W | 4-0 | | 7 | 8 | Carpenter | Clement | | 43-29 | 1st | +3.0 |
| 6-25 | At K.C. | W | 5-2 | | 10 | 6 | Morris | Greinke | Isringhausen | 44-29 | 1st | +3.0 |
| 6-26 | At K.C. | W | 3-1 | (10) | 9 | 11 | Tavarez | Seanez | Isringhausen | 45-29 | 1st | +4.0 |
| 6-27 | At K.C. | W | 10-3 | | 15 | 8 | Marquis | Gobble | | 46-29 | 1st | +5.0 |
| 6-28 | At Pit. | L | 1-2 | | 7 | 3 | Mesa | Tavarez | | 46-30 | 1st | +4.5 |
| 6-29 | At Pit. | L | 0-3 | | 6 | 6 | Burnett | Carpenter | Mesa | 46-31 | 1st | +3.5 |
| 6-30 | At Pit. | L | 5-6 | | 10 | 13 | Mesa | Tavarez | | 46-32 | 1st | +3.5 |
| 7-2 | Sea. | W | 11-2 | | 11 | 6 | Williams | Thornton | | 47-32 | 1st | +3.0 |
| 7-3 | Sea. | W | 8-1 | | 13 | 6 | Marquis | Franklin | | 48-32 | 1st | +3.0 |
| 7-4 | Sea. | W | 2-1 | | 6 | 6 | Suppan | Pineiro | Isringhausen | 49-32 | 1st | +3.0 |
| 7-5 | Cin. | W | 4-1 | | 11 | 5 | Carpenter | Lidle | Isringhausen | 50-32 | 1st | +4.0 |
| 7-6 | Cin. | W | 5-3 | | 7 | 8 | Morris | White | Kline | 51-32 | 1st | +5.0 |
| 7-7 | Cin. | W | 4-2 | | 10 | 4 | King | Riedling | Isringhausen | 52-32 | 1st | +6.0 |
| 7-9 | Chi. | W | 6-1 | | 12 | 9 | Marquis | Maddux | | 53-32 | 1st | +7.0 |
| 7-10 | Chi. | W | 5-2 | | 10 | 7 | Suppan | Clement | Isringhausen | 54-32 | 1st | +8.0 |
| 7-11 | Chi. | L | 4-8 | | 7 | 16 | Wood | Carpenter | | 54-33 | 1st | +7.0 |
| 7-15 | At Cin. | W | 7-2 | | 11 | 11 | Morris | Sanchez | | 55-33 | 1st | +7.0 |
| 7-16 | At Cin. | W | 7-5 | | 12 | 8 | Calero | Graves | Isringhausen | 56-33 | 1st | +8.0 |
| 7-17 | At Cin. | L | 5-7 | | 11 | 13 | Jones | Tavarez | Graves | 56-34 | 1st | +7.0 |
| 7-18 | At Cin. | W | 10-4 | | 13 | 9 | Suppan | Acevedo | | 57-34 | 1st | +8.0 |
| 7-19 | At Chi. | W | 5-4 | | 6 | 12 | Carpenter | Zambrano | Isringhausen | 58-34 | 1st | +9.0 |
| 7-20 | At Chi. | W | 11-8 | | 14 | 10 | King | Hawkins | Isringhausen | 59-34 | 1st | +9.5 |
| 7-21 | Mil. | W | 1-0 | | 3 | 5 | Williams | Santos | Isringhausen | 60-34 | 1st | +10.0 |
| 7-22 | Mil. | W | 4-0 | | 11 | 10 | Marquis | Sheets | | 61-34 | 1st | +10.0 |
| 7-23 | S.F | L | 2-7 | | 4 | 11 | Hermanson | Suppan | | 61-35 | 1st | +9.0 |
| 7-24 | S.F | L | 3-5 | (10) | 9 | 7 | Rodriguez | King | Christiansen | 61-36 | 1st | +9.0 |
| 7-25 | S.F | W | 6-0 | | 9 | 7 | Morris | Williams | | 62-36 | 1st | +10.0 |
| 7-26 | At Cin. | W | 9-6 | (11) | 12 | 7 | King | Norton | | 63-36 | 1st | +10.0 |
| 7-27 | At Cin. | W | 6-0 | | 13 | 3 | Marquis | Lidle | | 64-36 | 1st | +10.0 |
| 7-28 | At Cin. | W | 11-10 | | 19 | 9 | Eldred | Acevedo | Isringhausen | 65-36 | 1st | +11.0 |
| 7-30 | At S.F | W | 7-4 | | 11 | 10 | Carpenter | Brower | Isringhausen | 66-36 | 1st | +10.5 |
| 7-31 | At S.F | L | 7-8 | | 15 | 11 | Rueter | Morris | Christiansen | 66-37 | 1st | +10.5 |
| 8-1 | At S.F | W | 6-1 | | 13 | 5 | Williams | Schmidt | | 67-37 | 1st | +10.5 |
| 8-3 | Mon. | L | 6-10 | (12) | 12 | 16 | Cordero | Haren | | 67-38 | 1st | +9.5 |
| 8-4 | Mon. | W | 5-4 | | 13 | 11 | Tavarez | Cordero | | 68-38 | 1st | +9.5 |
| 8-5 | Mon. | W | 2-1 | | 6 | 5 | Carpenter | Ayala | Isringhausen | 69-38 | 1st | +9.5 |
| 8-6 | N.Y. | W | 6-4 | | 11 | 7 | Morris | Glavine | Isringhausen | 70-38 | 1st | +10.5 |
| 8-7 | N.Y. | W | 2-1 | | 5 | 3 | Tavarez | Stanton | | 71-38 | 1st | +10.5 |
| 8-8 | N.Y. | W | 6-2 | | 12 | 7 | Marquis | Leiter | Tavarez | 72-38 | 1st | +11.5 |
| 8-10 | At Fla. | W | 2-1 | (10) | 2 | 7 | Tavarez | Mota | Isringhausen | 73-38 | 1st | +12.5 |
| 8-11 | At Fla. | W | 1-0 | | 6 | 2 | Suppan | Pavano | Isringhausen | 74-38 | 1st | +12.5 |
| 8-12 | At Fla. | L | 2-8 | | 7 | 11 | Burnett | Morris | | 74-39 | 1st | +12.5 |
| 8-13 | At Atl. | W | 4-1 | | 8 | 3 | Williams | Byrd | Isringhausen | 75-39 | 1st | +13.5 |
| 8-14 | At Atl. | L | 7-9 | | 10 | 15 | Alfonseca | King | Smoltz | 75-40 | 1st | +12.5 |
| 8-15 | At Atl. | W | 10-4 | | 11 | 10 | Haren | Thomson | | 76-40 | 1st | +13.5 |
| 8-16 | Cin. | W | 10-5 | | 12 | 8 | Suppan | Harang | Isringhausen | 77-40 | 1st | +14.0 |
| 8-17 | Cin. | W | 7-2 | | 10 | 8 | Eldred | Graves | | 78-40 | 1st | +15.0 |
| 8-18 | Cin. | L | 4-5 | | 9 | 9 | Hancock | Williams | Graves | 78-41 | 1st | +14.0 |
| 8-19 | Pit. | L | 2-3 | (10) | 8 | 6 | Mesa | Kline | Grabow | 78-42 | 1st | +13.0 |
| 8-20# | Pit. | W | 5-4 | | 9 | 6 | Haren | Fogg | Isringhausen | 79-42 | | |
| 8-20$ | Pit. | W | 5-3 | | 11 | 8 | Carpenter | Gonzalez | Isringhausen | 80-42 | 1st | +13.5 |
| 8-21 | Pit. | W | 10-6 | | 13 | 9 | Suppan | Burnett | | 81-42 | 1st | +14.5 |
| 8-22 | Pit. | W | 11-4 | | 12 | 13 | Morris | Vogelsong | Kline | 82-42 | 1st | +14.5 |
| 8-24 | At Cin. | L | 3-4 | (10) | 9 | 7 | Valentine | Tavarez | | 82-43 | 1st | +13.0 |
| 8-25 | At Cin. | W | 6-5 | | 8 | 10 | Tavarez | Valentine | Isringhausen | 83-43 | 1st | +13.0 |
| 8-26 | At Cin. | L | 0-1 | | 3 | 3 | Harang | Carpenter | | 83-44 | 1st | +12.0 |
| 8-27 | At Pit. | W | 8-5 | | 12 | 10 | Suppan | Vogelsong | Isringhausen | 84-44 | 1st | +13.0 |
| 8-28 | At Pit. | W | 6-4 | | 8 | 8 | Morris | Figueroa | Isringhausen | 85-44 | 1st | +14.0 |
| 8-29 | At Pit. | W | 4-0 | | 7 | 4 | Marquis | Perez | Tavarez | 86-44 | 1st | +15.0 |
| 8-31 | S.D. | W | 9-3 | | 16 | 7 | Williams | Lawrence | | 87-44 | 1st | +15.5 |
| 9-1 | S.D. | W | 4-2 | | 6 | 9 | Carpenter | Eaton | Isringhausen | 88-44 | 1st | +15.5 |
| 9-2 | S.D. | W | 7-2 | | 12 | 10 | Suppan | Peavy | | 89-44 | 1st | +16.0 |
| 9-3 | L.A. | W | 3-0 | | 7 | 2 | Morris | Lima | | 90-44 | 1st | +16.5 |
| 9-4 | L.A. | W | 5-1 | | 2 | 10 | Marquis | Ishii | | 91-44 | 1st | +17.0 |

| Date | Opp. | Res. | Score | (inn.*) | Hits | Opp. hits | Winning pitcher | Losing pitcher | Save | Record | Pos. | GB |
|---|---|---|---|---|---|---|---|---|---|---|---|---|
| 9-5 | L.A. | W | 6-5 | (11) | 10 | 10 | King | Carrara | | 92-44 | 1st | +17.5 |
| 9-6 | At S.D. | L | 3-7 | | 9 | 9 | Linebrink | Eldred | Hoffman | 92-45 | 1st | +16.5 |
| 9-7 | At S.D. | W | 4-2 | | 8 | 7 | Suppan | Peavy | Isringhausen | 93-45 | 1st | +17.5 |
| 9-8 | At S.D. | L | 5-10 | | 7 | 12 | Wells | Morris | | 93-46 | 1st | +17.0 |
| 9-10 | At L.A. | L | 6-7 | | 10 | 11 | Carrara | Calero | Gagne | 93-47 | 1st | +17.0 |
| 9-11 | At L.A. | L | 5-6 | | 9 | 10 | Stewart | Eldred | Gagne | 93-48 | 1st | +16.0 |
| 9-12 | At L.A. | W | 7-6 | | 12 | 9 | Carpenter | Jackson | Isringhausen | 94-48 | 1st | +17.0 |
| 9-14 | Hou. | L | 5-7 | | 9 | 15 | Clemens | Suppan | Lidge | 94-49 | 1st | +15.5 |
| 9-15 | Hou. | W | 4-2 | | 8 | 4 | Calero | Springer | Isringhausen | 95-49 | 1st | +15.5 |
| 9-16 | Hou. | L | 3-8 | | 10 | 8 | Harville | Marquis | | 95-50 | 1st | +14.5 |
| 9-17 | Ari. | W | 4-3 | | 8 | 8 | Isringhausen | Service | | 96-50 | 1st | +14.5 |
| 9-18 | Ari. | W | 7-0 | | 9 | 6 | Haren | Fossum | | 97-50 | 1st | +15.5 |
| 9-19 | Ari. | L | 2-3 | | 8 | 3 | Gosling | Suppan | Aquino | 97-51 | 1st | +14.5 |
| 9-20 | At Mil. | W | 7-4 | | 13 | 9 | Tavarez | Kolb | Isringhausen | 98-51 | 1st | +15.0 |
| 9-21 | At Mil. | L | 4-6 | | 9 | 11 | Santos | Marquis | Kolb | 98-52 | 1st | +14.0 |
| 9-22 | At Mil. | W | 3-2 | | 7 | 11 | Williams | Sheets | Isringhausen | 99-52 | 1st | +14.0 |
| 9-23 | At Mil. | W | 4-2 | | 9 | 4 | Eldred | Wise | Isringhausen | 100-52 | 1st | +14.0 |
| 9-24 | At Col. | W | 5-4 | | 10 | 8 | Suppan | Jennings | Calero | 101-52 | 1st | +14.0 |
| 9-25 | At Col. | W | 10-6 | | 11 | 10 | Flores | Harikkala | Isringhausen | 102-52 | 1st | +15.0 |
| 9-26 | At Col. | W | 9-3 | | 16 | 8 | Marquis | Gissell | Eldred | 103-52 | 1st | +16.0 |
| 9-27 | At Hou. | L | 3-10 | | 12 | 14 | Oswalt | Williams | | 103-53 | 1st | +15.0 |
| 9-28 | At Hou. | L | 1-2 | | 5 | 8 | Backe | Haren | Lidge | 103-54 | 1st | +15.0 |
| 9-29 | At Hou. | L | 4-6 | | 6 | 9 | Qualls | Suppan | Lidge | 103-55 | 1st | +14.5 |
| 9-30 | Mil. | L | 6-7 | | 12 | 10 | Davis | Morris | Kolb | 103-56 | 1st | +14.0 |
| 10-1 | Mil. | W | 4-1 | | 8 | 3 | Ankiel | Hendrickson | Isringhausen | 104-56 | 1st | +14.0 |
| 10-2 | Mil. | L | 1-5 | | 8 | 8 | Sheets | Marquis | | 104-57 | 1st | +13.0 |
| 10-3 | Mil. | W | 9-4 | | 16 | 12 | Calero | de la Rosa | | 105-57 | 1st | +13.0 |

Monthly records: April (12-11), May (15-12), June (19-9), July (20-5), August (21-7), September (16-12), October (2-1).
*Innings, if other than nine. # Day separate admission. $ Night separate admission.

## RECORDS

**2004 regular-season record:** 105-57
**Position:** 1st in N.L. Central
**Home:** 53-28 **Road:** 52-29
**N.L. East:** 19-11 **N.L. Central:** 54-36
**N.L. West:** 21-9 **A.L.** 11-1
**Vs. LH starters:** 26-13
**Vs. RH starters:** 79-44
**Grass:** 104-55 **Artificial:** 1-2
**Day:** 36-21 **Night:** 69-36
**1-Run:** 29-20 **X-inn.:** 9-4
**Doubleheaders:** 0-0-0
**Team record past five years:** 475-335 (.586, ranks 2nd in league in that span)

## TEAM LEADERS

**Batting average**: Albert Pujols (.331).
**At-bats:** Albert Pujols (592).
**Runs:** Albert Pujols (133).
**Hits:** Albert Pujols (196).
**Total Bases:** Albert Pujols (389).
**Doubles:** Albert Pujols (51).
**Triples:** Scott Rolen (4).
**Home runs:** Albert Pujols (46).
**Runs batted in:** Scott Rolen (124).
**Stolen bases:** Tony Womack (26).
**Slugging percentage:** Albert Pujols (.657).
**On-base percentage:** Jim Edmonds (.418).
**Wins:** Jeff Suppan (16).
**Earned-run average:** Chris Carpenter (3.46).
**Complete games**: Matt Morris (3).
**Shutouts:** Matt Morris (2).
**Saves:** Jason Isringhausen (47).
**Innings pitched:** Matt Morris (202.0).
**Strikeouts:** Chris Carpenter (152).

## GAMES BY POSITION

**Catcher:** Mike Matheny 122, Yadier Molina 51, Cody McKay 18.
**First base:** Albert Pujols 150, John Mabry 14, Marlon Anderson 2, Jim Edmonds 1, Mike Matheny 1, Cody McKay 1.
**Second base:** Tony Womack 133, Marlon Anderson 37, Hector Luna 19, Bo Hart 4.
**Third base:** Scott Rolen 141, John Mabry 20, Hector Luna 16, Cody McKay 7.
**Shortstop:** Edgar Renteria 149, Hector Luna 24, Bo Hart 1.
**Outfield:** Jim Edmonds 146, Reggie Sanders 119, So Taguchi 103, Ray Lankford 70, John Mabry 57, Roger Cedeno 54, Larry Walker 41, Marlon Anderson 36, Colin Porter 14, Hector Luna 10, Jason Simontacchi 1.
**Designated hitter:** Albert Pujols 3, Marlon Anderson 1, Roger Cedeno 1, Jim Edmonds 1, Reggie Sanders 1.

## TOP DRAFT CHOICES

1. **Chris Lambert,** RHP, Boston College.
2. **Mike Ferris,** 1B, Miami (Ohio).
3. **Eric Haberer,** LHP, Southern Illinois-Carbondale.
4. **Donnie Smith,** RHP, Old Dominion.
5. **Wes Swackhamer,** OF, Tulane.
6. **Jarrett Hoffpauir,** 2B, Southern Mississippi.
7. **Buck Cody,** LHP, Texas.
8. **Matt Shepherd,** SS, Southern Mississippi.
9. **Mike Parisi,** RHP, Manhattan.
10. **Brady Toops,** C, Arkansas.

# SAN DIEGO PADRES
## NATIONAL LEAGUE WEST DIVISION

## 2005 SEASON

### Padres Schedule
Home games shaded.
All-Star Game July 12 at Detroit. Schedule subject to change.

**April**

| SUN | MON | TUE | WED | THU | FRI | SAT |
|---|---|---|---|---|---|---|
| 3 | 4 COL | 5 | 6 COL | 7 PIT | 8 PIT | 9 PIT |
| 10 PIT | 11 CHC | 12 CHC | 13 CHC | 14 | 15 LA | 16 LA |
| 17 LA | 18 SF | 19 SF | 20 LA | 21 LA | 22 ARI | 23 ARI |
| 24 ARI | 25 SF | 26 SF | 27 SF | 28 | 29 ARI | 30 ARI |

**May**

| SUN | MON | TUE | WED | THU | FRI | SAT |
|---|---|---|---|---|---|---|
| 1 ARI | 2 COL | 3 COL | 4 COL | 5 STL | 6 STL | 7 STL |
| 8 STL | 9 CIN | 10 CIN | 11 CIN | 12 | 13 FLA | 14 FLA |
| 15 FLA | 16 ATL | 17 ATL | 18 ATL | 19 | 20 SEA | 21 SEA |
| 22 SEA | 23 | 24 ARI | 25 ARI | 26 ARI | 27 SF | 28 SF |
| 29 SF | 30 MIL | 31 MIL | | | | |

**June**

| SUN | MON | TUE | WED | THU | FRI | SAT |
|---|---|---|---|---|---|---|
| | | | 1 MIL | 2 CHC | 3 CHC | 4 CHC |
| 5 CHC | 6 | 7 CLE | 8 CLE | 9 CLE | 10 CHW | 11 CHW |
| 12 CHW | 13 | 14 DET | 15 DET | 16 DET | 17 MIN | 18 MIN |
| 19 MIN | 20 LA | 21 LA | 22 LA | 23 LA | 24 SEA | 25 SEA |
| 26 SEA | 27 LA | 28 LA | 29 LA | 30 | | |

**July**

| SUN | MON | TUE | WED | THU | FRI | SAT |
|---|---|---|---|---|---|---|
| | | | | | 1 SF | 2 SF |
| 3 SF | 4 HOU | 5 HOU | 6 HOU | 7 HOU | 8 COL | 9 COL |
| 10 COL | 11 | 12 All-Star | 13 | 14 ARI | 15 ARI | 16 ARI |
| 17 ARI | 18 | 19 NYM | 20 NYM | 21 NYM | 22 PHI | 23 PHI |
| 24 PHI | 25 | 26 STL | 27 STL | 28 STL | 29 CIN | 30 CIN |
| 31 CIN | | | | | | |

**August**

| SUN | MON | TUE | WED | THU | FRI | SAT |
|---|---|---|---|---|---|---|
| | 1 | 2 PIT | 3 PIT | 4 PIT | 5 WAS | 6 WAS |
| 7 WAS | 8 | 9 NYM | 10 NYM | 11 NYM | 12 PHI | 13 PHI |
| 14 PHI | 15 | 16 FLA | 17 FLA | 18 FLA | 19 ATL | 20 ATL |
| 21 ATL | 22 HOU | 23 HOU | 24 HOU | 25 | 26 COL | 27 COL |
| 28 COL | 29 ARI | 30 ARI | 31 ARI | | | |

**September**

| SUN | MON | TUE | WED | THU | FRI | SAT |
|---|---|---|---|---|---|---|
| | | | | 1 MIL | 2 MIL | 3 MIL |
| 4 MIL | 5 | 6 COL | 7 COL | 8 COL | 9 LA | 10 LA |
| 11 LA | 12 SF | 13 SF | 14 SF | 15 | 16 WAS | 17 WAS |
| 18 WAS | 19 COL | 20 COL | 21 COL | 22 COL | 23 ARI | 24 ARI |
| 25 ARI | 26 SF | 27 SF | 28 SF | 29 SF | 30 LA | |

**October**

| SUN | MON | TUE | WED | THU | FRI | SAT |
|---|---|---|---|---|---|---|
| | | | | | | 1 LA |
| 2 LA | 3 | 4 | 5 | 6 | 7 | 8 |

Home games shaded. All-Star Game July 12 at Detroit. Schedule subject to change.

### CLUB DIRECTORY

**Chairman**
John Moores
**President and chief operating officer**
Dick Freeman
**Exec. v.p. & man. dir. of ballpark op.**
Richard Anderson
**Exec. v.p., baseball operations and g.m.**
Kevin Towers
**Vice president, community relations**
Michele Anderson
**Assistant general manager**
Fred Uhlman Jr.
**Director, scouting**
Bill Gayton
**Director, minor league operations**
Priscilla Oppenheimer
**Director, player development**
Tye Waller

### MINOR LEAGUE AFFILIATES

| Class | Team | League | Manager |
|---|---|---|---|
| AAA | Portland | Pacific Coast | Craig Colbert |
| AA | Mobile | Southern | Gary Jones |
| Advanced A | Lake Elsinore | California | Rick Renteria |
| A | Fort Wayne | Midwest | Randy Ready |
| Short-Season A | Eugene | Northwest | Roy Howell |
| Rookie | Arizona Padres | Arizona | Carlos Lezcano |

### BROADCAST INFORMATION

**Radio:** MIGHTY 1090, KURS-AM (1040, Spanish).
**Cable TV:** Channel 4 Padres.

### SPRING TRAINING

**Ballpark (city):** Peoria Stadium (Peoria, Ariz.).
**Ticket information:** 623-878-4337, 800-409-1511.

**For more on the Padres, go to msn.foxsports.com/mlb/teams.**

Burroughs

## SPRING TRAINING ROSTER

**Manager**—Bruce Bochy (15).
**Coaches**—Darrel Akerfelds (48), Darren Balsley (36), Davey Lopes (25), Dave Magadan (12), Tony Muser (40), Rob Picciolo (5).

| No. | PITCHERS | B/T | Ht./Wt. | Age* | 2004 Clubs |
|---|---|---|---|---|---|
| 43 | Ashby, Andy | R/R | 6-1/202 | 37 | San Diego |
| | Baker, Brad | R/R | 6-2/180 | 24 | Mobile, Portland |
| | Bukvich, Ryan | R/R | 6-2/250 | 26 | Kansas City, Omaha |
| 53 | Eaton, Adam | R/R | 6-2/196 | 27 | San Diego |
| 47 | Germano, Justin | R/R | 6-1/190 | 21 | Mobile, Portland, San Diego |
| 51 | Hoffman, Trevor | R/R | 6-0/215 | 37 | San Diego |
| 50 | Lawrence, Brian | R/R | 6-0/197 | 28 | San Diego |
| 38 | Linebrink, Scott | R/R | 6-3/208 | 28 | San Diego |
| | May, Darrell | L/L | 6-2/185 | 32 | Kansas City |
| 39 | Neal, Blaine | L/R | 6-5/248 | 26 | Portland, San Diego |
| 16 | Otsuka, Akinori | R/R | 6-0/200 | 33 | San Diego |
| | Oxspring, Chris | L/R | 6-0/180 | 27 | Portland |
| 44 | Peavy, Jake | R/R | 6-1/180 | 23 | Mobile, San Diego |
| | Reyes, Dennys | R/L | 6-3/245 | 27 | Kansas City |
| | Seanez, Rudy | R/R | 5-11/200 | 36 | Omaha, Kansas City, Florida |
| | Thompson, Sean | L/L | 5-11/160 | 22 | Fort Wayne |
| | Tucker, Rusty | L/L | 6-0/190 | 22 | Arizona Padres, Lake Elsinore |
| | Williams, Randy | L/L | 6-3/195 | 29 | Tacoma, Seattle |
| | Williams, Woody | R/R | 6-0/200 | 38 | St. Louis |

| No. | CATCHERS | B/T | Ht./Wt. | Age* | 2004 Clubs |
|---|---|---|---|---|---|
| 55 | Hernandez, Ramon | R/R | 6-0/210 | 28 | Portland, San Diego |
| 20 | Ojeda, Miguel | R/R | 6-2/190 | 30 | Portland, San Diego |
| 11 | Quintero, Humberto | R/R | 6-1/190 | 25 | Portland, San Diego |

| No. | INFIELDERS | B/T | Ht./Wt. | Age* | 2004 Clubs |
|---|---|---|---|---|---|
| | Barfield, Josh | R/R | 6-0/185 | 22 | Mobile |
| | Blum, Geoff | B/R | 6-3/200 | 31 | Tampa Bay |
| | Bozied, Tagg | R/R | 6-3/210 | 25 | Portland |
| 32 | Burroughs, Sean | L/R | 6-2/200 | 24 | San Diego |
| | Castro, Bernie | B/R | 5-10/165 | 25 | Portland |
| | Furmaniak, J.J. | R/R | 6-0/190 | 25 | Mobile, Portland |
| 3 | Greene, Khalil | R/R | 5-11/210 | 25 | San Diego |
| 8 | Loretta, Mark | R/R | 6-0/186 | 33 | San Diego |
| | McAnulty, Paul | L/R | 5-10/220 | 24 | Lake Elsinore |
| 23 | Nevin, Phil | R/R | 6-2/231 | 34 | San Diego |
| | Young, Eric | R/R | 5-8/186 | 37 | Texas |

| No. | OUTFIELDERS | B/T | Ht./Wt. | Age* | 2004 Clubs |
|---|---|---|---|---|---|
| 24 | Giles, Brian | L/L | 5-10/205 | 34 | San Diego |
| 7 | Guzman, Freddy | B/R | 5-10/165 | 24 | Mobile, Portland, San Diego |
| | Johnson, Ben | R/R | 6-1/200 | 23 | Mobile |
| 30 | Klesko, Ryan | L/L | 6-3/220 | 33 | San Diego |
| 10 | Knott, Jon | R/R | 6-3/220 | 26 | San Diego, Portland |
| 22 | Nady, Xavier | R/R | 6-2/205 | 26 | Portland, San Diego |
| | Roberts, Dave | L/L | 5-10/180 | 32 | Vero Beach, Los Angeles, Boston |
| | Sweeney, Mark | L/L | 6-1/215 | 35 | Colorado |

*Age as of April 1, 2005.

## BALLPARK INFORMATION

**Ballpark (capacity, surface)**
Petco Park (42,500, grass)

**Address**
100 Park Blvd.
San Diego, CA 92101

**Official website**
www.padres.com

**Business phone**
619-795-5000

**Ticket information**
1-877-FRIAR-TIX

**Field dimensions (from home plate)**
To left field at foul line, 334 feet
To center field, 396 feet
To right field at foul line, 322 feet

**First game played**
April 8, 2004, vs. San Francisco

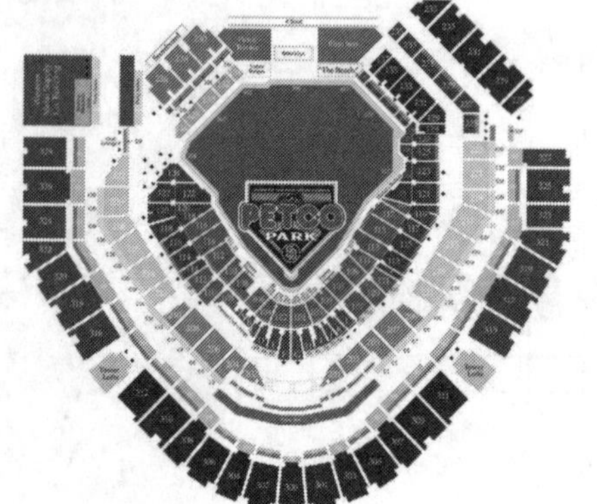

# 2004REVIEW

## DAY BY DAY



| Date | Opp. | Res. | Score | (inn.*) | Hits | Opp. hits | Winning pitcher | Losing pitcher | Save | Record | Pos. | GB |
|---|---|---|---|---|---|---|---|---|---|---|---|---|
| 4-5 | At L.A. | W | 8-2 | | 12 | 15 | Lawrence | Nomo | | 1-0 | T1st | ... |
| 4-6 | At L.A. | L | 4-5 | | 13 | 12 | Gagne | Otsuka | | 1-1 | T3rd | 1.0 |
| 4-7 | At L.A. | L | 1-2 | (11) | 10 | 6 | Lima | Oropesa | | 1-2 | 5th | 1.0 |
| 4-8 | S.F | W | 4-3 | (10) | 11 | 10 | Oropesa | Herges | | 2-2 | T3rd | 0.5 |
| 4-10 | S.F | W | 6-4 | | 14 | 8 | Linebrink | Brower | Hoffman | 3-2 | 2nd | 1.0 |
| 4-11 | S.F | L | 3-6 | | 5 | 11 | Christiansen | Witasick | Herges | 3-3 | T2nd | 1.0 |
| 4-13 | L.A. | W | 8-3 | | 10 | 7 | Eaton | Weaver | | 4-3 | T2nd | 0.5 |
| 4-14 | L.A. | L | 4-11 | | 7 | 13 | Ishii | Wells | | 4-4 | T3rd | 1.0 |
| 4-15 | L.A. | L | 5-7 | | 10 | 11 | Nomo | Lawrence | Gagne | 4-5 | T3rd | 2.0 |
| 4-16 | Ari. | L | 0-5 | | 2 | 7 | Johnson | Peavy | | 4-6 | T3rd | 3.0 |
| 4-17 | Ari. | W | 3-2 | | 3 | 6 | Valdez | Webb | Hoffman | 5-6 | T2nd | 3.0 |
| 4-18 | Ari. | W | 6-5 | | 13 | 8 | Oropesa | Mantei | | 6-6 | 2nd | 3.0 |
| 4-19 | At S.F | L | 3-4 | | 8 | 7 | Williams | Wells | Brower | 6-7 | T2nd | 3.5 |
| 4-20 | At S.F | W | 9-5 | | 15 | 11 | Lawrence | Hermanson | | 7-7 | 2nd | 2.5 |
| 4-21 | At S.F | W | 11-0 | | 17 | 4 | Peavy | Schmidt | | 8-7 | 2nd | 2.5 |
| 4-22 | At S.F | W | 9-4 | | 13 | 8 | Valdez | Rueter | | 9-7 | 2nd | 1.5 |
| 4-23 | At Ari. | L | 2-5 | | 4 | 9 | Koplove | Eaton | Mantei | 9-8 | 2nd | 2.5 |
| 4-24 | At Ari. | W | 4-2 | | 7 | 6 | Otsuka | Villarreal | Hoffman | 10-8 | 2nd | 1.5 |
| 4-25 | At Ari. | L | 7-12 | | 12 | 14 | Dessens | Lawrence | | 10-9 | 2nd | 2.5 |
| 4-26 | Mon. | W | 3-2 | | 8 | 8 | Otsuka | Ayala | | 11-9 | 2nd | 2.0 |
| 4-27 | Mon. | W | 3-0 | | 8 | 4 | Valdez | Patterson | Hoffman | 12-9 | 2nd | 1.0 |
| 4-28 | Mon. | W | 5-4 | | 8 | 13 | Osuna | Ayala | Hoffman | 13-9 | 2nd | 1.0 |
| 4-29 | Mon. | W | 2-1 | | 6 | 5 | Wells | Ohka | Hoffman | 14-9 | 2nd | ... |
| 4-30 | N.Y. | W | 7-6 | | 12 | 12 | Lawrence | Yates | Otsuka | 15-9 | 2nd | ... |
| 5-1 | N.Y. | W | 3-1 | | 7 | 10 | Peavy | Franco | Hoffman | 16-9 | 2nd | ... |
| 5-2 | N.Y. | L | 2-6 | | 6 | 9 | Glavine | Valdez | | 16-10 | 2nd | ... |
| 5-4 | At Atl. | L | 2-4 | | 7 | 7 | Ortiz | Eaton | Smoltz | 16-11 | 2nd | 1.0 |
| 5-5 | At Atl. | W | 2-0 | | 11 | 5 | Wells | Wright | Hoffman | 17-11 | 2nd | ... |
| 5-6 | At Atl. | W | 7-3 | | 13 | 6 | Lawrence | Hampton | | 18-11 | 2nd | ... |
| 5-7 | At Fla. | L | 1-3 | | 4 | 10 | Pavano | Peavy | Benitez | 18-12 | 2nd | 1.0 |
| 5-8 | At Fla. | W | 6-3 | (10) | 17 | 7 | Otsuka | Gracesqui | Hoffman | 19-12 | 2nd | 1.0 |
| 5-9 | At Fla. | L | 4-7 | | 9 | 12 | Beckett | Eaton | Benitez | 19-13 | 2nd | 2.0 |
| 5-11 | Cin. | L | 3-6 | | 8 | 8 | Harang | Wells | Graves | 19-14 | 2nd | 3.0 |
| 5-12 | Cin. | W | 2-1 | | 6 | 9 | Lawrence | Lidle | Hoffman | 20-14 | 2nd | 3.0 |
| 5-13 | Cin. | W | 8-2 | | 6 | 10 | Peavy | Acevedo | | 21-14 | 2nd | 2.0 |
| 5-14 | Chi. | L | 1-6 | | 5 | 12 | Maddux | Valdez | | 21-15 | 2nd | 2.0 |
| 5-15 | Chi. | L | 5-7 | | 9 | 14 | Mitre | Eaton | Hawkins | 21-16 | 2nd | 2.0 |
| 5-16 | Chi. | L | 2-4 | | 5 | 12 | Beltran | Wells | Borowski | 21-17 | 2nd | 2.0 |
| 5-19! | At Pit. | W | 6-3 | | 13 | 9 | Lawrence | Johnston | Hoffman | 22-17 | | |
| 5-19& | At Pit. | W | 7-3 | | 9 | 7 | Peavy | Perez | | 23-17 | 2nd | ... |
| 5-20 | At Pit. | L | 7-9 | | 7 | 14 | Gonzalez | Puffer | Mesa | 23-18 | 2nd | ... |
| 5-21 | At Phi. | L | 4-5 | | 8 | 7 | Madson | Otsuka | Worrell | 23-19 | 2nd | ... |
| 5-22 | At Phi. | W | 9-6 | | 11 | 12 | Germano | Hernandez | | 24-19 | 2nd | ... |
| 5-23 | At Phi. | L | 4-6 | | 11 | 8 | Padilla | Lawrence | Worrell | 24-20 | 2nd | ... |
| 5-25 | At Col. | W | 11-6 | | 16 | 13 | Linebrink | Fassero | | 25-20 | 2nd | ... |
| 5-26 | At Col. | L | 6-13 | | 13 | 14 | Jennings | Eaton | | 25-21 | 2nd | ... |
| 5-27 | At Col. | W | 4-3 | (10) | 13 | 4 | Otsuka | Nunez | Hoffman | 26-21 | 1st | +1.0 |
| 5-28 | At Mil. | W | 5-3 | | 8 | 5 | Lawrence | Davis | Hoffman | 27-21 | 1st | +2.0 |
| 5-29 | At Mil. | L | 3-4 | | 11 | 4 | Obermueller | Tankersley | Kolb | 27-22 | 1st | +1.0 |
| 5-30 | At Mil. | W | 5-2 | | 8 | 10 | Valdez | Santos | Hoffman | 28-22 | 1st | +1.0 |
| 5-31 | Col. | L | 1-7 | | 5 | 10 | Jennings | Eaton | | 28-23 | 2nd | ... |
| 6-1 | Col. | L | 1-7 | | 7 | 8 | Cook | Germano | | 28-24 | 2nd | ... |
| 6-2 | Col. | W | 2-1 | (10) | 7 | 6 | Hoffman | Fuentes | | 29-24 | 2nd | ... |
| 6-4 | Mil. | L | 1-3 | | 5 | 8 | Santos | Tankersley | Kolb | 29-25 | 2nd | 1.0 |
| 6-5 | Mil. | W | 4-0 | | 10 | 4 | Valdez | Obermueller | | 30-25 | 2nd | 1.0 |
| 6-6 | Mil. | W | 8-3 | | 12 | 5 | Eaton | Davis | | 31-25 | 2nd | ... |
| 6-8 | At Bos. | L | 0-1 | | 2 | 9 | Martinez | Osuna | Foulke | 31-26 | 2nd | ... |
| 6-9 | At Bos. | W | 8-1 | | 12 | 7 | Lawrence | Arroyo | | 32-26 | 1st | +1.0 |
| 6-10 | At Bos. | L | 3-9 | | 11 | 13 | Schilling | Valdez | | 32-27 | 2nd | ... |
| 6-11 | At N.Y. | W | 10-2 | | 12 | 4 | Eaton | Heredia | Otsuka | 33-27 | 1st | +1.0 |
| 6-12 | At N.Y. | L | 2-3 | | 13 | 8 | Lieber | Tankersley | Rivera | 33-28 | 2nd | ... |
| 6-13 | At N.Y. | L | 5-6 | (12) | 12 | 12 | Heredia | Beck | | 33-29 | 2nd | ... |
| 6-15 | T.B. | L | 2-5 | | 7 | 12 | Hendrickson | Lawrence | | 33-30 | 2nd | 1.0 |
| 6-16 | T.B. | L | 6-9 | | 11 | 15 | Zambrano | Linebrink | Baez | 33-31 | 3rd | 2.0 |
| 6-17 | T.B. | L | 1-4 | | 10 | 5 | Gaudin | Eaton | Baez | 33-32 | 3rd | 3.0 |

| Date | Opp. | Res. | Score | (inn.*) | Hits | Opp. hits | Winning pitcher | Losing pitcher | Save | Record | Pos. | GB |
|---|---|---|---|---|---|---|---|---|---|---|---|---|
| 6-18 | Tor. | L | 2-3 | | 6 | 7 | Lilly | Wells | Frasor | 33-33 | 3rd | 4.0 |
| 6-19 | Tor. | W | 3-2 | | 8 | 7 | Linebrink | Speier | Hoffman | 34-33 | 3rd | 3.0 |
| 6-20 | Tor. | L | 0-3 | | 7 | 10 | Batista | Lawrence | Frasor | 34-34 | 3rd | 4.0 |
| 6-21 | Ari. | W | 3-1 | | 9 | 7 | Valdez | Fossum | Hoffman | 35-34 | 3rd | 3.0 |
| 6-22 | Ari. | W | 2-1 | (10) | 5 | 7 | Hoffman | Koplove | | 36-34 | 3rd | 2.5 |
| 6-23 | Ari. | W | 4-3 | | 8 | 13 | Otsuka | Dessens | | 37-34 | 3rd | 2.5 |
| 6-25 | At Sea. | W | 3-2 | | 4 | 8 | Lawrence | Garcia | Hoffman | 38-34 | 2nd | 3.0 |
| 6-26 | At Sea. | L | 3-7 | | 8 | 13 | Mateo | Valdez | | 38-35 | 2nd | 3.0 |
| 6-27 | At Sea. | W | 5-1 | | 7 | 3 | Eaton | Moyer | | 39-35 | 2nd | 3.0 |
| 6-28 | At Ari. | W | 10-5 | | 17 | 13 | Wells | Reynolds | | 40-35 | 2nd | 2.5 |
| 6-29 | At Ari. | W | 3-2 | | 6 | 9 | Sweeney | Johnson | Hoffman | 41-35 | 2nd | 1.5 |
| 6-30 | At Ari. | L | 5-8 | | 11 | 10 | Randolph | Neal | Koplove | 41-36 | 2nd | 2.5 |
| 7-1 | At Ari. | L | 5-7 | | 7 | 9 | Fossum | Valdez | Koplove | 41-37 | 3rd | 2.5 |
| 7-2 | K.C. | W | 7-5 | | 12 | 7 | Peavy | Reyes | Hoffman | 42-37 | 2nd | 2.5 |
| 7-3 | K.C. | W | 5-4 | | 8 | 3 | Linebrink | Sullivan | Hoffman | 43-37 | 2nd | 1.5 |
| 7-4 | K.C. | W | 7-1 | | 13 | 6 | Wells | Wood | | 44-37 | 2nd | 0.5 |
| 7-5 | Hou. | W | 2-1 | | 5 | 5 | Lawrence | Miceli | Hoffman | 45-37 | 1st | +0.5 |
| 7-6 | Hou. | W | 5-3 | | 9 | 5 | Valdez | Munro | Hoffman | 46-37 | 1st | +1.0 |
| 7-7 | Hou. | L | 1-5 | | 7 | 12 | Oswalt | Peavy | Lidge | 46-38 | 2nd | ... |
| 7-8 | Col. | L | 1-5 | | 5 | 10 | Jennings | Eaton | | 46-39 | 2nd | 1.0 |
| 7-9 | Col. | L | 5-6 | | 10 | 9 | Harikkala | Hoffman | Chacon | 46-40 | 3rd | 1.0 |
| 7-10 | Col. | L | 2-6 | | 11 | 11 | Cook | Lawrence | | 46-41 | 3rd | 2.0 |
| 7-11 | Col. | W | 4-2 | | 7 | 8 | Valdez | Stark | Hoffman | 47-41 | 3rd | 2.0 |
| 7-16 | At Hou. | W | 5-1 | | 9 | 6 | Peavy | Pettitte | | 48-41 | 3rd | 2.5 |
| 7-17 | At Hou. | W | 7-4 | | 8 | 10 | Wells | Oswalt | Hoffman | 49-41 | 3rd | 2.5 |
| 7-18 | At Hou. | L | 3-5 | | 5 | 10 | Clemens | Lawrence | Lidge | 49-42 | 3rd | 3.5 |
| 7-19 | At Col. | W | 13-6 | | 18 | 12 | Valdez | Stark | | 50-42 | 3rd | 3.5 |
| 7-20 | At Col. | W | 9-7 | | 16 | 14 | Eaton | Jennings | Hoffman | 51-42 | 3rd | 3.5 |
| 7-21 | At S.F | W | 7-1 | | 16 | 5 | Peavy | Rueter | | 52-42 | 2nd | 2.5 |
| 7-22 | At S.F | W | 9-4 | | 10 | 12 | Wells | Schmidt | | 53-42 | 2nd | 2.5 |
| 7-23 | At L.A. | L | 2-3 | | 6 | 5 | Gagne | Beck | | 53-43 | 2nd | 3.5 |
| 7-24 | At L.A. | L | 2-12 | | 7 | 14 | Alvarez | Valdez | | 53-44 | 3rd | 4.5 |
| 7-25 | At L.A. | W | 3-0 | | 8 | 2 | Eaton | Weaver | Hoffman | 54-44 | 2nd | 3.5 |
| 7-26 | S.F | W | 3-2 | | 7 | 5 | Linebrink | Rodriguez | Hoffman | 55-44 | 2nd | 3.5 |
| 7-27 | S.F | L | 4-6 | | 10 | 11 | Schmidt | Wells | Herges | 55-45 | 2nd | 3.5 |
| 7-28 | S.F | W | 9-4 | | 12 | 5 | Lawrence | Hermanson | | 56-45 | 2nd | 2.5 |
| 7-29 | S.F | W | 7-4 | | 10 | 7 | Neal | Tomko | Hoffman | 57-45 | 2nd | 2.5 |
| 7-30 | L.A. | L | 3-12 | | 8 | 15 | Weaver | Eaton | | 57-46 | 2nd | 3.5 |
| 7-31 | L.A. | W | 3-2 | | 7 | 7 | Otsuka | Dreifort | Hoffman | 58-46 | 2nd | 2.5 |
| 8-1 | L.A. | L | 1-2 | (12) | 8 | 9 | Gagne | Stone | Dreifort | 58-47 | 2nd | 3.5 |
| 8-3 | Phi. | L | 2-5 | | 9 | 8 | Myers | Lawrence | | 58-48 | 2nd | 4.5 |
| 8-4 | Phi. | L | 5-7 | | 13 | 11 | Milton | Eaton | Worrell | 58-49 | 2nd | 5.5 |
| 8-5 | Phi. | L | 3-5 | (10) | 9 | 9 | Rodriguez | Hoffman | Worrell | 58-50 | 2nd | 6.5 |
| 8-6 | Pit. | W | 13-1 | | 11 | 5 | Peavy | Vogelsong | | 59-50 | 2nd | 5.5 |
| 8-7 | Pit. | L | 1-3 | | 4 | 12 | Wells | Wells | Mesa | 59-51 | 2nd | 6.5 |
| 8-8 | Pit. | L | 2-4 | | 8 | 12 | Perez | Lawrence | Mesa | 59-52 | 2nd | 6.5 |
| 8-10 | At Chi. | W | 8-6 | | 12 | 8 | Eaton | Prior | Hoffman | 60-52 | 2nd | 6.5 |
| 8-11 | At Chi. | L | 1-5 | | 6 | 8 | Zambrano | Hitchcock | | 60-53 | 2nd | 7.5 |
| 8-12 | At Chi. | W | 5-4 | (11) | 15 | 12 | Stone | Dempster | Hoffman | 61-53 | 2nd | 6.5 |
| 8-13 | At Cin. | W | 14-5 | | 17 | 8 | Wells | Wilson | Witasick | 62-53 | 2nd | 6.5 |
| 8-14 | At Cin. | L | 5-11 | | 9 | 16 | Acevedo | Lawrence | | 62-54 | 2nd | 6.5 |
| 8-15 | At Cin. | W | 7-2 | | 10 | 11 | Eaton | Hudson | | 63-54 | 2nd | 6.5 |
| 8-16 | Atl. | L | 4-5 | | 11 | 7 | Hampton | Hitchcock | Smoltz | 63-55 | 3rd | 6.5 |
| 8-17 | Atl. | W | 11-6 | | 17 | 8 | Peavy | Wright | | 64-55 | 3rd | 6.5 |
| 8-18 | Atl. | L | 5-6 | | 9 | 15 | Reitsma | Hoffman | Smoltz | 64-56 | 3rd | 6.5 |
| 8-20 | Fla. | W | 6-1 | | 10 | 5 | Lawrence | Willis | | 65-56 | 3rd | 6.0 |
| 8-21 | Fla. | L | 2-8 | | 6 | 15 | Beckett | Eaton | | 65-57 | 3rd | 7.0 |
| 8-22 | Fla. | L | 3-8 | | 7 | 14 | Pavano | Hitchcock | Mota | 65-58 | 3rd | 7.0 |
| 8-23 | At N.Y. | W | 9-4 | | 13 | 6 | Peavy | Heilman | | 66-58 | 3rd | 6.0 |
| 8-24 | At N.Y. | W | 3-1 | | 9 | 4 | Wells | Benson | Hoffman | 67-58 | 3rd | 6.0 |
| 8-25 | At N.Y. | W | 4-0 | | 10 | 6 | Lawrence | Leiter | | 68-58 | 3rd | 5.0 |
| 8-26 | At N.Y. | W | 10-3 | | 16 | 6 | Eaton | Trachsel | | 69-58 | 3rd | 5.0 |
| 8-27 | At Mon. | L | 3-10 | | 8 | 14 | Downs | Tankersley | | 69-59 | 3rd | 5.0 |
| 8-28 | At Mon. | W | 5-2 | | 9 | 6 | Peavy | Patterson | Hoffman | 70-59 | 2nd | 5.0 |
| 8-29 | At Mon. | W | 11-3 | | 14 | 10 | Wells | Kim | | 71-59 | 2nd | 5.0 |
| 8-31 | At StL. | L | 3-9 | | 7 | 16 | Williams | Lawrence | | 71-60 | 3rd | 6.0 |
| 9-1 | At StL. | L | 2-4 | | 9 | 6 | Carpenter | Eaton | Isringhausen | 71-61 | 3rd | 6.0 |
| 9-2 | At StL. | L | 2-7 | | 10 | 12 | Suppan | Peavy | | 71-62 | 3rd | 7.0 |

| Date | Opp. | Res. | Score | (inn.*) | Hits | Opp. hits | Winning pitcher | Losing pitcher | Save | Record | Pos. | GB |
|---|---|---|---|---|---|---|---|---|---|---|---|---|
| 9-3 | Col. | W | 7-6 | | 8 | 12 | Linebrink | Dohmann | Hoffman | 72-62 | 3rd | 6.0 |
| 9-4 | Col. | L | 2-8 | | 4 | 10 | Estes | Tankersley | | 72-63 | 3rd | 6.0 |
| 9-5 | Col. | L | 2-5 | | 10 | 9 | Francis | Lawrence | | 72-64 | 3rd | 6.0 |
| 9-6 | StL. | W | 7-3 | | 9 | 9 | Linebrink | Eldred | Hoffman | 73-64 | 3rd | 5.5 |
| 9-7 | StL. | L | 2-4 | | 7 | 8 | Suppan | Peavy | Isringhausen | 73-65 | 3rd | 6.5 |
| 9-8 | StL. | W | 10-5 | | 12 | 7 | Wells | Morris | | 74-65 | 3rd | 6.5 |
| 9-9 | At Col. | L | 7-9 | | 14 | 12 | Lopez | Linebrink | Chacon | 74-66 | 3rd | 7.5 |
| 9-10 | At Col. | W | 10-4 | | 13 | 8 | Lawrence | Harikkala | | 75-66 | 3rd | 7.5 |
| 9-11 | At Col. | L | 2-13 | | 8 | 18 | Francis | Eaton | | 75-67 | 3rd | 8.5 |
| 9-12 | At Col. | W | 15-2 | | 18 | 7 | Peavy | Reed | | 76-67 | 3rd | 7.5 |
| 9-13 | At L.A. | W | 9-7 | | 13 | 10 | Wells | Perez | Hoffman | 77-67 | 3rd | 6.5 |
| 9-14 | At L.A. | L | 3-6 | | 11 | 11 | Lima | Germano | Gagne | 77-68 | 3rd | 7.5 |
| 9-15 | At L.A. | W | 7-3 | | 13 | 8 | Lawrence | Alvarez | Hoffman | 78-68 | 3rd | 6.5 |
| 9-16 | At L.A. | W | 3-0 | | 9 | 7 | Eaton | Weaver | Hoffman | 79-68 | 3rd | 5.5 |
| 9-17 | At S.F | L | 1-4 | | 6 | 9 | Lowry | Peavy | Hermanson | 79-69 | 3rd | 6.5 |
| 9-18 | At S.F | W | 5-1 | | 7 | 7 | Wells | Schmidt | Hoffman | 80-69 | 3rd | 5.5 |
| 9-19 | At S.F | L | 2-4 | | 7 | 6 | Hermanson | Linebrink | | 80-70 | 3rd | 6.5 |
| 9-21 | L.A. | W | 9-4 | | 13 | 7 | Eaton | Weaver | | 81-70 | 3rd | 5.5 |
| 9-22 | L.A. | W | 4-0 | | 6 | 3 | Peavy | Penny | | 82-70 | 3rd | 4.5 |
| 9-23 | L.A. | L | 6-9 | | 10 | 14 | Brazoban | Lawrence | Gagne | 82-71 | 3rd | 5.5 |
| 9-24 | Ari. | W | 6-5 | | 10 | 13 | Otsuka | Aquino | | 83-71 | 3rd | 5.5 |
| 9-25 | Ari. | W | 6-5 | | 8 | 10 | Osuna | Durbin | Hoffman | 84-71 | 3rd | 4.5 |
| 9-26 | Ari. | W | 7-1 | | 12 | 6 | Peavy | Sparks | | 85-71 | 3rd | 4.5 |
| 9-28 | S.F | L | 5-7 | | 10 | 17 | Schmidt | Lawrence | Hermanson | 85-72 | 3rd | 6.0 |
| 9-29 | S.F | W | 4-3 | (10) | 7 | 7 | Hoffman | Hermanson | | 86-72 | 3rd | 5.0 |
| 9-30 | S.F | L | 1-4 | | 5 | 9 | Williams | Eaton | Hermanson | 86-73 | 3rd | 6.0 |
| 10-1 | At Ari. | W | 3-2 | | 7 | 5 | Peavy | Gosling | Hoffman | 87-73 | 3rd | 5.0 |
| 10-2 | At Ari. | L | 6-7 | | 10 | 11 | Johnson | Bynum | Aquino | 87-74 | 3rd | 6.0 |
| 10-3 | At Ari. | L | 1-4 | | 6 | 10 | Webb | Wells | Aquino | 87-75 | 3rd | 6.0 |

Monthly records: April (15-9), May (13-14), June (13-13), July (17-10), August (13-14), September (15-13), October (1-2).
*Innings, if other than nine. ! First game of a doubleheader. & Second game of a doubleheader.

## RECORDS

**2004 regular-season record:** 87-75
**Position:** 3rd in N.L. West
**Home:** 42-39 **Road:** 45-36
**N.L. East:** 18-14 **N.L. Central:** 19-17
**N.L. West:** 42-34 **A.L.** 8-10
**Vs. LH starters:** 29-23
**Vs. RH starters:** 58-52
**Grass:** 85-74 **Artificial:** 2-1
**Day:** 22-17 **Night:** 65-58
**1-Run:** 25-15 **X-inn.:** 7-4
**Doubleheaders:** 1-0-0
**Team record past five years:** 372-438 (.459, ranks 12th in league in that span)

## TEAM LEADERS

**Batting average**: Mark Loretta (.335).
**At-bats:** Mark Loretta (620).
**Runs:** Mark Loretta (108).
**Hits:** Mark Loretta (208).
**Total Bases:** Mark Loretta (307).
**Doubles:** Mark Loretta (47).
**Triples:** Brian Giles (7).
**Home runs:** Phil Nevin (26).
**Runs batted in:** Phil Nevin (105).
**Stolen bases:** Kerry Robinson (11).
**Slugging percentage:** Mark Loretta (.495).
**On-base percentage:** Ryan Klesko (.399).
**Wins:** Brian Lawrence, Jake Peavy (15).
**Earned-run average:** Jake Peavy (2.27).
**Complete games:** Brian Lawrence (2).
**Shutouts:** Brian Lawrence, Ismael Valdez (1).
**Saves:** Trevor Hoffman (41).
**Innings pitched:** Brian Lawrence (203.0).
**Strikeouts:** Jake Peavy (173).

## GAMES BY POSITION

**Catcher:** Ramon Hernandez 108, Miguel Ojeda 50, Humberto Quintero 21, Phil Nevin 1.
**First base:** Phil Nevin 144, Ryan Klesko 18, Jeff Cirillo 10, Dave Hansen 7, Brian Buchanan 3, Ramon Vazquez 3, Rich Aurilia 1, Robert Fick 1.
**Second base:** Mark Loretta 154, Ramon Vazquez 10, Rich Aurilia 7, Jeff Cirillo 4.
**Third base:** Sean Burroughs 125, Rich Aurilia 29, Jeff Cirillo 11, Ramon Vazquez 9, Dave Hansen 2.
**Shortstop:** Khalil Greene 136, Ramon Vazquez 22, Alex S. Gonzalez 11, Rich Aurilia 6.
**Outfield:** Brian Giles 159, Jay Payton 137, Ryan Klesko 104, Terrence Long 87, Kerry Robinson 49, Xavier Nady 22, Brian Buchanan 18, Freddy Guzman 17, Jon Knott 5, Jeff Cirillo 1.
**Designated hitter:** Ryan Klesko 3, Xavier Nady 2, Phil Nevin 2, Kerry Robinson 2, Terrence Long 1, Jay Payton 1.

## TOP DRAFT CHOICES

1. **Matt Bush,** SS, Mission Bay H.S., El Cajon, Calif.
3. **Billy Killian,** C, Chippewa Hills H.S., Stanwood, Mich.
4. **Daryl Jones,** 1B, Westchester H.S., Gardena, Calif.
5. **Sean Kazmar,** SS, CC of Southern Nevada.
6. **Jonathan Ellis,** RHP, The Citadel.
7. **Ricky Steik,** RHP, Golden West College (Calif.).
8. **Vern Sterry,** RHP, North Carolina State.
9. **David O'Hagan,** RHP, Stanford.
10. **Chris Kolkhorst,** OF, Rice.

# SAN FRANCISCO GIANTS
## *NATIONAL LEAGUE WEST DIVISION*

## 2005 SEASON

**Giants Schedule**
Home games shaded.
All-Star Game July 12 at Detroit. Schedule subject to change.

**April**

| SUN | MON | TUE | WED | THU | FRI | SAT |
|---|---|---|---|---|---|---|
| 3 | 4 | 5 LA | 6 LA | 7 LA | 8 COL | 9 COL |
| 10 COL | 11 | 12 LA | 13 LA | 14 | 15 COL | 16 COL |
| 17 COL | 18 SD | 19 SD | 20 ARI | 21 ARI | 22 MIL | 23 MIL |
| 24 MIL | 25 SD | 26 SD | 27 SD | 28 | 29 PIT | 30 PIT |

**May**

| SUN | MON | TUE | WED | THU | FRI | SAT |
|---|---|---|---|---|---|---|
| 1 PIT | 2 ARI | 3 ARI | 4 ARI | 5 | 6 WAS | 7 WAS |
| 8 WAS | 9 PIT | 10 PIT | 11 PIT | 12 HOU | 13 HOU | 14 HOU |
| 15 HOU | 16 | 17 COL | 18 COL | 19 COL | 20 OAK | 21 OAK |
| 22 OAK | 23 | 24 LA | 25 LA | 26 LA | 27 SD | 28 SD |
| 29 SD | 30 | 31 PHI | | | | |

**June**

| SUN | MON | TUE | WED | THU | FRI | SAT |
|---|---|---|---|---|---|---|
| | | | 1 PHI | 2 PHI | 3 NYM | 4 NYM |
| 5 NYM | 6 | 7 KC | 8 KC | 9 KC | 10 CLE | 11 CLE |
| 12 CLE | 13 | 14 MIN | 15 MIN | 16 MIN | 17 DET | 18 DET |
| 19 DET | 20 ARI | 21 ARI | 22 ARI | 23 ARI | 24 OAK | 25 OAK |
| 26 OAK | 27 | 28 ARI | 29 ARI | 30 ARI | | |

**July**

| SUN | MON | TUE | WED | THU | FRI | SAT |
|---|---|---|---|---|---|---|
| | | | | | 1 SD | 2 SD |
| 3 SD | 4 CIN | 5 CIN | 6 CIN | 7 CIN | 8 STL | 9 STL |
| 10 STL | 11 | 12 All-Star | 13 | 14 LA | 15 LA | 16 LA |
| 17 LA | 18 ATL | 19 ATL | 20 ATL | 21 | 22 FLA | 23 FLA |
| 24 FLA | 25 CHC | 26 CHC | 27 CHC | 28 MIL | 29 MIL | 30 MIL |
| 31 MIL | | | | | | |

**August**

| SUN | MON | TUE | WED | THU | FRI | SAT |
|---|---|---|---|---|---|---|
| | 1 | 2 COL | 3 COL | 4 COL | 5 HOU | 6 HOU |
| 7 HOU | 8 | 9 ATL | 10 ATL | 11 ATL | 12 FLA | 13 FLA |
| 14 FLA | 15 CIN | 16 CIN | 17 CIN | 18 CIN | 19 STL | 20 STL |
| 21 STL | 22 PHI | 23 PHI | 24 PHI | 25 | 26 NYM | 27 NYM |
| 28 NYM | 29 COL | 30 COL | 31 COL | | | |

**September**

| SUN | MON | TUE | WED | THU | FRI | SAT |
|---|---|---|---|---|---|---|
| | | | | 1 | 2 ARI | 3 ARI |
| 4 ARI | 5 LA | 6 LA | 7 LA | 8 CHC | 9 CHC | 10 CHC |
| 11 CHC | 12 SD | 13 SD | 14 SD | 15 LA | 16 LA | 17 LA |
| 18 LA | 19 | 20 WAS | 21 WAS | 22 WAS | 23 COL | 24 COL |
| 25 COL | 26 SD | 27 SD | 28 SD | 29 SD | 30 ARI | |

**October**

| SUN | MON | TUE | WED | THU | FRI | SAT |
|---|---|---|---|---|---|---|
| | | | | | | 1 ARI |
| 2 ARI | 3 | 4 | 5 | 6 | 7 | 8 |

Home games shaded. All-Star Game July 12 at Detroit. Schedule subject to change.

### CLUB DIRECTORY

**President and managing general partner**
Peter A. Magowan

**Executive vice president/COO**
Larry Baer

**Senior v.p. and general manager**
Brian Sabean

**Vice president and assistant g.m.**
Ned Colletti

**Vice president of player personnel**
Dick Tidrow

**Special assistant to the general manager**
Ron Perranoski

**Director of player development**
Jack Hiatt

**Coordinator of minor league instruction**
Fred Stanley

**Media relations manager**
Jim Moorehead

**Baseball information manager**
Blake Rhodes

**Director, broadcasting & media services**
Maria Jacinto

### MINOR LEAGUE AFFILIATES

| Class | Team | League | Manager |
|---|---|---|---|
| AAA | Fresno | Pacific Coast | Shane Turner |
| AA | Norwich | Eastern | Dave Machemer |
| Advanced A | San Jose | California | Lenn Sakata |
| A | Augusta | South Atlantic | Robert Kelly |
| Short-Season A | Salem-Keizer | Northwest | Steve Decker |
| Rookie | Arizona Giants | Arizona | Bert Hunter |

### BROADCAST INFORMATION

**Radio:** KNBR-AM (680).
**TV:** KTVU-TV (Channel 2).
**Cable TV:** Fox Sports Net.

### SPRING TRAINING

**Ballpark (city):** Scottsdale Stadium (Scottsdale, Ariz.).
**Ticket information:** 480-990-7972.

**For more on the Giants, go to msn.foxsports.com/mlb/teams.**

Bonds

## SPRING TRAINING ROSTER

**Manager**—Felipe Alou (23).
**Coaches**—Carlos Alfonso (17), Mark Gardner (26), Gene Glynn (15), Joe Lefebvre (18), Luis Pujols (55), Dave Righetti (19), Ron Wotus (10).

| No. | PITCHERS | B/T | Ht./Wt. | Age* | 2004 Clubs |
|---|---|---|---|---|---|
| 47 | Aardsma, David | R/R | 6-5/200 | 23 | San Francisco, Fresno |
| | Benitez, Armando | R/R | 6-4/229 | 32 | Florida |
| 38 | Brower, Jim | R/R | 6-3/215 | 32 | San Francisco |
| 34 | Burba, Dave | R/R | 6-4/255 | 38 | Milwaukee, San Francisco |
| | Burres, Brian | L/L | 6-1/175 | 23 | San Jose |
| 40 | Christiansen, Jason | R/L | 6-5/241 | 35 | San Francisco |
| 53 | Correia, Kevin | R/R | 6-3/200 | 24 | Fresno, San Francisco |
| 49 | Eyre, Scott | L/L | 6-1/210 | 32 | Fresno, San Francisco |
| 34 | Foppert, Jesse | R/R | 6-6/210 | 24 | Arizona Giants, San Jose, Fresno, San Francisco |
| 41 | Hennessey, Brad | R/R | 6-2/185 | 25 | Norwich, Fresno, San Francisco |
| 48 | Herges, Matt | L/R | 6-0/200 | 35 | San Francisco |
| 51 | Lowry, Noah | R/L | 6-2/210 | 24 | Fresno, San Francisco |
| | Munter, Scott | R/R | 6-6/235 | 25 | Norwich, Fresno |
| 46 | Rueter, Kirk | L/L | 6-2/212 | 34 | San Francisco |
| 29 | Schmidt, Jason | R/R | 6-5/205 | 32 | San Jose, San Francisco |
| | Simon, Alfredo | R/R | 6-4/215 | 23 | Clearwater, San Jose |
| | Threets, Erick | L/L | 6-5/240 | 23 | Did Not Play |
| 50 | Tomko, Brett | R/R | 6-4/215 | 31 | Fresno, San Francisco |
| 37 | Valdez, Merkin | R/R | 6-5/208 | 23 | Fresno, San Jose, San Francisco, Norwich |
| 45 | Walker, Tyler | R/R | 6-3/255 | 28 | Fresno, San Francisco |
| 57 | Williams, Jerome | R/R | 6-3/246 | 23 | San Francisco |

| No. | CATCHERS | B/T | Ht./Wt. | Age* | 2004 Clubs |
|---|---|---|---|---|---|
| 52 | Knoedler, Justin | R/R | 6-2/210 | 24 | Norwich, San Francisco |
| | Matheny, Mike | R/R | 6-3/220 | 34 | St. Louis |
| 8 | Torrealba, Yorvit | R/R | 5-11/190 | 26 | San Francisco |

| No. | INFIELDERS | B/T | Ht./Wt. | Age* | 2004 Clubs |
|---|---|---|---|---|---|
| 13 | Alfonzo, Edgardo | R/R | 5-11/226 | 31 | San Francisco |
| 8 | Cruz, Deivi | R/R | 6-0/207 | 32 | Fresno, San Francisco |
| 5 | Durham, Ray | B/R | 5-8/196 | 33 | San Jose, Fresno, San Francisco |
| 7 | Feliz, Pedro | R/R | 6-1/205 | 29 | San Francisco |
| 28 | Niekro, Lance | R/R | 6-3/210 | 26 | San Jose, Fresno |
| 6 | Snow, J.T. | L/L | 6-2/209 | 37 | Fresno, San Francisco |
| | Vizquel, Omar | B/R | 5-9/175 | 37 | Cleveland |

| No. | OUTFIELDERS | B/T | Ht./Wt. | Age* | 2004 Clubs |
|---|---|---|---|---|---|
| | Alou, Moises | R/R | 6-3/220 | 38 | Chicago N.L. |
| 25 | Bonds, Barry | L/L | 6-2/228 | 40 | San Francisco |
| 56 | Ellison, Jason | R/R | 5-10/180 | 26 | Fresno, San Francisco |
| 9 | Grissom, Marquis | R/R | 5-11/208 | 37 | San Francisco |
| | Lewis, Frederick | L/R | 6-2/190 | 24 | San Jose, Fresno |
| 39 | Linden, Todd | B/R | 6-3/210 | 24 | Fresno, San Francisco |
| | Ortmeier, Daniel | B/R | 6-4/220 | 23 | Norwich |
| 21 | Torcato, Tony | L/R | 6-1/219 | 25 | Fresno, San Francisco |
| 20 | Tucker, Michael | L/R | 6-2/195 | 33 | San Francisco |

*Age as of April 1, 2005.

## BALLPARK INFORMATION

**Ballpark (capacity, surface)**
SBC Park (41,584, grass)
**Address**
24 Willie Mays Plaza
San Francisco, CA 94107
**Official website**
www.sfgiants.com
**Business phone**
415-972-2000
**Ticket information**
415-972-2000
**Field dimensions (from home plate)**
To left field at foul line, 339 feet
To center field, 399 feet
To right field at foul line, 309 feet
**First game played**
April 11, 2000 (Dodgers 6, Giants 5)

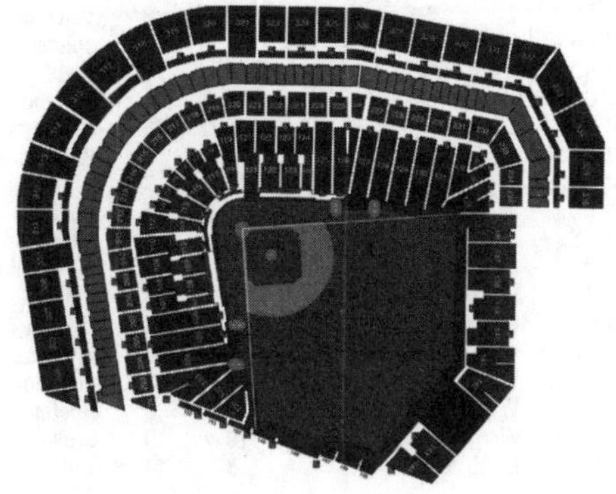

# 2004 REVIEW

## DAY BY DAY

| Date | Opp. | Res. | Score | (inn.*) | Hits | Opp. hits | Winning pitcher | Losing pitcher | Save | Record | Pos. | GB |
|---|---|---|---|---|---|---|---|---|---|---|---|---|
| 4-5 | At Hou. | W | 5-4 | | 10 | 9 | Rodriguez | Dotel | Herges | 1-0 | T1st | ... |
| 4-6 | At Hou. | W | 7-5 | | 15 | 15 | Aardsma | Pettitte | Herges | 2-0 | 1st | +0.5 |
| 4-7 | At Hou. | L | 1-10 | | 4 | 12 | Clemens | Williams | | 2-1 | T1st | ... |
| 4-8 | At S.D. | L | 3-4 | (10) | 10 | 11 | Oropesa | Herges | | 2-2 | T3rd | 0.5 |
| 4-10 | At S.D. | L | 4-6 | | 8 | 14 | Linebrink | Brower | Hoffman | 2-3 | T3rd | 2.0 |
| 4-11 | At S.D. | W | 6-3 | | 11 | 5 | Christiansen | Witasick | Herges | 3-3 | T2nd | 1.0 |
| 4-12 | Mil. | W | 7-5 | | 10 | 13 | Williams | Kinney | Herges | 4-3 | 2nd | 0.5 |
| 4-13 | Mil. | W | 4-2 | | 8 | 7 | Hermanson | Capuano | Herges | 5-3 | 1st | +0.5 |
| 4-14 | Mil. | L | 0-3 | | 4 | 6 | Obermueller | Cooper | Kolb | 5-4 | 2nd | 0.5 |
| 4-16 | L.A. | L | 2-3 | | 3 | 4 | Perez | Schmidt | Gagne | 5-5 | 2nd | 2.0 |
| 4-17 | L.A. | L | 4-5 | | 8 | 14 | Lima | Rueter | Gagne | 5-6 | T2nd | 3.0 |
| 4-18 | L.A. | L | 6-7 | | 12 | 13 | Weaver | Tomko | Gagne | 5-7 | T3rd | 4.0 |
| 4-19 | S.D. | W | 4-3 | | 7 | 8 | Williams | Wells | Brower | 6-7 | T2nd | 3.5 |
| 4-20 | S.D. | L | 5-9 | | 11 | 15 | Lawrence | Hermanson | | 6-8 | 4th | 3.5 |
| 4-21 | S.D. | L | 0-11 | | 4 | 17 | Peavy | Schmidt | | 6-9 | 4th | 4.5 |
| 4-22 | S.D. | L | 4-9 | | 8 | 13 | Valdez | Rueter | | 6-10 | 4th | 4.5 |
| 4-23 | At L.A. | L | 4-5 | (12) | 8 | 10 | Dreifort | Herges | | 6-11 | 5th | 5.5 |
| 4-24 | At L.A. | W | 5-3 | | 8 | 5 | Williams | Weaver | Herges | 7-11 | 4th | 4.5 |
| 4-25 | At L.A. | L | 0-9 | | 4 | 13 | Ishii | Cooper | | 7-12 | 5th | 5.5 |
| 4-26 | Atl. | W | 3-2 | | 6 | 6 | Schmidt | Ramirez | Herges | 8-12 | 5th | 5.0 |
| 4-27 | Atl. | L | 3-12 | | 10 | 18 | Wright | Rueter | | 8-13 | 5th | 5.0 |
| 4-28 | Atl. | W | 10-7 | | 14 | 12 | Tomko | Ortiz | | 9-13 | 5th | 5.0 |
| 4-29 | Fla. | L | 3-4 | | 9 | 6 | Wayne | Rodriguez | Gracesqui | 9-14 | 5th | 5.0 |
| 4-30 | Fla. | W | 12-9 | | 16 | 9 | Walker | Bump | Herges | 10-14 | 4th | 5.0 |
| 5-1 | Fla. | W | 6-3 | | 7 | 8 | Schmidt | Pavano | Herges | 11-14 | 3rd | 5.0 |
| 5-2 | Fla. | W | 9-8 | (11) | 16 | 11 | Walker | Perisho | | 12-14 | 3rd | 4.0 |
| 5-4 | At N.Y. | L | 2-6 | | 6 | 14 | Trachsel | Tomko | | 12-15 | 3rd | 5.0 |
| 5-5 | At N.Y. | L | 2-8 | | 6 | 11 | Weathers | Rodriguez | | 12-16 | 5th | 5.0 |
| 5-6 | At N.Y. | L | 1-2 | (11) | 7 | 5 | Weathers | Brower | | 12-17 | 5th | 6.0 |
| 5-7 | At Cin. | W | 6-1 | | 8 | 6 | Rueter | Lidle | Herges | 13-17 | 3rd | 6.0 |
| 5-8 | At Cin. | L | 3-5 | | 8 | 9 | Wilson | Hermanson | Graves | 13-18 | 4th | 7.0 |
| 5-9 | At Cin. | W | 7-6 | (10) | 9 | 9 | Brower | Graves | | 14-18 | 3rd | 7.0 |
| 5-11 | Phi. | L | 4-10 | | 9 | 15 | Millwood | Williams | | 14-19 | 4th | 8.0 |
| 5-12 | Phi. | W | 4-3 | | 8 | 7 | Schmidt | Wolf | Herges | 15-19 | 3rd | 8.0 |
| 5-13 | Phi. | L | 3-4 | | 10 | 7 | Padilla | Rueter | Madson | 15-20 | 3rd | 8.0 |
| 5-14 | Pit. | L | 2-4 | | 9 | 10 | Boehringer | Rodriguez | Mesa | 15-21 | 3rd | 8.0 |
| 5-15 | Pit. | L | 4-6 | | 11 | 9 | Fogg | Tomko | Mesa | 15-22 | 3rd | 8.0 |
| 5-16 | Pit. | L | 1-8 | | 8 | 15 | Wells | Williams | | 15-23 | 4th | 8.0 |
| 5-18 | At Chi. | W | 1-0 | | 6 | 1 | Schmidt | Clement | | 16-23 | 4th | 7.0 |
| 5-19 | At Chi. | L | 3-4 | (10) | 8 | 7 | Borowski | Brower | | 16-24 | 5th | 7.0 |
| 5-20 | At Chi. | W | 5-3 | (10) | 10 | 8 | Herges | Borowski | | 17-24 | 4th | 6.0 |
| 5-21@ | At Mon. | W | 6-5 | | 8 | 10 | Franklin | Hernandez | Herges | 18-24 | 3rd | 5.0 |
| 5-22@ | At Mon. | W | 7-2 | (11) | 7 | 9 | Walker | Fikac | | 19-24 | 3rd | 5.0 |
| 5-25 | Ari. | W | 4-1 | | 11 | 5 | Schmidt | Fossum | Herges | 20-24 | 3rd | 4.5 |
| 5-26 | Ari. | W | 4-3 | | 6 | 10 | Rodriguez | Bruney | Herges | 21-24 | 3rd | 3.5 |
| 5-27 | Ari. | W | 5-4 | (10) | 7 | 10 | Walker | Valverde | | 22-24 | 3rd | 3.5 |
| 5-28 | Col. | W | 4-2 | | 9 | 8 | Brower | Chacon | | 23-24 | 3rd | 3.5 |
| 5-29 | Col. | W | 5-3 | | 8 | 10 | Williams | Fassero | Herges | 24-24 | 3rd | 2.5 |
| 5-30 | Col. | W | 3-1 | | 8 | 3 | Schmidt | Kennedy | Herges | 25-24 | 3rd | 2.5 |
| 5-31 | At Ari. | W | 8-4 | | 9 | 11 | Rueter | Daigle | | 26-24 | 3rd | 1.5 |
| 6-1 | At Ari. | L | 5-6 | | 8 | 8 | Valverde | Christiansen | | 26-25 | 3rd | 1.5 |
| 6-2 | At Ari. | L | 6-8 | | 13 | 12 | Johnson | Tomko | Valverde | 26-26 | 3rd | 2.5 |
| 6-3 | At Ari. | L | 5-11 | | 7 | 16 | Webb | Williams | | 26-27 | 3rd | 3.0 |
| 6-4 | At Col. | W | 13-7 | | 14 | 11 | Schmidt | Fassero | | 27-27 | 3rd | 3.0 |
| 6-5 | At Col. | L | 2-11 | | 8 | 16 | Jennings | Rueter | | 27-28 | 3rd | 4.0 |
| 6-6 | At Col. | W | 16-4 | | 16 | 9 | Hermanson | Cook | | 28-28 | 3rd | 3.0 |
| 6-7 | At Col. | W | 10-5 | | 15 | 7 | Brower | Reed | | 29-28 | 3rd | 2.5 |
| 6-8 | At T.B. | W | 7-3 | | 10 | 6 | Williams | Waechter | | 30-28 | 3rd | 1.5 |
| 6-9 | At T.B. | L | 3-4 | (10) | 11 | 8 | Baez | Walker | | 30-29 | 3rd | 2.5 |
| 6-10 | At T.B. | L | 2-5 | | 5 | 9 | Zambrano | Rueter | Colome | 30-30 | 3rd | 2.5 |
| 6-12# | At Bal. | W | 9-6 | (11) | 12 | 10 | Herges | Julio | | 31-30 | | |
| 6-12$ | At Bal. | L | 4-5 | (12) | 5 | 14 | Parrish | Eyre | | 31-31 | 3rd | 2.5 |
| 6-13 | At Bal. | W | 7-3 | | 15 | 6 | Williams | Ponson | Walker | 32-31 | 3rd | 1.5 |
| 6-15 | Tor. | W | 4-3 | | 7 | 12 | Schmidt | Batista | Herges | 33-31 | 3rd | 1.5 |
| 6-16 | Tor. | W | 10-2 | | 13 | 9 | Rueter | Hentgen | | 34-31 | 2nd | 1.5 |
| 6-17 | Tor. | W | 8-5 | | 10 | 10 | Brower | Speier | Herges | 35-31 | 2nd | 1.5 |
| 6-18 | Bos. | L | 9-14 | | 8 | 14 | Timlin | Williams | | 35-32 | 2nd | 2.5 |

| Date | Opp. | Res. | Score | (inn.*) | Hits | Opp. hits | Winning pitcher | Losing pitcher | Save | Record | Pos. | GB |
|---|---|---|---|---|---|---|---|---|---|---|---|---|
| 6-19 | Bos. | W | 6-4 | | 8 | 10 | Herges | Embree | | 36-32 | 2nd | 1.5 |
| 6-20 | Bos. | W | 4-0 | | 6 | 1 | Schmidt | Arroyo | | 37-32 | 2nd | 1.5 |
| 6-21 | L.A. | W | 3-2 | | 9 | 9 | Herges | Mota | | 38-32 | 2nd | 0.5 |
| 6-22 | L.A. | W | 11-5 | | 16 | 7 | Brower | Alvarez | | 39-32 | 1st | +0.5 |
| 6-23 | L.A. | W | 3-2 | | 7 | 8 | Williams | Weaver | Herges | 40-32 | 1st | +1.5 |
| 6-24 | L.A. | W | 9-3 | | 12 | 8 | Tomko | Nomo | | 41-32 | 1st | +2.5 |
| 6-25 | At Oak. | W | 6-4 | | 8 | 8 | Schmidt | Zito | Herges | 42-32 | 1st | +3.0 |
| 6-26 | At Oak. | L | 7-8 | (10) | 12 | 15 | Dotel | Brower | | 42-33 | 1st | +3.0 |
| 6-27 | At Oak. | W | 5-2 | | 9 | 7 | Hermanson | Redman | Herges | 43-33 | 1st | +3.0 |
| 6-29 | At L.A. | L | 1-2 | | 8 | 4 | Mota | Brower | Gagne | 43-34 | 1st | +1.5 |
| 6-30 | At L.A. | W | 7-1 | | 10 | 7 | Tomko | Nomo | | 44-34 | 1st | +2.5 |
| 7-1 | At L.A. | L | 4-5 | | 7 | 7 | Mota | Rodriguez | Gagne | 44-35 | 1st | +2.5 |
| 7-2 | Oak. | W | 7-3 | | 7 | 8 | Rueter | Redman | | 45-35 | 1st | +2.5 |
| 7-3 | Oak. | L | 2-6 | | 4 | 13 | Duchscherer | Herges | | 45-36 | 1st | +1.5 |
| 7-4 | Oak. | L | 6-9 | | 12 | 13 | Mulder | Williams | | 45-37 | 1st | +0.5 |
| 7-5 | Col. | L | 4-7 | | 8 | 13 | Cook | Tomko | Chacon | 45-38 | 2nd | 0.5 |
| 7-6 | Col. | L | 6-8 | | 9 | 6 | Harikkala | Christiansen | Chacon | 45-39 | 3rd | 1.5 |
| 7-7 | Col. | W | 8-4 | | 13 | 7 | Rueter | Bernero | | 46-39 | 3rd | 0.5 |
| 7-8 | Ari. | L | 4-8 | | 12 | 13 | Good | Hermanson | | 46-40 | 3rd | 1.5 |
| 7-9 | Ari. | W | 8-3 | | 10 | 5 | Williams | Johnson | | 47-40 | 2nd | 0.5 |
| 7-10 | Ari. | W | 3-1 | | 8 | 5 | Tomko | Webb | Herges | 48-40 | 2nd | 0.5 |
| 7-11 | Ari. | W | 9-2 | | 12 | 5 | Schmidt | Fossum | | 49-40 | 2nd | 0.5 |
| 7-15 | At Col. | W | 7-5 | | 12 | 11 | Brower | Chacon | Eyre | 50-40 | 2nd | 0.5 |
| 7-16 | At Col. | L | 1-7 | | 8 | 11 | Estes | Rueter | | 50-41 | 2nd | 1.5 |
| 7-17 | At Col. | W | 4-0 | | 3 | 4 | Schmidt | Cook | | 51-41 | 2nd | 1.5 |
| 7-18 | At Col. | L | 9-10 | | 11 | 15 | Harikkala | Herges | | 51-42 | 2nd | 2.5 |
| 7-19 | At Ari. | W | 6-1 | | 8 | 10 | Tomko | Sparks | | 52-42 | 2nd | 2.5 |
| 7-20 | At Ari. | W | 3-1 | | 9 | 7 | Williams | Johnson | Christiansen | 53-42 | 2nd | 2.5 |
| 7-21 | S.D. | L | 1-7 | | 5 | 16 | Peavy | Rueter | | 53-43 | 3rd | 2.5 |
| 7-22 | S.D. | L | 4-9 | | 12 | 10 | Wells | Schmidt | | 53-44 | 3rd | 3.5 |
| 7-23 | At StL. | W | 7-2 | | 11 | 4 | Hermanson | Suppan | | 54-44 | 3rd | 3.5 |
| 7-24 | At StL. | W | 5-3 | (10) | 7 | 9 | Rodriguez | King | Christiansen | 55-44 | 2nd | 3.5 |
| 7-25 | At StL. | L | 0-6 | | 7 | 9 | Morris | Williams | | 55-45 | 3rd | 3.5 |
| 7-26 | At S.D. | L | 2-3 | | 5 | 7 | Linebrink | Rodriguez | Hoffman | 55-46 | 3rd | 4.5 |
| 7-27 | At S.D. | W | 6-4 | | 11 | 10 | Schmidt | Wells | Herges | 56-46 | 3rd | 3.5 |
| 7-28 | At S.D. | L | 4-9 | | 5 | 12 | Lawrence | Hermanson | | 56-47 | 3rd | 3.5 |
| 7-29 | At S.D. | L | 4-7 | | 7 | 10 | Neal | Tomko | Hoffman | 56-48 | 3rd | 4.5 |
| 7-30 | StL. | L | 4-7 | | 10 | 11 | Carpenter | Brower | Isringhausen | 56-49 | 3rd | 5.5 |
| 7-31 | StL. | W | 8-7 | | 11 | 15 | Rueter | Morris | Christiansen | 57-49 | 3rd | 4.5 |
| 8-1 | StL. | L | 1-6 | | 5 | 13 | Williams | Schmidt | | 57-50 | 3rd | 5.5 |
| 8-3 | Cin. | W | 11-0 | | 15 | 3 | Lowry | Lidle | | 58-50 | 3rd | 5.5 |
| 8-4 | Cin. | L | 7-8 | | 14 | 14 | Hancock | Eyre | Graves | 58-51 | 3rd | 6.5 |
| 8-5 | Cin. | L | 3-12 | | 6 | 13 | Harang | Rueter | | 58-52 | 3rd | 7.5 |
| 8-6 | Chi. | W | 6-2 | | 8 | 9 | Schmidt | Clement | | 59-52 | 3rd | 6.5 |
| 8-7 | Chi. | L | 4-8 | | 11 | 12 | Maddux | Hennessey | | 59-53 | 3rd | 7.5 |
| 8-8 | Chi. | W | 6-3 | | 11 | 8 | Lowry | Wood | Hermanson | 60-53 | 3rd | 6.5 |
| 8-10 | At Pit. | L | 7-8 | | 13 | 10 | Mesa | Herges | | 60-54 | 3rd | 7.5 |
| 8-11 | At Pit. | L | 6-8 | (11) | 11 | 12 | Grabow | Hermanson | | 60-55 | 3rd | 8.5 |
| 8-12 | At Pit. | W | 7-0 | | 10 | 4 | Schmidt | Vogelsong | | 61-55 | 3rd | 7.5 |
| 8-13 | At Phi. | W | 16-6 | | 18 | 9 | Hennessey | Myers | | 62-55 | 3rd | 7.5 |
| 8-14 | At Phi. | W | 7-6 | | 11 | 11 | Christiansen | Rodriguez | Hermanson | 63-55 | 3rd | 6.5 |
| 8-15 | At Phi. | W | 3-1 | | 5 | 6 | Tomko | Padilla | Hermanson | 64-55 | 3rd | 6.5 |
| 8-16 | Mon. | W | 8-5 | | 9 | 10 | Christiansen | Cordero | Hermanson | 65-55 | 2nd | 5.5 |
| 8-17 | Mon. | W | 5-4 | | 9 | 6 | Hermanson | Ayala | | 66-55 | 2nd | 5.5 |
| 8-18! | Mon. | L | 2-6 | | 10 | 10 | Biddle | Hennessey | | 66-56 | | |
| 8-18& | Mon. | W | 14-4 | | 14 | 8 | Franklin | Tucker | | 67-56 | 2nd | 5.0 |
| 8-20 | N.Y. | W | 7-3 | | 13 | 8 | Lowry | Trachsel | | 68-56 | 2nd | 4.5 |
| 8-21 | N.Y. | L | 9-11 | (12) | 15 | 17 | Stanton | Correia | Fortunato | 68-57 | 2nd | 5.5 |
| 8-22 | N.Y. | W | 3-1 | | 7 | 8 | Rueter | Ginter | Hermanson | 69-57 | 2nd | 4.5 |
| 8-24 | At Fla. | L | 1-9 | | 3 | 10 | Burnett | Franklin | | 69-58 | 2nd | 5.0 |
| 8-25 | At Fla. | W | 6-5 | (10) | 7 | 8 | Brower | Seanez | Hermanson | 70-58 | 2nd | 4.0 |
| 8-26 | At Fla. | W | 5-0 | | 8 | 4 | Tomko | Beckett | | 71-58 | 2nd | 4.0 |
| 8-27 | At Atl. | L | 3-5 | | 7 | 10 | Wright | Rueter | Smoltz | 71-59 | 2nd | 4.0 |
| 8-28 | At Atl. | L | 3-9 | | 6 | 15 | Byrd | Schmidt | | 71-60 | 3rd | 5.0 |
| 8-29 | At Atl. | W | 9-5 | | 14 | 12 | Christiansen | Ortiz | Hermanson | 72-60 | 3rd | 5.0 |
| 8-30 | At Atl. | L | 6-7 | | 9 | 13 | Colon | Hermanson | | 72-61 | 3rd | 5.5 |
| 8-31 | Col. | W | 9-5 | | 10 | 7 | Tomko | Francis | Hermanson | 73-61 | 2nd | 5.5 |
| 9-1 | Col. | L | 1-4 | | 4 | 13 | Wright | Rueter | Chacon | 73-62 | 2nd | 5.5 |
| 9-2 | Col. | L | 5-6 | | 9 | 9 | Kennedy | Schmidt | Chacon | 73-63 | 2nd | 6.5 |
| 9-3 | Ari. | W | 18-7 | | 18 | 15 | Burba | Gonzalez | | 74-63 | 2nd | 5.5 |

| Date | Opp. | Res. | Score | (inn.*) | Hits | Opp. hits | Winning pitcher | Losing pitcher | Save | Record | Pos. | GB |
|---|---|---|---|---|---|---|---|---|---|---|---|---|
| 9-4 | Ari. | W | 9-7 | | 11 | 13 | Eyre | Koplove | Hermanson | 75-63 | 2nd | 4.5 |
| 9-5 | Ari. | W | 4-1 | | 8 | 6 | Tomko | Johnson | Hermanson | 76-63 | 2nd | 3.5 |
| 9-7 | At Col. | L | 7-8 | | 13 | 7 | Harikkala | Christiansen | Chacon | 76-64 | 2nd | 4.5 |
| 9-8 | At Col. | W | 5-3 | | 16 | 5 | Walker | Reed | Hermanson | 77-64 | 2nd | 4.5 |
| 9-10 | At Ari. | L | 1-2 | | 5 | 4 | Johnson | Brower | Aquino | 77-65 | 2nd | 6.0 |
| 9-11 | At Ari. | W | 5-3 | | 9 | 7 | Lowry | Randolph | Hermanson | 78-65 | 2nd | 6.0 |
| 9-12 | At Ari. | W | 5-2 | | 8 | 4 | Schmidt | Choate | | 79-65 | 2nd | 5.0 |
| 9-14 | At Mil. | W | 3-2 | | 4 | 7 | Rueter | Davis | Hermanson | 80-65 | 2nd | 4.5 |
| 9-15 | At Mil. | W | 8-1 | | 11 | 4 | Tomko | Obermueller | | 81-65 | 2nd | 3.5 |
| 9-16 | At Mil. | W | 4-0 | | 9 | 3 | Hennessey | Santos | | 82-65 | 2nd | 2.5 |
| 9-17 | S.D. | W | 4-1 | | 9 | 6 | Lowry | Peavy | Hermanson | 83-65 | 2nd | 2.5 |
| 9-18 | S.D. | L | 1-5 | | 7 | 7 | Wells | Schmidt | Hoffman | 83-66 | 2nd | 2.5 |
| 9-19 | S.D. | W | 4-2 | | 6 | 7 | Hermanson | Linebrink | | 84-66 | 2nd | 2.5 |
| 9-21 | Hou. | W | 9-2 | | 13 | 4 | Tomko | Hernandez | | 85-66 | 2nd | 1.5 |
| 9-22 | Hou. | W | 5-1 | | 11 | 5 | Lowry | Oswalt | | 86-66 | 2nd | 0.5 |
| 9-23 | Hou. | L | 3-7 | | 10 | 10 | Miceli | Hermanson | | 86-67 | 2nd | 1.5 |
| 9-24 | L.A. | L | 2-3 | | 3 | 12 | Perez | Rueter | Gagne | 86-68 | 2nd | 2.5 |
| 9-25 | L.A. | W | 9-5 | | 11 | 9 | Eyre | Brazoban | | 87-68 | 2nd | 1.5 |
| 9-26 | L.A. | L | 4-7 | | 11 | 8 | Weaver | Tomko | Gagne | 87-69 | 2nd | 2.5 |
| 9-28 | At S.D. | W | 7-5 | | 17 | 10 | Schmidt | Lawrence | Hermanson | 88-69 | 2nd | 3.0 |
| 9-29 | At S.D. | L | 3-4 | (10) | 7 | 7 | Hoffman | Hermanson | | 88-70 | 2nd | 3.0 |
| 9-30 | At S.D. | W | 4-1 | | 9 | 5 | Williams | Eaton | Hermanson | 89-70 | 2nd | 3.0 |
| 10-1 | At L.A. | W | 4-2 | | 8 | 4 | Rueter | Weaver | Hermanson | 90-70 | 2nd | 2.0 |
| 10-2 | At L.A. | L | 3-7 | | 6 | 7 | Brazoban | Hermanson | | 90-71 | 2nd | 3.0 |
| 10-3 | At L.A. | W | 10-0 | | 15 | 3 | Schmidt | Ishii | | 91-71 | 2nd | 2.0 |

Monthly records: April (10-14), May (16-10), June (18-10), July (13-15), August (16-12), September (16-9), October (2-1).
*Innings, if other than nine. @ At Hiram Bithorn Stadium, San Juan, Puerto Rico. ! First game of a doubleheader. & Second game of a doubleheader. # Day separate admission. $ Night separate admission.

## RECORDS

**2004 regular-season record**: 91-71
**Position:** 2nd in N.L. West
**Home:** 47-35 **Road:** 44-36
**N.L. East:** 19-13 **N.L. Central:** 20-16
**N.L. West:** 41-35 **A.L.** 11-7
**Vs. LH starters:** 32-18
**Vs. RH starters:** 59-53
**Grass:** 88-69 **Artificial:** 3-2
**Day:** 28-25 **Night:** 63-46
**1-Run:** 18-25 **X-inn.:** 8-10
**Doubleheaders:** 0-0-1
**Team record past five years:** 473-335 (.585, ranks 3rd in league in that span)

## TEAM LEADERS

**Batting average:** Barry Bonds (.362).
**At-bats:** Marquis Grissom (562).
**Runs:** Barry Bonds (129).
**Hits:** Marquis Grissom (157).
**Total Bases:** Barry Bonds (303).
**Doubles:** Pedro Feliz (33).
**Triples:** Ray Durham (8).
**Home runs:** Barry Bonds (45).
**Runs batted in:** Barry Bonds (101).
**Stolen bases:** Ray Durham (10).
**Slugging percentage:** Barry Bonds (.812).
**On-base percentage:** Barry Bonds (.609).
**Wins:** Jason Schmidt (18).
**Earned-run average:** Jason Schmidt (3.20).
**Complete games:** Jason Schmidt (4).
**Shutouts:** Jason Schmidt (3).
**Saves:** Matt Herges (23).
**Innings pitched:** Jason Schmidt (225.0).
**Strikeouts:** Jason Schmidt (251).

## GAMES BY POSITION

**Catcher:** A.J. Pierzynski 118, Yorvit Torrealba 59, Justin Knoedler 1.
**First base:** J.T. Snow 100, Pedro Feliz 70, Damon Minor 17.
**Second base:** Ray Durham 118, Neifi Perez 39, Cody Ransom 16, Brian Dallimore 9, Edgardo Alfonzo 5, Deivi Cruz 2.
**Third base:** Edgardo Alfonzo 129, Pedro Feliz 51, Brian Dallimore 6, Neifi Perez 2, Deivi Cruz 1, Cody Ransom 1.
**Shortstop:** Deivi Cruz 104, Neifi Perez 57, Cody Ransom 45, Pedro Feliz 20.
**Outfield:** Marquis Grissom 142, Barry Bonds 133, Michael Tucker 124, Dustan Mohr 95, Jeffrey Hammonds 28, Ricky Ledee 15, Todd Linden 11, Jason Ellison 4, Pedro Feliz 4, Cody Ransom 1.
**Designated hitter:** Barry Bonds 7, Dustan Mohr 2, Damon Minor 1.

## TOP DRAFT CHOICES

2. **Eddy Martinez-Esteve,** OF, Florida State.
3. **John Bowker,** OF, Long Beach State.
4. **Clay Timpner,** OF, Central Florida.
5. **Garrett Broshuis,** RHP, Missouri.
6. **Justin Hedrick,** RHP, Northeastern.
7. **Will Thompson,** 1B, Santa Clara.
8. **Omar Aguilar,** RHP, Merced (Calif.) College.
9. **Jamie Arnesen,** LHP, Liberty H.S., Bakersfield, Calif.
10. **Spencer Grogan,** LHP, Oklahoma State.

# WASHINGTON NATIONALS

## *NATIONAL LEAGUE EAST DIVISION*

## 2005 SEASON

### Nationals Schedule

**Home games shaded.**
**All-Star Game July 12 at Detroit. Schedule subject to change.**

**April**

| SUN | MON | TUE | WED | THU | FRI | SAT |
|---|---|---|---|---|---|---|
| 3 | 4 PHI | 5 | 6 PHI | 7 PHI | 8 FLA | 9 FLA |
| 10 FLA | 11 ATL | 12 ATL | 13 ATL | 14 ARI | 15 | 16 ARI |
| 17 ARI | 18 FLA | 19 FLA | 20 ATL | 21 ATL | 22 NYM | 23 NYM |
| 24 NYM | 25 PHI | 26 PHI | 27 PHI | 28 | 29 NYM | 30 NYM |

**May**

| SUN | MON | TUE | WED | THU | FRI | SAT |
|---|---|---|---|---|---|---|
| 1 NYM | 2 LA | 3 LA | 4 LA | 5 | 6 SF | 7 SF |
| 8 SF | 9 ARI | 10 ARI | 11 ARI | 12 | 13 CHC | 14 CHC |
| 15 CHC | 16 MIL | 17 MIL | 18 MIL | 19 MIL | 20 TOR | 21 TOR |
| 22 TOR | 23 CIN | 24 CIN | 25 CIN | 26 | 27 STL | 28 STL |
| 29 STL | 30 ATL | 31 ATL | | | | |

**June**

| SUN | MON | TUE | WED | THU | FRI | SAT |
|---|---|---|---|---|---|---|
| | | | 1 ATL | 2 ATL | 3 FLA | 4 FLA |
| 5 FLA | 6 | 7 OAK | 8 OAK | 9 OAK | 10 SEA | 11 SEA |
| 12 SEA | 13 ANA | 14 ANA | 15 ANA | 16 | 17 TEX | 18 TEX |
| 19 TEX | 20 PIT | 21 PIT | 22 PIT | 23 | 24 TOR | 25 TOR |
| 26 TOR | 27 | 28 PIT | 29 PIT | 30 PIT | | |

**July**

| SUN | MON | TUE | WED | THU | FRI | SAT |
|---|---|---|---|---|---|---|
| | | | | | 1 CHC | 2 CHC |
| 3 CHC | 4 NYM | 5 NYM | 6 NYM | 7 NYM | 8 PHI | 9 PHI |
| 10 PHI | 11 | 12 All-Star | 13 | 14 MIL | 15 MIL | 16 MIL |
| 17 MIL | 18 COL | 19 COL | 20 COL | 21 HOU | 22 HOU | 23 HOU |
| 24 HOU | 25 | 26 ATL | 27 ATL | 28 ATL | 29 FLA | 30 FLA |
| 31 FLA | | | | | | |

**August**

| SUN | MON | TUE | WED | THU | FRI | SAT |
|---|---|---|---|---|---|---|
| | 1 | 2 LA | 3 LA | 4 LA | 5 SD | 6 SD |
| 7 SD | 8 | 9 HOU | 10 HOU | 11 HOU | 12 COL | 13 COL |
| 14 COL | 15 PHI | 16 PHI | 17 PHI | 18 PHI | 19 NYM | 20 NYM |
| 21 NYM | 22 CIN | 23 CIN | 24 CIN | 25 | 26 STL | 27 STL |
| 28 STL | 29 ATL | 30 ATL | 31 ATL | | | |

**September**

| SUN | MON | TUE | WED | THU | FRI | SAT |
|---|---|---|---|---|---|---|
| | | | | 1 ATL | 2 PHI | 3 PHI |
| 4 PHI | 5 FLA | 6 FLA | 7 FLA | 8 FLA | 9 ATL | 10 ATL |
| 11 ATL | 12 | 13 NYM | 14 NYM | 15 NYM | 16 SD | 17 SD |
| 18 SD | 19 | 20 SF | 21 SF | 22 SF | 23 NYM | 24 NYM |
| 25 NYM | 26 FLA | 27 FLA | 28 FLA | 29 | 30 PHI | |

**October**

| SUN | MON | TUE | WED | THU | FRI | SAT |
|---|---|---|---|---|---|---|
| | | | | | | 1 PHI |
| 2 PHI | 3 | 4 | 5 | 6 | 7 | 8 |

Home games shaded. All-Star Game July 12 at Detroit. Schedule subject to change.

### CLUB DIRECTORY

**President**
Tony Tavares

**General manager**
Jim Bowden

**Assistant general manager**
Tony Siegle

**Director, baseball administration**
Lee MacPhail IV

**Director, player development**
Adam Wogan

**Director of amateur, professional and international scouting**
Dana Brown

**Vice president, communications**
Chartese Berry

**Director, baseball information**
John Dever

### MINOR LEAGUE AFFILIATES

| Class | Team | League | Manager |
|---|---|---|---|
| AAA | New Orleans | Pacific Coast | TBA |
| AA | Harrisburg | Eastern | TBA |
| Advanced A | Potomac | Carolina | TBA |
| A | Savannah | South Atlantic | TBA |
| Short-Season A | Vermont | New York-Pennsylvania | TBA |
| Rookie | Gulf Coast Nationals | Gulf Coast | TBA |

### BROADCAST INFORMATION

**Radio:** TBA.
**TV:** TBA.

### SPRING TRAINING

**Ballpark (city):** Space Coast Stadium (Melbourne, Fla.).
**Ticket information:** 321-633-8119.

**For more on the Nationals, go to msn.foxsports.com/mlb/teams.**

Wilkerson

## SPRING TRAINING ROSTER

**Manager**—Frank Robinson (20).
**Coaches**—Don Buford, Tom McCraw (17), Dave Huppert, Bob Natal (13), Eddie Rodriguez (45), Randy St. Claire (46).

| No. | PITCHERS | B/T | Ht./Wt. | Age* | 2004 Clubs |
|---|---|---|---|---|---|
| 36 | Armas, Tony | R/R | 6-3/225 | 26 | Brevard County, Edmonton, Montreal |
| 56 | Ayala, Luis | R/R | 6-2/186 | 27 | Montreal |
| 55 | Beltran, Francis | R/R | 6-6/230 | 25 | Chicago N.L., Iowa, Edmonton, Montreal |
| 32 | Cordero, Chad | R/R | 6-0/198 | 23 | Montreal |
| 54 | Day, Zach | R/R | 6-4/216 | 26 | Montreal |
| 58 | Eischen, Joey | L/L | 6-0/214 | 34 | G.C. Expos, Brevard County, Montreal |
| 61 | Hernandez, Livan | R/R | 6-2/245 | 30 | Montreal |
| | Hinckley, Michael | R/L | 6-3/170 | 22 | Brevard County, Harrisburg |
| 59 | Horgan, Joe | L/L | 6-1/200 | 27 | Memphis, Edmonton, Montreal |
| | Karp, Josh | R/R | 6-5/210 | 25 | Edmonton |
| 31 | Kim, Sun-Woo | R/R | 6-1/185 | 27 | Montreal |
| 50 | Majewski, Gary | R/R | 6-1/215 | 25 | Charlotte, Edmonton, Montreal |
| 34 | Ohka, Tomo | R/R | 6-1/200 | 29 | Montreal |
| 21 | Patterson, John | R/R | 6-5/208 | 27 | Harrisburg, Brevard County, Montreal |
| | Rasner, Darrell | R/R | 6-3/210 | 24 | Brevard County, Harrisburg |
| 51 | Rauch, Jon | R/R | 6-11/260 | 26 | Chicago A.L., Charlotte, Edmonton, Montreal |
| | Rueckel, Danny | R/R | 6-0/175 | 25 | Harrisburg, Edmonton |
| 52 | Tucker, T.J. | R/R | 6-3/266 | 26 | Edmonton, Montreal |
| 33 | Vargas, Claudio | R/R | 6-3/228 | 26 | Montreal |

| No. | CATCHERS | B/T | Ht./Wt. | Age* | 2004 Clubs |
|---|---|---|---|---|---|
| | Bennett, Gary | R/R | 6-0/208 | 32 | Milwaukee |
| 23 | Schneider, Brian | L/R | 6-1/196 | 28 | Montreal |

| No. | INFIELDERS | B/T | Ht./Wt. | Age* | 2004 Clubs |
|---|---|---|---|---|---|
| | Blanco, Tony | R/R | 6-1/175 | 23 | Potomac, Chattanooga |
| | Broadway, Larry | L/L | 6-4/230 | 24 | Harrisburg |
| 5 | Carroll, Jamey | R/R | 5-9/170 | 31 | Montreal |
| | Castilla, Vinny | R/R | 6-1/205 | 37 | Colorado |
| | Cordero, Wil | R/R | 6-2/232 | 33 | Jupiter, Florida |
| | Guzman, Cristian | B/R | 6-0/205 | 27 | Minnesota |
| 12 | Harris, Brendan | R/R | 6-1/200 | 24 | Chicago N.L., Iowa, Edmonton, Montreal |
| 24 | Johnson, Nick | L/L | 6-3/224 | 26 | Brevard County, Edmonton, Montreal |
| | Machado, Alejandro | S/R | 6-0/160 | 22 | Brevard County, Harrisburg |
| 4 | Mateo, Henry | B/R | 6-0/176 | 28 | G.C. Expos., Edmonton, Montreal |
| 3 | Vidro, Jose | B/R | 5-11/193 | 30 | Montreal |
| 6 | Wilkerson, Brad | L/L | 6-0/206 | 27 | Montreal |

| No. | OUTFIELDERS | B/T | Ht./Wt. | Age* | 2004 Clubs |
|---|---|---|---|---|---|
| 19 | Chavez, Endy | L/L | 5-10/189 | 27 | Edmonton, Montreal |
| 38 | Church, Ryan | L/L | 6-1/190 | 26 | Edmonton, Montreal |
| | Davis, J.J. | R/R | 6-5/250 | 26 | Pittsburgh, Nashville |
| | Guillen, Jose | R/R | 5-11/190 | 28 | Anaheim |
| 48 | Sledge, Terrmel | L/L | 6-0/185 | 28 | Montreal |
| | Watson, Brandon | L/R | 6-1/170 | 23 | Edmonton |

*Age as of April 1, 2005.

## BALLPARK INFORMATION

**Ballpark (capacity, surface)**
RFK Stadium (capacity TBD, turf TBD)

**Address**
2400 East Capitol Street SE
Washington, DC 20003

**Official website**
www.nationals.com

**Business phone**
202-675-6287

**Ticket information**
202-675-6287

**Field dimensions (from home plate)**
TBD

**First game played**
Scheduled for April 15, 2005, vs. Arizona

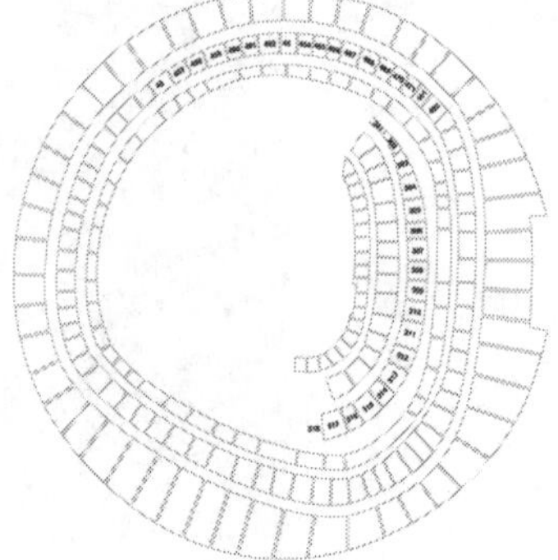

# 2004 REVIEW

## DAY BY DAY

| Date | Opp. | Res. | Score | (inn.*) | Hits | Opp. hits | Winning pitcher | Losing pitcher | Save | Record | Pos. | GB |
|---|---|---|---|---|---|---|---|---|---|---|---|---|
| 4-6 | At Fla. | L | 3-4 | | 8 | 10 | Perisho | Ayala | Benitez | 0-1 | T3rd | 1.0 |
| 4-7 | At Fla. | W | 3-2 | | 5 | 6 | Vargas | Penny | Biddle | 1-1 | T1st | ... |
| 4-8 | At Fla. | L | 0-3 | | 5 | 11 | Willis | Ohka | Benitez | 1-2 | T3rd | 1.0 |
| 4-9@ | N.Y. | L | 2-3 | (11) | 8 | 8 | Weathers | Ayala | Moreno | 1-3 | T4th | 2.0 |
| 4-10@ | N.Y. | W | 1-0 | | 7 | 3 | Patterson | Seo | Biddle | 2-3 | T3rd | 2.0 |
| 4-11@ | N.Y. | L | 1-4 | | 6 | 8 | Glavine | Hernandez | Looper | 2-4 | 4th | 3.0 |
| 4-13@ | Fla. | L | 0-5 | | 4 | 8 | Penny | Vargas | | 2-5 | 4th | 4.0 |
| 4-14@ | Fla. | L | 0-9 | | 8 | 15 | Willis | Ohka | | 2-6 | 4th | 5.0 |
| 4-15@ | Fla. | L | 0-3 | | 3 | 6 | Pavano | Day | Benitez | 2-7 | 5th | 6.0 |
| 4-16 | At Phi. | L | 2-4 | | 5 | 9 | Milton | Hernandez | Wagner | 2-8 | 5th | 6.0 |
| 4-17 | At Phi. | L | 3-6 | | 7 | 7 | Millwood | Patterson | Wagner | 2-9 | 5th | 6.0 |
| 4-18 | At Phi. | L | 4-5 | | 9 | 8 | Wagner | Biddle | | 2-10 | 5th | 6.0 |
| 4-19 | At N.Y. | L | 1-4 | | 10 | 8 | Yates | Ohka | Looper | 2-11 | 5th | 6.5 |
| 4-20 | At N.Y. | W | 2-1 | | 8 | 4 | Day | Weathers | Biddle | 3-11 | 5th | 6.5 |
| 4-21 | At N.Y. | W | 2-1 | | 6 | 8 | Hernandez | Glavine | Biddle | 4-11 | 5th | 6.5 |
| 4-22 | At N.Y. | L | 2-3 | | 5 | 6 | Trachsel | Bentz | Looper | 4-12 | 5th | 7.5 |
| 4-23 | Phi. | L | 6-8 | | 12 | 12 | Millwood | Bentz | Wagner | 4-13 | 5th | 7.5 |
| 4-24 | Phi. | L | 0-7 | | 4 | 17 | Wolf | Ohka | | 4-14 | 5th | 8.5 |
| 4-25 | Phi. | W | 2-0 | | 5 | 9 | Day | Padilla | Biddle | 5-14 | 5th | 7.5 |
| 4-26 | At S.D. | L | 2-3 | | 8 | 8 | Otsuka | Ayala | | 5-15 | 5th | 8.5 |
| 4-27 | At S.D. | L | 0-3 | | 4 | 8 | Valdez | Patterson | Hoffman | 5-16 | 5th | 8.5 |
| 4-28 | At S.D. | L | 4-5 | | 13 | 8 | Osuna | Ayala | Hoffman | 5-17 | 5th | 9.5 |
| 4-29 | At S.D. | L | 1-2 | | 5 | 6 | Wells | Ohka | Hoffman | 5-18 | 5th | 10.5 |
| 4-30 | At L.A. | L | 4-13 | | 9 | 15 | Ishii | Day | | 5-19 | 5th | 10.5 |
| 5-1 | At L.A. | L | 4-5 | | 7 | 11 | Mota | Ayala | Gagne | 5-20 | 5th | 10.5 |
| 5-2 | At L.A. | W | 6-4 | | 12 | 10 | Kim | Nomo | | 6-20 | 5th | 9.5 |
| 5-4 | Col. | W | 10-4 | | 14 | 8 | Vargas | Jennings | | 7-20 | 5th | 8.5 |
| 5-5 | Col. | L | 0-2 | | 5 | 9 | Kennedy | Day | Chacon | 7-21 | 5th | 9.5 |
| 5-6 | Col. | W | 3-1 | | 8 | 5 | Hernandez | Elarton | | 8-21 | 5th | 8.5 |
| 5-7 | StL. | W | 4-2 | | 7 | 9 | Kim | Morris | Biddle | 9-21 | 5th | 8.5 |
| 5-8 | StL. | W | 2-0 | | 8 | 3 | Ohka | Marquis | Biddle | 10-21 | 5th | 7.5 |
| 5-9 | StL. | L | 2-5 | | 5 | 8 | Carpenter | Vargas | Isringhausen | 10-22 | 5th | 8.5 |
| 5-11 | At Mil. | L | 5-8 | (14) | 11 | 16 | Burba | Tucker | | 10-23 | 5th | 8.5 |
| 5-12 | At Mil. | L | 3-4 | | 6 | 7 | Obermueller | Day | Kolb | 10-24 | 5th | 9.5 |
| 5-13 | At Mil. | L | 4-7 | | 5 | 11 | Davis | Kim | Kolb | 10-25 | 5th | 10.5 |
| 5-14 | At Ari. | W | 4-3 | | 7 | 6 | Cordero | Valverde | Biddle | 11-25 | 5th | 9.5 |
| 5-15 | At Ari. | W | 5-0 | | 9 | 7 | Vargas | Daigle | | 12-25 | 5th | 8.5 |
| 5-16 | At Ari. | W | 6-1 | | 11 | 6 | Hernandez | Sparks | | 13-25 | 5th | 8.5 |
| 5-18@ | Mil. | W | 3-2 | | 7 | 12 | Day | Davis | Biddle | 14-25 | 5th | 7.5 |
| 5-19@ | Mil. | L | 3-6 | | 10 | 11 | Santos | Kim | Kolb | 14-26 | 5th | 8.0 |
| 5-20@ | Mil. | L | 2-3 | | 8 | 6 | Adams | Biddle | Kolb | 14-27 | 5th | 9.0 |
| 5-21@ | S.F | L | 5-6 | | 10 | 8 | Franklin | Hernandez | Herges | 14-28 | 5th | 10.0 |
| 5-22@ | S.F | L | 2-7 | (11) | 9 | 7 | Walker | Fikac | | 14-29 | 5th | 10.5 |
| 5-24 | Atl. | L | 0-5 | | 11 | 9 | Thomson | Day | | 14-30 | 5th | 11.0 |
| 5-25 | Atl. | W | 3-1 | | 9 | 7 | Ohka | Ramirez | Biddle | 15-30 | 5th | 10.0 |
| 5-26 | Atl. | L | 1-6 | | 5 | 13 | Ortiz | Hernandez | | 15-31 | 5th | 11.0 |
| 5-28 | Cin. | L | 6-7 | | 7 | 14 | Lidle | Vargas | Graves | 15-32 | 5th | 12.5 |
| 5-29 | Cin. | L | 1-4 | | 5 | 6 | Acevedo | Day | Graves | 15-33 | 5th | 13.5 |
| 5-30 | Cin. | W | 6-2 | | 7 | 10 | Ohka | Valentine | Cordero | 16-33 | 5th | 13.5 |
| 5-31 | At Atl. | L | 2-8 | | 6 | 8 | Ortiz | Hernandez | | 16-34 | 5th | 13.5 |
| 6-1 | At Atl. | L | 6-7 | | 9 | 9 | Almanza | Biddle | | 16-35 | 5th | 13.5 |
| 6-2 | At Atl. | W | 8-4 | | 17 | 7 | Vargas | Hampton | | 17-35 | 5th | 12.5 |
| 6-4 | At Cin. | W | 4-2 | | 10 | 6 | Day | Acevedo | Biddle | 18-35 | 5th | 12.0 |
| 6-5 | At Cin. | L | 3-6 | (10) | 5 | 10 | Jones | Cordero | | 18-36 | 5th | 13.0 |
| 6-6 | At Cin. | L | 5-6 | | 9 | 10 | Matthews | Biddle | | 18-37 | 5th | 13.0 |
| 6-8 | At K.C. | L | 2-4 | | 7 | 5 | Greinke | Armas | Affeldt | 18-38 | 5th | 14.0 |
| 6-10! | At K.C. | W | 8-0 | | 16 | 6 | Day | Reyes | | 19-38 | | |
| 6-10& | At K.C. | W | 7-2 | | 8 | 6 | Kim | Gobble | | 20-38 | 5th | 13.0 |
| 6-11 | At Sea. | L | 0-1 | | 5 | 10 | Guardado | Hernandez | | 20-39 | 5th | 13.0 |
| 6-12 | At Sea. | L | 0-3 | | 8 | 5 | Moyer | Vargas | Guardado | 20-40 | 5th | 13.0 |
| 6-13 | At Sea. | L | 1-8 | | 6 | 14 | Pineiro | Armas | | 20-41 | 5th | 14.0 |
| 6-15 | Min. | L | 2-8 | | 4 | 9 | Santana | Day | | 20-42 | 5th | 14.0 |
| 6-16 | Min. | L | 4-5 | (11) | 8 | 9 | Rincon | Fikac | Nathan | 20-43 | 5th | 15.0 |
| 6-17 | Min. | L | 4-6 | | 11 | 10 | Fultz | Hernandez | Nathan | 20-44 | 5th | 16.0 |
| 6-18 | Chi. | L | 7-11 | | 12 | 18 | Cotts | Ayala | Marte | 20-45 | 5th | 16.0 |

| Date | Opp. | Res. | Score | (inn.*) | Hits | Opp. hits | Winning pitcher | Losing pitcher | Save | Record | Pos. | GB |
|---|---|---|---|---|---|---|---|---|---|---|---|---|
| 6-19 | Chi. | W | 17-14 | | 18 | 15 | Fikac | Munoz | Cordero | 21-45 | 5th | 15.0 |
| 6-20 | Chi. | W | 4-2 | | 3 | 8 | Cordero | Garland | | 22-45 | 5th | 14.0 |
| 6-22 | Phi. | W | 5-2 | | 10 | 4 | Hernandez | Myers | Cordero | 23-45 | 5th | 14.0 |
| 6-23 | Phi. | L | 2-5 | | 6 | 8 | Millwood | Kim | Wagner | 23-46 | 5th | 15.0 |
| 6-24 | Phi. | W | 3-2 | | 7 | 5 | Armas | Milton | Cordero | 24-46 | 5th | 14.0 |
| 6-25 | At Tor. | L | 1-3 | | 8 | 9 | Towers | Day | Frasor | 24-47 | 5th | 14.0 |
| 6-26 | At Tor. | L | 5-10 | | 9 | 13 | Batista | Downs | | 24-48 | 5th | 14.0 |
| 6-27 | At Tor. | W | 9-4 | | 8 | 9 | Hernandez | Hentgen | | 25-48 | 5th | 14.0 |
| 6-28 | At Phi. | L | 6-14 | | 6 | 15 | Millwood | Kim | | 25-49 | 5th | 14.0 |
| 6-29 | At Phi. | L | 7-17 | | 8 | 17 | Milton | Hill | | 25-50 | 5th | 15.0 |
| 6-30 | At Phi. | W | 6-3 | | 9 | 8 | Horgan | Worrell | Cordero | 26-50 | 5th | 14.0 |
| 7-1 | At Phi. | L | 5-10 | | 8 | 16 | Wolf | Downs | | 26-51 | 5th | 15.0 |
| 7-2@ | Tor. | W | 2-0 | | 7 | 4 | Hernandez | Bush | | 27-51 | 5th | 14.0 |
| 7-3@ | Tor. | L | 0-2 | | 6 | 8 | Halladay | Armas | Frasor | 27-52 | 5th | 15.0 |
| 7-4@ | Tor. | W | 6-4 | | 10 | 9 | Hill | Lilly | Horgan | 28-52 | 5th | 15.0 |
| 7-5@ | Atl. | L | 4-11 | | 11 | 13 | Byrd | Day | | 28-53 | 5th | 16.0 |
| 7-6@ | Atl. | L | 0-1 | | 5 | 7 | Ortiz | Downs | Smoltz | 28-54 | 5th | 16.0 |
| 7-7@ | Atl. | L | 2-14 | | 9 | 17 | Wright | Hernandez | | 28-55 | 5th | 16.0 |
| 7-8@ | Pit. | W | 2-1 | | 6 | 5 | Ayala | Grabow | Cordero | 29-55 | 5th | 16.0 |
| 7-9@ | Pit. | L | 0-11 | | 10 | 10 | Burnett | Hill | | 29-56 | 5th | 17.0 |
| 7-10@ | Pit. | W | 4-0 | | 7 | 4 | Biddle | Wells | | 30-56 | 5th | 16.0 |
| 7-11@ | Pit. | W | 2-1 | | 6 | 6 | Downs | Fogg | Cordero | 31-56 | 5th | 15.0 |
| 7-15 | At Atl. | L | 0-8 | | 5 | 11 | Wright | Hernandez | | 31-57 | 5th | 15.0 |
| 7-16 | At Atl. | W | 5-1 | | 8 | 6 | Horgan | Byrd | | 32-57 | 5th | 15.0 |
| 7-17 | At Atl. | L | 2-6 | | 2 | 9 | Ortiz | Bentz | Smoltz | 32-58 | 5th | 16.0 |
| 7-18 | At Atl. | L | 5-16 | | 13 | 15 | Thomson | Downs | | 32-59 | 5th | 16.0 |
| 7-19 | At Pit. | W | 6-2 | | 11 | 6 | Horgan | Grabow | | 33-59 | 5th | 16.0 |
| 7-20 | At Pit. | L | 1-2 | | 10 | 4 | Burnett | Hernandez | Mesa | 33-60 | 5th | 16.0 |
| 7-21 | At N.Y. | L | 4-5 | | 13 | 9 | Moreno | Horgan | Looper | 33-61 | 5th | 17.0 |
| 7-22 | At N.Y. | W | 4-1 | | 8 | 9 | Ayala | Franco | Cordero | 34-61 | 5th | 16.0 |
| 7-23 | Fla. | W | 2-1 | | 5 | 6 | Armas | Penny | Cordero | 35-61 | 5th | 15.5 |
| 7-24 | Fla. | W | 6-2 | | 6 | 10 | Biddle | Willis | | 36-61 | 5th | 15.5 |
| 7-25 | Fla. | W | 6-4 | | 9 | 8 | Hernandez | Wayne | Ayala | 37-61 | 5th | 15.5 |
| 7-26 | N.Y. | W | 19-10 | | 18 | 16 | Ayala | Erickson | | 38-61 | 5th | 15.5 |
| 7-27 | N.Y. | L | 2-4 | | 10 | 9 | Glavine | Day | Looper | 38-62 | 5th | 15.5 |
| 7-28 | N.Y. | W | 7-4 | | 8 | 6 | Tucker | Seo | Cordero | 39-62 | 5th | 15.5 |
| 7-29 | N.Y. | L | 1-10 | | 6 | 14 | Leiter | Biddle | | 39-63 | 5th | 16.5 |
| 7-30 | At Fla. | W | 9-0 | | 16 | 3 | Hernandez | Beckett | | 40-63 | 5th | 16.5 |
| 7-31 | At Fla. | W | 8-5 | | 10 | 11 | Biddle | Manzanillo | Cordero | 41-63 | 5th | 16.5 |
| 8-3 | At StL. | W | 10-6 | (12) | 16 | 12 | Cordero | Haren | | 42-63 | 5th | 16.0 |
| 8-4 | At StL. | L | 4-5 | | 11 | 13 | Tavarez | Cordero | | 42-64 | 5th | 17.0 |
| 8-5 | At StL. | L | 1-2 | | 5 | 6 | Carpenter | Ayala | Isringhausen | 42-65 | 5th | 18.0 |
| 8-6 | At Hou. | L | 0-4 | | 5 | 8 | Oswalt | Biddle | | 42-66 | 5th | 19.0 |
| 8-7 | At Hou. | W | 8-3 | | 13 | 10 | Rauch | Weathers | | 43-66 | 5th | 19.0 |
| 8-8 | At Hou. | W | 5-2 | | 11 | 7 | Tucker | Clemens | | 44-66 | 5th | 19.0 |
| 8-10 | Ari. | W | 4-0 | | 8 | 8 | Hernandez | Johnson | | 45-66 | 5th | 18.0 |
| 8-11 | Ari. | W | 7-3 | | 8 | 8 | Patterson | Webb | | 46-66 | 5th | 18.0 |
| 8-12 | Ari. | W | 7-5 | | 13 | 11 | Ayala | Cormier | Cordero | 47-66 | 5th | 18.0 |
| 8-13 | Hou. | W | 6-5 | (12) | 11 | 7 | Vargas | Harville | | 48-66 | 5th | 17.0 |
| 8-14 | Hou. | W | 8-3 | | 14 | 4 | Tucker | Hernandez | | 49-66 | 5th | 17.0 |
| 8-15 | Hou. | L | 4-5 | | 8 | 8 | Miceli | Ayala | Lidge | 49-67 | 5th | 17.0 |
| 8-16 | At S.F | L | 5-8 | | 10 | 9 | Christiansen | Cordero | Hermanson | 49-68 | 5th | 18.0 |
| 8-17 | At S.F | L | 4-5 | | 6 | 9 | Hermanson | Ayala | | 49-69 | 5th | 18.0 |
| 8-18! | At S.F | W | 6-2 | | 10 | 10 | Biddle | Hennessey | | 50-69 | | |
| 8-18& | At S.F | L | 4-14 | | 8 | 14 | Franklin | Tucker | | 50-70 | 5th | 18.5 |
| 8-20 | At Col. | W | 4-3 | | 8 | 8 | Ayala | Fuentes | Cordero | 51-70 | 5th | 18.0 |
| 8-21 | At Col. | L | 2-5 | | 6 | 8 | Kennedy | Hernandez | | 51-71 | 5th | 18.0 |
| 8-22 | At Col. | W | 8-2 | | 14 | 8 | Patterson | Jennings | | 52-71 | 5th | 18.0 |
| 8-23 | L.A. | W | 8-7 | | 11 | 10 | Cordero | Carrara | | 53-71 | 5th | 17.5 |
| 8-24 | L.A. | L | 2-10 | | 8 | 10 | Ishii | Biddle | | 53-72 | 5th | 18.5 |
| 8-25 | L.A. | W | 6-3 | | 10 | 9 | Horgan | Lima | Ayala | 54-72 | 5th | 18.5 |
| 8-26 | L.A. | L | 3-10 | | 8 | 10 | Weaver | Hernandez | | 54-73 | 5th | 19.5 |
| 8-27 | S.D. | W | 10-3 | | 14 | 8 | Downs | Tankersley | | 55-73 | 5th | 19.5 |
| 8-28 | S.D. | L | 2-5 | | 6 | 9 | Peavy | Patterson | Hoffman | 55-74 | 5th | 20.5 |
| 8-29 | S.D. | L | 3-11 | | 10 | 14 | Wells | Kim | | 55-75 | 5th | 20.5 |
| 8-30 | Chi. | L | 2-5 | | 7 | 9 | Maddux | Biddle | Hawkins | 55-76 | 5th | 21.5 |
| 8-31 | Chi. | W | 8-0 | | 12 | 4 | Hernandez | Prior | | 56-76 | 5th | 21.5 |
| 9-1 | Chi. | L | 1-2 | (11) | 7 | 11 | Hawkins | Vargas | | 56-77 | 5th | 22.5 |

| Date | Opp. | Res. | Score | (inn.*) | Hits | Opp. hits | Winning pitcher | Losing pitcher | Save | Record | Pos. | GB |
|---|---|---|---|---|---|---|---|---|---|---|---|---|
| 9-3 | Atl. | L | 1-7 | | 4 | 9 | Byrd | Downs | | 56-78 | 5th | 23.5 |
| 9-4 | Atl. | L | 0-9 | | 3 | 13 | Ortiz | Patterson | | 56-79 | 5th | 24.5 |
| 9-5 | Atl. | W | 4-3 | (12) | 12 | 6 | Tucker | Cruz | | 57-79 | 5th | 23.5 |
| 9-6 | At Chi. | L | 1-9 | | 4 | 9 | Zambrano | Armas | | 57-80 | 5th | 24.5 |
| 9-7 | At Chi. | W | 7-6 | (12) | 13 | 16 | Cordero | Wellemeyer | Horgan | 58-80 | 5th | 24.0 |
| 9-8 | At Chi. | W | 6-0 | | 6 | 5 | Downs | Maddux | | 59-80 | 5th | 22.5 |
| 9-10 | At Atl. | L | 3-4 | | 13 | 6 | Thomson | Patterson | Smoltz | 59-81 | 5th | 23.0 |
| 9-11 | At Atl. | L | 1-8 | | 6 | 11 | Cruz | Hernandez | | 59-82 | 5th | 24.0 |
| 9-12 | At Atl. | L | 8-9 | (12) | 14 | 15 | Cruz | Ayala | | 59-83 | 5th | 25.0 |
| 9-13 | At Fla. | L | 3-6 | | 5 | 11 | Perisho | Majewski | | 59-84 | 5th | 25.5 |
| 9-14 | At Fla. | L | 6-8 | | 11 | 13 | Seanez | Ayala | Mota | 59-85 | 5th | 25.5 |
| 9-15! | At Fla. | W | 6-2 | | 12 | 8 | Patterson | Pavano | | 60-85 | | |
| 9-15& | At Fla. | W | 10-4 | | 15 | 9 | Rauch | Bump | | 61-85 | 5th | 25.0 |
| 9-16 | At Fla. | L | 3-4 | | 7 | 8 | Willis | Hernandez | Benitez | 61-86 | 5th | 25.0 |
| 9-17 | At Phi. | W | 12-8 | | 12 | 10 | Ayala | Worrell | | 62-86 | 5th | 25.0 |
| 9-18 | At Phi. | W | 6-5 | (14) | 11 | 11 | Cordero | Myers | Beltran | 63-86 | 5th | 25.0 |
| 9-19 | At Phi. | L | 2-7 | | 8 | 14 | Floyd | Downs | | 63-87 | 5th | 25.0 |
| 9-21 | N.Y. | W | 6-1 | | 11 | 6 | Hernandez | Leiter | | 64-87 | 5th | 25.0 |
| 9-22 | N.Y. | L | 2-3 | | 6 | 9 | Fortunato | Ayala | Looper | 64-88 | 5th | 25.0 |
| 9-23 | N.Y. | L | 2-4 | | 7 | 9 | Glavine | Ohka | Looper | 64-89 | 5th | 25.0 |
| 9-24 | Phi. | W | 8-1 | | 11 | 7 | Kim | Myers | | 65-89 | 5th | 25.0 |
| 9-25 | Phi. | L | 3-4 | (10) | 6 | 10 | Worrell | Eischen | Wagner | 65-90 | 5th | 26.0 |
| 9-26 | Phi. | L | 1-2 | | 4 | 10 | Lidle | Hernandez | Wagner | 65-91 | 5th | 27.0 |
| 9-27 | Fla. | L | 1-4 | | 4 | 10 | Beckett | Patterson | Benitez | 65-92 | 5th | 27.5 |
| 9-28 | Fla. | L | 2-5 | | 3 | 8 | Valdez | Ohka | Benitez | 65-93 | 5th | 28.0 |
| 9-29 | Fla. | L | 1-9 | | 7 | 15 | Pavano | Kim | | 65-94 | 5th | 29.0 |
| 10-1 | At N.Y. | W | 4-2 | | 11 | 6 | Rauch | Feliciano | Cordero | 66-94 | 5th | 29.0 |
| 10-2 | At N.Y. | W | 6-3 | | 9 | 9 | Cordero | Looper | Majewski | 67-94 | 5th | 29.0 |
| 10-3 | At N.Y. | L | 1-8 | | 5 | 11 | Glavine | Patterson | | 67-95 | 5th | 29.0 |

Monthly records: April (5-19), May (11-15), June (10-16), July (15-13), August (15-13), September (9-18), October (2-1).
*Innings, if other than nine. @ At Hiram Bithorn Stadium, San Juan, Puerto Rico. ! First game of a doubleheader. & Second game of a doubleheader.

## RECORDS

**2004 regular-season record:** 67-95
**Position:** 5th in N.L. East
**Home:** 35-45 **Road:** 32-50
**N.L. East:** 28-48 **N.L. Central:** 17-19
**N.L. West:** 15-17 **A.L.** 7-11
**Vs. LH starters:** 21-28
**Vs. RH starters:** 46-67
**Grass:** 31-48 **Artificial:** 36-47
**Day:** 17-26 **Night:** 50-69
**1-Run:** 16-30 **X-inn.:** 5-8
**Doubleheaders:** 2-0-1
**Team record past five years:** 368-442 (.454, ranks 14th in league in that span)

## TEAM LEADERS

**Batting average:** Juan Rivera (.307).
**At-bats:** Tony Batista (606).
**Runs:** Brad Wilkerson (112).
**Hits:** Tony Batista, Brad Wilkerson (146).
**Total Bases:** Brad Wilkerson (285).
**Doubles:** Brad Wilkerson (39).
**Triples:** Endy Chavez, Terrmel Sledge (6).
**Home runs:** Tony Batista, Brad Wilkerson (32).
**Runs batted in:** Tony Batista (110).
**Stolen bases:** Endy Chavez (32).
**Slugging percentage:** Brad Wilkerson (.498).
**On-base percentage:** Brad Wilkerson (.374).
**Wins:** Livan Hernandez (11).
**Earned-run average:** Livan Hernandez (3.60).
**Complete games:** Livan Hernandez (9).
**Shutouts:** Livan Hernandez (2).
**Saves:** Chad Cordero (14).
**Innings pitched:** Livan Hernandez (255.0).
**Strikeouts:** Livan Hernandez (186).

## GAMES BY POSITION

**Catcher:** Brian Schneider 133, Einar Diaz 44.
**First base:** Brad Wilkerson 86, Nick Johnson 73, Terrmel Sledge 10, Luis Lopez 8, Val Pascucci 5, Andy Fox 1.
**Second base:** Jose Vidro 105, Jamey Carroll 51, Brendan Harris 11, Maicer Izturis 10, Henry Mateo 9, Andy Fox 3, Josh Labandeira 2.
**Third base:** Tony Batista 155, Jamey Carroll 13, Brendan Harris 4, Andy Fox 3, Einar Diaz 1.
**Shortstop:** Orlando Cabrera 101, Alex S. Gonzalez 33, Maicer Izturis 23, Jamey Carroll 10, Andy Fox 5, Josh Labandeira 3.
**Outfield:** Endy Chavez 127, Juan Rivera 121, Terrmel Sledge 114, Brad Wilkerson 80, Carl Everett 33, Ron Calloway 20, Ryan Church 18, Val Pascucci 17, Peter Bergeron 11, Matt Cepicky 11, Jamey Carroll 2, Henry Mateo 1.
**Designated hitter:** Jose Vidro 4, Carl Everett 3, Matt Cepicky 2, Juan Rivera 1.

## TOP DRAFT CHOICES

1. **Bill Bray,** LHP, William & Mary.
2. **Erick San Pedro,** C, Miami (Fla.).
3. **Ian Desmond,** SS, Sarasota (Fla.) H.S.
4. **Collin Balester,** RHP, Huntington Beach (Calif.) H.S.
5. **Greg Bunn,** RHP, East Carolina.
6. **Devin Ivany,** C, South Florida.
7. **Marvin Lowrance,** OF, Golden West College (Calif.).
8. **Leonard Davis,** 3B, Fresno (Calif.) City College.
9. **Brandon Conway,** SS, Frederick (Md.) CC.
10. **Duron Legrande**, OF, North Carolina A&T.

# 2004 REVIEW

# YEAR IN REVIEW

## THE TOP STORIES OF THE PAST YEAR

By STEVE GIETSCHIER
TSN Senior Managing Editor

A reasonable way to summarize the year in baseball would be to call 2004 a marvelous opportunity squandered. Ever since baseball endured "a series of unfortunate events" in the mid-1990s, the sport has struggled to repolish its image, reconnect with its traditional fan base, grow its business and restore some of the luster once part of its lure as the national pastime. The strike by the Major League Baseball Players Association that eliminated the end of the 1994 season and delayed the start of the 1995 season had put the sport into a deep funk. Chronic public complaints by commissioner Allan H. "Bud" Selig and club owners about the sport's economic woes, the lack of competitive balance between teams and the apparent need to contract teams deemed unable to prosper either on or off the field added to the sense of gloom. Over the past few seasons, though, the battle to overcome those difficulties was being won on many fronts. On the field, the game had been enlivened by a plethora of exciting pennant races—some involving teams that so recently had been branded incapable of competing at the highest level—gripping postseason play and record-setting individual accomplishments. Off the field, the collective bargaining agreement signed in 2002 without a work stoppage brought with it some economic adjustments that have silenced a good many critics.

2003 had been a very good year for baseball, and as the 2004 season unfolded, the promise of more of the same came true. One of the game's greatest pitchers emerged from a very brief retirement to earn a record seventh Cy Young Award, his first in the National League, and another pitched a perfect game at age 40. The game's greatest hitter extended some of his own remarkable records and closed in on the all-time home run mark, and another player, the best from Japan to play in the majors, broke the season record for hits—a standard often considered out of reach in the modern game. The 2004 postseason iced this delectable cake. The Boston Red Sox, a team that had for decades suffered "the slings and arrows of outrageous fortune," some self-imposed and some from the menacing New York Yankees, won their first World Series since 1918. They did it in unprecedented style, rebounding from a 3-0 deficit in the American League Championship Series to beat the Yankees in seven games and then sweeping the St. Louis Cardinals in the Series. These events not only were astounding in their own right, but they seemed to reinforce what Selig had told the *New York Daily News* in May: "Well, there's not much wrong with baseball today."

Just a few weeks later, much of the glow from these positive developments had vanished. The attempt to find a new home for the Montreal Expos found no easy resolution and led to much adverse publicity. Discussions between MLB officials and representatives from several cities interested in attracting the club had dragged on for months. When a decision finally was made, local politicians quickly took action that nearly sabotaged the deal. Simultaneously, publication of confidential grand jury testimony from an investigation of a company billing itself as a nutritional supplements business implicated prominent players for allegedly using performance-enhancing drugs, including anabolic steroids. Regardless of the truth of the many allegations associated with these revelations, baseball found itself with a massive public relations problem and, quite possibly, much more than that.

### OUTSTANDING PERFORMANCES

A pair of players who passed the 40-year-old marker continued to amaze fans with their excellence. San Francisco Giants outfielder Barry Bonds, who turned 40 in July, put together a fourth straight season of superlative statistics. He won the N.L. batting crown with a .362 average, hit 45 home runs and produced 101 RBIs. He set a major league record by walking 232 times, 120 of which were intentional, and passed Rickey Henderson for first place on the career walks list. Bonds' on-base percentage was .609, also a record, and his slugging percentage, .812, outpaced runner-up Albert Pujols by .155. Bonds hit more home runs than he had strikeouts, and he came close to scoring more runs than he had hits. On April 13, he hit the 661st home run of his career, moving past Willie Mays, his godfather, into third place on the all-time list behind only Henry Aaron (755) and Babe Ruth (714). He hit his 700th home run on September 17 in the third inning against young righthander Jake Peavy of the San Diego Padres. Bonds won his fourth straight N.L. MVP award, his seventh overall, and was voted TSN's Player of the Year by his peers.

Arizona Diamondbacks pitcher Randy Johnson, who turned 41 in September, became the oldest pitcher to throw a perfect game when he beat the Atlanta Braves, 2-0, on May 18. Johnson struck out 13 and went to three balls on just one hitter, Johnny Estrada (in the second inning). There were no controversial calls or close plays in the 17th nine-inning perfect game in major league history and the first one since David Cone's in 1999. This also was the second no-hitter of Johnson's career, the first having come in 1990, when he was with the Seattle Mariners. Johnson became the fourth pitcher in history to reach 4,000 career strikeouts on June 29. He struck out Jeff Cirillo of the Padres in the eighth inning of a game the Diamondbacks lost, 3-2.

### EXPOS MOVE TO WASHINGTON

Major League Baseball—that is, the other 29 clubs acting in concert—has owned the Expos since before the 2002 season, when MLB decided a team could no longer survive in Montreal. After missing target dates to sell the franchise that year and in 2003, MLB announced its intention to find a new home for the team by the 2004 All-Star break. Interested parties included groups from Las Vegas; Monterrey, Mexico; Washington, D.C.; Norfolk, Va.; northern Virginia; Portland, Ore.; and San Juan, Puerto Rico. MLB's goal was to select a city that would provide public funding for a new ballpark before picking an ownership group, but the All-Star Game came and went without a decision.

Washington seemed to become the leading candidate during the summer, but Peter Angelos, CEO of the Baltimore Orioles, emerged as an obstacle. He argued that moving the Expos to Washington would adversely affect his business, located only about 40 miles to the north. Still, on September 29, Selig announced an agreement to move the Expos to Washington, previously home to two editions of the Washington Senators, from 1901-1960 and 1961-1971. The deal was contingent upon approval by MLB owners and on passage of legislation by the District of Columbia Council to provide public funds to construct a ballpark on the Anacostia River waterfront in southeast Washington. Beginning in 2005, the team, subsequently named the Nationals, would play in a refurbished Robert F. Kennedy Stadium.

The agreement began to unravel when council chair Linda Cropp postponed a November 9 vote, declaring that the District government should spend additional time seeking private financing for part of the ballpark's costs. MLB's owners declined to approve the agreement on November 18 but did so on December 3, with Angelos dissenting. Eleven days later, the council voted 7-6 to approve a plan calling for substantial private financing, which was quite different from the September accord reached with mayor Anthony Williams. MLB officials reacted by halting season ticket sales, canceling a news conference to unveil the team's uniforms and logo and closing the stadium store. MLB gave the city 15 days to work out an arrangement suitable to baseball. After further negotiations involving both Cropp and Williams, the council backed down and approved a package whose terms called for the city to merely continue to search for private funds to cover up to 50 percent of the ballpark's costs and for the District and MLB to share the cost of insurance against cost overruns. MLB chief operating officer Robert DuPuy said he was pleased with the legislation, but three new council members who take office in January 2005 still could attempt to reopen negotiations.

### STEROIDS TAKE CENTER STAGE

On February 12, U.S. Attorney General John Ashcroft announced a 42-count indictment against four individuals connected to the Bay Area Laboratory Co-Operative (BALCO), the subject of an 18-month investigation by federal prosecutors and a grand jury in San Francisco. The four indicted were BALCO president and CEO Victor Conte Jr., vice president James J. Valente, track coach Remi Korchemny and Greg F. Anderson, Barry Bonds' personal trainer. The charges included possession of human growth hormone, mishandling of drugs with intent to defraud, money laundering and conspiracy to distribute anabolic steroids to track and field athletes and professional football and baseball players.

In the months leading up to the indictments, the grand jury had called many athletes to testify, including Bonds, Jason Giambi and Gary Sheffield, and throughout the season, as in seasons past, speculation raged that these players and many others had used performance-enhancing drugs. Players steadfastly denied doing so, even though more than 5 percent of the drug tests administered to players during 2003 had produced positive results. Testing continued during 2004, according to terms set forth in the collective bargaining agreement, and rumors continued to swirl, especially around batters putting up huge offensive numbers. Critics of baseball's testing policy continued to complain about its laxity.

In December, the *San Francisco Chronicle* published excerpts from confidential testimony before the grand jury in which Giambi admitted injecting himself with a human growth hormone and using steroids obtained from Anderson for at least three seasons. The *Chronicle* also published testimony in which Bonds said he used substances known as "the cream" and "the clear" but that he did not know if they were steroids. The cream was said to be a substance that included a steroid and a masking agent, and the clear was said to be a substance that could provide steroid-like effects without leading to a positive drug test. MLB and the players association had agreed in March to ban THG, a recently unmasked steroid, but the news reports on Giambi and Bonds led to a firestorm of outrage from the public and the media alike, as well as the threat of congressional intervention. In response, MLB and the players association announced near year's end that they were developing a tougher testing program.

### ROSE ADMITS GAMBLING ON BASEBALL

The *Philadelphia Inquirer* reported on January 3 that Pete Rose would admit in his soon-to-be-published autobiography that he had bet on baseball while serving as manager of the Cincinnati Reds, contrary to his previous statements. Other sources confirmed this over the next few days, and Rose appeared on numerous television interview shows to say so. According to Rose, he had talked with Selig in November 2002 and confessed to this behavior. Reaction to this announcement was quite negative. Some questioned Rose's sincerity and his motives while others complained about the timing of his admission, coming as it did just as the Hall of Fame was announcing the election of new members Paul Molitor and Dennis Eckersley. There was no immediate reaction from Selig, and at year's end, Rose still was on the permanently ineligible list.

### SEASON OPENS IN JAPAN

After a one-year hiatus caused by the imminent threat of war waged by the United States against Iraq, MLB resumed its practice of opening the regular season abroad, with games in Japan. The Yankees and the Tampa Bay Devil Rays played a two-game series in Tokyo on March 30 and 31. Tampa Bay won the opener, 8-3, and the Yankees came back to win the second game, 12-1.

The Expos scheduled 59 home games in Montreal and 22 at Hiram Bithorn Stadium in San Juan. The latter set of games was broken into three blocks: April 9-15 against the New York Mets and Florida Marlins; May 18-23 against the Milwaukee Brewers and Giants; and July 2-11 against the Toronto Blue Jays, Braves and Pittsburgh Pirates. The Expos played their final game in Montreal's Olympic Stadium on September 29, losing to the Marlins, 9-1, on the same day as the announcement that the team would move to Washington.

### TWO PARKS OPEN

Two new ballparks opened in 2004. After a protracted and contentious period of construction, the Padres opened Petco Park in downtown San Diego on April 8, beating the Giants, 4-3, in 10 innings before a crowd of 41,400. The Philadelphia Phillies, replacing Veterans Stadium, opened Citizens Bank Park on April 12, losing to the Reds, 4-1, before a crowd of 41,626. The Cardinals secured public and private financing for a new ballpark adjacent to the current Busch Stadium and broke ground in January. The team anticipates opening the new park, also to be called Busch Stadium, in 2006.

### EIGHTH YEAR OF INTERLEAGUE PLAY

Regular-season games between A.L. and N.L. clubs continued for the eighth consecutive season. Teams in the A.L. East played most of their games against the N.L. West, A.L. Central teams played the N.L. East, and A.L. West teams played the N.L. Central. There was one period of interleague play, June 7-20, followed by two weekends, June 25-27 and July 2-4, during which teams played their so-called traditional rivals. One game, postponed by rain, was made up in August. The schedule had all N.L. Central teams playing 12 interleague games and all other teams playing 18 interleague games.

Overall, A.L. teams won 127 games and lost 125, decreasing the N.L.'s lead to 988-960 in overall interleague play. The Devil Rays compiled the best interleague mark among A.L. teams (15-3), and the Orioles won only five games. In the N.L., the Cardinals finished with the best record (11-1), and the Giants were 11-7. The Pirates finished with the worst mark (2-10). Attendance at interleague games averaged 33,024, 6.1 percent higher than the 31,112 of 2003 and 13.3 percent higher than the average for intraleague games played to that point in the season.

### ATLANTA WINS DIVISION AGAIN

The Braves won the N.L. East title for the 10th year in a row. Leaving aside the incomplete 1994 season, Atlanta has won an unprecedented 13 straight division crowns. Although they were not favored to the win the division, the Braves had a relatively easy run to the title, finishing 10 games ahead of the Phillies. They clinched the division on September 24 by beating the Marlins, 8-7. Bobby Cox, who won his 2,000th game as a manager on September 29, was named TSN's N.L. Manager of the Year for the third straight season and for a record seventh time overall.

J.D. Drew, obtained in a trade with the Cardinals, led the Braves' offense. He batted .305 with an on-base percentage of .436 (fourth in the league) and a .569 slugging percentage (ninth in the league). He hit 31 home runs, drove in 93 runs and had a 22-game hitting streak. Estrada hit .314, and Marcus Giles hit .311. Chipper Jones added 30 homers and 96 RBIs, Andruw Jones drove in 91 runs, and Rafael Furcal stole 29 bases.

Despite the departure of Greg Maddux, the Braves' pitching staff led the N.L. in ERA (3.74). Russ Ortiz and Jaret Wright won 15 games each, and John Thomson added 14 victories. Wright's ERA was 3.28, and Thomson's was 3.72. John Smoltz ranked fourth in the league in saves (44).

The 2003 World Series champions, the Marlins, finished in third place (83-79), eight games worse than their record in '03.

### ST. LOUIS RUNS AWAY WITH CENTRAL TITLE

The Cardinals won 105 games to capture their second division title in three years and qualify for postseason play for the fifth time in Tony La Russa's nine years as manager. The team played sizzling baseball during the middle of the season (69-22, .758, from May 27 through September 5) and finished first easily. In first place from June 11 on, the Cardinals led by seven games at the All-Star break, 10½ games at the end of July and 15½ games at the end of August. The Cards clinched the division on September 18, beating the Diamondbacks, 7-0, while the Chicago Cubs lost to Cincinnati.

St. Louis led the league in batting (.278), hits (1,544) and runs (855) and finished second in doubles, total bases and stolen bases. Pujols put together his fourth consecutive marvelous season, batting .331 (fifth in the league) with 46 home runs (tied for second in the league) and 123 RBIs (third in the league). Scott Rolen hit .314 with 34 homers and 124 RBIs (second in the league), and Jim Edmonds hit .301 with 42 homers and 111 RBIs. Larry Walker joined the team on August 6 and batted .280 in 44 games.

The Cardinals' pitching staff included Jeff Suppan, who won 16 games, and three 15-game winners: Chris Carpenter, Jason Marquis and Matt Morris. Jason Isringhausen tied for first in the league in saves (47). The staff's ERA was 3.75, second best in the league.

### HOUSTON TAKES WILD CARD

The Astros finished second in the N.L. Central for the third straight year and qualified for postseason play for the first time since 2001. A .500 team at the All-Star break, Houston changed managers, and four weeks later, the team began a 36-10 run that vaulted it into wild-card contention. The Astros passed five teams in a close race and won the playoff spot by a single game over the Giants. Lance Berkman led the team in batting average (.316) and home runs (30), and Jeff Kent led in runs batted in (107). Roy Oswalt won 20 games, and Roger Clemens (18-4), who finished fifth in the league in strikeouts with 218, won the N.L. Cy Young Award.

### LOS ANGELES WINS N.L. WEST

The Dodgers qualified for postseason play for the first time since 1996 and won the N.L. West title for the first time since 1995. The team's season was keyed by timely offensive production and 53 come-from-behind wins, a franchise record. Los Angeles stayed close to the division lead in the early part of the season and never was more than 3½ games out of first place. The team took over first place on July 7 and never was headed. The Dodgers led the division by 2½ games at the end of July and 5½ games at the end of August. They clinched the title on October 2, beating the Giants, 7-3.

Los Angeles finished 10th in the league in batting average, fourth in home runs and eighth in RBIs. The team's offensive star was Adrian Beltre, who batted .334 (fourth in the league), hit 48 homers to lead the N.L. and drove in 121 runs (fourth in the league). No other Dodger hit 30 home runs or had even 90 RBIs.

The Dodgers' pitching staff finished fourth in the league in ERA. Odalis Perez was 10th in the N.L. in ERA but won only seven games. Kazuhisa Ishii, Jose Lima and Jeff Weaver each won 13 games, but no other pitcher won more than eight. Eric Gagne saved 45 games, third best in the league, and was named TSN's N.L. Reliever of the Year. After extending his record of consecutive saves to 84 on July 3, Gagne had the streak come to an end on July 5, when Arizona scored two runs in the ninth to tie the game, which the Dodgers won in extra innings.

### YANKEES WIN SEVENTH STRAIGHT

The Yankees won their seventh consecutive A.L. East title and their eighth in nine seasons. New York stood in second place at the end of May, then caught the Red Sox on May 31 and passed them the next day. By the end of June, the Yankees had a 7½-game lead. Boston won 21 games in August and another 21 in the season's final month, but the Red Sox could not regain the division lead. The Yankees clinched the title on September 30, beating the Minnesota Twins, 6-4.

New York's offense finished second in the league in runs and tied for first in home runs (242), but no Yankees regular batted better than .300. Hideki Matsui hit .298 with 31 home runs and 108 RBIs. Gary Sheffield batted .290 with 36 home runs and 121 RBIs (fifth in the league), and newly acquired Alex Rodriguez hit .286 with 36 homers and 106 RBIs.

Javier Vazquez and Jon Lieber both won 14 games, and Mike Mussina added 12. Paul Quantrill appeared in 86 games to lead the league, and Mariano Rivera had 53 saves, tops in the A.L. Rivera was named TSN's A.L. Reliever of the Year.

### BOSTON TAKES WILD CARD

The Red Sox won the wild-card spot by putting together another impressive offensive display augmented by fine pitching. Boston's hitters finished first in the league in slugging percentage (.472), runs (949), doubles (373) and total bases (2,702), tied for first in the league in batting average (.282) and were fourth in the league in home runs (222). Manny Ramirez hit 43 homers (tops in the A.L.), and David Ortiz drove in 139 runs (second in the league). Curt Schilling led the league with 21 wins and was second in ERA (3.26). Pedro Martinez won 16 games, Derek Lowe won 14, and Keith Foulke saved 32 games. The team clinched a playoff spot on September 27 by beating Tampa Bay, 7-3.

### TWINS SECURE THIRD STRAIGHT CROWN

The Minnesota Twins won their third straight A.L. Central title by a comfortable nine games over the Chicago White Sox. The Twins stood at or near the top of the division standings through the All-Star break. A three-game sweep of the White Sox in late July gave Minnesota a 3½-game lead that the team never relinquished. They led by seven games at the end of August and clinched the division pennant on September 20 by beating Chicago, 8-2. Ron Gardenhire was voted TSN's co-A.L. Manager of the Year by his peers, sharing the award with the Texas Rangers' Buck Showalter.

Minnesota's offense was mediocre, ranking eighth in the league in hits, 10th in runs and sixth in homers. Only one Twins regular, Shannon Stewart, batted over .300. He hit .304 with 11 home runs and 47 RBIs. No one hit more than 25 homers or drove in more than 81 runs. No Minnesota player finished in the top 10 of any major offensive category in the league except Torii Hunter, who was tied for eighth in stolen bases.

The Twins' pitching, by contrast, was the best in the league, ranking first in ERA (4.03), third in strikeouts, first in fewest walks (431) and fourth in fewest home runs allowed. Johan Santana, TSN's A.L. Pitcher of the Year, won 20 games (second in the league) and finished first in ERA (2.61) and strikeouts (265). He also had a 13-game winning streak. Carlos Silva won 14 games, and Brad Radke and Juan Rincon each won 11. Radke finished fourth in the league in ERA, and Joe Nathan finished third in saves with 44.

### ANAHEIM REBOUNDS TO WIN A.L. WEST

After missing the postseason in 2003, the year after they won the World Series, the Angels captured their first division title in 18 years, edging the defending champion Oakland A's by one game. The Angels stayed in first place or close to it through the first half of the season, but a swoon in July dropped them six games behind. The team was tied with Oakland going into the season's final weekend and won the pennant with victories on October 1 and 2.

Vladimir Guerrero led Anaheim's offense by batting .337 (third in the league), hitting 39 home runs (fourth in the A.L.) and driving in 126 runs (also fourth). He led the league in runs (124) and total bases (366) and was third in slugging percentage. Garret Anderson hit .301, and Jose Guillen had 104 RBIs. Chone Figgins stole 34 bases, ranking third in the league.

Anaheim's pitching staff compiled the league's fourth best ERA (4.28). Bartolo Colon won 18 games (tied for third in the league), and John Lackey won 14. Kelvim Escobar had an ERA of 3.93, and Troy Percival had 33 saves, fourth most in the league.

### OTHER FEATS AND EVENTS

Playing his fourth season in the United States, Seattle's Ichiro Suzuki set a major league record with 262 hits, surpassing George Sisler's 1920 total of 257. Suzuki produced his 257th and 258th hits on October 1, both against Ryan Drese of the Rangers. Suzuki is the first player to get more than 200 hits in each of his first four seasons. He had 225 singles (also a major league record) and 80 multihit games, including six four-hit games and four five-hit games. He led the majors with 704 at-bats and won the A.L. batting title (.372).

Maddux returned to the Cubs as a free agent and won his 300th game on August 7, defeating the Giants, 8-4. He ended the season with 305 wins. On June 20, Ken Griffey Jr. became the 20th player and the sixth youngest to reach 500 homers. He connected off Matt Morris in the sixth inning at St. Louis.

For the second year in a row, a Rockies player led the N.L. in RBIs. Vinny Castilla drove in 131 runs after Preston Wilson produced 141 in 2003. The Marlins' Juan Pierre led the league in hits (221) and multihit games (70). Scott Podsednik of the Brewers led the league in stolen bases with 70, and Kent had the N.L.'s longest hitting streak (25 games). Peavy won the N.L. ERA crown (2.27), Johnson led in strikeouts (290), and the Giants' Jason Schmidt, TSN's N.L. Pitcher of the Year, won 12 games in a row, the league's longest streak. In the A.L., Miguel Tejada of Baltimore led in RBIs (150), and Tampa Bay's Carl Crawford was first in stolen bases (59). Carlos Lee of the White Sox had the longest hitting streak (28 games).

Edgar Martinez retired at the end of the season after an 18-year career spent entirely with the Mariners. A third baseman and designated hitter, he had a career batting average of .312 with 309 home runs and 1,261 RBIs. Martinez was a seven-time member of the A.L. All-Star team, and he won the Silver Slugger award five times.



### DIVISION SERIES WINNERS

One division series was a three-game sweep, two others went four games and one went the maximum five games. The Red Sox won the first two games of their series in Anaheim and came home to finish off the Angels in extra innings. The Yankees dropped the first game to the Twins and won the next three. The Cardinals won the first two games in St. Louis, lost the third game in Los Angeles and won the fourth. The Astros and Braves alternated wins in the first four games before Houston won the deciding game, 12-3.

### CARDINALS DEFEAT ASTROS IN SEVEN

The N.L. Championship Series opened in St. Louis, and the Cardinals won both games. St. Louis batters struck out 11 times in Game 1, but the Cardinals scored six runs in the sixth inning to overcome four Houston homers, including one by Carlos Beltran, to win, 10-7. In Game 2, Beltran homered again, but the Cards hit four homers of their own, including a pair by Scott Rolen, and won, 6-4. Homers by Rolen and Pujols in the eighth inning broke a 4-4 tie.

After the series shifted to Minute Maid Park, the Astros swept Games 3, 4 and 5. Clemens pitched seven innings in Game 3, giving up only four hits, and his teammates, including Beltran again, hit three home runs in a 5-2 win. Houston won Game 4, 6-5. The Astros scored two runs in the sixth inning to tie the score, and Beltran hit his fourth series home run to give his team the lead. Brandon Backe pitched a one-hitter over eight innings to win Game 5, 3-0. Beltran did not homer, but Kent's three-run homer in the bottom of the ninth produced all of Houston's runs.

Back in Busch Stadium, the Cardinals rebounded to win Game 6, 6-4, in 12 innings. Pujols hit his fourth home run of the series in the first inning. Jeff Bagwell singled home the tying run in the ninth inning, but Edmonds hit a two-run homer in the 12th to win it. St. Louis won Game 7, 5-2, scoring three runs in the sixth on a Pujols double and a Rolen home run. The Cardinals thus advanced to the World Series for the first time since 1987.

### BOSTON STAGES UNPRECEDENTED COMEBACK

The Red Sox met the Yankees in the A.L. Championship Series for the second year in a row. This time, New York won the first three games, two in New York and the third in Boston. Matsui drove in five runs as the Yankees took Game 1, 10-7. They won Game 2, 3-1, with Lieber besting Martinez. John Olerud's two-run homer in the sixth inning proved to be the difference.

The Yankees pounded the Red Sox, 19-8, in Game 3 at Fenway Park. Matsui again drove in five runs, Sheffield drove in four, and Rodriguez and Bernie Williams both had three RBIs. New York took a 4-3 lead into the bottom of the ninth inning of Game 4 and was on the verge of a series sweep, but the Red Sox tied the score on a single by Bill Mueller. The Yankees put runners on base in each of the next three innings but did not score. Ramirez opened the bottom of the 12th with a single, and Ortiz hit a home run to win the game, 6-4, and give Boston a glimmer of hope.

No team in baseball's postseason history had ever won a series after being down 3-0, and only two had even forced a sixth game. The Red Sox did just that by winning Game 5, 5-4, in 14 innings. Boston scored two runs in the eighth to tie the score, and Ortiz's broken-bat single scored Johnny Damon to win the game. Back in New York, the Red Sox continued to make history by winning Game 6, 4-2. Schilling, his ankle having been surgically repaired, surrendered only four hits in seven innings, and Mark Bellhorn's three-run homer gave Boston a four-run lead. The Sox scored two runs in the first inning of Game 7 and four in the second on a Damon grand slam and went on to win, 10-3. Boston thus completed a comeback unique in baseball history and advanced to the World Series for the first time since 1986.

### BOSTON WINS FIRST SERIES SINCE 1918

Over the past decade or so, the popular way to explain the failure of the Red Sox to win the World Series since 1918 has been to blame the "Curse of the Bambino." It was retribution by the baseball gods, so it is said, for Boston's decision to sell young Babe Ruth to the Yankees in January 1920. The Red Sox lost the Series in 1946, 1967, 1975 and 1986, often quite painfully, and lost the ALCS in 1988, 1990, 1999 and 2003. But 2004 was different.

Since the A.L. squad had won the All-Star Game, 9-4, the Series opened in the home park of the Red Sox. They won Game 1, 11-9, in a game that included 24 hits and five errors, two by Ramirez on consecutive plays. The Cards tied the score in the eighth inning, but Bellhorn's two-run homer gave the game to Boston. The Sox won Game 2, 6-2, despite committing four more errors, three by Mueller. Schilling and three relievers held St. Louis to five hits.

After the Series moved to St. Louis, the Red Sox won Game 3, 4-1. The Cardinals got only four hits and scored their only run in the bottom of the ninth inning on a Walker home run. Martinez pitched seven innings for the winners, and Ramirez drove in a pair of runs. Boston completed its improbable triumph in Game 4, shutting out the Cardinals, 3-0. Lowe pitched a three-hitter for seven innings, and three relievers kept St. Louis off the board. Damon led off the game with a home run, and Trot Nixon doubled home two runs in the third inning to account for all of Boston's scoring.

The Red Sox awarded 58 full World Series shares, each worth $223,619.79 (down from $306,149.92 in 2003), 29 partial shares and eight cash awards. The Cardinals voted 51 full shares, each worth $163,378.53, 35 partial shares and 16 cash awards. The number of people watching the Series on television rose from 2003. The rating (the percentage of households with televisions watching the games), increased from 12.8 to 15.8 percent, and the share (the percentage of households watching a program among those with televisions in use at the time), grew from 22 to 25 percent.

### ATTENDANCE RISES TO HIGHEST LEVEL

According to figures released in November, major league baseball games drew 73,022,969 fans, the highest total ever and 8.1 percent above 2003's corrected figure of 67,568,397. Average attendance was 30,401, up from 28,013 in 2003. N.L. teams drew 40,221,301 people to their home games, and A.L. teams attracted 32,801,668.

All clubs except Montreal drew more than 1.2 million fans. Nine teams drew more than 3 million: the Yankees (who led both leagues with 3,775,292) and Angels in the A.L., and the Dodgers, Giants, Phillies, Cubs, Astros, Cardinals and Padres in the N.L. Eleven other teams exceeded 2 million, and seven clubs (the Angels, Red Sox, Yankees, Astros, Cubs, Padres and Phillies) set all-time franchise marks.

Eighteen teams, nine in the A.L. and nine in the N.L., had an increase in attendance. The Phillies had the greatest increase, up 990,189 to 3,250,092, and the Mariners declined the most, down 327,778 to 2,940,731. The Expos drew 748,550.

### SIX TEAMS CHANGE MANAGERS

Three teams replaced managers during the season, and three others made changes immediately thereafter. Arizona's saga was the most convoluted. The team fired Bob Brenly on July 2 and replaced him on an interim basis with third base coach Al Pedrique. The Diamondbacks had recently suffered an 11-game losing streak and stood fourth in the N.L. West with a record of 29-50. They went 22-61 under Pedrique, who was relieved of his duties after the season. Arizona hired minor league manager Wally Backman on November 1 but fired him four days later, after revelations in the media about his arrests and financial problems. The team then hired Bob Melvin, a former Diamondbacks coach who had just been fired as Seattle's manager.

The Astros fired Jimy Williams on July 14, at the conclusion of the All-Star break. The team, in fifth place in the N.L. Central with a record of 44-44, appointed Phil Garner as interim manager. The Astros finished strong (48-26) and captured the wild-card spot in the playoffs, and the club removed the "interim" tag before Garner's name on November 3. The Blue Jays fired Carlos Tosca on August 8 with the team at 47-64 (last place in the A.L. East) and replaced him with first base coach John Gibbons. He also had interim status through the rest of the season, and after finishing 20-30, was named manager on October 4.

The Mets announced on September 15 that Art Howe would not return as manager in 2005. He finished the season, however, as the Mets finished in fourth place in the N.L. East at 71-91. The team hired Yankees coach Willie Randolph on November 3. The Phillies fired Larry Bowa on October 2, the next-to-last day of the season, and the Mariners fired Melvin on October 4, the day after the end of the season. Philadelphia finished in second place in the N.L. East (86-76), and Seattle was last in the A.L. West at 63-99. The Mariners hired former Cleveland and Baltimore manager Mike Hargrove on October 20, and the Phillies hired former Indians manager Charlie Manuel on November 4.

### OWNERSHIP CHANGES

Owners delayed approval of the sale of the Dodgers from News Corp. to real estate developer Frank McCourt. Running up against a January 31 deadline to complete the purchase or risk having to pay a penalty, McCourt filed papers with MLB's ownership committee that seemed to suggest noncompliance with baseball's debt-servicing rules. After Selig postponed a vote set for mid-January, the sale was approved by conference call on January 29. McCourt bought the club for $430 million. In the aftermath, he fired general manager Dan Evans and hired Paul DePodesta as his replacement.

The Brewers, the team owned by Selig and his family since 1970, were put up for sale in January. Daniel Gilbert, chairman of Quicken Loans, made a bid, but in September the team announced an agreement with Mark L. Attanasio, an investment officer with the Trust Company of the West. Approval of the sale was pending at year's end.

In March, a group of three businessmen from the Phoenix area and one Canadian bought out the managing partners of the Diamondbacks, including Jerry Colangelo. The new group, whose members had owned smaller parts of the club for some time, pledged to raise $99 million over 10 years to restore the team to competitiveness.

### LUXURY TAX AND REVENUE SHARING

In the second year of the competitive balance tax (CBT), the so-called luxury tax, three teams were sent tax bills for exceeding the threshold on payrolls. The Yankees, the only team to pay the CBT for 2003, were assessed $25,026,352. Boston's bill was $3,155,234, and Anaheim owed $927,059. The Yankees also paid an estimated $60 million under the provisions of MLB's revenue-sharing plan. The Red Sox revenue-sharing payment was an estimated $42 million.

### SEVEN ARBITRATION CASES

Sixty-five players filed for salary arbitration by the January 15 deadline, but only seven cases proceeded through the hearing and decision stage. Before teams and players exchanged figures on January 20, Kerry Wood and Derrek Lee signed with the Cubs for $9.75 million and $6.9 million, respectively, and Alfonso Soriano signed with the Yankees for $5.4 million. Twenty-seven players and teams exchanged figures, led by Albert Pujols of the Cardinals, who asked for $10.5 million against the team's offer of $7 million. After the exchange of figures, Roy Halladay signed a four-year contract with Toronto for $42 million, and Kevin Millwood agreed to a one-year contract with the Phillies for $11 million.

The three players who won their cases were David Eckstein, A.J. Pierzynski and Jack Wilson. The four losers were Eric Gagne, Nick Johnson, Chris Reitsma and Johan Santana. Owners now lead players in winning arbitration cases, 263-197.

The 65 players who filed earned an average salary increase of 126 percent, up from 92 percent in 2003. They received an average salary in 2004 of $3.26 million, a record far above the previous mark, $2.76 million, set in 2003. Forty-two players at least doubled their salaries, including 15 who had a sixfold increase. Pujols garnered the largest increase, 1,404 percent, from $950,000 in 2003 to an average of $14.29 million, when he signed a seven-year contract worth $100 million two days before his hearing was scheduled. Only two players among the 65 failed to get raises.

### SALARIES DROP A BIT

According to figures compiled by the Players Association and released by The Associated Press in December, the average major league salary declined 2.5 percent to $2,313,535, the first drop since 1995 and only the third decline in nearly 40 years. (Salary calculations, it

## FINAL STANDINGS

### AMERICAN LEAGUE

#### EAST DIVISION

| Team | N.Y. | Bos. | Tor. | Bal. | TB. | Min. | Chi. | K.C. | Cle. | Det. | Oak. | Sea. | Ana. | Tex. | N.L. | W | L | Pct. | GB | LD1st | DIF | Lead |
|---|---|---|---|---|---|---|---|---|---|---|---|---|---|---|---|---|---|---|---|---|---|---|
| New York...... | ... | 8 | 14 | 15 | 12 | 4 | 4 | 4 | 3 | 5 | 4 | 7 | 5 | 6 | 10-8 | 101 | 61 | .623 | ... | 10/3 | 141 | 10.5 |
| Boston.......... | 11 | ... | 9 | 14 | 14 | 2 | 4 | 3 | 6 | 4 | 5 | 8 | 4 | 5 | 9-9 | 98 | 64 | .605 | 3.0 | 5/30 | 45 | 3.0 |
| Baltimore...... | 5 | 10 | ... | 11 | 11 | 4 | 2 | 3 | 6 | 6 | 3 | 0 | 5 | 7 | 5-13 | 78 | 84 | .481 | 23.0 | 4/23 | 15 | 1.0 |
| Tampa Bay.... | 4 | 5 | 8 | ... | 9 | 5 | 2 | 3 | 3 | 6 | 1 | 2 | 2 | 5 | 15-3 | 70 | 91 | .435 | 30.5 | 4/16 | 12 | 0.5 |
| Toronto......... | 7 | 5 | 8 | 9 | ... | 2 | 4 | 2 | 2 | 3 | 5 | 3 | 2 | 7 | 8-10 | 67 | 94 | .416 | 33.5 | 4/3 | 5 | 0.0 |

#### CENTRAL DIVISION

| Team | Min. | Chi. | K.C. | Cle. | Det. | N.Y. | Bos. | Tor. | Bal. | TB. | Oak. | Sea. | Ana. | Tex. | N.L. | W | L | Pct. | GB | LD1st | DIF | Lead |
|---|---|---|---|---|---|---|---|---|---|---|---|---|---|---|---|---|---|---|---|---|---|---|
| Minnesota .... | ... | 10 | 12 | 12 | 12 | 2 | 4 | 5 | 4 | 4 | 4 | 2 | 5 | 5 | 11-7 | 92 | 70 | .568 | ... | 10/3 | 135 | 13.5 |
| Chicago ........ | 9 | ... | 10 | 8 | 13 | 3 | 2 | 4 | 4 | 3 | 4 | 2 | 6 | 7 | 8-10 | 83 | 79 | .512 | 9.0 | 7/24 | 53 | 2.5 |
| Cleveland...... | 7 | 9 | ... | 9 | 11 | 2 | 4 | 3 | 3 | 5 | 5 | 6 | 1 | 5 | 10-8 | 80 | 82 | .494 | 12.0 | ... | ... | ... |
| Detroit .......... | 7 | 11 | 10 | ... | 8 | 4 | 1 | 0 | 3 | 4 | 2 | 4 | 4 | 5 | 9-9 | 72 | 90 | .444 | 20.0 | 4/17 | 13 | 2.0 |
| Kansas City .. | 7 | 6 | 8 | 11 | ... | 1 | 2 | 3 | 3 | 3 | 0 | 2 | 4 | 2 | 6-12 | 58 | 104 | .358 | 34.0 | 4/5 | 1 | 0.0 |

#### WEST DIVISION

| Team | Oak. | Sea. | Ana. | Tex. | N.Y. | Bos. | Tor. | Bal. | TB. | Min. | Chi. | K.C. | Cle. | Det. | N.L. | W | L | Pct. | GB | LD1st | DIF | Lead |
|---|---|---|---|---|---|---|---|---|---|---|---|---|---|---|---|---|---|---|---|---|---|---|
| Anaheim ....... | ... | 10 | 9 | 13 | 5 | 4 | 6 | 6 | 4 | 5 | 5 | 4 | 7 | 7 | 7-11 | 92 | 70 | .568 | ... | 10/3 | 52 | 3.5 |
| Oakland ........ | 9 | ... | 11 | 11 | 2 | 1 | 7 | 7 | 6 | 5 | 7 | 3 | 5 | 7 | 10-8 | 91 | 71 | .562 | 1.0 | 9/30 | 96 | 4.0 |
| Texas ........... | 10 | 9 | ... | 12 | 4 | 5 | 2 | 7 | 7 | 2 | 3 | 8 | 5 | 5 | 10-8 | 89 | 73 | .549 | 3.0 | 8/5 | 50 | 4.5 |
| Seattle ......... | 7 | 8 | 7 | ... | 3 | 4 | 2 | 2 | 2 | 4 | 2 | 4 | 4 | 5 | 9-9 | 63 | 99 | .389 | 29.0 | ... | ... | ... |

NOTE: Read across for wins, down for losses; final standings are shaded.

Abbreviations: LD1st denotes last date in 1st place; DIF denotes days in first place; Lead denotes largest lead.

### NATIONAL LEAGUE

#### EAST DIVISION

| Team | Atl. | Fla. | Phi. | Mon. | N.Y. | Chi. | Hou. | St.L. | Pit. | Cin. | Mil. | S.F. | L.A. | Ari. | Col. | S.D. | A.L. | W | L | Pct. | GB | LD1st | DIF | Lead |
|---|---|---|---|---|---|---|---|---|---|---|---|---|---|---|---|---|---|---|---|---|---|---|---|---|
| Atlanta ............ | ... | 10 | 14 | 12 | 15 | 2 | 3 | 3 | 2 | 4 | 4 | 4 | 4 | 3 | 4 | 4 | 8-10 | 96 | 66 | .593 | ... | 10/3 | 81 | 11.0 |
| Philadelphia ... | 9 | ... | 7 | 11 | 12 | 3 | 0 | 3 | 3 | 3 | 6 | 5 | 2 | 5 | 3 | 5 | 9-9 | 86 | 76 | .531 | 10.0 | 7/22 | 36 | 3.0 |
| Florida............ | 5 | 12 | ... | 15 | 11 | 2 | 3 | 3 | 2 | 1 | 4 | 3 | 2 | 4 | 5 | 4 | 7-11 | 83 | 79 | .512 | 13.0 | 6/27 | 73 | 3.5 |
| New York ....... | 7 | 8 | 4 | ... | 10 | 1 | 4 | 2 | 3 | 1 | 4 | 3 | 4 | 1 | 5 | 4 | 10-8 | 71 | 91 | .438 | 25.0 | 4/7 | 3 | 0.0 |
| Montreal ........ | 4 | 7 | 8 | 9 | ... | 3 | 4 | 3 | 2 | 4 | 1 | 3 | 1 | 1 | 4 | 6 | 7-11 | 67 | 95 | .414 | 29.0 | 4/7 | 2 | 0.0 |

#### CENTRAL DIVISION

| Team | Chi. | Hou. | St.L. | Pit. | Cin. | Mil. | Atl. | Fla. | Phi. | Mon. | N.Y. | S.F. | L.A. | Ari. | Col. | S.D. | A.L. | W | L | Pct. | GB | LD1st | DIF | Lead |
|---|---|---|---|---|---|---|---|---|---|---|---|---|---|---|---|---|---|---|---|---|---|---|---|---|
| St. Louis ......... | ... | 8 | 11 | 14 | 12 | 9 | 4 | 3 | 4 | 5 | 3 | 4 | 3 | 4 | 5 | 5 | 11-1 | 105 | 57 | .648 | ... | 10/3 | 116 | 17.5 |
| Houston ......... | 10 | ... | 9 | 11 | 12 | 13 | 3 | 6 | 3 | 2 | 2 | 1 | 2 | 2 | 5 | 4 | 7-5 | 92 | 70 | .568 | 13.0 | 5/22 | 29 | 3.0 |
| Chicago.......... | 8 | 10 | ... | 9 | 13 | 10 | 3 | 3 | 3 | 4 | 3 | 2 | 2 | 4 | 5 | 2 | 8-4 | 89 | 73 | .549 | 16.0 | 5/23 | 17 | 1.0 |
| Cincinnati....... | 5 | 6 | 8 | ... | 9 | 10 | 4 | 3 | 4 | 3 | 4 | 4 | 3 | 2 | 3 | 3 | 5-7 | 76 | 86 | .469 | 29.0 | 6/10 | 32 | 2.5 |
| Pittsburgh...... | 5 | 5 | 5 | 10 | ... | 12 | 2 | 3 | 5 | 5 | 2 | 0 | 5 | 3 | 4 | 4 | 2-10 | 72 | 89 | .447 | 32.5 | 4/5 | 1 | 0.0 |
| Milwaukee...... | 8 | 6 | 7 | 8 | 6 | ... | 2 | 0 | 2 | 2 | 5 | 3 | 1 | 2 | 4 | 3 | 8-4 | 67 | 94 | .416 | 37.5 | 4/8 | 4 | 0.5 |

#### WEST DIVISION

| Team | S.F. | L.A. | Ari. | Col. | S.D. | Atl. | Fla. | Phi. | Mon. | N.Y. | Chi. | Hou. | St.L. | Pit. | Cin. | Mil. | A.L. | W | L | Pct. | GB | LD1st | DIF | Lead |
|---|---|---|---|---|---|---|---|---|---|---|---|---|---|---|---|---|---|---|---|---|---|---|---|---|
| Los Angeles ..... | ... | 10 | 10 | 11 | 16 | 3 | 1 | 3 | 3 | 4 | 2 | 5 | 4 | 2 | 6 | 3 | 10-8 | 93 | 69 | .574 | ... | 10/3 | 158 | 7.5 |
| San Fran. ....... | 9 | ... | 7 | 11 | 14 | 3 | 4 | 5 | 2 | 5 | 3 | 4 | 4 | 3 | 1 | 5 | 11-7 | 91 | 71 | .562 | 2.0 | 7/4 | 17 | 3.0 |
| San Diego ...... | 9 | 12 | ... | 9 | 12 | 3 | 1 | 2 | 6 | 6 | 2 | 4 | 2 | 4 | 3 | 4 | 8-10 | 87 | 75 | .537 | 6.0 | 7/6 | 9 | 2.0 |
| Colorado ........ | 8 | 8 | 10 | ... | 13 | 2 | 5 | 1 | 1 | 2 | 1 | 1 | 1 | 3 | 2 | 2 | 8-10 | 68 | 94 | .420 | 25.0 | ... | ... | ... |
| Arizona........... | 3 | 5 | 7 | 6 | ... | 2 | 1 | 3 | 3 | 0 | 1 | 2 | 4 | 3 | 2 | 3 | 6-12 | 51 | 111 | .315 | 42.0 | 4/8 | 1 | 0.0 |

NOTE: Read across for wins, down for losses; final standings are shaded.

Abbreviations: LD1st denotes last date in 1st place; DIF denotes days in first place; Lead denotes largest lead.

should be noted, can differ, depending on what factors are included.) The Yankees had the highest average salary for the sixth consecutive year (a record $6,382,187), and the Pirates had the lowest ($917,126), although MLB's figures, released later, showed Tampa Bay with the lowest total payroll. The players association has been studying whether to file a new collusion grievance for two years but has taken no action. For 2005, a cost-of-living increase will boost the minimum salary from $300,000 to $316,000.

### CONCLUSION

In April 2003, Selig announced that he would not seek re-election beyond the end of his current term in December 2006. But he changed his mind, and in August 2004, the owners voted to extend his tenure through 2009. Baseball has its problems, to be sure, including most prominently how to deal with the repercussions of the BALCO investigation, but Selig has spoken optimistically about its future. In June, commenting on attendance, he said, "I can't tell you how good I feel about where we are and how we got there." However the remainder of Selig's term transpires, here (starting on page 166) is how the game on the field ended up in 2004:

## INTERLEAGUE RECORDS

### AMERICAN LEAGUE

#### EAST DIVISION

| A.L. team vs. | Ari. | Atl. | Chi. | Cin. | Col. | Fla. | Hou. | L.A. | Mil. | Mon. | N.Y. | Phi. | Pit. | St.L. | S.D. | S.F. | W | L | Pct. |
|---|---|---|---|---|---|---|---|---|---|---|---|---|---|---|---|---|---|---|---|
| New York........ | 2-1 | 0-0 | 0-0 | 0-0 | 3-0 | 0-0 | 0-0 | 1-2 | 0-0 | 0-0 | 2-4 | 0-0 | 0-0 | 0-0 | 2-1 | 0-0 | 10 | 8 | .556 |
| Boston............ | 0-0 | 1-2 | 0-0 | 0-0 | 1-2 | 0-0 | 0-0 | 2-1 | 0-0 | 0-0 | 0-0 | 2-1 | 0-0 | 0-0 | 2-1 | 1-2 | 9 | 9 | .500 |
| Baltimore........ | 1-2 | 1-2 | 0-0 | 0-0 | 1-2 | 0-0 | 0-0 | 0-3 | 0-0 | 0-0 | 0-0 | 1-2 | 0-0 | 0-0 | 0-0 | 1-2 | 5 | 13 | .278 |
| Tampa Bay ..... | 3-0 | 0-0 | 0-0 | 0-0 | 3-0 | 4-2 | 0-0 | 0-0 | 0-0 | 0-0 | 0-0 | 0-0 | 0-0 | 0-0 | 3-0 | 2-1 | 15 | 3 | .833 |
| Toronto .......... | 1-2 | 0-0 | 0-0 | 0-0 | 0-0 | 0-0 | 0-0 | 2-1 | 0-0 | 3-3 | 0-0 | 0-0 | 0-0 | 0-0 | 2-1 | 0-3 | 8 | 10 | .444 |

#### CENTRAL DIVISION

| A.L. team vs. | Ari. | Atl. | Chi. | Cin. | Col. | Fla. | Hou. | L.A. | Mil. | Mon. | N.Y. | Phi. | Pit. | St.L. | S.D. | S.F. | W | L | Pct. |
|---|---|---|---|---|---|---|---|---|---|---|---|---|---|---|---|---|---|---|---|
| Minnesota ...... | 2-1 | 0-0 | 0-0 | 0-0 | 0-0 | 0-0 | 0-0 | 0-0 | 2-4 | 3-0 | 3-0 | 1-2 | 0-0 | 0-0 | 0-0 | 0-0 | 11 | 7 | .611 |
| Chicago .......... | 0-0 | 2-1 | 2-4 | 0-0 | 0-0 | 1-2 | 0-0 | 0-0 | 0-0 | 1-2 | 0-0 | 2-1 | 0-0 | 0-0 | 0-0 | 0-0 | 8 | 10 | .444 |
| Cleveland........ | 0-0 | 2-1 | 0-0 | 4-2 | 2-1 | 1-2 | 0-0 | 0-0 | 0-0 | 0-0 | 1-2 | 0-0 | 0-0 | 0-0 | 0-0 | 0-0 | 10 | 8 | .556 |
| Detroit............ | 3-0 | 2-1 | 0-0 | 0-0 | 0-3 | 2-1 | 0-0 | 0-0 | 0-0 | 0-0 | 0-3 | 2-1 | 0-0 | 0-0 | 0-0 | 0-0 | 9 | 9 | .500 |
| Kansas City .... | 0-0 | 2-1 | 0-0 | 0-0 | 0-0 | 0-0 | 0-0 | 0-0 | 0-0 | 1-2 | 2-1 | 1-2 | 0-0 | 0-3 | 0-3 | 0-0 | 6 | 12 | .333 |

#### WEST DIVISION

| A.L. team vs. | Ari. | Atl. | Chi. | Cin. | Col. | Fla. | Hou. | L.A. | Mil. | Mon. | N.Y. | Phi. | Pit. | St.L. | S.D. | S.F. | W | L | Pct. |
|---|---|---|---|---|---|---|---|---|---|---|---|---|---|---|---|---|---|---|---|
| Anaheim......... | 0-0 | 0-0 | 1-2 | 0-0 | 0-0 | 0-0 | 1-2 | 3-3 | 1-2 | 0-0 | 0-0 | 0-0 | 1-2 | 0-0 | 0-0 | 0-0 | 7 | 11 | .389 |
| Oakland .......... | 0-0 | 0-0 | 1-2 | 3-0 | 0-0 | 0-0 | 0-0 | 0-0 | 0-0 | 0-0 | 0-0 | 0-0 | 3-0 | 0-3 | 0-0 | 3-3 | 10 | 8 | .556 |
| Texas.............. | 0-0 | 0-0 | 0-0 | 0-3 | 0-0 | 3-0 | 3-3 | 0-0 | 0-0 | 0-0 | 0-0 | 0-0 | 3-0 | 1-2 | 0-0 | 0-0 | 10 | 8 | .556 |
| Seattle............ | 0-0 | 0-0 | 0-0 | 0-0 | 0-0 | 0-0 | 1-2 | 0-0 | 1-2 | 3-0 | 0-0 | 0-0 | 3-0 | 0-3 | 1-2 | 0-0 | 9 | 9 | .500 |

NOTE: Teams are listed in order of their final standings, not by their interleague records.

### NATIONAL LEAGUE

#### EAST DIVISION

| N.L. team vs. | Ana. | Bal. | Bos. | Chi. | Cle. | Det. | K.C. | Min. | N.Y. | Oak. | Sea. | T.B. | Tex. | Tor. | W | L | Pct. |
|---|---|---|---|---|---|---|---|---|---|---|---|---|---|---|---|---|---|
| Atlanta............ | 0-0 | 2-1 | 2-1 | 1-2 | 1-2 | 1-2 | 1-2 | 0-0 | 0-0 | 0-0 | 0-0 | 0-0 | 0-0 | 0-0 | 8 | 10 | .444 |
| Philadelphia.... | 0-0 | 2-1 | 1-2 | 1-2 | 0-0 | 1-2 | 2-1 | 2-1 | 0-0 | 0-0 | 0-0 | 0-0 | 0-0 | 0-0 | 9 | 9 | .500 |
| Florida ............ | 0-0 | 0-0 | 0-0 | 2-1 | 2-1 | 1-2 | 0-0 | 0-0 | 0-0 | 0-0 | 0-0 | 2-4 | 0-3 | 0-0 | 7 | 11 | .389 |
| New York........ | 0-0 | 0-0 | 0-0 | 0-0 | 2-1 | 3-0 | 1-2 | 0-3 | 4-2 | 0-0 | 0-0 | 0-0 | 0-0 | 0-0 | 10 | 8 | .556 |
| Montreal......... | 0-0 | 0-0 | 0-0 | 2-1 | 0-0 | 0-0 | 2-1 | 0-3 | 0-0 | 0-0 | 0-3 | 0-0 | 0-0 | 3-3 | 7 | 11 | .389 |

#### CENTRAL DIVISION

| N.L. team vs. | Ana. | Bal. | Bos. | Chi. | Cle. | Det. | K.C. | Min. | N.Y. | Oak. | Sea. | T.B. | Tex. | Tor. | W | L | Pct. |
|---|---|---|---|---|---|---|---|---|---|---|---|---|---|---|---|---|---|
| St. Louis......... | 0-0 | 0-0 | 0-0 | 0-0 | 0-0 | 0-0 | 3-0 | 0-0 | 0-0 | 3-0 | 3-0 | 0-0 | 2-1 | 0-0 | 11 | 1 | .917 |
| Houston ......... | 2-1 | 0-0 | 0-0 | 0-0 | 0-0 | 0-0 | 0-0 | 0-0 | 0-0 | 0-0 | 2-1 | 0-0 | 3-3 | 0-0 | 7 | 5 | .583 |
| Chicago .......... | 2-1 | 0-0 | 0-0 | 4-2 | 0-0 | 0-0 | 0-0 | 0-0 | 0-0 | 2-1 | 0-0 | 0-0 | 0-0 | 0-0 | 8 | 4 | .667 |
| Cincinnati ....... | 0-0 | 0-0 | 0-0 | 0-0 | 2-4 | 0-0 | 0-0 | 0-0 | 0-0 | 0-3 | 0-0 | 0-0 | 3-0 | 0-0 | 5 | 7 | .417 |
| Pittsburgh ...... | 2-1 | 0-0 | 0-0 | 0-0 | 0-0 | 0-0 | 0-0 | 0-0 | 0-0 | 0-3 | 0-3 | 0-0 | 0-3 | 0-0 | 2 | 10 | .167 |
| Milwaukee ...... | 2-1 | 0-0 | 0-0 | 0-0 | 0-0 | 0-0 | 0-0 | 4-2 | 0-0 | 0-0 | 2-1 | 0-0 | 0-0 | 0-0 | 8 | 4 | .667 |

#### WEST DIVISION

| N.L. team vs. | Ana. | Bal. | Bos. | Chi. | Cle. | Det. | K.C. | Min. | N.Y. | Oak. | Sea. | T.B. | Tex. | Tor. | W | L | Pct. |
|---|---|---|---|---|---|---|---|---|---|---|---|---|---|---|---|---|---|
| Los Angeles ... | 3-3 | 3-0 | 1-2 | 0-0 | 0-0 | 0-0 | 0-0 | 0-0 | 2-1 | 0-0 | 0-0 | 0-0 | 0-0 | 1-2 | 10 | 8 | .556 |
| San Francisco | 0-0 | 2-1 | 2-1 | 0-0 | 0-0 | 0-0 | 0-0 | 0-0 | 0-0 | 3-3 | 0-0 | 1-2 | 0-0 | 3-0 | 11 | 7 | .611 |
| San Diego ...... | 0-0 | 0-0 | 1-2 | 0-0 | 0-0 | 0-0 | 3-0 | 0-0 | 1-2 | 0-0 | 2-1 | 0-3 | 0-0 | 1-2 | 8 | 10 | .444 |
| Colorado ........ | 0-0 | 2-1 | 2-1 | 0-0 | 1-2 | 3-0 | 0-0 | 0-0 | 0-3 | 0-0 | 0-0 | 0-3 | 0-0 | 0-0 | 8 | 10 | .444 |
| Arizona........... | 0-0 | 2-1 | 0-0 | 0-0 | 0-0 | 0-3 | 0-0 | 1-2 | 1-2 | 0-0 | 0-0 | 0-3 | 0-0 | 2-1 | 6 | 12 | .333 |

NOTE: Teams are listed in order of their final standings, not by their interleague records.

# A.L. DIVISION SERIES

## BOSTON VS. ANAHEIM

### RESULTS

| Day | Date | Place | Score |
|---|---|---|---|
| Tue. | Oct. 5 | Anaheim | Boston 9, Anaheim 3 |
| Wed. | Oct. 6 | Anaheim | Boston 8, Anaheim 3 |
| Fri. | Oct. 8 | Boston | Boston 8, Anaheim 6 |

### BOX SCORES

### GAME 1

**BOSTON 9, ANAHEIM 3**

TUESDAY, OCTOBER 5, AT ANAHEIM

| Boston | AB | R | H | BI | BB | SO | PO | A |
|---|---|---|---|---|---|---|---|---|
| Damon, cf | 5 | 2 | 2 | 0 | 0 | 1 | 2 | 0 |
| Bellhorn, 2b | 4 | 0 | 0 | 0 | 1 | 1 | 0 | 2 |
| Reese, 2b | 0 | 0 | 0 | 0 | 0 | 0 | 0 | 0 |
| M.Ramirez, lf | 5 | 2 | 2 | 3 | 0 | 1 | 2 | 0 |
| D.Ortiz, dh | 3 | 1 | 1 | 1 | 2 | 0 | 0 | 0 |
| Millar, 1b | 4 | 1 | 2 | 2 | 0 | 0 | 4 | 3 |
| Mientkiewicz, pr-1b | 1 | 0 | 1 | 1 | 0 | 0 | 2 | 0 |
| Varitek, c | 5 | 1 | 1 | 0 | 0 | 1 | 8 | 0 |
| O.Cabrera, ss | 3 | 1 | 1 | 0 | 2 | 0 | 1 | 3 |
| Mueller, 3b | 4 | 0 | 0 | 0 | 1 | 1 | 1 | 1 |
| Kapler, rf | 5 | 1 | 1 | 0 | 0 | 0 | 5 | 0 |
| Schilling, p | 0 | 0 | 0 | 0 | 0 | 0 | 2 | 0 |
| Embree, p | 0 | 0 | 0 | 0 | 0 | 0 | 0 | 0 |
| Timlin, p | 0 | 0 | 0 | 0 | 0 | 0 | 0 | 0 |
| **TOTALS** | 39 | 9 | 11 | 7 | 6 | 5 | 27 | 9 |

| Aanheim | AB | R | H | BI | BB | SO | PO | A |
|---|---|---|---|---|---|---|---|---|
| Figgins, 3b-2b | 5 | 0 | 1 | 0 | 0 | 2 | 0 | 3 |
| Erstad, 1b | 4 | 1 | 3 | 1 | 1 | 1 | 12 | 0 |
| V.Guerrero, rf | 5 | 0 | 0 | 0 | 0 | 2 | 3 | 0 |
| G.Anderson, cf | 4 | 1 | 0 | 0 | 0 | 0 | 4 | 0 |
| Glaus, dh | 3 | 1 | 3 | 2 | 1 | 0 | 0 | 0 |
| DaVanon, lf | 3 | 0 | 0 | 0 | 0 | 0 | 1 | 0 |
| Riggs, ph-lf | 1 | 0 | 0 | 0 | 0 | 0 | 0 | 0 |
| B.Molina, c | 4 | 0 | 1 | 0 | 0 | 0 | 5 | 1 |
| Eckstein, ss | 4 | 0 | 1 | 0 | 0 | 0 | 1 | 0 |
| Amezaga, 2b | 1 | 0 | 0 | 0 | 0 | 1 | 0 | 1 |
| McPherson, ph-3b | 3 | 0 | 0 | 0 | 0 | 1 | 1 | 2 |
| Washburn, p | 0 | 0 | 0 | 0 | 0 | 0 | 0 | 1 |
| Shields, p | 0 | 0 | 0 | 0 | 0 | 0 | 0 | 0 |
| Gregg, p | 0 | 0 | 0 | 0 | 0 | 0 | 0 | 0 |
| Ra.Ortiz, p | 0 | 0 | 0 | 0 | 0 | 0 | 0 | 1 |
| **TOTALS** | 37 | 3 | 9 | 3 | 2 | 7 | 27 | 9 |

| | | | | |
|---|---|---|---|---|
| Boston | 100 | 700 | 010—9 | 11 1 |
| Anaheim | 003 | 000 | 001—3 | 9 1 |

| Boston | IP | H | R | ER | HR | BB | SO |
|---|---|---|---|---|---|---|---|
| Schilling (W) | 6.2 | 9 | 3 | 2 | 2 | 2 | 4 |
| Embree | 0.1 | 0 | 0 | 0 | 0 | 0 | 0 |
| Timlin | 2.0 | 0 | 0 | 0 | 0 | 0 | 3 |

| Anaheim | IP | H | R | ER | HR | BB | SO |
|---|---|---|---|---|---|---|---|
| Washburn (L) | 3.1 | 5 | 7 | 3 | 1 | 3 | 3 |
| Shields | 1.2 | 1 | 1 | 1 | 1 | 1 | 2 |
| Gregg | 2.0 | 3 | 0 | 0 | 0 | 1 | 0 |
| Ra.Ortiz | 2.0 | 2 | 1 | 1 | 0 | 1 | 0 |

E—Schilling, Figgins. LOB—Boston 9, Anaheim 9. Scoring Position—Boston 4 for 13, Anaheim 2 for 9. 2B—Damon, M.Ramirez, Glaus 2. HR—Millar (4th inning, 0 out, 1 on) off Washburn, M.Ramirez (4th inning, 2 out, 2 on) off Shields, Glaus (4th inning, 0 out, 0 on) off Schilling, Erstad (7th inning, 1 out, 0 on) off Schilling. SB—Damon, Figgins. WP—Gregg. T—3:04. A—44,608. U—HP-Young, 1B-Meals, 2B-Runge, 3B-Cederstrom, LF-Montague, RF-Danley.

### HOW THEY SCORED

TOP OF 1

Red Sox first. Damon popped out to shortstop Eckstein. Bellhorn popped out to right fielder Guerrero. Ramirez infield double to third. Ortiz singled to right, Ramirez scored. Millar flied out to right fielder Guerrero. Runs: 1, Hits: 2, Errors: 0

TOP OF 4

Red Sox fourth. Ortiz walked on four pitches. Millar homered to left on a 0-1 count, Ortiz scored. Varitek singled to left. Cabrera walked, Varitek to second. Mueller struck out. Kapler singled to right, Varitek to third, Cabrera to second. Damon safe on fielder's choice and Figgins' error, Varitek scored, Cabrera scored, Kapler to third. Shields pitching. Bellhorn struck out. Ramirez homered to center on a 1-0 count, Kapler scored, Damon scored. Ortiz grounded out, second baseman Amezaga to first baseman Erstad. Runs: 7, Hits: 4, Errors: 1

BOTTOM OF 4

Angels fourth. Glaus homered to left on a 0-1 count. DaVanon grounded out, first baseman Millar to pitcher Schilling. B.Molina grounded out, shortstop Cabrera to first baseman Millar. Eckstein fouled out to third baseman Mueller. Runs: 1, Hits: 1, Errors: 0

BOTTOM OF 7

Angels seventh. Mientkiewicz in as first baseman. Figgins grounded out, second baseman Bellhorn to first baseman Mientkiewicz. Erstad homered to center on the first pitch. Guerrero flied out to right fielder Kapler. Anderson safe at third on Schilling's error. Glaus doubled to center, Anderson scored. Embree pitching. Riggs pinch-hitting for DaVanon. Riggs fouled out to catcher Varitek. Runs: 2, Hits: 2, Errors: 1

TOP OF 8

Red Sox eighth. Riggs in as left fielder. Ortiz pitching. Damon singled to right. Bellhorn fouled out to first baseman Erstad. Damon stole second. Ramirez grounded out, pitcher Ortiz to second baseman Figgins to first baseman Erstad, Damon to third. Ortiz was intentionally walked. Mientkiewicz bunt single to third, Damon scored, Ortiz to second. Varitek flied out to right fielder Guerrero. Runs: 1, Hits: 2, Errors: 0

### GAME 2

**BOSTON 8, ANAHEIM 3**

WEDNESDAY, OCTOBER 6, AT ANAHEIM

| Boston | AB | R | H | BI | BB | SO | PO | A |
|---|---|---|---|---|---|---|---|---|
| Damon, cf | 5 | 1 | 2 | 0 | 0 | 0 | 2 | 0 |
| Bellhorn, 2b | 3 | 0 | 1 | 0 | 2 | 0 | 0 | 3 |
| Reese, 2b | 0 | 0 | 0 | 0 | 0 | 0 | 0 | 1 |
| M.Ramirez, lf | 3 | 1 | 1 | 2 | 1 | 1 | 2 | 0 |
| D.Ortiz, dh | 2 | 1 | 1 | 0 | 3 | 0 | 0 | 0 |
| Nixon, rf | 5 | 0 | 1 | 1 | 0 | 0 | 0 | 0 |
| Kapler, pr-rf | 0 | 1 | 0 | 0 | 0 | 0 | 0 | 0 |
| Millar, 1b | 3 | 1 | 1 | 0 | 0 | 0 | 6 | 1 |
| Mientkiewicz, 1b | 2 | 0 | 1 | 0 | 0 | 0 | 2 | 0 |
| Varitek, c | 3 | 2 | 1 | 2 | 1 | 2 | 10 | 1 |
| O.Cabrera, ss | 5 | 0 | 1 | 3 | 0 | 1 | 1 | 0 |
| Mueller, 3b | 3 | 1 | 2 | 0 | 0 | 0 | 2 | 0 |
| D.Roberts, pr | 0 | 0 | 0 | 0 | 0 | 0 | 0 | 0 |

| Boston | AB | R | H | BI | BB | SO | PO | A |
|---|---|---|---|---|---|---|---|---|
| Youkilis, 3b | 2 | 0 | 0 | 0 | 0 | 1 | 0 | 0 |
| P.Martinez, p | 0 | 0 | 0 | 0 | 0 | 0 | 2 | 1 |
| Timlin, p | 0 | 0 | 0 | 0 | 0 | 0 | 0 | 0 |
| M.Myers, p | 0 | 0 | 0 | 0 | 0 | 0 | 0 | 0 |
| Foulke, p | 0 | 0 | 0 | 0 | 0 | 0 | 0 | 1 |
| **TOTALS** | 36 | 8 | 12 | 8 | 7 | 5 | 27 | 8 |

| Anaheim | AB | R | H | BI | BB | SO | PO | A |
|---|---|---|---|---|---|---|---|---|
| Figgins, 2b | 4 | 0 | 0 | 0 | 0 | 2 | 2 | 3 |
| Erstad, 1b | 3 | 0 | 1 | 0 | 0 | 0 | 9 | 0 |
| V.Guerrero, rf | 3 | 0 | 1 | 2 | 1 | 1 | 3 | 0 |
| G.Anderson, cf | 4 | 0 | 0 | 0 | 0 | 2 | 3 | 0 |
| Glaus, dh | 3 | 1 | 0 | 0 | 1 | 2 | 0 | 0 |
| DaVanon, lf | 4 | 0 | 2 | 0 | 0 | 0 | 2 | 0 |
| McPherson, 3b | 4 | 0 | 1 | 1 | 0 | 2 | 0 | 2 |
| J.Molina, c | 2 | 1 | 1 | 0 | 0 | 0 | 3 | 1 |
| Kotchman, ph | 1 | 0 | 0 | 0 | 0 | 0 | 0 | 0 |
| B.Molina, c | 0 | 0 | 0 | 0 | 0 | 0 | 2 | 0 |
| Pride, ph | 1 | 0 | 0 | 0 | 0 | 1 | 0 | 0 |
| Eckstein, ss | 3 | 1 | 1 | 0 | 0 | 0 | 3 | 4 |
| B.Colon, p | 0 | 0 | 0 | 0 | 0 | 0 | 0 | 0 |
| F.Rodriguez, p | 0 | 0 | 0 | 0 | 0 | 0 | 0 | 0 |
| Donnelly, p | 0 | 0 | 0 | 0 | 0 | 0 | 0 | 0 |
| **TOTALS** | 32 | 3 | 7 | 3 | 2 | 10 | 27 | 10 |

| | | | | | |
|---|---|---|---|---|---|
| Boston | 0 1 0 | 0 0 2 | 1 0 4—8 | 12 | 0 |
| Anaheim | 0 1 0 | 0 2 0 | 0 0 0—3 | 7 | 0 |

| Boston | IP | H | R | ER | HR | BB | SO |
|---|---|---|---|---|---|---|---|
| P.Martinez (W) | 7.0 | 6 | 3 | 3 | 0 | 2 | 6 |
| Timlin (HOLD) | 0.1 | 1 | 0 | 0 | 0 | 0 | 1 |
| M.Myers (HOLD) | 0.1 | 0 | 0 | 0 | 0 | 0 | 1 |
| Foulke (S) | 1.1 | 0 | 0 | 0 | 0 | 0 | 2 |

| Anaheim | IP | H | R | ER | HR | BB | SO |
|---|---|---|---|---|---|---|---|
| B.Colon | 6.0 | 7 | 3 | 3 | 1 | 3 | 3 |
| F.Rodriguez (L) | 2.0 | 2 | 1 | 1 | 0 | 2 | 2 |
| Donnelly | 1.0 | 3 | 4 | 4 | 0 | 2 | 0 |

DP—Boston 2, Anaheim 1. LOB—Boston 10, Anaheim 5. Scoring Position—Boston 2 for 11, Anaheim 2 for 7. 2B—M.Ramirez, O.Cabrera. HR—Varitek (6th inning, 2 out, 1 on) off B.Colon. SB—Damon. CS—DaVanon. S—M.Ramirez. WP—F.Rodriguez 2, Donnelly. HBP—Erstad by P.Martinez, Varitek by F.Rodriguez. T—3:48. A—45,118. U—HP-Meals, 1B-Runge, 2B-Cederstrom, 3B-Montague, LF-Danley, RF-Young.

## HOW THEY SCORED

### TOP OF 2

Red Sox second. Varitek struck out. Cabrera lined out to center fielder Anderson. Mueller singled to right. Damon singled to center, Mueller to third. Bellhorn walked, Damon to second. Ramirez walked on a full count, Mueller scored, Damon to third, Bellhorn to second. Bellhorn was picked off, catcher J.Molina to shortstop Eckstein, Bellhorn out. Runs: 1, Hits: 2, Errors: 0

### BOTTOM OF 2

Angels second. Glaus walked on a full count. DaVanon singled to left, Glaus to second. McPherson singled to left, Glaus scored, DaVanon to second. J.Molina grounded into fielder's choice, pitcher P.Martinez to third baseman Mueller, DaVanon out, McPherson to second. Eckstein flied out to center fielder Damon. Figgins struck out. Runs: 1, Hits: 2, Errors: 0

### BOTTOM OF 5

Angels fifth. J.Molina singled to center. Eckstein singled to center, J.Molina to second. Figgins flied out on a bunt to third baseman Mueller. Erstad was hit by a pitch, J.Molina to third, Eckstein to second. Guerrero singled to center, J.Molina scored, Eckstein scored, Erstad to third. Anderson lined into a double play, first baseman Millar unassisted, Guerrero out. Runs: 2, Hits: 3, Errors: 0

### TOP OF 6

Red Sox sixth. Ortiz infield single to short. Nixon grounded into a double play, second baseman Figgins to shortstop Eckstein to first baseman Erstad, Ortiz out. Millar singled to center. Varitek homered to right on the first pitch, Millar scored. Cabrera grounded out, third baseman McPherson to first baseman Erstad. Runs: 2, Hits: 3, Errors: 0

### TOP OF 7

Red Sox seventh. Rodriguez pitching. Mueller infield single to second. Roberts pinch-running for Mueller. Damon grounded into fielder's choice, shortstop Eckstein to second baseman Figgins, Roberts out. Damon stole second. Bellhorn walked on a full count. On Rodriguez's wild pitch, Damon to third, Bellhorn to second. Ramirez hit a sacrifice fly to center fielder Anderson, Damon scored. Ortiz was intentionally walked. Nixon grounded out, first baseman Erstad unassisted. Runs: 1, Hits: 1, Errors: 0

### TOP OF 9

Red Sox ninth. Donnelly pitching. Bellhorn flied out to right fielder Guerrero. Ramirez doubled to left. Ortiz was intentionally walked. Nixon singled to center, Ramirez scored, Ortiz to second. Kapler pinch-running for Nixon. On Donnelly's wild pitch, Ortiz to third, Kapler to second. Mientkiewicz grounded out, second baseman Figgins unassisted. Varitek was intentionally walked. Cabrera doubled to center, Ortiz scored, Kapler scored, Varitek scored. Cabrera to third. Youkilis flied out to right fielder Guerrero. Runs: 4, Hits: 3, Errors: 0

## GAME 3

### BOSTON 8, ANAHEIM 6

FRIDAY, OCTOBER 8, AT BOSTON

| Anaheim | AB | R | H | BI | BB | SO | PO | A |
|---|---|---|---|---|---|---|---|---|
| Figgins, 2b-3b | 5 | 0 | 1 | 0 | 0 | 1 | 2 | 4 |
| Erstad, 1b | 3 | 1 | 1 | 1 | 2 | 0 | 6 | 0 |
| V.Guerrero, rf | 4 | 1 | 1 | 4 | 1 | 1 | 0 | 0 |
| G.Anderson, cf | 5 | 0 | 2 | 0 | 0 | 1 | 1 | 0 |
| Glaus, dh | 5 | 1 | 1 | 1 | 0 | 2 | 0 | 0 |
| DaVanon, lf | 3 | 1 | 0 | 0 | 2 | 1 | 3 | 0 |
| B.Molina, c | 2 | 0 | 0 | 0 | 0 | 2 | 8 | 0 |
| Kotchman, ph | 0 | 0 | 0 | 0 | 0 | 0 | 0 | 0 |
| J.Molina, ph-c | 1 | 1 | 0 | 0 | 2 | 0 | 5 | 0 |
| McPherson, 3b | 2 | 0 | 0 | 0 | 0 | 1 | 2 | 0 |
| Riggs, ph | 0 | 0 | 0 | 0 | 0 | 0 | 0 | 0 |
| Pride, ph | 1 | 0 | 0 | 0 | 0 | 0 | 0 | 0 |
| Amezaga, 2b | 1 | 0 | 0 | 0 | 0 | 1 | 0 | 1 |
| Eckstein, ss | 5 | 1 | 2 | 0 | 0 | 1 | 2 | 1 |
| K.Escobar, p | 0 | 0 | 0 | 0 | 0 | 0 | 0 | 0 |
| Shields, p | 0 | 0 | 0 | 0 | 0 | 0 | 0 | 0 |
| Donnelly, p | 0 | 0 | 0 | 0 | 0 | 0 | 0 | 0 |
| F.Rodriguez, p | 0 | 0 | 0 | 0 | 0 | 0 | 0 | 0 |
| Washburn, p | 0 | 0 | 0 | 0 | 0 | 0 | 0 | 0 |
| **TOTALS** | 37 | 6 | 8 | 6 | 7 | 11 | 29 | 6 |

| Boston | AB | R | H | BI | BB | SO | PO | A |
|---|---|---|---|---|---|---|---|---|
| Damon, cf | 5 | 1 | 3 | 0 | 1 | 1 | 3 | 0 |
| Bellhorn, 2b | 4 | 2 | 0 | 0 | 2 | 3 | 1 | 3 |
| Reese, pr | 0 | 1 | 0 | 0 | 0 | 0 | 0 | 0 |
| M.Ramirez, lf | 5 | 0 | 2 | 2 | 0 | 2 | 4 | 0 |
| D.Ortiz, dh | 6 | 2 | 4 | 3 | 0 | 2 | 0 | 0 |
| Nixon, rf | 3 | 0 | 1 | 1 | 2 | 1 | 1 | 0 |
| Millar, 1b | 3 | 0 | 0 | 2 | 1 | 1 | 4 | 0 |
| Mientkiewicz, 1b | 1 | 0 | 0 | 0 | 0 | 0 | 3 | 0 |
| Varitek, c | 4 | 0 | 0 | 0 | 1 | 2 | 11 | 1 |
| O.Cabrera, ss | 5 | 0 | 0 | 0 | 0 | 1 | 1 | 2 |
| Mueller, 3b | 5 | 2 | 2 | 0 | 0 | 0 | 2 | 1 |
| Arroyo, p | 0 | 0 | 0 | 0 | 0 | 0 | 0 | 1 |
| M.Myers, p | 0 | 0 | 0 | 0 | 0 | 0 | 0 | 0 |
| Timlin, p | 0 | 0 | 0 | 0 | 0 | 0 | 0 | 0 |
| Embree, p | 0 | 0 | 0 | 0 | 0 | 0 | 0 | 0 |
| Foulke, p | 0 | 0 | 0 | 0 | 0 | 0 | 0 | 0 |
| Lowe, p | 0 | 0 | 0 | 0 | 0 | 0 | 0 | 0 |
| **TOTALS** | 41 | 8 | 12 | 8 | 7 | 13 | 30 | 8 |

| | | | | | | |
|---|---|---|---|---|---|---|
| Anaheim | 0 0 0 | 1 0 0 | 5 0 0 | 0—6 | 8 | 2 |
| Boston | 0 0 2 | 0 2 0 | 0 0 0 | 2—8 | 12 | 0 |

| Anaheim | IP | H | R | ER | HR | BB | SO |
|---|---|---|---|---|---|---|---|
| K.Escobar | 3.1 | 5 | 5 | 3 | 0 | 5 | 4 |
| Shields | 1.1 | 4 | 1 | 1 | 0 | 1 | 1 |
| Donnelly | 2.1 | 0 | 0 | 0 | 0 | 0 | 5 |
| F.Rodriguez (L) | 2.2 | 2 | 1 | 1 | 0 | 1 | 3 |
| Washburn | 0.0 | 1 | 1 | 1 | 1 | 0 | 0 |
| **Boston** | **IP** | **H** | **R** | **ER** | **HR** | **BB** | **SO** |
| Arroyo | 6.0 | 3 | 2 | 2 | 1 | 2 | 7 |
| M.Myers | 0.0 | 0 | 1 | 1 | 0 | 1 | 0 |
| Timlin | 0.2 | 2 | 3 | 3 | 1 | 1 | 1 |
| Embree | 0.2 | 0 | 0 | 0 | 0 | 1 | 0 |
| Foulke | 1.2 | 2 | 0 | 0 | 0 | 1 | 3 |
| Lowe (W) | 1.0 | 1 | 0 | 0 | 0 | 1 | 0 |

Washburn pitched to 1 batter in the 10th. Arroyo pitched to 1 batter in the 7th. M.Myers pitched to 1 batter in the 7th.

E—Figgins, Eckstein. DP—Anaheim 1. LOB—Anaheim 10, Boston 12. Scoring Position—Anaheim 3 for 9, Boston 4 for 14. 2B—Erstad, D.Ortiz 2. HR—Glaus (4th inning, 2 out, 0 on) off Arroyo, V.Guerrero (7th inning, 2 out, 3 on) off Timlin, D.Ortiz (10th inning, 2 out, 1 on) off Washburn. SB—Damon. S—M.Ramirez. SH—Amezaga. HBP—Figgins by Arroyo. T—4:11. A—35,547. U—HP-Runge, 1B-Cederstrom, 2B-Montague, 3B-Danley, LF-Young, RF-Meals.

## HOW THEY SCORED

BOTTOM OF 3

Red Sox third. Bellhorn walked on a full count. Ramirez flied out to center fielder Anderson. Ortiz doubled to left, Bellhorn to third. Nixon singled to right, Bellhorn scored, Ortiz to third. Millar grounded out, second baseman Figgins to first baseman Erstad, Ortiz scored, Nixon to second. Varitek was intentionally walked. Cabrera popped out to second baseman Figgins. Runs: 2, Hits: 2, Errors: 0

TOP OF 4

Angels fourth. Guerrero popped out to third baseman Mueller. Anderson popped out to third baseman Mueller. Glaus homered to left on a 0-1 count. DaVanon grounded out, first baseman Millar unassisted. Runs: 1, Hits: 1, Errors: 0

BOTTOM OF 4

Red Sox fourth. Mueller safe on Figgins' error. Damon singled to center, Mueller to second. Bellhorn walked, Mueller to third, Damon to second. Ramirez hit a sacrifice fly to left fielder DaVanon, Mueller scored. Shields pitching. Ortiz doubled to right, Damon scored, Bellhorn to third. Nixon was intentionally walked. Millar safe on fielder's choice and Eckstein's error, Bellhorn scored, Ortiz to third, Nixon to second. Varitek grounded into a double play, shortstop Eckstein to second baseman Figgins to first baseman Erstad, Millar out. Runs: 3, Hits: 2, Errors: 2

BOTTOM OF 5

Red Sox fifth. Cabrera grounded out, first baseman Erstad unassisted. Mueller singled to right. Damon singled to right, Mueller to second. Bellhorn struck out. Ramirez singled to right, Mueller scored, Damon to third. Donnelly pitching. Ortiz struck out. Runs: 1, Hits: 3, Errors: 0

TOP OF 7

Angels seventh. Mientkiewicz in as first baseman. DaVanon walked. Kotchman pinch-hitting for B.Molina. Myers pitching. J.Molina pinch-hitting for Kotchman. J.Molina walked, DaVanon to second. Riggs pinch-hitting for McPherson. Timlin pitching. Pride pinch-hitting for Riggs. Pride popped out to shortstop Cabrera. Eckstein singled to right, DaVanon to third, J.Molina to second. Figgins struck out. Erstad walked on a full count, DaVanon scored, J.Molina to third, Eckstein to second. Guerrero homered to right on a 0-1 count, J.Molina scored, Eckstein scored, Erstad scored. Embree pitching. Anderson grounded out, second baseman Bellhorn to first baseman Mientkiewicz. Runs: 5, Hits: 2, Errors: 0

BOTTOM OF 10

Red Sox tenth. Damon singled to center. Bellhorn grounded into fielder's choice, third baseman Figgins to shortstop Eckstein, Damon out. Reese pinch-running for Bellhorn. Ramirez struck out. Washburn pitching. Ortiz homered to left on the first pitch, Reese scored. Runs: 2, Hits: 2, Errors: 0



## STATISTICS

### BOSTON RED SOX' BATTING AND FIELDING AVERAGES

| | | BATTING | | | | | | | | | | | | | | FIELDING | | | |
|---|---|---|---|---|---|---|---|---|---|---|---|---|---|---|---|---|---|---|---|
| Player, position | G | AB | R | H | TB | 2B | 3B | HR | RBI | BB | IBB | SO | Avg. | OBP | Slg. | PO | A | E | Avg. |
| Ortiz,dh | 3 | 11 | 4 | 6 | 11 | 2 | 0 | 1 | 4 | 5 | 3 | 2 | .545 | .688 | 1.000 | 0 | 0 | 0 | .000 |
| Mientkiewicz,1b-pr | 3 | 4 | 0 | 2 | 2 | 0 | 0 | 0 | 1 | 0 | 0 | 0 | .500 | .500 | .500 | 7 | 0 | 0 | 1.000 |
| Damon,cf | 3 | 15 | 4 | 7 | 8 | 1 | 0 | 0 | 0 | 1 | 0 | 2 | .467 | .500 | .533 | 7 | 0 | 0 | 1.000 |
| Ramirez,lf | 3 | 13 | 3 | 5 | 10 | 2 | 0 | 1 | 7 | 1 | 0 | 4 | .385 | .375 | .769 | 8 | 0 | 0 | 1.000 |
| Mueller,3b | 3 | 12 | 3 | 4 | 4 | 0 | 0 | 0 | 0 | 1 | 0 | 1 | .333 | .385 | .333 | 5 | 2 | 0 | 1.000 |
| Millar,1b | 3 | 10 | 2 | 3 | 6 | 0 | 0 | 1 | 4 | 1 | 0 | 1 | .300 | .364 | .600 | 14 | 4 | 0 | 1.000 |
| Nixon,rf | 2 | 8 | 0 | 2 | 2 | 0 | 0 | 0 | 2 | 2 | 1 | 1 | .250 | .400 | .250 | 1 | 0 | 0 | 1.000 |
| Kapler,rf-pr | 2 | 5 | 2 | 1 | 1 | 0 | 0 | 0 | 0 | 0 | 0 | 0 | .200 | .200 | .200 | 5 | 0 | 0 | 1.000 |
| Varitek,c | 3 | 12 | 3 | 2 | 5 | 0 | 0 | 1 | 2 | 2 | 2 | 5 | .167 | .333 | .417 | 29 | 2 | 0 | 1.000 |
| Cabrera,ss | 3 | 13 | 1 | 2 | 3 | 1 | 0 | 0 | 3 | 2 | 0 | 2 | .154 | .267 | .231 | 3 | 5 | 0 | 1.000 |
| Bellhorn,2b | 3 | 11 | 2 | 1 | 1 | 0 | 0 | 0 | 0 | 5 | 0 | 4 | .091 | .375 | .091 | 1 | 8 | 0 | 1.000 |
| Arroyo,p | 1 | 0 | 0 | 0 | 0 | 0 | 0 | 0 | 0 | 0 | 0 | 0 | .000 | .000 | .000 | 0 | 1 | 0 | 1.000 |
| Embree,p | 2 | 0 | 0 | 0 | 0 | 0 | 0 | 0 | 0 | 0 | 0 | 0 | .000 | .000 | .000 | 0 | 0 | 0 | .000 |
| Foulke,p | 2 | 0 | 0 | 0 | 0 | 0 | 0 | 0 | 0 | 0 | 0 | 0 | .000 | .000 | .000 | 0 | 1 | 0 | 1.000 |
| Lowe,p | 1 | 0 | 0 | 0 | 0 | 0 | 0 | 0 | 0 | 0 | 0 | 0 | .000 | .000 | .000 | 0 | 0 | 0 | .000 |
| Martinez,p | 1 | 0 | 0 | 0 | 0 | 0 | 0 | 0 | 0 | 0 | 0 | 0 | .000 | .000 | .000 | 2 | 1 | 0 | 1.000 |
| Myers,p | 2 | 0 | 0 | 0 | 0 | 0 | 0 | 0 | 0 | 0 | 0 | 0 | .000 | .000 | .000 | 0 | 0 | 0 | .000 |
| Reese,2b-pr | 3 | 0 | 1 | 0 | 0 | 0 | 0 | 0 | 0 | 0 | 0 | 0 | .000 | .000 | .000 | 0 | 1 | 0 | 1.000 |
| Roberts,pr | 1 | 0 | 0 | 0 | 0 | 0 | 0 | 0 | 0 | 0 | 0 | 0 | .000 | .000 | .000 | 0 | 0 | 0 | .000 |
| Schilling,p | 1 | 0 | 0 | 0 | 0 | 0 | 0 | 0 | 0 | 0 | 0 | 0 | .000 | .000 | .000 | 2 | 0 | 1 | .667 |
| Timlin,p | 3 | 0 | 0 | 0 | 0 | 0 | 0 | 0 | 0 | 0 | 0 | 0 | .000 | .000 | .000 | 0 | 0 | 0 | .000 |
| Youkilis,3b | 1 | 2 | 0 | 0 | 0 | 0 | 0 | 0 | 0 | 0 | 0 | 1 | .000 | .000 | .000 | 0 | 0 | 0 | .000 |
| Totals | 3 | 116 | 25 | 35 | 53 | 6 | 0 | 4 | 23 | 20 | 6 | 23 | .302 | .403 | .457 | 84 | 25 | 1 | .991 |

## ANAHEIM ANGELS' BATTING AND FIELDING AVERAGES

| | BATTING | | | | | | | | | | | | | | | FIELDING | | | |
|---|---|---|---|---|---|---|---|---|---|---|---|---|---|---|---|---|---|---|---|
| Player, position | G | AB | R | H | TB | 2B | 3B | HR | RBI | BB | IBB | SO | Avg. | OBP | Slg. | PO | A | E | Avg. |
| Erstad,1b | 3 | 10 | 2 | 5 | 9 | 1 | 0 | 1 | 2 | 3 | 0 | 1 | .500 | .643 | .900 | 27 | 0 | 0 | 1.000 |
| Glaus,dh | 3 | 11 | 3 | 4 | 12 | 2 | 0 | 2 | 3 | 2 | 0 | 4 | .364 | .462 | 1.091 | 0 | 0 | 0 | .000 |
| Eckstein,ss | 3 | 12 | 2 | 4 | 4 | 0 | 0 | 0 | 0 | 0 | 0 | 1 | .333 | .333 | .333 | 6 | 5 | 1 | .917 |
| Molina,c-ph | 2 | 3 | 2 | 1 | 1 | 0 | 0 | 0 | 0 | 2 | 0 | 0 | .333 | .600 | .333 | 8 | 1 | 0 | 1.000 |
| DaVanon,lf | 3 | 10 | 1 | 2 | 2 | 0 | 0 | 0 | 0 | 2 | 0 | 1 | .200 | .333 | .200 | 6 | 0 | 0 | 1.000 |
| Guerrero,rf | 3 | 12 | 1 | 2 | 5 | 0 | 0 | 1 | 6 | 2 | 1 | 4 | .167 | .286 | .417 | 6 | 0 | 0 | 1.000 |
| Molina,c | 3 | 6 | 0 | 1 | 1 | 0 | 0 | 0 | 0 | 0 | 0 | 2 | .167 | .167 | .167 | 15 | 1 | 0 | 1.000 |
| Anderson,cf | 3 | 13 | 1 | 2 | 2 | 0 | 0 | 0 | 0 | 0 | 0 | 3 | .154 | .154 | .154 | 8 | 0 | 0 | 1.000 |
| Figgins,2b-3b | 3 | 14 | 0 | 2 | 2 | 0 | 0 | 0 | 0 | 0 | 0 | 5 | .143 | .200 | .143 | 4 | 10 | 2 | .875 |
| McPherson,3b-ph | 3 | 9 | 0 | 1 | 1 | 0 | 0 | 0 | 1 | 0 | 0 | 4 | .111 | .111 | .111 | 3 | 4 | 0 | 1.000 |
| Colon,p | 1 | 0 | 0 | 0 | 0 | 0 | 0 | 0 | 0 | 0 | 0 | 0 | .000 | .000 | .000 | 0 | 0 | 0 | .000 |
| Donnelly,p | 2 | 0 | 0 | 0 | 0 | 0 | 0 | 0 | 0 | 0 | 0 | 0 | .000 | .000 | .000 | 0 | 0 | 0 | .000 |
| Escobar,p | 1 | 0 | 0 | 0 | 0 | 0 | 0 | 0 | 0 | 0 | 0 | 0 | .000 | .000 | .000 | 0 | 0 | 0 | .000 |
| Gregg,p | 1 | 0 | 0 | 0 | 0 | 0 | 0 | 0 | 0 | 0 | 0 | 0 | .000 | .000 | .000 | 0 | 0 | 0 | .000 |
| Ortiz,p | 1 | 0 | 0 | 0 | 0 | 0 | 0 | 0 | 0 | 0 | 0 | 0 | .000 | .000 | .000 | 0 | 1 | 0 | 1.000 |
| Rodriguez,p | 2 | 0 | 0 | 0 | 0 | 0 | 0 | 0 | 0 | 0 | 0 | 0 | .000 | .000 | .000 | 0 | 0 | 0 | .000 |
| Shields,p | 2 | 0 | 0 | 0 | 0 | 0 | 0 | 0 | 0 | 0 | 0 | 0 | .000 | .000 | .000 | 0 | 0 | 0 | .000 |
| Washburn,p | 2 | 0 | 0 | 0 | 0 | 0 | 0 | 0 | 0 | 0 | 0 | 0 | .000 | .000 | .000 | 0 | 1 | 0 | 1.000 |
| Kotchman,ph | 2 | 1 | 0 | 0 | 0 | 0 | 0 | 0 | 0 | 0 | 0 | 0 | .000 | .000 | .000 | 0 | 0 | 0 | .000 |
| Riggs,lf-ph | 2 | 1 | 0 | 0 | 0 | 0 | 0 | 0 | 0 | 0 | 0 | 0 | .000 | .000 | .000 | 0 | 0 | 0 | .000 |
| Amezaga,2b | 2 | 2 | 0 | 0 | 0 | 0 | 0 | 0 | 0 | 0 | 0 | 2 | .000 | .000 | .000 | 0 | 2 | 0 | 1.000 |
| Pride,ph | 2 | 2 | 0 | 0 | 0 | 0 | 0 | 0 | 0 | 0 | 0 | 1 | .000 | .000 | .000 | 0 | 0 | 0 | .000 |
| Totals | 3 | 106 | 12 | 24 | 39 | 3 | 0 | 4 | 12 | 11 | 1 | 28 | .226 | .311 | .368 | 83 | 25 | 3 | .973 |

## BOSTON RED SOX' PITCHING RECORDS

| Pitcher | G | GS | CG | IP | H | R | ER | HR | BB | IBB | SO | HB | WP | W | L | Pct. | ERA |
|---|---|---|---|---|---|---|---|---|---|---|---|---|---|---|---|---|---|
| Foulke | 2 | 0 | 0 | 3.0 | 2 | 0 | 0 | 0 | 1 | 1 | 5 | 0 | 0 | 0 | 0 | .000 | 0.00 |
| Embree | 2 | 0 | 0 | 1.0 | 0 | 0 | 0 | 0 | 1 | 0 | 0 | 0 | 0 | 0 | 0 | .000 | 0.00 |
| Lowe | 1 | 0 | 0 | 1.0 | 1 | 0 | 0 | 0 | 1 | 0 | 0 | 0 | 0 | 1 | 0 | 1.000 | 0.00 |
| Schilling | 1 | 1 | 0 | 6.2 | 9 | 3 | 2 | 2 | 2 | 0 | 4 | 0 | 0 | 1 | 0 | 1.000 | 2.70 |
| Arroyo | 1 | 1 | 0 | 6.0 | 3 | 2 | 2 | 1 | 2 | 0 | 7 | 1 | 0 | 0 | 0 | .000 | 3.00 |
| Martinez | 1 | 1 | 0 | 7.0 | 6 | 3 | 3 | 0 | 2 | 0 | 6 | 1 | 0 | 1 | 0 | 1.000 | 3.86 |
| Timlin | 3 | 0 | 0 | 3.0 | 3 | 3 | 3 | 1 | 1 | 0 | 5 | 0 | 0 | 0 | 0 | .000 | 9.00 |
| Myers | 2 | 0 | 0 | 0.1 | 0 | 1 | 1 | 0 | 1 | 0 | 1 | 0 | 0 | 0 | 0 | .000 | 27.00 |
| Totals | 3 | 3 | 0 | 28.0 | 24 | 12 | 11 | 4 | 11 | 1 | 28 | 2 | 0 | 3 | 0 | 1.000 | 3.54 |

No shutouts. Saves- Foulke.

## ANAHEIM ANGELS' PITCHING RECORDS

| Pitcher | G | GS | CG | IP | H | R | ER | HR | BB | IBB | SO | HB | WP | W | L | Pct. | ERA |
|---|---|---|---|---|---|---|---|---|---|---|---|---|---|---|---|---|---|
| Gregg | 1 | 0 | 0 | 2.0 | 3 | 0 | 0 | 0 | 1 | 0 | 0 | 0 | 1 | 0 | 0 | .000 | 0.00 |
| Rodriguez | 2 | 0 | 0 | 4.2 | 4 | 2 | 2 | 0 | 3 | 1 | 5 | 1 | 2 | 0 | 2 | .000 | 3.86 |
| Colon | 1 | 1 | 0 | 6.0 | 7 | 3 | 3 | 1 | 3 | 0 | 3 | 0 | 0 | 0 | 0 | .000 | 4.50 |
| Ortiz | 1 | 0 | 0 | 2.0 | 2 | 1 | 1 | 0 | 1 | 1 | 0 | 0 | 0 | 0 | 0 | .000 | 4.50 |
| Shields | 2 | 0 | 0 | 3.0 | 5 | 2 | 2 | 1 | 2 | 1 | 3 | 0 | 0 | 0 | 0 | .000 | 6.00 |
| Escobar | 1 | 1 | 0 | 3.1 | 5 | 5 | 3 | 0 | 5 | 1 | 4 | 0 | 0 | 0 | 0 | .000 | 8.10 |
| Donnelly | 2 | 0 | 0 | 3.1 | 3 | 4 | 4 | 0 | 2 | 2 | 5 | 0 | 1 | 0 | 0 | .000 | 10.80 |
| Washburn | 2 | 1 | 0 | 3.1 | 6 | 8 | 4 | 2 | 3 | 0 | 3 | 0 | 0 | 0 | 1 | .000 | 10.80 |
| Totals | 3 | 3 | 0 | 27.2 | 35 | 25 | 18 | 4 | 20 | 6 | 23 | 1 | 4 | 0 | 3 | .000 | 5.86 |

No shutouts or saves.

## SCORE BY INNINGS

| | | | | | | | | | | |
|---|---|---|---|---|---|---|---|---|---|---|
| Boston | 1 | 1 | 2 | 10 | 1 | 2 | 1 | 1 | 4 | 2—25 |
| Anaheim | 0 | 1 | 0 | 2 | 2 | 0 | 7 | 0 | 0 | 0—12 |

## MISCELLANEOUS STATISTICS

Sacrifice hits—Amezaga.
Sacrifice flies—Ramirez 2.
Stolen bases—Damon 3, Figgins.
Caught stealing—DaVanon.
Double plays—Eckstein, Figgins and Erstad; Figgins, Eckstein and Erstad; Millar (unassisted).
Left on bases—Boston 9, 10, 12—31; Anaheim 9, 5, 10—24.
Scoring position—Boston 4 for 13, 2 for 11, 4 for 14—10 for 38; Anaheim 2 for 9, 2 for 7, 3 for 9—7 for 25.
Hit by pitcher—by Martinez (Erstad), by Arroyo (Figgins), by Rodriguez (Varitek).
Passed balls—None.
Balks—None.
Time of games—3:04, 3:48, 4:11—Avg.: 3:41.
Attendance—44,608, 45,118, 35,547—125,273.
Umpires—Young, Larry; Meals, Jerry; Runge, Brian; Cederstrom, Gary; Montague, Ed; Danley, Kerwin.

# MINNESOTA VS. NEW YORK

## RESULTS

| Day | Date | Place | Score |
|---|---|---|---|
| Tue. | Oct. 5 | New York | Minnesota 2, New York 0 |
| Wed. | Oct. 6 | New York | New York 7, Minnesota 6 |
| Fri. | Oct. 8 | Minnesota | New York 8, Minnesota 4 |
| Sat. | Oct. 9 | Minnesota | New York 6, Minnesota 5 |

## BOX SCORES

### GAME 1

**MINNESOTA 2, NEW YORK 0**

TUESDAY, OCTOBER 5, AT NEW YORK

| Minnesota | AB | R | H | BI | BB | SO | PO | A |
|---|---|---|---|---|---|---|---|---|
| Sh.Stewart, lf | 4 | 0 | 2 | 1 | 0 | 1 | 3 | 0 |
| J.Jones, rf | 4 | 1 | 1 | 1 | 0 | 1 | 2 | 0 |
| Hunter, cf | 4 | 0 | 1 | 0 | 0 | 0 | 4 | 1 |
| Morneau, 1b | 4 | 0 | 0 | 0 | 0 | 1 | 6 | 0 |
| Koskie, 3b | 3 | 0 | 1 | 0 | 1 | 0 | 2 | 0 |
| L.Ford, dh | 4 | 0 | 0 | 0 | 0 | 2 | 0 | 0 |
| C.Guzman, ss | 3 | 0 | 0 | 0 | 0 | 1 | 0 | 6 |
| Cuddyer, 2b | 3 | 1 | 2 | 0 | 0 | 1 | 3 | 3 |
| Rivas, 2b | 0 | 0 | 0 | 0 | 0 | 0 | 1 | 1 |
| H.Blanco, c | 2 | 0 | 0 | 0 | 0 | 1 | 6 | 1 |
| Santana, p | 0 | 0 | 0 | 0 | 0 | 0 | 0 | 0 |
| J.Rincon, p | 0 | 0 | 0 | 0 | 0 | 0 | 0 | 0 |
| Nathan, p | 0 | 0 | 0 | 0 | 0 | 0 | 0 | 0 |
| TOTALS | 31 | 2 | 7 | 2 | 1 | 8 | 27 | 12 |

| NY Yankees | AB | R | H | BI | BB | SO | PO | A |
|---|---|---|---|---|---|---|---|---|
| Jeter, ss | 4 | 0 | 1 | 0 | 0 | 0 | 1 | 1 |
| A.Rodriguez, 3b | 4 | 0 | 2 | 0 | 0 | 1 | 0 | 3 |
| Sheffield, rf | 2 | 0 | 0 | 0 | 2 | 0 | 1 | 0 |
| B.Williams, cf | 4 | 0 | 1 | 0 | 0 | 1 | 2 | 0 |
| Posada, c | 4 | 0 | 2 | 0 | 0 | 0 | 8 | 1 |
| H.Matsui, lf | 4 | 0 | 2 | 0 | 0 | 0 | 2 | 0 |
| Sierra, dh | 4 | 0 | 0 | 0 | 0 | 1 | 0 | 0 |
| Olerud, 1b | 2 | 0 | 0 | 0 | 0 | 0 | 8 | 2 |
| Cairo, 2b | 3 | 0 | 1 | 0 | 0 | 2 | 3 | 3 |
| Mussina, p | 0 | 0 | 0 | 0 | 0 | 0 | 1 | 1 |
| Gordon, p | 0 | 0 | 0 | 0 | 0 | 0 | 0 | 0 |
| M.Rivera, p | 0 | 0 | 0 | 0 | 0 | 0 | 1 | 1 |
| TOTALS | 31 | 0 | 9 | 0 | 2 | 5 | 27 | 12 |

Minnesota.................0 0 1 0 0 1 0 0 0—2 7 0
NY Yankees................0 0 0 0 0 0 0 0 0—0 9 0

| Minnesota | IP | H | R | ER | HR | BB | SO |
|---|---|---|---|---|---|---|---|
| Santana (W) | 7.0 | 9 | 0 | 0 | 0 | 1 | 5 |
| J.Rincon (HOLD) | 1.0 | 0 | 0 | 0 | 0 | 1 | 0 |
| Nathan (S) | 1.0 | 0 | 0 | 0 | 0 | 0 | 0 |

| NY Yankees | IP | H | R | ER | HR | BB | SO |
|---|---|---|---|---|---|---|---|
| Mussina (L) | 7.0 | 7 | 2 | 2 | 1 | 1 | 7 |
| Gordon | 1.0 | 0 | 0 | 0 | 0 | 0 | 0 |
| M.Rivera | 1.0 | 0 | 0 | 0 | 0 | 0 | 1 |

DP—Minnesota 5, NY Yankees 1. LOB—Minnesota 4, NY Yankees 7. Scoring Position—Minnesota 1 for 3, NY Yankees 0 for 6. 2B—H.Matsui, Cairo. HR—J.Jones (6th inning, 1 out, 0 on) off Mussina. SB—Hunter. CS—Cuddyer, A.Rodriguez. SH—H.Blanco. HBP—Olerud by Santana. T—2:53. A—55,749. U—HP-Reliford, 1B-Wegner, 2B-Gorman, 3B-Everitt, LF-Crawford, RF-Nauert.

### HOW THEY SCORED

TOP OF 3

Twins third. Cuddyer singled to center. Blanco sacrificed, pitcher Mussina to second baseman Cairo, Cuddyer to second. Stewart singled to left, Cuddyer scored. Jones grounded into a double play, second baseman Cairo to shortstop Jeter to first baseman Olerud, Stewart out. Runs: 1, Hits: 2, Errors: 0

TOP OF 6

Twins sixth. Stewart struck out. Jones homered to left on a 0-1 count. Hunter singled to left. Morneau struck out. Hunter stole second. Koskie walked. Ford grounded out, third baseman Rodriguez to first baseman Olerud. Runs: 1, Hits: 2, Errors: 0

### GAME 2

**NEW YORK 7, MINNESOTA 6**

WEDNESDAY, OCTOBER 6, AT NEW YORK

| Minnesota | AB | R | H | BI | BB | SO | PO | A |
|---|---|---|---|---|---|---|---|---|
| Sh.Stewart, lf | 6 | 0 | 0 | 0 | 0 | 1 | 2 | 0 |
| J.Jones, rf | 6 | 1 | 1 | 0 | 0 | 3 | 3 | 0 |
| Hunter, cf | 6 | 3 | 3 | 1 | 0 | 1 | 2 | 0 |
| Morneau, 1b | 4 | 0 | 2 | 2 | 0 | 0 | 10 | 1 |
| Rivas, pr-2b | 0 | 0 | 0 | 0 | 0 | 0 | 0 | 1 |
| LeCroy, ph-1b | 1 | 0 | 1 | 0 | 1 | 0 | 2 | 0 |
| Koskie, 3b | 4 | 1 | 1 | 1 | 2 | 2 | 2 | 3 |
| Kubel, dh | 6 | 0 | 0 | 0 | 0 | 2 | 0 | 0 |
| C.Guzman, ss | 4 | 1 | 2 | 0 | 1 | 0 | 1 | 5 |
| Cuddyer, 2b-1b-2b | 5 | 0 | 2 | 1 | 0 | 0 | 6 | 3 |
| H.Blanco, c | 1 | 0 | 0 | 1 | 0 | 0 | 0 | 0 |
| Offerman, ph | 1 | 0 | 0 | 0 | 0 | 0 | 0 | 0 |
| Borders, c | 2 | 0 | 0 | 0 | 0 | 1 | 7 | 0 |
| Radke, p | 0 | 0 | 0 | 0 | 0 | 0 | 0 | 1 |
| Balfour, p | 0 | 0 | 0 | 0 | 0 | 0 | 0 | 1 |
| J.Rincon, p | 0 | 0 | 0 | 0 | 0 | 0 | 0 | 0 |
| Nathan, p | 0 | 0 | 0 | 0 | 0 | 0 | 0 | 1 |
| Romero, p | 0 | 0 | 0 | 0 | 0 | 0 | 0 | 0 |
| TOTALS | 46 | 6 | 12 | 6 | 4 | 10 | 35 | 16 |

| NY Yankees | AB | R | H | BI | BB | SO | PO | A |
|---|---|---|---|---|---|---|---|---|
| Jeter, ss | 4 | 2 | 1 | 1 | 1 | 0 | 6 | 3 |
| A.Rodriguez, 3b | 6 | 2 | 4 | 3 | 0 | 0 | 2 | 2 |
| Sheffield, rf | 5 | 1 | 1 | 2 | 1 | 0 | 4 | 1 |
| H.Matsui, lf | 4 | 0 | 1 | 1 | 1 | 1 | 0 | 0 |
| B.Williams, cf | 4 | 0 | 1 | 0 | 1 | 0 | 0 | 0 |
| Posada, c | 5 | 0 | 0 | 0 | 0 | 2 | 9 | 1 |
| Sierra, dh | 4 | 0 | 0 | 0 | 1 | 2 | 0 | 0 |
| Olerud, 1b | 5 | 0 | 1 | 0 | 0 | 1 | 9 | 2 |
| Cairo, 2b | 3 | 2 | 0 | 0 | 2 | 1 | 4 | 5 |
| Lieber, p | 0 | 0 | 0 | 0 | 0 | 0 | 2 | 0 |
| Gordon, p | 0 | 0 | 0 | 0 | 0 | 0 | 0 | 0 |
| M.Rivera, p | 0 | 0 | 0 | 0 | 0 | 0 | 0 | 1 |
| Sturtze, p | 0 | 0 | 0 | 0 | 0 | 0 | 0 | 1 |
| Quantrill, p | 0 | 0 | 0 | 0 | 0 | 0 | 0 | 0 |
| TOTALS | 40 | 7 | 9 | 7 | 7 | 7 | 36 | 16 |

Minnesota..................1 2 0 0 0 0 0 2 0 0 0 1—6 12 0
NY Yankees.................1 0 2 0 1 0 1 0 0 0 0 2—7 9 0

| Minnesota | IP | H | R | ER | HR | BB | SO |
|---|---|---|---|---|---|---|---|
| Radke | 6.1 | 8 | 5 | 5 | 3 | 3 | 0 |
| Balfour | 0.2 | 0 | 0 | 0 | 0 | 0 | 0 |
| J.Rincon | 2.0 | 0 | 0 | 0 | 0 | 0 | 4 |
| Nathan (L) | 2.1 | 1 | 2 | 2 | 0 | 4 | 3 |
| Romero | 0.1 | 0 | 0 | 0 | 0 | 0 | 0 |

| NY Yankees | IP | H | R | ER | HR | BB | SO |
|---|---|---|---|---|---|---|---|
| Lieber | 6.2 | 7 | 3 | 3 | 0 | 1 | 4 |
| Gordon (HOLD) | 0.2 | 1 | 2 | 2 | 0 | 0 | 1 |
| M.Rivera (BS) | 1.2 | 2 | 0 | 0 | 0 | 0 | 1 |
| Sturtze | 2.2 | 2 | 1 | 1 | 1 | 3 | 4 |
| Quantrill (W) | 0.1 | 0 | 0 | 0 | 0 | 0 | 0 |

DP—Minnesota 2, NY Yankees 1. LOB—Minnesota 9, NY Yankees 7. Scoring Position—Minnesota 3 for 10, NY Yankees 2 for 5. 2B—Morneau, Koskie, A.Rodriguez, B.Williams, Olerud. HR—Jeter (1st inning, 0 out, 0 on) off Radke, Sheffield (3rd inning, 1 out, 1 on) off Radke, A.Rodriguez (5th inning, 1 out, 0 on) off Radke, Hunter (12th inning, 2 out, 0 on) off Sturtze. SB—Hunter, Sierra. S—H.Blanco, H.Matsui. SH—Jeter. WP—Gordon. PB—Posada. T—4:19. A—56,354. U—HP-Wegner, 1B-Gorman, 2B-Everitt, 3B-Crawford, LF-Nauert, RF-Reliford.

## HOW THEY SCORED

TOP OF 1

Twins first. Stewart flied out to right fielder Sheffield. Jones singled to right. Hunter grounded into fielder's choice, third baseman Rodriguez to second baseman Cairo, Jones out. Morneau doubled to right, Hunter scored. Morneau was out advancing, right fielder Sheffield to second baseman Cairo to catcher Posada to third baseman Rodriguez, Morneau out. Runs: 1, Hits: 2, Errors: 0

BOTTOM OF 1

Yankees first. Jeter homered to center on a 1-1 count. Rodriguez lined out to second baseman Cuddyer. Sheffield grounded out, third baseman Koskie to first baseman Morneau. Matsui walked on four pitches. Williams doubled to right, Matsui to third. Posada popped out to second baseman Cuddyer. Runs: 1, Hits: 2, Errors: 0

TOP OF 2

Twins second. Koskie walked. Kubel struck out. Guzman singled to right, Koskie to second. Cuddyer singled to center, Koskie scored, Guzman to third. Blanco hit a sacrifice fly to right fielder Sheffield, Guzman scored. Stewart grounded into fielder's choice, shortstop Jeter to second baseman Cairo, Cuddyer out. Runs: 2, Hits: 2, Errors: 0

BOTTOM OF 3

Yankees third. Jeter flied out to left fielder Stewart. Rodriguez singled to left. Sheffield homered to left on a 2-1 count, Rodriguez scored. Matsui singled to right. Williams grounded into a double play, first baseman Morneau to shortstop Guzman to first baseman Morneau, Matsui out. Runs: 2, Hits: 3, Errors: 0

BOTTOM OF 5

Yankees fifth. Jeter grounded out, third baseman Koskie to first baseman Morneau. Rodriguez homered to center on the first pitch. Sheffield popped out to third baseman Koskie. Matsui flied out to center fielder Hunter. Runs: 1, Hits: 1, Errors: 0

BOTTOM OF 7

Yankees seventh. Borders in as catcher. Cairo walked on a full count. Jeter sacrificed, third baseman Koskie to second baseman Cuddyer, Cairo to second. Rodriguez singled to left, Cairo scored. Balfour pitching. Sheffield grounded into a double play, pitcher Balfour to second baseman Cuddyer to first baseman Morneau, Rodriguez out. Runs: 1, Hits: 1, Errors: 0

TOP OF 8

Twins eighth. Stewart flied out to right fielder Sheffield. Jones struck out, safe on Gordon wild pitch. Hunter singled to center, Jones to second. Rivera pitching. Morneau singled to center, Jones scored, Hunter to third. Rivas pinch-running for Morneau. Koskie doubled to left, Hunter scored, Rivas to third. Kubel struck out. Guzman lined out to first baseman Olerud. Runs: 2, Hits: 3, Errors: 0

TOP OF 12

Twins twelfth. Stewart struck out. Jones popped out to second baseman Cairo. Hunter homered to left on a 1-0 count. LeCroy singled to left. Koskie walked, LeCroy to second. Quantrill pitching. Kubel grounded into fielder's choice, second baseman Cairo to shortstop Jeter, Koskie out. Runs: 1, Hits: 2, Errors: 0

BOTTOM OF 12

Yankees twelfth. Olerud struck out. Cairo walked. Jeter walked on four pitches, Cairo to second. Rodriguez doubled to center, Cairo scored, Jeter to third. Sheffield was intentionally walked. Romero pitching. Matsui hit a sacrifice fly to right fielder Jones, Jeter scored. Runs: 2, Hits: 1, Errors: 0

## GAME 3

### NEW YORK 8, MINNESOTA 4

FRIDAY, OCTOBER 8, AT MINNESOTA

| NY Yankees | AB | R | H | BI | BB | SO | PO | A |
|---|---|---|---|---|---|---|---|---|
| Jeter, ss | 5 | 0 | 3 | 3 | 0 | 0 | 1 | 5 |
| A.Rodriguez, 3b | 5 | 0 | 0 | 0 | 0 | 0 | 2 | 4 |
| Sheffield, rf | 5 | 0 | 2 | 0 | 0 | 0 | 0 | 0 |
| Bu.Crosby, rf | 0 | 0 | 0 | 0 | 0 | 0 | 0 | 0 |
| H.Matsui, lf | 5 | 2 | 3 | 1 | 0 | 0 | 3 | 1 |
| B.Williams, cf | 5 | 1 | 1 | 2 | 0 | 0 | 3 | 1 |
| Posada, c | 4 | 2 | 2 | 0 | 0 | 1 | 2 | 0 |
| Olerud, 1b | 3 | 2 | 1 | 0 | 1 | 0 | 13 | 1 |
| Cairo, 2b | 3 | 1 | 1 | 1 | 0 | 0 | 2 | 3 |
| Lofton, dh | 4 | 0 | 1 | 1 | 0 | 1 | 0 | 0 |
| K.Brown, p | 0 | 0 | 0 | 0 | 0 | 0 | 0 | 0 |
| Quantrill, p | 0 | 0 | 0 | 0 | 0 | 0 | 0 | 1 |
| Heredia, p | 0 | 0 | 0 | 0 | 0 | 0 | 0 | 0 |
| Sturtze, p | 0 | 0 | 0 | 0 | 0 | 0 | 0 | 0 |
| M.Rivera, p | 0 | 0 | 0 | 0 | 0 | 0 | 1 | 0 |
| **TOTALS** | 39 | 8 | 14 | 8 | 1 | 2 | 27 | 16 |

| Minnesota | AB | R | H | BI | BB | SO | PO | A |
|---|---|---|---|---|---|---|---|---|
| Sh.Stewart, lf | 4 | 0 | 1 | 1 | 0 | 0 | 1 | 0 |
| J.Jones, rf | 5 | 1 | 2 | 1 | 0 | 0 | 2 | 0 |
| Hunter, cf | 4 | 0 | 1 | 0 | 0 | 0 | 3 | 0 |
| Morneau, 1b | 4 | 0 | 0 | 0 | 0 | 0 | 12 | 0 |
| Koskie, 3b | 3 | 1 | 2 | 0 | 0 | 0 | 0 | 1 |
| L.Ford, dh | 3 | 1 | 1 | 0 | 0 | 0 | 0 | 0 |
| C.Guzman, ss | 4 | 1 | 3 | 0 | 0 | 0 | 4 | 7 |
| Cuddyer, 2b | 4 | 0 | 2 | 1 | 0 | 1 | 3 | 4 |
| H.Blanco, c | 2 | 0 | 0 | 0 | 0 | 0 | 2 | 1 |
| LeCroy, ph-c | 1 | 0 | 0 | 0 | 0 | 1 | 0 | 0 |
| Offerman, ph | 1 | 0 | 0 | 1 | 0 | 0 | 0 | 0 |
| C.Silva, p | 0 | 0 | 0 | 0 | 0 | 0 | 0 | 0 |
| Romero, p | 0 | 0 | 0 | 0 | 0 | 0 | 0 | 1 |
| Crain, p | 0 | 0 | 0 | 0 | 0 | 0 | 0 | 1 |
| Mulholland, p | 0 | 0 | 0 | 0 | 0 | 0 | 0 | 0 |
| **TOTALS** | 35 | 4 | 12 | 4 | 0 | 2 | 27 | 15 |

| | | | | |
|---|---|---|---|---|
| NY Yankees | 0 3 0 | 0 0 4 | 1 0 0—8 | 14 1 |
| Minnesota | 1 0 0 | 0 0 0 | 0 0 3—4 | 12 1 |

| NY Yankees | IP | H | R | ER | HR | BB | SO |
|---|---|---|---|---|---|---|---|
| K.Brown (W) | 6.0 | 8 | 1 | 1 | 1 | 0 | 1 |
| Quantrill | 1.2 | 2 | 0 | 0 | 0 | 0 | 1 |
| Heredia | 0.1 | 0 | 2 | 2 | 0 | 0 | 0 |
| Sturtze | 0.0 | 2 | 1 | 1 | 0 | 0 | 0 |
| M.Rivera | 1.0 | 0 | 0 | 0 | 0 | 0 | 0 |

| Minnesota | IP | H | R | ER | HR | BB | SO |
|---|---|---|---|---|---|---|---|
| C.Silva (L) | 5.0 | 10 | 6 | 6 | 1 | 0 | 1 |
| Romero | 0.2 | 0 | 1 | 1 | 0 | 1 | 1 |
| Crain | 0.1 | 1 | 0 | 0 | 0 | 0 | 0 |
| Mulholland | 3.0 | 3 | 1 | 1 | 1 | 0 | 0 |

Heredia pitched to 2 batters in the 9th. Sturtze pitched to 2 batters in the 9th. C.Silva pitched to 3 batters in the 6th.

E—Jeter, C.Guzman. DP—NY Yankees 1, Minnesota 2. LOB—NY Yankees 6, Minnesota 7. Scoring Position—NY Yankees 4 for 11, Minnesota 4 for 11. 2B—Jeter, Sheffield, J.Jones, Hunter. HR—J.Jones (1st inning, 1 out, 0 on) off K.Brown, B.Williams (6th inning, 0 out, 1 on) off C.Silva, H.Matsui (7th inning, 1 out, 0 on) off Mulholland. SB—Jeter, C.Guzman. CS—Sheffield. S—Sh.Stewart. SH—Cairo. HBP—Koskie by Heredia, L.Ford by Heredia. T—3:02. A—54,803. U—HP-Gorman, 1B-Everitt, 2B-Crawford, 3B-Nauert, LF-Reliford, RF-Wegner.

## HOW THEY SCORED

BOTTOM OF 1

Twins first. Stewart grounded out, shortstop Jeter to first baseman Olerud. Jones homered to center on a 2-2 count. Hunter flied out to left fielder Matsui. Morneau popped out to left fielder Matsui. Runs: 1, Hits: 1, Errors: 0

TOP OF 2

Yankees second. Matsui lined out to shortstop Guzman. Williams grounded out, second baseman Cuddyer to first baseman Morneau. Posada singled to center. Olerud infield single to short, Posada to second. Cairo singled to right, Posada scored, Olerud to third. Lofton singled to left, Olerud scored, Cairo to second. Jeter singled to left, Cairo scored, Lofton to second. Rodriguez popped out to second baseman Cuddyer. Runs: 3, Hits: 5, Errors: 0

TOP OF 6

Yankees sixth. Matsui singled to center. Williams homered to right on the first pitch, Matsui scored. Posada singled to left. Romero pitching. Olerud walked on a full count, Posada to second. Cairo sacrificed, pitcher Romero to second baseman Cuddyer, Posada to third, Olerud to second. Lofton struck out. Crain pitching. Jeter singled to center, Posada scored, Olerud scored. Jeter stole second. Rodriguez grounded out, pitcher Crain to first baseman Morneau. Runs: 4, Hits: 4, Errors: 0

TOP OF 7

Yankees seventh. Mulholland pitching. Sheffield grounded out, shortstop Guzman to first baseman Morneau. Matsui homered to center on a full count. Williams safe on Guzman's error. Posada flied out to right fielder Jones. Olerud grounded out, second baseman Cuddyer to first baseman Morneau. Runs: 1, Hits: 1, Errors: 1

BOTTOM OF 9

Twins ninth. Crosby in as right fielder. Koskie was hit by a pitch. Ford was hit by a pitch, Koskie to second. Sturtze pitching. Guzman infield single to first, Koskie to third, Ford to second. Cuddyer singled to center, Koskie scored, Ford to third, Guzman to second. Offerman pinch-hitting for LeCroy. Rivera pitching. Offerman grounded out, first baseman Olerud to pitcher Rivera, Ford scored, Guzman to third, Cuddyer to second. Stewart hit a sacrifice fly to center fielder Williams, Guzman scored, Cuddyer to third. Jones grounded out, third baseman Rodriguez to first baseman Olerud. Runs: 3, Hits: 2, Errors: 0

## GAME 4

### NEW YORK 6, MINNESOTA 5

SATURDAY, OCTOBER 9, AT MINNESOTA

| New York | AB | R | H | RBI | BB | SO | PO | A |
|---|---|---|---|---|---|---|---|---|
| Jeter, ss | 6 | 1 | 1 | 0 | 0 | 4 | 7 | 0 |
| A.Rodriguez, 3b | 4 | 1 | 2 | 0 | 2 | 0 | 1 | 2 |
| Sheffield, rf | 6 | 1 | 1 | 0 | 0 | 1 | 1 | 0 |
| H.Matsui, lf | 4 | 1 | 1 | 1 | 2 | 3 | 4 | 0 |
| B.Williams, cf | 5 | 1 | 2 | 1 | 0 | 1 | 0 | 0 |
| Posada, c | 5 | 0 | 0 | 0 | 0 | 3 | 8 | 3 |
| Sierra, dh | 4 | 1 | 2 | 3 | 1 | 0 | 0 | 0 |
| Olerud, 1b | 4 | 0 | 1 | 0 | 0 | 1 | 6 | 1 |
| Bu.Crosby, pr | 0 | 0 | 0 | 0 | 0 | 0 | 0 | 0 |
| T.Clark, 1b | 1 | 0 | 0 | 0 | 0 | 1 | 4 | 0 |
| Cairo, 2b | 5 | 0 | 1 | 0 | 0 | 2 | 1 | 4 |
| J.Vazquez, p | 0 | 0 | 0 | 0 | 0 | 0 | 1 | 0 |
| Loaiza, p | 0 | 0 | 0 | 0 | 0 | 0 | 0 | 0 |
| Gordon, p | 0 | 0 | 0 | 0 | 0 | 0 | 0 | 0 |
| M.Rivera, p | 0 | 0 | 0 | 0 | 0 | 0 | 0 | 1 |
| **TOTALS** | 44 | 6 | 11 | 5 | 5 | 16 | 33 | 11 |

| Minnesota | AB | R | H | BI | BB | SO | PO | A |
|---|---|---|---|---|---|---|---|---|
| Sh.Stewart, dh | 6 | 1 | 1 | 0 | 0 | 0 | 0 | 0 |
| J.Jones, rf | 5 | 0 | 2 | 0 | 0 | 2 | 1 | 0 |
| Hunter, cf | 3 | 2 | 1 | 1 | 1 | 0 | 4 | 0 |
| Morneau, 1b | 5 | 1 | 2 | 0 | 0 | 2 | 7 | 1 |
| Koskie, 3b | 3 | 0 | 0 | 1 | 0 | 0 | 0 | 0 |
| L.Ford, lf | 4 | 0 | 2 | 2 | 0 | 0 | 1 | 0 |
| C.Guzman, ss | 4 | 0 | 0 | 0 | 1 | 2 | 1 | 3 |
| Cuddyer, 2b | 3 | 0 | 1 | 0 | 0 | 1 | 0 | 2 |
| Rivas, 2b | 1 | 0 | 0 | 0 | 0 | 0 | 2 | 0 |
| Offerman, ph | 1 | 0 | 0 | 0 | 0 | 0 | 0 | 0 |
| H.Blanco, c | 3 | 1 | 2 | 1 | 0 | 1 | 12 | 0 |
| Kubel, ph | 1 | 0 | 1 | 0 | 0 | 0 | 0 | 0 |
| Borders, c | 0 | 0 | 0 | 0 | 0 | 0 | 5 | 0 |
| LeCroy, ph | 1 | 0 | 0 | 0 | 0 | 0 | 0 | 0 |
| Santana, p | 0 | 0 | 0 | 0 | 0 | 0 | 0 | 0 |
| Balfour, p | 0 | 0 | 0 | 0 | 0 | 0 | 0 | 0 |
| J.Rincon, p | 0 | 0 | 0 | 0 | 0 | 0 | 0 | 0 |
| Nathan, p | 0 | 0 | 0 | 0 | 0 | 0 | 0 | 0 |
| Lohse, p | 0 | 0 | 0 | 0 | 0 | 0 | 0 | 1 |
| **TOTALS** | 40 | 5 | 12 | 5 | 2 | 8 | 33 | 7 |

| | | | | | |
|---|---|---|---|---|---|
| NY Yankees | 0 0 1 | 0 0 0 | 0 4 0 | 0 1—6 | 11 0 |
| Minnesota | 1 0 0 | 1 3 0 | 0 0 0 | 0 0—5 | 12 0 |

| New York | IP | H | R | ER | HR | BB | SO |
|---|---|---|---|---|---|---|---|
| J.Vazquez | 5.0 | 7 | 5 | 5 | 1 | 2 | 6 |
| Loaiza | 2.0 | 4 | 0 | 0 | 0 | 0 | 0 |
| Gordon | 2.0 | 1 | 0 | 0 | 0 | 0 | 2 |
| M.Rivera (W) | 2.0 | 0 | 0 | 0 | 0 | 0 | 0 |

| Minnesota | IP | H | R | ER | HR | BB | SO |
|---|---|---|---|---|---|---|---|
| Santana | 5.0 | 5 | 1 | 1 | 0 | 3 | 7 |
| Balfour | 2.0 | 0 | 0 | 0 | 0 | 0 | 2 |
| J.Rincon | 0.1 | 4 | 4 | 4 | 1 | 1 | 1 |
| Nathan | 1.2 | 1 | 0 | 0 | 0 | 1 | 3 |
| Lohse (L) | 2.0 | 1 | 1 | 1 | 0 | 0 | 3 |

E—H.Blanco. DP—NY Yankees 1. LOB—NY Yankees 10, Minnesota 8. Scoring Position—NY Yankees 3 for 15, Minnesota 1 for 8. 2B—A.Rodriguez 2, Olerud, Morneau, L.Ford, Kubel. HR—H.Blanco (5th inning, 0 out, 0 on) off J.Vazquez, Sierra (8th inning, 1 out, 2 on) off J.Rincon. SB—A.Rodriguez 2, L.Ford. CS—J.Jones, L.Ford, Cuddyer. S—Hunter, Koskie. WP—J.Rincon, Lohse. PB—Borders. HBP—Koskie by J.Vazquez, L.Ford by J.Vazquez. T—4:16. A—52,498. U—HP-Everitt, 1B-Crawford, 2B-Nauert, 3B-Reliford, LF-Wegner, RF-Gorman.

## HOW THEY SCORED

BOTTOM OF 1

Twins first. Stewart singled to center. Jones singled to right, Stewart to third. Hunter hit a sacrifice fly to right fielder Sheffield, Stewart scored. Morneau struck out. Jones was caught stealing, catcher Posada to shortstop Jeter, Jones out. Runs: 1, Hits: 2, Errors: 0

TOP OF 3

Yankees third. Jeter singled to center. Rodriguez flied out to center fielder Hunter. Sheffield grounded out, second baseman Cuddyer to first baseman Morneau, Jeter to second. Matsui singled to right, Jeter scored. On Blanco's error, Matsui to second. Williams flied out to center fielder Hunter. Runs: 1, Hits: 2, Errors: 1

BOTTOM OF 4

Twins fourth. Hunter walked. Morneau doubled to right, Hunter to third. Koskie hit a sacrifice fly to left fielder Matsui, Hunter scored. Ford fouled out to third baseman Rodriguez. Guzman walked on a full count. Cuddyer grounded out, first baseman Olerud to pitcher Vazquez. Runs: 1, Hits: 1, Errors: 0

BOTTOM OF 5

Twins fifth. Blanco homered to left on a 3-1 count. Stewart grounded out, third baseman Rodriguez to first baseman Olerud. Jones struck out. Hunter singled to left. Morneau infield single to first, Hunter to second. Koskie was hit by a pitch, Hunter to third, Morneau to second. Ford doubled to left, Hunter scored, Morneau scored, Koskie to third. Guzman struck out. Runs: 3, Hits: 4, Errors: 0

TOP OF 8

Yankees eighth. Rincon pitching. Rivas in as second baseman. Sheffield infield single to third. On Rincon's wild pitch, Sheffield to second. Matsui walked. Williams singled to center, Sheffield scored, Matsui to third. Posada struck out. Sierra homered to right on a 2-2 count, Matsui scored, Williams scored. Olerud doubled to center. Crosby pinch-running for Olerud. Nathan pitching. Cairo struck out. Jeter grounded out, shortstop Guzman to first baseman Morneau. Runs: 4, Hits: 4, Errors: 0

TOP OF 11

Yankees eleventh. Jeter struck out. Rodriguez doubled to left. Rodriguez stole third. On Lohse's wild pitch, Rodriguez scored. Sheffield popped out to second baseman Rivas. Matsui struck out. Runs: 1, Hits: 1, Errors: 0

## NEW YORK YANKEES' BATTING AND FIELDING AVERAGES

| | | BATTING | | | | | | | | | | | | | FIELDING | | | |
|---|---|---|---|---|---|---|---|---|---|---|---|---|---|---|---|---|---|---|
| **Player, position** | **G** | **AB** | **R** | **H** | **TB** | **2B** | **3B** | **HR** | **RBI** | **BB** | **IBB** | **SO** | **Avg.** | **OBP** | **Slg.** | **PO** | **A** | **E** | **Avg.** |
| Rodriguez,3b | 4 | 19 | 3 | 8 | 14 | 3 | 0 | 1 | 3 | 2 | 0 | 1 | .421 | .476 | .737 | 5 | 11 | 0 | 1.000 |
| Matsui,lf | 4 | 17 | 3 | 7 | 11 | 1 | 0 | 1 | 3 | 3 | 1 | 4 | .412 | .476 | .647 | 9 | 1 | 0 | 1.000 |
| Jeter,ss | 4 | 19 | 3 | 6 | 10 | 1 | 0 | 1 | 4 | 1 | 0 | 4 | .316 | .350 | .526 | 15 | 9 | 1 | .960 |
| Williams,cf | 4 | 18 | 2 | 5 | 9 | 1 | 0 | 1 | 3 | 1 | 0 | 2 | .278 | .316 | .500 | 5 | 1 | 0 | 1.000 |
| Lofton,dh | 1 | 4 | 0 | 1 | 1 | 0 | 0 | 0 | 1 | 0 | 0 | 1 | .250 | .250 | .250 | 0 | 0 | 0 | .000 |
| Posada,c | 4 | 18 | 2 | 4 | 4 | 0 | 0 | 0 | 0 | 0 | 0 | 6 | .222 | .222 | .222 | 27 | 5 | 0 | 1.000 |
| Sheffield,rf | 4 | 18 | 2 | 4 | 8 | 1 | 0 | 1 | 2 | 3 | 1 | 1 | .222 | .333 | .444 | 6 | 1 | 0 | 1.000 |
| Cairo,2b | 4 | 14 | 3 | 3 | 4 | 1 | 0 | 0 | 1 | 2 | 0 | 5 | .214 | .313 | .286 | 10 | 15 | 0 | 1.000 |
| Olerud,1b | 4 | 14 | 2 | 3 | 5 | 2 | 0 | 0 | 0 | 1 | 0 | 2 | .214 | .313 | .357 | 36 | 6 | 0 | 1.000 |
| Sierra,dh | 3 | 12 | 1 | 2 | 5 | 0 | 0 | 1 | 3 | 2 | 0 | 3 | .167 | .286 | .417 | 0 | 0 | 0 | .000 |
| Brown,p | 1 | 0 | 0 | 0 | 0 | 0 | 0 | 0 | 0 | 0 | 0 | 0 | .000 | .000 | .000 | 0 | 0 | 0 | .000 |
| Crosby,rf-pr | 2 | 0 | 0 | 0 | 0 | 0 | 0 | 0 | 0 | 0 | 0 | 0 | .000 | .000 | .000 | 0 | 0 | 0 | .000 |
| Gordon,p | 3 | 0 | 0 | 0 | 0 | 0 | 0 | 0 | 0 | 0 | 0 | 0 | .000 | .000 | .000 | 0 | 0 | 0 | .000 |
| Heredia,p | 1 | 0 | 0 | 0 | 0 | 0 | 0 | 0 | 0 | 0 | 0 | 0 | .000 | .000 | .000 | 0 | 0 | 0 | .000 |
| Lieber,p | 1 | 0 | 0 | 0 | 0 | 0 | 0 | 0 | 0 | 0 | 0 | 0 | .000 | .000 | .000 | 2 | 0 | 0 | 1.000 |
| Loaiza,p | 1 | 0 | 0 | 0 | 0 | 0 | 0 | 0 | 0 | 0 | 0 | 0 | .000 | .000 | .000 | 0 | 0 | 0 | .000 |
| Mussina,p | 1 | 0 | 0 | 0 | 0 | 0 | 0 | 0 | 0 | 0 | 0 | 0 | .000 | .000 | .000 | 1 | 1 | 0 | 1.000 |
| Quantrill,p | 2 | 0 | 0 | 0 | 0 | 0 | 0 | 0 | 0 | 0 | 0 | 0 | .000 | .000 | .000 | 0 | 1 | 0 | 1.000 |
| Rivera,p | 4 | 0 | 0 | 0 | 0 | 0 | 0 | 0 | 0 | 0 | 0 | 0 | .000 | .000 | .000 | 2 | 3 | 0 | 1.000 |
| Sturtze,p | 2 | 0 | 0 | 0 | 0 | 0 | 0 | 0 | 0 | 0 | 0 | 0 | .000 | .000 | .000 | 0 | 1 | 0 | 1.000 |
| Vazquez,p | 1 | 0 | 0 | 0 | 0 | 0 | 0 | 0 | 0 | 0 | 0 | 0 | .000 | .000 | .000 | 1 | 0 | 0 | 1.000 |
| Clark,1b | 1 | 1 | 0 | 0 | 0 | 0 | 0 | 0 | 0 | 0 | 0 | 1 | .000 | .000 | .000 | 4 | 0 | 0 | 1.000 |
| Totals | 4 | 154 | 21 | 43 | 71 | 10 | 0 | 6 | 20 | 15 | 2 | 30 | .279 | .345 | .461 | 123 | 55 | 1 | .994 |

## MINNESOTA TWINS' BATTING AND FIELDING AVERAGES

| | | BATTING | | | | | | | | | | | | | FIELDING | | | |
|---|---|---|---|---|---|---|---|---|---|---|---|---|---|---|---|---|---|---|
| **Player, position** | **G** | **AB** | **R** | **H** | **TB** | **2B** | **3B** | **HR** | **RBI** | **BB** | **IBB** | **SO** | **Avg.** | **OBP** | **Slg.** | **PO** | **A** | **E** | **Avg.** |
| Cuddyer,2b-1b | 4 | 15 | 1 | 7 | 7 | 0 | 0 | 0 | 2 | 0 | 0 | 3 | .467 | .467 | .467 | 12 | 12 | 0 | 1.000 |
| Hunter,cf | 4 | 17 | 5 | 6 | 10 | 1 | 0 | 1 | 2 | 1 | 0 | 1 | .353 | .368 | .588 | 13 | 1 | 0 | 1.000 |
| Guzman,ss | 4 | 15 | 2 | 5 | 5 | 0 | 0 | 0 | 0 | 2 | 0 | 3 | .333 | .412 | .333 | 6 | 21 | 1 | .964 |
| LeCroy,1b-ph-c | 3 | 3 | 0 | 1 | 1 | 0 | 0 | 0 | 0 | 1 | 0 | 1 | .333 | .500 | .333 | 2 | 0 | 0 | 1.000 |
| Koskie,3b | 4 | 13 | 2 | 4 | 5 | 1 | 0 | 0 | 2 | 3 | 0 | 2 | .308 | .474 | .385 | 4 | 4 | 0 | 1.000 |
| Jones,rf | 4 | 20 | 3 | 6 | 13 | 1 | 0 | 2 | 2 | 0 | 0 | 6 | .300 | .300 | .650 | 8 | 0 | 0 | 1.000 |
| Ford,dh-lf | 3 | 11 | 1 | 3 | 4 | 1 | 0 | 0 | 2 | 0 | 0 | 2 | .273 | .385 | .364 | 1 | 0 | 0 | 1.000 |
| Blanco,c | 4 | 8 | 1 | 2 | 5 | 0 | 0 | 1 | 2 | 0 | 0 | 2 | .250 | .222 | .625 | 20 | 2 | 1 | .957 |
| Morneau,1b | 4 | 17 | 1 | 4 | 6 | 2 | 0 | 0 | 2 | 0 | 0 | 3 | .235 | .235 | .353 | 35 | 2 | 0 | 1.000 |
| Stewart,lf-dh | 4 | 20 | 1 | 4 | 4 | 0 | 0 | 0 | 2 | 0 | 0 | 2 | .200 | .190 | .200 | 6 | 0 | 0 | 1.000 |
| Kubel,dh-ph | 2 | 7 | 0 | 1 | 2 | 1 | 0 | 0 | 0 | 0 | 0 | 2 | .143 | .143 | .286 | 0 | 0 | 0 | .000 |
| Balfour,p | 2 | 0 | 0 | 0 | 0 | 0 | 0 | 0 | 0 | 0 | 0 | 0 | .000 | .000 | .000 | 0 | 1 | 0 | 1.000 |
| Crain,p | 1 | 0 | 0 | 0 | 0 | 0 | 0 | 0 | 0 | 0 | 0 | 0 | .000 | .000 | .000 | 0 | 1 | 0 | 1.000 |
| Lohse,p | 1 | 0 | 0 | 0 | 0 | 0 | 0 | 0 | 0 | 0 | 0 | 0 | .000 | .000 | .000 | 0 | 1 | 0 | 1.000 |
| Mulholland,p | 1 | 0 | 0 | 0 | 0 | 0 | 0 | 0 | 0 | 0 | 0 | 0 | .000 | .000 | .000 | 0 | 0 | 0 | .000 |
| Nathan,p | 3 | 0 | 0 | 0 | 0 | 0 | 0 | 0 | 0 | 0 | 0 | 0 | .000 | .000 | .000 | 0 | 1 | 0 | 1.000 |
| Radke,p | 1 | 0 | 0 | 0 | 0 | 0 | 0 | 0 | 0 | 0 | 0 | 0 | .000 | .000 | .000 | 0 | 1 | 0 | 1.000 |
| Rincon,p | 3 | 0 | 0 | 0 | 0 | 0 | 0 | 0 | 0 | 0 | 0 | 0 | .000 | .000 | .000 | 0 | 0 | 0 | .000 |
| Romero,p | 2 | 0 | 0 | 0 | 0 | 0 | 0 | 0 | 0 | 0 | 0 | 0 | .000 | .000 | .000 | 0 | 1 | 0 | 1.000 |
| Santana,p | 2 | 0 | 0 | 0 | 0 | 0 | 0 | 0 | 0 | 0 | 0 | 0 | .000 | .000 | .000 | 0 | 0 | 0 | .000 |
| Silva,p | 1 | 0 | 0 | 0 | 0 | 0 | 0 | 0 | 0 | 0 | 0 | 0 | .000 | .000 | .000 | 0 | 0 | 0 | .000 |
| Rivas,2b-pr | 3 | 1 | 0 | 0 | 0 | 0 | 0 | 0 | 0 | 0 | 0 | 0 | .000 | .000 | .000 | 3 | 2 | 0 | 1.000 |
| Borders,c | 2 | 2 | 0 | 0 | 0 | 0 | 0 | 0 | 0 | 0 | 0 | 1 | .000 | .000 | .000 | 12 | 0 | 0 | 1.000 |
| Offerman,ph | 3 | 3 | 0 | 0 | 0 | 0 | 0 | 0 | 1 | 0 | 0 | 0 | .000 | .000 | .000 | 0 | 0 | 0 | .000 |
| Totals | 4 | 152 | 17 | 43 | 62 | 7 | 0 | 4 | 17 | 7 | 0 | 28 | .283 | .323 | .408 | 122 | 50 | 2 | .989 |

## NEW YORK YANKEES' PITCHING RECORDS

| **Pitcher** | **G** | **GS** | **CG** | **IP** | **H** | **R** | **ER** | **HR** | **BB** | **IBB** | **SO** | **HB** | **WP** | **W** | **L** | **Pct.** | **ERA** |
|---|---|---|---|---|---|---|---|---|---|---|---|---|---|---|---|---|---|
| Rivera | 4 | 0 | 0 | 5.2 | 2 | 0 | 0 | 0 | 0 | 0 | 2 | 0 | 0 | 1 | 0 | 1.000 | 0.00 |
| Loaiza | 1 | 0 | 0 | 2.0 | 4 | 0 | 0 | 0 | 0 | 0 | 0 | 0 | 0 | 0 | 0 | .000 | 0.00 |
| Quantrill | 2 | 0 | 0 | 2.0 | 2 | 0 | 0 | 0 | 0 | 0 | 1 | 0 | 0 | 1 | 0 | 1.000 | 0.00 |
| Brown | 1 | 1 | 0 | 6.0 | 8 | 1 | 1 | 1 | 0 | 0 | 1 | 0 | 0 | 1 | 0 | 1.000 | 1.50 |
| Mussina | 1 | 1 | 0 | 7.0 | 7 | 2 | 2 | 1 | 1 | 0 | 7 | 0 | 0 | 0 | 1 | .000 | 2.57 |
| Lieber | 1 | 1 | 0 | 6.2 | 7 | 3 | 3 | 0 | 1 | 0 | 4 | 0 | 0 | 0 | 0 | .000 | 4.05 |
| Gordon | 3 | 0 | 0 | 3.2 | 2 | 2 | 2 | 0 | 0 | 0 | 3 | 0 | 1 | 0 | 0 | .000 | 4.91 |
| Sturtze | 2 | 0 | 0 | 2.2 | 4 | 2 | 2 | 1 | 3 | 0 | 4 | 0 | 0 | 0 | 0 | .000 | 6.75 |
| Vazquez | 1 | 1 | 0 | 5.0 | 7 | 5 | 5 | 1 | 2 | 0 | 6 | 2 | 0 | 0 | 0 | .000 | 9.00 |
| Heredia | 1 | 0 | 0 | 0.1 | 0 | 2 | 2 | 0 | 0 | 0 | 0 | 2 | 0 | 0 | 0 | .000 | 54.00 |
| Totals | 4 | 4 | 0 | 41.0 | 43 | 17 | 17 | 4 | 7 | 0 | 28 | 4 | 1 | 3 | 1 | .750 | 3.73 |

No shutouts or saves.

## MINNESOTA TWINS' PITCHING RECORDS

| Pitcher | G | GS | CG | IP | H | R | ER | HR | BB | IBB | SO | HB | WP | W | L | Pct. | ERA |
|---|---|---|---|---|---|---|---|---|---|---|---|---|---|---|---|---|---|
| Balfour | 2 | 0 | 0 | 2.2 | 0 | 0 | 0 | 0 | 0 | 0 | 2 | 0 | 0 | 0 | 0 | .000 | 0.00 |
| Crain | 1 | 0 | 0 | 0.1 | 1 | 0 | 0 | 0 | 0 | 0 | 0 | 0 | 0 | 0 | 0 | .000 | 0.00 |
| Santana | 2 | 2 | 0 | 12.0 | 14 | 1 | 1 | 0 | 4 | 0 | 12 | 1 | 0 | 1 | 0 | 1.000 | 0.75 |
| Mulholland | 1 | 0 | 0 | 3.0 | 3 | 1 | 1 | 1 | 0 | 0 | 0 | 0 | 0 | 0 | 0 | .000 | 3.00 |
| Nathan | 3 | 0 | 0 | 5.0 | 2 | 2 | 2 | 0 | 5 | 2 | 6 | 0 | 0 | 0 | 1 | .000 | 3.60 |
| Lohse | 1 | 0 | 0 | 2.0 | 1 | 1 | 1 | 0 | 0 | 0 | 3 | 0 | 1 | 0 | 1 | .000 | 4.50 |
| Radke | 1 | 1 | 0 | 6.1 | 8 | 5 | 5 | 3 | 3 | 0 | 0 | 0 | 0 | 0 | 0 | .000 | 7.11 |
| Romero | 2 | 0 | 0 | 1.0 | 0 | 1 | 1 | 0 | 1 | 0 | 1 | 0 | 0 | 0 | 0 | .000 | 9.00 |
| Silva | 1 | 1 | 0 | 5.0 | 10 | 6 | 6 | 1 | 0 | 0 | 1 | 0 | 0 | 0 | 1 | .000 | 10.80 |
| Rincon | 3 | 0 | 0 | 3.1 | 4 | 4 | 4 | 1 | 2 | 0 | 5 | 0 | 1 | 0 | 0 | .000 | 10.80 |
| Totals | 4 | 4 | 0 | 40.2 | 43 | 21 | 21 | 6 | 15 | 2 | 30 | 1 | 2 | 1 | 3 | .250 | 4.65 |

No shutouts. Saves- Nathan.

## SCORE BY INNINGS

| | | | | | | | | | | | | |
|---|---|---|---|---|---|---|---|---|---|---|---|---|
| New York | 1 | 3 | 3 | 0 | 1 | 4 | 2 | 4 | 0 | 0 | 1 | 2—21 |
| Minnesota | 3 | 2 | 1 | 1 | 3 | 1 | 0 | 2 | 3 | 0 | 0 | 1—17 |

## MISCELLANEOUS STATISTICS

Sacrifice hits—Blanco, Cairo, Jeter.
Sacrifice flies—Blanco, Hunter, Koskie, Matsui, Stewart.
Stolen bases—Hunter 2, Rodriguez 2, Ford, Guzman, Jeter, Sierra.
Caught stealing—Cuddyer 2, Ford, Jones, Rodriguez, Sheffield.
Double plays—Guzman, Cuddyer and Morneau 3; Jeter and Olerud 2; Balfour, Cuddyer and Morneau; Cairo, Jeter and Olerud; Guzman and Morneau; Guzman, Rivas and Morneau; Morneau, Guzman and Morneau.
Left on bases—New York 7, 7, 6, 10—30; Minnesota 4, 9, 7, 8—28.
Scoring position—New York 0 for 6, 2 for 5, 4 for 11, 3 for 15—9 for 37; Minnesota 1 for 3, 3 for 10, 4 for 11, 1 for 8—9 for 32.
Hit by pitcher—by Heredia 2 (Ford, Koskie), by Vazquez 2 (Ford,Koskie), by Santana (Olerud).
Passed balls—Borders, Posada.
Balks—None.
Time of games—2:53, 4:19, 3:02, 4:16—Avg.: 3:37.
Attendance—55,749, 56,354, 54,803, 52,498—219,404.
Umpires—Reliford, Charlie; Wegner, Mark; Gorman, Brian; Everitt, Mike; Crawford, Jerry; Nauert, Paul.

# N.L. DIVISION SERIES

## ST. LOUIS VS. LOS ANGELES

### RESULTS

| Day | Date | Place | Score |
|---|---|---|---|
| Tue. | Oct. 5 | St. Louis | St. Louis 8, Los Angeles 3 |
| Thu. | Oct. 7 | St. Louis | St. Louis 8, Los Angeles 3 |
| Sat. | Oct. 9 | Los Angeles | Los Angeles 4, St. Louis 0 |
| Sun. | Oct. 10 | Los Angeles | St. Louis 6, Los Angeles 2 |

### BOX SCORES

### GAME 1

**ST.LOUIS 8, LOS ANGELES 3**

TUESDAY, OCTOBER 5, AT ST. LOUIS

| Los Angels | AB | R | H | BI | BB | SO | PO | A |
|---|---|---|---|---|---|---|---|---|
| C.Izturis, ss | 5 | 1 | 2 | 0 | 0 | 1 | 3 | 4 |
| Werth, lf | 4 | 0 | 2 | 1 | 0 | 1 | 1 | 0 |
| Finley, cf | 4 | 0 | 0 | 0 | 0 | 0 | 1 | 0 |
| Beltre, 3b | 4 | 1 | 2 | 0 | 0 | 0 | 0 | 0 |
| Sh.Green, 1b | 4 | 0 | 0 | 0 | 0 | 1 | 8 | 0 |
| Bradley, rf | 3 | 0 | 1 | 0 | 1 | 0 | 0 | 0 |
| Cora, 2b | 4 | 0 | 1 | 1 | 0 | 1 | 2 | 1 |
| Mayne, c | 2 | 0 | 0 | 0 | 0 | 0 | 5 | 1 |
| Ventura, ph | 1 | 0 | 0 | 0 | 0 | 1 | 0 | 0 |
| T.Wilson, c | 1 | 1 | 1 | 1 | 0 | 0 | 4 | 0 |
| O.Perez, p | 1 | 0 | 0 | 0 | 0 | 0 | 0 | 1 |
| Dessens, p | 0 | 0 | 0 | 0 | 0 | 0 | 0 | 0 |
| Grabowski, ph | 1 | 0 | 0 | 0 | 0 | 0 | 0 | 0 |
| D.Sanchez, p | 0 | 0 | 0 | 0 | 0 | 0 | 0 | 0 |
| Venafro, p | 0 | 0 | 0 | 0 | 0 | 0 | 0 | 0 |
| Choi, ph | 1 | 0 | 0 | 0 | 0 | 0 | 0 | 0 |
| Carrara, p | 0 | 0 | 0 | 0 | 0 | 0 | 0 | 0 |
| Brazoban, p | 0 | 0 | 0 | 0 | 0 | 0 | 0 | 0 |
| J.Hernandez, ph | 0 | 0 | 0 | 0 | 1 | 0 | 0 | 0 |
| **TOTALS** | 35 | 3 | 9 | 3 | 2 | 5 | 24 | 7 |

| St. Louis | AB | R | H | BI | BB | SO | PO | A |
|---|---|---|---|---|---|---|---|---|
| Womack, 2b | 5 | 0 | 0 | 0 | 0 | 0 | 0 | 2 |
| L.Walker, rf | 4 | 2 | 2 | 2 | 0 | 2 | 0 | 0 |
| Pujols, 1b | 4 | 2 | 2 | 1 | 0 | 0 | 10 | 0 |
| Rolen, 3b | 2 | 1 | 0 | 0 | 2 | 0 | 2 | 2 |
| Renteria, ss | 2 | 1 | 1 | 2 | 2 | 1 | 4 | 3 |
| Edmonds, cf | 4 | 1 | 2 | 2 | 0 | 2 | 0 | 0 |
| R.Sanders, lf | 4 | 0 | 0 | 0 | 0 | 1 | 5 | 0 |
| Matheny, c | 4 | 1 | 1 | 1 | 0 | 2 | 6 | 0 |
| W.Williams, p | 2 | 0 | 0 | 0 | 0 | 0 | 0 | 0 |
| Cedeno, ph | 1 | 0 | 1 | 0 | 0 | 0 | 0 | 0 |
| Calero, p | 0 | 0 | 0 | 0 | 0 | 0 | 0 | 0 |
| King, p | 0 | 0 | 0 | 0 | 0 | 0 | 0 | 0 |
| Mar.Anderson, ph | 1 | 0 | 0 | 0 | 0 | 0 | 0 | 0 |
| Isringhausen, p | 0 | 0 | 0 | 0 | 0 | 0 | 0 | 0 |
| **TOTALS** | 33 | 8 | 9 | 8 | 4 | 8 | 27 | 7 |

| | | | | |
|---|---|---|---|---|
| Los Angeles | 0 0 0 | 0 1 1 | 0 0 1—3 | 9 1 |
| St. Louis | 1 0 5 | 1 0 0 | 1 0 x—8 | 9 0 |

| Los Angeles | IP | H | R | ER | HR | BB | SO |
|---|---|---|---|---|---|---|---|
| O.Perez (L) | 2.2 | 5 | 6 | 6 | 3 | 2 | 3 |
| Dessens | 1.1 | 1 | 1 | 1 | 1 | 0 | 1 |
| D.Sanchez | 1.2 | 1 | 0 | 0 | 0 | 1 | 3 |
| Venafro | 0.1 | 0 | 0 | 0 | 0 | 0 | 0 |
| Carrara | 1.0 | 2 | 1 | 1 | 1 | 1 | 1 |
| Brazoban | 1.0 | 0 | 0 | 0 | 0 | 0 | 0 |

| St. Louis | IP | H | R | ER | HR | BB | SO |
|---|---|---|---|---|---|---|---|
| W.Williams (W) | 6.0 | 8 | 2 | 2 | 0 | 1 | 2 |
| Calero | 1.0 | 0 | 0 | 0 | 0 | 0 | 2 |
| King | 1.0 | 0 | 0 | 0 | 0 | 0 | 1 |
| Isringhausen | 1.0 | 1 | 1 | 1 | 1 | 1 | 0 |

E—O.Perez. DP—St. Louis 1. LOB—Los Angeles 7, St. Louis 5. Scoring Position—Los Angeles 1 for 5, St. Louis 2 for 6. 2B—C.Izturis, Werth, Renteria. 3B—Cora. HR—Pujols (1st inning, 2 out, 0 on) off O.Perez, L.Walker (3rd inning, 2 out, 0 on) off O.Perez, Edmonds (3rd inning, 2 out, 1 on) off O.Perez, Matheny (4th inning, 0 out, 0 on) off Dessens, L.Walker (7th inning, 0 out, 0 on) off Carrara, T.Wilson (9th inning, 2 out, 0 on) off Isringhausen. SB—Bradley, Renteria. CS—Renteria. WP—Carrara. T—3:11. A—52,127. U—HP-Scott, 1B-Gibson, 2B-Meriwether, 3B-Dreckman, LF-Davis, RF-O'Nora.

### HOW THEY SCORED

BOTTOM OF 1

Cardinals first. Womack flied out to center fielder Finley. Walker struck out. Pujols homered to center on a 2-2 count. Rolen fouled out to first baseman Green. Runs: 1, Hits: 1, Errors: 0

BOTTOM OF 3

Cardinals third. Williams grounded out, shortstop Izturis to first baseman Green. Womack grounded out, pitcher O.Perez to first baseman Green. Walker homered to right on the first pitch. Pujols singled to center. Rolen walked, Pujols to second. Renteria doubled to left, Pujols scored, Rolen scored. Edmonds homered to right on the first pitch, Renteria scored. Dessens pitching. Sanders popped out to shortstop Izturis. Runs: 5, Hits: 4, Errors: 0

BOTTOM OF 4

Cardinals fourth. Matheny homered to left on the first pitch. Williams fouled out to catcher Mayne. Womack flied out to left fielder Werth. Walker struck out.
Runs: 1, Hits: 1, Errors: 0

TOP OF 5

Dodgers fifth. Mayne popped out to shortstop Renteria. Grabowski pinch-hitting for Dessens. Grabowski fouled out to catcher Matheny. Izturis doubled to right. Werth doubled to left, Izturis scored. Finley popped out to left fielder Sanders. Runs: 1, Hits: 2, Errors: 0

TOP OF 6

Dodgers sixth. Beltre singled to center. Green flied out to left fielder Sanders. Bradley flied out to left fielder Sanders. Cora tripled to center, Beltre scored. Ventura pinch-hitting for Mayne. Ventura struck out. Runs: 1, Hits: 2, Errors: 0

BOTTOM OF 7

Cardinals seventh. Carrara pitching. Walker homered to center on a 2-0 count. Pujols grounded out, shortstop Izturis to first baseman Green. Rolen walked on a full count. Renteria struck out. Edmonds singled to right, Rolen to third. On Carrara's wild pitch, Edmonds to second. Sanders grounded out, shortstop Izturis to first baseman Green. Runs: 1, Hits: 2, Errors: 0

TOP OF 9

Dodgers ninth. Isringhausen pitching. Bradley grounded out, first baseman Pujols unassisted. Cora grounded out, second baseman Womack to first baseman Pujols. Wilson homered to center on a 2-2 count. Hernandez pinch-hitting for Brazoban. Hernandez walked. Izturis grounded out, first baseman Pujols unassisted. Runs: 1, Hits: 1, Errors: 0

## GAME 2

### ST.LOUIS 8, LOS ANGELES 3

THURSDAY, OCTOBER 7, AT ST. LOUIS

| Los Angeles | AB | R | H | BI | BB | SO | PO | A |
|---|---|---|---|---|---|---|---|---|
| C.Izturis, ss | 4 | 0 | 0 | 0 | 1 | 1 | 1 | 1 |
| Werth, lf | 3 | 1 | 1 | 1 | 2 | 1 | 4 | 0 |
| Finley, cf | 4 | 0 | 0 | 0 | 1 | 0 | 5 | 0 |
| Beltre, 3b | 4 | 0 | 1 | 0 | 0 | 1 | 1 | 0 |
| Sh.Green, 1b | 4 | 1 | 1 | 1 | 0 | 0 | 1 | 0 |
| Bradley, rf | 3 | 1 | 2 | 1 | 1 | 1 | 1 | 0 |
| Cora, 2b | 4 | 0 | 0 | 0 | 0 | 1 | 1 | 0 |
| D.Ross, c | 2 | 0 | 0 | 0 | 1 | 0 | 8 | 0 |
| Ventura, ph | 1 | 0 | 0 | 0 | 0 | 0 | 0 | 0 |
| Gagne, p | 0 | 0 | 0 | 0 | 0 | 0 | 0 | 0 |
| Weaver, p | 2 | 0 | 0 | 0 | 0 | 0 | 0 | 1 |
| D.Sanchez, p | 0 | 0 | 0 | 0 | 0 | 0 | 0 | 0 |
| Grabowski, ph | 0 | 0 | 0 | 0 | 1 | 0 | 0 | 0 |
| W.Alvarez, p | 0 | 0 | 0 | 0 | 0 | 0 | 0 | 0 |
| Carrara, p | 0 | 0 | 0 | 0 | 0 | 0 | 0 | 0 |
| Mayne, c | 1 | 0 | 1 | 0 | 0 | 0 | 2 | 0 |
| **TOTALS** | 32 | 3 | 6 | 3 | 7 | 5 | 24 | 2 |

| St. Louis | AB | R | H | BI | BB | SO | PO | A |
|---|---|---|---|---|---|---|---|---|
| Womack, 2b | 5 | 1 | 1 | 1 | 0 | 1 | 0 | 4 |
| L.Walker, rf | 4 | 1 | 1 | 1 | 0 | 1 | 3 | 0 |
| Pujols, 1b | 3 | 1 | 1 | 0 | 2 | 0 | 11 | 0 |
| Rolen, 3b | 4 | 0 | 0 | 0 | 1 | 2 | 1 | 0 |
| Edmonds, cf | 4 | 0 | 0 | 0 | 0 | 3 | 3 | 0 |
| Renteria, ss | 4 | 3 | 3 | 1 | 0 | 0 | 1 | 4 |
| R.Sanders, lf | 3 | 2 | 3 | 0 | 0 | 0 | 3 | 0 |
| Matheny, c | 3 | 0 | 2 | 4 | 0 | 0 | 5 | 0 |
| Marquis, p | 1 | 0 | 0 | 0 | 0 | 0 | 0 | 0 |
| Eldred, p | 0 | 0 | 0 | 0 | 0 | 0 | 0 | 0 |
| Mar.Anderson, ph | 1 | 0 | 0 | 0 | 0 | 1 | 0 | 0 |
| Haren, p | 1 | 0 | 0 | 0 | 0 | 0 | 0 | 0 |
| King, p | 0 | 0 | 0 | 0 | 0 | 0 | 0 | 0 |
| Cedeno, ph | 1 | 0 | 0 | 0 | 0 | 0 | 0 | 0 |
| Tavarez, p | 0 | 0 | 0 | 0 | 0 | 0 | 0 | 0 |
| Kline, p | 0 | 0 | 0 | 0 | 0 | 0 | 0 | 0 |
| **TOTALS** | 34 | 8 | 11 | 7 | 3 | 8 | 27 | 8 |

| | | | | |
|---|---|---|---|---|
| Los Angeles | 1 0 0 | 2 0 0 | 0 0 0—3 | 6 1 |
| St. Louis | 0 3 0 | 0 3 0 | 2 0 x—8 | 11 0 |

| Los Angeles | IP | H | R | ER | HR | BB | SO |
|---|---|---|---|---|---|---|---|
| Weaver (L) | 4.2 | 8 | 6 | 6 | 0 | 2 | 4 |
| D.Sanchez | 0.1 | 0 | 0 | 0 | 0 | 0 | 0 |
| W.Alvarez | 1.2 | 1 | 1 | 1 | 0 | 0 | 2 |
| Carrara | 0.1 | 2 | 1 | 1 | 0 | 0 | 0 |
| Gagne | 1.0 | 0 | 0 | 0 | 0 | 1 | 2 |

| St. Louis | IP | H | R | ER | HR | BB | SO |
|---|---|---|---|---|---|---|---|
| Marquis | 3.1 | 4 | 3 | 3 | 3 | 4 | 0 |
| Eldred | 0.2 | 0 | 0 | 0 | 0 | 2 | 0 |
| Haren (W) | 2.0 | 1 | 0 | 0 | 0 | 1 | 3 |
| King (HOLD) | 1.0 | 0 | 0 | 0 | 0 | 0 | 0 |
| Tavarez | 1.2 | 1 | 0 | 0 | 0 | 0 | 2 |
| Kline | 0.1 | 0 | 0 | 0 | 0 | 0 | 0 |

E—Weaver. DP—St. Louis 1. LOB—Los Angeles 9, St. Louis 8. Scoring Position—Los Angeles 0 for 3, St. Louis 6 for 15. 2B—Bradley, L.Walker, Renteria. 3B—Womack. HR—Werth (1st inning, 1 out, 0 on) off Marquis, Sh.Green (4th inning, 0 out, 0 on) off Marquis, Bradley (4th inning, 0 out, 0 on) off Marquis. SB—R.Sanders. SH—Matheny. WP—Weaver. HBP—L.Walker by Weaver, R.Sanders by Weaver. T—3:36. A 52,228. U—HP-Gibson, 1B-Meriwether, 2B-Dreckman, 3B-Davis, LF-O'Nora, RF-Scott.

## HOW THEY SCORED

TOP OF 1

Dodgers first. Izturis flied out to center fielder Edmonds. Werth homered to center on a 2-1 count. Finley flied out to right fielder Walker. Beltre singled to left. Green grounded out, first baseman Pujols unassisted. Runs: 1, Hits: 2, Errors: 0

BOTTOM OF 2

Cardinals second. Renteria doubled to right. Sanders bunt single to first, Renteria to third. Matheny popped out to shortstop Izturis. On Weaver's error on a pickoff attempt, Renteria scored, Sanders to second. Marquis fouled out to catcher D.Ross. Womack tripled to right, Sanders scored. Walker doubled to right, Womack scored. On Weaver's wild pitch, Walker to third. Pujols grounded out, shortstop Izturis to first baseman Green. Runs: 3, Hits: 4, Errors: 1

TOP OF 4

Dodgers fourth. Green homered to right on a full count. Bradley homered to right on a full count. Cora flied out to left fielder Sanders. D.Ross walked. Eldred pitching. Weaver flied out on a bunt to first baseman Pujols. Izturis walked on a full count, D.Ross to second. Werth walked, D.Ross to third, Izturis to second. Finley flied out to center fielder Edmonds. Runs: 2, Hits: 2, Errors: 0

BOTTOM OF 5

Cardinals fifth. Walker was hit by a pitch. Pujols singled to center, Walker to second. Rolen flied out to center fielder Finley. Edmonds struck out. Renteria singled to center, Walker scored, Pujols to second. Sanders was hit by a pitch, Pujols to third, Renteria to second. Matheny singled to center, Pujols scored, Renteria scored, Sanders to third. Sanchez pitching. Haren flied out to left fielder Werth. Runs: 3, Hits: 3, Errors: 0

BOTTOM OF 7

Cardinals seventh. Rolen struck out. Edmonds struck out. Renteria singled to left. Carrara pitching. Sanders singled to center, Renteria to third. Sanders stole second. Matheny singled to left, Renteria scored, Sanders scored. Cedeno pinch-hitting for King. Cedeno flied out to center fielder Finley. Runs: 2, Hits: 3, Errors: 0

## GAME 3

### LOS ANGELES 4, ST. LOUIS 0

SATURDAY, OCTOBER 9, AT LOS ANGELES

| St. Louis | AB | R | H | BI | BB | SO | PO | A |
|---|---|---|---|---|---|---|---|---|
| Womack, 2b | 4 | 0 | 2 | 0 | 0 | 0 | 0 | 4 |
| L.Walker, rf | 4 | 0 | 0 | 0 | 0 | 2 | 2 | 0 |
| Pujols, 1b | 4 | 0 | 0 | 0 | 0 | 0 | 12 | 0 |
| Rolen, 3b | 4 | 0 | 0 | 0 | 0 | 1 | 0 | 1 |
| Edmonds, cf | 4 | 0 | 2 | 0 | 0 | 1 | 0 | 0 |
| Renteria, ss | 2 | 0 | 0 | 0 | 1 | 0 | 2 | 4 |
| R.Sanders, lf | 3 | 0 | 0 | 0 | 0 | 0 | 3 | 0 |
| Matheny, c | 3 | 0 | 1 | 0 | 0 | 0 | 5 | 0 |
| M.Morris, p | 2 | 0 | 0 | 0 | 0 | 0 | 0 | 2 |
| Mar.Anderson, ph | 1 | 0 | 0 | 0 | 0 | 0 | 0 | 0 |
| Eldred, p | 0 | 0 | 0 | 0 | 0 | 0 | 0 | 0 |
| Kline, p | 0 | 0 | 0 | 0 | 0 | 0 | 0 | 0 |
| **TOTALS** | 31 | 0 | 5 | 0 | 1 | 4 | 24 | 11 |

| Los Angeles | AB | R | H | BI | BB | SO | PO | A |
|---|---|---|---|---|---|---|---|---|
| C.Izturis, ss | 4 | 0 | 0 | 0 | 0 | 0 | 1 | 2 |
| Werth, lf | 4 | 0 | 0 | 0 | 0 | 1 | 2 | 0 |
| Finley, cf | 4 | 0 | 1 | 2 | 0 | 0 | 5 | 0 |
| Beltre, 3b | 4 | 0 | 1 | 0 | 0 | 2 | 3 | 1 |
| Sh.Green, 1b | 4 | 2 | 3 | 2 | 0 | 0 | 8 | 0 |
| Bradley, rf | 3 | 0 | 0 | 0 | 1 | 0 | 3 | 0 |
| Cora, 2b | 3 | 1 | 1 | 0 | 0 | 0 | 1 | 4 |
| Mayne, c | 2 | 1 | 1 | 0 | 1 | 0 | 4 | 0 |
| Lima, p | 2 | 0 | 0 | 0 | 0 | 2 | 0 | 0 |
| **TOTALS** | 30 | 4 | 7 | 4 | 2 | 5 | 27 | 7 |

| | | | | |
|---|---|---|---|---|
| St. Louis | 0 0 0 | 0 0 0 | 0 0 0—0 | 5 0 |
| Los Angeles | 0 0 2 | 1 0 1 | 0 0 x—4 | 8 1 |

| St. Louis | IP | H | R | ER | HR | BB | SO |
|---|---|---|---|---|---|---|---|
| M.Morris (L) | 7.0 | 6 | 4 | 4 | 2 | 2 | 5 |
| Eldred | 0.0 | 1 | 0 | 0 | 0 | 0 | 0 |
| Kline | 1.0 | 0 | 0 | 0 | 0 | 0 | 0 |

Eldred pitched to 1 batter in the 8th.

| Los Angeles | IP | H | R | ER | HR | BB | SO |
|---|---|---|---|---|---|---|---|
| Lima (W) | 9.0 | 5 | 0 | 0 | 0 | 1 | 4 |

DP—St. Louis 1, Los Angeles 1. LOB—St. Louis 5, Los Angeles 6. Scoring Position—St. Louis 0 for 3, Los Angeles 1 for 7. 2B—Finley. HR—Sh.Green (4th inning, 0 out, 0 on) off M.Morris, Sh.Green (6th inning, 2 out, 0 on) off M.Morris. SB—Womack. SH—Lima. HBP—Cora by M.Morris. T—2:23. A—55,992. U—HP-Meriwether, 1B-Dreckman, 2B-Davis, 3B-O'Nora, LF-Scott, RF-Gibson.

## HOW THEY SCORED

BOTTOM OF 3

Dodgers third. Cora was hit by a pitch. Mayne singled to center, Cora to third. Lima safe on sacrifice plus fielder's choice, Mayne to second. Izturis flied out to left fielder Sanders. Werth fouled out to first baseman Pujols. Finley doubled to left, Cora scored, Mayne scored, Lima to third. Beltre struck out. Runs: 2, Hits: 2, Errors: 0

BOTTOM OF 4

Dodgers fourth. Green homered to center on a 2-0 count. Bradley grounded out, shortstop Renteria to first baseman Pujols. Cora flied out to left fielder Sanders. Mayne grounded out, first baseman Pujols unassisted. Runs: 1, Hits: 1, Errors: 0

BOTTOM OF 6

Dodgers sixth. Finley flied out to left fielder Sanders. Beltre grounded out, shortstop Renteria to first baseman Pujols. Green homered to right on the first pitch. Bradley walked on a full count. Cora singled to center, Bradley to third. Mayne was intentionally walked, Cora to second. Lima struck out. Runs: 1, Hits: 2, Errors: 0

## GAME 4

### ST.LOUIS 6, LOS ANGELES 2

SUNDAY, OCTOBER 10, AT LOS ANGELES

| St. Louis | AB | R | H | BI | BB | SO | PO | A |
|---|---|---|---|---|---|---|---|---|
| Womack, 2b | 5 | 1 | 0 | 0 | 0 | 1 | 0 | 2 |
| L.Walker, rf | 3 | 3 | 2 | 0 | 2 | 0 | 2 | 0 |
| Pujols, 1b | 4 | 1 | 2 | 4 | 1 | 0 | 10 | 1 |
| Rolen, 3b | 2 | 0 | 0 | 0 | 3 | 0 | 0 | 0 |
| Renteria, ss | 3 | 0 | 1 | 1 | 0 | 0 | 3 | 1 |
| Edmonds, cf | 3 | 0 | 0 | 0 | 1 | 3 | 3 | 0 |
| R.Sanders, lf | 4 | 1 | 1 | 1 | 0 | 1 | 3 | 0 |
| Taguchi, lf | 0 | 0 | 0 | 0 | 0 | 0 | 0 | 0 |
| Matheny, c | 4 | 0 | 0 | 0 | 0 | 0 | 5 | 1 |
| Suppan, p | 3 | 0 | 2 | 0 | 0 | 0 | 1 | 3 |
| Mabry, ph | 1 | 0 | 0 | 0 | 0 | 1 | 0 | 0 |
| Tavarez, p | 0 | 0 | 0 | 0 | 0 | 0 | 0 | 0 |
| King, p | 0 | 0 | 0 | 0 | 0 | 0 | 0 | 0 |
| Isringhausen, p | 0 | 0 | 0 | 0 | 0 | 0 | 0 | 0 |
| **TOTALS** | 32 | 6 | 8 | 6 | 7 | 6 | 27 | 8 |

| Los Angeles | AB | R | H | BI | BB | SO | PO | A |
|---|---|---|---|---|---|---|---|---|
| C.Izturis, ss | 4 | 0 | 1 | 0 | 0 | 0 | 3 | 5 |
| Werth, lf | 3 | 2 | 1 | 1 | 1 | 1 | 1 | 0 |
| Finley, cf | 4 | 0 | 1 | 0 | 0 | 0 | 0 | 0 |
| Beltre, 3b | 3 | 0 | 0 | 1 | 0 | 0 | 0 | 1 |
| Sh.Green, 1b | 4 | 0 | 0 | 0 | 0 | 2 | 10 | 1 |
| Bradley, rf | 2 | 0 | 0 | 0 | 2 | 1 | 3 | 1 |
| Cora, 2b | 4 | 0 | 0 | 0 | 0 | 1 | 4 | 5 |
| Mayne, c | 1 | 0 | 0 | 0 | 1 | 0 | 2 | 1 |
| Brazoban, p | 0 | 0 | 0 | 0 | 0 | 0 | 0 | 0 |
| Venafro, p | 0 | 0 | 0 | 0 | 0 | 0 | 0 | 0 |
| Carrara, p | 0 | 0 | 0 | 0 | 0 | 0 | 0 | 0 |
| Grabowski, ph | 1 | 0 | 0 | 0 | 0 | 0 | 0 | 0 |
| Gagne, p | 0 | 0 | 0 | 0 | 0 | 0 | 0 | 0 |
| O.Perez, p | 1 | 0 | 0 | 0 | 0 | 0 | 0 | 1 |
| W.Alvarez, p | 0 | 0 | 0 | 0 | 0 | 0 | 0 | 0 |
| D.Ross, c | 1 | 0 | 0 | 0 | 0 | 0 | 4 | 0 |
| Ventura, ph | 1 | 0 | 0 | 0 | 0 | 0 | 0 | 0 |
| T.Wilson, c | 0 | 0 | 0 | 0 | 0 | 0 | 0 | 0 |
| **TOTALS** | 29 | 2 | 3 | 2 | 4 | 5 | 27 | 15 |

| | | | | |
|---|---|---|---|---|
| St. Louis | 0 1 1 | 3 0 0 | 1 0 0—6 | 8 0 |
| Los Angeles | 1 0 1 | 0 0 0 | 0 0 0—2 | 3 1 |

| St. Louis | IP | H | R | ER | HR | BB | SO |
|---|---|---|---|---|---|---|---|
| Suppan (W) | 7.0 | 2 | 2 | 2 | 1 | 3 | 2 |
| Tavarez | 0.2 | 1 | 0 | 0 | 0 | 0 | 1 |
| King | 0.1 | 0 | 0 | 0 | 0 | 0 | 0 |
| Isringhausen | 1.0 | 0 | 0 | 0 | 0 | 1 | 2 |

| Los Angeles | IP | H | R | ER | HR | BB | SO |
|---|---|---|---|---|---|---|---|
| O.Perez | 2.1 | 3 | 2 | 2 | 1 | 5 | 0 |
| W.Alvarez (L) | 1.2 | 3 | 3 | 3 | 1 | 0 | 2 |
| Brazoban | 2.0 | 1 | 1 | 1 | 0 | 2 | 2 |
| Venafro | 0.1 | 0 | 0 | 0 | 0 | 0 | 1 |
| Carrara | 0.2 | 0 | 0 | 0 | 0 | 0 | 0 |
| Gagne | 2.0 | 1 | 0 | 0 | 0 | 0 | 1 |

Brazoban pitched to 4 batters in the 7th.

E—D.Ross. DP—Los Angeles 2. LOB—St. Louis 7, Los Angeles 5. Scoring Position—St. Louis 3 for 8, Los Angeles 0 for 4. HR—Werth (1st inning,1 out, 0 on) off Suppan, R.Sanders (2nd inning, 1 out, 0 on) off O.Perez, Pujols (4th inning, 2 out, 2 on) off W.Alvarez. SB—L.Walker, Bradley. CS—Edmonds. S—Beltre. PB—D.Ross. HBP—Renteria by Brazoban. T—3:21. A—56,268. U—HP-Dreckman, 1B-Davis, 2B-O'Nora, 3B-Scott, LF-Gibson, RF-Meriwether.

## HOW THEY SCORED

BOTTOM OF 1

Dodgers first. Izturis popped out to first baseman Pujols. Werth homered to center on a full count. Finley grounded out, second baseman Womack to first baseman Pujols. Beltre lined out to shortstop Renteria. Runs: 1, Hits: 1, Errors: 0

TOP OF 2

Cardinals second. Edmonds walked. Edmonds was caught stealing, catcher Mayne to second baseman Cora, Edmonds out. Sanders homered to left on a 1-2 count. Matheny grounded out, shortstop Izturis to first baseman Green. Suppan singled to center. Womack grounded into fielder's choice, pitcher O.Perez to second baseman Cora to shortstop Izturis, Suppan out. Runs: 1, Hits: 2, Errors: 0

TOP OF 3

Cardinals third. Walker walked. Pujols grounded out, third baseman Beltre to first baseman Green, Walker to second. Rolen walked on a full count. Renteria singled to left, Walker scored, Rolen to second. Alvarez pitching. Edmonds struck out. Sanders struck out. Runs: 1, Hits: 1, Errors: 0

BOTTOM OF 3

Dodgers third. Izturis grounded out, shortstop Renteria to first baseman Pujols. Werth walked. Finley singled to right, Werth to third. Beltre hit a sacrifice fly to right fielder Walker, Werth scored. Green struck out. Runs: 1, Hits: 1, Errors: 0

TOP OF 4

Cardinals fourth. Matheny grounded out, second baseman Cora to first baseman Green. Suppan singled to left. Womack grounded into fielder's choice, right fielder Bradley to second baseman Cora to first baseman Green to shortstop Izturis, Suppan out. Walker singled to center, Womack to second. Pujols homered to left on a 3-1 count, Womack scored, Walker scored. Rolen grounded out, shortstop Izturis to first baseman Green. Runs: 3, Hits: 3, Errors: 0

TOP OF 7

Cardinals seventh. Walker walked on four pitches. Walker stole second, on catcher D.Ross' throwing error, Walker to third. Pujols singled to center, Walker scored. Rolen walked on a full count, Pujols to second. On D.Ross' passed ball, Pujols to third. Renteria was hit by a pitch, Rolen to second. Venafro pitching. Edmonds struck out. Carrara pitching. Sanders grounded into a double play, second baseman Cora to shortstop Izturis to first baseman Green, Renteria out. Runs: 1, Hits: 1, Errors: 1

# STATISTICS

## ST. LOUIS CARDINALS' BATTING AND FIELDING AVERAGES

| Player, position | G | AB | R | H | TB | 2B | 3B | HR | RBI | BB | IBB | SO | Avg. | OBP | Slg. | PO | A | E | Avg. |
|---|---|---|---|---|---|---|---|---|---|---|---|---|---|---|---|---|---|---|---|
| | BATTING | | | | | | | | | | | | | | | FIELDING | | | |
| Suppan,p | 1 | 3 | 0 | 2 | 2 | 0 | 0 | 0 | 0 | 0 | 0 | 0 | .667 | .667 | .667 | 1 | 3 | 0 | 1.000 |
| Cedeno,ph | 2 | 2 | 0 | 1 | 1 | 0 | 0 | 0 | 0 | 0 | 0 | 0 | .500 | .500 | .500 | 0 | 0 | 0 | .000 |
| Renteria,ss | 4 | 11 | 4 | 5 | 7 | 2 | 0 | 0 | 4 | 3 | 0 | 1 | .455 | .600 | .636 | 10 | 12 | 0 | 1.000 |
| Pujols,1b | 4 | 15 | 4 | 5 | 11 | 0 | 0 | 2 | 5 | 3 | 0 | 0 | .333 | .444 | .733 | 43 | 1 | 0 | 1.000 |
| Walker,rf | 4 | 15 | 6 | 5 | 12 | 1 | 0 | 2 | 3 | 2 | 0 | 5 | .333 | .444 | .800 | 7 | 0 | 0 | 1.000 |
| Matheny,c | 4 | 14 | 1 | 4 | 7 | 0 | 0 | 1 | 5 | 0 | 0 | 2 | .286 | .286 | .500 | 21 | 1 | 0 | 1.000 |
| Sanders,lf | 4 | 14 | 3 | 4 | 7 | 0 | 0 | 1 | 1 | 0 | 0 | 2 | .286 | .333 | .500 | 14 | 0 | 0 | 1.000 |
| Edmonds,cf | 4 | 15 | 1 | 4 | 7 | 0 | 0 | 1 | 2 | 1 | 0 | 9 | .267 | .313 | .467 | 6 | 0 | 0 | 1.000 |
| Womack,2b | 4 | 19 | 2 | 3 | 5 | 0 | 1 | 0 | 1 | 0 | 0 | 2 | .158 | .158 | .263 | 0 | 12 | 0 | 1.000 |
| Calero,p | 1 | 0 | 0 | 0 | 0 | 0 | 0 | 0 | 0 | 0 | 0 | 0 | .000 | .000 | .000 | 0 | 0 | 0 | .000 |
| Eldred,p | 2 | 0 | 0 | 0 | 0 | 0 | 0 | 0 | 0 | 0 | 0 | 0 | .000 | .000 | .000 | 0 | 0 | 0 | .000 |
| Isringhausen,p | 2 | 0 | 0 | 0 | 0 | 0 | 0 | 0 | 0 | 0 | 0 | 0 | .000 | .000 | .000 | 0 | 0 | 0 | .000 |
| King,p | 3 | 0 | 0 | 0 | 0 | 0 | 0 | 0 | 0 | 0 | 0 | 0 | .000 | .000 | .000 | 0 | 0 | 0 | .000 |
| Kline,p | 2 | 0 | 0 | 0 | 0 | 0 | 0 | 0 | 0 | 0 | 0 | 0 | .000 | .000 | .000 | 0 | 0 | 0 | .000 |
| Taguchi,lf | 1 | 0 | 0 | 0 | 0 | 0 | 0 | 0 | 0 | 0 | 0 | 0 | .000 | .000 | .000 | 0 | 0 | 0 | .000 |
| Tavarez,p | 2 | 0 | 0 | 0 | 0 | 0 | 0 | 0 | 0 | 0 | 0 | 0 | .000 | .000 | .000 | 0 | 0 | 0 | .000 |
| Haren,p | 1 | 1 | 0 | 0 | 0 | 0 | 0 | 0 | 0 | 0 | 0 | 0 | .000 | .000 | .000 | 0 | 0 | 0 | .000 |
| Mabry,ph | 1 | 1 | 0 | 0 | 0 | 0 | 0 | 0 | 0 | 0 | 0 | 1 | .000 | .000 | .000 | 0 | 0 | 0 | .000 |
| Marquis,p | 1 | 1 | 0 | 0 | 0 | 0 | 0 | 0 | 0 | 0 | 0 | 0 | .000 | .000 | .000 | 0 | 0 | 0 | .000 |
| Morris,p | 1 | 2 | 0 | 0 | 0 | 0 | 0 | 0 | 0 | 0 | 0 | 0 | .000 | .000 | .000 | 0 | 2 | 0 | 1.000 |
| Williams,p | 1 | 2 | 0 | 0 | 0 | 0 | 0 | 0 | 0 | 0 | 0 | 0 | .000 | .000 | .000 | 0 | 0 | 0 | .000 |
| Anderson,ph | 3 | 3 | 0 | 0 | 0 | 0 | 0 | 0 | 0 | 0 | 0 | 1 | .000 | .000 | .000 | 0 | 0 | 0 | .000 |
| Rolen,3b | 4 | 12 | 1 | 0 | 0 | 0 | 0 | 0 | 0 | 6 | 0 | 3 | .000 | .333 | .000 | 3 | 3 | 0 | 1.000 |
| Totals | 4 | 130 | 22 | 33 | 59 | 3 | 1 | 7 | 21 | 15 | 0 | 26 | .254 | .345 | .454 | 105 | 34 | 0 | 1.000 |

## LOS ANGELES DODGERS' BATTING AND FIELDING AVERAGES

| Player, position | G | AB | R | H | TB | 2B | 3B | HR | RBI | BB | IBB | SO | Avg. | OBP | Slg. | PO | A | E | Avg. |
|---|---|---|---|---|---|---|---|---|---|---|---|---|---|---|---|---|---|---|---|
| | BATTING | | | | | | | | | | | | | | | FIELDING | | | |
| Wilson,c | 2 | 1 | 1 | 1 | 4 | 0 | 0 | 1 | 1 | 0 | 0 | 0 | 1.000 | 1.000 | 4.000 | 4 | 0 | 0 | 1.000 |
| Mayne,c | 4 | 6 | 1 | 2 | 2 | 0 | 0 | 0 | 0 | 2 | 1 | 0 | .333 | .500 | .333 | 13 | 2 | 0 | 1.000 |
| Werth,lf | 4 | 14 | 3 | 4 | 11 | 1 | 0 | 2 | 3 | 3 | 0 | 4 | .286 | .412 | .786 | 8 | 0 | 0 | 1.000 |
| Bradley,rf | 4 | 11 | 1 | 3 | 7 | 1 | 0 | 1 | 1 | 5 | 0 | 2 | .273 | .500 | .636 | 7 | 1 | 0 | 1.000 |
| Beltre,3b | 4 | 15 | 1 | 4 | 4 | 0 | 0 | 0 | 1 | 0 | 0 | 3 | .267 | .250 | .267 | 4 | 2 | 0 | 1.000 |
| Green,1b | 4 | 16 | 3 | 4 | 13 | 0 | 0 | 3 | 3 | 0 | 0 | 3 | .250 | .250 | .813 | 27 | 1 | 0 | 1.000 |
| Izturis,ss | 4 | 17 | 1 | 3 | 4 | 1 | 0 | 0 | 0 | 1 | 0 | 2 | .176 | .222 | .235 | 8 | 12 | 0 | 1.000 |
| Cora,2b | 4 | 15 | 1 | 2 | 4 | 0 | 1 | 0 | 1 | 0 | 0 | 3 | .133 | .188 | .267 | 8 | 10 | 0 | 1.000 |
| Finley,cf | 4 | 16 | 0 | 2 | 3 | 1 | 0 | 0 | 2 | 1 | 0 | 0 | .125 | .176 | .188 | 11 | 0 | 0 | 1.000 |
| Alvarez,p | 2 | 0 | 0 | 0 | 0 | 0 | 0 | 0 | 0 | 0 | 0 | 0 | .000 | .000 | .000 | 0 | 0 | 0 | .000 |
| Brazoban,p | 2 | 0 | 0 | 0 | 0 | 0 | 0 | 0 | 0 | 0 | 0 | 0 | .000 | .000 | .000 | 0 | 0 | 0 | .000 |
| Carrara,p | 3 | 0 | 0 | 0 | 0 | 0 | 0 | 0 | 0 | 0 | 0 | 0 | .000 | .000 | .000 | 0 | 0 | 0 | .000 |
| Dessens,p | 1 | 0 | 0 | 0 | 0 | 0 | 0 | 0 | 0 | 0 | 0 | 0 | .000 | .000 | .000 | 0 | 0 | 0 | .000 |
| Gagne,p | 2 | 0 | 0 | 0 | 0 | 0 | 0 | 0 | 0 | 0 | 0 | 0 | .000 | .000 | .000 | 0 | 0 | 0 | .000 |
| Hernandez,ph | 1 | 0 | 0 | 0 | 0 | 0 | 0 | 0 | 0 | 1 | 0 | 0 | .000 | 1.000 | .000 | 0 | 0 | 0 | .000 |
| Sanchez,p | 2 | 0 | 0 | 0 | 0 | 0 | 0 | 0 | 0 | 0 | 0 | 0 | .000 | .000 | .000 | 0 | 0 | 0 | .000 |
| Venafro,p | 2 | 0 | 0 | 0 | 0 | 0 | 0 | 0 | 0 | 0 | 0 | 0 | .000 | .000 | .000 | 0 | 0 | 0 | .000 |
| Choi,ph | 1 | 1 | 0 | 0 | 0 | 0 | 0 | 0 | 0 | 0 | 0 | 0 | .000 | .000 | .000 | 0 | 0 | 0 | .000 |
| Grabowski,ph | 3 | 2 | 0 | 0 | 0 | 0 | 0 | 0 | 0 | 1 | 0 | 0 | .000 | .333 | .000 | 0 | 0 | 0 | .000 |
| Lima,p | 1 | 2 | 0 | 0 | 0 | 0 | 0 | 0 | 0 | 0 | 0 | 2 | .000 | .000 | .000 | 0 | 0 | 0 | .000 |
| Perez,p | 2 | 2 | 0 | 0 | 0 | 0 | 0 | 0 | 0 | 0 | 0 | 0 | .000 | .000 | .000 | 0 | 2 | 1 | .667 |
| Weaver,p | 1 | 2 | 0 | 0 | 0 | 0 | 0 | 0 | 0 | 0 | 0 | 0 | .000 | .000 | .000 | 0 | 1 | 1 | .500 |
| Ross,c | 2 | 3 | 0 | 0 | 0 | 0 | 0 | 0 | 0 | 1 | 0 | 0 | .000 | .250 | .000 | 12 | 0 | 1 | .923 |
| Ventura,ph | 3 | 3 | 0 | 0 | 0 | 0 | 0 | 0 | 0 | 0 | 0 | 1 | .000 | .000 | .000 | 0 | 0 | 0 | .000 |
| Totals | 4 | 126 | 12 | 25 | 52 | 4 | 1 | 7 | 12 | 15 | 1 | 20 | .198 | .287 | .413 | 102 | 31 | 3 | .978 |

## ST. LOUIS CARDINALS' PITCHING RECORDS

| Pitcher | G | GS | CG | IP | H | R | ER | HR | BB | IBB | SO | HB | WP | W | L | Pct. | ERA |
|---|---|---|---|---|---|---|---|---|---|---|---|---|---|---|---|---|---|
| King | 3 | 0 | 0 | 2.1 | 0 | 0 | 0 | 0 | 0 | 0 | 1 | 0 | 0 | 0 | 0 | .000 | 0.00 |
| Tavarez | 2 | 0 | 0 | 2.1 | 2 | 0 | 0 | 0 | 0 | 0 | 3 | 0 | 0 | 0 | 0 | .000 | 0.00 |
| Haren | 1 | 0 | 0 | 2.0 | 1 | 0 | 0 | 0 | 1 | 0 | 3 | 0 | 0 | 1 | 0 | 1.000 | 0.00 |
| Kline | 2 | 0 | 0 | 1.1 | 0 | 0 | 0 | 0 | 0 | 0 | 0 | 0 | 0 | 0 | 0 | .000 | 0.00 |
| Calero | 1 | 0 | 0 | 1.0 | 0 | 0 | 0 | 0 | 0 | 0 | 2 | 0 | 0 | 0 | 0 | .000 | 0.00 |
| Eldred | 2 | 0 | 0 | 0.2 | 1 | 0 | 0 | 0 | 2 | 0 | 0 | 0 | 0 | 0 | 0 | .000 | 0.00 |
| Suppan | 1 | 1 | 0 | 7.0 | 2 | 2 | 2 | 1 | 3 | 0 | 2 | 0 | 0 | 1 | 0 | 1.000 | 2.57 |
| Williams | 1 | 1 | 0 | 6.0 | 8 | 2 | 2 | 0 | 1 | 0 | 2 | 0 | 0 | 1 | 0 | 1.000 | 3.00 |
| Isringhausen | 2 | 0 | 0 | 2.0 | 1 | 1 | 1 | 1 | 2 | 0 | 2 | 0 | 0 | 0 | 0 | .000 | 4.50 |
| Morris | 1 | 1 | 0 | 7.0 | 6 | 4 | 4 | 2 | 2 | 1 | 5 | 1 | 0 | 0 | 1 | .000 | 5.14 |
| Marquis | 1 | 1 | 0 | 3.1 | 4 | 3 | 3 | 3 | 4 | 0 | 0 | 0 | 0 | 0 | 0 | .000 | 8.10 |
| Totals | 4 | 4 | 0 | 35.0 | 25 | 12 | 12 | 7 | 15 | 1 | 20 | 1 | 0 | 3 | 1 | .750 | 3.09 |

No shutouts or saves.

## LOS ANGELES DODGERS' PITCHING RECORDS

| Pitcher | G | GS | CG | IP | H | R | ER | HR | BB | IBB | SO | HB | WP | W | L | Pct. | ERA |
|---|---|---|---|---|---|---|---|---|---|---|---|---|---|---|---|---|---|
| Lima | 1 | 1 | 1 | 9.0 | 5 | 0 | 0 | 0 | 1 | 0 | 4 | 0 | 0 | 1 | 0 | 1.000 | 0.00 |
| Gagne | 2 | 0 | 0 | 3.0 | 1 | 0 | 0 | 0 | 1 | 0 | 3 | 0 | 0 | 0 | 0 | .000 | 0.00 |
| Sanchez | 2 | 0 | 0 | 2.0 | 1 | 0 | 0 | 0 | 1 | 0 | 3 | 0 | 0 | 0 | 0 | .000 | 0.00 |
| Venafro | 2 | 0 | 0 | 0.2 | 0 | 0 | 0 | 0 | 0 | 0 | 1 | 0 | 0 | 0 | 0 | .000 | 0.00 |
| Brazoban | 2 | 0 | 0 | 3.0 | 1 | 1 | 1 | 0 | 2 | 0 | 2 | 1 | 0 | 0 | 0 | .000 | 3.00 |
| Dessens | 1 | 0 | 0 | 1.1 | 1 | 1 | 1 | 1 | 0 | 0 | 1 | 0 | 0 | 0 | 0 | .000 | 6.75 |
| Carrara | 3 | 0 | 0 | 2.0 | 4 | 2 | 2 | 1 | 1 | 0 | 1 | 0 | 1 | 0 | 0 | .000 | 9.00 |
| Alvarez | 2 | 0 | 0 | 3.1 | 4 | 4 | 4 | 1 | 0 | 0 | 4 | 0 | 0 | 0 | 1 | .000 | 10.80 |
| Weaver | 1 | 1 | 0 | 4.2 | 8 | 6 | 6 | 0 | 2 | 0 | 4 | 2 | 1 | 0 | 1 | .000 | 11.57 |
| Perez | 2 | 2 | 0 | 5.0 | 8 | 8 | 8 | 4 | 7 | 0 | 3 | 0 | 0 | 0 | 1 | .000 | 14.40 |
| Totals | 4 | 4 | 1 | 34.0 | 33 | 22 | 22 | 7 | 15 | 0 | 26 | 3 | 2 | 1 | 3 | .250 | 5.82 |

No saves. Shutouts- Lima.

## SCORE BY INNINGS

| | | | | | | | | | | |
|---|---|---|---|---|---|---|---|---|---|---|
| St. Louis | 1 | 4 | 6 | 4 | 3 | 0 | 4 | 0 | 0 | —22 |
| Los Angeles | 2 | 0 | 3 | 3 | 1 | 2 | 0 | 0 | 1 | —12 |

## MISCELLANEOUS STATISTICS

Sacrifice hits—Lima, Matheny.
Sacrifice flies—Beltre.
Stolen bases—Bradley 2, Renteria, Sanders, Walker, Womack.
Caught stealing—Edmonds, Renteria.
Double plays—Izturis, Cora and Green 2; Cora, Izturis and Green; Morris, Renteria and Pujols; Renteria and Pujols; Womack, Renteria and Pujols.
Left on bases—St. Louis 5, 8, 5, 7—25; Los Angeles 7, 9, 6, 5—27.
Scoring position—St. Louis 2 for 6, 6 for 15, 0 for 3, 3 for 8—11 for 32; Los Angeles 1 for 5, 0 for 3, 1 for 7, 0 for 4—2 for 19.
Hit by pitcher—by Weaver 2 (Sanders, Walker), by Morris (Cora), by Brazoban (Renteria).
Passed balls—Ross.
Balks—None.
Time of games—3:11, 3:36, 2:23, 3:21—Avg.: 3:07.
Attendance—52,127, 52,228, 55,992, 56,268—216,615.
Umpires—Scott, Dale; Gibson, Greg; Meriwether, Chuck; Dreckman, Bruce; Davis, Gerry; O'Nora, Brian.

# HOUSTON VS. ATLANTA

## RESULTS

| Day | Date | Place | Score |
|---|---|---|---|
| Wed. | Oct. 6 | Atlanta | Houston 9, Atlanta 3 |
| Thu. | Oct. 7 | Atlanta | Atlanta 4, Houston 2 |
| Sat. | Oct. 9 | Houston | Houston 8, Atlanta 5 |
| Sun. | Oct. 10 | Houston | Atlanta 6, Houston 5 |
| Mon. | Oct. 11 | Atlanta | Houston 12, Atlanta 3 |

## BOX SCORES

### GAME 1

**HOUSTON 9, ATLANTA 3**

WEDNESDAY, OCTOBER 6, AT ATLANTA

| Houston | AB | R | H | BI | BB | SO | PO | A |
|---|---|---|---|---|---|---|---|---|
| Biggio, lf | 5 | 1 | 1 | 0 | 0 | 3 | 2 | 0 |
| Qualls, p | 0 | 0 | 0 | 0 | 0 | 0 | 0 | 1 |
| Gallo, p | 0 | 0 | 0 | 0 | 0 | 0 | 0 | 0 |
| C.Beltran, cf | 3 | 3 | 3 | 2 | 0 | 0 | 1 | 0 |
| Lane, rf | 1 | 1 | 1 | 1 | 0 | 0 | 1 | 0 |
| Bagwell, 1b | 5 | 2 | 2 | 1 | 0 | 1 | 11 | 1 |
| Berkman, rf-cf | 5 | 1 | 2 | 2 | 0 | 2 | 1 | 0 |
| Kent, 2b | 5 | 0 | 1 | 1 | 0 | 1 | 1 | 4 |
| Ensberg, 3b | 4 | 0 | 2 | 1 | 0 | 1 | 0 | 3 |
| J.Vizcaino, ss | 4 | 0 | 0 | 0 | 0 | 1 | 0 | 2 |
| A.Everett, ss | 0 | 0 | 0 | 0 | 0 | 0 | 0 | 0 |
| Ausmus, c | 4 | 1 | 1 | 1 | 0 | 2 | 9 | 0 |
| Clemens, p | 2 | 0 | 0 | 0 | 1 | 1 | 1 | 1 |
| O.Palmeiro, ph-lf | 1 | 0 | 0 | 0 | 0 | 0 | 0 | 0 |
| TOTALS | 39 | 9 | 13 | 9 | 1 | 12 | 27 | 12 |

| Atlanta | AB | R | H | RBI | BB | SO | PO | A |
|---|---|---|---|---|---|---|---|---|
| Furcal, ss | 3 | 1 | 1 | 0 | 2 | 1 | 0 | 1 |
| M.Giles, 2b | 5 | 1 | 1 | 1 | 0 | 0 | 1 | 6 |
| J.Drew, rf | 3 | 0 | 0 | 0 | 2 | 1 | 2 | 0 |
| C.Jones, 3b | 4 | 0 | 0 | 0 | 1 | 2 | 0 | 1 |
| Estrada, c | 4 | 0 | 1 | 1 | 0 | 0 | 12 | 1 |
| LaRoche, 1b | 3 | 0 | 0 | 0 | 1 | 1 | 8 | 0 |
| Marrero, ph | 1 | 0 | 0 | 0 | 0 | 1 | 0 | 0 |
| A.Jones, cf | 3 | 1 | 2 | 1 | 1 | 1 | 3 | 0 |
| C.Thomas, lf | 4 | 0 | 2 | 0 | 0 | 1 | 1 | 0 |
| Jar.Wright, p | 1 | 0 | 0 | 0 | 0 | 1 | 0 | 0 |
| Gryboski, p | 0 | 0 | 0 | 0 | 0 | 0 | 0 | 0 |
| D.Wise, ph | 1 | 0 | 0 | 0 | 0 | 0 | 0 | 0 |
| Ju.Cruz, p | 0 | 0 | 0 | 0 | 0 | 0 | 0 | 0 |
| Alfonseca, p | 0 | 0 | 0 | 0 | 0 | 0 | 0 | 0 |
| Ju.Franco, ph | 1 | 0 | 0 | 0 | 0 | 0 | 0 | 0 |
| Reitsma, p | 0 | 0 | 0 | 0 | 0 | 0 | 0 | 0 |
| TOTALS | 33 | 3 | 7 | 3 | 7 | 9 | 27 | 9 |

| | | | | R | H | E |
|---|---|---|---|---|---|---|
| Houston | 0 0 4 | 0 3 0 | 1 0 1 | 9 | 13 | 1 |
| Atlanta | 1 0 0 | 0 1 1 | 0 0 0 | 3 | 7 | 0 |

| Houston | IP | H | R | ER | HR | BB | SO |
|---|---|---|---|---|---|---|---|
| Clemens (W) | 7.0 | 6 | 3 | 2 | 1 | 6 | 7 |
| Qualls | 1.0 | 0 | 0 | 0 | 0 | 1 | 0 |
| Gallo | 1.0 | 1 | 0 | 0 | 0 | 0 | 2 |

| Atlanta | IP | H | R | ER | HR | BB | SO |
|---|---|---|---|---|---|---|---|
| Jar.Wright (L) | 4.1 | 8 | 6 | 6 | 3 | 0 | 6 |
| Gryboski | 0.2 | 2 | 1 | 1 | 0 | 0 | 1 |
| Ju.Cruz | 2.0 | 2 | 1 | 1 | 0 | 1 | 4 |
| Alfonseca | 1.0 | 0 | 0 | 0 | 0 | 0 | 0 |
| Reitsma | 1.0 | 1 | 1 | 1 | 1 | 0 | 1 |

E—Berkman. DP—Atlanta 1. LOB—Houston 5, Atlanta 12. Scoring Position—Houston 3 for 7, Atlanta 0 for 7. 2B—Bagwell, Kent. 3B—Furcal. HR—Ausmus (3rd inning, 0 out, 0 on) off Jar.Wright, Berkman (3rd inning, 2 out, 1 on) off Jar.Wright, C.Beltran (5th inning, 1 out, 1 on) off Jar.Wright, A.Jones (5th inning, 2 out, 0 on) off Clemens, Lane (9th inning, 0 out, 0 on) off Reitsma. SB—Biggio, C.Beltran, M.Giles. CS—Ensberg. S—Estrada. SH—Jar.Wright. WP—Clemens 2. HBP—C.Beltran by Ju.Cruz. T—3:08. A—41,464. U—HP-McClelland, 1B-Cuzzi, 2B-Bell, 3B-Culbreth, LF-Brinkman, RF-Randazzo.

### HOW THEY SCORED

BOTTOM OF 1

Braves first. Furcal was out bunting, pitcher Clemens to first baseman Bagwell. Giles safe on Berkman's error. Giles stole second. On Clemens' wild pitch, Giles to third. J.Drew walked. C.Jones walked on a full count, J.Drew to second. Estrada hit a sacrifice fly to right fielder Berkman, Giles scored. LaRoche grounded out, second baseman Kent to first baseman Bagwell. Runs: 1, Hits: 0, Errors: 1

TOP OF 3

Astros third. Ausmus homered to left on the first pitch. Clemens grounded out, second baseman Giles to first baseman LaRoche. Biggio struck out. Beltran singled to left. Bagwell doubled to center, Beltran scored. Berkman homered to right on a 2-0 count, Bagwell scored. Kent grounded out, second baseman Giles to first baseman LaRoche. Runs: 4, Hits: 4, Errors: 0

TOP OF 5

Astros fifth. Clemens struck out. Biggio infield single to second. Biggio stole second. Beltran homered to center on a full count, Biggio scored. Gryboski pitching. Bagwell singled to left. Berkman struck out. Kent doubled to left, Bagwell scored. Kent to third. Ensberg grounded out, third baseman C.Jones to first baseman LaRoche. Runs: 3, Hits: 4, Errors: 0

BOTTOM OF 5

Braves fifth. Estrada flied out to center fielder Beltran. LaRoche struck out. A.Jones homered to left on the first pitch. Thomas singled to center. Wise pinch-hitting for Gryboski. Wise flied out to left fielder Biggio. Runs: 1, Hits: 2, Errors: 0

BOTTOM OF 6

Braves sixth. Furcal tripled to center. Giles grounded out, shortstop Vizcaino to first baseman Bagwell, Furcal scored. J.Drew grounded out, third baseman Ensberg to first baseman Bagwell. C.Jones struck out. Runs: 1, Hits: 1, Errors: 0

TOP OF 7

Astros seventh. Beltran was hit by a pitch. Bagwell struck out. Berkman singled to center, Beltran to third. Kent popped out to right fielder J.Drew. Ensberg infield single to short, Beltran scored, Berkman to second. Vizcaino struck out. Runs: 1, Hits: 2, Errors: 0

TOP OF 9

Astros ninth. Reitsma pitching. Lane homered to left on the first pitch. Bagwell flied out to center fielder A.Jones. Berkman struck out. Kent flied out to right fielder J.Drew. Runs: 1, Hits: 1, Errors: 0

### GAME 2

**ATLANTA 4, HOUSTON 2**

THURSDAY, OCTOBER 7, AT ATLANTA

| Houston | AB | R | H | BI | BB | SO | PO | A |
|---|---|---|---|---|---|---|---|---|
| Biggio, lf | 3 | 0 | 0 | 0 | 1 | 0 | 1 | 0 |
| Lane, lf | 1 | 0 | 0 | 0 | 0 | 1 | 1 | 0 |
| C.Beltran, cf | 5 | 0 | 0 | 0 | 0 | 3 | 2 | 0 |
| Bagwell, 1b | 5 | 1 | 1 | 1 | 0 | 1 | 12 | 1 |
| Berkman, rf | 5 | 0 | 1 | 0 | 0 | 2 | 0 | 0 |
| Kent, 2b | 4 | 0 | 0 | 0 | 0 | 1 | 2 | 5 |
| Ensberg, 3b | 2 | 0 | 0 | 0 | 2 | 0 | 0 | 2 |
| J.Vizcaino, ss | 3 | 0 | 0 | 0 | 0 | 0 | 2 | 2 |

| Houston | AB | R | H | BI | BB | SO | PO | A |
|---|---|---|---|---|---|---|---|---|
| Lidge, p | 0 | 0 | 0 | 0 | 0 | 0 | 1 | 0 |
| O.Palmeiro, ph | 0 | 0 | 0 | 0 | 0 | 0 | 0 | 0 |
| Ausmus, c | 0 | 0 | 0 | 0 | 0 | 0 | 2 | 0 |
| R.Chavez, c | 3 | 1 | 2 | 1 | 0 | 0 | 7 | 4 |
| Lamb, ph | 1 | 0 | 0 | 0 | 0 | 0 | 0 | 0 |
| Miceli, p | 0 | 0 | 0 | 0 | 0 | 0 | 0 | 0 |
| Oswalt, p | 1 | 0 | 0 | 0 | 1 | 0 | 1 | 1 |
| Bruntlett, ss | 1 | 0 | 0 | 0 | 1 | 0 | 1 | 1 |
| **TOTALS** | 34 | 2 | 4 | 2 | 5 | 8 | 32 | 16 |

| Atlanta | AB | R | H | BI | BB | SO | PO | A |
|---|---|---|---|---|---|---|---|---|
| Furcal, ss | 5 | 1 | 3 | 3 | 0 | 0 | 2 | 4 |
| M.Giles, 2b | 5 | 0 | 1 | 0 | 0 | 1 | 5 | 4 |
| J.Drew, rf | 5 | 0 | 1 | 0 | 0 | 3 | 1 | 0 |
| C.Jones, 3b | 4 | 1 | 0 | 0 | 1 | 0 | 0 | 5 |
| Estrada, c | 3 | 0 | 1 | 0 | 1 | 0 | 6 | 0 |
| Betemit, pr | 0 | 0 | 0 | 0 | 0 | 0 | 0 | 0 |
| Ju.Franco, 1b | 1 | 0 | 0 | 0 | 0 | 0 | 2 | 0 |
| LaRoche, 1b | 4 | 0 | 3 | 1 | 0 | 1 | 11 | 1 |
| N.Green, pr | 0 | 0 | 0 | 0 | 0 | 0 | 0 | 0 |
| E.Perez, c | 1 | 0 | 0 | 0 | 0 | 0 | 2 | 0 |
| A.Jones, cf | 5 | 0 | 1 | 0 | 0 | 1 | 3 | 0 |
| C.Thomas, lf | 5 | 1 | 1 | 0 | 0 | 1 | 0 | 0 |
| Hampton, p | 2 | 0 | 1 | 0 | 0 | 1 | 0 | 1 |
| Gryboski, p | 0 | 0 | 0 | 0 | 0 | 0 | 0 | 0 |
| D.Wise, ph | 1 | 1 | 1 | 0 | 0 | 0 | 0 | 0 |
| Smoltz, p | 1 | 0 | 1 | 0 | 0 | 0 | 1 | 0 |
| Alfonseca, p | 0 | 0 | 0 | 0 | 0 | 0 | 0 | 0 |
| Marrero, ph | 1 | 0 | 0 | 0 | 0 | 0 | 0 | 0 |
| **TOTALS** | 43 | 4 | 14 | 4 | 2 | 8 | 33 | 15 |

| | | | | | | |
|---|---|---|---|---|---|---|
| Houston | 1 0 1 | 0 0 0 | 0 0 0 | 0 0—2 | 4 | 1 |
| Atlanta | 0 0 0 | 0 0 0 | 1 1 0 | 0 2—4 | 14 | 0 |

| Houston | IP | H | R | ER | HR | BB | SO |
|---|---|---|---|---|---|---|---|
| Oswalt | 6.1 | 8 | 1 | 1 | 0 | 1 | 4 |
| Lidge (BS) | 2.2 | 4 | 1 | 1 | 0 | 1 | 3 |
| Miceli (L) | 1.2 | 2 | 2 | 2 | 1 | 0 | 1 |

| Atlanta | IP | H | R | ER | HR | BB | SO |
|---|---|---|---|---|---|---|---|
| Hampton | 6.1 | 4 | 2 | 2 | 2 | 3 | 5 |
| Gryboski | 0.2 | 0 | 0 | 0 | 0 | 0 | 0 |
| Smoltz | 3.0 | 0 | 0 | 0 | 0 | 2 | 3 |
| Alfonseca (W) | 1.0 | 0 | 0 | 0 | 0 | 0 | 0 |

E—R.Chavez. DP—Atlanta 1. LOB—Houston 5, Atlanta 10. Scoring Position—Houston 0 for 4, Atlanta 3 for 13. 2B—LaRoche, D.Wise. HR—Bagwell (1st inning, 2 out, 0 on) off Hampton, R.Chavez (3rd inning, 0 out, 0 on) off Hampton, Furcal (11th inning, 2 out, 1 on) off Miceli. SB—Furcal, C.Thomas. CS—Berkman, J.Drew. SH—O.Palmeiro, Furcal. T—3:27. A—40,075. U—HP-Cuzzi, 1B-Bell, 2B-Culbreth, 3B-Brinkman, LF-Randazzo, RF-McClelland.

## HOW THEY SCORED

TOP OF 1

Astros first. Biggio popped out to second baseman Giles. Beltran grounded out, third baseman C.Jones to first baseman LaRoche. Bagwell homered to right on a full count. Berkman popped out to second baseman Giles. Runs: 1, Hits: 1, Errors: 0

TOP OF 3

Astros third. Chavez homered to left on the first pitch. Oswalt grounded out, shortstop Furcal to first baseman LaRoche. Biggio walked on four pitches. Beltran struck out. Bagwell struck out. Runs: 1, Hits: 1, Errors: 0

BOTTOM OF 7

Braves seventh. Thomas grounded out, second baseman Kent to first baseman Bagwell. Wise pinch-hitting for Gryboski. Wise doubled to right. Furcal singled to center, Wise scored. Lidge pitching. Bruntlett in as shortstop. Furcal stole second, on catcher Chavez's throwing error, Furcal to third. Giles struck out. Furcal was out advancing, catcher Chavez to pitcher Lidge, Furcal out. Runs: 1, Hits: 2, Errors: 1

BOTTOM OF 8

Braves eighth. Lane in as left fielder. J.Drew infield single to second. J.Drew was caught stealing, catcher Chavez to shortstop Bruntlett, J.Drew out. C.Jones walked on a full count. Estrada singled to right, C.Jones to third. Betemit pinch-running for Estrada. LaRoche doubled to center, C.Jones scored, Betemit to third. Green pinch-running for LaRoche. A.Jones grounded into fielder's choice, third baseman Ensberg to catcher Chavez, Betemit out, Green to third. Thomas struck out. Runs: 1, Hits: 3, Errors: 0

BOTTOM OF 11

Braves eleventh. A.Jones struck out. Thomas singled to right. Marrero pinch-hitting for Alfonseca. Marrero fouled out to catcher Ausmus. Thomas stole second. Furcal homered to right on a 1-2 count, Thomas scored. Runs: 2, Hits: 2, Errors: 0

## GAME 3

### HOUSTON 8, ATLANTA 5

SATURDAY, OCTOBER 9, AT HOUSTON

| Atlanta | AB | R | H | BI | BB | SO | PO | A |
|---|---|---|---|---|---|---|---|---|
| Furcal, ss | 5 | 0 | 1 | 0 | 0 | 0 | 2 | 7 |
| M.Giles, 2b | 5 | 0 | 0 | 0 | 0 | 2 | 3 | 4 |
| J.Drew, rf | 4 | 1 | 1 | 0 | 0 | 1 | 1 | 0 |
| C.Jones, 3b | 3 | 1 | 0 | 0 | 1 | 0 | 1 | 0 |
| Estrada, c | 3 | 1 | 1 | 1 | 1 | 2 | 5 | 0 |
| LaRoche, 1b | 3 | 0 | 0 | 0 | 0 | 1 | 7 | 0 |
| Reitsma, p | 0 | 0 | 0 | 0 | 0 | 0 | 1 | 0 |
| D.Wise, ph-lf | 1 | 0 | 0 | 0 | 0 | 1 | 0 | 0 |
| A.Jones, cf | 4 | 2 | 3 | 3 | 0 | 1 | 1 | 0 |
| C.Thomas, lf | 2 | 0 | 1 | 0 | 1 | 0 | 2 | 0 |
| Ju.Cruz, p | 0 | 0 | 0 | 0 | 0 | 0 | 0 | 0 |
| Thomson, p | 0 | 0 | 0 | 0 | 0 | 0 | 0 | 0 |
| P.Byrd, p | 2 | 0 | 1 | 1 | 0 | 1 | 0 | 0 |
| Gryboski, p | 0 | 0 | 0 | 0 | 0 | 0 | 0 | 0 |
| Alfonseca, p | 0 | 0 | 0 | 0 | 0 | 0 | 0 | 0 |
| Martin, p | 0 | 0 | 0 | 0 | 0 | 0 | 0 | 0 |
| Ju.Franco, 1b | 2 | 0 | 0 | 0 | 0 | 1 | 1 | 1 |
| **TOTALS** | 34 | 5 | 8 | 5 | 3 | 10 | 24 | 12 |

| Houston | AB | R | H | BI | BB | SO | PO | A |
|---|---|---|---|---|---|---|---|---|
| Biggio, lf | 3 | 1 | 1 | 0 | 1 | 1 | 0 | 0 |
| Qualls, p | 0 | 0 | 0 | 0 | 0 | 0 | 0 | 0 |
| Lamb, ph | 0 | 0 | 0 | 1 | 0 | 0 | 0 | 0 |
| Springer, p | 0 | 0 | 0 | 0 | 0 | 0 | 0 | 0 |
| Bruntlett, ss | 0 | 0 | 0 | 0 | 0 | 0 | 0 | 0 |
| C.Beltran, cf | 5 | 2 | 2 | 2 | 0 | 0 | 3 | 0 |
| Bagwell, 1b | 4 | 1 | 1 | 0 | 1 | 0 | 9 | 1 |
| Berkman, rf | 3 | 2 | 2 | 1 | 2 | 0 | 1 | 0 |
| Kent, 2b | 3 | 1 | 1 | 1 | 2 | 1 | 1 | 7 |
| Ensberg, 3b | 4 | 0 | 2 | 3 | 1 | 0 | 0 | 0 |
| J.Vizcaino, ss | 4 | 0 | 0 | 0 | 1 | 1 | 2 | 3 |
| Lidge, p | 0 | 0 | 0 | 0 | 0 | 0 | 0 | 0 |
| Ausmus, c | 3 | 1 | 1 | 0 | 1 | 1 | 10 | 0 |
| Backe, p | 1 | 0 | 0 | 0 | 0 | 0 | 1 | 0 |
| O.Palmeiro, ph | 1 | 0 | 1 | 0 | 0 | 0 | 0 | 0 |
| Lane, lf | 1 | 0 | 0 | 0 | 0 | 0 | 0 | 0 |
| **TOTALS** | 32 | 8 | 11 | 8 | 9 | 4 | 27 | 11 |

| | | | | | | |
|---|---|---|---|---|---|---|
| Atlanta | 0 0 0 | 2 0 0 | 0 3 0—5 | 8 | 0 | |
| Houston | 0 0 2 | 0 2 3 | 1 0 x—8 | 11 | 0 | |

| Atlanta | IP | H | R | ER | HR | BB | SO |
|---|---|---|---|---|---|---|---|
| Thomson | 0.1 | 1 | 0 | 0 | 0 | 1 | 0 |
| P.Byrd (L) | 4.1 | 7 | 4 | 4 | 1 | 3 | 3 |
| Gryboski | 0.1 | 0 | 0 | 0 | 0 | 0 | 0 |
| Alfonseca | 0.2 | 1 | 2 | 2 | 0 | 1 | 0 |
| Martin | 0.0 | 2 | 1 | 1 | 0 | 1 | 0 |
| Reitsma | 1.1 | 0 | 1 | 1 | 0 | 1 | 1 |
| Ju.Cruz | 1.0 | 0 | 0 | 0 | 0 | 2 | 0 |

| Houston | IP | H | R | ER | HR | BB | SO |
|---|---|---|---|---|---|---|---|
| Backe (W) | 6.0 | 5 | 2 | 2 | 1 | 2 | 5 |
| Qualls | 1.0 | 1 | 0 | 0 | 0 | 0 | 1 |
| Springer | 1.0 | 2 | 3 | 3 | 1 | 1 | 2 |
| Lidge (S) | 1.0 | 0 | 0 | 0 | 0 | 0 | 2 |

Martin pitched to 3 batters in the 6th.

DP—Houston 1. LOB—Atlanta 6, Houston 11. Scoring Position—Atlanta 2 for 8, Houston 4 for 18. 2B—A.Jones, C.Beltran, Bagwell, Kent, Ensberg. HR—C.Beltran (3rd inning, 0 out, 1 on) off P.Byrd, Estrada (4th inning, 1 out, 0 on) off Backe, A.Jones (8th inning, 2 out, 2 on) off Springer. SB—C.Beltran. S—Lamb. SH—Backe. WP—Reitsma. HBP—C.Thomas by Backe. T—3:19. A—43,547. U—HP-Bell, 1B-Culbreth, 2B-Brinkman, 3B-Randazzo, LF-McClelland, RF-Cuzzi. .

## HOW THEY SCORED

BOTTOM OF 3

Astros third. Biggio singled to center. Beltran homered to right on the first pitch, Biggio scored. Bagwell doubled to left. Berkman popped out to shortstop Furcal. Kent flied out to center fielder A.Jones. Ensberg grounded out, shortstop Furcal to first baseman LaRoche. Runs: 2, Hits: 3, Errors: 0

TOP OF 4

Braves fourth. C.Jones grounded out, second baseman Kent to first baseman Bagwell. Estrada homered to left on a 2-0 count. LaRoche grounded out, second baseman Kent to first baseman Bagwell. A.Jones doubled to left. Thomas was intentionally walked. Byrd singled to center, A.Jones scored, Thomas to third. Furcal grounded into fielder's choice, shortstop Vizcaino to second baseman Kent, Byrd out. Runs: 2, Hits: 3, Errors: 0

BOTTOM OF 5

Astros fifth. Beltran grounded out, second baseman Giles to first baseman LaRoche. Bagwell flied out to left fielder Thomas. Berkman walked. Kent doubled to left, Berkman scored. Ensberg singled to left, Kent scored. Ensberg to second. Vizcaino was intentionally walked. Gryboski pitching. Ausmus fouled out to third baseman C.Jones. Runs: 2, Hits: 2, Errors: 0



BOTTOM OF 6

Astros sixth. Alfonseca pitching. Palmeiro pinch-hitting for Backe. Palmeiro singled to left. Biggio walked, Palmeiro to second. Beltran grounded into fielder's choice, second baseman Giles to shortstop Furcal, Palmeiro to third, Biggio out. Beltran stole second. Bagwell grounded into fielder's choice, shortstop Furcal to catcher Estrada, Palmeiro out. Martin pitching. Berkman singled to left, Beltran scored, Bagwell to second. Kent walked on a full count, Bagwell to third, Berkman to second. Ensberg infield double to third, Bagwell scored, Berkman scored, Kent to third. Reitsma pitching. Franco in as first baseman. Vizcaino struck out. Runs: 3, Hits: 3, Errors: 0

BOTTOM OF 7

Astros seventh. Ausmus walked. On Reitsma's wild pitch, Ausmus to second. Lane grounded out, shortstop Furcal to first baseman Franco, Ausmus to third. Lamb pinch-hitting for Qualls. Lamb hit a sacrifice fly to left fielder Thomas, Ausmus scored. Beltran grounded out, first baseman Franco to pitcher Reitsma. Runs: 1, Hits: 0, Errors: 0

TOP OF 8

Braves eighth. Springer pitching. J.Drew infield single to second. C.Jones walked on a full count, J.Drew to second. Estrada struck out. Wise pinch-hitting for Reitsma. Wise struck out. A.Jones homered to left on a 0-2 count, J.Drew scored, C.Jones scored. Thomas grounded out, second baseman Kent to first baseman Bagwell. Runs: 3, Hits: 2, Errors: 0

## GAME 4

### ATLANTA 6, HOUSTON 5

SUNDAY, OCTOBER 10, AT HOUSTON

| Atlanta | AB | R | H | BI | BB | SO | PO | A |
|---|---|---|---|---|---|---|---|---|
| Furcal, ss | 4 | 1 | 1 | 0 | 0 | 2 | 3 | 4 |
| J.Drew, rf | 4 | 0 | 1 | 1 | 1 | 2 | 3 | 0 |
| M.Giles, 2b | 5 | 0 | 0 | 0 | 0 | 2 | 3 | 7 |
| C.Jones, 3b | 4 | 2 | 2 | 0 | 0 | 0 | 0 | 1 |
| Estrada, c | 3 | 1 | 1 | 0 | 1 | 1 | 3 | 0 |
| N.Green, pr | 0 | 0 | 0 | 0 | 0 | 0 | 0 | 0 |
| Smoltz, p | 0 | 0 | 0 | 0 | 0 | 0 | 1 | 0 |
| A.Jones, cf | 4 | 1 | 3 | 1 | 0 | 0 | 4 | 0 |
| LaRoche, 1b | 3 | 1 | 1 | 3 | 1 | 1 | 8 | 0 |
| Marrero, lf | 3 | 0 | 1 | 0 | 0 | 1 | 0 | 0 |
| Alfonseca, p | 0 | 0 | 0 | 0 | 0 | 0 | 0 | 0 |
| Hampton, p | 0 | 0 | 0 | 0 | 0 | 0 | 0 | 0 |
| E.Perez, c | 1 | 0 | 0 | 0 | 0 | 1 | 1 | 0 |
| Ru.Ortiz, p | 1 | 0 | 0 | 0 | 0 | 1 | 0 | 0 |
| D.Wise, ph | 1 | 0 | 0 | 0 | 0 | 0 | 0 | 0 |
| Gryboski, p | 0 | 0 | 0 | 0 | 0 | 0 | 0 | 0 |
| C.Thomas, ph-lf | 2 | 0 | 0 | 0 | 0 | 1 | 1 | 0 |
| **TOTALS** | 35 | 6 | 10 | 5 | 3 | 12 | 27 | 12 |

| Houston | AB | R | H | BI | BB | SO | PO | A |
|---|---|---|---|---|---|---|---|---|
| Biggio, lf | 4 | 1 | 3 | 3 | 0 | 0 | 0 | 0 |
| Gallo, p | 0 | 0 | 0 | 0 | 0 | 0 | 0 | 0 |
| Miceli, p | 0 | 0 | 0 | 0 | 0 | 0 | 0 | 0 |
| Lidge, p | 0 | 0 | 0 | 0 | 0 | 0 | 0 | 0 |
| O.Palmeiro, ph | 1 | 0 | 0 | 0 | 0 | 0 | 0 | 0 |
| Springer, p | 0 | 0 | 0 | 0 | 0 | 0 | 0 | 0 |
| C.Beltran, cf | 4 | 1 | 1 | 0 | 1 | 1 | 4 | 0 |
| Bagwell, 1b | 4 | 0 | 2 | 1 | 1 | 0 | 7 | 0 |
| A.Everett, pr | 0 | 0 | 0 | 0 | 0 | 0 | 0 | 0 |
| Berkman, rf | 5 | 0 | 2 | 0 | 0 | 2 | 0 | 0 |
| Kent, 2b | 5 | 1 | 1 | 0 | 0 | 1 | 2 | 4 |
| Ensberg, 3b | 4 | 0 | 1 | 0 | 0 | 0 | 0 | 1 |
| J.Vizcaino, ss | 4 | 1 | 1 | 0 | 0 | 0 | 0 | 2 |
| Ausmus, c | 2 | 1 | 1 | 0 | 2 | 0 | 13 | 0 |
| Clemens, p | 1 | 0 | 0 | 1 | 0 | 0 | 0 | 0 |
| Qualls, p | 0 | 0 | 0 | 0 | 0 | 0 | 0 | 1 |
| Lamb, ph | 1 | 0 | 0 | 0 | 0 | 0 | 0 | 0 |
| Lane, lf | 1 | 0 | 1 | 0 | 0 | 0 | 1 | 0 |
| **TOTALS** | 36 | 5 | 13 | 5 | 4 | 4 | 27 | 8 |

| | | | | |
|---|---|---|---|---|
| Atlanta | 0 2 0 | 0 0 3 | 0 0 1—6 | 10 0 |
| Houston | 0 5 0 | 0 0 0 | 0 0 0—5 | 13 0 |

| Atlanta | IP | H | R | ER | HR | BB | SO |
|---|---|---|---|---|---|---|---|
| Ru.Ortiz | 3.0 | 7 | 5 | 5 | 1 | 1 | 1 |
| Gryboski | 2.0 | 1 | 0 | 0 | 0 | 1 | 1 |
| Alfonseca | 1.0 | 1 | 0 | 0 | 0 | 1 | 0 |
| Hampton | 1.0 | 0 | 0 | 0 | 0 | 1 | 1 |
| Smoltz (W) | 2.0 | 4 | 0 | 0 | 0 | 0 | 1 |

| Houston | IP | H | R | ER | HR | BB | SO |
|---|---|---|---|---|---|---|---|
| Clemens | 5.0 | 6 | 2 | 2 | 0 | 2 | 5 |
| Qualls (BS) | 1.0 | 3 | 3 | 3 | 1 | 0 | 1 |
| Gallo | 0.2 | 0 | 0 | 0 | 0 | 0 | 2 |
| Miceli | 0.2 | 0 | 0 | 0 | 0 | 1 | 0 |
| Lidge | 0.2 | 0 | 0 | 0 | 0 | 0 | 1 |
| Springer (L) | 1.0 | 1 | 1 | 1 | 0 | 0 | 3 |

DP—Atlanta 2, Houston 2. LOB—Atlanta 6, Houston 9. Scoring Position—Atlanta 3 for 9, Houston 2 for 9. 2B—A.Jones, Biggio, C.Beltran. HR—Biggio (2nd inning, 2 out, 2 on) off Ru.Ortiz, LaRoche (6th inning, 1 out, 2 on) off Qualls. SB—Furcal 2, J.Drew, A.Jones. S—Clemens. WP—Clemens. HBP—Furcal by Springer. T—3:24. A—43,336. U—HP-Culbreth, 1B-Brinkman, 2B-Randazzo, 3B-McClelland, LF-Cuzzi, RF-Bell.

## HOW THEY SCORED

TOP OF 2

Braves second. C.Jones singled to right. Estrada singled to center, C.Jones to third. A.Jones singled to center, C.Jones scored, Estrada to third. LaRoche grounded into a double play, shortstop Vizcaino to second baseman Kent to first baseman Bagwell, Estrada scored, A.Jones out. Marrero infield single to third. Ortiz struck out. Runs: 2, Hits: 4, Errors: 0

BOTTOM OF 2

Astros second. Kent singled to left. Ensberg singled to center, Kent to second. Vizcaino grounded into fielder's choice, second baseman Giles to shortstop Furcal, Kent to third, Ensberg out. Ausmus walked, Vizcaino to second. Clemens hit a sacrifice fly to center fielder A.Jones, Kent scored. Biggio homered to left on a 3-1 count, Vizcaino scored, Ausmus scored. Beltran doubled to right. Bagwell singled to left, Beltran scored. Berkman struck out. Runs: 5, Hits: 5, Errors: 0

TOP OF 6

Braves sixth. Qualls pitching. C.Jones singled to center. Estrada struck out. A.Jones doubled to left, C.Jones to third. LaRoche homered to center on the first pitch, C.Jones scored, A.Jones scored. Marrero grounded out, pitcher Qualls to first baseman Bagwell. Thomas pinch-hitting for Gryboski. Thomas grounded out, second baseman Kent to first baseman Bagwell. Runs: 3, Hits: 3, Errors: 0

TOP OF 9

Braves ninth. Springer pitching. Perez struck out. Thomas struck out. Furcal was hit by a pitch. Furcal stole second. J.Drew singled to center, Furcal scored. J.Drew stole second. Giles struck out. Runs: 1, Hits: 1, Errors: 0

## GAME 5

### HOUSTON 12, ATLANTA 3

MONDAY, OCTOBER 11, AT ATLANTA

| Houston | AB | R | H | BI | BB | SO | PO | A |
|---|---|---|---|---|---|---|---|---|
| Biggio, lf | 5 | 2 | 3 | 1 | 0 | 0 | 2 | 0 |
| Miceli, p | 0 | 0 | 0 | 0 | 0 | 0 | 0 | 0 |
| Wheeler, p | 0 | 0 | 0 | 0 | 0 | 0 | 0 | 1 |
| C.Beltran, cf | 5 | 3 | 4 | 5 | 0 | 0 | 3 | 0 |
| Bagwell, 1b | 4 | 1 | 1 | 2 | 1 | 1 | 10 | 0 |
| Berkman, rf | 4 | 2 | 2 | 0 | 1 | 0 | 2 | 0 |
| Kent, 2b | 5 | 1 | 2 | 1 | 0 | 1 | 2 | 4 |
| Ensberg, 3b | 5 | 1 | 2 | 1 | 0 | 0 | 0 | 2 |
| J.Vizcaino, ss | 4 | 1 | 1 | 1 | 0 | 0 | 2 | 3 |
| R.Chavez, c | 2 | 0 | 1 | 0 | 0 | 0 | 5 | 0 |
| O.Palmeiro, ph | 1 | 0 | 0 | 0 | 0 | 0 | 0 | 0 |
| Ausmus, c | 0 | 0 | 0 | 0 | 0 | 0 | 0 | 1 |
| Oswalt, p | 2 | 0 | 0 | 0 | 0 | 0 | 0 | 0 |
| Qualls, p | 0 | 0 | 0 | 0 | 0 | 0 | 0 | 0 |
| Lamb, ph | 1 | 0 | 0 | 0 | 0 | 0 | 0 | 0 |
| Gallo, p | 0 | 0 | 0 | 0 | 0 | 0 | 0 | 0 |
| Harville, p | 0 | 0 | 0 | 0 | 0 | 0 | 0 | 0 |
| Lane, ph-lf | 1 | 1 | 1 | 1 | 0 | 0 | 1 | 0 |
| **TOTALS** | 39 | 12 | 17 | 12 | 2 | 2 | 27 | 11 |

| Atlanta | AB | R | H | BI | BB | SO | PO | A |
|---|---|---|---|---|---|---|---|---|
| Furcal, ss | 4 | 2 | 2 | 1 | 1 | 0 | 2 | 4 |
| J.Drew, rf | 4 | 0 | 1 | 0 | 1 | 0 | 1 | 0 |
| C.Jones, 3b | 5 | 0 | 2 | 0 | 0 | 0 | 2 | 1 |
| Estrada, c | 4 | 1 | 2 | 2 | 0 | 0 | 2 | 1 |
| P.Byrd, p | 0 | 0 | 0 | 0 | 0 | 0 | 0 | 0 |
| A.Jones, cf | 3 | 0 | 1 | 0 | 1 | 0 | 1 | 1 |
| LaRoche, 1b | 4 | 0 | 0 | 0 | 0 | 1 | 8 | 2 |
| M.Giles, 2b | 4 | 0 | 1 | 0 | 0 | 1 | 5 | 4 |
| C.Thomas, lf | 3 | 0 | 0 | 0 | 1 | 2 | 4 | 0 |
| Jar.Wright, p | 2 | 0 | 0 | 0 | 0 | 1 | 1 | 2 |
| Gryboski, p | 0 | 0 | 0 | 0 | 0 | 0 | 0 | 0 |
| D.Wise, ph | 1 | 0 | 0 | 0 | 0 | 1 | 0 | 0 |
| Reitsma, p | 0 | 0 | 0 | 0 | 0 | 0 | 0 | 1 |
| Martin, p | 0 | 0 | 0 | 0 | 0 | 0 | 0 | 0 |
| Ju.Cruz, p | 0 | 0 | 0 | 0 | 0 | 0 | 0 | 0 |
| E.Perez, c | 1 | 0 | 0 | 0 | 0 | 0 | 1 | 0 |
| **TOTALS** | 35 | 3 | 9 | 3 | 4 | 6 | 27 | 16 |

| | | | | | |
|---|---|---|---|---|---|
| Houston | 0 2 1 | 0 0 1 | 5 3 0—12 | 17 | 1 |
| Atlanta | 0 0 0 | 0 2 0 | 1 0 0— 3 | 9 | 1 |

| Houston | IP | H | R | ER | HR | BB | SO |
|---|---|---|---|---|---|---|---|
| Oswalt (W) | 5.0 | 7 | 2 | 2 | 2 | 3 | 4 |
| Qualls (HOLD) | 1.0 | 0 | 0 | 0 | 0 | 0 | 1 |
| Gallo | 0.1 | 2 | 1 | 1 | 0 | 1 | 0 |
| Harville | 0.2 | 0 | 0 | 0 | 0 | 0 | 0 |
| Miceli | 1.0 | 0 | 0 | 0 | 0 | 0 | 1 |
| Wheeler | 1.0 | 0 | 0 | 0 | 0 | 0 | 0 |

| Atlanta | IP | H | R | ER | HR | BB | SO |
|---|---|---|---|---|---|---|---|
| Jar.Wright (L) | 5.1 | 6 | 4 | 4 | 2 | 1 | 1 |
| Gryboski | 0.2 | 0 | 0 | 0 | 0 | 0 | 1 |
| Reitsma | 0.2 | 4 | 4 | 4 | 1 | 0 | 0 |
| Martin | 0.1 | 2 | 1 | 1 | 0 | 0 | 0 |
| Ju.Cruz | 0.2 | 4 | 3 | 3 | 0 | 1 | 0 |
| P.Byrd | 1.1 | 1 | 0 | 0 | 0 | 0 | 0 |

E—Bagwell, J.Drew. DP—Houston 1, Atlanta 2. LOB—Houston 4, Atlanta 9. Scoring Position—Houston 5 for 10, Atlanta 1 for 5. 2B—Biggio, Berkman, Kent, Ensberg. HR—C.Beltran (3rd inning, 2 out, 0 on) off Jar.Wright, Furcal (5th inning, 0 out, 0 on) off Oswalt, Estrada (5th inning, 2 out, 0 on) off Oswalt, C.Beltran (6th inning, 0 out, 0 on) off Jar.Wright, Bagwell (7th inning, 2 out, 1 on) off Reitsma. S—J.Vizcaino. SH—R.Chavez. T—3:12. A—54,068. U—HP-Brinkman, 1B-Randazzo, 2B-McClelland, 3B-Cuzzi, LF-Bell, RF-Culbreth.

## HOW THEY SCORED

TOP OF 2

Astros second. Berkman singled to right. Kent doubled to left, Berkman to third. Ensberg grounded out, shortstop Furcal to first baseman LaRoche, Berkman scored, Kent to third. Vizcaino hit a sacrifice fly to left fielder Thomas, Kent scored. Chavez popped out to second baseman Giles. Runs: 2, Hits: 2, Errors: 0

TOP OF 3

Astros third. Oswalt grounded out, first baseman LaRoche to pitcher Wright. Biggio flied out to left fielder Thomas. Beltran homered to center on a 3-1 count. Bagwell flied out to center fielder A.Jones. Runs: 1, Hits: 1, Errors: 0

BOTTOM OF 5

Braves fifth. Furcal homered to center on a 1-1 count. J.Drew grounded out, shortstop Vizcaino to first baseman Bagwell. C.Jones flied out to right fielder Berkman. Estrada homered to right on the first pitch. A.Jones walked on a full count. LaRoche flied out to center fielder Beltran. Runs: 2, Hits: 2, Errors: 0

TOP OF 6

Astros sixth. Beltran homered to right on a 2-2 count. Bagwell struck out. Berkman walked on a full count. Gryboski pitching. Kent struck out. Ensberg flied out to right fielder J.Drew. Runs: 1, Hits: 1, Errors: 0

TOP OF 7

Astros seventh. Reitsma pitching. Vizcaino singled to center. Chavez sacrificed, pitcher Reitsma to second baseman Giles, Vizcaino to second. Lamb pinch-hitting for Qualls. Lamb fouled out to third baseman C.Jones. Biggio singled to right, Vizcaino scored. Biggio to second. On J.Drew's error, Biggio to third. Beltran singled to right, Biggio scored. Bagwell homered to center on a 2-2 count, Beltran scored. Martin pitching. Berkman doubled to left. Kent singled to center, Berkman scored. Kent was out advancing, center fielder A.Jones to catcher Estrada to shortstop Furcal, Kent out. Runs: 5, Hits: 6, Errors: 1

BOTTOM OF 7

Braves seventh. Gallo pitching. Furcal singled to left. J.Drew walked on a full count, Furcal to second. C.Jones flied out to right fielder Berkman, Furcal to third. Estrada singled to center, Furcal scored, J.Drew to second. Harville pitching. A.Jones grounded into a double play, shortstop Vizcaino to second baseman Kent to first baseman Bagwell, Estrada out. Runs: 1, Hits: 2, Errors: 0

TOP OF 8

Astros eighth. Cruz pitching. Ensberg doubled to center. Vizcaino grounded out, second baseman Giles to first baseman LaRoche, Ensberg to third. Palmeiro pinch-hitting for Chavez. Palmeiro lined out to third baseman C.Jones. Lane pinch-hitting for Harville. Lane infield single to third, Ensberg scored. Biggio doubled to left, Lane to third. Beltran singled to center, Lane scored, Biggio scored. Bagwell walked on a full count, Beltran to second. Byrd pitching. Perez in as catcher. Berkman fouled out to catcher Perez. Runs: 3, Hits: 4, Errors: 0

# STATISTICS

## HOUSTON ASTROS' BATTING AND FIELDING AVERAGES

| | | | | | | | | | BATTING | | | | | | | FIELDING | | | |
|---|---|---|---|---|---|---|---|---|---|---|---|---|---|---|---|---|---|---|---|
| **Player, position** | **G** | **AB** | **R** | **H** | **TB** | **2B** | **3B** | **HR** | **RBI** | **BB** | **IBB** | **SO** | **Avg.** | **OBP** | **Slg.** | **PO** | **A** | **E** | **Avg.** |
| Chavez,c | 2 | 5 | 1 | 3 | 6 | 0 | 0 | 1 | 1 | 0 | 0 | 0 | .600 | .600 | 1.200 | 12 | 4 | 1 | .941 |
| Lane,rf-lf-ph | 5 | 5 | 2 | 3 | 6 | 0 | 0 | 1 | 2 | 0 | 0 | 1 | .600 | .600 | 1.200 | 4 | 0 | 0 | 1.000 |
| Beltran,cf | 5 | 22 | 9 | 10 | 24 | 2 | 0 | 4 | 9 | 1 | 0 | 4 | .455 | .500 | 1.091 | 13 | 0 | 0 | 1.000 |
| Berkman,cf-rf | 5 | 22 | 5 | 9 | 13 | 1 | 0 | 1 | 3 | 3 | 0 | 6 | .409 | .480 | .591 | 4 | 0 | 1 | .800 |
| Biggio,lf | 5 | 20 | 5 | 8 | 13 | 2 | 0 | 1 | 4 | 2 | 0 | 4 | .400 | .455 | .650 | 5 | 0 | 0 | 1.000 |
| Ensberg,3b | 5 | 19 | 1 | 7 | 9 | 2 | 0 | 0 | 5 | 3 | 0 | 1 | .368 | .455 | .474 | 0 | 8 | 0 | 1.000 |
| Ausmus,c | 5 | 9 | 3 | 3 | 6 | 0 | 0 | 1 | 1 | 3 | 0 | 3 | .333 | .500 | .667 | 34 | 1 | 0 | 1.000 |
| Bagwell,1b | 5 | 22 | 5 | 7 | 15 | 2 | 0 | 2 | 5 | 3 | 0 | 3 | .318 | .400 | .682 | 49 | 3 | 1 | .981 |
| Palmeiro,lf-ph | 5 | 4 | 0 | 1 | 1 | 0 | 0 | 0 | 0 | 0 | 0 | 0 | .250 | .250 | .250 | 0 | 0 | 0 | .000 |
| Kent,2b | 5 | 22 | 3 | 5 | 8 | 3 | 0 | 0 | 3 | 2 | 0 | 5 | .227 | .292 | .364 | 8 | 24 | 0 | 1.000 |
| Vizcaino,ss | 5 | 19 | 2 | 2 | 2 | 0 | 0 | 0 | 1 | 1 | 1 | 2 | .105 | .143 | .105 | 6 | 12 | 0 | 1.000 |
| Everett,ss-pr | 2 | 0 | 0 | 0 | 0 | 0 | 0 | 0 | 0 | 0 | 0 | 0 | .000 | .000 | .000 | 0 | 0 | 0 | .000 |
| Gallo,p | 3 | 0 | 0 | 0 | 0 | 0 | 0 | 0 | 0 | 0 | 0 | 0 | .000 | .000 | .000 | 0 | 0 | 0 | .000 |
| Harville,p | 1 | 0 | 0 | 0 | 0 | 0 | 0 | 0 | 0 | 0 | 0 | 0 | .000 | .000 | .000 | 0 | 0 | 0 | .000 |
| Lidge,p | 3 | 0 | 0 | 0 | 0 | 0 | 0 | 0 | 0 | 0 | 0 | 0 | .000 | .000 | .000 | 1 | 0 | 0 | 1.000 |
| Miceli,p | 3 | 0 | 0 | 0 | 0 | 0 | 0 | 0 | 0 | 0 | 0 | 0 | .000 | .000 | .000 | 0 | 0 | 0 | .000 |
| Qualls,p | 4 | 0 | 0 | 0 | 0 | 0 | 0 | 0 | 0 | 0 | 0 | 0 | .000 | .000 | .000 | 0 | 2 | 0 | 1.000 |
| Springer,p | 2 | 0 | 0 | 0 | 0 | 0 | 0 | 0 | 0 | 0 | 0 | 0 | .000 | .000 | .000 | 0 | 0 | 0 | .000 |
| Wheeler,p | 1 | 0 | 0 | 0 | 0 | 0 | 0 | 0 | 0 | 0 | 0 | 0 | .000 | .000 | .000 | 0 | 1 | 0 | 1.000 |
| Backe,p | 1 | 1 | 0 | 0 | 0 | 0 | 0 | 0 | 0 | 0 | 0 | 0 | .000 | .000 | .000 | 1 | 0 | 0 | 1.000 |
| Bruntlett,ss | 2 | 1 | 0 | 0 | 0 | 0 | 0 | 0 | 0 | 1 | 0 | 0 | .000 | .500 | .000 | 1 | 1 | 0 | 1.000 |
| Clemens,p | 2 | 3 | 0 | 0 | 0 | 0 | 0 | 0 | 1 | 1 | 0 | 1 | .000 | .200 | .000 | 1 | 1 | 0 | 1.000 |
| Lamb,ph | 4 | 3 | 0 | 0 | 0 | 0 | 0 | 0 | 1 | 0 | 0 | 0 | .000 | .000 | .000 | 0 | 0 | 0 | .000 |
| Oswalt,p | 2 | 3 | 0 | 0 | 0 | 0 | 0 | 0 | 0 | 1 | 0 | 0 | .000 | .250 | .000 | 1 | 1 | 0 | 1.000 |
| **Totals** | 5 | 180 | 36 | 58 | 103 | 12 | 0 | 11 | 36 | 21 | 1 | 30 | .322 | .390 | .572 | 140 | 58 | 3 | .985 |

## ATLANTA BRAVES' BATTING AND FIELDING AVERAGES

| | | | | | | | | | BATTING | | | | | | | FIELDING | | | |
|---|---|---|---|---|---|---|---|---|---|---|---|---|---|---|---|---|---|---|---|
| **Player, position** | **G** | **AB** | **R** | **H** | **TB** | **2B** | **3B** | **HR** | **RBI** | **BB** | **IBB** | **SO** | **Avg.** | **OBP** | **Slg.** | **PO** | **A** | **E** | **Avg.** |
| Smoltz,p | 2 | 1 | 0 | 1 | 1 | 0 | 0 | 0 | 0 | 0 | 0 | 0 | 1.000 | 1.000 | 1.000 | 2 | 0 | 0 | 1.000 |
| Jones,cf | 5 | 19 | 4 | 10 | 18 | 2 | 0 | 2 | 5 | 2 | 0 | 3 | .526 | .571 | .947 | 12 | 1 | 0 | 1.000 |
| Byrd,p | 2 | 2 | 0 | 1 | 1 | 0 | 0 | 0 | 1 | 0 | 0 | 1 | .500 | .500 | .500 | 0 | 0 | 0 | .000 |
| Hampton,p | 2 | 2 | 0 | 1 | 1 | 0 | 0 | 0 | 0 | 0 | 0 | 1 | .500 | .500 | .500 | 0 | 1 | 0 | 1.000 |
| Furcal,ss | 5 | 21 | 5 | 8 | 16 | 0 | 1 | 2 | 4 | 3 | 0 | 3 | .381 | .480 | .762 | 9 | 20 | 0 | 1.000 |
| Estrada,c | 5 | 17 | 3 | 6 | 12 | 0 | 0 | 2 | 4 | 3 | 0 | 3 | .353 | .429 | .706 | 28 | 2 | 0 | 1.000 |
| Thomas,lf-ph | 5 | 16 | 1 | 4 | 4 | 0 | 0 | 0 | 0 | 2 | 1 | 5 | .250 | .368 | .250 | 8 | 0 | 0 | 1.000 |
| LaRoche,1b | 5 | 17 | 1 | 4 | 8 | 1 | 0 | 1 | 4 | 2 | 0 | 5 | .235 | .316 | .471 | 42 | 3 | 0 | 1.000 |
| Drew,rf | 5 | 20 | 1 | 4 | 4 | 0 | 0 | 0 | 1 | 4 | 0 | 7 | .200 | .333 | .200 | 8 | 0 | 1 | .889 |
| Jones,3b | 5 | 20 | 4 | 4 | 4 | 0 | 0 | 0 | 0 | 3 | 0 | 2 | .200 | .304 | .200 | 3 | 8 | 0 | 1.000 |
| Marrero,ph-lf | 3 | 5 | 0 | 1 | 1 | 0 | 0 | 0 | 0 | 0 | 0 | 2 | .200 | .200 | .200 | 0 | 0 | 0 | .000 |
| Wise,ph-lf | 5 | 5 | 1 | 1 | 2 | 1 | 0 | 0 | 0 | 0 | 0 | 2 | .200 | .200 | .400 | 0 | 0 | 0 | .000 |
| Giles,2b | 5 | 24 | 1 | 3 | 3 | 0 | 0 | 0 | 1 | 0 | 0 | 6 | .125 | .125 | .125 | 17 | 25 | 0 | 1.000 |
| Alfonseca,p | 4 | 0 | 0 | 0 | 0 | 0 | 0 | 0 | 0 | 0 | 0 | 0 | .000 | .000 | .000 | 0 | 0 | 0 | .000 |
| Betemit,pr | 1 | 0 | 0 | 0 | 0 | 0 | 0 | 0 | 0 | 0 | 0 | 0 | .000 | .000 | .000 | 0 | 0 | 0 | .000 |
| Cruz,p | 3 | 0 | 0 | 0 | 0 | 0 | 0 | 0 | 0 | 0 | 0 | 0 | .000 | .000 | .000 | 0 | 0 | 0 | .000 |
| Green,pr | 2 | 0 | 0 | 0 | 0 | 0 | 0 | 0 | 0 | 0 | 0 | 0 | .000 | .000 | .000 | 0 | 0 | 0 | .000 |
| Gryboski,p | 5 | 0 | 0 | 0 | 0 | 0 | 0 | 0 | 0 | 0 | 0 | 0 | .000 | .000 | .000 | 0 | 0 | 0 | .000 |
| Martin,p | 2 | 0 | 0 | 0 | 0 | 0 | 0 | 0 | 0 | 0 | 0 | 0 | .000 | .000 | .000 | 0 | 0 | 0 | .000 |
| Reitsma,p | 3 | 0 | 0 | 0 | 0 | 0 | 0 | 0 | 0 | 0 | 0 | 0 | .000 | .000 | .000 | 1 | 1 | 0 | 1.000 |
| Thomson,p | 1 | 0 | 0 | 0 | 0 | 0 | 0 | 0 | 0 | 0 | 0 | 0 | .000 | .000 | .000 | 0 | 0 | 0 | .000 |
| Ortiz,p | 1 | 1 | 0 | 0 | 0 | 0 | 0 | 0 | 0 | 0 | 0 | 1 | .000 | .000 | .000 | 0 | 0 | 0 | .000 |
| Perez,c | 3 | 3 | 0 | 0 | 0 | 0 | 0 | 0 | 0 | 0 | 0 | 1 | .000 | .000 | .000 | 4 | 0 | 0 | 1.000 |
| Wright,p | 2 | 3 | 0 | 0 | 0 | 0 | 0 | 0 | 0 | 0 | 0 | 2 | .000 | .000 | .000 | 1 | 2 | 0 | 1.000 |
| Franco,ph-1b | 3 | 4 | 0 | 0 | 0 | 0 | 0 | 0 | 0 | 0 | 0 | 1 | .000 | .000 | .000 | 3 | 1 | 0 | 1.000 |
| **Totals** | 5 | 180 | 21 | 48 | 75 | 4 | 1 | 7 | 20 | 19 | 1 | 45 | .267 | .342 | .417 | 138 | 64 | 1 | .995 |

## HOUSTON ASTROS' PITCHING RECORDS

| **Pitcher** | **G** | **GS** | **CG** | **IP** | **H** | **R** | **ER** | **HR** | **BB** | **IBB** | **SO** | **HB** | **WP** | **W** | **L** | **Pct.** | **ERA** |
|---|---|---|---|---|---|---|---|---|---|---|---|---|---|---|---|---|---|
| Wheeler | 1 | 0 | 0 | 1.0 | 0 | 0 | 0 | 0 | 0 | 0 | 0 | 0 | 0 | 0 | 0 | .000 | 0.00 |
| Harville | 1 | 0 | 0 | 0.2 | 0 | 0 | 0 | 0 | 0 | 0 | 0 | 0 | 0 | 0 | 0 | .000 | 0.00 |
| Lidge | 3 | 0 | 0 | 4.1 | 4 | 1 | 1 | 0 | 1 | 0 | 6 | 0 | 0 | 0 | 0 | .000 | 2.08 |
| Oswalt | 2 | 2 | 0 | 11.1 | 15 | 3 | 3 | 2 | 4 | 0 | 8 | 0 | 0 | 1 | 0 | 1.000 | 2.38 |
| Clemens | 2 | 2 | 0 | 12.0 | 12 | 5 | 4 | 1 | 8 | 0 | 12 | 0 | 3 | 1 | 0 | 1.000 | 3.00 |
| Backe | 1 | 1 | 0 | 6.0 | 5 | 2 | 2 | 1 | 2 | 1 | 5 | 1 | 0 | 1 | 0 | 1.000 | 3.00 |
| Gallo | 3 | 0 | 0 | 2.0 | 3 | 1 | 1 | 0 | 1 | 0 | 4 | 0 | 0 | 0 | 0 | .000 | 4.50 |
| Miceli | 3 | 0 | 0 | 3.1 | 2 | 2 | 2 | 1 | 1 | 0 | 2 | 0 | 0 | 0 | 1 | .000 | 5.40 |
| Qualls | 4 | 0 | 0 | 4.0 | 4 | 3 | 3 | 1 | 1 | 0 | 3 | 0 | 0 | 0 | 0 | .000 | 6.75 |
| Springer | 2 | 0 | 0 | 2.0 | 3 | 4 | 4 | 1 | 1 | 0 | 5 | 1 | 0 | 0 | 1 | .000 | 18.00 |
| **Totals** | 5 | 5 | 0 | 46.2 | 48 | 21 | 20 | 7 | 19 | 1 | 45 | 2 | 3 | 3 | 2 | .600 | 3.86 |

No shutouts. Saves- Lidge.

## ATLANTA BRAVES' PITCHING RECORDS

| Pitcher | G | GS | CG | IP | H | R | ER | HR | BB | IBB | SO | HB | WP | W | L | Pct. | ERA |
|---|---|---|---|---|---|---|---|---|---|---|---|---|---|---|---|---|---|
| Smoltz | 2 | 0 | 0 | 5.0 | 4 | 0 | 0 | 0 | 2 | 0 | 4 | 0 | 0 | 1 | 0 | 1.000 | 0.00 |
| Thomson | 1 | 1 | 0 | 0.1 | 1 | 0 | 0 | 0 | 1 | 0 | 0 | 0 | 0 | 0 | 0 | .000 | 0.00 |
| Gryboski | 5 | 0 | 0 | 4.1 | 3 | 1 | 1 | 0 | 1 | 0 | 3 | 0 | 0 | 0 | 0 | .000 | 2.08 |
| Hampton | 2 | 1 | 0 | 7.1 | 4 | 2 | 2 | 2 | 4 | 0 | 6 | 0 | 0 | 0 | 0 | .000 | 2.45 |
| Alfonseca | 4 | 0 | 0 | 3.2 | 2 | 2 | 2 | 0 | 2 | 0 | 0 | 0 | 0 | 1 | 0 | 1.000 | 4.91 |
| Byrd | 2 | 0 | 0 | 5.2 | 8 | 4 | 4 | 1 | 3 | 1 | 3 | 0 | 0 | 0 | 1 | .000 | 6.35 |
| Wright | 2 | 2 | 0 | 9.2 | 14 | 10 | 10 | 5 | 1 | 0 | 7 | 0 | 0 | 0 | 2 | .000 | 9.31 |
| Cruz | 3 | 0 | 0 | 3.2 | 6 | 4 | 4 | 0 | 4 | 0 | 4 | 1 | 0 | 0 | 0 | .000 | 9.82 |
| Ortiz | 1 | 1 | 0 | 3.0 | 7 | 5 | 5 | 1 | 1 | 0 | 1 | 0 | 0 | 0 | 0 | .000 | 15.00 |
| Reitsma | 3 | 0 | 0 | 3.0 | 5 | 6 | 6 | 2 | 1 | 0 | 2 | 0 | 1 | 0 | 0 | .000 | 18.00 |
| Martin | 2 | 0 | 0 | 0.1 | 4 | 2 | 2 | 0 | 1 | 0 | 0 | 0 | 0 | 0 | 0 | .000 | 54.00 |
| **Totals** | 5 | 5 | 0 | 46.0 | 58 | 36 | 36 | 11 | 21 | 1 | 30 | 1 | 1 | 2 | 3 | .400 | 7.04 |

No shutouts or saves.

## SCORE BY INNINGS

| | | | | | | | | | | | |
|---|---|---|---|---|---|---|---|---|---|---|---|
| Houston | 1 | 7 | 8 | 0 | 5 | 4 | 7 | 3 | 1 | 0 | 0—36 |
| Atlanta | 1 | 2 | 0 | 2 | 3 | 4 | 2 | 4 | 1 | 0 | 2—21 |

## MISCELLANEOUS STATISTICS

Sacrifice hits—Backe, Chavez, Furcal, Palmeiro, Wright.
Sacrifice flies—Clemens, Estrada, Lamb, Vizcaino.
Stolen bases—Furcal 3, Beltran 2, Biggio, Drew, Giles, Jones, Thomas.
Caught stealing—Berkman, Drew, Ensberg.
Double plays—Jones, Giles and LaRoche 3; Vizcaino, Kent and Bagwell 3; Furcal, Giles and LaRoche 2; Furcal and LaRoche; Vizcaino and Bagwell.
Left on bases—Houston 5, 5, 11, 9, 4—34; Atlanta 12, 10, 6, 6, 9—43.
Scoring position—Houston 3 for 7, 0 for 4, 4 for 18, 2 for 9, 5 for 10—14 for 48; Atlanta 0 for 7, 3 for 13, 2 for 8, 3 for 9, 1 for 5—9 for 42.
Hit by pitcher—by Springer (Furcal), by Cruz (Beltran), by Backe (Thomas).
Passed balls—None.
Balks—None.
Time of games—3:08, 3:27, 3:19, 3:24, 3:12—Avg.: 3:18.
Attendance—41,464, 40,075, 43,547, 43,336, 54,068—222,490.
Umpires—McClelland, Tim; Cuzzi, Phil; Bell, Wally; Culbreth, Fieldin; Brinkman, Joe; Randazzo, Tony.

# A.L. CHAMPIONSHIP SERIES

## BOSTON VS. NEW YORK

### RESULTS

| Day | Date | Place | Score |
|---|---|---|---|
| Tue. | Oct. 12 | New York | New York 10, Boston 7 |
| Wed. | Oct. 13 | New York | New York 3, Boston 1 |
| Sat. | Oct. 16 | Boston | New York 19, Boston 8 |
| Sun. | Oct. 17 | Boston | Boston 6, New York 4 |
| Mon. | Oct 18 | Boston | Boston 5, New York 4 |
| Tue. | Oct. 19 | New York | Boston 4, New York 2 |
| Wed. | Oct 20 | New York | Boston 10, New York 3 |

### BOX SCORES

### GAME 1

**NEW YORK 10, BOSTON 7**

TUESDAY, OCTOBER 12, AT NEW YORK

| Boston | AB | R | H | BI | BB | SO | PO | A |
|---|---|---|---|---|---|---|---|---|
| Damon, cf | 4 | 0 | 0 | 0 | 0 | 4 | 2 | 0 |
| Bellhorn, 2b | 4 | 1 | 1 | 0 | 0 | 1 | 1 | 6 |
| M.Ramirez, lf | 4 | 1 | 1 | 0 | 0 | 1 | 5 | 0 |
| D.Ortiz, dh | 4 | 1 | 2 | 2 | 0 | 1 | 0 | 0 |
| Millar, 1b | 4 | 1 | 1 | 2 | 0 | 1 | 8 | 0 |
| Nixon, rf | 4 | 1 | 1 | 1 | 0 | 0 | 2 | 0 |
| Varitek, c | 4 | 1 | 2 | 2 | 0 | 1 | 3 | 0 |
| O.Cabrera, ss | 4 | 0 | 1 | 0 | 0 | 1 | 2 | 2 |
| Mueller, 3b | 4 | 1 | 1 | 0 | 0 | 0 | 1 | 1 |
| Schilling, p | 0 | 0 | 0 | 0 | 0 | 0 | 0 | 0 |
| Leskanic, p | 0 | 0 | 0 | 0 | 0 | 0 | 0 | 0 |
| Mendoza, p | 0 | 0 | 0 | 0 | 0 | 0 | 0 | 0 |
| Wakefield, p | 0 | 0 | 0 | 0 | 0 | 0 | 0 | 0 |
| Embree, p | 0 | 0 | 0 | 0 | 0 | 0 | 0 | 0 |
| Timlin, p | 0 | 0 | 0 | 0 | 0 | 0 | 0 | 0 |
| Foulke, p | 0 | 0 | 0 | 0 | 0 | 0 | 0 | 0 |
| **TOTALS** | 36 | 7 | 10 | 7 | 0 | 10 | 24 | 9 |

| NY Yankees | AB | R | H | BI | BB | SO | PO | A |
|---|---|---|---|---|---|---|---|---|
| Jeter, ss | 4 | 1 | 1 | 0 | 1 | 0 | 5 | 3 |
| A.Rodriguez, 3b | 5 | 2 | 2 | 0 | 0 | 1 | 0 | 0 |
| Sheffield, rf | 4 | 4 | 3 | 0 | 1 | 1 | 1 | 0 |
| H.Matsui, lf | 5 | 2 | 3 | 5 | 0 | 0 | 3 | 0 |
| B.Williams, cf | 5 | 0 | 2 | 3 | 0 | 0 | 1 | 0 |
| Posada, c | 3 | 0 | 0 | 1 | 0 | 0 | 9 | 1 |
| Olerud, 1b | 3 | 0 | 1 | 0 | 1 | 0 | 6 | 2 |
| Cairo, 2b | 4 | 0 | 1 | 0 | 0 | 0 | 0 | 0 |
| Lofton, dh | 3 | 1 | 1 | 1 | 1 | 1 | 0 | 0 |
| Mussina, p | 0 | 0 | 0 | 0 | 0 | 0 | 2 | 1 |
| Sturtze, p | 0 | 0 | 0 | 0 | 0 | 0 | 0 | 0 |
| Gordon, p | 0 | 0 | 0 | 0 | 0 | 0 | 0 | 0 |
| M.Rivera, p | 0 | 0 | 0 | 0 | 0 | 0 | 0 | 1 |
| **TOTALS** | 36 | 10 | 14 | 10 | 4 | 3 | 27 | 8 |

| | | | | | |
|---|---|---|---|---|---|
| Boston | 0 0 0 | 0 0 0 | 5 2 0— | 7 | 10 | 0 |
| NY Yankees | 2 0 4 | 0 0 2 | 0 2 x— | 10 | 14 | 0 |

| Boston | IP | H | R | ER | HR | BB | SO |
|---|---|---|---|---|---|---|---|
| Schilling (L) | 3.0 | 6 | 6 | 6 | 0 | 2 | 1 |
| Leskanic | 1.0 | 0 | 0 | 0 | 0 | 2 | 1 |
| Mendoza | 1.0 | 1 | 0 | 0 | 0 | 0 | 0 |
| Wakefield | 1.0 | 3 | 2 | 2 | 1 | 0 | 1 |
| Embree | 1.0 | 1 | 0 | 0 | 0 | 0 | 0 |
| Timlin | 0.2 | 3 | 2 | 2 | 0 | 0 | 0 |
| Foulke | 0.1 | 0 | 0 | 0 | 0 | 0 | 0 |

| NY Yankees | IP | H | R | ER | HR | BB | SO |
|---|---|---|---|---|---|---|---|
| Mussina (W) | 6.2 | 4 | 4 | 4 | 0 | 0 | 8 |
| Sturtze | 0.1 | 1 | 1 | 1 | 1 | 0 | 1 |
| Gordon (HOLD) | 0.2 | 3 | 2 | 2 | 0 | 0 | 1 |
| M.Rivera (S) | 1.1 | 2 | 0 | 0 | 0 | 0 | 0 |

DP—Boston 1. LOB—Boston 2, NY Yankees 8. Scoring Position—Boston 4 for 7, NY Yankees 5 for 11. 2B—Bellhorn, Millar, Sheffield 2, H.Matsui 2, B.Williams. 3B—D.Ortiz. HR—Lofton (6th inning, 0 out, 0 on) off Wakefield, Varitek (7th inning, 2 out, 1 on) off Sturtze. S—Posada. PB—Posada. HBP—Posada by Mendoza. T—3:20. A—56,135. U—HP-Marsh, 1B-Nelson, 2B-Hirschbeck, 3B-Joyce, LF-Kellogg, RF-West.

### HOW THEY SCORED

BOTTOM OF 1

Yankees first. Jeter flied out to right fielder Nixon. Rodriguez flied out to right fielder Nixon. Sheffield doubled to left. Matsui doubled to left, Sheffield scored. Williams singled to center, Matsui scored. Posada grounded out, second baseman Bellhorn to first baseman Millar. Runs: 2, Hits: 3, Errors: 0

BOTTOM OF 3

Yankees third. Jeter singled to center. Rodriguez infield single to third, Jeter to second. Sheffield walked on a full count, Jeter to third, Rodriguez to second. Matsui doubled to right, Jeter scored, Rodriguez scored, Sheffield scored. Williams grounded out, second baseman Bellhorn to first baseman Millar, Matsui to third. Posada hit a sacrifice fly to center fielder Damon, Matsui scored. Olerud walked on four pitches. Cairo flied out to center fielder Damon. Runs: 4, Hits: 3, Errors: 0

BOTTOM OF 6

Yankees sixth. Wakefield pitching. Lofton homered to right on a 2-2 count. Jeter grounded out, third baseman Mueller to first baseman Millar. Rodriguez struck out. Sheffield doubled to center. Matsui singled to right, Sheffield scored. Williams flied out to left fielder Ramirez. Runs: 2, Hits: 3, Errors: 0

TOP OF 7

Red Sox seventh. Damon struck out. Bellhorn doubled to left. Ramirez grounded out, shortstop Jeter to first baseman Olerud. Ortiz singled to right, Bellhorn to third. Millar doubled to left, Bellhorn scored, Ortiz scored. On Posada's passed ball, Millar to third. Nixon singled to right, Millar scored. Sturtze pitching. Varitek homered to right on a 0-2 count, Nixon scored. Cabrera struck out. Runs: 5, Hits: 5, Errors: 0

TOP OF 8

Red Sox eighth. Gordon pitching. Mueller infield single to second. Damon struck out. Bellhorn flied out to left fielder Matsui. Ramirez singled to center, Mueller to third. Ortiz tripled to center, Mueller scored, Ramirez scored. Rivera pitching. Millar popped out to shortstop Jeter. Runs: 2, Hits: 3, Errors: 0

BOTTOM OF 8

Yankees eighth. Timlin pitching. Jeter grounded out, shortstop Cabrera to first baseman Millar. Rodriguez singled to left. Sheffield singled to left, Rodriguez to second. Matsui popped out to shortstop Cabrera. Williams doubled to left, Rodriguez scored, Sheffield scored. Williams to third. Foulke pitching. Posada lined out to third baseman Mueller. Runs: 2, Hits: 3, Errors: 0

### GAME 2

**NEW YORK 3, BOSTON 1**

WEDNESDAY, OCTOBER 13, AT NEW YORK

| Boston | AB | R | H | BI | BB | SO | PO | A |
|---|---|---|---|---|---|---|---|---|
| Damon, cf | 4 | 0 | 0 | 0 | 0 | 1 | 3 | 0 |
| Bellhorn, 2b | 4 | 0 | 0 | 0 | 0 | 1 | 1 | 2 |
| M.Ramirez, lf | 4 | 0 | 1 | 0 | 0 | 1 | 1 | 0 |
| D.Ortiz, dh | 3 | 0 | 1 | 0 | 1 | 1 | 0 | 0 |
| Millar, 1b | 4 | 0 | 0 | 0 | 0 | 1 | 5 | 1 |

| Boston | AB | R | H | BI | BB | SO | PO | A |
|---|---|---|---|---|---|---|---|---|
| Nixon, rf | 3 | 1 | 1 | 0 | 0 | 0 | 2 | 0 |
| Varitek, c. | 3 | 0 | 1 | 0 | 0 | 0 | 8 | 0 |
| O.Cabrera, ss | 3 | 0 | 1 | 1 | 0 | 1 | 1 | 2 |
| Mueller, 3b | 3 | 0 | 0 | 0 | 0 | 0 | 2 | 0 |
| P.Martinez, p | 0 | 0 | 0 | 0 | 0 | 0 | 1 | 0 |
| Timlin, p | 0 | 0 | 0 | 0 | 0 | 0 | 0 | 0 |
| Embree, p | 0 | 0 | 0 | 0 | 0 | 0 | 0 | 0 |
| Foulke, p | 0 | 0 | 0 | 0 | 0 | 0 | 0 | 0 |
| **TOTALS** | 31 | 1 | 5 | 1 | 1 | 6 | 24 | 5 |

| NY Yankees | AB | R | H | BI | BB | SO | PO | A |
|---|---|---|---|---|---|---|---|---|
| Jeter, ss | 3 | 1 | 0 | 0 | 2 | 0 | 2 | 2 |
| A.Rodriguez, 3b | 4 | 0 | 1 | 0 | 0 | 1 | 1 | 1 |
| Sheffield, rf | 4 | 0 | 2 | 1 | 0 | 1 | 0 | 0 |
| H.Matsui, lf | 4 | 0 | 1 | 0 | 0 | 2 | 2 | 0 |
| B.Williams, cf | 4 | 0 | 0 | 0 | 0 | 1 | 3 | 0 |
| Posada, c | 2 | 1 | 1 | 0 | 2 | 0 | 6 | 0 |
| Olerud, 1b | 4 | 1 | 1 | 2 | 0 | 0 | 11 | 0 |
| Cairo, 2b | 2 | 0 | 0 | 0 | 1 | 1 | 2 | 4 |
| Lofton, dh | 4 | 0 | 1 | 0 | 0 | 2 | 0 | 0 |
| Lieber, p | 0 | 0 | 0 | 0 | 0 | 0 | 0 | 2 |
| Gordon, p | 0 | 0 | 0 | 0 | 0 | 0 | 0 | 0 |
| M.Rivera, p | 0 | 0 | 0 | 0 | 0 | 0 | 0 | 0 |
| **TOTALS** | 31 | 3 | 7 | 3 | 5 | 8 | 27 | 9 |

| | | | | |
|---|---|---|---|---|
| Boston | 0 0 0 | 0 0 0 | 0 1 0 | —1 5 0 |
| NY Yankees | 1 0 0 | 0 0 2 | 0 0 x | —3 7 0 |

| Boston | IP | H | R | ER | HR | BB | SO |
|---|---|---|---|---|---|---|---|
| P.Martinez (L) | 6.0 | 4 | 3 | 3 | 1 | 4 | 7 |
| Timlin | 0.2 | 1 | 0 | 0 | 0 | 0 | 0 |
| Embree | 0.2 | 2 | 0 | 0 | 0 | 0 | 0 |
| Foulke | 0.2 | 0 | 0 | 0 | 0 | 1 | 1 |

| NY Yankees | IP | H | R | ER | HR | BB | SO |
|---|---|---|---|---|---|---|---|
| Lieber (W) | 7.0 | 3 | 1 | 1 | 0 | 1 | 3 |
| Gordon (HOLD) | 0.2 | 1 | 0 | 0 | 0 | 0 | 0 |
| M.Rivera (S) | 1.1 | 1 | 0 | 0 | 0 | 0 | 3 |

Lieber pitched to 1 batter in the 8th.

DP—NY Yankees 1. LOB—Boston 4, NY Yankees 11. Scoring Position—Boston 0 for 7, NY Yankees 1 for 9. 2B—M.Ramirez, Varitek. HR—Olerud (6th inning, 1 out, 1 on) off P.Martinez. SB—Jeter. HBP—A.Rodriguez by P.Martinez, Cairo by Foulke. T—3:15. A—56,136. U—HP-Nelson, 1B-Hirschbeck, 2B-Joyce, 3B-Kellogg, LF-West, RF-Marsh.

## HOW THEY SCORED

BOTTOM OF 1

Yankees first. Jeter walked on four pitches. Jeter stole second. Rodriguez was hit by a pitch. Sheffield singled to center, Jeter scored, Rodriguez to second. Matsui struck out. Williams struck out. Posada grounded out, second baseman Bellhorn to first baseman Millar. Runs: 1, Hits: 1, Errors: 0

BOTTOM OF 6

Yankees sixth. Williams flied out to center fielder Damon. Posada walked. Olerud homered to right on a 1-2 count, Posada scored. Cairo struck out. Lofton popped out to third baseman Mueller. Runs: 2, Hits: 1, Errors: 0

TOP OF 8

Red Sox eighth. Nixon singled to right. Gordon pitching. Varitek doubled to center, Nixon to third. Cabrera grounded out, shortstop Jeter to first baseman Olerud, Nixon scored. Mueller grounded out, second baseman Cairo to first baseman Olerud, Varitek to third. Rivera pitching. Damon struck out. Runs: 1, Hits: 2, Errors: 0

## GAME 3

### NEW YORK 19, BOSTON 8

SATURDAY, OCTOBER 16, AT BOSTON

| NY Yankees | AB | R | H | BI | BB | SO | PO | A |
|---|---|---|---|---|---|---|---|---|
| Jeter, ss | 4 | 2 | 1 | 0 | 2 | 0 | 0 | 2 |
| A.Rodriguez, 3b | 5 | 5 | 3 | 3 | 1 | 0 | 1 | 1 |
| Sheffield, rf | 5 | 3 | 4 | 4 | 1 | 0 | 2 | 1 |
| Bu.Crosby, pr-rf | 0 | 1 | 0 | 0 | 0 | 0 | 0 | 0 |
| H.Matsui, lf | 6 | 5 | 5 | 5 | 0 | 0 | 1 | 0 |
| B.Williams, cf | 6 | 1 | 4 | 3 | 0 | 1 | 4 | 1 |
| Posada, c | 5 | 1 | 2 | 1 | 1 | 0 | 9 | 0 |
| Sierra, dh | 6 | 0 | 2 | 2 | 0 | 2 | 0 | 0 |
| Olerud, 1b | 4 | 0 | 0 | 0 | 0 | 0 | 6 | 1 |
| T.Clark, 1b | 2 | 0 | 0 | 0 | 0 | 1 | 1 | 0 |
| Cairo, 2b | 4 | 1 | 1 | 0 | 0 | 1 | 2 | 3 |
| K.Brown, p | 0 | 0 | 0 | 0 | 0 | 0 | 0 | 0 |
| J.Vazquez, p | 0 | 0 | 0 | 0 | 0 | 0 | 1 | 0 |
| Quantrill, p | 0 | 0 | 0 | 0 | 0 | 0 | 0 | 0 |
| Gordon, p | 0 | 0 | 0 | 0 | 0 | 0 | 0 | 0 |
| **TOTALS** | 47 | 19 | 22 | 18 | 5 | 5 | 27 | 9 |

| Boston | AB | R | H | BI | BB | SO | PO | A |
|---|---|---|---|---|---|---|---|---|
| Damon, cf | 5 | 1 | 1 | 1 | 0 | 0 | 4 | 0 |
| Bellhorn, 2b | 4 | 0 | 0 | 0 | 1 | 4 | 1 | 2 |
| M.Ramirez, lf | 4 | 0 | 1 | 0 | 1 | 1 | 1 | 0 |
| D.Ortiz, dh | 5 | 1 | 3 | 0 | 0 | 1 | 0 | 0 |
| Varitek, c | 3 | 3 | 2 | 2 | 1 | 0 | 2 | 0 |
| Mirabelli, c | 1 | 0 | 0 | 0 | 0 | 0 | 3 | 0 |
| Nixon, rf | 5 | 1 | 2 | 2 | 0 | 1 | 2 | 0 |
| Millar, 1b | 5 | 1 | 1 | 0 | 0 | 1 | 8 | 0 |
| Mueller, 3b | 4 | 1 | 2 | 0 | 1 | 0 | 1 | 1 |
| O.Cabrera, ss | 4 | 0 | 3 | 2 | 0 | 0 | 5 | 5 |
| Arroyo, p | 0 | 0 | 0 | 0 | 0 | 0 | 0 | 0 |
| Mendoza, p | 0 | 0 | 0 | 0 | 0 | 0 | 0 | 0 |
| Leskanic, p | 0 | 0 | 0 | 0 | 0 | 0 | 0 | 0 |
| Wakefield, p | 0 | 0 | 0 | 0 | 0 | 0 | 0 | 0 |
| Embree, p | 0 | 0 | 0 | 0 | 0 | 0 | 0 | 0 |
| M.Myers, p | 0 | 0 | 0 | 0 | 0 | 0 | 0 | 0 |
| **TOTALS** | 40 | 8 | 15 | 7 | 4 | 8 | 27 | 8 |

| | | | | |
|---|---|---|---|---|
| NY Yankees | 3 0 3 | 5 2 0 | 4 0 2 | —19 22 1 |
| Boston | 0 4 2 | 0 0 0 | 2 0 0 | — 8 15 0 |

| NY Yankees | IP | H | R | ER | HR | BB | SO |
|---|---|---|---|---|---|---|---|
| K.Brown | 2.0 | 5 | 4 | 3 | 1 | 2 | 1 |
| J.Vazquez (W) | 4.1 | 7 | 4 | 4 | 1 | 2 | 4 |
| Quantrill | 1.2 | 2 | 0 | 0 | 0 | 0 | 2 |
| Gordon | 1.0 | 1 | 0 | 0 | 0 | 0 | 1 |

| Boston | IP | H | R | ER | HR | BB | SO |
|---|---|---|---|---|---|---|---|
| Arroyo | 2.0 | 6 | 6 | 6 | 2 | 2 | 0 |
| Mendoza (L) | 1.0 | 1 | 1 | 1 | 0 | 0 | 1 |
| Leskanic | 0.1 | 2 | 3 | 3 | 1 | 1 | 0 |
| Wakefield | 3.1 | 5 | 5 | 5 | 0 | 2 | 1 |
| Embree | 0.1 | 3 | 2 | 2 | 0 | 0 | 0 |
| M.Myers | 2.0 | 5 | 2 | 2 | 1 | 0 | 3 |

Arroyo pitched to 3 batters in the 3rd. Mendoza pitched to 1 batter in the 4th.

E—Jeter. DP—NY Yankees 1, Boston 2. LOB—NY Yankees 7, Boston 9. Scoring Position—NY Yankees 8 for 22, Boston 2 for 13. 2B—A.Rodriguez 2, Sheffield, H.Matsui 2, B.Williams, Posada, Sierra, Nixon, Millar, Mueller, O.Cabrera 2. 3B—Sierra. HR—H.Matsui (1st inning, 1 out, 1 on) off Arroyo, Nixon (2nd inning, 0 out, 1 on) off K.Brown, A.Rodriguez (3rd inning, 0 out, 0 on) off Arroyo, Sheffield (4th inning, 1 out, 2 on) off Leskanic, Varitek (7th inning, 0 out, 1 on) off J.Vazquez, H.Matsui (9th inning, 0 out, 1 on) off M.Myers. WP—K.Brown, Gordon. BK—Mendoza. HBP—Cairo by Mendoza. T—4:20. A—35,126. U—HP-Hirschbeck, 1B-Joyce, 2B-Kellogg, 3B-West, LF-Marsh, RF-Nelson.

## HOW THEY SCORED

TOP OF 1

Yankees first. Jeter walked on a full count. Rodriguez doubled to left, Jeter scored. Sheffield flied out to center fielder Damon, Rodriguez to third. Matsui homered to right on a 1-2 count, Rodriguez scored. Williams singled to right. Posada grounded into a double play, shortstop Cabrera to first baseman Millar, Williams out. Runs: 3, Hits: 3, Errors: 0

BOTTOM OF 2

Red Sox second. Varitek walked. Nixon homered to right on a 2-

2 count, Varitek scored. Millar flied out to center fielder Williams. Mueller doubled to right. Cabrera grounded out, third baseman Rodriguez to first baseman Olerud. Damon infield single to first, Mueller scored. Damon to second. On Brown's wild pitch, Damon to third. Bellhorn walked on a full count. Ramirez safe on Jeter's error, Damon scored, Bellhorn to second. Ortiz grounded out, second baseman Cairo to first baseman Olerud. Runs: 4, Hits: 3, Errors: 1

TOP OF 3

Yankees third. Rodriguez homered to left on a 2-1 count. Sheffield walked. Matsui doubled to right, Sheffield to third. Mendoza pitching. Williams singled to center, Sheffield scored, Matsui to third. On Mendoza's balk, Matsui scored, Williams to second. Posada popped out to first baseman Millar. Sierra struck out. Olerud grounded out, shortstop Cabrera to first baseman Millar. Runs: 3, Hits: 3, Errors: 0

BOTTOM OF 3

Red Sox third. Vazquez pitching. Varitek singled to right. Nixon struck out. Millar doubled to left, Varitek to third. Mueller walked. Cabrera doubled to right, Varitek scored, Millar scored, Mueller to third. Mueller was out advancing, center fielder Williams to second baseman Cairo to catcher Posada, Mueller out, Cabrera to third. Damon grounded out, first baseman Olerud to pitcher Vazquez. Runs: 2, Hits: 3, Errors: 0

TOP OF 4

Yankees fourth. Cairo was hit by a pitch. Leskanic pitching. Jeter lined out to right fielder Nixon. Rodriguez walked on a full count, Cairo to second. Sheffield homered to left on a 1-0 count, Cairo scored, Rodriguez scored. Matsui doubled to left. Wakefield pitching. Williams popped out to first baseman Millar. Posada was intentionally walked. Sierra tripled to right, Matsui scored, Posada scored. Olerud lined out to shortstop Cabrera. Runs: 5, Hits: 3, Errors: 0

TOP OF 5

Yankees fifth. Cairo grounded out, shortstop Cabrera to first baseman Millar. Jeter walked on a full count. Rodriguez doubled to right, Jeter scored. Sheffield doubled to center, Rodriguez scored. Matsui flied out to left fielder Ramirez. Williams struck out. Runs: 2, Hits: 2, Errors: 0

TOP OF 7

Yankees seventh. Cairo infield single to short. Jeter flied out to center fielder Damon. Rodriguez grounded into fielder's choice, second baseman Bellhorn to shortstop Cabrera, Cairo out. Sheffield singled to left, Rodriguez to third. Embree pitching. Matsui singled to center, Rodriguez scored, Sheffield to third. Williams doubled to center, Sheffield scored, Matsui scored. Posada doubled to center, Williams scored. Sierra grounded out, shortstop Cabrera to first baseman Millar. Runs: 4, Hits: 5, Errors: 0

BOTTOM OF 7

Red Sox seventh. Ortiz singled to left. Varitek homered to center on a 1-1 count, Ortiz scored. Nixon flied out to right fielder Sheffield. Quantrill pitching. Millar grounded out, shortstop Jeter to first baseman Clark. Mueller singled to left. Cabrera singled to center, Mueller to second. Damon flied out to left fielder Matsui. Runs: 2, Hits: 4, Errors: 0

TOP OF 9

Yankees ninth. Sheffield singled to center. Crosby pinch-running for Sheffield. Matsui homered to center on a 1-1 count, Crosby scored. Williams singled to center. Posada singled to center, Williams to second. Sierra struck out. Clark lined into a double play, third baseman Mueller to second baseman Bellhorn, Williams out. Runs: 2, Hits: 4, Errors: 0

## GAME 4

### BOSTON 6, NEW YORK 4

SUNDAY, OCTOBER 17, AT BOSTON

| NY Yankees | AB | R | H | BI | BB | SO | PO | A |
|---|---|---|---|---|---|---|---|---|
| Jeter, ss | 4 | 1 | 1 | 0 | 1 | 0 | 2 | 3 |
| A.Rodriguez, 3b | 5 | 1 | 1 | 2 | 1 | 1 | 0 | 1 |
| Sheffield, rf | 5 | 0 | 0 | 0 | 1 | 1 | 2 | 0 |
| H.Matsui, lf | 5 | 1 | 2 | 0 | 1 | 1 | 4 | 0 |
| B.Williams, cf | 6 | 0 | 1 | 1 | 0 | 1 | 2 | 0 |
| Posada, c | 4 | 1 | 2 | 0 | 2 | 0 | 10 | 0 |
| Sierra, dh | 6 | 0 | 2 | 0 | 0 | 1 | 0 | 0 |
| T.Clark, 1b | 6 | 0 | 2 | 1 | 0 | 1 | 7 | 2 |
| Cairo, 2b | 4 | 0 | 1 | 0 | 1 | 1 | 5 | 2 |
| O.Hernandez, p | 0 | 0 | 0 | 0 | 0 | 0 | 0 | 0 |
| Sturtze, p | 0 | 0 | 0 | 0 | 0 | 0 | 0 | 1 |
| M.Rivera, p | 0 | 0 | 0 | 0 | 0 | 0 | 1 | 1 |
| Gordon, p | 0 | 0 | 0 | 0 | 0 | 0 | 0 | 0 |
| Quantrill, p | 0 | 0 | 0 | 0 | 0 | 0 | 0 | 0 |
| **TOTALS** | 45 | 4 | 12 | 4 | 7 | 7 | 33 | 10 |
| **Boston** | **AB** | **R** | **H** | **BI** | **BB** | **SO** | **PO** | **A** |
| Damon, cf | 5 | 1 | 0 | 0 | 1 | 0 | 4 | 0 |
| O.Cabrera, ss | 6 | 1 | 1 | 1 | 0 | 2 | 3 | 2 |
| M.Ramirez, lf | 3 | 1 | 2 | 0 | 3 | 1 | 3 | 0 |
| D.Ortiz, dh | 5 | 1 | 2 | 4 | 1 | 1 | 0 | 0 |
| Varitek, c | 5 | 0 | 0 | 0 | 0 | 3 | 9 | 1 |
| Nixon, rf | 5 | 0 | 0 | 0 | 0 | 0 | 2 | 0 |
| Millar, 1b | 2 | 0 | 1 | 0 | 2 | 0 | 9 | 1 |
| D.Roberts, pr | 0 | 1 | 0 | 0 | 0 | 0 | 0 | 0 |
| Reese, 2b | 1 | 0 | 0 | 0 | 0 | 1 | 0 | 0 |
| Mueller, 3b | 5 | 1 | 2 | 1 | 0 | 0 | 1 | 4 |
| Bellhorn, 2b | 2 | 0 | 0 | 0 | 1 | 2 | 2 | 4 |
| Mientkiewicz, ph-1b | 1 | 0 | 0 | 0 | 0 | 0 | 2 | 0 |
| Lowe, p | 0 | 0 | 0 | 0 | 0 | 0 | 1 | 2 |
| Timlin, p | 0 | 0 | 0 | 0 | 0 | 0 | 0 | 0 |
| Foulke, p | 0 | 0 | 0 | 0 | 0 | 0 | 0 | 0 |
| Embree, p | 0 | 0 | 0 | 0 | 0 | 0 | 0 | 1 |
| M.Myers, p | 0 | 0 | 0 | 0 | 0 | 0 | 0 | 0 |
| Leskanic, p | 0 | 0 | 0 | 0 | 0 | 0 | 0 | 1 |
| **TOTALS** | 40 | 6 | 8 | 6 | 8 | 10 | 36 | 16 |

| | | | | | | |
|---|---|---|---|---|---|---|
| NY Yankees | 0 0 2 | 0 0 2 | 0 0 0 | 0 0 0—4 | 12 | 1 |
| Boston | 0 0 0 | 0 3 0 | 0 0 1 | 0 0 2—6 | 8 | 0 |

| NY Yankees | IP | H | R | ER | HR | BB | SO |
|---|---|---|---|---|---|---|---|
| O.Hernandez | 5.0 | 3 | 3 | 3 | 0 | 5 | 6 |
| Sturtze (HOLD) | 2.0 | 1 | 0 | 0 | 0 | 0 | 1 |
| M.Rivera (BS) | 2.0 | 2 | 1 | 1 | 0 | 2 | 2 |
| Gordon | 2.0 | 0 | 0 | 0 | 0 | 1 | 1 |
| Quantrill (L) | 0.0 | 2 | 2 | 2 | 1 | 0 | 0 |
| **Boston** | **IP** | **H** | **R** | **ER** | **HR** | **BB** | **SO** |
| Lowe | 5.1 | 6 | 3 | 3 | 1 | 0 | 3 |
| Timlin (BS) | 1.0 | 3 | 1 | 1 | 0 | 3 | 0 |
| Foulke | 2.2 | 0 | 0 | 0 | 0 | 2 | 3 |
| Embree | 1.2 | 2 | 0 | 0 | 0 | 1 | 0 |
| M.Myers | 0.0 | 0 | 0 | 0 | 0 | 1 | 0 |
| Leskanic (W) | 1.1 | 1 | 0 | 0 | 0 | 0 | 1 |

Quantrill pitched to 2 batters in the 12th. M.Myers pitched to 1 batter in the 11th.

E—T.Clark. DP—NY Yankees 1. LOB—NY Yankees 14, Boston 10. Scoring Position—NY Yankees 3 for 13, Boston 3 for 11. 2B—H.Matsui. 3B—H.Matsui. HR—A.Rodriguez (3rd inning, 2 out, 1 on) off Lowe, D.Ortiz (12th inning, 0 out, 1 on) off Quantrill. SB—Damon, D.Roberts. SH—Jeter, Cairo, Mientkiewicz. WP—Timlin. T—5:02. A—34,826. U—HP-Joyce, 1B-Kellogg, 2B-West, 3B-Marsh, LF-Nelson, RF-Hirschbeck.

## HOW THEY SCORED

TOP OF 3

Yankees third. Clark flied out to center fielder Damon. Cairo grounded out, shortstop Cabrera to first baseman Millar. Jeter infield single to third. Rodriguez homered to center on the first pitch, Jeter scored. Sheffield struck out. Runs: 2, Hits: 2, Errors: 0

BOTTOM OF 5

Red Sox fifth. Millar walked on four pitches. Mueller grounded into fielder's choice, first baseman Clark to shortstop Jeter, Millar out. Bellhorn walked, Mueller to second. Damon grounded into fielder's choice, shortstop Jeter to second baseman Cairo, Mueller to third, Bellhorn out. Cabrera singled to right, Mueller scored, Damon to second. Ramirez walked, Damon to third, Cabrera to second. Ortiz singled to center, Damon scored, Cabrera scored, Ramirez to third. Varitek struck out. Runs: 3, Hits: 2, Errors: 0

TOP OF 6

Yankees sixth. Sheffield grounded out, third baseman Mueller to first baseman Millar. Matsui tripled to center. Timlin pitching. Williams infield single to short, Matsui scored. On Timlin's wild pitch, Williams to second. Posada walked on four pitches. Williams was out advancing, catcher Varitek to third baseman Mueller, Williams out, Posada to second. Sierra infield single to second, Posada to third. Clark infield single to first, Posada scored, Sierra to second. Cairo walked on a full count, Sierra to third, Clark to second. Jeter grounded out, second baseman Bellhorn to first baseman Millar. Runs: 2, Hits: 4, Errors: 0

BOTTOM OF 9

Red Sox ninth. Millar walked. Roberts pinch-running for Millar.Roberts stole second. Mueller singled to center, Roberts scored. Mientkiewicz pinch-hitting for Bellhorn. Mientkiewicz sacrificed, pitcher Rivera to second baseman Cairo, Mueller to second. Damon safe on Clark's error, Mueller to third. Cabrera struck out. On defensive indifference, Damon to second. Ramirez walked on a full count. Ortiz popped out to second baseman Cairo. Runs: 1, Hits: 1, Errors: 1

BOTTOM OF 12

Red Sox twelfth. Quantrill pitching. Ramirez singled to left. Ortiz homered to right on a 2-1 count, Ramirez scored. Runs: 2, Hits: 2, Errors: 0

## GAME 5

### BOSTON 5, NEW YORK 4

MONDAY, OCTOBER 15, AT BOSTON

| NY Yankees | AB | R | H | BI | BB | SO | PO | A |
|---|---|---|---|---|---|---|---|---|
| Jeter, ss | 7 | 0 | 1 | 3 | 0 | 2 | 4 | 4 |
| A.Rodriguez, 3b | 4 | 0 | 0 | 0 | 2 | 2 | 1 | 2 |
| Sheffield, rf | 4 | 0 | 0 | 0 | 3 | 3 | 0 | 0 |
| H.Matsui, lf | 7 | 0 | 1 | 0 | 0 | 1 | 2 | 0 |
| B.Williams, cf | 7 | 1 | 2 | 1 | 0 | 1 | 6 | 0 |
| Posada, c | 6 | 1 | 2 | 0 | 1 | 1 | 13 | 3 |
| Sierra, dh | 5 | 1 | 3 | 0 | 2 | 2 | 0 | 0 |
| T.Clark, 1b | 7 | 0 | 1 | 0 | 0 | 4 | 10 | 1 |
| Cairo, 2b | 6 | 1 | 2 | 0 | 0 | 0 | 4 | 5 |
| Mussina, p | 0 | 0 | 0 | 0 | 0 | 0 | 0 | 0 |
| Sturtze, p | 0 | 0 | 0 | 0 | 0 | 0 | 0 | 0 |
| Gordon, p | 0 | 0 | 0 | 0 | 0 | 0 | 0 | 0 |
| M.Rivera, p | 0 | 0 | 0 | 0 | 0 | 0 | 0 | 0 |
| Heredia, p | 0 | 0 | 0 | 0 | 0 | 0 | 0 | 0 |
| Quantrill, p | 0 | 0 | 0 | 0 | 0 | 0 | 0 | 0 |
| Loaiza, p | 0 | 0 | 0 | 0 | 0 | 0 | 1 | 0 |
| **TOTALS** | 53 | 4 | 12 | 4 | 8 | 16 | 41 | 15 |

| Boston | AB | R | H | BI | BB | SO | PO | A |
|---|---|---|---|---|---|---|---|---|
| Damon, cf | 6 | 1 | 1 | 0 | 1 | 2 | 3 | 0 |
| O.Cabrera, ss | 6 | 1 | 2 | 0 | 1 | 1 | 3 | 1 |
| M.Ramirez, lf | 6 | 0 | 2 | 0 | 1 | 0 | 4 | 0 |
| D.Ortiz, dh | 6 | 2 | 3 | 3 | 1 | 3 | 0 | 0 |
| Millar, 1b | 2 | 0 | 0 | 0 | 2 | 0 | 4 | 1 |
| D.Roberts, pr | 0 | 1 | 0 | 0 | 0 | 0 | 0 | 0 |
| Mientkiewicz, 1b | 2 | 0 | 1 | 0 | 0 | 1 | 4 | 0 |
| Nixon, rf | 4 | 0 | 1 | 0 | 0 | 1 | 4 | 0 |
| Kapler, pr-rf | 2 | 0 | 0 | 0 | 0 | 0 | 2 | 0 |
| Varitek, c | 4 | 0 | 0 | 2 | 1 | 1 | 15 | 0 |
| Mueller, 3b | 6 | 0 | 1 | 0 | 0 | 1 | 0 | 1 |
| Bellhorn, 2b | 6 | 0 | 2 | 0 | 0 | 2 | 2 | 4 |
| P.Martinez, p | 0 | 0 | 0 | 0 | 0 | 0 | 1 | 0 |
| Timlin, p | 0 | 0 | 0 | 0 | 0 | 0 | 0 | 1 |
| Foulke, p | 0 | 0 | 0 | 0 | 0 | 0 | 0 | 0 |
| Arroyo, p | 0 | 0 | 0 | 0 | 0 | 0 | 0 | 0 |
| M.Myers, p | 0 | 0 | 0 | 0 | 0 | 0 | 0 | 0 |
| Embree, p | 0 | 0 | 0 | 0 | 0 | 0 | 0 | 0 |
| Wakefield, p | 0 | 0 | 0 | 0 | 0 | 0 | 0 | 0 |
| **TOTALS** | 50 | 5 | 13 | 5 | 7 | 12 | 42 | 8 |

| | | | | | | | | |
|---|---|---|---|---|---|---|---|---|
| NY Yankees | 0 1 0 | 0 0 3 | 0 0 0 | 0 0 0 | 0 0—4 | 12 | 1 |
| Boston | 2 0 0 | 0 0 0 | 0 2 0 | 0 0 0 | 0 1—5 | 13 | 1 |

| NY Yankees | IP | H | R | ER | HR | BB | SO |
|---|---|---|---|---|---|---|---|
| Mussina | 6.0 | 6 | 2 | 2 | 0 | 2 | 7 |
| Sturtze (HOLD) | 0.1 | 0 | 0 | 0 | 0 | 1 | 0 |
| Gordon (HOLD) | 0.2 | 2 | 2 | 2 | 1 | 1 | 0 |
| M.Rivera (BS) | 2.0 | 1 | 0 | 0 | 0 | 0 | 1 |
| Heredia | 0.1 | 1 | 0 | 0 | 0 | 0 | 1 |
| Quantrill | 1.0 | 2 | 0 | 0 | 0 | 0 | 0 |
| Loaiza (L) | 3.1 | 1 | 1 | 1 | 0 | 3 | 3 |

| Boston | IP | H | R | ER | HR | BB | SO |
|---|---|---|---|---|---|---|---|
| P.Martinez | 6.0 | 7 | 4 | 4 | 1 | 5 | 6 |
| Timlin | 1.2 | 2 | 0 | 0 | 0 | 1 | 1 |
| Foulke | 1.1 | 1 | 0 | 0 | 0 | 1 | 0 |
| Arroyo | 1.0 | 0 | 0 | 0 | 0 | 0 | 2 |
| M.Myers | 0.1 | 0 | 0 | 0 | 0 | 0 | 1 |
| Embree | 0.2 | 1 | 0 | 0 | 0 | 0 | 2 |
| Wakefield (W) | 3.0 | 1 | 0 | 0 | 0 | 1 | 4 |

Mussina pitched to 1 batter in the 7th. Gordon pitched to 3 batters in the 8th.

E—Jeter, M.Ramirez. DP—NY Yankees 2, Boston 1. LOB—NY Yankees 18, Boston 12. Scoring Position—NY Yankees 1 for 13, Boston 2 for 13. 2B—Jeter, T.Clark, Cairo, Bellhorn, Mientkiewicz. HR—B.Williams (2nd inning, 0 out, 0 on) off P.Martinez, D.Ortiz (8th inning, 0 out, 0 on) off Gordon. CS—Damon, D.Ortiz. S—Varitek. SH—Jeter. PB—Varitek 3. HBP—A.Rodriguez by P.Martinez, Cairo by P.Martinez. T—5:49. A—35,120. U—HP-Kellogg, 1B-West, 2B-Marsh, 3B-Nelson, LF-Hirschbeck, RF-Joyce.

### HOW THEY SCORED

TOP OF 2

Yankees second. Williams homered to right on the first pitch. Posada grounded out, second baseman Bellhorn to first baseman Millar. Sierra singled to left. Clark flied out to left fielder Ramirez. Cairo grounded out, first baseman Millar unassisted. Runs: 1, Hits: 2, Errors: 0

TOP OF 6

Yankees sixth. Williams flied out to left fielder Ramirez. Posada infield single to second. Sierra singled to center, Posada to second. Clark struck out. Cairo was hit by a pitch, Posada to third, Sierra to second. Jeter doubled to right, Posada scored, Sierra scored, Cairo scored. Jeter to third. Rodriguez was hit by a pitch. Sheffield walked, Rodriguez to second. Matsui lined out to right fielder Nixon. Runs: 3, Hits: 3, Errors: 0

BOTTOM OF 8

Red Sox eighth. Ortiz homered to center on a 0-1 count. Millar walked on a full count. Roberts pinch-running for Millar. Nixon singled to center, Roberts to third. Kapler pinch-running for Nixon. Rivera pitching. Varitek hit a sacrifice fly to center fielder Williams, Roberts scored. Mueller grounded out, first baseman Clark unassisted, Kapler to second. Bellhorn struck out. Runs: 2, Hits: 2, Errors: 0

BOTTOM OF 14

Red Sox fourteenth. Bellhorn struck out. Damon walked. Cabrera struck out. Ramirez walked on a full count, Damon to second. Ortiz singled to center, Damon scored, Ramirez to second. Runs: 1, Hits: 1, Errors: 0

## GAME 6

### BOSTON 4, NEW YORK 2

TUESDAY, OCTOBER 19, AT NEW YORK

| Boston | AB | R | H | BI | BB | SO | PO | A |
|---|---|---|---|---|---|---|---|---|
| Damon, cf | 5 | 0 | 1 | 0 | 0 | 1 | 2 | 0 |
| Mueller, 3b | 4 | 0 | 0 | 0 | 0 | 0 | 2 | 0 |
| M.Ramirez, lf | 4 | 0 | 1 | 0 | 0 | 0 | 2 | 0 |
| D.Ortiz, dh | 4 | 0 | 0 | 0 | 0 | 0 | 0 | 0 |
| Nixon, rf | 3 | 0 | 0 | 0 | 0 | 1 | 3 | 0 |
| Kapler, ph-rf | 1 | 0 | 1 | 0 | 0 | 0 | 0 | 0 |
| Millar, 1b | 4 | 1 | 2 | 0 | 0 | 0 | 6 | 1 |
| Mientkiewicz, 1b | 0 | 0 | 0 | 0 | 0 | 0 | 0 | 0 |
| Varitek, c | 4 | 1 | 3 | 1 | 0 | 0 | 8 | 0 |
| O.Cabrera, ss | 4 | 1 | 2 | 0 | 0 | 0 | 1 | 1 |
| Bellhorn, 2b | 3 | 1 | 1 | 3 | 1 | 0 | 1 | 1 |

| Boston | AB | R | H | BI | BB | SO | PO | A |
|---|---|---|---|---|---|---|---|---|
| Reese, pr-2b | 0 | 0 | 0 | 0 | 0 | 0 | 0 | 0 |
| Schilling, p | 0 | 0 | 0 | 0 | 0 | 0 | 1 | 0 |
| Arroyo, p | 0 | 0 | 0 | 0 | 0 | 0 | 1 | 0 |
| Foulke, p | 0 | 0 | 0 | 0 | 0 | 0 | 0 | 0 |
| **TOTALS** | 36 | 4 | 11 | 4 | 1 | 2 | 27 | 3 |

| NY Yankees | AB | R | H | BI | BB | SO | PO | A |
|---|---|---|---|---|---|---|---|---|
| Jeter, ss | 4 | 0 | 1 | 1 | 0 | 0 | 5 | 3 |
| A.Rodriguez, 3b | 4 | 0 | 1 | 0 | 0 | 0 | 0 | 1 |
| Sheffield, rf | 4 | 0 | 1 | 0 | 0 | 0 | 4 | 0 |
| H.Matsui, lf | 3 | 0 | 0 | 0 | 1 | 0 | 2 | 0 |
| B.Williams, cf | 4 | 1 | 1 | 1 | 0 | 1 | 3 | 0 |
| Posada, c | 4 | 0 | 0 | 0 | 0 | 0 | 2 | 1 |
| Sierra, dh | 3 | 0 | 0 | 0 | 1 | 3 | 0 | 0 |
| T.Clark, 1b | 4 | 0 | 0 | 0 | 0 | 3 | 10 | 1 |
| Cairo, 2b | 3 | 1 | 2 | 0 | 0 | 0 | 0 | 5 |
| Lieber, p | 0 | 0 | 0 | 0 | 0 | 0 | 1 | 0 |
| Heredia, p | 0 | 0 | 0 | 0 | 0 | 0 | 0 | 0 |
| Quantrill, p | 0 | 0 | 0 | 0 | 0 | 0 | 0 | 0 |
| Sturtze, p | 0 | 0 | 0 | 0 | 0 | 0 | 0 | 0 |
| **TOTALS** | 33 | 2 | 6 | 2 | 2 | 7 | 27 | 11 |

| | | | | | | |
|---|---|---|---|---|---|---|
| Boston | 0 0 0 | 4 0 0 | 0 0 0 | —4 | 11 | 0 |
| NY Yankees | 0 0 0 | 0 0 0 | 1 1 0 | —2 | 6 | 0 |

| Boston | IP | H | R | ER | HR | BB | SO |
|---|---|---|---|---|---|---|---|
| Schilling (W) | 7.0 | 4 | 1 | 1 | 1 | 0 | 4 |
| Arroyo (HOLD) | 1.0 | 2 | 1 | 1 | 0 | 0 | 1 |
| Foulke (S) | 1.0 | 0 | 0 | 0 | 0 | 2 | 2 |

| NY Yankees | IP | H | R | ER | HR | BB | SO |
|---|---|---|---|---|---|---|---|
| Lieber (L) | 7.1 | 9 | 4 | 4 | 1 | 0 | 2 |
| Heredia | 0.1 | 0 | 0 | 0 | 0 | 0 | 0 |
| Quantrill | 0.2 | 2 | 0 | 0 | 0 | 0 | 0 |
| Sturtze | 0.2 | 0 | 0 | 0 | 0 | 1 | 0 |

DP—NY Yankees 2. LOB—Boston 7, NY Yankees 6. Scoring Position—Boston 3 for 7, NY Yankees 1 for 6. 2B—Millar, Cairo 2. HR—Bellhorn (4th inning, 2 out, 2 on) off Lieber, B.Williams (7th inning, 1 out, 0 on) off Schilling. SB—O.Cabrera. WP—Lieber. HBP—Mueller by Lieber. T—3:50. A—56,128. U—HP-West, 1B-Marsh, 2B-Nelson, 3B-Hirschbeck, LF-Joyce, RF-Kellogg.

## HOW THEY SCORED

TOP OF 4

Red Sox fourth. Ortiz grounded out, catcher Posada to first baseman Clark. Nixon grounded out, second baseman Cairo to first baseman Clark. Millar doubled to left. On Lieber's wild pitch, Millar to third. Varitek singled to center, Millar scored. Cabrera singled to left, Varitek to second. Bellhorn homered to left on a 1-2 count, Varitek scored, Cabrera scored. Damon flied out to left fielder Matsui. Runs: 4, Hits: 4, Errors: 0

BOTTOM OF 7

Yankees seventh. Matsui grounded out, first baseman Millar unassisted. Williams homered to right on a 3-1 count. Posada popped out to second baseman Bellhorn. Sierra struck out. Runs: 1, Hits: 1, Errors: 0

BOTTOM OF 8

Yankees eighth. Kapler in as right fielder. Mientkiewicz in as first baseman. Arroyo pitching. Clark struck out. Cairo doubled to right. Jeter singled to left, Cairo scored. Rodriguez was called out on obstruction. Sheffield fouled out to catcher Varitek. Runs: 1, Hits: 2, Errors: 0

## GAME 7

### BOSTON 10, NEW YORK 3

WEDNESDAY, OCTOBER 20, AT NEW YORK

| Boston | AB | R | H | BI | BB | SO | PO | A |
|---|---|---|---|---|---|---|---|---|
| Damon, cf | 6 | 2 | 3 | 6 | 0 | 0 | 1 | 0 |
| Bellhorn, 2b | 3 | 1 | 1 | 1 | 2 | 1 | 0 | 1 |
| Reese, 2b | 0 | 0 | 0 | 0 | 0 | 0 | 0 | 2 |
| M.Ramirez, lf | 5 | 1 | 1 | 0 | 0 | 0 | 2 | 0 |
| D.Ortiz, dh | 4 | 1 | 1 | 2 | 1 | 0 | 0 | 0 |
| Varitek, c | 5 | 0 | 1 | 0 | 0 | 1 | 5 | 1 |
| Nixon, rf | 5 | 1 | 1 | 0 | 0 | 2 | 1 | 0 |
| Millar, 1b | 3 | 1 | 1 | 0 | 1 | 1 | 9 | 3 |
| Mientkiewicz, 1b | 1 | 0 | 1 | 0 | 0 | 0 | 3 | 1 |
| Mueller, 3b | 4 | 1 | 2 | 0 | 1 | 0 | 0 | 3 |
| O.Cabrera, ss | 2 | 2 | 1 | 1 | 2 | 0 | 2 | 5 |
| Lowe, p | 0 | 0 | 0 | 0 | 0 | 0 | 3 | 1 |
| P.Martinez, p | 0 | 0 | 0 | 0 | 0 | 0 | 1 | 0 |
| Timlin, p | 0 | 0 | 0 | 0 | 0 | 0 | 0 | 0 |
| Embree, p | 0 | 0 | 0 | 0 | 0 | 0 | 0 | 0 |
| **TOTALS** | 38 | 10 | 13 | 10 | 7 | 5 | 27 | 17 |

| NY Yankees | AB | R | H | BI | BB | SO | PO | A |
|---|---|---|---|---|---|---|---|---|
| Jeter, ss | 4 | 0 | 1 | 1 | 0 | 0 | 5 | 3 |
| A.Rodriguez, 3b | 4 | 0 | 0 | 0 | 0 | 1 | 1 | 1 |
| Sheffield, rf | 4 | 0 | 0 | 0 | 0 | 2 | 0 | 0 |
| H.Matsui, lf | 4 | 1 | 2 | 0 | 0 | 0 | 1 | 1 |
| B.Williams, cf | 4 | 1 | 1 | 1 | 0 | 0 | 2 | 0 |
| Posada, c | 3 | 0 | 0 | 0 | 1 | 0 | 6 | 0 |
| Lofton, dh | 3 | 0 | 1 | 1 | 1 | 0 | 0 | 0 |
| T.Clark, 1b | 2 | 0 | 0 | 0 | 0 | 0 | 9 | 0 |
| Olerud, ph-1b | 1 | 0 | 0 | 0 | 0 | 1 | 2 | 0 |
| Sierra, ph | 1 | 0 | 0 | 0 | 0 | 0 | 0 | 0 |
| Cairo, 2b | 2 | 1 | 0 | 0 | 0 | 1 | 0 | 4 |
| K.Brown, p | 0 | 0 | 0 | 0 | 0 | 0 | 1 | 0 |
| J.Vazquez, p | 0 | 0 | 0 | 0 | 0 | 0 | 0 | 1 |
| Loaiza, p | 0 | 0 | 0 | 0 | 0 | 0 | 0 | 0 |
| Heredia, p | 0 | 0 | 0 | 0 | 0 | 0 | 0 | 1 |
| Gordon, p | 0 | 0 | 0 | 0 | 0 | 0 | 0 | 0 |
| M.Rivera, p | 0 | 0 | 0 | 0 | 0 | 0 | 0 | 1 |
| **TOTALS** | 32 | 3 | 5 | 3 | 2 | 5 | 27 | 12 |

| | | | | | | |
|---|---|---|---|---|---|---|
| Boston | 2 4 0 | 2 0 0 | 0 1 1 | —10 | 13 | 0 |
| NY Yankees | 0 0 1 | 0 0 0 | 2 0 0 | — 3 | 5 | 1 |

| Boston | IP | H | R | ER | HR | BB | SO |
|---|---|---|---|---|---|---|---|
| Lowe (W) | 6.0 | 1 | 1 | 1 | 0 | 1 | 3 |
| P.Martinez | 1.0 | 3 | 2 | 2 | 0 | 0 | 1 |
| Timlin | 1.2 | 1 | 0 | 0 | 0 | 1 | 1 |
| Embree | 0.1 | 0 | 0 | 0 | 0 | 0 | 0 |

| NY Yankees | IP | H | R | ER | HR | BB | SO |
|---|---|---|---|---|---|---|---|
| K.Brown (L) | 1.1 | 4 | 5 | 5 | 1 | 2 | 1 |
| J.Vazquez | 2.0 | 2 | 3 | 3 | 2 | 5 | 2 |
| Loaiza | 3.0 | 4 | 0 | 0 | 0 | 0 | 2 |
| Heredia | 0.2 | 0 | 0 | 0 | 0 | 0 | 0 |
| Gordon | 1.2 | 3 | 2 | 2 | 1 | 0 | 0 |
| M.Rivera | 0.1 | 0 | 0 | 0 | 0 | 0 | 0 |

E—Loaiza. DP—NY Yankees 1. LOB—Boston 9, NY Yankees 5. Scoring Position—Boston 3 for 11, NY Yankees 3 for 8. 2B—H.Matsui, B.Williams. HR—D.Ortiz (1st inning, 2 out, 1 on) off K.Brown, Damon (2nd inning, 1 out, 3 on) off J.Vazquez, Damon (4th inning, 0 out, 1 on) off J.Vazquez, Bellhorn (8th inning, 0 out, 0 on) off Gordon. SB—Damon, Lofton, Cairo.S—O.Cabrera. HBP—Cairo by Lowe. T—3:31. A—56,129. U—HP-Marsh, 1B-Nelson, 2B-Hirschbeck, 3B-Joyce, LF-Kellogg, RF-West.

## HOW THEY SCORED

TOP OF 1

Red Sox first. Damon singled to left. Damon stole second. Bellhorn struck out. Ramirez singled to center, Damon to third. Damon was out advancing, left fielder Matsui to shortstop Jeter to catcher Posada, Damon out. Ortiz homered to right on the first pitch, Ramirez scored. Varitek grounded out, pitcher Brown unassisted. Runs: 2, Hits: 3, Errors: 0

TOP OF 2

Red Sox second. Nixon grounded out, shortstop Jeter to first baseman Clark. Millar singled to center. Mueller walked, Millar to second. Cabrera walked on a full count, Millar to third, Mueller to second. Vazquez pitching. Damon homered to right on the first pitch, Millar scored, Mueller scored, Cabrera scored. Bellhorn walked. Ramirez popped out to shortstop Jeter. Ortiz grounded out, pitcher Vazquez to second baseman Cairo to first baseman Clark. Runs: 4, Hits: 2, Errors: 0

BOTTOM OF 3

Yankees third. Clark flied out to left fielder Ramirez. Cairo was hit by a pitch. Cairo stole second. Jeter singled to left, Cairo scored. Rodriguez grounded out, pitcher Lowe to first baseman Millar, Jeter to second. Sheffield grounded out, third baseman Mueller to first baseman Millar. Runs: 1, Hits: 1, Errors: 0

TOP OF 4

Red Sox fourth. Cabrera walked on a full count. Damon homered to right on the first pitch, Cabrera scored. Bellhorn walked on four pitches. Ramirez popped out to third baseman Rodriguez. Ortiz walked on a full count, Bellhorn to second. Loaiza pitching. Varitek singled to right, Bellhorn to third, Ortiz to second. Nixon struck out. Millar grounded out, second baseman Cairo to first baseman Clark. Runs: 2, Hits: 2, Errors: 0

BOTTOM OF 7

Yankees seventh. P.Martinez pitching. Mientkiewicz in as first baseman. Matsui doubled to left. Williams doubled to center, Matsui scored. Posada grounded out, first baseman Mientkiewicz to pitcher P.Martinez, Williams to third. Lofton singled to center, Williams scored. Olerud pinch-hitting for Clark.Lofton stole second. Olerud struck out. Cairo flied out to right fielder Nixon. Runs: 2, Hits: 3, Errors: 0

TOP OF 8

Red Sox eighth. Olerud in as first baseman. Gordon pitching. Bellhorn homered to left on a 1-1 count. Ramirez fouled out to first baseman Olerud. Ortiz popped out to shortstop Jeter. Varitek flied out to left fielder Matsui. Runs: 1, Hits: 1, Errors: 0

TOP OF 9

Red Sox ninth. Nixon singled to left. Mientkiewicz singled to left, Nixon to second. Mueller flied out to center fielder Williams, Nixon to third. Cabrera hit a sacrifice fly to center fielder Williams, Nixon scored. Rivera pitching. Damon grounded out, pitcher Rivera to first baseman Olerud. Runs: 1, Hits: 2, Errors: 0

# STATISTICS

## BOSTON RED SOX' BATTING AND FIELDING AVERAGES

| | | BATTING | | | | | | | | | | | | | | FIELDING | | | |
|---|---|---|---|---|---|---|---|---|---|---|---|---|---|---|---|---|---|---|---|
| **Player, position** | **G** | **AB** | **R** | **H** | **TB** | **2B** | **3B** | **HR** | **RBI** | **BB** | **IBB** | **SO** | **Avg.** | **OBP** | **Slg.** | **PO** | **A** | **E** | **Avg.** |
| Mientkiewicz,1b-ph | 4 | 4 | 0 | 2 | 3 | 1 | 0 | 0 | 0 | 0 | 0 | 1 | .500 | .500 | .750 | 9 | 1 | 0 | 1.000 |
| Ortiz,dh | 7 | 31 | 6 | 12 | 23 | 0 | 1 | 3 | 11 | 4 | 0 | 7 | .387 | .457 | .742 | 0 | 0 | 0 | .000 |
| Cabrera,ss | 7 | 29 | 5 | 11 | 13 | 2 | 0 | 0 | 5 | 3 | 0 | 5 | .379 | .424 | .448 | 17 | 18 | 0 | 1.000 |
| Kapler,rf-pr-ph | 2 | 3 | 0 | 1 | 1 | 0 | 0 | 0 | 0 | 0 | 0 | 0 | .333 | .333 | .333 | 2 | 0 | 0 | 1.000 |
| Varitek,c | 7 | 28 | 5 | 9 | 16 | 1 | 0 | 2 | 7 | 2 | 0 | 6 | .321 | .355 | .571 | 50 | 2 | 0 | 1.000 |
| Ramirez,lf | 7 | 30 | 3 | 9 | 10 | 1 | 0 | 0 | 0 | 5 | 0 | 4 | .300 | .400 | .333 | 18 | 0 | 1 | .947 |
| Mueller,3b | 7 | 30 | 4 | 8 | 9 | 1 | 0 | 0 | 1 | 2 | 0 | 1 | .267 | .333 | .300 | 7 | 10 | 0 | 1.000 |
| Millar,1b | 7 | 24 | 4 | 6 | 9 | 3 | 0 | 0 | 2 | 5 | 0 | 4 | .250 | .379 | .375 | 49 | 7 | 0 | 1.000 |
| Nixon,rf | 7 | 29 | 4 | 6 | 10 | 1 | 0 | 1 | 3 | 0 | 0 | 5 | .207 | .207 | .345 | 16 | 0 | 0 | 1.000 |
| Bellhorn,2b | 7 | 26 | 3 | 5 | 13 | 2 | 0 | 2 | 4 | 5 | 0 | 11 | .192 | .323 | .500 | 8 | 20 | 0 | 1.000 |
| Damon,cf | 7 | 35 | 5 | 6 | 12 | 0 | 0 | 2 | 7 | 2 | 0 | 8 | .171 | .216 | .343 | 19 | 0 | 0 | 1.000 |
| Arroyo,p | 3 | 0 | 0 | 0 | 0 | 0 | 0 | 0 | 0 | 0 | 0 | 0 | .000 | .000 | .000 | 1 | 0 | 0 | 1.000 |
| Embree,p | 6 | 0 | 0 | 0 | 0 | 0 | 0 | 0 | 0 | 0 | 0 | 0 | .000 | .000 | .000 | 0 | 1 | 0 | 1.000 |
| Foulke,p | 5 | 0 | 0 | 0 | 0 | 0 | 0 | 0 | 0 | 0 | 0 | 0 | .000 | .000 | .000 | 0 | 0 | 0 | .000 |
| Leskanic,p | 3 | 0 | 0 | 0 | 0 | 0 | 0 | 0 | 0 | 0 | 0 | 0 | .000 | .000 | .000 | 0 | 1 | 0 | 1.000 |
| Lowe,p | 2 | 0 | 0 | 0 | 0 | 0 | 0 | 0 | 0 | 0 | 0 | 0 | .000 | .000 | .000 | 4 | 3 | 0 | 1.000 |
| Martinez,p | 3 | 0 | 0 | 0 | 0 | 0 | 0 | 0 | 0 | 0 | 0 | 0 | .000 | .000 | .000 | 3 | 0 | 0 | 1.000 |
| Mendoza,p | 2 | 0 | 0 | 0 | 0 | 0 | 0 | 0 | 0 | 0 | 0 | 0 | .000 | .000 | .000 | 0 | 0 | 0 | .000 |
| Myers,p | 3 | 0 | 0 | 0 | 0 | 0 | 0 | 0 | 0 | 0 | 0 | 0 | .000 | .000 | .000 | 0 | 0 | 0 | .000 |
| Roberts,pr | 2 | 0 | 2 | 0 | 0 | 0 | 0 | 0 | 0 | 0 | 0 | 0 | .000 | .000 | .000 | 0 | 0 | 0 | .000 |
| Schilling,p | 2 | 0 | 0 | 0 | 0 | 0 | 0 | 0 | 0 | 0 | 0 | 0 | .000 | .000 | .000 | 1 | 0 | 0 | 1.000 |
| Timlin,p | 5 | 0 | 0 | 0 | 0 | 0 | 0 | 0 | 0 | 0 | 0 | 0 | .000 | .000 | .000 | 0 | 1 | 0 | 1.000 |
| Wakefield,p | 3 | 0 | 0 | 0 | 0 | 0 | 0 | 0 | 0 | 0 | 0 | 0 | .000 | .000 | .000 | 0 | 0 | 0 | .000 |
| Mirabelli,c | 1 | 1 | 0 | 0 | 0 | 0 | 0 | 0 | 0 | 0 | 0 | 0 | .000 | .000 | .000 | 3 | 0 | 0 | 1.000 |
| Reese,2b-pr | 3 | 1 | 0 | 0 | 0 | 0 | 0 | 0 | 0 | 0 | 0 | 1 | .000 | .000 | .000 | 0 | 2 | 0 | 1.000 |
| **Totals** | 7 | 271 | 41 | 75 | 119 | 12 | 1 | 10 | 40 | 28 | 0 | 53 | .277 | .344 | .439 | 207 | 66 | 1 | .996 |

## NEW YORK YANKEES' BATTING AND FIELDING AVERAGES

| | | BATTING | | | | | | | | | | | | | | FIELDING | | | |
|---|---|---|---|---|---|---|---|---|---|---|---|---|---|---|---|---|---|---|---|
| **Player, position** | **G** | **AB** | **R** | **H** | **TB** | **2B** | **3B** | **HR** | **RBI** | **BB** | **IBB** | **SO** | **Avg.** | **OBP** | **Slg.** | **PO** | **A** | **E** | **Avg.** |
| Matsui,lf | 7 | 34 | 9 | 14 | 28 | 6 | 1 | 2 | 10 | 2 | 0 | 4 | .412 | .444 | .824 | 15 | 1 | 0 | 1.000 |
| Sheffield,rf | 7 | 30 | 7 | 10 | 16 | 3 | 0 | 1 | 5 | 6 | 1 | 8 | .333 | .444 | .533 | 9 | 1 | 0 | 1.000 |
| Sierra,dh-ph | 5 | 21 | 1 | 7 | 10 | 1 | 1 | 0 | 2 | 3 | 0 | 8 | .333 | .417 | .476 | 0 | 0 | 0 | .000 |
| Williams,cf | 7 | 36 | 4 | 11 | 20 | 3 | 0 | 2 | 10 | 0 | 0 | 5 | .306 | .306 | .556 | 21 | 1 | 0 | 1.000 |
| Lofton,dh | 3 | 10 | 1 | 3 | 6 | 0 | 0 | 1 | 2 | 2 | 0 | 3 | .300 | .417 | .600 | 0 | 0 | 0 | .000 |
| Cairo,2b | 7 | 25 | 4 | 7 | 10 | 3 | 0 | 0 | 0 | 2 | 0 | 4 | .280 | .419 | .400 | 13 | 23 | 0 | 1.000 |
| Posada,c | 7 | 27 | 4 | 7 | 8 | 1 | 0 | 0 | 2 | 7 | 2 | 1 | .259 | .417 | .296 | 55 | 5 | 0 | 1.000 |
| Rodriguez,3b | 7 | 31 | 8 | 8 | 16 | 2 | 0 | 2 | 5 | 4 | 0 | 6 | .258 | .378 | .516 | 4 | 7 | 0 | 1.000 |
| Jeter,ss | 7 | 30 | 5 | 6 | 7 | 1 | 0 | 0 | 5 | 6 | 0 | 2 | .200 | .333 | .233 | 23 | 20 | 2 | .956 |
| Olerud,1b-ph | 4 | 12 | 1 | 2 | 5 | 0 | 0 | 1 | 2 | 1 | 0 | 1 | .167 | .231 | .417 | 25 | 3 | 0 | 1.000 |
| Clark,1b | 5 | 21 | 0 | 3 | 4 | 1 | 0 | 0 | 1 | 0 | 0 | 9 | .143 | .143 | .190 | 37 | 4 | 1 | .976 |
| Brown,p | 2 | 0 | 0 | 0 | 0 | 0 | 0 | 0 | 0 | 0 | 0 | 0 | .000 | .000 | .000 | 1 | 0 | 0 | 1.000 |
| Crosby,rf-pr | 1 | 0 | 1 | 0 | 0 | 0 | 0 | 0 | 0 | 0 | 0 | 0 | .000 | .000 | .000 | 0 | 0 | 0 | .000 |
| Gordon,p | 6 | 0 | 0 | 0 | 0 | 0 | 0 | 0 | 0 | 0 | 0 | 0 | .000 | .000 | .000 | 0 | 0 | 0 | .000 |
| Heredia,p | 3 | 0 | 0 | 0 | 0 | 0 | 0 | 0 | 0 | 0 | 0 | 0 | .000 | .000 | .000 | 0 | 1 | 0 | 1.000 |
| Hernandez,p | 1 | 0 | 0 | 0 | 0 | 0 | 0 | 0 | 0 | 0 | 0 | 0 | .000 | .000 | .000 | 0 | 0 | 0 | .000 |
| Lieber,p | 2 | 0 | 0 | 0 | 0 | 0 | 0 | 0 | 0 | 0 | 0 | 0 | .000 | .000 | .000 | 1 | 2 | 0 | 1.000 |
| Loaiza,p | 2 | 0 | 0 | 0 | 0 | 0 | 0 | 0 | 0 | 0 | 0 | 0 | .000 | .000 | .000 | 1 | 0 | 1 | .500 |

| Player, position | G | AB | R | H | TB | 2B | 3B | HR | RBI | BB | IBB | SO | Avg. | OBP | Slg. | PO | A | E | Avg. |
|---|---|---|---|---|---|---|---|---|---|---|---|---|---|---|---|---|---|---|---|
| | BATTING | | | | | | | | | | | | | | | FIELDING | | | |
| Mussina,p | 2 | 0 | 0 | 0 | 0 | 0 | 0 | 0 | 0 | 0 | 0 | 0 | .000 | .000 | .000 | 2 | 1 | 0 | 1.000 |
| Quantrill,p | 4 | 0 | 0 | 0 | 0 | 0 | 0 | 0 | 0 | 0 | 0 | 0 | .000 | .000 | .000 | 0 | 0 | 0 | .000 |
| Rivera,p | 5 | 0 | 0 | 0 | 0 | 0 | 0 | 0 | 0 | 0 | 0 | 0 | .000 | .000 | .000 | 1 | 3 | 0 | 1.000 |
| Sturtze,p | 4 | 0 | 0 | 0 | 0 | 0 | 0 | 0 | 0 | 0 | 0 | 0 | .000 | .000 | .000 | 0 | 1 | 0 | 1.000 |
| Vazquez,p | 2 | 0 | 0 | 0 | 0 | 0 | 0 | 0 | 0 | 0 | 0 | 0 | .000 | .000 | .000 | 1 | 1 | 0 | 1.000 |
| **Totals** | 7 | 277 | 45 | 78 | 130 | 21 | 2 | 9 | 44 | 33 | 3 | 51 | .282 | .371 | .469 | 209 | 74 | 4 | .986 |

## BOSTON RED SOX' PITCHING RECORDS

| Pitcher | G | GS | CG | IP | H | R | ER | HR | BB | IBB | SO | HB | WP | W | L | Pct. | ERA |
|---|---|---|---|---|---|---|---|---|---|---|---|---|---|---|---|---|---|
| Foulke | 5 | 0 | 0 | 6.0 | 1 | 0 | 0 | 0 | 6 | 0 | 6 | 1 | 0 | 0 | 0 | .000 | 0.00 |
| Lowe | 2 | 2 | 0 | 11.1 | 7 | 4 | 4 | 1 | 1 | 0 | 6 | 1 | 0 | 1 | 0 | 1.000 | 3.18 |
| Embree | 6 | 0 | 0 | 4.2 | 9 | 2 | 2 | 0 | 1 | 1 | 2 | 0 | 0 | 0 | 0 | .000 | 3.86 |
| Mendoza | 2 | 0 | 0 | 2.0 | 2 | 1 | 1 | 0 | 0 | 0 | 1 | 2 | 0 | 0 | 1 | .000 | 4.50 |
| Timlin | 5 | 0 | 0 | 5.2 | 10 | 3 | 3 | 0 | 5 | 0 | 2 | 0 | 1 | 0 | 0 | .000 | 4.76 |
| Martinez | 3 | 2 | 0 | 13.0 | 14 | 9 | 9 | 2 | 9 | 0 | 14 | 3 | 0 | 0 | 1 | .000 | 6.23 |
| Schilling | 2 | 2 | 0 | 10.0 | 10 | 7 | 7 | 1 | 2 | 0 | 5 | 0 | 0 | 1 | 1 | .500 | 6.30 |
| Myers | 3 | 0 | 0 | 2.1 | 5 | 2 | 2 | 1 | 1 | 0 | 4 | 0 | 0 | 0 | 0 | .000 | 7.71 |
| Wakefield | 3 | 0 | 0 | 7.1 | 9 | 7 | 7 | 1 | 3 | 2 | 6 | 0 | 0 | 1 | 0 | 1.000 | 8.59 |
| Leskanic | 3 | 0 | 0 | 2.2 | 3 | 3 | 3 | 1 | 3 | 0 | 2 | 0 | 0 | 1 | 0 | 1.000 | 10.13 |
| Arroyo | 3 | 1 | 0 | 4.0 | 8 | 7 | 7 | 2 | 2 | 0 | 3 | 0 | 0 | 0 | 0 | .000 | 15.75 |
| Totals | 7 | 7 | 0 | 69.0 | 78 | 45 | 45 | 9 | 33 | 3 | 51 | 7 | 1 | 4 | 3 | .571 | 5.87 |

No shutouts. Saves- Foulke.

## NEW YORK YANKEES' PITCHING RECORDS

| Pitcher | G | GS | CG | IP | H | R | ER | HR | BB | IBB | SO | HB | WP | W | L | Pct. | ERA |
|---|---|---|---|---|---|---|---|---|---|---|---|---|---|---|---|---|---|
| Heredia | 3 | 0 | 0 | 1.1 | 1 | 0 | 0 | 0 | 0 | 0 | 1 | 0 | 0 | 0 | 0 | .000 | 0.00 |
| Rivera | 5 | 0 | 0 | 7.0 | 6 | 1 | 1 | 0 | 2 | 0 | 6 | 0 | 0 | 0 | 0 | .000 | 1.29 |
| Loaiza | 2 | 0 | 0 | 6.1 | 5 | 1 | 1 | 0 | 3 | 0 | 5 | 0 | 0 | 0 | 1 | .000 | 1.42 |
| Sturtze | 4 | 0 | 0 | 3.1 | 2 | 1 | 1 | 1 | 2 | 0 | 2 | 0 | 0 | 0 | 0 | .000 | 2.70 |
| Lieber | 2 | 2 | 0 | 14.1 | 12 | 5 | 5 | 1 | 1 | 0 | 5 | 1 | 1 | 1 | 1 | .500 | 3.14 |
| Mussina | 2 | 2 | 0 | 12.2 | 10 | 6 | 6 | 0 | 2 | 0 | 15 | 0 | 0 | 1 | 0 | 1.000 | 4.26 |
| Hernandez | 1 | 1 | 0 | 5.0 | 3 | 3 | 3 | 0 | 5 | 0 | 6 | 0 | 0 | 0 | 0 | .000 | 5.40 |
| Quantrill | 4 | 0 | 0 | 3.1 | 8 | 2 | 2 | 1 | 0 | 0 | 2 | 0 | 0 | 0 | 1 | .000 | 5.40 |
| Gordon | 6 | 0 | 0 | 6.2 | 10 | 6 | 6 | 2 | 2 | 0 | 3 | 0 | 1 | 0 | 0 | .000 | 8.10 |
| Vazquez | 2 | 0 | 0 | 6.1 | 9 | 7 | 7 | 3 | 7 | 0 | 6 | 0 | 0 | 1 | 0 | 1.000 | 9.95 |
| Brown | 2 | 2 | 0 | 3.1 | 9 | 9 | 8 | 2 | 4 | 0 | 2 | 0 | 1 | 0 | 1 | .000 | 21.60 |
| Totals | 7 | 7 | 0 | 69.2 | 75 | 41 | 40 | 10 | 28 | 0 | 53 | 1 | 3 | 3 | 4 | .429 | 5.17 |

No shutouts. Saves- Rivera 2.

## SCORE BY INNINGS

| | | | | | | | | | | | | | | |
|---|---|---|---|---|---|---|---|---|---|---|---|---|---|---|
| Boston | 4 | 8 | 2 | 6 | 3 | 0 | 7 | 6 | 2 | 0 | 0 | 2 | 0 | 1—41 |
| New York | 6 | 1 | 10 | 5 | 2 | 9 | 7 | 3 | 2 | 0 | 0 | 0 | 0 | 0—45 |

## MISCELLANEOUS STATISTICS

Sacrifice hits—Jeter 2, Cairo, Mientkiewicz.

Sacrifice flies—Cabrera, Posada, Varitek.

Stolen bases—Damon 2, Cabrera, Cairo, Jeter, Lofton, Roberts.

Caught stealing—Damon, Ortiz.

Double plays—Jeter, Cairo and Clark 2; Cabrera and Millar; Cabrera, Bellhorn and Millar; Cairo, Jeter and Clark; Heredia, Jeter and Clark; Jeter and Clark; Mueller and Bellhorn; Mueller, Bellhorn and Millar; Olerud (unassisted); Rivera, Jeter and Olerud; Rodriguez, Cairo and Clark; Rodriguez, Cairo and Olerud.

Left on bases—Boston 2, 4, 9, 10, 12, 7, 9—53; New York 8, 11, 7, 14, 18, 6, 5—69.

Scoring position—Boston 4 for 7, 0 for 7, 2 for 13, 3 for 11, 2 for 13, 3 for 7, 3 for 11—17 for 69; New York 5 for 11, 1 for 9, 8 for 22, 3 for 13, 1 for 13, 1 for 6, 3 for 8—22 for 82.

Hit by pitcher—by Martinez 3 (Rodriguez 2, Cairo), by Mendoza 2 (Cairo, Posada), by Lieber (Mueller), by Lowe (Cairo), by Foulke (Cairo).

Passed balls—Varitek 3, Posada.

Balks—Mendoza.

Time of games—3:20, 3:15, 4:20, 5:02, 5:49, 3:50, 3:31—Avg.: 4:10.

Attendance—56,136, 35,126, 34,826, 35,120, 56,128, 56,129, 56,135—329,600.

Umpires—Nelson, Jeff; Hirschbeck, John; Joyce, Jim; Kellogg, Jeff; West, Joe; Marsh, Randy.

# N.L. CHAMPIONSHIP SERIES

## ST. LOUIS VS. HOUSTON

### RESULTS

| Day | Date | Place | Score |
|---|---|---|---|
| Wed. | Oct. 13 | St. Louis | St. Louis 10, Houston 7 |
| Thu. | Oct. 14 | St. Louis | St. Louis 6, Houston 4 |
| Sat. | Oct. 16 | Houston | Houston 5, St. Louis 2 |
| Sun. | Oct. 17 | Houston | Houston 6, St. Louis 5 |
| Mon. | Oct. 18 | Houston | Houston 3, St. Louis 0 |
| Wed. | Oct 20 | St. Louis | St. Louis 6, Houston 4 |
| Thu. | Oct. 21 | St. Louis | St. Louis 5, Houston 2 |

### BOX SCORES

#### GAME 1

**ST. LOUIS 10, HOUSTON 7**

WEDNESDAY, OCTOBER 13, AT ST. LOUIS

| Houston | AB | R | H | BI | BB | SO | PO | A |
|---|---|---|---|---|---|---|---|---|
| Biggio, lf | 5 | 1 | 2 | 0 | 0 | 1 | 1 | 0 |
| C.Beltran, cf | 5 | 2 | 2 | 2 | 0 | 1 | 1 | 0 |
| Bagwell, 1b | 3 | 0 | 0 | 0 | 1 | 2 | 9 | 0 |
| Berkman, rf | 4 | 2 | 1 | 2 | 0 | 1 | 0 | 0 |
| Kent, 2b | 4 | 1 | 1 | 2 | 0 | 1 | 2 | 2 |
| A.Everett, ss | 0 | 0 | 0 | 0 | 0 | 0 | 1 | 0 |
| Ensberg, 3b | 4 | 0 | 0 | 0 | 0 | 0 | 0 | 1 |
| J.Vizcaino, ss-2b | 4 | 0 | 2 | 0 | 0 | 0 | 0 | 4 |
| Ausmus, c | 4 | 0 | 0 | 0 | 0 | 2 | 10 | 1 |
| Backe, p | 2 | 0 | 0 | 0 | 0 | 1 | 0 | 1 |
| Qualls, p | 0 | 0 | 0 | 0 | 0 | 0 | 0 | 1 |
| Harville, p | 0 | 0 | 0 | 0 | 0 | 0 | 0 | 0 |
| O.Palmeiro, ph | 1 | 0 | 1 | 0 | 0 | 0 | 0 | 0 |
| Wheeler, p | 0 | 0 | 0 | 0 | 0 | 0 | 0 | 0 |
| Lamb, ph | 1 | 1 | 1 | 1 | 0 | 0 | 0 | 0 |
| **TOTALS** | 37 | 7 | 10 | 7 | 1 | 9 | 24 | 10 |

| St. Louis | AB | R | H | BI | BB | SO | PO | A |
|---|---|---|---|---|---|---|---|---|
| Womack, 2b | 5 | 1 | 1 | 1 | 0 | 1 | 1 | 5 |
| L.Walker, rf | 5 | 3 | 3 | 1 | 0 | 1 | 2 | 0 |
| Pujols, 1b | 3 | 2 | 2 | 2 | 2 | 1 | 11 | 0 |
| Rolen, 3b | 4 | 1 | 1 | 1 | 1 | 2 | 1 | 3 |
| Edmonds, cf | 3 | 0 | 2 | 3 | 0 | 1 | 1 | 0 |
| Renteria, ss | 3 | 1 | 1 | 0 | 1 | 1 | 2 | 1 |
| R.Sanders, lf | 4 | 1 | 1 | 0 | 0 | 2 | 1 | 0 |
| Matheny, c | 3 | 0 | 0 | 0 | 0 | 2 | 8 | 1 |
| W.Williams, p | 2 | 1 | 1 | 0 | 0 | 0 | 0 | 0 |
| Cedeno, ph | 1 | 0 | 0 | 1 | 0 | 0 | 0 | 0 |
| Calero, p | 0 | 0 | 0 | 0 | 0 | 0 | 0 | 0 |
| Mar.Anderson, ph | 1 | 0 | 0 | 0 | 0 | 0 | 0 | 0 |
| Haren, p | 0 | 0 | 0 | 0 | 0 | 0 | 0 | 0 |
| King, p | 0 | 0 | 0 | 0 | 0 | 0 | 0 | 0 |
| Tavarez, p | 0 | 0 | 0 | 0 | 0 | 0 | 0 | 0 |
| Isringhausen, p | 0 | 0 | 0 | 0 | 0 | 0 | 0 | 0 |
| **TOTALS** | 34 | 10 | 12 | 9 | 4 | 11 | 27 | 10 |

| | | | | |
|---|---|---|---|---|
| Houston | 2 0 0 | 2 0 0 | 0 2 1—7 | 10 1 |
| St. Louis | 2 0 0 | 0 2 6 | 0 0 x—10 | 12 0 |

| Houston | IP | H | R | ER | HR | BB | SO |
|---|---|---|---|---|---|---|---|
| Backe | 4.2 | 5 | 4 | 4 | 1 | 2 | 6 |
| Qualls (L) | 1.0 | 5 | 5 | 5 | 0 | 1 | 1 |
| Harville | 0.1 | 1 | 1 | 1 | 0 | 1 | 0 |
| Wheeler | 2.0 | 1 | 0 | 0 | 0 | 0 | 4 |

| St. Louis | IP | H | R | ER | HR | BB | SO |
|---|---|---|---|---|---|---|---|
| W.Williams (W) | 6.0 | 4 | 4 | 4 | 2 | 1 | 5 |
| Calero | 1.0 | 2 | 0 | 0 | 0 | 0 | 2 |
| Haren | 0.1 | 1 | 1 | 1 | 0 | 0 | 1 |
| King | 0.1 | 1 | 1 | 1 | 1 | 0 | 0 |
| Tavarez | 1.0 | 2 | 1 | 1 | 1 | 0 | 1 |
| Isringhausen (S) | 0.1 | 0 | 0 | 0 | 0 | 0 | 0 |

E—J.Vizcaino. DP—Houston 1. LOB—Houston 4, St. Louis 6. Scoring Position—Houston 0 for 2, St. Louis 6 for 11. 2B—Biggio, O.Palmeiro, L.Walker, Edmonds, W.Williams. 3B—L.Walker. HR—C.Beltran (1st inning, 0 out, 1 on) off W.Williams, Pujols (1st inning, 1 out, 1 on) off Backe, Kent (4th inning, 1 out, 1 on) off W.Williams, Berkman (8th inning, 1 out, 1 on) off King, Lamb (9th inning, 2 out, 0 on) off Tavarez. SB—Womack. SH—Matheny. HBP—Edmonds by Backe. T—3:15. A—52,323. U—HP-Welke, 1B-Cooper, 2B-Darling, 3B-Winters, LF-Hernandez, RF-Rapuano.

### HOW THEY SCORED

TOP OF 1

Astros first. Biggio singled to center. Beltran homered to right on a 2-2 count, Biggio scored. Bagwell grounded out, third baseman Rolen to first baseman Pujols. Berkman struck out. Kent popped out to second baseman Womack. Runs: 2, Hits: 2, Errors: 0

BOTTOM OF 1

Cardinals first. Womack lined out to left fielder Biggio. Walker tripled to right. Pujols homered to right on a 2-0 count, Walker scored. Rolen grounded out, shortstop Vizcaino to first baseman Bagwell. Edmonds singled to right. Renteria struck out. Runs: 2, Hits: 3, Errors: 0

TOP OF 4

Astros fourth. Bagwell walked on a full count. Berkman grounded into fielder's choice, second baseman Womack to shortstop Renteria, Bagwell out. Kent homered to left on a 1-2 count, Berkman scored. Ensberg flied out to right fielder Walker. Vizcaino singled to right. Ausmus grounded out, third baseman Rolen to first baseman Pujols. Runs: 2, Hits: 2, Errors: 0

BOTTOM OF 5

Cardinals fifth. Matheny grounded out, shortstop Vizcaino to first baseman Bagwell. Williams doubled to right. Womack grounded out, shortstop Vizcaino to first baseman Bagwell, Williams to third. Walker doubled to left, Williams scored. Pujols walked. Qualls pitching. Rolen singled to left, Walker scored, Pujols to second. Edmonds struck out. Runs: 2, Hits: 3, Errors: 0

BOTTOM OF 6

Cardinals sixth. Renteria singled to center. Sanders infield single to second, Renteria to second. Matheny sacrificed, pitcher Qualls to second baseman Kent, Renteria to third, Sanders to second. Cedeno pinch-hitting for Williams. Cedeno grounded out, first baseman Bagwell unassisted, Renteria scored, Sanders to third. Womack singled to center, Sanders scored. Womack stole second. Walker infield single to short, Womack to third. On Vizcaino's error, Womack scored. Pujols walked on four pitches, Walker to second. Harville pitching. Rolen walked, Walker to third, Pujols to second. Edmonds doubled to right, Walker scored, Pujols scored, Rolen scored. Renteria grounded out, second baseman Kent to first baseman Bagwell. Runs: 6, Hits: 5, Errors: 1

TOP OF 8

Astros eighth. Haren pitching. Beltran singled to right. Bagwell struck out. King pitching. Berkman homered to left on a 0-1 count, Beltran scored. Kent popped out to first baseman Pujols. Tavarez pitching. Ensberg lined out to third baseman Rolen. Runs: 2, Hits: 2, Errors: 0

TOP OF 9

Astros ninth. Vizcaino grounded out, second baseman Womack to first baseman Pujols. Ausmus struck out. Lamb pinch-hitting for Wheeler. Lamb homered to center on a 2-1 count. Biggio doubled to left. Isringhausen pitching. Beltran grounded out, first baseman Pujols unassisted. Runs: 1, Hits: 2, Errors: 0

## GAME 2

### ST. LOUIS 6, HOUSTON 4

THURSDAY, OCTOBER 14, AT ST. LOUIS

| Houston | AB | R | H | BI | BB | SO | PO | A |
|---|---|---|---|---|---|---|---|---|
| Biggio, lf | 5 | 1 | 1 | 0 | 0 | 1 | 0 | 0 |
| Miceli, p | 0 | 0 | 0 | 0 | 0 | 0 | 1 | 0 |
| C.Beltran, cf | 2 | 1 | 1 | 1 | 3 | 1 | 2 | 0 |
| Bagwell, 1b | 3 | 0 | 0 | 0 | 2 | 1 | 6 | 2 |
| Berkman, rf | 5 | 1 | 2 | 1 | 0 | 0 | 2 | 0 |
| Kent, 2b | 4 | 0 | 1 | 0 | 1 | 1 | 2 | 2 |
| A.Everett, pr | 0 | 0 | 0 | 0 | 0 | 0 | 0 | 0 |
| Ensberg, 3b | 5 | 1 | 2 | 2 | 0 | 1 | 1 | 1 |
| J.Vizcaino, ss | 4 | 0 | 2 | 0 | 0 | 0 | 1 | 3 |
| Ausmus, c | 3 | 0 | 1 | 0 | 1 | 1 | 7 | 0 |
| Munro, p | 1 | 0 | 0 | 0 | 1 | 0 | 1 | 0 |
| Harville, p | 0 | 0 | 0 | 0 | 0 | 0 | 0 | 0 |
| Bruntlett, ph | 1 | 0 | 0 | 0 | 0 | 0 | 0 | 0 |
| Wheeler, p | 0 | 0 | 0 | 0 | 0 | 0 | 1 | 0 |
| O.Palmeiro, ph-lf | 1 | 0 | 0 | 0 | 0 | 0 | 0 | 0 |
| **TOTALS** | 34 | 4 | 10 | 4 | 8 | 6 | 24 | 8 |

| St. Louis | AB | R | H | BI | BB | SO | PO | A |
|---|---|---|---|---|---|---|---|---|
| Womack, 2b | 4 | 1 | 1 | 0 | 0 | 0 | 2 | 2 |
| L.Walker, rf | 4 | 1 | 1 | 2 | 0 | 2 | 2 | 0 |
| Pujols, 1b | 4 | 2 | 3 | 1 | 0 | 0 | 4 | 2 |
| Rolen, 3b | 4 | 2 | 2 | 3 | 0 | 1 | 1 | 0 |
| Edmonds, cf | 4 | 0 | 1 | 0 | 0 | 1 | 4 | 0 |
| Renteria, ss | 4 | 0 | 0 | 0 | 0 | 0 | 5 | 3 |
| R.Sanders, lf | 4 | 0 | 0 | 0 | 0 | 0 | 3 | 1 |
| Isringhausen, p | 0 | 0 | 0 | 0 | 0 | 0 | 0 | 0 |
| Matheny, c | 3 | 0 | 1 | 0 | 0 | 2 | 6 | 2 |
| M.Morris, p | 0 | 0 | 0 | 0 | 0 | 0 | 0 | 0 |
| Mar.Anderson, ph | 0 | 0 | 0 | 0 | 1 | 0 | 0 | 0 |
| Kline, p | 0 | 0 | 0 | 0 | 0 | 0 | 0 | 0 |
| Calero, p | 0 | 0 | 0 | 0 | 0 | 0 | 0 | 0 |
| Cedeno, ph | 1 | 0 | 0 | 0 | 0 | 1 | 0 | 0 |
| Tavarez, p | 0 | 0 | 0 | 0 | 0 | 0 | 0 | 0 |
| Taguchi, lf | 0 | 0 | 0 | 0 | 0 | 0 | 0 | 0 |
| **TOTALS** | 32 | 6 | 9 | 6 | 1 | 7 | 27 | 10 |

| | | | | | | |
|---|---|---|---|---|---|---|
| Houston | 1 0 0 | 1 1 0 | 1 0 0—4 | 10 | 1 |
| St. Louis | 0 0 0 | 0 4 0 | 0 2 x—6 | 9 | 0 |

| Houston | IP | H | R | ER | HR | BB | SO |
|---|---|---|---|---|---|---|---|
| Munro | 4.2 | 6 | 3 | 3 | 1 | 1 | 4 |
| Harville | 0.1 | 1 | 1 | 1 | 1 | 0 | 1 |
| Wheeler | 2.0 | 0 | 0 | 0 | 0 | 0 | 2 |
| Miceli (L) | 1.0 | 2 | 2 | 2 | 2 | 0 | 0 |

| St. Louis | IP | H | R | ER | HR | BB | SO |
|---|---|---|---|---|---|---|---|
| M.Morris | 5.0 | 6 | 3 | 3 | 2 | 5 | 5 |
| Kline | 0.0 | 2 | 0 | 0 | 0 | 0 | 0 |
| Calero (BS) | 2.0 | 2 | 1 | 1 | 0 | 1 | 1 |
| Tavarez (W) | 1.0 | 0 | 0 | 0 | 0 | 0 | 0 |
| Isringhausen (S) | 1.0 | 0 | 0 | 0 | 0 | 2 | 0 |

Kline pitched to 2 batters in the 6th.

E—Munro. DP—St. Louis 1. LOB—Houston 11, St. Louis 4. Scoring Position—Houston 2 for 14, St. Louis 1 for 8. 2B—Berkman, Kent, Edmonds. HR—C.Beltran (1st inning, 1 out, 0 on) off M.Morris, Ensberg (4th inning, 0 out, 0 on) off M.Morris, L.Walker (5th inning, 2 out, 1 on) off Munro, Rolen (5th inning, 2 out, 1 on) off Harville, Pujols (8th inning, 0 out, 0 on) off Miceli, Rolen (8th inning, 0 out, 0 on) off Miceli. SB—Berkman, Womack. CS—Bagwell, Ensberg. SH—M.Morris. WP—M.Morris 2. BK—M.Morris. T—3:02. A—52,347. U—HP-Cooper, 1B-Darling, 2B-Winters, 3B-Hernandez, LF-Rapuano, RF-Welke.

## HOW THEY SCORED

TOP OF 1

Astros first. Biggio flied out to left fielder Sanders. Beltran homered to right on a 0-1 count. Bagwell struck out. Berkman flied out to left fielder Sanders. Runs: 1, Hits: 1, Errors: 0

TOP OF 4

Astros fourth. Ensberg homered to left on a 1-1 count. Vizcaino singled to center. Vizcaino was out advancing, left fielder Sanders to second baseman Womack, Vizcaino out. Ausmus struck out. Munro grounded out, second baseman Womack to first baseman Pujols. Runs: 1, Hits: 2, Errors: 0

TOP OF 5

Astros fifth. Biggio singled to left. Beltran struck out. On Morris' balk, Biggio to second. Bagwell walked on a full count. Berkman singled to right, Biggio scored, Bagwell to second. Kent popped out to shortstop Renteria. Ensberg flied out to center fielder Edmonds. Runs: 1, Hits: 2, Errors: 0

BOTTOM OF 5

Cardinals fifth. Matheny struck out. Anderson pinch-hitting for Morris. Anderson walked. Womack grounded into fielder's choice, third baseman Ensberg to second baseman Kent, Anderson out. Womack stole second. Walker homered to right on a 1-1 count, Womack scored. Pujols singled to center. Harville pitching. Rolen homered to left on a 0-1 count, Pujols scored. Edmonds struck out. Runs: 4, Hits: 3, Errors: 0

TOP OF 7

Astros seventh. Berkman doubled to center. Kent flied out to left fielder Sanders. Berkman stole third. Ensberg singled to center, Berkman scored. Ensberg was caught stealing, catcher Matheny to shortstop Renteria, Ensberg out. Vizcaino grounded out, shortstop Renteria to first baseman Pujols. Runs: 1, Hits: 2, Errors: 0

BOTTOM OF 8

Cardinals eighth. Miceli pitching. Palmeiro in as left fielder. Pujols homered to left on a 1-0 count. Rolen homered to left on a 0-2 count. Edmonds grounded out, first baseman Bagwell to pitcher Miceli. Renteria grounded out, shortstop Vizcaino to first baseman Bagwell. Sanders flied out to right fielder Berkman. Runs: 2, Hits: 2, Errors: 0

## GAME 3

### HOUSTON 5, ST. LOUIS 2

SATURDAY, OCTOBER 16, AT HOUSTON

| St. Louis | AB | R | H | BI | BB | SO | PO | A |
|---|---|---|---|---|---|---|---|---|
| Womack, 2b | 4 | 0 | 0 | 0 | 0 | 1 | 0 | 2 |
| L.Walker, rf | 4 | 1 | 1 | 1 | 0 | 1 | 1 | 0 |
| Pujols, 1b | 4 | 0 | 1 | 0 | 0 | 1 | 10 | 0 |
| Rolen, 3b | 3 | 0 | 1 | 0 | 1 | 1 | 3 | 2 |
| Edmonds, cf | 3 | 1 | 1 | 1 | 1 | 1 | 5 | 0 |
| Renteria, ss | 4 | 0 | 0 | 0 | 0 | 2 | 1 | 2 |
| R.Sanders, lf | 3 | 0 | 0 | 0 | 1 | 2 | 0 | 0 |
| Matheny, c | 3 | 0 | 1 | 0 | 0 | 1 | 4 | 1 |
| Mar.Anderson, ph | 0 | 0 | 0 | 0 | 0 | 0 | 0 | 0 |
| Suppan, p | 2 | 0 | 0 | 0 | 0 | 0 | 0 | 0 |
| Cedeno, ph | 1 | 0 | 0 | 0 | 0 | 1 | 0 | 0 |
| Haren, p | 0 | 0 | 0 | 0 | 0 | 0 | 0 | 1 |
| King, p | 0 | 0 | 0 | 0 | 0 | 0 | 0 | 0 |
| Eldred, p | 0 | 0 | 0 | 0 | 0 | 0 | 0 | 1 |
| Mabry, ph | 1 | 0 | 0 | 0 | 0 | 1 | 0 | 0 |
| **TOTALS** | 32 | 2 | 5 | 2 | 3 | 12 | 24 | 9 |

| Houston | AB | R | H | BI | BB | SO | PO | A |
|---|---|---|---|---|---|---|---|---|
| Biggio, lf | 4 | 0 | 1 | 0 | 0 | 1 | 2 | 0 |
| Lidge, p | 0 | 0 | 0 | 0 | 0 | 0 | 0 | 0 |
| C.Beltran, cf | 3 | 2 | 2 | 1 | 1 | 1 | 0 | 0 |
| Bagwell, 1b | 4 | 0 | 1 | 0 | 0 | 0 | 7 | 0 |
| Berkman, rf | 4 | 2 | 2 | 2 | 0 | 0 | 4 | 0 |
| Kent, 2b | 3 | 1 | 1 | 2 | 1 | 1 | 1 | 1 |
| Bruntlett, ss | 0 | 0 | 0 | 0 | 0 | 0 | 0 | 0 |
| Ensberg, 3b | 3 | 0 | 0 | 0 | 1 | 0 | 0 | 1 |
| J.Vizcaino, ss-2b | 4 | 0 | 0 | 0 | 0 | 0 | 1 | 4 |
| Ausmus, c | 3 | 0 | 0 | 0 | 0 | 1 | 12 | 0 |
| Clemens, p | 2 | 0 | 0 | 0 | 0 | 1 | 0 | 1 |
| O.Palmeiro, ph-lf | 1 | 0 | 1 | 0 | 0 | 0 | 0 | 0 |
| **TOTALS** | 31 | 5 | 8 | 5 | 3 | 5 | 27 | 7 |

| | | | | | | |
|---|---|---|---|---|---|---|
| St. Louis | 1 1 0 | 0 0 0 | 0 0 0—2 | 5 | 0 |
| Houston | 3 0 0 | 0 0 0 | 0 2 x—5 | 8 | 0 |

| St. Louis | IP | H | R | ER | HR | BB | SO |
|---|---|---|---|---|---|---|---|
| Suppan (L) | 6.0 | 5 | 3 | 3 | 1 | 2 | 3 |
| Haren | 1.1 | 2 | 1 | 1 | 1 | 0 | 1 |
| King | 0.1 | 1 | 1 | 1 | 1 | 0 | 1 |
| Eldred | 0.1 | 0 | 0 | 0 | 0 | 1 | 0 |

| Houston | IP | H | R | ER | HR | BB | SO |
|---|---|---|---|---|---|---|---|
| Clemens (W) | 7.0 | 4 | 2 | 2 | 2 | 2 | 7 |
| Lidge (S) | 2.0 | 1 | 0 | 0 | 0 | 1 | 5 |

DP—St. Louis 1. LOB—St. Louis 7, Houston 5. Scoring Position—St. Louis 0 for 5, Houston 2 for 5. 2B—C.Beltran. HR—L.Walker (1st inning, 1 out, 0 on) off Clemens, Kent (1st inning, 2 out, 1 on) off Suppan, Edmonds (2nd inning, 0 out, 0 on) off Clemens, C.Beltran (8th inning, 0 out, 0 on) off Haren, Berkman (8th inning, 1 out, 0 on) off King. WP—Clemens. HBP—Mar.Anderson by Lidge. T—2:57. A—42,896. U—HP-Darling, 1B-Winters, 2B-Hernandez, 3B-Rapuano, LF-Welke, RF-Cooper.

## HOW THEY SCORED

TOP OF 1

Cardinals first. Womack lined out to shortstop Vizcaino. Walker homered to center on the first pitch. Pujols grounded out, shortstop Vizcaino to first baseman Bagwell. Rolen popped out to second baseman Kent. Runs: 1, Hits: 1, Errors: 0

BOTTOM OF 1

Astros first. Biggio singled to left. Beltran walked, Biggio to second. Bagwell grounded into a double play, third baseman Rolen to first baseman Pujols, Biggio out, Beltran to second. Berkman singled to center, Beltran scored. Kent homered to left on a full count, Berkman scored. Ensberg flied out to center fielder Edmonds. Runs: 3, Hits: 3, Errors: 0

TOP OF 2

Cardinals second. Edmonds homered to right on a 2-2 count. Renteria grounded out, shortstop Vizcaino to first baseman Bagwell. Sanders grounded out, shortstop Vizcaino to first baseman Bagwell. Matheny singled to left. Suppan grounded out, third baseman Ensberg to first baseman Bagwell. Runs: 1, Hits: 2, Errors: 0

BOTTOM OF 8

Astros eighth. Beltran homered to center on a 1-0 count. Bagwell fouled out to first baseman Pujols. King pitching. Berkman homered to left on a 2-2 count. Kent struck out. Eldred pitching. Ensberg walked on a full count. Vizcaino grounded out, pitcher Eldred to first baseman Pujols. Runs: 2, Hits: 2, Errors: 0

## GAME 4

### HOUSTON 6, ST. LOUIS 5

SUNDAY, OCTOBER 17, AT HOUSTON

| St. Louis | AB | R | H | BI | BB | SO | PO | A |
|---|---|---|---|---|---|---|---|---|
| Womack, 2b | 4 | 1 | 0 | 0 | 1 | 0 | 1 | 2 |
| L.Walker, rf | 3 | 1 | 1 | 0 | 2 | 0 | 2 | 0 |
| Pujols, 1b | 4 | 2 | 3 | 3 | 1 | 0 | 7 | 0 |
| Rolen, 3b | 5 | 1 | 2 | 0 | 0 | 2 | 2 | 0 |
| Edmonds, cf | 3 | 0 | 0 | 1 | 0 | 0 | 2 | 0 |
| Renteria, ss | 3 | 0 | 0 | 0 | 1 | 0 | 1 | 2 |
| Tavarez, p | 0 | 0 | 0 | 0 | 0 | 0 | 0 | 0 |
| Matheny, c | 0 | 0 | 0 | 0 | 0 | 0 | 0 | 0 |
| Mabry, lf | 3 | 0 | 1 | 1 | 0 | 0 | 1 | 0 |
| Calero, p | 0 | 0 | 0 | 0 | 0 | 0 | 0 | 0 |
| King, p | 0 | 0 | 0 | 0 | 0 | 0 | 0 | 0 |
| Luna, ss | 1 | 0 | 0 | 0 | 0 | 1 | 1 | 0 |
| Y.Molina, c | 4 | 0 | 1 | 0 | 0 | 0 | 5 | 1 |
| Isringhausen, p | 0 | 0 | 0 | 0 | 0 | 0 | 0 | 0 |
| Marquis, p | 2 | 0 | 1 | 0 | 0 | 0 | 0 | 0 |
| Taguchi, lf | 0 | 0 | 0 | 0 | 0 | 0 | 2 | 0 |
| Cedeno, ph-lf | 1 | 0 | 0 | 0 | 0 | 0 | 0 | 0 |
| **TOTALS** | 33 | 5 | 9 | 5 | 5 | 3 | 24 | 5 |

| Houston | AB | R | H | BI | BB | SO | PO | A |
|---|---|---|---|---|---|---|---|---|
| Biggio, lf | 4 | 0 | 1 | 0 | 0 | 0 | 1 | 0 |
| Lane, lf | 0 | 0 | 0 | 0 | 0 | 0 | 1 | 0 |
| C.Beltran, cf | 3 | 3 | 2 | 1 | 1 | 1 | 4 | 0 |
| Bagwell, 1b | 3 | 1 | 2 | 1 | 1 | 1 | 12 | 0 |
| Berkman, rf | 2 | 1 | 2 | 3 | 2 | 0 | 2 | 1 |
| Kent, 2b | 3 | 0 | 0 | 0 | 0 | 2 | 2 | 4 |
| Lidge, p | 0 | 0 | 0 | 0 | 0 | 0 | 0 | 0 |
| Ensberg, 3b | 4 | 0 | 0 | 0 | 0 | 1 | 1 | 1 |
| J.Vizcaino, ss-2b | 4 | 1 | 1 | 0 | 0 | 0 | 1 | 2 |
| R.Chavez, c | 3 | 0 | 1 | 1 | 0 | 0 | 1 | 0 |
| Ausmus, c | 1 | 0 | 0 | 0 | 0 | 0 | 2 | 0 |
| Oswalt, p | 2 | 0 | 0 | 0 | 0 | 0 | 0 | 2 |
| O.Palmeiro, ph | 1 | 0 | 0 | 0 | 0 | 0 | 0 | 0 |
| Wheeler, p | 0 | 0 | 0 | 0 | 0 | 0 | 0 | 0 |
| Bruntlett, ss | 1 | 0 | 0 | 0 | 0 | 0 | 0 | 0 |
| **TOTALS** | 31 | 6 | 9 | 6 | 4 | 5 | 27 | 10 |

| | | | | |
|---|---|---|---|---|
| St. Louis | 3 0 1 | 1 0 0 | 0 0 0—5 9 0 |
| Houston | 1 0 2 | 0 0 2 | 1 0 x—6 9 0 |

| St. Louis | IP | H | R | ER | HR | BB | SO |
|---|---|---|---|---|---|---|---|
| Marquis | 4.0 | 5 | 3 | 3 | 0 | 2 | 2 |
| Calero | 1.2 | 3 | 2 | 2 | 1 | 0 | 3 |
| King | 0.1 | 0 | 0 | 0 | 0 | 0 | 0 |
| Tavarez (L) | 1.0 | 1 | 1 | 1 | 1 | 2 | 0 |
| Isringhausen | 1.0 | 0 | 0 | 0 | 0 | 0 | 0 |

Marquis pitched to 1 batter in the 5th.

| Houston | IP | H | R | ER | HR | BB | SO |
|---|---|---|---|---|---|---|---|
| Oswalt | 6.0 | 8 | 5 | 5 | 1 | 4 | 0 |
| Wheeler (W) | 1.0 | 1 | 0 | 0 | 0 | 0 | 1 |
| Lidge (S) | 2.0 | 0 | 0 | 0 | 0 | 1 | 2 |

DP—St. Louis 1. LOB—St. Louis 8, Houston 6. Scoring Position—St. Louis 2 for 10, Houston 2 for 7. 2B—Rolen, Bagwell, Berkman, J.Vizcaino. HR—Pujols (1st inning, 1 out, 1 on) off Oswalt, Berkman (6th inning, 0 out, 0 on) off Calero, C.Beltran (7th inning, 1 out, 0 on) off Tavarez. CS—Biggio. S—Edmonds. SH—Taguchi. WP—Tavarez. PB—R.Chavez. HBP—Kent by Tavarez. T—3:01. A—42,760. U—HP-Winters, 1B-Hernandez, 2B-Rapuano, 3B-Welke, LF-Cooper, RF-Darling.

## HOW THEY SCORED

TOP OF 1

Cardinals first. Womack grounded out, pitcher Oswalt to first baseman Bagwell. Walker walked on a full count. Pujols homered to left on a 2-0 count, Walker scored. Rolen doubled to left. Edmonds grounded out, first baseman Bagwell unassisted, Rolen to third. Renteria walked on a full count. Mabry singled to center, Rolen scored, Renteria to third. Molina grounded into fielder's choice, third baseman Ensberg to second baseman Kent, Mabry out. Runs: 3, Hits: 3, Errors: 0

BOTTOM OF 1

Astros first. Biggio grounded out, shortstop Renteria to first baseman Pujols. Beltran walked on four pitches. Bagwell doubled to center, Beltran scored. Berkman walked. Kent struck out. Ensberg flied out to center fielder Edmonds. Runs: 1, Hits: 1, Errors: 0

TOP OF 3

Cardinals third. Pujols walked on a full count. Rolen singled to center, Pujols to third. Edmonds hit a sacrifice fly to right fielder Berkman, Pujols scored. Renteria flied out to right fielder Berkman. Mabry grounded out, first baseman Bagwell unassisted. Runs: 1, Hits: 1, Errors: 0

BOTTOM OF 3

Astros third. Biggio popped out to third baseman Rolen. Beltran singled to center. Bagwell singled to center, Beltran to second. Berkman doubled to center, Beltran scored, Bagwell scored. Kent popped out to third baseman Rolen. Ensberg struck out. Runs: 2, Hits: 3, Errors: 0

TOP OF 4

Cardinals fourth. Molina flied out to center fielder Beltran. Marquis singled to right. Marquis was out advancing, right fielder Berkman to shortstop Vizcaino, Marquis out. Womack walked. Walker singled to center, Womack to third. Pujols singled to center, Womack scored, Walker to third. Rolen flied out to center fielder Beltran. Runs: 1, Hits: 3, Errors: 0

BOTTOM OF 6

Astros sixth. Berkman homered to left on a 3-1 count. Kent struck out. Ensberg flied out to left fielder Taguchi. Vizcaino doubled to left. Chavez singled to center, Vizcaino scored. King pitching. Palmeiro pinch-hitting for Oswalt. Palmeiro flied out to left fielder Taguchi. Runs: 2, Hits: 3, Errors: 0

BOTTOM OF 7

Astros seventh. Tavarez pitching. Luna in as shortstop. Biggio flied out to right fielder Walker. Beltran homered to right on a 2-2 count. Bagwell walked on four pitches. On Tavarez's wild pitch, Bagwell to second. Berkman was intentionally walked. Kent was hit by a pitch, Bagwell to third, Berkman to second. Ensberg grounded into a double play, second baseman Womack to first baseman Pujols, Kent out. Runs: 1, Hits: 1, Errors: 0

## GAME 5

### HOUSTON 3, ST. LOUIS 0

MONDAY, OCTOBER 18, AT HOUSTON

| St. Louis | AB | R | H | BI | BB | SO | PO | A |
|---|---|---|---|---|---|---|---|---|
| Womack, 2b | 4 | 0 | 1 | 0 | 0 | 0 | 3 | 1 |
| L.Walker, rf | 3 | 0 | 0 | 0 | 1 | 2 | 1 | 0 |
| Pujols, 1b | 4 | 0 | 0 | 0 | 0 | 1 | 6 | 3 |
| Rolen, 3b | 3 | 0 | 0 | 0 | 0 | 1 | 0 | 4 |
| Edmonds, cf | 2 | 0 | 0 | 0 | 1 | 0 | 2 | 0 |
| Renteria, ss | 3 | 0 | 0 | 0 | 0 | 1 | 3 | 0 |
| R.Sanders, lf | 3 | 0 | 0 | 0 | 0 | 0 | 2 | 0 |
| Matheny, c | 3 | 0 | 0 | 0 | 0 | 0 | 5 | 0 |
| W.Williams, p | 2 | 0 | 0 | 0 | 0 | 0 | 3 | 1 |
| Mabry, ph | 1 | 0 | 0 | 0 | 0 | 1 | 0 | 0 |
| Isringhausen, p | 0 | 0 | 0 | 0 | 0 | 0 | 0 | 0 |
| **TOTALS** | 28 | 0 | 1 | 0 | 2 | 6 | 25 | 9 |

| Houston | AB | R | H | BI | BB | SO | PO | A |
|---|---|---|---|---|---|---|---|---|
| Biggio, lf | 4 | 0 | 0 | 0 | 0 | 0 | 1 | 0 |
| Lidge, p | 0 | 0 | 0 | 0 | 0 | 0 | 0 | 0 |
| C.Beltran, cf | 4 | 1 | 1 | 0 | 0 | 0 | 3 | 0 |
| Bagwell, 1b | 4 | 0 | 1 | 0 | 0 | 1 | 9 | 0 |
| Berkman, rf | 2 | 1 | 0 | 0 | 2 | 0 | 2 | 0 |
| Kent, 2b | 4 | 1 | 1 | 3 | 0 | 0 | 3 | 4 |
| Ensberg, 3b | 2 | 0 | 0 | 0 | 0 | 1 | 2 | 3 |
| J.Vizcaino, ss | 3 | 0 | 0 | 0 | 0 | 1 | 1 | 1 |
| Ausmus, c | 2 | 0 | 0 | 0 | 1 | 1 | 6 | 0 |
| Backe, p | 2 | 0 | 0 | 0 | 0 | 1 | 0 | 1 |
| O.Palmeiro, ph-lf | 1 | 0 | 0 | 0 | 0 | 0 | 0 | 0 |
| **TOTALS** | 28 | 3 | 3 | 3 | 3 | 5 | 27 | 9 |

| | | | | |
|---|---|---|---|---|
| St. Louis | 0 0 0 | 0 0 0 | 0 0 0—0 | 1 0 |
| Houston | 0 0 0 | 0 0 0 | 0 0 3—3 | 3 0 |

| St. Louis | IP | H | R | ER | HR | BB | SO |
|---|---|---|---|---|---|---|---|
| W.Williams | 7.0 | 1 | 0 | 0 | 0 | 2 | 4 |
| Isringhausen (L) | 1.1 | 2 | 3 | 3 | 1 | 1 | 1 |

| Houston | IP | H | R | ER | HR | BB | SO |
|---|---|---|---|---|---|---|---|
| Backe | 8.0 | 1 | 0 | 0 | 0 | 2 | 4 |
| Lidge (W) | 1.0 | 0 | 0 | 0 | 0 | 0 | 2 |

LOB—St. Louis 3, Houston 4. Scoring Position—St. Louis 0 for 1, Houston 1 for 2. HR—Kent (9th inning, 1 out, 2 on) off Isringhausen. SB—C.Beltran. HBP—Ensberg by W.Williams. T—2:33. A—43,045. U—HP-Hernandez, 1B-Rapuano, 2B-Welke, 3B-Cooper, LF-Darling, RF-Winters.

## HOW THEY SCORED

BOTTOM OF 9

Astros ninth. Beltran singled to right. Bagwell flied out to center fielder Edmonds. Beltran stole second. Berkman was intentionally walked. Kent homered to left on the first pitch, Beltran scored, Berkman scored. Runs: 3, Hits: 2, Errors: 0

## GAME 6

### ST. LOUIS 6, HOUSTON 4

WEDNESDAY, OCTOBER 20, AT ST. LOUIS

| Houston | AB | R | H | BI | BB | SO | PO | A |
|---|---|---|---|---|---|---|---|---|
| Biggio, lf | 6 | 0 | 0 | 0 | 0 | 0 | 3 | 0 |
| C.Beltran, cf | 4 | 2 | 2 | 0 | 2 | 0 | 0 | 0 |
| Bagwell, 1b | 6 | 0 | 3 | 2 | 0 | 0 | 12 | 0 |
| Berkman, rf | 3 | 0 | 0 | 1 | 1 | 1 | 3 | 0 |
| Lidge, p | 0 | 0 | 0 | 0 | 0 | 0 | 0 | 0 |
| Backe, ph | 1 | 0 | 0 | 0 | 0 | 1 | 0 | 0 |
| Miceli, p | 0 | 0 | 0 | 0 | 0 | 0 | 0 | 0 |
| Kent, 2b | 5 | 0 | 2 | 0 | 0 | 0 | 0 | 2 |
| Lamb, 3b | 4 | 1 | 1 | 1 | 1 | 1 | 1 | 3 |
| J.Vizcaino, ss | 5 | 0 | 1 | 0 | 0 | 0 | 1 | 5 |
| Ausmus, c | 3 | 0 | 1 | 0 | 0 | 1 | 9 | 1 |
| Ensberg, ph | 0 | 1 | 0 | 0 | 0 | 0 | 0 | 0 |
| Lane, rf | 1 | 0 | 0 | 0 | 0 | 0 | 0 | 0 |
| Munro, p | 1 | 0 | 0 | 0 | 0 | 0 | 0 | 1 |
| Harville, p | 0 | 0 | 0 | 0 | 0 | 0 | 0 | 0 |
| A.Everett, ph | 1 | 0 | 0 | 0 | 0 | 0 | 0 | 0 |
| Qualls, p | 0 | 0 | 0 | 0 | 0 | 0 | 0 | 0 |
| O.Palmeiro, ph | 1 | 0 | 0 | 0 | 0 | 0 | 0 | 0 |
| Wheeler, p | 0 | 0 | 0 | 0 | 0 | 0 | 0 | 0 |
| Bruntlett, ph | 0 | 0 | 0 | 0 | 0 | 0 | 0 | 0 |
| R.Chavez, c | 1 | 0 | 0 | 0 | 0 | 1 | 5 | 2 |
| **TOTALS** | 42 | 4 | 10 | 4 | 4 | 5 | 34 | 14 |

| St. Louis | AB | R | H | BI | BB | SO | PO | A |
|---|---|---|---|---|---|---|---|---|
| Womack, 2b | 2 | 1 | 2 | 0 | 0 | 0 | 2 | 1 |
| Luna, 2b | 3 | 0 | 0 | 0 | 0 | 1 | 4 | 2 |
| Mar.Anderson, ph-2b | 1 | 0 | 0 | 0 | 0 | 0 | 0 | 0 |
| L.Walker, rf | 6 | 0 | 0 | 0 | 0 | 2 | 2 | 0 |
| Pujols, 1b | 5 | 3 | 3 | 2 | 1 | 0 | 9 | 2 |
| Rolen, 3b | 6 | 1 | 2 | 0 | 0 | 2 | 1 | 3 |
| Edmonds, cf | 6 | 1 | 2 | 2 | 0 | 2 | 2 | 0 |
| Renteria, ss | 5 | 0 | 3 | 2 | 0 | 1 | 5 | 3 |
| R.Sanders, lf | 4 | 0 | 3 | 0 | 0 | 0 | 2 | 0 |
| Isringhausen, p | 0 | 0 | 0 | 0 | 0 | 0 | 1 | 0 |
| Cedeno, ph | 1 | 0 | 0 | 0 | 0 | 0 | 0 | 0 |
| Tavarez, p | 0 | 0 | 0 | 0 | 0 | 0 | 0 | 0 |
| Matheny, c | 4 | 0 | 0 | 0 | 1 | 2 | 6 | 1 |
| M.Morris, p | 2 | 0 | 0 | 0 | 0 | 1 | 0 | 0 |
| Mabry, ph | 1 | 0 | 0 | 0 | 0 | 1 | 0 | 0 |
| King, p | 0 | 0 | 0 | 0 | 0 | 0 | 0 | 1 |
| Calero, p | 0 | 0 | 0 | 0 | 0 | 0 | 0 | 1 |
| Taguchi, lf | 2 | 0 | 0 | 0 | 0 | 1 | 2 | 0 |
| **TOTALS** | 48 | 6 | 15 | 6 | 2 | 13 | 36 | 14 |

| | | | | | |
|---|---|---|---|---|---|
| Houston | 1 0 1 | 1 0 0 | 0 0 1 | 0 0 0—4 | 10 0 |
| St. Louis | 2 0 2 | 0 0 0 | 0 0 0 | 0 0 2—6 | 15 0 |

| Houston | IP | H | R | ER | HR | BB | SO |
|---|---|---|---|---|---|---|---|
| Munro | 2.1 | 8 | 4 | 4 | 1 | 0 | 1 |
| Harville | 0.2 | 1 | 0 | 0 | 0 | 0 | 2 |
| Qualls | 3.0 | 3 | 0 | 0 | 0 | 1 | 3 |
| Wheeler | 2.0 | 2 | 0 | 0 | 0 | 0 | 2 |
| Lidge | 3.0 | 0 | 0 | 0 | 0 | 0 | 5 |
| Miceli (L) | 0.1 | 1 | 2 | 2 | 1 | 1 | 0 |

| St. Louis | IP | H | R | ER | HR | BB | SO |
|---|---|---|---|---|---|---|---|
| M.Morris | 5.0 | 5 | 3 | 3 | 1 | 3 | 1 |
| King (HOLD) | 0.2 | 2 | 0 | 0 | 0 | 0 | 0 |
| Calero (HOLD) | 1.1 | 1 | 0 | 0 | 0 | 0 | 0 |
| Isringhausen (BS) | 3.0 | 2 | 1 | 1 | 0 | 1 | 2 |
| Tavarez (W) | 2.0 | 0 | 0 | 0 | 0 | 0 | 2 |

DP—St. Louis 2. LOB—Houston 9, St. Louis 10. Scoring Position—Houston 2 for 7, St. Louis 3 for 9. 2B—Bagwell, Kent, Pujols, Rolen, R.Sanders 2. HR—Pujols (1st inning, 1 out, 1 on) off Munro, Lamb (4th inning, 0 out, 0 on) off M.Morris, Edmonds (12th inning, 1 out, 1 on) off Miceli. SB—C.Beltran 2, Bagwell. CS—J.Vizcaino. S—Berkman. SH—Bruntlett. HBP—Ensberg by Isringhausen. T—3:54. A—52,144. U—HP-Rapuano, 1B-Welke, 2B-Cooper, 3B-Darling, LF-Winters, RF-Hernandez.

## HOW THEY SCORED

TOP OF 1

Astros first. Biggio grounded out, third baseman Rolen to first baseman Pujols. Beltran walked on a full count. Beltran stole second. Bagwell singled to left, Beltran to third. Berkman hit a sacrifice fly to left fielder Sanders, Beltran scored. Kent grounded into fielder's choice, third baseman Rolen to second baseman Womack, Bagwell out. Runs: 1, Hits: 1, Errors: 0

BOTTOM OF 1

Cardinals first. Womack singled to right. Walker grounded out, third baseman Lamb to first baseman Bagwell, Womack to second. Pujols homered to left on a 1-2 count, Womack scored. Rolen struck out. Edmonds singled to right. Renteria singled to right, Edmonds to third. Sanders flied out to right fielder Berkman. Runs: 2, Hits: 4, Errors: 0

TOP OF 3

Astros third. Munro grounded out, first baseman Pujols unassisted. Biggio lined out to shortstop Renteria. Beltran singled to right. Bagwell doubled to left, Beltran scored. Berkman walked. Kent lined out to shortstop Renteria. Runs: 1, Hits: 2, Errors: 0

BOTTOM OF 3

Cardinals third. Pujols doubled to center. Rolen infield single to third. Edmonds flied out to left fielder Biggio, Pujols to third. Rolen to second. Renteria singled to center, Pujols scored, Rolen scored. Harville pitching. Sanders doubled to right, Renteria to third. Matheny struck out. Morris struck out. Runs: 2, Hits: 4, Errors: 0

TOP OF 4

Astros fourth. Luna in as second baseman. Lamb homered to right on a 2-2 count. Vizcaino popped out to third baseman Rolen. Ausmus singled to center. Everett pinch-hitting for Harville. Everett grounded into fielder's choice, shortstop Renteria to second baseman Luna, Ausmus out. Biggio flied out to right fielder Walker. Runs: 1, Hits: 2, Errors: 0

TOP OF 9

Astros ninth. Ensberg pinch-hitting for Ausmus. Ensberg was hit by a pitch. Bruntlett pinch-hitting for Wheeler. Bruntlett sacrificed, first baseman Pujols to second baseman Luna, Ensberg to second. Biggio flied out to left fielder Taguchi. Beltran was intentionally walked. Bagwell singled to left, Ensberg scored, Beltran to second. Beltran stole third.Bagwell stole second. Berkman struck out. Runs: 1, Hits: 1, Errors: 0

BOTTOM OF 12

Cardinals twelfth. Miceli pitching. Pujols walked on four pitches. Rolen fouled out to catcher Chavez. Edmonds homered to right on a 0-1 count, Pujols scored. Runs: 2, Hits: 1, Errors: 0

## GAME 7

### ST. LOUIS 5, HOUSTON 2

THURSDAY, OCTOBER 21, AT ST. LOUIS

| Houston | AB | R | H | BI | BB | SO | PO | A |
|---|---|---|---|---|---|---|---|---|
| Biggio, lf | 4 | 1 | 1 | 1 | 0 | 1 | 1 | 0 |
| Oswalt, p | 0 | 0 | 0 | 0 | 0 | 0 | 0 | 1 |
| C.Beltran, cf | 3 | 1 | 0 | 0 | 1 | 0 | 3 | 0 |
| Bagwell, 1b | 4 | 0 | 0 | 0 | 0 | 0 | 10 | 1 |
| Berkman, rf | 4 | 0 | 0 | 0 | 0 | 2 | 1 | 0 |
| Kent, 2b | 2 | 0 | 0 | 0 | 1 | 0 | 4 | 3 |
| Ensberg, 3b | 4 | 0 | 1 | 0 | 0 | 0 | 1 | 2 |
| J.Vizcaino, ss | 4 | 0 | 1 | 0 | 0 | 0 | 0 | 2 |
| Ausmus, c | 3 | 0 | 0 | 0 | 0 | 2 | 4 | 1 |
| Clemens, p | 2 | 0 | 0 | 0 | 0 | 2 | 0 | 3 |
| O.Palmeiro, ph-lf | 0 | 0 | 0 | 0 | 0 | 0 | 0 | 0 |
| TOTALS | 30 | 2 | 3 | 1 | 2 | 7 | 24 | 13 |

| St. Louis | AB | R | H | BI | BB | SO | PO | A |
|---|---|---|---|---|---|---|---|---|
| Renteria, ss | 2 | 0 | 0 | 0 | 0 | 0 | 2 | 3 |
| L.Walker, rf | 4 | 0 | 1 | 1 | 0 | 0 | 1 | 0 |
| Pujols, 1b | 4 | 1 | 2 | 1 | 0 | 0 | 6 | 1 |
| Rolen, 3b | 4 | 1 | 1 | 2 | 0 | 0 | 0 | 3 |
| Edmonds, cf | 3 | 0 | 1 | 0 | 0 | 1 | 4 | 0 |
| R.Sanders, lf | 3 | 0 | 0 | 0 | 0 | 1 | 4 | 0 |
| Womack, 2b | 3 | 1 | 2 | 0 | 0 | 1 | 3 | 1 |
| Matheny, c | 3 | 0 | 0 | 0 | 0 | 1 | 7 | 0 |
| Suppan, p | 0 | 0 | 0 | 1 | 0 | 0 | 0 | 0 |
| Cedeno, ph | 1 | 1 | 1 | 0 | 0 | 0 | 0 | 0 |
| Calero, p | 0 | 0 | 0 | 0 | 0 | 0 | 0 | 0 |
| Tavarez, p | 0 | 0 | 0 | 0 | 0 | 0 | 0 | 1 |
| Mar.Anderson, ph | 1 | 1 | 1 | 0 | 0 | 0 | 0 | 0 |
| Isringhausen, p | 0 | 0 | 0 | 0 | 0 | 0 | 0 | 0 |
| TOTALS | 28 | 5 | 9 | 5 | 0 | 4 | 27 | 9 |

| | | | | |
|---|---|---|---|---|
| Houston | 1 0 1 | 0 0 0 | 0 0 0—2 | 3 0 |
| St. Louis | 0 0 1 | 0 0 3 | 0 1 x—5 | 9 1 |

| Houston | IP | H | R | ER | HR | BB | SO |
|---|---|---|---|---|---|---|---|
| Clemens (L) | 6.0 | 6 | 4 | 4 | 1 | 0 | 2 |
| Oswalt | 2.0 | 3 | 1 | 1 | 0 | 0 | 2 |

| St. Louis | IP | H | R | ER | HR | BB | SO |
|---|---|---|---|---|---|---|---|
| Suppan (W) | 6.0 | 3 | 2 | 1 | 1 | 2 | 6 |
| Calero (HOLD) | 1.0 | 0 | 0 | 0 | 0 | 0 | 1 |
| Tavarez (HOLD) | 1.0 | 0 | 0 | 0 | 0 | 0 | 0 |
| Isringhausen (S) | 1.0 | 0 | 0 | 0 | 0 | 0 | 0 |

E—Edmonds. DP—Houston 1. LOB—Houston 5, St. Louis 2. Scoring Position—Houston 0 for 6, St. Louis 3 for 7. 2B—Pujols, Womack, Mar.Anderson. HR—Biggio (1st inning, 0 out, 0 on) off Suppan, Rolen (6th inning, 2 out, 1 on) off Clemens. SB—C.Beltran. SH—Renteria 2, Suppan. HBP—Kent by Suppan, O.Palmeiro by Calero. T—2:51. A—52,140. U—HP-Welke, 1B-Cooper, 2B-Darling, 3B-Winters, LF-Hernandez, RF-Rapuano.

## HOW THEY SCORED

TOP OF 1

Astros first. Biggio homered to left on a 1-2 count. Beltran popped out to second baseman Womack. Bagwell lined out to left fielder Sanders. Berkman struck out. Runs: 1, Hits: 1, Errors: 0

TOP OF 3

Astros third. Biggio lined out to left fielder Sanders. Beltran walked on four pitches. Beltran stole second. Bagwell flied out to center fielder Edmonds, Beltran to third. On Edmonds' error, Beltran scored. Berkman lined out to center fielder Edmonds. Runs: 1, Hits: 0, Errors: 1

BOTTOM OF 3

Cardinals third. Womack doubled to center. Matheny grounded out, first baseman Bagwell unassisted, Womack to third. Suppan sacrificed, first baseman Bagwell to second baseman Kent, Womack scored. Renteria grounded out, pitcher Clemens to first baseman Bagwell. Runs: 1, Hits: 1, Errors: 0

BOTTOM OF 6

Cardinals sixth. Cedeno pinch-hitting for Suppan. Cedeno singled to center. Renteria sacrificed, pitcher Clemens to second baseman Kent, Cedeno to second. Walker grounded out, pitcher Clemens to first baseman Bagwell, Cedeno to third. Pujols doubled to left, Cedeno scored. Rolen homered to left on the first pitch, Pujols scored. Edmonds struck out. Runs: 3, Hits: 3, Errors: 0

BOTTOM OF 8

Cardinals eighth. Anderson pinch-hitting for Tavarez. Anderson doubled to center. Renteria sacrificed, pitcher Oswalt to second baseman Kent, Anderson to third. Walker singled to right, Anderson scored. Pujols singled to center, Walker to second. Rolen grounded into a double play, shortstop Vizcaino to second baseman Kent to first baseman Bagwell, Pujols out. Runs: 1, Hits: 3, Errors: 0

## ST. LOUIS CARDINALS' BATTING AND FIELDING AVERAGES

| | | BATTING | | | | | | | | | | | | | | FIELDING | | | |
|---|---|---|---|---|---|---|---|---|---|---|---|---|---|---|---|---|---|---|---|
| Player, position | G | AB | R | H | TB | 2B | 3B | HR | RBI | BB | IBB | SO | Avg. | OBP | Slg. | PO | A | E | Avg. |
| Pujols,1b | 7 | 28 | 10 | 14 | 28 | 2 | 0 | 4 | 9 | 4 | 0 | 3 | .500 | .563 | 1.000 | 53 | 8 | 0 | 1.000 |
| Marquis,p | 1 | 2 | 0 | 1 | 1 | 0 | 0 | 0 | 0 | 0 | 0 | 0 | .500 | .500 | .500 | 0 | 0 | 0 | .000 |
| Anderson,ph-2b | 5 | 3 | 1 | 1 | 2 | 1 | 0 | 0 | 0 | 1 | 0 | 0 | .333 | .600 | .667 | 0 | 0 | 0 | .000 |
| Rolen,3b | 7 | 29 | 6 | 9 | 20 | 2 | 0 | 3 | 6 | 2 | 0 | 9 | .310 | .355 | .690 | 8 | 15 | 0 | 1.000 |
| Edmonds,cf | 7 | 24 | 2 | 7 | 15 | 2 | 0 | 2 | 7 | 2 | 0 | 6 | .292 | .357 | .625 | 20 | 0 | 1 | .952 |
| Womack,2b | 7 | 26 | 5 | 7 | 8 | 1 | 0 | 0 | 1 | 1 | 0 | 3 | .269 | .296 | .308 | 12 | 14 | 0 | 1.000 |
| Molina,c | 1 | 4 | 0 | 1 | 1 | 0 | 0 | 0 | 0 | 0 | 0 | 0 | .250 | .250 | .250 | 5 | 1 | 0 | 1.000 |
| Williams,p | 2 | 4 | 1 | 1 | 2 | 1 | 0 | 0 | 0 | 0 | 0 | 0 | .250 | .250 | .500 | 3 | 1 | 0 | 1.000 |
| Walker,rf | 7 | 29 | 6 | 7 | 16 | 1 | 1 | 2 | 5 | 3 | 0 | 8 | .241 | .313 | .552 | 11 | 0 | 0 | 1.000 |
| Sanders,lf | 6 | 21 | 1 | 4 | 6 | 2 | 0 | 0 | 0 | 1 | 0 | 5 | .190 | .227 | .286 | 12 | 1 | 0 | 1.000 |
| Renteria,ss | 7 | 24 | 1 | 4 | 4 | 0 | 0 | 0 | 2 | 2 | 0 | 5 | .167 | .231 | .167 | 19 | 14 | 0 | 1.000 |
| Cedeno,ph-lf | 6 | 6 | 1 | 1 | 1 | 0 | 0 | 0 | 1 | 0 | 0 | 2 | .167 | .167 | .167 | 0 | 0 | 0 | .000 |
| Mabry,ph-lf | 4 | 6 | 0 | 1 | 1 | 0 | 0 | 0 | 1 | 0 | 0 | 3 | .167 | .167 | .167 | 1 | 0 | 0 | 1.000 |
| Matheny,c | 7 | 19 | 0 | 2 | 2 | 0 | 0 | 0 | 0 | 1 | 1 | 8 | .105 | .150 | .105 | 36 | 5 | 0 | 1.000 |
| Calero,p | 5 | 0 | 0 | 0 | 0 | 0 | 0 | 0 | 0 | 0 | 0 | 0 | .000 | .000 | .000 | 0 | 1 | 0 | 1.000 |
| Eldred,p | 1 | 0 | 0 | 0 | 0 | 0 | 0 | 0 | 0 | 0 | 0 | 0 | .000 | .000 | .000 | 0 | 1 | 0 | 1.000 |
| Haren,p | 2 | 0 | 0 | 0 | 0 | 0 | 0 | 0 | 0 | 0 | 0 | 0 | .000 | .000 | .000 | 0 | 1 | 0 | 1.000 |
| Isringhausen,p | 6 | 0 | 0 | 0 | 0 | 0 | 0 | 0 | 0 | 0 | 0 | 0 | .000 | .000 | .000 | 1 | 0 | 0 | 1.000 |
| King,p | 4 | 0 | 0 | 0 | 0 | 0 | 0 | 0 | 0 | 0 | 0 | 0 | .000 | .000 | .000 | 0 | 1 | 0 | 1.000 |
| Kline,p | 1 | 0 | 0 | 0 | 0 | 0 | 0 | 0 | 0 | 0 | 0 | 0 | .000 | .000 | .000 | 0 | 0 | 0 | .000 |
| Tavarez,p | 5 | 0 | 0 | 0 | 0 | 0 | 0 | 0 | 0 | 0 | 0 | 0 | .000 | .000 | .000 | 0 | 1 | 0 | 1.000 |
| Morris,p | 2 | 2 | 0 | 0 | 0 | 0 | 0 | 0 | 0 | 0 | 0 | 1 | .000 | .000 | .000 | 0 | 0 | 0 | .000 |
| Suppan,p | 2 | 2 | 0 | 0 | 0 | 0 | 0 | 0 | 1 | 0 | 0 | 0 | .000 | .000 | .000 | 0 | 0 | 0 | .000 |
| Taguchi,lf | 3 | 2 | 0 | 0 | 0 | 0 | 0 | 0 | 0 | 0 | 0 | 1 | .000 | .000 | .000 | 4 | 0 | 0 | 1.000 |
| Luna,ss-2b | 2 | 4 | 0 | 0 | 0 | 0 | 0 | 0 | 0 | 0 | 0 | 2 | .000 | .000 | .000 | 5 | 2 | 0 | 1.000 |
| Totals | 7 | 235 | 34 | 60 | 107 | 12 | 1 | 11 | 33 | 17 | 1 | 56 | .255 | .310 | .455 | 190 | 66 | 1 | .996 |

## HOUSTON ASTROS' BATTING AND FIELDING AVERAGES

| | | BATTING | | | | | | | | | | | | | | FIELDING | | | |
|---|---|---|---|---|---|---|---|---|---|---|---|---|---|---|---|---|---|---|---|
| Player, position | G | AB | R | H | TB | 2B | 3B | HR | RBI | BB | IBB | SO | Avg. | OBP | Slg. | PO | A | E | Avg. |
| Beltran,cf | 7 | 24 | 12 | 10 | 23 | 1 | 0 | 4 | 5 | 8 | 1 | 4 | .417 | .563 | .958 | 13 | 0 | 0 | 1.000 |
| Lamb,ph-3b | 2 | 5 | 2 | 2 | 8 | 0 | 0 | 2 | 2 | 1 | 0 | 1 | .400 | .500 | 1.600 | 1 | 3 | 0 | 1.000 |
| Palmeiro,ph-lf | 7 | 6 | 0 | 2 | 3 | 1 | 0 | 0 | 0 | 0 | 0 | 0 | .333 | .429 | .500 | 0 | 0 | 0 | .000 |
| Berkman,rf | 7 | 24 | 7 | 7 | 18 | 2 | 0 | 3 | 9 | 5 | 2 | 4 | .292 | .400 | .750 | 14 | 1 | 0 | 1.000 |
| Bagwell,1b | 7 | 27 | 1 | 7 | 9 | 2 | 0 | 0 | 3 | 4 | 0 | 5 | .259 | .355 | .333 | 65 | 3 | 0 | 1.000 |
| Vizcaino,2b-ss | 7 | 28 | 1 | 7 | 8 | 1 | 0 | 0 | 0 | 0 | 0 | 1 | .250 | .250 | .286 | 5 | 21 | 1 | .963 |
| Chavez,c | 2 | 4 | 0 | 1 | 1 | 0 | 0 | 0 | 1 | 0 | 0 | 1 | .250 | .250 | .250 | 6 | 2 | 0 | 1.000 |
| Kent,2b | 7 | 25 | 3 | 6 | 17 | 2 | 0 | 3 | 7 | 3 | 0 | 5 | .240 | .367 | .680 | 14 | 18 | 0 | 1.000 |
| Biggio,lf | 7 | 32 | 3 | 6 | 10 | 1 | 0 | 1 | 1 | 0 | 0 | 4 | .188 | .188 | .313 | 9 | 0 | 0 | 1.000 |
| Ensberg,3b-ph | 7 | 22 | 2 | 3 | 6 | 0 | 0 | 1 | 2 | 1 | 0 | 3 | .136 | .240 | .273 | 5 | 9 | 0 | 1.000 |
| Ausmus,c | 7 | 19 | 0 | 2 | 2 | 0 | 0 | 0 | 0 | 2 | 1 | 8 | .105 | .190 | .105 | 50 | 3 | 0 | 1.000 |
| Harville,p | 3 | 0 | 0 | 0 | 0 | 0 | 0 | 0 | 0 | 0 | 0 | 0 | .000 | .000 | .000 | 0 | 0 | 0 | .000 |
| Lidge,p | 4 | 0 | 0 | 0 | 0 | 0 | 0 | 0 | 0 | 0 | 0 | 0 | .000 | .000 | .000 | 0 | 0 | 0 | .000 |
| Miceli,p | 2 | 0 | 0 | 0 | 0 | 0 | 0 | 0 | 0 | 0 | 0 | 0 | .000 | .000 | .000 | 1 | 0 | 0 | 1.000 |
| Qualls,p | 2 | 0 | 0 | 0 | 0 | 0 | 0 | 0 | 0 | 0 | 0 | 0 | .000 | .000 | .000 | 0 | 1 | 0 | 1.000 |
| Wheeler,p | 4 | 0 | 0 | 0 | 0 | 0 | 0 | 0 | 0 | 0 | 0 | 0 | .000 | .000 | .000 | 1 | 0 | 0 | 1.000 |
| Everett,ss-pr-ph | 3 | 1 | 0 | 0 | 0 | 0 | 0 | 0 | 0 | 0 | 0 | 0 | .000 | .000 | .000 | 1 | 0 | 0 | 1.000 |
| Lane,lf-rf | 2 | 1 | 0 | 0 | 0 | 0 | 0 | 0 | 0 | 0 | 0 | 0 | .000 | .000 | .000 | 1 | 0 | 0 | 1.000 |
| Bruntlett,ph-ss | 4 | 2 | 0 | 0 | 0 | 0 | 0 | 0 | 0 | 0 | 0 | 0 | .000 | .000 | .000 | 0 | 0 | 0 | .000 |
| Munro,p | 2 | 2 | 0 | 0 | 0 | 0 | 0 | 0 | 0 | 1 | 0 | 0 | .000 | .333 | .000 | 1 | 1 | 1 | .667 |
| Oswalt,p | 2 | 2 | 0 | 0 | 0 | 0 | 0 | 0 | 0 | 0 | 0 | 0 | .000 | .000 | .000 | 0 | 3 | 0 | 1.000 |
| Clemens,p | 2 | 4 | 0 | 0 | 0 | 0 | 0 | 0 | 0 | 0 | 0 | 3 | .000 | .000 | .000 | 0 | 4 | 0 | 1.000 |
| Backe,p-ph | 3 | 5 | 0 | 0 | 0 | 0 | 0 | 0 | 0 | 0 | 0 | 3 | .000 | .000 | .000 | 0 | 2 | 0 | 1.000 |
| Totals | 7 | 233 | 31 | 53 | 105 | 10 | 0 | 14 | 30 | 25 | 4 | 42 | .227 | .314 | .451 | 187 | 71 | 2 | .992 |

## ST. LOUIS CARDINALS' PITCHING RECORDS

| Pitcher | G | GS | CG | IP | H | R | ER | HR | BB | IBB | SO | HB | WP | W | L | Pct. | ERA |
|---|---|---|---|---|---|---|---|---|---|---|---|---|---|---|---|---|---|
| Eldred | 1 | 0 | 0 | 0.1 | 0 | 0 | 0 | 0 | 1 | 0 | 0 | 0 | 0 | 0 | 0 | .000 | 0.00 |
| Williams | 2 | 2 | 0 | 13.0 | 5 | 4 | 4 | 2 | 3 | 0 | 9 | 1 | 0 | 1 | 0 | 1.000 | 2.77 |
| Suppan | 2 | 2 | 0 | 12.0 | 8 | 5 | 4 | 2 | 4 | 0 | 9 | 1 | 0 | 1 | 1 | .500 | 3.00 |
| Tavarez | 5 | 0 | 0 | 6.0 | 3 | 2 | 2 | 2 | 2 | 1 | 3 | 1 | 1 | 2 | 1 | .667 | 3.00 |
| Calero | 5 | 0 | 0 | 7.0 | 8 | 3 | 3 | 1 | 1 | 0 | 7 | 1 | 0 | 0 | 0 | .000 | 3.86 |
| Isringhausen | 6 | 0 | 0 | 7.2 | 4 | 4 | 4 | 1 | 4 | 2 | 3 | 1 | 0 | 0 | 1 | .000 | 4.70 |
| Morris | 2 | 2 | 0 | 10.0 | 11 | 6 | 6 | 3 | 8 | 1 | 6 | 0 | 2 | 0 | 0 | .000 | 5.40 |
| Marquis | 1 | 1 | 0 | 4.0 | 5 | 3 | 3 | 0 | 2 | 0 | 2 | 0 | 0 | 0 | 0 | .000 | 6.75 |
| Haren | 2 | 0 | 0 | 1.2 | 3 | 2 | 2 | 1 | 0 | 0 | 2 | 0 | 0 | 0 | 0 | .000 | 10.80 |
| King | 4 | 0 | 0 | 1.2 | 4 | 2 | 2 | 2 | 0 | 0 | 1 | 0 | 0 | 0 | 0 | .000 | 10.80 |
| Kline | 1 | 0 | 0 | 0.0 | 2 | 0 | 0 | 0 | 0 | 0 | 0 | 0 | 0 | 0 | 0 | .000 | - |
| Totals | 7 | 7 | 0 | 63.1 | 53 | 31 | 30 | 14 | 25 | 4 | 42 | 5 | 3 | 4 | 3 | .571 | 4.26 |

No shutouts. Saves- Isringhausen 3.

## HOUSTON ASTROS' PITCHING RECORDS

| Pitcher | G | GS | CG | IP | H | R | ER | HR | BB | IBB | SO | HB | WP | W | L | Pct. | ERA |
|---|---|---|---|---|---|---|---|---|---|---|---|---|---|---|---|---|---|
| Lidge | 4 | 0 | 0 | 8.0 | 1 | 0 | 0 | 0 | 2 | 0 | 14 | 1 | 0 | 1 | 0 | 1.000 | 0.00 |
| Wheeler | 4 | 0 | 0 | 7.0 | 4 | 0 | 0 | 0 | 0 | 0 | 9 | 0 | 0 | 1 | 0 | 1.000 | 0.00 |
| Backe | 2 | 2 | 0 | 12.2 | 6 | 4 | 4 | 1 | 4 | 0 | 10 | 1 | 0 | 0 | 0 | .000 | 2.84 |
| Clemens | 2 | 2 | 0 | 13.0 | 10 | 6 | 6 | 3 | 2 | 0 | 9 | 0 | 1 | 1 | 1 | .500 | 4.15 |
| Oswalt | 2 | 1 | 0 | 8.0 | 11 | 6 | 6 | 1 | 4 | 0 | 2 | 0 | 0 | 0 | 0 | .000 | 6.75 |
| Munro | 2 | 2 | 0 | 7.0 | 14 | 7 | 7 | 2 | 1 | 0 | 5 | 0 | 0 | 0 | 0 | .000 | 9.00 |
| Qualls | 2 | 0 | 0 | 4.0 | 8 | 5 | 5 | 0 | 2 | 1 | 4 | 0 | 0 | 0 | 1 | .000 | 11.25 |
| Harville | 3 | 0 | 0 | 1.1 | 3 | 2 | 2 | 1 | 1 | 0 | 3 | 0 | 0 | 0 | 0 | .000 | 13.50 |
| Miceli | 2 | 0 | 0 | 1.1 | 3 | 4 | 4 | 3 | 1 | 0 | 0 | 0 | 0 | 0 | 2 | .000 | 27.00 |
| Totals | 7 | 7 | 0 | 62.1 | 60 | 34 | 34 | 11 | 17 | 1 | 56 | 2 | 1 | 3 | 4 | .429 | 4.91 |

No shutouts. Saves- Lidge 2.

## SCORE BY INNINGS

| | | | | | | | | | | | | | |
|---|---|---|---|---|---|---|---|---|---|---|---|---|---|
| St. Louis | 8 | 1 | 4 | 1 | 6 | 9 | 0 | 3 | 0 | 0 | 0 | 2 | —34 |
| Houston | 9 | 0 | 4 | 4 | 1 | 2 | 2 | 4 | 5 | 0 | 0 | 0 | —31 |

## MISCELLANEOUS STATISTICS

Sacrifice hits—Renteria 2, Bruntlett, Matheny, Morris, Suppan, Taguchi.
Sacrifice flies—Berkman, Edmonds.
Stolen bases—Beltran 4, Womack 2, Bagwell, Berkman.
Caught stealing—Bagwell, Biggio, Ensberg, Vizcaino.
Double plays—Ensberg, Kent and Bagwell; King, Renteria and Pujols; Rolen and Pujols; Vizcaino, Kent and Bagwell; Womack and Pujols.
Left on bases—St. Louis 6, 4, 7, 8, 3, 10, 2—40; Houston 4, 11, 5, 6, 4, 9, 5—44.
Scoring position—St. Louis 6 for 11, 1 for 8, 0 for 5, 2 for 10, 0 for 1, 3 for 9, 3 for 7—15 for 51; Houston 0 for 2, 2 for 14, 2 for 5, 2 for 7, 1 for 2, 2 for 7, 0 for 6—9 for 43.
Hit by pitcher—by Williams (Ensberg), by Tavarez (Kent), by Isringhausen (Ensberg), by Suppan (Kent), by Lidge (Anderson), by Backe (Edmonds), by Calero (Palmeiro).
Passed balls—Chavez.
Balks—Morris.
Time of games—3:15, 3:02, 2:57, 3:01, 2:33, 3:54, 2:51—Avg.: 3:04.
Attendance—52,323, 52,347, 42,896, 42,760, 43,045, 52,144, 52,140—337,655.
Umpires—Welke, Tim; Cooper, Eric; Darling, Gary; Winters, Mike; Hernandez, Angel; Rapuano, Ed.

# WORLD SERIES

## ST. LOUIS VS. BOSTON

### RESULTS

| Day | Date | Place | Score |
|---|---|---|---|
| Sat. | Oct. 23 | Boston | Boston 11, St. Louis 9 |
| Sun. | Oct. 24 | Boston | Boston 6, St. Louis 2 |
| Tue. | Oct. 26 | St. Louis | Boston 4, St. Louis 1 |
| Wed. | Oct. 27 | St. Louis | Boston 3, St. Louis 0 |

### BOX SCORES

#### GAME 1

**BOSTON 11, ST. LOUIS 9**

SATURDAY, OCTOBER 23, AT BOSTON

| St. Louis | AB | R | H | BI | BB | SO | PO | A |
|---|---|---|---|---|---|---|---|---|
| Renteria, ss | 4 | 1 | 2 | 1 | 1 | 1 | 2 | 3 |
| L.Walker, rf | 5 | 1 | 4 | 2 | 0 | 0 | 3 | 0 |
| Pujols, 1b | 3 | 0 | 0 | 0 | 1 | 1 | 8 | 0 |
| Rolen, 3b | 5 | 0 | 0 | 0 | 0 | 0 | 1 | 2 |
| Edmonds, cf | 4 | 2 | 1 | 0 | 1 | 2 | 1 | 0 |
| R.Sanders, dh | 3 | 1 | 0 | 0 | 2 | 2 | 0 | 0 |
| Womack, 2b | 1 | 1 | 0 | 0 | 1 | 0 | 1 | 2 |
| Mar.Anderson, 2b | 2 | 0 | 1 | 0 | 0 | 0 | 0 | 1 |
| Matheny, c | 2 | 0 | 1 | 2 | 0 | 1 | 4 | 0 |
| Marquis, pr | 0 | 1 | 0 | 0 | 0 | 0 | 0 | 0 |
| Y.Molina, c | 1 | 0 | 0 | 0 | 0 | 0 | 0 | 0 |
| Taguchi, lf | 3 | 1 | 1 | 1 | 0 | 1 | 4 | 0 |
| Cedeno, ph-lf | 2 | 1 | 1 | 0 | 0 | 1 | 0 | 0 |
| W.Williams, p | 0 | 0 | 0 | 0 | 0 | 0 | 0 | 0 |
| Haren, p | 0 | 0 | 0 | 0 | 0 | 0 | 0 | 1 |
| Calero, p | 0 | 0 | 0 | 0 | 0 | 0 | 0 | 0 |
| King, p | 0 | 0 | 0 | 0 | 0 | 0 | 0 | 0 |
| Eldred, p | 0 | 0 | 0 | 0 | 0 | 0 | 0 | 0 |
| Tavarez, p | 0 | 0 | 0 | 0 | 0 | 0 | 0 | 0 |
| **TOTALS** | 35 | 9 | 11 | 6 | 6 | 9 | 24 | 9 |

| Boston | AB | R | H | BI | BB | SO | PO | A |
|---|---|---|---|---|---|---|---|---|
| Damon, cf | 6 | 1 | 2 | 1 | 0 | 0 | 2 | 0 |
| O.Cabrera, ss | 4 | 2 | 1 | 1 | 1 | 0 | 1 | 1 |
| M.Ramirez, lf | 5 | 0 | 3 | 2 | 0 | 0 | 1 | 0 |
| D.Ortiz, dh | 3 | 1 | 2 | 4 | 2 | 0 | 0 | 0 |
| Millar, 1b | 5 | 1 | 1 | 0 | 0 | 0 | 4 | 0 |
| Mientkiewicz, 1b | 0 | 0 | 0 | 0 | 0 | 0 | 2 | 0 |
| Nixon, rf | 3 | 0 | 0 | 0 | 1 | 0 | 2 | 0 |
| Kapler, ph-rf | 1 | 0 | 0 | 0 | 0 | 1 | 0 | 0 |
| Mueller, 3b | 3 | 1 | 1 | 1 | 2 | 0 | 2 | 4 |
| Mirabelli, c | 3 | 1 | 1 | 0 | 0 | 1 | 6 | 0 |
| Varitek, ph-c | 2 | 1 | 0 | 0 | 0 | 1 | 3 | 0 |
| Bellhorn, 2b | 3 | 3 | 2 | 2 | 2 | 0 | 4 | 2 |
| Reese, 2b | 0 | 0 | 0 | 0 | 0 | 0 | 0 | 0 |
| Wakefield, p | 0 | 0 | 0 | 0 | 0 | 0 | 0 | 0 |
| Arroyo, p | 0 | 0 | 0 | 0 | 0 | 0 | 0 | 0 |
| Timlin, p | 0 | 0 | 0 | 0 | 0 | 0 | 0 | 1 |
| Embree, p | 0 | 0 | 0 | 0 | 0 | 0 | 0 | 0 |
| Foulke, p | 0 | 0 | 0 | 0 | 0 | 0 | 0 | 0 |
| **TOTALS** | 38 | 11 | 13 | 11 | 8 | 3 | 27 | 8 |

| | | | | |
|---|---|---|---|---|
| St. Louis | 0 1 1 | 3 0 2 | 0 2 0— | 9 11 1 |
| Boston | 4 0 3 | 0 0 0 | 2 2 x— | 11 13 4 |

| St. Louis | IP | H | R | ER | HR | BB | SO |
|---|---|---|---|---|---|---|---|
| W.Williams | 2.1 | 8 | 7 | 7 | 1 | 3 | 1 |
| Haren | 3.2 | 2 | 0 | 0 | 0 | 3 | 1 |
| Calero | 0.1 | 1 | 2 | 2 | 0 | 2 | 0 |
| King | 0.1 | 1 | 0 | 0 | 0 | 0 | 0 |
| Eldred | 0.1 | 0 | 0 | 0 | 0 | 0 | 1 |
| Tavarez (L) | 1.0 | 1 | 2 | 1 | 1 | 0 | 0 |

| Boston | IP | H | R | ER | HR | BB | SO |
|---|---|---|---|---|---|---|---|
| Wakefield | 3.2 | 3 | 5 | 5 | 1 | 5 | 2 |
| Arroyo | 2.1 | 4 | 2 | 2 | 0 | 0 | 4 |
| Timlin | 1.1 | 1 | 1 | 1 | 0 | 0 | 0 |
| Embree | 0.0 | 1 | 1 | 0 | 0 | 0 | 0 |
| Foulke (BS, W) | 1.2 | 2 | 0 | 0 | 0 | 1 | 3 |

Embree pitched to 1 batter in the 8th.

Bases on balls—Off W.Williams 3 (Mueller, Bellhorn, D.Ortiz), off Haren 3 (Mueller, Nixon, D.Ortiz), off Calero 2 (Bellhorn, O.Cabrera), off Wakefield 5 (R.Sanders 2, Edmonds, Womack, Renteria), off Foulke 1 (Pujols).

Strikeouts—By W.Williams 1 (Mirabelli), by Haren 1 (Varitek), by Eldred1 (Kapler), by Wakefield 2 (Renteria, Taguchi), by Arroyo 4 (R.Sanders, Edmonds, Matheny, Pujols), by Foulke 3 (R.Sanders, Edmonds, Cedeno).

E—Renteria, Arroyo, Millar, M.Ramirez 2. DP—Boston 1. LOB—St. Louis 9, Boston 12. Scoring Position—St. Louis 3 for 14, Boston 6 for 16. 2B—Renteria, L.Walker 2, Mar.Anderson, Damon, Millar. HR—D.Ortiz (1st inning, 1 out, 2 on) off W.Williams, L.Walker (3rd inning, 1 out, 0 on) off Wakefield, Bellhorn (8th inning, 1 out, 1 on) off Tavarez. S—Matheny 2. SH—Womack. PB—Mirabelli. HBP—O.Cabrera by W.Williams, Pujols by Wakefield. T—4:00. A—35,035. U—HP-Montague, 1B-Scott, 2B-Gorman, 3B-Meriwether, LF-Davis, RF-Reliford.

### PLAY BY PLAY

TOP OF 1

Cardinals first. Renteria struck out. Walker doubled to right. Pujols popped out to second baseman Bellhorn. Rolen fouled out to third baseman Mueller. Runs: 0, Hits: 1, Errors: 0

BOTTOM OF 1

Red Sox first. Damon doubled to left. Cabrera was hit by a pitch. Ramirez flied out to right fielder Walker, Damon to third. Ortiz homered to right on a 1-0 count, Damon scored, Cabrera scored. Millar doubled to left. Nixon flied out to right fielder Walker, Millar to third. Mueller singled to left, Millar scored. Mirabelli struck out. Runs: 4, Hits: 4, Errors: 0

TOP OF 2

Cardinals second. Edmonds bunt single to third. Sanders walked on a full count, Edmonds to second. Womack sacrificed, third baseman Mueller to second baseman Bellhorn, Edmonds to third, Sanders to second. Matheny hit a sacrifice fly to center fielder Damon, Edmonds scored, Sanders to third. Taguchi struck out. Runs: 1, Hits: 1, Errors: 0

BOTTOM OF 2

Red Sox second. Bellhorn singled to left. Damon lined out to shortstop Renteria. Cabrera lined out to left fielder Taguchi. Ramirez singled to left, Bellhorn to second. Ortiz walked on four pitches, Bellhorn to third, Ramirez to second. Millar grounded into fielder's choice, third baseman Rolen unassisted, Ramirez out, Ortiz to second. Runs: 0, Hits: 2, Errors: 0

TOP OF 3

Cardinals third. Renteria grounded out, third baseman Mueller to first baseman Millar. Walker homered to right on a 0-1 count. Pujols was hit by a pitch. Rolen grounded into a double play, third baseman Mueller to second baseman Bellhorn to first baseman Millar, Pujols out. Runs: 1, Hits: 1, Errors: 0

BOTTOM OF 3

Red Sox third. Nixon grounded out, second baseman Womack to first baseman Pujols. Mueller walked on a full count. Mirabelli singled to left, Mueller to third. Bellhorn walked on a full count, Mirabelli to second. Damon singled to right, Mueller scored, Mirabelli to third, Bellhorn to second. Haren pitching. Cabrera singled to left, Mirabelli scored, Bellhorn to third, Damon to second. Ramirez grounded into fielder's choice, shortstop Renteria to second baseman Womack, Bellhorn scored, Damon to third, Cabrera out. Ortiz walked on four pitches, Ramirez to second. Millar grounded out, shortstop Renteria to first baseman Pujols. Runs: 3, Hits: 3, Errors: 0

TOP OF 4

Cardinals fourth. Edmonds walked. On Mirabelli's passed ball, Edmonds to second. Sanders walked on four pitches. Womack walked, Edmonds to third, Sanders to second. Matheny hit a sacrifice fly to right fielder Nixon, Edmonds scored, Sanders to third. On Millar's error, Sanders scored, Womack to third. Taguchi grounded out, third baseman Mueller to first baseman Millar, Womack scored. Renteria walked. Arroyo pitching. Walker singled to right, Renteria to third. Pujols grounded into fielder's choice, shortstop Cabrera to second baseman Bellhorn, Walker out. Runs: 3, Hits: 1, Errors: 1

BOTTOM OF 4

Red Sox fourth. Nixon walked on a full count. Mueller walked on a full count, Nixon to second. Mirabelli flied out to left fielder Taguchi. Bellhorn popped out to right fielder Walker. Damon flied out to left fielder Taguchi. Runs: 0, Hits: 0, Errors: 0

TOP OF 5

Cardinals fifth. Rolen lined out to shortstop Cabrera. Edmonds struck out. Sanders struck out. Runs: 0, Hits: 0, Errors: 0

BOTTOM OF 5

Red Sox fifth. Cabrera grounded out, shortstop Renteria to first baseman Pujols. Ramirez singled to left. Ortiz flied out to left fielder Taguchi. Millar grounded out, third baseman Rolen to first baseman Pujols. Runs: 0, Hits: 1, Errors: 0

TOP OF 6

Cardinals sixth. Womack flied out to right fielder Nixon. Matheny struck out. Taguchi infield single to third. On Arroyo's error, Taguchi to second. Renteria doubled to center, Taguchi scored. Walker doubled to right, Renteria scored. Pujols struck out. Runs: 2, Hits: 3, Errors: 1

BOTTOM OF 6

Red Sox sixth. Nixon grounded out, pitcher Haren to first baseman Pujols. Mueller flied out to center fielder Edmonds. Varitek pinch-hitting for Mirabelli. Varitek struck out. Runs: 0, Hits: 0, Errors: 0

TOP OF 7

Cardinals seventh. Varitek in as catcher. Timlin pitching. Rolen flied out to center fielder Damon. Edmonds flied out to left fielder Ramirez. Sanders grounded out, pitcher Timlin to first baseman Millar. Runs: 0, Hits: 0, Errors: 0

BOTTOM OF 7

Red Sox seventh. Calero pitching. Bellhorn walked on a full count. Damon grounded out, second baseman Womack to first baseman Pujols, Bellhorn to second. Cabrera walked. Ramirez singled to left, Bellhorn scored, Cabrera to third. King pitching. Ortiz infield single to second, Cabrera scored, Ramirez to second. Anderson in as second baseman. Millar fouled out to catcher Matheny. Kapler pinch-hitting for Nixon. Eldred pitching. Kapler struck out. Runs: 2, Hits: 2, Errors: 0

TOP OF 8

Cardinals eighth. Mientkiewicz in as first baseman. Kapler in as right fielder. Anderson grounded out, second baseman Bellhorn to first baseman Mientkiewicz. Matheny singled to center. Marquis pinch-running for Matheny. Cedeno pinch-hitting for Taguchi. Embree pitching. Cedeno singled to right, Marquis to second. Foulke pitching. Renteria singled to left, Marquis to third, Cedeno to second. On Ramirez's error, Marquis scored. Walker safe at second on Ramirez's error, Cedeno scored, Renteria to third. Pujols was intentionally walked. Rolen popped out to third baseman Mueller. Edmonds struck out. Runs: 2, Hits: 3, Errors: 2

BOTTOM OF 8

Red Sox eighth. Molina in as catcher. Cedeno in as left fielder. Tavarez pitching. Mueller grounded out, second baseman Anderson to first baseman Pujols. Varitek safe on Renteria's error. Bellhorn homered to right on a 2-2 count, Varitek scored. Damon popped out to shortstop Renteria. Cabrera grounded out, third baseman Rolen to first baseman Pujols. Runs: 2, Hits: 1, Errors: 1

TOP OF 9

Cardinals ninth. Reese in as second baseman. Sanders struck out. Anderson doubled to left. Molina popped out to first baseman Mientkiewicz. Cedeno struck out. Runs: 0, Hits: 1, Errors: 0

## GAME 2

### BOSTON 6, ST. LOUIS 2

SUNDAY, OCTOBER 24, AT BOSTON

| St. Louis | AB | R | H | BI | BB | SO | PO | A |
|---|---|---|---|---|---|---|---|---|
| Renteria, ss | 3 | 1 | 0 | 0 | 1 | 0 | 2 | 3 |
| L.Walker, rf | 4 | 0 | 0 | 0 | 0 | 2 | 3 | 0 |
| Pujols, 1b | 4 | 1 | 3 | 0 | 0 | 0 | 11 | 0 |
| Rolen, 3b | 3 | 0 | 0 | 1 | 0 | 0 | 0 | 3 |
| Edmonds, cf | 4 | 0 | 0 | 0 | 0 | 2 | 2 | 0 |
| R.Sanders, lf | 3 | 0 | 0 | 0 | 1 | 1 | 0 | 0 |
| Womack, 2b | 4 | 0 | 1 | 0 | 0 | 1 | 0 | 4 |
| Matheny, c | 4 | 0 | 1 | 0 | 0 | 1 | 6 | 0 |
| Mar.Anderson, dh | 2 | 0 | 0 | 0 | 0 | 1 | 0 | 0 |
| Taguchi, ph-dh | 1 | 0 | 0 | 0 | 0 | 1 | 0 | 0 |
| M.Morris, p | 0 | 0 | 0 | 0 | 0 | 0 | 0 | 0 |
| Eldred, p | 0 | 0 | 0 | 0 | 0 | 0 | 0 | 0 |
| King, p | 0 | 0 | 0 | 0 | 0 | 0 | 0 | 0 |
| Marquis, p | 0 | 0 | 0 | 0 | 0 | 0 | 0 | 0 |
| A.Reyes, p | 0 | 0 | 0 | 0 | 0 | 0 | 0 | 0 |
| **TOTALS** | 32 | 2 | 5 | 1 | 2 | 9 | 24 | 10 |

| Boston | AB | R | H | BI | BB | SO | PO | A |
|---|---|---|---|---|---|---|---|---|
| Damon, cf | 5 | 1 | 1 | 0 | 0 | 1 | 1 | 0 |
| O.Cabrera, ss | 4 | 0 | 1 | 2 | 1 | 0 | 1 | 4 |
| M.Ramirez, lf | 4 | 1 | 1 | 0 | 1 | 1 | 0 | 0 |
| Kapler, lf | 0 | 0 | 0 | 0 | 0 | 0 | 0 | 0 |
| D.Ortiz, dh | 3 | 1 | 0 | 0 | 1 | 1 | 0 | 0 |
| Varitek, c | 3 | 0 | 1 | 2 | 0 | 0 | 9 | 0 |
| Millar, 1b | 1 | 1 | 0 | 0 | 2 | 1 | 5 | 0 |
| Mientkiewicz, pr-1b | 0 | 0 | 0 | 0 | 0 | 0 | 2 | 0 |
| Nixon, rf | 4 | 1 | 1 | 0 | 0 | 1 | 4 | 0 |
| Mueller, 3b | 3 | 1 | 2 | 0 | 1 | 0 | 4 | 0 |
| Bellhorn, 2b | 3 | 0 | 1 | 2 | 0 | 0 | 1 | 1 |
| Reese, 2b | 1 | 0 | 0 | 0 | 0 | 0 | 0 | 0 |
| Schilling, p | 0 | 0 | 0 | 0 | 0 | 0 | 0 | 0 |
| Embree, p | 0 | 0 | 0 | 0 | 0 | 0 | 0 | 0 |
| Timlin, p | 0 | 0 | 0 | 0 | 0 | 0 | 0 | 1 |
| Foulke, p | 0 | 0 | 0 | 0 | 0 | 0 | 0 | 0 |
| **TOTALS** | 31 | 6 | 8 | 6 | 6 | 5 | 27 | 6 |

| | | | | |
|---|---|---|---|---|
| St. Louis | 0 0 0 | 1 0 0 | 0 1 0—2 | 5 0 |
| Boston | 2 0 0 | 2 0 2 | 0 0 x—6 | 8 4 |

| St. Louis | IP | H | R | ER | HR | BB | SO |
|---|---|---|---|---|---|---|---|
| M.Morris (L) | 4.1 | 4 | 4 | 4 | 0 | 4 | 3 |
| Eldred | 1.1 | 4 | 2 | 2 | 0 | 0 | 1 |
| King | 0.1 | 0 | 0 | 0 | 0 | 0 | 1 |
| Marquis | 1.0 | 0 | 0 | 0 | 0 | 2 | 0 |
| A.Reyes | 1.0 | 0 | 0 | 0 | 0 | 0 | 0 |

| Boston | IP | H | R | ER | HR | BB | SO |
|---|---|---|---|---|---|---|---|
| Schilling (W) | 6.0 | 4 | 1 | 0 | 0 | 1 | 4 |
| Embree | 1.0 | 0 | 0 | 0 | 0 | 0 | 3 |
| Timlin | 0.2 | 1 | 1 | 1 | 0 | 1 | 0 |
| Foulke | 1.1 | 0 | 0 | 0 | 0 | 0 | 2 |

Bases on balls—Off M.Morris 4 (M.Ramirez, O.Cabrera, D.Ortiz, Millar), off Marquis 2 (Mueller, Millar), off Schilling 1 (R.Sanders), off Timlin1 (Renteria).

Strikeouts—By M.Morris 3 (M.Ramirez, Damon, Nixon), by Eldred 1 (Millar), by King 1 (D.Ortiz), by Schilling 4 (L.Walker 2, Edmonds, Mar.Anderson), by Embree 3 (Womack, Matheny, Taguchi), by Foulke 2 (R.Sanders, Edmonds).

E—Bellhorn, Mueller 3. DP—St. Louis 1, Boston 2. LOB—St. Louis 6, Boston 9. Scoring Position—St. Louis 1 for 7, Boston 3 for 8. 2B—Pujols 2, Mueller, Bellhorn. 3B—Varitek. S—Rolen. HBP—Varitek by Eldred, Millar by M.Morris. T—3:20. A—35,001. U—HP-Scott, 1B-Gorman, 2B-Meriwether, 3B-Davis, LF-Reliford, RF-Montague.

## PLAY BY PLAY

TOP OF 1

Cardinals first. Renteria grounded out, shortstop Cabrera to first baseman Millar. Walker flied out to right fielder Nixon. Pujols doubled to center. Rolen lined out to third baseman Mueller. Runs: 0, Hits: 1, Errors: 0

BOTTOM OF 1

Red Sox first. Damon grounded out, third baseman Rolen to first baseman Pujols. Cabrera grounded out, shortstop Renteria to first baseman Pujols. Ramirez walked on a full count. Ortiz walked on a full count, Ramirez to second. Varitek tripled to center, Ramirez scored, Ortiz scored. Millar walked. Nixon grounded out, third baseman Rolen to first baseman Pujols. Runs: 2, Hits: 1, Errors: 0

TOP OF 2

Cardinals second. Edmonds remained at bat on Mueller's fielding error, Edmonds grounded out, first baseman Millar unassisted. Sanders walked on a full count. Womack singled to center, Sanders to second. Matheny lined into a double play, third baseman Mueller unassisted, Sanders out. Runs: 0, Hits: 1, Errors: 1

BOTTOM OF 2

Red Sox second. Mueller singled to right. Bellhorn grounded into a double play, second baseman Womack to shortstop Renteria to first baseman Pujols, Mueller out. Damon struck out. Runs: 0, Hits: 1, Errors: 0

TOP OF 3

Cardinals third. Anderson popped out to first baseman Millar. Renteria grounded out, shortstop Cabrera to first baseman Millar. Walker struck out. Runs: 0, Hits: 0, Errors: 0

BOTTOM OF 3

Red Sox third. Cabrera grounded out, third baseman Rolen to first baseman Pujols. Ramirez struck out. Ortiz grounded out, first baseman Pujols unassisted. Runs: 0, Hits: 0, Errors: 0

TOP OF 4

Cardinals fourth. Pujols doubled to left. Rolen flied out to right fielder Nixon, Pujols to third. Edmonds struck out. Sanders safe on Mueller's error, Pujols scored. Womack grounded into fielder's choice, shortstop Cabrera unassisted, Sanders out. Runs: 1, Hits: 1, Errors: 1

BOTTOM OF 4

Red Sox fourth. Varitek grounded out, second baseman Womack to first baseman Pujols. Millar was hit by a pitch. Nixon struck out. Mueller doubled to right, Millar to third. Bellhorn doubled to center, Millar scored, Mueller scored. Damon grounded out, second baseman Womack to first baseman Pujols. Runs: 2, Hits: 2, Errors: 0

TOP OF 5

Cardinals fifth. Matheny singled to left. Anderson struck out. Renteria grounded into a double play, shortstop Cabrera to second baseman Bellhorn to first baseman Millar, Matheny out. Runs: 0, Hits: 1, Errors: 0

BOTTOM OF 5
Red Sox fifth. Cabrera walked. Ramirez flied out to right fielder Walker. Eldred pitching. Ortiz flied out to right fielder Walker. Varitek was hit by a pitch, Cabrera to second. Millar struck out. Runs: 0, Hits: 0, Errors: 0

TOP OF 6
Cardinals sixth. Walker struck out. Pujols flied out to right fielder Nixon. Rolen safe on Mueller's error. Edmonds safe on Bellhorn's error, Rolen to second. Sanders grounded into fielder's choice, third baseman Mueller unassisted, Rolen out, Edmonds to second. Runs: 0, Hits: 0, Errors: 2

BOTTOM OF 6
Red Sox sixth. Nixon singled to center. Mueller flied out to right fielder Walker. Bellhorn popped out to shortstop Renteria. Damon singled to left, Nixon to second. Cabrera singled to left, Nixon scored, Damon scored. Ramirez singled to center, Cabrera to third. King pitching. Ortiz struck out. Runs: 2, Hits: 4, Errors: 0

TOP OF 7
Cardinals seventh. Embree pitching. Reese in as second baseman. Womack struck out. Matheny struck out. Taguchi pinch-hitting for Anderson. Taguchi struck out. Runs: 0, Hits: 0, Errors: 0

BOTTOM OF 7
Red Sox seventh. Taguchi in as designated hitter. Marquis pitching. Varitek flied out to center fielder Edmonds. Millar walked on four pitches. Mientkiewicz pinch-running for Millar. Nixon flied out to center fielder Edmonds. Mueller walked on a full count, Mientkiewicz to second. Reese popped out to first baseman Pujols. Runs: 0, Hits: 0, Errors: 0

TOP OF 8
Cardinals eighth. Mientkiewicz in as first baseman. Timlin pitching. Renteria walked. Walker grounded out, pitcher Timlin to first baseman Mientkiewicz, Renteria to second. Pujols singled to left, Renteria to third. Rolen hit a sacrifice fly to center fielder Damon, Renteria scored. Foulke pitching. Edmonds struck out. Runs: 1, Hits: 1, Errors: 0

BOTTOM OF 8
Red Sox eighth. Reyes pitching. Damon grounded out, shortstop Renteria to first baseman Pujols. Cabrera fouled out to catcher Matheny. Ramirez grounded out, second baseman Womack to first baseman Pujols. Runs: 0, Hits: 0, Errors: 0

TOP OF 9
Cardinals ninth. Kapler in as left fielder. Sanders struck out. Womack lined out to right fielder Nixon. Matheny grounded out, shortstop Cabrera to first baseman Mientkiewicz. Runs: 0, Hits: 0, Errors: 0

## GAME 3

### BOSTON 4, ST. LOUIS 1

TUESDAY, OCTOBER 26, AT ST. LOUIS

| Boston | AB | R | H | BI | BB | SO | PO | A |
|---|---|---|---|---|---|---|---|---|
| Damon, cf | 5 | 1 | 1 | 0 | 0 | 0 | 1 | 0 |
| O.Cabrera, ss | 4 | 1 | 2 | 0 | 1 | 0 | 1 | 1 |
| M.Ramirez, lf | 4 | 1 | 2 | 2 | 1 | 1 | 3 | 1 |
| D.Ortiz, 1b | 4 | 0 | 1 | 0 | 0 | 0 | 6 | 1 |
| Mientkiewicz, 1b | 0 | 0 | 0 | 0 | 0 | 0 | 4 | 0 |
| Varitek, c | 3 | 0 | 0 | 0 | 1 | 1 | 9 | 0 |
| Mueller, 3b | 4 | 1 | 2 | 1 | 0 | 0 | 2 | 3 |
| Nixon, rf | 3 | 0 | 1 | 1 | 0 | 0 | 0 | 0 |
| Kapler, ph-rf | 1 | 0 | 0 | 0 | 0 | 0 | 0 | 0 |
| Bellhorn, 2b | 3 | 0 | 0 | 0 | 0 | 1 | 1 | 4 |
| Reese, 2b | 0 | 0 | 0 | 0 | 0 | 0 | 0 | 0 |
| P.Martinez, p | 2 | 0 | 0 | 0 | 1 | 2 | 0 | 0 |
| Millar, ph | 1 | 0 | 0 | 0 | 0 | 0 | 0 | 0 |
| Timlin, p | 0 | 0 | 0 | 0 | 0 | 0 | 0 | 0 |
| Foulke, p | 0 | 0 | 0 | 0 | 0 | 0 | 0 | 0 |
| TOTALS | 34 | 4 | 9 | 4 | 4 | 5 | 27 | 10 |

| St. Louis | AB | R | H | BI | BB | SO | PO | A |
|---|---|---|---|---|---|---|---|---|
| Renteria, ss | 4 | 0 | 1 | 0 | 0 | 1 | 4 | 1 |
| L.Walker, rf | 3 | 1 | 1 | 1 | 1 | 0 | 3 | 0 |
| Pujols, 1b | 4 | 0 | 1 | 0 | 0 | 1 | 8 | 1 |
| Rolen, 3b | 3 | 0 | 0 | 0 | 1 | 1 | 1 | 3 |
| Edmonds, cf | 3 | 0 | 0 | 0 | 0 | 1 | 5 | 0 |
| R.Sanders, lf | 3 | 0 | 0 | 0 | 0 | 2 | 1 | 0 |
| Womack, 2b | 3 | 0 | 0 | 0 | 0 | 1 | 0 | 3 |
| Matheny, c | 2 | 0 | 0 | 0 | 0 | 1 | 4 | 0 |
| Cedeno, ph | 1 | 0 | 0 | 0 | 0 | 0 | 0 | 0 |
| Tavarez, p | 0 | 0 | 0 | 0 | 0 | 0 | 0 | 0 |
| Suppan, p | 1 | 0 | 1 | 0 | 0 | 0 | 0 | 0 |
| A.Reyes, p | 0 | 0 | 0 | 0 | 0 | 0 | 0 | 0 |
| Mar.Anderson, ph | 1 | 0 | 0 | 0 | 0 | 0 | 0 | 0 |
| Calero, p | 0 | 0 | 0 | 0 | 0 | 0 | 0 | 0 |
| King, p | 0 | 0 | 0 | 0 | 0 | 0 | 0 | 0 |
| Mabry, ph | 1 | 0 | 0 | 0 | 0 | 0 | 0 | 0 |
| Y.Molina, c | 0 | 0 | 0 | 0 | 0 | 0 | 1 | 0 |
| TOTALS | 29 | 1 | 4 | 1 | 2 | 8 | 27 | 8 |

| | | | | | |
|---|---|---|---|---|---|
| Boston | 1 0 0 | 1 2 0 | 0 0 0—4 | 9 | 0 |
| St. Louis | 0 0 0 | 0 0 0 | 0 0 1—1 | 4 | 0 |

| Boston | IP | H | R | ER | HR | BB | SO |
|---|---|---|---|---|---|---|---|
| P.Martinez (W) | 7.0 | 3 | 0 | 0 | 0 | 2 | 6 |
| Timlin | 1.0 | 0 | 0 | 0 | 0 | 0 | 0 |
| Foulke | 1.0 | 1 | 1 | 1 | 1 | 0 | 2 |

| St. Louis | IP | H | R | ER | HR | BB | SO |
|---|---|---|---|---|---|---|---|
| Suppan (L) | 4.2 | 8 | 4 | 4 | 1 | 1 | 4 |
| A.Reyes | 0.1 | 0 | 0 | 0 | 0 | 0 | 0 |
| Calero | 1.0 | 1 | 0 | 0 | 0 | 2 | 0 |
| King | 2.0 | 0 | 0 | 0 | 0 | 1 | 0 |
| Tavarez | 1.0 | 0 | 0 | 0 | 0 | 0 | 1 |

Calero pitched to 2 batters in the 7th.

Bases on balls—Off P.Martinez 2 (L.Walker, Rolen), off Suppan 1 (O.Cabrera), off Calero 2 (P.Martinez, M.Ramirez), off King 1 (Varitek).

Strikeouts—By P.Martinez 6 (R.Sanders 2, Edmonds, Womack, Matheny, Pujols), by Foulke 2 (Renteria, Rolen), by Suppan 4 (P.Martinez 2, Bellhorn, Varitek), by Tavarez 1 (M.Ramirez).

DP—Boston 2, St. Louis 2. LOB—Boston 8, St. Louis 3. Scoring Position—Boston 4 for 10, St. Louis 0 for 3. 2B—Damon, O.Cabrera, Mueller, Renteria. HR—M.Ramirez (1st inning, 2 out, 0 on) off Suppan, L.Walker (9th inning, 1 out, 0 on) off Foulke. HBP—Bellhorn by Suppan. T—2:58. A—52,015. U—HP-Gorman, 1B-Meriwether, 2B-Davis, 3B-Reliford, LF-Montague, RF-Scott.

## PLAY BY PLAY

TOP OF 1
Red Sox first. Damon lined out to right fielder Walker. Cabrera lined out to center fielder Edmonds. Ramirez homered to left on a 2-2 count. Ortiz singled to right. Varitek grounded into fielder's choice, second baseman Womack to shortstop Renteria, Ortiz out. Runs: 1, Hits: 2, Errors: 0

BOTTOM OF 1
Cardinals first. Renteria grounded out, second baseman Bellhorn to first baseman Ortiz. Walker walked. Pujols infield single to third, Walker to second. Rolen walked, Walker to third, Pujols to second. Edmonds flied out to left fielder Ramirez. Walker was out advancing, left fielder Ramirez to catcher Varitek, Walker out. Runs: 0, Hits: 1, Errors: 0

TOP OF 2
Red Sox second. Mueller lined out to center fielder Edmonds. Nixon popped out to shortstop Renteria. Bellhorn struck out. Runs: 0, Hits: 0, Errors: 0

BOTTOM OF 2
Cardinals second. Sanders flied out to left fielder Ramirez. Womack grounded out, second baseman Bellhorn to first baseman Ortiz. Matheny struck out. Runs: 0, Hits: 0, Errors: 0

TOP OF 3
Red Sox third. P.Martinez struck out. Damon grounded out, second baseman Womack to first baseman Pujols. Cabrera walked on a full count. Ramirez flied out to right fielder Walker. Runs: 0, Hits: 0, Errors: 0

BOTTOM OF 3
Cardinals third. Suppan infield single to third. Renteria doubled to right, Suppan to third. Walker grounded out, second baseman Bellhorn to first baseman Ortiz. Suppan was out advancing, first baseman Ortiz to third baseman Mueller, Suppan out. Pujols grounded out, third baseman Mueller to first baseman Ortiz. Runs: 0, Hits: 2, Errors: 0

TOP OF 4
Red Sox fourth. Ortiz grounded out, first baseman Pujols unassisted. Varitek struck out. Mueller doubled to center. Nixon singled to right, Mueller scored. Bellhorn was hit by a pitch, Nixon to second. P.Martinez struck out. Runs: 1, Hits: 2, Errors: 0

BOTTOM OF 4
Cardinals fourth. Rolen grounded out, third baseman Mueller to first baseman Ortiz. Edmonds flied out to center fielder Damon. Sanders struck out. Runs: 0, Hits: 0, Errors: 0

TOP OF 5
Red Sox fifth. Damon doubled to right. Cabrera singled to right, Damon to third. Ramirez singled to left, Damon scored, Cabrera to second. Ortiz flied out to center fielder Edmonds. Varitek grounded into fielder's choice, first baseman Pujols to shortstop Renteria, Cabrera to third, Ramirez out. Mueller singled to right, Cabrera scored, Varitek to second. Reyes pitching. Nixon flied out to left fielder Sanders. Runs: 2, Hits: 4, Errors: 0

BOTTOM OF 5

Cardinals fifth. Womack struck out. Matheny popped out to shortstop Cabrera. Anderson pinch-hitting for Reyes. Anderson popped out to third baseman Mueller. Runs: 0, Hits: 0, Errors: 0

TOP OF 6

Red Sox sixth. Calero pitching. Bellhorn grounded out, first baseman Pujols unassisted. P.Martinez walked on a full count. Damon grounded into a double play, second baseman Womack to shortstop Renteria to first baseman Pujols, P.Martinez out. Runs: 0, Hits: 0, Errors: 0

BOTTOM OF 6

Cardinals sixth. Renteria grounded out, second baseman Bellhorn to first baseman Ortiz. Walker lined out to second baseman Bellhorn. Pujols struck out. Runs: 0, Hits: 0, Errors: 0

TOP OF 7

Red Sox seventh. Cabrera doubled to center. Ramirez walked on a full count. King pitching. Ortiz grounded out, first baseman Pujols unassisted, Cabrera to third, Ramirez to second. Varitek walked on four pitches. Mueller grounded into a double play, third baseman Rolen to first baseman Pujols, Ramirez out. Runs: 0, Hits: 1, Errors: 0

BOTTOM OF 7

Cardinals seventh. Mientkiewicz in as first baseman. Rolen grounded out, first baseman Mientkiewicz unassisted. Edmonds struck out. Sanders struck out. Runs: 0, Hits: 0, Errors: 0

TOP OF 8

Red Sox eighth. Kapler pinch-hitting for Nixon. Kapler grounded out, third baseman Rolen to first baseman Pujols. Bellhorn flied out to right fielder Walker. Millar pinch-hitting for P.Martinez. Millar grounded out, third baseman Rolen to first baseman Pujols. Runs: 0, Hits: 0, Errors: 0

BOTTOM OF 8

Cardinals eighth. Kapler in as right fielder. Reese in as second baseman. Timlin pitching. Womack grounded out, third baseman Mueller to first baseman Mientkiewicz. Cedeno pinch-hitting for Matheny. Cedeno grounded out, shortstop Cabrera to first baseman Mientkiewicz. Mabry pinch-hitting for King. Mabry grounded out, first baseman Mientkiewicz unassisted. Runs: 0, Hits: 0, Errors: 0

TOP OF 9

Red Sox ninth. Tavarez pitching. Molina in as catcher. Damon flied out to center fielder Edmonds. Cabrera lined out to center fielder Edmonds. Ramirez struck out. Runs: 0, Hits: 0, Errors: 0

BOTTOM OF 9

Cardinals ninth. Foulke pitching. Renteria struck out. Walker homered to center on a 0-2 count. Pujols flied out to left fielder Ramirez. Rolen struck out. Runs: 1, Hits: 1, Errors: 0

## GAME 4

### BOSTON 3, ST. LOUIS 0

WEDNESDAY, OCTOBER 27, AT ST. LOUIS

| Boston | AB | R | H | BI | BB | SO | PO | A |
|---|---|---|---|---|---|---|---|---|
| Damon, cf | 5 | 1 | 2 | 1 | 0 | 0 | 3 | 0 |
| O.Cabrera, ss | 5 | 0 | 0 | 0 | 0 | 1 | 1 | 3 |
| M.Ramirez, lf | 4 | 0 | 1 | 0 | 1 | 1 | 1 | 0 |
| D.Ortiz, 1b | 3 | 1 | 1 | 0 | 1 | 0 | 8 | 0 |
| Mientkiewicz, 1b | 1 | 0 | 0 | 0 | 0 | 0 | 1 | 0 |
| Varitek, c | 5 | 1 | 1 | 0 | 0 | 2 | 6 | 0 |
| Mueller, 3b | 4 | 0 | 1 | 0 | 1 | 0 | 1 | 1 |
| Nixon, rf | 4 | 0 | 3 | 2 | 0 | 0 | 2 | 0 |
| Kapler, pr-rf | 0 | 0 | 0 | 0 | 0 | 0 | 1 | 0 |
| Bellhorn, 2b | 1 | 0 | 0 | 0 | 3 | 1 | 1 | 1 |
| Reese, pr-2b | 0 | 0 | 0 | 0 | 0 | 0 | 1 | 0 |
| Lowe, p | 2 | 0 | 0 | 0 | 0 | 1 | 1 | 2 |
| Millar, ph | 1 | 0 | 0 | 0 | 0 | 1 | 0 | 0 |
| Arroyo, p | 0 | 0 | 0 | 0 | 0 | 0 | 0 | 0 |
| Embree, p | 0 | 0 | 0 | 0 | 0 | 0 | 0 | 0 |
| Foulke, p | 0 | 0 | 0 | 0 | 0 | 0 | 0 | 1 |
| **TOTALS** | 35 | 3 | 9 | 3 | 6 | 7 | 27 | 8 |

| St. Louis | AB | R | H | BI | BB | SO | PO | A |
|---|---|---|---|---|---|---|---|---|
| Womack, 2b | 3 | 0 | 1 | 0 | 0 | 0 | 1 | 3 |
| Luna, ph-2b | 1 | 0 | 0 | 0 | 0 | 1 | 0 | 0 |
| L.Walker, rf | 2 | 0 | 0 | 0 | 1 | 0 | 2 | 0 |
| Pujols, 1b | 4 | 0 | 1 | 0 | 0 | 1 | 7 | 3 |
| Rolen, 3b | 4 | 0 | 0 | 0 | 0 | 0 | 0 | 3 |
| Edmonds, cf | 4 | 0 | 0 | 0 | 0 | 1 | 4 | 0 |
| Renteria, ss | 4 | 0 | 2 | 0 | 0 | 0 | 1 | 0 |
| Mabry, lf | 3 | 0 | 0 | 0 | 0 | 2 | 2 | 0 |
| Isringhausen, p | 0 | 0 | 0 | 0 | 0 | 0 | 0 | 0 |
| Y.Molina, c | 2 | 0 | 0 | 0 | 0 | 1 | 9 | 0 |
| Cedeno, ph | 1 | 0 | 0 | 0 | 0 | 0 | 0 | 0 |
| Matheny, c | 0 | 0 | 0 | 0 | 0 | 0 | 0 | 0 |
| Marquis, p | 1 | 0 | 0 | 0 | 0 | 0 | 0 | 1 |
| Mar.Anderson, ph | 1 | 0 | 0 | 0 | 0 | 0 | 0 | 0 |
| Haren, p | 0 | 0 | 0 | 0 | 0 | 0 | 1 | 0 |
| R.Sanders, lf | 0 | 0 | 0 | 0 | 1 | 0 | 0 | 0 |
| **TOTALS** | 30 | 0 | 4 | 0 | 2 | 6 | 27 | 10 |

| | | | | |
|---|---|---|---|---|
| Boston | 1 0 2 | 0 0 0 | 0 0 0 | —3 9 0 |
| St. Louis | 0 0 0 | 0 0 0 | 0 0 0 | —0 4 0 |

| Boston | IP | H | R | ER | HR | BB | SO |
|---|---|---|---|---|---|---|---|
| Lowe (W) | 7.0 | 3 | 0 | 0 | 0 | 1 | 4 |
| Arroyo (HOLD) | 0.1 | 0 | 0 | 0 | 0 | 1 | 0 |
| Embree (HOLD) | 0.2 | 0 | 0 | 0 | 0 | 0 | 1 |
| Foulke (S) | 1.0 | 1 | 0 | 0 | 0 | 0 | 1 |

| St. Louis | IP | H | R | ER | HR | BB | SO |
|---|---|---|---|---|---|---|---|
| Marquis (L) | 6.0 | 6 | 3 | 3 | 1 | 5 | 4 |
| Haren | 1.0 | 2 | 0 | 0 | 0 | 0 | 1 |
| Isringhausen | 2.0 | 1 | 0 | 0 | 0 | 1 | 2 |

Haren pitched to 2 batters in the 8th.

Bases on balls—Off Lowe 1 (L.Walker), off Arroyo 1 (R.Sanders), off Marquis 5 (M.Ramirez, Mueller, Bellhorn 2, D.Ortiz), off Isringhausen 1 (Bellhorn).

Strikeouts—By Lowe 4 (Mabry 2, Pujols, Y.Molina), by Embree 1 (Luna), by Foulke 1 (Edmonds), by Marquis 4 (Lowe, Bellhorn, Varitek 2), by Haren 1 (M.Ramirez), by Isringhausen 2 (O.Cabrera, Millar).

LOB—Boston 12, St. Louis 6. Scoring Position—Boston 1 for 9, St. Louis 0 for 7. 2B—D.Ortiz, Nixon 3, Renteria. 3B—Damon. HR—Damon (1st inning, 0 out, 0 on) off Marquis. SB—R.Sanders. SH—Lowe, L.Walker. WP—Lowe. T—3:14. A—52,037. U—HP-Meriwether, 1B-Davis, 2B-Reliford, 3B-Montague, LF-Scott, RF-Gorman.

## PLAY BY PLAY

TOP OF 1

Red Sox first. Damon homered to right on a 2-1 count. Cabrera grounded out, third baseman Rolen to first baseman Pujols. Ramirez walked. Ortiz flied out to left fielder Mabry. Varitek struck out. Runs: 1, Hits: 1, Errors: 0

BOTTOM OF 1

Cardinals first. Womack singled to center. Walker sacrificed, pitcher Lowe to first baseman Ortiz, Womack to second. Pujols grounded out, second baseman Bellhorn to first baseman Ortiz, Womack to third. Rolen grounded out, pitcher Lowe unassisted. Runs: 0, Hits: 1, Errors: 0

TOP OF 2

Red Sox second. Mueller grounded out, second baseman Womack to first baseman Pujols. Nixon doubled to right. Bellhorn walked on a full count. Lowe sacrificed, third baseman Rolen to second baseman Womack, Nixon to third, Bellhorn to second. Damon grounded out, first baseman Pujols unassisted. Runs: 0, Hits: 1, Errors: 0

BOTTOM OF 2

Cardinals second. Edmonds flied out to left fielder Ramirez. Renteria grounded out, third baseman Mueller to first baseman Ortiz. Mabry flied out to right fielder Nixon. Runs: 0, Hits: 0, Errors: 0

TOP OF 3

Red Sox third. Cabrera flied out to left fielder Mabry. Ramirez singled to left. Ortiz doubled to right, Ramirez to third. Varitek grounded into fielder's choice, first baseman Pujols to catcher Molina, Ramirez out, Ortiz to third. Mueller walked on four pitches, Varitek to second. Nixon doubled to center, Ortiz scored, Varitek scored, Mueller to third. Bellhorn was intentionally walked. Lowe struck out. Runs: 2, Hits: 3, Errors: 0

BOTTOM OF 3

Cardinals third. Molina struck out. Marquis grounded out, shortstop Cabrera to first baseman Ortiz. Womack grounded out, shortstop Cabrera to first baseman Ortiz. Runs: 0, Hits: 0, Errors: 0

TOP OF 4

Red Sox fourth. Damon grounded out, second baseman Womack to first baseman Pujols. Cabrera flied out to center fielder Edmonds. Ramirez flied out to center fielder Edmonds. Runs: 0, Hits: 0, Errors: 0

BOTTOM OF 4

Cardinals fourth. Walker lined out to right fielder Nixon. Pujols struck out. Rolen fouled out to first baseman Ortiz. Runs: 0, Hits: 0, Errors: 0

TOP OF 5

Red Sox fifth. Ortiz walked on a full count. Varitek struck out. Mueller grounded out, second baseman Womack to first baseman Pujols, Ortiz to second. Nixon flied out to center fielder Edmonds. Runs: 0, Hits: 0, Errors: 0

BOTTOM OF 5

Cardinals fifth. Edmonds lined out to third baseman Mueller. Renteria doubled to center. On Lowe's wild pitch, Renteria to third. Mabry struck out. Molina grounded out, shortstop Cabrera to first baseman Ortiz. Runs: 0, Hits: 1, Errors: 0

TOP OF 6

Red Sox sixth. Bellhorn struck out. Lowe grounded out, pitcher Marquis to first baseman Pujols. Damon tripled to center. Cabrera flied out to right fielder Walker. Runs: 0, Hits: 1, Errors: 0

BOTTOM OF 6

Cardinals sixth. Anderson pinch-hitting for Marquis. Anderson was out bunting, pitcher Lowe to first baseman Ortiz. Womack flied out to center fielder Damon. Walker walked. Pujols popped out to second baseman Bellhorn. Runs: 0, Hits: 0, Errors: 0

TOP OF 7

Red Sox seventh. Haren pitching. Ramirez struck out. Ortiz grounded out, first baseman Pujols to pitcher Haren. Varitek flied out to center fielder Edmonds. Runs: 0, Hits: 0, Errors: 0

BOTTOM OF 7

Cardinals seventh. Mientkiewicz in as first baseman. Rolen flied out to center fielder Damon. Edmonds lined out to center fielder Damon. Renteria singled to right. Mabry struck out. Runs: 0, Hits: 1, Errors: 0

TOP OF 8

Red Sox eighth. Mueller singled to right. Nixon doubled to right, Mueller to third. Kapler pinch-running for Nixon. Isringhausen pitching. Sanders in as left fielder. Bellhorn walked on a full count. Reese pinch-running for Bellhorn. Millar pinch-hitting for Lowe. Millar struck out. Damon grounded into fielder's choice, first baseman Pujols to catcher Molina, Mueller out, Kapler to third, Reese to second. Cabrera struck out. Runs: 0, Hits: 2, Errors: 0

BOTTOM OF 8

Cardinals eighth. Kapler in as right fielder. Reese in as second baseman. Arroyo pitching. Cedeno pinch-hitting for Molina. Cedeno popped out to second baseman Reese. Sanders walked on a full count. Embree pitching. Luna pinch-hitting for Womack.Sanders stole second. Luna struck out. Walker popped out to shortstop Cabrera. Runs: 0, Hits: 0, Errors: 0

TOP OF 9

Red Sox ninth. Luna in as second baseman. Matheny in as catcher. Ramirez grounded out, third baseman Rolen to first baseman Pujols. Mientkiewicz popped out to right fielder Walker. Varitek singled to left. Mueller grounded into fielder's choice, shortstop Renteria unassisted, Varitek out. Runs: 0, Hits: 1, Errors: 0

BOTTOM OF 9

Cardinals ninth. Foulke pitching. Pujols singled to center. Rolen flied out to right fielder Kapler. Edmonds struck out. On defensive indifference, Pujols to second. Renteria grounded out, pitcher Foulke to first baseman Mientkiewicz. Runs: 0, Hits: 1, Errors: 0d to left on a full count. One run. Marlins 4, Yankees 3.

# STATISTICS

## BOSTON RED SOX' BATTING AND FIELDING AVERAGES

| | BATTING | | | | | | | | | | | | | | FIELDING | | | |
|---|---|---|---|---|---|---|---|---|---|---|---|---|---|---|---|---|---|---|
| **Player, position** | **G** | **AB** | **R** | **H** | **TB** | **2B** | **3B** | **HR** | **RBI** | **BB** | **IBB** | **SO** | **Avg.** | **OBP** | **Slg.** | **PO** | **A** | **E** | **Avg.** |
| Mueller,3b | 4 | 14 | 3 | 6 | 8 | 2 | 0 | 0 | 2 | 4 | 0 | 0 | .429 | .556 | .571 | 9 | 8 | 3 | .850 |
| Ramirez,lf | 4 | 17 | 2 | 7 | 10 | 0 | 0 | 1 | 4 | 3 | 0 | 3 | .412 | .500 | .588 | 5 | 1 | 2 | .750 |
| Nixon,rf | 4 | 14 | 1 | 5 | 8 | 3 | 0 | 0 | 3 | 1 | 0 | 1 | .357 | .400 | .571 | 8 | 0 | 0 | 1.000 |
| Mirabelli,c | 1 | 3 | 1 | 1 | 1 | 0 | 0 | 0 | 0 | 0 | 0 | 1 | .333 | .333 | .333 | 6 | 0 | 0 | 1.000 |
| Ortiz,dh-1b | 4 | 13 | 3 | 4 | 8 | 1 | 0 | 1 | 4 | 4 | 0 | 1 | .308 | .471 | .615 | 14 | 1 | 0 | 1.000 |
| Bellhorn,2b | 4 | 10 | 3 | 3 | 7 | 1 | 0 | 1 | 4 | 5 | 1 | 2 | .300 | .563 | .700 | 7 | 8 | 1 | .938 |
| Damon,cf | 4 | 21 | 4 | 6 | 13 | 2 | 1 | 1 | 2 | 0 | 0 | 1 | .286 | .286 | .619 | 7 | 0 | 0 | 1.000 |
| Cabrera,ss | 4 | 17 | 3 | 4 | 5 | 1 | 0 | 0 | 3 | 3 | 0 | 1 | .235 | .381 | .294 | 4 | 9 | 0 | 1.000 |
| Varitek,c-ph | 4 | 13 | 2 | 2 | 4 | 0 | 1 | 0 | 2 | 1 | 0 | 4 | .154 | .267 | .308 | 27 | 0 | 0 | 1.000 |
| Millar,1b-ph | 4 | 8 | 2 | 1 | 2 | 1 | 0 | 0 | 0 | 2 | 0 | 2 | .125 | .364 | .250 | 9 | 0 | 1 | .900 |
| Arroyo,p | 2 | 0 | 0 | 0 | 0 | 0 | 0 | 0 | 0 | 0 | 0 | 0 | .000 | .000 | .000 | 0 | 0 | 1 | .000 |
| Embree,p | 3 | 0 | 0 | 0 | 0 | 0 | 0 | 0 | 0 | 0 | 0 | 0 | .000 | .000 | .000 | 0 | 0 | 0 | .000 |
| Foulke,p | 4 | 0 | 0 | 0 | 0 | 0 | 0 | 0 | 0 | 0 | 0 | 0 | .000 | .000 | .000 | 0 | 1 | 0 | 1.000 |
| Schilling,p | 1 | 0 | 0 | 0 | 0 | 0 | 0 | 0 | 0 | 0 | 0 | 0 | .000 | .000 | .000 | 0 | 0 | 0 | .000 |
| Timlin,p | 3 | 0 | 0 | 0 | 0 | 0 | 0 | 0 | 0 | 0 | 0 | 0 | .000 | .000 | .000 | 0 | 2 | 0 | 1.000 |
| Wakefield,p | 1 | 0 | 0 | 0 | 0 | 0 | 0 | 0 | 0 | 0 | 0 | 0 | .000 | .000 | .000 | 0 | 0 | 0 | .000 |
| Mientkiewicz,1b-pr | 4 | 1 | 0 | 0 | 0 | 0 | 0 | 0 | 0 | 0 | 0 | 0 | .000 | .000 | .000 | 9 | 0 | 0 | 1.000 |
| Reese,2b-pr | 4 | 1 | 0 | 0 | 0 | 0 | 0 | 0 | 0 | 0 | 0 | 0 | .000 | .000 | .000 | 1 | 0 | 0 | 1.000 |
| Kapler,rf-ph-lf-pr | 4 | 2 | 0 | 0 | 0 | 0 | 0 | 0 | 0 | 0 | 0 | 1 | .000 | .000 | .000 | 1 | 0 | 0 | 1.000 |
| Lowe,p | 1 | 2 | 0 | 0 | 0 | 0 | 0 | 0 | 0 | 0 | 0 | 1 | .000 | .000 | .000 | 1 | 2 | 0 | 1.000 |
| Martinez,p | 1 | 2 | 0 | 0 | 0 | 0 | 0 | 0 | 0 | 1 | 0 | 2 | .000 | .333 | .000 | 0 | 0 | 0 | .000 |
| Totals | 4 | 138 | 24 | 39 | 66 | 11 | 2 | 4 | 24 | 24 | 1 | 20 | .283 | .404 | .478 | 108 | 32 | 8 | .946 |

## ST. LOUIS CARDINALS' BATTING AND FIELDING AVERAGES

| | BATTING | | | | | | | | | | | | | | FIELDING | | | |
|---|---|---|---|---|---|---|---|---|---|---|---|---|---|---|---|---|---|---|
| **Player, position** | **G** | **AB** | **R** | **H** | **TB** | **2B** | **3B** | **HR** | **RBI** | **BB** | **IBB** | **SO** | **Avg.** | **OBP** | **Slg.** | **PO** | **A** | **E** | **Avg.** |
| Suppan,p | 1 | 1 | 0 | 1 | 1 | 0 | 0 | 0 | 0 | 0 | 0 | 0 | 1.000 | 1.000 | 1.000 | 0 | 0 | 0 | .000 |
| Walker,rf | 4 | 14 | 2 | 5 | 13 | 2 | 0 | 2 | 3 | 2 | 0 | 2 | .357 | .438 | .929 | 11 | 0 | 0 | 1.000 |
| Pujols,1b | 4 | 15 | 1 | 5 | 7 | 2 | 0 | 0 | 0 | 1 | 1 | 3 | .333 | .412 | .467 | 34 | 4 | 0 | 1.000 |
| Renteria,ss | 4 | 15 | 2 | 5 | 8 | 3 | 0 | 0 | 1 | 2 | 0 | 2 | .333 | .412 | .533 | 9 | 7 | 1 | .941 |
| Matheny,c | 4 | 8 | 0 | 2 | 2 | 0 | 0 | 0 | 2 | 0 | 0 | 3 | .250 | .200 | .250 | 14 | 0 | 0 | 1.000 |
| Cedeno,lf-ph | 3 | 4 | 1 | 1 | 1 | 0 | 0 | 0 | 0 | 0 | 0 | 1 | .250 | .250 | .250 | 0 | 0 | 0 | .000 |
| Taguchi,lf-dh | 2 | 4 | 1 | 1 | 1 | 0 | 0 | 0 | 1 | 0 | 0 | 2 | .250 | .250 | .250 | 4 | 0 | 0 | 1.000 |
| Womack,2b | 4 | 11 | 1 | 2 | 2 | 0 | 0 | 0 | 0 | 1 | 0 | 2 | .182 | .250 | .182 | 2 | 12 | 0 | 1.000 |
| Anderson,2b-dh-ph | 4 | 6 | 0 | 1 | 2 | 1 | 0 | 0 | 0 | 0 | 0 | 1 | .167 | .167 | .333 | 0 | 1 | 0 | 1.000 |
| Edmonds,cf | 4 | 15 | 2 | 1 | 1 | 0 | 0 | 0 | 0 | 1 | 0 | 6 | .067 | .125 | .067 | 12 | 0 | 0 | 1.000 |
| Calero,p | 2 | 0 | 0 | 0 | 0 | 0 | 0 | 0 | 0 | 0 | 0 | 0 | .000 | .000 | .000 | 0 | 0 | 0 | .000 |
| Eldred,p | 2 | 0 | 0 | 0 | 0 | 0 | 0 | 0 | 0 | 0 | 0 | 0 | .000 | .000 | .000 | 0 | 0 | 0 | .000 |
| Haren,p | 2 | 0 | 0 | 0 | 0 | 0 | 0 | 0 | 0 | 0 | 0 | 0 | .000 | .000 | .000 | 1 | 1 | 0 | 1.000 |
| Isringhausen,p | 1 | 0 | 0 | 0 | 0 | 0 | 0 | 0 | 0 | 0 | 0 | 0 | .000 | .000 | .000 | 0 | 0 | 0 | .000 |
| King,p | 3 | 0 | 0 | 0 | 0 | 0 | 0 | 0 | 0 | 0 | 0 | 0 | .000 | .000 | .000 | 0 | 0 | 0 | .000 |
| Morris,p | 1 | 0 | 0 | 0 | 0 | 0 | 0 | 0 | 0 | 0 | 0 | 0 | .000 | .000 | .000 | 0 | 0 | 0 | .000 |
| Reyes,p | 2 | 0 | 0 | 0 | 0 | 0 | 0 | 0 | 0 | 0 | 0 | 0 | .000 | .000 | .000 | 0 | 0 | 0 | .000 |
| Tavarez,p | 2 | 0 | 0 | 0 | 0 | 0 | 0 | 0 | 0 | 0 | 0 | 0 | .000 | .000 | .000 | 0 | 0 | 0 | .000 |
| Williams,p | 1 | 0 | 0 | 0 | 0 | 0 | 0 | 0 | 0 | 0 | 0 | 0 | .000 | .000 | .000 | 0 | 0 | 0 | .000 |
| Luna,2b-ph | 1 | 1 | 0 | 0 | 0 | 0 | 0 | 0 | 0 | 0 | 0 | 1 | .000 | .000 | .000 | 0 | 0 | 0 | .000 |
| Marquis,pr-p | 3 | 1 | 1 | 0 | 0 | 0 | 0 | 0 | 0 | 0 | 0 | 0 | .000 | .000 | .000 | 0 | 1 | 0 | 1.000 |
| Molina,c | 3 | 3 | 0 | 0 | 0 | 0 | 0 | 0 | 0 | 0 | 0 | 1 | .000 | .000 | .000 | 10 | 0 | 0 | 1.000 |
| Mabry,ph-lf | 2 | 4 | 0 | 0 | 0 | 0 | 0 | 0 | 0 | 0 | 0 | 2 | .000 | .000 | .000 | 2 | 0 | 0 | 1.000 |

| Player, position | G | AB | R | H | TB | 2B | 3B | HR | RBI | BB | IBB | SO | Avg. | OBP | Slg. | PO | A | E | Avg. |
|---|---|---|---|---|---|---|---|---|---|---|---|---|---|---|---|---|---|---|---|
| | BATTING | | | | | | | | | | | | | | | FIELDING | | | |
| Sanders,dh-lf | 4 | 9 | 1 | 0 | 0 | 0 | 0 | 0 | 0 | 4 | 0 | 5 | .000 | .308 | .000 | 1 | 0 | 0 | 1.000 |
| Rolen,3b | 4 | 15 | 0 | 0 | 0 | 0 | 0 | 0 | 1 | 1 | 0 | 1 | .000 | .059 | .000 | 2 | 11 | 0 | 1.000 |
| Totals | 4 | 126 | 12 | 24 | 38 | 8 | 0 | 2 | 8 | 12 | 1 | 32 | .190 | .261 | .302 | 102 | 37 | 1 | .993 |

## BOSTON RED SOX' PITCHING RECORDS

| Pitcher | G | GS | CG | IP | H | R | ER | HR | BB | IBB | SO | HB | WP | W | L | Pct. | ERA |
|---|---|---|---|---|---|---|---|---|---|---|---|---|---|---|---|---|---|
| Lowe | 1 | 1 | 0 | 7.0 | 3 | 0 | 0 | 0 | 1 | 0 | 4 | 0 | 1 | 1 | 0 | 1.000 | 0.00 |
| Martinez | 1 | 1 | 0 | 7.0 | 3 | 0 | 0 | 0 | 2 | 0 | 6 | 0 | 0 | 1 | 0 | 1.000 | 0.00 |
| Schilling | 1 | 1 | 0 | 6.0 | 4 | 1 | 0 | 0 | 1 | 0 | 4 | 0 | 0 | 1 | 0 | 1.000 | 0.00 |
| Embree | 3 | 0 | 0 | 1.2 | 1 | 1 | 0 | 0 | 0 | 0 | 4 | 0 | 0 | 0 | 0 | .000 | 0.00 |
| Foulke | 4 | 0 | 0 | 5.0 | 4 | 1 | 1 | 1 | 1 | 1 | 8 | 0 | 0 | 1 | 0 | 1.000 | 1.80 |
| Timlin | 3 | 0 | 0 | 3.0 | 2 | 2 | 2 | 0 | 1 | 0 | 0 | 0 | 0 | 0 | 0 | .000 | 6.00 |
| Arroyo | 2 | 0 | 0 | 2.2 | 4 | 2 | 2 | 0 | 1 | 0 | 4 | 0 | 0 | 0 | 0 | .000 | 6.75 |
| Wakefield | 1 | 1 | 0 | 3.2 | 3 | 5 | 5 | 1 | 5 | 0 | 2 | 1 | 0 | 0 | 0 | .000 | 12.27 |
| Totals | 4 | 4 | 0 | 36.0 | 24 | 12 | 10 | 2 | 12 | 1 | 32 | 1 | 1 | 4 | 0 | 1.000 | 2.50 |

No shutouts. Saves- Foulke.

## ST. LOUIS CARDINALS' PITCHING RECORDS

| Pitcher | G | GS | CG | IP | H | R | ER | HR | BB | IBB | SO | HB | WP | W | L | Pct. | ERA |
|---|---|---|---|---|---|---|---|---|---|---|---|---|---|---|---|---|---|
| Haren | 2 | 0 | 0 | 4.2 | 4 | 0 | 0 | 0 | 3 | 0 | 2 | 0 | 0 | 0 | 0 | .000 | 0.00 |
| King | 3 | 0 | 0 | 2.2 | 1 | 0 | 0 | 0 | 1 | 0 | 1 | 0 | 0 | 0 | 0 | .000 | 0.00 |
| Isringhausen | 1 | 0 | 0 | 2.0 | 1 | 0 | 0 | 0 | 1 | 0 | 2 | 0 | 0 | 0 | 0 | .000 | 0.00 |
| Reyes | 2 | 0 | 0 | 1.1 | 0 | 0 | 0 | 0 | 0 | 0 | 0 | 0 | 0 | 0 | 0 | .000 | 0.00 |
| Marquis | 2 | 1 | 0 | 7.0 | 6 | 3 | 3 | 1 | 7 | 1 | 4 | 0 | 0 | 0 | 1 | .000 | 3.86 |
| Tavarez | 2 | 0 | 0 | 2.0 | 1 | 2 | 1 | 1 | 0 | 0 | 1 | 0 | 0 | 0 | 1 | .000 | 4.50 |
| Suppan | 1 | 1 | 0 | 4.2 | 8 | 4 | 4 | 1 | 1 | 0 | 4 | 1 | 0 | 0 | 1 | .000 | 7.71 |
| Morris | 1 | 1 | 0 | 4.1 | 4 | 4 | 4 | 0 | 4 | 0 | 3 | 1 | 0 | 0 | 1 | .000 | 8.31 |
| Eldred | 2 | 0 | 0 | 1.2 | 4 | 2 | 2 | 0 | 0 | 0 | 2 | 1 | 0 | 0 | 0 | .000 | 10.80 |
| Calero | 2 | 0 | 0 | 1.1 | 2 | 2 | 2 | 0 | 4 | 0 | 0 | 0 | 0 | 0 | 0 | .000 | 13.50 |
| Williams | 1 | 1 | 0 | 2.1 | 8 | 7 | 7 | 1 | 3 | 0 | 1 | 1 | 0 | 0 | 0 | .000 | 27.00 |
| Totals | 4 | 4 | 0 | 34.0 | 39 | 24 | 23 | 4 | 24 | 1 | 20 | 4 | 0 | 0 | 4 | .000 | 6.09 |

No shutouts or saves.

## SCORE BY INNINGS

| | | | | | | | | | | |
|---|---|---|---|---|---|---|---|---|---|---|
| Boston | 8 | 0 | 5 | 3 | 2 | 2 | 2 | 2 | 0 | —24 |
| St. Louis | 0 | 1 | 1 | 4 | 0 | 2 | 0 | 3 | 1 | —12 |

## MISCELLANEOUS STATISTICS

Sacrifice hits—Lowe, Walker, Womack.
Sacrifice flies—Matheny 2, Rolen.
Stolen bases—Sanders.
Caught stealing—None.
Double plays—Womack, Renteria and Pujols 2; Cabrera, Bellhorn and Millar; Mueller (unassisted); Mueller, Bellhorn and Millar; Rolen and Pujols.
Left on bases—Boston 12, 9, 8, 12—41; St. Louis 9, 6, 3, 6—24.
Scoring position—Boston 6 for 16, 3 for 8, 4 for 10, 1 for 9—14 for 43; St. Louis 3 for 14, 1 for 7, 0 for 3, 0 for 7—4 for 31.
Hit by pitcher—by Eldred (Varitek), by Wakefield (Pujols), by Williams (Cabrera), by Suppan (Bellhorn), by Morris (Millar).
Passed balls—Mirabelli.
Balks—None.
Time of games—4:00, 3:20, 2:58, 3:14—Avg.: 3:23.
Attendance—35,035, 35,001, 52,015, 52,037—174,088.
Umpires—Montague, Ed; Scott, Dale; Gorman, Brian; Meriwether, Chuck; Davis, Gerry; Reliford, Charlie.

# ALL-STAR GAME

## BOX SCORE

### AMERICAN 9, NATIONAL 4

TUESDAY, JULY 13, AT MINUTE MAID PARK, HOUSTON

| American League | AB | R | H | RBI | BB | SO | PO | A |
|---|---|---|---|---|---|---|---|---|
| Suzuki, cf (Mariners) | 4 | 1 | 1 | 0 | 0 | 0 | 1 | 0 |
| J.Vazquez, p (Yankees) | 0 | 0 | 0 | 0 | 0 | 0 | 0 | 0 |
| Belliard, 2b (Indians) | 1 | 0 | 0 | 0 | 0 | 1 | 1 | 1 |
| I.Rodriguez, c (Tigers) | 4 | 1 | 2 | 1 | 0 | 0 | 3 | 0 |
| V.Martinez, c (Indians) | 1 | 0 | 0 | 0 | 0 | 0 | 3 | 0 |
| V.Guerrero, rf (Angels) | 4 | 1 | 1 | 0 | 0 | 0 | 0 | 0 |
| Lilly, p (Blue Jays) | 0 | 0 | 0 | 0 | 0 | 0 | 0 | 0 |
| Tejada, ss (Orioles) | 1 | 0 | 0 | 0 | 0 | 0 | 2 | 0 |
| M.Ramirez, lf (Red Sox) | 2 | 1 | 1 | 2 | 0 | 0 | 0 | 0 |
| D.Ortiz, ph-1b (Red Sox) | 1 | 2 | 1 | 2 | 2 | 0 | 3 | 1 |
| A.Rodriguez, 3b (Yankees) | 3 | 0 | 1 | 1 | 0 | 1 | 0 | 3 |
| Blalock, ph-3b (Rangers) | 2 | 0 | 0 | 0 | 0 | 0 | 0 | 0 |
| Ja.Giambi, 1b (Yankees) | 2 | 1 | 1 | 0 | 0 | 0 | 6 | 0 |
| Crawford, ph-lf (Devil Rays) | 2 | 0 | 0 | 0 | 0 | 1 | 3 | 0 |
| H.Matsui, ph-lf (Yankees) | 1 | 0 | 0 | 0 | 0 | 1 | 0 | 0 |
| Jeter, ss (Yankees) | 3 | 1 | 3 | 0 | 0 | 0 | 1 | 0 |
| Lawton, cf (Indians) | 2 | 0 | 1 | 0 | 0 | 1 | 0 | 0 |
| A.Soriano, 2b (Rangers) | 3 | 1 | 2 | 3 | 0 | 1 | 1 | 1 |
| Sheffield, rf (Yankees) | 1 | 0 | 0 | 0 | 0 | 0 | 1 | 0 |
| Mulder, p (Athletics) | 1 | 0 | 0 | 0 | 0 | 1 | 0 | 0 |
| Harvey, ph (Royals) | 1 | 0 | 0 | 0 | 0 | 1 | 0 | 0 |
| Loaiza, p (White Sox) | 0 | 0 | 0 | 0 | 0 | 0 | 0 | 1 |
| Sabathia, p (Indians) | 0 | 0 | 0 | 0 | 0 | 0 | 0 | 0 |
| M.Young, ph-ss (Rangers) | 2 | 0 | 0 | 0 | 0 | 0 | 1 | 1 |
| Nathan, p (Twins) | 0 | 0 | 0 | 0 | 0 | 0 | 0 | 0 |
| Gordon, p (Yankees) | 0 | 0 | 0 | 0 | 0 | 0 | 0 | 1 |
| F.Rodriguez, p (Angels) | 0 | 0 | 0 | 0 | 0 | 0 | 1 | 0 |
| M.Rivera, p (Yankees) | 0 | 0 | 0 | 0 | 0 | 0 | 0 | 0 |
| **TOTALS** | 41 | 9 | 14 | 9 | 2 | 8 | 27 | 9 |

| National League | AB | R | H | BI | BB | SO | PO | A |
|---|---|---|---|---|---|---|---|---|
| Renteria, ss (Cardinals) | 3 | 1 | 1 | 1 | 0 | 0 | 1 | 1 |
| J.Wilson, ss (Pirates) | 2 | 0 | 0 | 0 | 0 | 0 | 1 | 1 |
| Pujols, 1b (Cardinals) | 3 | 1 | 2 | 2 | 0 | 0 | 5 | 1 |
| Thome, 1b (Phillies) | 2 | 0 | 0 | 0 | 0 | 1 | 6 | 0 |
| Bonds, lf (Giants) | 2 | 0 | 0 | 0 | 1 | 0 | 0 | 0 |
| Pavano, p (Marlins) | 0 | 0 | 0 | 0 | 0 | 0 | 0 | 0 |
| T.Glavine, p (Mets) | 0 | 0 | 0 | 0 | 0 | 0 | 0 | 0 |
| Abreu, ph (Phillies) | 1 | 0 | 0 | 0 | 0 | 1 | 0 | 0 |
| Sheets, p (Brewers) | 0 | 0 | 0 | 0 | 0 | 0 | 0 | 0 |
| Lo Duca, c (Dodgers) | 0 | 0 | 0 | 0 | 0 | 0 | 2 | 0 |
| Rolen, 3b (Cardinals) | 1 | 0 | 1 | 0 | 0 | 0 | 0 | 2 |
| Lowell, ph-3b (Marlins) | 2 | 0 | 0 | 0 | 0 | 1 | 0 | 0 |
| S.Sosa, rf (Cubs) | 2 | 0 | 1 | 1 | 0 | 0 | 0 | 0 |
| M.Cabrera, rf (Marlins) | 2 | 0 | 0 | 0 | 0 | 1 | 1 | 0 |
| Piazza, c (Mets) | 2 | 0 | 0 | 0 | 0 | 1 | 4 | 0 |
| Estrada, c (Braves) | 2 | 0 | 0 | 0 | 0 | 1 | 2 | 0 |
| Gagne, p (Dodgers) | 0 | 0 | 0 | 0 | 0 | 0 | 0 | 0 |
| Berkman, cf (Astros) | 2 | 0 | 0 | 0 | 0 | 0 | 1 | 0 |
| Alou, lf (Cubs) | 2 | 0 | 1 | 0 | 0 | 0 | 0 | 0 |
| Kent, 2b (Astros) | 2 | 1 | 1 | 0 | 0 | 0 | 2 | 4 |
| Loretta, ph-2b (Padres) | 2 | 0 | 1 | 0 | 0 | 0 | 1 | 3 |
| Clemens, p (Astros) | 0 | 0 | 0 | 0 | 0 | 0 | 0 | 1 |
| Kolb, p (Brewers) | 0 | 0 | 0 | 0 | 0 | 0 | 0 | 0 |
| Larkin, ph (Reds) | 1 | 0 | 0 | 0 | 0 | 0 | 0 | 0 |
| Ra.Johnson, p (Diamondbacks) | 0 | 0 | 0 | 0 | 0 | 0 | 1 | 0 |
| C.Zambrano, p (Cubs) | 0 | 0 | 0 | 0 | 0 | 0 | 0 | 0 |
| C.Beltran, ph-cf (Astros) | 2 | 1 | 1 | 0 | 0 | 0 | 0 | 0 |
| Helton, ph (Rockies) | 1 | 0 | 0 | 0 | 0 | 0 | 0 | 0 |
| **TOTALS** | 36 | 4 | 9 | 4 | 1 | 6 | 27 | 13 |

| | | | | | | |
|---|---|---|---|---|---|---|
| American League | 6 0 0 | 1 0 2 | 0 0 0—9 | 14 | 1 |
| National League | 1 0 0 | 3 0 0 | 0 0 0—4 | 9 | 1 |

| American League | IP | H | R | ER | HR | BB | SO |
|---|---|---|---|---|---|---|---|
| Mulder (Athletics) (W) | 2.0 | 2 | 1 | 1 | 0 | 0 | 1 |
| Loaiza (White Sox) | 1.0 | 1 | 0 | 0 | 0 | 1 | 0 |
| Sabathia (Indians) | 1.0 | 4 | 3 | 3 | 0 | 0 | 0 |
| J.Vazquez (Yankees) | 1.0 | 0 | 0 | 0 | 0 | 0 | 2 |
| Lilly (Blue Jays) | 1.0 | 2 | 0 | 0 | 0 | 0 | 1 |
| Nathan (Twins) | 1.0 | 0 | 0 | 0 | 0 | 0 | 2 |
| Gordon (Yankees) | 0.1 | 0 | 0 | 0 | 0 | 0 | 0 |
| F.Rodriguez (Angels) | 0.2 | 0 | 0 | 0 | 0 | 0 | 0 |
| M.Rivera (Yankees) | 1.0 | 0 | 0 | 0 | 0 | 0 | 0 |

| National League | IP | H | R | ER | HR | BB | SO |
|---|---|---|---|---|---|---|---|
| Clemens (Astros) (L) | 1.0 | 5 | 6 | 3 | 2 | 0 | 2 |
| Kolb (Brewers) | 1.0 | 1 | 0 | 0 | 0 | 0 | 0 |
| Ra.Johnson (Diamondbacks) | 1.0 | 3 | 0 | 0 | 0 | 0 | 1 |
| C.Zambrano (Cubs) | 1.0 | 1 | 1 | 1 | 0 | 1 | 1 |
| Pavano (Marlins) | 2.0 | 3 | 2 | 2 | 1 | 0 | 1 |
| T.Glavine (Mets) | 1.0 | 1 | 0 | 0 | 0 | 0 | 0 |
| Sheets (Brewers) | 1.0 | 0 | 0 | 0 | 0 | 0 | 1 |
| Gagne (Dodgers) | 1.0 | 0 | 0 | 0 | 0 | 1 | 2 |

E—Kent. DP—National League 1. LOB—American League 7, National League 7. Scoring Position—American League 4 for 8, National League 3 for 10. 2B—Suzuki, Renteria, Pujols 2. 3B—I.Rodriguez, A.Rodriguez. HR—M.Ramirez (1st inning, 1 out, 1 on) off Clemens, A.Soriano (1st inning, 2 out, 2 on) off Clemens, D.Ortiz (6th inning, 1 out, 1 on) off Pavano. HBP—Rolen by Mulder. T—2:59. A—41,886. U—HP-Montague, 1B-Hirschbeck, 2B-Eddings, 3B-Reynolds, LF-Hudson, RF-Holbrook.

## PLAY BY PLAY

### FIRST INNING

A.L.—Suzuki doubled to right. I.Rodriguez tripled to right, Suzuki scored. Guerrero grounded out, pitcher Clemens to first baseman Pujols. Ramirez homered to left on a 0-2 count, I.Rodriguez scored. A.Rodriguez struck out. Giambi safe on Kent's error. Jeter singled to right, Giambi to third. Soriano homered to left on the first pitch, Giambi scored, Jeter scored. Mulder struck out. Six runs. A.L. 6, N.L 0.

N.L.—Renteria grounded out, third baseman A.Rodriguez to first baseman Giambi. Pujols doubled to center. Bonds flied out to center fielder Suzuki. Rolen was hit by a pitch. Sosa singled to right, Pujols scored, Rolen to second. Piazza struck out. One run. A.L. 6, N.L 1.

### SECOND INNING

A.L.—Kolb pitching. Suzuki grounded out, first baseman Pujols unassisted. I.Rodriguez singled to center. Guerrero flied out to center fielder Berkman. Ramirez grounded into fielder's choice, shortstop Renteria to second baseman Kent, I.Rodriguez out.

N.L.—Berkman grounded out, first baseman Giambi unassisted. Kent lined out to second baseman Soriano. Larkin pinch-hitting for Kolb. Larkin grounded out, third baseman A.Rodriguez to first baseman Giambi.

### THIRD INNING

A.L.—Johnson pitching. A.Rodriguez grounded out, second baseman Kent to first baseman Pujols. Giambi singled to center. Jeter singled to right, Giambi to second. Soriano singled to left, Giambi to third, Jeter to second. Harvey pinch-hitting for Mulder. Harvey struck out. Suzuki grounded out, first baseman Pujols to pitcher Johnson.

N.L.—Loaiza pitching. Renteria grounded out, third baseman A.Rodriguez to first baseman Giambi. Pujols grounded out, pitcher Loaiza to first baseman Giambi. Bonds walked. Rolen singled to left, Bonds to second. Sosa grounded out, second baseman Soriano to first baseman Giambi.

FOURTH INNING

A.L.—Zambrano pitching. I.Rodriguez grounded out, third baseman Rolen to first baseman Pujols. Guerrero fouled out to first baseman Pujols. Ortiz pinch-hitting for Ramirez. Ortiz walked. A.Rodriguez tripled to center, Ortiz scored. Crawford pinch-hitting for Giambi. Crawford struck out. One run. A.L. 7, N.L. 1.

N.L.—Ortiz in as first baseman. Crawford in as left fielder. Sabathia pitching. Piazza popped out to left fielder Crawford. Berkman flied out to left fielder Crawford. Kent singled to left. Beltran pinch-hitting for Zambrano. Beltran singled to left, Kent to second. Renteria infield double to third, Kent scored, Beltran to third. Pujols doubled to left, Beltran scored, Renteria scored. Bonds popped out to shortstop Jeter. Three runs. A.L. 7, N.L. 4.

FIFTH INNING

A.L.—Pavano pitching. Cabrera in as right fielder. Estrada in as catcher. Alou in as left fielder. Beltran in as center fielder. Jeter infield single to first. Soriano struck out. Young pinch-hitting for Sabathia. Young grounded into fielder's choice, second baseman Kent to shortstop Renteria, Jeter out. Suzuki grounded into fielder's choice, third baseman Rolen to second baseman Kent, Young out.

N.L.—Vazquez pitching. Lawton in as center fielder. Young in as shortstop. Lowell pinch-hitting for Rolen. Lowell struck out. Cabrera grounded out, shortstop Young to first baseman Ortiz. Estrada struck out.

SIXTH INNING

A.L.—Wilson in as shortstop. Thome in as first baseman. Lowell in as third baseman. I.Rodriguez flied out to right fielder Cabrera. Guerrero singled to center. Ortiz homered to right on a 2-2 count, Guerrero scored. Blalock pinch-hitting for A.Rodriguez. Blalock grounded out, second baseman Kent to first baseman Thome. Crawford grounded out, second baseman Kent to first baseman Thome. Two runs. A.L. 9, N.L. 4.

N.L.—Belliard in as second baseman. Martinez in as catcher. Lilly pitching. Blalock in as third baseman. Sheffield in as right fielder. Alou singled to right. Loretta pinch-hitting for Kent. Loretta singled to center, Alou to second. Beltran popped out to shortstop Young. Wilson flied out to left fielder Crawford. Thome struck out.

SEVENTH INNING

A.L.—Glavine pitching. Loretta in as second baseman. Lawton infield single to short. Sheffield grounded into a double play, shortstop Wilson to second baseman Loretta to first baseman Thome, Lawton out. Young grounded out, first baseman Thome unassisted.

N.L.—Tejada in as shortstop. Nathan pitching. Abreu pinch-hitting for Glavine. Abreu struck out. Lowell popped out to right fielder Sheffield. Cabrera struck out.

EIGHTH INNING

A.L.—Sheets pitching. Belliard struck out. Martinez grounded out, second baseman Loretta to first baseman Thome. Tejada grounded out, second baseman Loretta to first baseman Thome.

N.L.—Gordon pitching. Estrada grounded out, pitcher Gordon to second baseman Belliard to first baseman Ortiz. F.Rodriguez pitching. Alou grounded out, first baseman Ortiz to pitcher F.Rodriguez. Loretta popped out to shortstop Tejada.

NINTH INNING

A.L.—Lo Duca in as catcher. Gagne pitching. Ortiz walked on a full count. Blalock popped out to shortstop Wilson. Matsui pinch-hitting for Crawford. Matsui struck out. Lawton struck out.

N.L.—Matsui in as left fielder. Rivera pitching. Helton pinch-hitting for Beltran. Helton fouled out to first baseman Ortiz. Wilson popped out to second baseman Belliard. Thome popped out to shortstop Tejada.

# NOTABLE PERFORMANCES

## BOX SCORES OF NO-HIT GAMES

### RANDY JOHNSON

ARIZONA 2, ATLANTA 0
TUESDAY, MAY 18, AT ATLANTA

| Arizona | AB | R | H | BI | BB | SO | PO | A |
|---|---|---|---|---|---|---|---|---|
| C.Tracy, 3b | 4 | 0 | 2 | 1 | 1 | 0 | 0 | 1 |
| Kata, 2b | 5 | 0 | 0 | 0 | 0 | 1 | 0 | 3 |
| L.Gonzalez, lf | 3 | 0 | 0 | 0 | 1 | 0 | 1 | 0 |
| Hillenbrand, 1b | 4 | 0 | 1 | 0 | 0 | 1 | 7 | 0 |
| Finley, cf | 4 | 0 | 1 | 0 | 0 | 0 | 3 | 0 |
| D.Bautista, rf | 4 | 1 | 1 | 0 | 0 | 0 | 3 | 0 |
| Cintron, ss | 4 | 1 | 3 | 1 | 0 | 0 | 0 | 2 |
| Hammock, c | 3 | 0 | 0 | 0 | 1 | 1 | 13 | 0 |
| Ra.Johnson, p | 4 | 0 | 0 | 0 | 0 | 2 | 0 | 0 |
| **TOTALS** | 35 | 2 | 8 | 2 | 3 | 5 | 27 | 6 |

| Atlanta | AB | R | H | BI | BB | SO | PO | A |
|---|---|---|---|---|---|---|---|---|
| Garcia, ss | 3 | 0 | 0 | 0 | 0 | 2 | 2 | 4 |
| Ju.Franco, 1b | 3 | 0 | 0 | 0 | 0 | 1 | 12 | 0 |
| C.Jones, lf | 3 | 0 | 0 | 0 | 0 | 3 | 2 | 0 |
| A.Jones, cf | 3 | 0 | 0 | 0 | 0 | 0 | 1 | 1 |
| Estrada, c | 3 | 0 | 0 | 0 | 0 | 2 | 5 | 0 |
| J.Drew, rf | 3 | 0 | 0 | 0 | 0 | 1 | 4 | 0 |
| DeRosa, 3b | 3 | 0 | 0 | 0 | 0 | 0 | 0 | 3 |
| N.Green, 2b | 3 | 0 | 0 | 0 | 0 | 2 | 1 | 2 |
| Hampton, p | 2 | 0 | 0 | 0 | 0 | 1 | 0 | 3 |
| E.Perez, ph | 1 | 0 | 0 | 0 | 0 | 1 | 0 | 0 |
| **TOTALS** | 27 | 0 | 0 | 0 | 0 | 13 | 27 | 13 |

| | | | | | | | | | | | | |
|---|---|---|---|---|---|---|---|---|---|---|---|---|
| Arizona | 0 | 1 | 0 | 0 | 0 | 0 | 1 | 0 | 0 | —2 | 8 | 0 |
| Atlanta | 0 | 0 | 0 | 0 | 0 | 0 | 0 | 0 | 0 | —0 | 0 | 3 |

| Arizona | IP | H | R | ER | HR | BB | SO |
|---|---|---|---|---|---|---|---|
| Ra.Johnson (W) | 9.0 | 0 | 0 | 0 | 0 | 0 | 13 |

| Atlanta | IP | H | R | ER | HR | BB | SO |
|---|---|---|---|---|---|---|---|
| Hampton (L) | 9.0 | 8 | 2 | 2 | 0 | 3 | 5 |

E—Hampton, Estrada, DeRosa. DP—Atlanta 1. LOB—Arizona 9. Scoring Position—Arizona 1 for 8, Atlanta 0 for 0. 2B—Cintron 2. T—2:13. A—23,381. U—HP-Gibson, 1B-Dreckman, 2B-Davis, 3B-Poncino.

## LOW-HIT GAMES

### AMERICAN LEAGUE

ONE-HIT GAMES

**Date Pitcher(s), Team, Opponent, Result—Player with hit**

6-25 Jason Johnson (8 inn.) and Ugueth Urbina (1 inn.), Detroit vs. Arizona, W 2-1—Luis Gonzalez (triple in fifth)
7-16 Mike Maroth, Detroit vs. New York, W 8-0—Gary Sheffield (double in fourth)
7-17 Johan Santana (8 inn.) and Joe Nathan (1 inn.), Minnesota at Kansas City, W 4-1—Angel Berroa (double in second)
7-27 Bartolo Colon (7 inn.), Francisco Rodriguez (1 inn.) and Troy Percival (1 inn.), Anaheim vs. Texas, W 2-0—Michael Young (single in third)

TWO-HIT GAMES

**Date Pitcher(s), Team, Opponent, Result—Player(s) with hit(s)**

4-16 Matt Riley (7 inn.), Rick Bauer (1 inn.) and John Parrish (1 inn.), Baltimore at Toronto, W 11-2—Josh Phelps (home run in second), Vernon Wells (double in ninth)
4-18 Esteban Loaiza, Chicago at Tampa Bay, W 5-0—Tino Martinez (single in fifth), Aubrey Huff (single in seventh)
4-25 Jake Westbrook, Cleveland at Detroit, W 3-2—Carlos Pena (home run in second), Bobby Higginson (single in seventh)
4-26 Ted Lilly, Toronto at Minnesota, W 6-1—Cristian Guzman (single in first), Michael Cuddyer (home run in sixth)
5-14 Gary Knotts (5 inn.) and Esteban Yan (4 inn.), Detroit vs. Texas, W 7-1—Mark Teixeira (double in fifth), Michael Young (triple in sixth)
6-8 Pedro Martinez (8 inn.) and Keith Foulke (1 inn.), Boston vs. San Diego, W 1-0—Mark Loretta (single in first), Terrence Long (double in fifth)
6-15 Jeremy Bonderman (7 inn.), Danny Patterson (.2 inn.), Jamie Walker (.1 inn.) and Ugueth Urbina (1 inn.), Detroit at Philadelphia, W 10-3—Bobby Abreu (home run in fourth), Jim Thome (home run in ninth)
6-25 Pedro Martinez (7 inn.) and Curtis Leskanic (1 inn.), Boston vs. Philadelphia, W 12-1—Placido Polanco (single in fourth), Jim Thome (home run in seventh)
6-25 Dewon Brazelton (7.2 inn.) and Danys Baez (1.1 inn.), Tampa Bay vs. Florida, W 2-0—Mike Lowell (double in eighth), Hee Seop Choi (single in ninth)
7-11 Johan Santana (8 inn.) and Joe Nathan (1 inn.), Minnesota vs. Detroit, L 0-2—Marcus Thames (double in second), Eric Munson (home run in second)

7-21 Mark Buehrle, Chicago at Cleveland, W 14-0—Omar Vizquel (single in seventh), Tim Laker (single in eighth)

7-25 Rich Harden (5 inn.), Justin Lehr (1 inn.), Chad Bradford (2 inn.) and Ricardo Rincon (1 inn.), Oakland vs. Texas, W 9-2—Gary Matthews Jr. (double in fourth), Michael Young (home run in fifth)

7-30 Josh Towers (7 inn.), Vinnie Chulk (1 inn.) and Jason Frasor (1 inn.), Toronto at Tampa Bay, W 3-0—Rocco Baldelli (single in first), Julio Lugo (single in seventh)

8-1 Johan Santana (8 inn.) and Joe Nathan (1 inn.), Minnesota vs. Boston, W 4-3—Orlando Cabrera (home run in first), Manny Ramirez (home run in fourth)

8-4 Brian Anderson, Kansas City vs. Chicago, W 11-0—Aaron Rowand (double in first and double in ninth)

8-6 Dewon Brazelton (8 inn.) and Travis Harper (2 inn.), Tampa Bay vs. Seattle, W 2-1—Bret Boone (single in third), Edgar Martinez (single in third)

8-29 Scott Elarton, Cleveland vs. Chicago, W 9-0—Willie Harris (single in fourth), Joe Crede (single in ninth)

9-1 Daniel Cabrera (6.1 inn.), Todd Williams (.2 inn.) and John Parrish (2 inn.), Baltimore at Tampa Bay, W 8-0—Rocco Baldelli (double in first), Julio Lugo (single in third)

9-3 Johan Santana (7 inn.), J.C. Romero (1 inn.) and Joe Nathan (1 inn.), Minnesota vs. Kansas City, W 2-0—Desi Relaford (sin gle in seventh), David DeJesus (single in eighth)

9-4 Sidney Ponson, Baltimore at New York, W 7-0—Miguel Cairo (single in third), Gary Sheffield (single in fourth)

9-5 John Lackey (7.1 inn.) and Francisco Rodriguez (1.2 inn.), Anaheim at Cleveland, W 2-1—Travis Hafner (double in sixth), Ronnie Belliard (double in eighth)

9-8 Justin Miller (8 inn.) and Justin Speier (1 inn.), Toronto at Anaheim, W 1-0—Vladimir Guerrero (single in fourth), Adam Kennedy (single in eighth)

9-15 Ryan Franklin, Seattle vs. Anaheim, W 1-0—Adam Kennedy (single in second), Darin Erstad (triple in third)

10-1 David Bush, Toronto vs. New York, W 7-0—Enrique Wilson (single in fifth), Dioner Navarro (single in eighth)

## NATIONAL LEAGUE

### NO-HIT GAMES

**Date Pitcher(s), Team, Opponent**

5-18 Randy Johnson, Arizona at Atlanta, W 2-0

### ONE-HIT GAMES

**Date Pitcher(s), Team, Opponent, Result—Player with hit**

5-7 Wilson Alvarez (7 inn.) and Guillermo Mota (2 inn.), Los Angeles at Pittsburgh, W 4-0—Chris Stynes (single in sixth)

5-18 Jason Schmidt, San Francisco at Chicago, W 1-0—Michael Barrett (single in fifth)

5-23 Tom Glavine, New York vs. Colorado, W 4-0—Kit Pellow (double in eighth)

5-26 Tommy Phelps (7 inn.), Matt Perisho (.2 inn.) and Armando Benitez (1.1 inn.), Florida at Cincinnati, W 3-0—Sean Casey (double in fourth)

6-20 Jason Schmidt, San Francisco vs. Boston, W 4-0—Kevin Youkilis (double in sixth)

7-7 Kazuhisa Ishii, Los Angeles vs. Arizona, W 11-0—Shea Hillenbrand (single in fifth)

### TWO-HIT GAMES

**Date Pitcher(s), Team, Opponent, Result—Player(s) with hit(s)**

4-16 Randy Johnson, Arizona at San Diego, W 5-0—Brian Buchanan (single in second), Ramon Hernandez (single in fourth)

4-22 Shawn Estes, Colorado vs. Los Angeles, W 7-1—Paul Lo Duca (single in fourth), Adrian Beltre (single in fourth)

4-25 Matt Clement (8 inn.) and Joe Borowski (1 inn.), Chicago vs. New York, W 4-1—Karim Garcia (home run in seventh), Eric Valent (single in seventh)

4-29 Andy Pettitte (6 inn.), Dan Miceli (1 inn.), Brad Lidge (1 inn.) and Octavio Dotel (1 inn.), Houston at Pittsburgh, W 2-0—Raul Mondesi (single in fourth), Bobby Hill (single in eighth)

5-7 Carlos Zambrano, Chicago vs. Colorado, W 11-0—Matt Holliday (single in fifth), Aaron Miles (single in ninth)

5-8 Adrian Hernandez (4.1 inn.), Matt Kinney (2.2 inn.), Luis Vizcaino (1 inn.) and Dan Kolb (1 inn.), Milwaukee at New York, W

6-4 Karim Garcia (single in fifth), Eric Valent (double in eighth)

6-15 Victor Santos (7 inn.), Luis Vizcaino (1 inn.) and Dan Kolb (1 inn.), Milwaukee vs. Seattle, W 3-0—Bret Boone (single in second), John Olerud (double in second)

7-17 Russ Ortiz (7.2 inn.) and John Smoltz (1.1 inn.), Atlanta vs. Montreal, W 6-2—Carl Everett (single in first), Tony Batista (single in ninth)

7-25 Adam Eaton (7 inn.), Akinori Otsuka (1 inn.) and Trevor Hoffman (1 inn.), San Diego at Los Angeles, W 3-0—Alex Cora (single in fourth), Cesar Izturis (double in ninth)

8-10 Josh Beckett (6 inn.), Rudy Seanez (3 inn.) and Guillermo Mota (1 inn.), Florida vs. St. Louis, L 1-2—Albert Pujols (home run in sixth), Jim Edmonds (home run in tenth)

8-11 Jeff Suppan (8 inn.), Steve Kline (.1 inn.) and Jason Isringhausen (.2 inn.), St. Louis at Florida, W 1-0—Alex Gonzalez (single in sixth), Juan Pierre (single in ninth)

8-12 Victor Zambrano (7 inn.), Ricky Bottalico (.2 inn.), Mike Stanton (.1 inn.) and Braden Looper (1 inn.), New York vs. Houston, W 2-1—Jose Vizcaino (single in fifth), Lance Berkman (single in sixth)

9-3 Matt Morris, St. Louis vs. Los Angeles, W 3-0—Jose Lima (single in third), Robin Ventura (single in fifth)

9-4 Kazuhisa Ishii (5.2 inn.), Elmer Dessens (.1 inn.), Duaner Sanchez (1.1 inn.) and Mike Venafro (.2 inn.), Los Angeles at St. Louis, L 1-5—Jim Edmonds (home run in second), Scott Rolen (single in sixth)

9-19 Aaron Heilman (7 inn.) and Ricky Bottalico (1 inn.), New York at Pittsburgh, L 0-1—Humberto Cota (home run in third and single in fifth)

9-19 Roger Clemens (8 inn.) and Brad Lidge (1 inn.), Houston vs. Milwaukee, W 1-0—Scott Podsednik (single in first), Brady Clark (double in fourth)

9-25 Carl Pavano (7 inn.) and Rudy Seanez (1 inn.), Florida at Atlanta, L 0-1—Adam LaRoche (single in fifth), Dewayne Wise (home run in seventh)

# 15-STRIKEOUT GAMES

## AMERICAN LEAGUE

No occurrences

## NATIONAL LEAGUE

| Date | Pitcher, Team, Opponent | IP | H | R | ER | BB | SO | Result |
|---|---|---|---|---|---|---|---|---|
| 5-16 | Ben Sheets, Milwaukee vs. Atlanta | 9 | 3 | 1 | 1 | 1 | 18 | W 4-1 |
| 8-31 | Randy Johnson, Arizona vs. Los Angeles | 8 | 3 | 1 | 1 | 1 | 15 | L 1-4 |
| 9-30 | Mark Prior, Chicago vs. Cincinnati | 9 | 3 | 1 | 1 | 1 | 16 | L 1-2 |

# 10-STRIKEOUT GAMES

## AMERICAN LEAGUE

| Team | No. | Pitchers |
|---|---|---|
| Minnesota | 12 | Johan Santana 12. |
| Boston | 11 | Pedro Martinez 6, Curt Schilling 4, Bronson Arroyo 1. |
| New York | 4 | Mike Mussina 2, Orlando Hernandez 1, Jose Contreras 1. |
| Anaheim | 3 | Kelvim Escobar 2, John Lackey 1. |
| Detroit | 3 | Jason Johnson 1, Nate Robertson 1, Jeremy Bonderman 1. |
| Toronto | 3 | Ted Lilly 2, David Bush 1. |
| Cleveland | 2 | C.C. Sabathia 1, Kazuhito Tadano 1. |
| Baltimore | 1 | Erik Bedard 1. |
| Oakland | 1 | Barry Zito 1. |
| Seattle | 1 | Gil Meche 1. |
| Tampa Bay | 1 | Victor Zambrano 1. |
| Chicago | 0 | None. |
| Kansas City | 0 | None. |
| Texas | 0 | None. |

## NATIONAL LEAGUE

| Team | No. | Pitchers |
|---|---|---|
| Arizona | 13 | Randy Johnson 13. |
| Chicago | 11 | Kerry Wood 4, Matt Clement 4, Carlos Zambrano 2, Mark Prior 1. |
| San Francisco | 11 | Jason Schmidt 9, Dustin Hermanson 1, Noah Lowry 1. |
| Milwaukee | 9 | Ben Sheets 9. |
| Pittsburgh | 9 | Oliver Perez 9. |
| Houston | 6 | Roger Clemens 4, Roy Oswalt 2. |
| Florida | 6 | Brad Penny 3, A.J. Burnett 1, Josh Beckett 1, Dontrelle Willis 1. |
| San Diego | 4 | Jake Peavy 2, Adam Eaton 1, Brian Lawrence 1. |
| St. Louis | 3 | Woody Williams 1, Chris Carpenter 1, Matt Morris 1. |
| Cincinnati | 2 | Jose Acevedo 1, Aaron Harang 1. |
| Los Angeles | 1 | Odalis Perez 1. |
| New York | 1 | Al Leiter 1. |
| Philadelphia | 1 | Eric Milton 1. |
| Atlanta | 0 | None. |
| Montreal | 0 | None. |
| Colorado | 0 | None. |

# 1-0 GAMES

## AMERICAN LEAGUE

| Date | Winner | Loser | Inn.* | Site |
|---|---|---|---|---|
| 5-1 | ~Francisco Rodriguez, Anaheim | ~Juan Rincon, Minnesota | 9 | Minnesota |
| 5-7 | John Lackey, Anaheim | ~Mark Hendrickson, Tampa Bay | 3 | Anaheim |
| 5-13 | ~Johan Santana, Minnesota | ~Ryan Franklin, Seattle | 2 | Minnesota |
| 5-13 | #~Daniel Cabrera, Baltimore | ~Jon Garland, Chicago | 1 | Chicago |
| 5-18 | ~Scot Shields, Anaheim | ~Paul Quantrill, New York | 11 | Anaheim |
| 5-28 | ~Jose Jimenez, Cleveland | ~Jim Mecir, Oakland | 9 | Cleveland |
| 6-8 | ~Pedro Martinez, Boston | ~Antonio Osuna, San Diego | 7 | Boston |
| 6-11 | ~Eddie Guardado, Seattle | Livan Hernandez, Montreal | 9 | Seattle |
| 7-20 | ~Justin Lehr, Oakland | ~Justin Speier, Toronto | 14 | Oakland |
| 7-22 | ~Mariano Rivera, New York | ~Vinnie Chulk, Toronto | 9 | New York |
| 9-1 | ~Zack Greinke, Kansas City | Mike Maroth, Detroit | 4 | Kansas City |
| 9-8 | ~Justin Miller, Toronto | ~Kelvim Escobar, Anaheim | 1 | Anaheim |
| 9-12 | ~Barry Zito, Oakland | Jake Westbrook, Cleveland | 2 | Oakland |
| 9-15 | Ryan Franklin, Seattle | ~John Lackey, Anaheim | 8 | Seattle |
| 9-19 | ~Chris Young, Texas | ~Jarrod Washburn, Anaheim | 4 | Anaheim |

PLAYERS HITTING HOME RUNS IN 1-0 GAMES: 5-28—Casey Blake, Cleveland; 7-22—Ruben Sierra, New York; 9-12—Erubiel Durazo, Oakland.

*Inning in which run scored. ~Did not pitch complete game. # First game of doubleheader.

## NATIONAL LEAGUE

| Date | Winner | Loser | Inn.* | Site |
|---|---|---|---|---|
| 4-10 | ~John Patterson, Montreal | ~Jae Weong Seo, New York | 7 | Montreal |
| 5-2 | ~Jason Isringhausen, St. Louis | ~Kyle Farnsworth, Chicago | 10 | St. Louis |
| 5-12 | ~Tom Glavine, New York | ~Randy Johnson, Arizona | 1 | Arizona |
| 5-18 | Jason Schmidt, San Francisco | ~Matt Clement, Chicago | 4 | Chicago |

| Date | Winner | Loser | Inn.* | Site |
|---|---|---|---|---|
| 5-19 | ~Cal Eldred, St. Louis | ~Mike Stanton, New York | 8 | New York |
| 6-8 | ~Matt Kinney, Milwaukee | ~Ramon Ortiz, Anaheim | 17 | Anaheim |
| 6-8 | ~Roger Clemens, Houston | ~Joel Pineiro, Seattle | 7 | Seattle |
| 6-26 | ~Mark Corey, Pittsburgh | ~Todd Jones, Cincinnati | 9 | Cincinnati |
| 6-27 | ~Roy Oswalt, Houston | Ryan Drese, Texas | 4 | Texas |
| 7-5 | ~Ben Sheets, Milwaukee | ~Matt Clement, Chicago | 1 | Milwaukee |
| 7-6 | ~Russ Ortiz, Atlanta | ~Scott Downs, Montreal | 7 | Montreal |
| 7-21 | ~Woody Williams, St. Louis | ~Victor Santos, Milwaukee | 6 | St. Louis |
| 7-28 | ~Russ Ortiz, Atlanta | ~Oliver Perez, Pittsburgh | 4 | Pittsburgh |
| 8-11 | ~Jeff Suppan, St. Louis | ~Carl Pavano, Florida | 6 | Florida |
| 8-26 | Aaron Harang, Cincinnati | Chris Carpenter, St. Louis | 6 | Cincinnati |
| 9-19 | ~Roger Clemens, Houston | ~Doug Davis, Milwaukee | 3 | Houston |
| 9-19 | #~Ryan Vogelsong, Pittsburgh | ~Aaron Heilman, New York | 3 | Pittsburgh |
| 9-22 | ~Carlos Zambrano, Chicago | ~Oliver Perez, Pittsburgh | 5 | Pittsburgh |
| 9-24 | ~Brad Lidge, Houston | ~Mike Adams, Milwaukee | 10 | Milwaukee |
| 9-25 | ~Mike Hampton, Atlanta | ~Carl Pavano, Florida | 7 | Atlanta |

PLAYERS HITTING HOME RUNS IN 1-0 GAMES: 5-12—Kazuo Matsui, New York; 6-26—Randall Simon, Pittsburgh; 7-5—Craig Counsell, Milwaukee; 7-28—Chipper Jones, Atlanta; 8-26—Sean Casey, Cincinnati; 9-19—Humberto Cota, Pittsburgh; 9-25 Dewayne Wise, Atlanta.

*Inning in which run scored. ~Did not pitch complete game. # First game of doubleheader.

## FOUR OR MORE HITS IN ONE GAME

### AMERICAN LEAGUE

| Team | No. | Hitters |
|---|---|---|
| Cleveland | 20 | Omar Vizquel 3, Jody Gerut 3, Travis Hafner 3, Ronnie Belliard 2, Ben Broussard 2, Victor Martinez 2, Coco Crisp 2, Matt Lawton 1, John McDonald 1, Casey Blake 1. |
| Baltimore | 19 | David Newhan 5, Miguel Tejada 3, Javy Lopez 2, Jerry Hairston Jr. 2, Melvin Mora 2, Brian Roberts 2, B.J. Surhoff 1, Jay Gibbons 1, Larry Bigbie 1. |
| Texas | 19 | Hank Blalock 4, Michael Young 3, Eric Young 2, David Dellucci 2, Alfonso Soriano 2, Mark Teixeira 2, Kevin Mench 2, Gary Matthews Jr. 1, Laynce Nix 1. |
| Anaheim | 16 | Vladimir Guerrero 5, Adam Kennedy 3, Garret Anderson 1, Darin Erstad 1, Jose Guillen 1, Bengie Molina 1, Jeff DaVanon 1, David Eckstein 1, Chone Figgins 1, Robb Quinlan 1. |
| Chicago | 16 | Willie Harris 4, Paul Konerko 3, Carlos Lee 3, Aaron Rowand 2, Frank Thomas 1, Jose Valentin 1, Magglio Ordonez 1, Joe Crede 1. |
| Detroit | 16 | Ivan Rodriguez 5, Dmitri Young 2, Carlos Pena 2, Brandon Inge 2, Bobby Higginson 1, Carlos Guillen 1, Alex Sanchez 1, Craig Monroe 1, Omar Infante 1. |
| Tampa Bay | 16 | Carl Crawford 5, Jose Cruz Jr. 3, Aubrey Huff 3, Julio Lugo 2, Geoff Blum 1, Rocco Baldelli 1, Jorge Cantu 1. |
| Kansas City | 15 | Joe Randa 3, Mike Sweeney 3, Angel Berroa 2, Juan Gonzalez 1, Dee Brown 1, Carlos Beltran 1, Abraham Nunez 1, Ken Harvey 1, John Buck 1, David DeJesus 1. |
| Seattle | 15 | Ichiro Suzuki 10, Randy Winn 3, Raul Ibanez 2. |
| Boston | 14 | Johnny Damon 4, Kevin Millar 3, Manny Ramirez 2, David Ortiz 2, Bill Mueller 1, Nomar Garciaparra 1, Mark Bellhorn 1. |
| Toronto | 14 | Frank Catalanotto 2, Chris Woodward 2, Chris Gomez 1, Carlos Delgado 1, Gregg Zaun 1, Vernon Wells 1, Frank Menechino 1, Eric Hinske 1, Orlando Hudson 1, Howie Clark 1, Kevin Cash 1, Alexis Rios 1. |
| Oakland | 10 | Mark Kotsay 3, Erubiel Durazo 3, Scott Hatteberg 2, Jermaine Dye 1, Bobby Crosby 1. |
| Minnesota | 9 | Cristian Guzman 3, Shannon Stewart 1, Henry Blanco 1, Torii Hunter 1, Luis Rivas 1, Lew Ford 1, Joe Mauer 1. |
| New York | 8 | Gary Sheffield 2, Bernie Williams 1, Alex Rodriguez 1, Derek Jeter 1, Jorge Posada 1, Tony Clark 1, Miguel Cairo 1. |

### NATIONAL LEAGUE

| Team | No. | Hitters |
|---|---|---|
| St. Louis | 21 | Albert Pujols 7, Tony Womack 3, Edgar Renteria 3, Hector Luna 2, Larry Walker 1, Jim Edmonds 1, John Mabry 1, Scott Rolen 1, So Taguchi 1, Cody McKay 1. |
| San Francisco | 19 | Barry Bonds 3, Marquis Grissom 2, J.T. Snow 2, Michael Tucker 2, Neifi Perez 2, Deivi Cruz 2, A.J. Pierzynski 2, Ray Durham 1, Edgardo Alfonzo 1, Pedro Feliz 1, Dustan Mohr 1. |
| Atlanta | 15 | J.D. Drew 4, Rafael Furcal 3, Johnny Estrada 3, Eddie Perez 2, Andruw Jones 1, Marcus Giles 1, Adam LaRoche 1. |
| Chicago | 15 | Derrek Lee 3, Aramis Ramirez 3, Moises Alou 2, Mark Grudzielanek 2, Todd Walker 2, Corey Patterson 2, Neifi Perez 1. |
| Pittsburgh | 15 | Jack Wilson 5, Jason Bay 4, Jason Kendall 3, Craig Wilson 2, Daryle Ward 1. |
| Milwaukee | 13 | Scott Podsednik 4, Brady Clark 3, Gary Bennett 1, Craig Counsell 1, Ben Grieve 1, Junior Spivey 1, Chad Moeller 1, Lyle Overbay 1. |
| Philadelphia | 13 | David Bell 3, Jimmy Rollins 3, Bobby Abreu 2, Pat Burrell 2, Jason Michaels 2, Jim Thome 1. |
| Los Angeles | 12 | Paul Lo Duca 3, Jose Hernandez 2, Adrian Beltre 2, Cesar Izturis 2, Shawn Green 1, Milton Bradley 1, Jayson Werth 1. |
| Montreal | 12 | Brad Wilkerson 3, Endy Chavez 3, Tony Batista 2, Jamey Carroll 2, Brian Schneider 1, Juan Rivera 1. |
| Cincinnati | 11 | Sean Casey 3, D'Angelo Jimenez 3, Ryan Freel 2, Javier Valentin 1, Wily Mo Pena 1, Austin Kearns 1. |
| Houston | 11 | Jose Vizcaino 3, Lance Berkman 2, Mike Lamb 2, Jeff Bagwell 1, Brad Ausmus 1, Carlos Beltran 1, Morgan Ensberg 1. |
| Colorado | 11 | Todd Helton 3, Royce Clayton 2, Aaron Miles 2, Luis A. Gonzalez 2, Larry Walker 1, Jeromy Burnitz 1. |
| Florida | 11 | Juan Pierre 4, Jeff Conine 2, Luis Castillo 2, Mike Mordecai 1, Mike Lowell 1, Miguel Cabrera 1. |
| New York | 8 | David Wright 2, Mike Piazza 1, Wilson Delgado 1, Vance Wilson 1, Eric Valent 1, Ty Wigginton 1, Jose Reyes 1. |
| San Diego | 8 | Mark Loretta 2, Jay Payton 2, Phil Nevin 1, Brian Giles 1, Sean Burroughs 1, Khalil Greene 1. |
| Arizona | 6 | Roberto Alomar 1, Danny Bautista 1, Scott Hairston 1, Chad Tracy 1, Koyie Hill 1, Robby Hammock 1. |

# FIVE OR MORE HITS IN ONE GAME

## AMERICAN LEAGUE

| Date | Player, Team, Opponent | AB | R | H | 2B | 3B | HR | RBI | Result |
|---|---|---|---|---|---|---|---|---|---|
| 4-7 | Johnny Damon, Boston at Baltimore | 5 | 2 | 5 | 1 | 0 | 0 | 2 | W 10-3 |
| 4-16 | Jody Gerut, Cleveland vs. Detroit | 5 | 3 | 5 | 3 | 0 | 1 | 3 | W 10-3 |
| 4-21 | Corey Patterson, Chicago at Pittsburgh | 6 | 2 | 5 | 2 | 0 | 0 | 1 | W 12-1 |
| 4-22 | Danny Bautista, Arizona at Milwaukee | 8 | 2 | 5 | 1 | 0 | 2 | 5 | W 11-9 |
| 5-1 | +Frank Catalanotto, Toronto at Chicago | 6 | 2 | 6 | 1 | 0 | 0 | 2 | W 10-6 |
| 5-6 | Derrek Lee, Chicago vs. Arizona | 5 | 2 | 5 | 0 | 0 | 1 | 5 | W 11-3 |
| 5-7 | Cristian Guzman, Minnesota at Oakland | 6 | 2 | 5 | 2 | 0 | 0 | 0 | L 9-11 |
| 5-8 | Alfonso Soriano, Texas vs. Detroit | 6 | 1 | 6 | 2 | 0 | 0 | 4 | W 16-15 |
| 5-10 | Ty Wigginton, New York at Arizona | 5 | 1 | 5 | 1 | 0 | 0 | 0 | L 8-12 |
| 5-14 | Chone Figgins, Anaheim at Baltimore | 6 | 2 | 5 | 0 | 1 | 1 | 6 | W 10-9 |
| 5-15 | Johnny Estrada, Atlanta at Milwaukee | 5 | 2 | 5 | 1 | 0 | 1 | 5 | W 11-6 |
| 5-27 | Carlos Pena, Detroit at Kansas City | 6 | 4 | 6 | 1 | 0 | 2 | 5 | W 17-7 |
| 6-1 | Albert Pujols, St. Louis at Pittsburgh | 5 | 3 | 5 | 2 | 0 | 1 | 3 | W 8-1 |
| 6-2 | David Eckstein, Anaheim vs. Boston | 5 | 4 | 5 | 1 | 0 | 0 | 1 | W 10-7 |
| 6-13 | Derrek Lee, Chicago at Anaheim | 5 | 2 | 5 | 1 | 0 | 1 | 2 | W 6-5 |
| 6-22 | Deivi Cruz, San Francisco vs. Los Angeles | 5 | 1 | 5 | 3 | 0 | 0 | 2 | W 11-5 |
| 6-23 | Sean Casey, Cincinnati at New York | 6 | 2 | 5 | 0 | 0 | 2 | 4 | W 6-4 |
| 6-24 | Julio Lugo, Tampa Bay at Toronto | 7 | 3 | 5 | 1 | 0 | 0 | 3 | W 19-13 |
| 6-30 | Brian Giles, San Diego at Arizona | 5 | 0 | 5 | 2 | 0 | 0 | 2 | L 5-8 |
| 7-6 | Johnny Damon, Boston vs. Oakland | 6 | 2 | 5 | 0 | 0 | 0 | 0 | W 11-0 |
| 7-11 | Eric Young, Texas at Boston | 5 | 1 | 5 | 1 | 0 | 0 | 0 | W 6-5 |
| 7-16 | Victor Martinez, Cleveland at Seattle | 5 | 3 | 5 | 0 | 0 | 3 | 7 | W 18-6 |
| 7-20 | Albert Pujols, St. Louis at Chicago | 5 | 4 | 5 | 1 | 0 | 3 | 5 | W 11-8 |
| 7-29 | Ichiro Suzuki, Seattle at Anaheim | 7 | 2 | 5 | 1 | 0 | 0 | 0 | W 6-5 |
| 7-31 | Jose Guillen, Anaheim vs. Seattle | 6 | 2 | 5 | 0 | 0 | 1 | 4 | W 9-8 |
| 8-3 | #Ichiro Suzuki, Seattle at Baltimore | 5 | 2 | 5 | 0 | 1 | 0 | 0 | L 7-9 |
| 8-4 | Casey Blake, Cleveland at Toronto | 6 | 1 | 5 | 1 | 1 | 0 | 1 | W 14-5 |
| 8-8 | Edgar Renteria, St. Louis vs. New York | 5 | 1 | 5 | 1 | 0 | 0 | 1 | W 6-2 |
| 8-10 | Willie Harris, Chicago vs. Kansas City | 5 | 2 | 5 | 3 | 0 | 0 | 1 | W 9-3 |
| 8-17 | Raul Ibanez, Seattle at Kansas City | 5 | 4 | 5 | 1 | 0 | 0 | 0 | W 16-3 |
| 8-21 | Randy Winn, Seattle at Detroit | 6 | 1 | 5 | 1 | 0 | 1 | 4 | L 10-11 |
| 8-28 | Adrian Beltre, Los Angeles at New York | 5 | 2 | 5 | 0 | 0 | 1 | 2 | W 4-2 |
| 8-31 | Omar Vizquel, Cleveland at New York | 7 | 3 | 6 | 2 | 0 | 0 | 4 | W 22-0 |
| 9-3 | Edgardo Alfonzo, San Francisco vs. Arizona | 6 | 4 | 5 | 1 | 0 | 1 | 2 | W 18-7 |
| 9-4 | Ichiro Suzuki, Seattle at Chicago | 5 | 3 | 5 | 0 | 0 | 0 | 1 | L 7-8 |
| 9-9 | #Joe Randa, Kansas City at Detroit | 7 | 6 | 6 | 1 | 0 | 0 | 2 | W 26-5 |
| 9-13 | Angel Berroa, Kansas City vs. New York | 5 | 5 | 5 | 0 | 0 | 0 | 1 | W 17-8 |
| 9-21 | Ichiro Suzuki, Seattle at Anaheim | 5 | 1 | 5 | 0 | 0 | 0 | 0 | W 7-3 |
| 9-22 | Raul Ibanez, Seattle at Anaheim | 6 | 1 | 6 | 0 | 0 | 0 | 5 | W 16-6 |
| 9-28 | Ray Durham, San Francisco at San Diego | 6 | 2 | 5 | 1 | 0 | 0 | 1 | W 7-5 |

# First game of doubleheader. + Second game of doubleheader.

## NATIONAL LEAGUE

| Date | Player, Team, Opponent | AB | R | H | 2B | 3B | HR | RBI | Result |
|---|---|---|---|---|---|---|---|---|---|
| 4-7 | Mike Piazza, New York at Atlanta | 5 | 2 | 5 | 1 | 0 | 2 | 4 | L 10-18 |
| 4-21 | Corey Patterson, Chicago at Pittsburgh | 6 | 2 | 5 | 2 | 0 | 0 | 1 | W 12-1 |
| 4-22 | Danny Bautista, Arizona at Milwaukee | 8 | 2 | 5 | 1 | 0 | 2 | 5 | W 11-9 |
| 5-6 | Derrek Lee, Chicago vs. Arizona | 5 | 2 | 5 | 0 | 0 | 1 | 5 | W 11-3 |
| 5-10 | Ty Wigginton, New York at Arizona | 5 | 1 | 5 | 1 | 0 | 0 | 0 | L 8-12 |
| 5-15 | Johnny Estrada, Atlanta at Milwaukee | 5 | 2 | 5 | 1 | 0 | 1 | 5 | W 11-6 |
| 6-1 | Albert Pujols, St. Louis at Pittsburgh | 5 | 3 | 5 | 2 | 0 | 1 | 3 | W 8-1 |
| 6-13 | Derrek Lee, Chicago at Anaheim | 5 | 2 | 5 | 1 | 0 | 1 | 2 | W 6-5 |
| 6-22 | Deivi Cruz, San Francisco vs. Los Angeles | 5 | 1 | 5 | 3 | 0 | 0 | 2 | W 11-5 |
| 6-23 | Sean Casey, Cincinnati at New York | 6 | 2 | 5 | 0 | 0 | 2 | 4 | W 6-4 |
| 6-30 | Brian Giles, San Diego at Arizona | 5 | 0 | 5 | 2 | 0 | 0 | 2 | L 5-8 |
| 7-20 | Albert Pujols, St. Louis at Chicago | 5 | 4 | 5 | 1 | 0 | 3 | 5 | W 11-8 |
| 8-8 | Edgar Renteria, St. Louis vs. New York | 5 | 1 | 5 | 1 | 0 | 0 | 1 | W 6-2 |
| 8-28 | Adrian Beltre, Los Angeles at New York | 5 | 2 | 5 | 0 | 0 | 1 | 2 | W 4-2 |
| 9-3 | Edgardo Alfonzo, San Francisco vs. Arizona | 6 | 4 | 5 | 1 | 0 | 1 | 2 | W 18-7 |
| 9-28 | Ray Durham, San Francisco at San Diego | 6 | 2 | 5 | 1 | 0 | 0 | 1 | W 7-5 |

# HITTING STREAKS OF 15 OR MORE GAMES

## AMERICAN LEAGUE

| G | Player, Team | Span of streak |
|---|---|---|
| 28 | Carlos Lee, Chicago | May 13-June 15 |
| 21 | Ichiro Suzuki, Seattle | July 4-July 29 |
| | Robb Quinlan, Anaheim | July 7-Aug. 10 |
| 19 | Miguel Tejada, Baltimore | June 15-July 4 |
| 18 | David Eckstein, Anaheim | May 14-June 3 |
| 17 | Jody Gerut, Cleveland | Apr. 25-May 15 |
| | Vernon Wells, Toronto | May 8-May 26 |
| | Derek Jeter, New York | July 30-Aug. 17 |
| 16 | Ichiro Suzuki, Seattle | Apr. 30-May 18 |
| | Matt Lawton, Cleveland | June 3-June 19 |
| | Johnny Damon, Boston | June 24-July 11 |
| | Eric Hinske, Toronto | June 28-July 18 |
| | Bret Boone, Seattle | July 26-Aug. 12 |
| | Ross Gload, Chicago | Sept. 17-Oct. 3 |
| 15 | Frank Thomas, Chicago | May 18-June 5 |
| | Aubrey Huff, Tampa Bay | May 22-June 8 |
| | Ken Harvey, Kansas City | May 22-June 6 |
| | Carlos Beltran, Kansas City-Houston | June 15-July 1 |
| | David Newhan, Baltimore | June 18-July 3 |
| | David DeJesus, Kansas City | July 30-Aug. 15 |
| | Jason Varitek, Boston | Aug. 17-Sept. 10 |
| | Mark Kotsay, Oakland | Sept. 13-Sept. 28 |
| | David DeJesus, Kansas City | Sept. 19-Oct. 3 |

## NATIONAL LEAGUE

| G | Player, Team | Span of streak |
|---|---|---|
| 25 | Jeff Kent, Houston | May 14-June 11 |
| 22 | J.D. Drew, Atlanta | June 30-July 26 |
| 21 | Danny Bautista, Arizona | Apr. 7-Apr. 30 |
| 20 | Jason Kendall, Pittsburgh | May 8-June 3 |
| 19 | Jose Vidro, Montreal | June 12-July 2 |
| 18 | Lyle Overbay, Milwaukee | Apr. 27-May 18 |
| 16 | Adrian Beltre, Los Angeles | Apr. 25-May 13 |
| | Sean Burroughs, San Diego | May 19-June 6 |
| | Lyle Overbay, Milwaukee | June 1-June 19 |
| | J.D. Drew, Atlanta | Aug. 20-Sept. 8 |
| | Juan Pierre, Florida | Aug. 20-Sept. 9 |
| 15 | Cesar Izturis, Los Angeles | May 22-June 8 |
| | Carlos Beltran, Kansas City-Houston | June 15-July 1 |

# MULTI-HOMER GAMES

## AMERICAN LEAGUE

| Team | No. | Hitters |
|---|---|---|
| Chicago | 16 | Paul Konerko 5, Carlos Lee 4, Juan Uribe 2, Aaron Rowand 2, Frank Thomas 1, Jose Valentin 1, Joe Crede 1. |
| Detroit | 16 | Carlos Pena 3, Bobby Higginson 2, Carlos Guillen 2, Eric Munson 2, Omar Infante 2, Ivan Rodriguez 1, Dmitri Young 1, Jason Smith 1, Craig Monroe 1, Marcus Thames 1. |
| Texas | 16 | David Dellucci 3, Hank Blalock 3, Rod Barajas 2, Mark Teixeira 2, Kevin Mench 2, Laynce Nix 2, Alfonso Soriano 1, Michael Young 1. |
| Boston | 15 | Manny Ramirez 4, Johnny Damon 3, David Ortiz 3, Doug Mirabelli 1, Pokey Reese 1, Jason Varitek 1, Kevin Millar 1, Kevin Youkilis 1. |
| Oakland | 14 | Eric Byrnes 3, Mark Kotsay 2, Eric Chavez 2, Erubiel Durazo 2, Scott Hatteberg 1, Jermaine Dye 1, Damian Miller 1, Bobby Kielty 1, Bobby Crosby 1. |
| New York | 13 | Alex Rodriguez 3, Tony Clark 3, Gary Sheffield 2, Derek Jeter 2, Ruben Sierra 1, Jorge Posada 1, Hideki Matsui 1. |
| Baltimore | 9 | Rafael Palmeiro 2, Miguel Tejada 2, Melvin Mora 2, Javy Lopez 1, Karim Garcia 1, Jay Gibbons 1. |
| Kansas City | 9 | Matt Stairs 2, Mike Sweeney 2, Juan Gonzalez 1, Calvin Pickering 1, Dee Brown 1, Carlos Beltran 1, John Buck 1. |
| Anaheim | 8 | Vladimir Guerrero 4, Garret Anderson 2, Jose Guillen 1, Troy Glaus 1. |
| Cleveland | 7 | Travis Hafner 4, Matt Lawton 1, Casey Blake 1, Victor Martinez 1. |
| Toronto | 7 | Vernon Wells 3, Josh Phelps 2, Carlos Delgado 1, Orlando Hudson 1. |
| Minnesota | 5 | Henry Blanco 1, Torii Hunter 1, Corey Koskie 1, Joe Mauer 1, Justin Morneau 1. |
| Seattle | 4 | Edgar Martinez 1, Bret Boone 1, Raul Ibanez 1, Miguel Olivo 1. |
| Tampa Bay | 4 | Aubrey Huff 2, Tino Martinez 1, Geoff Blum 1. |

## NATIONAL LEAGUE

| Team | No. | Hitters |
|---|---|---|
| Chicago | 18 | Moises Alou 4, Aramis Ramirez 4, Sammy Sosa 3, Michael Barrett 2, Corey Patterson 2, Mark Grudzielanek 1, Todd Walker 1, Derrek Lee 1. |
| Los Angeles | 18 | Adrian Beltre 7, Shawn Green 4, Milton Bradley 3, Steve Finley 1, Jose Hernandez 1, Jayson Werth 1, Jason Grabowski 1. |
| Cincinnati | 17 | Sean Casey 5, Adam Dunn 5, Wily Mo Pena 3, Ken Griffey Jr. 2, Javier Valentin 1, Jason LaRue 1. |
| St. Louis | 15 | Scott Rolen 5, Albert Pujols 4, Jim Edmonds 3, Reggie Sanders 2, Larry Walker 1. |
| New York | 12 | Mike Piazza 2, Mike Cameron 2, Richard Hidalgo 2, Todd Zeile 1, Cliff Floyd 1, Jason Phillips 1, Ty Wigginton 1, Kazuo Matsui 1, David Wright 1. |
| Philadelphia | 12 | Jim Thome 3, Bobby Abreu 3, Pat Burrell 2, David Bell 1, Ricky Ledee 1, Randy Wolf 1, Jason Michaels 1. |
| San Francisco | 12 | Barry Bonds 4, Pedro Feliz 3, Marquis Grissom 2, J.T. Snow 1, Michael Tucker 1, Ray Durham 1. |
| Colorado | 12 | Vinny Castilla 4, Jeromy Burnitz 4, Larry Walker 1, Todd Greene 1, Aaron Miles 1, Matt Holliday 1. |
| Houston | 11 | Craig Biggio 3, Jeff Kent 3, Carlos Beltran 3, Lance Berkman 1, Adam Everett 1. |
| Atlanta | 10 | Chipper Jones 2, Andruw Jones 2, Charles Thomas 2, Eddie Perez 1, J.D. Drew 1, Rafael Furcal 1, Adam LaRoche 1. |
| Pittsburgh | 9 | Jason Bay 3, Daryle Ward 2, Ruben Mateo 1, Tike Redman 1, Craig Wilson 1, Rob Mackowiak 1. |
| Arizona | 9 | Luis Gonzalez 3, Steve Finley 2, Danny Bautista 1, Richie Sexson 1, Alex Cintron 1, Chris Snyder 1. |
| Florida | 7 | Mike Lowell 4, Alex Gonzalez 1, Hee Seop Choi 1, Miguel Cabrera 1. |
| Montreal | 6 | Tony Batista 3, Brad Wilkerson 2, Juan Rivera 1. |
| San Diego | 6 | Phil Nevin 2, Khalil Greene 2, Mark Loretta 1, Brian Giles 1. |
| Milwaukee | 4 | Russell Branyan 2, Scott Podsednik 1, Brady Clark 1. |

# THREE-HOMER GAMES

| Date | Player, Team, Opponent | AB | R | H | 2B | 3B | HR | RBI | Result |
|---|---|---|---|---|---|---|---|---|---|
| 4-21 | Mike Lowell, Florida at Philadelphia | 6 | 3 | 4 | 0 | 0 | 3 | 4 | W 8-7 |
| 4-28 | Steve Finley, Arizona vs. Chicago | 4 | 3 | 3 | 0 | 0 | 3 | 3 | L 3-4 |
| 5-10 | Luis Gonzalez, Arizona vs. New York | 5 | 3 | 3 | 0 | 0 | 3 | 4 | W 12-8 |
| 6-25 | Larry Walker, Colorado at Cleveland | 4 | 4 | 4 | 1 | 0 | 3 | 5 | W 10-8 |
| 7-16 | Victor Martinez, Cleveland at Seattle | 5 | 3 | 5 | 0 | 0 | 3 | 7 | W 18-6 |
| 7-20 | Travis Hafner, Cleveland at Anaheim | 4 | 3 | 4 | 0 | 0 | 3 | 6 | W 14-5 |
| 7-20 | Albert Pujols, St. Louis at Chicago | 5 | 4 | 5 | 1 | 0 | 3 | 5 | W 11-8 |
| 7-23 | Kevin Millar, Boston vs. New York | 4 | 3 | 3 | 0 | 0 | 3 | 3 | L 7-8 |
| 7-30 | Aramis Ramirez, Chicago vs. Philadelphia | 4 | 3 | 3 | 0 | 0 | 3 | 3 | W 10-7 |
| 8-13 | J.T. Snow, San Francisco at Philadelphia | 4 | 5 | 3 | 0 | 0 | 3 | 4 | W 16-6 |
| 8-18 | Erubiel Durazo, Oakland at Baltimore | 4 | 3 | 4 | 0 | 0 | 3 | 5 | W 5-4 |
| 8-28 | Tony Clark, New York at Toronto | 5 | 3 | 3 | 0 | 0 | 3 | 5 | W 18-6 |
| 9-16 | Aramis Ramirez, Chicago at Cincinnati | 5 | 3 | 4 | 1 | 0 | 3 | 5 | W 5-4 |

# GRAND SLAMS

## AMERICAN LEAGUE

| Date | Batter, Team | Pitcher, Team | Inn.* | Site |
|---|---|---|---|---|
| 4-12 | Travis Hafner, Cleveland | Kyle Lohse, Minnesota | 3 | Cleveland |
| 4-20 | Matt Stairs, Kansas City | Jeriome Robertson, Cleveland | 6 | Cleveland |
| 4-22 | Chris Gomez, Toronto | Curt Schilling, Boston | 8 | Toronto |
| 4-23 | Brandon Inge, Detroit | Jason Anderson, Cleveland | 6 | Detroit |
| 4-27 | Brandon Inge, Detroit | Scot Shields, Anaheim | 7 | Detroit |
| 5-1 | Ruben Sierra, New York | Curtis Leskanic, Kansas City | 8 | New York |
| 5-1 | Erubiel Durazo, Oakland | Trever Miller, Tampa Bay | 9 | Tampa Bay |
| 5-8 | Shane Halter, Anaheim | Trever Miller, Tampa Bay | 7 | Anaheim |
| 5-14 | Chone Figgins, Anaheim | Kurt Ainsworth, Baltimore | 2 | Baltimore |
| 5-19 | Matthew LeCroy, Minnesota | Terry Adams, Toronto | 9 | Toronto |
| 5-28 | David Ortiz, Boston | Joel Pineiro, Seattle | 5 | Boston |
| 6-2 | Josh Phelps, Toronto | Joel Pineiro, Seattle | 2 | Seattle |
| 6-4 | Melvin Mora, Baltimore | Victor Zambrano, Tampa Bay | 3 | Baltimore |
| 6-7 | Scott Hatteberg, Oakland | Cory Lidle, Cincinnati | 2 | Oakland |
| 6-9 | Damian Miller, Oakland | Jose Acevedo, Cincinnati | 3 | Oakland |
| 6-10 | John Flaherty, New York | Scott Dohmann, Colorado | 6 | New York |
| 6-10 | +Brad Fullmer, Texas | Mike Johnston, Pittsburgh | 5 | Texas |
| 6-12 | Hank Blalock, Texas | Chris Carpenter, St. Louis | 4 | Texas |
| 6-13 | Adam Melhuse, Oakland | Kip Wells, Pittsburgh | 5 | Oakland |
| 6-20 | Brian Roberts, Baltimore | Shawn Chacon, Colorado | 9 | Colorado |
| 6-22 | Nomar Garciaparra, Boston | Joe Roa, Minnesota | 7 | Boston |
| 6-23 | Ben Broussard, Cleveland | Mike Jackson, Chicago | 8 | Chicago |
| 6-27 | Carlos Pena, Detroit | Mike Koplove, Arizona | 9 | Detroit |
| 6-27 | #Hideki Matsui, New York | Mike Stanton, New York | 8 | New York |
| 7-1 | Dmitri Young, Detroit | Cliff Lee, Cleveland | 5 | Detroit |
| 7-3 | Doug Mirabelli, Boston | John Thomson, Atlanta | 6 | Atlanta |
| 7-4 | Mark Teixeira, Texas | Chad Harville, Houston | 9 | Houston |
| 7-4 | Hank Blalock, Texas | Tim Redding, Houston | 6 | Houston |
| 7-7 | Josh Phelps, Toronto | Julio Mateo, Seattle | 6 | Toronto |
| 7-10 | Hank Blalock, Texas | Derek Lowe, Boston | 2 | Boston |
| 7-10 | Erubiel Durazo, Oakland | Cliff Bartosh, Cleveland | 6 | Cleveland |
| 7-10 | Bengie Molina, Anaheim | Kerry Ligtenberg, Toronto | 7 | Toronto |
| 7-16 | Dee Brown, Kansas City | Brad Radke, Minnesota | 3 | Kansas City |
| 7-18 | Mark Teixeira, Texas | Vinnie Chulk, Toronto | 8 | Texas |
| 7-19 | Bret Boone, Seattle | Curtis Leskanic, Boston | 11 | Seattle |
| 7-22 | Mike Sweeney, Kansas City | Gary Knotts, Detroit | 2 | Detroit |
| 7-22 | Rocco Baldelli, Tampa Bay | Juan Rincon, Minnesota | 8 | Minnesota |
| 7-22 | Nick Punto, Minnesota | Jesus Colome, Tampa Bay | 7 | Minnesota |
| 7-25 | Hideki Matsui, New York | Mike Timlin, Boston | 7 | Boston |
| 7-25 | Marcus Thames, Detroit | Mike Jackson, Chicago | 7 | Chicago |
| 7-26 | Jorge Posada, New York | Sean Douglass, Toronto | 1 | Toronto |
| 7-27 | Coco Crisp, Cleveland | Gary Knotts, Detroit | 2 | Cleveland |
| 8-3 | Paul Konerko, Chicago | Mike Wood, Kansas City | 5 | Kansas City |
| 8-4 | Toby Hall, Tampa Bay | Bronson Arroyo, Boston | 7 | Tampa Bay |
| 8-8 | Bernie Williams, New York | Miguel Batista, Toronto | 1 | New York |
| 8-9 | Ben Broussard, Cleveland | Felix Diaz, Chicago | 3 | Chicago |
| 8-12 | Ben Broussard, Cleveland | Vinnie Chulk, Toronto | 7 | Cleveland |
| 8-12 | Miguel Cairo, New York | Scott Erickson, Texas | 2 | Texas |
| 8-13 | Abraham Nunez, Kansas City | Mark Mulder, Oakland | 6 | Oakland |
| 8-13 | John Buck, Kansas City | Jairo Garcia, Oakland | 8 | Oakland |
| 8-13 | Ruben Sierra, New York | Scott Atchison, Seattle | 4 | Seattle |
| 8-17 | Scott Hatteberg, Oakland | Todd Williams, Baltimore | 6 | Baltimore |
| 8-18 | Aaron Rowand, Chicago | Jeremy Bonderman, Detroit | 1 | Chicago |
| 8-19 | Josh Paul, Anaheim | Travis Harper, Tampa Bay | 7 | Tampa Bay |
| 8-20 | Chris Woodward, Toronto | Eddy Rodriguez, Baltimore | 9 | Baltimore |
| 8-20 | Manny Ramirez, Boston | Mark Buehrle, Chicago | 2 | Chicago |
| 8-22 | Calvin Pickering, Kansas City | Scott Erickson, Texas | 3 | Kansas City |
| 8-24 | Carlos Pena, Detroit | Jon Garland, Chicago | 3 | Detroit |

| | | | | |
|---|---|---|---|---|
| 8-25 | Jose Molina, Anaheim | Scott Sullivan, Kansas City | 7 | Anaheim |
| 8-26 | Abraham Nunez, Kansas City | Jamie Moyer, Seattle | 1 | Seattle |
| 8-28 | Ruben Sierra, New York | Kerry Ligtenberg, Toronto | 9 | Toronto |
| 8-31 | Alfredo Amezaga, Anaheim | Mike Myers, Boston | 9 | Boston |
| 9-4 | Mark Bellhorn, Boston | Ron Mahay, Texas | 7 | Boston |
| 9-5 | Gabe Gross, Toronto | Justin Duchscherer, Oakland | 5 | Toronto |
| 9-10 | Manny Ramirez, Boston | Aaron Taylor, Seattle | 7 | Seattle |
| 9-20 | B.J. Surhoff, Baltimore | Tim Wakefield, Boston | 4 | Boston |
| 9-21 | Juan Uribe, Chicago | Jesse Crain, Minnesota | 7 | Chicago |
| 9-21 | Michael Young, Texas | Mark Mulder, Oakland | 4 | Texas |
| 9-29 | Carlos Lee, Chicago | John Ennis, Detroit | 9 | Detroit |
| 10-1 | Alfredo Amezaga, Anaheim | Joe Blanton, Oakland | 6 | Oakland |

*Inning in which grand slam was hit. # First game of doubleheader. + Second game of doubleheader.

## NATIONAL LEAGUE

| Date | Batter, Team | Pitcher, Team | Inn.* | Site |
|---|---|---|---|---|
| 4-5 | Phil Nevin, San Diego | Hideo Nomo, Los Angeles | 5 | Los Angeles |
| 4-7 | Charles Johnson, Colorado | Andrew Good, Arizona | 8 | Arizona |
| 4-9 | Jeff Bagwell, Houston | Brooks Kieschnick, Milwaukee | 6 | Milwaukee |
| 4-11 | Lance Berkman, Houston | Doug Davis, Milwaukee | 3 | Milwaukee |
| 4-19 | Derrek Lee, Chicago | Ryan Wagner, Cincinnati | 7 | Chicago |
| 4-21 | Jim Edmonds, St. Louis | Ricky Stone, Houston | 6 | Houston |
| 4-30 | Brian Dallimore, San Francisco | Dontrelle Willis, Florida | 2 | San Francisco |
| 5-2 | Yorvit Torrealba, San Francisco | Darren Oliver, Florida | 2 | San Francisco |
| 5-4 | Lyle Overbay, Milwaukee | Jimmy Haynes, Cincinnati | 3 | Cincinnati |
| 5-11 | Steve Finley, Arizona | Mike Stanton, New York | 6 | Arizona |
| 5-14 | Cliff Floyd, New York | Roy Oswalt, Houston | 3 | Houston |
| 5-22 | A.J. Pierzynski, San Francisco | Jeremy Fikac, Montreal | 11 | Montreal |
| 5-22 | Luis Castillo, Florida | Steve Sparks, Arizona | 3 | Florida |
| 5-27 | Andruw Jones, Atlanta | Kevin Millwood, Philadelphia | 4 | Philadelphia |
| 5-28 | #Rob Mackowiak, Pittsburgh | Joe Borowski, Chicago | 9 | Pittsburgh |
| 5-28 | #Michael Barrett, Chicago | Mike Johnston, Pittsburgh | 7 | Pittsburgh |
| 6-3 | Julio Franco, Atlanta | Josh Hancock, Philadelphia | 1 | Atlanta |
| 6-9 | Edgar Renteria, St. Louis | Mark Prior, Chicago | 4 | Chicago |
| 6-12 | Ruben Mateo, Pittsburgh | Mark Redman, Oakland | 5 | Oakland |
| 6-12 | Matt Holliday, Colorado | Rob Bell, Tampa Bay | 6 | Tampa Bay |
| 6-13 | Wily Mo Pena, Cincinnati | Cliff Lee, Cleveland | 1 | Cleveland |
| 6-19 | Juan Rivera, Montreal | Arnie Munoz, Chicago | 2 | Montreal |
| 6-20 | Edgardo Alfonzo, San Francisco | Mike Timlin, Boston | 7 | San Francisco |
| 6-23 | Jason Kendall, Pittsburgh | David Weathers, Houston | 7 | Houston |
| 6-25 | Wily Mo Pena, Cincinnati | Mike Gonzalez, Pittsburgh | 7 | Cincinnati |
| 6-29 | Chad Moeller, Milwaukee | Shawn Estes, Colorado | 3 | Colorado |
| 7-1 | Roberto Alomar, Arizona | Ismael Valdez, San Diego | 4 | Arizona |
| 7-2 | #Tony Alvarez, Pittsburgh | Doug Davis, Milwaukee | 3 | Pittsburgh |
| 7-3 | Morgan Ensberg, Houston | Ricardo Rodriguez, Texas | 5 | Houston |
| 7-11 | Paul Lo Duca, Los Angeles | David Weathers, Houston | 8 | Los Angeles |
| 7-11 | Jeff Conine, Florida | Al Leiter, New York | 3 | Florida |
| 7-15 | Shawn Green, Los Angeles | Randy Choate, Arizona | 8 | Arizona |
| 7-18 | Eli Marrero, Atlanta | Scott Downs, Montreal | 1 | Atlanta |
| 7-22 | Aramis Ramirez, Chicago | Ryan Wagner, Cincinnati | 6 | Chicago |
| 7-24 | Adrian Beltre, Los Angeles | Ismael Valdez, San Diego | 4 | Los Angeles |
| 7-28 | Barry Larkin, Cincinnati | Steve Kline, St. Louis | 5 | Cincinnati |
| 7-29 | Alex Gonzalez, Florida | Paul Abbott, Philadelphia | 3 | Florida |
| 7-31 | Terrmel Sledge, Montreal | Josias Manzanillo, Florida | 7 | Florida |
| 8-3 | Tony Batista, Montreal | Danny Haren, St. Louis | 12 | St. Louis |
| 8-7 | Jeff Conine, Florida | Wes Obermueller, Milwaukee | 1 | Florida |
| 8-11 | Brian Schneider, Montreal | Brandon Webb, Arizona | 4 | Montreal |
| 8-14 | Jeff Conine, Florida | Luis Vizcaino, Milwaukee | 9 | Milwaukee |
| 8-14 | Nick Johnson, Montreal | Chad Qualls, Houston | 7 | Montreal |
| 8-17 | Larry Walker, St. Louis | Danny Graves, Cincinnati | 8 | St. Louis |
| 8-21 | Shawn Green, Los Angeles | Mike Hampton, Atlanta | 1 | Los Angeles |
| 8-22 | Larry Walker, St. Louis | Brian Meadows, Pittsburgh | 8 | St. Louis |
| 8-24 | Derrek Lee, Chicago | Chris Capuano, Milwaukee | 2 | Chicago |
| 8-24 | Adrian Beltre, Los Angeles | Rocky Biddle, Montreal | 5 | Montreal |
| 8-29 | Robin Ventura, Los Angeles | Kris Benson, New York | 5 | New York |
| 8-29 | Marlon Byrd, Philadelphia | Pedro Liriano, Milwaukee | 7 | Philadelphia |
| 9-1 | Jeff Kent, Houston | Ryan Wagner, Cincinnati | 7 | Cincinnati |
| 9-4 | Andruw Jones, Atlanta | Joe Horgan, Montreal | 3 | Montreal |
| 9-4 | Marquis Grissom, San Francisco | Stephen Randolph, Arizona | 6 | San Francisco |
| 9-7 | Robin Ventura, Los Angeles | Chad Durbin, Arizona | 7 | Los Angeles |
| 9-7 | Mark Sweeney, Colorado | Jason Schmidt, San Francisco | 7 | Colorado |
| 9-8 | Olmedo Saenz, Los Angeles | Casey Fossum, Arizona | 5 | Los Angeles |
| 9-9 | Wes Helms, Milwaukee | Juan Padilla, Cincinnati | 7 | Cincinnati |
| 9-11 | Adam Dunn, Cincinnati | Victor Santos, Milwaukee | 3 | Cincinnati |
| 9-15 | Sammy Sosa, Chicago | Mark Corey, Pittsburgh | 8 | Chicago |
| 9-25 | Pedro Feliz, San Francisco | Yhency Brazoban, Los Angeles | 8 | San Francisco |
| 9-27 | Adrian Beltre, Los Angeles | Shawn Estes, Colorado | 2 | Los Angeles |
| 10-2 | Steve Finley, Los Angeles | Wayne Franklin, San Francisco | 9 | Los Angeles |
| 10-3 | Jimmy Rollins, Philadelphia | Matt Perisho, Florida | 8 | Philadelphia |

*Inning in which grand slam was hit. # First game of doubleheader.

# TRANSACTIONS

## JANUARY 1, 2004-DECEMBER 31, 2004

### JANUARY 5

**Indians** organization signed RHP Jeff D'Amico.
**Expos** traded LHP Scott Stewart to Indians for OF Ryan Church and INF Maicer Izturis.
**Rockies** signed SS Royce Clayton, 2B/OF Damian Jackson and OF/1B Mark Sweeney.
**Yankees** signed RHP Javier Vazquez.
**Rangers** signed 2B Eric Young.

### JANUARY 6

**Diamondbacks** signed 2B Roberto Alomar.
**Royals** signed OF Juan Gonzalez.
**Dodgers** signed OF Bubba Trammell.
**Expos** agreed to terms on deal with SS Orlando Cabrera.
**Mets** signed RHP Braden Looper.
**Athletics** signed INF Frank Menechino.
**Padres** traded RHP Kevin Jarvis, C Wiki Gonzalez, INF Dave Hansen and minor league OF Vince Faison to **Mariners** for 3B Jeff Cirillo, RHP Brian Sweeney and cash considerations.
**Cardinals** signed RHP Mike Lincoln.
**Devil Rays** signed RHP Danys Baez.

### JANUARY 7

**White Sox** agreed to terms on deal with RHP Cliff Politte.
**Marlins** organization signed INF Damion Easley.
**Padres** claimed C Tom Wilson off waivers from **Blue Jays**.
**Devil Rays** organization signed SS Deivi Cruz.
**Blue Jays** agreed to terms on deals with RHP Terry Adams and SS Chris Gomez.

### JANUARY 8

**Orioles** organization signed OF B.J. Surhoff.
**Indians** signed RHP Jose Jimenez.
**Mariners** traded SS Carlos Guillen to **Tigers** for SS Ramon Santiago and minor league SS Juan Gonzalez.
**Mariners** signed SS Rich Aurilia.

### JANUARY 9

**Braves** organization signed 1B Julio Franco.
**Cubs** organization signed LHP Jimmy Anderson.
**Reds** organization signed C Javier Valentin and OF Jermaine Clark.
**Rockies** organization signed INF Denny Hocking.
**Dodgers** signed OF Dave Roberts.
**Giants** signed RHP Brett Tomko.
**Cardinals** organization signed OF Ray Lankford.
**Cardinals** signed RHP Julian Tavarez and INF Marlon Anderson.

### JANUARY 10

**Orioles** signed 1B/DH Rafael Palmeiro.

### JANUARY 11

**Twins** organization signed LHP Aaron Fultz.

### JANUARY 12

**Angels** signed OF Vladimir Guerrero.
**White Sox** agreed to terms on deal with LHP Scott Schoeneweis.
**Reds** signed OF John Vander Wal.
**Indians** organization signed INF Lou Merloni.
**Rockies** signed LHP Jeff Fassero and RHP Vladimir Nunez.
**Astros** signed RHP Roger Clemens.
**Yankees** signed 1B Tony Clark.
**Phillies** signed OF Doug Glanville.
**Devil Rays** organization agreed to terms on deals with RHPs Todd Jones and Al Reyes and 3B Fernando Tatis.
**Rangers** signed RHP Jeff Nelson.

### JANUARY 13

**Padres** agreed to terms on deal with OF Jay Payton.
**Rangers** signed LHP Kenny Rogers.

### JANUARY 14

**Angels** agreed to terms on deal with INF Shane Halter.
**Braves** signed INF Mark DeRosa.
**Orioles** agreed to terms on deal with RHP Sidney Ponson.
**Tigers** organization signed INF Greg Norton and C Bobby Estalella.
**Blue Jays** agreed to terms on a deal with LHP Ted Lilly.

### JANUARY 15

**Angels** organization signed C Josh Paul and INF Adam Riggs.
**Phillies** signed SS Jimmy Rollins.
**Rangers** organization signed C Rod Barajas.

### JANUARY 16

**Orioles** organization signed C Keith Osik.
**Reds** organization signed LHP Mike Matthews.
**Astros** signed OF Orlando Palmeiro.
**Padres** agreed to terms on deal with INF Rey Ordonez.
**Mariners** organization signed LHPs Mike Myers, OF Hiram Bocachica and C Pat Borders.
**Rangers** signed RHP Francisco Cordero.

### JANUARY 17

**Expos** agreed to terms on deal with RHP Rocky Biddle.

### JANUARY 18

**Dodgers** organization signed OF Jeremy Giambi.

### JANUARY 19

**Red Sox** agreed to terms on deal with RHP Scott Williamson.
**Dodgers** signed 3B Adrian Beltre.
**Brewers** signed RHP Dan Kolb.
**Expos** agreed to terms on deals with RHPs Tomo Ohka and Tony Armas Jr.
**Giants** signed RHP Jim Brower and INF Pedro Feliz.

### JANUARY 20

**Braves** signed OF J.D. Drew and SS Rafael Furcal.
**Orioles** signed 2B Jerry Hairston Jr. and OF Luis Matos.
**Red Sox** signed OF Trot Nixon and RHP Byung-Hyun Kim.
**Tigers** organization signed RHP Esteban Yan.
**Marlins** signed RHPs Carl Pavano and Brad Penny.
**Royals** signed OF Carlos Beltran.
**Dodgers** signed LHP Odalis Perez.
**Brewers** signed RHP Ben Sheets.
**Mets** signed OF Karim Garcia.
**Yankees** signed 2B Alfonso Soriano.
**Devil Rays** signed RHP Jeremi Gonzalez.
**Blue Jays** signed RHP Justin Speier.

### JANUARY 21

**Diamondbacks** organization signed RHP Brandon Villafuerte and INF Russell Branyan.
**Cubs** signed RHP Ryan Dempster.

### JANUARY 22

**White Sox** signed RHP Shingo Takatsu.
**Devil Rays** agreed to terms on deal with INF/OF Damian Rolls.
**Devil Rays** signed LHP Damian Moss.
**Blue Jays** signed RHP Roy Halladay.

### JANUARY 23

**Rockies** organization signed LHP Shawn Estes.
**Royals** agreed to terms on deal with LHP Darrell May.

### JANUARY 24

**Red Sox** organization agreed to terms on deal with INF Tony Womack.

### JANUARY 26

**Rockies** agreed to terms on deal with RHP Shawn Chacon.
**Mets** traded LHP Jaime Cerda to **Royals** for minor league RHP Shawn Sedlacek.

### JANUARY 27

**Dodgers** organization signed INF Jose Hernandez and RHP Jose Lima.
**Pirates** organization agreed to terms on deal with OF Daryle Ward.

### JANUARY 28
**Orioles** signed 3B Melvin Mora.
**Mets** signed INF Todd Zeile.
**Yankees** organization signed OF Darren Bragg.

### JANUARY 29
**Marlins** signed LHP Darren Oliver.
**Mets** signed OF Shane Spencer.
**Pirates** organization agreed to terms on deal with RHP Jose Mesa.

### FEBRUARY 2
**Tigers** signed C Ivan Rodriguez.
**Twins** signed LHP J.C. Romero.
**Expos** agreed to terms on deal with OF Terrmel Sledge.
**Athletics** signed 1B Eric Karros.

### FEBRUARY 3
**Devil Rays** agreed to terms on deals with RHP Jesus Colome and LHP Mark Hendrickson.

### FEBRUARY 4
**Orioles** organization signed INF/OF Mark McLemore.
**Red Sox** signed DH David Ortiz.

### FEBRUARY 5
**Red Sox** signed DH Ellis Burks.
**Mets** signed RHP Scott Erickson.
**Yankees** released 3B Drew Henson.
**Yankees** organization signed OF Darren Bragg.
**Padres** signed RHP Antonio Osuna.

### FEBRUARY 6
**Yankees** traded 3B Mike Lamb to **Rangers** for minor league RHP Jose Garcia.

### FEBRUARY 9
**Twins** organization signed INF Jose Offerman.
**Pirates** organization signed OF Ruben Mateo.
**Mariners** signed LHP Ron Villone.

### FEBRUARY 10
**Brewers** signed RHP Wes Obermueller.
**Mariners** organization signed LHP Terry Mulholland.
**Devil Rays** organization signed INF/DH Fred McGriff.

### FEBRUARY 11
**Mets** organization signed RHP Ricky Bottalico.

### FEBRUARY 12
**Orioles** signed OF Jay Gibbons.
**Tigers** released C Bobby Estalella.
**Mets** organization signed RHP James Baldwin.
**Cardinals** organization signed OF John Mabry.
**Devil Rays** signed RHP Jorge Sosa and INF Antonio Perez.

### FEBRUARY 13
**Diamondbacks** agreed to terms on deal with 3B Shea Hillenbrand.
**Diamondbacks** organization signed C Bobby Estalella.
**Royals** organization signed RHP Rudy Seanez.

### FEBRUARY 16
**Twins** signed 1B Doug Mientkiewicz.
**Rangers** traded SS Alex Rodriguez to **Yankees** for 2B Alfonso Soriano and a player to be named.

### FEBRUARY 18
**Cubs** signed RHP Greg Maddux.

### FEBRUARY 19
**Pirates** signed 1B Randall Simon.

### FEBRUARY 20
**Angels** agreed to terms on deals with RHP Francisco Rodriguez and C Wil Nieves.
**Cardinals** agreed to terms on deal with 1B Albert Pujols.

### FEBRUARY 21
**Marlins** signed OF Abraham Nunez.
**Rangers** agreed to terms on deals with LHP Erasmo Ramirez and OF Kevin Mench.
**Rangers** signed 3B Hank Blalock.

### FEBRUARY 23
**Braves** signed UT Eli Marrero.
**Indians** signed RHP Rafael Betancourt and OF Grady Sizemore.
**Pirates** signed OF Raul Mondesi.

### FEBRUARY 24
**Tigers** signed OFs Craig Monroe and Alex Sanchez, RHP Nate Cornejo and LHP Nate Robertson.

### FEBRUARY 25
**Brewers** agreed to terms on deal with RHP Matt Kinney.
**Yankees** signed 1B Travis Lee.

### FEBRUARY 26
**Angels** agreed to terms on deal with OF Jeff DaVanon.
**Tigers** signed C Brandon Inge, INF Omar Infante, RHP Gary Knotts and LHPs Wilfredo Ledezma and Mike Maroth.
**Royals** signed RHPs Mike MacDougal and Ryan Bukvich, LHP Jimmy Gobble, OF David DeJesus and 1B Ken Harvey.
**Yankees** released 3B Aaron Boone.
**Rangers** agreed to terms on deals with RHPs R.A. Dickey and Ryan Drese and C Gerald Laird.

### FEBRUARY 27
**Angels** agreed to terms on deals with INF Alfredo Amezaga, INF/OF Chone Figgins, INF Dallas McPherson and C Jose Molina.
**Orioles** agreed to terms on deals with RHP Daniel Cabrera, LHPs Eric DuBose, Matt Riley and Erik Bedard, INF Jose Bautista and OF Tim Raines.
**Cubs** agreed to terms on deal with RHP Kerry Wood.
**Astros** agreed to terms on deals with RHP Ricky Stone.
**Expos** agreed to terms on deals with RHP Sun-Woo Kim and LHP Randy Choate.
**Devil Rays** agreed to terms on deal with RHP Travis Harper.

### FEBRUARY 28
**Cubs** agreed to terms on deal with INF Derrek Lee.
**Marlins** agreed to terms on deals with RHPs Nate Bump and Tim Spooneybarger, 1B Hee Seop Choi and INF Wilson Valdez.

### MARCH 1
**Orioles** agreed to terms on deals with 2B Brian Roberts, OF Larry Bigbie, RHP Denny Bautista and LHP John Parrish.
**Indians** agreed to terms on deals with INF Ben Broussard, OFs Alex Escobar and Ryan Ludwick and LHP Cliff Lee.
**Astros** agreed to terms on deal with OF Jason Lane.
**Expos** agreed to terms on deals with RHP Zach Day and OF Endy Chavez.

### MARCH 2
**White Sox** signed LHP Damaso Marte.
**Expos** agreed to terms on deals with RHP Luis Ayala, INF Henry Mateo and OFs Ron Calloway and Juan Rivera.

### MARCH 3
**Angels** agreed to terms on deals with RHPs Scot Shields and Brendan Donnelly.
**Orioles** agreed to terms on deals with RHPs Kurt Ainsworth, Jorge Julio, OF Jack Cust and C Geronimo Gil.
**White Sox** signed RHPs Matt Ginter and Jon Rauch, LHP Neal Cotts, Cs Jamie Burke and Miguel Olivo, INFs Joe Crede, Ross Gload, Willie Harris and Juan Uribe and OF Aaron Rowand.
**Brewers** agreed to terms on deal with OF Geoff Jenkins.
**Rangers** signed INF Michael Young.

### MARCH 4
**Angels** agreed to terms on deals with RHPs John Lackey and Kevin Gregg.

### MARCH 5
**Royals** signed LHP Jaime Cerda and RHP Jorge Vasquez.
**Dodgers** signed RHP Jason Frasor, C Koyie Hill, INF Cesar Izturis, C David Ross and RHP Yhency Brazoban.

### MARCH 10
**Expos** agreed to terms on deal with C Brian Schneider.

### MARCH 11
**Yankees** signed RHP Orlando Hernandez.

**MARCH 16**

**Brewers** released RHP Mike Crudale.

**MARCH 17**

**Reds** organization signed OF John Vander Wal.

**MARCH 21**

**Red Sox** traded INF Tony Womack to **Cardinals** for minor league RHP Matt Duff.

**MARCH 24**

**Devil Rays** released INFs Deivi Cruz, Fernando Tatis and RHP Todd Jones.

**MARCH 25**

**Expos** traded LHP Randy Choate to **Diamondbacks** for RHP John Patterson.
**Braves** traded LHP Andy Pratt and INF Richard Lewis to **Cubs** for RHP Juan Cruz and LHP Steve Smyth.
**Reds** organization signed RHP Todd Jones.
**Yankees** traded INF Mike Lamb to **Astros** for minor league RHP Juan DeLeon.

**MARCH 26**

**Reds** traded RHP Chris Reitsma to **Braves** for LHP Jung Keun Bong and RHP Bubba Nelson.
**Tigers** signed RHP Ugueth Urbina.

**MARCH 27**

**Mets** traded OF Timo Perez to **White Sox** for RHP Matt Ginter.
**Indians** released RHP Giovanni Carrara.
**Royals** organization signed RHP Jamey Wright.

**MARCH 28**

**Indians** traded INF Ricky Gutierrez and cash to **Mets** for a player to be named.
**Rockies** released INF Damian Jackson.

**MARCH 29**

**Padres** released LHP Kevin Walker and C Tom Wilson.
**Cardinals** traded OF Kerry Robinson to **Padres** for OF Brian Hunter.
**Rockies** released INF Benji Gil.

**MARCH 30**

**Blue Jays** traded OF Jayson Werth to **Dodgers** for RHP Jason Frasor.
**Athletics** traded OF Jason Grabowski to **Dodgers** for cash considerations.
**Dodgers** released RHP Tanyon Sturtze.
**Giants** organization signed RHPs Dave Veres and Mike Crudale and INF Deivi Cruz.

**MARCH 31**

**Braves** released OF Gary Matthews Jr.
**Dodgers** released OF Bubba Trammell.
**Pirates** released LHP Joe Beimel.
**Brewers** traded LHP Wayne Franklin and RHP Leo Estrella to **Giants** for minor league RHPs Carlos Villanueva and Glenn Woolard.

**APRIL 1**

**Cubs** organization signed LHP Glendon Rusch and INF Damian Jackson.

**APRIL 2**

**Marlins** released RHP Tanyon Sturtze and OF Gerald Williams.

**APRIL 3**

**Orioles** released INF/OF Mark McLemore.
**Tigers** released C Mike DiFelice.
**Marlins** traded RHP Blaine Neal to **Padres** for RHP Ben Howard.
**Dodgers** traded INF Jolbert Cabrera to **Mariners** for minor league RHP Aaron Looper and LHP Ryan Ketchner.
**Expos** traded C/INF Josh McKinley and RHP Chris Young to **Rangers** for C Einar Diaz, minor league RHP Justin Echols and cash.
**Mets** traded OF Roger Cedeno and cash to **Cardinals** for C Chris Widger and INF Wilson Delgado.

**APRIL 4**

**Indians** traded OF Milton Bradley to **Dodgers** for minor league OF Franklin Gutierrez and a player to be named.
**Athletics** signed INF Mark McLemore.

**APRIL 9**

**Blue Jays** organization signed C Gregg Zaun.

**APRIL 13**

**Angels** agreed to terms on deal with OF Garret Anderson.
**Tigers** signed C Mike DiFelice.
**Mariners** release LHP Terry Mulholland.
**Twins** signed LHP Terry Mulholland.

**APRIL 17**

**Athletics** traded RHP Chad Harville to **Astros** for RHP Kirk Saarloos.

**APRIL 25**

**Braves** traded UT Russell Branyan to **Indians** for a player to be named.
**Dodgers** traded RHP Rick White to **Indians** for minor league OF Trey Dyson

**MAY 7**

**Royals** signed SS Angel Berroa.

**MAY 8**

**Mets** organization signed C Tom Wilson.

**MAY 12**

**Cubs** organization signed INF Rey Ordonez.

**MAY 13**

**Athletics** traded INF Frank Menechino to **Blue Jays** for future considerations.

**MAY 15**

**Dodgers** traded RHP Tanyon Sturtze to **Yankees** for a player to be named.

**MAY 18**

**Tigers** organization signed RHP Jimmy Haynes.

**MAY 19**

**Blue Jays** organization signed C Bobby Estalella.

**MAY 29**

**Angels** signed OF Raul Mondesi.

**MAY 30**

**Angels** organization signed OF Curtis Pride.
**Cubs** traded INF Damian Jackson to **Royals** for INF Gookie Dawkins and a player to be named.

**JUNE 1**

**Twins** organization released RHP Pete Munro.

**JUNE 3**

**Astros** signed RHP Pete Munro.
**Devil Rays** claimed INF/OF Jose Bautista off waivers from **Orioles** and released RHP Paul Abbott.

**JUNE 6**

**Cardinals** organization signed RHP Al Reyes.

**JUNE 7**

**Twins** organization signed RHP Gary Glover.

**JUNE 9**

**Phillies** organization signed RHP Paul Abbott.

**JUNE 12**

**Diamondbacks** organization signed OF Quinton McCracken.

**JUNE 14**

**Cubs** organization signed INF Ricky Gutierrez.

**JUNE 16**

**Royals** released RHP Curtis Leskanic.

**JUNE 17**

**White Sox** traded RHP Billy Koch and cash considerations to **Marlins** for minor league SS Wilson Valdez.

**Astros** traded OF Richard Hidalgo to **Mets** for RHP David Weathers and minor league RHP Jeremy Griffiths.

**JUNE 18**

**Orioles** signed INF/OF David Newhan.
**Yankees** traded LHP Gabe White to **Reds** for minor league LHP Charlie Manning.

**JUNE 19**

**Padres** claimed RHP Ricky Stone off waivers from **Astros**.

**JUNE 21**

**Orioles** traded RHP Denny Bautista to **Royals** for RHP Jason Grimsley.

**JUNE 22**

**Red Sox** signed RHP Curtis Leskanic.

**JUNE 24**

**Royals** traded OF Carlos Beltran to **Astros** for RHP Octavio Dotel, minor league C John Buck and cash considerations.
**Royals** traded RHP Octavio Dotel to **Athletics** for 3B Mark Teahen and RHP Mike Wood.

**JUNE 26**

**Indians** signed INF Aaron Boone and released RHP Jeff D'Amico.

**JUNE 27**

**Mariners** traded RHP Freddy Garcia, C Ben Davis and cash considerations to **White Sox** for C Miguel Olivo and minor leaguers OF Jeremy Reed and INF Michael Morse.

**JUNE 30**

**Red Sox** organization signed RHP Pedro Astacio.

**JULY 2**

**Pirates** traded OF Ruben Mateo to **Royals** for cash considerations.

**JULY 11**

**Expos** released INF Andy Fox.

**JULY 14**

**Rangers** organization signed INF Andy Fox.

**JULY 18**

**Expos** traded OF Carl Everett and cash considerations to **White Sox** for RHP Gary Majewski and minor league RHP Jon Rauch.

**JULY 19**

**Mets** traded OF Karim Garcia to **Orioles** for RHP Mike DeJean.
**Mariners** traded SS Rich Aurilia to **Padres** for a player to be named or cash considerations.

**JULY 21**

**Cubs** traded INF Ricky Gutierrez to **Red Sox** for a player to be named or cash considerations.

**JULY 22**

**Rockies** signed RHP Jamey Wright.
**Marlins** traded LHP Darren Oliver to **Astros** for a player to be named or cash considerations.

**JULY 23**

**Cubs** organization signed INF Denny Hocking.
**Mariners** released 1B John Olerud.

**JULY 24**

**Blue Jays** traded RHP Terry Adams to **Red Sox** for minor league 3B John Hattig.

**JULY 26**

**Brewers** organization signed RHP Gary Glover.
**Devil Rays** released 1B Fred McGriff.

**JULY 27**

**Brewers** agreed to terms on deal with LHP Doug Davis.

**JULY 28**

**Reds** organization signed OF Darren Bragg.

**JULY 29**

**Athletics** released 1B/DH Eric Karros.
**Rangers** signed RHP Francisco Cordero.

**JULY 30**

**Phillies** traded minor leaguers RHP Josh Hancock and SS Anderson Machado to **Reds** for RHP Todd Jones and minor league OF Brad Correll.
**Dodgers** traded C Paul Lo Duca, OF Juan Encarnacion and RHP Guillermo Mota to **Marlins** for 1B Hee Seop Choi, RHP Brad Penny and minor league LHP Bill Murphy.
**Royals** traded INF Jose Bautista to **Pirates** for C Justin Huber.
**Pirates** traded RHP Kris Benson and minor league INF Jeff Keppinger to **Mets** for 3B Ty Wigginton, INF Jose Bautista and minor league RHP Matt Peterson.
**Devil Rays** traded RHP Victor Zambrano and minor league RHP Bartolome Fortunato to **Mets** for minor league LHP Scott Kazmir and minor league RHP Jose Diaz.
**Giants** traded RHP Felix Rodriguez to **Phillies** for OF Ricky Ledee and minor league RHP Alfredo Simon.
**Mariners** traded INF Dave Hansen to **Padres** for minor league RHP Jon Huber.

**JULY 31**

**Diamondbacks** traded OF Steve Finley and C Brent Mayne to **Dodgers** for minor leaguers C Koyie Hill, LHP Bill Murphy and OF Reggie Abercrombie.
**Expos** traded SS Orlando Cabrera to **Red Sox**. **Twins** traded 1B Doug Mientkiewicz to **Cubs**. **Cubs** traded Mientkiewicz to **Red Sox** and SS Alex Gonzalez, minor league RHP Francis Beltran and minor league INF Brendan Harris to **Expos** and minor league LHP Justin Jones to **Twins**. **Red Sox** traded SS Nomar Garciaparra, minor league OF Matt Murton and cash considerations to **Cubs**.
**Dodgers** traded OF Dave Roberts to **Red Sox** for minor league OF Henri Stanley.
**White Sox** traded RHP Esteban Loaiza to **Yankees** for RHP Jose Contreras and cash considerations.
**Padres** traded RHP Ismael Valdez to **Marlins** for minor league RHP Travis Chick.
**Royals** traded RHP Rudy Seanez to **Marlins** for OF Abraham Nunez.
**Mets** traded RHP Scott Erickson and cash considerations to **Rangers** for a player to be named.
**Pirates** released INF Chris Stynes.
**Dodgers** traded LHP Tom Martin to **Braves** for minor league LHP Matt Merricks.

**AUGUST 3**

**Yankees** signed 1B John Olerud.

**AUGUST 4**

**Angels** organization signed 1B Andres Galarraga.

**AUGUST 5**

**Diamondbacks** traded 2B Roberto Alomar to **White Sox** for cash considerations and a player to be named.

**AUGUST 6**

**Mariners** traded LHP Mike Myers to **Red Sox** for cash or a player to be named.
**Rockies** traded OF Larry Walker and cash considerations to **Cardinals** for minor league RHP Jason Burch and two players to be named.
**Mets** released OF Shane Spencer.

**AUGUST 9**

**Reds** traded RHP Cory Lidle to **Phillies** for minor leaguers OF Javon Moran and LHP Joe Wilson and a player to be named.

**AUGUST 12**

**Indians** released OF Alex Escobar.

**AUGUST 13**

**Royals** claimed RHP Matt Kinney off waivers from **Brewers**.
**Devil Rays** released OF Robert Fick.

**AUGUST 14**

**Pirates** released 1B Randall Simon.
**Devil Rays** released LHP Damian Moss.

**AUGUST 16**

**Reds** organization signed LHP Damian Moss.
**Yankees** organization signed OF Shane Spencer.
**Cardinals** organization signed RHP Danny Patterson.

**AUGUST 17**

**White Sox** claimed OF Alex Escobar off waivers from **Indians**.
**Mets** traded C Tom Wilson to **Dodgers** for minor league C Tony Socarras.

**AUGUST 19**

**Diamondbacks** traded RHP Elmer Dessens to **Dodgers** for minor league OF Jereme Milons.
**Cubs** organization signed INF Neifi Perez.
**Devil Rays** signed 1B Randall Simon.

**AUGUST 26**

**Orioles** released OF Karim Garcia.

**AUGUST 27**

**Mets** traded RHP **Dan Wheeler** to Astros for minor league OF Adam Seuss.

**AUGUST 31**

**Diamondbacks** claimed RHP Chad Durbin off waivers from **Indians**.
**Brewers** traded OF Ben Grieve to **Cubs** for a player to be named.
**Tigers** traded C Mike DiFelice to **Cubs** for a player to be named.
**Mariners** traded C Pat Borders to **Twins** for minor league OF B.J. Garbe.

**SEPTEMBER 2**

**Brewers** traded RHP Dave Burba to **Giants** for minor league LHP Josh Habel.

**SEPTEMBER 3**

**Red Sox** claimed INF Tim Hummel off waivers from **Reds**.
**Brewers** claimed LHP Andy Pratt off waivers from **Cubs**.

**SEPTEMBER 8**

**Devil Rays** released 1B Randall Simon.

**SEPTEMBER 10**

**Rangers** claimed LHP Michael Tejera off waivers from **Marlins.**

**SEPTEMBER 13**

**Blue Jays** signed OF/INF Frank Catalanotto.

**SEPTEMBER 15**

**Royals** signed OF Matt Stairs.

**SEPTEMBER 16**

**Expos** traded SS Alex Gonzalez to **Padres** for a player to be named or cash considerations.

**OCTOBER 4**

**White Sox** agreed to terms on deal with RHP Cliff Politte.

**OCTOBER 6**

**Athletics** claimed RHP Tim Harikkala off waivers from **Rockies**.
**Marlins** released RHP Billy Koch.

**OCTOBER 7**

**Padres** released RHP Jay Witasick.

**OCTOBER 15**

**Tigers** claimed OF Dewayne Wise off waivers from **Braves**.
**Phillies** claimed LHP Aaron Fultz off waivers from **Twins**.

**OCTOBER 22**

**Indians** agreed to terms on deal with RHP Bob Howry.

**OCTOBER 27**

**Orioles** signed INF Rafael Palmeiro.

**October 28**

**Indians** signed RHP Scott Elarton.

**OCTOBER 29**

**Tigers** signed LHP Jamie Walker.

**NOVEMBER 5**

**Cubs** agreed to terms on deal with INF Neifi Perez.

**NOVEMBER 8**

**Angels** organization signed OF Curtis Pride.
**Padres** traded OF Terrence Long, RHP Dennis Tankersley and cash to **Royals** for LHP Darrell May and RHP Ryan Bukvich.
**Expos** released RHP Rocky Biddle.

**NOVEMBER 11**

**Marlins** signed RHP Travis Smith.
**Pirates** agreed to terms on deals with RHPs Jose Mesa and Salomon Torres.

**NOVEMBER 12**

**Reds** signed C Jason LaRue.
**Rangers** signed RHP Doug Brocail.

**NOVEMBER 14**

**Giants** signed SS Omar Vizquel.

**NOVEMBER 16**

**Expos** agreed to terms on deals with 3B Vinny Castilla and INF Cristian Guzman.
**Phillies** signed RHP Cory Lidle.

**NOVEMBER 17**

**Tigers** signed RHP Troy Percival.
**Padres** organization signed INFs Damian Jackson and Jesse Garcia.

**NOVEMBER 19**

**Expos** traded INF Maicer Izturis and OF Juan Rivera to **Angels** for OF Jose Guillen.
**White Sox** agreed to terms on deal with RHP Jon Garland.
**Athletics** organization signed INF/OF Jermaine Clark and OFs Hiram Bocachica and Jack Cust.
**Devil Rays** released INF Geoff Blum, RHP Jeremi Gonzalez and INF/OF Damian Rolls.
**Rangers** organization signed RHPs John Wasdin and Vladimir Nunez, INF Esteban German, OFs Chad Allen and Jason Conti.
**Cardinals** released 2B Marlon Anderson and RHP Jason Simontacchi.

**NOVEMBER 20**

**Cubs** signed LHP Glendon Rusch.

**NOVEMBER 22**

**Marlins** signed INF Damion Easley.
**Mets** signed RHP Kris Benson.

**NOVEMBER 23**

**Twins** agreed to terms on deal with INF Juan Castro.
**Blue Jays** organization signed C Greg Myers.

**NOVEMBER 24**

**Indians** signed RHP Bob Wickman.
**Twins** signed C Mike Redmond.
**Padres** agreed to terms on deal with RHP Rudy Seanez.

**NOVEMBER 27**

**Pirates** traded C Jason Kendall to **Athletics** for LHPs Mark Redman and Arthur Rhodes and cash considerations.

**NOVEMBER 29**

**Red Sox** agreed to terms on deal with C Doug Mirabelli.
**Brewers** signed C Damian Miller.
**Padres** agreed to terms on deal with LHP Dennys Reyes.
**Expos** agreed to terms on deal with C Gary Bennett.

**NOVEMBER 30**

**Reds** signed RHP Paul Wilson.
**Marlins** organization signed INF/OF Lenny Harris.
**Giants** signed RHP Armando Benitez.
**Rangers** organization signed C Robert Machado.

**DECEMBER 2**

**Indians** traded INF John McDonald to **Blue Jays** for a player to be named.
**Pirates** released SS Abraham Nunez.
**Rangers** organization signed LHP Michael Tejera.
**Blue Jays** signed INF Frank Menechino.

**DECEMBER 3**

**Astros** signed INF Jose Vizcaino.
**Yankees** traded LHP Felix Heredia to **Mets** for LHP Mike Stanton and cash considerations.
**Yankees** signed C John Flaherty.
**Yankees** traded OF Kenny Lofton to **Phillies** for RHP Felix Rodriguez.

**DECEMBER 6**

**Dodgers** agreed to terms on deal with OF Ricky Ledee.
**Phillies** signed C Todd Pratt.

**DECEMBER 7**

**Cubs** agreed to terms on deals with C Henry Blanco, INF Todd Walker and SS Nomar Garciaparra.
**Astros** signed OF Orlando Palmeiro.
**Dodgers** signed RHP Elmer Dessens.
**Twins** signed RHP Brad Radke.
**Mariners** signed C Dan Wilson.

**DECEMBER 8**

**Orioles** signed OF B.J. Surhoff.
**White Sox** signed RHP Dustin Hermanson.
**Marlins** signed LHP Al Leiter.
**Brewers** signed C Chad Moeller.
**Mets** signed RHP Mike DeJean.
**Phillies** signed RHP Jon Lieber and LHP Rheal Cormier.
**Rangers** signed C Sandy Alomar Jr.
**Royals** organization signed RHP Kevin Appier.
**Padres** signed RHP Woody Williams and INF Geoff Blum.

**DECEMBER 9**

**Diamondbacks** signed 3B Troy Glaus.
**Braves** signed INF Julio Franco.
**Red Sox** signed RHP Matt Mantei.
**White Sox** signed OF Jermaine Dye.
**Dodgers** signed INF Jeff Kent.
**Padres** signed INF Eric Young.

**DECEMBER 10**

**Diamondbacks** signed RHP Russ Ortiz.
**Cardinals** signed RHPs Matt Morris and Cal Eldred and OF John Mabry.
**Rangers** signed OF Richard Hidalgo.

**DECEMBER 11**

**Brewers** traded RHP Dan Kolb to **Braves** for RHP Jose Capellan and a player to be named.
**Indians** traded OF Matt Lawton to **Pirates** for LHP Arthur Rhodes.
**Nationals** released LHP Chad Bentz.

**DECEMBER 12**

**Angels** agreed to terms on deal with OF Steve Finley.

**DECEMBER 13**

**Brewers** traded OF Scott Podsednik, RHP Luis Vizcaino and a player to be named to **White Sox** for OF Carlos Lee.
**Marlins** signed RHP Todd Jones.
**Devil Rays** traded RHP Chad Gaudin to **Blue Jays** for C Kevin Cash.
**Nationals** signed 1B Wil Cordero.
**Giants** signed C Mike Matheny.

**DECEMBER 14**

**Angels** agreed to terms on deal with RHP Paul Byrd.
**Reds** traded RHP Dustin Moseley to **Angels** for RHP Ramon Ortiz.
**Angels** signed RHP Esteban Yan.
**Diamondbacks** signed SS Royce Clayton.
**Red Sox** signed LHP David Wells.
**Indians** signed INF Jose Hernandez.
**Giants** released C A.J. Pierzynski.
**Blue Jays** signed 3B Corey Koskie.

**DECEMBER 15**

**Diamondbacks** signed INF Craig Counsell.
**Red Sox** signed LHP John Halama.
**Reds** signed RHPs David Weathers and Ben Weber.
**Athletics** traded RHP Justin Lehr and minor league OF Nelson Cruz to **Brewers** for INF Keith Ginter.
**Mariners** signed 1B Richie Sexon.
**Cardinals** signed C Einar Diaz.

**DECEMBER 16**

**Royals** traded minor league RHP Jorge Vasquez to **Braves** for OF Eli Marrero and cash considerations.
**Braves** traded RHP Juan Cruz, minor league LHP Dan Meyer and OF Charles Thomas to **Athletics** for RHP Tim Hudson.
**Braves** signed RHP John Smoltz.
**Twins** organization agreed to terms on deal with LHP Terry Mulholland.
**Mets** signed RHP Pedro Martinez.
**Pirates** traded minor league RHP Leo Nunez to **Royals** for C Benito Santiago and cash considerations.

**DECEMBER 17**

**Red Sox** signed SS Edgar Renteria.
**Marlins** organization signed LHP Chad Bentz, C Mike DiFelice and INF Wilson Delgado.
**Marlins** signed RHP Antonio Alfonseca.
**Giants** signed LHP Jason Christiansen.
**Mariners** signed 3B Adrian Beltre.
**Rangers** organization signed INF Greg Colbrunn.

**DECEMBER 18**

**Cardinals** traded RHPs Dan Haren and Kiko Calero and minor league C Daric Barton to **Athletics** for LHP Mark Mulder.

**DECEMBER 20**

**Phillies** traded INF Chris Gomez to **Orioles** for cash considerations.
**Reds** signed LHP Kent Mercker.
**Indians** signed INF Ronnie Belliard.
**Twins** signed OF Jacque Jones, INF Luis Rivas, C/DH Matthew LeCroy, OF Michael Ryan and RHP Matt Guerrier.
**Phillies** agreed to terms on deal with LHP Aaron Fultz.
**Red Sox** traded OF Dave Roberts to **Padres** for OF Jay Payton, INF Ramon Vazquez, minor league RHP David Pauley and cash.
**Rangers** signed OF David Dellucci.
**Mariners** traded RHP Aaron Taylor to **Rockies** for minor league RHP Sean Green.

**DECEMBER 21**

**Orioles** signed OF Jay Gibbons and LHP Bruce Chen.
**White Sox** agreed to terms on deal with C Ben Davis.
**Reds** signed 3B Joe Randa and agreed to terms on deal with 2B D'Angelo Jimenez.
**Rockies** signed C Todd Greene and RHP Jamey Wright.
**Dodgers** signed INF Jose Valentin and LHP Wilson Alvarez.
**Mets** agreed to terms on deal with C Vance Wilson.
**Yankees** signed 2B Tony Womack.
**Pirates** agreed to terms on deal with 1B/OF Daryle Ward.

**DECEMBER 22**

**Red Sox** agreed to terms on deal with RHP Matt Clement.
**White Sox** agreed to terms on deal with RHP Orlando Hernandez.
**Yankees** signed RHP Carl Pavano.
**Padres** agreed to terms on deals with OFs Dave Roberts and Mark Sweeney.
**Cardinals** agreed to terms on deals with OF So Taguchi and LHP Mike Myers.
**Nationals** agreed to terms on deal with C Brian Schneider.
**Devil Rays** signed 1B/DH Josh Phelps.

**DECEMBER 23**

**Dodgers** signed OF J.D. Drew.
**Red Sox** signed RHP Wade Miller.

**DECEMBER 25**

**Cardinals** organization signed INF Abraham Nunez.
**Royals** signed RHP Jose Lima.

**DECEMBER 27**

**Giants** signed OF Moises Alou.
**Reds** signed LHP Eric Milton.
**Cubs** signed OF Todd Hollandsworth.

**DECEMBER 29**

**Yankees** signed RHP Jaret Wright.

**DECEMBER 31**

**Yankees** signed 1B Tino Martinez.

# AWARD WINNERS

## THE SPORTING NEWS

### AMERICAN LEAGUE

**Pitcher of the Year:** Johan Santana, Minnesota
**Rookie Player of the Year:** Bobby Crosby, SS, Oakland
**Reliever of the Year:** Mariano Rivera, New York
**Comeback Player of the Year:** Paul Konerko, 1B, Chicago
**Managers of the Year:** Buck Showalter, Texas, and Ron Gardenhire, Minnesota

### MAJOR LEAGUE

**Player of the Year:** Barry Bonds, San Francisco
**Executive of the Year:** Walt Jocketty, St. Louis.

### NATIONAL LEAGUE

**Pitcher of the Year:** Jason Schmidt, San Francisco
**Rookie Player of the Year:** Jason Bay, OF, Pittsburgh
**Reliever of the Year:** Eric Gagne, Los Angeles
**Comeback Player of the Year:** Chris Carpenter, P, St. Louis
**Manager of the Year:** Bobby Cox, Atlanta

### MINOR LEAGUE

**Player of the Year:** Dallas McPherson, 3B, Arkansas, Texas, and Salt Lake, Pacific Coast

**Manager of the Year:** Wally Backman, Lancaster, California

**Executives of the Year:** Peter Bragan, president, Jacksonville, Southern, and Peter Bragan Jr., vice president/general manager, Jacksonville, Southern

## BASEBALL WRITERS' ASSOCIATION OF AMERICA

### AMERICAN LEAGUE

MOST VALUABLE PLAYER

| Player, Team | 1 | 2 | 3 | 4 | 5 | 6 | 7 | 8 | 9 | 10 | Pts. |
|---|---|---|---|---|---|---|---|---|---|---|---|
| Vladimir Guerrero, Anaheim | 21 | 5 | 1 | 1 | - | - | - | - | - | - | 354 |
| Gary Sheffied, New York | 5 | 8 | 9 | 4 | 2 | - | - | - | - | - | 254 |
| Manny Ramirez, Boston | 1 | 14 | 9 | 2 | 2 | - | - | - | - | - | 238 |
| David Ortiz, Boston | 1 | - | 5 | 9 | 2 | 5 | 5 | - | - | - | 174 |
| Miguel Tejada, Baltimore | - | 1 | - | 6 | 2 | 7 | 2 | 4 | 2 | 1 | 123 |
| Johan Santana, Minnesota | - | - | 2 | 1 | 7 | 5 | 4 | 2 | 2 | 1 | 117 |
| Ichiro Suzuki, Seattle | - | - | 1 | - | 6 | 2 | 6 | 4 | 1 | 6 | 98 |
| Michael Young, Texas | - | - | 1 | 4 | 2 | 2 | 4 | 4 | 3 | - | 92 |
| Mariano Rivera, New York | - | - | - | - | 2 | 3 | 3 | 3 | 3 | 5 | 59 |
| Ivan Rodriguez, Detroit | - | - | - | 1 | 1 | 1 | - | 2 | 5 | 2 | 36 |
| Curt Schilling, Boston | - | - | - | - | - | - | 2 | 2 | - | - | 14 |
| Joe Nathan, Minnesota | - | - | - | - | 1 | 1 | - | - | - | 1 | 12 |
| Derek Jeter, New York | - | - | - | - | 1 | - | - | 1 | 1 | - | 11 |
| Mark Kotsay, Oakland | - | - | - | - | - | 1 | - | - | 1 | 1 | 8 |
| Alex Rodriguez, New York | - | - | - | - | - | - | - | 2 | 1 | - | 8 |
| Johnny Damon, Boston | - | - | - | - | - | - | - | 1 | 2 | - | 7 |
| Paul Konerko, Chicago | - | - | - | - | - | - | - | - | 1 | 5 | 7 |
| Hank Blalock, Texas | - | - | - | - | - | 1 | - | - | - | - | 5 |
| Melvin Mora, Baltimore | - | - | - | - | - | - | - | 1 | 1 | - | 5 |
| Mark Teixeira, Texas | - | - | - | - | - | - | - | 1 | - | 2 | 5 |
| Torii Hunter, Minnesota | - | - | - | - | - | - | 1 | - | - | - | 4 |
| Victor Martinez, Cleveland | - | - | - | - | - | - | 1 | - | - | - | 4 |
| Erubiel Durazo, Oakland | - | - | - | - | - | - | - | 1 | - | - | 3 |
| Francisco Cordero, Texas | - | - | - | - | - | - | - | - | 1 | - | 2 |
| Lew Ford, Minnesota | - | - | - | - | - | - | - | - | 1 | - | 2 |
| Carlos Guillen, Detroit | - | - | - | - | - | - | - | - | 1 | - | 2 |
| Travis Hafner, Cleveland | - | - | - | - | - | - | - | - | 1 | - | 2 |
| Hideki Matsui, New York | - | - | - | - | - | - | - | - | 1 | - | 2 |
| Chone Figgins, Anaheim | - | - | - | - | - | - | - | - | - | 2 | 2 |
| Eric Chavez, Oakland | - | - | - | - | - | - | - | - | - | 1 | 1 |
| Jason Varitek, Boston | - | - | - | - | - | - | - | - | - | 1 | 1 |

Fourteen points awarded for a first-place vote, nine for second and down to one for 10th.

CY YOUNG AWARD

| Pitcher, Team | 1 | 2 | 3 | Pts. |
|---|---|---|---|---|
| Johan Santana, Minnesota | 28 | - | - | 140 |
| Curt Schilling, Boston | - | 27 | 1 | 82 |
| Mariano Rivera, New York | - | 1 | 24 | 27 |
| Pedro Martinez, Boston | - | - | 1 | 1 |
| Joe Nathan, Minnesota | - | - | 1 | 1 |
| Francisco Rodriguez, Anaheim | - | - | 1 | 1 |

Five points awarded for a first-place vote, three for second and one for third.

MANAGER OF THE YEAR

| Manager, Team | 1 | 2 | 3 | Pts. |
|---|---|---|---|---|
| Buck Showalter, Texas | 14 | 9 | 4 | 101 |
| Ron Gardenhire, Minnesota | 11 | 11 | 3 | 91 |
| Mike Scioscia, Anaheim | 2 | 4 | 9 | 31 |
| Joe Torre, New York | 1 | 2 | 7 | 18 |
| Terry Francona, Boston | - | 2 | 2 | 8 |
| Eric Wedge, Cleveland | - | - | 3 | 3 |

Five points awarded for a first-place vote, three for second and one for third.

### ROOKIE OF THE YEAR

| Player, Team | 1 | 2 | 3 | Pts. |
|---|---|---|---|---|
| Bobby Crosby, Oakland | 27 | 1 | - | 138 |
| Shingo Takatsu, Chicago | 1 | 11 | 6 | 44 |
| Daniel Cabrera. Baltimore | - | 7 | 8 | 29 |
| Zack Greinke, Kansas City | - | 4 | 4 | 16 |
| Alexis Rios, Toronto | - | 3 | 3 | 12 |
| David DeJesus, Kansas City | - | 1 | 3 | 6 |
| Ross Gload, Chicago | - | 1 | 1 | 4 |
| John Buck, Kansas City | - | - | 1 | 1 |
| David Bush, Toronto | - | - | 1 | 1 |
| Nate Robertson, Detroit | - | - | 1 | 1 |

Five points awarded for a first-place vote, three for second and one for third.

## NATIONAL LEAGUE

### MOST VALUABLE PLAYER

| Player, Team | 1 | 2 | 3 | 4 | 5 | 6 | 7 | 8 | 9 | 10 | Pts. |
|---|---|---|---|---|---|---|---|---|---|---|---|
| Barry Bonds, San Francisco | 24 | 7 | 1 | - | - | - | - | - | - | - | 407 |
| Adrian Beltre, Los Angeles | 6 | 21 | 3 | 2 | - | - | - | - | - | - | 311 |
| Albert Pujols, St. Louis | 1 | 1 | 20 | 5 | 4 | 1 | - | - | - | - | 247 |
| Scott Rolen, St. Louis | 1 | 3 | 7 | 12 | 5 | 3 | - | - | - | - | 226 |
| Jim Edmonds, St. Louis | - | - | - | 5 | 12 | 6 | 2 | 3 | 3 | - | 160 |
| J.D. Drew, Atlanta | - | - | - | 1 | 5 | 6 | 6 | 7 | - | 2 | 114 |
| Lance Berkman, Houston | - | - | - | 2 | 4 | 6 | 7 | 1 | - | 1 | 100 |
| Roger Clemens, Houston | - | - | 1 | 1 | - | 4 | 3 | 3 | 2 | 1 | 61 |
| Mark Loretta, San Diego | - | - | - | 1 | - | 1 | 3 | 5 | 5 | 1 | 50 |
| Aramis Ramirez, Chicago | - | - | - | 1 | 1 | - | 2 | 2 | 5 | 5 | 42 |
| Eric Gagne, Los Angeles | - | - | - | - | - | 3 | 3 | 1 | - | - | 30 |
| Carlos Beltran, Houston | - | - | - | 1 | - | - | 1 | 3 | - | - | 20 |
| Jeff Kent, Houston | - | - | - | 1 | - | 1 | - | 1 | 1 | 1 | 18 |
| Steve Finley, Arizona-Los Angeles | - | - | - | - | - | 1 | 2 | - | 1 | - | 15 |
| Moises Alou, Chicago | - | - | - | - | - | - | - | 3 | 2 | 2 | 15 |
| Juan Pierre, Florida | - | - | - | - | - | - | 1 | - | 1 | 3 | 9 |
| Todd Helton, Colorado | - | - | - | - | - | - | - | 1 | 1 | 4 | 9 |
| Johnny Estrada, Atlanta | - | - | - | - | - | - | 1 | - | 2 | - | 8 |
| Randy Johnson, Arizona | - | - | - | - | - | - | 1 | - | 1 | 1 | 7 |
| Jim Thome, Philadelphia | - | - | - | - | - | - | - | - | 2 | 3 | 7 |
| John Smoltz, Atlanta | - | - | - | - | 1 | - | - | - | - | - | 6 |
| Miguel Cabrera, Florida | - | - | - | - | - | - | - | - | 1 | 3 | 5 |
| Armando Benitez, Florida | - | - | - | - | - | - | - | 1 | - | - | 3 |
| Jeromy Burnitz, Colorado | - | - | - | - | - | - | - | 1 | - | - | 3 |
| Bobby Abreu, Philadelphia | - | - | - | - | - | - | - | - | 1 | 1 | 3 |
| Vinny Castilla, Colorado | - | - | - | - | - | - | - | - | 1 | 1 | 3 |
| Roy Oswalt, Houston | - | - | - | - | - | - | - | - | 1 | 1 | 3 |
| Adam Dunn, Cincinnati | - | - | - | - | - | - | - | - | 1 | - | 2 |
| Carlos Zambrano, Chicago | - | - | - | - | - | - | - | - | 1 | - | 2 |
| Phil Nevin, San Diego | - | - | - | - | - | - | - | - | - | 1 | 1 |
| Jimmy Rollins, Philadelphia | - | - | - | - | - | - | - | - | - | 1 | 1 |

Fourteen points awarded for a first-place vote, nine for second and down to one for 10th.

### CY YOUNG AWARD

| Pitcher, Team | 1 | 2 | 3 | Pts. |
|---|---|---|---|---|
| Roger Clemens, Houston | 23 | 8 | 1 | 140 |
| Randy Johnson, Arizona | 8 | 18 | 3 | 97 |
| Roy Oswalt, Houston | 1 | 3 | 5 | 19 |
| Jason Schmidt, San Francisco | - | 1 | 10 | 13 |
| Carlos Zambrano, Chicago | - | 1 | 5 | 8 |
| Carl Pavano, Florida | - | 1 | 3 | 6 |
| Eric Gagne, Los Angeles | - | - | 3 | 3 |
| Brad Lidge, Houston | - | - | 1 | 1 |
| Ben Sheets, Milwaukee | - | - | 1 | 1 |

Five points awarded for a first-place vote, three for second and one for third.

### MANAGER OF THE YEAR

| Manager, Team | 1 | 2 | 3 | Pts. |
|---|---|---|---|---|
| Bobby Cox, Atlanta | 22 | 10 | - | 140 |
| Tony La Russa, St. Louis | 4 | 9 | 15 | 62 |
| Jim Tracy, Los Angeles | 4 | 7 | 11 | 52 |
| Phil Garner, Houston | 2 | 4 | 5 | 27 |
| Felipe Alou, San Francisco | - | 1 | 1 | 4 |
| Bruce Bochy, San Diego | - | 1 | - | 3 |

Five points awarded for a first-place vote, three for second and one for third.

### ROOKIE OF THE YEAR

| Player, Team | 1 | 2 | 3 | Pts. |
|---|---|---|---|---|
| Jason Bay, Pittsburgh | 25 | 7 | - | 146 |
| Khalil Greene, San Diego | 7 | 24 | 1 | 108 |
| Akinori Otsuka, San Diego | - | 1 | 20 | 23 |
| Aaron Miles, Colorado | - | - | 6 | 6 |
| Matt Holliday, Colorado | - | - | 3 | 3 |
| Kazuo Matsui, New York | - | - | 1 | 1 |
| Terrmel Sledge, Montreal | - | - | 1 | 1 |

Five points awarded for a first-place vote, three for second and one for third.

# MISCELLANEOUS

## ATTENDANCE

### AMERICAN LEAGUE

| | 2004 | | | | 2003 | | | *Pct. |
|---|---|---|---|---|---|---|---|---|
| | Home | Road | Dates | Home Avg. | Home | Dates | Average | Change |
| New York | 3,775,292 | 3,308,666 | 79 | 47,789 | 3,465,585 | 81 | 42,785 | +11.7 |
| Anaheim | 3,375,677 | 2,391,458 | 81 | 41,675 | 3,061,090 | 81 | 37,791 | +10.3 |
| Seattle | 2,940,731 | 2,260,923 | 81 | 36,305 | 3,268,864 | 81 | 40,356 | -10.0 |
| Boston | 2,837,304 | 2,880,236 | 81 | 35,028 | 2,724,165 | 81 | 33,632 | +4.2 |
| Baltimore | 2,747,573 | 2,359,383 | 80 | 34,345 | 2,454,523 | 81 | 30,303 | +13.3 |
| Texas | 2,513,685 | 2,370,971 | 79 | 31,819 | 2,095,132 | 81 | 25,866 | +23.0 |
| Oakland | 2,201,516 | 2,585,067 | 81 | 27,179 | 2,216,596 | 81 | 27,365 | -0.7 |
| Chicago | 1,930,537 | 2,049,632 | 79 | 24,437 | 1,939,611 | 81 | 23,946 | +0.2 |
| Detroit | 1,917,004 | 2,188,739 | 80 | 23,963 | 1,368,285 | 80 | 17,104 | +40.1 |
| Minnesota | 1,911,418 | 2,144,301 | 81 | 23,598 | 1,946,011 | 81 | 24,025 | -1.8 |
| Toronto | 1,900,041 | 2,127,243 | 81 | 23,457 | 1,799,458 | 81 | 22,216 | +5.6 |
| Cleveland | 1,814,401 | 2,217,623 | 81 | 22,400 | 1,730,001 | 81 | 21,358 | +4.9 |
| Kansas City | 1,661,478 | 2,053,233 | 79 | 21,031 | 1,779,895 | 78 | 22,819 | -7.8 |
| Tampa Bay | 1,275,011 | 2,262,229 | 79 | 16,139 | 1,058,622 | 81 | 13,069 | +23.5 |
| **Totals** | 32,801,668 | 33,199,704 | 1,122 | 29,235 | 30,907,838 | 1130 | 27,352 | +6.9 |

*Percentage change refers to the change in average home attendance between 2004 and 2003.

### NATIONAL LEAGUE

| | 2004 | | | | 2003 | | | *Pct. |
|---|---|---|---|---|---|---|---|---|
| | Home | Road | Dates | Home Avg. | Home | Dates | Average | Change |
| Los Angeles | 3,488,283 | 2,578,981 | 81 | 43,065 | 3,138,626 | 81 | 38,748 | +11.1 |
| San Francisco | 3,256,858 | 2,895,206 | 81 | 40,208 | 3,264,903 | 81 | 40,307 | -0.2 |
| Philadelphia | 3,250,092 | 2,155,284 | 80 | 40,626 | 2,223,353 | 78 | 28,505 | +42.5 |
| Chicago | 3,170,184 | 2,893,837 | 81 | 39,138 | 2,962,630 | 80 | 37,033 | +5.7 |
| Houston | 3,087,872 | 2,461,031 | 81 | 38,122 | 2,454,038 | 81 | 30,297 | +25.8 |
| St. Louis | 3,048,427 | 2,484,345 | 81 | 37,635 | 2,910,371 | 81 | 35,931 | +4.7 |
| San Diego | 3,016,752 | 2,587,940 | 81 | 37,244 | 2,030,064 | 81 | 25,063 | +48.6 |
| Arizona | 2,519,560 | 2,475,873 | 81 | 31,106 | 2,805,202 | 81 | 34,632 | -10.2 |
| Colorado | 2,338,069 | 2,588,553 | 79 | 29,596 | 2,334,085 | 81 | 28,816 | +2.7 |
| Atlanta | 2,322,565 | 2,400,007 | 79 | 29,400 | 2,401,082 | 79 | 30,393 | -3.3 |
| New York | 2,318,321 | 2,406,142 | 80 | 28,979 | 2,132,341 | 77 | 27,693 | +4.6 |
| Cincinnati | 2,287,250 | 2,509,203 | 81 | 28,238 | 2,355,160 | 81 | 29,076 | -2.9 |
| Milwaukee | 2,062,382 | 2,350,028 | 81 | 25,462 | 1,685,049 | 81 | 20,803 | +22.4 |
| Florida | 1,723,105 | 2,355,110 | 78 | 22,091 | 1,303,214 | 80 | 16,290 | +35.6 |
| Pittsburgh | 1,583,031 | 2,366,479 | 75 | 21,107 | 1,636,761 | 78 | 20,984 | +0.6 |
| Montreal | 748,550 | 2,315,246 | 80 | 9,357 | 1,023,680 | 81 | 12,638 | -26.0 |
| **Totals** | 40,221,301 | 39,823,265 | 1,280 | 31,423 | 36,660,559 | 1282 | 28,596 | +9.9 |
| **Major League totals** | 73,022,969 | 73,022,969 | 2,402 | 30,401 | 67,568,397 | 2412 | 28,013 | +8.5 |

*Percentage change refers to the change in average home attendance between 2004 and 2003.

## DEBUTS

| Player | Pos. | Team | Birth date | Birthplace | Debut | *Age |
|---|---|---|---|---|---|---|
| Aardsma, David A. | P | San Francisco | 12-27-81 | Denver, Colorado | 4-6 | 22 |
| Adams, Jon Michael | P | Milwaukee | 7-29-78 | Corpus Christi, Texas | 5-18 | 25 |
| Adams, Russ Moore | PH | Toronto | 8-30-80 | Laurinburg, North Carolina | 9-3 | 24 |
| Aguila, Christopher Louis | PH | Florida | 2-23-79 | Redwood City, California | 6-28 | 25 |
| Alfaro, Jason | SS | Houston | 11-29-77 | San Antonio, Texas | 9-9 | 26 |
| Alvarez, Abraham | P | Boston | 10-17-82 | Los Angeles, California | 7-22 | 21 |
| Aquino, Gregori Emilio | P | Arizona | 1-11-78 | Palenque, Dominican Republic | 7-2 | 26 |
| Atchison, Scott Barhan | P | Seattle | 3-29-76 | Denton, Texas | 7-31 | 28 |
| Baek, Cha Seung | P | Seattle | 5-29-80 | Pusan, South Korea | 8-8 | 24 |
| Bajenaru, Jeffrey Michael | P | Chicago A.L. | 3-21-78 | Pomona, California | 9-4 | 26 |
| Bartlett, Jason Alan | SS | Minnesota | 10-30-79 | Mountain View, California | 8-3 | 24 |
| Bartosh, Clifford Paul | P | Cleveland | 9- 5-79 | West, Texas | 5-15 | 24 |
| Bautista, Denny M. | P | Baltimore | 8-23-80 | Sanchez, Dominican Republic | 5-25 | 23 |
| Bautista, Jose Antonio | PR | Baltimore | 10-19-80 | Santo Domingo, Dominican Republic | 4-4 | 23 |
| Bell, Heath Justin | P | New York N.L. | 9-29-77 | Oceanside, California | 8-24 | 26 |
| Bennett, David Jeffrey | P | Milwaukee | 6-10-80 | Donelson, Tennessee | 4-6 | 23 |
| Bentz, Chad Robert | P | Montreal | 5- 5-80 | Seward, Alaska | 4-7 | 23 |
| Bergman, Dustin Michael | P | Anaheim | 2- 1-78 | Carson City, Nevada | 6-9 | 26 |
| Blackley, Travis Jarrod | P | Seattle | 11- 4-82 | Melbourne, Australia | 7-1 | 21 |

| Player | Pos. | Team | Birth date | Birthplace | Debut | *Age |
|---|---|---|---|---|---|---|
| Blanco, Andres Eloy | SS | Kansas City | 4-11-84 | Moron, Venezuela | 4-17 | 20 |
| Blanton, Joseph Matthew | P | Oakland | 12-11-80 | Bowling Green, Kentucky | 9-21 | 23 |
| Brazell, Craig Walter | PH | New York N.L. | 5-10-80 | Montgomery, Alabama | 8-17 | 24 |
| Brazoban, Yhency Jose | P | Los Angeles | 6-11-80 | Santo Domingo, Dominican Republic | 8-5 | 24 |
| Brooks, Frank J. | P | Pittsburgh | 9- 6-78 | Brooklyn, New York | 8-27 | 25 |
| Brown, Jamie Monroe | P | Boston | 3-31-77 | Meridian, Mississippi | 5-20 | 27 |
| Bruney, Brian Anthony | P | Arizona | 2-17-82 | Astoria, Oregon | 5-8 | 22 |
| Buck, Johnathan R. | C | Kansas City | 7- 7-80 | Kemmerer, Wyoming | 6-25 | 23 |
| Burke, Christopher A. | 2B | Houston | 3-11-80 | Louisville, Kentucky | 7-4 | 24 |
| Burnett, Sean Richard | P | Pittsburgh | 9-17-82 | Dunedin, Florida | 5-30 | 21 |
| Bush, David T. | P | Toronto | 11- 9-79 | Pittsburgh, Pennsylvania | 7-2 | 24 |
| Cabrera, Daniel Alberto | P | Baltimore | 5-28-81 | San Pedro de Macoris, Dominican Rep. | 5-13 | 22 |
| Cabrera, Fernando Jose | P | Cleveland | 11-16-81 | Toja Baja, Puerto Rico | 8-20 | 22 |
| Cali, Carmen S. | P | St. Louis | 11- 2-78 | Cleveland, Ohio | 9-8 | 25 |
| Camp, Shawn Anthony | P | Kansas City | 11-18-75 | Fairfax, Virginia | 4-5 | 28 |
| Cantu, Jorge Luis | PH | Tampa Bay | 1-30-82 | Reynosa, Mexico | 7-17 | 22 |
| Capellan, Jose Francisco | P | Atlanta | 1-13-81 | Cotui, Dominican Republic | 9-12 | 23 |
| Castillo, Jose | 2B | Pittsburgh | 3-19-81 | Las Mercedes, Venezuela | 4-7 | 23 |
| Castro, Ramon Alfredo | PH | Oakland | 10-23-79 | Valencia, Venezuela | 6-21 | 24 |
| Chacin, Gustavo G. Adolfo | P | Toronto | 12- 4-80 | Maracaibo, Venezuela | 9-20 | 23 |
| Church, Ryan Matthew | PH | Montreal | 10-14-78 | Santa Barbara, California | 8-21 | 25 |
| Closser, Jeffrey Darrin | C | Colorado | 1-15-80 | Beech Grove, Indiana | 6-30 | 24 |
| Colon, Roman Benedicto | P | Atlanta | 8-13-79 | Montecristi, Dominican Republic | 8-21 | 25 |
| Cormier, Lance Robert | P | Arizona | 8-19-80 | Lafayette, Louisiana | 6-19 | 23 |
| Crain, Jesse Alan | P | Minnesota | 7- 5-81 | Toronto, Ontario | 8-5 | 23 |
| Crozier, Eric Le Roi | PH | Toronto | 8-11-78 | Columbus, Ohio | 9-4 | 26 |
| Cruceta, Francisco Alberto | P | Cleveland | 7- 4-81 | La Vega, Dominican Republic | 9-21 | 23 |
| Daigle, Sean Casey | P | Arizona | 4- 4-81 | Lake Charles, Louisiana | 4-9 | 23 |
| Dallimore, Brian Scott | PH | San Francisco | 11-15-73 | Las Vegas, Nevada | 4-29 | 30 |
| de la Rosa, Jorge Alberto | P | Milwaukee | 4- 5-81 | Monterrey, Mexico | 8-14 | 23 |
| Denney, Kyle Dean | P | Cleveland | 7-27-77 | Prague, Oklahoma | 9-14 | 27 |
| DeVore, Douglas Rinehart | PH | Arizona | 12-14-77 | Columbus, Ohio | 5-6 | 26 |
| Diaz, Felix Antonio | P | Chicago A.L. | 7-27-80 | Las Mata de Farfan, Dominican Republic | 5-13 | 23 |
| Diaz, Victor Israel | RF | New York N.L. | 12-10-81 | Santo Domingo, Dominican Republic | 9-11 | 22 |
| DiNardo, Leonard Edward | P | Boston | 9-19-79 | Miami, Florida | 4-23 | 24 |
| Dobbs, Gregory Stuart | PH | Seattle | 7- 2-78 | Los Angeles, California | 9-8 | 26 |
| Dohmann, Christopher Scott | P | Colorado | 2-13-78 | New Orleans, Louisiana | 5-15 | 26 |
| Dominique, Andrew John | 1B | Boston | 10-30-75 | Tarzana, California | 5-25 | 28 |
| Dubois, Jason Bradford | PH | Chicago N.L. | 3-26-79 | Virginia Beach, Virginia | 5-19 | 25 |
| Dunn, Scott Allen | P | Anaheim | 5-23-78 | San Antonio, Texas | 9-11 | 26 |
| Durbin, Joseph Adam | P | Minnesota | 2-24-82 | Portland, Oregon | 9-8 | 22 |
| Erickson, Matt | PH | Milwaukee | 7-30-75 | Appleton, Wisconsin | 7-9 | 28 |
| Floyd, Gavin Christopher | P | Philadelphia | 1-27-83 | Annapolis, Maryland | 9-3 | 21 |
| Fortunato, Bartolome | P | Tampa Bay | 8-24-74 | Santo Domingo, Dominican Republic | 6-29 | 29 |
| Francis, Jeffrey William | P | Colorado | 1- 8-81 | Vancouver, British Columbia | 8-25 | 23 |
| Francisco, Franklin | P | Texas | 9-11-79 | Santo Domingo, Dominican Republic | 5-14 | 24 |
| Frasor, Jason Andrew | P | Toronto | 8- 9-77 | Chicago, Illinois | 4-16 | 26 |
| Freeman, Raphael | CF | Colorado | 10-20-79 | Pine Bluff, Arkansas | 6-4 | 24 |
| Garcia, Jairo Paulino | P | Oakland | 3- 7-83 | Nizao, Dominican Republic | 8-9 | 21 |
| Gathright, Joey Renard | CF | Tampa Bay | 4-27-81 | Hattiesburg, Mississippi | 6-25 | 23 |
| Germano, Justin William | P | San Diego | 8- 6-82 | Pasadena, California | 5-22 | 21 |
| Gettis, Byron Earl | RF | Kansas City | 3-13-80 | Centreville, Illinois | 5-27 | 24 |
| Gil, Jerry Bienbenido | SS | Arizona | 10-14-82 | San Pedro de Macoris, Dominican Rep. | 8-22 | 21 |
| Gissell, Christopher Odell | P | Colorado | 1- 4-78 | Tacoma, Washington | 8-22 | 26 |
| Gonzalez, Adrian | 1B | Texas | 5- 8-82 | San Diego, California | 4-18 | 21 |
| Gonzalez, Luis Alberto | 2B | Colorado | 6-26-79 | Maracay, Venezuela | 4-6 | 24 |
| Gosling, Michael F. | P | Arizona | 9-23-80 | Madison, Wisconsin | 9-9 | 23 |
| Gotay, Ruben A. | 2B | Kansas City | 12-25-82 | Rio Piedras, Puerto Rico | 8-3 | 21 |
| Gracesqui, Franklyn Benjamin | P | Florida | 8-20-79 | Santo Domingo, Dominican Republic | 4-29 | 24 |
| Graman, Alex Joseph | P | New York A.L. | 11-17-77 | Huntingburg, Indiana | 4-20 | 26 |
| Granderson, Curtis | CF | Detroit | 3-16-81 | Blue Island, Illinois | 9-13 | 23 |
| Green, Andrew M. | PR | Arizona | 7- 7-77 | Lexington, Kentucky | 6-12 | 26 |
| Green, Nicholas Anthony | 2B | Atlanta | 9-10-78 | Pensacola, Florida | 5-15 | 25 |
| Greinke, Donald Zackary | P | Kansas City | 10-21-83 | Orlando, Florida | 5-22 | 20 |
| Gross, Gabriel Jordan | LF | Toronto | 10-21-79 | Baltimore, Maryland | 8-7 | 24 |
| Guerrier, Matthew Olson | P | Minnesota | 8- 2-78 | Cleveland, Ohio | 6-17 | 25 |
| Guthrie, Jeremy | P | Cleveland | 4- 8-79 | Roseburg, Oregon | 8-28 | 25 |
| Guzman, Freddy Antonio | CF | San Diego | 1-20-81 | Santo Domingo, Dominican Republic | 8-17 | 23 |
| Hairston, Scott Alexander | PH | Arizona | 5-25-80 | Fort Worth, Texas | 5-7 | 23 |
| Halsey, Bradford A. | P | New York A.L. | 2-14-81 | Houston, Texas | 6-19 | 23 |
| Harris, Brendan Michael | 3B | Chicago N.L. | 8-26-80 | Albany, New York | 7-6 | 23 |
| Hart, Jon Corey | PH | Milwaukee | 3-24-82 | Bowling Green, Kentucky | 5-25 | 22 |
| Hawpe, Bradley Bonte | PH | Colorado | 6-22-79 | Fort Worth, Texas | 5-1 | 24 |
| Hendrickson, Benjamin J. | P | Milwaukee | 2- 4-81 | St. Cloud, Minnesota | 6-2 | 23 |
| Hennessey, Brad Martin | P | San Francisco | 2- 7-80 | Toledo, Ohio | 8-7 | 24 |

| Player | Pos. | Team | Birth date | Birthplace | Debut | *Age |
|---|---|---|---|---|---|---|
| Hensley, Matthew Davis | P | Anaheim | 8-18-78 | San Diego, California | 5-4 | 25 |
| Hietpas, Joseph Carl | C | New York N.L. | 5- 1-79 | Appleton, Wisconsin | 10-3 | 25 |
| Hill, Shawn Richard | P | Montreal | 4-28-81 | Mississauga, Ontario | 6-29 | 23 |
| Holliday, Matthew Thomas | LF | Colorado | 1-15-80 | Stillwater, Oklahoma | 4-16 | 24 |
| Horgan, Joseph Paul | P | Montreal | 6- 7-77 | Sacramento, California | 6-12 | 27 |
| Howard, Ryan James | PH | Philadelphia | 11-19-79 | St. Louis, Missouri | 9-1 | 24 |
| Hughes, Travis Wade | P | Texas | 5-25-78 | Newton, Kansas | 9-26 | 26 |
| Huisman, Justin Ray | P | Kansas City | 4-16-79 | Harvey, Illinois | 4-25 | 25 |
| Izturis, Maicer E. | SS | Montreal | 9-12-80 | Barquisimeto, Venezuela | 8-27 | 23 |
| Jacobsen, Larry William | DH | Seattle | 8-30-75 | Riverton, Wyoming | 7-16 | 28 |
| Johnston, Michael Charles | P | Pittsburgh | 3-30-79 | Philadelphia, Pennsylvania | 4-7 | 25 |
| Kazmir, Scott E. | P | Tampa Bay | 1-24-84 | Houston, Texas | 8-23 | 20 |
| Kensing, Logan French | P | Florida | 7- 3-82 | San Antonio, Texas | 9-10 | 22 |
| Keppinger, Jeffrey Scott | PH | New York N.L. | 4-21-80 | Miami, Florida | 8-20 | 24 |
| Knoedler, Justin Joseph | C | San Francisco | 7-17-80 | Springfield, Illinois | 10-3 | 24 |
| Knott, Jonathan David | PH | San Diego | 8- 4-78 | Manassas, Virginia | 5-30 | 25 |
| Kotchman, Casey John | 1B | Anaheim | 2-22-83 | St. Petersburg, Florida | 5-9 | 21 |
| Kroeger, Joshua J. | LF | Arizona | 8-31-82 | Davenport, Iowa | 9-2 | 22 |
| Krynzel, David Benjamin | PH | Milwaukee | 11- 7-81 | Dayton, Ohio | 9-1 | 22 |
| Kubel, Jason James | PH | Minnesota | 5-25-82 | Belle Fourche, South Dakota | 8-31 | 22 |
| Labandeira, John Joshua | PH | Montreal | 2-25-79 | Tulare, California | 9-17 | 25 |
| LaRoche, David Adam | 1B | Atlanta | 11- 6-79 | Orange County, California | 4-7 | 24 |
| League, Brandon Paul | P | Toronto | 3-16-83 | Sacramento, California | 9-21 | 21 |
| Lehr, Charles Larry | P | Oakland | 8- 3-77 | Orange, California | 6-20 | 26 |
| Leicester, Jonathan David | P | Chicago N.L. | 2- 7-79 | Mariposa, California | 6-9 | 25 |
| Leone, Justin Paul | PH | Seattle | 7- 9-77 | Las Vegas, Nevada | 7-2 | 26 |
| Liriano, Pedro Antonio | P | Milwaukee | 10-23-80 | Fantino, Dominican Republic | 8-27 | 23 |
| Loe, Kameron D. | P | Texas | 9-10-81 | Simi Valley, California | 9-26 | 23 |
| Logan, Exavier Prente | CF | Detroit | 11-28-79 | Natchez, Mississippi | 7-21 | 24 |
| Lopez, Jose Celestino | SS | Seattle | 11-24-83 | Anzoategui, Venezuela | 7-31 | 20 |
| Lopez, Raymond Michael | PR | Seattle | 11-17-73 | Miami, Florida | 9-6 | 30 |
| Luna, Hector R. | 2B | St. Louis | 2- 1-80 | Montecristi, Dominican Republic | 4-8 | 24 |
| Madritsch, Robert A. | P | Seattle | 2-28-76 | Oak Lawn, Illinois | 7-21 | 28 |
| Maine, John K. | P | Baltimore | 5- 8-81 | Fredericksburg, Virginia | 7-23 | 23 |
| Majewski, Gary Wayne | P | Montreal | 2-26-80 | Houston, Texas | 8-26 | 24 |
| Majewski, Walter V. | PH | Baltimore | 6-19-81 | New Brunswick, New Jersey | 8-20 | 23 |
| Marsonek, Samuel R. | P | New York A.L. | 7-10-78 | Tampa, Florida | 7-11 | 26 |
| Martinez, Anastacio | P | Boston | 11- 3-78 | Santa Cruz de Villa Mella, Dominican Rep. | 5-22 | 25 |
| Matsui, Kazuo | SS | New York N.L. | 10-23-75 | Osaka, Japan | 4-6 | 28 |
| Mauer, Joseph Patrick | C | Minnesota | 4-19-83 | St. Paul, Minnesota | 4-5 | 20 |
| McConnell, John Samuel | P | Atlanta | 12-31-75 | Middletown, Ohio | 6-25 | 28 |
| McDonald, Darnell T. | RF | Baltimore | 11-17-78 | Fort Collins, Colorado | 4-30 | 25 |
| McLeary, Marty Lee | P | San Diego | 10-26-74 | Kettering, Ohio | 8-22 | 29 |
| McPherson, Dallas Lyle | PR | Anaheim | 7-23-80 | Greensboro, North Carolina | 9-10 | 24 |
| Meyer, Daniel L. | P | Atlanta | 7- 3-81 | Woodbury, New Jersey | 9-14 | 23 |
| Molina, Yadier B. | C | St. Louis | 7-13-82 | Bayamon, Puerto Rico | 6-3 | 21 |
| Munoz, Arnaldo Rafel | P | Chicago A.L. | 6-21-82 | Mao, Dominican Republic | 6-19 | 21 |
| Murphy, Donald Rex | 2B | Kansas City | 3-10-83 | Lakewood, California | 9-18 | 21 |
| Nageotte, Clinton Scott | P | Seattle | 10-25-80 | Parma, Ohio | 6-1 | 23 |
| Narron, Samuel Franklin | P | Texas | 7-12-81 | Goldsboro, North Carolina | 7-30 | 23 |
| Navarro, Dioner Faviau | C | New York A.L. | 2- 9-84 | Caracas, Venezuela | 9-7 | 20 |
| Novoa, Roberto | P | Detroit | 8-15-79 | Las Matas de Farfan, Dominican Republic | 7-29 | 24 |
| Nunez, Franklin | P | Tampa Bay | 1-18-77 | Nagua, Dominican Republic | 8-14 | 27 |
| Olson, Timothy Lane | 3B | Arizona | 8- 1-78 | Grand Forks, North Dakota | 5-30 | 25 |
| Otsuka, Akinori | P | San Diego | 1-13-72 | Chiba, Japan | 4-6 | 32 |
| Padilla, Juan Miguel | P | New York A.L. | 2-17-77 | Rio Piedras, Puerto Rico | 7-16 | 27 |
| Pascucci, Valentino Martin | RF | Montreal | 11-17-78 | Bellflower, California | 4-26 | 25 |
| Peterson, Adam L. | P | Toronto | 5-18-79 | Savannah, Georgia | 6-24 | 25 |
| Phillips, George Andrew | PR | New York A.L. | 4- 6-77 | Tuscaloosa, Alabama | 9-14 | 27 |
| Phillips, Paul Anthony | C | Kansas City | 4-15-77 | Demopolis, Alabama | 9-9 | 27 |
| Piedra, Jorge Moises | PH | Colorado | 4-17-79 | Sun Valley, California | 8-7 | 25 |
| Pond, Simon Emilio | RF | Toronto | 10-27-76 | North Vancouver, British Columbia | 4-7 | 27 |
| Proctor, Scott Christopher | P | New York A.L. | 1- 2-77 | Stuart, Florida | 4-20 | 27 |
| Qualls, Chad Michael | P | Houston | 8-17-78 | Lomita, California | 7-22 | 25 |
| Quiroz, Guillermo Antonio | DH | Toronto | 11-29-81 | Maracaibo, Venezuela | 9-4 | 22 |
| Raburn, Ryan N. | PH | Detroit | 4-17-81 | Tampa, Florida | 9-12 | 23 |
| Rakers, Aaron James | P | Baltimore | 1-22-77 | Highland, Illinois | 9-8 | 27 |
| Ramirez, Elizardo | P | Philadelphia | 1-28-83 | Villa Mella, Dominican Republic | 5-25 | 21 |
| Reed, Jeremy T. | PH | Seattle | 6-15-81 | San Dimas, California | 9-8 | 23 |
| Regilio, Nicholas D. | P | Texas | 9- 4-78 | Miami, Florida | 7-9 | 25 |
| Rios, Alexis Israel | RF | Toronto | 2-18-81 | Coffee, Alabama | 5-27 | 23 |
| Rivera, Rene | PH | Seattle | 7-31-83 | Bayamon, Puerto Rico | 9-22 | 21 |
| Robbins, Phillip Jacob | P | Cleveland | 5-23-76 | Charlotte, North Carolina | 9-20 | 28 |
| Rodriguez, Eddy | P | Baltimore | 8- 8-81 | San Pedro de Macoris, Dominican Rep. | 5-31 | 22 |
| Rose, Michael John-Ferrero | PH | Oakland | 8-25-76 | Sacramento, California | 10-1 | 28 |
| Saenz, Christopher Andrew | P | Milwaukee | 8-14-81 | Tuscon, Arizona | 4-24 | 22 |
| Seibel, Phillip Matthew | P | Boston | 1-28-79 | Louisville, Kentucky | 4-15 | 25 |
| Serrano, James | P | Kansas City | 5- 9-76 | Grand Junction, Colorado | 8-7 | 28 |

| Player | Pos. | Team | Birth date | Birthplace | Debut | *Age |
|---|---|---|---|---|---|---|
| Shelton, Christopher Bob | PH | Detroit | 6-26-80 | Salt Lake City, Utah | 4-15 | 23 |
| Sherrill, George Friederich | P | Seattle | 4-19-77 | Memphis, Tennessee | 7-16 | 27 |
| Simpson, Larry Allan | P | Colorado | 8-26-77 | Springfield, Illinois | 5-17 | 26 |
| Sizemore, Grady | CF | Cleveland | 8- 2-82 | Seattle, Washington | 7-21 | 21 |
| Sledge, Terrmel | LF | Montreal | 3-18-77 | Fayetteville, North Carolina | 4-6 | 27 |
| Snare, Ryan Delbert | P | Texas | 2- 8-79 | Clearwater, Florida | 8-6 | 25 |
| Snell, Ian Dante | P | Pittsburgh | 10-30-81 | Dover, Delaware | 8-20 | 22 |
| Snyder, Christopher Ryan | C | Arizona | 2-12-81 | Houston, Texas | 8-21 | 23 |
| Swisher, Nicolas Thompson | LF | Oakland | 11-25-80 | Parkersburg, West Virginia | 9-3 | 23 |
| Szuminski, Jason Ernest | P | San Diego | 12-11-78 | San Diego, California | 4-11 | 25 |
| Tadano, Kazuhito | P | Cleveland | 4-25-80 | Tokyo, Japan | 4-27 | 24 |
| Takatsu, Shingo | P | Chicago A.L. | 11-25-68 | Hiroshima, Japan | 4-9 | 35 |
| Taveras, Willy | CF | Houston | 12-25-81 | Tenares, Dominican Republic | 9-6 | 22 |
| Thomas, Charles Wesley | PH | Atlanta | 12-26-78 | Fairfield, California | 6-23 | 25 |
| Thompson, Richard Charles | PR | Kansas City | 4-23-79 | Reading, Pennsylvania | 4-7 | 24 |
| Thornton, Matthew J. | P | Seattle | 9-15-76 | Three Rivers, Michigan | 6-27 | 27 |
| Tiffee, Terry R. | 3B | Minnesota | 4-21-79 | North Little Rock, Arkansas | 9-1 | 25 |
| Tonis, Michael Timothy | C | Kansas City | 2- 9-79 | Sacramento, California | 6-20 | 25 |
| Tracy, Chad Austin | PH | Arizona | 5-22-80 | Charlotte, North Carolina | 4-21 | 23 |
| Treanor, Matthew Aaron | C | Florida | 3- 3-76 | Garden Grove, California | 6-2 | 28 |
| Upton, Melvin Emanuel | DH | Tampa Bay | 8-21-84 | Norfolk, Virginia | 8-2 | 19 |
| Urdaneta, Lino | P | Detroit | 11-20-79 | Caracas, Venezuela | 9-9 | 24 |
| Valdez, Merkin R. | P | San Francisco | 11-10-81 | San Cristobal, Dominican Republic | 8-1 | 22 |
| Valdez, Wilson Antonio | 2B | Chicago A.L. | 5-20-78 | Nizao, Dominican Republic | 9-7 | 26 |
| Van Benschoten, John Wesley | P | Pittsburgh | 4-14-80 | San Diego, California | 8-18 | 24 |
| Vasquez, Jorge Luis | P | Kansas City | 7-16-78 | Nagua, Dominican Republic | 8-13 | 26 |
| Villacis, Eduardo Enrique | P | Kansas City | 8-29-79 | Caracas, Venezuela | 5-1 | 24 |
| Watkins, Stephen Douglas | P | San Diego | 7-19-78 | Lubbock, Texas | 8-21 | 26 |
| Webb, John Floyd | P | Tampa Bay | 5-23-79 | Pensacola, Florida | 8-2 | 25 |
| Williams, Randall Duane | P | Seattle | 9-18-75 | Harlingen, Texas | 9-11 | 28 |
| Willingham, Joshua David | LF | Florida | 2-17-79 | Florence, Alabama | 7-6 | 25 |
| Wright, David Allen | 3B | New York N.L. | 12-20-82 | Norfolk, Virginia | 7-21 | 21 |
| Wuertz, Michael James | P | Chicago N.L. | 12-15-78 | Austin, Minnesota | 4-5 | 25 |
| Yates, Tyler Kali | P | New York N.L. | 8- 7-77 | Lihue, Hawaii | 4-9 | 26 |
| Youkilis, Kevin E. | 3B | Boston | 3-15-79 | Cincinnati, Ohio | 5-15 | 25 |
| Young, Christopher Ryan | P | Texas | 5-25-79 | Dallas, Texas | 8-24 | 25 |

* Denotes age on date of debut.

# 2004 FREE-AGENT FILINGS

## AMERICAN LEAGUE

**Anaheim:** Andres Galarraga, Troy Glaus, Shane Halter, Troy Percival, Aaron Sele.
**Baltimore:** Marty Cordova, Omar Daal, Buddy Groom, David Segui, B.J. Surhoff.
**Boston:** Terry Adams, Pedro Astacio, Ellis Burks, Orlando Cabrera, Ricky Gutierrez, Gabe Kapler, Curtis Leskanic, Derek Lowe, Pedro Martinez, Dave McCarty, Ramiro Mendoza, Doug Mirabelli, Mike Myers, Pokey Reese, Jason Varitek, Scott Williamson.
**Chicago:** Roberto Alomar, Sandy Alomar Jr., Magglio Ordonez, Jose Valentin.
**Cleveland:** Omar Vizquel, Rick White, Bob Wickman.
**Detroit:** Al Levine, Esteban Yan.
**Kansas City:** Kevin Appier, Juan Gonzalez, Joe Randa, Desi Relaford, Dennys Reyes, Kelly Stinnett.
**Minnesota:** Henry Blanco, Cristian Guzman, Corey Koskie, Terry Mulholland, Brad Radke.
**New York:** Miguel Cairo, Tony Clark, John Flaherty, Orlando Hernandez, Travis Lee, Jon Lieber, Esteban Loaiza, C.J. Nitkowski, John Olerud, Ruben Sierra, Enrique Wilson.
**Oakland:** Jermaine Dye, Chris Hammond, Jim Mecir, Mark McLemore, Damian Miller.
**Seattle:** Edgar Martinez, Ron Villone, Dan Wilson.
**Tampa Bay:** Brook Fordyce, John Halama, Tino Martinez, Todd Ritchie, Rey Sanchez.
**Texas:** Manny Alexander, Doug Brocail, David Dellucci, Andy Fox, Brad Fullmer, Rusty Greer, Brian Jordan, Jeff Nelson, Herbert Perry, Jay Powell, John Wasdin, Eric Young, Jeff Zimmerman.
**Toronto:** Dave Berg, Valerio de los Santos, Carlos Delgado, Chris Gomez, Pat Hentgen, Greg Myers, Gregg Zaun.

## NATIONAL LEAGUE

**Arizona:** Carlos Baerga, Danny Bautista, Greg Colbrunn, Jeff Fassero, Mike Fetters, Matt Mantei, Quinton McCracken, Shane Reynolds, Scott Service, Richie Sexson, Steve Sparks.
**Atlanta:** Antonio Alfonseca, Paul Byrd, J.D. Drew, Julio Franco, Russ Ortiz, Jaret Wright.
**Chicago:** Moises Alou, Paul Bako, Matt Clement, Nomar Garciaparra, Tom Goodwin, Ben Grieve, Mark Grudzielanek, Todd Hollandsworth, Ramon Martinez, Kent Mercker, Glendon Rusch, Todd Walker.
**Cincinnati:** Darren Bragg, Juan Castro, Barry Larkin, Todd Van Poppel, Gabe White, Paul Wilson.
**Colorado:** Jeromy Burnitz, Vinny Castilla, Royce Clayton, Shawn Estes, Todd Greene, Steve Reed, Mark Sweeney, Jamey Wright.
**Florida:** Armando Benitez, Wil Cordero, Damion Easley, Chad Fox, Lenny Harris, Josias Manzanillo, Mike Mordecai, Carl Pavano, Mike Redmond, Rudy Seanez, Ismael Valdez, David Weathers.
**Houston:** Carlos Beltran, Roger Clemens, Jeff Kent, Dan Miceli, Darren Oliver, Orlando Palmeiro, Russ Springer, Jose Vizcaino.
**Los Angeles:** Wilson Alvarez, Adrian Beltre, Elmer Dessens, Steve Finley, Jose Hernandez, Todd Hundley, Jose Lima, Brent Mayne, Hideo Nomo, Odalis Perez, Paul Shuey, Robin Ventura.
**Milwaukee:** Craig Counsell.
**Montreal:** Tony Batista, Einar Diaz.
**New York:** Kris Benson, Ricky Bottalico, Mike DeJean, John Franco, Richard Hidalgo, Al Leiter, Mo Vaughn, Todd Zeile.
**Philadelphia:** Rheal Cormier, Doug Glanville, Roberto Hernandez, Todd Jones, Cory Lidle, Kevin Millwood, Eric Milton, Todd Pratt, Placido Polanco.
**Pittsburgh:** Brian Boehringer.
**St. Louis:** Cal Eldred, Steve Kline, Ray Lankford, John Mabry, Mike Matheny, Matt Morris, Edgar Renteria, Woody Williams, Tony Womack.
**San Diego:** Andy Ashby, Rich Aurilia, Robert Fick, Alex Gonzalez, Dave Hansen, Antonio Osuna, David Wells.
**San Francisco:** Dave Burba, Jason Christiansen, Dustin Hermanson, Ricky Ledee, Robb Nen.

# MAJOR LEAGUE RULE 5 DRAFT

(Listed in order of selection)

| Player | Pos. | Drafted by | Drafted from (major league organization) |
|---|---|---|---|
| Angel Garcia | RHP | Arizona | Rochester, International League (Twins) |
| Andrew Sisco | LHP | Kansas City | Iowa, Pacific Coast League (Cubs) |
| Carlton "Tyrell" Godwin | OF | Washington | Syracuse, International League (Blue Jays) |
| Marcos Carvajal | RHP | Milwaukee | Las Vegas, Pacific Coast League (Dodgers) |
| Matthew Merricks | LHP | Colorado | Las Vegas, Pacific Coast League (Dodgers) |
| Luke Hagerty | LHP | Baltimore | Iowa, Pacific Coast League (Cubs) |
| Shane Victorino | OF | Philadelphia | Las Vegas, Pacific Coast League (Dodgers) |
| Tyler Johnson | LHP | Oakland | Memphis, Pacific Coast League (Cardinals) |
| Ryan Rowland-Smith | LHP | Minnesota | Tacoma, Pacific Coast League (Mariners) |
| D.J. Houlton | RHP | Los Angeles | New Orleans, Pacific Coast League (Astros) |
| Adam Stern | OF | Boston | Richmond, International League (Braves) |
| Tony Blanco | 3B | Washington | Louisville, International League (Reds) |

# NECROLOGY

## DEATHS

**Ted Abernathy**, 71, at Gastonia, N.C., on December 16. Abernathy, a sidearming righthander, led the National League in appearances three times and twice topped the N.L. in games saved (before saves became an official statistic). Abernathy established personal highs in 1965 when, as a member of the Cubs, he paced the league in games pitched (84) and saves (31). In 1967, he fashioned a 1.27 ERA in 70 appearances for the Reds. In 14 major league seasons with seven teams (he had two stints with the Cubs), the reliever compiled a 63-69 record with a 3.46 ERA and 148 saves.

**Doug Ault**, 54, at Tarpon Springs, Fla., on December 22. First baseman Ault hit two home runs for the Blue Jays in the first game in franchise history, against Chicago on April 7, 1977, in Toronto. Ault hit .245 with 11 home runs in '77, his only season as an everyday player in the majors. He played briefly for Texas in 1976 and saw part-time duty with the Jays in 1978 and 1980.

**Bobby Avila**, 80, at Veracruz, Mexico, on October 26. Cleveland's second baseman for most of the 1950s, Avila was a key player on an Indians team that established a longstanding American League record for victories in one season. Avila won the A.L. batting title with a .341 average and scored 112 runs in 1954, a year in which Cleveland set the league mark with 111 wins (unsurpassed for more than four decades). He batted .304 in 1951 and .300 in 1952. A .281 career hitter in the majors, Avila played for the Indians from 1949 through 1958 and then wound up his career in 1959, dividing that season between the Orioles, Red Sox and Braves.

**George Bamberger**, 80, at North Redington Beach, Fla., on April 4. Bamberger was a noted pitching coach for the Orioles, serving from 1968 through 1977 and producing four 20-game winners in one season (1971). He had two stints as manager of the Brewers (1978-1980, 1985-86) and also managed the Mets (1982-83). Although he had a losing record (458-478) as a manager, he led Milwaukee to 93-69 and 95-66 marks in '78 and '79. A longtime minor league pitcher, Bamberger appeared in a total of seven games for the Giants in 1951 and 1952 and in three games for the Orioles in 1959.

**Gene Bearden**, 83, at Alexander City, Ala., on March 18. A rookie in 1948, lefthander Bearden was a key contributor to Cleveland's World Series championship season. He won 20 games—No. 20 came when Bearden, on one day's rest, tossed a five-hitter in a one-game pennant playoff with the Red Sox—and led the A.L.with a 2.43 ERA. He also pitched six shutouts. In the Indians' six-game Series triumph over the Braves, Bearden threw a shutout in Game 3 and nailed down Game 6 in a relief role. He faded to an 8-8 record in 1949 and was sold to Washington during the 1950 season. Bearden also pitched for the Tigers, Browns and White Sox in a major league career in which he compiled a 45-38 record over seven years.

**Lou Berberet**, 74, at Las Vegas, Nev., on April 6. Catcher Berberet played in 448 games over seven major league seasons and hit .230. He saw his most extensive duty in 1959, appearing in 100 games for the Tigers and getting 338 at-bats. Berberet hit a career-high 13 homers in '59 but batted only .216. He reached the majors with the Yankees in 1954 and also played for the Senators and the Red Sox.

**Johnny Blatnik**, 82, at Lansing, Ohio, on January 21. Blatnik was the Phillies' No. 1 left fielder in 1948, getting 415 at-bats and hitting .260. He played in six games for the Philadelphia club in 1949 and appeared in a total of 11 games for the Phils and Cardinals in 1950.

**Cy Block**, 85, at Manhasset, N.Y., on September 22. Infielder Block appeared in only two regular-season games for the 1945 pennant-winning Cubs but nonetheless got into the '45 World Series against Detroit as a pinch runner in Game 6. He also played briefly for the Cubs in 1942 and 1946.

**Mike Blyzka**, 75, at Cheyenne, Wyo., on October 13. Righthander Blyzka pitched in 33 games for the St. Louis Browns in 1953 and in 37 games for the Baltimore Orioles (the relocated Browns franchise) in 1954. He was 3-11 overall with a 5.58 ERA.

**Ray Boone**, 81, at San Diego on October 17. The partriarch of the first three-generation family of players in major league history, infielder Boone was a .275 hitter over 13 seasons. He drove in 114 runs in 1953, a season during which he was traded from Cleveland to Detroit, and 116 in 1955 as a member of the Tigers. Boone also played for the White Sox, Athletics, Braves and Red Sox. Son Bob and grandsons Bret and Aaron followed Ray to the majors.

**Hank Borowy**, 88, at Brick, N.J., on August 23. Purchased in a waiver deal from the Yankees on July 27, 1945, righthander Borowy helped the Cubs to their most recent World Series appearance by going 11-2 with a 2.13 ERA over the final two months of the season. In the '45 Series against Detroit, Borowy started three games and relieved in another and split four decisions. A 21-game winner in '45 (he was 10-5 for New York), Borowy compiled a 108-82 record over 10 major league seasons. He pitched for the Phillies, Pirates and Tigers in the late stages of his career.

**Rex Bowen**, 93, at New Smyrna Beach, Fla., on December 30. Bowen signed Maury Wills for the Dodgers and Dick Groat and Bill Mazeroski for the Pirates in a long and notable career as a scout.

**Bob Boyd**, 84, at Wichita, Kan., on September 7. A quintessential line-drive hitter, first baseman Boyd batted .293 in a nine-season career in the big leagues. He hit .311 in part-time duty for the Orioles in 1956, then posted averages of .318 and .309 the next two years as Baltimore's No. 1 first baseman. Boyd collected 17 pinch hits for the Orioles in 1960, then wound up his major league career with the Athletics and Braves in 1961.

**Harry Brecheen**, 89, at Bethany, Okla., on January 17. Lefthander Brecheen fashioned a dazzling 2.92 earned-run average over 11 seasons with the Cardinals and one with the St. Louis Browns. "The Cat" went 31-9 overall for the Cardinals in 1944 and 1945, won three games for the Cards in the 1946 World Series, was a 20-game winner for the Cardinals in 1948 (a year in which he led the National League with a 2.24 ERA) and finished 133-92 in the majors. He then served 13 seasons as pitching coach for the Orioles, helping to make Baltimore's staff among the best in the majors.

**Jim Bucher**, 93, at Elizabethtown, Pa., on October 21. Bucher saw extensive duty for Brooklyn in the mid-1930s as a third baseman, second baseman, outfielder and pinch hitter. He had 473 at-bats for the Dodgers in 1935 and batted .302. He also played for the Cardinals and Red Sox over a seven-year career in which he hit .265.

**Ken Burkhart**, 88, at Knoxville, Tenn., on December 29. Righthander Burkhart won 18 games as a Cardinals rookie in 1945 and was 27-20 over five big-league seasons. He later turned to umpiring, calling games in the N.L. from 1957 through 1973.

**Ed Burtschy**, 82, at Delhi Township, Ohio, on May 2. Burtschy made 46 relief appearances for the 1954 Philadelphia Athletics, compiling a 5-4 record and a 3.80 ERA. He was a combined 5-1 for the Kansas City A's in 1955 and '56. The righthander was 10-6 overall in five seasons with the Athletics franchise.

**Ken Caminiti**, 41, at the Bronx, N.Y., on October 10. A 15-season major leaguer, third baseman Caminiti excelled in 1996 when he batted .326 with 40 home runs and 130 RBIs for the Padres and was named the N.L.'s Most Valuable Player. Caminiti, who spent his first eight big-league seasons with Houston and later played two additional years for the Astros, hit 121 homers and won three Gold Gloves in four years with San Diego. His final season was 2001, which he divided between Texas and Atlanta. He wound up with a .272 career average and 239 homers.

**Pete Center**, 92, at Campton, Ky., on August 8. Righthander Center compiled a 6-3 record for the Indians in 1945 and was 7-7 overall in four seasons with Cleveland.

**John Cerutti,** 44, at Toronto on October 3. A Blue Jays broadcaster at the time of his death, Cerutti spent six of his seven big-league seasons with Toronto. He was an 11-game winner for the Jays in 1987 and again in 1989 and twice posted nine victories. His final season in the majors was 1991, when he went 3-6 for the Tigers. Cerutti's overall record was 49-43.

**Walter "Rip" Coleman**, 72, at Wolfeboro, N.H., on May 14. As a rookie in 1955, lefthander Coleman was 2-1 in 10 games for the Yankees and made one relief appearance in the World Series. In his four other big-league seasons—with the Yanks, A's and Orioles—he struggled to a 5-24 mark overall.

**Willie Crawford**, 57, at Los Angeles on August 27. Crawford, who made his debut in the majors when he was barely 18 and delivered a pinch hit for the Dodgers in the 1965 World Series at age 19, batted .268 in a 1,210-game major league career that spanned 14 seasons. The outfielder hit .295 for Los Angeles in both 1973 and 1974, and he played in his second Series in '74. A Dodger from 1964 through 1975, he was with St. Louis in 1976 and divided the 1977 season between Houston and Oakland.

**Bob Cremins**, 98, at Pelham, N.Y., on March 27. Cremins made four relief appearances for the 1927 Red Sox.

**Victor Cruz**, 46, at Santo Domingo, Dominican Republic, on September 26. Cruz pitched in 187 games—all in relief—for four major league clubs from 1978 through 1981 and 1983. In his rookie year, with Toronto, he was 7-3 with a 1.71 earned-run average and nine saves in 32 games. Overall, the righthander had an 18-23 record, a 3.09 ERA and 37 saves.

**Al Cuccinello**, 89, at New York on March 29. Second baseman Cuccinello appeared in 54 games for the 1935 Giants. He was the brother of longtime major leaguer Tony Cuccinello.

**Harry Danning**, 93, at Valparaiso, Ind., on November 29. Catcher Danning, a member of New York's 1936 and 1937 N.L. pennant-winning teams, batted .300 or higher for the Giants in three consecutive seasons beginning in 1938. In 1939, he set career highs with a .313 average and 16 homers; in '40, he drove in a personal-best 91 runs. He was a .285 hitter over 10 seasons, all with the Giants.

**Russ Derry**, 88, at Princeton, Mo., on October 26. Outfielder Derry's most extensive duty in the majors came in 1945 when he appeared in 78 games for the Yankees. He hit 13 home runs that season. Derry also played for the Yanks in 1944, for the Athletics in 1946 and briefly for the Cardinals in 1949.

**Jim Devlin**, 81, at Bloomsburg, Pa., on January 15. Devlin, a catcher, appeared in one major league game—in 1944 with the Indians. He was 0-for-1 at the plate.

**Danny Doyle**, 87, at Stillwater, Okla., on December 14. Doyle, who as a Red Sox scout signed Jim Lonborg and Roger Clemens to Boston contracts, was a catcher in his playing days and appeared in 13 games for the Red Sox in 1943.

**Taylor Duncan**, 50, at Asheville, N.C., on January 3. Primarily a third baseman, Duncan batted .257 in 319 at-bats for the 1978 Athletics. In his only other major league experience, he appeared in eight games for the Cardinals in 1977.

**Joe Durso**, 80, at Stony Brook, N.Y., on December 31. Durso, voted into the writers wing of the Hall of Fame in 1995, covered the Yankees and Mets during his 51-year career with *The New York Times* and wrote numerous books on baseball.

**Hal Epps**, 90, at Houston on August 26. Outfielder Epps played in the majors in 1938, 1940, 1943 and 1944, appearing in a total of 125 games for the Cardinals, Browns and Athletics.

**Joe Falls**, 76, at Detroit on August 11. A longtime Detroit baseball writer and columnist, Falls was elected to the writers wing of the Baseball Hall of Fame in 2001.

**Charlie Fox**, 82, at Palo Alto, Calif., on February 16. Fox managed three full years in the majors—1971 through 1973, with San Francisco—and parts of four other seasons (with the Giants, Expos and Cubs). In '71, he guided the Giants to a 90-72 record and the N.L. West title. As a player, Fox was a catcher whose big-league career consisted of three games with the 1942 Giants.

**Hershell Freeman**, 75, at Orlando, Fla., on January 17. Reliever Freeman had a standout season in 1956 for a third-place Cincinnati Reds team that finished only two games out of first place. In 64 appearances out of the bullpen in '56, Freeman posted a 14-5 record and a 3.40 ERA. In 1955, he had fashioned a 2.16 ERA in 52 games for the Reds after being purchased from the Red Sox in May. The righthander also pitched for the Cubs in a six-year major league career in which he was 30-16.

**Floyd Giebell**, 94, at Wilkesboro, N.C., on April 28. Giebell won only three games in the majors, but victory No. 3 was a pennant-clinching triumph for the Tigers over Bob Feller and the Indians on September 27, 1940. A September call-up in '40, Giebell had defeated the Athletics on September 19 before pitching a six-hit shutout against Cleveland. The righthander was 3-1 overall for Detroit in 28 games over three seasons.

**Tony Giuliani**, 91, at St. Paul, Minn., on October 8. Giuliani was a backup catcher for the Browns, Senators (two stints) and Dodgers, appearing in 243 games over seven seasons in a major league career that began in 1936.

**Tom Glaviano**, 80, at Sacramento on January 19. Glaviano, who spent five seasons in the majors, was the Cardinals' No. 1 third baseman in 1950. He scored 92 runs, hit 11 homers and batted .285 in '50. Glaviano spent three other seasons with St. Louis and played for the Phillies in 1953.

**Mike Goliat**, 78, at Seven Hills, Ohio, on January 13. Goliat was a regular in one major league season—1950, when he was the second baseman for the National League pennant-winning Phillies. Goliat batted only .234 that year but hit 13 home runs and drove in 64 runs. He had a four-season major league career, playing 241 games for the Phils and eight for the St. Louis Browns.

**Ruben Gomez**, 77, at Arroyo, Puerto Rico, on July 26. Gomez won 17 games and had a 2.88 ERA for the 1954 World Series-winning New York Giants. In the '54 Series, he won Game 3 against Cleveland with 7⅓ innings of four-hit ball. Gomez was still a member of the Giants when the franchise moved to San Francisco after the 1957 season, and he pitched a six-hit shutout for San Francisco against the Los Angeles Dodgers in 1958 in the first West Coast game in major league history. Later a member of the Phillies, Indians and Twins, he went 76-86 over 10 big-league seasons.

**Jesse Gonder**, 68, at Oakland on November 14. Gonder was the Mets' No. 1 catcher in 1964, a year in which he batted .270 in 341 at-bats. He also played for the Yankees, Reds, Braves and Pirates in an eight-year major league career,

**Tom Haller**, 67, at Los Angeles on November 26. A major league catcher for 12 seasons, he hit 27 home runs for San Francisco in 1966 and 18 homers for the Giants' pennant-winning 1962 club. Haller, who spent seven seasons with the Giants, four with the Dodgers and one with the Tigers, had a .257 career batting average and played in two All-Star Games. He was a Giants coach from 1977 through 1979 and served as San Francisco's general manager for five years beginning in 1981.

**George Hausmann**, 88, at Boerne, Texas, on June 16. Hausmann was the Giants' regular second baseman in 1944 and 1945, batting .266 and .279 in those wartime years. Hausmann jumped to the Mexican League in 1946 and, like 17 other players, was banned from major league baseball. When the ban was lifted in 1949, Hausmann returned to the Giants and appeared in 16 games for the New Yorkers that season.

**Chuck Hiller**, 70, at St. Pete Beach, Fla., on October 20. The everyday second baseman for the 1962 Giants, Hiller batted .276 for that pennant-winning club. That fall, he became the first National Leaguer to hit a bases-loaded home run in the World Series, the grand slam coming in Game 4 against the Yankees. Hiller also played for the Mets, Phillies and Pirates in an eight-year big-league career. A coach in the majors for nine seasons, he was third base coach for the 1982 Series champions Cardinals.

**Vedie Himsl**, 86, at Chicago on March 15. When the Cubs eliminated the position of full-time manager and implemented a rotating College of Coaches before the 1961 season, Himsl was the first to serve as "head coach." Under Himsl, the Cubs went 10-21 in '61.

**Bill Hoffman**, 86, at Philadelphia on May 14. Hoffman made three relief appearances for the 1939 Phillies.

**Paul Hopkins**, 99, at Deep River, Conn., on January 2. Making his major league debut in a relief role for the Senators on September 29, 1927, Hopkins allowed the 59th home run of Babe Ruth's 60-homer season. The homer came with the bases loaded. Hopkins pitched in one other game in '27, then wound up his brief major league career in 1929 by appearing in seven games for Washington and two for the St. Louis Browns. He posted a 1-1 record overall.

**Connie Johnson**, 81, at Kansas City on November 25. A former Negro leagues standout, Johnson reached the majors at age 30 in 1953 and compiled a 40-39 record over five seasons. He went 14-11 with a 3.20 ERA and three shutouts for the 1957 Orioles.

**Darrell Johnson**, 75, at Fairfield, Calif., on May 3. Johnson was a major league manager for eight seasons, during which he guided the Red Sox to the A.L. pennant in 1975, served as the first manager in Mariners history (1977) and also piloted the Rangers (1982). As a player, Johnson was a reserve catcher over six big-league seasons and appeared in the 1961 World Series with the Reds.

**Ken Johnson**, 81, at Wichita, Kan., on April 6. Lefthander Johnson posted a 12-14 record in the majors from 1947 through 1952. In 1951, Johnson won only five games for the Phillies but tossed three shutouts. He broke into the big leagues with the Cardinals and also pitched for the Tigers.

**Mack Jones**, 65, at Atlanta on June 8. Breaking in with the Milwaukee Braves in 1961, Jones tied a modern record with four hits in his first big-league game. Four years later, the outfielder had a 31-homer season for the Braves and followed with 23 home runs in 1966 (the club's first season in Atlanta). Chosen off the Cincinnati roster in the expansion draft of October 1968, Jones was the cleanup hitter for Montreal in the Expos' first game in 1969 and went on to hit 22 homers that year. In 10 years in the majors, he batted .252 with 133 homers.

**Rod Kanehl**, 70, in Palm Springs, Calif., on December 14. Kanehl endeared himself to New York fans with his hustling play for the Mets in the team's first three years of existence. In the club's first season, 1962, he saw action in the outfield and at all four infield positions and batted .248 in 351 at-bats.

**Chris Kitsos**, 76, at Mobile, Ala., on June 7. In his only appearance in the majors, shortstop Kitsos was a late-game defensive replacement for the Cubs early in the 1954 season.

**Hub Kittle**, 86, at Yakima, Wash., on February 10. Kittle was pitching coach for the 1982 World Series champion Cardinals. He was a major league coach for eight seasons overall—with the Astros from 1971 through '75 and with the Cards from 1981 through '83. Kittle also was a longtime minor league player, manager and executive.

**Joe Lafata**, 82, at Roseville, Mich., on May 6. First baseman/outfielder Lafata played in 127 games for the Giants from 1947 through 1949. He batted .229.

**Tony Lupien**, 87, at Norwich, Vt., on July 9. Lupien was the regular first baseman for the Red Sox in 1942 and 1943, for the Phillies in 1944 and for the White Sox in 1948. His best years were '42, when he had a .281 batting average and drove in 70 runs, and '44, when he collected 169 hits and batted .283. He later was the longtime baseball coach at Dartmouth.

**Roger Marquis**, 67, at Holyoke, Mass., on July 19. Marquis' major league career consisted of one hitless at-bat in one game as a 18-year-old Orioles outfielder in 1955.

**Bobby Mattick**, 89, at Scottsdale, Ariz., on December 16. Mattick was a key member of the Blue Jays' scouting and player-development departments since the club's inception in 1977 and also managed Toronto in 1980 and 1981. In his playing days, Mattick was a regular player in one major league season, 1940, when he played shortstop for the Cubs and batted .218.

**Tug McGraw**, 59, at Nashville on January 5. The lefthander was a standout reliever and emotional leader for two World Series champion teams, the 1980 Phillies and the 1969 Mets; the 1973 pennant-winning Mets; and four other Phils teams that reached postseason play. He excelled in '80, posting a 1.46 ERA and making 20 saves in 57 appearances. He notched two saves for the Phillies against Kansas City in the Series, the second coming in decisive Game 6. McGraw, who had back-to-back 1.70 ERAs for the Mets in the early '70s, was 96-92 with 180 saves and a 3.14 ERA over 19 major league seasons (nine with the Mets, 10 with the Phillies).

**Wayne McLeland**, 79, at Friendswood, Texas, on May 9. McLeland pitched in six games for Detroit in 1951 and in four games for the Tigers in 1952.

**Lloyd Merriman**, 79, at Fresno, Calif., on January 20. Outfielder Merriman saw his most extensive duty in a five-year major league career in 1951, getting 359 at-bats for Cincinnati and batting .242. He spent four seasons with the Reds and was with the White Sox (one game) and Cubs (72 games) in his final year, 1955.

**Bob Murphy**, 79, at West Palm Beach, Fla., on August 3. Murphy was a broadcaster for the Mets from the team's inception in 1962 through the 2003 season. He earlier had called Red Sox and Orioles games. In 1994, Murphy was voted into the broadcasters wing of the Hall of Fame.

**Sam Nahem**, 88, at Berkeley, Calif., on April 19. Nahem posted a 10-8 record in 90 games over four major league seasons. Primarily a reliever, the righthander pitched for the Dodgers (1938), Cardinals (1941) and Phillies (1942, 1948).

**Leslie "Buster" Narum**, 63, at Clearwater, Fla., on May 17. Righhander Narum was 14-27 over five big-league seasons. He posted a 9-15 record in 1964 for a Washington Senators team that lost 100 games.

**Jim Nelson**, 57, at Sacramento on August 22. Righthander Nelson was 6-4 over two seasons with the Pirates. He was the starting and winning pitcher in the last game played at Forbes Field, going eight innings against the Cubs in a 4-1 victory in the second game of a June 28, 1970, doubleheader.

**Johnny Oates**, 58, at Richmond, Va., on December 24. Oates managed Texas to its only postseason appearances in franchise history, guiding the Rangers to A.L. West titles in 1996, 1998 and 1999. In '96, he shared A.L. Manager of the Year honors with New York's Joe Torre. Oates, who also managed Baltimore in a decade of managerial service in the majors, played 11 seasons in the big leagues and appeared in the 1977 and 1978 World Series as a backup catcher for the Dodgers.

**Ewald Pyle**, 93, at Du Quoin, Ill., on January 10. Pitching for the St. Louis Browns (1939, 1942), Washington Senators (1943), New York Giants (1944, 1945) and Boston Braves ('45), lefthander Pyle compiled an 11-21 record in the majors.

**Hal Reniff**, 66, at Ontario, Calif., on September 7. Reliever Reniff pitched in 247 games for the Yankees from 1961 to mid-1967, then wound up his big-league career with 29 appearances for the Mets in '67. He saved a team-leading 18 games for the Yanks in 1963 and worked in both the '63 and 1964 World Series. The righthander had an outstanding innings pitched/hits ratio of 471⅓/383 as a major leaguer.

**Lawrence Ritter**, 81, at New York on February 15. Noted baseball author Ritter won acclaim for his oral history of the game, *The Glory of Their Times: The Story of the Early Days of Baseball Told by the Men Who Played It.* The book was published in 1966 and expanded and republished in 1984.

**Andre Rodgers**, 70, in the Bahamas on December 13. When Ernie Banks moved from shortstop to first base on a full-time basis for the Cubs in 1962, it was Rodgers who took over at short for Chicago. A former cricket player, Rodgers was a Cubs regular for three years and a part-time player in eight other big-league seasons. Besides the Cubs, he played for the Giants and Pirates. His career batting average was .249.

**Jim Russo**, 81, at Wildwood, Mo., on February 8. Russo was a "super scout" for the Orioles for more than three decades, finding amateur talent and promoting trades that proved critical in turning Baltimore into an elite franchise that won World Series titles in the 1960s, 1970s and 1980s. He also stood out as an advance scout, his insight contributing to the Orioles' Series sweep of the defending champion Dodgers in 1966.

**Marge Schott**, 75, at Cincinnati on March 2. Schott was owner of the Reds from 1984 to 1999. It was a time frame during which her team captured a World Series championship (1990) but a period marred by Schott's racial and ethnic insensitivity (which resulted in suspensions that twice cost her daily control of the Cincinnati club).

**Andy Seminick**, 83, at Melbourne, Fla., on February 22. Seminick was a catcher for the Phillies from 1943 through 1951 and again in 1955, 1956 and, briefly, 1957. He batted .288 with 24 home runs for the 1950 pennant-winning Phils. Seminick, who also played three-plus seasons with the Reds, had double-figure homer totals in eight consecutive big-league seasons and finished a 15-year career in the majors with 164 homers and a .243 batting average.

**Frank Seward**, 83, at Elmira, N.Y., on April 12. Righthander Seward was 3-3 while pitching in a total of 26 games for the Giants in 1943 and 1944.

**John Stoneham**, 95, at Owasso, Okla., on January 1. Stoneham, an outfielder, appeared in 10 games for the 1933 White Sox and had three hits (one a home run) in 25 at-bats.

**Johnny Sturm**, 88, at St. Louis on October 8. In his only major league season, first baseman Sturm batted .239 in 124 games for the 1941 Yankees. He hit .286 in the '41 World Series, which New York won in five games over Brooklyn.

**Ed Sudol**, 84, at Daytona Beach, Fla., on December 10. Sudol was a National League umpire for 21 seasons, winding up his career in 1977. He was behind the plate in Atlanta on the night of April 8, 1974, when the Braves' Hank Aaron broke Babe Ruth's record with his 715th career home run.

**Gus Suhr**, 98, at Scottsdale, Ariz., on January 15. Suhr, a fixture at first base for Pittsburgh for most of the 1930s, once held the N.L. record for consecutive games played, 822. A career .279 hitter over 1,435 games (1,365 with the Pirates, 70 with the Phillies), Suhr had his best year in 1936 when he batted .312 with 118 RBIs for Pittsburgh. He had two other 100-plus RBI seasons.

**Ted Tappe**, 73, at Wenatchee, Wash., on February 13. Pinch hitting for Cincinnati in a 1950 game at Brooklyn, Tappe homered in his first major league at-bat. The outfielder wound up playing in only 34 games in the majors—a total of 11 for the Reds in '50 and '51 and 23 for the Cubs in 1955.

**Brian Traxler**, 37, at San Antonio on November 19. First baseman Traxler played in nine games for the 1990 Dodgers.

**Frenchy Uhalt**, 94, at Rossmoor, Calif., on September 3. Outfielder Uhalt had 165 at-bats for the 1934 White Sox. He hit .242.

**Glenn Vaughan**, 60, at Houston on December 18. At age 19, Vaughan, a shortstop, played in nine games for the Houston Colt .45s in 1963.

**Leon Wagner**, 69, at Los Angeles on January 3. Wagner was a power-hitting star for the Angels in the expansion team's first three years of existence, hitting a total of 91 homers for the club from 1961 through 1963. In 1962, he had career highs of 37 homers and 107 RBIs and helped the second-year Angels to a surprising third-place finish. The outfielder homered in the second All-Star Game of '62 and was 5-for-11 in three All-Star Games. Traded to the Indians, he had a 31-homer, 100-RBI season for Cleveland in 1964 and hit 28 home runs in 1965. Wagner connected for 211 homers in 12 years in the majors and batted .272 overall. Besides the Angels and Indians, he also played for the Giants (two stints), the Cardinals and the White Sox.

**Danny Whelan**, 84, at New York on January 2. Whelan was trainer for the 1960 World Series champion Pirates and also for the 1970 and 1973 NBA champion New York Knicks.

# 2004 A.L. STATISTICS

**Batting**

**Designated hitting**

**Pinch-hitting**

**Pitching**

**Fielding**

**Miscellaneous**

# BATTING

## TEAM

| Team | G | TPA | AB | R | H | TB | 2B | 3B | HR | RBI | SH | SF | HP | BB | IBB | SO | SB | CS | GDP | LOB | ShO | Avg. | OBP | Slg. |
|---|---|---|---|---|---|---|---|---|---|---|---|---|---|---|---|---|---|---|---|---|---|---|---|---|
| Anaheim | 162 | 6296 | 5675 | 836 | 1603 | 2435 | 272 | 37 | 162 | 783 | 56 | 41 | 73 | 450 | 43 | 942 | 143 | 46 | 123 | 1133 | 10 | .282 | .341 | .429 |
| Boston | 162 | 6515 | 5720 | 949 | 1613 | 2702 | 373 | 25 | 222 | 912 | 12 | 55 | 69 | 659 | 39 | 1189 | 68 | 30 | 123 | 1257 | 3 | .282 | .360 | .472 |
| Baltimore | 162 | 6431 | 5736 | 842 | 1614 | 2476 | 319 | 18 | 169 | 803 | 46 | 62 | 57 | 528 | 34 | 949 | 101 | 41 | 126 | 1216 | 12 | .281 | .345 | .432 |
| Cleveland | 162 | 6452 | 5676 | 858 | 1565 | 2520 | 345 | 29 | 184 | 820 | 47 | 42 | 78 | 606 | 41 | 1009 | 94 | 55 | 143 | 1197 | 6 | .276 | .351 | .444 |
| Detroit | 162 | 6285 | 5623 | 827 | 1531 | 2526 | 284 | 54 | 201 | 800 | 50 | 43 | 50 | 518 | 32 | 1144 | 86 | 50 | 110 | 1116 | 5 | .272 | .337 | .449 |
| Seattle | 162 | 6362 | 5722 | 698 | 1544 | 2268 | 276 | 20 | 136 | 658 | 46 | 48 | 54 | 492 | 49 | 1058 | 110 | 42 | 131 | 1241 | 12 | .270 | .331 | .396 |
| Oakland | 162 | 6459 | 5728 | 793 | 1545 | 2478 | 336 | 15 | 189 | 752 | 25 | 43 | 55 | 608 | 40 | 1061 | 47 | 22 | 142 | 1274 | 3 | .270 | .343 | .433 |
| New York | 162 | 6364 | 5527 | 897 | 1483 | 2530 | 281 | 20 | 242 | 863 | 37 | 50 | 80 | 670 | 40 | 982 | 84 | 33 | 157 | 1190 | 7 | .268 | .353 | .458 |
| Chicago | 162 | 6197 | 5534 | 865 | 1481 | 2529 | 284 | 19 | 242 | 823 | 58 | 42 | 63 | 499 | 25 | 1030 | 78 | 51 | 119 | 1031 | 8 | .268 | .333 | .457 |
| Texas | 162 | 6256 | 5615 | 860 | 1492 | 2564 | 323 | 34 | 227 | 825 | 23 | 57 | 61 | 500 | 41 | 1099 | 69 | 36 | 91 | 1098 | 9 | .266 | .329 | .457 |
| Minnesota | 162 | 6286 | 5623 | 780 | 1494 | 2425 | 310 | 24 | 191 | 735 | 46 | 40 | 64 | 513 | 42 | 982 | 116 | 46 | 130 | 1110 | 4 | .266 | .332 | .431 |
| Toronto | 161 | 6178 | 5531 | 719 | 1438 | 2231 | 290 | 34 | 145 | 680 | 20 | 42 | 71 | 513 | 25 | 1083 | 58 | 31 | 139 | 1164 | 12 | .260 | .328 | .403 |
| Kansas City | 162 | 6153 | 5538 | 720 | 1432 | 2201 | 261 | 29 | 150 | 675 | 40 | 38 | 76 | 461 | 28 | 1057 | 67 | 48 | 130 | 1099 | 13 | .259 | .322 | .397 |
| Tampa Bay | 161 | 6098 | 5483 | 714 | 1416 | 2221 | 278 | 46 | 145 | 685 | 35 | 56 | 55 | 469 | 33 | 944 | 132 | 42 | 97 | 1096 | 13 | .258 | .320 | .405 |
| **Totals** | 1133 | 88332 | 78731 | 11358 | 21251 | 34106 | 4232 | 404 | 2605 | 10814 | 541 | 659 | 906 | 7486 | 512 | 14529 | 1253 | 573 | 1761 | 16222 | 117 | .270 | .338 | .433 |

## INDIVIDUAL

### TOP QUALIFIERS FOR BATTING CHAMPIONSHIP

Minimum 502 plate appearances. *Lefthanded batter. †Switch-hitter.

| Player, Team | G | TPA | AB | R | H | TB | 2B | 3B | HR | RBI | SH | SF | HP | BB | IBB | SO | SB | CS | GDP | Avg. | OBP | Slg. |
|---|---|---|---|---|---|---|---|---|---|---|---|---|---|---|---|---|---|---|---|---|---|---|
| Suzuki, Ichiro, Sea.* | 161 | 762 | 704 | 101 | 262 | 320 | 24 | 5 | 8 | 60 | 2 | 3 | 4 | 49 | 19 | 63 | 36 | 11 | 6 | .372 | .414 | .455 |
| Mora, Melvin, Bal. | 140 | 636 | 550 | 111 | 187 | 309 | 41 | 0 | 27 | 104 | 6 | 3 | 11 | 66 | 0 | 95 | 11 | 6 | 10 | .340 | .419 | .562 |
| Guerrero, Vladimir, Ana. | 156 | 680 | 612 | 124 | 206 | 366 | 39 | 2 | 39 | 126 | 0 | 8 | 8 | 52 | 14 | 74 | 15 | 3 | 19 | .337 | .391 | .598 |
| Rodriguez, Ivan, Det. | 135 | 575 | 527 | 72 | 176 | 269 | 32 | 2 | 19 | 86 | 0 | 4 | 3 | 41 | 6 | 91 | 7 | 4 | 15 | .334 | .383 | .510 |
| Durazo, Erubiel, Oak.* | 142 | 578 | 511 | 80 | 164 | 267 | 35 | 1 | 22 | 88 | 0 | 2 | 9 | 56 | 9 | 104 | 3 | 2 | 7 | .321 | .396 | .523 |
| Guillen, Carlos, Det.† | 136 | 583 | 522 | 97 | 166 | 283 | 37 | 10 | 20 | 97 | 3 | 4 | 2 | 52 | 3 | 87 | 12 | 5 | 12 | .318 | .379 | .542 |
| Lopez, Javy, Bal. | 150 | 638 | 579 | 83 | 183 | 291 | 33 | 3 | 23 | 86 | 0 | 6 | 6 | 47 | 4 | 97 | 0 | 0 | 16 | .316 | .370 | .503 |
| Kotsay, Mark, Oak.* | 148 | 673 | 606 | 78 | 190 | 278 | 37 | 3 | 15 | 63 | 5 | 5 | 2 | 55 | 5 | 70 | 8 | 5 | 6 | .314 | .370 | .459 |
| Young, Michael, Tex. | 160 | 739 | 690 | 114 | 216 | 333 | 33 | 9 | 22 | 99 | 0 | 4 | 1 | 44 | 1 | 89 | 12 | 3 | 11 | .313 | .353 | .483 |
| Hafner, Travis, Cle.* | 140 | 576 | 482 | 96 | 150 | 281 | 41 | 3 | 28 | 109 | 0 | 6 | 17 | 68 | 7 | 111 | 3 | 2 | 11 | .311 | .410 | .583 |
| Tejada, Miguel, Bal. | 162 | 725 | 653 | 107 | 203 | 349 | 40 | 2 | 34 | 150 | 0 | 14 | 10 | 48 | 6 | 73 | 4 | 1 | 24 | .311 | .360 | .534 |
| Rowand, Aaron, Chi. | 140 | 534 | 487 | 94 | 151 | 265 | 38 | 2 | 24 | 69 | 5 | 2 | 10 | 30 | 1 | 91 | 17 | 5 | 5 | .310 | .361 | .544 |
| Ramirez, Manny, Bos. | 152 | 663 | 568 | 108 | 175 | 348 | 44 | 0 | 43 | 130 | 0 | 7 | 6 | 82 | 15 | 124 | 2 | 4 | 17 | .308 | .397 | .613 |
| Lee, Carlos, Chi. | 153 | 658 | 591 | 103 | 180 | 310 | 37 | 0 | 31 | 99 | 0 | 6 | 7 | 54 | 3 | 86 | 11 | 5 | 10 | .305 | .366 | .525 |
| Damon, Johnny, Bos.* | 150 | 702 | 621 | 123 | 189 | 296 | 35 | 6 | 20 | 94 | 0 | 3 | 2 | 76 | 1 | 71 | 19 | 8 | 8 | .304 | .380 | .477 |

DEPARTMENTAL LEADERS: G—Matsui, N.Y., Tejada, Bal., 162; AB—Suzuki, Sea., 704; R—Guerrero, Ana., 124; H—Suzuki, Sea., 262; TB—Guerrero, Ana., 366; 1B—Suzuki, Sea., 225; 2B—Roberts, Bal., 50; 3B—Crawford, TB., 19; HR—Ramirez, Bos., 43; RBI—Tejada, Bal., 150; SH—Vizquel, Cle., 20; SF—Tejada, Bal., 14; HP—Hafner, Cle., Millar, Bos., 17; BB—Chavez, Oak., 95; IBB—Suzuki, Sea., 19; SO—Bellhorn, Bos., 177; SB—Crawford, TB., 59; CS—Crawford, TB., 15; GDP—Posada, N.Y., Tejada, Bal., 24; Slg.—Ramirez, Bos., .613; OBP—Mora, Bal., .419.

### ALL PLAYERS

*Lefthanded batter. †Switch-hitter.

| Player, Team | G | TPA | AB | R | H | TB | 2B | 3B | HR | RBI | SH | SF | HP | BB | IBB | SO | SB | CS | GDP | Avg. | OBP | Slg. |
|---|---|---|---|---|---|---|---|---|---|---|---|---|---|---|---|---|---|---|---|---|---|---|
| Adams, Russ, Tor.* | 22 | 78 | 72 | 10 | 22 | 38 | 2 | 1 | 4 | 10 | 0 | 0 | 1 | 5 | 0 | 5 | 1 | 0 | 3 | .306 | .359 | .528 |
| Alexander, Manny, Tex. | 21 | 22 | 21 | 3 | 5 | 7 | 2 | 0 | 0 | 3 | 0 | 0 | 0 | 1 | 0 | 7 | 0 | 0 | 0 | .238 | .273 | .333 |
| Allen, Chad, Tex. | 20 | 63 | 58 | 4 | 14 | 20 | 4 | 1 | 0 | 6 | 2 | 1 | 0 | 2 | 0 | 13 | 0 | 1 | 1 | .241 | .262 | .345 |
| Alomar Jr., Sandy, Chi. | 50 | 164 | 146 | 15 | 35 | 45 | 4 | 0 | 2 | 14 | 3 | 2 | 2 | 11 | 2 | 13 | 0 | 0 | 4 | .240 | .298 | .308 |
| Alomar, Roberto, Chi.† | 18 | 65 | 61 | 4 | 11 | 15 | 1 | 0 | 1 | 8 | 1 | 1 | 0 | 2 | 0 | 13 | 0 | 0 | 2 | .180 | .203 | .246 |
| Amezaga, Alfredo, Ana.† | 73 | 105 | 93 | 12 | 15 | 23 | 2 | 0 | 2 | 11 | 6 | 0 | 3 | 3 | 0 | 24 | 3 | 2 | 2 | .161 | .212 | .247 |
| Anderson, Brian, K.C. | 35 | 2 | 1 | 0 | 0 | 0 | 0 | 0 | 0 | 0 | 1 | 0 | 0 | 0 | 0 | 0 | 0 | 0 | 0 | .000 | .000 | .000 |
| Anderson, Garret, Ana.* | 112 | 475 | 442 | 57 | 133 | 197 | 20 | 1 | 14 | 75 | 0 | 3 | 1 | 29 | 6 | 75 | 2 | 1 | 3 | .301 | .343 | .446 |
| Ardoin, Danny, Tex. | 6 | 11 | 8 | 1 | 1 | 1 | 0 | 0 | 0 | 1 | 0 | 0 | 0 | 3 | 0 | 2 | 0 | 0 | 0 | .125 | .364 | .125 |
| Arroyo, Bronson, Bos. | 32 | 7 | 6 | 0 | 0 | 0 | 0 | 0 | 0 | 0 | 1 | 0 | 0 | 0 | 0 | 5 | 0 | 0 | 0 | .000 | .000 | .000 |
| Aurilia, Rich, Sea. | 73 | 292 | 261 | 27 | 63 | 88 | 13 | 0 | 4 | 28 | 6 | 1 | 2 | 22 | 1 | 43 | 1 | 0 | 10 | .241 | .304 | .337 |
| Baldelli, Rocco, TB. | 136 | 565 | 518 | 79 | 145 | 226 | 27 | 3 | 16 | 74 | 3 | 6 | 8 | 30 | 2 | 88 | 17 | 4 | 12 | .280 | .326 | .436 |
| Barajas, Rod, Tex. | 108 | 389 | 358 | 50 | 89 | 162 | 26 | 1 | 15 | 58 | 8 | 7 | 3 | 13 | 0 | 63 | 0 | 1 | 3 | .249 | .276 | .453 |
| Bard, Josh, Cle.† | 7 | 23 | 19 | 5 | 8 | 13 | 2 | 0 | 1 | 4 | 0 | 1 | 0 | 3 | 0 | 0 | 0 | 0 | 0 | .421 | .478 | .684 |
| Bartlett, Jason, Min. | 8 | 14 | 12 | 2 | 1 | 1 | 0 | 0 | 0 | 1 | 1 | 0 | 0 | 1 | 0 | 1 | 2 | 0 | 0 | .083 | .154 | .083 |
| Batista, Miguel, Tor. | 38 | 5 | 5 | 0 | 0 | 0 | 0 | 0 | 0 | 0 | 0 | 0 | 0 | 0 | 0 | 3 | 0 | 0 | 0 | .000 | .000 | .000 |
| Bautista, Jose, Bal.-TB.-K.C. | 41 | 53 | 48 | 5 | 10 | 11 | 1 | 0 | 0 | 2 | 0 | 0 | 0 | 5 | 0 | 22 | 0 | 1 | 0 | .208 | .283 | .229 |
| Bedard, Erik, Bal.* | 27 | 5 | 4 | 0 | 0 | 0 | 0 | 0 | 0 | 0 | 0 | 0 | 0 | 1 | 0 | 3 | 0 | 0 | 0 | .000 | .200 | .000 |
| Bell, Rob, TB. | 24 | 5 | 5 | 1 | 1 | 2 | 1 | 0 | 0 | 0 | 0 | 0 | 0 | 0 | 0 | 2 | 0 | 0 | 0 | .200 | .200 | .400 |
| Bellhorn, Mark, Bos.† | 138 | 620 | 523 | 93 | 138 | 232 | 37 | 3 | 17 | 82 | 1 | 3 | 5 | 88 | 1 | 177 | 6 | 1 | 8 | .264 | .373 | .444 |
| Belliard, Ronnie, Cle. | 152 | 663 | 599 | 78 | 169 | 255 | 48 | 1 | 12 | 70 | 0 | 2 | 2 | 60 | 5 | 98 | 3 | 2 | 18 | .282 | .348 | .426 |
| Beltran, Carlos, K.C.† | 69 | 309 | 266 | 51 | 74 | 142 | 19 | 2 | 15 | 51 | 1 | 3 | 2 | 37 | 7 | 44 | 14 | 3 | 4 | .278 | .367 | .534 |
| Benoit, Joaquin, Tex. | 28 | 6 | 6 | 1 | 0 | 0 | 0 | 0 | 0 | 0 | 0 | 0 | 0 | 0 | 0 | 4 | 0 | 0 | 0 | .000 | .000 | .000 |
| Berg, Dave, Tor. | 58 | 162 | 154 | 13 | 39 | 52 | 4 | 0 | 3 | 23 | 0 | 2 | 2 | 4 | 0 | 27 | 0 | 1 | 4 | .253 | .278 | .338 |
| Berger, Brandon, K.C. | 11 | 36 | 35 | 5 | 7 | 9 | 2 | 0 | 0 | 2 | 1 | 0 | 0 | 0 | 0 | 7 | 1 | 1 | 1 | .200 | .200 | .257 |
| Berroa, Angel, K.C. | 134 | 554 | 512 | 72 | 134 | 197 | 27 | 6 | 8 | 43 | 5 | 2 | 12 | 23 | 0 | 87 | 14 | 8 | 10 | .262 | .308 | .385 |
| Bierbrodt, Nick, Tex.* | 4 | 3 | 2 | 0 | 0 | 0 | 0 | 0 | 0 | 0 | 1 | 0 | 0 | 0 | 0 | 2 | 0 | 0 | 0 | .000 | .000 | .000 |
| Bigbie, Larry, Bal.* | 139 | 531 | 478 | 76 | 134 | 204 | 23 | 1 | 15 | 68 | 3 | 4 | 1 | 45 | 0 | 113 | 8 | 3 | 7 | .280 | .341 | .427 |

| Player, Team | G | TPA | AB | R | H | TB | 2B | 3B | HR | RBI | SH | SF | HP | BB | IBB | SO | SB | CS | GDP | Avg. | OBP | Slg. |
|---|---|---|---|---|---|---|---|---|---|---|---|---|---|---|---|---|---|---|---|---|---|---|
| Blake, Casey, Cle. | 152 | 668 | 587 | 93 | 159 | 285 | 36 | 3 | 28 | 88 | 1 | 3 | 9 | 68 | 2 | 139 | 5 | 8 | 19 | .271 | .354 | .486 |
| Blalock, Hank, Tex.* | 159 | 713 | 624 | 107 | 172 | 312 | 38 | 3 | 32 | 110 | 0 | 8 | 6 | 75 | 7 | 149 | 2 | 2 | 13 | .276 | .355 | .500 |
| Blanco, Andres, K.C.† | 19 | 67 | 60 | 9 | 19 | 25 | 2 | 2 | 0 | 5 | 1 | 0 | 1 | 5 | 0 | 6 | 1 | 2 | 0 | .317 | .379 | .417 |
| Blanco, Henry, Min. | 114 | 353 | 315 | 36 | 65 | 116 | 19 | 1 | 10 | 37 | 11 | 3 | 3 | 21 | 0 | 56 | 0 | 3 | 8 | .206 | .260 | .368 |
| Bloomquist, Willie, Sea. | 93 | 201 | 188 | 27 | 46 | 62 | 10 | 0 | 2 | 18 | 3 | 0 | 0 | 10 | 0 | 48 | 13 | 2 | 2 | .245 | .283 | .330 |
| Blum, Geoff, TB.† | 112 | 369 | 339 | 38 | 73 | 118 | 21 | 0 | 8 | 35 | 4 | 2 | 0 | 24 | 1 | 58 | 2 | 3 | 4 | .215 | .266 | .348 |
| Bocachica, Hiram, Sea. | 50 | 107 | 90 | 9 | 22 | 36 | 5 | 0 | 3 | 6 | 3 | 1 | 1 | 12 | 0 | 27 | 5 | 4 | 1 | .244 | .337 | .400 |
| Bonderman, Jeremy, Det. | 33 | 7 | 7 | 0 | 0 | 0 | 0 | 0 | 0 | 0 | 0 | 0 | 0 | 0 | 0 | 4 | 0 | 0 | 0 | .000 | .000 | .000 |
| Boone, Bret, Sea. | 148 | 658 | 593 | 74 | 149 | 251 | 30 | 0 | 24 | 83 | 2 | 4 | 3 | 56 | 2 | 135 | 10 | 5 | 18 | .251 | .317 | .423 |
| Borchard, Joe, Chi.† | 63 | 222 | 201 | 26 | 35 | 68 | 4 | 1 | 9 | 20 | 1 | 0 | 1 | 19 | 1 | 57 | 1 | 0 | 4 | .174 | .249 | .338 |
| Borders, Pat, Sea.-Min. | 38 | 99 | 95 | 9 | 22 | 31 | 6 | 0 | 1 | 10 | 2 | 0 | 1 | 1 | 0 | 22 | 3 | 1 | 2 | .232 | .247 | .326 |
| Bowen, Rob, Min.† | 17 | 32 | 27 | 1 | 3 | 6 | 0 | 0 | 1 | 2 | 1 | 0 | 0 | 4 | 0 | 10 | 0 | 0 | 1 | .111 | .226 | .222 |
| Brazelton, Dewon, TB. | 22 | 1 | 1 | 0 | 0 | 0 | 0 | 0 | 0 | 0 | 0 | 0 | 0 | 0 | 0 | 0 | 0 | 0 | 0 | .000 | .000 | .000 |
| Broussard, Ben, Cle.* | 139 | 485 | 418 | 57 | 115 | 204 | 28 | 5 | 17 | 82 | 1 | 2 | 12 | 52 | 3 | 95 | 4 | 2 | 7 | .275 | .370 | .488 |
| Brown, Adrian, K.C.† | 5 | 11 | 11 | 0 | 3 | 3 | 0 | 0 | 0 | 0 | 0 | 0 | 0 | 0 | 0 | 2 | 0 | 0 | 0 | .273 | .273 | .273 |
| Brown, Dee, K.C.* | 59 | 209 | 195 | 19 | 49 | 68 | 7 | 0 | 4 | 24 | 1 | 1 | 1 | 11 | 0 | 50 | 2 | 2 | 1 | .251 | .293 | .349 |
| Buck, John, K.C. | 71 | 258 | 238 | 36 | 56 | 101 | 9 | 0 | 12 | 30 | 4 | 1 | 0 | 15 | 0 | 79 | 1 | 1 | 6 | .235 | .280 | .424 |
| Buehrle, Mark, Chi.* | 35 | 5 | 3 | 0 | 0 | 0 | 0 | 0 | 0 | 0 | 2 | 0 | 0 | 0 | 0 | 2 | 0 | 0 | 0 | .000 | .000 | .000 |
| Burke, Jamie, Chi. | 57 | 133 | 120 | 22 | 40 | 49 | 9 | 0 | 0 | 15 | 1 | 1 | 1 | 10 | 0 | 13 | 0 | 0 | 3 | .333 | .386 | .408 |
| Burks, Ellis, Bos. | 11 | 37 | 33 | 6 | 6 | 9 | 0 | 0 | 1 | 1 | 0 | 0 | 1 | 3 | 0 | 8 | 2 | 0 | 1 | .182 | .270 | .273 |
| Bush, David, Tor. | 16 | 2 | 2 | 0 | 0 | 0 | 0 | 0 | 0 | 0 | 0 | 0 | 0 | 0 | 0 | 0 | 0 | 0 | 0 | .000 | .000 | .000 |
| Bush, Homer, N.Y. | 9 | 8 | 7 | 2 | 0 | 0 | 0 | 0 | 0 | 0 | 0 | 0 | 1 | 0 | 0 | 2 | 1 | 0 | 1 | .000 | .125 | .000 |
| Byrnes, Eric, Oak. | 143 | 632 | 569 | 91 | 161 | 266 | 39 | 3 | 20 | 73 | 0 | 5 | 12 | 46 | 0 | 111 | 17 | 1 | 11 | .283 | .347 | .467 |
| Cabrera, Daniel, Bal. | 28 | 4 | 4 | 0 | 0 | 0 | 0 | 0 | 0 | 0 | 0 | 0 | 0 | 0 | 0 | 4 | 0 | 0 | 0 | .000 | .000 | .000 |
| Cabrera, Jolbert, Sea. | 113 | 391 | 359 | 38 | 97 | 138 | 19 | 2 | 6 | 47 | 3 | 5 | 8 | 16 | 1 | 70 | 10 | 3 | 13 | .270 | .312 | .384 |
| Cabrera, Orlando, Bos. | 58 | 248 | 228 | 33 | 67 | 106 | 19 | 1 | 6 | 31 | 1 | 7 | 1 | 11 | 0 | 23 | 4 | 1 | 4 | .294 | .320 | .465 |
| Cairo, Miguel, N.Y. | 122 | 408 | 360 | 48 | 105 | 150 | 17 | 5 | 6 | 42 | 12 | 4 | 14 | 18 | 1 | 49 | 11 | 3 | 7 | .292 | .346 | .417 |
| Cantu, Jorge, TB. | 50 | 185 | 173 | 25 | 52 | 80 | 20 | 1 | 2 | 17 | 0 | 1 | 2 | 9 | 0 | 44 | 0 | 0 | 5 | .301 | .341 | .462 |
| Cash, Kevin, Tor. | 60 | 197 | 181 | 18 | 35 | 56 | 9 | 0 | 4 | 21 | 0 | 2 | 4 | 10 | 0 | 59 | 0 | 0 | 3 | .193 | .249 | .309 |
| Castillo, Alberto, K.C. | 29 | 105 | 89 | 12 | 24 | 33 | 6 | 0 | 1 | 11 | 1 | 1 | 0 | 14 | 0 | 10 | 0 | 2 | 1 | .270 | .365 | .371 |
| Castro, Ramon A., Oak. | 9 | 16 | 15 | 2 | 2 | 3 | 1 | 0 | 0 | 3 | 0 | 0 | 0 | 1 | 1 | 3 | 0 | 0 | 1 | .133 | .188 | .200 |
| Catalanotto, Frank, Tor.* | 75 | 274 | 249 | 27 | 73 | 97 | 19 | 1 | 1 | 26 | 1 | 3 | 4 | 17 | 1 | 33 | 1 | 0 | 7 | .293 | .344 | .390 |
| Chavez, Eric, Oak.* | 125 | 577 | 475 | 87 | 131 | 238 | 20 | 0 | 29 | 77 | 0 | 4 | 3 | 95 | 10 | 99 | 6 | 3 | 21 | .276 | .397 | .501 |
| Clark, Howie, Tor.* | 40 | 133 | 115 | 17 | 25 | 40 | 6 | 0 | 3 | 12 | 3 | 2 | 0 | 13 | 0 | 15 | 0 | 0 | 2 | .217 | .292 | .348 |
| Clark, Tony, N.Y.† | 106 | 283 | 253 | 37 | 56 | 116 | 12 | 0 | 16 | 49 | 0 | 2 | 2 | 26 | 3 | 92 | 0 | 0 | 6 | .221 | .297 | .458 |
| Colome, Jesus, TB. | 33 | 2 | 1 | 0 | 0 | 0 | 0 | 0 | 0 | 0 | 1 | 0 | 0 | 0 | 0 | 1 | 0 | 0 | 0 | .000 | .000 | .000 |
| Colon, Bartolo, Ana. | 34 | 3 | 3 | 0 | 0 | 0 | 0 | 0 | 0 | 0 | 0 | 0 | 0 | 0 | 0 | 1 | 0 | 0 | 0 | .000 | .000 | .000 |
| Conti, Jason, Tex.* | 22 | 60 | 55 | 6 | 10 | 13 | 3 | 0 | 0 | 4 | 0 | 0 | 0 | 5 | 0 | 19 | 0 | 2 | 0 | .182 | .250 | .236 |
| Contreras, Jose, N.Y.-Chi. | 31 | 8 | 8 | 0 | 0 | 0 | 0 | 0 | 0 | 0 | 0 | 0 | 0 | 0 | 0 | 5 | 0 | 0 | 0 | .000 | .000 | .000 |
| Cotts, Neal, Chi.* | 56 | 1 | 1 | 0 | 1 | 2 | 1 | 0 | 0 | 0 | 0 | 0 | 0 | 0 | 0 | 0 | 0 | 0 | 0 | 1.000 | 1.000 | 2.000 |
| Crawford, Carl, TB.* | 152 | 672 | 626 | 104 | 185 | 282 | 26 | 19 | 11 | 55 | 4 | 6 | 1 | 35 | 2 | 81 | 59 | 15 | 2 | .296 | .331 | .450 |
| Crede, Joe, Chi. | 144 | 543 | 490 | 67 | 117 | 205 | 25 | 0 | 21 | 69 | 4 | 5 | 10 | 34 | 0 | 81 | 1 | 2 | 14 | .239 | .299 | .418 |
| Crespo, Cesar, Bos.† | 52 | 79 | 79 | 6 | 13 | 17 | 2 | 1 | 0 | 2 | 0 | 0 | 0 | 0 | 0 | 20 | 2 | 0 | 1 | .165 | .165 | .215 |
| Crisp, Coco, Cle.† | 139 | 538 | 491 | 78 | 146 | 219 | 24 | 2 | 15 | 71 | 9 | 2 | 0 | 36 | 4 | 69 | 20 | 13 | 8 | .297 | .344 | .446 |
| Crosby, Bobby, Oak. | 151 | 623 | 545 | 70 | 130 | 232 | 34 | 1 | 22 | 64 | 5 | 6 | 9 | 58 | 0 | 141 | 7 | 3 | 20 | .239 | .319 | .426 |
| Crosby, Bubba, N.Y.* | 55 | 58 | 53 | 8 | 8 | 16 | 2 | 0 | 2 | 7 | 2 | 0 | 1 | 2 | 0 | 13 | 2 | 0 | 0 | .151 | .196 | .302 |
| Crozier, Eric, Tor.* | 14 | 39 | 33 | 5 | 5 | 13 | 2 | 0 | 2 | 4 | 0 | 0 | 0 | 6 | 0 | 19 | 0 | 0 | 0 | .152 | .282 | .394 |
| Cruz Jr., Jose, TB.† | 153 | 636 | 545 | 76 | 132 | 236 | 25 | 8 | 21 | 78 | 5 | 8 | 2 | 76 | 8 | 117 | 11 | 6 | 6 | .242 | .333 | .433 |
| Cuddyer, Michael, Min. | 115 | 382 | 339 | 49 | 89 | 149 | 22 | 1 | 12 | 45 | 2 | 1 | 3 | 37 | 2 | 74 | 5 | 5 | 8 | .263 | .339 | .440 |
| Cummings, Midre, TB.* | 22 | 61 | 54 | 10 | 15 | 25 | 4 | 0 | 2 | 7 | 0 | 0 | 2 | 5 | 0 | 12 | 1 | 0 | 0 | .278 | .361 | .463 |
| Cust, Jack, Bal.* | 1 | 1 | 1 | 0 | 0 | 0 | 0 | 0 | 0 | 0 | 0 | 0 | 0 | 0 | 0 | 1 | 0 | 0 | 0 | .000 | .000 | .000 |
| Damon, Johnny, Bos.* | 150 | 702 | 621 | 123 | 189 | 296 | 35 | 6 | 20 | 94 | 0 | 3 | 2 | 76 | 1 | 71 | 19 | 8 | 8 | .304 | .380 | .477 |
| Daubach, Brian, Bos.* | 30 | 86 | 75 | 9 | 17 | 31 | 8 | 0 | 2 | 8 | 0 | 0 | 1 | 10 | 0 | 21 | 0 | 0 | 1 | .227 | .326 | .413 |
| DaVanon, Jeff, Ana.† | 108 | 337 | 285 | 41 | 79 | 119 | 11 | 4 | 7 | 34 | 1 | 5 | 0 | 46 | 2 | 54 | 18 | 3 | 2 | .277 | .372 | .418 |
| Davis, Ben, Sea.-Chi.† | 68 | 208 | 193 | 22 | 40 | 67 | 9 | 0 | 6 | 18 | 1 | 1 | 1 | 12 | 0 | 49 | 1 | 1 | 5 | .207 | .256 | .347 |
| Davis, Jason, Cle. | 26 | 5 | 5 | 1 | 1 | 4 | 0 | 0 | 1 | 1 | 0 | 0 | 0 | 0 | 0 | 2 | 0 | 0 | 0 | .200 | .200 | .800 |
| DeJean, Mike, Bal. | 37 | 1 | 1 | 0 | 0 | 0 | 0 | 0 | 0 | 0 | 0 | 0 | 0 | 0 | 0 | 1 | 0 | 0 | 0 | .000 | .000 | .000 |
| DeJesus, David, K.C.* | 96 | 413 | 363 | 58 | 104 | 146 | 15 | 3 | 7 | 39 | 8 | 0 | 9 | 33 | 0 | 53 | 8 | 11 | 6 | .287 | .360 | .402 |
| Delgado, Carlos, Tor.* | 128 | 551 | 458 | 74 | 123 | 245 | 26 | 0 | 32 | 99 | 0 | 11 | 13 | 69 | 12 | 115 | 0 | 1 | 11 | .269 | .372 | .535 |
| Dellucci, David, Tex.* | 107 | 387 | 331 | 59 | 80 | 146 | 13 | 1 | 17 | 61 | 1 | 3 | 5 | 47 | 3 | 88 | 9 | 4 | 4 | .242 | .342 | .441 |
| Diaz, Felix, Chi. | 18 | 1 | 1 | 0 | 0 | 0 | 0 | 0 | 0 | 0 | 0 | 0 | 0 | 0 | 0 | 0 | 0 | 0 | 0 | .000 | .000 | .000 |
| Diaz, Matt, TB. | 10 | 24 | 21 | 3 | 4 | 10 | 1 | 1 | 1 | 3 | 0 | 0 | 2 | 1 | 0 | 6 | 0 | 0 | 0 | .190 | .292 | .476 |
| DiFelice, Mike, Det. | 13 | 25 | 22 | 3 | 3 | 5 | 0 | 1 | 0 | 2 | 0 | 0 | 0 | 3 | 0 | 3 | 0 | 0 | 3 | .136 | .240 | .227 |
| Dobbs, Greg, Sea.* | 18 | 56 | 53 | 4 | 12 | 16 | 1 | 0 | 1 | 9 | 0 | 1 | 1 | 1 | 0 | 14 | 0 | 0 | 0 | .226 | .250 | .302 |
| Dominique, Andy, Bos. | 7 | 11 | 11 | 0 | 2 | 2 | 0 | 0 | 0 | 1 | 0 | 0 | 0 | 0 | 0 | 3 | 0 | 0 | 0 | .182 | .182 | .182 |
| Dransfeldt, Kelly, Chi. | 15 | 30 | 30 | 5 | 10 | 10 | 0 | 0 | 0 | 4 | 0 | 0 | 0 | 0 | 0 | 6 | 0 | 0 | 0 | .333 | .333 | .333 |
| Drese, Ryan, Tex. | 34 | 4 | 4 | 1 | 2 | 3 | 1 | 0 | 0 | 0 | 0 | 0 | 0 | 0 | 0 | 2 | 0 | 0 | 0 | .500 | .500 | .750 |
| DuBose, Eric, Bal.* | 14 | 2 | 2 | 0 | 0 | 0 | 0 | 0 | 0 | 0 | 0 | 0 | 0 | 0 | 0 | 2 | 0 | 0 | 0 | .000 | .000 | .000 |
| Durazo, Erubiel, Oak.* | 142 | 578 | 511 | 80 | 164 | 267 | 35 | 1 | 22 | 88 | 0 | 2 | 9 | 56 | 9 | 104 | 3 | 2 | 7 | .321 | .396 | .523 |
| Dye, Jermaine, Oak. | 137 | 590 | 532 | 87 | 141 | 247 | 29 | 4 | 23 | 80 | 0 | 5 | 4 | 49 | 4 | 128 | 4 | 2 | 16 | .265 | .329 | .464 |
| Eckstein, David, Ana. | 142 | 637 | 566 | 92 | 156 | 188 | 24 | 1 | 2 | 35 | 14 | 2 | 13 | 42 | 1 | 49 | 16 | 5 | 11 | .276 | .339 | .332 |
| Elarton, Scott, Cle. | 21 | 3 | 3 | 1 | 1 | 1 | 0 | 0 | 0 | 0 | 0 | 0 | 0 | 0 | 0 | 1 | 0 | 0 | 0 | .333 | .333 | .333 |
| Erstad, Darin, Ana.* | 125 | 543 | 495 | 79 | 146 | 198 | 29 | 1 | 7 | 69 | 3 | 4 | 4 | 37 | 1 | 74 | 16 | 1 | 9 | .295 | .346 | .400 |
| Escalona, Felix, N.Y. | 5 | 9 | 8 | 1 | 0 | 0 | 0 | 0 | 0 | 0 | 0 | 0 | 1 | 0 | 0 | 2 | 0 | 0 | 0 | .000 | .111 | .000 |
| Escobar, Alex, Cle. | 46 | 179 | 152 | 20 | 32 | 47 | 8 | 2 | 1 | 12 | 3 | 0 | 1 | 23 | 0 | 42 | 1 | 1 | 1 | .211 | .318 | .309 |
| Escobar, Kelvim, Ana. | 33 | 2 | 2 | 0 | 0 | 0 | 0 | 0 | 0 | 0 | 0 | 0 | 0 | 0 | 0 | 0 | 0 | 0 | 0 | .000 | .000 | .000 |
| Estalella, Bobby, Tor. | 5 | 17 | 13 | 1 | 3 | 3 | 0 | 0 | 0 | 0 | 0 | 0 | 1 | 3 | 0 | 5 | 0 | 0 | 1 | .231 | .412 | .231 |
| Everett, Carl, Chi.† | 43 | 169 | 154 | 21 | 41 | 65 | 7 | 1 | 5 | 21 | 0 | 2 | 5 | 8 | 1 | 26 | 1 | 0 | 3 | .266 | .320 | .422 |
| Fick, Robert, TB.* | 76 | 238 | 214 | 12 | 43 | 70 | 5 | 2 | 6 | 26 | 0 | 2 | 2 | 20 | 2 | 32 | 0 | 0 | 2 | .201 | .273 | .327 |
| Figgins, Chone, Ana.† | 148 | 638 | 577 | 83 | 171 | 242 | 22 | 17 | 5 | 60 | 10 | 2 | 0 | 49 | 0 | 94 | 34 | 13 | 6 | .296 | .350 | .419 |
| File, Bob, Tor. | 24 | 1 | 1 | 0 | 0 | 0 | 0 | 0 | 0 | 0 | 0 | 0 | 0 | 0 | 0 | 1 | 0 | 0 | 0 | .000 | .000 | .000 |
| Flaherty, John, N.Y. | 47 | 135 | 127 | 11 | 32 | 59 | 9 | 0 | 6 | 16 | 2 | 0 | 1 | 5 | 2 | 25 | 0 | 2 | 5 | .252 | .286 | .465 |

| Player, Team | G | TPA | AB | R | H | TB | 2B | 3B | HR | RBI | SH | SF | HP | BB | IBB | SO | SB | CS | GDP | Avg. | OBP | Slg. |
|---|---|---|---|---|---|---|---|---|---|---|---|---|---|---|---|---|---|---|---|---|---|---|
| Ford, Lew, Min. | 154 | 658 | 569 | 89 | 170 | 254 | 31 | 4 | 15 | 72 | 2 | 7 | 13 | 67 | 3 | 75 | 20 | 2 | 15 | .299 | .381 | .446 |
| Fordyce, Brook, TB. | 54 | 163 | 151 | 14 | 31 | 43 | 6 | 0 | 2 | 9 | 1 | 0 | 2 | 9 | 0 | 34 | 0 | 0 | 3 | .205 | .259 | .285 |
| Fox, Andy, Tex.* | 12 | 13 | 12 | 2 | 1 | 1 | 0 | 0 | 0 | 0 | 0 | 0 | 0 | 1 | 0 | 3 | 0 | 0 | 0 | .083 | .154 | .083 |
| Franklin, Ryan, Sea. | 32 | 5 | 3 | 0 | 0 | 0 | 0 | 0 | 0 | 0 | 1 | 0 | 0 | 1 | 0 | 2 | 0 | 0 | 0 | .000 | .250 | .000 |
| Fullmer, Brad, Tex.* | 76 | 290 | 258 | 41 | 60 | 114 | 19 | 1 | 11 | 33 | 0 | 2 | 3 | 27 | 1 | 30 | 1 | 2 | 7 | .233 | .310 | .442 |
| Galarraga, Andres, Ana. | 7 | 11 | 10 | 1 | 3 | 6 | 0 | 0 | 1 | 2 | 0 | 0 | 1 | 0 | 0 | 3 | 0 | 0 | 1 | .300 | .364 | .600 |
| Garcia, Freddy, Sea.-Chi. | 31 | 4 | 4 | 0 | 0 | 0 | 0 | 0 | 0 | 0 | 0 | 0 | 0 | 0 | 0 | 3 | 0 | 0 | 0 | .000 | .000 | .000 |
| Garcia, Karim, Bal.* | 23 | 73 | 66 | 9 | 14 | 23 | 0 | 0 | 3 | 11 | 0 | 3 | 0 | 4 | 1 | 15 | 0 | 0 | 1 | .212 | .247 | .348 |
| Garciaparra, Nomar, Bos. | 38 | 169 | 156 | 24 | 50 | 78 | 7 | 3 | 5 | 21 | 0 | 1 | 4 | 8 | 2 | 16 | 2 | 0 | 4 | .321 | .367 | .500 |
| Garland, Jon, Chi. | 34 | 5 | 4 | 0 | 1 | 1 | 0 | 0 | 0 | 0 | 1 | 0 | 0 | 0 | 0 | 0 | 0 | 0 | 0 | .250 | .250 | .250 |
| Gathright, Joey, TB.* | 19 | 57 | 52 | 11 | 13 | 13 | 0 | 0 | 0 | 1 | 0 | 0 | 3 | 2 | 0 | 14 | 6 | 1 | 2 | .250 | .316 | .250 |
| Gaudin, Chad, TB. | 28 | 2 | 1 | 0 | 0 | 0 | 0 | 0 | 0 | 0 | 1 | 0 | 0 | 0 | 0 | 0 | 0 | 0 | 0 | .000 | .000 | .000 |
| George, Chris, K.C.* | 10 | 3 | 2 | 0 | 0 | 0 | 0 | 0 | 0 | 0 | 0 | 0 | 0 | 1 | 0 | 0 | 0 | 0 | 0 | .000 | .333 | .000 |
| German, Esteban, Oak. | 31 | 65 | 60 | 9 | 15 | 18 | 1 | 1 | 0 | 7 | 1 | 0 | 0 | 4 | 0 | 13 | 0 | 1 | 1 | .250 | .297 | .300 |
| German, Franklyn, Det. | 16 | 1 | 1 | 0 | 0 | 0 | 0 | 0 | 0 | 0 | 0 | 0 | 0 | 0 | 0 | 1 | 0 | 0 | 0 | .000 | .000 | .000 |
| Gerut, Jody, Cle.* | 134 | 548 | 481 | 72 | 121 | 195 | 31 | 5 | 11 | 51 | 3 | 3 | 7 | 54 | 4 | 59 | 13 | 6 | 9 | .252 | .334 | .405 |
| Gettis, Byron, K.C. | 21 | 49 | 39 | 7 | 7 | 10 | 1 | 1 | 0 | 1 | 0 | 1 | 1 | 8 | 1 | 14 | 0 | 1 | 0 | .179 | .327 | .256 |
| Giambi, Jason, N.Y.* | 80 | 322 | 264 | 33 | 55 | 100 | 9 | 0 | 12 | 40 | 0 | 3 | 8 | 47 | 1 | 62 | 0 | 1 | 5 | .208 | .342 | .379 |
| Gibbons, Jay, Bal.* | 97 | 380 | 346 | 36 | 85 | 131 | 14 | 1 | 10 | 47 | 1 | 3 | 1 | 29 | 0 | 64 | 1 | 1 | 11 | .246 | .303 | .379 |
| Gil, Geronimo, Bal. | 12 | 35 | 32 | 1 | 9 | 11 | 2 | 0 | 0 | 4 | 0 | 0 | 0 | 3 | 1 | 5 | 0 | 0 | 0 | .281 | .343 | .344 |
| Gipson, Charles, TB. | 5 | 5 | 4 | 1 | 2 | 2 | 0 | 0 | 0 | 0 | 1 | 0 | 0 | 0 | 0 | 1 | 1 | 0 | 0 | .500 | .500 | .500 |
| Glaus, Troy, Ana. | 58 | 242 | 207 | 47 | 52 | 119 | 11 | 1 | 18 | 42 | 0 | 1 | 3 | 31 | 3 | 52 | 2 | 3 | 6 | .251 | .355 | .575 |
| Gload, Ross, Chi.* | 110 | 260 | 234 | 28 | 75 | 112 | 16 | 0 | 7 | 44 | 1 | 3 | 2 | 20 | 1 | 37 | 0 | 3 | 11 | .321 | .375 | .479 |
| Gobble, Jimmy, K.C.* | 25 | 2 | 2 | 0 | 0 | 0 | 0 | 0 | 0 | 0 | 0 | 0 | 0 | 0 | 0 | 1 | 0 | 0 | 0 | .000 | .000 | .000 |
| Gomes, Jonny, TB. | 5 | 15 | 14 | 0 | 1 | 1 | 0 | 0 | 0 | 1 | 0 | 0 | 0 | 1 | 0 | 6 | 0 | 0 | 0 | .071 | .133 | .071 |
| Gomez, Alexis, K.C.* | 13 | 31 | 29 | 1 | 8 | 9 | 1 | 0 | 0 | 4 | 0 | 0 | 0 | 2 | 0 | 8 | 0 | 0 | 1 | .276 | .323 | .310 |
| Gomez, Chris, Tor. | 109 | 377 | 341 | 41 | 96 | 118 | 11 | 1 | 3 | 37 | 3 | 3 | 2 | 28 | 0 | 41 | 3 | 2 | 4 | .282 | .337 | .346 |
| Gonzalez, Adrian, Tex.* | 16 | 44 | 42 | 7 | 10 | 16 | 3 | 0 | 1 | 7 | 0 | 0 | 0 | 2 | 0 | 6 | 0 | 0 | 0 | .238 | .273 | .381 |
| Gonzalez, Juan, K.C. | 33 | 138 | 127 | 17 | 35 | 56 | 4 | 1 | 5 | 17 | 0 | 1 | 1 | 9 | 1 | 19 | 0 | 1 | 3 | .276 | .326 | .441 |
| Gonzalez, Raul, Cle. | 7 | 11 | 11 | 0 | 1 | 1 | 0 | 0 | 0 | 0 | 0 | 0 | 0 | 0 | 0 | 4 | 0 | 0 | 0 | .091 | .091 | .091 |
| Gordon, Tom, N.Y. | 80 | 1 | 1 | 0 | 0 | 0 | 0 | 0 | 0 | 0 | 0 | 0 | 0 | 0 | 0 | 0 | 0 | 0 | 0 | .000 | .000 | .000 |
| Gotay, Ruben, K.C.† | 44 | 166 | 152 | 17 | 41 | 57 | 7 | 3 | 1 | 16 | 1 | 2 | 2 | 9 | 0 | 36 | 0 | 1 | 4 | .270 | .315 | .375 |
| Graffanino, Tony, K.C. | 75 | 314 | 278 | 37 | 73 | 93 | 11 | 0 | 3 | 26 | 4 | 2 | 3 | 27 | 0 | 38 | 10 | 2 | 5 | .263 | .332 | .335 |
| Granderson, Curtis, Det.* | 9 | 28 | 25 | 2 | 6 | 9 | 1 | 1 | 0 | 0 | 0 | 0 | 0 | 3 | 0 | 8 | 0 | 0 | 1 | .240 | .321 | .360 |
| Greinke, Zack, K.C. | 24 | 2 | 2 | 0 | 0 | 0 | 0 | 0 | 0 | 0 | 0 | 0 | 0 | 0 | 0 | 1 | 0 | 0 | 0 | .000 | .000 | .000 |
| Gross, Gabe, Tor.* | 44 | 149 | 129 | 18 | 27 | 40 | 4 | 0 | 3 | 16 | 0 | 0 | 0 | 19 | 0 | 31 | 2 | 2 | 1 | .209 | .311 | .310 |
| Guardado, Eddie, Sea. | 41 | 1 | 1 | 0 | 0 | 0 | 0 | 0 | 0 | 0 | 0 | 0 | 0 | 0 | 0 | 0 | 0 | 0 | 1 | .000 | .000 | .000 |
| Guerrero, Vladimir, Ana. | 156 | 680 | 612 | 124 | 206 | 366 | 39 | 2 | 39 | 126 | 0 | 8 | 8 | 52 | 14 | 74 | 15 | 3 | 19 | .337 | .391 | .598 |
| Guerrero, Wilton, K.C.† | 24 | 32 | 32 | 7 | 7 | 9 | 0 | 1 | 0 | 1 | 0 | 0 | 0 | 0 | 0 | 4 | 1 | 0 | 1 | .219 | .219 | .281 |
| Guerrier, Matt, Min. | 9 | 1 | 1 | 0 | 0 | 0 | 0 | 0 | 0 | 0 | 0 | 0 | 0 | 0 | 0 | 1 | 0 | 0 | 0 | .000 | .000 | .000 |
| Guiel, Aaron, K.C.* | 42 | 157 | 135 | 15 | 21 | 40 | 4 | 0 | 5 | 13 | 1 | 1 | 3 | 17 | 0 | 42 | 1 | 1 | 3 | .156 | .263 | .296 |
| Guillen, Carlos, Det.† | 136 | 583 | 522 | 97 | 166 | 283 | 37 | 10 | 20 | 97 | 3 | 4 | 2 | 52 | 3 | 87 | 12 | 5 | 12 | .318 | .379 | .542 |
| Guillen, Jose, Ana. | 148 | 621 | 565 | 88 | 166 | 281 | 28 | 3 | 27 | 104 | 0 | 3 | 15 | 37 | 5 | 92 | 5 | 4 | 14 | .294 | .352 | .497 |
| Gutierrez, Ricky, Bos. | 21 | 42 | 40 | 6 | 11 | 12 | 1 | 0 | 0 | 3 | 0 | 0 | 0 | 2 | 0 | 6 | 1 | 0 | 2 | .275 | .310 | .300 |
| Guzman, Cristian, Min.† | 145 | 624 | 576 | 84 | 158 | 221 | 31 | 4 | 8 | 46 | 13 | 4 | 1 | 30 | 4 | 64 | 10 | 5 | 15 | .274 | .309 | .384 |
| Hafner, Travis, Cle.* | 140 | 576 | 482 | 96 | 150 | 281 | 41 | 3 | 28 | 109 | 0 | 6 | 17 | 68 | 7 | 111 | 3 | 2 | 11 | .311 | .410 | .583 |
| Hairston Jr., Jerry, Bal. | 86 | 334 | 287 | 43 | 87 | 114 | 19 | 1 | 2 | 24 | 6 | 4 | 8 | 29 | 1 | 29 | 13 | 8 | 3 | .303 | .378 | .397 |
| Halama, John, TB.* | 34 | 3 | 3 | 0 | 0 | 0 | 0 | 0 | 0 | 0 | 0 | 0 | 0 | 0 | 0 | 1 | 0 | 0 | 1 | .000 | .000 | .000 |
| Hall, Toby, TB. | 119 | 441 | 404 | 35 | 103 | 148 | 21 | 0 | 8 | 60 | 1 | 7 | 5 | 24 | 1 | 41 | 0 | 2 | 20 | .255 | .300 | .366 |
| Halladay, Roy, Tor. | 21 | 6 | 6 | 0 | 0 | 0 | 0 | 0 | 0 | 0 | 0 | 0 | 0 | 0 | 0 | 3 | 0 | 0 | 0 | .000 | .000 | .000 |
| Halsey, Brad, N.Y.* | 8 | 2 | 2 | 0 | 1 | 1 | 0 | 0 | 0 | 0 | 0 | 0 | 0 | 0 | 0 | 1 | 0 | 0 | 0 | .500 | .500 | .500 |
| Halter, Shane, Ana. | 46 | 121 | 114 | 10 | 23 | 40 | 5 | 0 | 4 | 13 | 0 | 0 | 0 | 7 | 0 | 30 | 1 | 1 | 3 | .202 | .248 | .351 |
| Hansen, Dave, Sea.* | 57 | 97 | 78 | 14 | 22 | 33 | 5 | 0 | 2 | 12 | 0 | 1 | 0 | 18 | 3 | 16 | 0 | 0 | 3 | .282 | .412 | .423 |
| Harden, Rich, Oak.* | 31 | 5 | 5 | 0 | 0 | 0 | 0 | 0 | 0 | 0 | 0 | 0 | 0 | 0 | 0 | 3 | 0 | 0 | 0 | .000 | .000 | .000 |
| Harris, Willie, Chi.* | 129 | 472 | 409 | 68 | 107 | 132 | 15 | 2 | 2 | 27 | 7 | 3 | 1 | 51 | 0 | 79 | 19 | 7 | 4 | .262 | .343 | .323 |
| Harvey, Ken, K.C. | 120 | 494 | 456 | 47 | 131 | 192 | 20 | 1 | 13 | 55 | 0 | 2 | 8 | 28 | 2 | 89 | 1 | 1 | 14 | .287 | .338 | .421 |
| Hatteberg, Scott, Oak.* | 152 | 638 | 550 | 87 | 156 | 231 | 30 | 0 | 15 | 82 | 3 | 8 | 5 | 72 | 5 | 48 | 0 | 0 | 10 | .284 | .367 | .420 |
| Hendrickson, Mark, TB.* | 32 | 6 | 5 | 0 | 1 | 1 | 0 | 0 | 0 | 0 | 0 | 0 | 0 | 1 | 0 | 4 | 0 | 0 | 0 | .200 | .333 | .200 |
| Hensley, Matt, Ana. | 16 | 1 | 1 | 0 | 0 | 0 | 0 | 0 | 0 | 0 | 0 | 0 | 0 | 0 | 0 | 1 | 0 | 0 | 0 | .000 | .000 | .000 |
| Hentgen, Pat, Tor. | 18 | 1 | 1 | 0 | 0 | 0 | 0 | 0 | 0 | 0 | 0 | 0 | 0 | 0 | 0 | 0 | 0 | 0 | 1 | .000 | .000 | .000 |
| Hermansen, Chad, Tor. | 4 | 7 | 7 | 0 | 0 | 0 | 0 | 0 | 0 | 0 | 0 | 0 | 0 | 0 | 0 | 3 | 0 | 0 | 0 | .000 | .000 | .000 |
| Higginson, Bobby, Det.* | 131 | 531 | 448 | 63 | 110 | 174 | 24 | 2 | 12 | 64 | 2 | 4 | 7 | 70 | 5 | 84 | 5 | 2 | 10 | .246 | .353 | .388 |
| Hinske, Eric, Tor.* | 155 | 634 | 570 | 66 | 140 | 214 | 23 | 3 | 15 | 69 | 0 | 6 | 4 | 54 | 2 | 109 | 12 | 8 | 14 | .246 | .312 | .375 |
| Huckaby, Ken, Tex.-Bal. | 24 | 55 | 50 | 4 | 7 | 10 | 3 | 0 | 0 | 0 | 0 | 0 | 0 | 5 | 0 | 12 | 0 | 0 | 1 | .140 | .218 | .200 |
| Hudson, Orlando, Tor.† | 135 | 551 | 489 | 73 | 132 | 214 | 32 | 7 | 12 | 58 | 3 | 4 | 4 | 51 | 0 | 98 | 7 | 3 | 12 | .270 | .341 | .438 |
| Hudson, Tim, Oak. | 27 | 3 | 3 | 0 | 0 | 0 | 0 | 0 | 0 | 0 | 0 | 0 | 0 | 0 | 0 | 1 | 0 | 0 | 0 | .000 | .000 | .000 |
| Huff, Aubrey, TB.* | 157 | 667 | 600 | 92 | 178 | 296 | 27 | 2 | 29 | 104 | 0 | 5 | 6 | 56 | 6 | 74 | 5 | 1 | 9 | .297 | .360 | .493 |
| Hunter, Torii, Min. | 138 | 569 | 520 | 79 | 141 | 247 | 37 | 0 | 23 | 81 | 0 | 2 | 7 | 40 | 4 | 101 | 21 | 7 | 23 | .271 | .330 | .475 |
| Hyzdu, Adam, Bos. | 17 | 11 | 10 | 3 | 3 | 8 | 2 | 0 | 1 | 2 | 0 | 0 | 0 | 1 | 0 | 2 | 0 | 0 | 0 | .300 | .364 | .800 |
| Ibanez, Raul, Sea.* | 123 | 524 | 481 | 67 | 146 | 227 | 31 | 1 | 16 | 62 | 0 | 4 | 3 | 36 | 5 | 72 | 1 | 2 | 10 | .304 | .353 | .472 |
| Infante, Omar, Det. | 142 | 556 | 503 | 69 | 133 | 226 | 27 | 9 | 16 | 55 | 7 | 5 | 1 | 40 | 3 | 112 | 13 | 7 | 4 | .264 | .317 | .449 |
| Inge, Brandon, Det. | 131 | 458 | 408 | 43 | 117 | 185 | 15 | 7 | 13 | 64 | 8 | 6 | 4 | 32 | 0 | 72 | 5 | 4 | 4 | .287 | .340 | .453 |
| Jackson, Damian, K.C. | 14 | 16 | 15 | 1 | 2 | 4 | 2 | 0 | 0 | 2 | 0 | 0 | 0 | 1 | 0 | 6 | 0 | 0 | 0 | .133 | .188 | .267 |
| Jacobsen, Bucky, Sea. | 42 | 176 | 160 | 17 | 44 | 80 | 9 | 0 | 9 | 28 | 0 | 1 | 1 | 14 | 0 | 47 | 0 | 0 | 3 | .275 | .335 | .500 |
| Jeter, Derek, N.Y. | 154 | 721 | 643 | 111 | 188 | 303 | 44 | 1 | 23 | 78 | 16 | 2 | 14 | 46 | 1 | 99 | 23 | 4 | 19 | .292 | .352 | .471 |
| Johnson, Jason, Det. | 33 | 4 | 3 | 0 | 0 | 0 | 0 | 0 | 0 | 0 | 1 | 0 | 0 | 0 | 0 | 2 | 0 | 0 | 0 | .000 | .000 | .000 |
| Johnson, Reed, Tor. | 141 | 582 | 537 | 68 | 145 | 204 | 25 | 2 | 10 | 61 | 3 | 2 | 12 | 28 | 2 | 98 | 6 | 3 | 17 | .270 | .320 | .380 |
| Jones, Jacque, Min.* | 151 | 608 | 555 | 69 | 141 | 237 | 22 | 1 | 24 | 80 | 2 | 1 | 10 | 40 | 2 | 117 | 13 | 10 | 12 | .254 | .315 | .427 |
| Jordan, Brian, Tex. | 61 | 233 | 212 | 27 | 47 | 77 | 13 | 1 | 5 | 23 | 0 | 4 | 1 | 16 | 2 | 35 | 2 | 2 | 7 | .222 | .275 | .363 |
| Kapler, Gabe, Bos. | 136 | 310 | 290 | 51 | 79 | 113 | 14 | 1 | 6 | 33 | 1 | 2 | 2 | 15 | 0 | 49 | 5 | 4 | 5 | .272 | .311 | .390 |
| Karros, Eric, Oak. | 40 | 111 | 103 | 8 | 20 | 32 | 6 | 0 | 2 | 11 | 0 | 1 | 0 | 7 | 1 | 16 | 1 | 0 | 2 | .194 | .243 | .311 |
| Kennedy, Adam, Ana.* | 144 | 533 | 468 | 70 | 130 | 190 | 20 | 5 | 10 | 48 | 9 | 2 | 13 | 41 | 7 | 92 | 15 | 5 | 10 | .278 | .351 | .406 |
| Kielty, Bobby, Oak.† | 83 | 278 | 238 | 29 | 51 | 88 | 14 | 1 | 7 | 31 | 1 | 1 | 3 | 35 | 0 | 47 | 1 | 0 | 5 | .214 | .321 | .370 |

| Player, Team | G | TPA | AB | R | H | TB | 2B | 3B | HR | RBI | SH | SF | HP | BB | IBB | SO | SB | CS | GDP | Avg. | OBP | Slg. |
|---|---|---|---|---|---|---|---|---|---|---|---|---|---|---|---|---|---|---|---|---|---|---|
| Knotts, Gary, Det. | 36 | 5 | 3 | 2 | 1 | 1 | 0 | 0 | 0 | 0 | 1 | 0 | 0 | 1 | 0 | 1 | 0 | 0 | 0 | .333 | .500 | .333 |
| Konerko, Paul, Chi. | 155 | 643 | 563 | 84 | 156 | 301 | 22 | 0 | 41 | 117 | 0 | 5 | 6 | 69 | 5 | 107 | 1 | 0 | 23 | .277 | .359 | .535 |
| Koskie, Corey, Min.* | 118 | 488 | 422 | 68 | 106 | 209 | 24 | 2 | 25 | 71 | 0 | 5 | 12 | 49 | 10 | 103 | 9 | 3 | 6 | .251 | .342 | .495 |
| Kotchman, Casey, Ana.* | 38 | 128 | 116 | 7 | 26 | 32 | 6 | 0 | 0 | 15 | 0 | 1 | 4 | 7 | 3 | 11 | 3 | 0 | 3 | .224 | .289 | .276 |
| Kotsay, Mark, Oak.* | 148 | 673 | 606 | 78 | 190 | 278 | 37 | 3 | 15 | 63 | 5 | 5 | 2 | 55 | 5 | 70 | 8 | 5 | 6 | .314 | .370 | .459 |
| Kubel, Jason, Min.* | 23 | 67 | 60 | 10 | 18 | 26 | 2 | 0 | 2 | 7 | 0 | 1 | 0 | 6 | 0 | 9 | 1 | 1 | 0 | .300 | .358 | .433 |
| Lackey, John, Ana. | 33 | 2 | 2 | 0 | 0 | 0 | 0 | 0 | 0 | 0 | 0 | 0 | 0 | 0 | 0 | 1 | 0 | 0 | 0 | .000 | .000 | .000 |
| Laird, Gerald, Tex. | 49 | 168 | 147 | 20 | 33 | 42 | 6 | 0 | 1 | 16 | 4 | 3 | 2 | 12 | 0 | 35 | 0 | 1 | 5 | .224 | .287 | .286 |
| Laker, Tim, Cle. | 44 | 128 | 117 | 12 | 25 | 36 | 2 | 0 | 3 | 17 | 2 | 1 | 1 | 7 | 1 | 28 | 0 | 0 | 5 | .214 | .262 | .308 |
| Lawton, Matt, Cle.* | 150 | 680 | 591 | 109 | 164 | 249 | 25 | 0 | 20 | 70 | 0 | 4 | 11 | 74 | 3 | 84 | 23 | 9 | 21 | .277 | .366 | .421 |
| LeCroy, Matthew, Min. | 88 | 287 | 264 | 25 | 71 | 112 | 14 | 0 | 9 | 39 | 0 | 2 | 5 | 16 | 0 | 60 | 0 | 0 | 7 | .269 | .321 | .424 |
| Lee, Carlos, Chi. | 153 | 658 | 591 | 103 | 180 | 310 | 37 | 0 | 31 | 99 | 0 | 6 | 7 | 54 | 3 | 86 | 11 | 5 | 10 | .305 | .366 | .525 |
| Lee, Cliff, Cle.* | 33 | 3 | 3 | 0 | 1 | 1 | 0 | 0 | 0 | 0 | 0 | 0 | 0 | 0 | 0 | 0 | 0 | 0 | 0 | .333 | .333 | .333 |
| Lee, Travis, N.Y.* | 7 | 20 | 19 | 1 | 2 | 3 | 1 | 0 | 0 | 2 | 0 | 0 | 0 | 1 | 1 | 3 | 0 | 0 | 2 | .105 | .150 | .158 |
| Leon, Jose, Bal. | 31 | 69 | 66 | 4 | 12 | 20 | 2 | 0 | 2 | 8 | 0 | 1 | 0 | 2 | 0 | 19 | 0 | 0 | 6 | .182 | .203 | .303 |
| Leone, Justin, Sea. | 31 | 115 | 102 | 15 | 22 | 45 | 5 | 0 | 6 | 13 | 1 | 0 | 3 | 9 | 0 | 32 | 1 | 0 | 0 | .216 | .298 | .441 |
| Lieber, Jon, N.Y.* | 27 | 3 | 3 | 0 | 1 | 1 | 0 | 0 | 0 | 0 | 0 | 0 | 0 | 0 | 0 | 0 | 0 | 0 | 1 | .333 | .333 | .333 |
| Lilly, Ted, Tor.* | 32 | 4 | 3 | 0 | 0 | 0 | 0 | 0 | 0 | 0 | 1 | 0 | 0 | 0 | 0 | 2 | 0 | 0 | 0 | .000 | .000 | .000 |
| Little, Mark, Cle. | 11 | 23 | 20 | 0 | 4 | 4 | 0 | 0 | 0 | 2 | 0 | 1 | 2 | 0 | 0 | 7 | 0 | 0 | 0 | .200 | .261 | .200 |
| Loaiza, Esteban, Chi.-N.Y. | 31 | 5 | 5 | 0 | 0 | 0 | 0 | 0 | 0 | 0 | 0 | 0 | 0 | 0 | 0 | 2 | 0 | 0 | 1 | .000 | .000 | .000 |
| Lofton, Kenny, N.Y.* | 83 | 313 | 276 | 51 | 76 | 109 | 10 | 7 | 3 | 18 | 1 | 4 | 1 | 31 | 1 | 27 | 7 | 3 | 4 | .275 | .346 | .395 |
| Logan, Nook, Det.† | 47 | 152 | 133 | 12 | 37 | 46 | 5 | 2 | 0 | 10 | 5 | 1 | 0 | 13 | 0 | 24 | 8 | 2 | 1 | .278 | .340 | .346 |
| Lohse, Kyle, Min. | 35 | 4 | 3 | 0 | 0 | 0 | 0 | 0 | 0 | 0 | 1 | 0 | 0 | 0 | 0 | 3 | 0 | 0 | 0 | .000 | .000 | .000 |
| Lopez, Javy, Bal. | 150 | 638 | 579 | 83 | 183 | 291 | 33 | 3 | 23 | 86 | 0 | 6 | 6 | 47 | 4 | 97 | 0 | 0 | 16 | .316 | .370 | .503 |
| Lopez, Jose, Sea. | 57 | 218 | 207 | 28 | 48 | 76 | 13 | 0 | 5 | 22 | 1 | 1 | 1 | 8 | 0 | 31 | 0 | 1 | 1 | .232 | .263 | .367 |
| Lopez, Luis, Bal.† | 56 | 97 | 88 | 7 | 16 | 24 | 5 | 0 | 1 | 8 | 2 | 3 | 1 | 3 | 0 | 20 | 0 | 0 | 1 | .182 | .211 | .273 |
| Lopez, Mendy, K.C. | 18 | 44 | 38 | 4 | 4 | 7 | 0 | 0 | 1 | 4 | 1 | 0 | 1 | 4 | 0 | 9 | 0 | 0 | 3 | .105 | .209 | .184 |
| Lopez, Mickey, Sea.† | 6 | 6 | 4 | 1 | 1 | 1 | 0 | 0 | 0 | 0 | 0 | 0 | 1 | 1 | 0 | 0 | 0 | 0 | 0 | .250 | .500 | .250 |
| Lowe, Derek, Bos. | 33 | 5 | 4 | 0 | 1 | 2 | 1 | 0 | 0 | 1 | 1 | 0 | 0 | 0 | 0 | 1 | 0 | 0 | 0 | .250 | .250 | .500 |
| Ludwick, Ryan, Cle. | 15 | 54 | 50 | 3 | 11 | 19 | 2 | 0 | 2 | 4 | 0 | 0 | 2 | 2 | 0 | 14 | 0 | 0 | 0 | .220 | .278 | .380 |
| Lugo, Julio, TB. | 157 | 655 | 581 | 83 | 160 | 230 | 41 | 4 | 7 | 75 | 7 | 8 | 5 | 54 | 0 | 106 | 21 | 5 | 8 | .275 | .338 | .396 |
| Machado, Robert, Bal. | 37 | 77 | 73 | 5 | 11 | 17 | 3 | 0 | 1 | 3 | 0 | 0 | 0 | 4 | 0 | 18 | 0 | 0 | 2 | .151 | .195 | .233 |
| Mahay, Ron, Tex.* | 60 | 1 | 1 | 0 | 0 | 0 | 0 | 0 | 0 | 0 | 0 | 0 | 0 | 0 | 0 | 0 | 0 | 0 | 0 | .000 | .000 | .000 |
| Majewski, Val, Bal.* | 9 | 13 | 13 | 3 | 2 | 3 | 1 | 0 | 0 | 1 | 0 | 0 | 0 | 0 | 0 | 1 | 0 | 0 | 0 | .154 | .154 | .231 |
| Maroth, Mike, Det.* | 33 | 5 | 4 | 0 | 0 | 0 | 0 | 0 | 0 | 1 | 1 | 0 | 0 | 0 | 0 | 3 | 0 | 0 | 0 | .000 | .000 | .000 |
| Martinez, Edgar, Sea. | 141 | 549 | 486 | 45 | 128 | 187 | 23 | 0 | 12 | 63 | 0 | 3 | 2 | 58 | 10 | 107 | 1 | 0 | 15 | .263 | .342 | .385 |
| Martinez, Pedro, Bos. | 33 | 2 | 2 | 0 | 0 | 0 | 0 | 0 | 0 | 0 | 0 | 0 | 0 | 0 | 0 | 1 | 0 | 0 | 0 | .000 | .000 | .000 |
| Martinez, Sandy, Cle.-Bos.* | 4 | 6 | 6 | 0 | 0 | 0 | 0 | 0 | 0 | 0 | 0 | 0 | 0 | 0 | 0 | 3 | 0 | 0 | 0 | .000 | .000 | .000 |
| Martinez, Tino, TB.* | 138 | 538 | 458 | 63 | 120 | 211 | 20 | 1 | 23 | 76 | 0 | 5 | 9 | 66 | 9 | 72 | 3 | 1 | 10 | .262 | .362 | .461 |
| Martinez, Victor, Cle.† | 141 | 591 | 520 | 77 | 147 | 256 | 38 | 1 | 23 | 108 | 0 | 6 | 5 | 60 | 11 | 69 | 0 | 1 | 16 | .283 | .359 | .492 |
| Mateo, Ruben, K.C. | 32 | 98 | 93 | 9 | 18 | 28 | 4 | 3 | 0 | 7 | 0 | 0 | 2 | 3 | 0 | 20 | 1 | 1 | 2 | .194 | .235 | .301 |
| Matos, Luis, Bal. | 89 | 359 | 330 | 36 | 74 | 110 | 18 | 0 | 6 | 28 | 3 | 2 | 5 | 19 | 2 | 60 | 12 | 4 | 7 | .224 | .275 | .333 |
| Matsui, Hideki, N.Y.* | 162 | 680 | 584 | 109 | 174 | 305 | 34 | 2 | 31 | 108 | 0 | 5 | 3 | 88 | 2 | 103 | 3 | 0 | 11 | .298 | .390 | .522 |
| Matthews Jr., Gary, Tex.† | 87 | 317 | 280 | 37 | 77 | 129 | 17 | 1 | 11 | 36 | 0 | 3 | 1 | 33 | 5 | 64 | 5 | 1 | 1 | .275 | .350 | .461 |
| Mauer, Joe, Min.* | 35 | 122 | 107 | 18 | 33 | 61 | 8 | 1 | 6 | 17 | 0 | 3 | 1 | 11 | 0 | 14 | 1 | 0 | 1 | .308 | .369 | .570 |
| May, Darrell, K.C.* | 31 | 4 | 4 | 0 | 0 | 0 | 0 | 0 | 0 | 0 | 0 | 0 | 0 | 0 | 0 | 1 | 0 | 0 | 0 | .000 | .000 | .000 |
| McCarty, Dave, Bos. | 91 | 168 | 151 | 24 | 39 | 61 | 8 | 1 | 4 | 17 | 0 | 1 | 2 | 14 | 0 | 40 | 1 | 0 | 5 | .258 | .327 | .404 |
| McCracken, Quinton, Sea.† | 19 | 23 | 20 | 6 | 3 | 3 | 0 | 0 | 0 | 0 | 1 | 0 | 0 | 2 | 0 | 4 | 1 | 1 | 1 | .150 | .227 | .150 |
| McDonald, Darnell, Bal. | 17 | 34 | 32 | 3 | 5 | 6 | 1 | 0 | 0 | 1 | 0 | 0 | 0 | 2 | 0 | 6 | 1 | 0 | 0 | .156 | .206 | .188 |
| McDonald, John, Cle. | 66 | 100 | 93 | 17 | 19 | 32 | 5 | 1 | 2 | 7 | 3 | 0 | 0 | 4 | 0 | 11 | 0 | 0 | 2 | .204 | .237 | .344 |
| McGriff, Fred, TB.* | 27 | 81 | 72 | 7 | 13 | 22 | 3 | 0 | 2 | 7 | 0 | 0 | 0 | 9 | 2 | 19 | 0 | 0 | 1 | .181 | .272 | .306 |
| McLemore, Mark, Oak.† | 77 | 295 | 250 | 29 | 62 | 82 | 14 | 0 | 2 | 21 | 2 | 1 | 1 | 41 | 3 | 33 | 0 | 2 | 4 | .248 | .355 | .328 |
| McMillon, Billy, Oak.* | 52 | 102 | 92 | 10 | 17 | 30 | 4 | 0 | 3 | 11 | 0 | 1 | 1 | 8 | 0 | 22 | 0 | 1 | 2 | .185 | .255 | .326 |
| McPherson, Dallas, Ana.* | 16 | 43 | 40 | 5 | 9 | 19 | 1 | 0 | 3 | 6 | 0 | 0 | 0 | 3 | 0 | 17 | 1 | 0 | 0 | .225 | .279 | .475 |
| Melhuse, Adam, Oak.† | 69 | 231 | 214 | 23 | 55 | 99 | 11 | 0 | 11 | 31 | 1 | 0 | 0 | 16 | 1 | 47 | 0 | 1 | 4 | .257 | .309 | .463 |
| Mench, Kevin, Tex. | 125 | 481 | 438 | 69 | 122 | 236 | 30 | 3 | 26 | 71 | 0 | 4 | 6 | 33 | 2 | 63 | 0 | 0 | 6 | .279 | .335 | .539 |
| Menechino, Frank, Oak.-Tor. | 85 | 311 | 269 | 40 | 74 | 122 | 13 | 4 | 9 | 26 | 1 | 0 | 4 | 37 | 1 | 52 | 0 | 2 | 5 | .275 | .371 | .454 |
| Merloni, Lou, Cle. | 71 | 214 | 190 | 25 | 55 | 81 | 12 | 1 | 4 | 28 | 4 | 3 | 3 | 14 | 1 | 41 | 1 | 2 | 9 | .289 | .343 | .426 |
| Mientkiewicz, Doug, Min.-Bos.* | 127 | 447 | 391 | 47 | 93 | 137 | 24 | 1 | 6 | 35 | 2 | 2 | 4 | 48 | 2 | 56 | 2 | 3 | 12 | .238 | .326 | .350 |
| Millar, Kevin, Bos. | 150 | 588 | 508 | 74 | 151 | 241 | 36 | 0 | 18 | 74 | 0 | 6 | 17 | 57 | 0 | 91 | 1 | 1 | 16 | .297 | .383 | .474 |
| Miller, Damian, Oak. | 110 | 442 | 397 | 39 | 108 | 160 | 25 | 0 | 9 | 58 | 2 | 2 | 2 | 39 | 0 | 87 | 0 | 1 | 19 | .272 | .339 | .403 |
| Mirabelli, Doug, Bos. | 59 | 182 | 160 | 27 | 45 | 84 | 12 | 0 | 9 | 32 | 0 | 0 | 3 | 19 | 0 | 46 | 0 | 0 | 5 | .281 | .368 | .525 |
| Molina, Bengie, Ana. | 97 | 363 | 337 | 36 | 93 | 136 | 13 | 0 | 10 | 54 | 2 | 4 | 2 | 18 | 1 | 35 | 0 | 1 | 18 | .276 | .313 | .404 |
| Molina, Jose, Ana. | 73 | 218 | 203 | 26 | 53 | 76 | 10 | 2 | 3 | 25 | 5 | 0 | 0 | 10 | 0 | 52 | 4 | 1 | 6 | .261 | .296 | .374 |
| Mondesi, Raul, Ana. | 8 | 37 | 34 | 2 | 4 | 8 | 1 | 0 | 1 | 1 | 0 | 0 | 1 | 2 | 0 | 4 | 0 | 1 | 1 | .118 | .189 | .235 |
| Monroe, Craig, Det. | 128 | 481 | 447 | 65 | 131 | 218 | 27 | 3 | 18 | 72 | 0 | 3 | 2 | 29 | 1 | 79 | 3 | 4 | 8 | .293 | .337 | .488 |
| Mora, Melvin, Bal. | 140 | 636 | 550 | 111 | 187 | 309 | 41 | 0 | 27 | 104 | 6 | 3 | 11 | 66 | 0 | 95 | 11 | 6 | 10 | .340 | .419 | .562 |
| Morneau, Justin, Min.* | 74 | 312 | 280 | 39 | 76 | 150 | 17 | 0 | 19 | 58 | 0 | 2 | 2 | 28 | 8 | 54 | 0 | 0 | 4 | .271 | .340 | .536 |
| Mottola, Chad, Bal. | 6 | 16 | 14 | 2 | 2 | 6 | 1 | 0 | 1 | 3 | 0 | 0 | 0 | 2 | 0 | 3 | 0 | 0 | 1 | .143 | .250 | .429 |
| Moyer, Jamie, Sea.* | 34 | 2 | 2 | 0 | 1 | 1 | 0 | 0 | 0 | 2 | 0 | 0 | 0 | 0 | 0 | 1 | 0 | 0 | 0 | .500 | .500 | .500 |
| Mueller, Bill, Bos.† | 110 | 460 | 399 | 75 | 113 | 178 | 27 | 1 | 12 | 57 | 0 | 6 | 4 | 51 | 1 | 56 | 2 | 2 | 8 | .283 | .365 | .446 |
| Mulder, Mark, Oak.* | 33 | 6 | 4 | 2 | 0 | 0 | 0 | 0 | 0 | 0 | 0 | 0 | 1 | 1 | 0 | 3 | 0 | 0 | 0 | .000 | .333 | .000 |
| Mulholland, Terry, Min. | 39 | 2 | 2 | 0 | 0 | 0 | 0 | 0 | 0 | 0 | 0 | 0 | 0 | 0 | 0 | 0 | 0 | 0 | 0 | .000 | .000 | .000 |
| Munoz, Arnie, Chi.* | 11 | 1 | 1 | 0 | 0 | 0 | 0 | 0 | 0 | 0 | 0 | 0 | 0 | 0 | 0 | 0 | 0 | 0 | 0 | .000 | .000 | .000 |
| Munson, Eric, Det.* | 109 | 357 | 321 | 36 | 68 | 143 | 14 | 2 | 19 | 49 | 1 | 0 | 6 | 29 | 3 | 90 | 1 | 1 | 1 | .212 | .289 | .445 |
| Murphy, Donnie, K.C. | 7 | 27 | 27 | 1 | 5 | 8 | 3 | 0 | 0 | 3 | 0 | 0 | 0 | 0 | 0 | 7 | 1 | 0 | 1 | .185 | .185 | .296 |
| Mussina, Mike, N.Y.* | 27 | 1 | 1 | 0 | 0 | 0 | 0 | 0 | 0 | 0 | 0 | 0 | 0 | 0 | 0 | 0 | 0 | 0 | 0 | .000 | .000 | .000 |
| Myers, Greg, Tor.* | 8 | 20 | 18 | 0 | 4 | 6 | 2 | 0 | 0 | 1 | 0 | 0 | 0 | 2 | 0 | 4 | 0 | 0 | 1 | .222 | .300 | .333 |
| Nageotte, Clint, Sea. | 12 | 2 | 2 | 0 | 0 | 0 | 0 | 0 | 0 | 0 | 0 | 0 | 0 | 0 | 0 | 2 | 0 | 0 | 0 | .000 | .000 | .000 |
| Nathan, Joe, Min. | 73 | 1 | 1 | 0 | 0 | 0 | 0 | 0 | 0 | 0 | 0 | 0 | 0 | 0 | 0 | 0 | 0 | 0 | 0 | .000 | .000 | .000 |
| Navarro, Dioner, N.Y.† | 5 | 7 | 7 | 2 | 3 | 3 | 0 | 0 | 0 | 1 | 0 | 0 | 0 | 0 | 0 | 0 | 0 | 0 | 1 | .429 | .429 | .429 |
| Newhan, David, Bal.* | 95 | 412 | 373 | 66 | 116 | 169 | 15 | 7 | 8 | 54 | 5 | 3 | 4 | 27 | 0 | 72 | 11 | 1 | 4 | .311 | .361 | .453 |
| Nivar, Ramon, Tex. | 7 | 21 | 18 | 3 | 4 | 4 | 0 | 0 | 0 | 4 | 2 | 1 | 0 | 0 | 0 | 7 | 1 | 1 | 0 | .222 | .211 | .222 |

| Player, Team | G | TPA | AB | R | H | TB | 2B | 3B | HR | RBI | SH | SF | HP | BB | IBB | SO | SB | CS | GDP | Avg. | OBP | Slg. |
|---|---|---|---|---|---|---|---|---|---|---|---|---|---|---|---|---|---|---|---|---|---|---|
| Nix, Laynce, Tex.* | 115 | 400 | 371 | 58 | 92 | 162 | 20 | 4 | 14 | 46 | 1 | 3 | 2 | 23 | 4 | 113 | 1 | 1 | 6 | .248 | .293 | .437 |
| Nixon, Trot, Bos.* | 48 | 167 | 149 | 24 | 47 | 76 | 9 | 1 | 6 | 23 | 0 | 2 | 1 | 15 | 1 | 24 | 0 | 0 | 3 | .315 | .377 | .510 |
| Norton, Greg, Det.† | 41 | 99 | 86 | 9 | 15 | 22 | 1 | 0 | 2 | 2 | 1 | 0 | 0 | 12 | 1 | 21 | 0 | 0 | 3 | .174 | .276 | .256 |
| Nunez, Abraham, K.C.† | 59 | 247 | 221 | 31 | 50 | 74 | 9 | 0 | 5 | 29 | 0 | 1 | 0 | 25 | 1 | 48 | 0 | 1 | 4 | .226 | .304 | .335 |
| Offerman, Jose, Min.† | 77 | 202 | 172 | 22 | 44 | 68 | 14 | 2 | 2 | 22 | 1 | 0 | 0 | 29 | 2 | 31 | 1 | 1 | 1 | .256 | .363 | .395 |
| Ojeda, Augie, Min.† | 30 | 72 | 59 | 16 | 20 | 27 | 1 | 0 | 2 | 7 | 2 | 1 | 0 | 10 | 0 | 3 | 1 | 1 | 0 | .339 | .429 | .458 |
| Olerud, John, Sea.-N.Y.* | 127 | 500 | 425 | 45 | 110 | 159 | 20 | 1 | 9 | 48 | 1 | 5 | 8 | 61 | 4 | 61 | 0 | 0 | 11 | .259 | .359 | .374 |
| Olivo, Miguel, Chi.-Sea. | 96 | 329 | 301 | 46 | 70 | 132 | 15 | 4 | 13 | 40 | 4 | 1 | 3 | 20 | 2 | 84 | 7 | 6 | 4 | .233 | .286 | .439 |
| Ordonez, Magglio, Chi. | 52 | 222 | 202 | 32 | 59 | 98 | 8 | 2 | 9 | 37 | 0 | 1 | 3 | 16 | 2 | 22 | 0 | 2 | 4 | .292 | .351 | .485 |
| Ortiz, David, Bos.* | 150 | 669 | 582 | 94 | 175 | 351 | 47 | 3 | 41 | 139 | 0 | 8 | 4 | 75 | 8 | 133 | 0 | 0 | 12 | .301 | .380 | .603 |
| Ortiz, Ramon, Ana. | 34 | 3 | 3 | 0 | 0 | 0 | 0 | 0 | 0 | 0 | 0 | 0 | 0 | 0 | 0 | 0 | 0 | 0 | 1 | .000 | .000 | .000 |
| Osik, Keith, Bal. | 11 | 25 | 25 | 0 | 2 | 2 | 0 | 0 | 0 | 0 | 0 | 0 | 0 | 0 | 0 | 7 | 0 | 0 | 1 | .080 | .080 | .080 |
| Palmeiro, Rafael, Bal.* | 154 | 651 | 550 | 68 | 142 | 240 | 29 | 0 | 23 | 88 | 0 | 9 | 6 | 86 | 15 | 61 | 2 | 1 | 15 | .258 | .359 | .436 |
| Parrish, John, Bal.* | 56 | 1 | 1 | 0 | 0 | 0 | 0 | 0 | 0 | 0 | 0 | 0 | 0 | 0 | 0 | 0 | 0 | 0 | 0 | .000 | .000 | .000 |
| Paul, Josh, Ana. | 46 | 81 | 70 | 11 | 17 | 26 | 3 | 0 | 2 | 10 | 3 | 1 | 0 | 7 | 0 | 17 | 2 | 1 | 2 | .243 | .308 | .371 |
| Pena, Carlos, Det.* | 142 | 562 | 481 | 89 | 116 | 227 | 22 | 4 | 27 | 82 | 2 | 5 | 3 | 70 | 2 | 146 | 7 | 1 | 11 | .241 | .338 | .472 |
| Peralta, Jhonny, Cle. | 8 | 28 | 25 | 2 | 6 | 7 | 1 | 0 | 0 | 2 | 0 | 0 | 0 | 3 | 0 | 6 | 0 | 1 | 0 | .240 | .321 | .280 |
| Perez, Eduardo, TB. | 13 | 42 | 38 | 2 | 8 | 13 | 2 | 0 | 1 | 7 | 0 | 0 | 0 | 4 | 0 | 9 | 0 | 0 | 1 | .211 | .286 | .342 |
| Perez, Timo, Chi.* | 103 | 321 | 293 | 38 | 72 | 99 | 12 | 0 | 5 | 40 | 9 | 2 | 2 | 15 | 0 | 29 | 3 | 1 | 9 | .246 | .285 | .338 |
| Perry, Herbert, Tex. | 49 | 153 | 134 | 13 | 30 | 49 | 2 | 1 | 5 | 17 | 0 | 2 | 3 | 14 | 0 | 19 | 0 | 0 | 3 | .224 | .307 | .366 |
| Phelps, Josh, Tor.-Cle. | 103 | 401 | 371 | 51 | 93 | 167 | 19 | 2 | 17 | 61 | 0 | 1 | 7 | 22 | 2 | 93 | 0 | 0 | 13 | .251 | .304 | .450 |
| Phillips, Andy, N.Y. | 5 | 8 | 8 | 1 | 2 | 5 | 0 | 0 | 1 | 2 | 0 | 0 | 0 | 0 | 0 | 1 | 0 | 0 | 1 | .250 | .250 | .625 |
| Phillips, Brandon, Cle. | 6 | 24 | 22 | 1 | 4 | 6 | 2 | 0 | 0 | 1 | 0 | 0 | 0 | 2 | 0 | 5 | 0 | 2 | 1 | .182 | .250 | .273 |
| Phillips, Paul, K.C. | 4 | 6 | 5 | 2 | 1 | 1 | 0 | 0 | 0 | 0 | 0 | 0 | 1 | 0 | 0 | 1 | 0 | 0 | 0 | .200 | .333 | .200 |
| Pickering, Calvin, K.C.* | 35 | 142 | 122 | 21 | 30 | 61 | 8 | 1 | 7 | 26 | 0 | 2 | 0 | 18 | 1 | 42 | 0 | 0 | 6 | .246 | .338 | .500 |
| Pineiro, Joel, Sea. | 21 | 5 | 5 | 0 | 1 | 2 | 1 | 0 | 0 | 0 | 0 | 0 | 0 | 0 | 0 | 1 | 0 | 0 | 0 | .200 | .200 | .400 |
| Pond, Simon, Tor.* | 16 | 56 | 49 | 4 | 8 | 13 | 2 | 0 | 1 | 6 | 0 | 1 | 1 | 5 | 0 | 12 | 0 | 0 | 3 | .163 | .250 | .265 |
| Ponson, Sidney, Bal. | 33 | 5 | 5 | 0 | 0 | 0 | 0 | 0 | 0 | 0 | 0 | 0 | 0 | 0 | 0 | 4 | 0 | 0 | 0 | .000 | .000 | .000 |
| Posada, Jorge, N.Y.† | 137 | 547 | 449 | 72 | 122 | 216 | 31 | 0 | 21 | 81 | 0 | 1 | 9 | 88 | 5 | 92 | 1 | 3 | 24 | .272 | .400 | .481 |
| Pride, Curtis, Ana.* | 35 | 42 | 40 | 5 | 10 | 13 | 3 | 0 | 0 | 3 | 1 | 0 | 1 | 0 | 0 | 11 | 1 | 0 | 1 | .250 | .268 | .325 |
| Prieto, Alex, Min. | 16 | 36 | 32 | 4 | 8 | 12 | 1 | 0 | 1 | 4 | 0 | 1 | 0 | 3 | 0 | 9 | 0 | 1 | 1 | .250 | .306 | .375 |
| Punto, Nick, Min.† | 38 | 103 | 91 | 17 | 23 | 29 | 0 | 0 | 2 | 12 | 0 | 0 | 0 | 12 | 0 | 19 | 6 | 0 | 2 | .253 | .340 | .319 |
| Quantrill, Paul, N.Y.* | 86 | 1 | 1 | 0 | 0 | 0 | 0 | 0 | 0 | 0 | 0 | 0 | 0 | 0 | 0 | 0 | 0 | 0 | 1 | .000 | .000 | .000 |
| Quinlan, Robb, Ana. | 56 | 177 | 160 | 23 | 55 | 84 | 14 | 0 | 5 | 23 | 0 | 1 | 2 | 14 | 0 | 26 | 3 | 1 | 1 | .344 | .401 | .525 |
| Quiroz, Guillermo, Tor. | 17 | 57 | 52 | 2 | 11 | 13 | 2 | 0 | 0 | 6 | 0 | 1 | 2 | 2 | 0 | 8 | 1 | 0 | 1 | .212 | .263 | .250 |
| Raburn, Ryan, Det. | 12 | 31 | 29 | 4 | 4 | 5 | 1 | 0 | 0 | 1 | 0 | 0 | 0 | 2 | 0 | 15 | 1 | 0 | 0 | .138 | .194 | .172 |
| Radke, Brad, Min. | 34 | 3 | 2 | 0 | 0 | 0 | 0 | 0 | 0 | 0 | 1 | 0 | 0 | 0 | 0 | 1 | 0 | 0 | 0 | .000 | .000 | .000 |
| Raines Jr., Tim, Bal.† | 48 | 101 | 94 | 14 | 24 | 30 | 6 | 0 | 0 | 5 | 2 | 0 | 1 | 4 | 0 | 16 | 7 | 3 | 2 | .255 | .293 | .319 |
| Ramirez, Manny, Bos. | 152 | 663 | 568 | 108 | 175 | 348 | 44 | 0 | 43 | 130 | 0 | 7 | 6 | 82 | 15 | 124 | 2 | 4 | 17 | .308 | .397 | .613 |
| Randa, Joe, K.C. | 128 | 539 | 485 | 65 | 139 | 198 | 31 | 2 | 8 | 56 | 0 | 8 | 6 | 40 | 1 | 77 | 0 | 1 | 11 | .287 | .343 | .408 |
| Redman, Mark, Oak.* | 32 | 5 | 5 | 0 | 0 | 0 | 0 | 0 | 0 | 0 | 0 | 0 | 0 | 0 | 0 | 3 | 0 | 0 | 0 | .000 | .000 | .000 |
| Reed, Jeremy, Sea.* | 18 | 66 | 58 | 11 | 23 | 27 | 4 | 0 | 0 | 5 | 0 | 0 | 1 | 7 | 1 | 4 | 3 | 1 | 2 | .397 | .470 | .466 |
| Reese, Pokey, Bos. | 96 | 268 | 244 | 32 | 54 | 74 | 7 | 2 | 3 | 29 | 6 | 1 | 0 | 17 | 1 | 60 | 6 | 2 | 5 | .221 | .271 | .303 |
| Relaford, Desi, K.C.† | 114 | 430 | 380 | 45 | 84 | 116 | 14 | 0 | 6 | 34 | 4 | 4 | 8 | 34 | 3 | 56 | 5 | 4 | 10 | .221 | .296 | .305 |
| Restovich, Michael, Min. | 29 | 51 | 47 | 9 | 12 | 21 | 3 | 0 | 2 | 6 | 0 | 0 | 0 | 4 | 0 | 10 | 0 | 0 | 0 | .255 | .314 | .447 |
| Reyes, Dennys, K.C. | 40 | 6 | 6 | 0 | 0 | 0 | 0 | 0 | 0 | 0 | 0 | 0 | 0 | 0 | 0 | 3 | 0 | 0 | 0 | .000 | .000 | .000 |
| Riggs, Adam, Ana. | 16 | 37 | 36 | 2 | 7 | 10 | 3 | 0 | 0 | 3 | 0 | 0 | 0 | 1 | 0 | 10 | 1 | 0 | 2 | .194 | .216 | .278 |
| Riley, Matt, Bal.* | 14 | 2 | 2 | 0 | 0 | 0 | 0 | 0 | 0 | 0 | 0 | 0 | 0 | 0 | 0 | 2 | 0 | 0 | 0 | .000 | .000 | .000 |
| Rincon, Juan, Min. | 77 | 1 | 1 | 0 | 0 | 0 | 0 | 0 | 0 | 0 | 0 | 0 | 0 | 0 | 0 | 1 | 0 | 0 | 0 | .000 | .000 | .000 |
| Rios, Alexis, Tor. | 111 | 460 | 426 | 55 | 122 | 163 | 24 | 7 | 1 | 28 | 1 | 0 | 2 | 31 | 0 | 84 | 15 | 3 | 14 | .286 | .338 | .383 |
| Rivas, Luis, Min. | 109 | 358 | 336 | 44 | 86 | 145 | 19 | 5 | 10 | 34 | 5 | 3 | 1 | 13 | 0 | 53 | 15 | 1 | 8 | .256 | .283 | .432 |
| Rivera, Rene, Sea. | 2 | 3 | 3 | 0 | 0 | 0 | 0 | 0 | 0 | 0 | 0 | 0 | 0 | 0 | 0 | 1 | 0 | 0 | 0 | .000 | .000 | .000 |
| Roberts, Brian, Bal.† | 159 | 736 | 641 | 107 | 175 | 241 | 50 | 2 | 4 | 53 | 15 | 6 | 1 | 71 | 1 | 95 | 29 | 12 | 3 | .273 | .344 | .376 |
| Roberts, Dave, Bos.* | 45 | 101 | 86 | 19 | 22 | 38 | 10 | 0 | 2 | 14 | 1 | 3 | 1 | 10 | 0 | 17 | 5 | 2 | 2 | .256 | .330 | .442 |
| Robertson, Nate, Det. | 34 | 3 | 3 | 0 | 0 | 0 | 0 | 0 | 0 | 0 | 0 | 0 | 0 | 0 | 0 | 1 | 0 | 0 | 0 | .000 | .000 | .000 |
| Rodriguez, Alex, N.Y. | 155 | 698 | 601 | 112 | 172 | 308 | 24 | 2 | 36 | 106 | 0 | 7 | 10 | 80 | 6 | 131 | 28 | 4 | 18 | .286 | .375 | .512 |
| Rodriguez, Eddy, Bal. | 29 | 1 | 1 | 0 | 0 | 0 | 0 | 0 | 0 | 0 | 0 | 0 | 0 | 0 | 0 | 1 | 0 | 0 | 0 | .000 | .000 | .000 |
| Rodriguez, Ivan, Det. | 135 | 575 | 527 | 72 | 176 | 269 | 32 | 2 | 19 | 86 | 0 | 4 | 3 | 41 | 6 | 91 | 7 | 4 | 15 | .334 | .383 | .510 |
| Rodriguez, Ricardo, Tex. | 5 | 2 | 2 | 0 | 0 | 0 | 0 | 0 | 0 | 0 | 0 | 0 | 0 | 0 | 0 | 2 | 0 | 0 | 0 | .000 | .000 | .000 |
| Rogers, Kenny, Tex.* | 35 | 5 | 5 | 1 | 0 | 0 | 0 | 0 | 0 | 0 | 0 | 0 | 0 | 0 | 0 | 3 | 0 | 0 | 1 | .000 | .000 | .000 |
| Rolls, Damian, TB. | 53 | 132 | 117 | 12 | 19 | 24 | 5 | 0 | 0 | 9 | 2 | 2 | 1 | 10 | 0 | 36 | 2 | 1 | 4 | .162 | .231 | .205 |
| Romano, Jason, TB. | 4 | 8 | 8 | 0 | 1 | 1 | 0 | 0 | 0 | 1 | 0 | 0 | 0 | 0 | 0 | 2 | 0 | 0 | 0 | .125 | .125 | .125 |
| Rose, Mike, Oak.† | 2 | 2 | 2 | 1 | 0 | 0 | 0 | 0 | 0 | 0 | 0 | 0 | 0 | 0 | 0 | 2 | 0 | 0 | 0 | .000 | .000 | .000 |
| Rowand, Aaron, Chi. | 140 | 534 | 487 | 94 | 151 | 265 | 38 | 2 | 24 | 69 | 5 | 2 | 10 | 30 | 1 | 91 | 17 | 5 | 5 | .310 | .361 | .544 |
| Ryan, Michael, Min.* | 36 | 75 | 71 | 9 | 17 | 21 | 2 | 1 | 0 | 7 | 0 | 0 | 0 | 4 | 1 | 16 | 1 | 1 | 2 | .239 | .280 | .296 |
| Sabathia, C.C., Cle.* | 30 | 4 | 4 | 0 | 1 | 1 | 0 | 0 | 0 | 0 | 0 | 0 | 0 | 0 | 0 | 2 | 0 | 0 | 0 | .250 | .250 | .250 |
| Salmon, Tim, Ana. | 60 | 206 | 186 | 15 | 47 | 60 | 7 | 0 | 2 | 23 | 0 | 4 | 2 | 14 | 0 | 41 | 1 | 0 | 2 | .253 | .306 | .323 |
| Sanchez, Alex, Det.* | 79 | 352 | 332 | 41 | 107 | 128 | 9 | 3 | 2 | 26 | 12 | 1 | 0 | 7 | 0 | 50 | 19 | 13 | 5 | .322 | .335 | .386 |
| Sanchez, Rey, TB. | 91 | 307 | 285 | 23 | 70 | 96 | 14 | 3 | 2 | 26 | 4 | 3 | 3 | 12 | 0 | 28 | 0 | 1 | 6 | .246 | .281 | .337 |
| Santana, Johan, Min.* | 34 | 8 | 8 | 0 | 3 | 3 | 0 | 0 | 0 | 2 | 0 | 0 | 0 | 0 | 0 | 1 | 0 | 0 | 0 | .375 | .375 | .375 |
| Santiago, Benito, K.C. | 49 | 189 | 175 | 15 | 48 | 76 | 10 | 0 | 6 | 23 | 3 | 1 | 2 | 8 | 0 | 32 | 1 | 2 | 9 | .274 | .312 | .434 |
| Santiago, Ramon, Sea.† | 19 | 45 | 39 | 8 | 7 | 8 | 1 | 0 | 0 | 2 | 2 | 0 | 1 | 3 | 0 | 3 | 0 | 0 | 1 | .179 | .256 | .205 |
| Schilling, Curt, Bos. | 32 | 7 | 7 | 0 | 1 | 1 | 0 | 0 | 0 | 0 | 0 | 0 | 0 | 0 | 0 | 2 | 0 | 0 | 0 | .143 | .143 | .143 |
| Schoeneweis, Scott, Chi.* | 20 | 2 | 2 | 0 | 1 | 2 | 1 | 0 | 0 | 0 | 0 | 0 | 0 | 0 | 0 | 0 | 0 | 0 | 0 | .500 | .500 | 1.000 |
| Scutaro, Marco, Oak. | 137 | 477 | 455 | 50 | 124 | 179 | 32 | 1 | 7 | 43 | 5 | 1 | 0 | 16 | 1 | 58 | 0 | 0 | 9 | .273 | .297 | .393 |
| Segui, David, Bal.† | 18 | 65 | 59 | 8 | 20 | 26 | 3 | 0 | 1 | 7 | 0 | 0 | 1 | 5 | 1 | 13 | 0 | 1 | 3 | .339 | .400 | .441 |
| Sele, Aaron, Ana. | 28 | 1 | 1 | 0 | 0 | 0 | 0 | 0 | 0 | 0 | 0 | 0 | 0 | 0 | 0 | 1 | 0 | 0 | 0 | .000 | .000 | .000 |
| Sheffield, Gary, N.Y. | 154 | 684 | 573 | 117 | 166 | 306 | 30 | 1 | 36 | 121 | 0 | 8 | 11 | 92 | 7 | 83 | 5 | 6 | 16 | .290 | .393 | .534 |
| Shelton, Chris, Det. | 27 | 56 | 46 | 6 | 9 | 13 | 1 | 0 | 1 | 3 | 0 | 1 | 0 | 9 | 0 | 14 | 0 | 0 | 2 | .196 | .321 | .283 |
| Shields, Scot, Ana. | 60 | 1 | 1 | 0 | 0 | 0 | 0 | 0 | 0 | 0 | 0 | 0 | 0 | 0 | 0 | 1 | 0 | 0 | 0 | .000 | .000 | .000 |
| Sierra, Ruben, N.Y.† | 107 | 338 | 307 | 40 | 75 | 140 | 12 | 1 | 17 | 65 | 0 | 6 | 0 | 25 | 4 | 55 | 1 | 0 | 5 | .244 | .296 | .456 |
| Silva, Carlos, Min. | 33 | 3 | 3 | 0 | 0 | 0 | 0 | 0 | 0 | 0 | 0 | 0 | 0 | 0 | 0 | 1 | 0 | 0 | 0 | .000 | .000 | .000 |
| Simon, Randall, TB.* | 8 | 21 | 17 | 2 | 2 | 2 | 0 | 0 | 0 | 0 | 0 | 0 | 1 | 3 | 0 | 2 | 0 | 0 | 0 | .118 | .286 | .118 |

| Player, Team | G | TPA | AB | R | H | TB | 2B | 3B | HR | RBI | SH | SF | HP | BB | IBB | SO | SB | CS | GDP | Avg. | OBP | Slg. |
|---|---|---|---|---|---|---|---|---|---|---|---|---|---|---|---|---|---|---|---|---|---|---|
| Sizemore, Grady, Cle.* | 43 | 159 | 138 | 15 | 34 | 56 | 6 | 2 | 4 | 24 | 0 | 2 | 5 | 14 | 0 | 34 | 2 | 0 | 0 | .246 | .333 | .406 |
| Smith, Jason, Det.* | 61 | 169 | 155 | 20 | 37 | 67 | 7 | 4 | 5 | 19 | 5 | 0 | 1 | 8 | 0 | 37 | 1 | 2 | 0 | .239 | .280 | .432 |
| Snyder, Earl, Bos. | 1 | 4 | 4 | 0 | 1 | 1 | 0 | 0 | 0 | 0 | 0 | 0 | 0 | 0 | 0 | 1 | 0 | 0 | 1 | .250 | .250 | .250 |
| Soriano, Alfonso, Tex. | 145 | 658 | 608 | 77 | 170 | 294 | 32 | 4 | 28 | 91 | 0 | 7 | 10 | 33 | 4 | 121 | 18 | 5 | 7 | .280 | .324 | .484 |
| Speier, Justin, Tor. | 62 | 1 | 1 | 0 | 0 | 0 | 0 | 0 | 0 | 0 | 0 | 0 | 0 | 0 | 0 | 1 | 0 | 0 | 0 | .000 | .000 | .000 |
| Spiezio, Scott, Sea.† | 112 | 415 | 367 | 38 | 79 | 127 | 12 | 3 | 10 | 41 | 2 | 6 | 4 | 36 | 2 | 60 | 4 | 1 | 7 | .215 | .288 | .346 |
| Stairs, Matt, K.C.* | 126 | 496 | 439 | 48 | 117 | 198 | 21 | 3 | 18 | 66 | 0 | 3 | 5 | 49 | 2 | 92 | 1 | 0 | 15 | .267 | .345 | .451 |
| Stewart, Shannon, Min. | 92 | 430 | 378 | 46 | 115 | 169 | 17 | 2 | 11 | 47 | 1 | 3 | 1 | 47 | 4 | 44 | 6 | 3 | 5 | .304 | .380 | .447 |
| Stinnett, Kelly, K.C. | 20 | 69 | 59 | 10 | 18 | 27 | 0 | 0 | 3 | 7 | 3 | 0 | 2 | 5 | 0 | 16 | 0 | 0 | 0 | .305 | .379 | .458 |
| Sturtze, Tanyon, N.Y. | 28 | 3 | 3 | 0 | 0 | 0 | 0 | 0 | 0 | 0 | 0 | 0 | 0 | 0 | 0 | 1 | 0 | 0 | 0 | .000 | .000 | .000 |
| Surhoff, B.J., Bal.* | 100 | 378 | 343 | 49 | 106 | 144 | 12 | 1 | 8 | 50 | 3 | 1 | 1 | 30 | 2 | 46 | 2 | 0 | 9 | .309 | .365 | .420 |
| Suzuki, Ichiro, Sea.* | 161 | 762 | 704 | 101 | 262 | 320 | 24 | 5 | 8 | 60 | 2 | 3 | 4 | 49 | 19 | 63 | 36 | 11 | 6 | .372 | .414 | .455 |
| Sweeney, Mike, K.C. | 106 | 452 | 411 | 56 | 118 | 207 | 23 | 0 | 22 | 79 | 0 | 2 | 6 | 33 | 9 | 44 | 3 | 2 | 7 | .287 | .347 | .504 |
| Swisher, Nick, Oak.† | 20 | 71 | 60 | 11 | 15 | 25 | 4 | 0 | 2 | 8 | 0 | 1 | 2 | 8 | 0 | 11 | 0 | 0 | 2 | .250 | .352 | .417 |
| Tadano, Kazuhito, Cle. | 14 | 3 | 3 | 1 | 1 | 1 | 0 | 0 | 0 | 0 | 0 | 0 | 0 | 0 | 0 | 1 | 0 | 0 | 0 | .333 | .333 | .333 |
| Teixeira, Mark, Tex.† | 145 | 625 | 545 | 101 | 153 | 305 | 34 | 2 | 38 | 112 | 0 | 2 | 10 | 68 | 12 | 117 | 4 | 1 | 6 | .281 | .370 | .560 |
| Tejada, Miguel, Bal. | 162 | 725 | 653 | 107 | 203 | 349 | 40 | 2 | 34 | 150 | 0 | 14 | 10 | 48 | 6 | 73 | 4 | 1 | 24 | .311 | .360 | .534 |
| Thames, Marcus, Det. | 61 | 184 | 165 | 24 | 42 | 84 | 12 | 0 | 10 | 33 | 0 | 1 | 2 | 16 | 0 | 42 | 0 | 1 | 3 | .255 | .326 | .509 |
| Thomas, Frank, Chi. | 74 | 311 | 240 | 53 | 65 | 135 | 16 | 0 | 18 | 49 | 0 | 1 | 6 | 64 | 3 | 57 | 0 | 2 | 2 | .271 | .434 | .563 |
| Thompson, Rich, K.C.* | 6 | 1 | 1 | 1 | 0 | 0 | 0 | 0 | 0 | 0 | 0 | 0 | 0 | 0 | 0 | 0 | 1 | 0 | 1 | .000 | .000 | .000 |
| Tiffee, Terry, Min.† | 17 | 48 | 44 | 7 | 12 | 22 | 4 | 0 | 2 | 8 | 0 | 0 | 1 | 3 | 0 | 3 | 0 | 0 | 2 | .273 | .333 | .500 |
| Tonis, Mike, K.C. | 2 | 7 | 6 | 0 | 0 | 0 | 0 | 0 | 0 | 0 | 0 | 0 | 0 | 1 | 0 | 0 | 0 | 0 | 1 | .000 | .143 | .000 |
| Torres, Andres, Det.† | 3 | 0 | 0 | 1 | 0 | 0 | 0 | 0 | 0 | 0 | 0 | 0 | 0 | 0 | 0 | 0 | 1 | 0 | 0 | .000 | .000 | .000 |
| Towers, Josh, Tor. | 21 | 3 | 1 | 0 | 0 | 0 | 0 | 0 | 0 | 0 | 2 | 0 | 0 | 0 | 0 | 0 | 0 | 0 | 1 | .000 | .000 | .000 |
| Turnbow, Derrick, Ana. | 4 | 1 | 1 | 0 | 0 | 0 | 0 | 0 | 0 | 0 | 0 | 0 | 0 | 0 | 0 | 0 | 0 | 0 | 0 | .000 | .000 | .000 |
| Upton, B.J., TB. | 45 | 177 | 159 | 19 | 41 | 65 | 8 | 2 | 4 | 12 | 1 | 1 | 1 | 15 | 0 | 46 | 4 | 1 | 1 | .258 | .324 | .409 |
| Uribe, Juan, Chi. | 134 | 553 | 502 | 82 | 142 | 254 | 31 | 6 | 23 | 74 | 11 | 5 | 3 | 32 | 1 | 96 | 9 | 11 | 10 | .283 | .327 | .506 |
| Valdez, Wilson, Chi. | 19 | 46 | 43 | 8 | 10 | 14 | 1 | 0 | 1 | 4 | 1 | 0 | 0 | 2 | 0 | 5 | 1 | 2 | 1 | .233 | .267 | .326 |
| Valentin, Jose, Chi.* | 125 | 504 | 450 | 73 | 97 | 213 | 20 | 3 | 30 | 70 | 6 | 2 | 3 | 43 | 4 | 139 | 8 | 6 | 5 | .216 | .287 | .473 |
| Varitek, Jason, Bos.† | 137 | 536 | 463 | 67 | 137 | 223 | 30 | 1 | 18 | 73 | 0 | 1 | 10 | 62 | 9 | 126 | 10 | 3 | 11 | .296 | .390 | .482 |
| Vazquez, Javier, N.Y. | 32 | 5 | 4 | 1 | 1 | 2 | 1 | 0 | 0 | 0 | 1 | 0 | 0 | 0 | 0 | 0 | 0 | 0 | 1 | .250 | .250 | .500 |
| Vina, Fernando, Det.* | 29 | 131 | 115 | 21 | 26 | 31 | 5 | 0 | 0 | 7 | 1 | 1 | 5 | 9 | 0 | 9 | 2 | 1 | 6 | .226 | .308 | .270 |
| Vizquel, Omar, Cle.† | 148 | 651 | 567 | 82 | 165 | 220 | 28 | 3 | 7 | 59 | 20 | 6 | 1 | 57 | 0 | 62 | 19 | 6 | 12 | .291 | .353 | .388 |
| Wakefield, Tim, Bos. | 32 | 2 | 2 | 0 | 0 | 0 | 0 | 0 | 0 | 0 | 0 | 0 | 0 | 0 | 0 | 1 | 0 | 0 | 0 | .000 | .000 | .000 |
| Wasdin, John, Tex. | 15 | 3 | 3 | 0 | 0 | 0 | 0 | 0 | 0 | 0 | 0 | 0 | 0 | 0 | 0 | 3 | 0 | 0 | 0 | .000 | .000 | .000 |
| Washburn, Jarrod, Ana.* | 25 | 7 | 5 | 0 | 2 | 2 | 0 | 0 | 0 | 1 | 2 | 0 | 0 | 0 | 0 | 0 | 0 | 0 | 0 | .400 | .400 | .400 |
| Wells, Vernon, Tor. | 134 | 590 | 536 | 82 | 146 | 253 | 34 | 2 | 23 | 67 | 0 | 1 | 2 | 51 | 2 | 83 | 9 | 2 | 17 | .272 | .337 | .472 |
| Westbrook, Jake, Cle. | 33 | 4 | 3 | 0 | 0 | 0 | 0 | 0 | 0 | 0 | 1 | 0 | 0 | 0 | 0 | 2 | 0 | 0 | 0 | .000 | .000 | .000 |
| White, Rondell, Det. | 121 | 498 | 448 | 76 | 121 | 203 | 21 | 2 | 19 | 67 | 0 | 3 | 8 | 39 | 4 | 77 | 1 | 2 | 13 | .270 | .337 | .453 |
| Williams, Bernie, N.Y.† | 148 | 651 | 561 | 105 | 147 | 244 | 29 | 1 | 22 | 70 | 1 | 2 | 2 | 85 | 5 | 96 | 1 | 5 | 19 | .262 | .360 | .435 |
| Wilson, Dan, Sea. | 103 | 359 | 319 | 23 | 80 | 99 | 13 | 0 | 2 | 33 | 8 | 5 | 1 | 26 | 0 | 57 | 0 | 1 | 8 | .251 | .305 | .310 |
| Wilson, Enrique, N.Y.† | 93 | 262 | 240 | 19 | 51 | 78 | 9 | 0 | 6 | 31 | 2 | 5 | 0 | 15 | 0 | 20 | 1 | 2 | 5 | .213 | .254 | .325 |
| Winn, Randy, Sea.† | 157 | 703 | 626 | 84 | 179 | 267 | 34 | 6 | 14 | 81 | 9 | 7 | 8 | 53 | 1 | 98 | 21 | 7 | 16 | .286 | .346 | .427 |
| Wood, Mike, K.C. | 17 | 2 | 2 | 0 | 0 | 0 | 0 | 0 | 0 | 0 | 0 | 0 | 0 | 0 | 0 | 1 | 0 | 0 | 0 | .000 | .000 | .000 |
| Woodward, Chris, Tor. | 69 | 232 | 213 | 21 | 50 | 74 | 13 | 4 | 1 | 24 | 2 | 2 | 1 | 14 | 0 | 46 | 1 | 2 | 3 | .235 | .283 | .347 |
| Youkilis, Kevin, Bos. | 72 | 248 | 208 | 38 | 54 | 86 | 11 | 0 | 7 | 35 | 0 | 3 | 4 | 33 | 0 | 45 | 0 | 1 | 1 | .260 | .367 | .413 |
| Young, Dmitri, Det.† | 104 | 432 | 389 | 72 | 106 | 187 | 23 | 2 | 18 | 60 | 0 | 4 | 6 | 33 | 4 | 71 | 0 | 1 | 8 | .272 | .336 | .481 |
| Young, Eric, Tex. | 104 | 402 | 344 | 55 | 99 | 131 | 25 | 2 | 1 | 27 | 4 | 3 | 8 | 43 | 0 | 28 | 14 | 9 | 9 | .288 | .377 | .381 |
| Young, Ernie, Cle. | 3 | 5 | 4 | 0 | 2 | 2 | 0 | 0 | 0 | 0 | 0 | 0 | 0 | 1 | 0 | 2 | 0 | 0 | 0 | .500 | .600 | .500 |
| Young, Michael, Tex. | 160 | 739 | 690 | 114 | 216 | 333 | 33 | 9 | 22 | 99 | 0 | 4 | 1 | 44 | 1 | 89 | 12 | 3 | 11 | .313 | .353 | .483 |
| Zambrano, Victor, TB.† | 23 | 5 | 5 | 1 | 1 | 2 | 1 | 0 | 0 | 1 | 0 | 0 | 0 | 0 | 0 | 1 | 0 | 0 | 0 | .200 | .200 | .400 |
| Zaun, Gregg, Tor.† | 107 | 392 | 338 | 46 | 91 | 133 | 24 | 0 | 6 | 36 | 0 | 1 | 6 | 47 | 3 | 61 | 0 | 2 | 7 | .269 | .367 | .393 |
| Zito, Barry, Oak.* | 34 | 4 | 4 | 0 | 0 | 0 | 0 | 0 | 0 | 0 | 0 | 0 | 0 | 0 | 0 | 3 | 0 | 0 | 0 | .000 | .000 | .000 |

AWARDED FIRST BASE ON OBSTRUCTION OR CATCHER'S INTERFERENCE—Hafner, Cleveland 3 (Buck, Alomar Jr., Olivo); Roberts, Baltimore 2 (Laird, Laird); Gross, Toronto (Flaherty); Guillen, Anaheim (Buck); Harris, Chicago (Borders); Pena, Detroit (Stinnett).

## PLAYERS WITH TWO OR MORE TEAMS

| Player, Team | G | TPA | AB | R | H | TB | 2B | 3B | HR | RBI | SH | SF | HP | BB | IBB | SO | SB | CS | GDP | Avg. | OBP | Slg. |
|---|---|---|---|---|---|---|---|---|---|---|---|---|---|---|---|---|---|---|---|---|---|---|
| Bautista, Jose, Bal. | 16 | 12 | 11 | 3 | 3 | 3 | 0 | 0 | 0 | 0 | 0 | 0 | 0 | 1 | 0 | 3 | 0 | 0 | 0 | .273 | .333 | .273 |
| Bautista, Jose, TB. | 12 | 15 | 12 | 1 | 2 | 2 | 0 | 0 | 0 | 1 | 0 | 0 | 0 | 3 | 0 | 7 | 0 | 1 | 0 | .167 | .333 | .167 |
| Bautista, Jose, K.C. | 13 | 26 | 25 | 1 | 5 | 6 | 1 | 0 | 0 | 1 | 0 | 0 | 0 | 1 | 0 | 12 | 0 | 0 | 0 | .200 | .231 | .240 |
| Borders, Pat, Sea. | 19 | 55 | 53 | 6 | 10 | 15 | 2 | 0 | 1 | 5 | 1 | 0 | 0 | 1 | 0 | 12 | 1 | 1 | 2 | .189 | .204 | .283 |
| Borders, Pat, Min. | 19 | 44 | 42 | 3 | 12 | 16 | 4 | 0 | 0 | 5 | 1 | 0 | 1 | 0 | 0 | 10 | 2 | 0 | 0 | .286 | .302 | .381 |
| Contreras, Jose, N.Y. | 18 | 8 | 8 | 0 | 0 | 0 | 0 | 0 | 0 | 0 | 0 | 0 | 0 | 0 | 0 | 5 | 0 | 0 | 0 | .000 | .000 | .000 |
| Contreras, Jose, Chi. | 13 | 0 | 0 | 0 | 0 | 0 | 0 | 0 | 0 | 0 | 0 | 0 | 0 | 0 | 0 | 0 | 0 | 0 | 0 | – | – | – |
| Davis, Ben, Sea.† | 14 | 37 | 33 | 1 | 3 | 3 | 0 | 0 | 0 | 2 | 0 | 1 | 0 | 3 | 0 | 9 | 0 | 0 | 3 | .091 | .162 | .091 |
| Davis, Ben, Chi.† | 54 | 171 | 160 | 21 | 37 | 64 | 9 | 0 | 6 | 16 | 1 | 0 | 1 | 9 | 0 | 40 | 1 | 1 | 2 | .231 | .276 | .400 |
| Garcia, Freddy, Sea. | 15 | 4 | 4 | 0 | 0 | 0 | 0 | 0 | 0 | 0 | 0 | 0 | 0 | 0 | 0 | 3 | 0 | 0 | 0 | .000 | .000 | .000 |
| Garcia, Freddy, Chi. | 16 | 0 | 0 | 0 | 0 | 0 | 0 | 0 | 0 | 0 | 0 | 0 | 0 | 0 | 0 | 0 | 0 | 0 | 0 | – | – | – |
| Huckaby, Ken, Tex. | 16 | 43 | 38 | 3 | 5 | 7 | 2 | 0 | 0 | 0 | 0 | 0 | 0 | 5 | 0 | 12 | 0 | 0 | 1 | .132 | .233 | .184 |
| Huckaby, Ken, Bal. | 8 | 12 | 12 | 1 | 2 | 3 | 1 | 0 | 0 | 0 | 0 | 0 | 0 | 0 | 0 | 0 | 0 | 0 | 0 | .167 | .167 | .250 |
| Loaiza, Esteban, Chi. | 21 | 5 | 5 | 0 | 0 | 0 | 0 | 0 | 0 | 0 | 0 | 0 | 0 | 0 | 0 | 2 | 0 | 0 | 1 | .000 | .000 | .000 |
| Loaiza, Esteban, N.Y. | 10 | 0 | 0 | 0 | 0 | 0 | 0 | 0 | 0 | 0 | 0 | 0 | 0 | 0 | 0 | 0 | 0 | 0 | 0 | – | – | – |
| Martinez, Sandy, Cle.* | 1 | 2 | 2 | 0 | 0 | 0 | 0 | 0 | 0 | 0 | 0 | 0 | 0 | 0 | 0 | 1 | 0 | 0 | 0 | .000 | .000 | .000 |
| Martinez, Sandy, Bos.* | 3 | 4 | 4 | 0 | 0 | 0 | 0 | 0 | 0 | 0 | 0 | 0 | 0 | 0 | 0 | 2 | 0 | 0 | 0 | .000 | .000 | .000 |
| Menechino, Frank, Oak. | 13 | 35 | 33 | 0 | 3 | 3 | 0 | 0 | 0 | 1 | 0 | 0 | 1 | 1 | 0 | 8 | 0 | 0 | 2 | .091 | .143 | .091 |
| Menechino, Frank, Tor. | 71 | 276 | 236 | 40 | 71 | 119 | 13 | 4 | 9 | 25 | 1 | 0 | 3 | 36 | 1 | 44 | 0 | 2 | 3 | .301 | .400 | .504 |
| Mientkiewicz, Doug, Min.* | 78 | 328 | 284 | 34 | 70 | 103 | 18 | 0 | 5 | 25 | 2 | 1 | 3 | 38 | 2 | 38 | 2 | 2 | 9 | .246 | .340 | .363 |
| Mientkiewicz, Doug, Bos.* | 49 | 119 | 107 | 13 | 23 | 34 | 6 | 1 | 1 | 10 | 0 | 1 | 1 | 10 | 0 | 18 | 0 | 1 | 3 | .215 | .286 | .318 |
| Olerud, John, Sea.* | 78 | 312 | 261 | 29 | 64 | 94 | 13 | 1 | 5 | 22 | 1 | 4 | 6 | 40 | 3 | 41 | 0 | 0 | 6 | .245 | .354 | .360 |
| Olerud, John, N.Y.* | 49 | 188 | 164 | 16 | 46 | 65 | 7 | 0 | 4 | 26 | 0 | 1 | 2 | 21 | 1 | 20 | 0 | 0 | 5 | .280 | .367 | .396 |
| Olivo, Miguel, Chi. | 46 | 156 | 141 | 21 | 38 | 70 | 7 | 2 | 7 | 26 | 4 | 1 | 0 | 10 | 1 | 29 | 5 | 4 | 2 | .270 | .316 | .496 |
| Olivo, Miguel, Sea. | 50 | 173 | 160 | 25 | 32 | 62 | 8 | 2 | 6 | 14 | 0 | 0 | 3 | 10 | 1 | 55 | 2 | 2 | 2 | .200 | .260 | .388 |
| Phelps, Josh, Tor. | 79 | 321 | 295 | 38 | 70 | 123 | 13 | 2 | 12 | 51 | 0 | 1 | 7 | 18 | 2 | 73 | 0 | 0 | 9 | .237 | .296 | .417 |
| Phelps, Josh, Cle. | 24 | 80 | 76 | 13 | 23 | 44 | 6 | 0 | 5 | 10 | 0 | 0 | 0 | 4 | 0 | 20 | 0 | 0 | 4 | .303 | .338 | .579 |

# DESIGNATED HITTING

## TEAM

| Team | G | TPA | AB | R | H | TB | 2B | 3B | HR | RBI | SH | SF | HP | BB | IBB | SO | SB | CS | GDP | Avg. | OBP | Slg. |
|---|---|---|---|---|---|---|---|---|---|---|---|---|---|---|---|---|---|---|---|---|---|---|
| Oakland | 153 | 669 | 595 | 94 | 184 | 298 | 40 | 1 | 24 | 101 | 0 | 2 | 9 | 63 | 9 | 118 | 4 | 2 | 10 | .309 | .383 | .501 |
| Cleveland | 153 | 675 | 569 | 115 | 170 | 320 | 42 | 3 | 34 | 121 | 1 | 5 | 18 | 79 | 5 | 137 | 3 | 4 | 14 | .299 | .398 | .562 |
| Boston | 153 | 706 | 610 | 102 | 179 | 346 | 47 | 3 | 38 | 129 | 0 | 7 | 7 | 82 | 8 | 146 | 3 | 2 | 11 | .293 | .380 | .567 |
| Kansas City | 153 | 656 | 587 | 84 | 171 | 290 | 36 | 4 | 25 | 105 | 0 | 5 | 6 | 58 | 5 | 128 | 2 | 4 | 16 | .291 | .358 | .494 |
| Minnesota | 153 | 662 | 583 | 74 | 161 | 248 | 29 | 2 | 18 | 83 | 2 | 4 | 6 | 67 | 5 | 117 | 7 | 3 | 10 | .276 | .355 | .425 |
| Seattle | 153 | 690 | 607 | 68 | 165 | 243 | 30 | 0 | 16 | 80 | 0 | 5 | 3 | 75 | 14 | 138 | 4 | 0 | 17 | .272 | .352 | .400 |
| Texas | 153 | 653 | 571 | 90 | 145 | 252 | 34 | 5 | 21 | 80 | 1 | 7 | 7 | 67 | 1 | 72 | 6 | 4 | 14 | .254 | .336 | .441 |
| Detroit | 153 | 662 | 591 | 103 | 150 | 262 | 28 | 3 | 26 | 89 | 1 | 5 | 6 | 59 | 5 | 115 | 2 | 1 | 16 | .254 | .325 | .443 |
| Chicago | 153 | 661 | 556 | 95 | 138 | 253 | 32 | 1 | 27 | 93 | 0 | 4 | 10 | 91 | 3 | 119 | 2 | 1 | 13 | .248 | .362 | .455 |
| New York | 153 | 657 | 565 | 93 | 140 | 250 | 23 | 0 | 29 | 93 | 1 | 7 | 7 | 77 | 5 | 116 | 2 | 2 | 19 | .248 | .341 | .442 |
| Baltimore | 153 | 661 | 592 | 79 | 143 | 209 | 28 | 1 | 12 | 77 | 10 | 8 | 9 | 42 | 2 | 119 | 16 | 1 | 13 | .242 | .298 | .353 |
| Anaheim | 153 | 653 | 575 | 80 | 138 | 233 | 25 | 2 | 22 | 74 | 0 | 5 | 8 | 65 | 9 | 121 | 9 | 3 | 14 | .240 | .323 | .405 |
| Toronto | 152 | 648 | 574 | 78 | 132 | 215 | 23 | 3 | 18 | 69 | 2 | 1 | 12 | 59 | 3 | 143 | 1 | 2 | 15 | .230 | .314 | .375 |
| Tampa Bay | 152 | 649 | 571 | 61 | 127 | 209 | 22 | 3 | 18 | 79 | 4 | 5 | 8 | 61 | 6 | 112 | 4 | 0 | 9 | .222 | .304 | .366 |
| **Totals** | 2431 | 9302 | 8146 | 1216 | 2143 | 3628 | 439 | 31 | 328 | 1273 | 22 | 70 | 116 | 945 | 80 | 1701 | 65 | 29 | 191 | .263 | .345 | .445 |

## TOP DESIGNATED HITTERS

Minimum 100 at-bats. *Lefthanded batter. †Switch-hitter.

| Player, Team | G | TPA | AB | R | H | TB | 2B | 3B | HR | RBI | SH | SF | HP | BB | IBB | SO | SB | CS | GDP | Avg. | OBP | Slg. |
|---|---|---|---|---|---|---|---|---|---|---|---|---|---|---|---|---|---|---|---|---|---|---|
| Durazo, Erubiel, Oak.* | 132 | 561 | 494 | 79 | 162 | 263 | 33 | 1 | 22 | 88 | 0 | 2 | 9 | 56 | 9 | 98 | 3 | 2 | 6 | .328 | .405 | .532 |
| Hafner, Travis, Cle.* | 128 | 533 | 445 | 93 | 142 | 270 | 38 | 3 | 28 | 106 | 0 | 5 | 16 | 64 | 5 | 104 | 2 | 2 | 11 | .319 | .419 | .607 |
| Sweeney, Mike, K.C. | 48 | 210 | 192 | 30 | 61 | 105 | 14 | 0 | 10 | 41 | 0 | 1 | 2 | 15 | 2 | 19 | 2 | 2 | 5 | .318 | .371 | .547 |
| Ortiz, David, Bos.* | 115 | 522 | 450 | 78 | 139 | 278 | 34 | 3 | 33 | 109 | 0 | 6 | 4 | 62 | 7 | 112 | 0 | 0 | 8 | .309 | .393 | .618 |
| Harvey, Ken, K.C. | 41 | 170 | 154 | 16 | 47 | 75 | 11 | 1 | 5 | 22 | 0 | 2 | 2 | 12 | 1 | 31 | 0 | 1 | 1 | .305 | .359 | .487 |
| Young, Dmitri, Det.† | 74 | 313 | 283 | 56 | 78 | 142 | 17 | 1 | 15 | 47 | 0 | 3 | 3 | 24 | 3 | 49 | 0 | 0 | 7 | .276 | .335 | .502 |
| Everett, Carl, Chi.† | 41 | 165 | 151 | 21 | 41 | 65 | 7 | 1 | 5 | 21 | 0 | 2 | 5 | 7 | 1 | 25 | 1 | 0 | 3 | .272 | .321 | .430 |
| Newhan, David, Bal.* | 32 | 147 | 129 | 23 | 35 | 45 | 4 | 0 | 2 | 18 | 4 | 1 | 2 | 11 | 0 | 27 | 7 | 0 | 2 | .271 | .336 | .349 |
| Thomas, Frank, Chi. | 65 | 288 | 221 | 50 | 59 | 119 | 15 | 0 | 15 | 44 | 0 | 1 | 5 | 61 | 2 | 50 | 0 | 1 | 2 | .267 | .434 | .538 |
| Martinez, Edgar, Sea. | 122 | 530 | 469 | 44 | 121 | 175 | 21 | 0 | 11 | 61 | 0 | 3 | 2 | 56 | 10 | 103 | 1 | 0 | 15 | .258 | .338 | .373 |
| Phelps, Josh, Tor.-Cle. | 81 | 328 | 301 | 43 | 76 | 139 | 14 | 2 | 15 | 54 | 0 | 1 | 7 | 19 | 2 | 77 | 0 | 0 | 11 | .252 | .311 | .462 |
| White, Rondell, Det. | 43 | 178 | 163 | 31 | 41 | 76 | 7 | 2 | 8 | 24 | 0 | 0 | 2 | 13 | 1 | 28 | 0 | 0 | 3 | .252 | .315 | .466 |
| LeCroy, Matthew, Min. | 30 | 119 | 105 | 7 | 26 | 40 | 5 | 0 | 3 | 13 | 0 | 1 | 4 | 9 | 0 | 38 | 0 | 0 | 3 | .248 | .328 | .381 |
| Williams, Bernie, N.Y.† | 50 | 218 | 189 | 34 | 46 | 73 | 9 | 0 | 6 | 25 | 0 | 1 | 1 | 27 | 1 | 40 | 0 | 1 | 10 | .243 | .339 | .386 |
| Glaus, Troy, Ana. | 39 | 160 | 133 | 31 | 32 | 70 | 5 | 0 | 11 | 22 | 0 | 1 | 2 | 24 | 3 | 34 | 1 | 2 | 5 | .241 | .363 | .526 |

## ALL DESIGNATED HITTERS

*Lefthanded batter. †Switch-hitter.

| Player, Team | G | TPA | AB | R | H | TB | 2B | 3B | HR | RBI | SH | SF | HP | BB | IBB | SO | SB | CS | GDP | Avg. | OBP | Slg. |
|---|---|---|---|---|---|---|---|---|---|---|---|---|---|---|---|---|---|---|---|---|---|---|
| Allen, Chad, Tex. | 5 | 16 | 13 | 2 | 2 | 4 | 0 | 1 | 0 | 0 | 1 | 0 | 0 | 2 | 0 | 2 | 0 | 0 | 0 | .154 | .267 | .308 |
| Alomar Jr., Sandy, Chi. | 1 | 5 | 4 | 1 | 2 | 5 | 0 | 0 | 1 | 1 | 0 | 0 | 0 | 1 | 0 | 0 | 0 | 0 | 0 | .500 | .600 | 1.250 |
| Alomar, Roberto, Chi.† | 5 | 13 | 12 | 0 | 1 | 2 | 1 | 0 | 0 | 2 | 0 | 0 | 0 | 1 | 0 | 3 | 0 | 0 | 1 | .083 | .154 | .167 |
| Anderson, Garret, Ana.* | 18 | 74 | 69 | 5 | 19 | 27 | 5 | 0 | 1 | 7 | 0 | 0 | 0 | 5 | 3 | 14 | 0 | 0 | 1 | .275 | .324 | .391 |
| Baldelli, Rocco, TB. | 13 | 46 | 38 | 5 | 14 | 24 | 4 | 0 | 2 | 9 | 1 | 0 | 2 | 5 | 0 | 5 | 1 | 0 | 2 | .368 | .467 | .632 |
| Bartlett, Jason, Min. | 1 | 3 | 1 | 2 | 0 | 0 | 0 | 0 | 0 | 0 | 1 | 0 | 0 | 1 | 0 | 0 | 1 | 0 | 0 | .000 | .500 | .000 |
| Bautista, Jose, Bal. | 2 | 0 | 0 | 1 | 0 | 0 | 0 | 0 | 0 | 0 | 0 | 0 | 0 | 0 | 0 | 0 | 0 | 0 | 0 | .000 | .000 | .000 |
| Belliard, Ronnie, Cle. | 1 | 4 | 4 | 1 | 1 | 4 | 0 | 0 | 1 | 1 | 0 | 0 | 0 | 0 | 0 | 0 | 0 | 0 | 0 | .250 | .250 | 1.000 |
| Berg, Dave, Tor. | 7 | 13 | 11 | 0 | 1 | 2 | 1 | 0 | 0 | 0 | 0 | 0 | 0 | 2 | 0 | 1 | 0 | 0 | 1 | .091 | .231 | .182 |
| Bigbie, Larry, Bal.* | 2 | 1 | 1 | 1 | 1 | 1 | 0 | 0 | 0 | 2 | 0 | 0 | 0 | 0 | 0 | 0 | 0 | 0 | 0 | 1.000 | 1.000 | 1.000 |
| Bloomquist, Willie, Sea. | 6 | 1 | 1 | 1 | 0 | 0 | 0 | 0 | 0 | 0 | 0 | 0 | 0 | 0 | 0 | 1 | 2 | 0 | 0 | .000 | .000 | .000 |
| Blum, Geoff, TB.† | 2 | 2 | 2 | 0 | 0 | 0 | 0 | 0 | 0 | 0 | 0 | 0 | 0 | 0 | 0 | 1 | 0 | 0 | 0 | .000 | .000 | .000 |
| Bocachica, Hiram, Sea. | 3 | 1 | 1 | 0 | 0 | 0 | 0 | 0 | 0 | 0 | 0 | 0 | 0 | 0 | 0 | 0 | 0 | 0 | 0 | .000 | .000 | .000 |
| Borchard, Joe, Chi.† | 4 | 11 | 9 | 2 | 0 | 0 | 0 | 0 | 0 | 0 | 0 | 0 | 0 | 2 | 0 | 3 | 0 | 0 | 0 | .000 | .182 | .000 |
| Brown, Dee, K.C.* | 1 | 3 | 3 | 0 | 1 | 1 | 0 | 0 | 0 | 0 | 0 | 0 | 0 | 0 | 0 | 1 | 0 | 1 | 0 | .333 | .333 | .333 |
| Buck, John, K.C. | 3 | 11 | 11 | 2 | 3 | 7 | 1 | 0 | 1 | 2 | 0 | 0 | 0 | 0 | 0 | 4 | 0 | 0 | 0 | .273 | .273 | .636 |
| Burke, Jamie, Chi. | 3 | 7 | 6 | 0 | 0 | 0 | 0 | 0 | 0 | 0 | 0 | 0 | 0 | 1 | 0 | 3 | 0 | 0 | 0 | .000 | .143 | .000 |
| Burks, Ellis, Bos. | 9 | 35 | 32 | 6 | 5 | 8 | 0 | 0 | 1 | 1 | 0 | 0 | 0 | 3 | 0 | 8 | 2 | 0 | 1 | .156 | .229 | .250 |
| Bush, Homer, N.Y. | 2 | 0 | 0 | 1 | 0 | 0 | 0 | 0 | 0 | 0 | 0 | 0 | 0 | 0 | 0 | 0 | 0 | 0 | 0 | .000 | .000 | .000 |
| Byrnes, Eric, Oak. | 1 | 0 | 0 | 1 | 0 | 0 | 0 | 0 | 0 | 0 | 0 | 0 | 0 | 0 | 0 | 0 | 0 | 0 | 0 | .000 | .000 | .000 |
| Cabrera, Jolbert, Sea. | 5 | 1 | 1 | 1 | 0 | 0 | 0 | 0 | 0 | 0 | 0 | 0 | 0 | 0 | 0 | 0 | 0 | 0 | 0 | .000 | .000 | .000 |
| Cantu, Jorge, TB. | 4 | 11 | 11 | 2 | 4 | 7 | 3 | 0 | 0 | 0 | 0 | 0 | 0 | 0 | 0 | 2 | 0 | 0 | 0 | .364 | .364 | .636 |
| Castro, Ramon A., Oak. | 1 | 0 | 0 | 1 | 0 | 0 | 0 | 0 | 0 | 0 | 0 | 0 | 0 | 0 | 0 | 0 | 0 | 0 | 0 | .000 | .000 | .000 |
| Catalanotto, Frank, Tor.* | 29 | 106 | 96 | 10 | 19 | 22 | 3 | 0 | 0 | 4 | 0 | 0 | 3 | 7 | 0 | 14 | 0 | 0 | 3 | .198 | .274 | .229 |
| Clark, Howie, Tor.* | 4 | 9 | 6 | 2 | 0 | 0 | 0 | 0 | 0 | 1 | 2 | 0 | 0 | 1 | 0 | 4 | 0 | 0 | 0 | .000 | .143 | .000 |
| Clark, Tony, N.Y.† | 1 | 1 | 1 | 0 | 0 | 0 | 0 | 0 | 0 | 0 | 0 | 0 | 0 | 0 | 0 | 1 | 0 | 0 | 0 | .000 | .000 | .000 |
| Crawford, Carl, TB.* | 5 | 22 | 19 | 2 | 4 | 6 | 0 | 1 | 0 | 4 | 1 | 1 | 0 | 1 | 0 | 4 | 1 | 0 | 0 | .211 | .238 | .316 |
| Crisp, Coco, Cle.† | 6 | 14 | 12 | 1 | 3 | 3 | 0 | 0 | 0 | 1 | 0 | 0 | 0 | 2 | 0 | 5 | 0 | 2 | 0 | .250 | .357 | .250 |
| Crosby, Bubba, N.Y.* | 2 | 1 | 0 | 0 | 0 | 0 | 0 | 0 | 0 | 0 | 1 | 0 | 0 | 0 | 0 | 0 | 0 | 0 | 0 | .000 | .000 | .000 |
| Crozier, Eric, Tor.* | 8 | 24 | 20 | 2 | 2 | 3 | 1 | 0 | 0 | 0 | 0 | 0 | 0 | 4 | 0 | 11 | 0 | 0 | 0 | .100 | .250 | .150 |
| Cuddyer, Michael, Min. | 5 | 18 | 15 | 4 | 6 | 10 | 1 | 0 | 1 | 3 | 0 | 0 | 0 | 3 | 1 | 1 | 1 | 0 | 0 | .400 | .500 | .667 |
| Cummings, Midre, TB.* | 12 | 44 | 39 | 8 | 11 | 20 | 3 | 0 | 2 | 6 | 0 | 0 | 1 | 4 | 0 | 7 | 1 | 0 | 0 | .282 | .364 | .513 |
| Damon, Johnny, Bos.* | 1 | 4 | 4 | 0 | 0 | 0 | 0 | 0 | 0 | 0 | 0 | 0 | 0 | 0 | 0 | 1 | 0 | 0 | 0 | .000 | .000 | .000 |
| DaVanon, Jeff, Ana.† | 19 | 74 | 66 | 9 | 18 | 32 | 4 | 2 | 2 | 11 | 0 | 0 | 0 | 8 | 1 | 11 | 2 | 1 | 0 | .273 | .351 | .485 |
| Delgado, Carlos, Tor.* | 8 | 34 | 28 | 5 | 7 | 20 | 1 | 0 | 4 | 7 | 0 | 0 | 0 | 6 | 1 | 14 | 0 | 1 | 1 | .250 | .382 | .714 |
| Dellucci, David, Tex.* | 9 | 34 | 28 | 5 | 4 | 10 | 0 | 0 | 2 | 3 | 0 | 0 | 0 | 6 | 1 | 11 | 2 | 0 | 0 | .143 | .294 | .357 |

| Player, Team | G | TPA | AB | R | H | TB | 2B | 3B | HR | RBI | SH | SF | HP | BB | IBB | SO | SB | CS | GDP | Avg. | OBP | Slg. |
|---|---|---|---|---|---|---|---|---|---|---|---|---|---|---|---|---|---|---|---|---|---|---|
| Diaz, Matt, TB. | 4 | 9 | 7 | 2 | 2 | 5 | 0 | 0 | 1 | 1 | 0 | 0 | 2 | 0 | 0 | 2 | 0 | 0 | 0 | .286 | .444 | .714 |
| DiFelice, Mike, Det. | 1 | 1 | 1 | 0 | 0 | 0 | 0 | 0 | 0 | 0 | 0 | 0 | 0 | 0 | 0 | 0 | 0 | 0 | 0 | .000 | .000 | .000 |
| Dobbs, Greg, Sea.* | 1 | 4 | 4 | 0 | 1 | 1 | 0 | 0 | 0 | 0 | 0 | 0 | 0 | 0 | 0 | 1 | 0 | 0 | 0 | .250 | .250 | .250 |
| Dransfeldt, Kelly, Chi. | 1 | 1 | 1 | 0 | 0 | 0 | 0 | 0 | 0 | 0 | 0 | 0 | 0 | 0 | 0 | 1 | 0 | 0 | 0 | .000 | .000 | .000 |
| Durazo, Erubiel, Oak.* | 132 | 561 | 494 | 79 | 162 | 263 | 33 | 1 | 22 | 88 | 0 | 2 | 9 | 56 | 9 | 98 | 3 | 2 | 6 | .328 | .405 | .532 |
| Dye, Jermaine, Oak. | 2 | 9 | 8 | 3 | 3 | 4 | 1 | 0 | 0 | 0 | 0 | 0 | 0 | 1 | 0 | 0 | 0 | 0 | 0 | .375 | .444 | .500 |
| Eckstein, David, Ana. | 1 | 5 | 5 | 0 | 1 | 1 | 0 | 0 | 0 | 0 | 0 | 0 | 0 | 0 | 0 | 0 | 0 | 0 | 0 | .200 | .200 | .200 |
| Escobar, Alex, Cle. | 3 | 11 | 9 | 1 | 2 | 2 | 0 | 0 | 0 | 0 | 0 | 0 | 0 | 2 | 0 | 1 | 0 | 0 | 0 | .222 | .364 | .222 |
| Estalella, Bobby, Tor. | 2 | 5 | 3 | 0 | 0 | 0 | 0 | 0 | 0 | 0 | 0 | 0 | 0 | 2 | 0 | 2 | 0 | 0 | 0 | .000 | .400 | .000 |
| Everett, Carl, Chi.† | 41 | 165 | 151 | 21 | 41 | 65 | 7 | 1 | 5 | 21 | 0 | 2 | 5 | 7 | 1 | 25 | 1 | 0 | 3 | .272 | .321 | .430 |
| Fick, Robert, TB.* | 34 | 117 | 107 | 7 | 18 | 31 | 2 | 1 | 3 | 14 | 0 | 1 | 1 | 8 | 2 | 12 | 0 | 0 | 0 | .168 | .231 | .290 |
| Figgins, Chone, Ana.† | 1 | 0 | 0 | 1 | 0 | 0 | 0 | 0 | 0 | 0 | 0 | 0 | 0 | 0 | 0 | 0 | 2 | 0 | 0 | .000 | .000 | .000 |
| Ford, Lew, Min. | 26 | 108 | 96 | 13 | 29 | 43 | 6 | 1 | 2 | 16 | 0 | 1 | 1 | 10 | 0 | 10 | 3 | 0 | 2 | .302 | .370 | .448 |
| Fordyce, Brook, TB. | 1 | 1 | 0 | 0 | 0 | 0 | 0 | 0 | 0 | 0 | 0 | 0 | 0 | 1 | 0 | 0 | 0 | 0 | 0 | .000 | 1.000 | .000 |
| Fox, Andy, Tex.* | 1 | 1 | 1 | 1 | 0 | 0 | 0 | 0 | 0 | 0 | 0 | 0 | 0 | 0 | 0 | 0 | 0 | 0 | 0 | .000 | .000 | .000 |
| Fullmer, Brad, Tex.* | 66 | 273 | 242 | 40 | 56 | 105 | 17 | 1 | 10 | 30 | 0 | 2 | 3 | 26 | 0 | 28 | 1 | 2 | 7 | .231 | .311 | .434 |
| Galarraga, Andres, Ana. | 4 | 7 | 6 | 1 | 1 | 4 | 0 | 0 | 1 | 1 | 0 | 0 | 1 | 0 | 0 | 1 | 0 | 0 | 1 | .167 | .286 | .667 |
| Garciaparra, Nomar, Bos. | 1 | 6 | 5 | 3 | 4 | 8 | 1 | 0 | 1 | 3 | 0 | 0 | 0 | 1 | 0 | 0 | 0 | 0 | 0 | .800 | .833 | 1.600 |
| Gathright, Joey, TB.* | 1 | 0 | 0 | 0 | 0 | 0 | 0 | 0 | 0 | 0 | 0 | 0 | 0 | 0 | 0 | 0 | 1 | 0 | 0 | .000 | .000 | .000 |
| German, Esteban, Oak. | 2 | 0 | 0 | 2 | 0 | 0 | 0 | 0 | 0 | 0 | 0 | 0 | 0 | 0 | 0 | 0 | 0 | 0 | 0 | .000 | .000 | .000 |
| Gerut, Jody, Cle.* | 1 | 4 | 3 | 1 | 0 | 0 | 0 | 0 | 0 | 0 | 0 | 0 | 0 | 1 | 0 | 0 | 0 | 0 | 0 | .000 | .250 | .000 |
| Giambi, Jason, N.Y.* | 28 | 122 | 99 | 14 | 22 | 40 | 3 | 0 | 5 | 14 | 0 | 1 | 5 | 17 | 0 | 27 | 0 | 0 | 1 | .222 | .361 | .404 |
| Gibbons, Jay, Bal.* | 16 | 61 | 57 | 5 | 13 | 18 | 2 | 0 | 1 | 4 | 0 | 0 | 0 | 4 | 0 | 13 | 0 | 0 | 1 | .228 | .279 | .316 |
| Gipson, Charles, TB. | 1 | 1 | 0 | 0 | 0 | 0 | 0 | 0 | 0 | 0 | 1 | 0 | 0 | 0 | 0 | 0 | 0 | 0 | 0 | .000 | .000 | .000 |
| Glaus, Troy, Ana. | 39 | 160 | 133 | 31 | 32 | 70 | 5 | 0 | 11 | 22 | 0 | 1 | 2 | 24 | 3 | 34 | 1 | 2 | 5 | .241 | .363 | .526 |
| Gload, Ross, Chi.* | 13 | 35 | 32 | 4 | 8 | 13 | 5 | 0 | 0 | 5 | 0 | 0 | 0 | 3 | 0 | 6 | 0 | 0 | 3 | .250 | .314 | .406 |
| Gomes, Jonny, TB. | 4 | 14 | 13 | 0 | 1 | 1 | 0 | 0 | 0 | 1 | 0 | 0 | 0 | 1 | 0 | 5 | 0 | 0 | 0 | .077 | .143 | .077 |
| Gomez, Chris, Tor. | 5 | 11 | 9 | 3 | 3 | 7 | 1 | 0 | 1 | 4 | 0 | 0 | 0 | 2 | 0 | 2 | 0 | 1 | 0 | .333 | .455 | .778 |
| Gonzalez, Adrian, Tex.* | 1 | 1 | 1 | 0 | 0 | 0 | 0 | 0 | 0 | 0 | 0 | 0 | 0 | 0 | 0 | 0 | 0 | 0 | 0 | .000 | .000 | .000 |
| Gonzalez, Juan, K.C. | 4 | 18 | 16 | 1 | 3 | 6 | 1 | 1 | 0 | 2 | 0 | 0 | 1 | 1 | 0 | 5 | 0 | 0 | 0 | .188 | .278 | .375 |
| Gross, Gabe, Tor.* | 7 | 19 | 18 | 2 | 4 | 4 | 0 | 0 | 0 | 0 | 0 | 0 | 0 | 1 | 0 | 9 | 1 | 0 | 0 | .222 | .263 | .222 |
| Guerrero, Vladimir, Ana. | 13 | 54 | 49 | 9 | 13 | 22 | 3 | 0 | 2 | 6 | 0 | 0 | 1 | 4 | 1 | 3 | 1 | 0 | 1 | .265 | .333 | .449 |
| Guerrero, Wilton, K.C.† | 2 | 0 | 0 | 2 | 0 | 0 | 0 | 0 | 0 | 0 | 0 | 0 | 0 | 0 | 0 | 0 | 0 | 0 | 0 | .000 | .000 | .000 |
| Guiel, Aaron, K.C.* | 2 | 5 | 5 | 0 | 1 | 1 | 0 | 0 | 0 | 0 | 0 | 0 | 0 | 0 | 0 | 3 | 0 | 0 | 0 | .200 | .200 | .200 |
| Guillen, Jose, Ana. | 10 | 44 | 37 | 7 | 10 | 17 | 1 | 0 | 2 | 7 | 0 | 0 | 2 | 5 | 1 | 5 | 0 | 0 | 2 | .270 | .386 | .459 |
| Hafner, Travis, Cle.* | 128 | 533 | 445 | 93 | 142 | 270 | 38 | 3 | 28 | 106 | 0 | 5 | 16 | 64 | 5 | 104 | 2 | 2 | 11 | .319 | .419 | .607 |
| Hairston Jr., Jerry, Bal. | 21 | 81 | 67 | 10 | 21 | 25 | 4 | 0 | 0 | 11 | 3 | 3 | 2 | 6 | 0 | 8 | 4 | 1 | 0 | .313 | .372 | .373 |
| Halter, Shane, Ana. | 3 | 11 | 11 | 0 | 2 | 3 | 1 | 0 | 0 | 0 | 0 | 0 | 0 | 0 | 0 | 2 | 0 | 0 | 1 | .182 | .182 | .273 |
| Hansen, Dave, Sea.* | 8 | 29 | 22 | 4 | 9 | 12 | 3 | 0 | 0 | 3 | 0 | 1 | 0 | 6 | 2 | 2 | 0 | 0 | 0 | .409 | .517 | .545 |
| Harris, Willie, Chi.* | 2 | 1 | 0 | 1 | 0 | 0 | 0 | 0 | 0 | 0 | 0 | 0 | 0 | 1 | 0 | 0 | 0 | 0 | 0 | .000 | 1.000 | .000 |
| Harvey, Ken, K.C. | 41 | 170 | 154 | 16 | 47 | 75 | 11 | 1 | 5 | 22 | 0 | 2 | 2 | 12 | 1 | 31 | 0 | 1 | 1 | .305 | .359 | .487 |
| Hatteberg, Scott, Oak.* | 2 | 8 | 7 | 1 | 4 | 6 | 2 | 0 | 0 | 2 | 0 | 0 | 0 | 1 | 0 | 0 | 0 | 0 | 2 | .571 | .625 | .857 |
| Higginson, Bobby, Det.* | 10 | 42 | 34 | 4 | 12 | 13 | 1 | 0 | 0 | 10 | 1 | 2 | 0 | 5 | 0 | 5 | 0 | 0 | 0 | .353 | .415 | .382 |
| Hinske, Eric, Tor.* | 1 | 4 | 3 | 0 | 0 | 0 | 0 | 0 | 0 | 0 | 0 | 0 | 0 | 1 | 0 | 1 | 0 | 0 | 0 | .000 | .250 | .000 |
| Huff, Aubrey, TB.* | 34 | 141 | 127 | 15 | 30 | 49 | 4 | 0 | 5 | 25 | 0 | 2 | 0 | 12 | 2 | 21 | 0 | 0 | 5 | .236 | .298 | .386 |
| Hunter, Torii, Min. | 10 | 40 | 35 | 3 | 9 | 16 | 1 | 0 | 2 | 7 | 0 | 0 | 1 | 4 | 0 | 5 | 0 | 0 | 2 | .257 | .350 | .457 |
| Hyzdu, Adam, Bos. | 2 | 2 | 1 | 1 | 0 | 0 | 0 | 0 | 0 | 0 | 0 | 0 | 0 | 1 | 0 | 0 | 0 | 0 | 0 | .000 | .500 | .000 |
| Ibanez, Raul, Sea.* | 2 | 9 | 7 | 2 | 4 | 5 | 1 | 0 | 0 | 1 | 0 | 0 | 0 | 2 | 1 | 1 | 0 | 0 | 0 | .571 | .667 | .714 |
| Jackson, Damian, K.C. | 2 | 3 | 3 | 1 | 0 | 0 | 0 | 0 | 0 | 0 | 0 | 0 | 0 | 0 | 0 | 2 | 0 | 0 | 0 | .000 | .000 | .000 |
| Jacobsen, Bucky, Sea. | 20 | 85 | 75 | 9 | 21 | 39 | 3 | 0 | 5 | 12 | 0 | 0 | 1 | 9 | 0 | 25 | 0 | 0 | 1 | .280 | .365 | .520 |
| Johnson, Reed, Tor. | 4 | 11 | 11 | 2 | 4 | 4 | 0 | 0 | 0 | 1 | 0 | 0 | 0 | 0 | 0 | 3 | 0 | 0 | 0 | .364 | .364 | .364 |
| Jones, Jacque, Min.* | 3 | 11 | 11 | 1 | 3 | 4 | 1 | 0 | 0 | 2 | 0 | 0 | 0 | 0 | 0 | 1 | 0 | 0 | 0 | .273 | .273 | .364 |
| Jordan, Brian, Tex. | 17 | 66 | 62 | 6 | 11 | 18 | 2 | 1 | 1 | 8 | 0 | 2 | 0 | 2 | 0 | 9 | 0 | 0 | 1 | .177 | .197 | .290 |
| Kapler, Gabe, Bos. | 2 | 0 | 0 | 1 | 0 | 0 | 0 | 0 | 0 | 0 | 0 | 0 | 0 | 0 | 0 | 0 | 0 | 0 | 0 | .000 | .000 | .000 |
| Karros, Eric, Oak. | 10 | 31 | 29 | 3 | 6 | 12 | 3 | 0 | 1 | 4 | 0 | 0 | 0 | 2 | 0 | 6 | 1 | 0 | 0 | .207 | .258 | .414 |
| Kielty, Bobby, Oak.† | 11 | 39 | 36 | 4 | 8 | 12 | 1 | 0 | 1 | 7 | 0 | 0 | 0 | 3 | 0 | 6 | 0 | 0 | 1 | .222 | .282 | .333 |
| Konerko, Paul, Chi. | 16 | 67 | 55 | 8 | 16 | 27 | 2 | 0 | 3 | 11 | 0 | 1 | 0 | 11 | 0 | 13 | 0 | 0 | 2 | .291 | .403 | .491 |
| Koskie, Corey, Min.* | 1 | 5 | 4 | 0 | 0 | 0 | 0 | 0 | 0 | 1 | 0 | 1 | 0 | 0 | 0 | 2 | 0 | 0 | 0 | .000 | .000 | .000 |
| Kotchman, Casey, Ana.* | 2 | 2 | 1 | 0 | 1 | 1 | 0 | 0 | 0 | 1 | 0 | 0 | 0 | 1 | 0 | 0 | 1 | 0 | 0 | 1.000 | 1.000 | 1.000 |
| Kotsay, Mark, Oak.* | 1 | 1 | 1 | 0 | 0 | 0 | 0 | 0 | 0 | 0 | 0 | 0 | 0 | 0 | 0 | 0 | 0 | 0 | 0 | .000 | .000 | .000 |
| Kubel, Jason, Min.* | 9 | 31 | 28 | 7 | 11 | 18 | 1 | 0 | 2 | 6 | 0 | 0 | 0 | 3 | 0 | 3 | 1 | 0 | 0 | .393 | .452 | .643 |
| Lawton, Matt, Cle.* | 3 | 16 | 15 | 2 | 2 | 2 | 0 | 0 | 0 | 0 | 0 | 0 | 0 | 1 | 0 | 5 | 1 | 0 | 0 | .133 | .188 | .133 |
| LeCroy, Matthew, Min. | 30 | 119 | 105 | 7 | 26 | 40 | 5 | 0 | 3 | 13 | 0 | 1 | 4 | 9 | 0 | 38 | 0 | 0 | 3 | .248 | .328 | .381 |
| Lee, Carlos, Chi. | 5 | 20 | 19 | 5 | 7 | 14 | 1 | 0 | 2 | 6 | 0 | 0 | 0 | 1 | 0 | 4 | 0 | 0 | 1 | .368 | .400 | .737 |
| Leon, Jose, Bal. | 5 | 12 | 11 | 0 | 1 | 1 | 0 | 0 | 0 | 1 | 0 | 1 | 0 | 0 | 0 | 5 | 0 | 0 | 1 | .091 | .083 | .091 |
| Leone, Justin, Sea. | 1 | 1 | 1 | 0 | 1 | 2 | 1 | 0 | 0 | 0 | 0 | 0 | 0 | 0 | 0 | 0 | 0 | 0 | 0 | 1.000 | 1.000 | 2.000 |
| Lofton, Kenny, N.Y.* | 4 | 15 | 12 | 2 | 2 | 2 | 0 | 0 | 0 | 0 | 0 | 0 | 0 | 3 | 1 | 2 | 0 | 0 | 1 | .167 | .333 | .167 |
| Lopez, Javy, Bal. | 21 | 90 | 85 | 10 | 18 | 34 | 2 | 1 | 4 | 10 | 0 | 0 | 1 | 4 | 0 | 18 | 0 | 0 | 4 | .212 | .256 | .400 |
| Lopez, Luis, Bal.† | 8 | 25 | 21 | 0 | 1 | 2 | 1 | 0 | 0 | 2 | 2 | 2 | 0 | 0 | 0 | 9 | 0 | 0 | 0 | .048 | .043 | .095 |
| Lopez, Mickey, Sea.† | 3 | 1 | 1 | 1 | 0 | 0 | 0 | 0 | 0 | 0 | 0 | 0 | 0 | 0 | 0 | 0 | 0 | 0 | 0 | .000 | .000 | .000 |
| Lugo, Julio, TB. | 5 | 21 | 19 | 0 | 4 | 5 | 1 | 0 | 0 | 1 | 1 | 0 | 0 | 1 | 0 | 4 | 0 | 0 | 0 | .211 | .250 | .263 |
| Majewski, Val, Bal.* | 3 | 2 | 2 | 1 | 1 | 2 | 1 | 0 | 0 | 1 | 0 | 0 | 0 | 0 | 0 | 0 | 0 | 0 | 0 | .500 | .500 | 1.000 |
| Martinez, Edgar, Sea. | 122 | 530 | 469 | 44 | 121 | 175 | 21 | 0 | 11 | 61 | 0 | 3 | 2 | 56 | 10 | 103 | 1 | 0 | 15 | .258 | .338 | .373 |
| Martinez, Tino, TB.* | 19 | 79 | 65 | 8 | 15 | 26 | 0 | 1 | 3 | 11 | 0 | 1 | 1 | 12 | 0 | 12 | 0 | 0 | 1 | .231 | .354 | .400 |
| Martinez, Victor, Cle.† | 8 | 32 | 26 | 6 | 6 | 11 | 2 | 0 | 1 | 5 | 0 | 0 | 1 | 5 | 0 | 4 | 0 | 0 | 1 | .231 | .375 | .423 |
| Mauer, Joe, Min.* | 1 | 4 | 2 | 0 | 0 | 0 | 0 | 0 | 0 | 0 | 0 | 0 | 0 | 2 | 0 | 1 | 0 | 0 | 0 | .000 | .500 | .000 |
| McCarty, Dave, Bos. | 3 | 4 | 4 | 0 | 2 | 3 | 1 | 0 | 0 | 0 | 0 | 0 | 0 | 0 | 0 | 1 | 0 | 0 | 1 | .500 | .500 | .750 |
| McCracken, Quinton, Sea.† | 6 | 1 | 1 | 3 | 1 | 1 | 0 | 0 | 0 | 0 | 0 | 0 | 0 | 0 | 0 | 0 | 0 | 0 | 0 | 1.000 | 1.000 | 1.000 |
| McDonald, Darnell, Bal. | 1 | 1 | 1 | 0 | 0 | 0 | 0 | 0 | 0 | 0 | 0 | 0 | 0 | 0 | 0 | 0 | 0 | 0 | 0 | .000 | .000 | .000 |
| McDonald, John, Cle. | 8 | 1 | 0 | 1 | 0 | 0 | 0 | 0 | 0 | 0 | 1 | 0 | 0 | 0 | 0 | 0 | 0 | 0 | 0 | .000 | .000 | .000 |
| McGriff, Fred, TB.* | 14 | 50 | 44 | 4 | 6 | 10 | 1 | 0 | 1 | 4 | 0 | 0 | 0 | 6 | 2 | 13 | 0 | 0 | 1 | .136 | .240 | .227 |
| McMillon, Billy, Oak.* | 6 | 14 | 14 | 0 | 0 | 0 | 0 | 0 | 0 | 0 | 0 | 0 | 0 | 0 | 0 | 6 | 0 | 0 | 1 | .000 | .000 | .000 |
| Mench, Kevin, Tex. | 14 | 57 | 52 | 7 | 17 | 28 | 3 | 1 | 2 | 8 | 0 | 0 | 0 | 5 | 0 | 5 | 0 | 0 | 1 | .327 | .386 | .538 |
| Menechino, Frank, Tor. | 19 | 69 | 59 | 12 | 21 | 32 | 3 | 1 | 2 | 4 | 0 | 0 | 2 | 8 | 0 | 12 | 0 | 0 | 0 | .356 | .449 | .542 |
| Merloni, Lou, Cle. | 3 | 1 | 0 | 0 | 0 | 0 | 0 | 0 | 0 | 1 | 0 | 0 | 1 | 0 | 0 | 0 | 0 | 0 | 0 | .000 | 1.000 | .000 |

| Player, Team | G | TPA | AB | R | H | TB | 2B | 3B | HR | RBI | SH | SF | HP | BB | IBB | SO | SB | CS | GDP | Avg. | OBP | Slg. |
|---|---|---|---|---|---|---|---|---|---|---|---|---|---|---|---|---|---|---|---|---|---|---|
| Millar, Kevin, Bos. | 8 | 33 | 27 | 2 | 6 | 9 | 3 | 0 | 0 | 2 | 0 | 0 | 2 | 4 | 0 | 5 | 0 | 0 | 0 | .222 | .364 | .333 |
| Mirabelli, Doug, Bos. | 4 | 6 | 5 | 1 | 0 | 0 | 0 | 0 | 0 | 0 | 0 | 0 | 0 | 1 | 0 | 2 | 0 | 0 | 0 | .000 | .167 | .000 |
| Molina, Bengie, Ana. | 5 | 13 | 12 | 1 | 2 | 6 | 1 | 0 | 1 | 1 | 0 | 0 | 0 | 1 | 0 | 7 | 0 | 0 | 0 | .167 | .231 | .500 |
| Mondesi, Raul, Ana. | 1 | 3 | 2 | 0 | 0 | 0 | 0 | 0 | 0 | 0 | 0 | 0 | 0 | 1 | 0 | 0 | 0 | 0 | 0 | .000 | .333 | .000 |
| Monroe, Craig, Det. | 2 | 2 | 2 | 1 | 2 | 5 | 0 | 0 | 1 | 2 | 0 | 0 | 0 | 0 | 0 | 0 | 0 | 0 | 0 | 1.000 | 1.000 | 2.500 |
| Mora, Melvin, Bal. | 1 | 1 | 1 | 0 | 0 | 0 | 0 | 0 | 0 | 0 | 0 | 0 | 0 | 0 | 0 | 0 | 0 | 0 | 0 | .000 | .000 | .000 |
| Morneau, Justin, Min.* | 11 | 47 | 44 | 8 | 15 | 31 | 1 | 0 | 5 | 11 | 0 | 0 | 0 | 3 | 1 | 9 | 0 | 0 | 1 | .341 | .383 | .705 |
| Munson, Eric, Det.* | 7 | 11 | 9 | 0 | 0 | 0 | 0 | 0 | 0 | 0 | 0 | 0 | 1 | 1 | 0 | 3 | 0 | 0 | 0 | .000 | .182 | .000 |
| Myers, Greg, Tor.* | 1 | 2 | 2 | 0 | 1 | 2 | 1 | 0 | 0 | 0 | 0 | 0 | 0 | 0 | 0 | 0 | 0 | 0 | 0 | .500 | .500 | 1.000 |
| Newhan, David, Bal.* | 32 | 147 | 129 | 23 | 35 | 45 | 4 | 0 | 2 | 18 | 4 | 1 | 2 | 11 | 0 | 27 | 7 | 0 | 2 | .271 | .336 | .349 |
| Nixon, Trot, Bos.* | 3 | 6 | 6 | 0 | 1 | 1 | 0 | 0 | 0 | 0 | 0 | 0 | 0 | 0 | 0 | 1 | 0 | 0 | 0 | .167 | .167 | .167 |
| Norton, Greg, Det.† | 7 | 18 | 15 | 0 | 0 | 0 | 0 | 0 | 0 | 0 | 0 | 0 | 0 | 3 | 0 | 6 | 0 | 0 | 1 | .000 | .167 | .000 |
| Nunez, Abraham, K.C.† | 2 | 5 | 3 | 0 | 0 | 0 | 0 | 0 | 0 | 0 | 0 | 0 | 0 | 2 | 0 | 2 | 0 | 0 | 0 | .000 | .400 | .000 |
| Offerman, Jose, Min.† | 39 | 143 | 123 | 16 | 26 | 43 | 9 | 1 | 2 | 13 | 1 | 0 | 0 | 19 | 1 | 22 | 0 | 0 | 1 | .211 | .317 | .350 |
| Ordonez, Magglio, Chi. | 7 | 28 | 28 | 3 | 4 | 8 | 1 | 0 | 1 | 3 | 0 | 0 | 0 | 0 | 0 | 6 | 0 | 0 | 0 | .143 | .143 | .286 |
| Ortiz, David, Bos.* | 115 | 522 | 450 | 78 | 139 | 278 | 34 | 3 | 33 | 109 | 0 | 6 | 4 | 62 | 7 | 112 | 0 | 0 | 8 | .309 | .393 | .618 |
| Palmeiro, Rafael, Bal.* | 20 | 84 | 76 | 11 | 19 | 37 | 6 | 0 | 4 | 13 | 0 | 0 | 2 | 6 | 1 | 13 | 0 | 0 | 0 | .250 | .321 | .487 |
| Paul, Josh, Ana. | 2 | 6 | 4 | 2 | 1 | 4 | 0 | 0 | 1 | 2 | 0 | 0 | 0 | 2 | 0 | 1 | 0 | 0 | 1 | .250 | .500 | 1.000 |
| Pena, Carlos, Det.* | 5 | 16 | 13 | 2 | 2 | 2 | 0 | 0 | 0 | 0 | 0 | 0 | 0 | 3 | 0 | 5 | 0 | 0 | 1 | .154 | .313 | .154 |
| Perez, Eduardo, TB. | 3 | 10 | 9 | 0 | 2 | 2 | 0 | 0 | 0 | 2 | 0 | 0 | 0 | 1 | 0 | 2 | 0 | 0 | 0 | .222 | .300 | .222 |
| Perez, Timo, Chi.* | 6 | 9 | 9 | 0 | 0 | 0 | 0 | 0 | 0 | 0 | 0 | 0 | 0 | 0 | 0 | 2 | 0 | 0 | 1 | .000 | .000 | .000 |
| Perry, Herbert, Tex. | 21 | 76 | 65 | 9 | 18 | 31 | 1 | 0 | 4 | 13 | 0 | 1 | 2 | 8 | 0 | 9 | 0 | 0 | 2 | .277 | .368 | .477 |
| Phelps, Josh, Tor.-Cle. | 81 | 328 | 301 | 43 | 76 | 139 | 14 | 2 | 15 | 54 | 0 | 1 | 7 | 19 | 2 | 77 | 0 | 0 | 11 | .252 | .311 | .462 |
| Pickering, Calvin, K.C.* | 27 | 112 | 92 | 18 | 23 | 47 | 4 | 1 | 6 | 24 | 0 | 2 | 0 | 18 | 1 | 32 | 0 | 0 | 6 | .250 | .366 | .511 |
| Pond, Simon, Tor.* | 6 | 23 | 21 | 1 | 2 | 2 | 0 | 0 | 0 | 0 | 0 | 0 | 0 | 2 | 0 | 3 | 0 | 0 | 0 | .095 | .174 | .095 |
| Pride, Curtis, Ana.* | 2 | 3 | 3 | 0 | 1 | 2 | 1 | 0 | 0 | 0 | 0 | 0 | 0 | 0 | 0 | 0 | 0 | 0 | 0 | .333 | .333 | .667 |
| Prieto, Alex, Min. | 1 | 0 | 0 | 1 | 0 | 0 | 0 | 0 | 0 | 0 | 0 | 0 | 0 | 0 | 0 | 0 | 0 | 0 | 0 | .000 | .000 | .000 |
| Punto, Nick, Min.† | 3 | 1 | 1 | 1 | 0 | 0 | 0 | 0 | 0 | 0 | 0 | 0 | 0 | 0 | 0 | 1 | 0 | 0 | 0 | .000 | .000 | .000 |
| Quinlan, Robb, Ana. | 4 | 15 | 13 | 2 | 2 | 2 | 0 | 0 | 0 | 0 | 0 | 0 | 1 | 1 | 0 | 4 | 1 | 0 | 0 | .154 | .267 | .154 |
| Quiroz, Guillermo, Tor. | 2 | 7 | 6 | 0 | 2 | 2 | 0 | 0 | 0 | 0 | 0 | 0 | 0 | 1 | 0 | 0 | 0 | 0 | 0 | .333 | .429 | .333 |
| Raines Jr., Tim, Bal.† | 4 | 6 | 5 | 2 | 0 | 0 | 0 | 0 | 0 | 0 | 0 | 0 | 0 | 1 | 0 | 0 | 2 | 0 | 0 | .000 | .167 | .000 |
| Ramirez, Manny, Bos. | 19 | 80 | 69 | 10 | 21 | 38 | 8 | 0 | 3 | 14 | 0 | 1 | 1 | 9 | 1 | 14 | 0 | 2 | 1 | .304 | .388 | .551 |
| Randa, Joe, K.C. | 6 | 26 | 24 | 5 | 8 | 13 | 0 | 1 | 1 | 2 | 0 | 0 | 1 | 1 | 0 | 6 | 0 | 0 | 0 | .333 | .385 | .542 |
| Restovich, Michael, Min. | 5 | 8 | 8 | 1 | 2 | 3 | 1 | 0 | 0 | 0 | 0 | 0 | 0 | 0 | 0 | 2 | 0 | 0 | 0 | .250 | .250 | .375 |
| Riggs, Adam, Ana. | 4 | 16 | 15 | 1 | 2 | 3 | 1 | 0 | 0 | 1 | 0 | 0 | 0 | 1 | 0 | 6 | 0 | 0 | 0 | .133 | .188 | .200 |
| Roberts, Brian, Bal.† | 6 | 24 | 23 | 2 | 2 | 2 | 0 | 0 | 0 | 0 | 0 | 0 | 0 | 1 | 0 | 3 | 3 | 0 | 0 | .087 | .125 | .087 |
| Roberts, Dave, Bos.* | 1 | 0 | 0 | 0 | 0 | 0 | 0 | 0 | 0 | 0 | 0 | 0 | 0 | 0 | 0 | 0 | 1 | 0 | 0 | .000 | .000 | .000 |
| Rodriguez, Ivan, Det. | 8 | 34 | 29 | 2 | 10 | 15 | 2 | 0 | 1 | 4 | 0 | 0 | 0 | 5 | 1 | 4 | 1 | 0 | 3 | .345 | .441 | .517 |
| Rolls, Damian, TB. | 5 | 5 | 5 | 0 | 0 | 0 | 0 | 0 | 0 | 0 | 0 | 0 | 0 | 0 | 0 | 2 | 0 | 0 | 0 | .000 | .000 | .000 |
| Ryan, Michael, Min.* | 11 | 28 | 24 | 3 | 5 | 5 | 0 | 0 | 0 | 3 | 0 | 0 | 0 | 4 | 1 | 11 | 1 | 1 | 0 | .208 | .321 | .208 |
| Salmon, Tim, Ana. | 39 | 166 | 149 | 11 | 33 | 39 | 3 | 0 | 1 | 15 | 0 | 4 | 1 | 12 | 0 | 33 | 1 | 0 | 2 | .221 | .277 | .262 |
| Santiago, Ramon, Sea.† | 2 | 0 | 0 | 1 | 0 | 0 | 0 | 0 | 0 | 0 | 0 | 0 | 0 | 0 | 0 | 0 | 0 | 0 | 0 | .000 | .000 | .000 |
| Segui, David, Bal.† | 15 | 56 | 51 | 7 | 17 | 23 | 3 | 0 | 1 | 7 | 0 | 0 | 1 | 4 | 0 | 12 | 0 | 0 | 2 | .333 | .393 | .451 |
| Sheffield, Gary, N.Y. | 18 | 79 | 61 | 15 | 22 | 42 | 5 | 0 | 5 | 13 | 0 | 1 | 1 | 16 | 1 | 10 | 2 | 1 | 2 | .361 | .494 | .689 |
| Shelton, Chris, Det. | 11 | 34 | 29 | 5 | 5 | 9 | 1 | 0 | 1 | 2 | 0 | 0 | 0 | 5 | 0 | 11 | 0 | 0 | 1 | .172 | .294 | .310 |
| Sierra, Ruben, N.Y.† | 56 | 221 | 203 | 27 | 48 | 93 | 6 | 0 | 13 | 41 | 0 | 4 | 0 | 14 | 2 | 36 | 0 | 0 | 5 | .236 | .281 | .458 |
| Simon, Randall, TB.* | 6 | 19 | 15 | 2 | 2 | 2 | 0 | 0 | 0 | 0 | 0 | 0 | 1 | 3 | 0 | 2 | 0 | 0 | 0 | .133 | .316 | .133 |
| Smith, Jason, Det.* | 2 | 0 | 0 | 1 | 0 | 0 | 0 | 0 | 0 | 0 | 0 | 0 | 0 | 0 | 0 | 0 | 0 | 1 | 0 | .000 | .000 | .000 |
| Soriano, Alfonso, Tex. | 3 | 13 | 11 | 2 | 7 | 14 | 2 | 1 | 1 | 6 | 0 | 0 | 0 | 2 | 0 | 1 | 0 | 0 | 0 | .636 | .692 | 1.273 |
| Spiezio, Scott, Sea.† | 2 | 5 | 5 | 0 | 1 | 1 | 0 | 0 | 0 | 0 | 0 | 0 | 0 | 0 | 0 | 2 | 0 | 0 | 1 | .200 | .200 | .200 |
| Stairs, Matt, K.C.* | 22 | 93 | 84 | 9 | 24 | 35 | 5 | 0 | 2 | 12 | 0 | 0 | 0 | 9 | 1 | 23 | 0 | 0 | 4 | .286 | .355 | .417 |
| Stewart, Shannon, Min. | 21 | 93 | 83 | 7 | 28 | 33 | 2 | 0 | 1 | 8 | 0 | 1 | 0 | 9 | 1 | 11 | 0 | 2 | 1 | .337 | .398 | .398 |
| Surhoff, B.J., Bal.* | 18 | 70 | 62 | 6 | 14 | 19 | 5 | 0 | 0 | 8 | 1 | 1 | 1 | 5 | 1 | 11 | 0 | 0 | 3 | .226 | .290 | .306 |
| Suzuki, Ichiro, Sea.* | 3 | 11 | 9 | 1 | 3 | 3 | 0 | 0 | 0 | 0 | 0 | 0 | 0 | 2 | 1 | 1 | 1 | 0 | 0 | .333 | .455 | .333 |
| Sweeney, Mike, K.C. | 48 | 210 | 192 | 30 | 61 | 105 | 14 | 0 | 10 | 41 | 0 | 1 | 2 | 15 | 2 | 19 | 2 | 2 | 5 | .318 | .371 | .547 |
| Swisher, Nick, Oak.† | 2 | 6 | 6 | 0 | 1 | 1 | 0 | 0 | 0 | 0 | 0 | 0 | 0 | 0 | 0 | 2 | 0 | 0 | 0 | .167 | .167 | .167 |
| Teixeira, Mark, Tex.† | 2 | 8 | 7 | 1 | 3 | 3 | 0 | 0 | 0 | 0 | 0 | 0 | 0 | 1 | 0 | 2 | 0 | 0 | 0 | .429 | .500 | .429 |
| Thames, Marcus, Det. | 5 | 13 | 13 | 0 | 0 | 0 | 0 | 0 | 0 | 0 | 0 | 0 | 0 | 0 | 0 | 4 | 0 | 0 | 0 | .000 | .000 | .000 |
| Thomas, Frank, Chi. | 65 | 288 | 221 | 50 | 59 | 119 | 15 | 0 | 15 | 44 | 0 | 1 | 5 | 61 | 2 | 50 | 0 | 1 | 2 | .267 | .434 | .538 |
| Tiffee, Terry, Min.† | 1 | 3 | 3 | 0 | 1 | 2 | 1 | 0 | 0 | 0 | 0 | 0 | 0 | 0 | 0 | 0 | 0 | 0 | 0 | .333 | .333 | .667 |
| Torres, Andres, Det.† | 2 | 0 | 0 | 1 | 0 | 0 | 0 | 0 | 0 | 0 | 0 | 0 | 0 | 0 | 0 | 0 | 1 | 0 | 0 | .000 | .000 | .000 |
| Upton, B.J., TB. | 14 | 57 | 51 | 6 | 14 | 21 | 4 | 0 | 1 | 1 | 0 | 0 | 0 | 6 | 0 | 18 | 0 | 0 | 0 | .275 | .351 | .412 |
| Uribe, Juan, Chi. | 2 | 1 | 1 | 0 | 0 | 0 | 0 | 0 | 0 | 0 | 0 | 0 | 0 | 0 | 0 | 1 | 0 | 0 | 0 | .000 | .000 | .000 |
| Valentin, Jose, Chi.* | 2 | 10 | 8 | 0 | 0 | 0 | 0 | 0 | 0 | 0 | 0 | 0 | 0 | 2 | 0 | 2 | 1 | 0 | 0 | .000 | .200 | .000 |
| Varitek, Jason, Bos.† | 1 | 4 | 4 | 0 | 1 | 1 | 0 | 0 | 0 | 0 | 0 | 0 | 0 | 0 | 0 | 1 | 0 | 0 | 0 | .250 | .250 | .250 |
| Wells, Vernon, Tor. | 3 | 14 | 12 | 2 | 0 | 0 | 0 | 0 | 0 | 0 | 0 | 0 | 0 | 2 | 0 | 2 | 0 | 0 | 1 | .000 | .143 | .000 |
| White, Rondell, Det. | 43 | 178 | 163 | 31 | 41 | 76 | 7 | 2 | 8 | 24 | 0 | 0 | 2 | 13 | 1 | 28 | 0 | 0 | 3 | .252 | .315 | .466 |
| Williams, Bernie, N.Y.† | 50 | 218 | 189 | 34 | 46 | 73 | 9 | 0 | 6 | 25 | 0 | 1 | 1 | 27 | 1 | 40 | 0 | 1 | 10 | .243 | .339 | .386 |
| Winn, Randy, Sea.† | 2 | 11 | 10 | 1 | 3 | 4 | 1 | 0 | 0 | 3 | 0 | 1 | 0 | 0 | 0 | 2 | 0 | 0 | 0 | .300 | .273 | .400 |
| Woodward, Chris, Tor. | 2 | 4 | 4 | 1 | 1 | 1 | 0 | 0 | 0 | 1 | 0 | 0 | 0 | 0 | 0 | 0 | 0 | 0 | 0 | .250 | .250 | .250 |
| Youkilis, Kevin, Bos. | 2 | 4 | 3 | 0 | 0 | 0 | 0 | 0 | 0 | 0 | 0 | 0 | 0 | 1 | 0 | 1 | 0 | 0 | 0 | .000 | .250 | .000 |
| Young, Dmitri, Det.† | 74 | 313 | 283 | 56 | 78 | 142 | 17 | 1 | 15 | 47 | 0 | 3 | 3 | 24 | 3 | 49 | 0 | 0 | 7 | .276 | .335 | .502 |
| Young, Eric, Tex. | 23 | 99 | 81 | 15 | 22 | 30 | 8 | 0 | 0 | 8 | 0 | 2 | 2 | 14 | 0 | 5 | 3 | 1 | 3 | .272 | .384 | .370 |
| Young, Ernie, Cle. | 2 | 4 | 4 | 0 | 2 | 2 | 0 | 0 | 0 | 0 | 0 | 0 | 0 | 0 | 0 | 2 | 0 | 0 | 0 | .500 | .500 | .500 |
| Young, Michael, Tex. | 2 | 9 | 8 | 2 | 5 | 9 | 1 | 0 | 1 | 4 | 0 | 0 | 0 | 1 | 0 | 0 | 0 | 1 | 0 | .625 | .667 | 1.125 |
| Zaun, Gregg, Tor.† | 6 | 20 | 15 | 2 | 1 | 1 | 0 | 0 | 0 | 0 | 0 | 0 | 0 | 5 | 0 | 4 | 0 | 0 | 0 | .067 | .300 | .067 |

## DESIGNATED HITTERS WITH TWO OR MORE TEAMS

| Player, Team | G | TPA | AB | R | H | TB | 2B | 3B | HR | RBI | SH | SF | HP | BB | IBB | SO | SB | CS | GDP | Avg. | OBP | Slg. |
|---|---|---|---|---|---|---|---|---|---|---|---|---|---|---|---|---|---|---|---|---|---|---|
| Phelps, Josh, Tor. | 65 | 273 | 250 | 34 | 64 | 113 | 12 | 2 | 11 | 47 | 0 | 1 | 7 | 15 | 2 | 61 | 0 | 0 | 9 | .256 | .315 | .452 |
| Phelps, Josh, Cle. | 16 | 55 | 51 | 9 | 12 | 26 | 2 | 0 | 4 | 7 | 0 | 0 | 0 | 4 | 0 | 16 | 0 | 0 | 2 | .235 | .291 | .510 |

The following designated hitters, each of whom appeared in at least one game, had no plate appearances, runs scored or stolen base attempts: Amezaga, Alfredo, Anaheim; Bautista, Jose, Tampa Bay; Bellhorn, Mark, Boston; Bowen, Rob, Minnesota; Gomez, Alexis, Kansas City; Matthews Jr., Gary, Texas; Molina, Jose, Anaheim; Phillips, Andy, New York; Sanchez, Alex, Detroit; Thompson, Rich, Kansas City; Hall, Toby, Tampa Bay.

# PINCH-HITTING

## TEAM

| Team | G | TPA | AB | R | H | TB | 2B | 3B | HR | RBI | SH | SF | HP | BB | IBB | SO | SB | CS | GDP | Avg. | OBP | Slg. |
|---|---|---|---|---|---|---|---|---|---|---|---|---|---|---|---|---|---|---|---|---|---|---|
| New York | 62 | 86 | 78 | 12 | 24 | 41 | 2 | 0 | 5 | 20 | 0 | 2 | 0 | 6 | 2 | 18 | 1 | 0 | 1 | .308 | .349 | .526 |
| Chicago | 89 | 130 | 120 | 21 | 34 | 50 | 4 | 0 | 4 | 21 | 0 | 0 | 0 | 10 | 4 | 29 | 0 | 2 | 3 | .283 | .338 | .417 |
| Seattle | 83 | 109 | 96 | 12 | 26 | 44 | 6 | 0 | 4 | 19 | 0 | 0 | 0 | 13 | 0 | 27 | 0 | 0 | 3 | .271 | .358 | .458 |
| Cleveland | 64 | 89 | 72 | 8 | 19 | 34 | 3 | 0 | 4 | 21 | 2 | 2 | 2 | 11 | 1 | 15 | 0 | 0 | 1 | .264 | .368 | .472 |
| Boston | 74 | 112 | 99 | 10 | 26 | 40 | 6 | 1 | 2 | 20 | 0 | 3 | 1 | 9 | 0 | 30 | 0 | 0 | 1 | .263 | .321 | .404 |
| Anaheim | 62 | 91 | 77 | 13 | 20 | 30 | 4 | 0 | 2 | 11 | 4 | 1 | 2 | 7 | 1 | 26 | 4 | 1 | 0 | .260 | .333 | .390 |
| Minnesota | 88 | 125 | 105 | 17 | 27 | 55 | 8 | 1 | 6 | 26 | 0 | 0 | 1 | 19 | 1 | 25 | 2 | 0 | 5 | .257 | .376 | .524 |
| Toronto | 71 | 101 | 85 | 9 | 19 | 33 | 2 | 0 | 4 | 11 | 0 | 0 | 0 | 16 | 1 | 22 | 2 | 1 | 5 | .224 | .347 | .388 |
| Tampa Bay | 70 | 96 | 86 | 5 | 18 | 27 | 6 | 0 | 1 | 12 | 2 | 0 | 0 | 8 | 0 | 18 | 0 | 0 | 2 | .209 | .277 | .314 |
| Baltimore | 61 | 89 | 77 | 10 | 15 | 23 | 2 | 0 | 2 | 11 | 0 | 0 | 1 | 11 | 1 | 21 | 0 | 0 | 6 | .195 | .303 | .299 |
| Oakland | 82 | 120 | 110 | 10 | 20 | 32 | 3 | 0 | 3 | 17 | 0 | 0 | 0 | 10 | 1 | 24 | 0 | 0 | 3 | .182 | .250 | .291 |
| Detroit | 69 | 104 | 86 | 5 | 15 | 19 | 1 | 0 | 1 | 4 | 0 | 0 | 2 | 16 | 0 | 40 | 0 | 0 | 2 | .174 | .317 | .221 |
| Kansas City | 45 | 51 | 46 | 4 | 8 | 13 | 2 | 0 | 1 | 6 | 0 | 1 | 1 | 3 | 0 | 11 | 0 | 0 | 0 | .174 | .235 | .283 |
| Texas | 64 | 85 | 72 | 6 | 12 | 17 | 2 | 0 | 1 | 16 | 1 | 1 | 1 | 10 | 2 | 22 | 0 | 1 | 1 | .167 | .274 | .236 |
| **Totals** | 984 | 1388 | 1209 | 142 | 283 | 458 | 51 | 2 | 40 | 215 | 9 | 10 | 11 | 149 | 14 | 328 | 9 | 5 | 33 | .234 | .321 | .379 |

## TOP PINCH-HITTERS

Minimum 20 at-bats. *Lefthanded batter. †Switch-hitter.

| Player, Team | G | TPA | AB | R | H | TB | 2B | 3B | HR | RBI | SH | SF | HP | BB | IBB | SO | SB | CS | GDP | Avg. | OBP | Slg. |
|---|---|---|---|---|---|---|---|---|---|---|---|---|---|---|---|---|---|---|---|---|---|---|
| Offerman, Jose, Min.† | 36 | 36 | 29 | 3 | 12 | 17 | 3 | 1 | 0 | 7 | 0 | 0 | 0 | 7 | 1 | 5 | 1 | 0 | 0 | .414 | .528 | .586 |
| Martinez, Edgar, Sea. | 23 | 23 | 20 | 1 | 8 | 13 | 2 | 0 | 1 | 3 | 0 | 0 | 0 | 3 | 0 | 5 | 0 | 0 | 0 | .400 | .478 | .650 |
| Sierra, Ruben, N.Y.† | 31 | 31 | 26 | 3 | 10 | 17 | 1 | 0 | 2 | 11 | 0 | 2 | 0 | 3 | 0 | 4 | 1 | 0 | 0 | .385 | .419 | .654 |
| Gload, Ross, Chi.* | 30 | 29 | 29 | 2 | 10 | 13 | 0 | 0 | 1 | 5 | 0 | 0 | 0 | 0 | 0 | 5 | 0 | 1 | 1 | .345 | .345 | .448 |
| McCarty, Dave, Bos. | 23 | 23 | 21 | 1 | 7 | 10 | 1 | 1 | 0 | 3 | 0 | 1 | 0 | 1 | 0 | 5 | 0 | 0 | 0 | .333 | .348 | .476 |
| Perez, Timo, Chi.* | 27 | 26 | 26 | 3 | 5 | 6 | 1 | 0 | 0 | 1 | 0 | 0 | 0 | 0 | 0 | 7 | 0 | 0 | 1 | .192 | .192 | .231 |
| Hansen, Dave, Sea.* | 42 | 42 | 34 | 5 | 6 | 9 | 0 | 0 | 1 | 6 | 0 | 0 | 0 | 8 | 0 | 11 | 0 | 0 | 2 | .176 | .333 | .265 |
| McMillon, Billy, Oak.* | 32 | 30 | 27 | 2 | 2 | 5 | 0 | 0 | 1 | 2 | 0 | 0 | 0 | 3 | 0 | 7 | 0 | 0 | 1 | .074 | .167 | .185 |

**NOTE:** Only 8 batters (rather than the usual 15) are listed above since they are the only players to have the minimum 20 pinch-hit at-bats during the 2004 American League season.

## ALL PINCH-HITTERS

*Lefthanded batter. †Switch-hitter.

| Player, Team | G | TPA | AB | R | H | TB | 2B | 3B | HR | RBI | SH | SF | HP | BB | IBB | SO | SB | CS | GDP | Avg. | OBP | Slg. |
|---|---|---|---|---|---|---|---|---|---|---|---|---|---|---|---|---|---|---|---|---|---|---|
| Adams, Russ, Tor.* | 4 | 4 | 4 | 2 | 3 | 7 | 1 | 0 | 1 | 1 | 0 | 0 | 0 | 0 | 0 | 0 | 0 | 0 | 1 | .750 | .750 | 1.750 |
| Allen, Chad, Tex. | 5 | 5 | 4 | 1 | 2 | 3 | 1 | 0 | 0 | 0 | 0 | 0 | 0 | 1 | 0 | 1 | 0 | 1 | 0 | .500 | .600 | .750 |
| Alomar Jr., Sandy, Chi. | 1 | 1 | 1 | 0 | 0 | 0 | 0 | 0 | 0 | 0 | 0 | 0 | 0 | 0 | 0 | 0 | 0 | 0 | 0 | .000 | .000 | .000 |
| Amezaga, Alfredo, Ana.† | 5 | 5 | 4 | 0 | 1 | 1 | 0 | 0 | 0 | 0 | 1 | 0 | 0 | 0 | 0 | 1 | 0 | 0 | 0 | .250 | .250 | .250 |
| Anderson, Garret, Ana.* | 2 | 2 | 2 | 0 | 0 | 0 | 0 | 0 | 0 | 0 | 0 | 0 | 0 | 0 | 0 | 1 | 0 | 0 | 0 | .000 | .000 | .000 |
| Aurilia, Rich, Sea. | 1 | 1 | 1 | 1 | 1 | 1 | 0 | 0 | 0 | 0 | 0 | 0 | 0 | 0 | 0 | 0 | 0 | 0 | 0 | 1.000 | 1.000 | 1.000 |
| Baldelli, Rocco, TB. | 1 | 1 | 1 | 0 | 0 | 0 | 0 | 0 | 0 | 0 | 0 | 0 | 0 | 0 | 0 | 0 | 0 | 0 | 1 | .000 | .000 | .000 |
| Barajas, Rod, Tex. | 1 | 1 | 1 | 0 | 0 | 0 | 0 | 0 | 0 | 0 | 0 | 0 | 0 | 0 | 0 | 1 | 0 | 0 | 0 | .000 | .000 | .000 |
| Bartlett, Jason, Min. | 1 | 1 | 1 | 0 | 0 | 0 | 0 | 0 | 0 | 0 | 0 | 0 | 0 | 0 | 0 | 0 | 0 | 0 | 0 | .000 | .000 | .000 |
| Bautista, Jose, Bal.-TB.-K.C. | 5 | 5 | 4 | 0 | 1 | 1 | 0 | 0 | 0 | 0 | 0 | 0 | 0 | 1 | 0 | 0 | 0 | 0 | 0 | .250 | .400 | .250 |
| Bellhorn, Mark, Bos.† | 2 | 2 | 2 | 0 | 0 | 0 | 0 | 0 | 0 | 0 | 0 | 0 | 0 | 0 | 0 | 0 | 0 | 0 | 0 | .000 | .000 | .000 |
| Belliard, Ronnie, Cle. | 3 | 3 | 3 | 0 | 1 | 2 | 1 | 0 | 0 | 0 | 0 | 0 | 0 | 0 | 0 | 0 | 0 | 0 | 0 | .333 | .333 | .667 |
| Berg, Dave, Tor. | 10 | 10 | 9 | 0 | 1 | 1 | 0 | 0 | 0 | 1 | 0 | 0 | 0 | 1 | 0 | 2 | 0 | 0 | 0 | .111 | .200 | .111 |
| Bigbie, Larry, Bal.* | 3 | 3 | 2 | 0 | 0 | 0 | 0 | 0 | 0 | 0 | 0 | 0 | 0 | 1 | 0 | 2 | 0 | 0 | 0 | .000 | .333 | .000 |
| Blalock, Hank, Tex.* | 4 | 4 | 3 | 1 | 1 | 4 | 0 | 0 | 1 | 4 | 0 | 0 | 0 | 1 | 1 | 2 | 0 | 0 | 0 | .333 | .500 | 1.333 |
| Bloomquist, Willie, Sea. | 3 | 3 | 3 | 1 | 1 | 2 | 1 | 0 | 0 | 0 | 0 | 0 | 0 | 0 | 0 | 2 | 0 | 0 | 0 | .333 | .333 | .667 |
| Blum, Geoff, TB.† | 8 | 8 | 8 | 0 | 0 | 0 | 0 | 0 | 0 | 0 | 0 | 0 | 0 | 0 | 0 | 2 | 0 | 0 | 0 | .000 | .000 | .000 |
| Bocachica, Hiram, Sea. | 2 | 2 | 2 | 0 | 1 | 2 | 1 | 0 | 0 | 0 | 0 | 0 | 0 | 0 | 0 | 0 | 0 | 0 | 0 | .500 | .500 | 1.000 |
| Borchard, Joe, Chi.† | 6 | 6 | 5 | 2 | 2 | 5 | 0 | 0 | 1 | 1 | 0 | 0 | 0 | 1 | 0 | 2 | 0 | 0 | 0 | .400 | .500 | 1.000 |
| Bowen, Rob, Min.† | 1 | 1 | 1 | 1 | 1 | 4 | 0 | 0 | 1 | 2 | 0 | 0 | 0 | 0 | 0 | 0 | 0 | 0 | 0 | 1.000 | 1.000 | 4.000 |
| Broussard, Ben, Cle.* | 16 | 16 | 14 | 3 | 4 | 10 | 0 | 0 | 2 | 10 | 0 | 0 | 0 | 2 | 0 | 4 | 0 | 0 | 0 | .286 | .375 | .714 |
| Brown, Dee, K.C.* | 6 | 5 | 5 | 0 | 0 | 0 | 0 | 0 | 0 | 0 | 0 | 0 | 0 | 0 | 0 | 2 | 0 | 0 | 0 | .000 | .000 | .000 |
| Burke, Jamie, Chi. | 6 | 6 | 5 | 1 | 1 | 2 | 1 | 0 | 0 | 0 | 0 | 0 | 0 | 1 | 0 | 0 | 0 | 0 | 0 | .200 | .333 | .400 |
| Burks, Ellis, Bos. | 3 | 3 | 2 | 0 | 1 | 1 | 0 | 0 | 0 | 0 | 0 | 0 | 1 | 0 | 0 | 0 | 0 | 0 | 0 | .500 | .667 | .500 |
| Byrnes, Eric, Oak. | 2 | 2 | 2 | 0 | 1 | 2 | 1 | 0 | 0 | 2 | 0 | 0 | 0 | 0 | 0 | 0 | 0 | 0 | 0 | .500 | .500 | 1.000 |
| Cabrera, Jolbert, Sea. | 6 | 6 | 6 | 0 | 0 | 0 | 0 | 0 | 0 | 0 | 0 | 0 | 0 | 0 | 0 | 1 | 0 | 0 | 0 | .000 | .000 | .000 |
| Cairo, Miguel, N.Y. | 2 | 2 | 2 | 0 | 1 | 1 | 0 | 0 | 0 | 1 | 0 | 0 | 0 | 0 | 0 | 1 | 0 | 0 | 0 | .500 | .500 | .500 |
| Cantu, Jorge, TB. | 1 | 1 | 1 | 0 | 0 | 0 | 0 | 0 | 0 | 0 | 0 | 0 | 0 | 0 | 0 | 0 | 0 | 0 | 0 | .000 | .000 | .000 |
| Cash, Kevin, Tor. | 1 | 1 | 1 | 0 | 0 | 0 | 0 | 0 | 0 | 0 | 0 | 0 | 0 | 0 | 0 | 1 | 0 | 0 | 0 | .000 | .000 | .000 |
| Castro, Ramon A., Oak. | 2 | 2 | 2 | 0 | 0 | 0 | 0 | 0 | 0 | 1 | 0 | 0 | 0 | 0 | 0 | 0 | 0 | 0 | 0 | .000 | .000 | .000 |
| Catalanotto, Frank, Tor.* | 13 | 13 | 10 | 0 | 1 | 1 | 0 | 0 | 0 | 0 | 0 | 0 | 0 | 3 | 1 | 1 | 1 | 0 | 3 | .100 | .308 | .100 |
| Clark, Howie, Tor.* | 6 | 6 | 6 | 0 | 0 | 0 | 0 | 0 | 0 | 0 | 0 | 0 | 0 | 0 | 0 | 0 | 0 | 0 | 0 | .000 | .000 | .000 |
| Clark, Tony, N.Y.† | 10 | 10 | 10 | 0 | 2 | 2 | 0 | 0 | 0 | 1 | 0 | 0 | 0 | 0 | 0 | 2 | 0 | 0 | 0 | .200 | .200 | .200 |
| Conti, Jason, Tex.* | 1 | 1 | 1 | 0 | 0 | 0 | 0 | 0 | 0 | 0 | 0 | 0 | 0 | 0 | 0 | 0 | 0 | 0 | 0 | .000 | .000 | .000 |
| Crawford, Carl, TB.* | 4 | 4 | 4 | 0 | 0 | 0 | 0 | 0 | 0 | 0 | 0 | 0 | 0 | 0 | 0 | 1 | 0 | 0 | 0 | .000 | .000 | .000 |
| Crespo, Cesar, Bos.† | 3 | 3 | 3 | 0 | 0 | 0 | 0 | 0 | 0 | 0 | 0 | 0 | 0 | 0 | 0 | 2 | 0 | 0 | 0 | .000 | .000 | .000 |
| Crisp, Coco, Cle.† | 6 | 6 | 5 | 0 | 1 | 2 | 1 | 0 | 0 | 0 | 0 | 0 | 0 | 1 | 0 | 1 | 0 | 0 | 0 | .200 | .333 | .400 |
| Crosby, Bubba, N.Y.* | 6 | 6 | 5 | 1 | 0 | 0 | 0 | 0 | 0 | 0 | 0 | 0 | 0 | 1 | 0 | 3 | 0 | 0 | 0 | .000 | .167 | .000 |
| Crozier, Eric, Tor.* | 3 | 3 | 2 | 0 | 0 | 0 | 0 | 0 | 0 | 0 | 0 | 0 | 0 | 1 | 0 | 1 | 0 | 0 | 0 | .000 | .333 | .000 |

| Player, Team | G | TPA | AB | R | H | TB | 2B | 3B | HR | RBI | SH | SF | HP | BB | IBB | SO | SB | CS | GDP | Avg. | OBP | Slg. |
|---|---|---|---|---|---|---|---|---|---|---|---|---|---|---|---|---|---|---|---|---|---|---|
| Cruz Jr., Jose, TB.† | 3 | 3 | 2 | 1 | 0 | 0 | 0 | 0 | 0 | 0 | 0 | 0 | 0 | 1 | 0 | 0 | 0 | 0 | 0 | .000 | .333 | .000 |
| Cuddyer, Michael, Min. | 12 | 12 | 11 | 2 | 3 | 4 | 1 | 0 | 0 | 3 | 0 | 0 | 0 | 1 | 0 | 3 | 0 | 0 | 0 | .273 | .333 | .364 |
| Cummings, Midre, TB.* | 10 | 10 | 9 | 1 | 4 | 6 | 2 | 0 | 0 | 2 | 0 | 0 | 0 | 1 | 0 | 3 | 0 | 0 | 0 | .444 | .500 | .667 |
| Cust, Jack, Bal.* | 1 | 1 | 1 | 0 | 0 | 0 | 0 | 0 | 0 | 0 | 0 | 0 | 0 | 0 | 0 | 1 | 0 | 0 | 0 | .000 | .000 | .000 |
| Damon, Johnny, Bos.* | 3 | 3 | 2 | 0 | 0 | 0 | 0 | 0 | 0 | 1 | 0 | 1 | 0 | 0 | 0 | 1 | 0 | 0 | 0 | .000 | .000 | .000 |
| Daubach, Brian, Bos.* | 9 | 6 | 4 | 1 | 1 | 2 | 1 | 0 | 0 | 1 | 0 | 0 | 0 | 2 | 0 | 1 | 0 | 0 | 0 | .250 | .500 | .500 |
| DaVanon, Jeff, Ana.† | 18 | 18 | 15 | 3 | 2 | 3 | 1 | 0 | 0 | 0 | 0 | 0 | 0 | 3 | 1 | 3 | 1 | 0 | 0 | .133 | .278 | .200 |
| Davis, Ben, Sea.-Chi.† | 1 | 1 | 1 | 0 | 0 | 0 | 0 | 0 | 0 | 0 | 0 | 0 | 0 | 0 | 0 | 1 | 0 | 0 | 0 | .000 | .000 | .000 |
| DeJesus, David, K.C.* | 1 | 1 | 1 | 0 | 0 | 0 | 0 | 0 | 0 | 0 | 0 | 0 | 0 | 0 | 0 | 0 | 0 | 0 | 0 | .000 | .000 | .000 |
| Dellucci, David, Tex.* | 11 | 11 | 8 | 2 | 2 | 2 | 0 | 0 | 0 | 4 | 0 | 0 | 0 | 3 | 0 | 3 | 0 | 0 | 0 | .250 | .455 | .250 |
| Diaz, Matt, TB. | 3 | 3 | 3 | 0 | 0 | 0 | 0 | 0 | 0 | 0 | 0 | 0 | 0 | 0 | 0 | 0 | 0 | 0 | 0 | .000 | .000 | .000 |
| DiFelice, Mike, Det. | 1 | 1 | 1 | 0 | 0 | 0 | 0 | 0 | 0 | 0 | 0 | 0 | 0 | 0 | 0 | 0 | 0 | 0 | 0 | .000 | .000 | .000 |
| Dobbs, Greg, Sea.* | 5 | 5 | 5 | 2 | 2 | 6 | 1 | 0 | 1 | 4 | 0 | 0 | 0 | 0 | 0 | 3 | 0 | 0 | 0 | .400 | .400 | 1.200 |
| Dominique, Andy, Bos. | 3 | 3 | 3 | 0 | 1 | 1 | 0 | 0 | 0 | 1 | 0 | 0 | 0 | 0 | 0 | 1 | 0 | 0 | 0 | .333 | .333 | .333 |
| Dransfeldt, Kelly, Chi. | 5 | 5 | 5 | 3 | 2 | 2 | 0 | 0 | 0 | 2 | 0 | 0 | 0 | 0 | 0 | 1 | 0 | 0 | 0 | .400 | .400 | .400 |
| Durazo, Erubiel, Oak.* | 13 | 13 | 12 | 3 | 3 | 6 | 0 | 0 | 1 | 4 | 0 | 0 | 0 | 1 | 0 | 4 | 0 | 0 | 0 | .250 | .308 | .500 |
| Dye, Jermaine, Oak. | 2 | 2 | 2 | 0 | 0 | 0 | 0 | 0 | 0 | 0 | 0 | 0 | 0 | 0 | 0 | 0 | 0 | 0 | 0 | .000 | .000 | .000 |
| Eckstein, David, Ana. | 3 | 3 | 0 | 1 | 0 | 0 | 0 | 0 | 0 | 0 | 2 | 0 | 0 | 1 | 0 | 0 | 1 | 0 | 0 | .000 | 1.000 | .000 |
| Escalona, Felix, N.Y. | 1 | 1 | 1 | 1 | 0 | 0 | 0 | 0 | 0 | 0 | 0 | 0 | 0 | 0 | 0 | 0 | 0 | 0 | 0 | .000 | .000 | .000 |
| Escobar, Alex, Cle. | 1 | 1 | 1 | 0 | 0 | 0 | 0 | 0 | 0 | 0 | 0 | 0 | 0 | 0 | 0 | 1 | 0 | 0 | 0 | .000 | .000 | .000 |
| Estalella, Bobby, Tor. | 1 | 1 | 1 | 0 | 0 | 0 | 0 | 0 | 0 | 0 | 0 | 0 | 0 | 0 | 0 | 1 | 0 | 0 | 0 | .000 | .000 | .000 |
| Everett, Carl, Chi.† | 1 | 1 | 1 | 0 | 0 | 0 | 0 | 0 | 0 | 0 | 0 | 0 | 0 | 0 | 0 | 0 | 0 | 0 | 0 | .000 | .000 | .000 |
| Fick, Robert, TB.* | 17 | 17 | 15 | 1 | 5 | 11 | 3 | 0 | 1 | 4 | 0 | 0 | 0 | 2 | 0 | 4 | 0 | 0 | 0 | .333 | .412 | .733 |
| Figgins, Chone, Ana.† | 1 | 1 | 1 | 0 | 1 | 1 | 0 | 0 | 0 | 0 | 0 | 0 | 0 | 0 | 0 | 0 | 0 | 1 | 0 | 1.000 | 1.000 | 1.000 |
| Flaherty, John, N.Y. | 1 | 1 | 1 | 0 | 1 | 1 | 0 | 0 | 0 | 1 | 0 | 0 | 0 | 0 | 0 | 0 | 0 | 0 | 0 | 1.000 | 1.000 | 1.000 |
| Ford, Lew, Min. | 3 | 3 | 3 | 1 | 1 | 4 | 0 | 0 | 1 | 1 | 0 | 0 | 0 | 0 | 0 | 1 | 0 | 0 | 0 | .333 | .333 | 1.333 |
| Fordyce, Brook, TB. | 3 | 3 | 2 | 0 | 0 | 0 | 0 | 0 | 0 | 0 | 0 | 0 | 0 | 1 | 0 | 0 | 0 | 0 | 0 | .000 | .333 | .000 |
| Fox, Andy, Tex.* | 3 | 2 | 2 | 0 | 0 | 0 | 0 | 0 | 0 | 0 | 0 | 0 | 0 | 0 | 0 | 1 | 0 | 0 | 0 | .000 | .000 | .000 |
| Fullmer, Brad, Tex.* | 10 | 10 | 9 | 0 | 1 | 2 | 1 | 0 | 0 | 3 | 0 | 0 | 0 | 1 | 1 | 1 | 0 | 0 | 0 | .111 | .200 | .222 |
| Galarraga, Andres, Ana. | 5 | 4 | 4 | 1 | 1 | 4 | 0 | 0 | 1 | 1 | 0 | 0 | 0 | 0 | 0 | 2 | 0 | 0 | 0 | .250 | .250 | 1.000 |
| Garcia, Karim, Bal.* | 2 | 2 | 2 | 1 | 1 | 1 | 0 | 0 | 0 | 0 | 0 | 0 | 0 | 0 | 0 | 1 | 0 | 0 | 0 | .500 | .500 | .500 |
| Gathright, Joey, TB.* | 2 | 2 | 2 | 0 | 0 | 0 | 0 | 0 | 0 | 0 | 0 | 0 | 0 | 0 | 0 | 1 | 0 | 0 | 0 | .000 | .000 | .000 |
| German, Esteban, Oak. | 5 | 5 | 4 | 2 | 2 | 2 | 0 | 0 | 0 | 1 | 0 | 0 | 0 | 1 | 0 | 1 | 0 | 0 | 0 | .500 | .600 | .500 |
| Gerut, Jody, Cle.* | 7 | 7 | 6 | 0 | 1 | 1 | 0 | 0 | 0 | 0 | 1 | 0 | 0 | 0 | 0 | 1 | 0 | 0 | 0 | .167 | .167 | .167 |
| Giambi, Jason, N.Y.* | 5 | 5 | 4 | 0 | 1 | 2 | 1 | 0 | 0 | 0 | 0 | 0 | 0 | 1 | 1 | 2 | 0 | 0 | 0 | .250 | .400 | .500 |
| Gibbons, Jay, Bal.* | 4 | 4 | 3 | 1 | 0 | 0 | 0 | 0 | 0 | 0 | 0 | 0 | 0 | 1 | 0 | 1 | 0 | 0 | 0 | .000 | .250 | .000 |
| Gil, Geronimo, Bal. | 1 | 1 | 1 | 0 | 0 | 0 | 0 | 0 | 0 | 0 | 0 | 0 | 0 | 0 | 0 | 1 | 0 | 0 | 0 | .000 | .000 | .000 |
| Gipson, Charles, TB. | 1 | 1 | 0 | 0 | 0 | 0 | 0 | 0 | 0 | 0 | 1 | 0 | 0 | 0 | 0 | 0 | 0 | 0 | 0 | .000 | .000 | .000 |
| Gload, Ross, Chi.* | 30 | 29 | 29 | 2 | 10 | 13 | 0 | 0 | 1 | 5 | 0 | 0 | 0 | 0 | 0 | 5 | 0 | 1 | 1 | .345 | .345 | .448 |
| Gomes, Jonny, TB. | 1 | 1 | 1 | 0 | 0 | 0 | 0 | 0 | 0 | 0 | 0 | 0 | 0 | 0 | 0 | 1 | 0 | 0 | 0 | .000 | .000 | .000 |
| Gomez, Chris, Tor. | 8 | 8 | 8 | 2 | 4 | 10 | 0 | 0 | 2 | 5 | 0 | 0 | 0 | 0 | 0 | 0 | 0 | 0 | 0 | .500 | .500 | 1.250 |
| Gonzalez, Adrian, Tex.* | 5 | 5 | 5 | 0 | 0 | 0 | 0 | 0 | 0 | 0 | 0 | 0 | 0 | 0 | 0 | 2 | 0 | 0 | 0 | .000 | .000 | .000 |
| Gonzalez, Raul, Cle. | 4 | 4 | 4 | 0 | 0 | 0 | 0 | 0 | 0 | 0 | 0 | 0 | 0 | 0 | 0 | 2 | 0 | 0 | 0 | .000 | .000 | .000 |
| Gotay, Ruben, K.C.† | 1 | 1 | 1 | 0 | 0 | 0 | 0 | 0 | 0 | 0 | 0 | 0 | 0 | 0 | 0 | 1 | 0 | 0 | 0 | .000 | .000 | .000 |
| Graffanino, Tony, K.C. | 1 | 1 | 1 | 0 | 1 | 1 | 0 | 0 | 0 | 0 | 0 | 0 | 0 | 0 | 0 | 0 | 0 | 0 | 0 | 1.000 | 1.000 | 1.000 |
| Granderson, Curtis, Det.* | 1 | 1 | 1 | 1 | 1 | 1 | 0 | 0 | 0 | 0 | 0 | 0 | 0 | 0 | 0 | 0 | 0 | 0 | 0 | 1.000 | 1.000 | 1.000 |
| Gross, Gabe, Tor.* | 6 | 5 | 3 | 2 | 1 | 2 | 1 | 0 | 0 | 0 | 0 | 0 | 0 | 2 | 0 | 0 | 0 | 0 | 0 | .333 | .600 | .667 |
| Guerrero, Wilton, K.C.† | 1 | 1 | 1 | 0 | 0 | 0 | 0 | 0 | 0 | 0 | 0 | 0 | 0 | 0 | 0 | 0 | 0 | 0 | 0 | .000 | .000 | .000 |
| Guiel, Aaron, K.C.* | 3 | 3 | 2 | 0 | 1 | 1 | 0 | 0 | 0 | 0 | 0 | 0 | 1 | 0 | 0 | 1 | 0 | 0 | 0 | .500 | .667 | .500 |
| Guillen, Carlos, Det.† | 3 | 3 | 3 | 0 | 0 | 0 | 0 | 0 | 0 | 0 | 0 | 0 | 0 | 0 | 0 | 1 | 0 | 0 | 0 | .000 | .000 | .000 |
| Guillen, Jose, Ana. | 2 | 2 | 2 | 0 | 0 | 0 | 0 | 0 | 0 | 0 | 0 | 0 | 0 | 0 | 0 | 2 | 0 | 0 | 0 | .000 | .000 | .000 |
| Gutierrez, Ricky, Bos. | 3 | 3 | 3 | 0 | 0 | 0 | 0 | 0 | 0 | 0 | 0 | 0 | 0 | 0 | 0 | 1 | 0 | 0 | 0 | .000 | .000 | .000 |
| Hafner, Travis, Cle.* | 9 | 9 | 5 | 2 | 2 | 2 | 0 | 0 | 0 | 2 | 0 | 0 | 1 | 3 | 0 | 1 | 0 | 0 | 0 | .400 | .667 | .400 |
| Hairston Jr., Jerry, Bal. | 2 | 2 | 2 | 0 | 0 | 0 | 0 | 0 | 0 | 0 | 0 | 0 | 0 | 0 | 0 | 0 | 0 | 0 | 0 | .000 | .000 | .000 |
| Halter, Shane, Ana. | 3 | 3 | 3 | 1 | 2 | 5 | 0 | 0 | 1 | 4 | 0 | 0 | 0 | 0 | 0 | 0 | 0 | 0 | 0 | .667 | .667 | 1.667 |
| Hansen, Dave, Sea.* | 42 | 42 | 34 | 5 | 6 | 9 | 0 | 0 | 1 | 6 | 0 | 0 | 0 | 8 | 0 | 11 | 0 | 0 | 2 | .176 | .333 | .265 |
| Harris, Willie, Chi.* | 19 | 19 | 18 | 5 | 7 | 10 | 0 | 0 | 1 | 3 | 0 | 0 | 0 | 1 | 0 | 2 | 0 | 0 | 1 | .389 | .421 | .556 |
| Harvey, Ken, K.C. | 2 | 2 | 2 | 0 | 0 | 0 | 0 | 0 | 0 | 0 | 0 | 0 | 0 | 0 | 0 | 0 | 0 | 0 | 0 | .000 | .000 | .000 |
| Hatteberg, Scott, Oak.* | 6 | 6 | 5 | 1 | 2 | 5 | 0 | 0 | 1 | 3 | 0 | 0 | 0 | 1 | 1 | 1 | 0 | 0 | 1 | .400 | .500 | 1.000 |
| Hermansen, Chad, Tor. | 1 | 1 | 1 | 0 | 0 | 0 | 0 | 0 | 0 | 0 | 0 | 0 | 0 | 0 | 0 | 1 | 0 | 0 | 0 | .000 | .000 | .000 |
| Higginson, Bobby, Det.* | 6 | 6 | 4 | 0 | 0 | 0 | 0 | 0 | 0 | 0 | 0 | 0 | 0 | 2 | 0 | 1 | 0 | 0 | 0 | .000 | .333 | .000 |
| Hinske, Eric, Tor.* | 5 | 5 | 5 | 1 | 2 | 5 | 0 | 0 | 1 | 1 | 0 | 0 | 0 | 0 | 0 | 1 | 1 | 0 | 1 | .400 | .400 | 1.000 |
| Huckaby, Ken, Tex.-Bal. | 1 | 1 | 1 | 0 | 0 | 0 | 0 | 0 | 0 | 0 | 0 | 0 | 0 | 0 | 0 | 0 | 0 | 0 | 1 | .000 | .000 | .000 |
| Hudson, Orlando, Tor.† | 4 | 4 | 4 | 1 | 1 | 1 | 0 | 0 | 0 | 0 | 0 | 0 | 0 | 0 | 0 | 2 | 0 | 0 | 0 | .250 | .250 | .250 |
| Huff, Aubrey, TB.* | 2 | 2 | 2 | 0 | 0 | 0 | 0 | 0 | 0 | 1 | 0 | 0 | 0 | 0 | 0 | 0 | 0 | 0 | 0 | .000 | .000 | .000 |
| Hunter, Torii, Min. | 2 | 2 | 2 | 0 | 0 | 0 | 0 | 0 | 0 | 0 | 0 | 0 | 0 | 0 | 0 | 1 | 0 | 0 | 1 | .000 | .000 | .000 |
| Hyzdu, Adam, Bos. | 3 | 3 | 2 | 0 | 1 | 2 | 1 | 0 | 0 | 0 | 0 | 0 | 0 | 1 | 0 | 1 | 0 | 0 | 0 | .500 | .667 | 1.000 |
| Ibanez, Raul, Sea.* | 4 | 4 | 3 | 0 | 1 | 1 | 0 | 0 | 0 | 1 | 0 | 0 | 0 | 1 | 0 | 1 | 0 | 0 | 0 | .333 | .500 | .333 |
| Infante, Omar, Det. | 4 | 4 | 3 | 0 | 0 | 0 | 0 | 0 | 0 | 0 | 0 | 0 | 0 | 1 | 0 | 3 | 0 | 0 | 0 | .000 | .250 | .000 |
| Inge, Brandon, Det. | 4 | 4 | 3 | 0 | 2 | 3 | 1 | 0 | 0 | 1 | 0 | 0 | 0 | 1 | 0 | 0 | 0 | 0 | 0 | .667 | .750 | 1.000 |
| Jackson, Damian, K.C. | 9 | 9 | 8 | 0 | 1 | 2 | 1 | 0 | 0 | 2 | 0 | 0 | 0 | 1 | 0 | 1 | 0 | 0 | 0 | .125 | .222 | .250 |
| Jacobsen, Bucky, Sea. | 2 | 2 | 2 | 0 | 1 | 1 | 0 | 0 | 0 | 2 | 0 | 0 | 0 | 0 | 0 | 1 | 0 | 0 | 0 | .500 | .500 | .500 |
| Johnson, Reed, Tor. | 9 | 9 | 8 | 1 | 2 | 2 | 0 | 0 | 0 | 1 | 0 | 0 | 0 | 1 | 0 | 3 | 0 | 1 | 0 | .250 | .333 | .250 |
| Jones, Jacque, Min.* | 7 | 7 | 5 | 0 | 0 | 0 | 0 | 0 | 0 | 0 | 0 | 0 | 1 | 1 | 0 | 2 | 0 | 0 | 1 | .000 | .286 | .000 |
| Jordan, Brian, Tex. | 3 | 3 | 3 | 0 | 0 | 0 | 0 | 0 | 0 | 1 | 0 | 0 | 0 | 0 | 0 | 1 | 0 | 0 | 0 | .000 | .000 | .000 |
| Kapler, Gabe, Bos. | 7 | 7 | 6 | 2 | 2 | 2 | 0 | 0 | 0 | 1 | 0 | 0 | 0 | 1 | 0 | 2 | 0 | 0 | 0 | .333 | .429 | .333 |
| Karros, Eric, Oak. | 11 | 11 | 11 | 0 | 2 | 3 | 1 | 0 | 0 | 1 | 0 | 0 | 0 | 0 | 0 | 2 | 0 | 0 | 0 | .182 | .182 | .273 |
| Kennedy, Adam, Ana.* | 1 | 1 | 1 | 1 | 1 | 1 | 0 | 0 | 0 | 0 | 0 | 0 | 0 | 0 | 0 | 0 | 0 | 0 | 0 | 1.000 | 1.000 | 1.000 |
| Kielty, Bobby, Oak.† | 14 | 14 | 14 | 0 | 2 | 2 | 0 | 0 | 0 | 0 | 0 | 0 | 0 | 0 | 0 | 3 | 0 | 0 | 0 | .143 | .143 | .143 |
| Konerko, Paul, Chi. | 1 | 1 | 0 | 1 | 0 | 0 | 0 | 0 | 0 | 0 | 0 | 0 | 0 | 1 | 1 | 0 | 0 | 0 | 0 | .000 | 1.000 | .000 |
| Koskie, Corey, Min.* | 4 | 4 | 4 | 1 | 1 | 2 | 1 | 0 | 0 | 0 | 0 | 0 | 0 | 0 | 0 | 1 | 0 | 0 | 0 | .250 | .250 | .500 |
| Kotchman, Casey, Ana.* | 5 | 4 | 3 | 1 | 2 | 3 | 1 | 0 | 0 | 1 | 0 | 0 | 0 | 1 | 0 | 1 | 1 | 0 | 0 | .667 | .750 | 1.000 |

| Player, Team | G | TPA | AB | R | H | TB | 2B | 3B | HR | RBI | SH | SF | HP | BB | IBB | SO | SB | CS | GDP | Avg. | OBP | Slg. |
|---|---|---|---|---|---|---|---|---|---|---|---|---|---|---|---|---|---|---|---|---|---|---|
| Kotsay, Mark, Oak.* | 6 | 6 | 5 | 0 | 3 | 3 | 0 | 0 | 0 | 2 | 0 | 0 | 0 | 1 | 0 | 1 | 0 | 0 | 0 | .600 | .667 | .600 |
| Kubel, Jason, Min.* | 7 | 7 | 5 | 2 | 0 | 0 | 0 | 0 | 0 | 0 | 0 | 0 | 0 | 2 | 0 | 1 | 0 | 0 | 0 | .000 | .286 | .000 |
| Laker, Tim, Cle. | 1 | 1 | 1 | 0 | 0 | 0 | 0 | 0 | 0 | 0 | 0 | 0 | 0 | 0 | 0 | 0 | 0 | 0 | 0 | .000 | .000 | .000 |
| Lawton, Matt, Cle.* | 5 | 5 | 3 | 0 | 1 | 1 | 0 | 0 | 0 | 1 | 0 | 1 | 0 | 1 | 0 | 1 | 0 | 0 | 0 | .333 | .400 | .333 |
| LeCroy, Matthew, Min. | 19 | 19 | 15 | 4 | 5 | 18 | 1 | 0 | 4 | 9 | 0 | 0 | 0 | 4 | 0 | 4 | 0 | 0 | 3 | .333 | .474 | 1.200 |
| Lee, Travis, N.Y.* | 1 | 1 | 1 | 0 | 0 | 0 | 0 | 0 | 0 | 0 | 0 | 0 | 0 | 0 | 0 | 0 | 0 | 0 | 0 | .000 | .000 | .000 |
| Leon, Jose, Bal. | 7 | 7 | 6 | 0 | 1 | 1 | 0 | 0 | 0 | 2 | 0 | 0 | 0 | 1 | 0 | 2 | 0 | 0 | 1 | .167 | .286 | .167 |
| Leone, Justin, Sea. | 2 | 2 | 2 | 0 | 1 | 2 | 1 | 0 | 0 | 0 | 0 | 0 | 0 | 0 | 0 | 0 | 0 | 0 | 0 | .500 | .500 | 1.000 |
| Little, Mark, Cle. | 2 | 2 | 2 | 0 | 0 | 0 | 0 | 0 | 0 | 0 | 0 | 0 | 0 | 0 | 0 | 0 | 0 | 0 | 0 | .000 | .000 | .000 |
| Lofton, Kenny, N.Y.* | 9 | 9 | 8 | 3 | 3 | 6 | 0 | 0 | 1 | 1 | 0 | 0 | 0 | 1 | 1 | 1 | 0 | 0 | 0 | .375 | .444 | .750 |
| Lopez, Javy, Bal. | 4 | 4 | 4 | 1 | 1 | 2 | 1 | 0 | 0 | 2 | 0 | 0 | 0 | 0 | 0 | 0 | 0 | 0 | 1 | .250 | .250 | .500 |
| Lopez, Luis, Bal.† | 17 | 17 | 15 | 1 | 1 | 1 | 0 | 0 | 0 | 0 | 0 | 0 | 1 | 1 | 0 | 4 | 0 | 0 | 1 | .067 | .176 | .067 |
| Lopez, Mendy, K.C. | 2 | 2 | 2 | 1 | 1 | 4 | 0 | 0 | 1 | 3 | 0 | 0 | 0 | 0 | 0 | 0 | 0 | 0 | 0 | .500 | .500 | 2.000 |
| Lopez, Mickey, Sea.† | 3 | 3 | 2 | 0 | 0 | 0 | 0 | 0 | 0 | 0 | 0 | 0 | 0 | 1 | 0 | 0 | 0 | 0 | 0 | .000 | .333 | .000 |
| Lugo, Julio, TB | 2 | 2 | 2 | 0 | 0 | 0 | 0 | 0 | 0 | 0 | 0 | 0 | 0 | 0 | 0 | 1 | 0 | 0 | 0 | .000 | .000 | .000 |
| Machado, Robert, Bal. | 4 | 4 | 4 | 0 | 0 | 0 | 0 | 0 | 0 | 0 | 0 | 0 | 0 | 0 | 0 | 2 | 0 | 0 | 1 | .000 | .000 | .000 |
| Mahay, Ron, Tex.* | 1 | 1 | 1 | 0 | 0 | 0 | 0 | 0 | 0 | 0 | 0 | 0 | 0 | 0 | 0 | 0 | 0 | 0 | 0 | .000 | .000 | .000 |
| Majewski, Val, Bal.* | 3 | 3 | 3 | 1 | 1 | 2 | 1 | 0 | 0 | 1 | 0 | 0 | 0 | 0 | 0 | 0 | 0 | 0 | 0 | .333 | .333 | .667 |
| Martinez, Edgar, Sea. | 23 | 23 | 20 | 1 | 8 | 13 | 2 | 0 | 1 | 3 | 0 | 0 | 0 | 3 | 0 | 5 | 0 | 0 | 0 | .400 | .478 | .650 |
| Martinez, Sandy, Cle.-Bos.* | 1 | 1 | 1 | 0 | 0 | 0 | 0 | 0 | 0 | 0 | 0 | 0 | 0 | 0 | 0 | 1 | 0 | 0 | 0 | .000 | .000 | .000 |
| Martinez, Tino, TB.* | 8 | 8 | 5 | 2 | 2 | 3 | 1 | 0 | 0 | 2 | 0 | 0 | 0 | 3 | 0 | 0 | 0 | 0 | 1 | .400 | .625 | .600 |
| Martinez, Victor, Cle.† | 9 | 8 | 6 | 1 | 3 | 7 | 1 | 0 | 1 | 2 | 0 | 0 | 0 | 2 | 1 | 0 | 0 | 0 | 1 | .500 | .625 | 1.167 |
| Mateo, Ruben, K.C. | 2 | 2 | 2 | 0 | 0 | 0 | 0 | 0 | 0 | 0 | 0 | 0 | 0 | 0 | 0 | 1 | 0 | 0 | 0 | .000 | .000 | .000 |
| Matthews Jr., Gary, Tex.† | 2 | 2 | 2 | 0 | 1 | 1 | 0 | 0 | 0 | 1 | 0 | 0 | 0 | 0 | 0 | 1 | 0 | 0 | 0 | .500 | .500 | .500 |
| Mauer, Joe, Min.* | 5 | 5 | 4 | 0 | 0 | 0 | 0 | 0 | 0 | 0 | 0 | 0 | 0 | 1 | 0 | 2 | 0 | 0 | 0 | .000 | .200 | .000 |
| McCarty, Dave, Bos. | 23 | 23 | 21 | 1 | 7 | 10 | 1 | 1 | 0 | 3 | 0 | 1 | 0 | 1 | 0 | 5 | 0 | 0 | 0 | .333 | .348 | .476 |
| McDonald, Darnell, Bal. | 2 | 2 | 2 | 0 | 0 | 0 | 0 | 0 | 0 | 0 | 0 | 0 | 0 | 0 | 0 | 1 | 0 | 0 | 0 | .000 | .000 | .000 |
| McDonald, John, Cle. | 7 | 7 | 6 | 0 | 1 | 1 | 0 | 0 | 0 | 0 | 1 | 0 | 0 | 0 | 0 | 0 | 0 | 0 | 0 | .167 | .167 | .167 |
| McGriff, Fred, TB.* | 9 | 9 | 9 | 0 | 4 | 4 | 0 | 0 | 0 | 2 | 0 | 0 | 0 | 0 | 0 | 1 | 0 | 0 | 0 | .444 | .444 | .444 |
| McLemore, Mark, Oak.† | 8 | 8 | 7 | 0 | 1 | 1 | 0 | 0 | 0 | 0 | 0 | 0 | 0 | 1 | 0 | 0 | 0 | 0 | 0 | .143 | .250 | .143 |
| McMillon, Billy, Oak.* | 32 | 30 | 27 | 2 | 2 | 5 | 0 | 0 | 1 | 2 | 0 | 0 | 0 | 3 | 0 | 7 | 0 | 0 | 1 | .074 | .167 | .185 |
| McPherson, Dallas, Ana.* | 2 | 2 | 2 | 0 | 0 | 0 | 0 | 0 | 0 | 0 | 0 | 0 | 0 | 0 | 0 | 2 | 0 | 0 | 0 | .000 | .000 | .000 |
| Melhuse, Adam, Oak.† | 6 | 6 | 6 | 1 | 1 | 2 | 1 | 0 | 0 | 1 | 0 | 0 | 0 | 0 | 0 | 3 | 0 | 0 | 0 | .167 | .167 | .333 |
| Mench, Kevin, Tex. | 7 | 7 | 6 | 1 | 0 | 0 | 0 | 0 | 0 | 0 | 0 | 0 | 1 | 0 | 0 | 2 | 0 | 0 | 0 | .000 | .143 | .000 |
| Menechino, Frank, Oak.-Tor. | 9 | 9 | 7 | 0 | 1 | 1 | 0 | 0 | 0 | 1 | 0 | 0 | 0 | 2 | 0 | 4 | 0 | 0 | 0 | .143 | .333 | .143 |
| Merloni, Lou, Cle. | 10 | 9 | 6 | 0 | 2 | 2 | 0 | 0 | 0 | 5 | 0 | 1 | 1 | 1 | 0 | 1 | 0 | 0 | 0 | .333 | .444 | .333 |
| Mientkiewicz, Doug, Min.-Bos.* | 3 | 2 | 2 | 0 | 0 | 0 | 0 | 0 | 0 | 0 | 0 | 0 | 0 | 0 | 0 | 0 | 0 | 0 | 1 | .000 | .000 | .000 |
| Millar, Kevin, Bos. | 7 | 7 | 6 | 2 | 3 | 7 | 1 | 0 | 1 | 4 | 0 | 1 | 0 | 0 | 0 | 2 | 0 | 0 | 0 | .500 | .429 | 1.167 |
| Miller, Damian, Oak. | 1 | 1 | 1 | 0 | 1 | 1 | 0 | 0 | 0 | 0 | 0 | 0 | 0 | 0 | 0 | 0 | 0 | 0 | 0 | 1.000 | 1.000 | 1.000 |
| Mirabelli, Doug, Bos. | 4 | 4 | 4 | 0 | 0 | 0 | 0 | 0 | 0 | 0 | 0 | 0 | 0 | 0 | 0 | 2 | 0 | 0 | 0 | .000 | .000 | .000 |
| Molina, Bengie, Ana. | 6 | 6 | 5 | 0 | 0 | 0 | 0 | 0 | 0 | 0 | 0 | 0 | 0 | 1 | 0 | 4 | 0 | 0 | 0 | .000 | .167 | .000 |
| Monroe, Craig, Det. | 5 | 5 | 4 | 1 | 2 | 5 | 0 | 0 | 1 | 2 | 0 | 0 | 0 | 1 | 0 | 0 | 0 | 0 | 0 | .500 | .600 | 1.250 |
| Mora, Melvin, Bal. | 2 | 2 | 1 | 0 | 0 | 0 | 0 | 0 | 0 | 0 | 0 | 0 | 0 | 1 | 0 | 0 | 0 | 0 | 0 | .000 | .500 | .000 |
| Morneau, Justin, Min.* | 2 | 2 | 2 | 0 | 2 | 3 | 1 | 0 | 0 | 2 | 0 | 0 | 0 | 0 | 0 | 0 | 0 | 0 | 0 | 1.000 | 1.000 | 1.500 |
| Mottola, Chad, Bal. | 1 | 1 | 1 | 0 | 0 | 0 | 0 | 0 | 0 | 0 | 0 | 0 | 0 | 0 | 0 | 0 | 0 | 0 | 0 | .000 | .000 | .000 |
| Mueller, Bill, Bos.† | 1 | 1 | 1 | 0 | 1 | 1 | 0 | 0 | 0 | 0 | 0 | 0 | 0 | 0 | 0 | 0 | 0 | 0 | 0 | 1.000 | 1.000 | 1.000 |
| Munson, Eric, Det.* | 17 | 17 | 13 | 0 | 1 | 1 | 0 | 0 | 0 | 0 | 0 | 0 | 2 | 2 | 0 | 6 | 0 | 0 | 0 | .077 | .294 | .077 |
| Myers, Greg, Tor.* | 3 | 3 | 2 | 0 | 1 | 1 | 0 | 0 | 0 | 0 | 0 | 0 | 0 | 1 | 0 | 1 | 0 | 0 | 0 | .500 | .667 | .500 |
| Navarro, Dioner, N.Y.† | 1 | 1 | 1 | 1 | 1 | 1 | 0 | 0 | 0 | 1 | 0 | 0 | 0 | 0 | 0 | 0 | 0 | 0 | 0 | 1.000 | 1.000 | 1.000 |
| Newhan, David, Bal.* | 4 | 4 | 4 | 1 | 2 | 5 | 0 | 0 | 1 | 1 | 0 | 0 | 0 | 0 | 0 | 0 | 0 | 0 | 1 | .500 | .500 | 1.250 |
| Nix, Laynce, Tex.* | 8 | 8 | 6 | 1 | 0 | 0 | 0 | 0 | 0 | 0 | 0 | 0 | 0 | 2 | 0 | 3 | 0 | 0 | 0 | .000 | .250 | .000 |
| Nixon, Trot, Bos.* | 11 | 11 | 11 | 1 | 3 | 6 | 0 | 0 | 1 | 5 | 0 | 0 | 0 | 0 | 0 | 2 | 0 | 0 | 0 | .273 | .273 | .545 |
| Norton, Greg, Det.† | 15 | 15 | 12 | 1 | 3 | 3 | 0 | 0 | 0 | 0 | 0 | 0 | 0 | 3 | 0 | 4 | 0 | 0 | 1 | .250 | .400 | .250 |
| Nunez, Abraham, K.C.† | 1 | 1 | 1 | 0 | 0 | 0 | 0 | 0 | 0 | 0 | 0 | 0 | 0 | 0 | 0 | 1 | 0 | 0 | 0 | .000 | .000 | .000 |
| Offerman, Jose, Min.† | 36 | 36 | 29 | 3 | 12 | 17 | 3 | 1 | 0 | 7 | 0 | 0 | 0 | 7 | 1 | 5 | 1 | 0 | 0 | .414 | .528 | .586 |
| Olerud, John, Sea.-N.Y.* | 5 | 5 | 5 | 0 | 0 | 0 | 0 | 0 | 0 | 0 | 0 | 0 | 0 | 0 | 0 | 0 | 0 | 0 | 0 | .000 | .000 | .000 |
| Olivo, Miguel, Chi.-Sea. | 2 | 2 | 2 | 0 | 1 | 1 | 0 | 0 | 0 | 2 | 0 | 0 | 0 | 0 | 0 | 0 | 0 | 1 | 0 | .500 | .500 | .500 |
| Ordonez, Magglio, Chi. | 2 | 2 | 1 | 0 | 0 | 0 | 0 | 0 | 0 | 0 | 0 | 0 | 0 | 1 | 1 | 0 | 0 | 0 | 0 | .000 | .500 | .000 |
| Ortiz, David, Bos.* | 5 | 5 | 5 | 1 | 1 | 1 | 0 | 0 | 0 | 1 | 0 | 0 | 0 | 0 | 0 | 1 | 0 | 0 | 0 | .200 | .200 | .200 |
| Osik, Keith, Bal. | 1 | 1 | 1 | 0 | 0 | 0 | 0 | 0 | 0 | 0 | 0 | 0 | 0 | 0 | 0 | 1 | 0 | 0 | 0 | .000 | .000 | .000 |
| Palmeiro, Rafael, Bal.* | 7 | 7 | 6 | 2 | 2 | 5 | 0 | 0 | 1 | 2 | 0 | 0 | 0 | 1 | 0 | 0 | 0 | 0 | 1 | .333 | .429 | .833 |
| Paul, Josh, Ana. | 7 | 7 | 5 | 0 | 0 | 0 | 0 | 0 | 0 | 1 | 1 | 1 | 0 | 0 | 0 | 3 | 0 | 0 | 0 | .000 | .000 | .000 |
| Pena, Carlos, Det.* | 6 | 6 | 6 | 0 | 1 | 1 | 0 | 0 | 0 | 0 | 0 | 0 | 0 | 0 | 0 | 4 | 0 | 0 | 0 | .167 | .167 | .167 |
| Perez, Eduardo, TB. | 3 | 3 | 3 | 0 | 1 | 1 | 0 | 0 | 0 | 1 | 0 | 0 | 0 | 0 | 0 | 0 | 0 | 0 | 0 | .333 | .333 | .333 |
| Perez, Timo, Chi.* | 27 | 26 | 26 | 3 | 5 | 6 | 1 | 0 | 0 | 1 | 0 | 0 | 0 | 0 | 0 | 7 | 0 | 0 | 1 | .192 | .192 | .231 |
| Perry, Herbert, Tex. | 12 | 12 | 12 | 0 | 4 | 4 | 0 | 0 | 0 | 2 | 0 | 0 | 0 | 0 | 0 | 3 | 0 | 0 | 0 | .333 | .333 | .333 |
| Phelps, Josh, Tor.-Cle. | 6 | 6 | 5 | 1 | 1 | 4 | 0 | 0 | 1 | 1 | 0 | 0 | 0 | 1 | 0 | 2 | 0 | 0 | 0 | .200 | .333 | .800 |
| Phillips, Andy, N.Y. | 1 | 1 | 1 | 1 | 1 | 4 | 0 | 0 | 1 | 2 | 0 | 0 | 0 | 0 | 0 | 0 | 0 | 0 | 0 | 1.000 | 1.000 | 4.000 |
| Pond, Simon, Tor.* | 1 | 1 | 1 | 0 | 0 | 0 | 0 | 0 | 0 | 0 | 0 | 0 | 0 | 0 | 0 | 1 | 0 | 0 | 0 | .000 | .000 | .000 |
| Posada, Jorge, N.Y.† | 11 | 11 | 11 | 1 | 3 | 6 | 0 | 0 | 1 | 1 | 0 | 0 | 0 | 0 | 0 | 4 | 0 | 0 | 1 | .273 | .273 | .545 |
| Pride, Curtis, Ana.* | 12 | 11 | 11 | 2 | 3 | 4 | 1 | 0 | 0 | 0 | 0 | 0 | 0 | 0 | 0 | 4 | 0 | 0 | 0 | .273 | .273 | .364 |
| Prieto, Alex, Min. | 1 | 1 | 1 | 0 | 0 | 0 | 0 | 0 | 0 | 0 | 0 | 0 | 0 | 0 | 0 | 0 | 0 | 0 | 0 | .000 | .000 | .000 |
| Punto, Nick, Min.† | 4 | 4 | 2 | 1 | 0 | 0 | 0 | 0 | 0 | 0 | 0 | 0 | 0 | 2 | 0 | 1 | 1 | 0 | 0 | .000 | .500 | .000 |
| Quinlan, Robb, Ana. | 5 | 5 | 4 | 2 | 1 | 1 | 0 | 0 | 0 | 0 | 0 | 0 | 1 | 0 | 0 | 1 | 1 | 0 | 0 | .250 | .400 | .250 |
| Raburn, Ryan, Det. | 5 | 5 | 5 | 0 | 0 | 0 | 0 | 0 | 0 | 0 | 0 | 0 | 0 | 0 | 0 | 5 | 0 | 0 | 0 | .000 | .000 | .000 |
| Raines Jr., Tim, Bal.† | 4 | 4 | 3 | 1 | 2 | 2 | 0 | 0 | 0 | 1 | 0 | 0 | 0 | 1 | 0 | 1 | 0 | 0 | 0 | .667 | .750 | .667 |
| Ramirez, Manny, Bos. | 2 | 2 | 2 | 0 | 1 | 1 | 0 | 0 | 0 | 0 | 0 | 0 | 0 | 0 | 0 | 0 | 0 | 0 | 0 | .500 | .500 | .500 |
| Randa, Joe, K.C. | 2 | 2 | 2 | 0 | 0 | 0 | 0 | 0 | 0 | 0 | 0 | 0 | 0 | 0 | 0 | 1 | 0 | 0 | 0 | .000 | .000 | .000 |
| Reed, Jeremy, Sea.* | 3 | 3 | 3 | 1 | 1 | 1 | 0 | 0 | 0 | 0 | 0 | 0 | 0 | 0 | 0 | 0 | 0 | 0 | 0 | .333 | .333 | .333 |
| Relaford, Desi, K.C.† | 9 | 9 | 7 | 3 | 3 | 4 | 1 | 0 | 0 | 1 | 0 | 1 | 0 | 1 | 0 | 1 | 0 | 0 | 0 | .429 | .444 | .571 |
| Restovich, Michael, Min. | 5 | 5 | 4 | 0 | 0 | 0 | 0 | 0 | 0 | 0 | 0 | 0 | 0 | 1 | 0 | 1 | 0 | 0 | 0 | .000 | .200 | .000 |
| Riggs, Adam, Ana. | 3 | 3 | 3 | 0 | 1 | 1 | 0 | 0 | 0 | 0 | 0 | 0 | 0 | 0 | 0 | 0 | 0 | 0 | 0 | .333 | .333 | .333 |

| Player, Team | G | TPA | AB | R | H | TB | 2B | 3B | HR | RBI | SH | SF | HP | BB | IBB | SO | SB | CS | GDP | Avg. | OBP | Slg. |
|---|---|---|---|---|---|---|---|---|---|---|---|---|---|---|---|---|---|---|---|---|---|---|
| Rios, Alexis, Tor. | 1 | 1 | 1 | 0 | 0 | 0 | 0 | 0 | 0 | 0 | 0 | 0 | 0 | 0 | 0 | 1 | 0 | 0 | 0 | .000 | .000 | .000 |
| Rivera, Rene, Sea. | 2 | 2 | 2 | 0 | 0 | 0 | 0 | 0 | 0 | 0 | 0 | 0 | 0 | 0 | 0 | 1 | 0 | 0 | 0 | .000 | .000 | .000 |
| Roberts, Brian, Bal.† | 4 | 4 | 2 | 0 | 0 | 0 | 0 | 0 | 0 | 1 | 0 | 0 | 0 | 2 | 0 | 1 | 0 | 0 | 0 | .000 | .500 | .000 |
| Roberts, Dave, Bos.* | 2 | 2 | 1 | 0 | 0 | 0 | 0 | 0 | 0 | 0 | 0 | 0 | 0 | 1 | 0 | 1 | 0 | 0 | 0 | .000 | .500 | .000 |
| Rodriguez, Ivan, Det. | 3 | 3 | 3 | 0 | 1 | 1 | 0 | 0 | 0 | 1 | 0 | 0 | 0 | 0 | 0 | 1 | 0 | 0 | 0 | .333 | .333 | .333 |
| Rolls, Damian, TB. | 8 | 7 | 6 | 0 | 0 | 0 | 0 | 0 | 0 | 0 | 1 | 0 | 0 | 0 | 0 | 2 | 0 | 0 | 0 | .000 | .000 | .000 |
| Romano, Jason, TB. | 1 | 1 | 1 | 0 | 0 | 0 | 0 | 0 | 0 | 0 | 0 | 0 | 0 | 0 | 0 | 0 | 0 | 0 | 0 | .000 | .000 | .000 |
| Rose, Mike, Oak.† | 1 | 1 | 1 | 0 | 0 | 0 | 0 | 0 | 0 | 0 | 0 | 0 | 0 | 0 | 0 | 1 | 0 | 0 | 0 | .000 | .000 | .000 |
| Rowand, Aaron, Chi. | 10 | 10 | 8 | 2 | 2 | 3 | 1 | 0 | 0 | 2 | 0 | 0 | 0 | 2 | 0 | 3 | 0 | 0 | 0 | .250 | .400 | .375 |
| Ryan, Michael, Min.* | 14 | 13 | 13 | 2 | 2 | 3 | 1 | 0 | 0 | 2 | 0 | 0 | 0 | 0 | 0 | 2 | 0 | 0 | 0 | .154 | .154 | .231 |
| Salmon, Tim, Ana. | 14 | 14 | 12 | 1 | 5 | 6 | 1 | 0 | 0 | 4 | 0 | 0 | 1 | 1 | 0 | 2 | 0 | 0 | 0 | .417 | .500 | .500 |
| Sanchez, Rey, TB. | 4 | 4 | 4 | 0 | 0 | 0 | 0 | 0 | 0 | 0 | 0 | 0 | 0 | 0 | 0 | 1 | 0 | 0 | 0 | .000 | .000 | .000 |
| Scutaro, Marco, Oak. | 12 | 12 | 10 | 1 | 0 | 0 | 0 | 0 | 0 | 0 | 0 | 0 | 0 | 2 | 0 | 1 | 0 | 0 | 1 | .000 | .167 | .000 |
| Segui, David, Bal.† | 3 | 3 | 2 | 0 | 0 | 0 | 0 | 0 | 0 | 0 | 0 | 0 | 0 | 1 | 1 | 1 | 0 | 0 | 0 | .000 | .333 | .000 |
| Shelton, Chris, Det. | 7 | 7 | 6 | 0 | 1 | 1 | 0 | 0 | 0 | 0 | 0 | 0 | 0 | 1 | 0 | 3 | 0 | 0 | 0 | .167 | .286 | .167 |
| Sierra, Ruben, N.Y.† | 31 | 31 | 26 | 3 | 10 | 17 | 1 | 0 | 2 | 11 | 0 | 2 | 0 | 3 | 0 | 4 | 1 | 0 | 0 | .385 | .419 | .654 |
| Simon, Randall, TB.* | 3 | 3 | 3 | 0 | 0 | 0 | 0 | 0 | 0 | 0 | 0 | 0 | 0 | 0 | 0 | 1 | 0 | 0 | 0 | .000 | .000 | .000 |
| Sizemore, Grady, Cle.* | 1 | 1 | 1 | 1 | 1 | 1 | 0 | 0 | 0 | 0 | 0 | 0 | 0 | 0 | 0 | 0 | 0 | 0 | 0 | 1.000 | 1.000 | 1.000 |
| Smith, Jason, Det.* | 7 | 7 | 7 | 0 | 0 | 0 | 0 | 0 | 0 | 0 | 0 | 0 | 0 | 0 | 0 | 4 | 0 | 0 | 0 | .000 | .000 | .000 |
| Spiezio, Scott, Sea.† | 4 | 4 | 4 | 0 | 0 | 0 | 0 | 0 | 0 | 0 | 0 | 0 | 0 | 0 | 0 | 2 | 0 | 0 | 1 | .000 | .000 | .000 |
| Stairs, Matt, K.C.* | 9 | 8 | 8 | 0 | 1 | 1 | 0 | 0 | 0 | 0 | 0 | 0 | 0 | 0 | 0 | 2 | 0 | 0 | 0 | .125 | .125 | .125 |
| Surhoff, B.J., Bal.* | 9 | 9 | 9 | 1 | 3 | 3 | 0 | 0 | 0 | 1 | 0 | 0 | 0 | 0 | 0 | 2 | 0 | 0 | 0 | .333 | .333 | .333 |
| Sweeney, Mike, K.C. | 3 | 3 | 2 | 0 | 0 | 0 | 0 | 0 | 0 | 0 | 0 | 0 | 0 | 1 | 0 | 0 | 0 | 0 | 0 | .000 | .333 | .000 |
| Swisher, Nick, Oak.† | 1 | 1 | 1 | 0 | 0 | 0 | 0 | 0 | 0 | 0 | 0 | 0 | 0 | 0 | 0 | 0 | 0 | 0 | 0 | .000 | .000 | .000 |
| Teixeira, Mark, Tex.† | 1 | 1 | 1 | 0 | 0 | 0 | 0 | 0 | 0 | 0 | 0 | 0 | 0 | 0 | 0 | 0 | 0 | 0 | 0 | .000 | .000 | .000 |
| Thames, Marcus, Det. | 13 | 12 | 9 | 2 | 2 | 2 | 0 | 0 | 0 | 0 | 0 | 0 | 0 | 3 | 0 | 5 | 0 | 0 | 1 | .222 | .417 | .222 |
| Thomas, Frank, Chi. | 5 | 5 | 4 | 0 | 0 | 0 | 0 | 0 | 0 | 0 | 0 | 0 | 0 | 1 | 1 | 3 | 0 | 0 | 0 | .000 | .200 | .000 |
| Tiffee, Terry, Min.† | 3 | 3 | 3 | 0 | 0 | 0 | 0 | 0 | 0 | 0 | 0 | 0 | 0 | 0 | 0 | 1 | 0 | 0 | 0 | .000 | .000 | .000 |
| Upton, B.J., TB. | 3 | 3 | 3 | 0 | 2 | 2 | 0 | 0 | 0 | 0 | 0 | 0 | 0 | 0 | 0 | 0 | 0 | 0 | 0 | .667 | .667 | .667 |
| Uribe, Juan, Chi. | 8 | 8 | 7 | 1 | 3 | 7 | 1 | 0 | 1 | 5 | 0 | 0 | 0 | 1 | 0 | 3 | 0 | 0 | 0 | .429 | .500 | 1.000 |
| Valdez, Wilson, Chi. | 3 | 3 | 3 | 1 | 1 | 1 | 0 | 0 | 0 | 0 | 0 | 0 | 0 | 0 | 0 | 1 | 0 | 0 | 0 | .333 | .333 | .333 |
| Valentin, Jose, Chi.* | 5 | 5 | 4 | 0 | 0 | 0 | 0 | 0 | 0 | 0 | 0 | 0 | 0 | 1 | 1 | 1 | 0 | 0 | 0 | .000 | .200 | .000 |
| Varitek, Jason, Bos.† | 13 | 13 | 12 | 2 | 4 | 6 | 2 | 0 | 0 | 3 | 0 | 0 | 0 | 1 | 0 | 4 | 0 | 0 | 0 | .333 | .385 | .500 |
| Vizquel, Omar, Cle.† | 5 | 5 | 5 | 0 | 0 | 0 | 0 | 0 | 0 | 0 | 0 | 0 | 0 | 0 | 0 | 2 | 0 | 0 | 0 | .000 | .000 | .000 |
| Wells, Vernon, Tor. | 1 | 1 | 1 | 0 | 0 | 0 | 0 | 0 | 0 | 0 | 0 | 0 | 0 | 0 | 0 | 0 | 0 | 0 | 0 | .000 | .000 | .000 |
| White, Rondell, Det. | 5 | 5 | 4 | 0 | 1 | 1 | 0 | 0 | 0 | 0 | 0 | 0 | 0 | 1 | 0 | 2 | 0 | 0 | 0 | .250 | .400 | .250 |
| Williams, Bernie, N.Y.† | 3 | 3 | 3 | 1 | 1 | 1 | 0 | 0 | 0 | 1 | 0 | 0 | 0 | 0 | 0 | 1 | 0 | 0 | 0 | .333 | .333 | .333 |
| Wilson, Dan, Sea. | 2 | 2 | 2 | 0 | 2 | 2 | 0 | 0 | 0 | 1 | 0 | 0 | 0 | 0 | 0 | 0 | 0 | 0 | 0 | 1.000 | 1.000 | 1.000 |
| Wilson, Enrique, N.Y.† | 2 | 2 | 2 | 0 | 0 | 0 | 0 | 0 | 0 | 0 | 0 | 0 | 0 | 0 | 0 | 0 | 0 | 0 | 0 | .000 | .000 | .000 |
| Winn, Randy, Sea.† | 2 | 2 | 2 | 1 | 1 | 4 | 0 | 0 | 1 | 2 | 0 | 0 | 0 | 0 | 0 | 0 | 0 | 0 | 0 | .500 | .500 | 2.000 |
| Woodward, Chris, Tor. | 1 | 1 | 1 | 0 | 1 | 1 | 0 | 0 | 0 | 0 | 0 | 0 | 0 | 0 | 0 | 0 | 0 | 0 | 0 | 1.000 | 1.000 | 1.000 |
| Youkilis, Kevin, Bos. | 8 | 8 | 6 | 0 | 0 | 0 | 0 | 0 | 0 | 0 | 0 | 0 | 0 | 2 | 0 | 3 | 0 | 0 | 0 | .000 | .250 | .000 |
| Young, Dmitri, Det.† | 3 | 3 | 2 | 0 | 0 | 0 | 0 | 0 | 0 | 0 | 0 | 0 | 0 | 1 | 0 | 1 | 0 | 0 | 0 | .000 | .333 | .000 |
| Young, Eric, Tex. | 11 | 11 | 7 | 0 | 1 | 1 | 0 | 0 | 0 | 1 | 1 | 1 | 0 | 2 | 0 | 1 | 0 | 0 | 0 | .143 | .300 | .143 |
| Young, Ernie, Cle. | 2 | 2 | 1 | 0 | 1 | 1 | 0 | 0 | 0 | 0 | 0 | 0 | 0 | 1 | 0 | 0 | 0 | 0 | 0 | 1.000 | 1.000 | 1.000 |
| Zaun, Gregg, Tor.† | 12 | 12 | 8 | 0 | 1 | 1 | 0 | 0 | 0 | 1 | 0 | 0 | 0 | 4 | 0 | 1 | 0 | 0 | 0 | .125 | .417 | .125 |

## PINCH-HITTERS WITH TWO OR MORE TEAMS

| Player, Team | G | TPA | AB | R | H | TB | 2B | 3B | HR | RBI | SH | SF | HP | BB | IBB | SO | SB | CS | GDP | Avg. | OBP | Slg. |
|---|---|---|---|---|---|---|---|---|---|---|---|---|---|---|---|---|---|---|---|---|---|---|
| Bautista, Jose, Bal. | 4 | 4 | 3 | 0 | 1 | 1 | 0 | 0 | 0 | 0 | 0 | 0 | 0 | 1 | 0 | 0 | 0 | 0 | 0 | .333 | .500 | .333 |
| Bautista, Jose, K.C. | 1 | 1 | 1 | 0 | 0 | 0 | 0 | 0 | 0 | 0 | 0 | 0 | 0 | 0 | 0 | 0 | 0 | 0 | 0 | .000 | .000 | .000 |
| Olerud, John, Sea.* | 3 | 3 | 3 | 0 | 0 | 0 | 0 | 0 | 0 | 0 | 0 | 0 | 0 | 0 | 0 | 0 | 0 | 0 | 0 | .000 | .000 | .000 |
| Olerud, John, N.Y.* | 2 | 2 | 2 | 0 | 0 | 0 | 0 | 0 | 0 | 0 | 0 | 0 | 0 | 0 | 0 | 0 | 0 | 0 | 0 | .000 | .000 | .000 |
| Phelps, Josh, Tor. | 3 | 3 | 2 | 0 | 0 | 0 | 0 | 0 | 0 | 0 | 0 | 0 | 0 | 1 | 0 | 1 | 0 | 0 | 0 | .000 | .333 | .000 |
| Phelps, Josh, Cle. | 3 | 3 | 3 | 1 | 1 | 4 | 0 | 0 | 1 | 1 | 0 | 0 | 0 | 0 | 0 | 1 | 0 | 0 | 0 | .333 | .333 | 1.333 |

# PITCHING

## TEAM

| Team | W | L | Pct. | ERA | G | CG | ShO | Rel. | Sv.-Op. | IP | H | TBF | R | ER | HR | SH | SF | HB | BB | IBB | SO | WP | Bk. |
|---|---|---|---|---|---|---|---|---|---|---|---|---|---|---|---|---|---|---|---|---|---|---|---|
| Minnesota | 92 | 70 | .568 | 4.03 | 162 | 4 | 9 | 435 | 48-68 | 1476.0 | 1523 | 6269 | 715 | 661 | 167 | 46 | 35 | 54 | 431 | 27 | 1123 | 45 | 1 |
| Oakland | 91 | 71 | .562 | 4.17 | 162 | 10 | 8 | 414 | 35-63 | 1471.1 | 1466 | 6313 | 742 | 682 | 164 | 54 | 43 | 68 | 544 | 49 | 1034 | 39 | 5 |
| Boston | 98 | 64 | .605 | 4.18 | 162 | 4 | 12 | 436 | 36-49 | 1451.1 | 1430 | 6222 | 768 | 674 | 159 | 37 | 46 | 92 | 447 | 28 | 1132 | 39 | 1 |
| Anaheim | 92 | 70 | .568 | 4.28 | 162 | 2 | 11 | 343 | 50-67 | 1454.1 | 1476 | 6246 | 734 | 692 | 170 | 35 | 47 | 44 | 502 | 27 | 1164 | 61 | 7 |
| Texas | 89 | 73 | .549 | 4.53 | 162 | 5 | 9 | 468 | 52-66 | 1439.2 | 1536 | 6345 | 794 | 724 | 182 | 51 | 48 | 81 | 547 | 29 | 979 | 34 | 11 |
| New York | 101 | 61 | .623 | 4.69 | 162 | 1 | 5 | 436 | 59-76 | 1443.2 | 1532 | 6240 | 808 | 752 | 182 | 28 | 57 | 60 | 445 | 32 | 1058 | 57 | 4 |
| Baltimore | 78 | 84 | .481 | 4.70 | 162 | 8 | 10 | 452 | 27-47 | 1455.1 | 1488 | 6459 | 830 | 760 | 159 | 36 | 40 | 62 | 687 | 43 | 1090 | 68 | 9 |
| Seattle | 63 | 99 | .389 | 4.76 | 162 | 7 | 7 | 414 | 28-49 | 1459.1 | 1498 | 6389 | 823 | 772 | 212 | 43 | 48 | 72 | 575 | 32 | 1036 | 45 | 7 |
| Tampa Bay | 70 | 91 | .435 | 4.81 | 161 | 3 | 5 | 401 | 35-45 | 1417.0 | 1459 | 6261 | 842 | 757 | 192 | 30 | 52 | 93 | 580 | 35 | 923 | 55 | 7 |
| Cleveland | 80 | 82 | .494 | 4.81 | 162 | 8 | 8 | 479 | 32-60 | 1466.2 | 1553 | 6450 | 857 | 784 | 201 | 39 | 43 | 62 | 579 | 47 | 1115 | 43 | 6 |
| Toronto | 67 | 94 | .416 | 4.91 | 161 | 6 | 11 | 431 | 37-53 | 1421.0 | 1505 | 6281 | 823 | 775 | 181 | 42 | 56 | 58 | 608 | 47 | 956 | 60 | 11 |
| Chicago | 83 | 79 | .512 | 4.91 | 162 | 8 | 8 | 399 | 34-46 | 1432.1 | 1505 | 6189 | 831 | 782 | 224 | 39 | 46 | 48 | 527 | 36 | 1013 | 43 | 3 |
| Detroit | 72 | 90 | .444 | 4.93 | 162 | 7 | 9 | 432 | 35-63 | 1439.2 | 1542 | 6296 | 844 | 788 | 190 | 52 | 43 | 54 | 530 | 33 | 995 | 71 | 6 |
| Kansas City | 58 | 104 | .358 | 5.15 | 162 | 6 | 3 | 409 | 25-47 | 1420.1 | 1638 | 6320 | 905 | 813 | 208 | 38 | 57 | 56 | 518 | 49 | 887 | 60 | 10 |
| **Totals** | 1134 | 1132 | .500 | 4.63 | 1133 | 79 | 115 | 5949 | 533-799 | 20248.0 | 21151 | 88280 | 11316 | 10416 | 2591 | 570 | 661 | 904 | 7520 | 514 | 14505 | 720 | 88 |

**NOTE**—Totals for earned runs for several clubs do not agree with composite total for all pitchers of each respective club due to instances in which provisions of Section 10.18(i) of the Scoring Rules were applied. The following differences are to be noted: Minnesota pitchers add to 663; Boston pitchers add to 676; Texas pitchers add to 727; Baltimore pitchers add to 761; Tampa Bay pitchers add to 759; Cleveland pitchers add to 785; Toronto pitchers add to 778; Kansas City pitchers add to 815.

## TOP QUALIFIERS FOR EARNED-RUN AVERAGE TITLE

Minimum 162 innings. *Throws lefthanded.

| Pitcher, Team | W | L | Pct. | ERA | G | GS | CG | ShO | GF | Sv.-Op. | IP | H | TBF | R | ER | HR | SH | SF | HB | BB | IBB | SO | WP | Bk. |
|---|---|---|---|---|---|---|---|---|---|---|---|---|---|---|---|---|---|---|---|---|---|---|---|---|
| Santana, Johan, Min.* | 20 | 6 | .769 | 2.61 | 34 | 34 | 1 | 1 | 0 | 0-0 | 228.0 | 156 | 881 | 70 | 66 | 24 | 3 | 3 | 9 | 54 | 0 | 265 | 7 | 0 |
| Schilling, Curt, Bos. | 21 | 6 | .778 | 3.26 | 32 | 32 | 3 | 0 | 0 | 0-0 | 226.2 | 206 | 910 | 84 | 82 | 23 | 3 | 6 | 5 | 35 | 0 | 203 | 3 | 0 |
| Westbrook, Jake, Cle. | 14 | 9 | .609 | 3.38 | 33 | 30 | 5 | 1 | 2 | 0-0 | 215.2 | 208 | 895 | 95 | 81 | 19 | 6 | 6 | 5 | 61 | 3 | 116 | 4 | 1 |
| Radke, Brad, Min. | 11 | 8 | .579 | 3.48 | 34 | 34 | 1 | 1 | 0 | 0-0 | 219.2 | 229 | 901 | 92 | 85 | 23 | 5 | 5 | 6 | 26 | 1 | 143 | 2 | 0 |
| Hudson, Tim, Oak. | 12 | 6 | .667 | 3.53 | 27 | 27 | 3 | 2 | 0 | 0-0 | 188.2 | 194 | 793 | 82 | 74 | 8 | 7 | 4 | 12 | 44 | 3 | 103 | 4 | 1 |
| Lopez, Rodrigo, Bal. | 14 | 9 | .609 | 3.59 | 37 | 23 | 1 | 1 | 3 | 0-1 | 170.2 | 164 | 714 | 71 | 68 | 21 | 5 | 2 | 2 | 54 | 2 | 121 | 4 | 1 |
| Garcia, Freddy, Sea.-Chi. | 13 | 11 | .542 | 3.81 | 31 | 31 | 1 | 0 | 0 | 0-0 | 210.0 | 192 | 878 | 92 | 89 | 22 | 8 | 3 | 7 | 64 | 3 | 184 | 8 | 0 |
| Buehrle, Mark, Chi.* | 16 | 10 | .615 | 3.89 | 35 | 35 | 4 | 1 | 0 | 0-0 | 245.1 | 257 | 1016 | 119 | 106 | 33 | 4 | 6 | 8 | 51 | 2 | 165 | 0 | 0 |
| Martinez, Pedro, Bos. | 16 | 9 | .640 | 3.90 | 33 | 33 | 1 | 1 | 0 | 0-0 | 217.0 | 193 | 903 | 99 | 94 | 26 | 5 | 9 | 16 | 61 | 0 | 227 | 2 | 0 |
| Escobar, Kelvim, Ana. | 11 | 12 | .478 | 3.93 | 33 | 33 | 0 | 0 | 0 | 0-0 | 208.1 | 192 | 878 | 91 | 91 | 21 | 3 | 6 | 7 | 76 | 2 | 191 | 9 | 0 |
| Harden, Rich, Oak. | 11 | 7 | .611 | 3.99 | 31 | 31 | 0 | 0 | 0 | 0-0 | 189.2 | 171 | 803 | 90 | 84 | 16 | 5 | 6 | 3 | 81 | 6 | 167 | 4 | 1 |
| Arroyo, Bronson, Bos. | 10 | 9 | .526 | 4.03 | 32 | 29 | 0 | 0 | 0 | 0-0 | 178.2 | 171 | 764 | 99 | 80 | 17 | 5 | 4 | 20 | 47 | 3 | 142 | 5 | 0 |
| Lilly, Ted, Tor.* | 12 | 10 | .545 | 4.06 | 32 | 32 | 2 | 1 | 0 | 0-0 | 197.1 | 171 | 845 | 92 | 89 | 26 | 3 | 3 | 6 | 89 | 2 | 168 | 6 | 4 |
| Sabathia, C.C., Cle.* | 11 | 10 | .524 | 4.12 | 30 | 30 | 1 | 1 | 0 | 0-0 | 188.0 | 176 | 787 | 90 | 86 | 20 | 3 | 6 | 7 | 72 | 3 | 139 | 1 | 1 |
| Drese, Ryan, Tex. | 14 | 10 | .583 | 4.20 | 34 | 33 | 2 | 0 | 1 | 0-0 | 207.2 | 233 | 897 | 104 | 97 | 16 | 6 | 5 | 11 | 58 | 6 | 98 | 1 | 0 |

**DEPARTMENTAL LEADERS:** W—Schilling, Bos., 21; L—May, K.C., 19; G—Quantrill, N.Y., 86; GS—Buehrle, Chi., Rogers, Tex., 35; CG—Mulder, Oak., Ponson, Bal., Westbrook, Cle., 5; ShO—Bonderman, Det., Hudson, Oak., Ponson, Bal., 2; GF—Rivera, N.Y., 69; Sv.—Rivera, N.Y., 53; IP—Buehrle, Chi., 245.1; H—Ponson, Bal., 265; TBF—Buehrle, Chi., 1016; R—Lowe, Bos., 138; ER—Ponson, Bal., 127; HR—Moyer, Sea., 44; SH—Robertson, Det., 12; SF—Franklin, Sea., 11; HB—Arroyo, Bos., 20; TBB—Batista, Tor., Zambrano, TB., 96; IBB—Sullivan, K.C., 10; SO—Santana, Min., 265; WP—Contreras, N.Y.-Chi., 17; Bk.—Lilly, Tor., 4.

## ALL PITCHERS

*Throws lefthanded.

| Pitcher, Team | W | L | Pct. | ERA | G | GS | CG | ShO | GF | Sv.-Op. | IP | H | TBF | R | ER | HR | SH | SF | HB | BB | IBB | SO | WP | Bk. |
|---|---|---|---|---|---|---|---|---|---|---|---|---|---|---|---|---|---|---|---|---|---|---|---|---|
| Abbott, Paul, TB. | 2 | 5 | .286 | 6.70 | 10 | 9 | 0 | 0 | 0 | 0-0 | 47.0 | 49 | 222 | 39 | 35 | 8 | 0 | 1 | 3 | 27 | 0 | 25 | 3 | 0 |
| Adams, Terry, Tor.-Bos. | 6 | 4 | .600 | 4.76 | 61 | 0 | 0 | 0 | 21 | 3-6 | 70.0 | 84 | 316 | 39 | 37 | 10 | 3 | 5 | 2 | 28 | 3 | 56 | 8 | 0 |
| Adkins, Jon, Chi. | 2 | 3 | .400 | 4.65 | 50 | 0 | 0 | 0 | 19 | 0-0 | 62.0 | 75 | 271 | 35 | 32 | 13 | 3 | 1 | 1 | 20 | 3 | 44 | 1 | 0 |
| Affeldt, Jeremy, K.C.* | 3 | 4 | .429 | 4.95 | 38 | 8 | 0 | 0 | 26 | 13-17 | 76.1 | 91 | 344 | 49 | 42 | 6 | 4 | 4 | 3 | 32 | 2 | 49 | 4 | 3 |
| Ainsworth, Kurt, Bal. | 0 | 1 | .000 | 9.68 | 7 | 7 | 0 | 0 | 0 | 0-0 | 30.2 | 39 | 151 | 34 | 33 | 6 | 2 | 2 | 5 | 20 | 0 | 20 | 4 | 0 |
| Almanzar, Carlos, Tex. | 7 | 3 | .700 | 3.72 | 67 | 0 | 0 | 0 | 18 | 0-2 | 72.2 | 66 | 298 | 32 | 30 | 8 | 2 | 3 | 4 | 19 | 4 | 44 | 1 | 0 |
| Alvarez, Abe, Bos.* | 0 | 1 | .000 | 9.00 | 1 | 1 | 0 | 0 | 0 | 0-0 | 5.0 | 8 | 25 | 5 | 5 | 2 | 0 | 0 | 0 | 5 | 0 | 2 | 0 | 0 |
| Anderson, Brian, K.C.* | 6 | 12 | .333 | 5.64 | 35 | 26 | 2 | 1 | 2 | 0-0 | 166.0 | 217 | 745 | 123 | 104 | 33 | 5 | 7 | 1 | 53 | 4 | 70 | 2 | 0 |
| Anderson, Jason, Cle. | 0 | 0 | .000 | 45.00 | 1 | 0 | 0 | 0 | 0 | 0-0 | 1.0 | 1 | 8 | 5 | 5 | 1 | 0 | 0 | 0 | 4 | 1 | 1 | 0 | 0 |
| Anderson, Jimmy, Bos.* | 0 | 0 | .000 | 6.00 | 5 | 0 | 0 | 0 | 2 | 0-0 | 6.0 | 10 | 28 | 4 | 4 | 0 | 0 | 0 | 0 | 3 | 0 | 3 | 1 | 0 |
| Appier, Kevin, K.C. | 0 | 1 | .000 | 13.50 | 2 | 2 | 0 | 0 | 0 | 0-0 | 4.0 | 7 | 22 | 8 | 6 | 0 | 0 | 0 | 0 | 3 | 0 | 2 | 2 | 0 |
| Arroyo, Bronson, Bos. | 10 | 9 | .526 | 4.03 | 32 | 29 | 0 | 0 | 0 | 0-0 | 178.2 | 171 | 764 | 99 | 80 | 17 | 5 | 4 | 20 | 47 | 3 | 142 | 5 | 0 |
| Astacio, Pedro, Bos. | 0 | 0 | .000 | 10.38 | 5 | 1 | 0 | 0 | 1 | 0-0 | 8.2 | 13 | 43 | 10 | 10 | 2 | 0 | 0 | 0 | 5 | 0 | 6 | 1 | 0 |
| Atchison, Scott, Sea. | 2 | 3 | .400 | 3.52 | 25 | 0 | 0 | 0 | 8 | 0-0 | 30.2 | 29 | 133 | 12 | 12 | 4 | 2 | 1 | 0 | 14 | 2 | 36 | 2 | 0 |
| Bacsik, Mike, Tex.* | 1 | 1 | .500 | 4.60 | 3 | 3 | 0 | 0 | 0 | 0-0 | 15.2 | 16 | 63 | 8 | 8 | 2 | 0 | 0 | 2 | 1 | 0 | 6 | 0 | 0 |
| Baek, Cha Seung, Sea. | 2 | 4 | .333 | 5.52 | 7 | 5 | 0 | 0 | 2 | 0-0 | 31.0 | 35 | 139 | 23 | 19 | 5 | 0 | 0 | 2 | 11 | 1 | 20 | 2 | 0 |
| Baez, Danys, TB. | 4 | 4 | .500 | 3.57 | 62 | 0 | 0 | 0 | 59 | 30-33 | 68.0 | 60 | 295 | 31 | 27 | 6 | 5 | 1 | 7 | 29 | 4 | 52 | 3 | 1 |
| Bajenaru, Jeff, Chi. | 0 | 1 | .000 | 10.80 | 9 | 0 | 0 | 0 | 4 | 0-0 | 8.1 | 15 | 44 | 10 | 10 | 0 | 1 | 0 | 0 | 6 | 1 | 8 | 0 | 0 |
| Balfour, Grant, Min. | 4 | 1 | .800 | 4.35 | 36 | 0 | 0 | 0 | 14 | 0-1 | 39.1 | 35 | 172 | 19 | 19 | 4 | 2 | 0 | 2 | 21 | 1 | 42 | 3 | 0 |
| Bartosh, Cliff, Cle.* | 1 | 0 | 1.000 | 4.66 | 34 | 0 | 0 | 0 | 2 | 0-2 | 19.1 | 22 | 91 | 10 | 10 | 4 | 0 | 0 | 0 | 11 | 0 | 25 | 0 | 1 |
| Batista, Miguel, Tor. | 10 | 13 | .435 | 4.80 | 38 | 31 | 2 | 1 | 7 | 5-5 | 198.2 | 206 | 867 | 115 | 106 | 22 | 7 | 6 | 3 | 96 | 1 | 104 | 12 | 0 |
| Bauer, Rick, Bal. | 2 | 1 | .667 | 4.70 | 23 | 2 | 0 | 0 | 7 | 0-1 | 53.2 | 49 | 230 | 31 | 28 | 4 | 0 | 0 | 4 | 20 | 0 | 37 | 1 | 0 |
| Bautista, Denny, Bal.-K.C. | 0 | 4 | .000 | 8.49 | 7 | 5 | 0 | 0 | 0 | 0-0 | 29.2 | 44 | 142 | 28 | 28 | 3 | 0 | 1 | 3 | 13 | 1 | 19 | 3 | 2 |
| Bedard, Erik, Bal.* | 6 | 10 | .375 | 4.59 | 27 | 26 | 0 | 0 | 0 | 0-0 | 137.1 | 149 | 633 | 83 | 70 | 13 | 0 | 4 | 7 | 71 | 1 | 121 | 7 | 2 |

| Pitcher, Team | W | L | Pct. | ERA | G | GS | CG | ShO | GF | Sv.-Op. | IP | H | TBF | R | ER | HR | SH | SF | HB | BB | IBB | SO | WP | Bk. |
|---|---|---|---|---|---|---|---|---|---|---|---|---|---|---|---|---|---|---|---|---|---|---|---|---|
| Beimel, Joe, Min.* | 0 | 0 | .000 | 43.20 | 3 | 0 | 0 | 0 | 0 | 0-0 | 1.2 | 8 | 15 | 8 | 8 | 1 | 0 | 0 | 0 | 2 | 0 | 2 | 0 | 0 |
| Bell, Rob, TB | 8 | 8 | .500 | 4.46 | 24 | 19 | 1 | 0 | 3 | 0-0 | 123.0 | 121 | 529 | 71 | 61 | 16 | 2 | 2 | 5 | 41 | 0 | 57 | 10 | 0 |
| Benoit, Joaquin, Tex. | 3 | 5 | .375 | 5.68 | 28 | 15 | 0 | 0 | 2 | 0-0 | 103.0 | 113 | 456 | 67 | 65 | 19 | 2 | 10 | 8 | 31 | 0 | 95 | 3 | 0 |
| Bergman, Dusty, Ana.* | 0 | 0 | .000 | 13.50 | 1 | 0 | 0 | 0 | 1 | 0-0 | 2.0 | 4 | 11 | 3 | 3 | 0 | 0 | 1 | 0 | 1 | 0 | 1 | 1 | 0 |
| Betancourt, Rafael, Cle. | 5 | 6 | .455 | 3.92 | 68 | 0 | 0 | 0 | 21 | 4-11 | 66.2 | 71 | 286 | 32 | 29 | 7 | 1 | 2 | 0 | 18 | 6 | 76 | 5 | 1 |
| Bierbrodt, Nick, Tex.* | 1 | 1 | .500 | 5.82 | 4 | 4 | 0 | 0 | 0 | 0-0 | 17.0 | 14 | 81 | 11 | 11 | 4 | 2 | 1 | 2 | 19 | 0 | 10 | 2 | 0 |
| Blackley, Travis, Sea.* | 1 | 3 | .250 | 10.04 | 6 | 6 | 0 | 0 | 0 | 0-0 | 26.0 | 35 | 134 | 31 | 29 | 9 | 1 | 1 | 1 | 22 | 0 | 16 | 3 | 1 |
| Blanton, Joe, Oak. | 0 | 0 | .000 | 5.63 | 3 | 0 | 0 | 0 | 1 | 0-0 | 8.0 | 6 | 30 | 5 | 5 | 1 | 0 | 0 | 0 | 2 | 0 | 6 | 0 | 0 |
| Bonderman, Jeremy, Det. | 11 | 13 | .458 | 4.89 | 33 | 32 | 2 | 2 | 0 | 0-0 | 184.0 | 168 | 793 | 101 | 100 | 24 | 10 | 5 | 10 | 73 | 5 | 168 | 7 | 0 |
| Borkowski, Dave, Bal. | 3 | 4 | .429 | 5.14 | 17 | 8 | 0 | 0 | 2 | 0-1 | 56.0 | 65 | 247 | 37 | 32 | 6 | 2 | 2 | 3 | 15 | 1 | 45 | 2 | 1 |
| Bradford, Chad, Oak. | 5 | 7 | .417 | 4.42 | 68 | 0 | 0 | 0 | 16 | 1-4 | 59.0 | 51 | 251 | 32 | 29 | 5 | 3 | 1 | 5 | 24 | 9 | 34 | 0 | 0 |
| Brazelton, Dewon, TB. | 6 | 8 | .429 | 4.77 | 22 | 21 | 0 | 0 | 0 | 0-0 | 120.2 | 121 | 535 | 71 | 64 | 12 | 0 | 6 | 11 | 53 | 2 | 64 | 2 | 1 |
| Brocail, Doug, Tex. | 4 | 1 | .800 | 4.13 | 43 | 0 | 0 | 0 | 14 | 1-1 | 52.1 | 54 | 232 | 29 | 24 | 2 | 4 | 2 | 5 | 20 | 1 | 43 | 2 | 1 |
| Brown, Jamie, Bos. | 0 | 0 | .000 | 5.87 | 4 | 0 | 0 | 0 | 3 | 0-0 | 7.2 | 15 | 41 | 7 | 5 | 1 | 0 | 1 | 0 | 4 | 0 | 6 | 0 | 0 |
| Brown, Kevin, N.Y. | 10 | 6 | .625 | 4.09 | 22 | 22 | 0 | 0 | 0 | 0-0 | 132.0 | 132 | 551 | 65 | 60 | 14 | 0 | 9 | 3 | 35 | 0 | 83 | 6 | 0 |
| Buehrle, Mark, Chi.* | 16 | 10 | .615 | 3.89 | 35 | 35 | 4 | 1 | 0 | 0-0 | 245.1 | 257 | 1016 | 119 | 106 | 33 | 4 | 6 | 8 | 51 | 2 | 165 | 0 | 0 |
| Bukvich, Ryan, K.C. | 0 | 0 | .000 | 3.68 | 9 | 0 | 0 | 0 | 6 | 1-1 | 7.1 | 4 | 30 | 3 | 3 | 0 | 1 | 0 | 0 | 7 | 0 | 7 | 0 | 0 |
| Bush, David, Tor. | 5 | 4 | .556 | 3.69 | 16 | 16 | 1 | 1 | 0 | 0-0 | 97.2 | 95 | 412 | 47 | 40 | 11 | 4 | 4 | 6 | 25 | 2 | 64 | 3 | 0 |
| Cabrera, Daniel, Bal. | 12 | 8 | .600 | 5.00 | 28 | 27 | 1 | 1 | 1 | 1-1 | 147.2 | 145 | 662 | 85 | 82 | 14 | 4 | 7 | 2 | 89 | 2 | 76 | 12 | 0 |
| Cabrera, Fernando, Cle. | 0 | 0 | .000 | 3.38 | 4 | 0 | 0 | 0 | 2 | 0-0 | 5.1 | 3 | 20 | 3 | 2 | 0 | 0 | 1 | 0 | 1 | 0 | 6 | 0 | 0 |
| Callaway, Mickey, Tex. | 0 | 1 | .000 | 7.94 | 4 | 3 | 0 | 0 | 1 | 0-0 | 11.1 | 18 | 58 | 10 | 10 | 2 | 0 | 1 | 1 | 7 | 0 | 9 | 0 | 1 |
| Camp, Shawn, K.C. | 2 | 2 | .500 | 3.92 | 42 | 0 | 0 | 0 | 12 | 2-3 | 66.2 | 74 | 286 | 37 | 29 | 10 | 2 | 3 | 5 | 16 | 1 | 51 | 2 | 1 |
| Carrasco, D.J., K.C. | 2 | 2 | .500 | 4.84 | 30 | 0 | 0 | 0 | 11 | 0-3 | 35.1 | 41 | 163 | 22 | 19 | 5 | 1 | 1 | 3 | 15 | 3 | 22 | 2 | 0 |
| Carter, Lance, TB. | 3 | 3 | .500 | 3.47 | 56 | 0 | 0 | 0 | 27 | 0-1 | 80.1 | 77 | 336 | 32 | 31 | 12 | 1 | 5 | 1 | 23 | 2 | 36 | 1 | 0 |
| Castillo, Frank, Bos. | 0 | 0 | .000 | 0.00 | 2 | 0 | 0 | 0 | 2 | 0-0 | 1.0 | 1 | 4 | 0 | 0 | 0 | 0 | 0 | 0 | 1 | 0 | 0 | 0 | 0 |
| Cerda, Jaime, K.C.* | 1 | 4 | .200 | 3.15 | 53 | 0 | 0 | 0 | 16 | 2-3 | 45.2 | 41 | 206 | 21 | 16 | 1 | 2 | 3 | 3 | 30 | 3 | 33 | 4 | 0 |
| Chacin, Gustavo, Tor.* | 1 | 1 | .500 | 2.57 | 2 | 2 | 0 | 0 | 0 | 0-0 | 14.0 | 8 | 52 | 4 | 4 | 0 | 0 | 0 | 1 | 3 | 0 | 6 | 0 | 0 |
| Chen, Bruce, Bal.* | 2 | 1 | .667 | 3.02 | 8 | 7 | 1 | 0 | 0 | 0-0 | 47.2 | 39 | 196 | 19 | 16 | 7 | 2 | 1 | 0 | 16 | 0 | 32 | 0 | 0 |
| Chulk, Vinnie, Tor. | 1 | 3 | .250 | 4.66 | 47 | 0 | 0 | 0 | 10 | 2-5 | 56.0 | 59 | 248 | 30 | 29 | 6 | 1 | 1 | 1 | 27 | 1 | 44 | 2 | 0 |
| Colome, Jesus, TB. | 2 | 2 | .500 | 3.27 | 33 | 0 | 0 | 0 | 9 | 3-4 | 41.1 | 28 | 169 | 16 | 15 | 4 | 5 | 0 | 1 | 18 | 1 | 40 | 1 | 1 |
| Colon, Bartolo, Ana. | 18 | 12 | .600 | 5.01 | 34 | 34 | 0 | 0 | 0 | 0-0 | 208.1 | 215 | 897 | 122 | 116 | 38 | 5 | 8 | 3 | 71 | 1 | 158 | 1 | 0 |
| Colyer, Steve, Det.* | 1 | 0 | 1.000 | 6.47 | 41 | 0 | 0 | 0 | 9 | 0-0 | 32.0 | 33 | 147 | 24 | 23 | 8 | 0 | 0 | 1 | 24 | 1 | 31 | 3 | 0 |
| Contreras, Jose, N.Y.-Chi. | 13 | 9 | .591 | 5.50 | 31 | 31 | 0 | 0 | 0 | 0-0 | 170.1 | 166 | 758 | 114 | 104 | 31 | 3 | 6 | 8 | 84 | 1 | 150 | 17 | 0 |
| Cordero, Francisco, Tex. | 3 | 4 | .429 | 2.13 | 67 | 0 | 0 | 0 | 63 | 49-54 | 71.2 | 60 | 304 | 19 | 17 | 1 | 5 | 1 | 1 | 32 | 2 | 79 | 3 | 2 |
| Cornejo, Nate, Det. | 1 | 3 | .250 | 8.42 | 5 | 5 | 0 | 0 | 0 | 0-0 | 25.2 | 42 | 125 | 25 | 24 | 4 | 1 | 0 | 1 | 11 | 1 | 12 | 1 | 1 |
| Cotts, Neal, Chi.* | 4 | 4 | .500 | 5.65 | 56 | 1 | 0 | 0 | 12 | 0-2 | 65.1 | 61 | 281 | 45 | 41 | 13 | 0 | 1 | 3 | 30 | 2 | 58 | 8 | 0 |
| Crain, Jesse, Min. | 3 | 0 | 1.000 | 2.00 | 22 | 0 | 0 | 0 | 3 | 0-1 | 27.0 | 17 | 109 | 6 | 6 | 2 | 1 | 0 | 1 | 12 | 1 | 14 | 1 | 0 |
| Cressend, Jack, Cle. | 0 | 1 | .000 | 6.32 | 11 | 0 | 0 | 0 | 1 | 0-0 | 15.2 | 22 | 78 | 11 | 11 | 4 | 1 | 1 | 0 | 10 | 2 | 8 | 0 | 0 |
| Cruceta, Francisco, Cle. | 0 | 1 | .000 | 9.39 | 2 | 2 | 0 | 0 | 0 | 0-0 | 7.2 | 10 | 39 | 9 | 8 | 1 | 0 | 1 | 1 | 4 | 0 | 9 | 1 | 0 |
| Cubillan, Darwin, Bal. | 0 | 0 | .000 | 5.40 | 7 | 0 | 0 | 0 | 0 | 0-1 | 10.0 | 13 | 50 | 7 | 6 | 3 | 0 | 0 | 0 | 7 | 0 | 8 | 1 | 0 |
| D'Amico, Jeff, Cle. | 1 | 2 | .333 | 7.63 | 7 | 7 | 0 | 0 | 0 | 0-0 | 30.2 | 45 | 144 | 29 | 26 | 6 | 0 | 2 | 1 | 6 | 0 | 16 | 0 | 0 |
| Darensbourg, Vic, Chi.* | 0 | 0 | .000 | 0.00 | 2 | 0 | 0 | 0 | 2 | 0-0 | 1.1 | 1 | 4 | 0 | 0 | 0 | 0 | 0 | 0 | 1 | 0 | 0 | 0 | 0 |
| Davis, Jason, Cle. | 2 | 7 | .222 | 5.51 | 26 | 19 | 0 | 0 | 2 | 0-0 | 114.1 | 148 | 540 | 81 | 70 | 13 | 7 | 2 | 4 | 51 | 1 | 72 | 7 | 1 |
| Dawley, Joe, Cle. | 0 | 0 | .000 | 5.40 | 2 | 2 | 0 | 0 | 0 | 0-0 | 8.1 | 7 | 37 | 5 | 5 | 1 | 0 | 0 | 0 | 7 | 0 | 8 | 0 | 0 |
| de los Santos, Valerio, Tor.* | 0 | 0 | .000 | 6.17 | 17 | 0 | 0 | 0 | 1 | 0-1 | 11.2 | 11 | 56 | 8 | 8 | 0 | 1 | 1 | 0 | 10 | 2 | 10 | 3 | 0 |
| DeJean, Mike, Bal. | 0 | 5 | .000 | 6.13 | 37 | 0 | 0 | 0 | 12 | 0-0 | 39.2 | 49 | 197 | 29 | 27 | 2 | 2 | 2 | 6 | 28 | 6 | 36 | 2 | 0 |
| Denney, Kyle, Cle. | 1 | 2 | .333 | 9.56 | 4 | 4 | 0 | 0 | 0 | 0-0 | 16.0 | 32 | 86 | 17 | 17 | 3 | 1 | 1 | 0 | 8 | 0 | 13 | 1 | 0 |
| DePaula, Jorge, N.Y. | 0 | 1 | .000 | 5.00 | 3 | 1 | 0 | 0 | 0 | 0-0 | 9.0 | 9 | 38 | 6 | 5 | 2 | 0 | 2 | 0 | 4 | 0 | 2 | 0 | 0 |
| Diaz, Felix, Chi. | 2 | 5 | .286 | 6.75 | 18 | 7 | 0 | 0 | 3 | 0-0 | 49.1 | 62 | 226 | 38 | 37 | 13 | 2 | 3 | 3 | 16 | 1 | 33 | 0 | 0 |
| Dickey, R.A., Tex. | 6 | 7 | .462 | 5.61 | 25 | 15 | 0 | 0 | 2 | 1-1 | 104.1 | 136 | 480 | 77 | 65 | 17 | 3 | 3 | 4 | 33 | 1 | 57 | 5 | 1 |
| DiNardo, Lenny, Bos.* | 0 | 0 | .000 | 4.23 | 22 | 0 | 0 | 0 | 6 | 0-0 | 27.2 | 34 | 130 | 17 | 13 | 1 | 1 | 1 | 2 | 12 | 1 | 21 | 1 | 0 |
| Dingman, Craig, Det. | 2 | 2 | .500 | 6.75 | 24 | 0 | 0 | 0 | 5 | 0-2 | 29.1 | 33 | 141 | 22 | 22 | 3 | 1 | 2 | 4 | 22 | 3 | 16 | 1 | 0 |
| Dominguez, Juan, Tex. | 1 | 2 | .333 | 3.91 | 4 | 4 | 0 | 0 | 0 | 0-0 | 23.0 | 25 | 98 | 11 | 10 | 2 | 1 | 1 | 2 | 5 | 0 | 14 | 0 | 2 |
| Donnelly, Brendan, Ana. | 5 | 2 | .714 | 3.00 | 40 | 0 | 0 | 0 | 10 | 0-0 | 42.0 | 34 | 172 | 14 | 14 | 5 | 2 | 2 | 1 | 15 | 0 | 56 | 0 | 0 |
| Dotel, Octavio, Oak. | 6 | 2 | .750 | 4.09 | 45 | 0 | 0 | 0 | 41 | 22-28 | 50.2 | 41 | 210 | 23 | 23 | 9 | 2 | 1 | 3 | 18 | 3 | 72 | 1 | 0 |
| Douglass, Sean, Tor. | 0 | 2 | .000 | 6.28 | 14 | 3 | 0 | 0 | 4 | 0-0 | 38.2 | 37 | 179 | 27 | 27 | 6 | 0 | 2 | 2 | 28 | 4 | 36 | 2 | 0 |
| Drese, Ryan, Tex. | 14 | 10 | .583 | 4.20 | 34 | 33 | 2 | 0 | 1 | 0-0 | 207.2 | 233 | 897 | 104 | 97 | 16 | 6 | 5 | 11 | 58 | 6 | 98 | 1 | 0 |
| DuBose, Eric, Bal.* | 4 | 6 | .400 | 6.39 | 14 | 14 | 0 | 0 | 0 | 0-0 | 74.2 | 76 | 338 | 55 | 53 | 12 | 1 | 1 | 3 | 44 | 0 | 48 | 5 | 1 |
| Duchscherer, Justin, Oak. | 7 | 6 | .538 | 3.27 | 53 | 0 | 0 | 0 | 18 | 0-2 | 96.1 | 85 | 398 | 37 | 35 | 13 | 7 | 1 | 5 | 32 | 6 | 59 | 1 | 1 |
| Dunn, Scott, Ana. | 0 | 0 | .000 | 9.00 | 3 | 0 | 0 | 0 | 1 | 0-0 | 3.0 | 7 | 17 | 3 | 3 | 0 | 0 | 0 | 0 | 1 | 0 | 2 | 1 | 0 |
| Durbin, Chad, Cle. | 5 | 6 | .455 | 6.66 | 17 | 8 | 1 | 0 | 5 | 0-0 | 51.1 | 63 | 239 | 40 | 38 | 10 | 0 | 2 | 4 | 24 | 3 | 38 | 3 | 0 |
| Durbin, J.D., Min. | 0 | 1 | .000 | 7.36 | 4 | 1 | 0 | 0 | 2 | 0-0 | 7.1 | 12 | 38 | 6 | 6 | 0 | 0 | 1 | 0 | 6 | 0 | 6 | 1 | 0 |
| Elarton, Scott, Cle. | 3 | 5 | .375 | 4.53 | 21 | 21 | 1 | 1 | 0 | 0-0 | 117.1 | 107 | 498 | 62 | 59 | 25 | 3 | 4 | 4 | 42 | 2 | 80 | 3 | 0 |
| Embree, Alan, Bos.* | 2 | 2 | .500 | 4.13 | 71 | 0 | 0 | 0 | 11 | 0-1 | 52.1 | 49 | 217 | 28 | 24 | 7 | 2 | 2 | 1 | 11 | 1 | 37 | 0 | 0 |
| Ennis, John, Det. | 0 | 0 | .000 | 8.44 | 12 | 0 | 0 | 0 | 5 | 1-2 | 16.0 | 20 | 75 | 16 | 15 | 3 | 0 | 1 | 0 | 5 | 0 | 13 | 1 | 1 |
| Erickson, Scott, Tex. | 1 | 3 | .250 | 6.16 | 4 | 4 | 0 | 0 | 0 | 0-0 | 19.0 | 23 | 94 | 13 | 13 | 2 | 0 | 3 | 0 | 16 | 0 | 6 | 1 | 0 |
| Escobar, Kelvim, Ana. | 11 | 12 | .478 | 3.93 | 33 | 33 | 0 | 0 | 0 | 0-0 | 208.1 | 192 | 878 | 91 | 91 | 21 | 3 | 6 | 7 | 76 | 2 | 191 | 9 | 0 |
| Field, Nate, K.C. | 2 | 3 | .400 | 4.26 | 43 | 0 | 0 | 0 | 23 | 3-5 | 44.1 | 40 | 191 | 25 | 21 | 5 | 1 | 2 | 2 | 19 | 2 | 30 | 2 | 0 |
| File, Bob, Tor. | 1 | 0 | 1.000 | 4.81 | 24 | 0 | 0 | 0 | 6 | 0-0 | 33.2 | 45 | 154 | 19 | 18 | 4 | 0 | 4 | 2 | 12 | 2 | 15 | 1 | 0 |
| Fortunato, Bartolome, TB. | 0 | 0 | .000 | 3.68 | 3 | 0 | 0 | 0 | 1 | 0-0 | 7.1 | 10 | 30 | 3 | 3 | 1 | 0 | 0 | 0 | 2 | 0 | 5 | 1 | 0 |
| Foulke, Keith, Bos. | 5 | 3 | .625 | 2.17 | 72 | 0 | 0 | 0 | 61 | 32-39 | 83.0 | 63 | 333 | 22 | 20 | 8 | 2 | 4 | 6 | 15 | 5 | 79 | 3 | 0 |
| Francisco, Frank, Tex. | 5 | 1 | .833 | 3.33 | 45 | 0 | 0 | 0 | 7 | 0-3 | 51.1 | 36 | 216 | 19 | 19 | 4 | 2 | 1 | 3 | 28 | 2 | 60 | 4 | 1 |
| Franklin, Ryan, Sea. | 4 | 16 | .200 | 4.90 | 32 | 32 | 2 | 1 | 0 | 0-0 | 200.1 | 224 | 870 | 116 | 109 | 33 | 2 | 11 | 10 | 61 | 1 | 104 | 0 | 3 |
| Frasor, Jason, Tor. | 4 | 6 | .400 | 4.08 | 63 | 0 | 0 | 0 | 37 | 17-19 | 68.1 | 64 | 299 | 31 | 31 | 4 | 3 | 3 | 2 | 36 | 3 | 54 | 4 | 2 |
| Frederick, Kevin, Tor. | 0 | 2 | .000 | 6.59 | 22 | 0 | 0 | 0 | 4 | 0-1 | 28.2 | 32 | 133 | 21 | 21 | 4 | 0 | 3 | 1 | 16 | 1 | 22 | 0 | 0 |
| Fultz, Aaron, Min.* | 3 | 3 | .500 | 5.04 | 55 | 0 | 0 | 0 | 16 | 1-4 | 50.0 | 50 | 216 | 28 | 28 | 5 | 1 | 4 | 1 | 23 | 2 | 37 | 3 | 0 |
| Garcia, Freddy, Sea.-Chi. | 13 | 11 | .542 | 3.81 | 31 | 31 | 1 | 0 | 0 | 0-0 | 210.0 | 192 | 878 | 92 | 89 | 22 | 8 | 3 | 7 | 64 | 3 | 184 | 8 | 0 |
| Garcia, Jairo, Oak. | 0 | 0 | .000 | 12.71 | 4 | 0 | 0 | 0 | 2 | 0-0 | 5.2 | 5 | 32 | 8 | 8 | 3 | 0 | 0 | 1 | 9 | 0 | 5 | 0 | 0 |
| Garcia, Rosman, Tex. | 0 | 0 | .000 | 5.40 | 4 | 0 | 0 | 0 | 1 | 0-0 | 6.2 | 9 | 35 | 5 | 4 | 1 | 0 | 1 | 0 | 5 | 0 | 5 | 0 | 0 |
| Garland, Jon, Chi. | 12 | 11 | .522 | 4.89 | 34 | 33 | 1 | 0 | 0 | 0-0 | 217.0 | 223 | 923 | 125 | 118 | 34 | 9 | 5 | 4 | 76 | 2 | 113 | 3 | 0 |
| Gaudin, Chad, TB. | 1 | 2 | .333 | 4.85 | 26 | 4 | 0 | 0 | 5 | 0-1 | 42.2 | 59 | 201 | 27 | 23 | 4 | 2 | 4 | 4 | 16 | 4 | 30 | 0 | 0 |
| George, Chris, K.C.* | 1 | 2 | .333 | 7.23 | 10 | 7 | 0 | 0 | 1 | 0-0 | 42.1 | 60 | 207 | 39 | 34 | 1 | 0 | 1 | 0 | 25 | 1 | 15 | 0 | 0 |

| Pitcher, Team | W | L | Pct. | ERA | G | GS | CG | ShO | GF | Sv.-Op. | IP | H | TBF | R | ER | HR | SH | SF | HB | BB | IBB | SO | WP | Bk. |
|---|---|---|---|---|---|---|---|---|---|---|---|---|---|---|---|---|---|---|---|---|---|---|---|---|
| German, Franklyn, Det. | 1 | 0 | 1.000 | 7.36 | 16 | 0 | 0 | 0 | 5 | 0-1 | 14.2 | 17 | 73 | 15 | 12 | 4 | 1 | 0 | 0 | 11 | 1 | 8 | 2 | 0 |
| Glynn, Ryan, Tor. | 1 | 0 | 1.000 | 4.05 | 6 | 2 | 0 | 0 | 0 | 0-0 | 20.0 | 19 | 89 | 9 | 9 | 4 | 1 | 1 | 3 | 8 | 1 | 14 | 0 | 0 |
| Gobble, Jimmy, K.C.* | 9 | 8 | .529 | 5.35 | 25 | 24 | 1 | 0 | 0 | 0-0 | 148.0 | 157 | 638 | 94 | 88 | 24 | 4 | 7 | 3 | 43 | 0 | 49 | 4 | 0 |
| Gonzalez, Dicky, TB. | 0 | 0 | .000 | 6.14 | 4 | 0 | 0 | 0 | 1 | 0-0 | 7.1 | 9 | 32 | 5 | 5 | 1 | 0 | 1 | 0 | 2 | 0 | 7 | 2 | 0 |
| Gonzalez, Jeremi, TB. | 0 | 5 | .000 | 6.97 | 11 | 8 | 0 | 0 | 1 | 0-0 | 50.1 | 72 | 235 | 42 | 39 | 9 | 1 | 3 | 3 | 20 | 0 | 22 | 4 | 0 |
| Gordon, Tom, N.Y. | 9 | 4 | .692 | 2.21 | 80 | 0 | 0 | 0 | 15 | 4-10 | 89.2 | 56 | 342 | 23 | 22 | 5 | 5 | 2 | 1 | 23 | 5 | 96 | 3 | 0 |
| Graman, Alex, N.Y.* | 0 | 0 | .000 | 19.80 | 3 | 2 | 0 | 0 | 1 | 0-0 | 5.0 | 14 | 31 | 11 | 11 | 1 | 0 | 1 | 0 | 2 | 0 | 4 | 0 | 0 |
| Gregg, Kevin, Ana. | 5 | 2 | .714 | 4.21 | 55 | 0 | 0 | 0 | 23 | 1-2 | 87.2 | 86 | 377 | 43 | 41 | 6 | 4 | 5 | 3 | 28 | 3 | 84 | 13 | 1 |
| Greinke, Zack, K.C. | 8 | 11 | .421 | 3.97 | 24 | 24 | 0 | 0 | 0 | 0-0 | 145.0 | 143 | 599 | 64 | 64 | 26 | 3 | 2 | 8 | 26 | 3 | 100 | 1 | 1 |
| Greisinger, Seth, Min. | 2 | 5 | .286 | 6.18 | 12 | 9 | 0 | 0 | 1 | 0-0 | 51.0 | 68 | 233 | 40 | 35 | 12 | 1 | 2 | 2 | 15 | 1 | 36 | 1 | 0 |
| Grilli, Jason, Chi. | 2 | 3 | .400 | 7.40 | 8 | 8 | 1 | 0 | 0 | 0-0 | 45.0 | 52 | 203 | 38 | 37 | 11 | 2 | 1 | 3 | 20 | 0 | 26 | 2 | 0 |
| Grimsley, Jason, K.C.-Bal. | 5 | 7 | .417 | 3.86 | 73 | 0 | 0 | 0 | 7 | 0-9 | 63.0 | 61 | 285 | 36 | 27 | 4 | 3 | 1 | 3 | 35 | 6 | 39 | 6 | 0 |
| Groom, Buddy, Bal.* | 4 | 1 | .800 | 4.78 | 60 | 0 | 0 | 0 | 22 | 0-2 | 52.2 | 67 | 236 | 30 | 28 | 6 | 0 | 2 | 1 | 16 | 1 | 32 | 0 | 1 |
| Guardado, Eddie, Sea.* | 2 | 2 | .500 | 2.78 | 41 | 0 | 0 | 0 | 35 | 18-25 | 45.1 | 31 | 176 | 14 | 14 | 8 | 0 | 1 | 1 | 14 | 0 | 45 | 0 | 0 |
| Guerrier, Matt, Min. | 0 | 1 | .000 | 5.68 | 9 | 2 | 0 | 0 | 5 | 0-0 | 19.0 | 22 | 84 | 13 | 12 | 5 | 2 | 0 | 1 | 6 | 0 | 11 | 0 | 0 |
| Guthrie, Jeremy, Cle. | 0 | 0 | .000 | 4.63 | 6 | 0 | 0 | 0 | 2 | 0-0 | 11.2 | 9 | 49 | 6 | 6 | 1 | 0 | 0 | 1 | 6 | 0 | 7 | 1 | 0 |
| Halama, John, TB.* | 7 | 6 | .538 | 4.70 | 34 | 14 | 0 | 0 | 7 | 0-0 | 118.2 | 134 | 513 | 68 | 62 | 17 | 1 | 3 | 10 | 27 | 3 | 59 | 1 | 1 |
| Halladay, Roy, Tor. | 8 | 8 | .500 | 4.20 | 21 | 21 | 1 | 1 | 0 | 0-0 | 133.0 | 140 | 561 | 66 | 62 | 13 | 4 | 3 | 1 | 39 | 1 | 95 | 2 | 2 |
| Halsey, Brad, N.Y.* | 1 | 3 | .250 | 6.47 | 8 | 7 | 0 | 0 | 0 | 0-0 | 32.0 | 41 | 153 | 26 | 23 | 4 | 1 | 2 | 2 | 14 | 0 | 25 | 0 | 0 |
| Hammond, Chris, Oak.* | 4 | 1 | .800 | 2.68 | 41 | 0 | 0 | 0 | 9 | 1-3 | 53.2 | 56 | 224 | 21 | 16 | 4 | 3 | 3 | 3 | 13 | 1 | 34 | 0 | 0 |
| Harden, Rich, Oak. | 11 | 7 | .611 | 3.99 | 31 | 31 | 0 | 0 | 0 | 0-0 | 189.2 | 171 | 803 | 90 | 84 | 16 | 5 | 6 | 3 | 81 | 6 | 167 | 4 | 1 |
| Harper, Travis, TB. | 6 | 2 | .750 | 3.89 | 52 | 0 | 0 | 0 | 11 | 0-1 | 78.2 | 69 | 330 | 37 | 34 | 8 | 3 | 2 | 7 | 23 | 3 | 59 | 3 | 0 |
| Harville, Chad, Oak. | 0 | 0 | .000 | 3.38 | 3 | 0 | 0 | 0 | 1 | 0-0 | 2.2 | 2 | 11 | 1 | 1 | 0 | 0 | 0 | 0 | 1 | 0 | 0 | 0 | 0 |
| Hasegawa, Shigetoshi, Sea. | 4 | 6 | .400 | 5.16 | 68 | 0 | 0 | 0 | 19 | 0-5 | 68.0 | 67 | 300 | 42 | 39 | 5 | 5 | 4 | 2 | 31 | 4 | 46 | 1 | 1 |
| Hendrickson, Mark, TB.* | 10 | 15 | .400 | 4.81 | 32 | 30 | 2 | 0 | 1 | 0-0 | 183.1 | 211 | 803 | 113 | 98 | 21 | 4 | 5 | 7 | 46 | 5 | 87 | 5 | 2 |
| Hensley, Matt, Ana. | 0 | 2 | .000 | 4.88 | 16 | 0 | 0 | 0 | 13 | 0-0 | 27.2 | 32 | 120 | 15 | 15 | 5 | 1 | 1 | 2 | 7 | 1 | 30 | 0 | 0 |
| Hentgen, Pat, Tor. | 2 | 9 | .182 | 6.95 | 18 | 16 | 0 | 0 | 2 | 0-0 | 80.1 | 90 | 373 | 67 | 62 | 16 | 1 | 8 | 4 | 42 | 2 | 33 | 1 | 0 |
| Heredia, Felix, N.Y.* | 1 | 1 | .500 | 6.28 | 47 | 0 | 0 | 0 | 9 | 0-1 | 38.2 | 44 | 182 | 28 | 27 | 5 | 1 | 1 | 2 | 20 | 0 | 25 | 1 | 0 |
| Hernandez, Orlando, N.Y. | 8 | 2 | .800 | 3.30 | 15 | 15 | 0 | 0 | 0 | 0-0 | 84.2 | 73 | 359 | 31 | 31 | 9 | 0 | 1 | 5 | 36 | 0 | 84 | 3 | 0 |
| Howry, Bob, Cle. | 4 | 2 | .667 | 2.74 | 37 | 0 | 0 | 0 | 6 | 0-2 | 42.2 | 37 | 178 | 14 | 13 | 5 | 1 | 1 | 2 | 12 | 0 | 39 | 0 | 0 |
| Hudson, Tim, Oak. | 12 | 6 | .667 | 3.53 | 27 | 27 | 3 | 2 | 0 | 0-0 | 188.2 | 194 | 793 | 82 | 74 | 8 | 7 | 4 | 12 | 44 | 3 | 103 | 4 | 1 |
| Hughes, Travis, Tex. | 0 | 0 | .000 | 13.50 | 2 | 0 | 0 | 0 | 1 | 0-0 | 1.1 | 4 | 10 | 2 | 2 | 0 | 0 | 0 | 0 | 2 | 0 | 4 | 0 | 0 |
| Huisman, Justin, K.C. | 0 | 0 | .000 | 6.84 | 14 | 0 | 0 | 0 | 4 | 1-1 | 25.0 | 36 | 116 | 20 | 19 | 3 | 0 | 0 | 1 | 8 | 3 | 13 | 0 | 0 |
| Jackson, Mike, Chi. | 2 | 0 | 1.000 | 5.01 | 45 | 0 | 0 | 0 | 12 | 0-0 | 46.2 | 55 | 210 | 27 | 26 | 7 | 2 | 3 | 3 | 15 | 2 | 26 | 1 | 2 |
| Jarvis, Kevin, Sea. | 1 | 0 | 1.000 | 8.31 | 8 | 0 | 0 | 0 | 2 | 0-0 | 13.0 | 20 | 63 | 12 | 12 | 4 | 0 | 0 | 0 | 5 | 0 | 7 | 2 | 0 |
| Jimenez, Jose, Cle. | 1 | 7 | .125 | 8.42 | 31 | 0 | 0 | 0 | 18 | 8-11 | 36.1 | 45 | 170 | 37 | 34 | 6 | 0 | 0 | 4 | 14 | 2 | 21 | 0 | 0 |
| Johnson, Jason, Det. | 8 | 15 | .348 | 5.13 | 33 | 33 | 2 | 1 | 0 | 0-0 | 196.2 | 222 | 859 | 121 | 112 | 22 | 1 | 10 | 5 | 60 | 3 | 125 | 7 | 1 |
| Jones, Bobby M., Bos.* | 0 | 1 | .000 | 5.40 | 3 | 0 | 0 | 0 | 1 | 0-0 | 3.1 | 3 | 20 | 2 | 2 | 1 | 1 | 0 | 0 | 8 | 1 | 3 | 0 | 0 |
| Julio, Jorge, Bal. | 2 | 5 | .286 | 4.57 | 65 | 0 | 0 | 0 | 50 | 22-26 | 69.0 | 59 | 306 | 35 | 35 | 11 | 2 | 3 | 3 | 39 | 4 | 70 | 7 | 0 |
| Karsay, Steve, N.Y. | 0 | 0 | .000 | 2.70 | 7 | 0 | 0 | 0 | 6 | 0-0 | 6.2 | 5 | 27 | 3 | 2 | 2 | 0 | 2 | 0 | 2 | 0 | 4 | 1 | 0 |
| Kazmir, Scott, TB.* | 2 | 3 | .400 | 5.67 | 8 | 7 | 0 | 0 | 0 | 0-0 | 33.1 | 33 | 152 | 22 | 21 | 4 | 0 | 0 | 2 | 21 | 0 | 41 | 3 | 0 |
| Kershner, Jason, Tor.* | 0 | 1 | .000 | 6.04 | 24 | 2 | 0 | 0 | 2 | 0-0 | 22.1 | 30 | 103 | 16 | 15 | 3 | 0 | 0 | 0 | 8 | 0 | 15 | 3 | 1 |
| Kida, Masao, Sea. | 0 | 0 | .000 | 8.38 | 7 | 0 | 0 | 0 | 0 | 0-0 | 9.2 | 15 | 47 | 9 | 9 | 1 | 0 | 0 | 1 | 5 | 0 | 5 | 0 | 0 |
| Kim, Byung-Hyun, Bos. | 2 | 1 | .667 | 6.23 | 7 | 3 | 0 | 0 | 2 | 0-0 | 17.1 | 17 | 77 | 15 | 12 | 1 | 0 | 2 | 2 | 7 | 1 | 6 | 1 | 0 |
| Kinney, Matt, K.C. | 0 | 1 | .000 | 7.16 | 11 | 0 | 0 | 0 | 4 | 0-0 | 16.1 | 27 | 84 | 14 | 13 | 3 | 0 | 1 | 2 | 7 | 1 | 21 | 2 | 0 |
| Knotts, Gary, Det. | 7 | 6 | .538 | 5.25 | 36 | 19 | 0 | 0 | 6 | 2-2 | 135.1 | 142 | 599 | 83 | 79 | 20 | 4 | 2 | 4 | 58 | 3 | 81 | 11 | 0 |
| Koch, Billy, Chi. | 1 | 1 | .500 | 5.40 | 24 | 0 | 0 | 0 | 19 | 8-11 | 23.1 | 24 | 114 | 15 | 14 | 3 | 0 | 2 | 2 | 16 | 4 | 25 | 4 | 0 |
| Lackey, John, Ana. | 14 | 13 | .519 | 4.67 | 33 | 32 | 1 | 1 | 0 | 0-0 | 198.1 | 215 | 855 | 108 | 103 | 22 | 9 | 4 | 8 | 60 | 4 | 144 | 11 | 1 |
| Laker, Tim, Cle. | 0 | 0 | .000 | 0.00 | 1 | 0 | 0 | 0 | 1 | 0-0 | 1.0 | 1 | 4 | 0 | 0 | 0 | 0 | 0 | 0 | 1 | 0 | 0 | 0 | 0 |
| League, Brandon, Tor. | 1 | 0 | 1.000 | 0.00 | 3 | 0 | 0 | 0 | 0 | 0-0 | 4.2 | 3 | 18 | 0 | 0 | 0 | 0 | 0 | 0 | 1 | 0 | 2 | 0 | 0 |
| Ledezma, Wilfredo, Det.* | 4 | 3 | .571 | 4.39 | 15 | 8 | 0 | 0 | 1 | 0-1 | 53.1 | 55 | 225 | 28 | 26 | 3 | 0 | 3 | 2 | 18 | 0 | 29 | 3 | 1 |
| Lee, Cliff, Cle.* | 14 | 8 | .636 | 5.43 | 33 | 33 | 0 | 0 | 0 | 0-0 | 179.0 | 188 | 802 | 113 | 108 | 30 | 2 | 6 | 11 | 81 | 1 | 161 | 6 | 0 |
| Lee, Dave, Cle. | 0 | 0 | .000 | 10.38 | 4 | 0 | 0 | 0 | 2 | 0-0 | 4.1 | 8 | 27 | 7 | 5 | 0 | 0 | 0 | 0 | 4 | 0 | 4 | 1 | 0 |
| Lehr, Justin, Oak. | 1 | 1 | .500 | 5.23 | 27 | 0 | 0 | 0 | 11 | 0-1 | 32.2 | 35 | 144 | 19 | 19 | 3 | 1 | 2 | 2 | 14 | 2 | 16 | 2 | 0 |
| Leskanic, Curtis, K.C.-Bos. | 3 | 5 | .375 | 5.19 | 51 | 0 | 0 | 0 | 23 | 4-8 | 43.1 | 47 | 204 | 27 | 25 | 8 | 3 | 2 | 1 | 30 | 3 | 37 | 2 | 0 |
| Levine, Al, Det. | 3 | 4 | .429 | 4.58 | 65 | 0 | 0 | 0 | 14 | 0-1 | 70.2 | 83 | 310 | 37 | 36 | 10 | 2 | 2 | 1 | 24 | 1 | 32 | 3 | 0 |
| Lewis, Colby, Tex. | 1 | 1 | .500 | 4.11 | 3 | 3 | 0 | 0 | 0 | 0-0 | 15.1 | 13 | 71 | 7 | 7 | 1 | 0 | 0 | 1 | 13 | 0 | 11 | 0 | 0 |
| Lieber, Jon, N.Y. | 14 | 8 | .636 | 4.33 | 27 | 27 | 0 | 0 | 0 | 0-0 | 176.2 | 216 | 749 | 95 | 85 | 20 | 3 | 7 | 2 | 18 | 2 | 102 | 7 | 0 |
| Ligtenberg, Kerry, Tor. | 1 | 6 | .143 | 6.38 | 57 | 0 | 0 | 0 | 20 | 3-5 | 55.0 | 73 | 263 | 40 | 39 | 6 | 3 | 0 | 2 | 25 | 7 | 49 | 5 | 0 |
| Lilly, Ted, Tor.* | 12 | 10 | .545 | 4.06 | 32 | 32 | 2 | 1 | 0 | 0-0 | 197.1 | 171 | 845 | 92 | 89 | 26 | 3 | 3 | 6 | 89 | 2 | 168 | 6 | 4 |
| Loaiza, Esteban, Chi.-N.Y. | 10 | 7 | .588 | 5.70 | 31 | 27 | 2 | 1 | 1 | 0-0 | 183.0 | 217 | 818 | 124 | 116 | 32 | 1 | 10 | 3 | 71 | 5 | 117 | 4 | 0 |
| Loe, Kameron, Tex. | 0 | 0 | .000 | 5.40 | 2 | 1 | 0 | 0 | 0 | 0-0 | 6.2 | 6 | 29 | 5 | 4 | 0 | 0 | 0 | 1 | 6 | 0 | 3 | 0 | 0 |
| Lohse, Kyle, Min. | 9 | 13 | .409 | 5.34 | 35 | 34 | 1 | 1 | 1 | 0-0 | 194.0 | 240 | 883 | 128 | 115 | 28 | 5 | 7 | 7 | 76 | 5 | 111 | 6 | 0 |
| Lopez, Aquilino, Tor. | 1 | 1 | .500 | 6.00 | 18 | 0 | 0 | 0 | 6 | 0-0 | 21.0 | 21 | 95 | 15 | 14 | 5 | 0 | 1 | 2 | 13 | 3 | 13 | 0 | 0 |
| Lopez, Rodrigo, Bal. | 14 | 9 | .609 | 3.59 | 37 | 23 | 1 | 1 | 3 | 0-1 | 170.2 | 164 | 714 | 71 | 68 | 21 | 5 | 2 | 2 | 54 | 2 | 121 | 4 | 1 |
| Lowe, Derek, Bos. | 14 | 12 | .538 | 5.42 | 33 | 33 | 0 | 0 | 0 | 0-0 | 182.2 | 224 | 839 | 138 | 110 | 15 | 8 | 4 | 8 | 71 | 2 | 105 | 3 | 0 |
| MacDougal, Mike, K.C. | 1 | 1 | .500 | 5.56 | 13 | 0 | 0 | 0 | 8 | 1-3 | 11.1 | 16 | 61 | 8 | 7 | 2 | 0 | 0 | 1 | 9 | 0 | 14 | 2 | 0 |
| Madritsch, Bobby, Sea.* | 6 | 3 | .667 | 3.27 | 15 | 11 | 1 | 0 | 4 | 0-0 | 88.0 | 74 | 359 | 33 | 32 | 3 | 3 | 0 | 4 | 33 | 2 | 60 | 2 | 1 |
| Mahay, Ron, Tex.* | 3 | 0 | 1.000 | 2.55 | 60 | 0 | 0 | 0 | 12 | 0-2 | 67.0 | 60 | 290 | 23 | 19 | 5 | 4 | 0 | 2 | 29 | 5 | 54 | 2 | 0 |
| Maine, John, Bal. | 0 | 1 | .000 | 9.82 | 1 | 1 | 0 | 0 | 0 | 0-0 | 3.2 | 7 | 19 | 4 | 4 | 1 | 0 | 0 | 0 | 3 | 0 | 1 | 1 | 0 |
| Malaska, Mark, Bos.* | 1 | 1 | .500 | 4.50 | 19 | 0 | 0 | 0 | 8 | 0-0 | 20.0 | 21 | 93 | 11 | 10 | 2 | 1 | 0 | 1 | 12 | 1 | 12 | 0 | 0 |
| Maroth, Mike, Det.* | 11 | 13 | .458 | 4.31 | 33 | 33 | 2 | 1 | 0 | 0-0 | 217.0 | 244 | 928 | 112 | 104 | 25 | 11 | 4 | 7 | 59 | 1 | 108 | 10 | 1 |
| Marsonek, Sam, N.Y. | 0 | 0 | .000 | 0.00 | 1 | 0 | 0 | 0 | 1 | 0-0 | 1.1 | 2 | 6 | 0 | 0 | 0 | 0 | 0 | 0 | 0 | 0 | 0 | 0 | 0 |
| Marte, Damaso, Chi.* | 6 | 5 | .545 | 3.42 | 74 | 0 | 0 | 0 | 24 | 6-12 | 73.2 | 56 | 303 | 28 | 28 | 10 | 2 | 6 | 3 | 34 | 4 | 68 | 3 | 0 |
| Martinez, Anastacio, Bos. | 2 | 1 | .667 | 8.44 | 11 | 0 | 0 | 0 | 7 | 0-0 | 10.2 | 13 | 52 | 10 | 10 | 2 | 0 | 0 | 1 | 6 | 0 | 5 | 0 | 0 |
| Martinez, Pedro, Bos. | 16 | 9 | .640 | 3.90 | 33 | 33 | 1 | 1 | 0 | 0-0 | 217.0 | 193 | 903 | 99 | 94 | 26 | 5 | 9 | 16 | 61 | 0 | 227 | 2 | 0 |
| Mateo, Julio, Sea. | 1 | 2 | .333 | 4.68 | 45 | 0 | 0 | 0 | 9 | 1-4 | 57.2 | 56 | 248 | 30 | 30 | 11 | 0 | 4 | 5 | 16 | 3 | 43 | 2 | 0 |
| Maurer, Dave, Tor.* | 0 | 0 | .000 | 54.00 | 3 | 0 | 0 | 0 | 0 | 0-0 | 1.1 | 6 | 15 | 8 | 8 | 1 | 0 | 0 | 0 | 5 | 0 | 1 | 0 | 0 |
| May, Darrell, K.C.* | 9 | 19 | .321 | 5.61 | 31 | 31 | 3 | 1 | 0 | 0-0 | 186.0 | 234 | 832 | 130 | 116 | 38 | 1 | 9 | 2 | 55 | 4 | 120 | 2 | 0 |
| McCarty, Dave, Bos.* | 0 | 0 | .000 | 2.45 | 3 | 0 | 0 | 0 | 2 | 0-0 | 3.2 | 2 | 14 | 1 | 1 | 0 | 0 | 0 | 0 | 1 | 0 | 4 | 1 | 0 |
| Meche, Gil, Sea. | 7 | 7 | .500 | 5.01 | 23 | 23 | 1 | 1 | 0 | 0-0 | 127.2 | 139 | 565 | 73 | 71 | 21 | 1 | 3 | 5 | 47 | 0 | 99 | 4 | 0 |
| Mecir, Jim, Oak. | 0 | 5 | .000 | 3.59 | 65 | 0 | 0 | 0 | 17 | 2-7 | 47.2 | 45 | 212 | 21 | 19 | 5 | 1 | 0 | 4 | 19 | 2 | 49 | 1 | 0 |

| Pitcher, Team | W | L | Pct. | ERA | G | GS | CG | ShO | GF | Sv.-Op. | IP | H | TBF | R | ER | HR | SH | SF | HB | BB | IBB | SO | WP | Bk. |
|---|---|---|---|---|---|---|---|---|---|---|---|---|---|---|---|---|---|---|---|---|---|---|---|---|
| Mendoza, Ramiro, Bos. | 2 | 1 | .667 | 3.52 | 27 | 0 | 0 | 0 | 12 | 0-0 | 30.2 | 25 | 119 | 12 | 12 | 3 | 0 | 0 | 1 | 7 | 1 | 13 | 1 | 1 |
| Menechino, Frank, Tor. | 0 | 0 | .000 | 0.00 | 1 | 0 | 0 | 0 | 1 | 0-0 | 0.1 | 2 | 3 | 0 | 0 | 0 | 0 | 0 | 0 | 0 | 0 | 0 | 0 | 0 |
| Miller, Justin, Tor. | 3 | 4 | .429 | 6.06 | 19 | 15 | 0 | 0 | 0 | 0-0 | 81.2 | 101 | 375 | 58 | 55 | 14 | 2 | 6 | 5 | 42 | 3 | 47 | 3 | 1 |
| Miller, Matt, Cle. | 4 | 1 | .800 | 3.09 | 57 | 0 | 0 | 0 | 13 | 1-2 | 55.1 | 42 | 226 | 22 | 19 | 1 | 2 | 1 | 6 | 23 | 8 | 55 | 1 | 1 |
| Miller, Trever, TB.* | 1 | 1 | .500 | 3.12 | 60 | 0 | 0 | 0 | 15 | 1-3 | 49.0 | 48 | 208 | 21 | 17 | 3 | 3 | 0 | 3 | 15 | 4 | 43 | 2 | 0 |
| Moss, Damian, TB.* | 0 | 1 | .000 | 16.88 | 5 | 2 | 0 | 0 | 2 | 0-0 | 8.0 | 13 | 43 | 15 | 15 | 2 | 0 | 0 | 1 | 5 | 0 | 6 | 1 | 0 |
| Moyer, Jamie, Sea.* | 7 | 13 | .350 | 5.21 | 34 | 33 | 1 | 0 | 1 | 0-0 | 202.0 | 217 | 888 | 127 | 117 | 44 | 9 | 6 | 11 | 63 | 3 | 125 | 1 | 0 |
| Mulder, Mark, Oak.* | 17 | 8 | .680 | 4.43 | 33 | 33 | 5 | 1 | 0 | 0-0 | 225.2 | 223 | 952 | 119 | 111 | 25 | 7 | 6 | 12 | 83 | 1 | 140 | 10 | 0 |
| Mulholland, Terry, Min.* | 5 | 9 | .357 | 5.18 | 39 | 15 | 0 | 0 | 9 | 0-0 | 123.1 | 163 | 549 | 76 | 71 | 17 | 7 | 5 | 5 | 33 | 3 | 60 | 2 | 0 |
| Munoz, Arnie, Chi.* | 0 | 1 | .000 | 10.05 | 11 | 1 | 0 | 0 | 3 | 0-0 | 14.1 | 20 | 75 | 16 | 16 | 4 | 1 | 2 | 1 | 12 | 1 | 11 | 2 | 0 |
| Mussina, Mike, N.Y. | 12 | 9 | .571 | 4.59 | 27 | 27 | 1 | 0 | 0 | 0-0 | 164.2 | 178 | 697 | 91 | 84 | 22 | 5 | 4 | 2 | 40 | 1 | 132 | 5 | 0 |
| Myers, Mike, Sea.-Bos.* | 5 | 1 | .833 | 4.64 | 75 | 0 | 0 | 0 | 15 | 0-0 | 42.2 | 45 | 192 | 22 | 22 | 5 | 2 | 1 | 2 | 23 | 5 | 32 | 2 | 0 |
| Nageotte, Clint, Sea. | 1 | 6 | .143 | 7.36 | 12 | 5 | 0 | 0 | 4 | 0-0 | 36.2 | 48 | 185 | 31 | 30 | 3 | 4 | 2 | 4 | 27 | 1 | 24 | 3 | 0 |
| Nakamura, Mike, Tor. | 0 | 3 | .000 | 7.36 | 19 | 0 | 0 | 0 | 2 | 0-0 | 25.2 | 27 | 114 | 23 | 21 | 7 | 1 | 1 | 2 | 7 | 0 | 24 | 3 | 0 |
| Narron, Sam, Tex.* | 0 | 0 | .000 | 13.50 | 1 | 1 | 0 | 0 | 0 | 0-0 | 2.2 | 5 | 17 | 4 | 4 | 3 | 0 | 0 | 0 | 4 | 0 | 1 | 1 | 0 |
| Nathan, Joe, Min. | 1 | 2 | .333 | 1.62 | 73 | 0 | 0 | 0 | 63 | 44-47 | 72.1 | 48 | 284 | 14 | 13 | 3 | 2 | 0 | 2 | 23 | 3 | 89 | 5 | 0 |
| Nelson, Jeff, Tex. | 1 | 2 | .333 | 5.32 | 29 | 0 | 0 | 0 | 9 | 1-1 | 23.2 | 17 | 103 | 16 | 14 | 3 | 1 | 1 | 0 | 19 | 0 | 22 | 2 | 0 |
| Nelson, Joe, Bos. | 0 | 0 | .000 | 16.88 | 3 | 0 | 0 | 0 | 1 | 0-0 | 2.2 | 4 | 17 | 5 | 5 | 0 | 1 | 0 | 2 | 3 | 0 | 5 | 0 | 0 |
| Nitkowski, C.J., N.Y.* | 1 | 1 | .500 | 7.62 | 19 | 0 | 0 | 0 | 4 | 0-0 | 13.0 | 18 | 65 | 11 | 11 | 1 | 0 | 0 | 4 | 6 | 0 | 10 | 2 | 0 |
| Novoa, Roberto, Det. | 1 | 1 | .500 | 5.57 | 16 | 0 | 0 | 0 | 2 | 0-1 | 21.0 | 25 | 94 | 15 | 13 | 4 | 1 | 4 | 2 | 6 | 0 | 15 | 1 | 0 |
| Nunez, Franklin, TB. | 0 | 3 | .000 | 5.91 | 8 | 0 | 0 | 0 | 0 | 0-1 | 10.2 | 11 | 54 | 8 | 7 | 1 | 1 | 2 | 3 | 7 | 0 | 14 | 2 | 0 |
| Ortiz, Ramon, Ana. | 5 | 7 | .417 | 4.43 | 34 | 14 | 0 | 0 | 13 | 0-0 | 128.0 | 139 | 543 | 64 | 63 | 18 | 2 | 3 | 4 | 38 | 4 | 82 | 5 | 3 |
| Osborne, Donovan, N.Y.* | 2 | 0 | 1.000 | 7.13 | 9 | 2 | 0 | 0 | 2 | 0-0 | 17.2 | 25 | 79 | 16 | 14 | 3 | 0 | 0 | 2 | 5 | 0 | 10 | 0 | 0 |
| Padilla, Juan, N.Y. | 0 | 0 | .000 | 3.97 | 6 | 0 | 0 | 0 | 1 | 0-0 | 11.1 | 16 | 50 | 5 | 5 | 1 | 0 | 0 | 0 | 4 | 0 | 5 | 0 | 0 |
| Park, Chan Ho, Tex. | 4 | 7 | .364 | 5.46 | 16 | 16 | 0 | 0 | 0 | 0-0 | 95.2 | 105 | 428 | 63 | 58 | 22 | 4 | 4 | 13 | 33 | 0 | 63 | 1 | 1 |
| Parrish, John, Bal.* | 6 | 3 | .667 | 3.46 | 56 | 1 | 0 | 0 | 17 | 1-1 | 78.0 | 68 | 353 | 39 | 30 | 4 | 3 | 6 | 3 | 55 | 6 | 71 | 6 | 0 |
| Patterson, Danny, Det. | 0 | 4 | .000 | 4.75 | 37 | 0 | 0 | 0 | 16 | 2-4 | 41.2 | 44 | 179 | 24 | 22 | 7 | 2 | 0 | 5 | 16 | 2 | 24 | 3 | 0 |
| Percival, Troy, Ana. | 2 | 3 | .400 | 2.90 | 52 | 0 | 0 | 0 | 48 | 33-38 | 49.2 | 43 | 211 | 19 | 16 | 7 | 0 | 2 | 3 | 19 | 3 | 33 | 2 | 0 |
| Peterson, Adam, Tor. | 0 | 0 | .000 | 16.88 | 3 | 0 | 0 | 0 | 1 | 0-0 | 2.2 | 7 | 18 | 5 | 5 | 1 | 0 | 0 | 0 | 3 | 0 | 2 | 0 | 0 |
| Pineiro, Joel, Sea. | 6 | 11 | .353 | 4.67 | 21 | 21 | 1 | 0 | 0 | 0-0 | 140.2 | 144 | 596 | 77 | 73 | 21 | 1 | 5 | 4 | 43 | 1 | 111 | 4 | 0 |
| Politte, Cliff, Chi. | 0 | 3 | .000 | 4.38 | 54 | 0 | 0 | 0 | 9 | 1-1 | 51.1 | 52 | 225 | 26 | 25 | 6 | 0 | 2 | 2 | 22 | 5 | 48 | 2 | 0 |
| Ponson, Sidney, Bal. | 11 | 15 | .423 | 5.30 | 33 | 33 | 5 | 2 | 0 | 0-0 | 215.2 | 265 | 954 | 136 | 127 | 23 | 6 | 3 | 8 | 69 | 3 | 115 | 8 | 2 |
| Pote, Lou, Cle. | 0 | 0 | .000 | 9.00 | 2 | 0 | 0 | 0 | 1 | 0-0 | 3.0 | 3 | 13 | 3 | 3 | 0 | 0 | 0 | 0 | 1 | 0 | 5 | 0 | 0 |
| Powell, Jay, Tex. | 1 | 1 | .500 | 3.38 | 23 | 0 | 0 | 0 | 4 | 0-0 | 24.0 | 24 | 103 | 11 | 9 | 3 | 1 | 1 | 0 | 11 | 1 | 17 | 0 | 0 |
| Prinz, Bret, N.Y. | 1 | 0 | 1.000 | 5.08 | 26 | 0 | 0 | 0 | 10 | 0-0 | 28.1 | 28 | 124 | 17 | 16 | 5 | 0 | 1 | 1 | 14 | 0 | 22 | 2 | 0 |
| Proctor, Scott, N.Y. | 2 | 1 | .667 | 5.40 | 26 | 0 | 0 | 0 | 12 | 0-0 | 25.0 | 29 | 118 | 18 | 15 | 5 | 0 | 2 | 0 | 14 | 0 | 21 | 1 | 1 |
| Pulido, Carlos, Min.* | 0 | 0 | .000 | 8.74 | 6 | 0 | 0 | 0 | 3 | 0-0 | 11.1 | 16 | 55 | 13 | 11 | 2 | 0 | 2 | 1 | 4 | 1 | 9 | 0 | 0 |
| Putz, J.J., Sea. | 0 | 3 | .000 | 4.71 | 54 | 0 | 0 | 0 | 30 | 9-13 | 63.0 | 66 | 275 | 35 | 33 | 10 | 3 | 2 | 5 | 24 | 4 | 47 | 1 | 0 |
| Quantrill, Paul, N.Y. | 7 | 3 | .700 | 4.72 | 86 | 0 | 0 | 0 | 17 | 1-5 | 95.1 | 124 | 424 | 54 | 50 | 5 | 3 | 4 | 4 | 20 | 9 | 37 | 0 | 0 |
| Radke, Brad, Min. | 11 | 8 | .579 | 3.48 | 34 | 34 | 1 | 1 | 0 | 0-0 | 219.2 | 229 | 901 | 92 | 85 | 23 | 5 | 5 | 6 | 26 | 1 | 143 | 2 | 0 |
| Rakers, Aaron, Bal. | 0 | 0 | .000 | 4.15 | 3 | 0 | 0 | 0 | 1 | 0-0 | 4.1 | 5 | 19 | 2 | 2 | 0 | 0 | 0 | 0 | 1 | 0 | 3 | 0 | 0 |
| Ramirez, Erasmo, Tex.* | 5 | 3 | .625 | 4.29 | 34 | 0 | 0 | 0 | 6 | 0-2 | 35.2 | 34 | 148 | 19 | 17 | 5 | 2 | 1 | 3 | 7 | 1 | 21 | 1 | 0 |
| Rauch, Jon, Chi. | 1 | 1 | .500 | 6.23 | 2 | 2 | 0 | 0 | 0 | 0-0 | 8.2 | 16 | 43 | 6 | 6 | 0 | 1 | 1 | 0 | 4 | 0 | 4 | 1 | 0 |
| Redman, Mark, Oak.* | 11 | 12 | .478 | 4.71 | 32 | 32 | 2 | 0 | 0 | 0-0 | 191.0 | 218 | 832 | 110 | 100 | 28 | 5 | 7 | 6 | 68 | 6 | 102 | 6 | 1 |
| Regilio, Nick, Tex. | 0 | 4 | .000 | 6.05 | 6 | 4 | 0 | 0 | 1 | 0-0 | 19.1 | 20 | 91 | 16 | 13 | 3 | 1 | 1 | 2 | 15 | 1 | 12 | 1 | 0 |
| Reyes, Dennys, K.C.* | 4 | 8 | .333 | 4.75 | 40 | 12 | 0 | 0 | 5 | 0-1 | 108.0 | 114 | 483 | 64 | 57 | 12 | 7 | 5 | 4 | 50 | 3 | 91 | 6 | 2 |
| Rhodes, Arthur, Oak.* | 3 | 3 | .500 | 5.12 | 37 | 0 | 0 | 0 | 25 | 9-14 | 38.2 | 46 | 182 | 23 | 22 | 9 | 3 | 1 | 0 | 21 | 4 | 34 | 2 | 0 |
| Riley, Matt, Bal.* | 3 | 4 | .429 | 5.63 | 14 | 13 | 0 | 0 | 0 | 0-0 | 64.0 | 60 | 292 | 43 | 40 | 11 | 1 | 0 | 1 | 44 | 0 | 60 | 2 | 0 |
| Rincon, Juan, Min. | 11 | 6 | .647 | 2.63 | 77 | 0 | 0 | 0 | 18 | 2-6 | 82.0 | 52 | 327 | 27 | 24 | 5 | 3 | 3 | 2 | 32 | 1 | 106 | 2 | 0 |
| Rincon, Ricardo, Oak.* | 1 | 1 | .500 | 3.68 | 67 | 0 | 0 | 0 | 10 | 0-4 | 44.0 | 45 | 201 | 22 | 18 | 3 | 1 | 1 | 1 | 22 | 4 | 40 | 4 | 0 |
| Riske, David, Cle. | 7 | 3 | .700 | 3.72 | 72 | 0 | 0 | 0 | 27 | 5-12 | 77.1 | 69 | 336 | 32 | 32 | 11 | 3 | 2 | 2 | 41 | 4 | 78 | 3 | 0 |
| Ritchie, Todd, TB. | 0 | 2 | .000 | 9.00 | 4 | 2 | 0 | 0 | 2 | 0-0 | 8.0 | 12 | 42 | 9 | 8 | 4 | 0 | 0 | 1 | 6 | 0 | 4 | 0 | 0 |
| Rivera, Mariano, N.Y. | 4 | 2 | .667 | 1.94 | 74 | 0 | 0 | 0 | 69 | 53-57 | 78.2 | 65 | 316 | 17 | 17 | 3 | 2 | 0 | 5 | 20 | 3 | 66 | 0 | 0 |
| Roa, Joe, Min. | 2 | 3 | .400 | 4.50 | 48 | 0 | 0 | 0 | 11 | 0-1 | 70.0 | 84 | 318 | 38 | 35 | 9 | 4 | 2 | 5 | 24 | 0 | 47 | 1 | 0 |
| Robbins, Jake, Cle. | 0 | 0 | .000 | 5.40 | 2 | 0 | 0 | 0 | 0 | 0-0 | 1.2 | 3 | 8 | 1 | 1 | 1 | 0 | 0 | 0 | 0 | 0 | 0 | 0 | 0 |
| Robertson, Jeriome, Cle.* | 1 | 1 | .500 | 12.21 | 8 | 0 | 0 | 0 | 2 | 0-1 | 14.0 | 22 | 75 | 22 | 19 | 5 | 0 | 1 | 2 | 9 | 2 | 6 | 1 | 0 |
| Robertson, Nate, Det.* | 12 | 10 | .545 | 4.90 | 34 | 32 | 1 | 0 | 1 | 1-1 | 196.2 | 210 | 852 | 116 | 107 | 30 | 12 | 4 | 4 | 66 | 1 | 155 | 5 | 1 |
| Rodriguez, Eddy, Bal. | 1 | 0 | 1.000 | 4.78 | 29 | 0 | 0 | 0 | 10 | 0-0 | 43.1 | 36 | 193 | 23 | 23 | 5 | 1 | 1 | 5 | 30 | 5 | 37 | 2 | 1 |
| Rodriguez, Francisco, Ana. | 4 | 1 | .800 | 1.82 | 69 | 0 | 0 | 0 | 29 | 12-19 | 84.0 | 51 | 335 | 21 | 17 | 2 | 2 | 1 | 1 | 33 | 1 | 123 | 5 | 0 |
| Rodriguez, Ricardo, Tex. | 3 | 1 | .750 | 2.03 | 5 | 4 | 1 | 1 | 0 | 0-0 | 26.2 | 28 | 119 | 10 | 6 | 1 | 0 | 0 | 0 | 12 | 0 | 15 | 1 | 1 |
| Rogers, Kenny, Tex.* | 18 | 9 | .667 | 4.76 | 35 | 35 | 2 | 1 | 0 | 0-0 | 211.2 | 248 | 935 | 117 | 112 | 24 | 7 | 4 | 9 | 66 | 0 | 126 | 2 | 1 |
| Romero, J.C., Min.* | 7 | 4 | .636 | 3.51 | 74 | 0 | 0 | 0 | 12 | 1-8 | 74.1 | 61 | 319 | 32 | 29 | 4 | 3 | 1 | 5 | 38 | 6 | 69 | 5 | 0 |
| Ryan, B.J., Bal.* | 4 | 6 | .400 | 2.28 | 76 | 0 | 0 | 0 | 19 | 3-7 | 87.0 | 64 | 361 | 24 | 22 | 4 | 3 | 2 | 1 | 35 | 9 | 122 | 0 | 0 |
| Saarloos, Kirk, Oak. | 2 | 1 | .667 | 4.44 | 6 | 5 | 0 | 0 | 1 | 0-0 | 24.1 | 27 | 112 | 13 | 12 | 4 | 2 | 1 | 2 | 12 | 0 | 10 | 0 | 0 |
| Sabathia, C.C., Cle.* | 11 | 10 | .524 | 4.12 | 30 | 30 | 1 | 1 | 0 | 0-0 | 188.0 | 176 | 787 | 90 | 86 | 20 | 3 | 6 | 7 | 72 | 3 | 139 | 1 | 1 |
| Santana, Johan, Min.* | 20 | 6 | .769 | 2.61 | 34 | 34 | 1 | 1 | 0 | 0-0 | 228.0 | 156 | 881 | 70 | 66 | 24 | 3 | 3 | 9 | 54 | 0 | 265 | 7 | 0 |
| Schilling, Curt, Bos. | 21 | 6 | .778 | 3.26 | 32 | 32 | 3 | 0 | 0 | 0-0 | 226.2 | 206 | 910 | 84 | 82 | 23 | 3 | 6 | 5 | 35 | 0 | 203 | 3 | 0 |
| Schoeneweis, Scott, Chi.* | 6 | 9 | .400 | 5.59 | 20 | 19 | 0 | 0 | 0 | 0-0 | 112.2 | 129 | 500 | 74 | 70 | 17 | 3 | 2 | 3 | 49 | 0 | 69 | 3 | 0 |
| Seanez, Rudy, K.C. | 0 | 1 | .000 | 3.91 | 16 | 0 | 0 | 0 | 7 | 0-1 | 23.0 | 21 | 100 | 10 | 10 | 0 | 0 | 3 | 0 | 11 | 2 | 21 | 3 | 0 |
| Seay, Bobby, TB.* | 0 | 0 | .000 | 2.38 | 21 | 0 | 0 | 0 | 6 | 0-0 | 22.2 | 21 | 95 | 6 | 6 | 2 | 0 | 0 | 2 | 5 | 1 | 17 | 1 | 0 |
| Seibel, Phil, Bos.* | 0 | 0 | .000 | 0.00 | 2 | 0 | 0 | 0 | 0 | 0-0 | 3.2 | 0 | 18 | 0 | 0 | 0 | 0 | 0 | 1 | 5 | 0 | 1 | 0 | 0 |
| Sele, Aaron, Ana. | 9 | 4 | .692 | 5.05 | 28 | 24 | 0 | 0 | 1 | 0-0 | 132.0 | 163 | 593 | 84 | 74 | 16 | 3 | 8 | 5 | 51 | 2 | 51 | 4 | 2 |
| Serrano, Jimmy, K.C. | 1 | 2 | .333 | 4.68 | 10 | 5 | 0 | 0 | 2 | 0-0 | 32.2 | 35 | 141 | 17 | 17 | 5 | 0 | 3 | 1 | 12 | 0 | 25 | 2 | 0 |
| Sherrill, George, Sea.* | 2 | 1 | .667 | 3.80 | 21 | 0 | 0 | 0 | 4 | 0-0 | 23.2 | 24 | 104 | 12 | 10 | 3 | 0 | 1 | 1 | 9 | 1 | 16 | 4 | 1 |
| Shields, Scot, Ana. | 8 | 2 | .800 | 3.33 | 60 | 0 | 0 | 0 | 12 | 4-7 | 105.1 | 97 | 454 | 42 | 39 | 6 | 2 | 2 | 3 | 40 | 5 | 109 | 4 | 0 |
| Shouse, Brian, Tex.* | 2 | 0 | 1.000 | 2.23 | 53 | 0 | 0 | 0 | 14 | 0-0 | 44.1 | 36 | 184 | 12 | 11 | 3 | 2 | 2 | 1 | 18 | 3 | 34 | 0 | 0 |
| Silva, Carlos, Min. | 14 | 8 | .636 | 4.21 | 33 | 33 | 1 | 1 | 0 | 0-0 | 203.0 | 255 | 869 | 100 | 95 | 23 | 6 | 0 | 5 | 35 | 2 | 76 | 5 | 1 |
| Snare, Ryan, Tex.* | 0 | 0 | .000 | 10.80 | 1 | 0 | 0 | 0 | 0 | 0-0 | 3.1 | 5 | 17 | 5 | 4 | 3 | 0 | 0 | 0 | 2 | 0 | 0 | 0 | 0 |
| Soriano, Rafael, Sea. | 0 | 3 | .000 | 13.50 | 6 | 0 | 0 | 0 | 0 | 0-1 | 3.1 | 9 | 23 | 6 | 5 | 0 | 0 | 0 | 0 | 3 | 0 | 3 | 0 | 0 |
| Sosa, Jorge, TB. | 4 | 7 | .364 | 5.53 | 43 | 8 | 0 | 0 | 6 | 1-1 | 99.1 | 100 | 447 | 67 | 61 | 17 | 2 | 4 | 1 | 54 | 3 | 94 | 2 | 0 |
| Speier, Justin, Tor. | 3 | 8 | .273 | 3.91 | 62 | 0 | 0 | 0 | 32 | 7-11 | 69.0 | 61 | 294 | 32 | 30 | 8 | 6 | 3 | 5 | 25 | 6 | 52 | 4 | 0 |
| Standridge, Jason, TB. | 0 | 0 | .000 | 9.00 | 3 | 1 | 0 | 0 | 1 | 0-0 | 10.0 | 14 | 48 | 10 | 10 | 5 | 0 | 1 | 0 | 4 | 0 | 7 | 1 | 0 |

| Pitcher, Team | W | L | Pct. | ERA | G | GS | CG | ShO | GF | Sv.-Op. | IP | H | TBF | R | ER | HR | SH | SF | HB | BB | IBB | SO | WP | Bk. |
|---|---|---|---|---|---|---|---|---|---|---|---|---|---|---|---|---|---|---|---|---|---|---|---|---|
| Stanford, Jason, Cle.* | 0 | 1 | .000 | 0.82 | 2 | 2 | 0 | 0 | 0 | 0-0 | 11.0 | 12 | 50 | 1 | 1 | 0 | 1 | 0 | 1 | 5 | 0 | 5 | 1 | 0 |
| Stewart, Josh, Chi.* | 0 | 1 | .000 | 15.26 | 3 | 2 | 0 | 0 | 1 | 0-0 | 7.2 | 16 | 41 | 13 | 13 | 3 | 0 | 2 | 0 | 3 | 0 | 5 | 0 | 0 |
| Stewart, Scott, Cle.* | 0 | 2 | .000 | 7.24 | 23 | 0 | 0 | 0 | 5 | 0-2 | 13.2 | 23 | 70 | 14 | 11 | 2 | 0 | 1 | 0 | 6 | 2 | 18 | 0 | 0 |
| Sturtze, Tanyon, N.Y. | 6 | 2 | .750 | 5.47 | 28 | 3 | 0 | 0 | 7 | 1-1 | 77.1 | 75 | 337 | 49 | 47 | 9 | 2 | 1 | 6 | 33 | 2 | 56 | 2 | 1 |
| Sullivan, Scott, K.C. | 3 | 4 | .429 | 4.77 | 49 | 0 | 0 | 0 | 17 | 0-1 | 60.1 | 73 | 273 | 34 | 32 | 8 | 1 | 4 | 7 | 24 | 10 | 45 | 4 | 0 |
| Tadano, Kazuhito, Cle. | 1 | 1 | .500 | 4.65 | 14 | 4 | 0 | 0 | 1 | 0-0 | 50.1 | 55 | 225 | 30 | 26 | 6 | 2 | 0 | 3 | 18 | 0 | 39 | 2 | 0 |
| Takatsu, Shingo, Chi. | 6 | 4 | .600 | 2.31 | 59 | 0 | 0 | 0 | 45 | 19-20 | 62.1 | 40 | 245 | 17 | 16 | 6 | 2 | 0 | 2 | 21 | 3 | 50 | 1 | 0 |
| Taylor, Aaron, Sea. | 0 | 0 | .000 | 9.82 | 5 | 0 | 0 | 0 | 4 | 0-0 | 3.2 | 5 | 19 | 4 | 4 | 2 | 0 | 0 | 0 | 3 | 0 | 4 | 0 | 0 |
| Tejera, Michael, Tex.* | 0 | 0 | .000 | 10.13 | 6 | 0 | 0 | 0 | 1 | 0-0 | 5.1 | 9 | 29 | 6 | 6 | 1 | 0 | 0 | 1 | 3 | 0 | 7 | 0 | 0 |
| Thomas, Brad, Min.* | 0 | 0 | .000 | 16.88 | 3 | 0 | 0 | 0 | 0 | 0-0 | 2.2 | 7 | 16 | 5 | 5 | 0 | 1 | 0 | 0 | 1 | 0 | 0 | 1 | 0 |
| Thornton, Matt, Sea.* | 1 | 2 | .333 | 4.13 | 19 | 1 | 0 | 0 | 8 | 0-0 | 32.2 | 30 | 148 | 15 | 15 | 2 | 2 | 1 | 0 | 25 | 1 | 30 | 2 | 0 |
| Timlin, Mike, Bos. | 5 | 4 | .556 | 4.13 | 76 | 0 | 0 | 0 | 12 | 1-4 | 76.1 | 75 | 320 | 35 | 35 | 8 | 3 | 1 | 5 | 19 | 3 | 56 | 1 | 0 |
| Towers, Josh, Tor. | 9 | 9 | .500 | 5.11 | 21 | 21 | 0 | 0 | 0 | 0-0 | 116.1 | 148 | 518 | 70 | 66 | 16 | 2 | 4 | 9 | 26 | 4 | 51 | 0 | 1 |
| Turnbow, Derrick, Ana. | 0 | 0 | .000 | 0.00 | 4 | 0 | 0 | 0 | 4 | 0-0 | 6.1 | 2 | 26 | 0 | 0 | 0 | 0 | 0 | 0 | 7 | 0 | 3 | 0 | 0 |
| Urbina, Ugueth, Det. | 4 | 6 | .400 | 4.50 | 54 | 0 | 0 | 0 | 46 | 21-24 | 54.0 | 38 | 234 | 28 | 27 | 7 | 1 | 2 | 3 | 32 | 3 | 56 | 2 | 0 |
| Urdaneta, Lino, Det. | 0 | 0 | .000 | 0.00 | 1 | 0 | 0 | 0 | 0 | 0-0 | 0.0 | 5 | 6 | 6 | 6 | 0 | 0 | 0 | 0 | 1 | 0 | 0 | 0 | 0 |
| Vasquez, Jorge, K.C. | 0 | 0 | .000 | 8.10 | 2 | 0 | 0 | 0 | 1 | 0-0 | 3.1 | 4 | 17 | 4 | 3 | 1 | 0 | 0 | 1 | 1 | 0 | 4 | 1 | 0 |
| Vazquez, Javier, N.Y. | 14 | 10 | .583 | 4.91 | 32 | 32 | 0 | 0 | 0 | 0-0 | 198.0 | 195 | 849 | 114 | 108 | 33 | 4 | 8 | 11 | 60 | 3 | 150 | 12 | 2 |
| Villacis, Eduardo, K.C. | 0 | 1 | .000 | 13.50 | 1 | 1 | 0 | 0 | 0 | 0-0 | 3.1 | 6 | 20 | 5 | 5 | 1 | 0 | 0 | 0 | 4 | 0 | 0 | 1 | 0 |
| Villone, Ron, Sea.* | 8 | 6 | .571 | 4.08 | 56 | 10 | 0 | 0 | 14 | 0-1 | 117.0 | 102 | 523 | 64 | 53 | 12 | 4 | 4 | 12 | 64 | 3 | 86 | 6 | 0 |
| Waechter, Doug, TB. | 5 | 7 | .417 | 6.01 | 14 | 14 | 0 | 0 | 0 | 0-0 | 70.1 | 68 | 309 | 54 | 47 | 20 | 0 | 2 | 4 | 33 | 1 | 36 | 1 | 1 |
| Wakefield, Tim, Bos. | 12 | 10 | .545 | 4.87 | 32 | 30 | 0 | 0 | 0 | 0-0 | 188.1 | 197 | 831 | 121 | 102 | 29 | 2 | 4 | 16 | 63 | 3 | 116 | 9 | 0 |
| Walker, Jamie, Det.* | 3 | 4 | .429 | 3.20 | 70 | 0 | 0 | 0 | 18 | 1-7 | 64.2 | 69 | 277 | 28 | 23 | 8 | 1 | 1 | 1 | 12 | 3 | 53 | 4 | 0 |
| Wasdin, John, Tex. | 2 | 4 | .333 | 6.78 | 15 | 10 | 0 | 0 | 0 | 0-0 | 65.0 | 83 | 301 | 52 | 49 | 18 | 1 | 2 | 3 | 23 | 2 | 36 | 0 | 0 |
| Washburn, Jarrod, Ana.* | 11 | 8 | .579 | 4.64 | 25 | 25 | 1 | 1 | 0 | 0-0 | 149.1 | 159 | 640 | 81 | 77 | 20 | 2 | 4 | 4 | 40 | 1 | 86 | 5 | 0 |
| Webb, John, TB. | 0 | 0 | .000 | 7.00 | 4 | 0 | 0 | 0 | 1 | 0-0 | 9.0 | 12 | 45 | 7 | 7 | 2 | 0 | 0 | 1 | 7 | 0 | 9 | 1 | 0 |
| Weber, Ben, Ana. | 0 | 2 | .000 | 8.06 | 18 | 0 | 0 | 0 | 5 | 0-1 | 22.1 | 37 | 117 | 24 | 20 | 4 | 0 | 0 | 0 | 15 | 0 | 11 | 0 | 0 |
| Westbrook, Jake, Cle. | 14 | 9 | .609 | 3.38 | 33 | 30 | 5 | 1 | 2 | 0-0 | 215.2 | 208 | 895 | 95 | 81 | 19 | 6 | 6 | 5 | 61 | 3 | 116 | 4 | 1 |
| White, Gabe, N.Y.* | 0 | 1 | .000 | 8.27 | 24 | 0 | 0 | 0 | 6 | 0-2 | 20.2 | 33 | 104 | 19 | 19 | 2 | 1 | 1 | 2 | 7 | 4 | 8 | 0 | 0 |
| White, Rick, Cle. | 5 | 5 | .500 | 5.29 | 59 | 0 | 0 | 0 | 20 | 1-3 | 78.1 | 88 | 340 | 52 | 46 | 15 | 6 | 3 | 2 | 29 | 7 | 44 | 2 | 0 |
| Wickman, Bob, Cle. | 0 | 2 | .000 | 4.25 | 30 | 0 | 0 | 0 | 21 | 13-14 | 29.2 | 33 | 129 | 14 | 14 | 4 | 0 | 0 | 2 | 10 | 0 | 26 | 0 | 0 |
| Williams, Randy, Sea.* | 0 | 0 | .000 | 5.79 | 6 | 0 | 0 | 0 | 1 | 0-0 | 4.2 | 3 | 22 | 3 | 3 | 0 | 0 | 0 | 0 | 6 | 0 | 4 | 0 | 0 |
| Williams, Todd, Bal. | 2 | 0 | 1.000 | 2.87 | 29 | 0 | 0 | 0 | 7 | 0-0 | 31.1 | 26 | 126 | 10 | 10 | 2 | 0 | 0 | 5 | 9 | 0 | 13 | 1 | 0 |
| Williamson, Scott, Bos. | 0 | 1 | .000 | 1.26 | 28 | 0 | 0 | 0 | 5 | 1-2 | 28.2 | 11 | 120 | 6 | 4 | 0 | 0 | 3 | 3 | 18 | 1 | 28 | 4 | 0 |
| Wood, Mike, K.C. | 3 | 8 | .273 | 5.94 | 17 | 17 | 0 | 0 | 0 | 0-0 | 100.0 | 112 | 432 | 67 | 66 | 16 | 5 | 2 | 6 | 28 | 3 | 54 | 6 | 1 |
| Wright, Dan, Chi. | 0 | 4 | .000 | 8.15 | 4 | 4 | 0 | 0 | 0 | 0-0 | 17.2 | 24 | 88 | 17 | 16 | 5 | 0 | 0 | 2 | 11 | 1 | 6 | 0 | 1 |
| Wunsch, Kelly, Chi.* | 0 | 0 | .000 | 0.00 | 3 | 0 | 0 | 0 | 1 | 0-0 | 2.0 | 2 | 8 | 0 | 0 | 0 | 0 | 0 | 0 | 1 | 0 | 1 | 0 | 0 |
| Yan, Esteban, Det. | 3 | 6 | .333 | 3.83 | 69 | 0 | 0 | 0 | 27 | 7-17 | 87.0 | 92 | 379 | 43 | 37 | 8 | 4 | 3 | 4 | 32 | 5 | 69 | 7 | 0 |
| Young, Chris, Tex. | 3 | 2 | .600 | 4.71 | 7 | 7 | 0 | 0 | 0 | 0-0 | 36.1 | 36 | 158 | 21 | 19 | 7 | 1 | 0 | 2 | 10 | 0 | 27 | 1 | 0 |
| Zambrano, Victor, TB. | 9 | 7 | .563 | 4.43 | 23 | 22 | 0 | 0 | 0 | 0-0 | 128.0 | 107 | 588 | 68 | 63 | 13 | 0 | 10 | 16 | 96 | 2 | 109 | 5 | 0 |
| Zito, Barry, Oak.* | 11 | 11 | .500 | 4.48 | 34 | 34 | 0 | 0 | 0 | 0-0 | 213.0 | 216 | 926 | 116 | 106 | 28 | 7 | 9 | 9 | 81 | 2 | 163 | 4 | 1 |

## PITCHERS WITH TWO OR MORE TEAMS

| Pitcher, Team | W | L | Pct. | ERA | G | GS | CG | ShO | GF | Sv.-Op. | IP | H | TBF | R | ER | HR | SH | SF | HB | BB | IBB | SO | WP | Bk. |
|---|---|---|---|---|---|---|---|---|---|---|---|---|---|---|---|---|---|---|---|---|---|---|---|---|
| Adams, Terry, Tor. | 4 | 4 | .500 | 3.98 | 42 | 0 | 0 | 0 | 20 | 3-6 | 43.0 | 49 | 197 | 20 | 19 | 4 | 3 | 2 | 1 | 22 | 2 | 35 | 6 | 0 |
| Adams, Terry, Bos. | 2 | 0 | 1.000 | 6.00 | 19 | 0 | 0 | 0 | 1 | 0-0 | 27.0 | 35 | 119 | 19 | 18 | 6 | 0 | 3 | 1 | 6 | 1 | 21 | 2 | 0 |
| Bautista, Denny, Bal. | 0 | 0 | .000 | 36.00 | 2 | 0 | 0 | 0 | 0 | 0-0 | 2.0 | 6 | 15 | 8 | 8 | 1 | 0 | 1 | 1 | 2 | 0 | 1 | 1 | 0 |
| Bautista, Denny, K.C. | 0 | 4 | .000 | 6.51 | 5 | 5 | 0 | 0 | 0 | 0-0 | 27.2 | 38 | 127 | 20 | 20 | 2 | 0 | 0 | 2 | 11 | 1 | 18 | 2 | 2 |
| Contreras, Jose, N.Y. | 8 | 5 | .615 | 5.64 | 18 | 18 | 0 | 0 | 0 | 0-0 | 95.2 | 93 | 425 | 66 | 60 | 22 | 1 | 4 | 6 | 42 | 1 | 82 | 10 | 0 |
| Contreras, Jose, Chi. | 5 | 4 | .556 | 5.30 | 13 | 13 | 0 | 0 | 0 | 0-0 | 74.2 | 73 | 333 | 48 | 44 | 9 | 2 | 2 | 2 | 42 | 0 | 68 | 7 | 0 |
| Garcia, Freddy, Sea. | 4 | 7 | .364 | 3.20 | 15 | 15 | 1 | 0 | 0 | 0-0 | 107.0 | 96 | 446 | 39 | 38 | 8 | 4 | 1 | 2 | 32 | 1 | 82 | 5 | 0 |
| Garcia, Freddy, Chi. | 9 | 4 | .692 | 4.46 | 16 | 16 | 0 | 0 | 0 | 0-0 | 103.0 | 96 | 432 | 53 | 51 | 14 | 4 | 2 | 5 | 32 | 2 | 102 | 3 | 0 |
| Grimsley, Jason, K.C. | 3 | 3 | .500 | 3.38 | 32 | 0 | 0 | 0 | 4 | 0-3 | 26.2 | 24 | 118 | 11 | 10 | 1 | 1 | 0 | 1 | 15 | 3 | 18 | 4 | 0 |
| Grimsley, Jason, Bal. | 2 | 4 | .333 | 4.21 | 41 | 0 | 0 | 0 | 3 | 0-6 | 36.1 | 37 | 167 | 25 | 17 | 3 | 2 | 1 | 2 | 20 | 3 | 21 | 2 | 0 |
| Leskanic, Curtis, K.C. | 0 | 3 | .000 | 8.04 | 19 | 0 | 0 | 0 | 7 | 2-5 | 15.2 | 23 | 85 | 16 | 14 | 5 | 0 | 0 | 0 | 14 | 0 | 15 | 2 | 0 |
| Leskanic, Curtis, Bos. | 3 | 2 | .600 | 3.58 | 32 | 0 | 0 | 0 | 16 | 2-3 | 27.2 | 24 | 119 | 11 | 11 | 3 | 3 | 2 | 1 | 16 | 3 | 22 | 0 | 0 |
| Loaiza, Esteban, Chi. | 9 | 5 | .643 | 4.86 | 21 | 21 | 2 | 1 | 0 | 0-0 | 140.2 | 156 | 604 | 81 | 76 | 23 | 1 | 5 | 1 | 45 | 3 | 83 | 2 | 0 |
| Loaiza, Esteban, N.Y. | 1 | 2 | .333 | 8.50 | 10 | 6 | 0 | 0 | 1 | 0-0 | 42.1 | 61 | 214 | 43 | 40 | 9 | 0 | 5 | 2 | 26 | 2 | 34 | 2 | 0 |
| Myers, Mike, Sea.* | 4 | 1 | .800 | 4.88 | 50 | 0 | 0 | 0 | 10 | 0-0 | 27.2 | 29 | 126 | 15 | 15 | 3 | 2 | 1 | 2 | 17 | 4 | 23 | 1 | 0 |
| Myers, Mike, Bos.* | 1 | 0 | 1.000 | 4.20 | 25 | 0 | 0 | 0 | 5 | 0-0 | 15.0 | 16 | 66 | 7 | 7 | 2 | 0 | 0 | 0 | 6 | 1 | 9 | 1 | 0 |

**NOTE**—The following pitchers combined to pitch shutout games: Anaheim (9)—Sele, Gregg, Rodriguez and Percival; Sele, Rodriguez, Percival and Shields; Washburn and Turnbow; Colon, Rodriguez and Percival; Lackey and Percival; Escobar, Rodriguez and Percival; Ortiz and Percival; Colon, Gregg and Dunn; Colon, Donnelly and Ortiz; Baltimore (6)—DuBose, Ryan and Groom; Cabrera, Lopez and Julio; Ponson, Ryan, Grimsley and Julio; Riley, Groom, Grimsley and Ryan; Bauer, Groom, Grimsley and Ryan; Cabrera, Williams and Parrish; Boston (11)—P. Martinez and Williamson; Schilling, Embree and DiNardo; Kim, Wakefield, Timlin and Embree; Arroyo and Foulke; P. Martinez and Foulke; Lowe, Williamson and DiNardo; Wakefield and Anderson; Arroyo and Leskanic; Wakefield, Timlin and Embree; P. Martinez, Timlin, Embree and Foulke; Arroyo, Timlin and Embree; Chicago (6)—Buehrle and Adkins; Buehrle and Adkins; Loaiza and Takatsu; Buehrle, Adkins and Koch; Garcia, Politte and Takatsu; Contreras and Takatsu; Cleveland (5)—Sabathia and Miller; C. Lee, Betancourt, Miller and Jimenez; Sabathia, Riske and Miller; Durbin, Howry and Wickman; Westbrook and Guthrie; Detroit (5)—Johnson, Levine, Walker and Yan; Robertson, Levine and Urbina; Johnson, Patterson and Urbina; Knotts, Colyer and Urbina; Bonderman and Yan; Kansas City (1)—Greinke, Cerda, Carrasco and Affeldt; Minnesota (5)—Radke and Nathan; Santana, Mulholland, Romero and Nathan; Radke and Nathan; Santana, Romero and Nathan; Santana, Rincon and Durbin; New York (5)—Mussina and Quantrill; Hernandez, Gordon and Rivera; Hernandez and Proctor; Mussina and Gordon; Vazquez, Gordon and Rivera; Oakland (5)—Hudson, Rincon, Mecir and Rhodes; Harden, Dotel, Rincon and Lehr; Zito and Hammond; Harden and Dotel; Zito, Hammond, Bradford and Dotel; Seattle (5)—Moyer and Villone; Nageotte and Mateo; Franklin and Guardado; Baek and Atchison; Moyer, Villone, Hasegawa and Guardado; Tampa Bay (5)—Brazelton and Baez; Bell, Colome, Miller and Baez; Kazmir, Harper and Carter; Halama and Baez; Abbott, Miller, Gaudin and Baez; Texas (7)—Park and Almanzar; Benoit, Powell and Nelson; Rodriguez, Shouse, Francisco and Mahay; Bacsik, Almanzar and Benoit; Benoit, Ramirez, Nelson, Mahay, Brocail, Shouse and Cordero; Young, Almanzar, Shouse and Cordero; Park, Shouse, Brocail and Cordero; Toronto (7)—Batista, Chulk and Frasor; Lilly, Chulk and Frasor; Batista, Adams and Ligtenberg; Halladay, Chulk and Frasor; Towers, Chulk and Frasor; Miller and Speier; Lilly and Speier.

# FIELDING

## TEAM

| Team | G | PO | A | E | TC | DP | TP | PB | Pct. |
|---|---|---|---|---|---|---|---|---|---|
| Oakland | 162 | 4414 | 1809 | 91 | 6314 | 172 | 0 | 14 | .986 |
| Anaheim | 162 | 4363 | 1511 | 90 | 5964 | 126 | 0 | 11 | .985 |
| Toronto | 161 | 4263 | 1631 | 91 | 5985 | 150 | 0 | 11 | .985 |
| Minnesota | 162 | 4428 | 1658 | 101 | 6187 | 158 | 0 | 6 | .984 |
| Chicago | 162 | 4297 | 1667 | 100 | 6064 | 167 | 1 | 14 | .984 |
| New York | 162 | 4331 | 1571 | 99 | 6001 | 148 | 0 | 13 | .984 |
| Cleveland | 162 | 4400 | 1676 | 106 | 6182 | 152 | 0 | 15 | .983 |
| Seattle | 162 | 4378 | 1473 | 103 | 5954 | 140 | 0 | 11 | .983 |
| Baltimore | 162 | 4366 | 1683 | 110 | 6159 | 161 | 0 | 15 | .982 |
| Boston | 162 | 4354 | 1650 | 118 | 6122 | 129 | 0 | 21 | .981 |
| Texas | 162 | 4319 | 1604 | 117 | 6040 | 152 | 0 | 16 | .981 |
| Tampa Bay | 161 | 4251 | 1530 | 119 | 5900 | 139 | 0 | 8 | .980 |
| Kansas City | 162 | 4261 | 1635 | 131 | 6027 | 169 | 0 | 17 | .978 |
| Detroit | 162 | 4319 | 1712 | 144 | 6175 | 160 | 0 | 10 | .977 |
| **Totals** | 1133 | 60744 | 22810 | 1520 | 85074 | 2123 | 1 | 182 | .982 |

## INDIVIDUAL

### FIRST BASEMEN

NOTE: All caps denotes fielding-percentage leader based on 81 games for catchers, 108 for all other non-pitchers and 162 innings for pitchers. *Throws Lefthanded.

| Player, Team | G | GS | PO | A | E | TC | DP | Pct. |
|---|---|---|---|---|---|---|---|---|
| Barajas, Rod, Tex. | 2 | 0 | 3 | 1 | 0 | 4 | 0 | 1.000 |
| Berg, Dave, Tor. | 7 | 3 | 44 | 3 | 2 | 49 | 8 | .959 |
| Blake, Casey, Cle. | 8 | 0 | 12 | 0 | 0 | 12 | 2 | 1.000 |
| Bloomquist, Willie, Sea. | 19 | 11 | 70 | 8 | 2 | 80 | 11 | .975 |
| Blum, Geoff, TB. | 2 | 1 | 13 | 0 | 0 | 13 | 2 | 1.000 |
| Broussard, Ben, Cle.* | 133 | 107 | 991 | 77 | 6 | 1074 | 108 | .994 |
| Burke, Jamie, Chi. | 2 | 0 | 4 | 2 | 0 | 6 | 1 | 1.000 |
| Cabrera, Jolbert, Sea. | 23 | 17 | 151 | 7 | 0 | 158 | 18 | 1.000 |
| Cairo, Miguel, N.Y. | 1 | 0 | 2 | 0 | 0 | 2 | 0 | 1.000 |
| Clark, Howie, Tor. | 11 | 11 | 106 | 6 | 0 | 112 | 8 | 1.000 |
| Clark, Tony, N.Y. | 99 | 64 | 603 | 49 | 4 | 656 | 64 | .994 |
| Crozier, Eric, Tor.* | 5 | 4 | 33 | 2 | 1 | 36 | 2 | .972 |
| Cuddyer, Michael, Min. | 10 | 2 | 34 | 2 | 0 | 36 | 3 | 1.000 |
| Daubach, Brian, Bos. | 14 | 13 | 100 | 10 | 2 | 112 | 9 | .982 |
| Delgado, Carlos, Tor. | 120 | 120 | 1041 | 88 | 5 | 1134 | 98 | .996 |
| Dominique, Andy, Bos. | 5 | 1 | 25 | 1 | 1 | 27 | 2 | .963 |
| Durazo, Erubiel, Oak.* | 4 | 3 | 14 | 1 | 2 | 17 | 2 | .882 |
| Erstad, Darin, Ana.* | 124 | 124 | 986 | 66 | 4 | 1056 | 83 | .996 |
| Fick, Robert, TB. | 10 | 9 | 79 | 2 | 2 | 83 | 8 | .976 |
| Fullmer, Brad, Tex. | 4 | 3 | 15 | 0 | 0 | 15 | 5 | 1.000 |
| Galarraga, Andres, Ana. | 1 | 1 | 9 | 1 | 0 | 10 | 2 | 1.000 |
| Garcia, Karim, Bal.* | 1 | 1 | 10 | 1 | 0 | 11 | 0 | 1.000 |
| Giambi, Jason, N.Y. | 47 | 47 | 372 | 14 | 4 | 390 | 30 | .990 |
| Gibbons, Jay, Bal.* | 14 | 12 | 111 | 13 | 1 | 125 | 11 | .992 |
| Gload, Ross, Chi.* | 42 | 21 | 219 | 12 | 0 | 231 | 15 | 1.000 |
| Gomez, Chris, Tor. | 19 | 12 | 106 | 12 | 2 | 120 | 9 | .983 |
| Gonzalez, Adrian, Tex.* | 11 | 10 | 94 | 6 | 1 | 101 | 13 | .990 |
| Guerrero, Wilton, K.C. | 2 | 0 | 3 | 0 | 0 | 3 | 1 | 1.000 |
| Hafner, Travis, Cle. | 11 | 10 | 81 | 9 | 0 | 90 | 4 | 1.000 |
| Halter, Shane, Ana. | 4 | 1 | 10 | 1 | 0 | 11 | 2 | 1.000 |
| Hansen, Dave, Sea. | 7 | 3 | 25 | 4 | 0 | 29 | 1 | 1.000 |
| Harvey, Ken, K.C. | 73 | 73 | 610 | 52 | 4 | 666 | 73 | .994 |
| Hatteberg, Scott, Oak. | 148 | 143 | 1281 | 86 | 10 | 1377 | 135 | .993 |
| Huff, Aubrey, TB. | 38 | 30 | 262 | 27 | 1 | 290 | 24 | .997 |
| Ibanez, Raul, Sea. | 10 | 9 | 57 | 2 | 1 | 60 | 2 | .983 |
| Jacobsen, Bucky, Sea. | 21 | 21 | 169 | 12 | 3 | 184 | 12 | .984 |
| Karros, Eric, Oak. | 22 | 14 | 165 | 17 | 2 | 184 | 15 | .989 |
| Konerko, Paul, Chi. | 139 | 137 | 1150 | 78 | 6 | 1234 | 136 | .995 |
| Kotchman, Casey, Ana.* | 34 | 27 | 231 | 15 | 3 | 249 | 17 | .988 |
| LeCroy, Matthew, Min. | 23 | 20 | 172 | 3 | 1 | 176 | 17 | .994 |
| Lee, Travis, N.Y.* | 6 | 4 | 44 | 4 | 0 | 48 | 2 | 1.000 |
| Leon, Jose, Bal. | 16 | 12 | 83 | 10 | 0 | 93 | 9 | 1.000 |
| Lopez, Luis, Bal. | 6 | 2 | 22 | 0 | 1 | 23 | 1 | .957 |
| Lopez, Mendy, K.C. | 2 | 0 | 0 | 0 | 0 | 0 | 0 | .000 |
| Martinez, Tino, TB. | 114 | 110 | 876 | 67 | 3 | 946 | 85 | .997 |
| McCarty, Dave, Bos.* | 67 | 25 | 287 | 30 | 3 | 320 | 23 | .991 |
| McGriff, Fred, TB.* | 6 | 6 | 53 | 3 | 0 | 56 | 5 | 1.000 |
| McMillon, Billy, Oak.* | 3 | 0 | 4 | 1 | 0 | 5 | 1 | 1.000 |
| Melhuse, Adam, Oak. | 1 | 0 | 2 | 1 | 0 | 3 | 0 | 1.000 |
| Merloni, Lou, Cle. | 42 | 38 | 282 | 14 | 1 | 297 | 18 | .997 |
| Mientkiewicz, Doug, Min.-Bos. | 124 | 99 | 924 | 62 | 5 | 991 | 75 | .995 |
| Millar, Kevin, Bos. | 69 | 66 | 466 | 58 | 6 | 530 | 45 | .989 |
| Molina, Jose, Ana. | 2 | 0 | 5 | 1 | 0 | 6 | 2 | 1.000 |
| Morneau, Justin, Min. | 61 | 61 | 523 | 41 | 3 | 567 | 54 | .995 |
| Newhan, David, Bal. | 2 | 1 | 10 | 1 | 0 | 11 | 2 | 1.000 |
| Norton, Greg, Det. | 7 | 5 | 36 | 2 | 0 | 38 | 6 | 1.000 |
| Offerman, Jose, Min. | 7 | 5 | 52 | 6 | 1 | 59 | 11 | .983 |
| OLERUD, John, Sea.-N.Y.* | 124 | 118 | 915 | 77 | 2 | 994 | 92 | .998 |
| Ortiz, David, Bos.* | 34 | 31 | 253 | 21 | 4 | 278 | 23 | .986 |
| Palmeiro, Rafael, Bal.* | 130 | 128 | 1090 | 95 | 8 | 1193 | 114 | .993 |
| Pena, Carlos, Det.* | 135 | 131 | 1142 | 77 | 6 | 1225 | 128 | .995 |
| Perez, Eduardo, TB. | 5 | 5 | 43 | 2 | 0 | 45 | 6 | 1.000 |
| Perry, Herbert, Tex. | 15 | 11 | 104 | 3 | 0 | 107 | 12 | 1.000 |
| Phelps, Josh, Tor.-Cle. | 20 | 18 | 144 | 4 | 3 | 151 | 8 | .980 |
| Pickering, Calvin, K.C.* | 8 | 7 | 60 | 3 | 0 | 63 | 6 | 1.000 |
| Quinlan, Robb, Ana. | 13 | 9 | 96 | 7 | 0 | 103 | 7 | 1.000 |
| Randa, Joe, K.C. | 3 | 2 | 20 | 2 | 0 | 22 | 4 | 1.000 |
| Riggs, Adam, Ana. | 1 | 0 | 1 | 1 | 0 | 2 | 0 | 1.000 |
| Rolls, Damian, TB. | 1 | 0 | 0 | 0 | 0 | 0 | 0 | .000 |
| Segui, David, Bal.* | 2 | 2 | 17 | 0 | 0 | 17 | 1 | 1.000 |
| Shelton, Chris, Det. | 8 | 2 | 22 | 4 | 0 | 26 | 3 | 1.000 |
| Simon, Randall, TB.* | 1 | 0 | 0 | 0 | 0 | 0 | 0 | .000 |
| Spiezio, Scott, Sea. | 42 | 30 | 251 | 24 | 4 | 279 | 22 | .986 |
| Stairs, Matt, K.C. | 30 | 25 | 208 | 11 | 3 | 222 | 25 | .986 |
| Surhoff, B.J., Bal. | 10 | 4 | 46 | 4 | 0 | 50 | 6 | 1.000 |
| Sweeney, Mike, K.C. | 55 | 55 | 467 | 36 | 4 | 507 | 44 | .992 |
| Swisher, Nick, Oak.* | 3 | 2 | 19 | 0 | 0 | 19 | 3 | 1.000 |
| Teixeira, Mark, Tex. | 142 | 138 | 1210 | 98 | 10 | 1318 | 114 | .992 |
| Thomas, Frank, Chi. | 4 | 4 | 31 | 3 | 0 | 34 | 2 | 1.000 |
| Tiffee, Terry, Min. | 1 | 0 | 2 | 0 | 0 | 2 | 0 | 1.000 |
| Young, Dmitri, Det. | 25 | 24 | 203 | 17 | 0 | 220 | 15 | 1.000 |

#### FIRST BASEMEN WITH TWO OR MORE TEAMS

| Player, Team | G | GS | PO | A | E | TC | DP | Pct. |
|---|---|---|---|---|---|---|---|---|
| Mientkiewicz, Doug, Min. | 77 | 73 | 661 | 37 | 4 | 702 | 61 | .994 |
| Mientkiewicz, Doug, Bos. | 47 | 26 | 263 | 25 | 1 | 289 | 14 | .997 |
| Olerud, John, Sea.* | 77 | 71 | 548 | 52 | 1 | 601 | 58 | .998 |
| Olerud, John, N.Y.* | 47 | 47 | 367 | 25 | 1 | 393 | 34 | .997 |
| Phelps, Josh, Tor. | 12 | 11 | 101 | 2 | 2 | 105 | 7 | .981 |
| Phelps, Josh, Cle. | 8 | 7 | 43 | 2 | 1 | 46 | 1 | .978 |

### SECOND BASEMEN

| Player, Team | G | GS | PO | A | E | TC | DP | Pct. |
|---|---|---|---|---|---|---|---|---|
| Alexander, Manny, Tex. | 11 | 1 | 2 | 9 | 1 | 12 | 0 | .917 |
| Alomar, Roberto, Chi. | 13 | 13 | 23 | 32 | 1 | 56 | 14 | .982 |
| Amezaga, Alfredo, Ana. | 16 | 6 | 7 | 17 | 1 | 25 | 2 | .960 |
| Bartlett, Jason, Min. | 1 | 0 | 0 | 1 | 0 | 1 | 0 | 1.000 |
| Bellhorn, Mark, Bos. | 124 | 118 | 189 | 349 | 11 | 549 | 61 | .980 |
| Belliard, Ronnie, Cle. | 151 | 148 | 278 | 427 | 14 | 719 | 89 | .981 |
| Berg, Dave, Tor. | 4 | 3 | 5 | 9 | 0 | 14 | 1 | 1.000 |
| Bloomquist, Willie, Sea. | 1 | 0 | 0 | 0 | 0 | 0 | 0 | .000 |
| Blum, Geoff, TB. | 52 | 40 | 76 | 104 | 1 | 181 | 22 | .994 |
| Boone, Bret, Sea. | 148 | 148 | 280 | 350 | 14 | 644 | 90 | .978 |
| Bush, Homer, N.Y. | 4 | 2 | 7 | 4 | 0 | 11 | 3 | 1.000 |
| Cabrera, Jolbert, Sea. | 18 | 14 | 37 | 40 | 1 | 78 | 12 | .987 |
| Cairo, Miguel, N.Y. | 113 | 96 | 195 | 275 | 6 | 476 | 59 | .987 |
| Cantu, Jorge, TB. | 33 | 31 | 48 | 85 | 5 | 138 | 19 | .964 |
| Clark, Howie, Tor. | 1 | 1 | 0 | 0 | 0 | 0 | 0 | .000 |
| Crespo, Cesar, Bos. | 11 | 6 | 12 | 19 | 0 | 31 | 3 | 1.000 |
| Cuddyer, Michael, Min. | 48 | 40 | 54 | 113 | 3 | 170 | 17 | .982 |
| Figgins, Chone, Ana. | 20 | 15 | 27 | 42 | 1 | 70 | 8 | .986 |
| Fox, Andy, Tex. | 3 | 2 | 3 | 9 | 0 | 12 | 2 | 1.000 |
| German, Esteban, Oak. | 10 | 3 | 9 | 21 | 0 | 30 | 6 | 1.000 |
| Gomez, Chris, Tor. | 3 | 3 | 6 | 2 | 0 | 8 | 2 | 1.000 |
| Gotay, Ruben, K.C. | 42 | 41 | 78 | 97 | 3 | 178 | 29 | .983 |
| Graffanino, Tony, K.C. | 75 | 72 | 185 | 219 | 5 | 409 | 67 | .988 |
| Guerrero, Wilton, K.C. | 8 | 4 | 8 | 16 | 1 | 25 | 2 | .960 |
| Gutierrez, Ricky, Bos. | 14 | 5 | 15 | 24 | 0 | 39 | 6 | 1.000 |
| Hairston Jr., Jerry, Bal. | 12 | 12 | 22 | 37 | 1 | 60 | 9 | .983 |
| Halter, Shane, Ana. | 6 | 3 | 4 | 7 | 0 | 11 | 2 | 1.000 |
| Harris, Willie, Chi. | 92 | 76 | 163 | 223 | 4 | 390 | 46 | .990 |
| Hudson, Orlando, Tor. | 133 | 128 | 275 | 450 | 12 | 737 | 90 | .984 |

| Player, Team | G | GS | PO | A | E | TC | DP | Pct. |
|---|---|---|---|---|---|---|---|---|
| Infante, Omar, Det. | 105 | 97 | 204 | 281 | 12 | 497 | 73 | .976 |
| Jackson, Damian, K.C. | 1 | 0 | 0 | 0 | 0 | 0 | 0 | .000 |
| Kennedy, Adam, Ana. | 144 | 138 | 255 | 388 | 12 | 655 | 71 | .982 |
| Lopez, Luis, Bal. | 6 | 2 | 3 | 9 | 0 | 12 | 2 | 1.000 |
| Lopez, Mendy, K.C. | 6 | 4 | 10 | 6 | 1 | 17 | 2 | .941 |
| Lopez, Mickey, Sea. | 3 | 0 | 1 | 4 | 0 | 5 | 0 | 1.000 |
| Lugo, Julio, TB. | 8 | 8 | 16 | 16 | 1 | 33 | 3 | .970 |
| McDonald, John, Cle. | 12 | 4 | 10 | 23 | 0 | 33 | 5 | 1.000 |
| McLemore, Mark, Oak. | 47 | 44 | 113 | 123 | 6 | 242 | 37 | .975 |
| Menechino, Frank, Oak.-Tor. | 42 | 35 | 70 | 101 | 1 | 172 | 15 | .994 |
| Merloni, Lou, Cle. | 7 | 4 | 12 | 17 | 1 | 30 | 4 | .967 |
| Mientkiewicz, Doug, Bos. | 1 | 1 | 2 | 2 | 0 | 4 | 1 | 1.000 |
| Mueller, Bill, Bos. | 14 | 14 | 22 | 34 | 3 | 59 | 6 | .949 |
| Murphy, Donnie, K.C. | 7 | 7 | 12 | 17 | 0 | 29 | 8 | 1.000 |
| Offerman, Jose, Min. | 3 | 1 | 3 | 3 | 2 | 8 | 1 | .750 |
| Ojeda, Augie, Min. | 20 | 9 | 19 | 43 | 2 | 64 | 8 | .969 |
| Phillips, Brandon, Cle. | 6 | 6 | 17 | 19 | 1 | 37 | 4 | .973 |
| Prieto, Alex, Min. | 8 | 6 | 10 | 21 | 0 | 31 | 6 | 1.000 |
| Punto, Nick, Min. | 19 | 11 | 20 | 34 | 1 | 55 | 10 | .982 |
| Raburn, Ryan, Det. | 11 | 7 | 9 | 22 | 1 | 32 | 5 | .969 |
| Reese, Pokey, Bos. | 30 | 18 | 49 | 63 | 1 | 113 | 15 | .991 |
| Relaford, Desi, K.C. | 36 | 34 | 69 | 94 | 3 | 166 | 22 | .982 |
| Riggs, Adam, Ana. | 1 | 0 | 0 | 1 | 0 | 1 | 0 | 1.000 |
| Rivas, Luis, Min. | 109 | 95 | 176 | 317 | 3 | 496 | 75 | .994 |
| Roberts, Brian, Bal. | 150 | 148 | 235 | 426 | 8 | 669 | 92 | .988 |
| Rolls, Damian, TB. | 2 | 1 | 2 | 2 | 0 | 4 | 0 | 1.000 |
| Romano, Jason, TB. | 1 | 1 | 1 | 0 | 1 | 2 | 0 | .500 |
| Sanchez, Rey, TB. | 87 | 80 | 157 | 234 | 5 | 396 | 55 | .987 |
| SCUTARO, Marco, Oak. | 123 | 106 | 232 | 311 | 3 | 546 | 78 | .995 |
| Smith, Jason, Det. | 34 | 30 | 68 | 87 | 2 | 157 | 21 | .987 |
| Soriano, Alfonso, Tex. | 142 | 142 | 308 | 418 | 23 | 749 | 104 | .969 |
| Uribe, Juan, Chi. | 77 | 70 | 154 | 208 | 6 | 368 | 49 | .984 |
| Valdez, Wilson, Chi. | 5 | 3 | 9 | 4 | 0 | 13 | 3 | 1.000 |
| Vina, Fernando, Det. | 29 | 28 | 73 | 86 | 5 | 164 | 23 | .970 |
| Wilson, Enrique, N.Y. | 80 | 64 | 124 | 179 | 7 | 310 | 23 | .977 |
| Young, Eric, Tex. | 20 | 17 | 39 | 51 | 6 | 96 | 11 | .938 |

### SECOND BASEMEN WITH TWO OR MORE TEAMS

| Player, Team | G | GS | PO | A | E | TC | DP | Pct. |
|---|---|---|---|---|---|---|---|---|
| Menechino, Frank, Oak. | 12 | 9 | 16 | 29 | 1 | 46 | 2 | .978 |
| Menechino, Frank, Tor. | 30 | 26 | 54 | 72 | 0 | 126 | 13 | 1.000 |

## THIRD BASEMEN

| Player, Team | G | GS | PO | A | E | TC | DP | Pct. |
|---|---|---|---|---|---|---|---|---|
| Alexander, Manny, Tex. | 3 | 2 | 2 | 2 | 1 | 5 | 0 | .800 |
| Amezaga, Alfredo, Ana. | 26 | 2 | 3 | 9 | 1 | 13 | 3 | .923 |
| Bautista, Jose, Bal.-TB.-K.C. | 17 | 6 | 5 | 19 | 1 | 25 | 2 | .960 |
| Bellhorn, Mark, Bos. | 16 | 13 | 10 | 31 | 3 | 44 | 2 | .932 |
| Berg, Dave, Tor. | 3 | 2 | 0 | 3 | 2 | 5 | 0 | .600 |
| Blake, Casey, Cle. | 152 | 151 | 121 | 276 | 26 | 423 | 24 | .939 |
| Blalock, Hank, Tex. | 159 | 154 | 103 | 279 | 17 | 399 | 33 | .957 |
| Bloomquist, Willie, Sea. | 31 | 24 | 24 | 36 | 5 | 65 | 6 | .923 |
| Blum, Geoff, TB. | 59 | 40 | 35 | 78 | 8 | 121 | 8 | .934 |
| Burke, Jamie, Chi. | 2 | 0 | 0 | 0 | 0 | 0 | 0 | .000 |
| Cabrera, Jolbert, Sea. | 36 | 31 | 33 | 63 | 3 | 99 | 7 | .970 |
| Cairo, Miguel, N.Y. | 8 | 5 | 4 | 13 | 2 | 19 | 0 | .895 |
| Cantu, Jorge, TB. | 11 | 11 | 9 | 26 | 3 | 38 | 1 | .921 |
| Castro, Ramon A., Oak. | 6 | 3 | 1 | 4 | 0 | 5 | 0 | 1.000 |
| Chavez, Eric, Oak. | 125 | 125 | 113 | 276 | 13 | 402 | 31 | .968 |
| Clark, Howie, Tor. | 1 | 0 | 0 | 0 | 0 | 0 | 0 | .000 |
| Crede, Joe, Chi. | 144 | 142 | 91 | 243 | 12 | 346 | 23 | .965 |
| Cuddyer, Michael, Min. | 43 | 36 | 33 | 51 | 7 | 91 | 6 | .923 |
| Dobbs, Greg, Sea. | 14 | 12 | 5 | 21 | 2 | 28 | 3 | .929 |
| Dransfeldt, Kelly, Chi. | 3 | 1 | 2 | 0 | 0 | 2 | 0 | 1.000 |
| Escalona, Felix, N.Y. | 1 | 0 | 0 | 0 | 0 | 0 | 0 | .000 |
| Figgins, Chone, Ana. | 92 | 80 | 57 | 129 | 11 | 197 | 9 | .944 |
| Fox, Andy, Tex. | 2 | 0 | 0 | 0 | 0 | 0 | 0 | .000 |
| German, Esteban, Oak. | 15 | 10 | 8 | 21 | 2 | 31 | 3 | .935 |
| Glaus, Troy, Ana. | 19 | 19 | 11 | 27 | 2 | 40 | 2 | .950 |
| Gomez, Chris, Tor. | 5 | 4 | 2 | 8 | 0 | 10 | 1 | 1.000 |
| Guerrero, Wilton, K.C. | 2 | 0 | 0 | 0 | 0 | 0 | 0 | .000 |
| Hairston Jr., Jerry, Bal. | 1 | 1 | 0 | 1 | 0 | 1 | 0 | 1.000 |
| Halter, Shane, Ana. | 33 | 22 | 26 | 46 | 10 | 82 | 2 | .878 |
| Hansen, Dave, Sea. | 6 | 2 | 6 | 6 | 0 | 12 | 0 | 1.000 |
| HINSKE, Eric, Tor. | 153 | 148 | 107 | 242 | 8 | 357 | 23 | .978 |
| Huff, Aubrey, TB. | 86 | 85 | 69 | 129 | 12 | 210 | 12 | .943 |
| Infante, Omar, Det. | 10 | 2 | 2 | 8 | 0 | 10 | 2 | 1.000 |
| Inge, Brandon, Det. | 73 | 58 | 42 | 131 | 12 | 185 | 12 | .935 |
| Koskie, Corey, Min. | 115 | 112 | 79 | 207 | 11 | 297 | 14 | .963 |
| Leon, Jose, Bal. | 6 | 2 | 1 | 8 | 1 | 10 | 1 | .900 |
| Leone, Justin, Sea. | 28 | 28 | 25 | 48 | 8 | 81 | 2 | .901 |
| Lopez, Jose, Sea. | 1 | 0 | 0 | 0 | 0 | 0 | 0 | .000 |
| Lopez, Luis, Bal. | 11 | 6 | 6 | 15 | 4 | 25 | 2 | .840 |
| Lopez, Mendy, K.C. | 4 | 2 | 2 | 7 | 1 | 10 | 1 | .900 |
| McDonald, John, Cle. | 9 | 1 | 1 | 12 | 0 | 13 | 0 | 1.000 |
| McLemore, Mark, Oak. | 27 | 24 | 17 | 46 | 1 | 64 | 2 | .984 |
| McPherson, Dallas, Ana. | 14 | 11 | 9 | 22 | 0 | 31 | 1 | 1.000 |
| Melhuse, Adam, Oak. | 3 | 0 | 1 | 2 | 1 | 4 | 1 | .750 |
| Menechino, Frank, Tor. | 7 | 7 | 4 | 14 | 0 | 18 | 2 | 1.000 |
| Merloni, Lou, Cle. | 10 | 9 | 1 | 20 | 1 | 22 | 0 | .955 |
| Mora, Melvin, Bal. | 137 | 137 | 122 | 258 | 21 | 401 | 21 | .948 |
| Mueller, Bill, Bos. | 96 | 94 | 71 | 162 | 14 | 247 | 15 | .943 |
| Munson, Eric, Det. | 94 | 87 | 51 | 177 | 16 | 244 | 17 | .934 |
| Newhan, David, Bal. | 17 | 15 | 11 | 23 | 5 | 39 | 2 | .872 |
| Norton, Greg, Det. | 18 | 12 | 7 | 19 | 1 | 27 | 0 | .963 |
| Ojeda, Augie, Min. | 4 | 2 | 1 | 6 | 0 | 7 | 1 | 1.000 |
| Peralta, Jhonny, Cle. | 2 | 1 | 1 | 2 | 0 | 3 | 0 | 1.000 |
| Perez, Eduardo, TB. | 1 | 0 | 0 | 0 | 0 | 0 | 0 | .000 |
| Perry, Herbert, Tex. | 6 | 5 | 7 | 6 | 2 | 15 | 0 | .867 |
| Phillips, Andy, N.Y. | 4 | 2 | 2 | 5 | 0 | 7 | 0 | 1.000 |
| Prieto, Alex, Min. | 5 | 1 | 1 | 3 | 0 | 4 | 0 | 1.000 |
| Punto, Nick, Min. | 2 | 0 | 0 | 0 | 0 | 0 | 0 | .000 |
| Quinlan, Robb, Ana. | 32 | 28 | 13 | 44 | 1 | 58 | 1 | .983 |
| Randa, Joe, K.C. | 119 | 118 | 85 | 241 | 11 | 337 | 22 | .967 |
| Relaford, Desi, K.C. | 42 | 36 | 24 | 78 | 8 | 110 | 5 | .927 |
| Rodriguez, Alex, N.Y. | 155 | 155 | 100 | 262 | 13 | 375 | 25 | .965 |
| Rolls, Damian, TB. | 19 | 14 | 16 | 25 | 2 | 43 | 3 | .953 |
| Scutaro, Marco, Oak. | 1 | 0 | 0 | 0 | 0 | 0 | 0 | .000 |
| Sheffield, Gary, N.Y. | 2 | 0 | 0 | 0 | 1 | 1 | 0 | .000 |
| Smith, Jason, Det. | 5 | 2 | 5 | 5 | 2 | 12 | 2 | .833 |
| Snyder, Earl, Bos. | 1 | 1 | 2 | 3 | 0 | 5 | 0 | 1.000 |
| Spiezio, Scott, Sea. | 66 | 65 | 56 | 131 | 7 | 194 | 15 | .964 |
| Tiffee, Terry, Min. | 12 | 11 | 11 | 17 | 1 | 29 | 0 | .966 |
| Upton, B.J., TB. | 13 | 11 | 10 | 12 | 2 | 24 | 0 | .917 |
| Uribe, Juan, Chi. | 27 | 19 | 14 | 41 | 2 | 57 | 5 | .965 |
| Youkilis, Kevin, Bos. | 65 | 54 | 47 | 106 | 5 | 158 | 7 | .968 |
| Young, Dmitri, Det. | 1 | 1 | 1 | 1 | 0 | 2 | 0 | 1.000 |
| Young, Eric, Tex. | 1 | 1 | 0 | 1 | 0 | 1 | 0 | 1.000 |

### THIRD BASEMEN WITH TWO OR MORE TEAMS

| Player, Team | G | GS | PO | A | E | TC | DP | Pct. |
|---|---|---|---|---|---|---|---|---|
| Bautista, Jose, Bal. | 4 | 0 | 0 | 0 | 0 | 0 | 0 | .000 |
| Bautista, Jose, TB. | 2 | 0 | 0 | 2 | 0 | 2 | 0 | 1.000 |
| Bautista, Jose, K.C. | 11 | 6 | 5 | 17 | 1 | 23 | 2 | .957 |

## SHORTSTOPS

| Player, Team | G | GS | PO | A | E | TC | DP | Pct. |
|---|---|---|---|---|---|---|---|---|
| Adams, Russ, Tor. | 21 | 18 | 26 | 47 | 5 | 78 | 9 | .936 |
| Alexander, Manny, Tex. | 7 | 2 | 6 | 11 | 1 | 18 | 1 | .944 |
| Amezaga, Alfredo, Ana. | 32 | 14 | 38 | 58 | 1 | 97 | 5 | .990 |
| Aurilia, Rich, Sea. | 73 | 71 | 113 | 186 | 3 | 302 | 39 | .990 |
| Bartlett, Jason, Min. | 5 | 2 | 5 | 11 | 2 | 18 | 3 | .889 |
| Bellhorn, Mark, Bos. | 1 | 1 | 2 | 3 | 0 | 5 | 1 | 1.000 |
| Berroa, Angel, K.C. | 133 | 132 | 207 | 389 | 28 | 624 | 94 | .955 |
| Blanco, Andres, K.C. | 19 | 19 | 30 | 64 | 4 | 98 | 17 | .959 |
| Bloomquist, Willie, Sea. | 20 | 16 | 27 | 36 | 3 | 66 | 11 | .955 |
| Blum, Geoff, TB. | 1 | 0 | 1 | 0 | 0 | 1 | 0 | 1.000 |
| Cabrera, Jolbert, Sea. | 14 | 9 | 11 | 13 | 1 | 25 | 2 | .960 |
| Cabrera, Orlando, Bos. | 57 | 57 | 78 | 147 | 8 | 233 | 23 | .966 |
| Cairo, Miguel, N.Y. | 3 | 2 | 0 | 5 | 0 | 5 | 1 | 1.000 |
| Cantu, Jorge, TB. | 1 | 1 | 2 | 2 | 0 | 4 | 0 | 1.000 |
| Castro, Ramon A., Oak. | 1 | 0 | 0 | 2 | 0 | 2 | 0 | 1.000 |
| Crespo, Cesar, Bos. | 27 | 7 | 20 | 30 | 3 | 53 | 8 | .943 |
| Crosby, Bobby, Oak. | 151 | 151 | 241 | 505 | 19 | 765 | 107 | .975 |
| Dransfeldt, Kelly, Chi. | 8 | 4 | 4 | 14 | 1 | 19 | 1 | .947 |
| ECKSTEIN, David, Ana. | 138 | 136 | 198 | 309 | 6 | 513 | 75 | .988 |
| Escalona, Felix, N.Y. | 4 | 2 | 3 | 7 | 0 | 10 | 1 | 1.000 |
| Figgins, Chone, Ana. | 13 | 10 | 19 | 24 | 2 | 45 | 5 | .956 |
| Garciaparra, Nomar, Bos. | 37 | 37 | 52 | 81 | 6 | 139 | 17 | .957 |
| Gipson, Charles, TB. | 2 | 0 | 0 | 2 | 0 | 2 | 1 | 1.000 |
| Gomez, Chris, Tor. | 77 | 69 | 108 | 206 | 10 | 324 | 46 | .969 |
| Guerrero, Wilton, K.C. | 3 | 0 | 1 | 2 | 0 | 3 | 0 | 1.000 |
| Guillen, Carlos, Det. | 135 | 133 | 219 | 418 | 17 | 654 | 90 | .974 |
| Gutierrez, Ricky, Bos. | 6 | 3 | 7 | 9 | 1 | 17 | 3 | .941 |
| Guzman, Cristian, Min. | 145 | 143 | 234 | 440 | 12 | 686 | 103 | .983 |
| Halter, Shane, Ana. | 3 | 1 | 3 | 4 | 0 | 7 | 1 | 1.000 |
| Infante, Omar, Det. | 23 | 21 | 28 | 67 | 4 | 99 | 11 | .960 |
| Jackson, Damian, K.C. | 1 | 0 | 0 | 0 | 0 | 0 | 0 | .000 |
| Jeter, Derek, N.Y. | 154 | 154 | 273 | 392 | 13 | 678 | 96 | .981 |
| Leone, Justin, Sea. | 2 | 1 | 3 | 1 | 1 | 5 | 0 | .800 |
| Lopez, Jose, Sea. | 57 | 55 | 90 | 126 | 10 | 226 | 24 | .956 |
| Lopez, Luis, Bal. | 14 | 0 | 7 | 10 | 1 | 18 | 3 | .944 |

| Player, Team | G | GS | PO | A | E | TC | DP | Pct. |
|---|---|---|---|---|---|---|---|---|
| Lopez, Mendy, K.C. | 4 | 2 | 2 | 2 | 0 | 4 | 2 | 1.000 |
| Lugo, Julio, TB. | 143 | 142 | 236 | 422 | 25 | 683 | 91 | .963 |
| McDonald, John, Cle. | 30 | 15 | 25 | 65 | 5 | 95 | 16 | .947 |
| Menechino, Frank, Tor. | 14 | 14 | 26 | 26 | 1 | 53 | 9 | .981 |
| Mora, Melvin, Bal. | 1 | 0 | 0 | 0 | 0 | 0 | 0 | .000 |
| Ojeda, Augie, Min. | 7 | 5 | 8 | 14 | 0 | 22 | 4 | 1.000 |
| Peralta, Jhonny, Cle. | 7 | 6 | 7 | 17 | 3 | 27 | 2 | .889 |
| Prieto, Alex, Min. | 3 | 2 | 4 | 4 | 0 | 8 | 2 | 1.000 |
| Punto, Nick, Min. | 11 | 10 | 16 | 33 | 0 | 49 | 9 | 1.000 |
| Reese, Pokey, Bos. | 71 | 56 | 85 | 190 | 6 | 281 | 37 | .979 |
| Relaford, Desi, K.C. | 12 | 9 | 14 | 28 | 0 | 42 | 7 | 1.000 |
| Rodriguez, Alex, N.Y. | 2 | 0 | 1 | 1 | 0 | 2 | 1 | 1.000 |
| Sanchez, Rey, TB. | 4 | 2 | 5 | 15 | 0 | 20 | 1 | 1.000 |
| Santiago, Ramon, Sea. | 16 | 10 | 22 | 31 | 3 | 56 | 8 | .946 |
| Scutaro, Marco, Oak. | 16 | 11 | 25 | 42 | 2 | 69 | 9 | .971 |
| Smith, Jason, Det. | 20 | 8 | 16 | 35 | 1 | 52 | 5 | .981 |
| Tejada, Miguel, Bal. | 162 | 162 | 263 | 526 | 24 | 813 | 118 | .970 |
| Upton, B.J., TB. | 16 | 16 | 23 | 41 | 7 | 71 | 8 | .901 |
| Uribe, Juan, Chi. | 38 | 32 | 54 | 115 | 3 | 172 | 31 | .983 |
| Valdez, Wilson, Chi. | 12 | 9 | 13 | 23 | 1 | 37 | 3 | .973 |
| Valentin, Jose, Chi. | 122 | 117 | 186 | 373 | 20 | 579 | 85 | .965 |
| Vizquel, Omar, Cle. | 147 | 141 | 200 | 396 | 11 | 607 | 91 | .982 |
| Wilson, Enrique, N.Y. | 16 | 4 | 10 | 25 | 1 | 36 | 6 | .972 |
| Woodward, Chris, Tor. | 64 | 60 | 87 | 171 | 5 | 263 | 42 | .981 |
| Young, Eric, Tex. | 8 | 2 | 2 | 4 | 1 | 7 | 1 | .857 |
| Young, Michael, Tex. | 158 | 158 | 225 | 423 | 19 | 667 | 98 | .972 |

## OUTFIELDERS

| Player, Team | G | GS | PO | A | E | TC | DP | Pct. |
|---|---|---|---|---|---|---|---|---|
| Allen, Chad, Tex. | 13 | 11 | 14 | 0 | 0 | 14 | 0 | 1.000 |
| Anderson, Garret, Ana.* | 94 | 92 | 211 | 4 | 2 | 217 | 1 | .991 |
| Baldelli, Rocco, TB. | 124 | 120 | 342 | 11 | 8 | 361 | 2 | .978 |
| Bautista, Jose, Bal.-TB.-K.C. | 15 | 5 | 8 | 1 | 0 | 9 | 0 | 1.000 |
| Beltran, Carlos, K.C. | 69 | 69 | 197 | 4 | 3 | 204 | 1 | .985 |
| Berg, Dave, Tor. | 31 | 26 | 37 | 1 | 1 | 39 | 0 | .974 |
| Berger, Brandon, K.C. | 11 | 9 | 25 | 1 | 0 | 26 | 1 | 1.000 |
| Bigbie, Larry, Bal. | 134 | 131 | 289 | 3 | 2 | 294 | 0 | .993 |
| Bloomquist, Willie, Sea. | 9 | 4 | 14 | 0 | 0 | 14 | 0 | 1.000 |
| Blum, Geoff, TB. | 7 | 7 | 12 | 1 | 1 | 14 | 1 | .929 |
| Bocachica, Hiram, Sea. | 44 | 25 | 68 | 0 | 0 | 68 | 0 | 1.000 |
| Borchard, Joe, Chi. | 56 | 52 | 101 | 4 | 3 | 108 | 0 | .972 |
| Brown, Adrian, K.C. | 5 | 3 | 9 | 0 | 0 | 9 | 0 | 1.000 |
| Brown, Dee, K.C. | 53 | 49 | 93 | 4 | 3 | 100 | 0 | .970 |
| Burke, Jamie, Chi. | 2 | 1 | 2 | 0 | 0 | 2 | 0 | 1.000 |
| Byrnes, Eric, Oak. | 141 | 137 | 264 | 11 | 3 | 278 | 2 | .989 |
| Cabrera, Jolbert, Sea. | 23 | 19 | 46 | 2 | 1 | 49 | 1 | .980 |
| Catalanotto, Frank, Tor. | 41 | 34 | 67 | 1 | 2 | 70 | 1 | .971 |
| Chavez, Eric, Oak. | 1 | 0 | 2 | 0 | 0 | 2 | 0 | 1.000 |
| Clark, Howie, Tor. | 19 | 17 | 33 | 2 | 1 | 36 | 0 | .972 |
| Conti, Jason, Tex. | 21 | 14 | 45 | 0 | 0 | 45 | 0 | 1.000 |
| Crawford, Carl, TB.* | 145 | 140 | 350 | 5 | 2 | 357 | 1 | .994 |
| Crespo, Cesar, Bos. | 19 | 3 | 13 | 0 | 0 | 13 | 0 | 1.000 |
| Crisp, Coco, Cle. | 128 | 121 | 286 | 5 | 4 | 295 | 1 | .986 |
| Crosby, Bubba, N.Y.* | 45 | 6 | 36 | 0 | 1 | 37 | 0 | .973 |
| Cruz Jr., Jose, TB. | 152 | 148 | 315 | 10 | 10 | 335 | 0 | .970 |
| Cuddyer, Michael, Min. | 15 | 8 | 16 | 0 | 0 | 16 | 0 | 1.000 |
| Cummings, Midre, TB. | 2 | 2 | 3 | 0 | 0 | 3 | 0 | 1.000 |
| Damon, Johnny, Bos.* | 148 | 145 | 349 | 4 | 5 | 358 | 2 | .986 |
| Daubach, Brian, Bos. | 7 | 6 | 8 | 1 | 0 | 9 | 0 | 1.000 |
| DaVanon, Jeff, Ana. | 81 | 53 | 142 | 2 | 1 | 145 | 2 | .993 |
| DeJesus, David, K.C.* | 94 | 92 | 246 | 3 | 4 | 253 | 0 | .984 |
| Dellucci, David, Tex.* | 94 | 86 | 177 | 0 | 2 | 179 | 0 | .989 |
| Diaz, Matt, TB. | 4 | 4 | 11 | 0 | 0 | 11 | 0 | 1.000 |
| Dye, Jermaine, Oak. | 134 | 132 | 258 | 3 | 2 | 263 | 2 | .992 |
| Escobar, Alex, Cle. | 42 | 42 | 102 | 9 | 1 | 112 | 3 | .991 |
| Everett, Carl, Chi. | 1 | 1 | 1 | 1 | 0 | 2 | 0 | 1.000 |
| Fick, Robert, TB. | 21 | 18 | 40 | 0 | 1 | 41 | 0 | .976 |
| Figgins, Chone, Ana. | 57 | 37 | 100 | 1 | 1 | 102 | 0 | .990 |
| Ford, Lew, Min. | 126 | 121 | 268 | 7 | 4 | 279 | 0 | .986 |
| Fox, Andy, Tex. | 2 | 0 | 2 | 0 | 0 | 2 | 0 | 1.000 |
| Garcia, Karim, Bal.* | 19 | 16 | 33 | 0 | 0 | 33 | 0 | 1.000 |
| Gathright, Joey, TB. | 16 | 14 | 30 | 0 | 0 | 30 | 0 | 1.000 |
| Gerut, Jody, Cle.* | 131 | 121 | 267 | 7 | 4 | 278 | 2 | .986 |
| Gettis, Byron, K.C. | 21 | 15 | 38 | 2 | 3 | 43 | 1 | .930 |
| Gibbons, Jay, Bal.* | 66 | 63 | 116 | 6 | 2 | 124 | 1 | .984 |
| Gipson, Charles, TB. | 2 | 0 | 3 | 0 | 0 | 3 | 0 | 1.000 |
| Gload, Ross, Chi.* | 39 | 25 | 59 | 1 | 3 | 63 | 0 | .952 |
| Gomez, Alexis, K.C.* | 12 | 7 | 21 | 0 | 1 | 22 | 0 | .955 |
| Gonzalez, Juan, K.C. | 29 | 29 | 52 | 3 | 3 | 58 | 1 | .948 |
| Gonzalez, Raul, Cle. | 4 | 2 | 7 | 0 | 0 | 7 | 0 | 1.000 |
| Granderson, Curtis, Det. | 8 | 7 | 16 | 1 | 0 | 17 | 0 | 1.000 |
| Gross, Gabe, Tor. | 38 | 33 | 73 | 5 | 0 | 78 | 1 | 1.000 |
| Guerrero, Vladimir, Ana. | 143 | 143 | 308 | 13 | 9 | 330 | 2 | .973 |
| Guerrero, Wilton, K.C. | 3 | 0 | 2 | 0 | 0 | 2 | 0 | 1.000 |
| Guiel, Aaron, K.C. | 39 | 35 | 82 | 3 | 3 | 88 | 0 | .966 |
| Guillen, Jose, Ana. | 136 | 136 | 270 | 9 | 6 | 285 | 1 | .979 |
| Hairston Jr., Jerry, Bal. | 52 | 47 | 105 | 3 | 1 | 109 | 1 | .991 |
| Harris, Willie, Chi. | 30 | 25 | 57 | 1 | 1 | 59 | 0 | .983 |
| Harvey, Ken, K.C. | 4 | 4 | 4 | 0 | 0 | 4 | 0 | 1.000 |
| Hermansen, Chad, Tor. | 4 | 2 | 4 | 0 | 0 | 4 | 0 | 1.000 |
| Higginson, Bobby, Det. | 115 | 110 | 223 | 13 | 6 | 242 | 1 | .975 |
| Huff, Aubrey, TB. | 9 | 8 | 17 | 0 | 0 | 17 | 0 | 1.000 |
| Hunter, Torii, Min. | 126 | 124 | 311 | 5 | 4 | 320 | 0 | .988 |
| Hyzdu, Adam, Bos. | 14 | 0 | 6 | 0 | 0 | 6 | 0 | 1.000 |
| Ibanez, Raul, Sea. | 112 | 108 | 229 | 10 | 4 | 243 | 3 | .984 |
| Infante, Omar, Det. | 5 | 3 | 10 | 0 | 0 | 10 | 0 | 1.000 |
| Inge, Brandon, Det. | 26 | 20 | 43 | 5 | 1 | 49 | 1 | .980 |
| Jackson, Damian, K.C. | 5 | 0 | 2 | 0 | 0 | 2 | 0 | 1.000 |
| Johnson, Reed, Tor. | 137 | 123 | 266 | 9 | 3 | 278 | 1 | .989 |
| Jones, Jacque, Min.* | 142 | 139 | 318 | 5 | 2 | 325 | 1 | .994 |
| Jordan, Brian, Tex. | 44 | 40 | 94 | 1 | 1 | 96 | 0 | .990 |
| Kapler, Gabe, Bos. | 127 | 73 | 170 | 6 | 4 | 180 | 0 | .978 |
| Kielty, Bobby, Oak. | 67 | 50 | 97 | 1 | 1 | 99 | 0 | .990 |
| Kotsay, Mark, Oak.* | 145 | 140 | 347 | 11 | 6 | 364 | 4 | .984 |
| Kubel, Jason, Min. | 10 | 6 | 14 | 1 | 0 | 15 | 1 | 1.000 |
| Lawton, Matt, Cle. | 142 | 141 | 266 | 9 | 4 | 279 | 3 | .986 |
| LEE, Carlos, Chi. | 148 | 148 | 282 | 11 | 0 | 293 | 2 | 1.000 |
| Little, Mark, Cle. | 11 | 6 | 12 | 1 | 0 | 13 | 0 | 1.000 |
| Lofton, Kenny, N.Y.* | 74 | 67 | 180 | 4 | 2 | 186 | 4 | .989 |
| Logan, Nook, Det. | 46 | 41 | 117 | 3 | 2 | 122 | 1 | .984 |
| Lopez, Mendy, K.C. | 4 | 2 | 6 | 0 | 1 | 7 | 0 | .857 |
| Ludwick, Ryan, Cle.* | 15 | 13 | 32 | 0 | 1 | 33 | 0 | .970 |
| Majewski, Val, Bal.* | 4 | 3 | 11 | 0 | 0 | 11 | 0 | 1.000 |
| Mateo, Ruben, K.C. | 30 | 23 | 52 | 4 | 0 | 56 | 1 | 1.000 |
| Matos, Luis, Bal. | 89 | 85 | 220 | 3 | 1 | 224 | 1 | .996 |
| Matsui, Hideki, N.Y. | 160 | 160 | 307 | 8 | 7 | 322 | 2 | .978 |
| Matthews Jr., Gary, Tex. | 85 | 77 | 195 | 8 | 2 | 205 | 1 | .990 |
| McCarty, Dave, Bos.* | 17 | 6 | 13 | 1 | 0 | 14 | 1 | 1.000 |
| McCracken, Quinton, Sea. | 8 | 7 | 11 | 1 | 0 | 12 | 0 | 1.000 |
| McDonald, Darnell, Bal. | 13 | 9 | 21 | 0 | 0 | 21 | 0 | 1.000 |
| McLemore, Mark, Oak. | 1 | 0 | 0 | 0 | 0 | 0 | 0 | .000 |
| McMillon, Billy, Oak.* | 21 | 13 | 23 | 0 | 0 | 23 | 0 | 1.000 |
| Mench, Kevin, Tex. | 109 | 102 | 213 | 6 | 1 | 220 | 3 | .995 |
| Merloni, Lou, Cle. | 4 | 1 | 2 | 1 | 1 | 4 | 0 | .750 |
| Millar, Kevin, Bos. | 74 | 66 | 121 | 1 | 3 | 125 | 0 | .976 |
| Mondesi, Raul, Ana. | 7 | 7 | 20 | 1 | 0 | 21 | 0 | 1.000 |
| Monroe, Craig, Det. | 125 | 115 | 261 | 5 | 11 | 277 | 1 | .960 |
| Mottola, Chad, Bal. | 5 | 3 | 7 | 0 | 0 | 7 | 0 | 1.000 |
| Newhan, David, Bal. | 42 | 40 | 73 | 3 | 0 | 76 | 0 | 1.000 |
| Nivar, Ramon, Tex. | 6 | 6 | 12 | 1 | 0 | 13 | 0 | 1.000 |
| Nix, Laynce, Tex.* | 114 | 100 | 225 | 4 | 1 | 230 | 1 | .996 |
| Nixon, Trot, Bos.* | 40 | 36 | 63 | 1 | 1 | 65 | 0 | .985 |
| Norton, Greg, Det. | 6 | 0 | 2 | 0 | 0 | 2 | 0 | 1.000 |
| Nunez, Abraham, K.C. | 57 | 57 | 135 | 3 | 1 | 139 | 0 | .993 |
| Ordonez, Magglio, Chi. | 43 | 43 | 95 | 1 | 1 | 97 | 0 | .990 |
| Paul, Josh, Ana. | 4 | 1 | 2 | 0 | 0 | 2 | 0 | 1.000 |
| Perez, Eduardo, TB. | 3 | 3 | 5 | 0 | 0 | 5 | 0 | 1.000 |
| Perez, Timo, Chi.* | 80 | 69 | 135 | 8 | 2 | 145 | 4 | .986 |
| Pond, Simon, Tor. | 9 | 9 | 18 | 0 | 0 | 18 | 0 | 1.000 |
| Pride, Curtis, Ana. | 24 | 4 | 27 | 0 | 0 | 27 | 0 | 1.000 |
| Punto, Nick, Min. | 2 | 1 | 2 | 1 | 0 | 3 | 0 | 1.000 |
| Quinlan, Robb, Ana. | 9 | 1 | 4 | 0 | 0 | 4 | 0 | 1.000 |
| Raines Jr., Tim, Bal. | 38 | 21 | 61 | 2 | 0 | 63 | 0 | 1.000 |
| Ramirez, Manny, Bos. | 132 | 132 | 198 | 4 | 7 | 209 | 0 | .967 |
| Reed, Jeremy, Sea.* | 16 | 14 | 51 | 0 | 1 | 52 | 0 | .981 |
| Relaford, Desi, K.C. | 32 | 24 | 51 | 2 | 1 | 54 | 0 | .981 |
| Restovich, Michael, Min. | 19 | 9 | 20 | 0 | 0 | 20 | 0 | 1.000 |
| Riggs, Adam, Ana. | 8 | 5 | 11 | 1 | 0 | 12 | 0 | 1.000 |
| Rios, Alexis, Tor. | 111 | 109 | 218 | 11 | 2 | 231 | 4 | .991 |
| Roberts, Dave, Bos.* | 38 | 19 | 53 | 1 | 1 | 55 | 1 | .982 |
| Rolls, Damian, TB. | 24 | 13 | 35 | 1 | 0 | 36 | 0 | 1.000 |
| Romano, Jason, TB. | 1 | 1 | 2 | 1 | 0 | 3 | 0 | 1.000 |
| Rowand, Aaron, Chi. | 137 | 122 | 304 | 10 | 8 | 322 | 1 | .975 |
| Ryan, Michael, Min. | 15 | 7 | 18 | 0 | 1 | 19 | 0 | .947 |
| Salmon, Tim, Ana. | 8 | 7 | 15 | 1 | 0 | 16 | 0 | 1.000 |
| Sanchez, Alex, Det.* | 78 | 77 | 177 | 2 | 9 | 188 | 1 | .952 |
| Sheffield, Gary, N.Y. | 136 | 136 | 271 | 11 | 5 | 287 | 3 | .983 |
| Shelton, Chris, Det. | 1 | 0 | 1 | 0 | 0 | 1 | 0 | 1.000 |
| Sierra, Ruben, N.Y. | 29 | 22 | 41 | 1 | 1 | 43 | 0 | .977 |
| Sizemore, Grady, Cle.* | 42 | 38 | 105 | 0 | 1 | 106 | 0 | .991 |
| Stairs, Matt, K.C. | 71 | 68 | 131 | 5 | 2 | 138 | 2 | .986 |
| Stewart, Shannon, Min. | 71 | 71 | 103 | 2 | 3 | 108 | 0 | .972 |
| Surhoff, B.J., Bal. | 70 | 66 | 133 | 3 | 2 | 138 | 2 | .986 |

| Player, Team | G | GS | PO | A | E | TC | DP | Pct. |
|---|---|---|---|---|---|---|---|---|
| Suzuki, Ichiro, Sea. | 158 | 158 | 372 | 12 | 3 | 387 | 2 | .992 |
| Swisher, Nick, Oak.* | 16 | 14 | 24 | 0 | 3 | 27 | 0 | .889 |
| Teixeira, Mark, Tex. | 7 | 4 | 8 | 0 | 0 | 8 | 0 | 1.000 |
| Thames, Marcus, Det. | 52 | 38 | 94 | 3 | 0 | 97 | 1 | 1.000 |
| Thompson, Rich, K.C. | 3 | 0 | 2 | 0 | 0 | 2 | 0 | 1.000 |
| Torres, Andres, Det. | 1 | 0 | 0 | 0 | 0 | 0 | 0 | .000 |
| Upton, B.J., TB | 1 | 1 | 0 | 0 | 0 | 0 | 0 | .000 |
| Wells, Vernon, Tor. | 131 | 130 | 327 | 5 | 1 | 333 | 0 | .997 |
| White, Rondell, Det. | 74 | 73 | 127 | 2 | 3 | 132 | 0 | .977 |
| Williams, Bernie, N.Y. | 97 | 93 | 214 | 2 | 1 | 217 | 1 | .995 |
| Winn, Randy, Sea. | 154 | 151 | 416 | 5 | 4 | 425 | 1 | .991 |
| Young, Dmitri, Det. | 2 | 2 | 2 | 0 | 0 | 2 | 0 | 1.000 |
| Young, Eric, Tex. | 53 | 46 | 77 | 4 | 2 | 83 | 0 | .976 |

## OUTFIELDERS WITH TWO OR MORE TEAMS

| Player, Team | G | GS | PO | A | E | TC | DP | Pct. |
|---|---|---|---|---|---|---|---|---|
| Bautista, Jose, Bal. | 6 | 2 | 4 | 1 | 0 | 5 | 0 | 1.000 |
| Bautista, Jose, TB. | 8 | 3 | 4 | 0 | 0 | 4 | 0 | 1.000 |
| Bautista, Jose, K.C. | 1 | 0 | 0 | 0 | 0 | 0 | 0 | .000 |

# CATCHERS

| Player, Team | G | GS | PO | A | E | TC | DP | PB | Pct. |
|---|---|---|---|---|---|---|---|---|---|
| Alomar Jr., Sandy, Chi. | 49 | 46 | 278 | 15 | 3 | 296 | 2 | 4 | .990 |
| Ardoin, Danny, Tex. | 6 | 2 | 21 | 2 | 1 | 24 | 0 | 1 | .958 |
| Barajas, Rod, Tex. | 105 | 102 | 656 | 23 | 7 | 686 | 2 | 7 | .990 |
| Bard, Josh, Cle. | 7 | 6 | 47 | 4 | 0 | 51 | 1 | 0 | 1.000 |
| Blanco, Henry, Min. | 114 | 95 | 685 | 45 | 7 | 737 | 7 | 5 | .991 |
| Borders, Pat, Sea.-Min. | 38 | 31 | 203 | 18 | 4 | 225 | 4 | 1 | .982 |
| Bowen, Rob, Min. | 15 | 8 | 65 | 1 | 1 | 67 | 1 | 0 | .985 |
| Buck, John, K.C. | 68 | 66 | 376 | 14 | 3 | 393 | 4 | 7 | .992 |
| Burke, Jamie, Chi. | 45 | 32 | 215 | 11 | 3 | 229 | 1 | 1 | .987 |
| Cash, Kevin, Tor. | 60 | 50 | 316 | 36 | 2 | 354 | 5 | 5 | .994 |
| Castillo, Alberto, K.C. | 29 | 28 | 199 | 11 | 1 | 211 | 0 | 1 | .995 |
| Davis, Ben, Sea.-Chi. | 67 | 55 | 400 | 22 | 3 | 425 | 4 | 6 | .993 |
| DiFelice, Mike, Det. | 12 | 4 | 40 | 6 | 0 | 46 | 1 | 0 | 1.000 |
| Dominique, Andy, Bos. | 1 | 0 | 1 | 0 | 0 | 1 | 0 | 0 | 1.000 |
| Estalella, Bobby, Tor. | 3 | 3 | 20 | 1 | 0 | 21 | 0 | 0 | 1.000 |
| Fick, Robert, TB. | 3 | 0 | 3 | 1 | 0 | 4 | 0 | 0 | 1.000 |
| Flaherty, John, N.Y. | 46 | 35 | 255 | 19 | 3 | 277 | 3 | 4 | .989 |
| Fordyce, Brook, TB. | 51 | 46 | 274 | 11 | 3 | 288 | 3 | 1 | .990 |
| Gil, Geronimo, Bal. | 11 | 8 | 64 | 4 | 0 | 68 | 1 | 0 | 1.000 |
| Hall, Toby, TB. | 119 | 115 | 686 | 38 | 6 | 730 | 4 | 7 | .992 |
| Huckaby, Ken, Tex.-Bal. | 24 | 16 | 106 | 9 | 2 | 117 | 1 | 3 | .983 |
| Inge, Brandon, Det. | 39 | 34 | 209 | 30 | 3 | 242 | 1 | 4 | .988 |
| Laird, Gerald, Tex. | 49 | 46 | 275 | 19 | 5 | 299 | 6 | 6 | .983 |
| Laker, Tim, Cle. | 41 | 31 | 233 | 21 | 4 | 258 | 0 | 5 | .984 |
| LeCroy, Matthew, Min. | 26 | 16 | 114 | 4 | 4 | 122 | 0 | 1 | .967 |
| Lopez, Javy, Bal. | 132 | 125 | 848 | 49 | 5 | 902 | 11 | 10 | .994 |
| Machado, Robert, Bal. | 35 | 19 | 157 | 14 | 1 | 172 | 6 | 2 | .994 |
| Martinez, Sandy, Cle.-Bos. | 4 | 1 | 13 | 1 | 0 | 14 | 0 | 2 | 1.000 |
| Martinez, Victor, Cle. | 132 | 124 | 865 | 61 | 6 | 932 | 11 | 9 | .994 |
| Mauer, Joe, Min. | 32 | 29 | 212 | 10 | 2 | 224 | 0 | 0 | .991 |
| Melhuse, Adam, Oak. | 64 | 53 | 358 | 18 | 2 | 378 | 1 | 5 | .995 |
| MILLER, Damian, Oak. | 109 | 109 | 701 | 49 | 1 | 751 | 4 | 9 | .999 |
| Mirabelli, Doug, Bos. | 53 | 41 | 285 | 18 | 2 | 305 | 2 | 15 | .993 |
| Molina, Bengie, Ana. | 89 | 89 | 597 | 56 | 3 | 656 | 5 | 6 | .995 |
| Molina, Jose, Ana. | 70 | 57 | 441 | 37 | 3 | 481 | 4 | 3 | .994 |
| Munson, Eric, Det. | 1 | 0 | 0 | 0 | 0 | 0 | 0 | 0 | .000 |
| Myers, Greg, Tor. | 4 | 4 | 27 | 2 | 0 | 29 | 1 | 0 | 1.000 |
| Navarro, Dioner, N.Y. | 4 | 1 | 9 | 0 | 0 | 9 | 0 | 0 | 1.000 |
| Olivo, Miguel, Chi.-Sea. | 95 | 83 | 510 | 29 | 5 | 544 | 7 | 13 | .991 |
| Osik, Keith, Bal. | 11 | 6 | 43 | 3 | 0 | 46 | 1 | 2 | 1.000 |
| Paul, Josh, Ana. | 37 | 16 | 134 | 9 | 1 | 144 | 2 | 2 | .993 |
| Phillips, Paul, K.C. | 4 | 1 | 11 | 1 | 0 | 12 | 0 | 0 | 1.000 |
| Posada, Jorge, N.Y. | 134 | 126 | 835 | 53 | 9 | 897 | 13 | 9 | .990 |
| Quiroz, Guillermo, Tor. | 15 | 13 | 76 | 6 | 2 | 84 | 3 | 3 | .976 |
| Rivera, Rene, Sea. | 2 | 0 | 4 | 0 | 0 | 4 | 0 | 0 | 1.000 |
| Rodriguez, Ivan, Det. | 124 | 123 | 770 | 52 | 11 | 833 | 6 | 3 | .987 |
| Rose, Mike, Oak. | 2 | 0 | 1 | 0 | 0 | 1 | 0 | 0 | 1.000 |
| Santiago, Benito, K.C. | 49 | 48 | 228 | 18 | 1 | 247 | 3 | 6 | .996 |
| Shelton, Chris, Det. | 6 | 0 | 10 | 0 | 0 | 10 | 0 | 3 | 1.000 |
| Stinnett, Kelly, K.C. | 20 | 17 | 97 | 4 | 3 | 104 | 0 | 1 | .971 |
| Tonis, Mike, K.C. | 2 | 2 | 13 | 1 | 0 | 14 | 0 | 2 | 1.000 |
| Varitek, Jason, Bos. | 130 | 121 | 880 | 49 | 2 | 931 | 11 | 5 | .998 |
| Wilson, Dan, Sea. | 103 | 91 | 611 | 37 | 2 | 650 | 6 | 0 | .997 |
| Zaun, Gregg, Tor. | 97 | 91 | 547 | 46 | 8 | 601 | 5 | 3 | .987 |

## CATCHERS WITH TWO OR MORE TEAMS

| Player, Team | G | GS | PO | A | E | TC | DP | PB | Pct. |
|---|---|---|---|---|---|---|---|---|---|
| Borders, Pat, Sea. | 19 | 17 | 121 | 9 | 1 | 131 | 1 | 1 | .992 |
| Borders, Pat, Min. | 19 | 14 | 82 | 9 | 3 | 94 | 3 | 0 | .968 |
| Davis, Ben, Sea. | 14 | 11 | 71 | 5 | 0 | 76 | 3 | 1 | 1.000 |
| Davis, Ben, Chi. | 53 | 44 | 329 | 17 | 3 | 349 | 1 | 5 | .991 |
| Huckaby, Ken, Tex. | 16 | 12 | 81 | 7 | 2 | 90 | 1 | 2 | .978 |
| Huckaby, Ken, Bal. | 8 | 4 | 25 | 2 | 0 | 27 | 0 | 1 | 1.000 |
| Martinez, Sandy, Cle. | 1 | 1 | 7 | 1 | 0 | 8 | 0 | 1 | 1.000 |
| Martinez, Sandy, Bos. | 3 | 0 | 6 | 0 | 0 | 6 | 0 | 1 | 1.000 |
| Olivo, Miguel, Chi. | 46 | 40 | 237 | 10 | 4 | 251 | 5 | 4 | .984 |
| Olivo, Miguel, Sea. | 49 | 43 | 273 | 19 | 1 | 293 | 2 | 9 | .997 |

## CATCHERS—SPECIAL STATS*

| Player, Team | G | Inn. | SBA | CCS | PCS | CS% | ER | CERA |
|---|---|---|---|---|---|---|---|---|
| Alomar Jr.,Sandy, CWS | 49 | 377.0 | 45 | 7 | 11 | .21 | 209 | 4.99 |
| Ardoin,Danny, Tex | 6 | 25.0 | 4 | 0 | 0 | 0 | 7 | 2.52 |
| Barajas,Rod, Tex | 105 | 908.2 | 64 | 16 | 6 | .28 | 454 | 4.50 |
| Bard,Josh, Cle | 7 | 53.0 | 6 | 2 | 0 | .33 | 23 | 3.91 |
| Blanco,Henry, Min | 114 | 872.1 | 61 | 25 | 5 | .45 | 412 | 4.25 |
| Borders,Pat, TOT | 38 | 258.2 | 28 | 12 | 0 | .43 | 137 | 4.77 |
| Borders,Pat, Sea | 19 | 138.0 | 13 | 7 | 0 | .54 | 77 | 5.02 |
| Borders,Pat, Min | 19 | 120.2 | 15 | 5 | 0 | .33 | 60 | 4.48 |
| Bowen,Rob, Min | 15 | 81.2 | 7 | 1 | 0 | .14 | 36 | 3.97 |
| Buck,John, KC | 68 | 575.0 | 44 | 7 | 7 | .19 | 338 | 5.29 |
| Burke,Jamie, CWS | 45 | 292.0 | 19 | 7 | 1 | .39 | 155 | 4.78 |
| Cash,Kevin, Tor | 60 | 460.1 | 34 | 14 | 1 | .42 | 260 | 5.08 |
| Castillo,Alberto, KC | 29 | 242.1 | 22 | 5 | 3 | .26 | 136 | 5.05 |
| Davis,Ben, TOT | 67 | 494.0 | 48 | 11 | 3 | .24 | 286 | 5.21 |
| Davis,Ben, Sea | 14 | 97.0 | 4 | 2 | 0 | .50 | 59 | 5.47 |
| Davis,Ben, CWS | 53 | 397.0 | 44 | 9 | 3 | .22 | 227 | 5.15 |
| DiFelice,Mike, Det | 12 | 59.0 | 2 | 1 | 0 | .50 | 32 | 4.88 |
| Dominique,Andy, Bos | 1 | 2.0 | 0 | 0 | 0 | 0 | 1 | 4.50 |
| Estalella,Bobby, Tor | 3 | 25.0 | 4 | 0 | 0 | 0 | 18 | 6.48 |
| Fick,Robert, TB | 3 | 5.0 | 0 | 0 | 0 | 0 | 1 | 1.80 |
| Flaherty,John, NYY | 46 | 328.1 | 30 | 5 | 2 | .18 | 180 | 4.93 |
| Fordyce,Brook, TB | 51 | 400.2 | 32 | 5 | 4 | .18 | 226 | 5.08 |
| Gil,Geronimo, Bal | 11 | 78.0 | 8 | 3 | 1 | .43 | 31 | 3.58 |
| Hall,Toby, TB | 119 | 1011.1 | 67 | 17 | 6 | .28 | 530 | 4.72 |
| Huckaby,Ken, TOT | 24 | 146.0 | 15 | 4 | 0 | .27 | 89 | 5.49 |
| Huckaby,Ken, Tex | 16 | 109.0 | 11 | 3 | 0 | .27 | 69 | 5.70 |
| Huckaby,Ken, Bal | 8 | 37.0 | 4 | 1 | 0 | .25 | 20 | 4.86 |
| Inge,Brandon, Det | 39 | 312.2 | 51 | 18 | 3 | .38 | 177 | 5.09 |
| Laird,Gerald, Tex | 49 | 397.0 | 31 | 12 | 2 | .41 | 194 | 4.40 |
| Laker,Tim, Cle | 41 | 298.2 | 29 | 7 | 0 | .24 | 143 | 4.31 |
| LeCroy,Matthew, Min | 26 | 144.1 | 16 | 1 | 0 | .06 | 57 | 3.55 |
| Lopez,Javy, Bal | 132 | 1092.1 | 94 | 20 | 6 | .23 | 567 | 4.67 |
| Machado,Robert, Bal | 35 | 188.2 | 11 | 7 | 0 | .64 | 96 | 4.58 |
| Martinez,Sandy, TOT | 4 | 18.0 | 3 | 1 | 0 | .33 | 6 | 3.00 |
| Martinez,Sandy, Cle | 1 | 7.0 | 3 | 1 | 0 | .33 | 5 | 6.43 |
| Martinez,Sandy, Bos | 3 | 11.0 | 0 | 0 | 0 | 0 | 1 | 0.82 |
| Martinez,Victor, Cle | 132 | 1108.0 | 119 | 25 | 5 | .22 | 613 | 4.98 |
| Mauer,Joe, Min | 32 | 257.0 | 18 | 5 | 2 | .31 | 96 | 3.36 |
| Melhuse,Adam, Oak | 64 | 504.2 | 40 | 8 | 5 | .23 | 227 | 4.05 |
| Miller,Damian, Oak | 109 | 963.2 | 81 | 18 | 17 | .28 | 454 | 4.24 |
| Mirabelli,Doug, Bos | 53 | 375.2 | 54 | 7 | 1 | .13 | 178 | 4.26 |
| Molina,Bengie, Ana | 89 | 762.0 | 69 | 17 | 1 | .25 | 365 | 4.31 |
| Molina,Jose, Ana | 70 | 524.1 | 45 | 19 | 3 | .45 | 251 | 4.31 |
| Munson,Eric, Det | 1 | 1.0 | 0 | 0 | 0 | 0 | 0 | 0.00 |
| Myers,Greg, Tor | 4 | 32.0 | 4 | 1 | 0 | .25 | 12 | 3.38 |
| Navarro,Dioner, NYY | 4 | 13.0 | 0 | 0 | 0 | 0 | 2 | 1.38 |
| Olivo,Miguel, TOT | 95 | 760.1 | 49 | 11 | 6 | .26 | 383 | 4.53 |
| Olivo,Miguel, CWS | 46 | 366.1 | 30 | 7 | 3 | .26 | 191 | 4.69 |
| Olivo,Miguel, Sea | 49 | 394.0 | 19 | 4 | 3 | .25 | 192 | 4.39 |
| Osik,Keith, Bal | 11 | 59.1 | 4 | 1 | 0 | .25 | 46 | 6.98 |
| Paul,Josh, Ana | 37 | 168.0 | 17 | 4 | 0 | .24 | 76 | 4.07 |
| Phillips,Paul, KC | 4 | 15.0 | 0 | 0 | 0 | 0 | 12 | 7.20 |
| Posada,Jorge, NYY | 134 | 1102.1 | 92 | 23 | 2 | .26 | 570 | 4.65 |
| Quiroz,Guillermo, Tor | 15 | 114.2 | 7 | 2 | 0 | .29 | 68 | 5.34 |
| Rivera,Rene, Sea | 2 | 3.0 | 0 | 0 | 0 | 0 | 0 | 0.00 |
| Rodriguez,Ivan, Det | 124 | 1051.0 | 59 | 16 | 3 | .29 | 568 | 4.86 |
| Rose,Mike, Oak | 2 | 3.0 | 2 | 0 | 1 | 0 | 1 | 3.00 |
| Santiago,Benito, KC | 49 | 416.0 | 36 | 6 | 2 | .18 | 215 | 4.65 |
| Shelton,Chris, Det | 6 | 16.0 | 0 | 0 | 0 | 0 | 11 | 6.19 |
| Stinnett,Kelly, KC | 20 | 155.0 | 16 | 2 | 3 | .15 | 96 | 5.57 |
| Tonis,Mike, KC | 2 | 17.0 | 1 | 0 | 0 | 0 | 16 | 8.47 |
| Varitek,Jason, Bos | 130 | 1062.2 | 100 | 20 | 3 | .21 | 494 | 4.18 |
| Wilson,Dan, Sea | 103 | 827.1 | 66 | 17 | 5 | .28 | 444 | 4.83 |
| Zaun,Gregg, Tor | 97 | 789.0 | 83 | 21 | 2 | .26 | 417 | 4.76 |
| **Average** | 48 | 375.0 | 32 | 8 | 2 | .31 | 193 | 4.63 |

***Inn.** denotes the number of innings the catcher was behind the plate. **SBA** denotes stolen bases attempted. **CCS** denotes number of runners caught stealing by the catcher. **PCS** denotes number of runners caught stealing by the pitcher. **CS%** denotes the catcher's caught stealing percentage, figured by subtracting PCS from SBA and dividing this number into CCS. **ER** denotes number of earned runs scored when catcher was behind the plate. **CERA** denotes catcher's ERA when he was behind the plate, figured the same way a pitcher's ERA is completed (ER*9/IP).

## PITCHERS

| Player, Team | G | GS | PO | A | E | TC | DP | Pct. |
|---|---|---|---|---|---|---|---|---|
| Abbott, Paul, TB. | 10 | 9 | 3 | 7 | 2 | 12 | 0 | .833 |
| Adams, Terry, Tor.-Bos. | 61 | 0 | 9 | 4 | 2 | 15 | 1 | .867 |
| Adkins, Jon, Chi. | 50 | 0 | 4 | 8 | 1 | 13 | 1 | .923 |
| Affeldt, Jeremy, K.C.* | 38 | 8 | 3 | 12 | 2 | 17 | 2 | .882 |
| Ainsworth, Kurt, Bal. | 7 | 7 | 2 | 2 | 0 | 4 | 1 | 1.000 |
| Almanzar, Carlos, Tex. | 67 | 0 | 1 | 12 | 0 | 13 | 0 | 1.000 |
| Alvarez, Abe, Bos.* | 1 | 1 | 1 | 0 | 0 | 1 | 0 | 1.000 |
| Anderson, Brian, K.C.* | 35 | 26 | 5 | 24 | 2 | 31 | 2 | .935 |
| Anderson, Jason, Cle. | 1 | 0 | 0 | 0 | 0 | 0 | 0 | .000 |
| Anderson, Jimmy, Bos.* | 5 | 0 | 1 | 0 | 0 | 1 | 0 | 1.000 |
| Appier, Kevin, K.C. | 2 | 2 | 1 | 1 | 0 | 2 | 0 | 1.000 |
| Arroyo, Bronson, Bos. | 32 | 29 | 24 | 16 | 2 | 42 | 2 | .952 |
| Astacio, Pedro, Bos. | 5 | 1 | 1 | 0 | 0 | 1 | 0 | 1.000 |
| Atchison, Scott, Sea. | 25 | 0 | 2 | 6 | 0 | 8 | 1 | 1.000 |
| Bacsik, Mike, Tex.* | 3 | 3 | 1 | 2 | 0 | 3 | 0 | 1.000 |
| Baek, Cha Seung, Sea. | 7 | 5 | 3 | 2 | 0 | 5 | 0 | 1.000 |
| Baez, Danys, TB. | 62 | 0 | 1 | 10 | 0 | 11 | 0 | 1.000 |
| Bajenaru, Jeff, Chi. | 9 | 0 | 0 | 0 | 0 | 0 | 0 | .000 |
| Balfour, Grant, Min. | 36 | 0 | 3 | 4 | 0 | 7 | 0 | 1.000 |
| Bartosh, Cliff, Cle.* | 34 | 0 | 1 | 0 | 0 | 1 | 0 | 1.000 |
| Batista, Miguel, Tor. | 38 | 31 | 18 | 30 | 1 | 49 | 5 | .980 |
| Bauer, Rick, Bal. | 23 | 2 | 3 | 9 | 0 | 12 | 1 | 1.000 |
| Bautista, Denny, Bal.-K.C. | 7 | 5 | 0 | 1 | 0 | 1 | 0 | 1.000 |
| Bedard, Erik, Bal.* | 27 | 26 | 10 | 9 | 0 | 19 | 0 | 1.000 |
| Beimel, Joe, Min.* | 3 | 0 | 0 | 0 | 0 | 0 | 0 | .000 |
| Bell, Rob, TB. | 24 | 19 | 17 | 11 | 1 | 29 | 0 | .966 |
| Benoit, Joaquin, Tex. | 28 | 15 | 6 | 6 | 1 | 13 | 1 | .923 |
| Bergman, Dusty, Ana.* | 1 | 0 | 0 | 0 | 0 | 0 | 0 | .000 |
| Betancourt, Rafael, Cle. | 68 | 0 | 2 | 3 | 0 | 5 | 0 | 1.000 |
| Bierbrodt, Nick, Tex.* | 4 | 4 | 1 | 4 | 0 | 5 | 0 | 1.000 |
| Blackley, Travis, Sea.* | 6 | 6 | 2 | 4 | 0 | 6 | 0 | 1.000 |
| Blanton, Joe, Oak. | 3 | 0 | 1 | 0 | 0 | 1 | 0 | 1.000 |
| Bonderman, Jeremy, Det. | 33 | 32 | 14 | 15 | 3 | 32 | 1 | .906 |
| Borkowski, Dave, Bal. | 17 | 8 | 1 | 2 | 2 | 5 | 1 | .600 |
| Bradford, Chad, Oak. | 68 | 0 | 5 | 13 | 2 | 20 | 0 | .900 |
| Brazelton, Dewon, TB. | 22 | 21 | 5 | 8 | 0 | 13 | 1 | 1.000 |
| Brocail, Doug, Tex. | 43 | 0 | 8 | 8 | 1 | 17 | 2 | .941 |
| Brown, Jamie, Bos. | 4 | 0 | 0 | 0 | 0 | 0 | 0 | .000 |
| Brown, Kevin, N.Y. | 22 | 22 | 8 | 11 | 4 | 23 | 2 | .826 |
| Buehrle, Mark, Chi.* | 35 | 35 | 16 | 51 | 4 | 71 | 3 | .944 |
| Bukvich, Ryan, K.C. | 9 | 0 | 0 | 0 | 0 | 0 | 0 | .000 |
| Bush, David, Tor. | 16 | 16 | 9 | 5 | 0 | 14 | 0 | 1.000 |
| Cabrera, Daniel, Bal. | 28 | 27 | 9 | 6 | 1 | 16 | 0 | .938 |
| Cabrera, Fernando, Cle. | 4 | 0 | 1 | 0 | 0 | 1 | 0 | 1.000 |
| Callaway, Mickey, Tex. | 4 | 3 | 2 | 2 | 0 | 4 | 1 | 1.000 |
| Camp, Shawn, K.C. | 42 | 0 | 3 | 13 | 0 | 16 | 0 | 1.000 |
| Carrasco, D.J., K.C. | 30 | 0 | 7 | 6 | 0 | 13 | 0 | 1.000 |
| Carter, Lance, TB. | 56 | 0 | 4 | 8 | 0 | 12 | 0 | 1.000 |
| Castillo, Frank, Bos. | 2 | 0 | 0 | 0 | 0 | 0 | 0 | .000 |
| Cerda, Jaime, K.C.* | 53 | 0 | 7 | 8 | 1 | 16 | 0 | .938 |
| Chacin, Gustavo, Tor.* | 2 | 2 | 1 | 1 | 0 | 2 | 0 | 1.000 |
| Chen, Bruce, Bal.* | 8 | 7 | 4 | 7 | 0 | 11 | 1 | 1.000 |
| Chulk, Vinnie, Tor. | 47 | 0 | 3 | 6 | 0 | 9 | 0 | 1.000 |
| Colome, Jesus, TB. | 33 | 0 | 2 | 7 | 0 | 9 | 0 | 1.000 |
| Colon, Bartolo, Ana. | 34 | 34 | 8 | 30 | 3 | 41 | 4 | .927 |
| Colyer, Steve, Det.* | 41 | 0 | 1 | 5 | 0 | 6 | 2 | 1.000 |
| Contreras, Jose, N.Y.-Chi. | 31 | 31 | 7 | 12 | 2 | 21 | 0 | .905 |
| Cordero, Francisco, Tex. | 67 | 0 | 6 | 8 | 0 | 14 | 2 | 1.000 |
| Cornejo, Nate, Det. | 5 | 5 | 2 | 7 | 0 | 9 | 2 | 1.000 |
| Cotts, Neal, Chi.* | 56 | 1 | 1 | 8 | 1 | 10 | 1 | .900 |
| Crain, Jesse, Min. | 22 | 0 | 2 | 3 | 1 | 6 | 1 | .833 |
| Cressend, Jack, Cle. | 11 | 0 | 3 | 2 | 0 | 5 | 0 | 1.000 |
| Cruceta, Francisco, Cle. | 2 | 2 | 0 | 0 | 0 | 0 | 0 | .000 |
| Cubillan, Darwin, Bal. | 7 | 0 | 1 | 1 | 1 | 3 | 0 | .667 |
| D'Amico, Jeff, Cle. | 7 | 7 | 2 | 4 | 0 | 6 | 1 | 1.000 |
| Darensbourg, Vic, Chi.* | 2 | 0 | 0 | 1 | 0 | 1 | 0 | 1.000 |
| Davis, Jason, Cle. | 26 | 19 | 10 | 21 | 3 | 34 | 0 | .912 |
| Dawley, Joe, Cle. | 2 | 2 | 2 | 2 | 0 | 4 | 1 | 1.000 |
| de los Santos, Valerio, Tor.* | 17 | 0 | 0 | 2 | 0 | 2 | 0 | 1.000 |
| DeJean, Mike, Bal. | 37 | 0 | 2 | 3 | 0 | 5 | 1 | 1.000 |
| Denney, Kyle, Cle. | 4 | 4 | 0 | 2 | 0 | 2 | 0 | 1.000 |
| DePaula, Jorge, N.Y. | 3 | 1 | 1 | 2 | 0 | 3 | 0 | 1.000 |
| Diaz, Felix, Chi. | 18 | 7 | 2 | 4 | 0 | 6 | 0 | 1.000 |
| Dickey, R.A., Tex. | 25 | 15 | 7 | 22 | 2 | 31 | 0 | .935 |
| DiNardo, Lenny, Bos.* | 22 | 0 | 4 | 3 | 2 | 9 | 0 | .778 |
| Dingman, Craig, Det. | 24 | 0 | 2 | 1 | 0 | 3 | 0 | 1.000 |
| Dominguez, Juan, Tex. | 4 | 4 | 0 | 3 | 0 | 3 | 0 | 1.000 |
| Donnelly, Brendan, Ana. | 40 | 0 | 2 | 2 | 0 | 4 | 0 | 1.000 |
| Dotel, Octavio, Oak. | 45 | 0 | 2 | 5 | 0 | 7 | 1 | 1.000 |
| Douglass, Sean, Tor. | 14 | 3 | 3 | 2 | 0 | 5 | 0 | 1.000 |
| Drese, Ryan, Tex. | 34 | 33 | 15 | 31 | 2 | 48 | 5 | .958 |
| DuBose, Eric, Bal.* | 14 | 14 | 0 | 18 | 2 | 20 | 1 | .900 |
| Duchscherer, Justin, Oak. | 53 | 0 | 5 | 20 | 0 | 25 | 1 | 1.000 |
| Dunn, Scott, Ana. | 3 | 0 | 0 | 0 | 0 | 0 | 0 | .000 |
| Durbin, Chad, Cle. | 17 | 8 | 4 | 4 | 1 | 9 | 0 | .889 |
| Durbin, J.D., Min. | 4 | 1 | 0 | 2 | 0 | 2 | 0 | 1.000 |
| Elarton, Scott, Cle. | 21 | 21 | 5 | 8 | 1 | 14 | 1 | .929 |
| Embree, Alan, Bos.* | 71 | 0 | 5 | 7 | 0 | 12 | 0 | 1.000 |
| Ennis, John, Det. | 12 | 0 | 2 | 0 | 0 | 2 | 0 | 1.000 |
| Erickson, Scott, Tex. | 4 | 4 | 1 | 1 | 0 | 2 | 0 | 1.000 |
| Escobar, Kelvim, Ana. | 33 | 33 | 16 | 24 | 0 | 40 | 1 | 1.000 |
| Field, Nate, K.C. | 43 | 0 | 2 | 3 | 0 | 5 | 0 | 1.000 |
| File, Bob, Tor. | 24 | 0 | 3 | 8 | 0 | 11 | 2 | 1.000 |
| Fortunato, Bartolome, TB. | 3 | 0 | 0 | 1 | 0 | 1 | 1 | 1.000 |
| Foulke, Keith, Bos. | 72 | 0 | 5 | 11 | 0 | 16 | 1 | 1.000 |
| Francisco, Frank, Tex. | 45 | 0 | 4 | 2 | 0 | 6 | 0 | 1.000 |
| Franklin, Ryan, Sea. | 32 | 32 | 16 | 19 | 3 | 38 | 2 | .921 |
| Frasor, Jason, Tor. | 63 | 0 | 8 | 8 | 0 | 16 | 1 | 1.000 |
| Frederick, Kevin, Tor. | 22 | 0 | 3 | 0 | 0 | 3 | 0 | 1.000 |
| Fultz, Aaron, Min.* | 55 | 0 | 2 | 8 | 0 | 10 | 0 | 1.000 |
| GARCIA, Freddy, Sea.-Chi. | 31 | 31 | 12 | 37 | 0 | 49 | 3 | 1.000 |
| Garcia, Jairo, Oak. | 4 | 0 | 1 | 2 | 0 | 3 | 0 | 1.000 |
| Garcia, Rosman, Tex. | 4 | 0 | 0 | 1 | 0 | 1 | 0 | 1.000 |
| Garland, Jon, Chi. | 34 | 33 | 21 | 35 | 2 | 58 | 3 | .966 |
| Gaudin, Chad, TB. | 26 | 4 | 1 | 5 | 1 | 7 | 0 | .857 |
| George, Chris, K.C.* | 10 | 7 | 2 | 7 | 1 | 10 | 1 | .900 |
| German, Franklyn, Det. | 16 | 0 | 2 | 0 | 1 | 3 | 0 | .667 |
| Glynn, Ryan, Tor. | 6 | 2 | 2 | 1 | 2 | 5 | 0 | .600 |
| Gobble, Jimmy, K.C.* | 25 | 24 | 8 | 10 | 3 | 21 | 0 | .857 |
| Gonzalez, Dicky, TB. | 4 | 0 | 1 | 1 | 0 | 2 | 0 | 1.000 |
| Gonzalez, Jeremi, TB. | 11 | 8 | 2 | 5 | 2 | 9 | 0 | .778 |
| Gordon, Tom, N.Y. | 80 | 0 | 6 | 13 | 1 | 20 | 1 | .950 |
| Graman, Alex, N.Y.* | 3 | 2 | 0 | 0 | 0 | 0 | 0 | .000 |
| Gregg, Kevin, Ana. | 55 | 0 | 2 | 5 | 0 | 7 | 1 | 1.000 |
| Greinke, Zack, K.C. | 24 | 24 | 13 | 15 | 0 | 28 | 1 | 1.000 |
| Greisinger, Seth, Min. | 12 | 9 | 2 | 6 | 2 | 10 | 0 | .800 |
| Grilli, Jason, Chi. | 8 | 8 | 2 | 3 | 2 | 7 | 0 | .714 |
| Grimsley, Jason, K.C.-Bal. | 73 | 0 | 10 | 12 | 4 | 26 | 0 | .846 |
| Groom, Buddy, Bal.* | 60 | 0 | 4 | 3 | 0 | 7 | 0 | 1.000 |
| Guardado, Eddie, Sea.* | 41 | 0 | 0 | 4 | 0 | 4 | 0 | 1.000 |
| Guerrier, Matt, Min. | 9 | 2 | 2 | 3 | 0 | 5 | 0 | 1.000 |
| Guthrie, Jeremy, Cle. | 6 | 0 | 0 | 2 | 0 | 2 | 0 | 1.000 |
| Halama, John, TB.* | 34 | 14 | 2 | 14 | 0 | 16 | 0 | 1.000 |
| Halladay, Roy, Tor. | 21 | 21 | 10 | 21 | 1 | 32 | 1 | .969 |
| Halsey, Brad, N.Y.* | 8 | 7 | 0 | 3 | 1 | 4 | 0 | .750 |
| Hammond, Chris, Oak.* | 41 | 0 | 1 | 10 | 1 | 12 | 0 | .917 |
| Harden, Rich, Oak. | 31 | 31 | 15 | 18 | 1 | 34 | 2 | .971 |
| Harper, Travis, TB. | 52 | 0 | 9 | 8 | 0 | 17 | 1 | 1.000 |
| Harville, Chad, Oak. | 3 | 0 | 0 | 0 | 0 | 0 | 0 | .000 |
| Hasegawa, Shigetoshi, Sea. | 68 | 0 | 6 | 8 | 1 | 15 | 0 | .933 |
| Hendrickson, Mark, TB.* | 32 | 30 | 13 | 27 | 0 | 40 | 2 | 1.000 |
| Hensley, Matt, Ana. | 16 | 0 | 4 | 3 | 0 | 7 | 0 | 1.000 |
| Hentgen, Pat, Tor. | 18 | 16 | 3 | 8 | 1 | 12 | 0 | .917 |
| Heredia, Felix, N.Y.* | 47 | 0 | 3 | 7 | 1 | 11 | 0 | .909 |
| Hernandez, Orlando, N.Y. | 15 | 15 | 10 | 7 | 0 | 17 | 1 | 1.000 |
| Howry, Bob, Cle. | 37 | 0 | 2 | 7 | 0 | 9 | 0 | 1.000 |
| Hudson, Tim, Oak. | 27 | 27 | 22 | 26 | 1 | 49 | 3 | .980 |
| Hughes, Travis, Tex. | 2 | 0 | 0 | 0 | 0 | 0 | 0 | .000 |
| Huisman, Justin, K.C. | 14 | 0 | 3 | 2 | 0 | 5 | 0 | 1.000 |
| Jackson, Mike, Chi. | 45 | 0 | 2 | 8 | 0 | 10 | 0 | 1.000 |
| Jarvis, Kevin, Sea. | 8 | 0 | 0 | 2 | 0 | 2 | 0 | 1.000 |
| Jimenez, Jose, Cle. | 31 | 0 | 2 | 9 | 0 | 11 | 1 | 1.000 |
| Johnson, Jason, Det. | 33 | 33 | 10 | 17 | 3 | 30 | 1 | .900 |
| Jones, Bobby M., Bos.* | 3 | 0 | 0 | 1 | 0 | 1 | 0 | 1.000 |
| Julio, Jorge, Bal. | 65 | 0 | 3 | 3 | 0 | 6 | 0 | 1.000 |
| Karsay, Steve, N.Y. | 7 | 0 | 1 | 1 | 1 | 3 | 0 | .667 |
| Kazmir, Scott, TB.* | 8 | 7 | 2 | 3 | 1 | 6 | 0 | .833 |
| Kershner, Jason, Tor.* | 24 | 2 | 1 | 4 | 0 | 5 | 0 | 1.000 |
| Kida, Masao, Sea. | 7 | 0 | 1 | 0 | 0 | 1 | 1 | 1.000 |
| Kim, Byung-Hyun, Bos. | 7 | 3 | 3 | 3 | 1 | 7 | 0 | .857 |
| Kinney, Matt, K.C. | 11 | 0 | 1 | 0 | 0 | 1 | 0 | 1.000 |
| Knotts, Gary, Det. | 36 | 19 | 14 | 11 | 0 | 25 | 1 | 1.000 |
| Koch, Billy, Chi. | 24 | 0 | 1 | 1 | 1 | 3 | 0 | .667 |
| Lackey, John, Ana. | 33 | 32 | 15 | 23 | 0 | 38 | 1 | 1.000 |
| Laker, Tim, Cle. | 1 | 0 | 0 | 0 | 0 | 0 | 0 | .000 |
| League, Brandon, Tor. | 3 | 0 | 0 | 0 | 0 | 0 | 0 | .000 |
| Ledezma, Wilfredo, Det.* | 15 | 8 | 5 | 2 | 2 | 9 | 0 | .778 |
| Lee, Cliff, Cle.* | 33 | 33 | 5 | 7 | 0 | 12 | 0 | 1.000 |
| Lee, Dave, Cle. | 4 | 0 | 0 | 0 | 1 | 1 | 0 | .000 |
| Lehr, Justin, Oak. | 27 | 0 | 2 | 5 | 0 | 7 | 0 | 1.000 |
| Leskanic, Curtis, K.C.-Bos. | 51 | 0 | 1 | 3 | 0 | 4 | 0 | 1.000 |
| Levine, Al, Det. | 65 | 0 | 2 | 8 | 1 | 11 | 0 | .909 |
| Lewis, Colby, Tex. | 3 | 3 | 1 | 2 | 0 | 3 | 0 | 1.000 |
| Lieber, Jon, N.Y. | 27 | 27 | 10 | 19 | 4 | 33 | 1 | .879 |
| Ligtenberg, Kerry, Tor. | 57 | 0 | 1 | 5 | 0 | 6 | 0 | 1.000 |
| Lilly, Ted, Tor.* | 32 | 32 | 11 | 9 | 2 | 22 | 0 | .909 |

| Player, Team | G | GS | PO | A | E | TC | DP | Pct. |
|---|---|---|---|---|---|---|---|---|
| Loaiza, Esteban, Chi.-N.Y. | 31 | 27 | 13 | 29 | 0 | 42 | 4 | 1.000 |
| Loe, Kameron, Tex. | 2 | 1 | 0 | 1 | 1 | 2 | 0 | .500 |
| Lohse, Kyle, Min. | 35 | 34 | 12 | 22 | 0 | 34 | 1 | 1.000 |
| Lopez, Aquilino, Tor. | 18 | 0 | 0 | 3 | 0 | 3 | 0 | 1.000 |
| Lopez, Rodrigo, Bal. | 37 | 23 | 15 | 22 | 0 | 37 | 2 | 1.000 |
| Lowe, Derek, Bos. | 33 | 33 | 22 | 39 | 3 | 64 | 1 | .953 |
| MacDougal, Mike, K.C. | 13 | 0 | 2 | 1 | 0 | 3 | 0 | 1.000 |
| Madritsch, Bobby, Sea.* | 15 | 11 | 2 | 12 | 0 | 14 | 1 | 1.000 |
| Mahay, Ron, Tex.* | 60 | 0 | 3 | 9 | 0 | 12 | 1 | 1.000 |
| Maine, John, Bal. | 1 | 1 | 1 | 0 | 0 | 1 | 1 | 1.000 |
| Malaska, Mark, Bos.* | 19 | 0 | 1 | 6 | 1 | 8 | 0 | .875 |
| Maroth, Mike, Det.* | 33 | 33 | 11 | 37 | 0 | 48 | 5 | 1.000 |
| Marsonek, Sam, N.Y. | 1 | 0 | 0 | 0 | 0 | 0 | 0 | .000 |
| Marte, Damaso, Chi.* | 74 | 0 | 4 | 4 | 0 | 8 | 1 | 1.000 |
| Martinez, Anastacio, Bos. | 11 | 0 | 1 | 0 | 0 | 1 | 0 | 1.000 |
| Martinez, Pedro, Bos. | 33 | 33 | 16 | 16 | 1 | 33 | 0 | .970 |
| Mateo, Julio, Sea. | 45 | 0 | 3 | 1 | 3 | 7 | 1 | .571 |
| Maurer, Dave, Tor.* | 3 | 0 | 0 | 1 | 0 | 1 | 0 | 1.000 |
| May, Darrell, K.C.* | 31 | 31 | 8 | 12 | 0 | 20 | 0 | 1.000 |
| McCarty, Dave, Bos.* | 3 | 0 | 0 | 1 | 0 | 1 | 0 | 1.000 |
| Meche, Gil, Sea. | 23 | 23 | 5 | 7 | 1 | 13 | 0 | .923 |
| Mecir, Jim, Oak. | 65 | 0 | 1 | 3 | 0 | 4 | 0 | 1.000 |
| Mendoza, Ramiro, Bos. | 27 | 0 | 4 | 5 | 0 | 9 | 0 | 1.000 |
| Menechino, Frank, Tor. | 1 | 0 | 0 | 0 | 0 | 0 | 0 | .000 |
| Miller, Justin, Tor. | 19 | 15 | 9 | 7 | 1 | 17 | 1 | .941 |
| Miller, Matt, Cle. | 57 | 0 | 1 | 9 | 1 | 11 | 0 | .909 |
| Miller, Trever, TB.* | 60 | 0 | 4 | 9 | 0 | 13 | 1 | 1.000 |
| Moss, Damian, TB.* | 5 | 2 | 0 | 0 | 1 | 1 | 0 | .000 |
| Moyer, Jamie, Sea.* | 34 | 33 | 14 | 24 | 0 | 38 | 3 | 1.000 |
| Mulder, Mark, Oak.* | 33 | 33 | 6 | 51 | 3 | 60 | 3 | .950 |
| Mulholland, Terry, Min.* | 39 | 15 | 6 | 13 | 3 | 22 | 1 | .864 |
| Munoz, Arnie, Chi.* | 11 | 1 | 1 | 2 | 0 | 3 | 0 | 1.000 |
| Mussina, Mike, N.Y. | 27 | 27 | 11 | 28 | 2 | 41 | 1 | .951 |
| Myers, Mike, Sea.-Bos.* | 75 | 0 | 0 | 10 | 0 | 10 | 0 | 1.000 |
| Nageotte, Clint, Sea. | 12 | 5 | 4 | 8 | 0 | 12 | 0 | 1.000 |
| Nakamura, Mike, Tor. | 19 | 0 | 2 | 1 | 1 | 4 | 0 | .750 |
| Narron, Sam, Tex.* | 1 | 1 | 0 | 2 | 0 | 2 | 0 | 1.000 |
| Nathan, Joe, Min. | 73 | 0 | 1 | 6 | 0 | 7 | 1 | 1.000 |
| Nelson, Jeff, Tex. | 29 | 0 | 0 | 2 | 0 | 2 | 0 | 1.000 |
| Nelson, Joe, Bos. | 3 | 0 | 0 | 0 | 0 | 0 | 0 | .000 |
| Nitkowski, C.J., N.Y.* | 19 | 0 | 0 | 3 | 0 | 3 | 0 | 1.000 |
| Novoa, Roberto, Det. | 16 | 0 | 1 | 4 | 0 | 5 | 0 | 1.000 |
| Nunez, Franklin, TB. | 8 | 0 | 1 | 1 | 0 | 2 | 0 | 1.000 |
| Ortiz, Ramon, Ana. | 34 | 14 | 6 | 13 | 2 | 21 | 1 | .905 |
| Osborne, Donovan, N.Y.* | 9 | 2 | 1 | 6 | 0 | 7 | 1 | 1.000 |
| Padilla, Juan, N.Y. | 6 | 0 | 0 | 2 | 0 | 2 | 2 | 1.000 |
| Park, Chan Ho, Tex. | 16 | 16 | 6 | 10 | 2 | 18 | 0 | .889 |
| Parrish, John, Bal.* | 56 | 1 | 8 | 11 | 6 | 25 | 1 | .760 |
| Patterson, Danny, Det. | 37 | 0 | 3 | 1 | 2 | 6 | 0 | .667 |
| Percival, Troy, Ana. | 52 | 0 | 1 | 3 | 0 | 4 | 0 | 1.000 |
| Peterson, Adam, Tor. | 3 | 0 | 0 | 0 | 0 | 0 | 0 | .000 |
| Pineiro, Joel, Sea. | 21 | 21 | 12 | 11 | 1 | 24 | 1 | .958 |
| Politte, Cliff, Chi. | 54 | 0 | 0 | 4 | 0 | 4 | 0 | 1.000 |
| Ponson, Sidney, Bal. | 33 | 33 | 21 | 28 | 1 | 50 | 4 | .980 |
| Pote, Lou, Cle. | 2 | 0 | 0 | 1 | 0 | 1 | 0 | 1.000 |
| Powell, Jay, Tex. | 23 | 0 | 1 | 2 | 0 | 3 | 0 | 1.000 |
| Prinz, Bret, N.Y. | 26 | 0 | 0 | 3 | 0 | 3 | 0 | 1.000 |
| Proctor, Scott, N.Y. | 26 | 0 | 1 | 3 | 0 | 4 | 0 | 1.000 |
| Pulido, Carlos, Min.* | 6 | 0 | 0 | 0 | 0 | 0 | 0 | .000 |
| Putz, J.J., Sea. | 54 | 0 | 4 | 9 | 0 | 13 | 1 | 1.000 |
| Quantrill, Paul, N.Y. | 86 | 0 | 1 | 13 | 0 | 14 | 0 | 1.000 |
| Radke, Brad, Min. | 34 | 34 | 17 | 21 | 1 | 39 | 2 | .974 |
| Rakers, Aaron, Bal. | 3 | 0 | 0 | 1 | 0 | 1 | 0 | 1.000 |
| Ramirez, Erasmo, Tex.* | 34 | 0 | 2 | 3 | 0 | 5 | 0 | 1.000 |
| Rauch, Jon, Chi. | 2 | 2 | 0 | 0 | 0 | 0 | 0 | .000 |
| Redman, Mark, Oak.* | 32 | 32 | 9 | 25 | 1 | 35 | 2 | .971 |
| Regilio, Nick, Tex. | 6 | 4 | 2 | 4 | 0 | 6 | 1 | 1.000 |
| Reyes, Dennys, K.C.* | 40 | 12 | 4 | 17 | 5 | 26 | 0 | .808 |
| Rhodes, Arthur, Oak.* | 37 | 0 | 0 | 8 | 0 | 8 | 0 | 1.000 |
| Riley, Matt, Bal.* | 14 | 13 | 1 | 5 | 5 | 11 | 1 | .545 |
| Rincon, Juan, Min. | 77 | 0 | 3 | 6 | 3 | 12 | 0 | .750 |
| Rincon, Ricardo, Oak.* | 67 | 0 | 1 | 2 | 0 | 3 | 0 | 1.000 |
| Riske, David, Cle. | 72 | 0 | 7 | 4 | 0 | 11 | 1 | 1.000 |
| Ritchie, Todd, TB. | 4 | 2 | 0 | 0 | 0 | 0 | 0 | .000 |
| Rivera, Mariano, N.Y. | 74 | 0 | 9 | 31 | 1 | 41 | 1 | .976 |
| Roa, Joe, Min. | 48 | 0 | 5 | 9 | 1 | 15 | 1 | .933 |
| Robbins, Jake, Cle. | 2 | 0 | 0 | 0 | 0 | 0 | 0 | .000 |
| Robertson, Jeriome, Cle.* | 8 | 0 | 1 | 2 | 0 | 3 | 0 | 1.000 |
| Robertson, Nate, Det.* | 34 | 32 | 4 | 25 | 5 | 34 | 5 | .853 |
| Rodriguez, Eddy, Bal. | 29 | 0 | 0 | 5 | 0 | 5 | 1 | 1.000 |
| Rodriguez, Francisco, Ana. | 69 | 0 | 5 | 9 | 0 | 14 | 0 | 1.000 |
| Rodriguez, Ricardo, Tex. | 5 | 4 | 3 | 3 | 0 | 6 | 0 | 1.000 |

| Player, Team | G | GS | PO | A | E | TC | DP | Pct. |
|---|---|---|---|---|---|---|---|---|
| Rogers, Kenny, Tex.* | 35 | 35 | 16 | 48 | 1 | 65 | 2 | .985 |
| Romero, J.C., Min.* | 74 | 0 | 7 | 8 | 0 | 15 | 2 | 1.000 |
| Ryan, B.J., Bal.* | 76 | 0 | 3 | 6 | 1 | 10 | 0 | .900 |
| Saarloos, Kirk, Oak. | 6 | 5 | 2 | 9 | 0 | 11 | 1 | 1.000 |
| Sabathia, C.C., Cle.* | 30 | 30 | 1 | 17 | 0 | 18 | 2 | 1.000 |
| Santana, Johan, Min.* | 34 | 34 | 9 | 24 | 4 | 37 | 2 | .892 |
| Schilling, Curt, Bos. | 32 | 32 | 16 | 14 | 0 | 30 | 2 | 1.000 |
| Schoeneweis, Scott, Chi.* | 20 | 19 | 7 | 21 | 0 | 28 | 3 | 1.000 |
| Seanez, Rudy, K.C. | 16 | 0 | 5 | 2 | 0 | 7 | 0 | 1.000 |
| Seay, Bobby, TB.* | 21 | 0 | 1 | 3 | 0 | 4 | 0 | 1.000 |
| Seibel, Phil, Bos.* | 2 | 0 | 0 | 1 | 0 | 1 | 0 | 1.000 |
| Sele, Aaron, Ana. | 28 | 24 | 3 | 10 | 2 | 15 | 2 | .867 |
| Serrano, Jimmy, K.C. | 10 | 5 | 2 | 3 | 0 | 5 | 0 | 1.000 |
| Sherrill, George, Sea.* | 21 | 0 | 0 | 4 | 0 | 4 | 0 | 1.000 |
| Shields, Scot, Ana. | 60 | 0 | 6 | 13 | 1 | 20 | 0 | .950 |
| Shouse, Brian, Tex.* | 53 | 0 | 9 | 11 | 0 | 20 | 0 | 1.000 |
| Silva, Carlos, Min. | 33 | 33 | 11 | 25 | 2 | 38 | 1 | .947 |
| Snare, Ryan, Tex.* | 1 | 0 | 0 | 0 | 0 | 0 | 0 | .000 |
| Soriano, Rafael, Sea. | 6 | 0 | 0 | 0 | 1 | 1 | 0 | .000 |
| Sosa, Jorge, TB. | 43 | 8 | 2 | 7 | 0 | 9 | 1 | 1.000 |
| Speier, Justin, Tor. | 62 | 0 | 1 | 5 | 2 | 8 | 1 | .750 |
| Standridge, Jason, TB. | 3 | 1 | 2 | 1 | 0 | 3 | 0 | 1.000 |
| Stanford, Jason, Cle.* | 2 | 2 | 2 | 2 | 0 | 4 | 1 | 1.000 |
| Stewart, Josh, Chi.* | 3 | 2 | 0 | 1 | 0 | 1 | 0 | 1.000 |
| Stewart, Scott, Cle.* | 23 | 0 | 0 | 3 | 0 | 3 | 0 | 1.000 |
| Sturtze, Tanyon, N.Y. | 28 | 3 | 1 | 10 | 0 | 11 | 1 | 1.000 |
| Sullivan, Scott, K.C. | 49 | 0 | 1 | 5 | 1 | 7 | 3 | .857 |
| Tadano, Kazuhito, Cle. | 14 | 4 | 3 | 6 | 0 | 9 | 0 | 1.000 |
| Takatsu, Shingo, Chi. | 59 | 0 | 1 | 10 | 0 | 11 | 0 | 1.000 |
| Taylor, Aaron, Sea. | 5 | 0 | 1 | 0 | 0 | 1 | 0 | 1.000 |
| Tejera, Michael, Tex.* | 6 | 0 | 1 | 0 | 0 | 1 | 0 | 1.000 |
| Thomas, Brad, Min.* | 3 | 0 | 0 | 1 | 0 | 1 | 0 | 1.000 |
| Thornton, Matt, Sea.* | 19 | 1 | 0 | 4 | 0 | 4 | 1 | 1.000 |
| Timlin, Mike, Bos. | 76 | 0 | 9 | 6 | 0 | 15 | 0 | 1.000 |
| Towers, Josh, Tor. | 21 | 21 | 9 | 13 | 2 | 24 | 1 | .917 |
| Turnbow, Derrick, Ana. | 4 | 0 | 2 | 1 | 0 | 3 | 0 | 1.000 |
| Urbina, Ugueth, Det. | 54 | 0 | 2 | 2 | 0 | 4 | 0 | 1.000 |
| Urdaneta, Lino, Det. | 1 | 0 | 0 | 0 | 0 | 0 | 0 | .000 |
| Vasquez, Jorge, K.C. | 2 | 0 | 0 | 1 | 0 | 1 | 0 | 1.000 |
| Vazquez, Javier, N.Y. | 32 | 32 | 9 | 37 | 2 | 48 | 4 | .958 |
| Villacis, Eduardo, K.C. | 1 | 1 | 0 | 1 | 1 | 2 | 0 | .500 |
| Villone, Ron, Sea.* | 56 | 10 | 6 | 17 | 4 | 27 | 2 | .852 |
| Waechter, Doug, TB. | 14 | 14 | 5 | 5 | 1 | 11 | 0 | .909 |
| Wakefield, Tim, Bos. | 32 | 30 | 12 | 27 | 4 | 43 | 1 | .907 |
| Walker, Jamie, Det.* | 70 | 0 | 2 | 4 | 0 | 6 | 0 | 1.000 |
| Wasdin, John, Tex. | 15 | 10 | 3 | 6 | 0 | 9 | 0 | 1.000 |
| Washburn, Jarrod, Ana.* | 25 | 25 | 3 | 22 | 1 | 26 | 2 | .962 |
| Webb, John, TB. | 4 | 0 | 0 | 0 | 0 | 0 | 0 | .000 |
| Weber, Ben, Ana. | 18 | 0 | 0 | 0 | 0 | 0 | 0 | .000 |
| Westbrook, Jake, Cle. | 33 | 30 | 24 | 49 | 3 | 76 | 6 | .961 |
| White, Gabe, N.Y.* | 24 | 0 | 0 | 2 | 0 | 2 | 0 | 1.000 |
| White, Rick, Cle. | 59 | 0 | 6 | 14 | 0 | 20 | 1 | 1.000 |
| Wickman, Bob, Cle. | 30 | 0 | 3 | 3 | 0 | 6 | 1 | 1.000 |
| Williams, Randy, Sea.* | 6 | 0 | 0 | 1 | 0 | 1 | 1 | 1.000 |
| Williams, Todd, Bal. | 29 | 0 | 2 | 4 | 0 | 6 | 0 | 1.000 |
| Williamson, Scott, Bos. | 28 | 0 | 3 | 2 | 0 | 5 | 0 | 1.000 |
| Wood, Mike, K.C. | 17 | 17 | 8 | 19 | 3 | 30 | 1 | .900 |
| Wright, Dan, Chi. | 4 | 4 | 1 | 2 | 1 | 4 | 0 | .750 |
| Wunsch, Kelly, Chi.* | 3 | 0 | 0 | 1 | 0 | 1 | 0 | 1.000 |
| Yan, Esteban, Det. | 69 | 0 | 12 | 14 | 2 | 28 | 1 | .929 |
| Young, Chris, Tex. | 7 | 7 | 2 | 3 | 1 | 6 | 0 | .833 |
| Zambrano, Victor, TB. | 23 | 22 | 10 | 14 | 1 | 25 | 1 | .960 |
| Zito, Barry, Oak.* | 34 | 34 | 5 | 31 | 2 | 38 | 1 | .947 |

## PITCHERS WITH TWO OR MORE TEAMS

| Player, Team | G | GS | PO | A | E | TC | DP | Pct. |
|---|---|---|---|---|---|---|---|---|
| Adams, Terry, Tor. | 42 | 0 | 6 | 3 | 1 | 10 | 1 | .900 |
| Adams, Terry, Bos. | 19 | 0 | 3 | 1 | 1 | 5 | 0 | .800 |
| Bautista, Denny, Bal. | 2 | 0 | 0 | 0 | 0 | 0 | 0 | .000 |
| Bautista, Denny, K.C. | 5 | 5 | 0 | 1 | 0 | 1 | 0 | 1.000 |
| Contreras, Jose, N.Y. | 18 | 18 | 1 | 6 | 1 | 8 | 0 | .875 |
| Contreras, Jose, Chi. | 13 | 13 | 6 | 6 | 1 | 13 | 0 | .923 |
| Garcia, Freddy, Sea. | 15 | 15 | 6 | 24 | 0 | 30 | 1 | 1.000 |
| Garcia, Freddy, Chi. | 16 | 16 | 6 | 13 | 0 | 19 | 2 | 1.000 |
| Grimsley, Jason, K.C. | 32 | 0 | 3 | 7 | 2 | 12 | 0 | .833 |
| Grimsley, Jason, Bal. | 41 | 0 | 7 | 5 | 2 | 14 | 0 | .857 |
| Leskanic, Curtis, K.C. | 19 | 0 | 1 | 1 | 0 | 2 | 0 | 1.000 |
| Leskanic, Curtis, Bos. | 32 | 0 | 0 | 2 | 0 | 2 | 0 | 1.000 |
| Loaiza, Esteban, Chi. | 21 | 21 | 10 | 23 | 0 | 33 | 4 | 1.000 |
| Loaiza, Esteban, N.Y. | 10 | 6 | 3 | 6 | 0 | 9 | 0 | 1.000 |
| Myers, Mike, Sea.* | 50 | 0 | 0 | 5 | 0 | 5 | 0 | 1.000 |
| Myers, Mike, Bos.* | 25 | 0 | 0 | 5 | 0 | 5 | 0 | 1.000 |

# MISCELLANEOUS

## SHUTOUT GAMES

Read across for wins, down for losses.

| Team | Oak. | K.C. | N.Y. | Min. | Sea. | Cle. | Bos. | Tor. | Ana. | TB. | Chi. | Det. | Tex. | Bal. | N.L. | W | L | Pct. |
|---|---|---|---|---|---|---|---|---|---|---|---|---|---|---|---|---|---|---|
| Boston | .. | 1 | 0 | 0 | 0 | 0 | 2 | 0 | 1 | 1 | 1 | 1 | 3 | 0 | 2 | 12 | 3 | .800 |
| Oakland | 0 | .. | 0 | 0 | 1 | 1 | 0 | 0 | 2 | 2 | 0 | 0 | 1 | 1 | 0 | 8 | 3 | .727 |
| Minnesota | 0 | 0 | .. | 0 | 1 | 1 | 1 | 0 | 0 | 1 | 0 | 1 | 0 | 4 | 0 | 9 | 4 | .692 |
| Detroit | 0 | 0 | 2 | .. | 0 | 0 | 0 | 1 | 1 | 0 | 1 | 1 | 1 | 2 | 0 | 9 | 5 | .643 |
| Cleveland | 0 | 1 | 0 | 0 | .. | 1 | 0 | 1 | 1 | 1 | 1 | 1 | 1 | 0 | 0 | 8 | 6 | .571 |
| Anaheim | 0 | 1 | 1 | 0 | 0 | .. | 2 | 2 | 0 | 0 | 2 | 0 | 1 | 1 | 1 | 11 | 10 | .524 |
| Texas | 0 | 0 | 0 | 1 | 1 | 2 | .. | 0 | 1 | 0 | 0 | 3 | 1 | 0 | 0 | 9 | 9 | .500 |
| Chicago | 0 | 0 | 1 | 0 | 2 | 0 | 2 | .. | 0 | 1 | 0 | 0 | 1 | 1 | 0 | 8 | 8 | .500 |
| Toronto | 1 | 0 | 0 | 1 | 0 | 1 | 0 | 0 | .. | 1 | 1 | 0 | 3 | 0 | 3 | 11 | 12 | .478 |
| Baltimore | 0 | 0 | 0 | 2 | 0 | 1 | 0 | 1 | 3 | .. | 1 | 0 | 1 | 0 | 1 | 10 | 12 | .455 |
| New York | 0 | 0 | 0 | 0 | 0 | 0 | 0 | 0 | 2 | 0 | .. | 1 | 0 | 2 | 0 | 5 | 7 | .417 |
| Seattle | 1 | 0 | 0 | 0 | 0 | 1 | 1 | 0 | 0 | 1 | 0 | .. | 0 | 0 | 3 | 7 | 12 | .368 |
| Tampa Bay | 0 | 0 | 0 | 0 | 0 | 0 | 0 | 1 | 0 | 1 | 0 | 1 | .. | 1 | 1 | 5 | 13 | .278 |
| Kansas City | 0 | 0 | 0 | 1 | 0 | 0 | 0 | 1 | 0 | 1 | 0 | 0 | 0 | .. | 0 | 3 | 13 | .188 |
| N.L. Clubs | 1 | 0 | 0 | 0 | 1 | 2 | 1 | 1 | 1 | 2 | 0 | 3 | 0 | 1 | .. | .. | .. | .. |
| **Lost** | 3 | 3 | 4 | 5 | 6 | 10 | 9 | 8 | 12 | 12 | 7 | 12 | 13 | 13 | 11 | 115 | 117 | .496 |

A.L. shutouts vs N.L. clubs (11): Baltimore vs Atlanta, Boston vs San Diego, Boston vs Colorado, Anaheim vs Los Angeles, Seattle vs Houston, Seattle vs Montreal 2, Toronto vs Los Angeles, Toronto vs Montreal, Toronto vs San Diego, Tampa Bay vs Florida.

## HOME RECORD

Read across for home wins, down for road losses.

| Team | Oak. | Bos. | Chi. | Sea. | N.Y. | Min. | Ana. | Tex. | Tor. | Bal. | K.C. | Cle. | TB. | Det. | N.L. | W | L | Pct. |
|---|---|---|---|---|---|---|---|---|---|---|---|---|---|---|---|---|---|---|
| New York | .. | 5 | 5 | 2 | 3 | 2 | 2 | 2 | 10 | 6 | 7 | 1 | 2 | 3 | 7 | 57 | 24 | .704 |
| Boston | 7 | .. | 5 | 4 | 1 | 1 | 3 | 1 | 8 | 8 | 3 | 4 | 2 | 2 | 6 | 55 | 26 | .679 |
| Oakland | 1 | 0 | .. | 6 | 2 | 5 | 4 | 2 | 3 | 4 | 4 | 3 | 7 | 4 | 7 | 52 | 29 | .642 |
| Texas | 3 | 3 | 5 | .. | 2 | 2 | 5 | 3 | 5 | 6 | 2 | 1 | 7 | 1 | 6 | 51 | 30 | .630 |
| Minnesota | 2 | 2 | 1 | 3 | .. | 4 | 3 | 7 | 3 | 2 | 1 | 5 | 3 | 8 | 5 | 49 | 32 | .605 |
| Chicago | 1 | 0 | 1 | 2 | 3 | .. | 3 | 4 | 2 | 3 | 2 | 5 | 6 | 8 | 6 | 46 | 35 | .568 |
| Anaheim | 1 | 4 | 5 | 4 | 2 | 2 | .. | 1 | 4 | 1 | 4 | 5 | 6 | 3 | 3 | 45 | 36 | .556 |
| Cleveland | 1 | 2 | 5 | 1 | 5 | 3 | 0 | .. | 3 | 3 | 3 | 5 | 1 | 6 | 6 | 44 | 37 | .543 |
| Tampa Bay | 4 | 3 | 2 | 1 | 2 | 1 | 1 | 3 | .. | 6 | 4 | 1 | 2 | 4 | 7 | 41 | 39 | .513 |
| Toronto | 4 | 4 | 1 | 2 | 1 | 3 | 3 | 2 | 6 | .. | 2 | 0 | 5 | 2 | 5 | 40 | 41 | .494 |
| Baltimore | 2 | 4 | 0 | 4 | 2 | 1 | 1 | 3 | 5 | 4 | .. | 3 | 5 | 1 | 3 | 38 | 43 | .469 |
| Detroit | 2 | 1 | 1 | 2 | 2 | 7 | 1 | 5 | 1 | 1 | 0 | .. | 3 | 5 | 7 | 38 | 43 | .469 |
| Seattle | 2 | 3 | 5 | 5 | 4 | 2 | 3 | 2 | 0 | 1 | 1 | 1 | .. | 4 | 5 | 38 | 44 | .463 |
| Kansas City | 1 | 1 | 0 | 2 | 6 | 4 | 0 | 5 | 1 | 2 | 1 | 6 | 1 | .. | 3 | 33 | 47 | .413 |
| N.L. Clubs | 6 | 6 | 6 | 5 | 3 | 7 | 5 | 5 | 1 | 6 | 7 | 7 | 5 | 6 | .. | .. | .. | .. |
| **Lost on Road** | 37 | 38 | 42 | 43 | 38 | 44 | 34 | 45 | 52 | 53 | 41 | 47 | 55 | 57 | 76 | 627 | 506 | .553 |

## HOME RECORDS IN INTERLEAGUE GAMES

| Team | | | | Total | Team | | | | Total |
|---|---|---|---|---|---|---|---|---|---|
| Anaheim | 1-2 vs. Mil. | 1-2 vs. Chi. | 1-2 vs. L.A. | 3-6 | Minnesota | 1-2 vs. Mil. | 3-0 vs. N.Y. | 1-2 vs. Phi. | 5-4 |
| Baltimore | 1-2 vs. Atl. | 1-2 vs. S.F. | 1-2 vs. Ari. | 3-6 | New York | 2-1 vs. N.Y. | 2-1 vs. S.D. | 3-0 vs. Col. | 7-2 |
| Boston | 2-1 vs. L.A. | 2-1 vs. Phi. | 2-1 vs. S.D. | 6-3 | Oakland | 3-0 vs. Cin. | 3-0 vs. Pit. | 1-2 vs. S.F. | 7-2 |
| Chicago | 2-1 vs. Atl. | 2-1 vs. Chi. | 2-1 vs. Phi. | 6-3 | Seattle | 1-2 vs. Hou. | 3-0 vs. Mon. | 1-2 vs. S.D. | 5-4 |
| Cleveland | 3-0 vs. Cin. | 2-1 vs. Col. | 1-2 vs. Fla. | 6-3 | Tampa Bay | 2-1 vs. S.F. | 3-0 vs. Col. | 2-1 vs. Fla. | 7-2 |
| Detroit | 2-1 vs. Atl. | 2-1 vs. Fla. | 3-0 vs. Ari. | 7-2 | Texas | 2-1 vs. Hou. | 3-0 vs. Pit. | 1-2 vs. St.L. | 6-3 |
| Kansas City | 1-2 vs. Mon. | 2-1 vs. N.Y. | 0-3 vs. St.L. | 3-6 | Toronto | 2-1 vs. L.A. | 2-1 vs. Mon. | 1-2 vs. Ari. | 5-4 |

## ROAD RECORD

Read across for road wins, down for home losses.

| Team | N.Y. | Tor. | Sea. | K.C. | Bos. | Min. | Oak. | Chi. | Ana. | Bal. | Cle. | Tex. | TB. | Det. | N.L. | W | L | Pct. |
|---|---|---|---|---|---|---|---|---|---|---|---|---|---|---|---|---|---|---|
| Anaheim | .. | 4 | 0 | 3 | 2 | 5 | 5 | 3 | 3 | 2 | 2 | 3 | 7 | 4 | 4 | 47 | 34 | .580 |
| New York | 2 | .. | 3 | 1 | 7 | 2 | 3 | 2 | 2 | 2 | 5 | 6 | 4 | 2 | 3 | 44 | 37 | .543 |
| Boston | 2 | 4 | .. | 1 | 6 | 3 | 0 | 3 | 2 | 2 | 6 | 6 | 3 | 2 | 3 | 43 | 38 | .531 |
| Minnesota | 1 | 0 | 2 | .. | 4 | 1 | 2 | 6 | 5 | 7 | 1 | 2 | 2 | 4 | 6 | 43 | 38 | .531 |
| Baltimore | 2 | 3 | 6 | 2 | .. | 0 | 1 | 1 | 0 | 3 | 6 | 7 | 2 | 5 | 2 | 40 | 41 | .494 |
| Oakland | 5 | 1 | 1 | 3 | 3 | .. | 5 | 2 | 1 | 2 | 4 | 2 | 4 | 3 | 3 | 39 | 42 | .481 |
| Texas | 5 | 1 | 2 | 0 | 0 | 4 | .. | 1 | 5 | 4 | 2 | 1 | 5 | 4 | 4 | 38 | 43 | .469 |
| Chicago | 1 | 2 | 2 | 6 | 2 | 1 | 4 | .. | 6 | 3 | 2 | 0 | 1 | 5 | 2 | 37 | 44 | .457 |
| Cleveland | 5 | 1 | 2 | 2 | 0 | 1 | 0 | 6 | .. | 4 | 0 | 2 | 4 | 5 | 4 | 36 | 45 | .444 |
| Detroit | 1 | 2 | 0 | 5 | 0 | 3 | 2 | 4 | 5 | .. | 2 | 3 | 2 | 3 | 2 | 34 | 47 | .420 |
| Tampa Bay | 0 | 0 | 2 | 3 | 4 | 0 | 1 | 1 | 0 | 2 | .. | 3 | 3 | 2 | 8 | 29 | 52 | .358 |
| Toronto | 2 | 3 | 1 | 1 | 6 | 2 | 0 | 1 | 0 | 2 | 3 | .. | 2 | 1 | 3 | 27 | 53 | .338 |
| Seattle | 4 | 1 | 1 | 0 | 1 | 3 | 2 | 0 | 2 | 3 | 2 | 1 | .. | 1 | 4 | 25 | 55 | .313 |
| Kansas City | 0 | 0 | 1 | 1 | 2 | 2 | 2 | 2 | 3 | 5 | 2 | 1 | 1 | .. | 3 | 25 | 57 | .305 |
| N.L. Clubs | 6 | 2 | 3 | 4 | 6 | 2 | 3 | 3 | 3 | 2 | 2 | 4 | 4 | 6 | .. | .. | .. | .. |
| **Lost at home** | 36 | 24 | 26 | 32 | 43 | 29 | 30 | 35 | 37 | 43 | 39 | 41 | 44 | 47 | 51 | 507 | 626 | .447 |

# PITCHING AGAINST EACH CLUB

## ANAHEIM—92-70

| Pitcher | Bal. W-L | Bos. W-L | Chi. W-L | Cle. W-L | Det. W-L | K.C. W-L | Min. W-L | N.Y. W-L | Oak. W-L | Sea. W-L | T.B. W-L | Tex. W-L | Tor. W-L | N.L. W-L | Total W-L |
|---|---|---|---|---|---|---|---|---|---|---|---|---|---|---|---|
| Colon, Bartolo | 0-1 | 1-1 | 1-0 | 0-1 | 0-1 | 2-0 | 0-1 | 0-1 | 2-1 | 2-1 | 2-0 | 6-0 | 2-0 | 0-4 | 18-12 |
| Donnelly, Brendan | 0-0 | 0-0 | 0-1 | 0-0 | 0-0 | 1-0 | 0-0 | 0-0 | 1-1 | 2-0 | 0-0 | 0-0 | 0-0 | 1-0 | 5-2 |
| Escobar, Kelvim | 2-1 | 0-1 | 0-0 | 2-0 | 1-0 | 1-0 | 0-0 | 1-0 | 1-3 | 1-0 | 0-1 | 1-3 | 1-1 | 0-2 | 11-12 |
| Gregg, Kevin | 0-0 | 1-0 | 0-0 | 0-0 | 2-0 | 1-0 | 0-0 | 0-0 | 0-1 | 0-1 | 0-0 | 0-0 | 0-0 | 1-0 | 5-2 |
| Hensley, Matt | 0-0 | 0-0 | 0-0 | 0-0 | 0-0 | 0-0 | 0-0 | 0-0 | 0-0 | 0-0 | 0-0 | 0-0 | 0-0 | 0-2 | 0-2 |
| Lackey, John | 0-0 | 0-2 | 1-1 | 1-1 | 1-0 | 1-0 | 1-1 | 0-2 | 2-0 | 2-2 | 2-0 | 1-3 | 1-0 | 1-1 | 14-13 |
| Ortiz, Ramon | 0-0 | 1-0 | 0-1 | 0-0 | 0-0 | 1-0 | 0-2 | 1-0 | 1-0 | 0-1 | 0-0 | 0-2 | 0-0 | 1-1 | 5-7 |
| Percival, Troy | 1-0 | 0-0 | 0-0 | 0-1 | 0-1 | 0-0 | 0-0 | 0-0 | 0-0 | 1-0 | 0-0 | 0-0 | 0-1 | 0-0 | 2-3 |
| Rodriguez, Francisco | 0-0 | 0-0 | 1-0 | 0-1 | 0-0 | 0-0 | 2-0 | 0-0 | 1-0 | 0-0 | 0-0 | 0-0 | 0-0 | 0-0 | 4-1 |
| Sele, Aaron | 1-1 | 0-1 | 1-1 | 0-0 | 0-0 | 0-0 | 2-0 | 1-0 | 0-0 | 2-1 | 1-0 | 0-0 | 0-0 | 1-0 | 9-4 |
| Shields, Scot | 1-0 | 0-0 | 0-0 | 0-0 | 1-0 | 0-0 | 0-0 | 2-0 | 0-2 | 2-0 | 0-0 | 1-0 | 0-0 | 1-0 | 8-2 |
| Washburn, Jarrod | 1-0 | 1-0 | 1-0 | 1-1 | 2-0 | 0-0 | 0-0 | 0-0 | 2-1 | 1-1 | 1-0 | 0-2 | 0-2 | 1-1 | 11-8 |
| Weber, Ben | 0-0 | 0-0 | 0-0 | 0-0 | 0-0 | 0-0 | 0-0 | 0-1 | 0-0 | 0-0 | 0-0 | 0-0 | 0-1 | 0-0 | 0-2 |
| **Totals** | 6-3 | 4-5 | 5-4 | 4-5 | 7-2 | 7-0 | 5-4 | 5-4 | 10-9 | 13-7 | 6-1 | 9-10 | 4-5 | 7-11 | 92-70 |

No-decisions— Dusty Bergman, Scott Dunn, Derrick Turnbow.
INTERLEAGUE: John Lackey 1-0, Bartolo Colon 0-1, Matt Hensley 0-1 vs. Cubs; Kelvim Escobar 0-1, Matt Hensley 0-1, Ramon Ortiz 1-0 vs. Astros; Jarrod Washburn 1-0, Aaron Sele 1-0, Brendan Donnelly 1-0, Bartolo Colon 0-2, Kelvim Escobar 0-1 vs. Dodgers; Kevin Gregg 1-0, Ramon Ortiz 0-1, Jarrod Washburn 0-1 vs. Brewers; Scot Shields 1-0, John Lackey 0-1, Bartolo Colon 0-1 vs. Pirates. Total: 7-11.

## BALTIMORE—78-84

| Pitcher | Ana. W-L | Bos. W-L | Chi. W-L | Cle. W-L | Det. W-L | K.C. W-L | Min. W-L | N.Y. W-L | Oak. W-L | Sea. W-L | TB. W-L | Tex. W-L | Tor. W-L | N.L. W-L | Totals W-L |
|---|---|---|---|---|---|---|---|---|---|---|---|---|---|---|---|
| Ainsworth, Kurt | 0-0 | 0-1 | 0-0 | 0-0 | 0-0 | 0-0 | 0-0 | 0-0 | 0-0 | 0-0 | 0-0 | 0-0 | 0-0 | 0-0 | 0-1 |
| Bauer, Rick | 0-0 | 0-1 | 0-0 | 0-0 | 0-0 | 0-0 | 0-0 | 0-0 | 0-0 | 0-0 | 1-0 | 0-0 | 1-0 | 0-0 | 2-1 |
| Bedard, Erik | 0-0 | 1-1 | 0-1 | 0-0 | 0-0 | 1-1 | 0-1 | 1-2 | 0-1 | 1-0 | 1-1 | 1-1 | 0-1 | 0-0 | 6-10 |
| Borkowski, Dave | 0-0 | 1-1 | 0-0 | 0-0 | 0-0 | 0-0 | 0-0 | 0-0 | 0-0 | 0-0 | 1-1 | 1-0 | 0-2 | 0-0 | 3-4 |
| Cabrera, Daniel | 1-1 | 0-1 | 1-0 | 0-0 | 1-0 | 3-0 | 2-1 | 0-1 | 0-1 | 1-0 | 2-0 | 0-0 | 0-1 | 1-2 | 12-8 |
| Chen, Bruce | 0-0 | 1-0 | 0-0 | 0-0 | 0-0 | 0-0 | 0-1 | 0-0 | 0-0 | 0-0 | 0-0 | 0-0 | 1-0 | 0-0 | 2-1 |
| DeJean, Mike | 0-1 | 0-0 | 0-1 | 0-1 | 0-0 | 0-0 | 0-0 | 0-0 | 0-0 | 0-0 | 0-1 | 0-0 | 0-1 | 0-0 | 0-5 |
| DuBose, Eric | 0-1 | 0-1 | 0-0 | 0-1 | 1-0 | 0-0 | 0-0 | 0-1 | 0-0 | 1-0 | 0-1 | 0-0 | 2-0 | 0-1 | 4-6 |
| Grimsley, Jason | 0-1 | 1-1 | 0-0 | 0-0 | 0-0 | 0-0 | 0-0 | 0-0 | 0-0 | 1-0 | 0-0 | 0-0 | 0-0 | 0-2 | 2-4 |
| Groom, Buddy | 0-0 | 1-0 | 0-0 | 0-0 | 1-0 | 0-0 | 0-0 | 0-0 | 0-1 | 0-0 | 1-0 | 0-0 | 1-0 | 0-0 | 4-1 |
| Julio, Jorge | 0-1 | 0-0 | 0-0 | 1-0 | 0-0 | 0-0 | 0-1 | 0-2 | 0-0 | 1-0 | 0-0 | 0-0 | 0-0 | 0-1 | 2-5 |
| Lopez, Rodrigo | 1-0 | 3-1 | 1-0 | 1-0 | 1-0 | 1-1 | 0-0 | 2-1 | 0-1 | 0-2 | 2-1 | 1-0 | 1-0 | 0-2 | 14-9 |
| Maine, John | 0-0 | 0-0 | 0-0 | 0-0 | 0-0 | 0-0 | 0-1 | 0-0 | 0-0 | 0-0 | 0-0 | 0-0 | 0-0 | 0-0 | 0-1 |
| Parrish, John | 0-0 | 0-0 | 0-0 | 1-0 | 1-0 | 0-0 | 0-0 | 0-1 | 0-0 | 1-0 | 1-2 | 0-0 | 0-0 | 2-0 | 6-3 |
| Ponson, Sidney | 1-1 | 1-0 | 0-1 | 0-1 | 0-0 | 1-1 | 2-0 | 2-4 | 0-1 | 0-0 | 1-0 | 2-0 | 1-2 | 0-4 | 11-15 |
| Riley, Matt | 0-0 | 0-0 | 0-0 | 0-0 | 1-0 | 0-0 | 0-0 | 0-1 | 0-0 | 0-0 | 0-1 | 0-0 | 2-1 | 0-1 | 3-4 |
| Rodriguez, Eddy | 0-0 | 0-0 | 0-0 | 0-0 | 0-0 | 0-0 | 0-0 | 0-0 | 0-0 | 0-0 | 0-0 | 0-0 | 0-0 | 1-0 | 1-0 |
| Ryan, B.J. | 0-0 | 0-1 | 0-1 | 0-0 | 0-0 | 0-0 | 0-0 | 0-1 | 0-2 | 0-0 | 1-0 | 0-1 | 2-0 | 1-0 | 4-6 |
| Williams, Todd | 0-0 | 1-0 | 0-0 | 0-0 | 0-0 | 0-0 | 0-0 | 0-0 | 0-0 | 1-0 | 0-0 | 0-0 | 0-0 | 0-0 | 2-0 |
| **Totals** | 3-6 | 10-9 | 2-4 | 3-3 | 6-0 | 6-3 | 4-5 | 5-14 | 0-7 | 7-2 | 11-8 | 5-2 | 11-8 | 5-13 | 78-84 |

No-decisions— Denny Bautista, Darwin Cubillan, Aaron Rakers.
INTERLEAGUE: Sidney Ponson 0-1, John Parrish 1-0, Daniel Cabrera 0-1 vs. Diamondbacks; Daniel Cabrera 1-0, Rodrigo Lopez 0-1, Jason Grimsley 0-1 vs. Braves; Sidney Ponson 0-1, B.J. Ryan 1-0, Eric DuBose 0-1 vs. Rockies; Daniel Cabrera 0-1, Matt Riley 0-1, Rodrigo Lopez 0-1 vs. Dodgers; Jason Grimsley 0-1, Eddy Rodriguez 1-0, Sidney Ponson 0-1 vs. Phillies; John Parrish 1-0, Jorge Julio 0-1, Sidney Ponson 0-1 vs. Giants. Total: 5-13.

## BOSTON—98-64

| Pitcher | Ana. W-L | Bal. W-L | Chi. W-L | Cle. W-L | Det. W-L | K.C. W-L | Min. W-L | N.Y. W-L | Oak. W-L | Sea. W-L | TB. W-L | Tex. W-L | Tor. W-L | N.L. W-L | Totals W-L |
|---|---|---|---|---|---|---|---|---|---|---|---|---|---|---|---|
| Adams, Terry | 1-0 | 1-0 | 0-0 | 0-0 | 0-0 | 0-0 | 0-0 | 0-0 | 0-0 | 0-0 | 0-0 | 0-0 | 0-0 | 0-0 | 2-0 |
| Alvarez, Abe | 0-0 | 0-1 | 0-0 | 0-0 | 0-0 | 0-0 | 0-0 | 0-0 | 0-0 | 0-0 | 0-0 | 0-0 | 0-0 | 0-0 | 0-1 |
| Arroyo, Bronson | 0-1 | 0-1 | 1-1 | 1-0 | 1-0 | 0-0 | 1-0 | 0-0 | 1-1 | 1-0 | 2-1 | 1-0 | 1-0 | 0-4 | 10-9 |
| Embree, Alan | 0-0 | 0-0 | 0-0 | 1-0 | 0-0 | 0-0 | 0-1 | 0-0 | 0-0 | 0-0 | 0-0 | 0-0 | 1-0 | 0-1 | 2-2 |
| Foulke, Keith | 0-0 | 1-0 | 0-0 | 0-0 | 0-0 | 0-0 | 0-1 | 2-1 | 0-0 | 0-0 | 0-0 | 0-1 | 1-0 | 1-0 | 5-3 |
| Jones, Bobby M. | 0-0 | 0-1 | 0-0 | 0-0 | 0-0 | 0-0 | 0-0 | 0-0 | 0-0 | 0-0 | 0-0 | 0-0 | 0-0 | 0-0 | 0-1 |
| Kim, Byung-Hyun | 0-0 | 1-0 | 0-0 | 0-1 | 0-0 | 0-0 | 0-0 | 0-0 | 0-0 | 0-0 | 1-0 | 0-0 | 0-0 | 0-0 | 2-1 |
| Leskanic, Curtis | 0-0 | 1-0 | 1-0 | 0-0 | 0-0 | 0-0 | 0-0 | 0-1 | 1-0 | 0-1 | 0-0 | 0-0 | 0-0 | 0-0 | 3-2 |
| Lowe, Derek | 1-1 | 1-1 | 0-0 | 0-1 | 1-1 | 1-1 | 0-1 | 2-3 | 2-0 | 1-1 | 2-1 | 1-0 | 1-0 | 1-1 | 14-12 |
| Malaska, Mark | 0-0 | 0-0 | 0-0 | 0-0 | 0-0 | 0-0 | 0-0 | 0-0 | 0-0 | 0-0 | 0-0 | 0-1 | 1-0 | 0-0 | 1-1 |
| Martinez, Anastacio | 0-0 | 0-0 | 0-0 | 0-0 | 0-0 | 0-0 | 0-0 | 0-0 | 0-0 | 1-0 | 0-0 | 0-0 | 1-0 | 0-1 | 2-1 |
| Martinez, Pedro | 1-0 | 1-2 | 0-0 | 1-0 | 2-0 | 0-0 | 0-0 | 1-2 | 2-0 | 1-0 | 1-2 | 1-1 | 2-2 | 3-0 | 16-9 |
| Mendoza, Ramiro | 0-0 | 0-1 | 0-0 | 0-0 | 0-0 | 0-0 | 0-0 | 1-0 | 0-0 | 0-0 | 1-0 | 0-0 | 0-0 | 0-0 | 2-1 |
| Myers, Mike | 0-0 | 0-0 | 0-0 | 0-0 | 0-0 | 0-0 | 0-0 | 0-0 | 0-0 | 0-0 | 1-0 | 0-0 | 0-0 | 0-0 | 1-0 |
| Schilling, Curt | 2-0 | 1-1 | 2-0 | 0-1 | 0-0 | 2-0 | 1-0 | 2-0 | 1-0 | 1-0 | 4-1 | 1-0 | 1-2 | 3-1 | 21-6 |
| Timlin, Mike | 0-1 | 0-0 | 0-0 | 0-0 | 0-0 | 1-0 | 0-1 | 2-1 | 0-0 | 0-0 | 0-0 | 0-0 | 1-1 | 1-0 | 5-4 |
| Wakefield, Tim | 0-1 | 2-1 | 0-1 | 0-1 | 2-0 | 0-1 | 0-0 | 1-0 | 1-0 | 0-2 | 2-0 | 0-2 | 4-0 | 0-1 | 12-10 |
| Williamson, Scott | 0-0 | 0-1 | 0-0 | 0-0 | 0-0 | 0-0 | 0-0 | 0-0 | 0-0 | 0-0 | 0-0 | 0-0 | 0-0 | 0-0 | 0-1 |
| **Totals** | 5-4 | 9-10 | 4-2 | 3-4 | 6-1 | 4-2 | 2-4 | 11-8 | 8-1 | 5-4 | 14-5 | 4-5 | 14-5 | 9-9 | 98-64 |

No-decisions— Jimmy Anderson, Pedro Astacio, Jamie Brown, Frank Castillo, Lenny DiNardo, Dave McCarty, Joe Nelson, Phil Seibel.
INTERLEAGUE: Anastacio Martinez 0-1, Curt Schilling 1-0, Derek Lowe 0-1 vs. Braves; Bronson Arroyo 0-1, Curt Schilling 0-1, Derek Lowe 1-0 vs. Rockies; Keith Foulke 1-0, Tim Wakefield 0-1, Pedro Martinez 1-0 vs. Dodgers; Pedro Martinez 1-0, Bronson Arroyo 0-1, Curt Schilling 1-0 vs. Phillies; Pedro Martinez 1-0, Bronson Arroyo 0-1, Curt Schilling 1-0 vs. Padres; Mike Timlin 1-0, Alan Embree 0-1, Bronson Arroyo 0-1 vs. Giants. Total: 9-9.

## CHICAGO—83-79

| Pitcher | Ana. W-L | Bal. W-L | Bos. W-L | Cle. W-L | Det. W-L | K.C. W-L | Min. W-L | N.Y. W-L | Oak. W-L | Sea. W-L | TB. W-L | Tex. W-L | Tor. W-L | N.L. W-L | Totals W-L |
|---|---|---|---|---|---|---|---|---|---|---|---|---|---|---|---|
| Adkins, Jon | 0-0 | 0-0 | 0-1 | 0-1 | 0-0 | 1-0 | 0-0 | 0-0 | 0-1 | 0-0 | 1-0 | 0-0 | 0-0 | 0-0 | 2-3 |
| Bajenaru, Jeff | 0-1 | 0-0 | 0-0 | 0-0 | 0-0 | 0-0 | 0-0 | 0-0 | 0-0 | 0-0 | 0-0 | 0-0 | 0-0 | 0-0 | 0-1 |

| Pitcher | Ana. W-L | Bal. W-L | Bos. W-L | Cle. W-L | Det. W-L | K.C. W-L | Min. W-L | N.Y. W-L | Oak. W-L | Sea. W-L | TB. W-L | Tex. W-L | Tor. W-L | N.L. W-L | Totals W-L |
|---|---|---|---|---|---|---|---|---|---|---|---|---|---|---|---|
| Buehrle, Mark | 0-0 | 1-0 | 1-1 | 1-2 | 0-1 | 2-1 | 3-3 | 1-1 | 0-1 | 2-0 | 0-0 | 2-0 | 0-0 | 3-0 | 16-10 |
| Contreras, Jose | 0-1 | 0-0 | 1-0 | 1-0 | 1-1 | 2-0 | 0-0 | 0-0 | 0-1 | 0-0 | 0-0 | 0-1 | 0-0 | 0-0 | 5-4 |
| Cotts, Neal | 0-0 | 0-0 | 0-0 | 1-0 | 0-1 | 0-0 | 2-1 | 0-0 | 0-1 | 0-0 | 0-0 | 0-0 | 0-1 | 1-0 | 4-4 |
| Diaz, Felix | 0-0 | 0-0 | 0-0 | 0-2 | 0-0 | 0-1 | 0-0 | 0-0 | 0-1 | 1-0 | 0-0 | 0-0 | 0-0 | 1-1 | 2-5 |
| Garcia, Freddy | 0-1 | 0-0 | 0-0 | 1-0 | 3-1 | 1-0 | 1-2 | 0-0 | 1-0 | 1-0 | 0-0 | 1-0 | 0-0 | 0-0 | 9-4 |
| Garland, Jon | 0-0 | 0-1 | 0-0 | 1-1 | 1-2 | 3-1 | 2-1 | 1-1 | 0-1 | 3-0 | 0-0 | 0-0 | 1-0 | 0-3 | 12-11 |
| Grilli, Jason | 1-0 | 0-0 | 0-0 | 0-1 | 0-1 | 0-1 | 0-0 | 0-0 | 0-0 | 0-0 | 0-0 | 1-0 | 0-0 | 0-0 | 2-3 |
| Jackson, Mike | 0-0 | 1-0 | 0-0 | 1-0 | 0-0 | 0-0 | 0-0 | 0-0 | 0-0 | 0-0 | 0-0 | 0-0 | 0-0 | 0-0 | 2-0 |
| Koch, Billy | 0-0 | 0-0 | 0-0 | 0-0 | 0-0 | 0-0 | 0-0 | 0-0 | 0-0 | 0-1 | 1-0 | 0-0 | 0-0 | 0-0 | 1-1 |
| Loaiza, Esteban | 0-0 | 0-1 | 0-0 | 0-0 | 1-0 | 2-0 | 1-1 | 0-0 | 0-1 | 0-0 | 1-0 | 1-0 | 1-1 | 2-1 | 9-5 |
| Marte, Damaso | 1-0 | 0-0 | 0-1 | 0-0 | 2-1 | 2-1 | 0-1 | 0-0 | 0-0 | 0-0 | 0-0 | 0-1 | 0-0 | 1-0 | 6-5 |
| Munoz, Arnie | 0-0 | 0-0 | 0-0 | 0-0 | 0-0 | 0-0 | 0-0 | 0-0 | 0-0 | 0-0 | 0-0 | 0-0 | 0-0 | 0-1 | 0-1 |
| Politte, Cliff | 0-0 | 0-0 | 0-0 | 0-0 | 0-1 | 0-0 | 0-0 | 0-0 | 0-0 | 0-0 | 0-0 | 0-0 | 0-1 | 0-1 | 0-3 |
| Rauch, Jon | 0-1 | 0-0 | 0-0 | 1-0 | 0-0 | 0-0 | 0-0 | 0-0 | 0-0 | 0-0 | 0-0 | 0-0 | 0-0 | 0-0 | 1-1 |
| Schoeneweis, Scott | 1-1 | 1-0 | 0-0 | 1-1 | 0-1 | 0-1 | 0-0 | 1-1 | 0-0 | 0-1 | 1-0 | 1-1 | 0-0 | 0-2 | 6-9 |
| Stewart, Josh | 0-0 | 0-0 | 0-1 | 0-0 | 0-0 | 0-0 | 0-0 | 0-0 | 0-0 | 0-0 | 0-0 | 0-0 | 0-0 | 0-0 | 0-1 |
| Takatsu, Shingo | 1-0 | 1-0 | 0-0 | 2-1 | 0-1 | 0-0 | 0-1 | 0-0 | 1-0 | 0-0 | 0-0 | 0-0 | 1-0 | 0-1 | 6-4 |
| Wright, Dan | 0-0 | 0-0 | 0-0 | 0-0 | 0-0 | 0-0 | 0-0 | 0-1 | 0-0 | 0-0 | 0-2 | 0-0 | 0-1 | 0-0 | 0-4 |
| **Totals** | 4-5 | 4-2 | 2-4 | 10-9 | 8-11 | 13-6 | 9-10 | 3-4 | 2-7 | 7-2 | 4-2 | 6-3 | 3-4 | 8-10 | 83-79 |

No-decisions— Vic Darensbourg, Kelly Wunsch.

INTERLEAGUE: Scott Schoeneweis 0-1, Esteban Loaiza 1-0, Mark Buehrle 1-0 vs. Braves; Jon Garland 0-1, Felix Diaz 1-1, Shingo Takatsu 0-1, Esteban Loaiza 1-1 vs. Cubs; Cliff Politte 0-1, Damaso Marte 1-0, Scott Schoeneweis 0-1 vs. Marlins; Neal Cotts 1-0, Arnie Munoz 0-1, Jon Garland 0-1 vs. Expos; Mark Buehrle 2-0, Jon Garland 0-1 vs. Phillies. Total: 8-10.

## CLEVELAND—80-82

| Pitcher | Ana. W-L | Bal. W-L | Bos. W-L | Chi. W-L | Det. W-L | K.C. W-L | Min. W-L | N.Y. W-L | Oak. W-L | Sea. W-L | TB. W-L | Tex. W-L | Tor. W-L | N.L. W-L | Totals W-L |
|---|---|---|---|---|---|---|---|---|---|---|---|---|---|---|---|
| Bartosh, Cliff | 0-0 | 0-0 | 0-0 | 0-0 | 0-0 | 1-0 | 0-0 | 0-0 | 0-0 | 0-0 | 0-0 | 0-0 | 0-0 | 0-0 | 1-0 |
| Betancourt, Rafael | 0-0 | 0-0 | 0-0 | 1-2 | 0-1 | 2-1 | 0-0 | 0-0 | 0-0 | 0-0 | 0-0 | 0-1 | 1-1 | 1-0 | 5-6 |
| Cressend, Jack | 0-0 | 0-0 | 0-0 | 0-0 | 0-0 | 0-1 | 0-0 | 0-0 | 0-0 | 0-0 | 0-0 | 0-0 | 0-0 | 0-0 | 0-1 |
| Cruceta, Francisco | 0-0 | 0-0 | 0-0 | 0-0 | 0-0 | 0-0 | 0-1 | 0-0 | 0-0 | 0-0 | 0-0 | 0-0 | 0-0 | 0-0 | 0-1 |
| D'Amico, Jeff | 0-0 | 0-0 | 0-1 | 0-0 | 0-0 | 1-0 | 0-1 | 0-0 | 0-0 | 0-0 | 0-0 | 0-0 | 0-0 | 0-0 | 1-2 |
| Davis, Jason | 0-1 | 0-0 | 1-0 | 0-1 | 0-3 | 0-0 | 0-0 | 0-0 | 0-0 | 0-0 | 0-0 | 0-0 | 0-0 | 1-2 | 2-7 |
| Denney, Kyle | 0-0 | 0-0 | 0-0 | 0-0 | 0-1 | 1-0 | 0-1 | 0-0 | 0-0 | 0-0 | 0-0 | 0-0 | 0-0 | 0-0 | 1-2 |
| Durbin, Chad | 0-0 | 1-1 | 1-0 | 0-2 | 0-0 | 1-1 | 1-2 | 0-0 | 0-0 | 0-0 | 0-0 | 0-0 | 1-0 | 0-0 | 5-6 |
| Elarton, Scott | 0-1 | 0-0 | 0-0 | 1-0 | 1-1 | 0-0 | 1-0 | 0-0 | 0-0 | 0-0 | 0-0 | 0-2 | 0-0 | 0-1 | 3-5 |
| Howry, Bob | 0-0 | 0-0 | 0-0 | 0-0 | 2-0 | 0-0 | 1-1 | 0-0 | 1-1 | 0-0 | 0-0 | 0-0 | 0-0 | 0-0 | 4-2 |
| Jimenez, Jose | 0-0 | 0-0 | 0-1 | 0-1 | 0-1 | 0-1 | 0-0 | 0-0 | 1-0 | 0-1 | 0-0 | 0-0 | 0-0 | 0-2 | 1-7 |
| Lee, Cliff | 0-1 | 1-0 | 1-0 | 2-2 | 1-1 | 1-1 | 3-0 | 0-1 | 1-0 | 2-0 | 0-0 | 1-1 | 0-1 | 1-0 | 14-8 |
| Miller, Matt | 0-0 | 0-0 | 0-0 | 1-0 | 0-0 | 1-0 | 0-0 | 0-0 | 0-0 | 0-1 | 0-0 | 0-0 | 0-0 | 2-0 | 4-1 |
| Riske, David | 2-0 | 0-1 | 0-0 | 0-0 | 1-0 | 0-0 | 0-1 | 1-0 | 1-0 | 0-0 | 0-1 | 0-0 | 1-0 | 1-0 | 7-3 |
| Robertson, Jeriome | 0-0 | 0-0 | 0-0 | 0-0 | 0-0 | 0-0 | 0-0 | 0-0 | 0-0 | 0-0 | 0-0 | 0-1 | 0-0 | 1-0 | 1-1 |
| Sabathia, C.C. | 1-0 | 0-0 | 0-1 | 3-1 | 2-1 | 0-1 | 0-1 | 0-1 | 0-0 | 2-1 | 1-1 | 0-2 | 1-0 | 1-0 | 11-10 |
| Stanford, Jason | 0-0 | 0-0 | 0-0 | 0-0 | 0-0 | 0-0 | 0-1 | 0-0 | 0-0 | 0-0 | 0-0 | 0-0 | 0-0 | 0-0 | 0-1 |
| Stewart, Scott | 0-0 | 0-1 | 0-0 | 0-0 | 0-1 | 0-0 | 0-0 | 0-0 | 0-0 | 0-0 | 0-0 | 0-0 | 0-0 | 0-0 | 0-2 |
| Tadano, Kazuhito | 0-0 | 0-0 | 0-0 | 0-0 | 0-0 | 0-1 | 0-0 | 0-0 | 0-0 | 0-0 | 0-0 | 0-0 | 0-0 | 1-0 | 1-1 |
| Westbrook, Jake | 1-1 | 1-0 | 1-0 | 1-1 | 2-0 | 2-1 | 1-2 | 1-0 | 0-1 | 1-1 | 1-1 | 0-0 | 1-0 | 1-1 | 14-9 |
| White, Rick | 1-0 | 0-0 | 0-0 | 0-0 | 0-0 | 1-0 | 0-1 | 0-0 | 2-1 | 0-0 | 1-0 | 0-1 | 0-0 | 0-2 | 5-5 |
| Wickman, Bob | 0-0 | 0-0 | 0-0 | 0-0 | 0-0 | 0-0 | 0-0 | 0-2 | 0-0 | 0-0 | 0-0 | 0-0 | 0-0 | 0-0 | 0-2 |
| **Totals** | 5-4 | 3-3 | 4-3 | 9-10 | 9-10 | 11-8 | 7-12 | 2-4 | 6-3 | 5-4 | 3-3 | 1-8 | 5-2 | 10-8 | 80-82 |

No-decisions— Jason Anderson, Fernando Cabrera, Joe Dawley, Jeremy Guthrie, Tim Laker, Dave Lee, Lou Pote, Jake Robbins.

INTERLEAGUE: Cliff Lee 1-0, Jake Westbrook 0-1, Jason Davis 1-0 vs. Braves; Rick White 0-1, Matt Miller 1-0, David Riske 1-0, Scott Elarton 0-1, Rafael Betancourt 1-0, Kazuhito Tadano 1-0 vs. Reds; Matt Miller 1-0, Jose Jimenez 0-1, Jeriome Robertson 1-0 vs. Rockies; Jose Jimenez 0-1, Jake Westbrook 1-0, Jason Davis 0-1 vs. Marlins; Jason Davis 0-1, Rick White 0-1, C.C. Sabathia 1-0 vs. Mets. Total: 10-8.

## DETROIT—72-90

| Pitcher | Ana. W-L | Bal. W-L | Bos. W-L | Chi. W-L | Cle. W-L | K.C. W-L | Min. W-L | N.Y. W-L | Oak. W-L | Sea. W-L | TB. W-L | Tex. W-L | Tor. W-L | N.L. W-L | Totals W-L |
|---|---|---|---|---|---|---|---|---|---|---|---|---|---|---|---|
| Bonderman, Jeremy | 0-0 | 0-2 | 0-2 | 1-3 | 2-1 | 1-1 | 0-0 | 1-1 | 1-1 | 1-1 | 2-0 | 0-0 | 1-0 | 1-1 | 11-13 |
| Colyer, Steve | 0-0 | 0-0 | 0-0 | 0-0 | 0-0 | 0-0 | 1-0 | 0-0 | 0-0 | 0-0 | 0-0 | 0-0 | 0-0 | 0-0 | 1-0 |
| Cornejo, Nate | 0-1 | 0-0 | 0-0 | 0-0 | 0-1 | 0-0 | 1-0 | 0-0 | 0-0 | 0-1 | 0-0 | 0-0 | 0-0 | 0-0 | 1-3 |
| Dingman, Craig | 0-0 | 0-0 | 0-0 | 0-0 | 1-0 | 0-0 | 0-0 | 0-0 | 0-0 | 0-0 | 0-1 | 0-0 | 0-0 | 1-1 | 2-2 |
| German, Franklyn | 0-0 | 0-0 | 0-0 | 1-0 | 0-0 | 0-0 | 0-0 | 0-0 | 0-0 | 0-0 | 0-0 | 0-0 | 0-0 | 0-0 | 1-0 |
| Johnson, Jason | 0-2 | 0-1 | 0-1 | 1-1 | 0-1 | 1-1 | 1-4 | 1-0 | 0-1 | 1-0 | 0-0 | 1-1 | 1-1 | 1-1 | 8-15 |
| Knotts, Gary | 0-0 | 0-0 | 0-0 | 1-0 | 0-1 | 1-3 | 2-0 | 0-1 | 0-0 | 0-0 | 1-0 | 1-0 | 0-0 | 1-1 | 7-6 |
| Ledezma, Wilfredo | 0-0 | 0-0 | 0-1 | 2-1 | 0-1 | 1-0 | 0-0 | 0-0 | 1-0 | 0-0 | 0-0 | 0-0 | 0-0 | 0-0 | 4-3 |
| Levine, Al | 0-1 | 0-0 | 0-0 | 0-1 | 1-0 | 0-0 | 1-1 | 0-0 | 0-0 | 0-1 | 0-0 | 1-0 | 0-0 | 0-0 | 3-4 |
| Maroth, Mike | 1-0 | 0-1 | 0-1 | 1-0 | 3-0 | 1-3 | 0-3 | 1-0 | 2-1 | 0-1 | 0-1 | 0-0 | 1-0 | 1-2 | 11-13 |
| Novoa, Roberto | 0-1 | 0-0 | 1-0 | 0-0 | 0-0 | 0-0 | 0-0 | 0-0 | 0-0 | 0-0 | 0-0 | 0-0 | 0-0 | 0-0 | 1-1 |
| Patterson, Danny | 0-0 | 0-0 | 0-0 | 0-0 | 0-0 | 0-0 | 0-0 | 0-0 | 0-1 | 0-0 | 0-0 | 0-0 | 0-1 | 0-2 | 0-4 |
| Robertson, Nate | 0-2 | 0-0 | 0-1 | 1-1 | 1-0 | 3-1 | 1-1 | 1-1 | 0-0 | 2-0 | 0-1 | 1-2 | 1-0 | 1-0 | 12-10 |
| Urbina, Ugueth | 0-0 | 0-1 | 0-0 | 1-1 | 1-1 | 0-1 | 0-1 | 0-0 | 0-0 | 0-0 | 0-0 | 0-1 | 0-0 | 2-0 | 4-6 |
| Walker, Jamie | 0-0 | 0-0 | 0-0 | 0-0 | 1-1 | 0-0 | 0-1 | 0-0 | 0-1 | 1-0 | 0-0 | 0-0 | 0-0 | 1-1 | 3-4 |
| Yan, Esteban | 1-0 | 0-1 | 0-0 | 2-0 | 0-2 | 0-1 | 0-1 | 0-0 | 0-0 | 0-0 | 0-0 | 0-1 | 0-0 | 0-0 | 3-6 |
| **Totals** | 2-7 | 0-6 | 1-6 | 11-8 | 10-9 | 8-11 | 7-12 | 4-3 | 4-5 | 5-4 | 3-3 | 4-5 | 4-2 | 9-9 | 72-90 |

No-decisions— John Ennis, Lino Urdaneta.

INTERLEAGUE: Jason Johnson 1-0, Ugueth Urbina 1-0, Jamie Walker 1-0 vs. Diamondbacks; Danny Patterson 0-1, Craig Dingman 1-0, Mike Maroth 1-0 vs. Braves; Jamie Walker 0-1, Mike Maroth 0-1, Gary Knotts 0-1 vs. Rockies; Gary Knotts 1-0, Nate Robertson 1-0, Jason Johnson 0-1 vs. Marlins; Danny Patterson 0-1, Craig Dingman 0-1, Jeremy Bonderman 0-1 vs. Mets; Jeremy Bonderman 1-0, Ugueth Urbina 1-0, Mike Maroth 0-1 vs. Phillies. Total: 9-9.

## KANSAS CITY—58-104

| Pitcher | Ana. W-L | Bal. W-L | Bos. W-L | Chi. W-L | Cle. W-L | Det. W-L | Min. W-L | N.Y. W-L | Oak. W-L | Sea. W-L | TB. W-L | Tex. W-L | Tor. W-L | N.L. W-L | Totals W-L |
|---|---|---|---|---|---|---|---|---|---|---|---|---|---|---|---|
| Affeldt, Jeremy | 0-0 | 0-0 | 0-0 | 0-1 | 0-1 | 1-0 | 1-0 | 0-1 | 0-0 | 0-0 | 0-0 | 0-1 | 0-0 | 1-0 | 3-4 |
| Anderson, Brian | 0-0 | 0-2 | 0-0 | 2-1 | 1-0 | 0-1 | 0-1 | 1-1 | 0-3 | 1-0 | 1-0 | 0-1 | 0-2 | 0-0 | 6-12 |
| Appier, Kevin | 0-0 | 0-0 | 0-0 | 0-0 | 0-0 | 0-0 | 0-1 | 0-0 | 0-0 | 0-0 | 0-0 | 0-0 | 0-0 | 0-0 | 0-1 |
| Bautista, Denny | 0-0 | 0-0 | 0-0 | 0-1 | 0-1 | 0-1 | 0-0 | 0-0 | 0-0 | 0-0 | 0-1 | 0-0 | 0-0 | 0-0 | 0-4 |
| Camp, Shawn | 0-0 | 0-0 | 0-0 | 0-1 | 0-0 | 0-0 | 1-0 | 0-0 | 0-0 | 0-0 | 0-1 | 0-0 | 1-0 | 0-0 | 2-2 |
| Carrasco, D.J. | 0-0 | 0-0 | 0-0 | 1-1 | 0-0 | 0-0 | 0-0 | 0-0 | 0-0 | 1-1 | 0-0 | 0-0 | 0-0 | 0-0 | 2-2 |

| Pitcher | Ana. W-L | Bal. W-L | Bos. W-L | Chi. W-L | Cle. W-L | Det. W-L | Min. W-L | N.Y. W-L | Oak. W-L | Sea. W-L | TB. W-L | Tex. W-L | Tor. W-L | N.L. W-L | Totals W-L |
|---|---|---|---|---|---|---|---|---|---|---|---|---|---|---|---|
| Cerda, Jaime | 0-1 | 0-0 | 0-0 | 0-1 | 0-1 | 0-0 | 0-1 | 0-0 | 0-0 | 0-0 | 0-0 | 0-0 | 0-0 | 1-0 | 1-4 |
| Field, Nate | 0-1 | 0-0 | 0-0 | 0-0 | 0-1 | 0-0 | 0-0 | 0-0 | 0-1 | 0-0 | 0-0 | 0-0 | 2-0 | 0-0 | 2-3 |
| George, Chris | 0-0 | 0-0 | 0-0 | 0-0 | 0-1 | 0-1 | 0-0 | 0-0 | 0-0 | 0-0 | 0-0 | 0-0 | 0-0 | 1-0 | 1-2 |
| Gobble, Jimmy | 0-0 | 1-0 | 1-1 | 1-0 | 1-0 | 2-0 | 1-3 | 0-0 | 0-1 | 0-0 | 0-1 | 2-0 | 0-0 | 0-2 | 9-8 |
| Greinke, Zack | 0-0 | 0-2 | 0-0 | 1-2 | 1-1 | 2-1 | 1-1 | 0-1 | 1-0 | 0-0 | 0-0 | 1-0 | 0-0 | 1-3 | 8-11 |
| Grimsley, Jason | 0-0 | 0-0 | 0-1 | 0-0 | 1-1 | 2-0 | 0-0 | 0-0 | 0-0 | 0-0 | 0-0 | 0-0 | 0-0 | 0-1 | 3-3 |
| Kinney, Matt | 0-0 | 0-0 | 0-0 | 0-0 | 0-0 | 0-0 | 0-0 | 0-0 | 0-0 | 0-1 | 0-0 | 0-0 | 0-0 | 0-0 | 0-1 |
| Leskanic, Curtis | 0-0 | 0-0 | 0-0 | 0-1 | 0-0 | 0-0 | 0-1 | 0-0 | 0-0 | 0-0 | 0-0 | 0-1 | 0-0 | 0-0 | 0-3 |
| MacDougal, Mike | 0-0 | 0-0 | 0-1 | 0-0 | 0-0 | 0-0 | 0-0 | 0-0 | 0-0 | 0-0 | 1-0 | 0-0 | 0-0 | 0-0 | 1-1 |
| May, Darrell | 0-2 | 1-1 | 1-1 | 1-2 | 1-1 | 2-3 | 1-2 | 0-1 | 0-1 | 0-2 | 0-1 | 0-1 | 0-1 | 2-0 | 9-19 |
| Reyes, Dennys | 0-2 | 0-0 | 0-0 | 0-0 | 0-0 | 1-0 | 2-2 | 0-0 | 0-0 | 0-1 | 1-0 | 0-0 | 0-0 | 0-3 | 4-8 |
| Seanez, Rudy | 0-0 | 0-0 | 0-0 | 0-0 | 0-0 | 0-0 | 0-0 | 0-0 | 0-0 | 0-0 | 0-0 | 0-0 | 0-0 | 0-1 | 0-1 |
| Serrano, Jimmy | 0-0 | 0-0 | 0-0 | 0-1 | 0-0 | 1-0 | 0-0 | 0-0 | 0-0 | 0-0 | 0-1 | 0-0 | 0-0 | 0-0 | 1-2 |
| Sullivan, Scott | 0-0 | 0-0 | 0-0 | 0-0 | 2-2 | 0-0 | 0-0 | 0-0 | 0-1 | 0-0 | 0-0 | 1-0 | 0-0 | 0-1 | 3-4 |
| Villacis, Eduardo | 0-0 | 0-0 | 0-0 | 0-0 | 0-0 | 0-0 | 0-0 | 0-1 | 0-0 | 0-0 | 0-0 | 0-0 | 0-0 | 0-0 | 0-1 |
| Wood, Mike | 0-1 | 1-1 | 0-0 | 0-1 | 1-1 | 0-1 | 0-0 | 0-0 | 1-0 | 0-0 | 0-1 | 0-1 | 0-0 | 0-1 | 3-8 |
| **Totals** | 0-7 | 3-6 | 2-4 | 6-13 | 8-11 | 11-8 | 7-12 | 1-5 | 2-7 | 2-5 | 3-6 | 4-5 | 3-3 | 6-12 | 58-104 |

No-decisions— Ryan Bukvich, Justin Huisman, Jorge Vasquez.

INTERLEAGUE: Jason Grimsley 0-1, Jaime Cerda 1-0, Darrell May 1-0 vs. Braves; Zack Greinke 1-0, Dennys Reyes 0-1, Jimmy Gobble 0-1 vs. Expos; Darrell May 1-0, Jeremy Affeldt 1-0, Zack Greinke 0-1 vs. Mets; Chris George 1-0, Zack Greinke 0-1, Dennys Reyes 0-1 vs. Phillies; Dennys Reyes 0-1, Scott Sullivan 0-1, Mike Wood 0-1 vs. Padres; Zack Greinke 0-1, Rudy Seanez 0-1, Jimmy Gobble 0-1 vs. Cardinals. Total: 6-12.

## MINNESOTA—92-70

| Pitcher | Ana. W-L | Bal. W-L | Bos. W-L | Chi. W-L | Cle. W-L | Det. W-L | K.C. W-L | N.Y. W-L | Oak. W-L | Sea. W-L | TB. W-L | Tex. W-L | Tor. W-L | N.L. W-L | Totals W-L |
|---|---|---|---|---|---|---|---|---|---|---|---|---|---|---|---|
| Balfour, Grant | 0-0 | 0-0 | 1-0 | 0-0 | 0-0 | 2-0 | 0-1 | 0-0 | 0-0 | 0-0 | 0-0 | 0-0 | 0-0 | 1-0 | 4-1 |
| Crain, Jesse | 0-0 | 0-0 | 0-0 | 0-0 | 1-0 | 1-0 | 0-0 | 0-0 | 0-0 | 0-0 | 0-0 | 1-0 | 0-0 | 0-0 | 3-0 |
| Durbin, J.D. | 0-0 | 0-0 | 0-0 | 0-0 | 0-1 | 0-0 | 0-0 | 0-0 | 0-0 | 0-0 | 0-0 | 0-0 | 0-0 | 0-0 | 0-1 |
| Fultz, Aaron | 0-0 | 0-0 | 0-0 | 0-0 | 0-0 | 0-1 | 0-0 | 0-1 | 0-0 | 1-0 | 0-0 | 0-0 | 1-0 | 1-1 | 3-3 |
| Greisinger, Seth | 0-0 | 0-0 | 0-0 | 1-1 | 0-0 | 0-1 | 0-1 | 0-0 | 0-0 | 0-1 | 1-1 | 0-0 | 0-0 | 0-0 | 2-5 |
| Guerrier, Matt | 0-0 | 0-0 | 0-0 | 0-0 | 0-0 | 0-0 | 0-0 | 0-0 | 0-0 | 0-0 | 0-0 | 0-0 | 0-0 | 0-1 | 0-1 |
| Lohse, Kyle | 1-0 | 1-0 | 0-2 | 1-0 | 2-4 | 0-0 | 3-2 | 0-1 | 0-2 | 0-0 | 0-1 | 1-0 | 0-0 | 0-1 | 9-13 |
| Mulholland, Terry | 0-1 | 0-2 | 0-0 | 1-0 | 1-0 | 2-0 | 0-0 | 0-0 | 0-2 | 0-1 | 0-0 | 0-1 | 0-0 | 1-2 | 5-9 |
| Nathan, Joe | 0-0 | 0-0 | 0-0 | 0-0 | 0-0 | 1-0 | 0-0 | 0-1 | 0-0 | 0-0 | 0-0 | 0-1 | 0-0 | 0-0 | 1-2 |
| Radke, Brad | 0-1 | 0-1 | 0-0 | 2-1 | 2-0 | 2-2 | 1-1 | 1-0 | 0-0 | 1-0 | 1-1 | 1-0 | 0-1 | 0-0 | 11-8 |
| Rincon, Juan | 0-2 | 0-0 | 1-0 | 1-0 | 2-0 | 0-0 | 1-1 | 0-0 | 0-1 | 0-2 | 0-0 | 1-0 | 3-0 | 2-0 | 11-6 |
| Roa, Joe | 0-0 | 0-1 | 0-0 | 0-1 | 1-0 | 0-1 | 1-0 | 0-0 | 0-0 | 0-0 | 0-0 | 0-0 | 0-0 | 0-0 | 2-3 |
| Romero, J.C. | 0-1 | 1-0 | 0-0 | 0-1 | 0-1 | 1-0 | 2-0 | 0-1 | 1-0 | 0-0 | 1-0 | 0-0 | 0-0 | 1-0 | 7-4 |
| Santana, Johan | 1-0 | 2-0 | 1-0 | 2-2 | 1-0 | 1-1 | 3-1 | 1-0 | 1-0 | 2-0 | 0-1 | 1-0 | 0-1 | 4-0 | 20-6 |
| Silva, Carlos | 2-0 | 1-0 | 1-0 | 2-3 | 2-1 | 2-1 | 1-0 | 0-0 | 0-0 | 1-0 | 1-1 | 0-0 | 0-0 | 1-2 | 14-8 |
| **Totals** | 4-5 | 5-4 | 4-2 | 10-9 | 12-7 | 12-7 | 12-7 | 2-4 | 2-5 | 5-4 | 4-5 | 5-2 | 4-2 | 11-7 | 92-70 |

No-decisions— Joe Beimel, Carlos Pulido, Brad Thomas.

INTERLEAGUE: J.C. Romero 1-0, Terry Mulholland 1-0, Carlos Silva 0-1 vs. Diamondbacks; Carlos Silva 0-1, Terry Mulholland 0-1, Johan Santana 2-0, Matt Guerrier 0-1, Kyle Lohse 0-1 vs. Brewers; Johan Santana 1-0, Juan Rincon 1-0, Aaron Fultz 1-0 vs. Expos; Juan Rincon 1-0, Johan Santana 1-0, Grant Balfour 1-0 vs. Mets; Terry Mulholland 0-1, Carlos Silva 1-0, Aaron Fultz 0-1 vs. Phillies. Total: 11-7.

## NEW YORK—101-61

| Pitcher | Ana. W-L | Bal. W-L | Bos. W-L | Chi. W-L | Cle. W-L | Det. W-L | K.C. W-L | Min. W-L | Oak. W-L | Sea. W-L | TB. W-L | Tex. W-L | Tor. W-L | N.L. W-L | Totals W-L |
|---|---|---|---|---|---|---|---|---|---|---|---|---|---|---|---|
| Brown, Kevin | 0-1 | 1-1 | 0-1 | 0-0 | 0-0 | 0-0 | 0-0 | 0-0 | 2-0 | 1-0 | 4-0 | 1-2 | 1-1 | 0-0 | 10-6 |
| Contreras, Jose | 0-0 | 1-1 | 0-2 | 0-1 | 0-0 | 1-0 | 0-0 | 0-0 | 1-0 | 0-0 | 2-0 | 0-0 | 0-0 | 3-1 | 8-5 |
| DePaula, Jorge | 0-0 | 0-0 | 0-0 | 0-1 | 0-0 | 0-0 | 0-0 | 0-0 | 0-0 | 0-0 | 0-0 | 0-0 | 0-0 | 0-0 | 0-1 |
| Gordon, Tom | 1-0 | 1-0 | 3-1 | 0-0 | 2-1 | 0-0 | 0-0 | 2-0 | 0-0 | 0-0 | 0-0 | 0-1 | 0-0 | 0-1 | 9-4 |
| Halsey, Brad | 0-0 | 0-0 | 0-0 | 0-0 | 0-0 | 0-1 | 0-1 | 0-0 | 0-0 | 0-0 | 0-0 | 0-0 | 0-0 | 1-1 | 1-3 |
| Heredia, Felix | 0-0 | 0-0 | 0-0 | 0-0 | 0-0 | 0-0 | 0-0 | 0-0 | 0-0 | 0-0 | 0-0 | 0-0 | 0-0 | 1-1 | 1-1 |
| Hernandez, Orlando | 0-0 | 2-0 | 0-0 | 0-0 | 1-0 | 1-0 | 0-0 | 0-0 | 0-0 | 0-0 | 2-0 | 1-0 | 1-2 | 0-0 | 8-2 |
| Lieber, Jon | 2-1 | 1-1 | 1-0 | 0-0 | 1-0 | 1-1 | 1-0 | 1-0 | 0-1 | 1-1 | 3-1 | 0-1 | 1-0 | 1-1 | 14-8 |
| Loaiza, Esteban | 0-1 | 0-0 | 0-0 | 0-0 | 0-0 | 0-0 | 0-0 | 0-0 | 0-0 | 0-0 | 0-0 | 0-0 | 1-1 | 0-0 | 1-2 |
| Mussina, Mike | 1-0 | 2-1 | 1-1 | 1-1 | 0-0 | 0-1 | 2-0 | 0-1 | 0-0 | 2-0 | 1-2 | 1-0 | 0-1 | 1-1 | 12-9 |
| Nitkowski, C.J. | 0-0 | 0-0 | 0-0 | 0-0 | 0-0 | 0-0 | 0-0 | 0-0 | 0-0 | 0-1 | 0-0 | 0-0 | 1-0 | 0-0 | 1-1 |
| Osborne, Donovan | 0-0 | 0-0 | 0-0 | 0-0 | 0-0 | 0-0 | 0-0 | 0-0 | 2-0 | 0-0 | 0-0 | 0-0 | 0-0 | 0-0 | 2-0 |
| Prinz, Bret | 0-0 | 1-0 | 0-0 | 0-0 | 0-0 | 0-0 | 0-0 | 0-0 | 0-0 | 0-0 | 0-0 | 0-0 | 0-0 | 0-0 | 1-0 |
| Proctor, Scott | 0-0 | 0-0 | 0-0 | 0-0 | 0-0 | 0-0 | 0-0 | 0-0 | 0-0 | 0-0 | 0-0 | 0-0 | 2-1 | 0-0 | 2-1 |
| Quantrill, Paul | 0-1 | 0-0 | 1-2 | 1-0 | 0-0 | 0-0 | 0-0 | 1-0 | 1-0 | 2-0 | 0-0 | 0-0 | 0-0 | 1-0 | 7-3 |
| Rivera, Mariano | 0-0 | 1-0 | 0-2 | 0-0 | 0-0 | 0-0 | 0-0 | 0-0 | 1-0 | 0-0 | 0-0 | 0-0 | 2-0 | 0-0 | 4-2 |
| Sturtze, Tanyon | 0-0 | 1-0 | 1-0 | 0-0 | 0-0 | 0-0 | 0-0 | 0-0 | 0-0 | 0-0 | 1-1 | 1-0 | 1-0 | 1-1 | 6-2 |
| Vazquez, Javier | 0-1 | 3-1 | 1-2 | 2-0 | 0-1 | 0-1 | 2-0 | 0-1 | 0-1 | 0-0 | 2-0 | 1-0 | 2-1 | 1-1 | 14-10 |
| White, Gabe | 0-0 | 0-0 | 0-0 | 0-0 | 0-0 | 0-0 | 0-0 | 0-0 | 0-0 | 0-1 | 0-0 | 0-0 | 0-0 | 0-0 | 0-1 |
| **Totals** | 4-5 | 14-5 | 8-11 | 4-3 | 4-2 | 3-4 | 5-1 | 4-2 | 7-2 | 6-3 | 15-4 | 5-4 | 12-7 | 10-8 | 101-61 |

No-decisions— Alex Graman, Steve Karsay, Sam Marsonek, Juan Padilla.

INTERLEAGUE: Jose Contreras 1-0, Tanyon Sturtze 1-0, Jon Lieber 0-1 vs. Diamondbacks; Javier Vazquez 1-0, Paul Quantrill 1-0, Jose Contreras 1-0 vs. Rockies; Javier Vazquez 0-1, Brad Halsey 1-0, Jose Contreras 0-1 vs. Dodgers; Brad Halsey 0-1, Tanyon Sturtze 0-1, Jose Contreras 1-0, Tom Gordon 0-1, Mike Mussina 1-1 vs. Mets; Felix Heredia 1-1, Jon Lieber 1-0 vs. Padres. Total: 10-8.

## OAKLAND—96-66

| Pitcher | Ana. W-L | Bal. W-L | Bos. W-L | Chi. W-L | Cle. W-L | Det. W-L | K.C. W-L | Min. W-L | N.Y. W-L | Sea. W-L | TB. W-L | Tex. W-L | Tor. W-L | N.L. W-L | Totals W-L |
|---|---|---|---|---|---|---|---|---|---|---|---|---|---|---|---|
| Bradford, Chad | 1-1 | 0-0 | 0-0 | 0-0 | 0-0 | 0-0 | 0-0 | 1-0 | 0-1 | 0-1 | 0-0 | 2-1 | 1-1 | 0-2 | 5-7 |
| Dotel, Octavio | 0-0 | 1-0 | 0-0 | 0-0 | 0-1 | 0-0 | 0-0 | 1-0 | 0-0 | 2-0 | 1-0 | 0-1 | 0-0 | 1-0 | 6-2 |
| Duchscherer, Justin | 1-0 | 0-0 | 0-0 | 1-1 | 0-1 | 1-1 | 1-0 | 0-0 | 0-1 | 0-2 | 1-0 | 1-0 | 0-0 | 1-0 | 7-6 |
| Hammond, Chris | 0-0 | 0-0 | 0-0 | 0-0 | 0-0 | 0-0 | 0-0 | 1-0 | 0-0 | 1-1 | 1-0 | 0-0 | 1-0 | 0-0 | 4-1 |
| Harden, Rich | 1-2 | 0-0 | 0-0 | 2-0 | 0-0 | 1-1 | 1-0 | 1-0 | 1-0 | 0-1 | 1-0 | 2-1 | 0-1 | 1-1 | 11-7 |
| Hudson, Tim | 1-1 | 2-0 | 0-2 | 0-0 | 0-0 | 1-0 | 1-0 | 0-1 | 0-0 | 3-1 | 1-1 | 0-0 | 2-0 | 1-0 | 12-6 |
| Lehr, Justin | 0-0 | 0-0 | 0-1 | 0-0 | 0-0 | 0-0 | 0-0 | 0-0 | 0-0 | 0-0 | 0-0 | 0-0 | 1-0 | 0-0 | 1-1 |
| Mecir, Jim | 0-0 | 0-0 | 0-0 | 0-0 | 0-1 | 0-0 | 0-0 | 0-1 | 0-1 | 0-1 | 0-0 | 0-0 | 0-0 | 0-1 | 0-5 |

| Pitcher | Ana. W-L | Bal. W-L | Bos. W-L | Chi. W-L | Cle. W-L | Det. W-L | K.C. W-L | Min. W-L | N.Y. W-L | Sea. W-L | TB. W-L | Tex. W-L | Tor. W-L | N.L. W-L | Totals W-L |
|---|---|---|---|---|---|---|---|---|---|---|---|---|---|---|---|
| Mulder, Mark | 2-3 | 2-0 | 1-0 | 1-0 | 1-0 | 0-0 | 2-1 | 1-0 | 1-1 | 2-0 | 0-0 | 1-3 | 0-0 | 3-0 | 17-8 |
| Redman, Mark | 1-1 | 1-0 | 0-3 | 1-1 | 0-0 | 1-2 | 0-0 | 0-0 | 0-0 | 2-1 | 1-1 | 2-1 | 1-0 | 1-2 | 11-12 |
| Rhodes, Arthur | 0-0 | 0-0 | 0-0 | 1-0 | 0-2 | 0-0 | 1-0 | 0-0 | 0-1 | 0-0 | 0-0 | 0-0 | 0-0 | 1-0 | 3-3 |
| Rincon, Ricardo | 0-1 | 0-0 | 0-0 | 0-0 | 1-0 | 0-0 | 0-0 | 0-0 | 0-0 | 0-0 | 0-0 | 0-0 | 0-0 | 0-0 | 1-1 |
| Saarloos, Kirk | 1-0 | 0-0 | 0-0 | 0-0 | 0-0 | 0-0 | 0-0 | 0-0 | 0-0 | 0-0 | 0-0 | 1-0 | 0-1 | 0-0 | 2-1 |
| Zito, Barry | 1-1 | 1-0 | 0-2 | 1-0 | 1-1 | 1-0 | 1-1 | 0-0 | 0-2 | 1-0 | 1-0 | 2-2 | 0-0 | 1-2 | 11-11 |
| **Totals** | 9-10 | 7-0 | 1-8 | 7-2 | 3-6 | 5-4 | 7-2 | 5-2 | 2-7 | 11-8 | 7-2 | 11-9 | 6-3 | 10-8 | 91-71 |

No-decisions— Joe Blanton, Jairo Garcia, Chad Harville.

INTERLEAGUE: Mark Redman 1-0, Chad Bradford 0-1, Barry Zito 0-1 vs. Cubs; Mark Mulder 1-0, Barry Zito 1-0, Rich Harden 1-0 vs. Reds; Tim Hudson 1-0, Arthur Rhodes 1-0, Mark Mulder 1-0 vs. Pirates; Barry Zito 0-1, Justin Duchscherer 1-0, Octavio Dotel 1-0, Mark Redman 0-2, Mark Mulder 1-0 vs. Giants; Chad Bradford 0-1, Jim Mecir 0-1, Rich Harden 0-1 vs. Cardinals. Total: 10-8.

## SEATTLE—63-99

| Pitcher | Ana. W-L | Bal. W-L | Bos. W-L | Chi. W-L | Cle. W-L | Det. W-L | K.C. W-L | Min. W-L | N.Y. W-L | Oak. W-L | TB. W-L | Tex. W-L | Tor. W-L | N.L. W-L | Totals W-L |
|---|---|---|---|---|---|---|---|---|---|---|---|---|---|---|---|
| Atchison, Scott | 0-0 | 0-0 | 0-0 | 0-0 | 0-0 | 0-1 | 0-0 | 0-0 | 0-0 | 0-1 | 1-1 | 0-0 | 1-0 | 0-0 | 2-3 |
| Baek, Cha Seung | 0-1 | 0-0 | 0-0 | 0-0 | 0-1 | 0-0 | 1-0 | 0-0 | 0-0 | 0-1 | 0-0 | 1-0 | 0-1 | 0-0 | 2-4 |
| Blackley, Travis | 0-0 | 0-0 | 0-0 | 0-0 | 0-1 | 0-0 | 0-0 | 0-0 | 0-0 | 0-1 | 0-0 | 1-0 | 0-1 | 0-0 | 1-3 |
| Franklin, Ryan | 2-2 | 0-1 | 0-1 | 1-1 | 0-1 | 0-1 | 0-1 | 0-2 | 1-0 | 0-1 | 0-1 | 0-3 | 0-0 | 0-1 | 4-16 |
| Garcia, Freddy | 0-0 | 0-1 | 1-0 | 0-1 | 0-0 | 1-0 | 0-0 | 1-1 | 0-0 | 0-0 | 0-0 | 0-1 | 0-0 | 1-3 | 4-7 |
| Guardado, Eddie | 0-1 | 0-0 | 0-0 | 0-0 | 0-0 | 0-0 | 0-0 | 0-0 | 1-0 | 0-0 | 0-0 | 0-0 | 0-1 | 1-0 | 2-2 |
| Hasegawa, Shigetoshi | 0-2 | 0-2 | 0-0 | 1-0 | 1-0 | 0-0 | 0-0 | 0-0 | 0-1 | 2-0 | 0-0 | 0-1 | 0-0 | 0-0 | 4-6 |
| Jarvis, Kevin | 0-0 | 0-0 | 0-0 | 0-0 | 0-0 | 0-0 | 0-0 | 0-0 | 0-0 | 1-0 | 0-0 | 0-0 | 0-0 | 0-0 | 1-0 |
| Madritsch, Bobby | 2-0 | 0-0 | 1-0 | 0-1 | 0-0 | 0-0 | 1-0 | 0-0 | 0-0 | 2-1 | 0-1 | 0-0 | 0-0 | 0-0 | 6-3 |
| Mateo, Julio | 0-1 | 0-0 | 0-0 | 0-0 | 0-0 | 0-0 | 0-0 | 0-0 | 0-0 | 0-1 | 0-0 | 0-0 | 0-0 | 1-0 | 1-2 |
| Meche, Gil | 1-0 | 0-0 | 1-0 | 0-0 | 0-2 | 2-1 | 0-0 | 1-0 | 1-1 | 1-1 | 0-0 | 0-2 | 0-0 | 0-0 | 7-7 |
| Moyer, Jamie | 1-3 | 1-0 | 0-1 | 0-2 | 1-0 | 0-0 | 0-1 | 0-0 | 0-0 | 0-1 | 0-1 | 1-2 | 1-1 | 2-1 | 7-13 |
| Myers, Mike | 0-0 | 0-0 | 1-0 | 0-0 | 1-0 | 1-0 | 0-0 | 0-0 | 0-0 | 0-1 | 0-0 | 0-0 | 0-0 | 1-0 | 4-1 |
| Nageotte, Clint | 0-0 | 0-1 | 0-0 | 0-0 | 0-0 | 0-0 | 0-0 | 0-0 | 0-0 | 0-0 | 0-1 | 0-2 | 0-1 | 1-1 | 1-6 |
| Pineiro, Joel | 1-1 | 0-1 | 0-2 | 0-1 | 1-0 | 0-0 | 0-0 | 0-1 | 0-1 | 0-0 | 0-0 | 2-1 | 0-1 | 2-2 | 6-11 |
| Putz, J.J. | 0-1 | 0-0 | 0-1 | 0-0 | 0-0 | 0-1 | 0-0 | 0-0 | 0-0 | 0-0 | 0-0 | 0-0 | 0-0 | 0-0 | 0-3 |
| Sherrill, George | 0-0 | 0-1 | 0-0 | 0-0 | 0-0 | 0-0 | 1-0 | 1-0 | 0-0 | 0-0 | 0-0 | 0-0 | 0-0 | 0-0 | 2-1 |
| Soriano, Rafael | 0-1 | 0-0 | 0-0 | 0-0 | 0-0 | 0-0 | 0-0 | 0-0 | 0-1 | 0-1 | 0-0 | 0-0 | 0-0 | 0-0 | 0-3 |
| Thornton, Matt | 0-0 | 0-0 | 0-0 | 0-1 | 0-0 | 0-0 | 1-0 | 0-0 | 0-0 | 0-0 | 0-0 | 0-0 | 0-0 | 0-1 | 1-2 |
| Villone, Ron | 0-0 | 1-0 | 0-0 | 0-0 | 0-0 | 0-1 | 1-0 | 1-1 | 0-2 | 2-1 | 1-0 | 2-0 | 0-1 | 0-0 | 8-6 |
| **Totals** | 7-13 | 2-7 | 4-5 | 2-7 | 4-5 | 4-5 | 5-2 | 4-5 | 3-6 | 8-11 | 2-5 | 7-12 | 2-7 | 9-9 | 63-99 |

No-decisions— Masao Kida, Aaron Taylor, Randy Williams.

INTERLEAGUE: Clint Nageotte 1-0, Joel Pineiro 0-1, Freddy Garcia 0-1 vs. Astros; Freddy Garcia 0-1, Mike Myers 1-0, Clint Nageotte 0-1 vs. Brewers; Eddie Guardado 1-0, Jamie Moyer 1-0, Joel Pineiro 1-0 vs. Expos; Jamie Moyer 1-0, Joel Pineiro 1-0, Freddy Garcia 1-0 vs. Pirates; Freddy Garcia 0-1, Julio Mateo 1-0, Jamie Moyer 0-1 vs. Padres; Matt Thornton 0-1, Ryan Franklin 0-1, Joel Pineiro 0-1 vs. Cardinals. Total: 9-9.

## TAMPA BAY—70-91

| Pitcher | Ana. W-L | Bal. W-L | Bos. W-L | Chi. W-L | Cle. W-L | Det. W-L | K.C. W-L | Min. W-L | N.Y. W-L | Oak. W-L | Sea. W-L | Tex. W-L | Tor. W-L | N.L. W-L | Totals W-L |
|---|---|---|---|---|---|---|---|---|---|---|---|---|---|---|---|
| Abbott, Paul | 0-1 | 1-0 | 0-1 | 1-0 | 0-0 | 0-0 | 0-0 | 0-1 | 0-1 | 0-0 | 0-0 | 0-1 | 0-0 | 0-0 | 2-5 |
| Baez, Danys | 0-0 | 1-0 | 0-1 | 0-1 | 0-0 | 0-0 | 0-0 | 0-0 | 0-0 | 0-1 | 0-1 | 0-0 | 1-0 | 2-0 | 4-4 |
| Bell, Rob | 0-1 | 1-1 | 0-2 | 0-0 | 0-0 | 1-0 | 2-0 | 1-1 | 0-1 | 0-0 | 2-0 | 0-1 | 0-1 | 1-0 | 8-8 |
| Brazelton, Dewon | 1-0 | 0-3 | 0-1 | 0-0 | 0-0 | 0-1 | 1-0 | 0-0 | 0-2 | 1-1 | 0-0 | 0-0 | 2-0 | 1-0 | 6-8 |
| Carter, Lance | 0-0 | 1-1 | 0-0 | 0-0 | 0-1 | 0-0 | 0-0 | 0-0 | 1-0 | 0-1 | 0-0 | 1-0 | 0-0 | 0-0 | 3-3 |
| Colome, Jesus | 0-0 | 0-0 | 0-0 | 0-0 | 0-0 | 0-0 | 0-0 | 0-0 | 0-1 | 0-0 | 0-0 | 0-0 | 0-1 | 2-0 | 2-2 |
| Gaudin, Chad | 0-0 | 0-1 | 0-0 | 0-0 | 0-0 | 0-0 | 0-0 | 0-0 | 0-0 | 0-0 | 0-0 | 0-0 | 0-0 | 1-1 | 1-2 |
| Gonzalez, Jeremi | 0-1 | 0-2 | 0-0 | 0-1 | 0-0 | 0-0 | 0-0 | 0-0 | 0-1 | 0-0 | 0-0 | 0-0 | 0-0 | 0-0 | 0-5 |
| Halama, John | 0-0 | 1-0 | 1-0 | 0-0 | 0-0 | 1-0 | 0-0 | 1-1 | 0-0 | 0-1 | 0-0 | 0-1 | 1-2 | 2-1 | 7-6 |
| Harper, Travis | 0-0 | 0-1 | 1-0 | 0-0 | 1-0 | 1-0 | 0-0 | 0-1 | 0-0 | 0-0 | 2-0 | 0-0 | 1-0 | 0-0 | 6-2 |
| Hendrickson, Mark | 0-2 | 2-2 | 0-4 | 0-0 | 0-0 | 0-0 | 2-0 | 1-0 | 0-3 | 1-1 | 0-1 | 1-0 | 1-2 | 2-0 | 10-15 |
| Kazmir, Scott | 0-0 | 0-0 | 1-0 | 0-0 | 0-0 | 0-2 | 0-0 | 0-0 | 0-0 | 0-0 | 1-0 | 0-0 | 0-1 | 0-0 | 2-3 |
| Miller, Trever | 0-0 | 0-0 | 0-0 | 0-1 | 1-0 | 0-0 | 0-0 | 0-0 | 0-0 | 0-0 | 0-0 | 0-0 | 0-0 | 0-0 | 1-1 |
| Moss, Damian | 0-0 | 0-0 | 0-1 | 0-0 | 0-0 | 0-0 | 0-0 | 0-0 | 0-0 | 0-0 | 0-0 | 0-0 | 0-0 | 0-0 | 0-1 |
| Nunez, Franklin | 0-0 | 0-0 | 0-1 | 0-0 | 0-0 | 0-0 | 0-1 | 0-0 | 0-0 | 0-0 | 0-0 | 0-1 | 0-0 | 0-0 | 0-3 |
| Ritchie, Todd | 0-0 | 0-0 | 0-0 | 0-0 | 0-0 | 0-0 | 0-0 | 0-0 | 0-1 | 0-0 | 0-0 | 0-0 | 0-1 | 0-0 | 0-2 |
| Sosa, Jorge | 0-0 | 0-0 | 1-2 | 0-0 | 0-0 | 0-0 | 1-2 | 0-0 | 0-1 | 0-1 | 0-0 | 0-1 | 1-0 | 1-0 | 4-7 |
| Waechter, Doug | 0-0 | 0-0 | 1-0 | 1-0 | 1-1 | 0-0 | 0-0 | 1-0 | 0-2 | 0-1 | 0-0 | 0-2 | 1-0 | 0-1 | 5-7 |
| Zambrano, Victor | 0-1 | 1-0 | 0-1 | 0-1 | 0-1 | 0-0 | 0-0 | 1-0 | 3-2 | 0-0 | 0-0 | 0-0 | 1-1 | 3-0 | 9-7 |
| **Totals** | 1-6 | 8-11 | 5-14 | 2-4 | 3-3 | 3-3 | 6-3 | 5-4 | 4-15 | 2-7 | 5-2 | 2-7 | 9-9 | 15-3 | 70-91 |

No-decisions— Bartolome Fortunato, Dicky Gonzalez, Bobby Seay, Jason Standridge, John Webb.

INTERLEAGUE: John Halama 1-0, Rob Bell 1-0, Mark Hendrickson 1-0 vs. Diamondbacks; Danys Baez 1-0, John Halama 1-0, Jesus Colome 1-0 vs. Rockies; Dewon Brazelton 1-0, Jorge Sosa 1-0, Jesus Colome 1-0, Chad Gaudin 0-1, Victor Zambrano 1-0, John Halama 0-1 vs. Marlins; Mark Hendrickson 1-0, Victor Zambrano 1-0, Chad Gaudin 1-0 vs. Padres; Doug Waechter 0-1, Danys Baez 1-0, Victor Zambrano 1-0 vs. Giants. Total: 15-3.

## TEXAS—89-73

| Pitcher | Ana. W-L | Bal. W-L | Bos. W-L | Chi. W-L | Cle. W-L | Det. W-L | K.C. W-L | Min. W-L | N.Y. W-L | Oak. W-L | Sea. W-L | TB. W-L | Tor. W-L | N.L. W-L | Totals W-L |
|---|---|---|---|---|---|---|---|---|---|---|---|---|---|---|---|
| Almanzar, Carlos | 1-0 | 0-0 | 0-0 | 1-0 | 1-0 | 0-0 | 1-0 | 0-1 | 1-0 | 0-1 | 1-0 | 0-0 | 0-0 | 1-1 | 7-3 |
| Bacsik, Mike | 0-0 | 0-1 | 0-0 | 0-0 | 0-0 | 1-0 | 0-0 | 0-0 | 0-0 | 0-0 | 0-0 | 0-0 | 0-0 | 0-0 | 1-1 |
| Benoit, Joaquin | 0-0 | 0-0 | 1-1 | 0-2 | 0-0 | 0-1 | 0-0 | 0-0 | 1-0 | 0-0 | 0-1 | 0-0 | 0-0 | 1-0 | 3-5 |
| Bierbrodt, Nick | 0-0 | 0-0 | 0-0 | 0-0 | 0-1 | 0-0 | 0-0 | 0-0 | 0-0 | 0-0 | 1-0 | 0-0 | 0-0 | 0-0 | 1-1 |
| Brocail, Doug | 0-0 | 0-0 | 0-0 | 0-0 | 0-0 | 0-0 | 0-0 | 0-0 | 0-0 | 1-0 | 0-0 | 1-0 | 2-0 | 0-1 | 4-1 |
| Callaway, Mickey | 0-0 | 0-0 | 0-0 | 0-0 | 0-0 | 0-0 | 0-0 | 0-0 | 0-0 | 0-1 | 0-0 | 0-0 | 0-0 | 0-0 | 0-1 |
| Cordero, Francisco | 0-1 | 0-0 | 0-0 | 0-0 | 0-0 | 1-0 | 0-0 | 1-1 | 0-0 | 0-1 | 0-1 | 0-0 | 0-0 | 1-0 | 3-4 |
| Dickey, R.A. | 2-0 | 0-0 | 1-0 | 0-0 | 0-0 | 0-0 | 1-1 | 0-0 | 0-1 | 0-2 | 1-0 | 0-1 | 0-1 | 1-1 | 6-7 |
| Dominguez, Juan | 0-0 | 0-0 | 0-0 | 0-0 | 0-0 | 0-0 | 0-0 | 0-0 | 1-0 | 0-0 | 0-0 | 0-0 | 0-1 | 0-1 | 1-2 |
| Drese, Ryan | 2-0 | 0-0 | 0-1 | 0-1 | 0-0 | 1-1 | 1-0 | 0-1 | 1-1 | 2-1 | 2-2 | 2-0 | 2-0 | 1-2 | 14-10 |
| Erickson, Scott | 0-0 | 0-1 | 0-0 | 0-0 | 1-0 | 0-0 | 0-1 | 0-0 | 0-1 | 0-0 | 0-0 | 0-0 | 0-0 | 0-0 | 1-3 |
| Francisco, Frank | 0-0 | 1-0 | 0-0 | 0-0 | 0-0 | 1-0 | 1-0 | 0-0 | 0-0 | 1-0 | 0-0 | 0-0 | 0-0 | 1-1 | 5-1 |

| Pitcher | Ana. W-L | Bal. W-L | Bos. W-L | Chi. W-L | Cle. W-L | Det. W-L | K.C. W-L | Min. W-L | N.Y. W-L | Oak. W-L | Sea. W-L | TB. W-L | Tor. W-L | N.L. W-L | Totals W-L |
|---|---|---|---|---|---|---|---|---|---|---|---|---|---|---|---|
| Lewis, Colby | 0-0 | 0-0 | 0-0 | 0-0 | 0-0 | 0-0 | 0-0 | 0-0 | 0-0 | 1-0 | 0-1 | 0-0 | 0-0 | 0-0 | 1-1 |
| Mahay, Ron | 0-0 | 0-0 | 0-0 | 0-0 | 1-0 | 0-0 | 0-0 | 0-0 | 0-0 | 0-0 | 0-0 | 0-0 | 1-0 | 1-0 | 3-0 |
| Nelson, Jeff | 0-0 | 0-0 | 0-0 | 0-0 | 0-0 | 0-0 | 0-0 | 0-0 | 0-0 | 1-1 | 0-0 | 0-1 | 0-0 | 0-0 | 1-2 |
| Park, Chan Ho | 0-4 | 0-0 | 0-0 | 0-1 | 0-0 | 0-0 | 0-1 | 1-0 | 0-0 | 0-1 | 2-0 | 1-0 | 0-0 | 0-0 | 4-7 |
| Powell, Jay | 0-0 | 0-0 | 0-0 | 0-0 | 0-0 | 0-0 | 0-0 | 0-0 | 0-1 | 0-0 | 1-0 | 0-0 | 0-0 | 0-0 | 1-1 |
| Ramirez, Erasmo | 1-0 | 0-0 | 1-0 | 0-0 | 2-0 | 0-1 | 0-0 | 0-0 | 0-0 | 0-0 | 0-1 | 1-0 | 0-0 | 0-1 | 5-3 |
| Regilio, Nick | 0-1 | 0-1 | 0-0 | 0-0 | 0-0 | 0-0 | 0-0 | 0-0 | 0-1 | 0-1 | 0-0 | 0-0 | 0-0 | 0-0 | 0-4 |
| Rodriguez, Ricardo | 0-1 | 0-0 | 0-0 | 0-0 | 1-0 | 0-0 | 0-0 | 0-0 | 0-0 | 0-0 | 1-0 | 0-0 | 1-0 | 0-0 | 3-1 |
| Rogers, Kenny | 2-2 | 0-1 | 0-1 | 2-0 | 2-0 | 1-1 | 1-1 | 0-2 | 0-0 | 3-1 | 2-0 | 2-0 | 1-0 | 2-0 | 18-9 |
| Shouse, Brian | 0-0 | 0-0 | 1-0 | 0-0 | 0-0 | 0-0 | 0-0 | 0-0 | 0-0 | 0-0 | 1-0 | 0-0 | 0-0 | 0-0 | 2-0 |
| Wasdin, John | 0-0 | 1-0 | 0-1 | 0-1 | 0-0 | 0-0 | 0-0 | 0-0 | 0-0 | 0-1 | 0-1 | 0-0 | 0-0 | 1-0 | 2-4 |
| Young, Chris | 2-0 | 0-1 | 1-0 | 0-1 | 0-0 | 0-0 | 0-0 | 0-0 | 0-0 | 0-0 | 0-0 | 0-0 | 0-0 | 0-0 | 3-2 |
| **Totals** | 10-9 | 2-5 | 5-4 | 3-6 | 8-1 | 5-4 | 5-4 | 2-5 | 4-5 | 9-11 | 12-7 | 7-2 | 7-2 | 10-8 | 89-73 |

No-decisions— Rosman Garcia, Travis Hughes, Kameron Loe, Sam Narron, Ryan Snare, Michael Tejera.
INTERLEAGUE: Frank Francisco 0-1, Erasmo Ramirez 0-1, Ryan Drese 0-1 vs. Reds; John Wasdin 1-0, Ron Mahay 1-0, R.A. Dickey 1-0 vs. Marlins; Kenny Rogers 1-0, Doug Brocail 0-1, Carlos Almanzar 1-1, Ryan Drese 0-1, Joaquin Benoit 1-0 vs. Astros; Frank Francisco 1-0, Francisco Cordero 1-0, Kenny Rogers 1-0 vs. Pirates; Juan Dominguez 0-1, Ryan Drese 1-0, R.A. Dickey 0-1 vs. Cardinals. Total: 10-8.

## TORONTO—67-94

| Pitcher | Ana. W-L | Bal. W-L | Bos. W-L | Chi. W-L | Cle. W-L | Det. W-L | K.C. W-L | Min. W-L | N.Y. W-L | Oak. W-L | Sea. W-L | TB. W-L | Tex. W-L | N.L. W-L | Totals W-L |
|---|---|---|---|---|---|---|---|---|---|---|---|---|---|---|---|
| Adams, Terry | 1-0 | 0-0 | 1-0 | 1-0 | 0-0 | 1-0 | 0-2 | 0-1 | 0-0 | 0-1 | 0-0 | 0-0 | 0-0 | 0-0 | 4-4 |
| Batista, Miguel | 0-1 | 0-3 | 1-3 | 0-1 | 0-0 | 0-1 | 0-0 | 1-0 | 1-1 | 0-0 | 1-0 | 2-1 | 1-1 | 3-1 | 10-13 |
| Bush, David | 0-1 | 1-0 | 0-0 | 0-0 | 0-1 | 0-0 | 0-0 | 0-0 | 1-0 | 0-0 | 1-0 | 2-1 | 0-0 | 0-1 | 5-4 |
| Chacin, Gustavo | 0-0 | 0-1 | 0-0 | 0-0 | 0-0 | 0-0 | 0-0 | 0-0 | 1-0 | 0-0 | 0-0 | 0-0 | 0-0 | 0-0 | 1-1 |
| Chulk, Vinnie | 0-0 | 0-1 | 0-0 | 0-0 | 0-0 | 0-0 | 0-0 | 0-0 | 0-1 | 0-0 | 0-0 | 1-0 | 0-1 | 0-0 | 1-3 |
| Douglass, Sean | 0-0 | 0-0 | 0-0 | 0-0 | 0-0 | 0-0 | 0-0 | 0-0 | 0-1 | 0-0 | 0-0 | 0-1 | 0-0 | 0-0 | 0-2 |
| File, Bob | 0-0 | 0-0 | 0-0 | 0-0 | 0-0 | 0-0 | 0-0 | 0-0 | 0-0 | 0-0 | 1-0 | 0-0 | 0-0 | 0-0 | 1-0 |
| Frasor, Jason | 1-0 | 0-0 | 0-0 | 1-0 | 0-0 | 0-0 | 0-0 | 0-1 | 1-2 | 0-1 | 0-0 | 1-0 | 0-1 | 0-1 | 4-6 |
| Frederick, Kevin | 0-0 | 0-0 | 0-1 | 0-0 | 0-1 | 0-0 | 0-0 | 0-0 | 0-0 | 0-0 | 0-0 | 0-0 | 0-0 | 0-0 | 0-2 |
| Glynn, Ryan | 0-0 | 0-0 | 0-0 | 0-0 | 0-0 | 0-0 | 0-0 | 0-0 | 0-0 | 1-0 | 0-0 | 0-0 | 0-0 | 0-0 | 1-0 |
| Halladay, Roy | 1-1 | 1-0 | 1-2 | 0-0 | 0-0 | 1-1 | 1-1 | 0-0 | 1-1 | 0-0 | 0-0 | 0-1 | 0-1 | 2-0 | 8-8 |
| Hentgen, Pat | 0-0 | 0-1 | 0-1 | 0-0 | 0-0 | 0-1 | 2-0 | 0-0 | 0-1 | 0-1 | 0-1 | 0-1 | 0-0 | 0-2 | 2-9 |
| Kershner, Jason | 0-0 | 0-0 | 0-0 | 0-0 | 0-0 | 0-0 | 0-0 | 0-0 | 0-0 | 0-1 | 0-0 | 0-0 | 0-0 | 0-0 | 0-1 |
| League, Brandon | 0-0 | 1-0 | 0-0 | 0-0 | 0-0 | 0-0 | 0-0 | 0-0 | 0-0 | 0-0 | 0-0 | 0-0 | 0-0 | 0-0 | 1-0 |
| Ligtenberg, Kerry | 0-0 | 1-0 | 0-2 | 0-0 | 0-2 | 0-0 | 0-0 | 0-0 | 0-1 | 0-0 | 0-1 | 0-0 | 0-0 | 0-0 | 1-6 |
| Lilly, Ted | 1-1 | 1-0 | 1-1 | 1-0 | 1-0 | 0-1 | 0-0 | 1-0 | 1-2 | 0-1 | 1-0 | 1-1 | 1-1 | 2-2 | 12-10 |
| Lopez, Aquilino | 0-0 | 0-0 | 0-1 | 0-0 | 0-0 | 0-0 | 0-0 | 0-0 | 0-0 | 0-0 | 1-0 | 0-0 | 0-0 | 0-0 | 1-1 |
| Miller, Justin | 1-0 | 1-1 | 0-1 | 1-0 | 0-0 | 0-0 | 0-0 | 0-0 | 0-1 | 0-0 | 0-0 | 0-0 | 0-1 | 0-0 | 3-4 |
| Nakamura, Mike | 0-0 | 0-0 | 0-1 | 0-1 | 0-0 | 0-0 | 0-0 | 0-1 | 0-0 | 0-0 | 0-0 | 0-0 | 0-0 | 0-0 | 0-3 |
| Speier, Justin | 0-0 | 0-2 | 1-0 | 0-1 | 1-0 | 0-0 | 0-0 | 0-1 | 0-0 | 0-1 | 1-0 | 0-0 | 0-1 | 0-2 | 3-8 |
| Towers, Josh | 0-0 | 2-2 | 0-1 | 0-0 | 0-1 | 0-0 | 0-0 | 0-0 | 1-1 | 2-0 | 1-0 | 2-3 | 0-0 | 1-1 | 9-9 |
| **Totals** | 5-4 | 8-11 | 5-14 | 4-3 | 2-5 | 2-4 | 3-3 | 2-4 | 7-12 | 3-6 | 7-2 | 9-9 | 2-7 | 8-10 | 67-94 |

No-decisions— Valerio de los Santos, Dave Maurer, Frank Menechino, Adam Peterson.
INTERLEAGUE: Jason Frasor 0-1, Roy Halladay 1-0, Ted Lilly 0-1 vs. Diamondbacks; Ted Lilly 1-0, Miguel Batista 1-0, Josh Towers 0-1 vs. Dodgers; Josh Towers 1-0, Miguel Batista 1-0, Pat Hentgen 0-1, David Bush 0-1, Roy Halladay 1-0, Ted Lilly 0-1 vs. Expos; Ted Lilly 1-0, Justin Speier 0-1, Miguel Batista 1-0 vs. Padres; Miguel Batista 0-1, Justin Speier 0-1, Pat Hentgen 0-1 vs. Giants. Total: 8-10.

# HOME RUNS BY PARKS

| | At Ana. | At Bal. | At Bos. | At CWS. | At Cle. | At Det. | At KC. | At Min. | At NYY. | At Oak. | At Sea. | At TB. | At Tex. | At Tor. | At N.L. Parks | Totals 2004 | Totals 2003 | HR Allow. |
|---|---|---|---|---|---|---|---|---|---|---|---|---|---|---|---|---|---|---|
| Anaheim | 77 | 3 | 1 | 6 | 4 | 3 | 2 | 1 | 11 | 9 | 14 | 5 | 11 | 5 | 10 | 162 | 150 | 170 |
| Baltimore | 7 | 82 | 15 | 4 | 2 | 3 | 12 | 5 | 11 | 0 | 3 | 8 | 2 | 6 | 9 | 169 | 152 | 159 |
| Boston | 10 | 7 | 111 | 8 | 6 | 4 | 4 | 4 | 14 | 5 | 9 | 14 | 1 | 12 | 13 | 222 | 238 | 159 |
| Chicago | 1 | 3 | 5 | 145 | 9 | 12 | 17 | 15 | 5 | 9 | 1 | 2 | 9 | 2 | 7 | 242 | 220 | 224 |
| Cleveland | 14 | 3 | 2 | 18 | 70 | 8 | 9 | 12 | 4 | 4 | 18 | 4 | 2 | 7 | 9 | 184 | 158 | 201 |
| Detroit | 9 | 1 | 2 | 25 | 16 | 87 | 9 | 15 | 4 | 7 | 2 | 3 | 6 | 6 | 9 | 201 | 153 | 190 |
| Kansas City | 5 | 4 | 2 | 17 | 8 | 10 | 56 | 9 | 2 | 5 | 9 | 4 | 6 | 2 | 11 | 150 | 162 | 208 |
| Minnesota | 6 | 6 | 1 | 13 | 9 | 18 | 8 | 89 | 3 | 4 | 8 | 3 | 6 | 4 | 13 | 191 | 155 | 167 |
| New York | 3 | 15 | 9 | 3 | 4 | 8 | 2 | 4 | 126 | 4 | 10 | 16 | 8 | 18 | 12 | 242 | 230 | 182 |
| Oakland | 8 | 7 | 4 | 2 | 2 | 3 | 5 | 0 | 9 | 100 | 11 | 13 | 15 | 3 | 7 | 189 | 176 | 164 |
| Seattle | 8 | 4 | 4 | 5 | 4 | 8 | 4 | 1 | 1 | 6 | 71 | 1 | 8 | 5 | 6 | 136 | 139 | 212 |
| Tampa Bay | 2 | 8 | 8 | 2 | 2 | 1 | 2 | 8 | 7 | 3 | 2 | 74 | 7 | 12 | 7 | 145 | 137 | 192 |
| Texas | 8 | 4 | 8 | 2 | 14 | 7 | 7 | 0 | 4 | 11 | 14 | 8 | 116 | 2 | 22 | 227 | 239 | 182 |
| Toronto | 2 | 14 | 8 | 5 | 1 | 3 | 3 | 0 | 4 | 3 | 4 | 8 | 6 | 80 | 4 | 145 | 190 | 181 |
| N.L. clubs | 11 | 7 | 8 | 17 | 13 | 7 | 6 | 9 | 10 | 14 | 3 | 5 | 10 | 9 | .... | 129 | 136 | .... |
| **2004 Totals** | 171 | 168 | 188 | 272 | 164 | 182 | 146 | 172 | 215 | 184 | 179 | *168 | 213 | 173 | 139 | 2605 | .... | 2591 |
| **2003 Totals** | 152 | 177 | 185 | 218 | 141 | 162 | 182 | 171 | 182 | 159 | 158 | 152 | 245 | 201 | .... | .... | 2499 | .... |

* There were actually 161 home runs hit at Tampa Bay in 2004. The total also includes 7 home runs hit by teams when Tampa Bay played 2 "home" games at Tokyo, Japan vs. the Yankees.

## AT ANAHEIM (171):

Anaheim (77)—Guerrero 19, Guillen 13, Glaus 9, Kennedy 5, B. Molina 5, Anderson 4, DaVanon 4, Erstad 3, Figgins 3, Quinlan 3, Eckstein 2, Halter 2, McPherson 2, J. Molina 1, Mondesi 1, Salmon 1. Baltimore (7)—Mora 2, Bigbie 1, Gibbons 1, J. Lopez 1, Surhoff 1, Tejada 1. Boston (10)—Damon 2, Kapler 2, Ortiz 2, Daubach 1, Garciaparra 1, Millar 1, Ramirez 1. Chicago (4)—Hollandsworth 1, Lee 1, Ramirez 1, Walker 1. Chicago (1)—Gload 1. Cleveland (14)—Hafner 6, Blake 2, Crisp 2, Belliard 1, V. Martinez 1, McDonald 1, Vizquel 1. Detroit (9)—Pena 3, Rodriguez 3, White 3. Kansas City (5)—Buck 1, DeJesus 1, Guiel 1, Nunez 1, Pickering 1. Los Angeles (6)—Beltre 2, Bradley 1, Cora 1, Lo Duca 1, Ventura 1. Milwaukee (1)—Jenkins 1. Minnesota (6)—Jones 2, LeCroy 1, Morneau 1, Ojeda 1, Stewart 1. New York (3)—Giambi 1, Jeter 1, Matsui 1. Oakland (8)—Dye 3, Byrnes 2, Crosby 1, McMillon 1, Melhuse 1. Seattle (8)—Boone 2, Ibanez 1, Jacobsen 1, Leone 1, Martinez 1, Olivo 1, Suzuki 1. Tampa Bay (2)—Cruz Jr. 1, Martinez 1. Texas (8)—Dellucci 2, Blalock 1, Fullmer 1, Matthews Jr. 1, Nix 1, Teixeira 1, M. Young 1. Toronto (2)—Delgado 1, Zaun 1.

## AT BALTIMORE (168):

Anaheim (3)—Figgins 1, Guerrero 1, Halter 1. Arizona (1)—Finley 1. Atlanta (1)—J. Drew 1. Baltimore (82)—Tejada 17, Mora 15, J. Lopez 14, Palmeiro 12, Bigbie 8, Gibbons 4, Surhoff 4, Newhan 3, Leon 2, Matos 2, Garcia 1. Boston (7)—Ortiz 3, Burks 1, Cabrera 1, Damon 1, Millar 1. Chicago (3)—Crede 2, Ordonez 1. Cleveland (3)—Gerut 1, Hafner 1, Merloni 1. Detroit (1)—Pena 1. Kansas City (4)—Sweeney 3, Stairs 1. Minnesota (6)—Cuddyer 2, Jones 1, Koskie 1, LeCroy 1, Morneau 1. New York (15)—Rodriguez 5, Jeter 3, Matsui 2, Sheffield 2, Clark 1, Sierra 1, Wilson 1. Oakland (7)—Durazo 3, Byrnes 1, Dye 1, Hatteberg 1, Melhuse 1. San Francisco (5)—Bonds 2, Alfonzo 1, Pierzynski 1, Torrealba 1. Seattle (4)—Leone 1, Martinez 1, Wilson 1, Winn 1. Tampa Bay (8)—Baldelli 3, Martinez 3, Fick 1, Huff 1. Texas (4)—Soriano 2, Dellucci 1, Jordan 1. Toronto (14)—Delgado 4, Wells 3, Hinske 2, R. Adams 1, Cash 1, Menechino 1, Woodward 1, Zaun 1.

## AT BOSTON (188):

Anaheim (1)—Amezaga 1. Baltimore (15)—Mora 4, Tejada 3, Newhan 2, Surhoff 2, J. Lopez 1, Palmeiro 1, Roberts 1, Segui 1. Boston (111)—Ramirez 23, Ortiz 17, Millar 12, Bellhorn 11, Damon 9, Mueller 9, Varitek 8, Garciaparra 3, Kapler 3, Mirabelli 3, Nixon 3, Reese 3, McCarty 2, Youkilis 2, Cabrera 1, Daubach 1, Roberts 1. Chicago (5)—Lee 2, Rowand 2, Perez 1. Cleveland (2)—Laker 1, V. Martinez 1. Detroit (2)—Monroe 2. Kansas City (2)—Santiago 1, Stinnett 1. Los Angeles (3)—Encarnacion 1, Saenz 1, Werth 1. Minnesota (1)—Hunter 1. New York (9)—Matsui 3, Clark 1, Giambi 1, Phillips 1, Posada 1, Sheffield 1, Sierra 1. Oakland (4)—Chavez 2, Byrnes 1, Hatteberg 1. Philadelphia (4)—Thome 2, Bell 1, Burrell 1. San Diego (1)—Nevin 1. Seattle (4)—Ibanez 2, Aurilia 1, Boone 1. Tampa Bay (8)—Baldelli 2, Cantu 1, Crawford 1, Hall 1, Huff 1, Lugo 1, Martinez 1. Texas (8)—M. Young 3, Barajas 1, Blalock 1, Mench 1, Soriano 1, Teixeira 1. Toronto (8)—Hinske 2, Wells 2, Delgado 1, Hudson 1, Phelps 1, Pond 1.

## AT CHICAGO (272):

Anaheim (6)—Guillen 3, Anderson 1, DaVanon 1, Guerrero 1. Atlanta (3)—J. Drew 1, Furcal 1, C. Jones 1. Baltimore (4)—Hairston Jr. 1, Matos 1, Mora 1, Palmeiro 1. Boston (8)—Ramirez 3, Varitek 2, Cabrera 1, Mientkiewicz 1, Ortiz 1. Chicago (5)—Sosa 2, Grudzielanek 1, Martinez 1, Patterson 1. Chicago (145)—Konerko 29, Lee 17, Uribe 16, Valentin 16, Thomas 14, Crede 12, Rowand 12, Borchard 6, Olivo 4, Ordonez 4, Davis 3, Gload 3, Everett 2, Harris 2, Perez 2, Alomar 1, Alomar Jr. 1, Valdez 1. Cleveland (18)—Belliard 3, Blake 3, Broussard 2, Crisp 2, Lawton 2, V. Martinez 2, Vizquel 2, Hafner 1, Merloni 1. Detroit (25)—Higginson 5, Infante 4, Pena 4, Young 4, Guillen 3, Monroe 2, Thames 2, Inge 1. Kansas City (17)—Beltran 3, Sweeney 3, Buck 2, Stairs 2, Berroa 1, Gonzalez 1, Graffanino 1, Guiel 1, Pickering 1, Randa 1, Santiago 1. Minnesota (13)—Hunter 4, Blanco 2, Kubel 2, Ford 1, Jones 1, Koskie 1, Restovich 1, Rivas 1. New York (3)—Posada 2, Rodriguez 1. Oakland (2)—McMillon 1, Melhuse 1. Philadelphia (9)—Thome 4, Abreu 2, Michaels 2, Perez 1. Seattle (5)—Cabrera 2, Winn 2, Boone 1. Tampa Bay (2)—Hall 1, Huff 1. Texas (2)—Perry 1, Teixeira 1. Toronto (5)—Delgado 2, Hinske 1, Hudson 1, Zaun 1.

## AT CLEVELAND (164):

Anaheim (4)—Glaus 2, Anderson 1, B. Molina 1. Baltimore (2)—Matos 1, Mora 1. Boston (6)—Ortiz 2, Ramirez 2, Damon 1, Mueller 1. Chicago (9)—Gload 2, Lee 2, Davis 1, Everett 1, Konerko 1, Uribe 1, Valentin 1. Cincinnati (3)—Griffey Jr. 1, LaRue 1, Pena 1. Cleveland (70)—Blake 13, Lawton 10, Broussard 9, Crisp 8, V. Martinez 8, Hafner 7, Belliard 4, Gerut 3, Phelps 2, Sizemore 2, Vizquel 2, Bard 1, Merloni 1. Colorado (4)—Walker 3, Greene 1. Detroit (16)—Guillen 3, Infante 2, Pena 2, Smith 2, White 2, Inge 1, Munson 1, Rodriguez 1, Thames 1, Young 1. Florida (6)—Cabrera 2, Gonzalez 2, Easley 1, Nunez 1. Kansas City (8)—Stairs 2, Buck 1, Graffanino 1, Harvey 1, Nunez 1, Stinnett 1, Sweeney 1. Minnesota (9)—Jones 3, Koskie 3, Blanco 1, Morneau 1, Stewart 1. New York (4)—Clark 1, Jeter 1, Posada 1, Sheffield 1. Oakland (2)—Durazo 1, Melhuse 1. Seattle (4)—Martinez 2, Ibanez 1, Suzuki 1. Tampa Bay (2)—Cruz Jr. 1, Lugo 1. Texas (14)—Barajas 2, Dellucci 2, Matthews Jr. 2, Soriano 2, Teixeira 2, Blalock 1, Fullmer 1, Mench 1, M. Young 1. Toronto (1)—Hudson 1.

## AT DETROIT (182):

Anaheim (3)—Glaus 1, Guerrero 1, Guillen 1. Arizona (1)—Bautista 1. Atlanta (3)—C. Jones 2, Marrero 1. Baltimore (3)—Tejada 2, Matos 1. Boston (4)—Youkilis 2, Ortiz 1, Varitek 1. Chicago (12)—Crede 2, Lee 2, Rowand 2, Uribe 2, Borchard 1, Davis 1, Gload 1, Konerko 1. Cleveland (8)—Broussard 2, Gerut 2, Hafner 1, Lawton 1, V. Martinez 1, Phelps 1. Detroit (87)—Munson 13, Pena 10, Inge 9, Monroe 9, Young 8, Guillen 7, Infante 7, Rodriguez 7, Thames 5, White 5, Higginson 4, Norton 1, Sanchez 1, Shelton 1. Florida (3)—Cabrera 1, Castillo 1, Pierre 1. Kansas City (10)—Berroa 2, D. Brown 2, Harvey 2, Sweeney 2, Relaford 1, Stinnett 1. Minnesota (18)—Blanco 2, Ford 2, Guzman 2, Jones 2, Offerman 2, Bowen 1, Hunter 1, Koskie 1, Morneau 1, Ojeda 1, Rivas 1, Stewart 1, Tiffee 1. New York (8)—Rodriguez 2, Sierra 2, Jeter 1, Lofton 1, Matsui 1, Sheffield 1. Oakland (3)—Crosby 1, Dye 1, Melhuse 1. Seattle (8)—Ibanez 2, Winn 2, Bloomquist 1, Boone 1, Spiezio 1, Suzuki 1. Tampa Bay (1)—Baldelli 1. Texas (7)—Soriano 2, Blalock 1, Mench 1, Nix 1, Teixeira 1, M. Young 1. Toronto (3)—Cash 1, Hinske 1, Johnson 1.

## AT KANSAS CITY (146):

Anaheim (2)—Guillen 1, Quinlan 1. Baltimore (12)—Tejada 3, Garcia 2, Newhan 2, Bigbie 1, J. Lopez 1, Machado 1, Mottola 1, Palmeiro 1. Boston (4)—Bellhorn 1, Mirabelli 1, Ortiz 1, Youkilis 1. Chicago (17)—Rowand 4, Valentin 3, Borchard 2, Lee 2, Alomar Jr. 1, Crede 1, Konerko 1, Olivo 1, Ordonez 1, Uribe 1. Cleveland (9)—Blake 2, Hafner 2, Belliard 1, Broussard 1, Ludwick 1, Sizemore 1, Vizquel 1. Detroit (9)—Monroe 2, Pena 2, Rodriguez 2, Guillen 1, Infante 1, Young 1. Kansas City (56)—Beltran 8, Sweeney 8, Buck 6, Harvey 6, Stairs 6, Pickering 4, Berroa 3, Santiago 3, D. Brown 2, DeJesus 2, Guiel 2, Relaford 2, Gonzalez 1, Gotay 1, Lopez 1, Randa 1. Minnesota (8)—Ford 3, Cuddyer 1, Hunter 1, Morneau 1, Prieto 1, Stewart 1. Montreal (3)—Batista 2, Wilkerson 1. New York (1)—Piazza 1. New York (2)—Clark 1, Jeter 1. Oakland (5)—Chavez 1, Crosby 1, Durazo 1, Hatteberg 1, Karros 1. St. Louis (2)—Mabry 1, Rolen 1. Seattle (4)—Boone 2, Cabrera 1, Suzuki 1. Tampa Bay (2)—Baldelli 1, Martinez 1. Texas (7)—Dellucci 2, Barajas 1, Fullmer 1, Mench 1, Teixeira 1, M. Young 1. Toronto (3)—Hudson 2, Johnson 1.

## AT MINNESOTA (172):

Anaheim (1)—Guerrero 1. Baltimore (5)—Tejada 2, Bigbie 1, Palmeiro 1, Roberts 1. Boston (4)—Bellhorn 1, Cabrera 1, Ramirez 1, Varitek 1. Chicago (15)—Konerko 3, Valentin 3, Rowand 2, Uribe 2, Crede 1, Lee 1, Olivo 1, Perez 1, Thomas 1. Cleveland (12)—Broussard 2, Hafner 2, Phelps 2, Belliard 1, Gerut 1, Laker 1, Lawton 1, V. Martinez 1, Sizemore 1. Detroit (15)—Guillen 3, Smith 3, Rodriguez 2, Infante 1, Inge 1, Munson 1, Pena 1, Thames 1, White 1, Young 1. Kansas City (9)—Beltran 2, Gonzalez 2, Randa 2, Sweeney 2, DeJesus 1. Milwaukee (3)—Liefer 1, Overbay 1, Spivey 1. Minnesota (89)—Koskie 16, Hunter 9, Jones 9, Morneau 9, Cuddyer 8, Ford 6, Guzman 5, LeCroy 5, Stewart 5, Blanco 4, Mauer 4, Rivas 4, Punto 2, Mientkiewicz 1, Restovich 1, Tiffee 1. New York (2)—Floyd 1, Williams 1. New York (4)—Sheffield 3, Rodriguez 1. Philadelphia (4)—Ledee 2, Polanco 1, Thome 1. Seattle (1)—Martinez 1. Tampa Bay (8)—Martinez 2, Baldelli 1, Blum 1, Crawford 1, Fick 1, Huff 1, McGriff 1.

## AT NEW YORK (215):

Anaheim (11)—Guillen 3, Kennedy 2, B. Molina 2, Anderson 1, DaVanon 1, Glaus 1, Guerrero 1. Baltimore (11)—Palmeiro 3, J. Lopez 2, Gibbons 1, Hairston Jr. 1, Mora 1, Roberts 1, Surhoff 1, Tejada 1. Boston (14)—Ramirez 4, Damon 3, Ortiz 3, Bellhorn 1, Millar 1, Mueller 1, Roberts 1. Chicago (5)—Ordonez 2, Valentin 2, Crede 1. Cleveland (4)—V. Martinez 2, Crisp 1, Gerut 1. Colorado (3)—Freeman 1, Gonzalez 1, Helton 1. Detroit (4)—Guillen 1, Higginson 1, Monroe 1, White 1. Kansas City (2)—Harvey 1, Stairs 1. Minnesota (3)—Hunter 2, Morneau 1. New York (5)—Hidalgo 2, Cameron 1, Floyd 1, Valent 1. New York (126)—Sheffield 19, Matsui 18, Rodriguez 17, Williams 13, Jeter 11, Posada 11, Sierra 8, Flaherty 6, Clark 5, Giambi 5, Cairo 4, Olerud 3, Crosby 2, Lofton 2, Wilson 2. Oakland (9)—Chavez 3, Hatteberg 2, Byrnes 1, Crosby 1, Dye 1, Melhuse 1. San Diego (2)—Greene 1, Nevin 1. Seattle (1)—Spiezio 1. Tampa Bay (7)—Baldelli 1, Blum 1, Cantu 1, Cruz Jr. 1, Fick 1, Huff 1, Upton 1. Texas (4)—Teixeira 2, Fullmer 1, Soriano 1. Toronto (4)—R. Adams 2, Delgado 1, Gross 1.

## AT OAKLAND (184):

Anaheim (9)—Guerrero 2, Amezaga 1, Galarraga 1, Glaus 1, Guillen 1, Kennedy 1, J. Molina 1, Salmon 1. Boston (5)—Damon 1, Kapler 1, Millar 1, Ortiz 1, Ramirez 1. Chicago (9)—Konerko 2, Rowand 2, Valentin 2, Lee 1, Ordonez 1, Thomas 1. Cincinnati (5)—Casey 1, Cruz 1, Dunn 1, Larkin 1, LaRue 1. Cleveland (4)—Blake 1, Crisp 1, Hafner 1, Ludwick 1. Detroit (7)—White 3, Monroe 2, Pena 1, Young 1. Kansas City (5)—Sweeney 2, Buck 1, Nunez 1,

Randa 1. Minnesota (4)—Cuddyer 1, Jones 1, Mientkiewicz 1, Stewart 1. New York (4)—Rodriguez 2, Giambi 1, Sheffield 1. Oakland (100)—Chavez 15, Durazo 12, Dye 12, Crosby 11, Byrnes 10, Kotsay 9, Hatteberg 8, Kielty 6, Scutaro 6, Miller 5, Melhuse 3, Karros 1, McMillon 1, Swisher 1. Pittsburgh (4)—Mateo 2, Ward 1, C. Wilson 1. San Francisco (5)—Bonds 1, Cruz 1, Feliz 1, Grissom 1, Pierzynski 1. Seattle (6)—Boone 2, Leone 2, Bloomquist 1, Jacobsen 1. Tampa Bay (3)—Blum 1, Cruz Jr. 1, Huff 1. Texas (11)—Teixeira 4, Soriano 3, M. Young 2, Blalock 1, Mench 1. Toronto (3)—Delgado 1, Hinske 1, Wells 1.

## AT SEATTLE (179):

Anaheim (14)—Anderson 3, Glaus 2, Guillen 2, Erstad 1, Figgins 1, Guerrero 1, B. Molina 1, J. Molina 1, Paul 1, Quinlan 1. Baltimore (3)—Bigbie 1, Gibbons 1, Matos 1. Boston (9)—Ramirez 4, Ortiz 2, Bellhorn 1, Cabrera 1, Varitek 1. Chicago (1)—Thomas 1. Cleveland (18)—V. Martinez 4, Gerut 3, Hafner 3, Blake 2, Lawton 2, Belliard 1, Broussard 1, Merloni 1, Vizquel 1. Detroit (2)—Munson 1, Pena 1. Kansas City (9)—Nunez 2, Randa 2, Relaford 2, Buck 1, Castillo 1, DeJesus 1. Minnesota (8)—Hunter 2, Morneau 2, Ford 1, Guzman 1, Jones 1, Koskie 1. Montreal (1)—Sledge 1. New York (10)—Giambi 2, Williams 2, Jeter 1, Matsui 1, Posada 1, Rodriguez 1, Sheffield 1, Sierra 1. Oakland (11)—Chavez 3, Crosby 2, Miller 2, Dye 1, Hatteberg 1, Kotsay 1, McLemore 1. San Diego (2)—Cirillo 1, Nevin 1. Seattle (71)—Boone 12, Ibanez 9, Jacobsen 7, Winn 6, Martinez 5, Spiezio 5, J. Lopez 4, Olivo 4, Suzuki 4, Bocachica 3, Aurilia 2, Cabrera 2, Hansen 2, Leone 2, Olerud 2, Dobbs 1, Wilson 1. Tampa Bay (2)—Cruz Jr. 1, Martinez 1. Texas (14)—Blalock 4, Mench 3, Teixeira 3, Nix 2, Soriano 1, M. Young 1. Toronto (4)—Wells 2, Menechino 1, Phelps 1.

## AT TAMPA BAY (168):

Anaheim (5)—Erstad 2, Guerrero 2, Paul 1. Baltimore (8)—Mora 3, Bigbie 2, Gibbons 2, J. Lopez 1. Boston (14)—Varitek 3, Damon 2, McCarty 2, Ramirez 2, Bellhorn 1, Hyzdu 1, Millar 1, Mueller 1, Nixon 1. Chicago (2)—Konerko 1, Valentin 1. Cleveland (4)—Escobar 1, Hafner 1, Lawton 1, V. Martinez 1. Colorado (2)—Helton 1, Holliday 1. Detroit (3)—Pena 1, Rodriguez 1, Young 1. Florida (1)—Easley 1. Kansas City (4)—DeJesus 2, Pickering 1, Randa 1. Minnesota (3)—Jones 1, Koskie 1, Morneau 1. New York (16)—Sheffield 3, Sierra 3, Matsui 2, Posada 2, Clark 1, Giambi 1, Jeter 1, Rodriguez 1, Williams 1, Wilson 1. Oakland (13)—Durazo 4, Chavez 3, Crosby 2, Byrnes 1, Kotsay 1, Melhuse 1, Scutaro 1. San Francisco (2)—Tucker 2. Seattle (1)—Olivo 1. Tampa Bay (74)—Huff 16, Cruz Jr. 13, Martinez 9, Baldelli 6, Crawford 6, Hall 6, Fick 3, Lugo 3, Blum 2, Cummings 2, Fordyce 2, Sanchez 2, Upton 2, Diaz 1, Perez 1. Texas (8)—Blalock 3, Fullmer 1, Mench 1, Nix 1, Soriano 1, M. Young 1. Toronto (8)—Phelps 3, Delgado 2, Crozier 1, Hinske 1, Rios 1.

## AT TEXAS (213):

Anaheim (11)—Guerrero 6, Glaus 2, Anderson 1, Kennedy 1, McPherson 1. Baltimore (2)—Tejada 2. Boston (1)—Varitek 1. Chicago (9)—Everett 2, Konerko 2, Lee 2, Crede 1, Davis 1, Valentin 1. Cleveland (2)—Blake 1, V. Martinez 1. Detroit (6)—Higginson 2, Guillen 1, Norton 1, Rodriguez 1, Sanchez 1. Houston (2)—Biggio 1, Lamb 1. Kansas City (6)—Beltran 1, Berroa 1, Gonzalez 1, Harvey 1, Stairs 1, Sweeney 1. Minnesota (6)—Blanco 1, Hunter 1, Koskie 1, Morneau 1, Rivas 1, Stewart 1. New York (8)—Wilson 2, Cairo 1, Clark 1, Jeter 1, Olerud 1, Rodriguez 1, Williams 1. Oakland (15)—Dye 3, Byrnes 2, Chavez 2, Crosby 2, Kotsay 2, Durazo 1, McLemore 1, Melhuse 1, Miller 1. Pittsburgh (2)—C. Wilson 1, J. Wilson 1. St. Louis (6)—Mabry 2, Anderson 1, Cedeno 1, Rolen 1, Sanders 1. Seattle (8)—Martinez 2, Olerud 2, Aurilia 1, Boone 1, Ibanez 1, Spiezio 1. Tampa Bay (7)—Martinez 3, Blum 2, Huff 1, Lugo 1. Texas (116)—Teixeira 18, Blalock 16, Mench 14, Soriano 12, Dellucci 9, Nix 9, M. Young 9, Barajas 8, Matthews Jr. 7, Fullmer 4, Jordan 4, Perry 3, Gonzalez 1, Laird 1, E. Young 1. Toronto (6)—Delgado 2, Gomez 1, Hinske 1, Hudson 1, Wells 1.

## AT TORONTO (173):

Anaheim (5)—DaVanon 1, Guerrero 1, Guillen 1, Halter 1, B. Molina 1. Arizona (3)—L. Gonzalez 1, Hairston 1, Hillenbrand 1. Baltimore (6)—Palmeiro 3, Bigbie 1, Gibbons 1, J. Lopez 1. Boston (12)—Ortiz 5, Mirabelli 3, Bellhorn 1, Cabrera 1, Ramirez 1, Youkilis 1. Chicago (2)—Crede 1, Olivo 1. Cleveland (7)—Hafner 3, Blake 1, Laker 1, Lawton 1, McDonald 1. Detroit (6)—White 2, Guillen 1, Munson 1, Pena 1, Rodriguez 1. Kansas City (2)—Guiel 1, Stairs 1. Los Angeles (3)—Beltre 1, Encarnacion 1, Green 1. Minnesota (4)—Ford 1, Hunter 1, Jones 1, LeCroy 1. Montreal (3)—Batista 1, Vidro 1, Wilkerson 1. New York (18)—Clark 3, Posada 3, Rodriguez 3, Sheffield 3, Williams 3, Jeter 1, Matsui 1, Sierra 1. Oakland (3)—Crosby 1, Kielty 1, Swisher 1. Seattle (5)—Winn 2, Boone 1, J. Lopez 1, Spiezio 1. Tampa Bay (12)—Huff 4, Crawford 2, Baldelli 1, Blum 1, Cruz Jr. 1, Lugo 1, Martinez 1, Upton 1. Texas (2)—Barajas 1, Fullmer 1. Toronto (80)—Delgado 18, Wells 14, Johnson 8, Phelps 7, Hinske 6, Menechino 6, Hudson 5, Berg 3, Clark 3, Cash 2, Gross 2, Zaun 2, R. Adams 1, Catalanotto 1, Crozier 1, Gomez 1.

# PARK DATA (SELECTED BATTING CATEGORIES AT EACH STADIUM)

This section contains selected batting statistics for all American League parks for 2004. A key component of this section is an index number for each category, which is used to determine how a given park influences a particular statistic. For example, Chicago's U.S. Cellular Field has had a reputation as being pitcher-friendly, but last year's park index of 131 for home runs was the highest in the A.L. for a second straight year. The park has boosted homers, especially for righthanded batters, since the outfield fences were moved in in 2001.

For each A.L. park, we show how the home team and its opponents performed, both at home and on the road, with the exception being that we do not include data from interleague games. The differences in interleague opponents and ballparks would skew the data.

By comparing the per-game averages at the home park and on the road, we can evaluate the park's impact. This is done by simply dividing the home average by the road average and multiplying the result by 100, generating a park index. If the home and road per-game averages are equal, the index equals 100, and it can be concluded that the park had no impact. An index above 100 means that the park favors that particular statistic. The indexes for at-bats, runs, hits, errors and infield errors are determined on a per-game basis; all other stats are calculated on a per-at-bat basis. "E-infield" denotes infield *fielding* errors. "Alt." is the approximate elevation of the ballpark.

For most parks, data is presented both for 2004 and for the last three years overall. If the park's dimensions have changed over that time, however, the data from the old and new configurations will not be combined. Following all the teams' charts is a ranking section that shows which parks most inflate runs, home runs and batting average.

## ANAHEIM

**Home park:** Angel Stadium of Anaheim **Alt.:** 160 feet **Surface:** Grass

| | 2004 Season | | | | | | | 2002-04 Seasons | | | | | | |
|---|---|---|---|---|---|---|---|---|---|---|---|---|---|---|
| | Home Games | | | Road Games | | | | Home Games | | | Road Games | | | |
| **Category** | **Ana.** | **Opp.** | **Total** | **Ana.** | **Opp.** | **Total** | **Index** | **Ana.** | **Opp.** | **Total** | **Ana.** | **Opp.** | **Total** | **Index** |
| G | 72 | 72 | 144 | 72 | 72 | 144 | | 217 | 217 | 434 | 215 | 215 | 430 | |
| Avg | .287 | .268 | .278 | .282 | .262 | .272 | 102 | .277 | .258 | .268 | .278 | .258 | .269 | 100 |
| AB | 2429 | 2556 | 4985 | 2588 | 2408 | 4996 | 100 | 7294 | 7610 | 14904 | 7642 | 7116 | 14758 | 100 |
| R | 357 | 331 | 688 | 404 | 312 | 716 | 96 | 1035 | 927 | 1962 | 1126 | 963 | 2089 | 93 |
| H | 698 | 686 | 1384 | 730 | 630 | 1360 | 102 | 2024 | 1966 | 3990 | 2127 | 1838 | 3965 | 100 |
| 2B | 111 | 128 | 239 | 131 | 140 | 271 | 88 | 375 | 374 | 749 | 418 | 349 | 767 | 97 |
| 3B | 11 | 8 | 19 | 21 | 13 | 34 | 56 | 40 | 20 | 60 | 44 | 42 | 86 | 69 |
| HR | 73 | 83 | 156 | 75 | 63 | 138 | 113 | 194 | 226 | 420 | 210 | 238 | 448 | 93 |
| BB | 187 | 221 | 408 | 214 | 220 | 434 | 94 | 588 | 679 | 1267 | 648 | 671 | 1319 | 95 |
| SO | 405 | 524 | 929 | 421 | 507 | 928 | 100 | 1105 | 1455 | 2560 | 1177 | 1339 | 2516 | 101 |
| E | 45 | 41 | 86 | 37 | 63 | 100 | 86 | 129 | 119 | 248 | 124 | 161 | 285 | 86 |
| E-Infield | 32 | 35 | 67 | 32 | 57 | 89 | 75 | 102 | 98 | 200 | 109 | 132 | 241 | 82 |
| LHB-Avg | .277 | .282 | .280 | .291 | .261 | .275 | 102 | .279 | .257 | .267 | .291 | .256 | .274 | 98 |
| LHB-HR | 19 | 46 | 65 | 20 | 27 | 47 | 134 | 75 | 112 | 187 | 89 | 107 | 196 | 92 |
| RHB-Avg | .294 | .255 | .276 | .276 | .263 | .270 | 102 | .276 | .260 | .268 | .268 | .260 | .264 | 102 |
| RHB-HR | 54 | 37 | 91 | 55 | 36 | 91 | 103 | 119 | 114 | 233 | 121 | 131 | 252 | 94 |

## BALTIMORE

**Home park:** Oriole Park at Camden Yards **Alt.:** 20 feet **Surface:** Grass

| | 2004 Season | | | | | | | 2002-04 Seasons | | | | | | |
|---|---|---|---|---|---|---|---|---|---|---|---|---|---|---|
| | Home Games | | | Road Games | | | | Home Games | | | Road Games | | | |
| **Category** | **Bal.** | **Opp.** | **Total** | **Bal.** | **Opp.** | **Total** | **Index** | **Bal.** | **Opp.** | **Total** | **Bal.** | **Opp.** | **Total** | **Index** |
| G | 72 | 72 | 144 | 72 | 72 | 144 | | 216 | 216 | 432 | 217 | 217 | 434 | |
| Avg | .282 | .272 | .277 | .287 | .256 | .272 | 102 | .268 | .265 | .266 | .265 | .274 | .269 | 99 |
| AB | 2465 | 2591 | 5056 | 2613 | 2398 | 5011 | 101 | 7302 | 7657 | 14959 | 7662 | 7366 | 15028 | 100 |
| R | 375 | 411 | 786 | 397 | 322 | 719 | 109 | 992 | 1072 | 2064 | 1029 | 1076 | 2105 | 99 |
| H | 695 | 704 | 1399 | 750 | 613 | 1363 | 103 | 1958 | 2027 | 3985 | 2027 | 2020 | 4047 | 99 |
| 2B | 143 | 113 | 256 | 150 | 103 | 253 | 100 | 384 | 346 | 730 | 425 | 378 | 803 | 91 |
| 3B | 4 | 12 | 16 | 10 | 12 | 22 | 72 | 20 | 25 | 45 | 35 | 48 | 83 | 54 |
| HR | 74 | 79 | 153 | 78 | 65 | 143 | 106 | 223 | 270 | 493 | 207 | 241 | 448 | 111 |
| BB | 217 | 315 | 532 | 253 | 296 | 549 | 96 | 623 | 792 | 1415 | 637 | 761 | 1398 | 102 |
| SO | 371 | 471 | 842 | 455 | 484 | 939 | 89 | 1164 | 1337 | 2501 | 1302 | 1364 | 2666 | 94 |
| E | 59 | 52 | 111 | 34 | 56 | 90 | 123 | 137 | 162 | 299 | 124 | 144 | 268 | 112 |
| E-Infield | 54 | 44 | 98 | 32 | 48 | 80 | 123 | 118 | 132 | 250 | 108 | 125 | 233 | 108 |
| LHB-Avg | .263 | .278 | .270 | .295 | .256 | .278 | 97 | .261 | .269 | .265 | .277 | .270 | .273 | 97 |
| LHB-HR | 28 | 37 | 65 | 37 | 26 | 63 | 103 | 81 | 129 | 210 | 79 | 119 | 198 | 105 |
| RHB-Avg | .300 | .267 | .282 | .279 | .255 | .267 | 106 | .272 | .261 | .267 | .257 | .278 | .266 | 100 |
| RHB-HR | 46 | 42 | 88 | 41 | 39 | 80 | 108 | 142 | 141 | 283 | 128 | 122 | 250 | 115 |

## BOSTON

**Home park:** Fenway Park **Alt.:** 21 feet **Surface:** Grass

| | 2004 Season | | | | | | | 2002-04 Seasons | | | | | | |
|---|---|---|---|---|---|---|---|---|---|---|---|---|---|---|
| | Home Games | | | Road Games | | | | Home Games | | | Road Games | | | |
| **Category** | **Bos.** | **Opp.** | **Total** | **Bos.** | **Opp.** | **Total** | **Index** | **Bos.** | **Opp.** | **Total** | **Bos.** | **Opp.** | **Total** | **Index** |
| G | 72 | 72 | 144 | 72 | 72 | 144 | | 216 | 216 | 432 | 216 | 216 | 432 | |
| Avg | .306 | .255 | .280 | .257 | .256 | .257 | 109 | .298 | .255 | .276 | .268 | .252 | .260 | 106 |
| AB | 2534 | 2553 | 5087 | 2557 | 2430 | 4987 | 102 | 7429 | 7561 | 14990 | 7778 | 7316 | 15094 | 99 |
| R | 469 | 350 | 819 | 381 | 329 | 710 | 115 | 1279 | 1005 | 2284 | 1177 | 974 | 2151 | 106 |
| H | 776 | 650 | 1426 | 658 | 622 | 1280 | 111 | 2217 | 1927 | 4144 | 2084 | 1844 | 3928 | 105 |
| 2B | 193 | 164 | 357 | 138 | 123 | 261 | 134 | 530 | 455 | 985 | 439 | 370 | 809 | 123 |
| 3B | 8 | 12 | 20 | 13 | 16 | 29 | 68 | 39 | 35 | 74 | 36 | 52 | 88 | 85 |
| HR | 102 | 69 | 171 | 98 | 71 | 169 | 99 | 268 | 188 | 456 | 297 | 211 | 508 | 90 |
| BB | 291 | 196 | 487 | 297 | 192 | 489 | 98 | 827 | 560 | 1387 | 776 | 635 | 1411 | 99 |
| SO | 515 | 520 | 1035 | 533 | 480 | 1013 | 100 | 1274 | 1543 | 2817 | 1434 | 1504 | 2938 | 97 |
| E | 59 | 53 | 112 | 44 | 42 | 86 | 130 | 161 | 151 | 312 | 130 | 124 | 254 | 123 |
| E-Infield | 51 | 47 | 98 | 36 | 36 | 72 | 136 | 136 | 127 | 263 | 108 | 106 | 214 | 123 |
| LHB-Avg | .311 | .255 | .281 | .249 | .243 | .246 | 115 | .297 | .248 | .272 | .258 | .251 | .255 | 107 |
| LHB-HR | 44 | 28 | 72 | 47 | 29 | 76 | 94 | 114 | 77 | 191 | 144 | 109 | 253 | 76 |
| RHB-Avg | .302 | .255 | .279 | .265 | .271 | .267 | 104 | .300 | .261 | .281 | .277 | .253 | .266 | 106 |
| RHB-HR | 58 | 41 | 99 | 51 | 42 | 93 | 104 | 154 | 111 | 265 | 153 | 102 | 255 | 105 |

## CHICAGO

**Home park:** U.S. Cellular Field **Alt.:** 595 feet **Surface:** Grass

| | 2004 Season | | | | | | | 2002-04 Seasons | | | | | | |
|---|---|---|---|---|---|---|---|---|---|---|---|---|---|---|
| | Home Games | | | Road Games | | | | Home Games | | | Road Games | | | |
| **Category** | **Chi.** | **Opp.** | **Total** | **Chi.** | **Opp.** | **Total** | **Index** | **Chi.** | **Opp.** | **Total** | **Chi.** | **Opp.** | **Total** | **Index** |
| G | 72 | 72 | 144 | 72 | 72 | 144 | | 216 | 216 | 432 | 216 | 216 | 432 | |
| Avg | .268 | .279 | .274 | .262 | .260 | .261 | 105 | .273 | .261 | .267 | .263 | .261 | .262 | 102 |
| AB | 2421 | 2548 | 4969 | 2492 | 2367 | 4859 | 102 | 7171 | 7443 | 14614 | 7546 | 7101 | 14647 | 100 |
| R | 390 | 374 | 764 | 359 | 343 | 702 | 109 | 1180 | 1002 | 2182 | 1047 | 1055 | 2102 | 104 |
| H | 650 | 710 | 1360 | 652 | 615 | 1267 | 107 | 1957 | 1942 | 3899 | 1983 | 1851 | 3834 | 102 |
| 2B | 114 | 124 | 238 | 126 | 119 | 245 | 95 | 366 | 373 | 739 | 409 | 369 | 778 | 95 |
| 3B | 9 | 9 | 18 | 8 | 10 | 18 | 98 | 28 | 28 | 56 | 33 | 30 | 63 | 89 |
| HR | 121 | 110 | 231 | 90 | 82 | 172 | 131 | 356 | 268 | 624 | 246 | 232 | 478 | 131 |
| BB | 231 | 221 | 452 | 200 | 250 | 450 | 98 | 687 | 679 | 1366 | 661 | 726 | 1387 | 99 |
| SO | 427 | 479 | 906 | 465 | 427 | 892 | 99 | 1187 | 1405 | 2592 | 1325 | 1272 | 2597 | 100 |
| E | 42 | 45 | 87 | 47 | 56 | 103 | 84 | 104 | 140 | 244 | 152 | 143 | 295 | 83 |
| E-Infield | 32 | 40 | 72 | 43 | 49 | 92 | 78 | 89 | 124 | 213 | 133 | 114 | 247 | 86 |
| LHB-Avg | .239 | .287 | .268 | .256 | .256 | .256 | 105 | .264 | .269 | .267 | .249 | .273 | .263 | 102 |
| LHB-HR | 25 | 48 | 73 | 28 | 38 | 66 | 115 | 80 | 134 | 214 | 72 | 111 | 183 | 121 |
| RHB-Avg | .281 | .272 | .277 | .265 | .263 | .264 | 105 | .276 | .253 | .266 | .269 | .249 | .261 | 102 |
| RHB-HR | 96 | 62 | 158 | 62 | 44 | 106 | 140 | 276 | 134 | 410 | 174 | 121 | 295 | 137 |

## CLEVELAND

**Home park:** Jacobs Field **Alt.:** 660 feet **Surface:** Grass

| | 2004 Season | | | | | | | 2002-04 Seasons | | | | | | |
|---|---|---|---|---|---|---|---|---|---|---|---|---|---|---|
| | Home Games | | | Road Games | | | | Home Games | | | Road Games | | | |
| **Category** | **Cle.** | **Opp.** | **Total** | **Cle.** | **Opp.** | **Total** | **Index** | **Cle.** | **Opp.** | **Total** | **Cle.** | **Opp.** | **Total** | **Index** |
| G | 72 | 72 | 144 | 72 | 72 | 144 | | 216 | 216 | 432 | 216 | 216 | 432 | |
| Avg | .267 | .272 | .269 | .281 | .274 | .278 | 97 | .255 | .266 | .261 | .266 | .275 | .270 | 97 |
| AB | 2400 | 2578 | 4978 | 2632 | 2517 | 5149 | 97 | 7192 | 7637 | 14829 | 7641 | 7324 | 14965 | 99 |
| R | 357 | 380 | 737 | 403 | 396 | 799 | 92 | 991 | 1083 | 2074 | 1075 | 1145 | 2220 | 93 |
| H | 640 | 700 | 1340 | 740 | 690 | 1430 | 94 | 1835 | 2034 | 3869 | 2033 | 2011 | 4044 | 96 |
| 2B | 156 | 155 | 311 | 136 | 148 | 284 | 113 | 408 | 431 | 839 | 383 | 418 | 801 | 106 |
| 3B | 12 | 12 | 24 | 15 | 16 | 31 | 80 | 27 | 36 | 63 | 45 | 53 | 98 | 65 |
| HR | 62 | 81 | 143 | 105 | 98 | 203 | 73 | 210 | 218 | 428 | 284 | 252 | 536 | 81 |
| BB | 290 | 255 | 545 | 257 | 255 | 512 | 110 | 703 | 765 | 1468 | 714 | 735 | 1449 | 102 |
| SO | 437 | 507 | 944 | 459 | 470 | 929 | 105 | 1329 | 1501 | 2830 | 1386 | 1238 | 2624 | 109 |
| E | 45 | 68 | 113 | 46 | 42 | 88 | 128 | 138 | 193 | 331 | 162 | 112 | 274 | 121 |
| E-Infield | 35 | 53 | 88 | 41 | 34 | 75 | 117 | 117 | 164 | 281 | 141 | 97 | 238 | 118 |
| LHB-Avg | .278 | .268 | .274 | .283 | .264 | .275 | 99 | .261 | .269 | .264 | .267 | .275 | .270 | 98 |
| LHB-HR | 39 | 40 | 79 | 63 | 45 | 108 | 72 | 138 | 99 | 237 | 168 | 104 | 272 | 86 |
| RHB-Avg | .251 | .274 | .265 | .279 | .281 | .280 | 95 | .249 | .265 | .258 | .265 | .274 | .270 | 95 |
| RHB-HR | 23 | 41 | 64 | 42 | 53 | 95 | 73 | 72 | 119 | 191 | 116 | 148 | 264 | 74 |

## DETROIT

**Home park:** Comerica Park **Alt.:** 585 feet **Surface:** Grass

| | 2004 Season | | | | | | | 2002-03 Seasons | | | | | | |
|---|---|---|---|---|---|---|---|---|---|---|---|---|---|---|
| | Home Games | | | Road Games | | | | Home Games | | | Road Games | | | |
| **Category** | **Det.** | **Opp.** | **Total** | **Det.** | **Opp.** | **Total** | **Index** | **Det.** | **Opp.** | **Total** | **Det.** | **Opp.** | **Total** | **Index** |
| G | 72 | 72 | 144 | 72 | 72 | 144 | | 143 | 143 | 286 | 144 | 144 | 288 | |
| Avg | .271 | .277 | .274 | .271 | .277 | .274 | 100 | .242 | .275 | .259 | .245 | .297 | .271 | 96 |
| AB | 2444 | 2578 | 5022 | 2551 | 2425 | 4976 | 101 | 4756 | 5162 | 9918 | 4913 | 4858 | 9771 | 102 |
| R | 335 | 382 | 717 | 399 | 369 | 768 | 93 | 501 | 747 | 1248 | 554 | 877 | 1431 | 88 |
| H | 663 | 715 | 1378 | 691 | 671 | 1362 | 101 | 1150 | 1422 | 2572 | 1205 | 1444 | 2649 | 98 |
| 2B | 99 | 130 | 229 | 146 | 128 | 274 | 83 | 176 | 267 | 443 | 249 | 317 | 566 | 77 |
| 3B | 33 | 21 | 54 | 12 | 11 | 23 | 233 | 44 | 57 | 101 | 20 | 41 | 61 | 163 |
| HR | 76 | 88 | 164 | 105 | 85 | 190 | 86 | 119 | 142 | 261 | 130 | 187 | 317 | 81 |
| BB | 230 | 234 | 464 | 229 | 229 | 458 | 100 | 340 | 448 | 788 | 386 | 466 | 852 | 91 |
| SO | 462 | 450 | 912 | 551 | 421 | 972 | 93 | 860 | 733 | 1593 | 1013 | 665 | 1678 | 94 |
| E | 58 | 32 | 90 | 72 | 48 | 120 | 75 | 118 | 90 | 208 | 136 | 71 | 207 | 101 |
| E-Infield | 44 | 27 | 71 | 57 | 39 | 96 | 74 | 96 | 70 | 166 | 106 | 62 | 168 | 100 |
| LHB-Avg | .263 | .260 | .262 | .259 | .262 | .260 | 101 | .262 | .287 | .273 | .256 | .306 | .279 | 98 |
| LHB-HR | 34 | 34 | 68 | 49 | 29 | 78 | 86 | 76 | 79 | 155 | 75 | 87 | 162 | 95 |
| RHB-Avg | .279 | .289 | .284 | .281 | .287 | .284 | 100 | .217 | .267 | .246 | .233 | .290 | .264 | 93 |
| RHB-HR | 42 | 54 | 96 | 56 | 56 | 112 | 85 | 43 | 63 | 106 | 55 | 100 | 155 | 67 |

## KANSAS CITY

**Home park:** Ewing M. Kauffman Stadium **Alt.:** 750 feet **Surface:** Grass

| | 2004 Season | | | | | | | 2002-03 Seasons | | | | | | |
|---|---|---|---|---|---|---|---|---|---|---|---|---|---|---|
| | Home Games | | | Road Games | | | | Home Games | | | Road Games | | | |
| **Category** | **K.C.** | **Opp.** | **Total** | **K.C.** | **Opp.** | **Total** | **Index** | **K.C.** | **Opp.** | **Total** | **K.C.** | **Opp.** | **Total** | **Index** |
| G | 71 | 71 | 142 | 73 | 73 | 146 | | 143 | 143 | 286 | 145 | 145 | 290 | |
| Avg | .265 | .283 | .274 | .257 | .296 | .276 | 99 | .276 | .291 | .284 | .250 | .265 | .258 | 110 |
| AB | 2356 | 2530 | 4886 | 2572 | 2504 | 5076 | 99 | 4854 | 5220 | 10074 | 4986 | 4811 | 9797 | 104 |
| R | 313 | 378 | 691 | 336 | 433 | 769 | 92 | 754 | 891 | 1645 | 627 | 654 | 1281 | 130 |
| H | 624 | 717 | 1341 | 662 | 741 | 1403 | 98 | 1342 | 1520 | 2862 | 1248 | 1276 | 2524 | 115 |
| 2B | 105 | 163 | 268 | 131 | 159 | 290 | 96 | 267 | 301 | 568 | 225 | 265 | 490 | 113 |
| 3B | 13 | 18 | 31 | 10 | 13 | 23 | 140 | 38 | 30 | 68 | 34 | 30 | 64 | 103 |
| HR | 51 | 84 | 135 | 83 | 106 | 189 | 74 | 135 | 211 | 346 | 127 | 154 | 281 | 120 |
| BB | 215 | 209 | 424 | 201 | 235 | 436 | 101 | 451 | 491 | 942 | 432 | 486 | 918 | 100 |
| SO | 413 | 418 | 831 | 532 | 370 | 902 | 96 | 689 | 772 | 1461 | 939 | 838 | 1777 | 80 |
| E | 46 | 40 | 86 | 69 | 58 | 127 | 70 | 88 | 114 | 202 | 116 | 97 | 213 | 96 |
| E-Infield | 41 | 35 | 76 | 55 | 50 | 105 | 74 | 71 | 102 | 173 | 97 | 83 | 180 | 97 |
| LHB-Avg | .258 | .290 | .274 | .249 | .322 | .284 | 96 | .274 | .296 | .285 | .243 | .273 | .257 | 111 |
| LHB-HR | 21 | 28 | 49 | 30 | 40 | 70 | 76 | 64 | 90 | 154 | 67 | 65 | 132 | 112 |
| RHB-Avg | .269 | .280 | .275 | .263 | .280 | .271 | 101 | .279 | .287 | .283 | .257 | .259 | .258 | 110 |
| RHB-HR | 30 | 56 | 86 | 53 | 66 | 119 | 73 | 71 | 121 | 192 | 60 | 89 | 149 | 126 |

## MINNESOTA

**Home park:** Hubert H. Humphrey Metrodome **Alt.:** 815 feet **Surface:** Turf

| | 2004 Season | | | | | | | 2002-03 Seasons | | | | | | |
|---|---|---|---|---|---|---|---|---|---|---|---|---|---|---|
| | Home Games | | | Road Games | | | | Home Games | | | Road Games | | | |
| **Category** | **Min.** | **Opp.** | **Total** | **Min.** | **Opp.** | **Total** | **Index** | **Min.** | **Opp.** | **Total** | **Min.** | **Opp.** | **Total** | **Index** |
| G | 72 | 72 | 144 | 72 | 72 | 144 | | 144 | 144 | 288 | 143 | 143 | 286 | |
| Avg | .269 | .268 | .269 | .264 | .269 | .266 | 101 | .276 | .259 | .268 | .274 | .269 | .271 | 99 |
| AB | 2449 | 2600 | 5049 | 2541 | 2461 | 5002 | 101 | 4868 | 5145 | 10013 | 5100 | 4860 | 9960 | 100 |
| R | 373 | 320 | 693 | 327 | 320 | 647 | 107 | 710 | 628 | 1338 | 696 | 672 | 1368 | 97 |
| H | 660 | 696 | 1356 | 671 | 661 | 1332 | 102 | 1346 | 1333 | 2679 | 1397 | 1306 | 2703 | 98 |
| 2B | 137 | 106 | 243 | 137 | 116 | 253 | 95 | 313 | 274 | 587 | 280 | 244 | 524 | 111 |
| 3B | 9 | 9 | 18 | 11 | 9 | 20 | 89 | 46 | 30 | 76 | 25 | 21 | 46 | 164 |
| HR | 83 | 74 | 157 | 89 | 74 | 163 | 95 | 134 | 151 | 285 | 158 | 177 | 335 | 85 |
| BB | 240 | 174 | 414 | 224 | 219 | 443 | 93 | 462 | 373 | 835 | 414 | 375 | 789 | 105 |
| SO | 420 | 537 | 957 | 432 | 445 | 877 | 108 | 904 | 957 | 1861 | 949 | 806 | 1755 | 105 |
| E | 46 | 41 | 87 | 44 | 51 | 95 | 92 | 62 | 106 | 168 | 85 | 109 | 194 | 86 |
| E-Infield | 41 | 36 | 77 | 38 | 42 | 80 | 96 | 49 | 87 | 136 | 70 | 91 | 161 | 84 |
| LHB-Avg | .274 | .258 | .265 | .252 | .279 | .265 | 100 | .287 | .261 | .274 | .283 | .276 | .280 | 98 |
| LHB-HR | 39 | 34 | 73 | 41 | 41 | 82 | 87 | 64 | 78 | 142 | 79 | 80 | 159 | 89 |
| RHB-Avg | .266 | .276 | .271 | .273 | .260 | .267 | 102 | .265 | .258 | .261 | .263 | .263 | .263 | 99 |
| RHB-HR | 44 | 40 | 84 | 48 | 33 | 81 | 104 | 70 | 73 | 143 | 79 | 97 | 176 | 81 |

## NEW YORK

**Home park:** Yankee Stadium **Alt.:** 55 feet **Surface:** Grass

| | 2004 Season | | | | | | | 2002-04 Seasons | | | | | | |
|---|---|---|---|---|---|---|---|---|---|---|---|---|---|---|
| | Home Games | | | Road Games | | | | Home Games | | | Road Games | | | |
| **Category** | **N.Y.** | **Opp.** | **Total** | **N.Y.** | **Opp.** | **Total** | **Index** | **N.Y.** | **Opp.** | **Total** | **N.Y.** | **Opp.** | **Total** | **Index** |
| G | 72 | 72 | 144 | 70 | 70 | 140 | | 216 | 216 | 432 | 214 | 214 | 428 | |
| Avg | .271 | .263 | .267 | .267 | .279 | .273 | 98 | .269 | .258 | .263 | .273 | .269 | .271 | 97 |
| AB | 2386 | 2558 | 4944 | 2460 | 2396 | 4856 | 99 | 7203 | 7649 | 14852 | 7622 | 7384 | 15006 | 98 |
| R | 394 | 329 | 723 | 393 | 375 | 768 | 92 | 1129 | 963 | 2092 | 1230 | 989 | 2219 | 93 |
| H | 647 | 672 | 1319 | 656 | 669 | 1325 | 97 | 1940 | 1972 | 3912 | 2082 | 1989 | 4071 | 95 |
| 2B | 114 | 137 | 251 | 142 | 130 | 272 | 91 | 359 | 402 | 761 | 434 | 434 | 868 | 89 |
| 3B | 7 | 9 | 16 | 9 | 18 | 27 | 58 | 18 | 28 | 46 | 22 | 44 | 66 | 70 |
| HR | 111 | 79 | 190 | 99 | 77 | 176 | 106 | 300 | 211 | 511 | 310 | 190 | 500 | 103 |
| BB | 284 | 195 | 479 | 301 | 201 | 502 | 94 | 842 | 526 | 1368 | 910 | 563 | 1473 | 94 |
| SO | 421 | 505 | 926 | 444 | 416 | 860 | 106 | 1358 | 1564 | 2922 | 1454 | 1364 | 2818 | 105 |
| E | 41 | 52 | 93 | 40 | 44 | 84 | 108 | 145 | 157 | 302 | 149 | 123 | 272 | 110 |
| E-Infield | 34 | 41 | 75 | 37 | 40 | 77 | 95 | 124 | 120 | 244 | 128 | 105 | 233 | 104 |
| LHB-Avg | .259 | .268 | .264 | .261 | .279 | .270 | 98 | .262 | .259 | .261 | .270 | .262 | .267 | 98 |
| LHB-HR | 49 | 45 | 94 | 44 | 41 | 85 | 113 | 150 | 106 | 256 | 159 | 86 | 245 | 108 |
| RHB-Avg | .281 | .257 | .269 | .272 | .280 | .276 | 98 | .276 | .256 | .266 | .276 | .275 | .275 | 96 |
| RHB-HR | 62 | 34 | 96 | 55 | 36 | 91 | 100 | 150 | 105 | 255 | 151 | 104 | 255 | 99 |

## OAKLAND

**Home park:** Network Associates Coliseum **Alt.:** 25 feet **Surface:** Grass

| | 2004 Season | | | | | | | 2002-04 Seasons | | | | | | |
|---|---|---|---|---|---|---|---|---|---|---|---|---|---|---|
| | Home Games | | | Road Games | | | | Home Games | | | Road Games | | | |
| **Category** | **Oak.** | **Opp.** | **Total** | **Oak.** | **Opp.** | **Total** | **Index** | **Oak.** | **Opp.** | **Total** | **Oak.** | **Opp.** | **Total** | **Index** |
| G | 72 | 72 | 144 | 72 | 72 | 144 | | 216 | 216 | 432 | 216 | 216 | 432 | |
| Avg | .258 | .254 | .256 | .269 | .266 | .267 | 96 | .259 | .243 | .251 | .259 | .261 | .260 | 97 |
| AB | 2446 | 2546 | 4992 | 2631 | 2451 | 5082 | 98 | 7225 | 7461 | 14686 | 7696 | 7259 | 14955 | 98 |
| R | 320 | 318 | 638 | 352 | 331 | 683 | 93 | 1016 | 854 | 1870 | 1041 | 944 | 1985 | 94 |
| H | 631 | 647 | 1278 | 708 | 651 | 1359 | 94 | 1874 | 1811 | 3685 | 1991 | 1891 | 3882 | 95 |
| 2B | 124 | 141 | 265 | 165 | 116 | 281 | 96 | 388 | 376 | 764 | 423 | 345 | 768 | 101 |
| 3B | 5 | 8 | 13 | 5 | 12 | 17 | 78 | 28 | 24 | 52 | 29 | 38 | 67 | 79 |
| HR | 84 | 70 | 154 | 82 | 71 | 153 | 102 | 263 | 188 | 451 | 245 | 190 | 435 | 106 |
| BB | 277 | 237 | 514 | 269 | 240 | 509 | 103 | 791 | 647 | 1438 | 784 | 700 | 1484 | 99 |
| SO | 438 | 464 | 902 | 499 | 456 | 955 | 96 | 1252 | 1419 | 2671 | 1362 | 1317 | 2679 | 102 |
| E | 39 | 50 | 89 | 43 | 38 | 81 | 110 | 118 | 154 | 272 | 145 | 115 | 260 | 105 |
| E-Infield | 31 | 38 | 69 | 37 | 30 | 67 | 103 | 99 | 124 | 223 | 121 | 96 | 217 | 103 |
| LHB-Avg | .272 | .267 | .270 | .283 | .286 | .284 | 95 | .271 | .249 | .261 | .259 | .264 | .261 | 100 |
| LHB-HR | 43 | 18 | 61 | 46 | 25 | 71 | 91 | 138 | 58 | 196 | 136 | 75 | 211 | 97 |
| RHB-Avg | .244 | .247 | .246 | .254 | .253 | .254 | 97 | .247 | .239 | .243 | .258 | .258 | .258 | 94 |
| RHB-HR | 41 | 52 | 93 | 36 | 46 | 82 | 112 | 125 | 130 | 255 | 109 | 115 | 224 | 114 |

## SEATTLE

**Home park:** Safeco Field **Alt.:** -2 feet **Surface:** Grass

| | 2004 Season | | | | | | | 2002-04 Seasons | | | | | | |
|---|---|---|---|---|---|---|---|---|---|---|---|---|---|---|
| | Home Games | | | Road Games | | | | Home Games | | | Road Games | | | |
| **Category** | **Sea.** | **Opp.** | **Total** | **Sea.** | **Opp.** | **Total** | **Index** | **Sea.** | **Opp.** | **Total** | **Sea.** | **Opp.** | **Total** | **Index** |
| G | 73 | 73 | 146 | 71 | 71 | 142 | | 217 | 217 | 434 | 215 | 215 | 430 | |
| Avg | .253 | .256 | .255 | .292 | .284 | .288 | 88 | .263 | .249 | .256 | .285 | .271 | .279 | 92 |
| AB | 2473 | 2623 | 5096 | 2673 | 2456 | 5129 | 97 | 7251 | 7571 | 14822 | 7797 | 7302 | 15099 | 97 |
| R | 286 | 372 | 658 | 359 | 395 | 754 | 85 | 983 | 949 | 1932 | 1117 | 1058 | 2175 | 88 |
| H | 626 | 672 | 1298 | 781 | 697 | 1478 | 85 | 1905 | 1886 | 3791 | 2225 | 1982 | 4207 | 89 |
| 2B | 119 | 167 | 286 | 132 | 126 | 258 | 112 | 333 | 377 | 710 | 430 | 377 | 807 | 90 |
| 3B | 6 | 5 | 11 | 12 | 15 | 27 | 41 | 39 | 18 | 57 | 37 | 30 | 67 | 87 |
| HR | 65 | 105 | 170 | 59 | 92 | 151 | 113 | 184 | 259 | 443 | 203 | 261 | 464 | 97 |
| BB | 227 | 261 | 488 | 208 | 250 | 458 | 107 | 813 | 686 | 1499 | 710 | 649 | 1359 | 112 |
| SO | 493 | 509 | 1002 | 442 | 412 | 854 | 118 | 1357 | 1470 | 2827 | 1350 | 1275 | 2625 | 110 |
| E | 53 | 51 | 104 | 43 | 49 | 92 | 110 | 118 | 152 | 270 | 117 | 134 | 251 | 107 |
| E-Infield | 48 | 47 | 95 | 36 | 39 | 75 | 123 | 99 | 135 | 234 | 97 | 111 | 208 | 111 |
| LHB-Avg | .286 | .243 | .264 | .321 | .278 | .300 | 88 | .276 | .251 | .263 | .302 | .277 | .290 | 91 |
| LHB-HR | 24 | 50 | 74 | 21 | 31 | 52 | 146 | 71 | 141 | 212 | 77 | 115 | 192 | 113 |
| RHB-Avg | .229 | .266 | .248 | .270 | .288 | .279 | 89 | .252 | .247 | .249 | .272 | .266 | .269 | 93 |
| RHB-HR | 41 | 55 | 96 | 38 | 61 | 99 | 96 | 113 | 118 | 231 | 126 | 146 | 272 | 86 |

## TAMPA BAY

**Home park:** Tropicana Field **Alt.:** 15 feet **Surface:** Turf

| | 2004 Season | | | | | | | 2002-04 Seasons | | | | | | |
|---|---|---|---|---|---|---|---|---|---|---|---|---|---|---|
| | Home Games | | | Road Games | | | | Home Games | | | Road Games | | | |
| **Category** | **T.B.** | **Opp.** | **Total** | **T.B.** | **Opp.** | **Total** | **Index** | **T.B.** | **Opp.** | **Total** | **T.B.** | **Opp.** | **Total** | **Index** |
| G | 69 | 69 | 138 | 72 | 72 | 144 | | 213 | 213 | 426 | 215 | 215 | 430 | |
| Avg | .253 | .249 | .251 | .259 | .282 | .270 | 93 | .262 | .259 | .261 | .255 | .283 | .269 | 97 |
| AB | 2299 | 2416 | 4715 | 2501 | 2403 | 4904 | 100 | 7277 | 7534 | 14811 | 7516 | 7177 | 14693 | 102 |
| R | 302 | 323 | 625 | 308 | 438 | 746 | 87 | 929 | 1099 | 2028 | 926 | 1250 | 2176 | 94 |
| H | 581 | 602 | 1183 | 648 | 678 | 1326 | 93 | 1909 | 1951 | 3860 | 1917 | 2032 | 3949 | 99 |
| 2B | 110 | 129 | 239 | 129 | 156 | 285 | 87 | 368 | 413 | 781 | 383 | 453 | 836 | 93 |
| 3B | 22 | 10 | 32 | 13 | 12 | 25 | 133 | 55 | 37 | 92 | 41 | 32 | 73 | 125 |
| HR | 64 | 84 | 148 | 64 | 91 | 155 | 99 | 171 | 258 | 429 | 203 | 289 | 492 | 87 |
| BB | 203 | 231 | 434 | 197 | 278 | 475 | 95 | 604 | 794 | 1398 | 563 | 837 | 1400 | 99 |
| SO | 388 | 422 | 810 | 448 | 388 | 836 | 101 | 1326 | 1297 | 2623 | 1401 | 1116 | 2517 | 103 |
| E | 49 | 44 | 93 | 62 | 43 | 105 | 92 | 149 | 140 | 289 | 163 | 129 | 292 | 100 |
| E-Infield | 43 | 39 | 82 | 47 | 37 | 84 | 102 | 128 | 129 | 257 | 128 | 113 | 241 | 108 |
| LHB-Avg | .266 | .256 | .261 | .245 | .279 | .260 | 100 | .272 | .267 | .270 | .259 | .285 | .271 | 100 |
| LHB-HR | 41 | 46 | 87 | 40 | 38 | 78 | 111 | 111 | 131 | 242 | 109 | 132 | 241 | 98 |
| RHB-Avg | .239 | .244 | .242 | .273 | .285 | .279 | 87 | .253 | .252 | .253 | .251 | .282 | .267 | 95 |
| RHB-HR | 23 | 38 | 61 | 24 | 53 | 77 | 86 | 60 | 127 | 187 | 94 | 157 | 251 | 75 |

## TEXAS

**Home park:** The Ballpark in Arlington **Alt.:** 551 feet **Surface:** Grass

| | 2004 Season | | | | | | | 2002-04 Seasons | | | | | | |
|---|---|---|---|---|---|---|---|---|---|---|---|---|---|---|
| | Home Games | | | Road Games | | | | Home Games | | | Road Games | | | |
| **Category** | **Tex.** | **Opp.** | **Total** | **Tex.** | **Opp.** | **Total** | **Index** | **Tex.** | **Opp.** | **Total** | **Tex.** | **Opp.** | **Total** | **Index** |
| G | 72 | 72 | 144 | 72 | 72 | 144 | | 216 | 216 | 432 | 216 | 216 | 432 | |
| Avg | .287 | .273 | .280 | .245 | .276 | .260 | 108 | .285 | .279 | .282 | .247 | .275 | .261 | 108 |
| AB | 2470 | 2585 | 5055 | 2494 | 2405 | 4899 | 103 | 7375 | 7755 | 15130 | 7613 | 7261 | 14874 | 102 |
| R | 439 | 365 | 804 | 308 | 332 | 640 | 126 | 1303 | 1225 | 2528 | 931 | 1106 | 2037 | 124 |
| H | 708 | 706 | 1414 | 610 | 664 | 1274 | 111 | 2104 | 2167 | 4271 | 1881 | 1998 | 3879 | 110 |
| 2B | 154 | 136 | 290 | 144 | 122 | 266 | 106 | 420 | 471 | 891 | 395 | 405 | 800 | 109 |
| 3B | 20 | 17 | 37 | 12 | 10 | 22 | 163 | 55 | 54 | 109 | 34 | 45 | 79 | 136 |
| HR | 102 | 87 | 189 | 89 | 79 | 168 | 109 | 354 | 278 | 632 | 261 | 240 | 501 | 124 |
| BB | 238 | 244 | 482 | 212 | 251 | 463 | 101 | 719 | 792 | 1511 | 644 | 837 | 1481 | 100 |
| SO | 445 | 447 | 892 | 517 | 426 | 943 | 92 | 1324 | 1413 | 2737 | 1485 | 1282 | 2767 | 97 |
| E | 52 | 39 | 91 | 48 | 38 | 86 | 106 | 130 | 132 | 262 | 146 | 130 | 276 | 95 |
| E-Infield | 48 | 32 | 80 | 44 | 32 | 76 | 105 | 108 | 107 | 215 | 126 | 108 | 234 | 92 |
| LHB-Avg | .282 | .252 | .266 | .229 | .264 | .248 | 107 | .285 | .270 | .276 | .241 | .274 | .259 | 107 |
| LHB-HR | 51 | 40 | 91 | 40 | 33 | 73 | 118 | 156 | 127 | 283 | 104 | 114 | 218 | 124 |
| RHB-Avg | .290 | .291 | .290 | .254 | .287 | .269 | 108 | .286 | .288 | .287 | .251 | .276 | .262 | 109 |
| RHB-HR | 51 | 47 | 98 | 49 | 46 | 95 | 102 | 198 | 151 | 349 | 157 | 126 | 283 | 124 |

## TORONTO

**Home park:** SkyDome **Alt.:** 300 feet **Surface:** Turf

| | 2004 Season | | | | | | | 2002-04 Seasons | | | | | | |
|---|---|---|---|---|---|---|---|---|---|---|---|---|---|---|
| | Home Games | | | Road Games | | | | Home Games | | | Road Games | | | |
| **Category** | **Tor.** | **Opp.** | **Total** | **Tor.** | **Opp.** | **Total** | **Index** | **Tor.** | **Opp.** | **Total** | **Tor.** | **Opp.** | **Total** | **Index** |
| G | 72 | 72 | 144 | 71 | 71 | 142 | | 216 | 216 | 432 | 215 | 215 | 430 | |
| Avg | .263 | .284 | .273 | .257 | .267 | .262 | 105 | .272 | .278 | .275 | .262 | .268 | .265 | 104 |
| AB | 2406 | 2557 | 4963 | 2514 | 2357 | 4871 | 100 | 7309 | 7698 | 15007 | 7635 | 7230 | 14865 | 100 |
| R | 343 | 396 | 739 | 303 | 358 | 661 | 110 | 1119 | 1174 | 2293 | 1061 | 1057 | 2118 | 108 |
| H | 632 | 725 | 1357 | 645 | 629 | 1274 | 105 | 1988 | 2137 | 4125 | 1999 | 1941 | 3940 | 104 |
| 2B | 129 | 141 | 270 | 127 | 122 | 249 | 106 | 462 | 452 | 914 | 404 | 363 | 767 | 118 |
| 3B | 20 | 12 | 32 | 11 | 12 | 23 | 137 | 53 | 38 | 91 | 40 | 46 | 86 | 105 |
| HR | 71 | 84 | 155 | 61 | 85 | 146 | 104 | 239 | 261 | 500 | 217 | 233 | 450 | 110 |
| BB | 249 | 285 | 534 | 216 | 263 | 479 | 109 | 730 | 766 | 1496 | 682 | 741 | 1423 | 104 |
| SO | 463 | 454 | 917 | 509 | 396 | 905 | 99 | 1407 | 1395 | 2802 | 1574 | 1215 | 2789 | 100 |
| E | 44 | 56 | 100 | 35 | 50 | 85 | 116 | 135 | 153 | 288 | 142 | 133 | 275 | 104 |
| E-Infield | 41 | 50 | 91 | 29 | 42 | 71 | 126 | 123 | 128 | 251 | 123 | 111 | 234 | 107 |
| LHB-Avg | .248 | .290 | .271 | .260 | .278 | .269 | 101 | .268 | .281 | .275 | .264 | .272 | .268 | 103 |
| LHB-HR | 36 | 46 | 82 | 34 | 50 | 84 | 94 | 120 | 129 | 249 | 108 | 118 | 226 | 110 |
| RHB-Avg | .274 | .277 | .275 | .254 | .257 | .255 | 108 | .275 | .275 | .275 | .260 | .265 | .263 | 105 |
| RHB-HR | 35 | 38 | 73 | 27 | 35 | 62 | 118 | 119 | 132 | 251 | 109 | 115 | 224 | 110 |

# 2002-2004 A.L. BALLPARK INDEX RANKINGS

## RUNS PER GAME

| Team | Home Games | | | | Road Games | | | | Index |
|---|---|---|---|---|---|---|---|---|---|
| | Games | Team | Opp. | Total | Games | Team | Opp. | Total | |
| Tex | 216 | 1303 | 1225 | 2528 | 216 | 931 | 1106 | 2037 | 124 |
| Tor | 216 | 1119 | 1174 | 2293 | 215 | 1061 | 1057 | 2118 | 108 |
| Min* | 72 | 373 | 320 | 693 | 72 | 327 | 320 | 647 | 107 |
| Bos | 216 | 1279 | 1005 | 2284 | 216 | 1177 | 974 | 2151 | 106 |
| CWS | 216 | 1180 | 1002 | 2182 | 216 | 1047 | 1055 | 2102 | 104 |
| Bal | 216 | 992 | 1072 | 2064 | 217 | 1029 | 1076 | 2105 | 99 |
| Oak | 216 | 1016 | 854 | 1870 | 216 | 1041 | 944 | 1985 | 94 |
| TB | 213 | 929 | 1099 | 2028 | 215 | 926 | 1250 | 2176 | 94 |
| Ana | 217 | 1035 | 927 | 1962 | 215 | 1126 | 963 | 2089 | 93 |
| Cle | 216 | 991 | 1083 | 2074 | 216 | 1075 | 1145 | 2220 | 93 |
| Det* | 72 | 335 | 382 | 717 | 72 | 399 | 369 | 768 | 93 |
| NYY | 216 | 1129 | 963 | 2092 | 214 | 1230 | 989 | 2219 | 93 |
| KC* | 71 | 313 | 378 | 691 | 73 | 336 | 433 | 769 | 92 |
| Sea | 217 | 983 | 949 | 1932 | 215 | 1117 | 1058 | 2175 | 88 |

*Current dimensions began in 2004.

## HOME RUNS PER AT-BAT

| Team | Home Games | | | | Road Games | | | | Index |
|---|---|---|---|---|---|---|---|---|---|
| | Games | Team | Opp. | Total | Games | Team | Opp. | Total | |
| CWS | 216 | 356 | 268 | 624 | 216 | 246 | 232 | 478 | 131 |
| Tex | 216 | 354 | 278 | 632 | 216 | 261 | 240 | 501 | 124 |
| Bal | 216 | 223 | 270 | 493 | 217 | 207 | 241 | 448 | 111 |
| Tor | 216 | 239 | 261 | 500 | 215 | 217 | 233 | 450 | 110 |
| Oak | 216 | 263 | 188 | 451 | 216 | 245 | 190 | 435 | 106 |
| NYY | 216 | 300 | 211 | 511 | 214 | 310 | 190 | 500 | 103 |
| Sea | 217 | 184 | 259 | 443 | 215 | 203 | 261 | 464 | 97 |
| Min* | 72 | 83 | 74 | 157 | 72 | 89 | 74 | 163 | 95 |
| Ana | 217 | 194 | 226 | 420 | 215 | 210 | 238 | 448 | 93 |
| Bos | 216 | 268 | 188 | 456 | 216 | 297 | 211 | 508 | 90 |
| TB | 213 | 171 | 258 | 429 | 215 | 203 | 289 | 492 | 87 |
| Det* | 72 | 76 | 88 | 164 | 72 | 105 | 85 | 190 | 86 |
| Cle | 216 | 210 | 218 | 428 | 216 | 284 | 252 | 536 | 81 |
| KC* | 71 | 51 | 84 | 135 | 73 | 83 | 106 | 189 | 74 |

*Current dimensions began in 2004.

## BATTING AVERAGE

| Team | Home Games | | | | Road Games | | | | Index |
|---|---|---|---|---|---|---|---|---|---|
| | Games | Team | Opp. | Total | Games | Team | Opp. | Total | |
| Tex | 216 | .285 | .279 | .282 | 216 | .247 | .275 | .261 | 108 |
| Bos | 216 | .298 | .255 | .276 | 216 | .268 | .252 | .260 | 106 |
| Tor | 216 | .272 | .278 | .275 | 215 | .262 | .268 | .265 | 104 |
| CWS | 216 | .273 | .261 | .267 | 216 | .263 | .261 | .262 | 102 |
| Min* | 72 | .269 | .268 | .269 | 72 | .264 | .269 | .266 | 101 |
| Det* | 72 | .271 | .277 | .274 | 72 | .271 | .277 | .274 | 100 |
| Ana | 217 | .277 | .258 | .268 | 215 | .278 | .258 | .269 | 100 |
| KC* | 71 | .265 | .283 | .274 | 73 | .257 | .296 | .276 | 99 |
| Bal | 216 | .268 | .265 | .266 | 217 | .265 | .274 | .269 | 99 |
| NYY | 216 | .269 | .258 | .263 | 214 | .273 | .269 | .271 | 97 |
| TB | 213 | .262 | .259 | .261 | 215 | .255 | .283 | .269 | 97 |
| Oak | 216 | .259 | .243 | .251 | 216 | .259 | .261 | .260 | 97 |
| Cle | 216 | .255 | .266 | .261 | 216 | .266 | .275 | .270 | 97 |
| Sea | 217 | .263 | .249 | .256 | 215 | .285 | .271 | .279 | 92 |

*Current dimensions began in 2004.

# 2004 N.L. STATISTICS

Batting

Designated hitting

Pinch-hitting

Pitching

Fielding

Miscellaneous

# BATTING

## TEAM

| Team | G | TPA | AB | R | H | TB | 2B | 3B | HR | RBI | SH | SF | HP | BB | IBB | SO | SB | CS | GDP | LOB | ShO | Avg. | OBP | Slg. |
|---|---|---|---|---|---|---|---|---|---|---|---|---|---|---|---|---|---|---|---|---|---|---|---|---|
| St. Louis | 162 | 6297 | 5555 | 855 | 1544 | 2553 | 319 | 24 | 214 | 817 | 73 | 70 | 51 | 548 | 64 | 1085 | 111 | 47 | 121 | 1156 | 4 | .278 | .344 | .460 |
| Colorado | 162 | 6333 | 5577 | 833 | 1531 | 2536 | 331 | 34 | 202 | 795 | 97 | 37 | 54 | 568 | 51 | 1181 | 44 | 33 | 132 | 1167 | 6 | .275 | .345 | .455 |
| San Diego | 162 | 6313 | 5573 | 768 | 1521 | 2306 | 304 | 32 | 139 | 722 | 52 | 66 | 56 | 566 | 45 | 910 | 52 | 25 | 128 | 1235 | 3 | .273 | .342 | .414 |
| San Francisco | 162 | 6466 | 5546 | 850 | 1500 | 2429 | 314 | 33 | 183 | 805 | 92 | 51 | 72 | 705 | 153 | 874 | 43 | 23 | 142 | 1289 | 4 | .270 | .357 | .438 |
| Atlanta | 162 | 6339 | 5570 | 803 | 1503 | 2415 | 304 | 37 | 178 | 767 | 75 | 48 | 59 | 587 | 51 | 1158 | 86 | 32 | 123 | 1230 | 7 | .270 | .343 | .434 |
| Chicago | 162 | 6281 | 5628 | 789 | 1508 | 2579 | 308 | 29 | 235 | 755 | 78 | 48 | 38 | 489 | 46 | 1080 | 66 | 28 | 120 | 1121 | 12 | .268 | .328 | .458 |
| Philadelphia | 162 | 6456 | 5643 | 840 | 1505 | 2499 | 303 | 23 | 215 | 802 | 64 | 46 | 58 | 645 | 60 | 1133 | 100 | 27 | 123 | 1236 | 4 | .267 | .345 | .443 |
| Houston | 162 | 6269 | 5468 | 803 | 1458 | 2385 | 294 | 36 | 187 | 756 | 98 | 52 | 61 | 590 | 54 | 999 | 89 | 30 | 128 | 1175 | 3 | .267 | .342 | .436 |
| Florida | 162 | 6160 | 5486 | 718 | 1447 | 2230 | 275 | 32 | 148 | 677 | 77 | 40 | 58 | 499 | 37 | 968 | 96 | 43 | 142 | 1127 | 8 | .264 | .329 | .406 |
| Los Angeles | 162 | 6244 | 5542 | 761 | 1450 | 2345 | 226 | 30 | 203 | 731 | 69 | 35 | 62 | 536 | 45 | 1092 | 102 | 41 | 121 | 1152 | 12 | .262 | .332 | .423 |
| Pittsburgh | 161 | 6115 | 5483 | 680 | 1428 | 2199 | 267 | 39 | 142 | 648 | 79 | 42 | 95 | 415 | 33 | 1066 | 63 | 40 | 117 | 1123 | 8 | .260 | .321 | .401 |
| Arizona | 162 | 6114 | 5544 | 615 | 1401 | 2177 | 295 | 38 | 135 | 582 | 56 | 37 | 35 | 441 | 38 | 1022 | 53 | 32 | 137 | 1108 | 9 | .253 | .310 | .393 |
| Cincinnati | 162 | 6278 | 5518 | 750 | 1380 | 2305 | 287 | 28 | 194 | 713 | 55 | 25 | 81 | 599 | 38 | 1335 | 77 | 25 | 125 | 1176 | 10 | .250 | .331 | .418 |
| New York | 162 | 6209 | 5532 | 684 | 1376 | 2260 | 289 | 20 | 185 | 658 | 69 | 34 | 61 | 512 | 54 | 1159 | 107 | 23 | 129 | 1142 | 12 | .249 | .317 | .409 |
| Montreal | 162 | 6138 | 5474 | 635 | 1361 | 2144 | 276 | 27 | 151 | 605 | 100 | 33 | 35 | 496 | 51 | 925 | 109 | 38 | 115 | 1123 | 16 | .249 | .313 | .392 |
| Milwaukee | 161 | 6195 | 5483 | 634 | 1358 | 2122 | 295 | 32 | 135 | 601 | 56 | 40 | 68 | 540 | 49 | 1312 | 138 | 40 | 120 | 1199 | 16 | .248 | .321 | .387 |
| **Totals** | 1295 | 100207 | 88622 | 12018 | 23271 | 37484 | 4687 | 494 | 2846 | 11434 | 1190 | 704 | 944 | 8736 | 869 | 17299 | 1336 | 527 | 2023 | 18759 | 134 | .263 | .333 | .423 |

## INDIVIDUAL

### TOP QUALIFIERS FOR BATTING CHAMPIONSHIP

Minimum 502 plate appearances. *Lefthanded batter. †Switch-hitter.

| Player, Team | G | TPA | AB | R | H | TB | 2B | 3B | HR | RBI | SH | SF | HP | BB | IBB | SO | SB | CS | GDP | Avg. | OBP | Slg. |
|---|---|---|---|---|---|---|---|---|---|---|---|---|---|---|---|---|---|---|---|---|---|---|
| Bonds, Barry, S.F.* | 147 | 617 | 373 | 129 | 135 | 303 | 27 | 3 | 45 | 101 | 0 | 3 | 9 | 232 | 120 | 41 | 6 | 1 | 5 | .362 | .609 | .812 |
| Helton, Todd, Col.* | 154 | 683 | 547 | 115 | 190 | 339 | 49 | 2 | 32 | 96 | 0 | 6 | 3 | 127 | 19 | 72 | 3 | 0 | 12 | .347 | .469 | .620 |
| Loretta, Mark, S.D. | 154 | 707 | 620 | 108 | 208 | 307 | 47 | 2 | 16 | 76 | 4 | 16 | 9 | 58 | 3 | 45 | 5 | 3 | 10 | .335 | .391 | .495 |
| Beltre, Adrian, L.A. | 156 | 657 | 598 | 104 | 200 | 376 | 32 | 0 | 48 | 121 | 0 | 4 | 2 | 53 | 9 | 87 | 7 | 2 | 15 | .334 | .388 | .629 |
| Pujols, Albert, St.L. | 154 | 692 | 592 | 133 | 196 | 389 | 51 | 2 | 46 | 123 | 0 | 9 | 7 | 84 | 12 | 52 | 5 | 5 | 21 | .331 | .415 | .657 |
| Pierre, Juan, Fla.* | 162 | 748 | 678 | 100 | 221 | 276 | 22 | 12 | 3 | 49 | 15 | 2 | 8 | 45 | 1 | 35 | 45 | 24 | 9 | .326 | .374 | .407 |
| Casey, Sean, Cin.* | 146 | 633 | 571 | 101 | 185 | 305 | 44 | 2 | 24 | 99 | 0 | 6 | 10 | 46 | 5 | 36 | 2 | 0 | 16 | .324 | .381 | .534 |
| Kendall, Jason, Pit. | 147 | 658 | 574 | 86 | 183 | 224 | 32 | 0 | 3 | 51 | 1 | 4 | 19 | 60 | 2 | 41 | 11 | 8 | 12 | .319 | .399 | .390 |
| Ramirez, Aramis, Chi. | 145 | 606 | 547 | 99 | 174 | 316 | 32 | 1 | 36 | 103 | 0 | 7 | 3 | 49 | 6 | 62 | 0 | 2 | 25 | .318 | .373 | .578 |
| Berkman, Lance, Hou.† | 160 | 687 | 544 | 104 | 172 | 308 | 40 | 3 | 30 | 106 | 0 | 6 | 10 | 127 | 14 | 101 | 9 | 7 | 10 | .316 | .450 | .566 |
| Rolen, Scott, St.L. | 142 | 593 | 500 | 109 | 157 | 299 | 32 | 4 | 34 | 124 | 1 | 7 | 13 | 72 | 5 | 92 | 4 | 3 | 8 | .314 | .409 | .598 |
| Estrada, Johnny, Atl.† | 134 | 517 | 462 | 56 | 145 | 208 | 36 | 0 | 9 | 76 | 1 | 4 | 11 | 39 | 7 | 66 | 0 | 0 | 18 | .314 | .378 | .450 |
| Hillenbrand, Shea, Ari. | 148 | 604 | 562 | 68 | 174 | 261 | 36 | 3 | 15 | 80 | 0 | 6 | 12 | 24 | 2 | 49 | 2 | 0 | 18 | .310 | .348 | .464 |
| Wilson, Jack, Pit. | 157 | 693 | 652 | 82 | 201 | 299 | 41 | 12 | 11 | 59 | 7 | 5 | 3 | 26 | 0 | 71 | 8 | 4 | 15 | .308 | .335 | .459 |
| Womack, Tony, St.L.* | 145 | 606 | 553 | 91 | 170 | 213 | 22 | 3 | 5 | 38 | 8 | 6 | 3 | 36 | 1 | 60 | 26 | 5 | 6 | .307 | .349 | .385 |

DEPARTMENTAL LEADERS: G—Finley, Ari.-L.A., Pierre, Fla., 162; AB—Pierre, Fla., 678; R—Pujols, St.L., 133 H—Pierre, Fla., 221; TB—Pujols, St.L., 389; 1B—Pierre, Fla., 184; 2B—Overbay, Mil., 53; 3B—Pierre, Fla., Rollins, Phi., J. Wilson, Pit., 12; HR—Beltre, L.A., 48; RBI—Castilla, Col., 131; SH—Clayton, Col., 24; SF—Loretta, S.D., 16; HP—C. Wilson, Pit., 30; BB—Bonds, S.F., 232; IBB—Bonds, S.F., 120; SO—Dunn, Cin., 195; SB—Podsednik, Mil., 70; CS—Pierre, Fla., 24; GDP—Pierzynski, S.F., 27; Slg.—Bonds, S.F., .812; OBP—Bonds, S.F., .609.

### ALL PLAYERS

*Lefthanded batter. †Switch-hitter.

| Player, Team | G | TPA | AB | R | H | TB | 2B | 3B | HR | RBI | SH | SF | HP | BB | IBB | SO | SB | CS | GDP | Avg. | OBP | Slg. |
|---|---|---|---|---|---|---|---|---|---|---|---|---|---|---|---|---|---|---|---|---|---|---|
| Abbott, Paul, Phi. | 10 | 14 | 11 | 1 | 2 | 2 | 0 | 0 | 0 | 2 | 3 | 0 | 0 | 0 | 0 | 4 | 0 | 0 | 0 | .182 | .182 | .182 |
| Abreu, Bobby, Phi.* | 159 | 713 | 574 | 118 | 173 | 312 | 47 | 1 | 30 | 105 | 0 | 7 | 5 | 127 | 10 | 116 | 40 | 5 | 5 | .301 | .428 | .544 |
| Acevedo, Jose, Cin. | 39 | 52 | 43 | 0 | 2 | 2 | 0 | 0 | 0 | 1 | 5 | 1 | 0 | 3 | 0 | 26 | 0 | 0 | 1 | .047 | .106 | .047 |
| Aguila, Chris, Fla. | 29 | 48 | 45 | 10 | 10 | 23 | 2 | 1 | 3 | 5 | 1 | 0 | 0 | 2 | 0 | 12 | 0 | 0 | 0 | .222 | .255 | .511 |
| Alfaro, Jason, Hou. | 7 | 12 | 11 | 1 | 2 | 2 | 0 | 0 | 0 | 0 | 1 | 0 | 0 | 0 | 0 | 5 | 0 | 0 | 1 | .182 | .182 | .182 |
| Alfonseca, Antonio, Atl. | 79 | 1 | 1 | 0 | 0 | 0 | 0 | 0 | 0 | 0 | 0 | 0 | 0 | 0 | 0 | 1 | 0 | 0 | 0 | .000 | .000 | .000 |
| Alfonzo, Edgardo, S.F. | 139 | 576 | 519 | 66 | 150 | 211 | 26 | 1 | 11 | 77 | 2 | 4 | 5 | 46 | 2 | 40 | 1 | 1 | 15 | .289 | .350 | .407 |
| Almanza, Armando, Atl.* | 13 | 1 | 0 | 0 | 0 | 0 | 0 | 0 | 0 | 0 | 1 | 0 | 0 | 0 | 0 | 0 | 0 | 0 | 0 | .000 | .000 | .000 |
| Alomar, Roberto, Ari.† | 38 | 125 | 110 | 14 | 34 | 52 | 5 | 2 | 3 | 16 | 2 | 0 | 1 | 12 | 0 | 18 | 0 | 2 | 2 | .309 | .382 | .473 |
| Alou, Moises, Chi. | 155 | 675 | 601 | 106 | 176 | 335 | 36 | 3 | 39 | 106 | 0 | 6 | 0 | 68 | 2 | 80 | 3 | 0 | 12 | .293 | .361 | .557 |
| Alvarez, Tony, Pit. | 24 | 45 | 38 | 5 | 8 | 13 | 2 | 0 | 1 | 8 | 0 | 2 | 1 | 4 | 0 | 7 | 0 | 0 | 1 | .211 | .289 | .342 |
| Alvarez, Wilson, L.A.* | 40 | 34 | 31 | 4 | 5 | 5 | 0 | 0 | 0 | 0 | 2 | 0 | 0 | 1 | 0 | 14 | 0 | 0 | 2 | .161 | .188 | .161 |
| Anderson, Jimmy, Chi.* | 7 | 1 | 1 | 0 | 0 | 0 | 0 | 0 | 0 | 0 | 0 | 0 | 0 | 0 | 0 | 0 | 0 | 0 | 0 | .000 | .000 | .000 |
| Anderson, Marlon, St.L.* | 113 | 271 | 253 | 31 | 60 | 96 | 12 | 0 | 8 | 28 | 0 | 5 | 1 | 12 | 1 | 38 | 6 | 2 | 5 | .237 | .269 | .379 |
| Ankiel, Rick, St.L.* | 5 | 2 | 1 | 0 | 0 | 0 | 0 | 0 | 0 | 0 | 0 | 0 | 0 | 1 | 0 | 1 | 0 | 0 | 0 | .000 | .500 | .000 |
| Aquino, Greg, Ari. | 34 | 1 | 1 | 0 | 0 | 0 | 0 | 0 | 0 | 0 | 0 | 0 | 0 | 0 | 0 | 0 | 0 | 0 | 0 | .000 | .000 | .000 |
| Armas, Tony, Mon. | 17 | 21 | 16 | 0 | 0 | 0 | 0 | 0 | 0 | 0 | 5 | 0 | 0 | 0 | 0 | 5 | 0 | 0 | 0 | .000 | .000 | .000 |
| Atkins, Garrett, Col. | 15 | 33 | 28 | 3 | 10 | 15 | 2 | 0 | 1 | 8 | 0 | 1 | 0 | 4 | 0 | 3 | 0 | 0 | 0 | .357 | .424 | .536 |
| Aurilia, Rich, S.D. | 51 | 158 | 138 | 22 | 35 | 53 | 8 | 2 | 2 | 16 | 1 | 2 | 2 | 15 | 0 | 28 | 0 | 0 | 2 | .254 | .331 | .384 |
| Ausmus, Brad, Hou. | 129 | 448 | 403 | 38 | 100 | 131 | 14 | 1 | 5 | 31 | 7 | 3 | 2 | 33 | 11 | 56 | 2 | 2 | 13 | .248 | .306 | .325 |
| Ayala, Luis, Mon. | 81 | 10 | 9 | 0 | 3 | 4 | 1 | 0 | 0 | 0 | 1 | 0 | 0 | 0 | 0 | 3 | 0 | 0 | 0 | .333 | .333 | .444 |
| Backe, Brandon, Hou. | 34 | 21 | 16 | 3 | 5 | 8 | 0 | 0 | 1 | 6 | 3 | 0 | 1 | 1 | 0 | 8 | 0 | 0 | 0 | .313 | .389 | .500 |
| Baerga, Carlos, Ari.† | 79 | 94 | 85 | 6 | 20 | 28 | 2 | 0 | 2 | 11 | 0 | 0 | 3 | 6 | 0 | 12 | 0 | 0 | 7 | .235 | .309 | .329 |
| Bagwell, Jeff, Hou. | 156 | 679 | 572 | 104 | 152 | 266 | 29 | 2 | 27 | 89 | 0 | 3 | 8 | 96 | 6 | 131 | 6 | 4 | 12 | .266 | .377 | .465 |
| Bako, Paul, Chi.* | 49 | 157 | 138 | 13 | 28 | 39 | 8 | 0 | 1 | 10 | 1 | 1 | 2 | 15 | 3 | 29 | 1 | 0 | 4 | .203 | .288 | .283 |
| Baldwin, James, N.Y. | 2 | 2 | 2 | 0 | 0 | 0 | 0 | 0 | 0 | 0 | 0 | 0 | 0 | 0 | 0 | 1 | 0 | 0 | 0 | .000 | .000 | .000 |
| Barmes, Clint, Col. | 20 | 77 | 71 | 14 | 20 | 31 | 3 | 1 | 2 | 10 | 2 | 0 | 1 | 3 | 0 | 10 | 0 | 1 | 2 | .282 | .320 | .437 |

| Player, Team | G | TPA | AB | R | H | TB | 2B | 3B | HR | RBI | SH | SF | HP | BB | IBB | SO | SB | CS | GDP | Avg. | OBP | Slg. |
|---|---|---|---|---|---|---|---|---|---|---|---|---|---|---|---|---|---|---|---|---|---|---|
| Barrett, Michael, Chi. | 134 | 506 | 456 | 55 | 131 | 223 | 32 | 6 | 16 | 65 | 4 | 8 | 5 | 33 | 4 | 64 | 1 | 4 | 13 | .287 | .337 | .489 |
| Batista, Tony, Mon. | 157 | 650 | 606 | 76 | 146 | 276 | 30 | 2 | 32 | 110 | 4 | 10 | 4 | 26 | 4 | 78 | 14 | 6 | 14 | .241 | .272 | .455 |
| Bautista, Danny, Ari. | 141 | 582 | 539 | 64 | 154 | 216 | 27 | 1 | 11 | 65 | 1 | 3 | 4 | 35 | 2 | 66 | 6 | 2 | 20 | .286 | .332 | .401 |
| Bautista, Jose, Pit. | 23 | 43 | 40 | 1 | 8 | 10 | 2 | 0 | 0 | 0 | 1 | 0 | 0 | 2 | 0 | 18 | 0 | 0 | 1 | .200 | .238 | .250 |
| Bay, Jason, Pit. | 120 | 472 | 411 | 61 | 116 | 226 | 24 | 4 | 26 | 82 | 5 | 5 | 10 | 41 | 2 | 129 | 4 | 6 | 9 | .282 | .358 | .550 |
| Beckett, Josh, Fla. | 26 | 55 | 44 | 2 | 7 | 8 | 1 | 0 | 0 | 2 | 9 | 0 | 0 | 2 | 0 | 18 | 0 | 0 | 0 | .159 | .196 | .182 |
| Bell, David, Phi. | 143 | 603 | 533 | 67 | 155 | 244 | 33 | 1 | 18 | 77 | 2 | 5 | 6 | 57 | 4 | 75 | 1 | 1 | 14 | .291 | .363 | .458 |
| Bell, Heath, N.Y. | 17 | 1 | 1 | 0 | 0 | 0 | 0 | 0 | 0 | 0 | 0 | 0 | 0 | 0 | 0 | 0 | 0 | 0 | 0 | .000 | .000 | .000 |
| Beltran, Carlos, Hou.† | 90 | 399 | 333 | 70 | 86 | 186 | 17 | 7 | 23 | 53 | 2 | 4 | 5 | 55 | 3 | 57 | 28 | 0 | 4 | .258 | .368 | .559 |
| Beltran, Francis, Chi.-Mon. | 45 | 3 | 3 | 0 | 1 | 1 | 0 | 0 | 0 | 0 | 0 | 0 | 0 | 0 | 0 | 0 | 0 | 0 | 0 | .333 | .333 | .333 |
| Beltre, Adrian, L.A. | 156 | 657 | 598 | 104 | 200 | 376 | 32 | 0 | 48 | 121 | 0 | 4 | 2 | 53 | 9 | 87 | 7 | 2 | 15 | .334 | .388 | .629 |
| Benitez, Armando, Fla. | 64 | 1 | 1 | 0 | 0 | 0 | 0 | 0 | 0 | 0 | 0 | 0 | 0 | 0 | 0 | 1 | 0 | 0 | 0 | .000 | .000 | .000 |
| Bennett, Gary, Mil. | 75 | 246 | 219 | 18 | 49 | 72 | 14 | 0 | 3 | 20 | 0 | 3 | 2 | 22 | 3 | 32 | 1 | 0 | 9 | .224 | .297 | .329 |
| Bennett, Jeff, Mil. | 60 | 2 | 2 | 0 | 0 | 0 | 0 | 0 | 0 | 0 | 0 | 0 | 0 | 0 | 0 | 2 | 0 | 0 | 0 | .000 | .000 | .000 |
| Benson, Kris, Pit.-N.Y. | 31 | 75 | 58 | 3 | 8 | 8 | 0 | 0 | 0 | 5 | 15 | 0 | 0 | 2 | 0 | 26 | 0 | 0 | 0 | .138 | .167 | .138 |
| Bentz, Chad, Mon. | 36 | 2 | 2 | 0 | 1 | 1 | 0 | 0 | 0 | 0 | 0 | 0 | 0 | 0 | 0 | 0 | 0 | 0 | 0 | .500 | .500 | .500 |
| Bergeron, Peter, Mon.* | 11 | 45 | 42 | 2 | 9 | 9 | 0 | 0 | 0 | 1 | 1 | 0 | 0 | 2 | 0 | 16 | 0 | 1 | 0 | .214 | .250 | .214 |
| Berkman, Lance, Hou.† | 160 | 687 | 544 | 104 | 172 | 308 | 40 | 3 | 30 | 106 | 0 | 6 | 10 | 127 | 14 | 101 | 9 | 7 | 10 | .316 | .450 | .566 |
| Bernero, Adam, Col. | 16 | 6 | 5 | 1 | 0 | 0 | 0 | 0 | 0 | 0 | 1 | 0 | 0 | 0 | 0 | 3 | 0 | 0 | 0 | .000 | .000 | .000 |
| Betemit, Wilson, Atl.† | 22 | 52 | 47 | 2 | 8 | 8 | 0 | 0 | 0 | 3 | 0 | 1 | 0 | 4 | 0 | 16 | 0 | 1 | 0 | .170 | .231 | .170 |
| Biddle, Rocky, Mon. | 47 | 14 | 11 | 0 | 0 | 0 | 0 | 0 | 0 | 0 | 3 | 0 | 0 | 0 | 0 | 7 | 0 | 0 | 0 | .000 | .000 | .000 |
| Biggio, Craig, Hou. | 156 | 700 | 633 | 100 | 178 | 297 | 47 | 0 | 24 | 63 | 9 | 3 | 15 | 40 | 0 | 94 | 7 | 2 | 8 | .281 | .337 | .469 |
| Boehringer, Brian, Pit.† | 21 | 1 | 1 | 0 | 0 | 0 | 0 | 0 | 0 | 0 | 0 | 0 | 0 | 0 | 0 | 1 | 0 | 0 | 0 | .000 | .000 | .000 |
| Bonds, Barry, S.F.* | 147 | 617 | 373 | 129 | 135 | 303 | 27 | 3 | 45 | 101 | 0 | 3 | 9 | 232 | 120 | 41 | 6 | 1 | 5 | .362 | .609 | .812 |
| Bong, Jung Keun, Cin.* | 3 | 4 | 4 | 0 | 0 | 0 | 0 | 0 | 0 | 0 | 0 | 0 | 0 | 0 | 0 | 3 | 0 | 0 | 0 | .000 | .000 | .000 |
| Bottalico, Ricky, N.Y.* | 60 | 2 | 2 | 0 | 0 | 0 | 0 | 0 | 0 | 0 | 0 | 0 | 0 | 0 | 0 | 0 | 0 | 0 | 0 | .000 | .000 | .000 |
| Bradley, Milton, L.A.† | 141 | 597 | 516 | 72 | 138 | 219 | 24 | 0 | 19 | 67 | 3 | 1 | 6 | 71 | 3 | 123 | 15 | 11 | 12 | .267 | .362 | .424 |
| Bragg, Darren, S.D.-Cin.* | 47 | 112 | 101 | 13 | 19 | 36 | 3 | 1 | 4 | 9 | 1 | 0 | 0 | 10 | 1 | 31 | 1 | 0 | 2 | .188 | .261 | .356 |
| Branyan, Russell, Mil.* | 51 | 182 | 158 | 21 | 37 | 83 | 11 | 1 | 11 | 27 | 0 | 2 | 2 | 20 | 0 | 68 | 1 | 0 | 1 | .234 | .324 | .525 |
| Brazell, Craig, N.Y.* | 24 | 35 | 34 | 3 | 9 | 14 | 2 | 0 | 1 | 3 | 0 | 0 | 0 | 1 | 0 | 7 | 0 | 0 | 1 | .265 | .286 | .412 |
| Brazoban, Yhency, L.A. | 31 | 1 | 1 | 0 | 0 | 0 | 0 | 0 | 0 | 0 | 0 | 0 | 0 | 0 | 0 | 1 | 0 | 0 | 0 | .000 | .000 | .000 |
| Brito, Juan, Ari. | 54 | 184 | 171 | 17 | 35 | 51 | 7 | 0 | 3 | 12 | 1 | 2 | 1 | 9 | 1 | 41 | 1 | 0 | 6 | .205 | .246 | .298 |
| Brooks, Frank, Pit.* | 11 | 1 | 1 | 0 | 0 | 0 | 0 | 0 | 0 | 0 | 0 | 0 | 0 | 0 | 0 | 0 | 0 | 0 | 0 | .000 | .000 | .000 |
| Brower, Jim, S.F. | 89 | 3 | 2 | 1 | 1 | 1 | 0 | 0 | 0 | 0 | 0 | 0 | 0 | 1 | 0 | 1 | 0 | 0 | 0 | .500 | .667 | .500 |
| Bruntlett, Eric, Hou. | 45 | 61 | 52 | 14 | 13 | 27 | 2 | 0 | 4 | 8 | 0 | 2 | 0 | 7 | 0 | 13 | 4 | 0 | 0 | .250 | .328 | .519 |
| Buchanan, Brian, S.D.-N.Y. | 40 | 72 | 63 | 7 | 12 | 20 | 2 | 0 | 2 | 6 | 0 | 1 | 1 | 7 | 2 | 20 | 0 | 0 | 2 | .190 | .278 | .317 |
| Bullinger, Kirk, Hou. | 27 | 4 | 3 | 0 | 0 | 0 | 0 | 0 | 0 | 0 | 0 | 0 | 0 | 1 | 0 | 2 | 0 | 0 | 0 | .000 | .250 | .000 |
| Bump, Nate, Fla.* | 50 | 5 | 5 | 0 | 0 | 0 | 0 | 0 | 0 | 0 | 0 | 0 | 0 | 0 | 0 | 2 | 0 | 0 | 0 | .000 | .000 | .000 |
| Burba, Dave, Mil.-S.F. | 51 | 4 | 4 | 0 | 0 | 0 | 0 | 0 | 0 | 0 | 0 | 0 | 0 | 0 | 0 | 1 | 0 | 0 | 0 | .000 | .000 | .000 |
| Burke, Chris, Hou. | 17 | 20 | 17 | 2 | 1 | 1 | 0 | 0 | 0 | 0 | 0 | 0 | 0 | 3 | 0 | 3 | 0 | 0 | 0 | .059 | .200 | .059 |
| Burnett, A.J., Fla. | 20 | 37 | 29 | 4 | 4 | 4 | 0 | 0 | 0 | 1 | 8 | 0 | 0 | 0 | 0 | 11 | 0 | 0 | 1 | .138 | .138 | .138 |
| Burnett, Sean, Pit.* | 13 | 27 | 23 | 0 | 0 | 0 | 0 | 0 | 0 | 0 | 2 | 0 | 0 | 2 | 0 | 6 | 0 | 0 | 0 | .000 | .080 | .000 |
| Burnitz, Jeromy, Col.* | 150 | 606 | 540 | 94 | 153 | 302 | 30 | 4 | 37 | 110 | 0 | 3 | 5 | 58 | 7 | 124 | 5 | 6 | 7 | .283 | .356 | .559 |
| Burrell, Pat, Phi. | 127 | 534 | 448 | 66 | 115 | 204 | 17 | 0 | 24 | 84 | 0 | 6 | 2 | 78 | 7 | 130 | 2 | 0 | 10 | .257 | .365 | .455 |
| Burroughs, Sean, S.D.* | 130 | 564 | 523 | 76 | 156 | 191 | 23 | 3 | 2 | 47 | 1 | 0 | 9 | 31 | 4 | 52 | 5 | 4 | 6 | .298 | .348 | .365 |
| Byrd, Marlon, Phi. | 106 | 378 | 346 | 48 | 79 | 111 | 13 | 2 | 5 | 33 | 2 | 1 | 7 | 22 | 1 | 68 | 2 | 2 | 10 | .228 | .287 | .321 |
| Byrd, Paul, Atl. | 19 | 43 | 30 | 2 | 6 | 6 | 0 | 0 | 0 | 4 | 8 | 0 | 0 | 5 | 0 | 7 | 0 | 0 | 0 | .200 | .314 | .200 |
| Cabrera, Miguel, Fla. | 160 | 685 | 603 | 101 | 177 | 309 | 31 | 1 | 33 | 112 | 0 | 8 | 6 | 68 | 5 | 148 | 5 | 2 | 20 | .294 | .366 | .512 |
| Cabrera, Orlando, Mon. | 103 | 425 | 390 | 41 | 96 | 131 | 19 | 2 | 4 | 31 | 2 | 3 | 2 | 28 | 0 | 31 | 12 | 3 | 12 | .246 | .298 | .336 |
| Calero, Kiko, St.L. | 41 | 1 | 1 | 0 | 0 | 0 | 0 | 0 | 0 | 0 | 0 | 0 | 0 | 0 | 0 | 1 | 0 | 0 | 0 | .000 | .000 | .000 |
| Calloway, Ron, Mon.* | 46 | 91 | 84 | 4 | 14 | 19 | 2 | 0 | 1 | 10 | 1 | 1 | 0 | 5 | 0 | 22 | 2 | 0 | 3 | .167 | .211 | .226 |
| Cameron, Mike, N.Y. | 140 | 562 | 493 | 76 | 114 | 236 | 30 | 1 | 30 | 76 | 1 | 3 | 8 | 57 | 2 | 143 | 22 | 6 | 5 | .231 | .319 | .479 |
| Capellan, Jose, Atl. | 3 | 2 | 2 | 0 | 0 | 0 | 0 | 0 | 0 | 0 | 0 | 0 | 0 | 0 | 0 | 1 | 0 | 0 | 0 | .000 | .000 | .000 |
| Capuano, Chris, Mil.* | 17 | 32 | 30 | 0 | 6 | 8 | 2 | 0 | 0 | 2 | 0 | 0 | 1 | 1 | 0 | 10 | 0 | 0 | 0 | .200 | .250 | .267 |
| Carpenter, Chris, St.L. | 28 | 67 | 62 | 1 | 5 | 5 | 0 | 0 | 0 | 1 | 4 | 0 | 0 | 1 | 0 | 21 | 0 | 0 | 0 | .081 | .095 | .081 |
| Carrara, Giovanni, L.A. | 42 | 2 | 2 | 0 | 0 | 0 | 0 | 0 | 0 | 0 | 0 | 0 | 0 | 0 | 0 | 1 | 0 | 0 | 0 | .000 | .000 | .000 |
| Carroll, Jamey, Mon. | 102 | 256 | 218 | 36 | 63 | 81 | 14 | 2 | 0 | 16 | 2 | 3 | 1 | 32 | 1 | 21 | 5 | 1 | 3 | .289 | .378 | .372 |
| Casey, Sean, Cin.* | 146 | 633 | 571 | 101 | 185 | 305 | 44 | 2 | 24 | 99 | 0 | 6 | 10 | 46 | 5 | 36 | 2 | 0 | 16 | .324 | .381 | .534 |
| Castilla, Vinny, Col. | 148 | 648 | 583 | 93 | 158 | 312 | 43 | 3 | 35 | 131 | 0 | 8 | 6 | 51 | 6 | 113 | 0 | 0 | 22 | .271 | .332 | .535 |
| Castillo, Jose, Pit. | 129 | 414 | 383 | 44 | 98 | 141 | 15 | 2 | 8 | 39 | 5 | 2 | 1 | 23 | 5 | 92 | 3 | 2 | 12 | .256 | .298 | .368 |
| Castillo, Luis, Fla.† | 150 | 649 | 564 | 91 | 164 | 196 | 12 | 7 | 2 | 47 | 5 | 4 | 1 | 75 | 2 | 68 | 21 | 4 | 15 | .291 | .373 | .348 |
| Castro, Juan, Cin. | 111 | 316 | 299 | 36 | 73 | 113 | 21 | 2 | 5 | 26 | 2 | 1 | 0 | 14 | 1 | 51 | 1 | 0 | 11 | .244 | .277 | .378 |
| Castro, Ramon, Fla. | 32 | 108 | 96 | 9 | 13 | 25 | 3 | 0 | 3 | 8 | 0 | 0 | 1 | 11 | 2 | 30 | 0 | 0 | 1 | .135 | .231 | .260 |
| Cedeno, Roger, St.L.† | 95 | 223 | 200 | 22 | 53 | 75 | 9 | 2 | 3 | 23 | 3 | 1 | 0 | 19 | 2 | 41 | 5 | 1 | 5 | .265 | .327 | .375 |
| Cepicky, Matt, Mon.* | 32 | 61 | 60 | 4 | 13 | 20 | 4 | 0 | 1 | 3 | 0 | 0 | 0 | 1 | 0 | 18 | 1 | 0 | 1 | .217 | .230 | .333 |
| Chavez, Endy, Mon.* | 132 | 547 | 502 | 65 | 139 | 186 | 20 | 6 | 5 | 34 | 12 | 2 | 1 | 30 | 0 | 40 | 32 | 7 | 6 | .277 | .318 | .371 |
| Chavez, Raul, Hou. | 64 | 176 | 162 | 9 | 34 | 42 | 8 | 0 | 0 | 23 | 4 | 0 | 0 | 10 | 3 | 38 | 0 | 1 | 9 | .210 | .256 | .259 |
| Chen, Chin-Feng, L.A. | 8 | 10 | 8 | 1 | 0 | 0 | 0 | 0 | 0 | 0 | 0 | 0 | 0 | 2 | 0 | 3 | 0 | 0 | 1 | .000 | .200 | .000 |
| Choate, Randy, Ari.* | 74 | 1 | 1 | 0 | 0 | 0 | 0 | 0 | 0 | 0 | 0 | 0 | 0 | 0 | 0 | 1 | 0 | 0 | 0 | .000 | .000 | .000 |
| Choi, Hee Seop, Fla.-L.A.* | 126 | 416 | 343 | 53 | 86 | 154 | 21 | 1 | 15 | 46 | 2 | 4 | 4 | 63 | 6 | 96 | 1 | 0 | 6 | .251 | .370 | .449 |
| Church, Ryan, Mon.* | 30 | 71 | 63 | 6 | 11 | 15 | 1 | 0 | 1 | 6 | 1 | 0 | 0 | 7 | 1 | 16 | 0 | 0 | 3 | .175 | .257 | .238 |
| Cintron, Alex, Ari.† | 154 | 613 | 564 | 56 | 148 | 205 | 31 | 7 | 4 | 49 | 12 | 4 | 2 | 31 | 2 | 59 | 3 | 3 | 11 | .262 | .301 | .363 |
| Cirillo, Jeff, S.D. | 33 | 81 | 75 | 12 | 16 | 22 | 3 | 0 | 1 | 7 | 0 | 1 | 0 | 5 | 0 | 14 | 0 | 0 | 0 | .213 | .259 | .293 |
| Clark, Brady, Mil. | 138 | 420 | 353 | 41 | 99 | 140 | 18 | 1 | 7 | 46 | 1 | 3 | 9 | 53 | 2 | 48 | 15 | 8 | 9 | .280 | .385 | .397 |
| Clark, Jermaine, Cin.* | 14 | 34 | 30 | 4 | 4 | 5 | 1 | 0 | 0 | 2 | 1 | 0 | 2 | 1 | 0 | 8 | 1 | 0 | 0 | .133 | .212 | .167 |
| Claussen, Brandon, Cin. | 14 | 22 | 19 | 1 | 2 | 2 | 0 | 0 | 0 | 0 | 2 | 0 | 0 | 1 | 0 | 6 | 0 | 0 | 1 | .105 | .150 | .105 |
| Clayton, Royce, Col. | 146 | 652 | 574 | 95 | 160 | 228 | 36 | 4 | 8 | 54 | 24 | 2 | 4 | 48 | 0 | 125 | 10 | 5 | 13 | .279 | .338 | .397 |
| Clemens, Roger, Hou. | 33 | 78 | 72 | 1 | 12 | 13 | 1 | 0 | 0 | 7 | 3 | 0 | 0 | 3 | 0 | 24 | 0 | 0 | 2 | .167 | .200 | .181 |
| Clement, Matt, Chi. | 30 | 61 | 55 | 2 | 8 | 9 | 1 | 0 | 0 | 2 | 4 | 1 | 0 | 1 | 0 | 29 | 0 | 0 | 0 | .145 | .158 | .164 |
| Closser, J.D., Col.† | 36 | 124 | 113 | 5 | 36 | 45 | 6 | 0 | 1 | 10 | 3 | 0 | 2 | 6 | 0 | 22 | 0 | 0 | 3 | .319 | .364 | .398 |
| Colbrunn, Greg, Ari. | 20 | 28 | 27 | 1 | 3 | 3 | 0 | 0 | 0 | 1 | 0 | 0 | 0 | 1 | 0 | 5 | 0 | 0 | 0 | .111 | .143 | .111 |
| Collier, Lou, Phi. | 32 | 42 | 36 | 7 | 10 | 14 | 1 | 0 | 1 | 4 | 0 | 0 | 1 | 5 | 0 | 10 | 1 | 0 | 2 | .278 | .381 | .389 |
| Conine, Jeff, Fla. | 140 | 579 | 521 | 55 | 146 | 225 | 35 | 1 | 14 | 83 | 2 | 6 | 2 | 48 | 3 | 78 | 5 | 5 | 15 | .280 | .340 | .432 |

| Player, Team | G | TPA | AB | R | H | TB | 2B | 3B | HR | RBI | SH | SF | HP | BB | IBB | SO | SB | CS | GDP | Avg. | OBP | Slg. |
|---|---|---|---|---|---|---|---|---|---|---|---|---|---|---|---|---|---|---|---|---|---|---|
| Cook, Aaron, Col. | 16 | 37 | 34 | 1 | 4 | 4 | 0 | 0 | 0 | 1 | 2 | 0 | 0 | 1 | 0 | 10 | 0 | 0 | 1 | .118 | .143 | .118 |
| Cooper, Brian, S.F. | 5 | 3 | 3 | 0 | 0 | 0 | 0 | 0 | 0 | 0 | 0 | 0 | 0 | 0 | 0 | 1 | 0 | 0 | 0 | .000 | .000 | .000 |
| Cora, Alex, L.A.* | 138 | 484 | 405 | 47 | 107 | 154 | 9 | 4 | 10 | 47 | 12 | 2 | 18 | 47 | 10 | 41 | 3 | 4 | 9 | .264 | .364 | .380 |
| Cordero, Chad, Mon. | 69 | 3 | 2 | 0 | 0 | 0 | 0 | 0 | 0 | 0 | 1 | 0 | 0 | 0 | 0 | 2 | 0 | 0 | 0 | .000 | .000 | .000 |
| Cordero, Wil, Fla. | 27 | 72 | 66 | 6 | 13 | 19 | 3 | 0 | 1 | 6 | 0 | 1 | 2 | 3 | 0 | 19 | 1 | 0 | 2 | .197 | .250 | .288 |
| Corey, Mark, Pit. | 31 | 1 | 1 | 0 | 0 | 0 | 0 | 0 | 0 | 0 | 0 | 0 | 0 | 0 | 0 | 1 | 0 | 0 | 0 | .000 | .000 | .000 |
| Cormier, Lance, Ari. | 17 | 10 | 8 | 1 | 2 | 3 | 1 | 0 | 0 | 1 | 1 | 0 | 0 | 1 | 0 | 2 | 0 | 0 | 0 | .250 | .333 | .375 |
| Cormier, Rheal, Phi.* | 84 | 1 | 1 | 0 | 0 | 0 | 0 | 0 | 0 | 0 | 0 | 0 | 0 | 0 | 0 | 1 | 0 | 0 | 0 | .000 | .000 | .000 |
| Correia, Kevin, S.F. | 12 | 4 | 3 | 1 | 1 | 2 | 1 | 0 | 0 | 0 | 0 | 0 | 0 | 1 | 0 | 1 | 0 | 0 | 0 | .333 | .500 | .667 |
| Cota, Humberto, Pit. | 36 | 70 | 66 | 10 | 15 | 33 | 1 | 1 | 5 | 8 | 0 | 0 | 1 | 3 | 1 | 20 | 0 | 0 | 1 | .227 | .271 | .500 |
| Counsell, Craig, Mil.* | 140 | 551 | 473 | 59 | 114 | 149 | 19 | 5 | 2 | 23 | 5 | 3 | 5 | 59 | 9 | 88 | 17 | 4 | 5 | .241 | .330 | .315 |
| Cruz, Deivi, S.F. | 127 | 431 | 397 | 46 | 116 | 171 | 30 | 2 | 7 | 55 | 8 | 6 | 3 | 17 | 6 | 32 | 1 | 3 | 11 | .292 | .322 | .431 |
| Cruz, Jacob, Cin.* | 96 | 167 | 147 | 22 | 33 | 50 | 8 | 0 | 3 | 28 | 0 | 0 | 4 | 16 | 2 | 43 | 0 | 0 | 5 | .224 | .317 | .340 |
| Cruz, Juan, Atl. | 50 | 6 | 5 | 1 | 1 | 2 | 1 | 0 | 0 | 0 | 0 | 0 | 0 | 1 | 0 | 3 | 0 | 0 | 0 | .200 | .333 | .400 |
| Daigle, Casey, Ari. | 11 | 18 | 17 | 2 | 2 | 4 | 2 | 0 | 0 | 0 | 1 | 0 | 0 | 0 | 0 | 7 | 0 | 0 | 1 | .118 | .118 | .235 |
| Dallimore, Brian, S.F. | 20 | 49 | 43 | 8 | 12 | 17 | 2 | 0 | 1 | 7 | 0 | 1 | 1 | 4 | 0 | 7 | 0 | 1 | 0 | .279 | .347 | .395 |
| Davis, Doug, Mil. | 34 | 71 | 64 | 0 | 1 | 1 | 0 | 0 | 0 | 0 | 6 | 0 | 0 | 1 | 0 | 43 | 0 | 0 | 1 | .016 | .031 | .016 |
| Davis, J.J., Pit. | 25 | 40 | 35 | 4 | 5 | 6 | 1 | 0 | 0 | 3 | 0 | 1 | 0 | 4 | 0 | 10 | 2 | 0 | 0 | .143 | .225 | .171 |
| Day, Zach, Mon. | 19 | 32 | 29 | 1 | 1 | 4 | 0 | 0 | 1 | 1 | 3 | 0 | 0 | 0 | 0 | 17 | 0 | 0 | 0 | .034 | .034 | .138 |
| de la Rosa, Jorge, Mil.* | 5 | 7 | 6 | 0 | 0 | 0 | 0 | 0 | 0 | 0 | 1 | 0 | 0 | 0 | 0 | 6 | 0 | 0 | 0 | .000 | .000 | .000 |
| Delgado, Wilson, N.Y.† | 42 | 147 | 130 | 11 | 38 | 50 | 4 | 1 | 2 | 13 | 2 | 0 | 0 | 15 | 3 | 29 | 1 | 0 | 1 | .292 | .366 | .385 |
| Dempster, Ryan, Chi. | 23 | 1 | 1 | 0 | 0 | 0 | 0 | 0 | 0 | 0 | 0 | 0 | 0 | 0 | 0 | 1 | 0 | 0 | 0 | .000 | .000 | .000 |
| DeRosa, Mark, Atl. | 118 | 345 | 309 | 33 | 74 | 99 | 16 | 0 | 3 | 31 | 4 | 6 | 3 | 23 | 3 | 53 | 1 | 3 | 6 | .239 | .293 | .320 |
| Dessens, Elmer, Ari.-L.A. | 50 | 29 | 22 | 0 | 4 | 6 | 2 | 0 | 0 | 0 | 4 | 0 | 0 | 3 | 0 | 3 | 0 | 0 | 1 | .182 | .280 | .273 |
| DeVore, Doug, Ari.* | 50 | 114 | 107 | 5 | 24 | 40 | 3 | 2 | 3 | 13 | 0 | 0 | 0 | 7 | 0 | 31 | 1 | 1 | 1 | .224 | .272 | .374 |
| Diaz, Einar, Mon. | 55 | 159 | 139 | 9 | 31 | 42 | 6 | 1 | 1 | 11 | 2 | 3 | 4 | 11 | 3 | 10 | 2 | 0 | 6 | .223 | .293 | .302 |
| Diaz, Victor, N.Y. | 15 | 53 | 51 | 8 | 15 | 27 | 3 | 0 | 3 | 8 | 0 | 0 | 1 | 1 | 0 | 15 | 0 | 0 | 3 | .294 | .321 | .529 |
| DiFelice, Mike, Chi. | 4 | 3 | 3 | 0 | 0 | 0 | 0 | 0 | 0 | 0 | 0 | 0 | 0 | 0 | 0 | 1 | 0 | 0 | 0 | .000 | .000 | .000 |
| Dohmann, Scott, Col. | 41 | 3 | 1 | 0 | 0 | 0 | 0 | 0 | 0 | 0 | 1 | 0 | 1 | 0 | 0 | 1 | 0 | 0 | 0 | .000 | .500 | .000 |
| Downs, Scott, Mon.* | 12 | 22 | 15 | 1 | 1 | 1 | 0 | 0 | 0 | 0 | 6 | 0 | 0 | 1 | 0 | 7 | 0 | 0 | 0 | .067 | .125 | .067 |
| Dreifort, Darren, L.A. | 60 | 1 | 1 | 0 | 0 | 0 | 0 | 0 | 0 | 0 | 0 | 0 | 0 | 0 | 0 | 1 | 0 | 0 | 0 | .000 | .000 | .000 |
| Drew, J.D., Atl.* | 145 | 645 | 518 | 118 | 158 | 295 | 28 | 8 | 31 | 93 | 1 | 3 | 5 | 118 | 2 | 116 | 12 | 3 | 7 | .305 | .436 | .569 |
| Drew, Tim, Atl. | 12 | 3 | 2 | 1 | 0 | 0 | 0 | 0 | 0 | 0 | 0 | 0 | 0 | 1 | 0 | 1 | 0 | 0 | 0 | .000 | .333 | .000 |
| Driskill, Travis, Col. | 5 | 1 | 1 | 0 | 0 | 0 | 0 | 0 | 0 | 0 | 0 | 0 | 0 | 0 | 0 | 1 | 0 | 0 | 0 | .000 | .000 | .000 |
| Dubois, Jason, Chi. | 20 | 25 | 23 | 2 | 5 | 10 | 0 | 1 | 1 | 5 | 0 | 1 | 0 | 1 | 0 | 7 | 0 | 0 | 0 | .217 | .240 | .435 |
| Duckworth, Brandon, Hou. | 19 | 10 | 9 | 1 | 2 | 2 | 0 | 0 | 0 | 1 | 0 | 0 | 0 | 1 | 0 | 2 | 0 | 0 | 0 | .222 | .300 | .222 |
| Duncan, Jeff, N.Y.* | 13 | 17 | 15 | 2 | 1 | 1 | 0 | 0 | 0 | 1 | 1 | 0 | 0 | 1 | 0 | 5 | 3 | 0 | 0 | .067 | .125 | .067 |
| Dunn, Adam, Cin.* | 161 | 681 | 568 | 105 | 151 | 323 | 34 | 0 | 46 | 102 | 0 | 0 | 5 | 108 | 11 | 195 | 6 | 1 | 8 | .266 | .388 | .569 |
| Durbin, Chad, Ari.† | 7 | 1 | 1 | 0 | 0 | 0 | 0 | 0 | 0 | 0 | 0 | 0 | 0 | 0 | 0 | 0 | 0 | 0 | 0 | .000 | .000 | .000 |
| Durham, Ray, S.F.† | 120 | 542 | 471 | 95 | 133 | 228 | 28 | 8 | 17 | 65 | 4 | 4 | 6 | 57 | 3 | 60 | 10 | 4 | 6 | .282 | .364 | .484 |
| Durrington, Trent, Mil. | 53 | 87 | 82 | 13 | 19 | 33 | 2 | 3 | 2 | 4 | 1 | 0 | 0 | 4 | 0 | 23 | 4 | 0 | 1 | .232 | .267 | .402 |
| Easley, Damion, Fla. | 98 | 257 | 223 | 26 | 53 | 102 | 20 | 1 | 9 | 43 | 0 | 2 | 8 | 24 | 1 | 36 | 4 | 1 | 6 | .238 | .331 | .457 |
| Eaton, Adam, S.D. | 38 | 76 | 64 | 9 | 13 | 20 | 7 | 0 | 0 | 8 | 5 | 0 | 1 | 6 | 0 | 16 | 2 | 0 | 1 | .203 | .282 | .313 |
| Edmonds, Jim, St.L.* | 153 | 612 | 498 | 102 | 150 | 320 | 38 | 3 | 42 | 111 | 0 | 8 | 5 | 101 | 12 | 150 | 8 | 3 | 4 | .301 | .418 | .643 |
| Eischen, Joey, Mon.* | 22 | 4 | 3 | 2 | 2 | 2 | 0 | 0 | 0 | 0 | 1 | 0 | 0 | 0 | 0 | 0 | 0 | 0 | 0 | .667 | .667 | .667 |
| Elarton, Scott, Col. | 8 | 14 | 9 | 1 | 2 | 2 | 0 | 0 | 0 | 0 | 4 | 0 | 0 | 1 | 0 | 2 | 0 | 0 | 0 | .222 | .300 | .222 |
| Eldred, Cal, St.L. | 52 | 6 | 5 | 0 | 0 | 0 | 0 | 0 | 0 | 0 | 1 | 0 | 0 | 0 | 0 | 3 | 0 | 0 | 1 | .000 | .000 | .000 |
| Ellison, Jason, S.F. | 13 | 4 | 4 | 4 | 2 | 5 | 0 | 0 | 1 | 3 | 0 | 0 | 0 | 0 | 0 | 1 | 2 | 0 | 0 | .500 | .500 | 1.250 |
| Encarnacion, Juan, L.A.-Fla. | 135 | 532 | 484 | 63 | 114 | 196 | 30 | 2 | 16 | 62 | 1 | 2 | 7 | 38 | 2 | 86 | 5 | 4 | 11 | .236 | .299 | .405 |
| Ensberg, Morgan, Hou. | 131 | 456 | 411 | 51 | 113 | 169 | 20 | 3 | 10 | 66 | 5 | 4 | 0 | 36 | 1 | 46 | 6 | 4 | 17 | .275 | .330 | .411 |
| Erickson, Matt, Mil.* | 4 | 6 | 6 | 0 | 1 | 1 | 0 | 0 | 0 | 0 | 0 | 0 | 0 | 0 | 0 | 1 | 0 | 0 | 0 | .167 | .167 | .167 |
| Erickson, Scott, N.Y. | 2 | 3 | 3 | 0 | 0 | 0 | 0 | 0 | 0 | 0 | 0 | 0 | 0 | 0 | 0 | 2 | 0 | 0 | 0 | .000 | .000 | .000 |
| Estalella, Bobby, Ari. | 7 | 14 | 14 | 2 | 2 | 8 | 0 | 0 | 2 | 4 | 0 | 0 | 0 | 0 | 0 | 6 | 0 | 0 | 0 | .143 | .143 | .571 |
| Estes, Shawn, Col. | 36 | 80 | 72 | 13 | 17 | 22 | 3 | 1 | 0 | 2 | 7 | 0 | 0 | 1 | 0 | 11 | 0 | 0 | 0 | .236 | .247 | .306 |
| Estrada, Johnny, Atl.† | 134 | 517 | 462 | 56 | 145 | 208 | 36 | 0 | 9 | 76 | 1 | 4 | 11 | 39 | 7 | 66 | 0 | 0 | 18 | .314 | .378 | .450 |
| Everett, Adam, Hou. | 104 | 435 | 384 | 66 | 105 | 148 | 15 | 2 | 8 | 31 | 22 | 3 | 9 | 17 | 0 | 56 | 13 | 2 | 4 | .273 | .317 | .385 |
| Everett, Carl, Mon.† | 39 | 141 | 127 | 8 | 32 | 48 | 10 | 0 | 2 | 14 | 0 | 1 | 5 | 8 | 2 | 19 | 0 | 0 | 8 | .252 | .319 | .378 |
| Eyre, Scott, S.F.* | 83 | 2 | 2 | 0 | 0 | 0 | 0 | 0 | 0 | 0 | 0 | 0 | 0 | 0 | 0 | 1 | 0 | 0 | 0 | .000 | .000 | .000 |
| Falkenborg, Brian, L.A. | 6 | 3 | 2 | 1 | 0 | 0 | 0 | 0 | 0 | 0 | 0 | 0 | 0 | 1 | 0 | 2 | 0 | 0 | 0 | .000 | .333 | .000 |
| Farnsworth, Kyle, Chi. | 72 | 1 | 1 | 0 | 0 | 0 | 0 | 0 | 0 | 0 | 0 | 0 | 0 | 0 | 0 | 0 | 0 | 0 | 0 | .000 | .000 | .000 |
| Fassero, Jeff, Col.-Ari.* | 41 | 24 | 21 | 3 | 4 | 4 | 0 | 0 | 0 | 1 | 2 | 0 | 0 | 1 | 0 | 9 | 0 | 0 | 0 | .190 | .227 | .190 |
| Feliz, Pedro, S.F. | 144 | 531 | 503 | 72 | 139 | 244 | 33 | 3 | 22 | 84 | 0 | 5 | 0 | 23 | 1 | 85 | 5 | 2 | 18 | .276 | .305 | .485 |
| Fick, Robert, S.D.* | 13 | 15 | 12 | 2 | 2 | 2 | 0 | 0 | 0 | 0 | 0 | 0 | 1 | 2 | 0 | 4 | 0 | 0 | 0 | .167 | .333 | .167 |
| Figueroa, Nelson, Pit. | 10 | 7 | 7 | 0 | 1 | 1 | 0 | 0 | 0 | 1 | 0 | 0 | 0 | 0 | 0 | 2 | 0 | 0 | 0 | .143 | .143 | .143 |
| Finley, Steve, Ari.-L.A.* | 162 | 706 | 628 | 92 | 170 | 308 | 28 | 1 | 36 | 94 | 9 | 7 | 1 | 61 | 1 | 82 | 9 | 7 | 14 | .271 | .333 | .490 |
| Flores, Jose, L.A. | 9 | 5 | 4 | 0 | 1 | 1 | 0 | 0 | 0 | 0 | 0 | 0 | 0 | 1 | 0 | 2 | 0 | 0 | 0 | .250 | .400 | .250 |
| Flores, Randy, St.L.* | 9 | 2 | 2 | 0 | 0 | 0 | 0 | 0 | 0 | 0 | 0 | 0 | 0 | 0 | 0 | 1 | 0 | 0 | 0 | .000 | .000 | .000 |
| Floyd, Cliff, N.Y.* | 113 | 457 | 396 | 55 | 103 | 183 | 26 | 0 | 18 | 63 | 0 | 3 | 11 | 47 | 6 | 103 | 11 | 4 | 8 | .260 | .352 | .462 |
| Floyd, Gavin, Phi. | 6 | 10 | 10 | 0 | 0 | 0 | 0 | 0 | 0 | 0 | 0 | 0 | 0 | 0 | 0 | 5 | 0 | 0 | 0 | .000 | .000 | .000 |
| Fogg, Josh, Pit. | 32 | 64 | 53 | 1 | 4 | 5 | 1 | 0 | 0 | 3 | 11 | 0 | 0 | 0 | 0 | 13 | 0 | 0 | 0 | .075 | .075 | .094 |
| Fossum, Casey, Ari.* | 29 | 46 | 42 | 3 | 4 | 4 | 0 | 0 | 0 | 0 | 3 | 0 | 0 | 1 | 0 | 16 | 0 | 0 | 1 | .095 | .116 | .095 |
| Fox, Andy, Mon.* | 34 | 43 | 43 | 2 | 4 | 7 | 0 | 0 | 1 | 1 | 0 | 0 | 0 | 0 | 0 | 16 | 0 | 0 | 1 | .093 | .093 | .163 |
| Francis, Jeff, Col.* | 7 | 14 | 10 | 1 | 0 | 0 | 0 | 0 | 0 | 0 | 4 | 0 | 0 | 0 | 0 | 4 | 0 | 0 | 0 | .000 | .000 | .000 |
| Franco, Julio, Atl. | 125 | 361 | 320 | 37 | 99 | 141 | 18 | 3 | 6 | 57 | 1 | 3 | 1 | 36 | 4 | 68 | 4 | 2 | 10 | .309 | .378 | .441 |
| Franklin, Wayne, S.F.* | 43 | 5 | 3 | 2 | 1 | 1 | 0 | 0 | 0 | 2 | 0 | 1 | 0 | 1 | 0 | 0 | 0 | 0 | 0 | .333 | .400 | .333 |
| Freel, Ryan, Cin. | 143 | 592 | 505 | 74 | 140 | 186 | 21 | 8 | 3 | 28 | 8 | 0 | 12 | 67 | 0 | 88 | 37 | 10 | 7 | .277 | .375 | .368 |
| Freeman, Choo, Col. | 45 | 105 | 90 | 15 | 17 | 27 | 3 | 2 | 1 | 11 | 1 | 0 | 0 | 14 | 1 | 21 | 1 | 1 | 5 | .189 | .298 | .300 |
| Furcal, Rafael, Atl.† | 143 | 632 | 563 | 103 | 157 | 233 | 24 | 5 | 14 | 59 | 5 | 5 | 1 | 58 | 4 | 71 | 29 | 6 | 9 | .279 | .344 | .414 |
| Gagne, Eric, L.A. | 70 | 3 | 3 | 0 | 0 | 0 | 0 | 0 | 0 | 0 | 0 | 0 | 0 | 0 | 0 | 3 | 0 | 0 | 0 | .000 | .000 | .000 |
| Gallo, Mike, Hou.* | 69 | 1 | 1 | 0 | 0 | 0 | 0 | 0 | 0 | 0 | 0 | 0 | 0 | 0 | 0 | 0 | 0 | 0 | 0 | .000 | .000 | .000 |
| Garcia, Danny, N.Y. | 58 | 174 | 138 | 23 | 32 | 50 | 7 | 1 | 3 | 17 | 4 | 1 | 9 | 22 | 2 | 34 | 3 | 0 | 1 | .232 | .371 | .362 |
| Garcia, Jesse, Atl. | 50 | 118 | 115 | 14 | 29 | 38 | 4 | 1 | 1 | 10 | 1 | 0 | 1 | 1 | 0 | 16 | 1 | 2 | 2 | .252 | .265 | .330 |
| Garcia, Karim, N.Y.* | 62 | 202 | 192 | 24 | 45 | 77 | 7 | 2 | 7 | 22 | 0 | 0 | 0 | 10 | 0 | 35 | 3 | 0 | 6 | .234 | .272 | .401 |

| Player, Team | G | TPA | AB | R | H | TB | 2B | 3B | HR | RBI | SH | SF | HP | BB | IBB | SO | SB | CS | GDP | Avg. | OBP | Slg. |
|---|---|---|---|---|---|---|---|---|---|---|---|---|---|---|---|---|---|---|---|---|---|---|
| Garciaparra, Nomar, Chi. | 43 | 185 | 165 | 28 | 49 | 75 | 14 | 0 | 4 | 20 | 1 | 1 | 2 | 16 | 0 | 14 | 2 | 1 | 6 | .297 | .364 | .455 |
| Geary, Geoff, Phi. | 33 | 1 | 1 | 0 | 0 | 0 | 0 | 0 | 0 | 0 | 0 | 0 | 0 | 0 | 0 | 0 | 0 | 0 | 0 | .000 | .000 | .000 |
| Germano, Justin, S.D. | 7 | 8 | 7 | 0 | 0 | 0 | 0 | 0 | 0 | 0 | 1 | 0 | 0 | 0 | 0 | 3 | 0 | 0 | 0 | .000 | .000 | .000 |
| Gil, Jerry, Ari. | 29 | 88 | 86 | 3 | 15 | 19 | 2 | 1 | 0 | 8 | 0 | 1 | 1 | 0 | 0 | 33 | 2 | 0 | 2 | .174 | .182 | .221 |
| Giles, Brian, S.D.* | 159 | 711 | 609 | 97 | 173 | 289 | 33 | 7 | 23 | 94 | 0 | 9 | 4 | 89 | 6 | 80 | 10 | 3 | 12 | .284 | .374 | .475 |
| Giles, Marcus, Atl. | 102 | 434 | 379 | 61 | 118 | 168 | 22 | 2 | 8 | 48 | 3 | 7 | 9 | 36 | 0 | 70 | 17 | 4 | 6 | .311 | .378 | .443 |
| Ginter, Keith, Mil. | 113 | 437 | 386 | 47 | 101 | 185 | 23 | 2 | 19 | 60 | 4 | 4 | 6 | 37 | 2 | 100 | 8 | 1 | 9 | .262 | .333 | .479 |
| Ginter, Matt, N.Y. | 15 | 19 | 14 | 1 | 3 | 4 | 1 | 0 | 0 | 1 | 3 | 0 | 0 | 2 | 0 | 5 | 0 | 0 | 0 | .214 | .313 | .286 |
| Gissell, Chris, Col. | 5 | 1 | 1 | 0 | 0 | 0 | 0 | 0 | 0 | 0 | 0 | 0 | 0 | 0 | 0 | 0 | 0 | 0 | 0 | .000 | .000 | .000 |
| Glanville, Doug, Phi. | 87 | 175 | 162 | 21 | 34 | 43 | 1 | 1 | 2 | 14 | 3 | 2 | 0 | 8 | 1 | 21 | 8 | 0 | 5 | .210 | .244 | .265 |
| Glavine, Tom, N.Y.* | 35 | 72 | 54 | 5 | 11 | 13 | 2 | 0 | 0 | 8 | 8 | 0 | 0 | 10 | 0 | 10 | 0 | 0 | 2 | .204 | .328 | .241 |
| Glover, Gary, Mil. | 4 | 7 | 7 | 0 | 0 | 0 | 0 | 0 | 0 | 0 | 0 | 0 | 0 | 0 | 0 | 4 | 0 | 0 | 0 | .000 | .000 | .000 |
| Gonzalez, Alex, Fla. | 159 | 599 | 561 | 67 | 130 | 235 | 30 | 3 | 23 | 79 | 3 | 4 | 4 | 27 | 9 | 126 | 3 | 1 | 17 | .232 | .270 | .419 |
| Gonzalez, Alex S., Chi.-Mon.-S.D. | 83 | 304 | 285 | 36 | 64 | 105 | 18 | 1 | 7 | 27 | 4 | 0 | 1 | 14 | 0 | 64 | 2 | 2 | 7 | .225 | .263 | .368 |
| Gonzalez, Edgar, Ari. | 10 | 15 | 13 | 0 | 2 | 2 | 0 | 0 | 0 | 0 | 1 | 0 | 1 | 0 | 0 | 2 | 0 | 0 | 0 | .154 | .214 | .154 |
| Gonzalez, Luis, Ari.* | 105 | 451 | 379 | 69 | 98 | 187 | 28 | 5 | 17 | 48 | 0 | 2 | 2 | 68 | 11 | 58 | 2 | 2 | 9 | .259 | .373 | .493 |
| Gonzalez, Luis A., Col. | 102 | 351 | 322 | 42 | 94 | 151 | 17 | 2 | 12 | 40 | 9 | 1 | 4 | 15 | 1 | 67 | 1 | 5 | 5 | .292 | .330 | .469 |
| Gonzalez, Mike, Pit. | 47 | 1 | 1 | 0 | 1 | 2 | 1 | 0 | 0 | 2 | 0 | 0 | 0 | 0 | 0 | 0 | 0 | 0 | 0 | 1.000 | 1.000 | 2.000 |
| Good, Andrew, Ari. | 17 | 6 | 5 | 0 | 0 | 0 | 0 | 0 | 0 | 1 | 0 | 1 | 0 | 0 | 0 | 2 | 0 | 0 | 0 | .000 | .000 | .000 |
| Goodwin, Tom, Chi.* | 77 | 114 | 105 | 11 | 21 | 29 | 8 | 0 | 0 | 3 | 0 | 1 | 0 | 8 | 0 | 22 | 5 | 0 | 1 | .200 | .254 | .276 |
| Gosling, Mike, Ari.* | 6 | 8 | 6 | 0 | 0 | 0 | 0 | 0 | 0 | 0 | 1 | 0 | 0 | 1 | 0 | 4 | 0 | 0 | 0 | .000 | .143 | .000 |
| Grabow, John, Pit.* | 68 | 1 | 1 | 0 | 0 | 0 | 0 | 0 | 0 | 0 | 0 | 0 | 0 | 0 | 0 | 0 | 0 | 0 | 0 | .000 | .000 | .000 |
| Grabowski, Jason, L.A.* | 113 | 192 | 173 | 18 | 38 | 66 | 7 | 0 | 7 | 20 | 0 | 0 | 0 | 19 | 0 | 50 | 0 | 0 | 4 | .220 | .297 | .382 |
| Green, Andy, Ari. | 46 | 119 | 109 | 13 | 22 | 29 | 2 | 1 | 1 | 4 | 3 | 1 | 1 | 5 | 0 | 17 | 1 | 1 | 2 | .202 | .241 | .266 |
| Green, Nick, Atl. | 95 | 290 | 264 | 40 | 72 | 102 | 15 | 3 | 3 | 26 | 8 | 2 | 4 | 12 | 1 | 63 | 1 | 2 | 0 | .273 | .312 | .386 |
| Green, Shawn, L.A.* | 157 | 671 | 590 | 92 | 157 | 271 | 28 | 1 | 28 | 86 | 0 | 2 | 8 | 71 | 6 | 114 | 5 | 2 | 17 | .266 | .352 | .459 |
| Greene, Khalil, S.D. | 139 | 554 | 484 | 67 | 132 | 216 | 31 | 4 | 15 | 65 | 1 | 8 | 8 | 53 | 10 | 94 | 4 | 2 | 9 | .273 | .349 | .446 |
| Greene, Todd, Col. | 75 | 209 | 195 | 23 | 55 | 99 | 14 | 0 | 10 | 35 | 0 | 1 | 0 | 13 | 4 | 38 | 0 | 0 | 9 | .282 | .325 | .508 |
| Grieve, Ben, Mil.-Chi.* | 123 | 294 | 250 | 30 | 65 | 106 | 17 | 0 | 8 | 35 | 0 | 3 | 2 | 39 | 5 | 70 | 0 | 0 | 4 | .260 | .361 | .424 |
| Griffey Jr., Ken, Cin.* | 83 | 348 | 300 | 49 | 76 | 154 | 18 | 0 | 20 | 60 | 0 | 2 | 2 | 44 | 3 | 67 | 1 | 0 | 8 | .253 | .351 | .513 |
| Griffiths, Jeremy, Hou. | 1 | 2 | 1 | 0 | 0 | 0 | 0 | 0 | 0 | 0 | 0 | 0 | 0 | 1 | 0 | 1 | 0 | 0 | 0 | .000 | .500 | .000 |
| Grissom, Marquis, S.F. | 145 | 606 | 562 | 78 | 157 | 253 | 26 | 2 | 22 | 90 | 2 | 4 | 1 | 37 | 5 | 83 | 3 | 1 | 22 | .279 | .323 | .450 |
| Grudzielanek, Mark, Chi. | 81 | 278 | 257 | 32 | 79 | 111 | 12 | 1 | 6 | 23 | 4 | 1 | 1 | 15 | 0 | 32 | 1 | 1 | 7 | .307 | .347 | .432 |
| Gutierrez, Ricky, N.Y. | 24 | 70 | 63 | 2 | 11 | 13 | 2 | 0 | 0 | 5 | 0 | 0 | 1 | 6 | 0 | 8 | 0 | 0 | 3 | .175 | .257 | .206 |
| Guzman, Freddy, S.D.† | 20 | 80 | 76 | 8 | 16 | 19 | 3 | 0 | 0 | 5 | 0 | 0 | 1 | 3 | 0 | 13 | 5 | 2 | 0 | .211 | .250 | .250 |
| Hairston, Scott, Ari. | 101 | 364 | 339 | 39 | 84 | 150 | 15 | 6 | 13 | 29 | 2 | 1 | 1 | 21 | 0 | 88 | 3 | 3 | 4 | .248 | .293 | .442 |
| Hall, Bill, Mil. | 126 | 415 | 390 | 43 | 93 | 146 | 20 | 3 | 9 | 53 | 2 | 2 | 1 | 20 | 1 | 119 | 12 | 6 | 4 | .238 | .276 | .374 |
| Hammock, Robby, Ari. | 62 | 210 | 195 | 22 | 47 | 79 | 16 | 2 | 4 | 18 | 1 | 1 | 0 | 13 | 6 | 39 | 3 | 3 | 9 | .241 | .287 | .405 |
| Hammonds, Jeffrey, S.F. | 40 | 113 | 95 | 14 | 20 | 34 | 5 | 0 | 3 | 6 | 0 | 0 | 3 | 15 | 0 | 22 | 1 | 0 | 2 | .211 | .336 | .358 |
| Hampton, Mike, Atl. | 36 | 71 | 64 | 7 | 11 | 20 | 3 | 0 | 2 | 7 | 4 | 0 | 0 | 3 | 0 | 23 | 0 | 0 | 1 | .172 | .209 | .313 |
| Hancock, Josh, Phi.-Cin. | 16 | 21 | 17 | 1 | 2 | 2 | 0 | 0 | 0 | 1 | 1 | 0 | 0 | 3 | 0 | 12 | 0 | 0 | 0 | .118 | .250 | .118 |
| Hansen, Dave, S.D.* | 29 | 31 | 28 | 1 | 4 | 4 | 0 | 0 | 0 | 0 | 0 | 0 | 0 | 3 | 0 | 5 | 0 | 0 | 3 | .143 | .226 | .143 |
| Harang, Aaron, Cin. | 28 | 61 | 57 | 1 | 4 | 5 | 1 | 0 | 0 | 0 | 4 | 0 | 0 | 0 | 0 | 33 | 0 | 0 | 1 | .070 | .070 | .088 |
| Haren, Danny, St.L. | 14 | 14 | 12 | 1 | 0 | 0 | 0 | 0 | 0 | 0 | 2 | 0 | 0 | 0 | 0 | 6 | 0 | 0 | 1 | .000 | .000 | .000 |
| Harikkala, Tim, Col. | 55 | 4 | 3 | 0 | 0 | 0 | 0 | 0 | 0 | 0 | 1 | 0 | 0 | 0 | 0 | 3 | 0 | 0 | 0 | .000 | .000 | .000 |
| Harris, Brendan, Chi.-Mon. | 23 | 63 | 59 | 4 | 10 | 16 | 3 | 0 | 1 | 3 | 0 | 0 | 1 | 3 | 0 | 12 | 0 | 0 | 0 | .169 | .222 | .271 |
| Harris, Lenny, Fla.* | 79 | 99 | 95 | 7 | 20 | 28 | 5 | 0 | 1 | 17 | 0 | 1 | 0 | 3 | 0 | 8 | 0 | 0 | 2 | .211 | .232 | .295 |
| Hart, Bo, St.L. | 11 | 14 | 13 | 0 | 2 | 2 | 0 | 0 | 0 | 2 | 0 | 0 | 0 | 1 | 0 | 3 | 0 | 0 | 0 | .154 | .214 | .154 |
| Hart, Corey, Mil. | 1 | 1 | 1 | 0 | 0 | 0 | 0 | 0 | 0 | 0 | 0 | 0 | 0 | 0 | 0 | 1 | 0 | 0 | 0 | .000 | .000 | .000 |
| Harville, Chad, Hou. | 56 | 1 | 1 | 0 | 0 | 0 | 0 | 0 | 0 | 0 | 0 | 0 | 0 | 0 | 0 | 1 | 0 | 0 | 0 | .000 | .000 | .000 |
| Hawpe, Brad, Col.* | 42 | 118 | 105 | 12 | 26 | 42 | 3 | 2 | 3 | 9 | 0 | 1 | 1 | 11 | 3 | 34 | 1 | 1 | 4 | .248 | .322 | .400 |
| Haynes, Jimmy, Cin. | 5 | 4 | 4 | 0 | 0 | 0 | 0 | 0 | 0 | 0 | 0 | 0 | 0 | 0 | 0 | 4 | 0 | 0 | 0 | .000 | .000 | .000 |
| Heilman, Aaron, N.Y. | 5 | 10 | 7 | 0 | 0 | 0 | 0 | 0 | 0 | 0 | 3 | 0 | 0 | 0 | 0 | 3 | 0 | 0 | 0 | .000 | .000 | .000 |
| Helms, Wes, Mil. | 92 | 306 | 274 | 24 | 72 | 99 | 13 | 1 | 4 | 28 | 1 | 2 | 5 | 24 | 1 | 60 | 0 | 1 | 10 | .263 | .331 | .361 |
| Helton, Todd, Col.* | 154 | 683 | 547 | 115 | 190 | 339 | 49 | 2 | 32 | 96 | 0 | 6 | 3 | 127 | 19 | 72 | 3 | 0 | 12 | .347 | .469 | .620 |
| Hendrickson, Ben, Mil. | 10 | 17 | 16 | 0 | 2 | 2 | 0 | 0 | 0 | 0 | 1 | 0 | 0 | 0 | 0 | 9 | 0 | 0 | 0 | .125 | .125 | .125 |
| Hennessey, Brad, S.F. | 7 | 15 | 13 | 1 | 3 | 3 | 0 | 0 | 0 | 2 | 0 | 1 | 0 | 1 | 0 | 4 | 0 | 0 | 0 | .231 | .267 | .231 |
| Hermanson, Dustin, S.F. | 47 | 37 | 30 | 2 | 3 | 3 | 0 | 0 | 0 | 1 | 6 | 0 | 1 | 0 | 0 | 12 | 0 | 0 | 0 | .100 | .129 | .100 |
| Hernandez, Adrian, Mil. | 6 | 5 | 4 | 0 | 0 | 0 | 0 | 0 | 0 | 0 | 1 | 0 | 0 | 0 | 0 | 3 | 0 | 0 | 0 | .000 | .000 | .000 |
| Hernandez, Carlos, Hou.† | 9 | 16 | 12 | 0 | 1 | 1 | 0 | 0 | 0 | 1 | 4 | 0 | 0 | 0 | 0 | 4 | 0 | 0 | 0 | .083 | .083 | .083 |
| Hernandez, Jose, L.A. | 95 | 238 | 211 | 32 | 61 | 114 | 12 | 1 | 13 | 29 | 0 | 0 | 1 | 26 | 6 | 61 | 3 | 1 | 3 | .289 | .370 | .540 |
| Hernandez, Livan, Mon. | 36 | 97 | 81 | 2 | 20 | 30 | 7 | 0 | 1 | 10 | 15 | 0 | 0 | 1 | 0 | 8 | 0 | 0 | 1 | .247 | .256 | .370 |
| Hernandez, Ramon, S.D. | 111 | 432 | 384 | 45 | 106 | 183 | 23 | 0 | 18 | 63 | 4 | 4 | 5 | 35 | 0 | 45 | 1 | 0 | 16 | .276 | .341 | .477 |
| Hessman, Mike, Atl. | 29 | 71 | 69 | 8 | 9 | 18 | 3 | 0 | 2 | 5 | 0 | 0 | 1 | 1 | 0 | 24 | 0 | 0 | 0 | .130 | .155 | .261 |
| Hidalgo, Richard, Hou.-N.Y. | 144 | 579 | 523 | 67 | 125 | 232 | 26 | 3 | 25 | 82 | 0 | 6 | 5 | 44 | 7 | 129 | 4 | 4 | 19 | .239 | .301 | .444 |
| Hill, Bobby, Pit.† | 126 | 267 | 233 | 28 | 62 | 79 | 7 | 2 | 2 | 27 | 1 | 1 | 12 | 20 | 2 | 39 | 0 | 3 | 12 | .266 | .353 | .339 |
| Hill, Koyie, Ari.† | 13 | 38 | 36 | 3 | 9 | 13 | 1 | 0 | 1 | 6 | 0 | 0 | 0 | 2 | 1 | 6 | 1 | 0 | 1 | .250 | .289 | .361 |
| Hill, Shawn, Mon. | 3 | 3 | 2 | 0 | 0 | 0 | 0 | 0 | 0 | 0 | 1 | 0 | 0 | 0 | 0 | 2 | 0 | 0 | 0 | .000 | .000 | .000 |
| Hillenbrand, Shea, Ari. | 148 | 604 | 562 | 68 | 174 | 261 | 36 | 3 | 15 | 80 | 0 | 6 | 12 | 24 | 2 | 49 | 2 | 0 | 18 | .310 | .348 | .464 |
| Hinch, A.J., Phi. | 4 | 11 | 11 | 1 | 2 | 3 | 1 | 0 | 0 | 0 | 0 | 0 | 0 | 0 | 0 | 4 | 0 | 0 | 0 | .182 | .182 | .273 |
| Hitchcock, Sterling, S.D.* | 4 | 7 | 7 | 0 | 0 | 0 | 0 | 0 | 0 | 0 | 0 | 0 | 0 | 0 | 0 | 4 | 0 | 0 | 1 | .000 | .000 | .000 |
| Hocking, Denny, Col.† | 55 | 106 | 94 | 7 | 19 | 21 | 2 | 0 | 0 | 4 | 5 | 0 | 0 | 7 | 0 | 20 | 0 | 1 | 3 | .202 | .257 | .223 |
| Hollandsworth, Todd, Chi.* | 57 | 167 | 148 | 28 | 47 | 81 | 6 | 2 | 8 | 22 | 1 | 0 | 1 | 17 | 3 | 26 | 1 | 1 | 2 | .318 | .392 | .547 |
| Holliday, Matt, Col. | 121 | 439 | 400 | 65 | 116 | 195 | 31 | 3 | 14 | 57 | 1 | 1 | 6 | 31 | 0 | 86 | 3 | 3 | 9 | .290 | .349 | .488 |
| Hollins, Damon, Atl. | 7 | 23 | 22 | 3 | 8 | 10 | 2 | 0 | 0 | 5 | 1 | 0 | 0 | 0 | 0 | 4 | 0 | 0 | 0 | .364 | .364 | .455 |
| Horgan, Joe, Mon.* | 47 | 4 | 4 | 0 | 1 | 1 | 0 | 0 | 0 | 1 | 0 | 0 | 0 | 0 | 0 | 1 | 0 | 0 | 0 | .250 | .250 | .250 |
| House, J.R., Pit. | 5 | 9 | 9 | 1 | 1 | 2 | 1 | 0 | 0 | 0 | 0 | 0 | 0 | 0 | 0 | 2 | 0 | 0 | 1 | .111 | .111 | .222 |
| Howard, Ben, Fla. | 31 | 3 | 3 | 0 | 0 | 0 | 0 | 0 | 0 | 0 | 0 | 0 | 0 | 0 | 0 | 0 | 0 | 0 | 0 | .000 | .000 | .000 |
| Howard, Ryan, Phi.* | 19 | 42 | 39 | 5 | 11 | 22 | 5 | 0 | 2 | 5 | 0 | 0 | 1 | 2 | 0 | 13 | 0 | 0 | 2 | .282 | .333 | .564 |
| Hudson, Luke, Cin. | 9 | 18 | 16 | 1 | 2 | 2 | 0 | 0 | 0 | 2 | 0 | 1 | 0 | 1 | 0 | 3 | 0 | 0 | 0 | .125 | .167 | .125 |
| Hummel, Tim, Cin. | 56 | 125 | 110 | 10 | 24 | 31 | 4 | 0 | 1 | 7 | 4 | 1 | 2 | 8 | 2 | 17 | 1 | 0 | 2 | .218 | .281 | .282 |
| Ishii, Kazuhisa, L.A.* | 31 | 62 | 55 | 7 | 7 | 10 | 0 | 0 | 1 | 6 | 6 | 0 | 0 | 1 | 0 | 24 | 0 | 0 | 1 | .127 | .143 | .182 |
| Isringhausen, Jason, St.L. | 74 | 3 | 3 | 1 | 1 | 1 | 0 | 0 | 0 | 2 | 0 | 0 | 0 | 0 | 0 | 2 | 0 | 0 | 0 | .333 | .333 | .333 |

| Player, Team | G | TPA | AB | R | H | TB | 2B | 3B | HR | RBI | SH | SF | HP | BB | IBB | SO | SB | CS | GDP | Avg. | OBP | Slg. |
|---|---|---|---|---|---|---|---|---|---|---|---|---|---|---|---|---|---|---|---|---|---|---|
| Izturis, Cesar, L.A.† | 159 | 728 | 670 | 90 | 193 | 255 | 32 | 9 | 4 | 62 | 12 | 3 | 0 | 43 | 2 | 70 | 25 | 9 | 6 | .288 | .330 | .381 |
| Izturis, Maicer, Mon.† | 32 | 121 | 107 | 10 | 22 | 34 | 5 | 2 | 1 | 4 | 2 | 0 | 2 | 10 | 1 | 20 | 4 | 0 | 1 | .206 | .286 | .318 |
| Jackson, Damian, Chi. | 7 | 18 | 15 | 1 | 1 | 4 | 0 | 0 | 1 | 1 | 0 | 0 | 0 | 3 | 2 | 6 | 0 | 0 | 0 | .067 | .222 | .267 |
| Jackson, Edwin, L.A. | 8 | 6 | 4 | 0 | 1 | 1 | 0 | 0 | 0 | 1 | 2 | 0 | 0 | 0 | 0 | 1 | 0 | 0 | 0 | .250 | .250 | .250 |
| Jenkins, Geoff, Mil.* | 157 | 681 | 617 | 88 | 163 | 292 | 36 | 6 | 27 | 93 | 0 | 6 | 12 | 46 | 10 | 152 | 3 | 1 | 19 | .264 | .325 | .473 |
| Jennings, Jason, Col.* | 37 | 78 | 71 | 3 | 17 | 24 | 4 | 0 | 1 | 6 | 5 | 0 | 0 | 2 | 0 | 16 | 0 | 0 | 1 | .239 | .260 | .338 |
| Jimenez, D'Angelo, Cin.† | 152 | 652 | 563 | 76 | 152 | 222 | 28 | 3 | 12 | 67 | 3 | 2 | 2 | 82 | 1 | 99 | 13 | 7 | 15 | .270 | .364 | .394 |
| Johnson, Charles, Col. | 109 | 362 | 305 | 42 | 72 | 131 | 20 | 0 | 13 | 47 | 2 | 1 | 5 | 49 | 1 | 91 | 2 | 1 | 6 | .236 | .350 | .430 |
| Johnson, Mark, Mil.* | 7 | 15 | 11 | 1 | 1 | 1 | 0 | 0 | 0 | 2 | 0 | 1 | 0 | 3 | 1 | 2 | 0 | 0 | 0 | .091 | .267 | .091 |
| Johnson, Nick, Mon.* | 73 | 295 | 251 | 35 | 63 | 100 | 16 | 0 | 7 | 33 | 0 | 1 | 3 | 40 | 2 | 58 | 6 | 3 | 5 | .251 | .359 | .398 |
| Johnson, Randy, Ari. | 35 | 87 | 80 | 1 | 10 | 13 | 3 | 0 | 0 | 6 | 3 | 0 | 0 | 4 | 0 | 37 | 0 | 0 | 1 | .125 | .167 | .163 |
| Jones, Andruw, Atl. | 154 | 646 | 570 | 85 | 149 | 278 | 34 | 4 | 29 | 91 | 0 | 2 | 3 | 71 | 9 | 147 | 6 | 6 | 24 | .261 | .345 | .488 |
| Jones, Chipper, Atl.† | 137 | 567 | 472 | 69 | 117 | 229 | 20 | 1 | 30 | 96 | 0 | 7 | 4 | 84 | 8 | 96 | 2 | 0 | 14 | .248 | .362 | .485 |
| Jones, Todd, Cin.-Phi.* | 78 | 1 | 0 | 0 | 0 | 0 | 0 | 0 | 0 | 0 | 0 | 0 | 0 | 1 | 0 | 0 | 0 | 0 | 0 | .000 | 1.000 | .000 |
| Kata, Matt, Ari.† | 42 | 178 | 162 | 17 | 40 | 59 | 9 | 2 | 2 | 13 | 1 | 1 | 0 | 13 | 2 | 29 | 4 | 1 | 1 | .247 | .301 | .364 |
| Kearns, Austin, Cin. | 64 | 246 | 217 | 28 | 50 | 91 | 10 | 2 | 9 | 32 | 0 | 0 | 1 | 28 | 0 | 71 | 2 | 1 | 8 | .230 | .321 | .419 |
| Kelton, David, Chi. | 8 | 10 | 10 | 1 | 1 | 2 | 1 | 0 | 0 | 0 | 0 | 0 | 0 | 0 | 0 | 3 | 0 | 0 | 0 | .100 | .100 | .200 |
| Kendall, Jason, Pit. | 147 | 658 | 574 | 86 | 183 | 224 | 32 | 0 | 3 | 51 | 1 | 4 | 19 | 60 | 2 | 41 | 11 | 8 | 12 | .319 | .399 | .390 |
| Kennedy, Joe, Col. | 27 | 54 | 48 | 2 | 6 | 9 | 1 | 1 | 0 | 4 | 4 | 0 | 0 | 2 | 0 | 14 | 0 | 0 | 0 | .125 | .160 | .188 |
| Kensing, Logan, Fla. | 5 | 3 | 2 | 0 | 0 | 0 | 0 | 0 | 0 | 0 | 1 | 0 | 0 | 0 | 0 | 1 | 0 | 0 | 0 | .000 | .000 | .000 |
| Kent, Jeff, Hou. | 145 | 606 | 540 | 96 | 156 | 287 | 34 | 8 | 27 | 107 | 0 | 11 | 6 | 49 | 3 | 96 | 7 | 3 | 23 | .289 | .348 | .531 |
| Keppinger, Jeff, N.Y. | 33 | 123 | 116 | 9 | 33 | 44 | 2 | 0 | 3 | 9 | 0 | 1 | 0 | 6 | 0 | 7 | 2 | 1 | 6 | .284 | .317 | .379 |
| Kieschnick, Brooks, Mil.* | 77 | 68 | 63 | 2 | 17 | 23 | 3 | 0 | 1 | 7 | 0 | 0 | 0 | 5 | 1 | 16 | 0 | 0 | 3 | .270 | .324 | .365 |
| Kim, Sun-Woo, Mon. | 43 | 32 | 28 | 1 | 6 | 8 | 2 | 0 | 0 | 5 | 4 | 0 | 0 | 0 | 0 | 9 | 1 | 0 | 0 | .214 | .214 | .286 |
| King, Ray, St.L.* | 86 | 2 | 2 | 0 | 0 | 0 | 0 | 0 | 0 | 0 | 0 | 0 | 0 | 0 | 0 | 0 | 0 | 0 | 0 | .000 | .000 | .000 |
| Kinney, Matt, Mil. | 32 | 10 | 9 | 0 | 2 | 2 | 0 | 0 | 0 | 1 | 1 | 0 | 0 | 0 | 0 | 1 | 0 | 0 | 0 | .222 | .222 | .222 |
| Klesko, Ryan, S.D.* | 127 | 480 | 402 | 58 | 117 | 180 | 32 | 2 | 9 | 66 | 1 | 3 | 1 | 73 | 6 | 67 | 3 | 2 | 8 | .291 | .399 | .448 |
| Kline, Steve, St.L. | 67 | 1 | 0 | 1 | 0 | 0 | 0 | 0 | 0 | 0 | 1 | 0 | 0 | 0 | 0 | 0 | 0 | 0 | 0 | .000 | .000 | .000 |
| Knoedler, Justin, S.F. | 1 | 1 | 1 | 0 | 0 | 0 | 0 | 0 | 0 | 0 | 0 | 0 | 0 | 0 | 0 | 0 | 0 | 0 | 0 | .000 | .000 | .000 |
| Knott, Jon, S.D. | 9 | 15 | 14 | 1 | 3 | 5 | 2 | 0 | 0 | 1 | 0 | 0 | 0 | 1 | 0 | 5 | 0 | 0 | 0 | .214 | .267 | .357 |
| Kroeger, Josh, Ari.* | 22 | 55 | 54 | 5 | 9 | 12 | 3 | 0 | 0 | 2 | 0 | 0 | 0 | 1 | 0 | 21 | 0 | 1 | 2 | .167 | .182 | .222 |
| Krynzel, Dave, Mil.* | 16 | 47 | 41 | 6 | 9 | 10 | 1 | 0 | 0 | 3 | 0 | 0 | 3 | 3 | 0 | 15 | 0 | 0 | 0 | .220 | .319 | .244 |
| Labandeira, Josh, Mon. | 7 | 14 | 14 | 0 | 0 | 0 | 0 | 0 | 0 | 0 | 0 | 0 | 0 | 0 | 0 | 4 | 0 | 0 | 1 | .000 | .000 | .000 |
| Lamb, Mike, Hou.* | 112 | 312 | 278 | 38 | 80 | 142 | 14 | 3 | 14 | 58 | 0 | 3 | 0 | 31 | 3 | 63 | 1 | 1 | 4 | .288 | .356 | .511 |
| Lane, Jason, Hou. | 107 | 156 | 136 | 21 | 37 | 63 | 10 | 2 | 4 | 19 | 1 | 2 | 1 | 16 | 0 | 33 | 1 | 0 | 2 | .272 | .348 | .463 |
| Lankford, Ray, St.L.* | 92 | 235 | 200 | 36 | 51 | 85 | 14 | 1 | 6 | 22 | 0 | 4 | 2 | 29 | 4 | 55 | 2 | 2 | 6 | .255 | .349 | .425 |
| Larkin, Barry, Cin. | 111 | 386 | 346 | 55 | 100 | 145 | 15 | 3 | 8 | 44 | 2 | 3 | 1 | 34 | 1 | 39 | 2 | 0 | 16 | .289 | .352 | .419 |
| LaRoche, Adam, Atl.* | 110 | 356 | 324 | 45 | 90 | 158 | 27 | 1 | 13 | 45 | 2 | 2 | 1 | 27 | 1 | 78 | 0 | 0 | 10 | .278 | .333 | .488 |
| Larson, Brandon, Cin. | 40 | 135 | 118 | 13 | 25 | 40 | 6 | 0 | 3 | 14 | 0 | 1 | 2 | 14 | 0 | 35 | 1 | 0 | 2 | .212 | .304 | .339 |
| LaRue, Jason, Cin. | 114 | 445 | 390 | 46 | 98 | 168 | 24 | 2 | 14 | 55 | 2 | 3 | 24 | 26 | 5 | 108 | 0 | 2 | 7 | .251 | .334 | .431 |
| Lawrence, Brian, S.D. | 36 | 73 | 62 | 5 | 6 | 7 | 1 | 0 | 0 | 2 | 8 | 0 | 0 | 3 | 0 | 25 | 0 | 0 | 1 | .097 | .138 | .113 |
| Ledee, Ricky, Phi.-S.F.* | 104 | 205 | 176 | 25 | 41 | 71 | 9 | 0 | 7 | 30 | 0 | 1 | 1 | 27 | 2 | 47 | 3 | 0 | 6 | .233 | .337 | .403 |
| Lee, Derrek, Chi. | 161 | 688 | 605 | 90 | 168 | 305 | 39 | 1 | 32 | 98 | 2 | 5 | 8 | 68 | 4 | 128 | 12 | 5 | 14 | .278 | .356 | .504 |
| Leicester, Jon, Chi. | 32 | 1 | 1 | 0 | 0 | 0 | 0 | 0 | 0 | 0 | 0 | 0 | 0 | 0 | 0 | 0 | 0 | 0 | 0 | .000 | .000 | .000 |
| Leiter, Al, N.Y.* | 30 | 59 | 54 | 0 | 5 | 6 | 1 | 0 | 0 | 0 | 2 | 0 | 0 | 3 | 0 | 30 | 0 | 0 | 1 | .093 | .140 | .111 |
| Lidge, Brad, Hou. | 80 | 1 | 1 | 0 | 0 | 0 | 0 | 0 | 0 | 0 | 0 | 0 | 0 | 0 | 0 | 0 | 0 | 0 | 0 | .000 | .000 | .000 |
| Lidle, Cory, Cin.-Phi. | 34 | 75 | 62 | 3 | 9 | 16 | 4 | 0 | 1 | 6 | 8 | 0 | 0 | 5 | 0 | 36 | 0 | 0 | 0 | .145 | .209 | .258 |
| Lieberthal, Mike, Phi. | 131 | 529 | 476 | 58 | 129 | 213 | 31 | 1 | 17 | 61 | 1 | 4 | 11 | 37 | 2 | 69 | 1 | 1 | 19 | .271 | .335 | .447 |
| Liefer, Jeff, Mil.* | 16 | 31 | 28 | 2 | 6 | 11 | 2 | 0 | 1 | 5 | 0 | 1 | 0 | 2 | 0 | 8 | 0 | 0 | 2 | .214 | .258 | .393 |
| Lima, Jose, L.A. | 38 | 57 | 48 | 1 | 9 | 9 | 0 | 0 | 0 | 2 | 8 | 0 | 0 | 1 | 0 | 19 | 0 | 0 | 2 | .188 | .204 | .188 |
| Linden, Todd, S.F.† | 16 | 40 | 32 | 6 | 5 | 6 | 1 | 0 | 0 | 1 | 2 | 0 | 1 | 5 | 0 | 7 | 0 | 0 | 0 | .156 | .289 | .188 |
| Linebrink, Scott, S.D. | 73 | 3 | 2 | 0 | 0 | 0 | 0 | 0 | 0 | 0 | 1 | 0 | 0 | 0 | 0 | 2 | 0 | 0 | 0 | .000 | .000 | .000 |
| Liriano, Pedro, Mil. | 11 | 1 | 1 | 0 | 0 | 0 | 0 | 0 | 0 | 0 | 0 | 0 | 0 | 0 | 0 | 0 | 0 | 0 | 0 | .000 | .000 | .000 |
| Lo Duca, Paul, L.A.-Fla. | 143 | 594 | 535 | 68 | 153 | 225 | 29 | 2 | 13 | 80 | 8 | 6 | 9 | 36 | 0 | 49 | 4 | 5 | 22 | .286 | .338 | .421 |
| Long, Terrence, S.D.* | 136 | 313 | 288 | 31 | 85 | 121 | 19 | 4 | 3 | 28 | 0 | 5 | 1 | 19 | 4 | 51 | 3 | 2 | 13 | .295 | .335 | .420 |
| Looper, Braden, N.Y. | 71 | 2 | 2 | 0 | 0 | 0 | 0 | 0 | 0 | 0 | 0 | 0 | 0 | 0 | 0 | 1 | 0 | 0 | 0 | .000 | .000 | .000 |
| Lopez, Felipe, Cin.† | 79 | 295 | 264 | 35 | 64 | 107 | 18 | 2 | 7 | 31 | 2 | 1 | 3 | 25 | 0 | 81 | 1 | 1 | 1 | .242 | .314 | .405 |
| Lopez, Javier, Col.* | 64 | 3 | 2 | 0 | 0 | 0 | 0 | 0 | 0 | 0 | 1 | 0 | 0 | 0 | 0 | 2 | 0 | 0 | 0 | .000 | .000 | .000 |
| Lopez, Luis, Mon. | 11 | 27 | 26 | 0 | 4 | 4 | 0 | 0 | 0 | 0 | 0 | 0 | 1 | 0 | 0 | 9 | 0 | 0 | 1 | .154 | .185 | .154 |
| Loretta, Mark, S.D. | 154 | 707 | 620 | 108 | 208 | 307 | 47 | 2 | 16 | 76 | 4 | 16 | 9 | 58 | 3 | 45 | 5 | 3 | 10 | .335 | .391 | .495 |
| Lowell, Mike, Fla. | 158 | 671 | 598 | 87 | 175 | 302 | 44 | 1 | 27 | 85 | 0 | 3 | 6 | 64 | 8 | 77 | 5 | 1 | 17 | .293 | .365 | .505 |
| Lowry, Noah, S.F. | 16 | 36 | 33 | 2 | 6 | 8 | 2 | 0 | 0 | 0 | 3 | 0 | 0 | 0 | 0 | 10 | 0 | 0 | 1 | .182 | .182 | .242 |
| Luna, Hector, St.L. | 83 | 192 | 173 | 25 | 43 | 63 | 7 | 2 | 3 | 22 | 1 | 3 | 2 | 13 | 0 | 37 | 6 | 3 | 2 | .249 | .304 | .364 |
| Mabry, John, St.L.* | 87 | 275 | 240 | 32 | 71 | 121 | 11 | 0 | 13 | 40 | 5 | 3 | 1 | 26 | 5 | 63 | 0 | 1 | 6 | .296 | .363 | .504 |
| Machado, Anderson, Cin.† | 17 | 66 | 56 | 6 | 15 | 22 | 5 | 1 | 0 | 4 | 0 | 0 | 0 | 10 | 2 | 26 | 3 | 1 | 0 | .268 | .379 | .393 |
| Macias, Jose, Chi.† | 98 | 204 | 194 | 23 | 52 | 73 | 6 | 3 | 3 | 22 | 2 | 1 | 2 | 5 | 0 | 38 | 4 | 1 | 2 | .268 | .292 | .376 |
| Mackowiak, Rob, Pit.* | 155 | 555 | 491 | 65 | 121 | 206 | 22 | 6 | 17 | 75 | 1 | 7 | 6 | 50 | 2 | 114 | 13 | 4 | 3 | .246 | .319 | .420 |
| Maddux, Greg, Chi. | 34 | 79 | 69 | 5 | 11 | 11 | 0 | 0 | 0 | 5 | 9 | 0 | 0 | 1 | 0 | 12 | 1 | 0 | 1 | .159 | .171 | .159 |
| Madson, Ryan, Phi.* | 52 | 4 | 3 | 0 | 0 | 0 | 0 | 0 | 0 | 0 | 1 | 0 | 0 | 0 | 0 | 2 | 0 | 0 | 0 | .000 | .000 | .000 |
| Magruder, Chris, Mil.† | 56 | 101 | 89 | 11 | 21 | 35 | 6 | 1 | 2 | 10 | 1 | 1 | 2 | 8 | 2 | 21 | 0 | 1 | 3 | .236 | .310 | .393 |
| Majewski, Gary, Mon. | 16 | 2 | 2 | 0 | 0 | 0 | 0 | 0 | 0 | 0 | 0 | 0 | 0 | 0 | 0 | 2 | 0 | 0 | 0 | .000 | .000 | .000 |
| Manzanillo, Josias, Fla. | 26 | 1 | 1 | 0 | 0 | 0 | 0 | 0 | 0 | 0 | 0 | 0 | 0 | 0 | 0 | 1 | 0 | 0 | 0 | .000 | .000 | .000 |
| Marquis, Jason, St.L.* | 35 | 76 | 72 | 6 | 21 | 27 | 6 | 0 | 0 | 9 | 2 | 1 | 0 | 1 | 0 | 17 | 1 | 0 | 3 | .292 | .297 | .375 |
| Marrero, Eli, Atl. | 90 | 280 | 250 | 37 | 80 | 130 | 18 | 1 | 10 | 40 | 2 | 4 | 1 | 23 | 1 | 50 | 4 | 1 | 4 | .320 | .374 | .520 |
| Martinez, Ramon, Chi. | 102 | 298 | 260 | 22 | 64 | 90 | 15 | 1 | 3 | 30 | 7 | 4 | 1 | 26 | 3 | 40 | 1 | 0 | 5 | .246 | .313 | .346 |
| Mateo, Henry, Mon.† | 40 | 46 | 44 | 3 | 12 | 14 | 2 | 0 | 0 | 0 | 1 | 0 | 0 | 1 | 0 | 9 | 2 | 3 | 1 | .273 | .289 | .318 |
| Mateo, Ruben, Pit. | 19 | 39 | 33 | 4 | 8 | 17 | 0 | 0 | 3 | 7 | 0 | 0 | 1 | 5 | 1 | 6 | 0 | 0 | 1 | .242 | .359 | .515 |
| Matheny, Mike, St.L. | 122 | 419 | 385 | 28 | 95 | 134 | 22 | 1 | 5 | 50 | 5 | 3 | 3 | 23 | 7 | 83 | 0 | 2 | 12 | .247 | .292 | .348 |
| Matsui, Kazuo, N.Y.† | 114 | 509 | 460 | 65 | 125 | 182 | 32 | 2 | 7 | 44 | 5 | 2 | 2 | 40 | 4 | 97 | 14 | 3 | 3 | .272 | .331 | .396 |
| Mayne, Brent, Ari.-L.A.* | 83 | 224 | 190 | 14 | 42 | 50 | 6 | 1 | 0 | 15 | 4 | 3 | 0 | 27 | 8 | 41 | 1 | 0 | 7 | .221 | .314 | .263 |
| McConnell, Sam, Atl.* | 10 | 1 | 1 | 0 | 0 | 0 | 0 | 0 | 0 | 0 | 0 | 0 | 0 | 0 | 0 | 0 | 0 | 0 | 0 | .000 | .000 | .000 |
| McCracken, Quinton, Ari.† | 55 | 172 | 156 | 20 | 45 | 64 | 11 | 1 | 2 | 13 | 2 | 1 | 0 | 13 | 0 | 23 | 2 | 4 | 2 | .288 | .341 | .410 |
| McEwing, Joe, N.Y. | 75 | 154 | 138 | 17 | 35 | 43 | 3 | 1 | 1 | 16 | 6 | 1 | 0 | 9 | 4 | 32 | 4 | 1 | 0 | .254 | .297 | .312 |

| Player, Team | G | TPA | AB | R | H | TB | 2B | 3B | HR | RBI | SH | SF | HP | BB | IBB | SO | SB | CS | GDP | Avg. | OBP | Slg. |
|---|---|---|---|---|---|---|---|---|---|---|---|---|---|---|---|---|---|---|---|---|---|---|
| McKay, Cody, St.L.* | 35 | 79 | 74 | 7 | 17 | 19 | 2 | 0 | 0 | 6 | 1 | 0 | 2 | 2 | 0 | 14 | 0 | 0 | 3 | .230 | .269 | .257 |
| Meadows, Brian, Pit. | 68 | 4 | 3 | 0 | 0 | 0 | 0 | 0 | 0 | 1 | 0 | 0 | 0 | 1 | 0 | 3 | 0 | 0 | 0 | .000 | .250 | .000 |
| Mercker, Kent, Chi.* | 71 | 2 | 2 | 0 | 0 | 0 | 0 | 0 | 0 | 0 | 0 | 0 | 0 | 0 | 0 | 0 | 0 | 0 | 0 | .000 | .000 | .000 |
| Miceli, Dan, Hou. | 74 | 2 | 2 | 0 | 1 | 1 | 0 | 0 | 0 | 0 | 0 | 0 | 0 | 0 | 0 | 1 | 0 | 0 | 0 | .500 | .500 | .500 |
| Michaels, Jason, Phi. | 115 | 346 | 299 | 44 | 82 | 124 | 12 | 0 | 10 | 40 | 0 | 3 | 2 | 42 | 1 | 80 | 2 | 2 | 3 | .274 | .364 | .415 |
| Miles, Aaron, Col.† | 134 | 566 | 522 | 75 | 153 | 192 | 15 | 3 | 6 | 47 | 7 | 6 | 2 | 29 | 0 | 53 | 12 | 7 | 12 | .293 | .329 | .368 |
| Miller, Corky, Cin. | 13 | 49 | 39 | 2 | 1 | 1 | 0 | 0 | 0 | 3 | 0 | 1 | 3 | 6 | 0 | 12 | 0 | 0 | 3 | .026 | .204 | .026 |
| Miller, Wade, Hou. | 16 | 35 | 27 | 2 | 7 | 7 | 0 | 0 | 0 | 3 | 8 | 0 | 0 | 0 | 0 | 6 | 0 | 0 | 0 | .259 | .259 | .259 |
| Millwood, Kevin, Phi. | 25 | 53 | 46 | 0 | 8 | 10 | 2 | 0 | 0 | 1 | 5 | 0 | 0 | 2 | 0 | 26 | 0 | 0 | 1 | .174 | .208 | .217 |
| Milton, Eric, Phi.* | 34 | 75 | 65 | 4 | 10 | 11 | 1 | 0 | 0 | 5 | 5 | 1 | 0 | 4 | 0 | 29 | 0 | 0 | 0 | .154 | .200 | .169 |
| Minor, Damon, S.F.* | 24 | 74 | 58 | 8 | 14 | 16 | 2 | 0 | 0 | 6 | 0 | 0 | 4 | 12 | 0 | 18 | 0 | 0 | 2 | .241 | .405 | .276 |
| Mitre, Sergio, Chi. | 13 | 19 | 15 | 0 | 1 | 2 | 1 | 0 | 0 | 0 | 3 | 0 | 0 | 1 | 0 | 8 | 0 | 0 | 0 | .067 | .125 | .133 |
| Moeller, Chad, Mil. | 101 | 349 | 317 | 25 | 66 | 96 | 13 | 1 | 5 | 27 | 6 | 1 | 4 | 21 | 1 | 74 | 0 | 1 | 12 | .208 | .265 | .303 |
| Mohr, Dustan, S.F. | 117 | 324 | 263 | 52 | 72 | 115 | 20 | 1 | 7 | 28 | 4 | 3 | 8 | 46 | 3 | 64 | 0 | 3 | 5 | .274 | .394 | .437 |
| Molina, Yadier, St.L. | 51 | 151 | 135 | 12 | 36 | 48 | 6 | 0 | 2 | 15 | 2 | 1 | 0 | 13 | 3 | 20 | 0 | 1 | 4 | .267 | .329 | .356 |
| Mondesi, Raul, Pit. | 26 | 110 | 99 | 8 | 28 | 42 | 8 | 0 | 2 | 14 | 0 | 0 | 0 | 11 | 0 | 27 | 0 | 2 | 1 | .283 | .355 | .424 |
| Mordecai, Mike, Fla. | 69 | 90 | 84 | 7 | 19 | 25 | 3 | 0 | 1 | 5 | 0 | 0 | 0 | 6 | 0 | 18 | 0 | 1 | 1 | .226 | .278 | .298 |
| Moreno, Orber, N.Y. | 33 | 1 | 1 | 0 | 0 | 0 | 0 | 0 | 0 | 0 | 0 | 0 | 0 | 0 | 0 | 0 | 0 | 0 | 0 | .000 | .000 | .000 |
| Morris, Matt, St.L. | 32 | 75 | 62 | 4 | 10 | 11 | 1 | 0 | 0 | 6 | 8 | 1 | 0 | 4 | 0 | 26 | 0 | 0 | 0 | .161 | .209 | .177 |
| Mota, Guillermo, L.A.-Fla. | 78 | 12 | 12 | 1 | 2 | 3 | 1 | 0 | 0 | 1 | 0 | 0 | 0 | 0 | 0 | 7 | 0 | 0 | 0 | .167 | .167 | .250 |
| Munro, Pete, Hou. | 22 | 35 | 29 | 4 | 2 | 2 | 0 | 0 | 0 | 1 | 3 | 1 | 0 | 2 | 0 | 10 | 0 | 0 | 0 | .069 | .125 | .069 |
| Murray, Calvin, Chi. | 11 | 6 | 5 | 2 | 1 | 1 | 0 | 0 | 0 | 1 | 0 | 0 | 0 | 1 | 0 | 0 | 0 | 0 | 0 | .200 | .333 | .200 |
| Myers, Brett, Phi. | 32 | 61 | 51 | 6 | 10 | 14 | 4 | 0 | 0 | 1 | 8 | 0 | 0 | 2 | 0 | 17 | 0 | 0 | 2 | .196 | .226 | .275 |
| Nady, Xavier, S.D. | 34 | 84 | 77 | 7 | 19 | 32 | 4 | 0 | 3 | 9 | 1 | 0 | 1 | 5 | 0 | 13 | 0 | 0 | 4 | .247 | .301 | .416 |
| Nevin, Phil, S.D. | 147 | 623 | 547 | 78 | 158 | 269 | 31 | 1 | 26 | 105 | 0 | 5 | 5 | 66 | 5 | 121 | 0 | 0 | 16 | .289 | .368 | .492 |
| Nomo, Hideo, L.A. | 18 | 27 | 26 | 2 | 3 | 6 | 0 | 0 | 1 | 1 | 1 | 0 | 0 | 0 | 0 | 17 | 0 | 0 | 0 | .115 | .115 | .231 |
| Nunez, Abraham, Fla.† | 58 | 75 | 64 | 9 | 11 | 17 | 1 | 1 | 1 | 5 | 2 | 0 | 0 | 9 | 0 | 21 | 1 | 2 | 3 | .172 | .274 | .266 |
| Nunez, Abraham O., Pit.† | 112 | 195 | 182 | 17 | 43 | 58 | 9 | 0 | 2 | 13 | 2 | 1 | 0 | 10 | 0 | 36 | 1 | 3 | 8 | .236 | .275 | .319 |
| Obermueller, Wes, Mil. | 26 | 42 | 39 | 2 | 15 | 18 | 3 | 0 | 0 | 5 | 2 | 0 | 0 | 1 | 0 | 14 | 0 | 0 | 1 | .385 | .400 | .462 |
| Ohka, Tomo, Mon. | 15 | 26 | 25 | 0 | 2 | 2 | 0 | 0 | 0 | 0 | 0 | 0 | 0 | 1 | 0 | 8 | 1 | 0 | 0 | .080 | .115 | .080 |
| Ojeda, Miguel, S.D. | 62 | 174 | 156 | 23 | 40 | 67 | 3 | 0 | 8 | 26 | 0 | 2 | 1 | 15 | 1 | 34 | 0 | 0 | 1 | .256 | .322 | .429 |
| Oliver, Darren, Fla.-Hou. | 28 | 25 | 22 | 0 | 3 | 3 | 0 | 0 | 0 | 1 | 3 | 0 | 0 | 0 | 0 | 9 | 0 | 0 | 3 | .136 | .136 | .136 |
| Olmedo, Ray, Cin.† | 8 | 2 | 1 | 0 | 0 | 0 | 0 | 0 | 0 | 0 | 0 | 0 | 0 | 1 | 0 | 0 | 0 | 0 | 0 | .000 | .500 | .000 |
| Olson, Tim, Ari. | 48 | 114 | 97 | 8 | 18 | 31 | 7 | 0 | 2 | 5 | 1 | 0 | 0 | 16 | 0 | 18 | 1 | 0 | 4 | .186 | .301 | .320 |
| Ordonez, Rey, Chi. | 23 | 67 | 61 | 2 | 10 | 16 | 3 | 0 | 1 | 5 | 4 | 0 | 0 | 2 | 0 | 14 | 0 | 0 | 1 | .164 | .190 | .262 |
| Ortiz, Russ, Atl. | 34 | 71 | 59 | 1 | 6 | 8 | 2 | 0 | 0 | 1 | 10 | 0 | 1 | 1 | 0 | 17 | 0 | 0 | 1 | .102 | .131 | .136 |
| Oswalt, Roy, Hou. | 36 | 89 | 71 | 1 | 10 | 11 | 1 | 0 | 0 | 6 | 13 | 1 | 1 | 3 | 0 | 16 | 0 | 0 | 1 | .141 | .184 | .155 |
| Otsuka, Akinori, S.D. | 73 | 1 | 1 | 0 | 0 | 0 | 0 | 0 | 0 | 0 | 0 | 0 | 0 | 0 | 0 | 0 | 0 | 0 | 0 | .000 | .000 | .000 |
| Overbay, Lyle, Mil.* | 159 | 668 | 579 | 83 | 174 | 277 | 53 | 1 | 16 | 87 | 0 | 6 | 2 | 81 | 9 | 128 | 2 | 1 | 11 | .301 | .385 | .478 |
| Padilla, Vicente, Phi.† | 20 | 40 | 35 | 2 | 4 | 4 | 0 | 0 | 0 | 3 | 3 | 0 | 0 | 2 | 0 | 17 | 0 | 0 | 0 | .114 | .162 | .114 |
| Palmeiro, Orlando, Hou.* | 102 | 156 | 133 | 19 | 32 | 46 | 5 | 0 | 3 | 12 | 2 | 0 | 3 | 18 | 1 | 19 | 2 | 1 | 1 | .241 | .344 | .346 |
| Pascucci, Val, Mon. | 32 | 74 | 62 | 6 | 11 | 18 | 1 | 0 | 2 | 6 | 0 | 1 | 1 | 10 | 1 | 22 | 1 | 0 | 3 | .177 | .297 | .290 |
| Patterson, Corey, Chi.* | 157 | 687 | 631 | 91 | 168 | 285 | 33 | 6 | 24 | 72 | 5 | 1 | 5 | 45 | 7 | 168 | 32 | 9 | 7 | .266 | .320 | .452 |
| Patterson, John, Mon. | 19 | 39 | 33 | 0 | 4 | 4 | 0 | 0 | 0 | 1 | 5 | 0 | 0 | 1 | 0 | 17 | 0 | 0 | 2 | .121 | .147 | .121 |
| Pavano, Carl, Fla. | 31 | 79 | 68 | 4 | 13 | 22 | 3 | 0 | 2 | 6 | 9 | 0 | 1 | 1 | 0 | 24 | 0 | 0 | 1 | .191 | .214 | .324 |
| Payton, Jay, S.D. | 143 | 511 | 458 | 57 | 119 | 168 | 17 | 4 | 8 | 55 | 2 | 4 | 4 | 43 | 2 | 56 | 2 | 0 | 12 | .260 | .326 | .367 |
| Peavy, Jake, S.D. | 27 | 68 | 59 | 5 | 10 | 11 | 1 | 0 | 0 | 3 | 5 | 0 | 0 | 4 | 0 | 17 | 0 | 0 | 1 | .169 | .222 | .186 |
| Pellow, Kit, Col. | 59 | 133 | 121 | 15 | 29 | 42 | 5 | 1 | 2 | 10 | 0 | 0 | 4 | 8 | 1 | 43 | 1 | 0 | 3 | .240 | .308 | .347 |
| Pena, Wily Mo, Cin. | 110 | 364 | 336 | 45 | 87 | 177 | 10 | 1 | 26 | 66 | 0 | 0 | 6 | 22 | 1 | 108 | 5 | 2 | 7 | .259 | .316 | .527 |
| Penny, Brad, Fla.-L.A. | 24 | 52 | 51 | 1 | 3 | 3 | 0 | 0 | 0 | 1 | 1 | 0 | 0 | 0 | 0 | 15 | 0 | 0 | 1 | .059 | .059 | .059 |
| Perez, Antonio, L.A. | 13 | 14 | 13 | 5 | 3 | 4 | 1 | 0 | 0 | 0 | 0 | 0 | 1 | 0 | 0 | 5 | 1 | 0 | 0 | .231 | .286 | .308 |
| Perez, Eddie, Atl. | 74 | 188 | 170 | 14 | 39 | 60 | 12 | 0 | 3 | 13 | 3 | 1 | 3 | 11 | 1 | 29 | 0 | 0 | 5 | .229 | .286 | .353 |
| Perez, Neifi, S.F.-Chi.† | 126 | 420 | 381 | 40 | 97 | 128 | 17 | 1 | 4 | 39 | 11 | 4 | 0 | 24 | 3 | 41 | 1 | 1 | 8 | .255 | .296 | .336 |
| Perez, Odalis, L.A.* | 31 | 70 | 62 | 5 | 7 | 9 | 2 | 0 | 0 | 2 | 6 | 0 | 0 | 2 | 0 | 17 | 0 | 0 | 2 | .113 | .141 | .145 |
| Perez, Oliver, Pit.* | 31 | 72 | 58 | 2 | 11 | 11 | 0 | 0 | 0 | 0 | 10 | 0 | 0 | 4 | 0 | 22 | 0 | 0 | 0 | .190 | .242 | .190 |
| Perez, Tomas, Phi.† | 86 | 190 | 176 | 22 | 38 | 73 | 13 | 2 | 6 | 21 | 3 | 1 | 1 | 9 | 2 | 44 | 0 | 0 | 2 | .216 | .257 | .415 |
| Pettitte, Andy, Hou.* | 15 | 29 | 23 | 0 | 4 | 5 | 1 | 0 | 0 | 2 | 3 | 0 | 0 | 3 | 0 | 5 | 0 | 0 | 1 | .174 | .269 | .217 |
| Phelps, Tommy, Fla.* | 19 | 6 | 6 | 0 | 0 | 0 | 0 | 0 | 0 | 0 | 0 | 0 | 0 | 0 | 0 | 2 | 0 | 0 | 0 | .000 | .000 | .000 |
| Phelps, Travis, Mil. | 4 | 1 | 1 | 0 | 0 | 0 | 0 | 0 | 0 | 0 | 0 | 0 | 0 | 0 | 0 | 1 | 0 | 0 | 0 | .000 | .000 | .000 |
| Phillips, Jason, N.Y. | 128 | 412 | 362 | 34 | 79 | 118 | 18 | 0 | 7 | 34 | 2 | 5 | 8 | 35 | 4 | 42 | 0 | 1 | 11 | .218 | .298 | .326 |
| Piazza, Mike, N.Y. | 129 | 528 | 455 | 47 | 121 | 202 | 21 | 0 | 20 | 54 | 0 | 3 | 2 | 68 | 14 | 78 | 0 | 0 | 14 | .266 | .362 | .444 |
| Piedra, Jorge, Col.* | 38 | 98 | 91 | 15 | 27 | 44 | 8 | 0 | 3 | 10 | 1 | 0 | 1 | 5 | 0 | 19 | 0 | 1 | 1 | .297 | .340 | .484 |
| Pierre, Juan, Fla.* | 162 | 748 | 678 | 100 | 221 | 276 | 22 | 12 | 3 | 49 | 15 | 2 | 8 | 45 | 1 | 35 | 45 | 24 | 9 | .326 | .374 | .407 |
| Pierzynski, A.J., S.F.* | 131 | 510 | 471 | 45 | 128 | 193 | 28 | 2 | 11 | 77 | 2 | 3 | 15 | 19 | 4 | 27 | 0 | 1 | 27 | .272 | .319 | .410 |
| Podsednik, Scott, Mil.* | 154 | 713 | 640 | 85 | 156 | 233 | 27 | 7 | 12 | 39 | 6 | 1 | 7 | 58 | 2 | 105 | 70 | 13 | 7 | .244 | .313 | .364 |
| Polanco, Placido, Phi. | 126 | 555 | 503 | 74 | 150 | 222 | 21 | 0 | 17 | 55 | 7 | 6 | 12 | 27 | 0 | 39 | 7 | 4 | 13 | .298 | .345 | .441 |
| Porter, Colin, St.L.* | 23 | 35 | 35 | 3 | 11 | 15 | 1 | 0 | 1 | 2 | 0 | 0 | 0 | 0 | 0 | 13 | 0 | 0 | 2 | .314 | .314 | .429 |
| Powell, Brian, Phi. | 17 | 9 | 8 | 0 | 1 | 1 | 0 | 0 | 0 | 0 | 1 | 0 | 0 | 0 | 0 | 5 | 0 | 0 | 0 | .125 | .125 | .125 |
| Pratt, Todd, Phi. | 45 | 149 | 128 | 16 | 33 | 47 | 5 | 0 | 3 | 16 | 1 | 1 | 1 | 18 | 0 | 38 | 0 | 0 | 5 | .258 | .351 | .367 |
| Prior, Mark, Chi. | 21 | 44 | 36 | 5 | 5 | 5 | 0 | 0 | 0 | 0 | 6 | 0 | 0 | 2 | 0 | 20 | 0 | 0 | 0 | .139 | .184 | .139 |
| Pujols, Albert, St.L. | 154 | 692 | 592 | 133 | 196 | 389 | 51 | 2 | 46 | 123 | 0 | 9 | 7 | 84 | 12 | 52 | 5 | 5 | 21 | .331 | .415 | .657 |
| Qualls, Chad, Hou. | 25 | 1 | 1 | 0 | 0 | 0 | 0 | 0 | 0 | 0 | 0 | 0 | 0 | 0 | 0 | 1 | 0 | 0 | 0 | .000 | .000 | .000 |
| Quintero, Humberto, S.D. | 23 | 78 | 72 | 7 | 18 | 27 | 3 | 0 | 2 | 10 | 0 | 1 | 0 | 5 | 0 | 16 | 0 | 2 | 5 | .250 | .295 | .375 |
| Ramirez, Aramis, Chi. | 145 | 606 | 547 | 99 | 174 | 316 | 32 | 1 | 36 | 103 | 0 | 7 | 3 | 49 | 6 | 62 | 0 | 2 | 25 | .318 | .373 | .578 |
| Ramirez, Elizardo, Phi.† | 7 | 1 | 0 | 0 | 0 | 0 | 0 | 0 | 0 | 0 | 0 | 0 | 0 | 1 | 0 | 0 | 0 | 0 | 0 | .000 | 1.000 | .000 |
| Ramirez, Horacio, Atl.* | 11 | 22 | 21 | 0 | 2 | 2 | 0 | 0 | 0 | 1 | 1 | 0 | 0 | 0 | 0 | 5 | 0 | 0 | 0 | .095 | .095 | .095 |
| Randolph, Stephen, Ari.* | 47 | 12 | 12 | 4 | 5 | 8 | 3 | 0 | 0 | 3 | 0 | 0 | 0 | 0 | 0 | 3 | 0 | 0 | 0 | .417 | .417 | .667 |
| Ransom, Cody, S.F. | 78 | 78 | 68 | 13 | 17 | 26 | 6 | 0 | 1 | 11 | 3 | 0 | 1 | 6 | 0 | 20 | 2 | 2 | 2 | .250 | .320 | .382 |
| Rauch, Jon, Mon. | 9 | 6 | 6 | 1 | 1 | 4 | 0 | 0 | 1 | 2 | 0 | 0 | 0 | 0 | 0 | 4 | 0 | 0 | 0 | .167 | .167 | .667 |
| Redding, Tim, Hou. | 27 | 30 | 29 | 1 | 4 | 4 | 0 | 0 | 0 | 0 | 1 | 0 | 0 | 0 | 0 | 13 | 0 | 0 | 0 | .138 | .138 | .138 |
| Redman, Tike, Pit.* | 155 | 581 | 546 | 65 | 153 | 204 | 19 | 4 | 8 | 51 | 4 | 5 | 3 | 23 | 2 | 52 | 18 | 6 | 6 | .280 | .310 | .374 |
| Redmond, Mike, Fla. | 81 | 273 | 246 | 19 | 63 | 84 | 15 | 0 | 2 | 25 | 3 | 2 | 8 | 14 | 0 | 28 | 1 | 0 | 10 | .256 | .315 | .341 |
| Reed, Steve, Col. | 65 | 2 | 2 | 0 | 1 | 1 | 0 | 0 | 0 | 0 | 0 | 0 | 0 | 0 | 0 | 1 | 0 | 0 | 0 | .500 | .500 | .500 |

| Player, Team | G | TPA | AB | R | H | TB | 2B | 3B | HR | RBI | SH | SF | HP | BB | IBB | SO | SB | CS | GDP | Avg. | OBP | Slg. |
|---|---|---|---|---|---|---|---|---|---|---|---|---|---|---|---|---|---|---|---|---|---|---|
| Remlinger, Mike, Chi.* | 48 | 1 | 1 | 0 | 0 | 0 | 0 | 0 | 0 | 0 | 0 | 0 | 0 | 0 | 0 | 1 | 0 | 0 | 0 | .000 | .000 | .000 |
| Renteria, Edgar, St.L. | 149 | 642 | 586 | 84 | 168 | 235 | 37 | 0 | 10 | 72 | 6 | 10 | 1 | 39 | 5 | 78 | 17 | 11 | 14 | .287 | .327 | .401 |
| Reyes, Al, St.L. | 12 | 1 | 1 | 0 | 1 | 1 | 0 | 0 | 0 | 0 | 0 | 0 | 0 | 0 | 0 | 0 | 0 | 0 | 0 | 1.000 | 1.000 | 1.000 |
| Reyes, Jose, N.Y.† | 53 | 229 | 220 | 33 | 56 | 82 | 16 | 2 | 2 | 14 | 4 | 0 | 0 | 5 | 0 | 31 | 19 | 2 | 1 | .255 | .271 | .373 |
| Reyes, Rene, Col.† | 28 | 66 | 61 | 5 | 9 | 11 | 2 | 0 | 0 | 1 | 0 | 0 | 0 | 5 | 2 | 17 | 0 | 0 | 0 | .148 | .212 | .180 |
| Riedling, John, Cin. | 70 | 3 | 3 | 0 | 0 | 0 | 0 | 0 | 0 | 0 | 0 | 0 | 0 | 0 | 0 | 1 | 0 | 0 | 0 | .000 | .000 | .000 |
| Rivera, Carlos, Pit.* | 7 | 17 | 15 | 1 | 3 | 3 | 0 | 0 | 0 | 1 | 0 | 0 | 0 | 1 | 1 | 3 | 0 | 0 | 0 | .200 | .250 | .200 |
| Rivera, Juan, Mon. | 134 | 426 | 391 | 48 | 120 | 182 | 24 | 1 | 12 | 49 | 0 | 0 | 1 | 34 | 7 | 45 | 6 | 2 | 11 | .307 | .364 | .465 |
| Roberts, Dave, L.A.* | 68 | 270 | 233 | 45 | 59 | 83 | 4 | 7 | 2 | 21 | 2 | 3 | 4 | 28 | 0 | 31 | 33 | 1 | 2 | .253 | .340 | .356 |
| Roberts, Willis, Pit. | 9 | 1 | 1 | 0 | 0 | 0 | 0 | 0 | 0 | 0 | 0 | 0 | 0 | 0 | 0 | 1 | 0 | 0 | 0 | .000 | .000 | .000 |
| Robinson, Kerry, S.D.* | 80 | 101 | 92 | 20 | 27 | 31 | 4 | 0 | 0 | 5 | 1 | 2 | 1 | 5 | 0 | 8 | 11 | 4 | 0 | .293 | .330 | .337 |
| Rodriguez, Felix, S.F.-Phi. | 76 | 1 | 1 | 0 | 0 | 0 | 0 | 0 | 0 | 0 | 0 | 0 | 0 | 0 | 0 | 1 | 0 | 0 | 0 | .000 | .000 | .000 |
| Rolen, Scott, St.L. | 142 | 593 | 500 | 109 | 157 | 299 | 32 | 4 | 34 | 124 | 1 | 7 | 13 | 72 | 5 | 92 | 4 | 3 | 8 | .314 | .409 | .598 |
| Rollins, Jimmy, Phi.† | 154 | 725 | 657 | 119 | 190 | 299 | 43 | 12 | 14 | 73 | 6 | 2 | 3 | 57 | 3 | 73 | 30 | 9 | 4 | .289 | .348 | .455 |
| Romano, Jason, Cin. | 22 | 29 | 26 | 3 | 4 | 7 | 0 | 0 | 1 | 3 | 1 | 0 | 0 | 2 | 0 | 10 | 0 | 0 | 0 | .154 | .214 | .269 |
| Ross, David, L.A. | 70 | 190 | 165 | 13 | 28 | 48 | 3 | 1 | 5 | 15 | 0 | 5 | 5 | 15 | 1 | 62 | 0 | 0 | 3 | .170 | .253 | .291 |
| Rueter, Kirk, S.F.* | 34 | 67 | 61 | 4 | 8 | 10 | 2 | 0 | 0 | 2 | 3 | 0 | 0 | 3 | 0 | 7 | 0 | 0 | 0 | .131 | .172 | .164 |
| Rusch, Glendon, Chi.* | 33 | 46 | 39 | 3 | 6 | 13 | 1 | 0 | 2 | 3 | 7 | 0 | 0 | 0 | 0 | 11 | 0 | 0 | 0 | .154 | .154 | .333 |
| Sadler, Donnie, Ari. | 18 | 24 | 23 | 1 | 3 | 5 | 2 | 0 | 0 | 0 | 0 | 0 | 0 | 1 | 0 | 7 | 0 | 0 | 0 | .130 | .167 | .217 |
| Saenz, Chris, Mil. | 1 | 2 | 2 | 0 | 0 | 0 | 0 | 0 | 0 | 0 | 0 | 0 | 0 | 0 | 0 | 1 | 0 | 0 | 0 | .000 | .000 | .000 |
| Saenz, Olmedo, L.A. | 77 | 128 | 111 | 17 | 31 | 56 | 1 | 0 | 8 | 22 | 0 | 3 | 2 | 12 | 1 | 33 | 0 | 0 | 4 | .279 | .352 | .505 |
| Sanchez, Duaner, L.A. | 67 | 5 | 4 | 1 | 1 | 2 | 1 | 0 | 0 | 2 | 1 | 0 | 0 | 0 | 0 | 1 | 0 | 0 | 1 | .250 | .250 | .500 |
| Sanchez, Freddy, Pit. | 9 | 20 | 19 | 2 | 3 | 3 | 0 | 0 | 0 | 2 | 1 | 0 | 0 | 0 | 0 | 3 | 0 | 0 | 0 | .158 | .158 | .158 |
| Sanchez, Jesus, Cin.* | 3 | 5 | 4 | 0 | 0 | 0 | 0 | 0 | 0 | 0 | 1 | 0 | 0 | 0 | 0 | 3 | 0 | 0 | 0 | .000 | .000 | .000 |
| Sanders, Reggie, St.L. | 135 | 487 | 446 | 64 | 116 | 215 | 27 | 3 | 22 | 67 | 1 | 3 | 4 | 33 | 5 | 118 | 21 | 5 | 5 | .260 | .315 | .482 |
| Santos, Victor, Mil. | 31 | 47 | 39 | 0 | 2 | 3 | 1 | 0 | 0 | 1 | 6 | 0 | 0 | 2 | 0 | 20 | 0 | 0 | 0 | .051 | .098 | .077 |
| Schmidt, Jason, S.F. | 32 | 84 | 66 | 4 | 9 | 15 | 0 | 0 | 2 | 3 | 13 | 0 | 1 | 4 | 0 | 30 | 0 | 0 | 0 | .136 | .197 | .227 |
| Schneider, Brian, Mon.* | 135 | 488 | 436 | 40 | 112 | 174 | 20 | 3 | 12 | 49 | 5 | 2 | 3 | 42 | 10 | 63 | 0 | 1 | 8 | .257 | .325 | .399 |
| Seo, Jae Weong, N.Y. | 26 | 38 | 32 | 2 | 5 | 6 | 1 | 0 | 0 | 1 | 3 | 0 | 1 | 2 | 0 | 9 | 1 | 0 | 1 | .156 | .229 | .188 |
| Service, Scott, Ari. | 21 | 1 | 1 | 0 | 0 | 0 | 0 | 0 | 0 | 0 | 0 | 0 | 0 | 0 | 0 | 0 | 0 | 0 | 0 | .000 | .000 | .000 |
| Sexson, Richie, Ari. | 23 | 104 | 90 | 20 | 21 | 52 | 4 | 0 | 9 | 23 | 0 | 0 | 0 | 14 | 0 | 21 | 0 | 0 | 2 | .233 | .337 | .578 |
| Sheets, Ben, Mil. | 34 | 81 | 67 | 2 | 9 | 9 | 0 | 0 | 0 | 1 | 9 | 0 | 0 | 5 | 0 | 22 | 0 | 0 | 2 | .134 | .194 | .134 |
| Simon, Randall, Pit.* | 61 | 193 | 175 | 14 | 34 | 49 | 6 | 0 | 3 | 14 | 0 | 1 | 2 | 15 | 5 | 17 | 0 | 0 | 8 | .194 | .264 | .280 |
| Simontacchi, Jason, St.L. | 15 | 2 | 2 | 1 | 1 | 1 | 0 | 0 | 0 | 0 | 0 | 0 | 0 | 0 | 0 | 0 | 0 | 0 | 0 | .500 | .500 | .500 |
| Simpson, Allan, Col. | 32 | 1 | 1 | 0 | 0 | 0 | 0 | 0 | 0 | 0 | 0 | 0 | 0 | 0 | 0 | 0 | 0 | 0 | 0 | .000 | .000 | .000 |
| Sledge, Terrmel, Mon.* | 133 | 446 | 398 | 45 | 107 | 184 | 20 | 6 | 15 | 62 | 6 | 1 | 1 | 40 | 4 | 66 | 3 | 3 | 2 | .269 | .336 | .462 |
| Small, Aaron, Fla. | 7 | 2 | 2 | 0 | 0 | 0 | 0 | 0 | 0 | 0 | 0 | 0 | 0 | 0 | 0 | 2 | 0 | 0 | 0 | .000 | .000 | .000 |
| Smith, Travis, Atl. | 16 | 8 | 8 | 0 | 1 | 1 | 0 | 0 | 0 | 0 | 0 | 0 | 0 | 0 | 0 | 1 | 0 | 0 | 0 | .125 | .125 | .125 |
| Smoltz, John, Atl. | 73 | 2 | 2 | 0 | 0 | 0 | 0 | 0 | 0 | 0 | 0 | 0 | 0 | 0 | 0 | 2 | 0 | 0 | 0 | .000 | .000 | .000 |
| Snead, Esix, N.Y.† | 1 | 0 | 0 | 1 | 0 | 0 | 0 | 0 | 0 | 0 | 0 | 0 | 0 | 0 | 0 | 0 | 0 | 0 | 0 | .000 | .000 | .000 |
| Snell, Ian, Pit. | 3 | 3 | 2 | 0 | 0 | 0 | 0 | 0 | 0 | 0 | 1 | 0 | 0 | 0 | 0 | 2 | 0 | 0 | 0 | .000 | .000 | .000 |
| Snow, J.T., S.F.* | 107 | 417 | 346 | 62 | 113 | 183 | 32 | 1 | 12 | 60 | 2 | 4 | 7 | 58 | 0 | 61 | 4 | 0 | 5 | .327 | .429 | .529 |
| Snyder, Chris, Ari. | 29 | 110 | 96 | 10 | 23 | 44 | 6 | 0 | 5 | 15 | 0 | 1 | 0 | 13 | 1 | 25 | 0 | 0 | 0 | .240 | .327 | .458 |
| Sosa, Sammy, Chi. | 126 | 539 | 478 | 69 | 121 | 247 | 21 | 0 | 35 | 80 | 0 | 3 | 2 | 56 | 4 | 133 | 0 | 0 | 9 | .253 | .332 | .517 |
| Sparks, Steve, Ari. | 29 | 32 | 31 | 0 | 4 | 4 | 0 | 0 | 0 | 1 | 1 | 0 | 0 | 0 | 0 | 14 | 0 | 0 | 0 | .129 | .129 | .129 |
| Spencer, Shane, N.Y. | 74 | 204 | 185 | 21 | 52 | 76 | 10 | 1 | 4 | 26 | 2 | 2 | 2 | 13 | 0 | 37 | 6 | 0 | 1 | .281 | .332 | .411 |
| Spivey, Junior, Mil. | 59 | 263 | 228 | 33 | 62 | 96 | 13 | 0 | 7 | 28 | 1 | 2 | 7 | 25 | 0 | 48 | 5 | 3 | 7 | .272 | .359 | .421 |
| Stanton, Mike, N.Y.* | 83 | 2 | 2 | 0 | 1 | 1 | 0 | 0 | 0 | 1 | 0 | 0 | 0 | 0 | 0 | 1 | 0 | 0 | 0 | .500 | .500 | .500 |
| Stark, Denny, Col. | 6 | 9 | 8 | 0 | 0 | 0 | 0 | 0 | 0 | 0 | 0 | 0 | 0 | 1 | 0 | 3 | 0 | 0 | 0 | .000 | .111 | .000 |
| Stone, Ricky, Hou.-S.D. | 43 | 1 | 1 | 0 | 0 | 0 | 0 | 0 | 0 | 0 | 0 | 0 | 0 | 0 | 0 | 0 | 0 | 0 | 0 | .000 | .000 | .000 |
| Stynes, Chris, Pit. | 74 | 174 | 162 | 16 | 35 | 48 | 10 | 0 | 1 | 16 | 1 | 0 | 2 | 9 | 2 | 23 | 0 | 0 | 2 | .216 | .266 | .296 |
| Suppan, Jeff, St.L. | 31 | 65 | 57 | 3 | 4 | 4 | 0 | 0 | 0 | 0 | 7 | 0 | 0 | 1 | 0 | 11 | 0 | 0 | 1 | .070 | .086 | .070 |
| Sutton, Larry, Fla.* | 8 | 6 | 5 | 0 | 1 | 1 | 0 | 0 | 0 | 1 | 0 | 0 | 0 | 1 | 0 | 2 | 0 | 0 | 0 | .200 | .333 | .200 |
| Sweeney, Brian, S.D. | 7 | 4 | 4 | 0 | 0 | 0 | 0 | 0 | 0 | 0 | 0 | 0 | 0 | 0 | 0 | 2 | 0 | 0 | 0 | .000 | .000 | .000 |
| Sweeney, Mark, Col.* | 122 | 215 | 177 | 25 | 47 | 90 | 12 | 2 | 9 | 40 | 0 | 4 | 2 | 32 | 2 | 51 | 1 | 0 | 2 | .266 | .377 | .508 |
| Szuminski, Jason, S.D. | 7 | 1 | 1 | 0 | 0 | 0 | 0 | 0 | 0 | 0 | 0 | 0 | 0 | 0 | 0 | 1 | 0 | 0 | 0 | .000 | .000 | .000 |
| Taguchi, So, St.L. | 109 | 206 | 179 | 26 | 52 | 75 | 10 | 2 | 3 | 25 | 10 | 3 | 2 | 12 | 1 | 23 | 6 | 3 | 6 | .291 | .337 | .419 |
| Tankersley, Dennis, S.D. | 9 | 10 | 8 | 0 | 2 | 2 | 0 | 0 | 0 | 1 | 1 | 0 | 0 | 1 | 0 | 4 | 0 | 0 | 0 | .250 | .333 | .250 |
| Taveras, Willy, Hou. | 10 | 2 | 1 | 2 | 0 | 0 | 0 | 0 | 0 | 0 | 1 | 0 | 0 | 0 | 0 | 1 | 1 | 0 | 0 | .000 | .000 | .000 |
| Telemaco, Amaury, Phi. | 42 | 4 | 4 | 0 | 0 | 0 | 0 | 0 | 0 | 0 | 0 | 0 | 0 | 0 | 0 | 1 | 0 | 0 | 0 | .000 | .000 | .000 |
| Terrero, Luis, Ari. | 62 | 255 | 229 | 21 | 56 | 82 | 14 | 0 | 4 | 14 | 1 | 0 | 5 | 20 | 2 | 78 | 10 | 2 | 5 | .245 | .319 | .358 |
| Thomas, Charles, Atl.* | 83 | 267 | 236 | 35 | 68 | 105 | 8 | 4 | 7 | 31 | 1 | 0 | 9 | 21 | 9 | 45 | 3 | 1 | 3 | .288 | .368 | .445 |
| Thome, Jim, Phi.* | 143 | 618 | 508 | 97 | 139 | 295 | 28 | 1 | 42 | 105 | 0 | 4 | 2 | 104 | 26 | 144 | 0 | 2 | 10 | .274 | .396 | .581 |
| Thomson, John, Atl. | 33 | 76 | 66 | 3 | 13 | 14 | 1 | 0 | 0 | 4 | 10 | 0 | 0 | 0 | 0 | 24 | 0 | 0 | 2 | .197 | .197 | .212 |
| Thurston, Joe, L.A.* | 17 | 18 | 17 | 1 | 3 | 6 | 1 | 1 | 0 | 1 | 0 | 1 | 0 | 0 | 0 | 5 | 0 | 0 | 0 | .176 | .167 | .353 |
| Tomko, Brett, S.F. | 33 | 77 | 62 | 3 | 7 | 8 | 1 | 0 | 0 | 0 | 13 | 0 | 0 | 2 | 0 | 27 | 0 | 0 | 1 | .113 | .141 | .129 |
| Torcato, Tony, S.F.* | 13 | 12 | 9 | 1 | 5 | 5 | 0 | 0 | 0 | 2 | 0 | 1 | 1 | 1 | 0 | 0 | 0 | 0 | 0 | .556 | .583 | .556 |
| Torrealba, Yorvit, S.F. | 64 | 196 | 172 | 19 | 39 | 70 | 7 | 3 | 6 | 23 | 4 | 1 | 2 | 17 | 3 | 31 | 2 | 0 | 7 | .227 | .302 | .407 |
| Torres, Salomon, Pit. | 84 | 2 | 2 | 0 | 1 | 2 | 1 | 0 | 0 | 0 | 0 | 0 | 0 | 0 | 0 | 1 | 0 | 0 | 0 | .500 | .500 | 1.000 |
| Trachsel, Steve, N.Y. | 35 | 71 | 59 | 6 | 11 | 12 | 1 | 0 | 0 | 5 | 11 | 0 | 0 | 1 | 0 | 17 | 0 | 0 | 1 | .186 | .200 | .203 |
| Tracy, Andy, Col.* | 15 | 17 | 16 | 1 | 3 | 4 | 1 | 0 | 0 | 1 | 0 | 0 | 0 | 1 | 0 | 8 | 0 | 0 | 0 | .188 | .235 | .250 |
| Tracy, Chad, Ari.* | 143 | 532 | 481 | 45 | 137 | 196 | 29 | 3 | 8 | 53 | 1 | 5 | 0 | 45 | 3 | 60 | 2 | 3 | 11 | .285 | .343 | .407 |
| Treanor, Matt, Fla. | 29 | 61 | 55 | 7 | 13 | 15 | 2 | 0 | 0 | 1 | 0 | 0 | 2 | 4 | 0 | 13 | 0 | 0 | 3 | .236 | .311 | .273 |
| Tucker, Michael, S.F.* | 140 | 547 | 464 | 77 | 119 | 191 | 21 | 6 | 13 | 62 | 6 | 5 | 2 | 70 | 3 | 106 | 5 | 2 | 5 | .256 | .353 | .412 |
| Tucker, T.J., Mon. | 54 | 12 | 12 | 1 | 1 | 1 | 0 | 0 | 0 | 0 | 0 | 0 | 0 | 0 | 0 | 4 | 0 | 0 | 0 | .083 | .083 | .083 |
| Utley, Chase, Phi.* | 94 | 287 | 267 | 36 | 71 | 125 | 11 | 2 | 13 | 57 | 1 | 2 | 2 | 15 | 1 | 40 | 4 | 1 | 6 | .266 | .308 | .468 |
| Valdez, Ismael, S.D.-Fla. | 34 | 59 | 52 | 6 | 10 | 14 | 4 | 0 | 0 | 5 | 3 | 1 | 0 | 3 | 0 | 13 | 0 | 0 | 1 | .192 | .232 | .269 |
| Valent, Eric, N.Y.* | 130 | 300 | 270 | 39 | 72 | 130 | 15 | 2 | 13 | 34 | 0 | 1 | 1 | 28 | 4 | 61 | 0 | 1 | 10 | .267 | .337 | .481 |
| Valentin, Javier, Cin.† | 82 | 222 | 202 | 18 | 47 | 77 | 10 | 1 | 6 | 20 | 0 | 2 | 1 | 17 | 3 | 36 | 0 | 0 | 4 | .233 | .293 | .381 |
| Valentine, Joe, Cin. | 24 | 1 | 1 | 0 | 0 | 0 | 0 | 0 | 0 | 0 | 0 | 0 | 0 | 0 | 0 | 0 | 0 | 0 | 0 | .000 | .000 | .000 |
| Van Benschoten, John, Pit. | 6 | 11 | 8 | 2 | 1 | 4 | 0 | 0 | 1 | 2 | 2 | 0 | 0 | 1 | 0 | 3 | 0 | 0 | 0 | .125 | .222 | .500 |
| Van Poppel, Todd, Cin. | 48 | 23 | 17 | 1 | 3 | 3 | 0 | 0 | 0 | 1 | 5 | 0 | 0 | 1 | 0 | 6 | 0 | 0 | 0 | .176 | .222 | .176 |
| Vander Wal, John, Cin.* | 42 | 55 | 51 | 2 | 6 | 14 | 2 | 0 | 2 | 4 | 0 | 0 | 0 | 4 | 0 | 20 | 0 | 0 | 0 | .118 | .182 | .275 |

| Player, Team | G | TPA | AB | R | H | TB | 2B | 3B | HR | RBI | SH | SF | HP | BB | IBB | SO | SB | CS | GDP | Avg. | OBP | Slg. |
|---|---|---|---|---|---|---|---|---|---|---|---|---|---|---|---|---|---|---|---|---|---|---|
| Vargas, Claudio, Mon. | 45 | 29 | 22 | 0 | 1 | 1 | 0 | 0 | 0 | 0 | 7 | 0 | 0 | 0 | 0 | 8 | 0 | 0 | 1 | .045 | .045 | .045 |
| Vazquez, Ramon, S.D.* | 52 | 132 | 115 | 12 | 27 | 37 | 3 | 2 | 1 | 13 | 4 | 2 | 0 | 11 | 2 | 24 | 1 | 1 | 2 | .235 | .297 | .322 |
| Ventura, Robin, L.A.* | 102 | 175 | 152 | 19 | 37 | 55 | 3 | 0 | 5 | 28 | 0 | 1 | 0 | 22 | 1 | 31 | 0 | 0 | 3 | .243 | .337 | .362 |
| Vidro, Jose, Mon.† | 110 | 467 | 412 | 51 | 121 | 187 | 24 | 0 | 14 | 60 | 4 | 2 | 0 | 49 | 7 | 43 | 3 | 1 | 14 | .294 | .367 | .454 |
| Villafuerte, Brandon, Ari. | 20 | 1 | 1 | 0 | 0 | 0 | 0 | 0 | 0 | 0 | 0 | 0 | 0 | 0 | 0 | 1 | 0 | 0 | 0 | .000 | .000 | .000 |
| Vizcaino, Jose, Hou.† | 138 | 385 | 358 | 34 | 98 | 134 | 21 | 3 | 3 | 33 | 5 | 2 | 0 | 20 | 5 | 39 | 1 | 1 | 8 | .274 | .311 | .374 |
| Vogelsong, Ryan, Pit. | 33 | 44 | 31 | 2 | 7 | 9 | 2 | 0 | 0 | 3 | 10 | 1 | 0 | 2 | 0 | 13 | 0 | 0 | 1 | .226 | .265 | .290 |
| Wagner, Billy, Phi.* | 46 | 2 | 2 | 0 | 0 | 0 | 0 | 0 | 0 | 0 | 0 | 0 | 0 | 0 | 0 | 2 | 0 | 0 | 0 | .000 | .000 | .000 |
| Walker, Larry, Col.-St.L.* | 82 | 316 | 258 | 51 | 77 | 152 | 16 | 4 | 17 | 47 | 0 | 1 | 8 | 49 | 3 | 57 | 6 | 0 | 8 | .298 | .424 | .589 |
| Walker, Todd, Chi.* | 129 | 424 | 372 | 60 | 102 | 174 | 19 | 4 | 15 | 50 | 1 | 4 | 4 | 43 | 8 | 52 | 0 | 3 | 2 | .274 | .352 | .468 |
| Walker, Tyler, S.F. | 52 | 7 | 7 | 0 | 0 | 0 | 0 | 0 | 0 | 0 | 0 | 0 | 0 | 0 | 0 | 5 | 0 | 0 | 0 | .000 | .000 | .000 |
| Ward, Daryle, Pit.* | 79 | 321 | 293 | 39 | 73 | 139 | 17 | 2 | 15 | 57 | 0 | 3 | 3 | 22 | 3 | 45 | 0 | 0 | 8 | .249 | .305 | .474 |
| Wayne, Justin, Fla. | 19 | 4 | 3 | 0 | 0 | 0 | 0 | 0 | 0 | 0 | 1 | 0 | 0 | 0 | 0 | 1 | 0 | 0 | 0 | .000 | .000 | .000 |
| Weathers, David, N.Y.-Hou.-Fla. | 66 | 3 | 3 | 0 | 0 | 0 | 0 | 0 | 0 | 0 | 0 | 0 | 0 | 0 | 0 | 1 | 0 | 0 | 0 | .000 | .000 | .000 |
| Weaver, Jeff, L.A. | 35 | 78 | 70 | 3 | 15 | 19 | 2 | 1 | 0 | 2 | 7 | 0 | 0 | 1 | 0 | 26 | 0 | 0 | 0 | .214 | .225 | .271 |
| Webb, Brandon, Ari. | 35 | 71 | 64 | 3 | 6 | 6 | 0 | 0 | 0 | 4 | 4 | 0 | 0 | 3 | 0 | 36 | 0 | 0 | 0 | .094 | .134 | .094 |
| Wells, David, S.D.* | 31 | 69 | 57 | 2 | 6 | 6 | 0 | 0 | 0 | 3 | 8 | 0 | 1 | 3 | 0 | 24 | 0 | 0 | 1 | .105 | .164 | .105 |
| Wells, Kip, Pit. | 25 | 50 | 43 | 4 | 8 | 13 | 3 | 1 | 0 | 0 | 4 | 0 | 0 | 3 | 0 | 20 | 0 | 0 | 0 | .186 | .239 | .302 |
| Wendell, Turk, Col.* | 12 | 2 | 2 | 0 | 0 | 0 | 0 | 0 | 0 | 0 | 0 | 0 | 0 | 0 | 0 | 0 | 0 | 0 | 1 | .000 | .000 | .000 |
| Werth, Jayson, L.A. | 89 | 326 | 290 | 56 | 76 | 141 | 11 | 3 | 16 | 47 | 1 | 1 | 4 | 30 | 0 | 85 | 4 | 1 | 1 | .262 | .338 | .486 |
| Wheeler, Dan, N.Y.-Hou. | 46 | 6 | 5 | 1 | 1 | 1 | 0 | 0 | 0 | 0 | 1 | 0 | 0 | 0 | 0 | 1 | 0 | 0 | 0 | .200 | .200 | .200 |
| Wigginton, Ty, N.Y.-Pit. | 144 | 545 | 494 | 63 | 129 | 214 | 30 | 2 | 17 | 66 | 1 | 3 | 2 | 45 | 6 | 82 | 7 | 1 | 15 | .261 | .324 | .433 |
| Wilkerson, Brad, Mon.* | 160 | 688 | 572 | 112 | 146 | 285 | 39 | 2 | 32 | 67 | 3 | 3 | 4 | 106 | 8 | 152 | 13 | 6 | 6 | .255 | .374 | .498 |
| Williams, Dave, Pit.* | 10 | 9 | 9 | 0 | 1 | 1 | 0 | 0 | 0 | 0 | 0 | 0 | 0 | 0 | 0 | 3 | 0 | 0 | 0 | .111 | .111 | .111 |
| Williams, Gerald, N.Y. | 57 | 138 | 129 | 17 | 30 | 54 | 8 | 2 | 4 | 11 | 1 | 0 | 0 | 8 | 1 | 26 | 2 | 1 | 2 | .233 | .277 | .419 |
| Williams, Jerome, S.F. | 22 | 43 | 36 | 1 | 5 | 5 | 0 | 0 | 0 | 0 | 6 | 0 | 0 | 1 | 0 | 14 | 0 | 1 | 0 | .139 | .162 | .139 |
| Williams, Woody, St.L. | 34 | 70 | 61 | 3 | 11 | 15 | 4 | 0 | 0 | 2 | 5 | 2 | 1 | 1 | 0 | 22 | 0 | 0 | 0 | .180 | .200 | .246 |
| Willingham, Josh, Fla. | 12 | 29 | 25 | 2 | 5 | 8 | 0 | 0 | 1 | 1 | 0 | 0 | 0 | 4 | 0 | 8 | 0 | 0 | 1 | .200 | .310 | .320 |
| Willis, Dontrelle, Fla.* | 42 | 84 | 74 | 5 | 15 | 22 | 2 | 1 | 1 | 3 | 6 | 0 | 0 | 4 | 0 | 17 | 0 | 0 | 2 | .203 | .244 | .297 |
| Wilson, Craig, Pit. | 155 | 644 | 561 | 97 | 148 | 280 | 35 | 5 | 29 | 82 | 0 | 3 | 30 | 50 | 3 | 169 | 2 | 2 | 11 | .264 | .354 | .499 |
| Wilson, Jack, Pit. | 157 | 693 | 652 | 82 | 201 | 299 | 41 | 12 | 11 | 59 | 7 | 5 | 3 | 26 | 0 | 71 | 8 | 4 | 15 | .308 | .335 | .459 |
| Wilson, Paul, Cin. | 29 | 70 | 60 | 2 | 6 | 8 | 2 | 0 | 0 | 2 | 7 | 0 | 1 | 2 | 0 | 37 | 0 | 0 | 0 | .100 | .143 | .133 |
| Wilson, Preston, Col. | 58 | 222 | 202 | 24 | 50 | 79 | 11 | 0 | 6 | 29 | 0 | 0 | 3 | 17 | 2 | 49 | 2 | 1 | 9 | .248 | .315 | .391 |
| Wilson, Tom, N.Y.-L.A. | 13 | 13 | 12 | 1 | 2 | 2 | 0 | 0 | 0 | 0 | 0 | 0 | 0 | 1 | 0 | 5 | 0 | 0 | 0 | .167 | .231 | .167 |
| Wilson, Vance, N.Y. | 79 | 177 | 157 | 18 | 43 | 67 | 10 | 1 | 4 | 21 | 1 | 3 | 5 | 11 | 2 | 24 | 1 | 0 | 5 | .274 | .335 | .427 |
| Wise, Dewayne, Atl.* | 77 | 175 | 162 | 24 | 37 | 72 | 9 | 4 | 6 | 17 | 2 | 1 | 1 | 9 | 1 | 28 | 6 | 1 | 1 | .228 | .272 | .444 |
| Wise, Matt, Mil. | 30 | 5 | 4 | 0 | 0 | 0 | 0 | 0 | 0 | 0 | 1 | 0 | 0 | 0 | 0 | 1 | 0 | 0 | 0 | .000 | .000 | .000 |
| Witasick, Jay, S.D. | 44 | 5 | 5 | 0 | 0 | 0 | 0 | 0 | 0 | 0 | 0 | 0 | 0 | 0 | 0 | 1 | 0 | 0 | 1 | .000 | .000 | .000 |
| Wolf, Randy, Phi.* | 25 | 55 | 45 | 6 | 12 | 23 | 2 | 0 | 3 | 8 | 8 | 1 | 0 | 1 | 0 | 10 | 0 | 0 | 1 | .267 | .277 | .511 |
| Womack, Tony, St.L.* | 145 | 606 | 553 | 91 | 170 | 213 | 22 | 3 | 5 | 38 | 8 | 6 | 3 | 36 | 1 | 60 | 26 | 5 | 6 | .307 | .349 | .385 |
| Wood, Kerry, Chi. | 22 | 53 | 45 | 2 | 6 | 10 | 1 | 0 | 1 | 3 | 5 | 1 | 0 | 2 | 0 | 11 | 0 | 0 | 0 | .133 | .167 | .222 |
| Wooten, Shawn, Phi. | 33 | 57 | 53 | 2 | 9 | 12 | 3 | 0 | 0 | 2 | 0 | 0 | 2 | 2 | 0 | 9 | 0 | 0 | 4 | .170 | .228 | .226 |
| Wright, David, N.Y. | 69 | 283 | 263 | 41 | 77 | 138 | 17 | 1 | 14 | 40 | 0 | 3 | 3 | 14 | 0 | 40 | 6 | 0 | 7 | .293 | .332 | .525 |
| Wright, Jamey, Col. | 14 | 27 | 19 | 1 | 1 | 2 | 1 | 0 | 0 | 0 | 8 | 0 | 0 | 0 | 0 | 12 | 0 | 0 | 0 | .053 | .053 | .105 |
| Wright, Jaret, Atl. | 32 | 65 | 57 | 4 | 6 | 10 | 1 | 0 | 1 | 4 | 6 | 0 | 0 | 2 | 0 | 33 | 0 | 0 | 0 | .105 | .136 | .175 |
| Wuertz, Michael, Chi. | 31 | 1 | 1 | 0 | 0 | 0 | 0 | 0 | 0 | 0 | 0 | 0 | 0 | 0 | 0 | 1 | 0 | 0 | 0 | .000 | .000 | .000 |
| Yates, Tyler, N.Y. | 21 | 12 | 11 | 0 | 1 | 1 | 0 | 0 | 0 | 0 | 1 | 0 | 0 | 0 | 0 | 5 | 0 | 0 | 0 | .091 | .091 | .091 |
| Young, Jason, Col. | 2 | 5 | 2 | 0 | 0 | 0 | 0 | 0 | 0 | 1 | 2 | 1 | 0 | 0 | 0 | 0 | 0 | 0 | 0 | .000 | .000 | .000 |
| Zambrano, Carlos, Chi.† | 31 | 82 | 70 | 8 | 16 | 20 | 1 | 0 | 1 | 5 | 8 | 1 | 0 | 3 | 0 | 29 | 0 | 0 | 2 | .229 | .257 | .286 |
| Zambrano, Victor, N.Y.† | 3 | 7 | 6 | 0 | 1 | 1 | 0 | 0 | 0 | 0 | 1 | 0 | 0 | 0 | 0 | 1 | 0 | 0 | 0 | .167 | .167 | .167 |
| Zeile, Todd, N.Y. | 137 | 396 | 348 | 30 | 81 | 124 | 16 | 0 | 9 | 35 | 1 | 2 | 1 | 44 | 1 | 83 | 0 | 0 | 13 | .233 | .319 | .356 |
| Zinter, Alan, Ari.† | 28 | 40 | 34 | 2 | 7 | 12 | 2 | 0 | 1 | 6 | 0 | 1 | 0 | 5 | 0 | 15 | 0 | 0 | 0 | .206 | .300 | .353 |

AWARDED FIRST BASE ON OBSTRUCTION OR CATCHER'S INTERFERENCE—Counsell, Milwaukee 6 (Valentin, Hernandez, Wilson, Barrett, Bako, V. Wilson); Clark, Milwaukee (Cota); Hidalgo, Hou.-N.Y. (Willingham); Kata, Arizona (Lieberthal); Podsednik, Milwaukee (Paul, Haren); Rivera, Pittsburgh (LaRue).

## PLAYERS WITH TWO OR MORE TEAMS

| Player, Team | G | TPA | AB | R | H | TB | 2B | 3B | HR | RBI | SH | SF | HP | BB | IBB | SO | SB | CS | GDP | Avg. | OBP | Slg. |
|---|---|---|---|---|---|---|---|---|---|---|---|---|---|---|---|---|---|---|---|---|---|---|
| Beltran, Francis, Chi. | 34 | 1 | 1 | 0 | 0 | 0 | 0 | 0 | 0 | 0 | 0 | 0 | 0 | 0 | 0 | 0 | 0 | 0 | 0 | .000 | .000 | .000 |
| Beltran, Francis, Mon. | 11 | 2 | 2 | 0 | 1 | 1 | 0 | 0 | 0 | 0 | 0 | 0 | 0 | 0 | 0 | 0 | 0 | 0 | 0 | .500 | .500 | .500 |
| Benson, Kris, Pit. | 20 | 50 | 39 | 2 | 7 | 7 | 0 | 0 | 0 | 3 | 10 | 0 | 0 | 1 | 0 | 17 | 0 | 0 | 0 | .179 | .200 | .179 |
| Benson, Kris, N.Y. | 11 | 25 | 19 | 1 | 1 | 1 | 0 | 0 | 0 | 2 | 5 | 0 | 0 | 1 | 0 | 9 | 0 | 0 | 0 | .053 | .100 | .053 |
| Bragg, Darren, S.D.* | 9 | 9 | 7 | 2 | 1 | 1 | 0 | 0 | 0 | 0 | 0 | 0 | 0 | 2 | 0 | 2 | 0 | 0 | 0 | .143 | .333 | .143 |
| Bragg, Darren, Cin.* | 38 | 103 | 94 | 11 | 18 | 35 | 3 | 1 | 4 | 9 | 1 | 0 | 0 | 8 | 1 | 29 | 1 | 0 | 2 | .191 | .255 | .372 |
| Buchanan, Brian, S.D. | 38 | 68 | 60 | 7 | 12 | 20 | 2 | 0 | 2 | 6 | 0 | 1 | 1 | 6 | 2 | 19 | 0 | 0 | 2 | .200 | .279 | .333 |
| Buchanan, Brian, N.Y. | 2 | 4 | 3 | 0 | 0 | 0 | 0 | 0 | 0 | 0 | 0 | 0 | 0 | 1 | 0 | 1 | 0 | 0 | 0 | .000 | .250 | .000 |
| Burba, Dave, Mil. | 45 | 3 | 3 | 0 | 0 | 0 | 0 | 0 | 0 | 0 | 0 | 0 | 0 | 0 | 0 | 1 | 0 | 0 | 0 | .000 | .000 | .000 |
| Burba, Dave, S.F. | 6 | 1 | 1 | 0 | 0 | 0 | 0 | 0 | 0 | 0 | 0 | 0 | 0 | 0 | 0 | 0 | 0 | 0 | 0 | .000 | .000 | .000 |
| Choi, Hee Seop, Fla.* | 95 | 340 | 281 | 48 | 76 | 139 | 16 | 1 | 15 | 40 | 2 | 2 | 3 | 52 | 4 | 78 | 1 | 0 | 4 | .270 | .388 | .495 |
| Choi, Hee Seop, L.A.* | 31 | 76 | 62 | 5 | 10 | 15 | 5 | 0 | 0 | 6 | 0 | 2 | 1 | 11 | 2 | 18 | 0 | 0 | 2 | .161 | .289 | .242 |
| Dessens, Elmer, Ari. | 38 | 25 | 18 | 0 | 3 | 5 | 2 | 0 | 0 | 0 | 4 | 0 | 0 | 3 | 0 | 3 | 0 | 0 | 1 | .167 | .286 | .278 |
| Dessens, Elmer, L.A. | 12 | 4 | 4 | 0 | 1 | 1 | 0 | 0 | 0 | 0 | 0 | 0 | 0 | 0 | 0 | 0 | 0 | 0 | 0 | .250 | .250 | .250 |
| Encarnacion, Juan, L.A. | 86 | 350 | 324 | 42 | 76 | 135 | 18 | 1 | 13 | 43 | 0 | 1 | 4 | 21 | 0 | 53 | 3 | 3 | 9 | .235 | .289 | .417 |
| Encarnacion, Juan, Fla. | 49 | 182 | 160 | 21 | 38 | 61 | 12 | 1 | 3 | 19 | 1 | 1 | 3 | 17 | 2 | 33 | 2 | 1 | 2 | .238 | .320 | .381 |
| Fassero, Jeff, Col.* | 40 | 24 | 21 | 3 | 4 | 4 | 0 | 0 | 0 | 1 | 2 | 0 | 0 | 1 | 0 | 9 | 0 | 0 | 0 | .190 | .227 | .190 |
| Fassero, Jeff, Ari.* | 1 | 0 | 0 | 0 | 0 | 0 | 0 | 0 | 0 | 0 | 0 | 0 | 0 | 0 | 0 | 0 | 0 | 0 | 0 | — | — | — |
| Finley, Steve, Ari.* | 104 | 456 | 404 | 61 | 111 | 198 | 16 | 1 | 23 | 48 | 6 | 5 | 1 | 40 | 1 | 52 | 8 | 4 | 9 | .275 | .338 | .490 |
| Finley, Steve, L.A.* | 58 | 250 | 224 | 31 | 59 | 110 | 12 | 0 | 13 | 46 | 3 | 2 | 0 | 21 | 0 | 30 | 1 | 3 | 5 | .263 | .324 | .491 |
| Gonzalez, Alex S., Chi. | 37 | 135 | 129 | 15 | 28 | 47 | 10 | 0 | 3 | 8 | 2 | 0 | 0 | 4 | 0 | 26 | 1 | 1 | 6 | .217 | .241 | .364 |
| Gonzalez, Alex S., Mon. | 35 | 144 | 133 | 19 | 32 | 51 | 7 | 0 | 4 | 16 | 2 | 0 | 1 | 8 | 0 | 32 | 1 | 1 | 1 | .241 | .289 | .383 |
| Gonzalez, Alex S., S.D. | 11 | 25 | 23 | 2 | 4 | 7 | 1 | 1 | 0 | 3 | 0 | 0 | 0 | 2 | 0 | 6 | 0 | 0 | 0 | .174 | .240 | .304 |

| Player, Team | G | TPA | AB | R | H | TB | 2B | 3B | HR | RBI | SH | SF | HP | BB | IBB | SO | SB | CS | GDP | Avg. | OBP | Slg. |
|---|---|---|---|---|---|---|---|---|---|---|---|---|---|---|---|---|---|---|---|---|---|---|
| Grieve, Ben, Mil.* | 108 | 275 | 234 | 28 | 61 | 97 | 15 | 0 | 7 | 29 | 0 | 2 | 0 | 39 | 5 | 65 | 0 | 0 | 4 | .261 | .364 | .415 |
| Grieve, Ben, Chi.* | 15 | 19 | 16 | 2 | 4 | 9 | 2 | 0 | 1 | 6 | 0 | 1 | 2 | 0 | 0 | 5 | 0 | 0 | 0 | .250 | .316 | .563 |
| Hancock, Josh, Phi | 4 | 2 | 2 | 0 | 0 | 0 | 0 | 0 | 0 | 0 | 0 | 0 | 0 | 0 | 0 | 1 | 0 | 0 | 0 | .000 | .000 | .000 |
| Hancock, Josh, Cin | 12 | 19 | 15 | 1 | 2 | 2 | 0 | 0 | 0 | 1 | 1 | 0 | 0 | 3 | 0 | 11 | 0 | 0 | 0 | .133 | .278 | .133 |
| Harris, Brendan, Chi. | 3 | 10 | 9 | 0 | 2 | 3 | 1 | 0 | 0 | 1 | 0 | 0 | 0 | 1 | 0 | 1 | 0 | 0 | 0 | .222 | .300 | .333 |
| Harris, Brendan, Mon. | 20 | 53 | 50 | 4 | 8 | 13 | 2 | 0 | 1 | 2 | 0 | 0 | 1 | 2 | 0 | 11 | 0 | 0 | 0 | .160 | .208 | .260 |
| Hidalgo, Richard, Hou. | 58 | 220 | 199 | 21 | 51 | 82 | 15 | 2 | 4 | 30 | 0 | 4 | 0 | 17 | 4 | 53 | 1 | 2 | 7 | .256 | .309 | .412 |
| Hidalgo, Richard, N.Y. | 86 | 359 | 324 | 46 | 74 | 150 | 11 | 1 | 21 | 52 | 0 | 2 | 5 | 27 | 3 | 76 | 3 | 2 | 12 | .228 | .296 | .463 |
| Jones, Todd, Cin.* | 51 | 0 | 0 | 0 | 0 | 0 | 0 | 0 | 0 | 0 | 0 | 0 | 0 | 0 | 0 | 0 | 0 | 0 | 0 | _ | _ | _ |
| Jones, Todd, Phi.* | 27 | 1 | 0 | 0 | 0 | 0 | 0 | 0 | 0 | 0 | 0 | 0 | 0 | 1 | 0 | 0 | 0 | 0 | 0 | _ | 1.000 | _ |
| Ledee, Ricky, Phi.* | 73 | 145 | 123 | 19 | 35 | 63 | 7 | 0 | 7 | 26 | 0 | 0 | 0 | 22 | 2 | 27 | 2 | 0 | 5 | .285 | .393 | .512 |
| Ledee, Ricky, S.F.* | 31 | 60 | 53 | 6 | 6 | 8 | 2 | 0 | 0 | 4 | 0 | 1 | 1 | 5 | 0 | 20 | 1 | 0 | 1 | .113 | .200 | .151 |
| Lidle, Cory, Cin. | 24 | 51 | 42 | 2 | 6 | 8 | 2 | 0 | 0 | 2 | 4 | 0 | 0 | 5 | 0 | 23 | 0 | 0 | 0 | .143 | .234 | .190 |
| Lidle, Cory, Phi. | 10 | 24 | 20 | 1 | 3 | 8 | 2 | 0 | 1 | 4 | 4 | 0 | 0 | 0 | 0 | 13 | 0 | 0 | 0 | .150 | .150 | .400 |
| Lo Duca, Paul, L.A. | 91 | 381 | 349 | 41 | 105 | 155 | 18 | 1 | 10 | 49 | 2 | 2 | 6 | 22 | 0 | 27 | 2 | 4 | 15 | .301 | .351 | .444 |
| Lo Duca, Paul, Fla. | 52 | 213 | 186 | 27 | 48 | 70 | 11 | 1 | 3 | 31 | 6 | 4 | 3 | 14 | 0 | 22 | 2 | 1 | 7 | .258 | .314 | .376 |
| Mayne, Brent, Ari.* | 36 | 111 | 94 | 9 | 24 | 32 | 6 | 1 | 0 | 10 | 3 | 1 | 0 | 13 | 4 | 17 | 1 | 0 | 5 | .255 | .343 | .340 |
| Mayne, Brent, L.A.* | 47 | 113 | 96 | 5 | 18 | 18 | 0 | 0 | 0 | 5 | 1 | 2 | 0 | 14 | 4 | 24 | 0 | 0 | 2 | .188 | .286 | .188 |
| Mota, Guillermo, L.A. | 52 | 6 | 6 | 0 | 0 | 0 | 0 | 0 | 0 | 0 | 0 | 0 | 0 | 0 | 0 | 5 | 0 | 0 | 0 | .000 | .000 | .000 |
| Mota, Guillermo, Fla. | 26 | 6 | 6 | 1 | 2 | 3 | 1 | 0 | 0 | 1 | 0 | 0 | 0 | 0 | 0 | 2 | 0 | 0 | 0 | .333 | .333 | .500 |
| Oliver, Darren, Fla. | 18 | 21 | 19 | 0 | 3 | 3 | 0 | 0 | 0 | 1 | 2 | 0 | 0 | 0 | 0 | 8 | 0 | 0 | 2 | .158 | .158 | .158 |
| Oliver, Darren, Hou. | 10 | 4 | 3 | 0 | 0 | 0 | 0 | 0 | 0 | 0 | 1 | 0 | 0 | 0 | 0 | 1 | 0 | 0 | 1 | .000 | .000 | .000 |
| Penny, Brad, Fla. | 21 | 48 | 47 | 1 | 3 | 3 | 0 | 0 | 0 | 1 | 1 | 0 | 0 | 0 | 0 | 13 | 0 | 0 | 1 | .064 | .064 | .064 |
| Penny, Brad, L.A. | 3 | 4 | 4 | 0 | 0 | 0 | 0 | 0 | 0 | 0 | 0 | 0 | 0 | 0 | 0 | 2 | 0 | 0 | 0 | .000 | .000 | .000 |
| Perez, Neifi, S.F.† | 103 | 353 | 319 | 28 | 74 | 94 | 12 | 1 | 2 | 33 | 9 | 4 | 0 | 21 | 3 | 35 | 0 | 1 | 7 | .232 | .276 | .295 |
| Perez, Neifi, Chi.† | 23 | 67 | 62 | 12 | 23 | 34 | 5 | 0 | 2 | 6 | 2 | 0 | 0 | 3 | 0 | 6 | 1 | 0 | 1 | .371 | .400 | .548 |
| Rodriguez, Felix, S.F. | 53 | 1 | 1 | 0 | 0 | 0 | 0 | 0 | 0 | 0 | 0 | 0 | 0 | 0 | 0 | 1 | 0 | 0 | 0 | .000 | .000 | .000 |
| Rodriguez, Felix, Phi | 23 | 0 | 0 | 0 | 0 | 0 | 0 | 0 | 0 | 0 | 0 | 0 | 0 | 0 | 0 | 0 | 0 | 0 | 0 | _ | _ | _ |
| Stone, Ricky, Hou. | 16 | 0 | 0 | 0 | 0 | 0 | 0 | 0 | 0 | 0 | 0 | 0 | 0 | 0 | 0 | 0 | 0 | 0 | 0 | _ | _ | _ |
| Stone, Ricky, S.D. | 27 | 1 | 1 | 0 | 0 | 0 | 0 | 0 | 0 | 0 | 0 | 0 | 0 | 0 | 0 | 0 | 0 | 0 | 0 | .000 | .000 | .000 |
| Valdez, Ismael, S.D. | 23 | 41 | 35 | 4 | 6 | 9 | 3 | 0 | 0 | 5 | 3 | 1 | 0 | 2 | 0 | 9 | 0 | 0 | 1 | .171 | .211 | .257 |
| Valdez, Ismael, Fla. | 11 | 18 | 17 | 2 | 4 | 5 | 1 | 0 | 0 | 0 | 0 | 0 | 0 | 1 | 0 | 4 | 0 | 0 | 0 | .235 | .278 | .294 |
| Walker, Larry, Col.* | 38 | 138 | 108 | 22 | 35 | 68 | 9 | 3 | 6 | 20 | 0 | 1 | 4 | 25 | 2 | 23 | 2 | 0 | 2 | .324 | .464 | .630 |
| Walker, Larry, St.L.* | 44 | 178 | 150 | 29 | 42 | 84 | 7 | 1 | 11 | 27 | 0 | 0 | 4 | 24 | 1 | 34 | 4 | 0 | 6 | .280 | .393 | .560 |
| Weathers, David, N.Y. | 32 | 0 | 0 | 0 | 0 | 0 | 0 | 0 | 0 | 0 | 0 | 0 | 0 | 0 | 0 | 0 | 0 | 0 | 0 | _ | _ | _ |
| Weathers, David, Hou | 26 | 0 | 0 | 0 | 0 | 0 | 0 | 0 | 0 | 0 | 0 | 0 | 0 | 0 | 0 | 0 | 0 | 0 | 0 | _ | _ | _ |
| Weathers, David, Fla | 8 | 3 | 3 | 0 | 0 | 0 | 0 | 0 | 0 | 0 | 0 | 0 | 0 | 0 | 0 | 1 | 0 | 0 | 0 | .000 | .000 | .000 |
| Wheeler, Dan, N.Y. | 32 | 6 | 5 | 1 | 1 | 1 | 0 | 0 | 0 | 0 | 1 | 0 | 0 | 0 | 0 | 1 | 0 | 0 | 0 | .200 | .200 | .200 |
| Wheeler, Dan, Hou. | 14 | 0 | 0 | 0 | 0 | 0 | 0 | 0 | 0 | 0 | 0 | 0 | 0 | 0 | 0 | 0 | 0 | 0 | 0 | _ | _ | _ |
| Wigginton, Ty, N.Y. | 86 | 339 | 312 | 46 | 89 | 152 | 23 | 2 | 12 | 42 | 1 | 2 | 1 | 23 | 4 | 48 | 6 | 1 | 11 | .285 | .334 | .487 |
| Wigginton, Ty, Pit. | 58 | 206 | 182 | 17 | 40 | 62 | 7 | 0 | 5 | 24 | 0 | 1 | 1 | 22 | 2 | 34 | 1 | 0 | 4 | .220 | .306 | .341 |
| Wilson, Tom, N.Y. | 4 | 5 | 4 | 0 | 1 | 1 | 0 | 0 | 0 | 0 | 0 | 0 | 0 | 1 | 0 | 2 | 0 | 0 | 0 | .250 | .400 | .250 |
| Wilson, Tom, L.A. | 9 | 8 | 8 | 1 | 1 | 1 | 0 | 0 | 0 | 0 | 0 | 0 | 0 | 0 | 0 | 3 | 0 | 0 | 0 | .125 | .125 | .125 |

# DESIGNATED HITTING

## TEAM

| Team | G | TPA | AB | R | H | TB | 2B | 3B | HR | RBI | SH | SF | HP | BB | IBB | SO | SB | CS | GDP | Avg. | OBP | Slg. |
|---|---|---|---|---|---|---|---|---|---|---|---|---|---|---|---|---|---|---|---|---|---|---|
| Cincinnati | 6 | 28 | 27 | 4 | 9 | 18 | 3 | 0 | 2 | 7 | 0 | 0 | 0 | 1 | 0 | 5 | 0 | 0 | 0 | .333 | .357 | .667 |
| Montreal | 9 | 37 | 33 | 4 | 11 | 13 | 2 | 0 | 0 | 4 | 0 | 1 | 1 | 2 | 1 | 2 | 0 | 1 | 0 | .333 | .378 | .394 |
| Philadelphia | 9 | 41 | 37 | 11 | 12 | 34 | 1 | 0 | 7 | 12 | 0 | 0 | 0 | 4 | 0 | 9 | 0 | 0 | 0 | .324 | .390 | .919 |
| Chicago | 6 | 28 | 25 | 7 | 8 | 20 | 1 | 1 | 3 | 7 | 0 | 1 | 0 | 2 | 0 | 4 | 0 | 0 | 0 | .320 | .357 | .800 |
| Colorado | 9 | 39 | 38 | 5 | 10 | 12 | 2 | 0 | 0 | 1 | 0 | 0 | 0 | 1 | 0 | 14 | 0 | 0 | 0 | .263 | .282 | .316 |
| San Diego | 9 | 38 | 32 | 3 | 8 | 9 | 1 | 0 | 0 | 1 | 0 | 0 | 2 | 4 | 0 | 6 | 1 | 1 | 1 | .250 | .368 | .281 |
| San Francisco | 9 | 45 | 28 | 7 | 7 | 13 | 0 | 0 | 2 | 6 | 0 | 0 | 1 | 16 | 7 | 6 | 0 | 0 | 0 | .250 | .533 | .464 |
| Florida | 9 | 40 | 37 | 4 | 9 | 15 | 3 | 0 | 1 | 7 | 0 | 1 | 1 | 1 | 0 | 6 | 1 | 0 | 1 | .243 | .275 | .405 |
| Los Angeles | 9 | 37 | 33 | 3 | 8 | 12 | 1 | 0 | 1 | 5 | 0 | 0 | 2 | 2 | 0 | 12 | 0 | 0 | 0 | .242 | .324 | .364 |
| Pittsburgh | 6 | 26 | 21 | 3 | 5 | 8 | 0 | 0 | 1 | 2 | 1 | 0 | 1 | 3 | 1 | 3 | 0 | 0 | 0 | .238 | .360 | .381 |
| New York | 9 | 41 | 32 | 3 | 7 | 11 | 1 | 0 | 1 | 5 | 0 | 1 | 1 | 7 | 2 | 7 | 0 | 1 | 0 | .219 | .366 | .344 |
| Milwaukee | 6 | 29 | 25 | 2 | 5 | 8 | 0 | 0 | 1 | 5 | 0 | 1 | 0 | 3 | 0 | 9 | 0 | 0 | 1 | .200 | .276 | .320 |
| Atlanta | 9 | 40 | 36 | 4 | 7 | 17 | 1 | 0 | 3 | 6 | 0 | 0 | 0 | 4 | 0 | 6 | 0 | 0 | 3 | .194 | .275 | .472 |
| Houston | 6 | 24 | 19 | 1 | 3 | 6 | 3 | 0 | 0 | 1 | 0 | 1 | 0 | 4 | 0 | 4 | 1 | 0 | 0 | .158 | .292 | .316 |
| St. Louis | 6 | 28 | 26 | 4 | 4 | 4 | 0 | 0 | 0 | 3 | 0 | 0 | 0 | 2 | 1 | 4 | 0 | 1 | 0 | .154 | .214 | .154 |
| Arizona | 9 | 36 | 33 | 0 | 5 | 6 | 1 | 0 | 0 | 5 | 0 | 0 | 0 | 3 | 1 | 3 | 0 | 0 | 0 | .152 | .222 | .182 |
| **Totals** | 139 | 557 | 482 | 65 | 118 | 206 | 20 | 1 | 22 | 77 | 1 | 6 | 9 | 59 | 13 | 100 | 3 | 4 | 6 | .245 | .335 | .427 |

## TOP DESIGNATED HITTERS

Minimum 15 at-bats. *Lefthanded batter. †Switch-hitter.

| Player, Team | G | TPA | AB | R | H | TB | 2B | 3B | HR | RBI | SH | SF | HP | BB | IBB | SO | SB | CS | GDP | Avg. | OBP | Slg. |
|---|---|---|---|---|---|---|---|---|---|---|---|---|---|---|---|---|---|---|---|---|---|---|
| Vidro, Jose, Mon.† | 4 | 17 | 16 | 2 | 6 | 6 | 0 | 0 | 0 | 3 | 0 | 0 | 0 | 1 | 1 | 1 | 0 | 1 | 0 | .375 | .412 | .375 |
| Bonds, Barry, S.F.* | 7 | 35 | 20 | 6 | 6 | 12 | 0 | 0 | 2 | 6 | 0 | 0 | 1 | 14 | 7 | 1 | 0 | 0 | 0 | .300 | .600 | .600 |
| Sweeney, Mark, Col.* | 4 | 15 | 15 | 2 | 4 | 5 | 1 | 0 | 0 | 1 | 0 | 0 | 0 | 0 | 0 | 6 | 0 | 0 | 0 | .267 | .267 | .333 |
| Thome, Jim, Phi.* | 6 | 26 | 23 | 5 | 6 | 18 | 0 | 0 | 4 | 6 | 0 | 0 | 0 | 3 | 0 | 6 | 0 | 0 | 0 | .261 | .346 | .783 |
| Piazza, Mike, N.Y. | 8 | 37 | 29 | 2 | 6 | 10 | 1 | 0 | 1 | 5 | 0 | 1 | 0 | 7 | 2 | 7 | 0 | 0 | 0 | .207 | .351 | .345 |
| Jones, Chipper, Atl.† | 7 | 33 | 30 | 4 | 5 | 15 | 1 | 0 | 3 | 6 | 0 | 0 | 0 | 3 | 0 | 6 | 0 | 0 | 3 | .167 | .242 | .500 |

NOTE: Only 6 batters (rather than the usual 10) are listed above since they are the only players to have the minimum 15 Designated Hitter at-bats during the 2004 National League season.

## ALL DESIGNATED HITTERS

*Lefthanded batter. †Switch-hitter.

| Player, Team | G | TPA | AB | R | H | TB | 2B | 3B | HR | RBI | SH | SF | HP | BB | IBB | SO | SB | CS | GDP | Avg. | OBP | Slg. |
|---|---|---|---|---|---|---|---|---|---|---|---|---|---|---|---|---|---|---|---|---|---|---|
| Alomar, Roberto, Ari.† | 1 | 4 | 4 | 0 | 1 | 2 | 1 | 0 | 0 | 2 | 0 | 0 | 0 | 0 | 0 | 1 | 0 | 0 | 0 | .250 | .250 | .500 |
| Alou, Moises, Chi. | 1 | 7 | 6 | 1 | 0 | 0 | 0 | 0 | 0 | 0 | 0 | 0 | 0 | 1 | 0 | 1 | 0 | 0 | 0 | .000 | .143 | .000 |
| Anderson, Marlon, St.L.* | 1 | 4 | 4 | 0 | 0 | 0 | 0 | 0 | 0 | 0 | 0 | 0 | 0 | 0 | 0 | 0 | 0 | 0 | 0 | .000 | .000 | .000 |
| Baerga, Carlos, Ari.† | 2 | 6 | 6 | 0 | 2 | 2 | 0 | 0 | 0 | 1 | 0 | 0 | 0 | 0 | 0 | 1 | 0 | 0 | 0 | .333 | .333 | .333 |
| Bagwell, Jeff, Hou. | 2 | 8 | 7 | 1 | 1 | 2 | 1 | 0 | 0 | 0 | 0 | 0 | 0 | 1 | 0 | 2 | 0 | 0 | 0 | .143 | .250 | .286 |
| Bautista, Danny, Ari. | 1 | 5 | 5 | 0 | 0 | 0 | 0 | 0 | 0 | 0 | 0 | 0 | 0 | 0 | 0 | 0 | 0 | 0 | 0 | .000 | .000 | .000 |
| Biggio, Craig, Hou. | 1 | 5 | 5 | 0 | 1 | 2 | 1 | 0 | 0 | 0 | 0 | 0 | 0 | 0 | 0 | 2 | 0 | 0 | 0 | .200 | .200 | .400 |
| Bonds, Barry, S.F.* | 7 | 35 | 20 | 6 | 6 | 12 | 0 | 0 | 2 | 6 | 0 | 0 | 1 | 14 | 7 | 1 | 0 | 0 | 0 | .300 | .600 | .600 |
| Burnitz, Jeromy, Col.* | 3 | 14 | 14 | 2 | 2 | 2 | 0 | 0 | 0 | 0 | 0 | 0 | 0 | 0 | 0 | 6 | 0 | 0 | 0 | .143 | .143 | .143 |
| Cabrera, Miguel, Fla. | 1 | 4 | 4 | 0 | 1 | 1 | 0 | 0 | 0 | 0 | 0 | 0 | 0 | 0 | 0 | 2 | 1 | 0 | 1 | .250 | .250 | .250 |
| Casey, Sean, Cin.* | 1 | 4 | 4 | 1 | 1 | 4 | 0 | 0 | 1 | 1 | 0 | 0 | 0 | 0 | 0 | 1 | 0 | 0 | 0 | .250 | .250 | 1.000 |
| Cedeno, Roger, St.L.† | 1 | 2 | 1 | 0 | 0 | 0 | 0 | 0 | 0 | 0 | 0 | 0 | 0 | 1 | 1 | 1 | 0 | 1 | 0 | .000 | .500 | .000 |
| Cepicky, Matt, Mon.* | 2 | 6 | 6 | 0 | 2 | 3 | 1 | 0 | 0 | 0 | 0 | 0 | 0 | 0 | 0 | 1 | 0 | 0 | 0 | .333 | .333 | .500 |
| Colbrunn, Greg, Ari. | 2 | 7 | 7 | 0 | 1 | 1 | 0 | 0 | 0 | 1 | 0 | 0 | 0 | 0 | 0 | 0 | 0 | 0 | 0 | .143 | .143 | .143 |
| Cruz, Jacob, Cin.* | 2 | 10 | 10 | 2 | 4 | 7 | 0 | 0 | 1 | 6 | 0 | 0 | 0 | 0 | 0 | 3 | 0 | 0 | 0 | .400 | .400 | .700 |
| Drew, J.D., Atl.* | 1 | 4 | 3 | 0 | 0 | 0 | 0 | 0 | 0 | 0 | 0 | 0 | 0 | 1 | 0 | 0 | 0 | 0 | 0 | .000 | .250 | .000 |
| Dunn, Adam, Cin.* | 1 | 5 | 4 | 0 | 0 | 0 | 0 | 0 | 0 | 0 | 0 | 0 | 0 | 1 | 0 | 0 | 0 | 0 | 0 | .000 | .200 | .000 |
| Durrington, Trent, Mil. | 1 | 5 | 5 | 1 | 1 | 1 | 0 | 0 | 0 | 0 | 0 | 0 | 0 | 0 | 0 | 1 | 0 | 0 | 0 | .200 | .200 | .200 |
| Easley, Damion, Fla. | 3 | 13 | 11 | 2 | 4 | 9 | 2 | 0 | 1 | 5 | 0 | 0 | 1 | 1 | 0 | 0 | 0 | 0 | 0 | .364 | .462 | .818 |
| Edmonds, Jim, St.L.* | 1 | 3 | 2 | 0 | 1 | 1 | 0 | 0 | 0 | 0 | 0 | 0 | 0 | 1 | 0 | 1 | 0 | 0 | 0 | .500 | .667 | .500 |
| Everett, Carl, Mon.† | 3 | 13 | 10 | 2 | 2 | 2 | 0 | 0 | 0 | 1 | 0 | 1 | 1 | 1 | 0 | 0 | 0 | 0 | 0 | .200 | .308 | .200 |
| Finley, Steve, Ari.* | 1 | 4 | 4 | 0 | 0 | 0 | 0 | 0 | 0 | 0 | 0 | 0 | 0 | 0 | 0 | 0 | 0 | 0 | 0 | .000 | .000 | .000 |
| Floyd, Cliff, N.Y.* | 1 | 4 | 3 | 1 | 1 | 1 | 0 | 0 | 0 | 0 | 0 | 0 | 1 | 0 | 0 | 0 | 0 | 1 | 0 | .333 | .500 | .333 |
| Franco, Julio, Atl. | 1 | 3 | 3 | 0 | 2 | 2 | 0 | 0 | 0 | 0 | 0 | 0 | 0 | 0 | 0 | 0 | 0 | 0 | 0 | .667 | .667 | .667 |
| Ginter, Keith, Mil. | 2 | 6 | 5 | 0 | 1 | 1 | 0 | 0 | 0 | 1 | 0 | 0 | 0 | 1 | 0 | 1 | 0 | 0 | 0 | .200 | .333 | .200 |
| Gonzalez, Luis, Ari.* | 1 | 5 | 4 | 0 | 0 | 0 | 0 | 0 | 0 | 0 | 0 | 0 | 0 | 1 | 1 | 1 | 0 | 0 | 0 | .000 | .200 | .000 |
| Gonzalez, Luis A., Col. | 1 | 5 | 5 | 1 | 2 | 3 | 1 | 0 | 0 | 0 | 0 | 0 | 0 | 0 | 0 | 1 | 0 | 0 | 0 | .400 | .400 | .600 |
| Grabowski, Jason, L.A.* | 3 | 8 | 7 | 0 | 1 | 1 | 0 | 0 | 0 | 0 | 0 | 0 | 0 | 1 | 0 | 4 | 0 | 0 | 0 | .143 | .250 | .143 |
| Green, Shawn, L.A.* | 3 | 13 | 13 | 0 | 4 | 5 | 1 | 0 | 0 | 1 | 0 | 0 | 0 | 0 | 0 | 3 | 0 | 0 | 0 | .308 | .308 | .385 |
| Grieve, Ben, Mil.* | 1 | 7 | 6 | 0 | 0 | 0 | 0 | 0 | 0 | 0 | 0 | 0 | 0 | 1 | 0 | 5 | 0 | 0 | 0 | .000 | .143 | .000 |
| Griffey Jr., Ken, Cin.* | 1 | 5 | 5 | 1 | 3 | 5 | 2 | 0 | 0 | 0 | 0 | 0 | 0 | 0 | 0 | 0 | 0 | 0 | 0 | .600 | .600 | 1.000 |
| Harris, Lenny, Fla.* | 2 | 9 | 9 | 1 | 2 | 2 | 0 | 0 | 0 | 0 | 0 | 0 | 0 | 0 | 0 | 1 | 0 | 0 | 0 | .222 | .222 | .222 |
| Hollandsworth, Todd, Chi.* | 3 | 13 | 12 | 4 | 6 | 12 | 1 | 1 | 1 | 3 | 0 | 0 | 0 | 1 | 0 | 3 | 0 | 0 | 0 | .500 | .538 | 1.000 |
| Jones, Chipper, Atl.† | 7 | 33 | 30 | 4 | 5 | 15 | 1 | 0 | 3 | 6 | 0 | 0 | 0 | 3 | 0 | 6 | 0 | 0 | 3 | .167 | .242 | .500 |
| Kent, Jeff, Hou. | 2 | 7 | 4 | 0 | 1 | 2 | 1 | 0 | 0 | 1 | 0 | 1 | 0 | 2 | 0 | 0 | 1 | 0 | 0 | .250 | .429 | .500 |
| Klesko, Ryan, S.D.* | 3 | 12 | 8 | 0 | 1 | 1 | 0 | 0 | 0 | 0 | 0 | 0 | 1 | 3 | 0 | 2 | 0 | 0 | 1 | .125 | .417 | .125 |
| Lamb, Mike, Hou.* | 1 | 4 | 3 | 0 | 0 | 0 | 0 | 0 | 0 | 0 | 0 | 0 | 0 | 1 | 0 | 0 | 0 | 0 | 0 | .000 | .250 | .000 |
| LaRue, Jason, Cin. | 1 | 4 | 4 | 0 | 1 | 2 | 1 | 0 | 0 | 0 | 0 | 0 | 0 | 0 | 0 | 1 | 0 | 0 | 0 | .250 | .250 | .500 |
| Ledee, Ricky, Phi.* | 2 | 10 | 9 | 5 | 5 | 12 | 1 | 0 | 2 | 5 | 0 | 0 | 0 | 1 | 0 | 2 | 0 | 0 | 0 | .556 | .600 | 1.333 |

| | | | | | | | | | | | | | | | | | | | | | |
|---|---|---|---|---|---|---|---|---|---|---|---|---|---|---|---|---|---|---|---|---|---|
| Liefer, Jeff, Mil.* | 3 | 11 | 9 | 1 | 3 | 6 | 0 | 0 | 1 | 4 | 0 | 1 | 0 | 1 | 0 | 2 | 0 | 0 | 1 | .333 | .364 | .667 |
| Long, Terrence, S.D.* | 1 | 3 | 3 | 0 | 1 | 2 | 1 | 0 | 0 | 0 | 0 | 0 | 0 | 0 | 0 | 1 | 0 | 0 | 0 | .333 | .333 | .667 |
| Lowell, Mike, Fla | 3 | 14 | 13 | 1 | 2 | 3 | 1 | 0 | 0 | 2 | 0 | 1 | 0 | 0 | 0 | 3 | 0 | 0 | 0 | .154 | .143 | .231 |
| Mateo, Ruben, Pit | 1 | 1 | 0 | 0 | 0 | 0 | 0 | 0 | 0 | 0 | 0 | 0 | 0 | 1 | 1 | 0 | 0 | 0 | 0 | .000 | 1.000 | .000 |
| Michaels, Jason, Phi. | 1 | 5 | 5 | 1 | 1 | 4 | 0 | 0 | 1 | 1 | 0 | 0 | 0 | 0 | 0 | 1 | 0 | 0 | 0 | .200 | .200 | .800 |
| Minor, Damon, S.F.* | 1 | 4 | 3 | 0 | 1 | 1 | 0 | 0 | 0 | 0 | 0 | 0 | 0 | 1 | 0 | 1 | 0 | 0 | 0 | .333 | .500 | .333 |
| Mohr, Dustan, S.F. | 2 | 6 | 5 | 1 | 0 | 0 | 0 | 0 | 0 | 0 | 0 | 0 | 0 | 1 | 0 | 4 | 0 | 0 | 0 | .000 | .167 | .000 |
| Nady, Xavier, S.D. | 2 | 5 | 5 | 0 | 0 | 0 | 0 | 0 | 0 | 1 | 0 | 0 | 0 | 0 | 0 | 0 | 0 | 0 | 0 | .000 | .000 | .000 |
| Nevin, Phil, S.D. | 2 | 10 | 8 | 1 | 2 | 2 | 0 | 0 | 0 | 0 | 0 | 0 | 1 | 1 | 0 | 3 | 0 | 0 | 0 | .250 | .400 | .250 |
| Nunez, Abraham O., Pit.† | 1 | 1 | 0 | 0 | 0 | 0 | 0 | 0 | 0 | 0 | 1 | 0 | 0 | 0 | 0 | 0 | 0 | 0 | 0 | .000 | .000 | .000 |
| Payton, Jay, S.D. | 1 | 4 | 4 | 0 | 1 | 1 | 0 | 0 | 0 | 0 | 0 | 0 | 0 | 0 | 0 | 0 | 0 | 0 | 0 | .250 | .250 | .250 |
| Piazza, Mike, N.Y. | 8 | 37 | 29 | 2 | 6 | 10 | 1 | 0 | 1 | 5 | 0 | 1 | 0 | 7 | 2 | 7 | 0 | 0 | 0 | .207 | .351 | .345 |
| Pujols, Albert, St.L. | 3 | 14 | 14 | 2 | 1 | 1 | 0 | 0 | 0 | 1 | 0 | 0 | 0 | 0 | 0 | 1 | 0 | 0 | 0 | .071 | .071 | .071 |
| Rivera, Juan, Mon. | 1 | 1 | 1 | 0 | 1 | 2 | 1 | 0 | 0 | 0 | 0 | 0 | 0 | 0 | 0 | 0 | 0 | 0 | 0 | 1.000 | 1.000 | 2.000 |
| Robinson, Kerry, S.D.* | 2 | 4 | 4 | 2 | 3 | 3 | 0 | 0 | 0 | 0 | 0 | 0 | 0 | 0 | 0 | 0 | 1 | 1 | 0 | .750 | .750 | .750 |
| Saenz, Olmedo, L.A. | 4 | 16 | 13 | 2 | 3 | 6 | 0 | 0 | 1 | 4 | 0 | 0 | 2 | 1 | 0 | 5 | 0 | 0 | 0 | .231 | .375 | .462 |
| Sanders, Reggie, St.L. | 1 | 5 | 5 | 2 | 2 | 2 | 0 | 0 | 0 | 2 | 0 | 0 | 0 | 0 | 0 | 1 | 0 | 0 | 0 | .400 | .400 | .400 |
| Simon, Randall, Pit.* | 4 | 15 | 14 | 1 | 4 | 4 | 0 | 0 | 0 | 0 | 0 | 0 | 1 | 0 | 0 | 3 | 0 | 0 | 0 | .286 | .333 | .286 |
| Sosa, Sammy, Chi. | 2 | 8 | 7 | 2 | 2 | 8 | 0 | 0 | 2 | 4 | 0 | 1 | 0 | 0 | 0 | 0 | 0 | 0 | 0 | .286 | .250 | 1.143 |
| Sweeney, Mark, Col.* | 4 | 15 | 15 | 2 | 4 | 5 | 1 | 0 | 0 | 1 | 0 | 0 | 0 | 0 | 0 | 6 | 0 | 0 | 0 | .267 | .267 | .333 |
| Thome, Jim, Phi.* | 6 | 26 | 23 | 5 | 6 | 18 | 0 | 0 | 4 | 6 | 0 | 0 | 0 | 3 | 0 | 6 | 0 | 0 | 0 | .261 | .346 | .783 |
| Vidro, Jose, Mon.† | 4 | 17 | 16 | 2 | 6 | 6 | 0 | 0 | 0 | 3 | 0 | 0 | 0 | 1 | 1 | 1 | 0 | 1 | 0 | .375 | .412 | .375 |
| Walker, Larry, Col.* | 1 | 5 | 4 | 0 | 2 | 2 | 0 | 0 | 0 | 0 | 0 | 0 | 0 | 1 | 0 | 1 | 0 | 0 | 0 | .500 | .600 | .500 |
| Werth, Jayson, L.A. | 1 | 0 | 0 | 1 | 0 | 0 | 0 | 0 | 0 | 0 | 0 | 0 | 0 | 0 | 0 | 0 | 0 | 0 | 0 | .000 | .000 | .000 |
| Wilson, Craig, Pit. | 2 | 9 | 7 | 2 | 1 | 4 | 0 | 0 | 1 | 2 | 0 | 0 | 0 | 2 | 0 | 0 | 0 | 0 | 0 | .143 | .333 | .571 |
| Zinter, Alan, Ari.† | 2 | 5 | 3 | 0 | 1 | 1 | 0 | 0 | 0 | 1 | 0 | 0 | 0 | 2 | 0 | 0 | 0 | 0 | 0 | .333 | .600 | .333 |

The following designated hitters, each of whom appeared in at least one game, had no plate appearances, runs scored or stolen base attempts: Hummel, Tim, Cincinnati; Spencer, Shane, New York.

# PINCH-HITTING

## TEAM

| Team | G | TPA | AB | R | H | TB | 2B | 3B | HR | RBI | SH | SF | HP | BB | IBB | SO | SB | CS | GDP | Avg. | OBP | Slg. |
|---|---|---|---|---|---|---|---|---|---|---|---|---|---|---|---|---|---|---|---|---|---|---|
| San Francisco | 122 | 234 | 190 | 33 | 56 | 86 | 16 | 1 | 4 | 30 | 1 | 1 | 6 | 36 | 6 | 47 | 2 | 0 | 3 | .295 | .421 | .453 |
| Atlanta | 134 | 242 | 220 | 28 | 61 | 90 | 10 | 2 | 5 | 35 | 4 | 5 | 1 | 12 | 1 | 54 | 1 | 0 | 1 | .277 | .311 | .409 |
| St. Louis | 128 | 271 | 243 | 25 | 64 | 97 | 9 | 3 | 6 | 44 | 3 | 5 | 1 | 19 | 1 | 56 | 5 | 1 | 5 | .263 | .313 | .399 |
| Houston | 143 | 269 | 225 | 28 | 59 | 84 | 8 | 1 | 5 | 35 | 4 | 2 | 3 | 35 | 4 | 46 | 2 | 0 | 6 | .262 | .366 | .373 |
| Colorado | 142 | 286 | 244 | 34 | 62 | 112 | 15 | 1 | 11 | 47 | 2 | 4 | 5 | 31 | 5 | 79 | 1 | 0 | 2 | .254 | .345 | .459 |
| Philadelphia | 137 | 257 | 225 | 28 | 54 | 90 | 9 | 0 | 9 | 35 | 1 | 0 | 2 | 29 | 3 | 61 | 1 | 0 | 5 | .240 | .332 | .400 |
| Chicago | 135 | 253 | 228 | 17 | 54 | 78 | 12 | 0 | 4 | 30 | 2 | 6 | 1 | 16 | 3 | 53 | 4 | 0 | 3 | .237 | .283 | .342 |
| New York | 149 | 262 | 234 | 19 | 51 | 79 | 10 | 0 | 6 | 23 | 4 | 0 | 1 | 23 | 0 | 68 | 0 | 1 | 4 | .218 | .291 | .338 |
| Pittsburgh | 140 | 275 | 240 | 30 | 52 | 78 | 7 | 2 | 5 | 30 | 3 | 3 | 5 | 24 | 2 | 61 | 1 | 3 | 6 | .217 | .298 | .325 |
| Los Angeles | 139 | 286 | 246 | 30 | 52 | 88 | 7 | 1 | 9 | 39 | 1 | 5 | 1 | 33 | 2 | 82 | 2 | 1 | 6 | .211 | .302 | .358 |
| Arizona | 139 | 242 | 215 | 17 | 45 | 66 | 9 | 0 | 4 | 20 | 3 | 0 | 3 | 21 | 0 | 63 | 0 | 1 | 8 | .209 | .289 | .307 |
| Milwaukee | 144 | 280 | 249 | 19 | 51 | 85 | 11 | 1 | 7 | 30 | 0 | 2 | 4 | 25 | 0 | 87 | 2 | 0 | 4 | .205 | .286 | .341 |
| San Diego | 135 | 249 | 212 | 28 | 43 | 65 | 7 | 0 | 5 | 24 | 5 | 4 | 2 | 26 | 2 | 41 | 1 | 0 | 5 | .203 | .291 | .307 |
| Cincinnati | 141 | 258 | 224 | 27 | 43 | 70 | 4 | 1 | 7 | 31 | 4 | 0 | 6 | 24 | 1 | 74 | 2 | 0 | 7 | .192 | .287 | .313 |
| Montreal | 128 | 249 | 221 | 16 | 42 | 52 | 4 | 0 | 2 | 19 | 3 | 1 | 0 | 24 | 2 | 63 | 5 | 2 | 6 | .190 | .268 | .235 |
| Florida | 122 | 217 | 195 | 10 | 34 | 54 | 6 | 1 | 4 | 23 | 2 | 1 | 2 | 17 | 0 | 53 | 0 | 1 | 1 | .174 | .247 | .277 |
| **Totals** | 2178 | 4130 | 3611 | 389 | 823 | 1274 | 144 | 14 | 93 | 495 | 42 | 39 | 43 | 395 | 32 | 988 | 29 | 10 | 72 | .228 | .308 | .353 |

## TOP PINCH-HITTERS

Minimum 20 at-bats. *Lefthanded batter. †Switch-hitter.

| Player, Team | G | TPA | AB | R | H | TB | 2B | 3B | HR | RBI | SH | SF | HP | BB | IBB | SO | SB | CS | GDP | Avg. | OBP | Slg. |
|---|---|---|---|---|---|---|---|---|---|---|---|---|---|---|---|---|---|---|---|---|---|---|
| Utley, Chase, Phi.* | 34 | 34 | 31 | 5 | 11 | 22 | 2 | 0 | 3 | 10 | 0 | 0 | 0 | 3 | 1 | 10 | 0 | 0 | 0 | .355 | .412 | .710 |
| Franco, Julio, Atl. | 50 | 50 | 43 | 5 | 15 | 24 | 3 | 0 | 2 | 16 | 1 | 0 | 0 | 6 | 1 | 14 | 0 | 0 | 0 | .349 | .429 | .558 |
| Cruz, Deivi, S.F. | 24 | 24 | 23 | 4 | 8 | 11 | 3 | 0 | 0 | 5 | 0 | 0 | 1 | 0 | 0 | 1 | 0 | 0 | 0 | .348 | .375 | .478 |
| Long, Terrence, S.D.* | 58 | 54 | 50 | 5 | 17 | 22 | 2 | 0 | 1 | 8 | 0 | 2 | 0 | 2 | 1 | 5 | 0 | 0 | 0 | .340 | .352 | .440 |
| Anderson, Marlon, St.L.* | 54 | 54 | 51 | 8 | 17 | 28 | 2 | 0 | 3 | 10 | 0 | 0 | 0 | 3 | 0 | 10 | 1 | 0 | 0 | .333 | .370 | .549 |
| Lane, Jason, Hou. | 41 | 41 | 36 | 5 | 12 | 19 | 1 | 0 | 2 | 6 | 1 | 0 | 0 | 4 | 0 | 9 | 0 | 0 | 1 | .333 | .400 | .528 |
| Gonzalez, Luis A., Col. | 22 | 22 | 21 | 3 | 7 | 14 | 1 | 0 | 2 | 6 | 1 | 0 | 0 | 0 | 0 | 8 | 0 | 0 | 0 | .333 | .333 | .667 |
| Carroll, Jamey, Mon. | 34 | 31 | 25 | 6 | 8 | 9 | 1 | 0 | 0 | 2 | 1 | 0 | 0 | 5 | 0 | 4 | 0 | 0 | 1 | .320 | .433 | .360 |
| Saenz, Olmedo, L.A. | 55 | 55 | 48 | 6 | 15 | 25 | 1 | 0 | 3 | 13 | 0 | 3 | 0 | 4 | 1 | 17 | 0 | 0 | 2 | .313 | .345 | .521 |
| Lamb, Mike, Hou.* | 42 | 41 | 36 | 3 | 11 | 15 | 1 | 0 | 1 | 10 | 0 | 1 | 0 | 4 | 2 | 10 | 0 | 0 | 0 | .306 | .366 | .417 |
| Mateo, Henry, Mon.† | 28 | 28 | 27 | 2 | 8 | 8 | 0 | 0 | 0 | 0 | 1 | 0 | 0 | 0 | 0 | 5 | 2 | 2 | 0 | .296 | .296 | .296 |
| Lankford, Ray, St.L.* | 30 | 29 | 22 | 5 | 6 | 12 | 1 | 1 | 1 | 8 | 0 | 3 | 0 | 4 | 0 | 7 | 1 | 0 | 0 | .273 | .345 | .545 |
| Feliz, Pedro, S.F. | 25 | 25 | 22 | 2 | 6 | 8 | 0 | 1 | 0 | 4 | 0 | 0 | 0 | 3 | 0 | 6 | 2 | 0 | 1 | .273 | .360 | .364 |
| Ventura, Robin, L.A.* | 61 | 57 | 48 | 7 | 13 | 22 | 0 | 0 | 3 | 14 | 0 | 1 | 0 | 8 | 0 | 12 | 0 | 0 | 1 | .271 | .368 | .458 |
| Larkin, Barry, Cin. | 28 | 28 | 26 | 4 | 7 | 10 | 0 | 0 | 1 | 4 | 0 | 0 | 0 | 2 | 0 | 5 | 0 | 0 | 2 | .269 | .321 | .385 |

## ALL PINCH-HITTERS

*Lefthanded batter. †Switch-hitter.

| Player, Team | G | TPA | AB | R | H | TB | 2B | 3B | HR | RBI | SH | SF | HP | BB | IBB | SO | SB | CS | GDP | Avg. | OBP | Slg. |
|---|---|---|---|---|---|---|---|---|---|---|---|---|---|---|---|---|---|---|---|---|---|---|
| Abreu, Bobby, Phi.* | 2 | 2 | 2 | 0 | 0 | 0 | 0 | 0 | 0 | 0 | 0 | 0 | 0 | 0 | 0 | 0 | 0 | 0 | 0 | .000 | .000 | .000 |
| Aguila, Chris, Fla. | 8 | 8 | 8 | 0 | 0 | 0 | 0 | 0 | 0 | 0 | 0 | 0 | 0 | 0 | 0 | 5 | 0 | 0 | 0 | .000 | .000 | .000 |
| Alfaro, Jason, Hou. | 4 | 4 | 4 | 0 | 1 | 1 | 0 | 0 | 0 | 0 | 0 | 0 | 0 | 0 | 0 | 1 | 0 | 0 | 0 | .250 | .250 | .250 |
| Alfonzo, Edgardo, S.F. | 9 | 9 | 7 | 1 | 3 | 6 | 0 | 0 | 1 | 3 | 0 | 0 | 1 | 1 | 0 | 2 | 0 | 0 | 0 | .429 | .556 | .857 |
| Alomar, Roberto, Ari.† | 10 | 10 | 8 | 0 | 1 | 1 | 0 | 0 | 0 | 0 | 0 | 0 | 0 | 2 | 0 | 2 | 0 | 0 | 0 | .125 | .300 | .125 |
| Alou, Moises, Chi. | 1 | 1 | 1 | 0 | 0 | 0 | 0 | 0 | 0 | 0 | 0 | 0 | 0 | 0 | 0 | 0 | 0 | 0 | 1 | .000 | .000 | .000 |
| Alvarez, Tony, Pit. | 9 | 9 | 7 | 1 | 0 | 0 | 0 | 0 | 0 | 1 | 0 | 1 | 1 | 0 | 0 | 2 | 0 | 0 | 0 | .000 | .111 | .000 |
| Anderson, Marlon, St.L.* | 54 | 54 | 51 | 8 | 17 | 28 | 2 | 0 | 3 | 10 | 0 | 0 | 0 | 3 | 0 | 10 | 1 | 0 | 0 | .333 | .370 | .549 |
| Atkins, Garrett, Col. | 7 | 7 | 5 | 2 | 2 | 6 | 1 | 0 | 1 | 3 | 0 | 1 | 0 | 1 | 0 | 0 | 0 | 0 | 0 | .400 | .429 | 1.200 |
| Aurilia, Rich, S.D. | 10 | 10 | 9 | 2 | 1 | 1 | 0 | 0 | 0 | 0 | 0 | 0 | 0 | 1 | 0 | 2 | 0 | 0 | 0 | .111 | .200 | .111 |
| Ausmus, Brad, Hou. | 3 | 3 | 3 | 1 | 1 | 1 | 0 | 0 | 0 | 0 | 0 | 0 | 0 | 0 | 0 | 1 | 0 | 0 | 0 | .333 | .333 | .333 |
| Backe, Brandon, Hou. | 1 | 1 | 1 | 0 | 0 | 0 | 0 | 0 | 0 | 0 | 0 | 0 | 0 | 0 | 0 | 0 | 0 | 0 | 0 | .000 | .000 | .000 |
| Baerga, Carlos, Ari.† | 71 | 71 | 63 | 4 | 14 | 19 | 2 | 0 | 1 | 8 | 0 | 0 | 3 | 5 | 0 | 8 | 0 | 0 | 5 | .222 | .310 | .302 |
| Bagwell, Jeff, Hou. | 2 | 2 | 1 | 1 | 0 | 0 | 0 | 0 | 0 | 0 | 0 | 0 | 0 | 1 | 0 | 0 | 0 | 0 | 0 | .000 | .500 | .000 |
| Bako, Paul, Chi.* | 3 | 3 | 2 | 0 | 0 | 0 | 0 | 0 | 0 | 0 | 0 | 0 | 0 | 1 | 0 | 0 | 0 | 0 | 0 | .000 | .333 | .000 |
| Barmes, Clint, Col. | 1 | 1 | 1 | 0 | 0 | 0 | 0 | 0 | 0 | 0 | 0 | 0 | 0 | 0 | 0 | 0 | 0 | 0 | 0 | .000 | .000 | .000 |
| Barrett, Michael, Chi. | 11 | 11 | 8 | 1 | 2 | 6 | 1 | 0 | 1 | 7 | 0 | 3 | 0 | 0 | 0 | 2 | 0 | 0 | 0 | .250 | .182 | .750 |
| Batista, Tony, Mon. | 5 | 5 | 5 | 0 | 2 | 2 | 0 | 0 | 0 | 1 | 0 | 0 | 0 | 0 | 0 | 0 | 0 | 0 | 0 | .400 | .400 | .400 |
| Bautista, Danny, Ari. | 3 | 3 | 3 | 0 | 0 | 0 | 0 | 0 | 0 | 0 | 0 | 0 | 0 | 0 | 0 | 2 | 0 | 0 | 0 | .000 | .000 | .000 |
| Bautista, Jose, Pit. | 12 | 12 | 10 | 0 | 2 | 2 | 0 | 0 | 0 | 0 | 0 | 0 | 0 | 2 | 0 | 4 | 0 | 0 | 0 | .200 | .333 | .200 |
| Bay, Jason, Pit. | 6 | 6 | 5 | 1 | 0 | 0 | 0 | 0 | 0 | 0 | 0 | 0 | 0 | 1 | 0 | 1 | 0 | 0 | 0 | .000 | .167 | .000 |
| Bell, David, Phi. | 1 | 1 | 1 | 0 | 1 | 2 | 1 | 0 | 0 | 1 | 0 | 0 | 0 | 0 | 0 | 0 | 0 | 0 | 0 | 1.000 | 1.000 | 2.000 |
| Beltran, Carlos, Hou.† | 2 | 2 | 2 | 0 | 0 | 0 | 0 | 0 | 0 | 0 | 0 | 0 | 0 | 0 | 0 | 0 | 0 | 0 | 0 | .000 | .000 | .000 |
| Beltre, Adrian, L.A. | 1 | 1 | 0 | 1 | 0 | 0 | 0 | 0 | 0 | 0 | 0 | 0 | 0 | 1 | 0 | 0 | 0 | 0 | 0 | .000 | 1.000 | .000 |
| Berkman, Lance, Hou.† | 1 | 1 | 1 | 0 | 0 | 0 | 0 | 0 | 0 | 0 | 0 | 0 | 0 | 0 | 0 | 1 | 0 | 0 | 0 | .000 | .000 | .000 |
| Betemit, Wilson, Atl.† | 4 | 4 | 3 | 0 | 0 | 0 | 0 | 0 | 0 | 0 | 0 | 0 | 0 | 1 | 0 | 1 | 0 | 0 | 0 | .000 | .250 | .000 |
| Biggio, Craig, Hou. | 6 | 6 | 6 | 2 | 2 | 6 | 1 | 0 | 1 | 2 | 0 | 0 | 0 | 0 | 0 | 2 | 0 | 0 | 0 | .333 | .333 | 1.000 |
| Bonds, Barry, S.F.* | 8 | 8 | 2 | 2 | 0 | 0 | 0 | 0 | 0 | 0 | 0 | 0 | 0 | 6 | 5 | 0 | 0 | 0 | 0 | .000 | .750 | .000 |
| Bradley, Milton, L.A.† | 4 | 3 | 2 | 0 | 0 | 0 | 0 | 0 | 0 | 0 | 0 | 0 | 0 | 1 | 0 | 1 | 0 | 1 | 0 | .000 | .333 | .000 |
| Bragg, Darren, S.D.-Cin.* | 23 | 23 | 18 | 4 | 3 | 3 | 0 | 0 | 0 | 0 | 1 | 0 | 0 | 4 | 0 | 6 | 1 | 0 | 0 | .167 | .318 | .167 |
| Branyan, Russell, Mil.* | 8 | 8 | 5 | 0 | 0 | 0 | 0 | 0 | 0 | 0 | 0 | 0 | 1 | 2 | 0 | 5 | 0 | 0 | 0 | .000 | .375 | .000 |
| Brazell, Craig, N.Y.* | 18 | 17 | 17 | 1 | 5 | 7 | 2 | 0 | 0 | 2 | 0 | 0 | 0 | 0 | 0 | 4 | 0 | 0 | 1 | .294 | .294 | .412 |
| Bruntlett, Eric, Hou. | 5 | 5 | 3 | 0 | 1 | 1 | 0 | 0 | 0 | 0 | 0 | 0 | 0 | 2 | 0 | 0 | 0 | 0 | 0 | .333 | .600 | .333 |
| Buchanan, Brian, S.D.-N.Y. | 19 | 19 | 16 | 1 | 2 | 5 | 0 | 0 | 1 | 1 | 0 | 0 | 1 | 2 | 1 | 5 | 0 | 0 | 0 | .125 | .263 | .313 |

| Player, Team | G | TPA | AB | R | H | TB | 2B | 3B | HR | RBI | SH | SF | HP | BB | IBB | SO | SB | CS | GDP | Avg. | OBP | Slg. |
|---|---|---|---|---|---|---|---|---|---|---|---|---|---|---|---|---|---|---|---|---|---|---|
| Burke, Chris, Hou. | 10 | 10 | 7 | 2 | 1 | 1 | 0 | 0 | 0 | 0 | 0 | 0 | 0 | 3 | 0 | 1 | 0 | 0 | 0 | .143 | .400 | .143 |
| Burnitz, Jeromy, Col.* | 9 | 9 | 9 | 1 | 1 | 2 | 1 | 0 | 0 | 0 | 0 | 0 | 0 | 0 | 0 | 3 | 0 | 0 | 0 | .111 | .111 | .222 |
| Burrell, Pat, Phi. | 5 | 4 | 3 | 1 | 1 | 4 | 0 | 0 | 1 | 2 | 0 | 0 | 0 | 1 | 0 | 0 | 0 | 0 | 0 | .333 | .500 | 1.333 |
| Burroughs, Sean, S.D.* | 6 | 6 | 5 | 2 | 1 | 4 | 0 | 0 | 1 | 2 | 0 | 0 | 0 | 1 | 0 | 1 | 0 | 0 | 0 | .200 | .333 | .800 |
| Byrd, Marlon, Phi. | 12 | 12 | 11 | 4 | 4 | 6 | 2 | 0 | 0 | 0 | 0 | 0 | 0 | 1 | 0 | 2 | 0 | 0 | 0 | .364 | .417 | .545 |
| Cabrera, Miguel, Fla. | 1 | 1 | 1 | 0 | 0 | 0 | 0 | 0 | 0 | 0 | 0 | 0 | 0 | 0 | 0 | 0 | 0 | 0 | 0 | .000 | .000 | .000 |
| Cabrera, Orlando, Mon. | 2 | 2 | 2 | 0 | 0 | 0 | 0 | 0 | 0 | 0 | 0 | 0 | 0 | 0 | 0 | 0 | 0 | 0 | 0 | .000 | .000 | .000 |
| Calloway, Ron, Mon.* | 28 | 28 | 22 | 0 | 4 | 4 | 0 | 0 | 0 | 6 | 0 | 1 | 0 | 5 | 0 | 8 | 2 | 0 | 0 | .182 | .321 | .182 |
| Cameron, Mike, N.Y. | 2 | 2 | 2 | 0 | 0 | 0 | 0 | 0 | 0 | 0 | 0 | 0 | 0 | 0 | 0 | 1 | 0 | 0 | 0 | .000 | .000 | .000 |
| Carroll, Jamey, Mon. | 34 | 31 | 25 | 6 | 8 | 9 | 1 | 0 | 0 | 2 | 1 | 0 | 0 | 5 | 0 | 4 | 0 | 0 | 1 | .320 | .433 | .360 |
| Casey, Sean, Cin.* | 2 | 2 | 2 | 0 | 1 | 1 | 0 | 0 | 0 | 0 | 0 | 0 | 0 | 0 | 0 | 0 | 0 | 0 | 0 | .500 | .500 | .500 |
| Castilla, Vinny, Col. | 1 | 1 | 1 | 1 | 1 | 2 | 1 | 0 | 0 | 2 | 0 | 0 | 0 | 0 | 0 | 0 | 0 | 0 | 0 | 1.000 | 1.000 | 2.000 |
| Castillo, Jose, Pit. | 4 | 4 | 3 | 0 | 1 | 1 | 0 | 0 | 0 | 0 | 0 | 0 | 0 | 1 | 0 | 1 | 0 | 0 | 0 | .333 | .500 | .333 |
| Castillo, Luis, Fla.† | 2 | 2 | 1 | 0 | 0 | 0 | 0 | 0 | 0 | 1 | 0 | 1 | 0 | 0 | 0 | 1 | 0 | 0 | 0 | .000 | .000 | .000 |
| Castro, Juan, Cin. | 13 | 13 | 13 | 1 | 3 | 8 | 0 | 1 | 1 | 4 | 0 | 0 | 0 | 0 | 0 | 3 | 0 | 0 | 0 | .231 | .231 | .615 |
| Castro, Ramon, Fla. | 1 | 1 | 1 | 1 | 1 | 4 | 0 | 0 | 1 | 2 | 0 | 0 | 0 | 0 | 0 | 0 | 0 | 0 | 0 | 1.000 | 1.000 | 4.000 |
| Cedeno, Roger, St.L.† | 47 | 47 | 45 | 3 | 11 | 16 | 2 | 0 | 1 | 9 | 0 | 0 | 0 | 2 | 0 | 6 | 0 | 0 | 0 | .244 | .277 | .356 |
| Cepicky, Matt, Mon.* | 19 | 19 | 19 | 1 | 2 | 5 | 0 | 0 | 1 | 1 | 0 | 0 | 0 | 0 | 0 | 8 | 0 | 0 | 0 | .105 | .105 | .263 |
| Chavez, Endy, Mon.* | 5 | 5 | 4 | 1 | 2 | 4 | 2 | 0 | 0 | 1 | 0 | 0 | 0 | 1 | 0 | 0 | 1 | 0 | 0 | .500 | .600 | 1.000 |
| Chavez, Raul, Hou. | 3 | 3 | 2 | 0 | 0 | 0 | 0 | 0 | 0 | 0 | 0 | 0 | 0 | 1 | 0 | 1 | 0 | 0 | 0 | .000 | .333 | .000 |
| Chen, Chin-Feng, L.A. | 4 | 4 | 4 | 0 | 0 | 0 | 0 | 0 | 0 | 0 | 0 | 0 | 0 | 0 | 0 | 1 | 0 | 0 | 1 | .000 | .000 | .000 |
| Choi, Hee Seop, Fla.-L.A.* | 15 | 15 | 11 | 1 | 0 | 0 | 0 | 0 | 0 | 1 | 0 | 0 | 0 | 4 | 1 | 5 | 0 | 0 | 0 | .000 | .267 | .000 |
| Church, Ryan, Mon.* | 14 | 13 | 10 | 2 | 1 | 1 | 0 | 0 | 0 | 1 | 0 | 0 | 0 | 3 | 0 | 3 | 0 | 0 | 1 | .100 | .308 | .100 |
| Cintron, Alex, Ari.† | 8 | 8 | 8 | 1 | 2 | 3 | 1 | 0 | 0 | 0 | 0 | 0 | 0 | 0 | 0 | 0 | 0 | 0 | 0 | .250 | .250 | .375 |
| Cirillo, Jeff, S.D. | 11 | 11 | 9 | 1 | 2 | 3 | 1 | 0 | 0 | 0 | 0 | 0 | 0 | 2 | 0 | 2 | 0 | 0 | 0 | .222 | .364 | .333 |
| Clark, Brady, Mil. | 25 | 25 | 19 | 3 | 6 | 9 | 0 | 0 | 1 | 6 | 0 | 0 | 1 | 5 | 0 | 2 | 2 | 0 | 1 | .316 | .480 | .474 |
| Clark, Jermaine, Cin.* | 5 | 5 | 5 | 1 | 1 | 1 | 0 | 0 | 0 | 1 | 0 | 0 | 0 | 0 | 0 | 3 | 1 | 0 | 0 | .200 | .200 | .200 |
| Clayton, Royce, Col. | 3 | 3 | 3 | 1 | 1 | 1 | 0 | 0 | 0 | 1 | 0 | 0 | 0 | 0 | 0 | 1 | 0 | 0 | 0 | .333 | .333 | .333 |
| Closser, J.D., Col.† | 6 | 6 | 6 | 0 | 2 | 2 | 0 | 0 | 0 | 0 | 0 | 0 | 0 | 0 | 0 | 1 | 0 | 0 | 0 | .333 | .333 | .333 |
| Colbrunn, Greg, Ari. | 16 | 16 | 15 | 1 | 2 | 2 | 0 | 0 | 0 | 0 | 0 | 0 | 0 | 1 | 0 | 5 | 0 | 0 | 0 | .133 | .188 | .133 |
| Collier, Lou, Phi. | 22 | 22 | 17 | 3 | 2 | 3 | 1 | 0 | 0 | 1 | 0 | 0 | 1 | 4 | 0 | 5 | 1 | 0 | 1 | .118 | .318 | .176 |
| Conine, Jeff, Fla. | 2 | 2 | 2 | 0 | 1 | 1 | 0 | 0 | 0 | 1 | 0 | 0 | 0 | 0 | 0 | 0 | 0 | 0 | 0 | .500 | .500 | .500 |
| Cora, Alex, L.A.* | 5 | 5 | 4 | 0 | 0 | 0 | 0 | 0 | 0 | 0 | 1 | 0 | 0 | 0 | 0 | 0 | 0 | 0 | 0 | .000 | .000 | .000 |
| Cordero, Wil, Fla. | 11 | 11 | 10 | 0 | 1 | 1 | 0 | 0 | 0 | 1 | 0 | 0 | 1 | 0 | 0 | 5 | 0 | 0 | 0 | .100 | .182 | .100 |
| Cota, Humberto, Pit. | 12 | 12 | 11 | 1 | 2 | 2 | 0 | 0 | 0 | 1 | 0 | 0 | 1 | 0 | 0 | 3 | 0 | 0 | 0 | .182 | .250 | .182 |
| Counsell, Craig, Mil.* | 9 | 9 | 8 | 1 | 2 | 5 | 1 | 1 | 0 | 0 | 0 | 0 | 0 | 1 | 0 | 4 | 0 | 0 | 0 | .250 | .333 | .625 |
| Cruz, Deivi, S.F. | 24 | 24 | 23 | 4 | 8 | 11 | 3 | 0 | 0 | 5 | 0 | 0 | 1 | 0 | 0 | 1 | 0 | 0 | 0 | .348 | .375 | .478 |
| Cruz, Jacob, Cin.* | 67 | 66 | 55 | 10 | 14 | 21 | 4 | 0 | 1 | 8 | 0 | 0 | 2 | 9 | 1 | 13 | 0 | 0 | 2 | .255 | .379 | .382 |
| Daigle, Casey, Ari. | 1 | 1 | 1 | 0 | 0 | 0 | 0 | 0 | 0 | 0 | 0 | 0 | 0 | 0 | 0 | 1 | 0 | 0 | 0 | .000 | .000 | .000 |
| Dallimore, Brian, S.F. | 8 | 8 | 7 | 2 | 3 | 4 | 1 | 0 | 0 | 0 | 0 | 0 | 0 | 1 | 0 | 2 | 0 | 0 | 0 | .429 | .500 | .571 |
| Davis, J.J., Pit. | 7 | 7 | 6 | 1 | 0 | 0 | 0 | 0 | 0 | 0 | 0 | 0 | 0 | 1 | 0 | 4 | 0 | 0 | 0 | .000 | .143 | .000 |
| Delgado, Wilson, N.Y.† | 4 | 4 | 4 | 0 | 2 | 2 | 0 | 0 | 0 | 1 | 0 | 0 | 0 | 0 | 0 | 0 | 0 | 0 | 0 | .500 | .500 | .500 |
| DeRosa, Mark, Atl. | 32 | 32 | 27 | 4 | 7 | 8 | 1 | 0 | 0 | 2 | 1 | 1 | 1 | 2 | 0 | 4 | 0 | 0 | 0 | .259 | .323 | .296 |
| DeVore, Doug, Ari.* | 19 | 19 | 17 | 0 | 3 | 3 | 0 | 0 | 0 | 0 | 0 | 0 | 0 | 2 | 0 | 10 | 0 | 0 | 0 | .176 | .263 | .176 |
| Diaz, Einar, Mon. | 10 | 10 | 9 | 0 | 0 | 0 | 0 | 0 | 0 | 0 | 0 | 0 | 0 | 1 | 0 | 2 | 0 | 0 | 0 | .000 | .100 | .000 |
| Diaz, Victor, N.Y. | 2 | 2 | 2 | 1 | 2 | 2 | 0 | 0 | 0 | 0 | 0 | 0 | 0 | 0 | 0 | 0 | 0 | 0 | 0 | 1.000 | 1.000 | 1.000 |
| Drew, J.D., Atl.* | 1 | 1 | 1 | 0 | 0 | 0 | 0 | 0 | 0 | 0 | 0 | 0 | 0 | 0 | 0 | 1 | 0 | 0 | 0 | .000 | .000 | .000 |
| Dubois, Jason, Chi. | 16 | 16 | 14 | 0 | 3 | 3 | 0 | 0 | 0 | 1 | 0 | 1 | 0 | 1 | 0 | 2 | 0 | 0 | 0 | .214 | .250 | .214 |
| Duncan, Jeff, N.Y.* | 8 | 8 | 6 | 0 | 0 | 0 | 0 | 0 | 0 | 0 | 1 | 0 | 0 | 1 | 0 | 5 | 0 | 0 | 0 | .000 | .143 | .000 |
| Dunn, Adam, Cin.* | 2 | 2 | 2 | 0 | 1 | 1 | 0 | 0 | 0 | 0 | 0 | 0 | 0 | 0 | 0 | 1 | 0 | 0 | 0 | .500 | .500 | .500 |
| Durham, Ray, S.F.† | 5 | 5 | 4 | 1 | 1 | 2 | 1 | 0 | 0 | 0 | 0 | 0 | 0 | 1 | 0 | 2 | 0 | 0 | 0 | .250 | .400 | .500 |
| Durrington, Trent, Mil. | 30 | 30 | 28 | 4 | 4 | 10 | 0 | 0 | 2 | 2 | 0 | 0 | 0 | 2 | 0 | 8 | 0 | 0 | 0 | .143 | .200 | .357 |
| Easley, Damion, Fla. | 35 | 35 | 32 | 1 | 2 | 6 | 1 | 0 | 1 | 5 | 0 | 0 | 1 | 2 | 0 | 9 | 0 | 0 | 0 | .063 | .143 | .188 |
| Eaton, Adam, S.D. | 5 | 5 | 2 | 0 | 0 | 0 | 0 | 0 | 0 | 1 | 2 | 0 | 0 | 1 | 0 | 1 | 0 | 0 | 0 | .000 | .333 | .000 |
| Edmonds, Jim, St.L.* | 6 | 6 | 4 | 0 | 1 | 1 | 0 | 0 | 0 | 0 | 0 | 0 | 0 | 2 | 1 | 1 | 0 | 0 | 0 | .250 | .500 | .250 |
| Eischen, Joey, Mon.* | 1 | 1 | 1 | 1 | 1 | 1 | 0 | 0 | 0 | 0 | 0 | 0 | 0 | 0 | 0 | 0 | 0 | 0 | 0 | 1.000 | 1.000 | 1.000 |
| Ellison, Jason, S.F. | 1 | 1 | 1 | 0 | 0 | 0 | 0 | 0 | 0 | 0 | 0 | 0 | 0 | 0 | 0 | 1 | 0 | 0 | 0 | .000 | .000 | .000 |
| Encarnacion, Juan, L.A.-Fla. | 2 | 2 | 2 | 0 | 0 | 0 | 0 | 0 | 0 | 0 | 0 | 0 | 0 | 0 | 0 | 0 | 0 | 0 | 0 | .000 | .000 | .000 |
| Ensberg, Morgan, Hou. | 19 | 19 | 15 | 1 | 5 | 6 | 1 | 0 | 0 | 6 | 0 | 1 | 0 | 3 | 0 | 0 | 0 | 0 | 1 | .333 | .421 | .400 |
| Erickson, Matt, Mil.* | 2 | 2 | 2 | 0 | 0 | 0 | 0 | 0 | 0 | 0 | 0 | 0 | 0 | 0 | 0 | 1 | 0 | 0 | 0 | .000 | .000 | .000 |
| Estalella, Bobby, Ari. | 2 | 2 | 2 | 0 | 0 | 0 | 0 | 0 | 0 | 0 | 0 | 0 | 0 | 0 | 0 | 2 | 0 | 0 | 0 | .000 | .000 | .000 |
| Estrada, Johnny, Atl.† | 12 | 12 | 12 | 1 | 3 | 3 | 0 | 0 | 0 | 1 | 0 | 0 | 0 | 0 | 0 | 2 | 0 | 0 | 0 | .250 | .250 | .250 |
| Everett, Adam, Hou. | 4 | 4 | 1 | 1 | 0 | 0 | 0 | 0 | 0 | 0 | 1 | 0 | 2 | 0 | 0 | 0 | 0 | 0 | 0 | .000 | .667 | .000 |
| Everett, Carl, Mon.† | 3 | 3 | 3 | 0 | 1 | 1 | 0 | 0 | 0 | 2 | 0 | 0 | 0 | 0 | 0 | 1 | 0 | 0 | 0 | .333 | .333 | .333 |
| Feliz, Pedro, S.F. | 25 | 25 | 22 | 2 | 6 | 8 | 0 | 1 | 0 | 4 | 0 | 0 | 0 | 3 | 0 | 6 | 2 | 0 | 1 | .273 | .360 | .364 |
| Fick, Robert, S.D.* | 12 | 11 | 8 | 2 | 1 | 1 | 0 | 0 | 0 | 0 | 0 | 0 | 1 | 2 | 0 | 4 | 0 | 0 | 0 | .125 | .364 | .125 |
| Finley, Steve, Ari.-L.A.* | 3 | 3 | 2 | 0 | 1 | 1 | 0 | 0 | 0 | 1 | 0 | 1 | 0 | 0 | 0 | 1 | 0 | 0 | 0 | .500 | .333 | .500 |
| Flores, Jose, L.A. | 2 | 1 | 1 | 0 | 0 | 0 | 0 | 0 | 0 | 0 | 0 | 0 | 0 | 0 | 0 | 1 | 0 | 0 | 0 | .000 | .000 | .000 |
| Floyd, Cliff, N.Y.* | 5 | 5 | 5 | 0 | 0 | 0 | 0 | 0 | 0 | 0 | 0 | 0 | 0 | 0 | 0 | 4 | 0 | 0 | 0 | .000 | .000 | .000 |
| Fox, Andy, Mon.* | 21 | 21 | 21 | 0 | 1 | 1 | 0 | 0 | 0 | 0 | 0 | 0 | 0 | 0 | 0 | 11 | 0 | 0 | 1 | .048 | .048 | .048 |
| Franco, Julio, Atl. | 50 | 50 | 43 | 5 | 15 | 24 | 3 | 0 | 2 | 16 | 1 | 0 | 0 | 6 | 1 | 14 | 0 | 0 | 0 | .349 | .429 | .558 |
| Freel, Ryan, Cin. | 3 | 3 | 2 | 0 | 1 | 1 | 0 | 0 | 0 | 0 | 0 | 0 | 1 | 0 | 0 | 0 | 0 | 0 | 0 | .500 | .667 | .500 |
| Freeman, Choo, Col. | 4 | 4 | 3 | 1 | 1 | 2 | 1 | 0 | 0 | 2 | 0 | 0 | 0 | 1 | 0 | 1 | 0 | 0 | 0 | .333 | .500 | .667 |
| Furcal, Rafael, Atl.† | 10 | 10 | 10 | 0 | 4 | 4 | 0 | 0 | 0 | 0 | 0 | 0 | 0 | 0 | 0 | 0 | 0 | 0 | 1 | .400 | .400 | .400 |
| Garcia, Danny, N.Y. | 14 | 13 | 10 | 2 | 2 | 2 | 0 | 0 | 0 | 0 | 2 | 0 | 0 | 1 | 0 | 5 | 0 | 0 | 0 | .200 | .273 | .200 |
| Garcia, Jesse, Atl. | 14 | 14 | 14 | 4 | 5 | 7 | 2 | 0 | 0 | 1 | 0 | 0 | 0 | 0 | 0 | 2 | 0 | 0 | 0 | .357 | .357 | .500 |
| Garcia, Karim, N.Y.* | 15 | 13 | 12 | 2 | 3 | 4 | 1 | 0 | 0 | 1 | 0 | 0 | 0 | 1 | 0 | 5 | 0 | 0 | 1 | .250 | .308 | .333 |
| Garciaparra, Nomar, Chi. | 2 | 2 | 2 | 0 | 1 | 1 | 0 | 0 | 0 | 1 | 0 | 0 | 0 | 0 | 0 | 0 | 0 | 0 | 0 | .500 | .500 | .500 |
| Gil, Jerry, Ari. | 1 | 1 | 1 | 0 | 1 | 1 | 0 | 0 | 0 | 0 | 0 | 0 | 0 | 0 | 0 | 0 | 0 | 0 | 0 | 1.000 | 1.000 | 1.000 |
| Giles, Brian, S.D.* | 1 | 1 | 0 | 1 | 0 | 0 | 0 | 0 | 0 | 0 | 0 | 0 | 0 | 1 | 0 | 0 | 0 | 0 | 0 | .000 | 1.000 | .000 |
| Giles, Marcus, Atl. | 7 | 7 | 5 | 1 | 1 | 4 | 0 | 0 | 1 | 2 | 1 | 1 | 0 | 0 | 0 | 1 | 0 | 0 | 0 | .200 | .167 | .800 |
| Ginter, Keith, Mil. | 10 | 10 | 6 | 1 | 1 | 2 | 1 | 0 | 0 | 1 | 0 | 0 | 0 | 4 | 0 | 1 | 0 | 0 | 0 | .167 | .500 | .333 |
| Glanville, Doug, Phi. | 18 | 18 | 17 | 1 | 2 | 2 | 0 | 0 | 0 | 0 | 1 | 0 | 0 | 0 | 0 | 3 | 0 | 0 | 1 | .118 | .118 | .118 |
| Glavine, Tom, N.Y.* | 2 | 2 | 1 | 0 | 0 | 0 | 0 | 0 | 0 | 0 | 0 | 0 | 0 | 1 | 0 | 0 | 0 | 0 | 0 | .000 | .500 | .000 |
| Gonzalez, Alex, Fla. | 1 | 1 | 1 | 0 | 0 | 0 | 0 | 0 | 0 | 0 | 0 | 0 | 0 | 0 | 0 | 1 | 0 | 0 | 0 | .000 | .000 | .000 |

| Player, Team | G | TPA | AB | R | H | TB | 2B | 3B | HR | RBI | SH | SF | HP | BB | IBB | SO | SB | CS | GDP | Avg. | OBP | Slg. |
|---|---|---|---|---|---|---|---|---|---|---|---|---|---|---|---|---|---|---|---|---|---|---|
| Gonzalez, Alex S., Chi.-Mon.-S.D. | 4 | 4 | 4 | 1 | 2 | 5 | 0 | 0 | 1 | 1 | 0 | 0 | 0 | 0 | 0 | 2 | 0 | 0 | 0 | .500 | .500 | 1.250 |
| Gonzalez, Luis, Ari.* | 1 | 1 | 1 | 1 | 1 | 2 | 1 | 0 | 0 | 1 | 0 | 0 | 0 | 0 | 0 | 0 | 0 | 0 | 0 | 1.000 | 1.000 | 2.000 |
| Gonzalez, Luis A., Col. | 22 | 22 | 21 | 3 | 7 | 14 | 1 | 0 | 2 | 6 | 1 | 0 | 0 | 0 | 0 | 8 | 0 | 0 | 0 | .333 | .333 | .667 |
| Goodwin, Tom, Chi.* | 55 | 54 | 51 | 2 | 10 | 15 | 5 | 0 | 0 | 1 | 0 | 0 | 0 | 3 | 0 | 13 | 3 | 0 | 0 | .196 | .241 | .294 |
| Grabowski, Jason, L.A.* | 81 | 80 | 69 | 5 | 12 | 20 | 5 | 0 | 1 | 5 | 0 | 0 | 0 | 11 | 0 | 25 | 0 | 0 | 1 | .174 | .288 | .290 |
| Green, Andy, Ari. | 11 | 11 | 9 | 2 | 2 | 5 | 0 | 0 | 1 | 2 | 1 | 0 | 0 | 1 | 0 | 5 | 0 | 0 | 0 | .222 | .300 | .556 |
| Green, Nick, Atl. | 9 | 9 | 9 | 2 | 2 | 3 | 1 | 0 | 0 | 0 | 0 | 0 | 0 | 0 | 0 | 4 | 0 | 0 | 0 | .222 | .222 | .333 |
| Green, Shawn, L.A.* | 1 | 1 | 1 | 0 | 1 | 1 | 0 | 0 | 0 | 0 | 0 | 0 | 0 | 0 | 0 | 0 | 0 | 0 | 0 | 1.000 | 1.000 | 1.000 |
| Greene, Todd, Col. | 22 | 21 | 18 | 2 | 5 | 10 | 2 | 0 | 1 | 3 | 0 | 0 | 0 | 3 | 1 | 6 | 0 | 0 | 0 | .278 | .381 | .556 |
| Grieve, Ben, Mil.-Chi.* | 54 | 53 | 48 | 4 | 12 | 20 | 5 | 0 | 1 | 10 | 0 | 2 | 0 | 3 | 0 | 19 | 0 | 0 | 0 | .250 | .283 | .417 |
| Griffey Jr., Ken, Cin.* | 5 | 5 | 5 | 0 | 2 | 2 | 0 | 0 | 0 | 1 | 0 | 0 | 0 | 0 | 0 | 3 | 0 | 0 | 0 | .400 | .400 | .400 |
| Grissom, Marquis, S.F. | 5 | 5 | 5 | 0 | 1 | 2 | 1 | 0 | 0 | 2 | 0 | 0 | 0 | 0 | 0 | 2 | 0 | 0 | 0 | .200 | .200 | .400 |
| Grudzielanek, Mark, Chi. | 11 | 11 | 9 | 0 | 2 | 2 | 0 | 0 | 0 | 0 | 0 | 0 | 0 | 2 | 0 | 3 | 0 | 0 | 0 | .222 | .364 | .222 |
| Gutierrez, Ricky, N.Y. | 5 | 4 | 3 | 0 | 1 | 1 | 0 | 0 | 0 | 0 | 0 | 0 | 0 | 1 | 0 | 1 | 0 | 0 | 0 | .333 | .500 | .333 |
| Guzman, Freddy, S.D.† | 1 | 1 | 1 | 0 | 0 | 0 | 0 | 0 | 0 | 0 | 0 | 0 | 0 | 0 | 0 | 0 | 0 | 0 | 0 | .000 | .000 | .000 |
| Hairston, Scott, Ari. | 14 | 14 | 11 | 1 | 2 | 2 | 0 | 0 | 0 | 2 | 0 | 0 | 0 | 3 | 0 | 5 | 0 | 1 | 0 | .182 | .357 | .182 |
| Hall, Bill, Mil. | 30 | 30 | 29 | 3 | 7 | 13 | 0 | 0 | 2 | 5 | 0 | 0 | 0 | 1 | 0 | 11 | 0 | 0 | 0 | .241 | .267 | .448 |
| Hammock, Robby, Ari. | 4 | 4 | 4 | 0 | 1 | 2 | 1 | 0 | 0 | 0 | 0 | 0 | 0 | 0 | 0 | 0 | 0 | 0 | 1 | .250 | .250 | .500 |
| Hammonds, Jeffrey, S.F. | 13 | 13 | 11 | 3 | 2 | 3 | 1 | 0 | 0 | 2 | 0 | 0 | 2 | 0 | 0 | 4 | 0 | 0 | 0 | .182 | .308 | .273 |
| Hampton, Mike, Atl. | 3 | 3 | 3 | 0 | 0 | 0 | 0 | 0 | 0 | 0 | 0 | 0 | 0 | 0 | 0 | 2 | 0 | 0 | 0 | .000 | .000 | .000 |
| Hansen, Dave, S.D.* | 22 | 20 | 17 | 0 | 2 | 2 | 0 | 0 | 0 | 0 | 0 | 0 | 0 | 3 | 0 | 4 | 0 | 0 | 3 | .118 | .250 | .118 |
| Harris, Brendan, Chi.-Mon. | 7 | 7 | 7 | 0 | 0 | 0 | 0 | 0 | 0 | 0 | 0 | 0 | 0 | 0 | 0 | 3 | 0 | 0 | 0 | .000 | .000 | .000 |
| Harris, Lenny, Fla.* | 64 | 58 | 55 | 4 | 12 | 19 | 4 | 0 | 1 | 9 | 0 | 0 | 0 | 3 | 0 | 5 | 0 | 0 | 1 | .218 | .259 | .345 |
| Hart, Bo, St.L. | 6 | 5 | 4 | 0 | 1 | 1 | 0 | 0 | 0 | 1 | 0 | 0 | 0 | 1 | 0 | 0 | 0 | 0 | 0 | .250 | .400 | .250 |
| Hart, Corey, Mil. | 1 | 1 | 1 | 0 | 0 | 0 | 0 | 0 | 0 | 0 | 0 | 0 | 0 | 0 | 0 | 1 | 0 | 0 | 0 | .000 | .000 | .000 |
| Hawpe, Brad, Col.* | 10 | 10 | 8 | 2 | 2 | 5 | 0 | 0 | 1 | 1 | 0 | 0 | 0 | 2 | 0 | 4 | 0 | 0 | 0 | .250 | .400 | .625 |
| Helms, Wes, Mil. | 16 | 16 | 15 | 0 | 3 | 4 | 1 | 0 | 0 | 1 | 0 | 0 | 0 | 1 | 0 | 3 | 0 | 0 | 0 | .200 | .250 | .267 |
| Helton, Todd, Col.* | 3 | 3 | 2 | 1 | 0 | 0 | 0 | 0 | 0 | 0 | 0 | 0 | 0 | 1 | 1 | 0 | 0 | 0 | 0 | .000 | .333 | .000 |
| Hernandez, Jose, L.A. | 21 | 21 | 19 | 5 | 2 | 5 | 0 | 0 | 1 | 3 | 0 | 0 | 0 | 2 | 0 | 8 | 0 | 0 | 0 | .105 | .190 | .263 |
| Hernandez, Livan, Mon. | 1 | 1 | 0 | 0 | 0 | 0 | 0 | 0 | 0 | 0 | 1 | 0 | 0 | 0 | 0 | 0 | 0 | 0 | 0 | .000 | .000 | .000 |
| Hernandez, Ramon, S.D. | 4 | 3 | 3 | 1 | 1 | 4 | 0 | 0 | 1 | 2 | 0 | 0 | 0 | 0 | 0 | 1 | 0 | 0 | 0 | .333 | .333 | 1.333 |
| Hessman, Mike, Atl. | 9 | 9 | 9 | 1 | 2 | 3 | 1 | 0 | 0 | 2 | 0 | 0 | 0 | 0 | 0 | 3 | 0 | 0 | 0 | .222 | .222 | .333 |
| Hidalgo, Richard, Hou.-N.Y. | 3 | 3 | 3 | 0 | 0 | 0 | 0 | 0 | 0 | 0 | 0 | 0 | 0 | 0 | 0 | 0 | 0 | 0 | 1 | .000 | .000 | .000 |
| Hill, Bobby, Pit.† | 70 | 70 | 60 | 15 | 16 | 26 | 2 | 1 | 2 | 10 | 0 | 1 | 2 | 7 | 0 | 13 | 0 | 1 | 3 | .267 | .357 | .433 |
| Hill, Koyie, Ari.† | 2 | 2 | 2 | 0 | 0 | 0 | 0 | 0 | 0 | 0 | 0 | 0 | 0 | 0 | 0 | 0 | 0 | 0 | 1 | .000 | .000 | .000 |
| Hillenbrand, Shea, Ari. | 2 | 2 | 2 | 0 | 0 | 0 | 0 | 0 | 0 | 0 | 0 | 0 | 0 | 0 | 0 | 2 | 0 | 0 | 0 | .000 | .000 | .000 |
| Hocking, Denny, Col.† | 10 | 10 | 9 | 0 | 4 | 5 | 1 | 0 | 0 | 0 | 0 | 0 | 0 | 1 | 0 | 0 | 0 | 0 | 0 | .444 | .500 | .556 |
| Hollandsworth, Todd, Chi.* | 18 | 18 | 16 | 4 | 9 | 17 | 2 | 0 | 2 | 4 | 0 | 0 | 0 | 2 | 0 | 1 | 0 | 0 | 0 | .563 | .611 | 1.063 |
| Holliday, Matt, Col. | 10 | 10 | 9 | 0 | 1 | 1 | 0 | 0 | 0 | 0 | 0 | 0 | 0 | 1 | 0 | 3 | 0 | 0 | 0 | .111 | .200 | .111 |
| Hollins, Damon, Atl. | 2 | 2 | 2 | 1 | 1 | 1 | 0 | 0 | 0 | 0 | 0 | 0 | 0 | 0 | 0 | 0 | 0 | 0 | 0 | .500 | .500 | .500 |
| House, J.R., Pit. | 2 | 2 | 2 | 0 | 0 | 0 | 0 | 0 | 0 | 0 | 0 | 0 | 0 | 0 | 0 | 1 | 0 | 0 | 0 | .000 | .000 | .000 |
| Howard, Ryan, Phi.* | 11 | 11 | 10 | 2 | 5 | 13 | 2 | 0 | 2 | 4 | 0 | 0 | 0 | 1 | 0 | 4 | 0 | 0 | 1 | .500 | .545 | 1.300 |
| Hummel, Tim, Cin. | 18 | 17 | 12 | 1 | 0 | 0 | 0 | 0 | 0 | 0 | 2 | 0 | 1 | 2 | 0 | 2 | 0 | 0 | 1 | .000 | .200 | .000 |
| Izturis, Maicer, Mon.† | 1 | 1 | 1 | 0 | 0 | 0 | 0 | 0 | 0 | 0 | 0 | 0 | 0 | 0 | 0 | 1 | 0 | 0 | 0 | .000 | .000 | .000 |
| Jackson, Damian, Chi. | 2 | 2 | 2 | 0 | 0 | 0 | 0 | 0 | 0 | 0 | 0 | 0 | 0 | 0 | 0 | 1 | 0 | 0 | 0 | .000 | .000 | .000 |
| Jenkins, Geoff, Mil.* | 1 | 1 | 1 | 0 | 0 | 0 | 0 | 0 | 0 | 0 | 0 | 0 | 0 | 0 | 0 | 0 | 0 | 0 | 0 | .000 | .000 | .000 |
| Jennings, Jason, Col.* | 4 | 4 | 4 | 0 | 2 | 2 | 0 | 0 | 0 | 0 | 0 | 0 | 0 | 0 | 0 | 0 | 0 | 0 | 0 | .500 | .500 | .500 |
| Jimenez, D'Angelo, Cin.† | 4 | 4 | 3 | 1 | 1 | 1 | 0 | 0 | 0 | 0 | 0 | 0 | 0 | 1 | 0 | 2 | 0 | 0 | 0 | .333 | .500 | .333 |
| Johnson, Charles, Col. | 19 | 18 | 12 | 2 | 3 | 6 | 0 | 0 | 1 | 2 | 0 | 0 | 2 | 4 | 0 | 5 | 0 | 0 | 0 | .250 | .500 | .500 |
| Johnson, Mark, Mil.* | 2 | 2 | 2 | 0 | 0 | 0 | 0 | 0 | 0 | 0 | 0 | 0 | 0 | 0 | 0 | 0 | 0 | 0 | 0 | .000 | .000 | .000 |
| Johnson, Nick, Mon.* | 2 | 2 | 2 | 0 | 1 | 1 | 0 | 0 | 0 | 1 | 0 | 0 | 0 | 0 | 0 | 0 | 0 | 0 | 0 | .500 | .500 | .500 |
| Jones, Andruw, Atl. | 1 | 1 | 1 | 0 | 1 | 1 | 0 | 0 | 0 | 0 | 0 | 0 | 0 | 0 | 0 | 0 | 0 | 0 | 0 | 1.000 | 1.000 | 1.000 |
| Jones, Chipper, Atl.† | 7 | 7 | 6 | 0 | 0 | 0 | 0 | 0 | 0 | 1 | 0 | 1 | 0 | 0 | 0 | 4 | 0 | 0 | 0 | .000 | .000 | .000 |
| Kata, Matt, Ari.† | 1 | 1 | 1 | 0 | 0 | 0 | 0 | 0 | 0 | 0 | 0 | 0 | 0 | 0 | 0 | 0 | 0 | 0 | 0 | .000 | .000 | .000 |
| Kearns, Austin, Cin. | 4 | 4 | 4 | 1 | 2 | 5 | 0 | 0 | 1 | 2 | 0 | 0 | 0 | 0 | 0 | 2 | 0 | 0 | 0 | .500 | .500 | 1.250 |
| Kelton, David, Chi. | 6 | 6 | 6 | 0 | 0 | 0 | 0 | 0 | 0 | 0 | 0 | 0 | 0 | 0 | 0 | 2 | 0 | 0 | 0 | .000 | .000 | .000 |
| Kendall, Jason, Pit. | 2 | 2 | 1 | 0 | 0 | 0 | 0 | 0 | 0 | 0 | 0 | 0 | 0 | 1 | 1 | 0 | 0 | 0 | 0 | .000 | .500 | .000 |
| Kent, Jeff, Hou. | 4 | 4 | 2 | 0 | 1 | 2 | 1 | 0 | 0 | 0 | 0 | 0 | 0 | 2 | 1 | 1 | 0 | 0 | 0 | .500 | .750 | 1.000 |
| Keppinger, Jeff, N.Y. | 3 | 3 | 3 | 0 | 0 | 0 | 0 | 0 | 0 | 0 | 0 | 0 | 0 | 0 | 0 | 1 | 0 | 0 | 0 | .000 | .000 | .000 |
| Kieschnick, Brooks, Mil.* | 48 | 47 | 44 | 1 | 11 | 16 | 2 | 0 | 1 | 6 | 0 | 0 | 0 | 3 | 0 | 14 | 0 | 0 | 3 | .250 | .298 | .364 |
| Klesko, Ryan, S.D.* | 7 | 7 | 5 | 0 | 1 | 1 | 0 | 0 | 0 | 1 | 0 | 0 | 0 | 2 | 0 | 1 | 0 | 0 | 0 | .200 | .429 | .200 |
| Knott, Jon, S.D. | 6 | 6 | 6 | 1 | 1 | 2 | 1 | 0 | 0 | 1 | 0 | 0 | 0 | 0 | 0 | 2 | 0 | 0 | 0 | .167 | .167 | .333 |
| Kroeger, Josh, Ari.* | 2 | 2 | 2 | 0 | 0 | 0 | 0 | 0 | 0 | 0 | 0 | 0 | 0 | 0 | 0 | 0 | 0 | 0 | 1 | .000 | .000 | .000 |
| Krynzel, Dave, Mil.* | 6 | 6 | 6 | 0 | 0 | 0 | 0 | 0 | 0 | 0 | 0 | 0 | 0 | 0 | 0 | 3 | 0 | 0 | 0 | .000 | .000 | .000 |
| Labandeira, Josh, Mon. | 3 | 3 | 3 | 0 | 0 | 0 | 0 | 0 | 0 | 0 | 0 | 0 | 0 | 0 | 0 | 0 | 0 | 0 | 0 | .000 | .000 | .000 |
| Lamb, Mike, Hou.* | 42 | 41 | 36 | 3 | 11 | 15 | 1 | 0 | 1 | 10 | 0 | 1 | 0 | 4 | 2 | 10 | 0 | 0 | 0 | .306 | .366 | .417 |
| Lane, Jason, Hou. | 41 | 41 | 36 | 5 | 12 | 19 | 1 | 0 | 2 | 6 | 1 | 0 | 0 | 4 | 0 | 9 | 0 | 0 | 1 | .333 | .400 | .528 |
| Lankford, Ray, St.L.* | 30 | 29 | 22 | 5 | 6 | 12 | 1 | 1 | 1 | 8 | 0 | 3 | 0 | 4 | 0 | 7 | 1 | 0 | 0 | .273 | .345 | .545 |
| Larkin, Barry, Cin. | 28 | 28 | 26 | 4 | 7 | 10 | 0 | 0 | 1 | 4 | 0 | 0 | 0 | 2 | 0 | 5 | 0 | 0 | 2 | .269 | .321 | .385 |
| LaRoche, Adam, Atl.* | 18 | 18 | 17 | 1 | 5 | 8 | 0 | 0 | 1 | 3 | 0 | 1 | 0 | 0 | 0 | 2 | 0 | 0 | 0 | .294 | .278 | .471 |
| Larson, Brandon, Cin. | 6 | 4 | 4 | 1 | 1 | 4 | 0 | 0 | 1 | 2 | 0 | 0 | 0 | 0 | 0 | 2 | 0 | 0 | 0 | .250 | .250 | 1.000 |
| LaRue, Jason, Cin. | 2 | 2 | 2 | 0 | 0 | 0 | 0 | 0 | 0 | 0 | 0 | 0 | 0 | 0 | 0 | 2 | 0 | 0 | 0 | .000 | .000 | .000 |
| Lawrence, Brian, S.D. | 1 | 1 | 1 | 0 | 0 | 0 | 0 | 0 | 0 | 0 | 0 | 0 | 0 | 0 | 0 | 0 | 0 | 0 | 0 | .000 | .000 | .000 |
| Ledee, Ricky, Phi.-S.F.* | 67 | 63 | 53 | 7 | 11 | 19 | 2 | 0 | 2 | 11 | 0 | 0 | 0 | 10 | 2 | 16 | 0 | 0 | 1 | .208 | .333 | .358 |
| Lee, Derrek, Chi. | 1 | 1 | 1 | 0 | 1 | 1 | 0 | 0 | 0 | 0 | 0 | 0 | 0 | 0 | 0 | 0 | 0 | 0 | 0 | 1.000 | 1.000 | 1.000 |
| Lieberthal, Mike, Phi. | 5 | 5 | 5 | 0 | 1 | 1 | 0 | 0 | 0 | 0 | 0 | 0 | 0 | 0 | 0 | 1 | 0 | 0 | 0 | .200 | .200 | .200 |
| Liefer, Jeff, Mil.* | 9 | 8 | 8 | 1 | 2 | 3 | 1 | 0 | 0 | 0 | 0 | 0 | 0 | 0 | 0 | 3 | 0 | 0 | 0 | .250 | .250 | .375 |
| Linden, Todd, S.F.† | 6 | 6 | 5 | 0 | 0 | 0 | 0 | 0 | 0 | 0 | 0 | 0 | 0 | 1 | 0 | 1 | 0 | 0 | 0 | .000 | .167 | .000 |
| Lo Duca, Paul, L.A.-Fla. | 7 | 7 | 6 | 2 | 1 | 4 | 0 | 0 | 1 | 2 | 0 | 0 | 0 | 1 | 0 | 2 | 0 | 0 | 1 | .167 | .286 | .667 |
| Long, Terrence, S.D.* | 58 | 54 | 50 | 5 | 17 | 22 | 2 | 0 | 1 | 8 | 0 | 2 | 0 | 2 | 1 | 5 | 0 | 0 | 0 | .340 | .352 | .440 |
| Lopez, Felipe, Cin.† | 2 | 2 | 2 | 0 | 0 | 0 | 0 | 0 | 0 | 0 | 0 | 0 | 0 | 0 | 0 | 1 | 0 | 0 | 0 | .000 | .000 | .000 |
| Lopez, Luis, Mon. | 4 | 4 | 4 | 0 | 1 | 1 | 0 | 0 | 0 | 0 | 0 | 0 | 0 | 0 | 0 | 2 | 0 | 0 | 0 | .250 | .250 | .250 |
| Lowell, Mike, Fla. | 2 | 2 | 2 | 0 | 0 | 0 | 0 | 0 | 0 | 0 | 0 | 0 | 0 | 0 | 0 | 2 | 0 | 0 | 0 | .000 | .000 | .000 |
| Luna, Hector, St.L. | 28 | 27 | 24 | 2 | 4 | 6 | 2 | 0 | 0 | 1 | 1 | 0 | 0 | 2 | 0 | 11 | 1 | 0 | 1 | .167 | .231 | .250 |
| Mabry, John, St.L.* | 10 | 10 | 7 | 0 | 1 | 1 | 0 | 0 | 0 | 0 | 0 | 0 | 0 | 3 | 0 | 2 | 0 | 0 | 0 | .143 | .400 | .143 |

| Player, Team | G | TPA | AB | R | H | TB | 2B | 3B | HR | RBI | SH | SF | HP | BB | IBB | SO | SB | CS | GDP | Avg. | OBP | Slg. |
|---|---|---|---|---|---|---|---|---|---|---|---|---|---|---|---|---|---|---|---|---|---|---|
| Macias, Jose, Chi.† | 51 | 51 | 47 | 4 | 10 | 10 | 0 | 0 | 0 | 6 | 1 | 0 | 1 | 2 | 0 | 12 | 1 | 0 | 0 | .213 | .260 | .213 |
| Mackowiak, Rob, Pit.* | 24 | 24 | 22 | 1 | 4 | 7 | 1 | 1 | 0 | 4 | 0 | 0 | 1 | 1 | 0 | 6 | 0 | 0 | 0 | .182 | .250 | .318 |
| Maddux, Greg, Chi. | 1 | 1 | 0 | 0 | 0 | 0 | 0 | 0 | 0 | 0 | 1 | 0 | 0 | 0 | 0 | 0 | 0 | 0 | 0 | .000 | .000 | .000 |
| Magruder, Chris, Mil.† | 35 | 35 | 29 | 2 | 5 | 6 | 1 | 0 | 0 | 3 | 0 | 1 | 2 | 3 | 0 | 11 | 0 | 0 | 0 | .172 | .286 | .207 |
| Marrero, Eli, Atl. | 19 | 19 | 16 | 3 | 4 | 5 | 1 | 0 | 0 | 2 | 0 | 1 | 0 | 2 | 0 | 4 | 0 | 0 | 0 | .250 | .316 | .313 |
| Martinez, Ramon, Chi. | 12 | 12 | 11 | 0 | 2 | 3 | 1 | 0 | 0 | 0 | 0 | 0 | 0 | 1 | 0 | 4 | 0 | 0 | 0 | .182 | .250 | .273 |
| Mateo, Henry, Mon.† | 28 | 28 | 27 | 2 | 8 | 8 | 0 | 0 | 0 | 0 | 1 | 0 | 0 | 0 | 0 | 5 | 2 | 2 | 0 | .296 | .296 | .296 |
| Mateo, Ruben, Pit. | 9 | 6 | 4 | 0 | 1 | 1 | 0 | 0 | 0 | 1 | 0 | 0 | 0 | 2 | 1 | 0 | 0 | 0 | 1 | .250 | .500 | .250 |
| Matheny, Mike, St.L. | 2 | 2 | 2 | 0 | 0 | 0 | 0 | 0 | 0 | 0 | 0 | 0 | 0 | 0 | 0 | 1 | 0 | 0 | 0 | .000 | .000 | .000 |
| Matsui, Kazuo, N.Y.† | 2 | 2 | 2 | 0 | 1 | 1 | 0 | 0 | 0 | 0 | 0 | 0 | 0 | 0 | 0 | 1 | 0 | 0 | 0 | .500 | .500 | .500 |
| Mayne, Brent, Ari.-L.A.* | 9 | 9 | 7 | 0 | 1 | 1 | 0 | 0 | 0 | 1 | 2 | 0 | 0 | 0 | 0 | 3 | 0 | 0 | 0 | .143 | .143 | .143 |
| McCracken, Quinton, Ari.† | 19 | 19 | 16 | 2 | 5 | 9 | 1 | 0 | 1 | 3 | 0 | 0 | 0 | 3 | 0 | 6 | 0 | 0 | 0 | .313 | .421 | .563 |
| McEwing, Joe, N.Y. | 11 | 11 | 10 | 2 | 5 | 5 | 0 | 0 | 0 | 1 | 1 | 0 | 0 | 0 | 0 | 0 | 0 | 0 | 0 | .500 | .500 | .500 |
| McKay, Cody, St.L.* | 16 | 16 | 15 | 2 | 2 | 2 | 0 | 0 | 0 | 1 | 0 | 0 | 1 | 0 | 0 | 2 | 0 | 0 | 1 | .133 | .188 | .133 |
| Michaels, Jason, Phi. | 39 | 39 | 34 | 2 | 9 | 9 | 0 | 0 | 0 | 1 | 0 | 0 | 0 | 5 | 0 | 10 | 0 | 0 | 0 | .265 | .359 | .265 |
| Miles, Aaron, Col.† | 12 | 12 | 10 | 3 | 3 | 3 | 0 | 0 | 0 | 1 | 1 | 0 | 0 | 1 | 0 | 1 | 1 | 0 | 1 | .300 | .364 | .300 |
| Miller, Corky, Cin. | 1 | 1 | 1 | 0 | 0 | 0 | 0 | 0 | 0 | 0 | 0 | 0 | 0 | 0 | 0 | 0 | 0 | 0 | 0 | .000 | .000 | .000 |
| Miller, Wade, Hou. | 1 | 1 | 1 | 0 | 0 | 0 | 0 | 0 | 0 | 0 | 0 | 0 | 0 | 0 | 0 | 1 | 0 | 0 | 0 | .000 | .000 | .000 |
| Minor, Damon, S.F.* | 8 | 7 | 5 | 0 | 2 | 2 | 0 | 0 | 0 | 1 | 0 | 0 | 0 | 2 | 0 | 1 | 0 | 0 | 1 | .400 | .571 | .400 |
| Moeller, Chad, Mil. | 1 | 1 | 1 | 0 | 0 | 0 | 0 | 0 | 0 | 0 | 0 | 0 | 0 | 0 | 0 | 1 | 0 | 0 | 0 | .000 | .000 | .000 |
| Mohr, Dustan, S.F. | 26 | 26 | 18 | 8 | 7 | 17 | 4 | 0 | 2 | 3 | 0 | 0 | 1 | 7 | 0 | 5 | 0 | 0 | 0 | .389 | .577 | .944 |
| Molina, Yadier, St.L. | 1 | 1 | 1 | 0 | 1 | 1 | 0 | 0 | 0 | 0 | 0 | 0 | 0 | 0 | 0 | 0 | 0 | 0 | 0 | 1.000 | 1.000 | 1.000 |
| Mordecai, Mike, Fla. | 45 | 45 | 39 | 2 | 9 | 10 | 1 | 0 | 0 | 0 | 0 | 0 | 0 | 6 | 0 | 12 | 0 | 1 | 0 | .231 | .333 | .256 |
| Murray, Calvin, Chi. | 2 | 2 | 2 | 0 | 1 | 1 | 0 | 0 | 0 | 1 | 0 | 0 | 0 | 0 | 0 | 0 | 0 | 0 | 0 | .500 | .500 | .500 |
| Nady, Xavier, S.D. | 11 | 11 | 8 | 2 | 1 | 1 | 0 | 0 | 0 | 0 | 0 | 0 | 0 | 3 | 0 | 0 | 0 | 0 | 2 | .125 | .364 | .125 |
| Nevin, Phil, S.D. | 2 | 1 | 1 | 0 | 0 | 0 | 0 | 0 | 0 | 0 | 0 | 0 | 0 | 0 | 0 | 0 | 0 | 0 | 0 | .000 | .000 | .000 |
| Nunez, Abraham, Fla.† | 9 | 9 | 8 | 0 | 1 | 1 | 0 | 0 | 0 | 0 | 1 | 0 | 0 | 0 | 0 | 2 | 0 | 0 | 0 | .125 | .125 | .125 |
| Nunez, Abraham O., Pit.† | 68 | 68 | 62 | 4 | 15 | 20 | 2 | 0 | 1 | 6 | 1 | 1 | 0 | 4 | 0 | 16 | 0 | 2 | 1 | .242 | .284 | .323 |
| Obermueller, Wes, Mil. | 1 | 1 | 1 | 0 | 0 | 0 | 0 | 0 | 0 | 0 | 0 | 0 | 0 | 0 | 0 | 1 | 0 | 0 | 0 | .000 | .000 | .000 |
| Ojeda, Miguel, S.D. | 17 | 15 | 14 | 2 | 2 | 6 | 1 | 0 | 1 | 3 | 0 | 0 | 0 | 1 | 0 | 4 | 0 | 0 | 0 | .143 | .200 | .429 |
| Oliver, Darren, Fla.-Hou. | 2 | 2 | 2 | 0 | 0 | 0 | 0 | 0 | 0 | 0 | 0 | 0 | 0 | 0 | 0 | 1 | 0 | 0 | 1 | .000 | .000 | .000 |
| Olmedo, Ray, Cin.† | 1 | 1 | 0 | 0 | 0 | 0 | 0 | 0 | 0 | 0 | 0 | 0 | 0 | 1 | 0 | 0 | 0 | 0 | 0 | .000 | 1.000 | .000 |
| Olson, Tim, Ari. | 11 | 11 | 11 | 1 | 2 | 2 | 0 | 0 | 0 | 1 | 0 | 0 | 0 | 0 | 0 | 1 | 0 | 0 | 0 | .182 | .182 | .182 |
| Ordonez, Rey, Chi. | 1 | 1 | 1 | 0 | 0 | 0 | 0 | 0 | 0 | 0 | 0 | 0 | 0 | 0 | 0 | 0 | 0 | 0 | 0 | .000 | .000 | .000 |
| Overbay, Lyle, Mil.* | 4 | 4 | 4 | 0 | 1 | 2 | 1 | 0 | 0 | 1 | 0 | 0 | 0 | 0 | 0 | 2 | 0 | 0 | 0 | .250 | .250 | .500 |
| Palmeiro, Orlando, Hou.* | 76 | 73 | 61 | 9 | 15 | 20 | 2 | 0 | 1 | 4 | 2 | 0 | 1 | 9 | 0 | 12 | 2 | 0 | 0 | .246 | .352 | .328 |
| Pascucci, Val, Mon. | 13 | 13 | 10 | 0 | 2 | 2 | 0 | 0 | 0 | 0 | 0 | 0 | 0 | 3 | 1 | 7 | 0 | 0 | 1 | .200 | .385 | .200 |
| Patterson, Corey, Chi.* | 2 | 2 | 2 | 0 | 0 | 0 | 0 | 0 | 0 | 0 | 0 | 0 | 0 | 0 | 0 | 1 | 0 | 0 | 0 | .000 | .000 | .000 |
| Payton, Jay, S.D. | 11 | 10 | 10 | 1 | 2 | 3 | 1 | 0 | 0 | 2 | 0 | 0 | 0 | 0 | 0 | 2 | 0 | 0 | 0 | .200 | .200 | .300 |
| Pellow, Kit, Col. | 20 | 20 | 18 | 1 | 4 | 6 | 0 | 1 | 0 | 0 | 0 | 0 | 1 | 1 | 0 | 10 | 0 | 0 | 0 | .222 | .300 | .333 |
| Pena, Wily Mo, Cin. | 21 | 20 | 19 | 3 | 4 | 10 | 0 | 0 | 2 | 6 | 0 | 0 | 1 | 0 | 0 | 9 | 0 | 0 | 2 | .211 | .250 | .526 |
| Perez, Antonio, L.A. | 8 | 8 | 7 | 1 | 2 | 2 | 0 | 0 | 0 | 0 | 0 | 0 | 1 | 0 | 0 | 2 | 1 | 0 | 0 | .286 | .375 | .286 |
| Perez, Eddie, Atl. | 9 | 9 | 8 | 0 | 1 | 1 | 0 | 0 | 0 | 1 | 0 | 0 | 0 | 1 | 0 | 3 | 0 | 0 | 0 | .125 | .222 | .125 |
| Perez, Neifi, S.F.-Chi.† | 14 | 13 | 13 | 1 | 6 | 7 | 1 | 0 | 0 | 1 | 0 | 0 | 0 | 0 | 0 | 2 | 0 | 0 | 0 | .462 | .462 | .538 |
| Perez, Tomas, Phi.† | 29 | 29 | 28 | 4 | 5 | 8 | 0 | 0 | 1 | 5 | 0 | 0 | 0 | 1 | 0 | 11 | 0 | 0 | 0 | .179 | .207 | .286 |
| Phillips, Jason, N.Y. | 11 | 10 | 10 | 0 | 1 | 1 | 0 | 0 | 0 | 0 | 0 | 0 | 0 | 0 | 0 | 2 | 0 | 0 | 0 | .100 | .100 | .100 |
| Piazza, Mike, N.Y. | 6 | 6 | 5 | 0 | 0 | 0 | 0 | 0 | 0 | 0 | 0 | 0 | 0 | 1 | 0 | 2 | 0 | 0 | 0 | .000 | .167 | .000 |
| Piedra, Jorge, Col.* | 9 | 9 | 9 | 2 | 3 | 3 | 0 | 0 | 0 | 2 | 0 | 0 | 0 | 0 | 0 | 4 | 0 | 0 | 0 | .333 | .333 | .333 |
| Pierzynski, A.J., S.F.* | 14 | 13 | 12 | 2 | 3 | 4 | 1 | 0 | 0 | 2 | 0 | 0 | 0 | 1 | 0 | 1 | 0 | 0 | 1 | .250 | .308 | .333 |
| Podsednik, Scott, Mil.* | 2 | 2 | 2 | 0 | 0 | 0 | 0 | 0 | 0 | 0 | 0 | 0 | 0 | 0 | 0 | 0 | 0 | 0 | 0 | .000 | .000 | .000 |
| Polanco, Placido, Phi. | 8 | 8 | 8 | 1 | 2 | 2 | 0 | 0 | 0 | 1 | 0 | 0 | 0 | 0 | 0 | 1 | 0 | 0 | 0 | .250 | .250 | .250 |
| Porter, Colin, St.L.* | 12 | 12 | 12 | 1 | 4 | 7 | 0 | 0 | 1 | 1 | 0 | 0 | 0 | 0 | 0 | 3 | 0 | 0 | 1 | .333 | .333 | .583 |
| Pratt, Todd, Phi. | 2 | 2 | 1 | 0 | 0 | 0 | 0 | 0 | 0 | 0 | 0 | 0 | 0 | 1 | 0 | 1 | 0 | 0 | 0 | .000 | .500 | .000 |
| Pujols, Albert, St.L. | 1 | 1 | 1 | 0 | 0 | 0 | 0 | 0 | 0 | 0 | 0 | 0 | 0 | 0 | 0 | 1 | 0 | 0 | 0 | .000 | .000 | .000 |
| Quintero, Humberto, S.D. | 2 | 2 | 2 | 0 | 0 | 0 | 0 | 0 | 0 | 0 | 0 | 0 | 0 | 0 | 0 | 1 | 0 | 0 | 0 | .000 | .000 | .000 |
| Ramirez, Aramis, Chi. | 4 | 4 | 4 | 0 | 0 | 0 | 0 | 0 | 0 | 0 | 0 | 0 | 0 | 0 | 0 | 0 | 0 | 0 | 1 | .000 | .000 | .000 |
| Ransom, Cody, S.F. | 15 | 15 | 12 | 0 | 2 | 3 | 1 | 0 | 0 | 0 | 1 | 0 | 0 | 2 | 0 | 5 | 0 | 0 | 0 | .167 | .286 | .250 |
| Redman, Tike, Pit.* | 13 | 13 | 11 | 3 | 4 | 5 | 1 | 0 | 0 | 2 | 0 | 0 | 0 | 2 | 0 | 1 | 1 | 0 | 0 | .364 | .462 | .455 |
| Redmond, Mike, Fla. | 3 | 3 | 3 | 0 | 1 | 1 | 0 | 0 | 0 | 0 | 0 | 0 | 0 | 0 | 0 | 0 | 0 | 0 | 0 | .333 | .333 | .333 |
| Renteria, Edgar, St.L. | 1 | 1 | 1 | 1 | 1 | 1 | 0 | 0 | 0 | 0 | 0 | 0 | 0 | 0 | 0 | 0 | 0 | 0 | 0 | 1.000 | 1.000 | 1.000 |
| Reyes, Jose, N.Y.† | 4 | 4 | 4 | 0 | 1 | 2 | 1 | 0 | 0 | 0 | 0 | 0 | 0 | 0 | 0 | 0 | 0 | 0 | 0 | .250 | .250 | .500 |
| Reyes, Rene, Col.† | 8 | 8 | 7 | 1 | 1 | 2 | 1 | 0 | 0 | 0 | 0 | 0 | 0 | 1 | 0 | 0 | 0 | 0 | 0 | .143 | .250 | .286 |
| Rivera, Juan, Mon. | 21 | 21 | 18 | 1 | 2 | 6 | 1 | 0 | 1 | 2 | 0 | 0 | 0 | 3 | 1 | 4 | 0 | 0 | 2 | .111 | .238 | .333 |
| Roberts, Dave, L.A.* | 7 | 7 | 5 | 1 | 1 | 1 | 0 | 0 | 0 | 0 | 0 | 0 | 0 | 2 | 0 | 1 | 1 | 0 | 0 | .200 | .429 | .200 |
| Robinson, Kerry, S.D.* | 29 | 29 | 26 | 3 | 5 | 6 | 1 | 0 | 0 | 1 | 1 | 1 | 0 | 1 | 0 | 4 | 1 | 0 | 0 | .192 | .214 | .231 |
| Romano, Jason, Cin. | 11 | 11 | 9 | 1 | 0 | 0 | 0 | 0 | 0 | 0 | 1 | 0 | 0 | 1 | 0 | 2 | 0 | 0 | 0 | .000 | .100 | .000 |
| Ross, David, L.A. | 5 | 4 | 2 | 0 | 0 | 0 | 0 | 0 | 0 | 0 | 0 | 0 | 0 | 2 | 0 | 1 | 0 | 0 | 0 | .000 | .500 | .000 |
| Rueter, Kirk, S.F.* | 1 | 1 | 1 | 0 | 1 | 1 | 0 | 0 | 0 | 0 | 0 | 0 | 0 | 0 | 0 | 0 | 0 | 0 | 0 | 1.000 | 1.000 | 1.000 |
| Rusch, Glendon, Chi.* | 1 | 1 | 1 | 0 | 0 | 0 | 0 | 0 | 0 | 0 | 0 | 0 | 0 | 0 | 0 | 0 | 0 | 0 | 0 | .000 | .000 | .000 |
| Sadler, Donnie, Ari. | 6 | 6 | 5 | 1 | 1 | 2 | 1 | 0 | 0 | 0 | 0 | 0 | 0 | 1 | 0 | 0 | 0 | 0 | 0 | .200 | .333 | .400 |
| Saenz, Olmedo, L.A. | 55 | 55 | 48 | 6 | 15 | 25 | 1 | 0 | 3 | 13 | 0 | 3 | 0 | 4 | 1 | 17 | 0 | 0 | 2 | .313 | .345 | .521 |
| Sanchez, Freddy, Pit. | 3 | 3 | 3 | 0 | 0 | 0 | 0 | 0 | 0 | 0 | 0 | 0 | 0 | 0 | 0 | 1 | 0 | 0 | 0 | .000 | .000 | .000 |
| Sanders, Reggie, St.L. | 18 | 18 | 17 | 1 | 7 | 10 | 1 | 1 | 0 | 7 | 0 | 0 | 0 | 1 | 0 | 4 | 2 | 0 | 0 | .412 | .444 | .588 |
| Schneider, Brian, Mon.* | 5 | 5 | 4 | 0 | 1 | 1 | 0 | 0 | 0 | 0 | 0 | 0 | 0 | 1 | 0 | 0 | 0 | 0 | 0 | .250 | .400 | .250 |
| Simon, Randall, Pit.* | 14 | 14 | 12 | 1 | 1 | 2 | 1 | 0 | 0 | 2 | 0 | 0 | 0 | 2 | 0 | 1 | 0 | 0 | 1 | .083 | .214 | .167 |
| Simontacchi, Jason, St.L. | 1 | 1 | 1 | 0 | 0 | 0 | 0 | 0 | 0 | 0 | 0 | 0 | 0 | 0 | 0 | 0 | 0 | 0 | 0 | .000 | .000 | .000 |
| Sledge, Terrmel, Mon.* | 17 | 17 | 15 | 2 | 3 | 3 | 0 | 0 | 0 | 1 | 0 | 0 | 0 | 2 | 0 | 3 | 0 | 0 | 0 | .200 | .294 | .200 |
| Snow, J.T., S.F.* | 9 | 9 | 6 | 2 | 2 | 5 | 0 | 0 | 1 | 1 | 0 | 0 | 0 | 3 | 0 | 2 | 0 | 0 | 0 | .333 | .556 | .833 |
| Spencer, Shane, N.Y. | 21 | 21 | 21 | 1 | 4 | 5 | 1 | 0 | 0 | 2 | 0 | 0 | 0 | 0 | 0 | 4 | 0 | 0 | 0 | .190 | .190 | .238 |
| Spivey, Junior, Mil. | 1 | 1 | 1 | 0 | 0 | 0 | 0 | 0 | 0 | 0 | 0 | 0 | 0 | 0 | 0 | 1 | 0 | 0 | 0 | .000 | .000 | .000 |
| Stynes, Chris, Pit. | 6 | 6 | 6 | 0 | 2 | 2 | 0 | 0 | 0 | 1 | 0 | 0 | 0 | 0 | 0 | 1 | 0 | 0 | 0 | .333 | .333 | .333 |
| Sutton, Larry, Fla.* | 7 | 6 | 5 | 0 | 1 | 1 | 0 | 0 | 0 | 1 | 0 | 0 | 0 | 1 | 0 | 2 | 0 | 0 | 0 | .200 | .333 | .200 |
| Sweeney, Mark, Col.* | 82 | 82 | 65 | 10 | 16 | 36 | 5 | 0 | 5 | 23 | 0 | 3 | 2 | 12 | 2 | 21 | 0 | 0 | 1 | .246 | .366 | .554 |
| Taguchi, So, St.L. | 19 | 18 | 15 | 0 | 4 | 5 | 1 | 0 | 0 | 3 | 1 | 1 | 0 | 1 | 0 | 2 | 0 | 1 | 1 | .267 | .294 | .333 |
| Terrero, Luis, Ari. | 1 | 1 | 1 | 0 | 0 | 0 | 0 | 0 | 0 | 0 | 0 | 0 | 0 | 0 | 0 | 0 | 0 | 0 | 0 | .000 | .000 | .000 |

| Player, Team | G | TPA | AB | R | H | TB | 2B | 3B | HR | RBI | SH | SF | HP | BB | IBB | SO | SB | CS | GDP | Avg. | OBP | Slg. |
|---|---|---|---|---|---|---|---|---|---|---|---|---|---|---|---|---|---|---|---|---|---|---|
| Thomas, Charles, Atl.* | 9 | 9 | 9 | 2 | 4 | 6 | 0 | 1 | 0 | 0 | 0 | 0 | 0 | 0 | 0 | 1 | 1 | 0 | 0 | .444 | .444 | .667 |
| Thome, Jim, Phi.* | 3 | 2 | 0 | 0 | 0 | 0 | 0 | 0 | 0 | 1 | 0 | 0 | 0 | 2 | 0 | 0 | 0 | 0 | 0 | .000 | 1.000 | .000 |
| Thurston, Joe, L.A.* | 12 | 12 | 12 | 1 | 3 | 6 | 1 | 1 | 0 | 0 | 0 | 0 | 0 | 0 | 0 | 2 | 0 | 0 | 0 | .250 | .250 | .500 |
| Tomko, Brett, S.F. | 1 | 1 | 1 | 0 | 0 | 0 | 0 | 0 | 0 | 0 | 0 | 0 | 0 | 0 | 0 | 1 | 0 | 0 | 0 | .000 | .000 | .000 |
| Torcato, Tony, S.F.* | 12 | 12 | 9 | 0 | 5 | 5 | 0 | 0 | 0 | 2 | 0 | 1 | 1 | 1 | 0 | 0 | 0 | 0 | 0 | .556 | .583 | .556 |
| Torrealba, Yorvit, S.F. | 4 | 4 | 4 | 0 | 0 | 0 | 0 | 0 | 0 | 0 | 0 | 0 | 0 | 0 | 0 | 1 | 0 | 0 | 0 | .000 | .000 | .000 |
| Trachsel, Steve, N.Y. | 1 | 1 | 1 | 0 | 0 | 0 | 0 | 0 | 0 | 0 | 0 | 0 | 0 | 0 | 0 | 0 | 0 | 0 | 0 | .000 | .000 | .000 |
| Tracy, Andy, Col.* | 14 | 14 | 13 | 0 | 1 | 2 | 1 | 0 | 0 | 0 | 0 | 0 | 0 | 1 | 0 | 8 | 0 | 0 | 0 | .077 | .143 | .154 |
| Tracy, Chad, Ari.* | 10 | 10 | 9 | 3 | 5 | 9 | 1 | 0 | 1 | 1 | 0 | 0 | 0 | 1 | 0 | 3 | 0 | 0 | 0 | .556 | .600 | 1.000 |
| Treanor, Matt, Fla. | 3 | 3 | 3 | 0 | 1 | 1 | 0 | 0 | 0 | 1 | 0 | 0 | 0 | 0 | 0 | 0 | 0 | 0 | 0 | .333 | .333 | .333 |
| Tucker, Michael, S.F.* | 19 | 18 | 12 | 4 | 5 | 7 | 2 | 0 | 0 | 2 | 0 | 0 | 0 | 6 | 1 | 1 | 0 | 0 | 0 | .417 | .611 | .583 |
| Tucker, T.J., Mon. | 2 | 2 | 2 | 0 | 0 | 0 | 0 | 0 | 0 | 0 | 0 | 0 | 0 | 0 | 0 | 0 | 0 | 0 | 0 | .000 | .000 | .000 |
| Utley, Chase, Phi.* | 34 | 34 | 31 | 5 | 11 | 22 | 2 | 0 | 3 | 10 | 0 | 0 | 0 | 3 | 1 | 10 | 0 | 0 | 0 | .355 | .412 | .710 |
| Valent, Eric, N.Y.* | 64 | 59 | 50 | 3 | 10 | 20 | 1 | 0 | 3 | 7 | 0 | 0 | 0 | 9 | 0 | 16 | 0 | 1 | 0 | .200 | .322 | .400 |
| Valentin, Javier, Cin.† | 23 | 23 | 20 | 1 | 2 | 2 | 0 | 0 | 0 | 3 | 0 | 0 | 1 | 2 | 0 | 7 | 0 | 0 | 0 | .100 | .217 | .100 |
| Vander Wal, John, Cin.* | 32 | 31 | 27 | 0 | 1 | 1 | 0 | 0 | 0 | 0 | 0 | 0 | 0 | 4 | 0 | 13 | 0 | 0 | 0 | .037 | .161 | .037 |
| Vazquez, Ramon, S.D.* | 18 | 18 | 13 | 2 | 3 | 3 | 0 | 0 | 0 | 2 | 2 | 1 | 0 | 2 | 0 | 2 | 0 | 0 | 0 | .231 | .313 | .231 |
| Ventura, Robin, L.A.* | 61 | 57 | 48 | 7 | 13 | 22 | 0 | 0 | 3 | 14 | 0 | 1 | 0 | 8 | 0 | 12 | 0 | 0 | 1 | .271 | .368 | .458 |
| Vidro, Jose, Mon.† | 2 | 2 | 2 | 0 | 1 | 1 | 0 | 0 | 0 | 1 | 0 | 0 | 0 | 0 | 0 | 0 | 0 | 0 | 0 | .500 | .500 | .500 |
| Vizcaino, Jose, Hou.† | 45 | 45 | 39 | 3 | 9 | 12 | 1 | 1 | 0 | 7 | 0 | 0 | 0 | 6 | 1 | 6 | 0 | 0 | 2 | .231 | .333 | .308 |
| Vogelsong, Ryan, Pit. | 2 | 2 | 1 | 0 | 0 | 0 | 0 | 0 | 0 | 0 | 1 | 0 | 0 | 0 | 0 | 1 | 0 | 0 | 0 | .000 | .000 | .000 |
| Walker, Larry, Col.-St.L.* | 9 | 9 | 8 | 1 | 2 | 2 | 0 | 0 | 0 | 0 | 0 | 0 | 0 | 1 | 1 | 2 | 0 | 0 | 0 | .250 | .333 | .250 |
| Walker, Todd, Chi.* | 36 | 36 | 31 | 3 | 6 | 6 | 0 | 0 | 0 | 3 | 0 | 1 | 0 | 4 | 3 | 7 | 0 | 0 | 1 | .194 | .278 | .194 |
| Ward, Daryle, Pit.* | 5 | 5 | 5 | 0 | 0 | 0 | 0 | 0 | 0 | 0 | 0 | 0 | 0 | 0 | 0 | 2 | 0 | 0 | 0 | .000 | .000 | .000 |
| Wells, Kip, Pit. | 1 | 1 | 0 | 0 | 0 | 0 | 0 | 0 | 0 | 0 | 1 | 0 | 0 | 0 | 0 | 0 | 0 | 0 | 0 | .000 | .000 | .000 |
| Werth, Jayson, L.A. | 10 | 9 | 9 | 2 | 2 | 5 | 0 | 0 | 1 | 2 | 0 | 0 | 0 | 0 | 0 | 3 | 0 | 0 | 0 | .222 | .222 | .556 |
| Wigginton, Ty, N.Y.-Pit. | 6 | 6 | 5 | 0 | 2 | 2 | 0 | 0 | 0 | 2 | 0 | 0 | 0 | 1 | 0 | 0 | 0 | 0 | 0 | .400 | .500 | .400 |
| Wilkerson, Brad, Mon.* | 3 | 3 | 3 | 0 | 0 | 0 | 0 | 0 | 0 | 0 | 0 | 0 | 0 | 0 | 0 | 0 | 0 | 0 | 0 | .000 | .000 | .000 |
| Williams, Gerald, N.Y. | 14 | 14 | 13 | 3 | 3 | 7 | 1 | 0 | 1 | 3 | 0 | 0 | 0 | 1 | 0 | 3 | 0 | 0 | 0 | .231 | .286 | .538 |
| Williams, Woody, St.L. | 3 | 3 | 3 | 0 | 0 | 0 | 0 | 0 | 0 | 0 | 0 | 0 | 0 | 0 | 0 | 2 | 0 | 0 | 0 | .000 | .000 | .000 |
| Willingham, Josh, Fla. | 6 | 6 | 5 | 0 | 0 | 0 | 0 | 0 | 0 | 0 | 0 | 0 | 0 | 1 | 0 | 2 | 0 | 0 | 0 | .000 | .167 | .000 |
| Willis, Dontrelle, Fla.* | 10 | 10 | 8 | 0 | 3 | 5 | 0 | 1 | 0 | 0 | 1 | 0 | 0 | 1 | 0 | 3 | 0 | 0 | 0 | .375 | .444 | .625 |
| Wilson, Craig, Pit. | 4 | 4 | 4 | 2 | 2 | 8 | 0 | 0 | 2 | 2 | 0 | 0 | 0 | 0 | 0 | 2 | 0 | 0 | 0 | .500 | .500 | 2.000 |
| Wilson, Jack, Pit. | 2 | 2 | 2 | 0 | 1 | 1 | 0 | 0 | 0 | 0 | 0 | 0 | 0 | 0 | 0 | 1 | 0 | 0 | 0 | .500 | .500 | .500 |
| Wilson, Preston, Col. | 7 | 7 | 7 | 0 | 1 | 1 | 0 | 0 | 0 | 1 | 0 | 0 | 0 | 0 | 0 | 3 | 0 | 0 | 0 | .143 | .143 | .143 |
| Wilson, Tom, N.Y.-L.A. | 4 | 4 | 4 | 0 | 0 | 0 | 0 | 0 | 0 | 0 | 0 | 0 | 0 | 0 | 0 | 2 | 0 | 0 | 0 | .000 | .000 | .000 |
| Wilson, Vance, N.Y. | 13 | 13 | 10 | 3 | 4 | 8 | 1 | 0 | 1 | 2 | 0 | 0 | 1 | 2 | 0 | 1 | 0 | 0 | 0 | .400 | .538 | .800 |
| Wise, Dewayne, Atl.* | 27 | 26 | 25 | 3 | 6 | 12 | 1 | 1 | 1 | 4 | 1 | 0 | 0 | 0 | 0 | 6 | 0 | 0 | 0 | .240 | .240 | .480 |
| Wolf, Randy, Phi.* | 1 | 1 | 1 | 0 | 0 | 0 | 0 | 0 | 0 | 0 | 0 | 0 | 0 | 0 | 0 | 0 | 0 | 0 | 0 | .000 | .000 | .000 |
| Womack, Tony, St.L.* | 16 | 16 | 14 | 2 | 3 | 5 | 0 | 1 | 0 | 3 | 1 | 1 | 0 | 0 | 0 | 2 | 0 | 0 | 1 | .214 | .200 | .357 |
| Wooten, Shawn, Phi. | 19 | 19 | 17 | 0 | 2 | 2 | 0 | 0 | 0 | 0 | 0 | 0 | 1 | 1 | 0 | 4 | 0 | 0 | 1 | .118 | .211 | .118 |
| Zeile, Todd, N.Y. | 43 | 43 | 39 | 1 | 6 | 11 | 2 | 0 | 1 | 2 | 0 | 0 | 0 | 4 | 0 | 12 | 0 | 0 | 2 | .154 | .233 | .282 |
| Zinter, Alan, Ari.† | 19 | 19 | 17 | 0 | 2 | 3 | 1 | 0 | 0 | 1 | 0 | 0 | 0 | 2 | 0 | 9 | 0 | 0 | 0 | .118 | .211 | .176 |

## PINCH-HITTERS WITH TWO OR MORE TEAMS

| Player, Team | G | TPA | AB | R | H | TB | 2B | 3B | HR | RBI | SH | SF | HP | BB | IBB | SO | SB | CS | GDP | Avg. | OBP | Slg. |
|---|---|---|---|---|---|---|---|---|---|---|---|---|---|---|---|---|---|---|---|---|---|---|
| Bragg, Darren, S.D.* | 9 | 9 | 7 | 2 | 1 | 1 | 0 | 0 | 0 | 0 | 0 | 0 | 0 | 2 | 0 | 2 | 0 | 0 | 0 | .143 | .333 | .143 |
| Bragg, Darren, Cin.* | 14 | 14 | 11 | 2 | 2 | 2 | 0 | 0 | 0 | 0 | 1 | 0 | 0 | 2 | 0 | 4 | 1 | 0 | 0 | .182 | .308 | .182 |
| Buchanan, Brian, S.D. | 18 | 18 | 15 | 1 | 2 | 5 | 0 | 0 | 1 | 1 | 0 | 0 | 1 | 2 | 1 | 4 | 0 | 0 | 0 | .133 | .278 | .333 |
| Buchanan, Brian, N.Y. | 1 | 1 | 1 | 0 | 0 | 0 | 0 | 0 | 0 | 0 | 0 | 0 | 0 | 0 | 0 | 1 | 0 | 0 | 0 | .000 | .000 | .000 |
| Choi, Hee Seop, Fla.* | 7 | 7 | 5 | 0 | 0 | 0 | 0 | 0 | 0 | 0 | 0 | 0 | 0 | 2 | 0 | 2 | 0 | 0 | 0 | .000 | .286 | .000 |
| Choi, Hee Seop, L.A.* | 8 | 8 | 6 | 1 | 0 | 0 | 0 | 0 | 0 | 1 | 0 | 0 | 0 | 2 | 1 | 3 | 0 | 0 | 0 | .000 | .250 | .000 |
| Encarnacion, Juan, L.A. | 1 | 1 | 1 | 0 | 0 | 0 | 0 | 0 | 0 | 0 | 0 | 0 | 0 | 0 | 0 | 0 | 0 | 0 | 0 | .000 | .000 | .000 |
| Encarnacion, Juan, Fla. | 1 | 1 | 1 | 0 | 0 | 0 | 0 | 0 | 0 | 0 | 0 | 0 | 0 | 0 | 0 | 0 | 0 | 0 | 0 | .000 | .000 | .000 |
| Gonzalez, Alex S., Chi. | 2 | 2 | 2 | 1 | 1 | 4 | 0 | 0 | 1 | 1 | 0 | 0 | 0 | 0 | 0 | 1 | 0 | 0 | 0 | .500 | .500 | 2.000 |
| Gonzalez, Alex S., Mon. | 2 | 2 | 2 | 0 | 1 | 1 | 0 | 0 | 0 | 0 | 0 | 0 | 0 | 0 | 0 | 1 | 0 | 0 | 0 | .500 | .500 | .500 |
| Grieve, Ben, Mil.* | 42 | 41 | 37 | 3 | 9 | 15 | 3 | 0 | 1 | 5 | 0 | 1 | 0 | 3 | 0 | 15 | 0 | 0 | 0 | .243 | .293 | .405 |
| Grieve, Ben, Chi.* | 12 | 12 | 11 | 1 | 3 | 5 | 2 | 0 | 0 | 5 | 0 | 1 | 0 | 0 | 0 | 4 | 0 | 0 | 0 | .273 | .250 | .455 |
| Ledee, Ricky, Phi.* | 51 | 48 | 39 | 5 | 9 | 16 | 1 | 0 | 2 | 9 | 0 | 0 | 0 | 9 | 2 | 9 | 0 | 0 | 1 | .231 | .375 | .410 |
| Ledee, Ricky, S.F.* | 16 | 15 | 14 | 2 | 2 | 3 | 1 | 0 | 0 | 2 | 0 | 0 | 0 | 1 | 0 | 7 | 0 | 0 | 0 | .143 | .200 | .214 |
| Lo Duca, Paul, L.A. | 2 | 2 | 2 | 0 | 0 | 0 | 0 | 0 | 0 | 0 | 0 | 0 | 0 | 0 | 0 | 1 | 0 | 0 | 1 | .000 | .000 | .000 |
| Lo Duca, Paul, Fla. | 5 | 5 | 4 | 2 | 1 | 4 | 0 | 0 | 1 | 2 | 0 | 0 | 0 | 1 | 0 | 1 | 0 | 0 | 0 | .250 | .400 | 1.000 |
| Mayne, Brent, Ari.* | 8 | 8 | 6 | 0 | 1 | 1 | 0 | 0 | 0 | 1 | 2 | 0 | 0 | 0 | 0 | 2 | 0 | 0 | 0 | .167 | .167 | .167 |
| Mayne, Brent, L.A.* | 1 | 1 | 1 | 0 | 0 | 0 | 0 | 0 | 0 | 0 | 0 | 0 | 0 | 0 | 0 | 1 | 0 | 0 | 0 | .000 | .000 | .000 |
| Oliver, Darren, Fla. | 1 | 1 | 1 | 0 | 0 | 0 | 0 | 0 | 0 | 0 | 0 | 0 | 0 | 0 | 0 | 1 | 0 | 0 | 0 | .000 | .000 | .000 |
| Oliver, Darren, Hou. | 1 | 1 | 1 | 0 | 0 | 0 | 0 | 0 | 0 | 0 | 0 | 0 | 0 | 0 | 0 | 0 | 0 | 0 | 1 | .000 | .000 | .000 |
| Perez, Neifi, S.F.† | 10 | 9 | 9 | 0 | 3 | 3 | 0 | 0 | 0 | 1 | 0 | 0 | 0 | 0 | 0 | 2 | 0 | 0 | 0 | .333 | .333 | .333 |
| Perez, Neifi, Chi.† | 4 | 4 | 4 | 1 | 3 | 4 | 1 | 0 | 0 | 0 | 0 | 0 | 0 | 0 | 0 | 0 | 0 | 0 | 0 | .750 | .750 | 1.000 |
| Walker, Larry, Col.* | 5 | 5 | 4 | 1 | 1 | 1 | 0 | 0 | 0 | 0 | 0 | 0 | 0 | 1 | 1 | 0 | 0 | 0 | 0 | .250 | .400 | .250 |
| Walker, Larry, St.L.* | 4 | 4 | 4 | 0 | 1 | 1 | 0 | 0 | 0 | 0 | 0 | 0 | 0 | 0 | 0 | 2 | 0 | 0 | 0 | .250 | .250 | .250 |
| Wigginton, Ty, N.Y. | 3 | 3 | 2 | 0 | 1 | 1 | 0 | 0 | 0 | 2 | 0 | 0 | 0 | 1 | 0 | 0 | 0 | 0 | 0 | .500 | .667 | .500 |
| Wigginton, Ty, Pit. | 3 | 3 | 3 | 0 | 1 | 1 | 0 | 0 | 0 | 0 | 0 | 0 | 0 | 0 | 0 | 0 | 0 | 0 | 0 | .333 | .333 | .333 |
| Wilson, Tom, N.Y. | 1 | 1 | 1 | 0 | 0 | 0 | 0 | 0 | 0 | 0 | 0 | 0 | 0 | 0 | 0 | 0 | 0 | 0 | 0 | .000 | .000 | .000 |
| Wilson, Tom, L.A. | 3 | 3 | 3 | 0 | 0 | 0 | 0 | 0 | 0 | 0 | 0 | 0 | 0 | 0 | 0 | 2 | 0 | 0 | 0 | .000 | .000 | .000 |

# PITCHING

## TEAM

| Team | W | L | Pct. | ERA | G | CG | ShO | Rel. | Sv.-Op. | IP | H | TBF | R | ER | HR | SH | SF | HB | BB | IBB | SO | WP | Bk. |
|---|---|---|---|---|---|---|---|---|---|---|---|---|---|---|---|---|---|---|---|---|---|---|---|
| Atlanta | 96 | 66 | .593 | 3.74 | 162 | 4 | 13 | 483 | 48-68 | 1450.0 | 1475 | 6218 | 668 | 603 | 154 | 69 | 42 | 27 | 523 | 50 | 1025 | 36 | 6 |
| St. Louis | 105 | 57 | .648 | 3.75 | 162 | 4 | 12 | 469 | 57-73 | 1453.2 | 1378 | 6104 | 659 | 605 | 169 | 76 | 37 | 67 | 440 | 24 | 1041 | 42 | 4 |
| Chicago | 89 | 73 | .549 | 3.81 | 162 | 3 | 6 | 460 | 42-66 | 1465.1 | 1363 | 6262 | 665 | 621 | 169 | 78 | 44 | 76 | 545 | 33 | 1346 | 50 | 9 |
| Los Angeles | 93 | 69 | .574 | 4.01 | 162 | 2 | 6 | 459 | 51-60 | 1453.1 | 1386 | 6155 | 684 | 647 | 178 | 88 | 39 | 54 | 521 | 47 | 1066 | 43 | 2 |
| San Diego | 87 | 75 | .537 | 4.03 | 162 | 3 | 8 | 437 | 44-64 | 1441.0 | 1460 | 6135 | 705 | 645 | 184 | 73 | 41 | 48 | 422 | 39 | 1079 | 27 | 2 |
| Houston | 92 | 70 | .568 | 4.05 | 162 | 2 | 13 | 493 | 47-70 | 1443.0 | 1416 | 6201 | 698 | 650 | 174 | 74 | 35 | 68 | 525 | 61 | 1282 | 45 | 3 |
| New York | 71 | 91 | .438 | 4.09 | 162 | 2 | 6 | 474 | 31-52 | 1449.0 | 1452 | 6333 | 731 | 658 | 156 | 77 | 44 | 49 | 592 | 70 | 977 | 30 | 8 |
| Florida | 83 | 79 | .512 | 4.10 | 162 | 6 | 14 | 404 | 53-75 | 1439.0 | 1395 | 6110 | 700 | 655 | 166 | 55 | 36 | 51 | 513 | 61 | 1116 | 35 | 3 |
| Milwaukee | 67 | 94 | .416 | 4.24 | 161 | 6 | 10 | 423 | 42-64 | 1442.0 | 1440 | 6204 | 757 | 679 | 164 | 58 | 52 | 51 | 476 | 27 | 1098 | 59 | 5 |
| Pittsburgh | 72 | 89 | .447 | 4.29 | 161 | 3 | 8 | 464 | 46-69 | 1428.0 | 1451 | 6197 | 744 | 680 | 149 | 80 | 48 | 63 | 576 | 64 | 1079 | 45 | 3 |
| San Francisco | 91 | 71 | .562 | 4.29 | 162 | 8 | 8 | 521 | 46-74 | 1457.0 | 1481 | 6321 | 770 | 695 | 161 | 74 | 53 | 47 | 548 | 35 | 1020 | 52 | 2 |
| Montreal | 67 | 95 | .414 | 4.33 | 162 | 11 | 11 | 462 | 31-49 | 1447.0 | 1477 | 6307 | 769 | 696 | 191 | 54 | 36 | 79 | 582 | 78 | 1032 | 43 | 2 |
| Philadelphia | 86 | 76 | .531 | 4.45 | 162 | 4 | 5 | 476 | 43-68 | 1462.2 | 1488 | 6308 | 781 | 724 | 214 | 74 | 38 | 66 | 502 | 60 | 1070 | 40 | 3 |
| Arizona | 51 | 111 | .315 | 4.98 | 162 | 5 | 6 | 471 | 33-55 | 1436.0 | 1480 | 6418 | 899 | 794 | 197 | 74 | 47 | 75 | 668 | 79 | 1153 | 71 | 8 |
| Cincinnati | 76 | 86 | .469 | 5.19 | 162 | 5 | 8 | 497 | 47-77 | 1443.2 | 1595 | 6451 | 907 | 832 | 236 | 75 | 54 | 54 | 572 | 55 | 992 | 74 | 3 |
| Colorado | 68 | 94 | .420 | 5.54 | 162 | 3 | 2 | 473 | 36-70 | 1435.1 | 1634 | 6535 | 923 | 883 | 198 | 82 | 56 | 71 | 697 | 84 | 947 | 66 | 6 |
| **Totals** | 1294 | 1296 | .500 | 4.30 | 1295 | 71 | 136 | 7466 | 697-1054 | 23146.0 | 23371 | 100259 | 12060 | 11067 | 2860 | 1161 | 702 | 946 | 8702 | 867 | 17323 | 758 | 69 |

NOTE—Totals for earned runs for several clubs do not agree with composite total for all pitchers of each respective club due to instances in which provisions of Section 10.18(i) of the Scoring Rules were applied. The following differences are to be noted: Atlanta pitchers add to 604; Chicago pitchers add to 623; New York pitchers add to 660; Milwaukee pitchers add to 683; Pittsburgh pitchers add to 684; San Francisco pitchers add to 703; Philadelphia pitchers add to 726; Arizona pitchers add to 795; Cincinnati pitchers add to 836.

## INDIVIDUAL

### TOP QUALIFIERS FOR EARNED-RUN AVERAGE TITLE

Minimum 162 innings. *Throws lefthanded.

| Pitcher, Team | W | L | Pct. | ERA | G | GS | CG | ShO | GF | Sv.-Op. | IP | H | TBF | R | ER | HR | SH | SF | HB | BB | IBB | SO | WP | Bk. |
|---|---|---|---|---|---|---|---|---|---|---|---|---|---|---|---|---|---|---|---|---|---|---|---|---|
| Peavy, Jake, S.D. | 15 | 6 | .714 | 2.27 | 27 | 27 | 0 | 0 | 0 | 0-0 | 166.1 | 146 | 694 | 49 | 42 | 13 | 5 | 6 | 11 | 53 | 4 | 173 | 1 | 1 |
| Johnson, Randy, Ari.* | 16 | 14 | .533 | 2.60 | 35 | 35 | 4 | 2 | 0 | 0-0 | 245.2 | 177 | 964 | 88 | 71 | 18 | 7 | 5 | 10 | 44 | 1 | 290 | 3 | 1 |
| Sheets, Ben, Mil. | 12 | 14 | .462 | 2.70 | 34 | 34 | 5 | 0 | 0 | 0-0 | 237.0 | 201 | 937 | 85 | 71 | 25 | 6 | 4 | 4 | 32 | 1 | 264 | 8 | 1 |
| Zambrano, Carlos, Chi. | 16 | 8 | .667 | 2.75 | 31 | 31 | 1 | 1 | 0 | 0-0 | 209.2 | 174 | 887 | 73 | 64 | 14 | 10 | 3 | 20 | 81 | 4 | 188 | 6 | 2 |
| Clemens, Roger, Hou. | 18 | 4 | .818 | 2.98 | 33 | 33 | 0 | 0 | 0 | 0-0 | 214.1 | 169 | 878 | 76 | 71 | 15 | 8 | 7 | 6 | 79 | 5 | 218 | 5 | 0 |
| Perez, Oliver, Pit.* | 12 | 10 | .545 | 2.98 | 30 | 30 | 2 | 1 | 0 | 0-0 | 196.0 | 145 | 805 | 71 | 65 | 22 | 9 | 5 | 9 | 81 | 2 | 239 | 2 | 1 |
| Pavano, Carl, Fla. | 18 | 8 | .692 | 3.00 | 31 | 31 | 2 | 2 | 0 | 0-0 | 222.1 | 212 | 909 | 80 | 74 | 16 | 7 | 4 | 11 | 49 | 13 | 139 | 2 | 3 |
| Schmidt, Jason, S.F. | 18 | 7 | .720 | 3.20 | 32 | 32 | 4 | 3 | 0 | 0-0 | 225.0 | 165 | 907 | 84 | 80 | 18 | 7 | 3 | 3 | 77 | 3 | 251 | 7 | 1 |
| Leiter, Al, N.Y.* | 10 | 8 | .556 | 3.21 | 30 | 30 | 0 | 0 | 0 | 0-0 | 173.2 | 138 | 750 | 65 | 62 | 16 | 8 | 2 | 11 | 97 | 8 | 117 | 1 | 1 |
| Perez, Odalis, L.A.* | 7 | 6 | .538 | 3.25 | 31 | 31 | 0 | 0 | 0 | 0-0 | 196.1 | 180 | 787 | 76 | 71 | 26 | 16 | 3 | 3 | 44 | 4 | 128 | 2 | 2 |
| Wright, Jaret, Atl. | 15 | 8 | .652 | 3.28 | 32 | 32 | 0 | 0 | 0 | 0-0 | 186.1 | 168 | 781 | 79 | 68 | 11 | 8 | 6 | 3 | 70 | 5 | 159 | 3 | 0 |
| Davis, Doug, Mil.* | 12 | 12 | .500 | 3.39 | 34 | 34 | 0 | 0 | 0 | 0-0 | 207.1 | 192 | 880 | 84 | 78 | 14 | 11 | 5 | 7 | 79 | 3 | 166 | 4 | 1 |
| Carpenter, Chris, St.L. | 15 | 5 | .750 | 3.46 | 28 | 28 | 1 | 0 | 0 | 0-0 | 182.0 | 169 | 746 | 75 | 70 | 24 | 6 | 3 | 8 | 38 | 2 | 152 | 4 | 0 |
| Oswalt, Roy, Hou. | 20 | 10 | .667 | 3.49 | 36 | 35 | 2 | 2 | 0 | 0-0 | 237.0 | 233 | 983 | 100 | 92 | 17 | 11 | 4 | 11 | 62 | 5 | 206 | 5 | 1 |
| Webb, Brandon, Ari. | 7 | 16 | .304 | 3.59 | 35 | 35 | 1 | 0 | 0 | 0-0 | 208.0 | 194 | 933 | 111 | 83 | 17 | 14 | 6 | 11 | 119 | 11 | 164 | 17 | 1 |

DEPARTMENTAL LEADERS: W—Oswalt, Hou., 20; L—Webb, Ari., 16; G—Brower, S.F., 89; GS—Hernandez, Mon., Johnson, Ari., Oswalt, Hou., Webb, Ari., 35; CG—Hernandez, Mon., 9; ShO—Lidle, Cin.-Phi., Schmidt, S.F., 3; GF—Isringhausen, St.L., 66; Sv.—Benitez, Fla., Isringhausen, St.L., 47; IP—Hernandez, Mon., 255.0; H—Jennings, Col., 241; TBF—Hernandez, Mon., 1053; R—Estes, Col., 133; ER—Estes, Col., 131; HR—Milton, Phi., 43; SH—Perez, L.A., 16; SF—Glavine, N.Y., 10; HB—Zambrano, Chi., 20; TBB—Webb, Ari., 119; IBB—Jennings, Col., 14; SO—Johnson, Ari., 290; WP—Webb, Ari., 17; Bk.—Pavano, Fla., 3.

### ALL PITCHERS

*Throws lefthanded.

| Pitcher, Team | W | L | Pct. | ERA | G | GS | CG | ShO | GF | Sv.-Op. | IP | H | TBF | R | ER | HR | SH | SF | HB | BB | IBB | SO | WP | Bk. |
|---|---|---|---|---|---|---|---|---|---|---|---|---|---|---|---|---|---|---|---|---|---|---|---|---|
| Aardsma, David, S.F. | 1 | 0 | 1.000 | 6.75 | 11 | 0 | 0 | 0 | 5 | 0-1 | 10.2 | 20 | 61 | 8 | 8 | 1 | 0 | 1 | 2 | 10 | 0 | 5 | 0 | 0 |
| Abbott, Paul, Phi. | 1 | 6 | .143 | 6.24 | 10 | 10 | 0 | 0 | 0 | 0-0 | 49.0 | 57 | 229 | 37 | 34 | 14 | 1 | 0 | 1 | 31 | 1 | 21 | 3 | 0 |
| Acevedo, Jose, Cin. | 5 | 12 | .294 | 5.94 | 39 | 27 | 0 | 0 | 3 | 0-0 | 157.2 | 188 | 704 | 108 | 104 | 30 | 3 | 7 | 5 | 45 | 8 | 117 | 3 | 1 |
| Adams, Mike, Mil. | 2 | 3 | .400 | 3.40 | 46 | 0 | 0 | 0 | 13 | 0-5 | 53.0 | 50 | 225 | 21 | 20 | 5 | 5 | 2 | 2 | 14 | 2 | 39 | 2 | 0 |
| Alfonseca, Antonio, Atl. | 6 | 4 | .600 | 2.57 | 79 | 0 | 0 | 0 | 11 | 0-1 | 73.2 | 71 | 313 | 24 | 21 | 5 | 6 | 1 | 0 | 28 | 5 | 45 | 5 | 0 |
| Almanza, Armando, Atl.* | 1 | 1 | .500 | 6.17 | 13 | 0 | 0 | 0 | 5 | 0-0 | 11.2 | 9 | 54 | 8 | 8 | 3 | 0 | 1 | 1 | 7 | 2 | 13 | 0 | 1 |
| Alvarez, Wilson, L.A.* | 7 | 6 | .538 | 4.03 | 40 | 15 | 0 | 0 | 6 | 1-2 | 120.2 | 109 | 499 | 56 | 54 | 12 | 11 | 5 | 5 | 31 | 2 | 102 | 1 | 0 |
| Anderson, Jimmy, Chi.* | 0 | 0 | .000 | 4.66 | 7 | 0 | 0 | 0 | 2 | 1-1 | 9.2 | 9 | 42 | 5 | 5 | 0 | 0 | 0 | 2 | 3 | 0 | 3 | 1 | 0 |
| Ankiel, Rick, St.L.* | 1 | 0 | 1.000 | 5.40 | 5 | 0 | 0 | 0 | 0 | 0-0 | 10.0 | 10 | 43 | 6 | 6 | 2 | 1 | 0 | 2 | 1 | 0 | 9 | 1 | 0 |
| Aquino, Greg, Ari. | 0 | 2 | .000 | 3.06 | 34 | 0 | 0 | 0 | 26 | 16-19 | 35.1 | 24 | 147 | 15 | 12 | 4 | 2 | 2 | 2 | 17 | 2 | 26 | 4 | 0 |
| Armas, Tony, Mon. | 2 | 4 | .333 | 4.88 | 16 | 16 | 0 | 0 | 0 | 0-0 | 72.0 | 66 | 320 | 41 | 39 | 13 | 2 | 2 | 4 | 45 | 6 | 54 | 0 | 0 |
| Ashby, Andy, S.D. | 0 | 0 | .000 | 0.00 | 2 | 0 | 0 | 0 | 2 | 0-0 | 2.0 | 1 | 7 | 0 | 0 | 0 | 0 | 0 | 0 | 0 | 0 | 2 | 0 | 0 |
| Ayala, Luis, Mon. | 6 | 12 | .333 | 2.69 | 81 | 0 | 0 | 0 | 28 | 2-7 | 90.1 | 92 | 367 | 30 | 27 | 6 | 2 | 2 | 5 | 15 | 2 | 63 | 3 | 1 |
| Backe, Brandon, Hou. | 5 | 3 | .625 | 4.30 | 33 | 9 | 0 | 0 | 8 | 0-0 | 67.0 | 75 | 293 | 33 | 32 | 10 | 5 | 1 | 1 | 27 | 4 | 54 | 1 | 0 |
| Baldwin, James, N.Y. | 0 | 2 | .000 | 15.00 | 2 | 2 | 0 | 0 | 0 | 0-0 | 6.0 | 13 | 36 | 10 | 10 | 3 | 1 | 0 | 1 | 5 | 1 | 1 | 0 | 0 |
| Beck, Rod, S.D. | 0 | 2 | .000 | 6.38 | 26 | 0 | 0 | 0 | 10 | 0-0 | 24.0 | 27 | 108 | 18 | 17 | 8 | 0 | 2 | 0 | 9 | 0 | 15 | 1 | 0 |
| Beckett, Josh, Fla. | 9 | 9 | .500 | 3.79 | 26 | 26 | 1 | 1 | 0 | 0-0 | 156.2 | 137 | 654 | 72 | 66 | 16 | 9 | 3 | 6 | 54 | 3 | 152 | 5 | 0 |
| Bell, Heath, N.Y. | 0 | 2 | .000 | 3.33 | 17 | 0 | 0 | 0 | 2 | 0-1 | 24.1 | 22 | 94 | 9 | 9 | 5 | 1 | 0 | 0 | 6 | 0 | 27 | 0 | 0 |
| Beltran, Francis, Chi.-Mon. | 2 | 2 | .500 | 5.47 | 45 | 0 | 0 | 0 | 13 | 1-1 | 49.1 | 47 | 221 | 31 | 30 | 11 | 4 | 2 | 2 | 27 | 1 | 48 | 2 | 0 |
| Beltran, Rigo, Mon.* | 0 | 0 | .000 | 13.50 | 2 | 0 | 0 | 0 | 0 | 0-0 | 0.2 | 1 | 3 | 1 | 1 | 0 | 0 | 0 | 0 | 0 | 0 | 0 | 0 | 0 |
| Benitez, Armando, Fla. | 2 | 2 | .500 | 1.29 | 64 | 0 | 0 | 0 | 59 | 47-51 | 69.2 | 36 | 262 | 11 | 10 | 6 | 3 | 1 | 0 | 21 | 4 | 62 | 0 | 0 |
| Bennett, Jeff, Mil. | 1 | 5 | .167 | 4.79 | 60 | 0 | 0 | 0 | 20 | 0-1 | 71.1 | 78 | 316 | 43 | 38 | 12 | 2 | 5 | 2 | 26 | 2 | 45 | 6 | 0 |

| Pitcher, Team | W | L | Pct. | ERA | G | GS | CG | ShO | GF | Sv.-Op. | IP | H | TBF | R | ER | HR | SH | SF | HB | BB | IBB | SO | WP | Bk. |
|---|---|---|---|---|---|---|---|---|---|---|---|---|---|---|---|---|---|---|---|---|---|---|---|---|
| Benson, Kris, Pit.-N.Y. | 12 | 12 | .500 | 4.31 | 31 | 31 | 1 | 1 | 0 | 0-0 | 200.1 | 202 | 854 | 106 | 96 | 15 | 8 | 6 | 10 | 61 | 8 | 134 | 5 | 0 |
| Bentz, Chad, Mon.* | 0 | 3 | .000 | 5.86 | 36 | 0 | 0 | 0 | 5 | 0-0 | 27.2 | 23 | 126 | 19 | 18 | 5 | 0 | 0 | 2 | 23 | 3 | 18 | 1 | 0 |
| Bernero, Adam, Col. | 1 | 1 | .500 | 5.57 | 16 | 2 | 0 | 0 | 4 | 0-1 | 32.1 | 36 | 147 | 20 | 20 | 7 | 0 | 3 | 0 | 17 | 2 | 21 | 0 | 0 |
| Biddle, Rocky, Mon. | 4 | 8 | .333 | 6.92 | 47 | 9 | 0 | 0 | 19 | 11-15 | 78.0 | 98 | 364 | 69 | 60 | 15 | 3 | 3 | 8 | 31 | 3 | 51 | 5 | 0 |
| Boehringer, Brian, Pit. | 1 | 1 | .500 | 4.62 | 21 | 0 | 0 | 0 | 4 | 0-2 | 25.1 | 27 | 114 | 14 | 13 | 2 | 1 | 3 | 1 | 17 | 3 | 20 | 0 | 0 |
| Bong, Jung Keun, Cin.* | 1 | 1 | .500 | 4.70 | 3 | 3 | 0 | 0 | 0 | 0-0 | 15.1 | 17 | 75 | 13 | 8 | 3 | 2 | 0 | 0 | 10 | 0 | 11 | 1 | 0 |
| Borland, Toby, Fla. | 1 | 1 | .500 | 5.40 | 18 | 0 | 0 | 0 | 5 | 0-1 | 18.1 | 18 | 86 | 11 | 11 | 3 | 2 | 1 | 0 | 12 | 5 | 18 | 0 | 0 |
| Borowski, Joe, Chi. | 2 | 4 | .333 | 8.02 | 22 | 0 | 0 | 0 | 19 | 9-11 | 21.1 | 27 | 106 | 19 | 19 | 3 | 1 | 1 | 0 | 15 | 2 | 17 | 0 | 0 |
| Bottalico, Ricky, N.Y. | 3 | 2 | .600 | 3.38 | 60 | 0 | 0 | 0 | 8 | 0-4 | 69.1 | 54 | 296 | 30 | 26 | 3 | 3 | 4 | 4 | 34 | 7 | 61 | 3 | 0 |
| Boyd, Jason, Pit. | 1 | 0 | 1.000 | 5.54 | 12 | 0 | 0 | 0 | 4 | 0-0 | 13.0 | 13 | 64 | 9 | 8 | 4 | 3 | 0 | 3 | 8 | 1 | 12 | 0 | 0 |
| Brazoban, Yhency, L.A. | 6 | 2 | .750 | 2.48 | 31 | 0 | 0 | 0 | 10 | 0-0 | 32.2 | 25 | 133 | 9 | 9 | 2 | 4 | 0 | 0 | 15 | 2 | 27 | 1 | 0 |
| Brooks, Frank, Pit.* | 0 | 1 | .000 | 4.67 | 11 | 1 | 0 | 0 | 3 | 0-0 | 17.1 | 13 | 73 | 10 | 9 | 5 | 0 | 0 | 0 | 9 | 2 | 18 | 0 | 1 |
| Brower, Jim, S.F. | 7 | 7 | .500 | 3.29 | 89 | 0 | 0 | 0 | 21 | 1-5 | 93.0 | 90 | 401 | 42 | 34 | 6 | 11 | 2 | 4 | 36 | 2 | 63 | 10 | 0 |
| Bruney, Brian, Ari. | 3 | 4 | .429 | 4.31 | 30 | 0 | 0 | 0 | 14 | 0-1 | 31.1 | 20 | 135 | 16 | 15 | 2 | 1 | 0 | 1 | 27 | 5 | 34 | 2 | 0 |
| Bullinger, Kirk, Hou. | 1 | 0 | 1.000 | 6.16 | 27 | 0 | 0 | 0 | 7 | 1-2 | 30.2 | 36 | 140 | 22 | 21 | 5 | 2 | 1 | 1 | 10 | 2 | 11 | 0 | 0 |
| Bump, Nate, Fla. | 2 | 4 | .333 | 5.01 | 50 | 2 | 0 | 0 | 13 | 1-4 | 73.2 | 86 | 329 | 46 | 41 | 7 | 2 | 2 | 3 | 32 | 8 | 44 | 2 | 0 |
| Burba, Dave, Mil.-S.F. | 4 | 1 | .800 | 4.21 | 51 | 0 | 0 | 0 | 16 | 2-5 | 77.0 | 70 | 326 | 40 | 36 | 7 | 4 | 3 | 2 | 26 | 2 | 50 | 3 | 1 |
| Burnett, A.J., Fla. | 7 | 6 | .538 | 3.68 | 20 | 19 | 1 | 0 | 0 | 0-0 | 120.0 | 102 | 490 | 50 | 49 | 9 | 3 | 3 | 4 | 38 | 0 | 113 | 7 | 0 |
| Burnett, Sean, Pit.* | 5 | 5 | .500 | 5.02 | 13 | 13 | 1 | 1 | 0 | 0-0 | 71.2 | 86 | 318 | 41 | 40 | 9 | 2 | 1 | 1 | 28 | 2 | 30 | 2 | 0 |
| Bynum, Mike, S.D.* | 0 | 1 | .000 | 54.00 | 2 | 0 | 0 | 0 | 0 | 0-0 | 0.2 | 1 | 6 | 4 | 4 | 0 | 0 | 0 | 0 | 3 | 0 | 0 | 0 | 0 |
| Byrd, Paul, Atl. | 8 | 7 | .533 | 3.94 | 19 | 19 | 0 | 0 | 0 | 0-0 | 114.1 | 123 | 482 | 57 | 50 | 18 | 3 | 3 | 2 | 19 | 0 | 79 | 1 | 0 |
| Calero, Kiko, St.L. | 3 | 1 | .750 | 2.78 | 41 | 0 | 0 | 0 | 4 | 2-3 | 45.1 | 27 | 168 | 14 | 14 | 5 | 4 | 0 | 1 | 10 | 1 | 47 | 1 | 0 |
| Cali, Carmen, St.L.* | 0 | 0 | .000 | 8.59 | 10 | 0 | 0 | 0 | 2 | 0-0 | 7.1 | 13 | 40 | 7 | 7 | 1 | 0 | 1 | 0 | 6 | 1 | 8 | 1 | 0 |
| Capellan, Jose, Atl. | 0 | 1 | .000 | 11.25 | 3 | 2 | 0 | 0 | 0 | 0-0 | 8.0 | 14 | 42 | 10 | 10 | 2 | 1 | 1 | 0 | 5 | 0 | 4 | 0 | 0 |
| Capuano, Chris, Mil.* | 6 | 8 | .429 | 4.99 | 17 | 17 | 0 | 0 | 0 | 0-0 | 88.1 | 91 | 385 | 55 | 49 | 18 | 4 | 1 | 5 | 37 | 1 | 80 | 3 | 1 |
| Carpenter, Chris, St.L. | 15 | 5 | .750 | 3.46 | 28 | 28 | 1 | 0 | 0 | 0-0 | 182.0 | 169 | 746 | 75 | 70 | 24 | 6 | 3 | 8 | 38 | 2 | 152 | 4 | 0 |
| Carrara, Giovanni, L.A. | 5 | 2 | .714 | 2.18 | 42 | 0 | 0 | 0 | 15 | 2-3 | 53.2 | 46 | 227 | 15 | 13 | 1 | 4 | 0 | 1 | 20 | 3 | 48 | 1 | 0 |
| Chacon, Shawn, Col. | 1 | 9 | .100 | 7.11 | 66 | 0 | 0 | 0 | 60 | 35-44 | 63.1 | 71 | 316 | 52 | 50 | 12 | 7 | 0 | 5 | 52 | 7 | 52 | 9 | 0 |
| Choate, Randy, Ari.* | 2 | 4 | .333 | 4.62 | 74 | 0 | 0 | 0 | 17 | 0-2 | 50.2 | 52 | 232 | 26 | 26 | 1 | 0 | 4 | 5 | 28 | 11 | 49 | 1 | 1 |
| Christiansen, Jason, S.F.* | 4 | 3 | .571 | 4.50 | 60 | 0 | 0 | 0 | 11 | 3-6 | 36.0 | 34 | 167 | 20 | 18 | 3 | 0 | 2 | 3 | 26 | 1 | 22 | 3 | 0 |
| Claussen, Brandon, Cin.* | 2 | 8 | .200 | 6.14 | 14 | 14 | 0 | 0 | 0 | 0-0 | 66.0 | 80 | 313 | 50 | 45 | 9 | 5 | 3 | 2 | 35 | 2 | 45 | 3 | 0 |
| Clemens, Roger, Hou. | 18 | 4 | .818 | 2.98 | 33 | 33 | 0 | 0 | 0 | 0-0 | 214.1 | 169 | 878 | 76 | 71 | 15 | 8 | 7 | 6 | 79 | 5 | 218 | 5 | 0 |
| Clement, Matt, Chi. | 9 | 13 | .409 | 3.68 | 30 | 30 | 0 | 0 | 0 | 0-0 | 181.0 | 155 | 775 | 79 | 74 | 23 | 5 | 4 | 12 | 77 | 4 | 190 | 14 | 1 |
| Colon, Roman, Atl. | 2 | 1 | .667 | 3.32 | 18 | 0 | 0 | 0 | 7 | 0-1 | 19.0 | 18 | 82 | 9 | 7 | 0 | 1 | 2 | 0 | 8 | 1 | 15 | 0 | 0 |
| Cook, Aaron, Col. | 6 | 4 | .600 | 4.28 | 16 | 16 | 1 | 0 | 0 | 0-0 | 96.2 | 112 | 433 | 47 | 46 | 7 | 5 | 1 | 7 | 39 | 5 | 40 | 6 | 1 |
| Cooper, Brian, S.F. | 0 | 2 | .000 | 8.78 | 5 | 2 | 0 | 0 | 0 | 0-0 | 13.1 | 15 | 61 | 13 | 13 | 4 | 2 | 1 | 1 | 5 | 1 | 7 | 1 | 0 |
| Corcoran, Roy, Mon. | 0 | 0 | .000 | 6.75 | 5 | 0 | 0 | 0 | 3 | 0-0 | 5.1 | 7 | 28 | 4 | 4 | 0 | 0 | 0 | 0 | 5 | 0 | 4 | 0 | 0 |
| Cordero, Chad, Mon. | 7 | 3 | .700 | 2.94 | 69 | 0 | 0 | 0 | 40 | 14-18 | 82.2 | 68 | 357 | 28 | 27 | 8 | 2 | 4 | 1 | 43 | 4 | 83 | 5 | 0 |
| Corey, Mark, Pit. | 1 | 2 | .333 | 4.54 | 31 | 0 | 0 | 0 | 13 | 0-1 | 35.2 | 39 | 164 | 20 | 18 | 3 | 0 | 1 | 2 | 19 | 3 | 28 | 4 | 0 |
| Cormier, Lance, Ari. | 1 | 4 | .200 | 8.14 | 17 | 5 | 0 | 0 | 3 | 0-0 | 45.1 | 62 | 218 | 42 | 41 | 13 | 2 | 3 | 2 | 25 | 2 | 24 | 2 | 1 |
| Cormier, Rheal, Phi.* | 4 | 5 | .444 | 3.56 | 84 | 0 | 0 | 0 | 8 | 0-7 | 81.0 | 70 | 330 | 32 | 32 | 7 | 3 | 1 | 5 | 26 | 6 | 46 | 1 | 0 |
| Correia, Kevin, S.F. | 0 | 1 | .000 | 8.05 | 12 | 1 | 0 | 0 | 5 | 0-0 | 19.0 | 25 | 92 | 20 | 17 | 3 | 3 | 3 | 1 | 10 | 0 | 14 | 0 | 0 |
| Crowell, Jim, Phi.* | 0 | 0 | .000 | 3.00 | 4 | 0 | 0 | 0 | 0 | 0-0 | 3.0 | 6 | 18 | 2 | 1 | 0 | 0 | 0 | 0 | 0 | 0 | 1 | 0 | 0 |
| Cruz, Juan, Atl. | 6 | 2 | .750 | 2.75 | 50 | 0 | 0 | 0 | 22 | 0-0 | 72.0 | 59 | 300 | 24 | 22 | 7 | 4 | 1 | 2 | 30 | 1 | 70 | 1 | 0 |
| Cunnane, Will, Atl. | 1 | 1 | .500 | 7.30 | 9 | 0 | 0 | 0 | 5 | 0-1 | 12.1 | 18 | 59 | 10 | 10 | 3 | 0 | 2 | 1 | 4 | 1 | 11 | 0 | 0 |
| Daigle, Casey, Ari. | 2 | 3 | .400 | 7.16 | 10 | 10 | 0 | 0 | 0 | 0-0 | 49.0 | 63 | 230 | 41 | 39 | 9 | 3 | 1 | 2 | 27 | 3 | 17 | 1 | 1 |
| Darensbourg, Vic, N.Y.* | 0 | 1 | .000 | 7.94 | 5 | 0 | 0 | 0 | 2 | 0-0 | 5.2 | 10 | 28 | 5 | 5 | 1 | 1 | 2 | 0 | 2 | 0 | 1 | 0 | 0 |
| Davis, Doug, Mil.* | 12 | 12 | .500 | 3.39 | 34 | 34 | 0 | 0 | 0 | 0-0 | 207.1 | 192 | 880 | 84 | 78 | 14 | 11 | 5 | 7 | 79 | 3 | 166 | 4 | 1 |
| Day, Zach, Mon. | 5 | 10 | .333 | 3.93 | 19 | 19 | 1 | 1 | 0 | 0-0 | 116.2 | 117 | 496 | 53 | 51 | 13 | 4 | 1 | 4 | 45 | 7 | 61 | 5 | 0 |
| de la Rosa, Jorge, Mil.* | 0 | 3 | .000 | 6.35 | 5 | 5 | 0 | 0 | 0 | 0-0 | 22.2 | 29 | 113 | 20 | 16 | 1 | 1 | 3 | 1 | 14 | 0 | 5 | 3 | 0 |
| DeJean, Mike, N.Y. | 0 | 0 | .000 | 1.69 | 17 | 0 | 0 | 0 | 8 | 0-0 | 21.1 | 21 | 91 | 5 | 4 | 0 | 2 | 0 | 2 | 5 | 2 | 24 | 2 | 0 |
| Dempster, Ryan, Chi. | 1 | 1 | .500 | 3.92 | 23 | 0 | 0 | 0 | 8 | 2-2 | 20.2 | 16 | 93 | 9 | 9 | 1 | 1 | 0 | 2 | 13 | 0 | 18 | 1 | 0 |
| Dessens, Elmer, Ari.-L.A. | 2 | 6 | .250 | 4.46 | 50 | 10 | 0 | 0 | 9 | 2-5 | 105.0 | 123 | 468 | 61 | 52 | 15 | 4 | 3 | 1 | 31 | 4 | 73 | 2 | 0 |
| Dohmann, Scott, Col. | 0 | 3 | .000 | 4.11 | 41 | 0 | 0 | 0 | 13 | 0-4 | 46.0 | 41 | 198 | 22 | 21 | 8 | 2 | 3 | 0 | 19 | 0 | 49 | 3 | 0 |
| Dotel, Octavio, Hou. | 0 | 4 | .000 | 3.12 | 32 | 0 | 0 | 0 | 29 | 14-17 | 34.2 | 27 | 146 | 15 | 12 | 4 | 2 | 1 | 1 | 15 | 4 | 50 | 3 | 1 |
| Downs, Scott, Mon.* | 3 | 6 | .333 | 5.14 | 12 | 12 | 1 | 1 | 0 | 0-0 | 63.0 | 79 | 284 | 47 | 36 | 9 | 2 | 1 | 3 | 23 | 2 | 38 | 2 | 0 |
| Dreifort, Darren, L.A. | 1 | 4 | .200 | 4.44 | 60 | 0 | 0 | 0 | 9 | 1-4 | 50.2 | 43 | 227 | 25 | 25 | 5 | 4 | 2 | 0 | 36 | 2 | 63 | 5 | 0 |
| Drew, Tim, Atl. | 0 | 0 | .000 | 4.50 | 11 | 0 | 0 | 0 | 7 | 0-0 | 16.0 | 21 | 73 | 11 | 8 | 2 | 1 | 0 | 1 | 5 | 0 | 7 | 0 | 0 |
| Driskill, Travis, Col. | 0 | 0 | .000 | 6.48 | 5 | 0 | 0 | 0 | 1 | 0-1 | 8.1 | 13 | 39 | 6 | 6 | 0 | 0 | 0 | 0 | 3 | 0 | 6 | 0 | 0 |
| Duckworth, Brandon, Hou. | 1 | 2 | .333 | 6.86 | 19 | 6 | 0 | 0 | 6 | 0-0 | 39.1 | 55 | 180 | 30 | 30 | 11 | 3 | 1 | 0 | 13 | 3 | 23 | 3 | 0 |
| Durbin, Chad, Ari. | 1 | 1 | .500 | 8.68 | 7 | 0 | 0 | 0 | 0 | 0-0 | 9.1 | 9 | 52 | 10 | 9 | 1 | 2 | 0 | 1 | 11 | 0 | 10 | 2 | 0 |
| Durrington, Trent, Mil. | 0 | 0 | .000 | 0.00 | 1 | 0 | 0 | 0 | 1 | 0-0 | 0.1 | 0 | 1 | 0 | 0 | 0 | 0 | 0 | 0 | 0 | 0 | 0 | 0 | 0 |
| Eaton, Adam, S.D. | 11 | 14 | .440 | 4.61 | 33 | 33 | 0 | 0 | 0 | 0-0 | 199.1 | 204 | 848 | 113 | 102 | 28 | 12 | 7 | 10 | 52 | 3 | 153 | 5 | 0 |
| Eischen, Joey, Mon.* | 0 | 1 | .000 | 3.93 | 21 | 0 | 0 | 0 | 3 | 0-1 | 18.1 | 16 | 80 | 10 | 8 | 2 | 1 | 1 | 1 | 8 | 2 | 17 | 0 | 0 |
| Elarton, Scott, Col. | 0 | 6 | .000 | 9.80 | 8 | 8 | 0 | 0 | 0 | 0-0 | 41.1 | 57 | 199 | 45 | 45 | 8 | 2 | 3 | 0 | 20 | 1 | 23 | 5 | 0 |
| Eldred, Cal, St.L. | 4 | 2 | .667 | 3.76 | 52 | 0 | 0 | 0 | 10 | 1-3 | 67.0 | 71 | 282 | 31 | 28 | 11 | 5 | 2 | 1 | 17 | 1 | 54 | 3 | 0 |
| Erickson, Scott, N.Y. | 0 | 1 | .000 | 7.88 | 2 | 2 | 0 | 0 | 0 | 0-0 | 8.0 | 15 | 42 | 9 | 7 | 1 | 0 | 0 | 0 | 4 | 0 | 3 | 1 | 0 |
| Estes, Shawn, Col.* | 15 | 8 | .652 | 5.84 | 34 | 34 | 1 | 0 | 0 | 0-0 | 202.0 | 223 | 904 | 133 | 131 | 30 | 13 | 8 | 11 | 105 | 5 | 117 | 4 | 2 |
| Estrella, Leo, S.F. | 0 | 0 | .000 | 27.00 | 2 | 0 | 0 | 0 | 0 | 0-0 | 1.1 | 8 | 13 | 4 | 4 | 0 | 0 | 1 | 0 | 1 | 0 | 0 | 0 | 0 |
| Eyre, Scott, S.F.* | 2 | 2 | .500 | 4.10 | 83 | 0 | 0 | 0 | 12 | 1-5 | 52.2 | 43 | 229 | 26 | 24 | 8 | 3 | 3 | 0 | 27 | 3 | 49 | 3 | 0 |
| Falkenborg, Brian, L.A. | 1 | 0 | 1.000 | 7.53 | 6 | 0 | 0 | 0 | 1 | 0-0 | 14.1 | 19 | 73 | 14 | 12 | 2 | 2 | 0 | 3 | 9 | 0 | 11 | 1 | 0 |
| Farnsworth, Kyle, Chi. | 4 | 5 | .444 | 4.73 | 72 | 0 | 0 | 0 | 25 | 0-4 | 66.2 | 67 | 298 | 39 | 35 | 10 | 5 | 0 | 2 | 33 | 1 | 78 | 1 | 0 |
| Fassero, Jeff, Col.-Ari.* | 3 | 8 | .273 | 5.46 | 41 | 12 | 0 | 0 | 2 | 0-0 | 112.0 | 136 | 508 | 73 | 68 | 9 | 5 | 7 | 4 | 44 | 5 | 60 | 4 | 1 |
| Feliciano, Pedro, N.Y.* | 1 | 1 | .500 | 5.40 | 22 | 0 | 0 | 0 | 3 | 0-0 | 18.1 | 14 | 82 | 12 | 11 | 2 | 1 | 1 | 1 | 12 | 0 | 14 | 1 | 0 |
| Fernandez, Jared, Hou. | 0 | 0 | .000 | 54.00 | 2 | 1 | 0 | 0 | 0 | 0-0 | 1.0 | 6 | 14 | 6 | 6 | 0 | 0 | 1 | 0 | 5 | 0 | 0 | 0 | 0 |
| Fetters, Mike, Ari. | 0 | 1 | .000 | 8.68 | 23 | 0 | 0 | 0 | 6 | 1-1 | 18.2 | 23 | 94 | 22 | 18 | 2 | 0 | 2 | 1 | 14 | 2 | 14 | 4 | 0 |
| Figueroa, Nelson, Pit. | 0 | 3 | .000 | 5.72 | 10 | 3 | 0 | 0 | 0 | 0-0 | 28.1 | 32 | 121 | 18 | 18 | 4 | 4 | 0 | 0 | 11 | 1 | 10 | 3 | 0 |
| Fikac, Jeremy, Mon. | 1 | 2 | .333 | 5.40 | 19 | 0 | 0 | 0 | 6 | 0-0 | 25.0 | 26 | 112 | 16 | 15 | 5 | 3 | 1 | 0 | 13 | 4 | 22 | 1 | 0 |
| Flores, Randy, St.L.* | 1 | 0 | 1.000 | 1.93 | 9 | 1 | 0 | 0 | 3 | 0-0 | 14.0 | 13 | 57 | 3 | 3 | 0 | 1 | 1 | 3 | 3 | 1 | 7 | 0 | 0 |
| Floyd, Gavin, Phi. | 2 | 0 | 1.000 | 3.49 | 6 | 4 | 0 | 0 | 0 | 0-0 | 28.1 | 25 | 126 | 11 | 11 | 1 | 1 | 0 | 5 | 16 | 0 | 24 | 1 | 1 |
| Fogg, Josh, Pit. | 11 | 10 | .524 | 4.64 | 32 | 32 | 0 | 0 | 0 | 0-0 | 178.1 | 193 | 770 | 98 | 92 | 17 | 9 | 6 | 8 | 66 | 8 | 82 | 4 | 1 |
| Foppert, Jesse, S.F. | 0 | 0 | .000 | 0.00 | 1 | 0 | 0 | 0 | 0 | 0-0 | 1.0 | 1 | 4 | 0 | 0 | 0 | 0 | 0 | 0 | 0 | 0 | 2 | 0 | 0 |

| Pitcher, Team | W | L | Pct. | ERA | G | GS | CG | ShO | GF | Sv.-Op. | IP | H | TBF | R | ER | HR | SH | SF | HB | BB | IBB | SO | WP | Bk. |
|---|---|---|---|---|---|---|---|---|---|---|---|---|---|---|---|---|---|---|---|---|---|---|---|---|
| Ford, Ben, Mil. | 1 | 1 | .500 | 6.38 | 19 | 0 | 0 | 0 | 5 | 0-3 | 24.0 | 25 | 107 | 17 | 17 | 4 | 1 | 1 | 2 | 10 | 0 | 13 | 0 | 0 |
| Fortunato, Bartolome, N.Y. | 1 | 0 | 1.000 | 3.86 | 15 | 0 | 0 | 0 | 5 | 1-2 | 18.2 | 14 | 82 | 8 | 8 | 2 | 0 | 0 | 0 | 13 | 0 | 20 | 1 | 0 |
| Fossum, Casey, Ari.* | 4 | 15 | .211 | 6.65 | 27 | 27 | 0 | 0 | 0 | 0-0 | 142.0 | 171 | 652 | 111 | 105 | 31 | 8 | 4 | 10 | 63 | 5 | 117 | 4 | 2 |
| Fox, Chad, Fla. | 0 | 1 | .000 | 6.75 | 12 | 0 | 0 | 0 | 1 | 0-2 | 10.2 | 9 | 49 | 8 | 8 | 1 | 0 | 0 | 1 | 8 | 0 | 17 | 1 | 0 |
| Francis, Jeff, Col.* | 3 | 2 | .600 | 5.15 | 7 | 7 | 0 | 0 | 0 | 0-0 | 36.2 | 42 | 164 | 22 | 21 | 8 | 2 | 1 | 1 | 13 | 1 | 32 | 2 | 0 |
| Franco, John, N.Y.* | 2 | 7 | .222 | 5.28 | 52 | 0 | 0 | 0 | 16 | 0-1 | 46.0 | 46 | 207 | 28 | 27 | 6 | 2 | 2 | 1 | 24 | 2 | 36 | 2 | 0 |
| Franklin, Wayne, S.F.* | 2 | 1 | .667 | 6.39 | 43 | 2 | 0 | 0 | 8 | 0-1 | 50.2 | 55 | 227 | 37 | 36 | 11 | 4 | 2 | 3 | 22 | 2 | 40 | 0 | 0 |
| Fuentes, Brian, Col.* | 2 | 4 | .333 | 5.64 | 47 | 0 | 0 | 0 | 12 | 0-1 | 44.2 | 46 | 201 | 30 | 28 | 5 | 7 | 0 | 4 | 19 | 6 | 48 | 3 | 0 |
| Gagne, Eric, L.A. | 7 | 3 | .700 | 2.19 | 70 | 0 | 0 | 0 | 59 | 45-47 | 82.1 | 53 | 326 | 24 | 20 | 5 | 4 | 2 | 5 | 22 | 3 | 114 | 2 | 0 |
| Gallo, Mike, Hou.* | 2 | 0 | 1.000 | 4.74 | 69 | 0 | 0 | 0 | 5 | 0-1 | 49.1 | 55 | 223 | 27 | 26 | 12 | 2 | 1 | 6 | 20 | 7 | 34 | 3 | 0 |
| Geary, Geoff, Phi. | 1 | 0 | 1.000 | 5.44 | 33 | 0 | 0 | 0 | 16 | 0-0 | 44.2 | 52 | 200 | 29 | 27 | 8 | 1 | 2 | 3 | 16 | 3 | 30 | 2 | 1 |
| Germano, Justin, S.D. | 1 | 2 | .333 | 8.86 | 7 | 5 | 0 | 0 | 0 | 0-0 | 21.1 | 31 | 109 | 24 | 21 | 2 | 3 | 1 | 0 | 14 | 0 | 16 | 0 | 0 |
| Ginter, Matt, N.Y. | 1 | 3 | .250 | 4.54 | 15 | 14 | 0 | 0 | 0 | 0-0 | 69.1 | 82 | 313 | 41 | 35 | 8 | 3 | 1 | 5 | 20 | 5 | 38 | 1 | 0 |
| Gissell, Chris, Col. | 0 | 1 | .000 | 14.54 | 5 | 1 | 0 | 0 | 2 | 0-0 | 8.2 | 20 | 48 | 14 | 14 | 4 | 1 | 1 | 0 | 3 | 0 | 11 | 1 | 0 |
| Glavine, Tom, N.Y.* | 11 | 14 | .440 | 3.60 | 33 | 33 | 1 | 1 | 0 | 0-0 | 212.1 | 204 | 904 | 94 | 85 | 20 | 13 | 10 | 0 | 70 | 10 | 109 | 0 | 0 |
| Glover, Gary, Mil. | 2 | 1 | .667 | 3.50 | 4 | 3 | 0 | 0 | 0 | 0-0 | 18.0 | 18 | 82 | 9 | 7 | 2 | 2 | 2 | 2 | 8 | 1 | 8 | 1 | 0 |
| Gonzalez, Edgar, Ari. | 0 | 9 | .000 | 9.32 | 10 | 10 | 0 | 0 | 0 | 0-0 | 46.1 | 72 | 228 | 49 | 48 | 15 | 5 | 1 | 5 | 18 | 4 | 31 | 3 | 1 |
| Gonzalez, Mike, Pit.* | 3 | 1 | .750 | 1.25 | 47 | 0 | 0 | 0 | 12 | 1-4 | 43.1 | 32 | 169 | 7 | 6 | 2 | 3 | 0 | 1 | 6 | 0 | 55 | 4 | 0 |
| Good, Andrew, Ari. | 1 | 2 | .333 | 5.31 | 17 | 2 | 0 | 0 | 3 | 0-0 | 40.2 | 43 | 177 | 25 | 24 | 8 | 1 | 2 | 3 | 13 | 0 | 26 | 2 | 0 |
| Gosling, Mike, Ari.* | 1 | 1 | .500 | 4.62 | 6 | 4 | 0 | 0 | 0 | 0-0 | 25.1 | 26 | 112 | 13 | 13 | 5 | 2 | 0 | 2 | 13 | 1 | 14 | 2 | 0 |
| Grabow, John, Pit.* | 2 | 5 | .286 | 5.11 | 68 | 0 | 0 | 0 | 10 | 1-7 | 61.2 | 81 | 286 | 39 | 35 | 8 | 6 | 1 | 0 | 28 | 7 | 64 | 5 | 0 |
| Gracesqui, Franklyn, Fla.* | 0 | 1 | .000 | 11.25 | 7 | 0 | 0 | 0 | 5 | 1-1 | 4.0 | 6 | 23 | 5 | 5 | 0 | 0 | 0 | 2 | 3 | 0 | 1 | 0 | 0 |
| Graves, Danny, Cin. | 1 | 6 | .143 | 3.95 | 68 | 0 | 0 | 0 | 59 | 41-50 | 68.1 | 77 | 290 | 39 | 30 | 12 | 0 | 2 | 2 | 13 | 6 | 40 | 2 | 0 |
| Griffiths, Jeremy, Hou. | 0 | 0 | .000 | 10.38 | 1 | 1 | 0 | 0 | 0 | 0-0 | 4.1 | 4 | 20 | 5 | 5 | 1 | 0 | 0 | 0 | 3 | 0 | 5 | 0 | 0 |
| Gryboski, Kevin, Atl. | 3 | 2 | .600 | 2.84 | 69 | 0 | 0 | 0 | 10 | 2-4 | 50.2 | 54 | 217 | 22 | 16 | 2 | 1 | 0 | 0 | 23 | 4 | 24 | 5 | 0 |
| Hampton, Mike, Atl.* | 13 | 9 | .591 | 4.28 | 29 | 29 | 1 | 0 | 0 | 0-0 | 172.1 | 198 | 760 | 86 | 82 | 15 | 8 | 3 | 1 | 65 | 3 | 87 | 3 | 2 |
| Hancock, Josh, Phi.-Cin. | 5 | 2 | .714 | 5.09 | 16 | 11 | 0 | 0 | 2 | 0-0 | 63.2 | 73 | 293 | 43 | 36 | 17 | 3 | 2 | 1 | 28 | 2 | 36 | 5 | 0 |
| Harang, Aaron, Cin. | 10 | 9 | .526 | 4.86 | 28 | 28 | 1 | 1 | 0 | 0-0 | 161.0 | 177 | 711 | 90 | 87 | 26 | 13 | 6 | 5 | 53 | 5 | 125 | 7 | 0 |
| Haren, Danny, St.L. | 3 | 3 | .500 | 4.50 | 14 | 5 | 0 | 0 | 2 | 0-0 | 46.0 | 45 | 195 | 23 | 23 | 4 | 4 | 2 | 2 | 17 | 2 | 32 | 1 | 0 |
| Harikkala, Tim, Col. | 6 | 6 | .500 | 4.74 | 55 | 0 | 0 | 0 | 11 | 0-7 | 62.2 | 55 | 262 | 34 | 33 | 10 | 2 | 2 | 1 | 23 | 5 | 30 | 0 | 1 |
| Harville, Chad, Hou. | 3 | 2 | .600 | 4.75 | 56 | 0 | 0 | 0 | 14 | 0-4 | 53.0 | 54 | 238 | 35 | 28 | 8 | 2 | 0 | 2 | 26 | 2 | 46 | 5 | 0 |
| Hawkins, LaTroy, Chi. | 5 | 4 | .556 | 2.63 | 77 | 0 | 0 | 0 | 50 | 25-34 | 82.0 | 72 | 333 | 27 | 24 | 10 | 6 | 2 | 2 | 14 | 5 | 69 | 2 | 0 |
| Haynes, Jimmy, Cin. | 0 | 3 | .000 | 9.60 | 5 | 4 | 0 | 0 | 1 | 0-0 | 15.0 | 26 | 79 | 17 | 16 | 3 | 2 | 0 | 2 | 7 | 0 | 8 | 1 | 0 |
| Heilman, Aaron, N.Y. | 1 | 3 | .250 | 5.46 | 5 | 5 | 0 | 0 | 0 | 0-0 | 28.0 | 27 | 119 | 17 | 17 | 4 | 1 | 0 | 0 | 13 | 0 | 22 | 0 | 0 |
| Hendrickson, Ben, Mil. | 1 | 8 | .111 | 6.22 | 10 | 9 | 0 | 0 | 1 | 0-0 | 46.1 | 58 | 215 | 33 | 32 | 6 | 2 | 2 | 4 | 20 | 1 | 29 | 1 | 0 |
| Hennessey, Brad, S.F. | 2 | 2 | .500 | 4.98 | 7 | 7 | 0 | 0 | 0 | 0-0 | 34.1 | 42 | 163 | 24 | 19 | 2 | 4 | 1 | 0 | 15 | 1 | 25 | 1 | 0 |
| Herges, Matt, S.F. | 4 | 5 | .444 | 5.23 | 70 | 0 | 0 | 0 | 43 | 23-31 | 65.1 | 90 | 301 | 44 | 38 | 8 | 7 | 4 | 3 | 21 | 4 | 39 | 2 | 0 |
| Hermanson, Dustin, S.F. | 6 | 9 | .400 | 4.53 | 47 | 18 | 0 | 0 | 26 | 17-20 | 131.0 | 132 | 565 | 71 | 66 | 15 | 5 | 7 | 3 | 46 | 5 | 102 | 4 | 0 |
| Hernandez, Adrian, Mil. | 0 | 2 | .000 | 8.44 | 6 | 1 | 0 | 0 | 2 | 0-1 | 16.0 | 20 | 84 | 18 | 15 | 1 | 1 | 1 | 0 | 14 | 0 | 14 | 3 | 0 |
| Hernandez, Carlos, Hou.* | 1 | 3 | .250 | 6.43 | 9 | 9 | 0 | 0 | 0 | 0-0 | 42.0 | 50 | 200 | 31 | 30 | 11 | 4 | 3 | 5 | 23 | 0 | 26 | 1 | 0 |
| Hernandez, Livan, Mon. | 11 | 15 | .423 | 3.60 | 35 | 35 | 9 | 2 | 0 | 0-0 | 255.0 | 234 | 1053 | 105 | 102 | 26 | 11 | 4 | 10 | 83 | 9 | 186 | 1 | 0 |
| Hernandez, Roberto, Phi. | 3 | 5 | .375 | 4.76 | 63 | 0 | 0 | 0 | 11 | 0-4 | 56.2 | 66 | 260 | 39 | 30 | 9 | 7 | 1 | 1 | 29 | 3 | 44 | 3 | 0 |
| Hill, Shawn, Mon. | 1 | 2 | .333 | 16.00 | 3 | 3 | 0 | 0 | 0 | 0-0 | 9.0 | 17 | 51 | 16 | 16 | 1 | 0 | 2 | 1 | 7 | 0 | 10 | 0 | 0 |
| Hitchcock, Sterling, S.D.* | 0 | 3 | .000 | 6.33 | 4 | 4 | 0 | 0 | 0 | 0-0 | 21.1 | 22 | 91 | 15 | 15 | 5 | 0 | 0 | 0 | 8 | 0 | 14 | 1 | 0 |
| Hoffman, Trevor, S.D. | 3 | 3 | .500 | 2.30 | 55 | 0 | 0 | 0 | 51 | 41-45 | 54.2 | 42 | 209 | 14 | 14 | 5 | 2 | 0 | 0 | 8 | 1 | 53 | 2 | 0 |
| Horgan, Joe, Mon.* | 4 | 1 | .800 | 3.15 | 47 | 0 | 0 | 0 | 12 | 2-3 | 40.0 | 35 | 178 | 18 | 14 | 5 | 1 | 0 | 3 | 22 | 3 | 30 | 0 | 0 |
| Howard, Ben, Fla. | 1 | 1 | .500 | 5.50 | 31 | 0 | 0 | 0 | 7 | 0-0 | 37.2 | 37 | 167 | 23 | 23 | 6 | 1 | 2 | 1 | 21 | 3 | 33 | 3 | 0 |
| Hudson, Luke, Cin. | 4 | 2 | .667 | 2.42 | 9 | 9 | 0 | 0 | 0 | 0-0 | 48.1 | 36 | 204 | 16 | 13 | 3 | 2 | 2 | 2 | 25 | 1 | 38 | 5 | 0 |
| Ishii, Kazuhisa, L.A.* | 13 | 8 | .619 | 4.71 | 31 | 31 | 2 | 2 | 0 | 0-0 | 172.0 | 155 | 749 | 97 | 90 | 21 | 10 | 7 | 4 | 98 | 2 | 99 | 3 | 0 |
| Isringhausen, Jason, St.L. | 4 | 2 | .667 | 2.87 | 74 | 0 | 0 | 0 | 66 | 47-54 | 75.1 | 55 | 308 | 27 | 24 | 5 | 6 | 1 | 2 | 23 | 4 | 71 | 1 | 0 |
| Jackson, Edwin, L.A. | 2 | 1 | .667 | 7.30 | 8 | 5 | 0 | 0 | 1 | 0-0 | 24.2 | 31 | 113 | 20 | 20 | 7 | 1 | 0 | 0 | 11 | 1 | 16 | 0 | 0 |
| Jarvis, Kevin, Col. | 0 | 0 | .000 | 27.00 | 2 | 0 | 0 | 0 | 0 | 0-0 | 2.0 | 6 | 15 | 6 | 6 | 1 | 1 | 0 | 0 | 4 | 2 | 0 | 0 | 0 |
| Jennings, Jason, Col. | 11 | 12 | .478 | 5.51 | 33 | 33 | 0 | 0 | 0 | 0-0 | 201.0 | 241 | 925 | 125 | 123 | 27 | 9 | 3 | 7 | 101 | 14 | 133 | 6 | 1 |
| Johnson, Randy, Ari.* | 16 | 14 | .533 | 2.60 | 35 | 35 | 4 | 2 | 0 | 0-0 | 245.2 | 177 | 964 | 88 | 71 | 18 | 7 | 5 | 10 | 44 | 1 | 290 | 3 | 1 |
| Johnston, Mike, Pit.* | 0 | 3 | .000 | 4.37 | 24 | 0 | 0 | 0 | 5 | 0-1 | 22.2 | 29 | 110 | 16 | 11 | 2 | 1 | 0 | 2 | 15 | 1 | 18 | 0 | 0 |
| Jones, Todd, Cin.-Phi. | 11 | 5 | .688 | 4.15 | 78 | 0 | 0 | 0 | 16 | 2-8 | 82.1 | 84 | 358 | 39 | 38 | 7 | 5 | 6 | 6 | 33 | 5 | 59 | 2 | 0 |
| Kennedy, Joe, Col.* | 9 | 7 | .563 | 3.66 | 27 | 27 | 1 | 0 | 0 | 0-0 | 162.1 | 163 | 705 | 68 | 66 | 17 | 9 | 6 | 8 | 67 | 12 | 117 | 5 | 0 |
| Kensing, Logan, Fla. | 0 | 3 | .000 | 9.88 | 5 | 3 | 0 | 0 | 2 | 0-0 | 13.2 | 19 | 66 | 15 | 15 | 5 | 0 | 1 | 1 | 9 | 0 | 7 | 2 | 0 |
| Kida, Masao, L.A. | 0 | 0 | .000 | 0.00 | 3 | 0 | 0 | 0 | 1 | 0-0 | 4.2 | 4 | 19 | 0 | 0 | 0 | 0 | 0 | 1 | 1 | 0 | 5 | 0 | 0 |
| Kieschnick, Brooks, Mil. | 1 | 1 | .500 | 3.77 | 32 | 0 | 0 | 0 | 9 | 0-1 | 43.0 | 44 | 183 | 19 | 18 | 6 | 2 | 0 | 0 | 13 | 3 | 28 | 1 | 0 |
| Kim, Sun-Woo, Mon. | 4 | 6 | .400 | 4.58 | 43 | 17 | 0 | 0 | 3 | 0-0 | 135.2 | 145 | 603 | 80 | 69 | 17 | 5 | 3 | 13 | 55 | 11 | 87 | 6 | 0 |
| King, Ray, St.L.* | 5 | 2 | .714 | 2.61 | 86 | 0 | 0 | 0 | 9 | 0-1 | 62.0 | 43 | 248 | 19 | 18 | 1 | 2 | 1 | 3 | 24 | 0 | 40 | 2 | 0 |
| Kinney, Matt, Mil. | 3 | 4 | .429 | 5.78 | 32 | 6 | 0 | 0 | 10 | 0-0 | 62.1 | 77 | 286 | 41 | 40 | 8 | 2 | 3 | 2 | 23 | 1 | 52 | 5 | 0 |
| Kline, Steve, St.L.* | 2 | 2 | .500 | 1.79 | 67 | 0 | 0 | 0 | 22 | 3-4 | 50.1 | 37 | 202 | 12 | 10 | 3 | 3 | 1 | 4 | 17 | 4 | 35 | 1 | 0 |
| Koch, Billy, Fla. | 1 | 2 | .333 | 3.51 | 23 | 0 | 0 | 0 | 16 | 0-0 | 25.2 | 21 | 115 | 10 | 10 | 3 | 1 | 1 | 0 | 20 | 0 | 25 | 1 | 0 |
| Kolb, Dan, Mil. | 0 | 4 | .000 | 2.98 | 64 | 0 | 0 | 0 | 48 | 39-44 | 57.1 | 50 | 236 | 22 | 19 | 3 | 3 | 1 | 3 | 15 | 1 | 21 | 2 | 0 |
| Koplove, Mike, Ari. | 4 | 4 | .500 | 4.05 | 76 | 0 | 0 | 0 | 24 | 2-8 | 86.2 | 86 | 371 | 42 | 39 | 7 | 8 | 1 | 5 | 37 | 10 | 55 | 4 | 0 |
| Kroon, Marc, Col. | 0 | 0 | .000 | 6.00 | 6 | 0 | 0 | 0 | 1 | 0-0 | 6.0 | 7 | 32 | 4 | 4 | 1 | 1 | 1 | 0 | 10 | 0 | 3 | 1 | 0 |
| Lawrence, Brian, S.D. | 15 | 14 | .517 | 4.12 | 34 | 34 | 2 | 1 | 0 | 0-0 | 203.0 | 226 | 870 | 101 | 93 | 26 | 11 | 9 | 7 | 55 | 7 | 121 | 2 | 0 |
| Leicester, Jon, Chi. | 5 | 1 | .833 | 3.89 | 32 | 0 | 0 | 0 | 6 | 0-2 | 41.2 | 40 | 175 | 20 | 18 | 7 | 2 | 2 | 0 | 15 | 0 | 35 | 0 | 0 |
| Leiter, Al, N.Y.* | 10 | 8 | .556 | 3.21 | 30 | 30 | 0 | 0 | 0 | 0-0 | 173.2 | 138 | 750 | 65 | 62 | 16 | 8 | 2 | 11 | 97 | 8 | 117 | 1 | 1 |
| Lidge, Brad, Hou. | 6 | 5 | .545 | 1.90 | 80 | 0 | 0 | 0 | 44 | 29-33 | 94.2 | 57 | 369 | 21 | 20 | 8 | 3 | 2 | 6 | 30 | 5 | 157 | 3 | 1 |
| Lidle, Cory, Cin.-Phi. | 12 | 12 | .500 | 4.90 | 34 | 34 | 5 | 3 | 0 | 0-0 | 211.1 | 224 | 911 | 123 | 115 | 27 | 14 | 6 | 10 | 61 | 5 | 126 | 8 | 0 |
| Lima, Jose, L.A. | 13 | 5 | .722 | 4.07 | 36 | 24 | 0 | 0 | 3 | 0-0 | 170.1 | 178 | 702 | 81 | 77 | 33 | 9 | 1 | 1 | 34 | 6 | 93 | 3 | 0 |
| Lincoln, Mike, St.L. | 3 | 2 | .600 | 5.19 | 13 | 0 | 0 | 0 | 1 | 0-2 | 17.1 | 10 | 71 | 12 | 10 | 1 | 1 | 2 | 1 | 6 | 0 | 14 | 0 | 0 |
| Linebrink, Scott, S.D. | 7 | 3 | .700 | 2.14 | 73 | 0 | 0 | 0 | 7 | 0-5 | 84.0 | 61 | 326 | 22 | 20 | 8 | 2 | 3 | 3 | 26 | 2 | 83 | 3 | 0 |
| Liriano, Pedro, Mil. | 0 | 0 | .000 | 4.02 | 11 | 0 | 0 | 0 | 1 | 0-0 | 15.2 | 15 | 67 | 10 | 7 | 3 | 0 | 0 | 1 | 3 | 0 | 10 | 1 | 0 |
| Looper, Braden, N.Y. | 2 | 5 | .286 | 2.70 | 71 | 0 | 0 | 0 | 60 | 29-34 | 83.1 | 86 | 346 | 28 | 25 | 5 | 2 | 2 | 3 | 16 | 3 | 60 | 1 | 0 |
| Lopez, Javier, Col.* | 1 | 2 | .333 | 7.52 | 64 | 0 | 0 | 0 | 10 | 0-1 | 40.2 | 45 | 187 | 34 | 34 | 1 | 1 | 0 | 3 | 26 | 4 | 20 | 3 | 0 |
| Lowry, Noah, S.F.* | 6 | 0 | 1.000 | 3.82 | 16 | 14 | 2 | 1 | 0 | 0-0 | 92.0 | 91 | 383 | 41 | 39 | 10 | 2 | 1 | 0 | 28 | 1 | 72 | 2 | 0 |
| Maddux, Greg, Chi. | 16 | 11 | .593 | 4.02 | 33 | 33 | 2 | 1 | 0 | 0-0 | 212.2 | 218 | 872 | 103 | 95 | 35 | 12 | 8 | 9 | 33 | 4 | 151 | 2 | 0 |
| Madson, Ryan, Phi. | 9 | 3 | .750 | 2.34 | 52 | 1 | 0 | 0 | 14 | 1-2 | 77.0 | 68 | 312 | 23 | 20 | 6 | 1 | 1 | 5 | 19 | 4 | 55 | 7 | 0 |

| Pitcher, Team | W | L | Pct. | ERA | G | GS | CG | ShO | GF | Sv.-Op. | IP | H | TBF | R | ER | HR | SH | SF | HB | BB | IBB | SO | WP | Bk. |
|---|---|---|---|---|---|---|---|---|---|---|---|---|---|---|---|---|---|---|---|---|---|---|---|---|
| Majewski, Gary, Mon. | 0 | 1 | .000 | 3.86 | 16 | 0 | 0 | 0 | 7 | 1-2 | 21.0 | 28 | 95 | 15 | 9 | 2 | 1 | 1 | 2 | 5 | 1 | 12 | 0 | 0 |
| Mantei, Matt, Ari. | 0 | 3 | .000 | 11.81 | 12 | 0 | 0 | 0 | 9 | 4-7 | 10.2 | 17 | 55 | 15 | 14 | 5 | 0 | 1 | 0 | 6 | 1 | 13 | 0 | 0 |
| Manzanillo, Josias, Fla. | 3 | 3 | .500 | 6.12 | 26 | 0 | 0 | 0 | 7 | 1-4 | 32.1 | 38 | 151 | 24 | 22 | 6 | 2 | 1 | 3 | 15 | 2 | 27 | 0 | 0 |
| Marquis, Jason, St.L. | 15 | 7 | .682 | 3.71 | 32 | 32 | 0 | 0 | 0 | 0-0 | 201.1 | 215 | 874 | 90 | 83 | 26 | 5 | 6 | 10 | 70 | 1 | 138 | 6 | 0 |
| Martin, Tom, L.A.-Atl.* | 0 | 2 | .000 | 3.97 | 76 | 0 | 0 | 0 | 11 | 1-4 | 45.1 | 49 | 204 | 20 | 20 | 7 | 5 | 4 | 3 | 19 | 3 | 30 | 1 | 0 |
| Matthews, Mike, Cin.* | 2 | 1 | .667 | 6.30 | 35 | 0 | 0 | 0 | 6 | 0-0 | 30.0 | 31 | 137 | 22 | 21 | 7 | 1 | 1 | 2 | 16 | 1 | 15 | 4 | 1 |
| McConnell, Sam, Atl.* | 1 | 0 | 1.000 | 3.86 | 10 | 0 | 0 | 0 | 1 | 0-0 | 9.1 | 11 | 44 | 4 | 4 | 0 | 1 | 0 | 1 | 4 | 1 | 4 | 0 | 0 |
| McKay, Cody, St.L. | 0 | 0 | .000 | 0.00 | 1 | 0 | 0 | 0 | 1 | 0-0 | 2.0 | 0 | 7 | 0 | 0 | 0 | 0 | 0 | 0 | 1 | 0 | 0 | 0 | 0 |
| McLeary, Marty, S.D. | 0 | 0 | .000 | 14.73 | 3 | 0 | 0 | 0 | 2 | 0-0 | 3.2 | 7 | 20 | 6 | 6 | 2 | 1 | 1 | 0 | 2 | 0 | 4 | 0 | 0 |
| Meadows, Brian, Pit. | 2 | 4 | .333 | 3.58 | 68 | 0 | 0 | 0 | 15 | 1-2 | 78.0 | 76 | 323 | 40 | 31 | 7 | 6 | 5 | 0 | 19 | 7 | 46 | 5 | 0 |
| Mercker, Kent, Chi.* | 3 | 1 | .750 | 2.55 | 71 | 0 | 0 | 0 | 7 | 0-3 | 53.0 | 39 | 223 | 15 | 15 | 4 | 0 | 3 | 3 | 27 | 2 | 51 | 4 | 1 |
| Mesa, Jose, Pit. | 5 | 2 | .714 | 3.25 | 70 | 0 | 0 | 0 | 65 | 43-48 | 69.1 | 78 | 295 | 26 | 25 | 6 | 4 | 2 | 1 | 20 | 3 | 37 | 1 | 0 |
| Meyer, Dan, Atl.* | 0 | 0 | .000 | 0.00 | 2 | 0 | 0 | 0 | 1 | 0-0 | 2.0 | 2 | 8 | 0 | 0 | 0 | 0 | 0 | 0 | 1 | 1 | 1 | 0 | 0 |
| Miceli, Dan, Hou. | 6 | 6 | .500 | 3.59 | 74 | 0 | 0 | 0 | 15 | 2-8 | 77.2 | 74 | 336 | 34 | 31 | 10 | 5 | 3 | 2 | 27 | 12 | 83 | 4 | 0 |
| Miller, Wade, Hou. | 7 | 7 | .500 | 3.35 | 15 | 15 | 0 | 0 | 0 | 0-0 | 88.2 | 76 | 383 | 35 | 33 | 11 | 5 | 1 | 0 | 44 | 0 | 74 | 1 | 0 |
| Millwood, Kevin, Phi. | 9 | 6 | .600 | 4.85 | 25 | 25 | 0 | 0 | 0 | 0-0 | 141.0 | 155 | 628 | 81 | 76 | 14 | 11 | 2 | 7 | 51 | 5 | 125 | 4 | 0 |
| Milton, Eric, Phi.* | 14 | 6 | .700 | 4.75 | 34 | 34 | 0 | 0 | 0 | 0-0 | 201.0 | 196 | 862 | 110 | 106 | 43 | 11 | 6 | 1 | 75 | 6 | 161 | 3 | 0 |
| Mitre, Sergio, Chi. | 2 | 4 | .333 | 6.62 | 12 | 9 | 0 | 0 | 2 | 0-0 | 51.2 | 71 | 244 | 38 | 38 | 6 | 3 | 0 | 4 | 20 | 1 | 37 | 5 | 1 |
| Moreno, Orber, N.Y. | 3 | 1 | .750 | 3.38 | 33 | 0 | 0 | 0 | 8 | 1-3 | 34.2 | 29 | 146 | 17 | 13 | 0 | 1 | 0 | 3 | 11 | 0 | 29 | 2 | 1 |
| Morris, Matt, St.L. | 15 | 10 | .600 | 4.72 | 32 | 32 | 3 | 2 | 0 | 0-0 | 202.0 | 205 | 850 | 116 | 106 | 35 | 13 | 5 | 6 | 56 | 3 | 131 | 3 | 1 |
| Mota, Guillermo, L.A.-Fla. | 9 | 8 | .529 | 3.07 | 78 | 0 | 0 | 0 | 18 | 4-8 | 96.2 | 75 | 393 | 33 | 33 | 8 | 5 | 3 | 4 | 37 | 6 | 85 | 5 | 0 |
| Munro, Pete, Hou. | 4 | 7 | .364 | 5.15 | 21 | 19 | 0 | 0 | 1 | 0-0 | 99.2 | 120 | 446 | 59 | 57 | 12 | 9 | 4 | 10 | 26 | 2 | 63 | 2 | 0 |
| Myers, Brett, Phi. | 11 | 11 | .500 | 5.52 | 32 | 31 | 1 | 1 | 1 | 0-0 | 176.0 | 196 | 778 | 113 | 108 | 31 | 9 | 3 | 6 | 62 | 4 | 116 | 5 | 0 |
| Myers, Rodney, L.A. | 0 | 0 | .000 | 0.00 | 1 | 0 | 0 | 0 | 1 | 0-0 | 2.0 | 1 | 6 | 0 | 0 | 0 | 0 | 0 | 0 | 0 | 0 | 1 | 0 | 0 |
| Myette, Aaron, Cin. | 0 | 0 | .000 | 8.31 | 5 | 0 | 0 | 0 | 2 | 0-0 | 4.1 | 3 | 26 | 4 | 4 | 0 | 0 | 0 | 2 | 8 | 0 | 6 | 0 | 0 |
| Nance, Shane, Ari.* | 1 | 1 | .500 | 5.84 | 19 | 0 | 0 | 0 | 2 | 0-1 | 12.1 | 19 | 69 | 11 | 8 | 2 | 0 | 0 | 3 | 12 | 4 | 9 | 1 | 0 |
| Neal, Blaine, S.D. | 1 | 1 | .500 | 4.07 | 40 | 0 | 0 | 0 | 8 | 0-2 | 42.0 | 49 | 183 | 19 | 19 | 6 | 2 | 2 | 2 | 11 | 3 | 36 | 0 | 0 |
| Neu, Mike, Fla. | 0 | 0 | .000 | 4.50 | 1 | 0 | 0 | 0 | 0 | 0-0 | 4.0 | 5 | 18 | 2 | 2 | 1 | 0 | 0 | 0 | 2 | 0 | 2 | 0 | 0 |
| Nitkowski, C.J., Atl.* | 1 | 0 | 1.000 | 4.50 | 22 | 0 | 0 | 0 | 10 | 0-0 | 20.0 | 22 | 95 | 11 | 10 | 3 | 1 | 2 | 2 | 10 | 0 | 16 | 3 | 0 |
| Nomo, Hideo, L.A. | 4 | 11 | .267 | 8.25 | 18 | 18 | 0 | 0 | 0 | 0-0 | 84.0 | 105 | 393 | 77 | 77 | 19 | 7 | 3 | 4 | 42 | 1 | 54 | 3 | 0 |
| Norton, Phil, Cin.* | 2 | 5 | .286 | 5.07 | 69 | 0 | 0 | 0 | 14 | 0-2 | 65.2 | 71 | 296 | 41 | 37 | 5 | 4 | 2 | 2 | 38 | 7 | 48 | 2 | 0 |
| Nunez, Abraham O., Pit. | 0 | 0 | .000 | 0.00 | 1 | 0 | 0 | 0 | 1 | 0-0 | 0.1 | 0 | 1 | 0 | 0 | 0 | 0 | 0 | 0 | 0 | 0 | 0 | 0 | 0 |
| Nunez, Vladimir, Col. | 3 | 3 | .500 | 7.01 | 22 | 0 | 0 | 0 | 6 | 0-3 | 25.2 | 26 | 114 | 22 | 20 | 6 | 1 | 5 | 1 | 14 | 0 | 22 | 4 | 0 |
| Obermueller, Wes, Mil. | 6 | 8 | .429 | 5.80 | 25 | 20 | 1 | 1 | 1 | 0-0 | 118.0 | 138 | 529 | 80 | 76 | 15 | 4 | 5 | 3 | 42 | 0 | 59 | 4 | 0 |
| Ohka, Tomo, Mon. | 3 | 7 | .300 | 3.40 | 15 | 15 | 0 | 0 | 0 | 0-0 | 84.2 | 98 | 367 | 40 | 32 | 11 | 4 | 2 | 1 | 20 | 1 | 38 | 3 | 0 |
| Oliver, Darren, Fla.-Hou.* | 3 | 3 | .500 | 5.94 | 27 | 10 | 0 | 0 | 5 | 0-0 | 72.2 | 87 | 314 | 50 | 48 | 14 | 4 | 3 | 1 | 21 | 1 | 46 | 1 | 0 |
| Oropesa, Eddie, S.D.* | 2 | 1 | .667 | 11.00 | 16 | 0 | 0 | 0 | 4 | 0-0 | 9.0 | 6 | 45 | 12 | 11 | 1 | 0 | 0 | 0 | 13 | 3 | 6 | 1 | 0 |
| Ortiz, Russ, Atl. | 15 | 9 | .625 | 4.13 | 34 | 34 | 2 | 1 | 0 | 0-0 | 204.2 | 197 | 896 | 98 | 94 | 23 | 10 | 7 | 3 | 112 | 7 | 143 | 4 | 1 |
| Osuna, Antonio, S.D. | 2 | 1 | .667 | 2.45 | 31 | 0 | 0 | 0 | 6 | 0-2 | 36.2 | 32 | 151 | 11 | 10 | 3 | 0 | 1 | 1 | 11 | 0 | 36 | 0 | 0 |
| Oswalt, Roy, Hou. | 20 | 10 | .667 | 3.49 | 36 | 35 | 2 | 2 | 0 | 0-0 | 237.0 | 233 | 983 | 100 | 92 | 17 | 11 | 4 | 11 | 62 | 5 | 206 | 5 | 1 |
| Otsuka, Akinori, S.D. | 7 | 2 | .778 | 1.75 | 73 | 0 | 0 | 0 | 18 | 2-7 | 77.1 | 56 | 312 | 16 | 15 | 6 | 4 | 0 | 0 | 26 | 6 | 87 | 0 | 0 |
| Padilla, Juan, Cin. | 1 | 0 | 1.000 | 10.67 | 12 | 0 | 0 | 0 | 2 | 0-0 | 14.1 | 23 | 74 | 17 | 17 | 6 | 1 | 0 | 1 | 8 | 0 | 12 | 0 | 0 |
| Padilla, Vicente, Phi. | 7 | 7 | .500 | 4.53 | 20 | 20 | 0 | 0 | 0 | 0-0 | 115.1 | 119 | 503 | 63 | 58 | 16 | 7 | 5 | 10 | 36 | 6 | 82 | 2 | 0 |
| Parra, Jose, N.Y. | 1 | 0 | 1.000 | 3.21 | 13 | 0 | 0 | 0 | 7 | 0-0 | 14.0 | 14 | 61 | 6 | 5 | 2 | 0 | 0 | 0 | 6 | 1 | 14 | 0 | 0 |
| Patterson, John, Mon. | 4 | 7 | .364 | 5.03 | 19 | 19 | 0 | 0 | 0 | 0-0 | 98.1 | 100 | 445 | 58 | 55 | 18 | 4 | 2 | 8 | 46 | 4 | 99 | 0 | 0 |
| Pavano, Carl, Fla. | 18 | 8 | .692 | 3.00 | 31 | 31 | 2 | 2 | 0 | 0-0 | 222.1 | 212 | 909 | 80 | 74 | 16 | 7 | 4 | 11 | 49 | 13 | 139 | 2 | 3 |
| Pearce, Josh, St.L. | 0 | 0 | .000 | 3.86 | 3 | 0 | 0 | 0 | 1 | 0-0 | 2.1 | 3 | 9 | 1 | 1 | 0 | 1 | 0 | 0 | 0 | 0 | 0 | 0 | 0 |
| Peavy, Jake, S.D. | 15 | 6 | .714 | 2.27 | 27 | 27 | 0 | 0 | 0 | 0-0 | 166.1 | 146 | 694 | 49 | 42 | 13 | 5 | 6 | 11 | 53 | 4 | 173 | 1 | 1 |
| Penny, Brad, Fla.-L.A. | 9 | 10 | .474 | 3.15 | 24 | 24 | 0 | 0 | 0 | 0-0 | 143.0 | 130 | 590 | 55 | 50 | 12 | 3 | 3 | 3 | 45 | 6 | 111 | 5 | 0 |
| Perez, Odalis, L.A.* | 7 | 6 | .538 | 3.25 | 31 | 31 | 0 | 0 | 0 | 0-0 | 196.1 | 180 | 787 | 76 | 71 | 26 | 16 | 3 | 3 | 44 | 4 | 128 | 2 | 2 |
| Perez, Oliver, Pit.* | 12 | 10 | .545 | 2.98 | 30 | 30 | 2 | 1 | 0 | 0-0 | 196.0 | 145 | 805 | 71 | 65 | 22 | 9 | 5 | 9 | 81 | 2 | 239 | 2 | 1 |
| Perisho, Matt, Fla.* | 5 | 3 | .625 | 4.40 | 66 | 0 | 0 | 0 | 16 | 0-2 | 47.0 | 45 | 212 | 23 | 23 | 6 | 1 | 1 | 2 | 26 | 2 | 42 | 1 | 0 |
| Pettitte, Andy, Hou.* | 6 | 4 | .600 | 3.90 | 15 | 15 | 0 | 0 | 0 | 0-0 | 83.0 | 71 | 346 | 37 | 36 | 8 | 1 | 0 | 0 | 31 | 2 | 79 | 4 | 0 |
| Phelps, Tommy, Fla.* | 1 | 1 | .500 | 4.76 | 19 | 4 | 0 | 0 | 2 | 0-0 | 34.0 | 34 | 144 | 20 | 18 | 6 | 3 | 2 | 0 | 12 | 0 | 28 | 0 | 0 |
| Phelps, Travis, Mil. | 0 | 1 | .000 | 10.50 | 4 | 0 | 0 | 0 | 1 | 0-0 | 6.0 | 8 | 31 | 7 | 7 | 2 | 0 | 0 | 0 | 3 | 0 | 3 | 0 | 0 |
| Powell, Brian, Phi. | 1 | 2 | .333 | 5.03 | 17 | 2 | 0 | 0 | 9 | 0-0 | 39.1 | 39 | 166 | 23 | 22 | 5 | 2 | 5 | 1 | 16 | 4 | 24 | 3 | 0 |
| Pratt, Andy, Chi.* | 0 | 1 | .000 | 21.60 | 4 | 0 | 0 | 0 | 1 | 0-0 | 1.2 | 0 | 13 | 4 | 4 | 0 | 0 | 0 | 1 | 7 | 1 | 1 | 0 | 0 |
| Prior, Mark, Chi. | 6 | 4 | .600 | 4.02 | 21 | 21 | 0 | 0 | 0 | 0-0 | 118.2 | 112 | 510 | 53 | 53 | 14 | 8 | 4 | 3 | 48 | 2 | 139 | 2 | 1 |
| Puffer, Brandon, S.D. | 0 | 1 | .000 | 5.50 | 14 | 0 | 0 | 0 | 9 | 0-0 | 18.0 | 24 | 89 | 13 | 11 | 3 | 2 | 0 | 1 | 11 | 1 | 12 | 0 | 0 |
| Qualls, Chad, Hou. | 4 | 0 | 1.000 | 3.55 | 25 | 0 | 0 | 0 | 4 | 1-2 | 33.0 | 34 | 141 | 13 | 13 | 3 | 0 | 1 | 4 | 8 | 1 | 24 | 0 | 0 |
| Ramirez, Elizardo, Phi. | 0 | 0 | .000 | 4.80 | 7 | 0 | 0 | 0 | 5 | 0-0 | 15.0 | 17 | 67 | 8 | 8 | 3 | 0 | 1 | 1 | 5 | 1 | 9 | 1 | 0 |
| Ramirez, Horacio, Atl.* | 2 | 4 | .333 | 2.39 | 10 | 9 | 1 | 0 | 0 | 0-0 | 60.1 | 51 | 259 | 24 | 16 | 7 | 2 | 1 | 0 | 30 | 5 | 31 | 0 | 2 |
| Randolph, Stephen, Ari.* | 2 | 5 | .286 | 5.51 | 45 | 6 | 0 | 0 | 5 | 0-0 | 81.2 | 73 | 393 | 56 | 50 | 11 | 2 | 4 | 1 | 76 | 2 | 62 | 3 | 0 |
| Rauch, Jon, Mon. | 3 | 0 | 1.000 | 1.54 | 9 | 2 | 0 | 0 | 1 | 0-0 | 23.1 | 14 | 88 | 4 | 4 | 1 | 1 | 0 | 0 | 7 | 2 | 18 | 1 | 0 |
| Redding, Tim, Hou. | 5 | 7 | .417 | 5.72 | 27 | 17 | 0 | 0 | 2 | 0-0 | 100.2 | 125 | 465 | 73 | 64 | 15 | 10 | 3 | 5 | 43 | 3 | 56 | 2 | 0 |
| Reed, Steve, Col. | 3 | 8 | .273 | 3.68 | 65 | 0 | 0 | 0 | 18 | 0-4 | 66.0 | 72 | 285 | 29 | 27 | 7 | 4 | 1 | 7 | 17 | 7 | 38 | 1 | 0 |
| Reith, Brian, Cin. | 2 | 2 | .500 | 7.27 | 22 | 0 | 0 | 0 | 4 | 0-1 | 26.0 | 30 | 128 | 21 | 21 | 5 | 2 | 0 | 3 | 19 | 1 | 24 | 3 | 0 |
| Reitsma, Chris, Atl. | 6 | 4 | .600 | 4.07 | 84 | 0 | 0 | 0 | 12 | 2-9 | 79.2 | 89 | 344 | 38 | 36 | 9 | 2 | 6 | 3 | 20 | 3 | 60 | 1 | 0 |
| Remlinger, Mike, Chi.* | 1 | 2 | .333 | 3.44 | 48 | 0 | 0 | 0 | 6 | 2-6 | 36.2 | 33 | 156 | 16 | 14 | 3 | 1 | 4 | 1 | 16 | 3 | 35 | 1 | 0 |
| Reyes, Al, St.L. | 0 | 0 | .000 | 0.75 | 12 | 2 | 0 | 0 | 4 | 0-0 | 12.0 | 3 | 41 | 1 | 1 | 0 | 2 | 0 | 0 | 2 | 0 | 11 | 0 | 0 |
| Reynolds, Shane, Ari. | 0 | 1 | .000 | 4.50 | 1 | 1 | 0 | 0 | 0 | 0-0 | 2.0 | 6 | 14 | 6 | 1 | 0 | 0 | 0 | 0 | 2 | 0 | 0 | 0 | 0 |
| Riedling, John, Cin. | 5 | 3 | .625 | 5.10 | 70 | 0 | 0 | 0 | 15 | 0-7 | 77.2 | 90 | 365 | 54 | 44 | 10 | 3 | 3 | 4 | 40 | 5 | 46 | 6 | 0 |
| Roberts, Grant, N.Y. | 0 | 0 | .000 | 17.36 | 4 | 0 | 0 | 0 | 1 | 0-0 | 4.2 | 9 | 29 | 9 | 9 | 2 | 1 | 1 | 0 | 6 | 1 | 1 | 0 | 0 |
| Roberts, Willis, Pit. | 0 | 0 | .000 | 5.25 | 9 | 0 | 0 | 0 | 1 | 0-0 | 12.0 | 12 | 56 | 7 | 7 | 0 | 0 | 2 | 2 | 9 | 0 | 7 | 1 | 0 |
| Rodriguez, Felix, S.F.-Phi. | 5 | 8 | .385 | 3.29 | 76 | 0 | 0 | 0 | 13 | 1-4 | 65.2 | 61 | 289 | 25 | 24 | 8 | 4 | 1 | 5 | 29 | 4 | 59 | 4 | 0 |
| Rueter, Kirk, S.F.* | 9 | 12 | .429 | 4.73 | 33 | 33 | 0 | 0 | 0 | 0-0 | 190.1 | 225 | 840 | 108 | 100 | 21 | 9 | 4 | 1 | 66 | 5 | 56 | 1 | 0 |
| Rusch, Glendon, Chi.* | 6 | 2 | .750 | 3.47 | 32 | 16 | 0 | 0 | 5 | 2-2 | 129.2 | 127 | 545 | 54 | 50 | 10 | 8 | 2 | 4 | 33 | 1 | 90 | 1 | 1 |
| Saenz, Chris, Mil. | 1 | 0 | 1.000 | 0.00 | 1 | 1 | 0 | 0 | 0 | 0-0 | 6.0 | 2 | 24 | 0 | 0 | 0 | 0 | 0 | 1 | 3 | 0 | 7 | 0 | 0 |
| Sanchez, Duaner, L.A. | 3 | 1 | .750 | 3.38 | 67 | 0 | 0 | 0 | 27 | 0-1 | 80.0 | 81 | 342 | 34 | 30 | 9 | 2 | 3 | 6 | 27 | 2 | 44 | 6 | 0 |
| Sanchez, Jesus, Cin.* | 0 | 2 | .000 | 7.53 | 3 | 3 | 0 | 0 | 0 | 0-0 | 14.1 | 18 | 68 | 12 | 12 | 4 | 0 | 0 | 0 | 9 | 0 | 8 | 0 | 0 |
| Santos, Victor, Mil. | 11 | 12 | .478 | 4.97 | 31 | 28 | 0 | 0 | 2 | 0-0 | 154.0 | 169 | 684 | 95 | 85 | 18 | 6 | 7 | 7 | 57 | 5 | 115 | 2 | 1 |
| Schmidt, Jason, S.F. | 18 | 7 | .720 | 3.20 | 32 | 32 | 4 | 3 | 0 | 0-0 | 225.0 | 165 | 907 | 84 | 80 | 18 | 7 | 3 | 3 | 77 | 3 | 251 | 7 | 1 |
| Seanez, Rudy, Fla. | 3 | 1 | .750 | 2.74 | 23 | 0 | 0 | 0 | 8 | 0-1 | 23.0 | 18 | 93 | 7 | 7 | 3 | 0 | 0 | 0 | 8 | 1 | 25 | 1 | 0 |

| Pitcher, Team | W | L | Pct. | ERA | G | GS | CG | ShO | GF | Sv.-Op. | IP | H | TBF | R | ER | HR | SH | SF | HB | BB | IBB | SO | WP | Bk. |
|---|---|---|---|---|---|---|---|---|---|---|---|---|---|---|---|---|---|---|---|---|---|---|---|---|
| Seo, Jae Weong, N.Y. | 5 | 10 | .333 | 4.90 | 24 | 21 | 0 | 0 | 1 | 0-0 | 117.2 | 133 | 512 | 67 | 64 | 17 | 12 | 3 | 2 | 50 | 7 | 54 | 0 | 1 |
| Service, Scott, Ari. | 1 | 1 | .500 | 7.08 | 21 | 0 | 0 | 0 | 5 | 0-2 | 20.1 | 24 | 97 | 17 | 16 | 5 | 0 | 1 | 2 | 10 | 2 | 17 | 1 | 0 |
| Sheets, Ben, Mil. | 12 | 14 | .462 | 2.70 | 34 | 34 | 5 | 0 | 0 | 0-0 | 237.0 | 201 | 937 | 85 | 71 | 25 | 6 | 4 | 4 | 32 | 1 | 264 | 8 | 1 |
| Simontacchi, Jason, St.L. | 0 | 0 | .000 | 5.28 | 13 | 0 | 0 | 0 | 6 | 0-0 | 15.1 | 17 | 67 | 10 | 9 | 5 | 2 | 1 | 1 | 7 | 0 | 3 | 0 | 0 |
| Simpson, Allan, Col. | 2 | 1 | .667 | 5.08 | 32 | 0 | 0 | 0 | 9 | 0-1 | 39.0 | 44 | 183 | 26 | 22 | 4 | 3 | 4 | 4 | 20 | 0 | 46 | 3 | 0 |
| Small, Aaron, Fla. | 0 | 0 | .000 | 8.27 | 7 | 0 | 0 | 0 | 0 | 0-0 | 16.1 | 24 | 78 | 15 | 15 | 5 | 1 | 0 | 0 | 7 | 0 | 8 | 1 | 0 |
| Smith, Travis, Atl. | 2 | 3 | .400 | 6.20 | 16 | 4 | 0 | 0 | 4 | 0-0 | 40.2 | 48 | 180 | 28 | 28 | 12 | 3 | 0 | 1 | 12 | 2 | 26 | 1 | 0 |
| Smoltz, John, Atl. | 0 | 1 | .000 | 2.76 | 73 | 0 | 0 | 0 | 61 | 44-49 | 81.2 | 75 | 323 | 25 | 25 | 8 | 4 | 0 | 0 | 13 | 2 | 85 | 6 | 0 |
| Snell, Ian, Pit. | 0 | 1 | .000 | 7.50 | 3 | 1 | 0 | 0 | 1 | 0-0 | 12.0 | 14 | 56 | 10 | 10 | 2 | 0 | 0 | 0 | 9 | 0 | 9 | 0 | 0 |
| Sparks, Steve, Ari. | 3 | 7 | .300 | 6.04 | 29 | 18 | 0 | 0 | 6 | 0-0 | 120.2 | 139 | 545 | 89 | 81 | 18 | 6 | 5 | 5 | 45 | 2 | 57 | 4 | 0 |
| Springer, Russ, Hou. | 0 | 1 | .000 | 2.63 | 16 | 0 | 0 | 0 | 3 | 0-0 | 13.2 | 15 | 62 | 4 | 4 | 1 | 0 | 1 | 1 | 6 | 0 | 9 | 2 | 0 |
| Stanton, Mike, N.Y.* | 2 | 6 | .250 | 3.16 | 83 | 0 | 0 | 0 | 19 | 0-6 | 77.0 | 70 | 337 | 32 | 27 | 6 | 6 | 1 | 2 | 33 | 6 | 58 | 1 | 0 |
| Stark, Denny, Col. | 0 | 5 | .000 | 11.42 | 6 | 6 | 0 | 0 | 0 | 0-0 | 26.0 | 53 | 150 | 43 | 33 | 9 | 4 | 4 | 0 | 18 | 3 | 10 | 1 | 0 |
| Stewart, Scott, L.A.* | 1 | 0 | 1.000 | 5.84 | 11 | 0 | 0 | 0 | 2 | 0-0 | 12.1 | 20 | 60 | 8 | 8 | 3 | 1 | 2 | 0 | 6 | 3 | 8 | 0 | 0 |
| Stone, Ricky, Hou.-S.D. | 2 | 2 | .500 | 6.45 | 43 | 0 | 0 | 0 | 17 | 0-0 | 51.2 | 66 | 238 | 39 | 37 | 11 | 0 | 1 | 6 | 16 | 3 | 38 | 2 | 0 |
| Suppan, Jeff, St.L. | 16 | 9 | .640 | 4.16 | 31 | 31 | 0 | 0 | 0 | 0-0 | 188.0 | 192 | 811 | 98 | 87 | 25 | 8 | 5 | 8 | 65 | 1 | 110 | 4 | 1 |
| Sweeney, Brian, S.D. | 1 | 0 | 1.000 | 5.65 | 7 | 2 | 0 | 0 | 1 | 0-0 | 14.1 | 20 | 63 | 9 | 9 | 1 | 0 | 0 | 0 | 2 | 0 | 10 | 1 | 0 |
| Szuminski, Jason, S.D. | 0 | 0 | .000 | 7.20 | 7 | 0 | 0 | 0 | 2 | 0-0 | 10.0 | 12 | 57 | 9 | 8 | 3 | 2 | 0 | 2 | 11 | 2 | 5 | 0 | 0 |
| Tankersley, Dennis, S.D. | 0 | 5 | .000 | 5.14 | 9 | 6 | 0 | 0 | 0 | 0-0 | 35.0 | 35 | 157 | 25 | 20 | 3 | 1 | 0 | 1 | 17 | 3 | 29 | 2 | 0 |
| Tavarez, Julian, St.L. | 7 | 4 | .636 | 2.38 | 77 | 0 | 0 | 0 | 27 | 4-6 | 64.1 | 57 | 268 | 21 | 17 | 1 | 3 | 1 | 6 | 19 | 0 | 48 | 2 | 1 |
| Tejera, Michael, Fla.* | 0 | 1 | .000 | 18.00 | 2 | 2 | 0 | 0 | 0 | 0-0 | 4.0 | 6 | 23 | 8 | 8 | 0 | 0 | 0 | 1 | 6 | 0 | 3 | 0 | 0 |
| Telemaco, Amaury, Phi. | 0 | 2 | .000 | 4.31 | 42 | 0 | 0 | 0 | 9 | 0-0 | 54.1 | 51 | 225 | 27 | 26 | 12 | 1 | 0 | 0 | 19 | 2 | 32 | 2 | 1 |
| Thomson, John, Atl. | 14 | 8 | .636 | 3.72 | 33 | 33 | 0 | 0 | 0 | 0-0 | 198.1 | 210 | 834 | 93 | 82 | 20 | 11 | 4 | 6 | 52 | 5 | 133 | 3 | 0 |
| Tomko, Brett, S.F. | 11 | 7 | .611 | 4.04 | 32 | 31 | 2 | 1 | 1 | 0-0 | 194.0 | 196 | 825 | 98 | 87 | 19 | 7 | 1 | 0 | 64 | 3 | 108 | 10 | 0 |
| Torres, Salomon, Pit. | 7 | 7 | .500 | 2.64 | 84 | 0 | 0 | 0 | 20 | 0-4 | 92.0 | 87 | 380 | 33 | 27 | 6 | 9 | 3 | 6 | 22 | 6 | 62 | 5 | 0 |
| Trachsel, Steve, N.Y. | 12 | 13 | .480 | 4.00 | 33 | 33 | 0 | 0 | 0 | 0-0 | 202.2 | 203 | 881 | 104 | 90 | 25 | 11 | 8 | 5 | 83 | 9 | 117 | 4 | 2 |
| Tsao, Chin-hui, Col. | 0 | 0 | .000 | 3.86 | 10 | 0 | 0 | 0 | 5 | 1-2 | 9.1 | 7 | 37 | 4 | 4 | 2 | 1 | 0 | 0 | 1 | 0 | 11 | 0 | 0 |
| Tucker, T.J., Mon. | 4 | 2 | .667 | 3.72 | 54 | 1 | 0 | 0 | 15 | 0-2 | 67.2 | 73 | 291 | 28 | 28 | 5 | 3 | 2 | 4 | 17 | 6 | 44 | 1 | 1 |
| Valdez, Ismael, S.D.-Fla. | 14 | 9 | .609 | 5.19 | 34 | 31 | 1 | 1 | 2 | 0-0 | 170.0 | 202 | 751 | 105 | 98 | 33 | 10 | 4 | 2 | 49 | 3 | 67 | 1 | 0 |
| Valdez, Merkin, S.F. | 0 | 0 | .000 | 27.00 | 2 | 0 | 0 | 0 | 0 | 0-0 | 1.2 | 4 | 12 | 5 | 5 | 1 | 0 | 0 | 0 | 3 | 0 | 2 | 0 | 0 |
| Valentine, Joe, Cin. | 2 | 3 | .400 | 5.22 | 24 | 1 | 0 | 0 | 13 | 4-4 | 29.1 | 23 | 136 | 18 | 17 | 4 | 0 | 0 | 2 | 25 | 1 | 29 | 2 | 0 |
| Valverde, Jose, Ari. | 1 | 2 | .333 | 4.25 | 29 | 0 | 0 | 0 | 20 | 8-10 | 29.2 | 23 | 131 | 17 | 14 | 7 | 3 | 2 | 1 | 17 | 4 | 38 | 4 | 0 |
| Van Benschoten, John, Pit. | 1 | 3 | .250 | 6.91 | 6 | 5 | 0 | 0 | 0 | 0-0 | 28.2 | 33 | 135 | 27 | 22 | 3 | 2 | 2 | 2 | 19 | 0 | 18 | 1 | 0 |
| Van Poppel, Todd, Cin. | 4 | 6 | .400 | 6.09 | 48 | 11 | 0 | 0 | 12 | 0-1 | 115.1 | 136 | 502 | 80 | 78 | 22 | 6 | 4 | 3 | 32 | 3 | 72 | 6 | 1 |
| Vargas, Claudio, Mon. | 5 | 5 | .500 | 5.25 | 45 | 14 | 0 | 0 | 6 | 0-0 | 118.1 | 120 | 530 | 75 | 69 | 26 | 4 | 4 | 7 | 64 | 7 | 89 | 8 | 0 |
| Venafro, Mike, L.A.* | 0 | 0 | .000 | 4.00 | 17 | 0 | 0 | 0 | 2 | 0-0 | 9.0 | 11 | 42 | 5 | 4 | 1 | 1 | 0 | 2 | 3 | 1 | 6 | 0 | 0 |
| Ventura, Robin, L.A. | 0 | 0 | .000 | 0.00 | 1 | 0 | 0 | 0 | 1 | 0-0 | 1.0 | 1 | 4 | 0 | 0 | 0 | 0 | 0 | 0 | 0 | 0 | 0 | 0 | 0 |
| Villafuerte, Brandon, Ari. | 0 | 3 | .000 | 4.05 | 20 | 0 | 0 | 0 | 6 | 0-0 | 20.0 | 25 | 96 | 9 | 9 | 2 | 1 | 0 | 1 | 14 | 2 | 13 | 0 | 0 |
| Villarreal, Oscar, Ari. | 0 | 2 | .000 | 7.00 | 17 | 0 | 0 | 0 | 4 | 0-0 | 18.0 | 25 | 84 | 14 | 14 | 3 | 3 | 0 | 1 | 7 | 1 | 17 | 5 | 0 |
| Vizcaino, Luis, Mil. | 4 | 4 | .500 | 3.75 | 73 | 0 | 0 | 0 | 21 | 1-5 | 72.0 | 61 | 298 | 35 | 30 | 12 | 1 | 5 | 1 | 24 | 3 | 63 | 9 | 0 |
| Vogelsong, Ryan, Pit. | 6 | 13 | .316 | 6.50 | 31 | 26 | 0 | 0 | 4 | 0-0 | 133.0 | 148 | 610 | 97 | 96 | 22 | 8 | 6 | 10 | 67 | 7 | 92 | 3 | 0 |
| Wagner, Billy, Phi.* | 4 | 0 | 1.000 | 2.42 | 45 | 0 | 0 | 0 | 38 | 21-25 | 48.1 | 31 | 182 | 16 | 13 | 5 | 3 | 0 | 2 | 6 | 1 | 59 | 1 | 0 |
| Wagner, Ryan, Cin. | 3 | 2 | .600 | 4.70 | 49 | 0 | 0 | 0 | 5 | 0-3 | 51.2 | 59 | 242 | 31 | 27 | 7 | 2 | 3 | 2 | 27 | 2 | 37 | 6 | 0 |
| Walker, Kevin, S.F.* | 0 | 0 | .000 | 16.20 | 5 | 0 | 0 | 0 | 0 | 0-0 | 1.2 | 3 | 10 | 3 | 3 | 1 | 0 | 0 | 1 | 2 | 0 | 1 | 0 | 0 |
| Walker, Tyler, S.F. | 5 | 1 | .833 | 4.24 | 52 | 0 | 0 | 0 | 13 | 1-1 | 63.2 | 69 | 275 | 31 | 30 | 8 | 3 | 7 | 1 | 24 | 1 | 48 | 1 | 0 |
| Watkins, Steve, S.D. | 0 | 0 | .000 | 6.28 | 11 | 0 | 0 | 0 | 7 | 0-0 | 14.1 | 17 | 65 | 10 | 10 | 3 | 1 | 0 | 2 | 4 | 0 | 7 | 0 | 0 |
| Wayne, Justin, Fla. | 3 | 3 | .500 | 5.79 | 19 | 1 | 0 | 0 | 4 | 0-2 | 32.2 | 35 | 148 | 24 | 21 | 6 | 1 | 3 | 2 | 18 | 1 | 20 | 1 | 0 |
| Weathers, David, N.Y.-Hou.-Fla. | 7 | 7 | .500 | 4.15 | 66 | 2 | 0 | 0 | 20 | 0-4 | 82.1 | 85 | 357 | 44 | 38 | 12 | 5 | 2 | 5 | 35 | 2 | 61 | 1 | 1 |
| Weaver, Jeff, L.A. | 13 | 13 | .500 | 4.01 | 34 | 34 | 0 | 0 | 0 | 0-0 | 220.0 | 219 | 935 | 103 | 98 | 19 | 5 | 7 | 14 | 67 | 9 | 153 | 9 | 0 |
| Webb, Brandon, Ari. | 7 | 16 | .304 | 3.59 | 35 | 35 | 1 | 0 | 0 | 0-0 | 208.0 | 194 | 933 | 111 | 83 | 17 | 14 | 6 | 11 | 119 | 11 | 164 | 17 | 1 |
| Wellemeyer, Todd, Chi. | 2 | 1 | .667 | 5.92 | 20 | 0 | 0 | 0 | 7 | 0-0 | 24.1 | 27 | 119 | 16 | 16 | 1 | 3 | 2 | 0 | 20 | 2 | 30 | 0 | 1 |
| Wells, David, S.D.* | 12 | 8 | .600 | 3.73 | 31 | 31 | 0 | 0 | 0 | 0-0 | 195.2 | 203 | 804 | 85 | 81 | 23 | 14 | 4 | 2 | 20 | 1 | 101 | 2 | 1 |
| Wells, Kip, Pit. | 5 | 7 | .417 | 4.55 | 24 | 24 | 0 | 0 | 0 | 0-0 | 138.1 | 145 | 621 | 71 | 70 | 14 | 5 | 6 | 6 | 66 | 4 | 116 | 3 | 0 |
| Wendell, Turk, Col. | 0 | 0 | .000 | 7.02 | 12 | 0 | 0 | 0 | 5 | 0-1 | 16.2 | 21 | 80 | 13 | 13 | 4 | 0 | 2 | 2 | 12 | 1 | 11 | 1 | 0 |
| Wheeler, Dan, N.Y.-Hou. | 3 | 1 | .750 | 4.29 | 46 | 1 | 0 | 0 | 11 | 0-0 | 65.0 | 76 | 287 | 33 | 31 | 10 | 2 | 1 | 1 | 20 | 2 | 55 | 4 | 1 |
| White, Gabe, Cin.* | 1 | 2 | .333 | 6.23 | 40 | 0 | 0 | 0 | 9 | 1-3 | 39.0 | 39 | 161 | 27 | 27 | 12 | 2 | 2 | 0 | 5 | 0 | 33 | 1 | 0 |
| Williams, Dave, Pit.* | 2 | 3 | .400 | 4.42 | 10 | 6 | 0 | 0 | 0 | 0-0 | 38.2 | 31 | 162 | 21 | 19 | 4 | 1 | 1 | 3 | 13 | 2 | 33 | 0 | 0 |
| Williams, Jerome, S.F. | 10 | 7 | .588 | 4.24 | 22 | 22 | 0 | 0 | 0 | 0-0 | 129.1 | 123 | 559 | 69 | 61 | 14 | 4 | 9 | 17 | 44 | 1 | 80 | 2 | 1 |
| Williams, Woody, St.L. | 11 | 8 | .579 | 4.18 | 31 | 31 | 0 | 0 | 0 | 0-0 | 189.2 | 193 | 817 | 93 | 88 | 20 | 9 | 5 | 9 | 58 | 3 | 131 | 12 | 1 |
| Willis, Dontrelle, Fla.* | 10 | 11 | .476 | 4.02 | 32 | 32 | 2 | 0 | 0 | 0-0 | 197.0 | 210 | 848 | 99 | 88 | 20 | 8 | 2 | 8 | 61 | 8 | 139 | 2 | 0 |
| Wilson, Paul, Cin. | 11 | 6 | .647 | 4.36 | 29 | 29 | 1 | 0 | 0 | 0-0 | 183.2 | 192 | 798 | 93 | 89 | 26 | 10 | 8 | 8 | 63 | 5 | 117 | 7 | 0 |
| Wise, Matt, Mil. | 1 | 2 | .333 | 4.44 | 30 | 3 | 0 | 0 | 5 | 0-0 | 52.2 | 51 | 222 | 27 | 26 | 3 | 1 | 2 | 2 | 15 | 1 | 30 | 2 | 0 |
| Witasick, Jay, S.D. | 0 | 1 | .000 | 3.21 | 44 | 0 | 0 | 0 | 20 | 1-3 | 61.2 | 57 | 266 | 28 | 22 | 8 | 3 | 2 | 1 | 26 | 2 | 57 | 4 | 0 |
| Wolf, Randy, Phi.* | 5 | 8 | .385 | 4.28 | 23 | 23 | 1 | 1 | 0 | 0-0 | 136.2 | 145 | 585 | 73 | 65 | 20 | 6 | 3 | 5 | 36 | 4 | 89 | 2 | 0 |
| Wood, Kerry, Chi. | 8 | 9 | .471 | 3.72 | 22 | 22 | 0 | 0 | 0 | 0-0 | 140.1 | 127 | 595 | 62 | 58 | 16 | 6 | 6 | 11 | 51 | 0 | 144 | 7 | 0 |
| Worrell, Tim, Phi. | 5 | 6 | .455 | 3.68 | 77 | 0 | 0 | 0 | 36 | 19-27 | 78.1 | 75 | 327 | 36 | 32 | 10 | 4 | 5 | 2 | 21 | 4 | 64 | 0 | 0 |
| Wright, Jamey, Col. | 2 | 3 | .400 | 4.12 | 14 | 14 | 0 | 0 | 0 | 0-0 | 78.2 | 82 | 361 | 39 | 36 | 8 | 1 | 1 | 6 | 45 | 3 | 41 | 3 | 0 |
| Wright, Jaret, Atl. | 15 | 8 | .652 | 3.28 | 32 | 32 | 0 | 0 | 0 | 0-0 | 186.1 | 168 | 781 | 79 | 68 | 11 | 8 | 6 | 3 | 70 | 5 | 159 | 3 | 0 |
| Wuertz, Michael, Chi. | 1 | 0 | 1.000 | 4.34 | 31 | 0 | 0 | 0 | 11 | 1-1 | 29.0 | 22 | 124 | 14 | 14 | 4 | 4 | 2 | 0 | 17 | 1 | 30 | 2 | 1 |
| Yates, Tyler, N.Y. | 2 | 4 | .333 | 6.36 | 21 | 7 | 0 | 0 | 2 | 0-0 | 46.2 | 61 | 228 | 36 | 33 | 6 | 2 | 2 | 3 | 25 | 3 | 35 | 1 | 1 |
| Young, Jason, Col. | 0 | 1 | .000 | 12.96 | 2 | 2 | 0 | 0 | 0 | 0-0 | 8.1 | 15 | 45 | 12 | 12 | 3 | 1 | 0 | 0 | 5 | 1 | 7 | 1 | 0 |
| Zambrano, Carlos, Chi. | 16 | 8 | .667 | 2.75 | 31 | 31 | 1 | 1 | 0 | 0-0 | 209.2 | 174 | 887 | 73 | 64 | 14 | 10 | 3 | 20 | 81 | 4 | 188 | 6 | 2 |
| Zambrano, Victor, N.Y. | 2 | 0 | 1.000 | 3.86 | 3 | 3 | 0 | 0 | 0 | 0-0 | 14.0 | 12 | 62 | 9 | 6 | 0 | 1 | 0 | 0 | 6 | 0 | 14 | 1 | 0 |
| Zeile, Todd, N.Y. | 0 | 0 | .000 | 45.00 | 1 | 0 | 0 | 0 | 1 | 0-0 | 1.0 | 4 | 9 | 5 | 5 | 0 | 0 | 0 | 0 | 2 | 0 | 0 | 0 | 0 |

## PITCHERS WITH TWO OR MORE TEAMS

| Pitcher, Team | W | L | Pct. | ERA | G | GS | CG | ShO | GF | Sv.-Op. | IP | H | TBF | R | ER | HR | SH | SF | HB | BB | IBB | SO | WP | Bk. |
|---|---|---|---|---|---|---|---|---|---|---|---|---|---|---|---|---|---|---|---|---|---|---|---|---|
| Beltran, Francis, Chi. | 2 | 2 | .500 | 4.63 | 34 | 0 | 0 | 0 | 10 | 0-0 | 35.0 | 27 | 152 | 19 | 18 | 8 | 3 | 1 | 0 | 22 | 0 | 40 | 1 | 0 |
| Beltran, Francis, Mon. | 0 | 0 | .000 | 7.53 | 11 | 0 | 0 | 0 | 3 | 1-1 | 14.1 | 20 | 69 | 12 | 12 | 3 | 1 | 1 | 2 | 5 | 1 | 8 | 1 | 0 |
| Benson, Kris, Pit. | 8 | 8 | .500 | 4.22 | 20 | 20 | 0 | 0 | 0 | 0-0 | 132.1 | 137 | 564 | 69 | 62 | 7 | 7 | 4 | 6 | 44 | 5 | 83 | 2 | 0 |
| Benson, Kris, N.Y. | 4 | 4 | .500 | 4.50 | 11 | 11 | 1 | 1 | 0 | 0-0 | 68.0 | 65 | 290 | 37 | 34 | 8 | 1 | 2 | 4 | 17 | 3 | 51 | 3 | 0 |

| Pitcher, Team | W | L | Pct. | ERA | G | GS | CG | ShO | GF | Sv.-Op. | IP | H | TBF | R | ER | HR | SH | SF | HB | BB | IBB | SO | WP | Bk. |
|---|---|---|---|---|---|---|---|---|---|---|---|---|---|---|---|---|---|---|---|---|---|---|---|---|
| Burba, Dave, Mil. | 3 | 1 | .750 | 4.08 | 45 | 0 | 0 | 0 | 15 | 2-4 | 70.2 | 63 | 299 | 36 | 32 | 6 | 4 | 3 | 2 | 24 | 2 | 47 | 2 | 1 |
| Burba, Dave, S.F. | 1 | 0 | 1.000 | 5.68 | 6 | 0 | 0 | 0 | 1 | 0-1 | 6.1 | 7 | 27 | 4 | 4 | 1 | 0 | 0 | 0 | 2 | 0 | 3 | 1 | 0 |
| Dessens, Elmer, Ari. | 1 | 6 | .143 | 4.75 | 38 | 9 | 0 | 0 | 7 | 2-4 | 85.1 | 107 | 386 | 54 | 45 | 11 | 4 | 3 | 1 | 23 | 4 | 55 | 2 | 0 |
| Dessens, Elmer, L.A. | 1 | 0 | 1.000 | 3.20 | 12 | 1 | 0 | 0 | 2 | 0-1 | 19.2 | 16 | 82 | 7 | 7 | 4 | 0 | 0 | 0 | 8 | 0 | 18 | 0 | 0 |
| Fassero, Jeff, Col.* | 3 | 8 | .273 | 5.51 | 40 | 12 | 0 | 0 | 2 | 0-0 | 111.0 | 136 | 505 | 73 | 68 | 9 | 5 | 7 | 4 | 44 | 5 | 59 | 4 | 1 |
| Fassero, Jeff, Ari.* | 0 | 0 | .000 | 0.00 | 1 | 0 | 0 | 0 | 0 | 0-0 | 1.0 | 0 | 3 | 0 | 0 | 0 | 0 | 0 | 0 | 0 | 0 | 1 | 0 | 0 |
| Hancock, Josh, Phi. | 0 | 1 | .000 | 9.00 | 4 | 2 | 0 | 0 | 0 | 0-0 | 9.0 | 13 | 42 | 9 | 9 | 3 | 0 | 0 | 0 | 3 | 0 | 5 | 0 | 0 |
| Hancock, Josh, Cin. | 5 | 1 | .833 | 4.45 | 12 | 9 | 0 | 0 | 2 | 0-0 | 54.2 | 60 | 251 | 34 | 27 | 14 | 3 | 2 | 1 | 25 | 2 | 31 | 5 | 0 |
| Jones, Todd, Cin. | 8 | 2 | .800 | 3.79 | 51 | 0 | 0 | 0 | 10 | 1-6 | 57.0 | 49 | 235 | 25 | 24 | 4 | 2 | 5 | 1 | 25 | 2 | 37 | 2 | 0 |
| Jones, Todd, Phi. | 3 | 3 | .500 | 4.97 | 27 | 0 | 0 | 0 | 6 | 1-2 | 25.1 | 35 | 123 | 14 | 14 | 3 | 3 | 1 | 5 | 8 | 3 | 22 | 0 | 0 |
| Lidle, Cory, Cin. | 7 | 10 | .412 | 5.32 | 24 | 24 | 3 | 1 | 0 | 0-0 | 149.0 | 170 | 656 | 95 | 88 | 24 | 12 | 4 | 5 | 44 | 4 | 93 | 8 | 0 |
| Lidle, Cory, Phi. | 5 | 2 | .714 | 3.90 | 10 | 10 | 2 | 2 | 0 | 0-0 | 62.1 | 54 | 255 | 28 | 27 | 3 | 2 | 2 | 5 | 17 | 1 | 33 | 0 | 0 |
| Martin, Tom, L.A.* | 0 | 1 | .000 | 4.13 | 47 | 0 | 0 | 0 | 9 | 1-1 | 28.1 | 32 | 132 | 13 | 13 | 3 | 3 | 2 | 3 | 14 | 1 | 18 | 1 | 0 |
| Martin, Tom, Atl.* | 0 | 1 | .000 | 3.71 | 29 | 0 | 0 | 0 | 2 | 0-3 | 17.0 | 17 | 72 | 7 | 7 | 4 | 2 | 2 | 0 | 5 | 2 | 12 | 0 | 0 |
| Mota, Guillermo, L.A. | 8 | 4 | .667 | 2.14 | 52 | 0 | 0 | 0 | 11 | 1-1 | 63.0 | 51 | 259 | 15 | 15 | 4 | 4 | 2 | 2 | 27 | 5 | 52 | 5 | 0 |
| Mota, Guillermo, Fla. | 1 | 4 | .200 | 4.81 | 26 | 0 | 0 | 0 | 7 | 3-7 | 33.2 | 24 | 134 | 18 | 18 | 4 | 1 | 1 | 2 | 10 | 1 | 33 | 0 | 0 |
| Oliver, Darren, Fla.* | 2 | 3 | .400 | 6.44 | 18 | 8 | 0 | 0 | 3 | 0-0 | 58.2 | 75 | 260 | 44 | 42 | 13 | 4 | 3 | 1 | 17 | 1 | 33 | 1 | 0 |
| Oliver, Darren, Hou.* | 1 | 0 | 1.000 | 3.86 | 9 | 2 | 0 | 0 | 2 | 0-0 | 14.0 | 12 | 54 | 6 | 6 | 1 | 0 | 0 | 0 | 4 | 0 | 13 | 0 | 0 |
| Penny, Brad, Fla. | 8 | 8 | .500 | 3.15 | 21 | 21 | 0 | 0 | 0 | 0-0 | 131.1 | 124 | 545 | 50 | 46 | 10 | 3 | 3 | 3 | 39 | 6 | 105 | 5 | 0 |
| Penny, Brad, L.A. | 1 | 2 | .333 | 3.09 | 3 | 3 | 0 | 0 | 0 | 0-0 | 11.2 | 6 | 45 | 5 | 4 | 2 | 0 | 0 | 0 | 6 | 0 | 6 | 0 | 0 |
| Rodriguez, Felix, S.F. | 3 | 5 | .375 | 3.43 | 53 | 0 | 0 | 0 | 8 | 0-3 | 44.2 | 43 | 199 | 18 | 17 | 7 | 3 | 1 | 4 | 19 | 2 | 31 | 4 | 0 |
| Rodriguez, Felix, Phi. | 2 | 3 | .400 | 3.00 | 23 | 0 | 0 | 0 | 5 | 1-1 | 21.0 | 18 | 90 | 7 | 7 | 1 | 1 | 0 | 1 | 10 | 2 | 28 | 0 | 0 |
| Stone, Ricky, Hou. | 1 | 1 | .500 | 5.68 | 16 | 0 | 0 | 0 | 7 | 0-0 | 19.0 | 26 | 92 | 12 | 12 | 5 | 0 | 0 | 3 | 7 | 3 | 16 | 1 | 0 |
| Stone, Ricky, S.D. | 1 | 1 | .500 | 6.89 | 27 | 0 | 0 | 0 | 10 | 0-0 | 32.2 | 40 | 146 | 27 | 25 | 6 | 0 | 1 | 3 | 9 | 0 | 22 | 1 | 0 |
| Valdez, Ismael, S.D. | 9 | 6 | .600 | 5.53 | 23 | 20 | 1 | 1 | 2 | 0-0 | 114.0 | 141 | 509 | 75 | 70 | 21 | 8 | 2 | 2 | 31 | 1 | 37 | 1 | 0 |
| Valdez, Ismael, Fla. | 5 | 3 | .625 | 4.50 | 11 | 11 | 0 | 0 | 0 | 0-0 | 56.0 | 61 | 242 | 30 | 28 | 12 | 2 | 2 | 0 | 18 | 2 | 30 | 0 | 0 |
| Weathers, David, N.Y. | 5 | 3 | .625 | 4.28 | 32 | 0 | 0 | 0 | 10 | 0-1 | 33.2 | 41 | 156 | 19 | 16 | 5 | 2 | 2 | 2 | 15 | 0 | 25 | 1 | 1 |
| Weathers, David, Hou. | 1 | 4 | .200 | 4.78 | 26 | 0 | 0 | 0 | 9 | 0-3 | 32.0 | 31 | 137 | 20 | 17 | 5 | 2 | 0 | 3 | 13 | 1 | 26 | 0 | 0 |
| Weathers, David, Fla. | 1 | 0 | 1.000 | 2.70 | 8 | 2 | 0 | 0 | 1 | 0-0 | 16.2 | 13 | 64 | 5 | 5 | 2 | 1 | 0 | 0 | 7 | 1 | 10 | 0 | 0 |
| Wheeler, Dan, N.Y. | 3 | 1 | .750 | 4.80 | 32 | 1 | 0 | 0 | 7 | 0-0 | 50.2 | 65 | 232 | 29 | 27 | 9 | 2 | 1 | 0 | 17 | 2 | 46 | 4 | 1 |
| Wheeler, Dan, Hou. | 0 | 0 | .000 | 2.51 | 14 | 0 | 0 | 0 | 4 | 0-0 | 14.1 | 11 | 55 | 4 | 4 | 1 | 0 | 0 | 1 | 3 | 0 | 9 | 0 | 0 |

NOTE—The following pitchers combined to pitch shutout games: Arizona (4)—Daigle, Koplove, Choate, Villarreal and Valverde; Johnson and Choate; Fossum, Koplove and Valverde; Johnson and Aquino; Atlanta (12)—Ramirez and Smoltz; Ortiz, Reitsma and Smoltz; Thomson, Reitsma and Alfonseca; Byrd, Alfonseca and Smoltz; Ortiz and Smoltz; Ortiz, Reitsma and Smoltz; Hampton and Smoltz; Wright, Gryboski and Alfonseca; Ortiz, Reitsma and Smoltz; Wright, Gryboski and Cruz; Thomson, Reitsma and Smoltz; Hampton, Smith, Martin and Reitsma; Chicago (4)—Wood, Mercker and Hawkins; Zambrano and Farnsworth; Wood and Remlinger; Zambrano, Mercker and Remlinger; Cincinnati (6)—Van Poppel, Riedling, Jones and Graves; Bong, White, Riedling and Matthews; Lidle, Jones and Graves; Harang, White and Graves; Hudson, Wagner and Valentine; Hudson, Matthews, Norton and Myette; Colorado (2)—Kennedy, Harikkala, Fuentes, Nunez and Chacon; Cook and Chacon; Florida (11)—Willis, Fox and Benitez; Penny and Phelps; Willis, Wayne, Bump and Perisho; Pavano, Fox and Benitez; Penny, Perisho and Benitez; Phelps, Perisho and Benitez; Penny, Koch, Perisho and Howard; Valdez, Seanez, Koch and Bump; Valdez, Perisho, Mota and Benitez; Beckett and Benitez; Valdez, Mota and Benitez; Houston (11)—Pettitte, Miceli, Lidge and Dotel; Oswalt, Miceli and Dotel; Clemens, Lidge and Dotel; Miller, Miceli, Lidge and Dotel; Munro, Miceli, Lidge and Dotel; Oswalt and Lidge; Oliver, Gallo, Weathers and Bullinger; Oswalt, Gallo and Miceli; Backe, Qualls, Gallo and Wheeler; Clemens and Lidge; Clemens, Lidge and Miceli; Los Angeles (4)—Alvarez and Mota; Alvarez and Mota; Lima and Gagne; Ishii, Mota, Martin and Gagne; Milwaukee (9)—Obermueller, Bennett and Kolb; Sheets, Vizcaino, Adams, Bennett, Kinney and Kolb; Santos, Vizcaino and Kolb; Sheets, Vizcaino and Kolb; Davis and Adams; Sheets and Vizcaino; Davis, Adams and Vizcaino; Capuano, Adams and Kolb; Sheets, Vizcaino and Kolb; Montreal (7)—Patterson, Cordero and Biddle; Day and Biddle; Ohka and Biddle; Vargas and Ayala; Biddle, Vargas, Horgan and Ayala; Hernandez and Tucker; Hernandez and Ayala; New York (4)—Leiter, Weathers, Moreno and Looper; Trachsel, Stanton and Franco; Benson, Fortunato and Looper; Glavine and Looper; Philadelphia (1)—Wolf and Cormier; Pittsburgh (6)—Perez, Corey and Mesa; Burnett, Corey, Torres and Mesa; Fogg, Gonzalez, Torres and Mesa; Williams, Torres and Mesa; Vogelsong, Torres and Mesa; Perez, Torres and Mesa; San Diego (6)—Valdez and Hoffman; Wells, Otsuka and Hoffman; Eaton, Otsuka and Hoffman; Eaton, Otsuka and Hoffman; Peavy and Otsuka; Peavy, Witasick and Szuminski; San Francisco (3)—Schmidt, Brower and Eyre; Hennessey, Eyre and Brower; Schmidt, Foppert, T. Walker and Correia; St. Louis (10)—Morris and Isringhausen; Carpenter, Kline and Tavarez; Suppan, Eldred and Kline; Carpenter and Isringhausen; Williams, King and Isringhausen; Marquis and Tavarez; Marquis, Calero and Haren; Suppan, Kline and Isringhausen; Marquis, King and Tavarez; Carpenter, Haren, King, Eldred and Reyes.

# FIELDING

## TEAM

| Team | G | PO | A | E | TC | DP | TP | PB | Pct. |
|---|---|---|---|---|---|---|---|---|---|
| Los Angeles | 162 | 4360 | 1666 | 73 | 6099 | 145 | 0 | 15 | .988 |
| Philadelphia | 162 | 4388 | 1629 | 81 | 6098 | 142 | 0 | 7 | .987 |
| Chicago | 162 | 4396 | 1579 | 86 | 6061 | 126 | 0 | 9 | .986 |
| Colorado | 162 | 4306 | 1823 | 89 | 6218 | 161 | 0 | 15 | .986 |
| Florida | 162 | 4317 | 1603 | 86 | 6006 | 153 | 0 | 11 | .986 |
| St. Louis | 162 | 4361 | 1834 | 97 | 6292 | 154 | 0 | 9 | .985 |
| Montreal | 162 | 4341 | 1699 | 99 | 6139 | 172 | 0 | 7 | .984 |
| San Francisco | 162 | 4371 | 1737 | 101 | 6209 | 153 | 0 | 11 | .984 |
| Houston | 162 | 4329 | 1620 | 101 | 6050 | 136 | 1 | 4 | .983 |
| Pittsburgh | 161 | 4284 | 1693 | 103 | 6080 | 189 | 0 | 2 | .983 |
| San Diego | 162 | 4323 | 1602 | 108 | 6033 | 146 | 0 | 9 | .982 |
| Atlanta | 162 | 4350 | 1791 | 116 | 6257 | 171 | 1 | 10 | .981 |
| Cincinnati | 162 | 4331 | 1641 | 113 | 6085 | 123 | 0 | 17 | .981 |
| Milwaukee | 161 | 4326 | 1594 | 117 | 6037 | 132 | 0 | 7 | .981 |
| New York | 162 | 4347 | 1745 | 137 | 6229 | 144 | 0 | 12 | .978 |
| Arizona | 162 | 4308 | 1716 | 139 | 6163 | 144 | 0 | 18 | .977 |
| **Totals** | 1295 | 69438 | 26972 | 1646 | 98056 | 2391 | 2 | 163 | .983 |

## INDIVIDUAL

### FIRST BASEMEN

NOTE: All caps denotes fielding-percentage leader based on 81 games for catchers, 108 for all other non-pitchers and 162 innings for pitchers. *Throws Lefthanded.

| Player, Team | G | GS | PO | A | E | TC | DP | Pct. |
|---|---|---|---|---|---|---|---|---|
| Anderson, Marlon, St.L. | 2 | 0 | 3 | 0 | 0 | 3 | 0 | 1.000 |
| Atkins, Garrett, Col. | 3 | 2 | 22 | 1 | 0 | 23 | 6 | 1.000 |
| Aurilia, Rich, S.D. | 1 | 0 | 7 | 0 | 0 | 7 | 0 | 1.000 |
| Baerga, Carlos, Ari. | 6 | 4 | 32 | 4 | 0 | 36 | 2 | 1.000 |
| Bagwell, Jeff, Hou. | 152 | 151 | 1190 | 98 | 6 | 1294 | 109 | .995 |
| Berkman, Lance, Hou.* | 4 | 0 | 5 | 1 | 0 | 6 | 2 | 1.000 |
| Branyan, Russell, Mil. | 2 | 1 | 7 | 0 | 0 | 7 | 1 | 1.000 |
| Brazell, Craig, N.Y. | 7 | 3 | 34 | 4 | 1 | 39 | 1 | .974 |
| Buchanan, Brian, S.D.-N.Y. | 4 | 1 | 17 | 1 | 0 | 18 | 2 | 1.000 |
| Casey, Sean, Cin. | 145 | 142 | 1233 | 56 | 8 | 1297 | 86 | .994 |
| Castro, Juan, Cin. | 4 | 3 | 27 | 2 | 0 | 29 | 2 | 1.000 |
| Choi, Hee Seop, Fla.-L.A.* | 112 | 98 | 881 | 51 | 9 | 941 | 78 | .990 |
| Cirillo, Jeff, S.D. | 10 | 4 | 61 | 1 | 0 | 62 | 3 | 1.000 |
| Colbrunn, Greg, Ari. | 2 | 1 | 7 | 1 | 0 | 8 | 0 | 1.000 |
| Conine, Jeff, Fla. | 57 | 56 | 473 | 50 | 4 | 527 | 47 | .992 |
| Cordero, Wil, Fla. | 13 | 11 | 105 | 4 | 1 | 110 | 10 | .991 |
| Cruz, Jacob, Cin.* | 6 | 1 | 10 | 1 | 0 | 11 | 2 | 1.000 |
| Dubois, Jason, Chi. | 1 | 0 | 2 | 0 | 0 | 2 | 0 | 1.000 |
| Dunn, Adam, Cin. | 10 | 9 | 76 | 4 | 0 | 80 | 5 | 1.000 |
| Easley, Damion, Fla. | 18 | 16 | 119 | 8 | 2 | 129 | 16 | .984 |
| Edmonds, Jim, St.L.* | 1 | 1 | 9 | 1 | 0 | 10 | 0 | 1.000 |
| Feliz, Pedro, S.F. | 70 | 59 | 527 | 42 | 5 | 574 | 59 | .991 |
| Fick, Robert, S.D. | 1 | 1 | 9 | 0 | 0 | 9 | 1 | 1.000 |
| Fox, Andy, Mon. | 1 | 0 | 2 | 0 | 0 | 2 | 0 | 1.000 |
| Franco, Julio, Atl. | 84 | 71 | 627 | 48 | 2 | 677 | 68 | .997 |
| Grabowski, Jason, L.A. | 3 | 0 | 2 | 1 | 0 | 3 | 0 | 1.000 |
| Green, Shawn, L.A.* | 111 | 107 | 879 | 53 | 5 | 937 | 82 | .995 |
| Hansen, Dave, S.D. | 7 | 0 | 15 | 1 | 0 | 16 | 2 | 1.000 |
| Helms, Wes, Mil. | 10 | 10 | 68 | 3 | 2 | 73 | 7 | .973 |
| HELTON, Todd, Col.* | 153 | 151 | 1356 | 144 | 4 | 1504 | 130 | .997 |
| Hernandez, Jose, L.A. | 8 | 0 | 15 | 2 | 0 | 17 | 3 | 1.000 |
| Hessman, Mike, Atl. | 16 | 9 | 96 | 4 | 4 | 104 | 6 | .962 |
| Hillenbrand, Shea, Ari. | 131 | 129 | 1127 | 72 | 13 | 1212 | 105 | .989 |
| Hollandsworth, Todd, Chi.* | 3 | 3 | 16 | 4 | 1 | 21 | 1 | .952 |
| Howard, Ryan, Phi.* | 8 | 5 | 59 | 6 | 0 | 65 | 9 | 1.000 |
| Hummel, Tim, Cin. | 13 | 4 | 43 | 8 | 0 | 51 | 6 | 1.000 |
| Johnson, Nick, Mon.* | 73 | 70 | 618 | 43 | 4 | 665 | 69 | .994 |
| Klesko, Ryan, S.D.* | 18 | 15 | 138 | 16 | 2 | 156 | 19 | .987 |
| Lamb, Mike, Hou. | 10 | 7 | 76 | 4 | 0 | 80 | 7 | 1.000 |
| Lane, Jason, Hou.* | 3 | 1 | 13 | 1 | 1 | 15 | 3 | .933 |
| LaRoche, Adam, Atl.* | 98 | 82 | 740 | 41 | 5 | 786 | 87 | .994 |
| Lee, Derrek, Chi. | 161 | 159 | 1259 | 130 | 6 | 1395 | 113 | .996 |
| Lo Duca, Paul, L.A. | 3 | 2 | 11 | 1 | 0 | 12 | 1 | 1.000 |
| Lopez, Luis, Mon. | 8 | 6 | 53 | 2 | 0 | 55 | 5 | 1.000 |
| Mabry, John, St.L. | 14 | 11 | 90 | 16 | 2 | 108 | 6 | .981 |
| Mackowiak, Rob, Pit. | 1 | 0 | 0 | 0 | 0 | 0 | 0 | .000 |
| Matheny, Mike, St.L. | 1 | 0 | 1 | 0 | 0 | 1 | 0 | 1.000 |
| Mayne, Brent, Ari. | 1 | 0 | 2 | 0 | 0 | 2 | 0 | 1.000 |
| McEwing, Joe, N.Y. | 11 | 0 | 20 | 1 | 0 | 21 | 2 | 1.000 |
| McKay, Cody, St.L. | 1 | 0 | 2 | 0 | 0 | 2 | 0 | 1.000 |
| Minor, Damon, S.F.* | 17 | 15 | 131 | 9 | 0 | 140 | 12 | 1.000 |
| Nevin, Phil, S.D. | 144 | 142 | 1131 | 92 | 13 | 1236 | 108 | .989 |
| Overbay, Lyle, Mil.* | 158 | 150 | 1310 | 113 | 11 | 1434 | 110 | .992 |
| Pascucci, Val, Mon. | 5 | 2 | 14 | 0 | 1 | 15 | 1 | .933 |
| Pellow, Kit, Col. | 5 | 3 | 26 | 3 | 1 | 30 | 3 | .967 |
| Perez, Eddie, Atl. | 1 | 0 | 10 | 0 | 0 | 10 | 1 | 1.000 |
| Perez, Tomas, Phi. | 10 | 6 | 49 | 5 | 2 | 56 | 4 | .964 |
| Phillips, Jason, N.Y. | 38 | 29 | 259 | 16 | 0 | 275 | 20 | 1.000 |
| Piazza, Mike, N.Y. | 68 | 66 | 498 | 35 | 8 | 541 | 44 | .985 |
| Pujols, Albert, St.L. | 150 | 150 | 1458 | 114 | 10 | 1582 | 136 | .994 |
| Rivera, Carlos, Pit.* | 7 | 4 | 35 | 2 | 0 | 37 | 6 | 1.000 |
| Saenz, Olmedo, L.A. | 25 | 14 | 125 | 12 | 2 | 139 | 16 | .986 |
| Sexson, Richie, Ari. | 23 | 23 | 199 | 27 | 1 | 227 | 19 | .996 |
| Simon, Randall, Pit.* | 46 | 42 | 347 | 25 | 3 | 375 | 37 | .992 |
| Sledge, Terrmel, Mon.* | 10 | 6 | 63 | 6 | 0 | 69 | 3 | 1.000 |
| Snow, J.T., S.F.* | 100 | 88 | 801 | 55 | 4 | 860 | 69 | .995 |
| Spencer, Shane, N.Y. | 1 | 1 | 13 | 0 | 0 | 13 | 0 | 1.000 |
| Sutton, Larry, Fla.* | 1 | 0 | 1 | 0 | 0 | 1 | 0 | 1.000 |
| Sweeney, Mark, Col.* | 15 | 6 | 68 | 5 | 0 | 73 | 9 | 1.000 |
| Thome, Jim, Phi. | 134 | 134 | 1091 | 84 | 7 | 1182 | 103 | .994 |
| Tracy, Chad, Ari. | 11 | 2 | 29 | 3 | 1 | 33 | 2 | .970 |
| Utley, Chase, Phi. | 13 | 11 | 94 | 11 | 0 | 105 | 6 | 1.000 |
| Valent, Eric, N.Y.* | 27 | 23 | 202 | 21 | 1 | 224 | 21 | .996 |
| Valentin, Javier, Cin. | 7 | 3 | 37 | 1 | 0 | 38 | 5 | 1.000 |
| Vander Wal, John, Cin.* | 4 | 0 | 8 | 0 | 0 | 8 | 0 | 1.000 |
| Vazquez, Ramon, S.D. | 3 | 0 | 8 | 0 | 0 | 8 | 0 | 1.000 |
| Ventura, Robin, L.A. | 40 | 20 | 214 | 14 | 0 | 228 | 15 | 1.000 |
| Vizcaino, Jose, Hou. | 8 | 3 | 42 | 3 | 0 | 45 | 2 | 1.000 |
| Walker, Todd, Chi. | 5 | 0 | 7 | 1 | 0 | 8 | 1 | 1.000 |
| Ward, Daryle, Pit.* | 71 | 63 | 548 | 34 | 5 | 587 | 73 | .991 |
| Wigginton, Ty, N.Y. | 5 | 5 | 48 | 7 | 1 | 56 | 9 | .982 |
| Wilkerson, Brad, Mon.* | 86 | 78 | 694 | 67 | 4 | 765 | 68 | .995 |
| Wilson, Craig, Pit. | 65 | 52 | 460 | 34 | 3 | 497 | 53 | .994 |
| Wooten, Shawn, Phi. | 11 | 6 | 70 | 3 | 0 | 73 | 6 | 1.000 |
| Zeile, Todd, N.Y. | 67 | 34 | 386 | 23 | 2 | 411 | 35 | .995 |
| Zinter, Alan, Ari. | 8 | 3 | 41 | 3 | 1 | 45 | 1 | .978 |

#### FIRST BASEMEN WITH TWO OR MORE TEAMS

| Player, Team | G | GS | PO | A | E | TC | DP | Pct. |
|---|---|---|---|---|---|---|---|---|
| Buchanan, Brian, S.D. | 3 | 0 | 9 | 0 | 0 | 9 | 1 | 1.000 |
| Buchanan, Brian, N.Y. | 1 | 1 | 8 | 1 | 0 | 9 | 1 | 1.000 |
| Choi, Hee Seop, Fla.* | 89 | 79 | 720 | 41 | 8 | 769 | 59 | .990 |
| Choi, Hee Seop, L.A.* | 23 | 19 | 161 | 10 | 1 | 172 | 19 | .994 |

### SECOND BASEMEN

| Player, Team | G | GS | PO | A | E | TC | DP | Pct. |
|---|---|---|---|---|---|---|---|---|
| Alfonzo, Edgardo, S.F. | 5 | 5 | 5 | 10 | 2 | 17 | 2 | .882 |
| Alomar, Roberto, Ari. | 28 | 23 | 48 | 53 | 3 | 104 | 10 | .971 |
| Anderson, Marlon, St.L. | 37 | 24 | 55 | 70 | 4 | 129 | 20 | .969 |
| Aurilia, Rich, S.D. | 7 | 1 | 6 | 9 | 1 | 16 | 3 | .938 |
| Barmes, Clint, Col. | 9 | 8 | 19 | 27 | 1 | 47 | 5 | .979 |
| Bruntlett, Eric, Hou. | 5 | 1 | 3 | 5 | 0 | 8 | 0 | 1.000 |
| Burke, Chris, Hou. | 7 | 2 | 7 | 15 | 0 | 22 | 3 | 1.000 |
| Carroll, Jamey, Mon. | 51 | 36 | 84 | 97 | 1 | 182 | 32 | .995 |
| Castillo, Jose, Pit. | 123 | 105 | 230 | 301 | 11 | 542 | 81 | .980 |
| Castillo, Luis, Fla. | 148 | 147 | 275 | 406 | 6 | 687 | 97 | .991 |
| Castro, Juan, Cin. | 12 | 7 | 15 | 28 | 1 | 44 | 6 | .977 |
| Cintron, Alex, Ari. | 19 | 17 | 33 | 46 | 2 | 81 | 6 | .975 |
| Cirillo, Jeff, S.D. | 4 | 2 | 4 | 9 | 2 | 15 | 2 | .867 |
| Clark, Jermaine, Cin. | 2 | 2 | 4 | 3 | 0 | 7 | 1 | 1.000 |
| Cora, Alex, L.A. | 138 | 122 | 261 | 343 | 8 | 612 | 91 | .987 |
| Cruz, Deivi, S.F. | 2 | 0 | 0 | 0 | 0 | 0 | 0 | .000 |
| Dallimore, Brian, S.F. | 9 | 4 | 8 | 18 | 1 | 27 | 3 | .963 |
| DeRosa, Mark, Atl. | 5 | 3 | 3 | 11 | 0 | 14 | 4 | 1.000 |
| Durham, Ray, S.F. | 118 | 115 | 242 | 315 | 16 | 573 | 74 | .972 |
| Durrington, Trent, Mil. | 6 | 3 | 12 | 12 | 0 | 24 | 1 | 1.000 |
| Easley, Damion, Fla. | 25 | 15 | 29 | 53 | 3 | 85 | 11 | .965 |
| Erickson, Matt, Mil. | 1 | 1 | 1 | 3 | 0 | 4 | 1 | 1.000 |
| Flores, Jose, L.A. | 1 | 1 | 0 | 0 | 0 | 0 | 0 | .000 |
| Fox, Andy, Mon. | 3 | 1 | 0 | 5 | 0 | 5 | 0 | 1.000 |
| Freel, Ryan, Cin. | 15 | 10 | 25 | 23 | 0 | 48 | 4 | 1.000 |

| Player, Team | G | GS | PO | A | E | TC | DP | Pct. |
|---|---|---|---|---|---|---|---|---|
| Furcal, Rafael, Atl. | 1 | 0 | 0 | 0 | 0 | 0 | 0 | .000 |
| Garcia, Danny, N.Y. | 44 | 40 | 97 | 91 | 6 | 194 | 19 | .969 |
| Garcia, Jesse, Atl. | 11 | 4 | 16 | 19 | 2 | 37 | 5 | .946 |
| Giles, Marcus, Atl. | 97 | 94 | 186 | 289 | 12 | 487 | 69 | .975 |
| Ginter, Keith, Mil. | 54 | 52 | 91 | 127 | 6 | 224 | 19 | .973 |
| Gonzalez, Luis A., Col. | 40 | 33 | 84 | 96 | 1 | 181 | 27 | .994 |
| Green, Andy, Ari. | 14 | 4 | 16 | 15 | 1 | 32 | 4 | .969 |
| Green, Nick, Atl. | 75 | 61 | 137 | 203 | 8 | 348 | 44 | .977 |
| Grudzielanek, Mark, Chi. | 76 | 61 | 136 | 186 | 5 | 327 | 30 | .985 |
| Gutierrez, Ricky, N.Y. | 18 | 14 | 31 | 44 | 0 | 75 | 11 | 1.000 |
| Hairston, Scott, Ari. | 85 | 83 | 174 | 207 | 11 | 392 | 47 | .972 |
| Hall, Bill, Mil. | 50 | 47 | 95 | 113 | 9 | 217 | 29 | .959 |
| Harris, Brendan, Mon. | 11 | 10 | 15 | 20 | 1 | 36 | 3 | .972 |
| Hart, Bo, St.L. | 4 | 3 | 6 | 9 | 0 | 15 | 4 | 1.000 |
| Hernandez, Jose, L.A. | 50 | 39 | 80 | 113 | 4 | 197 | 21 | .980 |
| Hill, Bobby, Pit. | 40 | 31 | 70 | 89 | 1 | 160 | 22 | .994 |
| Hocking, Denny, Col. | 8 | 5 | 13 | 16 | 0 | 29 | 3 | 1.000 |
| Hummel, Tim, Cin. | 1 | 0 | 1 | 0 | 0 | 1 | 0 | 1.000 |
| Izturis, Maicer, Mon. | 10 | 10 | 18 | 25 | 1 | 44 | 6 | .977 |
| Jackson, Damian, Chi. | 5 | 3 | 8 | 14 | 1 | 23 | 5 | .957 |
| Jimenez, D'Angelo, Cin. | 146 | 143 | 297 | 388 | 7 | 692 | 74 | .990 |
| Kata, Matt, Ari. | 38 | 35 | 75 | 111 | 2 | 188 | 25 | .989 |
| Kent, Jeff, Hou. | 139 | 138 | 276 | 374 | 7 | 657 | 74 | .989 |
| Keppinger, Jeff, N.Y. | 32 | 27 | 61 | 86 | 2 | 149 | 20 | .987 |
| Labandeira, Josh, Mon. | 2 | 0 | 0 | 0 | 0 | 0 | 0 | .000 |
| Lamb, Mike, Hou. | 7 | 5 | 9 | 12 | 1 | 22 | 0 | .955 |
| Lopez, Felipe, Cin. | 2 | 0 | 1 | 1 | 1 | 3 | 1 | .667 |
| Loretta, Mark, S.D. | 154 | 154 | 288 | 451 | 10 | 749 | 101 | .987 |
| Luna, Hector, St.L. | 19 | 10 | 24 | 33 | 0 | 57 | 6 | 1.000 |
| Macias, Jose, Chi. | 16 | 8 | 15 | 24 | 0 | 39 | 3 | 1.000 |
| Martinez, Ramon, Chi. | 6 | 1 | 3 | 6 | 0 | 9 | 0 | 1.000 |
| Mateo, Henry, Mon. | 9 | 1 | 12 | 17 | 4 | 33 | 3 | .879 |
| Matsui, Kazuo, N.Y. | 3 | 3 | 4 | 8 | 1 | 13 | 3 | .923 |
| McEwing, Joe, N.Y. | 34 | 15 | 50 | 55 | 2 | 107 | 10 | .981 |
| Miles, Aaron, Col. | 128 | 116 | 273 | 353 | 10 | 636 | 70 | .984 |
| Mordecai, Mike, Fla. | 4 | 0 | 2 | 2 | 1 | 5 | 0 | .800 |
| Nunez, Abraham O., Pit. | 32 | 22 | 60 | 70 | 2 | 132 | 24 | .985 |
| Perez, Antonio, L.A. | 2 | 0 | 2 | 1 | 1 | 4 | 1 | .750 |
| Perez, Neifi, S.F.-Chi. | 41 | 32 | 84 | 119 | 1 | 204 | 26 | .995 |
| Perez, Tomas, Phi. | 17 | 11 | 26 | 32 | 0 | 58 | 7 | 1.000 |
| POLANCO, Placido, Phi. | 109 | 105 | 264 | 304 | 3 | 571 | 76 | .995 |
| Ransom, Cody, S.F. | 16 | 7 | 28 | 21 | 1 | 50 | 5 | .980 |
| Reyes, Jose, N.Y. | 43 | 41 | 75 | 117 | 4 | 196 | 26 | .980 |
| Sadler, Donnie, Ari. | 2 | 0 | 2 | 1 | 0 | 3 | 1 | 1.000 |
| Sanchez, Freddy, Pit. | 3 | 3 | 3 | 4 | 0 | 7 | 1 | 1.000 |
| Spivey, Junior, Mil. | 58 | 58 | 111 | 177 | 11 | 299 | 41 | .963 |
| Thurston, Joe, L.A. | 4 | 0 | 2 | 3 | 0 | 5 | 1 | 1.000 |
| Utley, Chase, Phi. | 50 | 46 | 100 | 123 | 4 | 227 | 29 | .982 |
| Vazquez, Ramon, S.D. | 10 | 5 | 13 | 17 | 0 | 30 | 4 | 1.000 |
| Vidro, Jose, Mon. | 105 | 104 | 176 | 270 | 6 | 452 | 71 | .987 |
| Vizcaino, Jose, Hou. | 37 | 16 | 45 | 51 | 0 | 96 | 17 | 1.000 |
| Walker, Todd, Chi. | 89 | 88 | 150 | 213 | 7 | 370 | 32 | .981 |
| Wigginton, Ty, N.Y. | 25 | 22 | 30 | 68 | 3 | 101 | 12 | .970 |
| Womack, Tony, St.L. | 133 | 125 | 225 | 391 | 15 | 631 | 81 | .976 |

### SECOND BASEMEN WITH TWO OR MORE TEAMS

| Player, Team | G | GS | PO | A | E | TC | DP | Pct. |
|---|---|---|---|---|---|---|---|---|
| Perez, Neifi, S.F. | 39 | 31 | 80 | 115 | 1 | 196 | 23 | .995 |
| Perez, Neifi, Chi. | 2 | 1 | 4 | 4 | 0 | 8 | 3 | 1.000 |

## THIRD BASEMEN

| Player, Team | G | GS | PO | A | E | TC | DP | Pct. |
|---|---|---|---|---|---|---|---|---|
| Alfonzo, Edgardo, S.F. | 129 | 122 | 88 | 246 | 12 | 346 | 20 | .965 |
| Atkins, Garrett, Col. | 4 | 3 | 2 | 4 | 0 | 6 | 1 | 1.000 |
| Aurilia, Rich, S.D. | 29 | 28 | 16 | 41 | 5 | 62 | 3 | .919 |
| Batista, Tony, Mon. | 155 | 149 | 82 | 308 | 19 | 409 | 35 | .954 |
| Bell, David, Phi. | 142 | 141 | 89 | 308 | 24 | 421 | 22 | .943 |
| Beltre, Adrian, L.A. | 155 | 154 | 120 | 322 | 10 | 452 | 32 | .978 |
| Betemit, Wilson, Atl. | 7 | 4 | 2 | 6 | 0 | 8 | 2 | 1.000 |
| Branyan, Russell, Mil. | 44 | 40 | 35 | 91 | 5 | 131 | 7 | .962 |
| Burroughs, Sean, S.D. | 125 | 119 | 100 | 209 | 14 | 323 | 25 | .957 |
| Carroll, Jamey, Mon. | 13 | 8 | 8 | 26 | 2 | 36 | 1 | .944 |
| CASTILLA, Vinny, Col. | 148 | 147 | 124 | 316 | 6 | 446 | 30 | .987 |
| Castro, Juan, Cin. | 78 | 35 | 38 | 75 | 5 | 118 | 7 | .958 |
| Cintron, Alex, Ari. | 1 | 0 | 1 | 0 | 0 | 1 | 0 | 1.000 |
| Cirillo, Jeff, S.D. | 11 | 8 | 8 | 10 | 0 | 18 | 1 | 1.000 |
| Collier, Lou, Phi. | 1 | 0 | 0 | 1 | 0 | 1 | 1 | 1.000 |
| Counsell, Craig, Mil. | 1 | 0 | 0 | 0 | 0 | 0 | 0 | .000 |
| Cruz, Deivi, S.F. | 1 | 0 | 0 | 0 | 0 | 0 | 0 | .000 |
| Dallimore, Brian, S.F. | 6 | 3 | 4 | 8 | 1 | 13 | 0 | .923 |
| DeRosa, Mark, Atl. | 72 | 62 | 27 | 126 | 10 | 163 | 7 | .939 |
| Diaz, Einar, Mon. | 1 | 0 | 0 | 0 | 0 | 0 | 0 | .000 |
| Durrington, Trent, Mil. | 11 | 7 | 3 | 12 | 4 | 19 | 0 | .789 |
| Easley, Damion, Fla. | 6 | 5 | 4 | 11 | 0 | 15 | 0 | 1.000 |
| Ensberg, Morgan, Hou. | 118 | 103 | 80 | 164 | 13 | 257 | 23 | .949 |
| Feliz, Pedro, S.F. | 51 | 37 | 32 | 85 | 3 | 120 | 7 | .975 |
| Flores, Jose, L.A. | 1 | 0 | 0 | 1 | 0 | 1 | 0 | 1.000 |
| Fox, Andy, Mon. | 3 | 2 | 1 | 6 | 0 | 7 | 0 | 1.000 |
| Freel, Ryan, Cin. | 56 | 51 | 42 | 107 | 12 | 161 | 11 | .925 |
| Garcia, Jesse, Atl. | 3 | 1 | 0 | 3 | 1 | 4 | 0 | .750 |
| Ginter, Keith, Mil. | 47 | 41 | 28 | 80 | 3 | 111 | 10 | .973 |
| Gonzalez, Luis A., Col. | 18 | 10 | 13 | 21 | 1 | 35 | 1 | .971 |
| Green, Andy, Ari. | 18 | 14 | 12 | 33 | 4 | 49 | 1 | .918 |
| Green, Nick, Atl. | 5 | 0 | 0 | 2 | 0 | 2 | 0 | 1.000 |
| Gutierrez, Ricky, N.Y. | 2 | 1 | 1 | 0 | 1 | 2 | 0 | .500 |
| Hall, Bill, Mil. | 11 | 7 | 6 | 22 | 2 | 30 | 4 | .933 |
| Hammock, Robby, Ari. | 1 | 0 | 1 | 0 | 0 | 1 | 0 | 1.000 |
| Hansen, Dave, S.D. | 2 | 2 | 0 | 1 | 0 | 1 | 0 | 1.000 |
| Harris, Brendan, Chi.-Mon. | 7 | 6 | 6 | 7 | 2 | 15 | 0 | .867 |
| Harris, Lenny, Fla. | 3 | 0 | 0 | 0 | 0 | 0 | 0 | .000 |
| Helms, Wes, Mil. | 66 | 65 | 45 | 105 | 16 | 166 | 10 | .904 |
| Hernandez, Jose, L.A. | 12 | 3 | 4 | 8 | 0 | 12 | 1 | 1.000 |
| Hessman, Mike, Atl. | 7 | 2 | 2 | 14 | 2 | 18 | 1 | .889 |
| Hill, Bobby, Pit. | 25 | 19 | 10 | 24 | 1 | 35 | 2 | .971 |
| Hillenbrand, Shea, Ari. | 17 | 15 | 6 | 29 | 3 | 38 | 3 | .921 |
| Hocking, Denny, Col. | 2 | 0 | 1 | 0 | 0 | 1 | 0 | 1.000 |
| Hummel, Tim, Cin. | 32 | 19 | 17 | 47 | 4 | 68 | 5 | .941 |
| Jones, Chipper, Atl. | 96 | 93 | 58 | 177 | 6 | 241 | 13 | .975 |
| Kata, Matt, Ari. | 3 | 2 | 4 | 4 | 0 | 8 | 0 | 1.000 |
| Lamb, Mike, Hou. | 57 | 53 | 41 | 106 | 13 | 160 | 9 | .919 |
| Larson, Brandon, Cin. | 35 | 33 | 24 | 50 | 5 | 79 | 4 | .937 |
| Lopez, Felipe, Cin. | 24 | 24 | 24 | 49 | 5 | 78 | 1 | .936 |
| Lowell, Mike, Fla. | 154 | 153 | 117 | 272 | 7 | 396 | 30 | .982 |
| Luna, Hector, St.L. | 16 | 8 | 4 | 19 | 2 | 25 | 3 | .920 |
| Mabry, John, St.L. | 20 | 14 | 10 | 27 | 3 | 40 | 3 | .925 |
| Macias, Jose, Chi. | 18 | 7 | 10 | 12 | 1 | 23 | 1 | .957 |
| Mackowiak, Rob, Pit. | 55 | 51 | 37 | 90 | 5 | 132 | 15 | .962 |
| Martinez, Ramon, Chi. | 24 | 11 | 12 | 21 | 3 | 36 | 4 | .917 |
| McEwing, Joe, N.Y. | 1 | 0 | 0 | 0 | 0 | 0 | 0 | .000 |
| McKay, Cody, St.L. | 7 | 0 | 1 | 2 | 1 | 4 | 0 | .750 |
| Mordecai, Mike, Fla. | 19 | 4 | 10 | 16 | 2 | 28 | 3 | .929 |
| Nunez, Abraham O., Pit. | 6 | 2 | 0 | 5 | 1 | 6 | 0 | .833 |
| Olson, Tim, Ari. | 19 | 11 | 17 | 35 | 2 | 54 | 2 | .963 |
| Pellow, Kit, Col. | 4 | 1 | 2 | 1 | 0 | 3 | 0 | 1.000 |
| Perez, Neifi, S.F. | 2 | 0 | 1 | 0 | 0 | 1 | 0 | 1.000 |
| Perez, Tomas, Phi. | 22 | 7 | 12 | 22 | 2 | 36 | 1 | .944 |
| Polanco, Placido, Phi. | 13 | 11 | 15 | 26 | 0 | 41 | 4 | 1.000 |
| Ramirez, Aramis, Chi. | 144 | 141 | 92 | 221 | 10 | 323 | 15 | .969 |
| Ransom, Cody, S.F. | 1 | 0 | 0 | 0 | 1 | 1 | 0 | .000 |
| Rolen, Scott, St.L. | 141 | 139 | 93 | 325 | 10 | 428 | 23 | .977 |
| Sadler, Donnie, Ari. | 2 | 0 | 1 | 0 | 0 | 1 | 0 | 1.000 |
| Saenz, Olmedo, L.A. | 2 | 0 | 0 | 2 | 0 | 2 | 0 | 1.000 |
| Sanchez, Freddy, Pit. | 1 | 0 | 0 | 0 | 0 | 0 | 0 | .000 |
| Stynes, Chris, Pit. | 71 | 39 | 28 | 89 | 1 | 118 | 9 | .992 |
| Tracy, Andy, Col. | 1 | 1 | 0 | 1 | 0 | 1 | 0 | 1.000 |
| Tracy, Chad, Ari. | 135 | 120 | 104 | 258 | 25 | 387 | 28 | .935 |
| Vazquez, Ramon, S.D. | 9 | 5 | 8 | 6 | 0 | 14 | 2 | 1.000 |
| Ventura, Robin, L.A. | 11 | 5 | 13 | 11 | 0 | 24 | 6 | 1.000 |
| Vizcaino, Jose, Hou. | 21 | 6 | 10 | 11 | 4 | 25 | 0 | .840 |
| Wigginton, Ty, N.Y.-Pit. | 122 | 104 | 63 | 208 | 18 | 289 | 16 | .938 |
| Wooten, Shawn, Phi. | 4 | 3 | 2 | 4 | 0 | 6 | 0 | 1.000 |
| Wright, David, N.Y. | 69 | 68 | 39 | 140 | 11 | 190 | 10 | .942 |
| Zeile, Todd, N.Y. | 46 | 39 | 38 | 73 | 8 | 119 | 7 | .933 |

### THIRD BASEMEN WITH TWO OR MORE TEAMS

| Player, Team | G | GS | PO | A | E | TC | DP | Pct. |
|---|---|---|---|---|---|---|---|---|
| Harris, Brendan, Chi. | 3 | 3 | 4 | 4 | 1 | 9 | 0 | .889 |
| Harris, Brendan, Mon. | 4 | 3 | 2 | 3 | 1 | 6 | 0 | .833 |
| Wigginton, Ty, N.Y. | 66 | 54 | 29 | 116 | 12 | 157 | 8 | .924 |
| Wigginton, Ty, Pit. | 56 | 50 | 34 | 92 | 6 | 132 | 8 | .955 |

## SHORTSTOPS

| Player, Team | G | GS | PO | A | E | TC | DP | Pct. |
|---|---|---|---|---|---|---|---|---|
| Alfaro, Jason, Hou. | 3 | 2 | 2 | 3 | 0 | 5 | 1 | 1.000 |
| Aurilia, Rich, S.D. | 6 | 5 | 8 | 17 | 1 | 26 | 2 | .962 |
| Barmes, Clint, Col. | 9 | 9 | 17 | 36 | 1 | 54 | 7 | .981 |
| Beltre, Adrian, L.A. | 1 | 0 | 0 | 1 | 0 | 1 | 0 | 1.000 |
| Betemit, Wilson, Atl. | 11 | 7 | 12 | 30 | 3 | 45 | 5 | .933 |
| Bruntlett, Eric, Hou. | 33 | 10 | 17 | 28 | 3 | 48 | 9 | .938 |
| Cabrera, Orlando, Mon. | 101 | 100 | 147 | 290 | 7 | 444 | 69 | .984 |
| Carroll, Jamey, Mon. | 10 | 6 | 11 | 16 | 0 | 27 | 4 | 1.000 |

| Player, Team | G | GS | PO | A | E | TC | DP | Pct. |
|---|---|---|---|---|---|---|---|---|
| Castillo, Jose, Pit. | 2 | 0 | 0 | 0 | 0 | 0 | 0 | .000 |
| Castro, Juan, Cin. | 31 | 21 | 32 | 72 | 2 | 106 | 16 | .981 |
| Cintron, Alex, Ari. | 133 | 125 | 141 | 382 | 15 | 538 | 61 | .972 |
| CLAYTON, Royce, Col. | 144 | 140 | 213 | 417 | 9 | 639 | 88 | .986 |
| Counsell, Craig, Mil. | 129 | 128 | 165 | 357 | 9 | 531 | 70 | .983 |
| Cruz, Deivi, S.F. | 104 | 95 | 127 | 267 | 8 | 402 | 59 | .980 |
| Delgado, Wilson, N.Y. | 39 | 37 | 49 | 128 | 8 | 185 | 28 | .957 |
| DeRosa, Mark, Atl. | 11 | 4 | 10 | 18 | 2 | 30 | 7 | .933 |
| Easley, Damion, Fla. | 15 | 5 | 6 | 24 | 1 | 31 | 3 | .968 |
| Ensberg, Morgan, Hou. | 1 | 0 | 0 | 0 | 0 | 0 | 0 | .000 |
| Erickson, Matt, Mil. | 1 | 0 | 0 | 4 | 0 | 4 | 0 | 1.000 |
| Everett, Adam, Hou. | 99 | 97 | 137 | 279 | 10 | 426 | 56 | .977 |
| Feliz, Pedro, S.F. | 20 | 14 | 17 | 48 | 5 | 70 | 9 | .929 |
| Fox, Andy, Mon. | 5 | 1 | 0 | 5 | 0 | 5 | 0 | 1.000 |
| Furcal, Rafael, Atl. | 131 | 130 | 190 | 411 | 24 | 625 | 101 | .962 |
| Garcia, Jesse, Atl. | 25 | 21 | 31 | 72 | 4 | 107 | 14 | .963 |
| Garciaparra, Nomar, Chi. | 42 | 41 | 69 | 94 | 3 | 166 | 17 | .982 |
| Gil, Jerry, Ari. | 28 | 24 | 34 | 73 | 5 | 112 | 18 | .955 |
| Gonzalez, Alex, Fla. | 158 | 155 | 225 | 425 | 16 | 666 | 99 | .976 |
| Gonzalez, Alex S., Chi.-Mon.-S.D. | 81 | 77 | 132 | 188 | 11 | 331 | 46 | .967 |
| Gonzalez, Luis A., Col. | 10 | 7 | 9 | 18 | 0 | 27 | 5 | 1.000 |
| Greene, Khalil, S.D. | 136 | 134 | 177 | 381 | 20 | 578 | 81 | .965 |
| Hall, Bill, Mil. | 37 | 33 | 59 | 116 | 8 | 183 | 23 | .956 |
| Hart, Bo, St.L. | 1 | 0 | 0 | 0 | 0 | 0 | 0 | .000 |
| Hernandez, Jose, L.A. | 13 | 6 | 8 | 26 | 1 | 35 | 5 | .971 |
| Hocking, Denny, Col. | 13 | 6 | 13 | 25 | 3 | 41 | 6 | .927 |
| Hummel, Tim, Cin. | 1 | 0 | 0 | 0 | 0 | 0 | 0 | .000 |
| Izturis, Cesar, L.A. | 159 | 156 | 234 | 430 | 10 | 674 | 96 | .985 |
| Izturis, Maicer, Mon. | 23 | 20 | 33 | 71 | 7 | 111 | 15 | .937 |
| Jimenez, D'Angelo, Cin. | 5 | 3 | 7 | 7 | 0 | 14 | 1 | 1.000 |
| Kata, Matt, Ari. | 1 | 1 | 3 | 5 | 0 | 8 | 2 | 1.000 |
| Labandeira, Josh, Mon. | 3 | 2 | 2 | 3 | 1 | 6 | 0 | .833 |
| Larkin, Barry, Cin. | 85 | 81 | 106 | 216 | 4 | 326 | 33 | .988 |
| Lopez, Felipe, Cin. | 51 | 41 | 65 | 137 | 9 | 211 | 25 | .957 |
| Luna, Hector, St.L. | 24 | 14 | 33 | 57 | 5 | 95 | 12 | .947 |
| Machado, Anderson, Cin. | 17 | 16 | 23 | 36 | 4 | 63 | 7 | .937 |
| Martinez, Ramon, Chi. | 73 | 57 | 80 | 174 | 6 | 260 | 34 | .977 |
| Matsui, Kazuo, N.Y. | 110 | 108 | 174 | 323 | 23 | 520 | 65 | .956 |
| McEwing, Joe, N.Y. | 13 | 10 | 19 | 36 | 1 | 56 | 5 | .982 |
| Mordecai, Mike, Fla. | 3 | 2 | 5 | 8 | 0 | 13 | 4 | 1.000 |
| Nunez, Abraham O., Pit. | 13 | 5 | 10 | 15 | 0 | 25 | 4 | 1.000 |
| Olmedo, Ray, Cin. | 7 | 0 | 4 | 4 | 0 | 8 | 1 | 1.000 |
| Olson, Tim, Ari. | 17 | 10 | 18 | 28 | 4 | 50 | 8 | .920 |
| Ordonez, Rey, Chi. | 22 | 17 | 31 | 39 | 3 | 73 | 9 | .959 |
| Perez, Antonio, L.A. | 1 | 0 | 1 | 2 | 0 | 3 | 1 | 1.000 |
| Perez, Neifi, S.F.-Chi. | 76 | 60 | 87 | 199 | 7 | 293 | 39 | .976 |
| Perez, Tomas, Phi. | 10 | 9 | 14 | 26 | 2 | 42 | 5 | .952 |
| Ransom, Cody, S.F. | 45 | 5 | 20 | 35 | 3 | 58 | 11 | .948 |
| Renteria, Edgar, St.L. | 149 | 148 | 222 | 419 | 11 | 652 | 92 | .983 |
| Reyes, Jose, N.Y. | 10 | 7 | 18 | 26 | 2 | 46 | 5 | .957 |
| Rollins, Jimmy, Phi. | 154 | 153 | 214 | 399 | 9 | 622 | 88 | .986 |
| Sadler, Donnie, Ari. | 3 | 2 | 3 | 3 | 0 | 6 | 1 | 1.000 |
| Sanchez, Freddy, Pit. | 4 | 1 | 1 | 3 | 1 | 5 | 0 | .800 |
| Spivey, Junior, Mil. | 1 | 0 | 1 | 1 | 0 | 2 | 0 | 1.000 |
| Vazquez, Ramon, S.D. | 22 | 14 | 22 | 35 | 1 | 58 | 5 | .983 |
| Vizcaino, Jose, Hou. | 64 | 53 | 65 | 153 | 7 | 225 | 27 | .969 |
| Wilson, Jack, Pit. | 156 | 155 | 234 | 492 | 17 | 743 | 129 | .977 |

## SHORTSTOPS WITH TWO OR MORE TEAMS

| Player, Team | G | GS | PO | A | E | TC | DP | Pct. |
|---|---|---|---|---|---|---|---|---|
| Gonzalez, Alex S., Chi. | 37 | 35 | 65 | 82 | 5 | 152 | 18 | .967 |
| Gonzalez, Alex S., Mon. | 33 | 33 | 57 | 88 | 6 | 151 | 24 | .960 |
| Gonzalez, Alex S., S.D. | 11 | 9 | 10 | 18 | 0 | 28 | 4 | 1.000 |
| Perez, Neifi, S.F. | 57 | 48 | 67 | 158 | 5 | 230 | 29 | .978 |
| Perez, Neifi, Chi. | 19 | 12 | 20 | 41 | 2 | 63 | 10 | .968 |

## OUTFIELDERS

| Player, Team | G | GS | PO | A | E | TC | DP | Pct. |
|---|---|---|---|---|---|---|---|---|
| Abreu, Bobby, Phi. | 158 | 157 | 311 | 13 | 6 | 330 | 4 | .982 |
| Aguila, Chris, Fla. | 20 | 7 | 19 | 1 | 2 | 22 | 0 | .909 |
| Alou, Moises, Chi. | 154 | 152 | 240 | 7 | 8 | 255 | 2 | .969 |
| Alvarez, Tony, Pit. | 16 | 10 | 17 | 0 | 0 | 17 | 0 | 1.000 |
| Anderson, Marlon, St.L. | 36 | 25 | 44 | 2 | 3 | 49 | 1 | .939 |
| Atkins, Garrett, Col. | 3 | 2 | 5 | 0 | 0 | 5 | 0 | 1.000 |
| Bautista, Danny, Ari. | 137 | 137 | 271 | 8 | 4 | 283 | 1 | .986 |
| Bautista, Jose, Pit. | 12 | 9 | 19 | 0 | 3 | 22 | 0 | .864 |
| Bay, Jason, Pit. | 119 | 110 | 211 | 3 | 2 | 216 | 0 | .991 |
| Beltran, Carlos, Hou. | 89 | 88 | 201 | 8 | 5 | 214 | 2 | .977 |
| Bergeron, Peter, Mon. | 11 | 11 | 21 | 0 | 2 | 23 | 0 | .913 |
| Berkman, Lance, Hou.* | 160 | 158 | 243 | 11 | 2 | 256 | 1 | .992 |
| Biggio, Craig, Hou. | 149 | 149 | 250 | 4 | 9 | 263 | 0 | .966 |
| Bonds, Barry, S.F.* | 133 | 132 | 214 | 11 | 4 | 229 | 0 | .983 |
| Bradley, Milton, L.A. | 138 | 137 | 332 | 8 | 8 | 348 | 1 | .977 |
| Bragg, Darren, Cin. | 26 | 18 | 61 | 2 | 1 | 64 | 0 | .984 |
| Bruntlett, Eric, Hou. | 2 | 1 | 1 | 0 | 0 | 1 | 0 | 1.000 |
| Buchanan, Brian, S.D. | 18 | 13 | 12 | 0 | 0 | 12 | 0 | 1.000 |
| Burnitz, Jeromy, Col. | 143 | 137 | 255 | 10 | 7 | 272 | 1 | .974 |
| Burrell, Pat, Phi. | 122 | 121 | 217 | 9 | 4 | 230 | 1 | .983 |
| Byrd, Marlon, Phi. | 92 | 86 | 195 | 4 | 2 | 201 | 1 | .990 |
| Cabrera, Miguel, Fla. | 158 | 158 | 262 | 13 | 9 | 284 | 1 | .968 |
| Calloway, Ron, Mon.* | 20 | 15 | 27 | 0 | 0 | 27 | 0 | 1.000 |
| Cameron, Mike, N.Y. | 135 | 132 | 354 | 6 | 8 | 368 | 2 | .978 |
| Carroll, Jamey, Mon. | 2 | 1 | 2 | 0 | 0 | 2 | 0 | 1.000 |
| Cedeno, Roger, St.L. | 54 | 40 | 47 | 2 | 0 | 49 | 0 | 1.000 |
| Cepicky, Matt, Mon. | 11 | 10 | 24 | 0 | 0 | 24 | 0 | 1.000 |
| Chavez, Endy, Mon.* | 127 | 122 | 301 | 9 | 5 | 315 | 5 | .984 |
| Chen, Chin-Feng, L.A. | 3 | 1 | 8 | 0 | 0 | 8 | 0 | 1.000 |
| Church, Ryan, Mon.* | 18 | 14 | 35 | 3 | 0 | 38 | 0 | 1.000 |
| Cirillo, Jeff, S.D. | 1 | 0 | 0 | 0 | 0 | 0 | 0 | .000 |
| Clark, Brady, Mil. | 133 | 86 | 248 | 5 | 4 | 257 | 3 | .984 |
| Clark, Jermaine, Cin. | 8 | 4 | 10 | 1 | 0 | 11 | 0 | 1.000 |
| Collier, Lou, Phi. | 8 | 4 | 3 | 0 | 0 | 3 | 0 | 1.000 |
| Conine, Jeff, Fla. | 83 | 82 | 174 | 5 | 1 | 180 | 2 | .994 |
| Cordero, Wil, Fla. | 3 | 3 | 5 | 0 | 0 | 5 | 0 | 1.000 |
| Cruz, Jacob, Cin.* | 29 | 19 | 36 | 1 | 0 | 37 | 0 | 1.000 |
| Davis, J.J., Pit. | 17 | 9 | 16 | 1 | 2 | 19 | 0 | .895 |
| DeRosa, Mark, Atl. | 3 | 2 | 0 | 0 | 0 | 0 | 0 | .000 |
| DeVore, Doug, Ari.* | 31 | 22 | 53 | 2 | 0 | 55 | 1 | 1.000 |
| Diaz, Victor, N.Y. | 14 | 12 | 29 | 0 | 2 | 31 | 0 | .935 |
| Drew, J.D., Atl. | 142 | 142 | 296 | 12 | 3 | 311 | 0 | .990 |
| Dubois, Jason, Chi. | 5 | 2 | 5 | 0 | 0 | 5 | 0 | 1.000 |
| Duncan, Jeff, N.Y.* | 4 | 2 | 7 | 0 | 0 | 7 | 0 | 1.000 |
| Dunn, Adam, Cin. | 156 | 146 | 250 | 10 | 8 | 268 | 1 | .970 |
| Easley, Damion, Fla. | 5 | 4 | 10 | 0 | 1 | 11 | 0 | .909 |
| Edmonds, Jim, St.L.* | 146 | 141 | 314 | 11 | 4 | 329 | 2 | .988 |
| Ellison, Jason, S.F. | 4 | 0 | 5 | 0 | 0 | 5 | 0 | 1.000 |
| Encarnacion, Juan, L.A.-Fla. | 133 | 131 | 257 | 5 | 6 | 268 | 0 | .978 |
| Everett, Carl, Mon. | 33 | 33 | 61 | 2 | 3 | 66 | 0 | .955 |
| Feliz, Pedro, S.F. | 4 | 0 | 1 | 0 | 0 | 1 | 0 | 1.000 |
| Finley, Steve, Ari.-L.A.* | 158 | 157 | 359 | 5 | 3 | 367 | 3 | .992 |
| Floyd, Cliff, N.Y. | 106 | 105 | 164 | 5 | 2 | 171 | 1 | .988 |
| Freel, Ryan, Cin. | 89 | 67 | 185 | 8 | 3 | 196 | 3 | .985 |
| Freeman, Choo, Col. | 41 | 24 | 69 | 1 | 1 | 71 | 0 | .986 |
| Garcia, Karim, N.Y.* | 51 | 44 | 91 | 0 | 3 | 94 | 0 | .968 |
| Giles, Brian, S.D.* | 159 | 158 | 322 | 8 | 7 | 337 | 3 | .979 |
| Ginter, Keith, Mil. | 2 | 2 | 5 | 0 | 0 | 5 | 0 | 1.000 |
| Glanville, Doug, Phi. | 68 | 30 | 112 | 0 | 0 | 112 | 0 | 1.000 |
| Gonzalez, Luis, Ari. | 104 | 103 | 162 | 2 | 6 | 170 | 0 | .965 |
| Gonzalez, Luis A., Col. | 29 | 20 | 33 | 0 | 0 | 33 | 0 | 1.000 |
| Goodwin, Tom, Chi. | 28 | 11 | 30 | 0 | 0 | 30 | 0 | 1.000 |
| Grabowski, Jason, L.A. | 31 | 23 | 42 | 0 | 1 | 43 | 0 | .977 |
| Green, Andy, Ari. | 9 | 4 | 10 | 1 | 0 | 11 | 0 | 1.000 |
| Green, Nick, Atl. | 1 | 0 | 0 | 0 | 0 | 0 | 0 | .000 |
| Green, Shawn, L.A.* | 52 | 46 | 81 | 2 | 2 | 85 | 1 | .976 |
| Grieve, Ben, Mil.-Chi. | 69 | 66 | 109 | 0 | 4 | 113 | 0 | .965 |
| Griffey Jr., Ken, Cin.* | 77 | 77 | 173 | 4 | 1 | 178 | 1 | .994 |
| Grissom, Marquis, S.F. | 142 | 138 | 341 | 3 | 2 | 346 | 2 | .994 |
| Guzman, Freddy, S.D. | 17 | 16 | 46 | 2 | 2 | 50 | 0 | .960 |
| Hairston, Scott, Ari. | 3 | 0 | 0 | 0 | 0 | 0 | 0 | .000 |
| Hammock, Robby, Ari. | 12 | 10 | 20 | 1 | 1 | 22 | 0 | .955 |
| Hammonds, Jeffrey, S.F. | 28 | 22 | 49 | 3 | 0 | 52 | 0 | 1.000 |
| Harris, Lenny, Fla. | 14 | 9 | 12 | 0 | 0 | 12 | 0 | 1.000 |
| Hawpe, Brad, Col.* | 34 | 30 | 54 | 1 | 1 | 56 | 1 | .982 |
| Hernandez, Jose, L.A. | 9 | 4 | 6 | 0 | 0 | 6 | 0 | 1.000 |
| Hessman, Mike, Atl. | 3 | 2 | 4 | 0 | 0 | 4 | 0 | 1.000 |
| Hidalgo, Richard, Hou.-N.Y. | 142 | 137 | 266 | 14 | 6 | 286 | 3 | .979 |
| Hocking, Denny, Col. | 30 | 5 | 39 | 0 | 1 | 40 | 0 | .975 |
| Hollandsworth, Todd, Chi.* | 36 | 29 | 59 | 2 | 0 | 61 | 0 | 1.000 |
| Holliday, Matt, Col. | 115 | 109 | 177 | 4 | 7 | 188 | 1 | .963 |
| Hollins, Damon, Atl.* | 6 | 5 | 8 | 1 | 0 | 9 | 0 | 1.000 |
| Jenkins, Geoff, Mil. | 156 | 154 | 261 | 10 | 1 | 272 | 3 | .996 |
| Jones, Andruw, Atl. | 154 | 153 | 389 | 10 | 3 | 402 | 2 | .993 |
| Jones, Chipper, Atl. | 29 | 29 | 35 | 2 | 0 | 37 | 1 | 1.000 |
| Kearns, Austin, Cin. | 60 | 59 | 118 | 1 | 3 | 122 | 0 | .975 |
| Kelton, David, Chi. | 3 | 1 | 2 | 0 | 0 | 2 | 0 | 1.000 |
| Klesko, Ryan, S.D.* | 104 | 102 | 135 | 2 | 2 | 139 | 0 | .986 |
| Knott, Jon, S.D. | 5 | 3 | 4 | 0 | 0 | 4 | 0 | 1.000 |
| Kroeger, Josh, Ari.* | 19 | 13 | 33 | 0 | 0 | 33 | 0 | 1.000 |
| Krynzel, Dave, Mil.* | 10 | 9 | 29 | 1 | 1 | 31 | 1 | .968 |
| Lane, Jason, Hou.* | 76 | 22 | 60 | 2 | 1 | 63 | 0 | .984 |
| Lankford, Ray, St.L.* | 70 | 45 | 85 | 1 | 4 | 90 | 0 | .956 |
| LaRue, Jason, Cin. | 1 | 0 | 1 | 0 | 0 | 1 | 0 | 1.000 |
| Ledee, Ricky, Phi.-S.F.* | 37 | 31 | 71 | 3 | 1 | 75 | 1 | .987 |

| Player, Team | G | GS | PO | A | E | TC | DP | Pct. |
|---|---|---|---|---|---|---|---|---|
| Liefer, Jeff, Mil. | 3 | 3 | 4 | 0 | 0 | 4 | 0 | 1.000 |
| Linden, Todd, S.F. | 11 | 6 | 9 | 0 | 0 | 9 | 0 | 1.000 |
| Lo Duca, Paul, L.A. | 9 | 8 | 13 | 0 | 0 | 13 | 0 | 1.000 |
| Long, Terrence, S.D.* | 87 | 56 | 140 | 2 | 2 | 144 | 0 | .986 |
| Luna, Hector, St.L. | 10 | 5 | 9 | 0 | 0 | 9 | 0 | 1.000 |
| Mabry, John, St.L. | 57 | 37 | 69 | 0 | 1 | 70 | 0 | .986 |
| Macias, Jose, Chi. | 28 | 13 | 30 | 2 | 0 | 32 | 0 | 1.000 |
| Mackowiak, Rob, Pit. | 118 | 71 | 138 | 9 | 4 | 151 | 3 | .974 |
| Magruder, Chris, Mil. | 24 | 13 | 32 | 1 | 0 | 33 | 0 | 1.000 |
| Marrero, Eli, Atl. | 73 | 60 | 121 | 6 | 1 | 128 | 1 | .992 |
| Mateo, Henry, Mon. | 1 | 0 | 1 | 0 | 0 | 1 | 0 | 1.000 |
| Mateo, Ruben, Pit. | 10 | 9 | 13 | 1 | 1 | 15 | 1 | .933 |
| McCracken, Quinton, Ari. | 37 | 34 | 45 | 2 | 1 | 48 | 0 | .979 |
| McEwing, Joe, N.Y. | 15 | 7 | 23 | 0 | 0 | 23 | 0 | 1.000 |
| Michaels, Jason, Phi. | 78 | 68 | 166 | 5 | 3 | 174 | 2 | .983 |
| Mohr, Dustan, S.F. | 95 | 63 | 153 | 6 | 3 | 162 | 2 | .981 |
| Mondesi, Raul, Pit. | 26 | 26 | 44 | 2 | 3 | 49 | 0 | .939 |
| Murray, Calvin, Chi. | 8 | 0 | 7 | 0 | 0 | 7 | 0 | 1.000 |
| Nady, Xavier, S.D. | 22 | 16 | 23 | 1 | 2 | 26 | 0 | .923 |
| Nunez, Abraham, Fla. | 48 | 12 | 43 | 0 | 0 | 43 | 0 | 1.000 |
| Olson, Tim, Ari. | 4 | 2 | 7 | 0 | 0 | 7 | 0 | 1.000 |
| Palmeiro, Orlando, Hou.* | 37 | 17 | 37 | 0 | 0 | 37 | 0 | 1.000 |
| Pascucci, Val, Mon. | 17 | 15 | 29 | 0 | 0 | 29 | 0 | 1.000 |
| PATTERSON, Corey, Chi. | 157 | 152 | 324 | 8 | 1 | 333 | 5 | .997 |
| Payton, Jay, S.D. | 137 | 115 | 342 | 11 | 4 | 357 | 2 | .989 |
| Pellow, Kit, Col. | 36 | 22 | 29 | 2 | 0 | 31 | 1 | 1.000 |
| Pena, Wily Mo, Cin. | 91 | 85 | 212 | 6 | 7 | 225 | 0 | .969 |
| Piedra, Jorge, Col.* | 34 | 22 | 49 | 1 | 0 | 50 | 1 | 1.000 |
| Pierre, Juan, Fla.* | 162 | 162 | 364 | 3 | 2 | 369 | 1 | .995 |
| Podsednik, Scott, Mil.* | 153 | 152 | 392 | 5 | 4 | 401 | 2 | .990 |
| Porter, Colin, St.L.* | 14 | 5 | 12 | 0 | 0 | 12 | 0 | 1.000 |
| Ransom, Cody, S.F. | 1 | 0 | 0 | 0 | 0 | 0 | 0 | .000 |
| Redman, Tike, Pit.* | 147 | 134 | 338 | 3 | 5 | 346 | 1 | .986 |
| Reyes, Rene, Col. | 21 | 12 | 31 | 1 | 0 | 32 | 1 | 1.000 |
| Rivera, Juan, Mon. | 121 | 93 | 192 | 14 | 3 | 209 | 3 | .986 |
| Roberts, Dave, L.A.* | 62 | 57 | 118 | 2 | 3 | 123 | 1 | .976 |
| Robinson, Kerry, S.D.* | 49 | 7 | 48 | 1 | 0 | 49 | 0 | 1.000 |
| Romano, Jason, Cin. | 11 | 4 | 9 | 1 | 0 | 10 | 0 | 1.000 |
| Sadler, Donnie, Ari. | 6 | 0 | 2 | 0 | 0 | 2 | 0 | 1.000 |
| Sanders, Reggie, St.L. | 119 | 112 | 198 | 6 | 4 | 208 | 1 | .981 |
| Simontacchi, Jason, St.L. | 1 | 0 | 0 | 0 | 0 | 0 | 0 | .000 |
| Sledge, Terrmel, Mon.* | 114 | 96 | 216 | 5 | 3 | 224 | 1 | .987 |
| Snead, Esix, N.Y. | 1 | 0 | 0 | 0 | 0 | 0 | 0 | .000 |
| Sosa, Sammy, Chi. | 124 | 124 | 238 | 5 | 4 | 247 | 2 | .984 |
| Spencer, Shane, N.Y. | 62 | 38 | 111 | 2 | 3 | 116 | 0 | .974 |
| Sweeney, Mark, Col.* | 28 | 23 | 42 | 3 | 0 | 45 | 1 | 1.000 |
| Taguchi, So, St.L. | 103 | 36 | 99 | 1 | 2 | 102 | 0 | .980 |
| Taveras, Willy, Hou. | 7 | 0 | 1 | 0 | 0 | 1 | 0 | 1.000 |
| Terrero, Luis, Ari. | 61 | 59 | 117 | 5 | 8 | 130 | 3 | .938 |
| Thomas, Charles, Atl.* | 71 | 62 | 138 | 7 | 1 | 146 | 2 | .993 |
| Tracy, Chad, Ari. | 1 | 0 | 2 | 0 | 0 | 2 | 0 | 1.000 |
| Tucker, Michael, S.F. | 124 | 114 | 262 | 2 | 6 | 270 | 2 | .978 |
| Valent, Eric, N.Y.* | 46 | 32 | 59 | 1 | 0 | 60 | 0 | 1.000 |
| Vander Wal, John, Cin.* | 7 | 7 | 12 | 1 | 0 | 13 | 0 | 1.000 |
| Walker, Larry, Col.-St.L. | 75 | 69 | 122 | 5 | 1 | 128 | 1 | .992 |
| Walker, Todd, Chi. | 1 | 0 | 1 | 0 | 0 | 1 | 0 | 1.000 |
| Ward, Daryle, Pit.* | 12 | 10 | 10 | 0 | 0 | 10 | 0 | 1.000 |
| Werth, Jayson, L.A. | 79 | 70 | 146 | 6 | 4 | 156 | 2 | .974 |
| Wilkerson, Brad, Mon.* | 80 | 76 | 159 | 8 | 3 | 170 | 3 | .982 |
| Williams, Gerald, N.Y. | 45 | 27 | 51 | 3 | 1 | 55 | 0 | .982 |
| Willingham, Josh, Fla. | 3 | 3 | 6 | 0 | 0 | 6 | 0 | 1.000 |
| Wilson, Craig, Pit. | 100 | 95 | 167 | 2 | 4 | 173 | 0 | .977 |
| Wilson, Preston, Col. | 52 | 51 | 119 | 3 | 6 | 128 | 1 | .953 |
| Wise, Dewayne, Atl.* | 56 | 30 | 61 | 2 | 0 | 63 | 0 | 1.000 |

## OUTFIELDERS WITH TWO OR MORE TEAMS

| Player, Team | G | GS | PO | A | E | TC | DP | Pct. |
|---|---|---|---|---|---|---|---|---|
| Encarnacion, Juan, L.A. | 85 | 85 | 161 | 3 | 4 | 168 | 0 | .976 |
| Encarnacion, Juan, Fla. | 48 | 46 | 96 | 2 | 2 | 100 | 0 | .980 |
| Finley, Steve, Ari.* | 103 | 102 | 214 | 5 | 2 | 221 | 3 | .991 |
| Finley, Steve, L.A.* | 55 | 55 | 145 | 0 | 1 | 146 | 0 | .993 |
| Grieve, Ben, Mil. | 65 | 64 | 106 | 0 | 4 | 110 | 0 | .964 |
| Grieve, Ben, Chi. | 4 | 2 | 3 | 0 | 0 | 3 | 0 | 1.000 |
| Hidalgo, Richard, Hou. | 56 | 51 | 107 | 4 | 2 | 113 | 0 | .982 |
| Hidalgo, Richard, N.Y. | 86 | 86 | 159 | 10 | 4 | 173 | 3 | .977 |
| Ledee, Ricky, Phi.* | 22 | 20 | 47 | 3 | 0 | 50 | 1 | 1.000 |
| Ledee, Ricky, S.F.* | 15 | 11 | 24 | 0 | 1 | 25 | 0 | .960 |
| Walker, Larry, Col. | 34 | 29 | 64 | 4 | 0 | 68 | 1 | 1.000 |
| Walker, Larry, St.L. | 41 | 40 | 58 | 1 | 1 | 60 | 0 | .983 |

# CATCHERS

| Player, Team | G | GS | PO | A | E | TC | DP | PB | Pct. |
|---|---|---|---|---|---|---|---|---|---|
| Ausmus, Brad, Hou. | 128 | 114 | 920 | 61 | 5 | 986 | 10 | 2 | .995 |
| Bako, Paul, Chi. | 47 | 43 | 332 | 30 | 4 | 366 | 2 | 1 | .989 |
| Barrett, Michael, Chi. | 130 | 119 | 1035 | 47 | 6 | 1088 | 9 | 8 | .994 |
| Bennett, Gary, Mil. | 75 | 65 | 379 | 31 | 3 | 413 | 3 | 3 | .993 |
| Brito, Juan, Ari. | 54 | 53 | 385 | 30 | 4 | 419 | 2 | 6 | .990 |
| Castro, Ramon, Fla. | 31 | 27 | 192 | 12 | 2 | 206 | 2 | 0 | .990 |
| Chavez, Raul, Hou. | 61 | 48 | 395 | 29 | 4 | 428 | 2 | 2 | .991 |
| Closser, J.D., Col. | 32 | 29 | 195 | 17 | 3 | 215 | 4 | 6 | .986 |
| Cota, Humberto, Pit. | 24 | 13 | 101 | 4 | 1 | 106 | 1 | 0 | .991 |
| Diaz, Einar, Mon. | 44 | 37 | 264 | 19 | 3 | 286 | 6 | 3 | .990 |
| DiFelice, Mike, Chi. | 4 | 0 | 6 | 0 | 0 | 6 | 0 | 0 | 1.000 |
| Estalella, Bobby, Ari. | 6 | 3 | 19 | 2 | 0 | 21 | 0 | 0 | 1.000 |
| Estrada, Johnny, Atl. | 133 | 120 | 776 | 44 | 9 | 829 | 8 | 8 | .989 |
| Greene, Todd, Col. | 53 | 48 | 258 | 15 | 3 | 276 | 1 | 2 | .989 |
| Hammock, Robby, Ari. | 46 | 42 | 313 | 21 | 1 | 335 | 8 | 5 | .997 |
| Hernandez, Ramon, S.D. | 108 | 106 | 753 | 35 | 6 | 794 | 7 | 7 | .992 |
| Hietpas, Joe, N.Y. | 1 | 0 | 2 | 0 | 0 | 2 | 0 | 0 | 1.000 |
| Hill, Koyie, Ari. | 11 | 10 | 57 | 5 | 1 | 63 | 0 | 0 | .984 |
| Hinch, A.J., Phi. | 4 | 1 | 14 | 5 | 0 | 19 | 0 | 0 | 1.000 |
| House, J.R., Pit. | 3 | 2 | 17 | 0 | 0 | 17 | 0 | 0 | 1.000 |
| Johnson, Charles, Col. | 91 | 85 | 523 | 44 | 7 | 574 | 8 | 7 | .988 |
| Johnson, Mark, Mil. | 5 | 4 | 18 | 2 | 1 | 21 | 0 | 0 | .952 |
| Kendall, Jason, Pit. | 146 | 145 | 998 | 78 | 10 | 1086 | 13 | 2 | .991 |
| Knoedler, Justin, S.F. | 1 | 0 | 2 | 0 | 0 | 2 | 0 | 0 | 1.000 |
| LaRue, Jason, Cin. | 111 | 106 | 648 | 59 | 8 | 715 | 8 | 15 | .989 |
| Lieberthal, Mike, Phi. | 129 | 123 | 859 | 43 | 6 | 908 | 7 | 6 | .993 |
| Lo Duca, Paul, L.A.-Fla. | 130 | 125 | 843 | 65 | 4 | 912 | 9 | 12 | .996 |
| MATHENY, Mike, St.L. | 122 | 110 | 742 | 58 | 1 | 801 | 10 | 2 | .999 |
| Mayne, Brent, Ari.-L.A. | 77 | 60 | 406 | 30 | 2 | 438 | 2 | 6 | .995 |
| McKay, Cody, St.L. | 18 | 13 | 75 | 12 | 0 | 87 | 1 | 3 | 1.000 |
| Miller, Corky, Cin. | 12 | 12 | 84 | 5 | 1 | 90 | 1 | 1 | .989 |
| Moeller, Chad, Mil. | 100 | 92 | 719 | 45 | 1 | 765 | 4 | 4 | .999 |
| Molina, Yadier, St.L. | 51 | 39 | 256 | 16 | 2 | 274 | 1 | 4 | .993 |
| Mordecai, Mike, Fla. | 1 | 0 | 9 | 0 | 0 | 9 | 0 | 0 | 1.000 |
| Nevin, Phil, S.D. | 1 | 0 | 4 | 0 | 0 | 4 | 0 | 0 | 1.000 |
| Ojeda, Miguel, S.D. | 50 | 37 | 240 | 18 | 1 | 259 | 2 | 2 | .996 |
| Pellow, Kit, Col. | 4 | 0 | 11 | 0 | 0 | 11 | 0 | 0 | 1.000 |
| Perez, Eddie, Atl. | 66 | 42 | 290 | 22 | 3 | 315 | 4 | 2 | .990 |
| Phillips, Jason, N.Y. | 87 | 72 | 486 | 37 | 1 | 524 | 4 | 3 | .998 |
| Piazza, Mike, N.Y. | 50 | 49 | 260 | 15 | 5 | 280 | 1 | 5 | .982 |
| Pierzynski, A.J., S.F. | 118 | 117 | 697 | 56 | 1 | 754 | 6 | 9 | .999 |
| Pratt, Todd, Phi. | 43 | 38 | 259 | 8 | 0 | 267 | 2 | 1 | 1.000 |
| Quintero, Humberto, S.D. | 21 | 19 | 130 | 10 | 0 | 140 | 0 | 0 | 1.000 |
| Redmond, Mike, Fla. | 79 | 71 | 488 | 34 | 2 | 524 | 7 | 4 | .996 |
| Ross, David, L.A. | 67 | 51 | 355 | 21 | 3 | 379 | 0 | 6 | .992 |
| Schneider, Brian, Mon. | 133 | 125 | 814 | 59 | 2 | 875 | 16 | 4 | .998 |
| Snyder, Chris, Ari. | 29 | 27 | 213 | 19 | 0 | 232 | 2 | 3 | 1.000 |
| Torrealba, Yorvit, S.F. | 59 | 45 | 349 | 18 | 2 | 369 | 4 | 2 | .995 |
| Treanor, Matt, Fla. | 27 | 14 | 117 | 6 | 3 | 126 | 0 | 0 | .976 |
| Tremie, Chris, Hou. | 1 | 0 | 0 | 0 | 0 | 0 | 0 | 0 | .000 |
| Valentin, Javier, Cin. | 55 | 44 | 305 | 31 | 4 | 340 | 2 | 1 | .988 |
| Willingham, Josh, Fla. | 5 | 3 | 15 | 0 | 1 | 16 | 0 | 2 | .938 |
| Wilson, Craig, Pit. | 4 | 1 | 11 | 0 | 0 | 11 | 0 | 0 | 1.000 |
| Wilson, Tom, N.Y.-L.A. | 10 | 1 | 22 | 0 | 0 | 22 | 0 | 0 | 1.000 |
| Wilson, Vance, N.Y. | 69 | 38 | 257 | 23 | 2 | 282 | 2 | 4 | .993 |
| Zeile, Todd, N.Y. | 2 | 2 | 12 | 0 | 0 | 12 | 0 | 0 | 1.000 |

## CATCHERS WITH TWO OR MORE TEAMS

| Player, Team | G | GS | PO | A | E | TC | DP | PB | Pct. |
|---|---|---|---|---|---|---|---|---|---|
| Lo Duca, Paul, L.A. | 81 | 78 | 513 | 42 | 3 | 558 | 4 | 7 | .995 |
| Lo Duca, Paul, Fla. | 49 | 47 | 330 | 23 | 1 | 354 | 5 | 5 | .997 |
| Mayne, Brent, Ari. | 30 | 27 | 182 | 18 | 2 | 202 | 0 | 4 | .990 |
| Mayne, Brent, L.A. | 47 | 33 | 224 | 12 | 0 | 236 | 2 | 2 | 1.000 |
| Wilson, Tom, N.Y. | 3 | 1 | 11 | 0 | 0 | 11 | 0 | 0 | 1.000 |
| Wilson, Tom, L.A. | 7 | 0 | 11 | 0 | 0 | 11 | 0 | 0 | 1.000 |

## CATCHERS—SPECIAL STATS*

| Player, Team | G | Inn. | SBA | CCS | PCS | CS% | ER | CERA |
|---|---|---|---|---|---|---|---|---|
| Ausmus,Brad, Hou | 128 | 1018.1 | 106 | 23 | 5 | .23 | 462 | 4.08 |
| Bako,Paul, ChC | 47 | 377.2 | 51 | 15 | 0 | .29 | 148 | 3.53 |
| Barrett,Michael, ChC | 130 | 1081.1 | 96 | 18 | 6 | .20 | 466 | 3.88 |
| Bennett,Gary, Mil | 75 | 584.0 | 44 | 9 | 2 | .21 | 328 | 5.05 |
| Brito,Juan, Ari | 54 | 461.2 | 51 | 12 | 4 | .26 | 233 | 4.54 |
| Castro,Ramon, Fla | 31 | 243.0 | 14 | 5 | 0 | .36 | 96 | 3.56 |
| Chavez,Raul, Hou | 61 | 423.2 | 34 | 10 | 1 | .30 | 187 | 3.97 |
| Closser,J.D, Col | 32 | 259.0 | 28 | 5 | 4 | .21 | 141 | 4.90 |
| Cota,Humberto, Pit | 24 | 133.0 | 5 | 1 | 0 | .20 | 53 | 3.59 |
| Diaz,Einar, Mon | 44 | 333.0 | 27 | 5 | 0 | .19 | 218 | 5.89 |
| DiFelice,Mike, ChC | 4 | 6.1 | 0 | 0 | 0 | 0 | 7 | 9.95 |
| Estalella,Bobby, Ari | 6 | 30.2 | 0 | 0 | 0 | 0 | 27 | 7.92 |

| Player, Team | G | Inn. | SBA | CCS | PCS | CS% | ER | CERA |
|---|---|---|---|---|---|---|---|---|
| Estrada,Johnny, Atl | 133 | 1042.0 | 86 | 15 | 1 | .18 | 436 | 3.77 |
| Greene,Todd, Col | 53 | 421.0 | 36 | 2 | 5 | .06 | 269 | 5.75 |
| Hammock,Robby, Ari | 46 | 376.2 | 39 | 10 | 2 | .27 | 164 | 3.92 |
| Hernandez,Ramon, SD | 108 | 925.1 | 74 | 18 | 3 | .25 | 414 | 4.03 |
| Hietpas,Joe, NYM | 1 | 1.0 | 0 | 0 | 0 | 0 | 0 | 0.00 |
| Hill,Koyie, Ari | 11 | 83.0 | 12 | 3 | 1 | .27 | 74 | 8.02 |
| Hinch,A.J., Phi | 4 | 25.2 | 3 | 2 | 0 | .67 | 8 | 2.81 |
| House,J.R., Pit | 3 | 19.0 | 0 | 0 | 0 | 0 | 2 | 0.95 |
| Johnson,Charles, Col | 91 | 746.1 | 79 | 12 | 4 | .16 | 471 | 5.68 |
| Johnson,Mark, Mil | 5 | 31.0 | 5 | 1 | 0 | .20 | 14 | 4.06 |
| Kendall,Jason, Pit | 146 | 1259.0 | 102 | 31 | 6 | .32 | 623 | 4.45 |
| Knoedler,Justin, SF | 1 | 2.0 | 0 | 0 | 0 | 0 | 0 | 0.00 |
| LaRue,Jason, Cin | 111 | 930.0 | 54 | 16 | 0 | .30 | 508 | 4.92 |
| Lieberthal,Mike, Phi | 129 | 1104.0 | 94 | 19 | 1 | .20 | 570 | 4.65 |
| Lo Duca,Paul, TOT | 130 | 1104.2 | 129 | 29 | 7 | .24 | 470 | 3.83 |
| Lo Duca,Paul, LA | 81 | 691.2 | 75 | 16 | 5 | .23 | 303 | 3.94 |
| Lo Duca,Paul, Fla | 49 | 413.0 | 54 | 13 | 2 | .25 | 167 | 3.64 |
| Matheny,Mike, StL | 122 | 977.2 | 54 | 15 | 1 | .28 | 422 | 3.88 |
| Mayne,Brent, TOT | 77 | 529.2 | 47 | 12 | 6 | .29 | 300 | 5.10 |
| Mayne,Brent, Ari | 30 | 236.2 | 26 | 8 | 4 | .36 | 177 | 6.73 |
| Mayne,Brent, LA | 47 | 293.0 | 21 | 4 | 2 | .21 | 123 | 3.78 |
| McKay,Cody, StL | 18 | 132.0 | 11 | 5 | 0 | .45 | 44 | 3.00 |
| Miller,Corky, Cin | 12 | 104.0 | 3 | 1 | 0 | .33 | 73 | 6.32 |
| Moeller,Chad, Mil | 100 | 827.0 | 69 | 13 | 4 | .20 | 337 | 3.67 |
| Molina,Yadier, StL | 51 | 344.0 | 17 | 8 | 0 | .47 | 139 | 3.64 |
| Mordecai,Mike, Fla | 1 | 8.0 | 4 | 0 | 0 | 0 | 4 | 4.50 |
| Nevin,Phil, SD | 1 | 4.0 | 0 | 0 | 0 | 0 | 0 | 0.00 |
| Ojeda,Miguel, SD | 50 | 340.0 | 11 | 3 | 0 | .27 | 161 | 4.26 |
| Pellow,Kit, Col | 4 | 9.0 | 0 | 0 | 0 | 0 | 2 | 2.00 |
| Perez,Eddie, Atl | 66 | 408.0 | 34 | 11 | 2 | .34 | 167 | 3.68 |
| Phillips,Jason, NYM | 87 | 650.1 | 61 | 12 | 7 | .22 | 278 | 3.85 |
| Piazza,Mike, NYM | 50 | 388.1 | 43 | 7 | 2 | .17 | 172 | 3.99 |
| Pierzynski,A.J., SF | 118 | 1022.0 | 66 | 11 | 4 | .18 | 480 | 4.23 |
| Pratt,Todd, Phi | 43 | 333.0 | 32 | 4 | 0 | .13 | 146 | 3.95 |
| Quintero,Humberto, SD | 21 | 171.2 | 9 | 1 | 0 | .11 | 70 | 3.67 |
| Redmond,Mike, Fla | 79 | 604.1 | 65 | 11 | 3 | .18 | 308 | 4.59 |
| Ross,David, LA | 67 | 451.2 | 39 | 11 | 1 | .29 | 213 | 4.24 |
| Schneider,Brian, Mon | 133 | 1114.0 | 72 | 33 | 3 | .48 | 478 | 3.86 |
| Snyder,Chris, Ari | 29 | 247.1 | 19 | 6 | 0 | .32 | 119 | 4.33 |
| Torrealba,Yorvit, SF | 59 | 433.0 | 30 | 6 | 3 | .22 | 215 | 4.47 |
| Treanor,Matt, Fla | 27 | 147.2 | 14 | 3 | 0 | .21 | 72 | 4.39 |
| Tremie,Chris, Hou | 1 | 1.0 | 0 | 0 | 0 | 0 | 1 | 9.00 |
| Valentin,Javier, Cin | 55 | 409.2 | 39 | 12 | 0 | .31 | 251 | 5.51 |
| Willingham,Josh, Fla | 5 | 23.0 | 5 | 0 | 1 | 0 | 8 | 3.13 |
| Wilson,Craig, Pit | 4 | 17.0 | 3 | 0 | 0 | 0 | 2 | 1.06 |
| Wilson,Tom, TOT | 10 | 28.2 | 4 | 0 | 1 | 0 | 19 | 5.97 |
| Wilson,Tom, NYM | 3 | 11.2 | 3 | 0 | 0 | 0 | 11 | 8.49 |
| Wilson,Tom, LA | 7 | 17.0 | 1 | 0 | 1 | 0 | 8 | 4.24 |
| Wilson,Vance, NYM | 69 | 383.2 | 32 | 10 | 1 | .32 | 190 | 4.46 |
| Zeile,Todd, NYM | 2 | 14.0 | 0 | 0 | 0 | 0 | 7 | 4.50 |
| **Average** | 53 | 413.1 | 35 | 8 | 2 | .29 | 198 | 4.31 |

***Inn.** denotes the number of innings the catcher was behind the plate. **SBA** denotes stolen bases attempted. **CCS** denotes number of runners caught stealing by the catcher. **PCS** denotes number of runners caught stealing by the pitcher. **CS%** denotes the catcher's caught stealing percentage, figured by subtracting PCS from SBA and dividing this number into CCS. **ER** denotes number of earned runs scored when catcher was behind the plate. **CERA** denotes catcher's ERA when he was behind the plate, figured the same way a pitcher's ERA is completed (ER*9/IP).

## PITCHERS

| Player, Team | G | GS | PO | A | E | TC | DP | Pct. |
|---|---|---|---|---|---|---|---|---|
| Aardsma, David, S.F. | 11 | 0 | 0 | 0 | 0 | 0 | 0 | .000 |
| Abbott, Paul, Phi. | 10 | 10 | 3 | 2 | 0 | 5 | 0 | 1.000 |
| Acevedo, Jose, Cin. | 39 | 27 | 4 | 18 | 0 | 22 | 0 | 1.000 |
| Adams, Mike, Mil. | 46 | 0 | 0 | 5 | 0 | 5 | 0 | 1.000 |
| Alfonseca, Antonio, Atl. | 79 | 0 | 3 | 7 | 0 | 10 | 0 | 1.000 |
| Almanza, Armando, Atl.* | 13 | 0 | 0 | 1 | 0 | 1 | 0 | 1.000 |
| Alvarez, Wilson, L.A.* | 40 | 15 | 3 | 16 | 0 | 19 | 0 | 1.000 |
| Anderson, Jimmy, Chi.* | 7 | 0 | 3 | 1 | 0 | 4 | 0 | 1.000 |
| Ankiel, Rick, St.L.* | 5 | 0 | 1 | 3 | 0 | 4 | 0 | 1.000 |
| Aquino, Greg, Ari. | 34 | 0 | 3 | 4 | 0 | 7 | 0 | 1.000 |
| Armas, Tony, Mon. | 16 | 16 | 2 | 13 | 0 | 15 | 3 | 1.000 |
| Ashby, Andy, S.D. | 2 | 0 | 0 | 0 | 0 | 0 | 0 | .000 |
| Ayala, Luis, Mon. | 81 | 0 | 9 | 21 | 0 | 30 | 4 | 1.000 |
| Backe, Brandon, Hou. | 33 | 9 | 4 | 10 | 0 | 14 | 1 | 1.000 |
| Baldwin, James, N.Y. | 2 | 2 | 0 | 2 | 0 | 2 | 0 | 1.000 |
| Beck, Rod, S.D. | 26 | 0 | 0 | 2 | 1 | 3 | 0 | .667 |
| Beckett, Josh, Fla. | 26 | 26 | 4 | 17 | 2 | 23 | 0 | .913 |
| Bell, Heath, N.Y. | 17 | 0 | 0 | 3 | 0 | 3 | 0 | 1.000 |
| Beltran, Francis, Chi.-Mon. | 45 | 0 | 0 | 5 | 1 | 6 | 1 | .833 |
| Beltran, Rigo, Mon.* | 2 | 0 | 0 | 0 | 0 | 0 | 0 | .000 |
| Benitez, Armando, Fla. | 64 | 0 | 4 | 3 | 1 | 8 | 0 | .875 |
| Bennett, Jeff, Mil. | 60 | 0 | 6 | 7 | 1 | 14 | 0 | .929 |
| Benson, Kris, Pit.-N.Y. | 31 | 31 | 17 | 25 | 1 | 43 | 2 | .977 |
| Bentz, Chad, Mon.* | 36 | 0 | 5 | 5 | 0 | 10 | 0 | 1.000 |
| Bernero, Adam, Col. | 16 | 2 | 1 | 4 | 0 | 5 | 0 | 1.000 |
| Biddle, Rocky, Mon. | 47 | 9 | 2 | 9 | 0 | 11 | 0 | 1.000 |
| Boehringer, Brian, Pit. | 21 | 0 | 0 | 3 | 0 | 3 | 1 | 1.000 |
| Bong, Jung Keun, Cin.* | 3 | 3 | 1 | 4 | 0 | 5 | 1 | 1.000 |
| Borland, Toby, Fla. | 18 | 0 | 2 | 2 | 1 | 5 | 0 | .800 |
| Borowski, Joe, Chi. | 22 | 0 | 0 | 1 | 0 | 1 | 0 | 1.000 |
| Bottalico, Ricky, N.Y. | 60 | 0 | 5 | 8 | 0 | 13 | 0 | 1.000 |
| Boyd, Jason, Pit. | 12 | 0 | 0 | 4 | 2 | 6 | 0 | .667 |
| Brazoban, Yhency, L.A. | 31 | 0 | 1 | 4 | 0 | 5 | 1 | 1.000 |
| Brooks, Frank, Pit.* | 11 | 1 | 0 | 0 | 0 | 0 | 0 | .000 |
| Brower, Jim, S.F. | 89 | 0 | 6 | 21 | 2 | 29 | 0 | .931 |
| Bruney, Brian, Ari. | 30 | 0 | 2 | 3 | 1 | 6 | 0 | .833 |
| Bullinger, Kirk, Hou. | 27 | 0 | 4 | 10 | 0 | 14 | 0 | 1.000 |
| Bump, Nate, Fla. | 50 | 2 | 2 | 9 | 1 | 12 | 0 | .917 |
| Burba, Dave, Mil.-S.F. | 51 | 0 | 6 | 13 | 2 | 21 | 0 | .905 |
| Burnett, A.J., Fla. | 20 | 19 | 10 | 18 | 0 | 28 | 0 | 1.000 |
| Burnett, Sean, Pit.* | 13 | 13 | 4 | 17 | 1 | 22 | 1 | .955 |
| Bynum, Mike, S.D.* | 2 | 0 | 0 | 0 | 0 | 0 | 0 | .000 |
| Byrd, Paul, Atl. | 19 | 19 | 7 | 15 | 3 | 25 | 2 | .880 |
| Calero, Kiko, St.L. | 41 | 0 | 2 | 9 | 0 | 11 | 0 | 1.000 |
| Cali, Carmen, St.L.* | 10 | 0 | 0 | 0 | 0 | 0 | 0 | .000 |
| Capellan, Jose, Atl. | 3 | 2 | 0 | 0 | 0 | 0 | 0 | .000 |
| Capuano, Chris, Mil.* | 17 | 17 | 3 | 16 | 0 | 19 | 0 | 1.000 |
| Carpenter, Chris, St.L. | 28 | 28 | 12 | 34 | 1 | 47 | 4 | .979 |
| Carrara, Giovanni, L.A. | 42 | 0 | 4 | 11 | 0 | 15 | 2 | 1.000 |
| Chacon, Shawn, Col. | 66 | 0 | 2 | 5 | 1 | 8 | 1 | .875 |
| Choate, Randy, Ari.* | 74 | 0 | 3 | 10 | 0 | 13 | 1 | 1.000 |
| Christiansen, Jason, S.F.* | 60 | 0 | 2 | 5 | 2 | 9 | 0 | .778 |
| Claussen, Brandon, Cin.* | 14 | 14 | 1 | 5 | 0 | 6 | 0 | 1.000 |
| Clemens, Roger, Hou. | 33 | 33 | 12 | 24 | 0 | 36 | 2 | 1.000 |
| Clement, Matt, Chi. | 30 | 30 | 16 | 21 | 3 | 40 | 3 | .925 |
| Colon, Roman, Atl. | 18 | 0 | 0 | 1 | 1 | 2 | 0 | .500 |
| Cook, Aaron, Col. | 16 | 16 | 11 | 21 | 0 | 32 | 4 | 1.000 |
| Cooper, Brian, S.F. | 5 | 2 | 1 | 1 | 0 | 2 | 0 | 1.000 |
| Corcoran, Roy, Mon. | 5 | 0 | 0 | 0 | 0 | 0 | 0 | .000 |
| Cordero, Chad, Mon. | 69 | 0 | 3 | 5 | 0 | 8 | 1 | 1.000 |
| Corey, Mark, Pit. | 31 | 0 | 2 | 4 | 0 | 6 | 1 | 1.000 |
| Cormier, Lance, Ari. | 17 | 5 | 1 | 4 | 0 | 5 | 0 | 1.000 |
| Cormier, Rheal, Phi.* | 84 | 0 | 13 | 14 | 0 | 27 | 3 | 1.000 |
| Correia, Kevin, S.F. | 12 | 1 | 2 | 1 | 0 | 3 | 0 | 1.000 |
| Crowell, Jim, Phi.* | 4 | 0 | 0 | 0 | 0 | 0 | 0 | .000 |
| Cruz, Juan, Atl. | 50 | 0 | 4 | 6 | 0 | 10 | 1 | 1.000 |
| Cunnane, Will, Atl. | 9 | 0 | 1 | 1 | 0 | 2 | 0 | 1.000 |
| Daigle, Casey, Ari. | 10 | 10 | 5 | 6 | 0 | 11 | 0 | 1.000 |
| Darensbourg, Vic, N.Y.* | 5 | 0 | 1 | 2 | 0 | 3 | 0 | 1.000 |
| Davis, Doug, Mil.* | 34 | 34 | 15 | 26 | 1 | 42 | 2 | .976 |
| Day, Zach, Mon. | 19 | 19 | 10 | 16 | 0 | 26 | 1 | 1.000 |
| de la Rosa, Jorge, Mil.* | 5 | 5 | 2 | 2 | 1 | 5 | 0 | .800 |
| DeJean, Mike, N.Y. | 17 | 0 | 1 | 3 | 0 | 4 | 0 | 1.000 |
| Dempster, Ryan, Chi. | 23 | 0 | 4 | 2 | 0 | 6 | 0 | 1.000 |
| Dessens, Elmer, Ari.-L.A. | 50 | 10 | 5 | 13 | 1 | 19 | 0 | .947 |
| Dohmann, Scott, Col. | 41 | 0 | 4 | 4 | 0 | 8 | 0 | 1.000 |
| Dotel, Octavio, Hou. | 32 | 0 | 4 | 0 | 0 | 4 | 0 | 1.000 |
| Downs, Scott, Mon.* | 12 | 12 | 3 | 11 | 0 | 14 | 1 | 1.000 |
| Dreifort, Darren, L.A. | 60 | 0 | 1 | 12 | 0 | 13 | 0 | 1.000 |
| Drew, Tim, Atl. | 11 | 0 | 2 | 3 | 0 | 5 | 1 | 1.000 |
| Driskill, Travis, Col. | 5 | 0 | 0 | 1 | 0 | 1 | 0 | 1.000 |
| Duckworth, Brandon, Hou. | 19 | 6 | 3 | 3 | 0 | 6 | 2 | 1.000 |
| Durbin, Chad, Ari. | 7 | 0 | 0 | 1 | 0 | 1 | 0 | 1.000 |
| Durrington, Trent, Mil. | 1 | 0 | 0 | 0 | 0 | 0 | 0 | .000 |
| Eaton, Adam, S.D. | 33 | 33 | 13 | 23 | 2 | 38 | 1 | .947 |
| Eischen, Joey, Mon.* | 21 | 0 | 0 | 1 | 1 | 2 | 0 | .500 |
| Elarton, Scott, Col. | 8 | 8 | 2 | 5 | 0 | 7 | 0 | 1.000 |
| Eldred, Cal, St.L. | 52 | 0 | 1 | 12 | 0 | 13 | 1 | 1.000 |
| Erickson, Scott, N.Y. | 2 | 2 | 0 | 1 | 0 | 1 | 0 | 1.000 |
| Estes, Shawn, Col.* | 34 | 34 | 14 | 27 | 1 | 42 | 4 | .976 |
| Estrella, Leo, S.F. | 2 | 0 | 0 | 0 | 0 | 0 | 0 | .000 |
| Eyre, Scott, S.F.* | 83 | 0 | 2 | 7 | 1 | 10 | 0 | .900 |
| Falkenborg, Brian, L.A. | 6 | 0 | 1 | 2 | 1 | 4 | 0 | .750 |
| Farnsworth, Kyle, Chi. | 72 | 0 | 7 | 10 | 1 | 18 | 0 | .944 |
| Fassero, Jeff, Col.-Ari.* | 41 | 12 | 7 | 24 | 0 | 31 | 2 | 1.000 |
| Feliciano, Pedro, N.Y.* | 22 | 0 | 2 | 4 | 0 | 6 | 0 | 1.000 |
| Fernandez, Jared, Hou. | 2 | 1 | 1 | 0 | 0 | 1 | 0 | 1.000 |
| Fetters, Mike, Ari. | 23 | 0 | 2 | 2 | 1 | 5 | 0 | .800 |
| Figueroa, Nelson, Pit. | 10 | 3 | 1 | 3 | 0 | 4 | 0 | 1.000 |
| Fikac, Jeremy, Mon. | 19 | 0 | 1 | 5 | 0 | 6 | 1 | 1.000 |
| Flores, Randy, St.L.* | 9 | 1 | 0 | 0 | 0 | 0 | 0 | .000 |
| Floyd, Gavin, Phi. | 6 | 4 | 1 | 3 | 0 | 4 | 0 | 1.000 |
| Fogg, Josh, Pit. | 32 | 32 | 13 | 36 | 2 | 51 | 5 | .961 |
| Foppert, Jesse, S.F. | 1 | 0 | 0 | 0 | 0 | 0 | 0 | .000 |
| Ford, Ben, Mil. | 19 | 0 | 0 | 3 | 0 | 3 | 1 | 1.000 |
| Fortunato, Bartolome, N.Y. | 15 | 0 | 2 | 0 | 0 | 2 | 0 | 1.000 |
| Fossum, Casey, Ari.* | 27 | 27 | 4 | 20 | 0 | 24 | 1 | 1.000 |
| Fox, Chad, Fla. | 12 | 0 | 1 | 1 | 0 | 2 | 0 | 1.000 |
| Francis, Jeff, Col.* | 7 | 7 | 2 | 6 | 0 | 8 | 1 | 1.000 |
| Franco, John, N.Y.* | 52 | 0 | 0 | 6 | 0 | 6 | 0 | 1.000 |

| Player, Team | G | GS | PO | A | E | TC | DP | Pct. |
|---|---|---|---|---|---|---|---|---|
| Franklin, Wayne, S.F.* | 43 | 2 | 2 | 5 | 0 | 7 | 0 | 1.000 |
| Fuentes, Brian, Col.* | 47 | 0 | 0 | 6 | 1 | 7 | 0 | .857 |
| Gagne, Eric, L.A. | 70 | 0 | 5 | 6 | 0 | 11 | 1 | 1.000 |
| Gallo, Mike, Hou.* | 69 | 0 | 4 | 9 | 0 | 13 | 2 | 1.000 |
| Geary, Geoff, Phi. | 33 | 0 | 3 | 3 | 1 | 7 | 0 | .857 |
| Germano, Justin, S.D. | 7 | 5 | 1 | 3 | 0 | 4 | 0 | 1.000 |
| Ginter, Matt, N.Y. | 15 | 14 | 4 | 4 | 2 | 10 | 0 | .800 |
| Gissell, Chris, Col. | 5 | 1 | 1 | 0 | 0 | 1 | 0 | 1.000 |
| Glavine, Tom, N.Y.* | 33 | 33 | 10 | 49 | 1 | 60 | 2 | .983 |
| Glover, Gary, Mil. | 4 | 3 | 3 | 3 | 1 | 7 | 0 | .857 |
| Gonzalez, Edgar, Ari. | 10 | 10 | 0 | 7 | 0 | 7 | 2 | 1.000 |
| Gonzalez, Mike, Pit.* | 47 | 0 | 1 | 5 | 1 | 7 | 0 | .857 |
| Good, Andrew, Ari. | 17 | 2 | 2 | 4 | 0 | 6 | 1 | 1.000 |
| Gosling, Mike, Ari.* | 6 | 4 | 2 | 1 | 1 | 4 | 0 | .750 |
| Grabow, John, Pit.* | 68 | 0 | 2 | 15 | 0 | 17 | 2 | 1.000 |
| Gracesqui, Franklyn, Fla.* | 7 | 0 | 0 | 1 | 0 | 1 | 0 | 1.000 |
| Graves, Danny, Cin. | 68 | 0 | 2 | 10 | 0 | 12 | 3 | 1.000 |
| Griffiths, Jeremy, Hou. | 1 | 1 | 0 | 1 | 0 | 1 | 0 | 1.000 |
| Gryboski, Kevin, Atl. | 69 | 0 | 2 | 6 | 0 | 8 | 3 | 1.000 |
| Hampton, Mike, Atl.* | 29 | 29 | 13 | 37 | 2 | 52 | 4 | .962 |
| Hancock, Josh, Phi.-Cin. | 16 | 11 | 3 | 5 | 2 | 10 | 0 | .800 |
| Harang, Aaron, Cin. | 28 | 28 | 10 | 21 | 0 | 31 | 1 | 1.000 |
| Haren, Danny, St.L. | 14 | 5 | 2 | 7 | 1 | 10 | 1 | .900 |
| Harikkala, Tim, Col. | 55 | 0 | 6 | 11 | 0 | 17 | 1 | 1.000 |
| Harville, Chad, Hou. | 56 | 0 | 2 | 8 | 3 | 13 | 2 | .769 |
| Hawkins, LaTroy, Chi. | 77 | 0 | 5 | 7 | 0 | 12 | 0 | 1.000 |
| Haynes, Jimmy, Cin. | 5 | 4 | 2 | 2 | 0 | 4 | 0 | 1.000 |
| Heilman, Aaron, N.Y. | 5 | 5 | 5 | 5 | 2 | 12 | 2 | .833 |
| Hendrickson, Ben, Mil. | 10 | 9 | 5 | 5 | 0 | 10 | 0 | 1.000 |
| Hennessey, Brad, S.F. | 7 | 7 | 3 | 8 | 0 | 11 | 0 | 1.000 |
| Herges, Matt, S.F. | 70 | 0 | 5 | 6 | 0 | 11 | 1 | 1.000 |
| Hermanson, Dustin, S.F. | 47 | 18 | 9 | 10 | 0 | 19 | 0 | 1.000 |
| Hernandez, Adrian, Mil. | 6 | 1 | 1 | 5 | 0 | 6 | 0 | 1.000 |
| Hernandez, Carlos, Hou.* | 9 | 9 | 4 | 6 | 0 | 10 | 0 | 1.000 |
| Hernandez, Livan, Mon. | 35 | 35 | 21 | 61 | 2 | 84 | 10 | .976 |
| Hernandez, Roberto, Phi. | 63 | 0 | 8 | 11 | 1 | 20 | 0 | .950 |
| Hill, Shawn, Mon. | 3 | 3 | 0 | 0 | 0 | 0 | 0 | .000 |
| Hitchcock, Sterling, S.D.* | 4 | 4 | 0 | 1 | 0 | 1 | 0 | 1.000 |
| Hoffman, Trevor, S.D. | 55 | 0 | 2 | 6 | 0 | 8 | 0 | 1.000 |
| Horgan, Joe, Mon.* | 47 | 0 | 3 | 6 | 0 | 9 | 0 | 1.000 |
| Howard, Ben, Fla. | 31 | 0 | 2 | 4 | 0 | 6 | 1 | 1.000 |
| Hudson, Luke, Cin. | 9 | 9 | 3 | 6 | 1 | 10 | 1 | .900 |
| Ishii, Kazuhisa, L.A.* | 31 | 31 | 5 | 16 | 0 | 21 | 0 | 1.000 |
| Isringhausen, Jason, St.L. | 74 | 0 | 3 | 18 | 0 | 21 | 0 | 1.000 |
| Jackson, Edwin, L.A. | 8 | 5 | 2 | 6 | 0 | 8 | 1 | 1.000 |
| Jarvis, Kevin, Col. | 2 | 0 | 0 | 1 | 0 | 1 | 0 | 1.000 |
| Jennings, Jason, Col. | 33 | 33 | 18 | 25 | 1 | 44 | 2 | .977 |
| Johnson, Randy, Ari.* | 35 | 35 | 5 | 20 | 0 | 25 | 0 | 1.000 |
| Johnston, Mike, Pit.* | 24 | 0 | 0 | 7 | 1 | 8 | 0 | .875 |
| Jones, Todd, Cin.-Phi. | 78 | 0 | 4 | 7 | 2 | 13 | 0 | .846 |
| Kennedy, Joe, Col.* | 27 | 27 | 9 | 33 | 4 | 46 | 1 | .913 |
| Kensing, Logan, Fla. | 5 | 3 | 0 | 1 | 0 | 1 | 0 | 1.000 |
| Kida, Masao, L.A. | 3 | 0 | 1 | 0 | 0 | 1 | 1 | 1.000 |
| Kieschnick, Brooks, Mil. | 32 | 0 | 4 | 2 | 0 | 6 | 0 | 1.000 |
| Kim, Sun-Woo, Mon. | 43 | 17 | 17 | 12 | 3 | 32 | 0 | .906 |
| King, Ray, St.L.* | 86 | 0 | 9 | 11 | 1 | 21 | 0 | .952 |
| Kinney, Matt, Mil. | 32 | 6 | 3 | 4 | 0 | 7 | 0 | 1.000 |
| Kline, Steve, St.L.* | 67 | 0 | 4 | 10 | 0 | 14 | 0 | 1.000 |
| Koch, Billy, Fla. | 23 | 0 | 2 | 1 | 0 | 3 | 2 | 1.000 |
| Kolb, Dan, Mil. | 64 | 0 | 2 | 10 | 1 | 13 | 1 | .923 |
| Koplove, Mike, Ari. | 76 | 0 | 6 | 23 | 2 | 31 | 4 | .935 |
| Kroon, Marc, Col. | 6 | 0 | 0 | 3 | 0 | 3 | 1 | 1.000 |
| Lawrence, Brian, S.D. | 34 | 34 | 11 | 38 | 0 | 49 | 3 | 1.000 |
| Leicester, Jon, Chi. | 32 | 0 | 0 | 4 | 0 | 4 | 0 | 1.000 |
| Leiter, Al, N.Y.* | 30 | 30 | 7 | 26 | 0 | 33 | 4 | 1.000 |
| Lidge, Brad, Hou. | 80 | 0 | 2 | 2 | 0 | 4 | 1 | 1.000 |
| Lidle, Cory, Cin.-Phi. | 34 | 34 | 17 | 44 | 1 | 62 | 2 | .984 |
| Lima, Jose, L.A. | 36 | 24 | 13 | 26 | 0 | 39 | 2 | 1.000 |
| Lincoln, Mike, St.L. | 13 | 0 | 1 | 2 | 1 | 4 | 0 | .750 |
| Linebrink, Scott, S.D. | 73 | 0 | 4 | 5 | 2 | 11 | 0 | .818 |
| Liriano, Pedro, Mil. | 11 | 0 | 1 | 1 | 0 | 2 | 0 | 1.000 |
| Looper, Braden, N.Y. | 71 | 0 | 5 | 12 | 0 | 17 | 1 | 1.000 |
| Lopez, Javier, Col.* | 64 | 0 | 6 | 17 | 1 | 24 | 2 | .958 |
| Lowry, Noah, S.F.* | 16 | 14 | 1 | 15 | 0 | 16 | 1 | 1.000 |
| Maddux, Greg, Chi. | 33 | 33 | 21 | 55 | 1 | 77 | 3 | .987 |
| Madson, Ryan, Phi. | 52 | 1 | 7 | 4 | 0 | 11 | 0 | 1.000 |
| Majewski, Gary, Mon. | 16 | 0 | 1 | 0 | 1 | 2 | 0 | .500 |
| Mantei, Matt, Ari. | 12 | 0 | 1 | 2 | 0 | 3 | 0 | 1.000 |
| Manzanillo, Josias, Fla. | 26 | 0 | 4 | 8 | 0 | 12 | 0 | 1.000 |
| Marquis, Jason, St.L. | 32 | 32 | 21 | 31 | 3 | 55 | 1 | .945 |
| Martin, Tom, L.A.-Atl.* | 76 | 0 | 1 | 7 | 0 | 8 | 1 | 1.000 |
| Matthews, Mike, Cin.* | 35 | 0 | 1 | 0 | 1 | 2 | 0 | .500 |
| McConnell, Sam, Atl.* | 10 | 0 | 0 | 1 | 0 | 1 | 0 | 1.000 |

| Player, Team | G | GS | PO | A | E | TC | DP | Pct. |
|---|---|---|---|---|---|---|---|---|
| McKay, Cody, St.L. | 1 | 0 | 1 | 0 | 0 | 1 | 0 | 1.000 |
| McLeary, Marty, S.D. | 3 | 0 | 0 | 1 | 0 | 1 | 0 | 1.000 |
| Meadows, Brian, Pit. | 68 | 0 | 4 | 13 | 1 | 18 | 0 | .944 |
| Mercker, Kent, Chi.* | 71 | 0 | 1 | 4 | 0 | 5 | 0 | 1.000 |
| Mesa, Jose, Pit. | 70 | 0 | 4 | 11 | 0 | 15 | 1 | 1.000 |
| Meyer, Dan, Atl.* | 2 | 0 | 0 | 0 | 0 | 0 | 0 | .000 |
| Miceli, Dan, Hou. | 74 | 0 | 5 | 10 | 0 | 15 | 1 | 1.000 |
| Miller, Wade, Hou. | 15 | 15 | 7 | 11 | 0 | 18 | 2 | 1.000 |
| Millwood, Kevin, Phi. | 25 | 25 | 10 | 19 | 0 | 29 | 0 | 1.000 |
| Milton, Eric, Phi.* | 34 | 34 | 4 | 23 | 0 | 27 | 0 | 1.000 |
| Mitre, Sergio, Chi. | 12 | 9 | 8 | 10 | 0 | 18 | 0 | 1.000 |
| Moreno, Orber, N.Y. | 33 | 0 | 3 | 4 | 0 | 7 | 0 | 1.000 |
| Morris, Matt, St.L. | 32 | 32 | 17 | 29 | 1 | 47 | 2 | .979 |
| Mota, Guillermo, L.A.-Fla. | 78 | 0 | 6 | 10 | 0 | 16 | 0 | 1.000 |
| Munro, Pete, Hou. | 21 | 19 | 11 | 21 | 0 | 32 | 1 | 1.000 |
| Myers, Brett, Phi. | 32 | 31 | 15 | 23 | 0 | 38 | 1 | 1.000 |
| Myers, Rodney, L.A. | 1 | 0 | 0 | 0 | 0 | 0 | 0 | .000 |
| Myette, Aaron, Cin. | 5 | 0 | 0 | 0 | 0 | 0 | 0 | .000 |
| Nance, Shane, Ari.* | 19 | 0 | 0 | 1 | 0 | 1 | 0 | 1.000 |
| Neal, Blaine, S.D. | 40 | 0 | 7 | 7 | 0 | 14 | 2 | 1.000 |
| Neu, Mike, Fla. | 1 | 0 | 0 | 1 | 0 | 1 | 0 | 1.000 |
| Nitkowski, C.J., Atl.* | 22 | 0 | 1 | 3 | 1 | 5 | 0 | .800 |
| Nomo, Hideo, L.A. | 18 | 18 | 5 | 14 | 0 | 19 | 1 | 1.000 |
| Norton, Phil, Cin.* | 69 | 0 | 2 | 11 | 0 | 13 | 2 | 1.000 |
| Nunez, Abraham O., Pit. | 1 | 0 | 0 | 0 | 0 | 0 | 0 | .000 |
| Nunez, Vladimir, Col. | 22 | 0 | 1 | 3 | 1 | 5 | 0 | .800 |
| Obermueller, Wes, Mil. | 25 | 20 | 11 | 12 | 0 | 23 | 0 | 1.000 |
| Ohka, Tomo, Mon. | 15 | 15 | 4 | 11 | 1 | 16 | 3 | .938 |
| Oliver, Darren, Fla.-Hou.* | 27 | 10 | 2 | 11 | 0 | 13 | 0 | 1.000 |
| Oropesa, Eddie, S.D.* | 16 | 0 | 0 | 2 | 0 | 2 | 0 | 1.000 |
| Ortiz, Russ, Atl. | 34 | 34 | 7 | 38 | 0 | 45 | 5 | 1.000 |
| Osuna, Antonio, S.D. | 31 | 0 | 2 | 5 | 0 | 7 | 0 | 1.000 |
| Oswalt, Roy, Hou. | 36 | 35 | 14 | 32 | 3 | 49 | 3 | .939 |
| Otsuka, Akinori, S.D. | 73 | 0 | 7 | 11 | 2 | 20 | 1 | .900 |
| Padilla, Juan, Cin. | 12 | 0 | 1 | 1 | 0 | 2 | 0 | 1.000 |
| Padilla, Vicente, Phi. | 20 | 20 | 9 | 16 | 0 | 25 | 0 | 1.000 |
| Parra, Jose, N.Y. | 13 | 0 | 1 | 0 | 0 | 1 | 0 | 1.000 |
| Patterson, John, Mon. | 19 | 19 | 8 | 11 | 1 | 20 | 0 | .950 |
| Pavano, Carl, Fla. | 31 | 31 | 9 | 31 | 0 | 40 | 3 | 1.000 |
| Pearce, Josh, St.L. | 3 | 0 | 0 | 1 | 0 | 1 | 0 | 1.000 |
| Peavy, Jake, S.D. | 27 | 27 | 10 | 24 | 1 | 35 | 4 | .971 |
| Penny, Brad, Fla.-L.A. | 24 | 24 | 15 | 15 | 1 | 31 | 1 | .968 |
| Perez, Odalis, L.A.* | 31 | 31 | 5 | 43 | 1 | 49 | 1 | .980 |
| Perez, Oliver, Pit.* | 30 | 30 | 7 | 21 | 0 | 28 | 2 | 1.000 |
| Perisho, Matt, Fla.* | 66 | 0 | 0 | 4 | 0 | 4 | 0 | 1.000 |
| Pettitte, Andy, Hou.* | 15 | 15 | 6 | 17 | 1 | 24 | 0 | .958 |
| Phelps, Tommy, Fla.* | 19 | 4 | 2 | 6 | 0 | 8 | 0 | 1.000 |
| Phelps, Travis, Mil. | 4 | 0 | 1 | 1 | 0 | 2 | 0 | 1.000 |
| Powell, Brian, Phi. | 17 | 2 | 2 | 3 | 1 | 6 | 0 | .833 |
| Pratt, Andy, Chi.* | 4 | 0 | 1 | 0 | 0 | 1 | 0 | 1.000 |
| Prior, Mark, Chi. | 21 | 21 | 4 | 18 | 0 | 22 | 3 | 1.000 |
| Puffer, Brandon, S.D. | 14 | 0 | 3 | 1 | 1 | 5 | 0 | .800 |
| Qualls, Chad, Hou. | 25 | 0 | 1 | 3 | 0 | 4 | 0 | 1.000 |
| Ramirez, Elizardo, Phi. | 7 | 0 | 3 | 4 | 0 | 7 | 0 | 1.000 |
| Ramirez, Horacio, Atl.* | 10 | 9 | 3 | 18 | 0 | 21 | 1 | 1.000 |
| Randolph, Stephen, Ari.* | 45 | 6 | 2 | 7 | 1 | 10 | 0 | .900 |
| Rauch, Jon, Mon. | 9 | 2 | 2 | 3 | 0 | 5 | 0 | 1.000 |
| Redding, Tim, Hou. | 27 | 17 | 7 | 18 | 1 | 26 | 3 | .962 |
| Reed, Steve, Col. | 65 | 0 | 0 | 7 | 2 | 9 | 0 | .778 |
| Reith, Brian, Cin. | 22 | 0 | 0 | 7 | 0 | 7 | 0 | 1.000 |
| Reitsma, Chris, Atl. | 84 | 0 | 3 | 7 | 0 | 10 | 1 | 1.000 |
| Remlinger, Mike, Chi.* | 48 | 0 | 3 | 7 | 0 | 10 | 1 | 1.000 |
| Reyes, Al, St.L. | 12 | 2 | 3 | 1 | 0 | 4 | 0 | 1.000 |
| Reynolds, Shane, Ari. | 1 | 1 | 0 | 0 | 0 | 0 | 0 | .000 |
| Riedling, John, Cin. | 70 | 0 | 4 | 17 | 0 | 21 | 1 | 1.000 |
| Roberts, Grant, N.Y. | 4 | 0 | 1 | 2 | 0 | 3 | 0 | 1.000 |
| Roberts, Willis, Pit. | 9 | 0 | 1 | 3 | 0 | 4 | 1 | 1.000 |
| Rodriguez, Felix, S.F.-Phi. | 76 | 0 | 1 | 7 | 1 | 9 | 1 | .889 |
| Rueter, Kirk, S.F.* | 33 | 33 | 18 | 51 | 1 | 70 | 6 | .986 |
| Rusch, Glendon, Chi.* | 32 | 16 | 6 | 16 | 1 | 23 | 4 | .957 |
| Saenz, Chris, Mil. | 1 | 1 | 0 | 0 | 0 | 0 | 0 | .000 |
| Sanchez, Duaner, L.A. | 67 | 0 | 9 | 11 | 0 | 20 | 0 | 1.000 |
| Sanchez, Jesus, Cin.* | 3 | 3 | 1 | 3 | 0 | 4 | 0 | 1.000 |
| Santos, Victor, Mil. | 31 | 28 | 13 | 4 | 3 | 20 | 1 | .850 |
| Schmidt, Jason, S.F. | 32 | 32 | 5 | 22 | 3 | 30 | 1 | .900 |
| Seanez, Rudy, Fla. | 23 | 0 | 1 | 2 | 1 | 4 | 0 | .750 |
| Seo, Jae Weong, N.Y. | 24 | 21 | 12 | 17 | 0 | 29 | 3 | 1.000 |
| Service, Scott, Ari. | 21 | 0 | 3 | 2 | 0 | 5 | 0 | 1.000 |
| Sheets, Ben, Mil. | 34 | 34 | 14 | 23 | 2 | 39 | 0 | .949 |
| Simontacchi, Jason, St.L. | 13 | 0 | 3 | 3 | 0 | 6 | 1 | 1.000 |
| Simpson, Allan, Col. | 32 | 0 | 0 | 4 | 2 | 6 | 0 | .667 |
| Small, Aaron, Fla. | 7 | 0 | 1 | 2 | 0 | 3 | 0 | 1.000 |
| Smith, Travis, Atl. | 16 | 4 | 3 | 4 | 1 | 8 | 0 | .875 |

| Player, Team | G | GS | PO | A | E | TC | DP | Pct. |
|---|---|---|---|---|---|---|---|---|
| Smoltz, John, Atl. | 73 | 0 | 9 | 9 | 0 | 18 | 0 | 1.000 |
| Snell, Ian, Pit. | 3 | 1 | 3 | 1 | 0 | 4 | 0 | 1.000 |
| Sparks, Steve, Ari. | 29 | 18 | 8 | 21 | 2 | 31 | 0 | .935 |
| Springer, Russ, Hou | 16 | 0 | 1 | 2 | 0 | 3 | 0 | 1.000 |
| Stanton, Mike, N.Y.* | 83 | 0 | 4 | 14 | 0 | 18 | 0 | 1.000 |
| Stark, Denny, Col. | 6 | 6 | 3 | 5 | 1 | 9 | 0 | .889 |
| Stewart, Scott, L.A.* | 11 | 0 | 0 | 2 | 0 | 2 | 0 | 1.000 |
| Stone, Ricky, Hou.-S.D. | 43 | 0 | 4 | 8 | 0 | 12 | 0 | 1.000 |
| Suppan, Jeff, St.L. | 31 | 31 | 10 | 30 | 1 | 41 | 0 | .976 |
| Sweeney, Brian, S.D. | 7 | 2 | 1 | 0 | 0 | 1 | 0 | 1.000 |
| Szuminski, Jason, S.D. | 7 | 0 | 1 | 3 | 1 | 5 | 0 | .800 |
| Tankersley, Dennis, S.D. | 9 | 6 | 7 | 1 | 0 | 8 | 0 | 1.000 |
| Tavarez, Julian, St.L. | 77 | 0 | 7 | 9 | 0 | 16 | 0 | 1.000 |
| Tejera, Michael, Fla.* | 2 | 2 | 0 | 1 | 0 | 1 | 0 | 1.000 |
| Telemaco, Amaury, Phi. | 42 | 0 | 2 | 6 | 0 | 8 | 0 | 1.000 |
| Thomson, John, Atl. | 33 | 33 | 12 | 27 | 1 | 40 | 2 | .975 |
| Tomko, Brett, S.F. | 32 | 31 | 13 | 25 | 2 | 40 | 2 | .950 |
| Torres, Salomon, Pit. | 84 | 0 | 6 | 16 | 0 | 22 | 0 | 1.000 |
| TRACHSEL, Steve, N.Y. | 33 | 33 | 13 | 37 | 0 | 50 | 4 | 1.000 |
| Tsao, Chin-hui, Col. | 10 | 0 | 0 | 0 | 1 | 1 | 0 | .000 |
| Tucker, T.J., Mon. | 54 | 1 | 2 | 10 | 0 | 12 | 1 | 1.000 |
| Valdez, Ismael, S.D.-Fla. | 34 | 31 | 12 | 19 | 1 | 32 | 0 | .969 |
| Valdez, Merkin, S.F. | 2 | 0 | 0 | 0 | 0 | 0 | 0 | .000 |
| Valentine, Joe, Cin. | 24 | 1 | 3 | 3 | 1 | 7 | 0 | .857 |
| Valverde, Jose, Ari. | 29 | 0 | 4 | 2 | 2 | 8 | 0 | .750 |
| Van Benschoten, John, Pit. | 6 | 5 | 1 | 4 | 0 | 5 | 1 | 1.000 |
| Van Poppel, Todd, Cin. | 48 | 11 | 5 | 10 | 1 | 16 | 0 | .938 |
| Vargas, Claudio, Mon. | 45 | 14 | 10 | 11 | 0 | 21 | 2 | 1.000 |
| Venafro, Mike, L.A.* | 17 | 0 | 0 | 1 | 0 | 1 | 0 | 1.000 |
| Ventura, Robin, L.A. | 1 | 0 | 0 | 0 | 0 | 0 | 0 | .000 |
| Villafuerte, Brandon, Ari. | 20 | 0 | 2 | 5 | 0 | 7 | 0 | 1.000 |
| Villarreal, Oscar, Ari. | 17 | 0 | 0 | 4 | 0 | 4 | 0 | 1.000 |
| Vizcaino, Luis, Mil. | 73 | 0 | 4 | 3 | 0 | 7 | 0 | 1.000 |
| Vogelsong, Ryan, Pit. | 31 | 26 | 8 | 14 | 0 | 22 | 1 | 1.000 |
| Wagner, Billy, Phi.* | 45 | 0 | 3 | 7 | 0 | 10 | 0 | 1.000 |
| Wagner, Ryan, Cin. | 49 | 0 | 2 | 10 | 2 | 14 | 0 | .857 |
| Walker, Kevin, S.F.* | 5 | 0 | 0 | 0 | 0 | 0 | 0 | .000 |
| Walker, Tyler, S.F. | 52 | 0 | 6 | 6 | 0 | 12 | 0 | 1.000 |
| Watkins, Steve, S.D. | 11 | 0 | 0 | 3 | 1 | 4 | 0 | .750 |
| Wayne, Justin, Fla. | 19 | 1 | 2 | 4 | 0 | 6 | 1 | 1.000 |
| Weathers, David, N.Y.-Hou.-Fla. | 66 | 2 | 3 | 7 | 0 | 10 | 0 | 1.000 |
| Weaver, Jeff, L.A. | 34 | 34 | 12 | 32 | 0 | 44 | 1 | 1.000 |
| Webb, Brandon, Ari. | 35 | 35 | 13 | 41 | 5 | 59 | 7 | .915 |
| Wellemeyer, Todd, Chi. | 20 | 0 | 0 | 2 | 0 | 2 | 1 | 1.000 |
| Wells, David, S.D.* | 31 | 31 | 7 | 38 | 1 | 46 | 1 | .978 |
| Wells, Kip, Pit. | 24 | 24 | 7 | 18 | 3 | 28 | 1 | .893 |
| Wendell, Turk, Col. | 12 | 0 | 2 | 2 | 0 | 4 | 0 | 1.000 |
| Wheeler, Dan, N.Y.-Hou | 46 | 1 | 4 | 6 | 2 | 12 | 0 | .833 |
| White, Gabe, Cin.* | 40 | 0 | 1 | 3 | 0 | 4 | 0 | 1.000 |
| Williams, Dave, Pit.* | 10 | 6 | 1 | 7 | 0 | 8 | 0 | 1.000 |
| Williams, Jerome, S.F. | 22 | 22 | 10 | 20 | 2 | 32 | 1 | .938 |
| Williams, Woody, St.L. | 31 | 31 | 20 | 31 | 3 | 54 | 2 | .944 |
| Willis, Dontrelle, Fla.* | 32 | 32 | 15 | 34 | 2 | 51 | 3 | .961 |
| Wilson, Paul, Cin. | 29 | 29 | 6 | 23 | 0 | 29 | 0 | 1.000 |
| Wise, Matt, Mil. | 30 | 3 | 3 | 12 | 0 | 15 | 1 | 1.000 |
| Witasick, Jay, S.D. | 44 | 0 | 2 | 7 | 0 | 9 | 0 | 1.000 |
| Wolf, Randy, Phi.* | 23 | 23 | 8 | 15 | 2 | 25 | 0 | .920 |
| Wood, Kerry, Chi. | 22 | 22 | 4 | 13 | 1 | 18 | 2 | .944 |
| Worrell, Tim, Phi. | 77 | 0 | 10 | 15 | 1 | 26 | 2 | .962 |
| Wright, Jamey, Col. | 14 | 14 | 7 | 18 | 0 | 25 | 3 | 1.000 |
| Wright, Jaret, Atl. | 32 | 32 | 15 | 25 | 2 | 42 | 2 | .952 |
| Wuertz, Michael, Chi. | 31 | 0 | 0 | 4 | 0 | 4 | 0 | 1.000 |
| Yates, Tyler, N.Y. | 21 | 7 | 1 | 6 | 0 | 7 | 1 | 1.000 |
| Young, Jason, Col. | 2 | 2 | 2 | 1 | 0 | 3 | 0 | 1.000 |
| Zambrano, Carlos, Chi. | 31 | 31 | 18 | 29 | 2 | 49 | 2 | .959 |
| Zambrano, Victor, N.Y. | 3 | 3 | 0 | 0 | 1 | 1 | 0 | .000 |
| Zeile, Todd, N.Y. | 1 | 0 | 0 | 0 | 0 | 0 | 0 | .000 |

## PITCHERS WITH TWO OR MORE TEAMS

| Player, Team | G | GS | PO | A | E | TC | DP | Pct. |
|---|---|---|---|---|---|---|---|---|
| Beltran, Francis, Chi. | 34 | 0 | 0 | 4 | 0 | 4 | 0 | 1.000 |
| Beltran, Francis, Mon. | 11 | 0 | 0 | 1 | 1 | 2 | 1 | .500 |
| Benson, Kris, Pit. | 20 | 20 | 12 | 19 | 0 | 31 | 2 | 1.000 |
| Benson, Kris, N.Y. | 11 | 11 | 5 | 6 | 1 | 12 | 0 | .917 |
| Burba, Dave, Mil. | 45 | 0 | 5 | 13 | 2 | 20 | 0 | .900 |
| Burba, Dave, S.F. | 6 | 0 | 1 | 0 | 0 | 1 | 0 | 1.000 |
| Dessens, Elmer, Ari. | 38 | 9 | 5 | 12 | 1 | 18 | 0 | .944 |
| Dessens, Elmer, L.A. | 12 | 1 | 0 | 1 | 0 | 1 | 0 | 1.000 |
| Fassero, Jeff, Col.* | 40 | 12 | 7 | 24 | 0 | 31 | 2 | 1.000 |
| Fassero, Jeff, Ari.* | 1 | 0 | 0 | 0 | 0 | 0 | 0 | .000 |
| Hancock, Josh, Phi. | 4 | 2 | 0 | 2 | 0 | 2 | 0 | 1.000 |
| Hancock, Josh, Cin. | 12 | 9 | 3 | 3 | 2 | 8 | 0 | .750 |
| Jones, Todd, Cin. | 51 | 0 | 3 | 5 | 1 | 9 | 0 | .889 |
| Jones, Todd, Phi. | 27 | 0 | 1 | 2 | 1 | 4 | 0 | .750 |
| Lidle, Cory, Cin. | 24 | 24 | 13 | 34 | 1 | 48 | 1 | .979 |
| Lidle, Cory, Phi. | 10 | 10 | 4 | 10 | 0 | 14 | 1 | 1.000 |
| Martin, Tom, L.A.* | 47 | 0 | 1 | 5 | 0 | 6 | 1 | 1.000 |
| Martin, Tom, Atl.* | 29 | 0 | 0 | 2 | 0 | 2 | 0 | 1.000 |
| Mota, Guillermo, L.A. | 52 | 0 | 4 | 6 | 0 | 10 | 0 | 1.000 |
| Mota, Guillermo, Fla. | 26 | 0 | 2 | 4 | 0 | 6 | 0 | 1.000 |
| Oliver, Darren, Fla.* | 18 | 8 | 1 | 11 | 0 | 12 | 0 | 1.000 |
| Oliver, Darren, Hou.* | 9 | 2 | 1 | 0 | 0 | 1 | 0 | 1.000 |
| Penny, Brad, Fla. | 21 | 21 | 14 | 15 | 1 | 30 | 1 | .967 |
| Penny, Brad, L.A. | 3 | 3 | 1 | 0 | 0 | 1 | 0 | 1.000 |
| Rodriguez, Felix, S.F. | 53 | 0 | 1 | 4 | 1 | 6 | 0 | .833 |
| Rodriguez, Felix, Phi. | 23 | 0 | 0 | 3 | 0 | 3 | 1 | 1.000 |
| Stone, Ricky, Hou. | 16 | 0 | 2 | 6 | 0 | 8 | 0 | 1.000 |
| Stone, Ricky, S.D. | 27 | 0 | 2 | 2 | 0 | 4 | 0 | 1.000 |
| Valdez, Ismael, S.D. | 23 | 20 | 6 | 15 | 1 | 22 | 0 | .955 |
| Valdez, Ismael, Fla. | 11 | 11 | 6 | 4 | 0 | 10 | 0 | 1.000 |
| Weathers, David, N.Y. | 32 | 0 | 2 | 7 | 0 | 9 | 0 | 1.000 |
| Weathers, David, Hou. | 26 | 0 | 1 | 0 | 0 | 1 | 0 | 1.000 |
| Weathers, David, Fla. | 8 | 2 | 0 | 0 | 0 | 0 | 0 | .000 |
| Wheeler, Dan, N.Y. | 32 | 1 | 4 | 6 | 2 | 12 | 0 | .833 |
| Wheeler, Dan, Hou. | 14 | 0 | 0 | 0 | 0 | 0 | 0 | .000 |

# MISCELLANEOUS

## SHUTOUT GAMES

Read across for wins, down for losses.

| Team | Atl. | S.F. | St.L. | Chi. | L.A. | Phi. | Mon. | Fla. | Pit. | S.D. | N.Y. | Hou. | Ari. | Cin. | Mil. | Col. | A.L. | W | L | Pct. |
|---|---|---|---|---|---|---|---|---|---|---|---|---|---|---|---|---|---|---|---|---|
| Houston | .. | 0 | 0 | 0 | 0 | 0 | 1 | 1 | 2 | 1 | 0 | 3 | 1 | 0 | 0 | 0 | 4 | 13 | 3 | .813 |
| St. Louis | 0 | .. | 0 | 1 | 0 | 2 | 0 | 1 | 1 | 0 | 1 | 2 | 2 | 1 | 1 | 0 | 0 | 12 | 4 | .750 |
| San Diego | 0 | 0 | .. | 1 | 1 | 0 | 0 | 0 | 0 | 1 | 0 | 1 | 0 | 3 | 1 | 0 | 0 | 8 | 3 | .727 |
| San Francisco | 0 | 0 | 0 | .. | 0 | 1 | 0 | 1 | 1 | 0 | 0 | 1 | 1 | 1 | 0 | 1 | 1 | 8 | 4 | .667 |
| Atlanta | 0 | 0 | 0 | 0 | .. | 1 | 1 | 1 | 0 | 4 | 0 | 1 | 0 | 1 | 2 | 0 | 2 | 13 | 7 | .650 |
| Florida | 0 | 0 | 0 | 0 | 2 | .. | 0 | 0 | 1 | 4 | 0 | 1 | 1 | 1 | 2 | 1 | 1 | 14 | 8 | .636 |
| Philadelphia | 0 | 0 | 0 | 0 | 0 | 0 | .. | 0 | 0 | 1 | 1 | 1 | 0 | 1 | 1 | 0 | 0 | 5 | 4 | .556 |
| Pittsburgh | 0 | 1 | 0 | 0 | 0 | 0 | 0 | .. | 3 | 1 | 0 | 1 | 0 | 0 | 1 | 1 | 0 | 8 | 8 | .500 |
| Cincinnati | 1 | 2 | 0 | 0 | 0 | 0 | 0 | 0 | .. | 0 | 1 | 2 | 0 | 1 | 1 | 0 | 0 | 8 | 10 | .444 |
| Montreal | 0 | 1 | 0 | 0 | 0 | 1 | 1 | 1 | 0 | .. | 2 | 0 | 2 | 0 | 1 | 0 | 2 | 11 | 16 | .407 |
| Arizona | 0 | 0 | 1 | 0 | 1 | 0 | 0 | 0 | 0 | 0 | .. | 0 | 2 | 0 | 1 | 0 | 1 | 6 | 9 | .400 |
| Milwaukee | 1 | 0 | 0 | 1 | 0 | 1 | 0 | 1 | 2 | 0 | 0 | .. | 2 | 0 | 0 | 0 | 2 | 10 | 16 | .385 |
| Chicago | 0 | 0 | 0 | 0 | 0 | 0 | 0 | 1 | 0 | 0 | 0 | 2 | .. | 1 | 1 | 1 | 0 | 6 | 12 | .333 |
| Los Angeles | 0 | 0 | 0 | 1 | 0 | 0 | 0 | 1 | 0 | 0 | 3 | 0 | 1 | .. | 0 | 0 | 0 | 6 | 12 | .333 |
| New York | 0 | 0 | 0 | 0 | 2 | 1 | 1 | 0 | 0 | 0 | 1 | 0 | 0 | 0 | .. | 1 | 0 | 6 | 12 | .333 |
| Colorado | 0 | 0 | 0 | 0 | 0 | 0 | 0 | 0 | 0 | 1 | 0 | 1 | 0 | 0 | 0 | .. | 0 | 2 | 6 | .250 |
| A.L. Clubs | 1 | 0 | 2 | 0 | 1 | 1 | 0 | 0 | 0 | 3 | 0 | 0 | 0 | 2 | 0 | 1 | .. | .. | .. | .. |
| **Lost** | 3 | 4 | 3 | 4 | 7 | 8 | 4 | 8 | 10 | 16 | 9 | 16 | 12 | 12 | 12 | 6 | 13 | 136 | 134 | .504 |

N.L. shutouts vs A.L. clubs (13): Milwaukee vs Anaheim, Milwaukee vs Seattle, Atlanta vs Baltimore, Atlanta vs Cleveland, Houston vs Anaheim, Houston vs Seattle 2, Houston vs Texas, Montreal vs Kansas City, Montreal vs Toronto, San Francisco vs Boston, Florida vs Chicago, Arizona vs Baltimore.

## HOME RECORD

Read across for home wins, down for road losses.

| Team | S.F. | Atl. | Fla. | Mon. | Phi. | Col. | Hou. | St.L. | L.A. | Ari. | Chi. | Pit. | Cin. | S.D. | N.Y. | Mil. | A.L. | W | L | Pct. |
|---|---|---|---|---|---|---|---|---|---|---|---|---|---|---|---|---|---|---|---|---|
| St. Louis | .. | 2 | 3 | 3 | 1 | 6 | 2 | 1 | 3 | 7 | 5 | 3 | 2 | 5 | 2 | 2 | 6 | 53 | 28 | .654 |
| Atlanta | 1 | .. | 2 | 1 | 3 | 1 | 9 | 4 | 1 | 1 | 1 | 7 | 3 | 2 | 8 | 1 | 4 | 49 | 32 | .605 |
| Los Angeles | 2 | 2 | .. | 3 | 5 | 2 | 1 | 1 | 5 | 0 | 3 | 1 | 6 | 2 | 2 | 8 | 6 | 49 | 32 | .605 |
| Houston | 4 | 1 | 0 | .. | 1 | 3 | 1 | 3 | 1 | 6 | 9 | 1 | 3 | 8 | 1 | 2 | 4 | 48 | 33 | .593 |
| San Francisco | 1 | 2 | 5 | 2 | .. | 2 | 3 | 1 | 3 | 1 | 0 | 2 | 5 | 2 | 3 | 9 | 6 | 47 | 35 | .573 |
| Chicago | 4 | 1 | 1 | 4 | 1 | .. | 2 | 2 | 1 | 5 | 7 | 3 | 2 | 5 | 1 | 1 | 5 | 45 | 37 | .549 |
| Florida | 1 | 4 | 1 | 1 | 1 | 1 | .. | 7 | 2 | 0 | 1 | 7 | 3 | 2 | 5 | 3 | 3 | 42 | 38 | .525 |
| Philadelphia | 1 | 3 | 3 | 0 | 0 | 2 | 4 | .. | 2 | 2 | 2 | 5 | 1 | 3 | 7 | 2 | 5 | 42 | 39 | .519 |
| San Diego | 2 | 1 | 4 | 2 | 6 | 0 | 1 | 0 | .. | 2 | 1 | 2 | 3 | 2 | 4 | 8 | 4 | 42 | 39 | .519 |
| Cincinnati | 3 | 2 | 1 | 5 | 1 | 3 | 1 | 2 | 1 | .. | 4 | 1 | 2 | 6 | 2 | 1 | 5 | 40 | 41 | .494 |
| Pittsburgh | 3 | 1 | 0 | 4 | 2 | 3 | 3 | 2 | 1 | 5 | .. | 2 | 2 | 6 | 1 | 2 | 2 | 39 | 41 | .488 |
| New York | 1 | 5 | 1 | 2 | 3 | 2 | 2 | 3 | 0 | 1 | 0 | .. | 3 | 1 | 4 | 2 | 8 | 38 | 43 | .469 |
| Colorado | 0 | 2 | 5 | 1 | 4 | 0 | 1 | 2 | 3 | 2 | 1 | 1 | .. | 0 | 1 | 8 | 7 | 38 | 43 | .469 |
| Milwaukee | 3 | 1 | 2 | 4 | 0 | 5 | 1 | 0 | 1 | 5 | 4 | 0 | 1 | .. | 3 | 2 | 4 | 36 | 45 | .444 |
| Montreal | 2 | 2 | 2 | 2 | 0 | 1 | 3 | 4 | 1 | 1 | 3 | 4 | 2 | 1 | .. | 3 | 4 | 35 | 45 | .438 |
| Arizona | 0 | 0 | 2 | 0 | 4 | 2 | 2 | 0 | 6 | 1 | 1 | 2 | 5 | 2 | 0 | .. | 2 | 29 | 52 | .358 |
| A.L. Clubs | 1 | 5 | 5 | 3 | 4 | 3 | 5 | 5 | 5 | 6 | 6 | 7 | 8 | 2 | 6 | 5 | .. | .. | .. | .. |
| **Lost on Road** | 29 | 34 | 37 | 37 | 36 | 36 | 41 | 37 | 36 | 45 | 48 | 48 | 51 | 49 | 50 | 59 | 75 | 672 | 623 | .519 |

## HOME RECORDS IN INTERLEAGUE GAMES

| Team | | | | Total | Team | | | | Total |
|---|---|---|---|---|---|---|---|---|---|
| Arizona | 1-2 vs. Min. | 1-2 vs. N.Y. | 0-3 vs. TB. | 2-7 | Milwaukee | 2-1 vs. Min. | 2-1 vs. Sea. | | 4-2 |
| Atlanta | 2-1 vs. Bos. | 1-2 vs. Cle. | 1-2 vs. K.C. | 4-5 | Montreal | 2-1 vs. Chi. | 0-3 vs. Min. | 2-1 vs. Tor. | 4-5 |
| Chicago | 3-0 vs. Chi. | 2-1 vs. Oak. | | 5-1 | New York | 2-1 vs. Cle. | 3-0 vs. Det. | 3-0 vs. N.Y. | 8-1 |
| Cincinnati | 2-1 vs. Cle. | 3-0 vs. Tex. | | 5-1 | Philadelphia | 2-1 vs. Bal. | 1-2 vs. Det. | 2-1 vs. K.C. | 5-4 |
| Colorado | 2-1 vs. Bal. | 2-1 vs. Bos. | 3-0 vs. Det. | 7-2 | Pittsburgh | 2-1 vs. Ana. | 0-3 vs. Sea. | | 2-4 |
| Florida | 2-1 vs. Chi. | 0-3 vs. Tex. | 1-2 vs. TB. | 3-6 | St. Louis | 3-0 vs. Oak. | 3-0 vs. Sea. | | 6-0 |
| Houston | 2-1 vs. Ana. | 2-1 vs. Tex. | | 4-2 | San Diego | 3-0 vs. K.C. | 1-2 vs. Tor. | 0-3 vs. TB. | 4-5 |
| Los Angeles | 3-0 vs. Bal. | 1-2 vs. Ana. | 2-1 vs. N.Y. | 6-3 | San Francisco | 2-1 vs. Bos. | 1-2 vs. Oak. | 3-0 vs. Tor. | 6-3 |

## ROAD RECORD

Read across for road wins, down for home losses.

| Team | Atl. | Chi. | S.F. | Hou. | L.A. | Ari. | Fla. | Mil. | Phi. | St.L. | Pit. | Cin. | N.Y. | Mon. | S.D. | Col. | A.L. | W | L | Pct. |
|---|---|---|---|---|---|---|---|---|---|---|---|---|---|---|---|---|---|---|---|---|
| St. Louis | .. | 2 | 1 | 5 | 2 | 5 | 1 | 2 | 2 | 7 | 2 | 7 | 1 | 4 | 3 | 3 | 5 | 52 | 29 | .642 |
| Atlanta | 1 | .. | 2 | 2 | 1 | 2 | 2 | 6 | 5 | 1 | 5 | 3 | 7 | 2 | 1 | 3 | 4 | 47 | 34 | .580 |
| San Diego | 0 | 2 | .. | 2 | 6 | 2 | 5 | 1 | 1 | 2 | 4 | 2 | 2 | 2 | 6 | 4 | 4 | 45 | 36 | .556 |
| Chicago | 4 | 2 | 3 | .. | 1 | 6 | 1 | 1 | 1 | 4 | 1 | 6 | 2 | 5 | 3 | 1 | 3 | 44 | 36 | .550 |
| San Francisco | 2 | 1 | 4 | 2 | .. | 2 | 4 | 3 | 2 | 2 | 0 | 1 | 2 | 3 | 6 | 5 | 5 | 44 | 36 | .550 |
| Houston | 6 | 2 | 1 | 6 | 1 | .. | 1 | 3 | 2 | 5 | 1 | 3 | 1 | 5 | 2 | 2 | 3 | 44 | 37 | .543 |
| Los Angeles | 0 | 1 | 5 | 2 | 5 | 2 | .. | 0 | 2 | 2 | 2 | 3 | 2 | 1 | 5 | 8 | 4 | 44 | 37 | .543 |
| Philadelphia | 2 | 6 | 3 | 1 | 2 | 0 | 2 | .. | 3 | 1 | 6 | 1 | 5 | 3 | 2 | 3 | 4 | 44 | 37 | .543 |
| Florida | 1 | 1 | 2 | 2 | 1 | 2 | 2 | 5 | .. | 2 | 8 | 0 | 6 | 2 | 2 | 1 | 4 | 41 | 41 | .500 |
| Cincinnati | 2 | 2 | 1 | 5 | 2 | 1 | 3 | 1 | 3 | .. | 2 | 5 | 2 | 4 | 1 | 2 | 0 | 36 | 45 | .444 |
| New York | 0 | 2 | 1 | 0 | 1 | 2 | 2 | 5 | 2 | 2 | .. | 1 | 6 | 3 | 2 | 2 | 2 | 33 | 48 | .407 |
| Pittsburgh | 2 | 1 | 2 | 2 | 3 | 1 | 0 | 1 | 2 | 5 | 3 | .. | 1 | 6 | 2 | 2 | 0 | 33 | 48 | .407 |
| Montreal | 1 | 2 | 0 | 2 | 1 | 2 | 1 | 3 | 5 | 1 | 5 | 1 | .. | 0 | 2 | 3 | 3 | 32 | 50 | .390 |
| Milwaukee | 5 | 1 | 1 | 2 | 1 | 2 | 1 | 0 | 1 | 3 | 2 | 2 | 2 | .. | 3 | 1 | 4 | 31 | 49 | .388 |

| Team | Atl. | Chi. | S.F. | Hou. | L.A. | Ari. | Fla. | Mil. | Phi. | St.L. | Pit. | Cin. | N.Y. | Mon. | S.D. | Col. | A.L. | W | L | Pct. |
|---|---|---|---|---|---|---|---|---|---|---|---|---|---|---|---|---|---|---|---|---|
| Colorado | 1 | 0 | 7 | 1 | 4 | 0 | 3 | 3 | 0 | 1 | 0 | 1 | 1 | 2 | .. | 5 | 1 | 30 | 51 | .370 |
| Arizona | 1 | 2 | 1 | 2 | 1 | 2 | 1 | 1 | 1 | 2 | 1 | 1 | 0 | 1 | 1 | .. | 4 | 22 | 59 | .272 |
| A.L. Clubs | 0 | 5 | 5 | 1 | 3 | 2 | 3 | 4 | 6 | 1 | 1 | 4 | 5 | 2 | 2 | 7 | .. | .. | .. | .. |
| **Lost at home** | 28 | 32 | 39 | 37 | 35 | 33 | 32 | 39 | 38 | 41 | 43 | 41 | 45 | 45 | 43 | 52 | 50 | 622 | 673 | .480 |

# PITCHING AGAINST EACH CLUB

## ARIZONA—51-111

| Pitcher | Atl. W-L | Chi. W-L | Cin. W-L | Col. W-L | Fla. W-L | Hou. W-L | L.A. W-L | Mil. W-L | Mon. W-L | N.Y. W-L | Phi. W-L | Pit. W-L | S.D. W-L | S.F. W-L | St.L. W-L | A.L. W-L | Totals W-L |
|---|---|---|---|---|---|---|---|---|---|---|---|---|---|---|---|---|---|
| Aquino, Greg | 0-0 | 0-0 | 0-0 | 0-0 | 0-0 | 0-0 | 0-0 | 0-0 | 0-0 | 0-0 | 0-0 | 0-1 | 0-1 | 0-0 | 0-0 | 0-0 | 0-2 |
| Bruney, Brian | 1-0 | 0-0 | 1-0 | 0-0 | 0-1 | 0-0 | 0-2 | 0-0 | 0-0 | 1-0 | 0-0 | 0-0 | 0-0 | 0-1 | 0-0 | 0-0 | 3-4 |
| Choate, Randy | 0-0 | 0-0 | 0-0 | 1-2 | 0-0 | 0-0 | 0-1 | 0-0 | 0-0 | 0-0 | 0-0 | 0-0 | 0-0 | 0-1 | 0-0 | 1-0 | 2-4 |
| Cormier, Lance | 0-0 | 0-0 | 0-0 | 0-1 | 0-1 | 1-0 | 0-0 | 0-0 | 0-1 | 0-0 | 0-0 | 0-0 | 0-0 | 0-0 | 0-0 | 0-1 | 1-4 |
| Daigle, Casey | 0-0 | 1-0 | 0-0 | 0-0 | 0-0 | 0-0 | 0-0 | 0-0 | 0-1 | 1-0 | 0-0 | 0-0 | 0-0 | 0-1 | 0-1 | 0-0 | 2-3 |
| Dessens, Elmer | 0-0 | 0-1 | 0-0 | 0-1 | 0-0 | 0-0 | 0-1 | 0-1 | 0-0 | 0-0 | 0-1 | 0-0 | 1-1 | 0-0 | 0-0 | 0-0 | 1-6 |
| Durbin, Chad | 0-0 | 0-0 | 0-0 | 1-0 | 0-0 | 0-0 | 0-0 | 0-0 | 0-0 | 0-0 | 0-0 | 0-0 | 0-1 | 0-0 | 0-0 | 0-0 | 1-1 |
| Fetters, Mike | 0-0 | 0-0 | 0-1 | 0-0 | 0-0 | 0-0 | 0-0 | 0-0 | 0-0 | 0-0 | 0-0 | 0-0 | 0-0 | 0-0 | 0-0 | 0-0 | 0-1 |
| Fossum, Casey | 0-2 | 0-0 | 1-0 | 0-2 | 0-0 | 0-1 | 0-3 | 0-1 | 0-0 | 0-1 | 0-0 | 1-0 | 1-1 | 0-2 | 0-1 | 1-1 | 4-15 |
| Gonzalez, Edgar | 0-1 | 0-0 | 0-0 | 0-1 | 0-0 | 0-2 | 0-2 | 0-0 | 0-0 | 0-1 | 0-0 | 0-1 | 0-0 | 0-1 | 0-0 | 0-0 | 0-9 |
| Good, Andrew | 0-0 | 0-0 | 0-0 | 0-0 | 0-0 | 0-0 | 0-0 | 0-0 | 0-0 | 0-0 | 0-0 | 0-0 | 0-0 | 1-0 | 0-0 | 0-2 | 1-2 |
| Gosling, Mike | 0-0 | 0-0 | 0-0 | 0-0 | 0-0 | 0-0 | 0-0 | 0-0 | 0-0 | 0-0 | 0-0 | 0-0 | 0-1 | 0-0 | 1-0 | 0-0 | 1-1 |
| Johnson, Randy | 1-0 | 1-0 | 0-1 | 1-3 | 2-0 | 0-0 | 1-0 | 1-1 | 0-1 | 1-1 | 1-1 | 0-1 | 2-1 | 2-3 | 0-0 | 3-1 | 16-14 |
| Koplove, Mike | 0-0 | 0-0 | 0-0 | 1-1 | 1-0 | 0-0 | 0-1 | 1-0 | 0-0 | 0-0 | 0-0 | 0-0 | 1-1 | 0-1 | 0-0 | 0-0 | 4-4 |
| Mantei, Matt | 0-0 | 0-1 | 0-0 | 0-0 | 0-0 | 0-0 | 0-0 | 0-0 | 0-0 | 0-0 | 0-0 | 0-0 | 0-1 | 0-0 | 0-1 | 0-0 | 0-3 |
| Nance, Shane | 0-0 | 0-0 | 0-0 | 0-0 | 0-0 | 0-0 | 0-1 | 0-0 | 0-0 | 0-0 | 0-0 | 1-0 | 0-0 | 0-0 | 0-0 | 0-0 | 1-1 |
| Randolph, Stephen | 0-0 | 0-0 | 0-1 | 1-0 | 0-0 | 0-0 | 0-0 | 0-0 | 0-0 | 0-0 | 0-0 | 0-1 | 1-0 | 0-1 | 0-0 | 0-2 | 2-5 |
| Reynolds, Shane | 0-0 | 0-0 | 0-0 | 0-0 | 0-0 | 0-0 | 0-0 | 0-0 | 0-0 | 0-0 | 0-0 | 0-0 | 0-1 | 0-0 | 0-0 | 0-0 | 0-1 |
| Service, Scott | 0-0 | 0-0 | 0-0 | 0-0 | 0-0 | 0-0 | 1-0 | 0-0 | 0-0 | 0-0 | 0-0 | 0-0 | 0-0 | 0-0 | 0-1 | 0-0 | 1-1 |
| Sparks, Steve | 0-0 | 1-0 | 0-0 | 0-0 | 0-1 | 0-0 | 0-1 | 1-0 | 0-1 | 0-0 | 0-1 | 0-0 | 0-1 | 0-1 | 0-1 | 1-0 | 3-7 |
| Valverde, Jose | 0-0 | 0-0 | 0-0 | 0-0 | 0-0 | 0-0 | 0-0 | 0-0 | 0-1 | 0-0 | 0-0 | 0-0 | 0-0 | 1-1 | 0-0 | 0-0 | 1-2 |
| Villafuerte, Brandon | 0-0 | 0-0 | 0-0 | 0-0 | 0-0 | 0-0 | 0-1 | 0-0 | 0-0 | 0-0 | 0-0 | 0-0 | 0-0 | 0-0 | 0-0 | 0-2 | 0-3 |
| Villarreal, Oscar | 0-0 | 0-0 | 0-0 | 0-0 | 0-0 | 0-0 | 0-0 | 0-0 | 0-0 | 0-0 | 0-1 | 0-0 | 0-1 | 0-0 | 0-0 | 0-0 | 0-2 |
| Webb, Brandon | 0-1 | 1-0 | 1-0 | 1-2 | 0-1 | 1-1 | 1-3 | 0-0 | 0-1 | 0-1 | 0-1 | 0-0 | 1-1 | 1-1 | 0-0 | 0-3 | 7-16 |
| **Totals** | 2-4 | 4-2 | 3-3 | 6-13 | 3-4 | 2-4 | 3-16 | 3-3 | 0-6 | 3-4 | 1-5 | 2-4 | 7-12 | 5-14 | 1-5 | 6-12 | 51-111 |

No-decisions— Jeff Fassero.

INTERLEAGUE: Randy Johnson 1-0, Stephen Randolph 0-1, Casey Fossum 1-0 vs. Orioles; Brandon Webb 0-1, Brandon Villafuerte 0-2 vs. Tigers; Stephen Randolph 0-1, Andrew Good 0-1, Randy Johnson 1-0 vs. Twins; Brandon Webb 0-1, Casey Fossum 0-1, Steve Sparks 1-0 vs. Yankees; Randy Johnson 0-1, Lance Cormier 0-1, Brandon Webb 0-1 vs. Devil Rays; Randy Choate 1-0, Andrew Good 0-1, Randy Johnson 1-0 vs. Blue Jays. Total: 6-12.

## ATLANTA—96-66

| Pitcher | Ari. W-L | Chi. W-L | Cin. W-L | Col. W-L | Fla. W-L | Hou. W-L | L.A. W-L | Mil. W-L | Mon. W-L | N.Y. W-L | Phi. W-L | Pit. W-L | S.D. W-L | S.F. W-L | St.L. W-L | A.L. W-L | Totals W-L |
|---|---|---|---|---|---|---|---|---|---|---|---|---|---|---|---|---|---|
| Alfonseca, Antonio | 0-0 | 1-0 | 0-0 | 0-0 | 1-0 | 1-0 | 0-0 | 1-0 | 0-0 | 0-0 | 0-3 | 0-0 | 0-0 | 0-0 | 2-0 | 0-1 | 6-4 |
| Almanza, Armando | 0-1 | 0-0 | 0-0 | 0-0 | 0-0 | 0-0 | 0-0 | 0-0 | 1-0 | 0-0 | 0-0 | 0-0 | 0-0 | 0-0 | 0-0 | 0-0 | 1-1 |
| Byrd, Paul | 1-0 | 0-1 | 0-0 | 0-0 | 1-0 | 0-0 | 0-0 | 0-0 | 2-1 | 2-1 | 0-1 | 0-1 | 0-0 | 1-0 | 0-1 | 1-1 | 8-7 |
| Capellan, Jose | 0-0 | 0-0 | 0-0 | 0-0 | 0-0 | 0-0 | 0-0 | 0-0 | 0-0 | 0-1 | 0-0 | 0-0 | 0-0 | 0-0 | 0-0 | 0-0 | 0-1 |
| Colon, Roman | 0-0 | 0-0 | 0-0 | 0-0 | 0-0 | 0-0 | 0-0 | 0-0 | 0-0 | 1-0 | 0-1 | 0-0 | 0-0 | 1-0 | 0-0 | 0-0 | 2-1 |
| Cruz, Juan | 0-0 | 0-0 | 0-0 | 0-0 | 0-0 | 1-0 | 0-1 | 0-0 | 2-1 | 0-0 | 0-0 | 1-0 | 0-0 | 0-0 | 0-0 | 2-0 | 6-2 |
| Cunnane, Will | 0-0 | 0-1 | 0-0 | 0-0 | 0-0 | 0-0 | 0-0 | 0-0 | 0-0 | 1-0 | 0-0 | 0-0 | 0-0 | 0-0 | 0-0 | 0-0 | 1-1 |
| Gryboski, Kevin | 0-0 | 1-0 | 0-0 | 1-0 | 0-1 | 0-0 | 0-0 | 0-0 | 0-0 | 1-0 | 0-0 | 0-1 | 0-0 | 0-0 | 0-0 | 0-0 | 3-2 |
| Hampton, Mike | 0-1 | 1-0 | 0-0 | 1-0 | 2-2 | 0-0 | 1-1 | 1-0 | 0-1 | 2-1 | 3-0 | 0-0 | 1-1 | 0-0 | 0-1 | 1-1 | 13-9 |
| Martin, Tom | 0-0 | 0-0 | 0-0 | 0-0 | 0-0 | 0-0 | 0-0 | 0-1 | 0-0 | 0-0 | 0-0 | 0-0 | 0-0 | 0-0 | 0-0 | 0-0 | 0-1 |
| McConnell, Sam | 0-0 | 0-0 | 0-0 | 0-0 | 1-0 | 0-0 | 0-0 | 0-0 | 0-0 | 0-0 | 0-0 | 0-0 | 0-0 | 0-0 | 0-0 | 0-0 | 1-0 |
| Nitkowski, C.J. | 0-0 | 0-0 | 0-0 | 1-0 | 0-0 | 0-0 | 0-0 | 0-0 | 0-0 | 0-0 | 0-0 | 0-0 | 0-0 | 0-0 | 0-0 | 0-0 | 1-0 |
| Ortiz, Russ | 1-0 | 0-1 | 0-0 | 0-0 | 3-1 | 0-1 | 1-0 | 0-0 | 5-0 | 1-2 | 1-1 | 1-0 | 1-0 | 0-2 | 0-0 | 1-1 | 15-9 |
| Ramirez, Horacio | 1-0 | 0-0 | 0-0 | 0-1 | 0-0 | 0-0 | 0-0 | 1-0 | 0-1 | 0-1 | 0-0 | 0-0 | 0-0 | 0-1 | 0-0 | 0-0 | 2-4 |
| Reitsma, Chris | 0-0 | 0-0 | 1-0 | 0-1 | 0-0 | 0-1 | 1-0 | 0-0 | 0-0 | 0-0 | 0-1 | 1-0 | 1-0 | 0-0 | 0-0 | 2-1 | 6-4 |
| Smith, Travis | 0-0 | 0-0 | 0-0 | 0-0 | 1-0 | 0-0 | 0-0 | 0-0 | 0-0 | 0-0 | 1-2 | 0-0 | 0-0 | 0-0 | 0-0 | 0-1 | 2-3 |
| Smoltz, John | 0-0 | 0-0 | 0-1 | 0-0 | 0-0 | 0-0 | 0-0 | 0-0 | 0-0 | 0-0 | 0-0 | 0-0 | 0-0 | 0-0 | 0-0 | 0-0 | 0-1 |
| Thomson, John | 0-0 | 0-0 | 1-1 | 1-0 | 3-1 | 1-1 | 0-0 | 0-0 | 3-0 | 3-0 | 2-0 | 0-0 | 0-0 | 0-0 | 0-1 | 0-4 | 14-8 |
| Wright, Jaret | 1-0 | 0-0 | 0-2 | 0-0 | 2-0 | 0-0 | 1-1 | 1-1 | 2-0 | 1-1 | 3-0 | 1-0 | 0-2 | 2-0 | 0-1 | 1-0 | 15-8 |
| **Totals** | 4-2 | 3-3 | 2-4 | 4-2 | 14-5 | 3-3 | 4-3 | 4-2 | 15-4 | 12-7 | 10-9 | 4-2 | 3-3 | 4-3 | 2-4 | 8-10 | 96-66 |

No-decisions— Tim Drew, Dan Meyer.

INTERLEAGUE: Paul Byrd 0-1, Russ Ortiz 1-0, Juan Cruz 1-0 vs. Orioles; Juan Cruz 1-0, John Thomson 0-1, Mike Hampton 1-0 vs. Red Sox; Jaret Wright 1-0, John Thomson 0-1, Travis Smith 0-1 vs. White Sox; Mike Hampton 0-1, Paul Byrd 1-0, Russ Ortiz 0-1 vs. Indians; Chris Reitsma 1-0, John Thomson 0-1, Antonio Alfonseca 0-1 vs. Tigers; Chris Reitsma 1-1, John Thomson 0-1 vs. Royals. Total: 8-10.

## CHICAGO—89-73

| Pitcher | Ari. W-L | Atl. W-L | Cin. W-L | Col. W-L | Fla. W-L | Hou. W-L | L.A. W-L | Mil. W-L | Mon. W-L | N.Y. W-L | Phi. W-L | Pit. W-L | S.D. W-L | S.F. W-L | St.L. W-L | A.L. W-L | Totals W-L |
|---|---|---|---|---|---|---|---|---|---|---|---|---|---|---|---|---|---|
| Beltran, Francis | 0-0 | 0-0 | 0-0 | 0-0 | 0-0 | 1-0 | 0-0 | 0-1 | 0-0 | 0-0 | 0-0 | 0-1 | 1-0 | 0-0 | 0-0 | 0-0 | 2-2 |
| Borowski, Joe | 0-0 | 0-0 | 1-1 | 0-0 | 0-0 | 0-0 | 0-0 | 0-0 | 0-0 | 0-0 | 0-0 | 0-2 | 0-0 | 1-1 | 0-0 | 0-0 | 2-4 |
| Clement, Matt | 1-0 | 0-0 | 1-1 | 0-0 | 0-1 | 0-2 | 0-1 | 2-2 | 0-0 | 1-0 | 0-1 | 1-0 | 0-0 | 0-2 | 3-2 | 0-1 | 9-13 |
| Dempster, Ryan | 0-0 | 0-0 | 0-0 | 0-0 | 1-0 | 0-0 | 0-0 | 0-0 | 0-0 | 0-0 | 0-0 | 0-0 | 0-1 | 0-0 | 0-0 | 0-0 | 1-1 |
| Farnsworth, Kyle | 0-0 | 0-1 | 0-0 | 1-0 | 0-0 | 1-1 | 0-1 | 0-0 | 0-0 | 0-0 | 0-0 | 0-0 | 0-0 | 0-0 | 1-2 | 1-0 | 4-5 |

| Pitcher | Ari. W-L | Atl. W-L | Cin. W-L | Col. W-L | Fla. W-L | Hou. W-L | L.A. W-L | Mil. W-L | Mon. W-L | N.Y. W-L | Phi. W-L | Pit. W-L | S.D. W-L | S.F. W-L | St.L. W-L | A.L. W-L | Totals W-L |
|---|---|---|---|---|---|---|---|---|---|---|---|---|---|---|---|---|---|
| Hawkins, LaTroy | 1-0 | 0-0 | 0-0 | 0-0 | 0-0 | 0-2 | 0-0 | 1-0 | 1-0 | 0-0 | 0-1 | 1-0 | 0-0 | 0-0 | 0-1 | 1-0 | 5-4 |
| Leicester, Jon | 0-0 | 0-0 | 1-1 | 0-0 | 0-0 | 2-0 | 0-0 | 0-0 | 0-0 | 0-0 | 1-0 | 0-0 | 0-0 | 0-0 | 0-0 | 1-0 | 5-1 |
| Maddux, Greg | 0-0 | 1-0 | 1-3 | 0-1 | 0-0 | 2-1 | 0-1 | 3-0 | 1-1 | 1-0 | 0-0 | 3-1 | 1-0 | 1-0 | 1-1 | 1-2 | 16-11 |
| Mercker, Kent | 0-0 | 1-0 | 0-0 | 0-0 | 0-0 | 0-0 | 0-0 | 1-0 | 0-0 | 0-1 | 1-0 | 0-0 | 0-0 | 0-0 | 0-0 | 0-0 | 3-1 |
| Mitre, Sergio | 0-2 | 0-0 | 0-0 | 0-0 | 0-0 | 0-0 | 0-0 | 0-0 | 0-0 | 0-0 | 0-0 | 1-1 | 1-0 | 0-0 | 0-1 | 0-0 | 2-4 |
| Pratt, Andy | 0-0 | 0-1 | 0-0 | 0-0 | 0-0 | 0-0 | 0-0 | 0-0 | 0-0 | 0-0 | 0-0 | 0-0 | 0-0 | 0-0 | 0-0 | 0-0 | 0-1 |
| Prior, Mark | 0-0 | 0-0 | 0-0 | 1-0 | 2-0 | 2-0 | 0-0 | 0-1 | 0-1 | 0-0 | 0-0 | 0-0 | 0-1 | 0-0 | 0-1 | 1-0 | 6-4 |
| Remlinger, Mike | 0-0 | 0-0 | 0-1 | 0-0 | 0-0 | 0-0 | 0-0 | 0-0 | 0-0 | 1-0 | 0-0 | 0-0 | 0-0 | 0-0 | 0-1 | 0-0 | 1-2 |
| Rusch, Glendon | 0-0 | 0-0 | 0-0 | 1-0 | 0-1 | 2-0 | 0-0 | 1-0 | 0-0 | 0-0 | 0-0 | 0-0 | 0-0 | 0-0 | 1-1 | 1-0 | 6-2 |
| Wellemeyer, Todd | 0-0 | 0-0 | 1-0 | 0-0 | 0-0 | 0-0 | 0-0 | 0-0 | 0-1 | 0-0 | 0-0 | 1-0 | 0-0 | 0-0 | 0-0 | 0-0 | 2-1 |
| Wood, Kerry | 0-1 | 1-1 | 2-1 | 1-0 | 0-1 | 0-1 | 1-1 | 0-1 | 0-0 | 1-1 | 1-0 | 0-0 | 0-0 | 0-1 | 1-0 | 0-0 | 8-9 |
| Wuertz, Michael | 0-0 | 0-0 | 0-0 | 0-0 | 0-0 | 0-0 | 0-0 | 0-0 | 0-0 | 0-0 | 0-0 | 1-0 | 0-0 | 0-0 | 0-0 | 0-0 | 1-0 |
| Zambrano, Carlos | 0-1 | 0-0 | 2-0 | 1-0 | 0-0 | 0-2 | 1-0 | 2-2 | 1-0 | 0-0 | 0-1 | 5-0 | 1-0 | 0-0 | 1-1 | 2-1 | 16-8 |
| **Totals** | 2-4 | 3-3 | 9-8 | 5-1 | 3-3 | 10-9 | 2-4 | 10-7 | 3-3 | 4-2 | 3-3 | 13-5 | 4-2 | 2-4 | 8-11 | 8-4 | 89-73 |

No-decisions— Jimmy Anderson.

INTERLEAGUE: Greg Maddux 0-1, Glendon Rusch 1-0, Jon Leicester 1-0 vs. Angels; Mark Prior 1-0, LaTroy Hawkins 1-0, Carlos Zambrano 1-1, Greg Maddux 1-1 vs. White Sox; Matt Clement 0-1, Kyle Farnsworth 1-0, Carlos Zambrano 1-0 vs. Athletics. Total: 8-4.

## CINCINNATI—76-86

| Pitcher | Ari. W-L | Atl. W-L | Chi. W-L | Col. W-L | Fla. W-L | Hou. W-L | L.A. W-L | Mil. W-L | Mon. W-L | N.Y. W-L | Phi. W-L | Pit. W-L | S.D. W-L | S.F. W-L | St.L. W-L | A.L. W-L | Totals W-L |
|---|---|---|---|---|---|---|---|---|---|---|---|---|---|---|---|---|---|
| Acevedo, Jose | 0-0 | 1-0 | 1-0 | 0-0 | 0-0 | 0-2 | 0-0 | 0-0 | 1-1 | 0-1 | 0-0 | 1-3 | 1-1 | 0-0 | 0-3 | 0-1 | 5-12 |
| Bong, Jung Keun | 0-0 | 0-0 | 0-0 | 0-0 | 0-0 | 0-0 | 0-0 | 0-0 | 0-0 | 0-0 | 0-0 | 0-0 | 0-0 | 0-0 | 1-0 | 0-1 | 1-1 |
| Claussen, Brandon | 1-0 | 0-1 | 0-1 | 0-1 | 0-0 | 0-1 | 0-1 | 1-1 | 0-0 | 0-0 | 0-1 | 0-1 | 0-0 | 0-0 | 0-0 | 0-0 | 2-8 |
| Graves, Danny | 0-0 | 0-0 | 0-2 | 0-0 | 0-0 | 0-0 | 0-0 | 1-1 | 0-0 | 0-0 | 0-0 | 0-0 | 0-0 | 0-1 | 0-2 | 0-0 | 1-6 |
| Hancock, Josh | 0-0 | 0-0 | 1-0 | 0-0 | 0-0 | 1-0 | 0-0 | 1-1 | 0-0 | 0-0 | 0-0 | 0-0 | 0-0 | 1-0 | 1-0 | 0-0 | 5-1 |
| Harang, Aaron | 0-1 | 0-0 | 1-0 | 0-0 | 0-1 | 0-3 | 1-1 | 2-1 | 0-0 | 0-0 | 0-0 | 3-1 | 1-0 | 1-0 | 1-1 | 0-0 | 10-9 |
| Haynes, Jimmy | 0-0 | 0-0 | 0-1 | 0-0 | 0-0 | 0-0 | 0-0 | 0-1 | 0-0 | 0-0 | 0-0 | 0-1 | 0-0 | 0-0 | 0-0 | 0-0 | 0-3 |
| Hudson, Luke | 1-0 | 1-0 | 0-1 | 0-0 | 0-0 | 0-0 | 0-0 | 2-0 | 0-0 | 0-0 | 0-0 | 0-0 | 0-1 | 0-0 | 0-0 | 0-0 | 4-2 |
| Jones, Todd | 0-0 | 0-0 | 1-0 | 0-0 | 0-0 | 1-1 | 0-0 | 2-0 | 1-0 | 0-0 | 0-0 | 0-1 | 0-0 | 0-0 | 1-0 | 2-0 | 8-2 |
| Lidle, Cory | 0-0 | 1-0 | 0-2 | 1-1 | 0-0 | 1-0 | 0-0 | 0-1 | 1-0 | 2-0 | 0-0 | 1-0 | 0-1 | 0-2 | 0-2 | 0-1 | 7-10 |
| Matthews, Mike | 0-0 | 0-0 | 0-0 | 0-0 | 0-0 | 0-0 | 0-0 | 0-0 | 1-0 | 1-0 | 0-0 | 0-0 | 0-0 | 0-0 | 0-1 | 0-0 | 2-1 |
| Norton, Phil | 0-1 | 1-0 | 0-0 | 0-0 | 0-0 | 0-1 | 0-0 | 0-0 | 0-0 | 0-0 | 0-0 | 0-0 | 0-0 | 0-0 | 0-1 | 1-2 | 2-5 |
| Padilla, Juan | 0-0 | 0-0 | 1-0 | 0-0 | 0-0 | 0-0 | 0-0 | 0-0 | 0-0 | 0-0 | 0-0 | 0-0 | 0-0 | 0-0 | 0-0 | 0-0 | 1-0 |
| Reith, Brian | 0-0 | 0-1 | 0-0 | 0-0 | 2-0 | 0-0 | 0-0 | 0-0 | 0-0 | 0-0 | 0-0 | 0-0 | 0-0 | 0-0 | 0-0 | 0-1 | 2-2 |
| Riedling, John | 0-0 | 0-0 | 1-0 | 1-0 | 1-0 | 2-1 | 0-0 | 0-0 | 0-0 | 0-0 | 0-1 | 0-0 | 0-0 | 0-0 | 0-1 | 0-0 | 5-3 |
| Sanchez, Jesus | 0-0 | 0-0 | 0-0 | 0-0 | 0-0 | 0-0 | 0-0 | 0-0 | 0-0 | 0-0 | 0-0 | 0-0 | 0-0 | 0-0 | 0-1 | 0-1 | 0-2 |
| Valentine, Joe | 0-1 | 0-0 | 0-0 | 0-0 | 0-0 | 0-0 | 0-0 | 0-0 | 0-1 | 0-0 | 1-0 | 0-0 | 0-0 | 0-0 | 1-1 | 0-0 | 2-3 |
| Van Poppel, Todd | 1-0 | 0-0 | 0-1 | 0-0 | 0-1 | 0-0 | 1-0 | 0-1 | 0-0 | 0-1 | 0-0 | 1-2 | 0-0 | 0-0 | 0-0 | 1-0 | 4-6 |
| Wagner, Ryan | 0-0 | 0-0 | 1-1 | 0-0 | 0-0 | 1-0 | 0-0 | 0-0 | 0-0 | 0-0 | 1-1 | 0-0 | 0-0 | 0-0 | 0-0 | 0-0 | 3-2 |
| White, Gabe | 0-0 | 0-0 | 0-0 | 0-0 | 0-0 | 0-0 | 1-0 | 0-1 | 0-0 | 0-0 | 0-0 | 0-0 | 0-0 | 0-0 | 0-1 | 0-0 | 1-2 |
| Wilson, Paul | 0-0 | 0-0 | 1-0 | 1-1 | 1-0 | 0-2 | 1-0 | 1-0 | 0-0 | 0-1 | 1-0 | 3-1 | 0-1 | 1-0 | 0-0 | 1-0 | 11-6 |
| **Totals** | 3-3 | 4-2 | 8-9 | 3-3 | 4-2 | 6-11 | 4-2 | 10-8 | 4-2 | 3-3 | 3-3 | 9-10 | 2-4 | 3-3 | 5-14 | 5-7 | 76-86 |

No-decisions— Aaron Myette.

INTERLEAGUE: Paul Wilson 1-0, Todd Jones 1-0, Phil Norton 0-2, Brian Reith 0-1, Jesus Sanchez 0-1 vs. Indians; Cory Lidle 0-1, Jung Keun Bong 0-1, Jose Acevedo 0-1 vs. Athletics; Todd Jones 1-0, Phil Norton 1-0, Todd Van Poppel 1-0 vs. Rangers. Total: 5-7.

## COLORADO—68-94

| Pitcher | Ari. W-L | Atl. W-L | Chi. W-L | Cin. W-L | Fla. W-L | Hou. W-L | L.A. W-L | Mil. W-L | Mon. W-L | N.Y. W-L | Phi. W-L | Pit. W-L | S.D. W-L | S.F. W-L | St.L. W-L | A.L. W-L | Totals W-L |
|---|---|---|---|---|---|---|---|---|---|---|---|---|---|---|---|---|---|
| Bernero, Adam | 0-0 | 0-0 | 0-0 | 0-0 | 0-0 | 0-0 | 0-0 | 0-0 | 0-0 | 0-0 | 0-0 | 0-0 | 0-0 | 0-1 | 0-0 | 1-0 | 1-1 |
| Chacon, Shawn | 0-1 | 0-0 | 0-1 | 0-0 | 0-0 | 0-0 | 0-2 | 0-0 | 0-0 | 0-0 | 0-0 | 0-0 | 0-0 | 0-2 | 0-0 | 1-3 | 1-9 |
| Cook, Aaron | 1-0 | 0-0 | 0-0 | 0-0 | 0-0 | 0-0 | 1-0 | 1-1 | 0-0 | 0-0 | 0-0 | 0-0 | 2-0 | 1-2 | 0-0 | 0-1 | 6-4 |
| Dohmann, Scott | 0-1 | 0-0 | 0-0 | 0-0 | 0-0 | 0-0 | 0-1 | 0-0 | 0-0 | 0-0 | 0-0 | 0-0 | 0-1 | 0-0 | 0-0 | 0-0 | 0-3 |
| Elarton, Scott | 0-1 | 0-0 | 0-0 | 0-0 | 0-1 | 0-0 | 0-2 | 0-0 | 0-1 | 0-0 | 0-1 | 0-0 | 0-0 | 0-0 | 0-0 | 0-0 | 0-6 |
| Estes, Shawn | 3-1 | 1-0 | 0-1 | 2-0 | 0-1 | 0-1 | 3-0 | 1-1 | 0-0 | 0-2 | 1-0 | 1-0 | 1-0 | 1-0 | 0-1 | 1-0 | 15-8 |
| Fassero, Jeff | 1-0 | 0-0 | 0-2 | 0-1 | 0-0 | 0-1 | 0-0 | 0-0 | 0-0 | 0-0 | 0-0 | 1-0 | 0-1 | 0-2 | 0-0 | 1-1 | 3-8 |
| Francis, Jeff | 1-0 | 0-1 | 0-0 | 0-0 | 0-0 | 0-0 | 0-0 | 0-0 | 0-0 | 0-0 | 0-0 | 0-0 | 2-0 | 0-1 | 0-0 | 0-0 | 3-2 |
| Fuentes, Brian | 0-0 | 0-0 | 0-0 | 0-1 | 0-0 | 0-0 | 1-1 | 0-0 | 0-1 | 0-0 | 1-0 | 0-0 | 0-1 | 0-0 | 0-0 | 0-0 | 2-4 |
| Gissell, Chris | 0-0 | 0-0 | 0-0 | 0-0 | 0-0 | 0-0 | 0-0 | 0-0 | 0-0 | 0-0 | 0-0 | 0-0 | 0-0 | 0-0 | 0-1 | 0-0 | 0-1 |
| Harikkala, Tim | 0-0 | 0-1 | 0-0 | 0-0 | 0-0 | 0-0 | 0-2 | 0-0 | 0-0 | 0-0 | 2-0 | 0-0 | 1-1 | 3-0 | 0-1 | 0-1 | 6-6 |
| Jennings, Jason | 2-1 | 0-0 | 1-1 | 0-0 | 0-1 | 0-1 | 0-0 | 0-0 | 0-2 | 1-0 | 0-1 | 0-1 | 3-1 | 1-0 | 1-1 | 2-2 | 11-12 |
| Kennedy, Joe | 2-0 | 0-0 | 0-0 | 0-1 | 0-1 | 1-1 | 2-0 | 0-0 | 2-0 | 0-0 | 0-1 | 0-1 | 0-0 | 1-1 | 0-0 | 1-1 | 9-7 |
| Lopez, Javier | 0-0 | 0-0 | 0-0 | 0-0 | 0-0 | 0-0 | 0-0 | 0-1 | 0-0 | 0-0 | 0-0 | 0-1 | 1-0 | 0-0 | 0-0 | 0-0 | 1-2 |
| Nunez, Vladimir | 1-0 | 1-1 | 0-0 | 0-0 | 1-0 | 0-0 | 0-0 | 0-0 | 0-0 | 0-1 | 0-0 | 0-0 | 0-1 | 0-0 | 0-0 | 0-0 | 3-3 |
| Reed, Steve | 0-1 | 0-0 | 0-0 | 0-0 | 0-1 | 0-0 | 1-1 | 0-0 | 0-0 | 0-1 | 1-0 | 0-0 | 0-1 | 0-2 | 0-0 | 1-1 | 3-8 |
| Simpson, Allan | 1-0 | 0-0 | 0-0 | 1-0 | 0-0 | 0-0 | 0-1 | 0-0 | 0-0 | 0-0 | 0-0 | 0-0 | 0-0 | 0-0 | 0-0 | 0-0 | 2-1 |
| Stark, Denny | 0-0 | 0-0 | 0-0 | 0-0 | 0-0 | 0-0 | 0-1 | 0-1 | 0-0 | 0-0 | 0-0 | 0-0 | 0-2 | 0-0 | 0-1 | 0-0 | 0-5 |
| Wright, Jamey | 1-0 | 0-1 | 0-0 | 0-0 | 0-0 | 0-1 | 0-0 | 0-0 | 0-0 | 0-0 | 0-0 | 0-1 | 0-0 | 1-0 | 0-0 | 0-0 | 2-3 |
| Young, Jason | 0-0 | 0-0 | 0-0 | 0-0 | 0-0 | 0-0 | 0-0 | 0-0 | 0-0 | 0-1 | 0-0 | 0-0 | 0-0 | 0-0 | 0-0 | 0-0 | 0-1 |
| **Totals** | 13-6 | 2-4 | 1-5 | 3-3 | 1-5 | 1-5 | 8-11 | 2-4 | 2-4 | 1-5 | 5-3 | 2-4 | 10-9 | 8-11 | 1-5 | 8-10 | 68-94 |

No-decisions— Travis Driskill, Kevin Jarvis, Marc Kroon, Chin-hui Tsao, Turk Wendell.

INTERLEAGUE: Shawn Estes 1-0, Shawn Chacon 0-1, Jeff Fassero 1-0 vs. Orioles; Joe Kennedy 1-0, Jason Jennings 1-0, Aaron Cook 0-1 vs. Red Sox; Steve Reed 1-1, Jason Jennings 0-1 vs. Indians; Adam Bernero 1-0, Shawn Chacon 1-0, Jason Jennings 1-0 vs. Tigers; Jeff Fassero 0-1, Joe Kennedy 0-1, Jason Jennings 0-1 vs. Yankees; Tim Harikkala 0-1, Shawn Chacon 0-2 vs. Devil Rays. Total: 8-10.

## FLORIDA—83-79

| Pitcher | Ari. W-L | Atl. W-L | Chi. W-L | Cin. W-L | Col. W-L | Hou. W-L | L.A. W-L | Mil. W-L | Mon. W-L | N.Y. W-L | Phi. W-L | Pit. W-L | S.D. W-L | S.F. W-L | St.L. W-L | A.L. W-L | Totals W-L |
|---|---|---|---|---|---|---|---|---|---|---|---|---|---|---|---|---|---|
| Beckett, Josh | 0-1 | 0-3 | 0-0 | 0-1 | 1-0 | 1-0 | 0-0 | 0-0 | 1-1 | 2-0 | 2-0 | 0-1 | 2-0 | 0-1 | 0-1 | 0-0 | 9-9 |
| Benitez, Armando | 1-0 | 0-0 | 0-0 | 0-0 | 0-0 | 0-0 | 0-0 | 0-0 | 0-0 | 0-0 | 0-1 | 0-1 | 0-0 | 0-0 | 0-0 | 1-0 | 2-2 |
| Borland, Toby | 0-0 | 0-0 | 0-0 | 0-0 | 0-0 | 0-0 | 0-0 | 0-0 | 0-0 | 1-0 | 0-0 | 0-0 | 0-0 | 0-0 | 0-0 | 0-1 | 1-1 |
| Bump, Nate | 0-0 | 0-1 | 0-0 | 0-1 | 0-0 | 0-0 | 0-0 | 0-0 | 0-1 | 0-0 | 0-0 | 1-0 | 0-0 | 0-1 | 0-0 | 1-0 | 2-4 |
| Burnett, A.J. | 0-0 | 0-0 | 1-0 | 0-0 | 1-0 | 0-0 | 0-1 | 0-0 | 0-0 | 1-1 | 1-1 | 0-1 | 0-0 | 1-0 | 1-0 | 1-2 | 7-6 |
| Fox, Chad | 0-0 | 0-0 | 0-0 | 0-0 | 0-1 | 0-0 | 0-0 | 0-0 | 0-0 | 0-0 | 0-0 | 0-0 | 0-0 | 0-0 | 0-0 | 0-0 | 0-1 |
| Gracesqui, Franklyn | 0-0 | 0-0 | 0-0 | 0-0 | 0-0 | 0-0 | 0-0 | 0-0 | 0-0 | 0-0 | 0-0 | 0-0 | 0-1 | 0-0 | 0-0 | 0-0 | 0-1 |
| Howard, Ben | 0-0 | 0-0 | 0-0 | 0-1 | 0-0 | 0-0 | 0-0 | 0-0 | 0-0 | 1-0 | 0-0 | 0-0 | 0-0 | 0-0 | 0-0 | 0-0 | 1-1 |
| Kensing, Logan | 0-0 | 0-1 | 0-1 | 0-0 | 0-0 | 0-0 | 0-0 | 0-0 | 0-0 | 0-0 | 0-1 | 0-0 | 0-0 | 0-0 | 0-0 | 0-0 | 0-3 |
| Koch, Billy | 0-0 | 0-0 | 0-0 | 0-0 | 0-0 | 0-0 | 0-0 | 1-0 | 0-0 | 0-0 | 0-0 | 0-1 | 0-0 | 0-0 | 0-0 | 0-1 | 1-2 |
| Manzanillo, Josias | 0-0 | 1-0 | 0-0 | 0-0 | 0-0 | 0-0 | 0-0 | 0-0 | 0-1 | 1-1 | 1-0 | 0-0 | 0-0 | 0-0 | 0-0 | 0-1 | 3-3 |
| Mota, Guillermo | 0-0 | 0-1 | 0-1 | 0-0 | 0-0 | 0-0 | 1-0 | 0-0 | 0-0 | 0-0 | 0-1 | 0-0 | 0-0 | 0-0 | 0-1 | 0-0 | 1-4 |
| Oliver, Darren | 0-0 | 0-2 | 0-0 | 0-0 | 0-0 | 0-0 | 0-0 | 0-0 | 0-0 | 0-0 | 2-0 | 0-0 | 0-0 | 0-0 | 0-1 | 0-0 | 2-3 |
| Pavano, Carl | 2-0 | 1-1 | 1-1 | 0-0 | 2-0 | 0-1 | 1-0 | 0-0 | 2-1 | 2-0 | 2-0 | 0-1 | 2-0 | 0-1 | 0-1 | 3-1 | 18-8 |
| Penny, Brad | 1-0 | 2-1 | 0-0 | 1-0 | 0-0 | 0-1 | 1-0 | 0-0 | 1-2 | 1-1 | 0-0 | 0-0 | 0-0 | 0-0 | 1-0 | 0-3 | 8-8 |
| Perisho, Matt | 0-0 | 0-1 | 0-0 | 0-0 | 0-0 | 1-0 | 0-0 | 0-0 | 2-0 | 1-0 | 1-1 | 0-0 | 0-0 | 0-1 | 0-0 | 0-0 | 5-3 |
| Phelps, Tommy | 0-0 | 0-0 | 0-0 | 1-0 | 0-0 | 0-0 | 0-0 | 0-0 | 0-0 | 0-0 | 0-0 | 0-0 | 0-0 | 0-0 | 0-0 | 0-1 | 1-1 |
| Seanez, Rudy | 0-0 | 0-0 | 0-0 | 0-0 | 0-0 | 0-0 | 0-0 | 1-0 | 1-0 | 1-0 | 0-0 | 0-0 | 0-0 | 0-1 | 0-0 | 0-0 | 3-1 |
| Tejera, Michael | 0-0 | 0-1 | 0-0 | 0-0 | 0-0 | 0-0 | 0-0 | 0-0 | 0-0 | 0-0 | 0-0 | 0-0 | 0-0 | 0-0 | 0-0 | 0-0 | 0-1 |
| Valdez, Ismael | 0-0 | 1-0 | 0-0 | 0-0 | 1-0 | 0-0 | 0-0 | 1-1 | 1-0 | 1-1 | 0-1 | 0-0 | 0-0 | 0-0 | 0-0 | 0-0 | 5-3 |
| Wayne, Justin | 0-0 | 0-0 | 0-0 | 0-1 | 0-0 | 0-0 | 0-1 | 0-0 | 0-1 | 1-0 | 1-0 | 0-0 | 0-0 | 1-0 | 0-0 | 0-0 | 3-3 |
| Weathers, David | 0-0 | 0-0 | 1-0 | 0-0 | 0-0 | 0-0 | 0-0 | 0-0 | 0-0 | 0-0 | 0-0 | 0-0 | 0-0 | 0-0 | 0-0 | 0-0 | 1-0 |
| Willis, Dontrelle | 0-2 | 0-2 | 0-0 | 0-0 | 0-0 | 1-1 | 0-1 | 1-1 | 3-1 | 2-0 | 2-1 | 0-0 | 0-1 | 0-0 | 0-0 | 1-1 | 10-11 |
| **Totals** | 4-3 | 5-14 | 3-3 | 2-4 | 5-1 | 3-3 | 3-3 | 4-2 | 11-8 | 15-4 | 12-7 | 1-5 | 4-2 | 2-5 | 2-4 | 7-11 | 83-79 |

No-decisions— Mike Neu, Aaron Small.

INTERLEAGUE: Armando Benitez 1-0, Toby Borland 0-1, Carl Pavano 1-0 vs. White Sox; Nate Bump 1-0, A.J. Burnett 0-1, Carl Pavano 1-0 vs. Indians; Tommy Phelps 0-1, Brad Penny 0-1, Dontrelle Willis 1-0 vs. Tigers; A.J. Burnett 1-1, Josias Manzanillo 0-1, Carl Pavano 1-1, Brad Penny 0-1 vs. Devil Rays; Brad Penny 0-1, Billy Koch 0-1, Dontrelle Willis 0-1 vs. Rangers. Total: 7-11.

## HOUSTON—92-70

| Pitcher | Ari. W-L | Atl. W-L | Chi. W-L | Cin. W-L | Col. W-L | Fla. W-L | L.A. W-L | Mil. W-L | Mon. W-L | N.Y. W-L | Phi. W-L | Pit. W-L | S.D. W-L | S.F. W-L | St.L. W-L | A.L. W-L | Totals W-L |
|---|---|---|---|---|---|---|---|---|---|---|---|---|---|---|---|---|---|
| Backe, Brandon | 0-0 | 0-0 | 0-1 | 2-0 | 1-0 | 0-0 | 0-0 | 1-0 | 0-0 | 0-1 | 0-0 | 0-1 | 0-0 | 0-0 | 1-0 | 0-0 | 5-3 |
| Bullinger, Kirk | 0-0 | 0-0 | 0-0 | 0-0 | 0-0 | 0-0 | 0-0 | 0-0 | 0-0 | 0-0 | 0-0 | 1-0 | 0-0 | 0-0 | 0-0 | 0-0 | 1-0 |
| Clemens, Roger | 1-0 | 0-0 | 2-1 | 2-0 | 1-0 | 1-0 | 0-1 | 2-0 | 0-1 | 0-0 | 1-0 | 3-0 | 1-0 | 1-0 | 2-0 | 1-1 | 18-4 |
| Dotel, Octavio | 0-0 | 0-0 | 0-1 | 0-0 | 0-0 | 0-1 | 0-0 | 0-0 | 0-0 | 0-0 | 0-0 | 0-0 | 0-0 | 0-1 | 0-1 | 0-0 | 0-4 |
| Duckworth, Brandon | 0-0 | 0-0 | 0-0 | 0-0 | 1-0 | 0-0 | 0-1 | 0-0 | 0-0 | 0-0 | 0-0 | 0-0 | 0-0 | 0-0 | 0-0 | 0-1 | 1-2 |
| Gallo, Mike | 0-0 | 0-0 | 0-0 | 0-0 | 1-0 | 0-0 | 0-0 | 0-0 | 0-0 | 0-0 | 0-0 | 1-0 | 0-0 | 0-0 | 0-0 | 0-0 | 2-0 |
| Harville, Chad | 0-0 | 0-0 | 0-0 | 0-1 | 0-0 | 0-0 | 0-0 | 1-0 | 0-1 | 0-0 | 1-0 | 0-0 | 0-0 | 0-0 | 1-0 | 0-0 | 3-2 |
| Hernandez, Carlos | 0-0 | 0-0 | 1-0 | 0-0 | 0-0 | 0-0 | 0-0 | 0-0 | 0-1 | 0-0 | 0-0 | 0-1 | 0-0 | 0-1 | 0-0 | 0-0 | 1-3 |
| Lidge, Brad | 0-0 | 0-0 | 3-1 | 0-3 | 0-0 | 0-0 | 0-0 | 1-1 | 0-0 | 1-0 | 0-0 | 1-0 | 0-0 | 0-0 | 0-0 | 0-0 | 6-5 |
| Miceli, Dan | 0-0 | 1-1 | 1-0 | 1-1 | 0-0 | 0-0 | 0-1 | 1-0 | 1-0 | 0-0 | 0-0 | 0-0 | 0-1 | 1-0 | 0-1 | 0-1 | 6-6 |
| Miller, Wade | 0-0 | 0-0 | 0-0 | 1-1 | 0-1 | 1-1 | 0-0 | 1-0 | 0-0 | 0-0 | 0-0 | 1-0 | 0-0 | 0-0 | 1-3 | 2-1 | 7-7 |
| Munro, Pete | 0-0 | 0-1 | 0-1 | 1-0 | 0-0 | 0-0 | 0-0 | 1-1 | 0-0 | 0-1 | 0-0 | 1-2 | 0-1 | 0-0 | 0-0 | 1-0 | 4-7 |
| Oliver, Darren | 0-0 | 0-0 | 0-0 | 1-0 | 0-0 | 0-0 | 0-0 | 0-0 | 0-0 | 0-0 | 0-0 | 0-0 | 0-0 | 0-0 | 0-0 | 0-0 | 1-0 |
| Oswalt, Roy | 2-0 | 0-0 | 2-3 | 3-0 | 1-0 | 0-1 | 0-1 | 3-1 | 1-0 | 0-1 | 2-0 | 1-1 | 1-1 | 0-1 | 2-0 | 2-0 | 20-10 |
| Pettitte, Andy | 1-1 | 1-0 | 0-0 | 0-0 | 0-0 | 0-0 | 1-0 | 0-0 | 0-0 | 1-0 | 0-0 | 2-0 | 0-1 | 0-1 | 0-0 | 0-1 | 6-4 |
| Qualls, Chad | 0-0 | 0-0 | 0-0 | 0-0 | 0-0 | 0-0 | 0-0 | 0-0 | 0-0 | 0-0 | 2-0 | 1-0 | 0-0 | 0-0 | 1-0 | 0-0 | 4-0 |
| Redding, Tim | 0-1 | 1-0 | 0-1 | 0-0 | 0-0 | 1-0 | 0-0 | 2-3 | 0-0 | 0-0 | 0-0 | 0-0 | 0-0 | 0-0 | 1-2 | 0-0 | 5-7 |
| Springer, Russ | 0-0 | 0-0 | 0-0 | 0-0 | 0-0 | 0-0 | 0-0 | 0-0 | 0-0 | 0-0 | 0-0 | 0-0 | 0-0 | 0-0 | 0-1 | 0-0 | 0-1 |
| Stone, Ricky | 0-0 | 0-1 | 0-0 | 0-0 | 0-0 | 0-0 | 0-0 | 0-0 | 0-0 | 0-0 | 0-0 | 0-0 | 0-0 | 0-0 | 1-0 | 0-0 | 1-1 |
| Weathers, David | 0-0 | 0-0 | 0-1 | 0-0 | 0-0 | 0-0 | 0-1 | 0-0 | 0-1 | 0-1 | 0-0 | 0-0 | 0-0 | 0-0 | 0-0 | 1-0 | 1-4 |
| **Totals** | 4-2 | 3-3 | 9-10 | 11-6 | 5-1 | 3-3 | 1-5 | 13-6 | 2-4 | 2-4 | 6-0 | 12-5 | 2-4 | 2-4 | 10-8 | 7-5 | 92-70 |

No-decisions— Jared Fernandez, Jeremy Griffiths, Dan Wheeler.

INTERLEAGUE: Pete Munro 1-0, Roger Clemens 0-1, Wade Miller 1-0 vs. Angels; Brandon Duckworth 0-1, Roger Clemens 1-0, Wade Miller 1-0 vs. Mariners; Wade Miller 0-1, David Weathers 1-0, Dan Miceli 0-1, Roy Oswalt 2-0, Andy Pettitte 0-1 vs. Rangers. Total: 7-5.

## LOS ANGELES—93-69

| Pitcher | Ari. W-L | Atl. W-L | Chi. W-L | Cin. W-L | Col. W-L | Fla. W-L | Hou. W-L | Mil. W-L | Mon. W-L | N.Y. W-L | Phi. W-L | Pit. W-L | S.D. W-L | S.F. W-L | St.L. W-L | A.L. W-L | Totals W-L |
|---|---|---|---|---|---|---|---|---|---|---|---|---|---|---|---|---|---|
| Alvarez, Wilson | 1-1 | 0-2 | 1-0 | 0-0 | 1-0 | 1-0 | 1-0 | 0-0 | 0-0 | 0-1 | 0-0 | 1-0 | 1-1 | 0-1 | 0-0 | 0-0 | 7-6 |
| Brazoban, Yhency | 1-0 | 0-0 | 0-0 | 0-0 | 3-1 | 0-0 | 0-0 | 0-0 | 0-0 | 0-0 | 0-0 | 0-0 | 1-0 | 1-1 | 0-0 | 0-0 | 6-2 |
| Carrara, Giovanni | 1-0 | 1-0 | 0-0 | 0-0 | 0-0 | 0-0 | 1-0 | 0-0 | 0-1 | 1-0 | 0-0 | 0-0 | 0-0 | 0-0 | 1-1 | 0-0 | 5-2 |
| Dessens, Elmer | 0-0 | 0-0 | 0-0 | 0-0 | 1-0 | 0-0 | 0-0 | 0-0 | 0-0 | 0-0 | 0-0 | 0-0 | 0-0 | 0-0 | 0-0 | 0-0 | 1-0 |
| Dreifort, Darren | 0-1 | 0-0 | 0-0 | 0-1 | 0-0 | 0-1 | 0-0 | 0-0 | 0-0 | 0-0 | 0-0 | 0-0 | 0-1 | 1-0 | 0-0 | 0-0 | 1-4 |
| Falkenborg, Brian | 0-0 | 0-0 | 0-0 | 0-0 | 0-0 | 0-0 | 0-0 | 0-0 | 0-0 | 0-0 | 0-0 | 1-0 | 0-0 | 0-0 | 0-0 | 0-0 | 1-0 |
| Gagne, Eric | 2-0 | 0-1 | 0-0 | 0-0 | 1-0 | 0-1 | 0-0 | 1-0 | 0-0 | 0-0 | 0-1 | 0-0 | 3-0 | 0-0 | 0-0 | 0-0 | 7-3 |
| Ishii, Kazuhisa | 4-0 | 0-0 | 0-1 | 0-1 | 1-2 | 1-0 | 0-0 | 0-0 | 2-0 | 1-0 | 0-1 | 0-0 | 1-0 | 1-1 | 0-1 | 2-1 | 13-8 |
| Jackson, Edwin | 0-0 | 0-0 | 0-0 | 0-0 | 0-0 | 0-0 | 1-0 | 1-0 | 0-0 | 0-0 | 0-0 | 0-0 | 0-0 | 0-0 | 0-1 | 0-0 | 2-1 |
| Lima, Jose | 4-0 | 0-0 | 0-0 | 1-0 | 0-1 | 0-0 | 1-0 | 1-0 | 0-1 | 0-0 | 0-0 | 1-0 | 2-0 | 1-0 | 0-1 | 2-2 | 13-5 |
| Martin, Tom | 0-0 | 0-0 | 0-0 | 0-0 | 0-0 | 0-0 | 0-0 | 0-0 | 0-0 | 0-0 | 0-0 | 0-0 | 0-0 | 0-0 | 0-0 | 0-1 | 0-1 |
| Mota, Guillermo | 1-0 | 0-0 | 0-0 | 0-0 | 1-1 | 0-0 | 0-0 | 0-0 | 1-0 | 0-0 | 0-1 | 1-0 | 0-0 | 2-1 | 0-0 | 2-1 | 8-4 |
| Nomo, Hideo | 1-1 | 0-0 | 0-1 | 0-0 | 2-0 | 0-0 | 0-0 | 0-0 | 0-1 | 0-1 | 0-1 | 0-0 | 1-1 | 0-2 | 0-0 | 0-3 | 4-11 |
| Penny, Brad | 0-0 | 0-0 | 0-0 | 0-0 | 0-0 | 0-0 | 0-0 | 0-0 | 0-0 | 0-0 | 0-1 | 1-0 | 0-1 | 0-0 | 0-0 | 0-0 | 1-2 |
| Perez, Odalis | 1-0 | 0-1 | 1-0 | 0-1 | 0-3 | 0-0 | 0-0 | 0-0 | 0-0 | 1-0 | 1-0 | 0-0 | 0-1 | 2-0 | 0-0 | 1-0 | 7-6 |
| Sanchez, Duaner | 0-0 | 0-0 | 1-0 | 0-0 | 1-0 | 1-0 | 0-0 | 0-1 | 0-0 | 0-0 | 0-0 | 0-0 | 0-0 | 0-0 | 0-0 | 0-0 | 3-1 |

| Pitcher | Ari. W-L | Atl. W-L | Chi. W-L | Cin. W-L | Col. W-L | Fla. W-L | Hou. W-L | Mil. W-L | Mon. W-L | N.Y. W-L | Phi. W-L | Pit. W-L | S.D. W-L | S.F. W-L | St.L. W-L | A.L. W-L | Totals W-L |
|---|---|---|---|---|---|---|---|---|---|---|---|---|---|---|---|---|---|
| Stewart, Scott | 0-0 | 0-0 | 0-0 | 0-0 | 0-0 | 0-0 | 0-0 | 0-0 | 0-0 | 0-0 | 0-0 | 0-0 | 0-0 | 0-0 | 1-0 | 0-0 | 1-0 |
| Weaver, Jeff | 0-0 | 2-0 | 1-0 | 1-1 | 0-0 | 0-1 | 1-1 | 0-2 | 1-0 | 0-1 | 0-0 | 1-0 | 1-4 | 2-3 | 0-0 | 3-0 | 13-13 |
| **Totals** | 16-3 | 3-4 | 4-2 | 2-4 | 11-8 | 3-3 | 5-1 | 3-3 | 4-3 | 3-3 | 1-5 | 6-0 | 10-9 | 10-9 | 2-4 | 10-8 | 93-69 |

No-decisions— Masao Kida, Rodney Myers, Mike Venafro, Robin Ventura.

INTERLEAGUE: Jose Lima 0-1, Guillermo Mota 1-1, Kazuhisa Ishii 1-1, Jeff Weaver 1-0 vs. Angels; Jose Lima 1-0, Guillermo Mota 1-0, Odalis Perez 1-0 vs. Orioles; Tom Martin 0-1, Jeff Weaver 1-0, Hideo Nomo 0-1 vs. Red Sox; Jeff Weaver 1-0, Hideo Nomo 0-1, Jose Lima 1-0 vs. Yankees; Hideo Nomo 0-1, Jose Lima 0-1, Kazuhisa Ishii 1-0 vs. Blue Jays. Total: 10-8.

## MILWAUKEE—67-94

| Pitcher | Ari. W-L | Atl. W-L | Chi. W-L | Cin. W-L | Col. W-L | Fla. W-L | Hou. W-L | L.A. W-L | Mon. W-L | N.Y. W-L | Phi. W-L | Pit. W-L | S.D. W-L | S.F. W-L | St.L. W-L | A.L. W-L | Totals W-L |
|---|---|---|---|---|---|---|---|---|---|---|---|---|---|---|---|---|---|
| Adams, Mike | 0-0 | 1-0 | 0-0 | 0-0 | 0-0 | 0-0 | 0-1 | 0-0 | 1-0 | 0-1 | 0-1 | 0-0 | 0-0 | 0-0 | 0-0 | 0-0 | 2-3 |
| Bennett, Jeff | 0-0 | 0-0 | 0-0 | 1-2 | 0-0 | 0-0 | 0-0 | 0-0 | 0-0 | 0-0 | 0-0 | 0-2 | 0-0 | 0-0 | 0-0 | 0-1 | 1-5 |
| Burba, Dave | 0-0 | 0-0 | 0-0 | 1-0 | 0-0 | 0-0 | 0-0 | 0-1 | 1-0 | 0-0 | 0-0 | 0-0 | 0-0 | 0-0 | 1-0 | 0-0 | 3-1 |
| Capuano, Chris | 0-0 | 0-0 | 2-2 | 0-1 | 1-1 | 1-0 | 1-1 | 0-0 | 0-0 | 0-1 | 0-0 | 0-1 | 0-0 | 0-1 | 1-0 | 0-0 | 6-8 |
| Davis, Doug | 0-0 | 0-0 | 1-1 | 1-1 | 1-0 | 0-0 | 1-4 | 1-0 | 1-1 | 1-0 | 0-1 | 1-1 | 0-2 | 0-1 | 2-0 | 2-0 | 12-12 |
| de la Rosa, Jorge | 0-0 | 0-0 | 0-0 | 0-1 | 0-0 | 0-1 | 0-0 | 0-0 | 0-0 | 0-0 | 0-0 | 0-0 | 0-0 | 0-0 | 0-1 | 0-0 | 0-3 |
| Ford, Ben | 1-0 | 0-0 | 0-0 | 0-0 | 0-0 | 0-0 | 0-0 | 0-0 | 0-0 | 0-1 | 0-0 | 0-0 | 0-0 | 0-0 | 0-0 | 0-0 | 1-1 |
| Glover, Gary | 1-0 | 0-0 | 0-0 | 0-0 | 0-0 | 0-0 | 0-1 | 0-0 | 0-0 | 0-0 | 0-0 | 1-0 | 0-0 | 0-0 | 0-0 | 0-0 | 2-1 |
| Hendrickson, Ben | 0-0 | 0-0 | 0-1 | 1-2 | 0-0 | 0-1 | 0-1 | 0-1 | 0-0 | 0-0 | 0-0 | 0-1 | 0-0 | 0-0 | 0-1 | 0-0 | 1-8 |
| Hernandez, Adrian | 0-1 | 0-0 | 0-0 | 0-0 | 0-0 | 0-0 | 0-0 | 0-0 | 0-0 | 0-0 | 0-0 | 0-0 | 0-0 | 0-0 | 0-1 | 0-0 | 0-2 |
| Kieschnick, Brooks | 0-1 | 0-0 | 0-0 | 0-0 | 0-0 | 0-0 | 0-0 | 0-0 | 0-0 | 0-0 | 0-0 | 0-0 | 0-0 | 0-0 | 1-0 | 0-0 | 1-1 |
| Kinney, Matt | 0-0 | 0-1 | 0-0 | 0-0 | 0-0 | 0-0 | 0-1 | 1-0 | 0-0 | 1-0 | 0-0 | 0-0 | 0-0 | 0-1 | 0-0 | 1-1 | 3-4 |
| Kolb, Dan | 0-0 | 0-0 | 0-0 | 0-1 | 0-0 | 0-1 | 0-0 | 0-0 | 0-0 | 0-0 | 0-1 | 0-0 | 0-0 | 0-0 | 0-1 | 0-0 | 0-4 |
| Obermueller, Wes | 0-0 | 0-0 | 0-0 | 1-1 | 0-0 | 1-1 | 1-1 | 0-0 | 1-0 | 0-0 | 0-1 | 0-1 | 1-1 | 1-1 | 0-0 | 0-1 | 6-8 |
| Phelps, Travis | 0-0 | 0-0 | 0-1 | 0-0 | 0-0 | 0-0 | 0-0 | 0-0 | 0-0 | 0-0 | 0-0 | 0-0 | 0-0 | 0-0 | 0-0 | 0-0 | 0-1 |
| Saenz, Chris | 0-0 | 0-0 | 0-0 | 0-0 | 0-0 | 0-0 | 0-0 | 0-0 | 0-0 | 0-0 | 0-0 | 0-0 | 0-0 | 0-0 | 1-0 | 0-0 | 1-0 |
| Santos, Victor | 0-0 | 0-1 | 3-1 | 1-1 | 1-0 | 0-0 | 0-1 | 0-1 | 1-0 | 0-1 | 0-1 | 0-1 | 1-1 | 0-1 | 1-1 | 3-1 | 11-12 |
| Sheets, Ben | 1-1 | 1-1 | 1-3 | 2-0 | 1-1 | 0-0 | 2-2 | 1-0 | 0-0 | 0-0 | 0-0 | 1-3 | 0-0 | 0-0 | 1-3 | 1-0 | 12-14 |
| Vizcaino, Luis | 0-0 | 0-1 | 0-1 | 0-0 | 0-0 | 0-0 | 1-0 | 0-0 | 0-0 | 0-0 | 0-1 | 2-1 | 0-0 | 0-0 | 0-0 | 1-0 | 4-4 |
| Wise, Matt | 0-0 | 0-0 | 0-0 | 0-0 | 0-0 | 0-0 | 0-0 | 0-0 | 0-0 | 0-0 | 0-0 | 1-1 | 0-0 | 0-0 | 0-1 | 0-0 | 1-2 |
| **Totals** | 3-3 | 2-4 | 7-10 | 8-10 | 4-2 | 2-4 | 6-13 | 3-3 | 5-1 | 2-4 | 0-6 | 6-12 | 2-4 | 1-5 | 8-9 | 8-4 | 67-94 |

No-decisions— Trent Durrington, Pedro Liriano.

INTERLEAGUE: Jeff Bennett 0-1, Matt Kinney 1-0, Victor Santos 1-0 vs. Angels; Ben Sheets 1-0, Wes Obermueller 0-1, Luis Vizcaino 1-0, Victor Santos 1-1, Doug Davis 1-0 vs. Twins; Victor Santos 1-0, Doug Davis 1-0, Matt Kinney 0-1 vs. Mariners. Total: 8-4.

## MONTREAL—67-95

| Pitcher | Ari. W-L | Atl. W-L | Chi. W-L | Cin. W-L | Col. W-L | Fla. W-L | Hou. W-L | L.A. W-L | Mil. W-L | N.Y. W-L | Phi. W-L | Pit. W-L | S.D. W-L | S.F. W-L | St.L. W-L | A.L. W-L | Totals W-L |
|---|---|---|---|---|---|---|---|---|---|---|---|---|---|---|---|---|---|
| Armas, Tony | 0-0 | 0-0 | 0-1 | 0-0 | 0-0 | 1-0 | 0-0 | 0-0 | 0-0 | 0-0 | 1-0 | 0-0 | 0-0 | 0-0 | 0-0 | 0-3 | 2-4 |
| Ayala, Luis | 1-0 | 0-1 | 0-0 | 0-0 | 1-0 | 0-2 | 0-1 | 0-1 | 0-0 | 2-2 | 1-0 | 1-0 | 0-2 | 0-1 | 0-1 | 0-1 | 6-12 |
| Bentz, Chad | 0-0 | 0-1 | 0-0 | 0-0 | 0-0 | 0-0 | 0-0 | 0-0 | 0-0 | 0-1 | 0-1 | 0-0 | 0-0 | 0-0 | 0-0 | 0-0 | 0-3 |
| Biddle, Rocky | 0-0 | 0-1 | 0-1 | 0-1 | 0-0 | 2-0 | 0-1 | 0-1 | 0-1 | 0-1 | 0-1 | 1-0 | 0-0 | 1-0 | 0-0 | 0-0 | 4-8 |
| Cordero, Chad | 1-0 | 0-0 | 1-0 | 0-1 | 0-0 | 0-0 | 0-0 | 1-0 | 0-0 | 1-0 | 1-0 | 0-0 | 0-0 | 0-1 | 1-1 | 1-0 | 7-3 |
| Day, Zach | 0-0 | 0-2 | 0-0 | 1-1 | 0-1 | 0-1 | 0-0 | 0-1 | 1-1 | 1-1 | 1-0 | 0-0 | 0-0 | 0-0 | 0-0 | 1-2 | 5-10 |
| Downs, Scott | 0-0 | 0-3 | 1-0 | 0-0 | 0-0 | 0-0 | 0-0 | 0-0 | 0-0 | 0-0 | 0-2 | 1-0 | 1-0 | 0-0 | 0-0 | 0-1 | 3-6 |
| Eischen, Joey | 0-0 | 0-0 | 0-0 | 0-0 | 0-0 | 0-0 | 0-0 | 0-0 | 0-0 | 0-0 | 0-1 | 0-0 | 0-0 | 0-0 | 0-0 | 0-0 | 0-1 |
| Fikac, Jeremy | 0-0 | 0-0 | 0-0 | 0-0 | 0-0 | 0-0 | 0-0 | 0-0 | 0-0 | 0-0 | 0-0 | 0-0 | 0-0 | 0-1 | 0-0 | 1-1 | 1-2 |
| Hernandez, Livan | 2-0 | 0-5 | 1-0 | 0-0 | 1-1 | 2-1 | 0-0 | 0-1 | 0-0 | 2-1 | 1-2 | 0-1 | 0-0 | 0-1 | 0-0 | 2-2 | 11-15 |
| Hill, Shawn | 0-0 | 0-0 | 0-0 | 0-0 | 0-0 | 0-0 | 0-0 | 0-0 | 0-0 | 0-0 | 0-1 | 0-1 | 0-0 | 0-0 | 0-0 | 1-0 | 1-2 |
| Horgan, Joe | 0-0 | 1-0 | 0-0 | 0-0 | 0-0 | 0-0 | 0-0 | 1-0 | 0-0 | 0-1 | 1-0 | 1-0 | 0-0 | 0-0 | 0-0 | 0-0 | 4-1 |
| Kim, Sun-Woo | 0-0 | 0-0 | 0-0 | 0-0 | 0-0 | 0-1 | 0-0 | 1-0 | 0-2 | 0-0 | 1-2 | 0-0 | 0-1 | 0-0 | 1-0 | 1-0 | 4-6 |
| Majewski, Gary | 0-0 | 0-0 | 0-0 | 0-0 | 0-0 | 0-1 | 0-0 | 0-0 | 0-0 | 0-0 | 0-0 | 0-0 | 0-0 | 0-0 | 0-0 | 0-0 | 0-1 |
| Ohka, Tomo | 0-0 | 1-0 | 0-0 | 1-0 | 0-0 | 0-3 | 0-0 | 0-0 | 0-0 | 0-2 | 0-1 | 0-0 | 0-1 | 0-0 | 1-0 | 0-0 | 3-7 |
| Patterson, John | 1-0 | 0-2 | 0-0 | 0-0 | 1-0 | 1-1 | 0-0 | 0-0 | 0-0 | 1-1 | 0-1 | 0-0 | 0-2 | 0-0 | 0-0 | 0-0 | 4-7 |
| Rauch, Jon | 0-0 | 0-0 | 0-0 | 0-0 | 0-0 | 1-0 | 1-0 | 0-0 | 0-0 | 1-0 | 0-0 | 0-0 | 0-0 | 0-0 | 0-0 | 0-0 | 3-0 |
| Tucker, T.J. | 0-0 | 1-0 | 0-0 | 0-0 | 0-0 | 0-0 | 2-0 | 0-0 | 0-1 | 1-0 | 0-0 | 0-0 | 0-0 | 0-1 | 0-0 | 0-0 | 4-2 |
| Vargas, Claudio | 1-0 | 1-0 | 0-1 | 0-1 | 1-0 | 1-1 | 1-0 | 0-0 | 0-0 | 0-0 | 0-0 | 0-0 | 0-0 | 0-0 | 0-1 | 0-1 | 5-5 |
| **Totals** | 6-0 | 4-15 | 3-3 | 2-4 | 4-2 | 8-11 | 4-2 | 3-4 | 1-5 | 9-10 | 7-12 | 4-2 | 1-6 | 1-5 | 3-3 | 7-11 | 67-95 |

No-decisions— Francis Beltran, Rigo Beltran, Roy Corcoran.

INTERLEAGUE: Luis Ayala 0-1, Jeremy Fikac 1-0, Chad Cordero 1-0 vs. White Sox; Tony Armas 0-1, Sun-Woo Kim 1-0, Zach Day 1-0 vs. Royals; Zach Day 0-1, Jeremy Fikac 0-1, Livan Hernandez 0-1 vs. Twins; Livan Hernandez 0-1, Claudio Vargas 0-1, Tony Armas 0-1 vs. Mariners; Zach Day 0-1, Scott Downs 0-1, Livan Hernandez 2-0, Tony Armas 0-1, Shawn Hill 1-0 vs. Blue Jays. Total: 7-11.

## NEW YORK—71-91

| Pitcher | Ari. W-L | Atl. W-L | Chi. W-L | Cin. W-L | Col. W-L | Fla. W-L | Hou. W-L | L.A. W-L | Mil. W-L | Mon. W-L | Phi. W-L | Pit. W-L | S.D. W-L | S.F. W-L | St.L. W-L | A.L. W-L | Totals W-L |
|---|---|---|---|---|---|---|---|---|---|---|---|---|---|---|---|---|---|
| Baldwin, James | 0-1 | 0-0 | 0-0 | 0-0 | 0-0 | 0-0 | 0-1 | 0-0 | 0-0 | 0-0 | 0-0 | 0-0 | 0-0 | 0-0 | 0-0 | 0-0 | 0-2 |
| Bell, Heath | 0-0 | 0-0 | 0-0 | 0-0 | 0-0 | 0-1 | 0-0 | 0-0 | 0-0 | 0-0 | 0-1 | 0-0 | 0-0 | 0-0 | 0-0 | 0-0 | 0-2 |
| Benson, Kris | 1-0 | 1-1 | 0-0 | 0-0 | 1-0 | 1-0 | 0-0 | 0-1 | 0-0 | 0-0 | 0-0 | 0-1 | 0-1 | 0-0 | 0-0 | 0-0 | 4-4 |
| Bottalico, Ricky | 0-0 | 0-0 | 0-0 | 0-0 | 0-0 | 0-0 | 0-0 | 0-0 | 0-0 | 0-0 | 1-1 | 0-0 | 0-0 | 0-0 | 1-0 | 1-1 | 3-2 |
| Darensbourg, Vic | 0-0 | 0-0 | 0-0 | 0-0 | 0-0 | 0-0 | 0-0 | 0-0 | 0-0 | 0-0 | 0-1 | 0-0 | 0-0 | 0-0 | 0-0 | 0-0 | 0-1 |
| Erickson, Scott | 0-0 | 0-0 | 0-0 | 0-0 | 0-0 | 0-0 | 0-0 | 0-0 | 0-0 | 0-1 | 0-0 | 0-0 | 0-0 | 0-0 | 0-0 | 0-0 | 0-1 |
| Feliciano, Pedro | 0-0 | 0-0 | 0-0 | 0-0 | 0-0 | 0-0 | 0-0 | 0-0 | 1-0 | 0-1 | 0-0 | 0-0 | 0-0 | 0-0 | 0-0 | 0-0 | 1-1 |
| Fortunato, Bartolome | 0-0 | 0-0 | 0-0 | 0-0 | 0-0 | 0-0 | 0-0 | 0-0 | 0-0 | 1-0 | 0-0 | 0-0 | 0-0 | 0-0 | 0-0 | 0-0 | 1-0 |
| Franco, John | 0-0 | 0-1 | 0-0 | 1-1 | 0-0 | 0-1 | 0-0 | 0-0 | 0-0 | 0-1 | 0-2 | 0-0 | 0-1 | 0-0 | 0-0 | 1-0 | 2-7 |
| Ginter, Matt | 0-0 | 0-0 | 0-0 | 0-0 | 1-0 | 0-0 | 0-0 | 0-0 | 0-0 | 0-0 | 0-0 | 0-0 | 0-0 | 0-1 | 0-0 | 0-2 | 1-3 |
| Glavine, Tom | 1-0 | 1-2 | 0-0 | 0-2 | 1-0 | 0-4 | 0-0 | 2-0 | 0-1 | 4-1 | 0-3 | 0-0 | 1-0 | 0-0 | 0-1 | 1-0 | 11-14 |

| Pitcher | Ari. W-L | Atl. W-L | Chi. W-L | Cin. W-L | Col. W-L | Fla. W-L | Hou. W-L | L.A. W-L | Mil. W-L | Mon. W-L | Phi. W-L | Pit. W-L | S.D. W-L | S.F. W-L | St.L. W-L | A.L. W-L | Totals W-L |
|---|---|---|---|---|---|---|---|---|---|---|---|---|---|---|---|---|---|
| Heilman, Aaron | 0-0 | 1-1 | 0-0 | 0-0 | 0-0 | 0-0 | 0-0 | 0-0 | 0-0 | 0-0 | 0-0 | 0-1 | 0-1 | 0-0 | 0-0 | 0-0 | 1-3 |
| Leiter, Al | 1-1 | 1-1 | 1-1 | 1-0 | 0-0 | 1-1 | 0-0 | 0-0 | 1-0 | 1-1 | 2-1 | 0-0 | 0-1 | 0-0 | 0-1 | 1-0 | 10-8 |
| Looper, Braden | 0-0 | 0-0 | 0-1 | 0-0 | 0-0 | 0-2 | 0-1 | 0-0 | 0-0 | 0-1 | 0-0 | 0-0 | 0-0 | 0-0 | 0-0 | 2-0 | 2-5 |
| Moreno, Orber | 0-0 | 0-0 | 0-0 | 0-0 | 0-0 | 0-0 | 0-0 | 0-0 | 0-0 | 1-0 | 1-0 | 0-1 | 0-0 | 0-0 | 0-0 | 1-0 | 3-1 |
| Parra, Jose | 0-0 | 0-0 | 0-0 | 0-0 | 0-0 | 0-0 | 0-0 | 0-0 | 0-0 | 0-0 | 1-0 | 0-0 | 0-0 | 0-0 | 0-0 | 0-0 | 1-0 |
| Seo, Jae Weong | 1-0 | 0-1 | 1-1 | 1-0 | 0-0 | 1-2 | 0-0 | 1-0 | 0-0 | 0-2 | 0-1 | 0-1 | 0-0 | 0-0 | 0-1 | 0-1 | 5-10 |
| Stanton, Mike | 0-0 | 0-1 | 0-0 | 0-0 | 1-0 | 0-1 | 0-0 | 0-1 | 0-0 | 0-0 | 0-0 | 0-0 | 0-0 | 1-0 | 0-2 | 0-1 | 2-6 |
| Trachsel, Steve | 0-1 | 3-3 | 0-0 | 0-0 | 0-0 | 0-2 | 2-0 | 0-1 | 0-0 | 1-0 | 2-1 | 0-1 | 0-1 | 1-1 | 0-0 | 3-2 | 12-13 |
| Weathers, David | 0-0 | 0-0 | 0-0 | 0-0 | 1-0 | 0-1 | 0-0 | 0-0 | 0-0 | 1-1 | 1-0 | 0-0 | 0-0 | 2-0 | 0-0 | 0-1 | 5-3 |
| Wheeler, Dan | 0-0 | 0-0 | 0-0 | 0-0 | 0-1 | 1-0 | 1-0 | 0-0 | 1-0 | 0-0 | 0-0 | 0-0 | 0-0 | 0-0 | 0-0 | 0-0 | 3-1 |
| Yates, Tyler | 0-0 | 0-1 | 0-1 | 0-0 | 0-0 | 0-0 | 0-0 | 0-0 | 0-1 | 1-0 | 0-0 | 1-0 | 0-1 | 0-0 | 0-0 | 0-0 | 2-4 |
| Zambrano, Victor | 0-0 | 0-0 | 0-0 | 0-0 | 0-0 | 0-0 | 1-0 | 0-0 | 1-0 | 0-0 | 0-0 | 0-0 | 0-0 | 0-0 | 0-0 | 0-0 | 2-0 |
| **Totals** | 4-3 | 7-12 | 2-4 | 3-3 | 5-1 | 4-15 | 4-2 | 3-3 | 4-2 | 10-9 | 8-11 | 1-5 | 1-6 | 4-2 | 1-5 | 10-8 | 71-91 |

No-decisions— Mike DeJean, Grant Roberts, Todd Zeile.

INTERLEAGUE: Steve Trachsel 1-0, Matt Ginter 0-1, Ricky Bottalico 1-0 vs. Indians; Braden Looper 2-0, Steve Trachsel 1-0 vs. Tigers; Jae Weong Seo 0-1, David Weathers 0-1, Tom Glavine 1-0 vs. Royals; Mike Stanton 0-1, Steve Trachsel 0-1, Ricky Bottalico 0-1 vs. Twins; Al Leiter 1-0, Steve Trachsel 1-1, Orber Moreno 1-0, Matt Ginter 0-1, John Franco 1-0 vs. Yankees. Total: 10-8.

## PHILADELPHIA—86-76

| Pitcher | Ari. W-L | Atl. W-L | Chi. W-L | Cin. W-L | Col. W-L | Fla. W-L | Hou. W-L | L.A. W-L | Mil. W-L | Mon. W-L | N.Y. W-L | Pit. W-L | S.D. W-L | S.F. W-L | St.L. W-L | A.L. W-L | Totals W-L |
|---|---|---|---|---|---|---|---|---|---|---|---|---|---|---|---|---|---|
| Abbott, Paul | 0-0 | 0-2 | 1-0 | 0-0 | 0-0 | 0-1 | 0-0 | 0-1 | 0-0 | 0-0 | 0-0 | 0-0 | 0-0 | 0-0 | 0-0 | 0-2 | 1-6 |
| Cormier, Rheal | 0-0 | 0-0 | 0-1 | 1-0 | 0-1 | 0-3 | 0-0 | 0-0 | 0-0 | 0-0 | 0-0 | 1-0 | 0-0 | 0-0 | 0-0 | 2-0 | 4-5 |
| Floyd, Gavin | 0-0 | 0-0 | 0-0 | 0-0 | 0-0 | 0-0 | 0-0 | 0-0 | 0-0 | 1-0 | 1-0 | 0-0 | 0-0 | 0-0 | 0-0 | 0-0 | 2-0 |
| Geary, Geoff | 0-0 | 0-0 | 0-0 | 0-0 | 0-0 | 0-0 | 0-0 | 0-0 | 1-0 | 0-0 | 0-0 | 0-0 | 0-0 | 0-0 | 0-0 | 0-0 | 1-0 |
| Hancock, Josh | 0-0 | 0-1 | 0-0 | 0-0 | 0-0 | 0-0 | 0-0 | 0-0 | 0-0 | 0-0 | 0-0 | 0-0 | 0-0 | 0-0 | 0-0 | 0-0 | 0-1 |
| Hernandez, Roberto | 0-0 | 0-0 | 0-0 | 0-0 | 0-0 | 0-0 | 0-1 | 1-0 | 0-0 | 0-0 | 2-2 | 0-0 | 0-1 | 0-0 | 0-0 | 0-1 | 3-5 |
| Jones, Todd | 0-0 | 1-0 | 0-0 | 0-0 | 0-1 | 1-0 | 0-2 | 0-0 | 0-0 | 0-0 | 1-0 | 0-0 | 0-0 | 0-0 | 0-0 | 0-0 | 3-3 |
| Lidle, Cory | 0-0 | 0-0 | 0-0 | 0-0 | 0-1 | 2-0 | 0-1 | 0-0 | 1-0 | 1-0 | 1-0 | 0-0 | 0-0 | 0-0 | 0-0 | 0-0 | 5-2 |
| Madson, Ryan | 1-0 | 2-0 | 1-0 | 1-1 | 0-0 | 0-1 | 0-0 | 0-0 | 0-0 | 0-0 | 1-0 | 0-0 | 1-0 | 0-0 | 1-0 | 1-1 | 9-3 |
| Millwood, Kevin | 0-0 | 0-2 | 1-0 | 0-0 | 0-0 | 1-2 | 0-0 | 0-0 | 0-0 | 4-0 | 1-0 | 0-1 | 0-0 | 1-0 | 1-0 | 0-1 | 9-6 |
| Milton, Eric | 1-0 | 2-2 | 0-0 | 0-0 | 1-0 | 1-1 | 0-0 | 1-0 | 1-0 | 2-1 | 0-1 | 0-1 | 1-0 | 0-0 | 1-0 | 3-0 | 14-6 |
| Myers, Brett | 1-0 | 1-0 | 0-1 | 1-0 | 1-0 | 1-1 | 0-0 | 2-0 | 0-0 | 0-3 | 1-3 | 1-0 | 1-0 | 0-1 | 0-1 | 1-1 | 11-11 |
| Padilla, Vicente | 1-1 | 0-2 | 0-0 | 0-0 | 0-0 | 0-1 | 0-0 | 1-0 | 1-0 | 0-1 | 1-0 | 1-1 | 1-0 | 1-1 | 0-0 | 0-0 | 7-7 |
| Powell, Brian | 0-0 | 0-0 | 0-0 | 0-0 | 0-0 | 0-0 | 0-0 | 0-0 | 0-0 | 0-0 | 0-0 | 0-0 | 0-0 | 0-0 | 0-0 | 1-2 | 1-2 |
| Rodriguez, Felix | 0-0 | 0-0 | 0-0 | 0-1 | 0-0 | 0-0 | 0-1 | 0-0 | 1-0 | 0-0 | 0-0 | 0-0 | 1-0 | 0-1 | 0-0 | 0-0 | 2-3 |
| Telemaco, Amaury | 0-0 | 0-0 | 0-0 | 0-0 | 0-0 | 0-0 | 0-0 | 0-0 | 0-0 | 0-0 | 0-0 | 0-0 | 0-0 | 0-0 | 0-1 | 0-1 | 0-2 |
| Wagner, Billy | 0-0 | 1-0 | 0-0 | 0-0 | 0-0 | 1-0 | 0-0 | 0-0 | 0-0 | 1-0 | 1-0 | 0-0 | 0-0 | 0-0 | 0-0 | 0-0 | 4-0 |
| Wolf, Randy | 1-0 | 0-1 | 0-1 | 0-1 | 1-0 | 0-1 | 0-1 | 0-0 | 0-0 | 2-0 | 1-1 | 0-0 | 0-0 | 0-1 | 0-1 | 0-0 | 5-8 |
| Worrell, Tim | 0-0 | 2-0 | 0-0 | 0-0 | 0-2 | 0-1 | 0-0 | 0-0 | 1-0 | 1-2 | 0-1 | 0-0 | 0-0 | 0-0 | 0-0 | 1-0 | 5-6 |
| **Totals** | 5-1 | 9-10 | 3-3 | 3-3 | 3-5 | 7-12 | 0-6 | 5-1 | 6-0 | 12-7 | 11-8 | 3-3 | 5-1 | 2-4 | 3-3 | 9-9 | 86-76 |

No-decisions— Jim Crowell, Elizardo Ramirez.

INTERLEAGUE: Rheal Cormier 1-0, Brian Powell 0-1, Eric Milton 1-0 vs. Orioles; Paul Abbott 0-1, Ryan Madson 1-0, Brett Myers 0-1 vs. Red Sox; Amaury Telemaco 0-1, Roberto Hernandez 0-1, Eric Milton 1-0 vs. White Sox; Brian Powell 0-1, Brett Myers 1-0, Ryan Madson 0-1 vs. Tigers; Paul Abbott 0-1, Eric Milton 1-0, Brian Powell 1-0 vs. Royals; Rheal Cormier 1-0, Tim Worrell 1-0, Kevin Millwood 0-1 vs. Twins. Total: 9-9.

## PITTSBURGH—72-89

| Pitcher | Ari. W-L | Atl. W-L | Chi. W-L | Cin. W-L | Col. W-L | Fla. W-L | Hou. W-L | L.A. W-L | Mil. W-L | Mon. W-L | N.Y. W-L | Phi. W-L | S.D. W-L | S.F. W-L | St.L. W-L | A.L. W-L | Totals W-L |
|---|---|---|---|---|---|---|---|---|---|---|---|---|---|---|---|---|---|
| Benson, Kris | 0-0 | 1-1 | 1-1 | 0-1 | 0-1 | 1-0 | 0-2 | 0-0 | 2-0 | 0-0 | 1-0 | 0-0 | 0-0 | 0-0 | 1-1 | 1-1 | 8-8 |
| Boehringer, Brian | 0-0 | 0-0 | 0-0 | 0-0 | 0-0 | 0-0 | 0-0 | 0-0 | 0-0 | 0-0 | 0-0 | 0-1 | 0-0 | 1-0 | 0-0 | 0-0 | 1-1 |
| Boyd, Jason | 0-0 | 0-0 | 0-0 | 0-0 | 0-0 | 0-0 | 0-0 | 0-0 | 1-0 | 0-0 | 0-0 | 0-0 | 0-0 | 0-0 | 0-0 | 0-0 | 1-0 |
| Brooks, Frank | 0-0 | 0-0 | 0-1 | 0-0 | 0-0 | 0-0 | 0-0 | 0-0 | 0-0 | 0-0 | 0-0 | 0-0 | 0-0 | 0-0 | 0-0 | 0-0 | 0-1 |
| Burnett, Sean | 0-0 | 0-0 | 0-0 | 1-0 | 0-0 | 0-0 | 0-1 | 0-1 | 1-1 | 2-0 | 0-0 | 0-0 | 0-0 | 0-0 | 1-1 | 0-1 | 5-5 |
| Corey, Mark | 0-0 | 0-0 | 0-0 | 1-0 | 0-0 | 0-1 | 0-0 | 0-0 | 0-0 | 0-0 | 0-0 | 0-0 | 0-0 | 0-0 | 0-0 | 0-1 | 1-2 |
| Figueroa, Nelson | 0-0 | 0-0 | 0-1 | 0-0 | 0-0 | 0-0 | 0-1 | 0-0 | 0-0 | 0-0 | 0-0 | 0-0 | 0-0 | 0-0 | 0-1 | 0-0 | 0-3 |
| Fogg, Josh | 1-0 | 0-0 | 1-2 | 3-1 | 1-0 | 0-0 | 0-3 | 0-1 | 3-0 | 0-1 | 0-0 | 0-0 | 0-0 | 1-0 | 0-1 | 1-1 | 11-10 |
| Gonzalez, Mike | 0-0 | 1-0 | 1-0 | 0-0 | 0-0 | 0-0 | 0-0 | 0-0 | 0-0 | 0-0 | 0-0 | 0-0 | 1-0 | 0-0 | 0-1 | 0-0 | 3-1 |
| Grabow, John | 0-1 | 0-0 | 0-1 | 1-0 | 0-0 | 0-0 | 0-0 | 0-1 | 0-0 | 0-2 | 0-0 | 0-0 | 0-0 | 1-0 | 0-0 | 0-0 | 2-5 |
| Johnston, Mike | 0-0 | 0-0 | 0-0 | 0-0 | 0-0 | 0-0 | 0-0 | 0-0 | 0-0 | 0-0 | 0-0 | 0-0 | 0-1 | 0-0 | 0-1 | 0-1 | 0-3 |
| Meadows, Brian | 0-0 | 0-0 | 0-1 | 0-0 | 0-0 | 0-0 | 0-0 | 0-0 | 1-2 | 0-0 | 1-0 | 0-0 | 0-0 | 0-0 | 0-0 | 0-1 | 2-4 |
| Mesa, Jose | 1-0 | 0-1 | 0-0 | 0-0 | 0-0 | 0-0 | 0-1 | 0-0 | 0-0 | 0-0 | 0-0 | 0-0 | 0-0 | 1-0 | 3-0 | 0-0 | 5-2 |
| Perez, Oliver | 1-0 | 0-1 | 0-2 | 4-0 | 2-0 | 1-0 | 1-1 | 0-2 | 1-0 | 0-0 | 0-0 | 1-0 | 1-1 | 0-0 | 0-2 | 0-1 | 12-10 |
| Snell, Ian | 0-0 | 0-0 | 0-0 | 0-0 | 0-0 | 0-0 | 0-0 | 0-0 | 0-0 | 0-0 | 0-0 | 0-1 | 0-0 | 0-0 | 0-0 | 0-0 | 0-1 |
| Torres, Salomon | 0-0 | 0-1 | 2-1 | 0-1 | 1-0 | 2-0 | 1-0 | 0-1 | 1-0 | 0-0 | 0-1 | 0-1 | 0-0 | 0-0 | 0-0 | 0-1 | 7-7 |
| Van Benschoten, John | 0-1 | 0-0 | 0-0 | 0-0 | 0-0 | 0-0 | 1-1 | 0-0 | 0-1 | 0-0 | 0-0 | 0-0 | 0-0 | 0-0 | 0-0 | 0-0 | 1-3 |
| Vogelsong, Ryan | 1-0 | 0-0 | 0-3 | 0-2 | 0-0 | 0-0 | 2-0 | 0-0 | 1-1 | 0-0 | 1-0 | 1-0 | 0-1 | 0-1 | 0-4 | 0-1 | 6-13 |
| Wells, Kip | 0-0 | 0-0 | 0-0 | 0-2 | 0-1 | 1-0 | 0-2 | 0-0 | 0-0 | 0-1 | 1-0 | 1-0 | 1-0 | 1-0 | 0-0 | 0-1 | 5-7 |
| Williams, Dave | 0-0 | 0-0 | 0-0 | 0-2 | 0-0 | 0-0 | 0-0 | 0-0 | 1-1 | 0-0 | 1-0 | 0-0 | 0-0 | 0-0 | 0-0 | 0-0 | 2-3 |
| **Totals** | 4-2 | 2-4 | 5-13 | 10-9 | 4-2 | 5-1 | 5-12 | 0-6 | 12-6 | 2-4 | 5-1 | 3-3 | 3-3 | 5-1 | 5-12 | 2-10 | 72-89 |

No-decisions— Abraham O. Nunez, Willis Roberts.

INTERLEAGUE: Salomon Torres 0-1, Josh Fogg 1-0, Kris Benson 1-0 vs. Angels; Kris Benson 0-1, Mark Corey 0-1, Kip Wells 0-1 vs. Athletics; Ryan Vogelsong 0-1, Sean Burnett 0-1, Oliver Perez 0-1 vs. Mariners; Mike Johnston 0-1, Brian Meadows 0-1, Josh Fogg 0-1 vs. Rangers. Total: 2-10

# SAN DIEGO—87-75

| Pitcher | Ari. W-L | Atl. W-L | Chi. W-L | Cin. W-L | Col. W-L | Fla. W-L | Hou. W-L | L.A. W-L | Mil. W-L | Mon. W-L | N.Y. W-L | Phi. W-L | Pit. W-L | S.F. W-L | St.L. W-L | A.L. W-L | Totals W-L |
|---|---|---|---|---|---|---|---|---|---|---|---|---|---|---|---|---|---|
| Beck, Rod | 0-0 | 0-0 | 0-0 | 0-0 | 0-0 | 0-0 | 0-0 | 0-1 | 0-0 | 0-0 | 0-0 | 0-0 | 0-0 | 0-0 | 0-0 | 0-1 | 0-2 |
| Bynum, Mike | 0-1 | 0-0 | 0-0 | 0-0 | 0-0 | 0-0 | 0-0 | 0-0 | 0-0 | 0-0 | 0-0 | 0-0 | 0-0 | 0-0 | 0-0 | 0-0 | 0-1 |
| Eaton, Adam | 0-1 | 0-1 | 1-1 | 1-0 | 1-4 | 0-2 | 0-0 | 4-1 | 1-0 | 0-0 | 1-0 | 0-1 | 0-0 | 0-1 | 0-1 | 2-1 | 11-14 |
| Germano, Justin | 0-0 | 0-0 | 0-0 | 0-0 | 0-1 | 0-0 | 0-0 | 0-1 | 0-0 | 0-0 | 0-0 | 1-0 | 0-0 | 0-0 | 0-0 | 0-0 | 1-2 |
| Hitchcock, Sterling | 0-0 | 0-1 | 0-1 | 0-0 | 0-0 | 0-1 | 0-0 | 0-0 | 0-0 | 0-0 | 0-0 | 0-0 | 0-0 | 0-0 | 0-0 | 0-0 | 0-3 |
| Hoffman, Trevor | 1-0 | 0-1 | 0-0 | 0-0 | 1-1 | 0-0 | 0-0 | 0-0 | 0-0 | 0-0 | 0-0 | 0-1 | 0-0 | 1-0 | 0-0 | 0-0 | 3-3 |
| Lawrence, Brian | 0-1 | 1-0 | 0-0 | 1-1 | 1-2 | 1-0 | 1-1 | 2-2 | 1-0 | 0-0 | 2-0 | 0-2 | 1-1 | 2-1 | 0-1 | 2-2 | 15-14 |
| Linebrink, Scott | 0-0 | 0-0 | 0-0 | 0-0 | 2-1 | 0-0 | 0-0 | 0-0 | 0-0 | 0-0 | 0-0 | 0-0 | 0-0 | 2-1 | 1-0 | 2-1 | 7-3 |
| Neal, Blaine | 0-1 | 0-0 | 0-0 | 0-0 | 0-0 | 0-0 | 0-0 | 0-0 | 0-0 | 0-0 | 0-0 | 0-0 | 0-0 | 1-0 | 0-0 | 0-0 | 1-1 |
| Oropesa, Eddie | 1-0 | 0-0 | 0-0 | 0-0 | 0-0 | 0-0 | 0-0 | 0-1 | 0-0 | 0-0 | 0-0 | 0-0 | 0-0 | 1-0 | 0-0 | 0-0 | 2-1 |
| Osuna, Antonio | 1-0 | 0-0 | 0-0 | 0-0 | 0-0 | 0-0 | 0-0 | 0-0 | 0-0 | 1-0 | 0-0 | 0-0 | 0-0 | 0-0 | 0-0 | 0-1 | 2-1 |
| Otsuka, Akinori | 3-0 | 0-0 | 0-0 | 0-0 | 1-0 | 1-0 | 0-0 | 1-1 | 0-0 | 1-0 | 0-0 | 0-1 | 0-0 | 0-0 | 0-0 | 0-0 | 7-2 |
| Peavy, Jake | 2-1 | 1-0 | 0-0 | 1-0 | 1-0 | 0-1 | 1-1 | 1-0 | 0-0 | 1-0 | 2-0 | 0-0 | 2-0 | 2-1 | 0-2 | 1-0 | 15-6 |
| Puffer, Brandon | 0-0 | 0-0 | 0-0 | 0-0 | 0-0 | 0-0 | 0-0 | 0-0 | 0-0 | 0-0 | 0-0 | 0-0 | 0-1 | 0-0 | 0-0 | 0-0 | 0-1 |
| Stone, Ricky | 0-0 | 0-0 | 1-0 | 0-0 | 0-0 | 0-0 | 0-0 | 0-1 | 0-0 | 0-0 | 0-0 | 0-0 | 0-0 | 0-0 | 0-0 | 0-0 | 1-1 |
| Sweeney, Brian | 1-0 | 0-0 | 0-0 | 0-0 | 0-0 | 0-0 | 0-0 | 0-0 | 0-0 | 0-0 | 0-0 | 0-0 | 0-0 | 0-0 | 0-0 | 0-0 | 1-0 |
| Tankersley, Dennis | 0-0 | 0-0 | 0-0 | 0-0 | 0-1 | 0-0 | 0-0 | 0-0 | 0-2 | 0-1 | 0-0 | 0-0 | 0-0 | 0-0 | 0-0 | 0-1 | 0-5 |
| Valdez, Ismael | 2-1 | 0-0 | 0-1 | 0-0 | 2-0 | 0-0 | 1-0 | 0-1 | 2-0 | 1-0 | 0-1 | 0-0 | 0-0 | 1-0 | 0-0 | 0-2 | 9-6 |
| Wells, David | 1-1 | 1-0 | 0-1 | 1-1 | 0-0 | 0-0 | 1-0 | 1-1 | 0-0 | 2-0 | 1-0 | 0-0 | 0-1 | 2-2 | 1-0 | 1-1 | 12-8 |
| Witasick, Jay | 0-0 | 0-0 | 0-0 | 0-0 | 0-0 | 0-0 | 0-0 | 0-0 | 0-0 | 0-0 | 0-0 | 0-0 | 0-0 | 0-1 | 0-0 | 0-0 | 0-1 |
| **Totals** | 12-7 | 3-3 | 2-4 | 4-2 | 9-10 | 2-4 | 4-2 | 9-10 | 4-2 | 6-1 | 6-1 | 1-5 | 3-3 | 12-7 | 2-4 | 8-10 | 87-75 |

No-decisions— Andy Ashby, Marty McLeary, Jason Szuminski, Steve Watkins.

INTERLEAGUE: Antonio Osuna 0-1, Brian Lawrence 1-0, Ismael Valdez 0-1 vs. Red Sox; Jake Peavy 1-0, Scott Linebrink 1-0, David Wells 1-0 vs. Royals; Adam Eaton 1-0, Dennis Tankersley 0-1, Rod Beck 0-1 vs. Yankees; Brian Lawrence 1-0, Ismael Valdez 0-1, Adam Eaton 1-0 vs. Mariners; Brian Lawrence 0-1, Scott Linebrink 0-1, Adam Eaton 0-1 vs. Devil Rays; David Wells 0-1, Scott Linebrink 1-0, Brian Lawrence 0-1 vs. Blue Jays. Total: 8-10.

# SAN FRANCISCO—91-71

| Pitcher | Ari. W-L | Atl. W-L | Chi. W-L | Cin. W-L | Col. W-L | Fla. W-L | Hou. W-L | L.A. W-L | Mil. W-L | Mon. W-L | N.Y. W-L | Phi. W-L | Pit. W-L | S.D. W-L | St.L. W-L | A.L. W-L | Totals W-L |
|---|---|---|---|---|---|---|---|---|---|---|---|---|---|---|---|---|---|
| Aardsma, David | 0-0 | 0-0 | 0-0 | 0-0 | 0-0 | 0-0 | 1-0 | 0-0 | 0-0 | 0-0 | 0-0 | 0-0 | 0-0 | 0-0 | 0-0 | 0-0 | 1-0 |
| Brower, Jim | 0-1 | 0-0 | 0-1 | 1-0 | 3-0 | 1-0 | 0-0 | 1-1 | 0-0 | 0-0 | 0-1 | 0-0 | 0-0 | 0-1 | 0-1 | 1-1 | 7-7 |
| Burba, Dave | 1-0 | 0-0 | 0-0 | 0-0 | 0-0 | 0-0 | 0-0 | 0-0 | 0-0 | 0-0 | 0-0 | 0-0 | 0-0 | 0-0 | 0-0 | 0-0 | 1-0 |
| Christiansen, Jason | 0-1 | 1-0 | 0-0 | 0-0 | 0-2 | 0-0 | 0-0 | 0-0 | 0-0 | 1-0 | 0-0 | 1-0 | 0-0 | 1-0 | 0-0 | 0-0 | 4-3 |
| Cooper, Brian | 0-0 | 0-0 | 0-0 | 0-0 | 0-0 | 0-0 | 0-0 | 0-1 | 0-1 | 0-0 | 0-0 | 0-0 | 0-0 | 0-0 | 0-0 | 0-0 | 0-2 |
| Correia, Kevin | 0-0 | 0-0 | 0-0 | 0-0 | 0-0 | 0-0 | 0-0 | 0-0 | 0-0 | 0-0 | 0-1 | 0-0 | 0-0 | 0-0 | 0-0 | 0-0 | 0-1 |
| Eyre, Scott | 1-0 | 0-0 | 0-0 | 0-1 | 0-0 | 0-0 | 0-0 | 1-0 | 0-0 | 0-0 | 0-0 | 0-0 | 0-0 | 0-0 | 0-0 | 0-1 | 2-2 |
| Franklin, Wayne | 0-0 | 0-0 | 0-0 | 0-0 | 0-0 | 0-1 | 0-0 | 0-0 | 0-0 | 2-0 | 0-0 | 0-0 | 0-0 | 0-0 | 0-0 | 0-0 | 2-1 |
| Hennessey, Brad | 0-0 | 0-0 | 0-1 | 0-0 | 0-0 | 0-0 | 0-0 | 0-0 | 1-0 | 0-1 | 0-0 | 1-0 | 0-0 | 0-0 | 0-0 | 0-0 | 2-2 |
| Herges, Matt | 0-0 | 0-0 | 1-0 | 0-0 | 0-1 | 0-0 | 0-0 | 1-1 | 0-0 | 0-0 | 0-0 | 0-0 | 0-1 | 0-1 | 0-0 | 2-1 | 4-5 |
| Hermanson, Dustin | 0-1 | 0-1 | 0-0 | 0-1 | 1-0 | 0-0 | 0-1 | 0-1 | 1-0 | 1-0 | 0-0 | 0-0 | 0-1 | 1-3 | 1-0 | 1-0 | 6-9 |
| Lowry, Noah | 1-0 | 0-0 | 1-0 | 1-0 | 0-0 | 0-0 | 1-0 | 0-0 | 0-0 | 0-0 | 1-0 | 0-0 | 0-0 | 1-0 | 0-0 | 0-0 | 6-0 |
| Rodriguez, Felix | 1-0 | 0-0 | 0-0 | 0-0 | 0-0 | 0-1 | 1-0 | 0-1 | 0-0 | 0-0 | 0-1 | 0-0 | 0-1 | 0-1 | 1-0 | 0-0 | 3-5 |
| Rueter, Kirk | 1-0 | 0-2 | 0-0 | 1-1 | 1-3 | 0-0 | 0-0 | 1-2 | 1-0 | 0-0 | 1-0 | 0-1 | 0-0 | 0-2 | 1-0 | 2-1 | 9-12 |
| Schmidt, Jason | 3-0 | 1-1 | 2-0 | 0-0 | 3-1 | 1-0 | 0-0 | 1-1 | 0-0 | 0-0 | 0-0 | 1-0 | 1-0 | 2-3 | 0-1 | 3-0 | 18-7 |
| Tomko, Brett | 3-1 | 1-0 | 0-0 | 0-0 | 1-1 | 1-0 | 1-0 | 2-2 | 1-0 | 0-0 | 0-1 | 1-0 | 0-1 | 0-1 | 0-0 | 0-0 | 11-7 |
| Walker, Tyler | 1-0 | 0-0 | 0-0 | 0-0 | 1-0 | 2-0 | 0-0 | 0-0 | 0-0 | 1-0 | 0-0 | 0-0 | 0-0 | 0-0 | 0-0 | 0-1 | 5-1 |
| Williams, Jerome | 2-1 | 0-0 | 0-0 | 0-0 | 1-0 | 0-0 | 0-1 | 2-0 | 1-0 | 0-0 | 0-0 | 0-1 | 0-1 | 2-0 | 0-1 | 2-2 | 10-7 |
| **Totals** | 14-5 | 3-4 | 4-2 | 3-3 | 11-8 | 5-2 | 4-2 | 9-10 | 5-1 | 5-1 | 2-4 | 4-2 | 1-5 | 7-12 | 3-3 | 11-7 | 91-71 |

No-decisions— Leo Estrella, Jesse Foppert, Merkin Valdez, Kevin Walker.

INTERLEAGUE: Scott Eyre 0-1, Matt Herges 1-0, Jerome Williams 1-0 vs. Orioles; Jerome Williams 0-1, Matt Herges 1-0, Jason Schmidt 1-0 vs. Red Sox; Jason Schmidt 1-0, Matt Herges 0-1, Kirk Rueter 1-0, Jim Brower 0-1, Dustin Hermanson 1-0, Jerome Williams 0-1 vs. Athletics; Jerome Williams 1-0, Tyler Walker 0-1, Kirk Rueter 0-1 vs. Devil Rays; Jason Schmidt 1-0, Kirk Rueter 1-0, Jim Brower 1-0 vs. Blue Jays. Total: 11-7.

# ST. LOUIS—105-57

| Pitcher | Ari. W-L | Atl. W-L | Chi. W-L | Cin. W-L | Col. W-L | Fla. W-L | Hou. W-L | L.A. W-L | Mil. W-L | Mon. W-L | N.Y. W-L | Phi. W-L | Pit. W-L | S.D. W-L | St.L. W-L | A.L. W-L | Totals W-L |
|---|---|---|---|---|---|---|---|---|---|---|---|---|---|---|---|---|---|
| Ankiel, Rick | 0-0 | 0-0 | 0-0 | 0-0 | 0-0 | 0-0 | 0-0 | 0-0 | 1-0 | 0-0 | 0-0 | 0-0 | 0-0 | 0-0 | 0-0 | 0-0 | 1-0 |
| Calero, Kiko | 0-0 | 0-0 | 0-0 | 1-0 | 0-0 | 0-0 | 1-0 | 0-1 | 1-0 | 0-0 | 0-0 | 0-0 | 0-0 | 0-0 | 0-0 | 0-0 | 3-1 |
| Carpenter, Chris | 1-0 | 0-0 | 4-1 | 1-1 | 0-0 | 1-0 | 0-1 | 1-0 | 0-0 | 2-0 | 0-0 | 1-0 | 2-1 | 1-0 | 1-0 | 0-1 | 15-5 |
| Eldred, Cal | 0-0 | 0-0 | 0-0 | 2-0 | 0-0 | 0-0 | 0-0 | 0-1 | 1-0 | 0-0 | 1-0 | 0-0 | 0-0 | 0-1 | 0-0 | 0-0 | 4-2 |
| Flores, Randy | 0-0 | 0-0 | 0-0 | 0-0 | 1-0 | 0-0 | 0-0 | 0-0 | 0-0 | 0-0 | 0-0 | 0-0 | 0-0 | 0-0 | 0-0 | 0-0 | 1-0 |
| Haren, Danny | 1-0 | 1-0 | 0-1 | 0-0 | 0-0 | 0-0 | 0-1 | 0-0 | 0-0 | 0-1 | 0-0 | 0-0 | 1-0 | 0-0 | 0-0 | 0-0 | 3-3 |
| Isringhausen, Jason | 1-0 | 0-0 | 1-1 | 0-0 | 0-0 | 0-0 | 2-0 | 0-0 | 0-0 | 0-0 | 0-1 | 0-0 | 0-0 | 0-0 | 0-0 | 0-0 | 4-2 |
| King, Ray | 0-0 | 0-1 | 1-0 | 2-0 | 0-0 | 0-0 | 0-0 | 1-0 | 0-0 | 0-0 | 0-0 | 0-0 | 0-0 | 0-0 | 0-1 | 1-0 | 5-2 |
| Kline, Steve | 0-0 | 0-0 | 2-0 | 0-0 | 0-0 | 0-0 | 0-0 | 0-0 | 0-1 | 0-0 | 0-0 | 0-0 | 0-1 | 0-0 | 0-0 | 0-0 | 2-2 |
| Lincoln, Mike | 1-0 | 0-0 | 0-0 | 0-0 | 0-0 | 0-0 | 0-1 | 0-0 | 1-0 | 0-0 | 0-0 | 1-1 | 0-0 | 0-0 | 0-0 | 0-0 | 3-2 |
| Marquis, Jason | 0-0 | 0-0 | 1-1 | 1-0 | 2-0 | 1-0 | 1-1 | 1-0 | 1-3 | 0-1 | 2-0 | 0-0 | 2-1 | 0-0 | 0-0 | 3-0 | 15-7 |
| Morris, Matt | 1-0 | 1-0 | 1-1 | 2-1 | 1-0 | 0-1 | 2-1 | 1-0 | 0-2 | 0-1 | 1-0 | 0-1 | 2-0 | 0-1 | 1-1 | 2-0 | 15-10 |
| Suppan, Jeff | 0-1 | 0-1 | 1-1 | 2-0 | 1-0 | 1-0 | 1-4 | 0-0 | 1-1 | 0-0 | 0-0 | 1-0 | 4-0 | 2-0 | 0-1 | 2-0 | 16-9 |
| Tavarez, Julian | 0-0 | 0-0 | 0-0 | 2-2 | 0-0 | 1-0 | 0-0 | 0-0 | 1-0 | 1-0 | 1-0 | 0-0 | 0-2 | 0-0 | 0-0 | 1-0 | 7-4 |
| Williams, Woody | 0-0 | 2-0 | 0-2 | 1-1 | 0-1 | 0-1 | 1-1 | 0-0 | 2-1 | 0-0 | 0-0 | 0-1 | 1-0 | 1-0 | 1-0 | 2-0 | 11-8 |
| **Totals** | 5-1 | 4-2 | 11-8 | 14-5 | 5-1 | 4-2 | 8-10 | 4-2 | 9-8 | 3-3 | 5-1 | 3-3 | 12-5 | 4-2 | 3-3 | 11-1 | 105-57 |

No-decisions— Carmen Cali, Cody McKay, Josh Pearce, Al Reyes, Jason Simontacchi.

INTERLEAGUE: Matt Morris 1-0, Julian Tavarez 1-0, Jason Marquis 1-0 vs. Royals; Matt Morris 1-0, Ray King 1-0, Jason Marquis 1-0 vs. Athletics; Woody Williams 1-0, Jason Marquis 1-0, Jeff Suppan 1-0 vs. Mariners; Jeff Suppan 1-0, Chris Carpenter 0-1, Woody Williams 1-0 vs. Rangers. Total: 11-1.

# HOME RUNS BY PARKS

| | At Ari. | At Atl. | At Chi. | At Cin. | At Col. | At Fla. | At Hou. | At L.A. | At Mil. | At Mon. | At N.Y. | At Phi. | At Pit. | At St.L. | At S.D. | At S.F. | At A.L. Parks | Totals 2004 | Totals 2003 | HR Allow. |
|---|---|---|---|---|---|---|---|---|---|---|---|---|---|---|---|---|---|---|---|---|
| Arizona | 78 | 4 | 2 | 2 | 7 | 6 | 3 | 8 | 3 | 0 | 4 | 2 | 1 | 0 | 5 | 5 | 5 | 135 | 152 | 197 |
| Atlanta | 6 | 92 | 7 | 4 | 1 | 6 | 1 | 3 | 5 | 16 | 4 | 13 | 2 | 2 | 6 | 3 | 7 | 178 | 235 | 154 |
| Chicago | 2 | 6 | 137 | 12 | 6 | 1 | 14 | 0 | 11 | 0 | 2 | 6 | 9 | 11 | 7 | 2 | 9 | 235 | 172 | 169 |
| Cincinnati | 2 | 1 | 19 | 92 | 7 | 9 | 8 | 1 | 11 | 4 | 5 | 4 | 9 | 8 | 2 | 4 | 8 | 194 | 182 | 236 |
| Colorado | 19 | 2 | 2 | 7 | 111 | 1 | 2 | 8 | 2 | 2 | 2 | 5 | 4 | 6 | 12 | 8 | 9 | 202 | 198 | 198 |
| Florida | 3 | 7 | 0 | 1 | 8 | 71 | 4 | 1 | 3 | 10 | 7 | 13 | 2 | 0 | 3 | 5 | 10 | 148 | 157 | 166 |
| Houston | 6 | 3 | 17 | 17 | 3 | 4 | 96 | 4 | 8 | 5 | 1 | 3 | 1 | 10 | 3 | 4 | 2 | 187 | 191 | 174 |
| Los Angeles | 14 | 2 | 2 | 7 | 14 | 4 | 4 | 100 | 2 | 5 | 4 | 5 | 5 | 1 | 10 | 12 | 12 | 203 | 124 | 178 |
| Milwaukee | 3 | 3 | 3 | 13 | 2 | 1 | 10 | 3 | 66 | 2 | 4 | 2 | 4 | 13 | 1 | 1 | 4 | 135 | 196 | 164 |
| Montreal | 3 | 7 | 2 | 4 | 3 | 15 | 4 | 4 | 3 | 69 | 9 | 16 | 0 | 3 | 1 | 1 | 7 | 151 | 144 | 191 |
| New York | 5 | 15 | 2 | 7 | 4 | 9 | 4 | 6 | 4 | 14 | 85 | 15 | 0 | 3 | 1 | 3 | 8 | 185 | 124 | 156 |
| Philadelphia | 3 | 12 | 8 | 5 | 6 | 9 | 2 | 7 | 3 | 7 | 11 | 113 | 1 | 4 | 4 | 3 | 17 | 215 | 166 | 214 |
| Pittsburgh | 5 | 1 | 5 | 7 | 5 | 2 | 5 | 1 | 7 | 2 | 2 | 3 | 78 | 5 | 2 | 6 | 6 | 142 | 163 | 149 |
| St. Louis | 10 | 7 | 21 | 19 | 4 | 3 | 14 | 5 | 8 | 3 | 3 | 1 | 10 | 93 | 2 | 3 | 8 | 214 | 196 | 169 |
| San Diego | 9 | 2 | 1 | 6 | 14 | 1 | 2 | 15 | 2 | 5 | 3 | 4 | 3 | 1 | 57 | 9 | 5 | 139 | 128 | 184 |
| San Francisco | 8 | 3 | 3 | 5 | 16 | 3 | 1 | 13 | 4 | 1 | 1 | 10 | 5 | 4 | 6 | 88 | 12 | 183 | 180 | 161 |
| A.L. clubs | 11 | 9 | 2 | 12 | 10 | 9 | 13 | 13 | 7 | 10 | 5 | 13 | 1 | 6 | 10 | 8 | .... | 139 | 150 | .... |
| **2004 Totals** | 187 | 176 | 233 | 220 | 221 | 154 | 187 | 192 | 149 | *155 | 152 | 228 | 135 | 170 | 132 | 165 | 129 | 2846 | .... | 2860 |
| **2003 Totals** | 162 | 179 | 153 | 215 | 230 | 120 | 186 | 140 | 232 | #197 | 132 | 144 | 161 | 178 | 150 | 143 | .... | .... | 2708 | .... |

* There were actually 131 home runs hit at Montreal in 2004. The total also includes 24 home runs hit by teams when Montreal played its 21 "home" games at Hiram Bithorn Stadium in San Juan, Puerto Rico.

# There were actually 122 home runs hit at Montreal in 2003. The total also includes 75 home runs hit by teams when Montreal played its 22 "home" games at Hiram Bithorn Stadium in San Juan, Puerto Rico.

## AT ARIZONA (187):

Arizona (78)—Finley 14, L. Gonzalez 10, Hillenbrand 9, Hairston 6, Sexson 6, Tracy 6, Bautista 4, Alomar 3, Brito 3, DeVore 3, McCracken 2, Olson 2, Terrero 2, Cintron 1, Estalella 1, Green 1, Hammock 1, Hill 1, Kata 1, Snyder 1, Zinter 1. Atlanta (6)—Perez 2, Furcal 1, C. Jones 1, LaRoche 1, Wright 1. Chicago (2)—Gonzalez 1, Hollandsworth 1. Cincinnati (2)—Casey 1, Jimenez 1. Colorado (19)—Castilla 5, Gonzalez 3, Burnitz 2, Johnson 2, Miles 2, Barmes 1, Greene 1, Hawpe 1, Helton 1, Walker 1. Florida (3)—Cabrera 1, Gonzalez 1, Lo Duca 1. Houston (6)—Beltran 3, Biggio 1, Everett 1, Lamb 1. Los Angeles (14)—Beltre 4, Finley 2, Lo Duca 2, Green 1, Hernandez 1, Izturis 1, Roberts 1, Ventura 1, Werth 1. Milwaukee (3)—Jenkins 2, Ginter 1. Minnesota (4)—Mientkiewicz 2, Mauer 1, Rivas 1. Montreal (3)—Schneider 2, Sledge 1. New York (5)—Cameron 1, D. Garcia 1, Matsui 1, Wigginton 1, V. Wilson 1. New York (5)—Rodriguez 2, Jeter 1, Sheffield 1, Williams 1. Philadelphia (3)—Byrd 1, Perez 1, Thome 1. Pittsburgh (5)—Bay 1, Redman 1, Ward 1, Wigginton 1, C. Wilson 1. St. Louis (10)—Rolen 3, Lankford 2, Pujols 2, Sanders 2, Anderson 1. San Diego (9)—Ojeda 3, Giles 1, Greene 1, Loretta 1, Nady 1, Nevin 1, Quintero 1. San Francisco (8)—Bonds 2, Feliz 2, Grissom 1, Pierzynski 1, Snow 1, Tucker 1. Tampa Bay (2)—Cruz Jr. 1, Martinez 1.

## AT ATLANTA (176):

Arizona (4)—L. Gonzalez 2, Finley 1, Hammock 1. Atlanta (92)—C. Jones 19, J. Drew 14, A. Jones 13, LaRoche 7, Giles 6, Marrero 6, Franco 5, Furcal 5, Estrada 4, Green 3, Wise 3, Hessman 2, Thomas 2, Garcia 1, Hampton 1, Perez 1. Boston (4)—Damon 1, Garciaparra 1, Mirabelli 1, Ortiz 1. Chicago (6)—Hollandsworth 2, Alou 1, Barrett 1, Gonzalez 1, Patterson 1. Cincinnati (1)—Valentin 1. Cleveland (2)—Blake 1, Davis 1. Colorado (2)—Burnitz 1, Piedra 1. Florida (7)—Cabrera 2, Gonzalez 2, Lowell 2, Castro 1. Houston (3)—Biggio 2, Kent 1. Kansas City (3)—Beltran 1, Berroa 1, Relaford 1. Los Angeles (2)—Cora 1, Grabowski 1. Milwaukee (3)—Jenkins 1, Magruder 1, Overbay 1. Montreal (7)—Batista 2, Wilkerson 2, Schneider 1, Sledge 1, Vidro 1. New York (15)—Cameron 3, Piazza 3, Wright 2, Diaz 1, Floyd 1, K. Garcia 1, Matsui 1, Valent 1, Wigginton 1, Williams 1. Philadelphia (12)—Thome 4, Lieberthal 3, Abreu 1, Burrell 1, Polanco 1, Rollins 1, Utley 1. Pittsburgh (1)—Redman 1. St. Louis (7)—Pujols 4, Rolen 2, Walker 1. San Diego (2)—Greene 1, Payton 1. San Francisco (3)—Bonds 3.

## AT CHICAGO (233):

Arizona (2)—Finley 2. Atlanta (7)—Thomas 2, Wise 2, Hampton 1, LaRoche 1, Marrero 1. Chicago (137)—Alou 29, Ramirez 22, Lee 18, Sosa 18, Patterson 14, Barrett 9, Walker 6, Garciaparra 3, Grudzielanek 3, Hollandsworth 3, Macias 2, Perez 2, Rusch 2, Bako 1, Dubois 1, Jackson 1, Martinez 1, Ordonez 1, Wood 1. Chicago (1)—Lee 1. Cincinnati (19)—Dunn 6, Kearns 3, Jimenez 2, Pena 2, Valentin 2, Bragg 1, Freel 1, Griffey Jr. 1, LaRue 1. Colorado (2)—Helton 1, Jennings 1. Houston (17)—Beltran 7, Bagwell 3, Berkman 3, Biggio 2, Kent 2. Los Angeles (2)—Beltre 1, Green 1. Milwaukee (3)—Hall 1, Jenkins 1, Podsednik 1. Montreal (2)—Sledge 2. New York (2)—Cameron 1, K. Garcia 1. Oakland (1)—Kotsay 1. Philadelphia (8)—Abreu 4, Burrell 2, Lieberthal 1, Rollins 1. Pittsburgh (5)—Bay 1, Cota 1, Mondesi 1, C. Wilson 1, J. Wilson 1. St. Louis (21)—Pujols 5, Rolen 5, Edmonds 4, Renteria 2, Sanders 2, Lankford 1, Mabry 1, Taguchi 1. San Diego (1)—Hernandez 1. San Francisco (3)—Feliz 1, Perez 1, Tucker 1.

## AT CINCINNATI (220):

Arizona (2)—Hairston 1, Terrero 1. Atlanta (4)—Furcal 1, Giles 1, A. Jones 1, LaRoche 1. Chicago (12)—Ramirez 3, Alou 2, Lee 2, Sosa 2, Grieve 1, Patterson 1, Zambrano 1. Cincinnati (92)—Dunn 25, Pena 13, Griffey Jr. 11, Casey 9, Jimenez 6, Larkin 5, Castro 3, Kearns 3, LaRue 3, Lopez 3, Bragg 2, Cruz 2, Valentin 2, Freel 1, Hummel 1, Larson 1, Romano 1, Vander Wal 1. Cleveland (6)—Lawton 2, Belliard 1, Blake 1, Crisp 1, V. Martinez 1. Colorado (7)—Burnitz 3, Castilla 2, Holliday 2. Florida (1)—Choi 1. Houston (17)—Berkman 6, Kent 3, Bagwell 2, Beltran 2, Lamb 2, Ausmus 1, Palmeiro 1. Los Angeles (7)—Beltre 2, Finley 1, Grabowski 1, Green 1, Hernandez 1, Ross 1. Milwaukee (13)—Branyan 3, Jenkins 3, Clark 2, Hall 2, Ginter 1, Helms 1, Overbay 1. Montreal (4)—Wilkerson 2, Batista 1, Johnson 1. New York (7)—Floyd 2, Hidalgo 1, Reyes 1, Spencer 1, Valent 1, Wigginton 1. Philadelphia (5)—Burrell 2, Abreu 1, Bell 1, Thome 1. Pittsburgh (7)—Bay 2, Castillo 2, Mackowiak 1, Simon 1, C. Wilson 1. St. Louis (19)—Edmonds 5, Pujols 4, Rolen 4, Sanders 3, Anderson 1, Renteria 1, Womack 1. San Diego (6)—Greene 2, Aurilia 1, Giles 1, Klesko 1, Ojeda 1. San Francisco (5)—Feliz 1, Grissom 1, Hammonds 1, Mohr 1, Snow 1. Texas (6)—Blalock 2, Perry 1, Soriano 1, Teixeira 1, M. Young 1.

## AT COLORADO (221):

Arizona (7)—Hillenbrand 2, Bautista 1, L. Gonzalez 1, Hairston 1, Hammock 1, Sexson 1. Atlanta (1)—Giles 1. Baltimore (3)—Newhan 1, Palmeiro 1, Roberts 1. Boston (4)—Nixon 1, Ortiz 1, Varitek 1, Youkilis 1. Chicago (6)—Lee 2, Patterson 1, Ramirez 1, Sosa 1, Walker 1. Cincinnati (7)—Dunn 2, Lopez 2, Pena 2, Vander Wal 1. Colorado (111)—Burnitz 24, Helton 21, Castilla 14, Holliday 10, Johnson 7, Clayton 6, Greene 6, Sweeney 6, Gonzalez 4, Miles 4, Wilson 3, Walker 2, Atkins 1, Hawpe 1, Pellow 1, Piedra 1. Detroit (3)—Munson 1, Thames 1, White 1. Florida (8)—Cabrera 3, Choi 2, Gonzalez 2, Lowell 1. Houston (3)—Berkman 1, Biggio 1, Palmeiro 1. Los Angeles (14)—Beltre 4, Bradley 2, Green 2, Hernandez 2, Lo Duca 1, Ross 1, Saenz 1, Werth 1. Milwaukee (2)—Moeller 1, Spivey 1. Montreal (3)—Batista 1, Rivera 1, Vidro 1. New York (4)—Cameron 1, Hidalgo 1, Valent 1, Wright 1. Philadelphia (6)—Abreu 2, Burrell 1, Ledee 1, Lieberthal 1, Utley 1. Pittsburgh (5)—C. Wilson 2, Hill 1, Redman 1, Ward 1. St. Louis (4)—Pujols 2, Cedeno 1, Mabry 1. San Diego (14)—Greene 6, Giles 2, Klesko 2, Long 1, Nady 1, Ojeda 1, Payton 1. San Francisco (16)—Bonds 4, Tucker 3, Feliz 2, Alfonzo 1, Cruz 1, Durham 1, Mohr 1, Perez 1, Pierzynski 1, Torrealba 1.

## AT FLORIDA (154):

Arizona (6)—Bautista 1, Finley 1, Hairston 1, Hillenbrand 1, Kata 1, Tracy 1. Atlanta (6)—J. Drew 2, DeRosa 1, Furcal 1, A. Jones 1, C. Jones 1. Chicago (1)—Barrett 1. Chicago (2)—Perez 1, Thomas 1. Cincinnati (9)—Casey 3, Dunn 2, Griffey Jr. 2, Larkin 1, Pena 1. Colorado (1)—Barmes 1. Florida (71)—Cabrera 14, Lowell 14, Gonzalez 13, Conine 9, Choi 8, Easley 5, Encarnacion 2, Lo Duca 2, Aguila 1, Castillo 1, Harris 1, Pierre 1. Houston (4)—Berkman 3, Ausmus 1. Los Angeles (4)—Green 2, Bradley 1, Encarnacion 1. Milwaukee (1)—Grieve 1. Montreal (15)—Batista 4, Wilkerson 2, Cabrera 1, Church 1, Everett 1, Harris 1, Johnson 1, Pascucci 1, Rivera 1, Sledge 1, Vidro 1. New York (9)—Wigginton 3, Phillips 2, Cameron 1, K. Garcia 1, Valent 1, Zeile 1. Philadelphia (9)—Rollins 2, Bell 1, Burrell 1, Lieberthal 1, Michaels 1, Polanco 1, Thome 1, Utley 1. Pittsburgh (2)—Castillo 1, C. Wilson 1. St. Louis (3)—Edmonds 1, Pujols 1, Walker 1. San Diego (1)—Hernandez 1. San Francisco (3)—Cruz 1, Durham 1, Feliz 1. Tampa Bay (2)—Crawford 1, Huff 1. Texas (5)—Barajas 2, Blalock 1, Fullmer 1, Mench 1.

## AT HOUSTON (187):

Anaheim (2)—Guerrero 1, Guillen 1. Arizona (3)—L. Gonzalez 1, Hairston 1, Hillenbrand 1. Atlanta (1)—Marrero 1. Chicago (14)—Alou 3, Grudzielanek 2, Ramirez 2, Walker 2, Garciaparra 1, Hollandsworth 1, Martinez 1, Patterson 1, Sosa 1. Cincinnati (8)—Casey 2, Castro 1, Dunn 1, Jimenez 1, Larson 1, LaRue 1, Valentin 1.

Colorado (2)—Castilla 1, Piedra 1. Florida (4)—Lowell 2, Castro 1, Conine 1. Houston (96)—Bagwell 18, Kent 14, Biggio 13, Ensberg 9, Berkman 8, Lamb 8, Beltran 7, Everett 5, Lane 4, Bruntlett 3, Ausmus 2, Hidalgo 2, Backe 1, Palmeiro 1, Vizcaino 1. Los Angeles (4)—Beltre 2, Bradley 1, Green 1. Milwaukee (10)—Podsednik 3, Clark 2, Ginter 2, Grieve 1, Jenkins 1, Overbay 1. Montreal (4)—Gonzalez 2, Batista 1, Schneider 1. New York (4)—Piazza 2, Floyd 1, Phillips 1. Philadelphia (2)—Polanco 1, Thome 1. Pittsburgh (5)—Bay 2, J. Wilson 2, Kendall 1. St. Louis (14)—Pujols 4, Rolen 3, Sanders 2, Anderson 1, Cedeno 1, Edmonds 1, Lankford 1, Walker 1. San Diego (2)—Klesko 1, Loretta 1. San Francisco (1)—Bonds 1. Texas (11)—Teixeira 3, Mench 2, Soriano 2, Blalock 1, Dellucci 1, Matthews Jr. 1, M. Young 1.

## AT LOS ANGELES (192):

Anaheim (7)—Anderson 2, Guerrero 2, Erstad 1, Guillen 1, Kennedy 1. Arizona (8)—Snyder 3, Finley 2, L. Gonzalez 1, Hammock 1, Hillenbrand 1. Atlanta (3)—J. Drew 1, Estrada 1, C. Jones 1. Baltimore (2)—J. Lopez 1, Tejada 1. Cincinnati (1)—Griffey Jr. 1. Colorado (8)—Castilla 4, Burnitz 2, Hawpe 1, Johnson 1. Florida (1)—Cabrera 1. Houston (4)—Beltran 2, Biggio 1, Everett 1. Los Angeles (100)—Beltre 23, Green 16, Werth 11, Finley 9, Bradley 8, Encarnacion 6, Lo Duca 6, Hernandez 5, Cora 4, Grabowski 3, Saenz 3, Ross 2, Izturis 1, Nomo 1, Roberts 1, Ventura 1. Milwaukee (3)—Podsednik 2, Jenkins 1. Montreal (4)—Batista 1, Cabrera 1, Rivera 1, Wilkerson 1. New York (6)—Cameron 1, K. Garcia 1, Matsui 1, Piazza 1, Spencer 1, Zeile 1. New York (4)—Matsui 2, Cairo 1, Giambi 1. Philadelphia (7)—Utley 2, Abreu 1, Byrd 1, Polanco 1, Rollins 1, Thome 1. Pittsburgh (1)—Bay 1. St. Louis (5)—Walker 2, Edmonds 1, Rolen 1, Sanders 1. San Diego (15)—Nevin 4, Giles 3, Payton 3, Hernandez 2, Burroughs 1, Klesko 1, Ojeda 1. San Francisco (13)—Durham 3, Grissom 3, Bonds 2, Cruz 1, Ellison 1, Feliz 1, Schmidt 1, Snow 1.

## AT MILWAUKEE (149):

Arizona (3)—Bautista 3. Atlanta (5)—A. Jones 2, J. Drew 1, Estrada 1, C. Jones 1. Chicago (11)—Sosa 4, Lee 3, Barrett 1, Patterson 1, Ramirez 1, Walker 1. Cincinnati (11)—Pena 3, Dunn 2, Kearns 2, LaRue 2, Freel 1, Griffey Jr. 1. Colorado (2)—Helton 1, Sweeney 1. Florida (3)—Cabrera 1, Conine 1, Gonzalez 1. Houston (8)—Berkman 3, Kent 3, Bagwell 1, Vizcaino 1. Los Angeles (2)—Bradley 1, Encarnacion 1. Milwaukee (66)—Jenkins 13, Ginter 9, Branyan 8, Overbay 6, Hall 5, Spivey 4, G. Bennett 3, Grieve 3, Helms 3, Moeller 3, Podsednik 3, Durrington 2, Clark 1, Counsell 1, Kieschnick 1, Magruder 1. Minnesota (3)—Jones 1, Mauer 1, Rivas 1. Montreal (3)—Day 1, Schneider 1, Sledge 1. New York (4)—Cameron 2, V. Wilson 1, Wright 1. Philadelphia (3)—Abreu 1, Glanville 1, Thome 1. Pittsburgh (7)—Ward 2, C. Wilson 2, Mackowiak 1, Simon 1, Wigginton 1. St. Louis (8)—Anderson 1, Edmonds 1, Luna 1, Mabry 1, Molina 1, Pujols 1, Sanders 1, Walker 1. San Diego (2)—Burroughs 1, Nevin 1. San Francisco (4)—Cruz 1, Feliz 1, Grissom 1, Snow 1. Seattle (4)—Borders 1, Cabrera 1, Spiezio 1, Winn 1.

## AT MONTREAL (155):

Atlanta (16)—A. Jones 6, J. Drew 3, Furcal 2, LaRoche 2, DeRosa 1, Marrero 1, Thomas 1. Chicago (4)—Konerko 1, Lee 1, Uribe 1, Valentin 1. Cincinnati (4)—Casey 1, Dunn 1, Griffey Jr. 1, Pena 1. Colorado (2)—Burnitz 1, Clayton 1. Florida (10)—Cabrera 5, Choi 2, Aguila 1, Conine 1, Willis 1. Houston (5)—Beltran 2, Bagwell 1, Ensberg 1, Kent 1. Los Angeles (5)—Beltre 3, Cora 1, Finley 1. Milwaukee (2)—Hall 1, Podsednik 1. Minnesota (6)—Ford 1, Hunter 1, Jones 1, LeCroy 1, Mientkiewicz 1, Rivas 1. Montreal (69)—Wilkerson 15, Batista 13, Rivera 6, Sledge 6, Vidro 6, Schneider 5, Chavez 4, Johnson 4, Gonzalez 2, Cabrera 1, Calloway 1, Cepicky 1, Diaz 1, Everett 1, Hernandez 1, Izturis 1, Rauch 1. New York (14)—Cameron 4, Hidalgo 3, Valent 2, Diaz 1, Floyd 1, Piazza 1, Williams 1, Wright 1. Philadelphia (7)—Thome 2, Abreu 1, Bell 1, Burrell 1, Lieberthal 1, Wolf 1. Pittsburgh (2)—Bay 2. St. Louis (3)—Edmonds 1, Porter 1, Pujols 1. San Diego (5)—Greene 1, Hernandez 1, Klesko 1, Nevin 1, Payton 1. San Francisco (1)—Pierzynski 1.

## AT NEW YORK (152):

Arizona (4)—Hairston 2, Baerga 1, Cintron 1. Atlanta (4)—J. Drew 2, Estrada 1, A. Jones 1. Chicago (2)—Ramirez 1, Walker 1. Cincinnati (5)—Casey 2, Dunn 1, Jimenez 1, Pena 1. Cleveland (1)—Blake 1. Colorado (2)—Johnson 1, Sweeney 1. Detroit (1)—Young 1. Florida (7)—Cabrera 2, Easley 2, Encarnacion 1, Gonzalez 1, Lowell 1. Houston (1)—Berkman 1. Los Angeles (4)—Beltre 1, Saenz 1, Ventura 1, Werth 1. Milwaukee (4)—Overbay 2, Ginter 1, Grieve 1. Montreal (9)—Wilkerson 3, Batista 1, Chavez 1, Pascucci 1, Rivera 1, Schneider 1, Vidro 1. New York (85)—Piazza 12, Cameron 11, Hidalgo 11, Wright 8, Floyd 7, Valent 5, Wigginton 5, Matsui 4, Zeile 4, K. Garcia 3, Keppinger 3, Delgado 2, Phillips 2, Spencer 2, Brazell 1, Diaz 1, D. Garcia 1, McEwing 1, Reyes 1, V. Wilson 1. New York (3)—Clark 2, Williams 1. Philadelphia (11)—Abreu 2, Bell 2, Thome 2, Burrell 1, Howard 1, Michaels 1, Polanco 1, Pratt 1. Pittsburgh (2)—Castillo 1, C. Wilson 1. St. Louis (3)—Matheny 1, Pujols 1, Rolen 1. San Diego (3)—Nevin 2, Hernandez 1. San Francisco (1)—Feliz 1.

## AT PHILADELPHIA (228):

Arizona (2)—Baerga 1, Finley 1. Atlanta (13)—Furcal 3, A. Jones 3, J. Drew 2, Thomas 2, Franco 1, C. Jones 1, Wise 1. Baltimore (4)—Tejada 2, J. Lopez 1, L. Lopez 1. Chicago (6)—Lee 2, Sosa 2, Alou 1, Ramirez 1. Cincinnati (4)—Casey 2, LaRue 2. Colorado (5)—Burnitz 1, Clayton 1, Gonzalez 1, Johnson 1, Wilson 1. Detroit (5)—Infante 1, Inge 1, Munson 1, Rodriguez 1, White 1. Florida (13)—Lowell 5, Redmond 2, Aguila 1, Cabrera 1, Conine 1, Cordero 1, Gonzalez 1, Mordecai 1. Houston (3)—Berkman 1, Biggio 1, Bruntlett 1. Kansas City (4)—Stairs 3, Santiago 1. Los Angeles (5)—Grabowski 2, Beltre 1, Izturis 1, Saenz 1. Milwaukee (2)—Jenkins 1, Overbay 1. Montreal (16)—Wilkerson 4, Batista 3, Rivera 2, Sledge 2, Vidro 2, Cabrera 1, Johnson 1, Schneider 1. New York (15)—Cameron 3, Zeile 3, Floyd 2, Phillips 2, Hidalgo 1, Valent 1, Wigginton 1, V. Wilson 1, Wright 1. Philadelphia (113)—Thome 19, Burrell 14, Abreu 13, Bell 10, Polanco 10, Lieberthal 8, Rollins 8, Utley 8, Michaels 5, Perez 4, Byrd 3, Ledee 3, Pratt 2, Wolf 2, Collier 1, Glanville 1, Howard 1, Lidle 1. Pittsburgh (3)—Wigginton 2, Bay 1. St. Louis (1)—Luna 1. San Diego (4)—Giles 2, Hernandez 1, Nevin 1. San Francisco (10)—Snow 3, Grissom 2, Bonds 1, Mohr 1, Pierzynski 1, Ransom 1, Torrealba 1.

## AT PITTSBURGH (135):

Anaheim (1)—Anderson 1. Arizona (1)—Snyder 1. Atlanta (2)—Estrada 1, C. Jones 1. Chicago (9)—Barrett 2, Patterson 2, Ramirez 2, Gonzalez 1, Lee 1, Walker 1. Cincinnati (9)—Casey 2, Dunn 1, Jimenez 1, Kearns 1, Larkin 1, LaRue 1, Lopez 1, Pena 1. Colorado (4)—Castilla 2, Gonzalez 1, Wilson 1. Florida (2)—Lowell 1, Willingham 1. Houston (1)—Biggio 1. Los Angeles (5)—Hernandez 2, Bradley 1, Green 1, Saenz 1. Milwaukee (4)—Jenkins 2, Ginter 1, Overbay 1. Philadelphia (1)—Lieberthal 1. Pittsburgh (78)—C. Wilson 16, Bay 15, Mackowiak 11, Ward 8, J. Wilson 7, Redman 5, Castillo 3, Cota 3, Kendall 2, Alvarez 1, Hill 1, Mateo 1, Mondesi 1, Nunez 1, Stynes 1, Van Benschoten 1, Wigginton 1. St. Louis (10)—Edmonds 3, Pujols 3, Sanders 2, Rolen 1, Womack 1. San Diego (3)—Giles 1, Hernandez 1, Loretta 1. San Francisco (5)—Tucker 2, Bonds 1, Durham 1, Pierzynski 1.

## AT SAN DIEGO (132):

Arizona (5)—Sexson 2, Estalella 1, Finley 1, L. Gonzalez 1. Atlanta (6)—A. Jones 2, C. Jones 2, J. Drew 1, LaRoche 1. Chicago (7)—Sosa 2, Alou 1, Barrett 1, Macias 1, Patterson 1, Ramirez 1. Cincinnati (2)—Dunn 1, Griffey Jr. 1. Colorado (12)—Castilla 3, Burnitz 2, Helton 2, Closser 1, Greene 1, Holliday 1, Sweeney 1, Wilson 1. Florida (3)—Conine 1, Pavano 1, Pierre 1. Houston (3)—Ausmus 1, Biggio 1, Vizcaino 1. Kansas City (4)—Harvey 2, Graffanino 1, Stairs 1. Los Angeles (10)—Beltre 2, Bradley 2, Encarnacion 1, Green 1, Hernandez 1, Ishii 1, Izturis 1, Ventura 1. Milwaukee (1)—Ginter 1. Montreal (1)—Fox 1. New York (1)—D. Garcia 1. Philadelphia (4)—Bell 1, Polanco 1, Rollins 1, Thome 1. Pittsburgh (2)—Cota 1, Simon 1. St. Louis (2)—Anderson 1, Taguchi 1. San Diego (57)—Nevin 12, Loretta 11, Giles 10, Hernandez 10, Greene 3, Klesko 3, Buchanan 2, Aurilia 1, Long 1, Nady 1, Ojeda 1, Quintero 1, Vazquez 1. San Francisco (6)—Durham 2, Bonds 1, Grissom 1, Mohr 1, Pierzynski 1. Tampa Bay (3)—Cruz Jr. 1, Huff 1, McGriff 1. Toronto (3)—Hudson 1, Menechino 1, Zaun 1.

## AT SAN FRANCISCO (165):

Arizona (5)—Cintron 2, Bautista 1, Terrero 1, Tracy 1. Atlanta (3)—DeRosa 1, J. Drew 1, Estrada 1. Boston (5)—Millar 1, Mirabelli 1, Nixon 1, Ortiz 1, Ramirez 1. Chicago (2)—Alou 1, Patterson 1. Cincinnati (4)—Dunn 3, Lopez 1. Colorado (8)—Castilla 2, Gonzalez 2, Burnitz 1, Greene 1, Helton 1, Johnson 1. Florida (5)—Choi 2, Castro 1, Lowell 1, Pavano 1. Houston (4)—Berkman 2, Bagwell 1, Kent 1. Los Angeles (12)—Cora 3, Bradley 2, Encarnacion 2, Beltre 1, Green 1, Hernandez 1, Ross 1, Werth 1. Milwaukee (1)—Jenkins 1. Montreal (1)—Vidro 1. New York (3)—Floyd 1, Hidalgo 1, Williams 1. Oakland (2)—Byrnes 2. Philadelphia (3)—Abreu 1, Bell 1, Michaels 1. Pittsburgh (6)—Mackowiak 3, Nunez 1, Ward 1, C. Wilson 1. St. Louis (3)—Rolen 2, Edmonds 1. San Diego (9)—Giles 2, Loretta 2, Payton 2, Long 1, Nevin 1, Ojeda 1. San Francisco (88)—Bonds 26, Feliz 11, Grissom 11, Alfonzo 8, Durham 8, Snow 5, Tucker 4, Mohr 3, Pierzynski 3, Torrealba 3, Cruz 2, Hammonds 2, Dallimore 1, Schmidt 1. Toronto (1)—Gomez 1.

## AT ST. LOUIS (170):

Atlanta (2)—J. Drew 2. Chicago (11)—Lee 3, Sosa 3, Walker 2, Alou 1, Barrett 1, Ramirez 1. Cincinnati (8)—LaRue 2, Bragg 1, Casey 1, Castro 1, Griffey Jr. 1, Larson 1, Pena 1. Colorado (6)—Helton 3, Castilla 2, Pellow 1. Houston (10)—Berkman 2, Hidalgo 2, Kent 2, Lamb 2, Bagwell 1, Everett 1. Los Angeles (1)—Beltre 1. Milwaukee (13)—Ginter 3, Clark 2, Overbay 2, Podsednik 2, Counsell 1, Grieve 1, Moeller 1, Spivey 1. Montreal (3)—Batista 2, Wilkerson 1. New York (3)—Cameron 1, Floyd 1, Hidalgo 1. Oakland (4)—Dye 1, Hatteberg 1, Kotsay 1, Miller 1. Philadelphia (4)—Abreu 1, Ledee 1, Lieberthal 1, Thome 1. Pittsburgh (5)—Bay 1, Castillo 1, Mackowiak 1, Ward 1, C. Wilson 1. St. Louis (93)—Edmonds 24, Pujols 18, Rolen 10, Sanders 8, Mabry 7, Renteria 7, Walker 5, Matheny 4, Womack 3, Anderson 2, Lankford 2, Luna 1, Molina 1, Taguchi 1. San Diego (1)—Giles 1. San Francisco (4)—Alfonzo 1, Bonds 1, Durham 1, Grissom 1. Seattle (2)—Boone 1, Olerud 1.

# PARK DATA (SELECTED BATTING CATEGORIES AT EACH STADIUM)

This section contains selected batting statistics for all National League parks for 2004. A key component of this section is an index number for each category, which is used to determine how a given park influences a particular statistic. To illustrate, see the indexes for runs and extra-base hits at Arizona's Bank One Ballpark, where the elevation ranks second only to Colorado's Coors Field and aids N.L. hitters. While Arizona and Milwaukee tied for the league's lowest home-run total in 2004, only five N.L. parks allowed more homers than BOB.

For each N.L. park, we show how the home team and its opponents performed, both at home and on the road, with the exception being that we do not include data from interleague games. The differences in interleague opponents and ballparks would skew the data.

By comparing the per-game averages at the home park and on the road, we can evaluate the park's impact. This is done by simply dividing the home average by the road average and multiplying the result by 100, generating a park index. If the home and road per-game averages are equal, the index equals 100, and it can be concluded that the park had no impact. An index above 100 means that the park favors that particular statistic. The indexes for at-bats, runs, hits, errors and infield errors are determined on a per-game basis; all other stats are calculated on a per-at-bat basis. "E-infield" denotes infield *fielding* errors. "Alt." is the approximate elevation of the ballpark.

For most parks, data is presented both for 2004 and for the last three years overall. If the park's dimensions have changed over that time, however, the data from the old and new configurations will not be combined. Following all the teams' charts is a ranking section that shows which parks most inflate runs, home runs and batting average.

## ARIZONA

**Home park:** Bank One Ballpark **Alt.:** 1,090 feet **Surface:** Grass

| | 2004 Season | | | | | | | 2002-04 Seasons | | | | | | |
|---|---|---|---|---|---|---|---|---|---|---|---|---|---|---|
| | Home Games | | | Road Games | | | | Home Games | | | Road Games | | | |
| Category | Ari. | Opp. | Total | Ari. | Opp. | Total | Index | Ari. | Opp. | Total | Ari. | Opp. | Total | Index |
| G | 72 | 72 | 144 | 72 | 72 | 144 | | 219 | 219 | 438 | 216 | 216 | 432 | |
| Avg | .265 | .261 | .263 | .241 | .272 | .256 | 103 | .274 | .254 | .264 | .245 | .254 | .250 | 106 |
| AB | 2436 | 2537 | 4973 | 2492 | 2405 | 4897 | 102 | 7370 | 7694 | 15064 | 7491 | 7149 | 14640 | 101 |
| R | 303 | 396 | 699 | 241 | 407 | 648 | 108 | 1083 | 1058 | 2141 | 824 | 971 | 1795 | 118 |
| H | 645 | 663 | 1308 | 601 | 653 | 1254 | 104 | 2020 | 1954 | 3974 | 1838 | 1819 | 3657 | 107 |
| 2B | 140 | 139 | 279 | 121 | 122 | 243 | 113 | 421 | 410 | 831 | 350 | 323 | 673 | 120 |
| 3B | 16 | 17 | 33 | 15 | 16 | 31 | 105 | 68 | 54 | 122 | 45 | 31 | 76 | 156 |
| HR | 72 | 98 | 170 | 52 | 77 | 129 | 130 | 224 | 250 | 474 | 191 | 213 | 404 | 114 |
| BB | 206 | 302 | 508 | 195 | 303 | 498 | 100 | 813 | 738 | 1551 | 667 | 721 | 1388 | 109 |
| SO | 420 | 551 | 971 | 496 | 489 | 985 | 97 | 1300 | 1779 | 3079 | 1461 | 1608 | 3069 | 98 |
| E | 56 | 39 | 95 | 64 | 29 | 93 | 102 | 143 | 125 | 268 | 153 | 132 | 285 | 93 |
| E-Infield | 48 | 33 | 81 | 53 | 21 | 74 | 109 | 120 | 107 | 227 | 128 | 108 | 236 | 95 |
| LHB-Avg | .286 | .265 | .276 | .244 | .306 | .272 | 101 | .284 | .273 | .279 | .254 | .270 | .261 | 107 |
| LHB-HR | 41 | 39 | 80 | 20 | 32 | 52 | 150 | 118 | 102 | 220 | 101 | 89 | 190 | 114 |
| RHB-Avg | .248 | .259 | .254 | .239 | .250 | .245 | 104 | .263 | .243 | .252 | .236 | .245 | .241 | 104 |
| RHB-HR | 31 | 59 | 90 | 32 | 45 | 77 | 116 | 106 | 148 | 254 | 90 | 124 | 214 | 114 |

## ATLANTA

**Home park:** Turner Field **Alt.:** 1,050 feet **Surface:** Grass

| | 2004 Season | | | | | | | 2002-04 Seasons | | | | | | |
|---|---|---|---|---|---|---|---|---|---|---|---|---|---|---|
| | Home Games | | | Road Games | | | | Home Games | | | Road Games | | | |
| Category | Atl. | Opp. | Total | Atl. | Opp. | Total | Index | Atl. | Opp. | Total | Atl. | Opp. | Total | Index |
| G | 72 | 72 | 144 | 69 | 69 | 138 | | 219 | 219 | 438 | 209 | 209 | 418 | |
| Avg | .268 | .258 | .263 | .273 | .264 | .269 | 98 | .272 | .250 | .261 | .270 | .260 | .265 | 98 |
| AB | 2418 | 2507 | 4925 | 2426 | 2299 | 4725 | 100 | 7309 | 7573 | 14882 | 7439 | 7006 | 14445 | 98 |
| R | 361 | 291 | 652 | 340 | 277 | 617 | 101 | 1074 | 888 | 1962 | 1044 | 871 | 1915 | 98 |
| H | 648 | 647 | 1295 | 663 | 607 | 1270 | 98 | 1988 | 1893 | 3881 | 2011 | 1819 | 3830 | 97 |
| 2B | 125 | 106 | 231 | 131 | 98 | 229 | 97 | 381 | 347 | 728 | 406 | 343 | 749 | 94 |
| 3B | 17 | 5 | 22 | 18 | 11 | 29 | 73 | 45 | 28 | 73 | 41 | 37 | 78 | 91 |
| HR | 81 | 75 | 156 | 72 | 59 | 131 | 114 | 256 | 197 | 453 | 244 | 186 | 430 | 102 |
| BB | 273 | 236 | 509 | 253 | 223 | 476 | 103 | 770 | 736 | 1506 | 729 | 722 | 1451 | 101 |
| SO | 529 | 498 | 1027 | 480 | 395 | 875 | 113 | 1375 | 1391 | 2766 | 1397 | 1296 | 2693 | 100 |
| E | 52 | 39 | 91 | 46 | 44 | 90 | 97 | 162 | 145 | 307 | 149 | 135 | 284 | 103 |
| E-Infield | 49 | 29 | 78 | 44 | 38 | 82 | 91 | 141 | 116 | 257 | 135 | 110 | 245 | 100 |
| LHB-Avg | .270 | .272 | .271 | .292 | .270 | .282 | 96 | .276 | .257 | .266 | .276 | .252 | .265 | 100 |
| LHB-HR | 40 | 34 | 74 | 37 | 22 | 59 | 118 | 87 | 69 | 156 | 69 | 63 | 132 | 113 |
| RHB-Avg | .267 | .247 | .257 | .258 | .260 | .259 | 99 | .270 | .246 | .258 | .267 | .264 | .265 | 97 |
| RHB-HR | 41 | 41 | 82 | 35 | 37 | 72 | 111 | 169 | 128 | 297 | 175 | 123 | 298 | 98 |

## CHICAGO

**Home park:** Wrigley Field  **Alt.:** 595 feet  **Surface:** Grass

| | 2004 Season | | | | | | | 2002-04 Seasons | | | | | | |
|---|---|---|---|---|---|---|---|---|---|---|---|---|---|---|
| | Home Games | | | Road Games | | | | Home Games | | | Road Games | | | |
| **Category** | **Chi.** | **Opp.** | **Total** | **Chi.** | **Opp.** | **Total** | **Index** | **Chi.** | **Opp.** | **Total** | **Chi.** | **Opp.** | **Total** | **Index** |
| G | 76 | 76 | 152 | 74 | 74 | 148 | | 223 | 223 | 446 | 218 | 218 | 436 | |
| Avg | .273 | .250 | .261 | .263 | .243 | .253 | 103 | .255 | .243 | .249 | .259 | .250 | .254 | 98 |
| AB | 2622 | 2671 | 5293 | 2597 | 2440 | 5037 | 102 | 7481 | 7703 | 15184 | 7620 | 7174 | 14794 | 100 |
| R | 404 | 339 | 743 | 331 | 281 | 612 | 118 | 1015 | 986 | 2001 | 1000 | 924 | 1924 | 102 |
| H | 715 | 668 | 1383 | 682 | 593 | 1275 | 106 | 1908 | 1872 | 3780 | 1971 | 1790 | 3761 | 98 |
| 2B | 138 | 121 | 259 | 151 | 107 | 258 | 96 | 371 | 352 | 723 | 416 | 341 | 757 | 93 |
| 3B | 12 | 14 | 26 | 13 | 14 | 27 | 92 | 33 | 33 | 66 | 40 | 41 | 81 | 79 |
| HR | 131 | 94 | 225 | 89 | 66 | 155 | 138 | 298 | 247 | 545 | 257 | 186 | 443 | 120 |
| BB | 234 | 255 | 489 | 220 | 257 | 477 | 98 | 761 | 803 | 1564 | 677 | 787 | 1464 | 104 |
| SO | 469 | 632 | 1101 | 537 | 604 | 1141 | 92 | 1609 | 1976 | 3585 | 1606 | 1730 | 3336 | 105 |
| E | 43 | 63 | 106 | 37 | 45 | 82 | 126 | 152 | 157 | 309 | 134 | 143 | 277 | 109 |
| E-Infield | 36 | 49 | 85 | 32 | 35 | 67 | 124 | 128 | 124 | 252 | 113 | 118 | 231 | 107 |
| LHB-Avg | .270 | .249 | .258 | .255 | .273 | .265 | 97 | .247 | .245 | .246 | .255 | .265 | .260 | 95 |
| LHB-HR | 27 | 49 | 76 | 22 | 41 | 63 | 113 | 79 | 107 | 186 | 87 | 98 | 185 | 98 |
| RHB-Avg | .274 | .251 | .263 | .266 | .221 | .246 | 107 | .259 | .241 | .251 | .261 | .239 | .251 | 100 |
| RHB-HR | 104 | 45 | 149 | 67 | 25 | 92 | 155 | 219 | 140 | 359 | 170 | 88 | 258 | 135 |

## CINCINNATI

**Home park:** Great American Ball Park  **Alt.:** 550 feet  **Surface:** Grass

| | 2004 Season | | | | | | | 2003-04 Seasons | | | | | | |
|---|---|---|---|---|---|---|---|---|---|---|---|---|---|---|
| | Home Games | | | Road Games | | | | Home Games | | | Road Games | | | |
| **Category** | **Cin.** | **Opp.** | **Total** | **Cin.** | **Opp.** | **Total** | **Index** | **Cin.** | **Opp.** | **Total** | **Cin.** | **Opp.** | **Total** | **Index** |
| G | 75 | 75 | 150 | 75 | 75 | 150 | | 150 | 150 | 300 | 147 | 147 | 294 | |
| Avg | .238 | .264 | .251 | .257 | .291 | .274 | 92 | .243 | .268 | .256 | .250 | .290 | .270 | 95 |
| AB | 2448 | 2658 | 5106 | 2646 | 2590 | 5236 | 98 | 4953 | 5333 | 10286 | 5150 | 5071 | 10221 | 99 |
| R | 308 | 393 | 701 | 379 | 418 | 797 | 88 | 630 | 798 | 1428 | 690 | 821 | 1511 | 93 |
| H | 582 | 702 | 1284 | 681 | 754 | 1435 | 89 | 1204 | 1427 | 2631 | 1288 | 1470 | 2758 | 93 |
| 2B | 119 | 160 | 279 | 142 | 174 | 316 | 91 | 236 | 314 | 550 | 247 | 325 | 572 | 96 |
| 3B | 11 | 9 | 20 | 17 | 22 | 39 | 53 | 16 | 15 | 31 | 32 | 49 | 81 | 38 |
| HR | 88 | 116 | 204 | 94 | 97 | 191 | 110 | 176 | 226 | 402 | 163 | 181 | 344 | 116 |
| BB | 259 | 246 | 505 | 283 | 271 | 554 | 93 | 500 | 501 | 1001 | 523 | 543 | 1066 | 93 |
| SO | 586 | 491 | 1077 | 656 | 431 | 1087 | 102 | 1172 | 940 | 2112 | 1268 | 817 | 2085 | 101 |
| E | 49 | 36 | 85 | 55 | 41 | 96 | 89 | 121 | 88 | 209 | 112 | 90 | 202 | 101 |
| E-Infield | 38 | 31 | 69 | 45 | 30 | 75 | 92 | 97 | 78 | 175 | 92 | 75 | 167 | 103 |
| LHB-Avg | .258 | .256 | .257 | .275 | .291 | .282 | 91 | .256 | .260 | .258 | .263 | .287 | .274 | 94 |
| LHB-HR | 58 | 47 | 105 | 57 | 41 | 98 | 111 | 97 | 86 | 183 | 89 | 76 | 165 | 113 |
| RHB-Avg | .220 | .270 | .248 | .241 | .291 | .268 | 92 | .233 | .272 | .254 | .240 | .292 | .267 | 95 |
| RHB-HR | 30 | 69 | 99 | 37 | 56 | 93 | 108 | 79 | 140 | 219 | 74 | 105 | 179 | 120 |

## COLORADO

**Home park:** Coors Field  **Alt.:** 5,280 feet  **Surface:** Grass

| | 2004 Season | | | | | | | 2002-04 Seasons | | | | | | |
|---|---|---|---|---|---|---|---|---|---|---|---|---|---|---|
| | Home Games | | | Road Games | | | | Home Games | | | Road Games | | | |
| **Category** | **Col.** | **Opp.** | **Total** | **Col.** | **Opp.** | **Total** | **Index** | **Col.** | **Opp.** | **Total** | **Col.** | **Opp.** | **Total** | **Index** |
| G | 72 | 72 | 144 | 72 | 72 | 144 | | 216 | 216 | 432 | 219 | 219 | 438 | |
| Avg | .302 | .307 | .304 | .245 | .267 | .256 | 119 | .302 | .291 | .296 | .239 | .275 | .256 | 116 |
| AB | 2490 | 2611 | 5101 | 2460 | 2367 | 4827 | 106 | 7382 | 7754 | 15136 | 7465 | 7257 | 14722 | 104 |
| R | 435 | 477 | 912 | 295 | 334 | 629 | 145 | 1328 | 1293 | 2621 | 859 | 1100 | 1959 | 136 |
| H | 751 | 801 | 1552 | 602 | 633 | 1235 | 126 | 2228 | 2259 | 4487 | 1782 | 1994 | 3776 | 120 |
| 2B | 166 | 163 | 329 | 127 | 127 | 254 | 123 | 476 | 447 | 923 | 372 | 398 | 770 | 117 |
| 3B | 18 | 20 | 38 | 12 | 13 | 25 | 144 | 67 | 58 | 125 | 29 | 43 | 72 | 169 |
| HR | 106 | 100 | 206 | 82 | 77 | 159 | 123 | 287 | 324 | 611 | 207 | 234 | 441 | 135 |
| BB | 272 | 329 | 601 | 229 | 285 | 514 | 111 | 795 | 790 | 1585 | 710 | 840 | 1550 | 99 |
| SO | 467 | 425 | 892 | 576 | 421 | 997 | 85 | 1309 | 1265 | 2574 | 1725 | 1162 | 2887 | 87 |
| E | 44 | 66 | 110 | 31 | 31 | 62 | 177 | 141 | 171 | 312 | 132 | 124 | 256 | 124 |
| E-Infield | 29 | 52 | 81 | 24 | 25 | 49 | 165 | 110 | 132 | 242 | 110 | 103 | 213 | 115 |
| LHB-Avg | .319 | .307 | .313 | .261 | .265 | .263 | 119 | .328 | .298 | .312 | .259 | .289 | .274 | 114 |
| LHB-HR | 56 | 39 | 95 | 33 | 28 | 61 | 144 | 127 | 131 | 258 | 85 | 85 | 170 | 147 |
| RHB-Avg | .289 | .306 | .298 | .233 | .269 | .252 | 119 | .286 | .287 | .287 | .227 | .266 | .246 | 117 |
| RHB-HR | 50 | 61 | 111 | 49 | 49 | 98 | 109 | 160 | 193 | 353 | 122 | 149 | 271 | 127 |

## FLORIDA

**Home park:** Pro Player Stadium **Alt.:** 10 feet **Surface:** Grass

| | 2004 Season | | | | | | | 2002-04 Seasons | | | | | | |
|---|---|---|---|---|---|---|---|---|---|---|---|---|---|---|
| | Home Games | | | Road Games | | | | Home Games | | | Road Games | | | |
| **Category** | **Fla.** | **Opp.** | **Total** | **Fla.** | **Opp.** | **Total** | **Index** | **Fla.** | **Opp.** | **Total** | **Fla.** | **Opp.** | **Total** | **Index** |
| G | 69 | 69 | 138 | 72 | 72 | 144 | | 213 | 213 | 426 | 216 | 216 | 432 | |
| Avg | .264 | .246 | .255 | .267 | .269 | .268 | 95 | .269 | .247 | .258 | .259 | .270 | .265 | 97 |
| AB | 2253 | 2364 | 4617 | 2507 | 2386 | 4893 | 98 | 7054 | 7387 | 14441 | 7474 | 7157 | 14631 | 100 |
| R | 293 | 279 | 572 | 339 | 339 | 678 | 88 | 975 | 865 | 1840 | 925 | 1038 | 1963 | 95 |
| H | 594 | 582 | 1176 | 669 | 643 | 1312 | 94 | 1897 | 1825 | 3722 | 1937 | 1935 | 3872 | 97 |
| 2B | 122 | 108 | 230 | 121 | 137 | 258 | 94 | 365 | 363 | 728 | 383 | 412 | 795 | 93 |
| 3B | 13 | 15 | 28 | 14 | 17 | 31 | 96 | 58 | 56 | 114 | 38 | 43 | 81 | 143 |
| HR | 58 | 72 | 130 | 64 | 79 | 143 | 96 | 185 | 175 | 360 | 205 | 226 | 431 | 85 |
| BB | 214 | 239 | 453 | 220 | 212 | 432 | 111 | 748 | 767 | 1515 | 665 | 726 | 1391 | 110 |
| SO | 408 | 522 | 930 | 447 | 434 | 881 | 112 | 1330 | 1649 | 2979 | 1415 | 1322 | 2737 | 110 |
| E | 28 | 53 | 81 | 48 | 55 | 103 | 82 | 104 | 146 | 250 | 138 | 167 | 305 | 83 |
| E-Infield | 23 | 43 | 66 | 37 | 42 | 79 | 87 | 82 | 119 | 201 | 117 | 141 | 258 | 79 |
| LHB-Avg | .280 | .252 | .263 | .293 | .269 | .279 | 94 | .282 | .246 | .261 | .270 | .280 | .276 | 95 |
| LHB-HR | 9 | 35 | 44 | 6 | 33 | 39 | 108 | 24 | 71 | 95 | 21 | 89 | 110 | 82 |
| RHB-Avg | .257 | .242 | .250 | .257 | .270 | .263 | 95 | .264 | .248 | .256 | .255 | .264 | .259 | 99 |
| RHB-HR | 49 | 37 | 86 | 58 | 46 | 104 | 92 | 161 | 104 | 265 | 184 | 137 | 321 | 86 |

## HOUSTON

**Home park:** Minute Maid Park **Alt.:** 22 feet **Surface:** Grass

| | 2004 Season | | | | | | | 2002-04 Seasons | | | | | | |
|---|---|---|---|---|---|---|---|---|---|---|---|---|---|---|
| | Home Games | | | Road Games | | | | Home Games | | | Road Games | | | |
| **Category** | **Hou.** | **Opp.** | **Total** | **Hou.** | **Opp.** | **Total** | **Index** | **Hou.** | **Opp.** | **Total** | **Hou.** | **Opp.** | **Total** | **Index** |
| G | 75 | 75 | 150 | 75 | 75 | 150 | | 222 | 222 | 444 | 222 | 222 | 444 | |
| Avg | .278 | .246 | .262 | .262 | .267 | .264 | 99 | .276 | .249 | .262 | .251 | .260 | .255 | 103 |
| AB | 2474 | 2564 | 5038 | 2602 | 2522 | 5124 | 98 | 7386 | 7592 | 14978 | 7720 | 7368 | 15088 | 99 |
| R | 373 | 309 | 682 | 385 | 335 | 720 | 95 | 1118 | 922 | 2040 | 1034 | 948 | 1982 | 103 |
| H | 687 | 631 | 1318 | 681 | 674 | 1355 | 97 | 2039 | 1889 | 3928 | 1936 | 1918 | 3854 | 102 |
| 2B | 128 | 123 | 251 | 146 | 140 | 286 | 89 | 401 | 369 | 770 | 415 | 406 | 821 | 94 |
| 3B | 21 | 19 | 40 | 14 | 12 | 26 | 156 | 57 | 47 | 104 | 33 | 41 | 74 | 142 |
| HR | 90 | 78 | 168 | 89 | 79 | 168 | 102 | 255 | 217 | 472 | 244 | 217 | 461 | 103 |
| BB | 272 | 214 | 486 | 272 | 271 | 543 | 91 | 812 | 654 | 1466 | 773 | 819 | 1592 | 93 |
| SO | 430 | 643 | 1073 | 498 | 550 | 1048 | 104 | 1335 | 1725 | 3060 | 1540 | 1589 | 3129 | 99 |
| E | 47 | 50 | 97 | 47 | 42 | 89 | 109 | 128 | 144 | 272 | 124 | 139 | 263 | 103 |
| E-Infield | 39 | 40 | 79 | 37 | 36 | 73 | 108 | 110 | 115 | 225 | 100 | 118 | 218 | 103 |
| LHB-Avg | .284 | .258 | .266 | .288 | .286 | .287 | 93 | .283 | .261 | .269 | .264 | .276 | .271 | 99 |
| LHB-HR | 19 | 29 | 48 | 43 | 38 | 81 | 60 | 77 | 75 | 152 | 85 | 96 | 181 | 84 |
| RHB-Avg | .276 | .236 | .259 | .252 | .253 | .252 | 103 | .273 | .240 | .258 | .245 | .250 | .247 | 105 |
| RHB-HR | 71 | 49 | 120 | 46 | 41 | 87 | 141 | 178 | 142 | 320 | 159 | 121 | 280 | 116 |

## LOS ANGELES

**Home park:** Dodger Stadium **Alt.:** 340 feet **Surface:** Grass

| | 2004 Season | | | | | | | 2002-04 Seasons | | | | | | |
|---|---|---|---|---|---|---|---|---|---|---|---|---|---|---|
| | Home Games | | | Road Games | | | | Home Games | | | Road Games | | | |
| **Category** | **L.A.** | **Opp.** | **Total** | **L.A.** | **Opp.** | **Total** | **Index** | **L.A.** | **Opp.** | **Total** | **L.A.** | **Opp.** | **Total** | **Index** |
| G | 72 | 72 | 144 | 72 | 72 | 144 | | 216 | 216 | 432 | 216 | 216 | 432 | |
| Avg | .259 | .246 | .252 | .265 | .263 | .264 | 95 | .250 | .234 | .242 | .266 | .253 | .260 | 93 |
| AB | 2393 | 2467 | 4860 | 2551 | 2391 | 4942 | 98 | 7081 | 7303 | 14384 | 7699 | 7134 | 14833 | 97 |
| R | 320 | 280 | 600 | 358 | 322 | 680 | 88 | 833 | 767 | 1600 | 1000 | 903 | 1903 | 84 |
| H | 619 | 607 | 1226 | 677 | 630 | 1307 | 94 | 1772 | 1707 | 3479 | 2045 | 1805 | 3850 | 90 |
| 2B | 88 | 95 | 183 | 113 | 132 | 245 | 76 | 305 | 267 | 572 | 386 | 370 | 756 | 78 |
| 3B | 10 | 8 | 18 | 19 | 15 | 34 | 54 | 29 | 15 | 44 | 48 | 50 | 98 | 46 |
| HR | 90 | 79 | 169 | 91 | 79 | 170 | 101 | 209 | 216 | 425 | 222 | 196 | 418 | 105 |
| BB | 226 | 213 | 439 | 260 | 258 | 518 | 86 | 598 | 694 | 1292 | 648 | 768 | 1416 | 94 |
| SO | 467 | 498 | 965 | 513 | 461 | 974 | 101 | 1292 | 1635 | 2927 | 1411 | 1483 | 2894 | 104 |
| E | 36 | 45 | 81 | 33 | 53 | 86 | 94 | 137 | 148 | 285 | 117 | 161 | 278 | 103 |
| E-Infield | 27 | 37 | 64 | 21 | 44 | 65 | 98 | 111 | 130 | 241 | 89 | 126 | 215 | 112 |
| LHB-Avg | .248 | .278 | .261 | .251 | .272 | .259 | 101 | .246 | .240 | .243 | .253 | .254 | .254 | 96 |
| LHB-HR | 39 | 33 | 72 | 39 | 32 | 71 | 98 | 84 | 73 | 157 | 94 | 70 | 164 | 98 |
| RHB-Avg | .271 | .224 | .244 | .281 | .259 | .269 | 91 | .254 | .230 | .241 | .277 | .252 | .264 | 91 |
| RHB-HR | 51 | 46 | 97 | 52 | 47 | 99 | 104 | 125 | 143 | 268 | 128 | 126 | 254 | 110 |

## MILWAUKEE

**Home park:** Miller Park **Alt.:** 635 feet **Surface:** Grass

| | 2004 Season | | | | | | | 2002-04 Seasons | | | | | | |
|---|---|---|---|---|---|---|---|---|---|---|---|---|---|---|
| | Home Games | | | Road Games | | | | Home Games | | | Road Games | | | |
| Category | Mil. | Opp. | Total | Mil. | Opp. | Total | Index | Mil. | Opp. | Total | Mil. | Opp. | Total | Index |
| G | 75 | 75 | 150 | 71 | 71 | 142 | | 225 | 225 | 450 | 221 | 221 | 442 | |
| Avg | .247 | .253 | .250 | .243 | .271 | .257 | 97 | .251 | .260 | .256 | .249 | .278 | .263 | 97 |
| AB | 2541 | 2672 | 5213 | 2409 | 2380 | 4789 | 103 | 7489 | 7992 | 15481 | 7574 | 7399 | 14973 | 102 |
| R | 315 | 358 | 673 | 251 | 355 | 606 | 105 | 910 | 1138 | 2048 | 885 | 1130 | 2015 | 100 |
| H | 627 | 675 | 1302 | 585 | 645 | 1230 | 100 | 1876 | 2080 | 3956 | 1885 | 2055 | 3940 | 99 |
| 2B | 152 | 163 | 315 | 117 | 137 | 254 | 114 | 394 | 448 | 842 | 369 | 405 | 774 | 105 |
| 3B | 17 | 17 | 34 | 13 | 14 | 27 | 116 | 37 | 51 | 88 | 40 | 47 | 87 | 98 |
| HR | 59 | 76 | 135 | 63 | 78 | 141 | 88 | 217 | 281 | 498 | 216 | 253 | 469 | 103 |
| BB | 284 | 223 | 507 | 209 | 215 | 424 | 110 | 786 | 789 | 1575 | 704 | 809 | 1513 | 101 |
| SO | 627 | 557 | 1184 | 555 | 453 | 1008 | 108 | 1657 | 1573 | 3230 | 1688 | 1345 | 3033 | 103 |
| E | 51 | 63 | 114 | 58 | 46 | 104 | 104 | 155 | 141 | 296 | 160 | 150 | 310 | 94 |
| E-Infield | 47 | 55 | 102 | 48 | 37 | 85 | 114 | 140 | 123 | 263 | 133 | 125 | 258 | 100 |
| LHB-Avg | .261 | .246 | .254 | .250 | .279 | .262 | 97 | .263 | .265 | .264 | .255 | .274 | .264 | 100 |
| LHB-HR | 32 | 27 | 59 | 38 | 27 | 65 | 84 | 82 | 115 | 197 | 83 | 92 | 175 | 106 |
| RHB-Avg | .231 | .257 | .246 | .234 | .266 | .253 | 97 | .242 | .257 | .250 | .244 | .280 | .263 | 95 |
| RHB-HR | 27 | 49 | 76 | 25 | 51 | 76 | 91 | 135 | 166 | 301 | 133 | 161 | 294 | 101 |

## MONTREAL

**Home park:** Olympic Stadium **Alt.:** 90 feet **Surface:** Turf

| | 2004 Season | | | | | | | 2002-04 Seasons | | | | | | |
|---|---|---|---|---|---|---|---|---|---|---|---|---|---|---|
| | Home Games | | | Road Games | | | | Home Games | | | Road Games | | | |
| Category | Mon. | Opp. | Total | Mon. | Opp. | Total | Index | Mon. | Opp. | Total | Mon. | Opp. | Total | Index |
| G | 53 | 53 | 106 | 73 | 73 | 146 | | 181 | 181 | 362 | 217 | 217 | 434 | |
| Avg | .248 | .260 | .254 | .252 | .273 | .262 | 97 | .267 | .260 | .264 | .247 | .271 | .259 | 102 |
| AB | 1733 | 1837 | 3570 | 2556 | 2485 | 5041 | 98 | 5985 | 6320 | 12305 | 7489 | 7292 | 14781 | 100 |
| R | 211 | 227 | 438 | 312 | 368 | 680 | 89 | 859 | 787 | 1646 | 864 | 996 | 1860 | 106 |
| H | 430 | 477 | 907 | 643 | 679 | 1322 | 94 | 1599 | 1644 | 3243 | 1853 | 1973 | 3826 | 102 |
| 2B | 108 | 98 | 206 | 119 | 124 | 243 | 120 | 388 | 369 | 757 | 346 | 374 | 720 | 126 |
| 3B | 10 | 8 | 18 | 12 | 14 | 26 | 98 | 39 | 29 | 68 | 36 | 42 | 78 | 105 |
| HR | 56 | 56 | 112 | 75 | 99 | 174 | 91 | 182 | 189 | 371 | 201 | 232 | 433 | 103 |
| BB | 176 | 196 | 372 | 225 | 265 | 490 | 107 | 621 | 546 | 1167 | 701 | 735 | 1436 | 98 |
| SO | 266 | 347 | 613 | 450 | 461 | 911 | 95 | 1030 | 1205 | 2235 | 1472 | 1367 | 2839 | 95 |
| E | 28 | 32 | 60 | 52 | 48 | 100 | 83 | 123 | 125 | 248 | 155 | 148 | 303 | 98 |
| E-Infield | 25 | 29 | 54 | 44 | 41 | 85 | 88 | 99 | 110 | 209 | 132 | 120 | 252 | 99 |
| LHB-Avg | .259 | .264 | .261 | .261 | .280 | .269 | 97 | .271 | .262 | .267 | .247 | .281 | .262 | 102 |
| LHB-HR | 34 | 20 | 54 | 43 | 42 | 85 | 93 | 85 | 71 | 156 | 89 | 97 | 186 | 104 |
| RHB-Avg | .236 | .256 | .248 | .241 | .268 | .256 | 97 | .264 | .259 | .261 | .248 | .263 | .256 | 102 |
| RHB-HR | 22 | 36 | 58 | 32 | 57 | 89 | 89 | 97 | 118 | 215 | 112 | 135 | 247 | 102 |

## NEW YORK

**Home park:** Shea Stadium **Alt.:** 20 feet **Surface:** Grass

| | 2004 Season | | | | | | | 2002-04 Seasons | | | | | | |
|---|---|---|---|---|---|---|---|---|---|---|---|---|---|---|
| | Home Games | | | Road Games | | | | Home Games | | | Road Games | | | |
| Category | N.Y. | Opp. | Total | N.Y. | Opp. | Total | Index | N.Y. | Opp. | Total | N.Y. | Opp. | Total | Index |
| G | 72 | 72 | 144 | 69 | 69 | 138 | | 218 | 218 | 436 | 208 | 208 | 416 | |
| Avg | .251 | .260 | .255 | .247 | .267 | .256 | 100 | .250 | .260 | .255 | .251 | .267 | .259 | 99 |
| AB | 2423 | 2550 | 4973 | 2385 | 2302 | 4687 | 102 | 7230 | 7669 | 14899 | 7160 | 6898 | 14058 | 101 |
| R | 288 | 321 | 609 | 300 | 326 | 626 | 93 | 869 | 968 | 1837 | 902 | 947 | 1849 | 95 |
| H | 608 | 662 | 1270 | 588 | 614 | 1202 | 101 | 1809 | 1993 | 3802 | 1798 | 1843 | 3641 | 100 |
| 2B | 128 | 125 | 253 | 125 | 129 | 254 | 94 | 352 | 384 | 736 | 351 | 371 | 722 | 96 |
| 3B | 7 | 5 | 12 | 11 | 17 | 28 | 40 | 27 | 32 | 59 | 33 | 59 | 92 | 61 |
| HR | 71 | 62 | 133 | 90 | 77 | 167 | 75 | 191 | 207 | 398 | 213 | 215 | 428 | 88 |
| BB | 223 | 266 | 489 | 215 | 262 | 477 | 97 | 674 | 762 | 1436 | 656 | 737 | 1393 | 97 |
| SO | 494 | 453 | 947 | 515 | 387 | 902 | 99 | 1400 | 1426 | 2826 | 1454 | 1200 | 2654 | 100 |
| E | 64 | 44 | 108 | 50 | 31 | 81 | 128 | 191 | 140 | 331 | 153 | 135 | 288 | 110 |
| E-Infield | 54 | 40 | 94 | 39 | 24 | 63 | 143 | 160 | 127 | 287 | 127 | 110 | 237 | 116 |
| LHB-Avg | .262 | .267 | .265 | .238 | .264 | .252 | 105 | .262 | .261 | .261 | .252 | .253 | .253 | 103 |
| LHB-HR | 18 | 27 | 45 | 19 | 29 | 48 | 91 | 81 | 80 | 161 | 69 | 64 | 133 | 114 |
| RHB-Avg | .247 | .255 | .251 | .250 | .268 | .259 | 97 | .243 | .259 | .251 | .250 | .275 | .263 | 96 |
| RHB-HR | 53 | 35 | 88 | 71 | 48 | 119 | 69 | 110 | 127 | 237 | 144 | 151 | 295 | 76 |

## PHILADELPHIA

**Home park:** Citizens Bank Park **Alt.:** 20 feet **Surface:** Grass

| | 2004 Season | | | | | | | 2002-03 Seasons (Veterans Stadium) | | | | | | |
|---|---|---|---|---|---|---|---|---|---|---|---|---|---|---|
| | Home Games | | | Road Games | | | | Home Games | | | Road Games | | | |
| **Category** | **Phi.** | **Opp.** | **Total** | **Phi.** | **Opp.** | **Total** | **Index** | **Phi.** | **Opp.** | **Total** | **Phi.** | **Opp.** | **Total** | **Index** |
| G | 72 | 72 | 144 | 72 | 72 | 144 | | 143 | 143 | 286 | 147 | 147 | 294 | |
| Avg | .269 | .259 | .264 | .264 | .259 | .261 | 101 | .258 | .234 | .246 | .265 | .274 | .269 | 91 |
| AB | 2438 | 2540 | 4978 | 2561 | 2413 | 4974 | 100 | 4717 | 4848 | 9565 | 5196 | 4934 | 10130 | 97 |
| R | 377 | 350 | 727 | 357 | 313 | 670 | 109 | 644 | 553 | 1197 | 720 | 734 | 1454 | 85 |
| H | 656 | 658 | 1314 | 675 | 625 | 1300 | 101 | 1216 | 1136 | 2352 | 1376 | 1351 | 2727 | 89 |
| 2B | 129 | 128 | 257 | 142 | 143 | 285 | 90 | 282 | 245 | 527 | 305 | 304 | 609 | 92 |
| 3B | 13 | 15 | 28 | 10 | 14 | 24 | 117 | 35 | 24 | 59 | 28 | 34 | 62 | 101 |
| HR | 100 | 102 | 202 | 85 | 79 | 164 | 123 | 141 | 121 | 262 | 153 | 149 | 302 | 92 |
| BB | 275 | 216 | 491 | 287 | 226 | 513 | 96 | 576 | 475 | 1051 | 573 | 511 | 1084 | 103 |
| SO | 462 | 495 | 957 | 524 | 448 | 972 | 98 | 983 | 1079 | 2062 | 1027 | 828 | 1855 | 118 |
| E | 35 | 40 | 75 | 38 | 46 | 84 | 89 | 71 | 73 | 144 | 99 | 94 | 193 | 77 |
| E-Infield | 29 | 34 | 63 | 30 | 42 | 72 | 88 | 61 | 60 | 121 | 81 | 73 | 154 | 81 |
| LHB-Avg | .273 | .283 | .278 | .273 | .268 | .270 | 103 | .255 | .234 | .245 | .273 | .285 | .278 | 88 |
| LHB-HR | 46 | 37 | 83 | 46 | 22 | 68 | 127 | 72 | 38 | 110 | 71 | 58 | 129 | 89 |
| RHB-Avg | .267 | .245 | .255 | .257 | .254 | .255 | 100 | .260 | .234 | .246 | .258 | .267 | .263 | 94 |
| RHB-HR | 54 | 65 | 119 | 39 | 57 | 96 | 121 | 69 | 83 | 152 | 82 | 91 | 173 | 94 |

## PITTSBURGH

**Home park:** PNC Park **Alt.:** 730 feet **Surface:** Grass

| | 2004 Season | | | | | | | 2002-04 Seasons | | | | | | |
|---|---|---|---|---|---|---|---|---|---|---|---|---|---|---|
| | Home Games | | | Road Games | | | | Home Games | | | Road Games | | | |
| **Category** | **Pit.** | **Opp.** | **Total** | **Pit.** | **Opp.** | **Total** | **Index** | **Pit.** | **Opp.** | **Total** | **Pit.** | **Opp.** | **Total** | **Index** |
| G | 74 | 74 | 148 | 71 | 71 | 142 | | 223 | 223 | 446 | 221 | 221 | 442 | |
| Avg | .265 | .263 | .264 | .261 | .267 | .264 | 100 | .265 | .268 | .266 | .251 | .266 | .258 | 103 |
| AB | 2474 | 2551 | 5025 | 2476 | 2348 | 4824 | 100 | 7373 | 7782 | 15155 | 7614 | 7260 | 14874 | 101 |
| R | 309 | 323 | 632 | 306 | 333 | 639 | 95 | 968 | 1042 | 2010 | 935 | 1010 | 1945 | 102 |
| H | 655 | 670 | 1325 | 646 | 627 | 1273 | 100 | 1952 | 2085 | 4037 | 1912 | 1929 | 3841 | 104 |
| 2B | 125 | 148 | 273 | 125 | 118 | 243 | 108 | 382 | 432 | 814 | 357 | 382 | 739 | 108 |
| 3B | 20 | 12 | 32 | 17 | 20 | 37 | 83 | 43 | 38 | 81 | 54 | 44 | 98 | 81 |
| HR | 67 | 56 | 123 | 56 | 79 | 135 | 87 | 198 | 210 | 408 | 210 | 236 | 446 | 90 |
| BB | 185 | 258 | 443 | 199 | 264 | 463 | 92 | 685 | 736 | 1421 | 690 | 776 | 1466 | 95 |
| SO | 459 | 489 | 948 | 509 | 480 | 989 | 92 | 1352 | 1370 | 2722 | 1636 | 1329 | 2965 | 90 |
| E | 41 | 46 | 87 | 51 | 39 | 90 | 93 | 166 | 139 | 305 | 149 | 131 | 280 | 108 |
| E-Infield | 31 | 36 | 67 | 42 | 31 | 73 | 88 | 141 | 117 | 258 | 126 | 113 | 239 | 107 |
| LHB-Avg | .254 | .291 | .273 | .249 | .270 | .259 | 105 | .273 | .288 | .281 | .259 | .272 | .266 | 106 |
| LHB-HR | 21 | 23 | 44 | 20 | 22 | 42 | 102 | 80 | 78 | 158 | 80 | 88 | 168 | 93 |
| RHB-Avg | .271 | .246 | .258 | .268 | .265 | .267 | 97 | .260 | .255 | .258 | .247 | .262 | .254 | 102 |
| RHB-HR | 46 | 33 | 79 | 36 | 57 | 93 | 81 | 118 | 132 | 250 | 130 | 148 | 278 | 88 |

## SAN DIEGO

**Home park:** Petco Park **Alt.:** 20 feet **Surface:** Grass

| | 2004 Season | | | | | | | 2002-03 Seasons (Qualcomm Stadium) | | | | | | |
|---|---|---|---|---|---|---|---|---|---|---|---|---|---|---|
| | Home Games | | | Road Games | | | | Home Games | | | Road Games | | | |
| **Category** | **S.D.** | **Opp.** | **Total** | **S.D.** | **Opp.** | **Total** | **Index** | **S.D.** | **Opp.** | **Total** | **S.D.** | **Opp.** | **Total** | **Index** |
| G | 72 | 72 | 144 | 72 | 72 | 144 | | 144 | 144 | 288 | 144 | 144 | 288 | |
| Avg | .254 | .263 | .258 | .293 | .269 | .281 | 92 | .263 | .259 | .261 | .251 | .284 | .267 | 98 |
| AB | 2353 | 2499 | 4852 | 2598 | 2438 | 5036 | 96 | 4844 | 5058 | 9902 | 4987 | 4806 | 9793 | 101 |
| R | 296 | 306 | 602 | 400 | 331 | 731 | 82 | 577 | 654 | 1231 | 608 | 834 | 1442 | 85 |
| H | 598 | 656 | 1254 | 760 | 655 | 1415 | 89 | 1273 | 1308 | 2581 | 1253 | 1363 | 2616 | 99 |
| 2B | 117 | 142 | 259 | 154 | 141 | 295 | 91 | 198 | 235 | 433 | 239 | 284 | 523 | 82 |
| 3B | 19 | 15 | 34 | 11 | 15 | 26 | 136 | 34 | 34 | 68 | 22 | 39 | 61 | 110 |
| HR | 48 | 65 | 113 | 77 | 100 | 177 | 66 | 105 | 160 | 265 | 127 | 192 | 319 | 82 |
| BB | 279 | 185 | 464 | 234 | 197 | 431 | 112 | 514 | 499 | 1013 | 465 | 564 | 1029 | 97 |
| SO | 392 | 492 | 884 | 409 | 472 | 881 | 104 | 911 | 1037 | 1948 | 1008 | 939 | 1947 | 99 |
| E | 36 | 44 | 80 | 59 | 54 | 113 | 71 | 99 | 99 | 198 | 100 | 87 | 187 | 106 |
| E-Infield | 30 | 33 | 63 | 48 | 45 | 93 | 68 | 84 | 76 | 160 | 85 | 70 | 155 | 103 |
| LHB-Avg | .275 | .262 | .268 | .287 | .272 | .279 | 96 | .270 | .270 | .270 | .257 | .302 | .277 | 97 |
| LHB-HR | 13 | 31 | 44 | 23 | 45 | 68 | 68 | 48 | 61 | 109 | 61 | 85 | 146 | 73 |
| RHB-Avg | .241 | .263 | .252 | .296 | .266 | .282 | 89 | .256 | .251 | .253 | .246 | .271 | .259 | 98 |
| RHB-HR | 35 | 34 | 69 | 54 | 55 | 109 | 65 | 57 | 99 | 156 | 66 | 107 | 173 | 90 |

## SAN FRANCISCO

**Home park:** SBC Park **Alt.:** 0 feet **Surface:** Grass

| | 2004 Season | | | | | | | 2002-03 Seasons | | | | | | |
|---|---|---|---|---|---|---|---|---|---|---|---|---|---|---|
| | Home Games | | | Road Games | | | | Home Games | | | Road Games | | | |
| **Category** | **S.F.** | **Opp.** | **Total** | **S.F.** | **Opp.** | **Total** | **Index** | **S.F.** | **Opp.** | **Total** | **S.F.** | **Opp.** | **Total** | **Index** |
| G | 73 | 73 | 146 | 69 | 69 | 138 | | 144 | 144 | 288 | 143 | 143 | 286 | |
| Avg | .286 | .273 | .279 | .259 | .255 | .257 | 109 | .267 | .244 | .255 | .262 | .254 | .258 | 99 |
| AB | 2441 | 2556 | 4997 | 2408 | 2321 | 4729 | 100 | 4720 | 4930 | 9650 | 4979 | 4650 | 9629 | 100 |
| R | 383 | 362 | 745 | 348 | 315 | 663 | 106 | 673 | 508 | 1181 | 697 | 596 | 1293 | 91 |
| H | 699 | 697 | 1396 | 624 | 592 | 1216 | 109 | 1259 | 1204 | 2463 | 1305 | 1179 | 2484 | 98 |
| 2B | 152 | 148 | 300 | 130 | 126 | 256 | 111 | 239 | 221 | 460 | 277 | 219 | 496 | 93 |
| 3B | 23 | 18 | 41 | 4 | 21 | 25 | 155 | 39 | 30 | 69 | 20 | 21 | 41 | 168 |
| HR | 76 | 69 | 145 | 82 | 74 | 156 | 88 | 132 | 89 | 221 | 202 | 130 | 332 | 66 |
| BB | 314 | 234 | 548 | 293 | 241 | 534 | 97 | 555 | 449 | 1004 | 543 | 497 | 1040 | 96 |
| SO | 367 | 466 | 833 | 402 | 407 | 809 | 97 | 811 | 921 | 1732 | 934 | 827 | 1761 | 98 |
| E | 47 | 49 | 96 | 41 | 35 | 76 | 119 | 86 | 110 | 196 | 70 | 82 | 152 | 128 |
| E-Infield | 37 | 38 | 75 | 38 | 30 | 68 | 104 | 67 | 88 | 155 | 56 | 72 | 128 | 120 |
| LHB-Avg | .290 | .279 | .285 | .279 | .269 | .274 | 104 | .262 | .240 | .249 | .275 | .264 | .269 | 93 |
| LHB-HR | 39 | 31 | 70 | 44 | 32 | 76 | 89 | 50 | 27 | 77 | 73 | 47 | 120 | 64 |
| RHB-Avg | .283 | .268 | .276 | .244 | .245 | .244 | 113 | .269 | .248 | .259 | .256 | .246 | .252 | 103 |
| RHB-HR | 37 | 38 | 75 | 38 | 42 | 80 | 87 | 82 | 62 | 144 | 129 | 83 | 212 | 68 |

## ST. LOUIS

**Home park:** Busch Stadium **Alt.:** 535 feet **Surface:** Grass

| | 2004 Season | | | | | | | 2002-04 Seasons | | | | | | |
|---|---|---|---|---|---|---|---|---|---|---|---|---|---|---|
| | Home Games | | | Road Games | | | | Home Games | | | Road Games | | | |
| **Category** | **St.L.** | **Opp.** | **Total** | **St.L.** | **Opp.** | **Total** | **Index** | **St.L.** | **Opp.** | **Total** | **St.L.** | **Opp.** | **Total** | **Index** |
| G | 75 | 75 | 150 | 75 | 75 | 150 | | 222 | 222 | 444 | 222 | 222 | 444 | |
| Avg | .281 | .252 | .266 | .270 | .255 | .263 | 101 | .276 | .248 | .262 | .269 | .267 | .268 | 98 |
| AB | 2501 | 2583 | 5084 | 2629 | 2487 | 5116 | 99 | 7429 | 7676 | 15105 | 7816 | 7426 | 15242 | 99 |
| R | 374 | 304 | 678 | 396 | 319 | 715 | 95 | 1104 | 891 | 1995 | 1148 | 1008 | 2156 | 93 |
| H | 704 | 650 | 1354 | 709 | 634 | 1343 | 101 | 2053 | 1906 | 3959 | 2099 | 1986 | 4085 | 97 |
| 2B | 150 | 137 | 287 | 144 | 136 | 280 | 103 | 437 | 404 | 841 | 418 | 401 | 819 | 104 |
| 3B | 14 | 10 | 24 | 9 | 8 | 17 | 142 | 27 | 24 | 51 | 47 | 30 | 77 | 67 |
| HR | 87 | 71 | 158 | 113 | 86 | 199 | 80 | 244 | 213 | 457 | 288 | 256 | 544 | 85 |
| BB | 255 | 218 | 473 | 244 | 205 | 449 | 106 | 784 | 696 | 1480 | 745 | 694 | 1439 | 104 |
| SO | 481 | 515 | 996 | 523 | 447 | 970 | 103 | 1293 | 1464 | 2757 | 1425 | 1319 | 2744 | 101 |
| E | 39 | 46 | 85 | 49 | 61 | 110 | 77 | 115 | 148 | 263 | 132 | 162 | 294 | 89 |
| E-Infield | 31 | 39 | 70 | 39 | 55 | 94 | 74 | 93 | 126 | 219 | 104 | 139 | 243 | 90 |
| LHB-Avg | .296 | .236 | .264 | .273 | .247 | .260 | 102 | .276 | .245 | .260 | .268 | .265 | .267 | 98 |
| LHB-HR | 40 | 30 | 70 | 41 | 46 | 87 | 80 | 107 | 82 | 189 | 104 | 105 | 209 | 92 |
| RHB-Avg | .272 | .264 | .268 | .268 | .261 | .265 | 101 | .276 | .250 | .263 | .269 | .269 | .269 | 98 |
| RHB-HR | 47 | 41 | 88 | 72 | 40 | 112 | 79 | 137 | 131 | 268 | 184 | 151 | 335 | 80 |

# 2002-2004 N.L. BALLPARK INDEX RANKINGS

## RUNS PER GAME

| Team | Home Games | | | | Road Games | | | | Index |
|---|---|---|---|---|---|---|---|---|---|
| | Games | Team | Opp. | Total | Games | Team | Opp. | Total | |
| Col | 216 | 1328 | 1293 | 2621 | 219 | 859 | 1100 | 1959 | 136 |
| Ari | 219 | 1083 | 1058 | 2141 | 216 | 824 | 971 | 1795 | 118 |
| Phi** | 72 | 377 | 350 | 727 | 72 | 357 | 313 | 670 | 109 |
| Mon | 181 | 859 | 787 | 1646 | 217 | 864 | 996 | 1860 | 106 |
| SF** | 73 | 383 | 362 | 745 | 69 | 348 | 315 | 663 | 106 |
| Hou | 222 | 1118 | 922 | 2040 | 222 | 1034 | 948 | 1982 | 103 |
| ChC | 223 | 1015 | 986 | 2001 | 218 | 1000 | 924 | 1924 | 102 |
| Pit | 223 | 968 | 1042 | 2010 | 221 | 935 | 1010 | 1945 | 102 |
| Mil | 225 | 910 | 1138 | 2048 | 221 | 885 | 1130 | 2015 | 100 |
| Atl | 219 | 1074 | 888 | 1962 | 209 | 1044 | 871 | 1915 | 98 |
| NYM | 218 | 869 | 968 | 1837 | 208 | 902 | 947 | 1849 | 95 |
| Fla | 213 | 975 | 865 | 1840 | 216 | 925 | 1038 | 1963 | 95 |
| Cin* | 150 | 630 | 798 | 1428 | 147 | 690 | 821 | 1511 | 93 |
| StL | 222 | 1104 | 891 | 1995 | 222 | 1148 | 1008 | 2156 | 93 |
| LA | 216 | 833 | 767 | 1600 | 216 | 1000 | 903 | 1903 | 84 |
| SD** | 72 | 296 | 306 | 602 | 72 | 400 | 331 | 731 | 82 |

*Current dimensions began 2003; **Current dimensions began 2004

## HOME RUNS PER AT-BAT

| Team | Home Games | | | | Road Games | | | | Index |
|---|---|---|---|---|---|---|---|---|---|
| | Games | Team | Opp. | Total | Games | Team | Opp. | Total | |
| Col | 216 | 287 | 324 | 611 | 219 | 207 | 234 | 441 | 135 |
| Phi** | 72 | 100 | 102 | 202 | 72 | 85 | 79 | 164 | 123 |
| ChC | 223 | 298 | 247 | 545 | 218 | 257 | 186 | 443 | 120 |
| Cin* | 150 | 176 | 226 | 402 | 147 | 163 | 181 | 344 | 116 |
| Ari | 219 | 224 | 250 | 474 | 216 | 191 | 213 | 404 | 114 |
| LA | 216 | 209 | 216 | 425 | 216 | 222 | 196 | 418 | 105 |
| Hou | 222 | 255 | 217 | 472 | 222 | 244 | 217 | 461 | 103 |
| Mon | 181 | 182 | 189 | 371 | 217 | 201 | 232 | 433 | 103 |
| Mil | 225 | 217 | 281 | 498 | 221 | 216 | 253 | 469 | 103 |
| Atl | 219 | 256 | 197 | 453 | 209 | 244 | 186 | 430 | 102 |
| Pit | 223 | 198 | 210 | 408 | 221 | 210 | 236 | 446 | 90 |
| SF** | 73 | 76 | 69 | 145 | 69 | 82 | 74 | 156 | 88 |
| NYM | 218 | 191 | 207 | 398 | 208 | 213 | 215 | 428 | 88 |
| StL | 222 | 244 | 213 | 457 | 222 | 288 | 256 | 544 | 85 |
| Fla | 213 | 185 | 175 | 360 | 216 | 205 | 226 | 431 | 85 |
| SD** | 72 | 48 | 65 | 113 | 72 | 77 | 100 | 177 | 66 |

*Current dimensions began 2003; **Current dimensions began 2004

## BATTING AVERAGE

| Team | Home Games | | | | Road Games | | | | Index |
|---|---|---|---|---|---|---|---|---|---|
| | Games | Team | Opp. | Total | Games | Team | Opp. | Total | |
| Col | 216 | .302 | .291 | .296 | 219 | .239 | .275 | .256 | 116 |
| SF** | 73 | .286 | .273 | .279 | 69 | .259 | .255 | .257 | 109 |
| Ari | 219 | .274 | .254 | .264 | 216 | .245 | .254 | .250 | 106 |
| Pit | 223 | .265 | .268 | .266 | 221 | .251 | .266 | .258 | 103 |
| Hou | 222 | .276 | .249 | .262 | 222 | .251 | .260 | .255 | 103 |
| Mon | 181 | .267 | .260 | .264 | 217 | .247 | .271 | .259 | 102 |
| Phi** | 72 | .269 | .259 | .264 | 72 | .264 | .259 | .261 | 101 |
| NYM | 218 | .250 | .260 | .255 | 208 | .251 | .267 | .259 | 99 |
| Atl | 219 | .272 | .250 | .261 | 209 | .270 | .260 | .265 | 98 |
| ChC | 223 | .255 | .243 | .249 | 218 | .259 | .250 | .254 | 98 |
| StL | 222 | .276 | .248 | .262 | 222 | .269 | .267 | .268 | 98 |
| Fla | 213 | .269 | .247 | .258 | 216 | .259 | .270 | .265 | 97 |
| Mil | 225 | .251 | .260 | .256 | 221 | .249 | .278 | .263 | 97 |
| Cin* | 150 | .243 | .268 | .256 | 147 | .250 | .290 | .270 | 95 |
| LA | 216 | .250 | .234 | .242 | 216 | .266 | .253 | .260 | 93 |
| SD** | 72 | .254 | .263 | .258 | 72 | .293 | .269 | .281 | 92 |

*Current dimensions began 2003; **Current dimensions began 2004

# 2004 STATISTICAL LEADERS

# 2004 AMERICAN LEAGUE LEADERS

## BATTING

### Batting Average

(minimum 502 PA)

| Player, Team | AB | H | Avg. |
|---|---|---|---|
| I Suzuki, Sea. | 704 | 262 | .372 |
| M Mora, Bal. | 550 | 187 | .340 |
| V Guerrero, Ana. | 612 | 206 | .337 |
| I Rodriguez, Det. | 527 | 176 | .334 |
| E Durazo, Oak. | 511 | 164 | .321 |
| C Guillen, Det. | 522 | 166 | .318 |
| J Lopez, Bal. | 579 | 183 | .316 |
| M Kotsay, Oak. | 606 | 190 | .314 |
| M Young, Tex. | 690 | 216 | .313 |
| T Hafner, Cle. | 482 | 150 | .311 |

### On-Base Percentage

(minimum 502 PA; *AB+BB+HBP+SF)

| Player, Team | AB | H | Avg. |
|---|---|---|---|
| M Mora, Bal. | 630 | 264 | .419 |
| I Suzuki, Sea. | 760 | 315 | .414 |
| T Hafner, Cle. | 573 | 235 | .410 |
| J Posada, N.Y. | 547 | 219 | .400 |
| E Chavez, Oak. | 577 | 229 | .397 |
| M Ramirez, Bos. | 663 | 263 | .397 |
| E Durazo, Oak. | 578 | 229 | .396 |
| G Sheffield, N.Y. | 684 | 269 | .393 |
| V Guerrero, Ana. | 680 | 266 | .391 |
| J Varitek, Bos. | 536 | 209 | .390 |

### Slugging Percentage

(minimum 502 PA)

| Player, Team | AB | H | Avg. |
|---|---|---|---|
| M Ramirez, Bos. | 568 | 348 | .613 |
| D Ortiz, Bos. | 582 | 351 | .603 |
| V Guerrero, Ana. | 612 | 366 | .598 |
| T Hafner, Cle. | 482 | 281 | .583 |
| M Mora, Bal. | 550 | 309 | .562 |
| M Teixeira, Tex. | 545 | 305 | .560 |
| A Rowand, Chi. | 487 | 265 | .544 |
| C Guillen, Det. | 522 | 283 | .542 |
| C Delgado, Tor. | 458 | 245 | .535 |
| P Konerko, Chi. | 563 | 301 | .535 |

### Games

H Matsui, N.Y. ....................162
M Tejada, Bal. ....................162
I Suzuki, Sea. ....................161
M Young, Tex. ....................160
2 tied with ....................159

### Plate Appearances

I Suzuki, Sea. ....................762
M Young, Tex. ....................739
B Roberts, Bal. ....................736
M Tejada, Bal. ....................725
D Jeter, N.Y. ....................721

### At-Bats

I Suzuki, Sea. ....................704
M Young, Tex. ....................690
M Tejada, Bal. ....................653
D Jeter, N.Y. ....................643
B Roberts, Bal. ....................641

### Hits

I Suzuki, Sea. ....................262
M Young, Tex. ....................216
V Guerrero, Ana. ....................206
M Tejada, Bal. ....................203
M Kotsay, Oak. ....................190

### Singles

I Suzuki, Sea. ....................225
M Young, Tex. ....................152
M Kotsay, Oak. ....................135
C Crawford, T.B. ....................129
D Eckstein, Ana. ....................129

### Doubles

B Roberts, Bal. ....................50
R Belliard, Cle. ....................48
D Ortiz, Bos. ....................47
D Jeter, N.Y. ....................44
M Ramirez, Bos. ....................44

### Triples

C Crawford, T.B. ....................19
C Figgins, Ana. ....................17
C Guillen, Det. ....................10
O Infante, Det. ....................9
M Young, Tex. ....................9

### Home Runs

M Ramirez, Bos. ....................43
P Konerko, Chi. ....................41
D Ortiz, Bos. ....................41
V Guerrero, Ana. ....................39
M Teixeira, Tex. ....................38

### Total Bases

V Guerrero, Ana. ....................366
D Ortiz, Bos. ....................351
M Tejada, Bal. ....................349
M Ramirez, Bos. ....................348
M Young, Tex. ....................333

### Runs Scored

V Guerrero, Ana. ....................124
J Damon, Bos. ....................123
G Sheffield, N.Y. ....................117
M Young, Tex. ....................114
A Rodriguez, N.Y. ....................112

### Runs Batted In

M Tejada, Bal. ....................150
D Ortiz, Bos. ....................139
M Ramirez, Bos. ....................130
V Guerrero, Ana. ....................126
G Sheffield, N.Y. ....................121

### GDP

J Posada, N.Y. ....................24
M Tejada, Bal. ....................24
T Hunter, Min. ....................23
P Konerko, Chi. ....................23
2 tied with ....................21

### Sacrifice Hits

O Vizquel, Cle. ....................20
D Jeter, N.Y. ....................16
B Roberts, Bal. ....................15
D Eckstein, Ana. ....................14
C Guzman, Min. ....................13

### Sacrifice Flies

M Tejada, Bal. ....................14
C Delgado, Tor. ....................11
R Palmeiro, Bal. ....................9
8 tied with ....................8

### Stolen Bases

C Crawford, T.B. ....................59
I Suzuki, Sea. ....................36
C Figgins, Ana. ....................34
B Roberts, Bal. ....................29
A Rodriguez, N.Y. ....................28

### Caught Stealing

C Crawford, T.B. ....................15
C Crisp, Cle. ....................13
C Figgins, Ana. ....................13
A Sanchez, Det. ....................13
B Roberts, Bal. ....................12

### Walks

E Chavez, Oak. ....................95
G Sheffield, N.Y. ....................92
M Bellhorn, Bos. ....................88
H Matsui, N.Y. ....................88
J Posada, N.Y. ....................88

### Intentional Walks

I Suzuki, Sea. ....................19
R Palmeiro, Bal. ....................15
M Ramirez, Bos. ....................15
V Guerrero, Ana. ....................14
2 tied with ....................12

### Hit by Pitch

T Hafner, Cle. ....................17
K Millar, Bos. ....................17
J Guillen, Ana. ....................15
M Cairo, N.Y. ....................14
D Jeter, N.Y. ....................14

### Strikeouts

M Bellhorn, Bos. ....................177
H Blalock, Tex. ....................149
C Pena, Det. ....................146
B Crosby, Oak. ....................141
2 tied with ....................139

# 2004 NATIONAL LEAGUE LEADERS

## BATTING

### Batting Average

(minimum 502 PA)

| Player, Team | AB | H | Avg. |
|---|---|---|---|
| B Bonds, S.F. | 373 | 135 | .362 |
| T Helton, Col. | 547 | 190 | .347 |
| M Loretta, S.D. | 620 | 208 | .335 |
| A Beltre, L.A. | 598 | 200 | .334 |
| A Pujols, St.L. | 592 | 196 | .331 |
| J Pierre, Fla. | 678 | 221 | .326 |
| S Casey, Cin. | 571 | 185 | .324 |
| J Kendall, Pit. | 574 | 183 | .319 |
| A Ramirez, Chi. | 547 | 174 | .318 |
| L Berkman, Hou. | 544 | 172 | .316 |

### On-Base Percentage

(minimum 502 PA; *AB+BB+HBP+SF)

| Player, Team | AB | H | Avg. |
|---|---|---|---|
| B Bonds, S.F. | 617 | 376 | .609 |
| T Helton, Col. | 683 | 320 | .469 |
| L Berkman, Hou. | 687 | 309 | .450 |
| J Drew, Atl. | 644 | 281 | .436 |
| B Abreu, Phi. | 713 | 305 | .428 |
| J Edmonds, St.L. | 612 | 256 | .418 |
| A Pujols, St.L. | 692 | 287 | .415 |
| S Rolen, St.L. | 592 | 242 | .409 |
| J Kendall, Pit. | 657 | 262 | .399 |
| J Thome, Phi. | 618 | 245 | .396 |

### Slugging Percentage

(minimum 502 PA)

| Player, Team | AB | H | Avg. |
|---|---|---|---|
| B Bonds, S.F. | 373 | 303 | .812 |
| A Pujols, St.L. | 592 | 389 | .657 |
| J Edmonds, St.L. | 498 | 320 | .643 |
| A Beltre, L.A. | 598 | 376 | .629 |
| T Helton, Col. | 547 | 339 | .620 |
| S Rolen, St.L. | 500 | 299 | .598 |
| J Thome, Phi. | 508 | 295 | .581 |
| A Ramirez, Chi. | 547 | 316 | .578 |
| J Drew, Atl. | 518 | 295 | .569 |
| A Dunn, Cin. | 568 | 323 | .569 |

### Games

S Finley, Ari.-L.A. ....162
J Pierre, Fla. ....162
A Dunn, Cin. ....161
D Lee, Chi. ....161
3 tied with ....160

### Plate Appearances

J Pierre, Fla. ....748
C Izturis, L.A. ....728
J Rollins, Phi. ....725
B Abreu, Phi. ....713
S Podsednik, Mil. ....713

### At-Bats

J Pierre, Fla. ....678
C Izturis, L.A. ....670
J Rollins, Phi. ....657
J Wilson, Pit. ....652
S Podsednik, Mil. ....640

### Hits

J Pierre, Fla. ....221
M Loretta, S.D. ....208
J Wilson, Pit. ....201
A Beltre, L.A. ....200
A Pujols, St.L. ....196

### Singles

J Pierre, Fla. ....184
C Izturis, L.A. ....148
J Kendall, Pit. ....148
L Castillo, Fla. ....143
M Loretta, S.D. ....143

### Doubles

L Overbay, Mil. ....53
A Pujols, St.L. ....51
T Helton, Col. ....49
3 tied with ....47

### Triples

J Pierre, Fla. ....12
J Rollins, Phi. ....12
J Wilson, Pit. ....12
C Izturis, L.A. ....9
4 tied with ....8

### Home Runs

A Beltre, L.A. ....48
A Dunn, Cin. ....46
A Pujols, St.L. ....46
B Bonds, S.F. ....45
2 tied with ....42

### Total Bases

A Pujols, St.L. ....389
A Beltre, L.A. ....376
T Helton, Col. ....339
M Alou, Chi. ....335
A Dunn, Cin. ....323

### Runs Scored

A Pujols, St.L. ....133
B Bonds, S.F. ....129
J Rollins, Phi. ....119
B Abreu, Phi. ....118
J Drew, Atl. ....118

### Runs Batted In

V Castilla, Col. ....131
S Rolen, St.L. ....124
A Pujols, St.L. ....123
A Beltre, L.A. ....121
M Cabrera, Fla. ....112

### GDP

A Pierzynski, S.F. ....27
A Ramirez, Chi. ....25
A Jones, Atl. ....24
J Kent, Hou. ....23
3 tied with ....22

### Sacrifice Hits

R Clayton, Col. ....24
A Everett, Hou. ....22
K Benson, Pit.-N.Y. ....15
L Hernandez, Mon. ....15
J Pierre, Fla. ....15

### Sacrifice Flies

M Loretta, S.D. ....16
J Kent, Hou. ....11
T Batista, Mon. ....10
E Renteria, St.L. ....10
2 tied with ....9

### Stolen Bases

S Podsednik, Mil. ....70
J Pierre, Fla. ....45
B Abreu, Phi. ....40
R Freel, Cin. ....37
D Roberts, L.A. ....33

### Caught Stealing

J Pierre, Fla. ....24
S Podsednik, Mil. ....13
M Bradley, L.A. ....11
E Renteria, St.L. ....11
R Freel, Cin. ....10

### Walks

B Bonds, S.F. ....232
B Abreu, Phi. ....127
L Berkman, Hou. ....127
T Helton, Col. ....127
J Drew, Atl. ....118

### Intentional Walks

B Bonds, S.F. ....120
J Thome, Phi. ....26
T Helton, Col. ....19
L Berkman, Hou. ....14
M Piazza, N.Y. ....14

### Hit by Pitch

C Wilson, Pit. ....30
J LaRue, Cin. ....24
J Kendall, Pit. ....19
A Cora, L.A. ....18
2 tied with ....15

### Strikeouts

A Dunn, Cin. ....195
C Wilson, Pit. ....169
C Patterson, Chi. ....168
G Jenkins, Mil. ....152
B Wilkerson, Mon. ....152

# AMERICAN LEAGUE PITCHING LEADERS

### Earned Run Average
(minimum 162 IP)

| Pitcher, Team | IP | ER | ERA |
|---|---|---|---|
| J Santana, Min. | 228.0 | 66 | 2.61 |
| C Schilling, Bos. | 226.2 | 82 | 3.26 |
| J Westbrook, Cle. | 215.2 | 81 | 3.38 |
| B Radke, Min. | 219.2 | 85 | 3.48 |
| T Hudson, Oak. | 188.2 | 74 | 3.53 |
| R Lopez, Bal. | 170.2 | 68 | 3.59 |
| F Garcia, Sea.-Chi. | 210.0 | 89 | 3.81 |
| M Buehrle, Chi. | 245.1 | 106 | 3.89 |
| P Martinez, Bos. | 217.0 | 94 | 3.90 |
| K Escobar, Ana. | 208.1 | 91 | 3.93 |

### Won-Lost Percentage
(minimum 15 decisions)

| Pitcher, Team | W | L | Pct. |
|---|---|---|---|
| C Schilling, Bos. | 21 | 6 | .778 |
| J Santana, Min. | 20 | 6 | .769 |
| M Mulder, Oak. | 17 | 8 | .680 |
| K Rogers, Tex. | 18 | 9 | .667 |
| T Hudson, Oak. | 12 | 6 | .667 |
| J Rincon, Min. | 11 | 6 | .647 |
| P Martinez, Bos. | 16 | 9 | .640 |
| C Lee, Cle. | 14 | 8 | .636 |
| J Lieber, N.Y. | 14 | 8 | .636 |
| C Silva, Min. | 14 | 8 | .636 |

### Opponents' Batting Average
(minimum 162 IP)

| Pitcher, Team | AB | H | Avg. |
|---|---|---|---|
| J Santana, Min. | 812 | 156 | .192 |
| T Lilly, Tor. | 744 | 171 | .230 |
| P Martinez, Bos. | 812 | 193 | .238 |
| C Schilling, Bos. | 861 | 206 | .239 |
| F Garcia, Sea.-Chi. | 795 | 192 | .242 |
| R Harden, Oak. | 708 | 171 | .242 |
| J Bonderman, Det. | 695 | 168 | .242 |
| K Escobar, Ana. | 786 | 192 | .244 |
| B Arroyo, Bos. | 688 | 171 | .249 |
| C Sabathia, Cle. | 699 | 176 | .252 |

### Games

| | |
|---|---|
| P Quantrill, N.Y. | 86 |
| T Gordon, N.Y. | 80 |
| J Rincon, Min. | 77 |
| B Ryan, Bal. | 76 |
| M Timlin, Bos. | 76 |

### Games Started

| | |
|---|---|
| M Buehrle, Chi. | 35 |
| K Rogers, Tex. | 35 |
| 5 tied with | 34 |

### Complete Games

| | |
|---|---|
| M Mulder, Oak. | 5 |
| S Ponson, Bal. | 5 |
| J Westbrook, Cle. | 5 |
| M Buehrle, Chi. | 4 |
| 3 tied with | 3 |

### Games Finished

| | |
|---|---|
| M Rivera, N.Y. | 69 |
| F Cordero, Tex. | 63 |
| J Nathan, Min. | 63 |
| K Foulke, Bos. | 61 |
| D Baez, T.B. | 59 |

### Wins

| | |
|---|---|
| C Schilling, Bos. | 21 |
| J Santana, Min. | 20 |
| B Colon, Ana. | 18 |
| K Rogers, Tex. | 18 |
| M Mulder, Oak. | 17 |

### Losses

| | |
|---|---|
| D May, K.C. | 19 |
| R Franklin, Sea. | 16 |
| M Hendrickson, T.B. | 15 |
| J Johnson, Det. | 15 |
| S Ponson, Bal. | 15 |

### Saves

| | |
|---|---|
| M Rivera, N.Y. | 53 |
| F Cordero, Tex. | 49 |
| J Nathan, Min. | 44 |
| T Percival, Ana. | 33 |
| K Foulke, Bos. | 32 |

### Shutouts

| | |
|---|---|
| J Bonderman, Det. | 2 |
| T Hudson, Oak. | 2 |
| S Ponson, Bal. | 2 |
| 27 tied with | 1 |

### Hits Allowed

| | |
|---|---|
| S Ponson, Bal. | 265 |
| M Buehrle, Chi. | 257 |
| C Silva, Min. | 255 |
| K Rogers, Tex. | 248 |
| M Maroth, Det. | 244 |

### Doubles Allowed

| | |
|---|---|
| K Rogers, Tex. | 59 |
| D May, K.C. | 58 |
| B Anderson, K.C. | 54 |
| C Schilling, Bos. | 54 |
| M Redman, Oak. | 51 |

### Triples Allowed

| | |
|---|---|
| D May, K.C. | 9 |
| P Martinez, Bos. | 8 |
| K Rogers, Tex. | 8 |
| J Johnson, Det. | 7 |
| M Maroth, Det. | 7 |

### Home Runs Allowed

| | |
|---|---|
| J Moyer, Sea. | 44 |
| B Colon, Ana. | 38 |
| D May, K.C. | 38 |
| J Garland, Chi. | 34 |
| 4 tied with | 33 |

### Batters Faced

| | |
|---|---|
| M Buehrle, Chi. | 1016 |
| S Ponson, Bal. | 954 |
| M Mulder, Oak. | 952 |
| K Rogers, Tex. | 935 |
| M Maroth, Det. | 928 |

### Innings Pitched

| | |
|---|---|
| M Buehrle, Chi. | 245.1 |
| J Santana, Min. | 228.0 |
| C Schilling, Bos. | 226.2 |
| M Mulder, Oak. | 225.2 |
| B Radke, Min. | 219.2 |

### Runs Allowed

| | |
|---|---|
| D Lowe, Bos. | 138 |
| S Ponson, Bal. | 136 |
| D May, K.C. | 130 |
| K Lohse, Min. | 128 |
| J Moyer, Sea. | 127 |

### Strikeouts

| | |
|---|---|
| J Santana, Min. | 265 |
| P Martinez, Bos. | 227 |
| C Schilling, Bos. | 203 |
| K Escobar, Ana. | 191 |
| F Garcia, Sea.-Chi. | 184 |

### Walks Allowed

| | |
|---|---|
| M Batista, Tor. | 96 |
| V Zambrano, T.B. | 96 |
| D Cabrera, Bal. | 89 |
| T Lilly, Tor. | 89 |
| J Contreras, N.Y.-Chi. | 84 |

### Hit Batsmen

| | |
|---|---|
| B Arroyo, Bos. | 20 |
| P Martinez, Bos. | 16 |
| T Wakefield, Bos. | 16 |
| V Zambrano, T.B. | 16 |
| C Park, Tex. | 13 |

### Wild Pitches

| | |
|---|---|
| J Contreras, N.Y.-Chi. | 17 |
| K Gregg, Ana. | 13 |
| M Batista, Tor. | 12 |
| D Cabrera, Bal. | 12 |
| J Vazquez, N.Y. | 12 |

### Balks

| | |
|---|---|
| T Lilly, Tor. | 4 |
| J Affeldt, K.C. | 3 |
| R Franklin, Sea. | 3 |
| R Ortiz, Ana. | 3 |
| 12 tied with | 2 |

# NATIONAL LEAGUE PITCHING LEADERS

### Earned Run Average

(minimum 162 IP)

| Pitcher, Team | IP | ER | ERA |
|---|---|---|---|
| J Peavy, S.D. | 166.1 | 42 | 2.27 |
| R Johnson, Ari. | 245.2 | 71 | 2.60 |
| B Sheets, Mil. | 237.0 | 71 | 2.70 |
| C Zambrano, Chi. | 209.2 | 64 | 2.75 |
| R Clemens, Hou. | 214.1 | 71 | 2.98 |
| O Perez, Pit. | 196.0 | 65 | 2.98 |
| C Pavano, Fla. | 222.1 | 74 | 3.00 |
| J Schmidt, S.F. | 225.0 | 80 | 3.20 |
| A Leiter, N.Y. | 173.2 | 62 | 3.21 |
| O Perez, L.A. | 196.1 | 71 | 3.25 |

### Won-Lost Percentage

(minimum 15 decisions)

| Pitcher, Team | W | L | Pct. |
|---|---|---|---|
| R Clemens, Hou. | 18 | 4 | .818 |
| C Carpenter, St.L. | 15 | 5 | .750 |
| J Lima, L.A. | 13 | 5 | .722 |
| J Schmidt, S.F. | 18 | 7 | .720 |
| J Peavy, S.D. | 15 | 6 | .714 |
| E Milton, Phi. | 14 | 6 | .700 |
| C Pavano, Fla. | 18 | 8 | .692 |
| T Jones, Cin.-Phi. | 11 | 5 | .688 |
| J Marquis, St.L. | 15 | 7 | .682 |
| 2 tied with | | | .667 |

### Opponents' Batting Average

(minimum 162 IP)

| Pitcher, Team | AB | H | Avg. |
|---|---|---|---|
| R Johnson, Ari. | 898 | 177 | .197 |
| J Schmidt, S.F. | 817 | 165 | .202 |
| O Perez, Pit. | 701 | 145 | .207 |
| R Clemens, Hou. | 778 | 169 | .217 |
| A Leiter, N.Y. | 632 | 138 | .218 |
| C Zambrano, Chi. | 773 | 174 | .225 |
| B Sheets, Mil. | 891 | 201 | .226 |
| M Clement, Chi. | 677 | 155 | .229 |
| J Peavy, S.D. | 619 | 146 | .236 |
| J Wright, Atl. | 694 | 168 | .242 |

### Games

J Brower, S.F. ....89
R King, St.L. ....86
R Cormier, Phi. ....84
C Reitsma, Atl. ....84
S Torres, Pit. ....84

### Games Started

L Hernandez, Mon. ....35
R Johnson, Ari. ....35
R Oswalt, Hou. ....35
B Webb, Ari. ....35
8 tied with ....34

### Complete Games

L Hernandez, Mon. ....9
C Lidle, Cin.-Phi. ....5
B Sheets, Mil. ....5
R Johnson, Ari. ....4
J Schmidt, S.F. ....4

### Games Finished

J Isringhausen, St.L. ....66
J Mesa, Pit. ....65
J Smoltz, Atl. ....61
S Chacon, Col. ....60
B Looper, N.Y. ....60

### Wins

R Oswalt, Hou. ....20
R Clemens, Hou. ....18
C Pavano, Fla. ....18
J Schmidt, S.F. ....18
4 tied with ....16

### Losses

B Webb, Ari. ....16
C Fossum, Ari. ....15
L Hernandez, Mon. ....15
5 tied with ....14

### Saves

A Benitez, Fla. ....47
J Isringhausen, St.L. ....47
E Gagne, L.A. ....45
J Smoltz, Atl. ....44
J Mesa, Pit. ....43

### Shutouts

C Lidle, Cin-Phi. ....3
J Schmidt, S.F. ....3
6 tied with ....2

### Hits Allowed

J Jennings, Col. ....241
L Hernandez, Mon. ....234
R Oswalt, Hou. ....233
B Lawrence, S.D. ....226
K Rueter, S.F. ....225

### Doubles Allowed

R Oswalt, Hou. ....57
B Sheets, Mil. ....57
W Williams, St.L. ....53
K Rueter, S.F. ....52
J Acevedo, Cin. ....51

### Triples Allowed

R Johnson, Ari. ....9
S Estes, Col. ....8
J Jennings, Col. ....8
B Tomko, S.F. ....8
4 tied with ....7

### Home Runs Allowed

E Milton, Phi. ....43
G Maddux, Chi. ....35
M Morris, St.L. ....35
J Lima, L.A. ....33
I Valdez, S.D.-Fla. ....33

### Batters Faced

L Hernandez, Mon. ....1053
R Oswalt, Hou. ....983
R Johnson, Ari. ....964
B Sheets, Mil. ....937
J Weaver, L.A. ....935

### Innings Pitched

L Hernandez, Mon. ....255.0
R Johnson, Ari. ....245.2
R Oswalt, Hou. ....237.0
B Sheets, Mil. ....237.0
J Schmidt, S.F. ....225.0

### Runs Allowed

S Estes, Col. ....133
J Jennings, Col. ....125
C Lidle, Cin.-Phi. ....123
M Morris, St.L. ....116
2 tied with ....113

### Strikeouts

R Johnson, Ari. ....290
B Sheets, Mil. ....264
J Schmidt, S.F. ....251
O Perez, Pit. ....239
R Clemens, Hou. ....218

### Walks Allowed

B Webb, Ari. ....119
R Ortiz, Atl. ....112
S Estes, Col. ....105
J Jennings, Col. ....101
K Ishii, L.A. ....98

### Hit Batsmen

C Zambrano, Chi. ....20
J Williams, S.F. ....17
J Weaver, L.A. ....14
S Kim, Mon. ....13
M Clement, Chi. ....12

### Wild Pitches

B Webb, Ari. ....17
M Clement, Chi. ....14
W Williams, St.L. ....12
J Brower, S.F. ....10
B Tomko, S.F. ....10

### Balks

C Pavano, Fla. ....3
7 tied with ....2

# AMERICAN LEAGUE SPECIAL BATTING LEADERS

### Scoring-Position Average†

(minimum 100 PA)

| Player, Team | AB | H | Avg. |
|---|---|---|---|
| I Suzuki, Sea. | 121 | 45 | .372 |
| I Rodriguez, Det. | 133 | 48 | .361 |
| S Stewart, Min. | 92 | 33 | .359 |
| J Damon, Bos. | 155 | 55 | .355 |
| D Ortiz, Bos. | 160 | 56 | .350 |
| D Newhan, Bal. | 99 | 34 | .343 |
| H Blalock, Tex. | 143 | 49 | .343 |
| M Young, Tex. | 161 | 55 | .342 |
| B Surhoff, Bal. | 94 | 32 | .340 |
| M Ramirez, Bos. | 156 | 53 | .340 |

### Leadoff OBP†

(minimum 150 PA; *AB+BB+HBP+SF)

| Player, Team | *PA | OB | OBP |
|---|---|---|---|
| I Suzuki, Sea. | 718 | 300 | .418 |
| J Damon, Bos. | 688 | 265 | .385 |
| R Belliard, Cle. | 250 | 96 | .384 |
| M Lawton, Cle. | 397 | 151 | .380 |
| S Stewart, Min. | 429 | 163 | .380 |
| D DeJesus, K.C. | 370 | 139 | .376 |
| B Williams, N.Y. | 224 | 83 | .371 |
| A Rowand, Chi. | 179 | 66 | .369 |
| E Byrnes, Oak. | 182 | 67 | .368 |
| M Young, Tex. | 424 | 156 | .368 |

### Cleanup Slugging†

(minimum 150 PA)

| Player, Team | AB | TB | Slg. |
|---|---|---|---|
| M Ramirez, Bos. | 380 | 236 | .621 |
| M Tejada, Bal. | 328 | 194 | .591 |
| D Ortiz, Bos. | 186 | 106 | .570 |
| C Lee, Chi. | 164 | 93 | .567 |
| V Guerrero, Ana. | 164 | 92 | .561 |
| C Delgado, Tor. | 458 | 245 | .535 |
| M Teixeira, Tex. | 283 | 150 | .530 |
| F Thomas, Chi. | 128 | 67 | .523 |
| J Morneau, Min. | 258 | 134 | .519 |
| G Anderson, Ana. | 304 | 150 | .493 |

### Avg. vs. LHP

(minimum 125 PA)

| Player, Team | |
|---|---|
| I Suzuki, Sea. | .404 |
| J Varitek, Bos. | .350 |
| A Sanchez, Det. | .348 |
| E Byrnes, Oak | 344 |
| I Rodriguez, Det. | .343 |

### Avg. vs. RHP

(minimum 377 PA)

| Player, Team | |
|---|---|
| I Suzuki, Sea | .359 |
| M Mora, Bal. | .352 |
| T Hafner, Cle. | .344 |
| E Durazo, Oak | .340 |
| V Guerrero, Ana. | .335 |

### Avg. at Home

(minimum 251 PA)

| Player, Team | |
|---|---|
| M Mora, Bal. | .356 |
| I Rodriguez, Det. | .354 |
| K Millar, Bos. | .350 |
| M Young, Tex. | .346 |
| M Kotsay, Oak. | .346 |

### Avg. on Road

(minimum 251 PA)

| Player, Team | |
|---|---|
| I Suzuki, Sea. | .405 |
| V Guerrero, Ana. | .335 |
| H Matsui, N.Y. | .327 |
| M Mora, Bal. | .327 |
| E Durazo, Oak. | .325 |

### OBP vs. LHP

(minimum 125 PA)

| Player, Team | |
|---|---|
| M Ramirez, Bos. | .446 |
| I Suzuki, Sea. | .444 |
| V Guerrero, Ana. | .434 |
| J Varitek, Bos. | .426 |
| G Sheffield, N.Y. | .423 |

### OBP vs. RHP

(minimum 377 PA)

| Player, Team | |
|---|---|
| T Hafner, Cle. | .433 |
| M Mora, Bal. | .419 |
| E Durazo, Oak. | .419 |
| D Ortiz, Bos. | .411 |
| J Posada, N.Y. | .407 |

### Late & Close Avg.†

(minimum 50 PA)

| Player, Team | |
|---|---|
| I Suzuki, Sea. | .393 |
| H Matsui, N.Y. | .378 |
| C Gomez, Tor. | .370 |
| K Harvey, K.C. | .358 |
| R Winn, Sea. | .347 |

### Bases Loaded Avg.

(minimum 10 PA)

| Player, Team | |
|---|---|
| C Guillen, Det. | .667 |
| B Broussard, Cle. | .636 |
| R Gload, Chi. | .615 |
| S Hatteberg, Oak. | .615 |
| I Suzuki, Sea. | .583 |

### Slg. vs. LHP

(minimum 125 PA)

| Player, Team | |
|---|---|
| V Guerrero, Ana. | .723 |
| A Rodriguez, N.Y. | .659 |
| K Mench, Tex. | .646 |
| M Ramirez, Bos. | .631 |
| J Phelps, Tor.-Cle. | .618 |

### Slg. vs. RHP

(minimum 377 PA)

| Player, Team | |
|---|---|
| T Hafner, Cle. | .690 |
| D Ortiz, Bos. | .671 |
| M Ramirez, Bos. | .605 |
| H Matsui, N.Y. | .572 |
| M Mora, Bal. | .567 |

### AB per Home Run

(minimum 502 PA)

| Player, Team | |
|---|---|
| M Ramirez, Bos. | 13.2 |
| P Konerko, Chi. | 13.7 |
| D Ortiz, Bos. | 14.2 |
| C Delgado, Tor. | 14.3 |
| M Teixeira, Tex. | 14.3 |

### Times on Base*

(*H+BB+HBP)

| Player, Team | |
|---|---|
| I Suzuki, Sea. | 315 |
| G Sheffield, N.Y. | 269 |
| J Damon, Bos. | 267 |
| V Guerrero, Ana. | 266 |
| H Matsui, N.Y. | 265 |

### Pitches Seen

| Player, Team | |
|---|---|
| B Roberts, Bal. | 2908 |
| J Damon, Bos. | 2893 |
| C Blake, Cle. | 2844 |
| H Blalock, Tex. | 2807 |
| A Rodriguez, N.Y. | 2747 |

### Pitches per PA

(minimum 502 PA)

| Player, Team | |
|---|---|
| C Blake, Cle. | 4.26 |
| J Dye, Oak. | 4.25 |
| B Crosby, Oak. | 4.17 |
| M Bellhorn, Bos. | 4.15 |
| J Damon, Bos. | 4.12 |

### Pct. of Pitches Taken

(minimum 1500 pitches)

| Player, Team | |
|---|---|
| J Olerud, Sea.-N.Y. | 64.7 |
| S Hatteberg, Oak. | 63.9 |
| B Higginson, Det. | 62.5 |
| E Chavez, Oak. | 62.2 |
| B Williams, N.Y. | 62.2 |

### Ground/Fly Ratio†

(minimum 502 PA)

| Player, Team | |
|---|---|
| I Suzuki, Sea. | 3.31 |
| R Johnson, Tor. | 2.12 |
| L Bigbie, Bal. | 2.08 |
| D Erstad, Ana. | 2.07 |
| C Guzman, Min. | 1.95 |

### GDP/GDP Opp.†

(minimum 50 PA)

| Player, Team | |
|---|---|
| E Munson, Det. | 0.02 |
| G Matthews Jr., Tex. | 0.02 |
| D Brown, K.C. | 0.02 |
| C Crawford, T.B. | 0.02 |
| B Roberts, Bal. | 0.03 |

### SB Success Pct.

(minimum 20 SB attempts)

| Player, Team | |
|---|---|
| L Ford, Min. | 90.9 |
| A Rodriguez, N.Y. | 87.5 |
| J DaVanon, Ana. | 85.7 |
| D Jeter, N.Y. | 85.2 |
| R Baldelli, T.B. | 81.0 |

### Steals of Third

| Player, Team | |
|---|---|
| D Jeter, N.Y. | 12 |
| C Figgins, Ana. | 10 |
| C Crawford, T.B. | 9 |
| R Winn, Sea. | 8 |
| J Lugo, T.B. | 7 |

### Pct. CS by Catchers

(minimum 50 SB attempts)

| Player, Team | |
|---|---|
| H Blanco, Min. | 44.6 |
| B Inge, Det. | 37.5 |
| I Rodriguez, Det. | 28.6 |
| D Miller, Oak. | 28.1 |
| T Hall, T.B. | 27.9 |

**†Scoring-Position Average** denotes batting average when a runner is at second and/or third base. **Leadoff OBP** denotes OBP for a player batting in the first position of the batting order. **Cleanup Slugging** denotes slugging percentage for a player batting in the fourth position of the batting order. **Late & Close Avg.** refers to batting average when the game is in the seventh inning or later and the batting team is either leading by one run, tied, or has the potential tying run on base, at bat or on deck (a batting situation coming close to a pitcher's save situation). **Ground/Fly Ratio** denotes ground balls hit divided by fly balls hit. All batted balls except line drives and bunts are included. **GDP/GDP Opp.** denotes the ratio of times grounding into double plays per opportunities to do so (any situation with a runner on first and less than two out).

# NATIONAL LEAGUE SPECIAL BATTING LEADERS

### Scoring-Position Average†
(minimum 100 PA)

| Player, Team | AB | H | Avg. |
|---|---|---|---|
| B Bonds, S.F. | 71 | 28 | .394 |
| J Snow, S.F. | 83 | 30 | .361 |
| S Rolen, St.L. | 151 | 54 | .358 |
| J Franco, Atl. | 95 | 33 | .347 |
| J Kendall, Pit. | 107 | 37 | .346 |
| A Pujols, St.L. | 143 | 49 | .343 |
| J Estrada, Atl. | 139 | 47 | .338 |
| T Sledge, Mon. | 95 | 32 | .337 |
| A Ramirez, Chi. | 122 | 41 | .336 |
| D Cruz, S.F. | 105 | 35 | .333 |

### Leadoff OBP†
(minimum 150 PA; *AB+BB+HBP+SF)

| Player, Team | *PA | OB | OBP |
|---|---|---|---|
| J Kendall, Pit. | 542 | 219 | .404 |
| R Freel, Cin. | 478 | 186 | .389 |
| J Pierre, Fla. | 641 | 245 | .382 |
| B Wilkerson, Mon. | 490 | 187 | .382 |
| T Walker, Chi. | 262 | 97 | .370 |
| R Durham, S.F. | 531 | 194 | .365 |
| J Rollins, Phi. | 547 | 197 | .360 |
| T Womack, St.L. | 577 | 203 | .352 |
| S Burroughs, S.D. | 460 | 158 | .343 |
| R Furcal, Atl. | 615 | 211 | .343 |

### Cleanup Slugging†
(minimum 150 PA)

| Player, Team | AB | TB | Slg. |
|---|---|---|---|
| B Bonds, S.F. | 371 | 303 | .817 |
| A Beltre, L.A. | 353 | 232 | .657 |
| M Alou, Chi. | 363 | 222 | .612 |
| S Rolen, St.L. | 386 | 233 | .604 |
| J Thome, Phi. | 459 | 265 | .577 |
| A Dunn, Cin. | 323 | 182 | .563 |
| V Castilla, Col. | 517 | 286 | .553 |
| M Lowell, Fla. | 268 | 145 | .541 |
| M Piazza, N.Y. | 223 | 119 | .534 |
| L Overbay, Mil. | 184 | 98 | .533 |

### Avg. vs. LHP
(minimum 125 PA)

| Player, Team | Avg. |
|---|---|
| A Pujols, St.L. | .379 |
| E Renteria, St.L. | .366 |
| M Loretta, S.D. | .352 |
| M Lowell, Fla. | .344 |
| R Durham, S.F. | .333 |

### Avg. vs. RHP
(minimum 377 PA)

| Player, Team | Avg. |
|---|---|
| B Bonds, S.F. | .395 |
| T Helton, Col. | .360 |
| A Beltre, L.A. | .347 |
| J Pierre, Fla. | .334 |
| S Casey, Cin. | .332 |

### Avg. at Home
(minimum 251 PA)

| Player, Team | Avg. |
|---|---|
| B Bonds, S.F. | .412 |
| T Helton, Col. | .368 |
| S Hillenbrand, Ari. | .347 |
| M Alou, Chi. | .339 |
| J Pierre, Fla. | .338 |

### Avg. on Road
(minimum 251 PA)

| Player, Team | Avg. |
|---|---|
| M Loretta, S.D. | .368 |
| S Casey, Cin. | .361 |
| J Estrada, Atl. | .351 |
| S Rolen, St.L. | .346 |
| A Beltre, L.A. | .342 |

### OBP vs. LHP
(minimum 125 PA)

| Player, Team | OBP |
|---|---|
| B Bonds, S.F. | .524 |
| A Pujols, St.L. | .465 |
| P Nevin, S.D. | .431 |
| M Loretta, S.D. | .431 |
| 2 tied with | .429 |

### OBP vs. RHP
(minimum 377 PA)

| Player, Team | OBP |
|---|---|
| B Bonds, S.F. | .652 |
| T Helton, Col. | .492 |
| L Berkman, Hou. | .463 |
| J Drew, Atl. | .450 |
| B Abreu, Phi. | .438 |

### Late & Close Avg.†
(minimum 50 PA)

| Player, Team | Avg. |
|---|---|
| M Grudzielanek, Chi. | .457 |
| D Bautista, Ari. | .386 |
| M Ensberg, Hou. | .383 |
| J Wilson, Pit. | .379 |
| S Burroughs, S.D. | .377 |

### Bases Loaded Avg.
(minimum 10 PA)

| Player, Team | Avg. |
|---|---|
| S Rolen, St.L. | .583 |
| P Lo Duca, L.A.-Fla. | .563 |
| P Nevin, S.D. | .556 |
| 4 tied with | .500 |

### Slg. vs. LHP
(minimum 125 PA)

| Player, Team | Slg. |
|---|---|
| A Pujols, St.L. | .741 |
| M Lowell, Fla. | .672 |
| J Hernandez, L.A. | .627 |
| D Lee, Chi. | .595 |
| P Nevin, S.D. | .582 |

### Slg. vs. RHP
(minimum 377 PA)

| Player, Team | Slg. |
|---|---|
| B Bonds, S.F. | .957 |
| A Beltre, L.A. | .672 |
| T Helton, Col. | .669 |
| J Edmonds, St.L. | .651 |
| J Thome, Phi. | .641 |

### AB per Home Run
(minimum 502 PA)

| Player, Team | AB/HR |
|---|---|
| B Bonds, S.F. | 8.3 |
| J Edmonds, St.L. | 11.9 |
| J Thome, Phi. | 12.1 |
| A Dunn, Cin. | 12.3 |
| A Beltre, L.A. | 12.5 |

### Times on Base*
(*H+BB+HBP)

| Player, Team | TOB |
|---|---|
| B Bonds, S.F. | 376 |
| T Helton, Col. | 320 |
| L Berkman, Hou. | 309 |
| B Abreu, Phi. | 305 |
| A Pujols, St.L. | 287 |

### Pitches Seen

| Player, Team | Pitches |
|---|---|
| B Abreu, Phi. | 3077 |
| B Wilkerson, Mon. | 2954 |
| A Dunn, Cin. | 2888 |
| S Podsednik, Mil. | 2837 |
| J Bagwell, Hou. | 2819 |

### Pitches per PA
(minimum 502 PA)

| Player, Team | P/PA |
|---|---|
| B Abreu, Phi. | 4.32 |
| B Wilkerson, Mon. | 4.29 |
| A Dunn, Cin. | 4.24 |
| J Edmonds, St.L. | 4.23 |
| J Kendall, Pit. | 4.21 |

### Pct. of Pitches Taken
(minimum 1500 pitches)

| Player, Team | Pct. |
|---|---|
| B Bonds, S.F. | 71.9 |
| T Zeile, N.Y. | 66.4 |
| D Jimenez, Cin. | 65.1 |
| B Abreu, Phi. | 64.8 |
| J Kendall, Pit. | 64.7 |

### Ground/Fly Ratio†
(minimum 502 PA)

| Player, Team | G/F |
|---|---|
| L Castillo, Fla. | 3.63 |
| J Pierre, Fla. | 2.36 |
| R Clayton, Col. | 2.34 |
| S Burroughs, S.D. | 2.18 |
| T Redman, Pit. | 1.96 |

### GDP/GDP Opp.†
(minimum 50 PA)

| Player, Team | Ratio |
|---|---|
| J Werth, L.A. | 0.01 |
| T Sledge, Mon. | 0.03 |
| R Mackowiak, Pit. | 0.03 |
| J Edmonds, St.L. | 0.03 |
| B Abreu, Phi. | 0.03 |

### SB Success Pct.
(minimum 20 SB attempts)

| Player, Team | Pct. |
|---|---|
| C Beltran, Hou. | 100.0 |
| D Roberts, L.A. | 97.1 |
| J Reyes, N.Y. | 90.5 |
| B Abreu, Phi. | 88.9 |
| S Podsednik, Mil. | 84.3 |

### Steals of Third

| Player, Team | SB |
|---|---|
| C Beltran, Hou. | 11 |
| S Podsednik, Mil. | 10 |
| J Pierre, Fla. | 8 |
| J Reyes, N.Y. | 6 |
| R Sanders, St.L. | 6 |

### Pct. CS by Catchers
(minimum 50 SB attempts)

| Player, Team | Pct. |
|---|---|
| B Schneider, Mon. | 47.8 |
| J Kendall, Pit. | 32.3 |
| J LaRue, Cin. | 29.6 |
| P Bako, Chi. | 29.4 |
| M Matheny, St.L. | 28.3 |

†**Scoring-Position Average** denotes batting average when a runner is at second and/or third base. **Leadoff OBP** denotes OBP for a player batting in the first position of the batting order. **Cleanup Slugging** denotes slugging percentage for a player batting in the fourth position of the batting order. **Late & Close Avg.** refers to batting average when the game is in the seventh inning or later and the batting team is either leading by one run, tied, or has the potential tying run on base, at bat or on deck (a batting situation coming close to a pitcher's save situation). **Ground/Fly Ratio** denotes ground balls hit divided by fly balls hit. All batted balls except line drives and bunts are included. **GDP/GDP Opp.** denotes the ratio of times grounding into double plays per opportunities to do so (any situation with a runner on first and less than two out).

# AMERICAN LEAGUE SPECIAL PITCHING LEADERS



### Baserunners per 9 IP
(minimum 162 IP)

| Pitcher, Team | IP | BR | BR/9 |
|---|---|---|---|
| J Santana, Min. | 228.0 | 219 | 8.64 |
| C Schilling, Bos. | 226.2 | 246 | 9.77 |
| B Radke, Min. | 219.2 | 261 | 10.69 |
| P Martinez, Bos. | 217.0 | 270 | 11.20 |
| F Garcia, Sea.-Chi. | 210.0 | 263 | 11.27 |
| J Westbrook, Cle. | 215.2 | 274 | 11.43 |
| M Buehrle, Chi. | 245.1 | 316 | 11.59 |
| R Lopez, Bal. | 170.2 | 220 | 11.60 |
| K Escobar, Ana. | 208.1 | 275 | 11.88 |
| T Hudson, Oak. | 188.2 | 250 | 11.93 |

### Strikeouts per 9 IP
(minimum 162 IP)

| Pitcher, Team | IP | SO | SO/9 |
|---|---|---|---|
| J Santana, Min. | 228.0 | 265 | 10.46 |
| P Martinez, Bos. | 217.0 | 227 | 9.41 |
| K Escobar, Ana. | 208.1 | 191 | 8.25 |
| J Bonderman, Det. | 184.0 | 168 | 8.22 |
| C Lee, Cle. | 179.0 | 161 | 8.09 |
| C Schilling, Bos. | 226.2 | 203 | 8.06 |
| J Contreras, N.Y.-Chi. | 170.1 | 150 | 7.93 |
| R Harden, Oak. | 189.2 | 167 | 7.92 |
| F Garcia, Sea.-Chi. | 210.0 | 184 | 7.89 |
| T Lilly, Tor. | 197.1 | 168 | 7.66 |

### Run Support per 9 IP†
(minimum 162 IP)

| Pitcher, Team | IP | R | RS/9 |
|---|---|---|---|
| C Schilling, Bos. | 226.2 | 190 | 7.54 |
| D Lowe, Bos. | 182.2 | 148 | 7.29 |
| B Colon, Ana. | 208.1 | 162 | 7.00 |
| K Rogers, Tex. | 211.2 | 161 | 6.85 |
| J Lieber, N.Y. | 176.2 | 134 | 6.83 |
| M Buehrle, Chi. | 245.1 | 181 | 6.64 |
| M Mulder, Oak. | 225.2 | 164 | 6.54 |
| J Westbrook, Cle. | 215.2 | 155 | 6.47 |
| N Robertson, Det. | 196.2 | 139 | 6.36 |
| J Contreras, N.Y.-Chi. | 170.1 | 120 | 6.34 |

### Opposition OBP
(minimum 162 IP)

| | |
|---|---|
| J Santana, Min. | .249 |
| C Schilling, Bos. | .271 |
| B Radke, Min. | .291 |
| P Martinez, Bos. | .301 |
| F Garcia, Sea.-Chi. | .303 |

### Opposition SLG
(minimum 162 IP)

| | |
|---|---|
| J Santana, Min. | .315 |
| R Harden, Oak. | .366 |
| T Hudson, Oak. | .366 |
| J Westbrook, Cle. | .386 |
| C Schilling, Bos. | .387 |

### Hits per 9 IP
(minimum 162 IP)

| | |
|---|---|
| J Santana, Min. | 6.16 |
| T Lilly, Tor. | 7.80 |
| P Martinez, Bos. | 8.00 |
| R Harden, Oak. | 8.11 |
| C Schilling, Bos. | 8.18 |

### Home Runs per 9 IP
(minimum 162 IP)

| | |
|---|---|
| T Hudson, Oak. | 0.38 |
| R Drese, Tex. | 0.69 |
| D Lowe, Bos. | 0.74 |
| R Harden, Oak. | 0.76 |
| J Westbrook, Cle. | 0.79 |

### Avg. vs. LHB
(minimum 125 BFP)

| | |
|---|---|
| J Rincon, Min. | .148 |
| K Foulke, Bos. | .185 |
| T Gordon, N.Y. | .185 |
| S Elarton, Cle. | .190 |
| J Santana, Min. | .196 |

### Avg. vs. RHB
(minimum 225 BFP)

| | |
|---|---|
| J Santana, Min. | .191 |
| V Zambrano, T.B. | .219 |
| J Bonderman, Det. | .223 |
| R Bell, T.B. | .226 |
| B Arroyo, Bos. | .227 |

### Avg. Allowed Sc. Pos.†
(minimum 125 BFP)

| | |
|---|---|
| V Zambrano, T.B. | .157 |
| J Santana, Min. | .165 |
| P Martinez, Bos. | .197 |
| R Lopez, Bal. | .197 |
| F Garcia, Sea.-Chi. | .218 |

### OBP Leading off Inn.
(minimum 150 BFP)

| | |
|---|---|
| C Schilling, Bos. | .223 |
| J Vazquez, N.Y. | .255 |
| J Santana, Min. | .264 |
| B Arroyo, Bos. | .275 |
| R Lopez, Bal. | .275 |

### SO/BB Ratio
(minimum 162 IP)

| | |
|---|---|
| C Schilling, Bos. | 5.80 |
| J Lieber, N.Y. | 5.67 |
| B Radke, Min. | 5.50 |
| J Santana, Min. | 4.91 |
| P Martinez, Bos. | 3.72 |

### Grd/Fly Ratio Off†
(minimum 162 IP)

| | |
|---|---|
| D Lowe, Bos. | 2.87 |
| J Westbrook, Cle. | 2.72 |
| T Hudson, Oak. | 2.53 |
| R Drese, Tex. | 2.20 |
| M Mulder, Oak. | 2.05 |

### Pitches per Start
(minimum 30 games started)

| | |
|---|---|
| B Zito, Oak. | 108.5 |
| C Schilling, Bos. | 106.6 |
| F Garcia, Sea.-Chi. | 106.1 |
| P Martinez, Bos. | 105.8 |
| M Buehrle, Chi. | 105.6 |

### Pitches per Batter
(minimum 162 IP)

| | |
|---|---|
| C Silva, Min. | 3.33 |
| J Lieber, N.Y. | 3.40 |
| R Drese, Tex. | 3.46 |
| M Mulder, Oak. | 3.46 |
| S Ponson, Bal. | 3.47 |

### Stolen Bases Allowed

| | |
|---|---|
| D Lowe, Bos. | 34 |
| T Wakefield, Bos. | 33 |
| J Contreras, N.Y.-Chi. | 29 |
| K Escobar, Ana. | 24 |
| 2 tied with | 19 |

### Caught Stealing Off

| | |
|---|---|
| M Mulder, Oak. | 13 |
| M Batista, Tor. | 11 |
| J Contreras, N.Y.-Chi. | 11 |
| M Maroth, Det. | 11 |
| A Sele, Ana. | 11 |

### SB Pct. Allowed
(minimum 162 IP)

| | |
|---|---|
| B Anderson, K.C. | 20.0 |
| K Rogers, Tex. | 28.6 |
| J Vazquez, N.Y. | 28.6 |
| B Colon, Ana. | 33.3 |
| 2 tied with | 38.5 |

### Pickoffs

| | |
|---|---|
| M Buehrle, Chi. | 10 |
| M Mulder, Oak. | 9 |
| M Redman, Oak. | 9 |
| K Rogers, Tex. | 6 |
| S Schoeneweis, Chi. | 6 |

### PkOf Throw/Runner†
(minimum 162 IP)

| | |
|---|---|
| R Franklin, Sea. | 1.06 |
| K Escobar, Ana. | 0.73 |
| D May, K.C. | 0.67 |
| B Zito, Oak. | 0.66 |
| M Redman, Oak. | 0.62 |

### GDP Induced

| | |
|---|---|
| M Mulder, Oak. | 37 |
| S Ponson, Bal. | 36 |
| M Buehrle, Chi. | 33 |
| J Westbrook, Cle. | 29 |
| 2 tied with | 28 |

### GDP per 9 IP
(minimum 162 IP)

| | |
|---|---|
| S Ponson, Bal. | 1.5 |
| M Mulder, Oak. | 1.5 |
| D Lowe, Bos. | 1.4 |
| C Silva, Min. | 1.2 |
| N Robertson, Det. | 1.2 |

### Quality Starts†

| | |
|---|---|
| J Santana, Min. | 25 |
| B Radke, Min. | 24 |
| M Buehrle, Chi. | 23 |
| P Martinez, Bos. | 22 |
| C Schilling, Bos. | 22 |

**†Run Support per 9 IP** denotes the number of runs scored by a pitcher's team while he was still in the game times nine divided by his innings pitched. **Avg. Allowed Sc. Pos.** denotes batting average allowed when a runner is at second and/or third base. **Grd/Fly Ratio Off** denotes ground balls allowed divided by fly balls allowed. All batted balls except line drives and bunts are included. **PkOf Throw/Runner** denotes the number of pickoff throws made by a pitcher divided by the number of runners on first base. **Quality Starts** denote the number of outings in which a starting pitcher works at least six innings and allows three or fewer earned runs.

# NATIONAL LEAGUE SPECIAL PITCHING LEADERS

### Baserunners per 9 IP
(minimum 162 IP)

| Pitcher, Team | IP | BR | BR/9 |
|---|---|---|---|
| R Johnson, Ari. | 245.2 | 231 | 8.46 |
| B Sheets, Mil. | 237.0 | 237 | 9.00 |
| J Schmidt, S.F. | 225.0 | 245 | 9.80 |
| D Wells, S.D. | 195.2 | 225 | 10.35 |
| O Perez, L.A. | 196.1 | 227 | 10.41 |
| C Carpenter, St.L. | 182.0 | 215 | 10.63 |
| R Clemens, Hou. | 214.1 | 254 | 10.67 |
| O Perez, Pit. | 196.0 | 235 | 10.79 |
| G Maddux, Chi. | 212.2 | 260 | 11.00 |
| C Pavano, Fla. | 222.1 | 272 | 11.01 |

### Strikeouts per 9 IP
(minimum 162 IP)

| Pitcher, Team | IP | SO | SO/9 |
|---|---|---|---|
| O Perez, Pit. | 196.0 | 239 | 10.97 |
| R Johnson, Ari. | 245.2 | 290 | 10.62 |
| J Schmidt, S.F. | 225.0 | 251 | 10.04 |
| B Sheets, Mil. | 237.0 | 264 | 10.03 |
| M Clement, Chi. | 181.0 | 190 | 9.45 |
| J Peavy, S.D. | 166.1 | 173 | 9.36 |
| R Clemens, Hou. | 214.1 | 218 | 9.15 |
| C Zambrano, Chi. | 209.2 | 188 | 8.07 |
| R Oswalt, Hou. | 237.0 | 206 | 7.82 |
| J Wright, Atl. | 186.1 | 159 | 7.68 |

### Run Support per 9 IP†
(minimum 162 IP)

| Pitcher, Team | IP | R | RS/9 |
|---|---|---|---|
| K Ishii, L.A. | 172.0 | 128 | 6.70 |
| S Estes, Col. | 202.0 | 147 | 6.55 |
| E Milton, Phi. | 201.0 | 146 | 6.54 |
| J Peavy, S.D. | 166.1 | 119 | 6.44 |
| B Myers, Phi. | 176.0 | 121 | 6.19 |
| C Zambrano, Chi. | 209.2 | 141 | 6.05 |
| R Oswalt, Hou. | 237.0 | 159 | 6.04 |
| B Tomko, S.F. | 194.0 | 129 | 5.98 |
| J Marquis, St.L. | 201.1 | 133 | 5.95 |
| J Thomson, Atl. | 198.1 | 130 | 5.90 |

### Opposition OBP
(minimum 162 IP)

R Johnson, Ari. .241
B Sheets, Mil. .255
J Schmidt, S.F. .272
D Wells, S.D. .285
C Carpenter, St.L. .291

### Opposition SLG
(minimum 162 IP)

R Johnson, Ari. .315
J Schmidt, S.F. .323
R Clemens, Hou. .329
J Wright, Atl. .337
C Zambrano, Chi. .338

### Hits per 9 IP
(minimum 162 IP)

R Johnson, Ari. 6.48
J Schmidt, S.F. 6.60
O Perez, Pit. 6.66
R Clemens, Hou. 7.10
A Leiter, N.Y. 7.15

### Home Runs per 9 IP
(minimum 162 IP)

J Wright, Atl. 0.53
C Zambrano, Chi. 0.60
D Davis, Mil. 0.61
R Clemens, Hou. 0.63
R Oswalt, Hou. 0.65

### Avg. vs. LHB
(minimum 125 BFP)

R King, St.L. .150
L Vizcaino, Mil. .163
R Johnson, Ari. .163
S Linebrink, S.D. .178
J Kennedy, Col. .184

### Avg. vs. RHB
(minimum 225 BFP)

J Beckett, Fla. .192
R Johnson, Ari. .204
O Perez, Pit. .204
A Pettitte, Hou. .208
A Burnett, Fla. .211

### Avg. Allowed Sc. Pos.†
(minimum 125 BFP)

A Leiter, N.Y. .173
C Zambrano, Chi. .179
O Perez, Pit. .180
J Schmidt, S.F. .180
J Peavy, S.D. .185

### OBP Leading off Inn.
(minimum 150 BFP)

R Johnson, Ari. .200
B Sheets, Mil. .218
C Carpenter, St.L. .250
D Wells, S.D. .260
E Milton, Phi. .266

### SO/BB Ratio
(minimum 162 IP)

B Sheets, Mil. 8.25
R Johnson, Ari. 6.59
D Wells, S.D. 5.05
G Maddux, Chi. 4.58
C Carpenter, St.L. 4.00

### Grd/Fly Ratio Off†
(minimum 162 IP)

B Webb, Ari. 3.55
J Marquis, St.L. 2.17
M Hampton, Atl. 2.01
C Carpenter, St.L. 1.93
B Lawrence, S.D. 1.82

### Pitches per Start
(minimum 30 games started)

J Schmidt, S.F. 112.8
L Hernandez, Mon. 112.2
C Zambrano, Chi. 111.9
A Leiter, N.Y. 108.3
B Sheets, Mil. 105.4

### Pitches per Batter
(minimum 162 IP)

G Maddux, Chi. 3.36
J Lima, L.A. 3.44
C Lidle, Cin.-Phi. 3.44
C Pavano, Fla. 3.47
B Lawrence, S.D. 3.47

### Stolen Bases Allowed

B Webb, Ari. 31
J Schmidt, S.F. 28
G Maddux, Chi. 26
R Clemens, Hou. 23
G Mota, L.A.-Fla. 21

### Caught Stealing Off

G Maddux, Chi. 12
R Clemens, Hou. 10
R Johnson, Ari. 10
B Webb, Ari. 10
2 tied with 9

### SB Pct. Allowed
(minimum 162 IP)

C Carpenter, St.L. 0.0
K Rueter, S.F. 25.0
T Glavine, N.Y. 46.7
O Perez, Pit. 50.0
P Wilson, Cin. 50.0

### Pickoffs

C Capuano, Mil. 6
5 tied with 5

### PkOf Throw/Runner†
(minimum 162 IP)

A Leiter, N.Y. 0.98
S Trachsel, N.Y. 0.90
R Clemens, Hou. 0.80
P Wilson, Cin. 0.73
R Ortiz, Atl. 0.64

### GDP Induced

S Estes, Col. 34
J Fogg, Pit. 27
M Morris, St.L. 26
O Perez, L.A. 25
K Rueter, S.F. 25

### GDP per 9 IP
(minimum 162 IP)

S Estes, Col. 1.5
J Fogg, Pit. 1.4
K Rueter, S.F. 1.2
M Morris, St.L. 1.2
O Perez, L.A. 1.1

### Quality Starts†

R Johnson, Ari. 26
J Weaver, L.A. 25
D Davis, Mil. 24
B Sheets, Mil. 24
2 tied with 23

**†Run Support per 9 IP** denotes the number of runs scored by a pitcher's team while he was still in the game times nine divided by his innings pitched. **Avg. Allowed Sc. Pos.** denotes batting average allowed when a runner is at second and/or third base. **Grd/Fly Ratio Off** denotes ground balls allowed divided by fly balls allowed. All batted balls except line drives and bunts are included. **PkOf Throw/Runner** denotes the number of pickoff throws made by a pitcher divided by the number of runners on first base. **Quality Starts** denote the number of outings in which a starting pitcher works at least six innings and allows three or fewer earned runs.

# AMERICAN LEAGUE RELIEF PITCHING LEADERS

## Saves

| Pitcher, Team | Saves |
|---|---|
| M Rivera, N.Y. | 53 |
| F Cordero, Tex. | 49 |
| J Nathan, Min. | 44 |
| T Percival, Ana. | 33 |
| K Foulke, Bos. | 32 |
| D Baez, T.B. | 30 |
| O Dotel, Oak. | 22 |
| J Julio, Bal. | 22 |
| U Urbina, Det. | 21 |
| S Takatsu, Chi. | 19 |

## Save Percentage

**(minimum 20 save opportunities)**

| Pitcher, Team | Opp. | Sv. | Pct. |
|---|---|---|---|
| S Takatsu, Chi. | 20 | 19 | 95.0 |
| J Nathan, Min. | 47 | 44 | 93.6 |
| M Rivera, N.Y. | 57 | 53 | 93.0 |
| D Baez, T.B. | 33 | 30 | 90.9 |
| F Cordero, Tex. | 54 | 49 | 90.7 |
| U Urbina, Det. | 24 | 21 | 87.5 |
| T Percival, Ana. | 38 | 33 | 86.8 |
| J Julio, Bal. | 26 | 22 | 84.6 |
| K Foulke, Bos. | 39 | 32 | 82.1 |
| O Dotel, Oak. | 28 | 22 | 78.6 |

## Relief ERA

**(minimum 50 relief IP)**

| Pitcher, Team | IP | ER | ERA |
|---|---|---|---|
| J Nathan, Min. | 72.1 | 13 | 1.62 |
| F Rodriguez, Ana. | 84.0 | 17 | 1.82 |
| M Rivera, N.Y. | 78.2 | 17 | 1.94 |
| F Cordero, Tex. | 71.2 | 17 | 2.13 |
| K Foulke, Bos. | 83.0 | 20 | 2.17 |
| T Gordon, N.Y. | 89.2 | 22 | 2.21 |
| B Ryan, Bal. | 87.0 | 22 | 2.28 |
| S Takatsu, Chi. | 62.1 | 16 | 2.31 |
| R Mahay, Tex. | 67.0 | 19 | 2.55 |
| J Rincon, Min. | 82.0 | 24 | 2.63 |

## Relief Wins

| | |
|---|---|
| J Rincon, Min. | 11 |
| T Gordon, N.Y. | 9 |
| S Shields, Ana. | 8 |
| 5 tied with | 7 |

## Relief Losses

| | |
|---|---|
| J Speier, Tor. | 8 |
| C Bradford, Oak. | 7 |
| J Grimsley, K.C.-Bal. | 7 |
| J Jimenez, Cle. | 7 |
| 9 tied with | 6 |

## Holds†

| | |
|---|---|
| T Gordon, N.Y. | 36 |
| F Rodriguez, Ana. | 27 |
| P Quantrill, N.Y. | 22 |
| 3 tied with | 21 |

## Blown Saves†

| | |
|---|---|
| E Yan, Det. | 10 |
| J Grimsley, K.C.-Bal. | 9 |
| 6 tied with | 7 |

## Relief Games

| | |
|---|---|
| P Quantrill, N.Y. | 86 |
| T Gordon, N.Y. | 80 |
| J Rincon, Min. | 77 |
| B Ryan, Bal. | 76 |
| M Timlin, Bos. | 76 |

## Games Finished

| | |
|---|---|
| M Rivera, N.Y. | 69 |
| F Cordero, Tex. | 63 |
| J Nathan, Min. | 63 |
| K Foulke, Bos. | 61 |
| D Baez, T.B. | 59 |

## Relief Innings

| | |
|---|---|
| S Shields, Ana. | 105.1 |
| J Duchscherer, Oak. | 96.1 |
| P Quantrill, N.Y. | 95.1 |
| T Gordon, N.Y. | 89.2 |
| K Gregg, Ana. | 87.2 |

## Pct. Inherited Scored†

**(minimum 30 inherited runners)**

| | |
|---|---|
| N Field, K.C. | 14.3 |
| D Brocail, Tex. | 15.2 |
| T Gordon, N.Y. | 16.2 |
| B Shouse, Tex. | 16.7 |
| J Cerda, K.C. | 17.4 |

## Opposition Avg.

**(minimum 50 relief IP)**

| | |
|---|---|
| F Rodriguez, Ana. | .172 |
| T Gordon, N.Y. | .180 |
| J Rincon, Min. | .181 |
| S Takatsu, Chi. | .182 |
| J Nathan, Min. | .187 |

## Opposition OBP

**(minimum 50 relief IP)**

| | |
|---|---|
| T Gordon, N.Y. | .237 |
| K Foulke, Bos. | .254 |
| F Rodriguez, Ana. | .256 |
| J Nathan, Min. | .259 |
| S Takatsu, Chi. | .259 |

## Opposition SLG

**(minimum 50 relief IP)**

| | |
|---|---|
| F Rodriguez, Ana. | .226 |
| J Nathan, Min. | .257 |
| J Rincon, Min. | .265 |
| B Ryan, Bal. | .272 |
| M Rivera, N.Y. | .280 |

## First Batter Avg.

**(minimum 40 first BFP)**

| | |
|---|---|
| R Villone, Sea. | .093 |
| S Takatsu, Chi. | .143 |
| C Bradford, Oak. | .145 |
| M Miller, Cle. | .163 |
| D Marte, Chi. | .169 |

## Avg. vs. LHB

**(minimum 50 relief IP)**

| | |
|---|---|
| B Ryan, Bal. | .094 |
| D Marte, Chi. | .143 |
| J Rincon, Min. | .148 |
| K Foulke, Bos. | .185 |
| T Gordon, N.Y. | .185 |

## Avg. vs. RHB

**(minimum 50 relief IP)**

| | |
|---|---|
| F Rodriguez, Ana. | .127 |
| S Takatsu, Chi. | .150 |
| J Nathan, Min. | .160 |
| F Francisco, Tex. | .165 |
| T Gordon, N.Y. | .174 |

## Avg., Runners On†

**(minimum 50 relief IP)**

| | |
|---|---|
| S Takatsu, Chi. | .155 |
| J Nathan, Min. | .159 |
| T Gordon, N.Y. | .162 |
| F Rodriguez, Ana. | .164 |
| O Dotel, Oak. | .176 |

## Avg., Scoring Pos.†

**(minimum 50 relief IP)**

| | |
|---|---|
| M Rivera, N.Y. | .139 |
| T Gordon, N.Y. | .153 |
| D Marte, Chi. | .161 |
| F Francisco, Tex. | .167 |
| J Nathan, Min. | .172 |

## Easy Saves†

| | |
|---|---|
| M Rivera, N.Y. | 36 |
| F Cordero, Tex. | 27 |
| J Nathan, Min. | 24 |
| T Percival, Ana. | 23 |
| K Foulke, Bos. | 20 |

## Regular Saves†

| | |
|---|---|
| F Cordero, Tex. | 20 |
| J Nathan, Min. | 19 |
| M Rivera, N.Y. | 15 |
| D Baez, T.B. | 13 |
| K Foulke, Bos. | 12 |

## Tough Saves†

| | |
|---|---|
| E Guardado, Sea. | 4 |
| F Rodriguez, Ana. | 4 |
| J Affeldt, K.C. | 3 |
| 4 tied with | 2 |

## Pitches per Batter

**(minimum 50 relief IP)**

| | |
|---|---|
| S Camp, K.C. | 3.35 |
| C Almanzar, Tex. | 3.44 |
| B Groom, Bal. | 3.48 |
| P Quantrill, N.Y. | 3.51 |
| J Walker, Det. | 3.52 |

**†Holds** denote the number of times a relief pitcher enters the game in a save situation, records at least one out and leaves the game never having relinquished the lead. A pitcher cannot finish the game and receive credit for a hold, nor can he earn a hold and a save in the same game. **Blown Saves** denote the number of times a relief pitcher enters a game in a save situation and allows the tying or go-ahead run to score. **Pct. Inherited Scored** denotes the percent of inherited runners (those on base when a reliever enters the game) that score. **Avg., Runners On** denotes batting average allowed when runners are on base. **Avg., Scoring Pos.** denotes batting average allowed when a runner is at second and/or third base. **Easy Saves** denote saves in which the first batter faced doesn't represent the tying run and the reliever pitches one inning or less. **Regular Saves** denote those saves that are not Easy Saves or Tough Saves. **Tough Saves** denote saves which occur after the reliever enters with the tying run anywhere on base.

# NATIONAL LEAGUE RELIEF PITCHING LEADERS

### Saves

| Pitcher, Team | Saves |
|---|---|
| A Benitez, Fla. | 47 |
| J Isringhausen, St.L. | 47 |
| E Gagne, L.A. | 45 |
| J Smoltz, Atl. | 44 |
| J Mesa, Pit. | 43 |
| D Graves, Cin. | 41 |
| T Hoffman, S.D. | 41 |
| D Kolb, Mil. | 39 |
| S Chacon, Col. | 35 |
| 2 tied with | 29 |

### Save Percentage

**(minimum 20 save opportunities)**

| Pitcher, Team | Opp. | Sv. | Pct. |
|---|---|---|---|
| E Gagne, L.A. | 47 | 45 | 95.7 |
| A Benitez, Fla. | 51 | 47 | 92.2 |
| T Hoffman, S.D. | 45 | 41 | 91.1 |
| J Smoltz, Atl. | 49 | 44 | 89.8 |
| J Mesa, Pit. | 48 | 43 | 89.6 |
| D Kolb, Mil. | 44 | 39 | 88.6 |
| B Lidge, Hou. | 33 | 29 | 87.9 |
| J Isringhausen, St.L. | 54 | 47 | 87.0 |
| B Looper, N.Y. | 34 | 29 | 85.3 |
| D Hermanson, S.F. | 20 | 17 | 85.0 |

### Relief ERA

**(minimum 50 relief IP)**

| Pitcher, Team | IP | ER | ERA |
|---|---|---|---|
| A Benitez, Fla. | 69.2 | 10 | 1.29 |
| R Madson, Phi. | 76.1 | 14 | 1.65 |
| A Otsuka, S.D. | 77.1 | 15 | 1.75 |
| S Kline, St.L. | 50.1 | 10 | 1.79 |
| B Lidge, Hou. | 94.2 | 20 | 1.90 |
| S Linebrink, S.D. | 84.0 | 20 | 2.14 |
| G Carrara, L.A. | 53.2 | 13 | 2.18 |
| E Gagne, L.A. | 82.1 | 20 | 2.19 |
| E Dessens, Ari.-L.A. | 60.0 | 15 | 2.25 |
| T Hoffman, S.D. | 54.2 | 14 | 2.30 |

### Relief Wins

| | |
|---|---|
| T Jones, Cin-Phi. | 11 |
| R Madson, Phi | 9 |
| G Mota, LA-Fla. | 9 |
| 7 tied with | 7 |

### Relief Losses

| | |
|---|---|
| L Ayala, Mon. | 12 |
| S Chacon, Col. | 9 |
| G Mota, LA-Fla. | 8 |
| S Reed, Col. | 8 |
| F Rodriguez, S.F.-Phi. | 8 |

### Holds†

| | |
|---|---|
| A Otsuka, S.D. | 34 |
| R King, St.L. | 31 |
| C Reitsma, Atl. | 31 |
| G Mota, L.A.-Fla. | 30 |
| S Torres, Pit. | 30 |

### Blown Saves†

| | |
|---|---|
| S Chacon, Col. | 9 |
| D Graves, Cin. | 9 |
| L Hawkins, Chi. | 9 |
| M Herges, S.F. | 8 |
| T Worrell, Phi. | 8 |

### Relief Games

| | |
|---|---|
| J Brower, S.F. | 89 |
| R King, St.L. | 86 |
| R Cormier, Phi. | 84 |
| C Reitsma, Atl. | 84 |
| S Torres, Pit. | 84 |

### Games Finished

| | |
|---|---|
| J Isringhausen, St.L. | 66 |
| J Mesa, Pit. | 65 |
| J Smoltz, Atl. | 61 |
| S Chacon, Col. | 60 |
| B Looper, N.Y. | 60 |

### Relief Innings

| | |
|---|---|
| G Mota, L.A.-Fla. | 96.2 |
| B Lidge, Hou. | 94.2 |
| J Brower, S.F. | 93.0 |
| S Torres, Pit. | 92.0 |
| L Ayala, Mon. | 90.1 |

### Pct. Inherited Scored†

**(minimum 30 inherited runners)**

| | |
|---|---|
| B Lidge, Hou. | 6.7 |
| J Lopez, Col. | 13.0 |
| S Eyre, S.F. | 15.6 |
| M Perisho, Fla. | 20.6 |
| W Franklin, S.F. | 20.9 |

### Opposition Avg.

**(minimum 50 relief IP)**

| | |
|---|---|
| A Benitez, Fla. | .152 |
| B Lidge, Hou. | .174 |
| E Gagne, L.A. | .181 |
| S Randolph, Ari. | .191 |
| R King, St.L. | .197 |

### Opposition OBP

**(minimum 50 relief IP)**

| | |
|---|---|
| A Benitez, Fla. | .220 |
| T Hoffman, S.D. | .242 |
| E Gagne, L.A. | .248 |
| B Lidge, Hou. | .254 |
| J Isringhausen, St.L. | .265 |

### Opposition SLG

**(minimum 50 relief IP)**

| | |
|---|---|
| R King, St.L. | .257 |
| A Benitez, Fla. | .257 |
| E Gagne, L.A. | .263 |
| R Madson, Phi. | .284 |
| B Lidge, Hou. | .290 |

### First Batter Avg.

**(minimum 40 first BFP)**

| | |
|---|---|
| J Horgan, Mon. | .100 |
| K Calero, St.L. | .108 |
| B Lidge, Hou. | .113 |
| J Isringhausen, St.L. | .116 |
| E Gagne, L.A. | .123 |

### Avg. vs. LHB

**(minimum 50 relief IP)**

| | |
|---|---|
| S Kline, St.L. | .143 |
| R King, St.L. | .150 |
| L Vizcaino, Mil. | .163 |
| A Benitez, Fla. | .168 |
| S Linebrink, S.D. | .178 |

### Avg. vs. RHB

**(minimum 50 relief IP)**

| | |
|---|---|
| E Gagne, L.A. | .129 |
| A Benitez, Fla. | .140 |
| B Lidge, Hou. | .155 |
| T Hoffman, S.D. | .161 |
| K Mercker, Chi. | .170 |

### Avg., Runners On†

**(minimum 50 relief IP)**

| | |
|---|---|
| B Lidge, Hou. | .141 |
| A Benitez, Fla. | .148 |
| T Hoffman, S.D. | .158 |
| S Linebrink, S.D. | .177 |
| J Cruz, Atl. | .186 |

### Avg., Scoring Pos.†

**(minimum 50 relief IP)**

| | |
|---|---|
| T Hoffman, S.D. | .087 |
| B Lidge, Hou. | .101 |
| K Mercker, Chi. | .148 |
| J Cruz, Atl. | .159 |
| R Madson, Phi. | .159 |

### Easy Saves†

| | |
|---|---|
| D Graves, Cin. | 31 |
| A Benitez, Fla. | 29 |
| J Mesa, Pit. | 29 |
| S Chacon, Col. | 28 |
| J Isringhausen, St.L. | 27 |

### Regular Saves†

| | |
|---|---|
| E Gagne, L.A. | 23 |
| J Smoltz, Atl. | 20 |
| T Hoffman, S.D. | 17 |
| A Benitez, Fla. | 15 |
| J Isringhausen, St.L. | 15 |

### Tough Saves†

| | |
|---|---|
| J Smoltz, Atl. | 6 |
| J Isringhausen, St.L. | 5 |
| M Herges, S.F. | 4 |
| B Lidge, Hou. | 4 |
| 2 tied with | 3 |

### Pitches per Batter

**(minimum 50 relief IP)**

| | |
|---|---|
| S Kim, Mon. | 3.28 |
| D Graves, Cin. | 3.34 |
| R Stone, Hou.-S.D. | 3.38 |
| B Meadows, Pit. | 3.44 |
| C Reitsma, Atl. | 3.53 |

**†Holds** denote the number of times a relief pitcher enters the game in a save situation, records at least one out and leaves the game never having relinquished the lead. A pitcher cannot finish the game and receive credit for a hold, nor can he earn a hold and a save in the same game. **Blown Saves** denote the number of times a relief pitcher enters a game in a save situation and allows the tying or go-ahead run to score. **Pct. Inherited Scored** denotes the percent of inherited runners (those on base when a reliever enters the game) that score. **Avg., Runners On** denotes batting average allowed when runners are on base. **Avg., Scoring Pos.** denotes batting average allowed when a runner is at second and/or third base. **Easy Saves** denote saves in which the first batter faced doesn't represent the tying run and the reliever pitches one inning or less. **Regular Saves** denote those saves that are not Easy Saves or Tough Saves. **Tough Saves** denote saves which occur after the reliever enters with the tying run anywhere on base.

# 2004 ACTIVE CAREER LEADERS

## BATTING

### Batting Average

(minimum 1000 PA)

| Rk. | Player | AB | H | Avg. |
|---|---|---|---|---|
| 1 | Ichiro Suzuki | 2722 | 924 | .339 |
| 2 | Todd Helton | 4051 | 1372 | .339 |
| 3 | Albert Pujols | 2363 | 787 | .333 |
| 4 | Vladimir Guerrero | 4375 | 1421 | .325 |
| 5 | Nomar Garciaparra | 4133 | 1330 | .322 |
| 6 | Manny Ramirez | 5572 | 1760 | .316 |
| 7 | Mike Piazza | 5805 | 1829 | .315 |
| 8 | Derek Jeter | 5513 | 1734 | .315 |
| 9 | Larry Walker | 6592 | 2069 | .314 |
| 10 | Juan Pierre | 2755 | 859 | .312 |
| 11 | Edgar Martinez | 7213 | 2247 | .312 |
| 12 | Frank Thomas | 6851 | 2113 | .308 |
| 13 | Magglio Ordonez | 3807 | 1167 | .307 |
| 14 | Ivan Rodriguez | 6694 | 2051 | .306 |
| 15 | Jason Kendall | 4606 | 1409 | .306 |
| 16 | Alex Rodriguez | 5590 | 1707 | .305 |
| 17 | Bobby Abreu | 4140 | 1264 | .305 |
| 18 | Mike Sweeney | 3717 | 1132 | .305 |
| 19 | Jose Vidro | 3485 | 1061 | .304 |
| 20 | Sean Casey | 3488 | 1060 | .304 |
| 21 | Chipper Jones | 5616 | 1705 | .304 |
| 22 | Lance Berkman | 2683 | 814 | .303 |
| 23 | Shannon Stewart | 4098 | 1242 | .303 |
| 24 | Mark Loretta | 3871 | 1172 | .303 |
| 25 | Bernie Williams | 6964 | 2097 | .301 |

### On-Base Percentage

(minimum 1000 PA; *AB+BB+HBP+SF)

| Rk. | Player | *PA | OB | OBP |
|---|---|---|---|---|
| 1 | Barry Bonds | 11580 | 5125 | .443 |
| 2 | Todd Helton | 4796 | 2070 | .432 |
| 3 | Frank Thomas | 8478 | 3634 | .429 |
| 4 | Edgar Martinez | 8662 | 3619 | .418 |
| 5 | Lance Berkman | 3247 | 1352 | .416 |
| 6 | Albert Pujols | 2727 | 1126 | .413 |
| 7 | Bobby Abreu | 4958 | 2042 | .412 |
| 8 | Brian Giles | 4982 | 2049 | .411 |
| 9 | Jason Giambi | 5782 | 2376 | .411 |
| 10 | Manny Ramirez | 6573 | 2701 | .411 |
| 11 | Jim Thome | 7038 | 2885 | .410 |
| 12 | Jeff Bagwell | 9305 | 3799 | .408 |
| 13 | Larry Walker | 7656 | 3070 | .401 |
| 14 | Chipper Jones | 6631 | 2656 | .401 |
| 15 | Gary Sheffield | 8710 | 3487 | .400 |
| 16 | John Olerud | 8859 | 3536 | .399 |
| 17 | Carlos Delgado | 6018 | 2362 | .392 |
| 18 | J.D. Drew | 2852 | 1114 | .391 |
| 19 | Vladimir Guerrero | 4900 | 1912 | .390 |
| 20 | Bernie Williams | 8035 | 3116 | .388 |
| 21 | Jason Kendall | 5273 | 2040 | .387 |
| 22 | Erubiel Durazo | 2124 | 821 | .387 |
| 23 | Tim Salmon | 6795 | 2623 | .386 |
| 24 | Mike Piazza | 6535 | 2519 | .385 |
| 25 | Derek Jeter | 6194 | 2385 | .385 |

### Slugging Percentage

(minimum 1000 PA)

| Rk. | Player | AB | TB | Slg. |
|---|---|---|---|---|
| 1 | Albert Pujols | 2363 | 1474 | .624 |
| 2 | Todd Helton | 4051 | 2497 | .616 |
| 3 | Barry Bonds | 9098 | 5556 | .611 |
| 4 | Manny Ramirez | 5572 | 3339 | .599 |
| 5 | Vladimir Guerrero | 4375 | 2577 | .589 |
| 6 | Alex Rodriguez | 5590 | 3207 | .574 |
| 7 | Jim Thome | 5726 | 3259 | .569 |
| 8 | Larry Walker | 6592 | 3746 | .568 |
| 9 | Frank Thomas | 6851 | 3887 | .567 |
| 10 | Lance Berkman | 2683 | 1511 | .563 |
| 11 | Mike Piazza | 5805 | 3260 | .562 |
| 12 | Juan Gonzalez | 6555 | 3676 | .561 |
| 13 | Ken Griffey Jr. | 7379 | 4131 | .560 |
| 14 | Carlos Delgado | 5008 | 2786 | .556 |
| 15 | Brian Giles | 4111 | 2259 | .550 |
| 16 | Nomar Garciaparra | 4133 | 2269 | .549 |
| 17 | Sammy Sosa | 8021 | 4368 | .545 |
| 18 | Jim Edmonds | 5090 | 2767 | .544 |
| 19 | Jeff Bagwell | 7697 | 4175 | .542 |
| 20 | Jason Giambi | 4757 | 2568 | .540 |
| 21 | Chipper Jones | 5616 | 3014 | .537 |
| 22 | Richie Sexson | 3065 | 1618 | .528 |
| 23 | Gary Sheffield | 7302 | 3854 | .528 |
| 24 | Magglio Ordonez | 3807 | 1998 | .525 |
| 25 | Mark Teixeira | 1074 | 559 | .520 |

### Hits

|  |  |
|---|---|
| Rafael Palmeiro | 2922 |
| Barry Bonds | 2730 |
| Roberto Alomar | 2724 |
| Craig Biggio | 2639 |
| Fred McGriff | 2490 |
| Julio Franco | 2457 |
| Barry Larkin | 2340 |
| Steve Finley | 2336 |
| Andres Galarraga | 2333 |
| Jeff Bagwell | 2289 |
| B.J. Surhoff | 2248 |
| Edgar Martinez | 2247 |
| Marquis Grissom | 2222 |
| Sammy Sosa | 2220 |
| John Olerud | 2189 |
| Gary Sheffield | 2175 |
| Ken Griffey Jr. | 2156 |
| Omar Vizquel | 2147 |
| Frank Thomas | 2113 |
| Ruben Sierra | 2108 |

### Home Runs

|  |  |
|---|---|
| Barry Bonds | 703 |
| Sammy Sosa | 574 |
| Rafael Palmeiro | 551 |
| Ken Griffey Jr. | 501 |
| Fred McGriff | 493 |
| Jeff Bagwell | 446 |
| Frank Thomas | 436 |
| Juan Gonzalez | 434 |
| Jim Thome | 423 |
| Gary Sheffield | 415 |
| Andres Galarraga | 399 |
| Manny Ramirez | 390 |
| Alex Rodriguez | 381 |
| Mike Piazza | 378 |
| Larry Walker | 368 |
| Ellis Burks | 352 |
| Carlos Delgado | 336 |
| Tino Martinez | 322 |
| Chipper Jones | 310 |
| Edgar Martinez | 309 |

### Runs Batted In

|  |  |
|---|---|
| Barry Bonds | 1843 |
| Rafael Palmeiro | 1775 |
| Fred McGriff | 1550 |
| Sammy Sosa | 1530 |
| Jeff Bagwell | 1510 |
| Ken Griffey Jr. | 1444 |
| Frank Thomas | 1439 |
| Andres Galarraga | 1425 |
| Juan Gonzalez | 1404 |
| Gary Sheffield | 1353 |
| Ruben Sierra | 1289 |
| Manny Ramirez | 1270 |
| Edgar Martinez | 1261 |
| Larry Walker | 1259 |
| Tino Martinez | 1222 |
| Jeff Kent | 1207 |
| Ellis Burks | 1206 |
| John Olerud | 1193 |
| Robin Ventura | 1182 |
| Luis Gonzalez | 1172 |

### Stolen Bases

|  |  |
|---|---|
| Kenny Lofton | 545 |
| Barry Bonds | 506 |
| Roberto Alomar | 474 |
| Eric Young | 450 |
| Marquis Grissom | 428 |
| Craig Biggio | 396 |
| Barry Larkin | 379 |
| Tom Goodwin | 369 |
| Tony Womack | 335 |
| Omar Vizquel | 318 |
| Steve Finley | 305 |
| Reggie Sanders | 283 |
| Mark McLemore | 272 |
| Luis Castillo | 271 |
| Julio Franco | 269 |
| Johnny Damon | 263 |
| Ray Lankford | 258 |
| Ray Durham | 242 |
| Edgar Renteria | 237 |
| Sammy Sosa | 233 |

## Seasons Played

Roger Clemens .................... 21
John Franco .......................... 20
Julio Franco .......................... 20
Barry Bonds .......................... 19
Andres Galarraga ................. 19
Barry Larkin .......................... 19
Greg Maddux ......................... 19
Fred McGriff .......................... 19
Mark McLemore .................... 19
Rafael Palmeiro ..................... 19
Benito Santiago ..................... 19

## Games

Rafael Palmeiro ................ 2721
Barry Bonds ...................... 2716
Fred McGriff ...................... 2460
Craig Biggio ....................... 2409
Roberto Alomar ................. 2379
Steve Finley ....................... 2289
Julio Franco ....................... 2269
Andres Galarraga .............. 2257
B.J. Surhoff ....................... 2222
Barry Larkin ....................... 2180

## At-Bats

Rafael Palmeiro ............. 10103
Craig Biggio ...................... 9221
Barry Bonds ...................... 9098
Roberto Alomar ................. 9073
Fred McGriff ...................... 8757
Steve Finley ....................... 8471
Julio Franco ....................... 8189
Marquis Grissom ............... 8138
Andres Galarraga .............. 8096
Sammy Sosa ..................... 8021

## Runs Scored

Barry Bonds ...................... 2070
Rafael Palmeiro ................ 1616
Craig Biggio ....................... 1603
Roberto Alomar ................. 1508
Jeff Bagwell ....................... 1506
Sammy Sosa ...................... 1383
Fred McGriff ....................... 1349
Barry Larkin ....................... 1329
Steve Finley ....................... 1327
Ken Griffey Jr. ................... 1320

## Doubles

Rafael Palmeiro ................... 572
Craig Biggio ......................... 564
Barry Bonds ......................... 563
Edgar Martinez .................... 514
Roberto Alomar .................... 504
John Olerud ......................... 493
Jeff Bagwell ......................... 484
Luis Gonzalez ...................... 458
Larry Walker ........................ 451
2 tied with ........................... 444

## Triples

Steve Finley ......................... 109
Kenny Lofton ......................... 93
Roberto Alomar ..................... 80
Barry Bonds ........................... 77
Barry Larkin ........................... 76
Johnny Damon ....................... 74
Jose Offerman ....................... 71
Ray Durham ........................... 70
Ellis Burks ............................. 63
Luis Gonzalez ........................ 63

## AB per HR

**(minimum 1000 AB)**

Barry Bonds ....................... 12.9
Jim Thome .......................... 13.5
Sammy Sosa ....................... 14.0
Manny Ramirez ................... 14.3
Adam Dunn .......................... 14.6
Alex Rodriguez ................... 14.7
Ken Griffey Jr. .................... 14.7
Albert Pujols ....................... 14.8
Carlos Delgado ................... 14.9
Juan Gonzalez .................... 15.1

## AB per RBI

**(minimum 1000 AB)**

Manny Ramirez ..................... 4.4
Juan Gonzalez ...................... 4.7
Albert Pujols ......................... 4.7
Carlos Delgado ..................... 4.7
Frank Thomas ........................ 4.8
Todd Helton ........................... 4.8
Jim Thome ............................. 4.9
Barry Bonds ........................... 4.9
Richie Sexson ........................ 5.0
Mike Piazza ........................... 5.0

## Total Bases

Barry Bonds ....................... 5556
Rafael Palmeiro ................. 5223
Fred McGriff ....................... 4458
Sammy Sosa ...................... 4368
Jeff Bagwell ....................... 4175
Ken Griffey Jr. ................... 4131
Andres Galarraga .............. 4038
Roberto Alomar ................. 4018
Craig Biggio ....................... 4007
Frank Thomas .................... 3887

## Walks

Barry Bonds ....................... 2302
Frank Thomas .................... 1450
Jeff Bagwell ....................... 1383
Rafael Palmeiro ................ 1310
Fred McGriff ...................... 1305
Edgar Martinez ................. 1283
John Olerud ...................... 1259
Jim Thome ........................ 1212
Gary Sheffield ................... 1202
Robin Ventura ................... 1075

## Intentional Walks

Barry Bonds ......................... 604
Ken Griffey Jr. ..................... 207
Fred McGriff ......................... 171
Rafael Palmeiro ................... 168
Frank Thomas ...................... 162
John Olerud ......................... 155
Jeff Bagwell ......................... 154
Sammy Sosa ........................ 148
Vladimir Guerrero ................ 144
Mike Piazza ......................... 138

## Hit by Pitch

Craig Biggio ......................... 256
Andres Galarraga ................ 178
Jason Kendall ...................... 177
Fernando Vina ..................... 157
Larry Walker ........................ 129
Jeff Bagwell ......................... 127
Carlos Delgado .................... 122
Damion Easley ..................... 111
Gary Sheffield ..................... 110
Jeff Kent ................................ 97

## Strikeouts

Sammy Sosa ...................... 2110
Andres Galarraga .............. 2003
Fred McGriff ....................... 1882
Jim Thome ......................... 1703
Ray Lankford ..................... 1550
Jeff Bagwell ....................... 1537
Craig Biggio ....................... 1467
Reggie Sanders ................. 1438
Barry Bonds ....................... 1428
Ellis Burks ......................... 1340

## SO/BB Ratio

**(minimum 1000 AB)**

Barry Bonds ...................... .620
Eric Young ........................ .689
Brian Giles ........................ .724
Gary Sheffield ................... .731
Frank Thomas ................... .782
John Olerud ...................... .791
Orlando Palmeiro .............. .798
Todd Helton ...................... .813
Barry Larkin ..................... .870
Matt Lawton ...................... .875

## Sacrifice Hits

Tom Glavine ......................... 186
Omar Vizquel ....................... 185
Greg Maddux ........................ 152
Roberto Alomar .................... 148
Mark McLemore .................... 105
Jose Vizcaino ....................... 104
Curt Schilling ....................... 102
Shane Reynolds ..................... 97
Royce Clayton ....................... 93
John Smoltz .......................... 92

## Sacrifice Flies

Ruben Sierra ......................... 117
Rafael Palmeiro .................... 111
Frank Thomas ...................... 106
B.J. Surhoff .......................... 100
Jeff Bagwell ........................... 98
Roberto Alomar ...................... 97
Gary Sheffield ........................ 96
John Olerud ........................... 93
Jeff Kent ................................ 88
Barry Bonds ........................... 87

## SB Success Pct.

**(minimum 100 SB attempts)**

Carlos Beltran ...................... 89.3
Pokey Reese ....................... 84.7
Tony Womack ...................... 83.1
Barry Larkin ........................ 83.1
Scott Podsednik .................. 83.1
Doug Glanville ..................... 82.4
Dave Roberts ....................... 80.8
Roberto Alomar .................... 80.6
Carl Crawford ...................... 80.4
Alex Rodriguez .................... 80.4

## Caught Stealing

Eric Young ........................... 160
Kenny Lofton ........................ 145
Barry Bonds ......................... 141
Omar Vizquel ........................ 129
Mark McLemore .................... 119
Craig Biggio ......................... 118
Tom Goodwin ....................... 118
Ray Lankford ........................ 117
Marquis Grissom .................. 115
2 tied with ............................ 114

## GDP

Julio Franco ......................... 289
Fred McGriff ......................... 226
John Olerud ......................... 226
Rafael Palmeiro ................... 223
Todd Zeile ............................ 223
Ivan Rodriguez ..................... 220
Jeff Bagwell ......................... 219
Roberto Alomar .................... 206
Benito Santiago ................... 203
Vinny Castilla ....................... 201

## AB per GDP

**(minimum 1000 AB)**

Dave Roberts ..................... 258.8
Carl Crawford ..................... 216.4
Rob Mackowiak ................... 180.6
Greg Maddux ...................... 166.3
Ichiro Suzuki ...................... 136.1
Peter Bergeron ................... 122.6
Joe McEwing ...................... 121.6
Russell Branyan ................. 114.7
Rafael Furcal ..................... 105.7
Tony Womack ...................... 99.3

# PITCHING

### Wins

|  |  |
|---|---|
| Roger Clemens | 328 |
| Greg Maddux | 305 |
| Tom Glavine | 262 |
| Randy Johnson | 246 |
| David Wells | 212 |
| Mike Mussina | 211 |
| Kevin Brown | 207 |
| Jamie Moyer | 192 |
| Curt Schilling | 184 |
| Pedro Martinez | 182 |

### Losses

| Player | Losses |
|---|---|
| Greg Maddux | 174 |
| Tom Glavine | 171 |
| Roger Clemens | 164 |
| Jamie Moyer | 145 |
| Terry Mulholland | 140 |
| Kevin Appier | 137 |
| Kevin Brown | 137 |
| David Wells | 136 |
| Scott Erickson | 132 |
| Steve Trachsel | 131 |

### Won-Lost Percentage
**(minimum 100 decisions)**

|  |  |
|---|---|
| Pedro Martinez | .705 |
| Tim Hudson | .702 |
| Roger Clemens | .667 |
| Mark Mulder | .659 |
| Randy Johnson | .658 |
| Andy Pettitte | .654 |
| Barry Zito | .643 |
| Mike Mussina | .639 |
| Greg Maddux | .637 |
| Roy Halladay | .632 |

### ERA
**(minimum 750 IP)**

| Player | ERA |
|---|---|
| Pedro Martinez | 2.71 |
| Trevor Hoffman | 2.74 |
| John Franco | 2.84 |
| Greg Maddux | 2.95 |
| Randy Johnson | 3.07 |
| Roger Clemens | 3.18 |
| Kevin Brown | 3.20 |
| John Smoltz | 3.27 |
| Tim Hudson | 3.30 |
| Rod Beck | 3.30 |

### Games

| Player | Games |
|---|---|
| John Franco | 1088 |
| Mike Jackson | 1005 |
| Mike Stanton | 968 |
| Jose Mesa | 832 |
| Roberto Hernandez | 825 |
| Mike Timlin | 812 |
| Steve Reed | 803 |
| Paul Quantrill | 791 |
| Todd Jones | 744 |
| Jeff Nelson | 743 |

### Games Started

|  |  |
|---|---|
| Roger Clemens | 639 |
| Greg Maddux | 604 |
| Tom Glavine | 570 |
| Randy Johnson | 479 |
| Kevin Brown | 463 |
| Jamie Moyer | 453 |
| David Wells | 417 |
| Mike Mussina | 413 |
| Kevin Appier | 402 |
| 2 tied with | 370 |

### Innings Pitched

|  |  |
|---|---|
| Roger Clemens | 4493.0 |
| Greg Maddux | 4181.1 |
| Tom Glavine | 3740.1 |
| Randy Johnson | 3368.0 |
| Kevin Brown | 3183.0 |
| David Wells | 3022.1 |
| Jamie Moyer | 2939.2 |
| Mike Mussina | 2833.1 |
| Curt Schilling | 2812.2 |
| John Smoltz | 2699.2 |

### Batters Faced

|  |  |
|---|---|
| Roger Clemens | 18531 |
| Greg Maddux | 16989 |
| Tom Glavine | 15725 |
| Randy Johnson | 13864 |
| Kevin Brown | 13196 |
| David Wells | 12615 |
| Jamie Moyer | 12473 |
| Mike Mussina | 11548 |
| Kenny Rogers | 11546 |
| Curt Schilling | 11399 |

### Complete Games

|  |  |
|---|---|
| Roger Clemens | 117 |
| Greg Maddux | 105 |
| Randy Johnson | 92 |
| Curt Schilling | 82 |
| Kevin Brown | 72 |
| Mike Mussina | 54 |
| Tom Glavine | 53 |
| David Wells | 52 |
| Scott Erickson | 51 |
| John Smoltz | 47 |

### Complete Game Pct.
**(minimum 100 games started)**

|  |  |
|---|---|
| Curt Schilling | 0.22 |
| Randy Johnson | 0.19 |
| Roger Clemens | 0.18 |
| Greg Maddux | 0.17 |
| Livan Hernandez | 0.16 |
| Kevin Brown | 0.16 |
| Mark Mulder | 0.15 |
| Scott Erickson | 0.14 |
| Terry Mulholland | 0.14 |
| Sidney Ponson | 0.14 |

### Shutouts

|  |  |
|---|---|
| Roger Clemens | 46 |
| Randy Johnson | 37 |
| Greg Maddux | 35 |
| Tom Glavine | 23 |
| Mike Mussina | 21 |
| Curt Schilling | 19 |
| Kevin Brown | 17 |
| Scott Erickson | 17 |
| Pedro Martinez | 16 |
| John Smoltz | 14 |

### Quality Start Pct.†
**(minimum 100 games started)**

|  |  |
|---|---|
| Pedro Martinez | 70.4 |
| Randy Johnson | 70.4 |
| Roy Oswalt | 68.2 |
| Curt Schilling | 68.1 |
| Greg Maddux | 67.9 |
| Kevin Brown | 67.0 |
| Tim Hudson | 66.1 |
| Barry Zito | 66.0 |
| Mark Buehrle | 65.5 |
| Roger Clemens | 65.3 |

### Strikeouts

|  |  |
|---|---|
| Roger Clemens | 4317 |
| Randy Johnson | 4161 |
| Greg Maddux | 2916 |
| Curt Schilling | 2745 |
| Pedro Martinez | 2653 |
| John Smoltz | 2398 |
| Kevin Brown | 2347 |
| Mike Mussina | 2258 |
| Tom Glavine | 2245 |
| Kevin Appier | 1994 |

### Walks Allowed

|  |  |
|---|---|
| Roger Clemens | 1458 |
| Randy Johnson | 1302 |
| Tom Glavine | 1276 |
| Al Leiter | 1065 |
| Kenny Rogers | 964 |
| Kevin Appier | 933 |
| Tom Gordon | 893 |
| Kevin Brown | 882 |
| Greg Maddux | 871 |
| Hideo Nomo | 853 |

### Strikeouts per 9 IP
**(minimum 750 IP)**

|  |  |
|---|---|
| Randy Johnson | 11.12 |
| Kerry Wood | 10.43 |
| Pedro Martinez | 10.40 |
| Trevor Hoffman | 10.13 |
| Hideo Nomo | 8.93 |
| Mike Remlinger | 8.81 |
| Arthur Rhodes | 8.80 |
| Curt Schilling | 8.78 |
| Roger Clemens | 8.65 |
| Darren Dreifort | 8.27 |

### Walks per 9 IP
**(minimum 750 IP)**

|  |  |
|---|---|
| Brad Radke | 1.68 |
| Jon Lieber | 1.76 |
| Greg Maddux | 1.87 |
| David Wells | 1.92 |
| Brian Anderson | 1.98 |
| Mike Mussina | 2.02 |
| Curt Schilling | 2.04 |
| Ramiro Mendoza | 2.05 |
| Jose Lima | 2.10 |
| Ben Sheets | 2.10 |

**†Quality Starts** denote the number of outings in which a starting pitcher works at least six innings and allows three or fewer earned runs.

## SO/BB Ratio
(minimum 750 IP)

Pedro Martinez ..........4.31
Curt Schilling ..........4.30
Trevor Hoffman ..........3.83
Jon Lieber ..........3.72
Ben Sheets ..........3.55
Mike Mussina ..........3.54
Rod Beck ..........3.37
Shane Reynolds ..........3.35
Greg Maddux ..........3.35
Brad Radke ..........3.25

## Hits per 9 IP
(minimum 750 IP)

Trevor Hoffman ..........6.77
Pedro Martinez ..........6.84
Kerry Wood ..........6.94
Randy Johnson ..........6.98
Mike Jackson ..........7.44
Barry Zito ..........7.63
Roger Clemens ..........7.70
John Smoltz ..........7.76
Mike Remlinger ..........7.83
Hideo Nomo ..........7.84

## Baserunners per 9 IP
(minimum 750 IP)

Trevor Hoffman ..........9.49
Pedro Martinez ..........9.71
Curt Schilling ..........10.16
Greg Maddux ..........10.40
Mike Mussina ..........10.63
John Smoltz ..........10.65
Rod Beck ..........10.71
Randy Johnson ..........10.88
Roger Clemens ..........10.92
Kevin Brown ..........11.27

## Home Runs per 9 IP
(minimum 750 IP)

Kevin Brown ..........0.57
Greg Maddux ..........0.58
John Franco ..........0.59
Terry Adams ..........0.63
Bob Wickman ..........0.66
Derek Lowe ..........0.66
Roger Clemens ..........0.67
Tim Hudson ..........0.68
Julian Tavarez ..........0.68
Pedro Martinez ..........0.69

## Opposition Avg.
(minimum 750 IP)

Trevor Hoffman .......... .206
Pedro Martinez .......... .209
Randy Johnson .......... .213
Kerry Wood .......... .214
Mike Jackson .......... .226
Barry Zito .......... .229
Roger Clemens .......... .230
John Smoltz .......... .232
Hideo Nomo .......... .235
Mike Remlinger .......... .235

## Opposition OBP
(minimum 750 IP)

Trevor Hoffman .......... .264
Pedro Martinez .......... .271
Curt Schilling .......... .281
Greg Maddux .......... .288
Rod Beck .......... .292
Mike Mussina .......... .292
John Smoltz .......... .292
Randy Johnson .......... .296
Roger Clemens .......... .296
Kevin Brown .......... .304

## Opposition Slg.
(minimum 750 IP)

Pedro Martinez .......... .323
Trevor Hoffman .......... .337
Randy Johnson .......... .337
John Franco .......... .342
Roger Clemens .......... .343
Greg Maddux .......... .345
Kevin Brown .......... .346
John Smoltz .......... .352
Kerry Wood .......... .353
Barry Zito .......... .354

## Home Runs Allowed

Jamie Moyer ..........358
David Wells ..........353
Roger Clemens ..........336
Randy Johnson ..........301
Mike Mussina ..........300
Steve Trachsel ..........290
Tom Glavine ..........288
Terry Mulholland ..........286
Curt Schilling ..........286
Kenny Rogers ..........271

## Hit Batsmen

Randy Johnson ..........156
Roger Clemens ..........147
Kevin Brown ..........132
Tim Wakefield ..........125
Greg Maddux ..........118
Pedro Martinez ..........115
Pedro Astacio ..........108
Chan Ho Park ..........106
Al Leiter ..........105
Aaron Sele ..........103

## Wild Pitches

Roger Clemens ..........130
John Smoltz ..........128
Kevin Appier ..........106
Hideo Nomo ..........105
Kevin Brown ..........102
Tom Gordon ..........101
David Wells ..........96
Randy Johnson ..........95
Jason Grimsley ..........94
Matt Clement ..........85

## GDP Induced

Greg Maddux ..........354
Tom Glavine ..........353
Kevin Brown ..........321
Scott Erickson ..........301
Roger Clemens ..........294
Kenny Rogers ..........267
Terry Mulholland ..........257
Mike Hampton ..........251
Jamie Moyer ..........239
David Wells ..........222

## GDP per 9 IP
(minimum 750 IP)

Shawn Estes ..........1.28
Scott Erickson ..........1.18
Julian Tavarez ..........1.17
Jamey Wright ..........1.17
Bob Wickman ..........1.16
Mike Hampton ..........1.13
Jon Garland ..........1.12
Derek Lowe ..........1.07
Danny Graves ..........1.06
Andy Pettitte ..........1.04

## Saves

John Franco ..........424
Trevor Hoffman ..........393
Mariano Rivera ..........336
Roberto Hernandez ..........320
Troy Percival ..........316
Jose Mesa ..........292
Rod Beck ..........286
Billy Wagner ..........246
Armando Benitez ..........244
Ugueth Urbina ..........227

## Save Percentage
(minimum 50 save opportunities)

Eric Gagne ..........96.2
John Smoltz ..........91.7
Trevor Hoffman ..........89.1
Mariano Rivera ..........87.5
Joe Nathan ..........86.5
Troy Percival ..........86.3
Armando Benitez ..........86.2
Dan Kolb ..........85.9
Jose Mesa ..........85.9
Billy Wagner ..........85.4

## Games Finished

John Franco ..........770
Roberto Hernandez ..........608
Trevor Hoffman ..........578
Jose Mesa ..........538
Rod Beck ..........519
Mariano Rivera ..........474
Troy Percival ..........466
Armando Benitez ..........441
Mike Jackson ..........422
2 tied with ..........417

## SB Pct. Allowed
(minimum 750 IP)

Kirk Rueter ..........35.1
Mark Buehrle ..........35.4
Terry Mulholland ..........41.0
Chris Carpenter ..........41.0
Kenny Rogers ..........41.8
Mark Redman ..........48.6
Brian Anderson ..........49.1
Wilson Alvarez ..........49.7
Jeff Weaver ..........51.2
Chan Ho Park ..........51.2

# HISTORY

**All-time results**

**Award winners**

**Hall of Fame**

# ALL-TIME RESULTS

## AMERICAN LEAGUE CHAMPIONS

| Year | Team | Manager |
|---|---|---|
| 1901 | Chicago | Clark Griffith |
| 1902 | Philadelphia | Connie Mack |
| 1903 | Boston | Jimmy Collins |
| 1904 | Boston | Jimmy Collins |
| 1905 | Philadelphia | Connie Mack |
| 1906 | Chicago | Fielder Jones |
| 1907 | Detroit | Hugh Jennings |
| 1908 | Detroit | Hugh Jennings |
| 1909 | Detroit | Hugh Jennings |
| 1910 | Philadelphia | Connie Mack |
| 1911 | Philadelphia | Connie Mack |
| 1912 | Boston | Jake Stahl |
| 1913 | Philadelphia | Connie Mack |
| 1914 | Philadelphia | Connie Mack |
| 1915 | Boston | Bill Carrigan |
| 1916 | Boston | Bill Carrigan |
| 1917 | Chicago | Pants Rowland |
| 1918 | Boston | Ed Barrow |
| 1919 | Chicago | Kid Gleason |
| 1920 | Cleveland | Tris Speaker |
| 1921 | New York | Miller Huggins |
| 1922 | New York | Miller Huggins |
| 1923 | New York | Miller Huggins |
| 1924 | Washington | Bucky Harris |
| 1925 | Washington | Bucky Harris |
| 1926 | New York | Miller Huggins |
| 1927 | New York | Miller Huggins |
| 1928 | New York | Miller Huggins |
| 1929 | Philadelphia | Connie Mack |
| 1930 | Philadelphia | Connie Mack |
| 1931 | Philadelphia | Connie Mack |
| 1932 | New York | Joe McCarthy |
| 1933 | Washington | Joe Cronin |
| 1934 | Detroit | Mickey Cochrane |
| 1935 | Detroit | Mickey Cochrane |
| 1936 | New York | Joe McCarthy |
| 1937 | New York | Joe McCarthy |
| 1938 | New York | Joe McCarthy |
| 1939 | New York | Joe McCarthy |
| 1940 | Detroit | Del Baker |
| 1941 | New York | Joe McCarthy |
| 1942 | New York | Joe McCarthy |
| 1943 | New York | Joe McCarthy |
| 1944 | St. Louis | Luke Sewell |
| 1945 | Detroit | Steve O'Neill |
| 1946 | Boston | Joe Cronin |
| 1947 | New York | Bucky Harris |
| 1948 | Cleveland* | Lou Boudreau |
| 1949 | New York | Casey Stengel |
| 1950 | New York | Casey Stengel |
| 1951 | New York | Casey Stengel |
| 1952 | New York | Casey Stengel |
| 1953 | New York | Casey Stengel |
| 1954 | Cleveland | Al Lopez |
| 1955 | New York | Casey Stengel |
| 1956 | New York | Casey Stengel |
| 1957 | New York | Casey Stengel |
| 1958 | New York | Casey Stengel |
| 1959 | Chicago | Al Lopez |
| 1960 | New York | Casey Stengel |
| 1961 | New York | Ralph Houk |
| 1962 | New York | Ralph Houk |
| 1963 | New York | Ralph Houk |
| 1964 | New York | Yogi Berra |
| 1965 | Minnesota | Sam Mele |
| 1966 | Baltimore | Hank Bauer |
| 1967 | Boston | Dick Williams |
| 1968 | Detroit | Mayo Smith |
| 1969 | Baltimore (East Division) | Earl Weaver |
| 1970 | Baltimore (East Division) | Earl Weaver |
| 1971 | Baltimore (East Division) | Earl Weaver |
| 1972 | Oakland (West Division) | Dick Williams |
| 1973 | Oakland (West Division) | Dick Williams |
| 1974 | Oakland (West Division) | Al Dark |
| 1975 | Boston (East Division) | Darrell Johnson |
| 1976 | New York (East Division) | Billy Martin |
| 1977 | New York (East Division) | Billy Martin |
| 1978 | New York (East Division) | Billy Martin, Bob Lemon |
| 1979 | Baltimore (East Division) | Earl Weaver |
| 1980 | Kansas City (West Division) | Jim Frey |
| 1981 | New York (East Division) | Gene Michael, Bob Lemon |
| 1982 | Milwaukee (East Division) | Buck Rodgers, Harvey Kuenn |
| 1983 | Baltimore (East Division) | Joe Altobelli |
| 1984 | Detroit (East Division) | Sparky Anderson |
| 1985 | Kansas City (West Division) | Dick Howser |
| 1986 | Boston (East Division) | John McNamara |
| 1987 | Minnesota (West Division) | Tom Kelly |
| 1988 | Oakland (West Division) | Tony La Russa |
| 1989 | Oakland (West Division) | Tony La Russa |
| 1990 | Oakland (West Division) | Tony La Russa |
| 1991 | Minnesota (West Division) | Tom Kelly |
| 1992 | Toronto (East Division) | Cito Gaston |
| 1993 | Toronto (East Division) | Cito Gaston |
| 1994 | None† | |
| 1995 | Cleveland (Central Division) | Mike Hargrove |
| 1996 | New York (East Division) | Joe Torre |
| 1997 | Cleveland (Central Division) | Mike Hargrove |
| 1998 | New York (East Division) | Joe Torre |
| 1999 | New York (East Division) | Joe Torre |
| 2000 | New York (East Division) | Joe Torre |
| 2001 | New York (East Division) | Joe Torre |
| 2002 | Anaheim (West Division) | Mike Scioscia |
| 2003 | New York (East Division) | Joe Torre |
| 2004 | Boston (East Division) | Terry Francona |

*Defeated Boston in one-game playoff. †New York finished the strike-shortened season with the league's best record.

## NATIONAL LEAGUE CHAMPIONS

| Year | Team | Manager |
|---|---|---|
| 1876 | Chicago | Albert Spalding |
| 1877 | Boston | Harry Wright |
| 1878 | Boston | Harry Wright |
| 1879 | Providence | George Wright |
| 1880 | Chicago | Cap Anson |
| 1881 | Chicago | Cap Anson |
| 1882 | Chicago | Cap Anson |
| 1883 | Boston | Jack Burdock, John Morrill |
| 1884 | Providence | Frank Bancroft |
| 1885 | Chicago | Cap Anson |
| 1886 | Chicago | Cap Anson |
| 1887 | Detroit | William Watkins |
| 1888 | New York | James Mutrie |
| 1889 | New York | James Mutrie |
| 1890 | Brooklyn | William McGunnigle |
| 1891 | Boston | Frank Selee |
| 1892 | Boston | Frank Selee |
| 1893 | Boston | Frank Selee |
| 1894 | Baltimore | Ned Hanlon |
| 1895 | Baltimore | Ned Hanlon |
| 1896 | Baltimore | Ned Hanlon |
| 1897 | Boston | Frank Selee |
| 1898 | Boston | Frank Selee |
| 1899 | Brooklyn | Ned Hanlon |

| Year | Team | Manager |
|---|---|---|
| 1900 | Brooklyn | Ned Hanlon |
| 1901 | Pittsburgh | Fred Clarke |
| 1902 | Pittsburgh | Fred Clarke |
| 1903 | Pittsburgh | Fred Clarke |
| 1904 | New York | John McGraw |
| 1905 | New York | John McGraw |
| 1906 | Chicago | Frank Chance |
| 1907 | Chicago | Frank Chance |
| 1908 | Chicago | Frank Chance |
| 1909 | Pittsburgh | Fred Clarke |
| 1910 | Chicago | Frank Chance |
| 1911 | New York | John McGraw |
| 1912 | New York | John McGraw |
| 1913 | New York | John McGraw |
| 1914 | Boston | George Stallings |
| 1915 | Philadelphia | Pat Moran |
| 1916 | Brooklyn | Wilbert Robinson |
| 1917 | New York | John McGraw |
| 1918 | Chicago | Fred Mitchell |
| 1919 | Cincinnati | Pat Moran |
| 1920 | Brooklyn | Wilbert Robinson |
| 1921 | New York | John McGraw |
| 1922 | New York | John McGraw |
| 1923 | New York | John McGraw |
| 1924 | New York | John McGraw |
| 1925 | Pittsburgh | Bill McKechnie |
| 1926 | St. Louis | Rogers Hornsby |
| 1927 | Pittsburgh | Donie Bush |
| 1928 | St. Louis | Bill McKechnie |
| 1929 | Chicago | Joe McCarthy |
| 1930 | St. Louis | Gabby Street |
| 1931 | St. Louis | Gabby Street |
| 1932 | Chicago | Rogers Hornsby, Charlie Grimm |
| 1933 | New York | Bill Terry |
| 1934 | St. Louis | Frank Frisch |
| 1935 | Chicago | Charlie Grimm |
| 1936 | New York | Bill Terry |
| 1937 | New York | Bill Terry |
| 1938 | Chicago | Charlie Grimm, Gabby Hartnett |
| 1939 | Cincinnati | Bill McKechnie |
| 1940 | Cincinnati | Bill McKechnie |
| 1941 | Brooklyn | Leo Durocher |
| 1942 | St. Louis | Billy Southworth |
| 1943 | St. Louis | Billy Southworth |
| 1944 | St. Louis | Billy Southworth |
| 1945 | Chicago | Charlie Grimm |
| 1946 | St. Louis* | Eddie Dyer |
| 1947 | Brooklyn | Clyde Sukeforth, Burt Shotton |
| 1948 | Boston | Billy Southworth |
| 1949 | Brooklyn | Burt Shotton |
| 1950 | Philadelphia | Eddie Sawyer |
| 1951 | New York† | Leo Durocher |
| 1952 | Brooklyn | Charlie Dressen |
| 1953 | Brooklyn | Charlie Dressen |
| 1954 | New York | Leo Durocher |
| 1955 | Brooklyn | Walter Alston |
| 1956 | Brooklyn | Walter Alston |
| 1957 | Milwaukee | Fred Haney |
| 1958 | Milwaukee | Fred Haney |
| 1959 | Los Angeles‡ | Walter Alston |
| 1960 | Pittsburgh | Danny Murtaugh |
| 1961 | Cincinnati | Fred Hutchinson |
| 1962 | San Francisco§ | Al Dark |
| 1963 | Los Angeles | Walter Alston |
| 1964 | St. Louis | Johnny Keane |
| 1965 | Los Angeles | Walter Alston |
| 1966 | Los Angeles | Walter Alston |
| 1967 | St. Louis | Red Schoendienst |
| 1968 | St. Louis | Red Schoendienst |
| 1969 | New York (East Division) | Gil Hodges |
| 1970 | Cincinnati (West Division) | Sparky Anderson |
| 1971 | Pittsburgh (East Division) | Danny Murtaugh |
| 1972 | Cincinnati (West Division) | Sparky Anderson |
| 1973 | New York (East Division) | Yogi Berra |
| 1974 | Los Angeles (West Division) | Walter Alston |
| 1975 | Cincinnati (West Division) | Sparky Anderson |
| 1976 | Cincinnati (West Division) | Sparky Anderson |
| 1977 | Los Angeles (West Division) | Tommy Lasorda |
| 1978 | Los Angeles (West Division) | Tommy Lasorda |
| 1979 | Pittsburgh (East Division) | Chuck Tanner |
| 1980 | Philadelphia (East Division) | Dallas Green |
| 1981 | Los Angeles (West Division) | Tommy Lasorda |
| 1982 | St. Louis (East Division) | Whitey Herzog |
| 1983 | Philadelphia (East Division) | Pat Corrales, Paul Owens |
| 1984 | San Diego (West Division) | Dick Williams |
| 1985 | St. Louis (East Division) | Whitey Herzog |
| 1986 | New York (East Division) | Dave Johnson |
| 1987 | St. Louis (East Division) | Whitey Herzog |
| 1988 | Los Angeles (West Division) | Tommy Lasorda |
| 1989 | San Francisco (West Division) | Roger Craig |
| 1990 | Cincinnati (West Division) | Lou Piniella |
| 1991 | Atlanta (West Division) | Bobby Cox |
| 1992 | Atlanta (West Division) | Bobby Cox |
| 1993 | Philadelphia (East Division) | Jim Fregosi |
| 1994 | None∞ | |
| 1995 | Atlanta (East Division) | Bobby Cox |
| 1996 | Atlanta (East Division) | Bobby Cox |
| 1997 | Florida (East Division) | Jim Leyland |
| 1998 | San Diego (West Division) | Bruce Bochy |
| 1999 | Atlanta (East Division) | Bobby Cox |
| 2000 | New York (East Division) | Bobby Valentine |
| 2001 | Arizona (West Division) | Bob Brenly |
| 2002 | San Francisco (West Division) | Dusty Baker |
| 2003 | Florida (East Division) | Jeff Torborg, Jack McKeon |
| 2004 | St. Louis (Central Division) | Tony La Russa |

*Defeated Brooklyn, two games to none, in playoff for pennant.
†Defeated Brooklyn, two games to one, in playoff for pennant.
‡Defeated Milwaukee, two games to none, in playoff for pennant.
§Defeated Los Angeles, two games to one, in playoff for pennant.
∞Montreal finished the strike-shortened season with the league's best record.

## WORLD SERIES

| Year | Winner | Loser | Games |
|---|---|---|---|
| 1903 | Boston A.L. | Pittsburgh N.L. | 5-3 |
| 1904 | No Series | | |
| 1905 | New York N.L. | Philadelphia A.L. | 4-1 |
| 1906 | Chicago A.L. | Chicago N.L. | 4-2 |
| 1907 | Chicago N.L. | Detroit A.L. | *4-0 |
| 1908 | Chicago N.L. | Detroit A.L. | 4-1 |
| 1909 | Pittsburgh N.L. | Detroit A.L. | 4-3 |
| 1910 | Philadelphia A.L. | Chicago N.L. | 4-1 |
| 1911 | Philadelphia A.L. | New York N.L. | 4-2 |
| 1912 | Boston A.L. | New York N.L. | *4-3 |
| 1913 | Philadelphia A.L. | New York N.L. | 4-1 |
| 1914 | Boston N.L. | Philadelphia A.L. | 4-0 |
| 1915 | Boston A.L. | Philadelphia N.L. | 4-1 |
| 1916 | Boston A.L. | Brooklyn N.L. | 4-1 |
| 1917 | Chicago A.L. | New York N.L. | 4-2 |
| 1918 | Boston A.L. | Chicago N.L. | 4-2 |
| 1919 | Cincinnati N.L. | Chicago A.L. | 5-3 |
| 1920 | Cleveland A.L. | Brooklyn N.L. | 5-2 |
| 1921 | New York N.L. | New York A.L. | 5-3 |
| 1922 | New York N.L. | New York A.L. | *4-0 |
| 1923 | New York A.L. | New York N.L. | 4-2 |
| 1924 | Washington A.L. | New York N.L. | 4-3 |
| 1925 | Pittsburgh N.L. | Washington A.L. | 4-3 |
| 1926 | St. Louis N.L. | New York A.L. | 4-3 |
| 1927 | New York A.L. | Pittsburgh, N.L. | 4-0 |
| 1928 | New York A.L. | St. Louis N.L. | 4-0 |
| 1929 | Philadelphia A.L. | Chicago N.L. | 4-1 |
| 1930 | Philadelphia A.L. | St. Louis N.L. | 4-2 |

| Year | Winner | Loser | Games |
|---|---|---|---|
| 1931— | St. Louis N.L. | Philadelphia A.L. | 4-3 |
| 1932— | New York A.L. | Chicago N.L. | 4-0 |
| 1933— | New York N.L. | Washington A.L. | 4-1 |
| 1934— | St. Louis N.L. | Detroit A.L. | 4-3 |
| 1935— | Detroit A.L. | Chicago N.L. | 4-2 |
| 1936— | New York A.L. | New York N.L. | 4-2 |
| 1937— | New York A.L. | New York N.L. | 4-1 |
| 1938— | New York A.L. | Chicago N.L. | 4-0 |
| 1939— | New York A.L. | Cincinnati N.L. | 4-0 |
| 1940— | Cincinnati N.L. | Detroit A.L. | 4-3 |
| 1941— | New York A.L. | Brooklyn N.L. | 4-1 |
| 1942— | St. Louis N.L. | New York A.L. | 4-1 |
| 1943— | New York A.L. | St. Louis N.L. | 4-1 |
| 1944— | St. Louis N.L. | St. Louis A.L. | 4-2 |
| 1945— | Detroit A.L. | Chicago N.L. | 4-3 |
| 1946— | St. Louis N.L. | Boston A.L. | 4-3 |
| 1947— | New York A.L. | Brooklyn, N.L. | 4-3 |
| 1948— | Cleveland A.L. | Boston N.L. | 4-2 |
| 1949— | New York A.L. | Brooklyn N.L. | 4-1 |
| 1950— | New York A.L. | Philadelphia N.L. | 4-0 |
| 1951— | New York A.L. | New York N.L. | 4-2 |
| 1952— | New York A.L. | Brooklyn N.L. | 4-3 |
| 1953— | New York A.L. | Brooklyn N.L. | 4-2 |
| 1954— | New York N.L. | Cleveland A.L. | 4-0 |
| 1955— | Brooklyn N.L. | New York A.L. | 4-3 |
| 1956— | New York A.L. | Brooklyn N.L. | 4-3 |
| 1957— | Milwaukee N.L. | New York A.L. | 4-3 |
| 1958— | New York A.L. | Milwaukee N.L. | 4-3 |
| 1959— | Los Angeles N.L. | Chicago A.L. | 4-2 |
| 1960— | Pittsburgh N.L. | New York A.L. | 4-3 |
| 1961— | New York A.L. | Cincinnati N.L. | 4-1 |
| 1962— | New York A.L. | San Francisco N.L. | 4-3 |
| 1963— | Los Angeles N.L. | New York A.L. | 4-0 |
| 1964— | St. Louis N.L. | New York A.L. | 4-3 |
| 1965— | Los Angeles N.L. | Minnesota A.L. | 4-3 |
| 1966— | Baltimore A.L. | Los Angeles N.L. | 4-0 |
| 1967— | St. Louis N.L. | Boston A.L. | 4-3 |
| 1968— | Detroit A.L. | St. Louis N.L. | 4-3 |
| 1969— | New York N.L. | Baltimore A.L. | 4-1 |
| 1970— | Baltimore A.L. | Cincinnati N.L. | 4-1 |
| 1971— | Pittsburgh N.L. | Baltimore A.L. | 4-3 |
| 1972— | Oakland A.L. | Cincinnati N.L. | 4-3 |
| 1973— | Oakland A.L. | New York N.L. | 4-3 |
| 1974— | Oakland A.L. | Los Angeles N.L. | 4-1 |
| 1975— | Cincinnati N.L. | Boston A.L. | 4-3 |
| 1976— | Cincinnati N.L. | New York A.L. | 4-0 |
| 1977— | New York A.L. | Los Angeles N.L. | 4-2 |
| 1978— | New York A.L. | Los Angeles N.L. | 4-2 |
| 1979— | Pittsburgh N.L. | Baltimore A.L. | 4-3 |
| 1980— | Philadelphia N.L. | Kansas City A.L. | 4-2 |
| 1981— | Los Angeles N.L. | New York A.L. | 4-2 |
| 1982— | St. Louis N.L. | Milwaukee A.L. | 4-3 |
| 1983— | Baltimore A.L. | Philadelphia N.L. | 4-1 |
| 1984— | Detroit A.L. | San Diego N.L. | 4-1 |
| 1985— | Kansas City A.L. | St. Louis N.L. | 4-3 |
| 1986— | New York N.L. | Boston A.L. | 4-3 |
| 1987— | Minnesota A.L. | St. Louis N.L. | 4-3 |
| 1988— | Los Angeles N.L. | Oakland A.L. | 4-1 |
| 1989— | Oakland A.L. | San Francisco N.L. | 4-0 |
| 1990— | Cincinnati N.L. | Oakland A.L. | 4-0 |
| 1991— | Minnesota A.L. | Atlanta N.L. | 4-3 |
| 1992— | Toronto A.L. | Atlanta N.L. | 4-2 |
| 1993— | Toronto A.L. | Philadelphia N.L. | 4-2 |
| 1994— | No Series | | |
| 1995— | Atlanta N.L. | Cleveland A.L. | 4-2 |
| 1996— | New York A.L. | Atlanta N.L. | 4-2 |
| 1997— | Florida N.L. | Cleveland A.L. | 4-3 |
| 1998— | New York A.L. | San Diego N.L. | 4-0 |
| 1999— | New York A.L. | Atlanta N.L. | 4-0 |
| 2000— | New York A.L. | New York N.L. | 4-1 |
| 2001— | Arizona N.L. | New York A.L. | 4-3 |
| 2002— | Anaheim A.L. | San Francisco N.L. | 4-3 |
| 2003— | Florida N.L. | New York A.L. | 4-2 |
| 2004— | Boston A.L. | St. Louis N.L. | 4-0 |

*Includes tie game.

# DIVISION SERIES

## AMERICAN LEAGUE

| Year | Winner (Division) | Loser (Division) | Games |
|---|---|---|---|
| 1981— | New York (East) | Milwaukee (East) | 3-2 |
| | Oakland (West) | Kansas City (West) | 3-0 |
| 1995— | Cleveland (Central) | Boston (East) | 3-0 |
| | Seattle (West) | New York* (East) | 3-2 |
| 1996— | New York (East) | Texas (West) | 3-1 |
| | Baltimore (East)* | Cleveland (Central) | 3-1 |
| 1997— | Baltimore (East) | Seattle (West) | 3-1 |
| | Cleveland (Central) | New York (East)* | 3-2 |
| 1998— | New York (East) | Texas (West) | 3-0 |
| | Cleveland (Central) | Boston (East)* | 3-1 |
| 1999— | New York (East) | Texas (West) | 3-0 |
| | Boston (East)* | Cleveland (Central) | 3-2 |
| 2000— | New York (East) | Oakland (West) | 3-2 |
| | Seattle (West)* | Chicago (Central) | 3-0 |
| 2001— | New York (East) | Oakland (West)* | 3-2 |
| | Seattle (West) | Cleveland (Central) | 3-2 |
| 2002— | Anaheim (West)* | New York (East) | 3-1 |
| | Minnesota (Central) | Oakland (West) | 3-2 |
| 2003— | Boston (East)* | Oakland (West) | 3-2 |
| | New York (East) | Minnesota (Central) | 3-1 |
| 2004— | Boston (East)* | Anaheim (West) | 3-0 |
| | New York (East) | Minnesota (Central) | 3-1 |

## NATIONAL LEAGUE

| Year | Winner (Division) | Loser (Division) | Games |
|---|---|---|---|
| 1981— | Montreal (East) | Philadelphia (East) | 3-2 |
| | Los Angeles (West) | Houston (West) | 3-2 |
| 1995— | Atlanta (East) | Colorado* (West) | 3-1 |
| | Cincinnati (Central) | Los Angeles (West) | 3-0 |
| 1996— | Atlanta (East) | Los Angeles (West)* | 3-0 |
| | St. Louis (Central) | San Diego (West) | 3-0 |
| 1997— | Atlanta (East) | Houston (Central) | 3-0 |
| | Florida (East)* | San Francisco (West) | 3-0 |
| 1998— | Atlanta (East) | Chicago (Central)* | 3-0 |
| | San Diego (West) | Houston (Central) | 3-1 |
| 1999— | Atlanta (East) | Houston (Central) | 3-1 |
| | New York (East)* | Arizona (West) | 3-1 |
| 2000— | St. Louis (Central) | Atlanta (East) | 3-0 |
| | New York (East)* | San Francisco (West) | 3-1 |
| 2001— | Arizona (West) | St. Louis (Central)* | 3-2 |
| | Atlanta (East) | Houston (Central) | 3-0 |
| 2002— | St. Louis (Central) | Arizona (West) | 3-0 |
| | San Francisco (West)* | Atlanta (East) | 3-2 |
| 2003— | Chicago (Central) | Atlanta (East) | 3-2 |
| | Florida (East)* | San Francisco (West) | 3-1 |
| 2004— | St. Louis (Central) | Los Angeles (West) | 3-1 |
| | Houston (Central)* | Atlanta (East) | 3-2 |

*Wild-card team.

# CHAMPIONSHIP SERIES

## AMERICAN LEAGUE

| Year | Winner (Division) | Loser (Division) | Games |
|---|---|---|---|
| 1969— | Baltimore (East) | Minnesota (West) | 3-0 |
| 1970— | Baltimore (East) | Minnesota (West) | 3-0 |
| 1971— | Baltimore (East) | Oakland (West) | 3-0 |
| 1972— | Oakland (West) | Detroit (East) | 3-2 |
| 1973— | Oakland (West) | Baltimore (East) | 3-2 |
| 1974— | Oakland (West) | Baltimore (East) | 3-1 |
| 1975— | Boston (East) | Oakland (West) | 3-0 |
| 1976— | New York (East) | Kansas City (West) | 3-2 |
| 1977— | New York (East) | Kansas City (West) | 3-2 |
| 1978— | New York (East) | Kansas City (West) | 3-1 |
| 1979— | Baltimore (East) | California (West) | 3-1 |
| 1980— | Kansas City (West) | New York (East) | 3-0 |

| Year | Winner (Division) | Loser (Division) | Games |
|---|---|---|---|
| 1981— | New York (East) | Oakland (West) | 3-0 |
| 1982— | Milwaukee (East) | California (West) | 3-2 |
| 1983— | Baltimore (East) | Chicago (West) | 3-1 |
| 1984— | Detroit (East) | Kansas City (West) | 3-0 |
| 1985— | Kansas City (West) | Toronto (East) | 4-3 |
| 1986— | Boston (East) | California (West) | 4-3 |
| 1987— | Minnesota (West) | Detroit (East) | 4-1 |
| 1988— | Oakland (West) | Boston (East) | 4-0 |
| 1989— | Oakland (West) | Toronto (East) | 4-1 |
| 1990— | Oakland (West) | Boston (East) | 4-0 |
| 1991— | Minnesota (West) | Toronto (East) | 4-1 |
| 1992— | Toronto (East) | Oakland (West) | 4-2 |
| 1993— | Toronto (East) | Chicago (West) | 4-2 |
| 1994— | No series | | |
| 1995— | Cleveland (Central) | Seattle (West) | 4-2 |
| 1996— | New York (East) | Baltimore (East)* | 4-1 |
| 1997— | Cleveland (Central) | Baltimore (East) | 4-2 |
| 1998— | New York (East) | Cleveland (Central) | 4-2 |
| 1999— | New York (East) | Boston (East)* | 4-1 |
| 2000— | New York (East) | Seattle (West) | 4-2 |
| 2001— | New York (East) | Seattle (West) | 4-1 |
| 2002— | Anaheim (West)* | Minnesota (Central) | 4-1 |
| 2003— | New York (East) | Boston (East)* | 4-3 |
| 2004— | Boston (East)* | New York (East) | 4-3 |

## NATIONAL LEAGUE

| Year | Winner (Division) | Loser (Division) | Games |
|---|---|---|---|
| 1969— | New York (East) | Atlanta (West) | 3-0 |
| 1970— | Cincinnati (West) | Pittsburgh (East) | 3-0 |
| 1971— | Pittsburgh (East) | San Francisco (West) | 3-1 |
| 1972— | Cincinnati (West) | Pittsburgh (East) | 3-2 |
| 1973— | New York (East) | Cincinnati (West) | 3-2 |
| 1974— | Los Angeles (West) | Pittsburgh (East) | 3-1 |
| 1975— | Cincinnati (West) | Pittsburgh (East) | 3-0 |
| 1976— | Cincinnati (West) | Philadelphia (East) | 3-0 |
| 1977— | Los Angeles (West) | Philadelphia (East) | 3-1 |
| 1978— | Los Angeles (West) | Philadelphia (East) | 3-1 |
| 1979— | Pittsburgh (East) | Cincinnati (West) | 3-0 |
| 1980— | Philadelphia (East) | Houston (West) | 3-2 |
| 1981— | Los Angeles (West) | Montreal (East) | 3-2 |
| 1982— | St. Louis (East) | Atlanta (West) | 3-0 |
| 1983— | Philadelphia (East) | Los Angeles (West) | 3-1 |
| 1984— | San Diego (West) | Chicago (East) | 3-2 |
| 1985— | St. Louis (East) | Los Angeles (West) | 4-2 |
| 1986— | New York (East) | Houston (West) | 4-2 |
| 1987— | St. Louis (East) | San Francisco (West) | 4-3 |
| 1988— | Los Angeles (West) | New York (East) | 4-3 |
| 1989— | San Francisco (West) | Chicago (East) | 4-1 |
| 1990— | Cincinnati (West) | Pittsburgh (East) | 4-2 |
| 1991— | Atlanta (West) | Pittsburgh (East) | 4-3 |
| 1992— | Atlanta (West) | Pittsburgh (East) | 4-3 |
| 1993— | Philadelphia (East) | Atlanta (West) | 4-2 |
| 1994— | No series | | |
| 1995— | Atlanta (East) | Cincinnati (Central) | 4-0 |
| 1996— | Atlanta (East) | St. Louis (Central) | 4-3 |
| 1997— | Florida (East)* | Atlanta (East) | 4-2 |
| 1998— | San Diego (West) | Atlanta (East) | 4-2 |
| 1999— | Atlanta (East) | New York (East)* | 4-2 |
| 2000— | New York (East)* | St. Louis (Central) | 4-1 |
| 2001— | Arizona (West) | Atlanta (East) | 4-1 |
| 2002— | San Francisco (West)* | St. Louis (Central) | 4-1 |
| 2003— | Florida (East)* | Chicago (Central) | 4-3 |
| 2004— | St. Louis (Central) | Houston (Central)* | 4-3 |

*Wild-card team.

# ALL-STAR GAME

| Date | Site | Score (Winner) | Winning pitcher (Losing pitcher) | Winning manager (Losing manager) | Att. |
|---|---|---|---|---|---|
| 7-6-33 | Comiskey Park<br>Chicago | 4-2<br>(A.L.) | Lefty Gomez, Yankees<br>(Bill Hallahan, Cardinals) | Connie Mack, Athletics<br>(John McGraw, Giants) | 47,595 |
| 7-10-34 | Polo Grounds<br>New York | 9-7<br>(A.L.) | Mel Harder, Indians<br>(Van Mungo, Dodgers) | Joe Cronin, Senators<br>(Bill Terry, Giants) | 48,363 |
| 7-8-35 | Municipal Stadium<br>Cleveland | 4-1<br>(A.L.) | Lefty Gomez, Yankees<br>(Bill Walker, Cardinals) | Mickey Cochrane, Tigers<br>(Frankie Frisch, Cardinals) | 69,831 |
| 7-7-36 | Braves Field<br>Boston | 4-3<br>(N.L.) | Dizzy Dean, Cardinals<br>(Lefty Grove, Red Sox) | Charlie Grimm, Cubs<br>(Joe McCarthy, Yankees) | 25,556 |
| 7-7-37 | Griffith Stadium<br>Washington | 8-3<br>(A.L.) | Lefty Gomez, Yankees<br>(Dizzy Dean, Cardinals) | Joe McCarthy, Yankees<br>(Bill Terry, Giants) | 31,391 |
| 7-6-38 | Crosley Field<br>Cincinnati | 4-1<br>(N.L.) | Johnny Vander Meer, Reds<br>(Lefty Gomez, Yankees) | Bill Terry, Giants<br>(Joe McCarthy, Yankees) | 27,067 |
| 7-11-39 | Yankee Stadium<br>New York | 3-1<br>(A.L.) | Tommy Bridges, Tigers<br>(Bill Lee, Cubs) | Joe McCarthy, Yankees<br>(Gabby Hartnett, Cubs) | 62,892 |
| 7-9-40 | Sportsman's Park<br>St. Louis | 4-0<br>(N.L.) | Paul Derringer, Reds<br>(Red Ruffing, Yankees) | Bill McKechnie, Reds<br>(Joe Cronin, Red Sox) | 32,373 |
| 7-8-41 | Briggs Stadium<br>Detroit | 7-5<br>(A.L.) | Ed Smith, White Sox<br>(Claude Passeau, Cubs) | Del Baker, Tigers<br>(Bill McKechnie, Reds) | 54,674 |
| 7-6-42 | Polo Grounds<br>New York | 3-1<br>(A.L.) | Spud Chandler, Yankees<br>(Mort Cooper, Cardinals) | Joe McCarthy, Yankees<br>(Leo Durocher, Dodgers) | 33,694 |
| 7-13-43 | Shibe Park<br>Philadelphia | 5-3<br>(A.L.) | Dutch Leonard, Senators<br>(Mort Cooper, Cardinals) | Joe McCarthy, Yankees<br>(Billy Southworth, Cardinals) | 31,938 |
| 7-11-44 | Forbes Field<br>Pittsburgh | 7-1<br>(N.L.) | Ken Raffensberger, Phillies<br>(Tex Hughson, Red Sox) | Billy Southworth, Cardinals<br>(Joe McCarthy, Yankees) | 29,589 |
| 1945 | No game played. | | | | |
| 7-9-46 | Fenway Park<br>Boston | 12-0<br>(A.L.) | Bob Feller, Indians<br>(Claude Passeau, Cubs) | Steve O'Neill, Tigers<br>(Charlie Grimm, Cubs) | 34,906 |
| 7-8-47 | Wrigley Field<br>Chicago | 2-1<br>(A.L.) | Frank Shea, Yankees<br>(Johnny Sain, Braves) | Joe Cronin, Red Sox<br>(Eddie Dyer, Cardinals) | 41,123 |
| 7-13-48 | Sportsman's Park<br>St. Louis | 5-2<br>(A.L.) | Vic Raschi, Yankees<br>(Johnny Schmitz, Cubs) | Bucky Harris, Yankees<br>(Leo Durocher, Dodgers) | 34,009 |
| 7-12-49 | Ebbets Field<br>Brooklyn | 11-7<br>(A.L.) | Virgil Trucks, Tigers<br>(Don Newcombe, Dodgers) | Lou Boudreau, Indians<br>(Billy Southworth, Braves) | 32,577 |
| 7-11-50 | Comiskey Park<br>Chicago | 4-3*<br>(N.L.) | Ewell Blackwell, Reds<br>(Ted Gray, Tigers) | Burt Shotton, Dodgers<br>(Casey Stengel, Yankees) | 46,127 |
| 7-10-51 | Briggs Stadium<br>Detroit | 8-3<br>(N.L.) | Sal Maglie, Giants<br>(Ed Lopat, Yankees) | Eddie Sawyer, Phillies<br>(Casey Stengel, Yankees) | 52,075 |

| Date | Site | Score (Winner) | Winning pitcher (Losing pitcher) | Winning manager (Losing manager) | Att. |
|---|---|---|---|---|---|
| 7-8-52 | Shibe Park | 3-2† | Bob Rush, Cubs | Leo Durocher, Giants | 32,785 |
| | Philadelphia | (N.L.) | (Bob Lemon, Indians) | (Casey Stengel, Yankees) | |
| 7-14-53 | Crosley Field | 5-1 | Warren Spahn, Braves | Chuck Dressen, Dodgers | 30,846 |
| | Cincinnati | (N.L.) | (Allie Reynolds, Yankees) | (Casey Stengel, Yankees) | |
| 7-13-54 | Municipal Stadium | 11-9 | Dean Stone, Senators | Casey Stengel, Yankees | 68,751 |
| | Cleveland | (A.L.) | (Gene Conley, Braves) | (Walter Alston, Dodgers) | |
| 7-12-55 | Milwaukee Co. Stadium | 6-5‡ | Gene Conley, Braves | Leo Durocher, Giants | 45,314 |
| | Milwaukee | (N.L.) | (Frank Sullivan, Red Sox) | (Al Lopez, Indians) | |
| 7-10-56 | Griffith Stadium | 7-3 | Bob Friend, Pirates | Walter Alston, Dodgers | 28,843 |
| | Washington | (N.L.) | (Billy Pierce, White Sox) | (Casey Stengel, Yankees) | |
| 7-9-57 | Busch Stadium | 6-5 | Jim Bunning, Tigers | Casey Stengel, Yankees | 30,693 |
| | St. Louis | (A.L.) | (Curt Simmons, Phillies) | (Walter Alston, Dodgers) | |
| 7-8-58 | Memorial Stadium | 4-3 | Early Wynn, White Sox | Casey Stengel, Yankees | 48,829 |
| | Baltimore | (A.L.) | (Bob Friend, Pirates) | (Fred Haney, Braves) | |
| 7-7-59 | Forbes Field | 5-4 | Johnny Antonelli, Giants | Fred Haney, Braves | 35,277 |
| | Pittsburgh | (N.L.) | (Whitey Ford, Yankees) | (Casey Stengel, Yankees) | |
| 8-3-59 | Memorial Coliseum | 5-3 | Jerry Walker, Orioles | Casey Stengel, Yankees | 55,105 |
| | Los Angeles | (A.L.) | (Don Drysdale, Dodgers) | (Fred Haney, Braves) | |
| 7-11-60 | Municipal Stadium | 5-3 | Bob Friend, Pirates | Walter Alston, Dodgers | 30,619 |
| | Kansas City | (N.L.) | (Bill Monbouquette, Red Sox) | (Al Lopez, White Sox) | |
| 7-13-60 | Yankee Stadium | 6-0 | Vernon Law, Pirates | Walter Alston, Dodgers | 38,362 |
| | New York | (N.L.) | (Whitey Ford, Yankees) | (Al Lopez, White Sox) | |
| 7-11-61 | Candlestick Park | 5-4§ | Stu Miller, Giants | Danny Murtaugh, Pirates | 44,115 |
| | San Francisco | (N.L.) | (Hoyt Wilhelm, Orioles) | (Paul Richards, Orioles) | |
| 7-31-61 | Fenway Park | 1-1 | | Paul Richards, Orioles (A.L.) | 31,851 |
| | Boston | (tie) | | Danny Murtaugh, Pirates (N.L.) | |
| 7-10-62 | District of Col. Stad. | 3-1 | Juan Marichal, Giants | Fred Hutchinson, Reds | 45,480 |
| | Washington | (N.L.) | (Camilo Pascual, Twins) | (Ralph Houk, Yankees) | |
| 7-30-62 | Wrigley Field | 9-4 | Ray Herbert, White Sox | Ralph Houk, Yankees | 38,359 |
| | Chicago | (A.L.) | (Art Mahaffey, Phillies) | (Fred Hutchinson, Reds) | |
| 7-9-63 | Municipal Stadium | 5-3 | Larry Jackson, Cubs | Alvin Dark, Giants | 44,160 |
| | Cleveland | (N.L.) | (Jim Bunning, Tigers) | (Ralph Houk, Yankees) | |
| 7-7-64 | Shea Stadium | 7-4 | Juan Marichal, Giants | Walter Alston, Dodgers | 50,850 |
| | New York | (N.L.) | (Dick Radatz, Red Sox) | (Al Lopez, White Sox) | |
| 7-13-65 | Metropolitan Stadium | 6-5 | Sandy Koufax, Dodgers | Gene Mauch, Phillies | 46,706 |
| | Bloomington, Minn. | (N.L.) | (Sam McDowell, Indians) | (Al Lopez, White Sox) | |
| 7-12-66 | Busch Stadium | 2-1§ | Gaylord Perry, Giants | Walter Alston, Dodgers | 49,936 |
| | St. Louis | (N.L.) | (Pete Richert, Senators) | (Sam Mele, Twins) | |
| 7-11-67 | Anaheim Stadium | 2-1∞ | Don Drysdale, Dodgers | Walter Alston, Dodgers | 46,309 |
| | Anaheim, Calif. | (N.L.) | (Jim Hunter, Athletics) | (Hank Bauer, Orioles) | |
| 7-9-68 | Astrodome | 1-0 | Don Drysdale, Dodgers | Red Schoendienst, Cardinals | 48,321 |
| | Houston | (N.L.) | (Luis Tiant, Indians) | (Dick Williams, Red Sox) | |
| 7-23-69 | R.F.K. Stadium | 9-3 | Steve Carlton, Cardinals | Red Schoendienst, Cardinals | 45,259 |
| | Washington | (N.L.) | (Mel Stottlemyre, Yankees) | (Mayo Smith, Tigers) | |
| 7-14-70 | Riverfront Stadium | 5-4‡ | Claude Osteen, Dodgers | Gil Hodges, Mets | 51,838 |
| | Cincinnati | (N.L.) | (Clyde Wright, Angels) | (Earl Weaver, Orioles) | |
| 7-13-71 | Tiger Stadium | 6-4 | Vida Blue, Athletics | Earl Weaver, Orioles | 53,559 |
| | Detroit | (A.L.) | (Dock Ellis, Pirates) | (Sparky Anderson, Reds) | |
| 7-25-72 | Atlanta Stadium | 4-3§ | Tug McGraw, Mets | Danny Murtaugh, Pirates | 53,107 |
| | Atlanta | (N.L.) | (Dave McNally, Orioles) | (Earl Weaver, Orioles) | |
| 7-24-73 | Royals Stadium | 7-1 | Rick Wise, Cardinals | Sparky Anderson, Reds | 40,849 |
| | Kansas City | (N.L.) | (Bert Blyleven, Twins) | (Dick Williams, Athletics) | |
| 7-23-74 | Three Rivers Stadium | 7-2 | Ken Brett, Pirates | Yogi Berra, Mets | 50,706 |
| | Pittsburgh | (N.L.) | (Luis Tiant, Red Sox) | (Dick Williams, Athletics) | |
| 7-15-75 | Milwaukee Co. Stadium | 6-3 | Jon Matlack, Mets | Walter Alston, Dodgers | 51,480 |
| | Milwaukee | (N.L.) | (Jim Hunter, Yankees) | (Alvin Dark, Athletics) | |
| 7-13-76 | Veterans Stadium | 7-1 | Randy Jones, Padres | Sparky Anderson, Reds | 63,974 |
| | Philadelphia | (N.L) | (Mark Fidrych, Tigers) | (Darrell Johnson, Red Sox) | |
| 7-19-77 | Yankee Stadium | 7-5 | Don Sutton, Dodgers | Sparky Anderson, Reds | 56,683 |
| | New York | (N.L.) | (Jim Palmer, Orioles) | (Billy Martin, Yankees) | |
| 7-11-78 | San Diego Stadium | 7-3 | Bruce Sutter, Cubs | Tommy Lasorda, Dodgers | 51,549 |
| | San Diego | (N.L.) | (Rich Gossage, Yankees) | (Billy Martin, Yankees) | |
| 7-17-79 | Kingdome | 7-6 | Bruce Sutter, Cubs | Tommy Lasorda, Dodgers | 58,905 |
| | Seattle | (N.L.) | (Jim Kern, Rangers) | (Bob Lemon, Yankees) | |
| 7-8-80 | Dodger Stadium | 4-2 | Jerry Reuss, Dodgers | Chuck Tanner, Pirates | 56,088 |
| | Los Angeles | (N.L.) | (Tommy John, Yankees) | (Earl Weaver, Orioles) | |
| 8-9-81 | Municipal Stadium | 5-4 | Vida Blue, Giants | Dallas Green, Phillies | 72,086 |
| | Cleveland | (N.L.) | (Rollie Fingers, Brewers) | (Jim Frey, Royals) | |
| 7-13-82 | Olympic Stadium | 4-1 | Steve Rogers, Expos | Tommy Lasorda, Dodgers | 59,057 |
| | Montreal | (N.L.) | (Dennis Eckersley, Red Sox) | (Billy Martin, Athletics) | |
| 7-6-83 | Comiskey Park | 13-3 | Dave Stieb, Blue Jays | Harvey Kuenn, Brewers | 43,801 |
| | Chicago | (A.L.) | (Mario Soto, Reds) | (Whitey Herzog, Cardinals) | |

| Date | Site | Score (Winner) | Winning pitcher (Losing pitcher) | Winning manager (Losing manager) | Att. |
|---|---|---|---|---|---|
| 7-10-84 | Candlestick Park<br>San Francisco | 3-1<br>(N.L.) | Charlie Lea, Expos<br>(Dave Stieb, Blue Jays) | Paul Owens, Phillies<br>(Joe Altobelli, Orioles) | 57,756 |
| 7-16-85 | Metrodome<br>Minneapolis | 6-1<br>(N.L.) | LaMarr Hoyt, Padres<br>(Jack Morris, Tigers) | Dick Williams, Padres<br>(Sparky Anderson, Tigers) | 54,960 |
| 7-15-86 | Astrodome<br>Houston | 3-2<br>(A.L.) | Roger Clemens, Red Sox<br>(Dwight Gooden, Mets) | Dick Howser, Royals<br>(Whitey Herzog, Cardinals) | 45,774 |
| 7-14-87 | Oak.-Alameda Co. Col.<br>Oakland | 2-0▲<br>(N.L.) | Lee Smith, Cubs<br>(Jay Howell, Athletics) | Dave Johnson, Mets<br>(John McNamara, Red Sox) | 49,671 |
| 7-12-88 | Riverfront Stadium<br>Cincinnati | 2-1<br>(A.L.) | Frank Viola, Twins<br>(Dwight Gooden, Mets) | Tom Kelly, Twins<br>(Whitey Herzog, Cardinals) | 55,837 |
| 7-11-89 | Anaheim Stadium<br>Anaheim, Calif. | 5-3<br>(A.L.) | Nolan Ryan, Rangers<br>(John Smoltz, Braves) | Tony La Russa, Athletics<br>(Tommy Lasorda, Dodgers) | 64,036 |
| 7-10-90 | Wrigley Field<br>Chicago | 2-0<br>(A.L.) | Bret Saberhagen, Royals<br>(Jeff Brantley, Giants) | Tony La Russa, Athletics<br>(Roger Craig, Giants) | 39,071 |
| 7-9-91 | SkyDome<br>Toronto | 4-2<br>(A.L.) | Jimmy Key, Blue Jays<br>(Dennis Martinez, Expos) | Tony La Russa, Athletics<br>(Lou Piniella, Reds) | 52,383 |
| 7-14-92 | Jack Murphy Stadium<br>San Diego | 13-6<br>(A.L.) | Kevin Brown, Rangers<br>(Tom Glavine, Braves) | Tom Kelly, Twins<br>(Bobby Cox, Braves) | 59,372 |
| 7-13-93 | Oriole Park at Camden<br>Yards, Baltimore | 9-3<br>(A.L.) | Jack McDowell, White Sox<br>(John Burkett, Giants) | Cito Gaston, Blue Jays<br>(Bobby Cox, Braves) | 48,147 |
| 7-12-94 | Three Rivers Stadium<br>Pittsburgh | 8-7§<br>(N.L.) | Doug Jones, Phillies<br>(Jason Bere, White Sox) | Jim Fregosi, Phillies<br>(Cito Gaston, Blue Jays) | 59,568 |
| 7-11-95 | Ballpark in Arlington<br>Arlington, Texas | 3-2<br>(N.L.) | Heathcliff Slocumb, Phillies<br>(Steve Ontiveros, A's) | Felipe Alou, Expos<br>(Buck Showalter, Yankees) | 50,920 |
| 7-9-96 | Veterans Stadium<br>Philadelphia | 6-0<br>(N.L.) | John Smoltz, Braves<br>(Charles Nagy, Indians) | Bobby Cox, Braves<br>(Mike Hargrove, Indians) | 62,670 |
| 7-8-97 | Jacobs Field<br>Cleveland | 3-1<br>(A.L.) | Jose Rosado, Royals<br>(Shawn Estes, Giants) | Joe Torre, Yankees<br>(Bobby Cox, Braves) | 44,916 |
| 7-7-98 | Coors Field<br>Colorado | 13-8<br>(A.L.) | Bartolo Colon, Indians<br>(Ugueth Urbina, Expos) | Mike Hargrove, Indians<br>(Jim Leyland, Marlins) | 51,267 |
| 7-13-99 | Fenway Park<br>Boston | 4-1<br>(A.L.) | Pedro Martinez, Red Sox<br>(Curt Schilling, Phillies) | Joe Torre, Yankees<br>(Bruce Bochy, Padres) | 34,187 |
| 7-11-00 | Turner Field<br>Atlanta | 6-3<br>(A.L.) | James Baldwin, White Sox<br>(Al Leiter, Mets) | Joe Torre, Yankees<br>(Bobby Cox, Braves) | 51,323 |
| 7-10-01 | Safeco Field<br>Seattle | 4-1<br>(A.L.) | Freddy Garcia, Mariners<br>(Chan Ho Park, Dodgers) | Joe Torre, Yankees<br>(Bobby Valentine, Mets) | 47,364 |
| 7-9-02 | Miller Park<br>Milwaukee | 7-7■<br>(tie) | | Joe Torre, Yankees<br>Bob Brenly, Diamondbacks | 41,871 |
| 7-15-03 | U.S. Cellular Field<br>Chicago | 7-6<br>(A.L.) | Brendan Donnelly, Angels<br>(Eric Gagne, Dodgers) | Mike Scioscia, Angels<br>(Dusty Baker, Cubs) | 47,609 |
| 7-13-04 | Minute Maid Park<br>Houston | 9-4<br>(A.L.) | Mark Mulder, Athletics<br>(Roger Clemens, Astros) | Joe Torre, Yankees<br>(Jack McKeon, Marlins) | 41,886 |

*14 innings. †5 innings (rain). ‡12 innings. §10 innings. ∞15 innings. ▲13 innings. ■11 innings.

# AWARD WINNERS

## THE SPORTING NEWS

### MOST VALUABLE PLAYER

#### AMERICAN LEAGUE

| Year | Player | Team | Pos. | Points |
|---|---|---|---|---|
| 1929— | Al Simmons | Philadelphia | OF | 40 |
| 1930— | Joe Cronin | Washington | SS | 52 |
| 1931— | Lou Gehrig | New York | 1B | 40 |
| 1932— | Jimmie Foxx | Philadelphia | 1B | 46 |
| 1933— | Jimmie Foxx | Philadelphia | 1B | 49 |
| 1934— | Lou Gehrig | New York | 1B | 51 |
| 1935— | Hank Greenberg | Detroit | 1B | 64 |
| 1936— | Lou Gehrig | New York | 1B | 55 |
| 1937— | Charlie Gehringer | Detroit | 2B | 78 |
| 1938— | Jimmie Foxx | Boston | 1B | 304 |
| 1939— | Joe DiMaggio | New York | OF | 280 |
| 1940— | Hank Greenberg | Detroit | OF | 292 |
| 1941— | Joe DiMaggio | New York | OF | 291 |
| 1942— | Joe Gordon | New York | 2B | 270 |
| 1943— | Spud Chandler | New York | P | 246 |
| 1944— | Bobby Doerr | Boston | 2B | |
| 1945— | Eddie Mayo | Detroit | 2B | |

#### NATIONAL LEAGUE

| Year | Player | Team | Pos. | Points |
|---|---|---|---|---|
| 1929— | No selection | | | |
| 1930— | Bill Terry | New York | 1B | 47 |
| 1931— | Chuck Klein | Philadelphia | OF | 40 |
| 1932— | Chuck Klein | Philadelphia | OF | 46 |
| 1933— | Carl Hubbell | New York | P | 64 |
| 1934— | Dizzy Dean | St. Louis | P | 57 |
| 1935— | Arky Vaughan | Pittsburgh | SS | 42 |
| 1936— | Carl Hubbell | New York | P | 61 |
| 1937— | Joe Medwick | St. Louis | OF | 70 |
| 1938— | Ernie Lombardi | Cincinnati | C | 229 |
| 1939— | Bucky Walters | Cincinnati | P | 303 |
| 1940— | Frank McCormick | Cincinnati | 1B | 274 |
| 1941— | Dolf Camilli | Brooklyn | 1B | 300 |
| 1942— | Mort Cooper | St. Louis | P | 263 |
| 1943— | Stan Musial | St. Louis | OF | 267 |
| 1944— | Marty Marion | St. Louis | SS | |
| 1945— | Tommy Holmes | Boston | OF | |

### PLAYER AND PITCHER OF THE YEAR

#### AMERICAN LEAGUE

| Year | Player | Team | Pos. |
|---|---|---|---|
| 1944— | Bobby Doerr | Boston | 2B |
| | Hal Newhouser | Detroit | P |
| 1945— | Eddie Mayo | Detroit | 2B |
| | Hal Newhouser | Detroit | P |
| 1946— | No selections | | |
| 1947— | No selections | | |
| 1948— | Lou Boudreau | Cleveland | SS |
| | Bob Lemon | Cleveland | P |
| 1949— | Ted Williams | Boston | OF |
| | Ellis Kinder | Boston | P |
| 1950— | Phil Rizzuto | New York | SS |
| | Bob Lemon | Cleveland | P |
| 1951— | Ferris Fain | Philadelphia | 1B |
| | Bob Feller | Cleveland | P |
| 1952— | Luke Easter | Cleveland | 1B |
| | Bobby Shantz | Philadelphia | P |
| 1953— | Al Rosen | Cleveland | 3B |
| | Bob Porterfield | Washington | P |
| 1954— | Bobby Avila | Cleveland | 2B |
| | Bob Lemon | Cleveland | P |
| 1955— | Al Kaline | Detroit | OF |
| | Whitey Ford | New York | P |
| 1956— | Mickey Mantle | New York | OF |
| | Billy Pierce | Chicago | P |
| 1957— | Ted Williams | Boston | OF |
| | Billy Pierce | Chicago | P |
| 1958— | Jackie Jensen | Boston | OF |
| | Bob Turley | New York | P |
| 1959— | Nellie Fox | Chicago | 2B |
| | Early Wynn | Chicago | P |
| 1960— | Roger Maris | New York | OF |
| | Chuck Estrada | Baltimore | P |
| 1961— | Roger Maris | New York | OF |
| | Whitey Ford | New York | P |
| 1962— | Mickey Mantle | New York | OF |
| | Dick Donovan | Cleveland | P |
| 1963— | Al Kaline | Detroit | OF |
| | Whitey Ford | New York | P |
| 1964— | Brooks Robinson | Baltimore | 3B |
| | Dean Chance | Los Angeles | P |
| 1965— | Tony Oliva | Minnesota | OF |
| | Jim Grant | Minnesota | P |
| 1966— | Frank Robinson | Baltimore | OF |
| | Jim Kaat | Minnesota | P |

#### NATIONAL LEAGUE

| Year | Player | Team | Pos. |
|---|---|---|---|
| 1944— | Marty Marion | St. Louis | SS |
| | Bill Voiselle | New York | P |
| 1945— | Tommy Holmes | Boston | OF |
| | Hank Borowy | Chicago | P |
| 1946— | No selections | | |
| 1947— | No selections | | |
| 1948— | Stan Musial | St. Louis | OF-1B |
| | Johnny Sain | Boston | P |
| 1949— | Enos Slaughter | St. Louis | OF |
| | Howard Pollet | St. Louis | P |
| 1950— | Ralph Kiner | Pittsburgh | OF |
| | Jim Konstanty | Philadelphia | P |
| 1951— | Stan Musial | St. Louis | OF |
| | Preacher Roe | Brooklyn | P |
| 1952— | Hank Sauer | Chicago | OF |
| | Robin Roberts | Philadelphia | P |
| 1953— | Roy Campanella | Brooklyn | C |
| | Warren Spahn | Milwaukee | P |
| 1954— | Willie Mays | New York | OF |
| | Johnny Antonelli | New York | P |
| 1955— | Duke Snider | Brooklyn | OF |
| | Robin Roberts | Philadelphia | P |
| 1956— | Hank Aaron | Milwaukee | OF |
| | Don Newcombe | Brooklyn | P |
| 1957— | Stan Musial | St. Louis | 1B |
| | Warren Spahn | Milwaukee | P |
| 1958— | Ernie Banks | Chicago | SS |
| | Warren Spahn | Milwaukee | P |
| 1959— | Ernie Banks | Chicago | SS |
| | Sam Jones | San Francisco | P |
| 1960— | Dick Groat | Pittsburgh | SS |
| | Vern Law | Pittsburgh | P |
| 1961— | Frank Robinson | Cincinnati | OF |
| | Warren Spahn | Milwaukee | P |
| 1962— | Maury Wills | Los Angeles | SS |
| | Don Drysdale | Los Angeles | P |
| 1963— | Hank Aaron | Milwaukee | OF |
| | Sandy Koufax | Los Angeles | P |
| 1964— | Ken Boyer | St. Louis | 3B |
| | Sandy Koufax | Los Angeles | P |
| 1965— | Willie Mays | San Francisco | OF |
| | Sandy Koufax | Los Angeles | P |
| 1966— | Roberto Clemente | Pittsburgh | OF |
| | Sandy Koufax | Los Angeles | P |

| Year | Player | Team | Pos. |
|---|---|---|---|
| 1967— | Carl Yastrzemski | Boston | OF |
| | Jim Lonborg | Boston | P |
| 1968— | Ken Harrelson | Boston | OF |
| | Denny McLain | Detroit | P |
| 1969— | Harmon Killebrew | Minnesota | 1B-3B |
| | Denny McLain | Detroit | P |
| 1970— | Harmon Killebrew | Minnesota | 3B |
| | Sam McDowell | Cleveland | P |
| 1971— | Tony Oliva | Minnesota | OF |
| | Vida Blue | Oakland | P |
| 1972— | Dick Allen | Chicago | 1B |
| | Wilbur Wood | Chicago | P |
| 1973— | Reggie Jackson | Oakland | OF |
| | Jim Palmer | Baltimore | P |
| 1974— | Jeff Burroughs | Texas | OF |
| | Jim Hunter | Oakland | P |
| 1975— | Fred Lynn | Boston | OF |
| | Jim Palmer | Baltimore | P |
| 1976— | Thurman Munson | New York | C |
| | Jim Palmer | Baltimore | P |
| 1977— | Rod Carew | Minnesota | 1B |
| | Nolan Ryan | California | P |
| 1978— | Jim Rice | Boston | OF |
| | Ron Guidry | New York | P |
| 1979— | Don Baylor | California | OF |
| | Mike Flanagan | Baltimore | P |
| 1980— | George Brett | Kansas City | 3B |
| | Steve Stone | Baltimore | P |
| 1981— | Tony Armas | Oakland | OF |
| | Jack Morris | Detroit | P |
| 1982— | Robin Yount | Milwaukee | SS |
| | Dave Stieb | Toronto | P |
| 1983— | Cal Ripken Jr. | Baltimore | SS |
| | LaMarr Hoyt | Chicago | P |
| 1984— | Don Mattingly | New York | 1B |
| | Willie Hernandez | Detroit | P |
| 1985— | Don Mattingly | New York | 1B |
| | Bret Saberhagen | Kansas City | P |
| 1986— | Don Mattingly | New York | 1B |
| | Roger Clemens | Boston | P |
| 1987— | George Bell | Toronto | OF |
| | Jimmy Key | Toronto | P |
| 1988— | Jose Canseco | Oakland | OF |
| | Frank Viola | Minnesota | P |
| 1989— | Ruben Sierra | Texas | OF |
| | Bret Saberhagen | Kansas City | P |
| 1990— | Cecil Fielder | Detroit | 1B |
| | Bob Welch | Oakland | P |
| 1991— | Cal Ripken Jr. | Baltimore | SS |
| | Roger Clemens | Boston | P |

| Year | Player | Team | Pos. |
|---|---|---|---|
| 1967— | Orlando Cepeda | St. Louis | 1B |
| | Mike McCormick | San Francisco | P |
| 1968— | Pete Rose | Cincinnati | OF |
| | Bob Gibson | St. Louis | P |
| 1969— | Willie McCovey | San Francisco | 1B |
| | Tom Seaver | New York | P |
| 1970— | Johnny Bench | Cincinnati | C |
| | Bob Gibson | St. Louis | P |
| 1971— | Joe Torre | St. Louis | 3B |
| | Ferguson Jenkins | Chicago | P |
| 1972— | Billy Williams | Chicago | OF |
| | Steve Carlton | Philadelphia | P |
| 1973— | Bobby Bonds | San Francisco | OF |
| | Ron Bryant | San Francisco | P |
| 1974— | Lou Brock | St. Louis | OF |
| | Mike Marshall | Los Angeles | P |
| 1975— | Joe Morgan | Cincinnati | 2B |
| | Tom Seaver | New York | P |
| 1976— | George Foster | Cincinnati | OF |
| | Randy Jones | San Diego | P |
| 1977— | George Foster | Cincinnati | OF |
| | Steve Carlton | Philadelphia | P |
| 1978— | Dave Parker | Pittsburgh | OF |
| | Vida Blue | San Francisco | P |
| 1979— | Keith Hernandez | St. Louis | 1B |
| | Joe Niekro | Houston | P |
| 1980— | Mike Schmidt | Philadelphia | 3B |
| | Steve Carlton | Philadelphia | P |
| 1981— | Andre Dawson | Montreal | OF |
| | Fernando Valenzuela | Los Angeles | P |
| 1982— | Dale Murphy | Atlanta | OF |
| | Steve Carlton | Philadelphia | P |
| 1983— | Dale Murphy | Atlanta | OF |
| | John Denny | Philadelphia | P |
| 1984— | Ryne Sandberg | Chicago | 2B |
| | Rick Sutcliffe | Chicago | P |
| 1985— | Willie McGee | St. Louis | OF |
| | Dwight Gooden | New York | P |
| 1986— | Mike Schmidt | Philadelphia | 3B |
| | Mike Scott | Houston | P |
| 1987— | Andre Dawson | Chicago | OF |
| | Rick Sutcliffe | Chicago | P |
| 1988— | Andy Van Slyke | Pittsburgh | OF |
| | Orel Hershiser | Los Angeles | P |
| 1989— | Kevin Mitchell | San Francisco | OF |
| | Mark Davis | San Diego | P |
| 1990— | Barry Bonds | Pittsburgh | OF |
| | Doug Drabek | Pittsburgh | P |
| 1991— | Barry Bonds | Pittsburgh | OF |
| | Tom Glavine | Atlanta | P |

## PITCHER OF THE YEAR

### AMERICAN LEAGUE

| Year | Pitcher | Team |
|---|---|---|
| 1992— | Dennis Eckersley | Oakland |
| 1993— | Jack McDowell | Chicago |
| 1994— | Jimmy Key | New York |
| 1995— | Randy Johnson | Seattle |
| 1996— | Pat Hentgen | Toronto |
| 1997— | Roger Clemens | Toronto |
| 1998— | Roger Clemens | Toronto |
| 1999— | Pedro Martinez | Boston |
| 2000— | Pedro Martinez | Boston |
| 2001— | Roger Clemens | New York |
| 2002— | Barry Zito | Oakland |
| 2003— | Roy Halladay | Toronto |
| 2004— | Johan Santana | Minnesota |

### NATIONAL LEAGUE

| Year | Pitcher | Team |
|---|---|---|
| 1992— | Greg Maddux | Chicago |
| 1993— | Greg Maddux | Atlanta |
| 1994— | Greg Maddux | Atlanta |
| 1995— | Greg Maddux | Atlanta |
| 1996— | John Smoltz | Atlanta |
| 1997— | Pedro Martinez | Montreal |
| 1998— | Kevin Brown | San Diego |
| 1999— | Mike Hampton | Houston |
| 2000— | Tom Glavine | Atlanta |
| 2001— | Curt Schilling | Arizona |
| 2002— | Curt Schilling | Arizona |
| 2003— | Eric Gagne | Los Angeles |
| 2004— | Jason Schmidt | San Francisco |

## ROOKIE OF THE YEAR

1946—Combined selection—Del Ennis, Philadelphia N.L., OF
1947—Combined selection—Jackie Robinson, Brooklyn N.L., 1B
1948—Combined selection—Richie Ashburn, Philadelphia N.L., OF

### AMERICAN LEAGUE

| Year | Player | Team | Pos. |
|---|---|---|---|
| 1949 | Roy Sievers | St. Louis | OF |
| 1950 | Whitey Ford | New York | P |
| 1951 | Minnie Minoso | Chicago | OF |
| 1952 | Clint Courtney | St. Louis | C |
| 1953 | Harvey Kuenn | Detroit | SS |
| 1954 | Bob Grim | New York | P |
| 1955 | Herb Score | Cleveland | P |
| 1956 | Luis Aparicio | Chicago | SS |
| 1957 | Tony Kubek | New York | IF-OF |
| | (No pitcher named) | | |
| 1958 | Albie Pearson | Washington | OF |
| | Ryne Duren | New York | P |
| 1959 | Bob Allison | Washington | OF |
| 1960 | Ron Hansen | Baltimore | SS |
| 1961 | Dick Howser | Kansas City | SS |
| | Don Schwall | Boston | P |
| 1962 | Tom Tresh | New York | OF-SS |
| 1963 | Pete Ward | Chicago | 3B |
| | Gary Peters | Chicago | P |
| 1964 | Tony Oliva | Minnesota | OF |
| | Wally Bunker | Baltimore | P |
| 1965 | Curt Blefary | Baltimore | OF |
| | Marcelino Lopez | California | P |
| 1966 | Tommie Agee | Chicago | OF |
| | Jim Nash | Kansas City | P |
| 1967 | Rod Carew | Minnesota | 2B |
| | Tom Phoebus | Baltimore | P |
| 1968 | Del Unser | Washington | OF |
| | Stan Bahnsen | New York | P |
| 1969 | Carlos May | Chicago | OF |
| | Mike Nagy | Boston | P |
| 1970 | Roy Foster | Cleveland | OF |
| | Bert Blyleven | Minnesota | P |
| 1971 | Chris Chambliss | Cleveland | 1B |
| | Bill Parsons | Milwaukee | P |
| 1972 | Carlton Fisk | Boston | C |
| | Dick Tidrow | Cleveland | P |
| 1973 | Al Bumbry | Baltimore | OF |
| | Steve Busby | Kansas City | P |
| 1974 | Mike Hargrove | Texas | 1B |
| | Frank Tanana | California | P |
| 1975 | Fred Lynn | Boston | OF |
| | Dennis Eckersley | Cleveland | P |
| 1976 | Butch Wynegar | Minnesota | C |
| | Mark Fidrych | Detroit | P |
| 1977 | Mitchell Page | Oakland | OF |
| | Dave Rozema | Detroit | P |
| 1978 | Paul Molitor | Milwaukee | 2B |
| | Rich Gale | Kansas City | P |
| 1979 | Pat Putnam | Texas | 1B |
| | Mark Clear | California | P |
| 1980 | Joe Charboneau | Cleveland | OF |
| | Britt Burns | Chicago | P |
| 1981 | Rich Gedman | Boston | C |
| | Dave Righetti | New York | P |
| 1982 | Cal Ripken Jr. | Baltimore | SS-3B |
| | Ed Vande Berg | Seattle | P |
| 1983 | Ron Kittle | Chicago | OF |
| | Mike Boddicker | Baltimore | P |
| 1984 | Alvin Davis | Seattle | 1B |
| | Mark Langston | Seattle | P |
| 1985 | Ozzie Gullen | Chicago | SS |
| | Teddy Higuera | Milwaukee | P |
| 1986 | Jose Canseco | Oakland | OF |
| | Mark Eichhorn | Toronto | P |
| 1987 | Mark McGwire | Oakland | 1B |
| | Mike Henneman | Detroit | P |
| 1988 | Walt Weiss | Oakland | SS |
| | Bryan Harvey | California | P |

### NATIONAL LEAGUE

| Year | Player | Team | Pos. |
|---|---|---|---|
| 1949 | Don Newcombe | Brooklyn | P |
| 1950 | Combined A.L.-N.L. selection | | |
| 1951 | Willie Mays | New York | OF |
| 1952 | Joe Black | Brooklyn | P |
| 1953 | Jim Gilliam | Brooklyn | 2B |
| 1954 | Wally Moon | St. Louis | OF |
| 1955 | Bill Virdon | St. Louis | OF |
| 1956 | Frank Robinson | Cincinnati | OF |
| 1957 | Ed Bouchee | Philadelphia | 1B |
| | Jack Sanford | Philadelphia | P |
| 1958 | Orlando Cepeda | San Francisco | 1B |
| | Carlton Willey | Milwaukee | P |
| 1959 | Willie McCovey | San Francisco | 1B |
| 1960 | Frank Howard | Los Angeles | OF |
| 1961 | Billy Williams | Chicago | OF |
| | Ken Hunt | Cincinnati | P |
| 1962 | Ken Hubbs | Chicago | 2B |
| 1963 | Pete Rose | Cincinnati | 2B |
| | Ray Culp | Philadelphia | P |
| 1964 | Dick Allen | Philadelphia | 3B |
| | Billy McCool | Cincinnati | P |
| 1965 | Joe Morgan | Houston | 2B |
| | Frank Linzy | San Francisco | P |
| 1966 | Tommy Helms | Cincinnati | 3B |
| | Don Sutton | Los Angéles | P |
| 1967 | Lee May | Cincinnati | 1B |
| | Dick Hughes | St. Louis | P |
| 1968 | Johnny Bench | Cincinnati | C |
| | Jerry Koosman | New York | P |
| 1969 | Coco Laboy | Montreal | 3B |
| | Tom Griffin | Houston | P |
| 1970 | Bernie Carbo | Cincinnati | OF |
| | Carl Morton | Montreal | P |
| 1971 | Earl Williams | Atlanta | C |
| | Reggie Cleveland | St. Louis | P |
| 1972 | Dave Rader | San Francisco | C |
| | Jon Matlack | New York | P |
| 1973 | Gary Matthews | San Francisco | OF |
| | Steve Rogers | Montreal | P |
| 1974 | Greg Gross | Houston | OF |
| | John D'Acquisto | San Francisco | P |
| 1975 | Gary Carter | Montreal | OF-C |
| | John Montefusco | San Francisco | P |
| 1976 | Larry Herndon | San Francisco | OF |
| | Butch Metzger | San Diego | P |
| 1977 | Andre Dawson | Montreal | OF |
| | Bob Owchinko | San Diego | P |
| 1978 | Bob Horner | Atlanta | 3B |
| | Don Robinson | Pittsburgh | P |
| 1979 | Jeff Leonard | Houston | OF |
| | Rick Sutcliffe | Los Angeles | P |
| 1980 | Lonnie Smith | Philadelphia | OF |
| | Bill Gullickson | Montreal | P |
| 1981 | Tim Raines | Montreal | OF |
| | Fernando Valenzuela | Los Angeles | P |
| 1982 | Johnny Ray | Pittsburgh | 2B |
| | Steve Bedrosian | Atlanta | P |
| 1983 | Darryl Strawberry | New York | OF |
| | Craig McMurtry | Atlanta | P |
| 1984 | Juan Samuel | Philadelphia | 2B |
| | Dwight Gooden | New York | P |
| 1985 | Vince Coleman | St. Louis | OF |
| | Tom Browning | Cincinnati | P |
| 1986 | Robby Thompson | San Francisco | 2B |
| | Todd Worrell | St. Louis | P |
| 1987 | Benito Santiago | San Diego | C |
| | Mike Dunne | Pittsburgh | P |
| 1988 | Mark Grace | Chicago | 1B |
| | Tim Belcher | Los Angeles | P |

| Year | Player | Team | Pos. |
|---|---|---|---|
| 1989— | Craig Worthington | Baltimore | 3B |
| | Tom Gordon | Kansas City | P |
| 1990— | Sandy Alomar Jr. | Cleveland | C |
| | Kevin Appier | Kansas City | P |
| 1991— | Chuck Knoblauch | Minnesota | 2B |
| | Juan Guzman | Toronto | P |
| 1992— | Pat Listach | Milwaukee | SS |
| | Cal Eldred | Milwaukee | P |
| 1993— | Tim Salmon | California | OF |
| | Aaron Sele | Boston | P |
| 1994— | Bob Hamelin | Kansas City | DH |
| | Brian Anderson | California | P |
| 1995— | Garret Anderson | California | OF |
| | Julian Tavarez | Cleveland | P |
| 1996— | Derek Jeter | New York | SS |
| | James Baldwin | Chicago | P |
| 1997— | Nomar Garciaparra | Boston | SS |
| | Jason Dickson | Anaheim | P |
| 1998— | Ben Grieve | Oakland | OF |
| | Rolando Arrojo | Tampa Bay | P |
| 1999— | Carlos Beltran | Kansas City | OF |
| | Tim Hudson | Oakland | P |
| 2000— | Mark Quinn | Kansas City | OF-DH |
| | Kazuhiro Sasaki | Seattle | P |
| 2001— | Ichiro Suzuki | Seattle | OF |
| | C.C. Sabathia | Cleveland | P |
| 2002— | Eric Hinske | Toronto | 3B |
| | Rodrigo Lopez | Baltimore | P |
| 2003— | Jody Gerut | Cleveland | OF |
| | Rafael Soriano | Seattle | P |
| 2004— | Bobby Crosby | Oakland | SS |

| Year | Player | Team | Pos. |
|---|---|---|---|
| 1989— | Jerome Walton | Chicago | OF |
| | Andy Benes | San Diego | P |
| 1990— | David Justice | Atlanta | OF |
| | Mike Harkey | Chicago | P |
| 1991— | Jeff Bagwell | Houston | 1B |
| | Al Osuna | Houston | P |
| 1992— | Eric Karros | Los Angeles | 1B |
| | Tim Wakefield | Pittsburgh | P |
| 1993— | Mike Piazza | Los Angeles | C |
| | Kirk Rueter | Montreal | P |
| 1994— | Raul Mondesi | Los Angeles | OF |
| | Steve Trachsel | Chicago | P |
| 1995— | Chipper Jones | Atlanta | 3B |
| | Hideo Nomo | Los Angeles | P |
| 1996— | Jason Kendall | Pittsburgh | C |
| | Alan Benes | St. Louis | P |
| 1997— | Scott Rolen | Philadelphia | 3B |
| | Matt Morris | St. Louis | P |
| 1998— | Todd Helton | Colorado | 1B |
| | Kerry Wood | Chicago | P |
| 1999— | Preston Wilson | Florida | OF |
| | Scott Williamson | Cincinnati | P |
| 2000— | Rafael Furcal | Atlanta | 2B-SS |
| | Rick Ankiel | St. Louis | P |
| 2001— | Albert Pujols | St. Louis | 0-3-1B |
| | Roy Oswalt | Houston | P |
| 2002— | Brad Wilkerson | Montreal | OF-1B |
| | Jason Jennings | Colorado | P |
| 2003— | Scott Podsednik | Milwaukee | OF |
| | Dontrelle Willis | Florida | P |
| 2004— | Jason Bay | Pittsburgh | OF |

## RELIEVER OF THE YEAR

### AMERICAN LEAGUE

| Year | Pitcher | Team |
|---|---|---|
| 1960— | Mike Fornieles | Boston |
| 1961— | Luis Arroyo | New York |
| 1962— | Dick Radatz | Boston |
| 1963— | Stu Miller | Baltimore |
| 1964— | Dick Radatz | Boston |
| 1965— | Eddie Fisher | Chicago |
| 1966— | Jack Aker | Kansas City |
| 1967— | Minnie Rojas | California |
| 1968— | Wilbur Wood | Chicago |
| 1969— | Ron Perranoski | Minnesota |
| 1970— | Ron Perranoski | Minnesota |
| 1971— | Ken Sanders | Milwaukee |
| 1972— | Sparky Lyle | New York |
| 1973— | John Hiller | Detroit |
| 1974— | Terry Forster | Chicago |
| 1975— | Rich Gossage | Chicago |
| 1976— | Bill Campbell | Minnesota |
| 1977— | Bill Campbell | Boston |
| 1978— | Rich Gossage | New York |
| 1979— | Mike Marshall | Minnesota |
| | Jim Kern | Texas |
| 1980— | Dan Quisenberry | Kansas City |
| 1981— | Rollie Fingers | Milwaukee |
| 1982— | Dan Quisenberry | Kansas City |
| 1983— | Dan Quisenberry | Kansas City |
| 1984— | Dan Quisenberry | Kansas City |
| 1985— | Dan Quisenberry | Kansas City |
| 1986— | Dave Righetti | New York |
| 1987— | Dave Righetti | New York |
| | Jeff Reardon | Minnesota |
| 1988— | Dennis Eckersley | Oakland |
| 1989— | Jeff Russell | Texas |
| 1990— | Bobby Thigpen | Chicago |
| 1991— | Dennis Eckersley | Oakland |
| | Bryan Harvey | California |
| 1992— | Dennis Eckersley | Oakland |
| 1993— | Jeff Montgomery | Kansas City |

### NATIONAL LEAGUE

| Year | Pitcher | Team |
|---|---|---|
| 1960— | Lindy McDaniel | St. Louis |
| 1961— | Stu Miller | San Francisco |
| 1962— | Roy Face | Pittsburgh |
| 1963— | Lindy McDaniel | Chicago |
| 1964— | Al McBean | Pittsburgh |
| 1965— | Ted Abernathy | Chicago |
| 1966— | Phil Regan | Los Angeles |
| 1967— | Ted Abernathy | Cincinnati |
| 1968— | Phil Regan | L.A.-Chicago |
| 1969— | Wayne Granger | Cincinnati |
| 1970— | Wayne Granger | Cincinnati |
| 1971— | Dave Giusti | Pittsburgh |
| 1972— | Clay Carroll | Cincinnati |
| 1973— | Mike Marshall | Montreal |
| 1974— | Mike Marshall | Los Angeles |
| 1975— | Al Hrabosky | St. Louis |
| 1976— | Rawly Eastwick | Cincinnati |
| 1977— | Rollie Fingers | San Diego |
| 1978— | Rollie Fingers | San Diego |
| 1979— | Bruce Sutter | Chicago |
| 1980— | Rollie Fingers | San Diego |
| | Tom Hume | Cincinnati |
| 1981— | Bruce Sutter | St. Louis |
| 1982— | Bruce Sutter | St. Louis |
| 1983— | Al Holland | Philadelphia |
| | Lee Smith | Chicago |
| 1984— | Bruce Sutter | St. Louis |
| 1985— | Jeff Reardon | Montreal |
| 1986— | Todd Worrell | St. Louis |
| 1987— | Steve Bedrosian | Philadelphia |
| 1988— | John Franco | Cincinnati |
| 1989— | Mark Davis | San Diego |
| 1990— | John Franco | New York |
| 1991— | Lee Smith | St. Louis |
| 1992— | Doug Jones | Houston |
| | Lee Smith | St. Louis |
| 1993— | Randy Myers | Chicago |

## AMERICAN LEAGUE

| Year Pitcher | Team |
|---|---|
| 1994—Lee Smith | Baltimore |
| 1995—Jose Mesa | Cleveland |
| 1996—John Wetteland | New York |
| 1997—Mariano Rivera | New York |
| 1998—Tom Gordon | Boston |
| 1999—Mariano Rivera | New York |
| 2000—Todd Jones | Detroit |
| 2001—Mariano Rivera | New York |
| 2002—Billy Koch | Oakland |
| 2003—Keith Foulke | Oakland |
| 2004—Mariano Rivera | New York |

## NATIONAL LEAGUE

| Year Pitcher | Team |
|---|---|
| 1994—John Franco | New York |
| 1995—Randy Myers | Chicago |
| 1996—Trevor Hoffman | San Diego |
| 1997—Jeff Shaw | Cincinnati |
| 1998—Trevor Hoffman | San Diego |
| 1999—Ugueth Urbina | Montreal |
| 2000—Antonio Alfonseca | Florida |
| 2001—Armando Benitez | New York |
| Robb Nen | San Francisco |
| 2002—John Smoltz | Atlanta |
| 2003—Eric Gagne | Los Angeles |
| 2004—Eric Gagne | Los Angeles |

# COMEBACK PLAYER OF THE YEAR

## AMERICAN LEAGUE

| Year Pitcher | Team |
|---|---|
| 1965—Norm Cash | Detroit |
| 1966—Boog Powell | Baltimore |
| 1967—Dean Chance | Minnesota |
| 1968—Ken Harrelson | Boston |
| 1969—Tony Conigliaro | Boston |
| 1970—Clyde Wright | California |
| 1971—Norm Cash | Detroit |
| 1972—Luis Tiant | Boston |
| 1973—John Hiller | Detroit |
| 1974—Ferguson Jenkins | Texas |
| 1975—Boog Powell | Cleveland |
| 1976—Dock Ellis | New York |
| 1977—Eric Soderholm | Chicago |
| 1978—Mike Caldwell | Milwaukee |
| 1979—Willie Horton | Seattle |
| 1980—Matt Keough | Oakland |
| 1981—Richie Zisk | Seattle |
| 1982—Andre Thornton | Cleveland |
| 1983—Alan Trammell | Detroit |
| 1984—Dave Kingman | Oakland |
| 1985—Gorman Thomas | Seattle |
| 1986—John Candelaria | California |
| 1987—Bret Saberhagen | Kansas City |
| 1988—Storm Davis | Oakland |
| 1989—Bert Blyleven | California |
| 1990—Dave Winfield | California |
| 1991—Jose Guzman | Texas |
| 1992—Rick Sutcliffe | Baltimore |
| 1993—Bo Jackson | Chicago |
| 1994—Jose Canseco | Texas |
| 1995—Tim Wakefield | Boston |
| 1996—Kevin Elster | Texas |
| 1997—David Justice | Cleveland |
| 1998—Bret Saberhagen | Boston |
| 1999—John Jaha | Oakland |
| 2000—Frank Thomas | Chicago |
| 2001—Ruben Sierra | Texas |
| 2002—Tim Salmon | Anaheim |
| 2003—Gil Meche | Seattle |
| 2004—Paul Konerko | Chicago |

## NATIONAL LEAGUE

| Year Pitcher | Team |
|---|---|
| 1965—Vernon Law | Pittsburgh |
| 1966—Phil Regan | Los Angeles |
| 1967—Mike McCormick | San Francisco |
| 1968—Alex Johnson | Cincinnati |
| 1969—Tommie Agee | New York |
| 1970—Jim Hickman | Chicago |
| 1971—Al Downing | Los Angeles |
| 1972—Bobby Tolan | Cincinnati |
| 1973—Dave Johnson | Atlanta |
| 1974—Jim Wynn | Los Angeles |
| 1975—Randy Jones | San Diego |
| 1976—Tommy John | Los Angeles |
| 1977—Willie McCovey | San Francisco |
| 1978—Willie Stargell | Pittsburgh |
| 1979—Lou Brock | St. Louis |
| 1980—Jerry Reuss | Los Angeles |
| 1981—Bob Knepper | Houston |
| 1982—Joe Morgan | San Francisco |
| 1983—John Denny | Philadelphia |
| 1984—Joaquin Andujar | St. Louis |
| 1985—Rick Reuschel | Pittsburgh |
| 1986—Ray Knight | New York |
| 1987—Rick Sutcliffe | Chicago |
| 1988—Tim Leary | Los Angeles |
| 1989—Lonnie Smith | Atlanta |
| 1990—John Tudor | St. Louis |
| 1991—Terry Pendleton | Atlanta |
| 1992—Gary Sheffield | San Diego |
| 1993—Andres Galarraga | Colorado |
| 1994—Tim Wallach | Los Angeles |
| 1995—Ron Gant | Cincinnati |
| 1996—Eric Davis | Cincinnati |
| 1997—Darren Daulton | Phi.-Fla. |
| 1998—Greg Vaughn | San Diego |
| 1999—Rickey Henderson | New York |
| 2000—Andres Galarraga | Atlanta |
| 2001—Matt Morris | St. Louis |
| 2002—Mike Lieberthal | Philadelphia |
| 2003—Javy Lopez | Atlanta |
| 2004—Chris Carpenter | St. Louis |

# MAJOR LEAGUE PLAYER OF THE YEAR

| Year Player | Team |
|---|---|
| 1936—Carl Hubbell | New York N.L. |
| 1937—Johnny Allen | Cleveland A.L. |
| 1938—Johnny Vander Meer | Cincinnati N.L. |
| 1939—Joe DiMaggio | New York A.L. |
| 1940—Bob Feller | Cleveland A.L. |
| 1941—Ted Williams | Boston A.L. |
| 1942—Ted Williams | Boston A.L. |
| 1943—Spud Chandler | New York A.L. |
| 1944—Marty Marion | St. Louis N.L. |
| 1945—Hal Newhouser | Detroit A.L. |
| 1946—Stan Musial | St. Louis N.L. |
| 1947—Ted Williams | Boston A.L. |
| 1948—Lou Boudreau | Cleveland A.L. |
| 1949—Ted Williams | Boston A.L. |

| Year Player | Team |
|---|---|
| 1950—Phil Rizzuto | New York A.L. |
| 1951—Stan Musial | St. Louis N.L. |
| 1952—Robin Roberts | Philadelphia N.L. |
| 1953—Al Rosen | Cleveland A.L. |
| 1954—Willie Mays | New York N.L. |
| 1955—Duke Snider | Brooklyn N.L. |
| 1956—Mickey Mantle | New York A.L. |
| 1957—Ted Williams | Boston A.L. |
| 1958—Bob Turley | New York A.L. |
| 1959—Early Wynn | Chicago A.L. |
| 1960—Bill Mazeroski | Pittsburgh N.L. |
| 1961—Roger Maris | New York A.L. |
| 1962—Maury Wills | Los Angeles N.L. |
| Don Drysdale | Los Angeles N.L. |

| Year Player | Team |
|---|---|
| 1963—Sandy Koufax | Los Angeles N.L. |
| 1964—Ken Boyer | St. Louis N.L. |
| 1965—Sandy Koufax | Los Angeles N.L. |
| 1966—Frank Robinson | Baltimore A.L. |
| 1967—Carl Yastrzemski | Boston A.L. |
| 1968—Denny McLain | Detroit A.L. |
| 1969—Willie McCovey | San Francisco N.L. |
| 1970—Johnny Bench | Cincinnati N.L. |
| 1971—Joe Torre | St. Louis N.L. |
| 1972—Billy Williams | Chicago N.L. |
| 1973—Reggie Jackson | Oakland A.L. |
| 1974—Lou Brock | St. Louis N.L. |
| 1975—Joe Morgan | Cincinnati N.L. |
| 1976—Joe Morgan | Cincinnati N.L. |

| Year | Player | Team |
|---|---|---|
| 1977 | Rod Carew | Minnesota A.L. |
| 1978 | Ron Guidry | New York A.L. |
| 1979 | Willie Stargell | Pittsburgh N.L. |
| 1980 | George Brett | Kansas City A.L. |
| 1981 | Fernando Valenzuela | Los Angeles N.L. |
| 1982 | Robin Yount | Milwaukee A.L. |
| 1983 | Cal Ripken Jr. | Baltimore A.L. |
| 1984 | Ryne Sandberg | Chicago N.L. |
| 1985 | Don Mattingly | New York A.L. |
| 1986 | Roger Clemens | Boston A.L. |
| 1987 | George Bell | Toronto A.L. |
| 1988 | Orel Hershiser | Los Angeles N.L. |
| 1989 | Kevin Mitchell | San Francisco N.L. |
| 1990 | Barry Bonds | Pittsburgh N.L. |
| 1991 | Cal Ripken Jr. | Baltimore A.L. |
| 1992 | Gary Sheffield | San Diego N.L. |
| 1993 | Frank Thomas | Chicago A.L. |
| 1994 | Jeff Bagwell | Houston N.L. |
| 1995 | Albert Belle | Cleveland A.L. |
| 1996 | Alex Rodriguez | Seattle A.L. |
| 1997 | Ken Griffey Jr. | Seattle A.L. |
| 1998 | Sammy Sosa | Chicago N.L. |
| 1999 | Rafael Palmeiro | Texas A.L. |
| 2000 | Carlos Delgado | Toronto A.L. |
| 2001 | Barry Bonds | San Francisco N.L. |
| 2002 | Alex Rodriguez | Texas A.L |
| 2003 | Albert Pujols | St. Louis N.L. |
| 2004 | Barry Bonds | San Francisco N.L. |

## MAJOR LEAGUE MANAGER OF THE YEAR

| Year | Manager | Team |
|---|---|---|
| 1936 | Joe McCarthy | New York A.L. |
| 1937 | Bill McKechnie | Boston N.L. |
| 1938 | Joe McCarthy | New York A.L. |
| 1939 | Leo Durocher | Brooklyn N.L. |
| 1940 | Bill McKechnie | Cincinnati N.L. |
| 1941 | Billy Southworth | St. Louis N.L. |
| 1942 | Billy Southworth | St. Louis N.L. |
| 1943 | Joe McCarthy | New York A.L. |
| 1944 | Luke Sewell | St. Louis A.L. |
| 1945 | Ossie Bluege | Washington A.L. |
| 1946 | Eddie Dyer | St. Louis N.L. |
| 1947 | Bucky Harris | New York A.L. |
| 1948 | Bill Meyer | Pittsburgh N.L. |
| 1949 | Casey Stengel | New York A.L. |
| 1950 | Red Rolfe | Detroit A.L. |
| 1951 | Leo Durocher | New York N.L. |
| 1952 | Eddie Stanky | St. Louis N.L. |
| 1953 | Casey Stengel | New York A.L. |
| 1954 | Leo Durocher | New York N.L. |
| 1955 | Walter Alston | Brooklyn N.L. |
| 1956 | Birdie Tebbetts | Cincinnati N.L. |
| 1957 | Fred Hutchinson | St. Louis N.L. |
| 1958 | Casey Stengel | New York A.L. |
| 1959 | Walter Alston | Los Angeles N.L. |
| 1960 | Danny Murtaugh | Pittsburgh N.L. |
| 1961 | Ralph Houk | New York A.L. |
| 1962 | Bill Rigney | Los Angeles A.L. |
| 1963 | Walter Alston | Los Angeles N.L. |
| 1964 | Johnny Keane | St. Louis N.L. |
| 1965 | Sam Mele | Minnesota A.L. |
| 1966 | Hank Bauer | Baltimore A.L. |
| 1967 | Dick Williams | Boston A.L. |
| 1968 | Mayo Smith | Detroit A.L. |
| 1969 | Gil Hodges | New York N.L. |
| 1970 | Danny Murtaugh | Pittsburgh N.L. |
| 1971 | Charlie Fox | San Francisco N.L. |
| 1972 | Chuck Tanner | Chicago A.L. |
| 1973 | Gene Mauch | Montreal N.L. |
| 1974 | Bill Virdon | New York A.L. |
| 1975 | Darrell Johnson | Boston A.L. |
| 1976 | Danny Ozark | Philadelphia N.L. |
| 1977 | Earl Weaver | Baltimore A.L. |
| 1978 | George Bamberger | Milwaukee A.L. |
| 1979 | Earl Weaver | Baltimore A.L. |
| 1980 | Bill Virdon | Houston N.L. |
| 1981 | Billy Martin | Oakland A.L. |
| 1982 | Whitey Herzog | St. Louis N.L. |
| 1983 | Tony La Russa | Chicago A.L. |
| 1984 | Jim Frey | Chicago N.L. |
| 1985 | Bobby Cox | Toronto A.L. |
| 1986 | John McNamara | Boston A.L. |
| | Hal Lanier | Houston N.L. |
| 1987 | Sparky Anderson | Detroit A.L. |
| | Buck Rodgers | Montreal N.L. |
| 1988 | Tony La Russa | Oakland A.L. |
| | Tommy Lasorda | L.A. N.L. (tie) |
| | Jim Leyland | Pit. N.L. (tie) |
| 1989 | Frank Robinson | Baltimore A.L. |
| | Don Zimmer | Chicago N.L. |
| 1990 | Jeff Torborg | Chicago A.L. |
| | Jim Leyland | Pittsburgh N.L. |
| 1991 | Tom Kelly | Minnesota A.L. |
| | Bobby Cox | Atlanta N.L. |
| 1992 | Tony La Russa | Oakland A.L. |
| | Jim Leyland | Pittsburgh N.L. |
| 1993 | Johnny Oates | Baltimore A.L. |
| | Bobby Cox | Atlanta N.L. |
| 1994 | Buck Showalter | New York A.L. |
| | Felipe Alou | Montreal N.L. |
| 1995 | Mike Hargrove | Cleveland A.L. |
| | Don Baylor | Colorado N.L. |
| 1996 | Johnny Oates | Texas A.L. |
| | Bruce Bochy | San Diego N.L. |
| 1997 | Dave Johnson | Baltimore A.L. |
| | Dusty Baker | San Fran. N.L. |
| 1998 | Joe Torre | New York A.L. |
| | Bruce Bochy | San Diego N.L. |
| 1999 | Jimy Williams | Boston A.L. |
| | Bobby Cox | Atlanta N.L. |
| 2000 | Jerry Manuel | Chicago A.L. |
| | Dusty Baker | San Fran. N.L. |
| 2001 | Lou Piniella | Seattle A.L. |
| | Larry Bowa | Philadelphia N.L. |
| 2002 | Mike Scioscia | Anaheim A.L. |
| | Bobby Cox | Atlanta N.L. |
| 2003 | Tony Pena | Kansas City A.L. |
| | Bobby Cox | Atlanta N.L. |
| 2004 | Buck Showalter | Texas A.L. |
| | Ron Gardenhire | Minnesota A.L. |
| | Bobby Cox | Atlanta N.L. |

## MAJOR LEAGUE EXECUTIVE OF THE YEAR

| Year | Executive | Team |
|---|---|---|
| 1936 | Branch Rickey | St. Louis N.L. |
| 1937 | Ed Barrow | New York A.L. |
| 1938 | Warren Giles | Cincinnati N.L. |
| 1939 | Larry MacPhail | Brooklyn N.L. |
| 1940 | Walter Briggs Sr. | Detroit A.L. |
| 1941 | Ed Barrow | New York A.L. |
| 1942 | Branch Rickey | St. Louis N.L. |
| 1943 | Clark Griffith | Washington A.L. |
| 1944 | Billy DeWitt | St. Louis A.L. |
| 1945 | Phil Wrigley | Chicago N.L. |
| 1946 | Tom Yawkey | Boston A.L. |
| 1947 | Branch Rickey | Brooklyn N.L. |
| 1948 | Bill Veeck | Cleveland A.L. |
| 1949 | Bob Carpenter | Philadelphia N.L. |
| 1950 | George Weiss | New York A.L. |
| 1951 | George Weiss | New York A.L. |
| 1952 | George Weiss | New York A.L. |
| 1953 | Lou Perini | Milwaukee N.L. |
| 1954 | Horace Stoneham | New York N.L. |
| 1955 | Walter O'Malley | Brooklyn N.L. |
| 1956 | Gabe Paul | Cincinnati N.L. |
| 1957 | Frank Lane | St. Louis N.L. |
| 1958 | Joe Brown | Pittsburgh N.L. |
| 1959 | Buzzie Bavasi | Los Angeles N.L. |
| 1960 | George Weiss | New York A.L. |
| 1961 | Dan Topping | New York A.L. |
| 1962 | Fred Haney | Los Angeles A.L. |
| 1963 | Bing Devine | St. Louis N.L. |
| 1964 | Bing Devine | St. Louis N.L. |
| 1965 | Cal Griffith | Minnesota A.L. |
| 1966 | Lee MacPhail | Commissioner's Off. |
| 1967 | Dick O'Connell | Boston A.L. |
| 1968 | Jim Campbell | Detroit A.L. |
| 1969 | John Murphy | New York N.L. |
| 1970 | Harry Dalton | Baltimore A.L. |
| 1971 | Cedric Tallis | Kansas City A.L. |
| 1972 | Roland Hemond | Chicago A.L. |
| 1973 | Bob Howsam | Cincinnati N.L. |
| 1974 | Gabe Paul | New York A.L. |
| 1975 | Dick O'Connell | Boston A.L. |
| 1976 | Joe Burke | Kansas City A.L. |
| 1977 | Bill Veeck | Chicago A.L. |
| 1978 | Spec Richardson | San Francisco N.L. |
| 1979 | Hank Peters | Baltimore A.L. |
| 1980 | Tal Smith | Houston N.L. |
| 1981 | John McHale | Montreal N.L. |
| 1982 | Harry Dalton | Milwaukee A.L. |
| 1983 | Hank Peters | Baltimore A.L. |
| 1984 | Dallas Green | Chicago N.L. |
| 1985 | John Schuerholz | Kansas City A.L. |
| 1986 | Frank Cashen | New York N.L. |
| 1987 | Al Rosen | San Francisco N.L. |
| 1988 | Fred Claire | Los Angeles N.L. |
| 1989 | Roland Hemond | Baltimore A.L. |
| 1990 | Bob Quinn | Cincinnati N.L. |
| 1991 | Andy MacPhail | Minnesota A.L. |
| 1992 | Dan Duquette | Montreal N.L. |
| 1993 | Lee Thomas | Philadelphia N.L. |
| 1994 | John Hart | Cleveland A.L. |
| 1995 | John Hart | Cleveland A.L. |
| 1996 | Doug Melvin | Texas A.L. |
| 1997 | Cam Bonifay | Pittsburgh N.L. |
| 1998 | Gerry Hunsicker | Houston N.L. |
| 1999 | Billy Beane | Oakland A.L. |
| 2000 | Walt Jocketty | St. Louis N.L. |
| 2001 | Pat Gillick | Seattle A.L. |
| 2002 | Terry Ryan | Minnesota A.L. |
| 2003 | Brian Sabean | San Francisco N.L. |
| 2004 | Walt Jocketty | St. Louis N.L. |

## 1925
1B— Jim Bottomley, St. Louis N.L.
2B— Rogers Hornsby, St. Louis N.L.
SS— Glenn Wright, Pittsburgh N.L.
3B— Pie Traynor, Pittsburgh N.L.
OF— Kiki Cuyler, Pittsburgh N.L.
OF— Max Carey, Pittsburgh N.L.
OF— Goose Goslin, Washington A.L.
C— Mickey Cochrane, Phil. A.L.
P— Walter Johnson, Washington A.L.
P— Ed Rommel, Philadelphia A.L.
P— Dazzy Vance, Brooklyn N.L.

## 1926
1B— George Burns, Cleveland A.L.
2B— Rogers Hornsby, St. Louis N.L.
SS— Joe Sewell, Cleveland A.L.
3B— Pie Traynor, Pittsburgh N.L.
OF— Goose Goslin, Washington A.L.
OF— John Mostil, Chicago A.L.
OF— Babe Ruth, New York A.L.
C— Bob O'Farrell, St. Louis N.L.
P— Herb Pennock, New York A.L.
P— George Uhle, Cleveland A.L.
P— Grover Alexander, St. Louis N.L.

## 1927
1B— Lou Gehrig, New York A.L.
2B— Rogers Hornsby, New York N.L.
SS— Travis Jackson, New York N.L.
3B— Pie Traynor, Pittsburgh N.L.
OF— Babe Ruth, New York A.L.
OF— Al Simmons, Philadelphia A.L.
OF— Paul Waner, Pittsburgh N.L.
C— Gabby Hartnett, Chicago N.L.
P— Charley Root, Chicago N.L.
P— Ted Lyons, Chicago A.L.

## 1928
1B— Lou Gehrig, New York A.L.
2B— Rogers Hornsby, Boston N.L.
SS— Travis Jackson, New York N.L.
3B— Fred Lindstrom, New York N.L.
OF— Babe Ruth, New York A.L.
OF— Heinie Manush, St. Louis A.L.
OF— Paul Waner, Pittsburgh N.L.
C— Mickey Cochrane, Phil. A.L.
P— Lefty Grove, Philadelphia A.L.
P— Waite Hoyt, New York A.L.

## 1929
1B— Jimmie Foxx, Philadelphia A.L.
2B— Rogers Hornsby, Chicago N.L.
SS— Travis Jackson, New York N.L.
3B— Pie Traynor, Pittsburgh, N.L.
OF— Al Simmons, Philadelphia A.L.
OF— Hack Wilson, Chicago N.L.
OF— Babe Ruth, New York A.L.
C— Mickey Cochrane, Phil. A.L.
P— Lefty Grove, Philadelphia A.L.
P— Burleigh Grimes, Pittsburgh N.L.

## 1930
1B— Bill Terry, New York N.L.
2B— Frank Frisch, St. Louis N.L.
SS— Joe Cronin, Washington A.L.
3B— Fred Lindstrom, New York N.L.
OF— Al Simmons, Philadelphia A.L.
OF— Hack Wilson, Chicago N.L.
OF— Babe Ruth, New York A.L.
C— Mickey Cochrane, Phil. A.L.
P— Lefty Grove, Philadelphia A.L.
P— Wes Ferrell, Cleveland A.L.

## 1931
1B— Lou Gehrig, New York A.L.
2B— Frank Frisch, St. Louis N.L.
SS— Joe Cronin, Washington A.L.
3B— Pie Traynor, Pittsburgh N.L.
OF— Al Simmons, Philadelphia A.L.
OF— Earl Averill, Cleveland A.L.
OF— Babe Ruth, New York A.L.
C— Mickey Cochrane, Phil. A.L.
P— Lefty Grove, Philadelphia A.L.
P— George Earnshaw, Phil. A.L.

## 1932
1B— Jimmie Foxx, Philadelphia A.L.
2B— Tony Lazzeri, New York A.L.
SS— Joe Cronin, Washington A.L.
3B— Pie Traynor, Pittsburgh N.L.
OF— Lefty O'Doul, Brooklyn N.L.
OF— Earl Averill, Cleveland A.L.
OF— Chuck Klein, Philadelphia N.L.
C— Bill Dickey, New York A.L.
P— Lefty Grove, Philadelphia A.L.
P— Lon Warneke, Chicago N.L.

## 1933
1B— Jimmie Foxx, Philadelphia A.L.
2B— Charley Gehringer, Detroit A.L.
SS— Joe Cronin, Washington A.L.
3B— Pie Traynor, Pittsburgh N.L.
OF— Al Simmons, Chicago A.L.
OF— Wally Berger, Boston N.L.
OF— Chuck Klein, Philadelphia N.L.
C— Bill Dickey, New York A.L.
P— Alvin Crowder, Washington A.L.
P— Carl Hubbell, New York N.L.

## 1934
1B— Lou Gehrig, New York A.L.
2B— Charley Gehringer, Detroit A.L.
SS— Joe Cronin, Washington A.L.
3B— Mike Higgins, Philadelphia A.L.
OF— Al Simmons, Chicago A.L.
OF— Earl Averill, Cleveland A.L.
OF— Mel Ott, New York N.L.
C— Mickey Cochrane, Detroit A.L.
P— Lefty Gomez, New York A.L.
P— Schoolboy Rowe, Detroit A.L.
P— Dizzy Dean, St. Louis N.L.

## 1935
1B— Hank Greenberg, Detroit A.L.
2B— Charley Gehringer, Detroit A.L.
SS— Arky Vaughan, Pittsburgh N.L.
3B— Pepper Martin, St. Louis N.L.
OF— Joe Medwick, St. Louis N.L.
OF— Doc Cramer, Philadelphia A.L.
OF— Mel Ott, New York N.L.
C— Mickey Cochrane, Detroit A.L.
P— Carl Hubbell, New York N.L.
P— Dizzy Dean, St. Louis N.L.

## 1936
1B— Lou Gehrig, New York A.L.
2B— Charley Gehringer, Detroit A.L.
SS— Luke Appling, Chicago A.L.
3B— Mike Higgins, Philadelphia A.L.
OF— Joe Medwick, St. Louis N.L.
OF— Earl Averill, Cleveland A.L.
OF— Mel Ott, New York N.L.
C— Bill Dickey, New York A.L.
P— Carl Hubbell, New York N.L.
P— Dizzy Dean, St. Louis N.L.

## 1937
1B— Lou Gehrig, New York A.L.
2B— Charley Gehringer, Detroit A.L.
SS— Dick Bartell, New York N.L.
3B— Red Rolfe, New York A.L.
OF— Joe Medwick, St. Louis N.L.
OF— Joe DiMaggio, New York A.L.
OF— Paul Waner, Pittsburgh N.L.
C— Gabby Hartnett, Chicago N.L.
P— Carl Hubbell, New York N.L.
P— Red Ruffing, New York A.L.

## 1938
1B— Jimmie Foxx, Boston A.L.
2B— Charley Gehringer, Detroit A.L.
SS— Joe Cronin, Boston A.L.
3B— Red Rolfe, New York A.L.
OF— Joe Medwick, St. Louis N.L.
OF— Joe DiMaggio, New York A.L.
OF— Mel Ott, New York N.L.
C— Bill Dickey, New York A.L.
P— Red Ruffing, New York A.L.
P— Lefty Gomez, New York A.L.
P— Johnny Vander Meer, Cin. N.L.

## 1939
1B— Jimmie Foxx, Boston A.L.
2B— Joe Gordon, New York A.L.
SS— Joe Cronin, Boston A.L.
3B— Red Rolfe, New York A.L.
OF— Joe Medwick, St. Louis N.L.
OF— Joe DiMaggio, New York A.L.
OF— Ted Williams, Boston A.L.
C— Bill Dickey, New York A.L.
P— Red Ruffing, New York A.L.
P— Bob Feller, Cleveland A.L.
P— Bucky Walters, Cincinnati N.L.

## 1940
1B— Frank McCormick, Cincinnati N.L.
2B— Joe Gordon, New York A.L.
SS— Luke Appling, Chicago A.L.
3B— Stan Hack, Chicago N.L.
OF— Hank Greenberg, Detroit A.L.
OF— Joe DiMaggio, New York A.L.
OF— Ted Williams, Boston A.L.
C— Harry Danning, New York N.L.
P— Bob Feller, Cleveland A.L.
P— Bucky Walters, Cincinnati N.L.
P— Paul Derringer, Cincinnati N.L.

## 1941
1B— Dolf Camilli, Brooklyn N.L.
2B— Joe Gordon, New York A.L.
SS— Cecil Travis, Washington A.L.
3B— Stan Hack, Chicago N.L.
OF— Ted Williams, Boston A.L.
OF— Joe DiMaggio, New York A.L.
OF— Pete Reiser, Brooklyn N.L.
C— Bill Dickey, New York A.L.
P— Bob Feller, Cleveland A.L.
P— Whitlow Wyatt, Brooklyn N.L.
P— Thornton Lee, Chicago A.L.

## 1942
1B— Johnny Mize, New York N.L.
2B— Joe Gordon, New York A.L.
SS— Johnny Pesky, Boston A.L.
3B— Stan Hack, Chicago N.L.
OF— Ted Williams, Boston A.L.
OF— Joe DiMaggio, New York A.L.
OF— Enos Slaughter, St. Louis N.L.
C— Mickey Owen, Brooklyn N.L.
P— Mort Cooper, St. Louis N.L.
P— Tiny Bonham, New York A.L.
P— Tex Hughson, Boston A.L.

## 1943
1B— Rudy York, Detroit A.L.
2B— Billy Herman, Brooklyn N.L.
SS— Luke Appling, Chicago A.L.
3B— Billy Johnson, New York A.L.
OF— Dick Wakefield, Detroit A.L.
OF— Stan Musial, St. Louis N.L.
OF— Bill Nicholson, Chicago N.L.
C— Walker Cooper, St. Louis N.L.
P— Spud Chandler, New York A.L.
P— Mort Cooper, St. Louis N.L.
P— Rip Sewell, Pittsburgh N.L.

## 1944
1B— Ray Sanders, St. Louis N.L.
2B— Bobby Doerr, Boston A.L.
SS— Marty Marion, St. Louis N.L.
3B— Bob Elliott, Pittsburgh N.L.
OF— Stan Musial, St. Louis N.L.
OF— Dick Wakefield, Detroit A.L.
OF— Dixie Walker, Brooklyn, N.L.
C— Walker Cooper, St. Louis N.L.
P— Hal Newhouser, Detroit A.L.
P— Mort Cooper, St. Louis N.L.
P— Dizzy Trout, Detroit A.L.

## 1945
1B— Phil Cavarretta, Chicago N.L.
2B— George Stirnweiss, N.Y. A.L.
SS— Marty Marion, St. Louis N.L.
3B— Whitey Kurowski, St. Louis N.L.
OF— Tommy Holmes, Boston N.L.
OF— Andy Pafko, Chicago N.L.
OF— Goody Rosen, Brooklyn N.L.
C— Paul Richards, Detroit A.L.
P— Hal Newhouser, Detroit A.L.
P— Boo Ferriss, Boston A.L.
P— Hank Borowy, Chicago N.L.

## 1946
1B— Stan Musial, St. Louis N.L.
2B— Bobby Doerr, Boston A.L.
SS— Johnny Pesky, Boston A.L.
3B— George Kell, Detroit A.L.
OF— Ted Williams, Boston A.L.
OF— Dom DiMaggio, Boston A.L.
OF— Enos Slaughter, St. Louis N.L.
C— Aaron Robinson, New York A.L.
P— Hal Newhouser, Detroit A.L.
P— Bob Feller, Cleveland A.L.
P— Boo Ferriss, Boston A.L.

## 1947
1B— Johnny Mize, New York N.L.
2B— Joe Gordon, Cleveland A.L.
SS— Lou Boudreau, Cleveland A.L.
3B— George Kell, Detroit A.L.
OF— Ted Williams, Boston A.L.
OF— Joe DiMaggio, New York A.L.
OF— Ralph Kiner, Pittsburgh N.L.
C— Walker Cooper, New York N.L.
P— Ewell Blackwell, Cincinnati N.L.
P— Bob Feller, Cleveland A.L.
P— Ralph Branca, Brooklyn N.L.

## 1948
1B— Johnny Mize, New York N.L.
2B— Joe Gordon, Cleveland A.L.
SS— Lou Boudreau, Cleveland A.L.
3B— Bob Elliott, Boston N.L.
OF— Ted Williams, Boston A.L.
OF— Joe DiMaggio, New York A.L.
OF— Stan Musial, St. Louis N.L.
C— Birdie Tebbetts, Boston A.L.
P— Johnny Sain, Boston N.L.
P— Bob Lemon, Cleveland A.L.
P— Harry Brecheen, St. Louis N.L.

## 1949
1B— Tommy Henrich, New York A.L.
2B— Jackie Robinson, Brooklyn N.L.
SS— Phil Rizzuto, New York A.L.
3B— George Kell, Detroit A.L.
OF— Ted Williams, Boston A.L.
OF— Stan Musial, St. Louis N.L.
OF— Ralph Kiner, Pittsburgh N.L.
C— Roy Campanella, Brooklyn N.L.
P— Mel Parnell, Boston A.L.
P— Ellis Kinder, Boston A.L.
P— Joe Page, New York A.L.

## 1950
1B— Walt Dropo, Boston A.L.
2B— Jackie Robinson, Brooklyn N.L.
SS— Phil Rizzuto, New York A.L.
3B— George Kell, Detroit A.L.
OF— Stan Musial, St. Louis N.L.
OF— Ralph Kiner, Pittsburgh N.L.
OF— Larry Doby, Cleveland A.L.
C— Yogi Berra, New York A.L.
P— Vic Raschi, New York A.L.
P— Bob Lemon, Cleveland A.L.
P— Jim Konstanty, Phil. N.L.

## 1951
1B— Ferris Fain, Philadelphia A.L.
2B— Jackie Robinson, Brooklyn N.L.
SS— Phil Rizzuto, New York A.L.
3B— George Kell, Detroit A.L.
OF— Stan Musial, St. Louis N.L.
OF— Ted Williams, Boston A.L.
OF— Ralph Kiner, Pittsburgh N.L.
C— Roy Campanella, Brooklyn N.L.
P— Sal Maglie, New York N.L.
P— Preacher Roe, Brooklyn N.L.
P— Allie Reynolds, New York A.L.

## 1952
1B— Ferris Fain, Philadelphia A.L.
2B— Jackie Robinson, Brooklyn N.L.
SS— Phil Rizzuto, New York A.L.
3B— George Kell, Boston A.L.
OF— Stan Musial, St. Louis N.L.
OF— Hank Sauer, Chicago N.L.
OF— Mickey Mantle, New York A.L.
C— Yogi Berra, New York A.L.
P— Robin Roberts, Philadelphia N.L.
P— Bobby Shantz, Philadelphia A.L.
P— Allie Reynolds, New York A.L.

## 1953
1B— Mickey Vernon, Washington A.L.
2B— Red Schoendienst, St. Louis N.L.
SS— Pee Wee Reese, Brooklyn N.L.
3B— Al Rosen, Cleveland A.L.
OF— Stan Musial, St. Louis N.L.
OF— Duke Snider, Brooklyn N.L.
OF— Carl Furillo, Brooklyn N.L.
C— Roy Campanella, Brooklyn N.L.
P— Robin Roberts, Philadelphia N.L.
P— Warren Spahn, Milwaukee N.L.
P— Bob Porterfield, Washington A.L.

## 1954
1B— Ted Kluszewski, Cincinnati N.L.
2B— Bobby Avila, Cleveland A.L.
SS— Alvin Dark, New York N.L.
3B— Al Rosen, Cleveland A.L.
OF— Willie Mays, New York N.L.
OF— Stan Musial, St. Louis N.L.
OF— Duke Snider, Brooklyn N.L.
C— Yogi Berra, New York A.L.
P— Bob Lemon, Cleveland A.L.
P— Johnny Antonelli, New York N.L.
P— Robin Roberts, Philadelphia N.L.

## 1955
1B— Ted Kluszewski, Cincinnati N.L.
2B— Nellie Fox, Chicago A.L.
SS— Ernie Banks, Chicago N.L.
3B— Ed Mathews, Milwaukee N.L.
OF— Duke Snider, Brooklyn N.L.
OF— Ted Williams, Boston A.L.
OF— Al Kaline, Detroit A.L.
C— Roy Campanella, Brooklyn N.L.
P— Robin Roberts, Philadelphia N.L.
P— Don Newcombe, Brooklyn N.L.
P— Whitey Ford, New York A.L.

## 1956
1B— Ted Kluszewski, Cincinnati N.L.
2B— Nellie Fox, Chicago A.L.
SS— Harvey Kuenn, Detroit A.L.
3B— Ken Boyer, St. Louis N.L.
OF— Mickey Mantle, New York A.L.
OF— Hank Aaron, Milwaukee N.L.
OF— Ted Williams, Boston A.L.
C— Yogi Berra, New York A.L.
P— Don Newcombe, Brooklyn N.L.
P— Whitey Ford, New York A.L.
P— Billy Pierce, Chicago A.L.

## 1957
1B— Stan Musial, St. Louis N.L.
2B— Red Schoendienst, N.Y.-Mil. N.L.
SS— Gil McDougald, New York A.L.
3B— Ed Mathews, Milwaukee N.L.
OF— Mickey Mantle, New York A.L.
OF— Ted Williams, Boston A.L.
OF— Willie Mays, New York N.L.
C— Yogi Berra, New York A.L.
P— Warren Spahn, Milwaukee N.L.
P— Billy Pierce, Chicago N.L.
P— Jim Bunning, Detroit A.L.

## 1958
1B— Stan Musial, St. Louis N.L.
2B— Nellie Fox, Chicago A.L.
SS— Ernie Banks, Chicago N.L.
3B— Frank Thomas, Pittsburgh N.L.
OF— Ted Williams, Boston A.L.
OF— Willie Mays, San Francisco N.L.
OF— Hank Aaron, Milwaukee N.L.
C— Del Crandall, Milwaukee N.L.
P— Bob Turley, New York A.L.
P— Warren Spahn, Milwaukee N.L.
P— Bob Friend, Pittsburgh N.L.

## 1959
1B— Orlando Cepeda, S.F. N.L.
2B— Nellie Fox, Chicago A.L.
SS— Ernie Banks, Chicago N.L.
3B— Ed Mathews, Milwaukee N.L.
OF— Minnie Minoso, Cleveland A.L.
OF— Willie Mays, San Francisco N.L.
OF— Hank Aaron, Milwaukee N.L.
C— Sherm Lollar, Chicago A.L.
P— Early Wynn, Chicago A.L.
P— Sam Jones, San Francisco N.L.
P— Johnny Antonelli, S.F. N.L.

## 1960
1B— Bill Skowron, New York A.L.
2B— Bill Mazeroski, Pittsburgh N.L.
SS— Ernie Banks, Chicago N.L.
3B— Ed Mathews, Milwaukee N.L.
OF— Minnie Minoso, Chicago A.L.
OF— Willie Mays, San Francisco N.L.
OF— Roger Maris, New York A.L.
C— Del Crandall, Milwaukee N.L.
P— Vernon Law, Pittsburgh N.L.
P— Warren Spahn, Milwaukee N.L.
P— Ernie Broglio, St. Louis N.L.

## 1961

### AMERICAN LEAGUE

1B— Norm Cash, Detroit
2B— Bobby Richardson, New York
SS— Tony Kubek, New York
3B— Brooks Robinson, Baltimore
OF— Mickey Mantle, New York
OF— Roger Maris, New York
OF— Rocky Colavito, Detroit
C— Elston Howard, New York
P— Whitey Ford, New York
P— Frank Lary, Detroit

### NATIONAL LEAGUE

1B— Orlando Cepeda, San Francisco
2B— Frank Bolling, Milwaukee
SS— Maury Wills, Los Angeles
3B— Ken Boyer, St. Louis
OF— Willie Mays, San Francisco
OF— Frank Robinson, Cincinnati
OF— Roberto Clemente, Pittsburgh
C— Smoky Burgess, Pittsburgh
P— Joey Jay, Cincinnati
P— Warren Spahn, Milwaukee

## 1962

### AMERICAN LEAGUE

1B— Norm Siebern, Kansas City
2B— Bobby Richardson, New York
SS— Tom Tresh, New York
3B— Brooks Robinson, Baltimore
OF— Leon Wagner, Los Angeles
OF— Mickey Mantle, New York
OF— Al Kaline, Detroit
C— Earl Battey, Minnesota
P— Ralph Terry, New York
P— Dick Donovan, Cleveland

### NATIONAL LEAGUE

1B— Orlando Cepeda, San Francisco
2B— Bill Mazeroski, Pittsburgh
SS— Maury Wills, Los Angeles
3B— Ken Boyer, St. Louis
OF— Tommy Davis, Los Angeles
OF— Willie Mays, San Francisco
OF— Frank Robinson, Cincinnati
C— Del Crandall, Milwaukee
P— Don Drysdale, Los Angeles
P— Bob Purkey, Cincinnati

## 1963

### AMERICAN LEAGUE

1B— Joe Pepitone, New York
2B— Bobby Richardson, New York
SS— Luis Aparicio, Baltimore
3B— Frank Malzone, Boston
OF— Carl Yastrzemski, Boston
OF— Albie Pearson, Los Angeles
OF— Al Kaline, Detroit
C— Elston Howard, New York
P— Whitey Ford, New York
P— Gary Peters, Chicago

### NATIONAL LEAGUE

1B— Bill White, St. Louis
2B— Jim Gilliam, Los Angeles
SS— Dick Groat, St. Louis
3B— Ken Boyer, St. Louis
OF— Tommy Davis, Los Angeles
OF— Willie Mays, San Francisco
OF— Hank Aaron, Milwaukee
C— John Edwards, Cincinnati
P— Sandy Koufax, Los Angeles
P— Juan Marichal, San Francisco

## 1964

### AMERICAN LEAGUE

1B— Dick Stuart, Boston
2B— Bobby Richardson, New York
SS— Jim Fregosi, Los Angeles
3B— Brooks Robinson, Baltimore
OF— Harmon Killebrew, Minnesota
OF— Mickey Mantle, New York
OF— Tony Oliva, Minnesota
C— Elston Howard, New York
P— Dean Chance, Los Angeles
P— Gary Peters, Chicago

### NATIONAL LEAGUE

1B— Bill White, St. Louis
2B— Ron Hunt, New York
SS— Dick Groat, St. Louis
3B— Ken Boyer, St. Louis
OF— Billy Williams, Chicago
OF— Willie Mays, San Francisco
OF— Roberto Clemente, Pittsburgh
C— Joe Torre, Milwaukee
P— Sandy Koufax, Los Angeles
P— Jim Bunning, Philadelphia

## 1965

### AMERICAN LEAGUE

1B— Fred Whitfield, Cleveland
2B— Bobby Richardson, New York
SS— Zoilo Versalles, Minnesota
3B— Brooks Robinson, Baltimore
OF— Carl Yastrzemski, Boston
OF— Jimmie Hall, Minnesota
OF— Tony Oliva, Minnesota
C— Earl Battey, Minnesota
P— Jim Grant, Minnesota
P— Mel Stottlemyre, New York

### NATIONAL LEAGUE

1B— Willie McCovey, San Francisco
2B— Pete Rose, Cincinnati
SS— Maury Wills, Los Angeles
3B— Deron Johnson, Cincinnati
OF— Willie Stargell, Pittsburgh
OF— Willie Mays, San Francisco
OF— Hank Aaron, Milwaukee
C— Joe Torre, Milwaukee
P— Sandy Koufax, Los Angeles
P— Juan Marichal, San Francisco

## 1966

### AMERICAN LEAGUE

1B— Boog Powell, Baltimore
2B— Bobby Richardson, New York
SS— Luis Aparicio, Baltimore
3B— Brooks Robinson, Baltimore
OF— Frank Robinson, Baltimore
OF— Al Kaline, Detroit
OF— Tony Oliva, Minnesota
C— Paul Casanova, Washington
P— Jim Kaat, Minnesota
P— Earl Wilson, Detroit

### NATIONAL LEAGUE

1B— Felipe Alou, Atlanta
2B— Pete Rose, Cincinnati
SS— Gene Alley, Pittsburgh
3B— Ron Santo, Chicago
OF— Willie Stargell, Pittsburgh
OF— Willie Mays, San Francisco
OF— Roberto Clemente, Pittsburgh
C— Joe Torre, Atlanta
P— Sandy Koufax, Los Angeles
P— Juan Marichal, San Francisco

## 1967

### AMERICAN LEAGUE

1B— Harmon Killebrew, Minnesota
2B— Rod Carew, Minnesota
SS— Jim Fregosi, California
3B— Brooks Robinson, Baltimore
OF— Carl Yastrzemski, Boston
OF— Al Kaline, Detroit
OF— Frank Robinson, Baltimore
C— Bill Freehan, Detroit
P— Jim Lonborg, Boston
P— Earl Wilson, Detroit

### NATIONAL LEAGUE

1B— Orlando Cepeda, St. Louis
2B— Bill Mazeroski, Pittsburgh
SS— Gene Alley, Pittsburgh
3B— Ron Santo, Chicago
OF— Hank Aaron, Atlanta
OF— Jim Wynn, Houston
OF— Roberto Clemente, Pittsburgh
C— Tim McCarver, St. Louis
P— Mike McCormick, San Francisco
P— Ferguson Jenkins, Chicago

## 1968

### AMERICAN LEAGUE

1B— Boog Powell, Baltimore
2B— Rod Carew, Minnesota
SS— Luis Aparicio, Chicago
3B— Brooks Robinson, Baltimore
OF— Ken Harrelson, Boston
OF— Willie Horton, Detroit
OF— Frank Howard, Washington
C— Bill Freehan, Detroit
P— Dave McNally, Baltimore
P— Denny McLain, Detroit

### NATIONAL LEAGUE

1B— Willie McCovey, San Francisco
2B— Tommy Helms, Cincinnati
SS— Don Kessinger, Chicago
3B— Ron Santo, Chicago
OF— Billy Williams, Chicago
OF— Curt Flood, St. Louis
OF— Pete Rose, Cincinnati
C— Johnny Bench, Cincinnati
P— Bob Gibson, St. Louis
P— Juan Marichal, San Francisco

## 1969

### AMERICAN LEAGUE

1B— Boog Powell, Baltimore
2B— Rod Carew, Minnesota
SS— Rico Petrocelli, Boston
3B— Harmon Killebrew, Minnesota
OF— Frank Howard, Washington
OF— Paul Blair, Baltimore
OF— Reggie Jackson, Oakland
C— Bill Freehan, Detroit
RHP— Denny McLain, Detroit
LHP— Mike Cuellar, Baltimore

### NATIONAL LEAGUE

1B— Willie McCovey, San Francisco
2B— Glenn Beckert, Chicago
SS— Don Kessinger, Chicago
3B— Ron Santo, Chicago
OF— Cleon Jones, New York
OF— Matty Alou, Pittsburgh
OF— Hank Aaron, Atlanta
C— Johnny Bench, Cincinnati
RHP— Tom Seaver, New York
LHP— Steve Carlton, St. Louis

## 1970

### AMERICAN LEAGUE

1B— Boog Powell, Baltimore
2B— Dave Johnson, Baltimore
SS— Luis Aparicio, Chicago
3B— Harmon Killebrew, Minnesota
OF— Frank Howard, Washington
OF— Reggie Smith, Boston
OF— Tony Oliva, Minnesota
C— Ray Fosse, Cleveland
RHP— Jim Perry, Minnesota
LHP— Sam McDowell, Cleveland

### NATIONAL LEAGUE

1B— Willie McCovey, San Francisco
2B— Glenn Beckert, Chicago
SS— Don Kessinger, Chicago
3B— Tony Perez, Cincinnati
OF— Billy Williams, Chicago
OF— Bobby Tolan, Cincinnati
OF— Hank Aaron, Atlanta
C— Johnny Bench, Cincinnati
RHP— Bob Gibson, St. Louis
LHP— Jim Merritt, Cincinnati

## 1971

### AMERICAN LEAGUE

1B— Norm Cash, Detroit
2B— Cookie Rojas, Kansas City
SS— Leo Cardenas, Minnesota
3B— Brooks Robinson, Baltimore
OF— Merv Rettenmund, Baltimore
OF— Bobby Murcer, New York
OF— Tony Oliva, Minnesota
C— Bill Freehan, Detroit
RHP— Jim Palmer, Baltimore
LHP— Vida Blue, Oakland

### NATIONAL LEAGUE

1B— Lee May, Cincinnati
2B— Glenn Beckett, Chicago
SS— Bud Harrelson, New York
3B— Joe Torre, St. Louis
OF— Willie Stargell, Pittsburgh
OF— Willie Davis, Los Angeles
OF— Hank Aaron, Atlanta
C— Manny Sanguillen, Pittsburgh
RHP— Ferguson Jenkins, Chicago
LHP— Steve Carlton, St. Louis

## 1972

### AMERICAN LEAGUE

1B— Dick Allen, Chicago
2B— Rod Carew, Minnesota
SS— Luis Aparicio, Boston
3B— Brooks Robinson, Baltimore
OF— Joe Rudi, Oakland
OF— Bobby Murcer, New York
OF— Richie Scheinblum, Kansas City
C— Carlton Fisk, Boston
RHP— Gaylord Perry, Cleveland
LHP— Wilbur Wood, Chicago

### NATIONAL LEAGUE

1B— Willie Stargell, Pittsburgh
2B— Joe Morgan, Cincinnati
SS— Chris Speier, San Francisco
3B— Ron Santo, Chicago
OF— Billy Williams, Chicago
OF— Cesar Cedeno, Houston
OF— Roberto Clemente, Pittsburgh
C— Johnny Bench, Cincinnati
RHP— Ferguson Jenkins, Chicago
LHP— Steve Carlton, Philadelphia

## 1973

### AMERICAN LEAGUE

1B— John Mayberry, Kansas City
2B— Rod Carew, Minnesota
SS— Bert Campaneris, Oakland
3B— Sal Bando, Oakland
OF— Reggie Jackson, Oakland
OF— Amos Otis, Kansas City
OF— Bobby Murcer, New York
C— Thurman Munson, New York
RHP— Jim Palmer, Baltimore
LHP— Ken Holtzman, Oakland

### NATIONAL LEAGUE

1B— Tony Perez, Cincinnati
2B— Dave Johnson, Atlanta
SS— Bill Russell, Los Angeles
3B— Darrell Evans, Atlanta
OF— Bobby Bonds, San Francisco
OF— Cesar Cedeno, Houston
OF— Pete Rose, Cincinnati
C— Johnny Bench, Cincinnati
RHP— Tom Seaver, New York
LHP— Ron Bryant, San Francisco

## 1974

### AMERICAN LEAGUE

1B— Dick Allen, Chicago
2B— Rod Carew, Minnesota
SS— Bert Campaneris, Oakland
3B— Sal Bando, Oakland
OF— Joe Rudi, Oakland
OF— Paul Blair, Baltimore
OF— Jeff Burroughs, Texas
C— Thurman Munson, New York
DH— Tommy Davis, Baltimore
RHP— Jim Hunter, Oakland
LHP— Mike Cuellar, Baltimore

### NATIONAL LEAGUE

1B— Steve Garvey, Los Angeles
2B— Joe Morgan, Cincinnati
SS— Dave Concepcion, Cincinnati
3B— Mike Schmidt, Philadelphia
OF— Lou Brock, St. Louis
OF— Jim Wynn, Los Angeles
OF— Richie Zisk, Pittsburgh
C— Johnny Bench, Cincinnati
RHP— Andy Messersmith, Los Angeles
LHP— Don Gullett, Cincinnati

## 1975

### AMERICAN LEAGUE

1B— John Mayberry, Kansas City
2B— Rod Carew, Minnesota
SS— Toby Harrah, Texas
3B— Graig Nettles, New York
OF— Jim Rice, Boston
OF— Fred Lynn, Boston
OF— Reggie Jackson, Oakland
C— Thurman Munson, New York
DH— Willie Horton, Detroit
RHP— Jim Palmer, Baltimore
LHP— Jim Kaat, Chicago

### NATIONAL LEAGUE

1B— Steve Garvey, Los Angeles
2B— Joe Morgan, Cincinnati
SS— Larry Bowa, Philadelphia
3B— Bill Madlock, Chicago
OF— Greg Luzinski, Philadelphia
OF— Al Oliver, Pittsburgh
OF— Dave Parker, Pittsburgh
C— Johnny Bench, Cincinnati
RHP— Tom Seaver, New York
LHP— Randy Jones, San Diego

## 1976

### AMERICAN LEAGUE

1B— Chris Chambliss, New York
2B— Bobby Grich, Baltimore
3B— George Brett, Kansas City
SS— Mark Belanger, Baltimore
OF— Joe Rudi, Oakland
OF— Mickey Rivers, New York
OF— Reggie Jackson, Baltimore
C— Thurman Munson, New York
DH— Hal McRae, Kansas City
RHP— Jim Palmer, Baltimore
LHP— Frank Tanana, California

### NATIONAL LEAGUE

1B— Willie Montanez, S.F.-Atl.
2B— Joe Morgan, Cincinnati
3B— Mike Schmidt, Philadelphia
SS— Dave Concepcion, Cincinnati
OF— George Foster, Cincinnati
OF— Cesar Cedeno, Houston
OF— Ken Griffey, Cincinnati
C— Bob Boone, Philadelphia
RHP— Don Sutton, Los Angeles
LHP— Randy Jones, San Diego

## 1977

### AMERICAN LEAGUE

1B— Rod Carew, Minnesota
2B— Willie Randolph, New York
3B— Graig Nettles, New York
SS— Rick Burleson, Boston
OF— Jim Rice, Boston
OF— Larry Hisle, Minnesota
OF— Bobby Bonds, California
C— Carlton Fisk, Boston
DH— Hal McRae, Kansas City
RHP— Nolan Ryan, California
LHP— Frank Tanana, California

### NATIONAL LEAGUE

1B— Steve Garvey, Los Angeles
2B— Joe Morgan, Cincinnati
3B— Mike Schmidt, Philadelphia
SS— Garry Templeton, St. Louis
OF— George Foster, Cincinnati
OF— Dave Parker, Pittsburgh
OF— Greg Luzinski, Philadelphia
C— Ted Simmons, St. Louis
RHP— Rick Reuschel, Chicago
LHP— Steve Carlton, Philadelphia

## 1978

### AMERICAN LEAGUE

1B— Rod Carew, Minnesota
2B— Frank White, Kansas City
3B— Graig Nettles, New York
SS— Robin Yount, Milwaukee
OF— Jim Rice, Boston
OF— Larry Hisle, Milwaukee
OF— Fred Lynn, Boston
C— Jim Sundberg, Texas
DH— Rusty Staub, Detroit
RHP— Jim Palmer, Baltimore
LHP— Ron Guidry, New York

### NATIONAL LEAGUE

1B— Steve Garvey, Los Angeles
2B— Dave Lopes, Los Angeles
3B— Pete Rose, Cincinnati
SS— Larry Bowa, Philadelphia
OF— George Foster, Cincinnati
OF— Dave Parker, Pittsburgh
OF— Jack Clark, San Francisco
C— Ted Simmons, St. Louis
RHP— Gaylord Perry, San Diego
LHP— Vida Blue, San Francisco

## 1979

### AMERICAN LEAGUE

1B— Cecil Cooper, Milwaukee
2B— Bobby Grich, California
3B— George Brett, Kansas City
SS— Roy Smalley, Minnesota
OF— Jim Rice, Boston
OF— Fred Lynn, Boston
OF— Ken Singleton, Baltimore
C— Darrell Porter, Kansas City
DH— Don Baylor, California
RHP— Jim Kern, Texas
LHP— Mike Flanagan, Baltimore

### NATIONAL LEAGUE

1B— Keith Hernandez, St. Louis
2B— Dave Lopes, Los Angeles
3B— Mike Schmidt, Philadelphia
SS— Garry Templeton, St. Louis
OF— Dave Kingman, Chicago
OF— Omar Moreno, Pittsburgh
OF— Dave Winfield, San Diego
C— Ted Simmons, St. Louis
RHP— Joe Niekro, Houston
LHP— Steve Carlton, Philadelphia

## 1980

### AMERICAN LEAGUE

1B— Cecil Cooper, Milwaukee
2B— Willie Randolph, New York
3B— George Brett, Kansas City
SS— Robin Yount, Milwaukee
OF— Ben Oglivie, Milwaukee
OF— Al Bumbry, Baltimore
OF— Reggie Jackson, New York
DH— Reggie Jackson, New York
C— Rick Cerone, New York
RHP— Steve Stone, Baltimore
LHP— Tommy John, New York

### NATIONAL LEAGUE

1B— Keith Hernandez, St. Louis
2B— Manny Trillo, Philadelphia
3B— Mike Schmidt, Philadelphia
SS— Garry Templeton, St. Louis
OF— Dusty Baker, Los Angeles
OF— Cesar Cedeno, Houston
OF— George Hendrick, St. Louis
C— Gary Carter, Montreal
RHP— Jim Bibby, Pittsburgh
LHP— Steve Carlton, Philadelphia

## 1981

### AMERICAN LEAGUE

1B— Cecil Cooper, Milwaukee
2B— Bobby Grich, California
3B— Buddy Bell, Texas
SS— Rick Burleson, California
OF— Rickey Henderson, Oakland
OF— Dwayne Murphy, Oakland
OF— Tony Armas, Oakland
C— Jim Sundberg, Texas
DH— Richie Zisk, Seattle
RHP— Jack Morris, Detroit
LHP— Ron Guidry, New York

### NATIONAL LEAGUE

1B— Pete Rose, Philadelphia
2B— Manny Trillo, Philadelphia
3B— Mike Schmidt, Philadelphia
SS— Dave Concepcion, Cincinnati
OF— George Foster, Cincinnati
OF— Andre Dawson, Montreal
OF— Pedro Guerrero, Los Angeles
C— Gary Carter, Montreal
RHP— Tom Seaver, Cincinnati
LHP— Fernando Valenzuela, Los Angeles

## 1982

### AMERICAN LEAGUE

1B— Cecil Cooper, Milwaukee
2B— Damaso Garcia, Toronto
3B— Doug DeCinces, California
SS— Robin Yount, Milwaukee
OF— Dave Winfield, New York
OF— Gorman Thomas, Milwaukee
OF— Dwight Evans, Boston
C— Lance Parrish, Detroit
DH— Hal McRae, Kansas City
RHP— Dave Stieb, Toronto
LHP— Geoff Zahn, California

### NATIONAL LEAGUE

1B— Al Oliver, Montreal
2B— Manny Trillo, Philadelphia
3B— Mike Schmidt, Philadelphia
SS— Ozzie Smith, St. Louis
OF— Lonnie Smith, St. Louis
OF— Dale Murphy, Atlanta
OF— Pedro Guerrero, Los Angeles
C— Gary Carter, Montreal
RHP— Steve Rogers, Montreal
LHP— Steve Carlton, Philadelphia

## 1983

### AMERICAN LEAGUE

1B— Eddie Murray, Baltimore
2B— Lou Whitaker, Detroit
3B— Wade Boggs, Boston
SS— Cal Ripken, Baltimore
OF— Jim Rice, Boston
OF— Dave Winfield, New York
OF— Lloyd Moseby, Toronto
C— Carlton Fisk, Chicago
DH— Greg Luzinski, Chicago
RHP— LaMarr Hoyt, Chicago
LHP— Ron Guidry, New York

### NATIONAL LEAGUE

1B— George Hendrick, St. Louis
2B— Glenn Hubbard, Atlanta
3B— Mike Schmidt, Philadelphia
SS— Dickie Thon, Houston
OF— Dale Murphy, Atlanta
OF— Andre Dawson, Montreal
OF— Tim Raines, Montreal
C— Tony Pena, Pittsburgh
RHP— John Denny, Philadelphia
LHP— Larry McWilliams, Pittsburgh

## 1984

### AMERICAN LEAGUE

1B— Don Mattingly, New York
2B— Lou Whitaker, Detroit
3B— Buddy Bell, Texas
SS— Cal Ripken, Baltimore
OF— Tony Armas, Boston
OF— Dwight Evans, Boston
OF— Dave Winfield, New York
C— Lance Parrish, Detroit
DH— Dave Kingman, Oakland
RHP— Mike Boddicker, Baltimore
LHP— Willie Hernandez, Detroit

### NATIONAL LEAGUE

1B— Keith Hernandez, New York
2B— Ryne Sandberg, Chicago
3B— Mike Schmidt, Philadelphia
SS— Ozzie Smith, St. Louis
OF— Dale Murphy, Atlanta
OF— Jose Cruz, Houston
OF— Tony Gwynn, San Diego
C— Gary Carter, Montreal
RHP— Rick Sutcliffe, Chicago
LHP— Mark Thurmond, San Diego

## 1985

### AMERICAN LEAGUE

1B— Don Mattingly, New York
2B— Damaso Garcia, Toronto
3B— Wade Boggs, Boston
SS— Cal Ripken, Baltimore
OF— Rickey Henderson, New York
OF— Harold Baines, Chicago
OF— Phil Bradley, Seattle
C— Carlton Fisk, Chicago
DH— Don Baylor, New York
RHP— Bret Saberhagen, Kansas City
LHP— Ron Guidry, New York

### NATIONAL LEAGUE

1B— Keith Hernandez, New York
2B— Tom Herr, St. Louis
3B— Tim Wallach, Montreal
SS— Ozzie Smith, St. Louis
OF— Dave Parker, Cincinnati
OF— Willie McGee, St. Louis
OF— Dale Murphy, Atlanta
C— Gary Carter, New York
RHP— Dwight Gooden, New York
LHP— John Tudor, St. Louis

## 1986

### AMERICAN LEAGUE

1B— Don Mattingly, New York
2B— Tony Bernazard, Cleveland
3B— Wade Boggs, Boston
SS— Tony Fernandez, Toronto
OF— Jim Rice, Boston
OF— George Bell, Toronto
OF— Kirby Puckett, Minnesota
C— Rich Gedman, Boston
DH— Don Baylor, Boston
RHP— Roger Clemens, Boston
LHP— Teddy Higuera, Milwaukee

### NATIONAL LEAGUE

1B— Keith Hernandez, New York
2B— Steve Sax, Los Angeles
3B— Mike Schmidt, Philadelphia
SS— Ozzie Smith, St. Louis
OF— Tim Raines, Montreal
OF— Tony Gwynn, San Diego
OF— Dave Parker, Cincinnati
C— Gary Carter, New York
RHP— Mike Scott, Houston
LHP— Fernando Valenzuela, Los Angeles

## 1987

### AMERICAN LEAGUE

1B— Don Mattingly, New York
2B— Willie Randolph, New York
3B— Wade Boggs, Boston
SS— Alan Trammell, Detroit
OF— George Bell, Toronto
OF— Kirby Puckett, Minnesota
OF— Dwight Evans, Boston
C— Matt Nokes, Detroit
DH— Paul Molitor, Milwaukee
RHP— Roger Clemens, Boston
LHP— Jimmy Key, Toronto

### NATIONAL LEAGUE

1B— Jack Clark, St. Louis
2B— Juan Samuel, Philadelphia
3B— Tim Wallach, Montreal
SS— Ozzie Smith, St. Louis
OF— Andre Dawson, Chicago
OF— Tony Gwynn, San Diego
OF— Eric Davis, Cincinnati
C— Benito Santiago, San Diego
RHP— Rick Sutcliffe, Chicago
LHP— Zane Smith, Atlanta

### 1988

**AMERICAN LEAGUE**

1B— George Brett, Kansas City
2B— Johnny Ray, California
3B— Wade Boggs, Boston
SS— Alan Trammell, Detroit
OF— Kirby Puckett, Minnesota
OF— Mike Greenwell, Boston
OF— Jose Canseco, Oakland
C— Ernie Whitt, Toronto
DH— Harold Baines, Chicago
RHP— Dave Stewart, Oakland
LHP— Frank Viola, Minnesota

**NATIONAL LEAGUE**

1B— Will Clark, San Francisco
2B— Ryne Sandberg, Chicago
3B— Bobby Bonilla, Pittsburgh
SS— Barry Larkin, Cincinnati
OF— Darryl Strawberry, New York
OF— Andy Van Slyke, Pittsburgh
OF— Kevin McReynolds, New York
C— Mike LaValliere, Pittsburgh
RHP— Orel Hershiser, Los Angeles
LHP— Danny Jackson, Cincinnati

### 1989

**AMERICAN LEAGUE**

1B— Fred McGriff, Toronto
2B— Julio Franco, Texas
3B— Carney Lansford, Oakland
SS— Cal Ripken, Baltimore
OF— Ruben Sierra, Texas
OF— Kirby Puckett, Minnesota
OF— Robin Yount, Milwaukee
C— Mickey Tettleton, Baltimore
DH— Harold Baines, Chi.-Tex.
RHP— Bret Saberhagen, Kansas City
LHP— Chuck Finley, California

**NATIONAL LEAGUE**

1B— Will Clark, San Francisco
2B— Ryne Sandberg, Chicago
3B— Howard Johnson, New York
SS— Shawon Dunston, Chicago
OF— Tony Gwynn, San Diego
OF— Kevin Mitchell, San Francisco
OF— Eric Davis, Cincinnati
C— Benito Santiago, San Diego
RHP— Mike Scott, Houston
LHP— Mark Davis, San Diego

### 1990

**AMERICAN LEAGUE**

1B— Cecil Fielder, Detroit
2B— Julio Franco, Texas
3B— Kelly Gruber, Toronto
SS— Alan Trammell, Detroit
OF— Rickey Henderson, Oakland
OF— Jose Canseco, Oakland
OF— Ellis Burks, Boston
C— Carlton Fisk, Chicago
DH— Dave Parker, Milwaukee
RHP— Bob Welch, Oakland
LHP— Chuck Finley, California

**NATIONAL LEAGUE**

1B— Eddie Murray, Los Angeles
2B— Ryne Sandberg, Chicago
3B— Matt Williams, San Francisco
SS— Barry Larkin, Cincinnati
OF— Barry Bonds, Pittsburgh
OF— Bobby Bonilla, Pittsburgh
OF— Darryl Strawberry, New York
C— Mike Scioscia, Los Angeles
RHP— Doug Drabek, Pittsburgh
LHP— Frank Viola, New York

### 1991

**AMERICAN LEAGUE**

1B— Cecil Fielder, Detroit
2B— Julio Franco, Texas
3B— Wade Boggs, Boston
SS— Cal Ripken, Baltimore
OF— Jose Canseco, Oakland
OF— Joe Carter, Toronto
OF— Ken Griffey Jr., Seattle
C— Mickey Tettleton, Detroit
RHP— Roger Clemens, Boston
LHP— Jim Abbott, California

**NATIONAL LEAGUE**

1B— Will Clark, San Francisco
2B— Ryne Sandberg, Chicago
3B— Terry Pendleton, Atlanta
SS— Barry Larkin, Cincinnati
OF— Barry Bonds, Pittsburgh
OF— Bobby Bonilla, Pittsburgh
OF— Ron Gant, Atlanta
C— Benito Santiago, San Diego
RHP— Jose Rijo, Cincinnati
LHP— Tom Glavine, Atlanta

### 1992

**AMERICAN LEAGUE**

1B— Mark McGwire, Oakland
2B— Roberto Alomar, Toronto
3B— Edgar Martinez, Seattle
SS— Travis Fryman, Detroit
OF— Joe Carter, Toronto
OF— Mike Devereaux, Baltimore
OF— Kirby Puckett, Minnesota
C— Mickey Tettleton, Detroit
RHP— Jack McDowell, Chicago
LHP— Dave Fleming, Seattle

**NATIONAL LEAGUE**

1B— Fred McGriff, San Diego
2B— Ryne Sandberg, Chicago
3B— Gary Sheffield, San Diego
SS— Barry Larkin, Cincinnati
OF— Barry Bonds, Pittsburgh
OF— Andy Van Slyke, Pittsburgh
OF— Larry Walker, Montreal
C— Darren Daulton, Philadelphia
RHP— Greg Maddux, Chicago
LHP— Tom Glavine, Atlanta

### 1993

**AMERICAN LEAGUE**

1B— Frank Thomas, Chicago
2B— Carlos Baerga, Cleveland
3B— Travis Fryman, Detroit
SS— Cal Ripken Jr., Baltimore
OF— Albert Belle, Cleveland
OF— Juan Gonzalez, Texas
OF— Ken Griffey Jr., Seattle
C— Mike Stanley, New York
DH— Paul Molitor, Toronto
RHP— Jack McDowell, Chicago
LHP— Jimmy Key, New York

**NATIONAL LEAGUE**

1B— Fred McGriff, S.D.-Atl.
2B— Robby Thompson, San Francisco
3B— Matt Williams, San Francisco
SS— Jay Bell, Pittsburgh
OF— Barry Bonds, San Francisco
OF— Lenny Dykstra, Philadelphia
OF— David Justice, Atlanta
C— Mike Piazza, Los Angeles
RHP— Greg Maddux, Atlanta
LHP— Steve Avery, Atlanta

### 1994

**AMERICAN LEAGUE**

1B— Frank Thomas, Chicago
2B— Chuck Knoblauch, Minnesota
3B— Wade Boggs, New York
SS— Cal Ripken Jr., Baltimore
OF— Albert Belle, Cleveland
OF— Ken Griffey Jr., Seattle
OF— Kirby Puckett, Minnesota
C— Ivan Rodriguez, Texas
DH— Paul Molitor, Toronto
RHP— David Cone, Kansas City
LHP— Jimmy Key, New York

**NATIONAL LEAGUE**

1B— Jeff Bagwell, Houston
2B— Craig Biggio, Houston
3B— Matt Williams, San Francisco
SS— Barry Larkin, Cincinnati
OF— Moises Alou, Montreal
OF— Barry Bonds, San Francisco
OF— Tony Gwynn, San Diego
C— Mike Piazza, Los Angeles
RHP— Greg Maddux, Atlanta
LHP— Danny Jackson, Philadelphia

### 1995

**AMERICAN LEAGUE**

1B— Mo Vaughn, Boston
2B— Carlos Baerga, Cleveland
3B— Jim Thome, Cleveland
SS— Cal Ripken Jr., Baltimore
OF— Albert Belle, Cleveland
OF— Tim Salmon, California
OF— Jim Edmonds, California
Manny Ramirez, Cleveland
C— Ivan Rodriguez, Texas
DH— Edgar Martinez, Seattle
RHP— Mike Mussina, Baltimore
LHP— Randy Johnson, Seattle

**NATIONAL LEAGUE**

1B— Eric Karros, Los Angeles
2B— Craig Biggio, Houston
3B— Vinny Castilla, Colorado
SS— Barry Larkin, Cincinnati
OF— Reggie Sanders, Cincinnati
OF— Dante Bichette, Colorado
OF— Sammy Sosa, Chicago
C— Mike Piazza, Los Angeles
RHP— Greg Maddux, Atlanta
LHP— Pete Schourek, Cincinnati

### 1996

**AMERICAN LEAGUE**

1B— Mark McGwire, Oakland
2B— Roberto Alomar, Baltimore
3B— Jim Thome, Cleveland
SS— Alex Rodriguez, Seattle
OF— Albert Belle, Cleveland
OF— Juan Gonzalez, Texas
OF— Ken Griffey Jr., Seattle
C— Ivan Rodriguez, Texas
DH— Paul Molitor, Minnesota
RHP— Pat Hentgen, Toronto
LHP— Andy Pettitte, New York

**NATIONAL LEAGUE**

1B— Jeff Bagwell, Houston
2B— Eric Young, Colorado
3B— Ken Caminiti, San Diego
SS— Barry Larkin, Cincinnati
OF— Barry Bonds, San Francisco
OF— Ellis Burks, Colorado
OF— Gary Sheffield, Florida
C— Mike Piazza, Los Angeles
RHP— John Smoltz, Atlanta
LHP— Al Leiter, Florida

## 1997

### AMERICAN LEAGUE

1B—Tino Martinez, New York
2B—Chuck Knoblauch, Minnesota
3B—Matt Williams, Cleveland
SS—Nomar Garciaparra, Boston
OF—Ken Griffey Jr., Seattle
OF—David Justice, Cleveland
OF—Tim Salmon, Anaheim
C—Ivan Rodriguez, Texas
DH—Edgar Martinez, Seattle
RHP—Roger Clemens, Toronto
LHP—Randy Johnson, Seattle

### NATIONAL LEAGUE

1B—Jeff Bagwell, Houston
2B—Craig Biggio, Houston
3B—Vinny Castillo, Colorado
SS—Jeff Blauser, Atlanta
OF—Barry Bonds, San Francisco
OF—Tony Gwynn, San Diego
OF—Larry Walker, Colorado
C—Mike Piazza, Los Angeles
RHP—Pedro Martinez, Montreal
LHP—Denny Neagle, Atlanta

## 1998

### AMERICAN LEAGUE

1B—Rafael Palmeiro, Baltimore
2B—Roberto Alomar, Baltimore
3B—Scott Brosius, New York
SS—Alex Rodriguez, Seattle
OF—Ken Griffey Jr., Seattle
OF—Juan Gonzalez, Texas
OF—Albert Belle, Chicago
C—Ivan Rodriguez, Texas
DH—Jose Canseco, Toronto
RHP—Pedro Martinez, Boston
LHP—David Wells, New York

### NATIONAL LEAGUE

1B—Mark McGwire, St. Louis
2B—Craig Biggio, Houston
3B—Vinny Castillo, Colorado
SS—Barry Larkin, Cincinnati
OF—Sammy Sosa, Chicago
OF—Moises Alou, Houston
OF—Greg Vaughn, San Diego
C—Mike Piazza, L.A.-Fla.-N.Y.
RHP—Kevin Brown, San Diego
LHP—Tom Glavine, Atlanta

## 1999

### AMERICAN LEAGUE

1B—Rafael Palmeiro, Texas
2B—Roberto Alomar, Cleveland
3B—Dean Palmer, Detroit
SS—Nomar Garciaparra, Boston
OF—Shawn Green, Toronto
OF—Ken Griffey Jr., Seattle
OF—Manny Ramirez, Cleveland
C—Ivan Rodriguez, Texas
RHP—Pedro Martinez, Boston
LHP—Jamie Moyer, Seattle

### NATIONAL LEAGUE

1B—Jeff Bagwell, Houston
2B—Edgardo Alfonzo, New York
3B—Chipper Jones, Atlanta
SS—Barry Larkin, Cincinnati
OF—Sammy Sosa, Chicago
OF—Vladimir Guerrero, Montreal
OF—Larry Walker, Colorado
C—Mike Piazza, New York
RHP—Jose Lima, Houston
LHP—Mike Hampton, Houston

## 2000

### AMERICAN LEAGUE

1B—Carlos Delgado, Toronto
2B—Roberto Alomar, Cleveland
3B—Travis Fryman, Cleveland
SS—Alex Rodriguez, Seattle
OF—Darin Erstad, Anaheim
OF—Magglio Ordonez, Chicago
OF—Bernie Williams, New York
C—Jorge Posada, New York
RHP—Pedro Martinez, Boston
LHP—David Wells, Toronto

### NATIONAL LEAGUE

1B—Todd Helton, Colorado
2B—Jeff Kent, San Francisco
3B—Chipper Jones, Atlanta
SS—Edgar Renteria, St. Louis
OF—Barry Bonds, San Francisco
OF—Vladimir Guerrero, Montreal
OF—Sammy Sosa, Chicago
C—Mike Piazza, New York
RHP—Greg Maddux, Atlanta
LHP—Tom Glavine, Atlanta

## 2001

### AMERICAN LEAGUE

1B—Jim Thome, Cleveland
2B—Bret Boone, Seattle
3B—Troy Glaus, Anaheim
SS—Alex Rodriguez, Texas
OF—Juan Gonzalez, Cleveland
OF—Manny Ramirez, Boston
OF—Ichiro Suzuki, Seattle
C—Jorge Posada, New York
RHP—Roger Clemens, New York
LHP—Mark Mulder, Oakland
DH—Edgar Martinez, Seattle

### NATIONAL LEAGUE

1B—Todd Helton, Colorado
2B—Craig Biggio, Houston
3B—Chipper Jones, Atlanta
SS—Rich Aurilia, San Francisco
OF—Barry Bonds, San Francisco
OF—Luis Gonzalez, Arizona
OF—Sammy Sosa, Chicago
C—Mike Piazza, New York
RHP—Curt Schilling, Arizona
LHP—Randy Johnson, Arizona

## 2002

### AMERICAN LEAGUE

1B—Jason Giambi, New York
2B—Alfonso Soriano, New York
3B—Eric Chavez, Oakland
SS—Alex Rodriguez, Texas
OF—Garret Anderson, Anaheim
OF—Torii Hunter, Minnesota
OF—Bernie Williams, New York
C—Jorge Posada, New York
RHP—Derek Lowe, Boston
LHP—Barry Zito, Oakland
DH—Manny Ramirez, Boston

### NATIONAL LEAGUE

1B—Todd Helton, Colorado
2B—Jeff Kent, San Francisco
3B—Scott Rolen, Phil.-St.L.
SS—Edgar Renteria, St. Louis
OF—Barry Bonds, San Francisco
OF—Vladimir Guerrero, Montreal
OF—Sammy Sosa, Chicago
C—Mike Piazza, New York
RHP—Curt Schilling, Arizona
LHP—Randy Johnson, Arizona

## 2003

### AMERICAN LEAGUE

1B—Carlos Delgado, Toronto
2B—Bret Boone, Seattle
3B—Bill Mueller, Boston
SS—Alex Rodriguez, Texas
OF—Garret Anderson, Anaheim
OF—Vernon Wells, Toronto
OF—Magglio Ordonez, White Sox
C—Jorge Posada, New York
RHP—Roy Halladay, Toronto
LHP—Andy Pettitte, New York
DH—Frank Thomas, Chicago

### NATIONAL LEAGUE

1B—Todd Helton, Colorado
2B—Marcus Giles, Atlanta
3B—Scott Rolen, St. Louis
SS—Edgar Renteria, St. Louis
OF—Barry Bonds, San Francisco
OF—Albert Pujols, St. Louis
OF—Gary Sheffield, Atlanta
C—Javy Lopez, Atlanta
RHP—Eric Gagne, Los Angeles
LHP—Randy Wolf, Philadelphia

## 2004

### AMERICAN LEAGUE

1B—Paul Konerko, Chicago
2B—Alfonso Soriano, Texas
3B—Melvin Mora, Baltimore
SS—Miguel Tejada, Baltimore
OF—Ichiro Suzuki, Seattle
OF—Manny Ramirez, Boston
OF—Vladimir Guerrero, Anaheim
C—Ivan Rodriguez, Detroit
P—Johan Santana, Minnesota
DH—David Ortiz, Boston

### NATIONAL LEAGUE

1B—Albert Pujols, St. Louis
2B—Mark Loretta, San Diego
3B—Scott Rolen, St. Louis
SS—Edgar Renteria, St. Louis
OF—Barry Bonds, San Francisco
OF—Jim Edmonds, St. Louis
OF—J.D. Drew, Atlanta
C—Johnny Estrada, Atlanta
P—Jason Schmidt, San Francisco

## MINOR LEAGUE PLAYER OF THE YEAR

**Year Player, Team, League**
1936—John Vander Meer, Durham, Piedmont
1937—Charlie Keller, Newark, International
1938—Fred Hutchinson, Seattle, Pacific Coast
1939—Lou Novikoff, Tulsa, Texas; Los Angeles, Pacific Coast
1940—Phil Rizzuto, Kansas City, American Association
1941—John Lindell, Newark, International
1942—Dick Barrett, Seattle, Pacific Coast
1943—Chet Covington, Scranton, Eastern

**Year Player, Team, League**
1944—Rip Collins, Albany, Eastern
1945—Gil Coan, Chattanooga, Southern
1946—Sibby Sisti, Indianapolis, American Association
1947—Hank Sauer, Syracuse, International
1948—Gene Woodling, San Francisco, Pacific Coast
1949—Orie Arntzen, Albany, Eastern
1950—Frank Saucier, San Antonio, Texas
1951—Gene Conley, Hartford, Eastern

Year Player, Team, League
1952—Bill Skowron, Kansas City, American Association
1953—Gene Conley, Toledo, American Association
1954—Herb Score, Indianapolis, American Association
1955—John Murff, Dallas, Texas
1956—Steve Bilko, Los Angeles, Pacific Coast
1957—Norm Siebern, Denver, American Association
1958—Jim O'Toole, Nashville, Southern
1959—Frank Howard, Victoria-Spokane
1960—Willie Davis, Spokane, Pacific Coast
1961—Howie Koplitz, Birmingham, Southern
1962—Bob Bailey, Columbus, International
1963—Don Buford, Indianapolis, International
1964—Mel Stottlemyre, Richmond, International
1965—Joe Foy, Toronto, International
1966—Mike Epstein, Rochester, International
1967—Johnny Bench, Buffalo, International
1968—Merv Rettenmund, Rochester, International
1969—Danny Walton, Oklahoma City, American Association
1970—Don Baylor, Rochester, International
1971—Bobby Grich, Rochester, International
1972—Tom Paciorek, Albuquerque, Pacific Coast
1973—Steve Ontiveros, Phoenix, Pacific Coast
1974—Jim Rice, Pawtucket, International
1975—Hector Cruz, Tulsa, American Association
1976—Pat Putnam, Asheville, Western Carolina
1977—Ken Landreaux, Salt Lake, Pacific Coast; El Paso, Texas
1978—Champ Summers, Indianapolis, American Association
1979—Mark Bomback, Vancouver, Pacific Coast
1980—Tim Raines, Denver, American Association

Year Player, Team, League
1981—Mike Marshall, Albuquerque, Pacific Coast
1982—Ron Kittle, Edmonton, Pacific Coast
1983—Kevin McReynolds, Las Vegas, Pacific Coast
1984—Alan Knicely, Wichita, American Association
1985—Jose Canseco, Huntsville, Southern; Tacoma., Pacific Coast
1986—Tim Pyznarski, Las Vegas, Pacific Coast
1987—Randy Milligan, Tidewater, International
1988—Sandy Alomar Jr., Las Vegas, Pacific Coast
Gary Sheffield, Denver, American Association (tie)
1989—Sandy Alomar Jr., Las Vegas, Pacific Coast
1990—Jose Offerman, Albuquerque, Pacific Coast
1991—Pedro Martinez, Albuquerque, Pacific Coast
1992—Tim Salmon, Edmonton, Pacific Coast
1993—Cliff Floyd, Harrisburg, Eastern
1994—Derek Jeter, Tampa, Florida State; Albany, Eastern; Columbus, International
1995—Karim Garcia, Albuquerque, Pacific Coast
1996—Vladimir Guerrero, West Palm Beach, Florida State; Harrisburg, Eastern
1997—Ben Grieve, Huntsville, Southern; Edmonton, Pacific Coast
1998—Gabe Kapler, Jacksonville, Southern
1999—Rick Ankiel, Arkansas, Texas; Memphis, Pacific Coast
2000—Jon Rauch, Win.-Salem, Carolina; Birmingham, Southern
2001—Josh Beckett, Brevard County, Fla. State; Portland, Eastern
2002—Jason Stokes, Kane County, Midwest
2003—Zack Greinke, Wilmington, Carolina; Wichita, Texas
2004—Dallas McPherson, Arkansas, Texas; Salt Lake, Pacific Coast

## MINOR LEAGUE MANAGER OF THE YEAR

Year Manager, Team, League
1936—Al Sothoron, Milwaukee, American Association
1937—Jake Flowers, Salisbury, Eastern Shore
1938—Paul Richards, Atlanta, Southern
1939—Bill Meyer, Kansas City, American Association
1940—Larry Gilbert, Nashville, Southern
1941—Burt Shotton, Columbus, American Association
1942—Eddie Dyer, Columbus, American Association
1943—Nick Cullop, Columbus, American Association
1944—Al Thomas, Baltimore, International
1945—Lefty O'Doul, San Francisco, Pacific Coast
1946—Clay Hopper, Montreal, International
1947—Nick Cullop, Milwaukee, American Association
1948—Casey Stengel, Oakland, Pacific Coast
1949—Fred Haney, Hollywood, Pacific Coast
1950—Rollie Hemsley, Columbus, American Association
1951—Charlie Grimm, Milwaukee, American Association
1952—Luke Appling, Memphis, Southern
1953—Bobby Bragan, Hollywood, Pacific Coast
1954—Kerby Farrell, Indianapolis, American Association
1955—Bill Rigney, Minneapolis, American Association
1956—Kerby Farrell, Indianapolis, American Association
1957—Ben Geraghty, Wichita, American Association
1958—Cal Ermer, Birmingham, Southern
1959—Pete Reiser, Victoria, Texas
1960—Mel McGaha, Toronto, International
1961—Kerby Farrell, Buffalo, International
1962—Ben Geraghty, Jacksonville, International
1963—Rollie Hemsley, Indianapolis, International
1964—Harry Walker, Jacksonville, International
1965—Grady Hatton, Oklahoma City, Pacific Coast
1966—Bob Lemon, Seattle, Pacific Coast
1967—Bob Skinner, San Diego, Pacific Coast
1968—Jack Tighe, Toledo, International
1969—Clyde McCullough, Tidewater, International
1970—Tommy Lasorda, Spokane, Pacific Coast
1971—Del Rice, Salt Lake City, Pacific Coast
1972—Hank Bauer, Tidewater, International
1973—Joe Morgan, Charleston, International
1974—Joe Altobelli, Rochester, International
1975—Joe Frazier, Tidewater, International
1976—Vern Rapp, Denver, American Association
1977—Tommy Thompson, Arkansas, Texas
1978—Les Moss, Evansville, American Association
1979—Vern Benson, Syracuse, International
1980—Hal Lanier, Springfield, American Association
1981—Del Crandall, Albuquerque, Pacific Coast
1982—George Scherger, Indianapolis, American Association
1983—Bill Dancy, Reading, Eastern
1984—Bob Rodgers, Indianapolis, American Association
1985—Jim Fregosi, Louisville, American Association
1986—Joe Sparks, Indianapolis, American Association
1987—Terry Collins, Albuquerque, Pacific Coast
1988—Joe Sparks, Indianapolis, American Association
1989—Bob Bailor, Syracuse, International
1990—Sal Rende, Omaha, American Association
1991—Chris Chambliss, Greenville, Southern
1992—Grady Little, Greenville, Southern
1993—Jim Tracy, Harrisburg, Eastern
1994—Mike Jirschele, Wilmington, Carolina
1995—Pete Mackanin, Ottawa, International
1996—John Mizerock, Wilmington, Carolina
1997—Marv Foley, Rochester, International
1998—Doug Davis, Columbia, South Atlantic
1999—DeMarlo Hale, Trenton, Eastern
2000—Joel Skinner, Buffalo, International
2001—Tony Pena, New Orleans, Pacific Coast
2002—Eric Wedge, Buffalo, International
2003—Tony DeFrancesco, Sacramento, Pacific Coast
2004—Wally Backman, Lancaster, California

## MINOR LEAGUE EXECUTIVE OF THE YEAR (HIGHER CLASSIFICATIONS, 1936-1992)

**(Restricted to Class AAA starting in 1963)**

Year Executive, Team, League
1936—Earl Mann, Atlanta, Southern
1937—Robert LaMotte, Savannah, Sally
1938—Louis McKenna, St. Paul, American Association
1939—Bruce Dudley, Louisville, American Association
1940—Roy Hamey, Kansas City, American Association
1941—Emil Sick, Seattle, Pacific Coast
1942—Bill Veeck, Milwaukee, American Association
1943—Clarence Rowland, Los Angeles, Pacific Coast

1944—William Mulligan, Seattle, Pacific Coast
1945—Bruce Dudley, Louisville, American Association
1946—Earl Mann, Atlanta, Southern
1947—William Purnhage, Waterloo, I.I.I.
1948—Edward Glennon, Birmingham, Southern
1949—Ted Sullivan, Indianapolis, American Association
1950—Clearnce (Brick) Laws, Oakland, Pacific Coast
1951—Robert Howsam, Denver, West
1952—Jack Cooke, Toronto, International
1953—Richard Burnett, Dallas, Texas
1954—Edward Stumpf, Indianapolis, American Association
1955—Dewey Soriano, Seattle, Pacific Coast
1956—Robert Howsam, Denver American Association
1957—John Stiglmeier, Buffalo, International
1958—Edward Glennon, Birmingham, Southern
1959—Edward Leishman, Salt Lake City, Pacific Coast
1960—Ray Winder, Little Rock, Southern
1961—Elten Schiller, Omaha, American Association
1962—George Sisler Jr., Rochester, International
1963—Lewis Matlin, Hawaii, Pacific Coast
1964—Edward Leishman, San Diego, Pacific Coast
1965—Harold Cooper, Columbus, International
1966—John Quinn Jr., Hawaii, Pacific Coast
1967—Hillman Lyons, Richmond, International
1968—Gabe Paul Jr., Tulsa, Pacific Coast
1969—Bill Gardner, Louisville, International
1970—Dick King, Wichita, American Association
1971—Carl Steinfeldt Jr., Rochester, International
1972—Don Labbruzzo, Evansville, American Association
1973—Merle Miller, Tucson, Pacific Coast
1974—John Carbray, Sacramento, Pacific Coast
1975—Stan Naccarato, Tacoma, Pacific Coast
1976—Art Teece, Salt Lake City, Pacific Coast
1977—George Sisler Jr., Columbus, International
1978—Willie Sanchez, Albuquerque, Pacific Coast
1979—George Sisler Jr., Columbus, International
1980—Jim Burris, Denver, American Association
1981—Pat McKernan, Albuquerque, Pacific Coast
1982—A. Ray Smith, Louisville, American Association
1983—A. Ray Smith, Louisville, American Association
1984—Mike Tamburro, Pawtucket, International
1985—Patty Cox Hampton, Oklahoma City, American Association
1986—Bob Goughan, Rochester, International
1987—Stu Kehoe, Vancouver, Pacific Coast
1988—Bob Rich, Buffalo, American Association
1989—Larry Schmittou, Nashville, American Association
1990—Greg Corns, Phoenix, Pacific Coast
1991—Tom Maloney, Denver, American Association
1992—Lou Schwechheimer, Pawtucket, International

## MINOR LEAGUE EXECUTIVE OF THE YEAR (LOWER CLASSIFICATIONS, 1950-1990)

**(Separate awards for Class AA and Class A started in 1963; for Short Class A in 1988)**

**Year Executive, Team, League**
1950—H. Cooper, Hutchinson, Western Association
1951—O. W. (Bill) Hayes, Triple, B.S.
1952—Hillman Lyons, Danville, MOV
1953—Carl Roth, Peoria, I.I.I.
1954—James Meagham, Cedar Rapids, I.I.I.
1955—John Petrakis, Dubuque, MOV
1956—Marvin Milkes, Fresno, California
1957—Richard Wagner, Lincoln, West.
1958—Gerald Waring, Macon, Sally
1959—Clay Dennis, Des Moines, I.I.I.
1960—Hubert Kittle, Yakima, Northwest
1961—David Steele, Fresno, California
1962—John Quinn Jr., San Jose, California
1963—Hugh Finnerty, Tulsa, Texas
Ben Jewell, M. Valley, Pioneer
1964—Glynn West, Birmingham, Southern
James Bayens, Rock Hill, W. Carolina
1965—Dick Butler, Dallas-Ft. Worth, Texas
Ken. Blackman, Quad Cities, Midwest
1966—Tom Fleming, Evansville, Southern
Cappy Harada, Lodi, California
1967—Robert Quinn, Reading, Eastern
Pat Williams, Spar'burg, W.C.
1968—Phil Howser, Charlotte, Southern
Merle Miller, Burlington, Midwest
1969—Charlie Blaney, Albuquerque, Texas
Bill Gorman, Visalia, California
1970—Carl Sawatski, Arkansas, Texas
Bob Williams, Bakersfield, California
1971—Miles Wolff, Savannah, Dixie Association
Ed Holtz, Appleton, Midwest
1972—John Begzos, S. Antonio, Texas
Bob Piccinini, Modesto, California
1973—Dick Kravitz, Jacksonville, Southern
Fritz Colschen, Clinton, Midwest

**Year Executive, Team, League**
1974—Jim Paul, El Paso, Texas
Bing Russell, Portland, Northwest
1975—Jim Paul, El Paso, Texas
Cordy Jensen, Eugene, Northwest
1976—Woodrow Reid, Chattanooga, Southern
Don Buchheister, Cedar Rapids, Midwest
1977—Jim Paul, El Paso, Texas
Harry Pells, Quad Cities, Midwest
1978—Larry Schmittou, Nashville, Southern
Dave Hersh, Appleton, Midwest
1979—Bill Rigney Jr., Midland, Texas
Tom Romenesko, Greensboro, W.C.
1980—Frances Crockett, Charlotte, Southern
Tom Romenesko, Greensboro, W.C.
1981—Allie Prescott, Memphis, Southern
Dan Overstreet, Hagerstown, Caro.
1982—Art Clarkson, Birmingham, Southern
Bob Carruesco, Stockton, California
1983—Edward Kenney, New Britain, Eastern
Terry Reynolds, Vero Beach, Florida State
1984—Bruce Baldwin, Greenville, Southern
Dave Tarrolly, Beloit, Midwest
1985—Ben Bernard, Albany-Colonie, Eastern
Pete Vonachen, Peoria, Midwest
1986—Bill Davidson, Midland, Texas
Rob Dlugozima, Durham, Carolina
1987—Joe Preseren, Tulsa, Texas
Skip Weisman, Greensboro, South Atlantic
1988—Bill Valentine, Arkansas, Texas
Dennis Bastien, Charleston (W.Va.), South Atlantic
Bob Beban, Eugene, Northwest
1989—Chuck Domino, Reading, Eastern
John Baxter, South Bend, Midwest
Bill Pereira, Boise, Northwest
1990—Joe Preseren, Tulsa, Texas
Dan Chapman, Stockton, California
Dave Baggott, Salt Lake City, Pioneer

## MINOR LEAGUE EXECUTIVE OF THE YEAR

**Year Executive, Team, League**
1993—Todd Vander Woude, Harrisburg, Eastern (AA)
1994—Scott Lane, West Michigan, Midwest (A)
1995—Jack and Mary Cain, Portland, Northwest (A)
1996—Wayne Hodes, Trenton, Eastern (AA)
1997—Andy Milovich, Erie, New York-Pennsylvania (A)
1998—Chuck Domino, Reading, Eastern (AA)
1999—Ben Mondor, Pawtucket, International (AAA)
2000—Art Savage, Sacramento, Pacific Coast (AAA)
2001—Jay Miller, Round Rock, Texas (AA)
2002—Gary Arthur, Sacramento, Pacific Coast (AAA)
2003—Jay Miller, Round Rock, Texas (AA)
2004—Peter Bragan and Peter Bragan Jr., Jacksonville, Southern (AA)

## 1957

**MAJORS**

P— Bobby Shantz, New York A.L.
C— Sherm Lollar, Chicago A.L.
1B— Gil Hodges, Brooklyn N.L.
2B— Nellie Fox, Chicago A.L.
3B— Frank Malzone, Boston A.L.
SS— Roy McMillan, Cincinnati N.L.
OF— Minnie Minoso, Chicago A.L.
OF— Willie Mays, New York N.L.
OF— Al Kaline, Detroit A.L.

## 1958

**AMERICAN LEAGUE**

P— Bobby Shantz, New York
C— Sherm Lollar, Chicago
1B— Vic Power, K.C.-Cle.
2B— Frank Bolling, Detroit
3B— Frank Malzone, Boston
SS— Luis Aparicio, Chicago
OF— Norm Siebern, New York
OF— Jimmy Piersall, Boston
OF— Al Kaline, Detroit

**NATIONAL LEAGUE**

P— Harvey Haddix, Cincinnati
C— Del Crandall, Milwaukee
1B— Gil Hodges, Los Angeles
2B— Bill Mazeroski, Pittsburgh
3B— Ken Boyer, St. Louis
SS— Roy McMillan, Cincinnati
OF— Frank Robinson, Cincinnati
OF— Willie Mays, San Francisco
OF— Hank Aaron, Milwaukee

## 1959

**AMERICAN LEAGUE**

P— Bobby Shantz, New York
C— Sherm Lollar, Chicago
1B— Vic Power, Cleveland
2B— Nellie Fox, Chicago
3B— Frank Malzone, Boston
SS— Luis Aparicio, Chicago
OF— Minnie Minoso, Cleveland
OF— Al Kaline, Detroit
OF— Jackie Jensen, Boston

**NATIONAL LEAGUE**

P— Harvey Haddix, Pittsburgh
C— Del Crandall, Milwaukee
1B— Gil Hodges, Los Angeles
2B— Charley Neal, Los Angeles
3B— Ken Boyer, St. Louis
SS— Roy McMillan, Cincinnati
OF— Jackie Brandt, San Francisco
OF— Willie Mays, San Francisco
OF— Hank Aaron, Milwaukee

## 1960

**AMERICAN LEAGUE**

P— Bobby Shantz, New York
C— Earl Battey, Washington
1B— Vic Power, Cleveland
2B— Nellie Fox, Chicago
3B— Brooks Robinson, Baltimore
SS— Luis Aparicio, Chicago
OF— Minnie Minoso, Chicago
OF— Jim Landis, Chicago
OF— Roger Maris, New York

**NATIONAL LEAGUE**

P— Harvey Haddix, Pittsburgh
C— Del Crandall, Milwaukee
1B— Bill White, St. Louis
2B— Bill Mazeroski, Pittsburgh
3B— Ken Boyer, St. Louis
SS— Ernie Banks, Chicago
OF— Wally Moon, Los Angeles
OF— Willie Mays, San Francisco
OF— Hank Aaron, Milwaukee

## 1961

**AMERICAN LEAGUE**

P— Frank Lary, Detroit
C— Earl Battey, Minnesota
1B— Vic Power, Cleveland
2B— Bobby Richardson, New York
3B— Brooks Robinson, Baltimore
SS— Luis Aparicio, Chicago
OF— Al Kaline, Detroit
OF— Jimmy Piersall, Cleveland
OF— Jim Landis, Chicago

**NATIONAL LEAGUE**

P— Bobby Shantz, Pittsburgh
C— John Roseboro, Los Angeles
1B— Bill White, St. Louis
2B— Bill Mazeroski, Pittsburgh
3B— Ken Boyer, St. Louis
SS— Maury Wills, Los Angeles
OF— Willie Mays, San Francisco
OF— Roberto Clemente, Pittsburgh
OF— Vada Pinson, Cincinnati

## 1962

**AMERICAN LEAGUE**

P— Jim Kaat, Minnesota
C— Earl Battey, Minnesota
1B— Vic Power, Minnesota
2B— Bobby Richardson, New York
3B— Brooks Robinson, Baltimore
SS— Luis Aparicio, Chicago
OF— Jim Landis, Chicago
OF— Mickey Mantle, New York
OF— Al Kaline, Detroit

**NATIONAL LEAGUE**

P— Bobby Shantz, Hou.-St.L.
C— Del Crandall, Milwaukee
1B— Bill White, St. Louis
2B— Ken Hubbs, Chicago
3B— Jim Davenport, San Francisco
SS— Maury Wills, Los Angeles
OF— Willie Mays, San Francisco
OF— Roberto Clemente, Pittsburgh
OF— Bill Virdon, Pittsburgh

## 1963

**AMERICAN LEAGUE**

P— Jim Kaat, Minnesota
C— Elston Howard, New York
1B— Vic Power, Minnesota
2B— Bobby Richardson, New York
3B— Brooks Robinson, Baltimore
SS— Zoilo Versalles, Minnesota
OF— Al Kaline, Detroit
OF— Carl Yastrzemski, Boston
OF— Jim Landis, Chicago

**NATIONAL LEAGUE**

P— Bobby Shantz, St. Louis
C— Johnny Edwards, Cincinnati
1B— Bill White, St. Louis
2B— Bill Mazeroski, Pittsburgh
3B— Ken Boyer, St. Louis
SS— Bobby Wine, Philadelphia
OF— Willie Mays, San Francisco
OF— Roberto Clemente, Pittsburgh
OF— Curt Flood, St. Louis

## 1964

**AMERICAN LEAGUE**

P— Jim Kaat, Minnesota
C— Elston Howard, New York
1B— Vic Power, Min.-L.A.
2B— Bobby Richardson, New York
3B— Brooks Robinson, Baltimore
SS— Luis Aparicio, Baltimore
OF— Al Kaline, Detroit
OF— Jim Landis, Chicago
OF— Vic Davalillo, Cleveland

**NATIONAL LEAGUE**

P— Bobby Shantz, St.L.-Chi.-Phi.
C— Johnny Edwards, Cincinnati
1B— Bill White, St. Louis
2B— Bill Mazeroski, Pittsburgh
3B— Ron Santo, Chicago
SS— Ruben Amaro, Philadelphia
OF— Willie Mays, San Francisco
OF— Roberto Clemente, Pittsburgh
OF— Curt Flood, St. Louis

## 1965

**AMERICAN LEAGUE**

P— Jim Kaat, Minnesota
C— Bill Freehan, Detroit
1B— Joe Pepitone, New York
2B— Bobby Richardson, New York
3B— Brooks Robinson, Baltimore
SS— Zoilo Versalles, Minnesota
OF— Al Kaline, Detroit
OF— Tom Tresh, New York
OF— Carl Yastrzemski, Boston

**NATIONAL LEAGUE**

P— Bob Gibson, St. Louis
C— Joe Torre, Milwaukee
1B— Bill White, St. Louis
2B— Bill Mazeroski, Pittsburgh
3B— Ron Santo, Chicago
SS— Leo Cardenas, Cincinnati
OF— Willie Mays, San Francisco
OF— Roberto Clemente, Pittsburgh
OF— Curt Flood, St. Louis

## 1966

**AMERICAN LEAGUE**

P— Jim Kaat, Minnesota
C— Bill Freehan, Detroit
1B— Joe Pepitone, New York
2B— Bobby Knoop, California
3B— Brooks Robinson, Baltimore
SS— Luis Aparicio, Baltimore
OF— Al Kaline, Detroit
OF— Tommie Agee, Chicago
OF— Tony Oliva, Minnesota

**NATIONAL LEAGUE**

P— Bob Gibson, St. Louis
C— John Roseboro, Los Angeles
1B— Bill White, Philadelphia
2B— Bill Mazeroski, Pittsburgh
3B— Ron Santo, Chicago
SS— Gene Alley, Pittsburgh
OF— Willie Mays, San Francisco
OF— Curt Flood, St. Louis
OF— Roberto Clemente, Pittsburgh

## 1967

**AMERICAN LEAGUE**

P— Jim Kaat, Minnesota
C— Bill Freehan, Detroit
1B— George Scott, Boston
2B— Bobby Knoop, California
3B— Brooks Robinson, Baltimore

SS— Jim Fregosi, California
OF— Carl Yastrzemski, Boston
OF— Paul Blair, Baltimore
OF— Al Kaline, Detroit

**NATIONAL LEAGUE**

P— Bob Gibson, St. Louis
C— Randy Hundley, Chicago
1B— Wes Parker, Los Angeles
2B— Bill Mazeroski, Pittsburgh
3B— Ron Santo, Chicago
SS— Gene Alley, Pittsburgh
OF— Roberto Clemente, Pittsburgh
OF— Curt Flood, St. Louis
OF— Willie Mays, San Francisco

## 1968

**AMERICAN LEAGUE**

P— Jim Kaat, Minnesota
C— Bill Freehan, Detroit
1B— George Scott, Boston
2B— Bobby Knoop, California
3B— Brooks Robinson, Baltimore
SS— Luis Aparicio, Chicago
OF— Mickey Stanley, Detroit
OF— Carl Yastrzemski, Boston
OF— Reggie Smith, Boston

**NATIONAL LEAGUE**

P— Bob Gibson, St. Louis
C— Johnny Bench, Cincinnati
1B— Wes Parker, Los Angeles
2B— Glenn Beckert, Chicago
3B— Ron Santo, Chicago
SS— Dal Maxvill, St. Louis
OF— Willie Mays, San Francisco
OF— Roberto Clemente, Pittsburgh
OF— Curt Flood, St. Louis

## 1969

**AMERICAN LEAGUE**

P— Jim Kaat, Minnesota
C— Bill Freehan, Detroit
1B— Joe Pepitone, New York
2B— Dave Johnson, Baltimore
3B— Brooks Robinson, Baltimore
SS— Mark Belanger, Baltimore
OF— Paul Blair, Baltimore
OF— Mickey Stanley, Detroit
OF— Carl Yastrzemski, Boston

**NATIONAL LEAGUE**

P— Bob Gibson, St. Louis
C— Johnny Bench, Cincinnati
1B— Wes Parker, Los Angeles
2B— Felix Millan, Atlanta
3B— Clete Boyer, Atlanta
SS— Don Kessinger, Chicago
OF— Roberto Clemente, Pittsburgh
OF— Curt Flood, St. Louis
OF— Pete Rose, Cincinnati

## 1970

**AMERICAN LEAGUE**

P— Jim Kaat, Minnesota
C— Ray Fosse, Cleveland
1B— Jim Spencer, California
2B— Dave Johnson, Baltimore
3B— Brooks Robinson, Baltimore
SS— Luis Aparicio, Chicago
OF— Mickey Stanley, Detroit
OF— Paul Blair, Baltimore
OF— Ken Berry, Chicago

**NATIONAL LEAGUE**

P— Bob Gibson, St. Louis
C— Johnny Bench, Cincinnati
1B— Wes Parker, Los Angeles
2B— Tommy Helms, Cincinnati
3B— Doug Rader, Houston
SS— Don Kessinger, Chicago
OF— Roberto Clemente, Pittsburgh
OF— Tommie Agee, New York
OF— Pete Rose, Cincinnati

## 1971

**AMERICAN LEAGUE**

P— Jim Kaat, Minnesota
C— Ray Fosse, Cleveland
1B— George Scott, Boston
2B— Dave Johnson, Baltimore
3B— Brooks Robinson, Baltimore
SS— Mark Belanger, Baltimore
OF— Paul Blair, Baltimore
OF— Amos Otis, Kansas City
OF— Carl Yastrzemski, Boston

**NATIONAL LEAGUE**

P— Bob Gibson, St. Louis
C— Johnny Bench, Cincinnati
1B— Wes Parker, Los Angeles
2B— Tommy Helms, Cincinnati
3B— Doug Rader, Houston
SS— Bud Harrelson, New York
OF— Roberto Clemente, Pittsburgh
OF— Bobby Bonds, San Francisco
OF— Willie Davis, Los Angeles

## 1972

**AMERICAN LEAGUE**

P— Jim Kaat, Minnesota
C— Carlton Fisk, Boston
1B— George Scott, Milwaukee
2B— Doug Griffin, Boston
3B— Brooks Robinson, Baltimore
SS— Ed Brinkman, Detroit
OF— Paul Blair, Baltimore
OF— Bobby Murcer, New York
OF— Ken Berry, California

**NATIONAL LEAGUE**

P— Bob Gibson, St. Louis
C— Johnny Bench, Cincinnati
1B— Wes Parker, Los Angeles
2B— Felix Millan, Atlanta
3B— Doug Rader, Houston
SS— Larry Bowa, Philadelphia
OF— Roberto Clemente, Pittsburgh
OF— Cesar Cedeno, Houston
OF— Willie Davis, Los Angeles

## 1973

**AMERICAN LEAGUE**

P— Jim Kaat, Chicago
C— Thurman Munson, New York
1B— George Scott, Milwaukee
2B— Bobby Grich, Baltimore
3B— Brooks Robinson, Baltimore
SS— Mark Belanger, Baltimore
OF— Paul Blair, Baltimore
OF— Amos Otis, Kansas City
OF— Mickey Stanley, Detroit

**NATIONAL LEAGUE**

P— Bob Gibson, St. Louis
C— Johnny Bench, Cincinnati
1B— Mike Jorgensen, Montreal
2B— Joe Morgan, Cincinnati
3B— Doug Rader, Houston
SS— Roger Metzger, Houston
OF— Bobby Bonds, San Francisco
OF— Cesar Cedeno, Houston
OF— Willie Davis, Los Angeles

## 1974

**AMERICAN LEAGUE**

P— Jim Kaat, Chicago
C— Thurman Munson, New York
1B— George Scott, Milwaukee
2B— Bobby Grich, Baltimore
3B— Brooks Robinson, Baltimore
SS— Mark Belanger, Baltimore
OF— Paul Blair, Baltimore
OF— Amos Otis, Kansas City
OF— Joe Rudi, Oakland

**NATIONAL LEAGUE**

P— Andy Messersmith, Los Angeles
C— Johnny Bench, Cincinnati
1B— Steve Garvey, Los Angeles
2B— Joe Morgan, Cincinnati
3B— Doug Rader, Houston
SS— Dave Concepcion, Cincinnati
OF— Cesar Cedeno, Houston
OF— Cesar Geronimo, Cincinnati
OF— Bobby Bonds, San Francisco

## 1975

**AMERICAN LEAGUE**

P— Jim Kaat, Chicago
C— Thurman Munson, New York
1B— George Scott, Milwaukee
2B— Bobby Grich, Baltimore
3B— Brooks Robinson, Baltimore
SS— Mark Belanger, Baltimore
OF— Paul Blair, Baltimore
OF— Joe Rudi, Oakland
OF— Fred Lynn, Boston

**NATIONAL LEAGUE**

P— Andy Messersmith, Los Angeles
C— Johnny Bench, Cincinnati
1B— Steve Garvey, Los Angeles
2B— Joe Morgan, Cincinnati
3B— Ken Reitz, St. Louis
SS— Dave Concepcion, Cincinnati
OF— Cesar Cedeno, Houston
OF— Cesar Geronimo, Cincinnati
OF— Garry Maddox, S.F.-Phi.

## 1976

**AMERICAN LEAGUE**

P— Jim Palmer, Baltimore
C— Jim Sundberg, Texas
1B— George Scott, Milwaukee
2B— Bobby Grich, Baltimore
3B— Aurelio Rodriguez, Detroit
SS— Mark Belanger, Baltimore
OF— Joe Rudi, Oakland
OF— Dwight Evans, Boston
OF— Rick Manning, Cleveland

**NATIONAL LEAGUE**

P— Jim Kaat, Philadelphia
C— Johnny Bench, Cincinnati
1B— Steve Garvey, Los Angeles
2B— Joe Morgan, Cincinnati
3B— Mike Schmidt, Philadelphia
SS— Dave Concepcion, Cincinnati
OF— Cesar Cedeno, Houston
OF— Cesar Geronimo, Cincinnati
OF— Garry Maddox, Philadelphia

## 1977

**AMERICAN LEAGUE**

P— Jim Palmer, Baltimore
C— Jim Sundberg, Texas
1B— Jim Spencer, Chicago
2B— Frank White, Kansas City
3B— Graig Nettles, New York
SS— Mark Belanger, Baltimore
OF— Juan Beniquez, Texas
OF— Carl Yastrzemski, Boston
OF— Al Cowens, Kansas City

NATIONAL LEAGUE
P— Jim Kaat, Philadelphia
C— Johnny Bench, Cincinnati
1B— Steve Garvey, Los Angeles
2B— Joe Morgan, Cincinnati
3B— Mike Schmidt, Philadelphia
SS— Dave Concepcion, Cincinnati
OF— Cesar Geronimo, Cincinnati
OF— Garry Maddox, Philadelphia
OF— Dave Parker, Pittsburgh

## 1978

AMERICAN LEAGUE
P— Jim Palmer, Baltimore
C— Jim Sundberg, Texas
1B— Chris Chambliss, New York
2B— Frank White, Kansas City
3B— Graig Nettles, New York
SS— Mark Belanger, Baltimore
OF— Fred Lynn, Boston
OF— Dwight Evans, Boston
OF— Rick Miller, California

NATIONAL LEAGUE
P— Phil Niekro, Atlanta
C— Bob Boone, Philadelphia
1B— Keith Hernandez, St. Louis
2B— Dave Lopes, Los Angeles
3B— Mike Schmidt, Philadelphia
SS— Larry Bowa, Philadelphia
OF— Garry Maddox, Philadelphia
OF— Dave Parker, Pittsburgh
OF— Ellis Valentine, Montreal

## 1979

AMERICAN LEAGUE
P— Jim Palmer, Baltimore
C— Jim Sundberg, Texas
1B— Cecil Cooper, Milwaukee
2B— Frank White, Kansas City
3B— Buddy Bell, Texas
SS— Rick Burleson, Boston
OF— Dwight Evans, Boston
OF— Sixto Lezcano, Milwaukee
OF— Fred Lynn, Boston

NATIONAL LEAGUE
P— Phil Niekro, Atlanta
C— Bob Boone, Philadelphia
1B— Keith Hernandez, St. Louis
2B— Manny Trillo, Philadelphia
3B— Mike Schmidt, Philadelphia
SS— Dave Concepcion, Cincinnati
OF— Garry Maddox, Philadelphia
OF— Dave Parker, Pittsburgh
OF— Dave Winfield, San Diego

## 1980

AMERICAN LEAGUE
P— Mike Norris, Oakland
C— Jim Sundberg, Texas
1B— Cecil Cooper, Milwaukee
2B— Frank White, Kansas City
3B— Buddy Bell, Texas
SS— Alan Trammell, Detroit
OF— Fred Lynn, Boston
OF— Dwayne Murphy, Oakland
OF— Willie Wilson, Kansas City

NATIONAL LEAGUE
P— Phil Niekro, Atlanta
C— Gary Carter, Montreal
1B— Keith Hernandez, St. Louis
2B— Doug Flynn, New York
3B— Mike Schmidt, Philadelphia
SS— Ozzie Smith, San Diego
OF— Andre Dawson, Montreal
OF— Garry Maddox, Philadelphia
OF— Dave Winfield, San Diego

## 1981

AMERICAN LEAGUE
P— Mike Norris, Oakland
C— Jim Sundberg, Texas
1B— Mike Squires, Chicago
2B— Frank White, Kansas City
3B— Buddy Bell, Texas
SS— Alan Trammell, Detroit
OF— Dwayne Murphy, Oakland
OF— Dwight Evans, Boston
OF— Rickey Henderson, Oakland

NATIONAL LEAGUE
P— Steve Carlton, Philadelphia
C— Gary Carter, Montreal
1B— Keith Hernandez, St. Louis
2B— Manny Trillo, Philadelphia
3B— Mike Schmidt, Philadelphia
SS— Ozzie Smith, San Diego
OF— Andre Dawson, Montreal
OF— Garry Maddox, Philadelphia
OF— Dusty Baker, Los Angeles

## 1982

AMERICAN LEAGUE
P— Ron Guidry, New York
C— Bob Boone, California
1B— Eddie Murray, Baltimore
2B— Frank White, Kansas City
3B— Buddy Bell, Texas
SS— Robin Yount, Milwaukee
OF— Dwight Evans, Boston
OF— Dave Winfield, New York
OF— Dwayne Murphy, Oakland

NATIONAL LEAGUE
P— Phil Niekro, Atlanta
C— Gary Carter, Montreal
1B— Keith Hernandez, St. Louis
2B— Manny Trillo, Philadelphia
3B— Mike Schmidt, Philadelphia
SS— Ozzie Smith, St. Louis
OF— Andre Dawson, Montreal
OF— Dale Murphy, Atlanta
OF— Garry Maddox, Philadelphia

## 1983

AMERICAN LEAGUE
P— Ron Guidry, New York
C— Lance Parrish, Detroit
1B— Eddie Murray, Baltimore
2B— Lou Whitaker, Detroit
3B— Buddy Bell, Texas
SS— Alan Trammell, Detroit
OF— Dwight Evans, Boston
OF— Dave Winfield, New York
OF— Dwayne Murphy, Oakland

NATIONAL LEAGUE
P— Phil Niekro, Atlanta
C— Tony Pena, Pittsburgh
1B— Keith Hernandez, St.L.-N.Y.
2B— Ryne Sandberg, Chicago
3B— Mike Schmidt, Philadelphia
SS— Ozzie Smith, St. Louis
OF— Andre Dawson, Montreal
OF— Dale Murphy, Atlanta
OF— Willie McGee, St. Louis

## 1984

AMERICAN LEAGUE
P— Ron Guidry, New York
C— Lance Parrish, Detroit
1B— Eddie Murray, Baltimore
2B— Lou Whitaker, Detroit
3B— Buddy Bell, Texas
SS— Alan Trammell, Detroit
OF— Dwight Evans, Boston
OF— Dave Winfield, New York
OF— Dwayne Murphy, Oakland

NATIONAL LEAGUE
P— Joaquin Andujar, St. Louis
C— Tony Pena, Pittsburgh
1B— Keith Hernandez, New York
2B— Ryne Sandberg, Chicago
3B— Mike Schmidt, Philadelphia
SS— Ozzie Smith, St. Louis
OF— Dale Murphy, Atlanta
OF— Bob Dernier, Chicago
OF— Andre Dawson, Montreal

## 1985

AMERICAN LEAGUE
P— Ron Guidry, New York
C— Lance Parrish, Detroit
1B— Don Mattingly, New York
2B— Lou Whitaker, Detroit
3B— George Brett, Kansas City
SS— Alfredo Griffin, Oakland
OF— Gary Pettis, California
OF— Dave Winfield, New York
OF— Dwight Evans, Boston (tie)
Dwayne Murphy, Oakland (tie)

NATIONAL LEAGUE
P— Rick Reuschel, Pittsburgh
C— Tony Pena, Pittsburgh
1B— Keith Hernandez, New York
2B— Ryne Sandberg, Chicago
3B— Tim Wallach, Montreal
SS— Ozzie Smith, St. Louis
OF— Willie McGee, St. Louis
OF— Dale Murphy, Atlanta
OF— Andre Dawson, Montreal

## 1986

AMERICAN LEAGUE
P— Ron Guidry, New York
C— Bob Boone, California
1B— Don Mattingly, New York
2B— Frank White, Kansas City
3B— Gary Gaetti, Minnesota
SS— Tony Fernandez, Toronto
OF— Gary Pettis, California
OF— Jesse Barfield, Toronto
OF— Kirby Puckett, Minnesota

NATIONAL LEAGUE
P— Fernando Valenzuela, Los Angeles
C— Jody Davis, Chicago
1B— Keith Hernandez, New York
2B— Ryne Sandberg, Chicago
3B— Mike Schmidt, Philadelphia
SS— Ozzie Smith, St. Louis
OF— Tony Gwynn, San Diego
OF— Dale Murphy, Atlanta
OF— Willie McGee, St. Louis

## 1987

AMERICAN LEAGUE
P— Mark Langston, Seattle
C— Bob Boone, California
1B— Don Mattingly, New York
2B— Frank White, Kansas City
3B— Gary Gaetti, Minnesota
SS— Tony Fernandez, Toronto
OF— Jesse Barfield, Toronto
OF— Kirby Puckett, Minnesota
OF— Dave Winfield, New York

NATIONAL LEAGUE
P— Rick Reuschel, Pit.-S.F.
C— Mike LaValliere, Pittsburgh
1B— Keith Hernandez, New York
2B— Ryne Sandberg, Chicago
3B— Terry Pendleton, St. Louis
SS— Ozzie Smith, St. Louis
OF— Eric Davis, Cincinnati
OF— Tony Gwynn, San Diego
OF— Andre Dawson, Chicago

### 1988
**AMERICAN LEAGUE**
P— Mark Langston, Seattle
C— Bob Boone, California
1B— Don Mattingly, New York
2B— Harold Reynolds, Seattle
3B— Gary Gaetti, Minnesota
SS— Tony Fernandez, Toronto
OF— Kirby Puckett, Minnesota
OF— Devon White, California
OF— Gary Pettis, Detroit

**NATIONAL LEAGUE**
P— Orel Hershiser, Los Angeles
C— Benito Santiago, San Diego
1B— Keith Hernandez, New York
2B— Ryne Sandberg, Chicago
3B— Tim Wallach, Montreal
SS— Ozzie Smith, St. Louis
OF— Andy Van Slyke, Pittsburgh
OF— Eric Davis, Cincinnati
OF— Andre Dawson, Chicago

### 1989
**AMERICAN LEAGUE**
P— Bret Saberhagen, Kansas City
C— Bob Boone, Kansas City
1B— Don Mattingly, New York
2B— Harold Reynolds, Seattle
3B— Gary Gaetti, Minnesota
SS— Tony Fernandez, Toronto
OF— Kirby Puckett, Minnesota
OF— Devon White, California
OF— Gary Pettis, Detroit

**NATIONAL LEAGUE**
P— Ron Darling, New York
C— Benito Santiago, San Diego
1B— Andres Galarraga, Montreal
2B— Ryne Sandberg, Chicago
3B— Terry Pendleton, St. Louis
SS— Ozzie Smith, St. Louis
OF— Andy Van Slyke, Pittsburgh
OF— Tony Gwynn, San Diego
OF— Eric Davis, Cincinnati

### 1990
**AMERICAN LEAGUE**
P— Mike Boddicker, Boston
C— Sandy Alomar Jr., Cleveland
1B— Mark McGwire, Oakland
2B— Harold Reynolds, Seattle
3B— Kelly Gruber, Toronto
SS— Ozzie Guillen, Chicago
OF— Ken Griffey Jr., Seattle
OF— Ellis Burks, Boston
OF— Gary Pettis, Texas

**NATIONAL LEAGUE**
P— Greg Maddux, Chicago
C— Benito Santiago, San Diego
1B— Andres Galarraga, Montreal
2B— Ryne Sandberg, Chicago
3B— Tim Wallach, Montreal
SS— Ozzie Smith, St. Louis
OF— Barry Bonds, Pittsburgh
OF— Andy Van Slyke, Pittsburgh
OF— Tony Gwynn, San Diego

### 1991
**AMERICAN LEAGUE**
P— Mark Langston, California
C— Tony Pena, Boston
1B— Don Mattingly, New York
2B— Roberto Alomar, Toronto
3B— Robin Ventura, Chicago
SS— Cal Ripken, Baltimore
OF— Ken Griffey Jr., Seattle
OF— Kirby Puckett, Minnesota
OF— Devon White, Toronto

**NATIONAL LEAGUE**
P— Greg Maddux, Chicago
C— Tom Pagnozzi, St. Louis
1B— Will Clark, San Francisco
2B— Ryne Sandberg, Chicago
3B— Matt Williams, San Francisco
SS— Ozzie Smith, St. Louis
OF— Barry Bonds, Pittsburgh
OF— Andy Van Slyke, Pittsburgh
OF— Tony Gwynn, San Diego

### 1992
**AMERICAN LEAGUE**
P— Mark Langston, California
C— Ivan Rodriguez, Texas
1B— Don Mattingly, New York
2B— Roberto Alomar, Toronto
3B— Robin Ventura, Chicago
SS— Cal Ripken, Baltimore
OF— Ken Griffey Jr., Seattle
OF— Kirby Puckett, Minnesota
OF— Devon White, Toronto

**NATIONAL LEAGUE**
P— Greg Maddux, Chicago
C— Tom Pagnozzi, St. Louis
1B— Mark Grace, Chicago
2B— Jose Lind, Pittsburgh
3B— Terry Pendleton, Atlanta
SS— Ozzie Smith, St. Louis
OF— Barry Bonds, Pittsburgh
OF— Andy Van Slyke, Pittsburgh
OF— Larry Walker, Montreal

### 1993
**AMERICAN LEAGUE**
P— Mark Langston, California
C— Ivan Rodriguez, Texas
1B— Don Mattingly, New York
2B— Roberto Alomar, Toronto
3B— Robin Ventura, Chicago
SS— Omar Vizquel, Seattle
OF— Ken Griffey Jr., Seattle
OF— Kenny Lofton, Cleveland
OF— Devon White, Toronto

**NATIONAL LEAGUE**
P— Greg Maddux, Atlanta
C— Kirt Manwaring, San Francisco
1B— Mark Grace, Chicago
2B— Robby Thompson, San Fran.
3B— Matt Williams, San Francisco
SS— Jay Bell, Pittsburgh
OF— Barry Bonds, San Francisco
OF— Marquis Grissom, Montreal
OF— Larry Walker, Montreal

### 1994
**AMERICAN LEAGUE**
P— Mark Langston, California
C— Ivan Rodriguez, Texas
1B— Don Mattingly, New York
2B— Roberto Alomar, Toronto
3B— Wade Boggs, New York
SS— Omar Vizquel, Cleveland
OF— Ken Griffey Jr., Seattle
OF— Kenny Lofton, Cleveland
OF— Devon White, Toronto

**NATIONAL LEAGUE**
P— Greg Maddux, Atlanta
C— Tom Pagnozzi, St. Louis
1B— Jeff Bagwell, Houston
2B— Craig Biggio, Houston
3B— Matt Williams, San Francisco
SS— Barry Larkin, Cincinnati
OF— Barry Bonds, San Francisco
OF— Marquis Grissom, Montreal
OF— Darren Lewis, San Francisco

### 1995
**AMERICAN LEAGUE**
P— Mark Langston, California
C— Ivan Rodriguez, Texas
1B— J.T. Snow, California
2B— Roberto Alomar, Toronto
3B— Wade Boggs, New York
SS— Omar Vizquel, Cleveland
OF— Ken Griffey Jr., Seattle
OF— Kenny Lofton, Cleveland
OF— Devon White, Toronto

**NATIONAL LEAGUE**
P— Greg Maddux, Atlanta
C— Charles Johnson, Florida
1B— Mark Grace, Chicago
2B— Craig Biggio, Houston
3B— Ken Caminiti, San Diego
SS— Barry Larkin, Cincinnati
OF— Raul Mondesi, Los Angeles
OF— Marquis Grissom, Atlanta
OF— Steve Finley, San Diego

### 1996
**AMERICAN LEAGUE**
P— Mike Mussina, Baltimore
C— Ivan Rodriguez, Texas
1B— J.T. Snow, California
2B— Roberto Alomar, Baltimore
3B— Robin Ventura, Chicago
SS— Omar Vizquel, Cleveland
OF— Jay Buhner, Seattle
OF— Ken Griffey Jr., Seattle
OF— Kenny Lofton, Cleveland

**NATIONAL LEAGUE**
P— Greg Maddux, Atlanta
C— Charles Johnson, Florida
1B— Mark Grace, Chicago
2B— Craig Biggio, Houston
3B— Ken Caminiti, San Diego
SS— Barry Larkin, Cincinnati
OF— Barry Bonds, San Francisco
OF— Marquis Grissom, Atlanta
OF— Steve Finley, San Diego

### 1997
**AMERICAN LEAGUE**
P— Mike Mussina, Baltimore
C— Ivan Rodriguez, Texas
1B— Rafael Palmeiro, Baltimore
2B— Chuck Knoblauch, Minnesota
3B— Matt Williams, Cleveland
SS— Omar Vizquel, Cleveland
OF— Jim Edmonds, Anaheim
OF— Ken Griffey Jr., Seattle
OF— Bernie Williams, New York

**NATIONAL LEAGUE**
P— Greg Maddux, Atlanta
C— Charles Johnson, Florida
1B— J.T. Snow, San Francisco
2B— Craig Biggio, Houston
3B— Ken Caminiti, San Diego
SS— Rey Ordonez, New York
OF— Barry Bonds, San Francisco
OF— Raul Mondesi, Los Angeles
OF— Larry Walker, Colorado

### 1998
**AMERICAN LEAGUE**
P— Mike Mussina, Baltimore
C— Ivan Rodriguez, Texas
1B— Rafael Palmeiro, Baltimore
2B— Roberto Alomar, Baltimore
3B— Robin Ventura, White Sox
SS— Omar Vizquel, Cleveland
OF— Jim Edmonds, Anaheim
OF— Ken Griffey Jr., Seattle
OF— Bernie Williams, New York

NATIONAL LEAGUE
P— Greg Maddux, Atlanta
C— Charles Johnson, Fla.-L.A.
1B— J.T. Snow, San Francisco
2B— Bret Boone, Cincinnati
3B— Scott Rolen, Philadelphia
SS— Rey Ordonez, New York
OF— Barry Bonds, San Francisco
OF— Andruw Jones, Atlanta
OF— Larry Walker, Colorado

## 1999

AMERICAN LEAGUE
P— Mike Mussina, Baltimore
C— Ivan Rodriguez, Texas
1B— Rafael Palmeiro, Texas
2B— Roberto Alomar, Cleveland
3B— Scott Brosius, New York
SS— Omar Vizquel, Cleveland
OF— Shawn Green, Toronto
OF— Ken Griffey Jr., Seattle
OF— Bernie Williams, New York

NATIONAL LEAGUE
P— Greg Maddux, Atlanta
C— Mike Lieberthal, Philadelphia
1B— J.T. Snow, San Francisco
2B— Pokey Reese, Cincinnati
3B— Robin Ventura, New York
SS— Rey Ordonez, New York
OF— Steve Finley, Arizona
OF— Andruw Jones, Atlanta
OF— Larry Walker, Colorado

## 2000

AMERICAN LEAGUE
P— Kenny Rogers, Texas
C— Ivan Rodriguez, Texas
1B— John Olerud, Seattle
2B— Roberto Alomar, Cleveland
3B— Travis Fryman, Cleveland
SS— Omar Vizquel, Cleveland
OF— Jermaine Dye, Kansas City
OF— Darin Erstad, Anaheim
OF— Bernie Williams, New York

NATIONAL LEAGUE
P— Greg Maddux, Atlanta
C— Mike Matheny, St. Louis
1B— J.T. Snow, San Francisco
2B— Pokey Reese, Cincinnati
3B— Scott Rolen, Philadelphia
SS— Neifi Perez, Colorado
OF— Jim Edmonds, St. Louis
OF— Steve Finley, Arizona
OF— Andruw Jones, Atlanta

## 2001

AMERICAN LEAGUE
P— Mike Mussina, New York
C— Ivan Rodriguez, Texas
1B— Doug Mientkiewicz, Minnesota
2B— Roberto Alomar, Cleveland
3B— Eric Chavez, Oakland
SS— Omar Vizquel, Cleveland
OF— Mike Cameron, Seattle
OF— Torii Hunter, Minnesota
OF— Ichiro Suzuki, Seattle

NATIONAL LEAGUE
P— Greg Maddux, Atlanta
C— Brad Ausmus, Houston
1B— Todd Helton, Colorado
2B— Fernando Vina, St. Louis
3B— Scott Rolen, Philadelphia
SS— Orlando Cabrera, Montreal
OF— Jim Edmonds, St. Louis
OF— Andruw Jones, Atlanta
OF— Larry Walker, Colorado

## 2002

AMERICAN LEAGUE
P— Kenny Rogers, Texas
C— Bengie Molina, Anaheim
1B— John Olerud, Seattle
2B— Bret Boone, Seattle
3B— Eric Chavez, Oakland
SS— Alex Rodriguez, Texas
OF— Darin Erstad, Anaheim
OF— Torii Hunter, Minnesota
OF— Ichiro Suzuki, Seattle

NATIONAL LEAGUE
P— Greg Maddux, Atlanta
C— Brad Ausmus, Houston
1B— Todd Helton, Colorado
2B— Fernando Vina, St. Louis
3B— Scott Rolen, Phil.-St.L.
SS— Edgar Renteria, St. Louis
OF— Jim Edmonds, St. Louis
OF— Andruw Jones, Atlanta
OF— Larry Walker, Colorado

## 2003

AMERICAN LEAGUE
P— Mike Mussina, New York
C— Bengie Molina, Anaheim
1B— John Olerud, Seattle
2B— Bret Boone, Seattle
3B— Eric Chavez, Oakland
SS— Alex Rodriguez, Texas
OF— Mike Cameron, Seattle
OF— Torii Hunter, Minnesota
OF— Ichiro Suzuki, Seattle

NATIONAL LEAGUE
P— Mike Hampton, Atlanta
C— Mike Matheny, St. Louis
1B— Derrek Lee, Florida
2B— Luis Castillo, Florida
3B— Scott Rolen, St. Louis
SS— Edgar Renteria, St. Louis
OF— Jim Edmonds, St. Louis
OF— Andruw Jones, Atlanta
OF— Jose Cruz Jr., San Francisco

## 2004

AMERICAN LEAGUE
P— Kenny Rogers, Texas
C— Ivan Rodriguez, Detroit
1B—Darin Erstad, Anaheim
2B—Bret Boone, Seattle
3B—Eric Chavez, Oakland
SS—Derek Jeter, New York
OF—Vernon Wells, Toronto
OF—Ichiro Suzuki, Seattle
OF— Torii Hunter, Minnesota

NATIONAL LEAGUE
P— Greg Maddux, Chicago
C—Mike Matheny, St. Louis
1B— Todd Helton, Colorado
2B—Luis Castillo, Florida
3B—Scott Rolen, St. Louis
SS—Cesar Izturis, Los Angeles
OF—Jim Edmonds, St. Louis
OF—Andruw Jones, Atlanta
OF—Steve Finley, Ariz.-Los Angeles

# HILLERICH & BRADSBY SILVER SLUGGER TEAMS

## 1980

AMERICAN LEAGUE
1B— Cecil Cooper, Milwaukee
2B— Willie Randolph, New York
3B— George Brett, Kansas City
SS— Robin Yount, Milwaukee
OF— Ben Oglivie, Milwaukee
OF— Al Oliver, Texas
OF— Willie Wilson, Kansas City
C— Lance Parrish, Detroit
DH— Reggie Jackson, New York

NATIONAL LEAGUE
1B— Keith Hernandez, St. Louis
2B— Manny Trillo, Philadelphia
3B— Mike Schmidt, Philadelphia
SS— Garry Templeton, St. Louis
OF— Dusty Baker, Los Angeles
OF— Andre Dawson, Montreal
OF— George Hendrick, St. Louis
C— Ted Simmons, St. Louis
P— Bob Forsch, St. Louis

## 1981

AMERICAN LEAGUE
1B— Cecil Cooper, Milwaukee
2B— Bobby Grich, California
3B— Carney Lansford, Boston
SS— Rick Burleson, California
OF— Rickey Henderson, Oakland
OF— Dwight Evans, Boston
OF— Dave Winfield, New York
C— Carlton Fisk, Chicago
DH— Al Oliver, Texas

NATIONAL LEAGUE
1B— Pete Rose, Philadelphia
2B— Manny Trillo, Philadelphia
3B— Mike Schmidt, Philadelphia
SS— Dave Concepcion, Cincinnati
OF— Andre Dawson, Montreal
OF— George Foster, Cincinnati
OF— Dusty Baker, Los Angeles
C— Gary Carter, Montreal
P— Fernando Valenzuela, Los Angeles

## 1982

AMERICAN LEAGUE
1B— Cecil Cooper, Milwaukee
2B— Damaso Garcia, Toronto
3B— Doug DeCinces, California
SS— Robin Yount, Milwaukee
OF— Dave Winfield, New York
OF— Willie Wilson, Kansas City
OF— Reggie Jackson, California
C— Lance Parrish, Detroit
DH— Hal McRae, Kansas City

NATIONAL LEAGUE
1B— Al Oliver, Montreal
2B— Joe Morgan, San Francisco
3B— Mike Schmidt, Philadelphia
SS— Dave Concepcion, Cincinnati
OF— Dale Murphy, Atlanta
OF— Pedro Guerrero, Los Angeles
OF— Leon Durham, Chicago
C— Gary Carter, Montreal
P— Don Robinson, Pittsburgh

## 1983

AMERICAN LEAGUE
1B— Eddie Murray, Baltimore
2B— Lou Whitaker, Detroit
3B— Wade Boggs, Boston
SS— Cal Ripken Jr., Baltimore
OF— Jim Rice, Boston
OF— Dave Winfield, New York
OF— Lloyd Moseby, Toronto
C— Lance Parrish, Detroit
DH— Don Baylor, New York

NATIONAL LEAGUE
1B— George Hendrick, St. Louis
2B— Johnny Ray, Pittsburgh

3B— Mike Schmidt, Philadelphia
SS— Dickie Thon, Houston
OF— Andre Dawson, Montreal
OF— Dale Murphy, Atlanta
OF— Jose Cruz, Houston
C— Terry Kennedy, San Diego
P— Fernando Valenzuela, Los Angeles

## 1984

### AMERICAN LEAGUE

1B— Eddie Murray, Baltimore
2B— Lou Whitaker, Detroit
3B— Buddy Bell, Texas
SS— Cal Ripken Jr., Baltimore
OF— Tony Armas, Boston
OF— Jim Rice, Boston
OF— Dave Winfield, New York
C— Lance Parrish, Detroit
DH— Andre Thornton, Cleveland

### NATIONAL LEAGUE

1B— Keith Hernandez, New York
2B— Ryne Sandberg, Chicago
3B— Mike Schmidt, Philadelphia
SS— Garry Templeton, San Diego
OF— Dale Murphy, Atlanta
OF— Jose Cruz, Houston
OF— Tony Gwynn, San Diego
C— Gary Carter, Montreal
P— Rick Rhoden, Pittsburgh

## 1985

### AMERICAN LEAGUE

1B— Don Mattingly, New York
2B— Lou Whitaker, Detroit
3B— George Brett, Kansas City
SS— Cal Ripken Jr., Baltimore
OF— Rickey Henderson, New York
OF— Dave Winfield, New York
OF— George Bell, Toronto
C— Carlton Fisk, Chicago
DH— Don Baylor, New York

### NATIONAL LEAGUE

1B— Jack Clark, St. Louis
2B— Ryne Sandberg, Chicago
3B— Tim Wallach, Montreal
SS— Hubie Brooks, Montreal
OF— Willie McGee, St. Louis
OF— Dale Murphy, Atlanta
OF— Dave Parker, Cincinnati
C— Gary Carter, New York
P— Rick Rhoden, Pittsburgh

## 1986

### AMERICAN LEAGUE

1B— Don Mattingly, New York
2B— Frank White, Kansas City
3B— Wade Boggs, Boston
SS— Cal Ripken Jr., Baltimore
OF— George Bell, Toronto
OF— Kirby Puckett, Minnesota
OF— Jesse Barfield, Toronto
C— Lance Parrish, Detroit
DH— Don Baylor, Boston

### NATIONAL LEAGUE

1B— Glenn Davis, Houston
2B— Steve Sax, Los Angeles
3B— Mike Schmidt, Philadelphia
SS— Hubie Brooks, Montreal
OF— Tony Gwynn, San Diego
OF— Tim Raines, Montreal
OF— Dave Parker, Cincinnati
C— Gary Carter, New York
P— Rick Rhoden, Pittsburgh

## 1987

### AMERICAN LEAGUE

1B— Don Mattingly, New York
2B— Lou Whitaker, Detroit
3B— Wade Boggs, Boston
SS— Alan Trammell, Detroit
OF— George Bell, Toronto
OF— Dwight Evans, Boston
OF— Kirby Puckett, Minnesota
C— Matt Nokes, Detroit
DH— Paul Molitor, Milwaukee

### NATIONAL LEAGUE

1B— Jack Clark, St. Louis
2B— Juan Samuel, Philadelphia
3B— Tim Wallach, Montreal
SS— Ozzie Smith, St. Louis
OF— Andre Dawson, Chicago
OF— Eric Davis, Cincinnati
OF— Tony Gwynn, San Diego
C— Benito Santiago, San Diego
P— Bob Forsch, St. Louis

## 1988

### AMERICAN LEAGUE

1B— George Brett, Kansas City
2B— Julio Franco, Cleveland
3B— Wade Boggs, Boston
SS— Alan Trammell, Detroit
OF— Kirby Puckett, Minnesota
OF— Jose Canseco, Oakland
OF— Mike Greenwell, Boston
C— Carlton Fisk, Chicago
DH— Paul Molitor, Milwaukee

### NATIONAL LEAGUE

1B— Andres Galarraga, Montreal
2B— Ryne Sandberg, Chicago
3B— Bobby Bonilla, Pittsburgh
SS— Barry Larkin, Cincinnati
OF— Darryl Strawberry, New York
OF— Andy Van Slyke, Pittsburgh
OF— Kirk Gibson, Los Angeles
C— Benito Santiago, San Diego
P— Tim Leary, Los Angeles

## 1989

### AMERICAN LEAGUE

1B— Fred McGriff, Toronto
2B— Julio Franco, Texas
3B— Wade Boggs, Boston
SS— Cal Ripken Jr., Baltimore
OF— Kirby Puckett, Minnesota
OF— Ruben Sierra, Texas
OF— Robin Yount, Milwaukee
C— Mickey Tettleton, Baltimore
DH— Harold Baines, Chi.-Tex.

### NATIONAL LEAGUE

1B— Will Clark, San Francisco
2B— Ryne Sandberg, Chicago
3B— Howard Johnson, New York
SS— Barry Larkin, Cincinnati
OF— Kevin Mitchell, San Francisco
OF— Tony Gwynn, San Diego
OF— Eric Davis, Cincinnati
C— Craig Biggio, Houston
P— Don Robinson, San Francisco

## 1990

### AMERICAN LEAGUE

1B— Cecil Fielder, Detroit
2B— Julio Franco, Texas
3B— Kelly Gruber, Toronto
SS— Alan Trammell, Detroit
OF— Rickey Henderson, Oakland
OF— Jose Canseco, Oakland
OF— Ellis Burks, Boston
C— Lance Parrish, California
DH— Dave Parker, Milwaukee

### NATIONAL LEAGUE

1B— Eddie Murray, Los Angeles
2B— Ryne Sandberg, Chicago
3B— Matt Williams, San Francisco
SS— Barry Larkin, Cincinnati
OF— Barry Bonds, Pittsburgh
OF— Bobby Bonilla, Pittsburgh
OF— Darryl Strawberry, New York
C— Benito Santiago, San Diego
P— Don Robinson, San Francisco

## 1991

### AMERICAN LEAGUE

1B— Cecil Fielder, Detroit
2B— Julio Franco, Texas
3B— Wade Boggs, Boston
SS— Cal Ripken Jr., Baltimore
OF— Jose Canseco, Oakland
OF— Joe Carter, Toronto
OF— Ken Griffey Jr., Seattle
C— Mickey Tettleton, Detroit
DH— Frank Thomas, Chicago

### NATIONAL LEAGUE

1B— Will Clark, San Francisco
2B— Ryne Sandberg, Chicago
3B— Howard Johnson, New York
SS— Barry Larkin, Cincinnati
OF— Barry Bonds, Pittsburgh
OF— Bobby Bonilla, Pittsburgh
OF— Ron Gant, Atlanta
C— Benito Santiago, San Diego
P— Tom Glavine, Atlanta

## 1992

### AMERICAN LEAGUE

1B— Mark McGwire, Oakland
2B— Roberto Alomar, Toronto
3B— Edgar Martinez, Seattle
SS— Travis Fryman, Detroit
OF— Joe Carter, Toronto
OF— Juan Gonzalez, Texas
OF— Kirby Puckett, Minnesota
C— Mickey Tettleton, Detroit
DH— Dave Winfield, Toronto

### NATIONAL LEAGUE

1B— Fred McGriff, San Diego
2B— Ryne Sandberg, Chicago
3B— Gary Sheffield, San Diego
SS— Barry Larkin, Cincinnati
OF— Barry Bonds, Pittsburgh
OF— Andy Van Slyke, Pittsburgh
OF— Larry Walker, Montreal
C— Darren Daulton, Philadelphia
P— Dwight Gooden, New York

## 1993

### AMERICAN LEAGUE

1B— Frank Thomas, Chicago
2B— Carlos Baerga, Cleveland
3B— Wade Boggs, New York
SS— Cal Ripken Jr., Baltimore
OF— Albert Belle, Cleveland
OF— Juan Gonzalez, Texas
OF— Ken Griffey Jr., Seattle
C— Mike Stanley, New York
DH— Paul Molitor, Toronto

### NATIONAL LEAGUE

1B— Fred McGriff, S.D.-Atl.
2B— Robby Thompson, San Fran.
3B— Matt Williams, San Francisco
SS— Jay Bell, Pittsburgh
OF— Barry Bonds, San Francisco
OF— Lenny Dykstra, Philadelphia
OF— David Justice, Atlanta
C— Mike Piazza, Los Angeles
P— Orel Hershiser, Los Angeles

## 1994

### AMERICAN LEAGUE

1B— Frank Thomas, Chicago
2B— Carlos Baerga, Cleveland
3B— Wade Boggs, New York
SS— Cal Ripken Jr., Baltimore
OF— Albert Belle, Cleveland
OF— Ken Griffey Jr., Seattle
OF— Kirby Puckett, Minnesota
C— Ivan Rodriguez, Texas
DH— Julio Franco, Chicago

**NATIONAL LEAGUE**
1B— Jeff Bagwell, Houston
2B— Craig Biggio, Houston
3B— Matt Williams, San Francisco
SS— Wil Cordero, Montreal
OF— Moises Alou, Montreal
OF— Barry Bonds, San Francisco
OF— Tony Gwynn, San Diego
C— Mike Piazza, Los Angeles
P— Mark Portugal, San Francisco

## 1995

**AMERICAN LEAGUE**
1B— Mo Vaughn, Boston
2B— Chuck Knoblauch, Minnesota
3B— Gary Gaetti, Kansas City
SS— John Valentin, Boston
OF— Albert Belle, Cleveland
OF— Tim Salmon, California
OF— Manny Ramirez, Cleveland
C— Ivan Rodriguez, Texas
DH— Edgar Martinez, Seattle

**NATIONAL LEAGUE**
1B— Eric Karros, Los Angeles
2B— Craig Biggio, Houston
3B— Vinny Castilla, Colorado
SS— Barry Larkin, Cincinnati
OF— Dante Bichette, Colorado
OF— Tony Gwynn, San Diego
OF— Sammy Sosa, Chicago
C— Mike Piazza, Los Angeles
P— Tom Glavine, Atlanta

## 1996

**AMERICAN LEAGUE**
1B— Mark McGwire, Oakland
2B— Roberto Alomar, Baltimore
3B— Jim Thome, Cleveland
SS— Alex Rodriguez, Seattle
OF— Albert Belle, Cleveland
OF— Juan Gonzalez, Texas
OF— Ken Griffey Jr., Seattle
C— Ivan Rodriguez, Texas
DH— Paul Molitor, Minnesota

**NATIONAL LEAGUE**
1B— Andres Galarraga, Colorado
2B— Eric Young, Colorado
3B— Ken Caminiti, San Diego
SS— Barry Larkin, Cincinnati
OF— Barry Bonds, San Francisco
OF— Ellis Burks, Colorado
OF— Gary Sheffield, Florida
C— Mike Piazza, Los Angeles
P— Tom Glavine, Atlanta

## 1997

**AMERICAN LEAGUE**
1B— Tino Martinez, New York
2B— Chuck Knoblauch, Minnesota
3B— Matt Williams, Cleveland
SS— Nomar Garciaparra, Boston
OF— Juan Gonzalez, Texas
OF— Ken Griffey Jr., Seattle
OF— David Justice, Cleveland
C— Ivan Rodriguez, Texas
DH— Edgar Martinez, Seattle

**NATIONAL LEAGUE**
1B— Jeff Bagwell, Houston
2B— Craig Biggio, Houston
3B— Vinny Castilla, Colorado
SS— Jeff Blauser, Atlanta
OF— Barry Bonds, San Francisco
OF— Tony Gwynn, San Diego
OF— Larry Walker, Colorado
C— Mike Piazza, Los Angeles
P— John Smoltz, Atlanta

## 1998

**AMERICAN LEAGUE**
1B— Rafael Palmeiro, Baltimore
2B— Damion Easley, Detroit
3B— Dean Palmer, Kansas City
SS— Alex Rodriguez, Seattle
OF— Juan Gonzalez, Texas
OF— Ken Griffey Jr., Seattle
OF— Albert Belle, Chicago
C— Ivan Rodriguez, Texas
DH— Jose Canseco, Toronto

**NATIONAL LEAGUE**
1B— Mark McGwire, St. Louis
2B— Craig Biggio, Houston
3B— Vinny Castilla, Colorado
SS— Barry Larkin, Cincinnati
OF— Sammy Sosa, Chicago
OF— Moises Alou, Houston
OF— Greg Vaughn, San Diego
C— Mike Piazza, L.A.-Fla.-N.Y.
P— Tom Glavine, Atlanta

## 1999

**AMERICAN LEAGUE**
1B— Carlos Delgado, Toronto
2B— Roberto Alomar, Cleveland
3B— Dean Palmer, Detroit
SS— Alex Rodriguez, Seattle
OF— Shawn Green, Toronto
OF— Ken Griffey Jr., Seattle
OF— Manny Ramirez, Cleveland
C— Ivan Rodriguez, Texas
DH— Rafael Palmeiro, Texas

**NATIONAL LEAGUE**
1B— Jeff Bagwell, Houston
2B— Edgardo Alfonzo, New York
3B— Chipper Jones, Atlanta
SS— Barry Larkin, Cincinnati
OF— Sammy Sosa, Chicago
OF— Vladimir Guerrero, Montreal
OF— Larry Walker, Colorado
C— Mike Piazza, New York
P— Mike Hampton, Houston

## 2000

**AMERICAN LEAGUE**
1B— Carlos Delgado, Toronto
2B— Roberto Alomar, Cleveland
3B— Troy Glaus, Anaheim
SS— Alex Rodriguez, Seattle
OF— Darin Erstad, Anaheim
OF— Manny Ramirez, Cleveland
OF— Magglio Ordonez, Chicago
C— Jorge Posada, New York
DH— Frank Thomas, Chicago

**NATIONAL LEAGUE**
1B— Todd Helton, Colorado
2B— Jeff Kent, San Francisco
3B— Chipper Jones, Atlanta
SS— Edgar Renteria, St. Louis
OF— Sammy Sosa, Chicago
OF— Barry Bonds, San Francisco
OF— Vladimir Guerrero, Montreal
C— Mike Piazza, New York
P— Mike Hampton, New York

## 2001

**AMERICAN LEAGUE**
1B— Jason Giambi, Oakland
2B— Bret Boone, Seattle
3B— Troy Glaus, Anaheim
SS— Alex Rodriguez, Texas
OF— Juan Gonzalez, Cleveland
OF— Manny Ramirez, Boston
OF— Ichiro Suzuki, Seattle
C— Jorge Posada, New York
DH— Edgar Martinez, Seattle

**NATIONAL LEAGUE**
1B— Todd Helton, Colorado
2B— Jeff Kent, San Francisco
3B— Albert Pujols, St. Louis
SS— Rich Aurilia, San Francisco
OF— Barry Bonds, San Francisco
OF— Luis Gonzalez, Arizona
OF— Sammy Sosa, Chicago
C— Mike Piazza, New York
P— Mike Hampton, Colorado

## 2002

**AMERICAN LEAGUE**
1B— Jason Giambi, New York
2B— Alfonso Soriano, New York
3B— Eric Chavez, Oakland
SS— Alex Rodriguez, Texas
OF— Garret Anderson, Anaheim
OF— Magglio Ordonez, Chicago
OF— Bernie Williams, New York
C— Jorge Posada, New York
DH— Manny Ramirez, Boston

**NATIONAL LEAGUE**
1B— Todd Helton, Colorado
2B— Jeff Kent, San Francisco
3B— Scott Rolen, Phi.-St.L.
SS— Edgar Renteria, St. Louis
OF— Barry Bonds, San Francisco
OF— Vladimir Guerrero, Montreal
OF— Sammy Sosa, Chicago
C— Mike Piazza, New York
P— Mike Hampton, Colorado

## 2003

**AMERICAN LEAGUE**
1B— Carlos Delgado, Toronto
2B— Bret Boone, Seattle
3B— Bill Mueller, Boston
SS— Alex Rodriguez, Texas
OF— Garret Anderson, Anaheim
OF— Vernon Wells, Toronto
OF— Manny Ramirez, Boston
C— Jorge Posada, New York
DH— Edgar Martinez, Seattle

**NATIONAL LEAGUE**
1B— Todd Helton, Colorado
2B— Jose Vidro, Montreal
3B— Mike Lowell, Florida
SS— Edgar Renteria, St. Louis
OF— Barry Bonds, San Francisco
OF— Albert Pujols, St. Louis
OF—Gary Sheffield, Atlanta
C— Javy Lopez, Atlanta
P— Mike Hampton, Atlanta

## 2004

**AMERICAN LEAGUE**
1B— Mark Teixeira, Texas
2B— Alfonso Soriano, Texas
3B—Melvin Mora, Baltimore
SS—Miguel Tejada, Baltimore
OF— Manny Ramirez, Boston
OF— Gary Sheffield, New York
OF— Vladimir Guerrero, Anaheim
C— Ivan Rodriguez, Detroit
Victor Martinez, Cleveland
DH—David Ortiz, Boston

**NATIONAL LEAGUE**
1B—Albert Pujols, St. Louis
2B—Mark Loretta, San Diego
3B—Adrian Beltre, Los Angeles
SS—Jack Wilson, Pittsburgh
OF—Barry Bonds, San Francisco
OF—Jim Edmonds, St. Louis
OF—Bobby Abreu, Philadelphia
C—Johnny Estrada, Atlanta
P—Livan Hernandez, Montreal

# BASEBALL WRITERS' ASSOCIATION OF AMERICA

## MOST VALUABLE PLAYER

### AMERICAN LEAGUE

| Year | Player | Team | Pos. | Points |
|---|---|---|---|---|
| 1931 | Lefty Grove | Philadelphia | P | 78 |
| 1932 | Jimmie Foxx | Philadelphia | 1B | 75 |
| 1933 | Jimmie Foxx | Philadelphia | 1B | 74 |
| 1934 | Mickey Cochrane | Detroit | C | 67 |
| 1935 | Hank Greenberg | Detroit | 1B | *80 |
| 1936 | Lou Gehrig | New York | 1B | 73 |
| 1937 | Charley Gehringer | Detroit | 2B | 78 |
| 1938 | Jimmie Foxx | Boston | 1B | 305 |
| 1939 | Joe DiMaggio | New York | OF | 280 |
| 1940 | Hank Greenberg | Detroit | OF | 292 |
| 1941 | Joe DiMaggio | New York | OF | 291 |
| 1942 | Joe Gordon | New York | 2B | 270 |
| 1943 | Spud Chandler | New York | P | 246 |
| 1944 | Hal Newhouser | Detroit | P | 236 |
| 1945 | Hal Newhouser | Detroit | P | 236 |
| 1946 | Ted Williams | Boston | OF | 224 |
| 1947 | Joe DiMaggio | New York | OF | 202 |
| 1948 | Lou Boudreau | Cleveland | SS | 324 |
| 1949 | Ted Williams | Boston | OF | 272 |
| 1950 | Phil Rizzuto | New York | SS | 284 |
| 1951 | Yogi Berra | New York | C | 184 |
| 1952 | Bobby Shantz | Philadelphia | P | 280 |
| 1953 | Al Rosen | Cleveland | 3B | *336 |
| 1954 | Yogi Berra | New York | C | 230 |
| 1955 | Yogi Berra | New York | C | 218 |
| 1956 | Mickey Mantle | New York | OF | *336 |
| 1957 | Mickey Mantle | New York | OF | 233 |
| 1958 | Jackie Jensen | Boston | OF | 233 |
| 1959 | Nellie Fox | Chicago | 2B | 295 |
| 1960 | Roger Maris | New York | OF | 225 |
| 1961 | Roger Maris | New York | OF | 202 |
| 1962 | Mickey Mantle | New York | OF | 234 |
| 1963 | Elston Howard | New York | C | 248 |
| 1964 | Brooks Robinson | Baltimore | 3B | 269 |
| 1965 | Zoilo Versalles | Minnesota | SS | 275 |
| 1966 | Frank Robinson | Baltimore | OF | *280 |
| 1967 | Carl Yastrzemski | Boston | OF | 275 |
| 1968 | Denny McLain | Detroit | P | *280 |
| 1969 | Harmon Killebrew | Minnesota | 1B-3B | 294 |
| 1970 | Boog Powell | Baltimore | 1B | 234 |
| 1971 | Vida Blue | Oakland | P | 268 |
| 1972 | Dick Allen | Chicago | 1B | 321 |
| 1973 | Reggie Jackson | Oakland | OF | *336 |
| 1974 | Jeff Burroughs | Texas | OF | 248 |
| 1975 | Fred Lynn | Boston | OF | 326 |
| 1976 | Thurman Munson | New York | C | 304 |
| 1977 | Rod Carew | Minnesota | 1B | 273 |
| 1978 | Jim Rice | Boston | OF | 352 |
| 1979 | Don Baylor | California | OF | 347 |
| | Keith Hernandez | St. Louis | 1B | 216 |
| 1980 | George Brett | Kansas City | 3B | 335 |
| 1981 | Rollie Fingers | Milwaukee | P | 319 |
| 1982 | Robin Yount | Milwaukee | SS | 385 |
| 1983 | Cal Ripken Jr. | Baltimore | SS | 322 |
| 1984 | Willie Hernandez | Detroit | P | 306 |
| 1985 | Don Mattingly | New York | 1B | 367 |
| 1986 | Roger Clemens | Boston | P | 339 |
| 1987 | George Bell | Toronto | OF | 332 |
| 1988 | Jose Canseco | Oakland | OF | *392 |
| 1989 | Robin Yount | Milwaukee | OF | 256 |
| 1990 | Rickey Henderson | Oakland | OF | 317 |
| 1991 | Cal Ripken Jr. | Baltimore | SS | 318 |
| 1992 | Dennis Eckersley | Oakland | P | 306 |
| 1993 | Frank Thomas | Chicago | 1B | *392 |
| 1994 | Frank Thomas | Chicago | 1B | 372 |
| 1995 | Mo Vaughn | Boston | 1B | 308 |
| 1996 | Juan Gonzalez | Texas | OF | 290 |
| 1997 | Ken Griffey Jr. | Seattle | OF | *392 |
| 1998 | Juan Gonzalez | Texas | OF | 357 |
| 1999 | Ivan Rodriguez | Texas | C | 252 |
| 2000 | Jason Giambi | Oakland | 1B | 317 |
| 2001 | Ichiro Suzuki | Seattle | OF | 289 |
| 2002 | Miguel Tejada | Oakland | SS | 356 |
| 2003 | Alex Rodriguez | Texas | SS | 242 |
| 2004 | Vladimir Guerrero | Anaheim | OF | 354 |

### NATIONAL LEAGUE

| Year | Player | Team | Pos. | Points |
|---|---|---|---|---|
| 1931 | Frank Frisch | St. Louis | 2B | 65 |
| 1932 | Chuck Klein | Philadelphia | OF | 78 |
| 1933 | Carl Hubbell | New York | P | 77 |
| 1934 | Dizzy Dean | St. Louis | P | 78 |
| 1935 | Gabby Hartnett | Chicago | C | 75 |
| 1936 | Carl Hubbell | New York | P | 60 |
| 1937 | Joe Medwick | St. Louis | OF | 70 |
| 1938 | Ernie Lombardi | Cincinnati | C | 229 |
| 1939 | Bucky Walters | Cincinnati | P | 303 |
| 1940 | Frank McCormick | Cincinnati | 1B | 274 |
| 1941 | Dolf Camilli | Brooklyn | 1B | 300 |
| 1942 | Mort Cooper | St. Louis | P | 263 |
| 1943 | Stan Musial | St. Louis | OF | 267 |
| 1944 | Marty Marion | St. Louis | SS | 190 |
| 1945 | Phil Cavarretta | Chicago | 1B | 279 |
| 1946 | Stan Musial | St. Louis | 1B | 319 |
| 1947 | Bob Elliott | Boston | 3B | 205 |
| 1948 | Stan Musial | St. Louis | OF | 303 |
| 1949 | Jackie Robinson | Brooklyn | 2B | 264 |
| 1950 | Jim Konstanty | Philadelphia | P | 286 |
| 1951 | Roy Campanella | Brooklyn | C | 243 |
| 1952 | Hank Sauer | Chicago | OF | 226 |
| 1953 | Roy Campanella | Brooklyn | C | 297 |
| 1954 | Willie Mays | New York | OF | 283 |
| 1955 | Roy Campanella | Brooklyn | C | 226 |
| 1956 | Don Newcombe | Brooklyn | P | 223 |
| 1957 | Hank Aaron | Milwaukee | OF | 239 |
| 1958 | Ernie Banks | Chicago | SS | 283 |
| 1959 | Ernie Banks | Chicago | SS | 232 1/2 |
| 1960 | Dick Groat | Pittsburgh | SS | 276 |
| 1961 | Frank Robinson | Cincinnati | OF | 219 |
| 1962 | Maury Wills | Los Angeles | SS | 209 |
| 1963 | Sandy Koufax | Los Angeles | P | 237 |
| 1964 | Ken Boyer | St. Louis | 3B | 243 |
| 1965 | Willie Mays | San Francisco | OF | 224 |
| 1966 | Roberto Clemente | Pittsburgh | OF | 218 |
| 1967 | Orlando Cepeda | St. Louis | 1B | *280 |
| 1968 | Bob Gibson | St. Louis | P | 242 |
| 1969 | Willie McCovey | San Francisco | 1B | 265 |
| 1970 | Johnny Bench | Cincinnati | C | 326 |
| 1971 | Joe Torre | St. Louis | 3B | 318 |
| 1972 | Johnny Bench | Cincinnati | C | 263 |
| 1973 | Pete Rose | Cincinnati | OF | 274 |
| 1974 | Steve Garvey | Los Angeles | 1B | 270 |
| 1975 | Joe Morgan | Cincinnati | 2B | 321 1/2 |
| 1976 | Joe Morgan | Cincinnati | 2B | 311 |
| 1977 | George Foster | Cincinnati | OF | 291 |
| 1978 | Dave Parker | Pittsburgh | OF | 320 |
| 1979 | Willie Stargell | Pittsburgh | 1B | 216 |
| 1980 | Mike Schmidt | Philadelphia | 3B | *336 |
| 1981 | Mike Schmidt | Philadelphia | 3B | 321 |
| 1982 | Dale Murphy | Atlanta | OF | 283 |
| 1983 | Dale Murphy | Atlanta | OF | 318 |
| 1984 | Ryne Sandberg | Chicago | 2B | 326 |
| 1985 | Willie McGee | St. Louis | OF | 280 |
| 1986 | Mike Schmidt | Philadelphia | 3B | 287 |
| 1987 | Andre Dawson | Chicago | OF | 269 |
| 1988 | Kirk Gibson | Los Angeles | OF | 272 |
| 1989 | Kevin Mitchell | San Francisco | OF | 314 |
| 1990 | Barry Bonds | Pittsburgh | OF | 331 |
| 1991 | Terry Pendleton | Atlanta | 3B | 274 |
| 1992 | Barry Bonds | Pittsburgh | OF | 304 |
| 1993 | Barry Bonds | San Francisco | OF | 372 |
| 1994 | Jeff Bagwell | Houston | 1B | *392 |
| 1995 | Barry Larkin | Cincinnati | SS | 281 |
| 1996 | Ken Caminiti | San Diego | 3B | *392 |
| 1997 | Larry Walker | Colorado | OF | 359 |
| 1998 | Sammy Sosa | Chicago | OF | 438 |
| 1999 | Chipper Jones | Atlanta | 3B | 432 |
| 2000 | Jeff Kent | San Francisco | 2B | 392 |
| 2001 | Barry Bonds | San Francisco | OF | 438 |
| 2002 | Barry Bonds | San Francisco | OF | *448 |
| 2003 | Barry Bonds | San Francisco | OF | 426 |
| 2004 | Barry Bonds | San Francisco | OF | 407 |

*Unanimous selection.

## CY YOUNG MEMORIAL AWARD

| Year | Pitcher | Team | Votes |
|---|---|---|---|
| 1956— | Don Newcombe | Brooklyn | 10 |
| 1957— | Warren Spahn | Milwaukee | 15 |
| 1958— | Bob Turley | New York A.L. | 5 |
| 1959— | Early Wynn | Chicago A.L. | 13 |
| 1960— | Vernon Law | Pittsburgh | 8 |
| 1961— | Whitey Ford | New York A.L. | 9 |
| 1962— | Don Drysdale | Los Angeles N.L. | 14 |
| 1963— | Sandy Koufax | Los Angeles N.L. | *20 |
| 1964— | Dean Chance | Los Angeles A.L. | 17 |
| 1965— | Sandy Koufax | Los Angeles N.L. | *20 |
| 1966— | Sandy Koufax | Los Angeles N.L. | *20 |
| 1967— | A.L.—Jim Lonborg | Boston | 18 |
| | N.L.—Mike McCormick | San Francisco | 18 |
| 1968— | A.L.—Denny McLain | Detroit | *20 |
| | N.L.—Bob Gibson | St. Louis | *20 |
| 1969— | A.L.—Denny McLain | Detroit | 10 |
| | Mike Cuellar | Baltimore | 10 |
| | N.L.—Tom Seaver | New York | 23 |
| 1970— | A.L.—Jim Perry | Minnesota | 55 |
| | N.L.—Bob Gibson | St. Louis | 118 |
| 1971— | A.L.—Vida Blue | Oakland | 98 |
| | N.L.—Fergie Jenkins | Chicago | 97 |
| 1972— | A.L.—Gaylord Perry | Cleveland | 64 |
| | N.L.—Steve Carlton | Philadelphia | *120 |
| 1973— | A.L.—Jim Palmer | Baltimore | 88 |
| | N.L.—Tom Seaver | New York | 71 |
| 1974— | A.L.—Jim Hunter | Oakland | 90 |
| | N.L.—Mike Marshall | Los Angeles | 96 |
| 1975— | A.L.—Jim Palmer | Baltimore | 98 |
| | N.L.—Tom Seaver | New York | 98 |
| 1976— | A.L.—Jim Palmer | Baltimore | 108 |
| | N.L.—Randy Jones | San Diego | 96 |
| 1977— | A.L.—Sparky Lyle | New York | 56½ |
| | N.L.—Steve Carlton | Philadelphia | 104 |
| 1978— | A.L.—Ron Guidry | New York | *140 |
| | N.L.—Gaylord Perry | San Diego | 116 |
| 1979— | A.L.—Mike Flanagan | Baltimore | 136 |
| | N.L.—Bruce Sutter | Chicago | 72 |
| 1980— | A.L.—Steve Stone | Baltimore | 100 |
| | N.L.—Steve Carlton | Philadelphia | 118 |
| 1981— | A.L.—Rollie Fingers | Milwaukee | 126 |
| | N.L.—Fernando Valenzuela | Los Angeles | 70 |
| 1982— | A.L.—Pete Vuckovich | Milwaukee | 87 |
| | N.L.—Steve Carlton | Philadelphia | 112 |
| 1983— | A.L.—LaMarr Hoyt | Chicago | 116 |
| | N.L.—John Denny | Philadelphia | 103 |
| 1984— | A.L.—Willie Hernandez | Detroit | 88 |
| | N.L.—Rick Sutcliffe | Chicago | *120 |
| 1985— | A.L.—Bret Saberhagen | Kansas City | 127 |
| | N.L.—Dwight Gooden | New York | *120 |
| 1986— | A.L.—Roger Clemens | Boston | *140 |
| | N.L.—Mike Scott | Houston | 98 |
| 1987— | A.L.—Roger Clemens | Boston | 124 |
| | N.L.—Steve Bedrosian | Philadelphia | 57 |
| 1988— | A.L.—Frank Viola | Minnesota | 138 |
| | N.L.—Orel Hershiser | Los Angeles | *120 |
| 1989— | A.L.—Bret Saberhagen | Kansas City | 138 |
| | N.L.—Mark Davis | San Diego | 107 |
| 1990— | A.L.—Bob Welch | Oakland | 107 |
| | N.L.—Doug Drabek | Pittsburgh | 118 |
| 1991— | A.L.—Roger Clemens | Boston | 119 |
| | N.L.—Tom Glavine | Atlanta | 110 |
| 1992— | A.L.—Dennis Eckersley | Oakland | 107 |
| | N.L.—Greg Maddux | Chicago | 112 |
| 1993— | A.L.—Jack McDowell | Chicago | 124 |
| | N.L.—Greg Maddux | Atlanta | 119 |
| 1994— | A.L.—David Cone | Kansas City | 108 |
| | N.L.—Greg Maddux | Atlanta | *140 |
| 1995— | A.L.—Randy Johnson | Seattle | 136 |
| | N.L.—Greg Maddux | Atlanta | *140 |
| 1996— | A.L.—Pat Hentgen | Toronto | 110 |
| | N.L.—John Smoltz | Atlanta | 136 |
| 1997— | A.L.—Roger Clemens | Toronto | 134 |
| | N.L.—Pedro Martinez | Montreal | 134 |
| 1998— | A.L.—Roger Clemens | Toronto | *140 |
| | N.L.—Tom Glavine | Atlanta | 99 |
| 1999— | A.L.—Pedro Martinez | Boston | *140 |
| | N.L.—Randy Johnson | Arizona | 134 |
| 2000— | A.L.—Pedro Martinez | Boston | *140 |
| | N.L.—Randy Johnson | Arizona | 133 |
| 2001— | A.L.—Roger Clemens | New York | 122 |
| | N.L.—Randy Johnson | Arizona | 156 |
| 2002— | A.L.—Barry Zito | Oakland | 114 |
| | N.L.—Randy Johnson | Arizona | *160 |
| 2003— | A.L.—Roy Halladay | Toronto | 136 |
| | N.L.—Eric Gagne | Los Angeles | 146 |
| 2004 | A.L.—Johan Santana | Minnesota | *140 |
| | N.L.—Roger Clemens | Houston | 140 |

*Unanimous selection.

## ROOKIE OF THE YEAR

1947—Combined selection—Jackie Robinson, Brooklyn N.L., 1B
1948—Combined selection—Alvin Dark, Boston N.L., SS

### AMERICAN LEAGUE

| Year | Player | Team | Pos. | Votes |
|---|---|---|---|---|
| 1949— | Roy Sievers | St. Louis | OF | 10 |
| 1950— | Walt Dropo | Boston | 1B | 15 |
| 1951— | Gil McDougald | New York | 3B | 13 |
| 1952— | Harry Byrd | Philadelphia | P | 9 |
| 1953— | Harvey Kuenn | Detroit | SS | 23 |
| 1954— | Bob Grim | New York | P | 15 |
| 1955— | Herb Score | Cleveland | P | 18 |
| 1956— | Luis Aparicio | Chicago | SS | 22 |
| 1957— | Tony Kubek | New York | IF-OF | 23 |
| 1958— | Albie Pearson | Washington | OF | 14 |
| 1959— | Bob Allison | Washington | OF | 18 |
| 1960— | Ron Hansen | Baltimore | SS | 22 |
| 1961— | Don Schwall | Boston | P | 7 |
| 1962— | Tom Tresh | New York | OF-SS | 13 |
| 1963— | Gary Peters | Chicago | P | 10 |
| 1964— | Tony Oliva | Minnesota | OF | 19 |
| 1965— | Curt Blefary | Baltimore | OF | 12 |
| 1966— | Tommie Agee | Chicago | OF | 16 |
| 1967— | Rod Carew | Minnesota | 2B | 19 |
| 1968— | Stan Bahnsen | New York | P | 17 |
| 1969— | Lou Piniella | Kansas City | OF | 9 |
| 1970— | Thurman Munson | New York | C | 23 |
| 1971— | Chris Chambliss | Cleveland | 1B | 11 |
| 1972— | Carlton Fisk | Boston | C | *24 |

### NATIONAL LEAGUE

| Year | Player | Team | Pos. | Votes |
|---|---|---|---|---|
| 1949— | Don Newcombe | Brooklyn | P | 21 |
| 1950— | Sam Jethroe | Boston | OF | 11 |
| 1951— | Willie Mays | New York | OF | 18 |
| 1952— | Joe Black | Brooklyn | P | 19 |
| 1953— | Jim Gilliam | Brooklyn | 2B | 11 |
| 1954— | Wally Moon | St. Louis | OF | 17 |
| 1955— | Bill Virdon | St. Louis | OF | 15 |
| 1956— | Frank Robinson | Cincinnati | OF | *24 |
| 1957— | Jack Sanford | Philadelphia | P | 16 |
| 1958— | Orlando Cepeda | San Francisco | 1B | *†21 |
| 1959— | Willie McCovey | San Francisco | 1B | *24 |
| 1960— | Frank Howard | Los Angeles | OF | 12 |
| 1961— | Billy Williams | Chicago | OF | 10 |
| 1962— | Ken Hubbs | Chicago | 2B | 19 |
| 1963— | Pete Rose | Cincinnati | 2B | 17 |
| 1964— | Dick Allen | Philadelphia | 3B | 18 |
| 1965— | Jim Lefebvre | Los Angeles | 2B | 13 |
| 1966— | Tommy Helms | Cincinnati | 3B | 12 |
| 1967— | Tom Seaver | New York | P | 11 |
| 1968— | Johnny Bench | Cincinnati | C | 10½ |
| 1969— | Ted Sizemore | Los Angeles | 2B | 14 |
| 1970— | Carl Morton | Montreal | P | 11 |
| 1971— | Earl Williams | Atlanta | C | 18 |
| 1972— | Jon Matlack | New York | P | 19 |

## AMERICAN LEAGUE

| Year | Player | Team | Pos. | Votes |
|---|---|---|---|---|
| 1973— | Al Bumbry | Baltimore | OF | 13½ |
| 1974— | Mike Hargrove | Texas | 1B | 16½ |
| 1975— | Fred Lynn | Boston | OF | 23½ |
| 1976— | Mark Fidrych | Detroit | P | 22 |
| 1977— | Eddie Murray | Baltimore | DH-1B | 12½ |
| 1978— | Lou Whitaker | Detroit | 2B | 21 |
| 1979— | John Castino | Minnesota | 3B | 7 |
| | Alfredo Griffin | Toronto | SS | 7 |
| 1980— | Joe Charboneau | Cleveland | OF | 102 |
| 1981— | Dave Righetti | New York | P | 127 |
| 1982— | Cal Ripken | Baltimore | SS-3B | 132 |
| 1983— | Ron Kittle | Chicago | OF | 104 |
| 1984— | Alvin Davis | Seattle | 1B | 134 |
| 1985— | Ozzie Guillen | Chicago | SS | 101 |
| 1986— | Jose Canseco | Oakland | OF | 110 |
| 1987— | Mark McGwire | Oakland | 1B | *140 |
| 1988— | Walt Weiss | Oakland | SS | 103 |
| 1989— | Gregg Olson | Baltimore | P | 136 |
| 1990— | Sandy Alomar Jr. | Cleveland | C | *140 |
| 1991— | Chuck Knoblauch | Minnesota | 2B | 136 |
| 1992— | Pat Listach | Milwaukee | SS | 122 |
| 1993— | Tim Salmon | California | OF | *140 |
| 1994— | Bob Hamelin | Kansas City | DH | 134 |
| 1995— | Marty Cordova | Minnesota | 3B | 105 |
| 1996— | Derek Jeter | New York | SS | *140 |
| 1997— | Nomar Garciaparra | Boston | SS | *140 |
| 1998— | Ben Grieve | Oakland | OF | 130 |
| 1999— | Carlos Beltran | Kansas City | OF | 133 |
| 2000— | Kazuhiro Sasaki | Seattle | P | 104 |
| 2001— | Ichiro Suzuki | Seattle | OF | 138 |
| 2002— | Eric Hinske | Toronto | 3B | 122 |
| 2003— | Angel Berroa | Kansas City | SS | 88 |
| 2004— | Bobby Crosby | Oakland | SS | 138 |

*Unanimous selection. †Three writers did not vote.

## NATIONAL LEAGUE

| Year | Player | Team | Pos. | Votes |
|---|---|---|---|---|
| 1973— | Gary Matthews | San Francisco | OF | 11 |
| 1974— | Bake McBride | St. Louis | OF | 16 |
| 1975— | John Montefusco | San Francisco | P | 12 |
| 1976— | Butch Metzger | San Diego | P | 11 |
| | Pat Zachry | Cincinnati | P | 11 |
| 1977— | Andre Dawson | Montreal | OF | 10 |
| 1978— | Bob Horner | Atlanta | 3B | 12½ |
| 1979— | Rick Sutcliffe | Los Angeles | P | 20 |
| 1980— | Steve Howe | Los Angeles | P | 80 |
| 1981— | Fernando Valenzuela | Los Angeles | P | 107 |
| 1982— | Steve Sax | Los Angeles | 2B | 63 |
| 1983— | Darryl Strawberry | New York | OF | 106 |
| 1984— | Dwight Gooden | New York | P | 118 |
| 1985— | Vince Coleman | St. Louis | OF | *120 |
| 1986— | Todd Worrell | St. Louis | P | 118 |
| 1987— | Benito Santiago | San Diego | C | *120 |
| 1988— | Chris Sabo | Cincinnati | 3B | 79 |
| 1989— | Jerome Walton | Chicago | OF | 116 |
| 1990— | Dave Justice | Atlanta | OF | 118 |
| 1991— | Jeff Bagwell | Houston | 1B | 118 |
| 1992— | Eric Karros | Los Angeles | 1B | 116 |
| 1993— | Mike Piazza | Los Angeles | C | *140 |
| 1994— | Raul Mondesi | Los Angeles | OF | *140 |
| 1995— | Hideo Nomo | Los Angeles | P | 118 |
| 1996— | Todd Hollandsworth | Los Angeles | OF | 105 |
| 1997— | Scott Rolen | Philadelphia | 3B | *140 |
| 1998— | Kerry Wood | Chicago | P | 128 |
| 1999— | Scott Williamson | Cincinnati | P | 118 |
| 2000— | Rafael Furcal | Atlanta | SS-2B | 144 |
| 2001— | Albert Pujols | St. Louis | OF-3B-1B | *160 |
| 2002— | Jason Jennings | Colorado | P | 150 |
| 2003— | Dontrelle Willis | Florida | P | 118 |
| 2004— | Jason Bay | Pittsburgh | OF | 146 |

# MANAGER OF THE YEAR

## AMERICAN LEAGUE

| Year | Manager | Team | Points |
|---|---|---|---|
| 1983— | Tony La Russa | Chicago | 17 |
| 1984— | Sparky Anderson | Detroit | 96 |
| 1985— | Bobby Cox | Toronto | 104 |
| 1986— | John McNamara | Boston | 95 |
| 1987— | Sparky Anderson | Detroit | 90 |
| 1988— | Tony La Russa | Oakland | 103 |
| 1989— | Frank Robinson | Baltimore | 125 |
| 1990— | Jeff Torborg | Chicago | 128 |
| 1991— | Tom Kelly | Minnesota | 138 |
| 1992— | Tony La Russa | Oakland | 132 |
| 1993— | Gene Lamont | Chicago | 72 |
| 1994— | Buck Showalter | New York | 132 |
| 1995— | Lou Piniella | Seattle | 86 |
| 1996— | Johnny Oates | Texas | 89 |
| | Joe Torre | New York | 89 |
| 1997— | Dave Johnson | Baltimore | 88 |
| 1998— | Joe Torre | New York | 128 |
| 1999— | Jimy Williams | Boston | 115 |
| 2000— | Jerry Manuel | Chicago | 134 |
| 2001— | Lou Piniella | Seattle | 128 |
| 2002— | Mike Scioscia | Anaheim | 116 |
| 2003— | Tony Pena | Kansas City | 130 |
| 2004— | Buck Showalter | Texas | 101 |

## NATIONAL LEAGUE

| Year | Manager | Team | Points |
|---|---|---|---|
| 1983— | Tommy Lasorda | Los Angeles | 10 |
| 1984— | Jim Frey | Chicago | 101 |
| 1985— | Whitey Herzog | St. Louis | 86 |
| 1986— | Hal Lanier | Houston | 108 |
| 1987— | Buck Rodgers | Montreal | 92 |
| 1988— | Tommy Lasorda | Los Angeles | 101 |
| 1989— | Don Zimmer | Chicago | 118 |
| 1990— | Jim Leyland | Pittsburgh | 99 |
| 1991— | Bobby Cox | Atlanta | 96 |
| 1992— | Jim Leyland | Pittsburgh | 109 |
| 1993— | Dusty Baker | San Francisco | 105 |
| 1994— | Felipe Alou | Montreal | 138 |
| 1995— | Don Baylor | Colorado | 122 |
| 1996— | Bruce Bochy | San Diego | 76 |
| 1997— | Dusty Baker | San Francisco | 110 |
| 1998— | Larry Dierker | Houston | 102 |
| 1999— | Jack McKeon | Cincinnati | 115 |
| 2000— | Dusty Baker | San Francisco | 154 |
| 2001— | Larry Bowa | Philadelphia | 113 |
| 2002— | Tony La Russa | St. Louis | 129 |
| 2003— | Jack McKeon | Florida | 116 |
| 2004— | Bobby Cox | Atlanta | 140 |

# EARLY MOST VALUABLE PLAYER AWARDS

## CHALMERS AWARD

### AMERICAN LEAGUE

| Year | Player | Team | Pos. | Points |
|---|---|---|---|---|
| 1911— | Ty Cobb | Detroit | OF | 64 |
| 1912— | Tris Speaker | Boston | OF | 59 |
| 1913— | Walter Johnson | Washington | P | 54 |
| 1914— | Eddie Collins | Philadelphia | 2B | 63 |

### NATIONAL LEAGUE

| Year | Player | Team | Pos. | Points |
|---|---|---|---|---|
| 1911— | Frank Schulte | Chicago | OF | 29 |
| 1912— | Larry Doyle | New York | 2B | 48 |
| 1913— | Jake Daubert | Brooklyn | 1B | 50 |
| 1914— | Johnny Evers | Boston | 2B | 50 |

## LEAGUE AWARDS

### AMERICAN LEAGUE

| Year | Player | Team | Pos. | Points |
|---|---|---|---|---|
| 1922— | George Sisler | St. Louis | 1B | 59 |
| 1923— | Babe Ruth | New York | OF | 64 |
| 1924— | Walter Johnson | Washington | P | 55 |
| 1925— | Roger Peckinpaugh | Washington | SS | 45 |
| 1926— | George Burns | Cleveland | 1B | 63 |
| 1927— | Lou Gehrig | New York | 1B | 56 |
| 1928— | Mickey Cochrane | Philadelphia | C | 53 |
| 1929— | No selection | | | |

### NATIONAL LEAGUE

| Year | Player | Team | Pos. | Points |
|---|---|---|---|---|
| 1922— | No selection | | | |
| 1923— | No selection | | | |
| 1924— | Dazzy Vance | Brooklyn | P | 74 |
| 1925— | Rogers Hornsby | St. Louis | 2B | 73 |
| 1926— | Bob O'Farrell | St. Louis | C | 79 |
| 1927— | Paul Waner | Pittsburgh | OF | 72 |
| 1928— | Jim Bottomley | St. Louis | 1B | 76 |
| 1929— | Rogers Hornsby | Chicago | 2B | 60 |

# HALL OF FAME

## ROSTER OF MEMBERS

| Name | Des.* | Elec. year | Votes rec.† | Votes cast‡ | % of vote | Teams as player |
|---|---|---|---|---|---|---|
| Aaron, Hank | P | 1982 | 406 | 415 | 97.8 | Milwaukee NL, Atlanta NL, Milwaukee AL |
| Alexander, Grover C. | P | 1938 | 212 | 262 | 80.9 | Philadelphia NL, Chicago NL, St. Louis NL |
| Alston, Walter | M | 1983 | CV | — | — | St. Louis NL |
| Anderson, Sparky | M | 2000 | CV | — | — | Philadelphia NL |
| Anson, Cap | P | 1939 | C1 | — | — | Chicago NL |
| Aparicio, Luis | P | 1984 | 341 | 403 | 84.6 | Chicago AL, Baltimore AL, Boston AL |
| Appling, Luke | P | 1964 | 189 | 225 | 84.0 | Chicago AL |
| Ashburn, Richie | P | 1995 | CV | — | — | Philadelphia NL, Chicago NL, New York NL |
| Averill, Earl | P | 1975 | CV | — | — | Cleveland AL, Detroit AL, Boston NL |
| Baker, Home Run | P | 1955 | CV | — | — | Philadelphia AL, New York AL |
| Bancroft, Dave | P | 1971 | CV | — | — | Philadelphia NL, New York NL, Boston NL, Brooklyn NL |
| Banks, Ernie | P | 1977 | 321 | 383 | 83.8 | Chicago NL |
| Barlick, Al | U | 1989 | CV | — | — | |
| Barrow, Ed | E | 1953 | CV | — | — | |
| Beckley, Jake | P | 1971 | CV | — | — | Pittsburgh NL, Pittsburgh PL, New York NL, Cincinnati NL, St. Louis NL |
| Bell, Cool Papa | P | 1974 | SCNL | — | — | Negro Leagues |
| Bench, Johnny | P | 1989 | 431 | 447 | 96.4 | Cincinnati NL |
| Bender, Chief | P | 1953 | CV | — | — | Philadelphia AL, Philadelphia NL, Chicago AL |
| Berra, Yogi | P | 1972 | 339 | 396 | 85.6 | New York AL, New York NL |
| Boggs, Wade | P | 2005 | 474 | 516 | 91.9 | Boston AL, New York AL, Tampa Bay NL |
| Bottomley, Jim | P | 1974 | CV | — | — | St. Louis NL, Cincinnati NL, St. Louis AL |
| Boudreau, Lou | P | 1970 | 232 | 300 | 77.3 | Cleveland AL, Boston AL |
| Bresnahan, Roger | P | 1945 | C2 | — | — | Washington NL, Chicago NL, Baltimore AL, New York NL, St. Louis NL |
| Brett, George | P | 1999 | 488 | 497 | 98.2 | Kansas City AL |
| Brock, Lou | P | 1985 | 315 | 395 | 79.7 | Chicago NL, St. Louis NL |
| Brouthers, Dan | P | 1945 | C2 | — | — | Troy NL, Buffalo NL, Detroit NL, Boston NL, Boston PL, Boston AA,Brooklyn NL, Baltimore NL,Louisville NL, Philadelphia NL, New York NL |
| Brown, Three Finger | P | 1949 | C2 | — | — | St. Louis NL, Chicago NL, Cincinnati NL |
| Bulkeley, Morgan | E | 1937 | CC | — | — | |
| Bunning, Jim | P | 1996 | CV | — | — | Detroit AL, Philadelphia NL, Pittsburgh NL, Los Angeles NL |
| Burkett, Jesse | P | 1946 | C2 | — | — | New York NL, Cleveland NL, St. Louis NL, St. Louis AL, Boston AL |
| Campanella, Roy | P | 1969 | 270 | 340 | 79.4 | Brooklyn NL |
| Carew, Rod | P | 1991 | 401 | 443 | 90.5 | Minnesota AL, California AL |
| Carey, Max | P | 1961 | CV | — | — | Pittsburgh NL, Brooklyn NL |
| Carlton, Steve | P | 1994 | 436 | 455 | 95.8 | St. Louis NL, Philadelphia NL, San Francisco NL, Chicago AL, Cleveland AL, Minnesota AL |
| Carter, Gary | P | 2003 | 387 | 496 | 78.0 | Montreal NL, New York NL, San Francisco NL, Los Angeles NL |
| Cartwright, Alexander | O | 1938 | CC | — | — | |
| Cepeda, Orlando | P | 1999 | CV | — | — | San Francisco NL, St. Louis NL, Atlanta NL, Oakland AL, Boston AL, Kansas City AL |
| Chadwick, Henry | O | 1938 | CC | — | — | |
| Chance, Frank | P | 1946 | C2 | — | — | Chicago NL, New York AL |
| Chandler, Happy | E | 1982 | CV | — | — | |
| Charleston, Oscar | P | 1976 | SCNL | — | — | Negro Leagues |
| Chesbro, Jack | P | 1946 | C2 | — | — | Pittsburgh NL, New York AL, Boston AL |
| Chylak, Nestor | U | 1999 | CV | — | — | |
| Clarke, Fred | P | 1945 | C2 | — | — | Louisville NL, Pittsburgh NL |
| Clarkson, John | P | 1963 | CV | — | — | Worcester NL, Chicago NL, Boston NL, Cleveland NL |
| Clemente, Roberto | P | 1973 | 393 | 424 | 92.7 | Pittsburgh NL |

HISTORY *Hall of Fame*

| Name | Des.* | Elec. year | Votes rec.† | Votes cast‡ | % of vote | Teams as player |
|---|---|---|---|---|---|---|
| Cobb, Ty | P | 1936 | 222 | 226 | 98.2 | Detroit AL, Philadelphia AL |
| Cochrane, Mickey | P | 1947 | 128 | 161 | 79.5 | Philadelphia AL, Detroit AL |
| Collins, Eddie | P | 1939 | 213 | 274 | 77.7 | Philadelphia AL, Chicago AL |
| Collins, Jimmy | P | 1945 | C2 | — | — | Boston NL, Louisville NL, Boston AL, Philadelphia AL |
| Combs, Earle | P | 1970 | CV | — | — | New York AL |
| Comiskey, Charley | F/P | 1939 | C1 | — | — | St. Louis AA, Chicago PL, Cincinnati NL |
| Conlan, Jocko | U | 1974 | CV | — | — | Chicago AL |
| Connolly, Tommy | U | 1953 | CV | — | — | |
| Connor, Roger | P | 1976 | CV | — | — | Troy NL, New York NL, New York PL, Philadelphia NL, St. Louis NL |
| Coveleski, Stan | P | 1969 | CV | — | — | Philadelphia AL, Cleveland AL, Washington AL, New York AL |
| Crawford, Sam | P | 1957 | CV | — | — | Cincinnati NL, Detroit AL |
| Cronin, Joe | P | 1956 | 152 | 193 | 78.8 | Pittsburgh NL, Washington AL, Boston AL |
| Cummings, Candy | P | 1939 | C1 | — | — | Hartford NL, Cincinnati NL |
| Cuyler, Kiki | P | 1968 | CV | — | — | Pittsburgh NL, Chicago NL, Cincinnati NL, Brooklyn NL |
| Dandridge, Ray | P | 1987 | CV | — | — | Negro Leagues |
| Davis, George S. | P | 1998 | CV | — | — | Cleveland NL, New York NL, Chicago AL |
| Day, Leon | P | 1995 | CV | — | — | Negro Leagues |
| Dean, Dizzy | P | 1953 | 209 | 264 | 79.2 | St. Louis NL, Chicago NL, St. Louis AL |
| Delahanty, Ed | P | 1945 | C2 | — | — | Philadelphia NL, Cleveland PL, Washington AL |
| Dickey, Bill | P | 1954 | 202 | 252 | 80.2 | New York AL |
| Dihigo, Martin | P | 1977 | SCNL | — | — | Negro Leagues |
| DiMaggio, Joe | P | 1955 | 223 | 251 | 88.8 | New York AL |
| Doby, Larry | P | 1998 | CV | — | — | Cleveland AL, Chicago AL, Detroit AL |
| Doerr, Bobby | P | 1986 | CV | — | — | Boston AL |
| Drysdale, Don | P | 1984 | 316 | 403 | 78.4 | Brooklyn NL, Los Angeles NL |
| Duffy, Hugh | P | 1945 | C2 | — | — | Chicago NL, Chicago PL, Boston AA, Boston NL, Milwaukee AL, Philadelphia NL |
| Durocher, Leo | M | 1994 | CV | — | — | New York AL, Cincinnati NL, St. Louis NL, Brooklyn NL |
| Eckersley, Dennis | P | 2004 | 421 | 506 | 83.2 | Cleveland AL, Boston AL, Chicago NL, Oakland AL, St. Louis NL |
| Evans, Billy | U | 1973 | CV | — | — | |
| Evers, Johnny | P | 1946 | C2 | — | — | Chicago NL, Boston NL, Philadelphia NL, Chicago AL |
| Ewing, Buck | P | 1939 | C1 | — | — | Troy NL, New York NL, New York PL, Cleveland NL, Cincinnati NL |
| Faber, Red | P | 1964 | CV | — | — | Chicago AL |
| Feller, Bob | P | 1962 | 150 | 160 | 93.8 | Cleveland AL |
| Ferrell, Rick | P | 1984 | CV | — | — | St. Louis AL, Boston AL, Washington AL |
| Fingers, Rollie | P | 1992 | 349 | 430 | 81.2 | Oakland AL, San Diego NL, Milwaukee AL |
| Fisk, Carlton | P | 2000 | 397 | 499 | 79.6 | Boston AL, Chicago AL |
| Flick, Elmer | P | 1963 | CV | — | — | Philadelphia NL, Philadelphia AL, Cleveland AL |
| Ford, Whitey | P | 1974 | 284 | 365 | 77.8 | New York AL |
| Foster, Bill | P | 1996 | CV | — | — | Negro Leagues |
| Foster, Rube | P | 1981 | CV | — | — | Negro Leagues |
| Fox, Nellie | P | 1997 | CV | — | — | Philadelphia AL, Chicago AL, Houston NL |
| Foxx, Jimmie | P | 1951 | 179 | 226 | 79.2 | Philadelphia AL, Boston AL, Chicago NL, Philadelphia NL |
| Frick, Ford | E | 1970 | CV | — | — | |
| Frisch, Frankie | P | 1947 | 136 | 161 | 84.5 | New York NL, St. Louis NL |
| Galvin, Pud | P | 1965 | CV | — | — | Buffalo NL, Pittsburgh AA, Pittsburgh NL, Pittsburgh PL, St. Louis NL |
| Gehrig, Lou | P | 1939 | SE | — | — | New York AL |
| Gehringer, Charlie | P | 1949 | 159 | 187 | 85.0 | Detroit AL |
| Gibson, Bob | P | 1981 | 337 | 401 | 84.0 | St. Louis NL |
| Gibson, Josh | P | 1972 | SCNL | — | — | Negro Leagues |
| Giles, Warren | E | 1979 | CV | — | — | |
| Gomez, Lefty | P | 1972 | CV | — | — | New York AL, Washington AL |
| Goslin, Goose | P | 1968 | CV | — | — | Washington AL, St. Louis AL, Detroit AL |
| Greenberg, Hank | P | 1956 | 164 | 193 | 85.0 | Detroit AL, Pittsburgh NL |
| Griffith, Clark | E | 1946 | C2 | — | — | St. Louis AA, Boston AA, Chicago NL, Chicago AL, New York AL, Cincinnati NL, Washington AL |
| Grimes, Burleigh | P | 1964 | CV | — | — | Pittsburgh NL, Brooklyn NL, New York NL, Boston NL, St. Louis NL, Chicago NL, New York AL |
| Grove, Lefty | P | 1947 | 123 | 161 | 76.4 | Philadelphia AL, Boston AL |
| Hafey, Chick | P | 1971 | CV | — | — | St. Louis NL, Cincinnati NL |
| Haines, Jesse | P | 1970 | CV | — | — | Cincinnati NL, St. Louis NL |
| Hamilton, Billy | P | 1961 | CV | — | — | Kansas City AA, Philadelphia NL, Boston NL |
| Hanlon, Ned | M | 1996 | CV | — | — | Cleveland NL, Detroit NL, Pittsburgh NL, Pittsburgh PL, Baltimore NL |
| Harridge, Will | E | 1972 | CV | — | — | |
| Harris, Bucky | M | 1975 | CV | — | — | Washington AL, Detroit AL |
| Hartnett, Gabby | P | 1955 | 195 | 251 | 77.7 | Chicago NL, New York NL |
| Heilmann, Harry | P | 1952 | 203 | 234 | 86.8 | Detroit AL, Cincinnati NL |

| Name | Des.* | Elec. year | Votes rec.† | Votes cast‡ | % of vote | Teams as player |
|---|---|---|---|---|---|---|
| Herman, Billy | P | 1975 | CV | — | — | Chicago NL, Brooklyn NL, Boston NL, Pittsburgh NL |
| Hooper, Harry | P | 1971 | CV | — | — | Boston AL, Chicago AL |
| Hornsby, Rogers | P | 1942 | 182 | 233 | 78.1 | St. Louis NL, New York NL, Boston NL, Chicago NL, St. Louis AL |
| Hoyt, Waite | P | 1969 | CV | — | — | New York NL, Boston AL, New York AL, Detroit AL, Philadelphia AL, Brooklyn NL, Pittsburgh NL |
| Hubbard, Cal | U | 1976 | CV | — | — | |
| Hubbell, Carl | P | 1947 | 140 | 161 | 87.0 | New York NL |
| Huggins, Miller | M | 1964 | CV | — | — | Cincinnati NL, St. Louis NL |
| Hulbert, William | F | 1995 | CV | — | — | |
| Hunter, Catfish | P | 1987 | 315 | 413 | 76.3 | Kansas City AL, Oakland AL, New York AL |
| Irvin, Monte | P | 1973 | SCNL | — | — | New York NL, Chicago NL, Negro Leagues |
| Jackson, Reggie | P | 1993 | 396 | 423 | 93.6 | Kansas City AL, Oakland AL, Baltimore AL, New York AL, California AL |
| Jackson, Travis | P | 1982 | CV | — | — | New York NL |
| Jenkins, Ferguson | P | 1991 | 334 | 443 | 75.4 | Philadelphia NL, Chicago NL, Texas AL, Boston AL |
| Jennings, Hugh | P | 1945 | C2 | — | — | Louisville AA, Louisville NL, Baltimore NL, Brooklyn NL, Philadelphia NL, Detroit AL |
| Johnson, Ban | E | 1937 | CC | — | — | |
| Johnson, Judy | P | 1975 | SCNL | — | — | Negro Leagues |
| Johnson, Walter | P | 1936 | 189 | 226 | 83.6 | Washington AL |
| Joss, Addie | P | 1978 | CV | — | — | Cleveland AL |
| Kaline, Al | P | 1980 | 340 | 385 | 88.3 | Detroit AL |
| Keefe, Tim | P | 1964 | CV | — | — | Troy NL, New York AA, New York NL, New York PL, Philadelphia NL |
| Keeler, Willie | P | 1939 | 207 | 274 | 75.5 | New York NL, Brooklyn NL, Baltimore NL, New York AL |
| Kell, George | P | 1983 | CV | — | — | Philadelphia AL, Detroit AL, Boston AL, Chicago AL, Baltimore AL |
| Kelley, Joe | P | 1971 | CV | — | — | Boston NL, Pittsburgh NL, Baltimore NL, Brooklyn NL, Baltimore AL, Cincinnati NL |
| Kelly, George | P | 1973 | CV | — | — | New York NL, Pittsburgh NL, Cincinnati NL, Chicago NL, Brooklyn NL |
| Kelly, King | P | 1945 | C2 | — | — | Cincinnati NL, Chicago NL, Boston NL, Boston PL, Cincinnati AA, Boston AA, New York NL |
| Killebrew, Harmon | P | 1984 | 335 | 403 | 83.1 | Washington AL, Minnesota AL, Kansas City AL |
| Kiner, Ralph | P | 1975 | 273 | 362 | 75.4 | Pittsburgh NL, Chicago NL, Cleveland AL |
| Klein, Chuck | P | 1980 | CV | — | — | Philadelphia NL, Chicago NL, Pittsburgh NL |
| Klem, Bill | U | 1953 | CV | — | — | |
| Koufax, Sandy | P | 1972 | 344 | 396 | 86.9 | Brooklyn NL, Los Angeles NL |
| Lajoie, Nap | P | 1937 | 168 | 201 | 83.6 | Philadelphia NL, Philadelphia AL, Cleveland AL |
| Landis, Kenesaw M. | E | 1944 | C2 | — | — | |
| Lasorda, Tommy | M | 1997 | CV | — | — | Brooklyn NL, Kansas City AL |
| Lazzeri, Tony | P | 1991 | CV | — | — | New York AL, Chicago NL, Brooklyn NL, New York NL |
| Lemon, Bob | P | 1976 | 305 | 388 | 78.6 | Cleveland AL |
| Leonard, Buck | P | 1972 | SCNL | — | — | Negro Leagues |
| Lindstrom, Fred | P | 1976 | CV | — | — | New York NL, Pittsburgh NL, Chicago NL, Brooklyn NL |
| Lloyd, John Henry | P | 1977 | SCNL | — | — | Negro Leagues |
| Lombardi, Ernie | P | 1986 | CV | — | — | Brooklyn NL, Cincinnati NL, Boston NL, New York NL |
| Lopez, Al | M | 1977 | CV | — | — | Brooklyn NL, Boston NL, Pittsburgh NL, Cleveland AL |
| Lyons, Ted | P | 1955 | 217 | 251 | 86.5 | Chicago AL |
| Mack, Connie | M | 1937 | CC | — | — | Washington NL, Buffalo PL, Pittsburgh NL |
| MacPhail, Larry | E | 1978 | CV | — | — | |
| MacPhail, Lee | E | 1998 | CV | — | — | |
| Mantle, Mickey | P | 1974 | 322 | 365 | 88.2 | New York AL |
| Manush, Heinie | P | 1964 | CV | — | — | Detroit AL, St. Louis AL, Washington AL, Boston AL, Brooklyn NL, Pittsburgh NL |
| Maranville, Rabbit | P | 1954 | 209 | 252 | 82.9 | Boston NL, Pittsburgh NL, Chicago NL, Brooklyn NL, St. Louis NL |
| Marichal, Juan | P | 1983 | 313 | 374 | 83.7 | San Francisco NL, Boston AL, Los Angeles NL |
| Marquard, Rube | P | 1971 | CV | — | — | New York NL, Brooklyn NL, Cincinnati NL, Boston NL |
| Mathews, Eddie | P | 1978 | 301 | 379 | 79.4 | Boston NL, Milwaukee NL, Atlanta NL, Houston NL, Detroit AL |
| Mathewson, Christy | P | 1936 | 205 | 226 | 90.7 | New York NL, Cincinnati NL |
| Mays, Willie | P | 1979 | 409 | 432 | 94.7 | New York (Giants) NL, San Francisco NL, New York (Mets) NL |
| Mazeroski, Bill | P | 2001 | CV | — | — | Pittsburgh NL |
| McCarthy, Joe | M | 1957 | CV | — | — | |
| McCarthy, Tommy | P | 1946 | C2 | — | — | Boston UA, Boston NL, Philadelphia NL, St. Louis AA, Brooklyn NL |
| McCovey, Willie | P | 1986 | 346 | 425 | 81.4 | San Francisco NL, San Diego NL, Oakland AL |
| McGinnity, Joe | P | 1946 | C2 | — | — | Baltimore NL, Brooklyn NL, Baltimore AL, New York NL |
| McGowan, Bill | U | 1992 | CV | — | — | |

| Name | Des.* | Elec. year | Votes rec.† | Votes cast‡ | % of vote | Teams as player |
|---|---|---|---|---|---|---|
| McGraw, John | M | 1937 | CC | — | — | Baltimore AA, Baltimore NL, St. Louis NL, Baltimore AL, New York NL |
| McKechnie, Bill | M | 1962 | CV | — | — | Pittsburgh NL, Boston NL, New York AL, New York NL, Cincinnati NL |
| McPhee, Bid | P | 2000 | CV | — | — | Cincinnati AA, Cincinnati NL |
| Medwick, Joe | P | 1968 | 240 | 283 | 84.8 | St. Louis NL, Brooklyn NL, New York NL, Boston NL |
| Mize, Johnny | P | 1981 | CV | — | — | St. Louis NL, New York NL, New York AL |
| Molitor, Paul | P | 2004 | 431 | 506 | 85.2 | Milwaukee AL, Toronto AL, Minnesota AL |
| Morgan, Joe | P | 1990 | 363 | 444 | 81.8 | Houston NL, Cincinnati NL, San Francisco NL, Philadelphia NL, Oakland AL |
| Murray, Eddie | P | 2003 | 423 | 496 | 85.3 | Baltimore AL, Los Angeles NL, New York NL, Cleveland AL, Anaheim AL |
| Musial, Stan | P | 1969 | 317 | 340 | 93.2 | St. Louis NL |
| Newhouser, Hal | P | 1992 | CV | — | — | Detroit AL, Cleveland AL |
| Nichols, Kid | P | 1949 | C2 | — | — | Boston NL, St. Louis NL, Philadelphia NL |
| Niekro, Phil | P | 1997 | 380 | 473 | 80.3 | Milwaukee NL, Atlanta NL, New York AL, Cleveland AL, Toronto AL |
| O'Rourke, Jim | P | 1945 | C2 | — | — | Boston NL, Providence NL, Buffalo NL, New York NL, New York PL, Washington NL |
| Ott, Mel | P | 1951 | 197 | 226 | 87.2 | New York NL |
| Paige, Satchel | P | 1971 | SCNL | — | — | Cleveland AL, St. Louis AL, Kansas City AL, Negro Leagues |
| Palmer, Jim | P | 1990 | 411 | 444 | 92.6 | Baltimore AL |
| Pennock, Herb | P | 1948 | 94 | 121 | 77.7 | Philadelphia AL, Boston AL, New York AL |
| Perez, Tony | P | 2000 | 385 | 499 | 77.2 | Cincinnati NL, Montreal NL, Boston AL, Philadelphia NL |
| Perry, Gaylord | P | 1991 | 342 | 443 | 77.2 | San Francisco NL, Cleveland AL, Texas AL, San Diego NL, New York AL, Atlanta NL, Seattle AL, Kansas City AL |
| Plank, Eddie | P | 1946 | C2 | — | — | Philadelphia AL, St. Louis AL |
| Puckett, Kirby | P | 2001 | 423 | 515 | 82.1 | Minnesota AL |
| Radbourn, Old Hoss | P | 1939 | C1 | — | — | Buffalo NL, Providence NL, Boston NL, Boston PL, Cincinnati NL |
| Reese, Pee Wee | P | 1984 | CV | — | — | Brooklyn NL, Los Angeles NL |
| Rice, Sam | P | 1963 | CV | — | — | Washington AL, Cleveland AL |
| Rickey, Branch | E | 1967 | CV | — | — | St. Louis AL, New York AL |
| Rixey, Eppa | P | 1963 | CV | — | — | Philadelphia NL, Cincinnati NL |
| Rizzuto, Phil | P | 1994 | CV | — | — | New York AL |
| Roberts, Robin | P | 1976 | 337 | 388 | 86.9 | Philadelphia NL, Baltimore AL, Houston NL, Chicago NL |
| Robinson, Brooks | P | 1983 | 344 | 374 | 92.0 | Baltimore AL |
| Robinson, Frank | P | 1982 | 370 | 415 | 89.2 | Cincinnati NL, Baltimore AL, Los Angeles NL, California AL, Cleveland AL |
| Robinson, Jackie | P | 1962 | 124 | 160 | 77.5 | Brooklyn NL |
| Robinson, Wilbert | M | 1945 | C2 | — | — | Philadelphia AA, Baltimore AA, Baltimore NL, St. Louis NL, Baltimore AL |
| Rogan, Bullet Joe | P | 1998 | CV | — | — | Negro Leagues |
| Roush, Edd | P | 1962 | CV | — | — | Chicago AL, New York NL, Cincinnati NL |
| Ruffing, Red | P | 1967 | 266 | 306 | 86.9 | Boston AL, New York AL, Chicago AL |
| Rusie, Amos | P | 1977 | CV | — | — | Indianapolis NL, New York NL, Cincinnati NL |
| Ruth, Babe | P | 1936 | 215 | 226 | 95.1 | Boston AL, New York AL, Boston NL |
| Ryan, Nolan | P | 1999 | 491 | 497 | 98.8 | New York NL, California AL, Houston NL, Texas AL |
| Sandberg, Ryne | P | 2005 | 393 | 516 | 76.2 | Philadelphia NL, Chicago NL |
| Schalk, Ray | P | 1955 | CV | — | — | Chicago AL, New York NL |
| Schmidt, Mike | P | 1995 | 444 | 460 | 96.5 | Philadelphia NL |
| Schoendienst, Red | P | 1989 | CV | — | — | St. Louis NL, New York (Giants) NL, Milwaukee NL |
| Seaver, Tom | P | 1992 | 425 | 430 | 98.8 | New York NL, Cincinnati NL, Chicago AL, Boston AL |
| Selee, Frank | M | 1999 | CV | — | — | |
| Sewell, Joe | P | 1977 | CV | — | — | Cleveland AL, New York AL |
| Simmons, Al | P | 1953 | 199 | 264 | 75.4 | Philadelphia AL, Chicago AL, Detroit AL, Washington AL, Boston NL, Cincinnati NL, Boston AL |
| Sisler, George | P | 1939 | 235 | 274 | 85.8 | St. Louis AL, Washington AL, Boston NL |
| Slaughter, Enos | P | 1985 | CV | — | — | St. Louis NL, New York AL, Kansas City AL, Milwaukee NL |
| Smith, Hilton | P | 2001 | CV | — | — | Negro Leagues |
| Smith, Ozzie | P | 2002 | 433 | 472 | 91.7 | San Diego NL, St. Louis NL |
| Snider, Duke | P | 1980 | 333 | 385 | 86.5 | Brooklyn NL, Los Angeles NL, New York NL, San Francisco NL |
| Spahn, Warren | P | 1973 | 316 | 380 | 83.2 | Boston NL, Milwaukee NL, New York NL, San Francisco NL |
| Spalding, Al | P | 1939 | C1 | — | — | Chicago NL |

| Name | Des.* | Elec. year | Votes rec.† | Votes cast‡ | % of vote | Teams as player |
|---|---|---|---|---|---|---|
| Speaker, Tris | P | 1937 | 165 | 201 | 82.1 | Boston AL, Cleveland AL, Washington AL, Philadelphia AL |
| Stargell, Willie | P | 1988 | 352 | 427 | 82.4 | Pittsburgh NL |
| Stearnes, Turkey | P | 2000 | CV | — | — | Negro Leagues |
| Stengel, Casey | M | 1966 | CV | — | — | Brooklyn NL, Pittsburgh NL, Philadelphia NL, New York NL, Boston NL |
| Sutton, Don | P | 1998 | 386 | 473 | 81.6 | Los Angeles NL, Houston NL, Milwaukee AL, Oakland AL, California AL |
| Terry, Bill | P | 1954 | 195 | 252 | 77.4 | New York NL |
| Thompson, Sam | P | 1974 | CV | — | — | Detroit NL, Philadelphia NL, Detroit AL |
| Tinker, Joe | P | 1946 | C2 | — | — | Chicago NL, Cincinnati NL |
| Traynor, Pie | P | 1948 | 93 | 121 | 76.9 | Pittsburgh NL |
| Vance, Dazzy | P | 1955 | 205 | 251 | 81.7 | Pittsburgh NL, New York AL, Brooklyn NL, St. Louis NL, Cincinnati NL |
| Vaughan, Arky | P | 1985 | CV | — | — | Pittsburgh NL, Brooklyn NL |
| Veeck, Bill | E | 1991 | CV | — | — | |
| Waddell, Rube | P | 1946 | C2 | — | — | Louisville NL, Pittsburgh NL, Chicago NL, Philadelphia AL, St. Louis AL |
| Wagner, Honus | P | 1936 | 215 | 226 | 95.1 | Louisville NL, Pittsburgh NL |
| Wallace, Bobby | P | 1953 | CV | — | — | Cleveland NL, St. Louis NL, St. Louis AL |
| Walsh, Ed | P | 1946 | C2 | — | — | Chicago AL, Boston NL |
| Waner, Lloyd | P | 1967 | CV | — | — | Pittsburgh NL, Boston NL, Cincinnati NL, Philadelphia NL, Brooklyn NL |
| Waner, Paul | P | 1952 | 195 | 234 | 83.3 | Pittsburgh NL, Brooklyn NL, Boston NL, New York AL |
| Ward, Monte | P | 1964 | CV | — | — | Providence NL, New York NL, Brooklyn PL, Brooklyn NL |
| Weaver, Earl | M | 1996 | CV | — | — | |
| Weiss, George | E | 1971 | CV | — | — | |
| Welch, Mickey | P | 1973 | CV | — | — | Troy NL, New York NL |
| Wells, Willie | P | 1997 | CV | — | — | Negro Leagues |
| Wheat, Zack | P | 1959 | CV | — | — | Brooklyn NL, Philadelphia AL |
| Wilhelm, Hoyt | P | 1985 | 331 | 395 | 83.8 | New York NL, St. Louis NL, Cleveland AL, Baltimore AL, Chicago AL, California AL, Atlanta NL, Chicago NL, Los Angeles NL |
| Williams, Billy | P | 1987 | 354 | 413 | 85.7 | Chicago NL, Oakland AL |
| Williams, Smokey Joe | P | 1999 | CV | — | — | Negro Leagues |
| Williams, Ted | P | 1966 | 282 | 302 | 93.4 | Boston AL |
| Willis, Vic | P | 1995 | CV | — | — | Boston NL, Pittsburgh NL, St. Louis NL |
| Wilson, Hack | P | 1979 | CV | — | — | New York NL, Chicago NL, Brooklyn NL, Philadelphia NL |
| Winfield, Dave | P | 2001 | 435 | 515 | 84.5 | San Diego NL, New York AL, California AL, Toronto AL, Minnesota AL, Cleveland AL |
| Wright, George | P | 1937 | CC | — | — | Boston NL, Providence NL |
| Wright, Harry | M | 1953 | CV | — | — | Boston NL |
| Wynn, Early | P | 1972 | 301 | 396 | 76.0 | Washington AL, Cleveland AL, Chicago AL |
| Yastrzemski, Carl | P | 1989 | 423 | 447 | 94.6 | Boston AL |
| Yawkey, Tom | E | 1980 | CV | — | — | |
| Young, Cy | P | 1937 | 153 | 201 | 76.1 | Cleveland NL, St. Louis NL, Boston AL, Cleveland AL, Boston NL |
| Youngs, Ross | P | 1972 | CV | — | — | New York NL |
| Yount, Robin | P | 1999 | 385 | 497 | 77.5 | Milwaukee AL |

*Designation for which he was honored. Abbreviations: E—executive; F—founder; M—manager; O—organizer; P—player; U—umpire.

†Where an abbreviation is listed rather than a vote total, the enshrinee was selected by one of the following groups: Centennial Commission (CC), committee of old-time players and writers (C1), committee on old-timers (C2), Committee on Veterans (CV), special election by Baseball Writers' Association of America (SE) or Special Committee on Negro Leagues (SCNL).

‡Votes cast by eligible members of the Baseball Writers' Association of America.

League abbreviations: AA—American Association; AL—American League; NL—National League; PL—Players League; UA—Union Association.

# MINOR LEAGUES

Farm systems

International League

Mexican League

Pacific Coast League

Eastern League

Southern League

Texas League

California League

Carolina League

Florida State League

Midwest League

South Atlantic League

New York-Pennsylvania League

Northwest League

Appalachian League

Pioneer League

Arizona League

Gulf Coast League

Minor league index

# 2005 FARM SYSTEMS

## AMERICAN LEAGUE

**ANAHEIM (6):** AAA—Salt Lake. AA—Arkansas. A—Rancho Cucamonga, Cedar Rapids. Rookie—Orem, Mesa Angels.
**BALTIMORE (7):** AAA—Ottawa. AA—Bowie. A—Frederick, Delmarva, Aberdeen. Rookie—Bluefield, Gulf Coast Orioles.
**BOSTON (6):** AAA—Pawtucket. AA—Portland (Maine). A—Wilmington, Capital City, Lowell. Rookie—Gulf Coast Red Sox.
**CHICAGO (6):** AAA—Charlotte. AA—Birmingham. A—Winston-Salem, Kannapolis. Rookie—Bristol, Great Falls.
**CLEVELAND (6):** AAA—Buffalo. AA—Akron. A—Kinston, Lake County, Mahoning Valley. Rookie—Burlington (N.C.).
**DETROIT (6):** AAA—Toledo. AA—Erie. A—Lakeland, West Michigan, Oneonta. Rookie—Gulf Coast Tigers.
**KANSAS CITY (6):** AAA—Omaha. AA—Wichita. A—High Desert, Burlington (Iowa). Rookie—Idaho Falls, Arizona Royals.
**MINNESOTA (6):** AAA—Rochester. AA—New Britain. A—Fort Myers, Beloit. Rookie—Elizabethton, Gulf Coast Twins.
**NEW YORK (6):** AAA—Columbus (Ohio). AA—Trenton. A—Tampa, Charleston (S.C.), Staten Island. Rookie—Gulf Coast Yankees.
**OAKLAND (6):** AAA—Sacramento. AA—Midland. A—Stockton, Kane County, Vancouver. Rookie—Scottsdale A's.
**SEATTLE (6):** AAA—Tacoma. AA—San Antonio. A—Inland Empire, Wisconsin, Everett. Rookie—Peoria (Ariz.) Mariners.
**TAMPA BAY (6):** AAA—Durham. AA—Montgomery. A—Visalia, Southwest Michigan, Hudson Valley. Rookie—Princeton.
**TEXAS (6):** AAA—Oklahoma. AA—Frisco. A—Bakersfield, Clinton, Spokane. Rookie—Arizona Rangers.
**TORONTO (6):** AAA—Syracuse. AA—New Hampshire. A—Dunedin, Lansing, Auburn. Rookie—Pulaski.

## NATIONAL LEAGUE

**ARIZONA (6):** AAA—Tucson. AA—Tennessee. A—Lancaster, South Bend, Yakima. Rookie—Missoula.
**ATLANTA (6):** AAA—Richmond. AA—Mississippi. A—Myrtle Beach, Rome. Rookie—Danville, Gulf Coast Braves.
**CHICAGO (6):** AAA—Iowa. AA—West Tenn. A—Daytona, Peoria (Ill.), Boise. Rookie—Mesa Cubs.
**CINCINNATI (6):** AAA—Louisville. AA—Chattanooga. A—Sarasota, Dayton. Rookie—Billings, Gulf Coast Reds.
**COLORADO (6):** AAA—Colorado Springs. AA—Tulsa. A—Modesto, Asheville, Tri-City (Wash.). Rookie—Casper.
**FLORIDA (6):** AAA—Albuquerque. AA—Carolina. A—Jupiter, Greensboro, Jamestown. Rookie—Gulf Coast Marlins.
**HOUSTON (6):** AAA—Round Rock. AA—Corpus Christi. A—Salem, Lexington, Tri-City (N.Y.). Rookie—Greeneville.
**LOS ANGELES (6):** AAA—Las Vegas. AA—Jacksonville. A—Vero Beach, Columbus (Ga.). Rookie—Ogden, Gulf Coast Dodgers.
**MILWAUKEE (6):** AAA—Nashville. AA—Huntsville. A—Brevard County, West Virginia. Rookie—Helena, Maryvale.
**NEW YORK (7):** AAA—Norfolk. AA—Binghamton. A—St. Lucie, Hagerstown, Brooklyn. Rookie—Kingsport, Gulf Coast Mets.
**PHILADELPHIA (6):** AAA—Scranton/Wilkes-Barre. AA—Reading. A—Clearwater, Lakewood, Batavia. Rookie—Gulf Coast Phillies.
**PITTSBURGH (6):** AAA—Indianapolis. AA—Altoona. A—Lynchburg, Hickory, Williamsport. Rookie—Gulf Coast Pirates.
**ST. LOUIS (6):** AAA—Memphis. AA—Springfield. A—Palm Beach, Quad Cities, New Jersey. Rookie—Johnson City.
**SAN DIEGO (6):** AAA—Portland (Ore.). AA—Mobile. A—Lake Elsinore, Fort Wayne, Eugene. Rookie—Arizona Padres.
**SAN FRANCISCO (6):** AAA—Fresno. AA—Norwich. A—San Jose, Augusta, Salem-Keizer. Rookie—Arizona Giants.
**WASHINGTON (6):** AAA—New Orleans. AA—Harrisburg. A—Potomac, Savannah, Vermont. Rookie—Gulf Coast Nationals.

# INTERNATIONAL LEAGUE

## LEAGUE OFFICE

**President**
Randy Mobley

**Address**
55 S. High St., Suite 202
Dublin, OH 43017

**Phone**
614-791-9300

## TEAMS

### BUFFALO BISONS

**General manager**
Mike Buczkowski
**Manager**
Marty Brown
**Ballpark (capacity, surface)**
Dunn Tire Park (18,500, grass)
**Affiliation**
Indians
**Address**
P.O. Box 450
Buffalo, NY 14205
**Phone**
716-846-2000

### CHARLOTTE KNIGHTS

**General manager**
Bill Blackwell
**Manager**
Nick Capra
**Ballpark (capacity, surface)**
Knights Stadium (10,000, grass)
**Affiliation**
White Sox
**Address**
2280 Deerfield Drive
Fort Mill, SC 29715
**Phone**
704-357-8071

### COLUMBUS CLIPPERS

**General manager/president**
Ken Schnacke
**Manager**
Bucky Dent
**Ballpark (capacity, surface)**
Cooper Stadium (15,000, grass)
**Affiliation**
Yankees
**Address**
1155 W. Mound St.
Columbus, OH 43223
**Phone**
614-462-5250

### DURHAM BULLS

**General manager**
Mike Birling
**Manager**
Bill Evers
**Ballpark (capacity, surface)**
Durham Bulls Athletic Park
(10,000, grass)
**Affiliation**
Devil Rays
**Address**
409 Blackwell St.
Durham, NC 27701
**Phone**
919-687-6500

### INDIANAPOLIS INDIANS

**General manager**
Cal Burleson
**Manager**
Trent Jewett
**Ballpark (capacity, surface)**
Victory Field (15,500, grass)
**Affiliation**
Pirates
**Address**
501 W. Maryland St.
Indianapolis, IN 46225
**Phone**
317-269-3542

### LOUISVILLE BATS

**President**
Gary Ulmer
**Manager**
Rick Sweet
**Ballpark (capacity, surface)**
Louisville Slugger Field (13,200, grass)
**Affiliation**
Reds
**Address**
401 E. Main Street
Louisville, KY 40202
**Phone**
502-212-2287

### NORFOLK TIDES

**General manager**
Dave Rosenfield
**Manager**
John Stearns
**Ballpark (capacity, surface)**
Harbor Park (12,067, grass)
**Affiliation**
Mets
**Address**
150 Park Ave.
Norfolk, VA 23510
**Phone**
757-622-2222

### OTTAWA LYNX

**General manager**
Kyle Bostwick
**Manager**
Dave Trembley
**Ballpark (capacity, surface)**
Lynx Stadium (10,332, grass)
**Affiliation**
Orioles
**Address**
300 Coventry Rd.
Ottawa, Ontario K1K 4P5
**Phone**
613-747-5969

### PAWTUCKET RED SOX

**President**
Mike Tamburro
**Manager**
Ron Johnson
**Ballpark (capacity, surface)**
McCoy Stadium (10,031, grass)
**Affiliation**
Red Sox
**Address**
P.O. Box 2365
Pawtucket, RI 02861
**Phone**
401-724-7303

### RICHMOND BRAVES

**General manager**
Bruce Baldwin
**Manager**
Pat Kelly
**Ballpark (capacity, surface)**
The Diamond (12,134, grass)
**Affiliation**
Braves
**Address**
P.O. Box 6667
Richmond, VA 23230
**Phone**
804-359-4444

### ROCHESTER RED WINGS

**General manager**
Dan Mason
**Manager**
Phil Roof
**Ballpark (capacity, surface)**
Frontier Field (10,840, grass)
**Affiliation**
Twins
**Address**
1 Morrie Silver Way
Rochester, NY 14608
**Phone**
585-454-1001

### SCRANTON/WILKES-BARRE RED BARONS

**General manager**
Tom Zunschaack
**Manager**
Gene Lamont
**Ballpark (capacity, surface)**
Lackawanna County Multi-Purpose
Stadium (10,982, artificial)
**Affiliation**
Phillies
**Address**
P.O. Box 3449
Scranton, PA 18505
**Phone**
570-969-2255

## SYRACUSE SKYCHIEFS

**General manager**
John Simone
**Manager**
Marty Pevey
**Ballpark (capacity, surface)**
TBA
**Affiliation**
Blue Jays
**Address**
One Tex Simone Dr.
Syracuse, NY 13208
**Phone**
315-474-7833

## TOLEDO MUD HENS

**General manager**
Joe Napoli
**Manager**
Larry Parrish
**Ballpark (capacity, surface)**
Fifth Third Field (8,943, grass)
**Affiliation**
Tigers
**Address**
406 Washington St.
Toledo, OH 43604
**Phone**
419-725-4367

# 2004 FINAL STANDINGS

### NORTH DIVISION

| Team | W | L | T | Pct. | GB |
|---|---|---|---|---|---|
| Buffalo (Indians) | 83 | 61 | - | .576 | ... |
| Pawtucket (Red Sox) | 73 | 71 | - | .507 | 10.0 |
| Rochester (Twins) | 73 | 71 | - | .507 | 10.0 |
| Scranton/Wilkes-Barre (Phillies) | 69 | 73 | - | .486 | 13.0 |
| Ottawa (Orioles) | 66 | 78 | - | .458 | 17.0 |
| Syracuse (Blue Jays) | 66 | 78 | - | .458 | 17.0 |

### SOUTH DIVISION

| Team | W | L | T | Pct. | GB |
|---|---|---|---|---|---|
| Richmond (Braves) | 79 | 62 | - | .560 | ... |
| Durham (Devil Rays) | 77 | 67 | - | .535 | 3.5 |
| Norfolk (Mets) | 72 | 72 | - | .500 | 8.5 |
| Charlotte (White Sox) | 68 | 74 | - | .479 | 11.5 |

### WEST DIVISION

| Team | W | L | T | Pct. | GB |
|---|---|---|---|---|---|
| Columbus (Yankees) | 80 | 64 | - | .556 | ... |
| Louisville (Reds) | 67 | 77 | - | .465 | 13.0 |
| Indianapolis (Brewers) | 66 | 78 | - | .458 | 14.0 |
| Toledo (Tigers) | 65 | 78 | - | .455 | 14.5 |

## COMPOSITE

| Team | W | L | T | PCT | GB | BUF | RMD | COL | DUR | PAW | ROC | NOR | SWB | CHR | LOU | IND | OTT | SYR | TOL |
|---|---|---|---|---|---|---|---|---|---|---|---|---|---|---|---|---|---|---|---|
| Buffalo (Indians) | 83 | 61 | - | .576 | ... | X | 4 | 1 | 5 | 8 | 10 | 4 | 11 | 6 | 5 | 6 | 10 | 10 | 3 |
| Richmond (Braves) | 79 | 62 | - | .560 | 21/2 | 4 | X | 7 | 9 | 7 | 6 | 9 | 3 | 8 | 3 | 7 | 4 | 5 | 7 |
| Columbus (Yankees) | 80 | 64 | - | .556 | 3 | 7 | 5 | X | 6 | 3 | 3 | 7 | 3 | 4 | 11 | 8 | 8 | 7 | 8 |
| Durham (Devil Rays) | 77 | 67 | - | .535 | 6 | 3 | 7 | 6 | X | 4 | 6 | 8 | 5 | 10 | 5 | 7 | 3 | 5 | 8 |
| Pawtucket (Red Sox) | 73 | 71 | - | .507 | 10 | 8 | 1 | 5 | 4 | X | 7 | 4 | 12 | 1 | 2 | 6 | 11 | 10 | 2 |
| Rochester (Twins) | 73 | 71 | - | .507 | 10 | 6 | 2 | 5 | 2 | 9 | X | 5 | 7 | 5 | 6 | 5 | 9 | 10 | 2 |
| Norfolk (Mets) | 72 | 72 | - | .500 | 11 | 4 | 7 | 5 | 8 | 4 | 3 | X | 4 | 8 | 8 | 5 | 3 | 5 | 8 |
| Scranton-WB (Phillies) | 69 | 73 | - | .486 | 13 | 5 | 3 | 5 | 3 | 4 | 9 | 4 | X | 5 | 6 | 7 | 6 | 9 | 3 |
| Charlotte (White Sox) | 68 | 74 | - | .479 | 14 | 2 | 7 | 8 | 6 | 7 | 3 | 8 | 3 | X | 6 | 7 | 3 | 2 | 6 |
| Louisville (Reds) | 67 | 77 | - | .465 | 16 | 3 | 9 | 5 | 7 | 6 | 2 | 4 | 2 | 6 | X | 7 | 2 | 4 | 10 |
| Indianapolis (Brewers) | 66 | 78 | - | .458 | 17 | 2 | 5 | 8 | 5 | 2 | 3 | 7 | 1 | 5 | 9 | X | 4 | 3 | 12 |
| Ottawa (Orioles) | 66 | 78 | - | .458 | 17 | 6 | 5 | 0 | 5 | 5 | 7 | 5 | 10 | 5 | 6 | 4 | X | 6 | 3 |
| Syracuse (Blue Jays) | 66 | 78 | - | .458 | 17 | 6 | 3 | 1 | 3 | 6 | 6 | 3 | 7 | 6 | 4 | 5 | 10 | X | 6 |
| Toledo (Tigers) | 65 | 78 | - | .455 | 171/2 | 5 | 4 | 8 | 4 | 6 | 6 | 4 | 5 | 5 | 6 | 4 | 5 | 2 | X |

Major league affiliations in parentheses.

PLAYOFFS: Buffalo defeated Durham, three games to two; Richmond defeated Columbus, three games to two; Buffalo defeated Richmond, three games to one, to win league championship.

REGULAR-SEASON ATTENDANCE: Buffalo, 604,159; Charlotte, 265,271; Columbus, 493,656; Durham, 493,629; Indianapolis, 576,067; Louisville, 648,092; Norfolk, 485,260; Ottawa, 159,619; Pawtucket, 657,067; Richmond, 375,029; Rochester, 437,088; Scranton/Wilkes-Barre, 402,676; Syracuse, 364,648; Toledo, 544,778. Total attendance—6,507,039. Playoffs (12 games)—44,992; Class AAA All-Star Game at Memphis—15,214.

MANAGERS: Buffalo, Marty Brown; Charlotte, Nick Capra; Columbus, Bucky Dent; Durham, Bill Evers; Indianapolis, Cecil Cooper; Louisville, Rick Burleson; Norfolk, John Stearns; Ottawa, Tim Leiper; Pawtucket, Buddy Bailey; Richmond, Pat Kelly; Rochester, Phil Roof; Scranton/Wilkes-Barre, Marc Bombard; Syracuse, Marty Pevey; Toledo, Larry Parrish. Managerial record of team with more than one manager: Louisville, Miley (63-47); Burleson (16-17).

ALL-STAR TEAM: 1B—Justin Morneau, Rochester; 2B—Pete Orr, Richmond; 3B—Earl Snyder, Pawtucket; SS—Johnny Peralta, Buffalo; OF—Matt Diaz, Durham; OF—Adam Hyzdu, Pawtucket; OF—Jason Kubel, Rochester; C—Kelly Shoppach, Pawtucket; DH—Ernie Young, Buffalo; Utility—Jorge Cantu, Durham; Starting pitcher—Ben Hendrickson, Indianapolis; Relief pitcher—Matt Whiteside, Richmond; Most Valuable Player—Jhonny Peralta, Buffalo; Most Valuable Pitcher—Ben Hendrickson, Indianapolis; Rookie of the Year—Jason Kubel, Rochester; Manager of the Year—Marty Brown, Buffalo.

# 2004 BATTING

## TEAM

| Team | G | TPA | AB | R | H | TB | 2B | 3B | HR | RBI | SH | SF | HP | BB | IBB | SO | SB | CS | GDP | LOB | ShO | Avg. | OBP | Slg. |
|---|---|---|---|---|---|---|---|---|---|---|---|---|---|---|---|---|---|---|---|---|---|---|---|---|
| Buffalo | 144 | 5597 | 4963 | 848 | 1472 | 2413 | 311 | 33 | 188 | 791 | 34 | 58 | 77 | 465 | 14 | 926 | 114 | 55 | 115 | 1013 | 6 | .297 | .362 | .486 |
| Richmond | 141 | 5212 | 4644 | 660 | 1300 | 2043 | 252 | 34 | 141 | 618 | 50 | 29 | 57 | 432 | 25 | 928 | 78 | 50 | 127 | 1001 | 9 | .280 | .347 | .440 |
| Columbus | 144 | 5435 | 4804 | 739 | 1328 | 2128 | 268 | 44 | 148 | 683 | 54 | 50 | 75 | 452 | 22 | 899 | 69 | 38 | 122 | 982 | 5 | .276 | .345 | .443 |
| Durham | 144 | 5330 | 4734 | 733 | 1308 | 2161 | 295 | 27 | 168 | 692 | 44 | 41 | 71 | 440 | 20 | 1034 | 119 | 50 | 105 | 950 | 8 | .276 | .344 | .456 |
| Rochester | 144 | 5545 | 4960 | 726 | 1352 | 2136 | 304 | 21 | 146 | 673 | 56 | 41 | 53 | 434 | 21 | 846 | 85 | 39 | 114 | 997 | 6 | .273 | .335 | .431 |
| Scranton-Wb. | 142 | 5408 | 4770 | 666 | 1297 | 1922 | 271 | 39 | 92 | 627 | 60 | 41 | 63 | 473 | 19 | 835 | 103 | 46 | 113 | 1036 | 6 | .272 | .343 | .403 |
| Louisville | 144 | 5376 | 4758 | 694 | 1269 | 1977 | 258 | 42 | 122 | 655 | 48 | 52 | 70 | 448 | 12 | 1060 | 110 | 52 | 98 | 969 | 11 | .267 | .335 | .416 |
| Syracuse | 144 | 5448 | 4844 | 661 | 1289 | 2002 | 294 | 31 | 119 | 620 | 31 | 48 | 57 | 467 | 15 | 940 | 52 | 40 | 117 | 1026 | 9 | .266 | .335 | .413 |
| Ottawa | 144 | 5388 | 4863 | 619 | 1289 | 1987 | 291 | 25 | 119 | 578 | 24 | 39 | 61 | 401 | 13 | 962 | 102 | 42 | 125 | 990 | 13 | .265 | .326 | .409 |
| Charlotte | 142 | 5298 | 4740 | 639 | 1258 | 2073 | 252 | 22 | 173 | 605 | 49 | 41 | 63 | 405 | 10 | 904 | 117 | 50 | 112 | 920 | 6 | .265 | .329 | .437 |
| Pawtucket | 144 | 5638 | 4927 | 763 | 1303 | 2235 | 310 | 23 | 192 | 716 | 31 | 35 | 68 | 577 | 17 | 1222 | 81 | 33 | 92 | 1090 | 5 | .264 | .347 | .454 |

| Team | G | TPA | AB | R | H | TB | 2B | 3B | HR | RBI | SH | SF | HP | BB | IBB | SO | SB | CS | GDP | LOB | ShO | Avg. | OBP | Slg. |
|---|---|---|---|---|---|---|---|---|---|---|---|---|---|---|---|---|---|---|---|---|---|---|---|---|
| Toledo | 143 | 5300 | 4827 | 626 | 1270 | 1973 | 262 | 36 | 123 | 575 | 32 | 45 | 42 | 354 | 14 | 986 | 120 | 47 | 92 | 926 | 6 | .263 | .316 | .409 |
| Norfolk | 144 | 5284 | 4740 | 590 | 1238 | 1898 | 253 | 28 | 117 | 535 | 87 | 43 | 41 | 373 | 18 | 1010 | 102 | 69 | 85 | 931 | 7 | .261 | .318 | .400 |
| Indianapolis | 144 | 5331 | 4730 | 620 | 1234 | 1845 | 269 | 33 | 92 | 576 | 70 | 40 | 53 | 438 | 26 | 845 | 106 | 70 | 74 | 939 | 10 | .261 | .328 | .390 |

## INDIVIDUAL

### TOP QUALIFIERS FOR BATTING CHAMPIONSHIP

Minimum 389 plate appearances. *Lefthanded batter. †Switch-hitter.

| Player, Team | G | TPA | AB | R | H | TB | 2B | 3B | HR | RBI | SH | SF | HP | BB | IBB | SO | SB | CS | GDP | Avg. | OBP | Slg. |
|---|---|---|---|---|---|---|---|---|---|---|---|---|---|---|---|---|---|---|---|---|---|---|
| Kubel, Jason, Rochester * | 90 | 390 | 350 | 71 | 120 | 196 | 28 | 0 | 16 | 71 | 1 | 4 | 1 | 34 | 2 | 40 | 16 | 3 | 2 | .343 | .398 | .560 |
| Diaz, Matt, Durham | 134 | 548 | 503 | 81 | 167 | 287 | 47 | 5 | 21 | 93 | 1 | 5 | 13 | 26 | 0 | 96 | 15 | 4 | 10 | .332 | .377 | .571 |
| Collier, Lou, Scranton-WB | 101 | 430 | 387 | 62 | 126 | 200 | 26 | 3 | 14 | 66 | 0 | 3 | 4 | 34 | 1 | 82 | 14 | 3 | 8 | .326 | .383 | .517 |
| Peralta, Jhonny, Buffalo | 138 | 623 | 556 | 109 | 181 | 274 | 44 | 2 | 15 | 86 | 0 | 9 | 4 | 54 | 0 | 126 | 8 | 4 | 16 | .326 | .384 | .493 |
| Orr, Pete, Richmond * | 115 | 491 | 460 | 69 | 147 | 186 | 16 | 10 | 1 | 35 | 7 | 2 | 2 | 20 | 0 | 59 | 24 | 11 | 7 | .320 | .349 | .404 |
| Phillips, Andy, Columbus | 115 | 493 | 434 | 83 | 138 | 247 | 19 | 6 | 26 | 85 | 1 | 5 | 2 | 51 | 5 | 60 | 2 | 1 | 18 | .318 | .388 | .569 |
| Clapinski, Chris, Buffalo † | 107 | 429 | 369 | 65 | 115 | 180 | 24 | 4 | 11 | 63 | 3 | 6 | 5 | 46 | 3 | 62 | 18 | 6 | 3 | .312 | .390 | .488 |
| Tyner, Jason, Richmond-Buffalo* | 102 | 435 | 382 | 65 | 118 | 141 | 16 | 2 | 1 | 32 | 6 | 5 | 9 | 33 | 0 | 37 | 23 | 6 | 4 | .309 | .373 | .369 |
| Escalona, Felix, Columbus | 130 | 513 | 448 | 79 | 138 | 193 | 32 | 1 | 7 | 59 | 11 | 6 | 17 | 31 | 0 | 56 | 2 | 4 | 20 | .308 | .371 | .431 |
| Ozuna, Pablo, Scranton-WB | 126 | 517 | 472 | 77 | 145 | 196 | 27 | 3 | 6 | 76 | 11 | 5 | 7 | 22 | 2 | 43 | 31 | 12 | 11 | .307 | .344 | .415 |
| Phillips, Brandon, Buffalo | 135 | 588 | 521 | 83 | 158 | 224 | 34 | 4 | 8 | 50 | 9 | 6 | 8 | 44 | 0 | 56 | 14 | 11 | 12 | .303 | .363 | .430 |
| Cantu, Jorge, Durham | 95 | 392 | 368 | 57 | 111 | 212 | 33 | 1 | 22 | 80 | 1 | 3 | 4 | 16 | 2 | 64 | 3 | 0 | 11 | .302 | .335 | .576 |
| Hyzdu, Adam, Pawtucket | 129 | 561 | 465 | 92 | 140 | 264 | 33 | 2 | 29 | 79 | 1 | 4 | 7 | 84 | 1 | 106 | 8 | 4 | 12 | .301 | .413 | .568 |
| Young, Ernie, Buffalo | 115 | 500 | 441 | 71 | 132 | 243 | 26 | 2 | 27 | 100 | 0 | 7 | 12 | 40 | 1 | 104 | 2 | 2 | 7 | .299 | .368 | .551 |
| Langerhans, Ryan, Richmond * | 135 | 538 | 456 | 103 | 136 | 236 | 34 | 3 | 20 | 72 | 4 | 2 | 6 | 70 | 3 | 113 | 5 | 9 | 6 | .298 | .397 | .518 |
| Garabito, Eddy, Ottawa † | 124 | 499 | 450 | 52 | 134 | 189 | 27 | 5 | 6 | 37 | 3 | 2 | 4 | 40 | 3 | 48 | 19 | 12 | 8 | .298 | .359 | .420 |

DEPARTMENTAL LEADERS: G—B. Nelson, 142; AB—B. Nelson, 560; R—Peralta, 109; H—Peralta, 181; TB—Snyder, 300; 2B—M. Diaz, 47; 3B—Budzinski, 15; HR—E. Snyder, 36; RBI—E. Snyder, 104; SH—L. Rodriguez, 18; SF—Peralta, V. Diaz, 9 each; HP—Gomes, 22; BB—Cummings, 86; IBB—Cummings, 12; SO—J. Owens, 140; SB—Snead, 40; CS—Holbert, 14; GIDP—B. Nelson, 20; Slg.—Cantu, .576; OBP—Hyzdu, .413.

### ALL PLAYERS

*Lefthanded batter. †Switch-hitter.

| Player, Team | G | TPA | AB | R | H | TB | 2B | 3B | HR | RBI | SH | SF | HP | BB | IBB | SO | SB | CS | GDP | Avg. | OBP | Slg. |
|---|---|---|---|---|---|---|---|---|---|---|---|---|---|---|---|---|---|---|---|---|---|---|
| Abernathy, Brent, Buffalo | 103 | 398 | 354 | 68 | 104 | 164 | 24 | 3 | 10 | 56 | 6 | 2 | 3 | 33 | 1 | 29 | 27 | 5 | 12 | .294 | .357 | .463 |
| Aceves, Jon, Charlotte | 49 | 171 | 151 | 22 | 43 | 74 | 10 | 0 | 7 | 17 | 0 | 1 | 4 | 15 | 0 | 35 | 1 | 1 | 5 | .285 | .363 | .490 |
| Adams, Mike, Indianapolis | 10 | 1 | 1 | 0 | 0 | 0 | 0 | 0 | 0 | 0 | 0 | 0 | 0 | 0 | 0 | 1 | 0 | 0 | 0 | .000 | .000 | .000 |
| Adams, Russ, Syracuse * | 122 | 540 | 483 | 58 | 139 | 197 | 37 | 3 | 5 | 54 | 2 | 5 | 5 | 45 | 1 | 62 | 6 | 2 | 9 | .288 | .351 | .408 |
| Aguilar, Ray, Richmond † | 9 | 3 | 3 | 0 | 0 | 0 | 0 | 0 | 0 | 0 | 0 | 0 | 0 | 0 | 0 | 0 | 0 | 0 | 0 | .000 | .000 | .000 |
| Alexander, Chad, Toledo | 60 | 226 | 203 | 26 | 52 | 81 | 14 | 3 | 3 | 16 | 1 | 1 | 0 | 21 | 0 | 36 | 2 | 0 | 4 | .256 | .324 | .399 |
| Almanza, Armando, Richmond * | 20 | 1 | 1 | 0 | 1 | 2 | 1 | 0 | 0 | 2 | 0 | 0 | 0 | 0 | 0 | 0 | 0 | 0 | 0 | 1.000 | 1.000 | 2.000 |
| Alvarez, Jimmy, Pawtucket † | 31 | 113 | 101 | 8 | 22 | 37 | 6 | 0 | 3 | 13 | 3 | 1 | 0 | 8 | 0 | 20 | 3 | 2 | 2 | .218 | .273 | .366 |
| Alviso, Jerome, Louisville † | 15 | 33 | 26 | 3 | 5 | 5 | 0 | 0 | 0 | 5 | 3 | 0 | 0 | 4 | 0 | 3 | 0 | 0 | 1 | .192 | .300 | .192 |
| Bacani, David, Norfolk | 44 | 166 | 144 | 20 | 38 | 59 | 9 | 3 | 2 | 14 | 3 | 0 | 2 | 17 | 0 | 34 | 4 | 2 | 4 | .264 | .350 | .410 |
| Badeaux, Brooks, Durham † | 58 | 215 | 193 | 26 | 63 | 78 | 8 | 2 | 1 | 18 | 3 | 2 | 1 | 16 | 0 | 23 | 1 | 2 | 6 | .326 | .377 | .404 |
| Bailey, Jeff, Pawtucket | 3 | 13 | 10 | 2 | 3 | 4 | 1 | 0 | 0 | 0 | 0 | 0 | 0 | 3 | 0 | 3 | 0 | 0 | 0 | .300 | .462 | .400 |
| Baldwin, James, Norfolk | 5 | 4 | 3 | 0 | 0 | 0 | 0 | 0 | 0 | 1 | 1 | 0 | 0 | 0 | 0 | 1 | 0 | 0 | 0 | .000 | .000 | .000 |
| Baldwin, James, Toledo | 18 | 0 | 0 | 0 | 0 | 0 | 0 | 0 | 0 | 0 | 0 | 0 | 0 | 0 | 0 | 0 | 0 | 0 | 0 | .000 | .000 | .000 |
| Bard, Josh, Buffalo † | 40 | 169 | 156 | 25 | 41 | 63 | 10 | 0 | 4 | 18 | 1 | 1 | 0 | 11 | 1 | 23 | 0 | 0 | 7 | .263 | .310 | .404 |
| Barker, Kevin, Scranton-WB * | 13 | 39 | 36 | 3 | 7 | 14 | 1 | 0 | 2 | 4 | 0 | 0 | 0 | 3 | 0 | 8 | 0 | 0 | 1 | .194 | .256 | .389 |
| Barkett, Andy, Toledo * | 114 | 462 | 413 | 59 | 117 | 205 | 29 | 1 | 19 | 66 | 2 | 5 | 4 | 38 | 2 | 80 | 6 | 4 | 6 | .283 | .346 | .496 |
| Barry, Kevin, Richmond | 30 | 1 | 1 | 0 | 0 | 0 | 0 | 0 | 0 | 0 | 0 | 0 | 0 | 0 | 0 | 1 | 0 | 0 | 0 | .000 | .000 | .000 |
| Bartlett, Jason, Rochester | 67 | 313 | 269 | 54 | 89 | 127 | 15 | 7 | 3 | 29 | 2 | 2 | 7 | 33 | 1 | 37 | 7 | 3 | 1 | .331 | .415 | .472 |
| Basak, Chris, Norfolk | 58 | 213 | 193 | 25 | 43 | 80 | 11 | 4 | 6 | 19 | 9 | 1 | 0 | 10 | 0 | 58 | 5 | 3 | 0 | .223 | .260 | .415 |
| Bautista, Rayner, Toledo | 63 | 229 | 211 | 19 | 46 | 67 | 16 | 1 | 1 | 19 | 4 | 0 | 5 | 9 | 0 | 58 | 3 | 1 | 3 | .218 | .267 | .318 |
| Belisle, Matt, Louisville † | 28 | 31 | 25 | 2 | 3 | 7 | 1 | 0 | 1 | 4 | 3 | 1 | 0 | 2 | 0 | 10 | 0 | 0 | 0 | .120 | .179 | .280 |
| Bell, Mike, Charlotte | 124 | 510 | 456 | 56 | 107 | 206 | 20 | 2 | 25 | 80 | 4 | 5 | 14 | 31 | 0 | 117 | 12 | 3 | 7 | .235 | .300 | .452 |
| Bellhorn, Mark, Pawtucket † | 2 | 6 | 6 | 1 | 1 | 2 | 1 | 0 | 0 | 0 | 0 | 0 | 0 | 0 | 0 | 2 | 0 | 0 | 0 | .167 | .167 | .333 |
| Bellinger, Clay, Ottawa | 67 | 236 | 218 | 29 | 50 | 93 | 15 | 2 | 8 | 27 | 1 | 1 | 2 | 14 | 0 | 48 | 2 | 0 | 3 | .229 | .281 | .427 |
| Benard, Marvin, Syracuse * | 33 | 135 | 123 | 15 | 26 | 47 | 5 | 2 | 4 | 18 | 0 | 0 | 3 | 9 | 1 | 21 | 0 | 1 | 3 | .211 | .281 | .382 |
| Bergeron, Peter, Indianapolis * | 82 | 346 | 317 | 46 | 86 | 120 | 9 | 8 | 3 | 22 | 7 | 1 | 1 | 20 | 1 | 39 | 12 | 7 | 2 | .271 | .316 | .379 |
| Bergman, Sean, Ottawa | 21 | 1 | 1 | 0 | 0 | 0 | 0 | 0 | 0 | 0 | 0 | 0 | 0 | 0 | 0 | 1 | 0 | 0 | 0 | .000 | .000 | .000 |
| Betemit, Wilson, Richmond † | 105 | 391 | 356 | 48 | 99 | 166 | 24 | 2 | 13 | 59 | 1 | 2 | 0 | 32 | 3 | 99 | 3 | 3 | 18 | .278 | .336 | .466 |
| Betts, Todd, Columbus * | 44 | 177 | 159 | 23 | 43 | 63 | 8 | 0 | 4 | 16 | 1 | 2 | 2 | 13 | 3 | 31 | 0 | 0 | 3 | .270 | .330 | .396 |
| Bikowski, Scott, Charlotte * | 21 | 75 | 66 | 8 | 13 | 17 | 1 | 0 | 1 | 4 | 0 | 0 | 0 | 9 | 0 | 18 | 0 | 1 | 2 | .197 | .293 | .258 |
| Bong, Jung, Louisville * | 19 | 13 | 10 | 1 | 4 | 7 | 1 | 1 | 0 | 2 | 2 | 0 | 0 | 1 | 0 | 1 | 0 | 0 | 1 | .400 | .455 | .700 |
| Borchard, Joe, Charlotte † | 82 | 336 | 301 | 44 | 80 | 149 | 21 | 0 | 16 | 48 | 0 | 3 | 2 | 30 | 1 | 68 | 4 | 3 | 8 | .266 | .333 | .495 |
| Boscan, Jean, Richmond | 21 | 72 | 61 | 4 | 19 | 21 | 2 | 0 | 0 | 6 | 0 | 1 | 1 | 9 | 0 | 14 | 0 | 1 | 2 | .311 | .403 | .344 |
| Bowers, Shane, Scranton-WB | 15 | 3 | 2 | 0 | 1 | 1 | 0 | 0 | 0 | 0 | 1 | 0 | 0 | 0 | 0 | 1 | 0 | 0 | 0 | .500 | .500 | .500 |
| Bragg, Darren, Louisville * | 13 | 51 | 46 | 4 | 11 | 18 | 1 | 0 | 2 | 4 | 0 | 0 | 0 | 5 | 0 | 13 | 1 | 0 | 2 | .239 | .314 | .391 |
| Bragg, Darren, Columbus * | 70 | 315 | 273 | 41 | 77 | 128 | 21 | 3 | 8 | 29 | 4 | 1 | 0 | 37 | 0 | 45 | 7 | 2 | 6 | .282 | .367 | .469 |
| Branyan, Russell, Richmond * | 11 | 42 | 28 | 5 | 5 | 8 | 0 | 0 | 1 | 4 | 0 | 0 | 1 | 13 | 2 | 11 | 1 | 0 | 0 | .179 | .452 | .286 |
| Branyan, Russell, Buffalo * | 82 | 366 | 313 | 58 | 90 | 185 | 16 | 2 | 25 | 75 | 0 | 6 | 5 | 42 | 4 | 102 | 5 | 2 | 5 | .288 | .374 | .591 |
| Brazell, Craig, Norfolk * | 121 | 505 | 475 | 66 | 126 | 221 | 22 | 2 | 23 | 67 | 5 | 1 | 3 | 21 | 5 | 99 | 1 | 2 | 5 | .265 | .300 | .465 |
| Budzinski, Mark, Scranton-WB * | 135 | 574 | 508 | 79 | 144 | 218 | 29 | 15 | 5 | 52 | 11 | 5 | 2 | 48 | 1 | 103 | 16 | 2 | 4 | .283 | .345 | .429 |
| Burke, Jamie, Charlotte | 37 | 150 | 134 | 12 | 31 | 43 | 6 | 0 | 2 | 12 | 3 | 2 | 2 | 9 | 0 | 15 | 0 | 0 | 5 | .231 | .286 | .321 |
| Burkhart, Morgan, Charlotte † | 6 | 20 | 18 | 1 | 2 | 3 | 1 | 0 | 0 | 0 | 0 | 0 | 0 | 2 | 0 | 9 | 0 | 0 | 0 | .111 | .200 | .167 |
| Burks, Ellis, Pawtucket | 1 | 3 | 2 | 1 | 0 | 0 | 0 | 0 | 0 | 0 | 0 | 0 | 1 | 0 | 0 | 0 | 0 | 0 | 0 | .000 | .333 | .000 |
| Burnham, Gary, Louisville * | 69 | 245 | 222 | 30 | 58 | 88 | 15 | 0 | 5 | 30 | 0 | 1 | 3 | 19 | 1 | 33 | 2 | 3 | 12 | .261 | .327 | .396 |

| Player, Team | G | TPA | AB | R | H | TB | 2B | 3B | HR | RBI | SH | SF | HP | BB | IBB | SO | SB | CS | GDP | Avg. | OBP | Slg. |
|---|---|---|---|---|---|---|---|---|---|---|---|---|---|---|---|---|---|---|---|---|---|---|
| Calzado, Napoleon, Richmond | 5 | 19 | 19 | 2 | 4 | 5 | 1 | 0 | 0 | 2 | 0 | 0 | 0 | 0 | 0 | 2 | 0 | 0 | 0 | .211 | .211 | .263 |
| Cancel, Robinson, Durham | 18 | 59 | 57 | 6 | 15 | 25 | 7 | 0 | 1 | 4 | 0 | 0 | 1 | 1 | 0 | 10 | 0 | 1 | 4 | .263 | .288 | .439 |
| Cano, Robinson, Columbus * | 61 | 240 | 216 | 22 | 56 | 87 | 9 | 2 | 6 | 30 | 3 | 2 | 1 | 18 | 1 | 27 | 0 | 1 | 7 | .259 | .316 | .403 |
| Cantu, Jorge, Durham | 95 | 392 | 368 | 57 | 111 | 212 | 33 | 1 | 22 | 80 | 1 | 3 | 4 | 16 | 2 | 64 | 3 | 0 | 11 | .302 | .335 | .576 |
| Capellan, Jose, Richmond | 7 | 4 | 3 | 0 | 0 | 0 | 0 | 0 | 0 | 0 | 1 | 0 | 0 | 0 | 0 | 0 | 0 | 0 | 0 | .000 | .000 | .000 |
| Cardona, Javier, Norfolk | 26 | 70 | 63 | 2 | 7 | 11 | 1 | 0 | 1 | 4 | 0 | 1 | 1 | 5 | 0 | 14 | 0 | 0 | 2 | .111 | .186 | .175 |
| Casanova, Raul, Pawtucket † | 23 | 85 | 74 | 4 | 20 | 27 | 2 | 1 | 1 | 9 | 0 | 1 | 0 | 10 | 1 | 15 | 0 | 0 | 2 | .270 | .353 | .365 |
| Castellano, John, Scranton-WB | 4 | 14 | 13 | 1 | 5 | 6 | 1 | 0 | 0 | 0 | 0 | 0 | 0 | 1 | 0 | 2 | 0 | 0 | 0 | .385 | .429 | .462 |
| Castro, Juan, Louisville | 5 | 20 | 18 | 1 | 3 | 4 | 1 | 0 | 0 | 3 | 0 | 1 | 0 | 1 | 0 | 2 | 0 | 0 | 0 | .167 | .200 | .222 |
| Cerros, Juan, Louisville | 30 | 5 | 4 | 0 | 1 | 1 | 0 | 0 | 0 | 0 | 1 | 0 | 0 | 0 | 0 | 1 | 0 | 0 | 1 | .250 | .250 | .250 |
| Cesar, Dionys, Louisville † | 18 | 60 | 54 | 7 | 10 | 14 | 4 | 0 | 0 | 6 | 1 | 0 | 1 | 4 | 0 | 8 | 1 | 0 | 0 | .185 | .254 | .259 |
| Cesar, Dionys, Charlotte † | 28 | 88 | 80 | 5 | 24 | 31 | 4 | 0 | 1 | 9 | 1 | 1 | 0 | 6 | 0 | 13 | 3 | 1 | 1 | .300 | .345 | .388 |
| Chamblee, Jim, Louisville | 123 | 468 | 397 | 73 | 104 | 170 | 23 | 5 | 11 | 63 | 1 | 4 | 14 | 52 | 0 | 117 | 3 | 2 | 3 | .262 | .364 | .428 |
| Chiaffredo, Paul, Syracuse | 34 | 127 | 114 | 12 | 25 | 40 | 3 | 0 | 4 | 14 | 1 | 3 | 1 | 8 | 0 | 31 | 0 | 1 | 3 | .219 | .270 | .351 |
| Childers, Matt, Indianapolis | 35 | 10 | 8 | 0 | 0 | 0 | 0 | 0 | 0 | 0 | 2 | 0 | 0 | 0 | 0 | 2 | 0 | 0 | 0 | .000 | .000 | .000 |
| Christensen, McKay, Louisville * | 5 | 18 | 17 | 1 | 5 | 6 | 1 | 0 | 0 | 3 | 0 | 0 | 0 | 1 | 0 | 4 | 1 | 0 | 0 | .294 | .333 | .353 |
| Clapinski, Chris, Buffalo † | 107 | 429 | 369 | 65 | 115 | 180 | 24 | 4 | 11 | 63 | 3 | 6 | 5 | 46 | 3 | 62 | 18 | 6 | 3 | .312 | .390 | .488 |
| Clapp, Stubby, Syracuse * | 29 | 106 | 87 | 13 | 25 | 37 | 8 | 2 | 0 | 6 | 1 | 0 | 3 | 15 | 1 | 18 | 0 | 2 | 1 | .287 | .410 | .425 |
| Clark, Howie, Syracuse * | 72 | 305 | 256 | 43 | 80 | 116 | 14 | 2 | 6 | 32 | 3 | 3 | 3 | 40 | 2 | 18 | 1 | 0 | 3 | .313 | .407 | .453 |
| Clark, Jermaine, Louisville * | 115 | 478 | 398 | 77 | 113 | 168 | 15 | 5 | 10 | 52 | 4 | 6 | 7 | 63 | 0 | 54 | 24 | 9 | 4 | .284 | .386 | .422 |
| Claussen, Brandon, Louisville | 18 | 13 | 8 | 0 | 0 | 0 | 0 | 0 | 0 | 1 | 5 | 0 | 0 | 0 | 0 | 2 | 0 | 0 | 0 | .000 | .000 | .000 |
| Cleveland, Russ, Toledo | 2 | 7 | 7 | 0 | 3 | 5 | 0 | 1 | 0 | 0 | 0 | 0 | 0 | 0 | 0 | 0 | 0 | 0 | 0 | .429 | .429 | .714 |
| Coggin, David, Scranton-WB | 16 | 2 | 2 | 0 | 0 | 0 | 0 | 0 | 0 | 0 | 0 | 0 | 0 | 0 | 0 | 0 | 0 | 0 | 0 | .000 | .000 | .000 |
| Collier, Lou, Scranton-WB | 101 | 430 | 387 | 62 | 126 | 200 | 26 | 3 | 14 | 66 | 0 | 3 | 4 | 34 | 1 | 82 | 14 | 3 | 8 | .326 | .383 | .517 |
| Collins, Mike, Norfolk | 35 | 83 | 74 | 1 | 12 | 15 | 3 | 0 | 0 | 5 | 3 | 3 | 0 | 3 | 0 | 16 | 0 | 2 | 2 | .162 | .188 | .203 |
| Colon, Roman, Richmond | 51 | 4 | 4 | 0 | 0 | 0 | 0 | 0 | 0 | 0 | 0 | 0 | 0 | 0 | 0 | 3 | 0 | 0 | 0 | .000 | .000 | .000 |
| Condrey, Clay, Scranton-WB | 27 | 13 | 11 | 0 | 2 | 3 | 1 | 0 | 0 | 3 | 2 | 0 | 0 | 0 | 0 | 3 | 0 | 0 | 0 | .182 | .182 | .273 |
| Cooper, Jason, Buffalo * | 16 | 60 | 51 | 6 | 9 | 19 | 1 | 0 | 3 | 7 | 0 | 0 | 0 | 9 | 0 | 15 | 1 | 1 | 0 | .176 | .300 | .373 |
| Coquillette, Trace, Pawtucket | 62 | 226 | 197 | 17 | 49 | 72 | 12 | 1 | 3 | 22 | 4 | 1 | 7 | 17 | 1 | 54 | 1 | 2 | 4 | .249 | .329 | .365 |
| Corporan, Elvis, Rochester † | 5 | 16 | 15 | 4 | 7 | 10 | 0 | 0 | 1 | 1 | 0 | 0 | 0 | 1 | 0 | 4 | 0 | 0 | 0 | .467 | .500 | .667 |
| Cosme, Caonabo, Columbus | 63 | 264 | 232 | 30 | 58 | 79 | 10 | 1 | 3 | 33 | 7 | 2 | 2 | 21 | 0 | 56 | 4 | 1 | 3 | .250 | .315 | .341 |
| Coste, Chris, Indianapolis | 78 | 291 | 262 | 34 | 77 | 106 | 21 | 1 | 2 | 26 | 2 | 2 | 5 | 20 | 0 | 37 | 2 | 3 | 6 | .294 | .353 | .405 |
| Crespo, Cesar, Pawtucket † | 55 | 245 | 221 | 30 | 60 | 91 | 13 | 3 | 4 | 19 | 2 | 1 | 0 | 21 | 0 | 53 | 10 | 2 | 2 | .271 | .333 | .412 |
| Crosby, Bubba, Columbus * | 33 | 138 | 116 | 18 | 32 | 44 | 5 | 2 | 1 | 15 | 1 | 3 | 4 | 14 | 0 | 26 | 3 | 3 | 2 | .276 | .365 | .379 |
| Crozier, Eric, Syracuse * | 25 | 113 | 94 | 12 | 26 | 37 | 8 | 0 | 1 | 16 | 1 | 0 | 2 | 16 | 1 | 27 | 3 | 2 | 2 | .277 | .393 | .394 |
| Crozier, Eric, Buffalo * | 84 | 334 | 296 | 55 | 88 | 169 | 21 | 0 | 20 | 53 | 1 | 0 | 1 | 36 | 0 | 67 | 5 | 1 | 8 | .297 | .375 | .571 |
| Cruz, Jacob, Louisville * | 17 | 65 | 54 | 12 | 17 | 30 | 4 | 0 | 3 | 7 | 0 | 1 | 0 | 10 | 1 | 10 | 0 | 0 | 2 | .315 | .415 | .556 |
| Cummings, Midre, Durham * | 119 | 507 | 414 | 83 | 118 | 231 | 26 | 3 | 27 | 89 | 0 | 4 | 3 | 86 | 12 | 107 | 13 | 2 | 6 | .285 | .408 | .558 |
| Cunnane, Will, Richmond | 35 | 1 | 1 | 0 | 1 | 1 | 0 | 0 | 0 | 0 | 0 | 0 | 0 | 0 | 0 | 0 | 0 | 0 | 0 | 1.000 | 1.000 | 1.000 |
| Curry, Mike, Pawtucket * | 50 | 192 | 164 | 29 | 43 | 48 | 5 | 0 | 0 | 16 | 0 | 2 | 2 | 24 | 1 | 43 | 12 | 4 | 5 | .262 | .359 | .293 |
| Curtis, Daniel, Richmond | 2 | 1 | 1 | 0 | 0 | 0 | 0 | 0 | 0 | 0 | 0 | 0 | 0 | 0 | 0 | 1 | 0 | 0 | 0 | .000 | .000 | .000 |
| Cust, Jack, Ottawa * | 102 | 413 | 344 | 55 | 81 | 149 | 15 | 1 | 17 | 55 | 0 | 2 | 2 | 65 | 3 | 127 | 4 | 0 | 7 | .235 | .358 | .433 |
| Daigle, Leo, Toledo | 1 | 1 | 1 | 0 | 0 | 0 | 0 | 0 | 0 | 0 | 0 | 0 | 0 | 0 | 0 | 1 | 0 | 0 | 0 | .000 | .000 | .000 |
| Darensbourg, Vic, Norfolk * | 18 | 1 | 1 | 0 | 1 | 1 | 0 | 0 | 0 | 0 | 0 | 0 | 0 | 0 | 0 | 0 | 0 | 0 | 0 | 1.000 | 1.000 | 1.000 |
| Darula, Bobby, Louisville * | 22 | 72 | 63 | 11 | 19 | 26 | 2 | 1 | 1 | 8 | 0 | 0 | 1 | 8 | 1 | 13 | 5 | 0 | 0 | .302 | .389 | .413 |
| Daubach, Brian, Pawtucket * | 93 | 412 | 336 | 63 | 91 | 177 | 23 | 0 | 21 | 81 | 0 | 2 | 3 | 71 | 7 | 93 | 0 | 1 | 1 | .271 | .400 | .527 |
| De La Rosa, Jorge, Indianapolis * | 20 | 14 | 12 | 1 | 0 | 0 | 0 | 0 | 0 | 1 | 1 | 1 | 0 | 0 | 0 | 6 | 0 | 0 | 0 | .000 | .000 | .000 |
| Deardorff, Jeff, Columbus | 122 | 491 | 432 | 68 | 117 | 190 | 13 | 3 | 18 | 76 | 1 | 5 | 3 | 50 | 1 | 112 | 10 | 6 | 9 | .271 | .347 | .440 |
| Delgado, Alex, Indianapolis | 65 | 219 | 206 | 9 | 46 | 56 | 10 | 0 | 0 | 28 | 5 | 1 | 2 | 5 | 0 | 21 | 1 | 1 | 2 | .223 | .248 | .272 |
| Delgado, Carlos, Syracuse * | 2 | 9 | 9 | 2 | 5 | 10 | 2 | 0 | 1 | 4 | 0 | 0 | 0 | 0 | 0 | 0 | 0 | 0 | 1 | .556 | .556 | 1.111 |
| Delgado, Wilson, Norfolk † | 108 | 389 | 352 | 40 | 92 | 129 | 18 | 5 | 3 | 23 | 7 | 1 | 2 | 27 | 1 | 73 | 1 | 6 | 7 | .261 | .317 | .366 |
| Depastino, Joe, Richmond | 93 | 340 | 299 | 34 | 69 | 101 | 12 | 1 | 6 | 43 | 5 | 3 | 4 | 29 | 2 | 52 | 2 | 2 | 18 | .231 | .304 | .338 |
| Detienne, Dave, Norfolk | 11 | 25 | 23 | 2 | 4 | 4 | 0 | 0 | 0 | 1 | 0 | 1 | 0 | 1 | 0 | 4 | 0 | 0 | 0 | .174 | .200 | .174 |
| DiFelice, Mike, Toledo | 64 | 254 | 237 | 20 | 64 | 93 | 14 | 0 | 5 | 36 | 0 | 2 | 1 | 14 | 0 | 37 | 1 | 0 | 7 | .270 | .311 | .392 |
| Diaz, Juan, Rochester | 39 | 153 | 137 | 23 | 37 | 75 | 5 | 0 | 11 | 24 | 0 | 0 | 2 | 14 | 0 | 43 | 0 | 0 | 2 | .270 | .346 | .547 |
| Diaz, Matt, Durham | 134 | 548 | 503 | 81 | 167 | 287 | 47 | 5 | 21 | 93 | 1 | 5 | 13 | 26 | 0 | 96 | 15 | 4 | 10 | .332 | .377 | .571 |
| Diaz, Victor, Norfolk | 141 | 578 | 528 | 81 | 154 | 259 | 31 | 1 | 24 | 94 | 5 | 9 | 5 | 31 | 1 | 133 | 6 | 7 | 12 | .292 | .332 | .491 |
| Dominique, Andy, Pawtucket | 111 | 486 | 419 | 54 | 112 | 185 | 28 | 0 | 15 | 69 | 0 | 4 | 8 | 55 | 1 | 87 | 0 | 2 | 11 | .267 | .360 | .442 |
| Done, Mike, Ottawa † | 1 | 1 | 1 | 0 | 1 | 2 | 1 | 0 | 0 | 0 | 0 | 0 | 0 | 0 | 0 | 0 | 0 | 0 | 0 | 1.000 | 1.000 | 2.000 |
| Dransfeldt, Kelly, Charlotte | 88 | 332 | 305 | 34 | 76 | 111 | 18 | 1 | 5 | 30 | 5 | 4 | 3 | 15 | 0 | 63 | 5 | 2 | 8 | .249 | .287 | .364 |
| Duncan, Jeff, Norfolk * | 55 | 234 | 203 | 26 | 52 | 72 | 12 | 1 | 2 | 14 | 7 | 1 | 0 | 23 | 0 | 52 | 11 | 5 | 1 | .256 | .330 | .355 |
| Dunwoody, Todd, Rochester * | 85 | 327 | 308 | 42 | 94 | 152 | 25 | 3 | 9 | 50 | 2 | 2 | 4 | 11 | 1 | 60 | 8 | 2 | 8 | .305 | .335 | .494 |
| Dunwoody, Todd, Buffalo * | 22 | 74 | 66 | 11 | 11 | 25 | 2 | 0 | 4 | 7 | 2 | 0 | 1 | 5 | 0 | 15 | 0 | 1 | 2 | .167 | .236 | .379 |
| Ellis, Robert, Buffalo | 10 | 0 | 0 | 0 | 0 | 0 | 0 | 0 | 0 | 0 | 0 | 0 | 0 | 0 | 0 | 0 | 0 | 0 | 0 | .000 | .000 | .000 |
| Ellis, Robert, Scranton-WB | 16 | 13 | 12 | 0 | 0 | 0 | 0 | 0 | 0 | 1 | 1 | 0 | 0 | 0 | 0 | 5 | 0 | 0 | 1 | .000 | .000 | .000 |
| Erickson, Matt, Indianapolis * | 122 | 470 | 402 | 57 | 109 | 144 | 27 | 1 | 2 | 34 | 11 | 1 | 11 | 45 | 0 | 68 | 12 | 10 | 5 | .271 | .359 | .358 |
| Erickson, Scott, Norfolk | 8 | 6 | 5 | 0 | 1 | 2 | 1 | 0 | 0 | 0 | 1 | 0 | 0 | 0 | 0 | 2 | 0 | 0 | 0 | .200 | .200 | .400 |
| Escalona, Felix, Columbus | 130 | 513 | 448 | 79 | 138 | 193 | 32 | 1 | 7 | 59 | 11 | 6 | 17 | 31 | 0 | 56 | 2 | 4 | 20 | .308 | .371 | .431 |
| Escobar, Alex, Buffalo | 16 | 69 | 63 | 10 | 18 | 35 | 5 | 0 | 4 | 10 | 0 | 0 | 2 | 4 | 0 | 15 | 0 | 1 | 0 | .286 | .348 | .556 |
| Estalella, Bobby, Syracuse | 6 | 25 | 24 | 3 | 6 | 12 | 0 | 0 | 2 | 3 | 0 | 0 | 0 | 1 | 0 | 6 | 0 | 0 | 0 | .250 | .280 | .500 |
| Etherton, Seth, Louisville | 19 | 10 | 9 | 0 | 1 | 1 | 0 | 0 | 0 | 0 | 1 | 0 | 0 | 0 | 0 | 1 | 0 | 0 | 0 | .111 | .111 | .111 |
| Evans, Lee, Richmond † | 58 | 203 | 180 | 25 | 43 | 72 | 8 | 0 | 7 | 20 | 0 | 1 | 1 | 21 | 0 | 57 | 0 | 1 | 4 | .239 | .320 | .400 |
| Evert, Brett, Richmond * | 7 | 2 | 2 | 1 | 1 | 1 | 0 | 0 | 0 | 0 | 0 | 0 | 0 | 0 | 0 | 0 | 0 | 0 | 0 | .500 | .500 | .500 |
| Fagan, Shawn, Syracuse | 95 | 377 | 329 | 45 | 78 | 116 | 12 | 1 | 8 | 45 | 2 | 1 | 3 | 42 | 1 | 72 | 0 | 2 | 12 | .237 | .328 | .353 |
| Farnsworth, Jeff, Indianapolis | 11 | 2 | 2 | 0 | 0 | 0 | 0 | 0 | 0 | 0 | 0 | 0 | 0 | 0 | 0 | 0 | 0 | 0 | 0 | .000 | .000 | .000 |
| Fasano, Sal, Columbus | 76 | 258 | 236 | 21 | 54 | 101 | 15 | 1 | 10 | 34 | 2 | 4 | 6 | 10 | 0 | 45 | 0 | 0 | 6 | .229 | .273 | .428 |
| Febles, Carlos, Pawtucket | 68 | 290 | 261 | 43 | 67 | 93 | 11 | 3 | 3 | 28 | 5 | 0 | 4 | 20 | 0 | 42 | 13 | 2 | 9 | .257 | .319 | .356 |
| Fesh, Sean, Richmond * | 40 | 3 | 3 | 0 | 1 | 1 | 0 | 0 | 0 | 0 | 0 | 0 | 0 | 0 | 0 | 0 | 0 | 0 | 0 | .333 | .333 | .333 |
| Figueroa, Luis, Indianapolis † | 116 | 418 | 383 | 44 | 104 | 133 | 14 | 0 | 5 | 48 | 7 | 3 | 1 | 24 | 1 | 24 | 5 | 6 | 6 | .272 | .314 | .347 |
| Fontenot, Mike, Ottawa * | 136 | 590 | 524 | 73 | 146 | 220 | 30 | 10 | 8 | 49 | 4 | 5 | 9 | 48 | 0 | 111 | 14 | 7 | 9 | .279 | .346 | .420 |
| Ford, Ben, Indianapolis | 32 | 2 | 2 | 0 | 0 | 0 | 0 | 0 | 0 | 0 | 0 | 0 | 0 | 0 | 0 | 2 | 0 | 0 | 0 | .000 | .000 | .000 |
| Ford, Lew, Rochester | 1 | 5 | 5 | 0 | 1 | 1 | 0 | 0 | 0 | 0 | 0 | 0 | 0 | 0 | 0 | 1 | 0 | 0 | 0 | .200 | .200 | .200 |
| French, Anton, Syracuse * | 36 | 167 | 149 | 37 | 52 | 87 | 10 | 2 | 7 | 23 | 4 | 2 | 0 | 12 | 1 | 33 | 13 | 6 | 1 | .349 | .393 | .584 |
| French, Anton, Durham * | 31 | 127 | 110 | 19 | 25 | 41 | 2 | 1 | 4 | 12 | 0 | 2 | 1 | 14 | 0 | 27 | 15 | 1 | 1 | .227 | .315 | .373 |
| Fuentes, Omar, Columbus | 5 | 10 | 9 | 0 | 1 | 1 | 0 | 0 | 0 | 0 | 0 | 0 | 1 | 0 | 0 | 1 | 0 | 0 | 0 | .111 | .200 | .111 |
| Garabito, Eddy, Ottawa † | 124 | 499 | 450 | 52 | 134 | 189 | 27 | 5 | 6 | 37 | 3 | 2 | 4 | 40 | 3 | 48 | 19 | 12 | 8 | .298 | .359 | .420 |

| Player, Team | G | TPA | AB | R | H | TB | 2B | 3B | HR | RBI | SH | SF | HP | BB | IBB | SO | SB | CS | GDP | Avg. | OBP | Slg. |
|---|---|---|---|---|---|---|---|---|---|---|---|---|---|---|---|---|---|---|---|---|---|---|
| Garcia, Danny, Norfolk | 63 | 269 | 242 | 28 | 63 | 85 | 14 | 1 | 2 | 19 | 5 | 0 | 7 | 15 | 0 | 35 | 9 | 5 | 5 | .260 | .322 | .351 |
| Garcia, Jesse, Richmond | 20 | 83 | 78 | 6 | 17 | 19 | 2 | 0 | 0 | 2 | 0 | 0 | 1 | 4 | 0 | 13 | 0 | 2 | 3 | .218 | .265 | .244 |
| Garciaparra, Nomar, Pawtucket | 6 | 22 | 21 | 1 | 5 | 9 | 1 | 0 | 1 | 3 | 0 | 0 | 0 | 1 | 0 | 3 | 0 | 0 | 0 | .238 | .273 | .429 |
| Garko, Ryan, Buffalo | 5 | 23 | 20 | 2 | 7 | 8 | 1 | 0 | 0 | 4 | 0 | 1 | 0 | 2 | 0 | 3 | 0 | 0 | 0 | .350 | .391 | .400 |
| Gathright, Joey, Durham * | 60 | 260 | 236 | 34 | 77 | 88 | 9 | 1 | 0 | 8 | 2 | 0 | 3 | 19 | 0 | 46 | 33 | 13 | 5 | .326 | .384 | .373 |
| Gemoll, Brandon, Indianapolis * | 80 | 263 | 248 | 30 | 68 | 97 | 18 | 1 | 3 | 34 | 1 | 0 | 1 | 13 | 2 | 65 | 3 | 2 | 5 | .274 | .313 | .391 |
| Giese, Dan, Scranton-WB | 54 | 3 | 3 | 1 | 1 | 1 | 0 | 0 | 0 | 1 | 0 | 0 | 0 | 0 | 0 | 1 | 0 | 0 | 0 | .333 | .333 | .333 |
| Gil, Benji, Toledo | 14 | 56 | 51 | 1 | 9 | 13 | 4 | 0 | 0 | 3 | 1 | 0 | 0 | 4 | 0 | 13 | 0 | 0 | 3 | .176 | .236 | .255 |
| Gil, Geronimo, Ottawa | 106 | 418 | 375 | 55 | 97 | 139 | 24 | 0 | 6 | 34 | 5 | 0 | 6 | 32 | 1 | 67 | 2 | 1 | 12 | .259 | .327 | .371 |
| Ginter, Keith, Indianapolis | 4 | 15 | 14 | 3 | 3 | 8 | 2 | 0 | 1 | 3 | 0 | 0 | 0 | 1 | 0 | 4 | 0 | 0 | 0 | .214 | .267 | .571 |
| Ginter, Matt, Norfolk | 11 | 4 | 3 | 0 | 1 | 1 | 0 | 0 | 0 | 0 | 1 | 0 | 0 | 0 | 0 | 1 | 0 | 0 | 0 | .333 | .333 | .333 |
| Gipson, Charles, Durham | 96 | 347 | 297 | 50 | 88 | 114 | 14 | 3 | 2 | 27 | 6 | 2 | 7 | 35 | 0 | 57 | 8 | 8 | 5 | .296 | .381 | .384 |
| Giron, Roberto, Indianapolis | 21 | 2 | 2 | 0 | 0 | 0 | 0 | 0 | 0 | 0 | 0 | 0 | 0 | 0 | 0 | 1 | 0 | 0 | 0 | .000 | .000 | .000 |
| Glavine, Mike, Norfolk * | 87 | 233 | 204 | 14 | 44 | 77 | 9 | 0 | 8 | 23 | 0 | 2 | 4 | 23 | 3 | 45 | 0 | 1 | 3 | .216 | .305 | .377 |
| Glover, Gary, Indianapolis | 8 | 2 | 2 | 0 | 0 | 0 | 0 | 0 | 0 | 0 | 0 | 0 | 0 | 0 | 0 | 1 | 0 | 0 | 0 | .000 | .000 | .000 |
| Gomes, Jonny, Durham | 114 | 470 | 390 | 73 | 100 | 207 | 27 | 1 | 26 | 78 | 0 | 7 | 22 | 51 | 0 | 136 | 8 | 5 | 6 | .256 | .368 | .531 |
| Gomez, Rich, Toledo | 75 | 274 | 249 | 37 | 65 | 95 | 9 | 3 | 5 | 25 | 0 | 4 | 4 | 17 | 0 | 56 | 19 | 4 | 2 | .261 | .314 | .382 |
| Gonzalez, Raul, Norfolk | 18 | 73 | 65 | 5 | 17 | 28 | 6 | 1 | 1 | 6 | 1 | 0 | 1 | 6 | 0 | 9 | 1 | 2 | 2 | .262 | .333 | .431 |
| Gonzalez, Raul, Buffalo | 56 | 247 | 232 | 36 | 72 | 114 | 13 | 1 | 9 | 40 | 1 | 1 | 0 | 13 | 0 | 19 | 5 | 5 | 11 | .310 | .346 | .491 |
| Graman, Alex, Columbus * | 24 | 2 | 2 | 0 | 1 | 1 | 0 | 0 | 0 | 0 | 0 | 0 | 0 | 0 | 0 | 0 | 0 | 0 | 0 | .500 | .500 | .500 |
| Green, Nick, Richmond | 22 | 89 | 77 | 8 | 29 | 35 | 4 | 1 | 0 | 11 | 1 | 1 | 4 | 6 | 0 | 9 | 0 | 3 | 3 | .377 | .443 | .455 |
| Griffiths, Jeremy, Norfolk | 13 | 3 | 2 | 1 | 0 | 0 | 0 | 0 | 0 | 0 | 0 | 0 | 0 | 1 | 0 | 1 | 0 | 0 | 0 | .000 | .333 | .000 |
| Grindell, Nate, Buffalo | 23 | 74 | 64 | 12 | 23 | 34 | 5 | 0 | 2 | 9 | 0 | 2 | 0 | 8 | 0 | 16 | 0 | 0 | 1 | .359 | .419 | .531 |
| Gross, Gabe, Syracuse * | 103 | 433 | 377 | 52 | 111 | 171 | 29 | 2 | 9 | 54 | 0 | 2 | 1 | 53 | 2 | 81 | 4 | 5 | 8 | .294 | .381 | .454 |
| Guiel, Jeff, Syracuse * | 68 | 253 | 228 | 28 | 45 | 78 | 13 | 1 | 6 | 26 | 3 | 1 | 2 | 19 | 1 | 63 | 1 | 0 | 2 | .197 | .264 | .342 |
| Gutierrez, Franklin, Buffalo | 7 | 28 | 27 | 4 | 4 | 8 | 1 | 0 | 1 | 3 | 0 | 0 | 0 | 1 | 0 | 11 | 0 | 0 | 0 | .148 | .179 | .296 |
| Guzman, Edwards, Durham * | 25 | 86 | 84 | 7 | 17 | 21 | 4 | 0 | 0 | 7 | 0 | 0 | 0 | 2 | 0 | 8 | 1 | 0 | 0 | .202 | .221 | .250 |
| Guzman, Edwards, Ottawa * | 62 | 260 | 248 | 22 | 63 | 80 | 11 | 0 | 2 | 32 | 1 | 0 | 0 | 11 | 0 | 28 | 3 | 2 | 8 | .254 | .286 | .323 |
| Hall, Noah, Syracuse | 58 | 209 | 176 | 28 | 41 | 56 | 3 | 3 | 2 | 15 | 0 | 0 | 8 | 25 | 1 | 38 | 4 | 4 | 3 | .233 | .354 | .318 |
| Hammond, Joey, Ottawa | 90 | 298 | 271 | 27 | 64 | 76 | 7 | 1 | 1 | 30 | 0 | 4 | 1 | 22 | 0 | 42 | 3 | 2 | 6 | .236 | .292 | .280 |
| Hancock, Josh, Scranton-WB | 18 | 14 | 12 | 0 | 0 | 0 | 0 | 0 | 0 | 1 | 0 | 0 | 0 | 2 | 0 | 8 | 0 | 0 | 0 | .000 | .143 | .000 |
| Hankins, Ryan, Charlotte | 89 | 342 | 301 | 35 | 89 | 141 | 25 | 3 | 7 | 34 | 3 | 3 | 5 | 30 | 1 | 33 | 5 | 1 | 7 | .296 | .366 | .468 |
| Hannahan, Buzz, Scranton-WB | 81 | 250 | 217 | 32 | 61 | 77 | 10 | 3 | 0 | 20 | 6 | 1 | 7 | 19 | 0 | 49 | 5 | 5 | 6 | .281 | .357 | .355 |
| Hardy, J.J., Indianapolis | 26 | 112 | 101 | 17 | 28 | 50 | 10 | 0 | 4 | 20 | 0 | 2 | 0 | 9 | 0 | 8 | 0 | 0 | 1 | .277 | .330 | .495 |
| Harper, Brandon, Toledo | 21 | 68 | 58 | 10 | 11 | 20 | 0 | 0 | 3 | 7 | 0 | 1 | 3 | 6 | 0 | 10 | 0 | 1 | 2 | .190 | .294 | .345 |
| Hart, Corey, Indianapolis | 121 | 491 | 441 | 68 | 124 | 214 | 29 | 8 | 15 | 67 | 0 | 6 | 3 | 41 | 3 | 92 | 17 | 7 | 7 | .281 | .342 | .485 |
| Hassey, Brad, Syracuse | 16 | 28 | 23 | 3 | 3 | 3 | 0 | 0 | 0 | 1 | 1 | 0 | 0 | 4 | 0 | 5 | 0 | 1 | 0 | .130 | .259 | .130 |
| Heilman, Aaron, Norfolk | 26 | 22 | 21 | 2 | 6 | 7 | 1 | 0 | 0 | 4 | 1 | 0 | 0 | 0 | 0 | 6 | 0 | 0 | 0 | .286 | .286 | .333 |
| Heintz, Chris, Rochester | 86 | 325 | 294 | 33 | 82 | 120 | 14 | 0 | 8 | 45 | 7 | 5 | 3 | 16 | 0 | 40 | 0 | 2 | 6 | .279 | .318 | .408 |
| Helms, Wes, Indianapolis | 6 | 22 | 19 | 4 | 6 | 7 | 1 | 0 | 0 | 1 | 0 | 0 | 0 | 3 | 0 | 4 | 0 | 0 | 0 | .316 | .409 | .368 |
| Hendrickson, Ben, Indianapolis | 21 | 15 | 15 | 1 | 2 | 2 | 0 | 0 | 0 | 0 | 0 | 0 | 0 | 0 | 0 | 8 | 0 | 0 | 0 | .133 | .133 | .133 |
| Hermansen, Chad, Syracuse | 42 | 166 | 146 | 18 | 35 | 64 | 9 | 1 | 6 | 18 | 0 | 4 | 0 | 16 | 0 | 52 | 0 | 0 | 1 | .240 | .307 | .438 |
| Hernandez, Adrian, Indianapolis | 22 | 12 | 11 | 1 | 2 | 2 | 0 | 0 | 0 | 0 | 1 | 0 | 0 | 0 | 0 | 5 | 0 | 0 | 0 | .182 | .182 | .182 |
| Hernandez, Michel, Scranton-WB | 77 | 264 | 232 | 34 | 59 | 86 | 9 | 0 | 6 | 31 | 2 | 3 | 2 | 25 | 0 | 24 | 0 | 1 | 8 | .254 | .328 | .371 |
| Hernandez, Yoel, Scranton-WB | 14 | 4 | 4 | 0 | 0 | 0 | 0 | 0 | 0 | 0 | 0 | 0 | 0 | 0 | 0 | 3 | 0 | 0 | 0 | .000 | .000 | .000 |
| Hessman, Mike, Richmond | 78 | 304 | 265 | 48 | 76 | 149 | 14 | 1 | 19 | 54 | 0 | 4 | 7 | 28 | 3 | 65 | 4 | 0 | 6 | .287 | .365 | .562 |
| Hill, Jason, Louisville | 3 | 8 | 7 | 0 | 1 | 1 | 0 | 0 | 0 | 0 | 0 | 0 | 1 | 0 | 0 | 1 | 0 | 0 | 0 | .143 | .250 | .143 |
| Hitchcox, Brian, Scranton-WB * | 47 | 160 | 136 | 22 | 32 | 47 | 10 | 1 | 1 | 5 | 1 | 0 | 5 | 18 | 1 | 16 | 3 | 0 | 4 | .235 | .346 | .346 |
| Hodges, Trey, Richmond | 10 | 3 | 3 | 0 | 0 | 0 | 0 | 0 | 0 | 0 | 0 | 0 | 0 | 0 | 0 | 1 | 0 | 0 | 0 | .000 | .000 | .000 |
| Holbert, Aaron, Louisville | 115 | 433 | 380 | 66 | 103 | 137 | 16 | 3 | 4 | 46 | 3 | 3 | 6 | 41 | 1 | 66 | 32 | 14 | 9 | .271 | .349 | .361 |
| Hollins, Damon, Richmond | 109 | 386 | 356 | 50 | 107 | 197 | 26 | 2 | 20 | 67 | 2 | 4 | 0 | 24 | 2 | 57 | 5 | 3 | 10 | .301 | .341 | .553 |
| Hooper, Kevin, Columbus | 29 | 95 | 87 | 6 | 17 | 18 | 1 | 0 | 0 | 4 | 3 | 0 | 0 | 5 | 0 | 11 | 3 | 1 | 1 | .195 | .239 | .207 |
| Hoover, Paul, Durham | 16 | 60 | 54 | 9 | 16 | 20 | 1 | 0 | 1 | 8 | 0 | 1 | 1 | 4 | 0 | 15 | 0 | 0 | 2 | .296 | .350 | .370 |
| Housman, Jeff, Indianapolis * | 5 | 5 | 4 | 0 | 1 | 1 | 0 | 0 | 0 | 1 | 0 | 1 | 0 | 0 | 0 | 1 | 0 | 0 | 0 | .250 | .200 | .250 |
| Howard, Ryan, Scranton-WB * | 29 | 127 | 111 | 21 | 30 | 67 | 10 | 0 | 9 | 29 | 0 | 0 | 2 | 14 | 1 | 37 | 0 | 0 | 4 | .270 | .362 | .604 |
| Huber, Justin, Norfolk | 5 | 19 | 16 | 3 | 5 | 7 | 2 | 0 | 0 | 3 | 0 | 0 | 0 | 3 | 0 | 3 | 0 | 0 | 0 | .313 | .421 | .438 |
| Hudson, Luke, Louisville | 3 | 2 | 2 | 0 | 0 | 0 | 0 | 0 | 0 | 0 | 0 | 0 | 0 | 0 | 0 | 0 | 0 | 0 | 0 | .000 | .000 | .000 |
| Hummel, Tim, Louisville | 42 | 168 | 152 | 18 | 44 | 63 | 13 | 0 | 2 | 20 | 0 | 2 | 2 | 12 | 1 | 27 | 2 | 0 | 4 | .289 | .345 | .414 |
| Hyzdu, Adam, Pawtucket | 129 | 561 | 465 | 92 | 140 | 264 | 33 | 2 | 29 | 79 | 1 | 4 | 7 | 84 | 1 | 106 | 8 | 4 | 12 | .301 | .413 | .568 |
| Jackson, Ryan, Richmond * | 16 | 59 | 58 | 7 | 13 | 22 | 3 | 0 | 2 | 4 | 0 | 0 | 0 | 1 | 1 | 15 | 2 | 0 | 1 | .224 | .237 | .379 |
| Jacobs, Mike, Norfolk * | 27 | 106 | 96 | 8 | 17 | 26 | 3 | 0 | 2 | 6 | 0 | 1 | 0 | 9 | 2 | 30 | 0 | 0 | 1 | .177 | .245 | .271 |
| Jacobson, Russ, Scranton-WB | 2 | 8 | 7 | 0 | 2 | 3 | 1 | 0 | 0 | 1 | 0 | 0 | 0 | 1 | 0 | 3 | 0 | 0 | 0 | .286 | .375 | .429 |
| Johnson, Mark, Indianapolis * | 88 | 326 | 278 | 39 | 72 | 105 | 18 | 0 | 5 | 38 | 2 | 2 | 1 | 43 | 1 | 41 | 3 | 2 | 4 | .259 | .358 | .378 |
| Joseph, Jake, Norfolk | 15 | 2 | 1 | 0 | 0 | 0 | 0 | 0 | 0 | 0 | 0 | 0 | 0 | 1 | 0 | 0 | 0 | 0 | 0 | .000 | .500 | .000 |
| Jurries, James, Richmond | 102 | 353 | 318 | 46 | 85 | 155 | 16 | 0 | 18 | 56 | 2 | 0 | 1 | 32 | 2 | 96 | 0 | 1 | 8 | .267 | .336 | .487 |
| Kearns, Austin, Louisville | 25 | 104 | 83 | 19 | 28 | 43 | 7 | 1 | 2 | 15 | 0 | 0 | 2 | 19 | 1 | 16 | 3 | 1 | 3 | .337 | .471 | .518 |
| Keene, Kurt, Scranton-WB | 6 | 11 | 8 | 2 | 2 | 2 | 0 | 0 | 0 | 2 | 1 | 1 | 0 | 1 | 0 | 2 | 1 | 0 | 0 | .250 | .300 | .250 |
| Keisler, Randy, Norfolk * | 26 | 21 | 14 | 1 | 5 | 7 | 2 | 0 | 0 | 1 | 5 | 0 | 0 | 2 | 0 | 6 | 0 | 0 | 0 | .357 | .438 | .500 |
| Kelly, Kenny, Louisville | 78 | 303 | 268 | 44 | 68 | 118 | 15 | 4 | 9 | 43 | 4 | 4 | 3 | 24 | 0 | 71 | 7 | 4 | 3 | .254 | .318 | .440 |
| Kelly, Mike, Columbus | 84 | 339 | 297 | 49 | 75 | 133 | 13 | 0 | 15 | 50 | 0 | 3 | 6 | 33 | 0 | 67 | 10 | 2 | 9 | .253 | .336 | .448 |
| Keppel, Bob, Norfolk | 17 | 7 | 6 | 0 | 2 | 2 | 0 | 0 | 0 | 1 | 1 | 0 | 0 | 0 | 0 | 2 | 0 | 0 | 0 | .333 | .333 | .333 |
| Keppinger, Jeff, Norfolk | 6 | 24 | 19 | 1 | 6 | 7 | 1 | 0 | 0 | 2 | 0 | 0 | 1 | 4 | 0 | 2 | 0 | 0 | 2 | .316 | .458 | .368 |
| Kilburg, Joe, Pawtucket * | 4 | 5 | 4 | 0 | 0 | 0 | 0 | 0 | 0 | 0 | 0 | 0 | 0 | 1 | 0 | 3 | 0 | 0 | 0 | .000 | .200 | .000 |
| Klassen, Danny, Toledo | 110 | 437 | 395 | 52 | 100 | 149 | 26 | 4 | 5 | 38 | 2 | 3 | 6 | 31 | 0 | 105 | 10 | 4 | 4 | .253 | .315 | .377 |
| Knox, Ryan, Indianapolis | 43 | 192 | 174 | 24 | 46 | 61 | 12 | 0 | 1 | 14 | 3 | 0 | 0 | 15 | 0 | 33 | 10 | 10 | 2 | .264 | .323 | .351 |
| Krynzel, Dave, Indianapolis * | 69 | 291 | 257 | 36 | 71 | 107 | 10 | 4 | 6 | 27 | 8 | 3 | 3 | 20 | 1 | 65 | 10 | 8 | 0 | .276 | .332 | .416 |
| Kubel, Jason, Rochester * | 90 | 390 | 350 | 71 | 120 | 196 | 28 | 0 | 16 | 71 | 1 | 4 | 1 | 34 | 2 | 40 | 16 | 3 | 2 | .343 | .398 | .560 |
| Kubes, Greg, Scranton-WB | 49 | 2 | 2 | 0 | 0 | 0 | 0 | 0 | 0 | 0 | 0 | 0 | 0 | 0 | 0 | 2 | 0 | 0 | 0 | .000 | .000 | .000 |
| LaForest, Pete, Durham * | 84 | 313 | 275 | 37 | 61 | 101 | 19 | 0 | 7 | 31 | 2 | 1 | 0 | 35 | 5 | 64 | 1 | 1 | 6 | .222 | .309 | .367 |

| Player, Team | G | TPA | AB | R | H | TB | 2B | 3B | HR | RBI | SH | SF | HP | BB | IBB | SO | SB | CS | GDP | Avg. | OBP | Slg. |
|---|---|---|---|---|---|---|---|---|---|---|---|---|---|---|---|---|---|---|---|---|---|---|
| LaRoche, Adam, Richmond * | 4 | 12 | 11 | 1 | 2 | 5 | 0 | 0 | 1 | 2 | 0 | 0 | 0 | 1 | 0 | 0 | 0 | 0 | 2 | .182 | .250 | .455 |
| LaRue, Jason, Louisville | 3 | 14 | 10 | 3 | 1 | 4 | 0 | 0 | 1 | 4 | 0 | 2 | 1 | 1 | 0 | 3 | 0 | 0 | 0 | .100 | .214 | .400 |
| Langerhans, Ryan, Richmond * | 135 | 538 | 456 | 103 | 136 | 236 | 34 | 3 | 20 | 72 | 4 | 2 | 6 | 70 | 3 | 113 | 5 | 9 | 6 | .298 | .397 | .518 |
| Larson, Brandon, Louisville | 32 | 124 | 117 | 14 | 33 | 65 | 5 | 0 | 9 | 25 | 0 | 1 | 1 | 5 | 1 | 39 | 0 | 0 | 4 | .282 | .315 | .556 |
| Lee, Seung, Scranton-WB | 35 | 3 | 3 | 0 | 1 | 1 | 0 | 0 | 0 | 1 | 0 | 0 | 0 | 0 | 0 | 2 | 0 | 0 | 0 | .333 | .333 | .333 |
| Leon, Jose, Ottawa | 83 | 319 | 283 | 45 | 91 | 167 | 21 | 2 | 17 | 55 | 0 | 5 | 7 | 24 | 2 | 68 | 1 | 1 | 11 | .322 | .382 | .590 |
| Levis, Jesse, Norfolk * | 10 | 28 | 27 | 3 | 10 | 12 | 2 | 0 | 0 | 3 | 0 | 0 | 0 | 1 | 0 | 0 | 0 | 0 | 1 | .370 | .393 | .444 |
| Liefer, Jeff, Indianapolis * | 106 | 425 | 368 | 60 | 104 | 191 | 25 | 1 | 20 | 83 | 0 | 6 | 4 | 47 | 6 | 62 | 1 | 0 | 12 | .283 | .365 | .519 |
| Liriano, Pedro, Indianapolis | 29 | 10 | 8 | 0 | 0 | 0 | 0 | 0 | 0 | 0 | 2 | 0 | 0 | 0 | 0 | 4 | 0 | 0 | 0 | .000 | .000 | .000 |
| Little, Mark, Buffalo | 68 | 262 | 239 | 37 | 75 | 133 | 17 | 4 | 11 | 39 | 1 | 6 | 7 | 9 | 0 | 40 | 4 | 6 | 3 | .314 | .349 | .556 |
| Logan, Nook, Toledo † | 105 | 462 | 427 | 67 | 112 | 150 | 14 | 9 | 2 | 27 | 7 | 2 | 3 | 23 | 0 | 95 | 38 | 11 | 3 | .262 | .303 | .351 |
| Lomasney, Steve, Louisville | 57 | 147 | 131 | 14 | 33 | 49 | 5 | 1 | 3 | 27 | 2 | 2 | 1 | 11 | 0 | 49 | 2 | 0 | 3 | .252 | .310 | .374 |
| Lombard, George, Pawtucket * | 55 | 224 | 192 | 38 | 53 | 76 | 8 | 3 | 3 | 23 | 3 | 0 | 9 | 20 | 0 | 33 | 16 | 3 | 1 | .276 | .371 | .396 |
| Lopez, Felipe, Louisville † | 75 | 326 | 293 | 50 | 80 | 124 | 11 | 3 | 9 | 44 | 1 | 5 | 2 | 25 | 0 | 71 | 2 | 3 | 2 | .273 | .329 | .423 |
| Lopez, Luis, Richmond | 68 | 266 | 231 | 37 | 77 | 122 | 18 | 0 | 9 | 51 | 0 | 2 | 3 | 30 | 1 | 27 | 0 | 0 | 11 | .333 | .414 | .528 |
| Luderer, Brian, Buffalo | 2 | 9 | 8 | 2 | 2 | 3 | 1 | 0 | 0 | 2 | 0 | 0 | 1 | 0 | 0 | 1 | 0 | 0 | 0 | .250 | .333 | .375 |
| Ludwick, Ryan, Buffalo | 44 | 188 | 166 | 25 | 45 | 84 | 15 | 0 | 8 | 30 | 0 | 2 | 4 | 16 | 0 | 52 | 0 | 0 | 4 | .271 | .346 | .506 |
| Machado, Andy, Louisville † | 31 | 123 | 109 | 14 | 25 | 34 | 5 | 2 | 0 | 12 | 1 | 2 | 1 | 10 | 0 | 26 | 3 | 2 | 1 | .229 | .295 | .312 |
| Machado, Andy, Scranton-WB † | 78 | 361 | 295 | 51 | 67 | 107 | 12 | 5 | 6 | 26 | 11 | 4 | 1 | 50 | 0 | 73 | 11 | 6 | 1 | .227 | .337 | .363 |
| Machado, Robert, Ottawa | 34 | 136 | 126 | 22 | 40 | 61 | 12 | 0 | 3 | 20 | 0 | 0 | 0 | 10 | 1 | 20 | 0 | 1 | 5 | .317 | .368 | .484 |
| Magruder, Chris, Indianapolis † | 79 | 339 | 305 | 37 | 83 | 126 | 17 | 4 | 6 | 39 | 1 | 2 | 10 | 21 | 4 | 55 | 7 | 4 | 4 | .272 | .337 | .413 |
| Marrero, Eli, Richmond | 6 | 25 | 24 | 1 | 5 | 7 | 2 | 0 | 0 | 3 | 0 | 0 | 0 | 1 | 0 | 3 | 0 | 0 | 0 | .208 | .240 | .292 |
| Marsters, Brandon, Rochester | 61 | 206 | 187 | 24 | 39 | 62 | 14 | 0 | 3 | 18 | 4 | 0 | 3 | 12 | 0 | 51 | 1 | 1 | 2 | .209 | .267 | .332 |
| Martinez, Octavio, Ottawa | 2 | 8 | 8 | 0 | 1 | 1 | 0 | 0 | 0 | 1 | 0 | 0 | 0 | 0 | 0 | 2 | 0 | 0 | 0 | .125 | .125 | .125 |
| Martinez, Sandy, Buffalo * | 62 | 213 | 197 | 29 | 54 | 115 | 8 | 1 | 17 | 47 | 4 | 0 | 0 | 12 | 2 | 44 | 2 | 0 | 7 | .274 | .316 | .584 |
| Massiatte, Danny, Durham | 32 | 110 | 89 | 6 | 13 | 19 | 4 | 1 | 0 | 5 | 8 | 2 | 1 | 10 | 0 | 30 | 0 | 0 | 2 | .146 | .235 | .213 |
| Matos, Julius, Syracuse | 73 | 323 | 297 | 49 | 87 | 128 | 18 | 1 | 7 | 42 | 1 | 8 | 2 | 15 | 0 | 20 | 1 | 1 | 16 | .293 | .323 | .431 |
| Matthews, Mike, Louisville * | 15 | 1 | 1 | 0 | 0 | 0 | 0 | 0 | 0 | 0 | 0 | 0 | 0 | 0 | 0 | 0 | 0 | 0 | 0 | .000 | .000 | .000 |
| Mauer, Joe, Rochester * | 5 | 21 | 19 | 1 | 6 | 9 | 3 | 0 | 0 | 2 | 0 | 1 | 0 | 1 | 0 | 4 | 0 | 0 | 1 | .316 | .333 | .474 |
| Maxwell, Jason, Durham | 100 | 394 | 363 | 41 | 96 | 150 | 13 | 1 | 13 | 55 | 5 | 4 | 2 | 20 | 1 | 55 | 0 | 1 | 8 | .264 | .303 | .413 |
| Maza, Luis, Rochester | 9 | 39 | 35 | 6 | 8 | 12 | 2 | 1 | 0 | 1 | 1 | 0 | 2 | 1 | 0 | 3 | 1 | 0 | 2 | .229 | .289 | .343 |
| McCarthy, Bill, Richmond | 54 | 200 | 178 | 26 | 63 | 96 | 13 | 1 | 6 | 23 | 1 | 3 | 4 | 14 | 1 | 32 | 0 | 2 | 7 | .354 | .407 | .539 |
| McCarty, Dave, Pawtucket | 3 | 12 | 7 | 2 | 2 | 2 | 0 | 0 | 0 | 1 | 0 | 0 | 1 | 4 | 0 | 2 | 0 | 0 | 0 | .286 | .583 | .286 |
| McConnell, Sam, Richmond * | 22 | 6 | 5 | 0 | 1 | 1 | 0 | 0 | 0 | 0 | 1 | 0 | 0 | 0 | 0 | 1 | 0 | 0 | 0 | .200 | .200 | .200 |
| McDonald, Donzell, Columbus † | 28 | 106 | 93 | 13 | 17 | 36 | 4 | 3 | 3 | 10 | 2 | 1 | 1 | 9 | 0 | 24 | 4 | 0 | 0 | .183 | .260 | .387 |
| McGee, Tom, Ottawa | 22 | 66 | 64 | 5 | 14 | 25 | 8 | 0 | 1 | 4 | 0 | 0 | 1 | 1 | 0 | 13 | 0 | 0 | 2 | .219 | .242 | .391 |
| McGinley, Blake, Norfolk | 13 | 4 | 4 | 0 | 0 | 0 | 0 | 0 | 0 | 0 | 0 | 0 | 0 | 0 | 0 | 3 | 0 | 0 | 0 | .000 | .000 | .000 |
| McGriff, Fred, Durham * | 7 | 26 | 21 | 4 | 5 | 8 | 0 | 0 | 1 | 4 | 0 | 0 | 0 | 5 | 0 | 6 | 0 | 0 | 0 | .238 | .385 | .381 |
| McNeal, Aaron, Charlotte | 32 | 122 | 111 | 9 | 27 | 38 | 2 | 0 | 3 | 13 | 0 | 0 | 2 | 9 | 0 | 30 | 0 | 0 | 7 | .243 | .311 | .342 |
| Medrano, Jesus, Pawtucket | 13 | 38 | 34 | 3 | 8 | 16 | 1 | 2 | 1 | 5 | 0 | 1 | 1 | 2 | 0 | 3 | 0 | 0 | 1 | .235 | .289 | .471 |
| Melian, Jackson, Columbus | 11 | 35 | 30 | 1 | 9 | 17 | 4 | 2 | 0 | 4 | 0 | 0 | 1 | 4 | 0 | 7 | 0 | 0 | 0 | .300 | .400 | .567 |
| Mendez, Carlos, Ottawa | 80 | 319 | 305 | 29 | 78 | 109 | 17 | 1 | 4 | 37 | 0 | 1 | 3 | 10 | 1 | 30 | 2 | 0 | 17 | .256 | .285 | .357 |
| Meyers, Mike, Norfolk | 16 | 2 | 1 | 0 | 1 | 1 | 0 | 0 | 0 | 0 | 1 | 0 | 0 | 0 | 0 | 0 | 0 | 0 | 0 | 1.000 | 1.000 | 1.000 |
| Michalak, Chris, Indianapolis * | 37 | 3 | 2 | 0 | 0 | 0 | 0 | 0 | 0 | 0 | 0 | 0 | 0 | 1 | 0 | 1 | 0 | 0 | 0 | .000 | .333 | .000 |
| Miller, Corky, Louisville | 74 | 267 | 227 | 31 | 50 | 82 | 14 | 0 | 6 | 37 | 1 | 5 | 9 | 25 | 0 | 44 | 0 | 0 | 4 | .220 | .316 | .361 |
| Monroe, Craig, Toledo | 6 | 26 | 25 | 4 | 8 | 18 | 4 | 0 | 2 | 6 | 0 | 1 | 0 | 0 | 0 | 6 | 0 | 0 | 0 | .320 | .308 | .720 |
| Moore, Mike, Charlotte | 9 | 26 | 24 | 1 | 2 | 3 | 1 | 0 | 0 | 0 | 0 | 0 | 0 | 2 | 0 | 10 | 0 | 0 | 1 | .083 | .154 | .125 |
| Morneau, Justin, Rochester * | 72 | 326 | 288 | 51 | 88 | 177 | 23 | 0 | 22 | 63 | 0 | 3 | 3 | 32 | 4 | 47 | 1 | 1 | 7 | .306 | .377 | .615 |
| Morris, Warren, Toledo * | 102 | 429 | 397 | 55 | 114 | 173 | 29 | 3 | 8 | 51 | 1 | 2 | 0 | 29 | 4 | 71 | 5 | 4 | 8 | .287 | .334 | .436 |
| Moseley, Dustin, Louisville | 12 | 7 | 7 | 0 | 1 | 1 | 0 | 0 | 0 | 0 | 0 | 0 | 0 | 0 | 0 | 4 | 0 | 0 | 0 | .143 | .143 | .143 |
| Moss, Damian, Louisville | 4 | 4 | 4 | 0 | 0 | 0 | 0 | 0 | 0 | 0 | 0 | 0 | 0 | 0 | 0 | 2 | 0 | 0 | 0 | .000 | .000 | .000 |
| Mottola, Chad, Ottawa | 117 | 493 | 457 | 60 | 121 | 209 | 22 | 0 | 22 | 69 | 0 | 5 | 9 | 22 | 0 | 90 | 8 | 0 | 13 | .265 | .308 | .457 |
| Mueller, Bill, Pawtucket † | 4 | 15 | 13 | 1 | 4 | 6 | 2 | 0 | 0 | 2 | 0 | 0 | 0 | 2 | 0 | 0 | 0 | 0 | 0 | .308 | .400 | .462 |
| Musser, Neal, Norfolk * | 7 | 9 | 7 | 0 | 1 | 1 | 0 | 0 | 0 | 0 | 2 | 0 | 0 | 0 | 0 | 3 | 0 | 0 | 0 | .143 | .143 | .143 |
| Myette, Aaron, Louisville | 41 | 2 | 2 | 0 | 0 | 0 | 0 | 0 | 0 | 0 | 0 | 0 | 0 | 0 | 0 | 1 | 0 | 0 | 0 | .000 | .000 | .000 |
| Myrow, Brian, Columbus * | 47 | 191 | 164 | 28 | 44 | 71 | 12 | 3 | 3 | 15 | 2 | 0 | 2 | 23 | 2 | 37 | 3 | 4 | 4 | .268 | .365 | .433 |
| Navarro, Dioner, Columbus † | 40 | 155 | 136 | 18 | 34 | 49 | 8 | 2 | 1 | 16 | 0 | 4 | 1 | 14 | 0 | 17 | 1 | 0 | 4 | .250 | .316 | .360 |
| Nelson, Bryant, Charlotte † | 142 | 625 | 560 | 81 | 161 | 272 | 37 | 4 | 22 | 83 | 3 | 5 | 1 | 56 | 5 | 50 | 13 | 8 | 20 | .288 | .350 | .486 |
| Nelson, Bubba, Louisville | 12 | 6 | 5 | 0 | 0 | 0 | 0 | 0 | 0 | 0 | 1 | 0 | 0 | 0 | 0 | 5 | 0 | 0 | 0 | .000 | .000 | .000 |
| Nicholson, Derek, Toledo * | 24 | 75 | 62 | 12 | 17 | 30 | 8 | 1 | 1 | 11 | 0 | 2 | 0 | 11 | 0 | 10 | 2 | 1 | 2 | .274 | .373 | .484 |
| Nicholson, Tommy, Charlotte * | 1 | 3 | 3 | 0 | 0 | 0 | 0 | 0 | 0 | 0 | 0 | 0 | 0 | 0 | 0 | 1 | 0 | 0 | 0 | .000 | .000 | .000 |
| Nilsson, Dave, Richmond * | 16 | 62 | 55 | 3 | 13 | 17 | 1 | 0 | 1 | 4 | 0 | 0 | 0 | 7 | 1 | 15 | 0 | 0 | 2 | .236 | .323 | .309 |
| Norton, Greg, Toledo † | 53 | 209 | 184 | 26 | 38 | 58 | 6 | 1 | 4 | 16 | 0 | 1 | 0 | 24 | 0 | 48 | 1 | 1 | 4 | .207 | .297 | .315 |
| Nunnally, Jon, Indianapolis * | 79 | 288 | 241 | 35 | 52 | 90 | 9 | 1 | 9 | 34 | 0 | 6 | 2 | 39 | 3 | 54 | 4 | 4 | 4 | .216 | .323 | .373 |
| Nye, Rodney, Norfolk | 130 | 475 | 423 | 44 | 117 | 159 | 27 | 0 | 5 | 50 | 8 | 7 | 4 | 33 | 0 | 81 | 0 | 4 | 9 | .277 | .330 | .376 |
| Obermueller, Wes, Indianapolis | 4 | 2 | 2 | 1 | 1 | 2 | 1 | 0 | 0 | 0 | 0 | 0 | 0 | 0 | 0 | 0 | 0 | 0 | 1 | .500 | .500 | 1.000 |
| Ojeda, Augie, Rochester † | 89 | 382 | 327 | 49 | 80 | 105 | 19 | 0 | 2 | 21 | 7 | 2 | 6 | 39 | 0 | 33 | 7 | 5 | 10 | .245 | .334 | .321 |
| Olmedo, Ray, Louisville † | 82 | 327 | 294 | 33 | 84 | 117 | 13 | 7 | 2 | 26 | 8 | 0 | 2 | 23 | 1 | 40 | 2 | 3 | 8 | .286 | .342 | .398 |
| Ordaz, Luis, Durham | 103 | 386 | 361 | 39 | 92 | 140 | 27 | 6 | 3 | 34 | 8 | 4 | 2 | 11 | 0 | 51 | 1 | 4 | 11 | .255 | .278 | .388 |
| Orr, Pete, Richmond * | 115 | 491 | 460 | 69 | 147 | 186 | 16 | 10 | 1 | 35 | 7 | 2 | 2 | 20 | 0 | 59 | 24 | 11 | 7 | .320 | .349 | .404 |
| Osik, Keith, Durham | 26 | 93 | 82 | 6 | 20 | 23 | 0 | 0 | 1 | 8 | 3 | 1 | 1 | 6 | 0 | 10 | 0 | 0 | 1 | .244 | .300 | .280 |
| Owens, Eric, Toledo | 120 | 475 | 443 | 37 | 111 | 133 | 11 | 1 | 3 | 32 | 8 | 3 | 2 | 19 | 0 | 50 | 15 | 6 | 17 | .251 | .283 | .300 |
| Owens, Jeremy, Pawtucket | 112 | 393 | 347 | 52 | 79 | 133 | 16 | 1 | 12 | 41 | 7 | 1 | 1 | 37 | 0 | 140 | 5 | 4 | 7 | .228 | .303 | .383 |
| Owens, Ryan, Rochester | 42 | 128 | 101 | 13 | 22 | 34 | 5 | 2 | 1 | 14 | 1 | 2 | 2 | 22 | 1 | 33 | 1 | 1 | 2 | .218 | .362 | .337 |
| Ozuna, Pablo, Scranton-WB | 126 | 517 | 472 | 77 | 145 | 196 | 27 | 3 | 6 | 76 | 11 | 5 | 7 | 22 | 2 | 43 | 31 | 12 | 11 | .307 | .344 | .415 |
| Pachot, John, Norfolk | 85 | 309 | 290 | 26 | 76 | 104 | 10 | 0 | 6 | 32 | 5 | 1 | 1 | 12 | 4 | 41 | 0 | 1 | 12 | .262 | .293 | .359 |
| Padilla, Jorge, Scranton-WB | 117 | 429 | 364 | 51 | 92 | 125 | 12 | 0 | 7 | 45 | 7 | 3 | 7 | 48 | 2 | 75 | 11 | 7 | 12 | .253 | .348 | .343 |
| Pagan, Angel, Norfolk † | 12 | 49 | 45 | 13 | 13 | 22 | 3 | 3 | 0 | 1 | 0 | 0 | 0 | 4 | 0 | 8 | 4 | 1 | 0 | .289 | .347 | .489 |
| Parker, Matt, Indianapolis | 1 | 1 | 1 | 0 | 0 | 0 | 0 | 0 | 0 | 0 | 0 | 0 | 0 | 0 | 0 | 1 | 0 | 0 | 0 | .000 | .000 | .000 |
| Parrish, Dave, Columbus | 32 | 105 | 97 | 12 | 26 | 35 | 7 | 1 | 0 | 12 | 1 | 0 | 0 | 7 | 0 | 23 | 0 | 0 | 5 | .268 | .317 | .361 |
| Patchett, Gary, Louisville | 4 | 2 | 2 | 1 | 0 | 0 | 0 | 0 | 0 | 0 | 0 | 0 | 0 | 0 | 0 | 0 | 0 | 0 | 0 | .000 | .000 | .000 |
| Paz, Rich, Charlotte | 29 | 114 | 95 | 10 | 25 | 33 | 2 | 0 | 2 | 7 | 1 | 0 | 1 | 17 | 0 | 11 | 0 | 0 | 1 | .263 | .381 | .347 |

| Player, Team | G | TPA | AB | R | H | TB | 2B | 3B | HR | RBI | SH | SF | HP | BB | IBB | SO | SB | CS | GDP | Avg. | OBP | Slg. |
|---|---|---|---|---|---|---|---|---|---|---|---|---|---|---|---|---|---|---|---|---|---|---|
| Peralta, Jhonny, Buffalo | 138 | 623 | 556 | 109 | 181 | 274 | 44 | 2 | 15 | 86 | 0 | 9 | 4 | 54 | 0 | 126 | 8 | 4 | 16 | .326 | .384 | .493 |
| Perez, Frank, Scranton-WB | 9 | 2 | 2 | 0 | 0 | 0 | 0 | 0 | 0 | 0 | 0 | 0 | 0 | 0 | 0 | 2 | 0 | 0 | 0 | .000 | .000 | .000 |
| Petrick, Ben, Toledo | 3 | 11 | 10 | 0 | 0 | 0 | 0 | 0 | 0 | 0 | 0 | 0 | 0 | 1 | 0 | 7 | 0 | 0 | 0 | .000 | .091 | .000 |
| Phelps, Travis, Indianapolis | 28 | 12 | 9 | 1 | 2 | 2 | 0 | 0 | 0 | 0 | 2 | 0 | 0 | 1 | 0 | 1 | 0 | 0 | 0 | .222 | .300 | .222 |
| Phillips, Andy, Columbus | 115 | 493 | 434 | 83 | 138 | 247 | 19 | 6 | 26 | 85 | 1 | 5 | 2 | 51 | 5 | 60 | 2 | 1 | 18 | .318 | .388 | .569 |
| Phillips, Brandon, Buffalo | 135 | 588 | 521 | 83 | 158 | 224 | 34 | 4 | 8 | 50 | 9 | 6 | 8 | 44 | 0 | 56 | 14 | 11 | 12 | .303 | .363 | .430 |
| Polanco, Placido, Scranton-WB | 1 | 4 | 3 | 1 | 0 | 0 | 0 | 0 | 0 | 0 | 0 | 0 | 0 | 1 | 0 | 0 | 0 | 0 | 0 | .000 | .250 | .000 |
| Pond, Simon, Syracuse * | 78 | 326 | 302 | 36 | 84 | 131 | 24 | 1 | 7 | 35 | 0 | 2 | 3 | 19 | 1 | 72 | 1 | 0 | 7 | .278 | .325 | .434 |
| Powell, Brian, Scranton-WB | 8 | 1 | 0 | 0 | 0 | 0 | 0 | 0 | 0 | 0 | 0 | 0 | 0 | 1 | 0 | 0 | 0 | 0 | 0 | .000 | 1.000 | .000 |
| Pratt, Scott, Buffalo * | 1 | 4 | 3 | 1 | 1 | 1 | 0 | 0 | 0 | 0 | 0 | 0 | 0 | 1 | 0 | 0 | 0 | 0 | 0 | .333 | .500 | .333 |
| Prieto, Alex, Rochester | 84 | 327 | 289 | 39 | 72 | 103 | 13 | 0 | 6 | 22 | 4 | 4 | 1 | 29 | 0 | 52 | 2 | 3 | 5 | .249 | .316 | .356 |
| Quiroz, Guillermo, Syracuse | 76 | 288 | 255 | 32 | 58 | 103 | 19 | 1 | 8 | 32 | 0 | 2 | 3 | 28 | 1 | 54 | 0 | 0 | 8 | .227 | .309 | .404 |
| Rabe, Josh, Rochester | 122 | 481 | 429 | 54 | 113 | 161 | 27 | 0 | 7 | 45 | 3 | 3 | 6 | 40 | 3 | 76 | 26 | 5 | 9 | .263 | .333 | .375 |
| Ragsdale, Corey, Norfolk | 6 | 21 | 20 | 1 | 5 | 6 | 1 | 0 | 0 | 1 | 0 | 0 | 0 | 1 | 0 | 4 | 1 | 0 | 0 | .250 | .286 | .300 |
| Raines, Tim, Ottawa | 72 | 303 | 267 | 32 | 70 | 88 | 13 | 1 | 1 | 23 | 7 | 6 | 5 | 18 | 0 | 69 | 24 | 7 | 4 | .262 | .314 | .330 |
| Ramirez, Horacio, Richmond * | 2 | 2 | 2 | 0 | 0 | 0 | 0 | 0 | 0 | 0 | 0 | 0 | 0 | 0 | 0 | 1 | 0 | 0 | 0 | .000 | .000 | .000 |
| Randall, Scott, Louisville | 27 | 1 | 0 | 0 | 0 | 0 | 0 | 0 | 0 | 0 | 1 | 0 | 0 | 0 | 0 | 0 | 0 | 0 | 0 | .000 | .000 | .000 |
| Redman, Prentice, Norfolk | 62 | 235 | 213 | 29 | 54 | 87 | 17 | 2 | 4 | 30 | 1 | 3 | 1 | 17 | 0 | 57 | 9 | 3 | 1 | .254 | .308 | .408 |
| Reed, Jeremy, Charlotte * | 73 | 324 | 276 | 44 | 76 | 116 | 14 | 1 | 8 | 37 | 2 | 7 | 3 | 36 | 0 | 34 | 12 | 7 | 7 | .275 | .357 | .420 |
| Reese, Kevin, Columbus * | 53 | 240 | 217 | 41 | 70 | 113 | 13 | 3 | 8 | 28 | 5 | 1 | 5 | 12 | 0 | 34 | 4 | 4 | 5 | .323 | .370 | .521 |
| Reichert, Dan, Indianapolis | 50 | 1 | 1 | 0 | 0 | 0 | 0 | 0 | 0 | 0 | 0 | 0 | 0 | 0 | 0 | 0 | 0 | 0 | 0 | .000 | .000 | .000 |
| Reyes, Guillermo, Charlotte † | 6 | 19 | 17 | 1 | 2 | 2 | 0 | 0 | 0 | 0 | 1 | 0 | 0 | 1 | 0 | 7 | 0 | 0 | 0 | .118 | .167 | .118 |
| Rios, Alexis, Syracuse | 46 | 195 | 185 | 14 | 48 | 69 | 10 | 1 | 3 | 23 | 0 | 1 | 0 | 9 | 0 | 30 | 2 | 1 | 10 | .259 | .292 | .373 |
| Rios, Armando, Ottawa * | 13 | 54 | 44 | 9 | 15 | 22 | 4 | 0 | 1 | 6 | 0 | 0 | 0 | 10 | 0 | 11 | 2 | 0 | 0 | .341 | .463 | .500 |
| Rivas, Luis, Rochester | 3 | 15 | 14 | 2 | 3 | 3 | 0 | 0 | 0 | 1 | 0 | 0 | 1 | 0 | 0 | 2 | 1 | 0 | 0 | .214 | .267 | .214 |
| Rivera, Mike, Charlotte | 11 | 45 | 40 | 3 | 4 | 6 | 0 | 1 | 0 | 2 | 0 | 1 | 1 | 3 | 0 | 12 | 0 | 0 | 0 | .100 | .178 | .150 |
| Roach, Jason, Norfolk | 42 | 8 | 8 | 0 | 2 | 2 | 0 | 0 | 0 | 1 | 0 | 0 | 0 | 0 | 0 | 3 | 0 | 0 | 0 | .250 | .250 | .250 |
| Roberge, J.P., Scranton-WB | 71 | 257 | 238 | 17 | 61 | 78 | 12 | 1 | 1 | 16 | 0 | 1 | 0 | 18 | 2 | 42 | 1 | 1 | 9 | .256 | .307 | .328 |
| Rodriguez, Guillermo, Toledo | 73 | 241 | 219 | 17 | 41 | 74 | 8 | 2 | 7 | 21 | 3 | 2 | 3 | 14 | 0 | 45 | 2 | 2 | 6 | .187 | .244 | .338 |
| Rodriguez, John, Columbus * | 112 | 438 | 378 | 78 | 111 | 205 | 26 | 10 | 16 | 68 | 1 | 3 | 8 | 48 | 7 | 84 | 10 | 3 | 7 | .294 | .382 | .542 |
| Rodriguez, Luis, Rochester † | 127 | 565 | 486 | 73 | 139 | 189 | 33 | 1 | 5 | 52 | 18 | 7 | 1 | 53 | 1 | 49 | 3 | 3 | 17 | .286 | .353 | .389 |
| Rodriguez, Luis, Toledo | 2 | 5 | 5 | 0 | 1 | 2 | 1 | 0 | 0 | 0 | 0 | 0 | 0 | 0 | 0 | 1 | 0 | 0 | 0 | .200 | .200 | .400 |
| Rolls, Damian, Durham | 23 | 107 | 97 | 23 | 27 | 43 | 7 | 0 | 3 | 14 | 0 | 0 | 3 | 7 | 0 | 17 | 2 | 1 | 2 | .278 | .346 | .443 |
| Romano, Jason, Louisville | 40 | 167 | 163 | 22 | 55 | 81 | 12 | 4 | 2 | 16 | 0 | 1 | 0 | 3 | 2 | 24 | 3 | 1 | 0 | .337 | .347 | .497 |
| Romano, Mike, Richmond | 40 | 21 | 16 | 1 | 1 | 1 | 0 | 0 | 0 | 1 | 2 | 0 | 0 | 3 | 0 | 6 | 0 | 0 | 0 | .063 | .211 | .063 |
| Rose, Brian, Louisville | 7 | 5 | 5 | 0 | 0 | 0 | 0 | 0 | 0 | 0 | 0 | 0 | 0 | 0 | 0 | 3 | 0 | 0 | 0 | .000 | .000 | .000 |
| Rushford, Jim, Scranton-WB * | 134 | 568 | 517 | 71 | 142 | 210 | 30 | 4 | 10 | 75 | 3 | 2 | 1 | 45 | 3 | 54 | 1 | 2 | 9 | .275 | .333 | .406 |
| Ryan, Michael, Rochester * | 50 | 196 | 175 | 29 | 37 | 64 | 7 | 1 | 6 | 16 | 4 | 0 | 1 | 16 | 1 | 38 | 3 | 4 | 3 | .211 | .281 | .366 |
| Sadler, Donnie, Charlotte | 3 | 9 | 7 | 0 | 1 | 1 | 0 | 0 | 0 | 0 | 1 | 0 | 0 | 1 | 0 | 3 | 0 | 0 | 0 | .143 | .250 | .143 |
| Sanchez, Alex, Toledo * | 2 | 10 | 10 | 0 | 0 | 0 | 0 | 0 | 0 | 0 | 0 | 0 | 0 | 0 | 0 | 6 | 0 | 0 | 0 | .000 | .000 | .000 |
| Sanchez, Jesus, Louisville * | 23 | 1 | 1 | 0 | 0 | 0 | 0 | 0 | 0 | 0 | 0 | 0 | 0 | 0 | 0 | 0 | 0 | 0 | 0 | .000 | .000 | .000 |
| Sandberg, Jared, Durham | 126 | 471 | 435 | 61 | 100 | 185 | 26 | 1 | 19 | 67 | 1 | 3 | 3 | 29 | 0 | 138 | 1 | 2 | 8 | .230 | .281 | .425 |
| Sanders, Anthony, Syracuse | 65 | 249 | 228 | 27 | 63 | 99 | 19 | 1 | 5 | 30 | 4 | 1 | 2 | 13 | 0 | 56 | 2 | 1 | 2 | .276 | .320 | .434 |
| Santos, Victor, Indianapolis | 3 | 2 | 2 | 1 | 1 | 1 | 0 | 0 | 0 | 0 | 0 | 0 | 0 | 0 | 0 | 0 | 0 | 0 | 0 | .500 | .500 | .500 |
| Sardinha, Dane, Louisville | 89 | 345 | 324 | 32 | 85 | 131 | 17 | 1 | 9 | 40 | 1 | 4 | 6 | 10 | 0 | 94 | 0 | 1 | 9 | .262 | .294 | .404 |
| Scanlon, Matt, Rochester * | 29 | 86 | 73 | 4 | 14 | 17 | 0 | 0 | 1 | 6 | 0 | 0 | 1 | 12 | 1 | 12 | 1 | 1 | 3 | .192 | .314 | .233 |
| Scarborough, Steve, Indianapolis | 113 | 395 | 342 | 39 | 84 | 131 | 27 | 4 | 4 | 37 | 3 | 0 | 7 | 43 | 4 | 72 | 2 | 0 | 5 | .246 | .342 | .383 |
| Schrager, Tony, Pawtucket | 122 | 494 | 436 | 63 | 116 | 190 | 29 | 0 | 15 | 49 | 2 | 4 | 5 | 47 | 0 | 88 | 2 | 2 | 8 | .266 | .341 | .436 |
| Seo, Jae, Norfolk | 4 | 1 | 1 | 1 | 1 | 1 | 0 | 0 | 0 | 0 | 0 | 0 | 0 | 0 | 0 | 0 | 0 | 0 | 0 | 1.000 | 1.000 | 1.000 |
| Sequea, Jorge, Syracuse | 97 | 381 | 335 | 53 | 89 | 123 | 16 | 3 | 4 | 31 | 4 | 1 | 6 | 35 | 0 | 63 | 10 | 6 | 7 | .266 | .345 | .367 |
| Shackelford, Brian, Louisville * | 60 | 5 | 5 | 0 | 1 | 1 | 0 | 0 | 0 | 0 | 0 | 0 | 0 | 0 | 0 | 1 | 0 | 0 | 0 | .200 | .200 | .200 |
| Sheldon, Scott, Indianapolis | 41 | 130 | 113 | 12 | 26 | 49 | 8 | 0 | 5 | 10 | 5 | 2 | 0 | 10 | 0 | 26 | 0 | 1 | 2 | .230 | .288 | .434 |
| Shelton, Chris, Toledo | 18 | 73 | 62 | 5 | 21 | 23 | 2 | 0 | 0 | 7 | 0 | 1 | 0 | 10 | 0 | 13 | 0 | 0 | 0 | .339 | .425 | .371 |
| Sherrod, Justin, Pawtucket | 104 | 373 | 341 | 55 | 91 | 172 | 20 | 5 | 17 | 51 | 1 | 2 | 4 | 25 | 1 | 108 | 6 | 2 | 2 | .267 | .323 | .504 |
| Shoppach, Kelly, Pawtucket | 113 | 454 | 399 | 62 | 93 | 184 | 25 | 0 | 22 | 64 | 1 | 2 | 6 | 46 | 0 | 138 | 0 | 0 | 7 | .233 | .320 | .461 |
| Simmons, Brian, Rochester † | 82 | 321 | 299 | 33 | 67 | 106 | 12 | 0 | 9 | 37 | 2 | 1 | 2 | 17 | 1 | 64 | 3 | 2 | 7 | .224 | .270 | .355 |
| Sizemore, Grady, Buffalo * | 101 | 473 | 418 | 73 | 120 | 183 | 23 | 8 | 8 | 51 | 1 | 4 | 8 | 42 | 0 | 72 | 15 | 10 | 6 | .287 | .360 | .438 |
| Slack, Jonathan, Norfolk * | 6 | 16 | 15 | 3 | 3 | 3 | 0 | 0 | 0 | 0 | 0 | 0 | 1 | 0 | 0 | 4 | 0 | 0 | 0 | .200 | .250 | .200 |
| Smith, Bobby, Charlotte | 134 | 559 | 508 | 84 | 138 | 263 | 37 | 2 | 28 | 89 | 1 | 2 | 8 | 40 | 2 | 117 | 12 | 4 | 10 | .272 | .333 | .518 |
| Smith, Chuck, Richmond | 30 | 18 | 16 | 0 | 1 | 1 | 0 | 0 | 0 | 0 | 2 | 0 | 0 | 0 | 0 | 2 | 0 | 0 | 1 | .063 | .063 | .063 |
| Smith, Corey, Buffalo | 5 | 20 | 18 | 0 | 2 | 3 | 1 | 0 | 0 | 1 | 0 | 0 | 1 | 1 | 0 | 6 | 0 | 0 | 1 | .111 | .200 | .167 |
| Smith, Jason, Toledo * | 33 | 130 | 122 | 18 | 33 | 54 | 8 | 2 | 3 | 13 | 0 | 2 | 0 | 6 | 1 | 26 | 5 | 1 | 1 | .270 | .300 | .443 |
| Smith, Mark, Scranton-WB | 116 | 454 | 398 | 54 | 112 | 176 | 29 | 1 | 11 | 62 | 0 | 5 | 9 | 42 | 4 | 69 | 3 | 1 | 11 | .281 | .359 | .442 |
| Smith, Travis, Richmond | 20 | 9 | 8 | 0 | 1 | 1 | 0 | 0 | 0 | 0 | 1 | 0 | 0 | 0 | 0 | 2 | 0 | 0 | 0 | .125 | .125 | .125 |
| Smitherman, Stephen, Louisville | 129 | 503 | 452 | 55 | 123 | 190 | 35 | 1 | 10 | 52 | 0 | 3 | 6 | 42 | 0 | 107 | 5 | 5 | 13 | .272 | .340 | .420 |
| Snead, Esix, Norfolk † | 79 | 314 | 269 | 42 | 71 | 85 | 10 | 2 | 0 | 21 | 4 | 4 | 2 | 35 | 0 | 53 | 40 | 10 | 2 | .264 | .348 | .316 |
| Snyder, Earl, Pawtucket | 136 | 586 | 538 | 85 | 147 | 300 | 43 | 1 | 36 | 104 | 0 | 6 | 7 | 35 | 3 | 128 | 1 | 1 | 14 | .273 | .323 | .558 |
| Socarras, Tony, Norfolk * | 13 | 24 | 22 | 3 | 6 | 10 | 1 | 0 | 1 | 3 | 0 | 1 | 0 | 1 | 0 | 10 | 0 | 1 | 0 | .273 | .292 | .455 |
| Solano, Danny, Syracuse | 9 | 30 | 25 | 3 | 5 | 6 | 1 | 0 | 0 | 3 | 0 | 0 | 1 | 4 | 0 | 6 | 0 | 0 | 0 | .200 | .333 | .240 |
| Sorensen, Zach, Buffalo † | 4 | 9 | 8 | 0 | 0 | 0 | 0 | 0 | 0 | 0 | 0 | 0 | 0 | 1 | 1 | 3 | 0 | 0 | 0 | .000 | .111 | .000 |
| Spencer, Shane, Columbus | 15 | 59 | 50 | 6 | 12 | 16 | 4 | 0 | 0 | 5 | 0 | 0 | 2 | 7 | 0 | 15 | 1 | 0 | 1 | .240 | .356 | .320 |
| Stanley, Henri, Pawtucket * | 51 | 189 | 164 | 30 | 49 | 77 | 17 | 1 | 3 | 17 | 1 | 1 | 0 | 23 | 0 | 27 | 2 | 2 | 3 | .299 | .383 | .470 |
| Stewart, Chris, Charlotte | 5 | 16 | 14 | 1 | 1 | 2 | 1 | 0 | 0 | 1 | 0 | 0 | 1 | 1 | 0 | 3 | 0 | 0 | 0 | .071 | .188 | .143 |
| Stewart, Shannon, Rochester | 3 | 10 | 9 | 3 | 3 | 4 | 1 | 0 | 0 | 0 | 0 | 0 | 0 | 1 | 0 | 2 | 0 | 0 | 0 | .333 | .400 | .444 |
| Strange, Pat, Norfolk | 31 | 16 | 15 | 0 | 2 | 3 | 1 | 0 | 0 | 0 | 1 | 0 | 0 | 0 | 0 | 7 | 1 | 0 | 0 | .133 | .133 | .200 |
| Stratton, Rob, Louisville | 34 | 130 | 119 | 23 | 42 | 92 | 10 | 2 | 12 | 34 | 0 | 2 | 0 | 9 | 0 | 35 | 0 | 1 | 3 | .353 | .392 | .773 |
| Swann, Pedro, Ottawa * | 126 | 511 | 458 | 59 | 124 | 203 | 32 | 1 | 15 | 54 | 1 | 3 | 9 | 40 | 2 | 84 | 5 | 3 | 8 | .271 | .339 | .443 |
| Taylor, Reggie, Louisville * | 61 | 211 | 191 | 28 | 49 | 87 | 9 | 1 | 9 | 24 | 4 | 2 | 1 | 13 | 1 | 46 | 10 | 3 | 5 | .257 | .304 | .455 |
| Taylor, Reggie, Charlotte * | 58 | 237 | 210 | 34 | 61 | 108 | 14 | 0 | 11 | 30 | 2 | 2 | 2 | 21 | 1 | 45 | 11 | 4 | 3 | .290 | .357 | .514 |
| Terveen, Bryce, Richmond * | 15 | 51 | 41 | 3 | 8 | 13 | 0 | 1 | 1 | 7 | 3 | 0 | 2 | 5 | 0 | 7 | 0 | 0 | 0 | .195 | .313 | .317 |
| Thames, Marcus, Toledo | 64 | 274 | 234 | 57 | 77 | 172 | 21 | 1 | 24 | 59 | 1 | 4 | 2 | 33 | 3 | 40 | 4 | 1 | 5 | .329 | .410 | .735 |
| Thomas, Charles, Richmond * | 61 | 240 | 215 | 31 | 77 | 115 | 18 | 4 | 4 | 32 | 2 | 1 | 6 | 16 | 0 | 40 | 7 | 5 | 4 | .358 | .416 | .535 |

| Player, Team | G | TPA | AB | R | H | TB | 2B | 3B | HR | RBI | SH | SF | HP | BB | IBB | SO | SB | CS | GDP | Avg. | OBP | Slg. |
|---|---|---|---|---|---|---|---|---|---|---|---|---|---|---|---|---|---|---|---|---|---|---|
| Tiffee, Terry, Rochester † | 82 | 342 | 316 | 42 | 97 | 165 | 26 | 3 | 12 | 68 | 0 | 1 | 4 | 21 | 2 | 26 | 0 | 0 | 9 | .307 | .357 | .522 |
| Timmons, Ozzie, Norfolk | 30 | 122 | 106 | 13 | 29 | 47 | 6 | 0 | 4 | 18 | 1 | 2 | 1 | 12 | 0 | 18 | 0 | 0 | 3 | .274 | .347 | .443 |
| Toca, Jorge, Toledo | 16 | 65 | 63 | 4 | 16 | 20 | 1 | 0 | 1 | 6 | 0 | 1 | 0 | 1 | 0 | 14 | 2 | 1 | 3 | .254 | .262 | .317 |
| Torrealba, Steve, Columbus | 4 | 13 | 13 | 3 | 6 | 13 | 1 | 0 | 2 | 4 | 0 | 0 | 0 | 0 | 0 | 3 | 0 | 0 | 0 | .462 | .462 | 1.000 |
| Torres, Andres, Charlotte | 87 | 371 | 322 | 49 | 95 | 138 | 11 | 4 | 8 | 26 | 7 | 2 | 5 | 35 | 0 | 74 | 23 | 7 | 3 | .295 | .371 | .429 |
| Torres, Gabby, Rochester | 10 | 32 | 31 | 1 | 7 | 11 | 4 | 0 | 0 | 3 | 0 | 0 | 1 | 0 | 0 | 6 | 0 | 0 | 0 | .226 | .250 | .355 |
| Trammell, Bubba, Durham | 10 | 46 | 41 | 6 | 15 | 31 | 4 | 0 | 4 | 14 | 0 | 0 | 0 | 5 | 0 | 2 | 0 | 0 | 2 | .366 | .435 | .756 |
| Tyner, Jason, Richmond * | 64 | 269 | 243 | 40 | 70 | 87 | 12 | 1 | 1 | 16 | 3 | 1 | 7 | 15 | 0 | 22 | 18 | 6 | 4 | .288 | .346 | .358 |
| Tyner, Jason, Buffalo * | 38 | 166 | 139 | 25 | 48 | 54 | 4 | 1 | 0 | 16 | 3 | 4 | 2 | 18 | 0 | 15 | 5 | 0 | 0 | .345 | .417 | .388 |
| Upton, B.J., Durham | 69 | 313 | 264 | 65 | 82 | 137 | 17 | 1 | 12 | 36 | 4 | 0 | 3 | 42 | 0 | 72 | 17 | 5 | 9 | .311 | .411 | .519 |
| Ust, Brant, Toledo | 111 | 430 | 406 | 47 | 103 | 154 | 17 | 2 | 10 | 41 | 2 | 4 | 3 | 15 | 2 | 97 | 3 | 3 | 7 | .254 | .283 | .379 |
| Utley, Chase, Scranton-WB * | 33 | 144 | 123 | 23 | 35 | 63 | 8 | 1 | 6 | 25 | 0 | 3 | 0 | 18 | 1 | 29 | 4 | 2 | 2 | .285 | .368 | .512 |
| Valdez, Wilson, Charlotte | 70 | 311 | 281 | 37 | 85 | 102 | 7 | 2 | 2 | 15 | 15 | 0 | 3 | 12 | 0 | 40 | 13 | 5 | 6 | .302 | .338 | .363 |
| Valentin, Jose, Charlotte † | 8 | 33 | 31 | 1 | 2 | 2 | 0 | 0 | 0 | 2 | 0 | 0 | 0 | 2 | 0 | 15 | 0 | 0 | 0 | .065 | .121 | .065 |
| Valentine, Joe, Louisville | 30 | 5 | 5 | 0 | 0 | 0 | 0 | 0 | 0 | 0 | 0 | 0 | 0 | 0 | 0 | 3 | 0 | 0 | 0 | .000 | .000 | .000 |
| Valenzuela, Mario, Charlotte | 119 | 460 | 429 | 67 | 113 | 212 | 20 | 2 | 25 | 66 | 0 | 3 | 6 | 22 | 0 | 81 | 3 | 3 | 11 | .263 | .307 | .494 |
| Vander Wal, John, Louisville * | 16 | 53 | 48 | 5 | 9 | 12 | 3 | 0 | 0 | 2 | 0 | 0 | 0 | 5 | 1 | 10 | 2 | 0 | 1 | .188 | .264 | .250 |
| Velandia, Jorge, Richmond | 129 | 447 | 391 | 39 | 83 | 124 | 21 | 1 | 6 | 25 | 7 | 2 | 6 | 41 | 3 | 67 | 1 | 1 | 8 | .212 | .295 | .317 |
| Velazquez, Gil, Norfolk | 17 | 40 | 33 | 4 | 3 | 4 | 1 | 0 | 0 | 0 | 2 | 0 | 0 | 5 | 0 | 12 | 1 | 0 | 1 | .091 | .211 | .121 |
| Velazquez, Juan, Richmond † | 13 | 46 | 41 | 4 | 6 | 6 | 0 | 0 | 0 | 1 | 0 | 0 | 1 | 4 | 0 | 9 | 1 | 0 | 1 | .146 | .239 | .146 |
| Vento, Michael, Columbus | 122 | 501 | 451 | 64 | 124 | 199 | 28 | 1 | 15 | 72 | 0 | 7 | 9 | 34 | 3 | 77 | 2 | 3 | 8 | .275 | .333 | .441 |
| Vitiello, Joe, Toledo | 86 | 360 | 323 | 52 | 106 | 173 | 19 | 0 | 16 | 70 | 0 | 4 | 6 | 27 | 2 | 61 | 2 | 2 | 5 | .328 | .386 | .536 |
| Walker, Matt, Ottawa | 3 | 8 | 8 | 1 | 3 | 3 | 0 | 0 | 0 | 1 | 0 | 0 | 0 | 0 | 0 | 3 | 1 | 0 | 0 | .375 | .375 | .375 |
| Wathan, Dusty, Buffalo | 77 | 271 | 238 | 41 | 72 | 92 | 15 | 1 | 1 | 24 | 2 | 1 | 13 | 17 | 1 | 30 | 3 | 0 | 10 | .303 | .379 | .387 |
| Weibl, Clint, Indianapolis | 24 | 9 | 8 | 0 | 0 | 0 | 0 | 0 | 0 | 0 | 1 | 0 | 0 | 0 | 0 | 5 | 0 | 0 | 0 | .000 | .000 | .000 |
| West, Kevin, Rochester | 20 | 85 | 79 | 10 | 22 | 42 | 8 | 0 | 4 | 22 | 0 | 2 | 0 | 4 | 0 | 19 | 0 | 0 | 4 | .278 | .306 | .532 |
| Whiteside, Matt, Richmond | 57 | 3 | 3 | 0 | 0 | 0 | 0 | 0 | 0 | 0 | 0 | 0 | 0 | 0 | 0 | 3 | 0 | 0 | 0 | .000 | .000 | .000 |
| Whittaker, Tim, Syracuse | 47 | 151 | 144 | 9 | 37 | 50 | 10 | 0 | 1 | 14 | 0 | 3 | 1 | 3 | 0 | 28 | 1 | 1 | 8 | .257 | .272 | .347 |
| Williams, Gerald, Norfolk | 63 | 266 | 246 | 37 | 75 | 112 | 10 | 3 | 7 | 28 | 6 | 2 | 3 | 9 | 0 | 35 | 6 | 9 | 4 | .305 | .335 | .455 |
| Williams, Glenn, Syracuse † | 117 | 486 | 432 | 65 | 114 | 214 | 23 | 4 | 23 | 79 | 4 | 8 | 8 | 34 | 1 | 79 | 2 | 4 | 9 | .264 | .324 | .495 |
| Wilson, Tom, Norfolk | 34 | 141 | 115 | 26 | 37 | 68 | 10 | 0 | 7 | 22 | 1 | 0 | 0 | 25 | 1 | 24 | 0 | 1 | 3 | .322 | .443 | .591 |
| Wilson, Vance, Norfolk | 1 | 4 | 4 | 1 | 2 | 5 | 0 | 0 | 1 | 1 | 0 | 0 | 0 | 0 | 0 | 0 | 0 | 0 | 0 | .500 | .500 | 1.250 |
| Wise, Dewayne, Richmond * | 34 | 127 | 118 | 18 | 37 | 68 | 4 | 6 | 5 | 16 | 4 | 0 | 0 | 5 | 1 | 19 | 5 | 0 | 1 | .314 | .341 | .576 |
| Wise, Matt, Indianapolis | 7 | 3 | 2 | 1 | 0 | 0 | 0 | 0 | 0 | 0 | 0 | 0 | 0 | 1 | 0 | 1 | 0 | 0 | 0 | .000 | .333 | .000 |
| Woolard, Glenn, Indianapolis | 1 | 3 | 3 | 0 | 0 | 0 | 0 | 0 | 0 | 0 | 0 | 0 | 0 | 0 | 0 | 1 | 0 | 0 | 0 | .000 | .000 | .000 |
| Wooten, Shawn, Scranton-WB | 61 | 254 | 225 | 28 | 66 | 100 | 22 | 0 | 4 | 34 | 0 | 1 | 4 | 24 | 0 | 29 | 0 | 1 | 11 | .293 | .370 | .444 |
| Wright, David, Norfolk | 31 | 134 | 114 | 18 | 34 | 66 | 8 | 0 | 8 | 17 | 0 | 2 | 2 | 16 | 1 | 19 | 2 | 4 | 3 | .298 | .388 | .579 |
| Yarnall, Ed, Pawtucket * | 2 | 0 | 0 | 0 | 0 | 0 | 0 | 0 | 0 | 0 | 0 | 0 | 0 | 0 | 0 | 0 | 0 | 0 | 0 | .000 | .000 | .000 |
| Yarnall, Ed, Pawtucket * | 2 | 0 | 0 | 0 | 0 | 0 | 0 | 0 | 0 | 0 | 0 | 0 | 0 | 0 | 0 | 0 | 0 | 0 | 0 | .000 | .000 | .000 |
| Yarnall, Ed, Scranton-WB * | 25 | 16 | 10 | 2 | 3 | 4 | 1 | 0 | 0 | 2 | 2 | 0 | 0 | 4 | 0 | 2 | 0 | 0 | 1 | .300 | .500 | .400 |
| Youkilis, Kevin, Pawtucket | 38 | 178 | 154 | 25 | 41 | 62 | 12 | 0 | 3 | 18 | 1 | 2 | 2 | 19 | 1 | 28 | 2 | 0 | 1 | .266 | .350 | .403 |
| Young, Dmitri, Toledo † | 2 | 11 | 10 | 1 | 5 | 11 | 1 | 1 | 1 | 5 | 0 | 0 | 0 | 1 | 0 | 0 | 0 | 0 | 0 | .500 | .545 | 1.100 |
| Young, Ernie, Buffalo | 115 | 500 | 441 | 71 | 132 | 243 | 26 | 2 | 27 | 100 | 0 | 7 | 12 | 40 | 1 | 104 | 2 | 2 | 7 | .299 | .368 | .551 |
| Zaun, Gregg, Syracuse † | 7 | 26 | 23 | 4 | 7 | 8 | 1 | 0 | 0 | 2 | 0 | 1 | 0 | 2 | 0 | 5 | 1 | 0 | 1 | .304 | .346 | .348 |

GRAND SLAMS—Clapinski, 4; Tiffee, 3; Branyan, M. Diaz, 2 each; Abernathy, Bell, Betemit, Borchard, Brazell, Cantu, Chamblee, Crozier, Cummings, Deardorff, DePastino, V. Diaz, D. Garcia, Gil, Glavine, Hardy, Heintz, M. Hernandez, Hessman, Kelly, Liefer, F. Lopez, Ludwick, Morneau, W. Morris, Nelson, Norton, Owens, Padilla, Schrager, Shoppach, Simmons, Sizemore, B. Smith, M. Smith, Snyder, G. Williams, Wooten.

AWARDED FIRST BASE ON CATCHER'S INTERFERENCE—Collier (Sardinha), Ojeda (Parrish), Sanders (Bard).

# 2004 PITCHING

## TEAM

| Team | W | L | Pct. | ERA | G | CG | ShO | Sv. | IP | H | TBF | R | ER | HR | SH | SF | HB | BB | IBB | SO | WP | Bk. |
|---|---|---|---|---|---|---|---|---|---|---|---|---|---|---|---|---|---|---|---|---|---|---|
| Richmond | 79 | 62 | .560 | 3.71 | 141 | 3 | 10 | 45 | 1190.0 | 1164 | 5095 | 543 | 491 | 94 | 49 | 35 | 62 | 445 | 22 | 976 | 42 | 12 |
| Norfolk | 72 | 72 | .500 | 4.03 | 144 | 5 | 5 | 43 | 1257.1 | 1272 | 5449 | 661 | 563 | 118 | 54 | 41 | 68 | 463 | 17 | 956 | 43 | 14 |
| Columbus | 80 | 64 | .556 | 4.20 | 144 | 8 | 12 | 37 | 1246.2 | 1294 | 5343 | 654 | 582 | 130 | 49 | 39 | 57 | 369 | 11 | 1034 | 42 | 4 |
| Durham | 77 | 67 | .535 | 4.24 | 144 | 3 | 9 | 37 | 1219.1 | 1264 | 5308 | 657 | 574 | 134 | 37 | 33 | 41 | 491 | 11 | 958 | 69 | 4 |
| Rochester | 73 | 71 | .507 | 4.26 | 144 | 2 | 9 | 39 | 1269.0 | 1352 | 5462 | 685 | 600 | 144 | 45 | 53 | 48 | 388 | 15 | 966 | 35 | 5 |
| Scranton-Wb | 69 | 73 | .486 | 4.39 | 142 | 8 | 8 | 33 | 1235.2 | 1316 | 5341 | 689 | 603 | 152 | 67 | 49 | 53 | 359 | 24 | 807 | 23 | 2 |
| Louisville | 67 | 77 | .465 | 4.40 | 144 | 5 | 9 | 33 | 1230.2 | 1261 | 5381 | 674 | 602 | 123 | 40 | 44 | 59 | 517 | 17 | 1010 | 56 | 5 |
| Pawtucket | 73 | 71 | .507 | 4.48 | 144 | 4 | 7 | 29 | 1257.2 | 1371 | 5464 | 697 | 626 | 179 | 45 | 41 | 66 | 365 | 12 | 901 | 46 | 5 |
| Charlotte | 68 | 74 | .479 | 4.56 | 142 | 4 | 5 | 37 | 1241.1 | 1252 | 5319 | 697 | 629 | 176 | 45 | 45 | 73 | 429 | 13 | 933 | 55 | 9 |
| Indianapolis | 66 | 78 | .458 | 4.59 | 144 | 4 | 7 | 33 | 1251.0 | 1353 | 5449 | 708 | 638 | 129 | 52 | 45 | 69 | 439 | 18 | 974 | 54 | 14 |
| Toledo | 65 | 78 | .455 | 4.63 | 143 | 7 | 10 | 41 | 1242.0 | 1329 | 5436 | 731 | 639 | 122 | 51 | 37 | 66 | 456 | 28 | 891 | 47 | 6 |
| Ottawa | 66 | 78 | .458 | 4.65 | 144 | 3 | 6 | 39 | 1260.1 | 1327 | 5555 | 726 | 651 | 146 | 50 | 42 | 59 | 520 | 23 | 1034 | 54 | 7 |
| Syracuse | 66 | 78 | .458 | 4.66 | 144 | 5 | 2 | 38 | 1247.1 | 1326 | 5450 | 738 | 646 | 163 | 53 | 50 | 62 | 424 | 13 | 995 | 70 | 4 |
| Buffalo | 83 | 61 | .576 | 4.71 | 144 | 3 | 8 | 32 | 1255.1 | 1326 | 5538 | 724 | 657 | 130 | 33 | 48 | 68 | 494 | 22 | 961 | 66 | 11 |

# INDIVIDUAL

## TOP QUALIFIERS FOR EARNED-RUN AVERAGE TITLE

Minimum 115 innings.*Lefthanded pitcher.

| Pitcher, Team | W | L | Pct. | ERA | G | GS | CG | ShO | GF | Sv. | IP | H | TBF | R | ER | HR | SH | SF | HB | BB | IBB | SO | WP | Bk. |
|---|---|---|---|---|---|---|---|---|---|---|---|---|---|---|---|---|---|---|---|---|---|---|---|---|
| Hendrickson, Ben, Indianapolis | 11 | 3 | .786 | 2.02 | 21 | 21 | 2 | 2 | 0 | 0 | 125.0 | 114 | 492 | 32 | 28 | 6 | 6 | 3 | 1 | 26 | 0 | 93 | 6 | 1 |
| Halsey, Brad, Columbus * | 11 | 4 | .733 | 2.63 | 24 | 23 | 3 | 2 | 0 | 0 | 144.0 | 128 | 589 | 46 | 42 | 8 | 8 | 3 | 7 | 37 | 0 | 109 | 2 | 1 |
| Diaz, Felix, Charlotte | 10 | 2 | .833 | 2.97 | 19 | 17 | 0 | 0 | 0 | 0 | 115.0 | 95 | 436 | 41 | 38 | 14 | 8 | 3 | 2 | 24 | 0 | 96 | 0 | 1 |
| Guerrier, Matt, Rochester | 5 | 10 | .333 | 3.19 | 24 | 23 | 0 | 0 | 1 | 0 | 144.0 | 135 | 579 | 65 | 51 | 15 | 8 | 9 | 5 | 25 | 0 | 97 | 2 | 0 |
| Graman, Alex, Columbus * | 11 | 6 | .647 | 3.37 | 24 | 22 | 1 | 1 | 0 | 0 | 131.0 | 115 | 550 | 56 | 49 | 12 | 10 | 5 | 3 | 53 | 0 | 129 | 7 | 0 |
| Gassner, Dave, Rochester * | 16 | 8 | .667 | 3.41 | 28 | 28 | 0 | 0 | 0 | 0 | 174.1 | 175 | 704 | 72 | 66 | 16 | 7 | 5 | 2 | 30 | 1 | 93 | 2 | 1 |
| Romano, Mike, Richmond | 13 | 5 | .722 | 3.42 | 40 | 16 | 0 | 0 | 9 | 0 | 123.2 | 130 | 537 | 51 | 47 | 13 | 8 | 7 | 7 | 51 | 6 | 99 | 6 | 3 |
| Baldwin, James, Norfolk-Toledo | 8 | 9 | .471 | 3.56 | 23 | 21 | 3 | 0 | 2 | 1 | 146.2 | 144 | 588 | 63 | 58 | 15 | 10 | 2 | 5 | 25 | 3 | 85 | 0 | 0 |
| Eyre, Willie, Rochester | 6 | 7 | .462 | 3.64 | 36 | 21 | 1 | 1 | 5 | 4 | 136.0 | 131 | 569 | 60 | 55 | 13 | 8 | 7 | 4 | 53 | 1 | 91 | 6 | 1 |
| Rayborn, Kenny, Buffalo | 8 | 2 | .800 | 3.64 | 23 | 22 | 0 | 0 | 0 | 0 | 123.2 | 122 | 524 | 57 | 50 | 13 | 7 | 5 | 12 | 40 | 0 | 65 | 4 | 0 |
| Smith, Chuck, Richmond | 9 | 4 | .692 | 3.72 | 29 | 24 | 1 | 1 | 3 | 0 | 142.2 | 125 | 597 | 62 | 59 | 8 | 8 | 5 | 8 | 47 | 1 | 129 | 5 | 4 |
| Keisler, Randy, Norfolk * | 6 | 7 | .462 | 3.81 | 22 | 21 | 1 | 0 | 0 | 0 | 130.0 | 145 | 566 | 72 | 55 | 13 | 4 | 4 | 2 | 45 | 1 | 110 | 2 | 2 |
| Standridge, Jason, Durham | 8 | 4 | .667 | 3.85 | 20 | 20 | 2 | 0 | 0 | 0 | 119.1 | 120 | 498 | 56 | 51 | 7 | 8 | 2 | 3 | 44 | 0 | 76 | 4 | 1 |
| Maine, John, Ottawa | 5 | 7 | .417 | 3.91 | 22 | 22 | 0 | 0 | 0 | 0 | 119.2 | 123 | 512 | 59 | 52 | 12 | 12 | 5 | 5 | 52 | 0 | 105 | 2 | 1 |

DEPARTMENTAL LEADERS: W—Gassner, 16; L—Ahearne, Ellis, 12; Pct.—F. Diaz, .833; G—Shackleford, 59; GS—Three tied with 28; CG—Four tied with three; ShO—Halsey, Hendrickson, 2; GF—Whiteside, 51; Sv.—Whiteside, 38; IP—Ahearne, 179.1; H—Condrey, 206; TBF—Ahearne, 751; R—Condrey, 106; ER—Belisle, 95; HR—Castillo, 28; SH—Three tied with 10; SF—Three tied with eight; HB—M. Smith, Rayborn, 12; BB—Moss, 80; IBB—Santiago, 8; SO—C. Smith, Graman 129; WP—Matos, 13; BK—Three tied with four.

## ALL PITCHERS

*Lefthanded pitcher.

| Pitcher, Team | W | L | Pct. | ERA | G | GS | CG | ShO | GF | Sv. | IP | H | TBF | R | ER | HR | SH | SF | HB | BB | IBB | SO | WP | Bk. |
|---|---|---|---|---|---|---|---|---|---|---|---|---|---|---|---|---|---|---|---|---|---|---|---|---|
| Abbott, Paul, Scranton-WB | 1 | 2 | .333 | 6.15 | 5 | 5 | 1 | 0 | 0 | 0 | 26.1 | 26 | 119 | 18 | 18 | 4 | 0 | 1 | 2 | 17 | 0 | 19 | 1 | 0 |
| Acosta, Anthony, Norfolk | 0 | 0 | .000 | 0.00 | 1 | 0 | 0 | 0 | 0 | 0 | 2.0 | 2 | 8 | 0 | 0 | 0 | 0 | 0 | 0 | 0 | 0 | 0 | 0 | 0 |
| Adams, Mike, Indianapolis | 2 | 0 | 1.000 | 2.61 | 10 | 2 | 0 | 0 | 1 | 0 | 31.0 | 23 | 116 | 10 | 9 | 3 | 1 | 0 | 2 | 4 | 0 | 37 | 0 | 0 |
| Adkins, Tim, Columbus * | 0 | 0 | .000 | 4.50 | 1 | 0 | 0 | 0 | 1 | 0 | 2.0 | 2 | 9 | 1 | 1 | 0 | 0 | 0 | 0 | 1 | 0 | 1 | 0 | 0 |
| Aguilar, Ray, Richmond * | 2 | 4 | .333 | 6.21 | 9 | 9 | 0 | 0 | 0 | 0 | 42.0 | 59 | 199 | 36 | 29 | 4 | 4 | 2 | 3 | 17 | 0 | 31 | 5 | 0 |
| Ahearne, Pat, Toledo | 9 | 12 | .429 | 4.01 | 28 | 28 | 3 | 1 | 0 | 0 | 179.1 | 182 | 751 | 101 | 80 | 15 | 10 | 5 | 5 | 45 | 2 | 123 | 1 | 0 |
| Ainsworth, Kurt, Ottawa | 0 | 0 | .000 | 9.00 | 1 | 1 | 0 | 0 | 0 | 0 | 4.0 | 7 | 18 | 4 | 4 | 1 | 0 | 0 | 1 | 1 | 0 | 6 | 0 | 0 |
| Almanza, Armando, Richmond * | 1 | 1 | .500 | 3.55 | 20 | 0 | 0 | 0 | 4 | 1 | 25.1 | 26 | 116 | 13 | 10 | 1 | 0 | 0 | 0 | 15 | 0 | 20 | 2 | 0 |
| Almonte, Edwin, Pawtucket | 5 | 6 | .455 | 5.50 | 51 | 0 | 0 | 0 | 29 | 7 | 72.0 | 89 | 328 | 49 | 44 | 15 | 2 | 1 | 3 | 22 | 0 | 37 | 4 | 2 |
| Alvarez, Oscar, Buffalo * | 0 | 0 | .000 | 0.00 | 1 | 0 | 0 | 0 | 0 | 0 | 3.1 | 4 | 14 | 0 | 0 | 0 | 0 | 0 | 0 | 2 | 0 | 0 | 0 | 0 |
| Anderson, Jason, Buffalo | 2 | 1 | .667 | 2.76 | 9 | 0 | 0 | 0 | 4 | 1 | 16.1 | 15 | 65 | 5 | 5 | 1 | 1 | 0 | 2 | 2 | 1 | 11 | 0 | 0 |
| Anderson, Jason, Columbus | 1 | 3 | .250 | 4.63 | 36 | 0 | 0 | 0 | 20 | 1 | 44.2 | 48 | 197 | 24 | 23 | 4 | 0 | 0 | 3 | 12 | 0 | 38 | 2 | 0 |
| Anderson, Jimmy, Pawtucket * | 0 | 0 | .000 | 5.40 | 1 | 0 | 0 | 0 | 0 | 0 | 1.2 | 1 | 7 | 1 | 1 | 0 | 0 | 0 | 0 | 1 | 0 | 1 | 0 | 0 |
| Anderson, Matt, Toledo | 0 | 5 | .000 | 5.82 | 34 | 0 | 0 | 0 | 14 | 1 | 34.0 | 41 | 167 | 26 | 22 | 5 | 0 | 0 | 2 | 23 | 3 | 25 | 5 | 1 |
| Arnold, Jason, Syracuse | 1 | 3 | .250 | 3.65 | 7 | 7 | 0 | 0 | 0 | 0 | 37.0 | 40 | 160 | 19 | 15 | 6 | 2 | 2 | 1 | 12 | 0 | 15 | 0 | 0 |
| Astacio, Pedro, Pawtucket | 0 | 1 | .000 | 2.89 | 2 | 2 | 0 | 0 | 0 | 0 | 9.1 | 9 | 35 | 4 | 3 | 1 | 1 | 0 | 1 | 1 | 0 | 7 | 0 | 0 |
| Bacani, David, Norfolk | 0 | 0 | .000 | 0.00 | 2 | 0 | 0 | 0 | 2 | 0 | 4.0 | 1 | 16 | 0 | 0 | 0 | 0 | 0 | 2 | 1 | 0 | 1 | 0 | 0 |
| Bajenaru, Jeff, Charlotte | 1 | 2 | .333 | 1.80 | 16 | 0 | 0 | 0 | 15 | 10 | 20.0 | 12 | 76 | 6 | 4 | 2 | 0 | 0 | 1 | 3 | 0 | 16 | 1 | 0 |
| Baker, Chris, Syracuse | 0 | 11 | .000 | 6.75 | 18 | 14 | 1 | 0 | 0 | 0 | 77.1 | 103 | 353 | 70 | 58 | 14 | 1 | 6 | 4 | 22 | 0 | 61 | 3 | 0 |
| Baker, Scott, Rochester | 1 | 3 | .250 | 4.97 | 9 | 9 | 0 | 0 | 0 | 0 | 54.1 | 65 | 241 | 31 | 30 | 3 | 0 | 2 | 4 | 15 | 1 | 36 | 0 | 0 |
| Baldwin, James, Norfolk | 3 | 2 | .600 | 2.90 | 5 | 5 | 0 | 0 | 0 | 0 | 31.0 | 34 | 131 | 11 | 10 | 3 | 3 | 0 | 2 | 5 | 0 | 24 | 0 | 0 |
| Baldwin, James, Toledo | 5 | 7 | .417 | 3.73 | 18 | 16 | 3 | 0 | 2 | 1 | 115.2 | 110 | 457 | 52 | 48 | 12 | 7 | 2 | 3 | 20 | 3 | 61 | 0 | 0 |
| Barker, Kevin, Scranton-WB * | 0 | 0 | .000 | 0.00 | 1 | 0 | 0 | 0 | 1 | 0 | 1.0 | 0 | 3 | 0 | 0 | 0 | 0 | 0 | 0 | 0 | 0 | 0 | 0 | 0 |
| Barry, Kevin, Richmond | 3 | 3 | .500 | 2.52 | 30 | 0 | 0 | 0 | 13 | 2 | 35.2 | 25 | 157 | 15 | 10 | 1 | 0 | 0 | 0 | 25 | 2 | 40 | 0 | 0 |
| Bartosh, Cliff, Buffalo * | 0 | 3 | .000 | 2.80 | 28 | 0 | 0 | 0 | 16 | 3 | 35.1 | 26 | 144 | 11 | 11 | 3 | 0 | 0 | 4 | 8 | 2 | 46 | 2 | 0 |
| Bauer, Rick, Ottawa | 3 | 5 | .375 | 4.00 | 11 | 11 | 0 | 0 | 0 | 0 | 63.0 | 69 | 266 | 28 | 28 | 3 | 4 | 3 | 4 | 19 | 0 | 42 | 1 | 2 |
| Beal, Andy, Columbus * | 4 | 6 | .400 | 5.29 | 28 | 16 | 1 | 0 | 3 | 0 | 114.0 | 145 | 511 | 76 | 67 | 15 | 5 | 2 | 2 | 38 | 2 | 50 | 2 | 0 |
| Bean, Colter, Columbus | 9 | 3 | .750 | 2.29 | 53 | 0 | 0 | 0 | 12 | 1 | 82.2 | 61 | 339 | 24 | 21 | 3 | 0 | 0 | 8 | 23 | 0 | 109 | 2 | 1 |
| Bedard, Erik, Ottawa * | 0 | 1 | .000 | 7.20 | 2 | 2 | 0 | 0 | 0 | 0 | 5.0 | 8 | 26 | 4 | 4 | 1 | 0 | 0 | 0 | 3 | 0 | 3 | 0 | 0 |
| Beech, Matt, Pawtucket * | 1 | 1 | .500 | 8.44 | 4 | 4 | 0 | 0 | 0 | 0 | 16.0 | 26 | 81 | 18 | 15 | 5 | 0 | 3 | 0 | 9 | 0 | 10 | 0 | 0 |
| Belisle, Matt, Louisville | 9 | 11 | .450 | 5.26 | 28 | 28 | 2 | 1 | 0 | 0 | 162.2 | 192 | 715 | 104 | 95 | 16 | 11 | 9 | 11 | 51 | 4 | 106 | 7 | 1 |
| Bell, Heath, Norfolk | 3 | 1 | .750 | 3.23 | 45 | 0 | 0 | 0 | 30 | 16 | 55.2 | 42 | 237 | 21 | 20 | 4 | 1 | 0 | 4 | 24 | 2 | 68 | 6 | 1 |
| Bell, Rob, Durham | 5 | 0 | 1.000 | 1.69 | 7 | 7 | 0 | 0 | 0 | 0 | 37.1 | 28 | 142 | 7 | 7 | 3 | 1 | 0 | 0 | 8 | 0 | 35 | 1 | 0 |
| Bergman, Sean, Ottawa | 7 | 10 | .412 | 4.94 | 20 | 18 | 2 | 0 | 0 | 0 | 102.0 | 119 | 462 | 68 | 56 | 20 | 2 | 3 | 8 | 33 | 1 | 89 | 3 | 0 |
| Bevis, P.J., Norfolk | 1 | 2 | .333 | 5.06 | 22 | 0 | 0 | 0 | 7 | 2 | 26.2 | 28 | 130 | 24 | 15 | 3 | 1 | 1 | 1 | 23 | 0 | 16 | 0 | 0 |
| Bong, Jung, Louisville * | 8 | 8 | .500 | 5.82 | 19 | 19 | 0 | 0 | 0 | 0 | 94.1 | 118 | 413 | 66 | 61 | 13 | 5 | 3 | 2 | 31 | 0 | 65 | 7 | 0 |
| Bonilla, Henry, Rochester | 1 | 2 | .333 | 3.24 | 3 | 2 | 0 | 0 | 0 | 0 | 16.2 | 16 | 67 | 8 | 6 | 1 | 0 | 0 | 1 | 2 | 1 | 11 | 0 | 0 |
| Bonser, Boof, Rochester | 1 | 0 | 1.000 | 1.29 | 1 | 1 | 0 | 0 | 0 | 0 | 7.0 | 5 | 26 | 1 | 1 | 1 | 0 | 0 | 0 | 1 | 0 | 7 | 0 | 0 |
| Booker, Chris, Louisville | 0 | 1 | .000 | 4.50 | 7 | 0 | 0 | 0 | 2 | 0 | 12.0 | 10 | 57 | 6 | 6 | 2 | 0 | 0 | 0 | 10 | 0 | 9 | 4 | 0 |
| Borkowski, Dave, Ottawa | 6 | 9 | .400 | 4.85 | 16 | 16 | 0 | 0 | 0 | 0 | 85.1 | 99 | 369 | 53 | 46 | 6 | 2 | 4 | 6 | 26 | 0 | 56 | 1 | 0 |
| Bottalico, Ricky, Norfolk | 0 | 0 | .000 | 0.00 | 5 | 0 | 0 | 0 | 2 | 0 | 7.1 | 7 | 32 | 1 | 0 | 0 | 0 | 0 | 0 | 4 | 0 | 8 | 1 | 0 |
| Bouknight, Kip, Syracuse | 0 | 1 | .000 | 3.60 | 1 | 1 | 0 | 0 | 0 | 0 | 5.0 | 6 | 21 | 3 | 2 | 0 | 0 | 0 | 1 | 1 | 0 | 5 | 1 | 0 |
| Bowers, Shane, Scranton-WB | 1 | 3 | .250 | 5.37 | 15 | 9 | 1 | 0 | 1 | 0 | 52.0 | 65 | 243 | 36 | 31 | 11 | 1 | 5 | 4 | 19 | 1 | 36 | 1 | 0 |
| Bowles, Brian, Indianapolis | 1 | 1 | .500 | 6.17 | 10 | 0 | 0 | 0 | 4 | 1 | 11.2 | 13 | 55 | 8 | 8 | 3 | 1 | 0 | 0 | 8 | 2 | 15 | 0 | 0 |
| Brazelton, Dewon, Durham | 4 | 4 | .500 | 4.71 | 10 | 10 | 0 | 0 | 0 | 0 | 49.2 | 61 | 221 | 35 | 26 | 0 | 1 | 3 | 1 | 15 | 0 | 38 | 2 | 0 |
| Brown, Andrew, Buffalo | 1 | 0 | 1.000 | 0.00 | 1 | 1 | 0 | 0 | 0 | 0 | 5.0 | 4 | 21 | 0 | 0 | 0 | 0 | 0 | 0 | 3 | 0 | 4 | 1 | 0 |
| Brown, Jamie, Pawtucket | 4 | 6 | .400 | 4.82 | 23 | 20 | 2 | 1 | 2 | 0 | 127.0 | 128 | 530 | 76 | 68 | 21 | 5 | 11 | 6 | 17 | 0 | 92 | 2 | 0 |
| Brown, Kevin J., Columbus | 0 | 0 | .000 | 4.50 | 1 | 1 | 0 | 0 | 0 | 0 | 4.0 | 5 | 18 | 2 | 2 | 1 | 0 | 0 | 0 | 1 | 0 | 3 | 1 | 0 |
| Burnside, Adrian, Toledo * | 4 | 7 | .364 | 6.13 | 26 | 14 | 0 | 0 | 2 | 0 | 76.1 | 87 | 351 | 61 | 52 | 11 | 2 | 4 | 7 | 40 | 0 | 62 | 7 | 3 |
| Bush, David, Syracuse | 6 | 6 | .500 | 4.06 | 16 | 16 | 2 | 1 | 0 | 0 | 99.2 | 108 | 426 | 52 | 45 | 7 | 7 | 5 | 6 | 20 | 1 | 88 | 4 | 1 |
| Byard, David, Norfolk | 0 | 0 | .000 | 6.00 | 2 | 0 | 0 | 0 | 1 | 0 | 3.0 | 5 | 16 | 2 | 2 | 0 | 0 | 0 | 0 | 2 | 0 | 0 | 1 | 0 |
| Byrd, Paul, Richmond | 0 | 1 | .000 | 7.71 | 1 | 1 | 0 | 0 | 0 | 0 | 4.2 | 3 | 20 | 4 | 4 | 0 | 0 | 0 | 0 | 2 | 0 | 5 | 0 | 0 |

| Pitcher, Team | W | L | Pct. | ERA | G | GS | CG | ShO | GF | Sv. | IP | H | TBF | R | ER | HR | SH | SF | HB | BB | IBB | SO | WP | Bk. |
|---|---|---|---|---|---|---|---|---|---|---|---|---|---|---|---|---|---|---|---|---|---|---|---|---|
| Byrdak, Tim, Ottawa * | 2 | 1 | .667 | 4.19 | 33 | 1 | 0 | 0 | 11 | 2 | 34.1 | 46 | 164 | 20 | 16 | 4 | 0 | 1 | 2 | 12 | 1 | 43 | 1 | 0 |
| Cabrera, Fernando, Buffalo | 4 | 3 | .571 | 3.84 | 44 | 0 | 0 | 0 | 17 | 5 | 75.0 | 57 | 328 | 37 | 32 | 9 | 0 | 1 | 3 | 43 | 3 | 92 | 5 | 1 |
| Cameron, Ryan, Pawtucket | 0 | 1 | .000 | 3.94 | 10 | 0 | 0 | 0 | 2 | 0 | 16.0 | 17 | 79 | 10 | 7 | 2 | 0 | 0 | 0 | 14 | 0 | 20 | 4 | 0 |
| Campos, Francisco, Charlotte | 2 | 3 | .400 | 4.26 | 5 | 5 | 0 | 0 | 0 | 0 | 31.2 | 36 | 125 | 16 | 15 | 7 | 1 | 1 | 0 | 5 | 0 | 16 | 1 | 0 |
| Capellan, Jose, Richmond | 4 | 2 | .667 | 2.51 | 7 | 7 | 0 | 0 | 0 | 0 | 43.0 | 33 | 172 | 13 | 12 | 0 | 3 | 1 | 0 | 15 | 1 | 37 | 3 | 0 |
| Capuano, Chris, Indianapolis * | 0 | 1 | .000 | 8.31 | 2 | 2 | 0 | 0 | 0 | 0 | 8.2 | 10 | 39 | 9 | 8 | 1 | 1 | 1 | 1 | 5 | 0 | 9 | 2 | 0 |
| Carlyle, Buddy, Columbus | 8 | 5 | .615 | 4.05 | 19 | 18 | 0 | 0 | 1 | 0 | 106.2 | 113 | 447 | 51 | 48 | 14 | 4 | 3 | 7 | 21 | 0 | 92 | 1 | 0 |
| Carmona, Fausto, Buffalo | 1 | 0 | 1.000 | 6.00 | 1 | 1 | 0 | 0 | 0 | 0 | 6.0 | 6 | 26 | 4 | 4 | 0 | 0 | 1 | 0 | 3 | 0 | 2 | 0 | 0 |
| Carnes, Matt, Durham | 4 | 2 | .667 | 3.02 | 28 | 1 | 0 | 0 | 9 | 2 | 53.2 | 58 | 239 | 23 | 18 | 3 | 0 | 2 | 1 | 22 | 1 | 43 | 5 | 0 |
| Cassidy, Scott, Pawtucket | 5 | 3 | .625 | 3.46 | 28 | 12 | 0 | 0 | 3 | 1 | 80.2 | 72 | 345 | 34 | 31 | 10 | 4 | 3 | 3 | 38 | 0 | 72 | 1 | 0 |
| Castillo, Frank, Pawtucket | 10 | 9 | .526 | 4.38 | 27 | 25 | 0 | 0 | 0 | 0 | 168.1 | 169 | 693 | 87 | 82 | 28 | 11 | 5 | 5 | 34 | 0 | 123 | 3 | 1 |
| Cerros, Juan, Louisville | 2 | 5 | .286 | 3.15 | 30 | 6 | 0 | 0 | 7 | 1 | 71.1 | 63 | 309 | 33 | 25 | 8 | 1 | 2 | 5 | 38 | 2 | 47 | 2 | 0 |
| Cesar, Dionys, Charlotte | 0 | 0 | .000 | 0.00 | 1 | 0 | 0 | 0 | 1 | 0 | 1.0 | 1 | 6 | 0 | 0 | 0 | 0 | 0 | 1 | 1 | 0 | 1 | 0 | 0 |
| Chacin, Gustavo, Syracuse * | 2 | 0 | 1.000 | 2.31 | 2 | 2 | 0 | 0 | 0 | 0 | 11.2 | 16 | 53 | 4 | 3 | 0 | 1 | 1 | 0 | 3 | 0 | 14 | 0 | 0 |
| Chen, Bruce, Syracuse * | 0 | 1 | .000 | 8.71 | 3 | 3 | 0 | 0 | 0 | 0 | 10.1 | 17 | 54 | 12 | 10 | 4 | 1 | 1 | 1 | 5 | 1 | 8 | 1 | 0 |
| Chen, Bruce, Ottawa * | 4 | 3 | .571 | 3.22 | 22 | 17 | 1 | 1 | 0 | 0 | 95.0 | 85 | 394 | 41 | 34 | 12 | 7 | 1 | 1 | 30 | 1 | 108 | 1 | 2 |
| Childers, Jason, Indianapolis | 1 | 0 | 1.000 | 1.26 | 24 | 0 | 0 | 0 | 22 | 15 | 28.2 | 20 | 115 | 4 | 4 | 0 | 1 | 0 | 3 | 9 | 0 | 27 | 0 | 0 |
| Childers, Matt, Indianapolis | 5 | 5 | .500 | 4.87 | 35 | 10 | 0 | 0 | 12 | 2 | 98.0 | 100 | 422 | 55 | 53 | 8 | 6 | 6 | 6 | 27 | 3 | 65 | 2 | 0 |
| Childs, Ryan, Ottawa | 0 | 1 | .000 | 12.00 | 1 | 1 | 0 | 0 | 0 | 0 | 3.0 | 5 | 15 | 4 | 4 | 2 | 0 | 0 | 1 | 2 | 0 | 0 | 0 | 0 |
| Chulk, Vinny, Syracuse | 4 | 2 | .667 | 2.83 | 18 | 0 | 0 | 0 | 11 | 3 | 28.2 | 27 | 129 | 13 | 9 | 5 | 0 | 2 | 1 | 11 | 2 | 26 | 0 | 0 |
| Claussen, Brandon, Louisville * | 8 | 6 | .571 | 4.66 | 18 | 18 | 0 | 0 | 0 | 0 | 100.1 | 98 | 437 | 56 | 52 | 10 | 3 | 6 | 5 | 47 | 0 | 111 | 1 | 1 |
| Cloude, Ken, Durham | 1 | 2 | .333 | 11.25 | 4 | 2 | 0 | 0 | 0 | 0 | 12.0 | 19 | 63 | 17 | 15 | 5 | 0 | 1 | 2 | 9 | 0 | 5 | 1 | 0 |
| Coffey, Todd, Louisville | 1 | 0 | 1.000 | 5.27 | 15 | 0 | 0 | 0 | 11 | 4 | 13.2 | 15 | 59 | 8 | 8 | 1 | 0 | 0 | 1 | 2 | 0 | 11 | 1 | 0 |
| Coggin, David, Scranton-WB | 2 | 3 | .400 | 4.73 | 16 | 8 | 0 | 0 | 2 | 0 | 53.1 | 50 | 222 | 30 | 28 | 9 | 3 | 1 | 2 | 18 | 0 | 39 | 0 | 1 |
| Cole, Joey, Norfolk | 1 | 0 | 1.000 | 0.00 | 1 | 0 | 0 | 0 | 1 | 0 | 1.0 | 0 | 4 | 0 | 0 | 0 | 0 | 0 | 0 | 1 | 0 | 2 | 0 | 0 |
| Colome, Jesus, Durham | 2 | 1 | .667 | 3.52 | 18 | 0 | 0 | 0 | 7 | 2 | 30.2 | 27 | 134 | 12 | 12 | 0 | 2 | 0 | 1 | 16 | 0 | 17 | 3 | 0 |
| Colon, Roman, Richmond | 4 | 1 | .800 | 3.65 | 51 | 0 | 0 | 0 | 11 | 0 | 74.0 | 72 | 318 | 33 | 30 | 4 | 1 | 1 | 3 | 22 | 1 | 64 | 1 | 0 |
| Colyer, Steve, Toledo * | 2 | 1 | .667 | 4.21 | 25 | 0 | 0 | 0 | 6 | 0 | 25.2 | 26 | 128 | 13 | 12 | 2 | 0 | 0 | 0 | 25 | 1 | 23 | 3 | 0 |
| Condrey, Clay, Scranton-WB | 9 | 9 | .500 | 5.46 | 27 | 27 | 2 | 0 | 0 | 0 | 155.0 | 205 | 699 | 106 | 94 | 23 | 16 | 8 | 6 | 34 | 1 | 70 | 1 | 0 |
| Contreras, Jose, Columbus | 2 | 0 | 1.000 | 3.29 | 2 | 2 | 0 | 0 | 0 | 0 | 13.2 | 11 | 58 | 5 | 5 | 2 | 0 | 0 | 2 | 5 | 0 | 19 | 4 | 0 |
| Coquillette, Trace, Pawtucket | 0 | 0 | .000 | 9.00 | 2 | 0 | 0 | 0 | 2 | 0 | 2.0 | 5 | 13 | 2 | 2 | 1 | 0 | 0 | 1 | 1 | 0 | 1 | 0 | 0 |
| Corcoran, Tim, Durham | 3 | 3 | .500 | 3.91 | 33 | 0 | 0 | 0 | 9 | 0 | 50.2 | 46 | 229 | 22 | 22 | 4 | 1 | 3 | 2 | 33 | 1 | 40 | 2 | 0 |
| Cornejo, Nate, Toledo | 0 | 0 | .000 | 4.15 | 4 | 3 | 0 | 0 | 0 | 0 | 8.2 | 11 | 38 | 4 | 4 | 2 | 0 | 1 | 0 | 2 | 0 | 8 | 0 | 0 |
| Cortes, David, Toledo | 1 | 0 | 1.000 | 3.95 | 14 | 0 | 0 | 0 | 4 | 0 | 13.2 | 12 | 58 | 6 | 6 | 0 | 0 | 0 | 1 | 6 | 2 | 10 | 1 | 0 |
| Crain, Jesse, Rochester | 3 | 2 | .600 | 2.49 | 41 | 0 | 0 | 0 | 33 | 19 | 50.2 | 38 | 204 | 20 | 14 | 5 | 1 | 0 | 1 | 17 | 2 | 64 | 1 | 0 |
| Cressend, Jack, Buffalo | 10 | 1 | .909 | 5.13 | 24 | 4 | 0 | 0 | 3 | 1 | 52.2 | 73 | 238 | 30 | 30 | 7 | 1 | 2 | 0 | 10 | 0 | 41 | 1 | 1 |
| Crowell, Jim, Scranton-WB * | 7 | 3 | .700 | 2.40 | 46 | 0 | 0 | 0 | 37 | 16 | 63.2 | 61 | 266 | 22 | 17 | 6 | 1 | 0 | 1 | 14 | 4 | 44 | 0 | 1 |
| Cruceta, Francisco, Buffalo | 6 | 5 | .545 | 3.25 | 14 | 14 | 1 | 0 | 0 | 0 | 83.0 | 78 | 341 | 35 | 30 | 6 | 2 | 2 | 0 | 36 | 0 | 62 | 9 | 1 |
| Cubillan, Darwin, Ottawa | 3 | 4 | .429 | 4.59 | 51 | 0 | 0 | 0 | 42 | 24 | 51.0 | 52 | 222 | 26 | 26 | 7 | 0 | 0 | 2 | 17 | 1 | 53 | 1 | 0 |
| Cuello, Felix, Toledo | 0 | 0 | .000 | 0.00 | 1 | 0 | 0 | 0 | 0 | 0 | 2.0 | 1 | 8 | 0 | 0 | 0 | 0 | 0 | 0 | 1 | 0 | 1 | 0 | 0 |
| Cunnane, Will, Richmond | 1 | 7 | .125 | 5.23 | 35 | 2 | 0 | 0 | 14 | 2 | 43.0 | 52 | 200 | 27 | 25 | 4 | 0 | 0 | 0 | 22 | 1 | 42 | 1 | 0 |
| Curtis, Daniel, Richmond | 0 | 1 | .000 | 5.40 | 2 | 2 | 0 | 0 | 0 | 0 | 8.1 | 8 | 36 | 5 | 5 | 1 | 1 | 0 | 0 | 5 | 0 | 8 | 0 | 1 |
| D'Amico, Jeff, Buffalo | 0 | 0 | .000 | 10.45 | 3 | 3 | 0 | 0 | 0 | 0 | 10.1 | 18 | 53 | 12 | 12 | 3 | 0 | 1 | 0 | 3 | 0 | 6 | 2 | 0 |
| Darensbourg, Vic, Norfolk * | 1 | 1 | .500 | 3.18 | 18 | 0 | 0 | 0 | 7 | 0 | 22.2 | 13 | 93 | 9 | 8 | 1 | 0 | 0 | 0 | 12 | 2 | 21 | 0 | 1 |
| Darensbourg, Vic, Charlotte * | 3 | 3 | .500 | 2.64 | 24 | 0 | 0 | 0 | 5 | 0 | 30.2 | 25 | 132 | 10 | 9 | 1 | 1 | 0 | 5 | 9 | 2 | 33 | 0 | 0 |
| Davies, Kyle, Richmond | 0 | 1 | .000 | 9.00 | 1 | 1 | 0 | 0 | 0 | 0 | 5.0 | 5 | 20 | 5 | 5 | 0 | 0 | 0 | 0 | 3 | 0 | 5 | 0 | 0 |
| Davis, Jason, Buffalo | 3 | 2 | .600 | 3.00 | 9 | 9 | 0 | 0 | 0 | 0 | 54.0 | 53 | 226 | 26 | 18 | 4 | 1 | 2 | 2 | 18 | 1 | 39 | 7 | 1 |
| Davis, Kane, Buffalo | 3 | 2 | .600 | 6.15 | 32 | 0 | 0 | 0 | 11 | 0 | 45.1 | 59 | 224 | 35 | 31 | 2 | 0 | 0 | 4 | 25 | 1 | 45 | 2 | 0 |
| Davis, Lance, Columbus * | 4 | 2 | .667 | 5.48 | 8 | 7 | 0 | 0 | 0 | 0 | 46.0 | 54 | 194 | 28 | 28 | 4 | 1 | 5 | 0 | 8 | 0 | 20 | 0 | 0 |
| Dawley, Joe, Buffalo | 0 | 0 | .000 | 0.00 | 1 | 1 | 0 | 0 | 0 | 0 | 5.2 | 4 | 23 | 3 | 0 | 0 | 0 | 1 | 0 | 1 | 0 | 7 | 0 | 0 |
| De La Rosa, Jorge, Indianapolis * | 5 | 6 | .455 | 4.52 | 20 | 20 | 0 | 0 | 0 | 0 | 85.2 | 80 | 368 | 45 | 43 | 9 | 4 | 4 | 8 | 36 | 1 | 86 | 5 | 2 |
| Dewitt, Matt, Ottawa | 2 | 4 | .333 | 7.88 | 25 | 5 | 0 | 0 | 4 | 1 | 53.2 | 70 | 248 | 47 | 47 | 12 | 1 | 3 | 1 | 20 | 2 | 25 | 0 | 0 |
| DiFelice, Mark, Ottawa | 9 | 4 | .692 | 3.44 | 36 | 4 | 0 | 0 | 3 | 1 | 89.0 | 73 | 365 | 42 | 34 | 10 | 1 | 1 | 2 | 27 | 1 | 70 | 3 | 1 |
| DiNardo, Lenny, Pawtucket * | 0 | 0 | .000 | 0.00 | 1 | 1 | 0 | 0 | 0 | 0 | 3.0 | 3 | 12 | 0 | 0 | 0 | 0 | 0 | 0 | 0 | 0 | 4 | 0 | 0 |
| Diaz, Felix, Charlotte | 10 | 2 | .833 | 2.97 | 19 | 17 | 0 | 0 | 0 | 0 | 115.0 | 95 | 436 | 41 | 38 | 14 | 8 | 3 | 2 | 24 | 0 | 96 | 0 | 1 |
| Dingman, Craig, Toledo | 1 | 2 | .333 | 4.56 | 21 | 0 | 0 | 0 | 7 | 0 | 25.2 | 26 | 115 | 14 | 13 | 5 | 0 | 1 | 1 | 11 | 2 | 31 | 0 | 0 |
| Donaldson, Bo, Pawtucket | 0 | 0 | .000 | 0.00 | 1 | 1 | 0 | 0 | 0 | 0 | 2.0 | 1 | 9 | 0 | 0 | 0 | 0 | 0 | 1 | 1 | 0 | 3 | 0 | 0 |
| Douglas, Shea, Buffalo * | 0 | 0 | .000 | 0.00 | 1 | 0 | 0 | 0 | 1 | 1 | 2.0 | 0 | 8 | 0 | 0 | 0 | 0 | 0 | 1 | 1 | 0 | 3 | 1 | 0 |
| Douglass, Sean, Syracuse | 5 | 6 | .455 | 4.75 | 18 | 18 | 1 | 0 | 0 | 0 | 89.0 | 92 | 382 | 53 | 47 | 7 | 8 | 4 | 3 | 37 | 0 | 74 | 6 | 0 |
| Duff, Matt, Pawtucket | 7 | 4 | .636 | 3.93 | 53 | 0 | 0 | 0 | 30 | 7 | 73.1 | 72 | 333 | 32 | 32 | 3 | 0 | 0 | 6 | 36 | 2 | 68 | 7 | 1 |
| Duncan, Courtney, Charlotte | 1 | 0 | 1.000 | 2.03 | 18 | 0 | 0 | 0 | 7 | 1 | 31.0 | 20 | 131 | 11 | 7 | 1 | 0 | 0 | 4 | 14 | 0 | 22 | 5 | 0 |
| Durbin, Chad, Buffalo | 3 | 3 | .500 | 3.46 | 9 | 9 | 0 | 0 | 0 | 0 | 52.0 | 55 | 216 | 22 | 20 | 7 | 2 | 1 | 0 | 16 | 0 | 40 | 1 | 0 |
| Durbin, J.D., Rochester | 3 | 2 | .600 | 4.54 | 7 | 7 | 0 | 0 | 0 | 0 | 35.2 | 49 | 168 | 27 | 18 | 4 | 0 | 0 | 1 | 16 | 0 | 38 | 1 | 0 |
| Eckenstahler, Eric, Toledo * | 1 | 2 | .333 | 5.15 | 42 | 0 | 0 | 0 | 12 | 0 | 43.2 | 58 | 226 | 32 | 25 | 5 | 1 | 1 | 4 | 30 | 0 | 45 | 4 | 0 |
| Elarton, Scott, Buffalo | 1 | 1 | .500 | 3.15 | 3 | 3 | 1 | 1 | 0 | 0 | 20.0 | 19 | 82 | 7 | 7 | 1 | 1 | 0 | 1 | 5 | 0 | 10 | 0 | 0 |
| Ellis, Robert, Buffalo | 3 | 4 | .429 | 6.83 | 10 | 10 | 0 | 0 | 0 | 0 | 55.1 | 65 | 240 | 42 | 42 | 7 | 3 | 2 | 1 | 16 | 0 | 35 | 3 | 0 |
| Ellis, Robert, Scranton-WB | 5 | 8 | .385 | 4.23 | 16 | 16 | 1 | 1 | 0 | 0 | 110.2 | 111 | 454 | 54 | 52 | 13 | 1 | 4 | 1 | 18 | 1 | 55 | 2 | 0 |
| Erdos, Todd, Indianapolis | 2 | 8 | .200 | 8.36 | 42 | 0 | 0 | 0 | 17 | 0 | 56.0 | 69 | 274 | 57 | 52 | 8 | 0 | 0 | 5 | 33 | 0 | 39 | 5 | 0 |
| Erdos, Todd, Rochester | 0 | 0 | .000 | 0.00 | 4 | 0 | 0 | 0 | 0 | 0 | 3.0 | 1 | 11 | 0 | 0 | 0 | 0 | 1 | 0 | 1 | 0 | 3 | 0 | 0 |
| Erickson, Scott, Norfolk | 3 | 3 | .500 | 4.50 | 8 | 8 | 0 | 0 | 0 | 0 | 52.0 | 56 | 217 | 30 | 26 | 5 | 1 | 2 | 4 | 12 | 0 | 30 | 0 | 0 |
| Etherton, Seth, Louisville | 5 | 6 | .455 | 3.47 | 19 | 19 | 3 | 1 | 0 | 0 | 111.2 | 107 | 467 | 45 | 43 | 13 | 4 | 3 | 3 | 32 | 1 | 110 | 1 | 0 |
| Evans, Kyle, Buffalo | 0 | 1 | .000 | 7.36 | 1 | 1 | 0 | 0 | 0 | 0 | 3.2 | 4 | 20 | 5 | 3 | 1 | 2 | 0 | 0 | 5 | 0 | 1 | 0 | 0 |
| Evert, Brett, Richmond | 2 | 1 | .667 | 7.03 | 7 | 5 | 0 | 0 | 0 | 0 | 24.1 | 26 | 113 | 19 | 19 | 5 | 1 | 2 | 4 | 15 | 0 | 20 | 0 | 1 |
| Eyre, Willie, Rochester | 6 | 7 | .462 | 3.64 | 36 | 21 | 1 | 1 | 5 | 4 | 136.0 | 131 | 569 | 60 | 55 | 13 | 8 | 7 | 4 | 53 | 1 | 91 | 6 | 1 |
| Farnsworth, Jeff, Indianapolis | 2 | 6 | .250 | 8.18 | 11 | 8 | 0 | 0 | 2 | 0 | 47.1 | 64 | 224 | 46 | 43 | 7 | 0 | 2 | 2 | 19 | 0 | 26 | 1 | 0 |
| Feliciano, Pedro, Norfolk * | 4 | 3 | .571 | 5.30 | 32 | 0 | 0 | 0 | 9 | 2 | 35.2 | 35 | 158 | 25 | 21 | 4 | 1 | 0 | 4 | 15 | 1 | 25 | 3 | 0 |
| Fesh, Sean, Richmond * | 1 | 5 | .167 | 3.74 | 40 | 1 | 0 | 0 | 11 | 0 | 53.0 | 50 | 238 | 27 | 22 | 4 | 3 | 0 | 5 | 28 | 4 | 41 | 4 | 0 |
| File, Bob, Syracuse | 3 | 3 | .500 | 2.57 | 24 | 0 | 0 | 0 | 17 | 7 | 35.0 | 31 | 145 | 11 | 10 | 2 | 0 | 0 | 2 | 7 | 0 | 11 | 2 | 0 |
| Fiore, Tony, Ottawa | 3 | 1 | .750 | 1.80 | 25 | 0 | 0 | 0 | 8 | 3 | 45.0 | 36 | 183 | 11 | 9 | 1 | 0 | 1 | 3 | 10 | 0 | 32 | 1 | 0 |
| Floyd, Gavin, Scranton-WB | 1 | 3 | .250 | 4.99 | 5 | 5 | 0 | 0 | 0 | 0 | 30.2 | 39 | 139 | 20 | 17 | 4 | 2 | 1 | 3 | 9 | 0 | 18 | 3 | 0 |
| Ford, Ben, Indianapolis | 2 | 2 | .500 | 4.85 | 32 | 1 | 0 | 0 | 23 | 9 | 42.2 | 52 | 199 | 25 | 23 | 2 | 0 | 0 | 1 | 21 | 2 | 36 | 3 | 0 |
| Fortunato, Bartolome, Durham | 4 | 3 | .571 | 2.42 | 34 | 0 | 0 | 0 | 24 | 9 | 44.2 | 28 | 182 | 14 | 12 | 4 | 0 | 1 | 0 | 21 | 1 | 54 | 2 | 0 |

| Pitcher, Team | W | L | Pct. | ERA | G | GS | CG | ShO | GF | Sv. | IP | H | TBF | R | ER | HR | SH | SF | HB | BB | IBB | SO | WP | Bk. |
|---|---|---|---|---|---|---|---|---|---|---|---|---|---|---|---|---|---|---|---|---|---|---|---|---|
| Fortunato, Bartolome, Norfolk | 0 | 0 | .000 | 3.38 | 6 | 0 | 0 | 0 | 1 | 0 | 5.1 | 4 | 24 | 2 | 2 | 0 | 0 | 0 | 1 | 3 | 0 | 5 | 0 | 1 |
| Forystek, Brian, Ottawa * | 3 | 5 | .375 | 5.58 | 12 | 11 | 0 | 0 | 0 | 0 | 61.1 | 71 | 275 | 46 | 38 | 6 | 7 | 4 | 4 | 32 | 1 | 43 | 1 | 0 |
| Frasor, Jason, Syracuse | 0 | 0 | .000 | 2.25 | 3 | 0 | 0 | 0 | 2 | 0 | 4.0 | 1 | 18 | 1 | 1 | 0 | 0 | 0 | 0 | 5 | 0 | 6 | 0 | 0 |
| Frederick, Kevin, Syracuse | 3 | 2 | .600 | 0.99 | 20 | 0 | 0 | 0 | 15 | 5 | 27.1 | 18 | 109 | 6 | 3 | 2 | 0 | 0 | 0 | 9 | 0 | 26 | 0 | 0 |
| Frendling, Neal, Durham | 0 | 0 | .000 | 3.00 | 1 | 0 | 0 | 0 | 0 | 0 | 3.0 | 5 | 13 | 1 | 1 | 0 | 0 | 0 | 0 | 2 | 0 | 2 | 0 | 0 |
| Fultz, Aaron, Rochester * | 0 | 0 | .000 | 0.00 | 7 | 0 | 0 | 0 | 1 | 0 | 8.1 | 6 | 36 | 1 | 0 | 0 | 0 | 0 | 0 | 5 | 0 | 5 | 0 | 0 |
| Gannon, Joe, Ottawa | 0 | 4 | .000 | 10.24 | 4 | 4 | 0 | 0 | 0 | 0 | 19.1 | 20 | 101 | 23 | 22 | 1 | 1 | 1 | 2 | 26 | 0 | 10 | 7 | 0 |
| Gassner, Dave, Rochester * | 16 | 8 | .667 | 3.41 | 28 | 28 | 0 | 0 | 0 | 0 | 174.1 | 175 | 704 | 72 | 66 | 16 | 7 | 5 | 2 | 30 | 1 | 93 | 2 | 1 |
| Gaudin, Chad, Durham | 1 | 3 | .250 | 4.72 | 17 | 7 | 0 | 0 | 7 | 2 | 47.2 | 48 | 205 | 26 | 25 | 8 | 2 | 1 | 2 | 17 | 0 | 52 | 0 | 1 |
| Geary, Geoff, Scranton-WB | 1 | 2 | .333 | 2.31 | 21 | 0 | 0 | 0 | 20 | 10 | 23.1 | 20 | 104 | 7 | 6 | 1 | 2 | 0 | 1 | 13 | 3 | 23 | 1 | 0 |
| Giese, Dan, Scranton-WB | 12 | 5 | .706 | 2.81 | 54 | 0 | 0 | 0 | 23 | 3 | 83.1 | 63 | 332 | 27 | 26 | 8 | 0 | 0 | 1 | 18 | 3 | 54 | 1 | 0 |
| Ginter, Matt, Norfolk | 1 | 5 | .167 | 2.95 | 11 | 11 | 0 | 0 | 0 | 0 | 64.0 | 55 | 255 | 26 | 21 | 4 | 5 | 2 | 1 | 8 | 1 | 49 | 1 | 2 |
| Giron, Roberto, Indianapolis | 5 | 0 | 1.000 | 1.86 | 21 | 0 | 0 | 0 | 11 | 3 | 29.0 | 25 | 122 | 11 | 6 | 3 | 0 | 0 | 2 | 7 | 2 | 18 | 1 | 1 |
| Glen, William, Durham | 0 | 1 | .000 | 12.27 | 2 | 0 | 0 | 0 | 0 | 0 | 3.2 | 5 | 18 | 5 | 5 | 3 | 0 | 0 | 0 | 2 | 0 | 4 | 0 | 0 |
| Glover, Gary, Rochester | 0 | 1 | .000 | 8.44 | 5 | 4 | 0 | 0 | 0 | 0 | 16.0 | 27 | 73 | 15 | 15 | 6 | 0 | 1 | 0 | 5 | 0 | 8 | 0 | 0 |
| Glover, Gary, Indianapolis | 3 | 3 | .500 | 3.98 | 8 | 6 | 0 | 0 | 0 | 0 | 40.2 | 47 | 172 | 19 | 18 | 1 | 3 | 4 | 1 | 11 | 0 | 18 | 2 | 0 |
| Glynn, Ryan, Richmond | 1 | 1 | .500 | 5.60 | 11 | 0 | 0 | 0 | 3 | 0 | 17.2 | 26 | 96 | 11 | 11 | 0 | 0 | 1 | 3 | 14 | 0 | 19 | 2 | 0 |
| Glynn, Ryan, Syracuse | 7 | 2 | .778 | 3.40 | 16 | 16 | 1 | 1 | 0 | 0 | 92.2 | 82 | 385 | 38 | 35 | 7 | 11 | 4 | 1 | 34 | 0 | 75 | 3 | 0 |
| Gonzalez, Dicky, Durham | 1 | 2 | .333 | 4.80 | 6 | 6 | 0 | 0 | 0 | 0 | 30.0 | 28 | 119 | 16 | 16 | 3 | 0 | 1 | 1 | 7 | 0 | 30 | 0 | 0 |
| Gonzalez, Jeremi, Durham | 4 | 2 | .667 | 3.97 | 18 | 8 | 0 | 0 | 4 | 1 | 56.2 | 50 | 231 | 27 | 25 | 7 | 1 | 1 | 1 | 18 | 0 | 44 | 4 | 0 |
| Graman, Alex, Columbus * | 11 | 6 | .647 | 3.37 | 24 | 22 | 1 | 1 | 0 | 0 | 131.0 | 115 | 550 | 56 | 49 | 12 | 10 | 5 | 3 | 53 | 0 | 129 | 7 | 0 |
| Greisinger, Seth, Rochester | 5 | 5 | .500 | 4.96 | 13 | 13 | 0 | 0 | 0 | 0 | 74.1 | 94 | 320 | 44 | 41 | 10 | 5 | 6 | 5 | 19 | 0 | 44 | 1 | 3 |
| Griffiths, Jeremy, Norfolk | 5 | 2 | .714 | 3.47 | 13 | 13 | 0 | 0 | 0 | 0 | 70.0 | 63 | 288 | 30 | 27 | 6 | 5 | 5 | 5 | 29 | 1 | 31 | 5 | 1 |
| Grilli, Jason, Charlotte | 9 | 9 | .500 | 4.83 | 25 | 25 | 2 | 1 | 0 | 0 | 152.2 | 163 | 665 | 95 | 82 | 22 | 5 | 6 | 11 | 58 | 0 | 101 | 9 | 4 |
| Gronkiewicz, Lee, Buffalo | 0 | 0 | .000 | 0.00 | 1 | 0 | 0 | 0 | 1 | 0 | 1.0 | 0 | 3 | 0 | 0 | 0 | 0 | 0 | 0 | 0 | 0 | 0 | 0 | 0 |
| Guerrier, Matt, Rochester | 5 | 10 | .333 | 3.19 | 24 | 23 | 0 | 0 | 1 | 0 | 144.0 | 135 | 579 | 65 | 51 | 15 | 8 | 9 | 5 | 25 | 0 | 97 | 2 | 0 |
| Guthrie, Jeremy, Buffalo | 1 | 2 | .333 | 7.91 | 4 | 4 | 0 | 0 | 0 | 0 | 19.1 | 23 | 99 | 19 | 17 | 0 | 0 | 1 | 4 | 18 | 0 | 10 | 2 | 1 |
| Hackman, Luther, Buffalo | 0 | 2 | .000 | 10.89 | 11 | 0 | 0 | 0 | 2 | 0 | 19.0 | 31 | 106 | 24 | 23 | 4 | 0 | 0 | 1 | 16 | 1 | 13 | 2 | 1 |
| Haines, Talley, Syracuse | 4 | 2 | .667 | 3.87 | 44 | 0 | 0 | 0 | 16 | 3 | 79.0 | 80 | 336 | 37 | 34 | 12 | 0 | 1 | 6 | 15 | 0 | 53 | 7 | 0 |
| Halsey, Brad, Columbus * | 11 | 4 | .733 | 2.63 | 24 | 23 | 3 | 2 | 0 | 0 | 144.0 | 128 | 589 | 46 | 42 | 8 | 8 | 3 | 7 | 37 | 0 | 109 | 2 | 1 |
| Hammond, Joey, Ottawa | 0 | 0 | .000 | 9.00 | 2 | 0 | 0 | 0 | 2 | 0 | 2.0 | 3 | 9 | 2 | 2 | 1 | 0 | 0 | 0 | 0 | 0 | 0 | 0 | 0 |
| Hamulack, Tim, Pawtucket * | 7 | 4 | .636 | 6.98 | 35 | 0 | 0 | 0 | 15 | 2 | 29.2 | 44 | 153 | 26 | 23 | 4 | 0 | 1 | 2 | 19 | 2 | 25 | 1 | 0 |
| Hancock, Josh, Scranton-WB | 8 | 7 | .533 | 4.01 | 18 | 18 | 1 | 0 | 0 | 0 | 107.2 | 106 | 443 | 52 | 48 | 10 | 12 | 8 | 1 | 21 | 1 | 65 | 2 | 0 |
| Hanson, Adam, Buffalo | 1 | 0 | 1.000 | 5.79 | 1 | 0 | 0 | 0 | 0 | 0 | 4.2 | 6 | 23 | 3 | 3 | 0 | 1 | 3 | 2 | 0 | 0 | 0 | 0 | 0 |
| Harang, Aaron, Louisville | 0 | 1 | .000 | 12.00 | 1 | 1 | 0 | 0 | 0 | 0 | 3.0 | 9 | 22 | 8 | 4 | 1 | 0 | 0 | 1 | 3 | 0 | 3 | 0 | 0 |
| Harper, Travis, Durham | 1 | 0 | 1.000 | 3.52 | 2 | 1 | 0 | 0 | 0 | 0 | 7.2 | 10 | 34 | 3 | 3 | 1 | 0 | 0 | 0 | 0 | 0 | 5 | 0 | 0 |
| Hartmann, Pete, Louisville * | 0 | 0 | .000 | 13.50 | 3 | 0 | 0 | 0 | 0 | 0 | 2.0 | 5 | 13 | 4 | 3 | 0 | 0 | 0 | 1 | 1 | 0 | 4 | 2 | 0 |
| Haynes, Jimmy, Toledo | 0 | 1 | .000 | 8.78 | 5 | 3 | 0 | 0 | 0 | 0 | 13.1 | 19 | 65 | 13 | 13 | 0 | 0 | 0 | 0 | 6 | 0 | 9 | 0 | 0 |
| Hebson, Bryan, Pawtucket | 1 | 0 | 1.000 | 5.73 | 7 | 0 | 0 | 0 | 0 | 0 | 11.0 | 13 | 51 | 7 | 7 | 2 | 0 | 0 | 1 | 4 | 0 | 9 | 0 | 0 |
| Heilman, Aaron, Norfolk | 7 | 10 | .412 | 4.33 | 26 | 26 | 1 | 0 | 0 | 0 | 151.2 | 156 | 668 | 88 | 73 | 15 | 8 | 4 | 10 | 66 | 0 | 123 | 5 | 0 |
| Helling, Rick, Rochester | 1 | 0 | 1.000 | 0.00 | 1 | 1 | 1 | 1 | 0 | 0 | 7.0 | 4 | 25 | 0 | 0 | 0 | 0 | 0 | 0 | 1 | 0 | 2 | 0 | 0 |
| Hendrickson, Ben, Indianapolis | 11 | 3 | .786 | 2.02 | 21 | 21 | 2 | 2 | 0 | 0 | 125.0 | 114 | 492 | 32 | 28 | 6 | 6 | 3 | 1 | 26 | 0 | 93 | 6 | 1 |
| Heredia, Felix, Columbus * | 0 | 0 | .000 | 0.00 | 3 | 0 | 0 | 0 | 0 | 0 | 3.2 | 2 | 14 | 0 | 0 | 0 | 0 | 0 | 0 | 1 | 0 | 5 | 0 | 0 |
| Hernandez, Adrian, Indianapolis | 0 | 8 | .000 | 5.72 | 20 | 15 | 0 | 0 | 0 | 0 | 94.1 | 111 | 415 | 61 | 60 | 9 | 9 | 6 | 9 | 39 | 2 | 83 | 2 | 4 |
| Hernandez, Buddy, Richmond | 7 | 2 | .778 | 2.42 | 47 | 0 | 0 | 0 | 11 | 0 | 67.0 | 45 | 273 | 21 | 18 | 5 | 0 | 0 | 3 | 26 | 1 | 60 | 2 | 0 |
| Hernandez, Orlando, Columbus | 2 | 1 | .667 | 5.60 | 3 | 3 | 0 | 0 | 0 | 0 | 17.2 | 17 | 72 | 11 | 11 | 3 | 0 | 0 | 0 | 3 | 0 | 16 | 0 | 0 |
| Hernandez, Yoel, Scranton-WB | 0 | 0 | .000 | 6.46 | 14 | 2 | 0 | 0 | 3 | 0 | 30.2 | 38 | 131 | 26 | 22 | 4 | 4 | 4 | 2 | 7 | 1 | 18 | 1 | 0 |
| Hodge, Kevin, Rochester | 3 | 6 | .333 | 3.41 | 49 | 1 | 0 | 0 | 24 | 4 | 74.0 | 78 | 309 | 34 | 28 | 10 | 3 | 2 | 2 | 9 | 2 | 63 | 2 | 0 |
| Hodges, Trey, Richmond | 5 | 2 | .714 | 4.82 | 10 | 10 | 0 | 0 | 0 | 0 | 52.1 | 51 | 219 | 29 | 28 | 9 | 1 | 0 | 6 | 18 | 0 | 41 | 1 | 1 |
| Holtz, Mike, Durham * | 1 | 2 | .333 | 3.80 | 17 | 0 | 0 | 0 | 3 | 0 | 23.2 | 17 | 96 | 10 | 10 | 4 | 1 | 0 | 1 | 8 | 0 | 27 | 1 | 0 |
| Hooper, Kevin, Columbus | 0 | 0 | .000 | 0.00 | 1 | 0 | 0 | 0 | 1 | 0 | 1.0 | 0 | 4 | 0 | 0 | 0 | 0 | 0 | 0 | 1 | 0 | 0 | 0 | 0 |
| House, Craig, Ottawa | 0 | 0 | .000 | 7.43 | 11 | 0 | 0 | 0 | 3 | 0 | 13.1 | 13 | 67 | 11 | 11 | 4 | 0 | 0 | 1 | 13 | 0 | 12 | 1 | 0 |
| Housman, Jeff, Indianapolis * | 1 | 1 | .500 | 8.20 | 5 | 3 | 0 | 0 | 0 | 0 | 18.2 | 33 | 98 | 17 | 17 | 4 | 1 | 2 | 0 | 13 | 0 | 14 | 0 | 0 |
| Howry, Bobby, Buffalo | 1 | 1 | .500 | 5.19 | 18 | 0 | 0 | 0 | 5 | 0 | 26.0 | 22 | 108 | 15 | 15 | 3 | 0 | 0 | 2 | 6 | 0 | 24 | 0 | 0 |
| Hudson, Luke, Louisville | 2 | 1 | .667 | 2.84 | 3 | 3 | 0 | 0 | 0 | 0 | 19.0 | 15 | 74 | 8 | 6 | 2 | 0 | 1 | 0 | 5 | 0 | 17 | 0 | 0 |
| Hutchison, Ryan, Scranton-WB | 1 | 0 | 1.000 | 2.84 | 4 | 0 | 0 | 0 | 1 | 0 | 6.1 | 8 | 28 | 2 | 2 | 0 | 0 | 0 | 1 | 0 | 0 | 2 | 1 | 0 |
| Izquierdo, Hansel, Columbus | 1 | 1 | .500 | 2.33 | 11 | 0 | 0 | 0 | 5 | 0 | 19.1 | 20 | 89 | 7 | 5 | 2 | 2 | 2 | 2 | 7 | 0 | 12 | 0 | 0 |
| Jimenez, Jason, Scranton-WB * | 0 | 2 | .000 | 5.33 | 14 | 0 | 0 | 0 | 1 | 0 | 27.0 | 32 | 129 | 23 | 16 | 2 | 1 | 1 | 3 | 14 | 0 | 20 | 1 | 0 |
| Jimenez, Jose, Buffalo | 0 | 0 | .000 | 0.00 | 2 | 0 | 0 | 0 | 0 | 0 | 3.0 | 3 | 13 | 0 | 0 | 0 | 0 | 0 | 0 | 1 | 0 | 3 | 0 | 0 |
| Johnson, Adam, Rochester | 5 | 4 | .556 | 6.07 | 38 | 6 | 0 | 0 | 10 | 1 | 83.0 | 100 | 380 | 59 | 56 | 10 | 4 | 4 | 6 | 30 | 2 | 86 | 2 | 0 |
| Johnson, James, Pawtucket * | 0 | 2 | .000 | 4.13 | 16 | 0 | 0 | 0 | 8 | 0 | 24.0 | 28 | 112 | 12 | 11 | 4 | 0 | 1 | 1 | 13 | 0 | 17 | 2 | 0 |
| Joseph, Jake, Norfolk | 1 | 1 | .500 | 4.08 | 15 | 1 | 0 | 0 | 4 | 0 | 28.2 | 37 | 134 | 15 | 13 | 3 | 0 | 0 | 2 | 7 | 0 | 15 | 1 | 0 |
| Junge, Eric, Scranton-WB | 0 | 4 | .000 | 9.91 | 9 | 5 | 0 | 0 | 3 | 0 | 26.1 | 42 | 130 | 29 | 29 | 1 | 0 | 3 | 1 | 16 | 1 | 17 | 1 | 0 |
| Karnuth, Jason, Toledo | 5 | 2 | .714 | 3.74 | 46 | 0 | 0 | 0 | 16 | 2 | 55.1 | 45 | 229 | 26 | 23 | 4 | 0 | 0 | 2 | 16 | 2 | 34 | 1 | 0 |
| Karsay, Steve, Columbus | 0 | 0 | .000 | 5.56 | 11 | 0 | 0 | 0 | 1 | 0 | 11.1 | 12 | 53 | 10 | 7 | 0 | 0 | 0 | 1 | 6 | 0 | 8 | 0 | 0 |
| Keisler, Randy, Norfolk * | 6 | 7 | .462 | 3.81 | 22 | 21 | 1 | 0 | 0 | 0 | 130.0 | 145 | 566 | 72 | 55 | 13 | 4 | 4 | 2 | 45 | 1 | 110 | 2 | 2 |
| Kemp, Beau, Rochester | 6 | 3 | .667 | 3.54 | 36 | 0 | 0 | 0 | 25 | 4 | 48.1 | 46 | 212 | 23 | 19 | 1 | 0 | 0 | 2 | 19 | 3 | 35 | 3 | 0 |
| Keppel, Bob, Norfolk | 3 | 7 | .300 | 4.71 | 17 | 16 | 1 | 0 | 0 | 0 | 93.2 | 111 | 402 | 51 | 49 | 8 | 8 | 6 | 9 | 22 | 1 | 42 | 2 | 1 |
| Kershner, Jason, Syracuse * | 3 | 2 | .600 | 5.20 | 28 | 0 | 0 | 0 | 11 | 4 | 36.1 | 45 | 167 | 23 | 21 | 6 | 0 | 0 | 3 | 10 | 2 | 31 | 1 | 0 |
| Kester, Tim, Pawtucket | 12 | 11 | .522 | 4.20 | 28 | 24 | 1 | 0 | 2 | 0 | 169.1 | 186 | 704 | 89 | 79 | 25 | 11 | 6 | 9 | 19 | 1 | 76 | 1 | 0 |
| Kieschnick, Brooks, Indianapolis | 0 | 0 | .000 | 0.00 | 2 | 2 | 0 | 0 | 0 | 0 | 2.0 | 1 | 7 | 0 | 0 | 0 | 0 | 0 | 0 | 0 | 0 | 1 | 0 | 0 |
| Kim, Byung-Hyun, Pawtucket | 2 | 6 | .250 | 5.34 | 22 | 19 | 0 | 0 | 0 | 0 | 60.2 | 71 | 262 | 43 | 36 | 6 | 2 | 2 | 6 | 12 | 0 | 39 | 0 | 1 |
| Kirsten, Rick, Toledo | 3 | 4 | .429 | 5.86 | 14 | 6 | 0 | 0 | 0 | 0 | 50.2 | 63 | 230 | 36 | 33 | 3 | 4 | 4 | 4 | 23 | 1 | 27 | 1 | 0 |
| Kohlmeier, Ryan, Charlotte | 3 | 10 | .231 | 6.24 | 23 | 17 | 1 | 0 | 2 | 0 | 102.1 | 116 | 441 | 75 | 71 | 27 | 2 | 8 | 4 | 23 | 0 | 74 | 5 | 0 |
| Kubes, Greg, Scranton-WB * | 5 | 3 | .625 | 3.84 | 49 | 0 | 0 | 0 | 14 | 0 | 75.0 | 95 | 346 | 44 | 32 | 13 | 1 | 1 | 3 | 26 | 4 | 46 | 0 | 0 |
| Larson, Adam, Charlotte | 0 | 2 | .000 | 7.36 | 6 | 1 | 0 | 0 | 4 | 0 | 14.2 | 18 | 67 | 12 | 12 | 3 | 0 | 0 | 2 | 5 | 1 | 6 | 1 | 0 |
| Lee, Dave, Buffalo | 2 | 4 | .333 | 4.88 | 51 | 0 | 0 | 0 | 37 | 9 | 66.1 | 63 | 302 | 37 | 36 | 6 | 1 | 0 | 5 | 35 | 3 | 55 | 2 | 0 |
| Lee, Seung, Scranton-WB | 2 | 4 | .333 | 4.57 | 35 | 6 | 0 | 0 | 8 | 1 | 80.2 | 89 | 349 | 45 | 41 | 12 | 3 | 5 | 5 | 24 | 0 | 67 | 1 | 0 |
| Leskanic, Curt, Pawtucket | 0 | 0 | .000 | 0.00 | 1 | 0 | 0 | 0 | 0 | 0 | 1.0 | 0 | 3 | 0 | 0 | 0 | 0 | 0 | 0 | 0 | 0 | 0 | 0 | 0 |
| Liriano, Pedro, Indianapolis | 3 | 10 | .231 | 5.20 | 29 | 21 | 1 | 0 | 2 | 1 | 126.1 | 149 | 555 | 81 | 73 | 21 | 4 | 4 | 5 | 50 | 1 | 97 | 7 | 3 |
| Lomasney, Steve, Louisville | 0 | 0 | .000 | 6.75 | 2 | 0 | 0 | 0 | 2 | 0 | 1.1 | 1 | 5 | 1 | 1 | 0 | 0 | 0 | 0 | 0 | 0 | 1 | 0 | 0 |
| Lopez, Aquilino, Syracuse | 1 | 6 | .143 | 7.17 | 32 | 0 | 0 | 0 | 17 | 5 | 42.2 | 58 | 198 | 36 | 34 | 8 | 0 | 0 | 2 | 10 | 0 | 32 | 4 | 0 |

| Pitcher, Team | W | L | Pct. | ERA | G | GS | CG | ShO | GF | Sv. | IP | H | TBF | R | ER | HR | SH | SF | HB | BB | IBB | SO | WP | Bk. |
|---|---|---|---|---|---|---|---|---|---|---|---|---|---|---|---|---|---|---|---|---|---|---|---|---|
| Lopez, Orionny, Charlotte | 1 | 0 | 1.000 | 6.00 | 2 | 1 | 0 | 0 | 1 | 0 | 6.0 | 7 | 27 | 4 | 4 | 2 | 0 | 0 | 0 | 3 | 0 | 7 | 1 | 0 |
| Lorraine, Andrew, Ottawa * | 5 | 4 | .556 | 4.50 | 28 | 19 | 0 | 0 | 3 | 0 | 120.0 | 137 | 524 | 65 | 60 | 11 | 8 | 6 | 3 | 36 | 3 | 74 | 4 | 0 |
| Loux, Shane, Toledo | 7 | 11 | .389 | 5.29 | 22 | 22 | 1 | 1 | 0 | 0 | 132.2 | 154 | 571 | 86 | 78 | 14 | 9 | 4 | 5 | 34 | 1 | 86 | 3 | 0 |
| Lukasiewicz, Mark, Syracuse * | 4 | 2 | .667 | 7.68 | 32 | 0 | 0 | 0 | 11 | 4 | 36.1 | 38 | 158 | 33 | 31 | 8 | 1 | 1 | 0 | 11 | 0 | 33 | 1 | 0 |
| Lundberg, Spike, Scranton-WB | 6 | 3 | .667 | 3.26 | 44 | 0 | 0 | 0 | 17 | 3 | 66.1 | 69 | 285 | 35 | 24 | 7 | 0 | 0 | 3 | 14 | 4 | 57 | 2 | 0 |
| Magrane, Jim, Durham | 8 | 5 | .615 | 3.93 | 25 | 21 | 1 | 0 | 0 | 0 | 132.2 | 160 | 574 | 67 | 58 | 18 | 3 | 1 | 3 | 42 | 1 | 65 | 7 | 0 |
| Maine, John, Ottawa | 5 | 7 | .417 | 3.91 | 22 | 22 | 0 | 0 | 0 | 0 | 119.2 | 123 | 512 | 59 | 52 | 12 | 12 | 5 | 5 | 52 | 0 | 105 | 2 | 1 |
| Majewski, Gary, Charlotte | 3 | 3 | .500 | 3.19 | 35 | 0 | 0 | 0 | 31 | 14 | 42.1 | 30 | 175 | 16 | 15 | 2 | 1 | 0 | 3 | 16 | 0 | 41 | 1 | 0 |
| Malaska, Mark, Pawtucket * | 1 | 1 | .500 | 4.21 | 33 | 0 | 0 | 0 | 8 | 1 | 36.1 | 42 | 163 | 17 | 17 | 7 | 0 | 0 | 3 | 11 | 2 | 31 | 1 | 0 |
| Mallette, Brian, Louisville | 1 | 0 | 1.000 | 2.27 | 40 | 0 | 0 | 0 | 24 | 5 | 43.2 | 35 | 178 | 12 | 11 | 1 | 0 | 0 | 0 | 12 | 1 | 36 | 3 | 0 |
| Mann, Jim, Columbus | 3 | 1 | .750 | 5.97 | 25 | 1 | 0 | 0 | 11 | 0 | 37.2 | 48 | 173 | 30 | 25 | 6 | 2 | 3 | 0 | 15 | 1 | 25 | 0 | 0 |
| Manning, Charlie, Columbus * | 1 | 1 | .500 | 3.65 | 11 | 0 | 0 | 0 | 4 | 0 | 12.1 | 10 | 54 | 6 | 5 | 0 | 0 | 0 | 1 | 6 | 0 | 11 | 0 | 0 |
| Marsonek, Sam, Columbus | 1 | 5 | .167 | 3.15 | 35 | 0 | 0 | 0 | 30 | 17 | 40.0 | 36 | 170 | 20 | 14 | 5 | 1 | 0 | 3 | 12 | 2 | 28 | 3 | 0 |
| Marsters, Brandon, Rochester | 0 | 0 | .000 | 0.00 | 1 | 0 | 0 | 0 | 1 | 0 | 0.1 | 1 | 2 | 0 | 0 | 0 | 0 | 0 | 0 | 0 | 0 | 0 | 0 | 0 |
| Martin, J.D., Buffalo | 0 | 0 | .000 | 10.80 | 1 | 1 | 0 | 0 | 0 | 0 | 5.0 | 9 | 26 | 6 | 6 | 1 | 0 | 0 | 0 | 2 | 0 | 2 | 0 | 1 |
| Martinez, Anastacio, Pawtucket | 3 | 3 | .500 | 3.74 | 38 | 0 | 0 | 0 | 12 | 1 | 67.1 | 73 | 308 | 37 | 28 | 5 | 0 | 2 | 3 | 31 | 2 | 57 | 9 | 0 |
| Martinez, Javier, Ottawa | 0 | 0 | .000 | 10.80 | 1 | 1 | 0 | 0 | 0 | 0 | 1.2 | 4 | 14 | 4 | 2 | 0 | 0 | 2 | 0 | 4 | 0 | 0 | 0 | 0 |
| Matos, Josue, Syracuse | 6 | 6 | .500 | 5.18 | 27 | 21 | 0 | 0 | 0 | 0 | 130.1 | 138 | 555 | 85 | 75 | 25 | 6 | 9 | 4 | 46 | 1 | 103 | 13 | 0 |
| Matos, Julius, Syracuse | 1 | 0 | 1.000 | 3.38 | 2 | 2 | 0 | 0 | 0 | 0 | 10.2 | 6 | 47 | 4 | 4 | 2 | 1 | 2 | 0 | 10 | 1 | 9 | 0 | 0 |
| Matthews, Mike, Louisville * | 1 | 0 | 1.000 | 1.53 | 15 | 0 | 0 | 0 | 3 | 1 | 17.2 | 12 | 69 | 3 | 3 | 1 | 0 | 0 | 0 | 5 | 0 | 16 | 3 | 0 |
| Maurer, Dave, Syracuse * | 0 | 0 | .000 | 3.56 | 43 | 4 | 0 | 0 | 9 | 2 | 65.2 | 58 | 278 | 27 | 26 | 7 | 1 | 1 | 5 | 26 | 0 | 64 | 3 | 0 |
| McClung, Seth, Durham | 2 | 1 | .667 | 3.29 | 11 | 0 | 0 | 0 | 2 | 0 | 13.2 | 10 | 58 | 5 | 5 | 0 | 0 | 0 | 0 | 7 | 0 | 12 | 2 | 0 |
| McConnell, Sam, Richmond * | 7 | 7 | .500 | 3.91 | 22 | 18 | 1 | 0 | 3 | 0 | 103.2 | 102 | 430 | 51 | 45 | 8 | 4 | 6 | 5 | 28 | 0 | 56 | 1 | 0 |
| McGinley, Blake, Norfolk * | 3 | 3 | .500 | 4.05 | 13 | 0 | 0 | 0 | 7 | 2 | 26.2 | 30 | 118 | 15 | 12 | 1 | 1 | 0 | 0 | 7 | 1 | 28 | 1 | 0 |
| McNichol, Brian, Charlotte * | 0 | 1 | .000 | 6.75 | 6 | 1 | 0 | 0 | 1 | 0 | 12.0 | 16 | 56 | 9 | 9 | 2 | 0 | 0 | 1 | 7 | 0 | 6 | 1 | 0 |
| Mears, Chris, Toledo | 1 | 1 | .500 | 3.83 | 30 | 1 | 0 | 0 | 5 | 0 | 40.0 | 37 | 186 | 21 | 17 | 1 | 0 | 1 | 8 | 20 | 2 | 29 | 1 | 0 |
| Mendoza, Ramiro, Pawtucket | 0 | 1 | .000 | 4.15 | 6 | 0 | 0 | 0 | 1 | 0 | 8.2 | 13 | 39 | 5 | 4 | 2 | 0 | 0 | 0 | 0 | 0 | 3 | 0 | 0 |
| Meyers, Mike, Norfolk | 3 | 1 | .750 | 5.54 | 16 | 4 | 0 | 0 | 6 | 0 | 39.0 | 44 | 177 | 26 | 24 | 4 | 1 | 4 | 4 | 17 | 1 | 20 | 2 | 0 |
| Michalak, Chris, Indianapolis * | 2 | 6 | .250 | 5.18 | 37 | 0 | 0 | 0 | 14 | 1 | 48.2 | 65 | 241 | 37 | 28 | 3 | 1 | 1 | 10 | 18 | 2 | 29 | 2 | 2 |
| Mieses, Jose, Charlotte | 0 | 0 | .000 | 1.80 | 2 | 0 | 0 | 0 | 1 | 0 | 5.0 | 2 | 21 | 1 | 1 | 0 | 0 | 0 | 1 | 3 | 0 | 4 | 0 | 0 |
| Miller, Justin, Syracuse | 1 | 1 | .500 | 2.16 | 3 | 3 | 0 | 0 | 0 | 0 | 16.2 | 16 | 70 | 6 | 4 | 2 | 0 | 0 | 0 | 4 | 0 | 21 | 1 | 0 |
| Miller, Matt, Buffalo | 1 | 2 | .333 | 1.93 | 13 | 0 | 0 | 0 | 9 | 2 | 14.0 | 10 | 59 | 4 | 3 | 0 | 0 | 1 | 1 | 6 | 1 | 17 | 0 | 0 |
| Mills, Ryan, Rochester * | 1 | 0 | 1.000 | 6.10 | 15 | 0 | 0 | 0 | 7 | 1 | 20.2 | 25 | 100 | 14 | 14 | 4 | 1 | 0 | 3 | 13 | 0 | 16 | 2 | 0 |
| Minix, Travis, Durham | 3 | 0 | 1.000 | 4.75 | 22 | 0 | 0 | 0 | 11 | 1 | 36.0 | 39 | 157 | 27 | 19 | 6 | 0 | 0 | 0 | 10 | 2 | 28 | 2 | 0 |
| Moreno, Victor, Rochester | 1 | 0 | 1.000 | 6.35 | 6 | 0 | 0 | 0 | 2 | 0 | 11.1 | 12 | 53 | 10 | 8 | 1 | 0 | 0 | 1 | 6 | 0 | 12 | 0 | 0 |
| Moseley, Dustin, Louisville | 2 | 4 | .333 | 4.65 | 12 | 12 | 0 | 0 | 0 | 0 | 71.2 | 78 | 312 | 38 | 37 | 7 | 4 | 5 | 4 | 34 | 0 | 48 | 2 | 0 |
| Moss, Damian, Durham * | 5 | 9 | .357 | 5.87 | 20 | 17 | 0 | 0 | 2 | 0 | 89.0 | 109 | 421 | 68 | 58 | 7 | 5 | 3 | 2 | 65 | 0 | 67 | 10 | 1 |
| Moss, Damian, Louisville * | 0 | 3 | .000 | 10.61 | 4 | 3 | 0 | 0 | 0 | 0 | 18.2 | 29 | 96 | 23 | 22 | 4 | 1 | 1 | 1 | 15 | 0 | 12 | 1 | 1 |
| Munoz, Arnie, Charlotte * | 2 | 6 | .250 | 5.68 | 13 | 13 | 0 | 0 | 0 | 0 | 69.2 | 81 | 316 | 48 | 44 | 11 | 3 | 2 | 2 | 29 | 0 | 60 | 6 | 2 |
| Munro, Pete, Rochester | 6 | 3 | .667 | 3.88 | 10 | 10 | 0 | 0 | 0 | 0 | 51.0 | 51 | 214 | 30 | 22 | 6 | 3 | 3 | 1 | 11 | 0 | 34 | 1 | 0 |
| Musser, Neal, Norfolk * | 2 | 4 | .333 | 6.25 | 7 | 7 | 0 | 0 | 0 | 0 | 36.0 | 39 | 161 | 30 | 25 | 4 | 5 | 5 | 0 | 17 | 2 | 24 | 3 | 0 |
| Mussina, Mike, Columbus | 0 | 0 | .000 | 0.00 | 1 | 1 | 0 | 0 | 0 | 0 | 3.0 | 2 | 11 | 0 | 0 | 0 | 0 | 0 | 0 | 0 | 0 | 5 | 0 | 0 |
| Myette, Aaron, Louisville | 3 | 3 | .500 | 2.89 | 41 | 1 | 0 | 0 | 32 | 19 | 62.1 | 45 | 270 | 27 | 20 | 2 | 0 | 0 | 4 | 36 | 4 | 58 | 3 | 0 |
| Nakamura, Micheal, Syracuse | 3 | 2 | .600 | 3.11 | 31 | 1 | 0 | 0 | 9 | 4 | 55.0 | 42 | 225 | 20 | 19 | 3 | 3 | 1 | 2 | 17 | 2 | 76 | 2 | 1 |
| Nelson, Bubba, Louisville | 1 | 10 | .091 | 7.09 | 12 | 12 | 0 | 0 | 0 | 0 | 59.2 | 74 | 268 | 56 | 47 | 12 | 4 | 6 | 5 | 26 | 0 | 45 | 3 | 0 |
| Nelson, Joe, Pawtucket | 0 | 0 | .000 | 4.64 | 16 | 0 | 0 | 0 | 2 | 0 | 21.1 | 27 | 102 | 14 | 11 | 1 | 0 | 0 | 2 | 9 | 0 | 31 | 1 | 0 |
| Nitkowski, C.J., Columbus * | 0 | 0 | .000 | 1.42 | 16 | 0 | 0 | 0 | 1 | 0 | 12.2 | 8 | 50 | 3 | 2 | 0 | 0 | 0 | 1 | 3 | 0 | 11 | 2 | 0 |
| Novinsky, John, Indianapolis | 0 | 0 | .000 | 0.00 | 1 | 0 | 0 | 0 | 0 | 0 | 0.1 | 1 | 2 | 0 | 0 | 0 | 0 | 0 | 0 | 0 | 0 | 0 | 0 | 0 |
| Obermueller, Wes, Indianapolis | 0 | 3 | .000 | 5.19 | 4 | 4 | 1 | 0 | 0 | 0 | 26.0 | 30 | 111 | 16 | 15 | 3 | 3 | 1 | 1 | 7 | 0 | 17 | 1 | 0 |
| Olson, Ryan, Norfolk * | 0 | 0 | .000 | 0.00 | 1 | 0 | 0 | 0 | 1 | 0 | 1.0 | 0 | 3 | 0 | 0 | 0 | 0 | 0 | 0 | 0 | 0 | 2 | 0 | 0 |
| Ormond, Rodney, Ottawa | 3 | 2 | .600 | 5.55 | 28 | 0 | 0 | 0 | 8 | 1 | 47.0 | 50 | 220 | 29 | 29 | 1 | 1 | 1 | 2 | 29 | 4 | 38 | 6 | 0 |
| Ortiz, Javier, Columbus | 1 | 5 | .167 | 7.50 | 9 | 9 | 0 | 0 | 0 | 0 | 42.0 | 66 | 204 | 38 | 35 | 10 | 1 | 0 | 4 | 19 | 1 | 33 | 0 | 0 |
| Orvella, Chad, Durham | 0 | 0 | .000 | 5.40 | 2 | 0 | 0 | 0 | 0 | 0 | 1.2 | 1 | 8 | 1 | 1 | 1 | 0 | 0 | 1 | 1 | 0 | 2 | 1 | 0 |
| Pacheco, Enemencio, Charlotte | 0 | 1 | .000 | 4.82 | 15 | 1 | 0 | 0 | 7 | 0 | 18.2 | 18 | 88 | 11 | 10 | 2 | 0 | 0 | 0 | 15 | 0 | 13 | 3 | 0 |
| Padilla, Juan, Columbus | 2 | 1 | .667 | 2.02 | 45 | 0 | 0 | 0 | 11 | 3 | 58.0 | 49 | 228 | 20 | 13 | 1 | 0 | 0 | 2 | 6 | 2 | 52 | 4 | 1 |
| Padilla, Vicente, Scranton-WB | 0 | 0 | .000 | 13.50 | 2 | 2 | 0 | 0 | 0 | 0 | 4.2 | 6 | 25 | 7 | 7 | 1 | 2 | 0 | 0 | 5 | 0 | 6 | 0 | 0 |
| Palki, Jeromy, Rochester | 2 | 0 | 1.000 | 4.44 | 42 | 1 | 0 | 0 | 8 | 3 | 73.0 | 74 | 331 | 40 | 36 | 5 | 0 | 0 | 5 | 37 | 0 | 74 | 5 | 0 |
| Paradis, Mike, Ottawa | 0 | 0 | .000 | 15.32 | 9 | 0 | 0 | 0 | 2 | 0 | 12.1 | 22 | 78 | 22 | 21 | 3 | 0 | 0 | 3 | 18 | 0 | 8 | 8 | 0 |
| Parker, Josh, Durham | 0 | 1 | .000 | 3.00 | 12 | 0 | 0 | 0 | 7 | 0 | 12.0 | 15 | 59 | 4 | 4 | 0 | 0 | 0 | 1 | 7 | 1 | 7 | 0 | 0 |
| Parker, Matt, Indianapolis | 0 | 1 | .000 | 7.36 | 1 | 0 | 0 | 0 | 0 | 0 | 3.2 | 7 | 18 | 3 | 3 | 0 | 0 | 1 | 0 | 1 | 1 | 3 | 2 | 0 |
| Parker, Matt, Durham | 0 | 0 | .000 | 5.79 | 1 | 1 | 0 | 0 | 0 | 0 | 4.2 | 8 | 23 | 3 | 3 | 2 | 0 | 0 | 0 | 1 | 0 | 7 | 0 | 0 |
| Parra, Jose, Norfolk | 2 | 1 | .667 | 1.63 | 24 | 0 | 0 | 0 | 22 | 16 | 27.2 | 19 | 111 | 6 | 5 | 1 | 0 | 1 | 0 | 10 | 1 | 35 | 0 | 0 |
| Patterson, Danny, Toledo | 1 | 0 | 1.000 | 4.15 | 3 | 0 | 0 | 0 | 1 | 0 | 4.1 | 3 | 18 | 2 | 2 | 0 | 0 | 0 | 0 | 2 | 1 | 3 | 1 | 1 |
| Paz, Rich, Charlotte | 0 | 0 | .000 | 9.00 | 1 | 0 | 0 | 0 | 1 | 0 | 1.0 | 2 | 5 | 1 | 1 | 1 | 0 | 0 | 0 | 0 | 0 | 1 | 0 | 0 |
| Perez, Carlos, Ottawa * | 0 | 0 | .000 | 36.00 | 1 | 0 | 0 | 0 | 0 | 0 | 1.0 | 4 | 7 | 4 | 4 | 1 | 0 | 0 | 0 | 1 | 0 | 1 | 0 | 0 |
| Perez, Frank, Scranton-WB | 0 | 5 | .000 | 6.00 | 9 | 6 | 0 | 0 | 1 | 0 | 39.0 | 49 | 173 | 32 | 26 | 8 | 2 | 2 | 6 | 5 | 0 | 23 | 2 | 0 |
| Peterson, Adam, Syracuse | 2 | 2 | .500 | 12.86 | 19 | 0 | 0 | 0 | 8 | 0 | 21.0 | 38 | 119 | 30 | 30 | 6 | 0 | 0 | 2 | 16 | 1 | 19 | 2 | 0 |
| Phelps, Travis, Indianapolis | 8 | 5 | .615 | 4.37 | 28 | 14 | 0 | 0 | 3 | 0 | 107.0 | 114 | 442 | 58 | 52 | 11 | 5 | 4 | 1 | 25 | 1 | 84 | 2 | 1 |
| Pineda, Luis, Norfolk | 0 | 0 | .000 | 2.00 | 5 | 0 | 0 | 0 | 1 | 0 | 9.0 | 5 | 41 | 4 | 2 | 1 | 0 | 1 | 3 | 5 | 1 | 13 | 0 | 0 |
| Porzio, Mike, Buffalo * | 0 | 0 | .000 | 6.00 | 1 | 1 | 0 | 0 | 0 | 0 | 3.0 | 7 | 18 | 6 | 2 | 1 | 0 | 0 | 0 | 2 | 0 | 0 | 2 | 0 |
| Powell, Brian, Scranton-WB | 3 | 1 | .750 | 1.62 | 8 | 8 | 2 | 1 | 0 | 0 | 44.1 | 27 | 165 | 11 | 8 | 2 | 2 | 0 | 0 | 6 | 0 | 29 | 0 | 0 |
| Prieto, Ariel, Toledo | 1 | 1 | .500 | 3.68 | 4 | 4 | 0 | 0 | 0 | 0 | 22.0 | 20 | 92 | 10 | 9 | 3 | 2 | 0 | 4 | 5 | 1 | 19 | 1 | 0 |
| Prinz, Bret, Columbus | 3 | 1 | .750 | 3.52 | 29 | 0 | 0 | 0 | 18 | 11 | 30.2 | 27 | 127 | 12 | 12 | 3 | 0 | 0 | 2 | 9 | 0 | 33 | 0 | 0 |
| Proctor, Scott, Columbus | 2 | 3 | .400 | 2.86 | 35 | 0 | 0 | 0 | 15 | 4 | 44.0 | 37 | 187 | 15 | 14 | 4 | 1 | 0 | 1 | 18 | 2 | 42 | 3 | 0 |
| Puffer, Brandon, Pawtucket | 3 | 2 | .600 | 3.26 | 24 | 0 | 0 | 0 | 21 | 10 | 30.1 | 31 | 134 | 11 | 11 | 1 | 0 | 0 | 1 | 11 | 3 | 21 | 4 | 0 |
| Pulido, Carlos, Rochester * | 1 | 3 | .250 | 11.72 | 5 | 5 | 0 | 0 | 0 | 0 | 17.2 | 29 | 90 | 24 | 23 | 7 | 0 | 5 | 0 | 7 | 0 | 12 | 1 | 0 |
| Purvis, Rob, Charlotte | 0 | 0 | .000 | 15.00 | 2 | 0 | 0 | 0 | 1 | 0 | 6.0 | 11 | 33 | 10 | 10 | 1 | 0 | 2 | 0 | 5 | 0 | 1 | 1 | 0 |
| Rakers, Aaron, Ottawa | 4 | 5 | .444 | 2.75 | 54 | 1 | 0 | 0 | 18 | 1 | 78.2 | 65 | 326 | 27 | 24 | 8 | 0 | 1 | 2 | 25 | 4 | 80 | 2 | 0 |
| Ramirez, Horacio, Richmond * | 0 | 0 | .000 | 8.00 | 2 | 2 | 0 | 0 | 0 | 0 | 9.0 | 15 | 42 | 8 | 8 | 1 | 2 | 2 | 0 | 1 | 0 | 3 | 0 | 0 |

| Pitcher, Team | W | L | Pct. | ERA | G | GS | CG | ShO | GF | Sv. | IP | H | TBF | R | ER | HR | SH | SF | HB | BB | IBB | SO | WP | Bk. |
|---|---|---|---|---|---|---|---|---|---|---|---|---|---|---|---|---|---|---|---|---|---|---|---|---|
| Ramirez, Ramon, Columbus | 0 | 3 | .000 | 8.50 | 4 | 4 | 0 | 0 | 0 | 0 | 18.0 | 25 | 87 | 19 | 17 | 3 | 0 | 3 | 0 | 8 | 1 | 17 | 1 | 0 |
| Ramsey, Keith, Buffalo * | 1 | 1 | .500 | 3.60 | 2 | 2 | 0 | 0 | 0 | 0 | 10.0 | 11 | 43 | 4 | 4 | 1 | 0 | 1 | 0 | 2 | 0 | 5 | 0 | 0 |
| Randall, Scott, Louisville | 1 | 4 | .200 | 4.98 | 27 | 1 | 0 | 0 | 12 | 0 | 43.1 | 49 | 199 | 29 | 24 | 4 | 1 | 1 | 6 | 19 | 1 | 30 | 1 | 0 |
| Rauch, Jon, Charlotte | 6 | 3 | .667 | 3.11 | 14 | 13 | 0 | 0 | 0 | 0 | 72.1 | 57 | 286 | 27 | 25 | 9 | 4 | 2 | 1 | 25 | 0 | 61 | 1 | 1 |
| Rayborn, Kenny, Buffalo | 8 | 2 | .800 | 3.64 | 23 | 22 | 0 | 0 | 0 | 0 | 123.2 | 122 | 524 | 57 | 50 | 13 | 7 | 5 | 12 | 40 | 0 | 65 | 4 | 0 |
| Reichert, Dan, Indianapolis | 7 | 4 | .636 | 3.70 | 50 | 0 | 0 | 0 | 22 | 1 | 87.2 | 90 | 392 | 44 | 36 | 6 | 0 | 1 | 4 | 38 | 1 | 74 | 9 | 0 |
| Reimers, Cameron, Syracuse | 2 | 7 | .222 | 5.05 | 12 | 12 | 0 | 0 | 0 | 0 | 66.0 | 82 | 301 | 43 | 37 | 8 | 5 | 2 | 5 | 20 | 1 | 28 | 3 | 2 |
| Reith, Brian, Louisville | 2 | 3 | .400 | 3.72 | 26 | 1 | 0 | 0 | 4 | 0 | 36.1 | 51 | 172 | 17 | 15 | 1 | 1 | 0 | 2 | 13 | 0 | 32 | 3 | 0 |
| Reyes, Al, Durham | 2 | 1 | .667 | 2.35 | 21 | 0 | 0 | 0 | 20 | 10 | 23.0 | 22 | 97 | 6 | 6 | 0 | 1 | 0 | 3 | 6 | 1 | 22 | 0 | 0 |
| Reyes, Carlos, Columbus | 2 | 1 | .667 | 5.88 | 5 | 5 | 0 | 0 | 0 | 0 | 26.0 | 43 | 120 | 17 | 17 | 3 | 0 | 0 | 0 | 10 | 0 | 12 | 3 | 1 |
| Ring, Royce, Norfolk * | 3 | 1 | .750 | 3.63 | 29 | 0 | 0 | 0 | 10 | 0 | 34.2 | 37 | 151 | 15 | 14 | 5 | 0 | 0 | 0 | 12 | 1 | 22 | 1 | 0 |
| Ritchie, Todd, Durham | 4 | 6 | .400 | 6.29 | 16 | 16 | 0 | 0 | 0 | 0 | 88.2 | 112 | 399 | 71 | 62 | 19 | 4 | 6 | 3 | 23 | 0 | 41 | 3 | 0 |
| Rivard, Reggie, Indianapolis | 1 | 0 | 1.000 | 9.00 | 1 | 0 | 0 | 0 | 0 | 0 | 2.0 | 2 | 9 | 2 | 2 | 0 | 0 | 0 | 0 | 1 | 0 | 0 | 1 | 0 |
| Roach, Jason, Norfolk | 2 | 5 | .286 | 3.47 | 39 | 8 | 1 | 0 | 9 | 0 | 90.2 | 90 | 393 | 44 | 35 | 12 | 2 | 2 | 3 | 30 | 1 | 80 | 4 | 1 |
| Robbins, Jake, Buffalo | 6 | 1 | .857 | 3.15 | 32 | 2 | 0 | 0 | 11 | 4 | 65.2 | 51 | 278 | 24 | 23 | 4 | 1 | 1 | 6 | 29 | 1 | 41 | 6 | 0 |
| Roberge, J.P., Scranton-WB | 0 | 0 | .000 | 0.00 | 1 | 0 | 0 | 0 | 1 | 0 | 0.1 | 0 | 1 | 0 | 0 | 0 | 0 | 0 | 0 | 0 | 0 | 0 | 0 | 0 |
| Robertson, Jeriome, Buffalo * | 4 | 5 | .444 | 7.27 | 14 | 12 | 0 | 0 | 0 | 0 | 64.1 | 91 | 300 | 58 | 52 | 10 | 2 | 5 | 3 | 22 | 1 | 28 | 4 | 1 |
| Rodriguez, Eddy, Ottawa | 1 | 0 | 1.000 | 5.12 | 28 | 0 | 0 | 0 | 17 | 3 | 31.2 | 34 | 152 | 19 | 18 | 4 | 0 | 1 | 3 | 18 | 0 | 31 | 1 | 0 |
| Rodriguez, Guillermo, Toledo | 0 | 0 | .000 | 9.00 | 1 | 0 | 0 | 0 | 1 | 0 | 1.0 | 3 | 6 | 1 | 1 | 0 | 0 | 0 | 0 | 0 | 0 | 0 | 1 | 0 |
| Rodriguez, Jose, Ottawa * | 2 | 0 | 1.000 | 7.56 | 20 | 0 | 0 | 0 | 8 | 0 | 25.0 | 30 | 121 | 25 | 21 | 8 | 0 | 1 | 1 | 16 | 1 | 17 | 2 | 1 |
| Rodriguez, Jose, Norfolk | 1 | 0 | 1.000 | 4.91 | 2 | 0 | 0 | 0 | 1 | 0 | 3.2 | 4 | 16 | 2 | 2 | 0 | 0 | 0 | 0 | 1 | 0 | 1 | 0 | 0 |
| Rodriguez, Nerio, Columbus | 2 | 6 | .250 | 8.36 | 12 | 11 | 0 | 0 | 1 | 0 | 51.2 | 71 | 238 | 54 | 48 | 13 | 2 | 5 | 3 | 19 | 0 | 48 | 4 | 0 |
| Rodriguez, Ryan, Charlotte * | 0 | 1 | .000 | 6.00 | 1 | 1 | 0 | 0 | 0 | 0 | 6.0 | 8 | 26 | 4 | 4 | 1 | 0 | 1 | 1 | 3 | 0 | 6 | 0 | 0 |
| Romano, Mike, Richmond | 13 | 5 | .722 | 3.42 | 40 | 16 | 0 | 0 | 9 | 0 | 123.2 | 130 | 537 | 51 | 47 | 13 | 8 | 7 | 7 | 51 | 6 | 99 | 6 | 3 |
| Romero, J.C., Rochester * | 0 | 0 | .000 | 2.25 | 3 | 3 | 0 | 0 | 0 | 0 | 8.0 | 4 | 32 | 2 | 2 | 1 | 2 | 2 | 1 | 5 | 0 | 11 | 0 | 0 |
| Roney, Matt, Toledo | 2 | 1 | .667 | 3.86 | 5 | 5 | 0 | 0 | 0 | 0 | 30.1 | 30 | 124 | 13 | 13 | 3 | 2 | 2 | 3 | 10 | 0 | 18 | 1 | 0 |
| Rose, Brian, Louisville | 3 | 2 | .600 | 3.31 | 6 | 6 | 0 | 0 | 0 | 0 | 35.1 | 39 | 150 | 13 | 13 | 2 | 3 | 1 | 2 | 10 | 1 | 26 | 1 | 0 |
| Sadler, Carl, Buffalo * | 0 | 1 | .000 | 12.46 | 3 | 0 | 0 | 0 | 1 | 0 | 4.1 | 5 | 24 | 6 | 6 | 0 | 0 | 0 | 0 | 6 | 1 | 4 | 2 | 0 |
| Sanches, Brian, Scranton-WB | 0 | 0 | .000 | 7.50 | 4 | 0 | 0 | 0 | 1 | 0 | 6.0 | 9 | 30 | 5 | 5 | 1 | 0 | 0 | 0 | 3 | 0 | 4 | 0 | 0 |
| Sanchez, Jesus, Syracuse * | 1 | 4 | .200 | 6.84 | 7 | 4 | 0 | 0 | 1 | 0 | 25.0 | 28 | 114 | 21 | 19 | 5 | 1 | 2 | 1 | 13 | 1 | 20 | 2 | 0 |
| Sanchez, Jesus, Louisville * | 3 | 2 | .600 | 3.00 | 22 | 5 | 0 | 0 | 6 | 1 | 60.0 | 49 | 254 | 22 | 20 | 6 | 0 | 0 | 1 | 28 | 2 | 51 | 1 | 0 |
| Sanders, Dave, Charlotte * | 2 | 2 | .500 | 6.06 | 40 | 0 | 0 | 0 | 18 | 2 | 52.0 | 61 | 243 | 38 | 35 | 7 | 1 | 0 | 3 | 24 | 0 | 45 | 3 | 0 |
| Santiago, Jose, Charlotte | 9 | 9 | .500 | 4.34 | 57 | 1 | 0 | 0 | 25 | 7 | 87.0 | 89 | 390 | 51 | 42 | 6 | 1 | 0 | 5 | 35 | 7 | 47 | 2 | 1 |
| Santos, Victor, Indianapolis | 0 | 0 | .000 | 3.48 | 3 | 3 | 0 | 0 | 0 | 0 | 10.1 | 12 | 45 | 4 | 4 | 1 | 1 | 1 | 0 | 4 | 0 | 11 | 0 | 0 |
| Scarborough, Steve, Indianapolis | 0 | 0 | .000 | 0.00 | 3 | 0 | 0 | 0 | 3 | 0 | 2.0 | 2 | 8 | 0 | 0 | 0 | 0 | 0 | 0 | 0 | 0 | 1 | 0 | 0 |
| Schmack, Brian, Toledo | 1 | 2 | .333 | 4.26 | 24 | 0 | 0 | 0 | 6 | 0 | 50.2 | 54 | 221 | 29 | 24 | 4 | 3 | 1 | 2 | 14 | 1 | 35 | 3 | 0 |
| Schmitt, Eric, Columbus | 5 | 5 | .500 | 6.05 | 20 | 16 | 1 | 0 | 0 | 0 | 86.1 | 103 | 383 | 66 | 58 | 10 | 10 | 8 | 4 | 17 | 0 | 69 | 1 | 0 |
| Schoening, Brent, Rochester | 4 | 8 | .333 | 4.56 | 44 | 8 | 0 | 0 | 10 | 1 | 94.2 | 103 | 424 | 51 | 48 | 13 | 0 | 4 | 2 | 37 | 1 | 80 | 3 | 0 |
| Seay, Bobby, Durham * | 2 | 1 | .667 | 1.72 | 29 | 0 | 0 | 0 | 11 | 1 | 36.2 | 26 | 144 | 9 | 7 | 3 | 0 | 0 | 1 | 9 | 0 | 35 | 4 | 0 |
| Seibel, Phil, Pawtucket * | 1 | 2 | .333 | 3.02 | 8 | 7 | 0 | 0 | 0 | 0 | 44.2 | 42 | 176 | 16 | 15 | 7 | 1 | 2 | 1 | 12 | 0 | 31 | 0 | 0 |
| Seo, Jae, Norfolk | 0 | 2 | .000 | 2.82 | 4 | 4 | 0 | 0 | 0 | 0 | 22.1 | 22 | 87 | 7 | 7 | 1 | 0 | 0 | 2 | 8 | 0 | 20 | 0 | 1 |
| Shackelford, Brian, Louisville * | 8 | 1 | .889 | 3.58 | 59 | 0 | 0 | 0 | 13 | 0 | 73.0 | 58 | 315 | 31 | 29 | 6 | 0 | 0 | 1 | 42 | 1 | 63 | 4 | 2 |
| Shearn, Tom, Louisville | 0 | 1 | .000 | 2.55 | 11 | 0 | 0 | 0 | 2 | 0 | 17.2 | 10 | 68 | 6 | 5 | 1 | 1 | 1 | 0 | 6 | 0 | 12 | 0 | 0 |
| Smith, Bud, Scranton-WB * | 0 | 1 | .000 | 6.00 | 1 | 1 | 0 | 0 | 0 | 0 | 3.0 | 3 | 15 | 4 | 2 | 0 | 0 | 0 | 0 | 2 | 0 | 0 | 0 | 0 |
| Smith, Chuck, Richmond | 9 | 4 | .692 | 3.72 | 29 | 24 | 1 | 1 | 3 | 0 | 142.2 | 125 | 597 | 62 | 59 | 8 | 8 | 5 | 8 | 47 | 1 | 129 | 5 | 4 |
| Smith, Mike, Syracuse | 4 | 6 | .400 | 5.28 | 35 | 15 | 0 | 0 | 12 | 1 | 109.0 | 123 | 508 | 80 | 64 | 12 | 2 | 5 | 12 | 53 | 0 | 72 | 9 | 0 |
| Smith, Travis, Richmond | 10 | 2 | .833 | 2.59 | 20 | 19 | 1 | 0 | 1 | 0 | 107.2 | 98 | 432 | 31 | 31 | 6 | 4 | 3 | 6 | 26 | 0 | 93 | 2 | 1 |
| Sosa, Jorge, Durham | 1 | 2 | .333 | 2.77 | 3 | 3 | 0 | 0 | 0 | 0 | 13.0 | 11 | 48 | 5 | 4 | 0 | 1 | 0 | 0 | 0 | 0 | 23 | 1 | 0 |
| Spencer, Sean, Ottawa * | 0 | 1 | .000 | 5.79 | 9 | 0 | 0 | 0 | 1 | 0 | 18.2 | 21 | 86 | 12 | 12 | 3 | 0 | 0 | 1 | 11 | 0 | 14 | 1 | 0 |
| Spradlin, Jerry, Ottawa * | 2 | 4 | .333 | 6.89 | 11 | 0 | 0 | 0 | 6 | 1 | 15.2 | 16 | 77 | 14 | 12 | 1 | 0 | 0 | 1 | 13 | 2 | 12 | 3 | 0 |
| Standridge, Jason, Durham | 8 | 4 | .667 | 3.85 | 20 | 20 | 2 | 0 | 0 | 0 | 119.1 | 120 | 498 | 56 | 51 | 7 | 8 | 2 | 3 | 44 | 0 | 76 | 4 | 1 |
| Stanford, Jason, Buffalo * | 0 | 0 | .000 | 0.00 | 1 | 1 | 0 | 0 | 0 | 0 | 3.1 | 2 | 16 | 0 | 0 | 0 | 0 | 0 | 0 | 3 | 0 | 4 | 0 | 0 |
| Stephens, John, Pawtucket | 9 | 6 | .600 | 4.47 | 24 | 21 | 1 | 0 | 2 | 0 | 143.0 | 148 | 594 | 74 | 71 | 23 | 5 | 4 | 10 | 32 | 0 | 101 | 5 | 0 |
| Stevens, Josh, Pawtucket | 1 | 0 | 1.000 | 5.00 | 5 | 4 | 0 | 0 | 0 | 0 | 27.0 | 45 | 123 | 16 | 15 | 5 | 3 | 0 | 0 | 4 | 0 | 11 | 0 | 0 |
| Stewart, Josh, Charlotte * | 8 | 7 | .533 | 3.93 | 25 | 25 | 0 | 0 | 0 | 0 | 148.2 | 155 | 617 | 70 | 65 | 20 | 8 | 10 | 8 | 44 | 0 | 82 | 4 | 0 |
| Stewart, Paul, Indianapolis | 0 | 2 | .000 | 10.80 | 6 | 1 | 0 | 0 | 1 | 0 | 11.2 | 20 | 63 | 16 | 14 | 4 | 0 | 0 | 2 | 6 | 0 | 8 | 0 | 0 |
| Stewart, Scott, Buffalo * | 3 | 1 | .750 | 4.22 | 27 | 0 | 0 | 0 | 14 | 6 | 32.0 | 37 | 143 | 15 | 15 | 4 | 0 | 0 | 1 | 9 | 1 | 21 | 2 | 0 |
| Strange, Pat, Norfolk | 10 | 9 | .526 | 5.25 | 29 | 19 | 1 | 0 | 5 | 1 | 135.1 | 152 | 608 | 85 | 79 | 18 | 8 | 4 | 6 | 53 | 0 | 88 | 2 | 2 |
| Tadano, Kazuhito, Buffalo | 2 | 4 | .333 | 5.44 | 12 | 8 | 0 | 0 | 2 | 0 | 44.2 | 49 | 195 | 28 | 27 | 9 | 1 | 3 | 2 | 14 | 0 | 39 | 3 | 1 |
| Tallet, Brian, Buffalo * | 0 | 0 | .000 | 4.15 | 5 | 0 | 0 | 0 | 1 | 0 | 8.2 | 7 | 36 | 4 | 4 | 0 | 0 | 0 | 0 | 3 | 1 | 7 | 1 | 0 |
| Telemaco, Amaury, Scranton-WB | 0 | 0 | .000 | 0.00 | 1 | 1 | 0 | 0 | 0 | 0 | 1.0 | 0 | 3 | 0 | 0 | 0 | 0 | 0 | 0 | 0 | 0 | 2 | 0 | 0 |
| Thomas, Brad, Pawtucket * | 0 | 1 | .000 | 10.38 | 4 | 1 | 0 | 0 | 0 | 0 | 4.1 | 6 | 25 | 9 | 5 | 0 | 0 | 0 | 0 | 6 | 0 | 1 | 0 | 0 |
| Thomas, Evan, Buffalo | 3 | 1 | .750 | 5.04 | 8 | 4 | 0 | 0 | 1 | 0 | 30.1 | 37 | 139 | 19 | 17 | 4 | 0 | 2 | 1 | 12 | 0 | 29 | 1 | 1 |
| Thurman, Mike, Columbus | 0 | 0 | .000 | 15.43 | 2 | 0 | 0 | 0 | 0 | 0 | 2.1 | 5 | 13 | 4 | 4 | 1 | 1 | 0 | 0 | 2 | 0 | 2 | 0 | 0 |
| Towers, Josh, Syracuse | 3 | 1 | .750 | 2.50 | 6 | 5 | 0 | 0 | 0 | 0 | 36.0 | 33 | 139 | 11 | 10 | 5 | 2 | 1 | 0 | 7 | 0 | 25 | 2 | 0 |
| Ulacia, Dennis, Charlotte * | 1 | 0 | 1.000 | 1.42 | 1 | 1 | 0 | 0 | 0 | 0 | 6.1 | 6 | 25 | 1 | 1 | 1 | 0 | 1 | 0 | 0 | 0 | 4 | 0 | 0 |
| Urdaneta, Lino, Toledo | 0 | 2 | .000 | 9.69 | 9 | 1 | 0 | 0 | 0 | 0 | 13.0 | 22 | 65 | 14 | 14 | 4 | 0 | 0 | 1 | 3 | 0 | 4 | 0 | 0 |
| Valentine, Joe, Louisville | 5 | 5 | .500 | 5.01 | 30 | 9 | 0 | 0 | 8 | 0 | 64.2 | 63 | 290 | 41 | 36 | 8 | 1 | 4 | 4 | 32 | 0 | 61 | 4 | 0 |
| Van Hekken, Andy, Toledo * | 9 | 7 | .563 | 4.96 | 28 | 27 | 0 | 0 | 0 | 0 | 152.1 | 179 | 672 | 97 | 84 | 13 | 8 | 9 | 8 | 59 | 1 | 101 | 8 | 0 |
| Velazquez, Juan, Richmond | 0 | 0 | .000 | 9.00 | 1 | 0 | 0 | 0 | 1 | 1 | 1.0 | 3 | 6 | 1 | 1 | 0 | 0 | 0 | 0 | 0 | 0 | 0 | 0 | 0 |
| Veras, Jose, Durham | 6 | 5 | .545 | 5.23 | 30 | 10 | 0 | 0 | 4 | 0 | 84.1 | 101 | 392 | 55 | 49 | 9 | 5 | 4 | 7 | 33 | 3 | 63 | 5 | 1 |
| Waechter, Doug, Durham | 0 | 2 | .000 | 6.75 | 8 | 8 | 0 | 0 | 0 | 0 | 29.1 | 33 | 135 | 22 | 22 | 11 | 0 | 1 | 1 | 17 | 0 | 22 | 1 | 0 |
| Wagner, Ryan, Louisville | 1 | 0 | 1.000 | 2.70 | 15 | 0 | 0 | 0 | 3 | 1 | 16.2 | 13 | 72 | 5 | 5 | 0 | 0 | 0 | 0 | 9 | 0 | 19 | 2 | 0 |
| Wang, Chien-Ming, Columbus | 5 | 1 | .833 | 2.01 | 6 | 5 | 2 | 1 | 1 | 0 | 40.1 | 31 | 154 | 9 | 9 | 3 | 1 | 0 | 1 | 8 | 0 | 35 | 0 | 0 |
| Wathan, Dusty, Buffalo | 0 | 0 | .000 | 0.00 | 2 | 0 | 0 | 0 | 2 | 0 | 2.0 | 0 | 8 | 0 | 0 | 0 | 0 | 0 | 0 | 2 | 0 | 0 | 0 | 0 |
| Watson, Mark, Louisville * | 1 | 0 | 1.000 | 4.71 | 23 | 0 | 0 | 0 | 10 | 1 | 21.0 | 23 | 97 | 12 | 11 | 2 | 0 | 1 | 0 | 10 | 0 | 17 | 0 | 0 |
| Webb, John, Durham | 1 | 3 | .250 | 3.27 | 6 | 6 | 0 | 0 | 0 | 0 | 33.0 | 31 | 142 | 19 | 12 | 5 | 1 | 3 | 4 | 14 | 0 | 22 | 3 | 0 |
| Weibl, Clint, Indianapolis | 4 | 3 | .571 | 3.94 | 24 | 9 | 0 | 0 | 3 | 0 | 80.0 | 84 | 349 | 44 | 35 | 13 | 5 | 4 | 4 | 26 | 0 | 59 | 1 | 0 |
| Wheeler, Dan, Norfolk | 1 | 0 | 1.000 | 2.45 | 5 | 0 | 0 | 0 | 1 | 0 | 7.1 | 8 | 32 | 2 | 2 | 0 | 0 | 0 | 0 | 2 | 0 | 10 | 0 | 1 |

| Pitcher, Team | W | L | Pct. | ERA | G | GS | CG | ShO | GF | Sv. | IP | H | TBF | R | ER | HR | SH | SF | HB | BB | IBB | SO | WP | Bk. |
|---|---|---|---|---|---|---|---|---|---|---|---|---|---|---|---|---|---|---|---|---|---|---|---|---|
| White, Matt, Buffalo * | 2 | 2 | .500 | 5.97 | 13 | 4 | 0 | 0 | 2 | 0 | 31.2 | 45 | 155 | 25 | 21 | 1 | 3 | 1 | 0 | 19 | 3 | 24 | 0 | 0 |
| Whiteside, Matt, Richmond | 2 | 4 | .333 | 3.23 | 57 | 0 | 0 | 0 | 51 | 38 | 64.0 | 56 | 265 | 23 | 23 | 9 | 0 | 1 | 2 | 16 | 3 | 59 | 2 | 0 |
| Wickman, Bob, Buffalo | 1 | 0 | 1.000 | 10.13 | 6 | 1 | 0 | 0 | 0 | 0 | 5.1 | 4 | 24 | 6 | 6 | 0 | 0 | 0 | 0 | 4 | 0 | 4 | 0 | 0 |
| Williams, Todd, Ottawa | 1 | 1 | .500 | 3.05 | 14 | 0 | 0 | 0 | 5 | 2 | 20.2 | 19 | 84 | 7 | 7 | 0 | 0 | 0 | 0 | 3 | 1 | 11 | 2 | 0 |
| Winkelsas, Joe, Charlotte | 0 | 0 | .000 | 6.30 | 5 | 0 | 0 | 0 | 1 | 0 | 10.0 | 15 | 48 | 7 | 7 | 1 | 0 | 0 | 0 | 3 | 0 | 5 | 1 | 0 |
| Wise, Matt, Indianapolis | 1 | 0 | 1.000 | 1.80 | 7 | 1 | 0 | 0 | 0 | 0 | 20.0 | 12 | 75 | 4 | 4 | 3 | 0 | 0 | 1 | 4 | 0 | 20 | 0 | 0 |
| Woolard, Glenn, Indianapolis | 0 | 0 | .000 | 0.00 | 1 | 1 | 0 | 0 | 0 | 0 | 6.0 | 3 | 21 | 0 | 0 | 0 | 0 | 0 | 0 | 1 | 0 | 4 | 0 | 0 |
| Wright, Danny, Charlotte | 0 | 2 | .000 | 28.69 | 2 | 2 | 0 | 0 | 0 | 0 | 5.1 | 17 | 41 | 19 | 17 | 4 | 0 | 2 | 1 | 6 | 0 | 3 | 1 | 0 |
| Wunsch, Kelly, Charlotte * | 1 | 0 | 1.000 | 2.93 | 27 | 0 | 0 | 0 | 6 | 2 | 27.2 | 21 | 123 | 9 | 9 | 1 | 0 | 0 | 7 | 12 | 0 | 29 | 4 | 0 |
| Wylie, Mitch, Charlotte | 1 | 4 | .200 | 5.74 | 28 | 1 | 0 | 0 | 11 | 1 | 53.1 | 63 | 248 | 41 | 34 | 8 | 1 | 1 | 4 | 24 | 2 | 42 | 0 | 0 |
| Yarnall, Ed, Pawtucket * | 0 | 1 | .000 | 4.26 | 2 | 2 | 0 | 0 | 0 | 0 | 6.1 | 7 | 29 | 3 | 3 | 1 | 0 | 0 | 0 | 2 | 0 | 4 | 0 | 0 |
| Yarnall, Ed, Scranton-WB * | 5 | 5 | .500 | 3.97 | 24 | 23 | 0 | 0 | 0 | 0 | 118.0 | 103 | 507 | 54 | 52 | 12 | 14 | 5 | 7 | 56 | 0 | 93 | 2 | 0 |
| Yates, Tyler, Norfolk | 6 | 2 | .750 | 3.18 | 30 | 1 | 0 | 0 | 12 | 4 | 39.2 | 28 | 172 | 18 | 14 | 2 | 0 | 0 | 3 | 22 | 0 | 43 | 3 | 0 |
| Yofu, Tetsu, Charlotte | 5 | 4 | .556 | 4.62 | 21 | 17 | 1 | 1 | 0 | 0 | 113.0 | 107 | 472 | 64 | 58 | 20 | 9 | 6 | 6 | 33 | 1 | 111 | 4 | 0 |
| Young, Tim, Buffalo * | 0 | 1 | .000 | 17.28 | 5 | 2 | 0 | 0 | 1 | 0 | 8.1 | 17 | 51 | 16 | 16 | 1 | 0 | 3 | 2 | 7 | 0 | 9 | 0 | 0 |

COMBINATION SHUTOUTS: **Buffalo** (6)—Stanford-M. White-Jimenez-M. Miller, Ramsey-Robbins-Cabrera, Rayborn-Bartosh-Cabrera-Stewart, Cressend-Robbins-Davis-Stewart-Lee, A. Brown-Cabrera-Lee-Bartosh-Robbins, Cruceta-Tallet. **Charlotte** (3)—F. Diaz-Darensbourg-Santiago, Kohlmeier-Duncan-Majewski, Grilli-Sanders. **Columbus** (8)—Halsey-Prinz-Marsonek, Carlyle-Bean-Nitkowski-Prinz-Karsay-Proctor, Wang-Prinz, Halsey-Bean-Padilla, Graman-Bean-Padilla, Halsey-Prinz, Carlyle-Bush-Beal, Carlyle-Bean-Proctor. **Durham** (9)—Brazelton-Holtz-Fortunato, Bell-Holtz-Reyes, Bell-Holtz-Seay, Moss-Veras-Seay-Fortunato, Moss-Nunez-Colome, Moss-Fortunato, J.Gonzalez-Nunez-Seay-Fortunato, Magrane-McClung-Gaudin, Standridge-Gaudin. **Indianapolis** (5)—Liriano-Reichert, Phelps-Weibl-Childers, Hendrickson-Phelps-Childers, De La Rosa-Weibl-Ford, Phelps-Liriano. **Louisville** (7)—Bong-Watson, Bong-Matthews-Mallette, Claussen-Reith-Myette, Etherton-Reith-Cerros-Myette, Belisle-Valentine, Moseley-Shearn, Moseley-Matthews-Mallette. **Norfolk** (5)—Ginter-Strange, Strange-Roach-Feliciano-Parra, Yates-Roach-Feliciano-Parra, Griffiths-Ring-Parra, Erickson-Feliciano-Bell. **Ottawa** (5)—Borkowski-Ormond-Rakers-Cubillan, DeWitt-Fiore-Cubillan, Lorraine-Cubillan, Maine-Fiore-House-Byrdak-Cubillan, Lorraine-Rakers-Cubillan. **Pawtucket** (5)—J. Brown-Hebson-Hamulack, Stephens-A. Martinez-Duff, Kester-Almonte-Hamulack, Kester-J. Johnson, Kester-Duff, Kim-Almonte. **Richmond** (9)—T. Smith-Drew-Romano-Fesh-Whiteside, T. Smith-Fesh-C. Smith, Romano-Cunnane-Whiteside, T. Smith-Colon-Whiteside, Romano-Colon-Whiteside, McConnell-Colon-Whiteside, Capellan-Fesh-Barry, Capellan-Whiteside, Romano-Barry. **Rochester** (7)—Schoening-A. Johnson-Crain, Gassner-Palki, Gassner-Crain, Schoening-Palki, Durbin-Kemp-Beimel, Gassner-Eyre, Gassner-Beimel-Eyre. **Scranton-WB** (6)—Powell-Kubes-Geary, Condrey-Giese, Hancock-Geary, Hancock-Kubes-Lundberg, Powell-Lee, Yarnall-Giese. **Toledo** (8)—Prieto-Mears-German, Mears-Karnuth-Cortes-M. Anderson-German, Ennis-Mears-German, Haynes-Mears-German, Burnside-M. Anderson-Karnuth, Van Hekken-German, Baldwin-Ennis-German, Roney-Schmack-Colyer-German.

NO-HIT GAMES: Ellis, Scranton-Wilkes Barre, defeated Louisville, 1-0, June 6; Yofu, Charlotte, defeated Durham, 5-0, August 1.

# 2004 FIELDING

## TEAM

| Team | G | PO | A | E | TC | DP | TP | PB | Pct. |
|---|---|---|---|---|---|---|---|---|---|
| Richmond | 141 | 3570 | 249 | 97 | 3916 | 146 | 0 | 16 | .975 |
| Charlotte | 142 | 3724 | 255 | 100 | 4079 | 142 | 0 | 21 | .975 |
| Indianapolis | 144 | 3753 | 225 | 112 | 4090 | 154 | 0 | 7 | .973 |
| Rochester | 144 | 3814 | 248 | 117 | 4179 | 123 | 0 | 12 | .972 |
| Pawtucket | 144 | 3780 | 272 | 119 | 4171 | 114 | 0 | 7 | .971 |
| Buffalo | 144 | 3766 | 206 | 118 | 4090 | 117 | 0 | 15 | .971 |
| Columbus | 144 | 3740 | 221 | 123 | 4084 | 138 | 0 | 13 | .970 |
| Toledo | 143 | 3726 | 275 | 126 | 4127 | 147 | 0 | 12 | .969 |
| Ottawa | 144 | 3781 | 273 | 135 | 4189 | 143 | 0 | 17 | .968 |
| Scranton-Wb | 142 | 3707 | 255 | 135 | 4097 | 152 | 0 | 9 | .967 |
| Syracuse | 144 | 3742 | 205 | 140 | 4087 | 143 | 0 | 18 | .966 |
| Norfolk | 144 | 3772 | 241 | 140 | 4153 | 139 | 0 | 15 | .966 |
| Louisville | 144 | 3699 | 263 | 143 | 4105 | 137 | 0 | 10 | .965 |
| Durham | 144 | 3658 | 223 | 144 | 4025 | 152 | 0 | 22 | .964 |

## INDIVIDUAL

### FIRST BASEMEN

NOTE: All caps denotes fielding-percentage leader based on 72 games for catchers, 96 for all other non-pitchers and 115 innings for pitchers. *Throws lefthanded.

| Player, Team | Pct. | G | PO | A | E | TC | DP |
|---|---|---|---|---|---|---|---|
| Aceves, Jonathan, CHR | 1.000 | 1 | 5 | 0 | 0 | 5 | 2 |
| Alviso, Jerome, LOU | 1.000 | 5 | 34 | 2 | 0 | 36 | 3 |
| Barker, Kevin, SWB* | 1.000 | 6 | 32 | 3 | 0 | 35 | 6 |
| BARKETT, ANDY, TOL* | .986 | 98 | 884 | 65 | 13 | 962 | 85 |
| Bell, Mike, CHR | .994 | 81 | 621 | 38 | 4 | 663 | 70 |
| Bellinger, Clay, OTT | .987 | 23 | 142 | 12 | 2 | 156 | 19 |
| Betts, Todd, COL* | 1.000 | 14 | 121 | 6 | 0 | 127 | 12 |
| Branyan, Russell, BUF* | .991 | 33 | 309 | 26 | 3 | 338 | 28 |
| Brazell, Craig, NOR* | .989 | 95 | 742 | 64 | 9 | 815 | 89 |
| Burnham, Gary, LOU* | .994 | 58 | 432 | 40 | 3 | 475 | 50 |
| Caligiuri, Jay, NOR | 1.000 | 2 | 16 | 2 | 0 | 18 | 3 |
| Cancel, Robinson, DUR | 1.000 | 1 | 1 | 0 | 0 | 1 | 0 |
| Casanova, Raul, PAW | 1.000 | 5 | 44 | 2 | 0 | 46 | 2 |
| Chamblee, Jim, LOU | 1.000 | 11 | 65 | 5 | 0 | 70 | 9 |
| Clapinski, Chris, BUF | 1.000 | 5 | 30 | 3 | 0 | 33 | 3 |
| Clark, Howie, SYR* | .966 | 6 | 52 | 5 | 2 | 59 | 5 |
| Collier, Lou, SWB | 1.000 | 2 | 10 | 0 | 0 | 10 | 1 |
| Coquillette, Trace, PAW | .991 | 16 | 101 | 7 | 1 | 109 | 5 |
| Coste, Chris, IND | 1.000 | 13 | 89 | 7 | 0 | 96 | 8 |
| Crozier, Eric, BUF* | .988 | 58 | 472 | 35 | 6 | 513 | 46 |
| Crozier, Eric, SYR* | .983 | 24 | 213 | 15 | 4 | 232 | 24 |
| Crozier, Eric, BUF-SYR* | .987 | 82 | 685 | 50 | 10 | 745 | 70 |
| Cruz, Jacob, LOU* | 1.000 | 4 | 29 | 3 | 0 | 32 | 3 |
| Cummings, Midre, DUR* | 1.000 | 1 | 1 | 0 | 0 | 1 | 0 |
| Daubach, Brian, PAW* | .992 | 78 | 609 | 41 | 5 | 655 | 55 |
| Deardorff, Jeff, COL | .984 | 9 | 56 | 6 | 1 | 63 | 4 |
| Delgado, Carlos, SYR* | 1.000 | 2 | 18 | 2 | 0 | 20 | 1 |
| DePastino, Joe, RMD | 1.000 | 5 | 25 | 4 | 0 | 29 | 2 |
| Detienne, David, NOR | 1.000 | 1 | 5 | 0 | 0 | 5 | 1 |
| Diaz, Juan, ROC | 1.000 | 1 | 6 | 0 | 0 | 6 | 0 |
| Dominique, Andy, PAW | 1.000 | 18 | 154 | 8 | 0 | 162 | 12 |
| Dunwoody, Todd, ROC* | .979 | 47 | 339 | 37 | 8 | 384 | 35 |
| Durrington, Trent, IND | 1.000 | 1 | 7 | 0 | 0 | 7 | 0 |
| Evans, Lee, RMD | .977 | 17 | 114 | 12 | 3 | 129 | 11 |
| Fagan, Shawn, SYR | .989 | 81 | 697 | 51 | 8 | 756 | 61 |
| Garcia, Danny, NOR | 1.000 | 2 | 13 | 1 | 0 | 14 | 1 |
| Garko, Ryan, BUF | 1.000 | 3 | 26 | 1 | 0 | 27 | 4 |
| Gemoll, Brandon, IND* | .997 | 52 | 351 | 31 | 1 | 383 | 41 |
| Gil, Benji, TOL | 1.000 | 2 | 22 | 1 | 0 | 23 | 0 |
| Gil, Geronimo, OTT | .957 | 4 | 21 | 1 | 1 | 23 | 1 |
| Glavine, Mike, NOR* | .989 | 53 | 343 | 27 | 4 | 374 | 35 |
| Grindell, Nate, BUF | 1.000 | 3 | 22 | 1 | 0 | 23 | 1 |
| Guiel, Jeff, SYR* | .947 | 3 | 17 | 1 | 1 | 19 | 0 |
| Guzman, Edwards, DUR* | 1.000 | 14 | 99 | 9 | 0 | 108 | 6 |
| Guzman, Edwards, OTT* | .986 | 26 | 192 | 15 | 3 | 210 | 21 |
| Guzman, Edwards, DUR-OTT* | .991 | 40 | 291 | 24 | 3 | 318 | 27 |
| Hammond, Joey, OTT | .995 | 28 | 165 | 22 | 1 | 188 | 24 |
| Hankins, Ryan, CHR | 1.000 | 6 | 51 | 4 | 0 | 55 | 6 |
| Hart, Corey, IND | .857 | 2 | 11 | 1 | 2 | 14 | 0 |
| Hassey, Brad, SYR | 1.000 | 1 | 2 | 0 | 0 | 2 | 1 |
| Hessman, Mike, RMD | .988 | 31 | 156 | 8 | 2 | 166 | 24 |
| Holbert, Aaron, LOU | .984 | 37 | 229 | 22 | 4 | 255 | 29 |
| Hoover, Paul, DUR | 1.000 | 4 | 42 | 3 | 0 | 45 | 4 |
| Howard, Ryan, SWB* | .977 | 29 | 232 | 21 | 6 | 259 | 22 |

| Player, Team | Pct. | G | PO | A | E | TC | DP |
|---|---|---|---|---|---|---|---|
| Hummel, Tim, LOU | 1.000 | 10 | 74 | 6 | 0 | 80 | 7 |
| Jackson, Ryan, RMD* | .962 | 11 | 95 | 7 | 4 | 106 | 11 |
| Jacobs, Mike, NOR* | 1.000 | 1 | 7 | 1 | 0 | 8 | 0 |
| Johnson, Mark, IND* | 1.000 | 9 | 51 | 2 | 0 | 53 | 6 |
| Jurries, James, RMD | .988 | 68 | 486 | 23 | 6 | 515 | 53 |
| Kilburg, Joe, PAW* | .900 | 1 | 9 | 0 | 1 | 10 | 0 |
| LaForest, Pete, DUR* | 1.000 | 1 | 9 | 0 | 0 | 9 | 1 |
| LaRoche, Adam, RMD* | 1.000 | 3 | 27 | 3 | 0 | 30 | 1 |
| Leon, Jose, OTT | 1.000 | 1 | 2 | 0 | 0 | 2 | 0 |
| Liefer, Jeff, IND* | .994 | 79 | 649 | 64 | 4 | 717 | 73 |
| Lomasney, Steve, LOU | .990 | 16 | 81 | 14 | 1 | 96 | 11 |
| Lopez, Luis, RMD | .988 | 24 | 152 | 10 | 2 | 164 | 15 |
| Matos, Julius, SYR | .993 | 17 | 127 | 11 | 1 | 139 | 17 |
| Maxwell, Jason, DUR | .993 | 63 | 535 | 32 | 4 | 571 | 59 |
| McCarty, David, PAW | 1.000 | 2 | 15 | 1 | 0 | 16 | 1 |
| McGriff, Fred, DUR* | .909 | 1 | 10 | 0 | 1 | 11 | 2 |
| McNeal, Aaron, CHR | 1.000 | 10 | 90 | 7 | 0 | 97 | 11 |
| Mendez, Carlos, OTT | .996 | 62 | 488 | 42 | 2 | 532 | 48 |
| Morneau, Justin, ROC* | .994 | 68 | 565 | 63 | 4 | 632 | 60 |
| Mottola, Chad, OTT | .977 | 18 | 123 | 6 | 3 | 132 | 12 |
| Myrow, Brian, COL* | .980 | 40 | 312 | 23 | 7 | 342 | 31 |
| Nicholson, Derek, TOL* | 1.000 | 1 | 4 | 0 | 0 | 4 | 0 |
| Nilsson, Dave, RMD* | 1.000 | 6 | 44 | 2 | 0 | 46 | 2 |
| Norton, Greg, TOL | 1.000 | 3 | 25 | 1 | 0 | 26 | 4 |
| Nye, Rodney, NOR | .929 | 3 | 11 | 2 | 1 | 14 | 0 |
| Owens, Ryan, ROC | .965 | 10 | 74 | 8 | 3 | 85 | 5 |
| Paz, Rich, CHR | .991 | 11 | 97 | 8 | 1 | 106 | 8 |
| Phillips, Andy, COL | .991 | 86 | 689 | 67 | 7 | 763 | 68 |
| Pond, Simon, SYR* | 1.000 | 7 | 57 | 3 | 0 | 60 | 5 |
| Prieto, Alex, ROC | .993 | 15 | 139 | 13 | 1 | 153 | 20 |
| Rivera, Mike, CHR | .974 | 9 | 72 | 3 | 2 | 77 | 5 |
| Roberge, JP, SWB | .986 | 35 | 268 | 15 | 4 | 287 | 19 |
| Rushford, Jim, SWB* | .993 | 73 | 654 | 44 | 5 | 703 | 63 |
| Sandberg, Jared, DUR | .990 | 58 | 447 | 32 | 5 | 484 | 63 |
| Sheldon, Scott, IND | 1.000 | 7 | 51 | 3 | 0 | 54 | 5 |
| Shelton, Chris, TOL | .973 | 9 | 64 | 8 | 2 | 74 | 11 |
| Smith, Bobby, CHR | .995 | 24 | 188 | 17 | 1 | 206 | 19 |
| Smitherman, Stephen, LOU | .984 | 18 | 117 | 7 | 2 | 126 | 16 |
| Snyder, Earl, PAW | .992 | 30 | 235 | 23 | 2 | 260 | 24 |
| Tiffee, Terry, ROC | .982 | 8 | 51 | 4 | 1 | 56 | 5 |
| Trammell, Bubba, DUR | .986 | 7 | 69 | 3 | 1 | 73 | 7 |
| Ust, Brant, TOL | 1.000 | 9 | 92 | 6 | 0 | 98 | 11 |
| Vander Wal, John, LOU* | 1.000 | 8 | 52 | 1 | 0 | 53 | 6 |
| Vitiello, Joe, TOL | .993 | 29 | 263 | 29 | 2 | 294 | 25 |
| Wathan, Dusty, BUF | 1.000 | 11 | 75 | 9 | 0 | 84 | 5 |
| Whittaker, Tim, SYR | .909 | 2 | 9 | 1 | 1 | 11 | 1 |
| Williams, Glenn, SYR | .984 | 8 | 56 | 4 | 1 | 61 | 9 |
| Wilson, Tom, NOR | .917 | 4 | 20 | 2 | 2 | 24 | 4 |
| Wooten, Shawn, SWB | 1.000 | 2 | 12 | 1 | 0 | 13 | 0 |
| Youkilis, Kevin, PAW | .929 | 2 | 13 | 0 | 1 | 14 | 3 |
| Young, Ernie, BUF | .997 | 33 | 272 | 15 | 1 | 288 | 33 |

## SECOND BASEMEN

| Player, Team | Pct. | G | PO | A | E | TC | DP |
|---|---|---|---|---|---|---|---|
| Abernathy, Brent, BUF | .975 | 58 | 100 | 168 | 7 | 275 | 41 |
| Alvarez, Jimmy, PAW | 1.000 | 7 | 12 | 21 | 0 | 33 | 4 |
| Alviso, Jerome, LOU | 1.000 | 1 | 3 | 3 | 0 | 6 | 0 |
| Bacani, David, NOR | .980 | 34 | 62 | 82 | 3 | 147 | 23 |
| Badeaux, Brooks, DUR | .994 | 46 | 68 | 110 | 1 | 179 | 32 |
| Bartlett, Jason, ROC | 1.000 | 1 | 1 | 8 | 0 | 9 | 1 |
| Basak, Chris, NOR | .976 | 27 | 54 | 68 | 3 | 125 | 23 |
| Bautista, Rayner, TOL | .985 | 30 | 49 | 80 | 2 | 131 | 15 |
| Bellhorn, Mark, PAW | 1.000 | 2 | 2 | 7 | 0 | 9 | 0 |
| Bellinger, Clay, OTT | 1.000 | 1 | 0 | 1 | 0 | 1 | 0 |
| Bush, Homer, COL | 1.000 | 17 | 44 | 43 | 0 | 87 | 9 |
| Cano, Robinson, COL* | .985 | 61 | 118 | 140 | 4 | 262 | 35 |
| Cantu, Jorge, DUR | .978 | 44 | 88 | 131 | 5 | 224 | 33 |
| Castro, Juan, LOU | 1.000 | 1 | 1 | 1 | 0 | 2 | 0 |
| Cesar, Dionys, LOU | 1.000 | 4 | 2 | 10 | 0 | 12 | 1 |
| Chamblee, Jim, LOU | .933 | 4 | 8 | 6 | 1 | 15 | 4 |
| Clapinski, Chris, BUF | .960 | 19 | 32 | 40 | 3 | 75 | 13 |
| Clapp, Stubby, SYR* | .928 | 12 | 28 | 36 | 5 | 69 | 9 |
| Clark, Howie, SYR* | .988 | 18 | 28 | 56 | 1 | 85 | 12 |
| Clark, Jermaine, LOU* | .991 | 31 | 53 | 58 | 1 | 112 | 21 |
| Collins, Mike, NOR | 1.000 | 24 | 48 | 51 | 0 | 99 | 16 |
| Coquillette, Trace, PAW | .989 | 21 | 38 | 53 | 1 | 92 | 13 |
| Cosme, Caonabo, COL | .978 | 45 | 96 | 126 | 5 | 227 | 27 |
| Coste, Chris, IND | 1.000 | 5 | 6 | 10 | 0 | 16 | 2 |
| Crespo, Cesar, PAW | .976 | 7 | 20 | 21 | 1 | 42 | 6 |
| Delgado, Wilson, NOR | 1.000 | 3 | 8 | 13 | 0 | 21 | 3 |
| Detienne, David, NOR | 1.000 | 4 | 0 | 6 | 0 | 6 | 1 |
| Done, Mike, OTT | 1.000 | 1 | 1 | 1 | 0 | 2 | 0 |
| Durrington, Trent, IND | .963 | 32 | 67 | 62 | 5 | 134 | 15 |
| Erickson, Matt, IND* | .990 | 69 | 115 | 186 | 3 | 304 | 45 |
| Febles, Carlos, PAW | .984 | 13 | 22 | 41 | 1 | 64 | 6 |
| Figueroa, Luis, IND | .984 | 31 | 62 | 62 | 2 | 126 | 16 |
| Fontenot, Mike, OTT* | .964 | 135 | 252 | 330 | 22 | 604 | 85 |
| Garabito, Eddy, OTT | 1.000 | 4 | 10 | 10 | 0 | 20 | 6 |
| Garcia, Danny, NOR | .955 | 48 | 72 | 97 | 8 | 177 | 26 |
| Garcia, Jesse, RMD | .942 | 20 | 37 | 44 | 5 | 86 | 16 |
| Gil, Benji, TOL | .944 | 7 | 13 | 21 | 2 | 36 | 6 |
| Ginter, Keith, IND | 1.000 | 2 | 3 | 3 | 0 | 6 | 1 |
| Gipson, Charles, DUR | .980 | 11 | 20 | 28 | 1 | 49 | 8 |
| Green, Nick, RMD | .967 | 20 | 34 | 55 | 3 | 92 | 14 |
| Grindell, Nate, BUF | 1.000 | 1 | 4 | 2 | 0 | 6 | 0 |
| Hammond, Joey, OTT | .947 | 6 | 6 | 12 | 1 | 19 | 6 |
| Hannahan, Buzz, SWB | .966 | 27 | 54 | 60 | 4 | 118 | 22 |
| Hassey, Brad, SYR | .929 | 4 | 7 | 6 | 1 | 14 | 1 |
| Hessman, Mike, RMD | 1.000 | 4 | 3 | 5 | 0 | 8 | 2 |
| Hitchcox, Brian, SWB* | .973 | 9 | 15 | 21 | 1 | 37 | 3 |
| Holbert, Aaron, LOU | .989 | 46 | 80 | 102 | 2 | 184 | 35 |
| Hooper, Kevin, COL | .991 | 18 | 37 | 69 | 1 | 107 | 20 |
| Hummel, Tim, LOU | 1.000 | 9 | 14 | 23 | 0 | 37 | 7 |
| Keene, Kurt, SWB | .957 | 4 | 11 | 11 | 1 | 23 | 3 |
| Keppinger, Jeff, NOR | 1.000 | 4 | 7 | 13 | 0 | 20 | 3 |
| Lopez, Felipe, LOU | .940 | 8 | 22 | 25 | 3 | 50 | 8 |
| Matos, Julius, SYR | 1.000 | 6 | 11 | 18 | 0 | 29 | 8 |
| Maxwell, Jason, DUR | .971 | 11 | 10 | 23 | 1 | 34 | 4 |
| Maza, Luis, ROC | .972 | 8 | 19 | 16 | 1 | 36 | 5 |
| Medrano, Jesus, PAW | .918 | 13 | 20 | 25 | 4 | 49 | 2 |
| Morris, Warren, TOL* | .972 | 90 | 155 | 266 | 12 | 433 | 62 |
| Nelson, Bryant, CHR | .977 | 109 | 202 | 256 | 11 | 469 | 68 |
| Nicholson, Tommy, CHR* | 1.000 | 1 | 1 | 6 | 0 | 7 | 1 |
| Nye, Rodney, NOR | .963 | 13 | 21 | 31 | 2 | 54 | 5 |
| Ojeda, Augie, ROC | 1.000 | 9 | 18 | 26 | 0 | 44 | 5 |
| Olmedo, Ray, LOU | .974 | 59 | 126 | 174 | 8 | 308 | 48 |
| Ordaz, Luis, DUR | .972 | 36 | 64 | 111 | 5 | 180 | 28 |
| Orr, Pete, RMD* | .993 | 92 | 150 | 251 | 3 | 404 | 56 |
| Owens, Ryan, ROC | 1.000 | 3 | 2 | 2 | 0 | 4 | 0 |
| Ozuna, Pablo, SWB | .975 | 58 | 132 | 145 | 7 | 284 | 32 |
| Patchett, Gary, LOU | 1.000 | 2 | 1 | 1 | 0 | 2 | 0 |
| Paz, Rich, CHR | 1.000 | 4 | 10 | 14 | 0 | 24 | 3 |
| Phillips, Andy, COL | .868 | 7 | 9 | 24 | 5 | 38 | 6 |
| Phillips, Brandon, BUF | .973 | 69 | 140 | 187 | 9 | 336 | 51 |
| Polanco, Placido, SWB | 1.000 | 1 | 1 | 1 | 0 | 2 | 0 |
| Pratt, Scott, BUF* | 1.000 | 1 | 1 | 2 | 0 | 3 | 1 |
| Prieto, Alex, ROC | .982 | 11 | 29 | 27 | 1 | 57 | 8 |
| Rivas, Luis, ROC | 1.000 | 3 | 5 | 13 | 0 | 18 | 2 |
| Roberge, JP, SWB | .989 | 19 | 38 | 51 | 1 | 90 | 10 |
| Rodriguez, Luis, ROC | .979 | 112 | 222 | 279 | 11 | 512 | 77 |
| Rolls, Damian, DUR | 1.000 | 3 | 5 | 11 | 0 | 16 | 1 |
| Scarborough, Stephen, IND | .937 | 23 | 48 | 56 | 7 | 111 | 17 |
| SCHRAGER, TONY, PAW | .995 | 96 | 196 | 208 | 2 | 406 | 56 |
| Sequea, Jorge, SYR | .969 | 87 | 152 | 220 | 12 | 384 | 57 |
| Smith, Bobby, CHR | .960 | 29 | 57 | 86 | 6 | 149 | 23 |
| Solano, Danny, SYR | 1.000 | 6 | 8 | 13 | 0 | 21 | 7 |
| Ust, Brant, TOL | .970 | 23 | 36 | 61 | 3 | 100 | 13 |
| Utley, Chase, SWB* | .970 | 33 | 70 | 93 | 5 | 168 | 20 |
| Velandia, Jorge, RMD | .933 | 5 | 4 | 10 | 1 | 15 | 1 |
| Velazquez, Gil, NOR | .939 | 9 | 14 | 17 | 2 | 33 | 1 |
| Velazquez, Juan, RMD | .972 | 8 | 20 | 15 | 1 | 36 | 6 |
| Williams, Glenn, SYR | .976 | 16 | 25 | 56 | 2 | 83 | 8 |

## THIRD BASEMEN

| Player, Team | Pct. | G | PO | A | E | TC | DP |
|---|---|---|---|---|---|---|---|
| Abernathy, Brent, BUF | .921 | 35 | 28 | 54 | 7 | 89 | 7 |
| Badeaux, Brooks, DUR | 1.000 | 3 | 3 | 1 | 0 | 4 | 0 |
| Basak, Chris, NOR | 1.000 | 6 | 1 | 13 | 0 | 14 | 2 |
| Bautista, Rayner, TOL | 1.000 | 8 | 1 | 13 | 0 | 14 | 3 |
| Bell, Mike, CHR | .921 | 35 | 19 | 63 | 7 | 89 | 7 |
| Bellinger, Clay, OTT | .930 | 17 | 9 | 31 | 3 | 43 | 2 |
| Betemit, Wilson, RMD | .945 | 89 | 68 | 121 | 11 | 200 | 9 |
| Branyan, Russell, BUF* | .964 | 29 | 21 | 59 | 3 | 83 | 4 |
| Bush, Homer, COL | .944 | 37 | 18 | 67 | 5 | 90 | 6 |
| Calzado, Napoleon, RMD | 1.000 | 2 | 2 | 3 | 0 | 5 | 0 |
| Cantu, Jorge, DUR | .923 | 12 | 4 | 20 | 2 | 26 | 0 |
| Cardona, Javier, NOR | .000 | 1 | 0 | 0 | 1 | 1 | 0 |
| Castro, Juan, LOU | 1.000 | 1 | 1 | 4 | 0 | 5 | 0 |
| 1Cesar, Dionys, LOU | 1.000 | 1 | 1 | 0 | 0 | 1 | 0 |
| 2Cesar, Dionys, CHR | 1.000 | 5 | 2 | 4 | 0 | 6 | 1 |
| TCesar, Dionys, LOU-CHR | 1.000 | 6 | 3 | 4 | 0 | 7 | 1 |
| Chamblee, Jim, LOU | .923 | 90 | 62 | 178 | 20 | 260 | 31 |
| Clapinski, Chris, BUF | .943 | 16 | 13 | 37 | 3 | 53 | 4 |
| Clapp, Stubby, SYR* | 1.000 | 2 | 0 | 1 | 0 | 1 | 0 |
| Clark, Howie, SYR* | .900 | 7 | 3 | 15 | 2 | 20 | 1 |
| Clark, Jermaine, LOU* | .909 | 6 | 3 | 7 | 1 | 11 | 1 |
| Collier, Lou, SWB | .888 | 45 | 25 | 70 | 12 | 107 | 3 |
| Coste, Chris, IND | .924 | 34 | 18 | 55 | 6 | 79 | 5 |
| Daubach, Brian, PAW* | 1.000 | 1 | 1 | 3 | 0 | 4 | 0 |
| Deardorff, Jeff, COL | .900 | 94 | 54 | 135 | 21 | 210 | 16 |
| Detienne, David, NOR | .875 | 4 | 5 | 2 | 1 | 8 | 0 |
| Dransfeldt, Kelly, CHR | .974 | 53 | 47 | 104 | 4 | 155 | 20 |
| Durrington, Trent, IND | .792 | 9 | 5 | 14 | 5 | 24 | 3 |
| Erickson, Matt, IND* | .978 | 41 | 17 | 72 | 2 | 91 | 6 |
| Escalona, Felix, COL | .920 | 9 | 2 | 21 | 2 | 25 | 3 |
| Figueroa, Luis, IND | .988 | 31 | 25 | 59 | 1 | 85 | 8 |
| Garcia, Danny, NOR | 1.000 | 3 | 0 | 4 | 0 | 4 | 0 |
| Ginter, Keith, IND | 1.000 | 1 | 1 | 1 | 0 | 2 | 0 |
| Gipson, Charles, DUR | .946 | 16 | 2 | 33 | 2 | 37 | 5 |
| Green, Nick, RMD | 1.000 | 1 | 2 | 2 | 0 | 4 | 0 |
| Grindell, Nate, BUF | 1.000 | 4 | 2 | 10 | 0 | 12 | 0 |
| Guzman, Edwards, DUR* | .889 | 5 | 1 | 7 | 1 | 9 | 2 |
| Guzman, Edwards, OTT* | .976 | 29 | 28 | 54 | 2 | 84 | 6 |
| Guzman, Edwards, DUR-OTT* | .968 | 34 | 29 | 61 | 3 | 93 | 8 |
| Hammond, Joey, OTT | .945 | 30 | 23 | 63 | 5 | 91 | 5 |
| Hankins, Ryan, CHR | .882 | 7 | 4 | 11 | 2 | 17 | 1 |
| Hannahan, Buzz, SWB | .982 | 19 | 13 | 41 | 1 | 55 | 1 |
| Heintz, Chris, ROC | .750 | 2 | 2 | 1 | 1 | 4 | 0 |
| Helms, Wes, IND | .857 | 5 | 3 | 9 | 2 | 14 | 2 |
| Hessman, Mike, RMD | .981 | 41 | 26 | 75 | 2 | 103 | 8 |
| Hitchcox, Brian, SWB* | .880 | 27 | 8 | 58 | 9 | 75 | 4 |
| Holbert, Aaron, LOU | 1.000 | 2 | 2 | 5 | 0 | 7 | 1 |
| Hoover, Paul, DUR | .882 | 5 | 5 | 10 | 2 | 17 | 0 |
| Hummel, Tim, LOU | .927 | 20 | 6 | 32 | 3 | 41 | 1 |
| Jones, Bobby, PAW* | 1.000 | 1 | 1 | 2 | 0 | 3 | 0 |
| Jurries, James, RMD | .857 | 4 | 1 | 5 | 1 | 7 | 0 |
| Larson, Brandon, LOU | .910 | 31 | 12 | 59 | 7 | 78 | 5 |
| Leon, Jose, OTT | .921 | 79 | 54 | 157 | 18 | 229 | 17 |
| Liefer, Jeff, IND* | 1.000 | 8 | 8 | 14 | 0 | 22 | 1 |
| Lopez, Felipe, LOU | 1.000 | 1 | 0 | 1 | 0 | 1 | 0 |
| Lopez, Luis, RMD | .926 | 9 | 9 | 16 | 2 | 27 | 0 |
| Matos, Julius, SYR | .967 | 21 | 12 | 47 | 2 | 61 | 0 |
| Maxwell, Jason, DUR | .960 | 17 | 10 | 38 | 2 | 50 | 7 |
| Mueller, Bill, PAW | .857 | 4 | 2 | 4 | 1 | 7 | 0 |
| Nakamura, Micheal, SYR | 1.000 | 1 | 0 | 3 | 0 | 3 | 0 |
| Nelson, Bryant, CHR | .875 | 4 | 2 | 5 | 1 | 8 | 1 |
| Nicholson, Derek, TOL* | .906 | 13 | 6 | 23 | 3 | 32 | 1 |
| Norton, Greg, TOL | .975 | 51 | 34 | 121 | 4 | 159 | 16 |
| NYE, RODNEY, NOR | .936 | 104 | 75 | 204 | 19 | 298 | 24 |
| Ojeda, Augie, ROC | .950 | 10 | 5 | 14 | 1 | 20 | 1 |
| Ordaz, Luis, DUR | .944 | 25 | 14 | 37 | 3 | 54 | 9 |
| Orr, Pete, RMD* | 1.000 | 12 | 6 | 36 | 0 | 42 | 4 |
| Owens, Ryan, ROC | .867 | 16 | 11 | 28 | 6 | 45 | 2 |
| Paz, Rich, CHR | 1.000 | 13 | 14 | 18 | 0 | 32 | 2 |
| Peralta, Jhonny, BUF | .923 | 59 | 38 | 130 | 14 | 182 | 12 |
| Phillips, Andy, COL | .941 | 7 | 4 | 12 | 1 | 17 | 2 |
| Pond, Simon, SYR* | .913 | 22 | 10 | 32 | 4 | 46 | 3 |
| Prieto, Alex, ROC | .920 | 45 | 23 | 69 | 8 | 100 | 9 |
| Reyes, Guillermo, CHR | .667 | 2 | 0 | 2 | 1 | 3 | 0 |
| Roberge, JP, SWB | 1.000 | 11 | 6 | 12 | 0 | 18 | 3 |
| Rodriguez, Guillermo, TOL | .333 | 1 | 0 | 1 | 2 | 3 | 0 |
| Rodriguez, Luis, ROC | 1.000 | 8 | 3 | 12 | 0 | 15 | 2 |
| Rolls, Damian, DUR | 1.000 | 4 | 4 | 7 | 0 | 11 | 2 |
| Sandberg, Jared, DUR | .935 | 65 | 54 | 134 | 13 | 201 | 14 |
| Scanlon, Matt, ROC* | .714 | 6 | 1 | 4 | 2 | 7 | 1 |
| Scarborough, Stephen, IND | .925 | 20 | 5 | 44 | 4 | 53 | 5 |
| Schrager, Tony, PAW | .976 | 21 | 14 | 26 | 1 | 41 | 1 |
| Sheldon, Scott, IND | .914 | 13 | 7 | 25 | 3 | 35 | 6 |
| Smith, Bobby, CHR | .922 | 31 | 16 | 55 | 6 | 77 | 7 |
| Smith, Corey, BUF | .667 | 5 | 3 | 3 | 3 | 9 | 1 |
| Smith, Jason, TOL* | .938 | 33 | 26 | 65 | 6 | 97 | 5 |
| Snyder, Earl, PAW | .958 | 94 | 60 | 189 | 11 | 260 | 16 |
| Solano, Danny, SYR | 1.000 | 3 | 2 | 4 | 0 | 6 | 0 |
| Tiffee, Terry, ROC | .930 | 67 | 53 | 119 | 13 | 185 | 12 |
| Ust, Brant, TOL | .917 | 43 | 21 | 101 | 11 | 133 | 10 |
| Velazquez, Gil, NOR | 1.000 | 4 | 0 | 3 | 0 | 3 | 0 |
| Williams, Glenn, SYR | .965 | 91 | 69 | 206 | 10 | 285 | 22 |
| Wilson, Tom, NOR | .750 | 3 | 1 | 5 | 2 | 8 | 1 |
| Wooten, Shawn, SWB | .935 | 50 | 29 | 86 | 8 | 123 | 6 |
| Wright, David, NOR | .933 | 31 | 27 | 71 | 7 | 105 | 5 |
| Youkilis, Kevin, PAW | .959 | 36 | 24 | 70 | 4 | 98 | 5 |

## SHORTSTOPS

| Player, Team | Pct. | G | PO | A | E | TC | DP |
|---|---|---|---|---|---|---|---|
| Adams, Russ, SYR* | .939 | 121 | 179 | 325 | 33 | 537 | 82 |
| Alvarez, Jimmy, PAW | .956 | 24 | 34 | 52 | 4 | 90 | 15 |
| Alviso, Jerome, LOU | .800 | 6 | 2 | 6 | 2 | 10 | 3 |
| Bacani, David, NOR | .857 | 2 | 3 | 9 | 2 | 14 | 1 |
| Bartlett, Jason, ROC | .944 | 65 | 107 | 216 | 19 | 342 | 42 |
| Basak, Chris, NOR | .963 | 26 | 31 | 73 | 4 | 108 | 21 |
| Bautista, Rayner, TOL | .975 | 22 | 30 | 49 | 2 | 81 | 9 |
| Bellinger, Clay, OTT | .975 | 18 | 33 | 44 | 2 | 79 | 16 |
| Betemit, Wilson, RMD | .917 | 19 | 20 | 35 | 5 | 60 | 6 |
| Bush, Homer, COL | 1.000 | 4 | 7 | 9 | 0 | 16 | 1 |
| Cantu, Jorge, DUR | .952 | 37 | 61 | 99 | 8 | 168 | 18 |
| Castro, Juan, LOU | .933 | 3 | 4 | 10 | 1 | 15 | 2 |
| Cesar, Dionys, LOU | .878 | 12 | 15 | 21 | 5 | 41 | 7 |
| Chamblee, Jim, LOU | 1.000 | 1 | 2 | 0 | 0 | 2 | 0 |
| Clapinski, Chris, BUF | 1.000 | 2 | 2 | 6 | 0 | 8 | 1 |
| Collins, Mike, NOR | 1.000 | 2 | 0 | 1 | 0 | 1 | 0 |
| Cosme, Caonabo, COL | .978 | 18 | 28 | 63 | 2 | 93 | 14 |
| Crespo, Cesar, PAW | .963 | 49 | 80 | 126 | 8 | 214 | 31 |
| DELGADO, WILSON, NOR | .977 | 104 | 149 | 285 | 10 | 444 | 62 |
| Dransfeldt, Kelly, CHR | .978 | 35 | 49 | 85 | 3 | 137 | 22 |
| Erickson, Matt, IND* | .976 | 11 | 13 | 28 | 1 | 42 | 5 |
| Escalona, Felix, COL | .960 | 120 | 144 | 354 | 21 | 519 | 67 |
| Febles, Carlos, PAW | .944 | 58 | 91 | 144 | 14 | 249 | 28 |
| Figueroa, Luis, IND | .991 | 52 | 92 | 132 | 2 | 226 | 31 |
| Garabito, Eddy, OTT | .957 | 117 | 174 | 295 | 21 | 490 | 67 |
| Garcia, Danny, NOR | .857 | 15 | 19 | 29 | 8 | 56 | 7 |
| Garcia, Jesse, RMD | 1.000 | 1 | 1 | 1 | 0 | 2 | 0 |
| Garciaparra, Nomar, PAW | 1.000 | 6 | 9 | 9 | 0 | 18 | 0 |
| Gil, Benji, TOL | .833 | 1 | 3 | 2 | 1 | 6 | 1 |
| Gipson, Charles, DUR | .667 | 1 | 0 | 2 | 1 | 3 | 1 |
| Hammond, Joey, OTT | .980 | 13 | 19 | 30 | 1 | 50 | 6 |
| Hannahan, Buzz, SWB | .938 | 11 | 12 | 18 | 2 | 32 | 6 |
| Hardy, JJ, IND | .953 | 25 | 29 | 72 | 5 | 106 | 16 |
| Hassey, Brad, SYR | 1.000 | 5 | 4 | 7 | 0 | 11 | 2 |
| Hitchcox, Brian, SWB* | .900 | 1 | 3 | 6 | 1 | 10 | 1 |
| Holbert, Aaron, LOU | .979 | 11 | 15 | 32 | 1 | 48 | 6 |
| Hooper, Kevin, COL | .960 | 9 | 8 | 16 | 1 | 25 | 1 |
| Klassen, Danny, TOL | .969 | 109 | 172 | 328 | 16 | 516 | 78 |
| Lopez, Felipe, LOU | .959 | 67 | 79 | 154 | 10 | 243 | 41 |
| Machado, Anderson, SWB | .943 | 78 | 111 | 220 | 20 | 351 | 43 |

| Player, Team | Pct. | G | PO | A | E | TC | DP |
|---|---|---|---|---|---|---|---|
| Machado, Anderson, LOU | .932 | 31 | 56 | 68 | 9 | 133 | 20 |
| Machado, Anderson, SWB-LOU | .940 | 109 | 167 | 288 | 29 | 484 | 63 |
| Matos, Julius, SYR | .935 | 23 | 32 | 68 | 7 | 107 | 11 |
| Maxwell, Jason, DUR | 1.000 | 1 | 1 | 1 | 0 | 2 | 0 |
| Ojeda, Augie, ROC | .978 | 64 | 93 | 180 | 6 | 279 | 45 |
| Olmedo, Ray, LOU | .947 | 24 | 33 | 56 | 5 | 94 | 16 |
| Ordaz, Luis, DUR | .968 | 41 | 58 | 121 | 6 | 185 | 28 |
| Orr, Pete, RMD* | 1.000 | 2 | 1 | 11 | 0 | 12 | 3 |
| Ozuna, Pablo, SWB | .968 | 56 | 84 | 160 | 8 | 252 | 32 |
| Patchett, Gary, LOU | 1.000 | 1 | 0 | 1 | 0 | 1 | 0 |
| Peralta, Jhonny, BUF | .962 | 77 | 106 | 221 | 13 | 340 | 51 |
| Phillips, Brandon, BUF | .932 | 66 | 94 | 168 | 19 | 281 | 36 |
| Prieto, Alex, ROC | .985 | 16 | 29 | 37 | 1 | 67 | 12 |
| Ragsdale, Corey, NOR | .933 | 6 | 15 | 13 | 2 | 30 | 4 |
| Reyes, Guillermo, CHR | 1.000 | 4 | 4 | 7 | 0 | 11 | 2 |
| Rodriguez, Luis, ROC | 1.000 | 2 | 3 | 8 | 0 | 11 | 1 |
| Scarborough, Stephen, IND | .955 | 65 | 86 | 190 | 13 | 289 | 40 |
| Schrager, Tony, PAW | .955 | 11 | 11 | 31 | 2 | 44 | 6 |
| Sequea, Jorge, SYR | 1.000 | 1 | 1 | 2 | 0 | 3 | 0 |
| Smith, Bobby, CHR | .971 | 32 | 57 | 77 | 4 | 138 | 19 |
| Snyder, Earl, PAW | .972 | 11 | 11 | 24 | 1 | 36 | 7 |
| Upton, BJ, DUR | .916 | 66 | 100 | 173 | 25 | 298 | 49 |
| Ust, Brant, TOL | .957 | 16 | 27 | 40 | 3 | 70 | 9 |
| Valdez, Wilson, CHR | .979 | 69 | 109 | 176 | 6 | 291 | 45 |
| Valentin, Jose, CHR | .895 | 4 | 7 | 10 | 2 | 19 | 2 |
| Velandia, Jorge, RMD | .959 | 126 | 161 | 325 | 21 | 507 | 80 |
| Velazquez, Gil, NOR | 1.000 | 3 | 1 | 3 | 0 | 4 | 1 |
| Velazquez, Juan, RMD | 1.000 | 5 | 7 | 8 | 0 | 15 | 2 |

## OUTFIELDERS

| Player, Team | Pct. | G | PO | A | E | TC | DP |
|---|---|---|---|---|---|---|---|
| Abernathy, Brent, BUF | 1.000 | 4 | 6 | 0 | 0 | 6 | 0 |
| Alexander, Chad, TOL | .968 | 58 | 114 | 7 | 4 | 125 | 2 |
| Badeaux, Brooks, DUR | 1.000 | 7 | 10 | 0 | 0 | 10 | 0 |
| Barker, Kevin, SWB* | 1.000 | 3 | 5 | 0 | 0 | 5 | 0 |
| Barkett, Andy, TOL* | 1.000 | 9 | 9 | 1 | 0 | 10 | 0 |
| Bellinger, Clay, OTT | .750 | 3 | 3 | 0 | 1 | 4 | 0 |
| Benard, Marvin, SYR* | .981 | 33 | 52 | 1 | 1 | 54 | 0 |
| Bergeron, Peter, IND* | .983 | 81 | 157 | 13 | 3 | 173 | 0 |
| Bikowski, Scott, CHR* | 1.000 | 8 | 20 | 0 | 0 | 20 | 0 |
| Borchard, Joe, CHR | .980 | 77 | 188 | 5 | 4 | 197 | 1 |
| Bragg, Darren, COL* | .991 | 65 | 102 | 3 | 1 | 106 | 0 |
| Bragg, Darren, LOU* | 1.000 | 12 | 33 | 0 | 0 | 33 | 0 |
| Bragg, Darren, COL-LOU* | .993 | 77 | 135 | 3 | 1 | 139 | 0 |
| Branyan, Russell, RMD* | 1.000 | 10 | 12 | 0 | 0 | 12 | 0 |
| Branyan, Russell, BUF* | 1.000 | 14 | 29 | 0 | 0 | 29 | 0 |
| Branyan, Russell, RMD-BUF* | 1.000 | 24 | 41 | 0 | 0 | 41 | 0 |
| Brazell, Craig, NOR* | 1.000 | 18 | 12 | 1 | 0 | 13 | 0 |
| Budzinski, Mark, SWB* | .987 | 132 | 287 | 7 | 4 | 298 | 0 |
| Byrd, Marlon, SWB | .980 | 37 | 97 | 2 | 2 | 101 | 0 |
| Calzado, Napoleon, RMD | .875 | 3 | 7 | 0 | 1 | 8 | 0 |
| Castellano, John, SWB | 1.000 | 2 | 4 | 0 | 0 | 4 | 0 |
| Cesar, Dionys, CHR | 1.000 | 17 | 31 | 0 | 0 | 31 | 0 |
| Chamblee, Jim, LOU | .962 | 15 | 23 | 2 | 1 | 26 | 0 |
| Christensen, McKay, LOU* | .889 | 4 | 8 | 0 | 1 | 9 | 0 |
| Clapinski, Chris, BUF | .984 | 62 | 112 | 11 | 2 | 125 | 2 |
| Clapp, Stubby, SYR* | 1.000 | 16 | 36 | 2 | 0 | 38 | 0 |
| Clark, Howie, SYR* | .937 | 38 | 69 | 5 | 5 | 79 | 3 |
| Clark, Jermaine, LOU* | 1.000 | 75 | 141 | 1 | 0 | 142 | 0 |
| Collier, Lou, SWB | .978 | 51 | 83 | 6 | 2 | 91 | 2 |
| Cooper, Jason, BUF* | .968 | 14 | 30 | 0 | 1 | 31 | 0 |
| Coquillette, Trace, PAW | 1.000 | 9 | 15 | 0 | 0 | 15 | 0 |
| Crosby, Bubba, COL* | 1.000 | 27 | 57 | 1 | 0 | 58 | 0 |
| Crozier, Eric, BUF* | 1.000 | 17 | 30 | 1 | 0 | 31 | 0 |
| Cruz, Jacob, LOU* | 1.000 | 9 | 9 | 1 | 0 | 10 | 0 |
| Cummings, Midre, DUR* | .982 | 29 | 54 | 2 | 1 | 57 | 0 |
| Curry, Mike, PAW* | .987 | 45 | 75 | 3 | 1 | 79 | 1 |
| Cust, Jack, OTT* | .966 | 34 | 55 | 1 | 2 | 58 | 0 |
| Darula, Bobby, LOU* | 1.000 | 10 | 8 | 0 | 0 | 8 | 0 |
| Daubach, Brian, PAW* | 1.000 | 4 | 6 | 0 | 0 | 6 | 0 |
| Diaz, Matt, DUR | .974 | 132 | 250 | 15 | 7 | 272 | 6 |
| Diaz, Victor, NOR | .969 | 131 | 267 | 12 | 9 | 288 | 4 |
| Duncan, Jeff, NOR* | .982 | 54 | 110 | 2 | 2 | 114 | 0 |
| Dunwoody, Todd, BUF* | 1.000 | 11 | 17 | 0 | 0 | 17 | 0 |
| Dunwoody, Todd, ROC* | 1.000 | 28 | 60 | 2 | 0 | 62 | 1 |
| Dunwoody, Todd, BUF-ROC* | 1.000 | 39 | 77 | 2 | 0 | 79 | 1 |
| Durrington, Trent, IND | 1.000 | 6 | 17 | 1 | 0 | 18 | 0 |
| Escobar, Alex, BUF | 1.000 | 14 | 22 | 2 | 0 | 24 | 0 |
| Fagan, Shawn, SYR | 1.000 | 4 | 5 | 0 | 0 | 5 | 0 |
| Figueroa, Luis, IND | 1.000 | 1 | 1 | 1 | 0 | 2 | 0 |
| Ford, Lew, ROC | 1.000 | 1 | 5 | 0 | 0 | 5 | 0 |
| French, Anton, DUR* | .981 | 29 | 50 | 3 | 1 | 54 | 0 |
| French, Anton, SYR* | .987 | 36 | 72 | 2 | 1 | 75 | 0 |
| French, Anton, DUR-SYR* | .984 | 65 | 122 | 5 | 2 | 129 | 0 |
| Garabito, Eddy, OTT | 1.000 | 1 | 1 | 0 | 0 | 1 | 0 |
| Garcia, Danny, NOR | 1.000 | 10 | 8 | 0 | 0 | 8 | 0 |
| Gathright, Joey, DUR* | .968 | 60 | 114 | 6 | 4 | 124 | 1 |
| Gemoll, Brandon, IND* | 1.000 | 11 | 10 | 1 | 0 | 11 | 0 |
| Gipson, Charles, DUR | .972 | 67 | 128 | 12 | 4 | 144 | 3 |
| Gomes, Jonny, DUR | .962 | 97 | 170 | 6 | 7 | 183 | 1 |
| Gomez, Rich, TOL | .957 | 31 | 45 | 0 | 2 | 47 | 0 |
| Gonzalez, Raul, NOR | 1.000 | 16 | 24 | 1 | 0 | 25 | 0 |
| Gonzalez, Raul, BUF | .984 | 54 | 116 | 10 | 2 | 128 | 3 |
| Gonzalez, Raul, NOR-BUF | .987 | 70 | 140 | 11 | 2 | 153 | 3 |
| Grindell, Nate, BUF | .962 | 14 | 24 | 1 | 1 | 26 | 0 |
| Gross, Gabe, SYR* | .957 | 34 | 64 | 3 | 3 | 70 | 0 |
| Guiel, Jeff, SYR* | .992 | 60 | 114 | 3 | 1 | 118 | 2 |
| Guzman, Edwards, DUR* | 1.000 | 3 | 1 | 0 | 0 | 1 | 0 |
| Hall, Noah, SYR | .980 | 56 | 93 | 3 | 2 | 98 | 1 |
| Hammond, Joey, OTT | 1.000 | 9 | 22 | 0 | 0 | 22 | 0 |
| Hannahan, Buzz, SWB | .983 | 18 | 55 | 2 | 1 | 58 | 1 |
| Hart, Corey, IND | .961 | 92 | 163 | 10 | 7 | 180 | 4 |
| Hermansen, Chad, SYR | 1.000 | 16 | 28 | 1 | 0 | 29 | 0 |
| Hernandez, Adrian, IND | 1.000 | 1 | 1 | 0 | 0 | 1 | 0 |
| Hessman, Mike, RMD | 1.000 | 13 | 13 | 2 | 0 | 15 | 1 |
| Holbert, Aaron, LOU | 1.000 | 10 | 14 | 2 | 0 | 16 | 0 |
| Hollins, Damon, RMD | .967 | 100 | 195 | 11 | 7 | 213 | 7 |
| Hoover, Paul, DUR | 1.000 | 1 | 2 | 0 | 0 | 2 | 0 |
| Hyzdu, Adam, PAW | .976 | 119 | 239 | 5 | 6 | 250 | 1 |
| Jackson, Ryan, RMD* | 1.000 | 1 | 1 | 1 | 0 | 2 | 0 |
| Kearns, Austin, LOU | .949 | 22 | 55 | 1 | 3 | 59 | 0 |
| Kelly, Kenny, LOU | .973 | 77 | 172 | 8 | 5 | 185 | 1 |
| Kelly, Mike, COL | 1.000 | 47 | 87 | 3 | 0 | 90 | 1 |
| Knox, Ryan, IND | .981 | 41 | 102 | 1 | 2 | 105 | 0 |
| Krynzel, Dave, IND* | .993 | 63 | 141 | 6 | 1 | 148 | 1 |
| Kubel, Jason, ROC* | .990 | 86 | 190 | 10 | 2 | 202 | 3 |
| Langerhans, Ryan, RMD* | .989 | 127 | 250 | 9 | 3 | 262 | 1 |
| Liefer, Jeff, IND* | 1.000 | 14 | 34 | 0 | 0 | 34 | 0 |
| Little, Mark, BUF | .984 | 67 | 120 | 4 | 2 | 126 | 0 |
| Logan, Nook, TOL | .979 | 105 | 228 | 7 | 5 | 240 | 1 |
| Lombard, George, PAW* | .991 | 48 | 112 | 1 | 1 | 114 | 0 |
| Ludwick, Ryan, BUF | .980 | 29 | 49 | 1 | 1 | 51 | 0 |
| Magruder, Chris, IND | 1.000 | 74 | 119 | 5 | 0 | 124 | 1 |
| Marrero, Eli, RMD | 1.000 | 6 | 13 | 1 | 0 | 14 | 0 |
| Matos, Julius, SYR | .905 | 9 | 18 | 1 | 2 | 21 | 0 |
| McCarthy, Bill, RMD | .987 | 46 | 76 | 2 | 1 | 79 | 1 |
| McDonald, Darnell, OTT | .973 | 104 | 246 | 4 | 7 | 257 | 1 |
| McDonald, Donzell, COL | .982 | 27 | 55 | 1 | 1 | 57 | 1 |
| Melian, Jackson, COL | 1.000 | 7 | 18 | 1 | 0 | 19 | 1 |
| Monroe, Craig, TOL | 1.000 | 5 | 9 | 1 | 0 | 10 | 0 |
| Moore, Michael, CHR | 1.000 | 7 | 9 | 2 | 0 | 11 | 0 |
| Morris, Warren, TOL* | 1.000 | 9 | 17 | 0 | 0 | 17 | 0 |
| Mottola, Chad, OTT | .980 | 91 | 188 | 9 | 4 | 201 | 1 |
| Nelson, Bryant, CHR | .938 | 12 | 15 | 0 | 1 | 16 | 0 |
| Nicholson, Derek, TOL* | 1.000 | 4 | 7 | 0 | 0 | 7 | 0 |
| Nixon, Trot, PAW* | .750 | 4 | 3 | 0 | 1 | 4 | 0 |
| Nunnally, Jon, IND* | .973 | 57 | 103 | 6 | 3 | 112 | 3 |
| Orr, Pete, RMD* | 1.000 | 8 | 12 | 0 | 0 | 12 | 0 |
| Owens, Eric, TOL | .987 | 118 | 214 | 13 | 3 | 230 | 2 |
| Owens, Jeremy, PAW | .993 | 104 | 261 | 6 | 2 | 269 | 3 |

| Player, Team | Pct. | G | PO | A | E | TC | DP |
|---|---|---|---|---|---|---|---|
| Owens, Ryan, ROC | 1.000 | 1 | 3 | 0 | 0 | 3 | 0 |
| Ozuna, Pablo, SWB | 1.000 | 3 | 9 | 0 | 0 | 9 | 0 |
| Padilla, Jorge, SWB | .977 | 115 | 288 | 9 | 7 | 304 | 4 |
| Pagan, Angel, NOR | 1.000 | 12 | 23 | 1 | 0 | 24 | 1 |
| Petrick, Ben, TOL | 1.000 | 3 | 4 | 0 | 0 | 4 | 0 |
| Pond, Simon, SYR* | .964 | 39 | 51 | 2 | 2 | 55 | 0 |
| Rabe, Josh, ROC | .989 | 101 | 173 | 4 | 2 | 179 | 0 |
| Raines, Jr, Tim, OTT | .982 | 70 | 160 | 3 | 3 | 166 | 1 |
| Redman, Prentice, NOR | .974 | 61 | 108 | 6 | 3 | 117 | 0 |
| Reed, Jeremy, CHR* | .995 | 72 | 180 | 6 | 1 | 187 | 1 |
| Reese, Kevin, COL* | .980 | 51 | 92 | 4 | 2 | 98 | 0 |
| Reichert, Dan, IND | 1.000 | 1 | 2 | 0 | 0 | 2 | 0 |
| Restovich, Michael, ROC | .975 | 98 | 189 | 6 | 5 | 200 | 3 |
| Rios, Alex, SYR | .964 | 46 | 101 | 6 | 4 | 111 | 0 |
| Rios, Armando, OTT* | 1.000 | 13 | 21 | 0 | 0 | 21 | 0 |
| Rodriguez, John, COL* | .969 | 102 | 217 | 4 | 7 | 228 | 1 |
| Rolls, Damian, DUR | 1.000 | 16 | 33 | 0 | 0 | 33 | 0 |
| Romano, Jason, LOU | .989 | 39 | 90 | 1 | 1 | 92 | 0 |
| Rushford, Jim, SWB* | .979 | 55 | 93 | 2 | 2 | 97 | 0 |
| Ryan, Michael, ROC* | .987 | 38 | 77 | 1 | 1 | 79 | 0 |
| Sanchez, Alex, TOL* | 1.000 | 2 | 6 | 0 | 0 | 6 | 0 |
| Sandberg, Jared, DUR | 1.000 | 2 | 4 | 0 | 0 | 4 | 0 |
| Sanders, Anthony, SYR | .977 | 61 | 126 | 4 | 3 | 133 | 1 |
| Scanlon, Matt, ROC* | 1.000 | 8 | 9 | 0 | 0 | 9 | 0 |
| Sherrod, Justin, PAW | .984 | 93 | 173 | 7 | 3 | 183 | 0 |
| Simmons, Brian, ROC | .995 | 79 | 195 | 7 | 1 | 203 | 0 |
| SIZEMORE, GRADY, BUF* | .996 | 100 | 252 | 7 | 1 | 260 | 2 |
| Slack, Jon, NOR* | 1.000 | 3 | 8 | 0 | 0 | 8 | 0 |
| Smith, Bobby, CHR | 1.000 | 2 | 4 | 0 | 0 | 4 | 0 |
| Smith, Mark, SWB | .983 | 28 | 55 | 3 | 1 | 59 | 0 |
| Smitherman, Stephen, LOU | .966 | 110 | 162 | 10 | 6 | 178 | 1 |
| Snead, Esix, NOR | .970 | 73 | 194 | 3 | 6 | 203 | 1 |
| Snyder, Earl, PAW | .917 | 8 | 11 | 0 | 1 | 12 | 0 |
| Sorensen, Zach, BUF | 1.000 | 3 | 8 | 0 | 0 | 8 | 0 |
| Spencer, Shane, COL | 1.000 | 10 | 13 | 0 | 0 | 13 | 0 |
| Stanley, Henri, PAW* | .984 | 36 | 62 | 1 | 1 | 64 | 1 |
| Stratton, Robert, LOU | .912 | 14 | 30 | 1 | 3 | 34 | 0 |
| Swann, Pedro, OTT* | .966 | 111 | 192 | 7 | 7 | 206 | 0 |
| Taylor, Reggie, LOU* | .973 | 55 | 101 | 6 | 3 | 110 | 1 |
| Taylor, Reggie, CHR* | .980 | 56 | 140 | 4 | 3 | 147 | 1 |
| Taylor, Reggie, LOU-CHR* | .977 | 111 | 241 | 10 | 6 | 257 | 2 |
| Thames, Marcus, TOL | .979 | 63 | 94 | 1 | 2 | 97 | 0 |
| Thomas, Charles, RMD* | .969 | 47 | 89 | 6 | 3 | 98 | 1 |
| Timmons, Ozzie, NOR | 1.000 | 23 | 28 | 1 | 0 | 29 | 0 |
| Toca, Jorge, TOL | 1.000 | 8 | 12 | 1 | 0 | 13 | 0 |
| Torres, Andres, CHR | .975 | 86 | 224 | 6 | 6 | 236 | 3 |
| Tyner, Jason, RMD* | 1.000 | 57 | 101 | 6 | 0 | 107 | 1 |
| Tyner, Jason, BUF* | 1.000 | 38 | 71 | 1 | 0 | 72 | 0 |
| Tyner, Jason, RMD-BUF* | 1.000 | 95 | 172 | 7 | 0 | 179 | 1 |
| Ust, Brant, TOL | 1.000 | 21 | 41 | 2 | 0 | 43 | 0 |
| Valenzuela, Mario, CHR | .990 | 97 | 183 | 15 | 2 | 200 | 5 |
| Vander Wal, John, LOU* | 1.000 | 4 | 4 | 0 | 0 | 4 | 0 |
| Vento, Michael, COL | .982 | 109 | 210 | 7 | 4 | 221 | 2 |
| Vitiello, Joe, TOL | 1.000 | 6 | 8 | 0 | 0 | 8 | 0 |
| Walker, Matt, OTT | 1.000 | 3 | 7 | 0 | 0 | 7 | 0 |
| West, Kevin, ROC | 1.000 | 2 | 4 | 0 | 0 | 4 | 0 |
| Williams, Gerald, NOR | .993 | 53 | 131 | 5 | 1 | 137 | 0 |
| Wise, DeWayne, RMD* | .986 | 30 | 72 | 1 | 1 | 74 | 1 |
| Young, Ernie, BUF | .944 | 6 | 16 | 1 | 1 | 18 | 1 |

## CATCHERS

| Player, Team | Pct. | G | PO | A | E | TC | DP | PB |
|---|---|---|---|---|---|---|---|---|
| Aceves, Jonathan, CHR | .997 | 41 | 284 | 20 | 1 | 305 | 5 | 6 |
| Bailey, Jeff, PAW | 1.000 | 1 | 6 | 0 | 0 | 6 | 0 | 0 |
| Bard, Josh, BUF | .988 | 33 | 238 | 19 | 3 | 260 | 1 | 3 |
| Boscan, JC, RMD | 1.000 | 21 | 137 | 10 | 0 | 147 | 2 | 3 |
| Burke, Jamie, CHR | .993 | 34 | 256 | 29 | 2 | 287 | 4 | 5 |
| Cancel, Robinson, DUR | 1.000 | 15 | 75 | 8 | 0 | 83 | 2 | 5 |
| Cardona, Javier, NOR | .980 | 19 | 132 | 16 | 3 | 151 | 5 | 3 |
| Casanova, Raul, PAW | .979 | 13 | 84 | 8 | 2 | 94 | 3 | 1 |
| Chiaffredo, Paul, SYR | .992 | 33 | 225 | 20 | 2 | 247 | 1 | 6 |
| Cleveland, Russ, TOL | 1.000 | 2 | 12 | 2 | 0 | 14 | 0 | 0 |
| Corporan, Elvis, ROC | 1.000 | 1 | 1 | 0 | 0 | 1 | 0 | 0 |
| Coste, Chris, IND | .985 | 27 | 180 | 15 | 3 | 198 | 2 | 0 |
| Delgado, Alex, IND | .988 | 61 | 382 | 35 | 5 | 422 | 5 | 5 |
| DePastino, Joe, RMD | .995 | 84 | 602 | 28 | 3 | 633 | 5 | 2 |
| DiFelice, Mike, TOL | .990 | 58 | 348 | 41 | 4 | 393 | 2 | 6 |
| Dominique, Andy, PAW | .975 | 36 | 213 | 17 | 6 | 236 | 2 | 3 |
| Estalella, Bobby, SYR | 1.000 | 5 | 37 | 5 | 0 | 42 | 0 | 0 |
| Evans, Lee, RMD | 1.000 | 27 | 178 | 15 | 0 | 193 | 3 | 4 |
| Fasano, Sal, COL | .993 | 76 | 524 | 49 | 4 | 577 | 2 | 7 |
| Fuentes, Omar, COL | .939 | 5 | 31 | 0 | 2 | 33 | 0 | 0 |
| Garko, Ryan, BUF | 1.000 | 2 | 19 | 0 | 0 | 19 | 0 | 0 |
| Gil, Geronimo, OTT | .991 | 95 | 715 | 46 | 7 | 768 | 8 | 9 |
| Guzman, Edwards, DUR* | 1.000 | 1 | 2 | 0 | 0 | 2 | 0 | 1 |
| Guzman, Edwards, OTT* | 1.000 | 2 | 8 | 0 | 0 | 8 | 0 | 0 |
| Guzman, Edwards, DUR-OTT* | 1.000 | 3 | 10 | 0 | 0 | 10 | 0 | 1 |
| Hankins, Ryan, CHR | 1.000 | 65 | 392 | 43 | 0 | 435 | 7 | 9 |
| Harper, Brandon, TOL | .978 | 20 | 120 | 12 | 3 | 135 | 1 | 2 |
| Heintz, Chris, ROC | .993 | 85 | 543 | 34 | 4 | 581 | 0 | 10 |
| Hernandez, Michel, SWB | .984 | 72 | 388 | 37 | 7 | 432 | 4 | 5 |
| Hill, Jason, LOU | 1.000 | 1 | 5 | 0 | 0 | 5 | 0 | 0 |
| Hinch, AJ, SWB | .992 | 75 | 435 | 34 | 4 | 473 | 3 | 3 |
| Hoover, Paul, DUR | 1.000 | 6 | 31 | 4 | 0 | 35 | 3 | 3 |
| Huber, Justin, NOR | 1.000 | 5 | 28 | 0 | 0 | 28 | 1 | 1 |
| Jacobs, Mike, NOR* | .992 | 16 | 118 | 3 | 1 | 122 | 1 | 1 |
| Jacobson, Russ, SWB | 1.000 | 2 | 19 | 1 | 0 | 20 | 0 | 1 |
| Johnson, Mark, IND* | .992 | 70 | 433 | 35 | 4 | 472 | 3 | 2 |
| LaForest, Pete, DUR* | .985 | 75 | 479 | 39 | 8 | 526 | 6 | 10 |
| LaRue, Jason, LOU | .917 | 3 | 11 | 0 | 1 | 12 | 0 | 0 |
| Levis, Jesse, NOR* | .946 | 8 | 32 | 3 | 2 | 37 | 0 | 1 |
| Lomasney, Steve, LOU | .987 | 23 | 142 | 9 | 2 | 153 | 0 | 2 |
| Luderer, Brian, BUF | 1.000 | 2 | 16 | 1 | 0 | 17 | 1 | 0 |
| Machado, Robert, OTT | .991 | 27 | 186 | 32 | 2 | 220 | 3 | 8 |
| Marsters, Brandon, ROC | .998 | 59 | 389 | 30 | 1 | 420 | 4 | 1 |
| Martinez, Octavio, OTT | 1.000 | 2 | 14 | 1 | 0 | 15 | 0 | 0 |
| Martinez, Sandy, BUF* | .992 | 52 | 327 | 28 | 3 | 358 | 3 | 9 |
| Massiatte, Dan, DUR | .992 | 30 | 233 | 22 | 2 | 257 | 3 | 2 |
| Mauer, Joe, ROC* | 1.000 | 2 | 8 | 1 | 0 | 9 | 0 | 0 |
| McGee, Tom, OTT | .992 | 22 | 117 | 11 | 1 | 129 | 1 | 1 |
| Mendez, Carlos, OTT | 1.000 | 5 | 22 | 0 | 0 | 22 | 0 | 0 |
| Miller, Corky, LOU | .990 | 52 | 384 | 31 | 4 | 419 | 6 | 7 |
| Navarro, Dioner, COL | .994 | 39 | 287 | 28 | 2 | 317 | 7 | 1 |
| Nilsson, Dave, RMD* | 1.000 | 1 | 1 | 1 | 0 | 2 | 0 | 0 |
| Osik, Keith, DUR | 1.000 | 25 | 166 | 8 | 0 | 174 | 0 | 1 |
| PACHOT, JOHN, NOR | .998 | 75 | 487 | 37 | 1 | 525 | 3 | 6 |
| Parrish, Dave, COL | .990 | 32 | 201 | 7 | 2 | 210 | 1 | 4 |
| Quiroz, Guillermo, SYR | .994 | 71 | 492 | 26 | 3 | 521 | 7 | 10 |
| Rodriguez, Guillermo, TOL | .985 | 70 | 407 | 44 | 7 | 458 | 5 | 4 |
| Rodriguez, Luis, TOL | 1.000 | 2 | 13 | 3 | 0 | 16 | 0 | 0 |
| Sardinha, Dane, LOU | .987 | 72 | 508 | 33 | 7 | 548 | 4 | 2 |
| Shoppach, Kelly, PAW | .988 | 101 | 621 | 61 | 8 | 690 | 7 | 3 |
| Socarras, Tony, NOR* | 1.000 | 10 | 42 | 1 | 0 | 43 | 0 | 1 |
| Stewart, Chris, CHR | .897 | 5 | 25 | 1 | 3 | 29 | 0 | 0 |
| Terveen, Bryce, RMD* | 1.000 | 14 | 95 | 9 | 0 | 104 | 1 | 7 |
| Torrealba, Steve, COL | 1.000 | 4 | 25 | 1 | 0 | 26 | 0 | 1 |
| Torres, Gabby, ROC | 1.000 | 9 | 61 | 6 | 0 | 67 | 1 | 1 |
| Wathan, Dusty, BUF | .991 | 64 | 401 | 26 | 4 | 431 | 4 | 3 |
| Whittaker, Tim, SYR | .983 | 35 | 218 | 19 | 4 | 241 | 3 | 2 |
| Wilson, Tom, NOR | .980 | 19 | 143 | 3 | 3 | 149 | 0 | 2 |
| Wilson, Vance, NOR | 1.000 | 1 | 10 | 1 | 0 | 11 | 0 | 0 |
| Zaun, Gregg, SYR | 1.000 | 5 | 42 | 1 | 0 | 43 | 0 | 0 |

## PITCHERS

| Player, Team | Pct. | G | PO | A | E | TC | DP |
|---|---|---|---|---|---|---|---|
| Abbott, Paul, SWB | 1.000 | 5 | 0 | 5 | 0 | 5 | 0 |
| Acosta, Domingo, NOR | 1.000 | 1 | 0 | 1 | 0 | 1 | 0 |
| Adams, Mike, IND | .833 | 10 | 3 | 2 | 1 | 6 | 1 |
| Adkins, Tim, COL* | .000 | 1 | 0 | 0 | 0 | 0 | 0 |
| Aguilar, Ray, RMD* | .889 | 9 | 3 | 5 | 1 | 9 | 0 |
| Ahearne, Pat, TOL | .981 | 28 | 12 | 41 | 1 | 54 | 1 |

| Player, Team | Pct. | G | PO | A | E | TC | DP |
|---|---|---|---|---|---|---|---|
| Ainsworth, Kurt, OTT | 1.000 | 1 | 0 | 1 | 0 | 1 | 0 |
| Almanza, Armando, RMD* | 1.000 | 20 | 0 | 2 | 0 | 2 | 0 |
| Almonte, Edwin, PAW | 1.000 | 51 | 6 | 17 | 0 | 23 | 2 |
| Anderson, Jason, BUF | 1.000 | 9 | 1 | 3 | 0 | 4 | 0 |
| Anderson, Jason, COL | 1.000 | 36 | 5 | 2 | 0 | 7 | 0 |
| Anderson, Jason,BUF-COL | 1.000 | 45 | 6 | 5 | 0 | 11 | 0 |
| Anderson, Matt, TOL | .333 | 34 | 1 | 1 | 4 | 6 | 0 |
| Arnold, Jason, SYR | .857 | 7 | 2 | 4 | 1 | 7 | 0 |
| Astacio, Pedro, PAW | 1.000 | 2 | 0 | 3 | 0 | 3 | 0 |
| Bajenaru, Jeff, CHR | 1.000 | 16 | 4 | 4 | 0 | 8 | 1 |
| Baker, Chris, SYR | 1.000 | 18 | 5 | 13 | 0 | 18 | 2 |
| Baker, Scott, ROC | 1.000 | 9 | 7 | 6 | 0 | 13 | 0 |
| Baldwin, James, NOR | .875 | 5 | 4 | 3 | 1 | 8 | 0 |
| Baldwin, James, TOL | 1.000 | 18 | 11 | 21 | 0 | 32 | 3 |
| Baldwin, James, NOR-TOL | .975 | 23 | 15 | 24 | 1 | 40 | 3 |
| Barry, Kevin, RMD | .909 | 30 | 4 | 6 | 1 | 11 | 1 |
| Bartosh, Cliff, BUF* | 1.000 | 28 | 1 | 0 | 0 | 1 | 0 |
| Bauer, Rick, OTT | .909 | 11 | 2 | 8 | 1 | 11 | 0 |
| Beal, Andy, COL* | .913 | 29 | 2 | 19 | 2 | 23 | 0 |
| Bean, Colter, COL | .846 | 53 | 2 | 9 | 2 | 13 | 0 |
| Bedard, Erik, OTT* | 1.000 | 2 | 0 | 1 | 0 | 1 | 0 |
| Beech, Matt, PAW* | .000 | 4 | 0 | 0 | 1 | 1 | 0 |
| Beimel, Joe, ROC* | 1.000 | 49 | 4 | 11 | 0 | 15 | 1 |
| Belisle, Matt, LOU | .939 | 28 | 14 | 17 | 2 | 33 | 2 |
| Bell, Heath, NOR | 1.000 | 45 | 3 | 6 | 0 | 9 | 1 |
| Bell, Rob, DUR | 1.000 | 7 | 4 | 3 | 0 | 7 | 1 |
| Bergman, Sean, OTT | .895 | 20 | 5 | 12 | 2 | 19 | 0 |
| Bevis, PJ, NOR | .600 | 22 | 1 | 2 | 2 | 5 | 0 |
| Bong, Jung Keun, LOU* | .947 | 19 | 6 | 12 | 1 | 19 | 3 |
| Bonilla, Henry, ROC | .000 | 3 | 0 | 0 | 0 | 0 | 0 |
| Bonser, Boof, ROC | 1.000 | 1 | 1 | 1 | 0 | 2 | 0 |
| Booker, Chris, LOU | 1.000 | 7 | 0 | 2 | 0 | 2 | 0 |
| Borkowski, Dave, OTT | .968 | 16 | 14 | 16 | 1 | 31 | 3 |
| Bouknight, Kip, SYR | .000 | 1 | 0 | 0 | 0 | 0 | 0 |
| Bowers, Shane, SWB | 1.000 | 15 | 0 | 4 | 0 | 4 | 1 |
| Bowles, Brian, IND | .750 | 10 | 2 | 1 | 1 | 4 | 0 |
| Brazelton, Dewon, DUR | .857 | 10 | 4 | 2 | 1 | 7 | 0 |
| Brown, Andrew, BUF | 1.000 | 1 | 1 | 0 | 0 | 1 | 0 |
| Brown, Jamie, PAW | .824 | 23 | 8 | 6 | 3 | 17 | 0 |
| Brown, Kevin, COL | 1.000 | 1 | 1 | 0 | 0 | 1 | 0 |
| Burnside, Adrian, TOL* | .833 | 26 | 4 | 6 | 2 | 12 | 0 |
| Bush, Dave, SYR | .933 | 16 | 7 | 7 | 1 | 15 | 0 |
| Byard, David, NOR | 1.000 | 2 | 0 | 1 | 0 | 1 | 0 |
| Byrd, Paul, RMD | .000 | 1 | 0 | 0 | 0 | 0 | 0 |
| Byrdak, Tim, OTT* | 1.000 | 33 | 2 | 3 | 0 | 5 | 0 |
| Cabrera, Fernando, BUF | 1.000 | 45 | 9 | 6 | 0 | 15 | 0 |
| Cameron, Ryan, PAW | 1.000 | 10 | 0 | 2 | 0 | 2 | 0 |
| Campos, Francisco, CHR | 1.000 | 5 | 0 | 1 | 0 | 1 | 0 |
| Capellan, Jose, RMD | 1.000 | 7 | 4 | 5 | 0 | 9 | 1 |
| Capuano, Chris, IND* | 1.000 | 2 | 0 | 4 | 0 | 4 | 0 |
| Carlyle, Buddy, COL | 1.000 | 19 | 5 | 12 | 0 | 17 | 0 |
| Carmona, Fausto, BUF | 1.000 | 1 | 0 | 3 | 0 | 3 | 0 |
| Carnes, Matt, DUR | 1.000 | 28 | 1 | 7 | 0 | 8 | 0 |
| Cassidy, Scott, PAW | .833 | 28 | 1 | 4 | 1 | 6 | 0 |
| Castillo, Frank, PAW | 1.000 | 27 | 14 | 30 | 0 | 44 | 2 |
| Cerros, Juan, LOU | 1.000 | 30 | 5 | 12 | 0 | 17 | 2 |
| Chacin, Gustavo, SYR* | 1.000 | 2 | 1 | 2 | 0 | 3 | 0 |
| Chen, Bruce, SYR* | .500 | 3 | 0 | 1 | 1 | 2 | 0 |
| Chen, Bruce, OTT* | .929 | 22 | 4 | 9 | 1 | 14 | 1 |
| Chen, Bruce, SYR-OTT* | .875 | 25 | 4 | 10 | 2 | 16 | 1 |
| Childers, Jason, IND | 1.000 | 24 | 2 | 5 | 0 | 7 | 0 |
| Childers, Matt, IND | 1.000 | 35 | 8 | 11 | 0 | 19 | 1 |
| Childs, Ryan, OTT | 1.000 | 1 | 0 | 1 | 0 | 1 | 0 |
| Chulk, Vinnie, SYR | .750 | 18 | 0 | 6 | 2 | 8 | 0 |
| Claussen, Brandon, LOU* | 1.000 | 18 | 1 | 15 | 0 | 16 | 0 |
| Cloude, Ken, DUR | .000 | 4 | 0 | 0 | 1 | 1 | 0 |
| Coffey, Todd, LOU | 1.000 | 15 | 0 | 2 | 0 | 2 | 1 |
| Coggin, David, SWB | 1.000 | 16 | 8 | 7 | 0 | 15 | 0 |
| Colome, Jesus, DUR | .857 | 18 | 0 | 6 | 1 | 7 | 0 |
| Colon, Roman, RMD | .923 | 51 | 5 | 7 | 1 | 13 | 1 |
| Colyer, Steve, TOL* | 1.000 | 25 | 0 | 2 | 0 | 2 | 0 |
| Condrey, Clay, SWB | .976 | 27 | 11 | 30 | 1 | 42 | 1 |
| Contreras, Jose, COL | 1.000 | 2 | 0 | 1 | 0 | 1 | 0 |
| Corcoran, Tim, DUR | 1.000 | 33 | 4 | 4 | 0 | 8 | 0 |
| Cornejo, Nate, TOL | 1.000 | 4 | 1 | 0 | 0 | 1 | 0 |
| Cortes, David, TOL | 1.000 | 14 | 1 | 0 | 0 | 1 | 0 |
| Crain, Jesse, ROC | .929 | 41 | 4 | 9 | 1 | 14 | 1 |
| Cressend, Jack, BUF | 1.000 | 24 | 6 | 4 | 0 | 10 | 0 |
| Crowell, Jim, SWB* | 1.000 | 46 | 5 | 11 | 0 | 16 | 0 |
| Cruceta, Francisco, BUF | 1.000 | 14 | 1 | 7 | 0 | 8 | 0 |
| Cubillan, Darwin, OTT | 1.000 | 51 | 2 | 5 | 0 | 7 | 0 |
| Cunnane, Will, RMD | .800 | 35 | 0 | 4 | 1 | 5 | 1 |
| Curtis, Daniel, RMD | 1.000 | 2 | 0 | 1 | 0 | 1 | 0 |
| D'Amico, Jeff, BUF | .000 | 3 | 0 | 0 | 0 | 0 | 0 |
| Darensbourg, Vic, CHR* | 1.000 | 24 | 1 | 8 | 0 | 9 | 0 |
| Darensbourg, Vic, NOR* | .833 | 18 | 0 | 5 | 1 | 6 | 1 |
| Darensbourg, Vic, CHR-NOR* | .933 | 42 | 1 | 13 | 1 | 15 | 1 |
| Davies, Kyle, RMD | 1.000 | 1 | 2 | 1 | 0 | 3 | 0 |
| Davis, Jason, BUF | .938 | 9 | 6 | 9 | 1 | 16 | 2 |
| Davis, Kane, BUF | 1.000 | 32 | 3 | 5 | 0 | 8 | 0 |
| Davis, Lance, COL* | 1.000 | 8 | 4 | 4 | 0 | 8 | 2 |
| Dawley, Joe, BUF | 1.000 | 1 | 0 | 1 | 0 | 1 | 0 |
| De La Rosa, Jorge, IND* | .933 | 20 | 5 | 9 | 1 | 15 | 0 |
| Denney, Kyle, BUF | .947 | 24 | 7 | 11 | 1 | 19 | 1 |
| DeWitt, Matt, OTT | .800 | 25 | 0 | 4 | 1 | 5 | 0 |
| Diaz, Felix, CHR | .958 | 19 | 7 | 16 | 1 | 24 | 1 |
| DiFelice, Mark, OTT | .952 | 36 | 8 | 12 | 1 | 21 | 1 |
| Dingman, Craig, TOL | 1.000 | 21 | 3 | 2 | 0 | 5 | 0 |
| Douglass, Sean, SYR | .929 | 18 | 2 | 11 | 1 | 14 | 0 |
| Drew, Tim, RMD | 1.000 | 19 | 9 | 15 | 0 | 24 | 1 |
| Duff, Matt, PAW | .867 | 53 | 4 | 9 | 2 | 15 | 0 |
| Duncan, Courtney, CHR | 1.000 | 18 | 3 | 2 | 0 | 5 | 0 |
| Durbin, Chad, BUF | 1.000 | 9 | 3 | 7 | 0 | 10 | 3 |
| Durbin, JD, ROC | .667 | 7 | 2 | 2 | 2 | 6 | 0 |
| Eckenstahler, Eric, TOL* | 1.000 | 42 | 1 | 6 | 0 | 7 | 1 |
| Elarton, Scott, BUF | 1.000 | 3 | 2 | 3 | 0 | 5 | 0 |
| Ellis, Robert, BUF | 1.000 | 10 | 3 | 4 | 0 | 7 | 0 |
| Ellis, Robert, SWB | .895 | 16 | 6 | 11 | 2 | 19 | 0 |
| TEllis, Robertk BUF-SWB | .923 | 26 | 9 | 15 | 2 | 26 | 0 |
| Ennis, John, TOL | .913 | 38 | 11 | 10 | 2 | 23 | 4 |
| Erdos, Todd, ROC | 1.000 | 4 | 0 | 1 | 0 | 1 | 0 |
| Erdos, Todd, IND | 1.000 | 42 | 2 | 6 | 0 | 8 | 1 |
| Erdos, Todd, ROC-IND | 1.000 | 46 | 2 | 7 | 0 | 9 | 1 |
| Erickson, Scott, NOR | .833 | 8 | 1 | 4 | 1 | 6 | 0 |
| Etherton, Seth, LOU | .926 | 19 | 6 | 19 | 2 | 27 | 1 |
| Evans, Kyle, BUF | 1.000 | 1 | 1 | 1 | 0 | 2 | 0 |
| Evert, Brett, RMD | 1.000 | 7 | 1 | 3 | 0 | 4 | 0 |
| Eyre, Willie, ROC | .865 | 36 | 12 | 20 | 5 | 37 | 2 |
| Farnsworth, Jeff, IND | 1.000 | 11 | 6 | 4 | 0 | 10 | 0 |
| Feliciano, Pedro, NOR* | .818 | 32 | 4 | 5 | 2 | 11 | 1 |
| Fesh, Sean, RMD* | 1.000 | 39 | 3 | 15 | 0 | 18 | 0 |
| File, Bob, SYR | 1.000 | 24 | 6 | 10 | 0 | 16 | 1 |
| Fiore, Tony, OTT | 1.000 | 25 | 5 | 7 | 0 | 12 | 1 |
| Floyd, Gavin, SWB | 1.000 | 5 | 2 | 2 | 0 | 4 | 0 |
| Ford, Ben, IND | .875 | 32 | 3 | 4 | 1 | 8 | 1 |
| Fortunato, Bartolome, DUR | .909 | 34 | 5 | 5 | 1 | 11 | 2 |
| Forystek, Brian, OTT* | .750 | 12 | 4 | 8 | 4 | 16 | 1 |
| Frasor, Jason, SYR | .000 | 3 | 0 | 0 | 0 | 0 | 0 |
| Frederick, Kevin, SYR | 1.000 | 20 | 2 | 3 | 0 | 5 | 0 |
| Frendling, Neal, DUR | 1.000 | 1 | 0 | 1 | 0 | 1 | 0 |
| Fultz, Aaron, ROC* | 1.000 | 7 | 1 | 2 | 0 | 3 | 0 |
| Gannon, Joe, OTT | 1.000 | 4 | 1 | 7 | 0 | 8 | 0 |
| Gassner, Dave, ROC* | 1.000 | 28 | 18 | 27 | 0 | 45 | 1 |
| Gaudin, Chad, DUR | .833 | 17 | 5 | 5 | 2 | 12 | 0 |
| Geary, Geoff, SWB | 1.000 | 21 | 0 | 5 | 0 | 5 | 0 |
| German, Franklyn, TOL | 1.000 | 49 | 0 | 4 | 0 | 4 | 0 |
| Giese, Dan, SWB | 1.000 | 54 | 3 | 9 | 0 | 12 | 1 |
| Ginter, Matt, NOR | 1.000 | 11 | 6 | 14 | 0 | 20 | 0 |
| Giron, Roberto, IND | 1.000 | 21 | 1 | 9 | 0 | 10 | 0 |
| Glover, Gary, ROC | 1.000 | 5 | 0 | 3 | 0 | 3 | 0 |
| Glover, Gary, IND | 1.000 | 8 | 2 | 9 | 0 | 11 | 1 |
| Glover, Gary, ROC-IND | 1.000 | 13 | 2 | 12 | 0 | 14 | 1 |

| Player, Team | Pct. | G | PO | A | E | TC | DP |
|---|---|---|---|---|---|---|---|
| Glynn, Ryan, RMD | 1.000 | 11 | 0 | 2 | 0 | 2 | 0 |
| Glynn, Ryan, SYR | .933 | 16 | 5 | 9 | 1 | 15 | 0 |
| Glynn, Ryan, RMD-SYR | .941 | 27 | 5 | 11 | 1 | 17 | 0 |
| Gonzalez, Dicky, DUR | 1.000 | 6 | 4 | 6 | 0 | 10 | 0 |
| Gonzalez, Jeremi, DUR | .833 | 19 | 3 | 7 | 2 | 12 | 1 |
| Graman, Alex, COL* | .900 | 24 | 7 | 11 | 2 | 20 | 0 |
| Greisinger, Seth, ROC | 1.000 | 13 | 3 | 10 | 0 | 13 | 0 |
| Griffiths, Jeremy, NOR | .917 | 13 | 7 | 4 | 1 | 12 | 2 |
| Grilli, Jason, CHR | 1.000 | 25 | 4 | 15 | 0 | 19 | 1 |
| Gronkiewicz, Lee, BUF | 1.000 | 1 | 1 | 1 | 0 | 2 | 0 |
| Guerrier, Matt, ROC | .956 | 24 | 17 | 26 | 2 | 45 | 1 |
| Guthrie, Jeremy, BUF | 1.000 | 4 | 1 | 3 | 0 | 4 | 0 |
| Hackman, Luther, BUF | 1.000 | 11 | 0 | 1 | 0 | 1 | 0 |
| Haines, Talley, SYR | 1.000 | 44 | 7 | 10 | 0 | 17 | 1 |
| Halsey, Brad, COL* | .923 | 24 | 5 | 19 | 2 | 26 | 0 |
| Hamulack, Tim, PAW* | .833 | 35 | 2 | 3 | 1 | 6 | 0 |
| Hancock, Josh, SWB | 1.000 | 18 | 4 | 13 | 0 | 17 | 1 |
| Hanson, Adam, BUF | .000 | 1 | 0 | 0 | 0 | 0 | 0 |
| Haynes, Jimmy, TOL | 1.000 | 5 | 2 | 3 | 0 | 5 | 0 |
| Hebson, Bryan, PAW | 1.000 | 7 | 1 | 0 | 0 | 1 | 0 |
| Heilman, Aaron, NOR | .906 | 26 | 13 | 16 | 3 | 32 | 2 |
| Helling, Rick, ROC | 1.000 | 1 | 2 | 0 | 0 | 2 | 0 |
| Hendrickson, Ben, IND | 1.000 | 21 | 9 | 18 | 0 | 27 | 3 |
| Heredia, Felix, COL* | .000 | 3 | 0 | 0 | 0 | 0 | 0 |
| Hernandez, Adrian, IND | .857 | 20 | 7 | 11 | 3 | 21 | 0 |
| Hernandez, Buddy, RMD | .889 | 47 | 5 | 3 | 1 | 9 | 0 |
| Hernandez, Orlando, COL | 1.000 | 3 | 4 | 1 | 0 | 5 | 0 |
| Hernandez, Yoel, SWB | .917 | 14 | 2 | 9 | 1 | 12 | 0 |
| Hodge, Kevin, ROC | .929 | 49 | 3 | 10 | 1 | 14 | 2 |
| Hodges, Trey, RMD | 1.000 | 10 | 0 | 6 | 0 | 6 | 0 |
| Holtz, Mike, DUR* | 1.000 | 17 | 1 | 4 | 0 | 5 | 1 |
| House, Craig, OTT | 1.000 | 11 | 1 | 0 | 0 | 1 | 0 |
| Housman, Jeff, IND* | 1.000 | 5 | 0 | 2 | 0 | 2 | 1 |
| Howry, Bob, BUF | 1.000 | 18 | 2 | 3 | 0 | 5 | 0 |
| Hudson, Luke, LOU | 1.000 | 3 | 2 | 4 | 0 | 6 | 0 |
| Hutchinson, Ryan, SWB | 1.000 | 4 | 0 | 2 | 0 | 2 | 1 |
| Hyzdu, Adam, PAW | 1.000 | 1 | 1 | 0 | 0 | 1 | 0 |
| Izquierdo, Hansel, COL | .889 | 11 | 1 | 7 | 1 | 9 | 0 |
| Jimenez, Jason, SWB* | .900 | 14 | 0 | 9 | 1 | 10 | 1 |
| Jimenez, Jose, BUF | 1.000 | 2 | 0 | 2 | 0 | 2 | 1 |
| Johnson, Adam, ROC | .857 | 38 | 4 | 8 | 2 | 14 | 1 |
| Johnson, James, PAW* | 1.000 | 16 | 2 | 2 | 0 | 4 | 0 |
| Joseph, Jake, NOR | 1.000 | 15 | 3 | 3 | 0 | 6 | 0 |
| Junge, Eric, SWB | 1.000 | 9 | 6 | 1 | 0 | 7 | 0 |
| Karnuth, Jason, TOL | .958 | 46 | 8 | 15 | 1 | 24 | 3 |
| Karsay, Steve, COL | 1.000 | 11 | 0 | 1 | 0 | 1 | 0 |
| Keisler, Randy, NOR* | .960 | 22 | 7 | 17 | 1 | 25 | 2 |
| Kemp, Beau, ROC | 1.000 | 36 | 13 | 11 | 0 | 24 | 0 |
| Keppel, Bobby, NOR* | .935 | 17 | 7 | 22 | 2 | 31 | 2 |
| Kershner, Jason, SYR* | 1.000 | 28 | 2 | 6 | 0 | 8 | 0 |
| Kester, Tim, PAW | .949 | 27 | 11 | 26 | 2 | 39 | 1 |
| Kieschnick, Brooks, IND | .000 | 2 | 0 | 0 | 1 | 1 | 0 |
| Kim, Byung-Hyun, PAW | .857 | 22 | 3 | 9 | 2 | 14 | 1 |
| Kirsten, Rick, TOL | 1.000 | 14 | 2 | 10 | 0 | 12 | 0 |
| Kohlmeier, Ryan, CHR | .923 | 23 | 6 | 6 | 1 | 13 | 0 |
| Kubes, Greg, SWB* | 1.000 | 49 | 4 | 13 | 0 | 17 | 0 |
| Larson, Adam, CHR | 1.000 | 6 | 2 | 1 | 0 | 3 | 0 |
| Lee, David, BUF | 1.000 | 51 | 1 | 5 | 0 | 6 | 0 |
| Lee, Seung, SWB | .900 | 35 | 5 | 4 | 1 | 10 | 2 |
| Leskanic, Curtis, PAW | 1.000 | 1 | 1 | 0 | 0 | 1 | 0 |
| Liriano, Pedro, IND | 1.000 | 29 | 8 | 29 | 0 | 37 | 2 |
| Lopez, Aquilino, SYR | 1.000 | 32 | 1 | 2 | 0 | 3 | 0 |
| Lorraine, Andrew, OTT* | 1.000 | 28 | 3 | 14 | 0 | 17 | 0 |
| Loux, Shane, TOL | .976 | 22 | 12 | 29 | 1 | 42 | 3 |
| Lukasiewicz, Mark, SYR* | 1.000 | 32 | 4 | 3 | 0 | 7 | 0 |
| Lundberg, Spike, SWB | .818 | 44 | 0 | 9 | 2 | 11 | 0 |
| Magrane, Jim, DUR | .968 | 25 | 11 | 19 | 1 | 31 | 6 |
| Maine, John, OTT | .960 | 22 | 12 | 12 | 1 | 25 | 1 |
| Majewski, Gary, CHR | 1.000 | 35 | 1 | 6 | 0 | 7 | 1 |
| Malaska, Mark, PAW* | .818 | 33 | 3 | 6 | 2 | 11 | 0 |
| Mallette, Brian, LOU | 1.000 | 40 | 3 | 7 | 0 | 10 | 0 |

| Player, Team | Pct. | G | PO | A | E | TC | DP |
|---|---|---|---|---|---|---|---|
| Mann, Jim, COL | 1.000 | 25 | 3 | 3 | 0 | 6 | 0 |
| Manning, Charlie, COL* | 1.000 | 11 | 1 | 2 | 0 | 3 | 1 |
| Marsonek, Sam, COL | .667 | 35 | 3 | 1 | 2 | 6 | 0 |
| Martin, JD, BUF | 1.000 | 1 | 0 | 1 | 0 | 1 | 0 |
| Martinez, Anastacio, PAW | .833 | 38 | 3 | 7 | 2 | 12 | 0 |
| Martinez, Javier, OTT | .000 | 1 | 0 | 0 | 0 | 0 | 0 |
| Matos, Josue, SYR | .955 | 29 | 6 | 15 | 1 | 22 | 0 |
| Matthews, Mike, LOU* | 1.000 | 15 | 2 | 0 | 0 | 2 | 0 |
| Maurer, Dave, SYR* | 1.000 | 43 | 4 | 6 | 0 | 10 | 1 |
| McClung, Seth, DUR | 1.000 | 11 | 0 | 5 | 0 | 5 | 1 |
| McConnell, Sam, RMD* | 1.000 | 22 | 5 | 15 | 0 | 20 | 0 |
| McGinley, Blake, NOR* | 1.000 | 13 | 2 | 8 | 0 | 10 | 1 |
| McNichol, Brian, CHR* | 1.000 | 6 | 0 | 2 | 0 | 2 | 1 |
| Mears, Chris, TOL | 1.000 | 30 | 5 | 7 | 0 | 12 | 2 |
| Mendoza, Ramiro, PAW | .500 | 6 | 0 | 1 | 1 | 2 | 0 |
| Meyer, Dan, RMD* | 1.000 | 12 | 0 | 4 | 0 | 4 | 0 |
| Meyers, Mike, NOR | .800 | 16 | 1 | 3 | 1 | 5 | 0 |
| Michalak, Chris, IND* | .941 | 37 | 3 | 13 | 1 | 17 | 0 |
| Mieses, Jose, CHR | .000 | 2 | 0 | 0 | 1 | 1 | 0 |
| Miller, Justin, SYR | 1.000 | 3 | 2 | 0 | 0 | 2 | 0 |
| Miller, Matt, BUF | .750 | 13 | 1 | 2 | 1 | 4 | 0 |
| Mills, Ryan, ROC* | .800 | 15 | 2 | 2 | 1 | 5 | 0 |
| Minix, Travis, DUR | .778 | 21 | 2 | 5 | 2 | 9 | 0 |
| Moreno, Victor, ROC | .000 | 6 | 0 | 0 | 0 | 0 | 0 |
| Moseley, Dustin, LOU | .909 | 12 | 5 | 15 | 2 | 22 | 1 |
| Moss, Damian, DUR* | 1.000 | 20 | 3 | 9 | 0 | 12 | 1 |
| Moss, Damian, LOU* | .800 | 4 | 1 | 3 | 1 | 5 | 1 |
| Moss, Damian, DUR-LOU* | .941 | 24 | 4 | 12 | 1 | 17 | 2 |
| Munoz, Arnie, CHR* | .786 | 13 | 1 | 10 | 3 | 14 | 0 |
| Munro, Pete, ROC | 1.000 | 10 | 5 | 11 | 0 | 16 | 2 |
| Musser, Neal, NOR* | .917 | 7 | 5 | 6 | 1 | 12 | 0 |
| Myette, Aaron, LOU | 1.000 | 41 | 10 | 6 | 0 | 16 | 1 |
| Nakamura, Micheal, SYR | 1.000 | 31 | 2 | 7 | 0 | 9 | 1 |
| Nelson, Bubba, LOU | .824 | 12 | 5 | 9 | 3 | 17 | 0 |
| Nelson, Joe, PAW | .500 | 16 | 0 | 1 | 1 | 2 | 0 |
| Nitkowski, CJ, COL* | 1.000 | 16 | 0 | 1 | 0 | 1 | 0 |
| Nunez, Franklin, DUR | .500 | 40 | 2 | 1 | 3 | 6 | 1 |
| Obermueller, Wes, IND | 1.000 | 4 | 2 | 5 | 0 | 7 | 0 |
| Ormond, Rodney, OTT | 1.000 | 28 | 3 | 5 | 0 | 8 | 0 |
| Ortiz, Javier, COL | .900 | 9 | 2 | 7 | 1 | 10 | 0 |
| Pacheco, Enemencio, CHR | .667 | 15 | 1 | 1 | 1 | 3 | 0 |
| Padilla, Juan, COL | 1.000 | 44 | 3 | 10 | 0 | 13 | 0 |
| Padilla, Vicente, SWB | .000 | 2 | 0 | 0 | 0 | 0 | 0 |
| Palki, Jeromy, ROC | 1.000 | 42 | 3 | 9 | 0 | 12 | 2 |
| Paradis, Mike, OTT | 1.000 | 9 | 1 | 2 | 0 | 3 | 0 |
| Parker, Josh, DUR | 1.000 | 12 | 0 | 3 | 0 | 3 | 0 |
| Parker, Matt, IND | 1.000 | 1 | 0 | 1 | 0 | 1 | 0 |
| Parker, Matt, DUR | .500 | 1 | 0 | 1 | 1 | 2 | 0 |
| Parker, Matt, IND-DUR | .667 | 2 | 0 | 2 | 1 | 3 | 0 |
| Parra, Jose, NOR | 1.000 | 24 | 2 | 2 | 0 | 4 | 0 |
| Perez, Carlos, OTT* | 1.000 | 1 | 0 | 1 | 0 | 1 | 0 |
| Perez, Franklin, SWB | 1.000 | 9 | 5 | 7 | 0 | 12 | 0 |
| Peterson, Adam, SYR | 1.000 | 19 | 0 | 1 | 0 | 1 | 0 |
| Phelps, Travis, IND | .833 | 28 | 6 | 9 | 3 | 18 | 2 |
| Porzio, Mike, BUF* | .000 | 1 | 0 | 0 | 0 | 0 | 0 |
| Powell, Brian, SWB | 1.000 | 8 | 5 | 7 | 0 | 12 | 0 |
| Prieto, Ariel, TOL | 1.000 | 4 | 4 | 4 | 0 | 8 | 0 |
| Prinz, Bret, COL | 1.000 | 29 | 0 | 5 | 0 | 5 | 2 |
| Proctor, Scott, COL | .900 | 35 | 6 | 3 | 1 | 10 | 1 |
| Puffer, Brandon, PAW | .800 | 24 | 2 | 2 | 1 | 5 | 0 |
| Pulido, Carlos, ROC* | 1.000 | 5 | 1 | 2 | 0 | 3 | 0 |
| Purvis, Rob, CHR | .000 | 2 | 0 | 0 | 0 | 0 | 0 |
| Rakers, Aaron, OTT | .944 | 54 | 4 | 13 | 1 | 18 | 2 |
| Ramirez, Horacio, RMD* | 1.000 | 2 | 0 | 2 | 0 | 2 | 1 |
| Ramirez, Ramon, COL | 1.000 | 4 | 1 | 0 | 0 | 1 | 0 |
| Ramsey, Keith, BUF* | 1.000 | 2 | 0 | 2 | 0 | 2 | 0 |
| Randall, Scott, LOU | .875 | 27 | 6 | 8 | 2 | 16 | 1 |
| Rauch, Jon, CHR | 1.000 | 14 | 1 | 9 | 0 | 10 | 1 |
| Rayborn, Kenny, BUF | .917 | 23 | 6 | 16 | 2 | 24 | 1 |
| Reichert, Dan, IND | .941 | 49 | 8 | 8 | 1 | 17 | 1 |

| Player, Team | Pct. | G | PO | A | E | TC | DP |
|---|---|---|---|---|---|---|---|
| Reimers, Cameron, SYR | 1.000 | 12 | 7 | 10 | 0 | 17 | 1 |
| Reith, Brian, LOU | 1.000 | 26 | 1 | 2 | 0 | 3 | 0 |
| Reyes, Al, DUR | 1.000 | 20 | 0 | 3 | 0 | 3 | 0 |
| Reyes, Carlos, COL | 1.000 | 5 | 1 | 1 | 0 | 2 | 0 |
| Riley, Matt, OTT* | 1.000 | 10 | 1 | 3 | 0 | 4 | 0 |
| Ring, Royce, NOR* | 1.000 | 29 | 0 | 3 | 0 | 3 | 1 |
| Ritchie, Todd, DUR | 1.000 | 16 | 3 | 8 | 0 | 11 | 0 |
| Roach, Jason, NOR | .905 | 39 | 11 | 8 | 2 | 21 | 1 |
| Robbins, Jake, BUF | 1.000 | 32 | 7 | 12 | 0 | 19 | 0 |
| Robertson, Jeriome, BUF* | 1.000 | 14 | 1 | 5 | 0 | 6 | 0 |
| Rodriguez, Eddy, OTT | 1.000 | 28 | 1 | 1 | 0 | 2 | 0 |
| Rodriguez, Joe, OTT* | 1.000 | 20 | 2 | 2 | 0 | 4 | 1 |
| Rodriguez, Jose, NOR | 1.000 | 2 | 0 | 1 | 0 | 1 | 0 |
| Rodriguez, Nerio, COL | .889 | 11 | 1 | 7 | 1 | 9 | 0 |
| Rodriguez, Ryan, CHR* | .000 | 1 | 0 | 0 | 1 | 1 | 0 |
| Romano, Mike, RMD | 1.000 | 40 | 4 | 16 | 0 | 20 | 0 |
| Romero, JC, ROC* | 1.000 | 3 | 1 | 2 | 0 | 3 | 0 |
| Roney, Matt, TOL | 1.000 | 5 | 1 | 7 | 0 | 8 | 1 |
| Rose, Brian, LOU | 1.000 | 6 | 0 | 5 | 0 | 5 | 1 |
| Sadler, Carl, BUF* | 1.000 | 3 | 0 | 1 | 0 | 1 | 0 |
| Sanches, Brian, SWB | 1.000 | 4 | 0 | 2 | 0 | 2 | 0 |
| Sanchez, Jesus, SYR* | .800 | 7 | 4 | 0 | 1 | 5 | 0 |
| Sanchez, Jesus, LOU* | 1.000 | 22 | 2 | 8 | 0 | 10 | 0 |
| Sanchez, Jesus, SYR-LOU* | .933 | 29 | 6 | 8 | 1 | 15 | 0 |
| Sanders, Dave, CHR* | 1.000 | 40 | 2 | 10 | 0 | 12 | 1 |
| Santiago, Jose, CHR | .917 | 57 | 4 | 18 | 2 | 24 | 1 |
| Santos, Victor, IND | .000 | 3 | 0 | 0 | 0 | 0 | 0 |
| Schmack, Brian, TOL | 1.000 | 24 | 3 | 7 | 0 | 10 | 0 |
| Schmitt, Eric, COL | 1.000 | 20 | 9 | 10 | 0 | 19 | 0 |
| Schoening, Brent, ROC | 1.000 | 44 | 4 | 9 | 0 | 13 | 2 |
| Seay, Bobby, DUR* | 1.000 | 29 | 3 | 3 | 0 | 6 | 0 |
| Seibel, Phil, PAW* | .917 | 8 | 2 | 9 | 1 | 12 | 0 |
| Seo, Jae, NOR | 1.000 | 4 | 1 | 3 | 0 | 4 | 1 |
| Shackelford, Brian, LOU* | .920 | 59 | 5 | 18 | 2 | 25 | 0 |
| Shearn, Tom, LOU | 1.000 | 11 | 1 | 4 | 0 | 5 | 0 |
| Smith, Bud, SWB* | .000 | 1 | 0 | 0 | 0 | 0 | 0 |
| Smith, Chuck, RMD | 1.000 | 29 | 12 | 17 | 0 | 29 | 1 |
| Smith, Mike, SYR | .958 | 35 | 9 | 14 | 1 | 24 | 1 |
| Smith, Travis, RMD | 1.000 | 20 | 6 | 11 | 0 | 17 | 0 |
| Sosa, Jorge, DUR | 1.000 | 3 | 1 | 0 | 0 | 1 | 0 |
| Spencer, Sean, OTT* | 1.000 | 9 | 0 | 4 | 0 | 4 | 1 |
| Spradlin, Jerry, OTT | 1.000 | 11 | 3 | 2 | 0 | 5 | 0 |
| Standridge, Jason, DUR | .880 | 20 | 7 | 15 | 3 | 25 | 2 |
| Stephens, John, PAW | 1.000 | 24 | 6 | 16 | 0 | 22 | 1 |
| Stevens, Josh, PAW | .667 | 5 | 1 | 3 | 2 | 6 | 2 |
| Stewart, Josh, CHR* | .903 | 25 | 3 | 25 | 3 | 31 | 1 |
| Stewart, Paul, IND | 1.000 | 6 | 1 | 2 | 0 | 3 | 0 |
| Stewart, Scott, BUF* | 1.000 | 27 | 1 | 1 | 0 | 2 | 0 |
| Strange, Pat, NOR | .971 | 29 | 14 | 19 | 1 | 34 | 1 |
| Tadano, Kazuhito, BUF | 1.000 | 12 | 5 | 6 | 0 | 11 | 1 |
| Thomas, Brad, PAW* | .500 | 4 | 0 | 1 | 1 | 2 | 0 |
| Thomas, Evan, BUF | .750 | 8 | 1 | 2 | 1 | 4 | 0 |
| Thurman, Mike, COL | 1.000 | 2 | 0 | 1 | 0 | 1 | 0 |
| Towers, Josh, SYR | 1.000 | 6 | 2 | 2 | 0 | 4 | 1 |
| Urdaneta, Lino, TOL | 1.000 | 9 | 1 | 1 | 0 | 2 | 0 |
| Valentine, Joe, LOU | .895 | 30 | 7 | 10 | 2 | 19 | 2 |
| Van Hekken, Andy, TOL* | .971 | 28 | 8 | 26 | 1 | 35 | 0 |
| Veras, Jose, DUR | .846 | 30 | 4 | 7 | 2 | 13 | 1 |
| Waechter, Doug, DUR | 1.000 | 8 | 2 | 1 | 0 | 3 | 0 |
| Wagner, Ryan, LOU | .800 | 15 | 1 | 3 | 1 | 5 | 0 |
| Wang, Chien-Ming, COL | .917 | 6 | 8 | 3 | 1 | 12 | 0 |
| Wathan, Dusty, BUF | 1.000 | 2 | 1 | 0 | 0 | 1 | 0 |
| Watson, Mark, LOU* | 1.000 | 23 | 0 | 5 | 0 | 5 | 0 |
| Webb, John, DUR | .900 | 6 | 2 | 7 | 1 | 10 | 1 |
| Weibl, Clint, IND | .941 | 24 | 6 | 10 | 1 | 17 | 2 |
| Wheeler, Dan, NOR | 1.000 | 5 | 0 | 1 | 0 | 1 | 1 |
| White, Matt, BUF* | 1.000 | 13 | 1 | 5 | 0 | 6 | 0 |
| Whiteside, Matt, RMD | .800 | 57 | 2 | 2 | 1 | 5 | 1 |
| Wickman, Bob, BUF | .000 | 6 | 0 | 0 | 0 | 0 | 0 |
| Williams, Todd, OTT | 1.000 | 14 | 4 | 10 | 0 | 14 | 0 |
| Williamson, Scott, PAW | .000 | 4 | 0 | 0 | 0 | 0 | 0 |
| Winkelsas, Joe, CHR | 1.000 | 5 | 1 | 2 | 0 | 3 | 1 |
| Wise, Matt, IND | 1.000 | 7 | 4 | 3 | 0 | 7 | 0 |
| Woolard, Glenn, IND | 1.000 | 1 | 1 | 0 | 0 | 1 | 0 |
| Wright, Dan, CHR | .000 | 2 | 0 | 0 | 0 | 0 | 0 |
| Wunsch, Kelly, CHR* | 1.000 | 27 | 0 | 4 | 0 | 4 | 0 |
| Wylie, Mitch, CHR | .909 | 28 | 2 | 8 | 1 | 11 | 0 |
| Yarnall, Ed, PAW* | 1.000 | 2 | 1 | 1 | 0 | 2 | 0 |
| Yarnall, Ed, SWB* | 1.000 | 24 | 3 | 13 | 0 | 16 | 1 |
| Yarnall, Ed, PAW-SWB* | 1.000 | 26 | 4 | 14 | 0 | 18 | 1 |
| Yates, Tyler, NOR | .909 | 30 | 5 | 5 | 1 | 11 | 0 |
| Yofu, Tetsu, CHR | .875 | 21 | 6 | 8 | 2 | 16 | 0 |
| Young, Tim, BUF* | 1.000 | 5 | 0 | 1 | 0 | 1 | 0 |

## LEAGUE CHAMPIONS

| Year | Team | Pct. |
|---|---|---|
| 1884— | Trenton | .520 |
| 1885— | Syracuse | .584 |
| 1886— | Utica | .646 |
| 1887— | Toronto | .644 |
| 1888— | Syracuse | .723 |
| 1889— | Detroit | .649 |
| 1890— | Detroit | .617 |
| 1891— | Buffalo (reg. season) | .727 |
| | Buffalo (supplemental) | .680 |
| 1892— | Providence | .615 |
| | Binghamton* | .667 |
| 1893— | Erie | .606 |
| 1894— | Providence | .696 |
| 1895— | Springfield | .687 |
| 1896— | Providence | .602 |
| 1897— | Syracuse | .632 |
| 1898— | Montreal | .586 |
| 1899— | Rochester | .624 |
| 1900— | Providence | .616 |
| 1901— | Rochester | .642 |
| 1902— | Toronto | .669 |
| 1903— | Jersey City | .742 |
| 1904— | Buffalo | .657 |
| 1905— | Providence | .638 |
| 1906— | Buffalo | .607 |
| 1907— | Toronto | .619 |
| 1908— | Baltimore | .593 |
| 1909— | Rochester | .596 |
| 1910— | Rochester | .601 |
| 1911— | Rochester | .645 |
| 1912— | Toronto | .595 |
| 1913— | Newark | .625 |
| 1914— | Providence | .617 |
| 1915— | Buffalo | .632 |
| 1916— | Buffalo | .586 |
| 1917— | Toronto | .604 |
| 1918— | Toronto | .693 |
| 1919— | Baltimore | .671 |
| 1920— | Baltimore | .719 |
| 1921— | Baltimore | .717 |
| 1922— | Baltimore | .689 |
| 1923— | Baltimore | .677 |
| 1924— | Baltimore | .709 |
| 1925— | Baltimore | .633 |
| 1926— | Toronto | .657 |
| 1927— | Buffalo | .667 |
| 1928— | Rochester | .549 |
| 1929— | Rochester | .613 |
| 1930— | Rochester | .629 |
| 1931— | Rochester | .601 |
| 1932— | Newark | .649 |
| 1933— | Newark | .622 |
| | Buffalo (4th)† | .494 |
| 1934— | Newark | .608 |
| | Toronto (3rd)† | .559 |
| 1935— | Montreal | .597 |
| | Syracuse (2nd)† | .565 |
| 1936— | Buffalo‡ | .610 |
| 1937— | Newark‡ | .717 |
| 1938— | Newark‡ | .684 |
| 1939— | Jersey City | .582 |
| | Rochester (2nd)† | .556 |
| 1940— | Rochester | .611 |
| | Newark (2nd)† | .594 |
| 1941— | Newark | .649 |
| | Montreal (2nd)† | .584 |
| 1942— | Newark | .601 |
| | Syracuse (3rd)† | .513 |
| 1943— | Toronto | .625 |
| | Syracuse (3rd)† | .536 |
| 1944— | Baltimore‡ | .553 |
| 1945— | Montreal | .621 |
| | Newark (2nd)† | .582 |
| 1946— | Montreal‡ | .649 |
| 1947— | Jersey City | .610 |
| | Syracuse (3rd)† | .575 |
| 1948— | Montreal‡ | .614 |
| 1949— | Buffalo | .584 |
| | Montreal (3rd)† | .545 |
| 1950— | Rochester | .609 |
| | Baltimore (3rd)† | .556 |
| 1951— | Montreal‡ | .617 |
| 1952— | Montreal | .629 |
| | Rochester (3rd)† | .619 |
| 1953— | Rochester | .630 |
| | Montreal (2nd)† | .586 |
| 1954— | Toronto | .630 |
| | Syracuse (4th)§ | .510 |

| Year | Team | Pct. |
|---|---|---|
| 1955— | Montreal | .617 |
| | Rochester (4th)† | .497 |
| 1956— | Toronto | .566 |
| | Rochester (2nd)† | .553 |
| 1957— | Toronto | .575 |
| | Buffalo (2nd)† | .571 |
| 1958— | Montreal‡ | .588 |
| 1959— | Buffalo | .582 |
| | Havana (3rd)† | .523 |
| 1960— | Toronto‡ | .649 |
| 1961— | Columbus | .597 |
| | Buffalo (3rd)† | .559 |
| 1962— | Jacksonville | .610 |
| | Atlanta (3rd)† | .539 |
| 1963— | Syracuse∞ | .533 |
| | Indianapolis‡ | .562 |
| 1964— | Jacksonville | .589 |
| | Rochester (4th)† | .532 |
| 1965— | Columbus | .582 |
| | Toronto (3rd)† | .556 |
| 1966— | Rochester | .565 |
| | Toronto (2nd-tied)† | .558 |
| 1967— | Richmond | .574 |
| | Toledo (3rd)† | .525 |
| 1968— | Toledo | .565 |
| | Jacksonville (4th)† | .514 |
| 1969— | Tidewater | .563 |
| | Syracuse (3rd)† | .536 |
| 1970— | Syracuse‡ | .600 |
| 1971— | Rochester‡ | .614 |
| 1972— | Louisville | .563 |
| | Tidewater (3rd)† | .545 |
| 1973— | Charleston | .586 |
| | Pawtuckets† | .534 |
| 1974— | Memphis | .613 |
| | Rochester ∞‡ | .611 |
| 1975— | Tidewater‡ | .610 |
| 1976— | Rochester | .638 |
| | Syracuse (2nd)† | .590 |
| 1977— | Pawtucket | .571 |
| | Charleston (2nd)‡ | .557 |
| 1978— | Charleston | .607 |
| | Richmond (4th)† | .511 |
| 1979— | Columbus‡ | .612 |
| 1980— | Columbus‡ | .593 |
| 1981— | Columbus‡ | .633 |
| 1982— | Richmond | .590 |
| | Tidewater (3rd)† | .540 |
| 1983— | Columbus | .593 |
| | Tidewater (4th)† | .511 |
| 1984— | Columbus | .590 |
| | Pawtucket (4th)† | .536 |
| 1985— | Syracuse | .564 |
| | Tidewater (4th)† | .540 |
| 1986— | Richmond‡ | .571 |
| 1987— | Tidewater | .579 |
| | Columbus† | .550 |
| 1988— | Rochester◆ | .546 |
| | Tidewater | .546 |
| 1989— | Syracuse | .572 |
| | Richmond◆ | .555 |
| 1990— | Rochester◆ | .614 |
| | Columbus | .596 |
| 1991— | Columbus◆ | .590 |
| | Pawtucket | .552 |
| 1992— | Columbus◆ | .660 |
| | Scr. W.B. | .592 |
| 1993— | Charlotte◆ | .610 |
| | Rochester | .525 |
| 1994— | Richmond◆ | .567 |
| | Pawtucket | .549 |
| 1995— | Norfolk | .606 |
| | Ottawa◆ | .507 |
| 1996— | Columbus◆ | .599 |
| | Rochester | .511 |
| 1997— | Rochester◆ | .589 |
| | Columbus | .556 |
| 1998— | Buffalo■ | .566 |
| 1999— | Columbus | .589 |
| | Charlotte▲ | .569 |
| 2000— | Buffalo | .593 |
| | Indianapolis▲ | .563 |
| 2001— | Buffalo | .641 |
| | Louisville▼ | .583 |
| 2002— | Scranton/Wilkes-Barre | .632 |
| | Durham▲ | .556 |
| 2003— | Pawtucket | .576 |
| | Durham▲ | .521 |
| 2004— | Buffalo▲ | .576 |

*Won split-season playoff. †Won four-team playoff. ‡Won championship and four-team playoff. §Defeated Havana in game to decide fourth place, then won four-team playoff. ∞League was divided into Northern, Southern divisions. ◆League divided into Eastern, Western divisions; won playoffs. ■League divided into Eastern, Northern and Southern divisions; won four-team playoff. ▲League divided into North, South and West divisions; won four-team playoff. ▼League divided into North, South and West divisions; was leading final series of four-team playoff and was declared champion when Professional Baseball declared a stoppage of play. (NOTE—Known as Eastern League in 1884, New York State League in 1885, International League in 1886-87, International Association in 1888, International League in 1889-90, Eastern Association in 1891 and Eastern League from 1892 until 1912.)

# MEXICAN LEAGUE

## 2004 FINAL STANDINGS

### FIRST HALF

#### NORTHERN DIVISION

| Team | W | L | T | Pct. | GB |
|---|---|---|---|---|---|
| Puebla | 33 | 16 | - | .673 | --- |
| Saltillo | 30 | 19 | - | .612 | 3 |
| Monterrey | 27 | 22 | - | .551 | 6 |
| Tijuana | 25 | 24 | - | .510 | 8 |
| Monclova | 23 | 28 | - | .451 | 11 |
| Laguna | 22 | 28 | - | .440 | 11 1/2 |
| Aguascalientes | 21 | 30 | - | .412 | 13 |
| San Luis Potosi | 18 | 32 | - | .360 | 15 1/2 |

#### SOUTHERN DIVISION

| Team | W | L | T | Pct. | GB |
|---|---|---|---|---|---|
| Mexico | 31 | 20 | - | .608 | --- |
| Tigres | 30 | 21 | - | .588 | 1 |
| Tabasco | 27 | 21 | - | .563 | 2 1/2 |
| Campeche | 25 | 25 | - | .500 | 5 1/2 |
| Oaxaca | 25 | 26 | - | .490 | 6 |
| Veracruz | 23 | 28 | - | .451 | 8 |
| Yucatan | 20 | 29 | - | .408 | 10 |
| Cancun | 20 | 31 | - | .392 | 11 |

### SECOND HALF

#### NORTHERN DIVISION

| Team | W | L | T | Pct. | GB |
|---|---|---|---|---|---|
| Saltillo | 33 | 15 | - | .688 | --- |
| Puebla | 30 | 18 | - | .625 | 3 |
| Monterrey | 29 | 19 | - | .604 | 4 |
| Tijuana | 24 | 24 | - | .500 | 9 |
| Aguascalientes | 24 | 25 | - | .490 | 9 1/2 |
| Laguna | 23 | 26 | - | .469 | 10 1/2 |
| Monclova | 16 | 32 | - | .333 | 17 |
| San Luis Potosi | 14 | 34 | - | .292 | 19 |

#### SOUTHERN DIVISION

| Team | W | L | T | Pct. | GB |
|---|---|---|---|---|---|
| Campeche | 30 | 17 | - | .638 | --- |
| Mexico | 29 | 20 | - | .592 | 2 |
| Oaxaca | 25 | 22 | - | .532 | 5 |
| Tigres | 24 | 24 | - | .500 | 6 1/2 |
| Yucatan | 23 | 26 | - | .469 | 8 |
| Tabasco | 21 | 27 | - | .438 | 9 1/2 |
| Veracruz | 21 | 28 | - | .429 | 10 |
| Cancun | 20 | 29 | - | .408 | 11 |

### COMPOSITE

| Teams | W | L | T | PCT | GB | PUE | SLT | MXO | MTY | CAM | TIG | OAX | TIJ | TAB | LAG | ASC | VER | YUC | CCN | MVA | SLP |
|---|---|---|---|---|---|---|---|---|---|---|---|---|---|---|---|---|---|---|---|---|---|
| Puebla | 63 | 34 | - | .649 | --- | X | 7 | 0 | 7 | 0 | 0 | 0 | 9 | 0 | 10 | 9 | 0 | 0 | 0 | 10 | 11 |
| Saltillo | 63 | 34 | - | .649 | 0 | 6 | X | 0 | 9 | 0 | 0 | 0 | 9 | 0 | 9 | 11 | 0 | 0 | 0 | 10 | 9 |
| Mexico | 60 | 40 | - | .600 | 4 1/2 | 0 | 0 | X | 0 | 5 | 10 | 9 | 0 | 8 | 0 | 0 | 9 | 7 | 12 | 0 | 0 |
| Monterrey | 56 | 41 | - | .577 | 7 | 7 | 5 | 0 | X | 0 | 0 | 0 | 9 | 0 | 7 | 9 | 0 | 0 | 0 | 8 | 11 |
| Campeche | 55 | 42 | - | .567 | 8 | 0 | 0 | 9 | 0 | X | 5 | 7 | 0 | 7 | 0 | 0 | 13 | 8 | 6 | 0 | 0 |
| Tigres | 54 | 45 | - | .545 | 10 | 0 | 0 | 6 | 0 | 9 | X | 5 | 0 | 9 | 0 | 0 | 9 | 7 | 9 | 0 | 0 |
| Oaxaca | 50 | 48 | - | .510 | 13 1/2 | 0 | 0 | 5 | 0 | 6 | 8 | X | 0 | 8 | 0 | 0 | 8 | 5 | 10 | 0 | 0 |
| Tijuana | 9 | 48 | - | .505 | 14 | 6 | 5 | 0 | 5 | 0 | 0 | 0 | X | 0 | 10 | 7 | 0 | 0 | 0 | 8 | 8 |
| Tabasco | 48 | 48 | - | .500 | 14 1/2 | 0 | 0 | 6 | 0 | 7 | 5 | 6 | 0 | X | 0 | 0 | 5 | 9 | 10 | 0 | 0 |
| Laguna | 45 | 54 | - | .455 | 19 | 4 | 5 | 0 | 7 | 0 | 0 | 0 | 3 | 0 | X | 8 | 0 | 0 | 0 | 8 | 10 |
| Aguascalientes | 45 | 55 | - | .450 | 19 1/2 | 5 | 3 | 0 | 5 | 0 | 0 | 0 | 7 | 0 | 6 | X | 0 | 0 | 0 | 8 | 11 |
| Veracruz | 44 | 56 | - | .440 | 20 1/2 | 0 | 0 | 5 | 0 | 1 | 5 | 8 | 0 | 9 | 0 | 0 | X | 9 | 7 | 0 | 0 |
| Yucatan | 43 | 55 | - | .439 | 20 1/2 | 0 | 0 | 7 | 0 | 6 | 7 | 9 | 0 | 3 | 0 | 0 | 5 | X | 6 | 0 | 0 |
| Cancun | 40 | 60 | - | .400 | 24 1/2 | 0 | 0 | 2 | 0 | 8 | 5 | 4 | 0 | 4 | 0 | 0 | 7 | 10 | X | 0 | 0 |
| Monclova | 39 | 60 | - | .394 | 25 | 4 | 4 | 0 | 5 | 0 | 0 | 0 | 6 | 0 | 8 | 6 | 0 | 0 | 0 | X | 6 |
| San Luis Potosi | 32 | 66 | - | .327 | 31 1/2 | 2 | 5 | 0 | 3 | 0 | 0 | 0 | 5 | 0 | 4 | 5 | 0 | 0 | 0 | 8 | X |

PLAYOFFS: Puebla defeated Aguascalientes, four games to none; Campeche defeated Tabasco, four games to one; Mexico City defeated Yucatan, four games to one; Angelopolis defeated Oaxaca, four games to one; Saltillo defeated Laguna, four games to none; Monterrey defeated Tijuana, four games to two; Campeche defeated Angelopolis, four games to one; Mexico City defeated Oaxaca, four games to none; Saltiillo defeated Monterrey, four games to two; Puebla defeated Tijuana, four games to one; Campeche defeated Mexico City, four games to three; Saltillo defeated Puebla, four games to two; Campeche defeated Saltillo, four games to one to win championship.

REGULAR-SEASON ATTENDANCE: Not available.

## 2004 BATTING

### TEAM

| Team | G | TPA | AB | R | H | TB | 2B | 3B | HR | RBI | SH | SF | HP | BB | IBB | SO | SB | CS | GDP | LOB | ShO | Avg. | OBP | Slg. |
|---|---|---|---|---|---|---|---|---|---|---|---|---|---|---|---|---|---|---|---|---|---|---|---|---|
| Puebla | 97 | 3695 | 3192 | 570 | 1015 | 1461 | 182 | 21 | 74 | 535 | 41 | 48 | 44 | 370 | 23 | 497 | 58 | 38 | 54 | 764 | 3 | .318 | .391 | .458 |
| Saltillo | 97 | 3735 | 3145 | 615 | 995 | 1490 | 157 | 10 | 106 | 586 | 42 | 36 | 54 | 458 | 23 | 493 | 38 | 28 | 88 | 764 | 5 | .316 | .408 | .474 |
| Monterrey | 97 | 3698 | 3152 | 550 | 994 | 1462 | 159 | 15 | 93 | 517 | 47 | 36 | 42 | 421 | 35 | 402 | 80 | 60 | 74 | 775 | 2 | .315 | .399 | .464 |
| Mexico | 102 | 3731 | 3237 | 581 | 984 | 1493 | 181 | 23 | 94 | 539 | 42 | 30 | 48 | 372 | 29 | 394 | 85 | 34 | 96 | 711 | 3 | .304 | .381 | .461 |
| Tigres | 97 | 3626 | 3235 | 558 | 985 | 1598 | 150 | 26 | 137 | 513 | 14 | 29 | 37 | 311 | 12 | 438 | 52 | 38 | 74 | 673 | 2 | .304 | .369 | .494 |
| Oaxaca | 97 | 3623 | 3129 | 495 | 951 | 1340 | 193 | 17 | 54 | 460 | 53 | 37 | 49 | 355 | 31 | 382 | 37 | 24 | 78 | 758 | 4 | .304 | .380 | .428 |
| Aguascalientes | 100 | 3709 | 3193 | 525 | 951 | 1394 | 173 | 21 | 76 | 495 | 55 | 37 | 54 | 370 | 27 | 492 | 93 | 43 | 78 | 727 | 5 | .298 | .376 | .437 |
| Vaqueros | 99 | 3610 | 3168 | 527 | 942 | 1397 | 153 | 10 | 94 | 498 | 25 | 21 | 34 | 360 | 15 | 444 | 28 | 26 | 94 | 684 | 5 | .297 | .373 | .441 |
| Tijuana | 97 | 3698 | 3133 | 535 | 917 | 1369 | 172 | 11 | 86 | 492 | 35 | 25 | 76 | 429 | 20 | 406 | 85 | 66 | 92 | 746 | 7 | .293 | .388 | .437 |
| Monclova | 99 | 3583 | 3108 | 415 | 882 | 1198 | 131 | 13 | 53 | 392 | 45 | 34 | 39 | 357 | 23 | 500 | 61 | 39 | 60 | 730 | 6 | .284 | .361 | .385 |
| Yucatan | 96 | 3491 | 3047 | 437 | 862 | 1212 | 148 | 11 | 60 | 388 | 45 | 28 | 50 | 320 | 21 | 366 | 65 | 44 | 89 | 658 | 4 | .283 | .358 | .398 |
| San Luis Potosi | 98 | 3608 | 3199 | 428 | 894 | 1331 | 160 | 14 | 83 | 395 | 36 | 18 | 32 | 323 | 17 | 519 | 58 | 21 | 72 | 734 | 9 | .279 | .350 | .416 |
| Campeche | 95 | 3478 | 3004 | 436 | 833 | 1209 | 167 | 10 | 63 | 398 | 40 | 35 | 54 | 345 | 29 | 424 | 32 | 32 | 87 | 693 | 6 | .277 | .358 | .402 |
| Tabasco | 91 | 3268 | 2812 | 398 | 774 | 1058 | 128 | 18 | 40 | 359 | 36 | 38 | 38 | 344 | 17 | 435 | 90 | 46 | 82 | 638 | 8 | .275 | .358 | .376 |
| Veracruz | 98 | 3485 | 3043 | 396 | 821 | 1111 | 142 | 11 | 42 | 359 | 43 | 27 | 50 | 322 | 33 | 410 | 60 | 28 | 82 | 695 | 4 | .270 | .347 | .365 |
| Cancun | 100 | 3453 | 3062 | 361 | 793 | 1123 | 139 | 13 | 55 | 339 | 38 | 22 | 49 | 282 | 25 | 445 | 23 | 27 | 100 | 649 | 10 | .259 | .329 | .367 |

# INDIVIDUAL

## TOP QUALIFIERS FOR BATTING CHAMPIONSHIP

Minimum 297 plate appearances. *Lefthanded batter. †Switch-hitter.

| Player, Team | G | TPA | AB | R | H | TB | 2B | 3B | HR | RBI | SH | SF | HP | BB | IBB | SO | SB | CS | GDP | Avg. | OBP | Slg. |
|---|---|---|---|---|---|---|---|---|---|---|---|---|---|---|---|---|---|---|---|---|---|---|
| Smith, Demond, Monterrey † | 78 | 349 | 298 | 82 | 121 | 195 | 19 | 5 | 15 | 52 | 4 | 4 | 7 | 36 | 3 | 44 | 30 | 18 | 1 | .406 | .475 | .654 |
| Munoz, Noe, Saltillo | 85 | 342 | 279 | 56 | 109 | 145 | 18 | 0 | 6 | 57 | 3 | 5 | 2 | 53 | 3 | 27 | 0 | 0 | 10 | .391 | .484 | .520 |
| Robles, Oscar, Mexico • | 97 | 407 | 335 | 72 | 128 | 185 | 23 | 5 | 8 | 64 | 5 | 5 | 0 | 62 | 8 | 11 | 8 | 6 | 8 | .382 | .473 | .552 |
| Bass, Jayson, Saltillo • | 86 | 372 | 308 | 93 | 115 | 188 | 19 | 3 | 16 | 62 | 1 | 3 | 3 | 57 | 3 | 55 | 13 | 6 | 5 | .373 | .472 | .610 |
| Flores, Miguel, Monterrey | 92 | 395 | 326 | 71 | 120 | 160 | 18 | 2 | 6 | 46 | 5 | 6 | 4 | 54 | 4 | 32 | 20 | 4 | 11 | .368 | .456 | .491 |
| White, Derrick, Tijuana | 88 | 362 | 288 | 65 | 104 | 169 | 20 | 0 | 15 | 76 | 0 | 7 | 6 | 61 | 3 | 38 | 9 | 6 | 7 | .361 | .472 | .587 |
| Burkhart, Morgan, Saltillo † | 95 | 416 | 309 | 98 | 110 | 198 | 19 | 0 | 23 | 90 | 0 | 4 | 7 | 96 | 5 | 58 | 0 | 1 | 10 | .356 | .512 | .641 |
| Bullett, Scott, Monterrey • | 85 | 356 | 319 | 58 | 113 | 165 | 14 | 4 | 10 | 69 | 0 | 4 | 2 | 31 | 6 | 52 | 10 | 7 | 5 | .354 | .410 | .517 |
| Martinez, Greg, Oaxaca † | 82 | 365 | 311 | 56 | 109 | 134 | 15 | 5 | 0 | 27 | 5 | 2 | 6 | 41 | 4 | 36 | 7 | 6 | 4 | .350 | .433 | .431 |
| Martinez, Manny, Tigres | 87 | 371 | 337 | 64 | 118 | 180 | 23 | 3 | 11 | 45 | 0 | 2 | 5 | 27 | 0 | 52 | 13 | 1 | 2 | .350 | .404 | .534 |
| Johnson, Rontrez, Agua. | 100 | 444 | 373 | 96 | 129 | 212 | 29 | 6 | 14 | 52 | 3 | 3 | 8 | 57 | 7 | 55 | 54 | 18 | 6 | .346 | .440 | .568 |
| Sherman, Darrell, Puebla • | 87 | 383 | 307 | 74 | 106 | 133 | 9 | 6 | 2 | 41 | 5 | 6 | 9 | 56 | 2 | 35 | 7 | 4 | 5 | .345 | .452 | .433 |
| Meyers, Chad, Mexico | 97 | 427 | 359 | 92 | 122 | 187 | 21 | 10 | 8 | 61 | 5 | 2 | 9 | 51 | 1 | 43 | 32 | 6 | 7 | .340 | .432 | .521 |
| Villalobos, Carlos, Puebla | 96 | 416 | 365 | 82 | 123 | 197 | 21 | 1 | 17 | 82 | 2 | 7 | 2 | 40 | 4 | 59 | 5 | 3 | 7 | .337 | .399 | .540 |
| Lara, Idelfonso, Vaqueros-Agua. | 86 | 314 | 267 | 44 | 90 | 143 | 17 | 0 | 12 | 55 | 3 | 2 | 4 | 38 | 4 | 59 | 1 | 1 | 8 | .337 | .424 | .536 |

DEPARTMENTAL LEADERS: G—Gastelum, 107; AB—Gastelum, 395; R—Burkhart, 100; H—Robles, R. Johnson, 129; TB—R. Johnson, 212; 2B—R. Johnson, Santana, 29; 3B—Meyers, 10; HR—Alcantara, 27; RBI—Saucedo, 97; SH—Meza, 18; SF—Yan, 11; HP—Arauz, 17; BB—Burkart, 95; IBB—Melo, 11; SO—O'Sullivan, 73; SB—R. Johnson, 54; CS—R. Johnson, D. Smith, 18; GIDP—L. Garcia, 16; Slg.—Burkhart, .658; OBP—Burkhart, .517.

## ALL PLAYERS

*Lefthanded batter. †Switch-hitter.

| Player, Team | G | TPA | AB | R | H | TB | 2B | 3B | HR | RBI | SH | SF | HP | BB | IBB | SO | SB | CS | GDP | Avg. | OBP | Slg. |
|---|---|---|---|---|---|---|---|---|---|---|---|---|---|---|---|---|---|---|---|---|---|---|
| Acuna, Jose, Cancun † | 77 | 247 | 204 | 30 | 59 | 67 | 8 | 0 | 0 | 8 | 2 | 0 | 2 | 39 | 2 | 29 | 4 | 2 | 3 | .289 | .408 | .328 |
| Adriana, Sharnol, Yucatan | 38 | 157 | 126 | 26 | 38 | 63 | 4 | 0 | 7 | 21 | 1 | 1 | 5 | 24 | 1 | 22 | 4 | 0 | 7 | .302 | .429 | .500 |
| Adriana, Sharnol, Monclova | 6 | 25 | 22 | 2 | 6 | 8 | 2 | 0 | 0 | 1 | 0 | 0 | 2 | 1 | 0 | 4 | 0 | 1 | 0 | .273 | .360 | .364 |
| Aganza, Ruben, Saltillo | 48 | 98 | 90 | 9 | 23 | 30 | 4 | 0 | 1 | 9 | 0 | 0 | 2 | 6 | 0 | 10 | 0 | 0 | 3 | .256 | .316 | .333 |
| Ahumada, Alex, Monterrey | 71 | 187 | 162 | 31 | 51 | 66 | 10 | 1 | 1 | 22 | 1 | 1 | 2 | 21 | 2 | 27 | 1 | 1 | 0 | .315 | .398 | .407 |
| Alcantara, Izzy, Vaqueros | 99 | 399 | 326 | 65 | 103 | 205 | 21 | 0 | 27 | 81 | 0 | 2 | 3 | 68 | 4 | 71 | 3 | 5 | 6 | .316 | .436 | .629 |
| Alejos, Fernando, Cancun | 63 | 221 | 203 | 17 | 46 | 67 | 6 | 3 | 3 | 17 | 1 | 3 | 3 | 11 | 1 | 33 | 2 | 4 | 8 | .227 | .273 | .330 |
| Alfonso, Manuel, Tabasco * | 47 | 116 | 108 | 20 | 20 | 25 | 3 | 1 | 0 | 9 | 2 | 0 | 1 | 5 | 0 | 22 | 4 | 2 | 4 | .185 | .228 | .231 |
| Almeida, Shammar, Oaxaca * | 53 | 84 | 58 | 10 | 13 | 18 | 2 | 0 | 1 | 10 | 2 | 0 | 3 | 21 | 1 | 17 | 0 | 0 | 1 | .224 | .451 | .310 |
| Alvarez, Hector, Oaxaca | 19 | 56 | 54 | 8 | 17 | 24 | 4 | 0 | 1 | 7 | 0 | 0 | 0 | 2 | 0 | 8 | 0 | 0 | 1 | .315 | .339 | .444 |
| Alvarez, Hector, Monterrey | 55 | 119 | 103 | 10 | 31 | 39 | 5 | 0 | 1 | 9 | 3 | 1 | 3 | 9 | 0 | 13 | 1 | 0 | 4 | .301 | .371 | .379 |
| Amador, Jose, Aguascalientes | 60 | 238 | 187 | 37 | 55 | 70 | 6 | 3 | 1 | 22 | 9 | 0 | 1 | 41 | 0 | 32 | 6 | 5 | 2 | .294 | .424 | .374 |
| Amezcua, Adan, San Luis Potosi | 65 | 257 | 221 | 32 | 59 | 89 | 16 | 1 | 4 | 29 | 0 | 1 | 3 | 32 | 3 | 25 | 4 | 2 | 5 | .267 | .366 | .403 |
| Andrews, Shane, San Luis Potosi | 38 | 150 | 125 | 12 | 27 | 40 | 4 | 0 | 3 | 15 | 1 | 1 | 2 | 21 | 0 | 28 | 1 | 1 | 4 | .216 | .336 | .320 |
| Angulo, Gregorio, Yucatan † | 16 | 22 | 20 | 6 | 4 | 11 | 1 | 0 | 2 | 4 | 0 | 0 | 0 | 1 | 0 | 3 | 0 | 0 | 1 | .200 | .238 | .550 |
| Arano, Eloy, Veracruz † | 97 | 364 | 323 | 43 | 87 | 98 | 9 | 1 | 0 | 24 | 6 | 1 | 8 | 26 | 1 | 31 | 10 | 4 | 3 | .269 | .338 | .303 |
| Arano, Wilfrido, Veracruz * | 22 | 59 | 51 | 4 | 14 | 19 | 2 | 0 | 1 | 11 | 1 | 1 | 2 | 4 | 0 | 2 | 0 | 0 | 1 | .275 | .345 | .373 |
| Arano, Wilfrido, Tijuana * | 33 | 45 | 38 | 5 | 10 | 11 | 1 | 0 | 0 | 3 | 0 | 0 | 1 | 6 | 0 | 1 | 0 | 1 | 0 | .263 | .378 | .289 |
| Arauz, Escarcega, Monclova | 21 | 47 | 42 | 1 | 9 | 10 | 1 | 0 | 0 | 1 | 0 | 0 | 1 | 4 | 0 | 11 | 0 | 0 | 1 | .214 | .298 | .238 |
| Arauz, Leobardo, Yucatan † | 87 | 305 | 247 | 37 | 55 | 90 | 12 | 1 | 7 | 29 | 1 | 1 | 17 | 39 | 3 | 45 | 4 | 3 | 6 | .223 | .365 | .364 |
| Arias, Francisco, Saltillo | 62 | 177 | 153 | 30 | 40 | 59 | 7 | 0 | 4 | 20 | 1 | 3 | 9 | 11 | 0 | 23 | 2 | 2 | 4 | .261 | .341 | .386 |
| Arredondo, Alan, Yucatan † | 79 | 205 | 182 | 41 | 47 | 54 | 7 | 0 | 0 | 16 | 5 | 0 | 2 | 16 | 1 | 28 | 11 | 5 | 2 | .258 | .325 | .297 |
| Arredondo, Eduardo, Tabasco * | 74 | 261 | 225 | 37 | 53 | 69 | 4 | 6 | 0 | 23 | 9 | 2 | 2 | 23 | 0 | 27 | 13 | 6 | 1 | .236 | .310 | .307 |
| Arredondo, Hernando, Tabasco | 78 | 281 | 260 | 21 | 77 | 102 | 14 | 1 | 3 | 33 | 3 | 5 | 0 | 13 | 2 | 50 | 7 | 6 | 6 | .296 | .324 | .392 |
| Arredondo, Jesus, Puebla * | 64 | 233 | 195 | 37 | 58 | 80 | 14 | 1 | 2 | 27 | 5 | 2 | 6 | 25 | 3 | 20 | 0 | 2 | 8 | .297 | .390 | .410 |
| Arredondo, Luis, Yucatan * | 90 | 384 | 342 | 53 | 104 | 130 | 13 | 2 | 3 | 29 | 3 | 0 | 2 | 37 | 1 | 33 | 26 | 13 | 6 | .304 | .375 | .380 |
| Avila, Carlos, Puebla * | 43 | 58 | 52 | 8 | 9 | 12 | 3 | 0 | 0 | 2 | 1 | 0 | 0 | 5 | 0 | 14 | 0 | 0 | 1 | .173 | .246 | .231 |
| Avila, Ignacio, Campeche | 40 | 14 | 13 | 6 | 2 | 3 | 1 | 0 | 0 | 0 | 0 | 0 | 0 | 1 | 0 | 5 | 0 | 1 | 0 | .154 | .214 | .231 |
| Aybar, Manny, Puebla | 18 | 1 | 1 | 0 | 0 | 0 | 0 | 0 | 0 | 0 | 0 | 0 | 0 | 0 | 0 | 1 | 0 | 0 | 0 | .000 | .000 | .000 |
| Baez, Carlos, Tabasco | 4 | 5 | 4 | 0 | 0 | 0 | 0 | 0 | 0 | 0 | 0 | 0 | 0 | 1 | 0 | 1 | 0 | 0 | 0 | .000 | .200 | .000 |
| Barajas, Edison, Aguascalientes * | 18 | 36 | 30 | 3 | 5 | 6 | 1 | 0 | 0 | 1 | 1 | 0 | 0 | 5 | 0 | 12 | 0 | 0 | 0 | .167 | .286 | .200 |
| Barajas, Edison, Vaqueros * | 31 | 49 | 43 | 5 | 13 | 18 | 5 | 0 | 0 | 7 | 0 | 1 | 3 | 2 | 0 | 11 | 0 | 0 | 2 | .302 | .367 | .419 |
| Bass, Jayson, Saltillo * | 86 | 372 | 308 | 93 | 115 | 188 | 19 | 3 | 16 | 62 | 1 | 3 | 3 | 57 | 3 | 55 | 13 | 6 | 5 | .373 | .472 | .610 |
| Beltran, Juan, Campeche | 52 | 114 | 104 | 16 | 17 | 28 | 5 | 0 | 2 | 13 | 4 | 0 | 1 | 5 | 0 | 33 | 1 | 0 | 6 | .163 | .209 | .269 |
| Bernal, Cosme, Monclova | 67 | 191 | 173 | 25 | 46 | 59 | 7 | 0 | 2 | 18 | 0 | 0 | 1 | 17 | 0 | 27 | 3 | 1 | 2 | .266 | .335 | .341 |
| Bojorquez, Victor, Mexico | 94 | 337 | 312 | 55 | 95 | 147 | 22 | 3 | 8 | 39 | 5 | 1 | 6 | 13 | 0 | 39 | 9 | 5 | 13 | .304 | .343 | .471 |
| Borges, Luis, Yucatan * | 84 | 284 | 263 | 32 | 76 | 91 | 10 | 1 | 1 | 28 | 8 | 2 | 1 | 10 | 0 | 9 | 1 | 4 | 7 | .289 | .315 | .346 |
| Brena, Jaime, Oaxaca | 81 | 267 | 227 | 22 | 57 | 67 | 8 | 1 | 0 | 20 | 9 | 3 | 5 | 23 | 1 | 23 | 3 | 3 | 5 | .251 | .329 | .295 |
| Brinkley, Darryl, Tijuana | 37 | 151 | 125 | 21 | 31 | 53 | 4 | 0 | 6 | 28 | 1 | 2 | 3 | 20 | 0 | 21 | 9 | 3 | 4 | .248 | .360 | .424 |
| Brinkley, Darryl, San Luis Potosi | 38 | 153 | 141 | 22 | 54 | 64 | 4 | 0 | 2 | 14 | 0 | 0 | 1 | 11 | 3 | 14 | 14 | 4 | 2 | .383 | .431 | .454 |
| Brown, Emil, Campeche | 28 | 119 | 101 | 23 | 32 | 64 | 8 | 0 | 8 | 24 | 0 | 2 | 1 | 15 | 2 | 16 | 0 | 0 | 1 | .317 | .403 | .634 |
| Buelna, Lorenzo, Puebla | 91 | 351 | 304 | 52 | 92 | 123 | 16 | 0 | 5 | 37 | 3 | 2 | 8 | 34 | 1 | 37 | 13 | 6 | 1 | .303 | .385 | .405 |
| Bullett, Scott, Monterrey * | 85 | 356 | 319 | 58 | 113 | 165 | 14 | 4 | 10 | 69 | 0 | 4 | 2 | 31 | 6 | 52 | 10 | 7 | 5 | .354 | .410 | .517 |
| Burkhart, Morgan, Saltillo † | 95 | 416 | 309 | 98 | 110 | 198 | 19 | 0 | 23 | 90 | 0 | 4 | 7 | 96 | 5 | 58 | 0 | 1 | 10 | .356 | .512 | .641 |
| Bustamante, Omar, Saltillo | 31 | 72 | 68 | 6 | 13 | 23 | 1 | 0 | 3 | 12 | 1 | 1 | 0 | 2 | 0 | 22 | 0 | 0 | 3 | .191 | .211 | .338 |
| Bustillos, Luis, San Luis Potosi | 67 | 240 | 212 | 27 | 56 | 86 | 16 | 1 | 4 | 23 | 5 | 0 | 3 | 20 | 0 | 53 | 1 | 1 | 7 | .264 | .336 | .406 |
| Camarero, Rafael, Veracruz | 42 | 77 | 71 | 4 | 12 | 15 | 3 | 0 | 0 | 7 | 2 | 0 | 1 | 3 | 0 | 19 | 0 | 0 | 3 | .169 | .213 | .211 |
| Canizalez, Juan, Campeche † | 40 | 167 | 151 | 20 | 38 | 48 | 7 | 0 | 1 | 16 | 2 | 1 | 2 | 11 | 0 | 15 | 1 | 1 | 6 | .252 | .309 | .318 |
| Canizalez, Juan, Yucatan † | 42 | 168 | 149 | 18 | 50 | 73 | 12 | 1 | 3 | 22 | 0 | 3 | 3 | 13 | 2 | 16 | 1 | 1 | 2 | .336 | .393 | .490 |
| Cansino, Jorge, Veracruz * | 5 | 9 | 9 | 0 | 1 | 2 | 1 | 0 | 0 | 0 | 0 | 0 | 0 | 0 | 0 | 2 | 0 | 0 | 0 | .111 | .111 | .222 |

| Player, Team | G | TPA | AB | R | H | TB | 2B | 3B | HR | RBI | SH | SF | HP | BB | IBB | SO | SB | CS | GDP | Avg. | OBP | Slg. |
|---|---|---|---|---|---|---|---|---|---|---|---|---|---|---|---|---|---|---|---|---|---|---|
| Carmona, Sergio, San Luis Potosi | 6 | 11 | 7 | 1 | 0 | 0 | 0 | 0 | 0 | 2 | 0 | 1 | 1 | 2 | 0 | 1 | 0 | 0 | 0 | .000 | .273 | .000 |
| Carrillo, Matias, Tigres * | 83 | 333 | 298 | 49 | 90 | 142 | 13 | 0 | 13 | 52 | 0 | 3 | 2 | 30 | 1 | 25 | 4 | 2 | 10 | .302 | .366 | .477 |
| Carrillo, Oscar, Mexico | 17 | 11 | 11 | 6 | 2 | 5 | 0 | 0 | 1 | 2 | 0 | 0 | 0 | 0 | 0 | 3 | 0 | 0 | 0 | .182 | .182 | .455 |
| Casillas, Uriel, Monclova | 2 | 4 | 4 | 0 | 0 | 0 | 0 | 0 | 0 | 0 | 0 | 0 | 0 | 0 | 0 | 1 | 0 | 0 | 0 | .000 | .000 | .000 |
| Castaneda, Federico, Vaqueros | 35 | 2 | 2 | 2 | 2 | 2 | 0 | 0 | 0 | 1 | 0 | 0 | 0 | 0 | 0 | 0 | 0 | 0 | 0 | 1.000 | 1.000 | 1.000 |
| Castaneda, Hector, Yucatan * | 76 | 238 | 190 | 30 | 59 | 84 | 13 | 0 | 4 | 37 | 0 | 4 | 2 | 42 | 2 | 25 | 1 | 0 | 12 | .311 | .433 | .442 |
| Castaneda, Rafael, Vaqueros | 44 | 160 | 139 | 21 | 45 | 72 | 9 | 0 | 6 | 26 | 3 | 2 | 3 | 13 | 0 | 14 | 0 | 1 | 3 | .324 | .389 | .518 |
| Castellano, Pedro, Mexico | 87 | 355 | 311 | 48 | 102 | 150 | 21 | 0 | 9 | 49 | 0 | 2 | 4 | 38 | 4 | 49 | 5 | 0 | 10 | .328 | .406 | .482 |
| Castro, Arnoldo, Cancun | 81 | 299 | 260 | 26 | 63 | 86 | 17 | 0 | 2 | 17 | 3 | 0 | 1 | 35 | 1 | 19 | 2 | 5 | 8 | .242 | .334 | .331 |
| Castro, Domingo, Monclova | 94 | 363 | 320 | 40 | 90 | 115 | 7 | 3 | 4 | 37 | 7 | 2 | 0 | 34 | 0 | 38 | 5 | 3 | 6 | .281 | .348 | .359 |
| Cazarin, Manuel, Veracruz | 80 | 263 | 238 | 24 | 59 | 86 | 15 | 0 | 4 | 30 | 2 | 5 | 3 | 15 | 0 | 19 | 0 | 2 | 9 | .248 | .295 | .361 |
| Cervantes, Ivan, Oaxaca | 93 | 394 | 358 | 45 | 116 | 148 | 22 | 2 | 2 | 51 | 10 | 1 | 7 | 18 | 1 | 28 | 0 | 2 | 9 | .324 | .367 | .413 |
| Cervantes, Refugio, Mexico * | 30 | 75 | 70 | 7 | 24 | 35 | 5 | 0 | 2 | 14 | 1 | 0 | 1 | 3 | 2 | 8 | 0 | 0 | 3 | .343 | .378 | .500 |
| Cervantes, Refugio, Cancun * | 36 | 137 | 128 | 15 | 27 | 49 | 7 | 0 | 5 | 16 | 1 | 0 | 0 | 8 | 2 | 23 | 0 | 0 | 4 | .211 | .257 | .383 |
| Cervera, Francisco, Yucatan | 60 | 149 | 129 | 16 | 37 | 50 | 7 | 0 | 2 | 24 | 2 | 1 | 4 | 13 | 1 | 22 | 0 | 1 | 7 | .287 | .367 | .388 |
| Chan, Armando, Yucatan * | 4 | 2 | 2 | 0 | 0 | 0 | 0 | 0 | 0 | 0 | 0 | 0 | 0 | 0 | 0 | 0 | 0 | 0 | 1 | .000 | .000 | .000 |
| Connell, Lino, Veracruz † | 98 | 410 | 365 | 52 | 116 | 159 | 27 | 2 | 4 | 48 | 9 | 4 | 2 | 30 | 3 | 51 | 15 | 5 | 13 | .318 | .369 | .436 |
| Contreras, Jose, Puebla | 84 | 306 | 252 | 50 | 85 | 129 | 16 | 8 | 4 | 45 | 3 | 5 | 8 | 38 | 1 | 43 | 19 | 4 | 2 | .337 | .432 | .512 |
| Contreras, Sergio, Tigres * | 66 | 195 | 181 | 32 | 59 | 94 | 16 | 2 | 5 | 19 | 2 | 1 | 0 | 11 | 0 | 23 | 4 | 5 | 3 | .326 | .363 | .519 |
| Crespo, Jorge, Oaxaca | 20 | 23 | 16 | 8 | 7 | 7 | 0 | 0 | 0 | 1 | 0 | 0 | 3 | 4 | 0 | 4 | 1 | 0 | 0 | .438 | .609 | .438 |
| Cruz, Fausto, Oaxaca | 60 | 245 | 201 | 47 | 76 | 117 | 17 | 0 | 8 | 28 | 2 | 1 | 4 | 37 | 2 | 34 | 4 | 2 | 4 | .378 | .481 | .582 |
| Cruz, Marco, Yucatan | 16 | 34 | 30 | 1 | 4 | 8 | 1 | 0 | 1 | 1 | 3 | 0 | 0 | 1 | 0 | 1 | 0 | 1 | 0 | .133 | .161 | .267 |
| Cruz, Marco, Campeche | 12 | 28 | 25 | 3 | 7 | 10 | 3 | 0 | 0 | 6 | 0 | 0 | 1 | 2 | 0 | 3 | 0 | 0 | 0 | .280 | .357 | .400 |
| Diaz, Eddy, Yucatan * | 65 | 260 | 233 | 26 | 72 | 107 | 11 | 0 | 8 | 36 | 2 | 3 | 4 | 18 | 1 | 24 | 5 | 1 | 4 | .309 | .364 | .459 |
| Diaz, Edwin, Veracruz | 93 | 360 | 307 | 37 | 85 | 107 | 13 | 0 | 3 | 40 | 4 | 6 | 8 | 35 | 4 | 39 | 5 | 2 | 3 | .277 | .360 | .349 |
| Diaz, Luis, Veracruz * | 25 | 59 | 48 | 7 | 10 | 12 | 2 | 0 | 0 | 4 | 0 | 0 | 0 | 11 | 1 | 8 | 0 | 0 | 0 | .208 | .356 | .250 |
| Diaz, Luis, Vaqueros * | 16 | 20 | 18 | 2 | 3 | 3 | 0 | 0 | 0 | 1 | 0 | 0 | 0 | 2 | 0 | 11 | 0 | 1 | 0 | .167 | .250 | .167 |
| Diaz, Pedro, Puebla | 54 | 141 | 123 | 23 | 41 | 51 | 2 | 1 | 2 | 23 | 2 | 2 | 1 | 13 | 0 | 16 | 1 | 0 | 0 | .333 | .396 | .415 |
| Diaz, Remigio, San Luis Potosi | 69 | 272 | 252 | 31 | 76 | 95 | 10 | 0 | 3 | 23 | 4 | 2 | 1 | 13 | 0 | 20 | 9 | 1 | 10 | .302 | .336 | .377 |
| Encarnacion, Mario, Cancun | 34 | 131 | 112 | 15 | 27 | 42 | 6 | 0 | 3 | 14 | 2 | 1 | 0 | 16 | 4 | 31 | 0 | 0 | 3 | .241 | .333 | .375 |
| Espino, Daniel, Cancun | 97 | 356 | 317 | 44 | 95 | 126 | 14 | 1 | 5 | 35 | 5 | 1 | 7 | 26 | 1 | 24 | 5 | 1 | 13 | .300 | .365 | .397 |
| Espinosa, Ramon, Vaqueros | 62 | 273 | 260 | 50 | 95 | 141 | 20 | 1 | 8 | 47 | 1 | 1 | 3 | 8 | 3 | 14 | 3 | 2 | 8 | .365 | .390 | .542 |
| Espinoza, Efren, Mexico | 49 | 146 | 129 | 25 | 40 | 61 | 4 | 1 | 5 | 12 | 3 | 0 | 4 | 10 | 0 | 22 | 6 | 2 | 1 | .310 | .378 | .473 |
| Espinoza, Jose, Tijuana † | 84 | 254 | 212 | 34 | 66 | 91 | 9 | 2 | 4 | 27 | 7 | 0 | 4 | 31 | 2 | 27 | 5 | 2 | 5 | .311 | .409 | .429 |
| Esqueda, Johnatan, Saltillo | 1 | 3 | 3 | 0 | 1 | 1 | 0 | 0 | 0 | 0 | 0 | 0 | 0 | 0 | 0 | 0 | 0 | 0 | 0 | .333 | .333 | .333 |
| Esquer, Ramon, Tabasco * | 31 | 70 | 61 | 9 | 13 | 15 | 2 | 0 | 0 | 2 | 0 | 0 | 0 | 9 | 0 | 13 | 3 | 0 | 6 | .213 | .314 | .246 |
| Estrada, Hector, Vaqueros | 63 | 190 | 172 | 21 | 40 | 66 | 5 | 0 | 7 | 25 | 1 | 1 | 2 | 13 | 0 | 19 | 1 | 0 | 7 | .233 | .293 | .384 |
| Evans, John, Tabasco | 86 | 350 | 259 | 69 | 85 | 142 | 22 | 4 | 9 | 44 | 1 | 4 | 12 | 74 | 6 | 64 | 4 | 0 | 9 | .328 | .490 | .548 |
| Felix, Alejandro, Vaqueros | 28 | 34 | 30 | 7 | 5 | 6 | 1 | 0 | 0 | 0 | 1 | 0 | 1 | 2 | 0 | 7 | 1 | 0 | 0 | .167 | .242 | .200 |
| Felix, Lorenzo, Cancun | 46 | 97 | 90 | 9 | 22 | 29 | 4 | 0 | 1 | 6 | 4 | 1 | 0 | 2 | 0 | 20 | 1 | 0 | 4 | .244 | .258 | .322 |
| Fentanes, Oscar, Veracruz | 87 | 285 | 247 | 21 | 64 | 72 | 2 | 0 | 2 | 26 | 6 | 2 | 10 | 20 | 2 | 24 | 2 | 2 | 5 | .259 | .337 | .291 |
| Fernandez, Dan, Mexico * | 82 | 333 | 280 | 53 | 75 | 85 | 7 | 0 | 1 | 18 | 10 | 0 | 6 | 37 | 1 | 28 | 10 | 5 | 2 | .268 | .365 | .304 |
| Figueroa, Marco, Veracruz | 22 | 26 | 25 | 6 | 2 | 2 | 0 | 0 | 0 | 3 | 1 | 0 | 0 | 0 | 0 | 14 | 0 | 0 | 1 | .080 | .080 | .080 |
| Flores, Kevin, Puebla | 52 | 135 | 115 | 17 | 31 | 37 | 4 | 1 | 0 | 7 | 7 | 0 | 2 | 11 | 0 | 27 | 2 | 1 | 2 | .270 | .344 | .322 |
| Flores, Miguel, Monterrey | 92 | 395 | 326 | 71 | 120 | 160 | 18 | 2 | 6 | 46 | 5 | 6 | 4 | 54 | 4 | 32 | 20 | 4 | 11 | .368 | .456 | .491 |
| Fornes, Daniel, Monterrey * | 87 | 308 | 278 | 44 | 78 | 120 | 15 | 0 | 9 | 46 | 1 | 2 | 2 | 25 | 7 | 13 | 2 | 5 | 9 | .281 | .342 | .432 |
| Freire, Alejandro, Veracruz | 25 | 106 | 80 | 12 | 16 | 20 | 1 | 0 | 1 | 11 | 0 | 1 | 6 | 19 | 2 | 14 | 2 | 0 | 2 | .200 | .387 | .250 |
| Gamez, Valentin, San Luis Potosi | 8 | 30 | 25 | 3 | 6 | 6 | 0 | 0 | 0 | 3 | 1 | 0 | 0 | 4 | 0 | 0 | 0 | 0 | 1 | .240 | .345 | .240 |
| Garcia, Carlos, Mexico | 4 | 0 | 0 | 0 | 0 | 0 | 0 | 0 | 0 | 0 | 0 | 0 | 0 | 0 | 0 | 0 | 0 | 0 | 0 | .000 | .000 | .000 |
| Garcia, Carlos, Vaqueros | 11 | 8 | 7 | 0 | 1 | 1 | 0 | 0 | 0 | 0 | 0 | 0 | 0 | 1 | 0 | 2 | 0 | 0 | 0 | .143 | .250 | .143 |
| Garcia, Cornelio, Vaqueros * | 50 | 184 | 152 | 24 | 50 | 59 | 4 | 1 | 1 | 17 | 3 | 0 | 0 | 29 | 0 | 21 | 1 | 0 | 7 | .329 | .436 | .388 |
| Garcia, Ernesto, Aguascalientes | 34 | 62 | 55 | 8 | 14 | 22 | 1 | 2 | 1 | 8 | 0 | 0 | 4 | 3 | 0 | 17 | 0 | 0 | 2 | .255 | .339 | .400 |
| Garcia, Guillermo, Tigres | 84 | 346 | 281 | 55 | 85 | 175 | 12 | 0 | 26 | 68 | 0 | 6 | 3 | 56 | 2 | 55 | 0 | 1 | 7 | .302 | .416 | .623 |
| Garcia, Hector, Tabasco | 65 | 217 | 205 | 31 | 56 | 62 | 6 | 0 | 0 | 16 | 1 | 1 | 2 | 8 | 1 | 13 | 6 | 3 | 5 | .273 | .306 | .302 |
| Garcia, Luis, Tigres † | 81 | 329 | 292 | 54 | 76 | 108 | 10 | 2 | 6 | 45 | 0 | 2 | 0 | 35 | 3 | 35 | 8 | 0 | 16 | .260 | .337 | .370 |
| Garcia, Nick, Saltillo | 87 | 298 | 269 | 35 | 77 | 99 | 14 | 1 | 2 | 36 | 11 | 3 | 2 | 13 | 1 | 41 | 2 | 3 | 3 | .286 | .321 | .368 |
| Garcia, Omar, Monclova † | 7 | 30 | 24 | 2 | 7 | 11 | 1 | 0 | 1 | 4 | 0 | 1 | 1 | 4 | 0 | 3 | 0 | 0 | 3 | .292 | .400 | .458 |
| Garcia, Omar, San Luis Potosi † | 22 | 93 | 84 | 9 | 23 | 37 | 5 | 0 | 3 | 13 | 0 | 1 | 0 | 8 | 0 | 8 | 0 | 0 | 2 | .274 | .333 | .440 |
| Garzon, Eliseo, Tijuana | 60 | 159 | 142 | 9 | 32 | 46 | 2 | 0 | 4 | 16 | 2 | 0 | 0 | 15 | 0 | 18 | 0 | 0 | 5 | .225 | .299 | .324 |
| Gastelum, Carlos, Tigres | 94 | 413 | 373 | 58 | 114 | 145 | 8 | 7 | 3 | 26 | 4 | 2 | 6 | 28 | 0 | 35 | 15 | 11 | 6 | .306 | .362 | .389 |
| Gastelum, Gato, Tigres | 16 | 25 | 24 | 1 | 1 | 1 | 0 | 0 | 0 | 0 | 0 | 0 | 0 | 1 | 0 | 6 | 0 | 0 | 0 | .042 | .080 | .042 |
| Gastelum, Sergio, Tigres | 13 | 59 | 50 | 8 | 14 | 18 | 2 | 1 | 0 | 4 | 1 | 0 | 0 | 8 | 0 | 3 | 0 | 1 | 1 | .280 | .379 | .360 |
| Gavia, Jesus, Aguascalientes | 36 | 89 | 83 | 11 | 25 | 38 | 7 | 0 | 2 | 15 | 2 | 2 | 1 | 1 | 0 | 10 | 0 | 0 | 5 | .301 | .310 | .458 |
| Gil, Benji, Tijuana | 33 | 141 | 126 | 26 | 35 | 50 | 9 | 0 | 2 | 21 | 1 | 1 | 0 | 13 | 0 | 29 | 10 | 0 | 2 | .278 | .343 | .397 |
| Gomez, Heber, Monterrey | 67 | 274 | 224 | 34 | 67 | 83 | 8 | 1 | 2 | 29 | 2 | 3 | 7 | 38 | 2 | 28 | 4 | 6 | 5 | .299 | .412 | .371 |
| Gonzalez, Fernando, San Luis Potosi | 36 | 90 | 83 | 7 | 23 | 32 | 3 | 0 | 2 | 11 | 1 | 0 | 1 | 5 | 0 | 11 | 1 | 3 | 2 | .277 | .326 | .386 |
| Gonzalez, Israel, Campeche | 56 | 124 | 105 | 9 | 30 | 33 | 3 | 0 | 0 | 11 | 1 | 2 | 2 | 14 | 1 | 14 | 0 | 0 | 3 | .286 | .374 | .314 |
| Gonzalez, Roman, Vaqueros | 54 | 75 | 63 | 13 | 14 | 17 | 3 | 0 | 0 | 4 | 0 | 0 | 2 | 10 | 1 | 10 | 2 | 3 | 1 | .222 | .347 | .270 |
| Gonzalez, Santiago, Veracruz | 78 | 230 | 215 | 30 | 65 | 90 | 10 | 3 | 3 | 15 | 1 | 2 | 3 | 9 | 1 | 38 | 6 | 5 | 3 | .302 | .336 | .419 |
| Grijak, Kevin, Vaqueros * | 29 | 114 | 98 | 13 | 30 | 44 | 5 | 0 | 3 | 20 | 0 | 2 | 0 | 14 | 1 | 14 | 2 | 0 | 5 | .306 | .386 | .449 |
| Grijak, Kevin, Campeche * | 14 | 54 | 45 | 2 | 12 | 12 | 0 | 0 | 0 | 2 | 0 | 2 | 1 | 6 | 0 | 5 | 1 | 0 | 0 | .267 | .352 | .267 |
| Guerrero, Sergio, Campeche | 94 | 363 | 309 | 37 | 82 | 110 | 18 | 2 | 2 | 26 | 5 | 4 | 11 | 34 | 1 | 18 | 1 | 1 | 15 | .265 | .355 | .356 |
| Guizar, Hector, Aguascalientes | 93 | 378 | 341 | 36 | 104 | 129 | 16 | 3 | 1 | 37 | 7 | 6 | 0 | 24 | 1 | 27 | 4 | 4 | 13 | .305 | .345 | .378 |
| Gutierrez, Said, Yucatan | 69 | 211 | 186 | 25 | 41 | 56 | 6 | 0 | 3 | 17 | 4 | 1 | 2 | 18 | 2 | 34 | 1 | 2 | 7 | .220 | .295 | .301 |
| Hadad, Jorge, Tijuana | 12 | 16 | 13 | 0 | 0 | 0 | 0 | 0 | 0 | 0 | 0 | 0 | 0 | 3 | 0 | 3 | 0 | 0 | 1 | .000 | .188 | .000 |
| Hernandez, Jose, Veracruz * | 32 | 3 | 3 | 0 | 0 | 0 | 0 | 0 | 0 | 0 | 0 | 0 | 0 | 0 | 0 | 0 | 0 | 0 | 0 | .000 | .000 | .000 |
| Hernandez, Julio, Tijuana | 95 | 418 | 337 | 79 | 109 | 154 | 25 | 1 | 6 | 34 | 6 | 1 | 13 | 61 | 0 | 26 | 4 | 9 | 7 | .323 | .444 | .457 |
| Hernandez, Kiki, Yucatan | 5 | 5 | 5 | 1 | 2 | 2 | 0 | 0 | 0 | 0 | 0 | 0 | 0 | 0 | 0 | 0 | 0 | 0 | 0 | .400 | .400 | .400 |
| Hernandez, Vladimir, Cancun | 21 | 81 | 73 | 5 | 17 | 20 | 3 | 0 | 0 | 10 | 3 | 2 | 2 | 1 | 1 | 7 | 0 | 0 | 0 | .233 | .256 | .274 |

| Player, Team | G | TPA | AB | R | H | TB | 2B | 3B | HR | RBI | SH | SF | HP | BB | IBB | SO | SB | CS | GDP | Avg. | OBP | Slg. |
|---|---|---|---|---|---|---|---|---|---|---|---|---|---|---|---|---|---|---|---|---|---|---|
| Herrera, Jose, Yucatan * | 26 | 100 | 90 | 3 | 20 | 25 | 5 | 0 | 0 | 10 | 5 | 2 | 0 | 3 | 0 | 9 | 2 | 0 | 2 | .222 | .242 | .278 |
| Higuera, Ottoniel, Oaxaca | 5 | 4 | 3 | 1 | 0 | 0 | 0 | 0 | 0 | 0 | 0 | 0 | 1 | 0 | 0 | 0 | 0 | 0 | 0 | .000 | .250 | .000 |
| Hurtado, Hector, Tijuana | 63 | 174 | 160 | 19 | 37 | 51 | 8 | 0 | 2 | 26 | 1 | 0 | 4 | 9 | 1 | 26 | 2 | 1 | 7 | .231 | .289 | .319 |
| Iturbe, Pedro, Puebla * | 77 | 318 | 296 | 51 | 92 | 146 | 20 | 2 | 10 | 53 | 0 | 7 | 2 | 13 | 3 | 35 | 2 | 4 | 10 | .311 | .336 | .493 |
| Jensen, Marcus, Cancun † | 16 | 56 | 47 | 3 | 9 | 9 | 0 | 0 | 0 | 3 | 0 | 1 | 0 | 8 | 0 | 11 | 0 | 0 | 3 | .191 | .304 | .191 |
| Jimenez, Eduardo, Saltillo * | 81 | 341 | 269 | 65 | 90 | 175 | 13 | 0 | 24 | 96 | 0 | 1 | 8 | 63 | 5 | 64 | 1 | 1 | 11 | .335 | .472 | .651 |
| Johnson, Rontrez, Aguascalientes | 100 | 444 | 373 | 96 | 129 | 212 | 29 | 6 | 14 | 52 | 3 | 3 | 8 | 57 | 7 | 55 | 54 | 18 | 6 | .346 | .440 | .568 |
| Jose, Felix, Mexico † | 4 | 14 | 14 | 0 | 2 | 4 | 2 | 0 | 0 | 0 | 0 | 0 | 0 | 0 | 0 | 1 | 0 | 0 | 1 | .143 | .143 | .286 |
| Landaeta, Luis, Tijuana * | 81 | 347 | 307 | 60 | 99 | 165 | 23 | 2 | 13 | 60 | 2 | 0 | 5 | 33 | 6 | 29 | 16 | 11 | 6 | .322 | .397 | .537 |
| Landaeta, Luis, Yucatan * | 15 | 57 | 50 | 4 | 12 | 19 | 1 | 0 | 2 | 4 | 0 | 0 | 1 | 6 | 1 | 4 | 2 | 0 | 0 | .240 | .333 | .380 |
| Lara, Idelfonso, Aguascalientes | 75 | 295 | 251 | 40 | 85 | 137 | 16 | 0 | 12 | 53 | 3 | 2 | 4 | 35 | 4 | 55 | 1 | 1 | 7 | .339 | .425 | .546 |
| Lara, Idelfonso, Vaqueros | 11 | 19 | 16 | 4 | 5 | 6 | 1 | 0 | 0 | 2 | 0 | 0 | 0 | 3 | 0 | 4 | 0 | 0 | 1 | .313 | .421 | .375 |
| LeBron, Juan, Cancun | 40 | 157 | 147 | 18 | 37 | 53 | 7 | 0 | 3 | 21 | 1 | 2 | 1 | 6 | 1 | 23 | 0 | 1 | 2 | .252 | .282 | .361 |
| Leach, Jalal, Yucatan * | 33 | 115 | 99 | 10 | 33 | 42 | 3 | 0 | 2 | 16 | 2 | 4 | 0 | 10 | 1 | 14 | 2 | 5 | 2 | .333 | .381 | .424 |
| Leach, Jalal, Monclova * | 19 | 71 | 58 | 9 | 13 | 15 | 2 | 0 | 0 | 6 | 1 | 0 | 0 | 12 | 0 | 12 | 1 | 0 | 0 | .224 | .357 | .259 |
| Leyva, Octavio, Tabasco * | 4 | 1 | 1 | 0 | 0 | 0 | 0 | 0 | 0 | 0 | 0 | 0 | 0 | 0 | 0 | 0 | 0 | 0 | 0 | .000 | .000 | .000 |
| Lizarraga, Norberto, Vaqueros | 7 | 12 | 11 | 2 | 2 | 2 | 0 | 0 | 0 | 0 | 0 | 0 | 0 | 1 | 0 | 7 | 0 | 0 | 1 | .182 | .250 | .182 |
| Lopez, Fausto, Tabasco | 61 | 173 | 152 | 19 | 35 | 37 | 2 | 0 | 0 | 6 | 4 | 0 | 1 | 16 | 0 | 28 | 9 | 4 | 4 | .230 | .308 | .243 |
| Lopez, Jose, San Luis Potosi | 27 | 32 | 26 | 4 | 5 | 9 | 1 | 0 | 1 | 3 | 1 | 0 | 2 | 3 | 0 | 12 | 1 | 0 | 0 | .192 | .323 | .346 |
| Lopez, Jose M., San Luis Potosi * | 64 | 178 | 159 | 18 | 46 | 55 | 3 | 3 | 0 | 16 | 5 | 1 | 2 | 11 | 0 | 25 | 4 | 2 | 6 | .289 | .341 | .346 |
| Lopez, Raul, Monclova * | 91 | 349 | 305 | 38 | 97 | 129 | 13 | 2 | 5 | 36 | 2 | 5 | 1 | 36 | 3 | 48 | 2 | 5 | 5 | .318 | .386 | .423 |
| Lucca, Lou, Cancun | 83 | 316 | 281 | 42 | 90 | 137 | 15 | 1 | 10 | 40 | 1 | 1 | 8 | 25 | 3 | 49 | 2 | 3 | 15 | .320 | .390 | .488 |
| Lugo, Roberto, Monterrey | 32 | 56 | 51 | 9 | 15 | 19 | 1 | 0 | 1 | 8 | 3 | 1 | 1 | 0 | 0 | 7 | 0 | 0 | 0 | .294 | .302 | .373 |
| Magallanes, Ever, Oaxaca * | 66 | 254 | 212 | 34 | 67 | 87 | 11 | 0 | 3 | 26 | 4 | 0 | 2 | 36 | 3 | 24 | 0 | 1 | 5 | .316 | .420 | .410 |
| Marrero, Oreste, Veracruz * | 18 | 76 | 63 | 8 | 15 | 30 | 1 | 1 | 4 | 12 | 0 | 1 | 0 | 12 | 0 | 10 | 0 | 0 | 2 | .238 | .355 | .476 |
| Marrero, Oreste, Oaxaca * | 20 | 82 | 73 | 9 | 17 | 30 | 4 | 0 | 3 | 16 | 0 | 1 | 0 | 8 | 1 | 9 | 0 | 0 | 3 | .233 | .305 | .411 |
| Martinez, Abel, Vaqueros | 80 | 272 | 246 | 47 | 81 | 120 | 10 | 1 | 9 | 45 | 2 | 3 | 5 | 14 | 0 | 33 | 4 | 5 | 5 | .329 | .373 | .488 |
| Martinez, Enrique, San Luis Potosi | 54 | 236 | 206 | 34 | 71 | 108 | 14 | 1 | 7 | 17 | 2 | 0 | 2 | 26 | 1 | 25 | 2 | 1 | 3 | .345 | .423 | .524 |
| Martinez, Gabby, Cancun | 15 | 58 | 53 | 5 | 10 | 10 | 0 | 0 | 0 | 4 | 2 | 0 | 1 | 2 | 0 | 3 | 1 | 1 | 1 | .189 | .232 | .189 |
| Martinez, Greg, Oaxaca † | 82 | 365 | 311 | 56 | 109 | 134 | 15 | 5 | 0 | 27 | 5 | 2 | 6 | 41 | 4 | 36 | 7 | 6 | 4 | .350 | .433 | .431 |
| Martinez, Grimaldo, Vaqueros | 72 | 289 | 251 | 36 | 67 | 81 | 8 | 0 | 2 | 19 | 1 | 1 | 3 | 33 | 0 | 26 | 1 | 1 | 6 | .267 | .358 | .323 |
| Martinez, Luis, Puebla | 79 | 291 | 269 | 43 | 97 | 126 | 17 | 0 | 4 | 31 | 5 | 3 | 0 | 14 | 0 | 28 | 1 | 7 | 4 | .361 | .388 | .468 |
| Martinez, Manny, Tigres | 87 | 371 | 337 | 64 | 118 | 180 | 23 | 3 | 11 | 45 | 0 | 2 | 5 | 27 | 0 | 52 | 13 | 1 | 2 | .350 | .404 | .534 |
| Martinez, Ray, Mexico | 87 | 334 | 284 | 43 | 79 | 121 | 11 | 2 | 9 | 53 | 2 | 1 | 7 | 40 | 1 | 53 | 0 | 2 | 15 | .278 | .380 | .426 |
| Mata, Noe, Aguascalientes | 77 | 255 | 230 | 38 | 66 | 105 | 11 | 2 | 8 | 37 | 7 | 2 | 2 | 14 | 0 | 55 | 8 | 2 | 5 | .287 | .331 | .457 |
| McDonald, Donzell, Tabasco † | 64 | 280 | 232 | 50 | 79 | 116 | 14 | 4 | 5 | 24 | 3 | 3 | 1 | 41 | 1 | 46 | 28 | 6 | 1 | .341 | .437 | .500 |
| Medina, Jose, Monclova | 56 | 131 | 103 | 20 | 30 | 44 | 7 | 2 | 1 | 17 | 4 | 0 | 3 | 21 | 2 | 17 | 3 | 5 | 3 | .291 | .425 | .427 |
| Mejia, Roberto, Campeche | 39 | 165 | 138 | 25 | 44 | 71 | 15 | 0 | 4 | 22 | 2 | 3 | 5 | 17 | 1 | 21 | 2 | 7 | 6 | .319 | .405 | .514 |
| Melo, Juan, Veracruz † | 92 | 371 | 318 | 55 | 96 | 160 | 21 | 2 | 13 | 61 | 0 | 1 | 3 | 49 | 10 | 46 | 10 | 1 | 13 | .302 | .399 | .503 |
| Mendez, Francisco, Monterrey * | 66 | 105 | 90 | 17 | 18 | 28 | 4 | 0 | 2 | 11 | 1 | 1 | 0 | 13 | 2 | 19 | 1 | 0 | 2 | .200 | .298 | .311 |
| Mendez, Roberto, Oaxaca * | 59 | 221 | 171 | 37 | 42 | 79 | 10 | 0 | 9 | 41 | 0 | 3 | 2 | 45 | 7 | 31 | 0 | 1 | 3 | .246 | .403 | .462 |
| Mendoza, Omar, San Luis Potosi | 78 | 302 | 270 | 44 | 74 | 112 | 15 | 1 | 7 | 32 | 8 | 2 | 1 | 21 | 2 | 37 | 3 | 1 | 7 | .274 | .327 | .415 |
| Mere, Pedro, Aguascalientes | 91 | 387 | 320 | 60 | 102 | 149 | 22 | 2 | 7 | 68 | 5 | 8 | 5 | 49 | 3 | 41 | 5 | 5 | 8 | .319 | .408 | .466 |
| Meyers, Chad, Mexico | 97 | 427 | 359 | 92 | 122 | 187 | 21 | 10 | 8 | 61 | 5 | 2 | 9 | 51 | 1 | 43 | 32 | 6 | 7 | .340 | .432 | .521 |
| Meza, Alfredo, Monterrey † | 86 | 276 | 249 | 23 | 47 | 60 | 7 | 0 | 2 | 27 | 18 | 0 | 1 | 8 | 0 | 28 | 0 | 0 | 7 | .189 | .217 | .241 |
| Meza, Gonzalo, Vaqueros * | 80 | 291 | 255 | 41 | 67 | 84 | 5 | 3 | 2 | 22 | 3 | 1 | 2 | 30 | 2 | 45 | 2 | 4 | 5 | .263 | .344 | .329 |
| Miller, Orlando, Aguascalientes | 33 | 133 | 121 | 20 | 38 | 56 | 9 | 0 | 3 | 17 | 1 | 1 | 1 | 9 | 0 | 13 | 3 | 1 | 2 | .314 | .364 | .463 |
| Miller, Orlando, Cancun | 2 | 5 | 5 | 1 | 1 | 2 | 1 | 0 | 0 | 0 | 0 | 0 | 0 | 0 | 0 | 0 | 0 | 0 | 1 | .200 | .200 | .400 |
| Montano, Angel, Tijuana * | 9 | 17 | 14 | 0 | 2 | 2 | 0 | 0 | 0 | 0 | 0 | 0 | 0 | 3 | 0 | 5 | 0 | 0 | 0 | .143 | .294 | .143 |
| Montenegro, Jose, Oaxaca | 52 | 179 | 155 | 18 | 41 | 64 | 11 | 0 | 4 | 23 | 5 | 0 | 0 | 19 | 2 | 31 | 0 | 0 | 4 | .265 | .345 | .413 |
| Montoya, Noel, Saltillo | 7 | 8 | 8 | 3 | 2 | 3 | 1 | 0 | 0 | 1 | 0 | 0 | 0 | 0 | 0 | 5 | 0 | 0 | 0 | .250 | .250 | .375 |
| Morales, Carlos, Yucatan | 1 | 3 | 3 | 0 | 1 | 2 | 1 | 0 | 0 | 0 | 0 | 0 | 0 | 0 | 0 | 0 | 0 | 0 | 0 | .333 | .333 | .667 |
| Morejon, Oswaldo, Yucatan | 95 | 398 | 355 | 61 | 106 | 151 | 18 | 3 | 7 | 48 | 3 | 3 | 2 | 35 | 1 | 36 | 4 | 3 | 15 | .299 | .362 | .425 |
| Mormolejo, Ivan, Cancun | 24 | 45 | 37 | 4 | 10 | 13 | 3 | 0 | 0 | 3 | 0 | 0 | 2 | 6 | 0 | 8 | 0 | 0 | 1 | .270 | .400 | .351 |
| Munoz, Adan, Tigres * | 70 | 246 | 220 | 33 | 68 | 121 | 17 | 0 | 12 | 48 | 4 | 2 | 4 | 16 | 1 | 25 | 1 | 3 | 9 | .309 | .364 | .550 |
| Munoz, Jose, Monclova * | 79 | 300 | 236 | 42 | 64 | 83 | 8 | 1 | 3 | 30 | 2 | 2 | 1 | 59 | 3 | 38 | 5 | 10 | 1 | .271 | .416 | .352 |
| Munoz, Noe, Saltillo | 85 | 342 | 279 | 56 | 109 | 145 | 18 | 0 | 6 | 57 | 3 | 5 | 2 | 53 | 3 | 27 | 0 | 0 | 10 | .391 | .484 | .520 |
| O'Sullivan, Patrick, San Luis Potosi | 96 | 381 | 334 | 55 | 103 | 199 | 27 | 0 | 23 | 62 | 0 | 1 | 5 | 41 | 2 | 73 | 5 | 2 | 2 | .308 | .391 | .596 |
| Ochoa, Edgar, Veracruz | 4 | 7 | 7 | 0 | 0 | 0 | 0 | 0 | 0 | 0 | 0 | 0 | 0 | 0 | 0 | 5 | 0 | 0 | 0 | .000 | .000 | .000 |
| Orantes, Ramon, Monterrey | 82 | 309 | 252 | 38 | 82 | 104 | 10 | 0 | 4 | 40 | 3 | 2 | 6 | 46 | 2 | 25 | 3 | 5 | 12 | .325 | .438 | .413 |
| Orrantia, Carlos, Monterrey | 57 | 112 | 96 | 12 | 23 | 30 | 5 | 1 | 0 | 8 | 4 | 1 | 1 | 10 | 0 | 13 | 1 | 5 | 3 | .240 | .315 | .313 |
| Ortiz, Alex, Tijuana | 29 | 71 | 61 | 4 | 11 | 12 | 1 | 0 | 0 | 4 | 1 | 0 | 0 | 9 | 0 | 9 | 0 | 2 | 1 | .180 | .286 | .197 |
| Otanez, Willis, Campeche | 34 | 148 | 134 | 23 | 52 | 88 | 12 | 0 | 8 | 27 | 0 | 1 | 1 | 12 | 1 | 17 | 1 | 0 | 4 | .388 | .439 | .657 |
| Pacho, Carlos, Vaqueros | 51 | 157 | 146 | 21 | 44 | 58 | 9 | 1 | 1 | 22 | 2 | 0 | 1 | 8 | 1 | 20 | 0 | 1 | 8 | .301 | .342 | .397 |
| Paez, Hector, Campeche * | 25 | 74 | 72 | 9 | 19 | 33 | 2 | 0 | 4 | 10 | 0 | 1 | 0 | 1 | 0 | 7 | 0 | 0 | 1 | .264 | .270 | .458 |
| Paez, Hector, Yucatan * | 25 | 71 | 66 | 4 | 18 | 26 | 5 | 0 | 1 | 7 | 1 | 1 | 0 | 3 | 1 | 8 | 0 | 0 | 1 | .273 | .300 | .394 |
| Paez, Raul, Tijuana * | 47 | 90 | 79 | 7 | 21 | 29 | 2 | 0 | 2 | 11 | 3 | 1 | 1 | 6 | 1 | 8 | 0 | 0 | 3 | .266 | .322 | .367 |
| Palafox, Sergio, Monclova | 79 | 271 | 249 | 41 | 73 | 106 | 12 | 0 | 7 | 38 | 1 | 4 | 1 | 16 | 1 | 27 | 4 | 3 | 8 | .293 | .333 | .426 |
| Pemberton, Rudy, Monclova | 85 | 342 | 298 | 42 | 96 | 146 | 12 | 1 | 12 | 53 | 0 | 7 | 6 | 31 | 4 | 40 | 8 | 0 | 8 | .322 | .389 | .490 |
| Perez, Alfredo, Cancun | 44 | 99 | 84 | 10 | 17 | 22 | 2 | 0 | 1 | 6 | 3 | 0 | 4 | 8 | 0 | 11 | 1 | 0 | 2 | .202 | .302 | .262 |
| Perez, Francisco, San Luis Potosi * | 52 | 124 | 110 | 11 | 24 | 32 | 5 | 0 | 1 | 9 | 0 | 1 | 1 | 12 | 2 | 32 | 1 | 0 | 1 | .218 | .298 | .291 |
| Perez, Jose, San Luis Potosi | 68 | 235 | 213 | 28 | 55 | 62 | 5 | 1 | 0 | 20 | 3 | 1 | 3 | 15 | 1 | 26 | 1 | 0 | 5 | .258 | .315 | .291 |
| Presichi, Cristian, Saltillo | 79 | 288 | 248 | 42 | 81 | 135 | 11 | 2 | 13 | 51 | 2 | 3 | 5 | 30 | 1 | 44 | 3 | 1 | 8 | .327 | .406 | .544 |
| Quinones, Ruben, Aguascalientes | 82 | 263 | 243 | 35 | 66 | 86 | 11 | 0 | 3 | 34 | 9 | 1 | 3 | 7 | 0 | 36 | 5 | 2 | 4 | .272 | .299 | .354 |
| Quintero, Christian, Oaxaca | 93 | 376 | 334 | 55 | 105 | 164 | 28 | 2 | 9 | 64 | 2 | 8 | 1 | 31 | 3 | 34 | 10 | 4 | 11 | .314 | .366 | .491 |
| Quintero, Edgar, Monterrey * | 70 | 187 | 165 | 33 | 62 | 100 | 12 | 1 | 8 | 28 | 2 | 0 | 1 | 19 | 2 | 30 | 5 | 7 | 3 | .376 | .443 | .606 |
| Quintero, Guillermo, San Luis Potosi | 6 | 4 | 3 | 1 | 1 | 1 | 0 | 0 | 0 | 0 | 0 | 0 | 0 | 1 | 0 | 2 | 0 | 0 | 0 | .333 | .500 | .333 |
| Ramirez, Jesus, Oaxaca | 40 | 89 | 79 | 14 | 17 | 21 | 4 | 0 | 0 | 4 | 2 | 2 | 1 | 5 | 0 | 4 | 0 | 3 | 0 | .215 | .264 | .266 |

| Player, Team | G | TPA | AB | R | H | TB | 2B | 3B | HR | RBI | SH | SF | HP | BB | IBB | SO | SB | CS | GDP | Avg. | OBP | Slg. |
|---|---|---|---|---|---|---|---|---|---|---|---|---|---|---|---|---|---|---|---|---|---|---|
| Ramirez, Omar, Veracruz | 95 | 403 | 342 | 60 | 106 | 141 | 21 | 1 | 4 | 30 | 6 | 1 | 4 | 50 | 4 | 40 | 8 | 6 | 12 | .310 | .403 | .412 |
| Ramirez, Oscar, Campeche | 88 | 345 | 307 | 43 | 84 | 126 | 19 | 1 | 7 | 42 | 3 | 5 | 4 | 26 | 5 | 63 | 5 | 4 | 11 | .274 | .333 | .410 |
| Resendez, Carlos, Monclova | 63 | 180 | 155 | 15 | 35 | 51 | 7 | 0 | 3 | 15 | 7 | 1 | 7 | 10 | 0 | 43 | 0 | 0 | 4 | .226 | .301 | .329 |
| Reyes, Julio, Aguascalientes * | 13 | 37 | 29 | 4 | 4 | 5 | 1 | 0 | 0 | 1 | 1 | 0 | 1 | 6 | 1 | 4 | 0 | 0 | 0 | .138 | .306 | .172 |
| Rincon, Isaias, Campeche | 59 | 128 | 112 | 16 | 31 | 48 | 3 | 1 | 4 | 12 | 5 | 1 | 3 | 7 | 0 | 19 | 0 | 3 | 2 | .277 | .333 | .429 |
| Rios, Armando, Tijuana * | 30 | 136 | 105 | 25 | 37 | 60 | 9 | 1 | 4 | 26 | 2 | 3 | 4 | 22 | 1 | 11 | 7 | 4 | 6 | .352 | .470 | .571 |
| Rios, Eduardo, Aguascalientes | 100 | 423 | 365 | 51 | 104 | 177 | 17 | 1 | 18 | 88 | 0 | 9 | 8 | 41 | 5 | 50 | 3 | 1 | 7 | .285 | .362 | .485 |
| Rivera, Francisco, Veracruz | 84 | 285 | 245 | 23 | 54 | 75 | 12 | 0 | 3 | 32 | 2 | 2 | 0 | 36 | 5 | 35 | 2 | 0 | 8 | .220 | .318 | .306 |
| Rivera, Jesus, Tabasco * | 34 | 67 | 58 | 2 | 20 | 23 | 3 | 0 | 0 | 10 | 0 | 3 | 1 | 5 | 0 | 6 | 0 | 0 | 0 | .345 | .388 | .397 |
| Rivera, Ruben, Campeche | 90 | 371 | 314 | 68 | 99 | 158 | 21 | 4 | 10 | 60 | 0 | 4 | 5 | 48 | 5 | 49 | 10 | 0 | 4 | .315 | .410 | .503 |
| Robles, Javier, Tigres | 90 | 359 | 318 | 69 | 106 | 183 | 20 | 6 | 15 | 68 | 0 | 3 | 5 | 33 | 1 | 21 | 5 | 6 | 4 | .333 | .401 | .575 |
| Robles, Juan, Tabasco | 37 | 114 | 99 | 7 | 25 | 36 | 3 | 1 | 2 | 18 | 4 | 0 | 2 | 9 | 0 | 17 | 1 | 3 | 2 | .253 | .327 | .364 |
| Robles, Oscar, Mexico * | 97 | 407 | 335 | 72 | 128 | 185 | 23 | 5 | 8 | 64 | 5 | 5 | 0 | 62 | 8 | 11 | 8 | 6 | 8 | .382 | .473 | .552 |
| Robles, Trinidad, Tigres | 62 | 184 | 161 | 20 | 37 | 62 | 4 | 0 | 7 | 24 | 1 | 3 | 2 | 17 | 0 | 24 | 1 | 0 | 3 | .230 | .306 | .385 |
| Rodarte, Raul, San Luis Potosi | 65 | 261 | 233 | 33 | 73 | 126 | 9 | 1 | 14 | 47 | 0 | 1 | 2 | 25 | 2 | 23 | 8 | 1 | 7 | .313 | .383 | .541 |
| Rodarte, Raul, Tabasco | 28 | 111 | 103 | 3 | 24 | 33 | 6 | 0 | 1 | 12 | 0 | 1 | 0 | 7 | 1 | 15 | 2 | 2 | 6 | .233 | .279 | .320 |
| Rodriguez, Armando, Monclova | 42 | 111 | 95 | 8 | 21 | 28 | 4 | 0 | 1 | 12 | 2 | 0 | 3 | 11 | 0 | 20 | 0 | 2 | 0 | .221 | .321 | .295 |
| Rodriguez, Boi, Campeche * | 30 | 114 | 86 | 7 | 22 | 30 | 6 | 1 | 0 | 9 | 1 | 1 | 0 | 26 | 6 | 19 | 1 | 5 | 2 | .256 | .425 | .349 |
| Rodriguez, Boi, Vaqueros * | 66 | 263 | 220 | 54 | 78 | 147 | 16 | 1 | 17 | 53 | 0 | 3 | 1 | 39 | 1 | 45 | 5 | 0 | 3 | .355 | .449 | .668 |
| Rodriguez, Carlos, San Luis Potosi | 65 | 217 | 193 | 22 | 47 | 73 | 11 | 3 | 3 | 20 | 0 | 0 | 1 | 23 | 0 | 59 | 0 | 0 | 6 | .244 | .327 | .378 |
| Rodriguez, Erick, Oaxaca | 59 | 194 | 173 | 16 | 53 | 68 | 10 | 1 | 1 | 32 | 4 | 4 | 0 | 13 | 1 | 11 | 0 | 0 | 11 | .306 | .347 | .393 |
| Rodriguez, Fernando, Vaqueros | 79 | 313 | 287 | 41 | 95 | 127 | 11 | 0 | 7 | 55 | 2 | 1 | 1 | 22 | 1 | 31 | 0 | 2 | 9 | .331 | .379 | .443 |
| Rodriguez, Jesus, Monclova | 22 | 1 | 1 | 0 | 0 | 0 | 0 | 0 | 0 | 0 | 0 | 0 | 0 | 0 | 0 | 1 | 0 | 0 | 0 | .000 | .000 | .000 |
| Rodriguez, Leonardo, Monterrey | 16 | 27 | 25 | 3 | 5 | 6 | 1 | 0 | 0 | 4 | 0 | 0 | 0 | 2 | 0 | 2 | 0 | 0 | 1 | .200 | .259 | .240 |
| Rodriguez, Liu, Tijuana † | 15 | 65 | 52 | 4 | 18 | 24 | 6 | 0 | 0 | 2 | 4 | 0 | 3 | 6 | 0 | 5 | 1 | 3 | 2 | .346 | .443 | .462 |
| Rodriguez, Serafin, Yucatan | 20 | 73 | 63 | 9 | 17 | 22 | 3 | 1 | 0 | 3 | 2 | 0 | 2 | 6 | 1 | 5 | 0 | 0 | 0 | .270 | .352 | .349 |
| Rodriguez, Serafin, Tigres | 14 | 24 | 23 | 5 | 5 | 9 | 1 | 0 | 1 | 3 | 0 | 1 | 0 | 0 | 0 | 1 | 0 | 0 | 0 | .217 | .208 | .391 |
| Rodriguez, Serafin, Monclova | 19 | 65 | 63 | 3 | 19 | 23 | 4 | 0 | 0 | 10 | 0 | 0 | 2 | 0 | 0 | 4 | 0 | 1 | 1 | .302 | .323 | .365 |
| Rojas, Homar, Oaxaca | 81 | 303 | 267 | 28 | 80 | 106 | 17 | 0 | 3 | 49 | 5 | 7 | 4 | 20 | 0 | 19 | 0 | 0 | 5 | .300 | .349 | .397 |
| Romero, Armando, Cancun † | 11 | 39 | 33 | 3 | 4 | 6 | 2 | 0 | 0 | 0 | 0 | 0 | 2 | 4 | 0 | 6 | 0 | 0 | 2 | .121 | .256 | .182 |
| Romero, Flavio, Saltillo * | 81 | 258 | 216 | 40 | 57 | 71 | 9 | 1 | 1 | 20 | 7 | 0 | 6 | 29 | 1 | 31 | 9 | 5 | 3 | .264 | .367 | .329 |
| Romero, Marco, Tijuana | 56 | 143 | 117 | 7 | 27 | 33 | 6 | 0 | 0 | 15 | 1 | 1 | 0 | 24 | 1 | 24 | 0 | 0 | 5 | .231 | .359 | .282 |
| Romero, Willie, Monclova | 95 | 389 | 326 | 53 | 106 | 147 | 21 | 1 | 6 | 39 | 2 | 5 | 3 | 53 | 6 | 45 | 21 | 5 | 7 | .325 | .419 | .451 |
| Rosas, Ezequiel, Oaxaca | 25 | 28 | 24 | 10 | 8 | 9 | 1 | 0 | 0 | 2 | 0 | 0 | 1 | 3 | 0 | 2 | 0 | 0 | 0 | .333 | .429 | .375 |
| Rose, Pete, Aguascalientes * | 54 | 207 | 177 | 16 | 47 | 61 | 8 | 0 | 2 | 23 | 0 | 2 | 3 | 25 | 4 | 26 | 0 | 1 | 7 | .266 | .362 | .345 |
| Ruiz, Juan, Monclova | 73 | 258 | 233 | 27 | 69 | 89 | 8 | 0 | 4 | 28 | 7 | 3 | 2 | 13 | 0 | 34 | 0 | 0 | 6 | .296 | .335 | .382 |
| Ruiz, Ricardo, Mexico | 23 | 11 | 10 | 4 | 1 | 1 | 0 | 0 | 0 | 0 | 1 | 0 | 0 | 0 | 0 | 1 | 0 | 0 | 0 | .100 | .100 | .100 |
| Saenz, Ricardo, Saltillo | 61 | 231 | 198 | 28 | 59 | 90 | 10 | 0 | 7 | 43 | 0 | 3 | 4 | 26 | 2 | 37 | 0 | 1 | 6 | .298 | .385 | .455 |
| Salas, Heriberto, Vaqueros | 92 | 324 | 282 | 42 | 66 | 89 | 10 | 2 | 3 | 35 | 4 | 3 | 3 | 32 | 0 | 26 | 2 | 0 | 6 | .234 | .316 | .316 |
| Salazar, Carlos, Aguascalientes | 38 | 51 | 39 | 14 | 14 | 15 | 1 | 0 | 0 | 5 | 2 | 1 | 3 | 6 | 0 | 5 | 1 | 0 | 0 | .359 | .469 | .385 |
| Salcedo, Eder, San Luis Potosi | 69 | 245 | 221 | 26 | 52 | 73 | 7 | 1 | 4 | 23 | 5 | 3 | 0 | 16 | 0 | 29 | 3 | 2 | 0 | .235 | .283 | .330 |
| Sanchez, Alejandro, Cancun | 37 | 11 | 8 | 1 | 1 | 1 | 0 | 0 | 0 | 0 | 1 | 0 | 1 | 1 | 0 | 3 | 0 | 1 | 0 | .125 | .300 | .125 |
| Sanchez, Jose, Tijuana | 59 | 63 | 57 | 11 | 7 | 10 | 0 | 0 | 1 | 2 | 1 | 0 | 0 | 5 | 0 | 13 | 4 | 2 | 2 | .123 | .194 | .175 |
| Sanchez, Orlando, San Luis Potosi | 16 | 27 | 25 | 4 | 6 | 12 | 1 | 1 | 1 | 3 | 0 | 0 | 0 | 2 | 0 | 5 | 0 | 0 | 1 | .240 | .296 | .480 |
| Sanchez, Raul, Cancun | 97 | 367 | 322 | 45 | 92 | 145 | 15 | 7 | 8 | 50 | 2 | 4 | 5 | 34 | 5 | 46 | 3 | 3 | 6 | .286 | .359 | .450 |
| Sanchez, Roque, Campeche | 71 | 192 | 178 | 16 | 53 | 75 | 14 | 1 | 2 | 24 | 1 | 0 | 3 | 10 | 3 | 15 | 0 | 1 | 9 | .298 | .346 | .421 |
| Sandoval, Jose, Mexico | 95 | 356 | 320 | 43 | 77 | 124 | 20 | 0 | 9 | 49 | 3 | 4 | 3 | 26 | 4 | 43 | 1 | 3 | 11 | .241 | .300 | .388 |
| Sandoval, Octavio, Tigres | 62 | 108 | 98 | 19 | 32 | 52 | 3 | 1 | 5 | 16 | 0 | 2 | 3 | 5 | 0 | 22 | 1 | 2 | 0 | .327 | .370 | .531 |
| Santana, Mario, Tabasco | 65 | 222 | 188 | 15 | 45 | 56 | 11 | 0 | 0 | 17 | 5 | 1 | 3 | 25 | 0 | 23 | 0 | 0 | 8 | .239 | .336 | .298 |
| Santana, Pedro, Oaxaca | 97 | 427 | 384 | 77 | 120 | 191 | 29 | 6 | 10 | 54 | 3 | 4 | 9 | 27 | 4 | 60 | 12 | 2 | 8 | .313 | .368 | .497 |
| Saucedo, Robert, Mexico | 99 | 420 | 353 | 69 | 108 | 190 | 22 | 0 | 20 | 97 | 0 | 10 | 4 | 51 | 4 | 43 | 7 | 1 | 12 | .306 | .390 | .538 |
| Sherman, Darrell, Puebla * | 87 | 383 | 307 | 74 | 106 | 133 | 9 | 6 | 2 | 41 | 5 | 6 | 9 | 56 | 2 | 35 | 7 | 4 | 5 | .345 | .452 | .433 |
| Sievers, Carlos, Tabasco * | 88 | 344 | 285 | 47 | 82 | 125 | 20 | 1 | 7 | 48 | 1 | 4 | 4 | 50 | 3 | 27 | 7 | 6 | 13 | .288 | .397 | .439 |
| Smith, Bubba, Monterrey | 95 | 405 | 332 | 58 | 108 | 184 | 25 | 0 | 17 | 77 | 0 | 8 | 3 | 62 | 2 | 44 | 1 | 1 | 8 | .325 | .427 | .554 |
| Smith, Demond, Monterrey † | 78 | 349 | 298 | 82 | 121 | 195 | 19 | 5 | 15 | 52 | 4 | 4 | 7 | 36 | 3 | 44 | 30 | 18 | 1 | .406 | .475 | .654 |
| Soriano, Ricardo, Aguascalientes * | 88 | 303 | 258 | 48 | 75 | 103 | 12 | 2 | 4 | 28 | 4 | 0 | 8 | 33 | 2 | 34 | 3 | 2 | 3 | .291 | .388 | .399 |
| Soto, Emison, Cancun | 8 | 22 | 19 | 3 | 7 | 10 | 0 | 0 | 1 | 2 | 0 | 0 | 1 | 2 | 0 | 3 | 0 | 0 | 1 | .368 | .455 | .526 |
| Soto, Saul, Mexico | 84 | 294 | 268 | 31 | 80 | 124 | 14 | 0 | 10 | 46 | 1 | 1 | 1 | 23 | 2 | 21 | 4 | 1 | 9 | .299 | .355 | .463 |
| Sotomayor, Gilberto, Saltillo * | 65 | 100 | 92 | 16 | 19 | 21 | 0 | 1 | 0 | 4 | 1 | 0 | 1 | 6 | 0 | 12 | 2 | 0 | 1 | .207 | .263 | .228 |
| Suarez, Luis, Tigres * | 65 | 212 | 192 | 30 | 57 | 92 | 10 | 2 | 7 | 22 | 1 | 0 | 0 | 19 | 4 | 25 | 0 | 2 | 4 | .297 | .360 | .479 |
| Tapia, Cesar, Puebla | 5 | 9 | 6 | 3 | 2 | 4 | 0 | 1 | 0 | 1 | 0 | 0 | 0 | 3 | 0 | 1 | 0 | 0 | 0 | .333 | .556 | .667 |
| Tellez, Alonso, Vaqueros | 9 | 20 | 17 | 0 | 1 | 1 | 0 | 0 | 0 | 2 | 0 | 0 | 0 | 3 | 0 | 3 | 0 | 0 | 2 | .059 | .200 | .059 |
| Tellez, Alonso, Aguascalientes | 20 | 75 | 63 | 4 | 13 | 16 | 3 | 0 | 0 | 4 | 0 | 0 | 0 | 12 | 0 | 13 | 0 | 0 | 4 | .206 | .333 | .254 |
| Tellez, Alonso, Monclova | 20 | 58 | 50 | 4 | 9 | 15 | 3 | 0 | 1 | 5 | 0 | 1 | 0 | 7 | 0 | 16 | 1 | 0 | 1 | .180 | .276 | .300 |
| Thomas, Juan, Yucatan | 34 | 136 | 123 | 20 | 37 | 63 | 11 | 0 | 5 | 22 | 0 | 1 | 2 | 10 | 2 | 17 | 0 | 1 | 6 | .301 | .360 | .512 |
| Trapaga, Julio, Puebla | 43 | 106 | 93 | 9 | 24 | 35 | 8 | 0 | 1 | 16 | 0 | 0 | 1 | 12 | 1 | 27 | 0 | 0 | 2 | .258 | .349 | .376 |
| Trejo, Jaime, Monclova | 55 | 127 | 111 | 16 | 30 | 43 | 5 | 1 | 2 | 16 | 4 | 1 | 4 | 7 | 1 | 28 | 2 | 0 | 1 | .270 | .333 | .387 |
| Valdez, Balthazar, Veracruz | 10 | 14 | 14 | 0 | 3 | 3 | 0 | 0 | 0 | 3 | 0 | 0 | 0 | 0 | 0 | 5 | 0 | 0 | 0 | .214 | .214 | .214 |
| Valdez, Emmanuel, Campeche | 27 | 94 | 77 | 18 | 21 | 35 | 5 | 0 | 3 | 14 | 0 | 0 | 0 | 17 | 0 | 25 | 0 | 0 | 0 | .273 | .404 | .455 |
| Valdez, Emmanuel, Tigres | 25 | 74 | 64 | 12 | 21 | 39 | 3 | 0 | 5 | 12 | 0 | 0 | 2 | 8 | 0 | 18 | 0 | 1 | 1 | .328 | .419 | .609 |
| Valdez, Francisco, Cancun | 42 | 143 | 129 | 13 | 32 | 45 | 7 | 0 | 2 | 17 | 1 | 0 | 4 | 9 | 1 | 13 | 2 | 2 | 7 | .248 | .317 | .349 |
| Valdez, Francisco, Mexico | 16 | 38 | 34 | 4 | 11 | 14 | 3 | 0 | 0 | 5 | 1 | 0 | 2 | 1 | 0 | 9 | 0 | 0 | 1 | .324 | .378 | .412 |
| Valdez, Mario, Monterrey * | 60 | 233 | 182 | 27 | 53 | 103 | 5 | 0 | 15 | 41 | 0 | 2 | 2 | 47 | 3 | 25 | 1 | 1 | 3 | .291 | .438 | .566 |
| Valdez, Ramon, Campeche * | 84 | 348 | 295 | 46 | 81 | 91 | 10 | 0 | 0 | 14 | 5 | 4 | 2 | 42 | 2 | 26 | 7 | 6 | 5 | .275 | .364 | .308 |
| Valdez, Uriel, Cancun * | 12 | 13 | 12 | 3 | 0 | 0 | 0 | 0 | 0 | 1 | 0 | 0 | 0 | 1 | 0 | 4 | 0 | 1 | 0 | .000 | .077 | .000 |
| Valencia, Abraham, Tijuana | 93 | 356 | 310 | 46 | 93 | 132 | 15 | 0 | 8 | 60 | 2 | 5 | 14 | 25 | 2 | 40 | 6 | 9 | 12 | .300 | .373 | .426 |
| Valencia, Carlos, Tijuana | 96 | 428 | 398 | 73 | 129 | 200 | 24 | 4 | 13 | 54 | 1 | 3 | 2 | 24 | 2 | 31 | 8 | 9 | 12 | .324 | .363 | .503 |
| Valenzuela, Irving, Monclova | 74 | 210 | 186 | 23 | 51 | 64 | 6 | 2 | 1 | 20 | 6 | 2 | 1 | 15 | 1 | 28 | 4 | 2 | 3 | .274 | .328 | .344 |

| Player, Team | G | TPA | AB | R | H | TB | 2B | 3B | HR | RBI | SH | SF | HP | BB | IBB | SO | SB | CS | GDP | Avg. | OBP | Slg. |
|---|---|---|---|---|---|---|---|---|---|---|---|---|---|---|---|---|---|---|---|---|---|---|
| Valle, Cosme, Cancun | 57 | 164 | 153 | 12 | 36 | 62 | 11 | 0 | 5 | 20 | 2 | 1 | 1 | 7 | 0 | 26 | 0 | 0 | 4 | .235 | .272 | .405 |
| Valle, Jorge, Cancun | 92 | 326 | 289 | 27 | 72 | 98 | 8 | 0 | 6 | 44 | 4 | 5 | 4 | 24 | 2 | 44 | 0 | 1 | 11 | .249 | .311 | .339 |
| Vazquez, Gregorio, Tabasco | 77 | 293 | 264 | 30 | 74 | 88 | 8 | 0 | 2 | 30 | 3 | 3 | 6 | 17 | 2 | 17 | 5 | 7 | 8 | .280 | .334 | .333 |
| Vazquez, Jorge, Tigres | 85 | 313 | 289 | 43 | 95 | 170 | 8 | 2 | 21 | 61 | 0 | 2 | 5 | 17 | 0 | 62 | 0 | 3 | 8 | .329 | .374 | .588 |
| Vazquez, Ricardo, Tigres | 23 | 35 | 34 | 6 | 7 | 7 | 0 | 0 | 0 | 0 | 1 | 0 | 0 | 0 | 0 | 6 | 0 | 0 | 0 | .206 | .206 | .206 |
| Vega, Edgar, Puebla | 69 | 256 | 221 | 25 | 57 | 70 | 10 | 0 | 1 | 38 | 6 | 1 | 0 | 28 | 0 | 32 | 4 | 7 | 7 | .258 | .340 | .317 |
| Vega, Jesus, Puebla | 45 | 133 | 116 | 20 | 38 | 64 | 8 | 0 | 6 | 20 | 2 | 0 | 3 | 12 | 0 | 28 | 1 | 0 | 1 | .328 | .405 | .552 |
| Velazquez, Guillermo, Puebla * | 92 | 357 | 301 | 48 | 96 | 153 | 24 | 0 | 11 | 59 | 0 | 6 | 0 | 50 | 5 | 65 | 3 | 0 | 4 | .319 | .409 | .508 |
| Velez, Manuel, Saltillo | 29 | 111 | 93 | 14 | 31 | 44 | 5 | 1 | 2 | 15 | 3 | 2 | 2 | 11 | 1 | 10 | 0 | 1 | 3 | .333 | .407 | .473 |
| Verdugo, Vincente, Saltillo | 73 | 259 | 237 | 25 | 69 | 83 | 11 | 0 | 1 | 28 | 8 | 3 | 1 | 10 | 0 | 20 | 1 | 1 | 11 | .291 | .319 | .350 |
| Villalobos, Carlos, Puebla | 96 | 416 | 365 | 82 | 123 | 197 | 21 | 1 | 17 | 82 | 2 | 7 | 2 | 40 | 4 | 59 | 5 | 3 | 7 | .337 | .399 | .540 |
| Villarreal, Alejandro, Tijuana | 22 | 48 | 36 | 6 | 8 | 8 | 0 | 0 | 0 | 2 | 0 | 0 | 2 | 10 | 1 | 6 | 0 | 1 | 1 | .222 | .417 | .222 |
| Villegas, Felipe, Aguascalientes | 5 | 6 | 6 | 0 | 1 | 1 | 0 | 0 | 0 | 0 | 0 | 0 | 0 | 0 | 0 | 4 | 0 | 0 | 0 | .167 | .167 | .167 |
| Villegas, Fernando, Aguascalientes | 16 | 27 | 22 | 4 | 4 | 6 | 2 | 0 | 0 | 2 | 1 | 0 | 2 | 2 | 0 | 3 | 0 | 1 | 3 | .182 | .308 | .273 |
| Vizcarra, Roberto, Campeche | 70 | 296 | 249 | 29 | 63 | 84 | 12 | 0 | 3 | 35 | 7 | 2 | 8 | 30 | 1 | 23 | 2 | 3 | 6 | .253 | .349 | .337 |
| White, Derrick, Tijuana | 88 | 362 | 288 | 65 | 104 | 169 | 20 | 0 | 15 | 76 | 0 | 7 | 6 | 61 | 3 | 38 | 9 | 6 | 7 | .361 | .472 | .587 |
| Yan, Julian, Tabasco | 89 | 363 | 308 | 38 | 86 | 129 | 10 | 0 | 11 | 67 | 0 | 11 | 3 | 41 | 1 | 66 | 1 | 1 | 9 | .279 | .358 | .419 |
| Yepez, Daniel, Puebla | 4 | 4 | 3 | 1 | 0 | 0 | 0 | 0 | 0 | 0 | 0 | 0 | 0 | 1 | 0 | 2 | 0 | 0 | 0 | .000 | .250 | .000 |
| Zambrano, Roberto, San Luis Potosi | 19 | 70 | 56 | 4 | 13 | 20 | 4 | 0 | 1 | 10 | 0 | 2 | 1 | 11 | 1 | 11 | 0 | 0 | 1 | .232 | .357 | .357 |
| Zambrano, Roberto, Tijuana | 42 | 166 | 113 | 27 | 30 | 53 | 5 | 0 | 6 | 20 | 0 | 1 | 13 | 39 | 0 | 30 | 1 | 0 | 3 | .265 | .494 | .469 |
| Zazueta, Juan, Saltillo † | 73 | 235 | 202 | 32 | 68 | 84 | 8 | 1 | 2 | 34 | 2 | 5 | 2 | 24 | 0 | 16 | 0 | 4 | 6 | .337 | .403 | .416 |
| Zazueta, Mauricio, Mexico † | 41 | 86 | 76 | 13 | 18 | 20 | 2 | 0 | 0 | 7 | 4 | 0 | 0 | 6 | 2 | 7 | 2 | 0 | 3 | .237 | .293 | .263 |
| Zuniga, Tony, Puebla | 55 | 197 | 173 | 27 | 64 | 101 | 10 | 0 | 9 | 53 | 0 | 7 | 2 | 15 | 3 | 27 | 0 | 0 | 0 | .370 | .411 | .584 |

GRAND SLAMS—Jimenez, 4; Burkhart, Landaeta, Robles, Saucedo, 2 each; Alcantara, Amezcua , Andrews, Brown, Bustamante , Castaneda , Cervera, Cobos, Contreras, Diaz, Espinosa, Estrada, Fornes, Guerrero, Inglin, Mata, Melo, Munoz , Paez, Presichi, Rivera, O. Robles, T. Robles, Romero, F. Rodriguez, Saenz, Salcedo, D. Smith, Soto, Valdez, Vizcarra, White, Yan, Zambrano, 1 each.

AWARDED FIRST BASE ON CATCHER'S INTERFERENCE—A. Martinez 2 (Murray, Picardo); Meyers 2 (V. Gonzalez, E. Perez); Arredondo (Alvarado); Estrada (Rios); Gomez (E. Rodriguez); Leach (Navarro); Saucedo (Salgado); Valdez (Salgado).

# 2004 PITCHING

## TEAM

| Team | W | L | Pct. | ERA | G | CG | ShO | Sv. | IP | H | TBF | R | ER | HR | SH | SF | HB | BB | IBB | SO | WP | Bk. |
|---|---|---|---|---|---|---|---|---|---|---|---|---|---|---|---|---|---|---|---|---|---|---|
| Tabasco | 46 | 45 | .505 | 3.53 | 91 | 9 | 6 | 16 | 745.0 | 811 | 3266 | 356 | 292 | 44 | 46 | 28 | 45 | 249 | 29 | 347 | 30 | 3 |
| Campeche | 54 | 41 | .568 | 4.06 | 95 | 16 | 5 | 23 | 787.1 | 746 | 3432 | 400 | 355 | 80 | 42 | 24 | 42 | 355 | 12 | 449 | 44 | 2 |
| Monterrey | 56 | 41 | .577 | 4.21 | 97 | 7 | 10 | 24 | 799.0 | 860 | 3542 | 426 | 374 | 52 | 52 | 33 | 41 | 347 | 30 | 475 | 35 | 2 |
| Cancun | 40 | 60 | .400 | 4.36 | 100 | 9 | 3 | 23 | 800.2 | 847 | 3540 | 456 | 388 | 65 | 39 | 29 | 47 | 391 | 29 | 356 | 51 | 2 |
| Puebla | 63 | 34 | .649 | 4.42 | 97 | 6 | 5 | 26 | 796.1 | 919 | 3544 | 444 | 391 | 91 | 31 | 22 | 44 | 343 | 22 | 406 | 47 | 2 |
| Saltillo | 63 | 34 | .649 | 4.52 | 97 | 1 | 4 | 31 | 805.0 | 878 | 3614 | 465 | 404 | 62 | 40 | 31 | 40 | 378 | 24 | 526 | 54 | 3 |
| Oaxaca | 50 | 47 | .515 | 4.53 | 97 | 6 | 7 | 24 | 789.0 | 875 | 3540 | 481 | 397 | 68 | 37 | 33 | 54 | 354 | 20 | 409 | 50 | 2 |
| Yucatan | 43 | 53 | .448 | 4.59 | 96 | 4 | 5 | 21 | 782.0 | 866 | 3525 | 452 | 399 | 75 | 42 | 19 | 46 | 333 | 45 | 448 | 51 | 5 |
| Mexico | 62 | 40 | .608 | 4.96 | 102 | 9 | 9 | 28 | 825.0 | 998 | 3671 | 499 | 455 | 68 | 32 | 37 | 44 | 300 | 14 | 445 | 49 | 2 |
| Veracruz | 42 | 56 | .429 | 5.01 | 98 | 7 | 1 | 29 | 792.1 | 965 | 3559 | 504 | 441 | 73 | 33 | 43 | 59 | 266 | 25 | 395 | 33 | 3 |
| Tigres | 52 | 45 | .536 | 5.05 | 97 | 5 | 5 | 29 | 804.1 | 898 | 3622 | 512 | 451 | 73 | 39 | 34 | 38 | 397 | 23 | 444 | 47 | 2 |
| Tijuana | 49 | 48 | .505 | 5.21 | 97 | 2 | 7 | 18 | 803.1 | 908 | 3676 | 518 | 465 | 96 | 44 | 31 | 41 | 426 | 43 | 566 | 51 | 3 |
| Aguascalientes | 45 | 55 | .450 | 5.74 | 100 | 10 | 2 | 26 | 816.1 | 973 | 3715 | 568 | 521 | 96 | 36 | 30 | 58 | 378 | 14 | 426 | 50 | 4 |
| Monclova | 39 | 60 | .394 | 5.81 | 99 | 3 | 6 | 19 | 790.0 | 1040 | 3776 | 562 | 510 | 67 | 42 | 35 | 46 | 426 | 19 | 418 | 51 | 3 |
| Vaqueros | 45 | 54 | .455 | 6.03 | 99 | 5 | 3 | 19 | 786.0 | 971 | 3700 | 584 | 527 | 108 | 35 | 30 | 57 | 414 | 13 | 453 | 59 | 2 |
| San Luis Potosi | 32 | 66 | .327 | 6.07 | 98 | 5 | 5 | 18 | 796.1 | 1041 | 3769 | 598 | 537 | 93 | 46 | 43 | 48 | 376 | 18 | 483 | 52 | 2 |

## INDIVIDUAL

### TOP QUALIFIERS FOR EARNED-RUN AVERAGE TITLE

Minimum 88 innings.*Lefthanded pitcher.

| Pitcher, Team | W | L | Pct. | ERA | G | GS | CG | ShO | GF | Sv. | IP | H | TBF | R | ER | HR | SH | SF | HB | BB | IBB | SO | WP | Bk. |
|---|---|---|---|---|---|---|---|---|---|---|---|---|---|---|---|---|---|---|---|---|---|---|---|---|
| Campos, Francisco, Campeche | 12 | 2 | .857 | 1.69 | 16 | 16 | 4 | 1 | 0 | 0 | 122.2 | 88 | 479 | 31 | 23 | 9 | 3 | 1 | 5 | 26 | 1 | 99 | 2 | 0 |
| Fernandez, Osvaldo, Tabasco | 8 | 6 | .571 | 2.69 | 18 | 18 | 3 | 1 | 0 | 0 | 123.2 | 117 | 516 | 51 | 37 | 7 | 9 | 7 | 1 | 34 | 0 | 68 | 5 | 0 |
| Loya, Rigoberto, Monterrey | 9 | 3 | .750 | 2.80 | 16 | 16 | 2 | 1 | 0 | 0 | 99.2 | 86 | 407 | 33 | 31 | 1 | 7 | 6 | 1 | 37 | 0 | 37 | 5 | 0 |
| Ward, Bryan, Monclova* | 7 | 7 | .500 | 2.83 | 18 | 18 | 1 | 1 | 0 | 0 | 108.0 | 118 | 461 | 37 | 34 | 4 | 5 | 3 | 7 | 34 | 0 | 68 | 2 | 1 |
| Perez, Edgar, Cancun | 3 | 7 | .300 | 3.11 | 19 | 13 | 2 | 1 | 3 | 0 | 89.2 | 97 | 382 | 40 | 31 | 3 | 7 | 3 | 6 | 29 | 2 | 43 | 2 | 0 |
| Ortega, Pablo, Puebla | 9 | 5 | .643 | 3.17 | 17 | 17 | 3 | 1 | 0 | 0 | 119.1 | 131 | 497 | 50 | 42 | 5 | 7 | 1 | 7 | 32 | 3 | 57 | 5 | 0 |
| Valdez, Armando, Puebla | 12 | 4 | .750 | 3.29 | 19 | 18 | 1 | 0 | 0 | 0 | 106.2 | 111 | 450 | 45 | 39 | 9 | 2 | 1 | 5 | 40 | 1 | 74 | 5 | 0 |
| Ochoa, Pablo, Monterrey | 6 | 2 | .750 | 3.36 | 18 | 18 | 1 | 1 | 0 | 0 | 109.2 | 114 | 476 | 46 | 41 | 6 | 6 | 5 | 7 | 47 | 0 | 71 | 1 | 1 |
| Mora, Eleazar, Oaxaca* | 7 | 4 | .636 | 3.46 | 18 | 16 | 1 | 1 | 0 | 0 | 88.1 | 104 | 378 | 45 | 34 | 2 | 7 | 3 | 5 | 16 | 0 | 35 | 3 | 0 |
| Magee, Danny, Campeche | 7 | 6 | .538 | 3.51 | 15 | 15 | 6 | 2 | 0 | 0 | 105.0 | 90 | 463 | 51 | 41 | 5 | 8 | 2 | 4 | 61 | 2 | 72 | 10 | 1 |
| Alvarez, Azael, Puebla* | 7 | 2 | .778 | 3.65 | 16 | 16 | 1 | 0 | 0 | 0 | 88.2 | 91 | 396 | 38 | 36 | 3 | 7 | 5 | 3 | 59 | 1 | 59 | 9 | 0 |
| Rivera, Francisco, Aguascalientes | 10 | 2 | .833 | 3.75 | 21 | 18 | 3 | 0 | 1 | 0 | 115.1 | 120 | 486 | 51 | 48 | 13 | 6 | 3 | 3 | 37 | 2 | 56 | 3 | 0 |
| Moreno, Angel, Veracruz* | 7 | 6 | .538 | 3.86 | 19 | 17 | 1 | 1 | 0 | 0 | 98.0 | 108 | 413 | 45 | 42 | 4 | 3 | 2 | 5 | 26 | 4 | 40 | 4 | 0 |
| Alvarez, Octavio, Tabasco | 7 | 7 | .500 | 3.90 | 17 | 17 | 1 | 1 | 0 | 0 | 99.1 | 127 | 439 | 55 | 43 | 8 | 8 | 3 | 6 | 17 | 2 | 37 | 0 | 0 |
| Ramirez, Roberto, Mexico* | 10 | 5 | .667 | 4.07 | 19 | 19 | 2 | 1 | 0 | 0 | 112.2 | 128 | 471 | 56 | 51 | 8 | 2 | 3 | 5 | 28 | 0 | 44 | 7 | 0 |

DEPARTMENTAL LEADERS: W—Three tied with 12; L—Three tied with 10; Pct.—Campos, .857; G—Flores, 52; GS—Six tied with 19; CG—Magee, 5; ShO—Magee, Moreno, 2; GF—Baez, Tovar, 30; Sv.—Baez, S. Hernandez, 26; IP—O. Fernandez, 123.2; H—Carrasco, 147; TBF—Moreno, 516; R—Carrasco, 80; ER—Carrasco, 73; HR—Navarro, 15; SH—Magee, Quintanilla, 9; SF—Three tied with eight; HB—Pina, 13; BB—Magee, 62; IBB—A. Sanchez, 9; SO—Campos, 99; WP—L. Gonzalez, 14; BK—Navarro, 3.

# ALL PITCHERS

*Lefthanded pitcher.

| Pitcher, Team | W | L | Pct. | ERA | G | GS | CG | ShO | GF | Sv. | IP | H | TBF | R | ER | HR | SH | SF | HB | BB | IBB | SO | WP | Bk. |
|---|---|---|---|---|---|---|---|---|---|---|---|---|---|---|---|---|---|---|---|---|---|---|---|---|
| Aceves, Alfredo, Yucatan | 4 | 2 | .667 | 4.55 | 17 | 11 | 0 | 0 | 2 | 0 | 65.1 | 64 | 296 | 33 | 33 | 4 | 6 | 0 | 6 | 37 | 3 | 37 | 7 | 0 |
| Acosta, Aaron, Veracruz | 0 | 0 | .000 | 10.00 | 5 | 0 | 0 | 0 | 0 | 0 | 9.0 | 17 | 49 | 11 | 10 | 1 | 0 | 0 | 1 | 4 | 0 | 7 | 0 | 0 |
| Acosta, Aaron, Campeche | 1 | 1 | .500 | 8.10 | 5 | 1 | 0 | 0 | 0 | 0 | 10.0 | 12 | 50 | 9 | 9 | 2 | 0 | 0 | 2 | 7 | 1 | 4 | 0 | 0 |
| Acosta, Jasiel, Monclova * | 4 | 6 | .400 | 5.12 | 19 | 19 | 0 | 0 | 0 | 0 | 103.2 | 110 | 457 | 60 | 59 | 14 | 8 | 5 | 5 | 54 | 0 | 66 | 2 | 0 |
| Aguilar, Hugo, Monclova * | 2 | 2 | .500 | 6.39 | 19 | 8 | 0 | 0 | 1 | 0 | 43.2 | 50 | 208 | 34 | 31 | 4 | 2 | 0 | 1 | 33 | 2 | 22 | 4 | 0 |
| Aguilar, Mario, Campeche * | 0 | 0 | .000 | 12.86 | 14 | 0 | 0 | 0 | 2 | 0 | 7.0 | 18 | 46 | 11 | 10 | 1 | 0 | 0 | 1 | 5 | 0 | 1 | 0 | 0 |
| Aguirre, Alejandro, Monclova | 0 | 3 | .000 | 9.15 | 10 | 3 | 0 | 0 | 1 | 0 | 19.2 | 30 | 103 | 22 | 20 | 5 | 2 | 5 | 2 | 16 | 1 | 14 | 1 | 0 |
| Aguirre, Gaudencio, Monterrey | 5 | 0 | 1.000 | 3.31 | 42 | 0 | 0 | 0 | 16 | 3 | 35.1 | 32 | 159 | 16 | 13 | 2 | 4 | 1 | 4 | 17 | 3 | 25 | 6 | 0 |
| Aguirre, Rodolfo, Puebla | 0 | 0 | .000 | 1.50 | 3 | 0 | 0 | 0 | 1 | 0 | 6.0 | 6 | 23 | 1 | 1 | 1 | 0 | 0 | 0 | 1 | 0 | 3 | 1 | 0 |
| Ahumada, Edgar, Monclova * | 1 | 0 | 1.000 | 5.96 | 19 | 0 | 0 | 0 | 8 | 0 | 22.2 | 35 | 115 | 16 | 15 | 0 | 0 | 0 | 3 | 16 | 0 | 6 | 4 | 0 |
| Aleman, Paulo, Campeche * | 0 | 0 | .000 | 4.50 | 2 | 0 | 0 | 0 | 1 | 0 | 2.0 | 4 | 11 | 1 | 1 | 1 | 0 | 0 | 0 | 1 | 0 | 0 | 1 | 0 |
| Alvarado, Carlos, Mexico | 0 | 0 | .000 | 8.31 | 2 | 0 | 0 | 0 | 1 | 0 | 4.1 | 6 | 22 | 4 | 4 | 1 | 1 | 0 | 1 | 2 | 0 | 3 | 1 | 0 |
| Alvarado, Carlos, Cancun | 0 | 1 | .000 | 4.15 | 4 | 4 | 0 | 0 | 0 | 0 | 17.1 | 18 | 87 | 9 | 8 | 0 | 3 | 2 | 0 | 17 | 0 | 10 | 4 | 0 |
| Alvarez, Antonio, Aguascalientes | 4 | 6 | .400 | 5.40 | 19 | 19 | 0 | 0 | 0 | 0 | 106.2 | 130 | 473 | 74 | 64 | 11 | 6 | 6 | 4 | 34 | 1 | 39 | 7 | 0 |
| Alvarez, Azael, Puebla * | 7 | 2 | .778 | 3.65 | 16 | 16 | 1 | 0 | 0 | 0 | 88.2 | 91 | 396 | 38 | 36 | 3 | 7 | 5 | 3 | 59 | 1 | 59 | 9 | 0 |
| Alvarez, Juan, Campeche | 5 | 5 | .500 | 6.81 | 18 | 15 | 1 | 0 | 0 | 0 | 72.2 | 92 | 327 | 56 | 55 | 10 | 7 | 5 | 2 | 35 | 1 | 44 | 8 | 0 |
| Alvarez, Octavio, Tabasco | 7 | 7 | .500 | 3.90 | 17 | 17 | 1 | 1 | 0 | 0 | 99.1 | 127 | 439 | 55 | 43 | 8 | 8 | 3 | 6 | 17 | 2 | 37 | 0 | 0 |
| Amarillas, Asdrubal, Vaqueros | 0 | 1 | .000 | 5.40 | 7 | 2 | 0 | 0 | 0 | 0 | 13.1 | 22 | 66 | 11 | 8 | 3 | 2 | 1 | 1 | 6 | 0 | 4 | 0 | 0 |
| Amarillas, Asdrubal, Cancun | 3 | 2 | .600 | 7.23 | 14 | 5 | 0 | 0 | 7 | 0 | 37.1 | 52 | 177 | 38 | 30 | 4 | 0 | 2 | 3 | 19 | 1 | 17 | 1 | 0 |
| Armenta, Alejandro, Tigres * | 0 | 0 | .000 | 9.00 | 2 | 2 | 0 | 0 | 0 | 0 | 5.0 | 8 | 26 | 5 | 5 | 1 | 0 | 0 | 0 | 3 | 0 | 3 | 1 | 0 |
| Avalos, Jose, Oaxaca | 4 | 1 | .800 | 3.12 | 36 | 0 | 0 | 0 | 17 | 0 | 34.2 | 39 | 168 | 16 | 12 | 0 | 1 | 1 | 5 | 21 | 4 | 18 | 7 | 0 |
| Aybar, Manny, Puebla | 2 | 2 | .500 | 4.64 | 18 | 0 | 0 | 0 | 15 | 7 | 21.1 | 25 | 95 | 12 | 11 | 5 | 0 | 0 | 1 | 5 | 2 | 21 | 6 | 0 |
| Baez, Sixto, Veracruz | 2 | 2 | .500 | 2.02 | 35 | 0 | 0 | 0 | 33 | 25 | 35.2 | 36 | 152 | 12 | 8 | 0 | 1 | 1 | 1 | 8 | 2 | 12 | 0 | 1 |
| Barradas, Roberto, Monclova | 1 | 0 | 1.000 | 6.38 | 22 | 0 | 0 | 0 | 7 | 0 | 36.2 | 54 | 187 | 28 | 26 | 5 | 0 | 0 | 4 | 21 | 2 | 14 | 5 | 0 |
| Barreras, Fernando, Vaqueros | 1 | 2 | .333 | 4.32 | 32 | 1 | 0 | 0 | 5 | 0 | 50.0 | 54 | 238 | 28 | 24 | 3 | 1 | 2 | 4 | 37 | 1 | 26 | 4 | 0 |
| Beltran, Alonso, Tijuana | 4 | 7 | .364 | 5.74 | 15 | 15 | 0 | 0 | 0 | 0 | 69.0 | 75 | 310 | 49 | 44 | 7 | 5 | 4 | 2 | 37 | 2 | 51 | 4 | 0 |
| Bernal, Manuel, Veracruz | 5 | 5 | .500 | 7.39 | 13 | 13 | 1 | 0 | 0 | 0 | 52.1 | 74 | 245 | 44 | 43 | 6 | 1 | 4 | 5 | 17 | 1 | 25 | 0 | 0 |
| Blancas, Rigoberto, Aguascalientes * | 2 | 0 | 1.000 | 7.02 | 39 | 0 | 0 | 0 | 4 | 0 | 16.2 | 30 | 86 | 15 | 13 | 4 | 1 | 0 | 1 | 5 | 0 | 7 | 3 | 0 |
| Bourgeois, Steve, Saltillo | 3 | 1 | .750 | 3.52 | 5 | 5 | 0 | 0 | 0 | 0 | 23.0 | 23 | 97 | 9 | 9 | 1 | 0 | 0 | 0 | 9 | 0 | 16 | 4 | 0 |
| Bullinger, Jim, Tijuana | 0 | 2 | .000 | 11.12 | 3 | 1 | 0 | 0 | 0 | 0 | 5.2 | 12 | 36 | 10 | 7 | 1 | 0 | 0 | 1 | 6 | 0 | 6 | 0 | 0 |
| Bustillos, Oscar, Tigres | 4 | 4 | .500 | 4.07 | 29 | 0 | 0 | 0 | 8 | 1 | 48.2 | 50 | 226 | 22 | 22 | 5 | 0 | 3 | 2 | 34 | 3 | 29 | 5 | 0 |
| Camara, Pedro, Yucatan * | 2 | 1 | .667 | 3.09 | 47 | 0 | 0 | 0 | 9 | 3 | 35.0 | 29 | 159 | 13 | 12 | 1 | 1 | 0 | 0 | 25 | 4 | 33 | 7 | 0 |
| Campillo, Jorge, Tigres | 5 | 5 | .500 | 5.38 | 17 | 16 | 1 | 0 | 0 | 0 | 98.2 | 120 | 435 | 67 | 59 | 14 | 7 | 5 | 3 | 28 | 2 | 66 | 3 | 0 |
| Campos, Francisco, Campeche | 12 | 2 | .857 | 1.69 | 16 | 16 | 4 | 1 | 0 | 0 | 122.2 | 88 | 479 | 31 | 23 | 9 | 3 | 1 | 5 | 26 | 1 | 99 | 2 | 0 |
| Canales, Julio, Tigres | 1 | 1 | .500 | 8.58 | 14 | 2 | 0 | 0 | 2 | 0 | 28.1 | 40 | 139 | 30 | 27 | 3 | 2 | 0 | 1 | 20 | 0 | 11 | 0 | 1 |
| Canto, Jafet, Cancun | 1 | 1 | .500 | 9.08 | 14 | 4 | 0 | 0 | 0 | 0 | 39.2 | 51 | 194 | 41 | 40 | 10 | 3 | 2 | 1 | 29 | 0 | 15 | 1 | 0 |
| Cantu, Jacobo, Tabasco | 0 | 0 | .000 | 23.63 | 3 | 0 | 0 | 0 | 0 | 0 | 2.2 | 8 | 17 | 7 | 7 | 0 | 0 | 0 | 0 | 1 | 0 | 2 | 2 | 0 |
| Carrasco, Alejandro, Monclova | 4 | 6 | .400 | 7.35 | 14 | 12 | 0 | 0 | 0 | 0 | 67.1 | 107 | 328 | 59 | 55 | 8 | 4 | 6 | 2 | 27 | 0 | 27 | 1 | 0 |
| Carrasco, Alejandro, Yucatan | 2 | 3 | .400 | 4.23 | 7 | 6 | 0 | 0 | 0 | 0 | 38.1 | 40 | 165 | 21 | 18 | 2 | 3 | 1 | 1 | 10 | 1 | 10 | 0 | 0 |
| Carrillo, Guillermo, Tijuana | 0 | 0 | .000 | 18.56 | 6 | 0 | 0 | 0 | 2 | 0 | 5.1 | 11 | 37 | 11 | 11 | 2 | 0 | 0 | 1 | 9 | 1 | 4 | 0 | 0 |
| Carrillo, Jose, San Luis Potosi | 1 | 0 | 1.000 | 2.77 | 8 | 0 | 0 | 0 | 4 | 0 | 13.0 | 11 | 53 | 4 | 4 | 0 | 1 | 2 | 0 | 7 | 0 | 8 | 0 | 0 |
| Carron, Uziel, Cancun | 5 | 2 | .714 | 4.46 | 30 | 1 | 0 | 0 | 8 | 0 | 40.1 | 44 | 187 | 22 | 20 | 7 | 0 | 1 | 2 | 18 | 0 | 12 | 1 | 0 |
| Castaneda, Federico, Vaqueros | 2 | 1 | .667 | 5.50 | 34 | 0 | 0 | 0 | 14 | 3 | 34.1 | 30 | 157 | 23 | 21 | 6 | 1 | 1 | 4 | 25 | 1 | 25 | 1 | 0 |
| Castellanos, Hugo, Tijuana | 4 | 2 | .667 | 3.15 | 44 | 0 | 0 | 0 | 6 | 0 | 60.0 | 42 | 250 | 23 | 21 | 4 | 2 | 1 | 3 | 30 | 5 | 47 | 1 | 0 |
| Castellanos, Jonathan, Monterrey | 0 | 3 | .000 | 4.81 | 22 | 1 | 0 | 0 | 7 | 0 | 33.2 | 43 | 160 | 22 | 18 | 6 | 1 | 0 | 2 | 16 | 5 | 23 | 0 | 0 |
| Castillo, Alberto, San Luis Potosi * | 1 | 4 | .200 | 4.22 | 6 | 6 | 1 | 0 | 0 | 0 | 32.0 | 34 | 150 | 19 | 15 | 3 | 2 | 0 | 0 | 27 | 0 | 18 | 1 | 0 |
| Castillo, Jorge, Mexico * | 0 | 1 | .000 | 2.08 | 7 | 1 | 0 | 0 | 0 | 0 | 17.1 | 14 | 74 | 7 | 4 | 0 | 1 | 1 | 0 | 10 | 0 | 11 | 1 | 0 |
| Castro, Luis, Oaxaca | 1 | 2 | .333 | 4.93 | 18 | 2 | 0 | 0 | 2 | 0 | 38.1 | 43 | 175 | 23 | 21 | 3 | 0 | 4 | 2 | 19 | 1 | 21 | 2 | 0 |
| Cazares, Rosario, Saltillo | 0 | 0 | .000 | 9.82 | 3 | 0 | 0 | 0 | 2 | 0 | 3.2 | 3 | 19 | 4 | 4 | 0 | 0 | 1 | 2 | 3 | 1 | 1 | 0 | 0 |
| Cervantes, Pedro, Puebla | 1 | 0 | 1.000 | 0.84 | 10 | 0 | 0 | 0 | 9 | 6 | 10.2 | 10 | 44 | 1 | 1 | 0 | 0 | 0 | 0 | 5 | 0 | 5 | 1 | 0 |
| Cervantes, Pedro, San Luis Potosi | 0 | 3 | .000 | 10.57 | 10 | 0 | 0 | 0 | 6 | 4 | 7.2 | 8 | 34 | 9 | 9 | 0 | 0 | 0 | 0 | 3 | 1 | 5 | 0 | 0 |
| Chantres, Carlos, Cancun | 4 | 3 | .571 | 3.47 | 10 | 10 | 1 | 0 | 0 | 0 | 57.0 | 45 | 244 | 26 | 22 | 2 | 3 | 1 | 4 | 35 | 1 | 33 | 9 | 0 |
| Chantres, Carlos, Aguascalientes | 1 | 2 | .333 | 7.63 | 4 | 4 | 0 | 0 | 0 | 0 | 15.1 | 21 | 75 | 13 | 13 | 1 | 0 | 1 | 1 | 11 | 0 | 9 | 1 | 0 |
| Chavarria, Hector, Vaqueros | 4 | 8 | .333 | 5.09 | 19 | 16 | 1 | 0 | 0 | 0 | 81.1 | 98 | 378 | 56 | 46 | 5 | 5 | 7 | 11 | 39 | 1 | 34 | 4 | 1 |
| Chavez, Alejandro, Vaqueros * | 1 | 2 | .333 | 8.80 | 29 | 4 | 0 | 0 | 0 | 0 | 29.2 | 48 | 169 | 31 | 29 | 5 | 2 | 1 | 5 | 30 | 0 | 25 | 5 | 0 |
| Chavez, Carlos, Tabasco | 0 | 1 | .000 | 5.29 | 15 | 0 | 0 | 0 | 14 | 7 | 17.0 | 21 | 82 | 10 | 10 | 1 | 0 | 1 | 0 | 12 | 1 | 13 | 1 | 0 |
| Cobos, Rogelio, San Luis Potosi | 0 | 0 | .000 | 27.00 | 2 | 0 | 0 | 0 | 1 | 0 | 1.0 | 3 | 7 | 3 | 3 | 0 | 0 | 0 | 0 | 1 | 0 | 1 | 1 | 0 |
| Coco, Pasqual, Saltillo | 3 | 1 | .750 | 4.42 | 10 | 10 | 0 | 0 | 0 | 0 | 59.0 | 68 | 263 | 32 | 29 | 6 | 4 | 1 | 5 | 34 | 1 | 64 | 6 | 0 |
| Cordova, Alejandro, San Luis Potosi | 0 | 0 | .000 | 8.31 | 3 | 0 | 0 | 0 | 1 | 0 | 4.1 | 7 | 25 | 6 | 4 | 1 | 0 | 0 | 1 | 4 | 0 | 1 | 0 | 0 |
| Cortes, David, Tijuana | 0 | 1 | .000 | 5.17 | 14 | 0 | 0 | 0 | 7 | 3 | 15.2 | 16 | 69 | 10 | 9 | 3 | 0 | 0 | 0 | 6 | 1 | 18 | 0 | 0 |
| Cortez, Jorge, Tigres * | 1 | 0 | 1.000 | 8.31 | 2 | 2 | 0 | 0 | 0 | 0 | 8.2 | 11 | 41 | 8 | 8 | 2 | 0 | 2 | 1 | 7 | 0 | 4 | 1 | 0 |
| Cortez, Jorge, Oaxaca * | 2 | 3 | .400 | 5.09 | 10 | 10 | 0 | 0 | 0 | 0 | 53.0 | 57 | 242 | 39 | 30 | 5 | 9 | 1 | 7 | 26 | 0 | 23 | 0 | 0 |
| Cortez, Martin, Yucatan * | 0 | 0 | .000 | 15.43 | 3 | 0 | 0 | 0 | 1 | 0 | 2.1 | 6 | 16 | 8 | 4 | 2 | 0 | 0 | 0 | 3 | 0 | 3 | 0 | 0 |
| Couoh, Enrique, Cancun | 0 | 0 | .000 | 0.00 | 1 | 0 | 0 | 0 | 1 | 0 | 1.0 | 1 | 4 | 0 | 0 | 0 | 0 | 0 | 0 | 0 | 0 | 0 | 0 | 0 |
| Cruz, Javier, Mexico | 2 | 4 | .333 | 6.39 | 32 | 1 | 0 | 0 | 13 | 0 | 38.0 | 49 | 177 | 29 | 27 | 5 | 1 | 1 | 8 | 11 | 2 | 23 | 1 | 1 |
| Daniel, Luis, Aguascalientes | 0 | 0 | .000 | 13.50 | 5 | 0 | 0 | 0 | 3 | 0 | 3.1 | 8 | 21 | 5 | 5 | 2 | 0 | 0 | 1 | 2 | 0 | 0 | 0 | 0 |
| De La Rosa, Maximo, Monclova | 1 | 4 | .200 | 2.62 | 29 | 0 | 0 | 0 | 29 | 16 | 34.1 | 44 | 151 | 12 | 10 | 1 | 2 | 0 | 2 | 7 | 2 | 18 | 2 | 0 |

| Pitcher, Team | W | L | Pct. | ERA | G | GS | CG | ShO | GF | Sv. | IP | H | TBF | R | ER | HR | SH | SF | HB | BB | IBB | SO | WP | Bk. |
|---|---|---|---|---|---|---|---|---|---|---|---|---|---|---|---|---|---|---|---|---|---|---|---|---|
| DeHart, Rick, Monterrey * | 8 | 6 | .571 | 4.42 | 18 | 17 | 3 | 0 | 0 | 0 | 89.2 | 105 | 402 | 55 | 44 | 3 | 7 | 8 | 1 | 34 | 0 | 60 | 5 | 1 |
| Deago, Roger, Tijuana * | 0 | 4 | .000 | 14.49 | 6 | 5 | 0 | 0 | 0 | 0 | 13.2 | 31 | 84 | 22 | 22 | 2 | 1 | 3 | 2 | 13 | 0 | 11 | 4 | 0 |
| Delahoya, Javier, Campeche | 3 | 3 | .500 | 3.30 | 8 | 8 | 0 | 0 | 0 | 0 | 46.1 | 42 | 212 | 21 | 17 | 3 | 5 | 2 | 4 | 26 | 0 | 22 | 0 | 0 |
| Delfin, Adolpho, Tijuana | 0 | 0 | .000 | 4.15 | 4 | 0 | 0 | 0 | 1 | 0 | 8.2 | 11 | 40 | 4 | 4 | 1 | 0 | 2 | 4 | 1 | 0 | 7 | 0 | 0 |
| Delgadillo, Juan, Yucatan | 1 | 4 | .200 | 6.05 | 13 | 11 | 0 | 0 | 1 | 0 | 55.0 | 59 | 244 | 44 | 37 | 8 | 5 | 2 | 2 | 23 | 2 | 29 | 8 | 0 |
| Diaz, Ralph, Saltillo | 2 | 1 | .667 | 2.63 | 7 | 7 | 0 | 0 | 0 | 0 | 37.2 | 30 | 142 | 12 | 11 | 1 | 3 | 2 | 0 | 10 | 0 | 28 | 1 | 0 |
| Dominguez, Carlos, Tijuana * | 0 | 2 | .000 | 16.20 | 9 | 2 | 0 | 0 | 0 | 0 | 6.2 | 11 | 33 | 12 | 12 | 3 | 0 | 0 | 1 | 4 | 1 | 2 | 1 | 0 |
| Dominguez, David, Mexico | 1 | 0 | 1.000 | 4.95 | 32 | 0 | 0 | 0 | 7 | 1 | 40.0 | 45 | 182 | 22 | 22 | 3 | 0 | 0 | 2 | 17 | 1 | 23 | 3 | 0 |
| Dorame, Randey, Monclova * | 1 | 4 | .200 | 9.00 | 7 | 7 | 0 | 0 | 0 | 0 | 24.0 | 41 | 126 | 25 | 24 | 3 | 1 | 3 | 0 | 18 | 0 | 9 | 0 | 0 |
| Dorame, Randey, Campeche * | 2 | 1 | .667 | 3.77 | 10 | 3 | 1 | 0 | 2 | 0 | 31.0 | 26 | 129 | 14 | 13 | 5 | 2 | 2 | 1 | 13 | 1 | 12 | 2 | 0 |
| Duarte, Miguel, Saltillo | 4 | 3 | .571 | 3.19 | 33 | 0 | 0 | 0 | 11 | 3 | 36.2 | 27 | 156 | 15 | 13 | 2 | 2 | 0 | 1 | 21 | 5 | 29 | 4 | 0 |
| Elizalde, Carlos, Oaxaca | 10 | 3 | .769 | 4.35 | 17 | 17 | 2 | 1 | 0 | 0 | 91.0 | 105 | 400 | 48 | 44 | 7 | 1 | 4 | 4 | 38 | 1 | 48 | 5 | 0 |
| Elvira, Abraham, Aguascalientes * | 4 | 10 | .286 | 6.26 | 17 | 17 | 1 | 0 | 0 | 0 | 82.0 | 93 | 372 | 62 | 57 | 8 | 3 | 3 | 2 | 56 | 1 | 46 | 4 | 0 |
| Elvira, Narciso, Campeche * | 6 | 3 | .667 | 3.94 | 15 | 14 | 3 | 1 | 0 | 0 | 82.1 | 75 | 350 | 39 | 36 | 10 | 8 | 5 | 4 | 36 | 1 | 54 | 6 | 0 |
| Escobedo, Edgar, Tijuana | 4 | 4 | .500 | 6.49 | 20 | 11 | 0 | 0 | 5 | 1 | 61.0 | 72 | 283 | 46 | 44 | 3 | 4 | 3 | 2 | 38 | 3 | 27 | 5 | 0 |
| Espadas, Gary, Yucatan | 4 | 1 | .800 | 3.98 | 19 | 4 | 0 | 0 | 1 | 0 | 40.2 | 48 | 184 | 19 | 18 | 3 | 0 | 0 | 4 | 11 | 1 | 21 | 0 | 0 |
| Esparza, Emerson, Vaqueros | 1 | 6 | .143 | 5.66 | 18 | 5 | 0 | 0 | 2 | 0 | 41.1 | 53 | 191 | 28 | 26 | 3 | 3 | 1 | 0 | 23 | 3 | 19 | 2 | 0 |
| Espinoza, Omar, Puebla | 1 | 1 | .500 | 5.32 | 23 | 5 | 0 | 0 | 7 | 0 | 44.0 | 54 | 208 | 30 | 26 | 7 | 2 | 1 | 6 | 22 | 2 | 13 | 3 | 0 |
| Esquer, Mercedes, San Luis Potosi * | 5 | 7 | .417 | 5.92 | 16 | 16 | 0 | 0 | 0 | 0 | 76.0 | 109 | 355 | 52 | 50 | 9 | 2 | 6 | 6 | 22 | 0 | 24 | 2 | 0 |
| Estrella, Luis, Puebla | 0 | 1 | .000 | 6.75 | 3 | 0 | 0 | 0 | 0 | 0 | 4.0 | 6 | 24 | 3 | 3 | 0 | 0 | 0 | 1 | 5 | 0 | 0 | 0 | 0 |
| Estrella, Luis, Tigres | 4 | 1 | .800 | 2.25 | 13 | 5 | 0 | 0 | 2 | 0 | 40.0 | 33 | 160 | 11 | 10 | 1 | 1 | 0 | 2 | 15 | 0 | 26 | 3 | 0 |
| Federico, Gustavo, Monclova | 0 | 5 | .000 | 3.89 | 37 | 0 | 0 | 0 | 10 | 0 | 37.0 | 44 | 177 | 18 | 16 | 1 | 0 | 1 | 4 | 19 | 2 | 13 | 1 | 1 |
| Federico, Gustavo, Saltillo | 0 | 0 | .000 | 6.23 | 2 | 0 | 0 | 0 | 1 | 0 | 4.1 | 7 | 21 | 4 | 3 | 1 | 0 | 1 | 1 | 0 | 0 | 1 | 0 | 0 |
| Fernandez, Osvaldo, Tabasco | 8 | 6 | .571 | 2.69 | 18 | 18 | 3 | 1 | 0 | 0 | 123.2 | 117 | 516 | 51 | 37 | 7 | 9 | 7 | 1 | 34 | 0 | 68 | 5 | 0 |
| Flores, Ignacio, Yucatan | 3 | 3 | .500 | 4.02 | 13 | 0 | 0 | 0 | 11 | 3 | 15.2 | 17 | 66 | 7 | 7 | 2 | 0 | 0 | 0 | 7 | 3 | 4 | 1 | 0 |
| Flores, Ignacio, Tigres | 1 | 2 | .333 | 4.81 | 17 | 0 | 0 | 0 | 8 | 1 | 24.1 | 26 | 107 | 14 | 13 | 6 | 0 | 0 | 0 | 8 | 1 | 14 | 0 | 0 |
| Flores, Javier, Saltillo | 0 | 0 | .000 | 0.00 | 1 | 1 | 0 | 0 | 0 | 0 | 6.0 | 2 | 20 | 0 | 0 | 0 | 0 | 0 | 0 | 0 | 0 | 3 | 0 | 0 |
| Flores, Jorge, Monclova * | 2 | 3 | .400 | 6.80 | 48 | 0 | 0 | 0 | 10 | 1 | 41.0 | 61 | 205 | 36 | 31 | 1 | 1 | 1 | 5 | 18 | 2 | 17 | 1 | 0 |
| Flores, Renato, Monclova | 2 | 1 | .667 | 3.96 | 32 | 0 | 0 | 0 | 8 | 0 | 38.2 | 33 | 174 | 18 | 17 | 1 | 0 | 0 | 0 | 27 | 3 | 26 | 6 | 0 |
| Flores, Wilfredo, Tabasco | 0 | 0 | .000 | 2.76 | 15 | 0 | 0 | 0 | 7 | 0 | 16.1 | 21 | 79 | 8 | 5 | 0 | 2 | 0 | 2 | 8 | 1 | 4 | 0 | 0 |
| Galindo, Erick, Monclova | 0 | 0 | .000 | 6.23 | 3 | 0 | 0 | 0 | 0 | 0 | 8.2 | 10 | 43 | 6 | 6 | 1 | 0 | 0 | 0 | 7 | 0 | 6 | 1 | 0 |
| Garcia, Adolfo, Veracruz | 3 | 4 | .429 | 3.42 | 27 | 1 | 0 | 0 | 6 | 0 | 50.0 | 63 | 227 | 26 | 19 | 4 | 3 | 3 | 4 | 13 | 1 | 14 | 5 | 1 |
| Garcia, Alfredo, Mexico | 3 | 7 | .300 | 5.19 | 16 | 15 | 0 | 0 | 0 | 0 | 76.1 | 90 | 336 | 50 | 44 | 6 | 4 | 4 | 5 | 27 | 1 | 29 | 4 | 0 |
| Garcia, Carlos, Mexico | 1 | 0 | 1.000 | 5.25 | 4 | 1 | 0 | 0 | 1 | 0 | 12.0 | 18 | 53 | 8 | 7 | 0 | 0 | 1 | 0 | 3 | 0 | 4 | 0 | 0 |
| Garcia, Carlos, Vaqueros | 2 | 2 | .500 | 5.93 | 9 | 9 | 0 | 0 | 0 | 0 | 44.0 | 56 | 189 | 32 | 29 | 9 | 4 | 0 | 0 | 14 | 0 | 22 | 1 | 0 |
| Garcia, Cornelio, Vaqueros * | 0 | 0 | .000 | 6.10 | 3 | 3 | 0 | 0 | 0 | 0 | 10.1 | 15 | 47 | 7 | 7 | 2 | 1 | 1 | 1 | 1 | 0 | 2 | 1 | 0 |
| Garcia, Humberto, San Luis Potosi * | 1 | 0 | 1.000 | 9.20 | 38 | 0 | 0 | 0 | 3 | 0 | 14.2 | 22 | 79 | 15 | 15 | 3 | 0 | 0 | 0 | 13 | 1 | 13 | 2 | 0 |
| Garcia, Jonathan, Campeche | 0 | 0 | .000 | 8.64 | 6 | 0 | 0 | 0 | 4 | 0 | 8.1 | 12 | 44 | 12 | 8 | 2 | 0 | 1 | 1 | 5 | 0 | 5 | 0 | 0 |
| Garcia, Jose, Tijuana | 1 | 0 | 1.000 | 7.94 | 12 | 0 | 0 | 0 | 0 | 0 | 5.2 | 9 | 27 | 5 | 5 | 2 | 0 | 0 | 0 | 2 | 1 | 6 | 0 | 0 |
| Garcia, Jose, Saltillo * | 5 | 2 | .714 | 4.31 | 49 | 1 | 0 | 0 | 9 | 2 | 48.0 | 59 | 227 | 26 | 23 | 4 | 1 | 1 | 2 | 22 | 4 | 35 | 2 | 0 |
| Garcia, Rafael, Saltillo | 3 | 1 | .750 | 4.08 | 7 | 6 | 0 | 0 | 0 | 0 | 35.1 | 33 | 148 | 16 | 16 | 3 | 4 | 0 | 2 | 15 | 0 | 22 | 3 | 0 |
| Garcia, Ramon, Monterrey | 0 | 0 | .000 | 6.75 | 8 | 0 | 0 | 0 | 3 | 0 | 6.2 | 9 | 33 | 5 | 5 | 1 | 1 | 1 | 1 | 4 | 1 | 2 | 0 | 0 |
| Garcia, Ramon, San Luis Potosi | 2 | 7 | .222 | 4.78 | 17 | 11 | 1 | 1 | 0 | 0 | 69.2 | 89 | 323 | 45 | 37 | 5 | 6 | 2 | 6 | 27 | 4 | 46 | 4 | 0 |
| Garibaldi, Cecilio, Tigres | 6 | 1 | .857 | 5.75 | 21 | 10 | 0 | 0 | 3 | 0 | 61.0 | 80 | 300 | 42 | 39 | 4 | 4 | 3 | 5 | 43 | 1 | 31 | 5 | 0 |
| Garibay, Salvador, Tijuana | 3 | 1 | .750 | 4.97 | 44 | 0 | 0 | 0 | 6 | 0 | 58.0 | 70 | 266 | 38 | 32 | 9 | 5 | 1 | 2 | 22 | 4 | 23 | 2 | 0 |
| Garza, Conrado, Cancun * | 3 | 3 | .500 | 3.66 | 39 | 0 | 0 | 0 | 9 | 3 | 32.0 | 25 | 139 | 13 | 13 | 1 | 0 | 0 | 1 | 22 | 5 | 15 | 2 | 0 |
| Garza, Luis, Cancun | 0 | 0 | .000 | 4.50 | 4 | 0 | 0 | 0 | 1 | 0 | 4.0 | 6 | 20 | 2 | 2 | 0 | 1 | 0 | 1 | 3 | 0 | 1 | 1 | 0 |
| Giron, Emiliano, Vaqueros | 7 | 5 | .583 | 4.27 | 38 | 6 | 1 | 0 | 21 | 5 | 65.1 | 60 | 280 | 40 | 31 | 7 | 0 | 1 | 5 | 26 | 3 | 59 | 6 | 0 |
| Giron, Isabel, Yucatan | 4 | 1 | .800 | 3.62 | 7 | 6 | 0 | 0 | 0 | 0 | 32.1 | 37 | 143 | 16 | 13 | 1 | 2 | 2 | 2 | 14 | 0 | 20 | 2 | 0 |
| Giron, Isabel, Vaqueros | 3 | 6 | .333 | 6.10 | 13 | 13 | 2 | 0 | 0 | 0 | 72.1 | 83 | 330 | 50 | 49 | 7 | 2 | 1 | 2 | 30 | 0 | 59 | 5 | 0 |
| Gomez, Alejandro, Cancun | 0 | 0 | .000 | 6.14 | 13 | 0 | 0 | 0 | 1 | 0 | 14.2 | 17 | 62 | 13 | 10 | 1 | 1 | 2 | 1 | 5 | 2 | 6 | 1 | 1 |
| Gomez, Alejandro, Oaxaca | 1 | 1 | .500 | 6.28 | 12 | 0 | 0 | 0 | 6 | 0 | 14.1 | 22 | 70 | 12 | 10 | 5 | 0 | 0 | 1 | 4 | 1 | 9 | 1 | 0 |
| Gomez, Martin, Vaqueros | 7 | 4 | .636 | 5.44 | 19 | 17 | 1 | 0 | 0 | 0 | 94.1 | 119 | 426 | 62 | 57 | 10 | 6 | 6 | 3 | 42 | 0 | 41 | 7 | 0 |
| Gonzalez, Carlos, Veracruz | 0 | 0 | .000 | 3.38 | 2 | 0 | 0 | 0 | 0 | 0 | 2.2 | 3 | 13 | 1 | 1 | 0 | 0 | 0 | 1 | 1 | 0 | 1 | 0 | 0 |
| Gonzalez, Erubiel, Veracruz | 1 | 1 | .500 | 3.00 | 14 | 0 | 0 | 0 | 3 | 0 | 24.0 | 19 | 99 | 8 | 8 | 1 | 1 | 1 | 4 | 8 | 2 | 13 | 0 | 0 |
| Gonzalez, Gilberto, San Luis Potosi * | 5 | 5 | .500 | 5.76 | 17 | 15 | 0 | 0 | 1 | 0 | 65.2 | 76 | 311 | 47 | 42 | 6 | 7 | 1 | 2 | 50 | 0 | 49 | 7 | 1 |
| Gonzalez, Leonardo, Tijuana | 4 | 6 | .400 | 4.80 | 18 | 18 | 1 | 1 | 0 | 0 | 93.2 | 107 | 422 | 52 | 50 | 12 | 8 | 1 | 3 | 58 | 1 | 80 | 14 | 0 |
| Gonzalez, Miguel, Saltillo | 3 | 4 | .429 | 4.50 | 25 | 9 | 0 | 0 | 7 | 0 | 72.0 | 73 | 335 | 46 | 36 | 6 | 8 | 10 | 5 | 45 | 2 | 49 | 11 | 0 |
| Gonzalez, Rudy, Mexico | 3 | 2 | .600 | 4.80 | 15 | 7 | 0 | 0 | 1 | 0 | 45.0 | 48 | 205 | 25 | 24 | 4 | 0 | 1 | 6 | 21 | 1 | 42 | 3 | 0 |
| Gonzalez, Vinicio, Tabasco | 3 | 4 | .429 | 2.09 | 11 | 8 | 0 | 0 | 1 | 0 | 51.2 | 52 | 226 | 18 | 12 | 1 | 2 | 0 | 3 | 18 | 2 | 30 | 4 | 0 |
| Grajales, Norberto, Campeche | 2 | 3 | .400 | 6.21 | 19 | 2 | 0 | 0 | 5 | 0 | 33.1 | 43 | 148 | 26 | 23 | 6 | 1 | 0 | 3 | 10 | 0 | 16 | 0 | 0 |
| Guerra, Pascual, Tabasco | 0 | 0 | .000 | 27.00 | 3 | 1 | 0 | 0 | 0 | 0 | 2.0 | 8 | 17 | 7 | 6 | 0 | 0 | 1 | 0 | 2 | 0 | 0 | 0 | 0 |
| Gutierrez, Carlos, Cancun | 0 | 2 | .000 | 4.50 | 5 | 3 | 0 | 0 | 1 | 0 | 18.0 | 27 | 88 | 10 | 9 | 0 | 1 | 2 | 1 | 8 | 0 | 2 | 2 | 0 |
| Gutierrez, Carlos, Vaqueros | 0 | 0 | .000 | 81.00 | 2 | 0 | 0 | 0 | 0 | 0 | 0.2 | 5 | 8 | 6 | 6 | 2 | 0 | 0 | 0 | 1 | 0 | 2 | 0 | 0 |
| Gutierrez, Israel, Tigres | 0 | 0 | .000 | 4.66 | 4 | 0 | 0 | 0 | 0 | 0 | 9.2 | 11 | 46 | 6 | 5 | 0 | 0 | 0 | 0 | 10 | 0 | 8 | 3 | 0 |
| Gutierrez, Israel, Puebla | 0 | 0 | .000 | 9.00 | 2 | 0 | 0 | 0 | 1 | 0 | 2.0 | 3 | 10 | 2 | 2 | 1 | 0 | 0 | 0 | 1 | 0 | 2 | 0 | 0 |
| Guzman, Christian, Saltillo | 3 | 1 | .750 | 4.13 | 20 | 0 | 0 | 0 | 5 | 0 | 28.1 | 29 | 128 | 19 | 13 | 1 | 0 | 0 | 2 | 13 | 2 | 16 | 4 | 0 |
| Guzman, Jesus, Tigres * | 5 | 7 | .417 | 5.02 | 18 | 17 | 1 | 0 | 0 | 0 | 80.2 | 103 | 369 | 61 | 45 | 9 | 5 | 4 | 6 | 32 | 4 | 35 | 4 | 0 |
| Hansell, Greg, Mexico | 2 | 2 | .500 | 4.08 | 35 | 1 | 0 | 0 | 31 | 19 | 39.2 | 42 | 172 | 18 | 18 | 5 | 1 | 0 | 1 | 13 | 0 | 25 | 1 | 0 |
| Haro, Esteban, Tigres | 2 | 2 | .500 | 6.17 | 17 | 5 | 0 | 0 | 5 | 0 | 42.1 | 50 | 196 | 31 | 29 | 2 | 0 | 1 | 0 | 27 | 0 | 16 | 1 | 0 |

| Pitcher, Team | W | L | Pct. | ERA | G | GS | CG | ShO | GF | Sv. | IP | H | TBF | R | ER | HR | SH | SF | HB | BB | IBB | SO | WP | Bk. |
|---|---|---|---|---|---|---|---|---|---|---|---|---|---|---|---|---|---|---|---|---|---|---|---|---|
| Henriquez, Oscar, Campeche | 2 | 0 | 1.000 | 1.59 | 8 | 0 | 0 | 0 | 2 | 0 | 11.1 | 7 | 49 | 2 | 2 | 0 | 0 | 0 | 2 | 9 | 0 | 3 | 1 | 0 |
| Hermosillo, Victor, Vaqueros | 0 | 1 | .000 | 9.95 | 13 | 1 | 0 | 0 | 6 | 0 | 19.0 | 23 | 93 | 22 | 21 | 6 | 0 | 0 | 3 | 16 | 0 | 19 | 5 | 0 |
| Hermosillo, Victor, Mexico | 0 | 0 | .000 | 10.57 | 11 | 0 | 0 | 0 | 5 | 1 | 7.2 | 15 | 49 | 11 | 9 | 0 | 0 | 2 | 2 | 7 | 0 | 4 | 4 | 0 |
| Hernandez, Esteban, Oaxaca | 1 | 1 | .500 | 4.08 | 22 | 0 | 0 | 0 | 8 | 0 | 46.1 | 54 | 209 | 31 | 21 | 5 | 0 | 2 | 4 | 15 | 1 | 15 | 1 | 0 |
| Hernandez, Jose, Veracruz * | 0 | 0 | .000 | 2.70 | 31 | 0 | 0 | 0 | 10 | 0 | 26.2 | 26 | 110 | 9 | 8 | 1 | 0 | 0 | 2 | 3 | 1 | 11 | 0 | 0 |
| Hernandez, Santos, Tigres | 3 | 2 | .600 | 2.55 | 36 | 0 | 0 | 0 | 35 | 26 | 42.1 | 35 | 166 | 13 | 12 | 4 | 0 | 0 | 1 | 5 | 1 | 33 | 4 | 0 |
| Herrera, Enrique, Tabasco | 3 | 3 | .500 | 1.76 | 37 | 0 | 0 | 0 | 20 | 3 | 46.0 | 49 | 197 | 14 | 9 | 0 | 0 | 1 | 2 | 14 | 7 | 16 | 3 | 0 |
| Hoil, Nelson, Tabasco * | 0 | 0 | .000 | 81.00 | 2 | 0 | 0 | 0 | 0 | 0 | 0.1 | 3 | 5 | 3 | 3 | 1 | 0 | 0 | 0 | 1 | 0 | 0 | 0 | 0 |
| Huerta, Amaya, Tabasco | 0 | 0 | .000 | 11.12 | 5 | 0 | 0 | 0 | 1 | 0 | 5.2 | 14 | 34 | 7 | 7 | 0 | 0 | 2 | 1 | 2 | 0 | 3 | 0 | 0 |
| Huerta, Luis, Tijuana | 0 | 2 | .000 | 7.81 | 10 | 5 | 0 | 0 | 1 | 0 | 27.2 | 41 | 138 | 28 | 24 | 9 | 1 | 1 | 1 | 16 | 1 | 12 | 1 | 0 |
| Hurtado, Edwin, Yucatan | 1 | 3 | .250 | 2.16 | 20 | 3 | 0 | 0 | 17 | 8 | 41.2 | 37 | 181 | 12 | 10 | 1 | 4 | 4 | 0 | 24 | 2 | 27 | 3 | 0 |
| Jacome, Victor, Veracruz * | 0 | 0 | .000 | 40.50 | 1 | 0 | 0 | 0 | 1 | 0 | 0.2 | 4 | 7 | 4 | 3 | 1 | 0 | 0 | 0 | 1 | 0 | 0 | 0 | 0 |
| Jimenez, Jose, Oaxaca * | 3 | 4 | .429 | 3.65 | 29 | 8 | 1 | 0 | 2 | 1 | 61.2 | 56 | 254 | 30 | 25 | 2 | 2 | 0 | 2 | 31 | 2 | 35 | 5 | 0 |
| Jimenez, Julio, Vaqueros * | 3 | 5 | .375 | 6.75 | 41 | 0 | 0 | 0 | 13 | 1 | 32.0 | 41 | 162 | 24 | 24 | 4 | 1 | 0 | 6 | 20 | 1 | 15 | 0 | 0 |
| Kamar, Emil, Monclova | 2 | 9 | .182 | 9.25 | 23 | 12 | 2 | 1 | 1 | 0 | 59.1 | 97 | 307 | 69 | 61 | 7 | 4 | 2 | 1 | 43 | 3 | 27 | 6 | 0 |
| Kelley, Rich, Veracruz * | 4 | 5 | .444 | 5.11 | 11 | 10 | 1 | 0 | 1 | 0 | 56.1 | 68 | 254 | 43 | 32 | 6 | 2 | 2 | 4 | 18 | 2 | 42 | 3 | 0 |
| Kelley, Rich, Puebla * | 3 | 1 | .750 | 4.57 | 8 | 7 | 0 | 0 | 0 | 0 | 41.1 | 52 | 192 | 24 | 21 | 6 | 3 | 1 | 2 | 22 | 0 | 27 | 3 | 0 |
| Kelly, John, Saltillo | 0 | 1 | .000 | 5.40 | 1 | 1 | 0 | 0 | 0 | 0 | 3.1 | 6 | 19 | 4 | 2 | 0 | 1 | 0 | 0 | 3 | 0 | 3 | 0 | 0 |
| Kelly, John, Yucatan | 1 | 2 | .333 | 5.82 | 5 | 5 | 0 | 0 | 0 | 0 | 21.2 | 30 | 98 | 17 | 14 | 4 | 0 | 1 | 0 | 10 | 1 | 16 | 2 | 0 |
| Lara, Jorge, Puebla | 2 | 3 | .400 | 7.47 | 24 | 1 | 0 | 0 | 4 | 1 | 31.1 | 42 | 141 | 30 | 26 | 10 | 0 | 0 | 2 | 10 | 1 | 16 | 2 | 0 |
| Lara, Mauricio, Monterrey * | 0 | 2 | .000 | 4.35 | 29 | 1 | 0 | 0 | 7 | 2 | 20.2 | 20 | 100 | 10 | 10 | 0 | 1 | 1 | 1 | 21 | 5 | 12 | 1 | 0 |
| Leon, Cupertino, Oaxaca | 1 | 2 | .333 | 3.27 | 34 | 0 | 0 | 0 | 15 | 2 | 44.0 | 42 | 195 | 21 | 16 | 3 | 2 | 1 | 4 | 18 | 2 | 26 | 2 | 0 |
| Leyva, Edgar, Tigres | 2 | 0 | 1.000 | 3.78 | 8 | 4 | 0 | 0 | 0 | 0 | 33.1 | 35 | 137 | 15 | 14 | 3 | 1 | 1 | 1 | 9 | 0 | 12 | 0 | 0 |
| Leyva, Edgar, Monterrey | 0 | 1 | .000 | 9.39 | 2 | 2 | 0 | 0 | 0 | 0 | 7.2 | 14 | 40 | 9 | 8 | 1 | 0 | 2 | 2 | 3 | 0 | 3 | 0 | 0 |
| Loaiza, Sabino, Tijuana | 0 | 0 | .000 | 9.39 | 6 | 0 | 0 | 0 | 3 | 0 | 7.2 | 14 | 40 | 8 | 8 | 2 | 0 | 0 | 0 | 5 | 1 | 5 | 1 | 0 |
| Lomeli, Israel, Oaxaca | 2 | 8 | .200 | 5.81 | 14 | 13 | 1 | 0 | 0 | 0 | 62.0 | 61 | 288 | 46 | 40 | 8 | 3 | 5 | 5 | 51 | 1 | 29 | 4 | 0 |
| Looney, Brian, San Luis Potosi * | 1 | 5 | .167 | 6.41 | 10 | 8 | 0 | 0 | 0 | 0 | 46.1 | 60 | 214 | 38 | 33 | 1 | 5 | 6 | 4 | 16 | 1 | 29 | 1 | 0 |
| Looney, Brian, Tigres * | 0 | 5 | .000 | 10.80 | 5 | 5 | 0 | 0 | 0 | 0 | 21.2 | 34 | 103 | 26 | 26 | 2 | 1 | 4 | 1 | 7 | 0 | 9 | 0 | 0 |
| Lopez, Emigdio, Veracruz | 7 | 7 | .500 | 5.30 | 17 | 17 | 2 | 0 | 0 | 0 | 91.2 | 132 | 419 | 62 | 54 | 8 | 5 | 7 | 4 | 26 | 3 | 48 | 1 | 0 |
| Lopez, Gilberto, Cancun | 0 | 0 | .000 | 0.00 | 2 | 0 | 0 | 0 | 0 | 0 | 0.0 | 1 | 3 | 2 | 2 | 0 | 0 | 0 | 1 | 1 | 0 | 0 | 0 | 0 |
| Lopez, Gilberto, Aguascalientes | 0 | 1 | .000 | 6.97 | 7 | 0 | 0 | 0 | 1 | 0 | 10.1 | 10 | 49 | 9 | 8 | 2 | 0 | 1 | 5 | 3 | 0 | 6 | 0 | 1 |
| Lopez, Jesus, Cancun | 1 | 2 | .333 | 3.54 | 7 | 2 | 0 | 0 | 1 | 0 | 20.1 | 18 | 82 | 10 | 8 | 2 | 2 | 1 | 2 | 12 | 0 | 12 | 0 | 0 |
| Lopez, Jose, San Luis Potosi | 0 | 2 | .000 | 6.16 | 16 | 0 | 0 | 0 | 14 | 6 | 19.0 | 27 | 84 | 13 | 13 | 5 | 0 | 0 | 0 | 0 | 0 | 12 | 0 | 0 |
| Lopez, Jose J., San Luis Potosi | 1 | 1 | .500 | 4.30 | 12 | 0 | 0 | 0 | 9 | 6 | 14.2 | 20 | 68 | 7 | 7 | 1 | 2 | 1 | 1 | 5 | 2 | 5 | 0 | 0 |
| Lopez, Miguel, Puebla | 2 | 4 | .333 | 5.09 | 42 | 0 | 0 | 0 | 24 | 7 | 40.2 | 50 | 196 | 26 | 23 | 5 | 0 | 0 | 3 | 22 | 6 | 23 | 1 | 0 |
| Lopez, Nain, Yucatan * | 0 | 0 | .000 | 7.20 | 4 | 0 | 0 | 0 | 2 | 0 | 5.0 | 12 | 29 | 9 | 4 | 2 | 0 | 0 | 0 | 2 | 0 | 2 | 1 | 0 |
| Lopez, Nain, Tijuana * | 0 | 1 | .000 | 5.40 | 22 | 2 | 0 | 0 | 4 | 0 | 18.1 | 25 | 88 | 12 | 11 | 2 | 2 | 0 | 0 | 9 | 3 | 10 | 0 | 1 |
| Loya, Rigoberto, Monterrey | 9 | 3 | .750 | 2.80 | 16 | 16 | 2 | 1 | 0 | 0 | 99.2 | 86 | 407 | 33 | 31 | 1 | 7 | 6 | 1 | 37 | 0 | 37 | 5 | 0 |
| Luevano, Juan, Aguascalientes | 5 | 5 | .500 | 5.79 | 32 | 0 | 0 | 0 | 7 | 1 | 37.1 | 50 | 176 | 27 | 24 | 5 | 1 | 0 | 5 | 15 | 3 | 17 | 3 | 0 |
| Macias, Luis, Puebla | 6 | 0 | 1.000 | 3.35 | 32 | 3 | 0 | 0 | 8 | 0 | 48.1 | 58 | 208 | 20 | 18 | 5 | 0 | 5 | 5 | 16 | 1 | 12 | 2 | 0 |
| Madero, Francisco, Vaqueros | 8 | 7 | .533 | 7.55 | 19 | 18 | 0 | 0 | 0 | 0 | 84.2 | 122 | 391 | 72 | 71 | 14 | 4 | 4 | 4 | 38 | 0 | 39 | 4 | 0 |
| Magee, Danny, Campeche | 7 | 6 | .538 | 3.51 | 15 | 15 | 6 | 2 | 0 | 0 | 105.0 | 90 | 463 | 51 | 41 | 5 | 8 | 2 | 4 | 61 | 2 | 72 | 10 | 1 |
| Mairena, Ozwaldo, Mexico * | 7 | 5 | .583 | 4.12 | 14 | 14 | 0 | 0 | 0 | 0 | 83.0 | 93 | 352 | 44 | 38 | 5 | 4 | 5 | 3 | 28 | 0 | 51 | 2 | 0 |
| Manrique, Alberto, Monterrey | 5 | 4 | .556 | 5.66 | 26 | 11 | 1 | 1 | 4 | 0 | 68.1 | 85 | 316 | 46 | 43 | 7 | 4 | 2 | 5 | 30 | 3 | 29 | 3 | 0 |
| Manzanillo, Ravelo, Puebla * | 2 | 1 | .667 | 6.59 | 5 | 5 | 0 | 0 | 0 | 0 | 27.1 | 34 | 132 | 21 | 20 | 6 | 3 | 3 | 2 | 21 | 0 | 20 | 3 | 0 |
| Manzanillo, Ravelo, Saltillo * | 4 | 0 | 1.000 | 5.33 | 5 | 5 | 0 | 0 | 0 | 0 | 25.1 | 30 | 121 | 17 | 15 | 4 | 2 | 0 | 0 | 16 | 0 | 14 | 0 | 0 |
| Manzano, Adrian, Tigres | 3 | 1 | .750 | 2.48 | 30 | 0 | 0 | 0 | 10 | 0 | 40.0 | 33 | 161 | 12 | 11 | 1 | 1 | 1 | 2 | 8 | 0 | 17 | 1 | 0 |
| Marquez, Isidro, Campeche | 2 | 3 | .400 | 2.91 | 34 | 0 | 0 | 0 | 30 | 21 | 34.0 | 31 | 149 | 11 | 11 | 1 | 1 | 2 | 3 | 11 | 2 | 21 | 2 | 0 |
| Marquez, Rob, Aguascalientes | 1 | 2 | .333 | 4.91 | 12 | 0 | 0 | 0 | 10 | 3 | 14.2 | 16 | 67 | 8 | 8 | 2 | 0 | 0 | 1 | 6 | 0 | 8 | 1 | 1 |
| Martinez, Cesar, Tijuana * | 5 | 4 | .556 | 4.69 | 20 | 15 | 0 | 0 | 0 | 0 | 71.0 | 76 | 325 | 48 | 37 | 5 | 2 | 7 | 7 | 49 | 5 | 42 | 3 | 2 |
| Martinez, Juan, Vaqueros-Aguascalientes | 0 | 0 | .000 | 3.38 | 16 | 1 | 0 | 0 | 8 | 0 | 18.2 | 22 | 90 | 9 | 7 | 0 | 0 | 0 | 1 | 12 | 0 | 6 | 2 | 0 |
| Martinez, Renan, Puebla * | 1 | 2 | .333 | 5.49 | 6 | 4 | 0 | 0 | 2 | 0 | 19.2 | 32 | 97 | 18 | 12 | 2 | 2 | 2 | 1 | 6 | 0 | 4 | 0 | 1 |
| McGlinchy, Kevin, Monterrey | 6 | 2 | .750 | 2.97 | 26 | 11 | 0 | 0 | 6 | 1 | 75.2 | 78 | 318 | 31 | 25 | 2 | 7 | 2 | 7 | 25 | 1 | 40 | 0 | 0 |
| Melendez, Nestor, San Luis Potosi * | 0 | 1 | .000 | 10.06 | 19 | 1 | 0 | 0 | 5 | 0 | 17.0 | 35 | 101 | 22 | 19 | 3 | 1 | 2 | 2 | 13 | 0 | 9 | 4 | 0 |
| Mendoza, Mario, Saltillo | 4 | 2 | .667 | 5.83 | 29 | 6 | 0 | 0 | 5 | 3 | 58.2 | 76 | 290 | 40 | 38 | 4 | 1 | 2 | 3 | 43 | 1 | 30 | 2 | 0 |
| Meyer, Jake, Tijuana | 2 | 1 | .667 | 2.93 | 6 | 6 | 0 | 0 | 0 | 0 | 30.2 | 25 | 134 | 11 | 10 | 3 | 1 | 1 | 2 | 18 | 0 | 29 | 1 | 0 |
| Meza, Jorge, Saltillo * | 0 | 1 | .000 | 8.83 | 18 | 1 | 0 | 0 | 5 | 1 | 17.1 | 34 | 96 | 17 | 17 | 1 | 1 | 1 | 0 | 10 | 0 | 10 | 1 | 0 |
| Montane, Ivan, Monclova | 3 | 2 | .600 | 4.32 | 11 | 10 | 0 | 0 | 0 | 0 | 58.1 | 65 | 262 | 36 | 28 | 2 | 6 | 2 | 5 | 34 | 0 | 38 | 10 | 0 |
| Montano, Ignacio, Aguascalientes * | 0 | 2 | .000 | 21.32 | 3 | 3 | 0 | 0 | 0 | 0 | 6.1 | 16 | 39 | 15 | 15 | 4 | 0 | 0 | 0 | 5 | 0 | 6 | 1 | 0 |
| Montano, Ignacio, Cancun * | 1 | 0 | 1.000 | 3.00 | 12 | 1 | 0 | 0 | 2 | 0 | 15.0 | 9 | 60 | 6 | 5 | 1 | 1 | 0 | 2 | 7 | 1 | 6 | 0 | 0 |
| Montemayor, Humberto, San Luis Potosi | 1 | 2 | .333 | 4.31 | 6 | 6 | 1 | 0 | 0 | 0 | 39.2 | 48 | 183 | 20 | 19 | 5 | 5 | 4 | 2 | 13 | 1 | 27 | 2 | 0 |
| Montemayor, Humberto, Monterrey | 0 | 0 | .000 | 4.15 | 5 | 0 | 0 | 0 | 1 | 0 | 8.2 | 9 | 36 | 4 | 4 | 0 | 1 | 0 | 0 | 3 | 2 | 6 | 1 | 0 |
| Montoya, Saul, San Luis Potosi | 3 | 3 | .500 | 4.18 | 41 | 1 | 0 | 0 | 14 | 1 | 51.2 | 51 | 227 | 27 | 24 | 3 | 0 | 2 | 3 | 26 | 2 | 31 | 6 | 1 |
| Mora, Eleazar, Oaxaca * | 7 | 4 | .636 | 3.46 | 18 | 16 | 1 | 1 | 0 | 0 | 88.1 | 104 | 378 | 45 | 34 | 2 | 7 | 3 | 5 | 16 | 0 | 35 | 3 | 0 |
| Mora, Sergio, Monterrey | 6 | 4 | .600 | 3.91 | 33 | 7 | 0 | 0 | 4 | 0 | 71.1 | 65 | 299 | 32 | 31 | 9 | 3 | 2 | 3 | 29 | 2 | 51 | 3 | 0 |
| Morales, Fernando, Cancun | 0 | 0 | .000 | 5.40 | 2 | 2 | 0 | 0 | 0 | 0 | 8.1 | 6 | 36 | 6 | 5 | 1 | 0 | 0 | 2 | 6 | 0 | 5 | 0 | 0 |
| Morales, Israel, Vaqueros | 3 | 0 | 1.000 | 6.58 | 24 | 0 | 0 | 0 | 5 | 1 | 26.0 | 31 | 131 | 22 | 19 | 5 | 1 | 0 | 3 | 19 | 1 | 12 | 4 | 1 |
| Morales, Luis, Cancun * | 0 | 1 | .000 | 11.57 | 5 | 2 | 0 | 0 | 1 | 0 | 7.0 | 8 | 34 | 10 | 9 | 3 | 0 | 0 | 3 | 5 | 1 | 3 | 1 | 0 |
| Morales, Luis, Saltillo * | 0 | 1 | .000 | 13.50 | 1 | 1 | 0 | 0 | 0 | 0 | 2.2 | 5 | 14 | 5 | 4 | 1 | 2 | 0 | 0 | 1 | 0 | 1 | 0 | 0 |
| Moreno, Angel, Veracruz * | 7 | 6 | .538 | 3.86 | 19 | 17 | 1 | 1 | 0 | 0 | 98.0 | 108 | 413 | 45 | 42 | 4 | 3 | 2 | 5 | 26 | 4 | 40 | 4 | 0 |

| Pitcher, Team | W | L | Pct. | ERA | G | GS | CG | ShO | GF | Sv. | IP | H | TBF | R | ER | HR | SH | SF | HB | BB | IBB | SO | WP | Bk. |
|---|---|---|---|---|---|---|---|---|---|---|---|---|---|---|---|---|---|---|---|---|---|---|---|---|
| Moreno, Claudio, Mexico | 8 | 7 | .533 | 4.56 | 21 | 18 | 4 | 2 | 0 | 0 | 108.2 | 128 | 474 | 61 | 55 | 9 | 5 | 3 | 4 | 38 | 3 | 47 | 4 | 0 |
| Moreno, Edgar, Veracruz | 1 | 0 | 1.000 | 5.31 | 12 | 2 | 0 | 0 | 3 | 0 | 20.1 | 26 | 91 | 13 | 12 | 3 | 0 | 0 | 1 | 6 | 0 | 8 | 2 | 0 |
| Moreno, Leobardo, Veracruz * | 1 | 7 | .125 | 5.43 | 20 | 9 | 1 | 0 | 4 | 0 | 56.1 | 64 | 245 | 40 | 34 | 7 | 2 | 4 | 0 | 22 | 0 | 40 | 3 | 0 |
| Mormolejo, Ivan, Cancun | 0 | 0 | .000 | 36.00 | 1 | 0 | 0 | 0 | 0 | 0 | 1.0 | 3 | 8 | 4 | 4 | 1 | 0 | 0 | 0 | 2 | 0 | 0 | 0 | 0 |
| Munoz, Leonardo, Tigres * | 2 | 2 | .500 | 4.67 | 24 | 0 | 0 | 0 | 5 | 0 | 17.1 | 16 | 76 | 10 | 9 | 1 | 2 | 0 | 0 | 9 | 0 | 7 | 3 | 0 |
| Munoz, Leonardo, Monterrey * | 0 | 1 | .000 | 2.45 | 4 | 0 | 0 | 0 | 1 | 0 | 3.2 | 3 | 13 | 1 | 1 | 0 | 1 | 0 | 0 | 1 | 1 | 0 | 0 | 0 |
| Munoz, Pablo, Aguascalientes * | 0 | 0 | .000 | 7.98 | 19 | 0 | 0 | 0 | 2 | 0 | 14.2 | 19 | 72 | 14 | 13 | 1 | 1 | 0 | 0 | 11 | 1 | 6 | 1 | 0 |
| Murguia, Edgar, Saltillo | 4 | 3 | .571 | 6.60 | 14 | 5 | 0 | 0 | 3 | 0 | 30.0 | 26 | 141 | 24 | 22 | 2 | 1 | 0 | 3 | 26 | 0 | 23 | 2 | 0 |
| Murillo, Felipe, Monclova | 0 | 0 | .000 | 7.71 | 9 | 0 | 0 | 0 | 1 | 0 | 7.0 | 10 | 32 | 6 | 6 | 3 | 0 | 0 | 0 | 3 | 0 | 4 | 1 | 0 |
| Murillo, Felipe, Yucatan | 0 | 2 | .000 | 3.43 | 20 | 0 | 0 | 0 | 5 | 0 | 21.0 | 31 | 101 | 9 | 8 | 1 | 0 | 0 | 3 | 7 | 2 | 8 | 1 | 0 |
| Murray, Dan, Aguascalientes | 1 | 3 | .250 | 7.38 | 8 | 8 | 1 | 0 | 0 | 0 | 39.0 | 40 | 183 | 33 | 32 | 5 | 1 | 1 | 4 | 36 | 0 | 24 | 6 | 0 |
| Navarro, Hector, Veracruz | 5 | 8 | .385 | 4.92 | 17 | 16 | 1 | 0 | 0 | 0 | 89.2 | 96 | 399 | 55 | 49 | 9 | 4 | 6 | 9 | 37 | 2 | 48 | 2 | 1 |
| Navarro, Joel, Oaxaca | 8 | 7 | .533 | 4.68 | 19 | 19 | 1 | 0 | 0 | 0 | 107.2 | 126 | 467 | 66 | 56 | 14 | 3 | 6 | 6 | 32 | 1 | 66 | 6 | 1 |
| Navarro, Jose, Puebla | 7 | 4 | .636 | 5.34 | 17 | 16 | 1 | 0 | 1 | 1 | 84.1 | 101 | 368 | 58 | 50 | 15 | 3 | 2 | 2 | 24 | 1 | 28 | 3 | 1 |
| Navarro, Luis, Yucatan * | 0 | 3 | .000 | 5.36 | 37 | 1 | 0 | 0 | 7 | 0 | 43.2 | 42 | 190 | 27 | 26 | 7 | 2 | 1 | 4 | 18 | 2 | 33 | 3 | 3 |
| Neri, Braulio, Tabasco * | 0 | 0 | .000 | 3.46 | 10 | 0 | 0 | 0 | 1 | 0 | 13.0 | 15 | 57 | 5 | 5 | 1 | 0 | 0 | 0 | 3 | 0 | 3 | 0 | 0 |
| Neri, Eduardo, Oaxaca * | 1 | 2 | .333 | 6.85 | 38 | 0 | 0 | 0 | 6 | 1 | 23.2 | 34 | 125 | 23 | 18 | 1 | 2 | 0 | 3 | 14 | 2 | 15 | 0 | 0 |
| Nieblas, Mauro, Monterrey * | 2 | 3 | .400 | 5.33 | 29 | 1 | 0 | 0 | 2 | 0 | 27.0 | 24 | 130 | 18 | 16 | 3 | 1 | 0 | 4 | 24 | 2 | 20 | 2 | 0 |
| Nieblas, Omar, Veracruz * | 0 | 1 | .000 | 13.50 | 5 | 0 | 0 | 0 | 1 | 0 | 2.2 | 4 | 17 | 4 | 4 | 2 | 1 | 0 | 0 | 5 | 1 | 1 | 3 | 0 |
| Nunez, Javier, Aguascalientes | 1 | 0 | 1.000 | 3.52 | 25 | 1 | 0 | 0 | 12 | 0 | 38.1 | 42 | 167 | 18 | 15 | 2 | 0 | 0 | 5 | 8 | 1 | 29 | 3 | 0 |
| Nunez, Jose, Puebla | 4 | 2 | .667 | 5.93 | 44 | 0 | 0 | 0 | 9 | 2 | 44.0 | 60 | 210 | 29 | 29 | 6 | 1 | 0 | 2 | 18 | 2 | 19 | 0 | 0 |
| Nunez, Jose, Tijuana | 4 | 2 | .667 | 2.73 | 11 | 11 | 1 | 0 | 0 | 0 | 62.2 | 52 | 245 | 24 | 19 | 5 | 3 | 2 | 0 | 14 | 2 | 48 | 2 | 0 |
| Ochoa, Pablo, Monterrey | 6 | 2 | .750 | 3.36 | 18 | 18 | 1 | 1 | 0 | 0 | 109.2 | 114 | 476 | 46 | 41 | 6 | 6 | 5 | 7 | 47 | 0 | 71 | 1 | 1 |
| Olague, Jesus, Tigres | 0 | 1 | .000 | 6.00 | 1 | 1 | 0 | 0 | 0 | 0 | 3.0 | 4 | 16 | 2 | 2 | 0 | 0 | 0 | 1 | 2 | 0 | 2 | 2 | 0 |
| Olague, Jesus, Monterrey | 4 | 2 | .667 | 3.99 | 13 | 11 | 0 | 0 | 0 | 0 | 65.1 | 74 | 286 | 37 | 29 | 6 | 5 | 2 | 0 | 20 | 1 | 37 | 1 | 0 |
| Orea, Flavio, Aguascalientes | 1 | 2 | .333 | 4.98 | 39 | 0 | 0 | 0 | 15 | 6 | 43.1 | 50 | 189 | 25 | 24 | 6 | 1 | 0 | 2 | 10 | 1 | 20 | 0 | 1 |
| Ortega, Pablo, Puebla | 9 | 5 | .643 | 3.17 | 17 | 17 | 3 | 1 | 0 | 0 | 119.1 | 131 | 497 | 50 | 42 | 5 | 7 | 1 | 7 | 32 | 3 | 57 | 5 | 0 |
| Ortega, Roberto, Puebla * | 3 | 0 | 1.000 | 3.38 | 42 | 0 | 0 | 0 | 6 | 2 | 24.0 | 20 | 107 | 10 | 9 | 1 | 0 | 0 | 2 | 14 | 2 | 13 | 1 | 0 |
| Ortega, Wilbert, Yucatan * | 1 | 0 | 1.000 | 8.69 | 32 | 0 | 0 | 0 | 5 | 0 | 19.2 | 26 | 96 | 19 | 19 | 3 | 1 | 0 | 4 | 9 | 2 | 19 | 1 | 0 |
| Osuna, Adrian, Vaqueros | 1 | 0 | 1.000 | 5.02 | 7 | 0 | 0 | 0 | 1 | 0 | 14.1 | 9 | 65 | 8 | 8 | 3 | 0 | 2 | 1 | 12 | 1 | 13 | 1 | 0 |
| Osuna, Adrian, Oaxaca | 0 | 0 | .000 | 10.13 | 3 | 0 | 0 | 0 | 1 | 0 | 2.2 | 2 | 16 | 3 | 3 | 1 | 0 | 1 | 0 | 6 | 0 | 2 | 0 | 0 |
| Osuna, Ricardo, Tabasco | 2 | 3 | .400 | 5.26 | 12 | 10 | 2 | 0 | 1 | 0 | 53.0 | 59 | 237 | 35 | 31 | 7 | 4 | 1 | 4 | 22 | 1 | 17 | 1 | 0 |
| Osuna, Ulises, Monterrey | 0 | 0 | .000 | 47.25 | 2 | 0 | 0 | 0 | 1 | 0 | 1.1 | 8 | 17 | 7 | 7 | 0 | 0 | 0 | 0 | 5 | 0 | 1 | 0 | 0 |
| Pablos, Rene, Tijuana * | 4 | 1 | .800 | 8.26 | 36 | 1 | 0 | 0 | 5 | 1 | 28.1 | 38 | 145 | 26 | 26 | 3 | 1 | 0 | 1 | 23 | 2 | 19 | 3 | 0 |
| Pacheco, Delvis, Tijuana | 0 | 1 | .000 | 13.50 | 1 | 1 | 0 | 0 | 0 | 0 | 2.0 | 4 | 12 | 4 | 3 | 0 | 0 | 0 | 1 | 1 | 0 | 1 | 1 | 0 |
| Palacios, Vicente, Tijuana | 3 | 0 | 1.000 | 2.98 | 23 | 1 | 0 | 0 | 4 | 0 | 42.1 | 45 | 184 | 17 | 14 | 3 | 3 | 2 | 1 | 15 | 3 | 21 | 0 | 0 |
| Palafox, Juan, Yucatan | 7 | 5 | .583 | 4.32 | 15 | 15 | 3 | 1 | 0 | 0 | 85.1 | 95 | 373 | 47 | 41 | 6 | 8 | 0 | 9 | 25 | 2 | 29 | 6 | 1 |
| Parra, Julio, Monterrey | 0 | 0 | .000 | 5.14 | 10 | 0 | 0 | 0 | 5 | 0 | 7.0 | 9 | 31 | 4 | 4 | 1 | 0 | 0 | 0 | 1 | 0 | 5 | 0 | 0 |
| Parra, Julio, Tijuana | 3 | 4 | .429 | 6.31 | 26 | 0 | 0 | 0 | 12 | 2 | 25.2 | 27 | 118 | 19 | 18 | 3 | 0 | 1 | 1 | 14 | 0 | 36 | 3 | 0 |
| Patrick, Bronswell, Mexico | 1 | 0 | 1.000 | 4.41 | 3 | 3 | 0 | 0 | 0 | 0 | 16.1 | 13 | 64 | 8 | 8 | 2 | 1 | 1 | 0 | 6 | 0 | 9 | 0 | 0 |
| Pena, Joel, San Luis Potosi | 0 | 1 | .000 | 5.59 | 2 | 2 | 0 | 0 | 0 | 0 | 9.2 | 13 | 47 | 7 | 6 | 2 | 2 | 0 | 1 | 4 | 0 | 7 | 0 | 0 |
| Perez, Alfredo, Cancun | 0 | 1 | .000 | 3.60 | 1 | 1 | 1 | 0 | 0 | 0 | 5.0 | 6 | 23 | 2 | 2 | 0 | 2 | 0 | 0 | 3 | 0 | 0 | 2 | 0 |
| Perez, Edgar, Cancun | 3 | 7 | .300 | 3.11 | 19 | 13 | 2 | 1 | 3 | 0 | 89.2 | 97 | 382 | 40 | 31 | 3 | 7 | 3 | 6 | 29 | 2 | 43 | 2 | 0 |
| Perez, Guadalupe, Veracruz | 0 | 2 | .000 | 5.29 | 19 | 3 | 0 | 0 | 6 | 0 | 34.0 | 41 | 157 | 21 | 20 | 3 | 4 | 2 | 3 | 17 | 0 | 15 | 1 | 0 |
| Perez, Sergio, San Luis Potosi | 2 | 2 | .500 | 4.70 | 23 | 0 | 0 | 0 | 7 | 0 | 38.1 | 54 | 185 | 31 | 20 | 5 | 2 | 4 | 3 | 17 | 0 | 26 | 3 | 0 |
| Pesqueira, Omar, Yucatan | 1 | 1 | .500 | 6.50 | 7 | 4 | 0 | 0 | 0 | 0 | 18.0 | 24 | 86 | 15 | 13 | 1 | 1 | 1 | 2 | 11 | 0 | 6 | 0 | 0 |
| Pichardo, Hipolito, Saltillo | 6 | 0 | 1.000 | 1.91 | 35 | 0 | 0 | 0 | 31 | 20 | 42.1 | 40 | 183 | 11 | 9 | 0 | 1 | 0 | 2 | 14 | 4 | 32 | 1 | 2 |
| Picota, Lenin, Yucatan | 2 | 4 | .333 | 3.80 | 11 | 11 | 0 | 0 | 0 | 0 | 66.1 | 75 | 292 | 34 | 28 | 5 | 5 | 2 | 6 | 19 | 3 | 37 | 2 | 0 |
| Picota, Lenin, San Luis Potosi | 1 | 3 | .250 | 6.00 | 6 | 6 | 1 | 0 | 0 | 0 | 36.0 | 43 | 160 | 27 | 24 | 5 | 2 | 1 | 6 | 9 | 0 | 33 | 0 | 0 |
| Pimentel, Roberto, Tabasco * | 4 | 1 | .800 | 3.86 | 27 | 4 | 0 | 0 | 8 | 0 | 42.0 | 52 | 181 | 20 | 18 | 2 | 2 | 1 | 3 | 6 | 1 | 23 | 0 | 0 |
| Pina, Rafael, Veracruz | 2 | 4 | .333 | 8.19 | 13 | 9 | 0 | 0 | 2 | 0 | 48.1 | 77 | 250 | 49 | 44 | 4 | 3 | 2 | 10 | 30 | 2 | 25 | 4 | 0 |
| Pina, Rafael, Tijuana | 2 | 1 | .667 | 3.68 | 13 | 3 | 0 | 0 | 5 | 0 | 29.1 | 31 | 133 | 13 | 12 | 4 | 2 | 0 | 3 | 13 | 0 | 28 | 3 | 0 |
| Pinales, Aquiles, Tabasco | 0 | 0 | .000 | 54.00 | 3 | 0 | 0 | 0 | 0 | 0 | 1.0 | 5 | 12 | 7 | 6 | 1 | 0 | 0 | 0 | 4 | 0 | 0 | 3 | 0 |
| Pinales, Aquiles, Campeche | 0 | 0 | .000 | 1.64 | 7 | 0 | 0 | 0 | 6 | 0 | 11.0 | 10 | 46 | 3 | 2 | 2 | 1 | 1 | 0 | 5 | 0 | 9 | 1 | 0 |
| Pineda, Jairo, Campeche | 0 | 1 | .000 | 5.17 | 8 | 2 | 0 | 0 | 3 | 1 | 15.2 | 22 | 73 | 9 | 9 | 0 | 0 | 0 | 0 | 6 | 0 | 8 | 2 | 1 |
| Posaadas, Obedt, Saltillo | 0 | 0 | .000 | 4.88 | 17 | 0 | 0 | 0 | 8 | 1 | 27.2 | 29 | 125 | 17 | 15 | 3 | 0 | 1 | 5 | 11 | 1 | 14 | 1 | 0 |
| Pulido, Raymundo, Campeche | 0 | 2 | .000 | 3.93 | 12 | 0 | 0 | 0 | 5 | 0 | 18.1 | 12 | 82 | 9 | 8 | 1 | 1 | 0 | 2 | 14 | 1 | 10 | 5 | 0 |
| Quinones, Enrique, San Luis Potosi | 0 | 4 | .000 | 10.80 | 10 | 6 | 0 | 0 | 3 | 0 | 30.0 | 52 | 153 | 41 | 36 | 11 | 1 | 3 | 2 | 9 | 0 | 9 | 1 | 0 |
| Quinones, Enrique, Yucatan | 0 | 1 | .000 | 9.00 | 8 | 2 | 0 | 0 | 0 | 0 | 8.0 | 12 | 38 | 8 | 8 | 3 | 0 | 0 | 0 | 3 | 1 | 3 | 0 | 0 |
| Quintanilla, Juan, Tijuana | 6 | 2 | .750 | 3.46 | 48 | 0 | 0 | 0 | 32 | 11 | 54.2 | 62 | 245 | 25 | 21 | 8 | 4 | 2 | 3 | 19 | 7 | 30 | 1 | 0 |
| Quiroz, Aaron, Saltillo | 6 | 4 | .600 | 4.21 | 15 | 15 | 0 | 0 | 0 | 0 | 72.2 | 84 | 318 | 37 | 34 | 7 | 5 | 4 | 4 | 17 | 0 | 43 | 1 | 0 |
| Ramirez, Adrian, Monclova * | 4 | 3 | .571 | 6.75 | 15 | 4 | 0 | 0 | 2 | 0 | 24.0 | 37 | 116 | 24 | 18 | 2 | 1 | 1 | 1 | 11 | 0 | 11 | 0 | 0 |
| Ramirez, Roberto, Mexico * | 10 | 5 | .667 | 4.07 | 19 | 19 | 2 | 1 | 0 | 0 | 112.2 | 128 | 471 | 56 | 51 | 8 | 2 | 3 | 5 | 28 | 0 | 44 | 7 | 0 |
| Renovato, Nestor, San Luis Potosi | 2 | 6 | .250 | 5.86 | 28 | 9 | 1 | 0 | 3 | 0 | 66.0 | 82 | 301 | 46 | 43 | 9 | 4 | 4 | 2 | 27 | 2 | 30 | 4 | 0 |
| Reyes, Nate, Saltillo * | 4 | 4 | .500 | 4.28 | 15 | 13 | 1 | 0 | 0 | 0 | 61.0 | 71 | 268 | 37 | 29 | 5 | 1 | 5 | 3 | 19 | 1 | 32 | 1 | 1 |
| Rios, Alejandro, Aguascalientes | 4 | 6 | .400 | 6.86 | 18 | 5 | 0 | 0 | 2 | 0 | 40.2 | 46 | 199 | 37 | 31 | 7 | 2 | 1 | 2 | 33 | 0 | 20 | 7 | 0 |
| Rios, Jesus, Tabasco | 5 | 4 | .556 | 2.81 | 14 | 14 | 1 | 1 | 0 | 0 | 80.0 | 59 | 333 | 30 | 25 | 4 | 8 | 5 | 12 | 32 | 4 | 42 | 4 | 0 |
| Rivera, Ben, Mexico | 0 | 1 | .000 | 31.50 | 4 | 0 | 0 | 0 | 2 | 1 | 2.0 | 7 | 13 | 7 | 7 | 1 | 0 | 1 | 0 | 1 | 0 | 1 | 0 | 0 |
| Rivera, Ben, Vaqueros | 1 | 1 | .500 | 3.50 | 16 | 0 | 0 | 0 | 14 | 9 | 18.0 | 15 | 74 | 7 | 7 | 1 | 0 | 0 | 0 | 5 | 0 | 12 | 2 | 0 |
| Rivera, Francisco, Aguascalientes | 10 | 2 | .833 | 3.75 | 21 | 18 | 3 | 0 | 1 | 0 | 115.1 | 120 | 486 | 51 | 48 | 13 | 6 | 3 | 3 | 37 | 2 | 56 | 3 | 0 |

| Pitcher, Team | W | L | Pct. | ERA | G | GS | CG | ShO | GF | Sv. | IP | H | TBF | R | ER | HR | SH | SF | HB | BB | IBB | SO | WP | Bk. |
|---|---|---|---|---|---|---|---|---|---|---|---|---|---|---|---|---|---|---|---|---|---|---|---|---|
| Rivera, Luis, Tigres | 0 | 1 | .000 | 15.43 | 3 | 1 | 0 | 0 | 0 | 0 | 4.2 | 6 | 26 | 8 | 8 | 0 | 1 | 0 | 0 | 7 | 0 | 2 | 1 | 0 |
| Rivera, Luis, Puebla | 0 | 2 | .000 | 9.87 | 5 | 5 | 0 | 0 | 0 | 0 | 17.1 | 19 | 84 | 22 | 19 | 4 | 1 | 1 | 0 | 16 | 0 | 5 | 2 | 0 |
| Rivera, Oscar, Yucatan * | 6 | 5 | .545 | 3.30 | 17 | 14 | 1 | 0 | 1 | 0 | 79.0 | 71 | 318 | 32 | 29 | 6 | 1 | 3 | 1 | 18 | 4 | 50 | 1 | 0 |
| Rivera, Oscar, Tigres | 2 | 4 | .333 | 7.11 | 7 | 6 | 0 | 0 | 1 | 0 | 25.1 | 27 | 113 | 23 | 20 | 2 | 0 | 2 | 0 | 19 | 1 | 10 | 4 | 0 |
| Rivera, Oscar, Campeche | 0 | 2 | .000 | 12.46 | 7 | 5 | 0 | 0 | 1 | 0 | 13.0 | 21 | 78 | 19 | 18 | 4 | 1 | 0 | 2 | 18 | 0 | 3 | 2 | 0 |
| Rivera, Paul, Tabasco * | 0 | 0 | .000 | 1.76 | 20 | 0 | 0 | 0 | 7 | 2 | 15.1 | 13 | 70 | 5 | 3 | 0 | 0 | 0 | 1 | 10 | 2 | 5 | 1 | 0 |
| Rodriguez, Enoc, Cancun * | 0 | 1 | .000 | 4.82 | 2 | 2 | 0 | 0 | 0 | 0 | 9.1 | 10 | 37 | 7 | 5 | 1 | 1 | 0 | 0 | 3 | 0 | 0 | 0 | 0 |
| Rodriguez, Enoc, Aguascalientes * | 0 | 0 | .000 | 7.36 | 6 | 0 | 0 | 0 | 0 | 0 | 3.2 | 4 | 19 | 3 | 3 | 1 | 0 | 0 | 0 | 4 | 0 | 2 | 0 | 0 |
| Rodriguez, Francisco, Tigres * | 1 | 0 | 1.000 | 4.55 | 10 | 4 | 0 | 0 | 1 | 1 | 31.2 | 42 | 151 | 21 | 16 | 2 | 4 | 3 | 0 | 12 | 1 | 8 | 1 | 0 |
| Rodriguez, Jesus, Monclova | 2 | 2 | .500 | 8.58 | 21 | 6 | 0 | 0 | 4 | 0 | 43.0 | 72 | 224 | 44 | 41 | 4 | 5 | 6 | 4 | 25 | 0 | 13 | 3 | 1 |
| Rodriguez, Manuel, Campeche | 4 | 4 | .500 | 4.97 | 30 | 0 | 0 | 0 | 11 | 1 | 38.0 | 35 | 165 | 22 | 21 | 4 | 0 | 0 | 1 | 17 | 0 | 15 | 1 | 0 |
| Romero, Josmir, Oaxaca | 3 | 5 | .375 | 4.10 | 15 | 6 | 0 | 0 | 7 | 2 | 48.1 | 52 | 212 | 26 | 22 | 7 | 2 | 1 | 1 | 23 | 2 | 23 | 2 | 0 |
| Roque, Jorge, Vaqueros | 0 | 3 | .000 | 7.20 | 20 | 4 | 0 | 0 | 5 | 0 | 35.0 | 44 | 157 | 31 | 28 | 10 | 2 | 2 | 2 | 11 | 0 | 9 | 2 | 0 |
| Roque, Rafael, Tigres * | 7 | 4 | .636 | 4.02 | 16 | 14 | 3 | 1 | 1 | 0 | 80.2 | 70 | 358 | 43 | 36 | 5 | 7 | 2 | 8 | 55 | 2 | 74 | 5 | 1 |
| Rubio, Miguel, Monterrey | 1 | 7 | .125 | 4.08 | 32 | 0 | 0 | 0 | 29 | 18 | 28.2 | 39 | 139 | 18 | 13 | 2 | 1 | 0 | 1 | 13 | 2 | 23 | 3 | 0 |
| Ruelas, Heriberto, Mexico * | 0 | 0 | .000 | 11.05 | 15 | 0 | 0 | 0 | 6 | 0 | 14.2 | 21 | 78 | 18 | 18 | 4 | 0 | 0 | 0 | 13 | 0 | 16 | 2 | 0 |
| Ruiz, Arturo, Saltillo * | 0 | 3 | .000 | 5.73 | 24 | 1 | 0 | 0 | 7 | 1 | 37.2 | 48 | 171 | 28 | 24 | 2 | 1 | 0 | 0 | 14 | 1 | 17 | 1 | 0 |
| Ruiz, Cecilio, Tabasco * | 4 | 3 | .571 | 3.42 | 13 | 8 | 0 | 0 | 2 | 0 | 50.0 | 63 | 209 | 20 | 19 | 4 | 7 | 0 | 1 | 8 | 0 | 18 | 0 | 1 |
| Ruiz, Miguel, Campeche | 0 | 0 | .000 | 0.00 | 4 | 1 | 0 | 0 | 2 | 0 | 5.2 | 4 | 23 | 1 | 0 | 0 | 0 | 0 | 0 | 2 | 0 | 3 | 1 | 0 |
| Sabido, Eduardo, Yucatan | 0 | 1 | .000 | 3.86 | 1 | 1 | 0 | 0 | 0 | 0 | 2.1 | 2 | 11 | 1 | 1 | 0 | 0 | 0 | 0 | 4 | 0 | 1 | 1 | 0 |
| Saenz, Alfredo, Aguascalientes * | 0 | 0 | .000 | 11.57 | 4 | 0 | 0 | 0 | 2 | 0 | 2.1 | 4 | 15 | 3 | 3 | 0 | 0 | 0 | 1 | 4 | 1 | 0 | 0 | 0 |
| Salas, Carlos, Saltillo | 1 | 0 | 1.000 | 0.00 | 1 | 0 | 0 | 0 | 0 | 0 | 1.2 | 2 | 8 | 1 | 0 | 0 | 0 | 0 | 0 | 1 | 0 | 0 | 0 | 0 |
| Salas, Noel, Saltillo | 0 | 0 | .000 | 0.00 | 1 | 0 | 0 | 0 | 1 | 0 | 1.0 | 1 | 4 | 0 | 0 | 0 | 0 | 0 | 0 | 0 | 0 | 0 | 0 | 0 |
| Salcido, Arturo, Saltillo | 1 | 0 | 1.000 | 7.24 | 9 | 0 | 0 | 0 | 1 | 0 | 13.2 | 12 | 67 | 14 | 11 | 2 | 0 | 0 | 0 | 16 | 1 | 13 | 3 | 0 |
| Saldana, Jose, Veracruz | 3 | 0 | 1.000 | 5.83 | 29 | 0 | 0 | 0 | 5 | 0 | 46.1 | 57 | 202 | 33 | 30 | 9 | 2 | 4 | 2 | 9 | 0 | 28 | 4 | 0 |
| Salgado, Eduardo, Cancun | 6 | 10 | .375 | 4.11 | 22 | 14 | 3 | 0 | 2 | 0 | 92.0 | 105 | 395 | 52 | 42 | 9 | 4 | 6 | 2 | 28 | 3 | 32 | 2 | 0 |
| Sanchez, Alejandro, Cancun | 4 | 4 | .500 | 4.12 | 34 | 0 | 0 | 0 | 15 | 1 | 39.1 | 40 | 178 | 21 | 18 | 3 | 0 | 0 | 2 | 20 | 7 | 15 | 2 | 1 |
| Sanchez, Claudio, Veracruz | 1 | 3 | .250 | 3.18 | 33 | 0 | 0 | 0 | 16 | 4 | 45.1 | 46 | 195 | 19 | 16 | 4 | 1 | 2 | 1 | 13 | 4 | 15 | 1 | 0 |
| Sanchez, Efrain, Campeche | 5 | 5 | .500 | 3.90 | 13 | 11 | 1 | 0 | 0 | 0 | 64.2 | 53 | 287 | 31 | 28 | 8 | 4 | 2 | 4 | 38 | 0 | 23 | 0 | 0 |
| Sanchez, Jose, Tijuana | 0 | 0 | .000 | 3.86 | 2 | 0 | 0 | 0 | 2 | 0 | 2.1 | 1 | 12 | 1 | 1 | 0 | 0 | 0 | 0 | 4 | 0 | 3 | 1 | 0 |
| Sangeado, Juan, Cancun | 1 | 2 | .333 | 4.40 | 18 | 4 | 0 | 0 | 5 | 0 | 45.0 | 46 | 205 | 24 | 22 | 5 | 1 | 1 | 2 | 32 | 0 | 26 | 5 | 0 |
| Silva, Jose, Mexico | 12 | 3 | .800 | 4.87 | 20 | 16 | 3 | 0 | 0 | 0 | 101.2 | 138 | 444 | 57 | 55 | 8 | 9 | 2 | 3 | 27 | 0 | 61 | 5 | 0 |
| Silva, Walter, San Luis Potosi | 2 | 5 | .286 | 4.04 | 29 | 1 | 0 | 0 | 11 | 1 | 35.2 | 32 | 156 | 17 | 16 | 5 | 0 | 0 | 1 | 18 | 2 | 36 | 4 | 0 |
| Silva, Walter, Monterrey | 3 | 1 | .750 | 7.50 | 13 | 0 | 0 | 0 | 2 | 0 | 18.0 | 21 | 87 | 16 | 15 | 1 | 2 | 1 | 2 | 9 | 1 | 13 | 1 | 0 |
| Sinohui, David, Oaxaca | 3 | 0 | 1.000 | 2.66 | 20 | 0 | 0 | 0 | 14 | 10 | 20.1 | 15 | 86 | 8 | 6 | 2 | 2 | 1 | 1 | 11 | 2 | 13 | 2 | 0 |
| Solano, Adrian, Tigres | 0 | 0 | .000 | 18.00 | 1 | 0 | 0 | 0 | 0 | 0 | 1.0 | 0 | 7 | 2 | 2 | 0 | 0 | 0 | 0 | 4 | 0 | 0 | 0 | 0 |
| Solis, Tomas, Puebla * | 0 | 0 | .000 | 5.40 | 7 | 0 | 0 | 0 | 0 | 0 | 1.2 | 3 | 9 | 1 | 1 | 0 | 0 | 0 | 0 | 2 | 0 | 2 | 0 | 0 |
| Solis, Tomas, Tigres * | 2 | 0 | 1.000 | 4.43 | 22 | 0 | 0 | 0 | 3 | 0 | 20.1 | 23 | 99 | 11 | 10 | 0 | 1 | 1 | 3 | 11 | 3 | 14 | 0 | 0 |
| Soto, Cruz, San Luis Potosi | 0 | 0 | .000 | 25.07 | 6 | 0 | 0 | 0 | 1 | 0 | 4.2 | 15 | 33 | 13 | 13 | 0 | 1 | 0 | 0 | 4 | 0 | 3 | 1 | 0 |
| Soto, Cruz, Puebla | 1 | 0 | 1.000 | 1.32 | 9 | 0 | 0 | 0 | 4 | 0 | 13.2 | 11 | 53 | 3 | 2 | 0 | 0 | 0 | 0 | 2 | 0 | 3 | 0 | 0 |
| Strong, Joe, Yucatan | 1 | 3 | .250 | 5.40 | 14 | 0 | 0 | 0 | 8 | 3 | 16.2 | 18 | 79 | 10 | 10 | 0 | 0 | 0 | 2 | 10 | 3 | 16 | 1 | 0 |
| Strong, Joe, Monclova | 3 | 3 | .500 | 4.84 | 15 | 0 | 0 | 0 | 14 | 2 | 22.1 | 22 | 100 | 12 | 12 | 1 | 1 | 0 | 0 | 13 | 2 | 19 | 1 | 0 |
| Tejeda, Felix, Yucatan * | 1 | 1 | .500 | 6.43 | 27 | 0 | 0 | 0 | 5 | 1 | 14.0 | 19 | 65 | 10 | 10 | 1 | 0 | 1 | 0 | 6 | 3 | 6 | 0 | 0 |
| Tequida, Mauricio, Mexico | 3 | 0 | 1.000 | 4.32 | 13 | 1 | 0 | 0 | 3 | 0 | 25.0 | 37 | 119 | 16 | 12 | 1 | 2 | 2 | 0 | 9 | 0 | 8 | 5 | 0 |
| Terrazas, J.C., Cancun * | 1 | 1 | .500 | 5.40 | 6 | 0 | 0 | 0 | 0 | 0 | 3.1 | 10 | 20 | 3 | 2 | 0 | 0 | 0 | 0 | 0 | 0 | 0 | 0 | 0 |
| Terrazas, J.C., Aguascalientes * | 0 | 0 | .000 | 16.20 | 3 | 0 | 0 | 0 | 2 | 0 | 1.2 | 3 | 12 | 3 | 3 | 0 | 0 | 0 | 1 | 3 | 0 | 1 | 0 | 0 |
| Torres, Melqui, Mexico | 0 | 0 | .000 | 6.43 | 7 | 0 | 0 | 0 | 2 | 0 | 7.0 | 10 | 35 | 5 | 5 | 0 | 0 | 0 | 2 | 3 | 0 | 9 | 1 | 0 |
| Torres, Melqui, Oaxaca | 0 | 0 | .000 | 3.12 | 10 | 0 | 0 | 0 | 9 | 8 | 8.2 | 7 | 35 | 3 | 3 | 0 | 0 | 0 | 0 | 2 | 0 | 4 | 0 | 0 |
| Tovar, Angel, Cancun | 2 | 3 | .400 | 1.88 | 36 | 0 | 0 | 0 | 34 | 19 | 38.1 | 34 | 169 | 11 | 8 | 0 | 2 | 3 | 2 | 21 | 6 | 25 | 4 | 0 |
| Trevino, Jesus, Mexico * | 0 | 0 | .000 | 13.50 | 8 | 0 | 0 | 0 | 2 | 0 | 6.2 | 13 | 36 | 12 | 10 | 0 | 0 | 2 | 0 | 5 | 0 | 4 | 0 | 0 |
| Trevino, Jesus, Oaxaca * | 0 | 1 | .000 | 18.90 | 3 | 1 | 0 | 0 | 0 | 0 | 3.1 | 6 | 20 | 9 | 7 | 2 | 1 | 1 | 0 | 5 | 0 | 3 | 3 | 0 |
| Valdez, Armando, Puebla | 12 | 4 | .750 | 3.29 | 19 | 18 | 1 | 0 | 0 | 0 | 106.2 | 111 | 450 | 45 | 39 | 9 | 2 | 1 | 5 | 40 | 1 | 74 | 5 | 0 |
| Valdez, Joel, Vaqueros | 1 | 0 | 1.000 | 6.41 | 20 | 0 | 0 | 0 | 3 | 0 | 19.2 | 34 | 102 | 18 | 14 | 3 | 0 | 0 | 1 | 12 | 1 | 9 | 3 | 0 |
| Valenzuela, Jose, Tigres | 0 | 0 | .000 | 10.13 | 4 | 0 | 0 | 0 | 0 | 0 | 5.1 | 4 | 25 | 8 | 6 | 1 | 0 | 0 | 1 | 7 | 0 | 2 | 0 | 0 |
| Valerio, Julio, Mexico * | 4 | 0 | 1.000 | 3.58 | 37 | 0 | 0 | 0 | 13 | 3 | 32.2 | 42 | 145 | 16 | 13 | 4 | 0 | 0 | 1 | 6 | 2 | 9 | 1 | 1 |
| Vargas, Joel, Tabasco | 4 | 8 | .333 | 3.33 | 18 | 11 | 2 | 0 | 6 | 2 | 83.2 | 90 | 359 | 38 | 31 | 2 | 4 | 3 | 3 | 26 | 2 | 35 | 2 | 1 |
| Vazquez, Adrian, Cancun | 2 | 7 | .222 | 4.71 | 11 | 11 | 0 | 0 | 0 | 0 | 57.1 | 53 | 248 | 35 | 30 | 3 | 0 | 2 | 6 | 29 | 0 | 20 | 2 | 0 |
| Vega, Obed, Cancun | 2 | 5 | .286 | 3.08 | 15 | 15 | 1 | 0 | 0 | 0 | 79.0 | 81 | 333 | 33 | 27 | 5 | 7 | 1 | 3 | 32 | 0 | 34 | 8 | 0 |
| Verdugo, Hugo, Aguascalientes | 5 | 3 | .625 | 5.26 | 32 | 7 | 0 | 0 | 0 | 0 | 78.2 | 88 | 353 | 49 | 46 | 4 | 7 | 4 | 8 | 46 | 2 | 40 | 5 | 1 |
| Verdugo, Orlando, San Luis Potosi | 1 | 2 | .333 | 7.40 | 14 | 10 | 0 | 0 | 1 | 0 | 48.2 | 71 | 242 | 40 | 40 | 3 | 3 | 3 | 3 | 29 | 1 | 24 | 2 | 0 |
| Verdugo, Oswaldo, Yucatan | 2 | 5 | .286 | 5.09 | 45 | 0 | 0 | 0 | 11 | 1 | 40.2 | 42 | 182 | 26 | 23 | 8 | 1 | 0 | 0 | 25 | 4 | 23 | 1 | 0 |
| Verdugo, Roberto, Tabasco | 6 | 5 | .545 | 3.19 | 41 | 0 | 0 | 0 | 14 | 2 | 42.1 | 35 | 196 | 16 | 15 | 5 | 0 | 3 | 6 | 29 | 6 | 31 | 4 | 1 |
| Villalobos, Fernando, Monterrey | 1 | 0 | 1.000 | 3.75 | 6 | 1 | 0 | 0 | 1 | 0 | 12.0 | 9 | 48 | 5 | 5 | 0 | 0 | 0 | 0 | 3 | 0 | 10 | 3 | 0 |
| Villarreal, Salvador, San Luis Potosi | 3 | 2 | .600 | 7.38 | 23 | 0 | 0 | 0 | 6 | 0 | 42.2 | 58 | 209 | 37 | 35 | 4 | 0 | 2 | 3 | 29 | 1 | 31 | 6 | 0 |
| Vizcarra, Ernesto, Campeche | 2 | 0 | 1.000 | 3.42 | 26 | 1 | 0 | 0 | 5 | 0 | 50.0 | 45 | 201 | 21 | 19 | 6 | 0 | 1 | 0 | 9 | 2 | 24 | 0 | 0 |
| Vizcarra, William, Yucatan | 0 | 2 | .000 | 7.45 | 6 | 1 | 0 | 0 | 1 | 0 | 9.2 | 14 | 45 | 8 | 8 | 2 | 0 | 1 | 0 | 5 | 0 | 2 | 1 | 1 |
| Ward, Bryan, Monclova * | 7 | 7 | .500 | 2.83 | 18 | 18 | 1 | 1 | 0 | 0 | 108.0 | 118 | 461 | 37 | 34 | 4 | 5 | 3 | 7 | 34 | 0 | 68 | 2 | 1 |
| Webster, Daniel, Campeche | 1 | 0 | 1.000 | 1.80 | 1 | 1 | 0 | 0 | 0 | 0 | 5.0 | 4 | 20 | 1 | 1 | 0 | 0 | 0 | 1 | 1 | 0 | 1 | 0 | 0 |
| Woodman, Hank, Mexico-Yucatan | 1 | 3 | .250 | 6.04 | 14 | 3 | 0 | 0 | 6 | 4 | 25.1 | 26 | 118 | 18 | 17 | 1 | 1 | 6 | 0 | 17 | 2 | 18 | 1 | 0 |
| Yepiz, Heriberto, Yucatan | 0 | 0 | .000 | 2.08 | 4 | 0 | 0 | 0 | 2 | 0 | 4.1 | 1 | 16 | 1 | 1 | 0 | 0 | 0 | 0 | 2 | 0 | 2 | 1 | 0 |

| Pitcher, Team | W | L | Pct. | ERA | G | GS | CG | ShO | GF | Sv. | IP | H | TBF | R | ER | HR | SH | SF | HB | BB | IBB | SO | WP | Bk. |
|---|---|---|---|---|---|---|---|---|---|---|---|---|---|---|---|---|---|---|---|---|---|---|---|---|
| Zambrano, Baudel, Tigres | 0 | 1 | .000 | 3.86 | 11 | 0 | 0 | 0 | 7 | 0 | 14.0 | 12 | 58 | 6 | 6 | 3 | 0 | 0 | 0 | 4 | 2 | 5 | 0 | 0 |
| Zambrano, Baudel, San Luis Potosi | 0 | 1 | .000 | 6.14 | 10 | 0 | 0 | 0 | 3 | 0 | 14.2 | 21 | 69 | 12 | 10 | 4 | 0 | 0 | 0 | 3 | 0 | 6 | 1 | 0 |
| Zavala, Marcos, Tigres * | 0 | 0 | .000 | 7.71 | 5 | 0 | 0 | 0 | 1 | 0 | 4.2 | 11 | 30 | 6 | 4 | 0 | 1 | 1 | 0 | 5 | 2 | 1 | 0 | 0 |
| Zavala, Marcos, Monterrey * | 0 | 0 | .000 | 11.00 | 20 | 0 | 0 | 0 | 1 | 0 | 9.0 | 13 | 45 | 11 | 11 | 1 | 0 | 0 | 0 | 5 | 1 | 7 | 0 | 0 |

COMBINATION SHUTOUTS: **Aguascalientes** (2)—F. Rivera-M. Diaz, Verdugo-Orea-M. Diaz. **Campeche** (1)—Campos-Pineda-M. Rodriguez. **Cancun** (1)—Vazquez-Couoh. **Laguna** (3)—I. Giron-E. Giron, Gomez-E. Giron-B. Rivera, Gomez-E. Giron-B. Rivera. **Mexico** (7)—J. Silva-Manning-Cruz-Valerio, Ramirez-Hansell, Mairena-Hansell, J. Silva-Dominguez, Mairena-Hansell, J. Castillo-Tequida-Valerio-Hansell, Ramirez-Hansell. **Monclova** (4)—Dorame-J. Flores-De la Rosa, Ward-J. Flores-Federico, Ward-De la Rosa, Ward-De la Rosa. **Monterrey** (7)—De Hart-W. Silva-R. Garcia, Ochoa-Castellanos-McGlinchy-Rubio, McGlinchy-Castellanos, Loya-S. Mora, De Hart-Aguirre, McGlinchy-Parra-Rubio, Manrique-S. Mora-Zavala-Rubio. **Oaxaca** (5)—Romero-Leon, E. Mora-Avalos, E. Mora-Leon, Jimenez-Leon-E. Hernandez, Elizalde-E. Hernandez-Neri-Avalos. **Puebla** (4)—P. Ortega-M. Lopez-Cervantes, Navarro-Espinoza, P.Ortega-R. Ortega-M. Lopez, Alvarez-Aybar. **Saltillo** (5)—I. Flores-J. Garcia-Duarte-Picardo, R. Diaz-Mendoza-M. Gonzalez, I. Flores-Picardo, Coco-N. Reyes-J. Garcia-Ruiz, Coco-Guzman-Mendoza. San Luis **Potosi** (4)—A. Castillo-Renovato-J. Lopez, Esquer-W. Silva, G. Gonzalez-Montoya-H. Garcia-Cervantes, Picota-W. Silva-H. Garcia-Cervantes. **Tabasco** (5)—V. Gonzalez-Osuna, Fernandez-R.Verdugo, Osuna-Herrera, Fernandez-Herrera-Pimentel-Verdugo, Rios-Herrera. **Tigres** (4)—Roque-Estrella-S. Hernandez, Estrella-Solis-Manzano-Munoz-S. Hernandez, Estrella-S. Hernandez, Campillo-S. Hernandez. **Tijuana** (6)—Nunez-Garibay-Quintanilla-Dominguez-Parra, C. Martinez-Quintanilla-Parra, Beltran-Castellanos-J. Garcia-Quintanilla, L. Gonzalez-Quintanilla, Beltran-Castellanos-N. Lopez-Cortes-Quintanilla, Escobedo-Pablos-Castellanos-Cortes. **Yucatan** (4)—Pesqueira-Verdugo, Palafox-C. Reyes-Tejeda, O. Rivera-Strong, Aceves-Woodman.

NO-HIT GAMES: Roque, Tigres, defeated Cancun, 1-0, April 11.

# 2004 FIELDING

## TEAM

| Team | G | PO | A | E | TC | DP | TP | PB | Pct. |
|---|---|---|---|---|---|---|---|---|---|
| Mexico | 102 | 2475 | 396 | 68 | 2939 | 131 | 0 | 1 | .977 |
| Monterrey | 97 | 2408 | 281 | 68 | 2757 | 92 | 0 | 7 | .975 |
| Yucatan | 96 | 2381 | 285 | 78 | 2744 | 85 | 0 | 4 | .972 |
| Puebla | 97 | 2389 | 356 | 85 | 2830 | 118 | 0 | 10 | .970 |
| Aguascalientes | 100 | 2449 | 346 | 86 | 2881 | 119 | 0 | 8 | .970 |
| Veracruz | 98 | 2377 | 350 | 90 | 2817 | 97 | 0 | 11 | .968 |
| Tijuana | 97 | 2417 | 306 | 93 | 2816 | 92 | 0 | 6 | .967 |
| Vaqueros | 99 | 2386 | 332 | 93 | 2811 | 92 | 0 | 11 | .967 |
| Saltillo | 97 | 2415 | 298 | 92 | 2805 | 99 | 0 | 7 | .967 |
| Tigres | 97 | 2413 | 315 | 92 | 2820 | 119 | 0 | 13 | .967 |
| Tabasco | 91 | 2235 | 304 | 90 | 2629 | 87 | 0 | 4 | .966 |
| Cancun | 100 | 2409 | 330 | 101 | 2840 | 116 | 0 | 8 | .964 |
| San Luis Potosi | 98 | 2396 | 287 | 100 | 2783 | 92 | 0 | 6 | .964 |
| Oaxaca | 97 | 2374 | 337 | 105 | 2816 | 111 | 0 | 5 | .963 |
| Monclova | 99 | 2398 | 339 | 107 | 2844 | 129 | 0 | 8 | .962 |
| Campeche | 95 | 2362 | 304 | 107 | 2773 | 75 | 0 | 7 | .961 |

## INDIVIDUAL

### FIRST BASEMEN

NOTE: All caps denotes fielding-percentage leader based on 55 games for catchers, 73 for all other non-pitchers and 88 innings for pitchers. *Throws lefthanded.

| Player, Team | Pct. | G | PO | A | E | TC | DP |
|---|---|---|---|---|---|---|---|
| Adriana, Sharnol, MVA | 1.000 | 2 | 16 | 1 | 0 | 17 | 2 |
| Adriana, Sharnol, LAG | .980 | 12 | 92 | 6 | 2 | 100 | 11 |
| Adriana, Sharnol, MVA-LAG | .983 | 14 | 108 | 7 | 2 | 117 | 13 |
| Aganza, Ruben, SLT | 1.000 | 16 | 83 | 4 | 0 | 87 | 10 |
| Almeida, Shammar, OAX* | 1.000 | 29 | 120 | 4 | 0 | 124 | 13 |
| Amezcua, Adan, SLP | 1.000 | 1 | 2 | 0 | 0 | 2 | 0 |
| Barajas, Edison, LAG* | 1.000 | 3 | 9 | 0 | 0 | 9 | 0 |
| Brena, Jaime, OAX | 1.000 | 1 | 1 | 0 | 0 | 1 | 0 |
| Burkhart, Morgan, SLT | .991 | 90 | 720 | 53 | 7 | 780 | 76 |
| Bustillos, Luis, SLP | 1.000 | 2 | 9 | 0 | 0 | 9 | 2 |
| Camarero, Rafael, VER | .988 | 20 | 76 | 9 | 1 | 86 | 6 |
| Canizalez, Juan, LAG | 1.000 | 6 | 43 | 2 | 0 | 45 | 2 |
| Carrillo, Matias, TIG* | 1.000 | 1 | 9 | 0 | 0 | 9 | 2 |
| Castaneda, Hector, YUC* | .984 | 50 | 338 | 36 | 6 | 380 | 36 |
| Castaneda, Rafael, LAG | 1.000 | 13 | 99 | 5 | 0 | 104 | 11 |
| Castellano, Pedro, MXO | .997 | 76 | 703 | 35 | 2 | 740 | 88 |
| Castro, Domingo, MVA | 1.000 | 1 | 2 | 0 | 0 | 2 | 0 |
| Cervantes, Refugio, CCN* | .985 | 30 | 247 | 13 | 4 | 264 | 39 |
| Cervantes, Refugio, MXO* | 1.000 | 18 | 148 | 8 | 0 | 156 | 17 |
| Cervantes, Refugio, CCN-MXO* | 990 | 1 | 395 | 21 | 4 | 420 | 56 |
| Chan, Armando, YUC* | 1.000 | 1 | 2 | 1 | 0 | 3 | 0 |
| Connell, Lino, VER | 1.000 | 12 | 58 | 1 | 0 | 59 | 4 |
| Contreras, Sergio, TIG* | .988 | 28 | 155 | 10 | 2 | 167 | 14 |
| Crespo, Jorge, OAX | 1.000 | 1 | 2 | 0 | 0 | 2 | 1 |
| Cruz, Fausto, OAX | .987 | 37 | 289 | 21 | 4 | 314 | 45 |
| Cruz, Marco, YUC | 1.000 | 2 | 6 | 1 | 0 | 7 | 0 |
| Diaz, Eddy, YUC* | .988 | 21 | 70 | 9 | 1 | 80 | 3 |
| Diaz, Luis, VER | .984 | 20 | 120 | 6 | 2 | 128 | 10 |
| Diaz, Luis, LAG | 1.000 | 1 | 4 | 0 | 0 | 4 | 1 |
| Diaz, Luis, VER-LAG | 985 | 8 | 124 | 6 | 2 | 132 | 11 |
| Diaz, Pedro, PUE | 1.000 | 2 | 1 | 0 | 0 | 1 | 1 |
| Espino, Daniel, CCN | .997 | 46 | 348 | 35 | 1 | 384 | 39 |
| Espinosa, Ramon, LAG | 1.000 | 5 | 38 | 5 | 0 | 43 | 2 |
| Esquer, Ramon, TAB | 1.000 | 3 | 11 | 2 | 0 | 13 | 0 |
| Estrada, Hector, LAG | 1.000 | 1 | 2 | 0 | 0 | 2 | 0 |
| Fentanes, Oscar, VER | .990 | 17 | 92 | 6 | 1 | 99 | 9 |
| Fornes, Daniel, MTY* | 1.000 | 11 | 105 | 6 | 0 | 111 | 7 |
| Freire, Alejandro, VER | .996 | 25 | 252 | 24 | 1 | 277 | 33 |
| Garcia, Carlos, LAG | 1.000 | 1 | 5 | 1 | 0 | 6 | 0 |
| Garcia, Cornelio, LAG* | .992 | 19 | 118 | 11 | 1 | 130 | 12 |
| Garcia, Ernesto, ASC | .967 | 7 | 27 | 2 | 1 | 30 | 2 |
| Garcia, Guillermo, TIG | .988 | 74 | 602 | 36 | 8 | 646 | 82 |
| Garcia, Luis, TIG | 1.000 | 1 | 9 | 1 | 0 | 10 | 0 |
| Garcia, Omar, MVA | 1.000 | 3 | 25 | 1 | 0 | 26 | 4 |
| Garcia, Omar, SLP | .986 | 8 | 63 | 5 | 1 | 69 | 6 |
| Garcia, Omar, MVA-SLP | .989 | 2 | 88 | 6 | 1 | 95 | 10 |
| Gavia, Jesus, ASC | 1.000 | 1 | 7 | 0 | 0 | 7 | 0 |
| Gonzalez, Roman, LAG | 1.000 | 2 | 2 | 0 | 0 | 2 | 0 |
| Grijak, Kevin, CAM* | 1.000 | 5 | 32 | 1 | 0 | 33 | 3 |
| Iturbe, Pedro, PUE* | .996 | 73 | 633 | 57 | 3 | 693 | 88 |
| Landaeta, Luis, TIJ* | .989 | 53 | 408 | 36 | 5 | 449 | 42 |
| Lara, Idelfonso, ASC | .989 | 13 | 85 | 7 | 1 | 93 | 8 |
| Lara, Idelfonso, LAG | 1.000 | 1 | 7 | 2 | 0 | 9 | 0 |
| Lara, Idelfonso, ASC-LAG | .990 | 34 | 92 | 9 | 1 | 102 | 8 |
| LeBron, Juan. CCN | 1.000 | 1 | 7 | 1 | 0 | 8 | 1 |
| Lopez, Raul, MVA* | .990 | 87 | 715 | 56 | 8 | 779 | 98 |
| Marrero, Oreste, OAX* | .990 | 20 | 185 | 14 | 2 | 201 | 18 |
| Marrero, Oreste, VER* | .989 | 19 | 160 | 15 | 2 | 177 | 20 |
| Marrero, Oreste, OAX-VER* | .989 | 1 | 345 | 29 | 4 | 378 | 38 |
| Martinez, Ray, MXO | 1.000 | 13 | 52 | 4 | 0 | 56 | 5 |
| Medina, Jose, MVA | 1.000 | 3 | 6 | 1 | 0 | 7 | 0 |
| Mendez, Francisco, MTY* | .985 | 25 | 124 | 5 | 2 | 131 | 14 |
| Montano, Angel, TIJ* | 1.000 | 3 | 7 | 0 | 0 | 7 | 0 |
| Montenegro, Jose, OAX | 1.000 | 3 | 22 | 2 | 0 | 24 | 3 |
| Morales, Carlos, LAG | 1.000 | 1 | 6 | 0 | 0 | 6 | 0 |
| Mosquera, Julio, CAM | .955 | 3 | 20 | 1 | 1 | 22 | 5 |

| Player, Team | Pct. | G | PO | A | E | TC | DP |
|---|---|---|---|---|---|---|---|
| Munoz, Adan, TIG* | 1.000 | 2 | 12 | 0 | 0 | 12 | 1 |
| Munoz, JosedeJ, MVA* | .938 | 2 | 13 | 2 | 1 | 16 | 0 |
| O`Sullivan, Patrick, SLP | .986 | 84 | 616 | 37 | 9 | 662 | 66 |
| Orantes, Ramon, MTY | 1.000 | 2 | 5 | 0 | 0 | 5 | 1 |
| Ortiz, Alejandro, TIJ | 968 | 5 | 28 | 2 | 1 | 31 | 5 |
| Otanez, Willis, CAM | 990 | 32 | 273 | 16 | 3 | 292 | 22 |
| Paez, Hector, YUC* | 1.000 | 1 | 1 | 0 | 0 | 1 | 0 |
| Paez, Hector, CAM* | 1.000 | 3 | 21 | 1 | 0 | 22 | 0 |
| Paez, Hector, YUC-CAM* | 1.000 | 1 | 22 | 1 | 0 | 23 | 0 |
| Paez, Raul, TIJ* | 981 | 14 | 47 | 5 | 1 | 53 | 4 |
| Palafox, Sergio, MVA | 1.000 | 1 | 10 | 1 | 0 | 11 | 1 |
| Perez, Francisco, SLP* | .982 | 12 | 51 | 4 | 1 | 56 | 3 |
| Rios, Eduardo, ASC | 996 | 56 | 467 | 31 | 2 | 500 | 52 |
| Rivera, Francisco, VER | 1.000 | 12 | 56 | 2 | 0 | 58 | 10 |
| Rivera, Jesus, TAB* | 1.000 | 2 | 2 | 0 | 0 | 2 | 2 |
| Rodarte, Raul, TAB | 1.000 | 1 | 7 | 0 | 0 | 7 | 0 |
| Rodarte, Raul, SLP | 1.000 | 2 | 7 | 0 | 0 | 7 | 1 |
| Rodarte, Raul, TAB-SLP | 1.000 | 89 | 14 | 0 | 0 | 14 | 1 |
| Rodriguez, Armando, MVA | 1.000 | 1 | 5 | 0 | 0 | 5 | 0 |
| Rodriguez, Boi, LAG* | 975 | 27 | 146 | 8 | 4 | 158 | 12 |
| Rodriguez, Boi, CAM* | .963 | 13 | 97 | 6 | 4 | 107 | 10 |
| Rodriguez, Boi, LAG-CAM* | .970 | 60 | 243 | 14 | 8 | 265 | 22 |
| Rodriguez, Carlos, SLP | 1.000 | 3 | 17 | 2 | 0 | 19 | 6 |
| Rodriguez, Fernando, LAG | .980 | 45 | 318 | 25 | 7 | 350 | 52 |
| Rodriguez, Leonardo, MTY | 1.000 | 1 | 8 | 0 | 0 | 8 | 0 |
| Rojas, Homar, OAX | .980 | 33 | 268 | 19 | 6 | 293 | 27 |
| Romero, Marco, TIJ | .996 | 33 | 230 | 13 | 1 | 244 | 24 |
| Romero, Wilfredo, MVA | 1.000 | 13 | 66 | 4 | 0 | 70 | 8 |
| Rose, Pete, ASC* | 1.000 | 33 | 323 | 11 | 0 | 334 | 42 |
| Sanchez, Roque, CAM | .982 | 11 | 51 | 5 | 1 | 57 | 4 |
| Saucedo, Roberto, MXO | .983 | 6 | 53 | 4 | 1 | 58 | 6 |
| Sievers, Carlos, TAB* | .990 | 22 | 168 | 23 | 2 | 193 | 18 |
| Smith, Charles, MTY | .989 | 60 | 520 | 27 | 6 | 553 | 53 |
| Soto, Saul, MXO | 1.000 | 5 | 23 | 3 | 0 | 26 | 2 |
| Tapia, Cesar, PUE | 1.000 | 2 | 4 | 2 | 0 | 6 | 0 |
| Thomas, Juan, YUC | .996 | 29 | 225 | 12 | 1 | 238 | 17 |
| Toca, Jorge, CCN | .984 | 7 | 57 | 4 | 1 | 62 | 6 |
| Valdez, Emmanuel, TIG | 1.000 | 1 | 3 | 0 | 0 | 3 | 1 |
| Valdez, Mario, MTY* | 1.000 | 11 | 79 | 2 | 0 | 81 | 13 |
| Valencia, Abraham, TIJ | 1.000 | 12 | 59 | 5 | 0 | 64 | 6 |
| Valle, Cosme, CCN | .990 | 12 | 99 | 2 | 1 | 102 | 15 |
| Valle, Jorge, CCN | .990 | 9 | 86 | 9 | 1 | 96 | 17 |
| Vazquez, Jorge, TIG | .965 | 11 | 50 | 5 | 2 | 57 | 7 |
| Vega, Jesus, PUE | 1.000 | 2 | 3 | 0 | 0 | 3 | 0 |
| Velazquez, Guillermo, PUE* | .992 | 14 | 111 | 7 | 1 | 119 | 12 |
| Villalobos, Carlos, PUE | .991 | 15 | 106 | 8 | 1 | 115 | 14 |
| Villarreal, Alejandr, TIJ | 1.000 | 3 | 21 | 1 | 0 | 22 | 4 |
| Vizcarra, Roberto, CAM | .995 | 42 | 364 | 38 | 2 | 404 | 35 |
| Yan, Julian, TAB | .990 | 72 | 635 | 75 | 7 | 717 | 60 |

## SECOND BASEMEN

| Player, Team | Pct. | G | PO | A | E | TC | DP |
|---|---|---|---|---|---|---|---|
| Ahumada, Alex, MTY | 1.000 | 1 | 2 | 3 | 0 | 5 | 0 |
| *Alfonso, Manuel, TAB | 1.000 | 4 | 2 | 1 | 0 | 3 | 1 |
| Amador, Jose, ASC | .979 | 12 | 19 | 27 | 1 | 47 | 6 |
| Arias, Francisco, SLT | .935 | 8 | 19 | 10 | 2 | 31 | 3 |
| Arredondo, Alan, LAG | 1.000 | 2 | 1 | 2 | 0 | 3 | 1 |
| *Arredondo, Jesus, PUE | .987 | 59 | 143 | 162 | 4 | 309 | 52 |
| *Borges, Luis, YUC | 1.000 | 2 | 4 | 5 | 0 | 9 | 1 |
| Brena, Jaime, OAX | .981 | 81 | 185 | 222 | 8 | 415 | 70 |
| Bustillos, Luis, SLP | .982 | 34 | 83 | 84 | 3 | 170 | 18 |
| *Cansino, Jorge, VER | 1.000 | 1 | 2 | 3 | 0 | 5 | 0 |
| Carrillo, Oscar, MXO | 1.000 | 2 | 1 | 0 | 0 | 1 | 0 |
| Casillas, Hector, MVA | 1.000 | 1 | 2 | 4 | 0 | 6 | 1 |
| Castro, Arnoldo, CCN | .991 | 81 | 194 | 232 | 4 | 430 | 70 |
| Castro, Domingo, MVA | 1.000 | 1 | 0 | 1 | 0 | 1 | 1 |
| Cervera, Francisco, YUC | 1.000 | 2 | 1 | 1 | 0 | 2 | 0 |
| Connell, Lino, VER | .966 | 85 | 193 | 202 | 14 | 409 | 60 |
| Contreras, Jose, PUE | 1.000 | 1 | 1 | 1 | 0 | 2 | 1 |
| *Diaz, Eddy, YUC | 1.000 | 1 | 0 | 1 | 0 | 1 | 0 |
| Esquer, Ramon, TAB | .960 | 21 | 41 | 55 | 4 | 100 | 19 |
| Evans, Tom, TAB | .966 | 77 | 178 | 223 | 14 | 415 | 42 |
| Felix, Alejandro, LAG | .971 | 17 | 20 | 13 | 1 | 34 | 5 |
| Flores, Kevin, PUE | .988 | 21 | 32 | 53 | 1 | 86 | 15 |
| Flores, Miguel, MTY | .990 | 90 | 235 | 244 | 5 | 484 | 64 |
| Gamez, Valentin, SLP | 1.000 | 8 | 9 | 15 | 0 | 24 | 3 |
| Gastelum, Carlos, TIG | 1.000 | 2 | 2 | 4 | 0 | 6 | 1 |
| Gastelum, CarlosA, TIG | .984 | 89 | 249 | 249 | 8 | 506 | 83 |
| Gonzalez, Santiago, VER | .960 | 7 | 14 | 10 | 1 | 25 | 3 |
| Guerrero, Sergio, CAM | .980 | 95 | 226 | 262 | 10 | 498 | 64 |
| Guizar, Hector, ASC | 1.000 | 3 | 7 | 4 | 0 | 11 | 1 |
| Hernandez, Hector, VER | .971 | 22 | 29 | 39 | 2 | 70 | 14 |
| **Player, Team** | **Pct.** | **G** | **PO** | **A** | **E** | **TC** | **DP** |
| Magallanes, Ever, OAX* | .976 | 31 | 61 | 63 | 3 | 127 | 18 |
| Martinez, Abel, LAG | .992 | 29 | 61 | 66 | 1 | 128 | 16 |
| Martinez, Grimaldo, LAG | .983 | 71 | 186 | 164 | 6 | 356 | 55 |
| Mejia, Roberto, CAM | 1.000 | 3 | 6 | 6 | 0 | 12 | 1 |
| Mendoza, Omar, SLP | .984 | 13 | 28 | 32 | 1 | 61 | 9 |
| Mere, Pedro, ASC | .980 | 91 | 220 | 275 | 10 | 505 | 79 |
| Morejon, Oswaldo, LAG | .982 | 97 | 248 | 241 | 9 | 498 | 57 |
| Orrantia, Carlos, MTY | .976 | 18 | 23 | 17 | 1 | 41 | 6 |
| Palafox, Sergio, MVA | .979 | 49 | 120 | 109 | 5 | 234 | 42 |
| Perez, Alfredo, CCN | .987 | 19 | 32 | 42 | 1 | 75 | 16 |
| Perez, Jose, SLP | .972 | 55 | 117 | 130 | 7 | 254 | 35 |
| Ramirez, Jesus, OAX | 1.000 | 6 | 7 | 15 | 0 | 22 | 2 |
| Rivera, Jesus, TAB* | .846 | 9 | 3 | 8 | 2 | 13 | 1 |
| Robles, Oscar, MXO* | .983 | 84 | 186 | 268 | 8 | 462 | 75 |
| Robles, Trinidad, TIG | .967 | 8 | 14 | 15 | 1 | 30 | 3 |
| Rodriguez, Liu, TIJ | .984 | 15 | 31 | 31 | 1 | 63 | 11 |
| Romero, Flavio, SLT* | .986 | 22 | 31 | 41 | 1 | 73 | 8 |
| Ruiz, JuandeD, MVA | .941 | 3 | 4 | 12 | 1 | 17 | 2 |
| Ruiz, Ricardo, MXO | 1.000 | 2 | 0 | 2 | 0 | 2 | 0 |
| Sanchez, Jose, TIJ | .909 | 3 | 5 | 5 | 1 | 11 | 2 |
| Sanchez, Orlando, SLP | 1.000 | 3 | 4 | 1 | 0 | 5 | 1 |
| Trapaga, Julio, PUE | .984 | 43 | 54 | 70 | 2 | 126 | 20 |
| Valencia, Abraham, TIJ | 1.000 | 1 | 5 | 4 | 0 | 9 | 3 |
| Valencia, Carlos, TIJ | .967 | 80 | 192 | 221 | 14 | 427 | 52 |
| Valenzuela, Irving, MVA | .972 | 62 | 129 | 149 | 8 | 286 | 40 |
| Valle, Jorge, CCN | 1.000 | 11 | 22 | 23 | 0 | 45 | 6 |
| Vazquez, Ricardo, TIG | .900 | 8 | 11 | 7 | 2 | 20 | 3 |
| Verdugo, Vincente, SLT | .985 | 73 | 144 | 179 | 5 | 328 | 45 |
| Villalobos, Carlos, PUE | 1.000 | 4 | 5 | 4 | 0 | 9 | 1 |
| Zazueta, Juan, SLT | .959 | 24 | 45 | 48 | 4 | 97 | 13 |
| Zazueta, Mauricio, MXO | .977 | 36 | 48 | 79 | 3 | 130 | 23 |

## THIRD BASEMEN

| Player, Team | Pct. | G | PO | A | E | TC | DP |
|---|---|---|---|---|---|---|---|
| Adriana, Sharnol, MVA | .900 | 4 | 4 | 5 | 1 | 10 | 1 |
| Aganza, Ruben, SLT | .923 | 7 | 3 | 9 | 1 | 13 | 0 |
| Ahumada, Alex, MTY | .977 | 29 | 6 | 36 | 1 | 43 | 1 |
| Andrews, Shane, SLP | .925 | 38 | 44 | 79 | 10 | 133 | 11 |
| Arano, Eloy, VER | 1.000 | 5 | 2 | 3 | 0 | 5 | 0 |
| Arauz, Ignacio, MVA | .857 | 1 | 0 | 6 | 1 | 7 | 0 |
| Arias, Francisco, SLT | .951 | 26 | 13 | 45 | 3 | 61 | 3 |
| Arredondo, Alan, LAG | 1.000 | 9 | 9 | 10 | 0 | 19 | 0 |
| Arredondo, Eduardo, TAB* | .875 | 1 | 0 | 7 | 1 | 8 | 0 |
| Arredondo, Hernando, TAB | .942 | 69 | 44 | 136 | 11 | 191 | 13 |
| Beltran, Juan, CAM | 1.000 | 3 | 1 | 2 | 0 | 3 | 0 |
| Castaneda, Rafael, LAG | .899 | 29 | 31 | 31 | 7 | 69 | 3 |
| Castellano, Pedro, MXO | .970 | 13 | 10 | 22 | 1 | 33 | 3 |
| Castillo, Jesus, LAG | .000 | 1 | 0 | 0 | 1 | 1 | 0 |
| Cervera, Francisco, YUC | .991 | 55 | 31 | 74 | 1 | 106 | 6 |
| Connell, Lino, VER | .842 | 7 | 6 | 10 | 3 | 19 | 4 |
| Cruz, Fausto, OAX | .960 | 32 | 17 | 55 | 3 | 75 | 7 |
| Diaz, Eddy, YUC* | .969 | 58 | 34 | 121 | 5 | 160 | 9 |
| Diaz, Edwin, VER | .958 | 94 | 82 | 190 | 12 | 284 | 11 |
| Diaz, Pedro, PUE | .912 | 40 | 20 | 73 | 9 | 102 | 10 |
| Evans, Tom, TAB | .897 | 18 | 11 | 24 | 4 | 39 | 5 |
| Felix, Alejandro, LAG | 1.000 | 5 | 2 | 1 | 0 | 3 | 0 |
| Fentanes, Oscar, VER | 1.000 | 1 | 0 | 1 | 0 | 1 | 0 |
| Flores, Kevin, PUE | 1.000 | 1 | 0 | 3 | 0 | 3 | 1 |
| Garcia, Ernesto, ASC | 1.000 | 13 | 4 | 16 | 0 | 20 | 2 |
| Gastelum, Sergio, TIG | .980 | 13 | 18 | 30 | 1 | 49 | 3 |
| Gil, Benji, TIJ | .955 | 31 | 38 | 69 | 5 | 112 | 6 |
| Gonzalez, Israel, CAM | .667 | 4 | 1 | 1 | 1 | 3 | 0 |
| Guizar, Hector, ASC | .957 | 56 | 57 | 122 | 8 | 187 | 15 |
| Lucca, Lou, CCN | .979 | 75 | 51 | 136 | 4 | 191 | 19 |
| Magallanes, Ever, OAX* | .966 | 47 | 39 | 102 | 5 | 146 | 18 |
| Martinez, Abel, LAG | .908 | 46 | 39 | 60 | 10 | 109 | 3 |
| Martinez, Ray, MXO | .948 | 82 | 46 | 190 | 13 | 249 | 26 |
| Mejia, Roberto, CAM | .948 | 24 | 21 | 52 | 4 | 77 | 2 |
| Mendez, Francisco, MTY* | 1.000 | 2 | 0 | 1 | 0 | 1 | 0 |
| Mendoza, Omar, SLP | .936 | 61 | 47 | 115 | 11 | 173 | 11 |
| Orantes, Ramon, MTY | .974 | 76 | 45 | 140 | 5 | 190 | 10 |
| Orrantia, Carlos, MTY | 1.000 | 13 | 6 | 15 | 0 | 21 | 2 |
| Ortiz, Alejandro, TIJ | .917 | 13 | 8 | 14 | 2 | 24 | 3 |
| Palafox, Sergio, MVA | 1.000 | 5 | 2 | 7 | 0 | 9 | 0 |
| Perez, Alfredo, CCN | .900 | 12 | 0 | 9 | 1 | 10 | 1 |
| Perez, Jose, SLP | 1.000 | 1 | 0 | 1 | 0 | 1 | 0 |
| Ramirez, Oscar, CAM | .954 | 34 | 29 | 54 | 4 | 87 | 5 |
| Rios, Eduardo, ASC | .946 | 47 | 40 | 100 | 8 | 148 | 7 |
| Rivera, Jesus, TAB* | 1.000 | 10 | 8 | 22 | 0 | 30 | 3 |
| Robles, Javier, TIG | .500 | 1 | 1 | 0 | 1 | 2 | 0 |
| Robles, Oscar, MXO* | .938 | 22 | 4 | 26 | 2 | 32 | 2 |

| Player, Team | Pct. | G | PO | A | E | TC | DP |
|---|---|---|---|---|---|---|---|
| Robles, Trinidad, TIG | .974 | 31 | 21 | 53 | 2 | 76 | 11 |
| Rodarte, Raul, TAB | 1.000 | 4 | 1 | 8 | 0 | 9 | 0 |
| Rodarte, Raul, SLP | 1.000 | 1 | 1 | 1 | 0 | 2 | 0 |
| Rodarte, Raul, TAB-SLP | 1.000 | 89 | 2 | 9 | 0 | 11 | 0 |
| Romero, Flavio, SLT* | .964 | 18 | 5 | 22 | 1 | 28 | 1 |
| Rosas, Ezequiel, OAX | 1.000 | 2 | 2 | 3 | 0 | 5 | 1 |
| Ruiz, JuandeD, MVA | .962 | 70 | 46 | 156 | 8 | 210 | 15 |
| Ruiz, Ricardo, MXO | 1.000 | 3 | 0 | 2 | 0 | 2 | 1 |
| Sanchez, Jose, TIJ | .953 | 27 | 7 | 34 | 2 | 43 | 5 |
| Sanchez, Roque, CAM | .932 | 39 | 37 | 72 | 8 | 117 | 6 |
| Santana, Pedro, OAX | .874 | 32 | 24 | 87 | 16 | 127 | 7 |
| Trapaga, Julio, PUE | 1.000 | 1 | 0 | 1 | 0 | 1 | 0 |
| Trejo, Jaime, MVA | .917 | 30 | 27 | 50 | 7 | 84 | 7 |
| Valencia, Abraham, TIJ | .873 | 26 | 17 | 38 | 8 | 63 | 4 |
| Valencia, Carlos, TIJ | .975 | 14 | 13 | 26 | 1 | 40 | 2 |
| Valle, Cosme, CCN | .800 | 7 | 5 | 7 | 3 | 15 | 0 |
| Valle, Jorge, CCN | .984 | 22 | 14 | 47 | 1 | 62 | 6 |
| Vazquez, Jorge, TIG | .899 | 58 | 35 | 116 | 17 | 168 | 19 |
| Vazquez, Ricardo, TIG | .846 | 10 | 0 | 11 | 2 | 13 | 1 |
| Velez, Manuel, SLT | .989 | 28 | 26 | 60 | 1 | 87 | 3 |
| Veraz, Wilton, LAG | .992 | 36 | 37 | 89 | 1 | 127 | 14 |
| Villalobos, Carlos, PUE | .932 | 32 | 20 | 49 | 5 | 74 | 4 |
| Villarreal, Alejandr, TIJ | 1.000 | 17 | 7 | 19 | 0 | 26 | 1 |
| Vizcarra, Roberto, CAM | .976 | 17 | 12 | 29 | 1 | 42 | 1 |
| Zazueta, Juan, SLT | .949 | 45 | 29 | 65 | 5 | 99 | 10 |
| Zuniga, Tony, PUE | .938 | 45 | 28 | 109 | 9 | 146 | 16 |

## SHORTSTOPS

| Player, Team | Pct. | G | PO | A | E | TC | DP |
|---|---|---|---|---|---|---|---|
| Ahumada, Alex, MTY | .949 | 33 | 40 | 90 | 7 | 137 | 16 |
| Alejos, Fernando, CCN | .937 | 64 | 100 | 197 | 20 | 317 | 49 |
| Alfonso, Manuel, TAB* | .957 | 41 | 57 | 100 | 7 | 164 | 20 |
| Amador, Jose, ASC | .954 | 46 | 77 | 151 | 11 | 239 | 32 |
| Arias, Francisco, SLT | .968 | 25 | 32 | 59 | 3 | 94 | 8 |
| Arredondo, Alan, LAG | .946 | 23 | 25 | 45 | 4 | 74 | 8 |
| Beltran, Juan, CAM | .935 | 48 | 57 | 117 | 12 | 186 | 20 |
| Borges, Luis, YUC* | .954 | 83 | 112 | 222 | 16 | 350 | 36 |
| Bustillos, Luis, SLP | .907 | 28 | 38 | 59 | 10 | 107 | 16 |
| Cansino, Jorge, VER* | .800 | 1 | 2 | 2 | 1 | 5 | 1 |
| Carrillo, Oscar, MXO | .900 | 10 | 1 | 8 | 1 | 10 | 1 |
| Castro, Domingo, MVA | .950 | 92 | 138 | 302 | 23 | 463 | 76 |
| Cervantes, Ivan, OAX | .954 | 95 | 169 | 309 | 23 | 501 | 62 |
| Connell, Lino, VER | .909 | 5 | 5 | 15 | 2 | 22 | 3 |
| Diaz, Remigio, SLP | .969 | 66 | 86 | 195 | 9 | 290 | 27 |
| Evans, Tom, TAB | 1.000 | 1 | 1 | 0 | 0 | 1 | 1 |
| Felix, Alejandro, LAG | .846 | 5 | 2 | 9 | 2 | 13 | 3 |
| Flores, Kevin, PUE | .968 | 31 | 24 | 66 | 3 | 93 | 14 |
| Garcia, Nick, SLT | .961 | 84 | 141 | 280 | 17 | 438 | 63 |
| Gastelum, CarlosA, TIG | 1.000 | 3 | 4 | 6 | 0 | 10 | 1 |
| Gil, Benji, TIJ | .875 | 2 | 3 | 4 | 1 | 8 | 0 |
| Gomez, Heber, MTY | .974 | 67 | 91 | 247 | 9 | 347 | 55 |
| Guizar, Hector, ASC | .986 | 43 | 68 | 150 | 3 | 221 | 33 |
| Hernandez, Hector, VER | 1.000 | 8 | 4 | 14 | 0 | 18 | 1 |
| Hernandez, Julio, TIJ | .962 | 95 | 153 | 297 | 18 | 468 | 59 |
| Hernandez, Vladimir, CCN | .982 | 12 | 21 | 33 | 1 | 55 | 9 |
| Lopez, Fausto, TAB | .948 | 60 | 95 | 162 | 14 | 271 | 36 |
| Martinez, Abel, LAG | .906 | 10 | 9 | 20 | 3 | 32 | 4 |
| Martinez, Luis, PUE | .953 | 79 | 134 | 253 | 19 | 406 | 61 |
| Melo, Juan, VER | .967 | 91 | 177 | 288 | 16 | 481 | 70 |
| Miller, Orlando, ASC | .935 | 18 | 27 | 45 | 5 | 77 | 8 |
| Morejon, Oswaldo, LAG | 1.000 | 1 | 0 | 1 | 0 | 1 | 0 |
| Orrantia, Carlos, MTY | 1.000 | 4 | 6 | 7 | 0 | 13 | 1 |
| Perez, Alfredo, CCN | 1.000 | 8 | 6 | 14 | 0 | 20 | 8 |
| Perez, Jose, SLP | .935 | 6 | 10 | 19 | 2 | 31 | 6 |
| Quintero, Mayque, SLP | .800 | 3 | 0 | 4 | 1 | 5 | 0 |
| Ramirez, Oscar, CAM | .936 | 67 | 89 | 174 | 18 | 281 | 32 |
| Rivera, Jesus, TAB* | .950 | 9 | 9 | 10 | 1 | 20 | 3 |
| Robles, Javier, TIG | .959 | 88 | 142 | 259 | 17 | 418 | 54 |
| Robles, Oscar, MXO* | 1.000 | 6 | 4 | 18 | 0 | 22 | 4 |
| Robles, Trinidad, TIG | .983 | 15 | 21 | 38 | 1 | 60 | 7 |
| Romero, Flavio, SLT* | 1.000 | 8 | 2 | 6 | 0 | 8 | 1 |
| Rosas, Ezequiel, OAX | 1.000 | 13 | 10 | 15 | 0 | 25 | 6 |
| Ruiz, Ricardo, MXO | 1.000 | 3 | 0 | 1 | 0 | 1 | 0 |
| Salas, Heriberto, LAG | .962 | 92 | 150 | 282 | 17 | 449 | 58 |
| Sanchez, Jose, TIJ | 1.000 | 3 | 3 | 1 | 0 | 4 | 0 |
| Sanchez, Orlando, SLP | 1.000 | 8 | 9 | 24 | 0 | 33 | 3 |
| Sandoval, Jose, MXO | .986 | 96 | 163 | 341 | 7 | 511 | 81 |
| Santana, Pedro, OAX | 1.000 | 1 | 0 | 1 | 0 | 1 | 1 |
| Trejo, Jaime, MVA | .968 | 17 | 18 | 42 | 2 | 62 | 15 |
| Valenzuela, Irving, MVA | 1.000 | 5 | 3 | 2 | 0 | 5 | 0 |
| Valle, Jorge, CCN | .985 | 29 | 44 | 89 | 2 | 135 | 21 |

## OUTFIELDERS

| Player, Team | Pct. | G | PO | A | E | TC | DP |
|---|---|---|---|---|---|---|---|
| Acuna, Jose, CCN | .952 | 68 | 110 | 8 | 6 | 124 | |
| Ahumada, Alex, MTY | .800 | 6 | 8 | 0 | 2 | 10 | 0 |
| Alcantara, Izzy, LAG | .954 | 79 | 141 | 4 | 7 | 152 | 1 |
| Alvarez, Hector, OAX | 1.000 | 17 | 29 | 3 | 0 | 32 | 0 |
| Alvarez, Hector, MTY | 1.000 | 50 | 53 | 3 | 0 | 56 | 1 |
| Alvarez, Hector, OAX-MTY | 1.000 | 67 | 82 | 6 | 0 | 88 | 1 |
| Amezcua, Adan, SLP | 1.000 | 8 | 9 | 1 | 0 | 10 | 0 |
| Angulo, Gregorio, LAG | .875 | 11 | 7 | 0 | 1 | 8 | 0 |
| Arano, Eloy, VER | .976 | 86 | 151 | 9 | 4 | 164 | 0 |
| Arano, Wilfrido, VER* | 1.000 | 5 | 6 | 1 | 0 | 7 | 0 |
| Arano, Wilfrido, TIJ* | 1.000 | 14 | 12 | 0 | 0 | 12 | 0 |
| Arano, Wilfrido, VER-TIJ* | 1.000 | 19 | 18 | 1 | 0 | 19 | 0 |
| Arauz, Ignacio, MVA | 1.000 | 1 | 1 | 0 | 0 | 1 | 0 |
| Arauz, Leobardo, LAG | .986 | 88 | 198 | 9 | 3 | 210 | 1 |
| Arredondo, Alan, LAG | .957 | 35 | 43 | 2 | 2 | 47 | 0 |
| Arredondo, Eduardo, TAB* | .993 | 71 | 141 | 4 | 1 | 146 | 0 |
| Arredondo, Hernando, TAB | 1.000 | 3 | 2 | 0 | 0 | 2 | 0 |
| Arredondo, Luis, LAG* | .973 | 90 | 172 | 7 | 5 | 184 | 0 |
| Avila, Carlos, PUE* | .971 | 31 | 32 | 1 | 1 | 34 | 0 |
| Avila, Ignacio, CAM | .923 | 28 | 12 | 0 | 1 | 13 | 0 |
| Avila, Rolando, YUC | 1.000 | 5 | 5 | 0 | 0 | 5 | 0 |
| Baertee, Kimera, SLT | .986 | 27 | 69 | 1 | 1 | 71 | 1 |
| Barajas, Edison, ASC* | .929 | 9 | 10 | 3 | 1 | 14 | 0 |
| Barajas, Edison, LAG* | 1.000 | 14 | 8 | 0 | 0 | 8 | 0 |
| Barajas, Edison, ASC-LAG* | .955 | 23 | 18 | 3 | 1 | 22 | 0 |
| Bass, Jayson, SLT* | .940 | 86 | 137 | 4 | 9 | 150 | 0 |
| Bernal, Cosme, MVA | .931 | 61 | 90 | 4 | 7 | 101 | 0 |
| Bojorquez, Victor, MXO | .983 | 94 | 161 | 10 | 3 | 174 | 2 |
| Brinkley, Darryl, SLP | 1.000 | 37 | 72 | 1 | 0 | 73 | 0 |
| Brinkley, Darryl, TIJ | 1.000 | 21 | 30 | 1 | 0 | 31 | 0 |
| Brinkley, Darryl, SLP-TIJ | 1.000 | 58 | 102 | 2 | 0 | 104 | 0 |
| Brown, Emil, CAM | .972 | 28 | 67 | 2 | 2 | 71 | 2 |
| Buelna, Lorenzo, PUE | .987 | 89 | 148 | 9 | 2 | 159 | 0 |
| Bullett, Scott, MTY* | .981 | 80 | 151 | 8 | 3 | 162 | 2 |
| Canizalez, Juan, LAG | 1.000 | 1 | 1 | 0 | 0 | 1 | 0 |
| Carmona, Sergio, SLP | .917 | 6 | 10 | 1 | 1 | 12 | 0 |
| Carrillo, Matias, TIG* | .981 | 59 | 98 | 6 | 2 | 106 | 1 |
| Connell, Lino, VER | .750 | 2 | 3 | 0 | 1 | 4 | 0 |
| Contreras, Jose, PUE | .975 | 81 | 143 | 10 | 4 | 157 | 2 |
| Contreras, Sergio, TIG* | .978 | 32 | 43 | 1 | 1 | 45 | 0 |
| Cookson, Brent, OAX | 1.000 | 3 | 5 | 0 | 0 | 5 | 0 |
| Crespo, Jorge, OAX | .833 | 6 | 5 | 0 | 1 | 6 | 0 |
| Diaz, Luis, VER | 1.000 | 3 | 2 | 0 | 0 | 2 | 0 |
| Diaz, Luis, LAG | 1.000 | 5 | 2 | 0 | 0 | 2 | 0 |
| Diaz, Luis, VER-LAG | 1.000 | 8 | 4 | 0 | 0 | 4 | 0 |
| Diaz, Pedro, PUE | 1.000 | 1 | 2 | 0 | 0 | 2 | 0 |
| Encarnacion, Mario, CCN | .927 | 16 | 35 | 3 | 3 | 41 | 0 |
| Espino, Daniel, CCN | .977 | 46 | 83 | 3 | 2 | 88 | 0 |
| Espinosa, Ramon, LAG | .986 | 53 | 141 | 3 | 2 | 146 | 0 |
| Espinoza, Efren, MXO | .929 | 46 | 60 | 5 | 5 | 70 | 1 |
| Espinoza, Jose, TIJ* | .980 | 64 | 93 | 5 | 2 | 100 | 0 |
| Felix, Lorenzo, CCN | 1.000 | 33 | 63 | 1 | 0 | 64 | 0 |
| Fentanes, Oscar, VER | .971 | 53 | 97 | 5 | 3 | 105 | 2 |
| Fernandez, Daniel, MXO* | .988 | 82 | 152 | 6 | 2 | 160 | 0 |
| Figueroa, Marco, VER | 1.000 | 11 | 12 | 0 | 0 | 12 | 0 |
| Fornes, Daniel, MTY* | .962 | 73 | 124 | 4 | 5 | 133 | 1 |
| Garcia, Amaury, CAM | .909 | 5 | 8 | 2 | 1 | 11 | 0 |
| Garcia, Cornelio, LAG* | .941 | 14 | 15 | 1 | 1 | 17 | 0 |
| Garcia, Hector, TAB | .964 | 64 | 103 | 4 | 4 | 111 | 0 |
| Garcia, Luis, TIG | .982 | 82 | 155 | 8 | 3 | 166 | 2 |
| Garcia, Omar, SLP | 1.000 | 2 | 2 | 0 | 0 | 2 | 0 |
| Gil, Benji, TIJ | 1.000 | 1 | 1 | 0 | 0 | 1 | 0 |
| Gonzalez, Israel, CAM | 1.000 | 16 | 19 | 2 | 0 | 21 | 0 |
| Gonzalez, Roman, LAG | .977 | 45 | 42 | 0 | 1 | 43 | 0 |
| Gonzalez, Santiago, VER | .986 | 69 | 132 | 7 | 2 | 141 | 3 |
| Grijak, Kevin, LAG* | 1.000 | 17 | 23 | 1 | 0 | 24 | 0 |
| Grijak, Kevin, CAM* | .913 | 10 | 19 | 2 | 2 | 23 | 0 |
| Grijak, Kevin, LAG-CAM* | .957 | 27 | 42 | 3 | 2 | 47 | 0 |
| Hernandez, Hector, VER | 1.000 | 4 | 6 | 0 | 0 | 6 | 0 |
| Hernandez, Vladimir, CCN | .833 | 6 | 9 | 1 | 2 | 12 | 0 |
| Herrera, Jose, YUC* | .957 | 25 | 66 | 1 | 3 | 70 | 0 |
| Hurst, James, MVA | 1.000 | 2 | 4 | 0 | 0 | 4 | 0 |
| Inglin, Jeff, YUC | 1.000 | 24 | 45 | 9 | 0 | 54 | 1 |
| Iturbe, Pedro, PUE* | 1.000 | 1 | 1 | 0 | 0 | 1 | 0 |
| Johnson, Rontrez, ASC | .977 | 100 | 212 | 4 | 5 | 221 | 0 |
| Jose, Felix, MXO | .833 | 3 | 5 | 0 | 1 | 6 | 0 |
| Landaeta, Luis, YUC* | .600 | 1 | 3 | 0 | 2 | 5 | 0 |
| Landaeta, Luis, TIJ* | .953 | 32 | 61 | 0 | 3 | 64 | 0 |
| Landaeta, Luis, YUC-TIJ* | .928 | 33 | 64 | 0 | 5 | 69 | 0 |
| Langaigne, Selwyn, TIJ* | .963 | 14 | 24 | 2 | 1 | 27 | 0 |
| Lara, Idelfonso, ASC | .903 | 31 | 26 | 2 | 3 | 31 | 0 |

| Player, Team | Pct. | G | PO | A | E | TC | DP |
|---|---|---|---|---|---|---|---|
| Lara, Idelfonso, LAG | 1.000 | 3 | 5 | 0 | 0 | 5 | 0 |
| Lara, Idelfonso, ASC-LAG | .917 | 34 | 31 | 2 | 3 | 36 | 0 |
| Leach, Jalal, MVA* | .970 | 19 | 31 | 1 | 1 | 33 | 0 |
| Leach, Jalal, YUC* | .983 | 31 | 57 | 0 | 1 | 58 | 0 |
| Leach, Jalal, MVA-YUC* | .978 | 50 | 88 | 1 | 2 | 91 | 0 |
| LeBron, Juan, CCN | .962 | 23 | 50 | 0 | 2 | 52 | 0 |
| Lopez, JM, SLP* | .952 | 10 | 20 | 0 | 1 | 21 | 0 |
| Lopez, Jose, SLP | .978 | 62 | 126 | 8 | 3 | 137 | 2 |
| Lopez, Raul, MVA* | .833 | 3 | 5 | 0 | 1 | 6 | 0 |
| Martinez, Enrique, SLP | .983 | 54 | 110 | 4 | 2 | 116 | 1 |
| Martinez, Gabby, CCN | 1.000 | 14 | 30 | 4 | 0 | 34 | 1 |
| Martinez, Greg, OAX | .974 | 81 | 141 | 7 | 4 | 152 | 0 |
| Martinez, Manny, TIG | .982 | 84 | 153 | 7 | 3 | 163 | 0 |
| Mata, Noe, ASC | .983 | 75 | 115 | 2 | 2 | 119 | 0 |
| McDonald, Donzell, TAB | .974 | 67 | 147 | 5 | 4 | 156 | 0 |
| Medina, Jose, MVA | 1.000 | 35 | 38 | 1 | 0 | 39 | 0 |
| Mejia, Roberto, CAM | .875 | 7 | 7 | 0 | 1 | 8 | 0 |
| Mendez, Francisco, MTY* | .500 | 2 | 1 | 0 | 1 | 2 | 0 |
| Mendez, Roberto, OAX* | .867 | 13 | 13 | 0 | 2 | 15 | 0 |
| Meyers, Chad, MXO | .966 | 97 | 135 | 7 | 5 | 147 | 1 |
| Meza, Gonzalo, LAG* | .977 | 78 | 119 | 6 | 3 | 128 | 2 |
| Miller, Orlando, CCN | .000 | 1 | 0 | 0 | 2 | 2 | 0 |
| Montoya, Noel, SLT | .750 | 6 | 3 | 0 | 1 | 4 | 0 |
| Munoz, JosedeJ, MVA* | .981 | 73 | 144 | 7 | 3 | 154 | 0 |
| O`Sullivan, Patrick, SLP | 1.000 | 9 | 6 | 0 | 0 | 6 | 0 |
| Orrantia, Carlos, MTY | 1.000 | 5 | 5 | 0 | 0 | 5 | 0 |
| Otanez, Willis, CAM | 1.000 | 1 | 4 | 0 | 0 | 4 | 0 |
| Paez, Hector, CAM* | 1.000 | 1 | 1 | 0 | 0 | 1 | 0 |
| Palafox, Sergio, MVA | 1.000 | 27 | 34 | 4 | 0 | 38 | 0 |
| Pemberton, Rudy, MVA | .905 | 14 | 19 | 0 | 2 | 21 | 0 |
| Perez, Jose, SLP | 1.000 | 5 | 4 | 0 | 0 | 4 | 1 |
| Presichi, Cristian, SLT | .993 | 76 | 130 | 8 | 1 | 139 | 0 |
| Quintero, Christian, OAX | .970 | 94 | 159 | 2 | 5 | 166 | 0 |
| Quintero, Edgar, MTY | .978 | 59 | 85 | 3 | 2 | 90 | 1 |
| Ramirez, Jesus, OAX | 1.000 | 27 | 44 | 4 | 0 | 48 | 2 |
| Ramirez, Omar, VER | .981 | 96 | 204 | 5 | 4 | 213 | 2 |
| Reyes, Julio, ASC* | 1.000 | 10 | 14 | 2 | 0 | 16 | 0 |
| Rincon, Isaias, CAM | .984 | 53 | 59 | 3 | 1 | 63 | 2 |
| Rios, Armando, TIJ* | .971 | 29 | 63 | 3 | 2 | 68 | 0 |
| Rivera, Ruben, CAM | .955 | 90 | 166 | 4 | 8 | 178 | 1 |
| Rodarte, Raul, TAB | .962 | 25 | 48 | 2 | 2 | 52 | 1 |
| Rodarte, Raul, SLP | .958 | 64 | 106 | 7 | 5 | 118 | 1 |
| Rodarte, Raul, TAB-SLP | .959 | 89 | 154 | 9 | 7 | 170 | 2 |
| Rodriguez, Boi, LAG* | .955 | 43 | 79 | 5 | 4 | 88 | 0 |
| Rodriguez, Boi, CAM* | .968 | 17 | 28 | 2 | 1 | 31 | 0 |
| Rodriguez, Boi, LAG-CAM* | .958 | 60 | 107 | 7 | 5 | 119 | 0 |
| Rodriguez, Jesus, MVA | 1.000 | 1 | 1 | 0 | 0 | 1 | 0 |
| Rodriguez, Serafin, TIG | 1.000 | 7 | 7 | 0 | 0 | 7 | 0 |
| Rodriguez, Serafin, MVA | .969 | 18 | 29 | 2 | 1 | 32 | 0 |
| Rodriguez, Serafin, YUC | .963 | 20 | 25 | 1 | 1 | 27 | 0 |
| TRodriguez, Serafin,TIG-MVA-YUC | .970 | 45 | 61 | 3 | 2 | 66 | 0 |
| Romero, Flavio, SLT* | .908 | 41 | 55 | 4 | 6 | 65 | 0 |
| Romero, Wilfredo, MVA | .971 | 90 | 158 | 11 | 5 | 174 | 4 |
| Ruiz, Ricardo, MXO | 1.000 | 3 | 1 | 0 | 0 | 1 | 0 |
| Saenz, Ricardo, SLT | .938 | 60 | 73 | 2 | 5 | 80 | 2 |
| Salazar, Carlos, ASC | 1.000 | 20 | 8 | 0 | 0 | 8 | 0 |
| Salcedo, Eder, SLP | .992 | 69 | 127 | 4 | 1 | 132 | 0 |
| Sanchez, Alejandro, CCN | 1.000 | 4 | 11 | 0 | 0 | 11 | 0 |
| Sanchez, Jose, TIJ | 1.000 | 8 | 5 | 0 | 0 | 5 | 0 |
| Sanchez, Raul, CCN | .969 | 96 | 232 | 16 | 8 | 256 | 5 |
| Sandoval, Octavio, TIG | .943 | 56 | 64 | 2 | 4 | 70 | 0 |
| Santana, Pedro, OAX | .972 | 67 | 128 | 12 | 4 | 144 | 2 |
| Sherman, Darrell, PUE* | .988 | 82 | 156 | 5 | 2 | 163 | 0 |
| Smith, Charles, MTY | 1.000 | 1 | 2 | 0 | 0 | 2 | 0 |
| Smith, Demond, MTY | .969 | 74 | 155 | 0 | 5 | 160 | 0 |
| Soriano, Ricardo, ASC* | .964 | 83 | 127 | 8 | 5 | 140 | 2 |
| Sotomayor, Gilberto, SLT* | 1.000 | 56 | 61 | 2 | 0 | 63 | 0 |
| Suarez, Luis, TIG | .946 | 33 | 48 | 5 | 3 | 56 | 2 |
| Toca, Jorge, CCN | .923 | 7 | 10 | 2 | 1 | 13 | 0 |
| Valdez, Mario, MTY* | 1.000 | 2 | 2 | 0 | 0 | 2 | 0 |
| Valdez, Ramon, CAM* | .977 | 85 | 165 | 6 | 4 | 175 | 1 |
| Valdez, Uriel, CCN | 1.000 | 7 | 7 | 0 | 0 | 7 | 0 |
| Valencia, Abraham, TIJ | .959 | 64 | 89 | 5 | 4 | 98 | 0 |
| Vazquez, Gregorio, TAB | .994 | 79 | 154 | 7 | 1 | 162 | 2 |
| Villalobos, Carlos, PUE | .965 | 49 | 78 | 5 | 3 | 86 | 1 |
| Villegas, Fernando, ASC | 1.000 | 11 | 14 | 0 | 0 | 14 | 0 |
| White, Derrick, TIJ | .992 | 85 | 117 | 5 | 1 | 123 | 0 |
| Zazueta, Juan, SLT | 1.000 | 5 | 4 | 0 | 0 | 4 | 0 |

## CATCHERS

| Player, Team | Pct. | G | PO | A | E | TC | DP | PB |
|---|---|---|---|---|---|---|---|---|
| Amezcua, Adan, SLP | .977 | 50 | 227 | 32 | 6 | 265 | 0 | 1 |
| Arauz, Ignacio, MVA | .953 | 19 | 55 | 6 | 3 | 64 | 0 | 1 |
| Baez, Carlos, TAB | 1.000 | 3 | 9 | 0 | 0 | 9 | 0 | 0 |
| Bustamante, Omar, SLT | .985 | 30 | 121 | 11 | 2 | 134 | 2 | 3 |
| Camarero, Rafael, VER | 1.000 | 1 | 2 | 0 | 0 | 2 | 0 | 0 |
| Castaneda, Hector, YUC* | .978 | 13 | 39 | 6 | 1 | 46 | 1 | 0 |
| Cazarin, Manuel, VER | .986 | 79 | 314 | 46 | 5 | 365 | 4 | 8 |
| Cobos, Rogelio, MXO | .986 | 25 | 57 | 12 | 1 | 70 | 3 | 0 |
| Cruz, Marco, YUC | .969 | 16 | 59 | 4 | 2 | 65 | 0 | 0 |
| Cruz, Marco, CAM | .976 | 12 | 35 | 5 | 1 | 41 | 1 | 1 |
| Cruz, Marco, YUC-CAM | .972 | 28 | 94 | 9 | 3 | 106 | 1 | 1 |
| Diaz, Luis, LAG | 1.000 | 3 | 1 | 2 | 0 | 3 | 0 | 0 |
| Esqueda, Jonathan, SLT | .833 | 1 | 5 | 0 | 1 | 6 | 0 | 0 |
| Estrada, Hector, LAG | .990 | 61 | 267 | 38 | 3 | 308 | 5 | 9 |
| Garcia, Ernesto, ASC | 1.000 | 1 | 2 | 0 | 0 | 2 | 0 | 0 |
| Garzon, Eliseo, TIJ | .987 | 55 | 286 | 29 | 4 | 319 | 2 | 1 |
| Gastelum, Carlos, TIG | 1.000 | 5 | 9 | 1 | 0 | 10 | 0 | 1 |
| Gastelum, CarlosA, TIG | .971 | 16 | 59 | 7 | 2 | 68 | 1 | 2 |
| Gavia, Jesus, ASC | .986 | 31 | 122 | 15 | 2 | 139 | 3 | 1 |
| Gonzalez, Fernando, SLP | .969 | 30 | 112 | 13 | 4 | 129 | 1 | 2 |
| Gutierrez, Said, LAG | .994 | 69 | 321 | 39 | 2 | 362 | 0 | 3 |
| Hadad, Jorge, TIJ | 1.000 | 12 | 26 | 1 | 0 | 27 | 0 | 0 |
| Hernandez, Enrique, YUC | 1.000 | 4 | 5 | 0 | 0 | 5 | 0 | 0 |
| Higuera, Ottoniel, OAX | 1.000 | 2 | 1 | 0 | 0 | 1 | 0 | 0 |
| Hurtado, Hector, TIJ | .976 | 62 | 281 | 40 | 8 | 329 | 0 | 5 |
| Jensen, Marcus, CCN | .974 | 16 | 73 | 3 | 2 | 78 | 1 | 1 |
| Lizarraga, Norberto, LAG | 1.000 | 6 | 14 | 0 | 0 | 14 | 0 | 1 |
| Lugo, Roberto, MTY | .978 | 26 | 83 | 7 | 2 | 92 | 1 | 3 |
| Marmolejo, Ivan, CCN | .978 | 18 | 42 | 3 | 1 | 46 | 0 | 0 |
| Medina, Jose, MVA | .900 | 6 | 9 | 0 | 1 | 10 | 0 | 1 |
| Mendez, Francisco, MTY* | 1.000 | 1 | 2 | 0 | 0 | 2 | 0 | 0 |
| Meza, Alfredo, MTY | .988 | 82 | 375 | 43 | 5 | 423 | 6 | 5 |
| Montenegro, Jose, OAX | .983 | 48 | 193 | 32 | 4 | 229 | 5 | 3 |
| Mosquera, Julio, CAM | .985 | 50 | 233 | 22 | 4 | 259 | 0 | 2 |
| Munoz, Adan, TIG* | .994 | 63 | 308 | 33 | 2 | 343 | 3 | 4 |
| Munoz, Noe, SLT | .991 | 82 | 418 | 37 | 4 | 459 | 2 | 4 |
| Ochoa, Edgar, VER | 1.000 | 3 | 4 | 0 | 0 | 4 | 0 | 1 |
| Pacho, Carlos, LAG | .983 | 52 | 201 | 25 | 4 | 230 | 2 | 1 |
| Paez, Hector, YUC* | .944 | 22 | 88 | 14 | 6 | 108 | 2 | 1 |
| Paez, Hector, CAM* | .963 | 20 | 96 | 9 | 4 | 109 | 2 | 0 |
| Paez, Hector, YUC-CAM* | .954 | 1 | 184 | 23 | 10 | 217 | 4 | 1 |
| Paez, Raul, TIJ* | 1.000 | 2 | 2 | 0 | 0 | 2 | 0 | 0 |
| Quinones, Ruben, ASC | .980 | 80 | 328 | 61 | 8 | 397 | 3 | 7 |
| Resendez, Carlos, MVA | .989 | 61 | 249 | 24 | 3 | 276 | 3 | 2 |
| Rivera, Francisco, VER | .951 | 24 | 106 | 10 | 6 | 122 | 1 | 2 |
| Robles, Juan, TAB | .993 | 37 | 136 | 15 | 1 | 152 | 1 | 1 |
| Rodriguez, Armando, MVA | .987 | 41 | 133 | 21 | 2 | 156 | 3 | 4 |
| Rodriguez, Carlos, SLP | .984 | 35 | 177 | 12 | 3 | 192 | 0 | 3 |
| Rodriguez, Erick, OAX | .989 | 59 | 257 | 23 | 3 | 283 | 2 | 2 |
| Rodriguez, Leonardo, MTY | .943 | 14 | 29 | 4 | 2 | 35 | 2 | 0 |
| Romero, Armando, CCN | .927 | 11 | 33 | 5 | 3 | 41 | 0 | 1 |
| Santana, Mario, TAB | .993 | 68 | 268 | 34 | 2 | 304 | 7 | 4 |
| Soto, Emison, CCN | .750 | 7 | 18 | 3 | 7 | 28 | 0 | 1 |
| Soto, Saul, MXO | .981 | 82 | 387 | 32 | 8 | 427 | 8 | 1 |
| Tapia, Cesar, PUE | 1.000 | 1 | 1 | 0 | 0 | 1 | 0 | 0 |
| Valdez, Baltazar, VER* | .929 | 6 | 13 | 0 | 1 | 14 | 0 | 0 |
| Valdez, Emmanuel, TIG | .978 | 22 | 80 | 10 | 2 | 92 | 0 | 2 |
| Valdez, Emmanuel, CAM | .973 | 25 | 131 | 11 | 4 | 146 | 1 | 4 |
| Valdez, Emmanuel, TIG-CAM | .975 | 1 | 211 | 21 | 6 | 238 | 1 | 6 |
| Valdez, Francisco, CCN | .973 | 43 | 155 | 27 | 5 | 187 | 1 | 2 |
| Valdez, Francisco, MXO | 1.000 | 16 | 37 | 3 | 0 | 40 | 2 | 0 |
| Valdez, Francisco, CCN-MXO | .978 | 59 | 192 | 30 | 5 | 227 | 3 | 2 |
| Valle, Cosme, CCN | .941 | 27 | 85 | 11 | 6 | 102 | 3 | 3 |
| Vazquez, Jorge, TIG | .975 | 10 | 34 | 5 | 1 | 40 | 0 | 4 |
| Vega, Edgar, PUE | .992 | 69 | 308 | 50 | 3 | 361 | 2 | 4 |
| Vega, Jesus, PUE | .981 | 37 | 136 | 20 | 3 | 159 | 3 | 6 |
| Villegas, Felipe, ASC | 1.000 | 5 | 8 | 2 | 0 | 10 | 0 | 0 |

## PITCHERS

| Player, Team | Pct. | G | PO | A | E | TC | DP |
|---|---|---|---|---|---|---|---|
| Aceves, Alfredo, LAG | .929 | 18 | 8 | 5 | 1 | 14 | 0 |
| Acosta, Aaron, VER | 1.000 | 5 | 1 | 2 | 0 | 3 | 0 |
| Acosta, Aaron, CAM | 1.000 | 5 | 0 | 3 | 0 | 3 | 0 |
| Acosta, Aaron, VER-CAM | 1.000 | 10 | 1 | 5 | 0 | 6 | 0 |
| Acosta, Jasiel, MVA* | 1.000 | 19 | 7 | 14 | 0 | 21 | 0 |
| Aguilar, Hugo, MVA* | .889 | 19 | 2 | 6 | 1 | 9 | 0 |
| Aguilar, Mario, CAM* | 1.000 | 14 | 0 | 2 | 0 | 2 | 0 |
| Aguirre, Alejandro, MVA | .857 | 10 | 2 | 4 | 1 | 7 | 0 |
| Aguirre, Gaudencio, MTY | .800 | 42 | 0 | 4 | 1 | 5 | 1 |
| Ahumada, Edgar, MVA* | 1.000 | 19 | 3 | 2 | 0 | 5 | 1 |
| Alexander, Jordy, CCN* | 1.000 | 6 | 0 | 4 | 0 | 4 | 0 |

| Player, Team | Pct. | G | PO | A | E | TC | DP |
|---|---|---|---|---|---|---|---|
| Alvarado, Giancarlo, CCN | .833 | 4 | 1 | 4 | 1 | 6 | 0 |
| Alvarado, Giancarlo, MXO | 1.000 | 2 | 0 | 1 | 0 | 1 | 0 |
| Alvarado, Giancarlo, CCN-MXO | .857 | 6 | 1 | 5 | 1 | 7 | 0 |
| Alvarez, Antonio, ASC | .906 | 19 | 6 | 23 | 3 | 32 | 4 |
| Alvarez, Azael, PUE* | 1.000 | 16 | 7 | 9 | 0 | 16 | 0 |
| Alvarez, Juan, CAM | .889 | 18 | 4 | 12 | 2 | 18 | 1 |
| Alvarez, Octavio, TAB | .880 | 17 | 6 | 16 | 3 | 25 | 1 |
| Amarillas, Asdrubal, CCN | .833 | 14 | 1 | 4 | 1 | 6 | 0 |
| Amarillas, Asdrubal, LAG | 1.000 | 7 | 0 | 2 | 0 | 2 | 0 |
| Amarillas, Asdrubal, CCN-LAG | .875 | 21 | 1 | 6 | 1 | 8 | 0 |
| Avalos, Jose, OAX | .929 | 38 | 6 | 7 | 1 | 14 | 2 |
| Aybar, Manny, PUE | 1.000 | 18 | 3 | 1 | 0 | 4 | 0 |
| Baez, Sixto, VER | .909 | 36 | 0 | 10 | 1 | 11 | 0 |
| Barradas, Roberto, MVA | .857 | 22 | 2 | 4 | 1 | 7 | 0 |
| Barreras, Fernando, LAG | .909 | 32 | 3 | 7 | 1 | 11 | 1 |
| Beltran, Alonso, TIJ | 1.000 | 15 | 3 | 8 | 0 | 11 | 1 |
| Bernal, Manuel, VER | .917 | 13 | 5 | 6 | 1 | 12 | 1 |
| Blancas, Rigoberto, ASC* | 1.000 | 39 | 2 | 4 | 0 | 6 | 0 |
| Bourgeois, Steve, SLT | 1.000 | 5 | 1 | 1 | 0 | 2 | 0 |
| Bullinger, Jim, TIJ | 1.000 | 3 | 1 | 1 | 0 | 2 | 0 |
| Bustillos, Oscar, TIG | 1.000 | 30 | 2 | 4 | 0 | 6 | 0 |
| Camara, Pedro, YUC* | 1.000 | 49 | 1 | 4 | 0 | 5 | 0 |
| Campillo, Jorge, TIG | 1.000 | 17 | 7 | 15 | 0 | 22 | 0 |
| Campos, Francisco, CAM | .963 | 16 | 12 | 14 | 1 | 27 | 3 |
| Canales, Julio, TIG | .875 | 14 | 2 | 5 | 1 | 8 | 0 |
| Canto, Jafet, CCN | 1.000 | 14 | 1 | 3 | 0 | 4 | 0 |
| Carrasco, Alejandro, MVA | 1.000 | 14 | 3 | 10 | 0 | 13 | 1 |
| Carrasco, Alejandro, LAG | 1.000 | 7 | 2 | 5 | 0 | 7 | 0 |
| Carrasco, Alejandro, MVA-YUC | 1.000 | 21 | 5 | 15 | 0 | 20 | 1 |
| Carreon, Uziel, CCN | 1.000 | 31 | 5 | 8 | 0 | 13 | 1 |
| Carrillo, Guillermo, TIJ | .000 | 6 | 0 | 0 | 0 | 0 | 0 |
| Castaneda, Federico, LAG | 1.000 | 34 | 1 | 0 | 0 | 1 | 0 |
| Castellanos, Hugo, TIJ | .955 | 44 | 2 | 19 | 1 | 22 | 2 |
| Castellanos, Jonatha, MTY | 1.000 | 22 | 2 | 3 | 0 | 5 | 0 |
| Castillo, Alberto, SLP* | 1.000 | 6 | 2 | 5 | 0 | 7 | 0 |
| Castillo, Jorge, MXO* | 1.000 | 7 | 0 | 5 | 0 | 5 | 1 |
| Castro, Luis, OAX | 1.000 | 18 | 2 | 4 | 0 | 6 | 0 |
| Cervantes, Pedro, SLP | .667 | 10 | 1 | 1 | 1 | 3 | 0 |
| Cervantes, Pedro, PUE | 1.000 | 10 | 1 | 4 | 0 | 5 | 0 |
| Cervantes, Pedro, SLP-PUE | .875 | 20 | 2 | 5 | 1 | 8 | 0 |
| Chantres, Carlos, ASC | 1.000 | 4 | 1 | 5 | 0 | 6 | 2 |
| Chantres, Carlos, CCN | .889 | 10 | 4 | 12 | 2 | 18 | 0 |
| Chavarria, Hector, LAG | .938 | 19 | 3 | 12 | 1 | 16 | 1 |
| Chavez, Alejandro, LAG* | .778 | 29 | 2 | 5 | 2 | 9 | 0 |
| Chavez, Carlos, TAB | .667 | 15 | 1 | 1 | 1 | 3 | 0 |
| Cobos, Jose, SLP | 1.000 | 10 | 1 | 0 | 0 | 1 | 0 |
| Coco, Pascual, SLT | .857 | 10 | 4 | 8 | 2 | 14 | 2 |
| Cortes, David, TIJ | 1.000 | 14 | 2 | 2 | 0 | 4 | 0 |
| Cortez, Jorge, TIG* | .000 | 2 | 0 | 0 | 0 | 0 | 0 |
| Cortez, Jorge, OAX* | 1.000 | 10 | 2 | 14 | 0 | 16 | 0 |
| Cortez, Jorge, TIG-OAX* | 1.000 | 12 | 2 | 14 | 0 | 16 | 0 |
| Cruz, Javier, MXO | 1.000 | 32 | 1 | 5 | 0 | 6 | 1 |
| Daniel, Luis, ASC | 1.000 | 4 | 0 | 1 | 0 | 1 | 0 |
| DeHart, Rickey, MTY* | .923 | 18 | 2 | 10 | 1 | 13 | 0 |
| DelaRosa, Maximo, MVA | 1.000 | 29 | 2 | 5 | 0 | 7 | 0 |
| Deago, Roger, TIJ* | .857 | 6 | 2 | 4 | 1 | 7 | 1 |
| Delahoya, Javier, CAM | 1.000 | 8 | 2 | 6 | 0 | 8 | 0 |
| Delfin, Adolfo, TIJ | .000 | 4 | 0 | 0 | 0 | 0 | 0 |
| Delgadillo, Juan, LAG | .889 | 13 | 3 | 5 | 1 | 9 | 0 |
| Diaz, Marco, ASC | .875 | 34 | 0 | 7 | 1 | 8 | 0 |
| Diaz, Rafael, SLT | 1.000 | 7 | 2 | 4 | 0 | 6 | 0 |
| Dominguez, Carlos, TIJ | 1.000 | 4 | 1 | 0 | 0 | 1 | 1 |
| Dominguez, Carlos, TIJ* | 1.000 | 5 | 0 | 2 | 0 | 2 | 0 |
| Dominguez, David, MXO | .909 | 32 | 3 | 7 | 1 | 11 | 0 |
| Dorame, Randey, MVA* | .875 | 7 | 1 | 6 | 1 | 8 | 0 |
| Dorame, Randey, CAM* | 1.000 | 11 | 0 | 4 | 0 | 4 | 1 |
| Dorame, Randey, MVA-CAM* | .917 | 18 | 1 | 10 | 1 | 12 | 1 |
| Duarte, Miguel, SLT | .800 | 33 | 2 | 2 | 1 | 5 | 0 |
| Elizalde, Carlos, OAX | 1.000 | 17 | 4 | 14 | 0 | 18 | 0 |
| Elvira, Abraham, ASC* | 1.000 | 17 | 2 | 11 | 0 | 13 | 2 |
| Elvira, Narciso, CAM* | 1.000 | 16 | 3 | 19 | 0 | 22 | 1 |
| Escobedo, Edgar, TIJ | 1.000 | 20 | 3 | 8 | 0 | 11 | 1 |
| Espadas, Gary, YUC | 1.000 | 21 | 2 | 3 | 0 | 5 | 0 |
| Esparza, Emerson, LAG | .875 | 18 | 4 | 3 | 1 | 8 | 3 |
| Espinoza, Omar, PUE | 1.000 | 23 | 3 | 3 | 0 | 6 | 0 |
| Esquer, Mercedes, SLP* | .938 | 16 | 2 | 13 | 1 | 16 | 1 |
| Estrella, Luis, TIG | .938 | 13 | 3 | 12 | 1 | 16 | 1 |
| Estrella, Luis, PUE | 1.000 | 3 | 0 | 3 | 0 | 3 | 0 |
| Estrella, Luis, TIG-PUE | .947 | 16 | 3 | 15 | 1 | 19 | 1 |
| Federico, Gustavo, MVA | 1.000 | 37 | 2 | 8 | 0 | 10 | 2 |
| Federico, Gustavo, SLT | 1.000 | 2 | 0 | 1 | 0 | 1 | 0 |
| Federico, Gustavo, MVA-SLT | 1.000 | 39 | 2 | 9 | 0 | 11 | 2 |

| Player, Team | Pct. | G | PO | A | E | TC | DP |
|---|---|---|---|---|---|---|---|
| Fernandez, Osvaldo, TAB | .964 | 18 | 7 | 20 | 1 | 28 | 0 |
| Flores, Ignacio, TIG | .875 | 11 | 1 | 6 | 1 | 8 | 1 |
| Flores, Ignacio, LAG | 1.000 | 13 | 0 | 3 | 0 | 3 | 1 |
| Flores, Ignacio, SLT | .750 | 5 | 0 | 3 | 1 | 4 | 1 |
| Flores, Ignacio, YUC-SLT | .867 | 0 | 1 | 12 | 2 | 15 | 3 |
| Flores, Ignacio, SLT | 1.000 | 6 | 1 | 1 | 0 | 2 | 0 |
| Flores, Jorge, MVA* | .952 | 52 | 5 | 15 | 1 | 21 | 1 |
| Flores, Renato, MVA | 1.000 | 28 | 3 | 1 | 0 | 4 | 1 |
| Flores, Wilfredo, TAB | 1.000 | 16 | 0 | 3 | 0 | 3 | 0 |
| Garcia, Adolfo, VER | 1.000 | 28 | 2 | 10 | 0 | 12 | 2 |
| Garcia, Alfredo, MXO | .944 | 16 | 2 | 15 | 1 | 18 | 0 |
| Garcia, Carlos, LAG | 1.000 | 9 | 3 | 1 | 0 | 4 | 1 |
| Garcia, Carlos, MXO | 1.000 | 4 | 0 | 1 | 0 | 1 | 0 |
| Garcia, Carlos, LAG-MXO | 1.000 | 1 | 3 | 2 | 0 | 5 | 1 |
| Garcia, Cornelio, LAG* | 1.000 | 3 | 0 | 3 | 0 | 3 | 0 |
| Garcia, Humberto, SLP* | .857 | 42 | 2 | 4 | 1 | 7 | 0 |
| Garcia, Jose, SLT* | .923 | 49 | 3 | 9 | 1 | 13 | 0 |
| Garcia, Rafael, SLT | 1.000 | 7 | 4 | 2 | 0 | 6 | 0 |
| Garcia, Ramon, MTY | .000 | 8 | 0 | 0 | 0 | 0 | 0 |
| Garcia, Ramon, SLP | 1.000 | 13 | 5 | 9 | 0 | 14 | 0 |
| Garcia, Ramon, MTY-SLP | 1.000 | 21 | 5 | 9 | 0 | 14 | 0 |
| Garibaldi, Cecilio, TIG | 1.000 | 21 | 5 | 11 | 0 | 16 | 1 |
| Garibay, Salvador, TIJ | .929 | 44 | 5 | 8 | 1 | 14 | 1 |
| Garza, Conrado, CCN* | 1.000 | 40 | 0 | 6 | 0 | 6 | 0 |
| Garza, Luis, CCN | 1.000 | 4 | 1 | 0 | 0 | 1 | 0 |
| Giron, Emiliano, LAG | .938 | 38 | 7 | 8 | 1 | 16 | 0 |
| Giron, Isabel, YUC | 1.000 | 7 | 1 | 2 | 0 | 3 | 0 |
| Giron, Isabel, LAG | 1.000 | 13 | 2 | 12 | 0 | 14 | 0 |
| Giron, Isabel, YUC-LAG | 1.000 | 20 | 3 | 14 | 0 | 17 | 0 |
| Gomez, Alejandro, OAX | .750 | 12 | 0 | 3 | 1 | 4 | 0 |
| Gomez, Alejandro, CCN | .800 | 13 | 2 | 2 | 1 | 5 | 1 |
| Gomez, Alejandro, OAX-CCN | .778 | 25 | 2 | 5 | 2 | 9 | 1 |
| Gomez, Martin, LAG | .929 | 19 | 9 | 17 | 2 | 28 | 1 |
| Gonzalez, Erubiel, VER | 1.000 | 14 | 2 | 3 | 0 | 5 | 0 |
| Gonzalez, Gilberto, SLP* | 1.000 | 17 | 4 | 8 | 0 | 12 | 1 |
| Gonzalez, Leonardo, TIJ | .941 | 18 | 5 | 11 | 1 | 17 | 1 |
| Gonzalez, Miguel, SLT | .800 | 26 | 3 | 9 | 3 | 15 | 2 |
| Gonzalez, Rudy, MXO | 1.000 | 15 | 1 | 2 | 0 | 3 | 0 |
| Gonzalez, Vinicio, TAB | 1.000 | 11 | 1 | 3 | 0 | 4 | 1 |
| Grajales, Norberto, CAM | 1.000 | 19 | 0 | 7 | 0 | 7 | 0 |
| Guerra, Pascual, TAB | .500 | 3 | 1 | 0 | 1 | 2 | 0 |
| Gutierrez, Carlos, CCN | 1.000 | 5 | 1 | 0 | 0 | 1 | 0 |
| Gutierrez, Israel, TIG | 1.000 | 4 | 1 | 0 | 0 | 1 | 0 |
| Gutierrez, Israel, PUE | 1.000 | 2 | 1 | 0 | 0 | 1 | 0 |
| Gutierrez, Israel, TIG-PUE | 1.000 | 6 | 2 | 0 | 0 | 2 | 0 |
| Gutierrez, Jorge, LAG | 1.000 | 3 | 0 | 1 | 0 | 1 | 0 |
| Guzman, Christian, SLT | 1.000 | 21 | 1 | 3 | 0 | 4 | 0 |
| Guzman, Jesus, TIG* | .909 | 19 | 1 | 9 | 1 | 11 | 1 |
| Hansell, Greg, MXO | 1.000 | 34 | 1 | 7 | 0 | 8 | 0 |
| Haro, Esteban, TIG | 1.000 | 17 | 5 | 5 | 0 | 10 | 3 |
| Henriquez, Oscar, CAM | 1.000 | 8 | 1 | 2 | 0 | 3 | 0 |
| Hermosillo, Victor, LAG | 1.000 | 13 | 1 | 0 | 0 | 1 | 0 |
| Hermosillo, Victor, MXO | 1.000 | 11 | 0 | 1 | 0 | 1 | 0 |
| Hermosillo, Victor, LAG-MXO | 1.000 | 24 | 1 | 1 | 0 | 2 | 0 |
| Hernandez, Esteban, OAX | 1.000 | 22 | 2 | 6 | 0 | 8 | 0 |
| Hernandez, Jose, VER* | 1.000 | 32 | 2 | 1 | 0 | 3 | 0 |
| Hernandez, Santos, TIG | 1.000 | 36 | 2 | 2 | 0 | 4 | 1 |
| Herrera, Enrique, TAB | 1.000 | 39 | 4 | 12 | 0 | 16 | 1 |
| Huerta, Francisco, TAB | 1.000 | 6 | 0 | 3 | 0 | 3 | 1 |
| Huerta, Luis, TIJ | 1.000 | 10 | 2 | 6 | 0 | 8 | 0 |
| Hurtado, Edwin, YUC | .917 | 21 | 4 | 7 | 1 | 12 | 0 |
| Jimenez, Jose, OAX* | .900 | 29 | 3 | 6 | 1 | 10 | 1 |
| Jimenez, Julio, LAG* | 1.000 | 41 | 0 | 4 | 0 | 4 | 0 |
| Kamar, Emil, MVA | .769 | 23 | 5 | 5 | 3 | 13 | 3 |
| Kelley, Rich, VER* | .905 | 11 | 4 | 15 | 2 | 21 | 0 |
| Kelley, Rich, PUE* | .818 | 8 | 1 | 8 | 2 | 11 | 0 |
| Kelley, Rich, VER-PUE* | .875 | 19 | 5 | 23 | 4 | 32 | 0 |
| Kelly, John, SLT | .000 | 1 | 0 | 0 | 0 | 0 | 0 |
| Kelly, John, YUC | .750 | 5 | 0 | 3 | 1 | 4 | 0 |
| Kelly, John, SLT-YUC | .750 | 6 | 0 | 3 | 1 | 4 | 0 |
| Lara, Jorge, PUE | 1.000 | 24 | 3 | 5 | 0 | 8 | 1 |
| Lara, Mauricio, MTY* | 1.000 | 29 | 2 | 5 | 0 | 7 | 1 |
| Leon, Cupertino, OAX | 1.000 | 36 | 1 | 11 | 0 | 12 | 1 |
| Leyva, Edgar, TIG | 1.000 | 8 | 0 | 4 | 0 | 4 | 0 |
| Leyva, Edgar, MTY | 1.000 | 2 | 0 | 1 | 0 | 1 | 0 |
| Leyva, Edgar, TIG-MTY | 1.000 | 10 | 0 | 5 | 0 | 5 | 0 |
| Loaiza, Sabino, TIJ | 1.000 | 6 | 1 | 1 | 0 | 2 | 1 |
| Lomeli, Israel, OAX | .875 | 15 | 9 | 5 | 2 | 16 | 0 |
| Looney, Brian, TIG* | .800 | 5 | 0 | 4 | 1 | 5 | 0 |
| Looney, Brian, SLP* | .923 | 10 | 4 | 8 | 1 | 13 | 0 |

| Player, Team | Pct. | G | PO | A | E | TC | DP |
|---|---|---|---|---|---|---|---|
| Looney, Brian, TIG-SLP* | .889 | 0 | 4 | 12 | 2 | 18 | 0 |
| Lopez, Emigdio, VER | 1.000 | 18 | 5 | 8 | 0 | 13 | 1 |
| Lopez, Gilberto, ASC | 1.000 | 7 | 1 | 1 | 0 | 2 | 0 |
| Lopez, Jesus, CCN | 1.000 | 8 | 2 | 2 | 0 | 4 | 1 |
| Lopez, JM, SLP* | .500 | 3 | 0 | 1 | 1 | 2 | 1 |
| Lopez, Jose, SLP | .875 | 25 | 0 | 7 | 1 | 8 | 0 |
| Lopez, Miguel, PUE | .909 | 42 | 5 | 5 | 1 | 11 | 0 |
| Lopez, Nain, TIJ* | 1.000 | 22 | 0 | 4 | 0 | 4 | 0 |
| Loya, Rigoberto, MTY | 1.000 | 16 | 5 | 16 | 0 | 21 | 2 |
| Luevano, Juan, ASC | .833 | 32 | 1 | 9 | 2 | 12 | 0 |
| Macias, Luis, PUE | 1.000 | 32 | 4 | 4 | 0 | 8 | 1 |
| Madero, Francisco, LAG | 1.000 | 19 | 5 | 6 | 0 | 11 | 1 |
| Magee, Danny, CAM | .929 | 16 | 3 | 23 | 2 | 28 | 1 |
| Mairena, Oswaldo, MXO* | 1.000 | 14 | 1 | 9 | 0 | 10 | 1 |
| Manning, David, MXO | 1.000 | 6 | 0 | 1 | 0 | 1 | 0 |
| Manrique, Alberto, MTY | 1.000 | 26 | 2 | 11 | 0 | 13 | 2 |
| Manzanillo, Ravelo, PUE* | 1.000 | 5 | 0 | 3 | 0 | 3 | 0 |
| Manzanillo, Ravelo, SLT* | 1.000 | 5 | 0 | 1 | 0 | 1 | 0 |
| Manzanillo, Ravelo, PUE-SLT* | 1.000 | 10 | 0 | 4 | 0 | 4 | 0 |
| Manzano, Adrian, TIG | 1.000 | 30 | 0 | 3 | 0 | 3 | 0 |
| Marquez, Isidro, CAM | 1.000 | 34 | 4 | 2 | 0 | 6 | 0 |
| Marquez, Robert, ASC | 1.000 | 12 | 1 | 1 | 0 | 2 | 0 |
| Martinez, Cesar, TIJ | 1.000 | 20 | 2 | 16 | 0 | 18 | 1 |
| Martinez, Juan, ASC | 1.000 | 9 | 0 | 2 | 0 | 2 | 0 |
| Martinez, Juan, LAG | 1.000 | 7 | 0 | 1 | 0 | 1 | 0 |
| Martinez, Juan, ASC-LAG | 1.000 | 16 | 0 | 3 | 0 | 3 | 0 |
| Martinez, Renan, PUE* | 1.000 | 6 | 1 | 2 | 0 | 3 | 0 |
| McGlinchy, Kevin, MTY | 1.000 | 26 | 3 | 16 | 0 | 19 | 1 |
| Melendez, Nestor, SLP | 1.000 | 19 | 1 | 1 | 0 | 2 | 0 |
| Mendoza, Mario, SLT | 1.000 | 28 | 5 | 8 | 0 | 13 | 1 |
| Meyer, Jake, TIJ | 1.000 | 6 | 0 | 2 | 0 | 2 | 0 |
| Meza, Jorge, SLT* | 1.000 | 17 | 1 | 1 | 0 | 2 | 0 |
| Montane, Ivan, MVA | .882 | 11 | 3 | 12 | 2 | 17 | 2 |
| Montano, Ignacio, ASC* | 1.000 | 3 | 1 | 0 | 0 | 1 | 0 |
| Montano, Ignacio, CCN* | 1.000 | 13 | 1 | 3 | 0 | 4 | 1 |
| Montano, Ignacio, ASC-CCN* | 1.000 | 16 | 2 | 3 | 0 | 5 | 1 |
| Montemayor, Humberto, MTY | 1.000 | 5 | 0 | 1 | 0 | 1 | 0 |
| Montemayor, Humberto, SLP | 1.000 | 7 | 0 | 8 | 0 | 8 | 2 |
| Montemayor, Humberto, MTY-SLP | 1.000 | 12 | 0 | 9 | 0 | 9 | 2 |
| Montoya, Saul, SLP | 1.000 | 40 | 5 | 9 | 0 | 14 | 2 |
| Mora, Eleazar, OAX* | .958 | 18 | 6 | 17 | 1 | 24 | 1 |
| Mora, Sergio, MTY | 1.000 | 33 | 0 | 10 | 0 | 10 | 1 |
| Morales, Fernando, CCN | 1.000 | 2 | 0 | 1 | 0 | 1 | 0 |
| Morales, Israel, LAG | .000 | 24 | 0 | 0 | 0 | 0 | 0 |
| Morales, Luis, CCN* | 1.000 | 5 | 0 | 1 | 0 | 1 | 0 |
| Morales, Luis, SLT* | 1.000 | 1 | 0 | 2 | 0 | 2 | 0 |
| Morales, Luis, CCN-SLT* | 1.000 | 6 | 0 | 3 | 0 | 3 | 0 |
| Moreno, Angel, VER* | 1.000 | 18 | 7 | 20 | 0 | 27 | 1 |
| Moreno, Claudio, MXO | .952 | 22 | 7 | 13 | 1 | 21 | 1 |
| Moreno, Edgar, VER | .750 | 13 | 0 | 3 | 1 | 4 | 0 |
| Moreno, Leo, VER* | 1.000 | 21 | 3 | 6 | 0 | 9 | 0 |
| Munoz, Leonardo, TIG* | 1.000 | 24 | 0 | 5 | 0 | 5 | 0 |
| Munoz, Leonardo, MTY* | .000 | 4 | 0 | 0 | 0 | 0 | 0 |
| Munoz, Leonardo, TIG-MTY* | 1.000 | 28 | 0 | 5 | 0 | 5 | 0 |
| Munoz, Pablo, ASC* | 1.000 | 15 | 1 | 1 | 0 | 2 | 0 |
| Munoz, Pablo, ASC* | 1.000 | 4 | 0 | 2 | 0 | 2 | 0 |
| Murguia, Edgar, SLT | .857 | 14 | 2 | 4 | 1 | 7 | 0 |
| Murillo, Felipe, MVA | 1.000 | 9 | 1 | 0 | 0 | 1 | 0 |
| Murillo, Felipe, LAG | 1.000 | 20 | 1 | 3 | 0 | 4 | 0 |
| Murillo, Felipe, MVA-YUC | 1.000 | 29 | 2 | 3 | 0 | 5 | 0 |
| Murray, Dan, ASC | 1.000 | 8 | 0 | 3 | 0 | 3 | 0 |
| Navarro, Hector, VER | .938 | 18 | 4 | 11 | 1 | 16 | 1 |
| Navarro, Joel, OAX | .905 | 19 | 5 | 14 | 2 | 21 | 0 |
| Navarro, Jose, PUE | .966 | 17 | 11 | 17 | 1 | 29 | 3 |
| Navarro, Luis, YUC | 1.000 | 38 | 1 | 6 | 0 | 7 | 0 |
| Neri, Braulio, TAB* | 1.000 | 11 | 0 | 1 | 0 | 1 | 0 |
| Neri, Eduardo, OAX | .900 | 39 | 1 | 8 | 1 | 10 | 0 |
| Nieblas, Mauro, MTY* | 1.000 | 29 | 0 | 4 | 0 | 4 | 2 |
| Nunez, Javier, ASC | 1.000 | 25 | 3 | 4 | 0 | 7 | 1 |
| Nunez, Jose, TIJ | 1.000 | 11 | 4 | 7 | 0 | 11 | 0 |
| Nunez, JoseJ, PUE | 1.000 | 44 | 4 | 5 | 0 | 9 | 0 |
| Ochoa, Pablo, MTY | .857 | 18 | 2 | 10 | 2 | 14 | 2 |
| Olague, Jesus, MTY | 1.000 | 13 | 2 | 8 | 0 | 10 | 0 |
| Orea, Flavio, ASC | 1.000 | 39 | 1 | 5 | 0 | 6 | 0 |
| Ortega, Pablo, PUE | .897 | 17 | 11 | 15 | 3 | 29 | 2 |
| Ortega, Roberto, PUE* | 1.000 | 43 | 2 | 6 | 0 | 8 | 2 |
| Ortega, Wilbert, LAG* | 1.000 | 34 | 0 | 5 | 0 | 5 | 0 |
| Osuna, Adrian, LAG | .000 | 7 | 0 | 0 | 0 | 0 | 0 |
| Osuna, Ricardo, TAB | 1.000 | 14 | 6 | 12 | 0 | 18 | 1 |
| Pablos, Rene, TIJ | 1.000 | 36 | 2 | 2 | 0 | 4 | 0 |
| Pacheco, Delvis, TIJ | .000 | 1 | 0 | 0 | 0 | 0 | 0 |
| Palacios, Vicente, TIJ | .900 | 24 | 5 | 4 | 1 | 10 | 0 |

| Player, Team | Pct. | G | PO | A | E | TC | DP |
|---|---|---|---|---|---|---|---|
| Palafox, Juan, YUC | .857 | 15 | 2 | 10 | 2 | 14 | 0 |
| Parra, Julio, MTY | 1.000 | 10 | 0 | 1 | 0 | 1 | 0 |
| Parra, Julio, TIJ | 1.000 | 26 | 1 | 1 | 0 | 2 | 0 |
| Parra, Julio, MTY-TIJ | 1.000 | 36 | 1 | 2 | 0 | 3 | 0 |
| Patrick, Bronswell, MXO | 1.000 | 3 | 0 | 1 | 0 | 1 | 0 |
| Pena, Juan, SLP | .750 | 2 | 1 | 2 | 1 | 4 | 0 |
| Perez, Alfredo, CCN | 1.000 | 1 | 0 | 2 | 0 | 2 | 0 |
| Perez, Edgar, CCN | 1.000 | 19 | 11 | 15 | 0 | 26 | 2 |
| Perez, Guadalupe, VER | 1.000 | 19 | 3 | 4 | 0 | 7 | 0 |
| Perez, Sergio, SLP | 1.000 | 23 | 5 | 7 | 0 | 12 | 0 |
| Pesqueira, Omar, LAG | 1.000 | 7 | 1 | 3 | 0 | 4 | 0 |
| Picardo, Hipolito, SLT | 1.000 | 35 | 4 | 14 | 0 | 18 | 0 |
| Picota, Lenin, SLP | .900 | 6 | 4 | 5 | 1 | 10 | 2 |
| Picota, Lenin, YUC | .929 | 11 | 4 | 9 | 1 | 14 | 2 |
| Picota, Lenin, SLP-YUC | .917 | 17 | 8 | 14 | 2 | 24 | 4 |
| Pimentel, Roberto, TAB* | 1.000 | 28 | 4 | 5 | 0 | 9 | 0 |
| Pina, Rafael, VER | .923 | 13 | 6 | 6 | 1 | 13 | 0 |
| Pina, Rafael, TIJ | 1.000 | 13 | 0 | 5 | 0 | 5 | 0 |
| Pina, Rafael, VER-TIJ | .944 | 26 | 6 | 11 | 1 | 18 | 0 |
| Pinales, Aquiles, TAB | .000 | 4 | 0 | 0 | 1 | 1 | 0 |
| Pinales, Aquiles, CAM | .800 | 7 | 2 | 2 | 1 | 5 | 0 |
| Pinales, Aquiles, TAB-CAM | .667 | 11 | 2 | 2 | 2 | 6 | 0 |
| Pineda, Jairo, CAM | 1.000 | 8 | 0 | 1 | 0 | 1 | 0 |
| Posadas, Obedt, SLT | 1.000 | 15 | 1 | 3 | 0 | 4 | 0 |
| Pulido, Raymundo, CAM | 1.000 | 12 | 1 | 1 | 0 | 2 | 0 |
| Quinones, Enrique, SLP | 1.000 | 10 | 2 | 7 | 0 | 9 | 1 |
| Quinones, Enrique, YUC | 1.000 | 9 | 0 | 1 | 0 | 1 | 0 |
| Quinones, Enrique, SLP-YUC | 1.000 | 19 | 2 | 8 | 0 | 10 | 1 |
| Quintanilla, Juan, TIJ | .944 | 48 | 4 | 13 | 1 | 18 | 0 |
| Quiroz, Aaron, SLT | .889 | 15 | 2 | 6 | 1 | 9 | 0 |
| Ramirez, Adrian, MVA* | 1.000 | 15 | 0 | 8 | 0 | 8 | 0 |
| Ramirez, Roberto, MXO* | .935 | 19 | 5 | 24 | 2 | 31 | 3 |
| Rekar, Bryan, TIG | .000 | 3 | 0 | 0 | 0 | 0 | 0 |
| Renovato, Nestor, SLP | 1.000 | 28 | 4 | 10 | 0 | 14 | 2 |
| Reyes, Carlos, YUC | 1.000 | 2 | 0 | 1 | 0 | 1 | 0 |
| Reyes, Natanael, SLT* | .917 | 15 | 4 | 7 | 1 | 12 | 1 |
| Rios, Alejandro, ASC | 1.000 | 16 | 1 | 6 | 0 | 7 | 0 |
| Rios, Eduardo, ASC | 1.000 | 2 | 0 | 1 | 0 | 1 | 0 |
| Rios, Jesus, TAB | .867 | 15 | 6 | 7 | 2 | 15 | 0 |
| Rivera, Ben, LAG | 1.000 | 16 | 0 | 2 | 0 | 2 | 0 |
| Rivera, Ben, MXO | .000 | 4 | 0 | 0 | 0 | 0 | 0 |
| Rivera, Ben, LAG-MXO | 1.000 | 20 | 0 | 2 | 0 | 2 | 0 |
| Rivera, Francisco, ASC | .955 | 21 | 8 | 13 | 1 | 22 | 0 |
| Rivera, Luis, TIG | 1.000 | 3 | 1 | 3 | 0 | 4 | 0 |
| Rivera, Luis, PUE | .667 | 5 | 1 | 1 | 1 | 3 | 0 |
| Rivera, Luis, TIG-PUE | .857 | 8 | 2 | 4 | 1 | 7 | 0 |
| Rivera, Oscar, TIG | 1.000 | 8 | 1 | 6 | 0 | 7 | 0 |
| Rivera, Oscar, YUC* | 1.000 | 17 | 5 | 11 | 0 | 16 | 0 |
| Rivera, Oscar, CAM | 1.000 | 7 | 1 | 4 | 0 | 5 | 0 |
| Rivera, Paul, TAB | .800 | 20 | 0 | 4 | 1 | 5 | 0 |
| Rodriguez, Enoc, CCN* | 1.000 | 2 | 0 | 1 | 0 | 1 | 1 |
| Rodriguez, Francisco, TIG* | 1.000 | 10 | 2 | 3 | 0 | 5 | 0 |
| Rodriguez, Jesus, MVA | .923 | 21 | 4 | 8 | 1 | 13 | 0 |
| Rodriguez, Manuel, CAM | 1.000 | 30 | 0 | 4 | 0 | 4 | 0 |
| Romero, Josmir, OAX | 1.000 | 16 | 3 | 8 | 0 | 11 | 1 |
| Roque, Jorge, LAG* | 1.000 | 20 | 0 | 4 | 0 | 4 | 0 |
| Roque, Rafael, TIG* | .895 | 16 | 3 | 14 | 2 | 19 | 1 |
| Rubio, Miguel, MTY | .667 | 32 | 3 | 1 | 2 | 6 | 1 |
| Ruelas, Heriberto, MXO* | 1.000 | 15 | 1 | 2 | 0 | 3 | 0 |
| Ruiz, Arturo, SLT* | .857 | 24 | 0 | 6 | 1 | 7 | 1 |
| Ruiz, Cecilio, TAB* | 1.000 | 14 | 3 | 4 | 0 | 7 | 0 |
| Sabido, Eduardo, LAG | .000 | 1 | 0 | 0 | 0 | 0 | 0 |
| Saenz, Alfredo, ASC* | 1.000 | 4 | 0 | 1 | 0 | 1 | 1 |
| Salas, Noel, SLT | 1.000 | 2 | 0 | 1 | 0 | 1 | 0 |
| Salcido, Arturo, SLT | 1.000 | 9 | 1 | 1 | 0 | 2 | 0 |
| Saldana, Jose, VER | 1.000 | 29 | 3 | 4 | 0 | 7 | 2 |
| Salgado, Eddie, CCN | 1.000 | 22 | 2 | 21 | 0 | 23 | 1 |
| Sanchez, Alejandro, CCN | .818 | 35 | 2 | 7 | 2 | 11 | 1 |
| Sanchez, Claudio, VER | 1.000 | 33 | 2 | 1 | 0 | 3 | 0 |
| Sanchez, Efrain, CAM | .889 | 14 | 7 | 9 | 2 | 18 | 0 |
| Sangeado, Juan, CCN | 1.000 | 18 | 8 | 6 | 0 | 14 | 0 |
| Serrano, Wascar, OAX | .875 | 8 | 3 | 4 | 1 | 8 | 0 |
| Silva, Jose, MXO | 1.000 | 20 | 5 | 15 | 0 | 20 | 3 |
| Silva, Walter, MTY | 1.000 | 13 | 1 | 1 | 0 | 2 | 0 |
| Silva, Walter, SLP | 1.000 | 29 | 1 | 3 | 0 | 4 | 0 |
| Silva, Walter, MTY-SLP | 1.000 | 0 | 2 | 4 | 0 | 6 | 0 |
| Simon, Benjamin, ASC | .800 | 14 | 2 | 10 | 3 | 15 | 0 |
| Sinohui, David, OAX | .800 | 20 | 2 | 2 | 1 | 5 | 0 |
| Solano, Adrian, TIG | 1.000 | 1 | 0 | 1 | 0 | 1 | 0 |
| Solis, Tomas, TIG* | 1.000 | 22 | 2 | 4 | 0 | 6 | 1 |

| Player, Team | Pct. | G | PO | A | E | TC | DP |
|---|---|---|---|---|---|---|---|
| Solis, Tomas, PUE* | .000 | 7 | 0 | 0 | 1 | 1 | 0 |
| Solis, Tomas, TIG-PUE* | .857 | 29 | 2 | 4 | 1 | 7 | 1 |
| Soto, Cruz, SLP | 1.000 | 6 | 0 | 2 | 0 | 2 | 0 |
| Soto, Cruz, PUE | 1.000 | 9 | 1 | 3 | 0 | 4 | 0 |
| Soto, Cruz, SLP-PUE | 1.000 | 15 | 1 | 5 | 0 | 6 | 0 |
| Strong, Joe, MVA | .500 | 15 | 0 | 2 | 2 | 4 | 1 |
| Strong, Joe, YUC | 1.000 | 14 | 1 | 3 | 0 | 4 | 0 |
| Strong, Joe, MVA-YUC | .750 | 29 | 1 | 5 | 2 | 8 | 1 |
| Tejeda, Felix, YUC* | 1.000 | 27 | 0 | 1 | 0 | 1 | 0 |
| Tequida, Mauricio, MXO | 1.000 | 13 | 3 | 5 | 0 | 8 | 2 |
| Terrazas, Juan, ASC* | 1.000 | 3 | 0 | 1 | 0 | 1 | 0 |
| Terrazas, Juan, CCN* | 1.000 | 6 | 0 | 1 | 0 | 1 | 0 |
| Terrazas, Juan, ASC-CCN* | 1.000 | 9 | 0 | 2 | 0 | 2 | 0 |
| Torres, Melqui, OAX | 1.000 | 11 | 0 | 1 | 0 | 1 | 0 |
| Torres, Melqui, MXO | 1.000 | 7 | 1 | 0 | 0 | 1 | 0 |
| Torres, Melqui, OAX-MXO | 1.000 | 18 | 1 | 1 | 0 | 2 | 0 |
| Tovar, Angel, CCN | .750 | 36 | 0 | 3 | 1 | 4 | 0 |
| Trevino, Jesus, OAX* | 1.000 | 3 | 0 | 1 | 0 | 1 | 0 |
| Valdez, Armando, PUE | .950 | 18 | 6 | 13 | 1 | 20 | 3 |
| Valdez, Joel, LAG | 1.000 | 20 | 3 | 7 | 0 | 10 | 1 |
| Valenzuela, Jose, TIG | 1.000 | 4 | 0 | 1 | 0 | 1 | 0 |
| Valerio, Julio, MXO* | 1.000 | 38 | 0 | 7 | 0 | 7 | 1 |
| Vargas, Joel, TAB | 1.000 | 19 | 10 | 10 | 0 | 20 | 1 |
| Vazquez, Adrian, CCN | 1.000 | 11 | 8 | 5 | 0 | 13 | 1 |
| Vega, Obed, CCN | 1.000 | 16 | 4 | 11 | 0 | 15 | 0 |
| Verdugo, Hugo, ASC | .933 | 32 | 4 | 10 | 1 | 15 | 0 |
| Verdugo, Orlando, SLP | 1.000 | 14 | 1 | 16 | 0 | 17 | 1 |
| Verdugo, Oswaldo, LAG | 1.000 | 45 | 4 | 6 | 0 | 10 | 1 |
| Verdugo, Roberto, TAB | 1.000 | 43 | 3 | 9 | 0 | 12 | 2 |
| Villalobos, Fernando, MTY | 1.000 | 6 | 1 | 3 | 0 | 4 | 0 |
| Villarreal, Salvador, SLP | 1.000 | 23 | 2 | 9 | 0 | 11 | 1 |
| Vizcarra, Ernesto, CAM | 1.000 | 26 | 4 | 10 | 0 | 14 | 1 |
| Vizcarra, William, YUC | 1.000 | 6 | 1 | 0 | 0 | 1 | 0 |
| Ward, Bryan, MVA* | 1.000 | 18 | 2 | 12 | 0 | 14 | 0 |
| Webster, Daniel, CAM | 1.000 | 1 | 0 | 1 | 0 | 1 | 0 |
| Woodman, Hank, MXO | 1.000 | 9 | 4 | 2 | 0 | 6 | 0 |
| Zambrano, Baudel, TIG | 1.000 | 11 | 0 | 2 | 0 | 2 | 0 |
| Zambrano, Baudel, SLP | .667 | 9 | 0 | 2 | 1 | 3 | 0 |
| Zambrano, Baudel, TIG-SLP | .800 | 20 | 0 | 4 | 1 | 5 | 0 |
| Zavala, Marco, MTY* | 1.000 | 20 | 1 | 1 | 0 | 2 | 0 |

## LEAGUE CHAMPIONS

| Year | Team | Pct. |
|---|---|---|
| 1955— | Mexico City Tigers* | .539 |
| 1956— | Mexico City Reds | .692 |
| 1957— | Yucatan | .567 |
| | Mex. C. Reds (2nd)† | .550 |
| 1958— | Nuevo Laredo | .625 |
| 1959— | Poza Rica | .575 |
| | Mex. C. Reds (3rd)† | .507 |
| 1960— | Mexico City Tigers | .538 |
| 1961— | Veracruz | .575 |
| 1962— | Monterrey | .592 |
| 1963— | Puebla | .606 |
| 1964— | Mexico City Reds | .586 |
| 1965— | Mexico City Tigers | .590 |
| 1966— | Mexico City Tigers‡ | .614 |
| | Mexico City Reds | .571 |
| 1967— | Jalisco | .607 |
| 1968— | Mexico City Reds | .586 |
| 1969— | Reynosa | .591 |
| 1970— | Aguila§ | .580 |
| | Mexico City Reds | .607 |
| 1971— | Jalisco§ | .558 |
| | Saltillo | .593 |
| 1972— | Saltillo | .636 |
| | Cordoba§ | .541 |
| 1973— | Saltillo | .656 |
| | Mexico City Reds∞ | .590 |
| 1974— | Jalisco | .627 |
| | Mexico City Reds∞ | .551 |
| 1975— | Tampico∞ | .541 |
| | Cordoba | .649 |
| 1976— | Mexico City Reds∞ | .543 |
| | Union Laguna | .547 |
| 1977— | Mexico City Reds | .623 |
| | Nuevo Laredo∞ | .507 |
| 1978— | Aguascalientes∞ | .589 |
| | Union Laguna | .523 |
| 1979— | Saltillo | .704 |
| | Puebla∞ | .628 |
| 1980— | No champion▲ | |
| 1981— | Mexico City Reds | .615 |
| | Reynosa | .492 |
| 1982— | Ciudad Juarez∞ | .570 |
| | Mexico City Tigers | .508 |
| 1983— | Campeche◆ | .614 |
| | Ciudad Juarez | .535 |
| 1984— | Yucatan◆ | .560 |
| | Ciudad Juarez | .509 |
| 1985— | Mexico City Reds◆ | .606 |
| | Nuevo Laredo | .5275 |
| 1986— | Puebla◆ | .682 |
| | Monclova | .598 |
| 1987— | Mexico City Reds◆ | .605 |
| | Monterrey | .536 |
| 1988— | Mexico City Reds◆ | .646 |
| | Nuevo Laredo | .602 |
| 1989— | Nuevo Laredo◆ | .621 |
| | Yucatan | .539 |
| 1990— | Nuevo Laredo | .618 |
| | Leon◆ | .565 |
| 1991— | Monterrey◆ | .683 |
| | Mexico City Reds | .627 |
| 1992— | Mexico City Tigers◆ | .594 |
| | Nuevo Laredo | .538 |
| 1993— | Nuevo Laredo | .589 |
| | Tabasco◆ | .528 |
| 1994— | Mexico City Red Devils◆ | .646 |
| | Monterrey Sultans | .608 |
| 1995— | Mexico City Red Devils | .708 |
| | Monterrey Sultans◆ | .570 |
| 1996— | Monterrey Sultans | .713 |
| | Mexico City Reds◆ | .619 |
| 1997— | Mexico City Red Devils | .686 |
| | Mexico City Tigers■ | .658 |
| 1998— | Monterrey | .672 |
| | Oaxaca■ | .576 |
| 1999— | Mexico City Tigers | .664 |
| | Mexico City Reds■ | .632 |
| 2000— | Saltillo | .647 |
| | Mexico City Tigers■ | .627 |
| 2001— | Mexico City Tigers■ | .632 |
| | Mexico City Reds | .575 |
| 2002— | Mexico City Reds▼ | .673 |
| 2003— | Mexico▼ | .630 |
| 2004— | Campeche▼▼ | .567 |

*Defeated Nuevo Laredo, two games to none, in playoff for pennant. †Won four-team playoff. ‡Won split-season playoff. §League divided into Northern, Southern divisions; won two-team playoff. ∞League divided into Northern, Southern zones; sub-divided into Eastern, Western divisions, won eight-team playoff. ▲ A players strike on July 1 forced the cancellation of the regular season and playoff schedule. ◆ League divided into Northern, Southern zones; four clubs from each zone qualified for postseason play. Won final series for league championship. ■ League divided into Northern, Central and Southern zones; played split season, with top eight teams qualifying for playoffs. Won final series for league championship. ▼ League divided into Northern and Southern divisions; played split season, with top eight teams qualifying for playoffs. Won final series for league championship. ▼▼ League divided into Northern and Southern divisions; played split season, with 12 teams qualifying for playoffs. Won final series for league championship.

# PACIFIC COAST LEAGUE



## LEAGUE OFFICE

**President**
Branch Rickey

**Address**
1631 Mesa Ave., Suite A
Colorado Springs, CO 80906-2917

**Phone**
719-636-3399

## TEAMS

### ALBUQUERQUE ISOTOPES

**General manager**
John Traub
**Manager**
Dean Treanor
**Ballpark (capacity, surface)**
Isotopes Park (11,124, grass)
**Affiliation**
Marlins
**Address**
1601 Avenida Cesar Chavez SE
Albuquerque, NM 87106
**Phone**
505-924-2255

### COLORADO SPRINGS SKY SOX

**General manager/president**
Tony Ensor
**Manager**
Marv Foley
**Ballpark (capacity, surface)**
Sky Sox Stadium (9,000, grass)
**Affiliation**
Rockies
**Address**
4385 Tutt Blvd.
Colorado Springs, CO 80922
**Phone**
719-597-1449

### FRESNO GRIZZLIES

**General manager**
TBA
**Manager**
TBA
**Ballpark (capacity, surface)**
Grizzlies Stadium (12,500, grass)
**Affiliation**
Giants
**Address**
1800 Tulari Ave.
Fresno, CA 93721
**Phone**
559-442-1994

### IOWA CUBS

**General manager**
Sam Bernabe
**Manager**
Mike Quade
**Ballpark (capacity, surface)**
Principal Park (10,500, grass)
**Affiliation**
Cubs
**Address**
One Line Drive
Des Moines, IA 50309
**Phone**
515-243-6111

### LAS VEGAS 51s

**General manager/president**
Don Logan
**Manager**
Jerry Royster
**Ballpark (capacity, surface)**
Cashman Field (9,334, grass)
**Affiliation**
Dodgers
**Address**
850 Las Vegas Blvd. N
Las Vegas, NV 89101
**Phone**
702-386-7200

### MEMPHIS REDBIRDS

**President/general manager**
Dave Chase
**Manager**
Danny Sheaffer
**Ballpark (capacity, surface)**
AutoZone Park (14,200; grass)
**Affiliation**
Cardinals
**Address**
175 Toyota Plaza, Suite 300
Memphis, TN 38103
**Phone**
901-721-6050

### NASHVILLE SOUNDS

**General manager**
Glenn Yaeger
**Manager**
Frank Kremblas
**Ballpark (capacity, surface)**
Greer Stadium (11,500, grass)
**Affiliation**
Brewers
**Address**
534 Chestnut Street
Nashville, TN 37203
**Phone**
615-242-4371

### NEW ORLEANS ZEPHYRS

**Vice president/general manager**
TBA
**Manager**
TBA
**Ballpark (capacity, surface)**
Zephyr Field (11,000, grass)
**Affiliation**
Nationals
**Address**
6000 Airline Dr.
Metairie, LA 70003
**Phone**
504-734-5155

### OKLAHOMA REDHAWKS

**President/general manager**
Scott Pruitt
**Manager**
Bobby Jones
**Ballpark (capacity, surface)**
SBC Bricktown Ballpark (13,066, grass)
**Affiliation**
Rangers
**Address**
2 South Mickey Mantle Dr.
Oklahoma City, OK 73104
**Phone**
405-218-1000

### OMAHA ROYALS

**Vice president/general manager**
Doug Stewart
**Manager**
Mike Jirschele
**Ballpark (capacity, surface)**
Omaha's Rosenblatt Stadium (24,000, grass)
**Affiliation**
Royals
**Address**
1202 Bert Murphy Ave.
Omaha, NE 68107
**Phone**
402-734-2550

### PORTLAND BEAVERS

**General manager**
Jack Cain
**Manager**
Craig Colbert
**Ballpark (capacity, surface)**
PGE Park (19,566, artificial)
**Affiliation**
Padres
**Address**
1844 SW Morrison
Portland Ore. 97205
**Phone**
503-553-5400

### ROUND ROCK EXPRESS

**President**
Dave Fendrick
**Manager**
Jackie Moore
**Ballpark (capacity, surface)**
The Dell Diamond (8,496, grass)
**Affiliation**
Astros
**Address**
3400 E. Palm Valley Blvd.
Round Rock, TX 78664
**Phone**
512-255-2255

## SACRAMENTO RIVER CATS

**General Manager**
Gary Arthur
**Manager**
Tony DeFrancesco
**Ballpark (capacity, surface)**
Raley Field (10,500, grass)
**Affiliation**
Athletics
**Address**
400 Ballpark Drive
West Sacramento, CA 95691
**Phone**
916-376-4700

## SALT LAKE STINGERS

**Vice president/ general manager**
Dorsena Picknell
**Manager**
Dino Ebel
**Ballpark (capacity, surface)**
Franklin Covey Field (15,500, grass)
**Affiliation**
Angels
**Address**
P.O. Box 4108
Salt Lake City, UT 84115
**Phone**
801-485-3800

## TACOMA RAINIERS

**General manager**
Dave Lewis
**Manager**
Dan Rohn
**Ballpark (capacity, surface)**
Cheney Stadium (10,106, grass)
**Affiliation**
Mariners
**Address**
P.O. Box 11087
Tacoma, WA 98411
**Phone**
253-752-7707

## TUCSON SIDEWINDERS

**General manager**
Rick Parr
**Manager**
Chip Hale
**Ballpark (capacity, surface)**
Tucson Electric Park (12,500, grass)
**Affiliation**
Diamondbacks
**Address**
P.O. Box 27045
Tucson, AZ 85726
**Phone**
520-434-1021

## 2004 FINAL STANDINGS

### EASTERN DIVISION

| Team | W | L | T | Pct. | GB |
|---|---|---|---|---|---|
| Oklahoma (Rangers) | 81 | 63 | - | .563 | ... |
| Memphis (Cardinals) | 73 | 71 | - | .507 | 8 |
| New Orleans (Astros) | 66 | 78 | - | .458 | 15 |
| Nashville (Pirates) | 63 | 79 | - | .444 | 17.0 |

### CENTRAL DIVISION

| Team | W | L | T | Pct. | GB |
|---|---|---|---|---|---|
| Iowa (Cubs) | 79 | 64 | - | .552 | ... |
| Colorado Springs (Rockies) | 78 | 65 | - | .545 | 1.0 |
| Omaha (Royals) | 71 | 73 | - | .493 | 8.5 |
| Albuquerque (Marlins) | 67 | 77 | - | .465 | 12.5 |

### NORTHERN DIVISION

| Team | W | L | T | Pct. | GB |
|---|---|---|---|---|---|
| Portland (Padres) | 84 | 60 | - | .583 | ... |
| Tacoma (Mariners) | 79 | 63 | - | .556 | 4.0 |
| Edmonton (Expos) | 69 | 74 | - | .483 | 14.5 |
| Salt Lake (Angels) | 56 | 88 | - | .389 | 28.0 |

### SOUTHERN DIVISION

| Team | W | L | T | Pct. | GB |
|---|---|---|---|---|---|
| Sacramento (A's) | 79 | 65 | - | .549 | ... |
| Tucson (Diamondbacks) | 74 | 70 | - | .514 | 5.0 |
| Las Vegas (Dodgers) | 67 | 76 | - | .469 | 11.5 |
| Fresno (Giants) | 62 | 82 | - | .431 | 17.0 |

## COMPOSITE

| Team | W | L | T | PCT | GB | POR | OKL | TAC | IWA | SCO | CSP | TCN | MEM | OMA | EDM | LVG | ABQ | NO | NVL | FRN | SLK |
|---|---|---|---|---|---|---|---|---|---|---|---|---|---|---|---|---|---|---|---|---|---|
| Portland | 84 | 60 | - | .583 | — | X | 2 | 9 | 1 | 9 | 4 | 8 | 1 | 2 | 9 | 8 | 3 | 2 | 2 | 11 | 13 |
| Oklahoma | 81 | 63 | - | .563 | 3 | 2 | X | 2 | 7 | 3 | 9 | 1 | 8 | 11 | 3 | 1 | 9 | 9 | 9 | 3 | 4 |
| Tacoma | 79 | 63 | - | .556 | 4 | 7 | 2 | X | 0 | 6 | 3 | 8 | 3 | 3 | 12 | 10 | 4 | 2 | 1 | 8 | 10 |
| Iowa | 79 | 64 | - | .552 | 41/2 | 3 | 9 | 3 | X | 2 | 6 | 2 | 9 | 8 | 4 | 1 | 10 | 9 | 9 | 2 | 2 |
| Sacramento | 79 | 65 | - | .549 | 5 | 7 | 1 | 10 | 2 | X | 1 | 6 | 3 | 3 | 9 | 8 | 2 | 2 | 3 | 11 | 11 |
| Colorado Springs | 78 | 65 | - | .545 | 51/2 | 0 | 7 | 1 | 10 | 3 | X | 3 | 6 | 8 | 1 | 3 | 11 | 11 | 9 | 2 | 3 |
| Tucson | 74 | 70 | - | .514 | 10 | 8 | 3 | 8 | 2 | 10 | 1 | X | 3 | 0 | 7 | 6 | 3 | 2 | 4 | 7 | 10 |
| Memphis | 73 | 71 | - | .507 | 11 | 3 | 8 | 1 | 7 | 1 | 10 | 1 | X | 7 | 2 | 4 | 7 | 9 | 9 | 1 | 3 |
| Omaha | 71 | 73 | - | .493 | 13 | 2 | 5 | 1 | 8 | 1 | 8 | 4 | 9 | X | 1 | 2 | 8 | 8 | 11 | 2 | 1 |
| Edmonton | 69 | 74 | - | .483 | 141/2 | 7 | 1 | 4 | 0 | 7 | 3 | 9 | 2 | 3 | X | 9 | 2 | 1 | 1 | 10 | 10 |
| Las Vegas | 67 | 76 | - | .469 | 161/2 | 8 | 3 | 6 | 3 | 8 | 1 | 10 | 0 | 2 | 6 | X | 0 | 2 | 3 | 8 | 7 |
| Albuquerque | 67 | 77 | - | .465 | 17 | 1 | 7 | 0 | 6 | 2 | 5 | 1 | 9 | 8 | 2 | 4 | X | 7 | 9 | 3 | 3 |
| New Orleans | 66 | 78 | - | .458 | 18 | 2 | 7 | 2 | 7 | 2 | 5 | 2 | 7 | 8 | 3 | 2 | 9 | X | 6 | 2 | 2 |
| Nashville | 63 | 79 | - | .444 | 20 | 2 | 7 | 2 | 7 | 1 | 6 | 0 | 7 | 5 | 3 | 1 | 7 | 10 | X | 2 | 3 |
| Fresno | 62 | 82 | - | .431 | 22 | 5 | 1 | 8 | 2 | 5 | 2 | 9 | 3 | 2 | 6 | 8 | 1 | 2 | 2 | X | 6 |
| Salt Lake | 56 | 88 | - | .389 | 28 | 3 | 0 | 6 | 2 | 5 | 1 | 6 | 1 | 3 | 6 | 9 | 1 | 2 | 1 | 10 | X |

Major league affiliations in parentheses.

PLAYOFFS: Iowa defeated Oklahoma, three games to two; Sacramento defeated Portland, three games to one; Sacramento defeated Iowa, three games to none, to win league championship.

REGULAR-SEASON ATTENDANCE: Albuquerque, 575,607; Colorado Springs, 236,022; Edmonton, 252,557; Fresno, 531,040; Iowa, 540,055; Las Vegas, 306,628; Memphis, 730,565; Nashville, 405,536; New Orleans, 324,324; Oklahoma, 474,206; Omaha, 318,537; Portland, 312,678; Sacramento, 751,156; Salt Lake, 448,153; Tacoma, 310,680; Tucson, 285,378; Total Attendance—6,567,100. All-Star game at McCoy Stadium—11,192.

MANAGERS: Albuquerque, Tracy Woodson; Colorado Springs, Marv Foley; Edmonton, Dave Huppert; Fresno, Fred Stanley; Iowa, Mike Quade; Las Vegas, Terry Kennedy; Memphis, Danny Sheaffer; Nashville, Trent Jewett; New Orleans, Chris Maloney; Oklahoma, Bobby Jones; Omaha, Mike Jirschele; Portland, Craig Colbert; Sacramento, Tony DeFrancesco; Salt Lake, Mike Brumley; Tacoma, Dan Rohn; Tucson, Chip Hale. Managerial record of team with more than one manager: Memphis, Spencer (23-42) and Sheaffer (41-37).

ALL-STAR TEAM: 1B—Dan Johnson, Sacramento; 2B—Chris Burke, New Orleans; 3B—Garrett Atkins, Colorado Springs; SS—Clint Barmes, Colorado Springs; OF—Chad Allen, Oklahoma; OF—Ryan Church, Edmonton; OF—Adam Riggs, Salt Lake; C—Mike Rose, Sacramento; DH—Calvin Pickering, Omaha; RHP—Brian Sweeney, Portland; LHP—Scott Downs, Edmonton; Relief pitcher—Al Reyes, Memphis; Most Valuable Player—Dan Johnson, Sacramento; Rookie of the Year—Chris Burke, New Orleans; Pitcher of the Year—Scott Downs, Edmonton; Manager of the Year—Dan Rohn, Tacoma.

# 2004 BATTING

## TEAM

| Team | G | TPA | AB | R | H | TB | 2B | 3B | HR | RBI | SH | SF | HP | BB | IBB | SO | SB | CS | GDP | LOB | ShO | Avg. | OBP | Slg. |
|---|---|---|---|---|---|---|---|---|---|---|---|---|---|---|---|---|---|---|---|---|---|---|---|---|
| Colorado Springs | 143 | 5532 | 4880 | 859 | 1496 | 2432 | 340 | 31 | 178 | 801 | 71 | 45 | 48 | 488 | 22 | 929 | 80 | 42 | 116 | 1041 | 3 | .307 | .372 | .498 |
| Oklahoma | 144 | 5718 | 5076 | 844 | 1504 | 2328 | 319 | 38 | 143 | 799 | 29 | 45 | 52 | 513 | 16 | 988 | 105 | 44 | 112 | 1108 | 4 | .296 | .364 | .459 |
| Tucson | 144 | 5597 | 5016 | 792 | 1453 | 2379 | 330 | 55 | 162 | 759 | 47 | 49 | 38 | 446 | 21 | 1175 | 97 | 38 | 87 | 1050 | 7 | .290 | .349 | .474 |
| Las Vegas | 143 | 5624 | 5036 | 806 | 1454 | 2383 | 307 | 35 | 184 | 758 | 56 | 41 | 58 | 433 | 23 | 963 | 92 | 47 | 105 | 1006 | 8 | .289 | .349 | .473 |
| Edmonton | 143 | 5516 | 4871 | 715 | 1410 | 2045 | 282 | 31 | 97 | 666 | 41 | 44 | 47 | 513 | 23 | 817 | 92 | 46 | 135 | 1121 | 8 | .289 | .360 | .420 |
| Salt Lake | 144 | 5554 | 5040 | 785 | 1458 | 2311 | 289 | 54 | 152 | 734 | 27 | 51 | 34 | 402 | 14 | 984 | 92 | 38 | 108 | 1002 | 6 | .289 | .343 | .459 |
| Fresno | 144 | 5659 | 5055 | 717 | 1421 | 2168 | 272 | 38 | 133 | 669 | 63 | 38 | 64 | 439 | 16 | 993 | 99 | 48 | 106 | 1072 | 5 | .281 | .344 | .429 |
| Albuquerque | 144 | 5643 | 4938 | 791 | 1383 | 2251 | 296 | 43 | 162 | 732 | 50 | 54 | 59 | 541 | 11 | 1067 | 90 | 53 | 105 | 1052 | 9 | .280 | .355 | .456 |
| Memphis | 144 | 5476 | 4942 | 723 | 1382 | 2195 | 247 | 22 | 174 | 675 | 53 | 39 | 67 | 373 | 14 | 869 | 82 | 35 | 114 | 984 | 4 | .280 | .336 | .444 |
| Iowa | 143 | 5430 | 4845 | 760 | 1357 | 2207 | 315 | 32 | 157 | 721 | 51 | 47 | 50 | 434 | 20 | 857 | 100 | 28 | 112 | 975 | 7 | .280 | .342 | .456 |
| Sacramento | 144 | 5819 | 4934 | 830 | 1377 | 2188 | 283 | 27 | 158 | 786 | 40 | 50 | 63 | 732 | 12 | 1021 | 70 | 29 | 126 | 1200 | 3 | .279 | .376 | .443 |
| Portland | 144 | 5531 | 4938 | 738 | 1370 | 2163 | 300 | 26 | 147 | 700 | 48 | 45 | 58 | 442 | 17 | 845 | 134 | 30 | 105 | 1006 | 8 | .277 | .341 | .438 |
| Omaha | 144 | 5511 | 4844 | 737 | 1344 | 2197 | 232 | 33 | 185 | 709 | 36 | 34 | 64 | 533 | 15 | 987 | 90 | 45 | 135 | 1054 | 11 | .277 | .355 | .454 |
| New Orleans | 144 | 5437 | 4820 | 665 | 1321 | 2078 | 264 | 26 | 147 | 620 | 49 | 46 | 71 | 450 | 20 | 937 | 100 | 41 | 131 | 1033 | 6 | .274 | .342 | .431 |
| Tacoma | 142 | 5365 | 4793 | 731 | 1306 | 2155 | 232 | 40 | 179 | 686 | 43 | 33 | 63 | 432 | 21 | 1037 | 132 | 65 | 81 | 960 | 7 | .272 | .338 | .450 |
| Nashville | 142 | 5343 | 4775 | 684 | 1300 | 2157 | 257 | 30 | 180 | 642 | 55 | 27 | 64 | 421 | 28 | 996 | 116 | 58 | 124 | 931 | 10 | .272 | .338 | .452 |

## INDIVIDUAL

### TOP QUALIFIERS FOR BATTING CHAMPIONSHIP

Minimum 389 plate appearances. *Lefthanded batter. †Switch-hitter.

| Player, Team | G | TPA | AB | R | H | TB | 2B | 3B | HR | RBI | SH | SF | HP | BB | IBB | SO | SB | CS | GDP | Avg. | OBP | Slg. |
|---|---|---|---|---|---|---|---|---|---|---|---|---|---|---|---|---|---|---|---|---|---|---|
| Atkins, Garrett, Colorado Springs | 122 | 516 | 445 | 88 | 163 | 257 | 43 | 3 | 15 | 94 | 0 | 10 | 4 | 57 | 4 | 45 | 0 | 0 | 20 | .366 | .434 | .578 |
| Allen, Chad, Oklahoma | 93 | 427 | 386 | 75 | 138 | 193 | 28 | 3 | 7 | 70 | 0 | 5 | 5 | 31 | 2 | 72 | 18 | 2 | 9 | .358 | .407 | .500 |
| Church, Ryan, Edmonton | 98 | 408 | 347 | 74 | 119 | 215 | 29 | 8 | 17 | 78 | 1 | 5 | 4 | 51 | 7 | 62 | 0 | 1 | 4 | .343 | .428 | .620 |
| Izturis, Maicer, Edmonton † | 99 | 443 | 376 | 65 | 127 | 159 | 19 | 2 | 3 | 36 | 4 | 2 | 4 | 57 | 1 | 30 | 14 | 12 | 12 | .338 | .428 | .423 |
| Piedra, Jorge, Colorado Springs | 99 | 412 | 377 | 71 | 126 | 210 | 29 | 5 | 15 | 55 | 3 | 6 | 3 | 23 | 1 | 56 | 4 | 3 | 7 | .334 | .372 | .557 |
| Riggs, Adam, Salt Lake | 112 | 493 | 450 | 104 | 149 | 285 | 33 | 8 | 29 | 90 | 2 | 7 | 4 | 30 | 2 | 80 | 8 | 3 | 5 | .331 | .373 | .633 |
| Hubbard, Trenidad, Iowa | 129 | 542 | 473 | 101 | 156 | 219 | 28 | 4 | 9 | 49 | 1 | 3 | 3 | 62 | 1 | 59 | 36 | 8 | 12 | .330 | .409 | .463 |
| Barmes, Clint, Colorado Springs | 125 | 589 | 533 | 104 | 175 | 269 | 42 | 2 | 16 | 51 | 9 | 4 | 15 | 28 | 1 | 61 | 20 | 8 | 5 | .328 | .376 | .505 |
| Conti, Jason, Oklahoma * | 104 | 470 | 421 | 63 | 138 | 198 | 26 | 5 | 8 | 61 | 3 | 3 | 5 | 33 | 1 | 84 | 5 | 1 | 8 | .328 | .381 | .470 |
| Alfaro, Jason, New Orleans | 126 | 501 | 465 | 62 | 151 | 222 | 32 | 0 | 13 | 67 | 3 | 3 | 4 | 26 | 1 | 58 | 3 | 6 | 11 | .325 | .363 | .477 |
| Dillon, Joe, Albuquerque | 108 | 468 | 403 | 96 | 131 | 268 | 33 | 7 | 30 | 86 | 0 | 9 | 10 | 46 | 0 | 85 | 12 | 3 | 7 | .325 | .400 | .665 |
| Dallimore, Brian, Fresno | 111 | 497 | 432 | 72 | 140 | 193 | 21 | 4 | 8 | 65 | 4 | 6 | 15 | 40 | 3 | 53 | 9 | 2 | 13 | .324 | .396 | .447 |
| Varner, Noochie, Tucson | 100 | 389 | 343 | 64 | 110 | 152 | 18 | 3 | 6 | 37 | 1 | 0 | 2 | 41 | 3 | 62 | 4 | 1 | 12 | .321 | .396 | .443 |
| Almonte, Erick, Colorado Springs | 123 | 522 | 450 | 91 | 143 | 228 | 26 | 4 | 17 | 74 | 5 | 2 | 1 | 64 | 3 | 87 | 14 | 8 | 14 | .318 | .402 | .507 |
| Dubois, Jason, Iowa | 109 | 437 | 386 | 76 | 122 | 243 | 26 | 1 | 31 | 99 | 0 | 3 | 7 | 41 | 2 | 97 | 2 | 0 | 10 | .316 | .389 | .630 |

DEPARTMENTAL LEADERS: G—Huffman, 144; AB—M. Edwards, 551; R—Swisher, 109; H—Barmes, 175; TB—Tracy, 293; 2B—Atkins, 43; 3B—Thompson, 13; HR—Witt, 36; RBI—Tracy, 120; SH—Pena, 13; SF—Zoccolillo, 11; HP—Thurston, 17; BB—Swisher, 103; IBB—Church, Zapp, 8; SO—Zapp, 184; SB—Thurston, 40; CS—Nivar, Thompson, 15; GIDP—Atkins, Short, 20; Slg.—Dillon, .665; OBP—Atkins, .434.

### ALL PLAYERS

*Lefthanded batter. †Switch-hitter.

| Player, Team | G | TPA | AB | R | H | TB | 2B | 3B | HR | RBI | SH | SF | HP | BB | IBB | SO | SB | CS | GDP | Avg. | OBP | Slg. |
|---|---|---|---|---|---|---|---|---|---|---|---|---|---|---|---|---|---|---|---|---|---|---|
| Aardsma, David, Fresno | 44 | 4 | 4 | 0 | 0 | 0 | 0 | 0 | 0 | 0 | 0 | 0 | 0 | 0 | 0 | 3 | 0 | 0 | 0 | .000 | .000 | .000 |
| Abad, Andy, Nashville * | 99 | 349 | 301 | 45 | 88 | 141 | 15 | 1 | 12 | 49 | 1 | 2 | 5 | 40 | 1 | 52 | 4 | 1 | 9 | .292 | .382 | .468 |
| Abreu, Winston, Tucson | 28 | 3 | 2 | 0 | 1 | 1 | 0 | 0 | 0 | 0 | 1 | 0 | 0 | 0 | 0 | 0 | 0 | 0 | 0 | .500 | .500 | .500 |
| Alfaro, Jason, New Orleans | 126 | 501 | 465 | 62 | 151 | 222 | 32 | 0 | 13 | 67 | 3 | 3 | 4 | 26 | 1 | 58 | 3 | 6 | 11 | .325 | .363 | .477 |
| Allen, Chad, Oklahoma | 93 | 427 | 386 | 75 | 138 | 193 | 28 | 3 | 7 | 70 | 0 | 5 | 5 | 31 | 2 | 72 | 18 | 2 | 9 | .358 | .407 | .500 |
| Allen, Luke, Nashville * | 123 | 450 | 414 | 53 | 107 | 180 | 18 | 2 | 17 | 43 | 1 | 2 | 0 | 33 | 3 | 94 | 3 | 6 | 12 | .258 | .312 | .435 |
| Almonte, Erick, Colorado Springs | 123 | 522 | 450 | 91 | 143 | 228 | 26 | 4 | 17 | 74 | 5 | 2 | 1 | 64 | 3 | 87 | 14 | 8 | 14 | .318 | .402 | .507 |
| Almonte, Hector, Colorado Springs | 12 | 2 | 2 | 0 | 0 | 0 | 0 | 0 | 0 | 0 | 0 | 0 | 0 | 0 | 0 | 1 | 0 | 0 | 0 | .000 | .000 | .000 |
| Alvarez, Juan, Albuquerque * | 49 | 4 | 4 | 0 | 1 | 1 | 0 | 0 | 0 | 0 | 0 | 0 | 0 | 0 | 0 | 0 | 0 | 0 | 0 | .250 | .250 | .250 |
| Alvarez, Tony, Nashville | 99 | 378 | 335 | 59 | 97 | 153 | 12 | 1 | 14 | 48 | 0 | 2 | 6 | 35 | 0 | 63 | 19 | 12 | 6 | .290 | .365 | .457 |
| Anderson, Jimmy, Iowa * | 16 | 28 | 23 | 4 | 5 | 6 | 1 | 0 | 0 | 5 | 4 | 0 | 0 | 1 | 0 | 3 | 0 | 0 | 0 | .217 | .250 | .261 |
| Ansman, Craig, Tucson | 104 | 386 | 342 | 59 | 87 | 165 | 19 | 1 | 19 | 58 | 0 | 4 | 4 | 36 | 0 | 117 | 1 | 1 | 4 | .254 | .329 | .482 |
| Ardoin, Danny, Oklahoma | 68 | 291 | 237 | 50 | 73 | 115 | 12 | 0 | 10 | 44 | 2 | 3 | 8 | 41 | 0 | 66 | 1 | 1 | 9 | .308 | .422 | .485 |
| Ashby, Chris, Albuquerque | 74 | 237 | 213 | 24 | 51 | 77 | 11 | 0 | 5 | 25 | 0 | 3 | 1 | 20 | 1 | 31 | 2 | 1 | 8 | .239 | .304 | .362 |
| Athas, Jamie, Fresno * | 124 | 474 | 419 | 58 | 107 | 143 | 16 | 4 | 4 | 45 | 8 | 3 | 6 | 38 | 0 | 91 | 13 | 11 | 9 | .255 | .324 | .341 |
| Atkins, Garrett, Colorado Springs | 122 | 516 | 445 | 88 | 163 | 257 | 43 | 3 | 15 | 94 | 0 | 10 | 4 | 57 | 4 | 45 | 0 | 0 | 20 | .366 | .434 | .578 |
| Baker, John, Sacramento * | 14 | 56 | 49 | 11 | 17 | 20 | 3 | 0 | 0 | 10 | 0 | 0 | 1 | 6 | 1 | 23 | 0 | 0 | 0 | .347 | .429 | .408 |
| Banks, Brian, Albuquerque † | 67 | 248 | 216 | 31 | 50 | 84 | 12 | 2 | 6 | 30 | 0 | 3 | 2 | 27 | 0 | 46 | 0 | 0 | 5 | .231 | .319 | .389 |
| Barden, Brian, Tucson | 89 | 360 | 332 | 50 | 94 | 158 | 30 | 5 | 8 | 50 | 2 | 4 | 5 | 17 | 0 | 83 | 3 | 1 | 6 | .283 | .324 | .476 |
| Barmes, Clint, Colorado Springs | 125 | 589 | 533 | 104 | 175 | 269 | 42 | 2 | 16 | 51 | 9 | 4 | 15 | 28 | 1 | 61 | 20 | 8 | 5 | .328 | .376 | .505 |
| Barzilla, Philip, New Orleans * | 27 | 2 | 2 | 0 | 0 | 0 | 0 | 0 | 0 | 0 | 0 | 0 | 0 | 0 | 0 | 1 | 0 | 0 | 0 | .000 | .000 | .000 |
| Bauer, Pete, Albuquerque | 1 | 3 | 2 | 1 | 1 | 2 | 1 | 0 | 0 | 0 | 0 | 0 | 0 | 1 | 0 | 1 | 1 | 0 | 0 | .500 | .667 | 1.000 |
| Bell, Rick, Las Vegas | 125 | 487 | 460 | 68 | 139 | 213 | 36 | 1 | 12 | 54 | 2 | 1 | 1 | 23 | 2 | 75 | 7 | 3 | 13 | .302 | .336 | .463 |
| Beltran, Rigo, Edmonton * | 26 | 9 | 8 | 0 | 1 | 2 | 1 | 0 | 0 | 2 | 0 | 0 | 0 | 1 | 0 | 1 | 0 | 0 | 0 | .125 | .222 | .250 |
| Benes, Alan, Memphis | 29 | 39 | 30 | 2 | 4 | 4 | 0 | 0 | 0 | 1 | 6 | 1 | 0 | 2 | 0 | 10 | 0 | 0 | 0 | .133 | .182 | .133 |
| Berger, Brandon, Omaha | 39 | 168 | 146 | 25 | 34 | 85 | 9 | 0 | 14 | 37 | 0 | 1 | 2 | 19 | 0 | 22 | 1 | 1 | 5 | .233 | .327 | .582 |
| Bernero, Adam, Colorado Springs | 9 | 17 | 12 | 1 | 3 | 5 | 0 | 1 | 0 | 0 | 3 | 0 | 0 | 2 | 0 | 3 | 0 | 0 | 0 | .250 | .357 | .417 |
| Bibee, Hal, Colorado Springs | 6 | 6 | 6 | 2 | 1 | 1 | 0 | 0 | 0 | 0 | 0 | 0 | 0 | 0 | 0 | 1 | 0 | 0 | 0 | .167 | .167 | .167 |
| Bland, Nate, Iowa * | 53 | 5 | 3 | 1 | 1 | 1 | 0 | 0 | 0 | 0 | 2 | 0 | 0 | 0 | 0 | 1 | 0 | 0 | 0 | .333 | .333 | .333 |
| Blank, Matt, Albuquerque * | 35 | 31 | 19 | 2 | 3 | 4 | 1 | 0 | 0 | 2 | 4 | 1 | 1 | 6 | 0 | 9 | 0 | 0 | 0 | .158 | .370 | .211 |
| Bowers, Jason, Memphis | 120 | 426 | 389 | 49 | 99 | 146 | 20 | 3 | 7 | 38 | 3 | 1 | 8 | 23 | 1 | 73 | 9 | 1 | 3 | .254 | .309 | .375 |

| Player, Team | G | TPA | AB | R | H | TB | 2B | 3B | HR | RBI | SH | SF | HP | BB | IBB | SO | SB | CS | GDP | Avg. | OBP | Slg. |
|---|---|---|---|---|---|---|---|---|---|---|---|---|---|---|---|---|---|---|---|---|---|---|
| Bowles, Brian, Colorado Springs | 13 | 3 | 2 | 0 | 0 | 0 | 0 | 0 | 0 | 0 | 0 | 0 | 0 | 1 | 0 | 1 | 0 | 0 | 0 | .000 | .333 | .000 |
| Boyd, Jason, Nashville | 11 | 3 | 3 | 0 | 0 | 0 | 0 | 0 | 0 | 0 | 0 | 0 | 0 | 0 | 0 | 2 | 0 | 0 | 0 | .000 | .000 | .000 |
| Bozied, Tagg, Portland | 57 | 239 | 213 | 41 | 67 | 134 | 17 | 1 | 16 | 58 | 1 | 3 | 4 | 18 | 1 | 29 | 0 | 0 | 3 | .315 | .374 | .629 |
| Brohawn, Troy, Las Vegas * | 72 | 9 | 8 | 3 | 3 | 4 | 1 | 0 | 0 | 4 | 0 | 0 | 0 | 1 | 0 | 1 | 0 | 0 | 0 | .375 | .444 | .500 |
| Brown, Adrian, Omaha † | 114 | 509 | 444 | 69 | 118 | 170 | 17 | 7 | 7 | 51 | 5 | 3 | 0 | 57 | 1 | 74 | 28 | 4 | 7 | .266 | .347 | .383 |
| Brown, Emil, New Orleans | 26 | 101 | 92 | 12 | 31 | 49 | 10 | 1 | 2 | 17 | 0 | 1 | 4 | 4 | 0 | 20 | 4 | 2 | 3 | .337 | .386 | .533 |
| Buchholz, Taylor, New Orleans | 20 | 18 | 15 | 1 | 0 | 0 | 0 | 0 | 0 | 0 | 2 | 0 | 0 | 1 | 0 | 6 | 0 | 0 | 0 | .000 | .063 | .000 |
| Bumatay, Mike, Colorado Springs * | 37 | 6 | 6 | 1 | 1 | 2 | 1 | 0 | 0 | 0 | 0 | 0 | 0 | 0 | 0 | 3 | 0 | 0 | 0 | .167 | .167 | .333 |
| Bumstead, Mike, Portland | 18 | 5 | 5 | 0 | 0 | 0 | 0 | 0 | 0 | 0 | 0 | 0 | 0 | 0 | 0 | 3 | 0 | 0 | 0 | .000 | .000 | .000 |
| Burnham, Gary, Memphis * | 36 | 97 | 89 | 15 | 26 | 40 | 5 | 0 | 3 | 13 | 0 | 0 | 1 | 7 | 0 | 13 | 1 | 1 | 3 | .292 | .351 | .449 |
| Bynum, Freddie, Sacramento * | 66 | 291 | 258 | 42 | 73 | 94 | 11 | 2 | 2 | 26 | 11 | 0 | 3 | 19 | 0 | 61 | 21 | 4 | 8 | .283 | .339 | .364 |
| Bynum, Mike, Portland * | 62 | 4 | 4 | 0 | 0 | 0 | 0 | 0 | 0 | 0 | 0 | 0 | 0 | 0 | 0 | 2 | 0 | 0 | 0 | .000 | .000 | .000 |
| Calloway, Ron, Edmonton * | 59 | 262 | 223 | 36 | 63 | 97 | 17 | 1 | 5 | 46 | 0 | 1 | 4 | 34 | 1 | 39 | 13 | 5 | 10 | .283 | .385 | .435 |
| Cannon, Jon, Tucson | 35 | 29 | 28 | 4 | 13 | 16 | 3 | 0 | 0 | 1 | 1 | 0 | 0 | 0 | 0 | 3 | 1 | 0 | 0 | .464 | .464 | .571 |
| Carrara, Giovanni, Iowa | 20 | 2 | 2 | 0 | 0 | 0 | 0 | 0 | 0 | 0 | 0 | 0 | 0 | 0 | 0 | 1 | 0 | 0 | 0 | .000 | .000 | .000 |
| Carrara, Giovanni, Las Vegas | 11 | 0 | 0 | 0 | 0 | 0 | 0 | 0 | 0 | 0 | 0 | 0 | 0 | 0 | 0 | 0 | 0 | 0 | 0 | .000 | .000 | .000 |
| Casanova, Raul, Omaha † | 58 | 243 | 223 | 37 | 72 | 114 | 12 | 0 | 10 | 49 | 0 | 2 | 3 | 15 | 0 | 36 | 1 | 0 | 10 | .323 | .370 | .511 |
| Cash, David, Iowa | 3 | 4 | 4 | 0 | 0 | 0 | 0 | 0 | 0 | 0 | 0 | 0 | 0 | 0 | 0 | 1 | 0 | 0 | 0 | .000 | .000 | .000 |
| Castillo, Wilkin, Tucson † | 6 | 24 | 20 | 2 | 3 | 4 | 1 | 0 | 0 | 2 | 1 | 0 | 0 | 3 | 0 | 3 | 0 | 0 | 0 | .150 | .261 | .200 |
| Castro, Bernabel, Portland † | 90 | 334 | 308 | 38 | 81 | 91 | 8 | 1 | 0 | 20 | 2 | 2 | 0 | 22 | 2 | 30 | 17 | 9 | 6 | .263 | .310 | .295 |
| Cepicky, Matt, Edmonton * | 82 | 334 | 312 | 51 | 83 | 149 | 15 | 3 | 15 | 67 | 0 | 4 | 0 | 18 | 2 | 75 | 2 | 1 | 4 | .266 | .302 | .478 |
| Cervenak, Mike, Fresno | 10 | 45 | 44 | 7 | 11 | 27 | 1 | 0 | 5 | 10 | 0 | 0 | 1 | 0 | 0 | 7 | 0 | 0 | 1 | .250 | .267 | .614 |
| Chavez, Wilton, Edmonton | 29 | 37 | 33 | 2 | 1 | 1 | 0 | 0 | 0 | 0 | 4 | 0 | 0 | 0 | 0 | 11 | 0 | 0 | 0 | .030 | .030 | .030 |
| Chen, Chin-Feng, Las Vegas | 81 | 351 | 308 | 59 | 89 | 180 | 19 | 6 | 20 | 65 | 0 | 6 | 2 | 35 | 1 | 78 | 6 | 2 | 4 | .289 | .359 | .584 |
| Chiasson, Scott, Iowa | 15 | 2 | 2 | 0 | 0 | 0 | 0 | 0 | 0 | 0 | 0 | 0 | 0 | 0 | 0 | 2 | 0 | 0 | 0 | .000 | .000 | .000 |
| Chiavacci, Ron, Edmonton | 25 | 14 | 11 | 1 | 2 | 5 | 0 | 0 | 1 | 1 | 3 | 0 | 0 | 0 | 0 | 2 | 0 | 0 | 0 | .182 | .182 | .455 |
| Childers, Jason, Edmonton | 14 | 1 | 1 | 0 | 0 | 0 | 0 | 0 | 0 | 0 | 0 | 0 | 0 | 0 | 0 | 0 | 0 | 0 | 0 | .000 | .000 | .000 |
| Choate, Randy, Tucson * | 15 | 1 | 1 | 0 | 1 | 1 | 0 | 0 | 0 | 0 | 0 | 0 | 0 | 0 | 0 | 0 | 0 | 0 | 0 | 1.000 | 1.000 | 1.000 |
| Christenson, Ryan, Albuquerque | 65 | 268 | 227 | 43 | 60 | 90 | 16 | 4 | 2 | 17 | 4 | 1 | 2 | 34 | 0 | 45 | 8 | 2 | 3 | .264 | .364 | .396 |
| Christianson, Ryan, Tacoma | 44 | 169 | 151 | 19 | 39 | 65 | 6 | 1 | 6 | 24 | 0 | 2 | 1 | 15 | 0 | 35 | 0 | 0 | 5 | .258 | .325 | .430 |
| Church, Ryan, Edmonton | 98 | 408 | 347 | 74 | 119 | 215 | 29 | 8 | 17 | 78 | 1 | 5 | 4 | 51 | 7 | 62 | 0 | 1 | 4 | .343 | .428 | .620 |
| Colangelo, Mike, Albuquerque | 97 | 352 | 292 | 64 | 95 | 174 | 27 | 2 | 16 | 73 | 1 | 6 | 8 | 45 | 1 | 66 | 0 | 3 | 10 | .325 | .422 | .596 |
| Colina, Javier, Memphis | 17 | 39 | 37 | 5 | 7 | 10 | 0 | 0 | 1 | 6 | 0 | 1 | 0 | 1 | 0 | 4 | 0 | 0 | 1 | .189 | .205 | .270 |
| Collins, Mike, Tacoma | 25 | 86 | 77 | 5 | 14 | 15 | 1 | 0 | 0 | 4 | 0 | 1 | 1 | 7 | 0 | 21 | 0 | 2 | 1 | .182 | .256 | .195 |
| Conti, Jason, Oklahoma * | 104 | 470 | 421 | 63 | 138 | 198 | 26 | 5 | 8 | 61 | 3 | 3 | 5 | 33 | 1 | 84 | 5 | 1 | 8 | .328 | .381 | .470 |
| Coolbaugh, Mike, New Orleans | 123 | 459 | 404 | 74 | 119 | 239 | 30 | 0 | 30 | 82 | 0 | 5 | 3 | 47 | 0 | 96 | 2 | 0 | 9 | .295 | .368 | .592 |
| Corcoran, Roy, Edmonton | 30 | 4 | 4 | 0 | 0 | 0 | 0 | 0 | 0 | 0 | 0 | 0 | 0 | 0 | 0 | 2 | 0 | 0 | 1 | .000 | .000 | .000 |
| Cruz, Nelson, Sacramento | 4 | 14 | 13 | 4 | 3 | 7 | 1 | 0 | 1 | 2 | 0 | 0 | 0 | 1 | 0 | 7 | 0 | 0 | 0 | .231 | .286 | .538 |
| Cummings, Jeremy, Memphis | 1 | 2 | 2 | 0 | 0 | 0 | 0 | 0 | 0 | 0 | 0 | 0 | 0 | 0 | 0 | 2 | 0 | 0 | 0 | .000 | .000 | .000 |
| Daigle, Casey, Tucson | 18 | 20 | 18 | 2 | 2 | 2 | 0 | 0 | 0 | 0 | 1 | 0 | 0 | 1 | 0 | 10 | 0 | 0 | 0 | .111 | .158 | .111 |
| Dallimore, Brian, Fresno | 111 | 497 | 432 | 72 | 140 | 193 | 21 | 4 | 8 | 65 | 4 | 6 | 15 | 40 | 3 | 53 | 9 | 2 | 13 | .324 | .396 | .447 |
| Davis, J.J., Nashville | 27 | 89 | 84 | 11 | 21 | 53 | 6 | 1 | 8 | 17 | 0 | 2 | 0 | 3 | 1 | 28 | 3 | 0 | 0 | .250 | .270 | .631 |
| Dawkins, Gookie, Iowa | 67 | 190 | 164 | 31 | 54 | 91 | 15 | 2 | 6 | 28 | 1 | 3 | 2 | 20 | 3 | 34 | 11 | 0 | 5 | .329 | .402 | .555 |
| Dawkins, Gookie, Omaha | 48 | 183 | 166 | 22 | 37 | 58 | 7 | 1 | 4 | 17 | 3 | 3 | 1 | 10 | 0 | 41 | 2 | 2 | 3 | .223 | .267 | .349 |
| De La Rosa, Tomas, Nashville | 63 | 194 | 173 | 22 | 48 | 79 | 6 | 2 | 7 | 29 | 2 | 3 | 0 | 16 | 0 | 34 | 3 | 0 | 4 | .277 | .333 | .457 |
| Deago, Roger, Portland | 5 | 1 | 1 | 0 | 0 | 0 | 0 | 0 | 0 | 0 | 0 | 0 | 0 | 0 | 0 | 0 | 0 | 0 | 1 | .000 | .000 | .000 |
| Dillon, Joe, Albuquerque | 108 | 468 | 403 | 96 | 131 | 268 | 33 | 7 | 30 | 86 | 0 | 9 | 10 | 46 | 0 | 85 | 12 | 3 | 7 | .325 | .400 | .665 |
| Dobbs, Greg, Tacoma * | 67 | 262 | 255 | 28 | 69 | 106 | 9 | 2 | 8 | 31 | 0 | 1 | 1 | 5 | 2 | 36 | 4 | 3 | 10 | .271 | .286 | .416 |
| Donnels, Chris, Colorado Springs * | 96 | 238 | 195 | 30 | 51 | 80 | 8 | 0 | 7 | 31 | 2 | 1 | 2 | 38 | 2 | 49 | 1 | 2 | 5 | .262 | .386 | .410 |
| Doster, Dave, Fresno | 120 | 464 | 424 | 50 | 132 | 195 | 36 | 0 | 9 | 66 | 2 | 7 | 5 | 26 | 3 | 42 | 2 | 5 | 18 | .311 | .353 | .460 |
| Driskill, Travis, Colorado Springs | 28 | 29 | 20 | 2 | 1 | 1 | 0 | 0 | 0 | 0 | 5 | 0 | 0 | 4 | 0 | 11 | 0 | 0 | 1 | .050 | .208 | .050 |
| Dubois, Jason, Iowa | 109 | 437 | 386 | 76 | 122 | 243 | 26 | 1 | 31 | 99 | 0 | 3 | 7 | 41 | 2 | 97 | 2 | 0 | 10 | .316 | .389 | .630 |
| Duckworth, Brandon, New Orleans | 14 | 19 | 14 | 0 | 3 | 3 | 0 | 0 | 0 | 0 | 4 | 0 | 0 | 1 | 0 | 4 | 0 | 0 | 0 | .214 | .267 | .214 |
| Eckelman, Alex, New Orleans | 76 | 198 | 185 | 23 | 54 | 74 | 10 | 2 | 2 | 16 | 1 | 1 | 1 | 10 | 0 | 24 | 2 | 3 | 6 | .292 | .330 | .400 |
| Eckert, Harold, Las Vegas | 31 | 15 | 13 | 1 | 3 | 3 | 0 | 0 | 0 | 0 | 2 | 0 | 0 | 0 | 0 | 3 | 0 | 0 | 0 | .231 | .231 | .231 |
| Edwards, Mike, Sacramento | 140 | 643 | 551 | 91 | 158 | 238 | 41 | 0 | 13 | 81 | 0 | 3 | 13 | 76 | 2 | 100 | 11 | 2 | 14 | .287 | .384 | .432 |
| Ellison, Josh, Tacoma | 8 | 24 | 22 | 1 | 5 | 6 | 1 | 0 | 0 | 0 | 1 | 0 | 0 | 1 | 0 | 10 | 0 | 0 | 0 | .227 | .261 | .273 |
| Enochs, Chris, New Orleans | 39 | 29 | 21 | 0 | 1 | 1 | 0 | 0 | 0 | 1 | 5 | 0 | 0 | 3 | 0 | 7 | 0 | 0 | 1 | .048 | .167 | .048 |
| Estrella, Leo, Fresno | 39 | 6 | 5 | 0 | 0 | 0 | 0 | 0 | 0 | 0 | 1 | 0 | 0 | 0 | 0 | 4 | 0 | 0 | 0 | .000 | .000 | .000 |
| Faison, Vince, Tacoma * | 10 | 33 | 30 | 7 | 8 | 18 | 2 | 1 | 2 | 3 | 1 | 0 | 0 | 2 | 0 | 12 | 0 | 0 | 0 | .267 | .313 | .600 |
| Falkenborg, Brian, Las Vegas | 18 | 18 | 15 | 2 | 2 | 3 | 1 | 0 | 0 | 1 | 1 | 0 | 0 | 2 | 0 | 7 | 0 | 0 | 0 | .133 | .235 | .200 |
| Falu, Irving, Omaha † | 3 | 6 | 6 | 1 | 3 | 3 | 0 | 0 | 0 | 0 | 0 | 0 | 0 | 0 | 0 | 1 | 0 | 0 | 0 | .500 | .500 | .500 |
| Farmer, Tom, Las Vegas | 47 | 10 | 8 | 1 | 0 | 0 | 0 | 0 | 0 | 1 | 1 | 0 | 0 | 1 | 0 | 2 | 0 | 0 | 0 | .000 | .111 | .000 |
| Fatheree, Danny, New Orleans | 23 | 40 | 36 | 4 | 9 | 13 | 1 | 0 | 1 | 2 | 0 | 0 | 0 | 4 | 0 | 9 | 0 | 1 | 3 | .250 | .325 | .361 |
| Fernandez, Alex, Portland * | 113 | 399 | 377 | 45 | 98 | 142 | 21 | 1 | 7 | 52 | 3 | 3 | 0 | 16 | 1 | 53 | 9 | 3 | 12 | .260 | .288 | .377 |
| Fernandez, Jared, New Orleans | 35 | 42 | 35 | 0 | 2 | 2 | 0 | 0 | 0 | 1 | 6 | 0 | 0 | 1 | 0 | 15 | 0 | 0 | 0 | .057 | .083 | .057 |
| Ferrari, Anthony, Edmonton * | 39 | 4 | 4 | 0 | 0 | 0 | 0 | 0 | 0 | 0 | 0 | 0 | 0 | 0 | 0 | 0 | 0 | 0 | 0 | .000 | .000 | .000 |
| Figueroa, Luis, Nashville | 103 | 351 | 321 | 40 | 95 | 128 | 13 | 1 | 6 | 44 | 0 | 1 | 4 | 25 | 0 | 37 | 2 | 2 | 14 | .296 | .353 | .399 |
| Fikac, Jeremy, Edmonton | 28 | 5 | 3 | 2 | 0 | 0 | 0 | 0 | 0 | 0 | 1 | 0 | 0 | 1 | 0 | 1 | 0 | 0 | 0 | .000 | .250 | .000 |
| Flores, Jose, Las Vegas | 99 | 377 | 319 | 64 | 100 | 143 | 20 | 1 | 7 | 51 | 1 | 4 | 4 | 49 | 1 | 30 | 6 | 2 | 6 | .313 | .407 | .448 |
| Florie, Bryce, Albuquerque | 11 | 2 | 2 | 1 | 0 | 0 | 0 | 0 | 0 | 0 | 0 | 0 | 0 | 0 | 0 | 1 | 0 | 0 | 0 | .000 | .000 | .000 |
| Foppert, Jesse, Fresno | 4 | 1 | 1 | 0 | 0 | 0 | 0 | 0 | 0 | 0 | 0 | 0 | 0 | 0 | 0 | 0 | 0 | 0 | 0 | .000 | .000 | .000 |
| Franklin, Micah, Tucson † | 29 | 79 | 67 | 10 | 19 | 36 | 5 | 0 | 4 | 12 | 1 | 2 | 1 | 8 | 1 | 21 | 4 | 0 | 0 | .284 | .359 | .537 |
| Freed, Mark, Tucson * | 57 | 3 | 3 | 0 | 0 | 0 | 0 | 0 | 0 | 0 | 0 | 0 | 0 | 0 | 0 | 1 | 0 | 0 | 0 | .000 | .000 | .000 |
| Furmaniak, J.J., Portland | 120 | 473 | 425 | 71 | 125 | 208 | 24 | 4 | 17 | 73 | 2 | 7 | 6 | 33 | 2 | 86 | 8 | 5 | 10 | .294 | .348 | .489 |
| Fussell, Chris, Nashville | 51 | 6 | 6 | 0 | 0 | 0 | 0 | 0 | 0 | 0 | 0 | 0 | 0 | 0 | 0 | 6 | 0 | 0 | 0 | .000 | .000 | .000 |
| Galarraga, Andres, Salt Lake | 25 | 111 | 102 | 10 | 31 | 46 | 3 | 0 | 4 | 19 | 0 | 2 | 1 | 6 | 1 | 24 | 0 | 0 | 8 | .304 | .342 | .451 |
| Gall, John, Memphis | 135 | 563 | 506 | 77 | 148 | 248 | 34 | 0 | 22 | 84 | 0 | 8 | 1 | 48 | 2 | 68 | 1 | 1 | 19 | .292 | .350 | .490 |
| Garcia, James, Fresno | 8 | 8 | 5 | 1 | 0 | 0 | 0 | 0 | 0 | 1 | 1 | 0 | 0 | 2 | 0 | 4 | 0 | 0 | 0 | .000 | .286 | .000 |
| Garcia, Luis, Las Vegas | 129 | 537 | 497 | 76 | 156 | 290 | 32 | 3 | 32 | 95 | 0 | 6 | 2 | 32 | 1 | 104 | 1 | 1 | 17 | .314 | .354 | .584 |
| Gardner, Lee, Fresno | 57 | 4 | 3 | 1 | 1 | 1 | 0 | 0 | 0 | 0 | 1 | 0 | 0 | 0 | 0 | 2 | 0 | 0 | 0 | .333 | .333 | .333 |

| Player, Team | G | TPA | AB | R | H | TB | 2B | 3B | HR | RBI | SH | SF | HP | BB | IBB | SO | SB | CS | GDP | Avg. | OBP | Slg. |
|---|---|---|---|---|---|---|---|---|---|---|---|---|---|---|---|---|---|---|---|---|---|---|
| Garrett, Shawn, Colorado Springs † | 30 | 125 | 116 | 25 | 43 | 64 | 12 | 0 | 3 | 22 | 0 | 0 | 0 | 9 | 0 | 28 | 5 | 2 | 2 | .371 | .416 | .552 |
| Gautreau, Jake, Portland * | 48 | 187 | 168 | 24 | 46 | 84 | 9 | 1 | 9 | 35 | 1 | 2 | 2 | 14 | 0 | 37 | 1 | 0 | 2 | .274 | .333 | .500 |
| Gerber, Joe, Portland * | 49 | 144 | 124 | 16 | 32 | 46 | 9 | 1 | 1 | 9 | 1 | 1 | 0 | 18 | 0 | 30 | 0 | 0 | 2 | .258 | .350 | .371 |
| Germano, Justin, Portland | 20 | 24 | 16 | 0 | 0 | 0 | 0 | 0 | 0 | 0 | 7 | 0 | 1 | 0 | 0 | 10 | 0 | 0 | 0 | .000 | .059 | .000 |
| Giambi, Jeremy, Las Vegas * | 11 | 26 | 23 | 3 | 3 | 6 | 0 | 0 | 1 | 1 | 0 | 0 | 0 | 3 | 0 | 8 | 0 | 0 | 0 | .130 | .231 | .261 |
| Gilfillan, Jason, Colorado Springs | 50 | 2 | 2 | 0 | 0 | 0 | 0 | 0 | 0 | 0 | 0 | 0 | 0 | 0 | 0 | 0 | 0 | 0 | 0 | .000 | .000 | .000 |
| Gissell, Chris, Colorado Springs | 25 | 20 | 17 | 4 | 3 | 4 | 1 | 0 | 0 | 1 | 1 | 0 | 0 | 2 | 0 | 5 | 0 | 0 | 1 | .176 | .263 | .235 |
| Gonzalez, Adrian, Oklahoma * | 123 | 508 | 457 | 61 | 139 | 209 | 28 | 3 | 12 | 88 | 2 | 4 | 6 | 39 | 1 | 73 | 1 | 1 | 17 | .304 | .364 | .457 |
| Gonzalez, Wiki, Tacoma | 13 | 54 | 52 | 9 | 16 | 36 | 5 | 0 | 5 | 14 | 0 | 0 | 0 | 2 | 0 | 3 | 0 | 0 | 0 | .308 | .333 | .692 |
| Good, Andrew, Tucson | 5 | 7 | 5 | 1 | 1 | 1 | 0 | 0 | 0 | 0 | 1 | 0 | 0 | 1 | 0 | 3 | 0 | 0 | 0 | .200 | .333 | .200 |
| Gordon, Brian, Salt Lake * | 127 | 517 | 475 | 80 | 123 | 221 | 24 | 4 | 22 | 70 | 3 | 5 | 4 | 30 | 1 | 145 | 6 | 2 | 5 | .259 | .305 | .465 |
| Gorneault, Nick, Salt Lake | 6 | 21 | 19 | 4 | 6 | 10 | 1 | 0 | 1 | 5 | 0 | 0 | 1 | 1 | 0 | 7 | 0 | 0 | 0 | .316 | .381 | .526 |
| Gosling, Mike, Tucson * | 24 | 28 | 22 | 1 | 2 | 2 | 0 | 0 | 0 | 1 | 2 | 1 | 0 | 3 | 0 | 11 | 0 | 0 | 0 | .091 | .192 | .091 |
| Greenberg, Adam, Iowa * | 1 | 5 | 4 | 0 | 0 | 0 | 0 | 0 | 0 | 0 | 0 | 0 | 0 | 1 | 0 | 0 | 0 | 0 | 0 | .000 | .200 | .000 |
| Gregorio, Tom, Salt Lake | 58 | 226 | 207 | 20 | 48 | 82 | 12 | 2 | 6 | 32 | 1 | 3 | 3 | 12 | 0 | 56 | 3 | 0 | 4 | .232 | .280 | .396 |
| Griffiths, Jeremy, New Orleans | 15 | 21 | 19 | 2 | 5 | 7 | 2 | 0 | 0 | 0 | 1 | 0 | 0 | 1 | 0 | 5 | 0 | 0 | 2 | .263 | .300 | .368 |
| Guiel, Aaron, Omaha * | 30 | 144 | 116 | 29 | 36 | 72 | 6 | 0 | 10 | 30 | 0 | 1 | 6 | 21 | 1 | 33 | 0 | 2 | 1 | .310 | .438 | .621 |
| Guzman, Elpidio, Tacoma * | 124 | 474 | 454 | 58 | 118 | 156 | 19 | 2 | 5 | 36 | 4 | 2 | 0 | 14 | 0 | 88 | 23 | 12 | 4 | .260 | .281 | .344 |
| Guzman, Freddy, Portland† | 66 | — | 264 | 48 | 77 | 100 | 12 | 4 | 1 | 19 | 4 | 1 | 0 | 30 | 1 | 46 | 48 | 5 | 1 | .292 | .365 | .379 |
| Haad, Yamid, Portland | 80 | 312 | 295 | 47 | 89 | 137 | 21 | 0 | 9 | 35 | 1 | 0 | 0 | 16 | 1 | 41 | 3 | 0 | 3 | .302 | .338 | .464 |
| Hackman, Luther, Nashville | 37 | 2 | 1 | 1 | 1 | 1 | 0 | 0 | 0 | 0 | 1 | 0 | 0 | 0 | 0 | 0 | 0 | 0 | 0 | 1.000 | 1.000 | 1.000 |
| Halter, Shane, Salt Lake | 35 | 146 | 131 | 18 | 36 | 63 | 7 | 1 | 6 | 18 | 0 | 0 | 0 | 15 | 0 | 21 | 2 | 3 | 5 | .275 | .349 | .481 |
| Hampton, Matt, Portland | 37 | 4 | 4 | 0 | 0 | 0 | 0 | 0 | 0 | 0 | 0 | 0 | 0 | 0 | 0 | 2 | 0 | 0 | 0 | .000 | .000 | .000 |
| Hanrahan, Joel, Las Vegas | 25 | 34 | 32 | 4 | 9 | 16 | 2 | 1 | 1 | 3 | 2 | 0 | 0 | 0 | 0 | 11 | 0 | 0 | 0 | .281 | .281 | .500 |
| Hansell, Greg, Tucson | 15 | 1 | 1 | 0 | 0 | 0 | 0 | 0 | 0 | 0 | 0 | 0 | 0 | 0 | 0 | 0 | 0 | 0 | 0 | .000 | .000 | .000 |
| Hansen, Jed, Omaha | 125 | 537 | 463 | 82 | 126 | 234 | 19 | 4 | 27 | 82 | 1 | 3 | 4 | 66 | 2 | 118 | 7 | 4 | 6 | .272 | .366 | .505 |
| Harris, Brendan, Edmonton | 33 | 140 | 123 | 20 | 35 | 59 | 6 | 0 | 6 | 24 | 1 | 3 | 3 | 10 | 2 | 21 | 0 | 1 | 3 | .285 | .345 | .480 |
| Harris, Brendan, Iowa | 69 | 275 | 254 | 48 | 79 | 135 | 21 | 1 | 11 | 35 | 3 | 1 | 1 | 16 | 1 | 40 | 0 | 2 | 8 | .311 | .353 | .531 |
| Harris, Brian, Edmonton † | 102 | 351 | 304 | 47 | 88 | 114 | 13 | 2 | 3 | 33 | 2 | 2 | 3 | 40 | 0 | 50 | 1 | 2 | 9 | .289 | .375 | .375 |
| Harris, Reggie, New Orleans | 7 | 1 | 1 | 0 | 0 | 0 | 0 | 0 | 0 | 0 | 0 | 0 | 0 | 0 | 0 | 1 | 0 | 0 | 0 | .000 | .000 | .000 |
| Hart, Bo, Memphis | 116 | 493 | 445 | 81 | 133 | 196 | 25 | 7 | 8 | 45 | 6 | 4 | 13 | 25 | 0 | 66 | 8 | 7 | 9 | .299 | .351 | .440 |
| Hawpe, Brad, Colorado Springs * | 92 | 388 | 345 | 62 | 111 | 225 | 19 | 1 | 31 | 86 | 3 | 3 | 1 | 36 | 1 | 91 | 3 | 2 | 10 | .322 | .384 | .652 |
| Haynes, Dee, Memphis | 58 | 192 | 182 | 29 | 61 | 108 | 5 | 0 | 14 | 33 | 0 | 2 | 1 | 7 | 0 | 25 | 1 | 0 | 7 | .335 | .359 | .593 |
| Haynes, Nathan, Fresno * | 1 | 4 | 4 | 1 | 1 | 3 | 0 | 1 | 0 | 0 | 0 | 0 | 0 | 0 | 0 | 1 | 1 | 0 | 0 | .250 | .250 | .750 |
| Henrie, Matt, Tucson * | 10 | 16 | 14 | 3 | 4 | 9 | 2 | 0 | 1 | 2 | 0 | 0 | 0 | 2 | 0 | 5 | 0 | 0 | 0 | .286 | .375 | .643 |
| Herrera, Alex, Colorado Springs * | 37 | 12 | 11 | 3 | 4 | 6 | 2 | 0 | 0 | 1 | 0 | 0 | 0 | 1 | 0 | 4 | 0 | 0 | 0 | .364 | .417 | .545 |
| Hiatt, Phil, New Orleans | 140 | 559 | 485 | 80 | 114 | 227 | 15 | 4 | 30 | 77 | 0 | 3 | 7 | 64 | 2 | 140 | 5 | 1 | 9 | .235 | .331 | .468 |
| Hill, Mike, New Orleans | 88 | 261 | 233 | 32 | 62 | 92 | 10 | 1 | 6 | 39 | 1 | 3 | 1 | 23 | 1 | 52 | 3 | 2 | 11 | .266 | .331 | .395 |
| Hocking, Denny, Iowa † | 39 | 117 | 104 | 20 | 30 | 51 | 12 | 0 | 3 | 22 | 0 | 1 | 1 | 11 | 0 | 20 | 0 | 2 | 1 | .288 | .359 | .490 |
| Hodges, Scott, Edmonton * | 38 | 136 | 118 | 12 | 25 | 34 | 6 | 0 | 1 | 18 | 0 | 5 | 2 | 11 | 1 | 29 | 1 | 0 | 3 | .212 | .279 | .288 |
| Hoffpauir, Micah, Iowa * | 1 | 4 | 3 | 0 | 1 | 2 | 1 | 0 | 0 | 1 | 0 | 0 | 0 | 1 | 0 | 0 | 0 | 0 | 0 | .333 | .500 | .667 |
| Hooper, Kevin, Omaha | 27 | 105 | 92 | 12 | 15 | 17 | 2 | 0 | 0 | 4 | 3 | 0 | 1 | 9 | 0 | 14 | 2 | 2 | 1 | .163 | .245 | .185 |
| Horgan, Joe, Memphis * | 11 | 1 | 1 | 0 | 1 | 1 | 0 | 0 | 0 | 0 | 0 | 0 | 0 | 0 | 0 | 0 | 0 | 0 | 0 | 1.000 | 1.000 | 1.000 |
| Horgan, Joe, Edmonton * | 13 | 1 | 1 | 0 | 0 | 0 | 0 | 0 | 0 | 0 | 0 | 0 | 0 | 0 | 0 | 0 | 0 | 0 | 0 | .000 | .000 | .000 |
| Horner, Jim, Tacoma | 39 | 135 | 127 | 9 | 24 | 41 | 5 | 0 | 4 | 15 | 0 | 1 | 1 | 6 | 0 | 23 | 0 | 1 | 4 | .189 | .230 | .323 |
| House, J.R., Nashville | 92 | 337 | 309 | 38 | 89 | 157 | 21 | 1 | 15 | 49 | 0 | 1 | 4 | 23 | 1 | 72 | 1 | 1 | 6 | .288 | .344 | .508 |
| Howard, Ben, Albuquerque | 23 | 6 | 6 | 0 | 2 | 3 | 1 | 0 | 0 | 1 | 0 | 0 | 0 | 0 | 0 | 3 | 0 | 0 | 0 | .333 | .333 | .500 |
| Hubbard, Trenidad, Iowa | 129 | 542 | 473 | 101 | 156 | 219 | 28 | 4 | 9 | 49 | 1 | 3 | 3 | 62 | 1 | 59 | 36 | 8 | 12 | .330 | .409 | .463 |
| Huckaby, Ken, Oklahoma | 35 | 141 | 127 | 18 | 35 | 51 | 8 | 1 | 2 | 20 | 2 | 3 | 0 | 9 | 0 | 18 | 0 | 0 | 6 | .276 | .317 | .402 |
| Huffman, Royce, New Orleans | 144 | 616 | 531 | 81 | 164 | 239 | 39 | 3 | 10 | 60 | 1 | 6 | 7 | 71 | 2 | 94 | 8 | 2 | 7 | .309 | .393 | .450 |
| Izquierdo, Hansel, Nashville | 5 | 7 | 6 | 0 | 0 | 0 | 0 | 0 | 0 | 0 | 1 | 0 | 0 | 0 | 0 | 3 | 0 | 0 | 1 | .000 | .000 | .000 |
| Izturis, Maicer, Edmonton † | 99 | 443 | 376 | 65 | 127 | 159 | 19 | 2 | 3 | 36 | 4 | 2 | 4 | 57 | 1 | 30 | 14 | 12 | 12 | .338 | .428 | .423 |
| Jackson, Damian, Omaha | 48 | 209 | 169 | 46 | 52 | 91 | 13 | 1 | 8 | 27 | 2 | 2 | 6 | 30 | 1 | 36 | 12 | 2 | 3 | .308 | .425 | .538 |
| Jackson, Damian, Iowa | 27 | 105 | 93 | 17 | 25 | 46 | 6 | 3 | 3 | 12 | 1 | 0 | 0 | 11 | 1 | 20 | 3 | 1 | 0 | .269 | .346 | .495 |
| Jackson, Edwin, Las Vegas | 21 | 23 | 21 | 5 | 8 | 17 | 0 | 0 | 3 | 7 | 2 | 0 | 0 | 0 | 0 | 2 | 0 | 0 | 0 | .381 | .381 | .810 |
| Jacobs, Greg, Tacoma * | 63 | 224 | 197 | 40 | 63 | 103 | 13 | 0 | 9 | 30 | 0 | 3 | 3 | 21 | 1 | 38 | 1 | 1 | 3 | .320 | .388 | .523 |
| Jacome, Jason, Fresno * | 37 | 12 | 9 | 1 | 0 | 0 | 0 | 0 | 0 | 0 | 2 | 0 | 0 | 1 | 0 | 4 | 0 | 0 | 1 | .000 | .100 | .000 |
| Jarvis, Kevin, Nashville | 12 | 9 | 8 | 0 | 0 | 0 | 0 | 0 | 0 | 1 | 1 | 0 | 0 | 0 | 0 | 4 | 0 | 0 | 1 | .000 | .000 | .000 |
| Jensen, Ryan, Fresno | 31 | 45 | 40 | 3 | 4 | 7 | 1 | 1 | 0 | 0 | 3 | 0 | 0 | 2 | 0 | 14 | 0 | 0 | 1 | .100 | .143 | .175 |
| Johnson, Dan, Sacramento * | 142 | 640 | 536 | 95 | 160 | 286 | 29 | 5 | 29 | 111 | 0 | 6 | 9 | 89 | 2 | 93 | 0 | 1 | 15 | .299 | .403 | .534 |
| Johnson, Gary, Salt Lake * | 91 | 347 | 304 | 44 | 77 | 118 | 13 | 5 | 6 | 36 | 0 | 0 | 4 | 39 | 1 | 71 | 1 | 2 | 10 | .253 | .346 | .388 |
| Johnson, Mark, Las Vegas | 37 | 24 | 19 | 0 | 3 | 3 | 0 | 0 | 0 | 0 | 4 | 0 | 0 | 1 | 0 | 9 | 0 | 0 | 0 | .158 | .200 | .158 |
| Johnson, Mike, Edmonton * | 32 | 28 | 24 | 3 | 7 | 8 | 1 | 0 | 0 | 5 | 3 | 0 | 0 | 1 | 0 | 12 | 0 | 0 | 0 | .292 | .320 | .333 |
| Johnson, Russ, Iowa | 129 | 491 | 415 | 71 | 122 | 206 | 38 | 2 | 14 | 78 | 1 | 3 | 2 | 70 | 2 | 63 | 7 | 3 | 8 | .294 | .396 | .496 |
| Jones, Jason, Oklahoma * | 81 | 344 | 300 | 45 | 79 | 135 | 15 | 1 | 13 | 45 | 1 | 2 | 1 | 40 | 1 | 68 | 2 | 1 | 4 | .263 | .350 | .450 |
| Jorgensen, Ryan, Albuquerque | 61 | 213 | 201 | 20 | 52 | 87 | 11 | 0 | 8 | 29 | 1 | 1 | 0 | 9 | 0 | 51 | 0 | 0 | 7 | .259 | .289 | .433 |
| Karp, Josh, Edmonton | 24 | 29 | 26 | 1 | 4 | 4 | 0 | 0 | 0 | 2 | 1 | 0 | 1 | 1 | 0 | 10 | 0 | 0 | 0 | .154 | .214 | .154 |
| Kellner, Ryan, Las Vegas | 65 | 207 | 187 | 20 | 35 | 60 | 7 | 0 | 6 | 23 | 7 | 1 | 2 | 10 | 1 | 56 | 0 | 0 | 6 | .187 | .235 | .321 |
| Kelton, Dave, Iowa | 121 | 462 | 420 | 57 | 103 | 188 | 26 | 1 | 19 | 68 | 0 | 5 | 4 | 33 | 1 | 92 | 7 | 2 | 10 | .245 | .303 | .448 |
| Kiger, Mark, Sacramento | 6 | 16 | 13 | 2 | 3 | 3 | 0 | 0 | 0 | 2 | 0 | 0 | 0 | 3 | 0 | 3 | 0 | 2 | 1 | .231 | .375 | .231 |
| Killian, William, Portland * | 3 | 8 | 7 | 0 | 1 | 1 | 0 | 0 | 0 | 0 | 0 | 0 | 0 | 1 | 0 | 0 | 0 | 0 | 2 | .143 | .250 | .143 |
| Knorr, Randy, Edmonton | 83 | 327 | 286 | 32 | 77 | 99 | 16 | 0 | 2 | 37 | 0 | 3 | 1 | 37 | 0 | 63 | 0 | 0 | 12 | .269 | .352 | .346 |
| Knott, Eric, Las Vegas * | 12 | 1 | 1 | 0 | 0 | 0 | 0 | 0 | 0 | 0 | 0 | 0 | 0 | 0 | 0 | 1 | 0 | 0 | 0 | .000 | .000 | .000 |
| Knott, Jon, Portland | 113 | 508 | 435 | 79 | 126 | 232 | 22 | 3 | 26 | 85 | 0 | 8 | 7 | 58 | 0 | 110 | 5 | 3 | 12 | .290 | .376 | .533 |
| Koonce, Graham, Sacramento * | 120 | 531 | 439 | 73 | 106 | 197 | 25 | 0 | 22 | 77 | 0 | 6 | 9 | 77 | 0 | 129 | 0 | 0 | 12 | .241 | .362 | .449 |
| Kopitzke, Casey, Iowa | 81 | 272 | 251 | 19 | 54 | 67 | 10 | 0 | 1 | 17 | 4 | 2 | 3 | 12 | 2 | 38 | 1 | 1 | 4 | .215 | .257 | .267 |
| Koronka, John, Iowa * | 29 | 38 | 34 | 2 | 2 | 3 | 1 | 0 | 0 | 1 | 4 | 0 | 0 | 0 | 0 | 17 | 0 | 0 | 0 | .059 | .059 | .088 |
| Kroon, Marc, Colorado Springs | 50 | 2 | 2 | 0 | 0 | 0 | 0 | 0 | 0 | 0 | 0 | 0 | 0 | 0 | 0 | 0 | 0 | 0 | 0 | .000 | .000 | .000 |
| Kuzmic, Craig, Fresno † | 78 | 271 | 228 | 33 | 54 | 87 | 7 | 1 | 8 | 31 | 1 | 2 | 5 | 35 | 0 | 61 | 0 | 2 | 3 | .237 | .348 | .382 |
| Leon, Donny, Iowa † | 118 | 443 | 397 | 49 | 110 | 175 | 26 | 0 | 13 | 60 | 0 | 4 | 6 | 30 | 0 | 54 | 0 | 0 | 12 | .277 | .334 | .441 |
| Lewis, Fred, Fresno * | 6 | 29 | 23 | 3 | 7 | 11 | 1 | 0 | 1 | 2 | 1 | 0 | 0 | 5 | 0 | 5 | 1 | 1 | 1 | .304 | .429 | .478 |
| Lewis, Richard, Iowa | 31 | 124 | 117 | 13 | 28 | 47 | 8 | 1 | 3 | 11 | 0 | 1 | 2 | 4 | 1 | 21 | 4 | 0 | 2 | .239 | .274 | .402 |
| Linden, Todd, Fresno † | 130 | 567 | 489 | 93 | 127 | 228 | 28 | 2 | 23 | 75 | 3 | 5 | 7 | 63 | 3 | 149 | 8 | 6 | 9 | .260 | .349 | .466 |

| Player, Team | G | TPA | AB | R | H | TB | 2B | 3B | HR | RBI | SH | SF | HP | BB | IBB | SO | SB | CS | GDP | Avg. | OBP | Slg. |
|---|---|---|---|---|---|---|---|---|---|---|---|---|---|---|---|---|---|---|---|---|---|---|
| Logan, Kyle, New Orleans * | 121 | 433 | 399 | 35 | 99 | 138 | 21 | 3 | 4 | 33 | 1 | 2 | 8 | 23 | 5 | 48 | 17 | 2 | 13 | .248 | .301 | .346 |
| Lopez, Mauber, Portland | 1 | 1 | 1 | 0 | 0 | 0 | 0 | 0 | 0 | 0 | 0 | 0 | 0 | 0 | 0 | 0 | 0 | 0 | 0 | .000 | .000 | .000 |
| Lopez, Mendy, Omaha | 31 | 133 | 123 | 20 | 36 | 83 | 6 | 1 | 13 | 26 | 1 | 0 | 0 | 9 | 0 | 31 | 1 | 2 | 6 | .293 | .341 | .675 |
| Lopez, Mickey, Tacoma † | 109 | 451 | 391 | 70 | 112 | 172 | 20 | 5 | 10 | 41 | 6 | 2 | 7 | 45 | 2 | 59 | 13 | 10 | 6 | .286 | .369 | .440 |
| Lunar, Fernando, Iowa | 78 | 276 | 254 | 30 | 64 | 87 | 8 | 0 | 5 | 23 | 4 | 1 | 7 | 10 | 0 | 46 | 0 | 0 | 10 | .252 | .298 | .343 |
| Lunsford, Trey, Fresno | 118 | 453 | 405 | 39 | 102 | 142 | 21 | 2 | 5 | 41 | 5 | 2 | 6 | 35 | 1 | 83 | 3 | 2 | 12 | .252 | .319 | .351 |
| Lyon, Brandon, Tucson | 6 | 2 | 2 | 0 | 0 | 0 | 0 | 0 | 0 | 0 | 0 | 0 | 0 | 0 | 0 | 0 | 0 | 0 | 0 | .000 | .000 | .000 |
| Maduro, Jorge, Tacoma | 9 | 30 | 29 | 4 | 5 | 8 | 1 | 1 | 0 | 2 | 0 | 0 | 0 | 1 | 0 | 9 | 0 | 0 | 0 | .172 | .200 | .276 |
| Magallanes, Ever, Tucson * | 16 | 43 | 38 | 7 | 10 | 11 | 1 | 0 | 0 | 3 | 0 | 0 | 1 | 4 | 0 | 5 | 2 | 0 | 1 | .263 | .349 | .289 |
| Mahomes, Pat, Edmonton | 20 | 0 | 0 | 0 | 0 | 0 | 0 | 0 | 0 | 0 | 0 | 0 | 0 | 0 | 0 | 0 | 0 | 0 | 0 | .000 | .000 | .000 |
| Mahomes, Pat, Albuquerque | 16 | 1 | 1 | 0 | 0 | 0 | 0 | 0 | 0 | 0 | 0 | 0 | 0 | 0 | 0 | 0 | 0 | 0 | 0 | .000 | .000 | .000 |
| Mahomes, Pat, Nashville | 26 | 8 | 8 | 1 | 1 | 1 | 0 | 0 | 0 | 2 | 0 | 0 | 0 | 0 | 0 | 3 | 1 | 0 | 1 | .125 | .125 | .125 |
| Mahoney, Mike, Memphis | 79 | 299 | 270 | 32 | 81 | 114 | 16 | 1 | 5 | 32 | 2 | 2 | 3 | 22 | 0 | 37 | 1 | 4 | 1 | .300 | .357 | .422 |
| Martin, Greg, Nashville * | 5 | 2 | 2 | 0 | 0 | 0 | 0 | 0 | 0 | 0 | 0 | 0 | 0 | 0 | 0 | 0 | 0 | 0 | 1 | .000 | .000 | .000 |
| Martinez, Felix, Iowa † | 7 | 21 | 21 | 1 | 4 | 8 | 1 | 0 | 1 | 3 | 0 | 0 | 0 | 0 | 0 | 3 | 0 | 0 | 2 | .190 | .190 | .381 |
| Martinez, Luis, Memphis * | 7 | 11 | 9 | 0 | 0 | 0 | 0 | 0 | 0 | 0 | 1 | 0 | 0 | 1 | 0 | 5 | 0 | 0 | 0 | .000 | .100 | .000 |
| Martinez, Luis, Colorado Springs | 5 | 7 | 6 | 0 | 0 | 0 | 0 | 0 | 0 | 0 | 0 | 0 | 1 | 0 | 0 | 2 | 0 | 0 | 0 | .000 | .143 | .000 |
| Matos, Pascual, Colorado Springs | 18 | 70 | 62 | 9 | 16 | 26 | 4 | 0 | 2 | 12 | 1 | 0 | 1 | 6 | 0 | 12 | 0 | 0 | 0 | .258 | .333 | .419 |
| Mazone, Brian, Fresno * | 5 | 7 | 5 | 1 | 2 | 3 | 1 | 0 | 0 | 1 | 1 | 1 | 0 | 0 | 0 | 2 | 0 | 0 | 0 | .400 | .333 | .600 |
| McDonald, Keith, Nashville | 92 | 317 | 274 | 29 | 70 | 104 | 16 | 0 | 6 | 30 | 1 | 4 | 4 | 34 | 3 | 58 | 1 | 2 | 11 | .255 | .342 | .380 |
| McDougall, Marshall, Oklahoma | 94 | 392 | 354 | 48 | 100 | 180 | 23 | 0 | 19 | 69 | 2 | 0 | 1 | 35 | 0 | 80 | 2 | 1 | 8 | .282 | .349 | .508 |
| McGlinchy, Kevin, Iowa | 7 | 6 | 5 | 0 | 0 | 0 | 0 | 0 | 0 | 0 | 0 | 0 | 0 | 1 | 0 | 1 | 0 | 0 | 0 | .000 | .167 | .000 |
| McLeary, Marty, Portland | 46 | 20 | 19 | 1 | 2 | 6 | 1 | 0 | 1 | 4 | 0 | 0 | 0 | 1 | 0 | 7 | 0 | 0 | 0 | .105 | .150 | .316 |
| McPherson, Dallas, Salt Lake * | 67 | 284 | 259 | 54 | 81 | 176 | 19 | 8 | 20 | 57 | 0 | 1 | 1 | 23 | 4 | 95 | 6 | 3 | 5 | .313 | .370 | .680 |
| Medrano, Anthony, Edmonton | 117 | 475 | 419 | 60 | 129 | 164 | 25 | 2 | 2 | 42 | 5 | 5 | 5 | 41 | 1 | 48 | 3 | 4 | 13 | .308 | .372 | .391 |
| Michalak, Chris, Albuquerque * | 17 | 3 | 2 | 0 | 1 | 1 | 0 | 0 | 0 | 1 | 0 | 0 | 0 | 1 | 0 | 0 | 0 | 0 | 0 | .500 | .667 | .500 |
| Minor, Damon, Fresno * | 97 | 396 | 338 | 48 | 102 | 182 | 23 | 3 | 17 | 56 | 0 | 2 | 6 | 50 | 2 | 78 | 0 | 0 | 7 | .302 | .399 | .538 |
| Mitre, Sergio, Iowa | 18 | 28 | 22 | 3 | 6 | 13 | 1 | 0 | 2 | 5 | 4 | 0 | 0 | 2 | 0 | 5 | 0 | 0 | 0 | .273 | .333 | .591 |
| Mondesi, Raul, Salt Lake | 2 | 7 | 6 | 1 | 2 | 5 | 0 | 0 | 1 | 2 | 0 | 0 | 0 | 1 | 0 | 2 | 0 | 0 | 0 | .333 | .429 | .833 |
| Morrissey, Adam, Sacramento | 109 | 439 | 392 | 61 | 114 | 169 | 26 | 1 | 9 | 56 | 1 | 3 | 3 | 40 | 1 | 89 | 1 | 1 | 14 | .291 | .358 | .431 |
| Motte, Jason, Memphis | 3 | 5 | 5 | 0 | 1 | 1 | 0 | 0 | 0 | 0 | 0 | 0 | 0 | 0 | 0 | 4 | 0 | 0 | 0 | .200 | .200 | .200 |
| Mottl, Ryan, Nashville † | 2 | 1 | 1 | 0 | 0 | 0 | 0 | 0 | 0 | 0 | 0 | 0 | 0 | 0 | 0 | 0 | 0 | 0 | 0 | .000 | .000 | .000 |
| Munhall, Brian, Fresno | 2 | 5 | 4 | 1 | 2 | 2 | 0 | 0 | 0 | 0 | 0 | 0 | 0 | 1 | 0 | 0 | 0 | 0 | 0 | .500 | .600 | .500 |
| Murray, Calvin, Iowa | 130 | 517 | 457 | 84 | 142 | 201 | 24 | 7 | 7 | 54 | 9 | 6 | 2 | 43 | 1 | 65 | 25 | 4 | 10 | .311 | .368 | .440 |
| Myers, Corey, Tucson | 57 | 204 | 180 | 25 | 52 | 87 | 12 | 1 | 7 | 25 | 1 | 0 | 1 | 22 | 1 | 43 | 0 | 1 | 4 | .289 | .369 | .483 |
| Myrow, Brian, Las Vegas * | 50 | 180 | 153 | 29 | 55 | 92 | 15 | 2 | 6 | 29 | 0 | 2 | 4 | 21 | 2 | 47 | 2 | 3 | 2 | .359 | .444 | .601 |
| Nady, Xavier, Portland | 74 | 320 | 291 | 52 | 96 | 183 | 19 | 1 | 22 | 70 | 0 | 0 | 7 | 22 | 2 | 42 | 3 | 0 | 8 | .330 | .391 | .629 |
| Nannini, Mike, Albuquerque | 32 | 40 | 35 | 1 | 5 | 5 | 0 | 0 | 0 | 2 | 4 | 0 | 1 | 0 | 0 | 14 | 0 | 0 | 0 | .143 | .167 | .143 |
| Neal, Steve, Tucson * | 119 | 421 | 373 | 52 | 104 | 177 | 22 | 3 | 15 | 58 | 0 | 2 | 1 | 45 | 3 | 109 | 2 | 2 | 6 | .279 | .356 | .475 |
| Neu, Mike, Albuquerque † | 35 | 3 | 2 | 0 | 0 | 0 | 0 | 0 | 0 | 0 | 0 | 0 | 0 | 1 | 0 | 0 | 0 | 0 | 0 | .000 | .333 | .000 |
| Nichols, Kyle, Tucson | 58 | 195 | 167 | 33 | 49 | 101 | 10 | 0 | 14 | 39 | 0 | 1 | 1 | 26 | 2 | 64 | 0 | 0 | 4 | .293 | .390 | .605 |
| Nickle, Doug, Las Vegas | 20 | 4 | 3 | 0 | 2 | 2 | 0 | 0 | 0 | 0 | 0 | 0 | 0 | 1 | 0 | 0 | 0 | 0 | 0 | .667 | .750 | .667 |
| Niekro, Lance, Fresno | 67 | 257 | 241 | 42 | 72 | 137 | 21 | 4 | 12 | 47 | 0 | 1 | 1 | 14 | 1 | 32 | 1 | 1 | 5 | .299 | .339 | .568 |
| Nieves, Jose, Portland | 80 | 313 | 288 | 35 | 78 | 111 | 19 | 1 | 4 | 31 | 1 | 5 | 2 | 17 | 0 | 30 | 5 | 3 | 6 | .271 | .311 | .385 |
| Nieves, Wil, Salt Lake | 108 | 435 | 421 | 60 | 125 | 193 | 22 | 8 | 10 | 53 | 1 | 1 | 0 | 12 | 0 | 64 | 3 | 6 | 11 | .297 | .316 | .458 |
| Niles, Drew, Albuquerque † | 111 | 329 | 278 | 39 | 72 | 97 | 9 | 2 | 4 | 29 | 5 | 3 | 2 | 41 | 1 | 73 | 3 | 3 | 5 | .259 | .355 | .349 |
| Nivar, Ramon, Oklahoma | 113 | 494 | 462 | 62 | 122 | 173 | 21 | 0 | 10 | 52 | 12 | 2 | 4 | 14 | 1 | 43 | 15 | 15 | 10 | .264 | .290 | .374 |
| Nunez, Vladimir, Colorado Springs | 22 | 4 | 4 | 0 | 1 | 1 | 0 | 0 | 0 | 0 | 0 | 0 | 0 | 0 | 0 | 1 | 0 | 0 | 0 | .250 | .250 | .250 |
| Nussbeck, Mark, Memphis * | 3 | 5 | 5 | 0 | 0 | 0 | 0 | 0 | 0 | 0 | 0 | 0 | 0 | 0 | 0 | 0 | 0 | 0 | 3 | .000 | .000 | .000 |
| Ohman, Will, Iowa * | 45 | 5 | 5 | 0 | 1 | 2 | 1 | 0 | 0 | 1 | 0 | 0 | 0 | 0 | 0 | 2 | 0 | 0 | 0 | .200 | .200 | .400 |
| Olsen, Kevin, Albuquerque | 10 | 16 | 13 | 0 | 1 | 1 | 0 | 0 | 0 | 0 | 2 | 0 | 0 | 1 | 0 | 5 | 0 | 0 | 0 | .077 | .143 | .077 |
| Olson, Tim, Tucson | 37 | 167 | 147 | 32 | 44 | 76 | 11 | 0 | 7 | 25 | 1 | 1 | 2 | 16 | 0 | 28 | 5 | 1 | 2 | .299 | .373 | .517 |
| Olszta, Eddie, Nashville | 16 | 21 | 17 | 2 | 2 | 2 | 0 | 0 | 0 | 0 | 0 | 0 | 0 | 4 | 0 | 8 | 0 | 1 | 0 | .118 | .286 | .118 |
| Oropesa, Eddie, Portland * | 37 | 2 | 2 | 0 | 0 | 0 | 0 | 0 | 0 | 0 | 0 | 0 | 0 | 0 | 0 | 1 | 0 | 0 | 0 | .000 | .000 | .000 |
| Ortiz, Hector, Colorado Springs | 46 | 169 | 155 | 18 | 41 | 51 | 7 | 0 | 1 | 15 | 1 | 1 | 2 | 10 | 2 | 26 | 1 | 1 | 8 | .265 | .315 | .329 |
| Ortiz, Luis, Edmonton | 22 | 59 | 51 | 2 | 10 | 13 | 1 | 1 | 0 | 4 | 1 | 0 | 1 | 6 | 0 | 5 | 0 | 0 | 6 | .196 | .293 | .255 |
| Osborne, Donovan, Portland * | 7 | 3 | 3 | 2 | 2 | 2 | 0 | 0 | 0 | 0 | 0 | 0 | 0 | 0 | 0 | 0 | 0 | 0 | 0 | .667 | .667 | .667 |
| Oxspring, Chris, Portland * | 17 | 22 | 17 | 3 | 1 | 1 | 0 | 0 | 0 | 0 | 2 | 0 | 0 | 3 | 0 | 9 | 0 | 0 | 0 | .059 | .200 | .059 |
| Padgett, Matt, Albuquerque * | 131 | 478 | 435 | 65 | 116 | 224 | 28 | 4 | 24 | 93 | 1 | 3 | 3 | 36 | 3 | 123 | 1 | 5 | 8 | .267 | .325 | .515 |
| Parker, Christian, Edmonton | 8 | 6 | 6 | 3 | 3 | 6 | 0 | 0 | 1 | 3 | 0 | 0 | 0 | 0 | 0 | 1 | 0 | 0 | 0 | .500 | .500 | 1.000 |
| Paronto, Chad, Memphis | 47 | 2 | 2 | 0 | 0 | 0 | 0 | 0 | 0 | 0 | 0 | 0 | 0 | 0 | 0 | 0 | 0 | 0 | 0 | .000 | .000 | .000 |
| Parque, Jim, Tucson * | 12 | 10 | 9 | 0 | 0 | 0 | 0 | 0 | 0 | 0 | 1 | 0 | 0 | 0 | 0 | 5 | 0 | 0 | 0 | .000 | .000 | .000 |
| Parrott, Rhett, Memphis | 7 | 13 | 10 | 0 | 2 | 3 | 1 | 0 | 0 | 2 | 3 | 0 | 0 | 0 | 0 | 1 | 0 | 0 | 0 | .200 | .200 | .300 |
| Patterson, Jarrod, Omaha * | 104 | 427 | 356 | 60 | 94 | 143 | 16 | 0 | 11 | 51 | 0 | 2 | 10 | 59 | 3 | 68 | 0 | 0 | 12 | .264 | .382 | .402 |
| Pavon, Julio, Fresno | 5 | 2 | 2 | 0 | 0 | 0 | 0 | 0 | 0 | 0 | 0 | 0 | 0 | 0 | 0 | 2 | 0 | 0 | 0 | .000 | .000 | .000 |
| Pearce, Josh, Memphis | 26 | 2 | 2 | 0 | 0 | 0 | 0 | 0 | 0 | 0 | 0 | 0 | 0 | 0 | 0 | 1 | 0 | 0 | 0 | .000 | .000 | .000 |
| Pelaez, Alex, Salt Lake | 92 | 381 | 353 | 43 | 112 | 161 | 18 | 2 | 9 | 60 | 0 | 7 | 1 | 20 | 2 | 48 | 1 | 1 | 10 | .317 | .349 | .456 |
| Pellow, Kit, Colorado Springs | 13 | 48 | 42 | 10 | 15 | 28 | 4 | 0 | 3 | 14 | 0 | 1 | 1 | 4 | 1 | 7 | 0 | 0 | 0 | .357 | .417 | .667 |
| Pena, Elvis, Colorado Springs † | 96 | 322 | 269 | 39 | 73 | 101 | 16 | 3 | 2 | 30 | 13 | 2 | 3 | 35 | 0 | 45 | 4 | 2 | 6 | .271 | .359 | .375 |
| Perez, Antonio, Las Vegas | 125 | 554 | 476 | 92 | 141 | 243 | 24 | 6 | 22 | 88 | 3 | 7 | 7 | 61 | 1 | 87 | 22 | 12 | 1 | .296 | .379 | .511 |
| Perez, Neifi, Iowa † | 10 | 34 | 34 | 1 | 7 | 8 | 1 | 0 | 0 | 3 | 0 | 0 | 0 | 0 | 0 | 5 | 0 | 0 | 0 | .206 | .206 | .235 |
| Perez, Santiago, Oklahoma † | 89 | 373 | 317 | 66 | 84 | 132 | 15 | 3 | 9 | 40 | 1 | 0 | 4 | 51 | 0 | 110 | 14 | 9 | 7 | .265 | .374 | .416 |
| Petrick, Ben, Portland | 24 | 93 | 80 | 14 | 18 | 32 | 6 | 1 | 2 | 11 | 0 | 1 | 1 | 11 | 1 | 18 | 0 | 0 | 2 | .225 | .323 | .400 |
| Phillips, Paul, Omaha | 86 | 335 | 311 | 40 | 97 | 134 | 17 | 1 | 6 | 41 | 0 | 1 | 3 | 20 | 0 | 36 | 4 | 3 | 10 | .312 | .358 | .431 |
| Pickford, Kevin, Fresno * | 1 | 2 | 2 | 0 | 1 | 1 | 0 | 0 | 0 | 0 | 0 | 0 | 0 | 0 | 0 | 0 | 0 | 0 | 0 | .500 | .500 | .500 |
| Pickler, Jeff, Oklahoma * | 86 | 391 | 354 | 64 | 110 | 145 | 22 | 5 | 1 | 51 | 1 | 2 | 0 | 34 | 1 | 49 | 15 | 3 | 9 | .311 | .369 | .410 |
| Piedra, Jorge, Colorado Springs | 99 | 412 | 377 | 71 | 126 | 210 | 29 | 5 | 15 | 55 | 3 | 6 | 3 | 23 | 1 | 56 | 4 | 3 | 7 | .334 | .372 | .557 |
| Porter, Colin, Memphis * | 101 | 359 | 330 | 46 | 86 | 140 | 20 | 2 | 10 | 34 | 1 | 1 | 2 | 25 | 5 | 75 | 13 | 5 | 5 | .261 | .316 | .424 |
| Powell, Greg, New Orleans | 5 | 4 | 3 | 0 | 0 | 0 | 0 | 0 | 0 | 0 | 1 | 0 | 0 | 0 | 0 | 2 | 0 | 0 | 0 | .000 | .000 | .000 |
| Prieto, Chris, Memphis * | 130 | 519 | 451 | 73 | 128 | 166 | 17 | 6 | 3 | 41 | 6 | 2 | 9 | 51 | 0 | 56 | 28 | 8 | 4 | .284 | .366 | .368 |
| Quinn, Mark, Memphis | 24 | 97 | 87 | 10 | 19 | 31 | 3 | 0 | 3 | 11 | 0 | 0 | 1 | 9 | 1 | 15 | 0 | 0 | 3 | .218 | .299 | .356 |

| Player, Team | G | TPA | AB | R | H | TB | 2B | 3B | HR | RBI | SH | SF | HP | BB | IBB | SO | SB | CS | GDP | Avg. | OBP | Slg. |
|---|---|---|---|---|---|---|---|---|---|---|---|---|---|---|---|---|---|---|---|---|---|---|
| Quintero, Humberto, Portland | 68 | 274 | 259 | 36 | 82 | 122 | 25 | 0 | 5 | 30 | 1 | 1 | 5 | 8 | 0 | 18 | 0 | 0 | 7 | .317 | .348 | .471 |
| Raggio, Brady, Tucson | 56 | 4 | 4 | 0 | 0 | 0 | 0 | 0 | 0 | 0 | 0 | 0 | 0 | 0 | 0 | 0 | 0 | 0 | 0 | .000 | .000 | .000 |
| Ramirez, Julio, Tucson | 125 | 474 | 441 | 67 | 120 | 185 | 26 | 9 | 7 | 64 | 3 | 4 | 4 | 22 | 1 | 118 | 21 | 11 | 5 | .272 | .310 | .420 |
| Redding, Tim, New Orleans | 5 | 8 | 6 | 1 | 0 | 0 | 0 | 0 | 0 | 0 | 2 | 0 | 0 | 0 | 0 | 4 | 0 | 0 | 0 | .000 | .000 | .000 |
| Reed, Jeremy, Tacoma * | 61 | 259 | 233 | 40 | 71 | 106 | 10 | 5 | 5 | 36 | 2 | 1 | 0 | 23 | 1 | 22 | 13 | 2 | 6 | .305 | .366 | .455 |
| Reid, Justin, Nashville | 32 | 28 | 24 | 1 | 2 | 2 | 0 | 0 | 0 | 0 | 3 | 0 | 0 | 1 | 0 | 11 | 0 | 0 | 0 | .083 | .120 | .083 |
| Repko, Jason, Las Vegas | 75 | 326 | 302 | 55 | 94 | 149 | 26 | 4 | 7 | 41 | 2 | 1 | 3 | 18 | 2 | 57 | 13 | 5 | 4 | .311 | .355 | .493 |
| Reyes, Rene, Colorado Springs † | 87 | 334 | 313 | 44 | 96 | 139 | 23 | 1 | 6 | 47 | 1 | 0 | 2 | 18 | 1 | 60 | 10 | 5 | 7 | .307 | .348 | .444 |
| Riggs, Adam, Salt Lake | 112 | 493 | 450 | 104 | 149 | 285 | 33 | 8 | 29 | 90 | 2 | 7 | 4 | 30 | 2 | 80 | 8 | 3 | 5 | .331 | .373 | .633 |
| Riggs, Eric, Las Vegas † | 52 | 155 | 130 | 14 | 30 | 45 | 6 | 0 | 3 | 14 | 1 | 0 | 4 | 20 | 3 | 21 | 1 | 2 | 0 | .231 | .351 | .346 |
| Rios, Armando, Memphis * | 9 | 27 | 25 | 4 | 8 | 12 | 1 | 0 | 1 | 6 | 0 | 0 | 0 | 2 | 1 | 5 | 2 | 0 | 0 | .320 | .370 | .480 |
| Risinger, Ben, Portland | 79 | 260 | 227 | 28 | 55 | 78 | 11 | 0 | 4 | 25 | 2 | 6 | 9 | 16 | 1 | 40 | 0 | 0 | 6 | .242 | .310 | .344 |
| Rivera, Carlos, Nashville * | 93 | 341 | 312 | 46 | 91 | 161 | 19 | 0 | 17 | 50 | 0 | 0 | 3 | 24 | 4 | 55 | 6 | 7 | 13 | .292 | .348 | .516 |
| Rivera, Mike, Sacramento | 49 | 184 | 170 | 12 | 38 | 64 | 7 | 2 | 5 | 20 | 1 | 3 | 0 | 10 | 0 | 34 | 1 | 1 | 2 | .224 | .262 | .376 |
| Rivera, Rene, Tacoma | 4 | 15 | 15 | 3 | 6 | 10 | 1 | 0 | 1 | 1 | 0 | 0 | 0 | 0 | 0 | 3 | 0 | 0 | 0 | .400 | .400 | .667 |
| Robertson, Jeriome, Edmonton * | 7 | 6 | 5 | 1 | 1 | 1 | 0 | 0 | 0 | 0 | 1 | 0 | 0 | 0 | 0 | 1 | 0 | 0 | 0 | .200 | .200 | .200 |
| Rodriguez, Nerio, Memphis | 16 | 18 | 17 | 0 | 2 | 2 | 0 | 0 | 0 | 2 | 1 | 0 | 0 | 0 | 0 | 7 | 0 | 0 | 1 | .118 | .118 | .118 |
| Rose, Mike, Sacramento † | 107 | 436 | 349 | 56 | 98 | 140 | 20 | 2 | 6 | 49 | 1 | 7 | 3 | 76 | 1 | 80 | 0 | 0 | 14 | .281 | .407 | .401 |
| Ross, Cody, Las Vegas | 60 | 259 | 238 | 44 | 65 | 128 | 17 | 2 | 14 | 49 | 0 | 1 | 2 | 18 | 0 | 43 | 2 | 0 | 11 | .273 | .328 | .538 |
| Rouse, Mike, Sacramento * | 99 | 391 | 323 | 53 | 89 | 134 | 11 | 2 | 10 | 40 | 11 | 2 | 5 | 50 | 0 | 68 | 0 | 4 | 5 | .276 | .379 | .415 |
| Rust, Evan, Memphis | 28 | 8 | 6 | 2 | 1 | 1 | 0 | 0 | 0 | 0 | 0 | 0 | 0 | 2 | 0 | 3 | 0 | 0 | 0 | .167 | .375 | .167 |
| Ryan, Jason, Memphis † | 15 | 21 | 20 | 2 | 4 | 5 | 1 | 0 | 0 | 2 | 1 | 0 | 0 | 0 | 0 | 3 | 0 | 0 | 1 | .200 | .200 | .250 |
| Ryan, Rob, Albuquerque * | 17 | 67 | 60 | 7 | 9 | 14 | 1 | 2 | 0 | 3 | 0 | 0 | 0 | 7 | 0 | 9 | 1 | 1 | 1 | .150 | .239 | .233 |
| Saarloos, Kirk, Sacramento | 5 | 0 | 0 | 0 | 0 | 0 | 0 | 0 | 0 | 0 | 0 | 0 | 0 | 0 | 0 | 0 | 0 | 0 | 0 | .000 | .000 | .000 |
| Saarloos, Kirk, New Orleans | 2 | 1 | 1 | 0 | 0 | 0 | 0 | 0 | 0 | 0 | 0 | 0 | 0 | 0 | 0 | 1 | 0 | 0 | 0 | .000 | .000 | .000 |
| Saladin, Miguel, New Orleans | 49 | 6 | 6 | 0 | 0 | 0 | 0 | 0 | 0 | 0 | 0 | 0 | 0 | 0 | 0 | 4 | 0 | 0 | 0 | .000 | .000 | .000 |
| Sanchez, Freddy, Nashville | 44 | 140 | 125 | 10 | 33 | 45 | 7 | 1 | 1 | 11 | 2 | 1 | 1 | 11 | 0 | 17 | 4 | 1 | 3 | .264 | .326 | .360 |
| Sandel, George, Tacoma * | 16 | 47 | 41 | 3 | 5 | 6 | 1 | 0 | 0 | 4 | 1 | 1 | 0 | 4 | 0 | 13 | 0 | 1 | 1 | .122 | .196 | .146 |
| Sanders, Scott, Albuquerque | 20 | 26 | 20 | 4 | 3 | 4 | 1 | 0 | 0 | 0 | 2 | 0 | 1 | 3 | 0 | 7 | 0 | 0 | 0 | .150 | .292 | .200 |
| Scales, Bobby, Portland † | 73 | 245 | 213 | 26 | 50 | 70 | 13 | 2 | 1 | 24 | 0 | 0 | 5 | 27 | 2 | 56 | 3 | 1 | 8 | .235 | .335 | .329 |
| Schroder, Chris, Edmonton | 17 | 2 | 1 | 0 | 0 | 0 | 0 | 0 | 0 | 0 | 1 | 0 | 0 | 0 | 0 | 1 | 0 | 0 | 0 | .000 | .000 | .000 |
| Seabol, Scott, Memphis | 138 | 562 | 514 | 92 | 156 | 277 | 26 | 1 | 31 | 78 | 0 | 4 | 7 | 37 | 0 | 93 | 6 | 3 | 17 | .304 | .356 | .539 |
| Sears, Todd, Portland | 1 | 3 | 3 | 0 | 0 | 0 | 0 | 0 | 0 | 0 | 0 | 0 | 0 | 0 | 0 | 1 | 0 | 0 | 0 | .000 | .000 | .000 |
| Sedlacek, Shawn, Iowa | 22 | 31 | 25 | 0 | 0 | 0 | 0 | 0 | 0 | 0 | 4 | 0 | 0 | 2 | 0 | 13 | 0 | 0 | 0 | .000 | .074 | .000 |
| Selby, Bill, Iowa * | 119 | 450 | 407 | 60 | 112 | 204 | 31 | 5 | 17 | 77 | 1 | 10 | 2 | 30 | 3 | 59 | 2 | 4 | 6 | .275 | .321 | .501 |
| Service, Scott, Tucson | 24 | 1 | 1 | 0 | 0 | 0 | 0 | 0 | 0 | 0 | 0 | 0 | 0 | 0 | 0 | 0 | 0 | 0 | 0 | .000 | .000 | .000 |
| Sessions, Doug, Edmonton | 7 | 5 | 4 | 1 | 3 | 3 | 0 | 0 | 0 | 1 | 0 | 0 | 0 | 1 | 0 | 0 | 0 | 0 | 0 | .750 | .800 | .750 |
| Shabala, Adam, Fresno * | 118 | 440 | 401 | 63 | 126 | 180 | 17 | 5 | 9 | 48 | 4 | 2 | 1 | 32 | 0 | 81 | 21 | 3 | 5 | .314 | .365 | .449 |
| Sheldon, Scott, Nashville | 34 | 116 | 113 | 8 | 25 | 38 | 7 | 0 | 2 | 13 | 0 | 0 | 1 | 2 | 1 | 31 | 0 | 0 | 7 | .221 | .241 | .336 |
| Shibilo, Andy, Iowa | 9 | 2 | 2 | 0 | 0 | 0 | 0 | 0 | 0 | 0 | 0 | 0 | 0 | 0 | 0 | 0 | 0 | 0 | 0 | .000 | .000 | .000 |
| Shibilo, Andy, Tacoma | 16 | 0 | 0 | 0 | 0 | 0 | 0 | 0 | 0 | 0 | 0 | 0 | 0 | 0 | 0 | 0 | 0 | 0 | 0 | .000 | .000 | .000 |
| Short, Rick, Edmonton | 40 | 164 | 152 | 13 | 51 | 70 | 13 | 0 | 2 | 19 | 0 | 1 | 1 | 10 | 0 | 7 | 1 | 1 | 5 | .336 | .378 | .461 |
| Short, Rick, Omaha | 89 | 339 | 316 | 30 | 89 | 126 | 16 | 0 | 7 | 48 | 1 | 3 | 4 | 15 | 0 | 39 | 1 | 1 | 15 | .282 | .320 | .399 |
| Shumpert, Terry, Nashville | 69 | 243 | 211 | 41 | 54 | 104 | 15 | 1 | 11 | 36 | 3 | 1 | 5 | 23 | 0 | 38 | 3 | 1 | 2 | .256 | .342 | .493 |
| Silva, Jose, Tucson | 9 | 7 | 7 | 0 | 0 | 0 | 0 | 0 | 0 | 0 | 0 | 0 | 0 | 0 | 0 | 3 | 0 | 0 | 0 | .000 | .000 | .000 |
| Simontacchi, Jason, Memphis | 33 | 16 | 13 | 2 | 1 | 1 | 0 | 0 | 0 | 0 | 2 | 0 | 0 | 1 | 0 | 5 | 0 | 0 | 0 | .077 | .143 | .077 |
| Simpson, Allan, Colorado Springs | 27 | 4 | 4 | 0 | 0 | 0 | 0 | 0 | 0 | 0 | 0 | 0 | 0 | 0 | 0 | 1 | 0 | 0 | 0 | .000 | .000 | .000 |
| Small, Aaron, Albuquerque | 28 | 40 | 37 | 4 | 9 | 13 | 1 | 0 | 1 | 2 | 2 | 0 | 0 | 1 | 0 | 9 | 0 | 0 | 0 | .243 | .263 | .351 |
| Smith, Casey, Salt Lake | 69 | 280 | 256 | 32 | 70 | 89 | 9 | 2 | 2 | 27 | 4 | 1 | 1 | 18 | 0 | 37 | 8 | 2 | 4 | .273 | .322 | .348 |
| Smith, Jeff, Oklahoma * | 13 | 41 | 35 | 3 | 7 | 9 | 2 | 0 | 0 | 3 | 1 | 0 | 1 | 4 | 0 | 4 | 0 | 0 | 2 | .200 | .300 | .257 |
| Smith, Roy, Las Vegas | 30 | 3 | 3 | 0 | 0 | 0 | 0 | 0 | 0 | 0 | 0 | 0 | 0 | 0 | 0 | 1 | 0 | 0 | 0 | .000 | .000 | .000 |
| Sodowsky, Clint, Albuquerque * | 48 | 2 | 1 | 0 | 0 | 0 | 0 | 0 | 0 | 0 | 1 | 0 | 0 | 0 | 0 | 1 | 0 | 0 | 0 | .000 | .000 | .000 |
| Sorensen, Zach, Salt Lake † | 95 | 416 | 359 | 73 | 111 | 144 | 16 | 4 | 3 | 37 | 6 | 6 | 0 | 45 | 0 | 58 | 22 | 5 | 6 | .309 | .380 | .401 |
| Specht, Brian, Salt Lake † | 54 | 209 | 190 | 30 | 45 | 68 | 10 | 2 | 3 | 15 | 0 | 0 | 2 | 17 | 0 | 45 | 8 | 1 | 2 | .237 | .306 | .358 |
| Stanifer, Rob, Edmonton | 37 | 3 | 3 | 0 | 0 | 0 | 0 | 0 | 0 | 0 | 0 | 0 | 0 | 0 | 0 | 1 | 0 | 0 | 0 | .000 | .000 | .000 |
| Stanley, Henri, Las Vegas * | 26 | 95 | 88 | 13 | 25 | 44 | 8 | 1 | 3 | 12 | 1 | 1 | 1 | 4 | 0 | 25 | 2 | 1 | 3 | .284 | .319 | .500 |
| Stark, Denny, Colorado Springs | 14 | 26 | 25 | 1 | 3 | 7 | 1 | 0 | 1 | 3 | 1 | 0 | 0 | 0 | 0 | 5 | 0 | 0 | 0 | .120 | .120 | .280 |
| Stauffer, Tim, Portland | 14 | 15 | 12 | 1 | 2 | 3 | 1 | 0 | 0 | 0 | 2 | 0 | 1 | 0 | 0 | 3 | 0 | 0 | 0 | .167 | .231 | .250 |
| Stegall, Ryan, New Orleans | 4 | 8 | 5 | 0 | 1 | 2 | 1 | 0 | 0 | 4 | 0 | 1 | 0 | 2 | 0 | 2 | 0 | 0 | 0 | .200 | .375 | .400 |
| Stemle, Steve, Memphis | 54 | 3 | 1 | 0 | 0 | 0 | 0 | 0 | 0 | 0 | 2 | 0 | 0 | 0 | 0 | 0 | 0 | 0 | 0 | .000 | .000 | .000 |
| Stocks, Nick, Memphis | 15 | 2 | 2 | 0 | 1 | 1 | 0 | 0 | 0 | 0 | 0 | 0 | 0 | 0 | 0 | 0 | 0 | 0 | 1 | .500 | .500 | .500 |
| Strong, Jamal, Tacoma | 64 | 286 | 238 | 46 | 77 | 101 | 11 | 2 | 3 | 24 | 6 | 1 | 3 | 38 | 0 | 28 | 19 | 6 | 3 | .324 | .421 | .424 |
| Sutton, Larry, Albuquerque * | 91 | 377 | 308 | 70 | 115 | 213 | 31 | 2 | 21 | 73 | 0 | 5 | 5 | 59 | 1 | 61 | 3 | 1 | 4 | .373 | .475 | .692 |
| Sweeney, Brian, Portland | 24 | 32 | 28 | 3 | 9 | 10 | 1 | 0 | 0 | 2 | 2 | 0 | 0 | 2 | 0 | 6 | 0 | 0 | 0 | .321 | .367 | .357 |
| Swisher, Nick, Sacramento † | 125 | 554 | 443 | 109 | 119 | 238 | 28 | 2 | 29 | 92 | 0 | — | 3 | 103 | 1 | 109 | 3 | 3 | 16 | .269 | .406 | .537 |
| Szuminski, Jason, Iowa | 41 | 2 | 2 | 0 | 0 | 0 | 0 | 0 | 0 | 0 | 0 | 0 | 0 | 0 | 0 | 1 | 0 | 0 | 0 | .000 | .000 | .000 |
| Taschner, Jack, Fresno * | 18 | 7 | 5 | 0 | 1 | 1 | 0 | 0 | 0 | 2 | 1 | 0 | 0 | 1 | 0 | 2 | 0 | 1 | 0 | .200 | .333 | .200 |
| Teahen, Mark, Omaha * | 66 | 274 | 246 | 33 | 69 | 110 | 15 | 1 | 8 | 31 | 1 | 2 | 4 | 21 | 0 | 69 | 0 | 0 | 4 | .280 | .344 | .447 |
| Tejera, Michael, Albuquerque * | 25 | 39 | 35 | 4 | 12 | 15 | 3 | 0 | 0 | 3 | 1 | 0 | 0 | 3 | 0 | 8 | 1 | 1 | 1 | .343 | .395 | .429 |
| Theodorou, Nick, Las Vegas † | 89 | 346 | 294 | 47 | 83 | 115 | 14 | 3 | 4 | 32 | 9 | 2 | 5 | 36 | 2 | 36 | 9 | 7 | 6 | .282 | .368 | .391 |
| Thompson, Rich, Nashville * | 112 | 461 | 411 | 73 | 118 | 166 | 7 | 13 | 5 | 36 | 10 | 1 | 13 | 26 | 1 | 62 | 40 | 15 | 0 | .287 | .348 | .404 |
| Thrower, Jake, Salt Lake † | 120 | 509 | 456 | 73 | 136 | 190 | 29 | 2 | 7 | 65 | 1 | 7 | 4 | 41 | 0 | 53 | 5 | 2 | 9 | .298 | .356 | .417 |
| Thurston, Joe, Las Vegas * | 101 | 360 | 317 | 38 | 90 | 125 | 17 | 3 | 4 | 23 | 3 | 3 | 17 | 20 | 3 | 46 | 7 | 2 | 5 | .284 | .356 | .394 |
| Tollberg, Brian, Colorado Springs | 28 | 48 | 42 | 4 | 6 | 8 | 2 | 0 | 0 | 0 | 5 | 0 | 0 | 1 | 0 | 9 | 0 | 0 | 0 | .143 | .163 | .190 |
| Totten, Heath, Las Vegas | 29 | 45 | 40 | 2 | 7 | 8 | 1 | 0 | 0 | 2 | 5 | 0 | 0 | 0 | 0 | 15 | 0 | 0 | 0 | .175 | .175 | .200 |
| Tracy, Andy, Colorado Springs * | 126 | 529 | 464 | 98 | 146 | 293 | 42 | 3 | 33 | 120 | 1 | 4 | 2 | 58 | 3 | 115 | 4 | 2 | 8 | .315 | .390 | .631 |
| Treanor, Matt, Albuquerque | 62 | 247 | 198 | 32 | 51 | 83 | 8 | 0 | 8 | 38 | 2 | 3 | 10 | 34 | 1 | 44 | 2 | 0 | 5 | .258 | .388 | .419 |
| Tremie, Chris, New Orleans | 70 | 230 | 195 | 23 | 47 | 61 | 6 | 1 | 2 | 24 | 0 | 5 | 5 | 24 | 1 | 30 | 0 | 1 | 7 | .241 | .332 | .313 |
| Truby, Chris, Nashville | 130 | 523 | 466 | 96 | 140 | 260 | 41 | 2 | 25 | 83 | 0 | 5 | 5 | 47 | 3 | 96 | 11 | 2 | 16 | .300 | .367 | .558 |
| Ugueto, Luis, Tacoma † | 101 | 401 | 361 | 53 | 98 | 159 | 18 | 8 | 9 | 50 | 2 | 0 | 0 | 38 | 0 | 98 | 25 | 7 | 4 | .271 | .341 | .440 |
| Urban, Jeff, Fresno | 47 | 7 | 5 | 0 | 1 | 2 | 1 | 0 | 0 | 0 | 1 | 0 | 0 | 1 | 0 | 3 | 0 | 0 | 0 | .200 | .333 | .400 |
| Varner, Noochie, Tucson | 100 | 389 | 343 | 64 | 110 | 152 | 18 | 3 | 6 | 37 | 1 | 0 | 2 | 41 | 3 | 62 | 4 | 1 | 12 | .321 | .396 | .443 |
| Villarreal, Oscar, Tucson * | 6 | 1 | 1 | 0 | 0 | 0 | 0 | 0 | 0 | 0 | 0 | 0 | 0 | 0 | 0 | 1 | 0 | 0 | 0 | .000 | .000 | .000 |

| Player, Team | G | TPA | AB | R | H | TB | 2B | 3B | HR | RBI | SH | SF | HP | BB | IBB | SO | SB | CS | GDP | Avg. | OBP | Slg. |
|---|---|---|---|---|---|---|---|---|---|---|---|---|---|---|---|---|---|---|---|---|---|---|
| Wainwright, Adam, Memphis | 12 | 24 | 17 | 1 | 3 | 5 | 2 | 0 | 0 | 0 | 6 | 0 | 1 | 0 | 0 | 6 | 0 | 0 | 1 | .176 | .222 | .294 |
| Waldron, Jeff, Oklahoma * | 34 | 117 | 101 | 9 | 23 | 28 | 3 | 1 | 0 | 8 | 0 | 1 | 3 | 12 | 0 | 35 | 0 | 0 | 1 | .228 | .325 | .277 |
| Waldron, Jeff, Tucson * | 3 | 3 | 2 | 0 | 0 | 0 | 0 | 0 | 0 | 0 | 0 | 0 | 0 | 1 | 0 | 1 | 0 | 0 | 0 | .000 | .333 | .000 |
| Walker, Kevin, Fresno * | 48 | 5 | 5 | 0 | 1 | 1 | 0 | 0 | 0 | 0 | 0 | 0 | 0 | 0 | 0 | 1 | 0 | 0 | 0 | .200 | .200 | .200 |
| Ware, Jeremy, Edmonton | 26 | 71 | 64 | 5 | 16 | 18 | 2 | 0 | 0 | 5 | 0 | 1 | 1 | 5 | 2 | 6 | 0 | 0 | 2 | .250 | .310 | .281 |
| Wathan, Derek, Albuquerque † | 106 | 452 | 414 | 74 | 125 | 191 | 26 | 5 | 10 | 47 | 3 | 1 | 1 | 33 | 0 | 74 | 15 | 10 | 8 | .302 | .354 | .461 |
| Watson, Brandon, Edmonton * | 139 | 566 | 526 | 74 | 154 | 183 | 17 | 3 | 2 | 41 | 6 | 2 | 1 | 31 | 2 | 68 | 22 | 10 | 3 | .293 | .332 | .348 |
| Watson, Matt, Sacramento * | 125 | 541 | 476 | 79 | 145 | 245 | 37 | 3 | 19 | 96 | 2 | 5 | 4 | 54 | 2 | 75 | 3 | 4 | 12 | .305 | .377 | .515 |
| Wayne, Justin, Albuquerque | 13 | 17 | 14 | 0 | 1 | 2 | 1 | 0 | 0 | 0 | 1 | 0 | 0 | 2 | 0 | 11 | 0 | 0 | 0 | .071 | .188 | .143 |
| Webb, Alan, Portland * | 8 | 1 | 1 | 0 | 1 | 1 | 0 | 0 | 0 | 0 | 0 | 0 | 0 | 0 | 0 | 0 | 0 | 0 | 0 | 1.000 | 1.000 | 1.000 |
| Wendell, Turk, Colorado Springs * | 12 | 3 | 3 | 1 | 0 | 0 | 0 | 0 | 0 | 0 | 0 | 0 | 0 | 0 | 0 | 1 | 0 | 0 | 0 | .000 | .000 | .000 |
| Whiteman, Tommy, New Orleans | 25 | 110 | 98 | 11 | 27 | 33 | 6 | 0 | 0 | 9 | 3 | 0 | 1 | 8 | 0 | 21 | 2 | 2 | 4 | .276 | .336 | .337 |
| Wilson, John, Edmonton | 37 | 130 | 117 | 10 | 30 | 46 | 7 | 0 | 3 | 11 | 1 | 1 | 1 | 10 | 0 | 11 | 2 | 0 | 7 | .256 | .318 | .393 |
| Wilson, Josh, Albuquerque | 56 | 263 | 240 | 32 | 67 | 98 | 12 | 2 | 5 | 23 | 2 | 0 | 2 | 19 | 0 | 51 | 6 | 1 | 5 | .279 | .337 | .408 |
| Witt, Kevin, Memphis * | 131 | 517 | 477 | 81 | 146 | 286 | 30 | 1 | 36 | 107 | 0 | 2 | 8 | 28 | 1 | 112 | 2 | 0 | 12 | .306 | .353 | .600 |
| Wood, Jason, Albuquerque | 102 | 426 | 375 | 44 | 92 | 141 | 21 | 2 | 8 | 49 | 0 | 6 | 5 | 40 | 2 | 74 | 2 | 1 | 5 | .245 | .322 | .376 |
| Woodard, Steve, Memphis * | 4 | 2 | 2 | 0 | 0 | 0 | 0 | 0 | 0 | 0 | 0 | 0 | 0 | 0 | 0 | 1 | 0 | 0 | 0 | .000 | .000 | .000 |
| Wuertz, Mike, Iowa | 37 | 1 | 1 | 0 | 0 | 0 | 0 | 0 | 0 | 0 | 0 | 0 | 0 | 0 | 0 | 0 | 0 | 0 | 0 | .000 | .000 | .000 |
| Zapp, A.J., Tacoma * | 136 | 574 | 509 | 78 | 148 | 266 | 27 | 2 | 29 | 101 | 0 | 3 | 5 | 56 | 8 | 184 | 0 | 0 | 5 | .291 | .365 | .523 |
| Zerbe, Chad, Fresno * | 33 | 22 | 18 | 0 | 1 | 1 | 0 | 0 | 0 | 0 | 2 | 0 | 0 | 2 | 0 | 9 | 0 | 0 | 1 | .056 | .150 | .056 |
| Zoccolillo, Peter, Oklahoma * | 128 | 566 | 484 | 83 | 142 | 250 | 37 | 1 | 23 | 96 | 1 | 11 | 5 | 65 | 6 | 94 | 4 | 2 | 5 | .293 | .375 | .517 |
| Zuniga, Tony, Tacoma | 9 | 29 | 25 | 3 | 7 | 9 | 0 | 1 | 0 | 3 | 0 | 0 | 1 | 3 | 0 | 8 | 0 | 1 | 0 | .280 | .379 | .360 |

GRAND SLAMS—Colangelo, House, D. Johnson, Padgett, Patterson, 3 each; Ansman, Bocachica, Bozied, Casanova, Dillon, Hawpe, Myrow, R. Thompson, A. Tracy, Zapp, Zoccolillo, 2 each; Allen, Atkins, D. Brown, Cervenak, Chen, Church, Coolbaugh, DeVore, Gautreau, A. Gonzalez, A. Green, Halter, Hiatt, G. Johnson, Kelton, Koonce, McDougall, Morrissey, Murray, Newhan, L. Ortiz, Pellow, Perez, Pickering, Quinn, Rusch, Sutton, Swisher, C. Tracy, Wesson.

AWARDED FIRST BASE ON CATCHER'S INTERFERENCE—Conti 3 (Jorgensen, Kopitzke, Kuzmic); Leon 3 (Buck, Ardoin, Ardoin); Bowers (House); A. Gonzalez (Kopitzke); Piedra (Horner); Reed (Haad); Rivera (Tremie); Tremie (Blanton); Varner (Gregorio); Witt (Tremie).

# 2004 PITCHING

## TEAM

| Team | W | L | Pct. | ERA | G | CG | ShO | Sv. | IP | H | TBF | R | ER | HR | SH | SF | HB | BB | IBB | SO | WP | Bk. |
|---|---|---|---|---|---|---|---|---|---|---|---|---|---|---|---|---|---|---|---|---|---|---|
| Portland | 84 | 60 | .583 | 3.85 | 144 | 2 | 11 | 40 | 1275.0 | 1253 | 5522 | 635 | 545 | 119 | 54 | 30 | 49 | 491 | 23 | 1041 | 45 | 5 |
| Sacramento | 79 | 65 | .549 | 4.55 | 144 | 3 | 10 | 35 | 1270.2 | 1428 | 5612 | 746 | 643 | 142 | 42 | 50 | 56 | 381 | 27 | 1071 | 59 | 9 |
| Iowa | 79 | 64 | .552 | 4.56 | 143 | 4 | 12 | 41 | 1242.2 | 1327 | 5501 | 717 | 629 | 150 | 52 | 39 | 65 | 543 | 33 | 1024 | 55 | 10 |
| Tacoma | 79 | 63 | .556 | 4.59 | 142 | 4 | 8 | 45 | 1232.2 | 1276 | 5501 | 707 | 629 | 131 | 35 | 49 | 64 | 585 | 9 | 1014 | 74 | 4 |
| Oklahoma | 81 | 64 | .559 | 4.60 | 144 | 6 | 9 | 34 | 1266.2 | 1396 | 5511 | 724 | 647 | 153 | 38 | 40 | 46 | 448 | 17 | 878 | 48 | 1 |
| Omaha | 71 | 73 | .493 | 4.67 | 144 | 5 | 7 | 34 | 1240.1 | 1370 | 5479 | 728 | 644 | 171 | 39 | 38 | 71 | 425 | 8 | 969 | 62 | 9 |
| Memphis | 73 | 71 | .507 | 4.75 | 144 | 3 | 7 | 41 | 1254.0 | 1401 | 5537 | 728 | 662 | 183 | 63 | 40 | 63 | 461 | 23 | 1010 | 55 | 2 |
| New Orleans | 66 | 78 | .458 | 4.86 | 144 | 6 | 6 | 35 | 1239.1 | 1318 | 5407 | 732 | 669 | 139 | 56 | 58 | 52 | 426 | 19 | 901 | 56 | 5 |
| Edmonton | 69 | 74 | .483 | 4.90 | 143 | 6 | 3 | 26 | 1221.0 | 1382 | 5421 | 728 | 665 | 154 | 48 | 51 | 57 | 456 | 17 | 899 | 66 | 6 |
| Nashville | 63 | 79 | .444 | 4.92 | 142 | 4 | 7 | 33 | 1234.0 | 1364 | 5435 | 722 | 674 | 148 | 49 | 41 | 54 | 437 | 29 | 1011 | 43 | 6 |
| Fresno | 62 | 82 | .431 | 4.94 | 144 | 1 | 7 | 27 | 1281.1 | 1476 | 5736 | 789 | 703 | 159 | 63 | 51 | 40 | 503 | 25 | 880 | 65 | 2 |
| Colorado Springs | 78 | 65 | .545 | 5.06 | 143 | 2 | 7 | 36 | 1218.1 | 1366 | 5411 | 775 | 685 | 165 | 39 | 34 | 68 | 455 | 10 | 1010 | 76 | 9 |
| Tucson | 74 | 70 | .514 | 5.38 | 144 | 4 | 6 | 34 | 1253.1 | 1494 | 5664 | 835 | 749 | 169 | 44 | 45 | 51 | 483 | 19 | 898 | 77 | 4 |
| Las Vegas | 67 | 76 | .469 | 5.44 | 143 | 1 | 2 | 27 | 1262.2 | 1482 | 5717 | 849 | 763 | 183 | 57 | 45 | 57 | 512 | 16 | 999 | 81 | 4 |
| Albuquerque | 67 | 77 | .465 | 5.67 | 144 | 4 | 3 | 30 | 1262.1 | 1488 | 5631 | 862 | 795 | 209 | 53 | 33 | 62 | 448 | 15 | 905 | 56 | 4 |
| Salt Lake | 56 | 88 | .389 | 5.70 | 144 | 5 | 1 | 24 | 1238.2 | 1515 | 5670 | 900 | 785 | 163 | 27 | 43 | 45 | 538 | 3 | 955 | 59 | 86 |

## INDIVIDUAL

### TOP QUALIFIERS FOR EARNED-RUN AVERAGE TITLE

Minimum 115 innings. *Lefthanded pitcher.

| Pitcher, Team | W | L | Pct. | ERA | G | GS | CG | ShO | GF | Sv. | IP | H | TBF | R | ER | HR | SH | SF | HB | BB | IBB | SO | WP | Bk. |
|---|---|---|---|---|---|---|---|---|---|---|---|---|---|---|---|---|---|---|---|---|---|---|---|---|
| Walrond, Les, Omaha * | 11 | 5 | .688 | 3.06 | 19 | 19 | 1 | 1 | 0 | 0 | 123.2 | 114 | 515 | 46 | 42 | 12 | 6 | 4 | 3 | 41 | 0 | 107 | 7 | 2 |
| Tankersley, Dennis, Portland | 7 | 4 | .636 | 3.15 | 19 | 19 | 0 | 0 | 0 | 0 | 120.0 | 114 | 495 | 52 | 42 | 10 | 4 | 3 | 2 | 37 | 1 | 86 | 1 | 0 |
| Germano, Justin, Portland | 9 | 5 | .643 | 3.38 | 20 | 20 | 2 | 2 | 0 | 0 | 122.2 | 113 | 496 | 48 | 46 | 12 | 5 | 6 | 5 | 25 | 0 | 98 | 3 | 0 |
| Williams, Dave, Nashville | 6 | 2 | .750 | 3.47 | 21 | 21 | 0 | 0 | 0 | 0 | 116.2 | 113 | 486 | 52 | 45 | 10 | 7 | 4 | 4 | 33 | 2 | 103 | 2 | 0 |
| Downs, Scott, Edmonton | 10 | 6 | .625 | 3.52 | 22 | 22 | 2 | 2 | 0 | 0 | 135.1 | 143 | 559 | 57 | 53 | 16 | 10 | 3 | 3 | 26 | 0 | 67 | 1 | 1 |
| Hernandez, Carlos, New Orleans | 9 | 4 | .692 | 3.60 | 23 | 23 | 0 | 0 | 0 | 0 | 127.2 | 115 | 528 | 54 | 51 | 9 | 11 | 8 | 5 | 46 | 1 | 81 | 3 | 0 |
| Flores, Randy, Memphis | 5 | 7 | .417 | 3.82 | 36 | 15 | 1 | 1 | 4 | 2 | 122.2 | 115 | 512 | 60 | 52 | 10 | 8 | 4 | 3 | 46 | 1 | 99 | 1 | 0 |
| Sweeney, Brian, Portland | 11 | 4 | .733 | 3.83 | 24 | 23 | 0 | 0 | 1 | 0 | 138.2 | 130 | 577 | 65 | 59 | 16 | 9 | 6 | 1 | 42 | 1 | 110 | 6 | 0 |
| Reid, Justin, Nashville | 5 | 3 | .625 | 3.96 | 32 | 16 | 0 | 0 | 6 | 2 | 122.2 | 112 | 504 | 56 | 54 | 18 | 10 | 6 | 2 | 35 | 3 | 121 | 3 | 0 |
| Haren, Danny, Memphis | 11 | 4 | .733 | 4.15 | 21 | 21 | 0 | 0 | 0 | 0 | 128.0 | 136 | 540 | 60 | 59 | 19 | 7 | 3 | 3 | 33 | 1 | 150 | 2 | 0 |
| Blanton, Joe, Sacramento | 11 | 8 | .579 | 4.19 | 28 | 26 | 1 | 0 | 0 | 0 | 176.1 | 199 | 756 | 101 | 82 | 13 | 5 | 14 | 6 | 34 | 2 | 143 | 6 | 0 |
| Figueroa, Nelson, Nashville | 12 | 8 | .600 | 4.19 | 25 | 23 | 3 | 1 | 1 | 0 | 152.1 | 168 | 648 | 79 | 71 | 20 | 6 | 3 | 4 | 36 | 1 | 129 | 2 | 0 |
| Cannon, Jon, Tucson * | 9 | 8 | .529 | 4.29 | 33 | 19 | 0 | 0 | 2 | 1 | 121.2 | 127 | 535 | 65 | 58 | 15 | 1 | 4 | 5 | 54 | 1 | 98 | 7 | 0 |
| Sedlacek, Shawn, Iowa | 10 | 7 | .588 | 4.32 | 22 | 22 | 1 | 1 | 0 | 0 | 131.1 | 151 | 577 | 70 | 63 | 21 | 9 | 4 | 8 | 42 | 2 | 95 | 3 | 1 |
| Koronka, John, Iowa * | 12 | 9 | .571 | 4.34 | 29 | 23 | 2 | 2 | 1 | 0 | 153.1 | 164 | 666 | 86 | 74 | 19 | 8 | 9 | 5 | 65 | 3 | 116 | 6 | 5 |

DEPARTMENTAL LEADERS: W—Gissell, 14; L—S. Green, 17; Pct.—Gissell, .875; G—Brohawn, 72; GS—S. Green, Middlebrook, 29; CG—Three tied with 3; ShO—Four tied with two; GF—Clontz, 48; Sv.—Reyes, 23; IP—Fernandez, 196.1; H—Middlebrook, 220; TBF—Fernandez, 833; R—S. Green, 131; ER—Middlebrook, 120; HR—K. Wilson, 39; SH—Hernandez, 11; SF—Blanton, 14; HB—Rheinecker, 15; BB—S. Green, 85; IBB—Bynum, Bland, 8; SO—Haren, 150; WP—Jensen, 14; BK—Koronka, 5.

### ALL PITCHERS

*Lefthanded pitcher.

| Pitcher, Team | W | L | Pct. | ERA | G | GS | CG | ShO | GF | Sv. | IP | H | TBF | R | ER | HR | SH | SF | HB | BB | IBB | SO | WP | Bk. |
|---|---|---|---|---|---|---|---|---|---|---|---|---|---|---|---|---|---|---|---|---|---|---|---|---|
| Aardsma, David, Fresno | 6 | 4 | .600 | 3.09 | 44 | 0 | 0 | 0 | 29 | 11 | 55.1 | 46 | 245 | 21 | 19 | 2 | 0 | 0 | 4 | 29 | 3 | 53 | 1 | 0 |

| Pitcher, Team | W | L | Pct. | ERA | G | GS | CG | ShO | GF | Sv. | IP | H | TBF | R | ER | HR | SH | SF | HB | BB | IBB | SO | WP | Bk. |
|---|---|---|---|---|---|---|---|---|---|---|---|---|---|---|---|---|---|---|---|---|---|---|---|---|
| Abreu, Winston, Tucson | 1 | 0 | 1.000 | 5.68 | 28 | 0 | 0 | 0 | 9 | 3 | 44.1 | 44 | 205 | 28 | 28 | 10 | 0 | 1 | 2 | 25 | 1 | 41 | 6 | 0 |
| Allen, Luke, Nashville | 0 | 0 | .000 | 9.00 | 1 | 0 | 0 | 0 | 1 | 0 | 1.0 | 1 | 5 | 1 | 1 | 0 | 0 | 0 | 0 | 1 | 0 | 2 | 1 | 0 |
| Almonte, Hector, Colorado Springs | 3 | 2 | .600 | 8.57 | 12 | 0 | 0 | 0 | 3 | 0 | 21.0 | 29 | 109 | 22 | 20 | 4 | 0 | 0 | 3 | 15 | 1 | 12 | 4 | 0 |
| Alvarez, Juan, Albuquerque * | 2 | 3 | .400 | 5.87 | 48 | 0 | 0 | 0 | 19 | 1 | 53.2 | 75 | 255 | 38 | 35 | 7 | 0 | 0 | 1 | 19 | 2 | 42 | 1 | 1 |
| Anderson, Craig, Tacoma * | 4 | 8 | .333 | 5.65 | 26 | 13 | 0 | 0 | 7 | 2 | 92.1 | 115 | 427 | 63 | 58 | 18 | 4 | 9 | 8 | 42 | 0 | 65 | 4 | 0 |
| Anderson, Jimmy, Iowa * | 6 | 5 | .545 | 4.28 | 16 | 15 | 0 | 0 | 0 | 0 | 94.2 | 108 | 411 | 54 | 45 | 7 | 6 | 6 | 2 | 35 | 1 | 42 | 2 | 0 |
| Ankiel, Rick, Memphis * | 1 | 0 | 1.000 | 0.00 | 1 | 1 | 0 | 0 | 0 | 0 | 6.0 | 1 | 20 | 1 | 0 | 0 | 0 | 0 | 1 | 0 | 0 | 5 | 0 | 0 |
| Appier, Kevin, Omaha | 0 | 0 | .000 | 6.75 | 1 | 1 | 0 | 0 | 0 | 0 | 4.0 | 7 | 20 | 3 | 3 | 1 | 0 | 1 | 0 | 2 | 0 | 2 | 0 | 0 |
| Ashby, Chris, Albuquerque | 0 | 0 | .000 | 9.45 | 6 | 0 | 0 | 0 | 4 | 0 | 6.2 | 10 | 34 | 7 | 7 | 3 | 0 | 0 | 2 | 2 | 0 | 2 | 0 | 0 |
| Bacsik, Mike, Oklahoma * | 8 | 6 | .571 | 4.55 | 34 | 9 | 0 | 0 | 3 | 0 | 95.0 | 106 | 426 | 58 | 48 | 16 | 5 | 1 | 1 | 23 | 1 | 50 | 0 | 0 |
| Baker, Brad, Portland | 1 | 0 | 1.000 | 0.93 | 8 | 0 | 0 | 0 | 6 | 4 | 9.2 | 5 | 38 | 2 | 1 | 0 | 0 | 0 | 0 | 4 | 0 | 17 | 0 | 0 |
| Barber, Scott, Tucson | 0 | 0 | .000 | 6.75 | 2 | 0 | 0 | 0 | 1 | 0 | 5.1 | 8 | 26 | 4 | 4 | 0 | 0 | 0 | 1 | 1 | 1 | 2 | 0 | 0 |
| Barzilla, Philip, New Orleans * | 1 | 1 | .500 | 4.28 | 27 | 0 | 0 | 0 | 11 | 0 | 33.2 | 42 | 165 | 21 | 16 | 4 | 0 | 0 | 1 | 21 | 1 | 22 | 2 | 0 |
| Bauer, Pete, Albuquerque | 1 | 0 | 1.000 | 1.29 | 1 | 1 | 0 | 0 | 0 | 0 | 7.0 | 6 | 28 | 1 | 1 | 0 | 0 | 0 | 1 | 3 | 0 | 4 | 0 | 0 |
| Beltran, Rigo, Edmonton * | 3 | 2 | .600 | 3.58 | 26 | 8 | 0 | 0 | 9 | 3 | 65.1 | 65 | 271 | 27 | 26 | 5 | 3 | 6 | 0 | 17 | 1 | 54 | 0 | 1 |
| Benes, Alan, Memphis | 8 | 10 | .444 | 5.60 | 28 | 27 | 0 | 0 | 0 | 0 | 160.2 | 193 | 726 | 102 | 100 | 27 | 10 | 11 | 5 | 79 | 2 | 94 | 12 | 0 |
| Bergman, Dusty, Salt Lake * | 1 | 2 | .333 | 2.85 | 45 | 0 | 0 | 0 | 16 | 1 | 72.2 | 82 | 313 | 35 | 23 | 2 | 0 | 1 | 2 | 13 | 0 | 54 | 1 | 0 |
| Bernero, Adam, Colorado Springs | 3 | 2 | .600 | 3.17 | 9 | 8 | 0 | 0 | 0 | 0 | 48.1 | 57 | 204 | 23 | 17 | 0 | 3 | 4 | 1 | 10 | 0 | 48 | 0 | 0 |
| Bierbrodt, Nick, Oklahoma * | 1 | 3 | .250 | 7.30 | 5 | 5 | 0 | 0 | 0 | 0 | 24.2 | 26 | 120 | 21 | 20 | 5 | 2 | 1 | 2 | 22 | 0 | 26 | 0 | 0 |
| Blackley, Travis, Tacoma * | 8 | 6 | .571 | 3.83 | 19 | 18 | 2 | 2 | 0 | 0 | 110.1 | 100 | 455 | 49 | 47 | 14 | 6 | 1 | 3 | 47 | 0 | 80 | 9 | 3 |
| Bland, Nate, Iowa * | 8 | 5 | .615 | 4.68 | 53 | 0 | 0 | 0 | 13 | 1 | 73.0 | 82 | 338 | 51 | 38 | 9 | 1 | 0 | 4 | 33 | 8 | 45 | 5 | 1 |
| Blank, Matt, Albuquerque * | 4 | 8 | .333 | 6.44 | 34 | 23 | 1 | 0 | 1 | 1 | 138.1 | 180 | 615 | 105 | 99 | 29 | 10 | 10 | 4 | 47 | 1 | 75 | 4 | 0 |
| Blanton, Joe, Sacramento | 11 | 8 | .579 | 4.19 | 28 | 26 | 1 | 0 | 0 | 0 | 176.1 | 199 | 756 | 101 | 82 | 13 | 5 | 14 | 6 | 34 | 2 | 143 | 6 | 0 |
| Bootcheck, Chris, Salt Lake | 11 | 9 | .550 | 5.12 | 28 | 28 | 3 | 1 | 0 | 0 | 163.1 | 202 | 734 | 109 | 93 | 22 | 4 | 4 | 6 | 60 | 2 | 105 | 7 | 0 |
| Borland, Toby, Albuquerque | 4 | 2 | .667 | 2.29 | 34 | 0 | 0 | 0 | 28 | 11 | 39.1 | 24 | 155 | 10 | 10 | 2 | 2 | 0 | 2 | 12 | 2 | 38 | 1 | 0 |
| Borowski, Joe, Iowa | 0 | 3 | .000 | 8.22 | 7 | 3 | 0 | 0 | 0 | 0 | 7.2 | 9 | 36 | 8 | 7 | 1 | 0 | 0 | 0 | 4 | 0 | 2 | 0 | 0 |
| Bost, Heath, New Orleans | 4 | 1 | .800 | 4.41 | 44 | 0 | 0 | 0 | 13 | 3 | 49.0 | 41 | 210 | 25 | 24 | 6 | 0 | 0 | 1 | 21 | 0 | 40 | 1 | 0 |
| Bowles, Brian, Colorado Springs | 2 | 0 | 1.000 | 3.91 | 13 | 0 | 0 | 0 | 6 | 0 | 23.0 | 28 | 111 | 14 | 10 | 2 | 0 | 0 | 2 | 12 | 1 | 17 | 1 | 0 |
| Boyd, Jason, Nashville | 1 | 3 | .250 | 3.86 | 11 | 0 | 0 | 0 | 5 | 0 | 16.1 | 23 | 76 | 7 | 7 | 2 | 0 | 0 | 1 | 3 | 1 | 11 | 2 | 0 |
| Brohawn, Troy, Las Vegas * | 7 | 5 | .583 | 5.42 | 72 | 1 | 0 | 0 | 24 | 5 | 91.1 | 122 | 423 | 58 | 55 | 20 | 1 | 0 | 4 | 26 | 4 | 74 | 6 | 0 |
| Brunet, Mike, Salt Lake | 2 | 8 | .200 | 6.51 | 13 | 12 | 0 | 0 | 1 | 0 | 65.0 | 85 | 299 | 57 | 47 | 6 | 0 | 2 | 3 | 29 | 0 | 49 | 2 | 1 |
| Buchholz, Taylor, New Orleans | 6 | 7 | .462 | 5.23 | 20 | 17 | 1 | 0 | 0 | 0 | 98.0 | 107 | 425 | 60 | 57 | 16 | 2 | 8 | 2 | 29 | 0 | 74 | 8 | 0 |
| Bukvich, Ryan, Omaha | 3 | 4 | .429 | 4.37 | 38 | 0 | 0 | 0 | 24 | 7 | 47.1 | 33 | 211 | 25 | 23 | 4 | 0 | 2 | 6 | 30 | 0 | 60 | 5 | 0 |
| Bumatay, Mike, Colorado Springs * | 2 | 4 | .333 | 6.28 | 37 | 0 | 0 | 0 | 10 | 0 | 53.0 | 60 | 267 | 38 | 37 | 7 | 0 | 0 | 4 | 44 | 2 | 45 | 6 | 0 |
| Bumstead, Mike, Portland | 4 | 0 | 1.000 | 2.57 | 18 | 5 | 0 | 0 | 3 | 0 | 49.0 | 43 | 205 | 14 | 14 | 4 | 1 | 0 | 0 | 18 | 0 | 38 | 1 | 0 |
| Burnham, Gary, Memphis * | 0 | 0 | .000 | 18.00 | 1 | 0 | 0 | 0 | 1 | 0 | 1.0 | 2 | 5 | 2 | 2 | 1 | 0 | 0 | 0 | 0 | 0 | 1 | 0 | 0 |
| Bynum, Mike, Portland * | 6 | 6 | .500 | 3.19 | 62 | 0 | 0 | 0 | 33 | 6 | 79.0 | 72 | 356 | 33 | 28 | 6 | 2 | 1 | 4 | 44 | 8 | 75 | 2 | 1 |
| Cali, Carmen, Memphis * | 1 | 1 | .500 | 2.70 | 17 | 0 | 0 | 0 | 7 | 3 | 20.0 | 17 | 81 | 6 | 6 | 4 | 0 | 0 | 0 | 4 | 0 | 20 | 2 | 0 |
| Cammack, Eric, Sacramento | 3 | 2 | .600 | 5.61 | 47 | 1 | 0 | 0 | 12 | 2 | 67.1 | 75 | 312 | 51 | 42 | 9 | 0 | 3 | 4 | 31 | 3 | 64 | 5 | 0 |
| Cannon, Jon, Tucson * | 9 | 8 | .529 | 4.29 | 33 | 19 | 0 | 0 | 2 | 1 | 121.2 | 127 | 535 | 65 | 58 | 15 | 1 | 4 | 5 | 54 | 1 | 98 | 7 | 0 |
| Carrara, Giovanni, Iowa | 1 | 2 | .333 | 3.81 | 20 | 0 | 0 | 0 | 4 | 1 | 28.1 | 29 | 120 | 12 | 12 | 3 | 1 | 1 | 3 | 8 | 1 | 23 | 0 | 0 |
| Carrara, Giovanni, Las Vegas | 0 | 1 | .000 | 2.51 | 11 | 0 | 0 | 0 | 5 | 2 | 14.1 | 11 | 62 | 4 | 4 | 1 | 0 | 0 | 0 | 8 | 2 | 15 | 1 | 0 |
| Cash, David, Iowa | 1 | 0 | 1.000 | 1.59 | 3 | 3 | 0 | 0 | 0 | 0 | 17.0 | 12 | 67 | 4 | 3 | 0 | 0 | 0 | 1 | 4 | 0 | 14 | 1 | 0 |
| Chavez, Wilton, Edmonton | 5 | 12 | .294 | 4.64 | 29 | 27 | 3 | 0 | 1 | 0 | 165.0 | 178 | 704 | 104 | 85 | 21 | 5 | 8 | 14 | 43 | 1 | 114 | 6 | 1 |
| Chiasson, Scott, Iowa | 1 | 0 | 1.000 | 3.15 | 15 | 0 | 0 | 0 | 2 | 0 | 20.0 | 16 | 84 | 7 | 7 | 2 | 0 | 0 | 1 | 7 | 0 | 20 | 1 | 1 |
| Chiavacci, Ron, Edmonton | 4 | 6 | .400 | 5.11 | 25 | 8 | 0 | 0 | 4 | 0 | 79.1 | 73 | 357 | 48 | 45 | 9 | 2 | 7 | 2 | 52 | 2 | 73 | 2 | 0 |
| Childers, Jason, Edmonton | 0 | 3 | .000 | 4.50 | 14 | 0 | 0 | 0 | 13 | 5 | 14.0 | 15 | 66 | 8 | 7 | 1 | 0 | 0 | 0 | 9 | 0 | 13 | 1 | 0 |
| Choate, Randy, Tucson * | 0 | 0 | .000 | 5.68 | 15 | 0 | 0 | 0 | 4 | 1 | 12.2 | 10 | 57 | 8 | 8 | 1 | 0 | 0 | 1 | 8 | 1 | 7 | 0 | 0 |
| Christman, Tim, Tacoma * | 2 | 0 | 1.000 | 4.62 | 30 | 0 | 0 | 0 | 11 | 2 | 39.0 | 44 | 176 | 24 | 20 | 3 | 0 | 0 | 1 | 15 | 2 | 45 | 1 | 0 |
| Clontz, Brad, Oklahoma | 2 | 6 | .250 | 4.47 | 59 | 0 | 0 | 0 | 48 | 18 | 56.1 | 57 | 252 | 35 | 28 | 10 | 1 | 0 | 5 | 19 | 2 | 51 | 2 | 0 |
| Corcoran, Roy, Edmonton | 5 | 1 | .833 | 3.05 | 30 | 0 | 0 | 0 | 17 | 5 | 44.1 | 39 | 198 | 16 | 15 | 0 | 1 | 0 | 2 | 24 | 1 | 35 | 1 | 0 |
| Corey, Mark, Nashville | 1 | 4 | .200 | 4.42 | 34 | 0 | 0 | 0 | 25 | 16 | 38.2 | 40 | 171 | 21 | 19 | 4 | 1 | 0 | 2 | 15 | 1 | 39 | 2 | 0 |
| Creek, Doug, Memphis * | 2 | 1 | .667 | 4.71 | 33 | 0 | 0 | 0 | 5 | 0 | 28.2 | 28 | 129 | 16 | 15 | 1 | 0 | 0 | 4 | 11 | 0 | 39 | 6 | 0 |
| Crudale, Mike, Nashville | 0 | 1 | .000 | 9.00 | 5 | 0 | 0 | 0 | 1 | 0 | 7.0 | 8 | 34 | 7 | 7 | 1 | 0 | 0 | 1 | 4 | 0 | 5 | 1 | 0 |
| Cummings, Jeremy, Memphis | 0 | 1 | .000 | 4.50 | 1 | 1 | 0 | 0 | 0 | 0 | 6.0 | 9 | 28 | 7 | 3 | 2 | 0 | 0 | 0 | 1 | 0 | 5 | 0 | 0 |
| Daigle, Casey, Tucson | 4 | 9 | .308 | 6.88 | 18 | 15 | 0 | 0 | 0 | 0 | 100.2 | 154 | 474 | 85 | 77 | 21 | 4 | 4 | 5 | 24 | 0 | 51 | 3 | 0 |
| Deago, Roger, Portland * | 0 | 0 | .000 | 4.66 | 5 | 0 | 0 | 0 | 1 | 0 | 9.2 | 13 | 48 | 6 | 5 | 0 | 0 | 0 | 1 | 5 | 0 | 6 | 0 | 0 |
| Dickson, Jason, Omaha | 4 | 5 | .444 | 6.93 | 13 | 12 | 0 | 0 | 0 | 0 | 61.0 | 95 | 289 | 53 | 47 | 14 | 3 | 2 | 7 | 13 | 0 | 26 | 3 | 1 |
| Donnels, Chris, Colorado Springs | 0 | 0 | .000 | 27.00 | 1 | 0 | 0 | 0 | 1 | 0 | 1.1 | 5 | 9 | 4 | 4 | 2 | 0 | 0 | 0 | 0 | 0 | 1 | 0 | 0 |
| Downs, Scott, Edmonton | 10 | 6 | .625 | 3.52 | 22 | 22 | 2 | 2 | 0 | 0 | 135.1 | 143 | 559 | 57 | 53 | 16 | 10 | 3 | 3 | 26 | 0 | 67 | 1 | 1 |
| Driskill, Travis, Colorado Springs | 5 | 5 | .500 | 5.40 | 28 | 13 | 0 | 0 | 4 | 2 | 111.2 | 141 | 491 | 70 | 67 | 18 | 8 | 4 | 5 | 24 | 0 | 81 | 10 | 0 |
| Duckworth, Brandon, New Orleans | 5 | 5 | .500 | 5.53 | 14 | 13 | 0 | 0 | 0 | 0 | 70.0 | 81 | 314 | 44 | 43 | 10 | 5 | 4 | 4 | 28 | 1 | 63 | 3 | 0 |
| Dunn, Scott, Salt Lake | 10 | 4 | .714 | 3.21 | 46 | 6 | 0 | 0 | 9 | 1 | 89.2 | 72 | 393 | 36 | 32 | 6 | 1 | 3 | 3 | 56 | 0 | 84 | 4 | 0 |
| Eckelman, Alex, New Orleans | 0 | 0 | .000 | 24.00 | 2 | 0 | 0 | 0 | 1 | 0 | 3.0 | 11 | 20 | 8 | 8 | 2 | 0 | 0 | 0 | 0 | 0 | 1 | 0 | 0 |
| Eckenstahler, Eric, Iowa * | 2 | 0 | 1.000 | 3.60 | 8 | 0 | 0 | 0 | 5 | 0 | 10.0 | 11 | 44 | 4 | 4 | 0 | 0 | 0 | 1 | 2 | 0 | 10 | 0 | 0 |
| Eckert, Harold, Las Vegas | 4 | 3 | .571 | 6.35 | 31 | 9 | 0 | 0 | 5 | 0 | 83.2 | 103 | 389 | 66 | 59 | 14 | 2 | 3 | 5 | 42 | 1 | 81 | 2 | 0 |
| Emanuel, Brandon, Salt Lake | 5 | 8 | .385 | 6.08 | 38 | 7 | 0 | 0 | 10 | 3 | 84.1 | 115 | 389 | 68 | 57 | 14 | 2 | 2 | 0 | 26 | 0 | 75 | 3 | 0 |
| Enochs, Chris, New Orleans | 6 | 8 | .429 | 4.15 | 38 | 14 | 1 | 0 | 5 | 0 | 112.2 | 114 | 487 | 61 | 52 | 11 | 5 | 9 | 8 | 35 | 2 | 92 | 5 | 1 |
| Erickson, Scott, Oklahoma * | 0 | 1 | .000 | 9.82 | 2 | 2 | 0 | 0 | 0 | 0 | 11.0 | 17 | 59 | 13 | 12 | 1 | 0 | 1 | 2 | 9 | 0 | 11 | 1 | 0 |
| Estrella, Leo, Fresno | 0 | 8 | .000 | 7.65 | 38 | 5 | 0 | 0 | 8 | 0 | 77.2 | 125 | 383 | 71 | 66 | 15 | 2 | 1 | 3 | 33 | 0 | 34 | 6 | 0 |
| Evert, Brett, Tacoma | 0 | 2 | .000 | 6.48 | 2 | 2 | 0 | 0 | 0 | 0 | 8.1 | 6 | 41 | 8 | 6 | 1 | 0 | 0 | 1 | 10 | 0 | 7 | 1 | 0 |
| Falkenborg, Brian, Las Vegas | 4 | 6 | .400 | 6.17 | 18 | 16 | 0 | 0 | 2 | 1 | 89.0 | 104 | 394 | 66 | 61 | 17 | 5 | 6 | 4 | 25 | 0 | 87 | 3 | 0 |
| Farmer, Tom, Las Vegas | 7 | 7 | .500 | 4.59 | 47 | 7 | 0 | 0 | 15 | 3 | 82.1 | 105 | 387 | 54 | 42 | 9 | 2 | 0 | 3 | 34 | 1 | 70 | 8 | 0 |
| Fatheree, Danny, New Orleans | 0 | 0 | .000 | 18.00 | 1 | 0 | 0 | 0 | 1 | 0 | 1.0 | 2 | 5 | 2 | 2 | 2 | 0 | 0 | 0 | 0 | 0 | 0 | 0 | 0 |
| Fernandez, Jared, New Orleans | 7 | 11 | .389 | 4.77 | 35 | 28 | 3 | 0 | 3 | 0 | 196.1 | 208 | 822 | 120 | 104 | 27 | 9 | 7 | 5 | 46 | 2 | 98 | 7 | 0 |
| Ferrari, Anthony, Edmonton * | 3 | 2 | .600 | 5.43 | 39 | 0 | 0 | 0 | 12 | 0 | 64.2 | 80 | 311 | 41 | 39 | 12 | 0 | 0 | 7 | 30 | 1 | 31 | 10 | 0 |
| Figueroa, Nelson, Nashville | 12 | 8 | .600 | 4.19 | 25 | 23 | 3 | 1 | 1 | 0 | 152.1 | 168 | 648 | 79 | 71 | 20 | 6 | 3 | 4 | 36 | 1 | 129 | 2 | 0 |
| Fikac, Jeremy, Edmonton | 5 | 5 | .500 | 6.02 | 28 | 0 | 0 | 0 | 10 | 1 | 40.1 | 44 | 189 | 30 | 27 | 9 | 0 | 0 | 2 | 21 | 1 | 33 | 3 | 0 |
| Flores, Randy, Memphis | 5 | 7 | .417 | 3.82 | 36 | 15 | 1 | 1 | 4 | 2 | 122.2 | 115 | 512 | 60 | 52 | 10 | 8 | 4 | 3 | 46 | 1 | 99 | 1 | 0 |
| Flores, Ron, Sacramento * | 4 | 3 | .571 | 3.83 | 55 | 0 | 0 | 0 | 13 | 1 | 54.0 | 60 | 241 | 27 | 23 | 5 | 0 | 1 | 0 | 19 | 4 | 55 | 3 | 0 |
| Florie, Bryce, Albuquerque | 1 | 1 | .500 | 2.45 | 11 | 0 | 0 | 0 | 2 | 0 | 14.2 | 12 | 60 | 4 | 4 | 1 | 0 | 0 | 0 | 5 | 0 | 9 | 0 | 0 |

| Pitcher, Team | W | L | Pct. | ERA | G | GS | CG | ShO | GF | Sv. | IP | H | TBF | R | ER | HR | SH | SF | HB | BB | IBB | SO | WP | Bk. |
|---|---|---|---|---|---|---|---|---|---|---|---|---|---|---|---|---|---|---|---|---|---|---|---|---|
| Foppert, Jesse, Fresno | 0 | 2 | .000 | 5.52 | 4 | 4 | 0 | 0 | 0 | 0 | 14.2 | 14 | 66 | 11 | 9 | 2 | 3 | 1 | 0 | 9 | 0 | 13 | 3 | 0 |
| Freed, Mark, Tucson * | 3 | 2 | .600 | 4.35 | 57 | 0 | 0 | 0 | 16 | 2 | 70.1 | 74 | 317 | 37 | 34 | 4 | 2 | 1 | 2 | 35 | 5 | 45 | 2 | 0 |
| Fulmer, T.A., Tacoma | 0 | 0 | .000 | 0.00 | 3 | 0 | 0 | 0 | 2 | 2 | 6.0 | 2 | 23 | 0 | 0 | 0 | 0 | 0 | 0 | 3 | 0 | 4 | 0 | 0 |
| Fussell, Chris, Nashville | 2 | 5 | .286 | 4.97 | 51 | 1 | 0 | 0 | 18 | 2 | 67.0 | 73 | 307 | 39 | 37 | 10 | 1 | 0 | 5 | 32 | 2 | 50 | 5 | 0 |
| Garcia, Jairo, Sacramento | 1 | 2 | .333 | 3.95 | 11 | 0 | 0 | 0 | 10 | 1 | 13.2 | 10 | 60 | 6 | 6 | 1 | 0 | 0 | 0 | 9 | 1 | 21 | 0 | 0 |
| Garcia, James, Fresno | 0 | 1 | .000 | 5.19 | 8 | 7 | 0 | 0 | 0 | 0 | 34.2 | 35 | 150 | 20 | 20 | 7 | 1 | 4 | 5 | 16 | 1 | 34 | 2 | 0 |
| Garcia, Luis, Las Vegas | 0 | 0 | .000 | 0.00 | 1 | 0 | 0 | 0 | 1 | 0 | 1.0 | 1 | 4 | 0 | 0 | 0 | 0 | 0 | 0 | 0 | 0 | 1 | 0 | 0 |
| Garcia, Rosman, Oklahoma | 4 | 6 | .400 | 4.65 | 41 | 0 | 0 | 0 | 10 | 2 | 71.2 | 87 | 348 | 41 | 37 | 6 | 0 | 0 | 3 | 36 | 3 | 49 | 5 | 0 |
| Gardner, Lee, Fresno | 7 | 4 | .636 | 4.46 | 57 | 0 | 0 | 0 | 16 | 1 | 70.2 | 79 | 313 | 40 | 35 | 8 | 1 | 2 | 1 | 22 | 3 | 42 | 5 | 0 |
| George, Chris, Omaha * | 8 | 6 | .571 | 3.42 | 20 | 19 | 2 | 1 | 0 | 0 | 105.1 | 97 | 435 | 45 | 40 | 7 | 6 | 5 | 2 | 40 | 0 | 74 | 4 | 1 |
| Germano, Justin, Portland | 9 | 5 | .643 | 3.38 | 20 | 20 | 2 | 2 | 0 | 0 | 122.2 | 113 | 496 | 48 | 46 | 12 | 5 | 6 | 5 | 25 | 0 | 98 | 3 | 0 |
| Gilfillan, Jason, Colorado Springs | 6 | 3 | .667 | 5.37 | 50 | 0 | 0 | 0 | 15 | 1 | 68.2 | 67 | 325 | 49 | 41 | 8 | 1 | 0 | 7 | 45 | 2 | 65 | 9 | 2 |
| Gissell, Chris, Colorado Springs | 14 | 2 | .875 | 3.67 | 24 | 8 | 0 | 0 | 2 | 0 | 90.2 | 80 | 366 | 41 | 37 | 11 | 3 | 3 | 5 | 17 | 0 | 74 | 1 | 2 |
| Gomes, Wayne, Sacramento | 3 | 2 | .600 | 3.81 | 51 | 0 | 0 | 0 | 15 | 2 | 78.0 | 99 | 360 | 41 | 33 | 6 | 2 | 1 | 4 | 26 | 1 | 54 | 4 | 2 |
| Good, Andrew, Tucson | 3 | 2 | .600 | 3.04 | 5 | 3 | 0 | 0 | 0 | 0 | 23.2 | 25 | 98 | 12 | 8 | 4 | 0 | 0 | 1 | 4 | 0 | 17 | 2 | 0 |
| Gosling, Mike, Tucson * | 9 | 5 | .643 | 5.82 | 24 | 21 | 0 | 0 | 0 | 0 | 128.1 | 160 | 581 | 101 | 83 | 16 | 5 | 8 | 3 | 53 | 0 | 67 | 12 | 0 |
| Green, Steve, Salt Lake | 5 | 17 | .227 | 7.66 | 29 | 29 | 1 | 0 | 0 | 0 | 136.1 | 186 | 665 | 131 | 116 | 14 | 8 | 12 | 5 | 85 | 0 | 93 | 8 | 1 |
| Griffiths, Jeremy, New Orleans | 3 | 6 | .333 | 5.85 | 15 | 14 | 0 | 0 | 0 | 0 | 80.0 | 95 | 349 | 55 | 52 | 9 | 6 | 9 | 3 | 26 | 1 | 58 | 5 | 0 |
| Hackman, Luther, Nashville | 1 | 5 | .167 | 5.36 | 37 | 0 | 0 | 0 | 12 | 1 | 43.2 | 42 | 190 | 29 | 26 | 6 | 0 | 0 | 2 | 15 | 2 | 45 | 1 | 1 |
| Hampton, Matt, Portland * | 2 | 2 | .500 | 4.88 | 37 | 1 | 0 | 0 | 10 | 0 | 59.0 | 59 | 257 | 35 | 32 | 7 | 0 | 0 | 5 | 17 | 1 | 51 | 2 | 0 |
| Hanrahan, Joel, Las Vegas | 7 | 7 | .500 | 5.05 | 25 | 22 | 0 | 0 | 1 | 0 | 119.1 | 128 | 548 | 78 | 67 | 22 | 9 | 7 | 7 | 75 | 0 | 97 | 9 | 0 |
| Hansell, Greg, Tucson | 1 | 0 | 1.000 | 4.87 | 15 | 0 | 0 | 0 | 3 | 0 | 20.1 | 25 | 101 | 11 | 11 | 5 | 0 | 0 | 2 | 13 | 0 | 23 | 3 | 0 |
| Haren, Danny, Memphis | 11 | 4 | .733 | 4.15 | 21 | 21 | 0 | 0 | 0 | 0 | 128.0 | 136 | 540 | 60 | 59 | 19 | 7 | 3 | 3 | 33 | 1 | 150 | 2 | 0 |
| Harris, Jeff, Tacoma | 5 | 3 | .625 | 4.34 | 26 | 8 | 1 | 1 | 4 | 1 | 74.2 | 60 | 302 | 37 | 36 | 6 | 1 | 2 | 4 | 26 | 0 | 53 | 4 | 0 |
| Harris, Reggie, New Orleans | 2 | 0 | 1.000 | 7.04 | 7 | 0 | 0 | 0 | 2 | 0 | 7.2 | 3 | 33 | 6 | 6 | 1 | 0 | 0 | 1 | 6 | 0 | 11 | 2 | 0 |
| Heaverlo, Jeff, Tacoma | 1 | 0 | 1.000 | 4.76 | 5 | 0 | 0 | 0 | 1 | 0 | 5.2 | 5 | 26 | 3 | 3 | 0 | 0 | 0 | 1 | 2 | 0 | 7 | 0 | 0 |
| Helling, Rick, Oklahoma | 1 | 4 | .200 | 9.00 | 6 | 6 | 0 | 0 | 0 | 0 | 31.0 | 59 | 149 | 35 | 31 | 8 | 3 | 1 | 0 | 11 | 0 | 20 | 1 | 0 |
| Henrie, Matt, Tucson | 1 | 4 | .200 | 6.70 | 8 | 7 | 0 | 0 | 1 | 0 | 44.1 | 63 | 192 | 34 | 33 | 5 | 1 | 1 | 0 | 10 | 0 | 17 | 1 | 0 |
| Hensley, Matt, Salt Lake | 1 | 3 | .250 | 2.93 | 30 | 0 | 0 | 0 | 23 | 5 | 43.0 | 29 | 170 | 16 | 14 | 6 | 0 | 0 | 2 | 12 | 0 | 49 | 0 | 0 |
| Herrera, Alex, Colorado Springs * | 6 | 3 | .667 | 5.24 | 37 | 7 | 0 | 0 | 8 | 1 | 77.1 | 77 | 362 | 49 | 45 | 10 | 3 | 1 | 3 | 57 | 1 | 72 | 4 | 1 |
| Hernandez, Carlos, New Orleans* | 9 | 4 | .692 | 3.60 | 23 | 23 | 0 | 0 | 8 | 0 | 127.2 | 115 | 528 | 54 | 51 | 9 | — | — | 5 | 46 | 1 | 81 | 3 | — |
| Hoerman, Jared, Tacoma | 5 | 1 | .833 | 4.91 | 39 | 1 | 0 | 0 | 13 | 1 | 62.1 | 68 | 301 | 38 | 34 | 7 | 0 | 0 | 6 | 40 | 1 | 34 | 2 | 0 |
| Horgan, Joe, Memphis * | 0 | 1 | .000 | 6.52 | 10 | 0 | 0 | 0 | 6 | 0 | 9.2 | 14 | 45 | 7 | 7 | 3 | 1 | 1 | 0 | 3 | 0 | 8 | 1 | 0 |
| Horgan, Joe, Edmonton * | 1 | 0 | 1.000 | 3.18 | 13 | 0 | 0 | 0 | 4 | 0 | 17.0 | 15 | 70 | 6 | 6 | 2 | 0 | 0 | 2 | 4 | 0 | 11 | 1 | 0 |
| Howard, Ben, Albuquerque | 3 | 0 | 1.000 | 3.67 | 23 | 0 | 0 | 0 | 4 | 1 | 34.1 | 29 | 151 | 16 | 14 | 3 | 0 | 0 | 0 | 22 | 2 | 28 | 4 | 0 |
| Hudgins, John, Oklahoma | 0 | 1 | .000 | 7.50 | 3 | 2 | 0 | 0 | 0 | 0 | 12.0 | 19 | 61 | 10 | 10 | 1 | 0 | 1 | 1 | 5 | 0 | 8 | 0 | 0 |
| Huerta, Edgar, Portland * | 1 | 0 | 1.000 | 1.17 | 6 | 0 | 0 | 0 | 1 | 0 | 7.2 | 4 | 32 | 1 | 1 | 0 | 3 | 0 | 0 | 6 | 1 | 4 | 1 | 0 |
| Hughes, Travis, Oklahoma | 1 | 2 | .333 | 5.26 | 13 | 0 | 0 | 0 | 2 | 0 | 25.2 | 21 | 107 | 15 | 15 | 2 | 0 | 0 | 0 | 9 | 0 | 24 | 2 | 0 |
| Huisman, Justin, Omaha | 4 | 2 | .667 | 3.61 | 32 | 0 | 0 | 0 | 21 | 6 | 42.1 | 49 | 197 | 23 | 17 | 3 | 0 | 0 | 1 | 18 | 2 | 37 | 2 | 0 |
| Izquierdo, Hansel, Nashville | 1 | 1 | .500 | 4.26 | 5 | 4 | 0 | 0 | 0 | 0 | 19.0 | 24 | 85 | 10 | 9 | 0 | 0 | 3 | 2 | 4 | 0 | 20 | 1 | 0 |
| Jackson, Edwin, Las Vegas | 6 | 4 | .600 | 5.86 | 19 | 19 | 0 | 0 | 0 | 0 | 90.2 | 90 | 410 | 65 | 59 | 4 | 9 | 6 | 8 | 55 | 1 | 70 | 10 | 0 |
| Jacome, Jason, Fresno * | 0 | 2 | .000 | 3.49 | 35 | 2 | 0 | 0 | 6 | 0 | 67.0 | 81 | 300 | 29 | 26 | 6 | 1 | 1 | 3 | 17 | 0 | 43 | 4 | 0 |
| Jarvis, Kevin, Nashville | 2 | 5 | .286 | 4.11 | 11 | 11 | 1 | 0 | 0 | 0 | 65.2 | 93 | 288 | 31 | 30 | 3 | 4 | 3 | 2 | 12 | 1 | 46 | 0 | 0 |
| Jensen, Ryan, Fresno | 10 | 7 | .588 | 5.36 | 30 | 26 | 0 | 0 | 1 | 0 | 169.2 | 178 | 745 | 105 | 101 | 23 | 8 | 13 | 2 | 81 | 2 | 127 | 14 | 0 |
| Johnson, Mark, Las Vegas | 6 | 12 | .333 | 5.39 | 37 | 21 | 0 | 0 | 9 | 2 | 140.1 | 171 | 622 | 91 | 84 | 16 | 8 | 10 | 3 | 42 | 2 | 89 | 11 | 0 |
| Johnson, Mike, Edmonton | 6 | 6 | .500 | 5.93 | 30 | 14 | 1 | 0 | 3 | 0 | 101.2 | 128 | 455 | 70 | 67 | 17 | 4 | 5 | 4 | 29 | 1 | 77 | 7 | 0 |
| Johnson, Russ, Iowa | 0 | 0 | .000 | 6.75 | 2 | 0 | 0 | 0 | 2 | 0 | 4.0 | 5 | 19 | 3 | 3 | 1 | 0 | 0 | 0 | 2 | 0 | 1 | 0 | 0 |
| Johnston, Mike, Nashville * | 0 | 0 | .000 | 8.40 | 19 | 0 | 0 | 0 | 1 | 0 | 15.0 | 19 | 79 | 14 | 14 | 3 | 0 | 0 | 2 | 13 | 1 | 6 | 0 | 0 |
| Jones, Greg, Salt Lake | 1 | 4 | .200 | 5.74 | 36 | 0 | 0 | 0 | 11 | 3 | 53.1 | 63 | 244 | 38 | 34 | 11 | 0 | 0 | 2 | 19 | 0 | 43 | 2 | 0 |
| Journell, Jimmy, Memphis | 0 | 0 | .000 | 0.00 | 4 | 0 | 0 | 0 | 2 | 1 | 2.2 | 4 | 13 | 0 | 0 | 0 | 0 | 0 | 0 | 1 | 0 | 5 | 0 | 0 |
| Karp, Josh, Edmonton | 4 | 10 | .286 | 5.95 | 24 | 24 | 0 | 0 | 0 | 0 | 127.0 | 147 | 557 | 91 | 84 | 17 | 9 | 7 | 9 | 51 | 1 | 102 | 11 | 1 |
| Kelly, John, Tacoma | 1 | 2 | .333 | 5.23 | 7 | 2 | 0 | 0 | 1 | 0 | 20.2 | 25 | 91 | 12 | 12 | 1 | 1 | 0 | 0 | 8 | 0 | 27 | 2 | 0 |
| Ketchner, Ryan, Las Vegas * | 0 | 0 | .000 | 1.29 | 1 | 1 | 0 | 0 | 0 | 0 | 7.0 | 5 | 25 | 1 | 1 | 1 | 0 | 0 | 0 | 0 | 0 | 4 | 0 | 0 |
| Knott, Eric, Las Vegas * | 0 | 2 | .000 | 5.00 | 12 | 0 | 0 | 0 | 3 | 0 | 18.0 | 18 | 77 | 13 | 10 | 4 | 0 | 0 | 1 | 6 | 0 | 9 | 0 | 0 |
| Koronka, John, Iowa * | 12 | 9 | .571 | 4.34 | 29 | 23 | 2 | 2 | 1 | 0 | 153.1 | 164 | 666 | 86 | 74 | 19 | 8 | 9 | 5 | 65 | 3 | 116 | 6 | 5 |
| Kroon, Marc, Colorado Springs | 2 | 3 | .400 | 2.72 | 50 | 0 | 0 | 0 | 44 | 20 | 49.2 | 44 | 220 | 23 | 15 | 3 | 0 | 0 | 1 | 26 | 0 | 72 | 9 | 0 |
| Lehr, Justin, Sacramento | 4 | 2 | .667 | 2.65 | 32 | 0 | 0 | 0 | 28 | 13 | 37.1 | 37 | 159 | 14 | 11 | 1 | 0 | 1 | 1 | 10 | 0 | 40 | 6 | 0 |
| Linton, Doug, Omaha | 3 | 9 | .250 | 7.59 | 27 | 13 | 1 | 0 | 7 | 1 | 99.2 | 143 | 465 | 86 | 84 | 23 | 4 | 3 | 6 | 18 | 1 | 81 | 9 | 0 |
| Lizarraga, Sergio, Tucson | 1 | 1 | .500 | 9.90 | 3 | 2 | 0 | 0 | 0 | 0 | 10.0 | 19 | 53 | 14 | 11 | 5 | 0 | 1 | 0 | 7 | 0 | 9 | 1 | 0 |
| Loe, Kameron, Oklahoma | 5 | 2 | .714 | 3.27 | 8 | 8 | 0 | 0 | 0 | 0 | 52.1 | 52 | 206 | 20 | 19 | 6 | 1 | 0 | 2 | 13 | 0 | 42 | 2 | 0 |
| Looper, Aaron, Tacoma | 1 | 0 | 1.000 | 4.26 | 8 | 0 | 0 | 0 | 2 | 0 | 12.2 | 15 | 59 | 6 | 6 | 1 | 2 | 0 | 2 | 3 | 0 | 13 | 0 | 0 |
| Lyon, Brandon, Tucson | 2 | 3 | .400 | 15.12 | 6 | 3 | 0 | 0 | 1 | 0 | 8.1 | 15 | 45 | 14 | 14 | 3 | 0 | 0 | 0 | 4 | 0 | 4 | 0 | 0 |
| Mabeus, Chris, Sacramento | 7 | 2 | .778 | 3.00 | 38 | 0 | 0 | 0 | 17 | 4 | 51.0 | 45 | 211 | 18 | 17 | 6 | 0 | 0 | 1 | 12 | 1 | 61 | 0 | 2 |
| Mahomes, Pat, Edmonton | 4 | 4 | .500 | 4.88 | 20 | 0 | 0 | 0 | 20 | 6 | 24.0 | 25 | 111 | 14 | 13 | 1 | 0 | 0 | 0 | 14 | 1 | 19 | 1 | 0 |
| Mahomes, Pat, Albuquerque | 0 | 4 | .000 | 7.29 | 16 | 0 | 0 | 0 | 4 | 0 | 21.0 | 31 | 104 | 19 | 17 | 6 | 0 | 0 | 1 | 9 | 1 | 15 | 0 | 0 |
| Mahomes, Pat, Nashville | 2 | 4 | .333 | 5.77 | 24 | 2 | 0 | 0 | 12 | 2 | 34.1 | 36 | 151 | 23 | 22 | 0 | 0 | 1 | 0 | 14 | 0 | 31 | 0 | 0 |
| Mann, Jim, Nashville | 1 | 3 | .250 | 11.47 | 20 | 0 | 0 | 0 | 6 | 0 | 24.1 | 40 | 127 | 32 | 31 | 8 | 0 | 0 | 5 | 9 | 3 | 25 | 0 | 0 |
| Martin, Greg, Nashville * | 0 | 1 | .000 | 7.50 | 5 | 1 | 0 | 0 | 1 | 0 | 12.0 | 15 | 57 | 10 | 10 | 0 | 0 | 1 | 0 | 7 | 0 | 7 | 4 | 0 |
| Martinez, Gustavo, Tacoma | 6 | 7 | .462 | 4.89 | 18 | 17 | 0 | 0 | 1 | 0 | 99.1 | 118 | 455 | 61 | 54 | 9 | 5 | 5 | 8 | 55 | 0 | 70 | 7 | 1 |
| Martinez, Luis, Memphis * | 0 | 5 | .000 | 5.06 | 7 | 7 | 0 | 0 | 0 | 0 | 42.2 | 53 | 196 | 26 | 24 | 7 | 6 | 0 | 2 | 23 | 1 | 35 | 5 | 0 |
| Martinez, Luis, Colorado Springs | 2 | 2 | .500 | 6.83 | 5 | 4 | 0 | 0 | 0 | 0 | 27.2 | 34 | 131 | 22 | 21 | 4 | 2 | 1 | 1 | 16 | 0 | 21 | 2 | 1 |
| Mathews, T.J., Las Vegas | 1 | 0 | 1.000 | 4.50 | 13 | 0 | 0 | 0 | 7 | 5 | 18.0 | 17 | 75 | 9 | 9 | 2 | 0 | 0 | 0 | 4 | 1 | 12 | 0 | 0 |
| Mazone, Brian, Fresno * | 1 | 0 | 1.000 | 4.63 | 2 | 2 | 0 | 0 | 0 | 0 | 11.2 | 17 | 53 | 6 | 6 | 3 | 0 | 0 | 0 | 3 | 0 | 6 | 1 | 0 |
| McGlinchy, Kevin, Iowa | 0 | 4 | .000 | 5.45 | 7 | 6 | 0 | 0 | 0 | 0 | 36.1 | 54 | 162 | 22 | 22 | 7 | 2 | 3 | 2 | 8 | 0 | 29 | 0 | 0 |
| McLeary, Marty, Portland | 5 | 4 | .556 | 2.99 | 44 | 7 | 0 | 0 | 23 | 13 | 84.1 | 65 | 357 | 30 | 28 | 4 | 3 | 0 | 5 | 42 | 1 | 81 | 5 | 1 |
| Medders, Brandon, Tucson | 0 | 0 | .000 | 4.26 | 11 | 0 | 0 | 0 | 3 | 0 | 12.2 | 15 | 60 | 7 | 6 | 3 | 1 | 0 | 0 | 4 | 1 | 17 | 0 | 0 |
| Miadich, Bart, Oklahoma | 1 | 0 | 1.000 | 4.45 | 20 | 0 | 0 | 0 | 13 | 2 | 28.1 | 23 | 129 | 14 | 14 | 3 | 0 | 0 | 1 | 20 | 0 | 34 | 5 | 0 |
| Michalak, Chris, Albuquerque * | 1 | 1 | .500 | 6.35 | 17 | 1 | 0 | 0 | 4 | 0 | 34.0 | 44 | 155 | 24 | 24 | 9 | 0 | 0 | 1 | 15 | 0 | 20 | 1 | 2 |
| Middlebrook, Jason, Salt Lake | 7 | 10 | .412 | 6.94 | 29 | 29 | 0 | 0 | 0 | 0 | 155.2 | 220 | 706 | 126 | 120 | 31 | 5 | 9 | 2 | 50 | 0 | 93 | 6 | 2 |

| Pitcher, Team | W | L | Pct. | ERA | G | GS | CG | ShO | GF | Sv. | IP | H | TBF | R | ER | HR | SH | SF | HB | BB | IBB | SO | WP | Bk. |
|---|---|---|---|---|---|---|---|---|---|---|---|---|---|---|---|---|---|---|---|---|---|---|---|---|
| Mitchell, Nathan, Iowa | 0 | 0 | .000 | 9.00 | 1 | 0 | 0 | 0 | 0 | 0 | 1.0 | 2 | 7 | 1 | 1 | 0 | 0 | 0 | 0 | 2 | 1 | 1 | 0 | 0 |
| Mitre, Sergio, Iowa | 6 | 3 | .667 | 2.98 | 18 | 15 | 1 | 1 | 1 | 1 | 102.2 | 97 | 424 | 38 | 34 | 9 | 8 | 0 | 6 | 39 | 1 | 95 | 7 | 1 |
| Mottl, Ryan, Nashville | 2 | 0 | 1.000 | 3.86 | 2 | 2 | 0 | 0 | 0 | 0 | 11.2 | 12 | 54 | 6 | 5 | 3 | 0 | 1 | 3 | 2 | 1 | 9 | 0 | 0 |
| Munter, Scott, Fresno | 1 | 1 | .500 | 3.45 | 13 | 0 | 0 | 0 | 6 | 1 | 15.2 | 20 | 71 | 8 | 6 | 1 | 0 | 0 | 0 | 4 | 0 | 5 | 1 | 0 |
| Nannini, Mike, Albuquerque | 9 | 10 | .474 | 5.29 | 29 | 25 | 1 | 1 | 1 | 0 | 151.1 | 156 | 637 | 99 | 89 | 31 | 7 | 6 | 5 | 42 | 0 | 111 | 3 | 0 |
| Narron, Sam, Oklahoma * | 8 | 2 | .800 | 4.43 | 17 | 16 | 1 | 1 | 0 | 0 | 101.2 | 123 | 436 | 55 | 50 | 14 | 8 | 7 | 4 | 24 | 0 | 31 | 1 | 1 |
| Neu, Mike, Albuquerque | 1 | 2 | .333 | 6.57 | 35 | 0 | 0 | 0 | 17 | 6 | 38.1 | 47 | 192 | 33 | 28 | 2 | 0 | 0 | 6 | 24 | 1 | 28 | 4 | 0 |
| Nickle, Doug, Las Vegas | 2 | 2 | .500 | 4.73 | 20 | 1 | 0 | 0 | 6 | 2 | 32.1 | 35 | 148 | 19 | 17 | 0 | 2 | 0 | 0 | 21 | 0 | 19 | 3 | 0 |
| Nina, Elvin, Omaha | 0 | 1 | .000 | 6.75 | 6 | 0 | 0 | 0 | 2 | 0 | 5.1 | 8 | 27 | 4 | 4 | 0 | 0 | 0 | 0 | 3 | 0 | 5 | 2 | 0 |
| Nunez, Victor, Colorado Springs | 0 | 1 | .000 | 9.00 | 1 | 1 | 0 | 0 | 0 | 0 | 5.0 | 7 | 24 | 5 | 5 | 3 | 0 | 0 | 0 | 4 | 0 | 5 | 0 | 0 |
| Nunez, Vladimir, Colorado Springs | 2 | 4 | .333 | 5.40 | 22 | 7 | 0 | 0 | 12 | 3 | 58.1 | 69 | 255 | 39 | 35 | 4 | 1 | 1 | 2 | 18 | 0 | 55 | 3 | 0 |
| Nussbeck, Mark, Memphis | 2 | 1 | .667 | 3.50 | 3 | 3 | 1 | 0 | 0 | 0 | 18.0 | 21 | 78 | 7 | 7 | 1 | 0 | 0 | 2 | 4 | 1 | 14 | 0 | 0 |
| Ohman, Will, Iowa * | 3 | 3 | .500 | 4.30 | 45 | 1 | 0 | 0 | 6 | 0 | 52.1 | 53 | 245 | 28 | 25 | 6 | 0 | 1 | 2 | 29 | 1 | 75 | 4 | 0 |
| Olsen, Kevin, Albuquerque | 3 | 3 | .500 | 4.37 | 10 | 10 | 0 | 0 | 0 | 0 | 55.2 | 58 | 232 | 30 | 27 | 4 | 4 | 2 | 1 | 13 | 0 | 47 | 3 | 0 |
| Oropesa, Eddie, Portland * | 3 | 3 | .500 | 2.33 | 37 | 0 | 0 | 0 | 12 | 1 | 46.1 | 31 | 192 | 15 | 12 | 2 | 0 | 0 | 3 | 19 | 1 | 54 | 3 | 0 |
| Osborne, Donovan, Portland * | 2 | 2 | .500 | 8.56 | 7 | 2 | 0 | 0 | 2 | 0 | 13.2 | 26 | 71 | 14 | 13 | 4 | 1 | 1 | 1 | 5 | 0 | 12 | 1 | 0 |
| Oxspring, Chris, Portland | 6 | 4 | .600 | 3.99 | 17 | 17 | 0 | 0 | 0 | 0 | 85.2 | 82 | 378 | 45 | 38 | 7 | 7 | 3 | 2 | 44 | 1 | 81 | 5 | 0 |
| Parker, Christian, Edmonton | 1 | 3 | .250 | 8.07 | 8 | 7 | 0 | 0 | 0 | 0 | 29.0 | 46 | 135 | 26 | 26 | 4 | 2 | 3 | 0 | 13 | 0 | 17 | 3 | 1 |
| Paronto, Chad, Memphis | 5 | 3 | .625 | 2.13 | 47 | 0 | 0 | 0 | 20 | 4 | 55.0 | 46 | 241 | 20 | 13 | 3 | 0 | 0 | 5 | 25 | 3 | 38 | 1 | 1 |
| Parque, Jim, Tucson * | 3 | 2 | .600 | 6.30 | 12 | 8 | 0 | 0 | 0 | 0 | 50.0 | 73 | 231 | 39 | 35 | 8 | 4 | 1 | 1 | 14 | 1 | 17 | 1 | 0 |
| Parrott, Rhett, Memphis | 2 | 2 | .500 | 5.29 | 7 | 7 | 1 | 1 | 0 | 0 | 34.0 | 44 | 151 | 21 | 20 | 7 | 2 | 1 | 2 | 15 | 0 | 15 | 2 | 0 |
| Patterson, Danny, Memphis | 0 | 0 | .000 | 6.75 | 9 | 0 | 0 | 0 | 3 | 0 | 6.2 | 8 | 38 | 5 | 5 | 0 | 0 | 0 | 3 | 7 | 0 | 7 | 0 | 0 |
| Pavon, Julio, Fresno | 1 | 1 | .500 | 5.52 | 5 | 2 | 0 | 0 | 0 | 0 | 14.2 | 19 | 64 | 9 | 9 | 2 | 1 | 1 | 0 | 3 | 0 | 11 | 0 | 0 |
| Pearce, Josh, Memphis | 3 | 2 | .600 | 3.56 | 26 | 0 | 0 | 0 | 13 | 1 | 30.1 | 34 | 132 | 12 | 12 | 1 | 2 | 0 | 2 | 6 | 1 | 31 | 1 | 0 |
| Pelaez, Alex, Salt Lake | 0 | 0 | .000 | 18.00 | 1 | 0 | 0 | 0 | 1 | 0 | 1.0 | 3 | 6 | 2 | 2 | 1 | 0 | 0 | 0 | 0 | 0 | 0 | 0 | 0 |
| Pettyjohn, Adam, Sacramento * | 3 | 1 | .750 | 6.32 | 10 | 9 | 1 | 0 | 0 | 0 | 52.2 | 55 | 222 | 38 | 37 | 10 | 2 | 3 | 3 | 14 | 0 | 44 | 3 | 1 |
| Pickford, Kevin, Fresno * | 0 | 0 | .000 | 6.23 | 1 | 1 | 0 | 0 | 0 | 0 | 4.1 | 7 | 23 | 3 | 3 | 1 | 0 | 0 | 0 | 5 | 0 | 2 | 0 | 0 |
| Pinto, Renyel, Iowa * | 1 | 1 | .500 | 7.71 | 2 | 2 | 0 | 0 | 0 | 0 | 9.1 | 9 | 43 | 9 | 8 | 2 | 0 | 0 | 0 | 8 | 0 | 9 | 1 | 0 |
| Pote, Lou, Portland | 1 | 0 | 1.000 | 7.20 | 4 | 0 | 0 | 0 | 3 | 1 | 5.0 | 5 | 23 | 4 | 4 | 1 | 0 | 0 | 0 | 3 | 0 | 6 | 2 | 0 |
| Powell, Greg, New Orleans | 0 | 0 | .000 | 7.59 | 5 | 0 | 0 | 0 | 0 | 0 | 10.2 | 13 | 50 | 9 | 9 | 1 | 1 | 1 | 0 | 6 | 0 | 5 | 2 | 0 |
| Prieto, Chris, Memphis * | 0 | 0 | .000 | 0.00 | 1 | 0 | 0 | 0 | 1 | 0 | 2.0 | 0 | 7 | 0 | 0 | 0 | 0 | 0 | 0 | 1 | 0 | 0 | 0 | 0 |
| Pulsipher, Bill, Tacoma * | 1 | 1 | .500 | 2.92 | 2 | 2 | 0 | 0 | 0 | 0 | 12.1 | 13 | 54 | 5 | 4 | 0 | 0 | 1 | 1 | 4 | 0 | 5 | 0 | 0 |
| Raggio, Brady, Tucson | 5 | 6 | .455 | 5.81 | 56 | 2 | 0 | 0 | 18 | 2 | 83.2 | 113 | 384 | 65 | 54 | 17 | 1 | 3 | 2 | 23 | 2 | 68 | 5 | 1 |
| Ramos, Mario, Sacramento * | 4 | 7 | .364 | 6.08 | 29 | 16 | 0 | 0 | 1 | 0 | 94.2 | 119 | 432 | 73 | 64 | 15 | 5 | 5 | 5 | 35 | 1 | 90 | 2 | 3 |
| Randall, Scott, Omaha | 1 | 2 | .333 | 5.14 | 12 | 1 | 0 | 0 | 7 | 5 | 35.0 | 39 | 159 | 22 | 20 | 4 | 0 | 1 | 1 | 14 | 0 | 21 | 1 | 0 |
| Rawson, Anthony, Memphis * | 1 | 0 | 1.000 | 0.00 | 3 | 0 | 0 | 0 | 2 | 0 | 3.0 | 0 | 10 | 0 | 0 | 0 | 0 | 0 | 0 | 1 | 0 | 1 | 0 | 0 |
| Reames, Britt, Sacramento | 3 | 5 | .375 | 4.67 | 34 | 3 | 0 | 0 | 16 | 8 | 52.0 | 55 | 240 | 27 | 27 | 5 | 0 | 0 | 2 | 28 | 5 | 57 | 5 | 0 |
| Redding, Tim, New Orleans | 1 | 3 | .250 | 6.04 | 5 | 5 | 0 | 0 | 0 | 0 | 28.1 | 30 | 127 | 21 | 19 | 2 | 1 | 1 | 2 | 12 | 0 | 26 | 3 | 1 |
| Regilio, Nick, Oklahoma | 6 | 5 | .545 | 4.71 | 17 | 17 | 0 | 0 | 0 | 0 | 91.2 | 98 | 399 | 49 | 48 | 6 | 2 | 3 | 3 | 46 | 0 | 72 | 4 | 0 |
| Reid, Justin, Nashville | 5 | 3 | .625 | 3.96 | 32 | 16 | 0 | 0 | 6 | 2 | 122.2 | 112 | 504 | 56 | 54 | 18 | 10 | 6 | 2 | 35 | 3 | 121 | 3 | 0 |
| Reyes, Al, Memphis | 2 | 2 | .500 | 2.95 | 37 | 0 | 0 | 0 | 33 | 23 | 39.2 | 32 | 168 | 13 | 13 | 7 | 0 | 0 | 3 | 14 | 3 | 47 | 0 | 0 |
| Rheinecker, John, Sacramento * | 11 | 9 | .550 | 4.44 | 28 | 27 | 0 | 0 | 1 | 0 | 172.1 | 192 | 757 | 102 | 85 | 22 | 9 | 5 | 15 | 51 | 3 | 129 | 8 | 0 |
| Risinger, Ben, Portland | 0 | 0 | .000 | 9.00 | 1 | 0 | 0 | 0 | 1 | 0 | 1.0 | 2 | 6 | 1 | 1 | 0 | 0 | 0 | 0 | 1 | 0 | 1 | 0 | 0 |
| Robertson, Jeriome, Edmonton * | 1 | 3 | .250 | 5.73 | 7 | 7 | 0 | 0 | 0 | 0 | 33.0 | 44 | 143 | 21 | 21 | 6 | 2 | 2 | 0 | 10 | 0 | 22 | 1 | 0 |
| Rodriguez, Nerio, Memphis | 5 | 3 | .625 | 5.67 | 16 | 13 | 0 | 0 | 1 | 0 | 73.0 | 80 | 317 | 50 | 46 | 13 | 5 | 3 | 7 | 30 | 0 | 46 | 2 | 0 |
| Rojas, Chris, Portland | 1 | 2 | .333 | 12.71 | 6 | 2 | 0 | 0 | 2 | 0 | 11.1 | 19 | 61 | 22 | 16 | 6 | 0 | 0 | 1 | 9 | 0 | 5 | 1 | 0 |
| Rueckel, Danny, Edmonton | 1 | 0 | 1.000 | 2.89 | 7 | 0 | 0 | 0 | 3 | 1 | 9.1 | 14 | 49 | 3 | 3 | 0 | 0 | 0 | 0 | 7 | 1 | 10 | 1 | 0 |
| Runion, Tony, Tacoma | 1 | 0 | 1.000 | 5.93 | 12 | 0 | 0 | 0 | 10 | 5 | 13.2 | 14 | 65 | 9 | 9 | 2 | 0 | 0 | 1 | 9 | 1 | 16 | 2 | 0 |
| Rust, Evan, Memphis | 3 | 1 | .750 | 5.74 | 28 | 5 | 0 | 0 | 7 | 0 | 47.0 | 57 | 221 | 35 | 30 | 6 | 0 | 3 | 4 | 21 | 2 | 37 | 1 | 0 |
| Ryan, Jason, Memphis | 1 | 7 | .125 | 7.36 | 14 | 13 | 0 | 0 | 0 | 0 | 66.0 | 98 | 317 | 62 | 54 | 18 | 6 | 2 | 3 | 30 | 0 | 34 | 6 | 0 |
| Ryan, Jason, Omaha * | 1 | 3 | .250 | 6.55 | 8 | 6 | 0 | 0 | 0 | 0 | 34.1 | 46 | 157 | 26 | 25 | 6 | 0 | 4 | 1 | 9 | 0 | 23 | 1 | 0 |
| Ryu, Jae-Kuk, Iowa | 0 | 0 | .000 | 40.50 | 1 | 0 | 0 | 0 | 0 | 0 | 0.2 | 2 | 5 | 4 | 3 | 1 | 0 | 0 | 0 | 1 | 0 | 0 | 0 | 0 |
| Saarloos, Kirk, Sacramento | 2 | 0 | 1.000 | 3.54 | 5 | 5 | 0 | 0 | 0 | 0 | 20.1 | 19 | 88 | 8 | 8 | 1 | 1 | 0 | 1 | 9 | 0 | 17 | 0 | 0 |
| Saarloos, Kirk, New Orleans | 0 | 2 | .000 | 15.43 | 2 | 2 | 0 | 0 | 0 | 0 | 7.0 | 17 | 40 | 15 | 12 | 4 | 0 | 1 | 0 | 1 | 0 | 6 | 0 | 0 |
| Saladin, Miguel, New Orleans | 1 | 6 | .143 | 4.04 | 49 | 0 | 0 | 0 | 27 | 6 | 64.2 | 51 | 274 | 30 | 29 | 3 | 0 | 0 | 1 | 30 | 1 | 42 | 3 | 3 |
| Sanders, Scott, Albuquerque | 3 | 10 | .231 | 7.90 | 20 | 20 | 0 | 0 | 0 | 0 | 98.0 | 151 | 465 | 90 | 86 | 21 | 8 | 3 | 6 | 29 | 1 | 72 | 5 | 0 |
| Schroder, Chris, Edmonton | 2 | 1 | .667 | 4.39 | 17 | 1 | 0 | 0 | 5 | 0 | 26.2 | 24 | 120 | 13 | 13 | 3 | 0 | 0 | 1 | 15 | 0 | 32 | 2 | 0 |
| Sedlacek, Shawn, Iowa | 10 | 7 | .588 | 4.32 | 22 | 22 | 1 | 1 | 0 | 0 | 131.1 | 151 | 577 | 70 | 63 | 21 | 9 | 4 | 8 | 42 | 2 | 95 | 3 | 1 |
| Service, Scott, Tucson | 5 | 0 | 1.000 | 3.24 | 24 | 0 | 0 | 0 | 22 | 9 | 25.0 | 28 | 108 | 9 | 9 | 2 | 1 | 0 | 0 | 6 | 0 | 28 | 1 | 0 |
| Sessions, Doug, Edmonton | 1 | 1 | .500 | 4.07 | 7 | 3 | 0 | 0 | 2 | 0 | 24.1 | 31 | 104 | 13 | 11 | 3 | 2 | 1 | 0 | 6 | 1 | 11 | 1 | 0 |
| Shibilo, Andy, Iowa | 0 | 0 | .000 | 6.23 | 9 | 0 | 0 | 0 | 3 | 0 | 13.0 | 17 | 65 | 11 | 9 | 1 | 1 | 0 | 1 | 9 | 2 | 9 | 3 | 0 |
| Shibilo, Andy, Tacoma | 1 | 1 | .500 | 8.74 | 16 | 0 | 0 | 0 | 10 | 0 | 22.2 | 35 | 124 | 23 | 22 | 3 | 0 | 0 | 2 | 20 | 0 | 21 | 4 | 0 |
| Shuey, Paul, Las Vegas | 0 | 1 | .000 | 18.00 | 3 | 0 | 0 | 0 | 0 | 0 | 3.0 | 9 | 20 | 6 | 6 | 2 | 0 | 0 | 0 | 2 | 0 | 2 | 0 | 0 |
| Silva, Jose, Tucson | 2 | 3 | .400 | 7.07 | 9 | 8 | 0 | 0 | 1 | 0 | 42.0 | 59 | 195 | 33 | 33 | 5 | 4 | 4 | 3 | 18 | 0 | 31 | 5 | 0 |
| Simas, Bill, Tacoma | 1 | 1 | .500 | 3.86 | 9 | 0 | 0 | 0 | 5 | 0 | 11.2 | 10 | 48 | 5 | 5 | 3 | 0 | 0 | 1 | 2 | 0 | 8 | 0 | 0 |
| Simontacchi, Jason, Memphis | 7 | 4 | .636 | 4.33 | 33 | 8 | 0 | 0 | 9 | 2 | 81.0 | 101 | 356 | 44 | 39 | 8 | 6 | 6 | 4 | 12 | 2 | 55 | 5 | 0 |
| Simpson, Allan, Colorado Springs | 2 | 1 | .667 | 2.80 | 27 | 0 | 0 | 0 | 19 | 4 | 35.1 | 30 | 154 | 14 | 11 | 1 | 1 | 0 | 7 | 10 | 0 | 43 | 4 | 1 |
| Small, Aaron, Albuquerque | 9 | 9 | .500 | 5.06 | 27 | 24 | 2 | 0 | 1 | 0 | 154.2 | 199 | 671 | 95 | 87 | 18 | 5 | 4 | 3 | 29 | 2 | 109 | 5 | 0 |
| Smith, Roy, Las Vegas | 0 | 3 | .000 | 6.23 | 30 | 3 | 0 | 0 | 13 | 0 | 47.2 | 70 | 242 | 38 | 33 | 6 | 2 | 1 | 2 | 27 | 1 | 40 | 5 | 0 |
| Snare, Ryan, Oklahoma * | 11 | 6 | .647 | 4.72 | 26 | 24 | 0 | 0 | 0 | 0 | 137.1 | 171 | 608 | 88 | 72 | 16 | 8 | 8 | 3 | 49 | 0 | 79 | 9 | 0 |
| Sodowsky, Clint, Albuquerque | 9 | 7 | .563 | 5.40 | 48 | 0 | 0 | 0 | 12 | 2 | 68.1 | 76 | 318 | 45 | 41 | 8 | 0 | 1 | 5 | 32 | 1 | 39 | 3 | 0 |
| Soriano, Rafael, Tacoma | 0 | 0 | .000 | 2.45 | 3 | 3 | 0 | 0 | 0 | 0 | 3.2 | 2 | 15 | 1 | 1 | 1 | 0 | 0 | 0 | 2 | 0 | 5 | 0 | 0 |
| Stamler, Keith, Oklahoma | 7 | 3 | .700 | 3.35 | 48 | 1 | 0 | 0 | 17 | 3 | 83.1 | 79 | 359 | 39 | 31 | 8 | 0 | 0 | 4 | 26 | 6 | 40 | 3 | 0 |
| Stanifer, Rob, Edmonton | 5 | 4 | .556 | 4.27 | 37 | 0 | 0 | 0 | 11 | 1 | 59.0 | 65 | 263 | 29 | 28 | 4 | 0 | 0 | 3 | 18 | 1 | 46 | 3 | 0 |
| Stark, Denny, Colorado Springs | 8 | 2 | .800 | 3.50 | 14 | 13 | 0 | 0 | 0 | 0 | 79.2 | 73 | 331 | 36 | 31 | 9 | 0 | 4 | 3 | 26 | 0 | 51 | 1 | 1 |
| Stauffer, Tim, Portland | 6 | 3 | .667 | 3.54 | 14 | 14 | 0 | 0 | 0 | 0 | 81.1 | 83 | 345 | 46 | 32 | 15 | 4 | 3 | 3 | 26 | 1 | 50 | 1 | 1 |
| Steik, Richard, Portland | 1 | 0 | 1.000 | 37.80 | 2 | 0 | 0 | 0 | 0 | 0 | 1.2 | 7 | 15 | 7 | 7 | 0 | 0 | 0 | 0 | 3 | 0 | 1 | 0 | 0 |

CLASS AAA *Pacific Coast League*

| Pitcher, Team | W | L | Pct. | ERA | G | GS | CG | ShO | GF | Sv. | IP | H | TBF | R | ER | HR | SH | SF | HB | BB | IBB | SO | WP | Bk. |
|---|---|---|---|---|---|---|---|---|---|---|---|---|---|---|---|---|---|---|---|---|---|---|---|---|
| Stemle, Steve, Memphis | 6 | 3 | .667 | 3.30 | 54 | 0 | 0 | 0 | 11 | 3 | 76.1 | 85 | 332 | 28 | 28 | 7 | 1 | 0 | 3 | 12 | 2 | 42 | 1 | 0 |
| Stevenson, Jason, Edmonton * | 0 | 0 | .000 | 3.60 | 3 | 0 | 0 | 0 | 2 | 0 | 5.0 | 7 | 23 | 2 | 2 | 1 | 0 | 0 | 0 | 1 | 1 | 3 | 0 | 0 |
| Stocks, Nick, Memphis | 1 | 0 | 1.000 | 7.24 | 15 | 1 | 0 | 0 | 1 | 1 | 27.1 | 30 | 128 | 22 | 22 | 2 | 0 | 1 | 1 | 19 | 2 | 24 | 2 | 0 |
| Street, Huston, Sacramento | 0 | 0 | .000 | 0.00 | 2 | 0 | 0 | 0 | 1 | 1 | 2.0 | 2 | 8 | 0 | 0 | 0 | 0 | 0 | 0 | 0 | 0 | 2 | 0 | 0 |
| Sweeney, Brian, Portland | 11 | 4 | .733 | 3.83 | 24 | 23 | 0 | 0 | 1 | 0 | 138.2 | 130 | 577 | 65 | 59 | 16 | 9 | 6 | 1 | 42 | 1 | 110 | 6 | 0 |
| Sylvester, Billy, Oklahoma | 1 | 4 | .200 | 6.05 | 19 | 5 | 0 | 0 | 7 | 0 | 41.2 | 49 | 195 | 28 | 28 | 7 | 1 | 2 | 3 | 22 | 1 | 53 | 2 | 0 |
| Szuminski, Jason, Iowa | 3 | 2 | .600 | 4.94 | 41 | 2 | 0 | 0 | 24 | 8 | 51.0 | 57 | 248 | 40 | 28 | 6 | 1 | 1 | 3 | 35 | 5 | 31 | 1 | 0 |
| Tankersley, Dennis, Portland | 7 | 4 | .636 | 3.15 | 19 | 19 | 0 | 0 | 0 | 0 | 120.0 | 114 | 495 | 52 | 42 | 10 | 4 | 3 | 2 | 37 | 1 | 86 | 1 | 0 |
| Taschner, Jack, Fresno * | 4 | 7 | .364 | 9.28 | 18 | 9 | 0 | 0 | 4 | 0 | 53.1 | 71 | 258 | 59 | 55 | 14 | 1 | 2 | 3 | 32 | 1 | 44 | 3 | 0 |
| Tejera, Michael, Albuquerque * | 8 | 4 | .667 | 3.97 | 22 | 19 | 0 | 0 | 1 | 0 | 113.1 | 109 | 476 | 56 | 50 | 17 | 4 | 3 | 6 | 39 | 0 | 88 | 3 | 0 |
| Tolar, Kevin, Iowa * | 4 | 0 | 1.000 | 3.45 | 51 | 0 | 0 | 0 | 11 | 0 | 57.1 | 55 | 263 | 30 | 22 | 2 | 1 | 0 | 3 | 40 | 4 | 77 | 3 | 0 |
| Tollberg, Brian, Colorado Springs | 6 | 13 | .316 | 6.86 | 28 | 26 | 0 | 0 | 0 | 0 | 149.2 | 199 | 657 | 122 | 114 | 33 | 5 | 8 | 7 | 27 | 0 | 99 | 4 | 0 |
| Totten, Heath, Las Vegas | 8 | 11 | .421 | 5.40 | 28 | 27 | 1 | 0 | 1 | 0 | 160.0 | 212 | 700 | 107 | 96 | 28 | 9 | 6 | 4 | 29 | 0 | 93 | 2 | 0 |
| Tremie, Chris, New Orleans | 0 | 0 | .000 | 0.00 | 1 | 0 | 0 | 0 | 1 | 0 | 1.0 | 0 | 3 | 0 | 0 | 0 | 0 | 0 | 0 | 0 | 0 | 0 | 0 | 0 |
| Tsao, Chin-Hui, Colorado Springs | 1 | 1 | .500 | 8.53 | 4 | 4 | 0 | 0 | 0 | 0 | 12.2 | 22 | 64 | 12 | 12 | 5 | 0 | 1 | 0 | 5 | 0 | 14 | 0 | 0 |
| Turnbow, Derrick, Salt Lake | 2 | 6 | .250 | 5.06 | 46 | 3 | 0 | 0 | 23 | 6 | 74.2 | 75 | 336 | 46 | 42 | 8 | 2 | 3 | 3 | 42 | 0 | 56 | 7 | 0 |
| Urban, Jeff, Fresno * | 5 | 4 | .556 | 4.07 | 46 | 0 | 0 | 0 | 15 | 1 | 66.1 | 69 | 295 | 35 | 30 | 7 | 3 | 1 | 3 | 23 | 3 | 56 | 1 | 0 |
| Vaillancourt, Tim, Tucson | 0 | 1 | .000 | 4.15 | 1 | 1 | 0 | 0 | 0 | 0 | 4.1 | 5 | 18 | 2 | 2 | 0 | 0 | 0 | 0 | 0 | 0 | 7 | 0 | 0 |
| Valverde, Jose, Tucson | 1 | 1 | .500 | 4.22 | 10 | 1 | 0 | 0 | 4 | 3 | 10.2 | 9 | 48 | 5 | 5 | 0 | 0 | 0 | 2 | 5 | 0 | 5 | 1 | 0 |
| Van Buren, Jermaine, Iowa | 0 | 0 | .000 | 2.08 | 3 | 0 | 0 | 0 | 2 | 1 | 4.1 | 3 | 16 | 1 | 1 | 1 | 0 | 0 | 0 | 0 | 0 | 5 | 0 | 0 |
| Veres, Dave, Fresno | 0 | 4 | .000 | 5.97 | 29 | 0 | 0 | 0 | 24 | 12 | 28.2 | 34 | 131 | 22 | 19 | 5 | 0 | 1 | 0 | 9 | 2 | 22 | 2 | 1 |
| Villarreal, Oscar, Tucson | 0 | 2 | .000 | 14.34 | 6 | 5 | 0 | 0 | 0 | 0 | 10.2 | 20 | 55 | 17 | 17 | 3 | 0 | 0 | 0 | 4 | 0 | 12 | 2 | 0 |
| Wainwright, Adam, Memphis | 4 | 4 | .500 | 5.37 | 12 | 12 | 0 | 0 | 0 | 0 | 63.2 | 68 | 282 | 47 | 38 | 12 | 7 | 1 | 3 | 28 | 0 | 64 | 2 | 1 |
| Walker, Kevin, Fresno * | 1 | 3 | .250 | 4.26 | 48 | 1 | 0 | 0 | 16 | 1 | 69.2 | 79 | 325 | 33 | 33 | 8 | 0 | 0 | 4 | 35 | 4 | 62 | 8 | 0 |
| Walrond, Les, Omaha * | 11 | 5 | .688 | 3.06 | 19 | 19 | 1 | 1 | 0 | 0 | 123.2 | 114 | 515 | 46 | 42 | 12 | 6 | 4 | 3 | 41 | 0 | 107 | 7 | 2 |
| Ward, Bryan, Tacoma * | 1 | 1 | .500 | 4.10 | 7 | 7 | 0 | 0 | 0 | 0 | 41.2 | 46 | 182 | 25 | 19 | 5 | 0 | 4 | 0 | 12 | 0 | 34 | 1 | 0 |
| Wayne, Justin, Albuquerque | 1 | 5 | .167 | 6.58 | 13 | 13 | 0 | 0 | 0 | 0 | 65.2 | 82 | 303 | 53 | 48 | 11 | 7 | 2 | 7 | 34 | 1 | 43 | 6 | 0 |
| Webb, Alan, Portland * | 0 | 0 | .000 | 3.86 | 8 | 0 | 0 | 0 | 3 | 0 | 11.2 | 12 | 57 | 5 | 5 | 0 | 0 | 0 | 2 | 8 | 0 | 8 | 2 | 1 |
| Weber, Ben, Salt Lake | 0 | 2 | .000 | 8.64 | 15 | 0 | 0 | 0 | 6 | 1 | 16.2 | 27 | 87 | 25 | 16 | 3 | 0 | 0 | 1 | 9 | 1 | 18 | 0 | 0 |
| Wendell, Turk, Colorado Springs | 0 | 1 | .000 | 5.79 | 12 | 8 | 0 | 0 | 1 | 0 | 14.0 | 19 | 68 | 10 | 9 | 2 | 0 | 0 | 3 | 4 | 0 | 8 | 0 | 0 |
| Westmoreland, Clay, Albuquerque | 0 | 0 | .000 | 5.14 | 5 | 0 | 0 | 0 | 2 | 0 | 7.0 | 4 | 34 | 4 | 4 | 0 | 0 | 0 | 1 | 8 | 0 | 6 | 1 | 0 |
| White, Matt, Omaha * | 2 | 2 | .500 | 6.18 | 23 | 4 | 0 | 0 | 8 | 1 | 55.1 | 71 | 266 | 45 | 38 | 12 | 3 | 1 | 1 | 34 | 2 | 43 | 2 | 3 |
| Williams, Dave, Nashville | 6 | 2 | .750 | 3.47 | 21 | 21 | 0 | 0 | 0 | 0 | 116.2 | 113 | 486 | 52 | 45 | 10 | 7 | 4 | 4 | 33 | 2 | 103 | 2 | 0 |
| Williams, Randy, Tacoma * | 7 | 2 | .778 | 3.63 | 50 | 0 | 0 | 0 | 16 | 8 | 79.1 | 68 | 355 | 37 | 32 | 6 | 0 | 1 | 3 | 46 | 0 | 64 | 4 | 0 |
| Wilson, Kris, Omaha | 10 | 13 | .435 | 5.65 | 28 | 28 | 0 | 0 | 0 | 0 | 167.1 | 201 | 715 | 116 | 105 | 39 | 4 | 8 | 14 | 28 | 1 | 97 | 3 | 1 |
| Woodard, Steve, Memphis | 1 | 3 | .250 | 10.02 | 4 | 4 | 0 | 0 | 0 | 0 | 20.2 | 37 | 104 | 27 | 23 | 7 | 0 | 1 | 1 | 5 | 0 | 13 | 1 | 0 |
| Woods, Jake, Salt Lake * | 6 | 4 | .600 | 6.07 | 15 | 14 | 1 | 0 | 1 | 0 | 83.0 | 107 | 389 | 67 | 56 | 13 | 2 | 3 | 4 | 42 | 0 | 60 | 2 | 1 |
| Wuertz, Mike, Iowa | 1 | 1 | .500 | 2.42 | 37 | 0 | 0 | 0 | 35 | 19 | 44.2 | 30 | 179 | 13 | 12 | 4 | 0 | 0 | 0 | 15 | 2 | 59 | 0 | 0 |
| Young, Tim, Memphis * | 0 | 2 | .000 | 9.00 | 8 | 0 | 0 | 0 | 1 | 0 | 12.0 | 16 | 57 | 12 | 12 | 6 | 0 | 0 | 1 | 4 | 0 | 12 | 0 | 0 |
| Zerbe, Chad, Fresno * | 6 | 6 | .500 | 4.29 | 33 | 14 | 0 | 0 | 4 | 0 | 107.0 | 131 | 476 | 63 | 51 | 7 | 9 | 2 | 3 | 35 | 1 | 51 | 3 | 0 |
| Ziegler, Mike, Sacramento | 2 | 8 | .200 | 6.46 | 18 | 16 | 0 | 0 | 0 | 0 | 92.0 | 118 | 418 | 69 | 66 | 15 | 5 | 7 | 3 | 26 | 1 | 70 | 6 | 0 |

COMBINATION SHUTOUTS: **Albuquerque** (2)—Nannini-Neu-Manzanillo, Baker-Michalak. **Colorado Springs** (6)—Cook-Herrera-Simpson-Kroon, Stark-Dohmann-Kroon, Stark-Gissell-Simpson, Francis-Driskill, Francis-Herrera-Kroon, Bernero-Stark-Bumatay-Kroon-Simpson. **Edmonton** (1)—Sessions-Beltran. **Fresno** (6)—J. Garcia-Estrella-L. Anderson–Urban-T. Walker, Pettyjohn-Urban-Veres, Begg-Gardner-Veres, Zerbe-Correia-Jacome-Aardsma-Urban, Hennessey-Walker-Aardsma, Taschner-Estrella-Urban-Correia. **Iowa** (8)—Leicester-Bland-Beltran, Cash-Corey-Beltran, Rusch-Carrara-Bland-Corey, Cash-Carrara, Sedlacek-Glover-Wuertz, J. Anderson-Izquierdo, Mitre-Tolar-Izquierdo, Sedlacek-Tolar-Eckenstahler. **Las Vegas** (2)—Sturtze-Myers-Brohawn, E. Jackson-Carrara. **Memphis** (5)—Wainwright-Flores-Journell, Haren-Simontacchi-Paronto, Haren-Reyes-Creek, Benes-Stemle-Reyes, Benes-Rust-Paronto. **Nashville** (6)—Reid-Brooks, VanBenschoten-Hackman-Roberts, Almonte-Fussell-Corey, Figueroa-Mahomes-Corey, Izquierdo-Fussell-Mahomes, Mahomes-Fussell. **New Orleans** (6)—Qualls-Chouinard-Bullinger, C. Hernandez-Babula-Gallo, Hernandez-Backe, Hernandez-Enochs-Barzilla-Qualls, Hernandez-Springer, Enochs-Harris-Saladin. **Oklahoma** (7)—Regilio-Wasdin-Bacsik, Regilio-Burke-T. Williams, Dominguez-T. Williams, Regilio-Clontz, Narron-Bacsik-Miadich, Wasdin-Stamler, Loe-Stamler-Clontz. **Omaha** (4)—Voyles-Venafro-Camp, Wilson-Venafro, Ryan-Huisman, George-White. **Portland** (9)—Oxspring-McLeary-Byrdak, Tankersley-Neal-Miadich, Sweeney-Puffer-Bynum, McLeary-Oropesa-Bynum, Sweeney-Oropesa, Oxspring-Bynum-McLeary, Stauffer-Watkins-Hampton, Tankersley-Bynum-McLeary, Oxspring-Huerta-Webb. **Sacramento** (10)—Rheinecker-Pote-Lehr, Blanton-Cammack-Kohn, Wood-Pote-Ramos-Lehr, Wood-Reames-Gomes, Ramos-Cammack-Reames-Lehr, Rheinecker-Gomes, Saarloos-Ramos-Reames, Pettyjohn-Mabeus-Reames, Rhodes-Pettyjohn-Gwyn, Reames-Ramos-Cammack-Flores. **Tacoma** (5)—Thornton-R. Williams-Sherrill, Blackley-Atchison-Williams, G. Martinez-Hoerman, Harris-Christman-Runion, Kelly-Hoerman-Fulmer. **Tucson** (3)—Good-Villafuerte-Nance, Parque-Aquino-Nance, Cannon-Fetters.

NO-HIT GAMES: Downs, Edmonton, defeated Las Vegas, 4-0, June 11.

## 2004 FIELDING

### TEAM

| Team | G | PO | A | E | TC | DP | TP | PB | Pct. |
|---|---|---|---|---|---|---|---|---|---|
| Memphis | 144 | 3762 | 239 | 96 | 4097 | 152 | 0 | 17 | .977 |
| Albuquerque | 144 | 3787 | 274 | 99 | 4160 | 146 | 0 | 13 | .976 |
| Nashville | 142 | 3709 | 285 | 101 | 4095 | 123 | 0 | 11 | .975 |
| New Orleans | 144 | 3725 | 276 | 115 | 4116 | 132 | 0 | 15 | .972 |
| Edmonton | 143 | 3663 | 250 | 112 | 4025 | 145 | 0 | 11 | .972 |
| Iowa | 143 | 3728 | 258 | 120 | 4106 | 160 | 0 | 10 | .971 |
| Fresno | 144 | 3844 | 237 | 125 | 4206 | 151 | 0 | 15 | .970 |
| Colorado Springs | 143 | 3655 | 243 | 120 | 4018 | 128 | 0 | 14 | .970 |
| Tucson | 144 | 3760 | 244 | 129 | 4133 | 123 | 0 | 11 | .969 |
| Las Vegas | 143 | 3788 | 272 | 128 | 4188 | 125 | 0 | 24 | .969 |
| Oklahoma | 144 | 3800 | 287 | 134 | 4221 | 183 | 0 | 13 | .968 |
| Omaha | 144 | 3721 | 243 | 134 | 4098 | 128 | 0 | 15 | .967 |
| Portland | 144 | 3825 | 245 | 137 | 4207 | 125 | 0 | 12 | .967 |
| Sacramento | 144 | 3812 | 278 | 144 | 4234 | 93 | 0 | 8 | .966 |
| Tacoma | 142 | 3698 | 240 | 138 | 4076 | 125 | 0 | 11 | .966 |
| Salt Lake | 144 | 3716 | 284 | 139 | 4139 | 140 | 0 | 16 | .966 |

## INDIVIDUAL

### FIRST BASEMEN

NOTE: All caps denotes fielding-percentage leader based on 72 games for catchers, 96 for all other non-pitchers and 115 innings for pitchers. *Throws lefthanded.

| Player, Team | Pct. | G | PO | A | E | TC | DP |
|---|---|---|---|---|---|---|---|
| Abad, Andy, NVL* | .983 | 9 | 54 | 5 | 1 | 60 | 8 |
| Allen, Chad, OKL | 1.000 | 1 | 9 | 1 | 0 | 10 | 2 |
| Ashby, Chris, ABQ | .996 | 32 | 236 | 18 | 1 | 255 | 27 |
| Atkins, Garrett, CSP | 1.000 | 7 | 58 | 2 | 0 | 60 | 7 |
| Banks, Brian, ABQ | .991 | 15 | 98 | 10 | 1 | 109 | 16 |
| Bell, Rick, LVG | .981 | 34 | 231 | 23 | 5 | 259 | 24 |
| Bocachica, Hiram, TAC | .938 | 2 | 15 | 0 | 1 | 16 | 1 |
| Bozied, Tagg, POR | .994 | 57 | 435 | 45 | 3 | 483 | 35 |
| Buchanan, Brian, POR | .983 | 11 | 104 | 9 | 2 | 115 | 9 |
| Burnham, Gary, MEM* | .984 | 20 | 120 | 7 | 2 | 129 | 17 |
| Casanova, Raul, OMA | .991 | 14 | 102 | 6 | 1 | 109 | 13 |

| Player, Team | Pct. | G | PO | A | E | TC | DP |
|---|---|---|---|---|---|---|---|
| Castillo, Alberto, OMA | 1.000 | 1 | 6 | 0 | 0 | 6 | 0 |
| Cepicky, Matt, EDM* | 1.000 | 1 | 1 | 0 | 0 | 1 | 1 |
| Chen, Chin-Feng, LVG | 1.000 | 2 | 16 | 0 | 0 | 16 | 5 |
| Cirillo, Jeff, POR | 1.000 | 1 | 10 | 0 | 0 | 10 | 0 |
| Colbrunn, Greg, TCN | 1.000 | 1 | 7 | 1 | 0 | 8 | 0 |
| Coolbaugh, Mike, NO | .967 | 5 | 27 | 2 | 1 | 30 | 4 |
| Creighton, Matt, IWA | 1.000 | 14 | 106 | 9 | 0 | 115 | 10 |
| Dillon, Joe, ABQ | 1.000 | 2 | 18 | 0 | 0 | 18 | 0 |
| Donnels, Chris, CSP* | 1.000 | 36 | 280 | 10 | 0 | 290 | 31 |
| Doster, Dave, FRN | 1.000 | 1 | 2 | 0 | 0 | 2 | 0 |
| Dubois, Jason, IWA | .978 | 25 | 165 | 10 | 4 | 179 | 20 |
| Erstad, Darin, SLK* | .963 | 4 | 21 | 5 | 1 | 27 | 3 |
| Fick, Robert, POR* | .990 | 12 | 87 | 10 | 1 | 98 | 8 |
| Fox, Andy, OKL* | .977 | 4 | 42 | 0 | 1 | 43 | 3 |
| Franklin, Micah, TCN | 1.000 | 1 | 11 | 1 | 0 | 12 | 0 |
| Galarraga, Andres, SLK | 1.000 | 4 | 26 | 1 | 0 | 27 | 3 |
| Gall, John, MEM | .991 | 17 | 104 | 7 | 1 | 112 | 6 |
| Garcia, Luis, LVG | .987 | 95 | 785 | 72 | 11 | 868 | 78 |
| Gerber, Joseph, POR* | .989 | 27 | 162 | 14 | 2 | 178 | 15 |
| Gonzalez, Adrian, OKL* | .995 | 123 | 1112 | 99 | 6 | 1217 | 141 |
| Greene, Todd, CSP | 1.000 | 1 | 1 | 0 | 0 | 1 | 1 |
| Haad, Yamid, POR | .990 | 10 | 97 | 3 | 1 | 101 | 10 |
| Halter, Shane, SLK | 1.000 | 4 | 32 | 3 | 0 | 35 | 2 |
| Hansen, Jed, OMA | .996 | 29 | 242 | 16 | 1 | 259 | 21 |
| Hiatt, Phil, NO | .985 | 15 | 123 | 7 | 2 | 132 | 11 |
| Hill, Koyie, LVG | .909 | 2 | 10 | 0 | 1 | 11 | 1 |
| Hoffpauir, Micah, IWA* | .857 | 1 | 6 | 0 | 1 | 7 | 1 |
| Hoover, Paul, EDM | 1.000 | 4 | 24 | 2 | 0 | 26 | 6 |
| House, JR, NVL | .992 | 19 | 120 | 1 | 1 | 122 | 8 |
| Huckaby, Ken, OKL | .983 | 6 | 58 | 1 | 1 | 60 | 8 |
| Huffman, Royce, NO | .997 | 130 | 1174 | 78 | 4 | 1256 | 102 |
| Jackson, Steve, SCO | 1.000 | 1 | 10 | 1 | 0 | 11 | 0 |
| Jacobsen, Bucky, TAC | .976 | 5 | 39 | 1 | 1 | 41 | 2 |
| Johnson, Dan*, SCO | .990 | 98 | 835 | 59 | 9 | 903 | 59 |
| Johnson, Nick, EDM* | 1.000 | 3 | 24 | 2 | 0 | 26 | 3 |
| Johnson, Russ, IWA | .989 | 34 | 265 | 14 | 3 | 282 | 35 |
| Jones, Jason, OKL | 1.000 | 4 | 27 | 1 | 0 | 28 | 4 |
| Kelton, David, IWA | 1.000 | 1 | 10 | 0 | 0 | 10 | 0 |
| Knott, Jon, POR | 1.000 | 1 | 4 | 2 | 0 | 6 | 0 |
| Koonce, Graham*, SCO | .993 | 49 | 414 | 34 | 3 | 451 | 31 |
| Kopitzke, Casey, IWA | 1.000 | 1 | 2 | 0 | 0 | 2 | 1 |
| Kotchman, Casey, SLK* | .992 | 42 | 340 | 26 | 3 | 369 | 42 |
| Leon, Donny, IWA | 1.000 | 19 | 140 | 12 | 0 | 152 | 13 |
| Lopez, Luis, EDM | 1.000 | 16 | 134 | 11 | 0 | 145 | 18 |
| Mabry, John, MEM* | .994 | 23 | 159 | 14 | 1 | 174 | 22 |
| Matos, Julius, EDM | 1.000 | 1 | 8 | 1 | 0 | 9 | 1 |
| Minor, Damon, FRN* | .994 | 62 | 509 | 33 | 3 | 545 | 50 |
| Morales, Willie, CSP | 1.000 | 5 | 41 | 1 | 0 | 42 | 3 |
| Myers, Cory, TCN | .971 | 5 | 33 | 1 | 1 | 35 | 5 |
| Myrow, Brian, LVG* | .988 | 25 | 219 | 18 | 3 | 240 | 17 |
| Nady, Xavier, POR | .990 | 13 | 90 | 7 | 1 | 98 | 9 |
| Neal, Steve, TCN* | .998 | 105 | 816 | 78 | 2 | 896 | 75 |
| Newhan, David, OKL* | .986 | 7 | 69 | 3 | 1 | 73 | 9 |
| Nichols, Kyle, TCN | .995 | 26 | 180 | 11 | 1 | 192 | 19 |
| Niekro, Lance, FRN | .991 | 34 | 310 | 20 | 3 | 333 | 31 |
| Nieves, Jose, POR | .956 | 5 | 40 | 3 | 2 | 45 | 5 |
| Nieves, Wil, SLK | .990 | 23 | 187 | 9 | 2 | 198 | 23 |
| Niles, Drew, ABQ | 1.000 | 4 | 38 | 5 | 0 | 43 | 2 |
| Norris, Dax, NO | 1.000 | 2 | 5 | 0 | 0 | 5 | 1 |
| Ortiz, Luis, EDM | .983 | 10 | 53 | 5 | 1 | 59 | 6 |
| Ortiz, Luis, MEM | 1.000 | 29 | 195 | 16 | 0 | 211 | 15 |
| Ortiz, Luis, EDM-MEM | .996 | 39 | 248 | 21 | 1 | 270 | 21 |
| Pascucci, Val, EDM | .990 | 75 | 622 | 55 | 7 | 684 | 70 |
| Patterson, Jarrod, OMA* | .994 | 55 | 452 | 30 | 3 | 485 | 35 |
| Pelaez, Alex, SLK | .991 | 28 | 188 | 22 | 2 | 212 | 13 |
| Pellow, Kit, CSP | 1.000 | 2 | 19 | 4 | 0 | 23 | 0 |
| Petrick, Ben, POR | .992 | 14 | 117 | 5 | 1 | 123 | 6 |
| Pickering, Calvin, OMA* | .975 | 55 | 441 | 26 | 12 | 479 | 47 |
| Quinlan, Robb, SLK | .996 | 23 | 200 | 25 | 1 | 226 | 19 |
| Riggs, Adam, SLK | .972 | 11 | 96 | 10 | 3 | 109 | 10 |
| Risinger, Ben, POR | .987 | 12 | 72 | 6 | 1 | 79 | 11 |
| Rivera, Carlos, NVL* | .992 | 76 | 574 | 30 | 5 | 609 | 56 |
| Rivera, Mike, SCO | 1.000 | 1 | 2 | 0 | 0 | 2 | 0 |
| Rodriguez, Javy, SLK | 1.000 | 1 | 7 | 0 | 0 | 7 | 1 |
| Santos, Francisco, FRN* | .993 | 37 | 266 | 25 | 2 | 293 | 31 |
| Seabol, Scott, MEM | 1.000 | 2 | 2 | 0 | 0 | 2 | 1 |
| Sears, Todd, POR* | .875 | 1 | 6 | 1 | 1 | 8 | 1 |
| Selby, Bill, IWA* | .988 | 73 | 547 | 39 | 7 | 593 | 64 |
| Sheldon, Scott, NVL | 1.000 | 9 | 39 | 9 | 0 | 48 | 5 |
| Short, Rick, EDM | .991 | 13 | 108 | 4 | 1 | 113 | 8 |
| Simon, Randall, NVL* | 1.000 | 11 | 76 | 6 | 0 | 82 | 9 |
| Smith, Casey, SLK | .976 | 8 | 76 | 4 | 2 | 82 | 8 |
| Snow, JT, FRN* | 1.000 | 2 | 14 | 2 | 0 | 16 | 1 |
| Sutton, Larry, ABQ* | .990 | 70 | 630 | 48 | 7 | 685 | 60 |
| Swisher, Nick, SCO | 1.000 | 1 | 1 | 0 | 0 | 1 | 0 |
| Thrower, Jake, SLK | 1.000 | 7 | 38 | 4 | 0 | 42 | 4 |
| Toca, Jorge, EDM | .987 | 28 | 204 | 28 | 3 | 235 | 17 |
| Torcato, Tony, FRN* | .994 | 23 | 160 | 8 | 1 | 169 | 22 |
| Tracy, Andy, CSP* | .993 | 100 | 788 | 56 | 6 | 850 | 80 |
| Truby, Chris, NVL | .976 | 22 | 148 | 14 | 4 | 166 | 8 |
| Ugueto, Luis, TAC | 1.000 | 1 | 3 | 1 | 0 | 4 | 0 |
| Ullery, Dave, OMA* | 1.000 | 2 | 9 | 2 | 0 | 11 | 1 |
| Ward, Daryle, NVL* | 1.000 | 22 | 164 | 14 | 0 | 178 | 15 |
| Wathan, Derek, ABQ | 1.000 | 3 | 13 | 5 | 0 | 18 | 0 |
| Wilson, Tom, SCO | 1.000 | 2 | 2 | 0 | 0 | 2 | 1 |
| Witt, Kevin, MEM* | .994 | 85 | 623 | 43 | 4 | 670 | 73 |
| Wood, Jason, ABQ | .997 | 36 | 272 | 17 | 1 | 290 | 35 |
| Zapp, AJ, TAC* | .992 | 135 | 1047 | 101 | 9 | 1157 | 112 |
| Zinter, Alan, TCN | .986 | 28 | 196 | 20 | 3 | 219 | 15 |
| Zoccolillo, Peter, OKL* | 1.000 | 2 | 16 | 0 | 0 | 16 | 2 |
| Zuniga, Tony, TAC | 1.000 | 1 | 7 | 1 | 0 | 8 | 0 |

## SECOND BASEMEN

| Player, Team | Pct. | G | PO | A | E | TC | DP |
|---|---|---|---|---|---|---|---|
| Alfaro, Jason, NO | .938 | 8 | 8 | 22 | 2 | 32 | 3 |
| Almonte, Erick, CSP | .976 | 72 | 131 | 200 | 8 | 339 | 43 |
| Alomar, Roberto, TCN | 1.000 | 2 | 9 | 2 | 0 | 11 | 0 |
| Alviso, Jerome, MEM | .985 | 19 | 31 | 33 | 1 | 65 | 10 |
| Athas, Jamie, FRN* | .955 | 12 | 16 | 26 | 2 | 44 | 5 |
| Barden, Brian, TCN | .982 | 25 | 41 | 70 | 2 | 113 | 17 |
| Barmes, Clint, CSP | .963 | 5 | 10 | 16 | 1 | 27 | 4 |
| Bell, Rick, LVG | 1.000 | 2 | 4 | 3 | 0 | 7 | 0 |
| Bowers, Jason, MEM | .875 | 1 | 2 | 5 | 1 | 8 | 0 |
| Boyer, Billy, SLK | 1.000 | 7 | 8 | 10 | 0 | 18 | 2 |
| Bruntlett, Eric, NO | 1.000 | 5 | 8 | 10 | 0 | 18 | 2 |
| Burke, Chris, NO | .983 | 121 | 265 | 377 | 11 | 653 | 86 |
| Bynum, Freddie, SCO* | .966 | 11 | 11 | 17 | 1 | 29 | 3 |
| Castro, Bernie, POR | .978 | 64 | 115 | 147 | 6 | 268 | 30 |
| Castro, Ramon, SCO | .889 | 3 | 3 | 5 | 1 | 9 | 2 |
| Cirillo, Jeff, POR | 1.000 | 1 | 2 | 1 | 0 | 3 | 0 |
| Colina, Javier, MEM | 1.000 | 3 | 5 | 7 | 0 | 12 | 3 |
| Collins, Mike, TAC | 1.000 | 3 | 8 | 11 | 0 | 19 | 4 |
| Cruz, Deivi, FRN | 1.000 | 6 | 8 | 12 | 0 | 20 | 3 |
| Dallimore, Brian, FRN | .982 | 49 | 98 | 126 | 4 | 228 | 29 |
| Dawkins, Gookie, IWA | 1.000 | 2 | 4 | 2 | 0 | 6 | 0 |
| de la Rosa, Tomas, NVL | .978 | 15 | 14 | 30 | 1 | 45 | 6 |
| DeRenne, Keoni, TCN | .988 | 64 | 117 | 200 | 4 | 321 | 47 |
| Dillon, Joe, ABQ | .956 | 25 | 57 | 51 | 5 | 113 | 17 |
| Doster, Dave, FRN | .979 | 67 | 113 | 166 | 6 | 285 | 38 |
| Durham, Ray, FRN | .944 | 5 | 11 | 23 | 2 | 36 | 6 |
| Eckelman, Alex, NO | .985 | 16 | 24 | 43 | 1 | 68 | 11 |
| Falu, Irving, OMA | .909 | 3 | 3 | 7 | 1 | 11 | 1 |
| Flores, Jose, LVG | 1.000 | 5 | 3 | 17 | 0 | 20 | 1 |
| Garcia, Sergio, LVG | 1.000 | 4 | 9 | 13 | 0 | 22 | 7 |
| Garrabrants, Steve, TCN | 1.000 | 5 | 7 | 11 | 0 | 18 | 2 |
| German, Esteban, SCO | .977 | 40 | 56 | 112 | 4 | 172 | 23 |
| Gil, Benji, IWA | 1.000 | 4 | 6 | 15 | 0 | 21 | 2 |
| Gomez, FrancisSCO | 1.000 | 5 | 5 | 13 | 0 | 18 | 4 |
| Graffanino, Tony, OMA | 1.000 | 3 | 4 | 12 | 0 | 16 | 1 |
| Green, Andy, TCN | .979 | 30 | 62 | 80 | 3 | 145 | 16 |
| Grudzielanek, Mark, IWA | 1.000 | 7 | 5 | 6 | 0 | 11 | 2 |
| Guerrero, Wilton, OMA | .959 | 55 | 83 | 130 | 9 | 222 | 31 |
| Gutierrez, Ricky, IWA | 1.000 | 4 | 10 | 12 | 0 | 22 | 5 |
| Gutierrez, Victor, SLK | 1.000 | 4 | 5 | 8 | 0 | 13 | 4 |
| Hairston, Scott, TCN | .933 | 21 | 36 | 47 | 6 | 89 | 7 |
| Halter, Shane, SLK | 1.000 | 6 | 10 | 8 | 0 | 18 | 2 |
| Hansen, Jed, OMA | 1.000 | 23 | 47 | 60 | 0 | 107 | 11 |
| Harris, Brendan, IWA | .992 | 53 | 103 | 157 | 2 | 262 | 42 |
| Harris, Brian, EDM | .983 | 62 | 111 | 171 | 5 | 287 | 45 |
| Hart, Bo, MEM | .978 | 97 | 183 | 260 | 10 | 453 | 67 |
| Hart, Corey, OMA | .969 | 16 | 26 | 37 | 2 | 65 | 12 |
| Hocking, Denny, IWA | 1.000 | 5 | 10 | 13 | 0 | 23 | 4 |
| Hooper, Kevin, ABQ | .984 | 38 | 66 | 115 | 3 | 184 | 22 |
| Hooper, Kevin, OMA | .978 | 25 | 51 | 81 | 3 | 135 | 21 |
| Hooper, Kevin, ABQ-OMA | .981 | 63 | 117 | 196 | 6 | 319 | 43 |
| Izturis, Maicer, EDM | .978 | 9 | 14 | 31 | 1 | 46 | 11 |
| Jackson, Damian, IWA | 1.000 | 1 | 3 | 1 | 0 | 4 | 0 |
| Jackson, Damian, OMA | 1.000 | 3 | 10 | 16 | 0 | 26 | 4 |
| Jackson, Damian, IWA-OMA | 1.000 | 4 | 13 | 17 | 0 | 30 | 4 |
| Johnson, Russ, IWA | .986 | 50 | 96 | 109 | 3 | 208 | 33 |
| Kiger, Mark, SCO | 1.000 | 6 | 6 | 8 | 0 | 14 | 2 |
| Kuzmic, Craig, FRN | 1.000 | 2 | 1 | 1 | 0 | 2 | 0 |
| Lewis, Richard, IWA | .986 | 31 | 62 | 82 | 2 | 146 | 20 |
| Lopez, Jose, TAC | 1.000 | 9 | 21 | 16 | 0 | 37 | 3 |

| Player, Team | Pct. | G | PO | A | E | TC | DP |
|---|---|---|---|---|---|---|---|
| Lopez, Mendy, OMA | 1.000 | 5 | 7 | 15 | 0 | 22 | 3 |
| Lopez, Mickey, TAC | .974 | 100 | 212 | 304 | 14 | 530 | 62 |
| Magallanes, Ever, TCN* | .960 | 8 | 8 | 16 | 1 | 25 | 0 |
| Mateo, Henry, EDM | .937 | 27 | 51 | 67 | 8 | 126 | 13 |
| McLemore, Mark, SCO | .933 | 3 | 7 | 7 | 1 | 15 | 3 |
| Medrano, Anthony, EDM | .991 | 48 | 76 | 133 | 2 | 211 | 27 |
| Menechino, Frank, SCO | 1.000 | 2 | 4 | 6 | 0 | 10 | 1 |
| Miles, Aaron, CSP | .968 | 12 | 35 | 25 | 2 | 62 | 11 |
| Moriarty, Mike, NVL | 1.000 | 49 | 71 | 100 | 0 | 171 | 27 |
| Morrissey, Adam, SCO | .977 | 79 | 98 | 202 | 7 | 307 | 27 |
| Newhan, David, OKL* | .966 | 36 | 85 | 113 | 7 | 205 | 33 |
| Nieves, Jose, POR | .979 | 16 | 21 | 25 | 1 | 47 | 9 |
| Niles, Drew, ABQ | .982 | 48 | 95 | 128 | 4 | 227 | 34 |
| Nivar, Ramon, OKL | .987 | 43 | 85 | 142 | 3 | 230 | 36 |
| Olson, Tim, TCN | 1.000 | 2 | 2 | 3 | 0 | 5 | 0 |
| Ordonez, Rey, IWA | 1.000 | 1 | 2 | 0 | 0 | 2 | 0 |
| Pelaez, Alex, SLK | 1.000 | 7 | 11 | 16 | 0 | 27 | 6 |
| Pena, Elvis, CSP | .989 | 61 | 120 | 150 | 3 | 273 | 34 |
| Perez, Antonio, LVG | .978 | 48 | 84 | 140 | 5 | 229 | 32 |
| Perez, Santiago, OKL | .960 | 6 | 14 | 10 | 1 | 25 | 6 |
| Pickler, Jeff, OKL* | .985 | 63 | 138 | 195 | 5 | 338 | 57 |
| Ransom, Cody, FRN | .984 | 28 | 48 | 72 | 2 | 122 | 20 |
| Relaford, Desi, OMA | 1.000 | 1 | 4 | 0 | 0 | 4 | 0 |
| Riggs, Adam, SLK | .909 | 4 | 5 | 5 | 1 | 11 | 0 |
| Riggs, Eric, LVG | 1.000 | 1 | 1 | 1 | 0 | 2 | 1 |
| Risinger, Ben, POR | .971 | 17 | 29 | 38 | 2 | 69 | 5 |
| Rodriguez, Javy, SLK | .909 | 5 | 15 | 15 | 3 | 33 | 6 |
| Rouse, Mike, SCO* | .953 | 12 | 18 | 23 | 2 | 43 | 3 |
| Sanchez, Freddy, NVL | .989 | 25 | 40 | 49 | 1 | 90 | 11 |
| Sandel, George, TAC | .923 | 13 | 12 | 24 | 3 | 39 | 3 |
| Santiago, Ramon, TAC | 1.000 | 10 | 19 | 25 | 0 | 44 | 8 |
| Scales, Bobby, POR | .965 | 15 | 21 | 34 | 2 | 57 | 8 |
| Seabol, Scott, MEM | .983 | 44 | 71 | 104 | 3 | 178 | 25 |
| Selby, Bill, IWA* | .956 | 11 | 16 | 27 | 2 | 45 | 6 |
| Sheldon, Scott, NVL | .941 | 7 | 7 | 9 | 1 | 17 | 3 |
| Short, Rick, EDM | 1.000 | 10 | 21 | 24 | 0 | 45 | 7 |
| Short, Rick, OMA | .990 | 20 | 42 | 56 | 1 | 99 | 8 |
| Short, Rick, EDM-OMA | .993 | 6 | 63 | 80 | 1 | 144 | 15 |
| Shumpert, Terry, NVL | .981 | 45 | 82 | 128 | 4 | 214 | 26 |
| Skrehot, Shaun, NVL | 1.000 | 1 | 1 | 2 | 0 | 3 | 1 |
| Smith, Casey, SLK | .987 | 14 | 28 | 46 | 1 | 75 | 10 |
| Sorensen, Zach, SLK | .981 | 12 | 21 | 32 | 1 | 54 | 2 |
| Specht, Brian, SLK | .973 | 53 | 96 | 155 | 7 | 258 | 34 |
| Theodorou, Nick, LVG | 1.000 | 11 | 19 | 27 | 0 | 46 | 6 |
| Thrower, Jake, SLK | .972 | 41 | 69 | 103 | 5 | 177 | 21 |
| Thurston, Joe, LVG* | .977 | 85 | 171 | 249 | 10 | 430 | 47 |
| Truby, Chris, NVL | .993 | 38 | 64 | 78 | 1 | 143 | 18 |
| Ugueto, Luis, TAC | .932 | 15 | 20 | 35 | 4 | 59 | 8 |
| Vazquez, Ramon, POR* | .995 | 46 | 69 | 117 | 1 | 187 | 19 |
| Wathan, Derek, ABQ | .984 | 42 | 79 | 106 | 3 | 188 | 23 |
| Wood, Jason, ABQ | 1.000 | 7 | 20 | 20 | 0 | 40 | 5 |

## THIRD BASEMEN

| Player, Team | Pct. | G | PO | A | E | TC | DP |
|---|---|---|---|---|---|---|---|
| Alfaro, Jason, NO | .983 | 43 | 38 | 80 | 2 | 120 | 7 |
| Allen, Luke, NVL* | .882 | 8 | 3 | 12 | 2 | 17 | 0 |
| Almonte, Erick, CSP | .951 | 23 | 17 | 60 | 4 | 81 | 9 |
| Alviso, Jerome, MEM | 1.000 | 7 | 0 | 4 | 0 | 4 | 0 |
| Atkins, Garrett, CSP | .917 | 105 | 46 | 187 | 21 | 254 | 19 |
| Barden, Brian, TCN | .970 | 67 | 37 | 127 | 5 | 169 | 17 |
| Beinbrink, Andrew, OKL | .963 | 10 | 5 | 21 | 1 | 27 | 3 |
| Bell, Rick, LVG | .941 | 89 | 53 | 169 | 14 | 236 | 10 |
| Bowers, Jason, MEM | 1.000 | 1 | 1 | 1 | 0 | 2 | 0 |
| Bynum, Freddie, SCO* | .840 | 12 | 4 | 17 | 4 | 25 | 1 |
| Carroll, Wes, EDM | .833 | 9 | 5 | 10 | 3 | 18 | 1 |
| Castillo, Wilkin, TCN | 1.000 | 4 | 4 | 3 | 0 | 7 | 0 |
| Castro, Ramon, SCO | 1.000 | 3 | 1 | 2 | 0 | 3 | 0 |
| Cervenak, Michael, FRN | .967 | 10 | 8 | 21 | 1 | 30 | 2 |
| Cirillo, Jeff, POR | .917 | 3 | 2 | 9 | 1 | 12 | 0 |
| Colina, Javier, MEM | 1.000 | 10 | 5 | 10 | 0 | 15 | 0 |
| Coolbaugh, Mike, NO | .967 | 98 | 51 | 211 | 9 | 271 | 13 |
| Dallimore, Brian, FRN | .941 | 35 | 25 | 71 | 6 | 102 | 7 |
| Dawkins, Gookie, IWA | 1.000 | 3 | 2 | 3 | 0 | 5 | 0 |
| DeRenne, Keoni, TCN | .938 | 8 | 1 | 14 | 1 | 16 | 0 |
| Dillon, Joe, ABQ | .943 | 65 | 27 | 122 | 9 | 158 | 12 |
| Dobbs, Greg, TAC* | .931 | 64 | 54 | 121 | 13 | 188 | 14 |
| Doster, Dave, FRN | .968 | 60 | 44 | 107 | 5 | 156 | 7 |
| Eckelman, Alex, NO | 1.000 | 17 | 5 | 25 | 0 | 30 | 4 |
| Edwards, Mike, SCO | .907 | 88 | 40 | 164 | 21 | 225 | 11 |
| Figueroa, Luis, NVL | .948 | 79 | 43 | 122 | 9 | 174 | 10 |
| Figueroa, Luis, NVL | 1.000 | 1 | 0 | 1 | 0 | 1 | 0 |
| Flores, Jose, LVG | .953 | 32 | 16 | 45 | 3 | 64 | 2 |
| Fox, Andy, OKL* | .914 | 17 | 10 | 22 | 3 | 35 | 0 |
| Garcia, Sergio, LVG | .909 | 4 | 1 | 9 | 1 | 11 | 1 |
| Gautreau, Jake, POR* | .948 | 45 | 28 | 63 | 5 | 96 | 6 |
| Gil, Benji, IWA | .864 | 16 | 7 | 31 | 6 | 44 | 4 |
| Green, Andy, TCN | .922 | 34 | 23 | 71 | 8 | 102 | 3 |
| Gutierrez, Ricky, IWA | 1.000 | 1 | 0 | 1 | 0 | 1 | 0 |
| Gutierrez, Victor, SLK | .800 | 4 | 1 | 3 | 1 | 5 | 0 |
| Hall, Billy, ABQ | .950 | 9 | 3 | 16 | 1 | 20 | 3 |
| Halter, Shane, SLK | 1.000 | 3 | 2 | 8 | 0 | 10 | 0 |
| Hansen, Jed, OMA | .818 | 5 | 1 | 8 | 2 | 11 | 0 |
| Harris, Brendan, EDM | .943 | 34 | 21 | 62 | 5 | 88 | 4 |
| Harris, Brendan, IWA | 1.000 | 7 | 0 | 6 | 0 | 6 | 0 |
| Harris, Brendan, EDM-IWA | .947 | 41 | 21 | 68 | 5 | 94 | 4 |
| Harris, Brian, EDM | .872 | 22 | 7 | 27 | 5 | 39 | 2 |
| Hart, Corey, OMA | 1.000 | 5 | 2 | 9 | 0 | 11 | 0 |
| Hill, Koyie, LVG | 1.000 | 1 | 1 | 2 | 0 | 3 | 0 |
| Hocking, Denny, IWA | 1.000 | 13 | 5 | 27 | 0 | 32 | 4 |
| Hodges, Scott, EDM* | .898 | 29 | 15 | 38 | 6 | 59 | 4 |
| Hoover, Paul, EDM | .842 | 19 | 8 | 24 | 6 | 38 | 2 |
| Huffman, Royce, NO | 1.000 | 1 | 0 | 1 | 0 | 1 | 0 |
| Johnson, Russ, IWA | .883 | 28 | 14 | 39 | 7 | 60 | 3 |
| Kuzmic, Craig, FRN | .924 | 35 | 23 | 50 | 6 | 79 | 3 |
| Leon, Donny, IWA | .932 | 92 | 59 | 148 | 15 | 222 | 22 |
| Leone, Justin, TAC | .900 | 45 | 42 | 75 | 13 | 130 | 3 |
| Lopez, Jose, TAC | .920 | 22 | 11 | 35 | 4 | 50 | 2 |
| Lopez, Mickey, TAC | 1.000 | 2 | 0 | 1 | 0 | 1 | 0 |
| Mabry, John, MEM* | .941 | 5 | 5 | 11 | 1 | 17 | 2 |
| Magallanes, Ever, TCN* | .500 | 2 | 0 | 1 | 1 | 2 | 0 |
| Martinez, Felix, IWA | 1.000 | 1 | 0 | 2 | 0 | 2 | 0 |
| Matos, Julius, EDM | .900 | 28 | 23 | 40 | 7 | 70 | 9 |
| McDougall, Marshall, OKL | .941 | 77 | 49 | 191 | 15 | 255 | 30 |
| McKay, Cody, MEM* | .938 | 7 | 4 | 11 | 1 | 16 | 1 |
| McPherson, Dallas, SLK* | .885 | 62 | 39 | 92 | 17 | 148 | 8 |
| Medrano, Anthony, EDM | 1.000 | 9 | 5 | 14 | 0 | 19 | 1 |
| Morrissey, Adam, SCO | .957 | 27 | 17 | 50 | 3 | 70 | 2 |
| Myers, Cory, TCN | .918 | 22 | 10 | 35 | 4 | 49 | 5 |
| Newhan, David, OKL* | .929 | 8 | 5 | 21 | 2 | 28 | 1 |
| Niekro, Lance, FRN | .950 | 24 | 20 | 37 | 3 | 60 | 7 |
| Nieves, Jose, POR | .956 | 42 | 37 | 72 | 5 | 114 | 3 |
| Niles, Drew, ABQ | .895 | 18 | 2 | 15 | 2 | 19 | 0 |
| Olson, Tim, TCN | .895 | 8 | 0 | 17 | 2 | 19 | 1 |
| Pascucci, Val, EDM | 1.000 | 3 | 0 | 4 | 0 | 4 | 0 |
| Patterson, Jarrod, OMA* | .929 | 11 | 6 | 20 | 2 | 28 | 2 |
| Pelaez, Alex, SLK | .962 | 36 | 20 | 56 | 3 | 79 | 4 |
| Pellow, Kit, CSP | .333 | 2 | 0 | 1 | 2 | 3 | 0 |
| Perez, Santiago, OKL | .882 | 31 | 17 | 73 | 12 | 102 | 7 |
| Pickler, Jeff, OKL* | 1.000 | 5 | 2 | 7 | 0 | 9 | 1 |
| Quinlan, Robb, SLK | .818 | 5 | 3 | 6 | 2 | 11 | 0 |
| Ransom, Cody, FRN | .857 | 2 | 1 | 5 | 1 | 7 | 0 |
| Riggs, Adam, SLK | 1.000 | 8 | 4 | 18 | 0 | 22 | 3 |
| Riggs, Eric, LVG | .955 | 28 | 15 | 48 | 3 | 66 | 4 |
| Risinger, Ben, POR | .977 | 32 | 28 | 58 | 2 | 88 | 8 |
| Rodriguez, Javy, SLK | .933 | 6 | 5 | 9 | 1 | 15 | 1 |
| Scales, Bobby, POR | 1.000 | 6 | 6 | 9 | 0 | 15 | 0 |
| Seabol, Scott, MEM | .955 | 98 | 63 | 149 | 10 | 222 | 18 |
| Selby, Bill, IWA* | .833 | 5 | 4 | 1 | 1 | 6 | 0 |
| Sheldon, Scott, NVL | .909 | 5 | 2 | 8 | 1 | 11 | 0 |
| Short, Rick, EDM | 1.000 | 10 | 10 | 14 | 0 | 24 | 1 |
| Short, Rick, OMA | .950 | 58 | 42 | 129 | 9 | 180 | 10 |
| Short, Rick, EDM-OMA | .956 | 6 | 52 | 143 | 9 | 204 | 11 |
| Smith, Casey, SLK | .913 | 11 | 9 | 12 | 2 | 23 | 0 |
| Specht, Brian, SLK | .833 | 1 | 0 | 5 | 1 | 6 | 0 |
| Strong, Zach, FRN | 1.000 | 3 | 1 | 1 | 0 | 2 | 0 |
| Teahen, Mark, OMA* | .932 | 66 | 41 | 136 | 13 | 190 | 9 |
| Teahen, Mark, SCO* | .983 | 20 | 18 | 39 | 1 | 58 | 3 |
| Teahen, Mark, OMA-SCO* | .944 | 86 | 59 | 175 | 14 | 248 | 12 |
| Theodorou, Nick, LVG | .789 | 7 | 4 | 11 | 4 | 19 | 1 |
| Thrower, Jake, SLK | .973 | 14 | 15 | 21 | 1 | 37 | 2 |
| Tracy, Andy, CSP* | .872 | 14 | 7 | 34 | 6 | 47 | 2 |
| Tracy, Chad, TCN* | .909 | 8 | 7 | 23 | 3 | 33 | 1 |
| Truby, Chris, NVL | .961 | 79 | 54 | 142 | 8 | 204 | 18 |
| Ugueto, Luis, TAC | .895 | 8 | 5 | 12 | 2 | 19 | 2 |
| Vazquez, Ramon, POR* | 1.000 | 4 | 1 | 7 | 0 | 8 | 2 |
| Washington, Rico, POR* | .894 | 29 | 12 | 64 | 9 | 85 | 9 |
| Wathan, Derek, ABQ | 1.000 | 17 | 6 | 34 | 0 | 40 | 5 |
| Wilson, Tom, SCO | .833 | 3 | 2 | 3 | 1 | 6 | 0 |
| Witt, Kevin, MEM* | .893 | 43 | 18 | 49 | 8 | 75 | 7 |
| Wood, Jason, ABQ | .940 | 55 | 34 | 108 | 9 | 151 | 11 |
| Zinter, Alan, TCN | .947 | 10 | 3 | 15 | 1 | 19 | 0 |
| Zuniga, Tony, TAC | .909 | 6 | 3 | 7 | 1 | 11 | 1 |

## SHORTSTOPS

| Player, Team | Pct. | G | PO | A | E | TC | DP |
|---|---|---|---|---|---|---|---|
| Alexander, Manny, OKL | .965 | 93 | 169 | 334 | 18 | 521 | 81 |
| Alfaro, Jason, NO | .959 | 53 | 76 | 132 | 9 | 217 | 32 |
| Almonte, Erick, CSP | .973 | 24 | 40 | 67 | 3 | 110 | 17 |
| Alviso, Jerome, MEM | .989 | 25 | 34 | 55 | 1 | 90 | 14 |
| Amezaga, Alfredo, SLK | .961 | 32 | 53 | 118 | 7 | 178 | 23 |
| Arteaga, Joshua, IWA | .983 | 14 | 17 | 42 | 1 | 60 | 8 |
| Athas, Jamie, FRN* | .952 | 112 | 151 | 343 | 25 | 519 | 74 |
| Barmes, Clint, CSP | .964 | 118 | 164 | 342 | 19 | 525 | 60 |
| Bloomquist, Willie, TAC | 1.000 | 2 | 1 | 2 | 0 | 3 | 0 |
| Bowers, Jason, MEM | .976 | 113 | 170 | 322 | 12 | 504 | 79 |
| Bruntlett, Eric, NO | .967 | 64 | 99 | 221 | 11 | 331 | 43 |
| Bynum, Freddie, SCO* | .960 | 19 | 23 | 49 | 3 | 75 | 5 |
| Castro, Ramon, SCO | .956 | 33 | 42 | 89 | 6 | 137 | 17 |
| Colina, Javier, MEM | .933 | 5 | 8 | 6 | 1 | 15 | 2 |
| Collins, Mike, TAC | .968 | 22 | 41 | 51 | 3 | 95 | 17 |
| Coolbaugh, Mike, NO | .952 | 6 | 7 | 13 | 1 | 21 | 3 |
| Cruz, Deivi, FRN | .955 | 7 | 7 | 14 | 1 | 22 | 2 |
| Dallimore, Brian, FRN | .960 | 32 | 43 | 78 | 5 | 126 | 14 |
| Dawkins, Gookie, IWA | .948 | 49 | 74 | 125 | 11 | 210 | 37 |
| Dawkins, Gookie, OMA | .955 | 48 | 78 | 133 | 10 | 221 | 33 |
| Dawkins, Gookie, IWA-OMA | .951 | 97 | 152 | 258 | 21 | 431 | 70 |
| de la Rosa, Tomas, NVL | .922 | 46 | 52 | 101 | 13 | 166 | 10 |
| DeRenne, Keoni, TCN | .950 | 13 | 13 | 25 | 2 | 40 | 3 |
| Flores, Jose, LVG | .955 | 56 | 82 | 150 | 11 | 243 | 36 |
| Fox, Andy, OKL* | .882 | 3 | 3 | 12 | 2 | 17 | 1 |
| Furmaniak, JJ, POR | .954 | 117 | 183 | 357 | 26 | 566 | 67 |
| Garcia, Sergio, LVG | 1.000 | 1 | 1 | 2 | 0 | 3 | 0 |
| German, Esteban, SCO | .914 | 13 | 17 | 36 | 5 | 58 | 5 |
| Gil, Benji, IWA | 1.000 | 13 | 17 | 48 | 0 | 65 | 11 |
| Gil, Jerry, TCN | .946 | 111 | 195 | 317 | 29 | 541 | 67 |
| Gomez, Francis, SCO | 1.000 | 1 | 2 | 1 | 0 | 3 | 0 |
| Gonzalez, Alex, IWA | 1.000 | 8 | 10 | 12 | 0 | 22 | 4 |
| Green, Andy, TCN | 1.000 | 8 | 10 | 17 | 0 | 27 | 2 |
| Guerrero, Wilton, OMA | .909 | 3 | 4 | 6 | 1 | 11 | 0 |
| Gutierrez, Ricky, IWA | .962 | 15 | 15 | 36 | 2 | 53 | 11 |
| Gutierrez, Victor, SLK | .929 | 15 | 22 | 43 | 5 | 70 | 10 |
| Halter, Shane, SLK | .971 | 7 | 9 | 25 | 1 | 35 | 3 |
| Hansen, Jed, OMA | .907 | 23 | 27 | 80 | 11 | 118 | 15 |
| Harris, Brendan, IWA | .912 | 12 | 12 | 19 | 3 | 34 | 1 |
| Hart, Bo, MEM | .963 | 21 | 28 | 49 | 3 | 80 | 15 |
| Hocking, Denny, IWA | .951 | 13 | 15 | 43 | 3 | 61 | 10 |
| Hooper, Kevin, ABQ | 1.000 | 3 | 1 | 5 | 0 | 6 | 0 |
| Hooper, Kevin, OMA | 1.000 | 4 | 3 | 3 | 0 | 6 | 0 |
| Hooper, Kevin, ABQ-OMA | 1.000 | 7 | 4 | 8 | 0 | 12 | 0 |
| Izturis, Maicer, EDM | .968 | 89 | 117 | 217 | 11 | 345 | 47 |
| Jackson, Damian, IWA | .989 | 22 | 31 | 60 | 1 | 92 | 14 |
| Jackson, Damian, OMA | .956 | 44 | 69 | 125 | 9 | 203 | 26 |
| Jackson, Damian, IWA-OMA | .966 | 66 | 100 | 185 | 10 | 295 | 40 |
| Leone, Justin, TAC | .961 | 12 | 16 | 33 | 2 | 51 | 9 |
| Lopez, Jose, TAC | .926 | 42 | 78 | 121 | 16 | 215 | 31 |
| Lopez, Mendy, OMA | .964 | 27 | 33 | 74 | 4 | 111 | 15 |
| Lopez, Mickey, TAC | 1.000 | 4 | 4 | 10 | 0 | 14 | 1 |
| Martinez, Felix, IWA | .850 | 4 | 7 | 10 | 3 | 20 | 3 |
| Matos, Julius, EDM | 1.000 | 4 | 7 | 7 | 0 | 14 | 6 |
| McDougall, Marshall, OKL | .961 | 16 | 26 | 47 | 3 | 76 | 12 |
| McLemore, Mark, SCO | 1.000 | 1 | 1 | 1 | 0 | 2 | 0 |
| Medrano, Anthony, EDM | .976 | 56 | 93 | 151 | 6 | 250 | 46 |
| Moriarty, Mike, NVL | .990 | 53 | 63 | 135 | 2 | 200 | 29 |
| Morrissey, Adam, SCO | 1.000 | 1 | 0 | 2 | 0 | 2 | 0 |
| Nieves, Jose, POR | .957 | 19 | 26 | 41 | 3 | 70 | 4 |
| Niles, Drew, ABQ | 1.000 | 14 | 22 | 38 | 0 | 60 | 6 |
| Olson, Tim, TCN | .966 | 20 | 37 | 48 | 3 | 88 | 12 |
| Ordonez, Rey, IWA | .969 | 6 | 8 | 23 | 1 | 32 | 4 |
| Pena, Elvis, CSP | .933 | 2 | 5 | 9 | 1 | 15 | 4 |
| Perez, Antonio, LVG | .952 | 79 | 97 | 201 | 15 | 313 | 46 |
| Perez, Neifi, IWA | 1.000 | 10 | 11 | 23 | 0 | 34 | 3 |
| Perez, Santiago, OKL | .945 | 33 | 66 | 105 | 10 | 181 | 26 |
| Ransom, Cody, FRN | .967 | 7 | 4 | 25 | 1 | 30 | 5 |
| Relaford, Desi, OMA | 1.000 | 1 | 3 | 3 | 0 | 6 | 1 |
| Riggs, Eric, LVG | .957 | 7 | 9 | 13 | 1 | 23 | 6 |
| Risinger, Ben, POR | .893 | 11 | 8 | 17 | 3 | 28 | 2 |
| Rodriguez, Javy, SLK | .923 | 6 | 11 | 25 | 3 | 39 | 6 |
| Rouse, Mike, SCO* | .967 | 85 | 107 | 249 | 12 | 368 | 42 |
| Sanchez, Freddy, NVL | .968 | 9 | 10 | 20 | 1 | 31 | 6 |
| Santiago, Ramon, TAC | .978 | 61 | 91 | 177 | 6 | 274 | 27 |
| Sheldon, Scott, NVL | .750 | 2 | 1 | 2 | 1 | 4 | 1 |
| Shumpert, Terry, NVL | 1.000 | 7 | 8 | 19 | 0 | 27 | 3 |
| Skrehot, Shaun, NVL | .955 | 38 | 51 | 99 | 7 | 157 | 24 |
| Smith, Casey, SLK | .961 | 26 | 46 | 77 | 5 | 128 | 17 |
| Sorensen, Zach, SLK | .954 | 27 | 55 | 89 | 7 | 151 | 25 |
| Stegall, Ryan, NO | 1.000 | 3 | 1 | 2 | 0 | 3 | 1 |
| Theodorou, Nick, LVG | .962 | 16 | 24 | 27 | 2 | 53 | 7 |
| Thrower, Jake, SLK | .958 | 34 | 46 | 90 | 6 | 142 | 16 |
| Truby, Chris, NVL | .966 | 6 | 12 | 16 | 1 | 29 | 5 |
| Ugueto, Luis, TAC | .917 | 6 | 3 | 8 | 1 | 12 | 0 |
| Valdez, Wilson, ABQ | .982 | 65 | 108 | 221 | 6 | 335 | 51 |
| Vazquez, Ramon, POR* | .950 | 4 | 4 | 15 | 1 | 20 | 1 |
| Wathan, Derek, ABQ | .978 | 10 | 13 | 32 | 1 | 46 | 7 |
| Whiteman, Tommy, NO | .972 | 25 | 38 | 66 | 3 | 107 | 11 |
| Wilson, Josh, ABQ | .972 | 56 | 97 | 178 | 8 | 283 | 36 |

## OUTFIELDERS

| Player, Team | Pct. | G | PO | A | E | TC | DP |
|---|---|---|---|---|---|---|---|
| Abad, Andy, NVL* | .992 | 75 | 125 | 2 | 1 | 128 | 0 |
| Aguila, Chris, ABQ | .986 | 94 | 199 | 8 | 3 | 210 | 1 |
| Alfaro, Jason, NO | .978 | 22 | 43 | 1 | 1 | 45 | 0 |
| Allen, Chad, OKL | .992 | 80 | 122 | 3 | 1 | 126 | 0 |
| Allen, Luke, NVL* | .974 | 110 | 216 | 7 | 6 | 229 | 2 |
| Alvarez, Tony, NVL | .980 | 91 | 138 | 6 | 3 | 147 | 0 |
| Alviso, Jerome, MEM | 1.000 | 2 | 3 | 0 | 0 | 3 | 0 |
| Asadoorian, Rick, OKL | 1.000 | 15 | 25 | 1 | 0 | 26 | 0 |
| Ashby, Chris, ABQ | .929 | 11 | 13 | 0 | 1 | 14 | 0 |
| Banks, Brian, ABQ | .983 | 41 | 58 | 0 | 1 | 59 | 0 |
| Barnes, John, LVG | .991 | 51 | 98 | 7 | 1 | 106 | 1 |
| Bay, Jason, NVL | 1.000 | 3 | 3 | 0 | 0 | 3 | 0 |
| Berger, Brandon, OMA | .983 | 31 | 56 | 3 | 1 | 60 | 0 |
| Bergeron, Peter, EDM* | 1.000 | 11 | 16 | 2 | 0 | 18 | 0 |
| Bloomquist, Willie, TAC | 1.000 | 1 | 1 | 0 | 0 | 1 | 0 |
| Bocachica, Hiram, TAC | .957 | 36 | 66 | 1 | 3 | 70 | 1 |
| Bowers, Jason, MEM | 1.000 | 1 | 1 | 0 | 0 | 1 | 0 |
| Brown, Adrian, OMA | .987 | 108 | 225 | 10 | 3 | 238 | 2 |
| Brown, Dee, OMA* | .875 | 6 | 7 | 0 | 1 | 8 | 0 |
| Brown, Emil, NO | .981 | 25 | 51 | 1 | 1 | 53 | 0 |
| Brown, Emil, MEM | 1.000 | 17 | 30 | 0 | 0 | 30 | 0 |
| Brown, Emil, NO-MEM | .988 | 42 | 81 | 1 | 1 | 83 | |
| Bruntlett, Eric, NO | .978 | 19 | 42 | 2 | 1 | 45 | 0 |
| Burnham, Gary, MEM* | 1.000 | 5 | 2 | 1 | 0 | 3 | 0 |
| Bynum, Freddie, SCO* | 1.000 | 31 | 58 | 1 | 0 | 59 | 0 |
| Calloway, Ron, EDM* | .982 | 56 | 105 | 7 | 2 | 114 | 1 |
| Castillo, Wilkin, TCN | 1.000 | 2 | 4 | 0 | 0 | 4 | 0 |
| Castro, Bernie, POR | 1.000 | 3 | 11 | 0 | 0 | 11 | 0 |
| Cedeno, Roger, MEM | 1.000 | 7 | 10 | 0 | 0 | 10 | 0 |
| Cepicky, Matt, EDM* | .975 | 75 | 154 | 4 | 4 | 162 | 0 |
| Chavez, Endy, EDM* | 1.000 | 14 | 27 | 2 | 0 | 29 | 0 |
| Chen, Chin-Feng, LVG | .967 | 74 | 112 | 5 | 4 | 121 | 0 |
| Christenson, Ryan, ABQ | .979 | 62 | 138 | 2 | 3 | 143 | 0 |
| Church, Ryan, EDM* | .990 | 91 | 184 | 6 | 2 | 192 | 3 |
| Colangelo, Mike, ABQ | .979 | 69 | 85 | 10 | 2 | 97 | 0 |
| Conti, Jason, OKL* | .979 | 99 | 210 | 22 | 5 | 237 | 9 |
| Cookson, Brent, IWA | 1.000 | 6 | 12 | 0 | 0 | 12 | 0 |
| Cruz, Nelson, SCO | 1.000 | 4 | 12 | 0 | 0 | 12 | 0 |
| Dallimore, Brian, FRN | 1.000 | 2 | 2 | 0 | 0 | 2 | 0 |
| DaVanon, Jeff, SLK | 1.000 | 3 | 7 | 0 | 0 | 7 | 0 |
| Davis, JJ, NVL | 1.000 | 20 | 31 | 1 | 0 | 32 | 1 |
| DeJesus, David, OMA* | .991 | 50 | 107 | 1 | 1 | 109 | 1 |
| DeVore, Doug, TCN* | .951 | 55 | 76 | 2 | 4 | 82 | 0 |
| Dillon, Joe, ABQ | .935 | 27 | 38 | 5 | 3 | 46 | 1 |
| Donnels, Chris, CSP* | 1.000 | 7 | 8 | 1 | 0 | 9 | 0 |
| Dubois, Jason, IWA | 1.000 | 81 | 120 | 5 | 0 | 125 | 1 |
| Eckelman, Alex, NO | 1.000 | 11 | 10 | 1 | 0 | 11 | 0 |
| Edwards, Mike, SCO | .967 | 53 | 88 | 1 | 3 | 92 | 0 |
| Ellison, Jason, FRN | .983 | 119 | 343 | 14 | 6 | 363 | 2 |
| Ellison, Josh, TAC* | .923 | 8 | 12 | 0 | 1 | 13 | 0 |
| Faison, Vince, TAC* | 1.000 | 8 | 11 | 3 | 0 | 14 | 2 |
| Fernandez, Alex, POR* | .959 | 99 | 156 | 8 | 7 | 171 | 4 |
| Fox, Andy, OKL* | 1.000 | 4 | 4 | 0 | 0 | 4 | 0 |
| Franklin, Micah, TCN | 1.000 | 8 | 14 | 3 | 0 | 17 | 0 |
| Freeman, Choo, CSP | .983 | 102 | 223 | 7 | 4 | 234 | 2 |
| Gall, John, MEM | .975 | 119 | 150 | 4 | 4 | 158 | 1 |
| Garcia, Luis, LVG | 1.000 | 4 | 5 | 1 | 0 | 6 | 0 |
| Garcia, Sergio, LVG | 1.000 | 2 | 2 | 0 | 0 | 2 | 0 |
| Garrett, Shawn, CSP | .978 | 29 | 44 | 1 | 1 | 46 | 0 |
| Gerber, Joseph, POR* | 1.000 | 13 | 11 | 1 | 0 | 12 | 0 |
| Gerez, Francisco, TAC | .500 | 2 | 1 | 0 | 1 | 2 | 0 |
| Gettis, Byron, OMA | .966 | 51 | 78 | 6 | 3 | 87 | 1 |
| Giambi, Jeremy, LVG* | 1.000 | 6 | 8 | 0 | 0 | 8 | 0 |
| Gibson, Derrick, SLK | .967 | 38 | 53 | 6 | 2 | 61 | 1 |
| Gomez, Alexis, OMA* | .971 | 107 | 197 | 3 | 6 | 206 | 2 |
| Gordon, Brian, SLK* | .970 | 126 | 249 | 14 | 8 | 271 | 6 |
| Gorneault, Nick, SLK | .909 | 6 | 10 | 0 | 1 | 11 | 0 |
| Green, Andy, TCN | 1.000 | 6 | 7 | 0 | 0 | 7 | 0 |
| Greenberg, Adam, IWA* | 1.000 | 1 | 4 | 0 | 0 | 4 | 0 |
| Guerrero, Wilton, OMA | 1.000 | 2 | 1 | 0 | 0 | 1 | 0 |

| Player, Team | Pct. | G | PO | A | E | TC | DP |
|---|---|---|---|---|---|---|---|
| Guiel, Aaron, OMA* | .980 | 28 | 43 | 6 | 1 | 50 | 0 |
| Guzman, Elpidio, TAC* | .970 | 121 | 212 | 13 | 7 | 232 | 5 |
| Guzman, Freddy, POR | .983 | 66 | 166 | 3 | 3 | 172 | 2 |
| Hairston, Scott, TCN | 1.000 | 5 | 11 | 0 | 0 | 11 | 0 |
| Hall, Billy, ABQ | 1.000 | 4 | 2 | 0 | 0 | 2 | 0 |
| Hall, Victor, TCN* | .984 | 33 | 60 | 3 | 1 | 64 | 0 |
| Halter, Shane, SLK | .972 | 17 | 35 | 0 | 1 | 36 | 0 |
| Hansen, Jed, OMA | .989 | 50 | 84 | 2 | 1 | 87 | 1 |
| Hawpe, Brad, CSP* | .984 | 86 | 172 | 7 | 3 | 182 | 3 |
| Haynes, Dee, MEM | .986 | 42 | 69 | 4 | 1 | 74 | 1 |
| Haynes, Nathan, FRN* | .667 | 1 | 2 | 0 | 1 | 3 | 0 |
| Hiatt, Phil, NO | .989 | 119 | 177 | 8 | 2 | 187 | 0 |
| Hill, Mike, NO | .978 | 61 | 85 | 3 | 2 | 90 | 1 |
| Hocking, Denny, IWA | 1.000 | 2 | 5 | 1 | 0 | 6 | 0 |
| Holliday, Matt, CSP | 1.000 | 6 | 9 | 0 | 0 | 9 | 0 |
| Holt, Daylan, LVG | 1.000 | 27 | 37 | 5 | 0 | 42 | 1 |
| Horner, Jim, TAC | 1.000 | 4 | 6 | 0 | 0 | 6 | 0 |
| House, JR, NVL | 1.000 | 5 | 5 | 1 | 0 | 6 | 0 |
| Hubbard, Trenidad, IWA | .974 | 113 | 177 | 11 | 5 | 193 | 0 |
| Huffman, Royce, NO | 1.000 | 10 | 13 | 0 | 0 | 13 | 0 |
| Hunter, Brian, MEM | 1.000 | 14 | 29 | 0 | 0 | 29 | 0 |
| Ibanez, Raul, TAC* | 1.000 | 2 | 2 | 0 | 0 | 2 | 0 |
| Jackson, Damian, IWA | 1.000 | 3 | 4 | 1 | 0 | 5 | 1 |
| Jacobs, Greg, TAC* | .980 | 54 | 96 | 4 | 2 | 102 | 2 |
| Johnson, Dan, SCO* | .900 | 15 | 27 | 0 | 3 | 30 | 0 |
| Johnson, Gary, SLK* | .991 | 67 | 107 | 6 | 1 | 114 | 2 |
| Jones, Jason, OKL | .978 | 52 | 85 | 3 | 2 | 90 | 0 |
| Jordan, Brian, OKL | 1.000 | 4 | 7 | 0 | 0 | 7 | 0 |
| Kelton, David, IWA | .983 | 105 | 169 | 5 | 3 | 177 | 1 |
| Kingsale, Eugene, POR | .939 | 15 | 30 | 1 | 2 | 33 | 0 |
| Knott, Jon, POR | .989 | 106 | 171 | 3 | 2 | 176 | 0 |
| Kroeger, Josh, TCN* | .964 | 56 | 132 | 3 | 5 | 140 | 0 |
| Lankford, Ray, MEM* | 1.000 | 3 | 5 | 0 | 0 | 5 | 0 |
| Leone, Justin, TAC | 1.000 | 13 | 16 | 0 | 0 | 16 | 0 |
| Lewis, Fred, FRN* | .923 | 6 | 12 | 0 | 1 | 13 | 0 |
| Linden, Todd, FRN | .976 | 126 | 262 | 19 | 7 | 288 | 1 |
| Lockwood, Mike, SCO* | 1.000 | 34 | 52 | 1 | 0 | 53 | 0 |
| Logan, Kyle, NO* | .962 | 114 | 216 | 9 | 9 | 234 | 3 |
| Lopez, Mickey, TAC | 1.000 | 1 | 2 | 0 | 0 | 2 | 0 |
| Mabry, John, MEM* | 1.000 | 18 | 24 | 3 | 0 | 27 | 0 |
| Mateo, Ruben, NVL | .981 | 30 | 50 | 1 | 1 | 52 | 1 |
| Matos, Julius, EDM | 1.000 | 13 | 21 | 2 | 0 | 23 | 0 |
| Matos, Pascual, CSP | 1.000 | 2 | 2 | 0 | 0 | 2 | 0 |
| Matthews, Gary, OKL | .971 | 37 | 66 | 1 | 2 | 69 | 0 |
| McCracken, Quinton, TCN | 1.000 | 13 | 22 | 2 | 0 | 24 | 0 |
| McMillon, Billy, SCO* | 1.000 | 5 | 6 | 0 | 0 | 6 | 0 |
| McPherson, Dallas, SLK* | 1.000 | 1 | 1 | 1 | 0 | 2 | 0 |
| Michaelis, Derek, LVG* | 1.000 | 4 | 6 | 0 | 0 | 6 | 0 |
| Mondesi, Raul, SLK | .800 | 2 | 3 | 1 | 1 | 5 | 0 |
| Murray, Calvin, IWA | .992 | 118 | 244 | 7 | 2 | 253 | 4 |
| Myrow, Brian, LVG* | 1.000 | 16 | 22 | 0 | 0 | 22 | 0 |
| Nady, Xavier, POR | .974 | 61 | 111 | 3 | 3 | 117 | 0 |
| Neal, Steve, TCN* | 1.000 | 6 | 8 | 0 | 0 | 8 | 0 |
| Nesbit, Michael, TAC | 1.000 | 6 | 14 | 0 | 0 | 14 | 0 |
| Nivar, Ramon, OKL | .988 | 67 | 156 | 5 | 2 | 163 | 1 |
| Olson, Tim, TCN | 1.000 | 9 | 16 | 0 | 0 | 16 | 0 |
| Olszta, Eddie, NVL | 1.000 | 4 | 4 | 0 | 0 | 4 | 0 |
| Padgett, Matthew, ABQ* | .990 | 116 | 196 | 8 | 2 | 206 | 3 |
| Pascucci, Val, EDM | .964 | 30 | 50 | 4 | 2 | 56 | 3 |
| Pellow, Kit, CSP | 1.000 | 4 | 8 | 0 | 0 | 8 | 0 |
| Pena, Elvis, CSP | .933 | 14 | 13 | 1 | 1 | 15 | 1 |
| Perez, Santiago, OKL | 1.000 | 13 | 24 | 1 | 0 | 25 | 1 |
| Petrick, Ben, POR | 1.000 | 10 | 13 | 0 | 0 | 13 | 0 |
| Phillips, Paul, OMA | 1.000 | 1 | 1 | 0 | 0 | 1 | 0 |
| Piedra, Jorge, CSP* | .978 | 92 | 168 | 7 | 4 | 179 | 0 |
| Porter, Colin, MEM* | .995 | 94 | 200 | 6 | 1 | 207 | 2 |
| Pride, Curtis, SLK* | 1.000 | 16 | 38 | 0 | 0 | 38 | 0 |
| Prieto, Chris, MEM* | .985 | 123 | 248 | 10 | 4 | 262 | 3 |
| Quinlan, Robb, SLK | 1.000 | 2 | 2 | 0 | 0 | 2 | 0 |
| Quinn, Mark, MEM | .969 | 20 | 30 | 1 | 1 | 32 | 0 |
| Ramirez, Julio, TCN | .978 | 117 | 261 | 10 | 6 | 277 | 2 |
| Reed, Jeremy, TAC* | .982 | 61 | 159 | 6 | 3 | 168 | 2 |
| Repko, Jason, LVG | .988 | 69 | 162 | 4 | 2 | 168 | 0 |
| Reyes, Rene, CSP | .957 | 72 | 128 | 7 | 6 | 141 | 0 |
| Riggs, Adam, SLK | .982 | 64 | 105 | 6 | 2 | 113 | 0 |
| Riggs, Eric, LVG | 1.000 | 5 | 7 | 1 | 0 | 8 | 0 |
| Rios, Armando, MEM* | 1.000 | 3 | 5 | 0 | 0 | 5 | 0 |
| Rivera, Carlos, NVL* | .947 | 14 | 18 | 0 | 1 | 19 | 0 |
| Robinson, Kerry, POR* | .986 | 40 | 66 | 2 | 1 | 69 | 0 |
| Rodriguez, Javy, SLK | 1.000 | 2 | 3 | 0 | 0 | 3 | 0 |
| Ross, Cody, LVG | .972 | 57 | 99 | 4 | 3 | 106 | 0 |
| Ryan, Rob, NO* | .974 | 39 | 73 | 3 | 2 | 78 | 0 |
| Ryan, Rob, ABQ* | 1.000 | 16 | 36 | 0 | 0 | 36 | 0 |
| Ryan, Rob, NO-ABQ* | .982 | 55 | 109 | 3 | 2 | 114 | 0 |
| Sandel, George, TAC | 1.000 | 2 | 2 | 1 | 0 | 3 | 0 |
| Sanders, Anthony, CSP | .969 | 24 | 31 | 0 | 1 | 32 | 0 |
| Santos, Francisco, FRN* | 1.000 | 15 | 14 | 2 | 0 | 16 | 0 |
| Scales, Bobby, POR | .893 | 18 | 24 | 1 | 3 | 28 | 0 |
| Selby, Bill, IWA* | .949 | 26 | 35 | 2 | 2 | 39 | 0 |
| Shabala, Adam, FRN* | .985 | 100 | 181 | 16 | 3 | 200 | 1 |
| Sheldon, Scott, NVL | 1.000 | 15 | 20 | 0 | 0 | 20 | 0 |
| Short, Rick, OMA | 1.000 | 6 | 8 | 0 | 0 | 8 | 0 |
| Shumpert, Terry, NVL | .000 | 3 | 0 | 0 | 1 | 1 | 0 |
| Sorensen, Zach, SLK | .978 | 57 | 127 | 6 | 3 | 136 | 1 |
| Stanley, Henri, POR* | .971 | 27 | 66 | 0 | 2 | 68 | 0 |
| Stanley, Henri, LVG* | .975 | 21 | 39 | 0 | 1 | 40 | 0 |
| Stanley, Henri, POR-LVG* | .972 | 48 | 105 | 0 | 3 | 108 | 0 |
| Stanley, Steve, SCO* | .973 | 65 | 140 | 2 | 4 | 146 | 0 |
| Stratton, Robert, FRN | 1.000 | 23 | 45 | 2 | 0 | 47 | 1 |
| Strong, Jamal, TAC | .985 | 61 | 127 | 3 | 2 | 132 | 1 |
| Sutton, Larry, ABQ* | 1.000 | 5 | 4 | 0 | 0 | 4 | 0 |
| Swisher, Nick, SCO | .977 | 121 | 287 | 6 | 7 | 300 | 0 |
| Taguchi, So, MEM | 1.000 | 16 | 30 | 0 | 0 | 30 | 0 |
| Terrero, Luis, TCN | .978 | 57 | 127 | 5 | 3 | 135 | 0 |
| Theodorou, Nick, LVG | .989 | 50 | 88 | 3 | 1 | 92 | 0 |
| Thompson, Rich, NVL* | .974 | 109 | 253 | 5 | 7 | 265 | 0 |
| Thompson, Ryan, NO | .938 | 51 | 89 | 2 | 6 | 97 | 2 |
| Thrower, Jake, SLK | .909 | 8 | 9 | 1 | 1 | 11 | 0 |
| Toca, Jorge, EDM | 1.000 | 3 | 2 | 0 | 0 | 2 | 0 |
| Torcato, Tony, FRN* | .991 | 65 | 109 | 4 | 1 | 114 | 0 |
| Tracy, Andy, CSP* | 1.000 | 3 | 5 | 1 | 0 | 6 | 1 |
| Tracy, Chad, TCN* | 1.000 | 3 | 5 | 0 | 0 | 5 | 0 |
| Ugueto, Luis, TAC | .948 | 72 | 105 | 5 | 6 | 116 | 0 |
| Varner, Noochie, TCN | .994 | 87 | 151 | 5 | 1 | 157 | 2 |
| Victorino, Shane, LVG | .984 | 50 | 118 | 9 | 2 | 129 | 1 |
| Ward, Daryle, NVL* | 1.000 | 2 | 1 | 0 | 0 | 1 | 0 |
| Ware, Jeremy, EDM | .972 | 22 | 35 | 0 | 1 | 36 | 0 |
| Wathan, Derek, ABQ | .985 | 37 | 62 | 2 | 1 | 65 | 0 |
| Watson, Brandon, EDM* | .981 | 130 | 310 | 6 | 6 | 322 | 2 |
| Watson, Matt, SCO* | .955 | 123 | 223 | 10 | 11 | 244 | 0 |
| Weber, Jon, SCO* | 1.000 | 14 | 19 | 0 | 0 | 19 | 0 |
| Werth, Jayson, LVG | 1.000 | 12 | 14 | 0 | 0 | 14 | 0 |
| Wesson, Barry, SLK | 1.000 | 44 | 102 | 1 | 0 | 103 | 0 |
| Zoccolillo, Peter, OKL* | .985 | 72 | 128 | 3 | 2 | 133 | 1 |

## CATCHERS

| Player, Team | Pct. | G | PO | A | E | TC | DP | PB |
|---|---|---|---|---|---|---|---|---|
| Ansman, Craig, TCN | .990 | 93 | 547 | 45 | 6 | 598 | 7 | 6 |
| Ardoin, Danny, OKL | .976 | 68 | 403 | 48 | 11 | 462 | 7 | 10 |
| Ashby, Chris, ABQ | .991 | 16 | 96 | 9 | 1 | 106 | 1 | 1 |
| Baker, John, SCO* | 1.000 | 12 | 101 | 7 | 0 | 108 | 0 | 1 |
| Borders, Pat, TAC | .996 | 36 | 248 | 21 | 1 | 270 | 3 | 1 |
| Brito, Juan, TCN | .995 | 31 | 168 | 14 | 1 | 183 | 0 | 0 |
| Brown, Jason, EDM | 1.000 | 5 | 24 | 5 | 0 | 29 | 0 | 0 |
| Buck, John, NO | .971 | 61 | 330 | 34 | 11 | 375 | 8 | 7 |
| Budde, Ryan, SLK | 1.000 | 4 | 27 | 1 | 0 | 28 | 0 | 0 |
| Casanova, Raul, OMA | .988 | 26 | 151 | 8 | 2 | 161 | 0 | 0 |
| Castillo, Alberto, OMA | .985 | 41 | 300 | 20 | 5 | 325 | 2 | 7 |
| Closser, JD, CSP | .983 | 76 | 544 | 44 | 10 | 598 | 3 | 6 |
| Conway, Dan, CSP | 1.000 | 6 | 46 | 3 | 0 | 49 | 0 | 2 |
| Cota, Humberto, NVL | 1.000 | 7 | 43 | 7 | 0 | 50 | 1 | 0 |
| Cresse, Brad, MEM | .984 | 17 | 109 | 15 | 2 | 126 | 2 | 1 |
| Davis, Ben, TAC | .997 | 38 | 299 | 13 | 1 | 313 | 3 | 4 |
| Del Chiaro, Brent, SLK | 1.000 | 3 | 12 | 2 | 0 | 14 | 1 | 0 |
| Donnels, Chris, CSP* | 1.000 | 1 | 3 | 1 | 0 | 4 | 0 | 1 |
| Eckelman, Alex, NO | 1.000 | 2 | 12 | 1 | 0 | 13 | 1 | 0 |
| Esposito, Brian, OKL | 1.000 | 1 | 6 | 0 | 0 | 6 | 0 | 0 |
| Fatheree, Danny, NO | .970 | 8 | 32 | 0 | 1 | 33 | 0 | 0 |
| Fick, Robert, POR* | 1.000 | 1 | 1 | 0 | 0 | 1 | 0 | 0 |
| Gonzalez, Wiki, TAC | .991 | 12 | 105 | 5 | 1 | 111 | 1 | 1 |
| Greene, Todd, CSP | 1.000 | 3 | 14 | 2 | 0 | 16 | 0 | 0 |
| Gregorio, Tom, SLK | .981 | 55 | 326 | 37 | 7 | 370 | 5 | 7 |
| Haad, Yamid, POR | .987 | 69 | 491 | 30 | 7 | 528 | 4 | 7 |
| Hammock, Robby, TCN | .968 | 6 | 29 | 1 | 1 | 31 | 0 | 0 |
| Hatcher, Justin, OKL | 1.000 | 2 | 10 | 0 | 0 | 10 | 0 | 0 |
| Hernandez, Ramon, POR | .938 | 7 | 24 | 6 | 2 | 32 | 0 | 0 |
| Hill, Koyie, LVG | .994 | 81 | 562 | 56 | 4 | 622 | 4 | 10 |
| Hoover, Paul, EDM | .990 | 33 | 190 | 17 | 2 | 209 | 1 | 5 |
| Horner, Jim, TAC | .996 | 33 | 213 | 11 | 1 | 225 | 2 | 3 |
| House, JR, NVL | .993 | 63 | 428 | 29 | 3 | 460 | 1 | 6 |
| Huckaby, Ken, OKL | .989 | 29 | 171 | 16 | 2 | 189 | 0 | 1 |
| Jackson, Steve, SCO | 1.000 | 3 | 4 | 0 | 0 | 4 | 0 | 0 |
| Jorgensen, Ryan, ABQ | .989 | 56 | 336 | 31 | 4 | 371 | 4 | 3 |
| Kellner, Ryan, LVG | .977 | 56 | 355 | 28 | 9 | 392 | 3 | 10 |

| Player, Team | Pct. | G | PO | A | E | TC | DP | PB |
|---|---|---|---|---|---|---|---|---|
| Knorr, Randy, EDM | .992 | 75 | 460 | 24 | 4 | 488 | 6 | 4 |
| Kopitzke, Casey, IWA | .989 | 79 | 492 | 49 | 6 | 547 | 5 | 5 |
| Kuzmic, Craig, FRN | .991 | 38 | 215 | 11 | 2 | 228 | 0 | 3 |
| Laird, Gerald, OKL | .955 | 4 | 21 | 0 | 1 | 22 | 0 | 1 |
| Langill, Eric, LVG | 1.000 | 8 | 39 | 1 | 0 | 40 | 0 | 0 |
| Lunar, Fernando, IWA | .993 | 77 | 542 | 55 | 4 | 601 | 11 | 5 |
| Lunsford, Trey, FRN | .991 | 116 | 697 | 47 | 7 | 751 | 4 | 14 |
| Maduro, Jorge, TAC | 1.000 | 9 | 52 | 2 | 0 | 54 | 0 | 1 |
| Mahoney, Mike, MEM | .986 | 76 | 530 | 46 | 8 | 584 | 3 | 5 |
| Matos, Pascual, CSP | .983 | 16 | 113 | 4 | 2 | 119 | 1 | 2 |
| Mayne, Brent, TCN* | 1.000 | 5 | 14 | 3 | 0 | 17 | 0 | 1 |
| McDonald, Keith, NVL | .997 | 80 | 546 | 33 | 2 | 581 | 8 | 4 |
| McKay, Cody, MEM* | .991 | 19 | 111 | 5 | 1 | 117 | 1 | 2 |
| Molina, Yadier, MEM | 1.000 | 36 | 266 | 35 | 0 | 301 | 3 | 9 |
| Moon, Brian, TAC | 1.000 | 16 | 81 | 17 | 0 | 98 | 1 | 1 |
| Morales, Willie, CSP | 1.000 | 2 | 10 | 2 | 0 | 12 | 0 | 1 |
| Motte, Jason, MEM | 1.000 | 2 | 12 | 2 | 0 | 14 | 0 | 0 |
| Munhall, Brian, FRN | 1.000 | 1 | 2 | 0 | 0 | 2 | 0 | 0 |
| Myers, Cory, TCN | .981 | 30 | 142 | 16 | 3 | 161 | 1 | 3 |
| Nieves, Wil, SLK | .992 | 85 | 602 | 58 | 5 | 665 | 4 | 9 |
| Norris, Dax, NO | .994 | 22 | 154 | 7 | 1 | 162 | 0 | 1 |
| Ojeda, Miguel, POR | .974 | 5 | 36 | 1 | 1 | 38 | 0 | 0 |
| Olszta, Eddie, NVL | 1.000 | 3 | 4 | 0 | 0 | 4 | 0 | 0 |
| Ortiz, Hector, CSP | .997 | 42 | 275 | 22 | 1 | 298 | 0 | 2 |
| Osik, Keith, ABQ | 1.000 | 18 | 109 | 12 | 0 | 121 | 3 | 2 |
| Pellow, Kit, CSP | .947 | 3 | 17 | 1 | 1 | 19 | 0 | 1 |
| Phillips, Paul, OMA | .995 | 77 | 522 | 44 | 3 | 569 | 2 | 8 |
| Quintero, Humberto, POR | .989 | 67 | 489 | 50 | 6 | 545 | 5 | 4 |
| Richardson, Mike, POR | 1.000 | 1 | 6 | 1 | 0 | 7 | 0 | 1 |
| Risinger, Ben, POR | .975 | 8 | 38 | 1 | 1 | 40 | 0 | 0 |
| Rivera, Mike, SCO | .980 | 45 | 325 | 22 | 7 | 354 | 1 | 3 |
| Rivera, Rene, TAC | 1.000 | 4 | 36 | 1 | 0 | 37 | 0 | 0 |
| Rose, Mike, SCO | .988 | 86 | 611 | 33 | 8 | 652 | 0 | 3 |
| Smith, Jeff, OKL* | 1.000 | 13 | 86 | 5 | 0 | 91 | 0 | 1 |
| Snusz, Chris, NVL | 1.000 | 6 | 16 | 0 | 0 | 16 | 0 | 1 |
| Treanor, Matt, ABQ | .991 | 61 | 399 | 30 | 4 | 433 | 2 | 6 |
| Tremie, Chris, NO | .982 | 65 | 387 | 38 | 8 | 433 | 3 | 7 |
| Ullery, Dave, OMA* | 1.000 | 5 | 24 | 0 | 0 | 24 | 0 | 0 |
| Waldron, Jeff, OKL* | .995 | 34 | 207 | 10 | 1 | 218 | 3 | 0 |
| Wilson, John, EDM | .996 | 33 | 234 | 24 | 1 | 259 | 3 | 2 |
| Wilson, Tom, SCO | 1.000 | 5 | 29 | 2 | 0 | 31 | 0 | 1 |
| Wilson, Tom, LVG | .986 | 9 | 65 | 6 | 1 | 72 | 1 | 4 |
| Wilson, Tom, SCO-LVG | .990 | 0 | 94 | 8 | 1 | 103 | 1 | 5 |
| Zinter, Alan, TCN | 1.000 | 2 | 16 | 1 | 0 | 17 | 0 | |

## PITCHERS

| Player, Team | Pct. | G | PO | A | E | TC | DP |
|---|---|---|---|---|---|---|---|
| Aardsma, Dave, FRN | 1.000 | 44 | 0 | 2 | 0 | 2 | 0 |
| Abreu, Winston, TCN | .889 | 28 | 7 | 1 | 1 | 9 | 1 |
| Abreu, Winston, LVG | 1.000 | 14 | 0 | 3 | 0 | 3 | 0 |
| Abreu, Winston, TCN-LVG | .917 | 42 | 7 | 4 | 1 | 12 | 1 |
| Acevedo, Juan, NVL | 1.000 | 18 | 2 | 3 | 0 | 5 | 0 |
| Affeldt, Jeremy, OMA* | 1.000 | 4 | 0 | 1 | 0 | 1 | 0 |
| Almonte, Hector, CSP | 1.000 | 12 | 0 | 1 | 0 | 1 | 0 |
| Almonte, Hector, NVL | 1.000 | 29 | 1 | 3 | 0 | 4 | 0 |
| Almonte, Hector, CSP-NVL | 1.000 | 41 | 1 | 4 | 0 | 5 | 0 |
| Alvarez, Juan, ABQ* | 1.000 | 48 | 0 | 6 | 0 | 6 | 1 |
| Anderson, Craig, TAC* | 1.000 | 26 | 4 | 12 | 0 | 16 | 0 |
| Anderson, Jimmy, IWA* | .966 | 16 | 9 | 19 | 1 | 29 | 1 |
| Anderson, Luke, FRN | .000 | 4 | 0 | 0 | 1 | 1 | 0 |
| Andrade, Steve, SLK | .750 | 12 | 1 | 2 | 1 | 4 | 0 |
| Andrew, Jason, OKL | 1.000 | 1 | 0 | 1 | 0 | 1 | 1 |
| Ankiel, Rick, MEM* | 1.000 | 1 | 0 | 2 | 0 | 2 | 0 |
| Appier, Kevin, OMA | 1.000 | 1 | 1 | 0 | 0 | 1 | 0 |
| Aquino, Greg, TCN | .923 | 21 | 3 | 9 | 1 | 13 | 1 |
| Armas, Tony, EDM | 1.000 | 2 | 1 | 1 | 0 | 2 | 0 |
| Atchison, Scott, TAC | 1.000 | 40 | 6 | 9 | 0 | 15 | 2 |
| Babula, Shaun, NO* | 1.000 | 26 | 1 | 6 | 0 | 7 | 0 |
| Backe, Brandon, NO | .933 | 19 | 3 | 11 | 1 | 15 | 3 |
| Bacsik, Mike, OKL* | 1.000 | 34 | 3 | 9 | 0 | 12 | 0 |
| Baek, Cha-Seung, TAC | .909 | 14 | 11 | 9 | 2 | 22 | 1 |
| Barber, Scott, TCN | 1.000 | 2 | 2 | 0 | 0 | 2 | 0 |
| Barzilla, Philip, NO* | .750 | 27 | 1 | 5 | 2 | 8 | 0 |
| Bauer, Peter, ABQ | 1.000 | 1 | 0 | 1 | 0 | 1 | 0 |
| Begg, Chris, FRN | 1.000 | 9 | 1 | 5 | 0 | 6 | 1 |
| Beltran, Francis, EDM | 1.000 | 6 | 1 | 2 | 0 | 3 | 0 |
| Beltran, Rigo, EDM* | 1.000 | 25 | 4 | 12 | 0 | 16 | 2 |
| Benes, Alan, MEM | .973 | 28 | 9 | 27 | 1 | 37 | 3 |
| Bentz, Chad, EDM* | 1.000 | 5 | 1 | 3 | 0 | 4 | 1 |
| Bergman, Dusty, SLK* | .905 | 45 | 3 | 16 | 2 | 21 | 2 |
| Bernero, Adam, CSP | 1.000 | 9 | 3 | 7 | 0 | 10 | 0 |
| Bierbrodt, Nick, OKL* | 1.000 | 5 | 1 | 6 | 0 | 7 | 1 |
| Billingsley, Brent, CSP* | 1.000 | 5 | 0 | 2 | 0 | 2 | 0 |
| Blackley, Travis, TAC* | .935 | 19 | 6 | 23 | 2 | 31 | 0 |
| Bland, Nate, IWA* | .875 | 53 | 2 | 12 | 2 | 16 | 2 |
| Blank, Matt, ABQ* | .955 | 34 | 16 | 26 | 2 | 44 | 4 |
| Blanton, Joe, SCO | .941 | 28 | 10 | 22 | 2 | 34 | 1 |
| Bootcheck, Chris, SLK | .936 | 28 | 21 | 23 | 3 | 47 | 4 |
| Borbon, Pedro, EDM* | 1.000 | 8 | 1 | 4 | 0 | 5 | 1 |
| Borland, Toby, ABQ | 1.000 | 34 | 4 | 5 | 0 | 9 | 2 |
| Borowski, Joe, IWA | .000 | 7 | 0 | 0 | 0 | 0 | 0 |
| Bost, Heath, NO | 1.000 | 44 | 2 | 4 | 0 | 6 | 0 |
| Bouknight, Kip, CSP | 1.000 | 19 | 4 | 5 | 0 | 9 | 1 |
| Bowles, Brian, CSP | 1.000 | 13 | 2 | 4 | 0 | 6 | 1 |
| Boyd, Jason, NVL | .667 | 11 | 1 | 1 | 1 | 3 | 0 |
| Bradford, Chad, SCO | 1.000 | 2 | 0 | 1 | 0 | 1 | 0 |
| Brazoban, Yhency, LVG | 1.000 | 10 | 2 | 2 | 0 | 4 | 0 |
| Brocail, Doug, OKL | 1.000 | 12 | 1 | 5 | 0 | 6 | 1 |
| Brohawn, Troy, LVG* | 1.000 | 72 | 4 | 11 | 0 | 15 | 1 |
| Brooks, Frank, NVL* | 1.000 | 42 | 2 | 10 | 0 | 12 | 0 |
| Bruback, Matt, POR | 1.000 | 14 | 4 | 11 | 0 | 15 | 0 |
| Brunet, Mike, SLK | 1.000 | 13 | 3 | 8 | 0 | 11 | 0 |
| Bruney, Brian, TCN | 1.000 | 31 | 1 | 3 | 0 | 4 | 1 |
| Buchholz, Taylor, NO | .958 | 20 | 10 | 13 | 1 | 24 | 0 |
| Bukvich, Ryan, OMA | 1.000 | 38 | 2 | 2 | 0 | 4 | 0 |
| Bullinger, Kirk, NO | .889 | 28 | 0 | 8 | 1 | 9 | 1 |
| Bumatay, Mike, CSP* | 1.000 | 37 | 1 | 6 | 0 | 7 | 1 |
| Bump, Nate, ABQ | 1.000 | 3 | 2 | 0 | 0 | 2 | 0 |
| Bumstead, Mike, POR | 1.000 | 18 | 5 | 2 | 0 | 7 | 0 |
| Burke, Erick, OKL* | .667 | 24 | 0 | 2 | 1 | 3 | 0 |
| Burnett, AJ, ABQ | .500 | 1 | 0 | 1 | 1 | 2 | 0 |
| Burnett, Sean, NVL* | 1.000 | 10 | 1 | 14 | 0 | 15 | 0 |
| Bynum, Mike, POR* | 1.000 | 62 | 7 | 16 | 0 | 23 | 2 |
| Byrdak, Tim, POR* | .778 | 20 | 2 | 5 | 2 | 9 | 1 |
| Calero, Kiko, MEM | .833 | 12 | 3 | 2 | 1 | 6 | 1 |
| Cali, Carmen, MEM* | 1.000 | 17 | 0 | 3 | 0 | 3 | 0 |
| Cammack, Eric, SCO | 1.000 | 47 | 7 | 5 | 0 | 12 | 0 |
| Camp, Shawn, OMA | 1.000 | 15 | 1 | 4 | 0 | 5 | 0 |
| Cannon, Jon, TCN* | .968 | 33 | 8 | 22 | 1 | 31 | 0 |
| Carrara, Giovanni, IWA | 1.000 | 20 | 1 | 2 | 0 | 3 | 1 |
| Carrara, Giovanni, LVG | .500 | 11 | 1 | 0 | 1 | 2 | 1 |
| Carrara, Giovanni, IWA-LVG | .800 | 31 | 2 | 2 | 1 | 5 | 2 |
| Carrasco, DJ, OMA | .941 | 32 | 4 | 12 | 1 | 17 | 1 |
| Cash, David, IWA | .750 | 3 | 1 | 2 | 1 | 4 | 1 |
| Cerda, Jaime, OMA* | 1.000 | 4 | 0 | 2 | 0 | 2 | 1 |
| Cervantes, Chris, TCN* | 1.000 | 5 | 1 | 0 | 0 | 1 | 0 |
| Chavez, Wilton, EDM | .950 | 28 | 18 | 20 | 2 | 40 | 2 |
| Chiasson, Scott, IWA | 1.000 | 15 | 0 | 3 | 0 | 3 | 0 |
| Chiavacci, Ron, EDM | 1.000 | 25 | 4 | 5 | 0 | 9 | 0 |
| Childers, Jason, EDM | 1.000 | 14 | 0 | 2 | 0 | 2 | 0 |
| Choate, Randy, TCN* | 1.000 | 15 | 1 | 4 | 0 | 5 | 1 |
| Chouinard, Bobby, NO | 1.000 | 26 | 2 | 5 | 0 | 7 | 1 |
| Christman, Tim, TAC* | .778 | 30 | 3 | 4 | 2 | 9 | 0 |
| Clontz, Brad, OKL | .833 | 59 | 0 | 5 | 1 | 6 | 0 |
| Coco, Pasqual, EDM | 1.000 | 4 | 0 | 1 | 0 | 1 | 0 |
| Cook, Aaron, CSP | .889 | 7 | 6 | 10 | 2 | 18 | 0 |
| Cooper, Brian, FRN | 1.000 | 4 | 0 | 2 | 0 | 2 | 0 |
| Corcoran, Roy, EDM | 1.000 | 30 | 3 | 5 | 0 | 8 | 0 |
| Corey, Bryan, IWA | 1.000 | 10 | 2 | 2 | 0 | 4 | 0 |
| Corey, Mark, NVL | .667 | 34 | 1 | 3 | 2 | 6 | 0 |
| Cormier, Lance, TCN | 1.000 | 8 | 6 | 9 | 0 | 15 | 0 |
| Correia, Kevin, FRN | .864 | 29 | 10 | 9 | 3 | 22 | 1 |
| Cosgrove, Mike, CSP | .000 | 1 | 0 | 0 | 0 | 0 | 0 |
| Creek, Doug, MEM* | 1.000 | 33 | 0 | 5 | 0 | 5 | 0 |
| Crudale, Mike, FRN | .000 | 4 | 0 | 0 | 2 | 2 | 0 |
| Crudale, Mike, NVL | .000 | 5 | 0 | 0 | 0 | 0 | 0 |
| Crudale, Mike, FRN-NVL | .000 | 9 | 0 | 0 | 2 | 2 | 0 |
| Cumberland, Chris, OMA* | 1.000 | 4 | 1 | 0 | 0 | 1 | 0 |
| Cummings, Jeremy, MEM | 1.000 | 1 | 0 | 1 | 0 | 1 | 0 |
| Daigle, Casey, TCN | .947 | 18 | 8 | 10 | 1 | 19 | 1 |
| Dawley, Joe, OMA | 1.000 | 9 | 0 | 1 | 0 | 1 | 0 |
| Deago, Roger, POR* | 1.000 | 5 | 0 | 2 | 0 | 2 | 1 |
| Dempster, Ryan, IWA | 1.000 | 6 | 1 | 1 | 0 | 2 | 0 |
| Dickson, Jason, OMA | 1.000 | 13 | 5 | 9 | 0 | 14 | 1 |

| Player, Team | Pct. | G | PO | A | E | TC | DP |
|---|---|---|---|---|---|---|---|
| Dohmann, Scott, CSP | .000 | 18 | 0 | 0 | 0 | 0 | 0 |
| Dominguez, Juan, OKL | 1.000 | 9 | 2 | 5 | 0 | 7 | 0 |
| Donnelly, Brendan, SLK | .000 | 3 | 0 | 0 | 0 | 0 | 0 |
| Downs, Scott, EDM* | .946 | 22 | 7 | 28 | 2 | 37 | 2 |
| Drese, Ryan, OKL | 1.000 | 1 | 0 | 3 | 0 | 3 | 1 |
| Driskill, Travis, CSP | 1.000 | 28 | 4 | 14 | 0 | 18 | 0 |
| Duckworth, Brandon, NO | 1.000 | 14 | 4 | 5 | 0 | 9 | 0 |
| Dunn, Scott, SLK | .938 | 46 | 9 | 6 | 1 | 16 | 1 |
| Eckelman, Alex, NO | 1.000 | 2 | 1 | 0 | 0 | 1 | 0 |
| Eckenstahler, Eric, IWA* | 1.000 | 8 | 1 | 1 | 0 | 2 | 0 |
| Eckert, Harold, LVG | 1.000 | 31 | 6 | 9 | 0 | 15 | 0 |
| Emanuel, Brandon, SLK | .813 | 38 | 4 | 9 | 3 | 16 | 0 |
| Enochs, Chris, NO | .923 | 38 | 7 | 17 | 2 | 26 | 2 |
| Erickson, Scott, OKL | 1.000 | 2 | 0 | 1 | 0 | 1 | 1 |
| Esslinger, Cameron, SLK | 1.000 | 8 | 0 | 1 | 0 | 1 | 0 |
| Estrella, Leo, FRN | .846 | 38 | 4 | 7 | 2 | 13 | 0 |
| Evert, Brett, TAC | 1.000 | 2 | 1 | 1 | 0 | 2 | 0 |
| Falkenborg, Brian, LVG | .923 | 18 | 7 | 5 | 1 | 13 | 0 |
| Farmer, Tom, LVG | .933 | 47 | 6 | 8 | 1 | 15 | 0 |
| Fernandez, Alfredo, POR | 1.000 | 1 | 0 | 3 | 0 | 3 | 0 |
| Fernandez, Jared, NO | .933 | 35 | 9 | 33 | 3 | 45 | 0 |
| Ferrari, Anthony, EDM* | 1.000 | 39 | 6 | 13 | 0 | 19 | 1 |
| Fetters, Mike, TCN | 1.000 | 7 | 1 | 2 | 0 | 3 | 0 |
| Figueroa, Nelson, NVL | .912 | 25 | 11 | 20 | 3 | 34 | 3 |
| Fikac, Jeremy, EDM | 1.000 | 28 | 7 | 6 | 0 | 13 | 0 |
| Fiore, Tony, NO | .889 | 23 | 3 | 5 | 1 | 9 | 1 |
| Flannery, Mike, ABQ | 1.000 | 29 | 1 | 3 | 0 | 4 | 1 |
| Flores, Randy, MEM* | .958 | 36 | 7 | 16 | 1 | 24 | 2 |
| Flores, Ron, SCO* | 1.000 | 55 | 1 | 3 | 0 | 4 | 0 |
| Flury, Patrick, ABQ | 1.000 | 9 | 0 | 1 | 0 | 1 | 0 |
| Foppert, Jesse, FRN | 1.000 | 4 | 3 | 1 | 0 | 4 | 0 |
| Fossum, Casey, TCN* | 1.000 | 3 | 1 | 2 | 0 | 3 | 0 |
| Francis, Jeff, CSP* | 1.000 | 7 | 1 | 1 | 0 | 2 | 0 |
| Freed, Mark, TCN* | .909 | 57 | 3 | 7 | 1 | 11 | 1 |
| Fuentes, Brian, CSP* | .000 | 5 | 0 | 0 | 0 | 0 | 0 |
| Fulmer, TA, TAC | 1.000 | 3 | 0 | 1 | 0 | 1 | 0 |
| Fussell, Chris, NVL | .938 | 51 | 5 | 10 | 1 | 16 | 1 |
| Gallo, Mike, NO* | 1.000 | 3 | 1 | 0 | 0 | 1 | 0 |
| Garcia, Jairo, SCO | 1.000 | 11 | 0 | 1 | 0 | 1 | 0 |
| Garcia, James, FRN | 1.000 | 8 | 4 | 3 | 0 | 7 | 0 |
| Garcia, Rosman, OKL | .944 | 41 | 4 | 13 | 1 | 18 | 2 |
| Gardner, Lee, FRN | 1.000 | 57 | 4 | 7 | 0 | 11 | 0 |
| George, Chris, OMA* | 1.000 | 20 | 5 | 9 | 0 | 14 | 0 |
| Gerk, Jordan, IWA* | .000 | 1 | 0 | 0 | 0 | 0 | 0 |
| Germano, Justin, POR | .957 | 20 | 10 | 12 | 1 | 23 | 2 |
| Gilfillan, Jason, CSP | .929 | 50 | 4 | 9 | 1 | 14 | 0 |
| Gissell, Chris, CSP | .938 | 24 | 2 | 13 | 1 | 16 | 0 |
| Glover, Gary, IWA | .714 | 20 | 3 | 2 | 2 | 7 | 0 |
| Gobble, Jimmy, OMA* | 1.000 | 4 | 1 | 1 | 0 | 2 | 0 |
| Gomes, Wayne, SCO | .833 | 52 | 2 | 13 | 3 | 18 | 1 |
| Gonzalez, Edgar, TCN | .950 | 15 | 7 | 12 | 1 | 20 | 1 |
| Gonzalez, Mike, NVL* | 1.000 | 14 | 1 | 3 | 0 | 4 | 0 |
| Good, Andrew, TCN | .800 | 5 | 3 | 1 | 1 | 5 | 0 |
| Gosling, Mike, TCN* | .920 | 24 | 3 | 20 | 2 | 25 | 2 |
| Gracesqui, Franklyn, ABQ* | 1.000 | 19 | 1 | 3 | 0 | 4 | 0 |
| Green, Steve, SLK | .968 | 29 | 5 | 25 | 1 | 31 | 0 |
| Greinke, Zack, OMA | 1.000 | 6 | 2 | 3 | 0 | 5 | 0 |
| Griffiths, Jeremy, NO | 1.000 | 15 | 2 | 4 | 0 | 6 | 0 |
| Gwyn, Marcus, SCO | 1.000 | 12 | 1 | 1 | 0 | 2 | 0 |
| Hackman, Luther, NVL | 1.000 | 37 | 0 | 4 | 0 | 4 | 0 |
| Hamilton, Joey, POR | .909 | 11 | 2 | 8 | 1 | 11 | 1 |
| Hammond, Chris, SCO* | 1.000 | 3 | 0 | 1 | 0 | 1 | 0 |
| Hampton, Matt, POR* | 1.000 | 37 | 1 | 5 | 0 | 6 | 1 |
| Hanrahan, Joel, LVG | .967 | 25 | 11 | 18 | 1 | 30 | 2 |
| Hansell, Greg, TCN | 1.000 | 15 | 2 | 2 | 0 | 4 | 0 |
| Harden, Rich, SCO | 1.000 | 1 | 0 | 1 | 0 | 1 | 0 |
| Haren, Danny, MEM | .960 | 21 | 9 | 15 | 1 | 25 | 2 |
| Harikkala, Tim, CSP | 1.000 | 4 | 0 | 1 | 0 | 1 | 0 |
| Harris, Jeff, TAC | 1.000 | 26 | 9 | 3 | 0 | 12 | 2 |
| Harris, Reggie, NO | 1.000 | 7 | 0 | 1 | 0 | 1 | 0 |
| Hartmann, Pete, ABQ* | 1.000 | 25 | 1 | 6 | 0 | 7 | 1 |
| Heaverlo, Jeff, TAC | .500 | 5 | 1 | 0 | 1 | 2 | 0 |
| Helling, Rick, OKL | 1.000 | 6 | 2 | 9 | 0 | 11 | 0 |
| Hennessey, Brad, FRN | 1.000 | 5 | 2 | 5 | 0 | 7 | 0 |
| Henrie, Matt, TCN | .833 | 8 | 4 | 6 | 2 | 12 | 0 |

| Player, Team | Pct. | G | PO | A | E | TC | DP |
|---|---|---|---|---|---|---|---|
| Hensley, Matt, SLK | 1.000 | 30 | 3 | 4 | 0 | 7 | 0 |
| Hernandez, Carlos, NO* | 1.000 | 23 | 6 | 11 | 0 | 17 | 1 |
| Herrera, Alex, CSP* | .857 | 37 | 0 | 6 | 1 | 7 | 1 |
| Hitchcock, Sterling, POR* | .600 | 3 | 1 | 2 | 2 | 5 | 0 |
| Hoerman, Jared, TAC | 1.000 | 39 | 3 | 8 | 0 | 11 | 0 |
| Horgan, Joe, EDM* | 1.000 | 13 | 1 | 1 | 0 | 2 | 0 |
| Horgan, Joe, MEM* | .800 | 10 | 1 | 3 | 1 | 5 | 0 |
| Horgan, Joe*, EDM-MEM | .857 | 23 | 2 | 4 | 1 | 7 | 0 |
| Howard, Ben, ABQ | 1.000 | 23 | 3 | 1 | 0 | 4 | 1 |
| Hudgins, John, OKL | 1.000 | 3 | 1 | 0 | 0 | 1 | 0 |
| Hudson, Tim, SCO | 1.000 | 1 | 1 | 0 | 0 | 1 | 0 |
| Huerta, Edgar, POR* | 1.000 | 6 | 0 | 3 | 0 | 3 | 0 |
| Hughes, Travis, OKL | .600 | 13 | 1 | 2 | 2 | 5 | 0 |
| Huisman, Justin, OMA | 1.000 | 32 | 3 | 7 | 0 | 10 | 1 |
| Izquierdo, Hansel, IWA | 1.000 | 21 | 1 | 0 | 0 | 1 | 0 |
| Izquierdo, Hansel, NVL | 1.000 | 5 | 1 | 2 | 0 | 3 | 0 |
| Izquierdo, Hansel, IWA-NVL | 1.000 | 26 | 2 | 2 | 0 | 4 | 0 |
| Jackson, Edwin, LVG | 1.000 | 19 | 9 | 16 | 0 | 25 | 3 |
| Jacome, Jason, FRN* | .929 | 35 | 4 | 9 | 1 | 14 | 0 |
| James, Delvin, SLK | 1.000 | 4 | 2 | 3 | 0 | 5 | 0 |
| Jarvis, Kevin, CSP | .833 | 6 | 1 | 4 | 1 | 6 | 0 |
| Jarvis, Kevin, NVL | 1.000 | 11 | 5 | 17 | 0 | 22 | 1 |
| Jarvis, Kevin, CSP-NVL | .964 | 17 | 6 | 21 | 1 | 28 | 1 |
| Jarvis, Matt, LVG* | 1.000 | 2 | 0 | 1 | 0 | 1 | 0 |
| Jenks, Bobby, SLK | 1.000 | 3 | 1 | 0 | 0 | 1 | 0 |
| Jensen, Ryan, FRN | 1.000 | 30 | 13 | 21 | 0 | 34 | 2 |
| Johnson, Mark, LVG | 1.000 | 37 | 10 | 15 | 0 | 25 | 1 |
| Johnson, Mike, EDM | .909 | 30 | 6 | 14 | 2 | 22 | 1 |
| Johnston, Mike, NVL* | .857 | 19 | 2 | 4 | 1 | 7 | 0 |
| Jones, Greg, SLK | 1.000 | 36 | 2 | 5 | 0 | 7 | 1 |
| Journell, Jimmy, MEM | .000 | 4 | 0 | 0 | 0 | 0 | 0 |
| Karp, Josh, EDM | .963 | 24 | 12 | 14 | 1 | 27 | 0 |
| Kelly, John, TAC | 1.000 | 7 | 1 | 2 | 0 | 3 | 0 |
| Kennedy, Joe, CSP* | 1.000 | 3 | 0 | 3 | 0 | 3 | 0 |
| Ketchner, Ryan, LVG* | 1.000 | 1 | 0 | 2 | 0 | 2 | 0 |
| Kida, Masao, LVG | 1.000 | 9 | 1 | 8 | 0 | 9 | 0 |
| Knott, Eric, LVG* | .667 | 12 | 0 | 2 | 1 | 3 | 1 |
| Kohn, Shawn, SCO | 1.000 | 24 | 2 | 2 | 0 | 4 | 0 |
| Koronka, John, IWA* | .921 | 29 | 7 | 28 | 3 | 38 | 0 |
| Kroon, Marc, CSP | 1.000 | 50 | 2 | 5 | 0 | 7 | 1 |
| Lee, Corey, SLK* | 1.000 | 4 | 0 | 3 | 0 | 3 | 0 |
| Lehr, Justin, SCO | 1.000 | 32 | 3 | 7 | 0 | 10 | 0 |
| Leicester, Jon, IWA | .882 | 12 | 3 | 12 | 2 | 17 | 2 |
| Linton, Doug, OMA | .913 | 27 | 7 | 14 | 2 | 23 | 1 |
| Lizarraga, Sergio, TCN | 1.000 | 3 | 1 | 0 | 0 | 1 | 0 |
| Loe, Kameron, OKL | 1.000 | 8 | 5 | 5 | 0 | 10 | 0 |
| Looper, Aaron, TAC | 1.000 | 8 | 0 | 1 | 0 | 1 | 0 |
| Lopez, Javier, CSP* | 1.000 | 8 | 0 | 2 | 0 | 2 | 0 |
| Lowry, Noah, FRN* | .889 | 17 | 3 | 13 | 2 | 18 | 0 |
| Lyon, Brandon, TCN | 1.000 | 6 | 2 | 0 | 0 | 2 | 0 |
| Mabeus, Chris, SCO | .933 | 37 | 2 | 12 | 1 | 15 | 1 |
| MacDougal, Mike, OMA | .000 | 14 | 0 | 0 | 0 | 0 | 0 |
| Madritsch, Bobby, TAC* | .889 | 12 | 3 | 5 | 1 | 9 | 0 |
| Mahomes, Pat, EDM | 1.000 | 20 | 1 | 5 | 0 | 6 | 1 |
| Mahomes, Pat, ABQ | 1.000 | 16 | 2 | 1 | 0 | 3 | 1 |
| Mahomes, Pat, NVL | 1.000 | 24 | 5 | 1 | 0 | 6 | 0 |
| Mahomes, Pat, EDM-ABQ-NVL | 1.000 | 60 | 8 | 7 | 0 | 15 | 2 |
| Majewski, Gary, EDM | .750 | 15 | 0 | 3 | 1 | 4 | 0 |
| Mann, Jim, NVL | 1.000 | 20 | 0 | 2 | 0 | 2 | 0 |
| Manning, David, IWA | 1.000 | 7 | 2 | 1 | 0 | 3 | 0 |
| Manzanillo, Josias, ABQ | 1.000 | 11 | 0 | 2 | 0 | 2 | 0 |
| Martin, Greg, NVL* | 1.000 | 5 | 1 | 0 | 0 | 1 | 0 |
| Martinez, Gustavo, TAC | .923 | 18 | 8 | 4 | 1 | 13 | 1 |
| Martinez, Luis, CSP* | .750 | 5 | 1 | 2 | 1 | 4 | 0 |
| Martinez, Luis, MEM* | 1.000 | 7 | 0 | 5 | 0 | 5 | 0 |
| Martinez, Luis*, CSP-MEM | .889 | 12 | 1 | 7 | 1 | 9 | 0 |
| Mathews, TJ, LVG | 1.000 | 13 | 1 | 2 | 0 | 3 | 0 |
| Maynard, Scott, TAC | 1.000 | 3 | 1 | 0 | 0 | 1 | 0 |
| Mazone, Brian, FRN* | 1.000 | 2 | 1 | 1 | 0 | 2 | 1 |
| McGlinchy, Kevin, IWA | 1.000 | 7 | 2 | 3 | 0 | 5 | 1 |
| McKay, Cody, MEM* | 1.000 | 1 | 1 | 0 | 0 | 1 | 0 |
| McLeary, Marty, POR | .962 | 44 | 7 | 18 | 1 | 26 | 1 |
| McLeary, Marty, ABQ | 1.000 | 1 | 0 | 1 | 0 | 1 | 0 |
| McLeary, Marty, POR-ABQ | .963 | 45 | 7 | 19 | 1 | 27 | 1 |
| McNutt, Mike, ABQ | .750 | 12 | 1 | 2 | 1 | 4 | 1 |
| Meche, Gil, TAC | 1.000 | 10 | 4 | 6 | 0 | 10 | 1 |

| Player, Team | Pct. | G | PO | A | E | TC | DP |
|---|---|---|---|---|---|---|---|
| Medders, Brandon, TCN | 1.000 | 11 | 0 | 3 | 0 | 3 | 0 |
| Meyer, Jake, IWA | 1.000 | 4 | 2 | 0 | 0 | 2 | 0 |
| Miadich, Bart, POR | 1.000 | 31 | 1 | 2 | 0 | 3 | 0 |
| Miadich, Bart, OKL | 1.000 | 21 | 0 | 2 | 0 | 2 | 0 |
| Miadich, Bart, POR-OKL | 1.000 | 52 | 1 | 4 | 0 | 5 | 0 |
| Michalak, Chris, ABQ* | .933 | 17 | 4 | 10 | 1 | 15 | 0 |
| Middlebrook, Jason, SLK | .962 | 29 | 7 | 18 | 1 | 26 | 1 |
| Mitchell, Nathan, IWA | 1.000 | 1 | 0 | 1 | 0 | 1 | 0 |
| Mitre, Sergio, IWA | 1.000 | 18 | 3 | 13 | 0 | 16 | 1 |
| Mizuo, Yoshitaka, SLK* | .875 | 24 | 2 | 5 | 1 | 8 | 1 |
| Montero, Agustin, LVG | .909 | 42 | 4 | 6 | 1 | 11 | 0 |
| Mottl, Ryan, NVL | .000 | 2 | 0 | 0 | 0 | 0 | 0 |
| Munter, Scott, FRN | 1.000 | 13 | 2 | 5 | 0 | 7 | 0 |
| Myers, Rodney, LVG | 1.000 | 24 | 4 | 5 | 0 | 9 | 0 |
| Nageotte, Clint, TAC | 1.000 | 14 | 9 | 8 | 0 | 17 | 2 |
| Nance, Shane, TCN* | .909 | 46 | 3 | 7 | 1 | 11 | 2 |
| Nannini, Mike, ABQ | .957 | 29 | 8 | 14 | 1 | 23 | 1 |
| Narron, Sam, OKL* | .955 | 17 | 5 | 16 | 1 | 22 | 0 |
| Neal, Blaine, POR | 1.000 | 27 | 2 | 2 | 0 | 4 | 0 |
| Neu, Mike, ABQ | .900 | 35 | 1 | 8 | 1 | 10 | 0 |
| Nickle, Doug, LVG | .875 | 19 | 0 | 7 | 1 | 8 | 0 |
| Nina, Elvin, OMA | 1.000 | 6 | 0 | 1 | 0 | 1 | 0 |
| Nina, Elvin, LVG | .667 | 10 | 2 | 0 | 1 | 3 | 0 |
| Nina, Elvin, OMA-LVG | .750 | 16 | 2 | 1 | 1 | 4 | 0 |
| Nolasco, Ricky, IWA | .500 | 9 | 0 | 1 | 1 | 2 | 0 |
| Nomo, Hideo, LVG | 1.000 | 4 | 0 | 1 | 0 | 1 | 0 |
| Nunez, Vladimir, CSP | .929 | 23 | 3 | 10 | 1 | 14 | 1 |
| Nussbeck, Mark, MEM | 1.000 | 3 | 1 | 1 | 0 | 2 | 0 |
| O`Brien, Matt, SCO* | 1.000 | 4 | 0 | 3 | 0 | 3 | 1 |
| O`Malley, Ryan, IWA* | 1.000 | 8 | 0 | 3 | 0 | 3 | 0 |
| Ohman, Will, IWA* | .750 | 45 | 2 | 4 | 2 | 8 | 0 |
| Olsen, Kevin, ABQ | 1.000 | 10 | 4 | 7 | 0 | 11 | 0 |
| Oropesa, Eddie, POR* | .889 | 37 | 1 | 7 | 1 | 9 | 0 |
| Osborne, Donovan, POR* | 1.000 | 7 | 2 | 3 | 0 | 5 | 0 |
| Osoria, Franquelis, LVG | 1.000 | 4 | 0 | 1 | 0 | 1 | 0 |
| Oxspring, Chris, POR | 1.000 | 17 | 9 | 10 | 0 | 19 | 1 |
| Park, Chan Ho, OKL | .800 | 4 | 2 | 2 | 1 | 5 | 1 |
| Parker, Christian, EDM | 1.000 | 8 | 2 | 3 | 0 | 5 | 0 |
| Paronto, Chad, MEM | 1.000 | 47 | 0 | 11 | 0 | 11 | 1 |
| Parque, Jim, TCN* | 1.000 | 12 | 0 | 11 | 0 | 11 | 0 |
| Parrott, Rhett, MEM | 1.000 | 7 | 1 | 3 | 0 | 4 | 1 |
| Patterson, Danny, MEM | 1.000 | 9 | 0 | 1 | 0 | 1 | 0 |
| Pavon, Julio, FRN | 1.000 | 5 | 0 | 2 | 0 | 2 | 0 |
| Pearce, Josh, MEM | 1.000 | 26 | 3 | 5 | 0 | 8 | 0 |
| Pearson, Jason, MEM* | 1.000 | 26 | 1 | 6 | 0 | 7 | 1 |
| Peralta, Joel, SLK | 1.000 | 39 | 5 | 1 | 0 | 6 | 0 |
| Perrault, Josh, TCN | 1.000 | 1 | 0 | 1 | 0 | 1 | 0 |
| Pettyjohn, Adam, FRN* | 1.000 | 21 | 2 | 21 | 0 | 23 | 0 |
| Pettyjohn, Adam, SCO* | 1.000 | 10 | 5 | 6 | 0 | 11 | 0 |
| Pettyjohn, Adam*, FRN-SCO | 1.000 | 31 | 7 | 27 | 0 | 34 | 0 |
| Pote, Lou, POR | 1.000 | 4 | 0 | 1 | 0 | 1 | 0 |
| Pote, Lou, SCO | 1.000 | 19 | 2 | 1 | 0 | 3 | 0 |
| Pote, Lou, POR-SCO | 1.000 | 23 | 2 | 2 | 0 | 4 | 0 |
| Powell, Greg, NO | 1.000 | 5 | 0 | 2 | 0 | 2 | 0 |
| Pratt, Andy, IWA* | 1.000 | 4 | 1 | 1 | 0 | 2 | 0 |
| Prior, Mark, IWA | 1.000 | 1 | 1 | 2 | 0 | 3 | 0 |
| Puffer, Brandon, POR | 1.000 | 22 | 4 | 4 | 0 | 8 | 0 |
| Pulsipher, Bill, TAC* | 1.000 | 2 | 0 | 1 | 0 | 1 | 0 |
| Putz, JJ, TAC | 1.000 | 7 | 0 | 1 | 0 | 1 | 0 |
| Qualls, Chad, NO | .964 | 32 | 4 | 23 | 1 | 28 | 1 |
| Raggio, Brady, TCN | 1.000 | 56 | 4 | 5 | 0 | 9 | 0 |
| Ramirez, Erasmo, OKL* | 1.000 | 14 | 4 | 5 | 0 | 9 | 0 |
| Ramos, Mario, SCO* | 1.000 | 29 | 5 | 17 | 0 | 22 | 1 |
| Randall, Scott, EDM | .000 | 3 | 0 | 0 | 0 | 0 | 0 |
| Randall, Scott, OMA | 1.000 | 12 | 2 | 5 | 0 | 7 | 0 |
| Randall, Scott, EDM-OMA | 1.000 | 15 | 2 | 5 | 0 | 7 | 0 |
| Rauch, Jon, EDM | 1.000 | 3 | 3 | 1 | 0 | 4 | 0 |
| Reames, Britt, SCO | .938 | 34 | 5 | 10 | 1 | 16 | 1 |
| Redding, Tim, NO | 1.000 | 5 | 0 | 2 | 0 | 2 | 0 |
| Regilio, Nick, OKL | .929 | 17 | 4 | 9 | 1 | 14 | 0 |
| Reid, Justin, NVL | 1.000 | 32 | 6 | 15 | 0 | 21 | 0 |
| Reyes, Al, MEM | 1.000 | 37 | 2 | 4 | 0 | 6 | 0 |
| Reynolds, Shane, TCN | 1.000 | 5 | 1 | 2 | 0 | 3 | 0 |
| Rheinecker, John, SCO* | .950 | 28 | 11 | 27 | 2 | 40 | 2 |
| Rhodes, Arthur, SCO* | .000 | 2 | 0 | 0 | 0 | 0 | 0 |
| Roberts, Willis, NVL | 1.000 | 35 | 0 | 9 | 0 | 9 | 1 |
| Robertson, Jeriome, EDM* | 1.000 | 7 | 1 | 4 | 0 | 5 | 0 |
| Rodriguez, Nerio, MEM | .923 | 16 | 3 | 9 | 1 | 13 | 0 |
| Rodriguez, Ricardo, OKL | 1.000 | 6 | 1 | 7 | 0 | 8 | 0 |
| Rojas, Chris, POR | .500 | 5 | 1 | 0 | 1 | 2 | 0 |
| Ruhl, Nathan, LVG | 1.000 | 6 | 2 | 0 | 0 | 2 | 0 |
| Runion, Tony, TAC | 1.000 | 12 | 0 | 1 | 0 | 1 | 0 |
| Rusch, Glendon, IWA* | .833 | 4 | 0 | 5 | 1 | 6 | 1 |
| Rust, Evan, MEM | .769 | 28 | 1 | 9 | 3 | 13 | 0 |
| Ryan, Jason, OMA | 1.000 | 8 | 22 | 3 | 0 | 4 | 0 |
| Ryan, Jason, MEM | .889 | 14 | 5 | 11 | 2 | 18 | 0 |
| Ryan, Jason, OMA-MEM | .909 | 22 | 6 | 14 | 2 | 22 | 0 |
| Ryu, JK, IWA | .000 | 1 | 0 | 0 | 0 | 0 | 0 |
| Saarloos, Kirk, SCO | 1.000 | 5 | 4 | 6 | 0 | 10 | 0 |
| Saladin, Miguel, NO | .923 | 49 | 5 | 7 | 1 | 13 | 1 |
| Sanders, Scott, ABQ | .870 | 20 | 6 | 14 | 3 | 23 | 3 |
| Schroder, Chris, EDM | 1.000 | 17 | 2 | 2 | 0 | 4 | 0 |
| Schultz, Mike, TCN | 1.000 | 7 | 0 | 2 | 0 | 2 | 0 |
| Seanez, Rudy, OMA | 1.000 | 24 | 3 | 3 | 0 | 6 | 0 |
| Sedlacek, Shawn, IWA | .963 | 22 | 8 | 18 | 1 | 27 | 0 |
| Serrano, Jimmy, OMA | 1.000 | 16 | 1 | 5 | 0 | 6 | 0 |
| Service, Scott, TCN | 1.000 | 24 | 3 | 2 | 0 | 5 | 0 |
| Sessions, Doug, EDM | 1.000 | 7 | 1 | 6 | 0 | 7 | 2 |
| Sessions, Doug, NO | .000 | 5 | 0 | 0 | 0 | 0 | 0 |
| Sessions, Doug, EDM-NO | 1.000 | 12 | 1 | 6 | 0 | 7 | 2 |
| Sherrill, George, TAC* | .500 | 36 | 0 | 1 | 1 | 2 | 0 |
| Shibilo, Andy, TAC | .600 | 16 | 1 | 2 | 2 | 5 | 0 |
| Shibilo, Andy, IWA | .833 | 9 | 2 | 3 | 1 | 6 | 1 |
| Shibilo, Andy, TAC-IWA | .727 | 25 | 3 | 5 | 3 | 11 | 1 |
| Shouse, Brian, OKL* | 1.000 | 9 | 1 | 1 | 0 | 2 | 0 |
| Shuey, Paul, LVG | 1.000 | 3 | 1 | 0 | 0 | 1 | 0 |
| Silva, Jose, TCN | 1.000 | 9 | 2 | 6 | 0 | 8 | 0 |
| Simas, Bill, TAC | 1.000 | 9 | 1 | 2 | 0 | 3 | 0 |
| Simontacchi, Jason, MEM | 1.000 | 33 | 7 | 14 | 0 | 21 | 0 |
| Simpson, Allan, CSP | 1.000 | 27 | 2 | 6 | 0 | 8 | 2 |
| Small, Aaron, ABQ | .971 | 27 | 13 | 21 | 1 | 35 | 3 |
| Smith, Roy, LVG | .889 | 30 | 3 | 5 | 1 | 9 | 1 |
| Snare, Ryan, OKL* | .944 | 26 | 3 | 14 | 1 | 18 | 0 |
| Sodowsky, Clint, ABQ | 1.000 | 48 | 4 | 8 | 0 | 12 | 0 |
| Song, Seung, EDM | .813 | 13 | 3 | 10 | 3 | 16 | 0 |
| Soriano, Rafael, TAC | .000 | 3 | 0 | 0 | 0 | 0 | 0 |
| Springer, Russ, NO | 1.000 | 26 | 1 | 1 | 0 | 2 | 0 |
| Stamler, Keith, OKL | .895 | 48 | 8 | 9 | 2 | 19 | 2 |
| Stanifer, Rob, EDM | 1.000 | 37 | 2 | 6 | 0 | 8 | 0 |
| Stark, Denny, CSP | .857 | 14 | 4 | 8 | 2 | 14 | 0 |
| Stauffer, Tim, POR | 1.000 | 14 | 15 | 12 | 0 | 27 | 2 |
| Steik, Richard, POR | .000 | 2 | 0 | 0 | 0 | 0 | 0 |
| Stein, Blake, NVL | 1.000 | 8 | 0 | 3 | 0 | 3 | 0 |
| Stemle, Steve, MEM | 1.000 | 54 | 8 | 16 | 0 | 24 | 1 |
| Stevenson, Jason, EDM* | 1.000 | 3 | 0 | 4 | 0 | 4 | 0 |
| Stewart, Cory, NVL* | .882 | 18 | 1 | 14 | 2 | 17 | 2 |
| Stewart, Scott, LVG* | 1.000 | 4 | 0 | 2 | 0 | 2 | 0 |
| Stockman, Phil, TCN | .900 | 12 | 0 | 9 | 1 | 10 | 0 |
| Stocks, Nick, MEM | .750 | 15 | 0 | 3 | 1 | 4 | 0 |
| Stone, Ricky, POR | .000 | 3 | 0 | 0 | 1 | 1 | 0 |
| Sturtze, Tanyon, LVG | .875 | 6 | 2 | 5 | 1 | 8 | 0 |
| Sweeney, Brian, POR | .960 | 24 | 9 | 15 | 1 | 25 | 1 |
| Sylvester, Billy, OKL | 1.000 | 19 | 4 | 5 | 0 | 9 | 0 |
| Szuminski, Jason, IWA | .938 | 41 | 1 | 14 | 1 | 16 | 1 |
| Tankersley, Dennis, POR | .903 | 19 | 12 | 16 | 3 | 31 | 0 |
| Taschner, Jack, FRN* | .667 | 18 | 2 | 2 | 2 | 6 | 0 |
| Tejera, Michael, ABQ* | 1.000 | 22 | 5 | 24 | 0 | 29 | 1 |
| Thompson, Brad, MEM | .500 | 3 | 1 | 0 | 1 | 2 | 0 |
| Thornton, Matt, TAC* | .882 | 16 | 3 | 12 | 2 | 17 | 1 |
| Tolar, Kevin, IWA* | .857 | 51 | 0 | 6 | 1 | 7 | 0 |
| Tollberg, Brian, CSP | .964 | 28 | 15 | 12 | 1 | 28 | 0 |
| Tomko, Brett, FRN | .000 | 1 | 0 | 0 | 0 | 0 | 0 |
| Totten, Heath, LVG | 1.000 | 28 | 18 | 18 | 0 | 36 | 2 |
| Tsao, Chin-hui, CSP | 1.000 | 4 | 1 | 2 | 0 | 3 | 0 |
| Tucker, TJ, EDM | 1.000 | 3 | 2 | 2 | 0 | 4 | 0 |
| Turnbow, Derrick, SLK | .923 | 46 | 5 | 7 | 1 | 13 | 1 |
| Urban, Jeff, FRN* | .882 | 46 | 2 | 13 | 2 | 17 | 0 |
| Valdez, Merkin, FRN | 1.000 | 1 | 0 | 3 | 0 | 3 | 1 |
| Valverde, Jose, TCN | 1.000 | 10 | 2 | 0 | 0 | 2 | 0 |
| Van Buren, Jermaine, IWA | .000 | 3 | 0 | 0 | 0 | 0 | 0 |
| VanBenschoten, John, NVL | 1.000 | 23 | 6 | 17 | 0 | 23 | 1 |
| Vance, Cory, OKL* | .833 | 8 | 2 | 3 | 1 | 6 | 0 |
| Venafro, Mike, OMA* | 1.000 | 35 | 0 | 13 | 0 | 13 | 2 |
| Venafro, Mike, LVG* | 1.000 | 5 | 0 | 3 | 0 | 3 | 0 |
| Venafro, Mike, OMA-LVG* | 1.000 | 40 | 0 | 16 | 0 | 16 | 2 |

| Player, Team | Pct. | G | PO | A | E | TC | DP |
|---|---|---|---|---|---|---|---|
| Veres, Dave, FRN | 1.000 | 29 | 3 | 2 | 0 | 5 | 0 |
| Villafuerte, Brandon, TCN | 1.000 | 23 | 5 | 3 | 0 | 8 | 0 |
| Villarreal, Oscar, TCN | 1.000 | 6 | 0 | 1 | 0 | 1 | 0 |
| Voyles, Brad, OMA | 1.000 | 10 | 1 | 2 | 0 | 3 | 1 |
| Wainwright, Adam, MEM | 1.000 | 12 | 2 | 7 | 0 | 9 | 0 |
| Walker, Kevin, FRN* | 1.000 | 48 | 4 | 10 | 0 | 14 | 1 |
| Walker, Tyler, FRN | 1.000 | 9 | 4 | 1 | 0 | 5 | 1 |
| Walrond, Les, OMA* | .957 | 19 | 8 | 14 | 1 | 23 | 0 |
| Ward, Bryan, TAC* | 1.000 | 7 | 0 | 3 | 0 | 3 | 0 |
| Ward, Jeremy, TCN | 1.000 | 6 | 1 | 0 | 0 | 1 | 0 |
| Wasdin, John, OKL | .938 | 18 | 6 | 9 | 1 | 16 | 0 |
| Watkins, Steve, POR | 1.000 | 22 | 5 | 7 | 0 | 12 | 1 |
| Wayne, Justin, ABQ | .947 | 13 | 5 | 13 | 1 | 19 | 0 |
| Wear, Greg, TAC | 1.000 | 7 | 0 | 4 | 0 | 4 | 0 |
| Webb, Alan, POR* | .000 | 8 | 0 | 0 | 0 | 0 | 0 |
| Weber, Ben, SLK | 1.000 | 15 | 2 | 1 | 0 | 3 | 0 |
| Wellemeyer, Todd, IWA | 1.000 | 14 | 1 | 2 | 0 | 3 | 0 |
| Wendell, Turk, CSP | 1.000 | 12 | 1 | 4 | 0 | 5 | 0 |
| Westmoreland, Clay, ABQ | .000 | 5 | 0 | 0 | 0 | 0 | 0 |
| White, Matt, OMA* | 1.000 | 23 | 1 | 8 | 0 | 9 | 0 |
| White, Rick, LVG | 1.000 | 6 | 1 | 1 | 0 | 2 | 0 |
| Williams, Dave, NVL* | .905 | 20 | 3 | 16 | 2 | 21 | 0 |
| Williams, Randy, TAC* | .950 | 50 | 6 | 13 | 1 | 20 | 1 |
| Williams, Todd, OKL | .667 | 27 | 0 | 4 | 2 | 6 | 0 |
| Wilson, Kris, OMA | .915 | 28 | 18 | 25 | 4 | 47 | 4 |
| Wood, Kerry, IWA | 1.000 | 1 | 0 | 1 | 0 | 1 | 0 |
| Wood, Mike, SCO | .889 | 15 | 12 | 20 | 4 | 36 | 0 |
| Woodard, Steve, SCO | .893 | 18 | 10 | 15 | 3 | 28 | 0 |
| Woodard, Steve, MEM | 1.000 | 4 | 2 | 3 | 0 | 5 | 0 |
| Woodard, Steve, SCO-MEM | .909 | 22 | 12 | 18 | 3 | 33 | 0 |
| Woods, Jake, SLK* | 1.000 | 15 | 4 | 4 | 0 | 8 | 2 |
| Wright, Jamey, OMA | .892 | 18 | 12 | 21 | 4 | 37 | 3 |
| Wuertz, Michael, IWA | 1.000 | 37 | 2 | 3 | 0 | 5 | 0 |
| Young, Chris, OKL | 1.000 | 5 | 2 | 4 | 0 | 6 | 1 |
| Young, Jason, CSP | 1.000 | 7 | 3 | 3 | 0 | 6 | 0 |
| Young, Tim, MEM* | .500 | 8 | 0 | 1 | 1 | 2 | 0 |
| Zerbe, Chad, FRN* | .962 | 33 | 9 | 16 | 1 | 26 | 1 |
| Ziegler, Mike, SCO | 1.000 | 18 | 1 | 11 | 0 | 12 | 1 |

## LEAGUE CHAMPIONS

| Year | Team | Pct. |
|---|---|---|
| 1903— | Los Angeles | .630 |
| 1904— | Tacoma | .589 |
| | Tacoma§ | .571 |
| | Los Angeles§ | .571 |
| 1905— | Tacoma | .583 |
| | Los Angeles* | .604 |
| 1906— | Portland | .657 |
| 1907— | Los Angeles | .608 |
| 1908— | Los Angeles | .585 |
| 1909— | San Francisco | .623 |
| 1910— | Portland | .567 |
| 1911— | Portland | .589 |
| 1912— | Oakland | .591 |
| 1913— | Portland | .559 |
| 1914— | Portland | .574 |
| 1915— | San Francisco | .570 |
| 1916— | Los Angeles | .601 |
| 1917— | San Francisco | .561 |
| 1918— | Vernon | .569 |
| | Los Angeles (2nd)◆ | .548 |
| 1919— | Vernon | .613 |
| 1920— | Vernon | .556 |
| 1921— | Los Angeles | .574 |
| 1922— | San Francisco | .638 |
| 1923— | San Francisco | .617 |
| 1924— | Seattle | .545 |
| 1925— | San Francisco | .643 |
| 1926— | Los Angeles | .599 |
| 1927— | Oakland | .615 |
| 1928— | San Francisco* | .630 |
| | Sacramento∞ | .626 |
| | San Francisco∞ | .626 |
| 1929— | Mission | .643 |
| | Hollywood* | .592 |
| 1930— | Los Angeles | .576 |
| | Hollywood* | .650 |
| 1931— | Hollywood | .626 |
| | San Francisco* | .608 |
| 1932— | Portland | .587 |
| 1933— | Los Angeles | .610 |
| 1934— | Los Angeles▼ | .786 |
| | Los Angeles▼ | .689 |
| 1935— | Los Angeles | .648 |
| | San Francisco* | .608 |
| 1936— | Portland‡ | .549 |
| 1937— | Sacramento | .573 |
| | San Diego (3rd)† | .545 |
| 1938— | Los Angeles | .590 |
| | Sacramento (3rd)† | .537 |
| 1939— | Seattle | .589 |
| | Sacramento (4th)† | .500 |
| 1940— | Seattle‡ | .629 |
| 1941— | Seattle‡ | .598 |
| 1942— | Sacramento | .590 |
| | Seattle (3rd)† | .539 |
| 1943— | Los Angeles | .710 |
| | S. Francisco (2nd)† | .574 |
| 1944— | Los Angeles | .586 |
| | S. Francisco (3rd)† | .509 |
| 1945— | Portland | .622 |
| | S. Francisco (4th)† | .525 |
| 1946— | San Francisco‡ | .628 |
| 1947— | Los Angeles▲ | .567 |
| 1948— | Oakland‡ | .606 |
| 1949— | Hollywood‡ | .583 |
| 1950— | Oakland | .590 |
| 1951— | Seattle‡ | .593 |
| 1952— | Hollywood | .606 |
| 1953— | Hollywood | .589 |
| 1954— | San Diego■ | .604 |
| 1955— | Seattle | .552 |
| 1956— | Los Angeles | .637 |
| 1957— | San Francisco | .601 |
| 1958— | Phoenix | .578 |
| 1959— | Salt Lake City | .552 |
| 1960— | Spokane | .601 |
| 1961— | Tacoma | .630 |
| 1962— | San Diego | .604 |
| 1963— | Spokane | .620 |
| | Oklahoma City• | .632 |
| 1964— | Arkansas | .609 |
| | San Diego• | .576 |
| 1965— | Oklahoma City | .628 |
| | Portland | .547 |
| 1966— | Seattle• | .561 |
| | Tulsa | .578 |
| 1967— | San Diego• | .574 |
| | Spokane | .541 |
| 1968— | Tulsa• | .642 |
| | Spokane | .586 |
| 1969— | Tacoma• | .589 |
| | Eugene | .603 |
| 1970— | Spokane• | .644 |
| | Hawaii | .671 |
| 1971— | Salt Lake City | .534 |
| | Tacoma | .545 |
| 1972— | Albuquerque | .622 |
| | Eugene | .534 |
| 1973— | Tucson | .583 |
| | Spokane• | .563 |
| 1974— | Spokane• | .549 |
| | Albuquerque | .535 |
| 1975— | Salt Lake City | .556 |
| | Hawaii• | .611 |
| 1976— | Salt Lake City | .625 |
| | Hawaii• | .531 |
| 1977— | Phoenix• | .579 |
| | Hawaii | .541 |
| 1978— | Tacoma†† | .584 |
| | Albuquerque†† | .557 |
| 1979— | Albuquerque | .581 |
| | Salt Lake City‡‡ | .541 |
| 1980— | Albuquerque | .578 |
| | Hawaii | .539 |
| 1981— | Albuquerque* | .712 |
| | Tacoma | .561 |
| 1982— | Albuquerque* | .594 |
| | Spokane | .545 |
| 1983— | Albuquerque | .594 |
| | Portland* | .528 |
| 1984— | Hawaii | .621 |
| | Edmonton* | .486 |
| 1985— | Vancouver* | .522 |
| | Phoenix | .563 |
| 1986— | Vancouver | .616 |
| | Las Vegas* | .563 |
| 1987— | Calgary | .596 |
| | Albuquerque* | .542 |
| 1988— | Vancouver | .599 |
| | Las Vegas* | .529 |
| 1989— | Albuquerque | .563 |
| | Vancouver* | .514 |
| 1990— | Albuquerque* | .641 |
| | Edmonton | .553 |
| 1991— | Albuquerque | .580 |
| | Tucson* | .564 |
| 1992— | Colorado Springs* | .596 |
| | Portland | .576 |
| 1993— | Portland | .608 |
| | Tucson* | .580 |
| 1994— | Albuquerque* | .597 |
| | Vancouver | .542 |
| 1995— | Salt Lake | .549 |
| | Colorado Springs* | .538 |
| 1996— | Edmonton* | .592 |
| | Phoenix | .479 |
| 1997— | Phoenix | .615 |
| | Edmonton* | .556 |
| 1998— | Iowa | .590 |
| | New Orleans† | .535 |
| 1999— | Vancouver‡ | .592 |
| 2000— | Salt Lake | .629 |
| | Memphis‡ | .576 |

| Year | Team | Pct. |
|---|---|---|
| 2001— | Tacoma§§ | .590 |
| | New Orleans§§ | .590 |
| 2002— | Las Vegas | .590 |
| | Edmonton† | .579 |
| 2003— | Sacramento‡ | .639 |
| 2004— | Sacramento† | .549 |

*Won split-season playoff. †Won four-team playoff. ‡Won pennant and four-team playoff. §Tied for second-half title with Tacoma winning playoff. ∞Tied for second-half title, with Sacramento winning playoff. ▲Ended regular season in tie with San Francisco and won one-game playoff for pennant, then won four-club playoff. ◆Won playoff from first-place Vernon and awarded championship. ■Defeated Hollywood in one-game playoff for pennant. ▼Won both halves, no playoff. •League was divided into Northern, Southern divisions in 1963, 1969-70-71, and Eastern, Western divisions in 1964 through 1968 and 1972 through 1977, won two-team playoff. ††League divided into Eastern and Western divisions, Tacoma and Albuquerque declared co-champions following cancellation of four-team playoff due to continuing rain and wet grounds. ‡‡Won second-half title and defeated Hawaii in four-team playoff. §§Were entering finals of four-team playoff and were declared co-champions when Professional Baseball declared a stoppage of play.

# EASTERN LEAGUE

## LEAGUE OFFICE

**President**
Joe McEacharn

**Address**
30 Danforth St., Suite 208
Portland, ME 04101

**Phone**
207-761-2700

## TEAMS

### AKRON AEROS
**General manager/vice president**
Jeff Auman
**Manager**
Torey Lovullo
**Ballpark (capacity, surface)**
Canal Park (9,097, grass)
**Affiliation**
Indians
**Address**
300 S. Main St.
Akron, OH 44308
**Phone**
330-253-5151

### ALTOONA CURVE
**General manager**
Todd Parnell
**Manager**
Tony Beasley
**Ballpark (capacity, surface)**
Blair County Ballpark (7,200, grass)
**Affiliation**
Pirates
**Address**
1000 Park Avenue
Altoona, PA 16602
**Phone**
814-943-5400

### BINGHAMTON METS
**General manager**
Scott Brown
**Manager**
TBA
**Ballpark (capacity, surface)**
NYSEG Stadium (6,012, grass)
**Affiliation**
Mets
**Address**
211 Henry Street
Binghamton, NY 13901
**Phone**
607-723-6387

### BOWIE BAYSOX
**General manager**
Brian Shallcross
**Manager**
Don Werner
**Ballpark (capacity, surface)**
Prince George's Stadium
(10,000, grass)
**Affiliation**
Orioles
**Address**
4101 NE Crain Highway
Bowie, MD 20716
**Phone**
301-805-6000

### ERIE SEAWOLVES
**General manager**
John Frey
**Manager**
Duffy Dyer
**Ballpark (capacity, surface)**
Jerry Uht Park (6,000, grass)
**Affiliation**
Tigers
**Address**
110 E. 10th Street
Erie, PA 16501
**Phone**
814-456-1300

### HARRISBURG SENATORS
**General manager**
Todd Vander Woude
**Manager**
TBA
**Ballpark (capacity, surface)**
Commerce Bank Park/City Island
(6,300, grass)
**Affiliation**
Nationals
**Address**
RiverSide Stadium/City Island
Harrisburg, PA 17101
**Phone**
717-231-4444

### NEW BRITAIN ROCK CATS
**General manager/president**
Bill Dowling
**Manager**
Stan Cliburn
**Ballpark (capacity, surface)**
New Britain Stadium (6,146, grass)
**Affiliation**
Twins
**Address**
230 John Karbonic Way
New Britain, CT 06051
**Phone**
860-224-8383

### NEW HAMPSHIRE FISHER CATS
**General manager**
Shawn Smith
**Manager**
Mike Basso
**Ballpark (capacity, surface)**
TBA (6,500, grass)
**Affiliation**
Blue Jays
**Address**
One Line Drive
Manchester, NH 03101
**Phone**
603-641-2005

### NORWICH NAVIGATORS
**General manager**
Keith Hallal
**Manager**
Dave Machemer
**Ballpark (capacity, surface)**
Thomas J. Dodd Memorial Stadium
(6,695, grass)
**Affiliation**
Giants
**Address**
14 Stott Ave.
Norwich, CT 06360
**Phone**
860-887-7962

### PORTLAND SEA DOGS
**General manager/president**
Charlie Eshbach
**Manager**
Todd Claus
**Ballpark (capacity, surface)**
Hadlock Field (6,975, grass)
**Affiliation**
Red Sox
**Address**
271 Park Avenue
Portland, ME 04102
**Phone**
207-874-9300

### READING PHILLIES
**General manager**
Chuck Domino
**Manager**
Steve Swisher
**Ballpark (capacity, surface)**
First Energy Stadium (9,100, grass)
**Affiliation**
Phillies
**Address**
Route 61 South/1900 South Centre Ave.
Reading, PA 19605
**Phone**
610-375-8469

### TRENTON THUNDER
**General manager**
Rick Brenner
**Manager**
Bill Masse
**Ballpark (capacity, surface)**
Samuel J. Plumeri Sr. Field at Mercer
County Waterfront Park (6,440, grass)
**Affiliation**
Yankees
**Address**
One Thunder Road
Trenton, NJ 08611
**Phone**
609-394-3300

# 2004 FINAL STANDINGS

## NORTHERN DIVISION

| Team | W | L | T | Pct. | GB |
|---|---|---|---|---|---|
| New Hampshire (Blue Jays) | 84 | 57 | - | .596 | ... |
| Binghamton (Mets) | 76 | 66 | - | .535 | 8.5 |
| New Britain (Twins) | 70 | 70 | - | .500 | 13.5 |
| Norwich (Giants) | 69 | 73 | - | .486 | 15.5 |
| Portland (Red Sox) | 69 | 73 | - | .486 | 15.5 |
| Trenton (Yankees) | 64 | 78 | - | .451 | 20.5 |

## SOUTHERN DIVISION

| Team | W | L | T | Pct. | GB |
|---|---|---|---|---|---|
| Altoona (Pirates) | 85 | 56 | - | .603 | ... |
| Erie (Tigers) | 80 | 62 | - | .563 | 5.5 |
| Bowie (Orioles) | 73 | 69 | - | .514 | 12.5 |
| Reading (Phillies) | 64 | 77 | 1 | .454 | 21.0 |
| Akron (Indians) | 63 | 78 | 1 | .447 | 22.0 |
| Harrisburg (Expos) | 52 | 90 | - | .366 | 33.5 |

## COMPOSITE

| Team | W | L | T | PCT | GB | ALT | NHF | ERI | BNG | BOW | NBR | NRW | PRT | REA | TRE | AKR | HRB |
|---|---|---|---|---|---|---|---|---|---|---|---|---|---|---|---|---|---|
| Altoona (Pirates) | 85 | 56 | - | .603 | ... | X | 3 | 7 | 4 | 10 | 5 | 3 | 6 | 15 | 4 | 16 | 13 |
| New Hampshire | 84 | 57 | - | .596 | 1 | 3 | X | 2 | 12 | 5 | 11 | 11 | 12 | 5 | 16 | 3 | 4 |
| Erie (Tigers) | 80 | 62 | - | .563 | 51/2 | 13 | 4 | X | 1 | 8 | 3 | 6 | 4 | 12 | 4 | 12 | 13 |
| Binghamton (Mets) | 76 | 66 | - | .535 | 91/2 | 2 | 8 | 5 | X | 5 | 12 | 13 | 9 | 2 | 11 | 4 | 5 |
| Bowie (Orioles) | 73 | 69 | - | .514 | 121/2 | 10 | 3 | 12 | 3 | X | 3 | 4 | 4 | 10 | 4 | 9 | 11 |
| New Britain (Twins) | 70 | 70 | - | .500 | 141/2 | 3 | 8 | 3 | 8 | 3 | X | 8 | 10 | 5 | 11 | 3 | 8 |
| Norwich (Giants) | 69 | 73 | - | .486 | 161/2 | 3 | 9 | 2 | 7 | 4 | 12 | X | 11 | 4 | 9 | 4 | 4 |
| Portland (Red Sox) | 69 | 73 | - | .486 | 161/2 | 2 | 8 | 4 | 11 | 2 | 10 | 9 | X | 2 | 12 | 4 | 5 |
| Reading (Phillies) | 64 | 77 | - | .454 | 21 | 5 | 3 | 8 | 6 | 10 | 3 | 2 | 4 | X | 3 | 9 | 11 |
| Trenton (Yankees) | 64 | 78 | - | .451 | 211/2 | 4 | 4 | 4 | 9 | 2 | 9 | 11 | 8 | 3 | X | 5 | 5 |
| Akron (Indians) | 63 | 78 | - | .447 | 22 | 4 | 3 | 8 | 2 | 11 | 2 | 4 | 4 | 11 | 3 | X | 11 |
| Harrisburg (Expos) | 52 | 90 | - | .366 | 331/2 | 7 | 4 | 7 | 3 | 9 | 0 | 2 | 1 | 9 | 1 | 9 | X |

Major league affiliations in parentheses.

PLAYOFFS: Altoona defeated Erie, three games to zero; New Hampshire defeated Binghamton, three games to one; New Hampshire defeated Altoona, three games to none, to win league championship.

REGULAR-SEASON ATTENDANCE: Akron, 478,611; Altoona, 394,062; Binghamton, 216,493; Bowie, 312,354; Erie, 245,117; Harrisburg, 255,978; New Britain, 311,671; New Hampshire, 216,381; Norwich, 168,559; Portland, 434,684; Reading, 478,257; Trenton, 402,280. Total attendance—3,914,447. Playoffs (12 games)—68,146. All-Star Game at New Britain—7,168.

MANAGERS: Akron, Brad Komminsk; Altoona, Tony Beasley; Binghamton, Ken Oberkfell; Bowie, Dave Trembley; Erie, Rick Sweet; Harrisburg, Dave Machemer; New Britain, Stan Cliburn; New Hampshire, Mike Basso; Norwich, Shane Turner; Portland, Ron Johnson; Reading, Greg Legg; Trenton, Stump Merrill.

ALL-STAR TEAM: 1B—Ryan Howard, Reading; 2B—Jeff Keppinger, Altoona-Birmingham; 3B—Mike Cervenak, Norwich; SS—Aaron Hill, New Hampshire; OF—Curits Granderson, Erie; OF—Val Majewski, Bowie; OF—Kevin West, New Britain; C—Ronny Paulino, Altoona; DH—Mitch Jones, Trenton; Utility—John Castellano, Reading; RHP—Ian Snell, Altoona; LHP—Gustavo Chacin, New Hampshire; Relief pitcher—Bobby Korecky, New Britain; Most Valuable Player—Ryan Howard, Reading; Pitcher of the Year—Gustavo Chacin, New Hampshire; Rookie of the Year—Ryan Howard, Reading; Manager of the Year—Mike Basso, New Hampshire.

# 2004 BATTING

## TEAM

| Team | G | TPA | AB | R | H | TB | 2B | 3B | HR | RBI | SH | SF | HP | BB | IBB | SO | SB | CS | GDP | LOB | ShO | Avg. | OBP | Slg. |
|---|---|---|---|---|---|---|---|---|---|---|---|---|---|---|---|---|---|---|---|---|---|---|---|---|
| Altoona | 141 | 5284 | 4695 | 697 | 1279 | 2010 | 270 | 28 | 135 | 656 | 57 | 45 | 86 | 400 | 17 | 871 | 115 | 39 | 96 | 959 | 11 | .272 | .338 | .428 |
| Binghamton | 142 | 5469 | 4790 | 696 | 1300 | 1943 | 296 | 40 | 89 | 640 | 56 | 37 | 68 | 517 | 18 | 1135 | 193 | 74 | 69 | 1070 | 9 | .271 | .348 | .406 |
| Trenton | 142 | 5435 | 4793 | 684 | 1288 | 2039 | 266 | 31 | 141 | 648 | 32 | 49 | 51 | 510 | 26 | 904 | 93 | 49 | 85 | 1030 | 6 | .269 | .342 | .425 |
| Erie | 142 | 5489 | 4749 | 734 | 1264 | 2132 | 254 | 37 | 180 | 681 | 37 | 40 | 72 | 590 | 23 | 1079 | 101 | 37 | 91 | 1074 | 5 | .266 | .353 | .449 |
| Reading | 141 | 5273 | 4654 | 644 | 1240 | 1999 | 225 | 30 | 158 | 602 | 63 | 41 | 67 | 447 | 21 | 923 | 74 | 45 | 87 | 1005 | 9 | .266 | .337 | .430 |
| Bowie | 142 | 5256 | 4684 | 660 | 1237 | 1907 | 252 | 17 | 128 | 605 | 52 | 46 | 54 | 414 | 13 | 922 | 87 | 45 | 81 | 950 | 6 | .264 | .328 | .407 |
| Norwich | 142 | 5335 | 4777 | 622 | 1250 | 1870 | 263 | 39 | 93 | 577 | 35 | 35 | 69 | 418 | 22 | 1026 | 122 | 33 | 87 | 1035 | 11 | .262 | .328 | .391 |
| Portland | 142 | 5462 | 4782 | 664 | 1247 | 1987 | 280 | 41 | 126 | 625 | 46 | 37 | 66 | 531 | 11 | 1011 | 116 | 56 | 106 | 1036 | 5 | .261 | .340 | .416 |
| Akron | 141 | 5352 | 4742 | 689 | 1224 | 1914 | 256 | 46 | 114 | 638 | 19 | 43 | 64 | 484 | 13 | 952 | 98 | 42 | 92 | 972 | 9 | .258 | .332 | .404 |
| New Britain | 140 | 5138 | 4586 | 626 | 1181 | 1854 | 245 | 28 | 124 | 587 | 65 | 44 | 71 | 371 | 6 | 855 | 81 | 46 | 85 | 874 | 6 | .258 | .320 | .404 |
| New Hamp. | 141 | 5202 | 4642 | 645 | 1179 | 1823 | 230 | 36 | 114 | 602 | 23 | 40 | 46 | 449 | 17 | 1032 | 79 | 29 | 99 | 931 | 7 | .254 | .323 | .393 |
| Harrisburg | 142 | 5309 | 4695 | 565 | 1176 | 1712 | 218 | 27 | 88 | 522 | 55 | 37 | 53 | 468 | 20 | 975 | 99 | 54 | 114 | 1007 | 17 | .250 | .323 | .365 |

## INDIVIDUAL

### TOP QUALIFIERS FOR BATTING CHAMPIONSHIP

Minimum 383 plate appearances. *Lefthanded batter. †Switch-hitter.

| Player, Team | G | TPA | AB | R | H | TB | 2B | 3B | HR | RBI | SH | SF | HP | BB | IBB | SO | SB | CS | GDP | Avg. | OBP | Slg. |
|---|---|---|---|---|---|---|---|---|---|---|---|---|---|---|---|---|---|---|---|---|---|---|
| Keppinger, Jeff, Altoona-Binghamton | 96 | 406 | 370 | 59 | 125 | 154 | 20 | 3 | 1 | 38 | 2 | 3 | 0 | 33 | 2 | 19 | 12 | 7 | 15 | .338 | .389 | .416 |
| Castellano, John, Reading | 103 | 406 | 368 | 50 | 125 | 205 | 24 | 1 | 18 | 68 | 0 | 4 | 2 | 32 | 2 | 55 | 0 | 3 | 7 | .340 | .392 | .557 |
| Cervenak, Mike, Norwich | 110 | 473 | 410 | 77 | 138 | 239 | 36 | 1 | 21 | 88 | 0 | 5 | 6 | 52 | 5 | 53 | 6 | 1 | 7 | .337 | .414 | .583 |
| McLouth, Nate, Altoona * | 133 | 592 | 515 | 93 | 166 | 238 | 40 | 4 | 8 | 73 | 14 | 7 | 8 | 48 | 2 | 62 | 31 | 7 | 8 | .322 | .384 | .462 |
| Jones, Garrett, New Britain * | 122 | 495 | 450 | 68 | 140 | 267 | 33 | 2 | 30 | 92 | 1 | 7 | 7 | 28 | 0 | 98 | 10 | 4 | 5 | .311 | .356 | .593 |
| Maza, Luis, New Britain | 126 | 541 | 492 | 84 | 153 | 231 | 26 | 8 | 12 | 66 | 4 | 2 | 15 | 28 | 0 | 70 | 5 | 6 | 12 | .311 | .365 | .470 |
| Duffy, Chris, Altoona * | 113 | 509 | 453 | 84 | 140 | 199 | 23 | 6 | 8 | 41 | 6 | 0 | 17 | 33 | 2 | 77 | 30 | 8 | 4 | .309 | .378 | .439 |
| Majewski, Val, Bowie | 112 | 476 | 433 | 71 | 133 | 212 | 24 | 5 | 15 | 80 | 0 | 5 | 5 | 33 | 3 | 68 | 14 | 4 | 7 | .307 | .359 | .490 |
| Granderson, Curtis, Erie * | 123 | 553 | 462 | 89 | 140 | 238 | 19 | 8 | 21 | 93 | 3 | 4 | 4 | 80 | 3 | 95 | 14 | 8 | 3 | .303 | .407 | .515 |
| Raburn, Ryan, Erie | 98 | 422 | 366 | 66 | 110 | 195 | 29 | 4 | 16 | 63 | 1 | 1 | 7 | 47 | 1 | 96 | 3 | 0 | 9 | .301 | .390 | .533 |
| Pressley, Josh, Binghamton * | 101 | 394 | 340 | 44 | 102 | 141 | 30 | 0 | 3 | 62 | 2 | 4 | 2 | 46 | 2 | 64 | 0 | 0 | 10 | .300 | .383 | .415 |
| Acuna, Ron, Binghamton | 129 | 534 | 500 | 61 | 150 | 188 | 27 | 4 | 1 | 57 | 3 | 4 | 1 | 26 | 0 | 99 | 22 | 12 | 5 | .300 | .333 | .376 |
| Howard, Ryan, Reading | 102 | 433 | 374 | 73 | 111 | 242 | 18 | 1 | 37 | 102 | 0 | 3 | 10 | 46 | 6 | 129 | 1 | 2 | 2 | .297 | .386 | .647 |
| Reed, Keith, Bowie | 121 | 505 | 464 | 62 | 137 | 217 | 32 | 0 | 16 | 65 | 1 | 3 | 6 | 31 | 2 | 101 | 3 | 6 | 12 | .295 | .345 | .468 |
| Lane, Rich, Harrisburg * | 128 | 539 | 488 | 67 | 143 | 197 | 29 | 2 | 7 | 58 | 3 | 2 | 2 | 43 | 2 | 90 | 4 | 4 | 19 | .293 | .351 | .404 |
| Grove, Jason, Trenton * | 119 | 422 | 375 | 47 | 110 | 171 | 24 | 2 | 11 | 68 | 1 | 5 | 9 | 32 | 2 | 90 | 2 | 2 | 4 | .293 | .359 | .456 |

DEPARTMENTAL LEADERS: G—D. Clark, 140; AB—D. Clark, 537; R—McLouth, 93; H—McLouth, 166; TB—M. Jones, 272; 2B—McLouth, 40; 3B—D. Clark, 13; HR—M. Jones, 39; RBI—Howard, 102; SH—Tomlin, 19; SF—A. Hill, 11; HP—Tousa, Duffy, 17; BB—Airoso, 82; IBB—N/A; SO—Singleton, M. Jones, 152; SB—Lydon, 65; CS—Lydon, 20; GIDP—N/A; Slg.—Howard, .647; OBP—Cervenak, .414.

## ALL PLAYERS

*Lefthanded batter. †Switch-hitter.

| Player, Team | G | TPA | AB | R | H | TB | 2B | 3B | HR | RBI | SH | SF | HP | BB | IBB | SO | SB | CS | GDP | Avg. | OBP | Slg. |
|---|---|---|---|---|---|---|---|---|---|---|---|---|---|---|---|---|---|---|---|---|---|---|
| Acuna, Ron, Binghamton | 129 | 534 | 500 | 61 | 150 | 188 | 27 | 4 | 1 | 57 | 3 | 4 | 1 | 26 | 0 | 99 | 22 | 12 | 5 | .300 | .333 | .376 |
| Airoso, Kurt, Erie | 122 | 521 | 427 | 78 | 111 | 234 | 15 | 3 | 34 | 94 | 0 | 6 | 5 | 82 | 5 | 127 | 7 | 0 | 10 | .260 | .381 | .548 |
| Anderson, Luke, Norwich | 35 | 2 | 2 | 0 | 0 | 0 | 0 | 0 | 0 | 0 | 0 | 0 | 0 | 0 | 0 | 2 | 0 | 0 | 0 | .000 | .000 | .000 |
| Aubrey, Michael, Akron * | 38 | 156 | 134 | 13 | 35 | 57 | 7 | 0 | 5 | 22 | 0 | 4 | 3 | 15 | 0 | 18 | 0 | 0 | 3 | .261 | .340 | .425 |
| Bailey, Jeff, Portland | 91 | 359 | 299 | 57 | 88 | 156 | 23 | 3 | 13 | 58 | 0 | 3 | 11 | 46 | 0 | 80 | 2 | 0 | 7 | .294 | .404 | .522 |
| Bailie, Stefan, Portland | 37 | 154 | 139 | 23 | 43 | 82 | 15 | 0 | 8 | 28 | 0 | 2 | 3 | 10 | 0 | 34 | 0 | 0 | 1 | .309 | .364 | .590 |
| Baldiris, Aarom, Binghamton | 21 | 89 | 81 | 8 | 18 | 23 | 3 | 1 | 0 | 8 | 1 | 1 | 0 | 6 | 0 | 13 | 0 | 0 | 0 | .222 | .273 | .284 |
| Bannister, Brian, Binghamton | 8 | 6 | 5 | 0 | 1 | 1 | 0 | 0 | 0 | 0 | 1 | 0 | 0 | 0 | 0 | 0 | 0 | 0 | 0 | .200 | .200 | .200 |
| Basak, Chris, Binghamton | 80 | 323 | 276 | 42 | 71 | 126 | 21 | 5 | 8 | 41 | 2 | 2 | 3 | 39 | 1 | 67 | 10 | 5 | 4 | .257 | .353 | .457 |
| Bateman, Joe, Norwich | 12 | 1 | 1 | 1 | 1 | 4 | 0 | 0 | 1 | 1 | 0 | 0 | 0 | 0 | 0 | 0 | 0 | 0 | 0 | 1.000 | 1.000 | 4.000 |
| Begg, Chris, Norwich | 16 | 11 | 8 | 0 | 2 | 2 | 0 | 0 | 0 | 1 | 3 | 0 | 0 | 0 | 0 | 0 | 0 | 0 | 0 | .250 | .250 | .250 |
| Belcher, Jason, Harrisburg * | 70 | 267 | 244 | 23 | 68 | 92 | 18 | 0 | 2 | 33 | 1 | 3 | 2 | 17 | 2 | 35 | 2 | 2 | 8 | .279 | .327 | .377 |
| Benavidez, Julian, Norwich | 65 | 244 | 217 | 27 | 59 | 94 | 12 | 1 | 7 | 37 | 0 | 1 | 3 | 23 | 1 | 67 | 0 | 0 | 4 | .272 | .348 | .433 |
| Bonifay, Josh, Altoona | 96 | 397 | 343 | 52 | 95 | 168 | 16 | 0 | 19 | 76 | 3 | 4 | 7 | 40 | 4 | 96 | 5 | 1 | 6 | .277 | .360 | .490 |
| Borner, Brady, Altoona * | 39 | 14 | 13 | 1 | 1 | 1 | 0 | 0 | 0 | 0 | 0 | 0 | 0 | 1 | 0 | 2 | 0 | 0 | 0 | .077 | .143 | .077 |
| Bowen, Rob, New Britain † | 77 | 285 | 249 | 28 | 49 | 86 | 10 | 0 | 9 | 24 | 1 | 1 | 3 | 31 | 1 | 76 | 3 | 0 | 3 | .197 | .292 | .345 |
| Bowers, Shane, Reading | 4 | 3 | 3 | 0 | 0 | 0 | 0 | 0 | 0 | 0 | 0 | 0 | 0 | 0 | 0 | 2 | 0 | 0 | 0 | .000 | .000 | .000 |
| Bridges, Donnie, Harrisburg | 45 | 99 | 87 | 9 | 12 | 21 | 2 | 2 | 1 | 7 | 2 | 1 | 0 | 9 | 0 | 19 | 0 | 1 | 1 | .138 | .216 | .241 |
| Brito, Eude, Reading * | 45 | 11 | 8 | 1 | 1 | 2 | 1 | 0 | 0 | 1 | 2 | 0 | 0 | 1 | 0 | 4 | 0 | 0 | 0 | .125 | .222 | .250 |
| Broadway, Larry, Harrisburg * | 131 | 556 | 477 | 70 | 129 | 215 | 20 | 0 | 22 | 72 | 0 | 7 | 4 | 68 | 4 | 103 | 2 | 3 | 9 | .270 | .362 | .451 |
| Brown, Jason, Harrisburg | 46 | 129 | 120 | 16 | 34 | 60 | 11 | 0 | 5 | 18 | 1 | 1 | 2 | 5 | 0 | 32 | 0 | 0 | 3 | .283 | .320 | .500 |
| Bucktrot, Keith, Reading * | 21 | 16 | 13 | 0 | 1 | 2 | 1 | 0 | 0 | 2 | 3 | 0 | 0 | 0 | 0 | 4 | 0 | 0 | 0 | .077 | .077 | .154 |
| Bullington, Bryan, Altoona | 26 | 26 | 22 | 1 | 3 | 3 | 0 | 0 | 0 | 0 | 4 | 0 | 0 | 0 | 0 | 7 | 0 | 0 | 0 | .136 | .136 | .136 |
| Cain, Matt, Norwich | 15 | 4 | 3 | 0 | 0 | 0 | 0 | 0 | 0 | 0 | 1 | 0 | 0 | 0 | 0 | 1 | 0 | 0 | 0 | .000 | .000 | .000 |
| Camacaro, Armando, Akron | 18 | 68 | 60 | 5 | 10 | 15 | 2 | 0 | 1 | 6 | 1 | 1 | 1 | 5 | 0 | 13 | 0 | 0 | 2 | .167 | .239 | .250 |
| Camilo, Juan, Harrisburg * | 117 | 412 | 363 | 54 | 95 | 153 | 19 | 3 | 11 | 52 | 1 | 3 | 2 | 43 | 1 | 98 | 12 | 6 | 5 | .262 | .341 | .421 |
| Cannizaro, Andy, Trenton | 85 | 379 | 328 | 44 | 103 | 130 | 18 | 0 | 3 | 44 | 5 | 5 | 5 | 36 | 1 | 31 | 7 | 9 | 7 | .314 | .385 | .396 |
| Carroll, Wes, Harrisburg | 23 | 65 | 59 | 2 | 14 | 16 | 2 | 0 | 0 | 3 | 1 | 0 | 0 | 5 | 0 | 5 | 2 | 1 | 5 | .237 | .297 | .271 |
| Carter, Bryan, Norwich * | 117 | 435 | 389 | 42 | 87 | 131 | 24 | 4 | 4 | 32 | 3 | 6 | 8 | 29 | 2 | 104 | 10 | 4 | 8 | .224 | .287 | .337 |
| Castellano, John, Reading | 103 | 406 | 368 | 50 | 125 | 205 | 24 | 1 | 18 | 68 | 0 | 4 | 2 | 32 | 2 | 55 | 0 | 3 | 7 | .340 | .392 | .557 |
| Cates, Gary, Bowie | 111 | 442 | 400 | 52 | 102 | 134 | 18 | 1 | 4 | 40 | 15 | 3 | 3 | 21 | 0 | 51 | 12 | 6 | 6 | .255 | .295 | .335 |
| Cervenak, Mike, Norwich | 110 | 473 | 410 | 77 | 138 | 239 | 36 | 1 | 21 | 88 | 0 | 5 | 6 | 52 | 5 | 53 | 6 | 1 | 7 | .337 | .414 | .583 |
| Chantres, Carlos, Reading | 6 | 6 | 5 | 1 | 1 | 1 | 0 | 0 | 0 | 0 | 0 | 0 | 0 | 1 | 0 | 2 | 0 | 0 | 0 | .200 | .333 | .200 |
| Chauncey, Clint, Portland | 29 | 108 | 98 | 11 | 19 | 28 | 6 | 0 | 1 | 8 | 0 | 1 | 2 | 7 | 0 | 36 | 0 | 0 | 1 | .194 | .259 | .286 |
| Chaves, Brandon, Altoona † | 41 | 134 | 108 | 16 | 24 | 35 | 2 | 3 | 1 | 15 | 3 | 2 | 2 | 19 | 1 | 20 | 2 | 0 | 4 | .222 | .344 | .324 |
| Chavez, Angel, Norwich | 89 | 339 | 308 | 22 | 61 | 73 | 8 | 2 | 0 | 21 | 2 | 2 | 3 | 24 | 2 | 53 | 6 | 4 | 10 | .198 | .261 | .237 |
| Chenard, Ken, Binghamton | 27 | 15 | 14 | 1 | 2 | 3 | 1 | 0 | 0 | 0 | 1 | 0 | 0 | 0 | 0 | 5 | 0 | 0 | 0 | .143 | .143 | .214 |
| Chiaffredo, Paul, New Hampshire | 63 | 242 | 228 | 32 | 58 | 97 | 12 | 0 | 9 | 29 | 0 | 1 | 3 | 10 | 0 | 54 | 1 | 0 | 2 | .254 | .293 | .425 |
| Clark, Doug, Norwich * | 140 | 587 | 537 | 82 | 157 | 236 | 23 | 13 | 10 | 71 | 1 | 2 | 3 | 44 | 1 | 103 | 33 | 8 | 9 | .292 | .348 | .439 |
| Clark, Jeff, Norwich | 4 | 4 | 4 | 1 | 1 | 1 | 0 | 0 | 0 | 0 | 0 | 0 | 0 | 0 | 0 | 1 | 0 | 0 | 0 | .250 | .250 | .250 |
| Clements, Zac, Binghamton | 9 | 30 | 27 | 5 | 5 | 8 | 0 | 0 | 1 | 1 | 0 | 0 | 1 | 2 | 0 | 12 | 0 | 0 | 1 | .185 | .267 | .296 |
| Connolly, Mike, Altoona * | 21 | 16 | 12 | 0 | 0 | 0 | 0 | 0 | 0 | 0 | 2 | 0 | 0 | 2 | 0 | 8 | 0 | 0 | 0 | .000 | .143 | .000 |
| Cortes, Jorge, Altoona * | 37 | 158 | 139 | 17 | 39 | 67 | 8 | 1 | 6 | 19 | 1 | 4 | 1 | 13 | 0 | 24 | 0 | 1 | 4 | .281 | .338 | .482 |
| Cosbey, Chris, Reading * | 56 | 166 | 148 | 16 | 36 | 48 | 6 | 3 | 0 | 16 | 5 | 2 | 2 | 9 | 0 | 28 | 6 | 4 | 0 | .243 | .292 | .324 |
| Culp, Brandon, Reading | 4 | 4 | 2 | 0 | 1 | 1 | 0 | 0 | 0 | 1 | 1 | 0 | 0 | 1 | 0 | 0 | 0 | 0 | 0 | .500 | .667 | .500 |
| Curry, Chris, Norwich | 88 | 328 | 299 | 32 | 76 | 120 | 18 | 1 | 8 | 40 | 5 | 2 | 6 | 16 | 1 | 81 | 0 | 0 | 6 | .254 | .303 | .401 |
| Davidson, Seth, New Britain | 94 | 296 | 272 | 50 | 64 | 94 | 16 | 7 | 0 | 8 | 7 | 0 | 5 | 12 | 0 | 32 | 7 | 4 | 5 | .235 | .280 | .346 |
| De Caster, Yurendell, Altoona | 97 | 360 | 330 | 54 | 92 | 157 | 18 | 1 | 15 | 42 | 1 | 2 | 5 | 22 | 1 | 78 | 4 | 2 | 11 | .279 | .331 | .476 |
| Deschaine, Jim, Reading | 79 | 326 | 277 | 36 | 78 | 123 | 16 | 1 | 9 | 38 | 0 | 7 | 7 | 35 | 0 | 38 | 3 | 1 | 5 | .282 | .368 | .444 |
| Dorta, Melvin, Harrisburg | 72 | 249 | 226 | 20 | 59 | 74 | 11 | 2 | 0 | 22 | 4 | 2 | 2 | 15 | 3 | 24 | 12 | 4 | 6 | .261 | .310 | .327 |
| Dougherty, Kevin, Reading * | 11 | 9 | 8 | 0 | 3 | 3 | 0 | 0 | 0 | 0 | 1 | 0 | 0 | 0 | 0 | 3 | 0 | 0 | 0 | .375 | .375 | .375 |
| Douglass, Ryan, Harrisburg | 36 | 4 | 4 | 0 | 0 | 0 | 0 | 0 | 0 | 0 | 0 | 0 | 0 | 0 | 0 | 1 | 0 | 0 | 1 | .000 | .000 | .000 |
| Doumit, Ryan, Altoona † | 67 | 255 | 221 | 31 | 58 | 108 | 20 | 0 | 10 | 34 | 1 | 4 | 8 | 21 | 2 | 49 | 0 | 1 | 4 | .262 | .343 | .489 |
| Duffy, Chris, Altoona * | 113 | 509 | 453 | 84 | 140 | 199 | 23 | 6 | 8 | 41 | 6 | 0 | 17 | 33 | 2 | 77 | 30 | 8 | 4 | .309 | .378 | .439 |
| Duke, Zach, Altoona * | 9 | 8 | 8 | 1 | 1 | 2 | 1 | 0 | 0 | 0 | 0 | 0 | 0 | 0 | 0 | 5 | 0 | 0 | 0 | .125 | .125 | .250 |
| Duncan, Jeff, Binghamton * | 38 | 159 | 133 | 19 | 34 | 42 | 6 | 1 | 0 | 9 | 1 | 1 | 3 | 21 | 0 | 38 | 10 | 2 | 4 | .256 | .367 | .316 |
| Echols, Justin, Harrisburg | 21 | 11 | 11 | 2 | 3 | 4 | 1 | 0 | 0 | 2 | 0 | 0 | 0 | 0 | 0 | 4 | 0 | 0 | 0 | .273 | .273 | .364 |
| Eldred, Brad, Altoona | 39 | 158 | 147 | 24 | 41 | 101 | 9 | 0 | 17 | 60 | 0 | 0 | 5 | 6 | 0 | 51 | 0 | 0 | 3 | .279 | .329 | .687 |
| Espinosa, David, Erie † | 134 | 603 | 511 | 89 | 135 | 225 | 23 | 5 | 19 | 52 | 7 | 2 | 3 | 80 | 3 | 134 | 20 | 7 | 5 | .264 | .366 | .440 |
| Evans, Tom, Altoona | 33 | 141 | 120 | 25 | 37 | 60 | 9 | 1 | 4 | 22 | 0 | 1 | 2 | 18 | 1 | 20 | 4 | 1 | 5 | .308 | .404 | .500 |
| Fahey, Brandon, Bowie * | 63 | 232 | 208 | 20 | 49 | 61 | 7 | 1 | 1 | 15 | 7 | 0 | 0 | 17 | 0 | 27 | 3 | 1 | 5 | .236 | .293 | .293 |
| Fleming, Ryan, Reading * | 110 | 450 | 388 | 56 | 101 | 150 | 14 | 7 | 7 | 38 | 7 | 4 | 3 | 48 | 1 | 47 | 17 | 4 | 12 | .260 | .343 | .387 |
| Florence, Branden, Bowie | 11 | 38 | 35 | 3 | 10 | 14 | 1 | 0 | 1 | 4 | 0 | 0 | 2 | 1 | 0 | 3 | 0 | 0 | 2 | .286 | .342 | .400 |
| Francisco, Ben, Akron | 133 | 563 | 497 | 72 | 126 | 206 | 29 | 3 | 15 | 71 | 4 | 6 | 6 | 50 | 2 | 86 | 21 | 5 | 10 | .254 | .326 | .414 |
| Franco, Martire, Reading | 48 | 1 | 1 | 0 | 0 | 0 | 0 | 0 | 0 | 1 | 0 | 0 | 0 | 0 | 0 | 0 | 0 | 0 | 0 | .000 | .000 | .000 |
| Fuentes, Omar, Trenton | 68 | 245 | 211 | 23 | 53 | 79 | 11 | 0 | 5 | 31 | 2 | 5 | 2 | 25 | 1 | 30 | 0 | 1 | 3 | .251 | .329 | .374 |
| Gardner, Hayden, Reading | 7 | 1 | 1 | 0 | 0 | 0 | 0 | 0 | 0 | 0 | 0 | 0 | 0 | 0 | 0 | 0 | 0 | 0 | 0 | .000 | .000 | .000 |
| Garko, Ryan, Akron | 43 | 194 | 172 | 29 | 57 | 90 | 15 | 0 | 6 | 38 | 0 | 2 | 6 | 14 | 0 | 28 | 1 | 0 | 3 | .331 | .397 | .523 |
| Garrido, Tomas, Norwich | 6 | 13 | 13 | 0 | 2 | 2 | 0 | 0 | 0 | 0 | 0 | 0 | 0 | 0 | 0 | 4 | 0 | 0 | 0 | .154 | .154 | .154 |
| Gibbs, Kevin, Reading † | 3 | 10 | 10 | 3 | 3 | 6 | 0 | 0 | 1 | 1 | 0 | 0 | 0 | 0 | 0 | 6 | 0 | 0 | 0 | .300 | .300 | .600 |
| Godwin, Tyrell, New Hampshire * | 133 | 584 | 521 | 85 | 132 | 185 | 21 | 7 | 6 | 40 | 4 | 2 | 5 | 52 | 0 | 110 | 42 | 12 | 6 | .253 | .326 | .355 |
| Gonzalez, Danny, Reading † | 134 | 534 | 461 | 62 | 121 | 160 | 23 | 2 | 4 | 41 | 9 | 2 | 10 | 52 | 2 | 95 | 2 | 4 | 10 | .262 | .349 | .347 |
| Gonzalez, Jimmy, Binghamton | 20 | 64 | 56 | 7 | 15 | 18 | 3 | 0 | 0 | 4 | 0 | 0 | 3 | 5 | 0 | 13 | 0 | 0 | 0 | .268 | .359 | .321 |
| Granderson, Curtis, Erie * | 123 | 553 | 462 | 89 | 140 | 238 | 19 | 8 | 21 | 93 | 3 | 4 | 4 | 80 | 3 | 95 | 14 | 8 | 3 | .303 | .407 | .515 |
| Griffin, John-Ford, New Hampshire * | 129 | 533 | 467 | 66 | 116 | 212 | 28 | 1 | 22 | 81 | 0 | 6 | 4 | 56 | 2 | 128 | 1 | 1 | 15 | .248 | .330 | .454 |
| Griffin, Nathan, Trenton | 1 | 3 | 3 | 0 | 0 | 0 | 0 | 0 | 0 | 0 | 0 | 0 | 0 | 0 | 0 | 1 | 0 | 0 | 0 | .000 | .000 | .000 |
| Grove, Jason, Trenton * | 119 | 422 | 375 | 47 | 110 | 171 | 24 | 2 | 11 | 68 | 1 | 5 | 9 | 32 | 2 | 90 | 2 | 2 | 4 | .293 | .359 | .456 |

| Player, Team | G | TPA | AB | R | H | TB | 2B | 3B | HR | RBI | SH | SF | HP | BB | IBB | SO | SB | CS | GDP | Avg. | OBP | Slg. |
|---|---|---|---|---|---|---|---|---|---|---|---|---|---|---|---|---|---|---|---|---|---|---|
| Gutierrez, Franklin, Akron | 70 | 298 | 262 | 38 | 79 | 122 | 24 | 2 | 5 | 35 | 0 | 4 | 9 | 23 | 3 | 77 | 6 | 3 | 4 | .302 | .372 | .466 |
| Habel, Josh, Norwich * | 27 | 13 | 11 | 0 | 0 | 0 | 0 | 0 | 0 | 0 | 1 | 0 | 0 | 1 | 0 | 7 | 0 | 0 | 0 | .000 | .083 | .000 |
| Hannahan, Jack, Erie * | 108 | 431 | 374 | 48 | 102 | 149 | 21 | 1 | 8 | 39 | 1 | 1 | 2 | 53 | 4 | 60 | 7 | 3 | 9 | .273 | .365 | .398 |
| Harper, Brandon, Erie | 48 | 188 | 166 | 26 | 48 | 87 | 12 | 0 | 9 | 29 | 0 | 0 | 6 | 16 | 1 | 31 | 2 | 1 | 2 | .289 | .372 | .524 |
| Hassey, Brad, New Hampshire | 23 | 70 | 65 | 6 | 10 | 17 | 1 | 0 | 2 | 6 | 1 | 0 | 1 | 3 | 0 | 14 | 0 | 0 | 2 | .154 | .203 | .262 |
| Hattig, John, New Hampshire † | 40 | 159 | 142 | 24 | 42 | 79 | 7 | 0 | 10 | 30 | 0 | 3 | 2 | 12 | 1 | 41 | 0 | 1 | 3 | .296 | .352 | .556 |
| Headley, Justin, Portland * | 17 | 71 | 60 | 9 | 14 | 19 | 3 | 1 | 0 | 2 | 0 | 0 | 1 | 10 | 0 | 10 | 0 | 0 | 0 | .233 | .352 | .317 |
| Hernandez, Anderson, Erie † | 101 | 440 | 394 | 65 | 108 | 148 | 19 | 3 | 5 | 29 | 13 | 2 | 5 | 26 | 0 | 89 | 17 | 6 | 5 | .274 | .326 | .376 |
| Hietpas, Joe, Binghamton | 43 | 162 | 139 | 13 | 32 | 51 | 10 | 0 | 3 | 19 | 1 | 0 | 3 | 19 | 0 | 41 | 0 | 2 | 6 | .230 | .335 | .367 |
| Hiles, Cary, Reading | 13 | 3 | 2 | 0 | 0 | 0 | 0 | 0 | 0 | 0 | 1 | 0 | 0 | 0 | 0 | 1 | 0 | 0 | 0 | .000 | .000 | .000 |
| Hill, Aaron, New Hampshire | 135 | 567 | 480 | 78 | 134 | 197 | 26 | 2 | 11 | 80 | 0 | 11 | 11 | 63 | 2 | 61 | 3 | 2 | 12 | .279 | .368 | .410 |
| Hill, Jeremy, Binghamton | 25 | 2 | 0 | 0 | 0 | 0 | 0 | 0 | 0 | 0 | 2 | 0 | 0 | 0 | 0 | 0 | 0 | 0 | 0 | .000 | .000 | .000 |
| Hill, Shawn, Harrisburg | 17 | 12 | 12 | 3 | 3 | 7 | 1 | 0 | 1 | 3 | 0 | 0 | 0 | 0 | 0 | 3 | 0 | 0 | 0 | .250 | .250 | .583 |
| Hinckley, Mike, Harrisburg | 16 | 20 | 13 | 0 | 5 | 7 | 2 | 0 | 0 | 1 | 4 | 1 | 0 | 2 | 0 | 2 | 0 | 0 | 1 | .385 | .438 | .538 |
| Howard, Ryan, Reading | 102 | 433 | 374 | 73 | 111 | 242 | 18 | 1 | 37 | 102 | 0 | 3 | 10 | 46 | 6 | 129 | 1 | 2 | 2 | .297 | .386 | .647 |
| Huggins, Mike, Bowie | 76 | 287 | 249 | 22 | 59 | 87 | 16 | 0 | 4 | 30 | 0 | 1 | 4 | 33 | 0 | 53 | 2 | 4 | 5 | .237 | .334 | .349 |
| Hutchison, Ryan, Reading | 12 | 1 | 1 | 0 | 1 | 1 | 0 | 0 | 0 | 1 | 0 | 0 | 0 | 0 | 0 | 0 | 0 | 0 | 0 | 1.000 | 1.000 | 1.000 |
| Inglett, Joe, Akron * | 66 | 300 | 266 | 49 | 85 | 121 | 19 | 7 | 1 | 20 | 2 | 0 | 1 | 31 | 2 | 28 | 3 | 5 | 1 | .320 | .393 | .455 |
| Jacobsen, Landon, Altoona | 15 | 10 | 10 | 0 | 1 | 1 | 0 | 0 | 0 | 1 | 0 | 0 | 0 | 0 | 0 | 3 | 0 | 0 | 0 | .100 | .100 | .100 |
| Jacobson, Russ, Reading | 54 | 193 | 174 | 12 | 31 | 45 | 8 | 0 | 2 | 17 | 2 | 3 | 3 | 11 | 0 | 37 | 0 | 0 | 6 | .178 | .236 | .259 |
| Jimenez, Jason, Reading | 17 | 1 | 1 | 0 | 0 | 0 | 0 | 0 | 0 | 0 | 0 | 0 | 0 | 0 | 0 | 1 | 0 | 0 | 0 | .000 | .000 | .000 |
| Jones, Garrett, New Britain * | 122 | 495 | 450 | 68 | 140 | 267 | 33 | 2 | 30 | 92 | 1 | 7 | 7 | 28 | 0 | 98 | 10 | 4 | 5 | .311 | .356 | .593 |
| Jones, Mitch, Trenton | 137 | 569 | 496 | 92 | 122 | 272 | 25 | 4 | 39 | 97 | 0 | 5 | 4 | 64 | 4 | 152 | 8 | 1 | 6 | .246 | .334 | .548 |
| Jova, Maikel, New Hampshire | 122 | 479 | 462 | 46 | 128 | 190 | 28 | 2 | 10 | 63 | 0 | 3 | 2 | 12 | 0 | 90 | 1 | 1 | 16 | .277 | .296 | .411 |
| Keene, Kurt, Reading | 111 | 422 | 391 | 56 | 110 | 166 | 12 | 4 | 12 | 41 | 4 | 3 | 3 | 21 | 0 | 54 | 6 | 4 | 7 | .281 | .321 | .425 |
| Kennedy, Bryan, New Britain * | 67 | 222 | 203 | 17 | 51 | 73 | 4 | 0 | 6 | 24 | 1 | 1 | 2 | 15 | 0 | 30 | 2 | 0 | 5 | .251 | .308 | .360 |
| Keppinger, Jeff, Altoona | 82 | 352 | 323 | 45 | 108 | 132 | 17 | 2 | 1 | 33 | 2 | 2 | 0 | 27 | 1 | 17 | 10 | 6 | 13 | .334 | .384 | .409 |
| Keppinger, Jeff, Binghamton | 14 | 54 | 47 | 14 | 17 | 22 | 3 | 1 | 0 | 5 | 0 | 1 | 0 | 6 | 1 | 2 | 2 | 1 | 1 | .362 | .426 | .468 |
| Kilburg, Joe, Portland * | 95 | 352 | 303 | 37 | 79 | 109 | 17 | 2 | 3 | 38 | 7 | 0 | 4 | 38 | 1 | 71 | 8 | 4 | 2 | .261 | .351 | .360 |
| Knoedler, Justin, Norwich | 115 | 454 | 409 | 64 | 112 | 173 | 28 | 3 | 9 | 47 | 0 | 5 | 8 | 32 | 0 | 98 | 5 | 3 | 7 | .274 | .335 | .423 |
| Labandeira, Josh, Harrisburg | 134 | 589 | 514 | 72 | 139 | 196 | 22 | 4 | 9 | 33 | 6 | 0 | 16 | 53 | 1 | 92 | 9 | 5 | 10 | .270 | .357 | .381 |
| Lambin, Chase, Binghamton † | 121 | 467 | 410 | 64 | 100 | 160 | 22 | 4 | 10 | 64 | 2 | 1 | 6 | 48 | 4 | 103 | 4 | 2 | 5 | .244 | .331 | .390 |
| Lane, Rich, Harrisburg * | 128 | 539 | 488 | 67 | 143 | 197 | 29 | 2 | 7 | 58 | 3 | 2 | 2 | 43 | 2 | 90 | 4 | 4 | 19 | .293 | .351 | .404 |
| Lavigne, Tim, Binghamton | 40 | 3 | 3 | 1 | 2 | 3 | 1 | 0 | 0 | 2 | 0 | 0 | 0 | 0 | 0 | 0 | 0 | 0 | 0 | .667 | .667 | 1.000 |
| Leon, Carlos, Reading † | 26 | 91 | 78 | 7 | 10 | 14 | 2 | 1 | 0 | 6 | 5 | 1 | 1 | 6 | 0 | 12 | 4 | 2 | 2 | .128 | .198 | .179 |
| Lockwood, Luke, Harrisburg * | 33 | 14 | 12 | 0 | 2 | 2 | 0 | 0 | 0 | 0 | 1 | 0 | 1 | 0 | 0 | 2 | 0 | 0 | 1 | .167 | .231 | .167 |
| Lockwood, Mike, Portland * | 74 | 341 | 296 | 46 | 83 | 135 | 21 | 2 | 9 | 39 | 5 | 2 | 4 | 34 | 0 | 46 | 2 | 4 | 4 | .280 | .360 | .456 |
| Lofton, James, Bowie | 29 | 118 | 101 | 13 | 27 | 37 | 4 | 0 | 2 | 13 | 3 | 4 | 3 | 7 | 0 | 12 | 0 | 1 | 1 | .267 | .322 | .366 |
| Lontayo, Alex, Erie * | 37 | 1 | 1 | 0 | 0 | 0 | 0 | 0 | 0 | 0 | 0 | 0 | 0 | 0 | 0 | 1 | 0 | 0 | 0 | .000 | .000 | .000 |
| Lopez-Cao, Mike, Portland * | 21 | 71 | 55 | 9 | 14 | 26 | 3 | 0 | 3 | 11 | 0 | 3 | 0 | 13 | 0 | 16 | 0 | 0 | 2 | .255 | .380 | .473 |
| Luderer, Brian, Akron | 44 | 156 | 140 | 13 | 29 | 36 | 7 | 0 | 0 | 13 | 0 | 0 | 4 | 12 | 0 | 15 | 0 | 2 | 6 | .207 | .288 | .257 |
| Lunetta, Anthony, Akron | 7 | 15 | 13 | 1 | 4 | 6 | 2 | 0 | 0 | 1 | 0 | 0 | 0 | 2 | 0 | 3 | 0 | 0 | 1 | .308 | .400 | .462 |
| Lydon, Wayne, Binghamton | 123 | 570 | 506 | 78 | 137 | 182 | 18 | 6 | 5 | 43 | 11 | 1 | 3 | 49 | 0 | 119 | 65 | 20 | 2 | .271 | .338 | .360 |
| Machado, Alejandro, Harrisburg † | 93 | 404 | 346 | 54 | 97 | 122 | 5 | 4 | 4 | 26 | 10 | 2 | 5 | 41 | 1 | 39 | 19 | 9 | 8 | .280 | .363 | .353 |
| Majewski, Val, Bowie | 112 | 476 | 433 | 71 | 133 | 212 | 24 | 5 | 15 | 80 | 0 | 5 | 5 | 33 | 3 | 68 | 14 | 4 | 7 | .307 | .359 | .490 |
| Malek, Bobby, Binghamton * | 14 | 58 | 54 | 7 | 12 | 17 | 2 | 0 | 1 | 1 | 1 | 0 | 1 | 2 | 0 | 13 | 0 | 0 | 1 | .222 | .263 | .315 |
| Mangrum, Micah, Binghamton | 14 | 1 | 1 | 0 | 0 | 0 | 0 | 0 | 0 | 0 | 0 | 0 | 0 | 0 | 0 | 1 | 0 | 0 | 0 | .000 | .000 | .000 |
| Markert, Jackson, Norwich | 15 | 1 | 1 | 0 | 0 | 0 | 0 | 0 | 0 | 0 | 0 | 0 | 0 | 0 | 0 | 1 | 0 | 0 | 0 | .000 | .000 | .000 |
| Mauer, Jake, New Britain | 101 | 329 | 283 | 29 | 73 | 88 | 11 | 2 | 0 | 31 | 12 | 4 | 6 | 24 | 0 | 25 | 3 | 0 | 7 | .258 | .325 | .311 |
| Maust, David, Harrisburg * | 44 | 7 | 7 | 0 | 0 | 0 | 0 | 0 | 0 | 0 | 0 | 0 | 0 | 0 | 0 | 2 | 0 | 0 | 0 | .000 | .000 | .000 |
| Maza, Luis, New Britain | 126 | 541 | 492 | 84 | 153 | 231 | 26 | 8 | 12 | 66 | 4 | 2 | 15 | 28 | 0 | 70 | 5 | 6 | 12 | .311 | .365 | .470 |
| McDade, Neal, Altoona | 32 | 11 | 9 | 1 | 1 | 1 | 0 | 0 | 0 | 0 | 2 | 0 | 0 | 0 | 0 | 4 | 0 | 0 | 0 | .111 | .111 | .111 |
| McGowan, Sean, Portland | 69 | 298 | 275 | 31 | 72 | 94 | 13 | 0 | 3 | 32 | 0 | 2 | 1 | 20 | 0 | 46 | 0 | 2 | 8 | .262 | .312 | .342 |
| McKinley, Josh, Harrisburg † | 83 | 353 | 296 | 39 | 71 | 122 | 16 | 4 | 9 | 42 | 1 | 4 | 2 | 50 | 5 | 72 | 10 | 5 | 6 | .240 | .349 | .412 |
| McLouth, Nate, Altoona * | 133 | 592 | 515 | 93 | 166 | 238 | 40 | 4 | 8 | 73 | 14 | 7 | 8 | 48 | 2 | 62 | 31 | 7 | 8 | .322 | .384 | .462 |
| McMains, Derin, Norwich † | 110 | 471 | 436 | 58 | 118 | 158 | 23 | 1 | 5 | 55 | 3 | 3 | 0 | 29 | 1 | 40 | 12 | 2 | 6 | .271 | .314 | .362 |
| McMillan, Drew, Harrisburg | 54 | 191 | 173 | 13 | 37 | 51 | 8 | 0 | 2 | 17 | 2 | 1 | 3 | 12 | 0 | 45 | 0 | 0 | 4 | .214 | .275 | .295 |
| Mendez, Donaldo, Altoona | 23 | 87 | 76 | 7 | 10 | 15 | 5 | 0 | 0 | 3 | 0 | 0 | 5 | 6 | 0 | 22 | 0 | 1 | 2 | .132 | .241 | .197 |
| Meyers, Chad, Erie | 34 | 152 | 134 | 26 | 42 | 78 | 10 | 1 | 8 | 17 | 0 | 0 | 2 | 16 | 1 | 18 | 11 | 3 | 3 | .313 | .395 | .582 |
| Miller, Jeff, Altoona | 52 | 4 | 4 | 0 | 0 | 0 | 0 | 0 | 0 | 0 | 0 | 0 | 0 | 0 | 0 | 2 | 0 | 0 | 0 | .000 | .000 | .000 |
| Minges, Tyler, Akron | 89 | 339 | 307 | 44 | 82 | 142 | 13 | 7 | 11 | 40 | 3 | 0 | 3 | 26 | 0 | 46 | 6 | 1 | 6 | .267 | .330 | .463 |
| Misch, Pat, Norwich | 26 | 14 | 11 | 0 | 0 | 0 | 0 | 0 | 0 | 0 | 2 | 0 | 0 | 1 | 0 | 5 | 0 | 0 | 0 | .000 | .083 | .000 |
| Montes, Albert, Norwich | 53 | 2 | 2 | 0 | 0 | 0 | 0 | 0 | 0 | 0 | 0 | 0 | 0 | 0 | 0 | 1 | 0 | 0 | 0 | .000 | .000 | .000 |
| Morban, Jose, Bowie | 67 | 272 | 243 | 35 | 51 | 91 | 9 | 2 | 9 | 23 | 3 | 2 | 3 | 21 | 0 | 74 | 9 | 3 | 3 | .210 | .279 | .374 |
| Moriarty, Mike, Altoona | 20 | 82 | 66 | 17 | 20 | 29 | 9 | 0 | 0 | 6 | 1 | 0 | 4 | 11 | 0 | 13 | 1 | 0 | 1 | .303 | .432 | .439 |
| Mota, Tony, Bowie † | 83 | 325 | 291 | 39 | 78 | 108 | 18 | 3 | 2 | 37 | 0 | 6 | 2 | 25 | 0 | 54 | 6 | 2 | 3 | .268 | .324 | .371 |
| Musser, Neal, Binghamton * | 20 | 13 | 12 | 1 | 1 | 1 | 0 | 0 | 0 | 2 | 0 | 0 | 0 | 1 | 0 | 2 | 0 | 0 | 0 | .083 | .154 | .083 |
| Nathans, John, Portland | 1 | 1 | 1 | 0 | 0 | 0 | 0 | 0 | 0 | 0 | 0 | 0 | 0 | 0 | 0 | 1 | 0 | 0 | 0 | .000 | .000 | .000 |
| Nicholson, Derek, Erie * | 61 | 247 | 221 | 31 | 60 | 105 | 13 | 1 | 10 | 37 | 1 | 2 | 0 | 23 | 0 | 47 | 1 | 0 | 4 | .271 | .337 | .475 |
| Nicholson, Kevin, Altoona † | 77 | 289 | 258 | 28 | 56 | 85 | 13 | 2 | 4 | 36 | 1 | 4 | 1 | 23 | 0 | 37 | 2 | 0 | 3 | .217 | .280 | .329 |
| Nieves, Raul, Portland † | 99 | 357 | 311 | 37 | 69 | 92 | 9 | 1 | 4 | 19 | 13 | 2 | 3 | 28 | 0 | 54 | 5 | 4 | 11 | .222 | .291 | .296 |
| Norman, Zach, Reading | 1 | 5 | 5 | 0 | 0 | 0 | 0 | 0 | 0 | 0 | 0 | 0 | 0 | 0 | 0 | 2 | 0 | 0 | 0 | .000 | .000 | .000 |
| Norris, Shawn, Harrisburg * | 37 | 156 | 124 | 16 | 39 | 62 | 10 | 2 | 3 | 33 | 2 | 3 | 2 | 25 | 0 | 37 | 1 | 1 | 2 | .315 | .429 | .500 |
| O'Keefe, Mike, Portland * | 133 | 541 | 472 | 50 | 117 | 203 | 21 | 4 | 19 | 68 | 0 | 2 | 4 | 63 | 0 | 99 | 2 | 4 | 8 | .248 | .340 | .430 |
| Olivares, Teuris, Trenton | 72 | 204 | 179 | 25 | 36 | 63 | 7 | 1 | 6 | 27 | 2 | 3 | 1 | 19 | 0 | 29 | 1 | 1 | 0 | .201 | .277 | .352 |
| Ortmeier, Daniel, Norwich † | 106 | 438 | 377 | 55 | 95 | 160 | 23 | 6 | 10 | 48 | 0 | 2 | 12 | 47 | 4 | 110 | 18 | 2 | 5 | .252 | .352 | .424 |
| Owens, Ryan, New Britain | 63 | 235 | 206 | 24 | 42 | 78 | 12 | 0 | 8 | 31 | 1 | 4 | 1 | 23 | 0 | 43 | 4 | 0 | 7 | .204 | .282 | .379 |
| Pagan, Angel, Binghamton † | 112 | 501 | 449 | 71 | 129 | 182 | 25 | 8 | 4 | 63 | 4 | 5 | 1 | 42 | 1 | 96 | 29 | 5 | 6 | .287 | .346 | .405 |
| Palmer, Matt, Norwich | 42 | 3 | 3 | 0 | 0 | 0 | 0 | 0 | 0 | 0 | 0 | 0 | 0 | 0 | 0 | 2 | 0 | 0 | 0 | .000 | .000 | .000 |
| Parrish, Dave, Trenton | 38 | 129 | 117 | 8 | 27 | 32 | 2 | 0 | 1 | 14 | 1 | 2 | 0 | 9 | 0 | 23 | 1 | 1 | 7 | .231 | .281 | .274 |
| Paulino, Ronny, Altoona | 99 | 408 | 369 | 54 | 105 | 177 | 23 | 2 | 15 | 60 | 1 | 3 | 3 | 32 | 1 | 62 | 3 | 2 | 7 | .285 | .344 | .480 |
| Pecci, Jay, Norwich † | 63 | 221 | 190 | 22 | 46 | 54 | 5 | 0 | 1 | 19 | 3 | 0 | 9 | 19 | 0 | 26 | 7 | 4 | 6 | .242 | .339 | .284 |
| Pena, Rodolfo, Altoona | 1 | 4 | 4 | 0 | 2 | 2 | 0 | 0 | 0 | 0 | 0 | 0 | 0 | 0 | 0 | 1 | 0 | 0 | 0 | .500 | .500 | .500 |
| Perez, Kenny, Portland † | 109 | 437 | 400 | 47 | 112 | 168 | 31 | 5 | 5 | 61 | 6 | 4 | 4 | 23 | 2 | 59 | 12 | 4 | 9 | .280 | .323 | .420 |
| Peterson, Matt, Altoona | 7 | 3 | 2 | 1 | 0 | 0 | 0 | 0 | 0 | 0 | 0 | 0 | 0 | 1 | 0 | 2 | 0 | 0 | 0 | .000 | .333 | .000 |
| Phelps, Jeff, Reading | 87 | 321 | 282 | 39 | 73 | 108 | 17 | 0 | 6 | 29 | 6 | 1 | 3 | 29 | 1 | 70 | 3 | 4 | 6 | .259 | .333 | .383 |

| Player, Team | G | TPA | AB | R | H | TB | 2B | 3B | HR | RBI | SH | SF | HP | BB | IBB | SO | SB | CS | GDP | Avg. | OBP | Slg. |
|---|---|---|---|---|---|---|---|---|---|---|---|---|---|---|---|---|---|---|---|---|---|---|
| Pinckney, Brandon, Akron | 68 | 263 | 244 | 32 | 76 | 93 | 9 | 1 | 2 | 33 | 1 | 1 | 3 | 14 | 0 | 30 | 4 | 3 | 3 | .311 | .355 | .381 |
| Pratt, Scott, Akron * | 114 | 453 | 405 | 73 | 108 | 157 | 27 | 5 | 4 | 44 | 0 | 7 | 10 | 31 | 0 | 90 | 22 | 8 | 7 | .267 | .329 | .388 |
| Pressley, Josh, Binghamton * | 101 | 394 | 340 | 44 | 102 | 141 | 30 | 0 | 3 | 62 | 2 | 4 | 2 | 46 | 2 | 64 | 0 | 0 | 10 | .300 | .383 | .415 |
| Raburn, Ryan, Erie | 98 | 422 | 366 | 66 | 110 | 195 | 29 | 4 | 16 | 63 | 1 | 1 | 7 | 47 | 1 | 96 | 3 | 0 | 9 | .301 | .390 | .533 |
| Ramirez, Hanley, Portland † | 32 | 139 | 129 | 26 | 40 | 66 | 7 | 2 | 5 | 15 | 0 | 0 | 0 | 10 | 0 | 26 | 12 | 3 | 0 | .310 | .360 | .512 |
| Ramirez, Ramon, Trenton | 18 | 2 | 2 | 1 | 1 | 1 | 0 | 0 | 0 | 0 | 0 | 0 | 0 | 0 | 0 | 1 | 1 | 0 | 0 | .500 | .500 | .500 |
| Rasner, Darrell, Harrisburg | 5 | 5 | 5 | 0 | 0 | 0 | 0 | 0 | 0 | 0 | 0 | 0 | 0 | 0 | 0 | 4 | 0 | 0 | 0 | .000 | .000 | .000 |
| Raymundo, G.J., Harrisburg | 35 | 113 | 103 | 13 | 31 | 44 | 7 | 0 | 2 | 13 | 0 | 1 | 2 | 7 | 0 | 14 | 0 | 0 | 6 | .301 | .354 | .427 |
| Reed, Keith, Bowie | 121 | 505 | 464 | 62 | 137 | 217 | 32 | 0 | 16 | 65 | 1 | 3 | 6 | 31 | 2 | 101 | 3 | 6 | 12 | .295 | .345 | .468 |
| Rich, Dominic, New Hampshire * | 136 | 582 | 513 | 79 | 142 | 202 | 30 | 3 | 8 | 71 | 4 | 4 | 8 | 53 | 4 | 72 | 3 | 2 | 13 | .277 | .351 | .394 |
| Richardson, Juan, Reading | 18 | 74 | 71 | 10 | 20 | 36 | 1 | 0 | 5 | 13 | 0 | 1 | 1 | 1 | 0 | 16 | 0 | 1 | 2 | .282 | .297 | .507 |
| Rifkin, Aaron, Trenton * | 127 | 530 | 468 | 62 | 118 | 216 | 27 | 1 | 23 | 82 | 0 | 10 | 3 | 49 | 3 | 118 | 4 | 1 | 6 | .252 | .321 | .462 |
| Ring, Royce, Binghamton * | 19 | 1 | 1 | 0 | 0 | 0 | 0 | 0 | 0 | 0 | 0 | 0 | 0 | 0 | 0 | 1 | 0 | 0 | 0 | .000 | .000 | .000 |
| Rogers, Ed, Bowie | 124 | 539 | 482 | 71 | 137 | 183 | 32 | 1 | 4 | 37 | 15 | 1 | 4 | 37 | 2 | 78 | 20 | 7 | 4 | .284 | .340 | .380 |
| Rogers, Omar, Bowie | 7 | 22 | 18 | 1 | 1 | 1 | 0 | 0 | 0 | 2 | 1 | 0 | 0 | 3 | 0 | 4 | 0 | 1 | 0 | .056 | .190 | .056 |
| Roman, Orlando, Binghamton | 8 | 6 | 3 | 0 | 1 | 1 | 0 | 0 | 0 | 1 | 2 | 1 | 0 | 0 | 0 | 0 | 0 | 0 | 0 | .333 | .250 | .333 |
| Roneberg, Brett, Portland * | 124 | 542 | 474 | 67 | 132 | 219 | 30 | 3 | 17 | 77 | 1 | 4 | 4 | 59 | 5 | 74 | 9 | 3 | 21 | .278 | .360 | .462 |
| Ruiz, Carlos, Reading | 101 | 384 | 349 | 45 | 99 | 169 | 15 | 2 | 17 | 50 | 1 | 3 | 8 | 22 | 1 | 37 | 8 | 4 | 15 | .284 | .338 | .484 |
| Rundles, Rich, Harrisburg * | 20 | 11 | 10 | 0 | 0 | 0 | 0 | 0 | 0 | 0 | 0 | 0 | 0 | 1 | 0 | 3 | 0 | 0 | 2 | .000 | .091 | .000 |
| Sadler, Billy, Norwich | 17 | 1 | 1 | 0 | 0 | 0 | 0 | 0 | 0 | 0 | 0 | 0 | 0 | 0 | 0 | 0 | 0 | 0 | 0 | .000 | .000 | .000 |
| Sadler, Ray, Altoona | 120 | 460 | 429 | 61 | 115 | 202 | 25 | 1 | 20 | 72 | 1 | 4 | 3 | 23 | 1 | 89 | 16 | 6 | 6 | .268 | .307 | .471 |
| Santos, Francisco, Norwich * | 28 | 108 | 102 | 8 | 32 | 42 | 5 | 1 | 1 | 13 | 0 | 0 | 0 | 6 | 1 | 12 | 0 | 0 | 3 | .314 | .352 | .412 |
| Sardinha, Bronson, Trenton * | 72 | 303 | 266 | 37 | 71 | 102 | 11 | 1 | 6 | 29 | 0 | 0 | 0 | 37 | 3 | 65 | 4 | 1 | 8 | .267 | .356 | .383 |
| Scanlon, Matt, New Britain * | 74 | 281 | 248 | 29 | 57 | 83 | 7 | 2 | 5 | 33 | 2 | 5 | 4 | 22 | 0 | 65 | 0 | 1 | 3 | .230 | .297 | .335 |
| Schneidmiller, Gary, Portland | 8 | 37 | 30 | 4 | 7 | 9 | 2 | 0 | 0 | 6 | 1 | 2 | 0 | 4 | 0 | 10 | 1 | 0 | 1 | .233 | .306 | .300 |
| Scobie, Jason, Binghamton | 26 | 15 | 11 | 1 | 2 | 2 | 0 | 0 | 0 | 0 | 1 | 0 | 0 | 3 | 0 | 6 | 0 | 0 | 0 | .182 | .357 | .182 |
| Serrano, Elio, Altoona | 45 | 3 | 2 | 2 | 1 | 1 | 0 | 0 | 0 | 0 | 1 | 0 | 0 | 0 | 0 | 0 | 0 | 0 | 0 | .500 | .500 | .500 |
| Shaffar, Ben, Altoona † | 8 | 2 | 1 | 0 | 0 | 0 | 0 | 0 | 0 | 0 | 1 | 0 | 0 | 0 | 0 | 0 | 0 | 0 | 0 | .000 | .000 | .000 |
| Shepard, David, Trenton | 51 | 1 | 1 | 0 | 0 | 0 | 0 | 0 | 0 | 0 | 0 | 0 | 0 | 0 | 0 | 1 | 0 | 0 | 0 | .000 | .000 | .000 |
| Sherrill, J.J., Akron † | 20 | 70 | 64 | 6 | 10 | 15 | 2 | 0 | 1 | 4 | 0 | 0 | 1 | 5 | 0 | 25 | 3 | 0 | 1 | .156 | .229 | .234 |
| Singleton, Justin, New Hampshire * | 129 | 482 | 441 | 54 | 104 | 193 | 19 | 11 | 16 | 50 | 4 | 2 | 2 | 33 | 3 | 152 | 7 | 4 | 5 | .236 | .291 | .438 |
| Skrehot, Shaun, Altoona | 67 | 267 | 243 | 33 | 64 | 81 | 12 | 1 | 1 | 16 | 3 | 0 | 6 | 15 | 0 | 24 | 5 | 2 | 5 | .263 | .322 | .333 |
| Smith, Corey, Akron | 128 | 525 | 454 | 79 | 113 | 190 | 14 | 3 | 19 | 66 | 0 | 2 | 6 | 63 | 0 | 106 | 3 | 2 | 11 | .249 | .347 | .419 |
| Snell, Ian, Altoona | 26 | 17 | 14 | 1 | 2 | 2 | 0 | 0 | 0 | 1 | 2 | 0 | 0 | 1 | 0 | 6 | 0 | 0 | 0 | .143 | .200 | .143 |
| Snusz, Chris, Altoona | 36 | 133 | 120 | 11 | 22 | 28 | 4 | 1 | 0 | 6 | 3 | 0 | 1 | 9 | 0 | 29 | 0 | 0 | 0 | .183 | .246 | .233 |
| Snyder, Mike, New Hampshire * | 79 | 292 | 261 | 32 | 55 | 94 | 9 | 3 | 8 | 36 | 1 | 2 | 0 | 28 | 1 | 79 | 2 | 2 | 3 | .211 | .285 | .360 |
| Solano, Danny, New Hampshire | 103 | 424 | 359 | 51 | 84 | 110 | 19 | 2 | 1 | 26 | 4 | 1 | 4 | 56 | 2 | 73 | 2 | 2 | 6 | .234 | .343 | .306 |
| Spilman, Ryan, Akron | 2 | 3 | 2 | 1 | 0 | 0 | 0 | 0 | 0 | 0 | 0 | 0 | 0 | 1 | 0 | 2 | 0 | 0 | 0 | .000 | .333 | .000 |
| Squires, Matt, Reading * | 26 | 1 | 1 | 0 | 0 | 0 | 0 | 0 | 0 | 0 | 0 | 0 | 0 | 0 | 0 | 1 | 0 | 0 | 0 | .000 | .000 | .000 |
| St. Pierre, Maxim, Erie | 84 | 322 | 290 | 31 | 72 | 111 | 15 | 0 | 8 | 33 | 1 | 2 | 4 | 25 | 0 | 41 | 2 | 1 | 7 | .248 | .315 | .383 |
| Stein, Blake, Altoona | 36 | 2 | 1 | 0 | 0 | 0 | 0 | 0 | 0 | 0 | 0 | 0 | 0 | 1 | 0 | 1 | 0 | 0 | 0 | .000 | .500 | .000 |
| Tejeda, Juan, Erie | 125 | 522 | 457 | 71 | 132 | 236 | 29 | 3 | 23 | 92 | 2 | 7 | 5 | 51 | 1 | 102 | 0 | 0 | 10 | .289 | .362 | .516 |
| Tejeda, Rob, Reading | 27 | 23 | 21 | 1 | 1 | 1 | 0 | 0 | 0 | 0 | 1 | 0 | 0 | 1 | 0 | 13 | 0 | 0 | 0 | .048 | .091 | .048 |
| Thomas, Gary, Altoona | 30 | 104 | 93 | 13 | 21 | 39 | 8 | 2 | 2 | 8 | 1 | 0 | 1 | 9 | 1 | 14 | 0 | 0 | 3 | .226 | .301 | .419 |
| Thompson, Kevin, Trenton | 69 | 306 | 270 | 43 | 76 | 120 | 17 | 0 | 9 | 17 | 2 | 0 | 4 | 30 | 1 | 40 | 29 | 10 | 8 | .281 | .362 | .444 |
| Thurman, Corey, Harrisburg | 5 | 1 | 1 | 0 | 1 | 1 | 0 | 0 | 0 | 0 | 0 | 0 | 0 | 0 | 0 | 0 | 0 | 0 | 0 | 1.000 | 1.000 | 1.000 |
| Tomlin, James, New Britain | 138 | 537 | 490 | 58 | 106 | 129 | 18 | 1 | 1 | 34 | 19 | 3 | 2 | 23 | 0 | 75 | 13 | 9 | 9 | .216 | .253 | .263 |
| Torres, Gabby, New Britain | 54 | 191 | 173 | 14 | 46 | 67 | 12 | 0 | 3 | 18 | 2 | 0 | 7 | 9 | 2 | 22 | 0 | 0 | 2 | .266 | .328 | .387 |
| Tousa, Scott, Erie * | 95 | 321 | 259 | 38 | 57 | 85 | 10 | 3 | 4 | 27 | 5 | 5 | 17 | 35 | 1 | 56 | 2 | 4 | 5 | .220 | .345 | .328 |
| Treadway, Brion, Norwich | 7 | 2 | 1 | 0 | 0 | 0 | 0 | 0 | 0 | 0 | 1 | 0 | 0 | 0 | 0 | 1 | 0 | 0 | 0 | .000 | .000 | .000 |
| Umbria, Jose, New Hampshire | 58 | 226 | 211 | 17 | 54 | 61 | 4 | 0 | 1 | 20 | 2 | 2 | 1 | 10 | 0 | 45 | 0 | 0 | 8 | .256 | .290 | .289 |
| Valderrama, Carlos, Norwich | 93 | 419 | 381 | 59 | 110 | 161 | 24 | 3 | 7 | 37 | 2 | 1 | 2 | 31 | 1 | 82 | 20 | 1 | 5 | .289 | .345 | .423 |
| Valdez, Merkin, Norwich | 10 | 4 | 4 | 0 | 1 | 1 | 0 | 0 | 0 | 0 | 0 | 0 | 0 | 0 | 0 | 2 | 0 | 0 | 0 | .250 | .250 | .250 |
| Valencia, Vic, Akron | 15 | 59 | 48 | 10 | 11 | 21 | 4 | 0 | 2 | 5 | 2 | 1 | 2 | 6 | 0 | 16 | 0 | 0 | 0 | .229 | .333 | .438 |
| Valencia, Vic, New Hampshire | 32 | 106 | 95 | 11 | 17 | 30 | 1 | 0 | 4 | 14 | 0 | 1 | 1 | 9 | 1 | 31 | 0 | 0 | 3 | .179 | .255 | .316 |
| Velazquez, Gil, Binghamton | 105 | 401 | 359 | 42 | 86 | 123 | 16 | 3 | 5 | 37 | 6 | 2 | 2 | 32 | 1 | 94 | 4 | 3 | 3 | .240 | .304 | .343 |
| Vericker, Brad, Norwich * | 17 | 63 | 52 | 6 | 10 | 13 | 3 | 0 | 0 | 2 | 0 | 1 | 0 | 10 | 0 | 20 | 0 | 0 | 1 | .192 | .317 | .250 |
| Villegas, Felix, Reading | 31 | 3 | 2 | 0 | 0 | 0 | 0 | 0 | 0 | 0 | 0 | 0 | 0 | 1 | 0 | 2 | 0 | 0 | 0 | .000 | .333 | .000 |
| Von Schell, Tyler, Norwich | 64 | 274 | 247 | 25 | 65 | 98 | 16 | 1 | 5 | 39 | 0 | 2 | 2 | 23 | 1 | 60 | 0 | 1 | 7 | .263 | .328 | .397 |
| Wald, Jake, Norwich | 52 | 187 | 162 | 19 | 34 | 50 | 8 | 1 | 2 | 13 | 2 | 2 | 4 | 17 | 1 | 49 | 0 | 3 | 2 | .210 | .297 | .309 |
| Walk, Mitch, Norwich * | 47 | 7 | 7 | 1 | 0 | 0 | 0 | 0 | 0 | 0 | 0 | 0 | 0 | 0 | 0 | 2 | 0 | 0 | 0 | .000 | .000 | .000 |
| Wallace, David, Akron | 47 | 168 | 141 | 19 | 30 | 52 | 4 | 0 | 6 | 19 | 0 | 1 | 1 | 25 | 2 | 58 | 0 | 0 | 0 | .213 | .333 | .369 |
| Walsh, Sean, Reading | 46 | 143 | 126 | 9 | 29 | 40 | 8 | 0 | 1 | 11 | 0 | 0 | 3 | 14 | 1 | 26 | 2 | 1 | 1 | .230 | .322 | .317 |
| Walter, Randy, Norwich | 13 | 48 | 45 | 1 | 5 | 5 | 0 | 0 | 0 | 2 | 1 | 0 | 0 | 2 | 0 | 15 | 0 | 0 | 1 | .111 | .149 | .111 |
| Watkins, Tommy, New Britain | 116 | 463 | 397 | 64 | 106 | 153 | 21 | 1 | 8 | 47 | 12 | 4 | 5 | 45 | 0 | 77 | 20 | 9 | 5 | .267 | .346 | .385 |
| Weber, Jake, Trenton * | 111 | 402 | 363 | 52 | 95 | 137 | 18 | 3 | 6 | 38 | 5 | 2 | 3 | 29 | 2 | 47 | 4 | 5 | 4 | .262 | .320 | .377 |
| Whiteside, Eli, Bowie | 90 | 334 | 297 | 41 | 75 | 147 | 18 | 0 | 18 | 60 | 0 | 3 | 1 | 25 | 0 | 65 | 2 | 2 | 3 | .253 | .310 | .495 |
| Wilson, Craig, Trenton | 80 | 336 | 268 | 49 | 82 | 103 | 12 | 0 | 3 | 27 | 5 | 1 | 6 | 56 | 3 | 35 | 3 | 3 | 4 | .306 | .435 | .384 |
| Young, Walter, Bowie * | 133 | 548 | 486 | 88 | 133 | 262 | 28 | 1 | 33 | 98 | 0 | 7 | 8 | 47 | 3 | 145 | 2 | 3 | 11 | .274 | .343 | .539 |
| Youngbauer, Scott, Akron † | 61 | 249 | 219 | 41 | 49 | 86 | 11 | 4 | 6 | 28 | 2 | 0 | 0 | 28 | 1 | 41 | 5 | 2 | 5 | .224 | .312 | .393 |

GRAND SLAMS—Eldred, Jenkins, Sadler, 2 each; Airoso, Aubrey, Basak, Bonifay, Broadway, Curry, Francisco, Garbe, Granderson, G. Jones, M. Jones, McMains, Reese, Redman, Rifkin, Roneberg, Tejeda, Von Schell, Weber, Whiteside, 1 each.

AWARDED FIRST BASE ON CATCHER'S INTERFERENCE—Whiteside 10 (Wilson, Wilson, Doumit, Camacaro, E. Martinez, Doumit, Fuentes, Parrish, Paulino, Umbria, Curry); Hill 3 (Castellano, Jacobson, J. Gonzalez); Airoso (Wilson); Basak (Curry); Campo (Valencia); French (Navarro); Griffin (E. Martinez); G. Jones (Knoedler); Keppinger (Luderer); Lane (Burkhart); Mota (E. Martinez); Nicholson (Jacobson); Ruiz (Madera); Valderrama (Wilson) .

# 2004 PITCHING

## TEAM

| Team | W | L | Pct. | ERA | G | CG | ShO | Sv. | IP | H | TBF | R | ER | HR | SH | SF | HB | BB | IBB | SO | WP | Bk. |
|---|---|---|---|---|---|---|---|---|---|---|---|---|---|---|---|---|---|---|---|---|---|---|
| New Hampshire | 84 | 57 | .596 | 3.48 | 141 | 3 | 13 | 46 | 1223.2 | 1096 | 5127 | 534 | 473 | 114 | 31 | 23 | 60 | 438 | 11 | 975 | 56 | 5 |
| Norwich | 69 | 73 | .486 | 3.64 | 142 | 5 | 11 | 35 | 1228.1 | 1170 | 5197 | 564 | 497 | 98 | 55 | 39 | 36 | 427 | 17 | 912 | 55 | 6 |
| New Britain | 70 | 70 | .500 | 4.09 | 140 | 3 | 9 | 47 | 1214.0 | 1214 | 5263 | 610 | 552 | 110 | 42 | 37 | 68 | 479 | 31 | 989 | 43 | 5 |
| Erie | 80 | 62 | .563 | 4.10 | 142 | 6 | 16 | 32 | 1239.1 | 1288 | 5389 | 665 | 564 | 139 | 51 | 39 | 75 | 411 | 10 | 872 | 48 | 6 |
| Altoona | 85 | 56 | .603 | 4.16 | 141 | 3 | 11 | 46 | 1222.2 | 1223 | 5279 | 644 | 565 | 140 | 54 | 54 | 52 | 438 | 21 | 992 | 62 | 3 |
| Binghamton | 76 | 66 | .535 | 4.21 | 142 | 1 | 2 | 42 | 1236.2 | 1149 | 5357 | 658 | 579 | 113 | 52 | 40 | 79 | 534 | 4 | 1007 | 74 | 11 |
| Bowie | 73 | 69 | .514 | 4.23 | 142 | 0 | 8 | 34 | 1216.0 | 1187 | 5314 | 642 | 571 | 128 | 38 | 38 | 68 | 519 | 26 | 1108 | 75 | 6 |
| Reading | 64 | 77 | .454 | 4.54 | 141 | 4 | 9 | 35 | 1200.1 | 1256 | 5296 | 683 | 605 | 147 | 40 | 53 | 63 | 484 | 18 | 917 | 48 | 12 |
| Akron | 63 | 78 | .447 | 4.59 | 141 | 4 | 5 | 32 | 1220.2 | 1290 | 5442 | 719 | 622 | 118 | 50 | 44 | 74 | 490 | 17 | 942 | 51 | 9 |
| Harrisburg | 52 | 90 | .366 | 4.69 | 142 | 3 | 6 | 28 | 1228.0 | 1338 | 5396 | 729 | 640 | 150 | 48 | 44 | 84 | 451 | 18 | 846 | 57 | 11 |
| Trenton | 64 | 78 | .451 | 4.72 | 142 | 6 | 7 | 33 | 1231.0 | 1335 | 5419 | 721 | 646 | 99 | 45 | 41 | 49 | 450 | 17 | 1072 | 83 | 5 |
| Portland | 69 | 73 | .486 | 4.82 | 142 | 1 | 4 | 40 | 1250.0 | 1319 | 5528 | 757 | 669 | 134 | 35 | 43 | 59 | 478 | 17 | 1053 | 62 | 15 |

## INDIVIDUAL

### TOP QUALIFIERS FOR EARNED-RUN AVERAGE TITLE

Minimum 114 innings. *Lefthanded pitcher.

| Pitcher, Team | W | L | Pct. | ERA | G | GS | CG | ShO | GF | Sv. | IP | H | TBF | R | ER | HR | SH | SF | HB | BB | IBB | SO | WP | Bk. |
|---|---|---|---|---|---|---|---|---|---|---|---|---|---|---|---|---|---|---|---|---|---|---|---|---|
| Floyd, Gavin, Reading | 6 | 6 | .500 | 2.57 | 20 | 20 | 2 | 1 | 0 | 0 | 119.0 | 93 | 496 | 39 | 34 | 5 | 6 | 5 | 9 | 46 | 1 | 94 | 1 | 2 |
| Scobie, Jason, Binghamton | 5 | 5 | .500 | 2.82 | 26 | 24 | 0 | 0 | 1 | 1 | 147.0 | 137 | 618 | 57 | 46 | 11 | 8 | 3 | 11 | 49 | 0 | 95 | 5 | 2 |
| Chacin, Gustavo, New Hampshire * | 16 | 2 | .889 | 2.86 | 25 | 25 | 0 | 0 | 0 | 0 | 141.2 | 113 | 577 | 53 | 45 | 15 | 4 | 1 | 5 | 49 | 0 | 109 | 3 | 0 |
| Larrison, Preston, Erie | 5 | 4 | .556 | 3.05 | 20 | 20 | 0 | 0 | 0 | 0 | 118.0 | 122 | 516 | 54 | 40 | 12 | 7 | 7 | 5 | 36 | 1 | 59 | 6 | 1 |
| Misch, Pat, Norwich * | 7 | 6 | .538 | 3.06 | 26 | 26 | 4 | 3 | 0 | 0 | 159.0 | 138 | 623 | 61 | 54 | 13 | 10 | 6 | 3 | 35 | 0 | 123 | 4 | 1 |
| Snell, Ian, Altoona | 11 | 7 | .611 | 3.16 | 26 | 26 | 3 | 2 | 0 | 0 | 151.0 | 147 | 624 | 54 | 53 | 16 | 9 | 6 | 5 | 40 | 2 | 142 | 6 | 0 |
| Alvarez, Abe, Portland * | 10 | 9 | .526 | 3.66 | 26 | 26 | 0 | 0 | 0 | 0 | 135.1 | 133 | 562 | 65 | 55 | 13 | 4 | 3 | 5 | 32 | 0 | 108 | 2 | 0 |
| Baugh, Kenny, Erie | 8 | 8 | .500 | 3.72 | 24 | 24 | 1 | 0 | 0 | 0 | 142.2 | 154 | 611 | 70 | 59 | 13 | 8 | 5 | 7 | 41 | 0 | 107 | 3 | 0 |
| Stevenson, Jason, Harrisburg | 8 | 10 | .444 | 4.06 | 24 | 22 | 0 | 0 | 1 | 1 | 135.1 | 132 | 570 | 66 | 61 | 20 | 8 | 6 | 12 | 46 | 1 | 75 | 5 | 4 |
| Bullington, Bryan, Altoona | 12 | 7 | .632 | 4.10 | 26 | 26 | 0 | 0 | 0 | 0 | 145.0 | 160 | 629 | 77 | 66 | 18 | 10 | 9 | 9 | 47 | 1 | 100 | 5 | 0 |
| Guthrie, Jeremy, Akron | 8 | 8 | .500 | 4.21 | 23 | 21 | 1 | 0 | 1 | 0 | 130.1 | 145 | 587 | 76 | 61 | 16 | 6 | 5 | 16 | 42 | 0 | 94 | 5 | 0 |
| Habel, Josh, Norwich * | 4 | 10 | .286 | 4.36 | 27 | 25 | 1 | 0 | 0 | 0 | 136.1 | 130 | 580 | 76 | 66 | 21 | 12 | 6 | 5 | 50 | 0 | 123 | 4 | 1 |
| Bonser, Boof, New Britain | 12 | 9 | .571 | 4.37 | 27 | 27 | 0 | 0 | 0 | 0 | 154.1 | 160 | 658 | 89 | 75 | 22 | 2 | 8 | 3 | 56 | 1 | 146 | 4 | 0 |
| Henn, Sean, Trenton * | 6 | 8 | .429 | 4.41 | 27 | 27 | 0 | 0 | 0 | 0 | 163.1 | 173 | 707 | 94 | 80 | 11 | 10 | 8 | 6 | 63 | 2 | 118 | 12 | 1 |
| Chenard, Ken, Binghamton | 9 | 6 | .600 | 4.45 | 27 | 17 | 0 | 0 | 3 | 3 | 123.1 | 101 | 523 | 66 | 61 | 17 | 5 | 3 | 11 | 48 | 0 | 122 | 15 | 1 |

DEPARTMENTAL LEADERS: W—Chacin, 16; L—Lockwood, 17; Pct.—Chacin, .889; G—Sequea, 59; GS—three pitchers with, 27; CG—Misch, 4; ShO—Misch, 3; GF—Sequea, 53; Sv.—Korecky, 31; IP—Henn, 163.1; H—Bonilla, 180; TBF—Henn, 707; R—Henn, 94; ER—Tejeda, 86; HR—Tejeda, 29; SH—Habel, 12; SF—Bullington, 9; HB—Guthrie, 16; BB—Zink, 72; IBB—J. Miller, 5; SO—Bonser, 146; WP—Chenard, 15; BK—C. Young, 6.

### ALL PITCHERS

*Lefthanded pitcher.

| Pitcher, Team | W | L | Pct. | ERA | G | GS | CG | ShO | GF | Sv. | IP | H | TBF | R | ER | HR | SH | SF | HB | BB | IBB | SO | WP | Bk. |
|---|---|---|---|---|---|---|---|---|---|---|---|---|---|---|---|---|---|---|---|---|---|---|---|---|
| Abbott, Jim, New Britain | 3 | 6 | .333 | 5.06 | 21 | 17 | 0 | 0 | 1 | 0 | 94.1 | 101 | 410 | 54 | 53 | 13 | 8 | 2 | 6 | 31 | 2 | 38 | 5 | 0 |
| Adkins, Tim, Trenton * | 1 | 4 | .200 | 4.63 | 52 | 1 | 0 | 0 | 17 | 1 | 56.1 | 65 | 260 | 38 | 29 | 1 | 0 | 0 | 1 | 27 | 4 | 44 | 4 | 0 |
| Agamennone, Brandon, Altoona | 3 | 1 | .750 | 4.29 | 20 | 0 | 0 | 0 | 5 | 0 | 35.2 | 36 | 156 | 18 | 17 | 4 | 0 | 0 | 1 | 12 | 2 | 39 | 1 | 0 |
| Alvarez, Abe, Portland * | 10 | 9 | .526 | 3.66 | 26 | 26 | 0 | 0 | 0 | 0 | 135.1 | 133 | 562 | 65 | 55 | 13 | 4 | 3 | 5 | 32 | 0 | 108 | 2 | 0 |
| Alvarez, Oscar, Akron * | 7 | 2 | .778 | 3.36 | 23 | 5 | 0 | 0 | 6 | 1 | 67.0 | 62 | 280 | 26 | 25 | 6 | 0 | 1 | 2 | 24 | 1 | 50 | 2 | 0 |
| Anderson, Luke, Norwich | 7 | 2 | .778 | 4.11 | 35 | 0 | 0 | 0 | 16 | 2 | 50.1 | 53 | 222 | 24 | 23 | 3 | 0 | 0 | 1 | 15 | 0 | 52 | 1 | 0 |
| Arnold, Jason, New Hampshire | 0 | 1 | .000 | 3.15 | 4 | 4 | 0 | 0 | 0 | 0 | 20.0 | 17 | 80 | 7 | 7 | 4 | 3 | 0 | 2 | 5 | 0 | 14 | 0 | 0 |
| Averette, Robert, Bowie | 5 | 1 | .833 | 3.02 | 10 | 9 | 0 | 0 | 0 | 0 | 50.2 | 54 | 210 | 20 | 17 | 5 | 4 | 4 | 1 | 14 | 1 | 27 | 0 | 0 |
| Baker, Chris, New Hampshire | 5 | 1 | .833 | 3.09 | 11 | 11 | 0 | 0 | 0 | 0 | 70.0 | 56 | 270 | 26 | 24 | 7 | 3 | 1 | 1 | 13 | 0 | 61 | 3 | 0 |
| Banks, Joshua, New Hampshire | 6 | 6 | .500 | 5.03 | 18 | 17 | 1 | 0 | 0 | 0 | 91.1 | 89 | 381 | 54 | 51 | 15 | 2 | 3 | 0 | 28 | 0 | 76 | 1 | 1 |
| Bannister, Brian, Binghamton | 3 | 3 | .500 | 4.06 | 8 | 8 | 0 | 0 | 0 | 0 | 44.1 | 45 | 180 | 23 | 20 | 2 | 2 | 0 | 2 | 17 | 0 | 28 | 4 | 0 |
| Bateman, Joe, Norwich | 1 | 3 | .250 | 2.78 | 12 | 1 | 0 | 0 | 7 | 0 | 22.2 | 20 | 96 | 7 | 7 | 1 | 0 | 0 | 0 | 8 | 1 | 17 | 0 | 0 |
| Baugh, Kenny, Erie | 8 | 8 | .500 | 3.72 | 24 | 24 | 1 | 0 | 0 | 0 | 142.2 | 154 | 611 | 70 | 59 | 13 | 8 | 5 | 7 | 41 | 0 | 107 | 3 | 0 |
| Begg, Chris, Norwich | 9 | 1 | .900 | 2.30 | 16 | 14 | 0 | 0 | 1 | 0 | 94.0 | 87 | 367 | 27 | 24 | 3 | 3 | 2 | 1 | 11 | 0 | 61 | 1 | 0 |
| Bentz, Chad, Harrisburg * | 0 | 1 | .000 | 8.59 | 5 | 1 | 0 | 0 | 2 | 1 | 7.1 | 5 | 32 | 7 | 7 | 2 | 0 | 0 | 1 | 8 | 0 | 2 | 0 | 0 |
| Bere, Jason, Akron | 0 | 1 | .000 | 11.12 | 2 | 2 | 0 | 0 | 0 | 0 | 5.2 | 10 | 29 | 7 | 7 | 0 | 0 | 1 | 0 | 4 | 0 | 4 | 2 | 0 |
| Bergmann, Jay, Harrisburg | 0 | 2 | .000 | 9.00 | 2 | 0 | 0 | 0 | 1 | 0 | 4.0 | 7 | 21 | 5 | 4 | 3 | 0 | 0 | 0 | 2 | 1 | 3 | 1 | 0 |
| Bevis, P.J., Binghamton | 1 | 2 | .333 | 3.06 | 27 | 0 | 0 | 0 | 25 | 12 | 32.1 | 26 | 131 | 12 | 11 | 3 | 0 | 0 | 0 | 8 | 1 | 32 | 0 | 0 |
| Birtwell, John, Erie | 0 | 0 | .000 | 3.52 | 6 | 0 | 0 | 0 | 3 | 1 | 7.2 | 6 | 32 | 3 | 3 | 1 | 0 | 0 | 1 | 2 | 0 | 7 | 0 | 0 |
| Blackwell, Brad, Trenton | 0 | 0 | .000 | 18.00 | 1 | 0 | 0 | 0 | 1 | 0 | 1.0 | 3 | 6 | 2 | 2 | 1 | 0 | 0 | 0 | 0 | 0 | 2 | 0 | 0 |
| Bonilla, Henry, New Britain | 11 | 10 | .524 | 4.54 | 25 | 22 | 1 | 0 | 1 | 0 | 142.2 | 180 | 612 | 75 | 72 | 14 | 3 | 6 | 6 | 36 | 3 | 67 | 2 | 1 |
| Bonser, Boof, New Britain | 12 | 9 | .571 | 4.37 | 27 | 27 | 0 | 0 | 0 | 0 | 154.1 | 160 | 658 | 89 | 75 | 22 | 2 | 8 | 3 | 56 | 1 | 146 | 4 | 0 |
| Borner, Brady, Altoona * | 5 | 6 | .455 | 5.47 | 39 | 9 | 0 | 0 | 7 | 1 | 100.1 | 120 | 450 | 76 | 61 | 17 | 2 | 6 | 1 | 30 | 2 | 62 | 1 | 0 |
| Bouknight, Kip, New Hampshire | 0 | 0 | .000 | 3.86 | 3 | 1 | 0 | 0 | 1 | 1 | 9.1 | 10 | 41 | 5 | 4 | 1 | 0 | 0 | 0 | 4 | 0 | 4 | 2 | 0 |
| Bowers, Shane, Reading | 1 | 0 | 1.000 | 1.20 | 4 | 4 | 0 | 0 | 0 | 0 | 15.0 | 12 | 60 | 2 | 2 | 0 | 0 | 0 | 0 | 4 | 0 | 14 | 0 | 0 |
| Bowyer, Travis, New Britain | 6 | 3 | .667 | 1.76 | 31 | 0 | 0 | 0 | 14 | 3 | 61.1 | 42 | 263 | 17 | 12 | 3 | 0 | 0 | 2 | 38 | 1 | 65 | 2 | 1 |
| Bridges, Donnie, Harrisburg | 3 | 5 | .375 | 5.07 | 18 | 12 | 0 | 0 | 1 | 0 | 76.1 | 65 | 336 | 52 | 43 | 9 | 3 | 5 | 11 | 45 | 0 | 56 | 4 | 1 |
| Brito, Eude, Reading * | 8 | 6 | .571 | 4.42 | 43 | 7 | 1 | 0 | 15 | 4 | 97.2 | 95 | 425 | 56 | 48 | 10 | 3 | 5 | 4 | 42 | 2 | 84 | 7 | 3 |
| Brown, Andrew, Akron | 3 | 6 | .333 | 4.66 | 17 | 17 | 0 | 0 | 0 | 0 | 77.1 | 66 | 335 | 44 | 40 | 7 | 7 | 7 | 3 | 36 | 1 | 67 | 4 | 0 |
| Bruback, Matt, Bowie | 5 | 5 | .500 | 4.32 | 14 | 13 | 0 | 0 | 0 | 0 | 75.0 | 80 | 330 | 41 | 36 | 7 | 3 | 4 | 3 | 36 | 0 | 83 | 2 | 0 |
| Bucktrot, Keith, Reading | 4 | 7 | .364 | 4.87 | 20 | 20 | 0 | 0 | 0 | 0 | 105.1 | 140 | 477 | 65 | 57 | 16 | 2 | 6 | 5 | 39 | 0 | 60 | 3 | 0 |
| Bullington, Bryan, Altoona | 12 | 7 | .632 | 4.10 | 26 | 26 | 0 | 0 | 0 | 0 | 145.0 | 160 | 629 | 77 | 66 | 18 | 10 | 9 | 9 | 47 | 1 | 100 | 5 | 0 |
| Cain, Matt, Norwich | 6 | 4 | .600 | 3.35 | 15 | 15 | 0 | 0 | 0 | 0 | 86.0 | 73 | 363 | 44 | 32 | 7 | 1 | 7 | 3 | 40 | 0 | 72 | 4 | 0 |
| Cameron, Kevin, New Britain | 1 | 3 | .250 | 2.33 | 26 | 0 | 0 | 0 | 10 | 3 | 46.1 | 47 | 209 | 20 | 12 | 1 | 0 | 0 | 2 | 21 | 2 | 47 | 2 | 0 |
| Cameron, Ryan, Portland | 4 | 6 | .400 | 4.30 | 23 | 15 | 0 | 0 | 0 | 0 | 90.0 | 94 | 396 | 50 | 43 | 8 | 1 | 3 | 6 | 37 | 0 | 83 | 10 | 0 |
| Carmona, Fausto, Akron | 4 | 8 | .333 | 4.97 | 15 | 15 | 0 | 0 | 0 | 0 | 87.0 | 114 | 381 | 52 | 48 | 3 | 7 | 5 | 2 | 21 | 0 | 63 | 4 | 1 |

| Pitcher, Team | W | L | Pct. | ERA | G | GS | CG | ShO | GF | Sv. | IP | H | TBF | R | ER | HR | SH | SF | HB | BB | IBB | SO | WP | Bk. |
|---|---|---|---|---|---|---|---|---|---|---|---|---|---|---|---|---|---|---|---|---|---|---|---|---|
| Chacin, Gustavo, New Hampshire * | 16 | 2 | .889 | 2.86 | 25 | 25 | 0 | 0 | 0 | 0 | 141.2 | 113 | 577 | 53 | 45 | 15 | 4 | 1 | 5 | 49 | 0 | 109 | 3 | 0 |
| Chantres, Carlos, Reading | 1 | 3 | .250 | 5.97 | 6 | 5 | 0 | 0 | 0 | 0 | 28.2 | 35 | 138 | 23 | 19 | 4 | 2 | 1 | 1 | 19 | 0 | 25 | 2 | 0 |
| Chenard, Ken, Binghamton | 9 | 6 | .600 | 4.45 | 27 | 17 | 0 | 0 | 3 | 3 | 123.1 | 101 | 523 | 66 | 61 | 17 | 5 | 3 | 11 | 48 | 0 | 122 | 15 | 1 |
| Clark, Jeff, Norwich | 2 | 0 | 1.000 | 4.50 | 4 | 4 | 0 | 0 | 0 | 0 | 18.0 | 24 | 84 | 9 | 9 | 2 | 0 | 0 | 2 | 4 | 0 | 17 | 2 | 0 |
| Connolly, Mike, Altoona * | 8 | 7 | .533 | 4.71 | 21 | 21 | 0 | 0 | 0 | 0 | 112.2 | 124 | 501 | 65 | 59 | 10 | 8 | 6 | 6 | 41 | 0 | 103 | 5 | 0 |
| Cooper, Chris, Akron * | 5 | 1 | .833 | 1.77 | 26 | 0 | 0 | 0 | 10 | 2 | 35.2 | 37 | 154 | 11 | 7 | 1 | 0 | 0 | 0 | 10 | 2 | 27 | 0 | 0 |
| Cordova, Jorge, Erie | 2 | 1 | .667 | 6.12 | 23 | 3 | 0 | 0 | 5 | 0 | 42.2 | 58 | 208 | 33 | 29 | 10 | 3 | 1 | 4 | 21 | 1 | 32 | 4 | 0 |
| Crouthers, Dave, Bowie | 9 | 9 | .500 | 5.03 | 27 | 27 | 0 | 0 | 0 | 0 | 139.2 | 134 | 604 | 81 | 78 | 23 | 5 | 6 | 3 | 68 | 2 | 138 | 8 | 1 |
| Cuello, Felix, Erie | 1 | 0 | 1.000 | 5.66 | 9 | 1 | 0 | 0 | 1 | 0 | 20.2 | 18 | 96 | 14 | 13 | 2 | 0 | 0 | 2 | 16 | 0 | 12 | 1 | 0 |
| Culp, Brandon, Reading | 2 | 1 | .667 | 4.38 | 4 | 4 | 0 | 0 | 0 | 0 | 24.2 | 23 | 101 | 12 | 12 | 7 | 1 | 1 | 0 | 8 | 0 | 28 | 2 | 0 |
| Currier, Rik, Trenton | 4 | 6 | .400 | 6.06 | 34 | 8 | 0 | 0 | 10 | 0 | 81.2 | 91 | 384 | 65 | 55 | 11 | 1 | 6 | 6 | 51 | 2 | 74 | 4 | 0 |
| DeJong, Jordan, New Hampshire | 6 | 2 | .750 | 2.86 | 57 | 0 | 0 | 0 | 29 | 14 | 69.1 | 69 | 317 | 24 | 22 | 2 | 1 | 1 | 7 | 30 | 2 | 57 | 9 | 0 |
| DeSalvo, Matt, Trenton | 2 | 2 | .500 | 6.59 | 5 | 5 | 0 | 0 | 0 | 0 | 27.1 | 27 | 116 | 20 | 20 | 3 | 1 | 1 | 1 | 10 | 0 | 24 | 5 | 0 |
| Denham, Dan, Akron | 5 | 4 | .556 | 5.33 | 14 | 14 | 1 | 1 | 0 | 0 | 76.0 | 88 | 347 | 55 | 45 | 12 | 6 | 5 | 7 | 31 | 0 | 50 | 4 | 0 |
| Deschenes, Marc, Portland | 1 | 1 | .500 | 2.45 | 27 | 0 | 0 | 0 | 25 | 11 | 33.0 | 29 | 141 | 9 | 9 | 5 | 0 | 0 | 1 | 12 | 3 | 34 | 0 | 0 |
| DiNardo, Lenny, Portland * | 1 | 0 | 1.000 | 9.53 | 3 | 0 | 0 | 0 | 0 | 0 | 5.2 | 8 | 26 | 6 | 6 | 1 | 0 | 0 | 0 | 1 | 0 | 4 | 1 | 0 |
| Diaz, Pedro, Erie | 1 | 1 | .500 | 4.42 | 4 | 3 | 0 | 0 | 1 | 0 | 18.1 | 21 | 83 | 13 | 9 | 4 | 1 | 1 | 3 | 6 | 0 | 14 | 0 | 0 |
| Dittler, Jake, Akron | 5 | 12 | .294 | 5.02 | 21 | 20 | 1 | 1 | 0 | 0 | 107.2 | 119 | 486 | 73 | 60 | 7 | 6 | 5 | 7 | 40 | 1 | 85 | 4 | 0 |
| Donaldson, Bo, Portland | 4 | 3 | .571 | 5.05 | 30 | 2 | 0 | 0 | 7 | 0 | 73.0 | 72 | 311 | 45 | 41 | 10 | 0 | 2 | 5 | 24 | 0 | 72 | 5 | 1 |
| Dougherty, Kevin, Reading * | 1 | 4 | .200 | 6.85 | 11 | 7 | 0 | 0 | 0 | 0 | 44.2 | 60 | 208 | 39 | 34 | 8 | 7 | 4 | 0 | 28 | 2 | 26 | 2 | 0 |
| Douglas, Shea, Akron * | 1 | 0 | 1.000 | 3.44 | 9 | 0 | 0 | 0 | 3 | 0 | 18.1 | 17 | 83 | 9 | 7 | 2 | 1 | 1 | 1 | 7 | 1 | 15 | 0 | 0 |
| Douglass, Ryan, Harrisburg | 2 | 4 | .333 | 6.23 | 36 | 0 | 0 | 0 | 21 | 0 | 65.0 | 93 | 310 | 56 | 45 | 6 | 0 | 0 | 4 | 23 | 1 | 53 | 7 | 2 |
| Duke, Zach, Altoona * | 5 | 1 | .833 | 1.58 | 9 | 9 | 0 | 0 | 0 | 0 | 51.1 | 41 | 193 | 11 | 9 | 2 | 6 | 2 | 1 | 10 | 0 | 36 | 1 | 1 |
| Echols, Justin, Harrisburg | 3 | 8 | .273 | 6.94 | 21 | 11 | 1 | 0 | 4 | 0 | 72.2 | 88 | 341 | 57 | 56 | 13 | 6 | 3 | 3 | 42 | 0 | 60 | 9 | 1 |
| Edwards, Bryan, Binghamton | 1 | 0 | 1.000 | 3.00 | 2 | 1 | 0 | 0 | 1 | 0 | 9.0 | 6 | 37 | 3 | 3 | 0 | 1 | 0 | 0 | 6 | 0 | 2 | 1 | 0 |
| Ehrlich, Andrew, Portland | 1 | 0 | 1.000 | 2.45 | 2 | 0 | 0 | 0 | 0 | 0 | 3.2 | 5 | 18 | 1 | 1 | 0 | 0 | 0 | 0 | 2 | 0 | 3 | 0 | 0 |
| Elder, Dave, Trenton | 2 | 2 | .500 | 2.55 | 17 | 0 | 0 | 0 | 8 | 1 | 17.2 | 12 | 80 | 7 | 5 | 0 | 0 | 0 | 0 | 15 | 0 | 24 | 1 | 0 |
| Evans, Kyle, Akron | 1 | 3 | .250 | 7.71 | 8 | 7 | 0 | 0 | 0 | 0 | 32.2 | 39 | 155 | 36 | 28 | 7 | 5 | 2 | 2 | 16 | 0 | 24 | 2 | 0 |
| Floyd, Gavin, Reading | 6 | 6 | .500 | 2.57 | 20 | 20 | 2 | 1 | 0 | 0 | 119.0 | 93 | 496 | 39 | 34 | 5 | 6 | 5 | 9 | 46 | 1 | 94 | 1 | 2 |
| Forystek, Brian, Bowie * | 5 | 5 | .500 | 5.74 | 15 | 15 | 0 | 0 | 0 | 0 | 84.2 | 94 | 382 | 57 | 54 | 16 | 5 | 3 | 8 | 41 | 2 | 75 | 7 | 1 |
| Franco, Martire, Reading | 4 | 4 | .500 | 3.30 | 48 | 0 | 0 | 0 | 29 | 15 | 84.2 | 73 | 345 | 31 | 31 | 4 | 0 | 2 | 3 | 20 | 2 | 63 | 6 | 1 |
| Gabbard, Kason, Portland * | 3 | 6 | .333 | 6.28 | 14 | 14 | 0 | 0 | 0 | 0 | 53.0 | 61 | 242 | 42 | 37 | 5 | 1 | 3 | 2 | 26 | 0 | 35 | 4 | 0 |
| Gamble, Jerome, Portland | 4 | 2 | .667 | 3.94 | 14 | 10 | 0 | 0 | 0 | 0 | 61.2 | 62 | 267 | 32 | 27 | 3 | 5 | 5 | 4 | 18 | 0 | 36 | 4 | 1 |
| Gardner, Hayden, Reading | 2 | 1 | .667 | 3.09 | 7 | 0 | 0 | 0 | 5 | 1 | 11.2 | 13 | 51 | 4 | 4 | 1 | 0 | 0 | 0 | 3 | 0 | 6 | 1 | 0 |
| Glaser, Eric, Portland | 7 | 6 | .538 | 4.67 | 31 | 12 | 0 | 0 | 10 | 2 | 96.1 | 98 | 407 | 55 | 50 | 5 | 2 | 5 | 1 | 26 | 1 | 78 | 1 | 0 |
| Goetz, Geoff, Trenton * | 0 | 0 | .000 | 5.19 | 9 | 0 | 0 | 0 | 3 | 0 | 8.2 | 11 | 40 | 5 | 5 | 2 | 0 | 0 | 0 | 3 | 0 | 6 | 1 | 0 |
| Gronkiewicz, Lee, Akron | 1 | 4 | .200 | 3.03 | 52 | 0 | 0 | 0 | 45 | 20 | 65.1 | 65 | 288 | 24 | 22 | 5 | 0 | 0 | 4 | 21 | 3 | 68 | 1 | 0 |
| Guthrie, Jeremy, Akron | 8 | 8 | .500 | 4.21 | 23 | 21 | 1 | 0 | 1 | 0 | 130.1 | 145 | 587 | 76 | 61 | 16 | 6 | 5 | 16 | 42 | 0 | 94 | 5 | 0 |
| Habel, Josh, Norwich * | 4 | 10 | .286 | 4.36 | 27 | 25 | 1 | 0 | 0 | 0 | 136.1 | 130 | 580 | 76 | 66 | 21 | 12 | 6 | 5 | 50 | 0 | 123 | 4 | 1 |
| Hamman, Corey, Erie * | 0 | 0 | .000 | 6.75 | 2 | 1 | 0 | 0 | 0 | 0 | 6.2 | 10 | 35 | 6 | 5 | 2 | 0 | 0 | 0 | 3 | 0 | 3 | 0 | 0 |
| Hamulack, Tim, Portland * | 2 | 0 | 1.000 | 3.52 | 7 | 0 | 0 | 0 | 2 | 0 | 15.1 | 16 | 69 | 6 | 6 | 0 | 0 | 0 | 0 | 7 | 0 | 16 | 1 | 0 |
| Harris, Josh, Akron | 2 | 0 | 1.000 | 0.00 | 2 | 0 | 0 | 0 | 0 | 0 | 3.1 | 3 | 13 | 0 | 0 | 0 | 0 | 0 | 0 | 0 | 0 | 2 | 0 | 0 |
| Harts, Jeremy, Altoona * | 0 | 2 | .000 | 5.28 | 9 | 0 | 0 | 0 | 6 | 1 | 15.1 | 12 | 73 | 12 | 9 | 0 | 0 | 0 | 2 | 13 | 0 | 10 | 3 | 0 |
| Hassey, Brad, New Hampshire | 0 | 0 | .000 | 9.00 | 1 | 0 | 0 | 0 | 1 | 0 | 1.0 | 1 | 4 | 1 | 1 | 0 | 0 | 0 | 0 | 0 | 0 | 0 | 0 | 0 |
| Hebson, Bryan, Portland | 1 | 0 | 1.000 | 4.26 | 12 | 0 | 0 | 0 | 3 | 2 | 25.1 | 19 | 106 | 14 | 12 | 2 | 0 | 0 | 0 | 11 | 0 | 20 | 0 | 0 |
| Henkel, Rob, Erie * | 1 | 1 | .500 | 4.70 | 3 | 3 | 0 | 0 | 0 | 0 | 15.1 | 14 | 66 | 9 | 8 | 3 | 0 | 0 | 0 | 8 | 0 | 10 | 0 | 0 |
| Henn, Sean, Trenton * | 6 | 8 | .429 | 4.41 | 27 | 27 | 0 | 0 | 0 | 0 | 163.1 | 173 | 707 | 94 | 80 | 11 | 10 | 8 | 6 | 63 | 2 | 118 | 12 | 1 |
| Heredia, Felix, Trenton * | 0 | 1 | .000 | 5.40 | 3 | 1 | 0 | 0 | 1 | 0 | 5.0 | 7 | 23 | 6 | 3 | 0 | 0 | 0 | 1 | 0 | 0 | 8 | 0 | 0 |
| Hernandez, Yoel, Reading | 1 | 2 | .333 | 2.01 | 20 | 0 | 0 | 0 | 15 | 6 | 31.1 | 24 | 136 | 12 | 7 | 0 | 1 | 0 | 2 | 15 | 2 | 33 | 3 | 0 |
| Hiles, Cary, Reading | 1 | 1 | .500 | 4.58 | 13 | 0 | 0 | 0 | 4 | 0 | 19.2 | 20 | 88 | 12 | 10 | 2 | 0 | 0 | 1 | 8 | 0 | 17 | 1 | 0 |
| Hill, Jeremy, Binghamton | 2 | 3 | .400 | 2.23 | 25 | 0 | 0 | 0 | 20 | 10 | 32.1 | 23 | 139 | 11 | 8 | 0 | 0 | 0 | 2 | 19 | 0 | 36 | 3 | 0 |
| Hill, Shawn, Harrisburg | 5 | 7 | .417 | 3.39 | 17 | 17 | 2 | 0 | 0 | 0 | 87.2 | 90 | 357 | 39 | 33 | 4 | 4 | 0 | 5 | 20 | 0 | 53 | 2 | 1 |
| Hinckley, Mike, Harrisburg * | 5 | 2 | .714 | 2.87 | 16 | 16 | 0 | 0 | 0 | 0 | 94.0 | 83 | 376 | 34 | 30 | 5 | 8 | 5 | 7 | 23 | 0 | 80 | 1 | 0 |
| Houston, Ryan, New Hampshire | 7 | 4 | .636 | 4.33 | 34 | 8 | 0 | 0 | 6 | 0 | 97.2 | 93 | 429 | 50 | 47 | 13 | 8 | 2 | 5 | 50 | 0 | 102 | 5 | 0 |
| Hundley, Jeff, Bowie * | 1 | 3 | .250 | 2.90 | 35 | 4 | 0 | 0 | 8 | 0 | 62.0 | 55 | 259 | 23 | 20 | 2 | 1 | 1 | 5 | 17 | 0 | 52 | 2 | 0 |
| Hutchison, Ryan, Reading | 1 | 1 | .500 | 3.18 | 12 | 1 | 0 | 0 | 4 | 0 | 22.2 | 25 | 101 | 9 | 8 | 3 | 0 | 0 | 1 | 6 | 0 | 15 | 1 | 0 |
| Jackson, Dan, New Hampshire | 3 | 10 | .231 | 4.80 | 53 | 0 | 0 | 0 | 18 | 3 | 69.1 | 63 | 307 | 42 | 37 | 6 | 0 | 0 | 9 | 30 | 3 | 66 | 7 | 0 |
| Jacobsen, Landon, Altoona | 5 | 2 | .714 | 4.99 | 15 | 14 | 0 | 0 | 0 | 0 | 70.1 | 83 | 317 | 46 | 39 | 8 | 2 | 5 | 3 | 23 | 0 | 47 | 4 | 0 |
| Jimenez, Jason, Reading * | 3 | 2 | .600 | 5.68 | 17 | 0 | 0 | 0 | 14 | 3 | 25.1 | 36 | 122 | 18 | 16 | 3 | 0 | 0 | 0 | 10 | 2 | 20 | 1 | 2 |
| Johnson, James, Portland * | 0 | 2 | .000 | 7.65 | 21 | 0 | 0 | 0 | 7 | 0 | 37.2 | 49 | 176 | 35 | 32 | 9 | 0 | 1 | 0 | 15 | 0 | 38 | 4 | 1 |
| Joseph, Jake, Binghamton | 6 | 0 | 1.000 | 3.32 | 25 | 0 | 0 | 0 | 9 | 1 | 43.1 | 32 | 177 | 18 | 16 | 3 | 1 | 1 | 3 | 14 | 0 | 28 | 4 | 1 |
| Kleine, Victor, Akron * | 4 | 4 | .500 | 4.95 | 25 | 9 | 0 | 0 | 4 | 0 | 87.1 | 91 | 385 | 55 | 48 | 8 | 3 | 5 | 6 | 40 | 0 | 54 | 0 | 3 |
| Korecky, Bobby, New Britain | 3 | 4 | .429 | 3.36 | 55 | 0 | 0 | 0 | 48 | 31 | 67.0 | 52 | 275 | 29 | 25 | 5 | 1 | 0 | 3 | 20 | 2 | 58 | 3 | 0 |
| Larrison, Preston, Erie | 5 | 4 | .556 | 3.05 | 20 | 20 | 0 | 0 | 0 | 0 | 118.0 | 122 | 516 | 54 | 40 | 12 | 7 | 7 | 5 | 36 | 1 | 59 | 6 | 1 |
| Larson, Ryan, Portland | 6 | 3 | .667 | 5.36 | 26 | 0 | 0 | 0 | 13 | 3 | 40.1 | 49 | 192 | 26 | 24 | 5 | 2 | 0 | 1 | 20 | 3 | 36 | 1 | 0 |
| Lavigne, Tim, Binghamton | 4 | 5 | .444 | 5.70 | 40 | 4 | 0 | 0 | 16 | 2 | 83.2 | 94 | 381 | 62 | 53 | 5 | 1 | 1 | 1 | 39 | 0 | 44 | 3 | 0 |
| League, Brandon, New Hampshire | 6 | 4 | .600 | 3.38 | 41 | 10 | 0 | 0 | 6 | 2 | 104.0 | 92 | 441 | 44 | 39 | 3 | 2 | 1 | 8 | 41 | 1 | 90 | 8 | 0 |
| Lee, Derek, New Hampshire * | 1 | 3 | .250 | 3.38 | 12 | 9 | 1 | 0 | 0 | 0 | 56.0 | 59 | 226 | 22 | 21 | 4 | 3 | 4 | 2 | 14 | 0 | 19 | 1 | 0 |
| Liriano, Francisco, New Britain * | 3 | 2 | .600 | 3.18 | 7 | 7 | 0 | 0 | 0 | 0 | 39.2 | 45 | 180 | 14 | 14 | 4 | 3 | 1 | 2 | 17 | 0 | 49 | 3 | 0 |
| Lockwood, Luke, Harrisburg * | 3 | 17 | .150 | 4.95 | 33 | 19 | 0 | 0 | 4 | 1 | 136.1 | 168 | 596 | 83 | 75 | 20 | 4 | 6 | 4 | 30 | 2 | 86 | 2 | 0 |
| Lohse, Erik, New Britain | 1 | 1 | .500 | 5.04 | 7 | 4 | 0 | 0 | 2 | 0 | 25.0 | 29 | 119 | 18 | 14 | 5 | 2 | 2 | 4 | 11 | 2 | 13 | 2 | 0 |
| Lontayo, Alex, Erie * | 3 | 4 | .429 | 5.28 | 36 | 7 | 0 | 0 | 9 | 0 | 73.1 | 82 | 340 | 50 | 43 | 10 | 2 | 3 | 7 | 41 | 2 | 61 | 8 | 3 |
| Luderer, Brian, Akron | 0 | 0 | .000 | 27.00 | 1 | 0 | 0 | 0 | 1 | 0 | 1.0 | 2 | 7 | 3 | 3 | 1 | 0 | 0 | 0 | 3 | 0 | 0 | 0 | 0 |
| Madson, Ryan, Reading | 0 | 0 | .000 | 4.50 | 2 | 1 | 0 | 0 | 0 | 0 | 2.0 | 3 | 11 | 2 | 1 | 1 | 0 | 0 | 0 | 2 | 0 | 1 | 0 | 0 |
| Mangrum, Micah, Binghamton | 1 | 0 | 1.000 | 4.88 | 14 | 0 | 0 | 0 | 3 | 0 | 31.1 | 33 | 134 | 17 | 17 | 3 | 0 | 0 | 2 | 4 | 0 | 22 | 2 | 0 |
| Manning, Charlie, Trenton * | 2 | 1 | .667 | 4.07 | 15 | 1 | 0 | 0 | 3 | 0 | 24.1 | 31 | 109 | 11 | 11 | 1 | 0 | 1 | 3 | 6 | 0 | 19 | 0 | 1 |
| Markert, Jackson, Norwich | 0 | 1 | .000 | 5.61 | 15 | 0 | 0 | 0 | 7 | 0 | 25.2 | 36 | 126 | 18 | 16 | 0 | 2 | 0 | 0 | 15 | 2 | 9 | 0 | 0 |
| Martinez, Dave, Akron * | 0 | 0 | .000 | 0.00 | 1 | 1 | 0 | 0 | 0 | 0 | 5.0 | 5 | 21 | 1 | 0 | 0 | 0 | 0 | 0 | 1 | 0 | 1 | 0 | 0 |
| Mata, Gustavo, Harrisburg | 0 | 0 | .000 | 9.00 | 1 | 0 | 0 | 0 | 0 | 0 | 3.0 | 6 | 16 | 3 | 3 | 1 | 0 | 0 | 0 | 1 | 0 | 2 | 0 | 0 |
| Maust, David, Harrisburg * | 3 | 8 | .273 | 6.43 | 44 | 7 | 0 | 0 | 10 | 0 | 85.1 | 107 | 406 | 65 | 61 | 10 | 3 | 2 | 10 | 37 | 3 | 44 | 6 | 0 |
| McDade, Neal, Altoona | 8 | 1 | .889 | 3.36 | 32 | 7 | 0 | 0 | 4 | 1 | 85.2 | 70 | 350 | 35 | 32 | 7 | 2 | 2 | 4 | 26 | 1 | 53 | 1 | 0 |
| McDowell, Kevin, Erie * | 1 | 0 | 1.000 | 1.69 | 7 | 0 | 0 | 0 | 1 | 0 | 10.2 | 7 | 53 | 2 | 2 | 0 | 0 | 0 | 1 | 13 | 0 | 7 | 2 | 0 |
| McGowan, Dustin, New Hampshire | 2 | 0 | 1.000 | 4.06 | 6 | 6 | 0 | 0 | 0 | 0 | 31.0 | 24 | 130 | 14 | 14 | 4 | 0 | 0 | 0 | 15 | 0 | 29 | 2 | 0 |
| Mears, Chris, Erie | 4 | 1 | .800 | 3.54 | 13 | 0 | 0 | 0 | 8 | 0 | 20.1 | 21 | 89 | 10 | 8 | 1 | 0 | 0 | 2 | 5 | 0 | 12 | 0 | 0 |

| Pitcher, Team | W | L | Pct. | ERA | G | GS | CG | ShO | GF | Sv. | IP | H | TBF | R | ER | HR | SH | SF | HB | BB | IBB | SO | WP | Bk. |
|---|---|---|---|---|---|---|---|---|---|---|---|---|---|---|---|---|---|---|---|---|---|---|---|---|
| Miller, Colby, New Britain | 3 | 7 | .300 | 5.83 | 14 | 14 | 0 | 0 | 0 | 0 | 78.2 | 87 | 345 | 55 | 51 | 9 | 2 | 4 | 8 | 31 | 3 | 39 | 1 | 0 |
| Miller, Jason, New Britain * | 0 | 2 | .000 | 4.28 | 33 | 1 | 0 | 0 | 7 | 2 | 40.0 | 33 | 174 | 19 | 19 | 2 | 0 | 0 | 2 | 21 | 1 | 42 | 2 | 2 |
| Miller, Jeff, Altoona | 5 | 4 | .556 | 2.91 | 52 | 0 | 0 | 0 | 37 | 18 | 68.0 | 48 | 285 | 25 | 22 | 8 | 2 | 1 | 5 | 28 | 5 | 79 | 4 | 0 |
| Misch, Pat, Norwich * | 7 | 6 | .538 | 3.06 | 26 | 26 | 4 | 3 | 0 | 0 | 159.0 | 138 | 623 | 61 | 54 | 13 | 10 | 6 | 3 | 35 | 0 | 123 | 4 | 1 |
| Mitchell, Andy, Bowie | 3 | 2 | .600 | 2.95 | 54 | 0 | 0 | 0 | 17 | 0 | 97.2 | 77 | 411 | 35 | 32 | 9 | 1 | 1 | 5 | 35 | 6 | 78 | 4 | 1 |
| Montalbano, Greg, Portland * | 0 | 2 | .000 | 4.50 | 6 | 5 | 0 | 0 | 0 | 0 | 18.0 | 22 | 88 | 11 | 9 | 0 | 1 | 2 | 1 | 8 | 0 | 11 | 0 | 0 |
| Montes, Albert, Norwich | 6 | 5 | .545 | 3.56 | 53 | 0 | 0 | 0 | 35 | 16 | 65.2 | 68 | 283 | 28 | 26 | 4 | 0 | 0 | 3 | 16 | 2 | 36 | 2 | 3 |
| Moreno, Victor, New Britain | 7 | 2 | .778 | 2.27 | 33 | 5 | 0 | 0 | 11 | 2 | 75.1 | 56 | 316 | 20 | 19 | 4 | 0 | 1 | 1 | 42 | 1 | 86 | 5 | 0 |
| Musser, Neal, Binghamton * | 9 | 6 | .600 | 3.41 | 19 | 19 | 0 | 0 | 0 | 0 | 108.1 | 103 | 458 | 52 | 41 | 7 | 8 | 5 | 4 | 40 | 0 | 70 | 3 | 1 |
| Nicholson, Derek, Erie | 0 | 0 | .000 | 22.50 | 2 | 0 | 0 | 0 | 2 | 0 | 2.0 | 7 | 14 | 5 | 5 | 0 | 0 | 0 | 0 | 1 | 0 | 0 | 0 | 0 |
| Nieves, Raul, Portland | 0 | 0 | .000 | 13.50 | 1 | 0 | 0 | 0 | 1 | 0 | 0.2 | 2 | 6 | 1 | 1 | 0 | 0 | 0 | 1 | 1 | 0 | 0 | 1 | 0 |
| Novoa, Roberto, Erie | 7 | 0 | 1.000 | 2.96 | 41 | 0 | 0 | 0 | 11 | 4 | 79.0 | 63 | 317 | 32 | 26 | 7 | 2 | 2 | 1 | 18 | 1 | 59 | 4 | 1 |
| O'Brien, Patrick, Altoona | 1 | 0 | 1.000 | 0.00 | 2 | 0 | 0 | 0 | 0 | 0 | 4.1 | 1 | 17 | 0 | 0 | 0 | 0 | 0 | 0 | 3 | 0 | 1 | 0 | 0 |
| Ogiltree, John, New Hampshire | 2 | 4 | .333 | 2.64 | 45 | 0 | 0 | 0 | 22 | 3 | 61.1 | 48 | 266 | 22 | 18 | 4 | 0 | 0 | 2 | 32 | 3 | 36 | 1 | 1 |
| Ormond, Rodney, Bowie | 2 | 0 | 1.000 | 3.32 | 32 | 0 | 0 | 0 | 13 | 1 | 40.2 | 42 | 184 | 20 | 15 | 3 | 0 | 0 | 4 | 16 | 1 | 44 | 4 | 0 |
| Ortiz, Javier, Trenton | 6 | 7 | .462 | 4.10 | 19 | 18 | 1 | 1 | 0 | 0 | 105.1 | 110 | 455 | 54 | 48 | 7 | 2 | 8 | 3 | 33 | 0 | 77 | 9 | 0 |
| Ozias, Todd, New Hampshire | 8 | 4 | .667 | 3.43 | 18 | 17 | 0 | 0 | 0 | 0 | 89.1 | 86 | 367 | 43 | 34 | 6 | 1 | 4 | 1 | 29 | 0 | 74 | 3 | 2 |
| Palma, Rick, Erie * | 2 | 11 | .154 | 4.34 | 53 | 3 | 0 | 0 | 30 | 10 | 66.1 | 67 | 281 | 35 | 32 | 7 | 3 | 1 | 2 | 15 | 0 | 55 | 4 | 0 |
| Palmer, Matt, Norwich | 4 | 7 | .364 | 3.06 | 42 | 5 | 0 | 0 | 17 | 8 | 79.1 | 66 | 358 | 35 | 27 | 4 | 4 | 4 | 7 | 51 | 4 | 81 | 7 | 0 |
| Parcus, Kyle, Reading * | 0 | 1 | .000 | 6.75 | 5 | 0 | 0 | 0 | 3 | 0 | 5.1 | 8 | 28 | 4 | 4 | 0 | 0 | 0 | 0 | 4 | 1 | 2 | 0 | 0 |
| Parra, Jose, Binghamton | 0 | 0 | .000 | 0.00 | 1 | 0 | 0 | 0 | 0 | 0 | 1.0 | 0 | 3 | 0 | 0 | 0 | 0 | 0 | 0 | 0 | 0 | 2 | 0 | 0 |
| Penn, Hayden, Bowie | 3 | 0 | 1.000 | 4.87 | 4 | 4 | 0 | 0 | 0 | 0 | 20.1 | 22 | 89 | 12 | 11 | 0 | 0 | 0 | 1 | 9 | 0 | 20 | 0 | 0 |
| Perez, Juan, Portland * | 5 | 1 | .833 | 4.14 | 46 | 0 | 0 | 0 | 18 | 6 | 78.1 | 72 | 345 | 46 | 36 | 12 | 1 | 1 | 2 | 37 | 5 | 79 | 7 | 0 |
| Peterson, Matt, Altoona | 3 | 2 | .600 | 6.25 | 7 | 7 | 0 | 0 | 0 | 0 | 36.0 | 36 | 158 | 25 | 25 | 7 | 2 | 2 | 2 | 22 | 0 | 29 | 7 | 0 |
| Petit, Yusmeiro, Binghamton | 1 | 1 | .500 | 4.50 | 2 | 2 | 0 | 0 | 0 | 0 | 12.0 | 10 | 49 | 6 | 6 | 0 | 1 | 0 | 0 | 5 | 0 | 16 | 0 | 0 |
| Piersoll, Chris, Bowie | 2 | 8 | .200 | 3.99 | 16 | 10 | 0 | 0 | 1 | 0 | 56.1 | 64 | 245 | 28 | 25 | 5 | 3 | 4 | 2 | 20 | 0 | 39 | 2 | 0 |
| Pope, Justin, Trenton | 5 | 3 | .625 | 4.06 | 18 | 10 | 2 | 1 | 4 | 0 | 75.1 | 78 | 315 | 37 | 34 | 12 | 5 | 1 | 1 | 18 | 1 | 53 | 4 | 0 |
| Prahm, Ryan, Akron | 0 | 0 | .000 | 2.22 | 15 | 0 | 0 | 0 | 6 | 1 | 24.1 | 19 | 114 | 9 | 6 | 1 | 0 | 0 | 2 | 20 | 0 | 22 | 1 | 0 |
| Pridie, Jonathon, New Britain | 3 | 6 | .333 | 5.44 | 36 | 7 | 0 | 0 | 7 | 1 | 92.2 | 100 | 409 | 57 | 56 | 8 | 5 | 4 | 3 | 40 | 2 | 81 | 2 | 0 |
| Ramirez, Ramon, Trenton | 4 | 6 | .400 | 4.62 | 18 | 18 | 2 | 0 | 0 | 0 | 115.0 | 116 | 485 | 60 | 59 | 11 | 6 | 4 | 3 | 32 | 0 | 128 | 9 | 3 |
| Rasner, Darrell, Harrisburg | 1 | 1 | .500 | 1.21 | 5 | 5 | 0 | 0 | 0 | 0 | 29.2 | 21 | 111 | 4 | 4 | 1 | 3 | 2 | 2 | 9 | 1 | 15 | 0 | 0 |
| Raymundo, G.J., Harrisburg | 0 | 0 | .000 | 18.00 | 1 | 0 | 0 | 0 | 1 | 0 | 1.0 | 3 | 6 | 2 | 2 | 1 | 0 | 0 | 0 | 0 | 0 | 0 | 0 | 0 |
| Rice, Scott, Bowie * | 6 | 5 | .545 | 3.66 | 41 | 10 | 0 | 0 | 5 | 1 | 96.0 | 94 | 419 | 48 | 39 | 3 | 1 | 4 | 6 | 40 | 2 | 61 | 11 | 2 |
| Ring, Royce, Binghamton * | 2 | 2 | .500 | 3.77 | 19 | 0 | 0 | 0 | 8 | 2 | 28.2 | 25 | 123 | 13 | 12 | 5 | 0 | 0 | 1 | 11 | 1 | 23 | 0 | 0 |
| Rleal, Sendy, Bowie | 4 | 0 | 1.000 | 2.66 | 39 | 0 | 0 | 0 | 21 | 3 | 47.1 | 41 | 197 | 16 | 14 | 7 | 1 | 0 | 3 | 12 | 0 | 60 | 2 | 0 |
| Rodney, Lee, Erie | 4 | 1 | .800 | 3.13 | 24 | 0 | 0 | 0 | 14 | 1 | 37.1 | 40 | 162 | 17 | 13 | 4 | 0 | 0 | 2 | 8 | 0 | 19 | 1 | 0 |
| Roman, Orlando, Binghamton | 2 | 2 | .500 | 4.35 | 8 | 5 | 0 | 0 | 1 | 0 | 31.0 | 26 | 133 | 16 | 15 | 3 | 1 | 2 | 0 | 15 | 0 | 31 | 4 | 0 |
| Rosario, Francisco, New Hampshire | 2 | 4 | .333 | 4.31 | 12 | 12 | 0 | 0 | 0 | 0 | 48.0 | 48 | 199 | 25 | 23 | 6 | 1 | 3 | 2 | 16 | 0 | 45 | 1 | 0 |
| Rundles, Rich, Harrisburg * | 3 | 6 | .333 | 3.42 | 20 | 20 | 0 | 0 | 0 | 0 | 102.2 | 107 | 441 | 50 | 39 | 7 | 3 | 5 | 8 | 35 | 2 | 65 | 8 | 0 |
| Sadler, Billy, Norwich | 0 | 3 | .000 | 3.86 | 17 | 0 | 0 | 0 | 6 | 0 | 30.1 | 22 | 134 | 16 | 13 | 3 | 0 | 0 | 3 | 18 | 0 | 24 | 8 | 0 |
| Sadler, Carl, Akron * | 1 | 1 | .500 | 2.93 | 23 | 0 | 0 | 0 | 11 | 3 | 43.0 | 36 | 182 | 17 | 14 | 1 | 0 | 0 | 2 | 15 | 1 | 41 | 5 | 0 |
| Sanchez, Felix, Erie * | 2 | 2 | .500 | 7.24 | 14 | 0 | 0 | 0 | 6 | 0 | 13.2 | 18 | 66 | 11 | 11 | 2 | 0 | 0 | 1 | 6 | 0 | 12 | 1 | 1 |
| Sanchez, Humberto, Erie | 1 | 0 | 1.000 | 2.13 | 2 | 2 | 0 | 0 | 0 | 0 | 12.2 | 10 | 56 | 5 | 3 | 1 | 0 | 1 | 2 | 6 | 0 | 15 | 1 | 0 |
| Scobie, Jason, Binghamton | 5 | 5 | .500 | 2.82 | 26 | 24 | 0 | 0 | 1 | 1 | 147.0 | 137 | 618 | 57 | 46 | 11 | 8 | 3 | 11 | 49 | 0 | 95 | 5 | 2 |
| Searles, Jon, Harrisburg | 3 | 3 | .500 | 5.05 | 30 | 0 | 0 | 0 | 16 | 0 | 46.1 | 45 | 210 | 32 | 26 | 8 | 0 | 0 | 1 | 25 | 1 | 27 | 0 | 0 |
| Seibel, Phil, Portland * | 0 | 1 | .000 | 7.50 | 3 | 1 | 0 | 0 | 0 | 0 | 6.0 | 8 | 28 | 5 | 5 | 3 | 0 | 0 | 1 | 2 | 0 | 6 | 1 | 0 |
| Sequea, Jacobo, Bowie | 3 | 5 | .375 | 2.62 | 59 | 0 | 0 | 0 | 53 | 27 | 65.1 | 51 | 272 | 25 | 19 | 5 | 0 | 1 | 1 | 25 | 2 | 53 | 0 | 0 |
| Serrano, Elio, Altoona | 3 | 5 | .375 | 5.63 | 45 | 0 | 0 | 0 | 35 | 14 | 56.0 | 73 | 258 | 44 | 35 | 11 | 1 | 3 | 4 | 15 | 3 | 39 | 0 | 0 |
| Shaffar, Ben, Altoona | 0 | 1 | .000 | 7.40 | 8 | 2 | 0 | 0 | 0 | 0 | 20.2 | 28 | 100 | 20 | 17 | 4 | 0 | 1 | 1 | 10 | 0 | 23 | 1 | 1 |
| Shepard, David, Trenton | 4 | 7 | .364 | 3.54 | 51 | 0 | 0 | 0 | 37 | 20 | 68.2 | 58 | 293 | 30 | 27 | 3 | 0 | 0 | 3 | 28 | 4 | 52 | 2 | 0 |
| Skrmetta, Matt, Harrisburg | 0 | 1 | .000 | 5.40 | 5 | 0 | 0 | 0 | 3 | 1 | 6.2 | 5 | 31 | 4 | 4 | 2 | 0 | 0 | 0 | 6 | 0 | 8 | 1 | 0 |
| Sleeth, Kyle, Erie | 4 | 4 | .500 | 6.30 | 13 | 13 | 0 | 0 | 0 | 0 | 80.0 | 93 | 352 | 58 | 56 | 14 | 4 | 3 | 4 | 34 | 0 | 57 | 5 | 0 |
| Smith, Chris, Portland | 5 | 2 | .714 | 3.75 | 14 | 14 | 0 | 0 | 0 | 0 | 74.1 | 77 | 317 | 34 | 31 | 10 | 4 | 1 | 2 | 21 | 0 | 85 | 1 | 3 |
| Smith, Matt, Trenton * | 4 | 4 | .500 | 4.96 | 14 | 11 | 0 | 0 | 0 | 0 | 61.2 | 67 | 271 | 34 | 34 | 5 | 2 | 2 | 1 | 31 | 1 | 56 | 3 | 0 |
| Snell, Ian, Altoona | 11 | 7 | .611 | 3.16 | 26 | 26 | 3 | 2 | 0 | 0 | 151.0 | 147 | 624 | 54 | 53 | 16 | 9 | 6 | 5 | 40 | 2 | 142 | 6 | 0 |
| Snusz, Chris, Altoona | 0 | 0 | .000 | 9.00 | 1 | 0 | 0 | 0 | 1 | 0 | 1.0 | 1 | 6 | 1 | 1 | 0 | 0 | 0 | 1 | 1 | 0 | 0 | 0 | 0 |
| Spradlin, Jerry, Bowie | 3 | 1 | .750 | 2.60 | 14 | 0 | 0 | 0 | 3 | 0 | 17.1 | 10 | 73 | 6 | 5 | 2 | 0 | 0 | 1 | 10 | 1 | 25 | 2 | 0 |
| Squires, Matt, Reading * | 0 | 1 | .000 | 3.62 | 26 | 0 | 0 | 0 | 9 | 1 | 32.1 | 35 | 148 | 17 | 13 | 1 | 1 | 1 | 3 | 15 | 0 | 26 | 2 | 2 |
| Stein, Blake, Altoona | 5 | 2 | .714 | 3.52 | 36 | 0 | 0 | 0 | 18 | 7 | 61.1 | 51 | 260 | 27 | 24 | 6 | 1 | 0 | 1 | 25 | 2 | 62 | 2 | 0 |
| Stevens, Josh, Portland | 6 | 9 | .400 | 5.24 | 20 | 20 | 1 | 0 | 0 | 0 | 125.1 | 148 | 541 | 80 | 73 | 11 | 7 | 8 | 5 | 20 | 0 | 107 | 2 | 0 |
| Stevenson, Jason, Harrisburg | 8 | 10 | .444 | 4.06 | 24 | 22 | 0 | 0 | 1 | 1 | 135.1 | 132 | 570 | 66 | 61 | 20 | 8 | 6 | 12 | 46 | 1 | 75 | 5 | 4 |
| Strayhorn, Kole, Binghamton | 5 | 4 | .556 | 5.22 | 39 | 0 | 0 | 0 | 25 | 8 | 50.0 | 49 | 228 | 34 | 29 | 10 | 1 | 2 | 2 | 27 | 1 | 43 | 3 | 0 |
| Tejeda, Rob, Reading | 8 | 14 | .364 | 5.15 | 27 | 26 | 0 | 0 | 0 | 0 | 150.1 | 148 | 657 | 93 | 86 | 29 | 6 | 8 | 6 | 59 | 0 | 133 | 6 | 1 |
| Thompson, Travis, New Hampshire | 4 | 3 | .571 | 5.61 | 22 | 0 | 0 | 0 | 7 | 1 | 33.2 | 38 | 158 | 25 | 21 | 4 | 0 | 0 | 1 | 21 | 2 | 27 | 0 | 0 |
| Thurman, Corey, Harrisburg | 1 | 2 | .333 | 9.31 | 5 | 5 | 0 | 0 | 0 | 0 | 19.1 | 31 | 92 | 22 | 20 | 8 | 1 | 2 | 0 | 6 | 0 | 15 | 0 | 1 |
| Tousa, Scott, Erie | 0 | 0 | .000 | 0.00 | 1 | 0 | 0 | 0 | 1 | 0 | 1.0 | 0 | 6 | 0 | 0 | 0 | 0 | 0 | 0 | 3 | 0 | 0 | 0 | 0 |
| Treadway, Brion, Norwich | 1 | 4 | .200 | 6.03 | 7 | 7 | 0 | 0 | 0 | 0 | 37.1 | 44 | 167 | 25 | 25 | 6 | 2 | 4 | 0 | 17 | 0 | 29 | 2 | 0 |
| Valdez, Merkin, Norwich | 1 | 4 | .200 | 4.32 | 10 | 7 | 0 | 0 | 1 | 1 | 41.2 | 35 | 172 | 21 | 20 | 3 | 1 | 3 | 0 | 15 | 0 | 31 | 1 | 0 |
| Vargas, Jose, Akron | 3 | 3 | .500 | 3.51 | 33 | 0 | 0 | 0 | 14 | 2 | 56.1 | 46 | 248 | 22 | 22 | 5 | 1 | 0 | 8 | 27 | 2 | 64 | 2 | 0 |
| Vermilyea, Jamie, New Hampshire | 3 | 2 | .600 | 2.51 | 20 | 6 | 1 | 1 | 10 | 5 | 57.1 | 43 | 223 | 20 | 16 | 2 | 1 | 0 | 3 | 12 | 0 | 39 | 1 | 0 |
| Villegas, Felix, Reading | 3 | 1 | .750 | 3.35 | 31 | 0 | 0 | 0 | 8 | 0 | 48.1 | 35 | 212 | 19 | 18 | 5 | 0 | 0 | 5 | 28 | 1 | 37 | 1 | 0 |
| Walk, Mitch, Norwich * | 6 | 8 | .429 | 5.09 | 47 | 4 | 0 | 0 | 18 | 2 | 88.1 | 94 | 407 | 56 | 50 | 4 | 4 | 1 | 2 | 46 | 2 | 53 | 4 | 0 |
| Ward, Jeremy, Trenton | 3 | 3 | .500 | 4.97 | 40 | 0 | 0 | 0 | 11 | 3 | 41.2 | 46 | 189 | 28 | 23 | 3 | 0 | 0 | 6 | 12 | 2 | 33 | 2 | 0 |
| Warden, Jim Ed, Akron | 0 | 1 | .000 | 9.53 | 4 | 0 | 0 | 0 | 3 | 0 | 5.2 | 7 | 31 | 7 | 6 | 1 | 0 | 0 | 0 | 7 | 1 | 5 | 1 | 0 |
| Wilson, Jeff, Bowie * | 2 | 0 | 1.000 | 3.75 | 10 | 1 | 0 | 0 | 1 | 0 | 24.0 | 22 | 104 | 11 | 10 | 5 | 0 | 1 | 1 | 10 | 0 | 18 | 0 | 0 |
| Wolfe, Brian, New Britain | 1 | 1 | .500 | 8.18 | 7 | 0 | 0 | 0 | 1 | 0 | 11.0 | 16 | 50 | 10 | 10 | 3 | 1 | 0 | 0 | 3 | 0 | 6 | 0 | 0 |
| Woodyard, Mark, Erie | 6 | 4 | .600 | 3.52 | 43 | 9 | 0 | 0 | 14 | 5 | 102.1 | 102 | 440 | 53 | 40 | 5 | 5 | 3 | 9 | 37 | 3 | 55 | 5 | 0 |
| Young, Colin, Portland * | 1 | 1 | .500 | 5.68 | 36 | 0 | 0 | 0 | 17 | 2 | 58.2 | 67 | 279 | 39 | 37 | 8 | 1 | 1 | 6 | 28 | 2 | 36 | 1 | 6 |
| Zink, Charlie, Portland | 1 | 8 | .111 | 5.79 | 18 | 18 | 0 | 0 | 0 | 0 | 93.1 | 101 | 442 | 70 | 60 | 3 | — | — | 7 | 72 | 0 | 50 | 4 | — |
| Zumaya, Joel, Erie | 2 | 2 | .500 | 6.30 | 4 | 4 | 0 | 0 | 0 | 0 | 20.0 | 19 | 90 | 20 | 14 | 6 | 1 | 1 | 2 | 10 | 0 | 29 | 0 | 0 |

COMBINATION SHUTOUTS: **Akron** (3)—Cruceta-Rayborn-Van Dusen, A. Brown-Sadler-Van Dusen, A. Brown-Tallet. **Altoona** (9)—Bullington-Lorraine-Serrano, Snell-Miller-Serrano, Snell-Stein, McDade-Stein-Crudale, Connolly-Crudale-Miller, McDade–O'Brien-Miller, Duke-Candelario, Snell-Stein-Crudale-Harts, McDade-Harts. **Binghamton** (3)—J. Diaz-Chenard, Chenard-Bevis, Musser-Ring-Bevis. **Bowie** (8)—Crouthers-Rice, Cabrera-Jacquez, Rice-Mitchell-Rleal, Crouthers-Jacquez-Sequea, Crouthers-Rice-Ormond-Sequea, Piersoll-Rice-Sequea, Hundley-Mitchell-House, Crouthers-Mitchell-Sequea. **Erie** (14) Roney-Novoa-Palma-Karnuth, Larrison-

Schmack-Palma, Woodyard-Cordova-Palma, Roney-Palma, Larrison-Novoa, Ledezma-Woodyard-Lontayo, Ledezma-Novoa, Baugh-Novoa, Woodyard-Novoa-Schmack, Larrison-Lontayo-Palma-Schmack, Lontayo-Rodney-Birtwell, Cuello-McDowell-Rodney, Lontayo-Woodyard, Cordova-Mears. **Harrisburg** (6)—Hill-Schroder-Rivera, Stevenson-Rueckel-Rivera, Patterson-Echols-Schroder-Maust-Rueckel, Bridges-Schroder, Hinckley-Ferrari, Rundles-Stevenson. **New Britain** (7)—Durbin-Moreno-Neshek, Richardson-Moreno, Helling-Korecky-Gutierrez, Bonilla-Miller-Korecky, Bonilla-Miller, Miller-Korecky, Liriano-Korecky. **New Hampshire** (13)—McGowan-League-Frederick-Peterson, Chacin-DeJong-Frederick-Peterson, Rosario-Houston-Frederick, Ozias-Ogiltree-Jackson-Peterson, Chacin-Thompson-DeJong, Rosario-Houston-DeJong, Chacin-Thompson-DeJong, Chacin-Vermilyea, Chacin-Jackson-Vermilyea, Rosario-Vermilyea, Banks-Vermilyea, Chacin-Vermilyea-DeJong, Rosario-Vermilyea-League. **Norwich** (8)—Begg-Munter, Clark-Walk, Taschner-Walk-Montes-Markert, Taschner-Palmer-Montes, Begg-L. Anderson, Misch-Accardo, Walk-Munter-Montes, Mazone-L. Anderson. **Portland** (4)—C. Smith-Glaser-Young, Zink-Nelson, Alvarez-C. Young-Larson, Gabbard-Seibel-J. Perez. **Reading** (8)—Bucktrot-Y. Hernandez, Tejeda-Brito-Y. Hernandez, Tejeda-Candelario, F. Perez-Squires, F. Perez–Villegas-Jimenez, Bowers-Brito-Villegas-Franco, Chantres-Brito, Tejeda-Villegas-Franco. **Trenton** (6)—J. Ortiz-Izquierdo, Carlyle-Ward-Wiggins, J. Ortiz-Shepard-Wiggins, Carlyle-Shepard, Carlyle-Wiggins-Ward-Shepard, Reimers-Ogiltree-Peterson.

NO-HIT GAMES: Song, Harrisburg, defeated Erie, 2-1, April 28; Keppel, Binghamton, defeated Portland, 3-0, August 2; Estrada, New Britain, defeated Reading, 10-0, August 24. Vermilyea, New Hampshire, defeated New Britian, 2-0, June 28; Crouthers, Bowie, defeated Altoona, 2-0, August 19.

# 2004 FIELDING

## TEAM

| Team | G | PO | A | E | TC | DP | TP | PB | Pct. |
|---|---|---|---|---|---|---|---|---|---|
| Norwich | 142 | 3685 | 269 | 108 | 4062 | 126 | 0 | 21 | .973 |
| New Britain | 140 | 3642 | 251 | 109 | 4002 | 116 | 0 | 19 | .973 |
| New Hamp. | 141 | 3671 | 223 | 122 | 4016 | 135 | 0 | 13 | .970 |
| Reading | 141 | 3601 | 238 | 120 | 3959 | 113 | 0 | 14 | .970 |
| Altoona | 141 | 3668 | 215 | 125 | 4008 | 111 | 0 | 14 | .969 |
| Trenton | 142 | 3700 | 214 | 125 | 4039 | 119 | 0 | 27 | .969 |
| Bowie | 142 | 3648 | 218 | 134 | 4000 | 113 | 0 | 25 | .967 |
| Binghamton | 142 | 3710 | 254 | 137 | 4101 | 120 | 0 | 18 | .967 |
| Portland | 142 | 3750 | 195 | 140 | 4085 | 114 | 0 | 16 | .966 |
| Harrisburg | 142 | 3684 | 250 | 145 | 4079 | 140 | 0 | 9 | .964 |
| Erie | 142 | 3718 | 235 | 147 | 4100 | 137 | 0 | 11 | .964 |
| Akron | 141 | 3669 | 234 | 174 | 4077 | 102 | 0 | 17 | .957 |

## INDIVIDUAL

### FIRST BASEMEN

NOTE: All caps denotes fielding-percentage leader based on 72 games for catchers, 96 for all other non-pitchers and 115 innings for pitchers. *Throws lefthanded.

| Player, Team | Pct. | G | PO | A | E | TC | DP |
|---|---|---|---|---|---|---|---|
| Aubrey, Michael, AKR* | .976 | 27 | 185 | 19 | 5 | 209 | 16 |
| Bailey, Jeff, PRT | .973 | 4 | 31 | 5 | 1 | 37 | 3 |
| Bailie, Stefan, PRT | .982 | 26 | 205 | 14 | 4 | 223 | 16 |
| Barker, Kevin, REA* | .991 | 19 | 102 | 14 | 1 | 117 | 9 |
| Benavidez, Julian, NRW | .985 | 54 | 418 | 39 | 7 | 464 | 45 |
| Bonifay, Josh, ALT | .993 | 73 | 546 | 50 | 4 | 600 | 47 |
| Broadway, Larry, HRB* | .993 | 121 | 1069 | 93 | 8 | 1170 | 111 |
| Cardona, Javier, BNG | 1.000 | 1 | 2 | 0 | 0 | 2 | 0 |
| Cervenak, Michael, NRW | .975 | 14 | 108 | 8 | 3 | 119 | 13 |
| Chiaffredo, Paul, NHF | 1.000 | 1 | 10 | 0 | 0 | 10 | 1 |
| Cleveland, Russ, ERI | 1.000 | 1 | 1 | 0 | 0 | 1 | 0 |
| Cordido, Julio, NRW | 1.000 | 1 | 12 | 0 | 0 | 12 | 1 |
| Curry, Chris, NRW | 1.000 | 3 | 19 | 1 | 0 | 20 | 0 |
| DeCaster, Yurendell, ALT | .980 | 6 | 44 | 5 | 1 | 50 | 4 |
| Detienne, David, BNG | .996 | 31 | 202 | 22 | 1 | 225 | 16 |
| Eldred, Brad, ALT | .994 | 38 | 331 | 17 | 2 | 350 | 34 |
| Fuentes, Omar, TRE | 1.000 | 3 | 27 | 0 | 0 | 27 | 3 |
| Garcia, Karim, BNG* | .955 | 3 | 20 | 1 | 1 | 22 | 1 |
| Garko, Ryan, AKR | .979 | 16 | 129 | 12 | 3 | 144 | 18 |
| Gonzalez, Jimmy, BNG | 1.000 | 1 | 2 | 0 | 0 | 2 | 0 |
| Griffin, John-Ford, NHF* | .978 | 16 | 127 | 8 | 3 | 138 | 15 |
| Grindell, Nate, AKR | .987 | 66 | 554 | 52 | 8 | 614 | 42 |
| Hammond, Joey, BOW | 1.000 | 2 | 13 | 0 | 0 | 13 | 1 |
| Harper, Brandon, ERI | 1.000 | 1 | 1 | 0 | 0 | 1 | 0 |
| Harper, Brett, BNG* | .985 | 41 | 354 | 28 | 6 | 388 | 36 |
| Hitchcox, Brian, REA* | 1.000 | 1 | 3 | 1 | 0 | 4 | 1 |
| Howard, Ryan, REA* | .992 | 97 | 786 | 53 | 7 | 846 | 75 |
| Huber, Justin, BNG | .971 | 5 | 33 | 0 | 1 | 34 | 4 |
| Huggins, Michael, BOW | .988 | 54 | 459 | 43 | 6 | 508 | 44 |
| Jacobson, Russ, REA | .958 | 4 | 22 | 1 | 1 | 24 | 1 |
| Jenkins, Neil, ERI | .970 | 3 | 29 | 3 | 1 | 33 | 2 |
| Jones, Garrett, NBR* | .983 | 121 | 875 | 127 | 17 | 1019 | 90 |
| Jones, Mitch, TRE | 1.000 | 21 | 141 | 10 | 0 | 151 | 18 |
| Keene, Kurt, REA | 1.000 | 26 | 173 | 20 | 0 | 193 | 15 |
| Kilburg, Joe, PRT* | 1.000 | 4 | 21 | 1 | 0 | 22 | 3 |
| Lane, Rich, HRB* | .978 | 24 | 163 | 17 | 4 | 184 | 20 |
| Logan, Matt, NHF* | .991 | 51 | 417 | 21 | 4 | 442 | 42 |
| Luderer, Brian, AKR | .982 | 6 | 49 | 7 | 1 | 57 | 4 |
| Mauer, Jake, NBR | 1.000 | 1 | 1 | 1 | 0 | 2 | 0 |
| McGowan, Sean, PRT | .990 | 25 | 189 | 19 | 2 | 210 | 10 |
| Munoz, Billy, NBR* | 1.000 | 19 | 152 | 26 | 0 | 178 | 16 |
| Navarrete, Ray, ALT | .993 | 20 | 145 | 6 | 1 | 152 | 10 |
| Nicholson, Derek, ERI* | .989 | 21 | 170 | 12 | 2 | 184 | 18 |
| O'Keefe, Mike, PRT* | .989 | 80 | 592 | 44 | 7 | 643 | 50 |
| Paulino, Ronny, ALT | .985 | 8 | 60 | 6 | 1 | 67 | 6 |
| Phillips, Andy, TRE | 1.000 | 5 | 34 | 6 | 0 | 40 | 3 |
| Pressley, Josh, BNG* | .988 | 75 | 583 | 57 | 8 | 648 | 51 |
| Rifkin, Aaron, TRE* | .987 | 118 | 956 | 60 | 13 | 1029 | 79 |
| Roneberg, Brett, PRT* | .987 | 12 | 65 | 10 | 1 | 76 | 6 |
| Salazar, Oscar, AKR | 1.000 | 7 | 47 | 7 | 0 | 54 | 4 |
| Santos, Francisco, NRW* | .987 | 18 | 145 | 8 | 2 | 155 | 14 |
| Snyder, Michael, NHF* | .994 | 75 | 636 | 57 | 4 | 697 | 60 |
| Tejeda, Juan, ERI | .986 | 122 | 1091 | 75 | 16 | 1182 | 93 |
| Tousa, Scott, ERI* | 1.000 | 6 | 28 | 1 | 0 | 29 | 4 |
| Umbria, Jose, NHF | 1.000 | 3 | 24 | 1 | 0 | 25 | 2 |
| Vericker, Brad, NRW* | .968 | 3 | 26 | 4 | 1 | 31 | 3 |
| Von Schell, Tyler, NRW | .992 | 54 | 470 | 26 | 4 | 500 | 34 |
| Walsh, Sean, REA | 1.000 | 2 | 9 | 0 | 0 | 9 | 1 |
| Wilken, Kris, BOW | .994 | 24 | 162 | 16 | 1 | 179 | 14 |
| Wilson, Craig, TRE | 1.000 | 7 | 33 | 0 | 0 | 33 | 2 |
| Young, Walter, BOW* | .983 | 66 | 480 | 42 | 9 | 531 | 44 |
| Youngbauer, Scott, AKR | .989 | 25 | 170 | 16 | 2 | 188 | 15 |

### SECOND BASEMEN

| Player, Team | Pct. | G | PO | A | E | TC | DP |
|---|---|---|---|---|---|---|---|
| Alvarez, Jimmy, PRT | .981 | 12 | 20 | 32 | 1 | 53 | 7 |
| Bacani, David, BNG | .979 | 32 | 53 | 90 | 3 | 146 | 15 |
| Basak, Chris, BNG | 1.000 | 4 | 7 | 5 | 0 | 12 | 3 |
| Bautista, Rayner, ERI | .985 | 15 | 18 | 49 | 1 | 68 | 6 |
| Cano, Robinson, TRE* | .967 | 70 | 126 | 201 | 11 | 338 | 44 |
| Carroll, Wes, HRB | .929 | 8 | 12 | 14 | 2 | 28 | 3 |
| Cates, Gary, BOW | .970 | 75 | 111 | 180 | 9 | 300 | 36 |
| Cervenak, Michael, NRW | 1.000 | 1 | 3 | 4 | 0 | 7 | 1 |
| Choy Foo, Rodney, AKR | .974 | 43 | 63 | 122 | 5 | 190 | 20 |
| Clapp, Stubby, NHF* | .967 | 5 | 11 | 18 | 1 | 30 | 5 |
| Cosme, Caonabo, TRE | .978 | 12 | 21 | 24 | 1 | 46 | 5 |
| Davidson, Seth, NBR | .989 | 23 | 31 | 56 | 1 | 88 | 9 |
| Detienne, David, BNG | 1.000 | 2 | 2 | 9 | 0 | 11 | 1 |
| Done, Mike, BOW | 1.000 | 1 | 1 | 3 | 0 | 4 | 0 |
| Dorta, Melvin, HRB | .970 | 28 | 45 | 86 | 4 | 135 | 23 |
| Garrido, Tomas, NRW | 1.000 | 4 | 6 | 10 | 0 | 16 | 2 |
| Gonzalez, Patrick, BOW | 1.000 | 1 | 1 | 1 | 0 | 2 | 1 |
| Guerrero, Francisco, BOW | 1.000 | 2 | 4 | 3 | 0 | 7 | 0 |
| Hairston Jr., Jerry, BOW | .929 | 5 | 5 | 8 | 1 | 14 | 3 |
| Hassey, Brad, NHF | 1.000 | 13 | 18 | 41 | 0 | 59 | 8 |
| Hitchcox, Brian, REA* | .970 | 44 | 70 | 125 | 6 | 201 | 24 |
| Inglett, Joe, AKR* | .954 | 51 | 97 | 129 | 11 | 237 | 26 |
| Keene, Kurt, REA | .932 | 25 | 53 | 57 | 8 | 118 | 13 |

| Player, Team | Pct. | G | PO | A | E | TC | DP |
|---|---|---|---|---|---|---|---|
| Kelly, Dustin, PRT | 1.000 | 3 | 6 | 5 | 0 | 11 | 1 |
| Keppinger, Jeff, ALT | .982 | 80 | 142 | 193 | 6 | 341 | 31 |
| Keppinger, Jeff, BNG | 1.000 | 11 | 19 | 25 | 0 | 44 | 5 |
| Keppinger, Jeff, ALT-BNG | .984 | 91 | 161 | 218 | 6 | 385 | 36 |
| Kilburg, Joe, PRT* | .958 | 29 | 35 | 56 | 4 | 95 | 11 |
| Knowlton, Jay, NRW | 1.000 | 5 | 7 | 12 | 0 | 19 | 0 |
| Lambin, Chase, BNG | .946 | 96 | 166 | 258 | 24 | 448 | 55 |
| Leon, Carlos, REA | 1.000 | 8 | 16 | 23 | 0 | 39 | 5 |
| Liriano, Pedro, HRB | .980 | 30 | 52 | 96 | 3 | 151 | 24 |
| Lofton, James, BOW | .963 | 20 | 23 | 56 | 3 | 82 | 4 |
| Lopez-Cao, Mike, PRT* | .900 | 4 | 1 | 8 | 1 | 10 | 1 |
| Machado, Alejandro, HRB | .992 | 80 | 154 | 226 | 3 | 383 | 57 |
| Maza, Luis, NBR | .989 | 124 | 214 | 330 | 6 | 550 | 67 |
| McMains, Derin, NRW | .992 | 103 | 218 | 310 | 4 | 532 | 64 |
| Medrano, Jesus, PRT | .957 | 53 | 87 | 112 | 9 | 208 | 20 |
| Mendez, Donaldo, ALT | .953 | 16 | 31 | 51 | 4 | 86 | 10 |
| Meyers, Chad, ERI | .000 | 1 | 0 | 0 | 1 | 1 | 0 |
| Morban, Jose, BOW | 1.000 | 1 | 4 | 6 | 0 | 10 | 2 |
| Moriarty, Mike, ALT | .986 | 15 | 25 | 48 | 1 | 74 | 12 |
| Navarrete, Ray, ALT | .952 | 17 | 22 | 38 | 3 | 63 | 7 |
| Nicholson, Kevin, ALT | .957 | 12 | 12 | 32 | 2 | 46 | 8 |
| Nieves, Raul, PRT | .982 | 43 | 75 | 90 | 3 | 168 | 20 |
| Olivares, Teuris, TRE | .991 | 35 | 30 | 84 | 1 | 115 | 17 |
| Pecci, Jay, NRW | .957 | 27 | 46 | 65 | 5 | 116 | 11 |
| Perez, Kenny, PRT | .935 | 14 | 25 | 33 | 4 | 62 | 5 |
| Phelps, Jeff, REA | .973 | 10 | 11 | 25 | 1 | 37 | 2 |
| Polanco, Placido, REA | 1.000 | 1 | 1 | 2 | 0 | 3 | 0 |
| Pratt, Scott, AKR* | .938 | 20 | 24 | 51 | 5 | 80 | 5 |
| Raburn, Ryan, ERI | .950 | 95 | 189 | 306 | 26 | 521 | 63 |
| Raymundo, GJ, HRB | 1.000 | 1 | 2 | 0 | 0 | 2 | 0 |
| Reyes, Jose, BNG | 1.000 | 4 | 8 | 12 | 0 | 20 | 4 |
| Rich, Dominic, NHF* | .971 | 124 | 236 | 365 | 18 | 619 | 69 |
| Rogers, Ed, BOW | .980 | 51 | 67 | 127 | 4 | 198 | 24 |
| Salazar, Oscar, AKR | .926 | 11 | 19 | 31 | 4 | 54 | 7 |
| Sheldon, Scott, ALT | .975 | 7 | 16 | 23 | 1 | 40 | 4 |
| Skrehot, Shaun, ALT | 1.000 | 4 | 11 | 13 | 0 | 24 | 4 |
| Solano, Danny, NHF | 1.000 | 4 | 15 | 13 | 0 | 28 | 3 |
| Taylor, Seth, HRB | 1.000 | 2 | 3 | 6 | 0 | 9 | 0 |
| Tousa, Scott, ERI* | .988 | 36 | 66 | 96 | 2 | 164 | 28 |
| Wald, Jacob, NRW | .960 | 8 | 11 | 13 | 1 | 25 | 3 |
| West, Todd, AKR | 1.000 | 1 | 1 | 3 | 0 | 4 | 1 |
| Wilson, Craig, TRE | .994 | 44 | 73 | 102 | 1 | 176 | 25 |
| Youngbauer, Scott, AKR | .969 | 18 | 36 | 57 | 3 | 96 | 15 |
| Youngbauer, Scott, REA | .967 | 59 | 126 | 168 | 10 | 304 | 41 |
| Youngbauer, Scott, AKR-REA | .968 | 77 | 162 | 225 | 13 | 400 | 56 |

## THIRD BASEMEN

| Player, Team | Pct. | G | PO | A | E | TC | DP |
|---|---|---|---|---|---|---|---|
| Alvarez, Jimmy, PRT | 1.000 | 1 | 2 | 0 | 0 | 2 | 0 |
| Bacani, David, BNG | 1.000 | 1 | 0 | 1 | 0 | 1 | 0 |
| Baldiris, Aarom, BNG | .946 | 21 | 17 | 36 | 3 | 56 | 2 |
| Basak, Chris, BNG | .957 | 45 | 26 | 85 | 5 | 116 | 7 |
| Bautista, Rayner, ERI | .846 | 6 | 1 | 10 | 2 | 13 | 0 |
| Belcher, Jason, HRB* | .714 | 3 | 0 | 5 | 2 | 7 | 0 |
| Benavidez, Julian, NRW | .943 | 12 | 13 | 20 | 2 | 35 | 2 |
| Cano, Robinson, TRE* | .909 | 4 | 3 | 7 | 1 | 11 | 0 |
| Cervenak, Michael, NRW | .970 | 95 | 67 | 162 | 7 | 236 | 14 |
| Choy Foo, Rodney, AKR | 1.000 | 1 | 1 | 0 | 0 | 1 | 0 |
| Clapp, Stubby, NHF* | 1.000 | 5 | 1 | 13 | 0 | 14 | 1 |
| Cockrell, Mike, ALT | .500 | 3 | 0 | 1 | 1 | 2 | 0 |
| Cordido, Julio, NRW | .902 | 18 | 9 | 28 | 4 | 41 | 1 |
| Cosby, Robert, NHF | 1.000 | 5 | 2 | 9 | 0 | 11 | 0 |
| Cosme, Caonabo, TRE | 1.000 | 1 | 1 | 1 | 0 | 2 | 0 |
| Curry, Chris, NRW | 1.000 | 1 | 0 | 1 | 0 | 1 | 1 |
| DeCaster, Yurendell, ALT | .919 | 85 | 69 | 123 | 17 | 209 | 16 |
| Detienne, David, BNG | .961 | 18 | 14 | 35 | 2 | 51 | 1 |
| Dorta, Melvin, HRB | .947 | 33 | 20 | 52 | 4 | 76 | 4 |
| Evans, Tom, ALT | .951 | 30 | 23 | 55 | 4 | 82 | 7 |
| Hammond, Joey, BOW | 1.000 | 2 | 4 | 1 | 0 | 5 | 0 |
| Hannahan, Jack, ERI* | .951 | 102 | 65 | 228 | 15 | 308 | 27 |
| Hassey, Brad, NHF | .857 | 7 | 7 | 11 | 3 | 21 | 0 |
| Hattig, John, NHF | .990 | 35 | 28 | 68 | 1 | 97 | 4 |
| Hattig, John, PRT | .944 | 71 | 44 | 124 | 10 | 178 | 10 |
| Hattig, John, NHF-PRT | .960 | 106 | 72 | 192 | 11 | 275 | 14 |
| Huggins, Michael, BOW | 1.000 | 1 | 0 | 3 | 0 | 3 | 0 |
| Keene, Kurt, REA | .981 | 27 | 19 | 33 | 1 | 53 | 5 |
| Keppinger, Jeff, BNG | .889 | 2 | 1 | 7 | 1 | 9 | 0 |
| Kilburg, Joe, PRT* | .919 | 36 | 18 | 61 | 7 | 86 | 5 |
| Knowlton, Jay, NRW | 1.000 | 1 | 2 | 1 | 0 | 3 | 0 |
| Kouzmanoff, Kevin, AKR | .813 | 7 | 5 | 8 | 3 | 16 | 0 |
| Leon, Carlos, REA | 1.000 | 10 | 5 | 10 | 0 | 15 | 1 |
| Mauer, Jake, NBR | .943 | 91 | 61 | 105 | 10 | 176 | 15 |
| Maza, Luis, NBR | 1.000 | 1 | 1 | 3 | 0 | 4 | 0 |
| McKinley, Josh, HRB | .333 | 2 | 0 | 1 | 2 | 3 | 0 |
| Navarrete, Ray, ALT | 1.000 | 4 | 0 | 3 | 0 | 3 | 0 |
| Nicholson, Derek, ERI* | .909 | 3 | 2 | 8 | 1 | 11 | 2 |
| Nicholson, Kevin, ALT | .891 | 25 | 11 | 30 | 5 | 46 | 4 |
| Nieves, Raul, PRT | .901 | 31 | 29 | 44 | 8 | 81 | 3 |
| Norris, Shawn, HRB* | .972 | 37 | 33 | 73 | 3 | 109 | 9 |
| Olivares, Teuris, TRE | .929 | 7 | 6 | 7 | 1 | 14 | 1 |
| Owens, Ryan, NBR | .951 | 34 | 26 | 52 | 4 | 82 | 4 |
| Pecci, Jay, NRW | .963 | 20 | 14 | 38 | 2 | 54 | 5 |
| Phelps, Jeff, REA | .949 | 71 | 51 | 134 | 10 | 195 | 15 |
| Phillips, Andy, TRE | .933 | 6 | 5 | 9 | 1 | 15 | 1 |
| Pratt, Scott, AKR* | 1.000 | 5 | 4 | 5 | 0 | 9 | 0 |
| Raymundo, GJ, HRB | .935 | 20 | 16 | 27 | 3 | 46 | 3 |
| Richardson, Juan, REA | .853 | 15 | 12 | 17 | 5 | 34 | 2 |
| Rogers, Ed, BOW | .946 | 66 | 54 | 105 | 9 | 168 | 8 |
| Rogers, Omar, BOW | .571 | 3 | 1 | 3 | 3 | 7 | 0 |
| Rooi, Vince, HRB | .938 | 34 | 23 | 68 | 6 | 97 | 3 |
| Salazar, Oscar, AKR | 1.000 | 2 | 3 | 3 | 0 | 6 | 0 |
| Sardinha, Bronson, TRE* | .831 | 57 | 30 | 68 | 20 | 118 | 7 |
| Scanlon, Matt, NBR* | 1.000 | 4 | 7 | 5 | 0 | 12 | 0 |
| Schneidmiller, Gary, PRT | 1.000 | 8 | 7 | 21 | 0 | 28 | 3 |
| Sheldon, Scott, ALT | 1.000 | 3 | 3 | 3 | 0 | 6 | 1 |
| Singleton, Justin, NHF* | 1.000 | 1 | 1 | 1 | 0 | 2 | 0 |
| Smith, Corey, AKR | .891 | 125 | 108 | 195 | 37 | 340 | 18 |
| Solano, Danny, NHF | .975 | 90 | 57 | 213 | 7 | 277 | 23 |
| Storey, Eric, HRB | 1.000 | 5 | 1 | 5 | 0 | 6 | 0 |
| Stotts, JT, TRE | .925 | 45 | 18 | 68 | 7 | 93 | 3 |
| Taylor, Seth, HRB | .914 | 12 | 12 | 20 | 3 | 35 | 0 |
| Tousa, Scott, ERI* | .967 | 39 | 28 | 88 | 4 | 120 | 13 |
| Walsh, Sean, REA | .947 | 30 | 21 | 50 | 4 | 75 | 3 |
| Watkins, Tommy, NBR | .956 | 20 | 12 | 31 | 2 | 45 | 0 |
| Wilken, Kris, BOW | .938 | 81 | 48 | 104 | 10 | 162 | 10 |
| Wilson, Craig, TRE | .986 | 34 | 18 | 54 | 1 | 73 | 5 |
| Wilson, John, HRB | 1.000 | 1 | 0 | 2 | 0 | 2 | 0 |
| Wright, David, BNG | .943 | 59 | 40 | 92 | 8 | 140 | 5 |
| Youngbauer, Scott, AKR | 1.000 | 77 | 2 | 3 | 0 | 5 | 0 |

## SHORTSTOPS

| Player, Team | Pct. | G | PO | A | E | TC | DP |
|---|---|---|---|---|---|---|---|
| Alvarez, Jimmy, PRT | 1.000 | 2 | 2 | 6 | 0 | 8 | 1 |
| Basak, Chris, BNG | .965 | 33 | 42 | 95 | 5 | 142 | 23 |
| Bautista, Rayner, ERI | .927 | 14 | 7 | 31 | 3 | 41 | 5 |
| Cannizaro, Andy, TRE | .962 | 84 | 116 | 240 | 14 | 370 | 55 |
| Chaves, Brandon, ALT | .952 | 40 | 53 | 85 | 7 | 145 | 18 |
| Chavez, Angel, NRW | .962 | 88 | 141 | 240 | 15 | 396 | 58 |
| Cockrell, Mike, ALT | .917 | 6 | 5 | 6 | 1 | 12 | 0 |
| Cordido, Julio, NRW | 1.000 | 5 | 7 | 14 | 0 | 21 | 2 |
| Cosme, Caonabo, TRE | 1.000 | 1 | 1 | 3 | 0 | 4 | 1 |
| Davidson, Seth, NBR | .969 | 51 | 92 | 129 | 7 | 228 | 35 |
| de la Rosa, Tomas, ALT | .692 | 7 | 4 | 5 | 4 | 13 | 0 |
| Detienne, David, BNG | .952 | 8 | 7 | 13 | 1 | 21 | 4 |
| Dorta, Melvin, HRB | .857 | 4 | 6 | 6 | 2 | 14 | 4 |
| Fahey, Brandon, BOW* | .976 | 63 | 93 | 189 | 7 | 289 | 39 |
| Gonzalez, Danny, REA | .945 | 133 | 199 | 297 | 29 | 525 | 71 |
| Hammond, Joey, BOW | 1.000 | 1 | 3 | 2 | 0 | 5 | 0 |
| Hannahan, Jack, ERI* | 1.000 | 1 | 0 | 2 | 0 | 2 | 0 |
| Hernandez, Anderson, ERI | .966 | 99 | 160 | 291 | 16 | 467 | 57 |
| Hill, Aaron, NHF | .959 | 134 | 236 | 375 | 26 | 637 | 82 |
| Keene, Kurt, REA | 1.000 | 7 | 8 | 8 | 0 | 16 | 3 |
| Kelly, Don, ERI* | .931 | 27 | 29 | 79 | 8 | 116 | 13 |
| Kelly, Dustin, PRT | 1.000 | 1 | 1 | 5 | 0 | 6 | 1 |
| Knowlton, Jay, NRW | .947 | 4 | 4 | 14 | 1 | 19 | 1 |
| Kuhaulua, Kaulana, NBR | 1.000 | 7 | 9 | 12 | 0 | 21 | 4 |
| Labandeira, Josh, HRB | .952 | 128 | 226 | 394 | 31 | 651 | 83 |
| Leon, Carlos, REA | .975 | 10 | 21 | 18 | 1 | 40 | 3 |
| Lunetta, Anthony, AKR | 1.000 | 4 | 5 | 13 | 0 | 18 | 3 |
| Machado, Alejandro, HRB | .982 | 13 | 17 | 39 | 1 | 57 | 10 |

| Player, Team | Pct. | G | PO | A | E | TC | DP |
|---|---|---|---|---|---|---|---|
| Mauer, Jake, NBR | .920 | 7 | 7 | 16 | 2 | 25 | 5 |
| McMains, Derin, NRW | 1.000 | 1 | 0 | 2 | 0 | 2 | 0 |
| Mendez, Donaldo, ALT | .905 | 5 | 8 | 11 | 2 | 21 | 5 |
| Morban, Jose, BOW | .965 | 65 | 108 | 143 | 9 | 260 | 31 |
| Moriarty, Mike, ALT | 1.000 | 5 | 8 | 16 | 0 | 24 | 3 |
| Nicholson, Kevin, ALT | .923 | 30 | 31 | 53 | 7 | 91 | 11 |
| Nieves, Raul, PRT | .979 | 25 | 35 | 60 | 2 | 97 | 14 |
| Olivares, Teuris, TRE | .972 | 27 | 37 | 68 | 3 | 108 | 9 |
| Pecci, Jay, NRW | .909 | 6 | 8 | 12 | 2 | 22 | 3 |
| Perez, Kenny, PRT | .938 | 89 | 136 | 199 | 22 | 357 | 35 |
| Pinckney, Brandon, AKR | .950 | 67 | 87 | 162 | 13 | 262 | 38 |
| Pratt, Scott, AKR* | .931 | 18 | 23 | 44 | 5 | 72 | 4 |
| Ramirez, Hanley, PRT | .978 | 32 | 52 | 82 | 3 | 137 | 12 |
| Rogers, Ed, BOW | 1.000 | 15 | 25 | 39 | 0 | 64 | 13 |
| Salazar, Oscar, AKR | .936 | 20 | 34 | 39 | 5 | 78 | 10 |
| Scanlon, Matt, NBR* | 1.000 | 1 | 1 | 4 | 0 | 5 | 0 |
| Skrehot, Shaun, ALT | .980 | 62 | 79 | 163 | 5 | 247 | 38 |
| Solano, Danny, NHF | .968 | 7 | 11 | 19 | 1 | 31 | 5 |
| Sorensen, Zach, AKR | .981 | 25 | 41 | 63 | 2 | 106 | 21 |
| Stotts, JT, TRE | .963 | 9 | 10 | 16 | 1 | 27 | 4 |
| Tejeda, Ferdin, TRE | .974 | 30 | 42 | 72 | 3 | 117 | 18 |
| Tousa, Scott, ERI* | .885 | 5 | 6 | 17 | 3 | 26 | 1 |
| Velazquez, Gil, BNG | .974 | 105 | 183 | 306 | 13 | 502 | 62 |
| Wald, Jacob, NRW | .940 | 44 | 60 | 113 | 11 | 184 | 22 |
| Watkins, Tommy, NBR | .957 | 79 | 118 | 196 | 14 | 328 | 46 |
| West, Todd, AKR | 1.000 | 2 | 4 | 5 | 0 | 9 | 1 |
| Youngbauer, Scott, AKR | .976 | 12 | 16 | 24 | 1 | 41 | 4 |

## OUTFIELDERS

| Player, Team | Pct. | G | PO | A | E | TC | DP |
|---|---|---|---|---|---|---|---|
| Acuna, Ron, BNG | .957 | 97 | 149 | 7 | 7 | 163 | 1 |
| Airoso, Kurt, ERI | .968 | 21 | 27 | 3 | 1 | 31 | 1 |
| Ambrosini, Dominick, HRB* | .987 | 42 | 72 | 3 | 1 | 76 | 0 |
| Bailey, Jeff, PRT | 1.000 | 21 | 27 | 2 | 0 | 29 | 0 |
| Barker, Kevin, REA* | .994 | 79 | 160 | 7 | 1 | 168 | 2 |
| Belcher, Jason, HRB* | .952 | 33 | 59 | 1 | 3 | 63 | 0 |
| Bonifay, Josh, ALT | 1.000 | 11 | 19 | 1 | 0 | 20 | 0 |
| Bridges, Donnie, HRB | 1.000 | 11 | 12 | 1 | 0 | 13 | 0 |
| Brown, Jason, HRB | 1.000 | 1 | 1 | 0 | 0 | 1 | 0 |
| Burrell, Pat, REA | .923 | 4 | 12 | 0 | 1 | 13 | 0 |
| Calzado, Napoleon, BOW | .750 | 4 | 3 | 0 | 1 | 4 | 0 |
| Camilo, Juan, HRB* | .959 | 103 | 178 | 8 | 8 | 194 | 1 |
| Campo, Mike, PRT* | .963 | 23 | 50 | 2 | 2 | 54 | 0 |
| Carroll, Wes, HRB | 1.000 | 13 | 17 | 1 | 0 | 18 | 0 |
| Carter, Bryan, NRW* | .973 | 90 | 174 | 4 | 5 | 183 | 1 |
| Castellano, John, REA | .988 | 46 | 82 | 3 | 1 | 86 | 1 |
| Cates, Gary, BOW | 1.000 | 34 | 56 | 2 | 0 | 58 | 0 |
| Clapp, Stubby, NHF* | 1.000 | 1 | 2 | 0 | 0 | 2 | 0 |
| Clark, Doug, NRW* | .989 | 134 | 269 | 10 | 3 | 282 | 0 |
| Clements, Zack, BNG | .875 | 8 | 7 | 0 | 1 | 8 | 0 |
| Cliffords, Woody, BOW* | .978 | 32 | 44 | 1 | 1 | 46 | 0 |
| Cooper, Jason, AKR* | .984 | 91 | 177 | 4 | 3 | 184 | 2 |
| Cordido, Julio, NRW | 1.000 | 1 | 1 | 0 | 0 | 1 | 0 |
| Cortes, Jorge, ALT* | .988 | 36 | 78 | 1 | 1 | 80 | 0 |
| Cosbey, Chris, REA* | .963 | 47 | 73 | 6 | 3 | 82 | 0 |
| DeCaster, Yurendell, ALT | 1.000 | 8 | 4 | 0 | 0 | 4 | 0 |
| Deschaine, Jim, REA | .991 | 67 | 97 | 8 | 1 | 106 | 1 |
| Detienne, David, BNG | 1.000 | 2 | 4 | 0 | 0 | 4 | 0 |
| Dorta, Melvin, HRB | 1.000 | 4 | 8 | 1 | 0 | 9 | 0 |
| Duffy, Chris, ALT* | .993 | 113 | 289 | 8 | 2 | 299 | 2 |
| Duncan, Jeff, BNG* | .972 | 38 | 69 | 1 | 2 | 72 | 0 |
| Espinosa, David, ERI | .970 | 133 | 249 | 14 | 8 | 271 | 2 |
| Fleming, Ryan, REA* | .981 | 106 | 252 | 6 | 5 | 263 | 4 |
| Florence, Branden, BOW | 1.000 | 8 | 5 | 0 | 0 | 5 | 0 |
| Francisco, Ben, AKR | .984 | 131 | 292 | 9 | 5 | 306 | 2 |
| French, Anton, NHF* | .970 | 31 | 61 | 4 | 2 | 67 | 0 |
| Fulse, Sheldon, PRT | .979 | 102 | 279 | 4 | 6 | 289 | 0 |
| Garbe, BJ, NBR | .981 | 113 | 256 | 7 | 5 | 268 | 1 |
| Gibbons, Jay, BOW* | 1.000 | 4 | 4 | 0 | 0 | 4 | 0 |
| Gibbs, Kevin, REA | 1.000 | 3 | 6 | 0 | 0 | 6 | 0 |
| Godwin, Tyrell, NHF* | .973 | 129 | 208 | 11 | 6 | 225 | 2 |
| Gomez, Rich, ERI | 1.000 | 20 | 34 | 1 | 0 | 35 | 0 |
| Granderson, Curtis, ERI* | .991 | 123 | 303 | 10 | 3 | 316 | 2 |
| Griffin, John-Ford, NHF* | 1.000 | 29 | 36 | 2 | 0 | 38 | 1 |
| Grindell, Nate, AKR | 1.000 | 13 | 13 | 0 | 0 | 13 | 0 |
| Grove, Jason, TRE* | .969 | 106 | 181 | 6 | 6 | 193 | 1 |
| Gutierrez, Franklin, AKR | .969 | 52 | 121 | 5 | 4 | 130 | 0 |
| Hassey, Brad, NHF | 1.000 | 3 | 2 | 0 | 0 | 2 | 0 |
| Headley, Justin, PRT* | 1.000 | 14 | 23 | 0 | 0 | 23 | 0 |
| Jenkins, Neil, ERI | .991 | 58 | 106 | 3 | 1 | 110 | 0 |
| Jiannetti, Joe, BNG | 1.000 | 2 | 2 | 0 | 0 | 2 | 0 |
| Johnson, Eric, PRT | 1.000 | 37 | 83 | 2 | 0 | 85 | 1 |
| Johnson, James, PRT* | 1.000 | 4 | 5 | 0 | 0 | 5 | 0 |
| Jones, Mitch, TRE | .973 | 119 | 202 | 13 | 6 | 221 | 2 |
| Jova, Maikel, NHF | .956 | 108 | 186 | 8 | 9 | 203 | 1 |
| Keene, Kurt, REA | .960 | 28 | 42 | 6 | 2 | 50 | 1 |
| Kilburg, Joe, PRT* | .966 | 24 | 27 | 1 | 1 | 29 | 0 |
| Kingsale, Eugene, BOW | .989 | 42 | 86 | 1 | 1 | 88 | 0 |
| Knoedler, Jason, ERI | .979 | 23 | 43 | 3 | 1 | 47 | 0 |
| Knoedler, Justin, NRW | 1.000 | 1 | 1 | 0 | 0 | 1 | 0 |
| Kubel, Jason, NBR* | .961 | 36 | 70 | 4 | 3 | 77 | 0 |
| Lane, Rich, HRB* | .974 | 94 | 178 | 9 | 5 | 192 | 1 |
| Lockwood, Mike, PRT* | .993 | 74 | 138 | 6 | 1 | 145 | 2 |
| Lofton, James, BOW | .889 | 4 | 7 | 1 | 1 | 9 | 0 |
| Lofton, Kenny, TRE* | 1.000 | 4 | 6 | 0 | 0 | 6 | 0 |
| Lombard, George, PRT* | .968 | 15 | 30 | 0 | 1 | 31 | 0 |
| Lopez-Cao, Mike, PRT* | 1.000 | 2 | 4 | 0 | 0 | 4 | 0 |
| Ludwick, Ryan, AKR | 1.000 | 5 | 6 | 0 | 0 | 6 | 0 |
| Lydon, Wayne, BNG | .952 | 119 | 213 | 7 | 11 | 231 | 0 |
| Majewski, Val, BOW* | .978 | 108 | 211 | 7 | 5 | 223 | 2 |
| Malek, Bobby, BNG* | 1.000 | 14 | 24 | 2 | 0 | 26 | 1 |
| McKinley, Josh, HRB | .948 | 62 | 124 | 3 | 7 | 134 | 1 |
| McLouth, Nate, ALT* | .969 | 126 | 250 | 3 | 8 | 261 | 0 |
| Melian, Jackson, TRE | 1.000 | 15 | 15 | 0 | 0 | 15 | 0 |
| Meyers, Chad, ERI | 1.000 | 34 | 56 | 3 | 0 | 59 | 0 |
| Minges, Tyler, AKR | .973 | 82 | 165 | 12 | 5 | 182 | 2 |
| Mota, Tony, BOW | .984 | 69 | 119 | 1 | 2 | 122 | 0 |
| Nicholson, Derek, ERI* | .964 | 23 | 27 | 0 | 1 | 28 | 0 |
| O'Keefe, Mike, PRT* | .976 | 25 | 40 | 0 | 1 | 41 | 0 |
| Ortmeier, Daniel, NRW | .990 | 98 | 192 | 4 | 2 | 198 | 1 |
| Owens, Ryan, NBR | .927 | 25 | 38 | 0 | 3 | 41 | 0 |
| Pagan, Angel, BNG | .991 | 102 | 215 | 11 | 2 | 228 | 2 |
| Perez, Josue, REA | .976 | 23 | 39 | 2 | 1 | 42 | 1 |
| Pratt, Scott, AKR* | 1.000 | 35 | 88 | 1 | 0 | 89 | 1 |
| Pressley, Josh, BNG* | 1.000 | 1 | 4 | 0 | 0 | 4 | 0 |
| Quintana, Miguel, REA* | .989 | 46 | 89 | 1 | 1 | 91 | 0 |
| Raymundo, GJ, HRB | 1.000 | 4 | 6 | 0 | 0 | 6 | 0 |
| Redman, Prentice, BNG | .973 | 56 | 107 | 1 | 3 | 111 | 0 |
| Reed, Keith, BOW | .961 | 118 | 211 | 10 | 9 | 230 | 4 |
| Reese, Kevin, TRE* | .988 | 78 | 165 | 6 | 2 | 173 | 2 |
| Rombley, Danny, HRB | .976 | 39 | 75 | 5 | 2 | 82 | 0 |
| Roneberg, Brett, PRT* | .981 | 108 | 202 | 6 | 4 | 212 | 1 |
| Sadler, Ray, ALT | .979 | 114 | 216 | 12 | 5 | 233 | 1 |
| Salazar, Oscar, AKR | 1.000 | 1 | 1 | 0 | 0 | 1 | 0 |
| Santos, Francisco, NRW* | 1.000 | 7 | 11 | 1 | 0 | 12 | 0 |
| Scanlon, Matt, NBR* | .947 | 40 | 68 | 4 | 4 | 76 | 0 |
| Sheldon, Scott, ALT | 1.000 | 4 | 6 | 1 | 0 | 7 | 0 |
| Sherrill, JJ, AKR | .953 | 20 | 40 | 1 | 2 | 43 | 0 |
| Singleton, Justin, NHF* | .977 | 129 | 248 | 6 | 6 | 260 | 2 |
| Sorensen, Zach, AKR | 1.000 | 2 | 3 | 0 | 0 | 3 | 0 |
| Storey, Eric, HRB | 1.000 | 2 | 1 | 0 | 0 | 1 | 0 |
| Thomas, Gary, ALT | 1.000 | 24 | 52 | 1 | 0 | 53 | 0 |
| Thompson, Kevin, TRE | .992 | 65 | 115 | 4 | 1 | 120 | 0 |
| Tomlin, James, NBR | .991 | 137 | 312 | 11 | 3 | 326 | 2 |
| Tousa, Scott, ERI* | 1.000 | 4 | 6 | 0 | 0 | 6 | 0 |
| Valderrama, Carlos, NRW | .995 | 88 | 180 | 2 | 1 | 183 | 1 |
| Walker, Matt, BOW | 1.000 | 12 | 20 | 1 | 0 | 21 | 0 |
| Walsh, Sean, REA | 1.000 | 8 | 7 | 0 | 0 | 7 | 0 |
| Walter, Randy, NRW | .947 | 13 | 34 | 2 | 2 | 38 | 0 |
| Ware, Jeremy, HRB | .990 | 45 | 100 | 1 | 1 | 102 | 0 |
| Watkins, Tommy, NBR | .933 | 15 | 25 | 3 | 2 | 30 | 1 |
| Waugh, Jason, NHF | 1.000 | 3 | 4 | 0 | 0 | 4 | 0 |
| Weber, Jake, TRE* | 1.000 | 51 | 88 | 5 | 0 | 93 | 2 |
| West, Kevin, NBR | 1.000 | 71 | 103 | 9 | 0 | 112 | 1 |
| Wilken, Kris, BOW | 1.000 | 8 | 10 | 0 | 0 | 10 | 0 |
| Winrow, Tommy, TRE* | 1.000 | 15 | 34 | 2 | 0 | 36 | 2 |
| Youngbauer, Scott, AKR | 1.000 | 3 | 6 | 0 | 0 | 6 | 0 |

## CATCHERS

| Player, Team | Pct. | G | PO | A | E | TC | DP | PB |
|---|---|---|---|---|---|---|---|---|
| Anderson, Jimmy, BNG | 1.000 | 3 | 20 | 1 | 0 | 21 | 0 | 0 |
| Bailey, Jeff, PRT | .987 | 66 | 441 | 19 | 6 | 466 | 6 | 5 |
| Bard, Josh, AKR | 1.000 | 4 | 20 | 3 | 0 | 23 | 0 | 0 |

| Player, Team | Pct. | G | PO | A | E | TC | DP | PB |
|---|---|---|---|---|---|---|---|---|
| Belcher, Jason, HRB* | .955 | 19 | 97 | 8 | 5 | 110 | 0 | 2 |
| Bowen, Rob, NBR | .985 | 66 | 484 | 32 | 8 | 524 | 3 | 7 |
| Brown, Jason, HRB | .965 | 28 | 127 | 9 | 5 | 141 | 1 | 2 |
| Burkhart, Lance, BOW | .991 | 43 | 320 | 29 | 3 | 352 | 3 | 4 |
| Camacaro, Armando, AKR | .969 | 17 | 111 | 16 | 4 | 131 | 2 | 3 |
| Cardona, Javier, BNG | .987 | 20 | 138 | 11 | 2 | 151 | 1 | 3 |
| Castellano, John, REA | .989 | 15 | 82 | 4 | 1 | 87 | 1 | 2 |
| Chauncey, Clint, PRT | .992 | 29 | 219 | 26 | 2 | 247 | 3 | 3 |
| Chiaffredo, Paul, NHF | .990 | 60 | 447 | 33 | 5 | 485 | 5 | 4 |
| Clements, Zack, BNG | 1.000 | 1 | 8 | 1 | 0 | 9 | 0 | 0 |
| Clendenin, Morgan, BOW* | 1.000 | 4 | 12 | 1 | 0 | 13 | 0 | 1 |
| Cleveland, Russ, ERI | .947 | 17 | 84 | 6 | 5 | 95 | 0 | 2 |
| Concepcion, Alberto, PRT | .949 | 4 | 37 | 0 | 2 | 39 | 0 | 1 |
| Corporan, Elvis, NBR | 1.000 | 4 | 20 | 5 | 0 | 25 | 0 | 1 |
| Curry, Chris, NRW | .982 | 44 | 250 | 18 | 5 | 273 | 1 | 6 |
| Doumit, Ryan, ALT | .983 | 25 | 159 | 14 | 3 | 176 | 2 | 3 |
| Fuentes, Omar, TRE | .990 | 63 | 452 | 34 | 5 | 491 | 2 | 9 |
| Garko, Ryan, AKR | .993 | 24 | 138 | 12 | 1 | 151 | 1 | 1 |
| Gonzalez, Jimmy, BNG | .982 | 15 | 104 | 8 | 2 | 114 | 1 | 1 |
| Griffin, Nate, TRE* | 1.000 | 1 | 6 | 0 | 0 | 6 | 0 | 0 |
| Harper, Brandon, ERI | .981 | 41 | 290 | 19 | 6 | 315 | 6 | 2 |
| Herrera, Javier, AKR | 1.000 | 5 | 38 | 3 | 0 | 41 | 0 | 1 |
| Hietpas, Joe, BNG | .982 | 43 | 298 | 23 | 6 | 327 | 4 | 4 |
| Huber, Justin, BNG | .992 | 66 | 461 | 37 | 4 | 502 | 3 | 10 |
| Jacobson, Russ, REA | .980 | 47 | 282 | 18 | 6 | 306 | 3 | 3 |
| Kennedy, Bryan, NBR* | .990 | 51 | 289 | 22 | 3 | 314 | 3 | 8 |
| Knoedler, Justin, NRW | .991 | 102 | 681 | 64 | 7 | 752 | 2 | 15 |
| Kratz, Erik, NHF | 1.000 | 3 | 24 | 2 | 0 | 26 | 0 | 1 |
| Lopez-Cao, Mike, PRT* | .982 | 11 | 54 | 1 | 1 | 56 | 0 | 0 |
| Luderer, Brian, AKR | .981 | 37 | 240 | 13 | 5 | 258 | 1 | 5 |
| Madera, Sandy, TRE | .923 | 6 | 19 | 5 | 2 | 26 | 1 | 0 |
| Manriquez, Salomon, HRB | 1.000 | 6 | 22 | 3 | 0 | 25 | 0 | 0 |
| Martinez, Edgar, PRT | .962 | 52 | 321 | 38 | 14 | 373 | 2 | 9 |
| Martinez, Octavio, BOW | .979 | 19 | 130 | 11 | 3 | 144 | 1 | 6 |
| McKinley, Josh, HRB | .984 | 10 | 57 | 4 | 1 | 62 | 1 | 1 |
| McMillan, Andrew, HRB | .991 | 52 | 299 | 33 | 3 | 335 | 1 | 3 |
| Navarro, Dioner, TRE | .984 | 54 | 394 | 37 | 7 | 438 | 5 | 13 |
| Parrish, Dave, TRE | .984 | 32 | 225 | 18 | 4 | 247 | 5 | 5 |
| Paulino, Ronny, ALT | .986 | 80 | 585 | 52 | 9 | 646 | 2 | 9 |
| Pena, Rudy, ALT | 1.000 | 1 | 10 | 2 | 0 | 12 | 0 | 0 |
| Rabelo, Mike, ERI | 1.000 | 5 | 32 | 4 | 0 | 36 | 0 | 0 |
| Ruiz, Carlos, REA | .988 | 86 | 596 | 53 | 8 | 657 | 8 | 10 |
| Snusz, Chris, ALT | .984 | 36 | 228 | 23 | 4 | 255 | 3 | 1 |
| Spilman, Ryan, AKR | 1.000 | 2 | 4 | 1 | 0 | 5 | 0 | 0 |
| St. Pierre, Maxim, ERI | .996 | 84 | 487 | 54 | 2 | 543 | 1 | 7 |
| Storey, Eric, HRB | 1.000 | 3 | 13 | 4 | 0 | 17 | 0 | 0 |
| Torres, Gabby, NBR | 1.000 | 31 | 222 | 12 | 0 | 234 | 3 | 4 |
| Umbria, Jose, NHF | .992 | 54 | 365 | 26 | 3 | 394 | 1 | 5 |
| Valencia, Victor, NHF | .977 | 26 | 160 | 10 | 4 | 174 | 2 | 3 |
| Valencia, Victor, AKR | .974 | 15 | 103 | 8 | 3 | 114 | 1 | 1 |
| Valencia, Victor, NHF-AKR | .976 | 0 | 263 | 18 | 7 | 288 | 3 | 4 |
| Wallace, David, AKR | .979 | 45 | 314 | 19 | 7 | 340 | 2 | 6 |
| Whiteside, Eli, BOW | .986 | 86 | 660 | 48 | 10 | 718 | 3 | 14 |
| Whittaker, Tim, NHF | 1.000 | 1 | 12 | 0 | 0 | 12 | 0 | 0 |
| Wilson, John, HRB | .976 | 41 | 259 | 25 | 7 | 291 | 4 | 2 |
| Wilson, Vance, BNG | 1.000 | 1 | 5 | 1 | 0 | 6 | 0 | 0 |

## PITCHERS

| Player, Team | Pct. | G | PO | A | E | TC | DP |
|---|---|---|---|---|---|---|---|
| Abbott, Jim, NBR | 1.000 | 21 | 7 | 11 | 0 | 18 | 0 |
| Accardo, Jeremy, NRW | 1.000 | 7 | 0 | 1 | 0 | 1 | 1 |
| Adkins, Tim, TRE* | .950 | 52 | 2 | 17 | 1 | 20 | 0 |
| Agamennone, Brandon, ALT | 1.000 | 19 | 1 | 2 | 0 | 3 | 0 |
| Alvarez, Abe, PRT* | 1.000 | 26 | 13 | 21 | 0 | 34 | 3 |
| Alvarez, Oscar, AKR* | 1.000 | 23 | 3 | 12 | 0 | 15 | 1 |
| Anderson, Luke, NRW | 1.000 | 35 | 3 | 2 | 0 | 5 | 0 |
| Arnold, Jason, NHF | 1.000 | 4 | 1 | 3 | 0 | 4 | 1 |
| Astacio, Pedro, PRT | .000 | 1 | 0 | 0 | 0 | 0 | 0 |
| Averette, Robert, BOW | .778 | 10 | 3 | 4 | 2 | 9 | 0 |
| Baker, Chris, NHF | 1.000 | 11 | 8 | 8 | 0 | 16 | 0 |
| Baker, Scott, NBR | 1.000 | 10 | 17 | 7 | 0 | 24 | 0 |
| Banks, Josh, NHF | .938 | 18 | 7 | 8 | 1 | 16 | 1 |
| Bannister, Brian, BNG | 1.000 | 8 | 6 | 8 | 0 | 14 | 0 |
| Bateman, Joe, NRW | 1.000 | 12 | 1 | 4 | 0 | 5 | 1 |
| Bauer, Rick, BOW | .000 | 1 | 0 | 0 | 0 | 0 | 0 |
| Baugh, Kenny, ERI | .931 | 24 | 10 | 17 | 2 | 29 | 2 |
| Bautista, Denny, BOW | 1.000 | 14 | 4 | 10 | 0 | 14 | 0 |
| Begg, Chris, NRW | .971 | 16 | 14 | 20 | 1 | 35 | 2 |
| Bell, Heath, BNG | 1.000 | 1 | 0 | 1 | 0 | 1 | 0 |
| Bentz, Chad, HRB* | .000 | 5 | 0 | 0 | 0 | 0 | 0 |
| Bere, Jason, AKR | 1.000 | 2 | 0 | 1 | 0 | 1 | 0 |
| Bergmann, Jason, HRB | 1.000 | 2 | 0 | 1 | 0 | 1 | 0 |
| Bevis, PJ, BNG | 1.000 | 27 | 1 | 0 | 0 | 1 | 0 |
| Birtwell, John, ERI | 1.000 | 6 | 2 | 0 | 0 | 2 | 0 |
| Blankenship, John, TRE* | .000 | 13 | 0 | 0 | 0 | 0 | 0 |
| Bonilla, Henry, NBR | .978 | 25 | 21 | 23 | 1 | 45 | 3 |
| Bonser, Boof, NBR | .880 | 27 | 12 | 10 | 3 | 25 | 1 |
| Borner, Brady, ALT* | .938 | 38 | 5 | 10 | 1 | 16 | 0 |
| Bouknight, Kip, NHF | .500 | 3 | 0 | 1 | 1 | 2 | 1 |
| Bowers, Shane, REA | 1.000 | 4 | 2 | 3 | 0 | 5 | 0 |
| Bowyer, Travis, NBR | .923 | 31 | 8 | 16 | 2 | 26 | 1 |
| Bradley, Bobby, ALT | .939 | 19 | 17 | 14 | 2 | 33 | 2 |
| Brannon, Nick, AKR* | 1.000 | 1 | 0 | 1 | 0 | 1 | 0 |
| Bridges, Donnie, HRB | 1.000 | 18 | 6 | 5 | 0 | 11 | 0 |
| Brito, Eude, REA* | 1.000 | 43 | 4 | 21 | 0 | 25 | 1 |
| Brown, Andrew, AKR | .900 | 17 | 5 | 4 | 1 | 10 | 0 |
| Brown, Kevin, TRE | 1.000 | 1 | 2 | 0 | 0 | 2 | 0 |
| Bruback, Matt, BOW | .818 | 14 | 4 | 5 | 2 | 11 | 1 |
| Bucktrot, Keith, REA | 1.000 | 20 | 5 | 9 | 0 | 14 | 0 |
| Bullington, Bryan, ALT | .941 | 26 | 9 | 23 | 2 | 34 | 2 |
| Cabrera, Daniel, BOW | .500 | 5 | 0 | 1 | 1 | 2 | 0 |
| Cain, Matthew, NRW | .846 | 15 | 5 | 6 | 2 | 13 | 0 |
| Cameron, Kevin, NBR | .875 | 26 | 6 | 8 | 2 | 16 | 1 |
| Cameron, Ryan, PRT | .867 | 23 | 4 | 9 | 2 | 15 | 1 |
| Candelario, Eddie, ALT | 1.000 | 21 | 2 | 3 | 0 | 5 | 0 |
| Candelario, Eddie, REA | 1.000 | 16 | 4 | 2 | 0 | 6 | 0 |
| Candelario, Eddie, ALT-REA | 1.000 | 37 | 6 | 5 | 0 | 11 | 0 |
| Caracioli, Lance, BNG* | .941 | 29 | 6 | 10 | 1 | 17 | 0 |
| Carlyle, Buddy, TRE | 1.000 | 8 | 0 | 2 | 0 | 2 | 0 |
| Carmona, Fausto, AKR | .906 | 15 | 9 | 20 | 3 | 32 | 3 |
| Casadiego, Gerardo, HRB | 1.000 | 10 | 0 | 1 | 0 | 1 | 0 |
| Chacin, Gustavo, NHF* | .852 | 25 | 4 | 19 | 4 | 27 | 0 |
| Chantres, Carlos, REA | 1.000 | 6 | 2 | 2 | 0 | 4 | 0 |
| Chenard, Ken, BNG | .941 | 27 | 6 | 10 | 1 | 17 | 1 |
| Clark, Jeff, NRW | 1.000 | 4 | 1 | 2 | 0 | 3 | 0 |
| Cole, Joe, BNG | 1.000 | 7 | 2 | 2 | 0 | 4 | 0 |
| Connolly, Mike, ALT* | .846 | 20 | 6 | 5 | 2 | 13 | 0 |
| Cooper, Chris, AKR* | 1.000 | 27 | 2 | 4 | 0 | 6 | 0 |
| Cordova, Jorge, ERI | .833 | 22 | 1 | 4 | 1 | 6 | 0 |
| Corona, Ronnie, NBR | 1.000 | 3 | 1 | 1 | 0 | 2 | 0 |
| Crouthers, Dave, BOW | .632 | 27 | 8 | 4 | 7 | 19 | 1 |
| Cruceta, Francisco, AKR | .889 | 15 | 7 | 9 | 2 | 18 | 1 |
| Crudale, Mike, ALT | .667 | 23 | 2 | 2 | 2 | 6 | 0 |
| Crumpton, Chuck, HRB | 1.000 | 6 | 0 | 2 | 0 | 2 | 0 |
| Cuello, Felix, ERI | 1.000 | 9 | 0 | 3 | 0 | 3 | 0 |
| Culp, Brandon, REA | 1.000 | 4 | 1 | 2 | 0 | 3 | 0 |
| Currier, Rik, TRE | .889 | 34 | 7 | 9 | 2 | 18 | 1 |
| Dawley, Joe, AKR | .000 | 1 | 0 | 0 | 0 | 0 | 0 |
| Dawson, Layne, REA | 1.000 | 9 | 1 | 0 | 0 | 1 | 0 |
| DeJong, Jordan, NHF | 1.000 | 57 | 3 | 9 | 0 | 12 | 0 |
| Denham, Dan, AKR | .867 | 14 | 5 | 8 | 2 | 15 | 0 |
| DeSalvo, Matthew, TRE | 1.000 | 5 | 0 | 2 | 0 | 2 | 1 |
| Deschenes, Marc, PRT | .750 | 27 | 1 | 2 | 1 | 4 | 1 |
| Diaz, Jose, BNG | 1.000 | 21 | 2 | 7 | 0 | 9 | 0 |
| Diaz, Pedro, ERI | 1.000 | 4 | 1 | 1 | 0 | 2 | 0 |
| Dinardo, Lenny, PRT* | 1.000 | 3 | 2 | 3 | 0 | 5 | 0 |
| Dittler, Jake, AKR | .960 | 21 | 12 | 12 | 1 | 25 | 2 |
| Donaldson, Bo, PRT | .900 | 30 | 4 | 5 | 1 | 10 | 1 |
| Dougherty, Kevin, REA* | 1.000 | 11 | 0 | 13 | 0 | 13 | 0 |
| Douglas, Shea, AKR* | .800 | 9 | 2 | 2 | 1 | 5 | 0 |
| Douglass, Ryan, HRB | 1.000 | 36 | 0 | 6 | 0 | 6 | 0 |
| Duke, Zach, ALT* | 1.000 | 9 | 5 | 13 | 0 | 18 | 0 |
| Durbin, JD, NBR | .952 | 13 | 8 | 12 | 1 | 21 | 2 |
| Echols, Justin, HRB | .867 | 21 | 3 | 10 | 2 | 15 | 0 |
| Edwards, Brian, BNG | 1.000 | 2 | 2 | 1 | 0 | 3 | 0 |
| Elder, Dave, TRE | 1.000 | 17 | 0 | 4 | 0 | 4 | 0 |
| Evans, Kyle, AKR | .900 | 8 | 5 | 4 | 1 | 10 | 0 |
| Ferrari, Anthony, HRB* | 1.000 | 3 | 0 | 1 | 0 | 1 | 0 |
| Finch, Brian, BOW | 1.000 | 11 | 6 | 4 | 0 | 10 | 0 |
| Floyd, Gavin, REA | .923 | 20 | 11 | 13 | 2 | 26 | 0 |

| Player, Team | Pct. | G | PO | A | E | TC | DP |
|---|---|---|---|---|---|---|---|
| Foley, Travis, AKR | 1.000 | 7 | 2 | 10 | 0 | 12 | 0 |
| Forystek, Brian, BOW* | 1.000 | 15 | 4 | 10 | 0 | 14 | 1 |
| Franco, Martire, REA | 1.000 | 48 | 10 | 10 | 0 | 20 | 1 |
| Frederick, Kevin, NHF | .875 | 18 | 2 | 5 | 1 | 8 | 0 |
| Gabbard, Kason, PRT* | 1.000 | 14 | 5 | 9 | 0 | 14 | 1 |
| Gamble, Jerome, PRT | 1.000 | 14 | 4 | 9 | 0 | 13 | 1 |
| Gannon, Joe, BOW | .000 | 1 | 0 | 0 | 0 | 0 | 0 |
| Gardner, Hayden, REA | 1.000 | 7 | 3 | 0 | 0 | 3 | 0 |
| Gardner, Jarrett, PRT | .000 | 1 | 0 | 0 | 1 | 1 | 0 |
| Glaser, Eric, PRT | .909 | 31 | 11 | 9 | 2 | 22 | 0 |
| Goetz, Geoff, TRE* | 1.000 | 9 | 2 | 1 | 0 | 3 | 0 |
| Gomez, Mariano, AKR* | 1.000 | 7 | 1 | 6 | 0 | 7 | 0 |
| Gronkiewicz, Lee, AKR | 1.000 | 52 | 3 | 11 | 0 | 14 | 0 |
| Guthrie, Jeremy, AKR | .833 | 23 | 6 | 19 | 5 | 30 | 1 |
| Gutierrez, Jannio, NBR | 1.000 | 10 | 2 | 1 | 0 | 3 | 1 |
| Gwaltney, Lee, REA | 1.000 | 4 | 1 | 2 | 0 | 3 | 0 |
| Habel, Josh, NRW* | .864 | 27 | 3 | 16 | 3 | 22 | 0 |
| Hamman, Corey, ERI* | .000 | 2 | 0 | 0 | 0 | 0 | 0 |
| Hamulack, Tim, PRT* | 1.000 | 7 | 0 | 4 | 0 | 4 | 0 |
| Hanson, Adam, AKR | 1.000 | 1 | 0 | 1 | 0 | 1 | 0 |
| Harts, Jeremy, ALT* | .667 | 9 | 0 | 2 | 1 | 3 | 0 |
| Helling, Rick, NBR | 1.000 | 5 | 2 | 2 | 0 | 4 | 0 |
| Henkel, Rob, ERI* | .800 | 3 | 2 | 2 | 1 | 5 | 0 |
| Henn, Sean, TRE* | .941 | 27 | 7 | 25 | 2 | 34 | 1 |
| Hennessey, Brad, NRW | .960 | 17 | 5 | 19 | 1 | 25 | 3 |
| Heredia, Felix, TRE* | .667 | 3 | 1 | 1 | 1 | 3 | 0 |
| Hernandez, Yoel, REA | 1.000 | 20 | 6 | 7 | 0 | 13 | 0 |
| Hiles, Cary, REA | 1.000 | 13 | 2 | 1 | 0 | 3 | 0 |
| Hill, Jeremy, BNG | 1.000 | 25 | 4 | 2 | 0 | 6 | 0 |
| Hill, Shawn, HRB | .907 | 17 | 13 | 26 | 4 | 43 | 1 |
| Hinckley, Michael, HRB* | .926 | 16 | 6 | 19 | 2 | 27 | 2 |
| Hoard, Brent, NBR* | 1.000 | 1 | 1 | 0 | 0 | 1 | 0 |
| House, Craig, BOW | 1.000 | 18 | 3 | 5 | 0 | 8 | 2 |
| Houston, Ryan, NHF | .846 | 34 | 2 | 9 | 2 | 13 | 2 |
| Howell, Jason, PRT* | 1.000 | 23 | 1 | 6 | 0 | 7 | 0 |
| Hundley, Jeff, BOW* | .875 | 35 | 4 | 10 | 2 | 16 | 2 |
| Hutchinson, Ryan, REA | 1.000 | 12 | 3 | 6 | 0 | 9 | 0 |
| Isaacson, Charlie, TRE | 1.000 | 10 | 3 | 1 | 0 | 4 | 0 |
| Izquierdo, Hansel, TRE | 1.000 | 11 | 1 | 3 | 0 | 4 | 0 |
| Jackson, Dan, NHF | .880 | 53 | 5 | 17 | 3 | 25 | 0 |
| Jacobsen, Landon, ALT | 1.000 | 15 | 6 | 12 | 0 | 18 | 1 |
| Jacquez, Tom, BOW* | .909 | 21 | 1 | 9 | 1 | 11 | 0 |
| Jimenez, Jason, REA* | 1.000 | 17 | 1 | 6 | 0 | 7 | 1 |
| Johnson, James, PRT* | 1.000 | 21 | 2 | 4 | 0 | 6 | 0 |
| Joseph, Jake, BNG | 1.000 | 25 | 3 | 6 | 0 | 9 | 0 |
| Julianel, Ben, TRE* | 1.000 | 6 | 0 | 2 | 0 | 2 | 0 |
| Karnuth, Jason, ERI | .857 | 10 | 2 | 4 | 1 | 7 | 0 |
| Karsay, Steve, TRE | 1.000 | 4 | 1 | 1 | 0 | 2 | 0 |
| Kaye, Justin, TRE | 1.000 | 3 | 0 | 1 | 0 | 1 | 0 |
| Kazmir, Scott, BNG* | .800 | 4 | 2 | 6 | 2 | 10 | 0 |
| Kemp, Beau, NBR | .909 | 18 | 5 | 5 | 1 | 11 | 1 |
| Kennard, Jeff, TRE | 1.000 | 7 | 3 | 2 | 0 | 5 | 0 |
| King, Jeremy, TRE | .000 | 2 | 0 | 0 | 0 | 0 | 0 |
| Kirsten, Rick, ERI | .929 | 17 | 5 | 8 | 1 | 14 | 1 |
| Kleine, Victor, AKR* | 1.000 | 25 | 5 | 13 | 0 | 18 | 1 |
| Korecky, Bobby, NBR | .958 | 55 | 4 | 19 | 1 | 24 | 0 |
| Kratz, Erik, NHF | .000 | 1 | 0 | 0 | 0 | 0 | 0 |
| Lambert, Jeremy, PRT | 1.000 | 4 | 1 | 2 | 0 | 3 | 0 |
| Larrison, Preston, ERI | .958 | 20 | 9 | 14 | 1 | 24 | 0 |
| Larson, Ryan, PRT | 1.000 | 26 | 1 | 8 | 0 | 9 | 0 |
| Lavigne, Tim, BNG | .970 | 40 | 12 | 20 | 1 | 33 | 3 |
| League, Brandon, NHF | .889 | 41 | 7 | 17 | 3 | 27 | 1 |
| Ledezma, Wilfredo, ERI* | .864 | 17 | 7 | 12 | 3 | 22 | 0 |
| Lee, Derek, NHF* | .938 | 12 | 8 | 7 | 1 | 16 | 0 |
| Lee, Seung, REA | 1.000 | 3 | 0 | 1 | 0 | 1 | 0 |
| Liriano, Francisco, NBR* | 1.000 | 7 | 2 | 2 | 0 | 4 | 0 |
| Lockwood, Luke, HRB* | .941 | 33 | 11 | 21 | 2 | 34 | 1 |
| Lohse, Erik, NBR | .875 | 7 | 2 | 5 | 1 | 8 | 0 |
| Lontayo, Alex, ERI* | 1.000 | 37 | 5 | 11 | 0 | 16 | 1 |
| Lorraine, Andrew, ALT* | 1.000 | 6 | 1 | 2 | 0 | 3 | 0 |
| Lundberg, Spike, REA | 1.000 | 12 | 2 | 3 | 0 | 5 | 0 |
| Lundquist, Dave, ALT | 1.000 | 15 | 2 | 3 | 0 | 5 | 0 |
| Madson, Ryan, REA | 1.000 | 2 | 0 | 1 | 0 | 1 | 0 |
| Maine, John, BOW | 1.000 | 5 | 1 | 5 | 0 | 6 | 1 |
| Mangrum, Micah, BNG | 1.000 | 14 | 3 | 10 | 0 | 13 | 0 |

| Player, Team | Pct. | G | PO | A | E | TC | DP |
|---|---|---|---|---|---|---|---|
| Manning, Charlie, TRE* | 1.000 | 15 | 1 | 7 | 0 | 8 | 0 |
| Markert, Jackson, NRW | .833 | 15 | 1 | 4 | 1 | 6 | 0 |
| Marrero, Darwin, HRB | 1.000 | 2 | 1 | 0 | 0 | 1 | 0 |
| Martinez, Dave, AKR* | .500 | 1 | 1 | 0 | 1 | 2 | 0 |
| Martinez, Javier, BOW | 1.000 | 11 | 0 | 1 | 0 | 1 | 1 |
| Mata, Gustavo, HRB | 1.000 | 1 | 2 | 0 | 0 | 2 | 1 |
| Maust, David, HRB* | 1.000 | 44 | 6 | 8 | 0 | 14 | 2 |
| Mazone, Brian, NRW* | 1.000 | 7 | 1 | 1 | 0 | 2 | 0 |
| McDade, Neal, ALT | .933 | 32 | 4 | 24 | 2 | 30 | 1 |
| McDowell, Kevin, ERI* | .000 | 7 | 0 | 0 | 0 | 0 | 0 |
| McGinley, Blake, BNG* | .875 | 33 | 7 | 7 | 2 | 16 | 0 |
| McGowan, Dustin, NHF | 1.000 | 6 | 1 | 3 | 0 | 4 | 0 |
| Mears, Chris, ERI | 1.000 | 13 | 0 | 3 | 0 | 3 | 0 |
| Mendoza, Marcos, AKR* | .000 | 1 | 0 | 0 | 1 | 1 | 0 |
| Meyers, Mike, BNG | 1.000 | 5 | 1 | 2 | 0 | 3 | 0 |
| Miller, Colby, NBR | 1.000 | 14 | 19 | 9 | 0 | 28 | 1 |
| Miller, Jason, NBR* | 1.000 | 31 | 4 | 5 | 0 | 9 | 0 |
| Miller, Jeff, ALT | 1.000 | 52 | 1 | 9 | 0 | 10 | 0 |
| Misch, Patrick, NRW* | .972 | 26 | 8 | 27 | 1 | 36 | 3 |
| Mitchell, Andy, BOW | .977 | 54 | 9 | 33 | 1 | 43 | 4 |
| Montalbano, Greg, PRT* | 1.000 | 6 | 1 | 2 | 0 | 3 | 0 |
| Montes, Alberto, NRW | .941 | 53 | 5 | 11 | 1 | 17 | 1 |
| Moreno, Victor, NBR | .944 | 33 | 10 | 7 | 1 | 18 | 0 |
| Morris, Cory, BOW | .727 | 12 | 2 | 6 | 3 | 11 | 0 |
| Munter, Scott, NRW | .955 | 42 | 6 | 15 | 1 | 22 | 0 |
| Musser, Neal, BNG* | .955 | 19 | 4 | 17 | 1 | 22 | 1 |
| Nelson, Joe, PRT | 1.000 | 25 | 3 | 2 | 0 | 5 | 0 |
| Neshek, Pat, NBR | 1.000 | 26 | 2 | 6 | 0 | 8 | 0 |
| Novoa, Roberto, ERI | .923 | 41 | 3 | 9 | 1 | 13 | 0 |
| O'Brien, Patrick, ALT | 1.000 | 2 | 0 | 1 | 0 | 1 | 0 |
| Ogiltree, John, NHF | 1.000 | 45 | 5 | 21 | 0 | 26 | 2 |
| Orloski, Joe, TRE | 1.000 | 6 | 1 | 1 | 0 | 2 | 0 |
| Ormond, Rodney, BOW | 1.000 | 32 | 6 | 5 | 0 | 11 | 0 |
| Ortiz, Javier, TRE | 1.000 | 19 | 8 | 13 | 0 | 21 | 0 |
| Ough, Wayne, BNG | .938 | 16 | 6 | 9 | 1 | 16 | 1 |
| Ozias, Todd, NHF | 1.000 | 18 | 3 | 7 | 0 | 10 | 0 |
| Padilla, Juan, TRE | 1.000 | 3 | 1 | 1 | 0 | 2 | 0 |
| Palma, Rick, ERI* | .933 | 53 | 2 | 12 | 1 | 15 | 1 |
| Palmer, Matt, NRW | .938 | 42 | 5 | 10 | 1 | 16 | 1 |
| Parcus, Kyle, REA* | .000 | 5 | 0 | 0 | 0 | 0 | 0 |
| Parra, Jose, BNG | 1.000 | 1 | 0 | 1 | 0 | 1 | 0 |
| Pavon, Julio, NRW | 1.000 | 17 | 8 | 7 | 0 | 15 | 1 |
| Penn, Hayden, BOW | 1.000 | 4 | 3 | 1 | 0 | 4 | 0 |
| Perez, Franklin, REA | 1.000 | 15 | 5 | 6 | 0 | 11 | 2 |
| Perez, Juan, PRT* | .909 | 46 | 2 | 8 | 1 | 11 | 0 |
| Pesco, Nick, AKR | .000 | 1 | 0 | 0 | 0 | 0 | 0 |
| Peterson, Adam, NHF | 1.000 | 27 | 0 | 2 | 0 | 2 | 0 |
| Peterson, Matt, ALT | 1.000 | 7 | 2 | 3 | 0 | 5 | 1 |
| Peterson, Matt, BNG | .909 | 19 | 6 | 14 | 2 | 22 | 1 |
| Peterson, Matt, ALT-BNG | .926 | 26 | 8 | 17 | 2 | 27 | 2 |
| Petit, Yusmeiro, BNG | 1.000 | 2 | 2 | 1 | 0 | 3 | 0 |
| Piersoll, Chris, BOW | 1.000 | 16 | 6 | 3 | 0 | 9 | 0 |
| Pope, Justin, TRE | .960 | 18 | 5 | 19 | 1 | 25 | 2 |
| Prahm, Ryan, AKR | .857 | 15 | 4 | 2 | 1 | 7 | 0 |
| Pridie, Jon, NBR | 1.000 | 36 | 14 | 15 | 0 | 29 | 2 |
| Puello, Ignacio, HRB | .000 | 10 | 0 | 0 | 0 | 0 | 0 |
| Ramirez, Elizardo, REA | 1.000 | 8 | 3 | 4 | 0 | 7 | 0 |
| Ramirez, Ramon, TRE | 1.000 | 18 | 3 | 8 | 0 | 11 | 0 |
| Rasner, Darrell, HRB | 1.000 | 5 | 2 | 2 | 0 | 4 | 0 |
| Rayborn, Kenny, AKR | 1.000 | 6 | 1 | 4 | 0 | 5 | 1 |
| Raymundo, GJ, HRB | 1.000 | 1 | 0 | 1 | 0 | 1 | 0 |
| Reid, Justin, ALT | 1.000 | 1 | 1 | 0 | 0 | 1 | 0 |
| Reimers, Cameron, NHF | 1.000 | 15 | 8 | 12 | 0 | 20 | 0 |
| Reyes, Carlos, TRE | .941 | 15 | 1 | 15 | 1 | 17 | 0 |
| Rice, Scott, BOW* | .917 | 41 | 8 | 14 | 2 | 24 | 0 |
| Richardson, Jason, NBR | .800 | 11 | 1 | 7 | 2 | 10 | 2 |
| Rijo, Fernando, HRB | 1.000 | 4 | 0 | 2 | 0 | 2 | 0 |
| Ring, Royce, BNG* | 1.000 | 19 | 1 | 3 | 0 | 4 | 0 |
| Rivera, Saul, HRB | 1.000 | 18 | 3 | 6 | 0 | 9 | 1 |
| Rleal, Sendy, BOW | 1.000 | 39 | 4 | 4 | 0 | 8 | 0 |
| Robbins, Jake, AKR | 1.000 | 12 | 4 | 4 | 0 | 8 | 0 |
| Rodney, Lee, ERI | .889 | 24 | 1 | 7 | 1 | 9 | 0 |
| Rodriguez, Joe, BOW* | .700 | 12 | 2 | 5 | 3 | 10 | 1 |
| Rodriguez, Wilfredo, HRB* | 1.000 | 4 | 1 | 0 | 0 | 1 | 0 |
| Rogers, Joe, PRT* | .667 | 5 | 0 | 2 | 1 | 3 | 0 |

| Player, Team | Pct. | G | PO | A | E | TC | DP |
|---|---|---|---|---|---|---|---|
| Roman, Orlando, BNG | .857 | 8 | 5 | 1 | 1 | 7 | 0 |
| Roney, Matt, ERI | 1.000 | 22 | 10 | 9 | 0 | 19 | 0 |
| Rosario, Francisco, NHF | 1.000 | 12 | 4 | 5 | 0 | 9 | 1 |
| Rueckel, Daniel, HRB | 1.000 | 41 | 7 | 4 | 0 | 11 | 1 |
| Rundles, Rich, HRB* | 1.000 | 19 | 13 | 24 | 0 | 37 | 1 |
| Sadler, Billy, NRW | 1.000 | 17 | 3 | 4 | 0 | 7 | 0 |
| Sadler, Carl, AKR* | .889 | 23 | 0 | 8 | 1 | 9 | 0 |
| Sanches, Brian, REA | 1.000 | 41 | 5 | 8 | 0 | 13 | 1 |
| Sanchez, Felix, ERI* | 1.000 | 14 | 2 | 0 | 0 | 2 | 0 |
| Sanchez, Humberto, ERI | .500 | 2 | 1 | 0 | 1 | 2 | 0 |
| Schmack, Brian, ERI | 1.000 | 26 | 2 | 3 | 0 | 5 | 0 |
| Schroder, Chris, HRB | 1.000 | 32 | 3 | 10 | 0 | 13 | 1 |
| Scobie, Jason, BNG | .936 | 25 | 16 | 28 | 3 | 47 | 2 |
| Searles, Jonathan, HRB | 1.000 | 30 | 5 | 1 | 0 | 6 | 3 |
| Sedlacek, Shawn, BNG | 1.000 | 8 | 0 | 3 | 0 | 3 | 1 |
| Seibel, Phil, PRT* | .000 | 2 | 0 | 0 | 0 | 0 | 0 |
| Sequea, Jacobo, BOW | .833 | 59 | 4 | 6 | 2 | 12 | 0 |
| Serrano, Elio, ALT | 1.000 | 44 | 2 | 2 | 0 | 4 | 0 |
| Sessions, Doug, HRB | 1.000 | 5 | 1 | 9 | 0 | 10 | 0 |
| Shaffar, Ben, ALT | 1.000 | 8 | 1 | 3 | 0 | 4 | 1 |
| Shepard, David, TRE | 1.000 | 51 | 8 | 17 | 0 | 25 | 0 |
| Skrmetta, Matt, HRB | 1.000 | 5 | 1 | 2 | 0 | 3 | 0 |
| Sleeth, Kyle, ERI | .882 | 13 | 8 | 7 | 2 | 17 | 0 |
| Smith, Chris, PRT | 1.000 | 14 | 8 | 9 | 0 | 17 | 1 |
| Smith, Matt, TRE* | 1.000 | 14 | 3 | 10 | 0 | 13 | 1 |
| Snell, Ian, ALT | .935 | 26 | 10 | 19 | 2 | 31 | 1 |
| Spencer, Sean, BOW* | .000 | 9 | 0 | 0 | 0 | 0 | 0 |
| Spiegel, Mike, REA* | 1.000 | 6 | 0 | 2 | 0 | 2 | 0 |
| Spradlin, Jerry, BOW | 1.000 | 14 | 0 | 2 | 0 | 2 | 0 |
| Squires, Matt, REA | 1.000 | 26 | 1 | 1 | 0 | 2 | 0 |
| Stein, Blake, ALT | 1.000 | 36 | 0 | 5 | 0 | 5 | 0 |
| Stevens, Josh, PRT* | .971 | 20 | 14 | 19 | 1 | 34 | 3 |
| Stevenson, Jason, HRB* | .906 | 24 | 11 | 18 | 3 | 32 | 1 |
| Strayhorn, Kole, BNG | 1.000 | 39 | 4 | 4 | 0 | 8 | 0 |
| Sturkie, Scott, AKR | 1.000 | 13 | 3 | 2 | 0 | 5 | 0 |
| Tallet, Brian, AKR* | 1.000 | 14 | 0 | 1 | 0 | 1 | 1 |
| Taschner, Jack, NRW* | 1.000 | 14 | 1 | 6 | 0 | 7 | 0 |
| Tejeda, Robinson, REA | .833 | 27 | 1 | 14 | 3 | 18 | 0 |
| Templet, Jordy, NHF | 1.000 | 2 | 1 | 0 | 0 | 1 | 0 |
| Thompson, Travis, NHF | .714 | 22 | 2 | 3 | 2 | 7 | 0 |
| Thurman, Corey, HRB | 1.000 | 5 | 2 | 4 | 0 | 6 | 0 |
| Torres, Andy, NHF | 1.000 | 9 | 4 | 4 | 0 | 8 | 0 |
| Tousa, Scott, ERI* | .000 | 1 | 0 | 0 | 0 | 0 | 0 |
| Treadway, Brion, NRW | 1.000 | 7 | 3 | 2 | 0 | 5 | 0 |
| Valdez, Merkin, NRW | 1.000 | 10 | 1 | 6 | 0 | 7 | 0 |
| Van Dusen, Derrick, AKR* | 1.000 | 26 | 2 | 11 | 0 | 13 | 0 |
| Vargas, Jose, AKR | .833 | 33 | 0 | 5 | 1 | 6 | 0 |
| Vaughan, Beau, PRT | .000 | 1 | 0 | 0 | 0 | 0 | 0 |
| Vermilyea, James, NHF | .900 | 21 | 4 | 5 | 1 | 10 | 2 |
| Villegas, Felix, REA | 1.000 | 31 | 1 | 10 | 0 | 11 | 1 |
| Villegas, Francisco, TRE | .833 | 20 | 3 | 2 | 1 | 6 | 0 |
| Wagner, Billy, REA* | .000 | 1 | 0 | 0 | 0 | 0 | 0 |
| Walk, Mitch, NRW* | 1.000 | 47 | 4 | 20 | 0 | 24 | 1 |
| Wang, Chien-Ming, TRE | 1.000 | 18 | 4 | 18 | 0 | 22 | 2 |
| Ward, Jeremy, TRE | .750 | 41 | 3 | 6 | 3 | 12 | 1 |
| Warden, Jim Ed, AKR | .000 | 4 | 0 | 0 | 0 | 0 | 0 |
| Weatherby, Charles, PRT | 1.000 | 9 | 1 | 3 | 0 | 4 | 0 |
| Wickman, Bob, AKR | .000 | 1 | 0 | 0 | 0 | 0 | 0 |
| Wiggins, Scott, TRE* | 1.000 | 16 | 0 | 2 | 0 | 2 | 0 |
| Wilken, Kris, BOW | .000 | 1 | 0 | 0 | 0 | 0 | 0 |
| Wilson, Jeff, BOW* | 1.000 | 10 | 2 | 2 | 0 | 4 | 0 |
| Wolfe, Brian, NBR | 1.000 | 7 | 1 | 3 | 0 | 4 | 0 |
| Woodyard, Mark, ERI | 1.000 | 43 | 8 | 13 | 0 | 21 | 2 |
| Young, Colin, PRT* | 1.000 | 36 | 4 | 7 | 0 | 11 | 0 |
| Zink, Charlie, PRT | .963 | 18 | 10 | 16 | 1 | 27 | 3 |
| Zumaya, Joel, ERI | .667 | 4 | 2 | 0 | 1 | 3 | 0 |

## LEAGUE CHAMPIONS

| Year | Team | Pct. |
|---|---|---|
| 1923— | Williamsport | .661 |
| 1924— | Williamsport | .654 |
| 1925— | York§ | .583 |
| | Williamsport§ | .583 |
| 1926— | Scranton | .627 |
| 1927— | Harrisburg | .630 |
| 1928— | Harrisburg | .603 |
| 1929— | Binghamton | .597 |
| 1930— | Wilkes-Barre | .572 |
| 1931— | Harrisburg | .597 |
| 1932— | Wilkes-Barre | .561 |
| 1933— | Binghamton | .690 |
| 1934— | Binghamton | .694 |
| | Williamsport* | .603 |
| 1935— | Scranton | .657 |
| | Binghamton* | .580 |
| 1936— | Scranton* | .609 |
| | Elmira | .629 |
| 1937— | Elmira† | .622 |
| 1938— | Binghamton | .622 |
| | Elmira (3rd)‡ | .522 |
| 1939— | Scranton† | .571 |
| 1940— | Scranton | .568 |
| | Binghamton (2nd)‡ | .554 |
| 1941— | Wilkes-Barre | .630 |
| | Elmira (3rd)‡ | .514 |
| 1942— | Albany | .600 |
| | Scranton (2nd)‡ | .593 |
| 1943— | Scranton | .630 |
| | Elmira (2nd)‡ | .568 |
| 1944— | Hartford | .723 |
| | Binghamton (4th)‡ | .474 |
| 1945— | Utica | .615 |
| | Albany (3rd)‡ | .564 |
| 1946— | Scranton† | .691 |
| 1947— | Utica† | .652 |
| 1948— | Scranton† | .636 |
| 1949— | Albany | .664 |
| | Binghamton (4th)‡ | .500 |
| 1950— | Wilkes-Barre‡ | .652 |
| 1951— | Wilkes-Barre‡ | .612 |
| | Scranton (2nd)† | .562 |
| 1952— | Albany | .603 |
| | Binghamton (2nd)‡ | .562 |
| 1953— | Reading | .682 |
| | Binghamton (2nd)‡ | .636 |
| 1954— | Wilkes-Barre | .576 |
| | Albany (3rd)‡ | .540 |
| 1955— | Reading | .613 |
| | Allentown (2nd)‡ | .565 |
| 1956— | Schenectady† | .609 |
| 1957— | Binghamton | .607 |
| | Reading (3rd)‡ | .529 |
| 1958— | Lancaster∞ | .568 |
| | Binghamton (6th)‡ | .493 |
| 1959— | Springfield† | .607 |
| 1960— | Williamsport▲ | .551 |
| | Springfield (3rd)▲ | .496 |
| 1961— | Springfield | .612 |
| 1962— | Williamsport | .593 |
| | Elmira (2nd)‡ | .514 |
| 1963— | Charleston | .593 |
| 1964— | Elmira | .586 |
| 1965— | Pittsfield | .607 |
| 1966— | Elmira | .633 |
| 1967— | Binghamton◆ | .586 |
| | Elmira | .532 |
| 1968— | Pittsfield | .604 |
| | Reading (2nd)‡ | .579 |
| 1969— | York | .640 |
| 1970— | Waterbury■ | .560 |
| | Reading■ | .553 |
| 1971— | Three Rivers | .569 |
| | Elmira▼ | .561 |
| 1972— | West Haven▼ | .600 |
| | Three Rivers | .559 |
| 1973— | Reading▼ | .551 |
| | Pittsfield | .551 |
| 1974— | Thetford Miners (2nd)• | .536 |
| | Pittsfield (2nd) | .496 |
| 1975— | Reading | .613 |
| | Bristol* | .587 |
| 1976— | Three Rivers | .601 |
| | West Haven†† | .576 |
| 1977— | West Haven‡‡ | .623 |
| | Three Rivers | .551 |
| 1978— | Reading | .642 |
| | Bristol* | .580 |
| 1979— | West Haven§§ | .597 |
| 1980— | Holyoke* | .561 |
| | Waterbury | .540 |
| 1981— | Glens Falls | .615 |
| | Bristol* | .577 |
| 1982— | West Haven* | .614 |
| | Lynn | .590 |
| 1983— | Lynn | .554 |
| | New Britain‡ | .518 |
| 1984— | Waterbury | .543 |
| | Vermont‡ | .536 |
| 1985— | Albany | .540 |
| | Vermont‡ | .514 |
| 1986— | Reading | .566 |
| | Vermont‡ | .554 |
| 1987— | Pittsfield | .630 |
| | Harrisburg‡ | .550 |
| 1988— | Glens Falls | .584 |
| | Albany‡ | .522 |
| 1989— | Albany‡ | .657 |
| | Harrisburg | .522 |
| 1990— | Albany | .568 |
| | London‡ | .547 |
| 1991— | Harrisburg | .621 |
| | Albany‡ | .543 |
| 1992— | Canton/Akron | .580 |
| | Binghamton‡ | .572 |
| 1993— | Harrisburg‡ | .681 |
| | Canton/Akron | .543 |
| 1994— | Harrisburg | .633 |
| | Binghamton‡ | .582 |
| 1995— | New Haven | .556 |
| | Reading‡ | .514 |
| 1996— | Portland | .589 |
| | Harrisburg‡ | .521 |
| 1997— | Harrisburg‡ | .606 |
| | Portland | .556 |
| 1998— | New Britain | .585 |
| | Harrisburg‡ | .514 |
| 1999— | Trenton | .648 |
| | Harrisburg‡ | .535 |

| Year | Team | Pct. |
|---|---|---|
| 2000— | Reading | .599 |
| | New Haven‡ | .577 |
| 2001— | New Britain∞∞ | .613 |
| | Reading∞∞ | .542 |
| 2002— | Akron | .660 |
| | Norwich‡ | .543 |
| 2003— | Akron† | .624 |
| 2004— | New Hampshire‡ | .596 |

*Won split-season playoff. †Won championship and four-team playoff. ‡Won four-team playoff. §Tied for pennant, York winning playoff. ∞League was divided into Northern, Southern divisions and played a split season; Lancaster was overall season leader. ▲Playoff finals canceled after one game because of rain with Williamsport and Springfield declared playoff co-champions. ◆League was divided into Eastern, Western divisions; Binghamton won playoff. ■Tied for pennant, Waterbury winning playoff. ▼League was divided into American, National divisions; won playoff. •League was divided into American and National divisions; won four-team playoff. ††League was divided into Northern, Southern divisions, won playoff. ‡‡League was divided into New England and Canadian-American divisions; won playoff. §§Won both halves of split season (no playoffs). ∞∞Were entering finals of four-team playoff and were declared co-champions when Professional Baseball declared a stoppage of play. (NOTE—Known as New York-Pennsylvania League prior to 1938.)

# SOUTHERN LEAGUE

## LEAGUE OFFICE

**President**
Don Mincher
**Vice president/operations**
Lori Webb

**Media coordinator**
Jason Risley
**Address**
2551 Roswell Road, Suite 330
Marietta, GA 30062

**Phone**
770-321-0400

## TEAMS

### BIRMINGHAM BARONS

**General manager**
Jonathan Nelson
**Manager**
Razor Shines
**Ballpark (capacity, surface)**
Hoover Metropolitan Stadium (10,800, grass)
**Affiliation**
White Sox
**Address**
P.O. Box 360007
Birmingham, AL 35236
**Phone**
205-988-3200

### CAROLINA MUDCATS

**General manager**
Joe Kremer
**Manager**
Gary Allenson
**Ballpark (capacity, surface)**
Five County Stadium (6,500, grass)
**Affiliation**
Marlins
**Address**
P.O. Drawer 1218
Zebulon, NC 27597
**Phone**
919-269-2287

### CHATTANOOGA LOOKOUTS

**President/general manager**
J. Frank Burke
**Manager**
Jayhawk Owens
**Ballpark (capacity, surface)**
BellSouth Park (6,100, grass)
**Affiliation**
Reds
**Address**
201 Power Alley
Chattanooga, TN 37402
**Phone**
423-267-2208

### HUNTSVILLE STARS

**General manager**
Bryan Dingo
**Manager**
Don Money
**Ballpark (capacity, surface)**
Joe W. Davis Stadium (10,400, grass)
**Affiliation**
Brewers
**Address**
3125 Leeman Ferry Road
Huntsville, AL 35801
**Phone**
256-882-2562

### JACKSONVILLE SUNS

**Vice president/general manager**
Peter Bragan Jr.
**Manager**
John Shoemaker
**Ballpark (capacity, surface)**
Baseball Grounds of Jacksonville (11,000, grass)
**Affiliation**
Dodgers
**Address**
301 A. Philip Randolph Blvd.
Jacksonville FL 32202
**Phone**
904-358-2846

### MISSISSIPPI BRAVES

**General manager**
Steve DeSalvo
**Manager**
Brian Snitker
**Ballpark (capacity, surface)**
Mississippi Braves Stadium (6,006, grass)
**Affiliation**
Braves
**Address**
P.O. Box 97389
Pearl, MS 39288
**Phone**
888-272-8374

### MOBILE BAYBEARS

**President/general manager**
Bill Shanahan
**Manager**
Gary Jones
**Ballpark (capacity, surface)**
Hank Aaron Stadium (6,000, grass)
**Affiliation**
Padres
**Address**
755 Bolling Brothers Blvd.
Mobile, AL 36606
**Phone**
251-479-2327

### MONTGOMERY BISCUITS

**General manager/operations**
Greg Rauch
**Manager**
Charlie Montoyo
**Ballpark (capacity, surface)**
Montgomery Riverwalk Stadium (7,000, grass)
**Affiliation**
Devil Rays
**Address**
200 Coosa St.
Montgomery, AL 36104
**Phone**
334-323-2255

### TENNESSEE SMOKIES

**General manager**
Brian Cox
**Manager**
Tony Perezchica
**Ballpark (capacity, surface)**
Smokies Park (6,000, grass)
**Affiliation**
Diamondbacks
**Address**
3540 Line Drive
Kodak, TN 37764
**Phone**
865-637-9494

### WEST TENN DIAMOND JAXX

**General manager**
Jeff Parker
**Manager**
Bobby Dickerson
**Ballpark (capacity, surface)**
Pringles Park (6,000, grass)
**Affiliation**
Cubs
**Address**
4 Fun Place
Jackson, TN 38305
**Phone**
731-664-2020

# 2004 FINAL STANDINGS

## FIRST HALF

### EAST DIVISION

| Team | W | L | T | Pct. | GB |
|---|---|---|---|---|---|
| Tennessee (Cardinals) | 39 | 31 | - | .557 | ... |
| Chattanooga (Reds) | 38 | 32 | - | .543 | 1.0 |
| Carolina (Marlins) | 37 | 33 | - | .529 | 2.0 |
| Jacksonville (Dodgers) | 35 | 34 | - | .507 | 3.5 |
| Greenville (Braves) | 26 | 43 | - | .377 | 12.5 |

### WEST DIVISION

| Team | W | L | T | Pct. | GB |
|---|---|---|---|---|---|
| Mobile (Padres) | 40 | 30 | - | .571 | ... |
| West Tenn (Cubs) | 37 | 32 | - | .536 | 2.5 |
| Birmingham (White Sox) | 35 | 34 | - | .507 | 4.5 |
| Huntsville (Brewers) | 32 | 38 | - | .457 | 8.0 |
| Montgomery (Devil Rays) | 29 | 41 | - | .414 | 11.0 |

## SECOND HALF

### EAST DIVISION

| Team | W | L | T | Pct. | GB |
|---|---|---|---|---|---|
| Chattanooga (Reds) | 49 | 21 | - | .700 | ... |
| Greenville (Braves) | 37 | 33 | - | .529 | 12.0 |
| Carolina (Marlins) | 36 | 33 | - | .522 | 12.5 |
| Jacksonville (Dodgers) | 31 | 37 | - | .456 | 17.0 |
| Tennessee (Cardinals) | 30 | 40 | - | .429 | 19.0 |

### WEST DIVISION

| Team | W | L | T | Pct. | GB |
|---|---|---|---|---|---|
| Birmingham (White Sox) | 38 | 32 | - | .543 | ... |
| West Tenn (Cubs) | 33 | 36 | - | .478 | 4.5 |
| Huntsville (Brewers) | 33 | 37 | - | .471 | 5.0 |
| Mobile (Padres) | 33 | 37 | - | .471 | 5.0 |
| Montgomery (Devil Rays) | 28 | 42 | - | .400 | 10.0 |

## COMPOSITE

| Team | W | L | T | PCT | GB | CNG | BIR | CAR | MOB | WTE | TEN | JAX | HVL | GRV | MON |
|---|---|---|---|---|---|---|---|---|---|---|---|---|---|---|---|
| Chattanooga (Reds) | 87 | 53 | - | .621 | ... | X | 9 | 16 | 3 | 6 | 12 | 13 | 7 | 15 | 6 |
| Birmingham (White Sox) | 73 | 66 | - | .525 | 131/2 | 3 | X | 3 | 14 | 14 | 4 | 6 | 14 | 3 | 13 |
| Carolina (Marlins) | 73 | 66 | - | .525 | 131/2 | 11 | 4 | X | 3 | 6 | 15 | 11 | 5 | 14 | 4 |
| Mobile (Padres) | 73 | 67 | - | .521 | 14 | 5 | 6 | 5 | X | 12 | 5 | 7 | 11 | 5 | 17 |
| West Tenn (Cubs) | 70 | 68 | - | .507 | 16 | 2 | 10 | 6 | 10 | X | 7 | 3 | 15 | 1 | 16 |
| Tennessee (Cardinals) | 69 | 71 | - | .493 | 18 | 10 | 4 | 13 | 6 | 5 | X | 8 | 6 | 13 | 4 |
| Jacksonville (Dodgers) | 66 | 71 | - | .482 | 191/2 | 7 | 5 | 11 | 9 | 3 | 8 | X | 4 | 15 | 4 |
| Huntsville (Brewers) | 65 | 75 | - | .464 | 22 | 5 | 10 | 2 | 13 | 9 | 5 | 4 | X | 3 | 14 |
| Greenville (Braves) | 63 | 76 | - | .453 | 231/2 | 8 | 5 | 6 | 3 | 6 | 11 | 15 | 4 | X | 5 |
| Montgomery (Devil Rays) | 57 | 83 | - | .407 | 30 | 2 | 13 | 4 | 6 | 8 | 4 | 4 | 9 | 7 | X |

Major league affiliations in parentheses.

PLAYOFFS: Mobile defeated Birmingham, three games to one; Tennessee defeated Chattanooga, three games to one; championship final cancelled due to weather, Mobile and Tennessee declared co-champions.

REGULAR-SEASON ATTENDANCE: Birmingham, 280,873; Carolina, 245,810; Chattanooga, 244,960; Greenville, 143,443; Huntsville, 180,506; Jacksonville, 420,495; Mobile, 193,885; Montgomery, 322,946; Tennessee, 251,282; West Tennessee, 159,308. Total attendance—2,443,508. All-Star game at Bell South Park—5,857.

MANAGERS: Birmingham, Razor Shines; Carolina, Ron Hassey; Chattanooga, Jayhawk Owens; Greenville, Brian Snitker; Huntsville, Frank Kremblas; Jacksonville, Dino Ebel; Mobile, Gary Jones; Montgomery, Charlie Montoyo; Tennessee, Mark DeJohn; West Tenn, Bobby Dickerson.

ALL-STAR TEAM: 1B—Jesse Gutierrez, Chattanooga; 2B—Richard Lewis, West Tenn; 3B—Edwin Encarnacion, Chattanooga; SS—Josh Wilson, Carolina; OF—Skip Schumaker, Tennessee; OF—Adam Stern, Greenville; OF—Napoleon Calzado, Greenville; OF—Brad Nelson, Huntsville; C—Josh Willingham, Carolina; DH—Greg Sain, Mobile; Utility—William Bergolla, Chattanooga; RHP—Brian Rose, Chattanooga; LHP—Renyel Pinto, West Tenn; Relief pitcher—Brad Baker, Mobile; Most Valuable Player—Richard Lewis, West Tenn; Most Outstanding Pitcher—Brad Baker, Mobile; Manager of the Year—Jayhawk Owens, Chattanooga.

# 2004 BATTING

## TEAM

| Team | G | TPA | AB | R | H | TB | 2B | 3B | HR | RBI | SH | SF | HP | BB | IBB | SO | SB | CS | GDP | LOB | ShO | Avg. | OBP | Slg. |
|---|---|---|---|---|---|---|---|---|---|---|---|---|---|---|---|---|---|---|---|---|---|---|---|---|
| Chattanooga | 140 | ---- | 4775 | 688 | 1318 | 1997 | 285 | 32 | 110 | 628 | 76 | 39 | 46 | 473 | 37 | 963 | 128 | 38 | 94 | --- | --- | .276 | .344 | .418 |
| Greenville | 139 | ---- | 4694 | 593 | 1268 | 1963 | 254 | 33 | 125 | 551 | 60 | 37 | 38 | 409 | 31 | 1045 | 106 | 62 | 66 | --- | --- | .270 | .331 | .418 |
| West Tenn | 138 | ---- | 4446 | 619 | 1177 | 1801 | 232 | 61 | 90 | 572 | 56 | 50 | 67 | 433 | 28 | 1047 | 116 | 72 | 63 | --- | --- | .265 | .336 | .405 |
| Birmingham | 139 | ---- | 4628 | 635 | 1214 | 1839 | 224 | 43 | 105 | 570 | 61 | 38 | 60 | 494 | 27 | 956 | 123 | 69 | 78 | --- | --- | .262 | .339 | .397 |
| Tennessee | 140 | ---- | 4593 | 634 | 1200 | 1870 | 237 | 23 | 129 | 593 | 37 | 29 | 45 | 525 | 37 | 1015 | 134 | 56 | 44 | --- | --- | .261 | .341 | .407 |
| Carolina | 139 | ---- | 4545 | 646 | 1170 | 1879 | 270 | 23 | 131 | 605 | 75 | 49 | 62 | 537 | 28 | 1080 | 126 | 57 | 74 | --- | --- | .257 | .341 | .413 |
| Montgomery | 140 | ---- | 4542 | 523 | 1148 | 1697 | 225 | 42 | 80 | 477 | 53 | 33 | 59 | 371 | 22 | 1001 | 49 | 37 | 76 | --- | --- | .253 | .315 | .374 |
| Jacksonville | 137 | ---- | 4582 | 567 | 1145 | 1176 | 222 | 26 | 119 | 517 | 62 | 26 | 56 | 388 | 26 | 1088 | 84 | 62 | 66 | --- | --- | .250 | .315 | .388 |
| Huntsville | 140 | ---- | 4497 | 510 | 1085 | 1618 | 219 | 25 | 88 | 457 | 38 | 37 | 75 | 438 | 31 | 998 | 128 | 91 | 57 | --- | --- | .241 | .317 | .360 |
| Mobile | 140 | ---- | 4529 | 601 | 1091 | 1749 | 212 | 25 | 132 | 556 | 58 | 41 | 66 | 461 | 23 | 1140 | 78 | 45 | 32 | --- | --- | .241 | .317 | .386 |

## INDIVIDUAL

### TOP QUALIFIERS FOR BATTING CHAMPIONSHIP

Minimum 378 plate appearances. *Lefthanded batter. †Switch-hitter.

| Player, Team | G | TPA | AB | R | H | TB | 2B | 3B | HR | RBI | SH | SF | HP | BB | IBB | SO | SB | CS | GDP | Avg. | OBP | Slg. |
|---|---|---|---|---|---|---|---|---|---|---|---|---|---|---|---|---|---|---|---|---|---|---|
| Calzado, Napoleon, Greenville | 119 | 485 | 449 | 68 | 161 | 227 | 28 | 7 | 8 | 59 | 2 | 4 | 8 | 22 | 1 | 59 | 18 | 8 | 10 | .359 | .395 | .506 |
| Lewis, Richard, West Tenn | 99 | 425 | 380 | 68 | 125 | 202 | 27 | 10 | 10 | 59 | 0 | 4 | 4 | 37 | 4 | 94 | 7 | 6 | 2 | .329 | .391 | .532 |
| Stern, Adam, Greenville * | 102 | 435 | 394 | 64 | 127 | 189 | 26 | 6 | 8 | 47 | 1 | 3 | 2 | 35 | 2 | 58 | 27 | 10 | 2 | .322 | .378 | .480 |
| Schumaker, Skip, Tennessee * | 138 | 583 | 516 | 78 | 163 | 216 | 29 | 6 | 4 | 43 | 4 | 1 | 2 | 60 | 3 | 61 | 19 | 14 | 7 | .316 | .389 | .419 |
| Hoffpauir, Micah, West Tenn | 94 | 381 | 340 | 58 | 104 | 169 | 20 | 6 | 11 | 75 | 1 | 12 | 1 | 27 | 6 | 61 | 1 | 4 | 4 | .306 | .347 | .497 |
| Spidale, Mike, Birmingham | 126 | 572 | 484 | 87 | 147 | 209 | 27 | 7 | 7 | 47 | 10 | 5 | 12 | 61 | 1 | 72 | 26 | 15 | 4 | .304 | .391 | .432 |

| Player, Team | G | TPA | AB | R | H | TB | 2B | 3B | HR | RBI | SH | SF | HP | BB | IBB | SO | SB | CS | GDP | Avg. | OBP | Slg. |
|---|---|---|---|---|---|---|---|---|---|---|---|---|---|---|---|---|---|---|---|---|---|---|
| Hall, Billy, Carolina † | 95 | 397 | 350 | 53 | 105 | 143 | 18 | 4 | 4 | 29 | 2 | 2 | 1 | 42 | 6 | 46 | 40 | 15 | 3 | .300 | .375 | .409 |
| Beattie, Andrew, Chattanooga † | 101 | 404 | 347 | 51 | 104 | 152 | 18 | 6 | 6 | 43 | 5 | 4 | 1 | 47 | 2 | 67 | 8 | 4 | 1 | .300 | .381 | .438 |
| Bolivar, Papo, Tennessee | 126 | 510 | 451 | 71 | 133 | 207 | 25 | 2 | 15 | 60 | 0 | 2 | 2 | 55 | 3 | 86 | 51 | 17 | 5 | .295 | .373 | .459 |
| Gutierrez, Jesse, Chattanooga | 127 | 542 | 487 | 74 | 142 | 233 | 32 | 4 | 17 | 82 | 0 | 6 | 13 | 36 | 3 | 64 | 0 | 0 | 14 | .292 | .352 | .478 |
| Duncan, Chris, Tennessee * | 120 | 455 | 387 | 57 | 112 | 183 | 23 | 0 | 16 | 65 | 0 | 1 | 3 | 64 | 8 | 94 | 8 | 4 | 6 | .289 | .393 | .473 |
| Weston, Aron, West Tenn * | 123 | 466 | 425 | 62 | 122 | 172 | 20 | 9 | 4 | 46 | 3 | 4 | 3 | 31 | 4 | 90 | 10 | 9 | 5 | .287 | .337 | .405 |
| Cortez, Fernando, Montgomery * | 94 | 400 | 359 | 51 | 103 | 142 | 20 | 5 | 3 | 30 | 6 | 2 | 1 | 32 | 1 | 60 | 7 | 7 | 3 | .287 | .345 | .396 |
| Bergolla, William, Chattanooga | 116 | 526 | 466 | 79 | 132 | 172 | 26 | 1 | 4 | 38 | 15 | 2 | 3 | 40 | 1 | 63 | 36 | 6 | 14 | .283 | .342 | .369 |
| Johnson, Kelly, Greenville * | 135 | 536 | 479 | 70 | 135 | 224 | 35 | 3 | 16 | 50 | 0 | 3 | 3 | 49 | 2 | 102 | 9 | 9 | 5 | .282 | .350 | .468 |

DEPARTMENTAL LEADERS: G—four players with 138; AB—Gwynn, 534; R—Spidale, 87; H—Schumaker, 163; TB—Fielder, 235; 2B—three players with 35; 3B—Bacon, 11; HR—Sain, 28; RBI—Barfield, 90; SH—Yan, 17; SF—Hoffpauir, 12; HP—Weeks, 28; BB—Willingham, 91; IBB—N/A; SO—Nelson, 146; SB—Bacon, 60; CS—Bacon, 20; GIDP—N/A; Slg.—Willingham, .565; OBP—Willingham, .449.

## ALL PLAYERS

*Lefthanded batter. †Switch-hitter.

| Player, Team | G | TPA | AB | R | H | TB | 2B | 3B | HR | RBI | SH | SF | HP | BB | IBB | SO | SB | CS | GDP | Avg. | OBP | Slg. |
|---|---|---|---|---|---|---|---|---|---|---|---|---|---|---|---|---|---|---|---|---|---|---|
| Adams, Brian, Huntsville * | 52 | 8 | 7 | 0 | 0 | 0 | 0 | 0 | 0 | 0 | 0 | 0 | 0 | 1 | 0 | 3 | 0 | 0 | 0 | .000 | .125 | .000 |
| Aguilar, Ray, Greenville † | 8 | 16 | 13 | 0 | 2 | 2 | 0 | 0 | 0 | 0 | 2 | 0 | 0 | 1 | 0 | 1 | 0 | 0 | 0 | .154 | .214 | .154 |
| Alvarado, Joel, Huntsville | 69 | 241 | 205 | 15 | 29 | 41 | 9 | 0 | 1 | 13 | 3 | 0 | 1 | 32 | 1 | 49 | 2 | 2 | 4 | .141 | .261 | .200 |
| Alvarez, Nick, Jacksonville | 80 | 239 | 217 | 30 | 54 | 86 | 11 | 0 | 7 | 29 | 1 | 0 | 4 | 17 | 0 | 32 | 5 | 3 | 6 | .249 | .315 | .396 |
| Ambres, Chip, Carolina | 137 | 546 | 452 | 81 | 109 | 203 | 28 | 3 | 20 | 62 | 4 | 8 | 6 | 76 | 2 | 117 | 26 | 9 | 7 | .241 | .352 | .449 |
| Anderson, Brian, Birmingham | 48 | 209 | 185 | 26 | 50 | 77 | 9 | 3 | 4 | 27 | 1 | 1 | 3 | 19 | 3 | 30 | 3 | 2 | 3 | .270 | .346 | .416 |
| Anderson, Bryan, Chattanooga | 35 | 77 | 61 | 7 | 17 | 26 | 7 | 1 | 0 | 9 | 3 | 3 | 0 | 10 | 0 | 16 | 0 | 0 | 1 | .279 | .365 | .426 |
| Anderson, Dennis, Carolina † | 91 | 256 | 221 | 15 | 51 | 69 | 10 | 1 | 2 | 29 | 2 | 4 | 2 | 27 | 2 | 44 | 1 | 1 | 3 | .231 | .315 | .312 |
| Arteaga, Josh, West Tenn | 82 | 250 | 224 | 20 | 49 | 78 | 18 | 1 | 3 | 27 | 4 | 4 | 4 | 14 | 0 | 59 | 1 | 1 | 0 | .219 | .272 | .348 |
| Axelson, Josh, Tennessee | 34 | 33 | 26 | 3 | 5 | 6 | 1 | 0 | 0 | 5 | 4 | 0 | 0 | 3 | 0 | 7 | 0 | 0 | 1 | .192 | .276 | .231 |
| Aybar, Willy, Jacksonville † | 126 | 537 | 482 | 56 | 133 | 205 | 27 | 0 | 15 | 77 | 0 | 2 | 3 | 50 | 4 | 77 | 8 | 10 | 11 | .276 | .346 | .425 |
| Bacon, Dwaine, West Tenn † | 129 | 541 | 444 | 80 | 110 | 151 | 10 | 11 | 3 | 32 | 5 | 2 | 9 | 81 | 2 | 139 | 60 | 20 | 2 | .248 | .373 | .340 |
| Baez, Benito, Chattanooga * | 12 | 1 | 1 | 0 | 0 | 0 | 0 | 0 | 0 | 0 | 0 | 0 | 0 | 0 | 0 | 1 | 0 | 0 | 0 | .000 | .000 | .000 |
| Baker, Ryan, Carolina | 40 | 7 | 6 | 0 | 1 | 1 | 0 | 0 | 0 | 0 | 0 | 0 | 0 | 1 | 0 | 2 | 0 | 0 | 1 | .167 | .286 | .167 |
| Bannon, Jeff, Chattanooga | 134 | 528 | 473 | 68 | 119 | 193 | 31 | 2 | 13 | 73 | 2 | 6 | 4 | 43 | 4 | 111 | 5 | 2 | 7 | .252 | .316 | .408 |
| Barfield, Josh, Mobile | 138 | 581 | 521 | 79 | 129 | 217 | 28 | 3 | 18 | 90 | 0 | 7 | 5 | 48 | 4 | 119 | 4 | 2 | 6 | .248 | .313 | .417 |
| Barnwell, Chris, Huntsville | 138 | 543 | 484 | 43 | 119 | 169 | 24 | 4 | 6 | 51 | 5 | 6 | 12 | 36 | 3 | 76 | 11 | 14 | 3 | .246 | .310 | .349 |
| Bauer, Greg, Tennessee | 10 | 1 | 1 | 0 | 0 | 0 | 0 | 0 | 0 | 0 | 0 | 0 | 0 | 0 | 0 | 1 | 0 | 0 | 0 | .000 | .000 | .000 |
| Bauer, Peter, Carolina * | 27 | 45 | 38 | 0 | 3 | 3 | 0 | 0 | 0 | 0 | 3 | 0 | 0 | 4 | 0 | 19 | 0 | 0 | 1 | .079 | .167 | .079 |
| Beattie, Andrew, Chattanooga † | 101 | 404 | 347 | 51 | 104 | 152 | 18 | 6 | 6 | 43 | 5 | 4 | 1 | 47 | 2 | 67 | 8 | 4 | 1 | .300 | .381 | .438 |
| Becker, Brian, Birmingham | 25 | 104 | 93 | 14 | 22 | 42 | 8 | 0 | 4 | 17 | 0 | 3 | 0 | 8 | 0 | 21 | 0 | 0 | 4 | .237 | .288 | .452 |
| Beech, Matt, Chattanooga * | 6 | 2 | 2 | 0 | 0 | 0 | 0 | 0 | 0 | 0 | 0 | 0 | 0 | 0 | 0 | 1 | 0 | 0 | 0 | .000 | .000 | .000 |
| Bellorin, Edwin, Jacksonville | 86 | 310 | 285 | 27 | 80 | 100 | 15 | 1 | 1 | 30 | 2 | 1 | 4 | 18 | 0 | 51 | 1 | 0 | 5 | .281 | .331 | .351 |
| Bergolla, William, Chattanooga | 116 | 526 | 466 | 79 | 132 | 172 | 26 | 1 | 4 | 38 | 15 | 2 | 3 | 40 | 1 | 63 | 36 | 6 | 14 | .283 | .342 | .369 |
| Bikowski, Scott, Birmingham * | 73 | 305 | 257 | 48 | 79 | 111 | 15 | 1 | 5 | 40 | 1 | 1 | 1 | 45 | 4 | 48 | 4 | 3 | 6 | .307 | .411 | .432 |
| Billingsley, Chad, Jacksonville | 8 | 16 | 12 | 2 | 0 | 0 | 0 | 0 | 0 | 1 | 3 | 0 | 0 | 1 | 0 | 5 | 0 | 0 | 0 | .000 | .077 | .000 |
| Blair, Tom, Tennessee * | 3 | 3 | 3 | 0 | 1 | 1 | 0 | 0 | 0 | 0 | 0 | 0 | 0 | 0 | 0 | 0 | 0 | 0 | 0 | .333 | .333 | .333 |
| Blanco, Tony, Chattanooga | 58 | 237 | 220 | 25 | 54 | 100 | 8 | 1 | 12 | 31 | 0 | 0 | 2 | 15 | 2 | 53 | 0 | 0 | 8 | .245 | .300 | .455 |
| Blasdell, Jared, West Tenn | 49 | 6 | 6 | 0 | 0 | 0 | 0 | 0 | 0 | 0 | 0 | 0 | 0 | 0 | 0 | 5 | 0 | 0 | 0 | .000 | .000 | .000 |
| Blasko, Chadd, West Tenn | 13 | 20 | 18 | 2 | 6 | 7 | 1 | 0 | 0 | 1 | 1 | 0 | 0 | 1 | 0 | 9 | 0 | 0 | 0 | .333 | .368 | .389 |
| Bolivar, Papo, Tennessee | 126 | 510 | 451 | 71 | 133 | 207 | 25 | 2 | 15 | 60 | 0 | 2 | 2 | 55 | 3 | 86 | 51 | 17 | 5 | .295 | .373 | .459 |
| Booker, Chris, Chattanooga | 28 | 1 | 1 | 0 | 0 | 0 | 0 | 0 | 0 | 0 | 0 | 0 | 0 | 0 | 0 | 1 | 0 | 0 | 0 | .000 | .000 | .000 |
| Bott, Glenn, Jacksonville * | 28 | 39 | 35 | 0 | 3 | 3 | 0 | 0 | 0 | 1 | 3 | 0 | 0 | 1 | 0 | 10 | 0 | 0 | 0 | .086 | .111 | .086 |
| Bowser, Matt, Montgomery * | 16 | 58 | 53 | 5 | 6 | 10 | 4 | 0 | 0 | 6 | 0 | 0 | 0 | 5 | 0 | 13 | 0 | 0 | 2 | .113 | .190 | .189 |
| Brewer, Jace, Montgomery | 110 | 441 | 404 | 44 | 102 | 156 | 18 | 3 | 10 | 49 | 14 | 1 | 3 | 19 | 1 | 78 | 1 | 3 | 11 | .252 | .290 | .386 |
| Brownlie, Bobby, West Tenn | 26 | 33 | 29 | 0 | 4 | 4 | 0 | 0 | 0 | 2 | 4 | 0 | 0 | 0 | 0 | 8 | 0 | 0 | 0 | .138 | .138 | .138 |
| Butler, Brent, Greenville | 70 | 221 | 196 | 22 | 48 | 69 | 9 | 0 | 4 | 23 | 0 | 3 | 2 | 19 | 0 | 34 | 0 | 1 | 3 | .245 | .314 | .352 |
| Calzado, Napoleon, Greenville | 119 | 485 | 449 | 68 | 161 | 227 | 28 | 7 | 8 | 59 | 2 | 4 | 8 | 22 | 1 | 59 | 18 | 8 | 10 | .359 | .395 | .506 |
| Caraccioli, Lance, Chattanooga * | 13 | 9 | 7 | 0 | 1 | 2 | 1 | 0 | 0 | 0 | 2 | 0 | 0 | 0 | 0 | 2 | 0 | 0 | 0 | .143 | .143 | .286 |
| Cassel, Jack, Mobile | 57 | 3 | 2 | 1 | 0 | 0 | 0 | 0 | 0 | 0 | 0 | 0 | 0 | 1 | 0 | 1 | 0 | 0 | 0 | .000 | .333 | .000 |
| Castellanos, Hugo, West Tenn | 22 | 2 | 2 | 0 | 0 | 0 | 0 | 0 | 0 | 0 | 0 | 0 | 0 | 0 | 0 | 2 | 0 | 0 | 0 | .000 | .000 | .000 |
| Castro, Nelson, Jacksonville † | 118 | 439 | 399 | 48 | 97 | 151 | 15 | 3 | 11 | 45 | 6 | 0 | 5 | 29 | 5 | 99 | 17 | 7 | 6 | .243 | .303 | .378 |
| Cedeno, Ronny, West Tenn | 116 | 432 | 384 | 39 | 107 | 154 | 19 | 5 | 6 | 48 | 8 | 8 | 8 | 24 | 3 | 74 | 10 | 10 | 10 | .279 | .328 | .401 |
| Chavez, Ozzie, Huntsville † | 85 | 296 | 269 | 18 | 57 | 75 | 10 | 1 | 2 | 18 | 3 | 2 | 1 | 21 | 5 | 59 | 1 | 4 | 4 | .212 | .270 | .279 |
| Childress, Daylan, Chattanooga | 29 | 16 | 14 | 0 | 0 | 0 | 0 | 0 | 0 | 0 | 1 | 0 | 0 | 1 | 0 | 10 | 0 | 0 | 0 | .000 | .067 | .000 |
| Clark, Aaron, Montgomery * | 115 | 326 | 299 | 36 | 60 | 113 | 12 | 4 | 11 | 28 | 2 | 0 | 5 | 20 | 1 | 113 | 3 | 1 | 2 | .201 | .262 | .378 |
| Clements, Jason, Mobile † | 99 | 270 | 233 | 33 | 62 | 80 | 7 | 1 | 3 | 21 | 5 | 1 | 5 | 25 | 1 | 63 | 5 | 1 | 2 | .266 | .348 | .343 |
| Coenen, Matt, Greenville * | 36 | 19 | 16 | 2 | 3 | 6 | 0 | 0 | 1 | 3 | 2 | 0 | 0 | 1 | 0 | 7 | 0 | 0 | 0 | .188 | .235 | .375 |
| Connolly, Jon, West Tenn | 1 | 3 | 3 | 0 | 0 | 0 | 0 | 0 | 0 | 1 | 0 | 0 | 0 | 0 | 0 | 1 | 0 | 0 | 0 | .000 | .000 | .000 |
| Cook, Jeremy, Tennessee | 29 | 40 | 36 | 1 | 3 | 3 | 0 | 0 | 0 | 0 | 3 | 0 | 1 | 0 | 0 | 17 | 0 | 0 | 0 | .083 | .108 | .083 |
| Cortez, Fernando, Montgomery * | 94 | 400 | 359 | 51 | 103 | 142 | 20 | 5 | 3 | 30 | 6 | 2 | 1 | 32 | 1 | 60 | 7 | 7 | 3 | .287 | .345 | .396 |
| Costello, Ryan, Huntsville | 24 | 27 | 25 | 1 | 2 | 2 | 0 | 0 | 0 | 0 | 2 | 0 | 0 | 0 | 0 | 12 | 0 | 0 | 0 | .080 | .080 | .080 |
| Craig, Matt, West Tenn † | 112 | 430 | 375 | 63 | 103 | 191 | 20 | 4 | 20 | 62 | 0 | 2 | 4 | 49 | 2 | 101 | 3 | 2 | 8 | .275 | .363 | .509 |
| Crawford, Paxton, Chattanooga | 18 | 2 | 2 | 0 | 1 | 1 | 0 | 0 | 0 | 0 | 0 | 0 | 0 | 0 | 0 | 0 | 0 | 0 | 0 | .500 | .500 | .500 |
| Creighton, Matt, West Tenn | 76 | 248 | 233 | 29 | 58 | 89 | 18 | 2 | 3 | 25 | 0 | 0 | 7 | 8 | 1 | 45 | 2 | 0 | 5 | .249 | .294 | .382 |
| Cresse, Brad, Tennessee | 49 | 188 | 164 | 25 | 48 | 87 | 12 | 0 | 9 | 27 | 0 | 2 | 2 | 20 | 2 | 41 | 0 | 0 | 0 | .293 | .372 | .530 |
| Curtis, Daniel, Greenville | 33 | 29 | 21 | 3 | 4 | 4 | 0 | 0 | 0 | 2 | 2 | 1 | 0 | 5 | 0 | 8 | 0 | 0 | 0 | .190 | .333 | .190 |
| Darula, Bobby, Chattanooga * | 48 | 173 | 153 | 38 | 56 | 82 | 8 | 0 | 6 | 27 | 2 | 1 | 1 | 16 | 3 | 16 | 8 | 2 | 5 | .366 | .427 | .536 |
| Davies, Kyle, Greenville | 11 | 24 | 22 | 0 | 4 | 4 | 0 | 0 | 0 | 0 | 2 | 0 | 0 | 0 | 0 | 5 | 0 | 0 | 1 | .182 | .182 | .182 |
| DeHart, Casey, Chattanooga * | 49 | 12 | 11 | 1 | 5 | 6 | 1 | 0 | 0 | 2 | 0 | 0 | 0 | 1 | 0 | 2 | 0 | 0 | 0 | .455 | .500 | .545 |
| DeMent, Dan, Montgomery | 98 | 379 | 336 | 45 | 86 | 149 | 25 | 7 | 8 | 34 | 5 | 5 | 3 | 30 | 2 | 82 | 1 | 2 | 5 | .256 | .318 | .443 |
| Demarco, Matt, Carolina * | 106 | 404 | 359 | 47 | 98 | 138 | 24 | 2 | 4 | 45 | 12 | 6 | 7 | 20 | 1 | 51 | 1 | 5 | 6 | .273 | .319 | .384 |
| Denorfia, Chris, Chattanooga | 61 | 256 | 221 | 30 | 55 | 87 | 10 | 2 | 6 | 27 | 3 | 1 | 1 | 30 | 1 | 42 | 5 | 2 | 1 | .249 | .340 | .394 |
| Donovan, Todd, Mobile | 52 | 234 | 201 | 38 | 60 | 79 | 7 | 3 | 2 | 19 | 1 | 2 | 6 | 24 | 0 | 44 | 20 | 9 | 1 | .299 | .386 | .393 |
| Dowdy, Brett, Jacksonville | 36 | 75 | 66 | 9 | 18 | 21 | 1 | 1 | 0 | 5 | 0 | 1 | 0 | 8 | 0 | 20 | 0 | 0 | 1 | .273 | .347 | .318 |
| Duncan, Chris, Tennessee * | 120 | 455 | 387 | 57 | 112 | 183 | 23 | 0 | 16 | 65 | 0 | 1 | 3 | 64 | 8 | 94 | 8 | 4 | 6 | .289 | .393 | .473 |

| Player, Team | G | TPA | AB | R | H | TB | 2B | 3B | HR | RBI | SH | SF | HP | BB | IBB | SO | SB | CS | GDP | Avg. | OBP | Slg. |
|---|---|---|---|---|---|---|---|---|---|---|---|---|---|---|---|---|---|---|---|---|---|---|
| Dzurilla, Mike, West Tenn | 120 | 436 | 381 | 49 | 93 | 145 | 21 | 5 | 7 | 59 | 0 | 4 | 6 | 45 | 0 | 54 | 5 | 8 | 5 | .244 | .330 | .381 |
| Ehrnsberger, Chad, Tennessee | 47 | 151 | 129 | 14 | 28 | 55 | 7 | 1 | 6 | 17 | 1 | 1 | 2 | 18 | 1 | 29 | 0 | 1 | 0 | .217 | .320 | .426 |
| Emiliano, Jamie, Greenville | 51 | 1 | 1 | 0 | 0 | 0 | 0 | 0 | 0 | 0 | 0 | 0 | 0 | 0 | 0 | 0 | 0 | 0 | 0 | .000 | .000 | .000 |
| Encarnacion, Edwin, Chattanooga | 120 | 526 | 469 | 73 | 132 | 208 | 35 | 1 | 13 | 76 | 1 | 3 | 0 | 53 | 3 | 79 | 17 | 3 | 5 | .281 | .352 | .443 |
| Erickson, Corey, Tennessee | 100 | 335 | 293 | 38 | 53 | 111 | 17 | 1 | 13 | 45 | 1 | 5 | 5 | 31 | 3 | 82 | 4 | 0 | 3 | .181 | .266 | .379 |
| Espada, Joe, Montgomery | 27 | 109 | 98 | 8 | 26 | 29 | 1 | 1 | 0 | 5 | 1 | 0 | 3 | 7 | 0 | 14 | 2 | 2 | 0 | .265 | .333 | .296 |
| Espy, Nate, Tennessee | 114 | 325 | 277 | 45 | 76 | 132 | 15 | 4 | 11 | 38 | 0 | 2 | 7 | 39 | 1 | 50 | 5 | 2 | 3 | .274 | .375 | .477 |
| Estrada, Kevin, Tennessee † | 2 | 4 | 4 | 0 | 0 | 0 | 0 | 0 | 0 | 0 | 0 | 0 | 0 | 0 | 0 | 1 | 0 | 0 | 0 | .000 | .000 | .000 |
| Evans, Lee, Greenville † | 21 | 81 | 72 | 7 | 15 | 30 | 3 | 0 | 4 | 14 | 0 | 2 | 1 | 6 | 0 | 26 | 1 | 0 | 0 | .208 | .272 | .417 |
| Eveland, Dana, Huntsville * | 4 | 5 | 5 | 0 | 0 | 0 | 0 | 0 | 0 | 0 | 0 | 0 | 0 | 0 | 0 | 3 | 0 | 0 | 0 | .000 | .000 | .000 |
| Fahrner, Evan, West Tenn | 58 | 3 | 2 | 0 | 0 | 0 | 0 | 0 | 0 | 1 | 1 | 0 | 0 | 0 | 0 | 1 | 0 | 0 | 0 | .000 | .000 | .000 |
| Fielder, Prince, Huntsville * | 135 | 577 | 497 | 70 | 135 | 235 | 29 | 1 | 23 | 78 | 0 | 4 | 11 | 65 | 6 | 93 | 11 | 7 | 11 | .272 | .366 | .473 |
| Flannery, Mike, Carolina | 25 | 4 | 2 | 0 | 1 | 1 | 0 | 0 | 0 | 0 | 2 | 0 | 0 | 0 | 0 | 1 | 0 | 0 | 0 | .500 | .500 | .500 |
| Flury, Pat, Carolina | 42 | 7 | 7 | 0 | 0 | 0 | 0 | 0 | 0 | 0 | 0 | 0 | 0 | 0 | 0 | 4 | 0 | 0 | 0 | .000 | .000 | .000 |
| Ford, Matt, Huntsville † | 21 | 20 | 20 | 0 | 0 | 0 | 0 | 0 | 0 | 0 | 0 | 0 | 0 | 0 | 0 | 9 | 0 | 0 | 0 | .000 | .000 | .000 |
| Franco, Iker, Montgomery | 63 | 205 | 187 | 17 | 39 | 54 | 6 | 0 | 3 | 14 | 2 | 0 | 1 | 15 | 0 | 32 | 1 | 0 | 3 | .209 | .271 | .289 |
| Francoeur, Jeff, Greenville | 18 | 76 | 76 | 8 | 15 | 26 | 2 | 0 | 3 | 9 | 0 | 0 | 0 | 0 | 0 | 14 | 1 | 0 | 0 | .197 | .197 | .342 |
| Fuell, Jerrod, Carolina | 17 | 1 | 1 | 0 | 0 | 0 | 0 | 0 | 0 | 0 | 0 | 0 | 0 | 0 | 0 | 1 | 0 | 0 | 0 | .000 | .000 | .000 |
| Fulchino, Jeff, Carolina | 17 | 37 | 29 | 1 | 2 | 6 | 1 | 0 | 1 | 1 | 6 | 0 | 0 | 2 | 0 | 19 | 0 | 0 | 1 | .069 | .129 | .207 |
| Gann, Jamie, Huntsville | 59 | 210 | 195 | 21 | 50 | 79 | 7 | 2 | 6 | 28 | 0 | 1 | 1 | 13 | 0 | 54 | 6 | 4 | 3 | .256 | .305 | .405 |
| Garcia, Sergio, Jacksonville | 83 | 199 | 169 | 24 | 43 | 58 | 3 | 0 | 4 | 18 | 3 | 1 | 3 | 23 | 0 | 40 | 4 | 2 | 0 | .254 | .352 | .343 |
| Gardner, Richie, Chattanooga | 11 | 18 | 16 | 1 | 2 | 2 | 0 | 0 | 0 | 0 | 2 | 0 | 0 | 0 | 0 | 8 | 0 | 0 | 0 | .125 | .125 | .125 |
| German, Amado, Montgomery † | 104 | 415 | 359 | 34 | 78 | 113 | 15 | 4 | 4 | 30 | 5 | 2 | 1 | 48 | 4 | 93 | 4 | 5 | 5 | .217 | .310 | .315 |
| Goelz, Jim, Carolina | 56 | 167 | 154 | 14 | 29 | 37 | 5 | 0 | 1 | 10 | 4 | 0 | 0 | 9 | 0 | 34 | 1 | 1 | 1 | .188 | .233 | .240 |
| Gomes, Joey, Montgomery | 25 | 96 | 89 | 12 | 24 | 37 | 7 | 0 | 2 | 8 | 0 | 1 | 0 | 6 | 0 | 17 | 0 | 0 | 3 | .270 | .313 | .416 |
| Gonzalez, Luis, Jacksonville * | 45 | 4 | 3 | 1 | 0 | 0 | 0 | 0 | 0 | 0 | 0 | 0 | 0 | 1 | 0 | 2 | 0 | 0 | 0 | .000 | .250 | .000 |
| Gorecki, Reid, Tennessee | 7 | 27 | 25 | 1 | 8 | 11 | 3 | 0 | 0 | 1 | 0 | 0 | 0 | 2 | 0 | 3 | 1 | 0 | 0 | .320 | .370 | .440 |
| Greenberg, Adam, West Tenn * | 32 | 133 | 112 | 22 | 31 | 51 | 7 | 2 | 3 | 10 | 2 | 2 | 3 | 14 | 1 | 30 | 3 | 0 | 1 | .277 | .366 | .455 |
| Grzecka, Casey, Carolina | 15 | 36 | 30 | 2 | 9 | 12 | 3 | 0 | 0 | 3 | 1 | 2 | 0 | 3 | 0 | 3 | 0 | 0 | 2 | .300 | .343 | .400 |
| Gutierrez, Jesse, Chattanooga | 127 | 542 | 487 | 74 | 142 | 233 | 32 | 4 | 17 | 82 | 0 | 6 | 13 | 36 | 3 | 64 | 0 | 0 | 14 | .292 | .352 | .478 |
| Guzman, Angel, West Tenn | 4 | 4 | 3 | 0 | 0 | 0 | 0 | 0 | 0 | 0 | 1 | 0 | 0 | 0 | 0 | 1 | 0 | 0 | 0 | .000 | .000 | .000 |
| Guzman, Joel, Jacksonville | 46 | 200 | 182 | 25 | 51 | 95 | 11 | 3 | 9 | 35 | 0 | 4 | 1 | 13 | 0 | 44 | 1 | 2 | 4 | .280 | .325 | .522 |
| Gwynn, Anthony, Huntsville * | 138 | 598 | 534 | 74 | 130 | 166 | 20 | 5 | 2 | 37 | 4 | 1 | 6 | 53 | 0 | 95 | 34 | 16 | 4 | .243 | .318 | .311 |
| Hall, Billy, Carolina † | 95 | 397 | 350 | 53 | 105 | 143 | 18 | 4 | 4 | 29 | 2 | 2 | 1 | 42 | 6 | 46 | 40 | 15 | 3 | .300 | .375 | .409 |
| Hamilton, Jon, Tennessee * | 114 | 349 | 316 | 37 | 76 | 111 | 15 | 1 | 6 | 32 | 3 | 2 | 0 | 28 | 2 | 73 | 16 | 5 | 3 | .241 | .301 | .351 |
| Harrison, Vince, Montgomery | 57 | 219 | 184 | 21 | 49 | 74 | 6 | 2 | 5 | 27 | 1 | 2 | 8 | 24 | 1 | 34 | 5 | 3 | 3 | .266 | .372 | .402 |
| Hensley, Clay, Mobile | 32 | 45 | 42 | 6 | 9 | 14 | 2 | 0 | 1 | 3 | 2 | 0 | 0 | 1 | 0 | 14 | 0 | 0 | 0 | .214 | .233 | .333 |
| Herr, Aaron, Greenville | 94 | 317 | 283 | 37 | 77 | 122 | 20 | 2 | 7 | 32 | 3 | 1 | 2 | 28 | 7 | 88 | 7 | 3 | 6 | .272 | .341 | .431 |
| Hill, Jason, Chattanooga | 78 | 261 | 232 | 30 | 69 | 94 | 16 | 0 | 3 | 30 | 4 | 4 | 1 | 20 | 1 | 32 | 1 | 0 | 9 | .297 | .350 | .405 |
| Hoffpauir, Micah, West Tenn | 94 | 381 | 340 | 58 | 104 | 169 | 20 | 6 | 11 | 75 | 1 | 12 | 1 | 27 | 6 | 61 | 1 | 4 | 4 | .306 | .347 | .497 |
| Holt, Daylan, Jacksonville | 75 | 196 | 178 | 22 | 38 | 78 | 8 | 1 | 10 | 22 | 0 | 1 | 2 | 15 | 1 | 49 | 2 | 0 | 0 | .213 | .281 | .438 |
| Hull, Eric, Jacksonville | 21 | 16 | 11 | 2 | 1 | 1 | 0 | 0 | 0 | 0 | 5 | 0 | 0 | 0 | 0 | 2 | 0 | 0 | 0 | .091 | .091 | .091 |
| Hutchinson, Trevor, Carolina | 24 | 34 | 31 | 1 | 6 | 7 | 1 | 0 | 0 | 2 | 2 | 0 | 0 | 1 | 0 | 10 | 0 | 0 | 0 | .194 | .219 | .226 |
| Iehl, Jay, Carolina | 4 | 4 | 3 | 0 | 0 | 0 | 0 | 0 | 0 | 0 | 1 | 0 | 0 | 0 | 0 | 2 | 0 | 0 | 0 | .000 | .000 | .000 |
| Inglin, Jeff, Carolina | 80 | 313 | 263 | 46 | 76 | 111 | 17 | 0 | 6 | 35 | 2 | 3 | 6 | 39 | 1 | 30 | 1 | 2 | 6 | .289 | .389 | .422 |
| Isenia, Chairon, Montgomery | 57 | 213 | 195 | 22 | 59 | 80 | 13 | 1 | 2 | 24 | 0 | 1 | 7 | 10 | 1 | 34 | 0 | 0 | 4 | .303 | .357 | .410 |
| Jansen, Archi, Greenville | 5 | 16 | 12 | 3 | 6 | 11 | 2 | 0 | 1 | 2 | 0 | 1 | 0 | 3 | 1 | 2 | 0 | 0 | 0 | .500 | .563 | .917 |
| Jaramillo, Milko, Tennessee † | 69 | 209 | 184 | 22 | 41 | 59 | 3 | 0 | 5 | 29 | 4 | 1 | 0 | 20 | 1 | 37 | 1 | 1 | 1 | .223 | .298 | .321 |
| Johnson, Ben, Mobile | 136 | 544 | 475 | 80 | 119 | 228 | 28 | 6 | 23 | 85 | 2 | 5 | 7 | 55 | 3 | 136 | 5 | 6 | 0 | .251 | .334 | .480 |
| Johnson, Gabe, Tennessee | 127 | 507 | 450 | 64 | 120 | 201 | 27 | 0 | 18 | 66 | 1 | 7 | 6 | 43 | 1 | 118 | 7 | 1 | 6 | .267 | .334 | .447 |
| Johnson, Kade, Huntsville | 69 | 253 | 224 | 26 | 58 | 84 | 9 | 1 | 5 | 28 | 4 | 2 | 2 | 21 | 5 | 41 | 6 | 2 | 4 | .259 | .325 | .375 |
| Johnson, Kelly, Greenville * | 135 | 536 | 479 | 70 | 135 | 224 | 35 | 3 | 16 | 50 | 0 | 3 | 3 | 49 | 2 | 102 | 9 | 9 | 5 | .282 | .350 | .468 |
| Johnson, Tyler, Tennessee † | 53 | 1 | 0 | 0 | 0 | 0 | 0 | 0 | 0 | 0 | 0 | 0 | 0 | 1 | 0 | 0 | 0 | 0 | 0 | .000 | 1.000 | .000 |
| Jones, Kennard, Mobile * | 82 | 339 | 304 | 35 | 71 | 89 | 14 | 2 | 0 | 9 | 3 | 0 | 5 | 25 | 0 | 76 | 6 | 3 | 0 | .234 | .302 | .293 |
| Jones, Mike, Huntsville | 6 | 2 | 0 | 0 | 0 | 0 | 0 | 0 | 0 | 0 | 0 | 0 | 0 | 2 | 0 | 0 | 0 | 0 | 0 | .000 | 1.000 | .000 |
| Kelly, Steve, Chattanooga | 28 | 50 | 41 | 4 | 3 | 4 | 1 | 0 | 0 | 3 | 5 | 0 | 0 | 4 | 0 | 20 | 0 | 0 | 1 | .073 | .156 | .098 |
| King, Brennan, Jacksonville | 131 | 528 | 480 | 61 | 132 | 202 | 29 | 1 | 13 | 47 | 4 | 3 | 11 | 30 | 2 | 109 | 1 | 6 | 11 | .275 | .330 | .421 |
| Kinney, Josh, Tennessee | 50 | 1 | 1 | 0 | 0 | 0 | 0 | 0 | 0 | 0 | 0 | 0 | 0 | 0 | 0 | 0 | 0 | 0 | 0 | .000 | .000 | .000 |
| Langen, Brian, Greenville * | 15 | 4 | 2 | 2 | 1 | 1 | 0 | 0 | 0 | 1 | 0 | 0 | 0 | 2 | 0 | 0 | 0 | 0 | 0 | .500 | .750 | .500 |
| Langill, Eric, Jacksonville | 6 | 15 | 15 | 1 | 2 | 3 | 1 | 0 | 0 | 0 | 0 | 0 | 0 | 0 | 0 | 4 | 0 | 0 | 0 | .133 | .133 | .200 |
| Leek, Randy, Tennessee * | 17 | 26 | 21 | 2 | 5 | 6 | 1 | 0 | 0 | 0 | 3 | 0 | 0 | 2 | 0 | 6 | 1 | 0 | 0 | .238 | .304 | .286 |
| Lewis, Richard, West Tenn | 99 | 425 | 380 | 68 | 125 | 202 | 27 | 10 | 10 | 59 | 0 | 4 | 4 | 37 | 4 | 94 | 7 | 6 | 2 | .329 | .391 | .532 |
| Loney, James, Jacksonville * | 104 | 442 | 395 | 39 | 94 | 129 | 19 | 2 | 4 | 35 | 0 | 2 | 3 | 42 | 6 | 75 | 5 | 5 | 7 | .238 | .314 | .327 |
| Lopez, Pedro, Birmingham | 7 | 31 | 23 | 3 | 5 | 7 | 0 | 1 | 0 | 0 | 2 | 0 | 1 | 5 | 0 | 2 | 2 | 0 | 0 | .217 | .379 | .304 |
| MacRae, Scott, Chattanooga | 5 | 6 | 5 | 0 | 0 | 0 | 0 | 0 | 0 | 0 | 1 | 0 | 0 | 0 | 0 | 1 | 0 | 0 | 0 | .000 | .000 | .000 |
| Maldonado, Carlos, Birmingham | 108 | 448 | 388 | 48 | 103 | 171 | 30 | 1 | 12 | 68 | 1 | 4 | 3 | 52 | 1 | 81 | 0 | 3 | 10 | .265 | .353 | .441 |
| Mallory, Mike, West Tenn | 104 | 321 | 290 | 30 | 75 | 118 | 20 | 1 | 7 | 36 | 1 | 1 | 7 | 22 | 0 | 80 | 2 | 3 | 6 | .259 | .325 | .407 |
| Marshall, Sean, West Tenn * | 6 | 6 | 4 | 0 | 0 | 0 | 0 | 0 | 0 | 0 | 1 | 0 | 0 | 1 | 0 | 3 | 0 | 0 | 0 | .000 | .200 | .000 |
| Marte, Andy, Greenville | 107 | 450 | 387 | 52 | 104 | 203 | 28 | 1 | 23 | 68 | 0 | 3 | 2 | 58 | 4 | 105 | 1 | 1 | 8 | .269 | .364 | .525 |
| Martel, Normand, Birmingham * | 89 | 309 | 279 | 38 | 84 | 133 | 15 | 2 | 10 | 35 | 0 | 4 | 1 | 25 | 6 | 35 | 5 | 3 | 8 | .301 | .356 | .477 |
| Martin, Brian, Montgomery | 115 | 418 | 367 | 40 | 94 | 150 | 25 | 2 | 9 | 37 | 3 | 5 | 5 | 38 | 2 | 102 | 5 | 3 | 8 | .256 | .330 | .409 |
| Massiatte, Danny, Montgomery | 20 | 67 | 57 | 6 | 14 | 24 | 4 | 0 | 2 | 10 | 2 | 0 | 2 | 6 | 0 | 15 | 1 | 0 | 0 | .246 | .338 | .421 |
| McBride, Macay, Greenville * | 38 | 27 | 23 | 2 | 3 | 5 | 2 | 0 | 0 | 0 | 3 | 0 | 0 | 1 | 0 | 6 | 0 | 0 | 0 | .130 | .167 | .217 |
| McCoy, Mike, Tennessee | 3 | 6 | 6 | 0 | 0 | 0 | 0 | 0 | 0 | 0 | 0 | 0 | 0 | 0 | 0 | 3 | 0 | 0 | 0 | .000 | .000 | .000 |
| McNeal, Aaron, Birmingham | 93 | 381 | 350 | 39 | 91 | 152 | 16 | 0 | 15 | 53 | 1 | 2 | 1 | 27 | 2 | 105 | 2 | 4 | 9 | .260 | .313 | .434 |
| McNutt, Mike, Carolina | 24 | 15 | 13 | 1 | 2 | 2 | 0 | 0 | 0 | 0 | 1 | 0 | 0 | 1 | 0 | 4 | 0 | 0 | 0 | .154 | .214 | .154 |
| Melian, Jackson, Greenville | 52 | 181 | 161 | 18 | 31 | 54 | 8 | 3 | 3 | 13 | 1 | 2 | 3 | 14 | 2 | 38 | 2 | 0 | 5 | .193 | .267 | .335 |
| Merrill, Ronnie, Mobile † | 91 | 370 | 325 | 41 | 82 | 127 | 21 | 3 | 6 | 32 | 7 | 3 | 4 | 31 | 2 | 58 | 5 | 4 | 1 | .252 | .322 | .391 |
| Messenger, Randy, Carolina | 58 | 6 | 5 | 0 | 1 | 1 | 0 | 0 | 0 | 0 | 0 | 0 | 0 | 1 | 0 | 2 | 0 | 0 | 0 | .200 | .333 | .200 |
| Meyer, Jake, Chattanooga | 4 | 3 | 3 | 0 | 0 | 0 | 0 | 0 | 0 | 0 | 0 | 0 | 0 | 0 | 0 | 3 | 0 | 0 | 0 | .000 | .000 | .000 |
| Michaelis, Derek, Jacksonville * | 110 | 375 | 330 | 47 | 87 | 145 | 26 | 1 | 10 | 41 | 0 | 2 | 4 | 38 | 0 | 104 | 5 | 5 | 2 | .264 | .345 | .439 |
| Miller, Ryan, Huntsville | 6 | 2 | 1 | 0 | 0 | 0 | 0 | 0 | 0 | 1 | 0 | 1 | 0 | 0 | 0 | 1 | 0 | 0 | 0 | .000 | .000 | .000 |
| Miner, Zach, Greenville | 28 | 40 | 33 | 2 | 3 | 6 | 0 | 0 | 1 | 2 | 3 | 1 | 0 | 3 | 0 | 12 | 0 | 0 | 0 | .091 | .162 | .182 |
| Miniel, Rene, Mobile | 30 | 3 | 3 | 0 | 0 | 0 | 0 | 0 | 0 | 0 | 0 | 0 | 0 | 0 | 0 | 1 | 0 | 0 | 0 | .000 | .000 | .000 |

| Player, Team | G | TPA | AB | R | H | TB | 2B | 3B | HR | RBI | SH | SF | HP | BB | IBB | SO | SB | CS | GDP | Avg. | OBP | Slg. |
|---|---|---|---|---|---|---|---|---|---|---|---|---|---|---|---|---|---|---|---|---|---|---|
| Minor, Ryan, Carolina | 48 | 194 | 176 | 23 | 44 | 84 | 14 | 1 | 8 | 33 | 0 | 3 | 3 | 12 | 0 | 51 | 1 | 1 | 3 | .250 | .304 | .477 |
| Moehler, Brian, Greenville | 20 | 33 | 25 | 1 | 3 | 3 | 0 | 0 | 0 | 1 | 4 | 0 | 1 | 3 | 0 | 8 | 0 | 0 | 0 | .120 | .241 | .120 |
| Moore, Frank, Montgomery * | 47 | 201 | 183 | 19 | 49 | 68 | 7 | 3 | 2 | 19 | 2 | 1 | 3 | 12 | 1 | 40 | 0 | 0 | 4 | .268 | .322 | .372 |
| Morales, Steve, Mobile † | 56 | 171 | 156 | 14 | 35 | 56 | 6 | 0 | 5 | 17 | 2 | 2 | 2 | 9 | 0 | 30 | 0 | 0 | 6 | .224 | .272 | .359 |
| Moreta, Ramon, Chattanooga | 91 | 259 | 234 | 31 | 54 | 80 | 14 | 3 | 2 | 19 | 1 | 2 | 0 | 22 | 3 | 46 | 9 | 7 | 5 | .231 | .295 | .342 |
| Morton, Colt, Mobile | 1 | 4 | 3 | 1 | 1 | 4 | 0 | 0 | 1 | 1 | 0 | 0 | 0 | 1 | 0 | 0 | 0 | 0 | 0 | .333 | .500 | 1.333 |
| Moser, Todd, Tennessee * | 11 | 17 | 15 | 2 | 4 | 4 | 0 | 0 | 0 | 3 | 1 | 0 | 0 | 1 | 0 | 5 | 0 | 0 | 0 | .267 | .313 | .267 |
| Moylan, Dan, Tennessee * | 104 | 371 | 316 | 39 | 91 | 113 | 16 | 0 | 2 | 38 | 1 | 1 | 5 | 48 | 3 | 54 | 1 | 1 | 2 | .288 | .389 | .358 |
| Murphy, Nate, Birmingham * | 90 | 369 | 335 | 49 | 93 | 151 | 11 | 4 | 13 | 45 | 6 | 3 | 3 | 22 | 1 | 104 | 10 | 3 | 3 | .278 | .325 | .451 |
| Nall, T.J., Jacksonville | 32 | 36 | 27 | 1 | 2 | 3 | 1 | 0 | 0 | 2 | 4 | 0 | 0 | 5 | 0 | 6 | 0 | 0 | 0 | .074 | .219 | .111 |
| Nelson, Brad, Huntsville * | 137 | 558 | 500 | 61 | 127 | 217 | 31 | 1 | 19 | 77 | 0 | 6 | 5 | 47 | 3 | 146 | 11 | 10 | 9 | .254 | .321 | .434 |
| Nelson, Bubba, Chattanooga | 10 | 15 | 13 | 0 | 1 | 1 | 0 | 0 | 0 | 0 | 2 | 0 | 0 | 0 | 0 | 3 | 0 | 0 | 0 | .077 | .077 | .077 |
| Nelson, John, Tennessee | 63 | 242 | 206 | 41 | 62 | 108 | 16 | 3 | 8 | 29 | 2 | 1 | 2 | 31 | 0 | 56 | 6 | 2 | 0 | .301 | .396 | .524 |
| Nettles, Marcus, Mobile * | 55 | 158 | 138 | 18 | 34 | 39 | 3 | 1 | 0 | 9 | 9 | 0 | 3 | 8 | 0 | 42 | 7 | 3 | 0 | .246 | .302 | .283 |
| Nicholson, Tommy, Birmingham * | 38 | 131 | 115 | 11 | 32 | 46 | 14 | 0 | 0 | 13 | 1 | 1 | 2 | 12 | 1 | 32 | 2 | 0 | 0 | .278 | .354 | .400 |
| Nolasco, Ricky, West Tenn | 19 | 32 | 25 | 0 | 3 | 3 | 0 | 0 | 0 | 0 | 5 | 0 | 0 | 2 | 0 | 11 | 0 | 0 | 0 | .120 | .185 | .120 |
| O'Malley, Ryan, West Tenn | 17 | 12 | 12 | 2 | 2 | 2 | 0 | 0 | 0 | 0 | 0 | 0 | 0 | 0 | 0 | 8 | 0 | 0 | 1 | .167 | .167 | .167 |
| O'Toole, Paul, West Tenn * | 63 | 208 | 183 | 22 | 47 | 70 | 9 | 1 | 4 | 20 | 5 | 2 | 2 | 16 | 3 | 41 | 5 | 2 | 4 | .257 | .320 | .383 |
| Osoria, Franquelis, Jacksonville | 51 | 4 | 4 | 0 | 0 | 0 | 0 | 0 | 0 | 0 | 0 | 0 | 0 | 0 | 0 | 3 | 0 | 0 | 0 | .000 | .000 | .000 |
| Parra, Manny, Huntsville * | 3 | 2 | 1 | 0 | 1 | 1 | 0 | 0 | 0 | 0 | 0 | 0 | 0 | 1 | 0 | 0 | 0 | 0 | 0 | 1.000 | 1.000 | 1.000 |
| Paz, Rich, Birmingham | 66 | 265 | 215 | 27 | 50 | 60 | 7 | 0 | 1 | 23 | 2 | 4 | 9 | 35 | 2 | 39 | 2 | 1 | 5 | .233 | .357 | .279 |
| Pena, Brayan, Greenville † | 77 | 299 | 277 | 30 | 87 | 111 | 10 | 4 | 2 | 30 | 4 | 2 | 1 | 15 | 2 | 29 | 3 | 4 | 6 | .314 | .349 | .401 |
| Pena, Tony, Greenville | 130 | 527 | 495 | 65 | 126 | 181 | 22 | 0 | 11 | 34 | 9 | 3 | 4 | 16 | 0 | 108 | 25 | 13 | 6 | .255 | .282 | .366 |
| Perez, Nestor, Montgomery | 42 | 139 | 131 | 18 | 42 | 52 | 8 | 1 | 0 | 11 | 3 | 2 | 1 | 2 | 0 | 10 | 1 | 0 | 3 | .321 | .331 | .397 |
| Peterson, Brian, Chattanooga | 93 | 348 | 313 | 40 | 94 | 139 | 21 | 3 | 6 | 40 | 2 | 2 | 7 | 24 | 3 | 61 | 3 | 1 | 5 | .300 | .361 | .444 |
| Phillips, Heath, Birmingham * | 27 | 1 | 1 | 0 | 0 | 0 | 0 | 0 | 0 | 0 | 0 | 0 | 0 | 0 | 0 | 0 | 0 | 0 | 0 | .000 | .000 | .000 |
| Pignatiello, Carmen, West Tenn | 27 | 32 | 23 | 2 | 5 | 5 | 0 | 0 | 0 | 0 | 7 | 0 | 0 | 2 | 0 | 4 | 0 | 0 | 0 | .217 | .280 | .217 |
| Pineda, Isauro, Greenville | 32 | 20 | 20 | 0 | 4 | 5 | 1 | 0 | 0 | 1 | 0 | 0 | 0 | 0 | 0 | 6 | 0 | 0 | 0 | .200 | .200 | .250 |
| Pratt, Andy, West Tenn * | 6 | 4 | 4 | 0 | 0 | 0 | 0 | 0 | 0 | 0 | 0 | 0 | 0 | 0 | 0 | 2 | 0 | 0 | 0 | .000 | .000 | .000 |
| Pratt, Andy, Huntsville * | 1 | 2 | 2 | 0 | 0 | 0 | 0 | 0 | 0 | 0 | 0 | 0 | 0 | 0 | 0 | 1 | 0 | 0 | 0 | .000 | .000 | .000 |
| Raburn, Johnny, Huntsville † | 115 | 364 | 314 | 38 | 77 | 98 | 12 | 3 | 1 | 23 | 5 | 6 | 2 | 37 | 2 | 53 | 16 | 8 | 2 | .245 | .323 | .312 |
| Ramirez, Elizardo, Chattanooga | 5 | 6 | 5 | 0 | 1 | 1 | 0 | 0 | 0 | 0 | 1 | 0 | 0 | 0 | 0 | 1 | 0 | 0 | 0 | .200 | .200 | .200 |
| Reece, Eric, Montgomery * | 58 | 235 | 216 | 22 | 51 | 76 | 11 | 1 | 4 | 26 | 0 | 3 | 5 | 11 | 0 | 49 | 1 | 0 | 5 | .236 | .285 | .352 |
| Reed, Eric, Carolina * | 55 | 239 | 222 | 32 | 68 | 98 | 9 | 6 | 3 | 14 | 1 | 2 | 0 | 14 | 1 | 55 | 24 | 6 | 2 | .306 | .345 | .441 |
| Reyes, Anthony, Tennessee | 12 | 23 | 19 | 2 | 4 | 10 | 0 | 0 | 2 | 5 | 2 | 0 | 1 | 1 | 0 | 9 | 0 | 0 | 0 | .211 | .286 | .526 |
| Reyes, Guillermo, Birmingham † | 40 | 134 | 124 | 17 | 34 | 37 | 3 | 0 | 0 | 7 | 0 | 0 | 0 | 10 | 1 | 13 | 8 | 1 | 2 | .274 | .328 | .298 |
| Ribas, Gabe, Mobile | 13 | 10 | 9 | 0 | 0 | 0 | 0 | 0 | 0 | 0 | 1 | 0 | 0 | 0 | 0 | 6 | 0 | 0 | 0 | .000 | .000 | .000 |
| Riggans, Shawn, Montgomery | 10 | 39 | 36 | 3 | 8 | 15 | 1 | 0 | 2 | 7 | 0 | 0 | 1 | 2 | 0 | 14 | 0 | 0 | 2 | .222 | .282 | .417 |
| Rijo, Fernando, Huntsville | 40 | 13 | 11 | 2 | 3 | 3 | 0 | 0 | 0 | 0 | 2 | 0 | 0 | 0 | 0 | 2 | 0 | 0 | 0 | .273 | .273 | .273 |
| Rivera, Saul, Huntsville | 26 | 3 | 3 | 0 | 0 | 0 | 0 | 0 | 0 | 0 | 0 | 0 | 0 | 0 | 0 | 2 | 0 | 0 | 0 | .000 | .000 | .000 |
| Rodriguez, Jose, Carolina * | 7 | 1 | 0 | 0 | 0 | 0 | 0 | 0 | 0 | 0 | 1 | 0 | 0 | 0 | 0 | 0 | 0 | 0 | 0 | .000 | .000 | .000 |
| Rohleder, Andy, Carolina | 66 | 204 | 183 | 18 | 47 | 71 | 16 | 1 | 2 | 26 | 4 | 1 | 3 | 13 | 0 | 49 | 1 | 1 | 6 | .257 | .315 | .388 |
| Rohlicek, Russ, West Tenn | 61 | 4 | 3 | 0 | 0 | 0 | 0 | 0 | 0 | 0 | 1 | 0 | 0 | 0 | 0 | 1 | 0 | 0 | 0 | .000 | .000 | .000 |
| Rojas, Jose, Jacksonville | 28 | 4 | 4 | 1 | 2 | 2 | 0 | 0 | 0 | 0 | 0 | 0 | 0 | 0 | 0 | 1 | 0 | 0 | 0 | .500 | .500 | .500 |
| Roman, Jesse, Mobile * | 69 | 190 | 173 | 16 | 29 | 49 | 5 | 0 | 5 | 14 | 0 | 1 | 0 | 16 | 2 | 39 | 0 | 1 | 3 | .168 | .237 | .283 |
| Rundgren, Rex, Carolina | 44 | 153 | 142 | 12 | 38 | 47 | 7 | 1 | 0 | 12 | 3 | 0 | 2 | 6 | 0 | 36 | 2 | 0 | 2 | .268 | .307 | .331 |
| Ryu, Jae-Kuk, West Tenn | 14 | 2 | 1 | 1 | 0 | 0 | 0 | 0 | 0 | 0 | 0 | 0 | 0 | 1 | 0 | 1 | 0 | 0 | 0 | .000 | .500 | .000 |
| Saenz, Chris, Huntsville | 15 | 28 | 28 | 2 | 10 | 16 | 3 | 0 | 1 | 2 | 0 | 0 | 0 | 0 | 0 | 11 | 1 | 0 | 0 | .357 | .357 | .571 |
| Sain, Greg, Mobile | 133 | 537 | 456 | 64 | 107 | 213 | 22 | 0 | 28 | 74 | 1 | 6 | 8 | 66 | 2 | 140 | 1 | 0 | 1 | .235 | .338 | .467 |
| Sarfate, Dennis, Huntsville | 29 | 31 | 29 | 1 | 6 | 8 | 2 | 0 | 0 | 2 | 1 | 0 | 0 | 1 | 0 | 12 | 1 | 0 | 1 | .207 | .233 | .276 |
| Sasser, Rob, Birmingham | 121 | 479 | 418 | 57 | 101 | 161 | 24 | 3 | 10 | 55 | 3 | 5 | 2 | 51 | 0 | 80 | 11 | 6 | 11 | .242 | .324 | .385 |
| Schmoll, Steve, Jacksonville | 11 | 3 | 1 | 0 | 0 | 0 | 0 | 0 | 0 | 0 | 1 | 0 | 0 | 1 | 0 | 0 | 0 | 0 | 0 | .000 | .500 | .000 |
| Schumaker, Skip, Tennessee * | 138 | 583 | 516 | 78 | 163 | 216 | 29 | 6 | 4 | 43 | 4 | 1 | 2 | 60 | 3 | 61 | 19 | 14 | 7 | .316 | .389 | .419 |
| Sevier, Nate, Mobile | 11 | 2 | 2 | 0 | 0 | 0 | 0 | 0 | 0 | 0 | 0 | 0 | 0 | 0 | 0 | 1 | 0 | 0 | 0 | .000 | .000 | .000 |
| Shanks, James, Carolina | 13 | 30 | 23 | 3 | 10 | 14 | 1 | 0 | 1 | 7 | 0 | 1 | 0 | 6 | 0 | 6 | 1 | 1 | 0 | .435 | .533 | .609 |
| Shelley, Jason, Huntsville | 17 | 9 | 9 | 1 | 0 | 0 | 0 | 0 | 0 | 0 | 0 | 0 | 0 | 0 | 0 | 3 | 0 | 0 | 0 | .000 | .000 | .000 |
| Soto, Geovany, West Tenn | 104 | 381 | 332 | 47 | 90 | 133 | 16 | 0 | 9 | 48 | 1 | 3 | 5 | 40 | 1 | 71 | 1 | 2 | 10 | .271 | .355 | .401 |
| Spidale, Mike, Birmingham | 126 | 572 | 484 | 87 | 147 | 209 | 27 | 7 | 7 | 47 | 10 | 5 | 12 | 61 | 1 | 72 | 26 | 15 | 4 | .304 | .391 | .432 |
| Steffek, Brian, Jacksonville | 36 | 4 | 4 | 0 | 0 | 0 | 0 | 0 | 0 | 0 | 0 | 0 | 0 | 0 | 0 | 2 | 0 | 0 | 0 | .000 | .000 | .000 |
| Stern, Adam, Greenville * | 102 | 435 | 394 | 64 | 127 | 189 | 26 | 6 | 8 | 47 | 1 | 3 | 2 | 35 | 2 | 58 | 27 | 10 | 2 | .322 | .378 | .480 |
| Stewart, Chris, Birmingham | 83 | 301 | 260 | 26 | 60 | 78 | 11 | 2 | 1 | 17 | 13 | 2 | 4 | 22 | 0 | 59 | 2 | 4 | 3 | .231 | .299 | .300 |
| Stewart, Paul, Huntsville | 41 | 16 | 15 | 1 | 3 | 4 | 1 | 0 | 0 | 1 | 1 | 0 | 0 | 0 | 0 | 9 | 0 | 0 | 0 | .200 | .200 | .267 |
| Strelitz, Brian, Carolina | 30 | 9 | 8 | 0 | 0 | 0 | 0 | 0 | 0 | 0 | 1 | 0 | 0 | 0 | 0 | 6 | 0 | 0 | 0 | .000 | .000 | .000 |
| Tavares, Anderson, West Tenn | 1 | 1 | 1 | 0 | 0 | 0 | 0 | 0 | 0 | 0 | 0 | 0 | 0 | 0 | 0 | 1 | 0 | 0 | 0 | .000 | .000 | .000 |
| Thompson, Bradley, Tennessee | 13 | 24 | 19 | 1 | 3 | 3 | 0 | 0 | 0 | 2 | 3 | 0 | 0 | 2 | 0 | 6 | 0 | 0 | 0 | .158 | .238 | .158 |
| Thompson, Derek, Jacksonville * | 22 | 33 | 27 | 0 | 1 | 1 | 0 | 0 | 0 | 0 | 3 | 0 | 0 | 3 | 0 | 11 | 0 | 0 | 1 | .037 | .133 | .037 |
| Thompson, Mike, Mobile | 35 | 24 | 21 | 1 | 1 | 2 | 1 | 0 | 0 | 1 | 2 | 0 | 0 | 1 | 0 | 7 | 0 | 0 | 0 | .048 | .091 | .095 |
| Thorman, Scott, Greenville * | 94 | 387 | 345 | 31 | 87 | 140 | 14 | 3 | 11 | 51 | 0 | 3 | 0 | 39 | 1 | 73 | 5 | 3 | 3 | .252 | .326 | .406 |
| Trzesniak, Nick, Mobile | 108 | 388 | 346 | 26 | 73 | 116 | 18 | 2 | 7 | 42 | 1 | 4 | 9 | 28 | 2 | 91 | 2 | 3 | 3 | .211 | .284 | .335 |
| Ungs, Nic, Carolina | 28 | 51 | 40 | 3 | 8 | 11 | 0 | 0 | 1 | 2 | 7 | 0 | 0 | 4 | 0 | 8 | 0 | 1 | 0 | .200 | .273 | .275 |
| Van Iderstine, Ben, Huntsville | 17 | 52 | 52 | 1 | 15 | 20 | 2 | 0 | 1 | 3 | 0 | 0 | 0 | 0 | 0 | 12 | 0 | 1 | 0 | .288 | .288 | .385 |
| Victorino, Shane, Jacksonville | 75 | 328 | 293 | 70 | 96 | 171 | 13 | 7 | 16 | 43 | 5 | 5 | 5 | 20 | 0 | 64 | 9 | 7 | 0 | .328 | .375 | .584 |
| Washington, Rico, Mobile * | 68 | 283 | 244 | 36 | 71 | 112 | 12 | 1 | 9 | 45 | 1 | 3 | 2 | 33 | 0 | 42 | 0 | 2 | 0 | .291 | .376 | .459 |
| Weeks, Rickie, Huntsville | 133 | 568 | 479 | 67 | 124 | 195 | 35 | 6 | 8 | 42 | 3 | 3 | 28 | 55 | 1 | 107 | 11 | 12 | 5 | .259 | .366 | .407 |
| Weston, Aron, West Tenn * | 123 | 466 | 425 | 62 | 122 | 172 | 20 | 9 | 4 | 46 | 3 | 4 | 3 | 31 | 4 | 90 | 10 | 9 | 5 | .287 | .337 | .405 |
| Whitaker, Brian, Mobile | 23 | 39 | 30 | 3 | 5 | 5 | 0 | 0 | 0 | 2 | 5 | 1 | 1 | 2 | 0 | 7 | 0 | 0 | 0 | .167 | .235 | .167 |
| Willingham, Josh, Carolina | 112 | 455 | 338 | 81 | 95 | 191 | 24 | 0 | 24 | 76 | 1 | 7 | 18 | 91 | 8 | 87 | 6 | 3 | 7 | .281 | .449 | .565 |
| Wilson, Travis, Chattanooga | 109 | 293 | 264 | 28 | 73 | 109 | 16 | 1 | 6 | 36 | 3 | 1 | 4 | 21 | 1 | 76 | 3 | 0 | 8 | .277 | .338 | .413 |
| Wodnicki, Mike, Tennessee | 12 | 5 | 5 | 0 | 0 | 0 | 0 | 0 | 0 | 0 | 0 | 0 | 0 | 0 | 0 | 3 | 0 | 0 | 0 | .000 | .000 | .000 |
| Woolard, Glenn, Huntsville | 24 | 23 | 21 | 1 | 4 | 4 | 0 | 0 | 0 | 1 | 1 | 0 | 0 | 1 | 0 | 7 | 0 | 1 | 1 | .190 | .227 | .190 |
| Yan, Ruddy, Birmingham † | 128 | 547 | 494 | 56 | 132 | 167 | 12 | 10 | 1 | 48 | 17 | 1 | 4 | 31 | 0 | 82 | 35 | 19 | 4 | .267 | .315 | .338 |
| Zumwalt, Alec, Greenville | 46 | 11 | 11 | 1 | 5 | 6 | 1 | 0 | 0 | 2 | 0 | 0 | 0 | 0 | 0 | 3 | 0 | 0 | 0 | .455 | .455 | .545 |

GRAND SLAMS—Alvarez, Bannon, Castro, Cresse, Dillon, Duncan, Denorfia, Furmaniak, Hall, Hoffpauir, Horrelbeke, B. Johnson, G. Johnson, King, Maldonado, McNeal, Moore, Sasser, Washington, J. Wilson, 1 each.

AWARDED FIRST BASE ON CATCHER'S INTERFERENCE—Butler 3 (Morales, Craig, G. Johnson); Barnwell (Morales); Clements (Isenia); Craig (Stewart); Creighton (Peterson); K. Johnson (Alvarado); Lewis (Isenia); Michaelis (Pena); Riggs (Stewart)

# 2004 PITCHING

| Team | W | L | Pct. | ERA | G | CG | ShO | Sv. | IP | H | TBF | R | ER | HR | SH | SF | HB | BB | IBB | SO | WP | Bk. |
|---|---|---|---|---|---|---|---|---|---|---|---|---|---|---|---|---|---|---|---|---|---|---|
| Chattanooga | 87 | 53 | .621 | 3.33 | 140 | 2 | 6 | 46 | 1247.2 | 1161 | 5259 | 540 | 461 | 111 | 58 | 37 | 60 | 395 | 20 | 1131 | 73 | 5 |
| Birmingham | 73 | 66 | .525 | 3.43 | 139 | 0 | 8 | 34 | 1224.0 | 1170 | 5148 | 535 | 466 | 80 | 37 | 38 | 49 | 391 | 47 | 969 | 57 | 14 |
| Huntsville | 65 | 75 | .464 | 3.57 | 140 | 1 | 10 | 35 | 1208.2 | 1156 | 5186 | 590 | 479 | 107 | 53 | 36 | 69 | 447 | 15 | 1050 | 74 | 10 |
| Mobile | 73 | 67 | .521 | 3.82 | 140 | 4 | 9 | 35 | 1220.1 | 1192 | 5165 | 584 | 518 | 109 | 60 | 36 | 63 | 424 | 36 | 911 | 55 | 7 |
| Greenville | 63 | 76 | .453 | 3.88 | 139 | 3 | 10 | 30 | 1216.0 | 1172 | 5228 | 623 | 524 | 94 | 61 | 37 | 42 | 502 | 21 | 1073 | 51 | 4 |
| Jacksonville | 66 | 71 | .482 | 3.88 | 137 | 3 | 9 | 30 | 1214.2 | 1201 | 5231 | 601 | 524 | 108 | 66 | 24 | 45 | 499 | 33 | 1102 | 53 | 5 |
| West Tenn | 70 | 68 | .507 | 3.99 | 138 | 3 | 8 | 27 | 1179.2 | 1094 | 5090 | 597 | 523 | 118 | 60 | 35 | 69 | 511 | 20 | 1142 | 49 | 3 |
| Tennessee | 69 | 71 | .493 | 4.27 | 140 | 6 | 10 | 31 | 1198.0 | 1198 | 5174 | 635 | 569 | 125 | 71 | 31 | 64 | 447 | 30 | 989 | 74 | 3 |
| Carolina | 73 | 66 | .525 | 4.34 | 139 | 0 | 9 | 33 | 1208.2 | 1235 | 5283 | 639 | 583 | 129 | 69 | 41 | 50 | 488 | 54 | 991 | 62 | 10 |
| Montgomery | 57 | 83 | .407 | 4.53 | 140 | 6 | 10 | 34 | 1187.1 | 1237 | 5136 | 672 | 597 | 128 | 41 | 64 | 63 | 425 | 14 | 975 | 72 | 7 |

## INDIVIDUAL

### TOP QUALIFIERS FOR EARNED-RUN AVERAGE TITLE

Minimum 112 innings. *Lefthanded pitcher.

| Pitcher, Team | W | L | Pct. | ERA | G | GS | CG | ShO | GF | Sv. | IP | H | TBF | R | ER | HR | SH | SF | HB | BB | IBB | SO | WP | Bk. |
|---|---|---|---|---|---|---|---|---|---|---|---|---|---|---|---|---|---|---|---|---|---|---|---|---|
| Pinto, Renyel, West Tenn | 11 | 8 | .579 | 2.92 | 25 | 25 | 0 | 0 | 0 | 0 | 141.2 | 107 | 587 | 50 | 46 | 10 | 8 | 5 | 6 | 72 | 0 | 179 | 9 | 1 |
| Kelly, Steve, Chattanooga | 12 | 7 | .632 | 2.96 | 28 | 28 | 0 | 0 | 0 | 0 | 161.1 | 156 | 684 | 69 | 53 | 12 | 12 | 9 | 4 | 48 | 2 | 116 | 13 | 0 |
| Ketchner, Ryan, Jacksonville | 8 | 7 | .533 | 3.02 | 21 | 21 | 1 | 0 | 0 | 0 | 119.1 | 118 | 479 | 43 | 40 | 10 | 12 | 1 | 3 | 36 | 1 | 98 | 1 | 0 |
| Housman, Jeff, Huntsville | 5 | 8 | .385 | 3.13 | 23 | 20 | 0 | 0 | 2 | 1 | 112.0 | 108 | 486 | 55 | 39 | 10 | 7 | 8 | 7 | 38 | 0 | 121 | 6 | 1 |
| Brownlie, Bobby, West Tenn | 9 | 9 | .500 | 3.36 | 26 | 26 | 2 | 0 | 0 | 0 | 147.1 | 127 | 584 | 62 | 55 | 15 | 10 | 5 | 6 | 36 | 1 | 114 | 10 | 0 |
| Thompson, Mike, Mobile | 10 | 2 | .833 | 3.41 | 35 | 18 | 0 | 0 | 4 | 0 | 121.1 | 128 | 498 | 50 | 46 | 13 | 14 | 3 | 8 | 31 | 2 | 69 | 2 | 0 |
| Bullard, Jim, Birmingham * | 8 | 4 | .667 | 3.47 | 37 | 15 | 0 | 0 | 9 | 0 | 114.0 | 107 | 482 | 52 | 44 | 8 | 4 | 3 | 4 | 44 | 2 | 74 | 7 | 1 |
| Thompson, Derek, Jacksonville * | 5 | 7 | .417 | 3.72 | 22 | 22 | 0 | 0 | 0 | 0 | 118.2 | 132 | 519 | 53 | 49 | 3 | 7 | 5 | 5 | 51 | 2 | 100 | 5 | 0 |
| Whitaker, Brian, Mobile | 8 | 9 | .471 | 3.73 | 23 | 23 | 1 | 0 | 0 | 0 | 137.2 | 128 | 561 | 68 | 57 | 9 | 16 | 6 | 7 | 36 | 3 | 82 | 3 | 0 |
| Ulacia, Dennis, Birmingham * | 8 | 8 | .500 | 3.77 | 28 | 23 | 0 | 0 | 1 | 0 | 129.0 | 137 | 555 | 63 | 54 | 8 | 5 | 7 | 6 | 36 | 4 | 107 | 5 | 0 |
| Costello, Ryan, Huntsville * | 8 | 8 | .500 | 3.89 | 24 | 23 | 1 | 1 | 0 | 0 | 125.0 | 124 | 542 | 66 | 54 | 9 | 9 | 6 | 5 | 49 | 2 | 105 | 9 | 0 |
| Phillips, Heath, Birmingham * | 12 | 10 | .545 | 4.02 | 27 | 26 | 0 | 0 | 1 | 0 | 154.1 | 179 | 649 | 78 | 69 | 12 | 5 | 12 | 4 | 36 | 3 | 107 | 5 | 2 |
| Meaux, Ryan, Birmingham * | 7 | 9 | .438 | 4.04 | 29 | 21 | 0 | 0 | 1 | 0 | 140.1 | 163 | 604 | 68 | 63 | 4 | 10 | 2 | 3 | 46 | 5 | 103 | 5 | 4 |
| Sarfate, Dennis, Huntsville | 7 | 12 | .368 | 4.05 | 28 | 25 | 0 | 0 | 2 | 0 | 129.0 | 128 | 566 | 71 | 58 | 12 | 10 | 8 | 9 | 78 | 0 | 113 | 6 | 2 |
| Nall, T.J., Jacksonville | 8 | 9 | .471 | 4.14 | 32 | 20 | 1 | 0 | 2 | 1 | 143.1 | 146 | 594 | 74 | 66 | 19 | 8 | 1 | 5 | 36 | 4 | 123 | 2 | 0 |

DEPARTMENTAL LEADERS: W—S. Kelly, Phillips, 12; L—Sarfate, 12; Pct.—S. Kelly, .632; G—M. Smith, 70; GS—S. Kelly, Ungs, 28; CG—Five pitchers with 2; ShO—Thompson, 2; GF—N/A; Sv.—Baker, 30; IP—S. Kelly, Ungs, 161.1; H—Cromer, 180; TBF—N/A; R—Pignatiello, 89; ER—Hensley, Ungs, 76; HR—Ungs, 24; SH—N/A; SF—N/A; HB—Hutchinson, Rose 11; BB—Sarfate, 78; IBB—N/A; SO—Pinto, 179; WP—S. Kelly, 13; BK—Meaux, 4.

### ALL PITCHERS

*Lefthanded pitcher.

| Pitcher, Team | W | L | Pct. | ERA | G | GS | CG | ShO | GF | Sv. | IP | H | TBF | R | ER | HR | SH | SF | HB | BB | IBB | SO | WP | Bk. |
|---|---|---|---|---|---|---|---|---|---|---|---|---|---|---|---|---|---|---|---|---|---|---|---|---|
| Adams, Brian, Huntsville * | 3 | 2 | .600 | 4.25 | 52 | 0 | 0 | 0 | 18 | 3 | 84.2 | 92 | 375 | 47 | 40 | 9 | 2 | 0 | 6 | 26 | 2 | 68 | 4 | 1 |
| Aguilar, Ray, Greenville * | 2 | 3 | .400 | 2.29 | 8 | 7 | 1 | 1 | 1 | 0 | 51.0 | 35 | 202 | 17 | 13 | 7 | 4 | 4 | 2 | 8 | 0 | 32 | 2 | 0 |
| Allen, Wyatt, Birmingham | 0 | 4 | .000 | 4.93 | 33 | 2 | 0 | 0 | 9 | 0 | 49.1 | 52 | 219 | 30 | 27 | 8 | 0 | 0 | 4 | 19 | 0 | 55 | 5 | 0 |
| Arteaga, Josh, West Tenn. | 1 | 0 | 1.000 | 33.75 | 2 | 0 | 0 | 0 | 0 | 0 | 1.1 | 4 | 11 | 5 | 5 | 1 | 0 | 0 | 0 | 3 | 0 | 1 | 0 | 0 |
| Axelson, Josh, Tennessee | 6 | 5 | .545 | 4.80 | 34 | 14 | 0 | 0 | 5 | 0 | 105.0 | 97 | 436 | 58 | 56 | 19 | 8 | 5 | 4 | 39 | 3 | 76 | 4 | 0 |
| Baez, Benito, Chattanooga * | 3 | 1 | .750 | 2.12 | 12 | 0 | 0 | 0 | 3 | 1 | 17.0 | 13 | 71 | 4 | 4 | 3 | 0 | 0 | 0 | 7 | 2 | 18 | 0 | 0 |
| Baker, Brad, Mobile | 2 | 1 | .667 | 1.57 | 55 | 0 | 0 | 0 | 49 | 30 | 57.1 | 37 | 232 | 11 | 10 | 2 | — | — | 0 | 24 | 1 | 68 | 4 | — |
| Baker, Ryan, Carolina | 5 | 3 | .625 | 3.34 | 40 | 1 | 0 | 0 | 9 | 0 | 64.2 | 65 | 286 | 27 | 24 | 3 | 1 | 1 | 3 | 29 | 5 | 46 | 1 | 0 |
| Bauer, Greg, Tennessee | 1 | 0 | 1.000 | 0.00 | 10 | 0 | 0 | 0 | 2 | 0 | 13.1 | 8 | 53 | 2 | 0 | 0 | 0 | 0 | 0 | 5 | 0 | 11 | 4 | 0 |
| Bauer, Peter, Carolina | 5 | 10 | .333 | 4.35 | 27 | 25 | 0 | 0 | 0 | 0 | 155.1 | 161 | 649 | 83 | 75 | 11 | 19 | 7 | 7 | 40 | 2 | 103 | 5 | 0 |
| Beech, Matt, Chattanooga * | 3 | 0 | 1.000 | 0.64 | 6 | 1 | 0 | 0 | 1 | 1 | 14.0 | 5 | 58 | 1 | 1 | 1 | 0 | 1 | 1 | 10 | 0 | 17 | 1 | 0 |
| Benedetti, John, Montgomery | 2 | 0 | 1.000 | 2.52 | 28 | 0 | 0 | 0 | 17 | 0 | 39.1 | 35 | 168 | 17 | 11 | 2 | 0 | 0 | 2 | 13 | 1 | 29 | 5 | 0 |
| Billingsley, Chad, Jacksonville | 4 | 0 | 1.000 | 2.98 | 8 | 8 | 0 | 0 | 0 | 0 | 42.1 | 32 | 169 | 16 | 14 | 1 | 1 | 0 | 1 | 22 | 0 | 47 | 2 | 0 |
| Blair, Tom, Tennessee * | 0 | 1 | .000 | 6.75 | 3 | 3 | 0 | 0 | 0 | 0 | 9.1 | 14 | 43 | 7 | 7 | 0 | 2 | 0 | 0 | 5 | 0 | 5 | 1 | 0 |
| Blasdell, Jared, West Tenn | 2 | 4 | .333 | 4.80 | 49 | 0 | 0 | 0 | 26 | 2 | 60.0 | 59 | 286 | 40 | 32 | 8 | 1 | 0 | 7 | 43 | 4 | 60 | 4 | 0 |
| Blasko, Chadd, West Tenn. | 5 | 4 | .556 | 5.67 | 13 | 13 | 0 | 0 | 0 | 0 | 66.2 | 77 | 302 | 45 | 42 | 12 | 3 | 4 | 6 | 24 | 0 | 65 | 5 | 0 |
| Booker, Chris, Chattanooga | 2 | 0 | 1.000 | 1.38 | 28 | 0 | 0 | 0 | 12 | 5 | 39.0 | 26 | 169 | 6 | 6 | 0 | 0 | 0 | 1 | 25 | 4 | 57 | 5 | 0 |
| Bott, Glenn, Jacksonville * | 4 | 11 | .267 | 4.37 | 28 | 27 | 1 | 0 | 1 | 0 | 146.1 | 143 | 638 | 81 | 71 | 14 | 17 | 8 | 1 | 75 | 1 | 120 | 3 | 1 |
| Brownlie, Bobby, West Tenn | 9 | 9 | .500 | 3.36 | 26 | 26 | 2 | 0 | 0 | 0 | 147.1 | 127 | 584 | 62 | 55 | 15 | 10 | 5 | 6 | 36 | 1 | 114 | 10 | 0 |
| Bullard, Jim, Birmingham * | 8 | 4 | .667 | 3.47 | 37 | 15 | 0 | 0 | 9 | 0 | 114.0 | 107 | 482 | 52 | 44 | 8 | 4 | 3 | 4 | 44 | 2 | 74 | 7 | 1 |
| Caraccioli, Lance, Chattanooga * | 2 | 1 | .667 | 3.00 | 12 | 6 | 0 | 0 | 2 | 0 | 39.0 | 29 | 167 | 14 | 13 | 3 | 2 | 3 | 1 | 29 | 1 | 37 | 3 | 0 |
| Carvajal, Marcos, Jacksonville | 0 | 0 | .000 | 0.00 | 1 | 0 | 0 | 0 | 0 | 0 | 3.0 | 2 | 13 | 0 | 0 | 0 | 0 | 0 | 0 | 2 | 0 | 2 | 1 | 0 |
| Cassel, Jack, Mobile | 4 | 2 | .667 | 3.74 | 57 | 0 | 0 | 0 | 19 | 1 | 74.2 | 76 | 333 | 35 | 31 | 4 | 1 | 2 | 8 | 27 | 2 | 52 | 6 | 1 |
| Castellanos, Hugo, West Tenn. | 1 | 0 | 1.000 | 3.52 | 22 | 0 | 0 | 0 | 4 | 1 | 23.0 | 21 | 109 | 9 | 9 | 1 | 0 | 0 | 3 | 16 | 0 | 14 | 0 | 0 |
| Cavazos, Andy, Tennessee | 2 | 5 | .286 | 6.14 | 46 | 0 | 0 | 0 | 14 | 1 | 51.1 | 67 | 253 | 40 | 35 | 6 | 0 | 0 | 1 | 32 | 3 | 41 | 2 | 0 |
| Childress, Daylan, Chattanooga | 3 | 5 | .375 | 3.42 | 29 | 9 | 0 | 0 | 11 | 7 | 81.2 | 73 | 351 | 37 | 31 | 9 | 3 | 6 | 8 | 31 | 0 | 77 | 3 | 0 |
| Coenen, Matt, Greenville * | 3 | 5 | .375 | 3.09 | 36 | 6 | 0 | 0 | 12 | 2 | 78.2 | 77 | 349 | 28 | 27 | 3 | 3 | 1 | 4 | 42 | 5 | 54 | 5 | 0 |

| Pitcher, Team | W | L | Pct. | ERA | G | GS | CG | ShO | GF | Sv. | IP | H | TBF | R | ER | HR | SH | SF | HB | BB | IBB | SO | WP | Bk. |
|---|---|---|---|---|---|---|---|---|---|---|---|---|---|---|---|---|---|---|---|---|---|---|---|---|
| Colon, Roman, Greenville | 1 | 0 | 1.000 | 0.00 | 3 | 0 | 0 | 0 | 2 | 0 | 3.0 | 1 | 11 | 1 | 0 | 0 | 0 | 0 | 1 | 0 | 0 | 5 | 0 | 0 |
| Connolly, Jon, West Tenn * | 1 | 0 | 1.000 | 1.50 | 1 | 1 | 0 | 0 | 0 | 0 | 6.0 | 4 | 22 | 1 | 1 | 0 | 0 | 0 | 0 | 1 | 0 | 8 | 0 | 0 |
| Cook, Jeremy, Tennessee | 8 | 3 | .727 | 4.19 | 29 | 16 | 0 | 0 | 3 | 0 | 116.0 | 118 | 477 | 59 | 54 | 12 | 4 | 5 | 4 | 21 | 0 | 67 | 3 | 0 |
| Coose, Austin, Montgomery | 5 | 4 | .556 | 3.18 | 43 | 0 | 0 | 0 | 11 | 2 | 56.2 | 51 | 248 | 22 | 20 | 4 | 2 | 2 | 4 | 23 | 3 | 60 | 4 | 1 |
| Costello, Ryan, Huntsville * | 8 | 8 | .500 | 3.89 | 24 | 23 | 1 | 1 | 0 | 0 | 125.0 | 124 | 542 | 66 | 54 | 9 | 9 | 6 | 5 | 49 | 2 | 105 | 9 | 0 |
| Crawford, Paxton, Chattanooga | 1 | 1 | .500 | 3.93 | 18 | 0 | 0 | 0 | 7 | 0 | 34.1 | 33 | 144 | 21 | 15 | 5 | 0 | 0 | 1 | 10 | 1 | 27 | 0 | 0 |
| Cromer, Jason, Montgomery * | 9 | 11 | .450 | 4.15 | 27 | 26 | 2 | 1 | 0 | 0 | 147.1 | 180 | 640 | 79 | 68 | 8 | 7 | 11 | 4 | 46 | 1 | 86 | 4 | 1 |
| Curtis, Daniel, Greenville | 7 | 3 | .700 | 3.12 | 33 | 6 | 0 | 0 | 6 | 0 | 95.1 | 90 | 402 | 39 | 33 | 7 | 5 | 1 | 1 | 35 | 1 | 88 | 1 | 0 |
| Davies, Kyle, Greenville | 4 | 0 | 1.000 | 2.32 | 11 | 10 | 0 | 0 | 0 | 0 | 62.0 | 40 | 238 | 18 | 16 | 9 | 3 | 0 | 2 | 22 | 0 | 73 | 3 | 0 |
| DeHart, Casey, Chattanooga * | 6 | 6 | .500 | 4.26 | 48 | 0 | 0 | 0 | 14 | 1 | 76.0 | 72 | 342 | 41 | 36 | 5 | 1 | 0 | 3 | 37 | 3 | 76 | 8 | 0 |
| Diaz, Jose, Montgomery | 1 | 3 | .250 | 5.40 | 7 | 6 | 0 | 0 | 0 | 0 | 30.0 | 26 | 143 | 19 | 18 | 4 | 1 | 2 | 7 | 27 | 0 | 37 | 3 | 0 |
| Dzurilla, Mike, West Tenn | 0 | 0 | .000 | 5.40 | 2 | 0 | 0 | 0 | 2 | 0 | 1.2 | 4 | 10 | 1 | 1 | 0 | 0 | 0 | 0 | 1 | 0 | 0 | 1 | 0 |
| Ehrnsberger, Chad, Tennessee | 0 | 0 | .000 | 0.00 | 1 | 0 | 0 | 0 | 1 | 0 | 1.1 | 2 | 7 | 0 | 0 | 0 | 0 | 0 | 1 | 0 | 0 | 0 | 0 | 0 |
| Emiliano, Jamie, Greenville | 4 | 3 | .571 | 3.50 | 51 | 0 | 0 | 0 | 29 | 11 | 61.2 | 59 | 281 | 34 | 24 | 3 | 0 | 0 | 6 | 35 | 4 | 53 | 6 | 1 |
| Erickson, Corey, Tennessee | 0 | 1 | .000 | 0.00 | 1 | 0 | 0 | 0 | 1 | 0 | 0.2 | 1 | 3 | 1 | 0 | 0 | 0 | 0 | 0 | 0 | 0 | 0 | 0 | 0 |
| Eveland, Dana, Huntsville * | 0 | 2 | .000 | 2.28 | 4 | 4 | 0 | 0 | 0 | 0 | 23.2 | 23 | 99 | 9 | 6 | 0 | 5 | 1 | 1 | 4 | 0 | 14 | 1 | 0 |
| Fahrner, Evan, West Tenn | 2 | 4 | .333 | 3.39 | 58 | 0 | 0 | 0 | 23 | 0 | 77.0 | 70 | 337 | 35 | 29 | 6 | 0 | 1 | 4 | 34 | 1 | 85 | 4 | 0 |
| Fields, Josh, Birmingham | 3 | 4 | .429 | 2.55 | 52 | 0 | 0 | 0 | 23 | 3 | 74.0 | 54 | 301 | 22 | 21 | 4 | 0 | 0 | 5 | 21 | 4 | 72 | 4 | 0 |
| Flannery, Mike, Carolina | 4 | 2 | .667 | 5.29 | 25 | 0 | 0 | 0 | 11 | 2 | 32.1 | 40 | 150 | 21 | 19 | 4 | 0 | 0 | 0 | 13 | 4 | 23 | 9 | 2 |
| Flury, Pat, Carolina | 3 | 4 | .429 | 2.56 | 42 | 0 | 0 | 0 | 13 | 1 | 59.2 | 42 | 258 | 19 | 17 | 1 | 0 | 0 | 0 | 38 | 5 | 68 | 5 | 1 |
| Ford, Matt, Huntsville * | 2 | 6 | .250 | 3.94 | 21 | 18 | 0 | 0 | 1 | 0 | 91.1 | 89 | 400 | 50 | 40 | 8 | 8 | 8 | 4 | 49 | 2 | 47 | 10 | 0 |
| Frendling, Neal, Montgomery | 1 | 1 | .500 | 7.15 | 6 | 1 | 0 | 0 | 2 | 0 | 11.1 | 18 | 58 | 10 | 9 | 1 | 1 | 1 | 1 | 2 | 0 | 7 | 1 | 0 |
| Fuell, Jerrod, Carolina | 0 | 1 | .000 | 4.15 | 17 | 0 | 0 | 0 | 5 | 1 | 21.2 | 18 | 90 | 10 | 10 | 3 | 0 | 1 | 0 | 6 | 0 | 17 | 0 | 0 |
| Fulchino, Jeff, Carolina | 6 | 5 | .545 | 4.47 | 17 | 17 | 0 | 0 | 0 | 0 | 90.2 | 93 | 391 | 45 | 45 | 5 | 5 | 3 | 3 | 37 | 3 | 84 | 3 | 0 |
| Gardner, Richie, Chattanooga | 5 | 2 | .714 | 2.56 | 11 | 11 | 0 | 0 | 0 | 0 | 70.1 | 68 | 296 | 24 | 20 | 7 | 6 | 1 | 3 | 13 | 0 | 59 | 3 | 1 |
| Glen, William, Montgomery | 4 | 4 | .500 | 4.48 | 29 | 8 | 0 | 0 | 6 | 0 | 78.1 | 81 | 350 | 41 | 39 | 9 | 1 | 4 | 3 | 33 | 3 | 81 | 2 | 0 |
| Gonzalez, Luis, Jacksonville * | 1 | 3 | .250 | 4.73 | 45 | 1 | 0 | 0 | 14 | 0 | 64.2 | 73 | 313 | 41 | 34 | 9 | 1 | 0 | 2 | 47 | 3 | 66 | 4 | 2 |
| Grzecka, Casey, Carolina | 0 | 0 | .000 | 0.00 | 1 | 0 | 0 | 0 | 1 | 0 | 1.0 | 1 | 5 | 0 | 0 | 0 | 0 | 0 | 0 | 1 | 0 | 0 | 0 | 0 |
| Guzman, Angel, West Tenn | 0 | 3 | .000 | 5.60 | 4 | 4 | 0 | 0 | 0 | 0 | 17.2 | 20 | 74 | 11 | 11 | 2 | 3 | 0 | 0 | 4 | 0 | 13 | 0 | 0 |
| Hamilton, Clayton, Mobile | 1 | 0 | 1.000 | 1.80 | 1 | 1 | 0 | 0 | 0 | 0 | 5.0 | 5 | 22 | 2 | 1 | 0 | 1 | 0 | 0 | 2 | 0 | 6 | 0 | 0 |
| Harper, Jesse, Huntsville | 0 | 0 | .000 | 3.18 | 1 | 1 | 0 | 0 | 0 | 0 | 5.2 | 6 | 27 | 2 | 2 | 0 | 2 | 0 | 0 | 0 | 0 | 4 | 0 | 0 |
| Henderson, Brian, Montgomery * | 1 | 0 | 1.000 | 2.91 | 20 | 0 | 0 | 0 | 2 | 2 | 21.2 | 26 | 101 | 14 | 7 | 1 | 0 | 0 | 3 | 7 | 1 | 15 | 0 | 0 |
| Hensley, Clay, Mobile | 11 | 10 | .524 | 4.30 | 27 | 27 | 2 | 1 | 0 | 0 | 159.0 | 167 | 666 | 84 | 76 | 14 | 8 | 7 | 8 | 48 | 2 | 125 | 6 | 0 |
| Hines, Carlos, Montgomery | 4 | 2 | .667 | 4.41 | 43 | 1 | 0 | 0 | 10 | 5 | 79.2 | 82 | 343 | 43 | 39 | 4 | 0 | 0 | 2 | 22 | 0 | 64 | 8 | 0 |
| Housman, Jeff, Huntsville | 5 | 8 | .385 | 3.13 | 23 | 20 | 0 | 0 | 2 | 1 | 112.0 | 108 | 486 | 55 | 39 | 10 | 7 | 8 | 7 | 38 | 0 | 121 | 6 | 1 |
| Hull, Eric, Jacksonville | 4 | 3 | .571 | 4.18 | 21 | 8 | 0 | 0 | 2 | 0 | 60.1 | 70 | 268 | 29 | 28 | 5 | 6 | 1 | 1 | 26 | 3 | 39 | 3 | 0 |
| Hutchinson, Trevor, Carolina | 10 | 7 | .588 | 4.23 | 24 | 24 | 0 | 0 | 0 | 0 | 123.1 | 133 | 531 | 70 | 58 | 11 | 10 | 4 | 11 | 38 | 2 | 86 | 4 | 0 |
| Iehl, Jay, Carolina | 1 | 0 | 1.000 | 3.14 | 4 | 3 | 0 | 0 | 0 | 0 | 14.1 | 13 | 64 | 5 | 5 | 0 | 3 | 1 | 0 | 10 | 2 | 7 | 1 | 1 |
| Johnson, Tyler, Tennessee * | 2 | 2 | .500 | 4.79 | 53 | 0 | 0 | 0 | 21 | 4 | 56.1 | 48 | 257 | 32 | 30 | 4 | 0 | 0 | 3 | 37 | 1 | 77 | 8 | 0 |
| Jones, Geoffrey, Mobile * | 0 | 0 | .000 | 3.00 | 6 | 0 | 0 | 0 | 3 | 0 | 9.0 | 6 | 38 | 3 | 3 | 0 | 0 | 0 | 0 | 5 | 1 | 13 | 0 | 1 |
| Jones, Mike, Huntsville | 1 | 4 | .200 | 4.18 | 6 | 6 | 0 | 0 | 0 | 0 | 23.2 | 22 | 106 | 14 | 11 | 0 | 0 | 0 | 3 | 13 | 0 | 16 | 2 | 0 |
| Kelly, Steve, Chattanooga | 12 | 7 | .632 | 2.96 | 28 | 28 | 0 | 0 | 0 | 0 | 161.1 | 156 | 684 | 69 | 53 | 12 | 12 | 9 | 4 | 48 | 2 | 116 | 13 | 0 |
| Ketchner, Ryan, Jacksonville | 8 | 7 | .533 | 3.02 | 21 | 21 | 1 | 0 | 0 | 0 | 119.1 | 118 | 479 | 43 | 40 | 10 | 12 | 1 | 3 | 36 | 1 | 98 | 1 | 0 |
| Kinney, Josh, Tennessee | 3 | 8 | .273 | 5.50 | 50 | 0 | 0 | 0 | 25 | 4 | 55.2 | 67 | 270 | 40 | 34 | 6 | 0 | 0 | 3 | 34 | 6 | 48 | 6 | 0 |
| LaMura, B.J., Birmingham | 4 | 4 | .500 | 3.69 | 24 | 2 | 0 | 0 | 5 | 2 | 39.0 | 31 | 165 | 19 | 16 | 4 | 2 | 5 | 0 | 21 | 1 | 39 | 3 | 0 |
| Langen, Brian, Greenville * | 1 | 0 | 1.000 | 4.91 | 15 | 0 | 0 | 0 | 7 | 2 | 18.1 | 14 | 84 | 11 | 10 | 1 | 0 | 1 | 0 | 15 | 0 | 18 | 3 | 0 |
| Leek, Randy, Tennessee * | 1 | 7 | .125 | 4.42 | 14 | 13 | 1 | 0 | 0 | 0 | 75.1 | 86 | 323 | 41 | 37 | 15 | 10 | 3 | 2 | 25 | 2 | 34 | 1 | 1 |
| Lubisich, Nik, Birmingham * | 0 | 0 | .000 | 2.42 | 10 | 3 | 0 | 0 | 1 | 0 | 26.0 | 30 | 109 | 8 | 7 | 2 | 1 | 1 | 0 | 3 | 2 | 15 | 0 | 3 |
| MacRae, Scott, Chattanooga | 2 | 0 | 1.000 | 3.00 | 5 | 4 | 0 | 0 | 0 | 0 | 21.0 | 25 | 88 | 9 | 7 | 1 | 1 | 0 | 1 | 6 | 0 | 12 | 0 | 0 |
| Marshall, Sean, West Tenn * | 2 | 2 | .500 | 5.90 | 6 | 6 | 0 | 0 | 0 | 0 | 29.0 | 36 | 131 | 20 | 19 | 2 | 2 | 2 | 2 | 12 | 0 | 23 | 3 | 0 |
| Matthews, Jarod, Montgomery | 3 | 7 | .300 | 3.67 | 24 | 15 | 1 | 0 | 4 | 0 | 100.2 | 85 | 404 | 49 | 41 | 12 | 4 | 6 | 5 | 25 | 0 | 84 | 2 | 0 |
| McBride, Macay, Greenville * | 1 | 7 | .125 | 4.44 | 38 | 12 | 0 | 0 | 5 | 0 | 103.1 | 113 | 464 | 59 | 51 | 9 | 5 | 5 | 0 | 46 | 0 | 102 | 5 | 0 |
| McCarthy, Brandon, Birmingham | 3 | 1 | .750 | 3.46 | 4 | 4 | 0 | 0 | 0 | 0 | 26.0 | 23 | 106 | 10 | 10 | 2 | 0 | 1 | 2 | 6 | 1 | 29 | 1 | 0 |
| McNutt, Mike, Carolina | 4 | 1 | .800 | 4.89 | 24 | 5 | 0 | 0 | 1 | 0 | 57.0 | 51 | 242 | 33 | 31 | 9 | 1 | 1 | 1 | 23 | 2 | 53 | 5 | 1 |
| Meaux, Ryan, Birmingham * | 7 | 9 | .438 | 4.04 | 29 | 21 | 0 | 0 | 1 | 0 | 140.1 | 163 | 604 | 68 | 63 | 4 | 10 | 2 | 3 | 46 | 5 | 103 | 5 | 4 |
| Messenger, Randy, Carolina | 6 | 3 | .667 | 2.58 | 58 | 0 | 0 | 0 | 45 | 21 | 69.2 | 67 | 306 | 21 | 20 | 4 | 1 | 2 | 0 | 29 | 3 | 71 | 4 | 0 |
| Meyer, Jake, Chattanooga | 1 | 1 | .500 | 3.15 | 4 | 4 | 0 | 0 | 0 | 0 | 20.0 | 21 | 86 | 8 | 7 | 3 | 4 | 2 | 1 | 3 | 0 | 16 | 1 | 0 |
| Miller, Ryan, Huntsville | 1 | 1 | .500 | 2.19 | 6 | 0 | 0 | 0 | 0 | 0 | 12.1 | 9 | 49 | 3 | 3 | 1 | 0 | 0 | 0 | 4 | 0 | 20 | 1 | 0 |
| Miner, Zach, Greenville | 6 | 10 | .375 | 5.22 | 27 | 22 | 1 | 0 | 1 | 0 | 129.1 | 132 | 552 | 87 | 75 | 14 | 9 | 9 | 5 | 55 | 0 | 111 | 1 | 1 |
| Miniel, Rene, Mobile | 1 | 2 | .333 | 4.64 | 30 | 0 | 0 | 0 | 5 | 0 | 42.2 | 39 | 193 | 26 | 22 | 4 | 0 | 0 | 4 | 22 | 1 | 38 | 7 | 0 |
| Moehler, Brian, Greenville | 3 | 9 | .250 | 4.17 | 20 | 20 | 0 | 0 | 0 | 0 | 108.0 | 113 | 449 | 58 | 50 | 8 | 9 | 2 | 2 | 27 | 1 | 57 | 2 | 0 |
| Montero, Agustin, Jacksonville | 2 | 0 | 1.000 | 2.40 | 21 | 0 | 0 | 0 | 13 | 4 | 30.0 | 20 | 128 | 10 | 8 | 1 | 0 | 0 | 2 | 16 | 0 | 36 | 4 | 1 |
| Moser, Todd, Tennessee * | 2 | 5 | .286 | 5.36 | 10 | 9 | 1 | 0 | 0 | 0 | 48.2 | 63 | 223 | 31 | 29 | 4 | 6 | 3 | 3 | 18 | 1 | 29 | 5 | 0 |
| Murray, Brad, Birmingham * | 0 | 4 | .000 | 9.50 | 11 | 0 | 0 | 0 | 6 | 1 | 18.0 | 31 | 95 | 20 | 19 | 1 | 0 | 0 | 1 | 9 | 4 | 7 | 0 | 1 |
| Nall, T.J., Jacksonville | 8 | 9 | .471 | 4.14 | 32 | 20 | 1 | 0 | 2 | 1 | 143.1 | 146 | 594 | 74 | 66 | 19 | 8 | 1 | 5 | 36 | 4 | 123 | 2 | 0 |
| Nelson, Bubba, Chattanooga | 1 | 2 | .333 | 4.08 | 10 | 9 | 0 | 0 | 0 | 0 | 53.0 | 61 | 223 | 32 | 24 | 5 | 4 | 0 | 1 | 12 | 0 | 35 | 4 | 0 |
| Nolasco, Ricky, West Tenn | 6 | 4 | .600 | 3.70 | 19 | 19 | 0 | 0 | 0 | 0 | 107.0 | 104 | 454 | 50 | 44 | 13 | 7 | 4 | 6 | 37 | 3 | 115 | 5 | 1 |
| O'Malley, Ryan, West Tenn * | 2 | 3 | .400 | 3.72 | 16 | 7 | 0 | 0 | 3 | 0 | 55.2 | 49 | 233 | 25 | 23 | 6 | 4 | 2 | 4 | 20 | 1 | 37 | 2 | 0 |
| Osoria, Franquelis, Jacksonville | 8 | 5 | .615 | 3.67 | 51 | 0 | 0 | 0 | 24 | 5 | 81.0 | 71 | 335 | 36 | 33 | 2 | 2 | 0 | 5 | 18 | 4 | 73 | 3 | 0 |
| Osting, Jimmy, Montgomery * | 0 | 3 | .000 | 9.90 | 4 | 4 | 0 | 0 | 0 | 0 | 10.0 | 14 | 51 | 11 | 11 | 0 | 0 | 1 | 3 | 8 | 0 | 9 | 2 | 0 |
| Pacheco, Enemencio, Birmingham | 0 | 0 | .000 | 3.55 | 5 | 2 | 0 | 0 | 0 | 0 | 12.2 | 10 | 53 | 6 | 5 | 2 | 0 | 0 | 0 | 5 | 0 | 3 | 0 | 0 |
| Parker, Matt, Montgomery | 1 | 6 | .143 | 5.01 | 12 | 6 | 0 | 0 | 1 | 0 | 41.1 | 42 | 180 | 26 | 23 | 3 | 2 | 4 | 0 | 20 | 0 | 22 | 3 | 1 |
| Parra, Manny, Huntsville * | 0 | 1 | .000 | 3.00 | 3 | 3 | 0 | 0 | 0 | 0 | 6.0 | 5 | 23 | 3 | 2 | 0 | 0 | 0 | 0 | 0 | 0 | 10 | 1 | 0 |
| Pearson, Jason, Carolina * | 0 | 1 | .000 | 1.88 | 16 | 0 | 0 | 0 | 6 | 0 | 14.1 | 15 | 63 | 5 | 3 | 1 | 0 | 0 | 1 | 4 | 0 | 14 | 1 | 0 |
| Phillips, Heath, Birmingham * | 12 | 10 | .545 | 4.02 | 27 | 26 | 0 | 0 | 1 | 0 | 154.1 | 179 | 649 | 78 | 69 | 12 | 5 | 12 | 4 | 36 | 3 | 107 | 5 | 2 |

| Pitcher, Team | W | L | Pct. | ERA | G | GS | CG | ShO | GF | Sv. | IP | H | TBF | R | ER | HR | SH | SF | HB | BB | IBB | SO | WP | Bk. |
|---|---|---|---|---|---|---|---|---|---|---|---|---|---|---|---|---|---|---|---|---|---|---|---|---|
| Pignatiello, Carmen, West Tenn * | 9 | 7 | .563 | 4.56 | 27 | 27 | 1 | 0 | 0 | 0 | 148.0 | 167 | 637 | 89 | 75 | 16 | 16 | 7 | 9 | 39 | 1 | 137 | 5 | 0 |
| Pineda, Isauro, Greenville | 5 | 7 | .417 | 4.48 | 32 | 10 | 1 | 1 | 8 | 5 | 76.1 | 77 | 345 | 51 | 38 | 5 | 6 | 5 | 3 | 38 | 1 | 79 | 0 | 1 |
| Pinto, Renyel, West Tenn | 11 | 8 | .579 | 2.92 | 25 | 25 | 0 | 0 | 0 | 0 | 141.2 | 107 | 587 | 50 | 46 | 10 | 8 | 5 | 6 | 72 | 0 | 179 | 9 | 1 |
| Pratt, Andy, West Tenn * | 0 | 5 | .000 | 9.28 | 6 | 5 | 0 | 0 | 0 | 0 | 21.1 | 24 | 107 | 27 | 22 | 6 | 1 | 4 | 0 | 21 | 0 | 26 | 5 | 0 |
| Pratt, Andy, Huntsville * | 1 | 0 | 1.000 | 1.80 | 1 | 1 | 0 | 0 | 0 | 0 | 5.0 | 5 | 18 | 1 | 1 | 1 | 0 | 0 | 0 | 0 | 0 | 6 | 0 | 0 |
| Prochaska, Mike, Montgomery * | 4 | 10 | .286 | 5.48 | 16 | 16 | 1 | 0 | 0 | 0 | 92.0 | 112 | 404 | 60 | 56 | 14 | 5 | 8 | 2 | 28 | 0 | 68 | 5 | 0 |
| Pruett, Jason, Montgomery * | 0 | 1 | .000 | 6.14 | 8 | 0 | 0 | 0 | 2 | 0 | 7.1 | 13 | 34 | 5 | 5 | 3 | 0 | 0 | 1 | 1 | 0 | 9 | 0 | 0 |
| Raburn, Johnny, Huntsville | 1 | 0 | 1.000 | 0.00 | 3 | 0 | 0 | 0 | 3 | 0 | 4.0 | 3 | 16 | 0 | 0 | 0 | 0 | 0 | 0 | 1 | 0 | 2 | 0 | 0 |
| Ramirez, Elizardo, Chattanooga | 1 | 0 | 1.000 | 3.19 | 5 | 5 | 1 | 1 | 0 | 0 | 31.0 | 35 | 129 | 11 | 11 | 6 | 1 | 1 | 2 | 4 | 1 | 23 | 0 | 0 |
| Reece, Eric, Montgomery | 0 | 0 | .000 | 0.00 | 1 | 0 | 0 | 0 | 1 | 0 | 0.1 | 0 | 1 | 0 | 0 | 0 | 0 | 0 | 0 | 0 | 0 | 0 | 1 | 0 |
| Reyes, Anthony, Tennessee | 6 | 2 | .750 | 2.91 | 12 | 12 | 0 | 0 | 0 | 0 | 74.1 | 62 | 294 | 27 | 24 | 3 | 6 | 1 | 5 | 13 | 1 | 102 | 3 | 1 |
| Ribas, Gabe, Mobile | 2 | 7 | .222 | 8.35 | 13 | 12 | 0 | 0 | 0 | 0 | 50.2 | 78 | 242 | 49 | 47 | 10 | 6 | 5 | 7 | 25 | 1 | 18 | 1 | 0 |
| Rijo, Fernando, Huntsville | 3 | 5 | .375 | 3.67 | 39 | 0 | 0 | 0 | 19 | 2 | 61.1 | 52 | 262 | 29 | 25 | 9 | 0 | 0 | 4 | 23 | 0 | 57 | 5 | 0 |
| Rivera, Saul, Huntsville | 2 | 1 | .667 | 1.62 | 26 | 0 | 0 | 0 | 10 | 1 | 33.1 | 30 | 146 | 11 | 6 | 1 | 0 | 0 | 0 | 16 | 1 | 25 | 0 | 0 |
| Rodriguez, Jose, Carolina * | 0 | 0 | .000 | 3.18 | 7 | 0 | 0 | 0 | 2 | 0 | 5.2 | 6 | 28 | 2 | 2 | 0 | 0 | 0 | 0 | 5 | 0 | 4 | 2 | 0 |
| Rohlicek, Russ, West Tenn * | 5 | 5 | .500 | 2.09 | 60 | 0 | 0 | 0 | 14 | 2 | 69.0 | 44 | 298 | 19 | 16 | 1 | 0 | 0 | 5 | 42 | 3 | 67 | 7 | 1 |
| Rojas, Jose, Jacksonville | 1 | 0 | 1.000 | 4.65 | 28 | 0 | 0 | 0 | 4 | 0 | 50.1 | 44 | 235 | 28 | 26 | 5 | 0 | 0 | 3 | 37 | 2 | 46 | 11 | 0 |
| Ryu, Jae-Kuk, West Tenn | 1 | 0 | 1.000 | 2.95 | 14 | 0 | 0 | 0 | 1 | 0 | 18.1 | 22 | 88 | 8 | 6 | 0 | 0 | 0 | 1 | 10 | 3 | 19 | 2 | 0 |
| Saenz, Chris, Huntsville | 5 | 5 | .500 | 4.15 | 14 | 14 | 0 | 0 | 0 | 0 | 84.2 | 76 | 340 | 41 | 39 | 10 | 2 | 2 | 5 | 18 | 1 | 84 | 2 | 3 |
| Sarfate, Dennis, Huntsville | 7 | 12 | .368 | 4.05 | 28 | 25 | 0 | 0 | 2 | 0 | 129.0 | 128 | 566 | 71 | 58 | 12 | 10 | 8 | 9 | 78 | 0 | 113 | 6 | 2 |
| Schmoll, Steve, Jacksonville | 0 | 2 | .000 | 1.83 | 11 | 0 | 0 | 0 | 7 | 2 | 19.2 | 14 | 81 | 7 | 4 | 0 | 0 | 0 | 3 | 7 | 1 | 18 | 2 | 0 |
| Seddon, Chris, Montgomery * | 9 | 10 | .474 | 4.39 | 21 | 21 | 1 | 0 | 0 | 0 | 119.0 | 129 | 516 | 67 | 58 | 19 | 5 | 6 | 6 | 44 | 0 | 102 | 5 | 0 |
| Sevier, Nate, Mobile | 0 | 0 | .000 | 1.47 | 11 | 0 | 0 | 0 | 2 | 0 | 18.1 | 10 | 73 | 4 | 3 | 0 | 0 | 0 | 0 | 7 | 1 | 13 | 3 | 0 |
| Shelley, Jason, Huntsville | 2 | 4 | .333 | 4.09 | 15 | 2 | 0 | 0 | 3 | 0 | 33.0 | 33 | 153 | 18 | 15 | 5 | 1 | 1 | 5 | 17 | 1 | 29 | 2 | 0 |
| Smith, Matt, Birmingham | 3 | 4 | .429 | 1.83 | 70 | 0 | 0 | 0 | 36 | 13 | 78.2 | 58 | 318 | 21 | 16 | 2 | 1 | 0 | 1 | 26 | 3 | 50 | 3 | 0 |
| Spiehs, R.D., Mobile | 5 | 6 | .455 | 2.88 | 59 | 0 | 0 | 0 | 21 | 3 | 65.2 | 59 | 276 | 24 | 21 | 7 | 0 | 0 | 1 | 19 | 3 | 60 | 2 | 0 |
| Steffek, Brian, Jacksonville | 4 | 7 | .364 | 4.87 | 36 | 1 | 0 | 0 | 19 | 3 | 57.1 | 69 | 271 | 38 | 31 | 10 | 1 | 0 | 3 | 27 | 5 | 49 | 2 | 0 |
| Stewart, Paul, Huntsville | 5 | 3 | .625 | 3.17 | 41 | 2 | 0 | 0 | 12 | 2 | 93.2 | 93 | 390 | 36 | 33 | 9 | 1 | 0 | 4 | 16 | 2 | 74 | 8 | 0 |
| Strelitz, Brian, Carolina | 5 | 1 | .833 | 6.33 | 30 | 0 | 0 | 0 | 6 | 0 | 48.1 | 66 | 224 | 35 | 34 | 8 | 2 | 1 | 2 | 16 | 6 | 24 | 1 | 1 |
| Tavares, Anderson, West Tenn | 0 | 1 | .000 | 17.18 | 1 | 1 | 0 | 0 | 0 | 0 | 3.2 | 6 | 21 | 9 | 7 | 1 | 1 | 1 | 1 | 3 | 0 | 3 | 0 | 0 |
| Thayer, Dale, Mobile | 1 | 1 | .500 | 3.68 | 8 | 0 | 0 | 0 | 4 | 0 | 7.1 | 8 | 31 | 3 | 3 | 1 | 0 | 0 | 0 | 1 | 0 | 7 | 0 | 0 |
| Thompson, Bradley, Tennessee | 8 | 2 | .800 | 2.36 | 13 | 12 | 2 | 2 | 0 | 0 | 72.1 | 56 | 284 | 19 | 19 | 6 | 4 | 3 | 9 | 11 | 0 | 57 | 1 | 0 |
| Thompson, Derek, Jacksonville * | 5 | 7 | .417 | 3.72 | 22 | 22 | 0 | 0 | 0 | 0 | 118.2 | 132 | 519 | 53 | 49 | 3 | 7 | 5 | 5 | 51 | 2 | 100 | 5 | 0 |
| Thompson, Mike, Mobile | 10 | 2 | .833 | 3.41 | 35 | 18 | 0 | 0 | 4 | 0 | 121.1 | 128 | 498 | 50 | 46 | 13 | 14 | 3 | 8 | 31 | 2 | 69 | 2 | 0 |
| Ulacia, Dennis, Birmingham * | 8 | 8 | .500 | 3.77 | 28 | 23 | 0 | 0 | 1 | 0 | 129.0 | 137 | 555 | 63 | 54 | 8 | 5 | 7 | 6 | 36 | 4 | 107 | 5 | 0 |
| Ungs, Nic, Carolina | 11 | 8 | .579 | 4.24 | 28 | 28 | 0 | 0 | 0 | 0 | 161.1 | 178 | 696 | 85 | 76 | 24 | 11 | 7 | 3 | 35 | 1 | 134 | 2 | 0 |
| Villacis, Eduardo, Birmingham | 6 | 4 | .600 | 3.28 | 19 | 18 | 0 | 0 | 0 | 0 | 96.0 | 93 | 409 | 40 | 35 | 9 | 5 | 3 | 8 | 34 | 4 | 71 | 10 | 1 |
| Walton, Sam, Montgomery * | 0 | 1 | .000 | 6.32 | 10 | 1 | 0 | 0 | 3 | 0 | 15.2 | 15 | 77 | 11 | 11 | 0 | 1 | 0 | 1 | 14 | 0 | 13 | 7 | 0 |
| Whitaker, Brian, Mobile | 8 | 9 | .471 | 3.73 | 23 | 23 | 1 | 0 | 0 | 0 | 137.2 | 128 | 561 | 68 | 57 | 9 | 16 | 6 | 7 | 36 | 3 | 82 | 3 | 0 |
| Wilson, Travis, Chattanooga | 0 | 1 | .000 | 3.38 | 3 | 0 | 0 | 0 | 3 | 0 | 8.0 | 5 | 37 | 5 | 3 | 2 | 0 | 0 | 2 | 6 | 0 | 3 | 0 | 0 |
| Wodnicki, Mike, Tennessee | 0 | 2 | .000 | 10.67 | 12 | 2 | 0 | 0 | 1 | 0 | 27.0 | 45 | 131 | 33 | 32 | 9 | 1 | 2 | 5 | 6 | 0 | 9 | 0 | 0 |
| Woolard, Glenn, Huntsville | 6 | 2 | .750 | 2.73 | 23 | 11 | 0 | 0 | 3 | 1 | 82.1 | 61 | 339 | 29 | 25 | 2 | 0 | 0 | 5 | 35 | 1 | 67 | 3 | 1 |
| Zumwalt, Alec, Greenville | 3 | 7 | .300 | 5.09 | 46 | 0 | 0 | 0 | 22 | 1 | 76.0 | 84 | 352 | 52 | 43 | 5 | 2 | 0 | 1 | 38 | 4 | 67 | 6 | 1 |

COMBINATION SHUTOUTS: **Birmingham** (8)—Munoz-M. Smith-McNichol-Bajenaru, Meaux-M. Smith-Bajenaru, Ulacia-Keller-McNichol, Munoz-Allen-Bajenaru, Bullard-Allen-McNichol-M. Smith-Bajenaru, Bullard-McNichol-M. Smith, Phillips-Fields-McNichol, Villacis-McNichol-Fields-M. Smith. **Carolina** (9)—Bauer-McNutt-Fuell, Hutchinson-Cave, Ungs-Flury-Cave, Murphy-Fuell-Moser, Murphy-Cave-Gaal-Messenger, Fulchino-Moser-Strelitz, Fulchino-Messenger, Hutchinson-Messenger, McNutt-Baker. **Chattanooga** (5)—Etherton-Coffey, Rose-Booker-Coffey, Rose-Booker, Rose-DeHart-Coffey, Hudson-Shearn. **Greenville** (8)—Meyer-Zumwalt-Roberts, Meyer-Emiliano-Barry, Meyer-Sturkie, Capellan-Sturkie, Coenen-Zumwalt, Capellan-Coenen-Emiliano, Coenen-Curtis-Pineda, H. Ramirez-Davies-McBride. **Huntsville** (9)—Rivard-Giron, Costello-Rijo-Giron, Woolard-Stewart-Rivera, Sarfate-Rivera-Giron-Novinsky, Woolard-Adams, Woolard-Giron, Woolard-Rivera-Novinsky, Woolard-Rivera, Parra-Ford. **Jacksonville** (9)—Ketchner-Nall, Bott-Rojas-Brazoban, Bott-Brazoban, Nall-Rojas-Nina, Nall-Osoria, Billingsley-Hull-Montero, Bott-Hull-Montero, Nall-Hull-Schmoll, Ketchner-Montero-L. Gonzalez. **Mobile** (8)—McAdoo-Cassel-Hampton-Baker, Whitaker-Webb-Spiehs, Stauffer-Baker, Rojas-Webb-Spiehs-Baker, Thompson-Ribas-Cassel, Watkins-Baker, Hensley-Spiehs-Sevier, Deago-Miniel-Baker. **Montgomery** (9)—Matthews-Hines-Nunez-Parker, Cromer-Hines, Ritchie-Minix, Seddon-Coose-Parker, Prochaska-Coose-Parker, Cromer-Coose-Parker, Prochaska-Coose-Henderson, McClung-Parker-Coose-Parker, Webb-Henderson-Coose-Parker. **Tennessee** (7)—Thompson-Parker, Thompson-Rust, Thompson-Johnson-Parker, Narveson-Rust-Stocks-Cali, L. Martinez-Parker-T. Johnson, Cook-Cali, Narveson-Stocks. **West Tenn** (8)—Pinto-Van Buren, Pinto-Blasdell, Gerk-Rohlicek-Van Buren, Brownlie-Gerk-Fahrner-Van Buren, Pinto-Mitchell-Van Buren, Pinto-Rohlicek-Van Buren, Pinto-Rohlicek-Van Buren, O'Malley-Fahrner-Blasdell.

NO-HIT GAMES: Hutchinson, Carolina, defeated Huntsville, 5-0, April 14.

# 2004 FIELDING

## TEAM

| Team | G | PO | A | E | TC | DP | TP | PB | Pct. |
|---|---|---|---|---|---|---|---|---|---|
| Carolina | 139 | 3626 | 1349 | 112 | 5087 | 117 | --- | 16 | .978 |
| Mobile | 140 | 3661 | 1533 | 119 | 5313 | 136 | --- | 14 | .978 |
| Montgomery | 138 | 3562 | 1276 | 111 | 4949 | 95 | --- | 20 | .978 |
| West Tenn | 138 | 3539 | 1331 | 112 | 4982 | 109 | --- | 17 | .978 |
| Tennessee | 140 | 3594 | 1452 | 117 | 5163 | 126 | --- | 13 | .977 |
| Jacksonville | 137 | 3644 | 1388 | 123 | 5155 | 130 | --- | 10 | .976 |
| Birmingham | 139 | 3672 | 1415 | 129 | 5216 | 104 | --- | 18 | .975 |
| Greenville | 139 | 3648 | 1411 | 138 | 5197 | 143 | --- | 9 | .973 |
| Chattanooga | 140 | 3743 | 1342 | 150 | 5235 | 118 | --- | 15 | .971 |
| Huntsville | 140 | 3626 | 1390 | 154 | 5170 | 114 | --- | 20 | .970 |

## INDIVIDUAL

### FIRST BASEMEN

NOTE: All caps denotes fielding-percentage leader based on 70 games for catchers, 93 for all other non-pitchers and 112 innings for pitchers. *Throws lefthanded.

| Player, Team | Pct. | G | PO | A | E | TC | DP |
|---|---|---|---|---|---|---|---|
| Alvarado, Joel, HVL | 1.000 | 2 | 9 | 0 | 0 | 9 | 0 |
| Alvarez, Nick, JAX | .972 | 12 | 63 | 6 | 2 | 71 | 6 |
| Becker, Brian, BIR | 1.000 | 22 | 208 | 10 | 0 | 218 | 13 |
| Boscan, JC, GRV | .917 | 2 | 10 | 1 | 1 | 12 | 2 |
| Bowser, Matt, MON* | 1.000 | 6 | 39 | 2 | 0 | 41 | 3 |

| Player, Team | Pct. | G | PO | A | E | TC | DP |
|---|---|---|---|---|---|---|---|
| Brewer, Jace, MON | .800 | 1 | 4 | 0 | 1 | 5 | 0 |
| Butler, Brent, GRV | 1.000 | 2 | 4 | 0 | 0 | 4 | 1 |
| Calzado, Napoleon, GRV | .970 | 29 | 214 | 12 | 7 | 233 | 25 |
| Cancel, Robinson, MON | 1.000 | 6 | 33 | 1 | 0 | 34 | 4 |
| Clark, Aaron, MON* | .990 | 19 | 96 | 6 | 1 | 103 | 9 |
| Craig, Matt, WTE | .973 | 10 | 66 | 5 | 2 | 73 | 6 |
| Creighton, Matt, WTE | .975 | 35 | 245 | 23 | 7 | 275 | 23 |
| Darula, Bobby, CNG* | 1.000 | 1 | 7 | 0 | 0 | 7 | 3 |
| Duncan, Chris, TEN* | .990 | 87 | 687 | 35 | 7 | 729 | 70 |
| Dzurilla, Mike, WTE | .984 | 19 | 113 | 9 | 2 | 124 | 9 |
| Erickson, Corey, TEN | 1.000 | 3 | 2 | 0 | 0 | 2 | 0 |
| Espy, Nate, TEN | .989 | 68 | 513 | 25 | 6 | 544 | 39 |
| Fielder, Prince, HVL* | .987 | 133 | 1079 | 56 | 15 | 1150 | 96 |
| Gemoll, Brandon, HVL* | 1.000 | 1 | 9 | 0 | 0 | 9 | 1 |
| Gerber, Joseph, MOB* | .991 | 12 | 95 | 10 | 1 | 106 | 13 |
| Gutierrez, Jesse, CNG | .994 | 124 | 984 | 87 | 7 | 1078 | 84 |
| Hamilton, Jon, TEN* | 1.000 | 3 | 17 | 2 | 0 | 19 | 0 |
| Hill, Jason, CNG | 1.000 | 2 | 3 | 0 | 0 | 3 | 1 |
| Hoffpauir, Micah, WTE* | .996 | 86 | 636 | 62 | 3 | 701 | 60 |
| Hood, Donny, WTE | .500 | 1 | 1 | 0 | 1 | 2 | 0 |
| Hoorelbeke, Jesse, JAX | .986 | 17 | 134 | 12 | 2 | 148 | 9 |
| Iorg, Isaac, GRV | 1.000 | 3 | 18 | 1 | 0 | 19 | 1 |
| Jurries, James, GRV | .993 | 17 | 137 | 5 | 1 | 143 | 13 |
| Loney, James, JAX* | .987 | 102 | 778 | 86 | 11 | 875 | 86 |
| Magness, Pat, CAR* | .992 | 19 | 112 | 6 | 1 | 119 | 5 |
| Maldonado, Carlos, BIR | .974 | 5 | 34 | 3 | 1 | 38 | 0 |
| McNeal, Aaron, BIR | .993 | 84 | 660 | 56 | 5 | 721 | 60 |
| Michaelis, Derek, JAX* | .978 | 13 | 85 | 6 | 2 | 93 | 10 |
| Moore, Frank, MON* | .978 | 32 | 216 | 9 | 5 | 230 | 15 |
| Moylan, Dan, TEN* | 1.000 | 2 | 3 | 0 | 0 | 3 | 0 |
| Murphy, Nate, BIR* | 1.000 | 1 | 11 | 0 | 0 | 11 | 3 |
| Nelson, Brad, HVL | .900 | 1 | 9 | 0 | 1 | 10 | 0 |
| O'Toole, Paul, WTE* | 1.000 | 1 | 9 | 0 | 0 | 9 | 0 |
| Raburn, Johnny, HVL | 1.000 | 6 | 41 | 1 | 0 | 42 | 1 |
| Reece, Eric, MON* | .990 | 40 | 274 | 13 | 3 | 290 | 22 |
| Roman, Jesse, MOB* | .988 | 18 | 159 | 7 | 2 | 168 | 16 |
| Sain, Greg, MOB | .992 | 113 | 993 | 64 | 8 | 1065 | 97 |
| Sasser, Rob, BIR | .990 | 31 | 269 | 22 | 3 | 294 | 18 |
| Soto, Geovany, WTE | 1.000 | 1 | 3 | 0 | 0 | 3 | 0 |
| Stokes, Jason, CAR | .992 | 103 | 861 | 55 | 7 | 923 | 83 |
| Thorman, Scott, GRV* | .994 | 94 | 796 | 42 | 5 | 843 | 86 |
| Tucker, Michael, CAR | 1.000 | 7 | 44 | 5 | 0 | 49 | 1 |
| Velazquez, Jose, MON* | .993 | 54 | 409 | 22 | 3 | 434 | 33 |
| Washington, Rico, MOB* | 1.000 | 1 | 2 | 0 | 0 | 2 | 0 |
| Willingham, Josh, CAR | 1.000 | 17 | 143 | 10 | 0 | 153 | 14 |
| Wilson, Travis, CNG | .985 | 18 | 121 | 10 | 2 | 133 | 15 |

## SECOND BASEMEN

| Player, Team | Pct. | G | PO | A | E | TC | DP |
|---|---|---|---|---|---|---|---|
| Anderson, Bryan, CNG | .962 | 14 | 20 | 30 | 2 | 52 | 7 |
| Arteaga, Joshua, WTE | .936 | 15 | 23 | 21 | 3 | 47 | 4 |
| Aybar, Willy, JAX | .975 | 125 | 267 | 319 | 15 | 601 | 86 |
| Bannon, Jeff, CNG | .977 | 14 | 37 | 47 | 2 | 86 | 11 |
| Barfield, Josh, MOB | .981 | 136 | 293 | 396 | 13 | 702 | 95 |
| Beattie, Andrew, CNG | .980 | 13 | 25 | 23 | 1 | 49 | 6 |
| Bergolla, William, CNG | .965 | 92 | 183 | 208 | 14 | 405 | 51 |
| Butler, Brent, GRV | .968 | 40 | 79 | 103 | 6 | 188 | 33 |
| Calzado, Napoleon, GRV | 1.000 | 3 | 4 | 9 | 0 | 13 | 1 |
| Cesar, Dionys, CNG | 1.000 | 12 | 25 | 23 | 0 | 48 | 5 |
| Clements, Jason, MOB | 1.000 | 3 | 4 | 9 | 0 | 13 | 0 |
| Colina, Javier, TEN | .967 | 75 | 152 | 167 | 11 | 330 | 40 |
| Cortez, Fernando, MON* | .976 | 94 | 196 | 219 | 10 | 425 | 38 |
| Creighton, Matt, WTE | .889 | 8 | 13 | 11 | 3 | 27 | 2 |
| Demarco, Matt, CAR* | .974 | 75 | 136 | 168 | 8 | 312 | 44 |
| DeMent, Dan, MON | .968 | 19 | 24 | 37 | 2 | 63 | 6 |
| Dowdy, Brett, JAX | 1.000 | 1 | 0 | 2 | 0 | 2 | 0 |
| Dzurilla, Mike, WTE | 1.000 | 18 | 33 | 39 | 0 | 72 | 9 |
| Ehrnsberger, Chad, TEN | .977 | 35 | 80 | 87 | 4 | 171 | 29 |
| Erickson, Corey, TEN | .980 | 39 | 58 | 88 | 3 | 149 | 16 |
| Espada, Joe, MON | .984 | 25 | 61 | 59 | 2 | 122 | 12 |
| Garcia, Sergio, JAX | 1.000 | 18 | 28 | 39 | 0 | 67 | 11 |
| Goelz, Jimmy, CAR | .993 | 36 | 53 | 89 | 1 | 143 | 12 |
| Hall, Billy, CAR | .965 | 34 | 61 | 76 | 5 | 142 | 19 |
| Herr, Aaron, GRV | .955 | 74 | 128 | 168 | 14 | 310 | 45 |
| Jaramillo, Milko, TEN | .967 | 6 | 11 | 18 | 1 | 30 | 2 |
| Lewis, Richard, WTE | .995 | 98 | 182 | 229 | 2 | 413 | 54 |
| McCoy, Mike, TEN | 1.000 | 2 | 0 | 3 | 0 | 3 | 2 |
| Moore, Frank, MON* | 1.000 | 2 | 3 | 2 | 0 | 5 | 0 |
| Nicholson, Tommy, BIR* | 1.000 | 8 | 14 | 30 | 0 | 44 | 5 |
| Niles, Drew, CAR | 1.000 | 2 | 5 | 0 | 0 | 5 | 1 |
| Perez, Nestor, MON | 1.000 | 5 | 6 | 11 | 0 | 17 | 5 |
| Raburn, Johnny, HVL | .950 | 12 | 23 | 34 | 3 | 60 | 4 |
| Reyes, Guillermo, BIR | .957 | 6 | 11 | 11 | 1 | 23 | 2 |
| Scales, Bobby, MOB | 1.000 | 1 | 2 | 5 | 0 | 7 | 1 |
| Schifano, Tony, JAX | 1.000 | 1 | 1 | 2 | 0 | 3 | 0 |
| Shaffer, Josh, BIR* | 1.000 | 2 | 0 | 1 | 0 | 1 | 0 |
| Spearman, Jemel, WTE | .931 | 11 | 12 | 15 | 2 | 29 | 3 |
| Tucker, Michael, CAR | 1.000 | 14 | 17 | 21 | 0 | 38 | 6 |
| Velazquez, Juan, GRV | .986 | 39 | 66 | 79 | 2 | 147 | 20 |
| Weeks, Rickie, HVL | .969 | 131 | 238 | 293 | 17 | 548 | 69 |
| Yan, Ruddy, BIR | .980 | 127 | 226 | 323 | 11 | 560 | 56 |

## THIRD BASEMEN

| Player, Team | Pct. | G | PO | A | E | TC | DP |
|---|---|---|---|---|---|---|---|
| Alvarado, Joel, HVL | 1.000 | 1 | 2 | 0 | 0 | 2 | 0 |
| Anderson, Dennis, CAR | 1.000 | 1 | 0 | 1 | 0 | 1 | 0 |
| Arteaga, Joshua, WTE | .935 | 22 | 17 | 41 | 4 | 62 | 2 |
| Bannon, Jeff, CNG | .870 | 9 | 8 | 12 | 3 | 23 | 2 |
| Barnwell, Chris, HVL | .943 | 138 | 127 | 271 | 24 | 422 | 26 |
| Beattie, Andrew, CNG | .923 | 5 | 4 | 8 | 1 | 13 | 1 |
| Brewer, Jace, MON | 1.000 | 1 | 1 | 4 | 0 | 5 | 0 |
| Butler, Brent, GRV | .875 | 6 | 4 | 10 | 2 | 16 | 1 |
| Calzado, Napoleon, GRV | .962 | 24 | 18 | 57 | 3 | 78 | 8 |
| Castro, Nelson, JAX | 1.000 | 5 | 0 | 12 | 0 | 12 | 2 |
| Cesar, Dionys, CNG | .813 | 6 | 3 | 10 | 3 | 16 | 0 |
| Clements, Jason, MOB | .950 | 9 | 5 | 14 | 1 | 20 | 0 |
| Colina, Javier, TEN | .970 | 10 | 10 | 22 | 1 | 33 | 2 |
| Craig, Matt, WTE | .933 | 90 | 51 | 172 | 16 | 239 | 11 |
| Demarco, Matt, CAR* | .935 | 15 | 9 | 20 | 2 | 31 | 5 |
| DeMent, Dan, MON | .727 | 10 | 1 | 7 | 3 | 11 | 0 |
| Dillon, Joe, CAR | .973 | 33 | 22 | 85 | 3 | 110 | 4 |
| Dowdy, Brett, JAX | .500 | 3 | 1 | 0 | 1 | 2 | 0 |
| Dzurilla, Mike, WTE | 1.000 | 4 | 1 | 4 | 0 | 5 | 0 |
| Encarnacion, Edwin, CNG | .921 | 119 | 97 | 196 | 25 | 318 | 11 |
| Erickson, Corey, TEN | .953 | 24 | 12 | 49 | 3 | 64 | 7 |
| Garcia, Sergio, JAX | 1.000 | 10 | 4 | 9 | 0 | 13 | 2 |
| Gautreau, Jake, MOB* | .940 | 63 | 40 | 116 | 10 | 166 | 8 |
| Gonzalez, Andy, BIR | .833 | 1 | 2 | 3 | 1 | 6 | 1 |
| Hall, Billy, CAR | .931 | 37 | 25 | 56 | 6 | 87 | 4 |
| Harrison, Vince, MON | .936 | 57 | 32 | 114 | 10 | 156 | 10 |
| Hood, Donny, WTE | 1.000 | 1 | 2 | 0 | 0 | 2 | 0 |
| Iorg, Isaac, GRV | .833 | 4 | 0 | 10 | 2 | 12 | 3 |
| Johnson, Gabe, TEN | .937 | 113 | 63 | 204 | 18 | 285 | 17 |
| Johnson, Kelly, GRV* | .900 | 3 | 2 | 7 | 1 | 10 | 0 |
| King, Brennan, JAX | .949 | 128 | 82 | 197 | 15 | 294 | 22 |
| Marte, Andy, GRV | .941 | 106 | 69 | 202 | 17 | 288 | 20 |
| Minor, Ryan, CAR | .960 | 41 | 24 | 72 | 4 | 100 | 7 |
| Nicholson, Tommy, BIR* | .952 | 24 | 17 | 43 | 3 | 63 | 5 |
| Paz, Rich, BIR | .943 | 52 | 35 | 98 | 8 | 141 | 12 |
| Raburn, Johnny, HVL | 1.000 | 3 | 1 | 7 | 0 | 8 | 0 |
| Reyes, Guillermo, BIR | .833 | 5 | 2 | 8 | 2 | 12 | 0 |
| Riggs, Eric, JAX | .500 | 2 | 1 | 0 | 1 | 2 | 0 |
| Sain, Greg, MOB | 1.000 | 7 | 3 | 14 | 0 | 17 | 0 |

| Player, Team | Pct. | G | PO | A | E | TC | DP |
|---|---|---|---|---|---|---|---|
| Salas, Juan, MON | .938 | 78 | 54 | 111 | 11 | 176 | 11 |
| Sasser, Rob, BIR | .889 | 55 | 29 | 83 | 14 | 126 | 12 |
| Schumaker, Skip, TEN* | .857 | 6 | 4 | 8 | 2 | 14 | 0 |
| Shaffer, Josh, BIR* | .886 | 16 | 10 | 21 | 4 | 35 | 2 |
| Spearman, Jemel, WTE | .908 | 26 | 12 | 47 | 6 | 65 | 3 |
| Tucker, Michael, CAR | .959 | 22 | 12 | 35 | 2 | 49 | 3 |
| Velazquez, Juan, GRV | 1.000 | 1 | 0 | 1 | 0 | 1 | 0 |
| Washington, Rico, MOB* | .960 | 65 | 48 | 143 | 8 | 199 | 19 |
| Wilson, Travis, CNG | .944 | 8 | 6 | 11 | 1 | 18 | 2 |

## SHORTSTOPS

| Player, Team | Pct. | G | PO | A | E | TC | DP |
|---|---|---|---|---|---|---|---|
| Agramonte, Marcos, MOB | 1.000 | 2 | 2 | 6 | 0 | 8 | 3 |
| Arteaga, Joshua, WTE | .989 | 26 | 38 | 53 | 1 | 92 | 15 |
| Bannon, Jeff, CNG | .937 | 93 | 142 | 244 | 26 | 412 | 53 |
| Beattie, Andrew, CNG | .935 | 8 | 13 | 16 | 2 | 31 | 2 |
| Bergolla, William, CNG | .944 | 23 | 28 | 57 | 5 | 90 | 15 |
| Brewer, Jace, MON | .969 | 82 | 99 | 211 | 10 | 320 | 37 |
| Butler, Brent, GRV | 1.000 | 6 | 6 | 16 | 0 | 22 | 2 |
| Castro, Nelson, JAX | .968 | 82 | 123 | 211 | 11 | 345 | 45 |
| Cedeno, Ronny, WTE | .963 | 116 | 168 | 303 | 18 | 489 | 60 |
| Cesar, Dionys, CNG | .944 | 19 | 26 | 59 | 5 | 90 | 9 |
| Chavez, Anthony, HVL | 1.000 | 1 | 0 | 2 | 0 | 2 | 0 |
| Chavez, Ozzie, HVL | .944 | 77 | 104 | 200 | 18 | 322 | 39 |
| Clements, Jason, MOB | .945 | 38 | 56 | 98 | 9 | 163 | 24 |
| Colina, Javier, TEN | 1.000 | 2 | 2 | 1 | 0 | 3 | 0 |
| Cruz, Enrique, HVL | .921 | 32 | 28 | 89 | 10 | 127 | 15 |
| *Demarco, Matt, CAR | 1.000 | 14 | 15 | 37 | 0 | 52 | 10 |
| Erickson, Corey, TEN | .980 | 38 | 38 | 106 | 3 | 147 | 18 |
| Espada, Joe, MON | 1.000 | 2 | 1 | 2 | 0 | 3 | 0 |
| Estrada, Kevin, TEN | 1.000 | 1 | 0 | 2 | 0 | 2 | 1 |
| Furmaniak, JJ, MOB | .970 | 14 | 23 | 42 | 2 | 67 | 8 |
| Garcia, Sergio, JAX | .913 | 6 | 11 | 10 | 2 | 23 | 4 |
| Goelz, Jimmy, CAR | .946 | 9 | 10 | 25 | 2 | 37 | 6 |
| Gonzalez, Andy, BIR | .941 | 34 | 59 | 84 | 9 | 152 | 16 |
| Guzman, Joel, JAX | .949 | 44 | 55 | 111 | 9 | 175 | 24 |
| Hall, Billy, CAR | .818 | 3 | 2 | 7 | 2 | 11 | 2 |
| Jaramillo, Milko, TEN | .963 | 59 | 64 | 168 | 9 | 241 | 36 |
| Knox, Ryan, HVL | .857 | 1 | 1 | 5 | 1 | 7 | 2 |
| Lopez, Pedro, BIR | .969 | 7 | 10 | 21 | 1 | 32 | 3 |
| Merrill, Ronnie, MOB | .961 | 89 | 125 | 274 | 16 | 415 | 59 |
| *Moore, Frank, MON | .000 | 1 | 0 | 0 | 2 | 2 | 0 |
| Morse, Michael, BIR | .944 | 54 | 59 | 125 | 11 | 195 | 21 |
| Nelson, John, TEN | .967 | 60 | 63 | 170 | 8 | 241 | 28 |
| *Nicholson, Tommy, BIR | 1.000 | 1 | 0 | 2 | 0 | 2 | 0 |
| Paz, Rich, BIR | .975 | 17 | 30 | 48 | 2 | 80 | 6 |
| Pena, Tony, GRV | .954 | 128 | 167 | 371 | 26 | 564 | 82 |
| Perez, Nestor, MON | .991 | 36 | 32 | 80 | 1 | 113 | 7 |
| Raburn, Johnny, HVL | .934 | 39 | 41 | 115 | 11 | 167 | 16 |
| Reyes, Guillermo, BIR | .958 | 27 | 29 | 62 | 4 | 95 | 9 |
| Riggs, Eric, JAX | .913 | 6 | 8 | 13 | 2 | 23 | 1 |
| Rundgren, Rex, CAR | .969 | 43 | 66 | 124 | 6 | 196 | 29 |
| Schifano, Tony, JAX | .958 | 4 | 6 | 17 | 1 | 24 | 3 |
| *Shaffer, Josh, BIR | 1.000 | 10 | 12 | 17 | 0 | 29 | 3 |
| Spearman, Jemel, WTE | 1.000 | 2 | 2 | 4 | 0 | 6 | 1 |
| Upton, BJ, MON | .900 | 23 | 29 | 61 | 10 | 100 | 16 |
| Velazquez, Juan, GRV | .966 | 10 | 7 | 21 | 1 | 29 | 4 |
| Wilson, Josh, CAR | .949 | 80 | 96 | 201 | 16 | 313 | 33 |

## OUTFIELDERS

| Player, Team | Pct. | G | PO | A | E | TC | DP |
|---|---|---|---|---|---|---|---|
| Abercrombie, Reggie, JAX | .958 | 40 | 90 | 2 | 4 | 96 | 1 |
| Aldridge, Cory, GRV* | .975 | 28 | 37 | 2 | 1 | 40 | 1 |
| Alvarez, Nick, JAX | .931 | 42 | 50 | 4 | 4 | 58 | 0 |
| Ambres, Chip, CAR | .984 | 130 | 291 | 8 | 5 | 304 | 2 |
| Anderson, Brian, BIR | .990 | 44 | 95 | 2 | 1 | 98 | 1 |
| Anderson, Bryan, CNG | 1.000 | 1 | 2 | 0 | 0 | 2 | 0 |
| Bacon, Dwaine, WTE | .960 | 122 | 261 | 3 | 11 | 275 | 0 |
| Bannon, Jeff, CNG | 1.000 | 11 | 15 | 0 | 0 | 15 | 0 |
| Barnwell, Chris, HVL | 1.000 | 1 | 0 | 1 | 0 | 1 | 0 |
| Beattie, Andrew, CNG | .967 | 64 | 108 | 8 | 4 | 120 | 4 |
| Belcher, Jason, HVL* | 1.000 | 25 | 37 | 1 | 0 | 38 | 0 |
| Bikowski, Scott, BIR* | .987 | 64 | 141 | 7 | 2 | 150 | 2 |
| Blakely, Darren, BIR | 1.000 | 27 | 52 | 2 | 0 | 54 | 0 |
| Blanco, Tony, CNG | .961 | 51 | 73 | 0 | 3 | 76 | 0 |
| Bolivar, Papo, TEN | .976 | 119 | 194 | 6 | 5 | 205 | 1 |
| Boyd, Shaun, TEN | .981 | 45 | 51 | 1 | 1 | 53 | 0 |
| Brewer, Jace, MON | 1.000 | 26 | 39 | 6 | 0 | 45 | 1 |
| Calzado, Napoleon, GRV | .989 | 56 | 79 | 10 | 1 | 90 | 2 |
| Cancel, Robinson, MON | 1.000 | 2 | 3 | 0 | 0 | 3 | 0 |
| Carter, Josh, MOB | 1.000 | 19 | 20 | 2 | 0 | 22 | 1 |
| Castro, Nelson, JAX | 1.000 | 24 | 39 | 3 | 0 | 42 | 0 |
| Clark, Aaron, MON* | .978 | 90 | 134 | 1 | 3 | 138 | 0 |
| Clements, Jason, MOB | 1.000 | 17 | 17 | 0 | 0 | 17 | 0 |
| Creighton, Matt, WTE | 1.000 | 2 | 2 | 0 | 0 | 2 | 0 |
| Darula, Bobby, CNG* | 1.000 | 33 | 50 | 2 | 0 | 52 | 0 |
| DeMent, Dan, MON | .969 | 40 | 58 | 5 | 2 | 65 | 0 |
| Denorfia, Chris, CNG | .987 | 60 | 151 | 5 | 2 | 158 | 3 |
| Donovan, Todd, MOB | .983 | 52 | 111 | 2 | 2 | 115 | 0 |
| Dowdy, Brett, JAX | 1.000 | 16 | 17 | 1 | 0 | 18 | 0 |
| Duncan, Chris, TEN* | .971 | 30 | 32 | 2 | 1 | 35 | 0 |
| Durham, Chad, CNG | 1.000 | 61 | 106 | 7 | 0 | 113 | 1 |
| Dzurilla, Mike, WTE | .984 | 58 | 59 | 4 | 1 | 64 | 0 |
| Ehrnsberger, Chad, TEN | 1.000 | 8 | 6 | 0 | 0 | 6 | 0 |
| Feliciano, Jesus, MON* | 1.000 | 28 | 66 | 2 | 0 | 68 | 1 |
| Fielder, Prince, HVL* | 1.000 | 2 | 1 | 0 | 0 | 1 | 0 |
| Francoeur, Jeff, GRV | .978 | 18 | 41 | 3 | 1 | 45 | 1 |
| Franklin, Micah, BIR | .947 | 15 | 17 | 1 | 1 | 19 | 0 |
| Frazier, Charles, CAR | 1.000 | 21 | 30 | 1 | 0 | 31 | 0 |
| Gann, Jamie, HVL | .970 | 52 | 93 | 4 | 3 | 100 | 2 |
| Garcia, Sergio, JAX | .911 | 30 | 38 | 3 | 4 | 45 | 0 |
| Gathright, Joey, MON* | .985 | 22 | 63 | 2 | 1 | 66 | 0 |
| Gemoll, Brandon, HVL* | 1.000 | 15 | 22 | 0 | 0 | 22 | 0 |
| Gerber, Joseph, MOB* | .949 | 20 | 35 | 2 | 2 | 39 | 1 |
| German, Amado, MON | .989 | 104 | 266 | 6 | 3 | 275 | 1 |
| Goelz, Jimmy, CAR | 1.000 | 2 | 3 | 0 | 0 | 3 | 0 |
| Gomes, Joey, MON | 1.000 | 6 | 17 | 1 | 0 | 18 | 0 |
| Gorecki, Reid, TEN | 1.000 | 7 | 16 | 0 | 0 | 16 | 0 |
| Greenberg, Adam, WTE* | .962 | 32 | 46 | 5 | 2 | 53 | 0 |
| Guzman, Freddy, MOB | .989 | 34 | 81 | 5 | 1 | 87 | 0 |
| Gwynn, Anthony, HVL* | .974 | 135 | 324 | 10 | 9 | 343 | 0 |
| Hall, Billy, CAR | 1.000 | 23 | 38 | 3 | 0 | 41 | 0 |
| Hamilton, Jon, TEN* | .992 | 89 | 123 | 7 | 1 | 131 | 1 |
| Haynes, Dee, TEN | .952 | 26 | 38 | 2 | 2 | 42 | 0 |
| Hill, Jason, CNG | 1.000 | 2 | 5 | 0 | 0 | 5 | 0 |
| Hoffpauir, Micah, WTE* | .917 | 11 | 8 | 3 | 1 | 12 | 0 |
| Holt, Daylan, JAX | 1.000 | 50 | 59 | 6 | 0 | 65 | 2 |
| Hoorelbeke, Jesse, JAX | .800 | 3 | 4 | 0 | 1 | 5 | 0 |
| Inglin, Jeff, CAR | .974 | 65 | 110 | 4 | 3 | 117 | 1 |
| Jansen, Ardley, GRV | .750 | 5 | 3 | 0 | 1 | 4 | 0 |
| Johnson, Ben, MOB | .963 | 130 | 226 | 10 | 9 | 245 | 1 |
| Johnson, Kelly, GRV* | .956 | 125 | 203 | 16 | 10 | 229 | 2 |
| Jones, Kennard, MOB* | .980 | 81 | 187 | 7 | 4 | 198 | 1 |
| Kavourias, Jim, CAR | .969 | 16 | 30 | 1 | 1 | 32 | 0 |
| Kelly, Kenny, CNG | 1.000 | 51 | 117 | 3 | 0 | 120 | 0 |
| Knox, Ryan, HVL | .984 | 43 | 58 | 4 | 1 | 63 | 0 |
| Magness, Pat, CAR* | .979 | 37 | 45 | 1 | 1 | 47 | 1 |
| Mallory, Mike, WTE | .978 | 89 | 131 | 3 | 3 | 137 | 0 |
| Marrero, Eli, GRV | 1.000 | 3 | 5 | 0 | 0 | 5 | 0 |
| Martel, Normand, BIR* | .971 | 65 | 128 | 5 | 4 | 137 | 0 |
| Martin, Brian, MON | .974 | 112 | 218 | 11 | 6 | 235 | 1 |

| Player, Team | Pct. | G | PO | A | E | TC | DP |
|---|---|---|---|---|---|---|---|
| McCarthy, Bill, GRV | .970 | 62 | 93 | 3 | 3 | 99 | 2 |
| Melian, Jackson, GRV | .979 | 46 | 93 | 1 | 2 | 96 | 0 |
| Michaelis, Derek, JAX* | .955 | 76 | 102 | 3 | 5 | 110 | 1 |
| Minor, Ryan, CAR | 1.000 | 6 | 10 | 0 | 0 | 10 | 0 |
| Moore, Frank, MON* | 1.000 | 20 | 36 | 3 | 0 | 39 | 0 |
| Moreta, Ramon, CNG | .983 | 70 | 111 | 4 | 2 | 117 | 2 |
| Moylan, Dan, TEN* | 1.000 | 15 | 18 | 2 | 0 | 20 | 0 |
| Murphy, Nate, BIR* | .984 | 81 | 175 | 4 | 3 | 182 | 2 |
| Nelson, Brad, HVL | .982 | 131 | 199 | 17 | 4 | 220 | 2 |
| Nettles, Marcus, MOB* | .964 | 37 | 52 | 2 | 2 | 56 | 0 |
| O'Toole, Paul, WTE* | 1.000 | 12 | 11 | 1 | 0 | 12 | 0 |
| Raburn, Johnny, HVL | .978 | 27 | 41 | 3 | 1 | 45 | 1 |
| Reed, Eric, CAR* | .982 | 53 | 105 | 4 | 2 | 111 | 0 |
| Repko, Jason, JAX | .966 | 45 | 81 | 4 | 3 | 88 | 2 |
| Richardson, Mike, MOB | 1.000 | 13 | 28 | 2 | 0 | 30 | 0 |
| Riggs, Eric, JAX | .957 | 10 | 21 | 1 | 1 | 23 | 0 |
| Rohleder, Andy, CAR | .981 | 52 | 98 | 5 | 2 | 105 | 0 |
| Roman, Jesse, MOB* | .969 | 24 | 30 | 1 | 1 | 32 | 0 |
| Ruan, Wilkin, JAX | .973 | 45 | 104 | 5 | 3 | 112 | 0 |
| Ryan, Rob, CAR* | 1.000 | 29 | 57 | 0 | 0 | 57 | 0 |
| Sasser, Rob, BIR | 1.000 | 14 | 24 | 0 | 0 | 24 | 0 |
| Scales, Bobby, MOB | .893 | 18 | 24 | 1 | 3 | 28 | 0 |
| Schumaker, Skip, TEN* | .982 | 130 | 272 | 7 | 5 | 284 | 3 |
| Senjem, Guye, CNG* | 1.000 | 6 | 9 | 0 | 0 | 9 | 0 |
| Shanks, James, CAR | 1.000 | 7 | 11 | 0 | 0 | 11 | 0 |
| Spearman, Jemel, WTE | 1.000 | 7 | 11 | 1 | 0 | 12 | 0 |
| Spidale, Mike, BIR | .985 | 122 | 252 | 4 | 4 | 260 | 0 |
| Stern, Adam, GRV* | .990 | 96 | 198 | 10 | 2 | 210 | 2 |
| Trzesniak, Nick, MOB | 1.000 | 1 | 2 | 0 | 0 | 2 | 0 |
| Van Iderstine, Ben, HVL* | 1.000 | 7 | 13 | 0 | 0 | 13 | 0 |
| Velazquez, Juan, GRV | 1.000 | 1 | 1 | 1 | 0 | 2 | 0 |
| Victorino, Shane, JAX | .989 | 74 | 179 | 9 | 2 | 190 | 2 |
| Weston, Aron, WTE* | .962 | 114 | 167 | 11 | 7 | 185 | 2 |
| Willingham, Josh, CAR | .933 | 8 | 13 | 1 | 1 | 15 | 0 |
| Wilson, Travis, CNG | .948 | 40 | 54 | 1 | 3 | 58 | 0 |
| Yan, Ruddy, BIR | 1.000 | 1 | 1 | 0 | 0 | 1 | 0 |

## CATCHERS

| Player, Team | Pct. | G | PO | A | E | TC | DP | PB |
|---|---|---|---|---|---|---|---|---|
| Aceves, Jonathan, BIR | .983 | 8 | 53 | 6 | 1 | 60 | 0 | 1 |
| Alvarado, Joel, HVL | .992 | 66 | 467 | 59 | 4 | 530 | 6 | 12 |
| Alvarez, Nick, JAX | 1.000 | 1 | 2 | 0 | 0 | 2 | 0 | 0 |
| Anderson, Dennis, CAR | .993 | 60 | 373 | 35 | 3 | 411 | 3 | 6 |
| Bellorin, Edwin, JAX | .990 | 83 | 653 | 58 | 7 | 718 | 8 | 4 |
| Boscan, JC, GRV | .993 | 50 | 385 | 36 | 3 | 424 | 5 | 5 |
| Cancel, Robinson, MON | .992 | 33 | 212 | 28 | 2 | 242 | 1 | 4 |
| Corredor, Nestor, HVL | .980 | 6 | 44 | 5 | 1 | 50 | 1 | 2 |
| Cresse, Brad, TEN | .991 | 45 | 301 | 27 | 3 | 331 | 3 | 4 |
| Delgado, Alex, HVL | .977 | 5 | 38 | 4 | 1 | 43 | 0 | 0 |
| Dzurilla, Mike, WTE | 1.000 | 1 | 2 | 1 | 0 | 3 | 0 | 0 |
| Eickhorst, Chris, TEN | 1.000 | 12 | 70 | 5 | 0 | 75 | 1 | 2 |
| Evans, Lee, GRV | .989 | 20 | 156 | 17 | 2 | 175 | 3 | 0 |
| Franco, Iker, MON | .986 | 60 | 387 | 51 | 6 | 444 | 3 | 8 |
| Grzecka, Casey, CAR | .957 | 11 | 43 | 2 | 2 | 47 | 0 | 0 |
| Hill, Jason, CNG | .989 | 58 | 425 | 39 | 5 | 469 | 6 | 5 |
| Isenia, Chairon, MON | .977 | 30 | 196 | 14 | 5 | 215 | 0 | 8 |
| Johnson, Gabe, TEN | .982 | 18 | 94 | 13 | 2 | 109 | 0 | 2 |
| Johnson, Kade, HVL | .987 | 63 | 503 | 42 | 7 | 552 | 4 | 6 |
| Langill, Eric, JAX | 1.000 | 5 | 29 | 1 | 0 | 30 | 0 | 0 |
| Maldonado, Carlos, BIR | 1.000 | 61 | 391 | 34 | 0 | 425 | 5 | 3 |
| Massiatte, Dan, MON | .979 | 20 | 126 | 14 | 3 | 143 | 1 | 0 |
| McGee, Tom, JAX | 1.000 | 10 | 65 | 5 | 0 | 70 | 1 | 0 |
| Morales, Steve, MOB | .986 | 44 | 257 | 29 | 4 | 290 | 0 | 4 |
| Morton, Colt, MOB | 1.000 | 1 | 10 | 0 | 0 | 10 | 0 | 1 |
| Moylan, Dan, TEN* | .988 | 78 | 547 | 40 | 7 | 594 | 6 | 5 |
| O'Toole, Paul, WTE* | .988 | 45 | 310 | 31 | 4 | 345 | 3 | 3 |
| Pena, Brayan, GRV | .988 | 73 | 568 | 28 | 7 | 603 | 4 | 4 |
| Peterson, Brian, CNG | .986 | 87 | 714 | 69 | 11 | 794 | 8 | 10 |
| Raburn, Johnny, HVL | 1.000 | 3 | 14 | 0 | 0 | 14 | 0 | 0 |
| Reece, Eric, MON* | 1.000 | 8 | 51 | 1 | 0 | 52 | 0 | 0 |
| Richardson, Mike, MOB | 1.000 | 2 | 9 | 1 | 0 | 10 | 0 | 1 |
| Riggans, Shawn, MON | 1.000 | 6 | 34 | 6 | 0 | 40 | 0 | 0 |
| Sain, Greg, MOB | .950 | 3 | 18 | 1 | 1 | 20 | 1 | 2 |
| Socarras, Tony, JAX* | .991 | 47 | 389 | 29 | 4 | 422 | 2 | 6 |
| Soto, Geovany, WTE | .994 | 102 | 837 | 89 | 6 | 932 | 11 | 14 |
| Stewart, Chris, BIR | .985 | 76 | 555 | 41 | 9 | 605 | 4 | 14 |
| Trzesniak, Nick, MOB | .990 | 101 | 645 | 84 | 7 | 736 | 4 | 6 |
| Velazquez, Juan, GRV | 1.000 | 1 | 2 | 0 | 0 | 2 | 0 | 0 |
| Willingham, Josh, CAR | .994 | 78 | 590 | 50 | 4 | 644 | 4 | 10 |

## PITCHERS

| Player, Team | Pct. | G | PO | A | E | TC | DP |
|---|---|---|---|---|---|---|---|
| Abreu, Winston, JAX | 1.000 | 3 | 0 | 1 | 0 | 1 | 0 |
| Adams, Brian, HVL* | .944 | 52 | 5 | 12 | 1 | 18 | 0 |
| Aguilar, Ray, GRV* | 1.000 | 8 | 0 | 11 | 0 | 11 | 0 |
| Allen, Wyatt, BIR | .818 | 33 | 1 | 8 | 2 | 11 | 0 |
| Almanza, Armando, GRV* | 1.000 | 5 | 0 | 2 | 0 | 2 | 1 |
| Ankiel, Rick, TEN* | 1.000 | 2 | 1 | 2 | 0 | 3 | 0 |
| Autrey, Scott, MON | 1.000 | 9 | 1 | 3 | 0 | 4 | 0 |
| Axelson, Josh, TEN | .950 | 34 | 4 | 15 | 1 | 20 | 0 |
| Baez, Benito, CNG* | 1.000 | 12 | 1 | 1 | 0 | 2 | 0 |
| Bajenaru, Jeff, BIR | 1.000 | 32 | 0 | 4 | 0 | 4 | 0 |
| Baker, Brad, MOB | 1.000 | 55 | 3 | 6 | 0 | 9 | 0 |
| Baker, Ryan, CAR | .750 | 40 | 4 | 5 | 3 | 12 | 1 |
| Barry, Kevin, GRV | 1.000 | 20 | 3 | 1 | 0 | 4 | 0 |
| Bauer, Greg, TEN | .750 | 10 | 2 | 1 | 1 | 4 | 0 |
| Bauer, Peter, CAR | .972 | 27 | 10 | 25 | 1 | 36 | 1 |
| Bausher, Tim, HVL | .625 | 11 | 2 | 3 | 3 | 8 | 0 |
| Beech, Matt, CNG* | 1.000 | 6 | 0 | 2 | 0 | 2 | 0 |
| Belizario, Ronald, CAR | .813 | 15 | 4 | 9 | 3 | 16 | 1 |
| Benedetti, John, MON | 1.000 | 28 | 4 | 8 | 0 | 12 | 0 |
| Billingsley, Chad, JAX | 1.000 | 8 | 2 | 3 | 0 | 5 | 0 |
| Blair, Buddy, TEN* | 1.000 | 3 | 1 | 0 | 0 | 1 | 0 |
| Blasdell, Jared, WTE | .933 | 49 | 4 | 10 | 1 | 15 | 0 |
| Blasko, Chadd, WTE | 1.000 | 13 | 4 | 6 | 0 | 10 | 0 |
| Booker, Chris, CNG | 1.000 | 28 | 1 | 4 | 0 | 5 | 0 |
| Bott, Glenn, JAX* | 1.000 | 28 | 4 | 16 | 0 | 20 | 0 |
| Brazoban, Yhency, JAX | 1.000 | 36 | 5 | 3 | 0 | 8 | 1 |
| Brown, Andrew, JAX | .889 | 8 | 3 | 5 | 1 | 9 | 0 |
| Brownlie, Bobby, WTE | 1.000 | 26 | 19 | 15 | 0 | 34 | 1 |
| Bullard, Jim, BIR* | .824 | 37 | 3 | 11 | 3 | 17 | 0 |
| Bumstead, Mike, MOB | 1.000 | 19 | 2 | 5 | 0 | 7 | 1 |
| Byrd, Paul, GRV | 1.000 | 3 | 1 | 4 | 0 | 5 | 0 |
| Cali, Carmen, TEN* | 1.000 | 38 | 0 | 5 | 0 | 5 | 0 |
| Cancel, Robinson, MON | 1.000 | 1 | 0 | 1 | 0 | 1 | 0 |
| Capellan, Jose, GRV | .800 | 9 | 1 | 3 | 1 | 5 | 1 |
| Caracioli, Lance, CNG* | .800 | 12 | 4 | 8 | 3 | 15 | 0 |
| Cassel, Jack, MOB | .935 | 57 | 6 | 23 | 2 | 31 | 5 |
| Castellanos, Hugo, WTE | 1.000 | 22 | 1 | 5 | 0 | 6 | 1 |
| Cavazos, Andy, TEN | .923 | 46 | 4 | 8 | 1 | 13 | 1 |
| Cave, Kevin, CAR | 1.000 | 20 | 2 | 4 | 0 | 6 | 0 |
| Chiasson, Scott, WTE | 1.000 | 12 | 2 | 1 | 0 | 3 | 0 |
| Childress, Daylan, CNG | 1.000 | 29 | 0 | 7 | 0 | 7 | 0 |
| Christensen, Ben, WTE | 1.000 | 9 | 1 | 1 | 0 | 2 | 0 |
| Ciprian, Wilson, TEN | .714 | 14 | 1 | 4 | 2 | 7 | 0 |
| Coenen, Matt, GRV* | .818 | 36 | 1 | 8 | 2 | 11 | 0 |
| Coffey, Todd, CNG | 1.000 | 40 | 4 | 2 | 0 | 6 | 0 |
| Colon, Roman, GRV | .000 | 3 | 0 | 0 | 1 | 1 | 0 |
| Conden, Greg, MOB | 1.000 | 1 | 0 | 1 | 0 | 1 | 0 |
| Connolly, Jon, WTE* | 1.000 | 1 | 0 | 1 | 0 | 1 | 0 |
| Cook, Jeremy, TEN | 1.000 | 29 | 5 | 23 | 0 | 28 | 3 |

| Player, Team | Pct. | G | PO | A | E | TC | DP |
|---|---|---|---|---|---|---|---|
| Coose, Austin, MON | 1.000 | 43 | 1 | 2 | 0 | 3 | 0 |
| Corcoran, Tim, MON | 1.000 | 6 | 0 | 2 | 0 | 2 | 0 |
| Costello, Ryan, HVL* | 1.000 | 24 | 2 | 12 | 0 | 14 | 1 |
| Crawford, Paxton, CNG | 1.000 | 18 | 2 | 3 | 0 | 5 | 0 |
| Cromer, Jason, MON* | .938 | 27 | 3 | 27 | 2 | 32 | 1 |
| Cueto, Jose, WTE | .000 | 4 | 0 | 0 | 0 | 0 | 0 |
| Cummings, Jeremy, TEN | 1.000 | 17 | 3 | 21 | 0 | 24 | 0 |
| Curtis, Daniel, GRV | .900 | 33 | 2 | 16 | 2 | 20 | 2 |
| Davies, Kyle, GRV | 1.000 | 11 | 3 | 2 | 0 | 5 | 0 |
| Deago, Roger, MOB* | 1.000 | 22 | 1 | 15 | 0 | 16 | 0 |
| DeHart, Casey, CNG* | .929 | 48 | 1 | 12 | 1 | 14 | 0 |
| Diaz, Jose, MON | 1.000 | 7 | 0 | 2 | 0 | 2 | 0 |
| Duncan, Courtney, BIR | .833 | 4 | 4 | 1 | 1 | 6 | 0 |
| Eckert, Harold, JAX | 1.000 | 3 | 0 | 6 | 0 | 6 | 0 |
| Elder, Dave, GRV | 1.000 | 8 | 1 | 2 | 0 | 3 | 0 |
| Emiliano, Jamie, GRV | .893 | 51 | 5 | 20 | 3 | 28 | 3 |
| Etherton, Seth, CNG | .833 | 7 | 1 | 4 | 1 | 6 | 0 |
| Eveland, Dana, HVL* | 1.000 | 4 | 2 | 0 | 0 | 2 | 0 |
| Evert, Brett, GRV | 1.000 | 22 | 2 | 9 | 0 | 11 | 0 |
| Fahrner, Evan, WTE | 1.000 | 58 | 3 | 9 | 0 | 12 | 0 |
| Fesh, Sean, GRV* | .000 | 1 | 0 | 0 | 1 | 1 | 0 |
| Fields, Josh, BIR | 1.000 | 52 | 4 | 16 | 0 | 20 | 1 |
| Flannery, Mike, CAR | .500 | 25 | 2 | 1 | 3 | 6 | 0 |
| Flinn, Chris, MON | 1.000 | 21 | 3 | 4 | 0 | 7 | 0 |
| Flury, Patrick, CAR | 1.000 | 42 | 5 | 5 | 0 | 10 | 1 |
| Ford, Matt, HVL* | .958 | 21 | 4 | 19 | 1 | 24 | 1 |
| Frendling, Neal, MON | 1.000 | 6 | 0 | 2 | 0 | 2 | 0 |
| Fuell, Jerrod, CAR | 1.000 | 17 | 0 | 2 | 0 | 2 | 0 |
| Fulchino, Jeff, CAR | 1.000 | 17 | 2 | 7 | 0 | 9 | 0 |
| Gaal, Bryan, CAR | 1.000 | 24 | 0 | 2 | 0 | 2 | 0 |
| Gardner, Richard, CNG | .955 | 11 | 9 | 12 | 1 | 22 | 1 |
| Gerk, Jordan, WTE* | 1.000 | 24 | 2 | 4 | 0 | 6 | 0 |
| Germano, Justin, MOB | 1.000 | 5 | 1 | 4 | 0 | 5 | 0 |
| Gil, David, CNG | .667 | 17 | 1 | 1 | 1 | 3 | 0 |
| Giron, Roberto, HVL | 1.000 | 31 | 2 | 7 | 0 | 9 | 0 |
| Glen, William, MON | 1.000 | 29 | 1 | 3 | 0 | 4 | 0 |
| Gonzalez, Luis, JAX* | .800 | 45 | 1 | 7 | 2 | 10 | 0 |
| Gregg, Grant, MOB* | 1.000 | 1 | 1 | 0 | 0 | 1 | 0 |
| Guzman, Angel, WTE | 1.000 | 4 | 2 | 0 | 0 | 2 | 0 |
| Hamilton, Clayton, MOB | 1.000 | 1 | 1 | 0 | 0 | 1 | 0 |
| Hampton, Matt, MOB* | 1.000 | 13 | 1 | 2 | 0 | 3 | 0 |
| Harper, Jesse, HVL | 1.000 | 1 | 0 | 1 | 0 | 1 | 0 |
| Hartmann, Pete, CAR* | 1.000 | 5 | 0 | 5 | 0 | 5 | 0 |
| Henderson, Brian, MON* | 1.000 | 20 | 1 | 4 | 0 | 5 | 0 |
| Hensley, Clay, MOB | .917 | 27 | 9 | 24 | 3 | 36 | 1 |
| Hines, Carlos, MON | 1.000 | 43 | 4 | 14 | 0 | 18 | 2 |
| Honel, Kris, BIR | 1.000 | 3 | 0 | 1 | 0 | 1 | 0 |
| Housman, Jeff, HVL* | .917 | 23 | 1 | 10 | 1 | 12 | 0 |
| Hudson, Luke, CNG | .933 | 16 | 7 | 7 | 1 | 15 | 0 |
| Huerta, Edgar, MOB* | .000 | 6 | 0 | 0 | 0 | 0 | 0 |
| Hull, Eric, JAX | 1.000 | 21 | 6 | 8 | 0 | 14 | 0 |
| Hutchinson, Trevor, CAR | 1.000 | 23 | 10 | 12 | 0 | 22 | 2 |
| Iehl, Jason, CAR | .000 | 4 | 0 | 0 | 0 | 0 | 0 |
| Johnson, Tyler, TEN* | .818 | 53 | 2 | 7 | 2 | 11 | 0 |
| Jones, Geoff, MOB* | 1.000 | 6 | 0 | 1 | 0 | 1 | 0 |
| Jones, Mike, HVL | .750 | 6 | 2 | 7 | 3 | 12 | 1 |
| Kazmir, Scott, MON* | 1.000 | 4 | 3 | 4 | 0 | 7 | 2 |
| Keller, Kris, BIR | .800 | 15 | 0 | 4 | 1 | 5 | 0 |
| Kelly, Steve, CNG | .923 | 28 | 13 | 23 | 3 | 39 | 1 |
| Ketchner, Ryan, JAX* | 1.000 | 21 | 0 | 26 | 0 | 26 | 0 |
| Kingrey, Jarrod, TEN | .000 | 3 | 0 | 0 | 0 | 0 | 0 |
| Kinney, Josh, TEN | 1.000 | 50 | 1 | 6 | 0 | 7 | 0 |
| LaMura, BJ, BIR | .857 | 24 | 3 | 3 | 1 | 7 | 0 |
| Langen, Brian, GRV* | 1.000 | 15 | 1 | 3 | 0 | 4 | 0 |
| Leek, Randy, JAX* | 1.000 | 9 | 3 | 9 | 0 | 12 | 0 |
| Leek, Randy, TEN* | 1.000 | 14 | 2 | 12 | 0 | 14 | 0 |
| Leek, Randy, JAX-TEN* | 1.000 | 25 | 5 | 21 | 0 | 26 | 0 |
| Lubisich, Nik, BIR* | 1.000 | 10 | 2 | 7 | 0 | 9 | 0 |
| Lugo, Ruddy, CAR | 1.000 | 8 | 1 | 2 | 0 | 3 | 0 |
| MacRae, Scott, CNG | 1.000 | 5 | 1 | 4 | 0 | 5 | 1 |
| Magrane, Jim, MON | 1.000 | 3 | 0 | 2 | 0 | 2 | 0 |
| Manning, Charlie, CNG* | 1.000 | 13 | 2 | 15 | 0 | 17 | 0 |
| Marshall, Sean, WTE* | 1.000 | 6 | 1 | 4 | 0 | 5 | 0 |
| Martinez, Luis, TEN* | .923 | 16 | 1 | 11 | 1 | 13 | 0 |
| Matthews, Jarod, MON | 1.000 | 24 | 6 | 5 | 0 | 11 | 0 |
| McAdoo, Duncan, MOB | .800 | 6 | 1 | 3 | 1 | 5 | 1 |
| McBride, Macay, GRV* | 1.000 | 38 | 3 | 12 | 0 | 15 | 2 |
| McCarthy, Brandon, BIR | 1.000 | 4 | 1 | 3 | 0 | 4 | 1 |
| McClung, Seth, MON | .000 | 3 | 0 | 0 | 0 | 0 | 0 |
| McNichol, Brian, BIR* | 1.000 | 42 | 1 | 12 | 0 | 13 | 0 |
| McNutt, Mike, CAR | .455 | 24 | 3 | 2 | 6 | 11 | 0 |
| Meaux, Ryan, BIR* | .980 | 29 | 7 | 41 | 1 | 49 | 2 |
| Merricks, Matt, GRV* | .333 | 6 | 0 | 1 | 2 | 3 | 0 |
| Messenger, Randy, CAR | .846 | 58 | 0 | 11 | 2 | 13 | 1 |
| Meyer, Dan, GRV* | .929 | 14 | 4 | 9 | 1 | 14 | 1 |
| Meyer, Jake, CNG | 1.000 | 4 | 3 | 4 | 0 | 7 | 0 |
| Miller, Ryan, HVL | 1.000 | 6 | 0 | 4 | 0 | 4 | 0 |
| Miner, Zach, GRV | .913 | 27 | 6 | 15 | 2 | 23 | 2 |
| Miniel, Rene, MOB | 1.000 | 30 | 4 | 3 | 0 | 7 | 0 |
| Minix, Travis, MON | 1.000 | 12 | 0 | 1 | 0 | 1 | 0 |
| Mitchell, Nathan, WTE | 1.000 | 26 | 3 | 3 | 0 | 6 | 1 |
| Moehler, Brian, GRV | 1.000 | 20 | 7 | 19 | 0 | 26 | 0 |
| Montero, Agustin, JAX | 1.000 | 21 | 1 | 5 | 0 | 6 | 0 |
| Moseley, Dustin, CNG | .923 | 8 | 5 | 7 | 1 | 13 | 0 |
| Moser, Todd, CAR* | 1.000 | 20 | 1 | 2 | 0 | 3 | 0 |
| Moser, Todd, TEN* | .923 | 10 | 2 | 10 | 1 | 13 | 2 |
| Moser, Todd, CAR-TEN* | .938 | 30 | 3 | 12 | 1 | 16 | 2 |
| Munoz, Arnie, BIR* | .889 | 13 | 2 | 22 | 3 | 27 | 1 |
| Murphy, Bill, CAR* | .957 | 20 | 3 | 19 | 1 | 23 | 0 |
| Murray, Brad, BIR* | .667 | 11 | 0 | 4 | 2 | 6 | 0 |
| Nall, TJ, JAX | .971 | 32 | 16 | 18 | 1 | 35 | 0 |
| Narveson, Chris, TEN* | .895 | 23 | 5 | 12 | 2 | 19 | 2 |
| Nelson, Bubba, CNG | .600 | 10 | 2 | 4 | 4 | 10 | 0 |
| Nina, Elvin, JAX | .917 | 33 | 5 | 17 | 2 | 24 | 1 |
| Nolasco, Ricky, WTE | .933 | 19 | 3 | 11 | 1 | 15 | 0 |
| Novinsky, John, HVL | .900 | 45 | 1 | 8 | 1 | 10 | 0 |
| Nunez, Franklin, MON | 1.000 | 6 | 1 | 2 | 0 | 3 | 0 |
| O`Malley, Ryan, WTE* | 1.000 | 16 | 6 | 4 | 0 | 10 | 1 |
| Orvella, Chad, MON | 1.000 | 6 | 1 | 1 | 0 | 2 | 0 |
| Osoria, Franquelis, JAX | .967 | 51 | 9 | 20 | 1 | 30 | 0 |
| Osting, Jimmy, MON* | 1.000 | 4 | 0 | 3 | 0 | 3 | 0 |
| Pacheco, Enemencio, BIR | .800 | 5 | 1 | 3 | 1 | 5 | 0 |
| Parker, Josh, MON | 1.000 | 42 | 3 | 5 | 0 | 8 | 0 |
| Parker, Matt, TEN | 1.000 | 25 | 3 | 2 | 0 | 5 | 0 |
| Parker, Matt, MON | .818 | 12 | 1 | 8 | 2 | 11 | 0 |
| Parker, Matt, TEN-MON | .875 | 37 | 4 | 10 | 2 | 16 | 0 |
| Pearson, Jason, CAR* | 1.000 | 16 | 1 | 0 | 0 | 1 | 0 |
| Peavy, Jake, MOB | .500 | 1 | 0 | 1 | 1 | 2 | 0 |
| Phillips, Heath, BIR* | .955 | 27 | 7 | 35 | 2 | 44 | 2 |
| Pignatiello, Carmen, WTE* | .964 | 27 | 5 | 22 | 1 | 28 | 0 |
| Pineda, Isauro, GRV | 1.000 | 32 | 4 | 6 | 0 | 10 | 1 |
| Pinto, Renyel, WTE* | .909 | 25 | 2 | 18 | 2 | 22 | 1 |
| Pratt, Andy, WTE* | .500 | 6 | 1 | 0 | 1 | 2 | 0 |
| Prochaska, Mike, MON* | 1.000 | 16 | 3 | 15 | 0 | 18 | 1 |
| Pruett, Jason, MON* | .000 | 8 | 0 | 0 | 0 | 0 | 0 |
| Purvis, Rob, BIR | 1.000 | 11 | 1 | 2 | 0 | 3 | 0 |
| Raburn, Johnny, HVL | 1.000 | 3 | 0 | 3 | 0 | 3 | 0 |
| Ramirez, Elizardo, CNG | .900 | 5 | 1 | 8 | 1 | 10 | 0 |
| Ramirez, Horacio, GRV* | 1.000 | 3 | 0 | 2 | 0 | 2 | 1 |
| Ransom, Robert, WTE | .000 | 1 | 0 | 0 | 0 | 0 | 0 |

| Player, Team | Pct. | G | PO | A | E | TC | DP |
|---|---|---|---|---|---|---|---|
| Reina, Dimas, JAX | .900 | 9 | 3 | 6 | 1 | 10 | 1 |
| Reyes, Anthony, TEN | .938 | 12 | 4 | 11 | 1 | 16 | 0 |
| Ribas, Gabe, MOB | 1.000 | 13 | 2 | 8 | 0 | 10 | 1 |
| Richardson, Jason, GRV | 1.000 | 4 | 0 | 1 | 0 | 1 | 0 |
| Rijo, Fernando, HVL | .917 | 39 | 5 | 6 | 1 | 12 | 0 |
| Ritchie, Todd, MON | 1.000 | 2 | 2 | 2 | 0 | 4 | 0 |
| Rivard, Reggie, HVL | .923 | 21 | 2 | 10 | 1 | 13 | 0 |
| Rivera, Homero, MOB* | 1.000 | 8 | 1 | 1 | 0 | 2 | 0 |
| Rivera, Saul, HVL | 1.000 | 26 | 3 | 9 | 0 | 12 | 2 |
| Roberts, Ralph, GRV | .000 | 8 | 0 | 0 | 0 | 0 | 0 |
| Rodriguez, Joe, CAR* | 1.000 | 7 | 2 | 1 | 0 | 3 | 1 |
| Rohlicek, Russ, WTE* | 1.000 | 60 | 3 | 16 | 0 | 19 | 0 |
| Rojas, Chris, MOB | .938 | 19 | 3 | 12 | 1 | 16 | 0 |
| Rojas, Jose, JAX | .938 | 28 | 4 | 11 | 1 | 16 | 1 |
| Rose, Brian, CNG | 1.000 | 20 | 4 | 14 | 0 | 18 | 1 |
| Ruhl, Nathan, JAX | 1.000 | 9 | 0 | 2 | 0 | 2 | 0 |
| Rust, Evan, TEN | 1.000 | 22 | 2 | 3 | 0 | 5 | 0 |
| Ryu, JK, WTE | .800 | 14 | 1 | 3 | 1 | 5 | 0 |
| Saenz, Chris, HVL | .917 | 14 | 4 | 7 | 1 | 12 | 0 |
| Salmon, Brad, CNG | 1.000 | 39 | 4 | 8 | 0 | 12 | 0 |
| Sanchez, Felix, WTE* | 1.000 | 7 | 1 | 0 | 0 | 1 | 0 |
| Sarfate, Dennis, HVL | .806 | 28 | 5 | 20 | 6 | 31 | 1 |
| Schmoll, Steve, JAX | 1.000 | 11 | 3 | 6 | 0 | 9 | 0 |
| Seddon, Chris, MON* | 1.000 | 21 | 5 | 14 | 0 | 19 | 1 |
| Sevier, Nate, MOB | 1.000 | 11 | 0 | 4 | 0 | 4 | 1 |
| Shearn, Tom, CNG | 1.000 | 37 | 2 | 7 | 0 | 9 | 0 |
| Shelley, Jason, HVL | 1.000 | 15 | 3 | 4 | 0 | 7 | 0 |
| Shields, Jamie, MON | 1.000 | 4 | 0 | 4 | 0 | 4 | 0 |
| Smith, Matt, BIR | 1.000 | 70 | 2 | 8 | 0 | 10 | 1 |
| Smyth, Steve, GRV* | 1.000 | 7 | 0 | 6 | 0 | 6 | 0 |
| Sodowsky, Clint, CAR | .750 | 8 | 2 | 1 | 1 | 4 | 0 |
| Spiehs, RD, MOB | 1.000 | 59 | 1 | 3 | 0 | 4 | 0 |
| Standridge, Jason, MON | 1.000 | 2 | 0 | 1 | 0 | 1 | 0 |
| Stauffer, Tim, MOB | .923 | 8 | 4 | 8 | 1 | 13 | 1 |
| Steffek, Brian, JAX | 1.000 | 36 | 2 | 10 | 0 | 12 | 0 |
| Stewart, Paul, HVL | .938 | 41 | 3 | 12 | 1 | 16 | 2 |
| Stocks, Nick, TEN | .929 | 31 | 4 | 9 | 1 | 14 | 1 |
| Strelitz, Brian, CAR | .889 | 30 | 2 | 6 | 1 | 9 | 0 |
| Sturkie, Scott, GRV | 1.000 | 19 | 4 | 6 | 0 | 10 | 1 |
| Tavarez, Anderson, WTE | 1.000 | 1 | 1 | 1 | 0 | 2 | 0 |
| Thayer, Dale, MOB | 1.000 | 8 | 0 | 1 | 0 | 1 | 0 |
| Thompson, Brad, TEN | .962 | 13 | 5 | 20 | 1 | 26 | 1 |
| Thompson, Derek, JAX* | .939 | 22 | 8 | 23 | 2 | 33 | 2 |
| Thompson, Mike, MOB | .875 | 35 | 4 | 17 | 3 | 24 | 0 |
| Thompson, Travis, CNG | .727 | 18 | 2 | 6 | 3 | 11 | 0 |
| Ulacia, Dennis, BIR* | .946 | 28 | 9 | 26 | 2 | 37 | 2 |
| Ungs, Nic, CAR | .941 | 28 | 12 | 20 | 2 | 34 | 0 |
| Van Buren, Jermaine, WTE | 1.000 | 51 | 2 | 7 | 0 | 9 | 2 |
| Veras, Jose, MON | 1.000 | 3 | 0 | 3 | 0 | 3 | 0 |
| Villacis, Eduardo, BIR | .839 | 19 | 10 | 16 | 5 | 31 | 1 |
| Waligora, TP, MON | 1.000 | 13 | 0 | 2 | 0 | 2 | 0 |
| Walton, Samuel, MON* | .750 | 10 | 1 | 2 | 1 | 4 | 0 |
| Watkins, Steve, MOB | 1.000 | 10 | 7 | 4 | 0 | 11 | 0 |
| Webb, Alan, MOB* | 1.000 | 42 | 1 | 7 | 0 | 8 | 0 |
| Webb, John, MON | .909 | 9 | 2 | 8 | 1 | 11 | 1 |
| Whitaker, Brian, MOB | .974 | 23 | 5 | 32 | 1 | 38 | 1 |
| Wilson, Travis, CNG | .500 | 3 | 1 | 0 | 1 | 2 | 0 |
| Wodnicki, Mike, MOB | 1.000 | 5 | 1 | 1 | 0 | 2 | 0 |
| Wodnicki, Mike, TEN | 1.000 | 12 | 1 | 3 | 0 | 4 | 1 |
| Wodnicki, Mike, MOB-TEN | 1.000 | 17 | 2 | 4 | 0 | 6 | 1 |
| Woolard, Glenn, HVL | .889 | 23 | 12 | 12 | 3 | 27 | 1 |
| Yofu, Tetsu, BIR | 1.000 | 7 | 3 | 11 | 0 | 14 | 1 |
| Zamora, Peter, HVL* | 1.000 | 10 | 2 | 3 | 0 | 5 | 0 |
| Zumwalt, Alec, GRV* | .900 | 46 | 7 | 11 | 2 | 20 | 0 |

## LEAGUE CHAMPIONS

| Year | Team | Pct. |
|---|---|---|
| 1904— | Macon | .598 |
| 1905— | Macon | .625 |
| 1906— | Savannah | .637 |
| 1907— | Charleston | .620 |
| 1908— | Jacksonville | .694 |
| 1909— | Chattanooga* | .738 |
| | Augusta | .702 |
| 1910— | Columbus | .588 |
| 1911— | Columbus* | .681 |
| | Columbia | .710 |
| 1912— | Jacksonville* | .679 |
| | Columbus | .632 |
| 1913— | Savannah | .754 |
| | Savannah | .593 |
| 1914— | Savannah* | .667 |
| | Albany | .650 |
| 1915— | Macon | .588 |
| | Columbus* | .686 |
| 1916— | Augusta* | .617 |
| | Columbia | .631 |
| 1917— | Charleston | .741 |
| | Columbia* | .667 |
| 1918— | Did not operate. | |
| 1919— | Columbia | .585 |
| 1920— | Columbia | .633 |
| 1921— | Columbia | .642 |
| 1922— | Charleston | .625 |
| 1923— | Charlotte* | .653 |
| | Macon | .580 |
| 1924— | Augusta | .612 |
| 1925— | Spartanburg | .620 |
| 1926— | Greenville | .662 |
| 1927— | Greenville | .622 |
| 1928— | Asheville | .664 |
| 1929— | Asheville | .605 |
| | Knoxville* | .634 |
| 1930— | Greenville* | .620 |
| | Macon | .643 |
| 1931-35— | Did not operate. | |
| 1936— | Jacksonville | .652 |
| | Columbus* | .650 |
| 1937— | Columbus | .572 |
| | Savannah (3rd)† | .565 |
| 1938— | Savannah | .574 |
| | Macon (2nd)† | .570 |
| 1939— | Columbus | .601 |
| | Augusta (2nd)† | .597 |
| 1940— | Savannah | .627 |
| | Columbus (2nd)† | .583 |
| 1941— | Macon | .643 |
| | Columbia (2nd)† | .636 |
| 1942— | Charleston | .620 |
| | Macon (2nd)† | .585 |
| 1943-45— | Did not operate. | |
| 1946— | Columbus | .568 |
| | Augusta (4th)† | .547 |
| 1947— | Columbus | .575 |
| | Savannah (2nd)† | .563 |
| 1948— | Charleston | .572 |
| | Greenville (3rd)† | .549 |
| 1949— | Macon‡ | .623 |
| 1950— | Macon‡ | .588 |
| 1951— | Montgomery | .607 |
| 1952— | Columbia | .649 |
| | Montgomery (3rd)† | .558 |
| 1953— | Jacksonville | .679 |
| | Savannah (2nd)† | .571 |
| 1954— | Jacksonville | .593 |
| | Savannah (2nd)† | .571 |
| 1955— | Columbia | .636 |
| | Augusta (3rd)† | .543 |
| 1956— | Jacksonville‡ | .621 |
| 1957— | Augusta | .636 |
| | Charlotte (2nd)† | .562 |
| 1958— | Augusta | .550 |
| | Macon (3rd)† | .500 |
| 1959— | Knoxville | .557 |
| | Gastonia (4th)† | .504 |
| 1960— | Columbia | .597 |
| | Savannah (3rd)† | .561 |
| 1961— | Asheville | .635 |
| 1962— | Savannah | .662 |
| | Macon (3rd)† | .576 |
| 1963— | Augusta* | .661 |
| | Lynchburg | .662 |
| 1964— | Lynchburg | .579 |
| 1965— | Columbus | .572 |
| 1966— | Mobile | .629 |
| 1967— | Birmingham | .604 |
| 1968— | Asheville | .614 |
| 1969— | Charlotte | .579 |
| 1970— | Columbus | .569 |
| 1971— | Did not operate as league—clubs were members of Dixie Association. | |
| 1972— | Asheville | .583 |
| | Montgomery§ | .561 |
| 1973— | Montgomery§ | .580 |
| | Jacksonville | .559 |
| 1974— | Jacksonville | .565 |
| | Knoxville§ | .533 |
| 1975— | Orlando | .587 |
| | Montgomery§ | .545 |
| 1976— | Montgomery∞ | .591 |
| | Orlando | .540 |
| 1977— | Montgomery∞ | .628 |
| | Jacksonville | .522 |
| 1978— | Knoxville∞ | .611 |
| | Savannah | .500 |
| 1979— | Columbus | .587 |
| | Nashville∞ | .576 |
| 1980— | Memphis | .576 |
| | Charlotte∞ | .500 |
| 1981— | Nashville | .566 |
| | Orlando∞ | .556 |

1982— Jacksonville .576
Nashville∞ .535
1983— Birmingham∞ .628
Jacksonville .531
1984— Charlotte∞ .510
Knoxville .483
1985— Charlotte .545
Huntsville∞ .542
1986— Huntsville .553
Columbus∞ .500
1987— Charlotte .586
Birmingham∞ .476
1988— Greenville .604
Chattanooga∞ .566
1989— Birmingham∞ .615
Greenville .504
1990— Orlando .590
Memphis∞ .507
1991— Greenville .611
Orlando∞ .535
1992— Greenville∞ .699
Chattanooga .629
1993— Birmingham∞ .549
Knoxville .500
1994— Huntsville∞ .587
Carolina .529
1995— Carolina∞ .618
Chattanooga .580
1996— Chattanooga .579
Jacksonville∞ .543
1997— Huntsville .554
Greenville∞ .529
1998— Mobile∞ .614
Jacksonville .614
1999— West Tenn .596
Orlando∞ .507
2000— West Tenn∞ .580
Jacksonville .493
2001— Jacksonville▲ .597
Huntsville▲ .543
2002— Birmingham∞ .564
2003— Carolina∞ .580
2004— Mobile▲▲ .521
Tennessee▲▲ .493

*Won split season playoff. †Won four-club playoff. ‡Won championship and four-club playoff. §League was divided into Eastern and Western divisions; won playoff. ∞League was divided into Eastern and Western divisions and played split season; won playoff. ▲Were entering finals of four-team playoff and were declared co-champions when Professional Baseball declared a stoppage of play.▲▲Were entering finals of four-team playoff and were declared co-champions when the championship series was canceled because of the threat of a hurricane.

# TEXAS LEAGUE

## LEAGUE OFFICE

**President/treasurer**
Tom Kayser

**Address**
2442 Facet Oak
San Antonio, TX 78232

**Phone**
210-545-5297

## TEAMS

### ARKANSAS TRAVELERS

**Vice president/general manager**
Bill Valentine
**Manager**
TBA
**Ballpark (capacity, surface)**
Ray Winder Field (6,083, grass)
**Affiliation**
Angels
**Address**
P.O. Box 55066
Little Rock, AR 72215
**Phone**
501-664-1555

### CORPUS CHRISTI HOOKS

**General manager/vice president**
Ken Schrom
**Manager**
Dave Clark
**Ballpark (capacity, surface)**
Whataburger Field
(7,500, grass)
**Affiliation**
Astros
**Address**
734 E. Port Ave.
Corpus Christi, TX 78401
**Phone**
361-866-8326

### FRISCO ROUGHRIDERS

**General manager/president**
Mike McCall
**Manager**
Darryl Kennedy
**Ballpark (capacity, surface)**
Dr Pepper/Seven Up Ballpark (8,000, grass)
**Affiliation**
Rangers
**Address**
7300 Roughriders Trail
Frisco, TX 75034
**Phone**
972-731-9200

### MIDLAND ROCKHOUNDS

**General manager**
Monty Hoppel
**Manager**
Von Hayes
**Ballpark (capacity, surface)**
First American Bank Ballpark (5,000, grass)
**Affiliation**
Athletics
**Address**
5514 Champions Dr.
Midland, TX 79706
**Phone**
432-520-2255

### SAN ANTONIO MISSIONS

**President**
Burl Yarbrough
**Manager**
Dave Brundage
**Ballpark (capacity, surface)**
Nelson Wolff Stadium (6,300, grass)
**Affiliation**
Mariners
**Address**
5757 Highway 90 West
San Antonio, TX 78227
**Phone**
210-675-7275

### SPRINGFIELD CARDINALS

**General manager**
Matt Gifford
**Manager**
Chris Maloney
**Ballpark (capacity, surface)**
Hammons Field (TBA)
**Affiliation**
Cardinals
**Address**
955 E.Trafficway
Springfield, MO 65802
**Phone**
417-863-2143

### TULSA DRILLERS

**Executive v.p./general manager**
Chuck Lamson
**Manager**
Tom Runnells
**Ballpark (capacity, surface)**
Drillers Stadium (10,997, grass)
**Affiliation**
Rockies
**Address**
4802 E. 15th St.
Tulsa, OK 74112
**Phone**
918-744-5998

### WICHITA WRANGLERS

**General manager**
Eric Edelstein
**Manager**
Frank White
**Ballpark (capacity, surface)**
Lawrence-Dumont Stadium (6,111, artificial infield, grass outfield)
**Affiliation**
Royals
**Address**
300 S. Sycamore
Wichita, KS 67213
**Phone**
316-267-3372



## 2004 FINAL STANDINGS

### FIRST HALF

#### EAST DIVISION

| Team | W | L | T | Pct. | GB |
|---|---|---|---|---|---|
| Tulsa (Rockies) | 38 | 31 | - | .551 | ... |
| Wichita (Royals) | 37 | 32 | - | .536 | 1.0 |
| Frisco (Rangers) | 36 | 34 | - | .514 | 2.5 |
| Arkansas (Angels) | 33 | 36 | - | .478 | 5.0 |

#### WEST DIVISION

| Team | W | L | T | Pct. | GB |
|---|---|---|---|---|---|
| Round Rock (Astros) | 45 | 25 | - | .643 | ... |
| Midland (A's) | 35 | 35 | - | .500 | 10.0 |
| San Antonio (Mariners) | 30 | 40 | - | .429 | 15.0 |
| El Paso (Diamondbacks) | 24 | 45 | - | .348 | 20.5 |

### SECOND HALF

#### EAST DIVISION

| Team | W | L | T | Pct. | GB |
|---|---|---|---|---|---|
| Frisco | 45 | 25 | - | .643 | ... |
| Wichita | 36 | 34 | - | .514 | 9.0 |
| Tulsa | 33 | 37 | - | .471 | 12.0 |
| Arkansas | 26 | 44 | - | .371 | 19.0 |

#### WEST DIVISION

| Team | W | L | T | Pct. | GB |
|---|---|---|---|---|---|
| Round Rock | 41 | 29 | - | .586 | ... |
| San Antonio | 36 | 32 | - | .529 | 4.0 |
| Midland | 37 | 33 | - | .529 | 4.0 |
| El Paso | 24 | 44 | - | .353 | 16.0 |

## COMPOSITE

| Team | W | L | T | PCT | GB | ROU | FRI | WCH | MDL | TUL | SAN | ARK | ELP |
|---|---|---|---|---|---|---|---|---|---|---|---|---|---|
| Round Rock | 86 | 54 | - | .614 | ... | X | 5 | 9 | 14 | 11 | 17 | 8 | 22 |
| Frisco | 81 | 59 | - | .579 | 5 | 11 | X | 13 | 5 | 11 | 11 | 16 | 14 |
| Wichita | 73 | 66 | - | .525 | 121/2 | 7 | 13 | X | 10 | 10 | 9 | 15 | 9 |
| Midland | 72 | 68 | - | .514 | 14 | 10 | 11 | 6 | X | 8 | 16 | 8 | 13 |
| Tulsa | 71 | 68 | - | .511 | 141/2 | 5 | 15 | 13 | 8 | X | 6 | 14 | 10 |
| San Antonio | 66 | 72 | - | .478 | 19 | 7 | 5 | 7 | 12 | 10 | X | 10 | 15 |
| Arkansas | 59 | 80 | - | .424 | 261/2 | 8 | 8 | 11 | 8 | 12 | 6 | X | 6 |
| El Paso | 48 | 89 | - | .350 | 361/2 | 6 | 2 | 7 | 11 | 6 | 8 | 10 | X |

Major league affiliations in parentheses.

PLAYOFFS: Frisco defeated Tulsa, three games to none; (Round Rock won both halves); Frisco defeated Round Rock, four games to one.

REGULAR-SEASON ATTENDANCE: Arkansas, 178,655; El Paso, 229,243; Frisco, 553,312; Midland, 256,110; Round Rock, 689,286; San Antonio, 278,080; Tulsa, 320,733; Wichita, 443,508. Total attendance—2,666,404. All-Star game at First American Bank Ballpark—7,112.

MANAGERS: Arkansas, Tyrone Boykin; El Paso, Scott Coolbaugh; Frisco, Tim Ireland; Midland, Webster Garrison; Round Rock, Jackie Moore; San Antonio, Dave Brundage; Tulsa, Tom Runnells; Wichita, Frank White.

ALL-STAR TEAM: 1B—Ryan Shealy, Tulsa; 2B—Ruben Gotay, Wichita; 3B—Dallas McPherson, Arkansas; SS—Danny Sandoval, Tulsa; OF—Shin-soo Choo, San Antonio; OF—Nick Gorneault, Arkansas; OF—Willy Taveras, Round Rock; C—Chris Snyder, El Paso; DH—Jason Botts, Frisco; Utility—Brooks Conrad, Round Rock; P—Ezequiel Astacio, Round Rock; P—Shane Bazzell, Midland; P—Jeff Francis, Tulsa; P—D.J. Houlton, Round Rock; P—Kameron Loe, Frisco; P—Santiago Ramirez, Round Rock; P—Ryan Speier, Tulsa; Player of the Year—Ryan Shealy, Tulsa; Pitcher of the Year—Jeff Francis, Tulsa; Manager of the Year—Jackie Moore, Round Rock.

# 2004 BATTING

## TEAM

| Team | G | TPA | AB | R | H | TB | 2B | 3B | HR | RBI | SH | SF | HP | BB | IBB | SO | SB | CS | GDP | LOB | ShO | Avg. | OBP | Slg. |
|---|---|---|---|---|---|---|---|---|---|---|---|---|---|---|---|---|---|---|---|---|---|---|---|---|
| Frisco | 142 | --- | 4820 | 736 | 1331 | 2015 | 243 | 45 | 117 | 681 | 22 | 34 | 77 | 505 | 12 | 1050 | 120 | 57 | 106 | --- | --- | .276 | .352 | .418 |
| El Paso | 137 | --- | 4676 | 668 | 1291 | 1950 | 273 | 52 | 94 | 624 | 41 | 43 | 64 | 419 | 9 | 980 | 119 | 59 | 114 | --- | --- | .276 | .341 | .417 |
| Midland | 140 | --- | 4834 | 716 | 1329 | 1991 | 279 | 43 | 99 | 661 | 28 | 41 | 62 | 524 | 15 | 1040 | 92 | 47 | 129 | --- | --- | .275 | .351 | .412 |
| Round Rock | 140 | --- | 4750 | 744 | 1299 | 2004 | 276 | 27 | 125 | 690 | 49 | 56 | 57 | 491 | 22 | 1002 | 160 | 50 | 88 | --- | --- | .273 | .345 | .422 |
| Arkansas | 140 | --- | 4681 | 641 | 1246 | 1913 | 249 | 38 | 114 | 582 | 58 | 35 | 57 | 389 | 14 | 916 | 88 | 53 | 96 | --- | --- | .266 | .328 | .409 |
| Wichita | 140 | --- | 4639 | 652 | 1226 | 1842 | 206 | 31 | 116 | 603 | 54 | 42 | 68 | 486 | 25 | 857 | 82 | 60 | 120 | --- | --- | .264 | .340 | .397 |
| San Antonio | 138 | --- | 4616 | 589 | 1211 | 1769 | 222 | 30 | 92 | 535 | 40 | 37 | 81 | 395 | 14 | 851 | 125 | 71 | 96 | --- | --- | .262 | .329 | .383 |
| Tulsa | 139 | --- | 4622 | 628 | 1199 | 1833 | 234 | 26 | 116 | 586 | 62 | 24 | 76 | 455 | 37 | 1052 | 121 | 63 | 86 | --- | --- | .259 | .334 | .397 |

## INDIVIDUAL

### TOP QUALIFIERS FOR BATTING CHAMPIONSHIP

Minimum 378 plate appearances. *Lefthanded batter. †Switch-hitter.

| Player, Team | G | TPA | AB | R | H | TB | 2B | 3B | HR | RBI | SH | SF | HP | BB | IBB | SO | SB | CS | GDP | Avg. | OBP | Slg. |
|---|---|---|---|---|---|---|---|---|---|---|---|---|---|---|---|---|---|---|---|---|---|---|
| Taveras, Willy, Round Rock | 103 | 464 | 409 | 76 | 137 | 158 | 13 | 1 | 2 | 27 | 6 | 2 | 9 | 38 | 2 | 76 | 55 | 11 | 2 | .335 | .402 | .386 |
| Sandoval, Danny, Tulsa | 133 | 580 | 530 | 73 | 169 | 238 | 37 | 4 | 8 | 66 | 10 | 1 | 2 | 37 | 3 | 64 | 22 | 10 | 12 | .319 | .365 | .449 |
| Shealy, Ryan, Tulsa | 132 | 552 | 469 | 88 | 149 | 274 | 32 | 3 | 29 | 99 | 2 | 4 | 16 | 61 | 7 | 123 | 1 | 1 | 10 | .318 | .411 | .584 |
| Choo, Shin-soo, San Antonio * | 132 | 579 | 517 | 89 | 163 | 239 | 17 | 7 | 15 | 84 | 1 | 3 | 2 | 56 | 4 | 97 | 40 | 8 | 8 | .315 | .382 | .462 |
| Self, Todd, Round Rock * | 131 | 571 | 476 | 86 | 150 | 219 | 34 | 1 | 11 | 81 | 0 | 5 | 1 | 89 | 6 | 95 | 8 | 0 | 8 | .315 | .420 | .460 |
| Garrett, Shawn, Tulsa † | 103 | 424 | 374 | 73 | 115 | 173 | 16 | 3 | 12 | 51 | 0 | 3 | 6 | 41 | 11 | 104 | 14 | 10 | 7 | .307 | .382 | .463 |
| Snyder, Chris, El Paso | 99 | 401 | 346 | 66 | 104 | 180 | 31 | 0 | 15 | 57 | 0 | 3 | 6 | 46 | 1 | 57 | 3 | 1 | 7 | .301 | .389 | .520 |
| Botts, Jason, Frisco † | 133 | 573 | 481 | 85 | 141 | 244 | 25 | 3 | 24 | 92 | 1 | 4 | 10 | 77 | 4 | 126 | 7 | 4 | 18 | .293 | .399 | .507 |
| Cota, Jesus, El Paso * | 94 | 389 | 366 | 50 | 106 | 165 | 21 | 4 | 10 | 59 | 0 | 3 | 2 | 18 | 0 | 61 | 2 | 2 | 18 | .290 | .324 | .451 |
| Gonzalez, Edgar, Frisco | 106 | 443 | 397 | 58 | 115 | 173 | 26 | 4 | 8 | 55 | 1 | 3 | 6 | 36 | 0 | 84 | 6 | 2 | 12 | .290 | .355 | .436 |
| Gotay, Ruben, Wichita † | 106 | 475 | 404 | 71 | 117 | 178 | 22 | 6 | 9 | 68 | 9 | 5 | 6 | 51 | 0 | 60 | 9 | 10 | 9 | .290 | .373 | .441 |
| Conrad, Brooks, Round Rock † | 129 | 561 | 480 | 84 | 139 | 228 | 38 | 6 | 13 | 83 | 5 | 12 | 1 | 63 | 1 | 105 | 8 | 7 | 8 | .290 | .365 | .475 |
| Brown, Hunter, San Antonio | 124 | 520 | 441 | 69 | 126 | 192 | 19 | 4 | 13 | 52 | 4 | 4 | 13 | 56 | 1 | 80 | 20 | 8 | 8 | .286 | .379 | .435 |
| Meadows, Tydus, Frisco | 99 | 405 | 344 | 55 | 98 | 176 | 20 | 2 | 18 | 69 | 0 | 5 | 9 | 47 | 2 | 72 | 3 | 1 | 13 | .285 | .380 | .512 |
| Eldridge, Rashad, Frisco † | 108 | 408 | 348 | 64 | 99 | 131 | 16 | 5 | 2 | 31 | 4 | 1 | 5 | 50 | 0 | 94 | 14 | 5 | 8 | .284 | .381 | .376 |

DEPARTMENTAL LEADERS: G—Bourgeois, 138; AB—Callaspo, 550; R—Gorneault, 91; H—Sandoval, 169; TB—Shealy, 274; 2B—Conrad, 39; 3B—M. Williams, 10; HR—Shealy, 29; RBI—Shealy, 99; SH—Piniella, 15; SF—Conrad, 12; HP—Matranga, Baker, 17; BB—Self, 89; IBB—Garrett, 11; SO—Jimerson, 163; SB—Taveras, 55; CS—Deluchi, 15; GIDP—J. Brown, 20; Slg.—Shealy, .584; OBP—Self, .420.

### ALL PLAYERS

*Lefthanded batter. †Switch-hitter.

| Player, Team | G | TPA | AB | R | H | TB | 2B | 3B | HR | RBI | SH | SF | HP | BB | IBB | SO | SB | CS | GDP | Avg. | OBP | Slg. |
|---|---|---|---|---|---|---|---|---|---|---|---|---|---|---|---|---|---|---|---|---|---|---|
| Acevedo, Anthony, Round Rock * | 10 | 29 | 25 | 2 | 4 | 5 | 1 | 0 | 0 | 3 | 0 | 0 | 0 | 4 | 0 | 6 | 0 | 1 | 1 | .160 | .276 | .200 |
| Acosta, Jesse, Midland | 9 | 18 | 17 | 5 | 2 | 2 | 0 | 0 | 0 | 2 | 0 | 1 | 0 | 0 | 0 | 2 | 0 | 0 | 0 | .118 | .111 | .118 |
| Aguirre, Rodrigo, El Paso * | 2 | 8 | 7 | 3 | 3 | 4 | 1 | 0 | 0 | 1 | 1 | 0 | 0 | 0 | 0 | 0 | 1 | 0 | 0 | .429 | .429 | .571 |
| Aldridge, Cory, Wichita * | 79 | 328 | 280 | 49 | 67 | 143 | 12 | 5 | 18 | 45 | 1 | 2 | 4 | 41 | 3 | 87 | 9 | 7 | 1 | .239 | .343 | .511 |
| Allegra, Matt, Midland | 18 | 73 | 68 | 10 | 26 | 39 | 8 | 1 | 1 | 13 | 0 | 0 | 1 | 4 | 0 | 19 | 1 | 1 | 3 | .382 | .425 | .574 |
| Anderson, Travis, Tulsa | 11 | 2 | 1 | 0 | 0 | 0 | 0 | 0 | 0 | 0 | 1 | 0 | 0 | 0 | 0 | 1 | 0 | 0 | 0 | .000 | .000 | .000 |
| Arnerich, Tony, Wichita | 2 | 7 | 6 | 0 | 0 | 0 | 0 | 0 | 0 | 0 | 1 | 0 | 0 | 0 | 0 | 4 | 0 | 0 | 0 | .000 | .000 | .000 |
| Arroyo, Jack, San Antonio | 4 | 6 | 4 | 1 | 0 | 0 | 0 | 0 | 0 | 0 | 0 | 0 | 0 | 2 | 0 | 0 | 0 | 0 | 0 | .000 | .333 | .000 |
| Asadoorian, Rick, Frisco | 81 | 247 | 229 | 28 | 66 | 103 | 14 | 7 | 3 | 27 | 3 | 1 | 1 | 13 | 0 | 60 | 9 | 0 | 1 | .288 | .328 | .450 |
| Aspito, Jason, Arkansas * | 89 | 330 | 296 | 36 | 68 | 104 | 10 | 1 | 8 | 42 | 3 | 0 | 8 | 23 | 1 | 59 | 1 | 4 | 4 | .230 | .303 | .351 |
| Astacio, Ezequiel, Round Rock | 28 | 23 | 22 | 1 | 5 | 7 | 2 | 0 | 0 | 2 | 1 | 0 | 0 | 0 | 0 | 8 | 0 | 0 | 0 | .227 | .227 | .318 |
| Baker, Jeffrey, Tulsa | 24 | 99 | 91 | 10 | 27 | 46 | 5 | 1 | 4 | 20 | 0 | 1 | 0 | 7 | 1 | 22 | 1 | 0 | 3 | .297 | .343 | .505 |
| Baker, John, Midland * | 117 | 499 | 440 | 67 | 123 | 210 | 32 | 5 | 15 | 78 | 0 | 5 | 17 | 37 | 2 | 95 | 1 | 2 | 16 | .280 | .355 | .477 |
| Balfe, Ryan, San Antonio † | 36 | 151 | 141 | 10 | 30 | 33 | 3 | 0 | 0 | 12 | 0 | 2 | 1 | 7 | 1 | 42 | 1 | 0 | 5 | .213 | .252 | .234 |
| Barber, Scott, El Paso | 40 | 12 | 12 | 2 | 3 | 3 | 0 | 0 | 0 | 0 | 0 | 0 | 0 | 0 | 0 | 2 | 0 | 0 | 2 | .250 | .250 | .250 |

| Player, Team | G | TPA | AB | R | H | TB | 2B | 3B | HR | RBI | SH | SF | HP | BB | IBB | SO | SB | CS | GDP | Avg. | OBP | Slg. |
|---|---|---|---|---|---|---|---|---|---|---|---|---|---|---|---|---|---|---|---|---|---|---|
| Barden, Brian, El Paso | 48 | 213 | 195 | 33 | 59 | 90 | 10 | 6 | 3 | 28 | 1 | 5 | 2 | 10 | 1 | 48 | 1 | 2 | 3 | .303 | .335 | .462 |
| Barker, Sean, Tulsa | 22 | 91 | 83 | 9 | 19 | 28 | 3 | 0 | 2 | 12 | 1 | 0 | 0 | 7 | 0 | 24 | 2 | 0 | 2 | .229 | .289 | .337 |
| Barzilla, Philip, Round Rock * | 17 | 2 | 2 | 0 | 0 | 0 | 0 | 0 | 0 | 0 | 0 | 0 | 0 | 0 | 0 | 2 | 0 | 0 | 0 | .000 | .000 | .000 |
| Bastida-Martinez, Evel, San Antonio * | 12 | 40 | 37 | 3 | 8 | 9 | 1 | 0 | 0 | 1 | 0 | 1 | 1 | 1 | 0 | 8 | 1 | 0 | 0 | .216 | .250 | .243 |
| Bausher, Tim, Tulsa | 16 | 5 | 5 | 1 | 1 | 1 | 0 | 0 | 0 | 0 | 0 | 0 | 0 | 0 | 0 | 1 | 0 | 0 | 0 | .200 | .200 | .200 |
| Beinbrink, Andrew, Frisco | 60 | 211 | 178 | 24 | 45 | 63 | 9 | 0 | 3 | 25 | 2 | 3 | 1 | 27 | 0 | 42 | 5 | 5 | 4 | .253 | .349 | .354 |
| Berger, Brandon, Wichita | 70 | 308 | 267 | 42 | 75 | 133 | 18 | 2 | 12 | 50 | 0 | 5 | 2 | 34 | 1 | 40 | 3 | 2 | 6 | .281 | .360 | .498 |
| Berroa, Angel, Wichita | 11 | 53 | 51 | 8 | 16 | 26 | 1 | 0 | 3 | 10 | 0 | 0 | 0 | 2 | 0 | 8 | 3 | 2 | 0 | .314 | .340 | .510 |
| Bibee, Hal, Tulsa | 2 | 4 | 4 | 1 | 1 | 1 | 0 | 0 | 0 | 0 | 0 | 0 | 0 | 0 | 0 | 2 | 0 | 0 | 0 | .250 | .250 | .250 |
| Biggs, Billy, El Paso | 14 | 1 | 1 | 0 | 0 | 0 | 0 | 0 | 0 | 0 | 0 | 0 | 0 | 0 | 0 | 1 | 0 | 0 | 0 | .000 | .000 | .000 |
| Blanco, Andres, Wichita † | 93 | 359 | 324 | 34 | 80 | 94 | 10 | 2 | 0 | 21 | 8 | 2 | 7 | 18 | 2 | 44 | 7 | 6 | 14 | .247 | .299 | .290 |
| Bohn, T.J., San Antonio | 62 | 249 | 220 | 24 | 58 | 96 | 9 | 4 | 7 | 29 | 2 | 2 | 3 | 22 | 0 | 46 | 6 | 1 | 1 | .264 | .336 | .436 |
| Botts, Jason, Frisco † | 133 | 573 | 481 | 85 | 141 | 244 | 25 | 3 | 24 | 92 | 1 | 4 | 10 | 77 | 4 | 126 | 7 | 4 | 18 | .293 | .399 | .507 |
| Bourgeois, Jason, Frisco | 138 | 583 | 530 | 73 | 135 | 174 | 19 | 7 | 2 | 58 | 2 | 4 | 3 | 44 | 0 | 81 | 30 | 10 | 8 | .255 | .313 | .328 |
| Boyd, Patrick, Frisco † | 68 | 251 | 220 | 27 | 42 | 76 | 7 | 3 | 7 | 28 | 0 | 2 | 9 | 20 | 0 | 73 | 5 | 2 | 4 | .191 | .283 | .345 |
| Brooks, Cedric, El Paso | 16 | 51 | 46 | 7 | 13 | 20 | 5 | 1 | 0 | 8 | 0 | 0 | 2 | 3 | 0 | 13 | 0 | 0 | 0 | .283 | .353 | .435 |
| Brown, Dee, Wichita * | 61 | 270 | 241 | 42 | 73 | 132 | 19 | 2 | 12 | 50 | 0 | 3 | 2 | 24 | 8 | 38 | 1 | 4 | 4 | .303 | .367 | .548 |
| Brown, Hunter, San Antonio | 124 | 520 | 441 | 69 | 126 | 192 | 19 | 4 | 13 | 52 | 4 | 4 | 13 | 56 | 1 | 80 | 20 | 8 | 8 | .286 | .379 | .435 |
| Brown, Jeremy, Midland | 122 | 526 | 446 | 59 | 114 | 159 | 27 | 0 | 6 | 49 | 3 | 2 | 4 | 71 | 0 | 80 | 1 | 1 | 20 | .256 | .361 | .357 |
| Brown, Neb, El Paso * | 21 | 90 | 80 | 8 | 23 | 27 | 4 | 0 | 0 | 7 | 1 | 0 | 0 | 9 | 0 | 13 | 6 | 2 | 2 | .288 | .360 | .338 |
| Bubela, Jaime, San Antonio * | 46 | 178 | 166 | 13 | 37 | 46 | 3 | 0 | 2 | 15 | 2 | 0 | 2 | 8 | 0 | 42 | 2 | 2 | 2 | .223 | .267 | .277 |
| Burns, Mike, Round Rock | 56 | 3 | 2 | 0 | 0 | 0 | 0 | 0 | 0 | 0 | 1 | 0 | 0 | 0 | 0 | 1 | 0 | 0 | 0 | .000 | .000 | .000 |
| Bynum, Freddie, Midland * | 65 | 297 | 265 | 38 | 71 | 95 | 13 | 4 | 1 | 22 | 5 | 1 | 2 | 24 | 0 | 56 | 18 | 7 | 1 | .268 | .332 | .358 |
| Callaspo, Alberto, Arkansas † | 136 | 612 | 550 | 76 | 155 | 205 | 28 | 2 | 6 | 48 | 11 | 4 | 0 | 47 | 1 | 25 | 15 | 14 | 16 | .282 | .336 | .373 |
| Carlson, Jesse, Round Rock * | 41 | 1 | 0 | 0 | 0 | 0 | 0 | 0 | 0 | 0 | 1 | 0 | 0 | 0 | 0 | 0 | 0 | 0 | 0 | .000 | .000 | .000 |
| Castro, Ramon, Midland | 28 | 113 | 93 | 16 | 23 | 31 | 2 | 3 | 0 | 12 | 1 | 3 | 4 | 12 | 0 | 18 | 3 | 2 | 1 | .247 | .348 | .333 |
| Cervantes, Chris, El Paso * | 21 | 3 | 2 | 0 | 0 | 0 | 0 | 0 | 0 | 0 | 1 | 0 | 0 | 0 | 0 | 1 | 0 | 0 | 0 | .000 | .000 | .000 |
| Chico, Matt, El Paso * | 15 | 4 | 3 | 0 | 0 | 0 | 0 | 0 | 0 | 0 | 1 | 0 | 0 | 0 | 0 | 1 | 0 | 0 | 0 | .000 | .000 | .000 |
| Choo, Shin-soo, San Antonio * | 132 | 579 | 517 | 89 | 163 | 239 | 17 | 7 | 15 | 84 | 1 | 3 | 2 | 56 | 4 | 97 | 40 | 8 | 8 | .315 | .382 | .462 |
| Christianson, Ryan, San Antonio | 34 | 144 | 132 | 15 | 37 | 49 | 9 | 0 | 1 | 13 | 1 | 1 | 0 | 10 | 1 | 25 | 2 | 1 | 3 | .280 | .329 | .371 |
| Clark, Daryl, Frisco * | 21 | 63 | 54 | 2 | 12 | 15 | 3 | 0 | 0 | 4 | 0 | 1 | 0 | 8 | 0 | 16 | 0 | 1 | 2 | .222 | .317 | .278 |
| Coffie, Ivanon, Round Rock * | 71 | 239 | 214 | 30 | 44 | 87 | 8 | 1 | 11 | 37 | 0 | 2 | 5 | 18 | 1 | 43 | 2 | 1 | 4 | .206 | .280 | .407 |
| Colamarino, Brant, Midland * | 77 | 333 | 304 | 39 | 83 | 133 | 22 | 2 | 8 | 50 | 0 | 1 | 1 | 27 | 1 | 61 | 0 | 0 | 9 | .273 | .333 | .438 |
| Conrad, Brooks, Round Rock † | 129 | 561 | 480 | 84 | 139 | 228 | 38 | 6 | 13 | 83 | 5 | 12 | 1 | 63 | 1 | 105 | 8 | 7 | 8 | .290 | .365 | .475 |
| Conway, Dan, Tulsa | 78 | 275 | 242 | 24 | 63 | 89 | 14 | 0 | 4 | 24 | 2 | 0 | 7 | 24 | 0 | 70 | 3 | 2 | 5 | .260 | .344 | .368 |
| Cormier, Lance, El Paso | 10 | 5 | 4 | 0 | 0 | 0 | 0 | 0 | 0 | 0 | 1 | 0 | 0 | 0 | 0 | 1 | 0 | 0 | 1 | .000 | .000 | .000 |
| Cosgrove, Mike, Tulsa | 21 | 2 | 1 | 0 | 0 | 0 | 0 | 0 | 0 | 0 | 0 | 0 | 0 | 1 | 0 | 1 | 0 | 0 | 0 | .000 | .500 | .000 |
| Cota, Jesus, El Paso * | 94 | 389 | 366 | 50 | 106 | 165 | 21 | 4 | 10 | 59 | 0 | 3 | 2 | 18 | 0 | 61 | 2 | 2 | 18 | .290 | .324 | .451 |
| Cruz, Nelson, Midland | 67 | 289 | 262 | 51 | 82 | 142 | 14 | 2 | 14 | 45 | 0 | 0 | 1 | 26 | 0 | 69 | 8 | 3 | 4 | .313 | .377 | .542 |
| Curry, Mike, Frisco * | 54 | 220 | 199 | 38 | 54 | 70 | 7 | 0 | 3 | 17 | 0 | 0 | 1 | 20 | 1 | 44 | 20 | 6 | 1 | .271 | .341 | .352 |
| D'Antona, Jamie, El Paso | 19 | 74 | 71 | 2 | 15 | 20 | 3 | 1 | 0 | 7 | 0 | 1 | 0 | 2 | 0 | 16 | 0 | 0 | 1 | .211 | .230 | .282 |
| DeRenne, Keoni, El Paso | 17 | 78 | 61 | 16 | 22 | 30 | 4 | 2 | 0 | 9 | 0 | 1 | 1 | 15 | 0 | 4 | 1 | 1 | 1 | .361 | .487 | .492 |
| Del Chiaro, Brent, Arkansas | 40 | 128 | 114 | 14 | 26 | 41 | 3 | 0 | 4 | 14 | 3 | 1 | 3 | 7 | 1 | 52 | 1 | 0 | 0 | .228 | .288 | .360 |
| Delucchi, Dustin, San Antonio * | 127 | 576 | 486 | 82 | 132 | 171 | 23 | 2 | 4 | 32 | 5 | 3 | 11 | 71 | 0 | 75 | 23 | 15 | 3 | .272 | .375 | .352 |
| DiRosa, Mike, El Paso | 65 | 236 | 192 | 27 | 41 | 64 | 12 | 1 | 3 | 31 | 1 | 5 | 2 | 36 | 0 | 63 | 1 | 0 | 4 | .214 | .336 | .333 |
| Dobbs, Greg, San Antonio * | 51 | 220 | 203 | 25 | 66 | 103 | 14 | 4 | 5 | 34 | 0 | 1 | 5 | 11 | 2 | 23 | 5 | 4 | 5 | .325 | .373 | .507 |
| Duenas, Tommy, Arkansas | 3 | 9 | 8 | 0 | 0 | 0 | 0 | 0 | 0 | 0 | 0 | 0 | 1 | 0 | 0 | 5 | 0 | 0 | 0 | .000 | .111 | .000 |
| Duncan, Carlos, Arkansas | 46 | 163 | 153 | 20 | 40 | 59 | 7 | 3 | 2 | 16 | 2 | 0 | 2 | 6 | 1 | 43 | 4 | 2 | 2 | .261 | .298 | .386 |
| Eldridge, Rashad, Frisco † | 108 | 408 | 348 | 64 | 99 | 131 | 16 | 5 | 2 | 31 | 4 | 1 | 5 | 50 | 0 | 94 | 14 | 5 | 8 | .284 | .381 | .376 |
| Ellison, Josh, San Antonio | 1 | 4 | 4 | 0 | 2 | 2 | 0 | 0 | 0 | 1 | 0 | 0 | 0 | 0 | 0 | 0 | 1 | 0 | 0 | .500 | .500 | .500 |
| Esposito, Brian, Frisco | 31 | 101 | 92 | 11 | 19 | 26 | 4 | 0 | 1 | 11 | 2 | 3 | 0 | 4 | 0 | 27 | 0 | 1 | 3 | .207 | .232 | .283 |
| Esposito, Mike, Tulsa | 24 | 15 | 14 | 2 | 2 | 2 | 0 | 0 | 0 | 1 | 1 | 0 | 0 | 0 | 0 | 3 | 1 | 0 | 1 | .143 | .143 | .143 |
| Eylward, Mike, Arkansas | 115 | 448 | 392 | 36 | 102 | 135 | 15 | 0 | 6 | 58 | 6 | 4 | 11 | 35 | 1 | 77 | 3 | 1 | 9 | .260 | .335 | .344 |
| Faison, Vince, San Antonio * | 17 | 69 | 59 | 8 | 17 | 32 | 6 | 0 | 3 | 11 | 1 | 0 | 1 | 8 | 1 | 13 | 0 | 2 | 1 | .288 | .382 | .542 |
| Fenster, Darren, Wichita | 30 | 126 | 111 | 14 | 34 | 40 | 3 | 0 | 1 | 11 | 0 | 0 | 1 | 14 | 0 | 14 | 0 | 1 | 3 | .306 | .389 | .360 |
| Fossum, Casey, El Paso † | 2 | 1 | 1 | 1 | 1 | 1 | 0 | 0 | 0 | 0 | 0 | 0 | 0 | 0 | 0 | 0 | 0 | 0 | 0 | 1.000 | 1.000 | 1.000 |
| Francis, Jeff, Tulsa * | 17 | 7 | 7 | 0 | 0 | 0 | 0 | 0 | 0 | 0 | 0 | 0 | 0 | 0 | 0 | 4 | 0 | 0 | 0 | .000 | .000 | .000 |
| Gandolfo, Rob, San Antonio * | 99 | 354 | 323 | 28 | 72 | 80 | 6 | 1 | 0 | 20 | 6 | 3 | 5 | 17 | 1 | 42 | 6 | 3 | 12 | .223 | .270 | .248 |
| Garbe, B.J., San Antonio | 3 | 9 | 8 | 0 | 3 | 3 | 0 | 0 | 0 | 0 | 0 | 0 | 0 | 1 | 0 | 1 | 0 | 1 | 0 | .375 | .444 | .375 |
| Garrabrants, Steve, El Paso | 31 | 127 | 112 | 20 | 28 | 43 | 7 | 1 | 2 | 12 | 3 | 0 | 2 | 10 | 0 | 29 | 6 | 3 | 1 | .250 | .323 | .384 |
| Garrett, Shawn, Tulsa † | 103 | 424 | 374 | 73 | 115 | 173 | 16 | 3 | 12 | 51 | 0 | 3 | 6 | 41 | 11 | 104 | 14 | 10 | 7 | .307 | .382 | .463 |
| Garthwaite, Jay, El Paso | 42 | 131 | 122 | 9 | 23 | 38 | 5 | 2 | 2 | 13 | 0 | 2 | 2 | 5 | 1 | 37 | 2 | 0 | 4 | .189 | .229 | .311 |
| Gemoll, Justin, Wichita | 124 | 487 | 421 | 60 | 114 | 158 | 16 | 2 | 8 | 37 | 6 | 4 | 12 | 44 | 1 | 80 | 8 | 4 | 14 | .271 | .353 | .375 |
| Gerez, Francisco, San Antonio | 1 | 1 | 1 | 0 | 0 | 0 | 0 | 0 | 0 | 0 | 0 | 0 | 0 | 0 | 0 | 1 | 0 | 0 | 0 | .000 | .000 | .000 |
| Gettis, Byron, Wichita | 17 | 67 | 58 | 6 | 21 | 33 | 4 | 1 | 2 | 11 | 0 | 0 | 1 | 8 | 1 | 12 | 0 | 1 | 1 | .362 | .448 | .569 |
| Gibson, Derrick, Arkansas | 50 | 204 | 185 | 29 | 43 | 84 | 11 | 0 | 10 | 26 | 0 | 2 | 6 | 11 | 0 | 47 | 1 | 1 | 4 | .232 | .294 | .454 |
| Gimenez, Hector, Round Rock † | 97 | 359 | 331 | 38 | 81 | 121 | 16 | 3 | 6 | 45 | 3 | 5 | 2 | 18 | 0 | 64 | 2 | 0 | 3 | .245 | .284 | .366 |
| Gomez, Francis, Midland | 103 | 384 | 347 | 48 | 82 | 113 | 13 | 3 | 4 | 39 | 4 | 2 | 4 | 27 | 1 | 84 | 10 | 4 | 9 | .236 | .297 | .326 |
| Gomez, Rudy, Arkansas | 119 | 492 | 439 | 56 | 116 | 162 | 25 | 3 | 5 | 38 | 3 | 3 | 6 | 41 | 0 | 41 | 4 | 4 | 16 | .264 | .333 | .369 |
| Gonzalez, Edgar, Frisco | 106 | 443 | 397 | 58 | 115 | 173 | 26 | 4 | 8 | 55 | 1 | 3 | 6 | 36 | 0 | 84 | 6 | 2 | 12 | .290 | .355 | .436 |
| Goocher, Clint, El Paso * | 17 | 7 | 5 | 1 | 2 | 2 | 0 | 0 | 0 | 0 | 1 | 0 | 0 | 1 | 0 | 1 | 0 | 0 | 0 | .400 | .500 | .400 |
| Good, Andrew, El Paso | 4 | 1 | 1 | 0 | 0 | 0 | 0 | 0 | 0 | 0 | 0 | 0 | 0 | 0 | 0 | 1 | 0 | 0 | 0 | .000 | .000 | .000 |
| Gorneault, Nick, Arkansas | 130 | 554 | 496 | 91 | 139 | 238 | 28 | 4 | 21 | 81 | 5 | 5 | 3 | 45 | 2 | 128 | 7 | 5 | 8 | .280 | .341 | .480 |
| Goss, Mike, El Paso * | 12 | 41 | 40 | 1 | 13 | 15 | 2 | 0 | 0 | 6 | 0 | 0 | 0 | 1 | 0 | 7 | 1 | 2 | 4 | .325 | .341 | .375 |
| Gotay, Ruben, Wichita † | 106 | 475 | 404 | 71 | 117 | 178 | 22 | 6 | 9 | 68 | 9 | 5 | 6 | 51 | 0 | 60 | 9 | 10 | 9 | .290 | .373 | .441 |
| Gothreaux, Jared, Round Rock | 27 | 17 | 17 | 0 | 0 | 0 | 0 | 0 | 0 | 0 | 0 | 0 | 0 | 0 | 0 | 8 | 0 | 0 | 0 | .000 | .000 | .000 |
| Green, Sean, Tulsa | 52 | 3 | 2 | 0 | 1 | 1 | 0 | 0 | 0 | 0 | 0 | 0 | 0 | 1 | 0 | 1 | 0 | 0 | 0 | .500 | .667 | .500 |
| Groves, Brett, Wichita | 27 | 99 | 84 | 9 | 20 | 24 | 4 | 0 | 0 | 4 | 3 | 0 | 1 | 11 | 0 | 18 | 0 | 3 | 3 | .238 | .333 | .286 |
| Guerrero, Cristian, Arkansas | 54 | 204 | 192 | 18 | 53 | 83 | 13 | 4 | 3 | 23 | 0 | 0 | 0 | 12 | 0 | 42 | 4 | 2 | 3 | .276 | .319 | .432 |
| Guerrero, Cristian, San Antonio | 56 | 208 | 196 | 28 | 44 | 77 | 7 | 1 | 8 | 23 | 1 | 2 | 1 | 8 | 0 | 50 | 7 | 5 | 2 | .224 | .256 | .393 |
| Guiel, Aaron, Wichita * | 6 | 31 | 20 | 7 | 5 | 5 | 0 | 0 | 0 | 0 | 0 | 0 | 3 | 8 | 0 | 6 | 2 | 0 | 0 | .250 | .516 | .250 |
| Gutierrez, Vic, Arkansas | 58 | 205 | 190 | 15 | 53 | 76 | 13 | 2 | 2 | 16 | 3 | 0 | 0 | 12 | 0 | 24 | 4 | 2 | 6 | .279 | .322 | .400 |
| Haley, Adam, El Paso * | 42 | 170 | 153 | 16 | 35 | 47 | 6 | 3 | 0 | 18 | 2 | 0 | 3 | 12 | 0 | 27 | 0 | 2 | 9 | .229 | .298 | .307 |

| Player, Team | G | TPA | AB | R | H | TB | 2B | 3B | HR | RBI | SH | SF | HP | BB | IBB | SO | SB | CS | GDP | Avg. | OBP | Slg. |
|---|---|---|---|---|---|---|---|---|---|---|---|---|---|---|---|---|---|---|---|---|---|---|
| Hall, Victor, El Paso * | 58 | 222 | 192 | 27 | 66 | 92 | 8 | 6 | 2 | 18 | 6 | 1 | 0 | 23 | 0 | 36 | 11 | 9 | 0 | .344 | .412 | .479 |
| Hampson, Justin, Tulsa * | 27 | 17 | 14 | 0 | 1 | 1 | 0 | 0 | 0 | 1 | 2 | 0 | 0 | 1 | 0 | 10 | 0 | 0 | 0 | .071 | .133 | .071 |
| Harrison, Adonis, Tulsa * | 106 | 361 | 318 | 39 | 72 | 103 | 14 | 1 | 5 | 28 | 4 | 1 | 0 | 38 | 0 | 58 | 9 | 6 | 10 | .226 | .308 | .324 |
| Hart, Corey, Wichita † | 75 | 291 | 240 | 37 | 55 | 71 | 13 | 0 | 1 | 29 | 1 | 5 | 3 | 42 | 0 | 52 | 0 | 6 | 4 | .229 | .345 | .296 |
| Henrie, Matt, El Paso * | 17 | 18 | 18 | 2 | 5 | 9 | 1 | 0 | 1 | 3 | 0 | 0 | 0 | 0 | 0 | 6 | 0 | 0 | 1 | .278 | .278 | .500 |
| Hill, Mike, Round Rock | 22 | 97 | 88 | 8 | 25 | 30 | 5 | 0 | 0 | 11 | 0 | 1 | 1 | 7 | 0 | 20 | 2 | 1 | 2 | .284 | .340 | .341 |
| Hopper, Norris, Wichita | 98 | 413 | 363 | 48 | 101 | 112 | 5 | 3 | 0 | 40 | 10 | 2 | 5 | 33 | 0 | 44 | 17 | 7 | 10 | .278 | .345 | .309 |
| Horner, Jim, San Antonio | 18 | 75 | 67 | 8 | 19 | 28 | 9 | 0 | 0 | 5 | 0 | 1 | 3 | 4 | 0 | 10 | 2 | 1 | 2 | .284 | .347 | .418 |
| Houlton, D.J., Round Rock | 28 | 25 | 24 | 2 | 6 | 8 | 2 | 0 | 0 | 1 | 1 | 0 | 0 | 0 | 0 | 5 | 0 | 0 | 0 | .250 | .250 | .333 |
| Howe, Matt, Midland | 9 | 35 | 31 | 0 | 4 | 5 | 1 | 0 | 0 | 1 | 0 | 0 | 0 | 4 | 0 | 5 | 0 | 0 | 1 | .129 | .229 | .161 |
| Jackson, Conor, El Paso | 60 | 256 | 226 | 33 | 68 | 103 | 13 | 2 | 6 | 37 | 0 | 4 | 2 | 24 | 0 | 36 | 3 | 3 | 4 | .301 | .367 | .456 |
| Jackson, Steve, Midland | 73 | 268 | 246 | 28 | 60 | 105 | 12 | 0 | 11 | 39 | 1 | 0 | 3 | 18 | 0 | 61 | 0 | 2 | 2 | .244 | .303 | .427 |
| Jacobs, Greg, San Antonio * | 42 | 173 | 155 | 27 | 48 | 78 | 13 | 1 | 5 | 31 | 0 | 2 | 0 | 16 | 1 | 20 | 1 | 3 | 1 | .310 | .370 | .503 |
| Jimerson, Charlton, Round Rock | 131 | 528 | 488 | 78 | 116 | 202 | 22 | 5 | 18 | 53 | 3 | 1 | 5 | 31 | 5 | 163 | 39 | 6 | 8 | .238 | .290 | .414 |
| Jones, Jaime, Wichita * | 69 | 287 | 251 | 32 | 68 | 94 | 6 | 1 | 6 | 38 | 1 | 1 | 4 | 30 | 1 | 56 | 0 | 0 | 8 | .271 | .357 | .375 |
| Jordan, Brian, Frisco | 6 | 19 | 19 | 1 | 3 | 4 | 1 | 0 | 0 | 0 | 0 | 0 | 0 | 0 | 0 | 6 | 0 | 0 | 0 | .158 | .158 | .211 |
| Juarez, William, El Paso | 13 | 14 | 13 | 0 | 0 | 0 | 0 | 0 | 0 | 0 | 1 | 0 | 0 | 0 | 0 | 3 | 0 | 0 | 1 | .000 | .000 | .000 |
| Kent, Steve, Tulsa * | 39 | 1 | 0 | 0 | 0 | 0 | 0 | 0 | 0 | 0 | 1 | 0 | 0 | 0 | 0 | 0 | 0 | 0 | 0 | .000 | .000 | .000 |
| Keppinger, Billy, Wichita * | 49 | 1 | 1 | 1 | 1 | 1 | 0 | 0 | 0 | 0 | 0 | 0 | 0 | 0 | 0 | 0 | 0 | 0 | 0 | 1.000 | 1.000 | 1.000 |
| Kiger, Mark, Midland | 126 | 577 | 488 | 78 | 128 | 173 | 24 | 3 | 5 | 47 | 3 | 2 | 5 | 77 | 1 | 97 | 12 | 6 | 19 | .262 | .367 | .355 |
| Kinsler, Ian, Frisco | 71 | 326 | 277 | 51 | 83 | 133 | 21 | 1 | 9 | 46 | 1 | 1 | 15 | 32 | 1 | 47 | 7 | 4 | 5 | .300 | .400 | .480 |
| Kotchman, Casey, Arkansas * | 28 | 130 | 114 | 19 | 42 | 62 | 11 | 0 | 3 | 18 | 0 | 1 | 5 | 10 | 0 | 7 | 0 | 0 | 6 | .368 | .438 | .544 |
| Kroeger, Josh, El Paso * | 65 | 272 | 245 | 44 | 81 | 144 | 28 | 4 | 9 | 46 | 0 | 1 | 5 | 21 | 3 | 48 | 2 | 1 | 7 | .331 | .393 | .588 |
| Leclair, Aric, El Paso * | 29 | 2 | 1 | 0 | 0 | 0 | 0 | 0 | 0 | 0 | 1 | 0 | 0 | 0 | 0 | 1 | 0 | 0 | 0 | .000 | .000 | .000 |
| Lindsey, John, San Antonio | 123 | 525 | 457 | 68 | 129 | 221 | 31 | 2 | 19 | 72 | 2 | 4 | 14 | 48 | 0 | 98 | 1 | 7 | 9 | .282 | .365 | .484 |
| Lizarraga, Sergio, El Paso | 29 | 18 | 16 | 1 | 4 | 4 | 0 | 0 | 0 | 2 | 2 | 0 | 0 | 0 | 0 | 5 | 0 | 0 | 2 | .250 | .250 | .250 |
| Luellwitz, Sean, El Paso | 26 | 100 | 86 | 12 | 17 | 30 | 4 | 0 | 3 | 7 | 1 | 0 | 4 | 9 | 1 | 19 | 0 | 0 | 1 | .198 | .303 | .349 |
| Mathis, Jeff, Arkansas | 117 | 494 | 432 | 57 | 98 | 170 | 24 | 3 | 14 | 55 | 4 | 4 | 5 | 49 | 1 | 101 | 2 | 1 | 5 | .227 | .310 | .394 |
| Matranga, Dave, Round Rock | 112 | 451 | 392 | 61 | 95 | 140 | 20 | 2 | 7 | 48 | 4 | 4 | 17 | 34 | 1 | 81 | 14 | 4 | 7 | .242 | .327 | .357 |
| McClaskey, Tim, Round Rock | 35 | 11 | 11 | 0 | 1 | 1 | 0 | 0 | 0 | 0 | 0 | 0 | 0 | 0 | 0 | 6 | 0 | 0 | 0 | .091 | .091 | .091 |
| McClellan, Zach, Tulsa | 26 | 8 | 7 | 1 | 3 | 3 | 0 | 0 | 0 | 0 | 0 | 0 | 0 | 1 | 0 | 2 | 0 | 0 | 0 | .429 | .500 | .429 |
| McCurdy, John, Midland | 100 | 373 | 349 | 40 | 87 | 127 | 20 | 1 | 6 | 43 | 3 | 3 | 1 | 17 | 0 | 100 | 4 | 4 | 14 | .249 | .284 | .364 |
| McDaniel, Denny, Round Rock * | 48 | 4 | 3 | 0 | 0 | 0 | 0 | 0 | 0 | 0 | 1 | 0 | 0 | 0 | 0 | 3 | 0 | 0 | 0 | .000 | .000 | .000 |
| McDougall, Marshall, Frisco | 18 | 81 | 73 | 17 | 23 | 36 | 7 | 0 | 2 | 14 | 0 | 0 | 0 | 8 | 0 | 12 | 0 | 0 | 3 | .315 | .383 | .493 |
| McKinley, Josh, Frisco † | 45 | 159 | 137 | 18 | 29 | 50 | 4 | 1 | 5 | 18 | 0 | 0 | 2 | 20 | 1 | 44 | 0 | 3 | 0 | .212 | .321 | .365 |
| McPherson, Dallas, Arkansas * | 68 | 302 | 262 | 53 | 84 | 173 | 17 | 6 | 20 | 69 | 0 | 2 | 4 | 34 | 5 | 74 | 6 | 5 | 2 | .321 | .404 | .660 |
| Meadows, Tydus, Frisco | 99 | 405 | 344 | 55 | 98 | 176 | 20 | 2 | 18 | 69 | 0 | 5 | 9 | 47 | 2 | 72 | 3 | 1 | 13 | .285 | .380 | .512 |
| Mench, Kevin, Frisco | 4 | 17 | 16 | 3 | 5 | 8 | 0 | 0 | 1 | 1 | 0 | 0 | 0 | 1 | 0 | 0 | 0 | 0 | 0 | .313 | .353 | .500 |
| Menchaca, Eriberto, San Antonio | 125 | 452 | 419 | 43 | 89 | 112 | 19 | 2 | 0 | 33 | 8 | 2 | 5 | 18 | 0 | 83 | 7 | 3 | 11 | .212 | .252 | .267 |
| Menechino, Frank, Midland | 4 | 15 | 13 | 1 | 4 | 4 | 0 | 0 | 0 | 0 | 0 | 0 | 0 | 2 | 0 | 1 | 0 | 0 | 0 | .308 | .400 | .308 |
| Meyer, Drew, Frisco * | 59 | 257 | 232 | 35 | 56 | 72 | 6 | 2 | 2 | 13 | 1 | 1 | 1 | 22 | 1 | 43 | 4 | 2 | 2 | .241 | .309 | .310 |
| Miller, Tony, Tulsa | 112 | 494 | 414 | 61 | 114 | 168 | 17 | 2 | 11 | 36 | 3 | 1 | 8 | 68 | 2 | 99 | 20 | 12 | 4 | .275 | .387 | .406 |
| Moon, Brian, San Antonio † | 37 | 132 | 119 | 5 | 20 | 26 | 4 | 1 | 0 | 10 | 2 | 3 | 2 | 6 | 0 | 22 | 0 | 1 | 7 | .168 | .215 | .218 |
| Morales, Willie, Tulsa | 11 | 37 | 35 | 2 | 8 | 11 | 0 | 0 | 1 | 4 | 0 | 0 | 0 | 2 | 0 | 9 | 1 | 0 | 2 | .229 | .270 | .314 |
| Morgan, Matt, El Paso | 19 | 68 | 55 | 8 | 9 | 14 | 5 | 0 | 0 | 7 | 0 | 1 | 0 | 12 | 0 | 13 | 0 | 0 | 1 | .164 | .309 | .255 |
| Morse, Michael, San Antonio | 41 | 173 | 157 | 18 | 43 | 73 | 10 | 1 | 6 | 33 | 1 | 2 | 4 | 9 | 0 | 27 | 0 | 2 | 8 | .274 | .326 | .465 |
| Mosquera, Julio, Frisco | 31 | 129 | 116 | 23 | 36 | 64 | 4 | 0 | 8 | 36 | 1 | 0 | 3 | 9 | 0 | 17 | 0 | 0 | 5 | .310 | .375 | .552 |
| Murphy, Bill, El Paso * | 7 | 4 | 3 | 1 | 0 | 0 | 0 | 0 | 0 | 0 | 0 | 0 | 0 | 1 | 0 | 0 | 0 | 0 | 1 | .000 | .250 | .000 |
| Murphy, Tommy, Arkansas | 129 | 528 | 477 | 77 | 124 | 181 | 24 | 6 | 7 | 45 | 9 | 5 | 1 | 36 | 1 | 113 | 27 | 5 | 9 | .260 | .310 | .379 |
| Myers, Casey, Midland | 10 | 36 | 34 | 3 | 7 | 7 | 0 | 0 | 0 | 2 | 0 | 0 | 1 | 1 | 0 | 9 | 0 | 0 | 0 | .206 | .250 | .206 |
| Narveson, Chris, Tulsa * | 4 | 1 | 0 | 0 | 0 | 0 | 0 | 0 | 0 | 0 | 1 | 0 | 0 | 0 | 0 | 0 | 0 | 0 | 0 | .000 | .000 | .000 |
| Nichols, Kyle, El Paso | 49 | 170 | 144 | 23 | 42 | 72 | 9 | 0 | 7 | 35 | 0 | 4 | 1 | 21 | 0 | 43 | 0 | 2 | 3 | .292 | .376 | .500 |
| Nieve, Fernando, Round Rock | 3 | 2 | 1 | 1 | 0 | 0 | 0 | 0 | 0 | 1 | 1 | 0 | 0 | 0 | 0 | 0 | 0 | 0 | 0 | .000 | .000 | .000 |
| Nippert, Dustin, El Paso | 14 | 9 | 8 | 1 | 1 | 2 | 1 | 0 | 0 | 2 | 0 | 0 | 0 | 1 | 0 | 6 | 0 | 0 | 0 | .125 | .222 | .250 |
| Nix, Jayson, Tulsa | 123 | 511 | 456 | 58 | 97 | 158 | 17 | 1 | 14 | 58 | 1 | 2 | 12 | 40 | 1 | 100 | 14 | 3 | 9 | .213 | .292 | .346 |
| Nix, Laynce, Frisco * | 7 | 27 | 26 | 2 | 7 | 8 | 1 | 0 | 0 | 2 | 0 | 0 | 0 | 1 | 0 | 10 | 0 | 1 | 1 | .269 | .296 | .308 |
| Norris, Dax, Round Rock | 57 | 222 | 204 | 24 | 65 | 96 | 13 | 0 | 6 | 33 | 1 | 3 | 1 | 13 | 1 | 24 | 0 | 0 | 8 | .319 | .357 | .471 |
| Obradovich, Mark, Round Rock † | 11 | 41 | 33 | 8 | 6 | 10 | 1 | 0 | 1 | 3 | 0 | 0 | 0 | 8 | 0 | 13 | 1 | 0 | 0 | .182 | .341 | .303 |
| Oliveros, Luis, San Antonio | 80 | 304 | 279 | 24 | 64 | 95 | 19 | 0 | 4 | 22 | 4 | 1 | 7 | 13 | 1 | 42 | 0 | 4 | 8 | .229 | .280 | .341 |
| Orie, Kevin, Round Rock | 22 | 86 | 76 | 12 | 25 | 44 | 7 | 0 | 4 | 20 | 0 | 2 | 1 | 7 | 0 | 12 | 1 | 0 | 1 | .329 | .384 | .579 |
| Parker, Zach, Tulsa | 22 | 10 | 8 | 0 | 2 | 2 | 0 | 0 | 0 | 0 | 2 | 0 | 0 | 0 | 0 | 2 | 0 | 0 | 0 | .250 | .250 | .250 |
| Perez, Beltran, El Paso | 37 | 6 | 6 | 0 | 1 | 1 | 0 | 0 | 0 | 0 | 0 | 0 | 0 | 0 | 0 | 0 | 0 | 0 | 0 | .167 | .167 | .167 |
| Perez, Santiago, Frisco † | 28 | 125 | 111 | 28 | 43 | 77 | 11 | 4 | 5 | 19 | 1 | 0 | 2 | 11 | 0 | 30 | 4 | 3 | 0 | .387 | .452 | .694 |
| Perry, Herbert, Frisco | 8 | 33 | 29 | 4 | 12 | 15 | 3 | 0 | 0 | 4 | 0 | 1 | 0 | 3 | 0 | 7 | 0 | 0 | 0 | .414 | .455 | .517 |
| Perry, Jason, Midland * | 28 | 92 | 81 | 11 | 16 | 26 | 5 | 1 | 1 | 11 | 1 | 1 | 5 | 4 | 0 | 23 | 3 | 1 | 3 | .198 | .275 | .321 |
| Phillips, Dan, Tulsa | 10 | 31 | 30 | 2 | 7 | 9 | 2 | 0 | 0 | 2 | 0 | 0 | 1 | 0 | 0 | 9 | 0 | 0 | 1 | .233 | .258 | .300 |
| Piniella, Juan, Tulsa | 113 | 419 | 370 | 51 | 85 | 133 | 17 | 2 | 9 | 45 | 15 | 2 | 3 | 29 | 1 | 89 | 15 | 6 | 4 | .230 | .290 | .359 |
| Poland, Trey, Round Rock * | 6 | 1 | 1 | 0 | 0 | 0 | 0 | 0 | 0 | 0 | 0 | 0 | 0 | 0 | 0 | 0 | 0 | 0 | 0 | .000 | .000 | .000 |
| Powell, Greg, Round Rock | 26 | 8 | 7 | 0 | 0 | 0 | 0 | 0 | 0 | 0 | 1 | 0 | 0 | 0 | 0 | 2 | 0 | 0 | 0 | .000 | .000 | .000 |
| Quentin, Carlos, El Paso | 60 | 246 | 210 | 39 | 75 | 112 | 19 | 0 | 6 | 38 | 0 | 2 | 16 | 18 | 1 | 23 | 0 | 6 | 6 | .357 | .443 | .533 |
| Quintanilla, Omar, Midland * | 23 | 105 | 94 | 20 | 33 | 49 | 10 | 0 | 2 | 20 | 0 | 0 | 1 | 10 | 0 | 9 | 2 | 0 | 1 | .351 | .419 | .521 |
| Ramirez, Santiago, Round Rock | 55 | 6 | 5 | 1 | 0 | 0 | 0 | 0 | 0 | 1 | 0 | 1 | 0 | 0 | 0 | 0 | 0 | 0 | 0 | .000 | .000 | .000 |
| Raymundo, G.J., Frisco | 19 | 59 | 52 | 5 | 15 | 22 | 0 | 2 | 1 | 15 | 0 | 0 | 2 | 5 | 0 | 11 | 0 | 1 | 1 | .288 | .373 | .423 |
| Richar, Danny, El Paso | 26 | 91 | 82 | 6 | 17 | 20 | 3 | 0 | 0 | 5 | 0 | 0 | 2 | 7 | 0 | 17 | 2 | 0 | 0 | .207 | .286 | .244 |
| Rodrigues, Rich, San Antonio | 7 | 20 | 17 | 1 | 4 | 4 | 0 | 0 | 0 | 2 | 0 | 0 | 1 | 2 | 0 | 1 | 0 | 0 | 0 | .235 | .350 | .235 |
| Rodriguez, Javy, Arkansas | 37 | 153 | 140 | 14 | 42 | 57 | 7 | 1 | 2 | 11 | 3 | 1 | 0 | 9 | 0 | 28 | 6 | 3 | 3 | .300 | .340 | .407 |
| Rodriguez, Mike, Round Rock * | 105 | 453 | 397 | 59 | 106 | 151 | 23 | 5 | 4 | 53 | 10 | 4 | 1 | 39 | 0 | 55 | 16 | 10 | 4 | .267 | .331 | .380 |
| Rodriguez, Wandy, Round Rock † | 28 | 20 | 13 | 0 | 2 | 3 | 1 | 0 | 0 | 3 | 6 | 1 | 0 | 0 | 0 | 5 | 0 | 0 | 0 | .154 | .143 | .231 |
| Rosamond, Mike, Tulsa | 60 | 196 | 178 | 23 | 44 | 71 | 10 | 1 | 5 | 30 | 1 | 1 | 4 | 12 | 1 | 52 | 3 | 4 | 3 | .247 | .308 | .399 |
| Rosario, Adriano, El Paso | 7 | 5 | 3 | 0 | 0 | 0 | 0 | 0 | 0 | 0 | 2 | 0 | 0 | 0 | 0 | 1 | 0 | 0 | 0 | .000 | .000 | .000 |
| Ruan, Wilkin, Wichita | 54 | 215 | 196 | 26 | 54 | 74 | 7 | 2 | 3 | 15 | 7 | 1 | 1 | 10 | 0 | 21 | 11 | 3 | 1 | .276 | .313 | .378 |
| Salazar, Jeff, Tulsa * | 58 | 270 | 224 | 39 | 50 | 70 | 13 | 2 | 1 | 17 | 7 | 2 | 2 | 35 | 0 | 31 | 10 | 3 | 1 | .223 | .331 | .313 |
| Sandel, George, San Antonio * | 3 | 6 | 5 | 0 | 0 | 0 | 0 | 0 | 0 | 0 | 0 | 0 | 0 | 1 | 0 | 2 | 0 | 0 | 0 | .000 | .167 | .000 |

| Player, Team | G | TPA | AB | R | H | TB | 2B | 3B | HR | RBI | SH | SF | HP | BB | IBB | SO | SB | CS | GDP | Avg. | OBP | Slg. |
|---|---|---|---|---|---|---|---|---|---|---|---|---|---|---|---|---|---|---|---|---|---|---|
| Sandoval, Danny, Tulsa | 133 | 580 | 530 | 73 | 169 | 238 | 37 | 4 | 8 | 66 | 10 | 1 | 2 | 37 | 3 | 64 | 22 | 10 | 12 | .319 | .365 | .449 |
| Santana, Mayobanex, El Paso | 15 | 29 | 27 | 2 | 6 | 7 | 1 | 0 | 0 | 2 | 1 | 0 | 0 | 1 | 0 | 6 | 0 | 1 | 2 | .222 | .250 | .259 |
| Santos, Chad, Wichita * | 130 | 524 | 471 | 59 | 123 | 219 | 27 | 3 | 21 | 68 | 0 | 3 | 4 | 46 | 5 | 119 | 3 | 1 | 14 | .261 | .330 | .465 |
| Santos, Sergio, El Paso | 89 | 377 | 347 | 53 | 98 | 160 | 19 | 5 | 11 | 52 | 1 | 2 | 3 | 24 | 1 | 89 | 3 | 2 | 7 | .282 | .332 | .461 |
| Scott, Luke, Round Rock * | 63 | 253 | 208 | 45 | 62 | 136 | 17 | 0 | 19 | 62 | 1 | 5 | 6 | 33 | 1 | 43 | 0 | 2 | 4 | .298 | .401 | .654 |
| Self, Todd, Round Rock * | 131 | 571 | 476 | 86 | 150 | 219 | 34 | 1 | 11 | 81 | 0 | 5 | 1 | 89 | 6 | 95 | 8 | 0 | 8 | .315 | .420 | .460 |
| Sellier, Brian, Midland * | 130 | 571 | 491 | 75 | 137 | 191 | 30 | 6 | 4 | 62 | 2 | 7 | 4 | 67 | 3 | 86 | 12 | 4 | 7 | .279 | .366 | .389 |
| Senjem, Guye, Tulsa * | 40 | 118 | 103 | 13 | 23 | 33 | 7 | 0 | 1 | 11 | 0 | 2 | 1 | 12 | 3 | 29 | 0 | 1 | 1 | .223 | .305 | .320 |
| Senreiso, Juan, Frisco | 11 | 48 | 46 | 7 | 16 | 25 | 1 | 1 | 2 | 5 | 0 | 0 | 0 | 2 | 0 | 7 | 0 | 1 | 3 | .348 | .375 | .543 |
| Shealy, Ryan, Tulsa | 132 | 552 | 469 | 88 | 149 | 274 | 32 | 3 | 29 | 99 | 2 | 4 | 16 | 61 | 7 | 123 | 1 | 1 | 10 | .318 | .411 | .584 |
| Sikaras, Pete, El Paso | 38 | 3 | 3 | 0 | 0 | 0 | 0 | 0 | 0 | 0 | 0 | 0 | 0 | 0 | 0 | 2 | 0 | 0 | 0 | .000 | .000 | .000 |
| Simpson, Gerrit, Tulsa | 39 | 5 | 5 | 0 | 1 | 1 | 0 | 0 | 0 | 0 | 0 | 0 | 0 | 0 | 0 | 2 | 0 | 0 | 0 | .200 | .200 | .200 |
| Slavik, Corey, Tulsa * | 113 | 398 | 364 | 32 | 83 | 118 | 16 | 5 | 3 | 47 | 5 | 1 | 7 | 21 | 1 | 79 | 3 | 2 | 5 | .228 | .282 | .324 |
| Slee, Gregory, San Antonio * | 1 | 1 | 1 | 0 | 0 | 0 | 0 | 0 | 0 | 0 | 0 | 0 | 0 | 0 | 0 | 1 | 0 | 0 | 0 | .000 | .000 | .000 |
| Smith, Casey, Arkansas | 44 | 185 | 170 | 25 | 48 | 63 | 9 | 3 | 0 | 19 | 4 | 1 | 0 | 10 | 0 | 24 | 3 | 3 | 3 | .282 | .320 | .371 |
| Smith, Dustin, Frisco | 16 | 39 | 37 | 2 | 3 | 3 | 0 | 0 | 0 | 2 | 0 | 0 | 0 | 2 | 0 | 11 | 0 | 0 | 1 | .081 | .128 | .081 |
| Smith, Jeff, Frisco * | 69 | 245 | 221 | 23 | 73 | 97 | 15 | 0 | 3 | 28 | 1 | 1 | 2 | 20 | 1 | 32 | 0 | 0 | 7 | .330 | .389 | .439 |
| Smith, Sam, El Paso | 18 | 5 | 4 | 0 | 0 | 0 | 0 | 0 | 0 | 0 | 1 | 0 | 0 | 0 | 0 | 1 | 0 | 0 | 0 | .000 | .000 | .000 |
| Smith, Will, Frisco * | 87 | 343 | 315 | 48 | 90 | 139 | 19 | 3 | 8 | 57 | 2 | 3 | 2 | 21 | 0 | 46 | 6 | 5 | 4 | .286 | .331 | .441 |
| Snyder, Chris, El Paso | 99 | 401 | 346 | 66 | 104 | 180 | 31 | 0 | 15 | 57 | 0 | 3 | 6 | 46 | 1 | 57 | 3 | 1 | 7 | .301 | .389 | .520 |
| Speier, Ryan, Tulsa | 62 | 1 | 0 | 0 | 0 | 0 | 0 | 0 | 0 | 1 | 0 | 0 | 0 | 1 | 0 | 0 | 0 | 0 | 0 | .000 | 1.000 | .000 |
| Stanley, Steve, Midland * | 36 | 176 | 148 | 32 | 62 | 75 | 7 | 3 | 0 | 21 | 3 | 4 | 1 | 20 | 0 | 20 | 6 | 5 | 0 | .419 | .480 | .507 |
| Stocker, Mel, Wichita † | 14 | 48 | 40 | 7 | 6 | 7 | 1 | 0 | 0 | 1 | 1 | 0 | 3 | 4 | 0 | 5 | 3 | 1 | 3 | .150 | .277 | .175 |
| Stockman, Phil, El Paso | 6 | 3 | 2 | 0 | 0 | 0 | 0 | 0 | 0 | 0 | 1 | 0 | 0 | 0 | 0 | 0 | 0 | 0 | 0 | .000 | .000 | .000 |
| Sugden, Jason, Arkansas † | 2 | 7 | 6 | 0 | 0 | 0 | 0 | 0 | 0 | 0 | 0 | 0 | 1 | 0 | 0 | 3 | 0 | 0 | 0 | .000 | .143 | .000 |
| Taveras, Willy, Round Rock | 103 | 464 | 409 | 76 | 137 | 158 | 13 | 1 | 2 | 27 | 6 | 2 | 9 | 38 | 2 | 76 | 55 | 11 | 2 | .335 | .402 | .386 |
| Teahen, Mark, Midland * | 53 | 229 | 197 | 31 | 66 | 107 | 15 | 4 | 6 | 36 | 0 | 2 | 1 | 29 | 3 | 44 | 0 | 0 | 12 | .335 | .419 | .543 |
| Teixeira, Mark, Frisco † | 1 | 4 | 3 | 0 | 0 | 0 | 0 | 0 | 0 | 0 | 0 | 0 | 1 | 0 | 0 | 1 | 0 | 0 | 0 | .000 | .250 | .000 |
| Terrell, Jim, Wichita * | 28 | 108 | 96 | 14 | 25 | 34 | 3 | 0 | 2 | 12 | 0 | 2 | 0 | 10 | 0 | 13 | 1 | 0 | 2 | .260 | .324 | .354 |
| Tonis, Mike, Wichita | 78 | 292 | 263 | 24 | 60 | 84 | 13 | 1 | 3 | 29 | 1 | 4 | 1 | 23 | 1 | 53 | 0 | 0 | 10 | .228 | .289 | .319 |
| Topolski, Jon, Round Rock * | 81 | 273 | 226 | 42 | 52 | 96 | 17 | 0 | 9 | 33 | 2 | 2 | 3 | 40 | 3 | 64 | 4 | 4 | 9 | .230 | .351 | .425 |
| Tsao, Chin-Hui, Tulsa | 2 | 2 | 2 | 0 | 0 | 0 | 0 | 0 | 0 | 0 | 0 | 0 | 0 | 0 | 0 | 1 | 0 | 0 | 0 | .000 | .000 | .000 |
| Turner, Justin, Arkansas * | 21 | 72 | 66 | 5 | 12 | 18 | 3 | 0 | 1 | 3 | 2 | 1 | 1 | 2 | 0 | 22 | 0 | 1 | 0 | .182 | .214 | .273 |
| Uggla, Dan, El Paso | 83 | 317 | 294 | 29 | 76 | 104 | 12 | 2 | 4 | 30 | 2 | 2 | 4 | 15 | 0 | 55 | 10 | 7 | 6 | .259 | .302 | .354 |
| Ullery, Dave, Wichita * | 18 | 65 | 57 | 8 | 13 | 19 | 0 | 0 | 2 | 8 | 1 | 0 | 0 | 7 | 0 | 17 | 0 | 0 | 0 | .228 | .313 | .333 |
| Varner, Noochie, El Paso | 32 | 126 | 115 | 15 | 38 | 47 | 4 | 1 | 1 | 10 | 1 | 0 | 0 | 10 | 0 | 23 | 2 | 1 | 2 | .330 | .384 | .409 |
| Waldron, Jeff, El Paso * | 16 | 56 | 50 | 4 | 16 | 23 | 4 | 0 | 1 | 6 | 0 | 0 | 0 | 6 | 0 | 9 | 0 | 1 | 1 | .320 | .393 | .460 |
| Waldron, Jeff, Frisco * | 12 | 45 | 41 | 4 | 13 | 14 | 1 | 0 | 0 | 4 | 0 | 0 | 2 | 2 | 1 | 8 | 0 | 0 | 0 | .317 | .378 | .341 |
| Walker, Larry, Tulsa * | 5 | 13 | 9 | 3 | 2 | 5 | 0 | 0 | 1 | 2 | 0 | 0 | 2 | 2 | 0 | 1 | 0 | 0 | 1 | .222 | .462 | .556 |
| Walter, Scott, Wichita | 104 | 428 | 387 | 53 | 96 | 159 | 22 | 1 | 13 | 55 | 4 | 3 | 8 | 26 | 1 | 65 | 5 | 2 | 13 | .248 | .307 | .411 |
| Weber, Jonathan, Midland * | 111 | 482 | 420 | 64 | 118 | 197 | 24 | 5 | 15 | 68 | 2 | 7 | 6 | 47 | 3 | 102 | 10 | 5 | 6 | .281 | .356 | .469 |
| West, Todd, El Paso | 66 | 244 | 214 | 24 | 54 | 66 | 10 | 1 | 0 | 24 | 7 | 3 | 2 | 18 | 0 | 36 | 12 | 3 | 5 | .252 | .312 | .308 |
| White, Bill, El Paso * | 32 | 3 | 3 | 0 | 0 | 0 | 0 | 0 | 0 | 0 | 0 | 0 | 0 | 0 | 0 | 2 | 0 | 0 | 0 | .000 | .000 | .000 |
| Whiteman, Tommy, Round Rock | 68 | 302 | 277 | 39 | 93 | 131 | 14 | 0 | 8 | 45 | 0 | 3 | 2 | 20 | 0 | 45 | 5 | 3 | 9 | .336 | .381 | .473 |
| Wilkerson, Wes, Wichita | 51 | 6 | 6 | 1 | 2 | 2 | 0 | 0 | 0 | 1 | 0 | 0 | 0 | 0 | 0 | 1 | 0 | 0 | 0 | .333 | .333 | .333 |
| Williams, Marland, El Paso | 121 | 534 | 487 | 82 | 125 | 190 | 21 | 10 | 8 | 43 | 1 | 3 | 3 | 40 | 0 | 116 | 48 | 8 | 8 | .257 | .315 | .390 |
| Wilson, Preston, Tulsa | 6 | 21 | 17 | 4 | 7 | 11 | 1 | 0 | 1 | 2 | 0 | 0 | 1 | 3 | 0 | 4 | 1 | 1 | 1 | .412 | .524 | .647 |
| Winchester, Jeff, Tulsa | 79 | 264 | 243 | 19 | 54 | 84 | 13 | 1 | 5 | 29 | 3 | 3 | 4 | 11 | 3 | 52 | 0 | 2 | 4 | .222 | .264 | .346 |
| Zamora, Junior, Round Rock | 95 | 353 | 318 | 47 | 84 | 128 | 20 | 3 | 6 | 44 | 1 | 3 | 2 | 29 | 0 | 53 | 3 | 0 | 10 | .264 | .327 | .4038 |

GRAND SLAMS—Aldridge, Aspito, Baker, Barker, Berger, Botts, Boyd, Bynum, Coffie, Conrad, Gomez, Harrison, Jackson, Jacobs, Jimerson, Kinsler, Matranga, McPherson, Morse, Raymundo, Santos, Walter, 1 each.

AWARDED FIRST BASE ON CATCHER'S INTERFERENCE—H. Brown 2 (Conway, J. Brown); D. Brown (Norris); Kiger (Norris); Quentin (Conway); M. Rodriguez (J. Brown); Sellier (Snyder).

# 2004 PITCHING

## TEAM

| Team | W | L | Pct. | ERA | G | CG | ShO | Sv. | IP | H | TBF | R | ER | HR | SH | SF | HB | BB | IBB | SO | WP | Bk. |
|---|---|---|---|---|---|---|---|---|---|---|---|---|---|---|---|---|---|---|---|---|---|---|
| Tulsa | 71 | 68 | .511 | 3.67 | 139 | 5 | 15 | 42 | 1209.0 | 1142 | 5120 | 573 | 493 | 117 | 47 | 62 | 74 | 407 | 11 | 958 | 73 | 4 |
| Frisco | 81 | 59 | .579 | 3.74 | 140 | 1 | 9 | 39 | 1242.2 | 1186 | 5322 | 608 | 516 | 119 | 40 | 38 | 65 | 462 | 35 | 1004 | 72 | 11 |
| Round Rock | 86 | 54 | .614 | 3.86 | 140 | 7 | 14 | 47 | 1227.2 | 1217 | 5226 | 589 | 526 | 100 | 44 | 27 | 63 | 398 | 23 | 1066 | 44 | 8 |
| Wichita | 73 | 66 | .525 | 4.30 | 139 | 4 | 9 | 34 | 1218.0 | 1287 | 5281 | 661 | 582 | 109 | 27 | 34 | 64 | 404 | 9 | 960 | 66 | 1 |
| Midland | 72 | 68 | .514 | 4.47 | 140 | 3 | 8 | 36 | 1235.0 | 1310 | 5360 | 695 | 613 | 102 | 45 | 45 | 61 | 463 | 9 | 908 | 61 | 4 |
| San Antonio | 66 | 72 | .478 | 4.53 | 138 | 3 | 8 | 40 | 1208.0 | 1254 | 5336 | 684 | 608 | 109 | 49 | 43 | 66 | 547 | 22 | 1037 | 73 | 15 |
| Arkansas | 59 | 80 | .424 | 4.96 | 139 | 4 | 11 | 26 | 1209.1 | 1353 | 5433 | 777 | 666 | 118 | 49 | 44 | 78 | 465 | 5 | 865 | 71 | 4 |
| El Paso | 48 | 89 | .350 | 5.04 | 137 | 5 | 4 | 25 | 1193.2 | 1383 | 5437 | 787 | 669 | 99 | 53 | 49 | 71 | 518 | 34 | 950 | 80 | 4 |

## INDIVIDUAL

### TOP QUALIFIERS FOR EARNED-RUN AVERAGE TITLE

Minimum 112 innings.*Lefthanded pitcher.

| Pitcher, Team | W | L | Pct. | ERA | G | GS | CG | ShO | GF | Sv. | IP | H | TBF | R | ER | HR | SH | SF | HB | BB | IBB | SO | WP | Bk. |
|---|---|---|---|---|---|---|---|---|---|---|---|---|---|---|---|---|---|---|---|---|---|---|---|---|
| Francis, Jeff, Tulsa * | 13 | 1 | .929 | 1.98 | 17 | 17 | 1 | 1 | 0 | 0 | 113.2 | 73 | 435 | 26 | 25 | 9 | 4 | 1 | 5 | 22 | 0 | 147 | 2 | 0 |
| Houlton, D.J., Round Rock | 12 | 5 | .706 | 2.94 | 28 | 28 | 3 | 1 | 0 | 0 | 159.0 | 141 | 654 | 59 | 52 | 14 | 7 | 2 | 12 | 47 | 2 | 159 | 4 | 0 |
| Bazzell, Shane, Midland | 15 | 3 | .833 | 3.03 | 34 | 14 | 0 | 0 | 8 | 2 | 119.0 | 105 | 487 | 52 | 40 | 11 | 5 | 4 | 7 | 36 | 0 | 86 | 1 | 0 |
| Loe, Kameron, Frisco | 7 | 7 | .500 | 3.12 | 19 | 19 | 0 | 0 | 0 | 0 | 112.2 | 122 | 478 | 42 | 39 | 5 | 6 | 4 | 6 | 29 | 3 | 97 | 5 | 1 |
| Esposito, Mike, Tulsa | 10 | 6 | .625 | 3.33 | 24 | 24 | 1 | 0 | 0 | 0 | 143.1 | 138 | 576 | 57 | 53 | 12 | 5 | 3 | 4 | 35 | 1 | 90 | 8 | 0 |
| Hampson, Justin, Tulsa * | 10 | 9 | .526 | 3.49 | 27 | 27 | 1 | 0 | 0 | 0 | 170.1 | 176 | 718 | 82 | 66 | 22 | 13 | 1 | 8 | 63 | 0 | 104 | 5 | 1 |
| Buglovsky, Chris, San Antonio | 6 | 8 | .429 | 3.64 | 24 | 21 | 1 | 1 | 0 | 0 | 121.0 | 121 | 515 | 68 | 49 | 7 | 14 | 4 | 6 | 45 | 2 | 81 | 6 | 0 |

| Pitcher, Team | W | L | Pct. | ERA | G | GS | CG | ShO | GF | Sv. | IP | H | TBF | R | ER | HR | SH | SF | HB | BB | IBB | SO | WP | Bk. |
|---|---|---|---|---|---|---|---|---|---|---|---|---|---|---|---|---|---|---|---|---|---|---|---|---|
| Astacio, Ezequiel, Round Rock | 13 | 10 | .565 | 3.89 | 28 | 28 | 1 | 0 | 0 | 0 | 176.0 | 155 | 724 | 89 | 76 | 12 | 11 | 4 | 8 | 56 | 1 | 185 | 11 | 1 |
| Tamayo, Danny, Wichita | 12 | 7 | .632 | 3.92 | 25 | 25 | 0 | 0 | 0 | 0 | 142.1 | 165 | 604 | 66 | 62 | 15 | 4 | 7 | 8 | 36 | 0 | 123 | 7 | 0 |
| Gothreaux, Jared, Round Rock | 9 | 7 | .563 | 3.96 | 27 | 24 | 2 | 0 | 1 | 0 | 157.0 | 173 | 661 | 82 | 69 | 16 | 6 | 4 | 4 | 35 | 0 | 110 | 3 | 0 |
| McClellan, Zach, Tulsa | 4 | 7 | .364 | 4.15 | 26 | 23 | 1 | 0 | 1 | 1 | 138.2 | 145 | 593 | 69 | 64 | 17 | 8 | 6 | 10 | 36 | 0 | 111 | 5 | 1 |
| Rodriguez, Wandy, Round Rock * | 11 | 6 | .647 | 4.48 | 26 | 25 | 1 | 0 | 0 | 0 | 142.2 | 159 | 632 | 77 | 71 | 15 | 6 | 6 | 7 | 57 | 1 | 115 | 2 | 6 |
| Jimenez, Kelvin, Frisco | 3 | 5 | .375 | 4.53 | 26 | 21 | 0 | 0 | 0 | 0 | 129.0 | 135 | 584 | 76 | 65 | 13 | 6 | 6 | 7 | 67 | 1 | 101 | 12 | 1 |
| Bittner, Tim, Arkansas * | 8 | 6 | .571 | 4.54 | 22 | 22 | 0 | 0 | 0 | 0 | 119.0 | 113 | 518 | 65 | 60 | 10 | 4 | 6 | 4 | 57 | 0 | 82 | 3 | 0 |
| McClaskey, Tim, Round Rock | 7 | 9 | .438 | 4.62 | 34 | 19 | 0 | 0 | 3 | 2 | 140.1 | 148 | 590 | 81 | 72 | 17 | 3 | 4 | 10 | 36 | 1 | 94 | 5 | 0 |

DEPARTMENTAL LEADERS: W—Bazzell, 15; L—Weis, 12; Pct.—Francis, .929; G—Speier, 61; GS—Three tied with 28; CG—Three tied with three; ShO—Collazo, 2; GF—Speier, 59; Sv.—Speier, 37; IP—Astacio, 176.0; H—Dickinson, 198; TBF—Hampson, 718; R—Weis, 106; ER—Weis, 94; HR—Hampson, 22; SH—Three tied with 10; SF—Six tied with six; HB—Weis, 15; BB—Done, 70; IBB—Lizarraga, Hughes, 7; SO—Astacio, 185; WP—Three with 12; BK—W. Rodriguez, 6.

## ALL PITCHERS

*Lefthanded pitcher.

| Pitcher, Team | W | L | Pct. | ERA | G | GS | CG | ShO | GF | Sv. | IP | H | TBF | R | ER | HR | SH | SF | HB | BB | IBB | SO | WP | Bk. |
|---|---|---|---|---|---|---|---|---|---|---|---|---|---|---|---|---|---|---|---|---|---|---|---|---|
| Anderson, Travis, Tulsa | 0 | 1 | .000 | 7.25 | 11 | 2 | 0 | 0 | 5 | 0 | 22.1 | 25 | 111 | 23 | 18 | 7 | 1 | 2 | 3 | 15 | 0 | 14 | 3 | 0 |
| Andrade, Steve, Arkansas | 2 | 2 | .500 | 2.44 | 35 | 0 | 0 | 0 | 24 | 9 | 48.0 | 37 | 196 | 16 | 13 | 4 | 0 | 0 | 3 | 12 | 0 | 59 | 4 | 0 |
| Andrew, Jason, Frisco | 3 | 0 | 1.000 | 3.31 | 24 | 2 | 0 | 0 | 13 | 1 | 49.0 | 46 | 213 | 22 | 18 | 7 | 2 | 0 | 2 | 21 | 3 | 36 | 7 | 1 |
| Appier, Kevin, Wichita | 0 | 0 | .000 | 4.91 | 4 | 4 | 0 | 0 | 0 | 0 | 14.2 | 19 | 67 | 9 | 8 | 1 | 2 | 0 | 0 | 4 | 0 | 3 | 2 | 0 |
| Astacio, Ezequiel, Round Rock | 13 | 10 | .565 | 3.89 | 28 | 28 | 1 | 0 | 0 | 0 | 176.0 | 155 | 724 | 89 | 76 | 12 | 11 | 4 | 8 | 56 | 1 | 185 | 11 | 1 |
| Astacio, Hector, Arkansas | 0 | 0 | .000 | 5.02 | 6 | 0 | 0 | 0 | 0 | 0 | 14.1 | 15 | 66 | 10 | 8 | 1 | 0 | 0 | 0 | 10 | 0 | 10 | 5 | 0 |
| Babula, Shaun, Round Rock * | 0 | 1 | .000 | 7.04 | 4 | 0 | 0 | 0 | 1 | 0 | 7.2 | 9 | 33 | 7 | 6 | 2 | 0 | 1 | 0 | 0 | 0 | 5 | 0 | 0 |
| Baek, Cha-Sueng, San Antonio | 0 | 0 | .000 | 0.00 | 1 | 1 | 0 | 0 | 0 | 0 | 5.0 | 2 | 15 | 0 | 0 | 0 | 1 | 0 | 0 | 0 | 0 | 5 | 0 | 0 |
| Baerlocher, Ryan, Wichita | 5 | 2 | .714 | 5.26 | 19 | 5 | 0 | 0 | 1 | 1 | 53.0 | 59 | 233 | 35 | 31 | 7 | 0 | 1 | 4 | 20 | 0 | 47 | 2 | 0 |
| Barber, Scott, El Paso | 1 | 3 | .250 | 5.47 | 38 | 1 | 0 | 0 | 12 | 1 | 80.2 | 98 | 365 | 51 | 49 | 6 | 2 | 1 | 5 | 24 | 3 | 47 | 6 | 0 |
| Barzilla, Philip, Round Rock * | 3 | 1 | .750 | 2.54 | 17 | 1 | 0 | 0 | 2 | 0 | 39.0 | 33 | 166 | 13 | 11 | 2 | 1 | 1 | 1 | 17 | 2 | 32 | 3 | 0 |
| Bass, Brian, Wichita | 0 | 4 | .000 | 7.43 | 10 | 10 | 0 | 0 | 0 | 0 | 36.1 | 53 | 179 | 30 | 30 | 4 | 3 | 0 | 3 | 22 | 0 | 20 | 1 | 0 |
| Bausher, Tim, Tulsa | 4 | 8 | .333 | 4.20 | 16 | 13 | 1 | 0 | 1 | 0 | 81.1 | 84 | 334 | 39 | 38 | 12 | 2 | 3 | 1 | 21 | 0 | 84 | 5 | 0 |
| Bautista, Denny, Wichita | 4 | 3 | .571 | 2.53 | 12 | 12 | 2 | 0 | 0 | 0 | 81.2 | 68 | 341 | 32 | 23 | 3 | 4 | 3 | 4 | 32 | 0 | 73 | 10 | 1 |
| Bazzell, Shane, Midland | 15 | 3 | .833 | 3.03 | 34 | 14 | 0 | 0 | 8 | 2 | 119.0 | 105 | 487 | 52 | 40 | 11 | 5 | 4 | 7 | 36 | 0 | 86 | 1 | 0 |
| Beasley, Ray, Frisco * | 3 | 0 | 1.000 | 3.00 | 42 | 0 | 0 | 0 | 19 | 8 | 51.0 | 43 | 213 | 22 | 17 | 4 | 0 | 0 | 0 | 17 | 3 | 43 | 2 | 1 |
| Benoit, Joaquin, Frisco | 0 | 0 | .000 | 0.00 | 1 | 1 | 0 | 0 | 0 | 0 | 2.0 | 0 | 6 | 0 | 0 | 0 | 0 | 0 | 0 | 0 | 0 | 6 | 0 | 0 |
| Bernero, Adam, Tulsa | 1 | 0 | 1.000 | 0.00 | 1 | 1 | 0 | 0 | 0 | 0 | 6.0 | 2 | 21 | 0 | 0 | 0 | 0 | 0 | 1 | 1 | 1 | 3 | 0 | 0 |
| Bierbrodt, Nick, Frisco * | 1 | 2 | .333 | 4.68 | 5 | 5 | 0 | 0 | 0 | 0 | 25.0 | 29 | 116 | 14 | 13 | 1 | 0 | 0 | 3 | 11 | 2 | 21 | 2 | 0 |
| Biggs, Billy, El Paso | 0 | 1 | .000 | 1.35 | 14 | 0 | 0 | 0 | 7 | 0 | 20.0 | 15 | 83 | 5 | 3 | 0 | 0 | 0 | 2 | 6 | 0 | 16 | 2 | 0 |
| Bilke, Austin, Arkansas | 0 | 0 | .000 | 4.50 | 2 | 0 | 0 | 0 | 0 | 0 | 2.0 | 3 | 11 | 3 | 1 | 0 | 0 | 0 | 1 | 1 | 0 | 0 | 0 | 0 |
| Bittner, Tim, Arkansas * | 8 | 6 | .571 | 4.54 | 22 | 22 | 0 | 0 | 0 | 0 | 119.0 | 113 | 518 | 65 | 60 | 10 | 4 | 6 | 4 | 57 | 0 | 82 | 3 | 0 |
| Bondurant, Steven, Midland * | 2 | 3 | .400 | 6.39 | 7 | 7 | 0 | 0 | 0 | 0 | 38.0 | 43 | 161 | 29 | 27 | 1 | 3 | 5 | 1 | 14 | 0 | 29 | 1 | 0 |
| Bott, Glenn, San Antonio * | 0 | 0 | .000 | 3.86 | 1 | 1 | 0 | 0 | 0 | 0 | 4.2 | 4 | 20 | 2 | 2 | 0 | 0 | 0 | 0 | 2 | 0 | 4 | 0 | 0 |
| Bouknight, Kip, Tulsa | 1 | 2 | .333 | 5.55 | 6 | 6 | 0 | 0 | 0 | 0 | 35.2 | 50 | 167 | 29 | 22 | 1 | 2 | 4 | 4 | 11 | 0 | 19 | 0 | 0 |
| Brocail, Doug, Frisco | 0 | 0 | .000 | 2.08 | 1 | 1 | 0 | 0 | 0 | 0 | 4.1 | 2 | 14 | 1 | 1 | 1 | 0 | 0 | 0 | 0 | 0 | 6 | 0 | 0 |
| Brunet, Mike, Arkansas | 1 | 1 | .500 | 1.42 | 2 | 2 | 0 | 0 | 0 | 0 | 12.2 | 8 | 49 | 2 | 2 | 1 | 0 | 0 | 0 | 4 | 0 | 8 | 0 | 0 |
| Buglovsky, Chris, San Antonio | 6 | 8 | .429 | 3.64 | 24 | 21 | 1 | 1 | 0 | 0 | 121.0 | 121 | 515 | 68 | 49 | 7 | 14 | 4 | 6 | 45 | 2 | 81 | 6 | 0 |
| Bulger, Jason, El Paso | 0 | 3 | .000 | 3.91 | 24 | 0 | 0 | 0 | 22 | 8 | 25.1 | 24 | 121 | 12 | 11 | 0 | 0 | 0 | 2 | 19 | 2 | 25 | 7 | 0 |
| Bumatay, Mike, Tulsa * | 1 | 0 | 1.000 | 3.18 | 12 | 0 | 0 | 0 | 4 | 0 | 11.1 | 10 | 56 | 4 | 4 | 1 | 1 | 0 | 1 | 9 | 1 | 12 | 1 | 0 |
| Burke, Erick, Frisco * | 4 | 2 | .667 | 1.77 | 25 | 0 | 0 | 0 | 5 | 0 | 40.2 | 32 | 175 | 11 | 8 | 2 | 2 | 0 | 2 | 20 | 1 | 35 | 2 | 1 |
| Burns, Mike, Round Rock | 11 | 3 | .786 | 1.67 | 56 | 0 | 0 | 0 | 35 | 9 | 80.2 | 63 | 321 | 18 | 15 | 1 | 0 | 0 | 4 | 15 | 3 | 94 | 1 | 0 |
| Callaway, Mickey, Frisco | 2 | 0 | 1.000 | 0.00 | 2 | 2 | 0 | 0 | 0 | 0 | 12.0 | 3 | 39 | 0 | 0 | 0 | 0 | 0 | 0 | 4 | 0 | 9 | 0 | 0 |
| Carlson, Jesse, Round Rock * | 5 | 0 | 1.000 | 5.04 | 41 | 0 | 0 | 0 | 19 | 1 | 55.1 | 57 | 248 | 33 | 31 | 5 | 0 | 0 | 4 | 21 | 3 | 51 | 2 | 0 |
| Cate, Troy, San Antonio * | 2 | 5 | .286 | 6.35 | 12 | 12 | 0 | 0 | 0 | 0 | 56.2 | 74 | 256 | 44 | 40 | 7 | 2 | 3 | 2 | 20 | 0 | 35 | 1 | 1 |
| Cervantes, Chris, El Paso * | 1 | 1 | .500 | 8.53 | 21 | 3 | 0 | 0 | 3 | 1 | 44.1 | 64 | 227 | 47 | 42 | 8 | 1 | 4 | 3 | 25 | 1 | 28 | 3 | 0 |
| Chico, Matt, El Paso * | 3 | 7 | .300 | 5.78 | 14 | 12 | 0 | 0 | 0 | 0 | 62.1 | 82 | 300 | 53 | 40 | 7 | 3 | 5 | 2 | 36 | 1 | 59 | 7 | 1 |
| Christensen, Ben, San Antonio | 0 | 0 | .000 | 9.35 | 5 | 0 | 0 | 0 | 2 | 0 | 8.2 | 13 | 50 | 9 | 9 | 1 | 0 | 0 | 1 | 10 | 1 | 5 | 1 | 0 |
| Coleman, Jeff, Midland | 0 | 0 | .000 | 15.63 | 5 | 0 | 0 | 0 | 1 | 0 | 6.1 | 16 | 38 | 13 | 11 | 1 | 0 | 0 | 0 | 2 | 0 | 5 | 1 | 0 |
| Collazo, William, Arkansas * | 6 | 10 | .375 | 4.62 | 32 | 20 | 3 | 2 | 2 | 0 | 148.0 | 157 | 642 | 88 | 76 | 11 | 3 | 6 | 12 | 38 | 0 | 100 | 8 | 0 |
| Cormier, Lance, El Paso | 2 | 3 | .400 | 2.29 | 10 | 8 | 0 | 0 | 0 | 0 | 63.0 | 66 | 259 | 19 | 16 | 3 | 8 | 2 | 2 | 17 | 0 | 58 | 3 | 1 |
| Cortez, Renee, San Antonio | 2 | 5 | .286 | 4.44 | 36 | 0 | 0 | 0 | 12 | 3 | 52.2 | 61 | 246 | 29 | 26 | 7 | 0 | 0 | 3 | 24 | 3 | 46 | 7 | 3 |
| Cosgrove, Mike, Tulsa | 1 | 4 | .200 | 4.71 | 21 | 0 | 0 | 0 | 13 | 1 | 28.2 | 37 | 133 | 18 | 15 | 4 | 0 | 0 | 3 | 7 | 0 | 15 | 2 | 0 |
| Crowell, Kyle, Midland | 2 | 0 | 1.000 | 4.54 | 40 | 0 | 0 | 0 | 17 | 0 | 67.1 | 78 | 306 | 40 | 34 | 4 | 1 | 2 | 3 | 29 | 1 | 70 | 7 | 0 |
| Cyr, Eric, Arkansas * | 4 | 3 | .571 | 3.17 | 11 | 8 | 0 | 0 | 0 | 0 | 54.0 | 48 | 223 | 23 | 19 | 5 | 1 | 1 | 4 | 15 | 0 | 44 | 0 | 0 |
| Del Chiaro, Brent, Arkansas | 0 | 0 | .000 | 0.00 | 2 | 0 | 0 | 0 | 2 | 0 | 0.2 | 1 | 3 | 0 | 0 | 0 | 0 | 0 | 0 | 0 | 0 | 0 | 0 | 0 |
| Devey, Phil, San Antonio * | 2 | 6 | .250 | 4.76 | 13 | 13 | 0 | 0 | 0 | 0 | 70.0 | 75 | 306 | 42 | 37 | 8 | 2 | 4 | 4 | 25 | 1 | 71 | 1 | 0 |
| DiRosa, Mike, El Paso | 0 | 0 | .000 | 36.00 | 1 | 0 | 0 | 0 | 1 | 0 | 1.0 | 5 | 8 | 4 | 4 | 0 | 0 | 0 | 0 | 0 | 0 | 0 | 0 | 0 |
| Dickey, R.A., Frisco | 1 | 1 | .500 | 1.98 | 4 | 4 | 0 | 0 | 0 | 0 | 13.2 | 16 | 58 | 5 | 3 | 0 | 0 | 1 | 0 | 1 | 0 | 9 | 0 | 0 |
| Dickinson, Drew, Midland * | 8 | 11 | .421 | 4.84 | 27 | 26 | 2 | 1 | 0 | 0 | 147.0 | 197 | 656 | 90 | 79 | 16 | 7 | 5 | 4 | 46 | 2 | 75 | 6 | 0 |
| Dittfurth, Ryan, Frisco | 0 | 0 | .000 | 12.60 | 3 | 0 | 0 | 0 | 0 | 0 | 5.0 | 8 | 33 | 7 | 7 | 1 | 2 | 0 | 3 | 6 | 2 | 4 | 1 | 0 |
| Dominguez, Juan, Frisco | 0 | 0 | .000 | 1.08 | 3 | 2 | 0 | 0 | 0 | 0 | 8.1 | 4 | 30 | 1 | 1 | 0 | 0 | 0 | 0 | 1 | 0 | 11 | 0 | 0 |
| Done, Juan, San Antonio | 10 | 10 | .500 | 5.34 | 27 | 27 | 0 | 0 | 0 | 0 | 153.1 | 165 | 668 | 99 | 91 | 19 | 6 | 11 | 14 | 70 | 4 | 86 | 6 | 0 |
| Dorman, Rich, San Antonio | 8 | 4 | .667 | 3.48 | 20 | 20 | 1 | 0 | 0 | 0 | 108.2 | 93 | 469 | 44 | 42 | 8 | 6 | 6 | 3 | 64 | 1 | 137 | 12 | 1 |
| Doyle, Jared, El Paso * | 0 | 1 | .000 | 3.97 | 11 | 0 | 0 | 0 | 3 | 0 | 11.1 | 10 | 55 | 6 | 5 | 0 | 0 | 0 | 1 | 10 | 3 | 9 | 2 | 0 |
| Emanuel, Brandon, Arkansas | 0 | 0 | .000 | 4.50 | 1 | 1 | 0 | 0 | 0 | 0 | 4.0 | 5 | 18 | 2 | 2 | 0 | 0 | 0 | 0 | 1 | 0 | 5 | 0 | 1 |
| Esposito, Mike, Tulsa | 10 | 6 | .625 | 3.33 | 24 | 24 | 1 | 0 | 0 | 0 | 143.1 | 138 | 576 | 57 | 53 | 12 | 5 | 3 | 4 | 35 | 1 | 90 | 8 | 0 |
| Esslinger, Cam, Arkansas | 2 | 4 | .333 | 3.60 | 44 | 0 | 0 | 0 | 21 | 5 | 60.0 | 53 | 274 | 27 | 24 | 4 | 0 | 0 | 5 | 36 | 1 | 44 | 7 | 2 |
| Fischer, Rich, Arkansas | 3 | 8 | .273 | 9.57 | 19 | 9 | 0 | 0 | 1 | 0 | 52.2 | 88 | 263 | 66 | 56 | 10 | 2 | 4 | 4 | 19 | 1 | 33 | 3 | 0 |
| Fischer, Steve, Midland | 0 | 1 | .000 | 13.50 | 6 | 0 | 0 | 0 | 2 | 0 | 7.1 | 12 | 41 | 12 | 11 | 1 | 1 | 1 | 1 | 6 | 1 | 6 | 1 | 0 |
| Flores, Ruben, San Antonio | 0 | 0 | .000 | 5.40 | 1 | 0 | 0 | 0 | 0 | 0 | 1.2 | 0 | 8 | 1 | 1 | 0 | 0 | 0 | 0 | 3 | 0 | 2 | 0 | 0 |
| Fossum, Casey, El Paso * | 0 | 0 | .000 | 2.08 | 2 | 2 | 0 | 0 | 0 | 0 | 4.1 | 3 | 19 | 1 | 1 | 0 | 0 | 0 | 0 | 3 | 0 | 5 | 0 | 0 |
| Francis, Jeff, Tulsa * | 13 | 1 | .929 | 1.98 | 17 | 17 | 1 | 1 | 0 | 0 | 113.2 | 73 | 435 | 26 | 25 | 9 | 4 | 1 | 5 | 22 | 0 | 147 | 2 | 0 |
| Francisco, Frank, Frisco | 1 | 3 | .250 | 2.55 | 15 | 0 | 0 | 0 | 14 | 6 | 17.2 | 7 | 72 | 6 | 5 | 1 | 0 | 0 | 2 | 10 | 1 | 30 | 4 | 1 |
| Fritz, Ben, Midland | 7 | 4 | .636 | 5.63 | 20 | 20 | 1 | 0 | 0 | 0 | 104.0 | 118 | 462 | 69 | 65 | 5 | 3 | 6 | 6 | 50 | 0 | 77 | 6 | 0 |
| Fruto, Emiliano, San Antonio | 3 | 3 | .500 | 5.66 | 43 | 1 | 0 | 0 | 13 | 1 | 68.1 | 77 | 322 | 47 | 43 | 6 | 3 | 3 | 5 | 37 | 0 | 56 | 7 | 1 |
| Fulmer, T.A., San Antonio | 0 | 2 | .000 | 5.58 | 9 | 4 | 0 | 0 | 2 | 0 | 30.2 | 33 | 134 | 21 | 19 | 2 | 0 | 2 | 2 | 12 | 1 | 31 | 2 | 1 |

| Pitcher, Team | W | L | Pct. | ERA | G | GS | CG | ShO | GF | Sv. | IP | H | TBF | R | ER | HR | SH | SF | HB | BB | IBB | SO | WP | Bk. |
|---|---|---|---|---|---|---|---|---|---|---|---|---|---|---|---|---|---|---|---|---|---|---|---|---|
| Gandolfo, Rob, San Antonio | 0 | 0 | .000 | 4.50 | 2 | 0 | 0 | 0 | 1 | 0 | 2.0 | 1 | 10 | 1 | 1 | 0 | 0 | 0 | 0 | 3 | 0 | 0 | 0 | 0 |
| Garcia, Jairo, Midland | 2 | 0 | 1.000 | 1.50 | 13 | 0 | 0 | 0 | 9 | 2 | 18.0 | 10 | 80 | 3 | 3 | 0 | 0 | 0 | 1 | 15 | 0 | 32 | 2 | 0 |
| Gardner, Hayden, Frisco | 1 | 0 | 1.000 | 9.00 | 9 | 0 | 0 | 0 | 4 | 0 | 13.0 | 14 | 65 | 14 | 13 | 2 | 0 | 0 | 2 | 12 | 0 | 8 | 1 | 0 |
| Gil, Dave, San Antonio | 1 | 1 | .500 | 6.35 | 5 | 0 | 0 | 0 | 2 | 0 | 5.2 | 9 | 27 | 4 | 4 | 1 | 0 | 0 | 1 | 0 | 0 | 7 | 0 | 0 |
| Gil, Dave, Arkansas | 1 | 6 | .143 | 7.29 | 11 | 11 | 0 | 0 | 0 | 0 | 54.1 | 89 | 268 | 58 | 44 | 8 | 3 | 4 | 3 | 24 | 0 | 30 | 1 | 0 |
| Gomez, Rudy, Arkansas | 0 | 0 | .000 | 18.00 | 1 | 0 | 0 | 0 | 1 | 0 | 1.0 | 2 | 6 | 3 | 2 | 1 | 0 | 0 | 0 | 1 | 0 | 0 | 0 | 0 |
| Goocher, Clint, El Paso * | 6 | 10 | .375 | 5.27 | 17 | 13 | 0 | 0 | 2 | 0 | 85.1 | 103 | 382 | 61 | 50 | 10 | 8 | 3 | 5 | 27 | 4 | 41 | 6 | 1 |
| Good, Andrew, El Paso | 0 | 0 | .000 | 0.93 | 4 | 4 | 0 | 0 | 0 | 0 | 9.2 | 7 | 39 | 2 | 1 | 0 | 0 | 0 | 0 | 3 | 0 | 9 | 0 | 0 |
| Gothreaux, Jared, Round Rock | 9 | 7 | .563 | 3.96 | 27 | 24 | 2 | 0 | 1 | 0 | 157.0 | 173 | 661 | 82 | 69 | 16 | 6 | 4 | 4 | 35 | 0 | 110 | 3 | 0 |
| Green, Sean, Tulsa | 4 | 3 | .571 | 3.03 | 52 | 0 | 0 | 0 | 19 | 2 | 77.1 | 63 | 330 | 32 | 26 | 5 | 0 | 1 | 7 | 29 | 1 | 50 | 6 | 0 |
| Grezlovski, Ben, Arkansas | 0 | 2 | .000 | 6.60 | 11 | 0 | 0 | 0 | 5 | 0 | 15.0 | 14 | 75 | 17 | 11 | 0 | 0 | 0 | 3 | 13 | 0 | 5 | 2 | 0 |
| Griffin, Colt, Wichita | 1 | 1 | .500 | 4.02 | 26 | 0 | 0 | 0 | 7 | 1 | 31.1 | 29 | 140 | 14 | 14 | 2 | 0 | 0 | 1 | 16 | 0 | 26 | 2 | 0 |
| Griffith, Dustin, Arkansas | 0 | 0 | .000 | 4.50 | 3 | 0 | 0 | 0 | 1 | 0 | 4.0 | 5 | 21 | 2 | 2 | 0 | 0 | 0 | 1 | 3 | 0 | 3 | 0 | 0 |
| Guttormson, Rick, San Antonio | 5 | 4 | .556 | 3.29 | 54 | 0 | 0 | 0 | 44 | 25 | 65.2 | 68 | 290 | 28 | 24 | 6 | 0 | 0 | 3 | 24 | 2 | 56 | 1 | 0 |
| Gwyn, Marc, Midland | 3 | 4 | .429 | 2.94 | 44 | 0 | 0 | 0 | 27 | 13 | 67.1 | 59 | 279 | 25 | 22 | 3 | 0 | 0 | 5 | 19 | 0 | 72 | 2 | 1 |
| Hampson, Justin, Tulsa * | 10 | 9 | .526 | 3.49 | 27 | 27 | 1 | 0 | 0 | 0 | 170.1 | 176 | 718 | 82 | 66 | 22 | 13 | 1 | 8 | 63 | 0 | 104 | 5 | 1 |
| Hart, Corey, Wichita | 0 | 0 | .000 | 0.00 | 1 | 0 | 0 | 0 | 1 | 0 | 1.0 | 1 | 4 | 0 | 0 | 0 | 0 | 0 | 0 | 0 | 0 | 1 | 0 | 0 |
| Harville, Chad, Round Rock | 0 | 0 | .000 | 0.00 | 2 | 2 | 0 | 0 | 0 | 0 | 3.0 | 0 | 11 | 0 | 0 | 0 | 0 | 0 | 0 | 2 | 0 | 2 | 1 | 0 |
| Henrie, Matt, El Paso | 9 | 4 | .692 | 5.28 | 17 | 15 | 1 | 0 | 1 | 0 | 102.1 | 128 | 442 | 68 | 60 | 8 | 6 | 5 | 8 | 20 | 0 | 60 | 2 | 0 |
| Hernandez, Felix, San Antonio | 5 | 1 | .833 | 3.30 | 10 | 10 | 1 | 1 | 0 | 0 | 57.1 | 47 | 235 | 23 | 21 | 3 | 6 | 0 | 4 | 21 | 0 | 58 | 2 | 2 |
| Herndon, Junior, Wichita | 7 | 3 | .700 | 3.38 | 12 | 11 | 1 | 0 | 0 | 0 | 69.1 | 69 | 283 | 34 | 26 | 7 | 0 | 4 | 3 | 12 | 0 | 41 | 1 | 0 |
| Hoerman, Jared, San Antonio | 0 | 1 | .000 | 3.00 | 11 | 0 | 0 | 0 | 11 | 8 | 12.0 | 13 | 53 | 4 | 4 | 0 | 0 | 1 | 1 | 4 | 1 | 10 | 0 | 0 |
| Hogan, Gary, Frisco | 0 | 0 | .000 | 0.00 | 2 | 0 | 0 | 0 | 2 | 0 | 4.0 | 1 | 16 | 0 | 0 | 0 | 0 | 0 | 0 | 3 | 0 | 3 | 0 | 0 |
| Houlton, D.J., Round Rock | 12 | 5 | .706 | 2.94 | 28 | 28 | 3 | 1 | 0 | 0 | 159.0 | 141 | 654 | 59 | 52 | 14 | 7 | 2 | 12 | 47 | 2 | 159 | 4 | 0 |
| Hudgins, John, Frisco | 5 | 3 | .625 | 3.13 | 12 | 12 | 0 | 0 | 0 | 0 | 69.0 | 57 | 275 | 29 | 24 | 12 | 5 | 2 | 4 | 18 | 1 | 64 | 0 | 1 |
| Hughes, Travis, Frisco | 3 | 6 | .333 | 3.73 | 40 | 0 | 0 | 0 | 19 | 7 | 62.2 | 63 | 282 | 34 | 26 | 4 | 0 | 1 | 1 | 33 | 5 | 66 | 6 | 1 |
| Jimenez, Kelvin, Frisco | 3 | 5 | .375 | 4.53 | 26 | 21 | 0 | 0 | 0 | 0 | 129.0 | 135 | 584 | 76 | 65 | 13 | 6 | 6 | 7 | 67 | 1 | 101 | 12 | 1 |
| Juarez, William, El Paso | 3 | 7 | .300 | 5.00 | 13 | 13 | 0 | 0 | 0 | 0 | 75.2 | 80 | 329 | 47 | 42 | 4 | 4 | 6 | 6 | 22 | 2 | 68 | 4 | 0 |
| Keller, Kris, Frisco | 1 | 0 | 1.000 | 7.79 | 14 | 0 | 0 | 0 | 8 | 1 | 17.1 | 25 | 82 | 15 | 15 | 2 | 0 | 0 | 1 | 4 | 2 | 13 | 0 | 0 |
| Kent, Steve, Tulsa * | 3 | 1 | .750 | 2.03 | 39 | 0 | 0 | 0 | 10 | 1 | 31.0 | 27 | 132 | 7 | 7 | 1 | 0 | 0 | 1 | 11 | 0 | 23 | 7 | 0 |
| Keppinger, Billy, Wichita * | 3 | 3 | .500 | 6.08 | 48 | 2 | 0 | 0 | 14 | 2 | 74.0 | 95 | 333 | 54 | 50 | 9 | 1 | 2 | 5 | 17 | 1 | 50 | 3 | 0 |
| Key, Chris, San Antonio * | 5 | 4 | .556 | 4.76 | 36 | 12 | 0 | 0 | 7 | 1 | 102.0 | 119 | 441 | 66 | 54 | 7 | 6 | 3 | 1 | 27 | 0 | 63 | 7 | 1 |
| Komine, Shane, Midland | 4 | 5 | .444 | 4.77 | 17 | 17 | 0 | 0 | 0 | 0 | 94.1 | 103 | 409 | 56 | 50 | 10 | 5 | 5 | 3 | 28 | 0 | 65 | 6 | 1 |
| Kozlowski, Ben, Frisco * | 3 | 2 | .600 | 4.89 | 8 | 7 | 0 | 0 | 1 | 1 | 38.2 | 38 | 163 | 25 | 21 | 5 | 3 | 5 | 0 | 20 | 0 | 23 | 0 | 1 |
| Leclair, Aric, El Paso * | 4 | 2 | .667 | 4.50 | 29 | 0 | 0 | 0 | 10 | 0 | 38.0 | 41 | 175 | 20 | 19 | 2 | 0 | 0 | 1 | 20 | 2 | 32 | 1 | 0 |
| Lee, Corey, Arkansas * | 2 | 6 | .250 | 4.27 | 14 | 14 | 0 | 0 | 0 | 0 | 65.1 | 63 | 287 | 40 | 31 | 3 | 4 | 8 | 5 | 30 | 0 | 53 | 1 | 0 |
| Levrault, Allen, San Antonio | 1 | 0 | 1.000 | 8.00 | 11 | 0 | 0 | 0 | 3 | 0 | 9.0 | 14 | 47 | 9 | 8 | 1 | 0 | 1 | 2 | 6 | 0 | 8 | 0 | 0 |
| Linton, Doug, Wichita | 1 | 0 | 1.000 | 1.69 | 1 | 1 | 0 | 0 | 0 | 0 | 5.1 | 8 | 25 | 2 | 1 | 0 | 0 | 0 | 0 | 0 | 0 | 4 | 0 | 0 |
| Lizarraga, Sergio, El Paso | 4 | 10 | .286 | 5.04 | 29 | 17 | 3 | 1 | 3 | 0 | 123.1 | 140 | 537 | 71 | 69 | 14 | 6 | 7 | 9 | 36 | 6 | 101 | 4 | 0 |
| Loe, Kameron, Frisco | 7 | 7 | .500 | 3.12 | 19 | 19 | 0 | 0 | 0 | 0 | 112.2 | 122 | 478 | 42 | 39 | 5 | 6 | 4 | 6 | 29 | 3 | 97 | 5 | 1 |
| Mabeus, Chris, Midland | 4 | 0 | 1.000 | 1.99 | 20 | 0 | 0 | 0 | 18 | 11 | 22.2 | 23 | 94 | 5 | 5 | 0 | 0 | 1 | 0 | 2 | 1 | 27 | 4 | 0 |
| MacDougal, Mike, Wichita | 1 | 0 | 1.000 | 1.47 | 17 | 2 | 0 | 0 | 5 | 1 | 18.1 | 14 | 83 | 7 | 3 | 0 | 0 | 0 | 0 | 14 | 0 | 13 | 2 | 0 |
| Marcano, Luis, Frisco | 2 | 2 | .500 | 5.52 | 18 | 0 | 0 | 0 | 9 | 0 | 29.1 | 33 | 141 | 19 | 18 | 1 | 0 | 0 | 3 | 17 | 0 | 13 | 2 | 0 |
| Markray, Thad, Wichita | 1 | 5 | .167 | 3.86 | 8 | 8 | 0 | 0 | 0 | 0 | 42.0 | 37 | 172 | 20 | 18 | 7 | 2 | 3 | 3 | 10 | 0 | 40 | 0 | 0 |
| Martinez, Gustavo, San Antonio | 2 | 3 | .400 | 3.75 | 10 | 8 | 0 | 0 | 0 | 0 | 50.1 | 42 | 208 | 23 | 21 | 3 | 1 | 2 | 1 | 27 | 0 | 39 | 1 | 0 |
| Masset, Nicholas, Frisco | 1 | 0 | 1.000 | 1.80 | 2 | 1 | 0 | 0 | 0 | 0 | 10.0 | 8 | 37 | 2 | 2 | 0 | 0 | 1 | 2 | 4 | 0 | 8 | 1 | 0 |
| Mattioni, Nick, Midland | 1 | 3 | .250 | 2.93 | 19 | 0 | 0 | 0 | 9 | 3 | 30.2 | 24 | 133 | 12 | 10 | 3 | 0 | 0 | 0 | 17 | 2 | 15 | 1 | 0 |
| McClaskey, Tim, Round Rock | 7 | 9 | .438 | 4.62 | 34 | 19 | 0 | 0 | 3 | 2 | 140.1 | 148 | 590 | 81 | 72 | 17 | 3 | 4 | 10 | 36 | 1 | 94 | 5 | 0 |
| McClellan, Zach, Tulsa | 4 | 7 | .364 | 4.15 | 26 | 23 | 1 | 0 | 1 | 1 | 138.2 | 145 | 593 | 69 | 64 | 17 | 8 | 6 | 10 | 36 | 0 | 111 | 5 | 1 |
| McDaniel, Denny, Round Rock * | 4 | 3 | .571 | 3.48 | 48 | 0 | 0 | 0 | 11 | 2 | 75.0 | 67 | 319 | 30 | 29 | 5 | 0 | 0 | 5 | 24 | 1 | 69 | 3 | 1 |
| Menchaca, Eriberto, San Antonio | 0 | 0 | .000 | 27.00 | 1 | 0 | 0 | 0 | 1 | 0 | 1.0 | 3 | 8 | 3 | 3 | 0 | 0 | 0 | 0 | 2 | 0 | 0 | 0 | 0 |
| Middleton, Kyle, Wichita | 8 | 8 | .500 | 4.73 | 28 | 27 | 0 | 0 | 1 | 0 | 161.2 | 177 | 700 | 97 | 85 | 16 | 5 | 4 | 9 | 55 | 0 | 89 | 8 | 0 |
| Mizuo, Yoshitaka, Arkansas | 1 | 1 | .500 | 6.48 | 9 | 2 | 0 | 0 | 1 | 0 | 16.2 | 23 | 76 | 13 | 12 | 1 | 0 | 0 | 0 | 4 | 0 | 9 | 0 | 0 |
| Moreno, Edwin, Frisco | 5 | 6 | .455 | 6.01 | 18 | 13 | 0 | 0 | 1 | 0 | 70.1 | 90 | 313 | 51 | 47 | 8 | 4 | 3 | 4 | 18 | 0 | 37 | 6 | 0 |
| Morgan, Matt, El Paso | 0 | 0 | .000 | 13.50 | 1 | 0 | 0 | 0 | 1 | 0 | 2.0 | 3 | 11 | 4 | 3 | 1 | 0 | 0 | 0 | 2 | 0 | 1 | 0 | 0 |
| Mozingo, Dan, Arkansas * | 0 | 5 | .000 | 5.85 | 11 | 4 | 0 | 0 | 4 | 0 | 32.1 | 43 | 158 | 24 | 21 | 4 | 3 | 3 | 4 | 12 | 1 | 14 | 3 | 0 |
| Murphy, Bill, El Paso * | 3 | 3 | .500 | 6.68 | 6 | 6 | 0 | 0 | 0 | 0 | 31.0 | 41 | 141 | 28 | 23 | 6 | 0 | 2 | 1 | 17 | 0 | 24 | 2 | 1 |
| Narron, Sam, Frisco * | 6 | 0 | 1.000 | 2.36 | 13 | 8 | 0 | 0 | 0 | 0 | 53.1 | 56 | 223 | 23 | 14 | 6 | 2 | 1 | 0 | 10 | 0 | 27 | 0 | 2 |
| Narveson, Chris, Tulsa * | 0 | 3 | .000 | 3.15 | 4 | 4 | 0 | 0 | 0 | 0 | 20.0 | 16 | 87 | 14 | 7 | 1 | 1 | 3 | 2 | 13 | 0 | 14 | 2 | 0 |
| Natale, Mike, Wichita | 8 | 5 | .615 | 6.21 | 44 | 3 | 0 | 0 | 12 | 0 | 84.0 | 110 | 380 | 65 | 58 | 8 | 2 | 3 | 3 | 23 | 0 | 72 | 9 | 0 |
| Nelson, Jeff, Frisco | 0 | 0 | .000 | 2.45 | 3 | 3 | 0 | 0 | 0 | 0 | 3.2 | 2 | 15 | 1 | 1 | 0 | 0 | 0 | 1 | 1 | 0 | 3 | 0 | 0 |
| Nieve, Fernando, Round Rock | 2 | 0 | 1.000 | 1.56 | 3 | 3 | 0 | 0 | 0 | 0 | 17.1 | 12 | 69 | 4 | 3 | 0 | 1 | 0 | 1 | 8 | 0 | 17 | 0 | 0 |
| Nippert, Dustin, El Paso | 2 | 5 | .286 | 3.64 | 14 | 14 | 0 | 0 | 0 | 0 | 71.2 | 77 | 335 | 45 | 29 | 0 | 6 | 3 | 4 | 40 | 1 | 73 | 4 | 0 |
| Nunez, Jose, San Antonio * | 1 | 0 | 1.000 | 6.19 | 10 | 0 | 0 | 0 | 4 | 0 | 16.0 | 21 | 82 | 13 | 11 | 2 | 0 | 1 | 2 | 12 | 0 | 11 | 0 | 0 |
| O'Sullivan, Mark, Arkansas | 5 | 5 | .500 | 7.46 | 45 | 4 | 0 | 0 | 12 | 1 | 79.2 | 117 | 401 | 74 | 66 | 10 | 2 | 2 | 2 | 46 | 1 | 53 | 6 | 0 |
| Obenchain, Steve, Midland | 2 | 2 | .500 | 5.11 | 17 | 2 | 0 | 0 | 3 | 1 | 37.0 | 42 | 161 | 22 | 21 | 2 | 0 | 2 | 0 | 11 | 0 | 32 | 1 | 0 |
| Oquist, Mike, Midland | 2 | 5 | .286 | 6.11 | 27 | 7 | 0 | 0 | 11 | 0 | 63.1 | 76 | 291 | 47 | 43 | 7 | 2 | 3 | 2 | 24 | 0 | 34 | 2 | 0 |
| Park, Chan Ho, Frisco | 0 | 2 | .000 | 8.74 | 2 | 2 | 0 | 0 | 0 | 0 | 11.1 | 16 | 51 | 11 | 11 | 1 | 1 | 2 | 0 | 5 | 0 | 5 | 0 | 0 |
| Parker, Zach, Tulsa * | 4 | 8 | .333 | 5.84 | 22 | 17 | 0 | 0 | 2 | 0 | 91.0 | 108 | 419 | 67 | 59 | 7 | 4 | 3 | 11 | 33 | 0 | 45 | 6 | 0 |
| Perez, Beltran, El Paso | 2 | 6 | .250 | 4.41 | 37 | 8 | 0 | 0 | 8 | 3 | 104.0 | 102 | 454 | 56 | 51 | 14 | 2 | 1 | 6 | 46 | 1 | 77 | 2 | 0 |
| Perez, Elvis, San Antonio | 1 | 6 | .143 | 7.56 | 10 | 7 | 0 | 0 | 1 | 0 | 33.1 | 47 | 161 | 31 | 28 | 2 | 2 | 2 | 3 | 18 | 0 | 35 | 6 | 3 |
| Pettitte, Andy, Round Rock * | 0 | 0 | .000 | 2.25 | 2 | 2 | 0 | 0 | 0 | 0 | 8.0 | 4 | 29 | 2 | 2 | 1 | 1 | 0 | 0 | 2 | 0 | 9 | 0 | 0 |
| Poland, Trey, Round Rock * | 0 | 0 | .000 | 3.09 | 6 | 0 | 0 | 0 | 2 | 0 | 11.2 | 11 | 50 | 4 | 4 | 1 | 1 | 0 | 0 | 5 | 0 | 7 | 2 | 0 |
| Powell, Greg, Round Rock | 2 | 5 | .286 | 8.26 | 26 | 8 | 0 | 0 | 6 | 0 | 68.2 | 110 | 346 | 65 | 63 | 7 | 7 | 4 | 5 | 33 | 2 | 28 | 3 | 0 |
| Rall, Tim, San Antonio * | 3 | 5 | .375 | 4.57 | 56 | 0 | 0 | 0 | 16 | 1 | 65.0 | 62 | 293 | 34 | 33 | 12 | 0 | 0 | 3 | 35 | 2 | 78 | 5 | 1 |
| Ramirez, Emmanuel, Tulsa | 3 | 5 | .375 | 3.58 | 48 | 0 | 0 | 0 | 10 | 0 | 65.1 | 46 | 291 | 29 | 26 | 4 | 0 | 1 | 9 | 42 | 4 | 68 | 12 | 1 |
| Ramirez, Santiago, Round Rock | 6 | 4 | .600 | 2.63 | 55 | 0 | 0 | 0 | 50 | 32 | 78.2 | 71 | 345 | 24 | 23 | 2 | 0 | 1 | 1 | 38 | 6 | 83 | 3 | 0 |
| Reynolds, Shane, El Paso | 0 | 1 | .000 | 5.79 | 2 | 2 | 0 | 0 | 0 | 0 | 4.2 | 7 | 23 | 3 | 3 | 0 | 0 | 0 | 0 | 2 | 0 | 3 | 0 | 0 |
| Roberts, Nick, Arkansas | 2 | 3 | .400 | 5.54 | 12 | 11 | 0 | 0 | 0 | 0 | 66.2 | 78 | 280 | 42 | 41 | 11 | 6 | 3 | 4 | 12 | 0 | 33 | 1 | 0 |
| Rodriguez, Javy, Arkansas | 0 | 0 | .000 | 0.00 | 1 | 0 | 0 | 0 | 1 | 0 | 0.1 | 0 | 2 | 0 | 0 | 0 | 0 | 0 | 1 | 0 | 0 | 0 | 0 | 0 |
| Rodriguez, Wandy, Round Rock * | 11 | 6 | .647 | 4.48 | 26 | 25 | 1 | 0 | 0 | 0 | 142.2 | 159 | 632 | 77 | 71 | 15 | 6 | 6 | 7 | 57 | 1 | 115 | 2 | 6 |
| Rosario, Adriano, El Paso | 3 | 3 | .500 | 5.44 | 7 | 7 | 0 | 0 | 0 | 0 | 43.0 | 47 | 174 | 27 | 26 | 4 | 0 | 0 | 1 | 5 | 0 | 36 | 0 | 0 |
| Rose, Brad, San Antonio | 0 | 0 | .000 | 4.50 | 1 | 0 | 0 | 0 | 0 | 0 | 2.0 | 2 | 12 | 1 | 1 | 0 | 0 | 0 | 0 | 4 | 1 | 2 | 0 | 0 |

| Pitcher, Team | W | L | Pct. | ERA | G | GS | CG | ShO | GF | Sv. | IP | H | TBF | R | ER | HR | SH | SF | HB | BB | IBB | SO | WP | Bk. |
|---|---|---|---|---|---|---|---|---|---|---|---|---|---|---|---|---|---|---|---|---|---|---|---|---|
| Rouwenhorst, Jonathon, Arkansas * | 4 | 7 | .364 | 4.06 | 52 | 0 | 0 | 0 | 37 | 10 | 68.2 | 67 | 306 | 39 | 31 | 6 | 1 | 0 | 2 | 32 | 1 | 65 | 5 | 0 |
| Rowe, Steven, Frisco | 8 | 2 | .800 | 3.59 | 54 | 0 | 0 | 0 | 19 | 3 | 82.2 | 63 | 350 | 38 | 33 | 12 | 0 | 2 | 5 | 34 | 2 | 72 | 8 | 0 |
| Rupe, Josh, Frisco | 2 | 2 | .500 | 4.38 | 7 | 6 | 0 | 0 | 0 | 0 | 37.0 | 41 | 172 | 23 | 18 | 5 | 1 | 4 | 5 | 16 | 1 | 16 | 2 | 0 |
| Saladin, Miguel, Round Rock | 1 | 0 | 1.000 | 0.00 | 3 | 0 | 0 | 0 | 2 | 1 | 5.0 | 3 | 19 | 1 | 0 | 0 | 0 | 0 | 1 | 2 | 0 | 6 | 1 | 0 |
| Sampson, Chris, Round Rock | 0 | 0 | .000 | 0.00 | 1 | 0 | 0 | 0 | 0 | 0 | 2.0 | 3 | 9 | 0 | 0 | 0 | 0 | 0 | 0 | 0 | 0 | 1 | 0 | 0 |
| Sansom, Trevor, Midland | 0 | 2 | .000 | 2.70 | 16 | 2 | 0 | 0 | 5 | 0 | 33.1 | 27 | 136 | 12 | 10 | 3 | 1 | 1 | 0 | 15 | 0 | 29 | 1 | 0 |
| Santana, Ervin, Arkansas | 2 | 1 | .667 | 3.30 | 8 | 8 | 0 | 0 | 0 | 0 | 43.2 | 41 | 191 | 19 | 16 | 3 | 3 | 0 | 4 | 18 | 0 | 48 | 5 | 0 |
| Saunders, Joe, Arkansas * | 4 | 3 | .571 | 5.77 | 8 | 8 | 0 | 0 | 0 | 0 | 39.0 | 51 | 182 | 26 | 25 | 5 | 5 | 2 | 5 | 14 | 0 | 25 | 2 | 0 |
| Schneider, Scott, Arkansas | 3 | 5 | .375 | 5.29 | 54 | 2 | 0 | 0 | 16 | 0 | 95.1 | 110 | 437 | 63 | 56 | 10 | 4 | 1 | 4 | 34 | 0 | 67 | 9 | 1 |
| Schultz, Mike, El Paso | 0 | 0 | .000 | 4.61 | 12 | 0 | 0 | 0 | 7 | 1 | 13.2 | 16 | 70 | 7 | 7 | 0 | 0 | 0 | 0 | 13 | 0 | 14 | 2 | 0 |
| Serrano, Alex, Tulsa | 3 | 4 | .429 | 3.38 | 14 | 0 | 0 | 0 | 3 | 0 | 24.0 | 22 | 99 | 9 | 9 | 2 | 2 | 1 | 0 | 4 | 1 | 27 | 0 | 0 |
| Serrano, Jim, Wichita | 3 | 1 | .750 | 1.96 | 11 | 11 | 1 | 1 | 0 | 0 | 64.1 | 42 | 247 | 18 | 14 | 6 | 1 | 4 | 2 | 18 | 0 | 74 | 2 | 0 |
| Shiery, Shaun, Wichita * | 2 | 0 | 1.000 | 4.67 | 5 | 3 | 0 | 0 | 0 | 0 | 17.1 | 21 | 86 | 11 | 9 | 1 | 0 | 0 | 1 | 14 | 0 | 4 | 1 | 0 |
| Sikaras, Pete, El Paso | 0 | 3 | .000 | 3.80 | 38 | 0 | 0 | 0 | 22 | 9 | 45.0 | 50 | 220 | 28 | 19 | 3 | 1 | 1 | 5 | 28 | 0 | 46 | 7 | 0 |
| Simpson, Gerrit, Tulsa | 5 | 4 | .556 | 4.42 | 39 | 3 | 0 | 0 | 7 | 0 | 73.1 | 75 | 320 | 50 | 36 | 8 | 3 | 2 | 1 | 27 | 1 | 51 | 5 | 0 |
| Slaten, Doug, El Paso * | 0 | 1 | .000 | 10.00 | 11 | 0 | 0 | 0 | 2 | 0 | 9.0 | 16 | 53 | 13 | 10 | 1 | 1 | 1 | 0 | 10 | 0 | 6 | 0 | 0 |
| Smith, Cliff, Arkansas | 0 | 0 | .000 | 9.00 | 18 | 0 | 0 | 0 | 8 | 0 | 22.0 | 37 | 114 | 26 | 22 | 5 | 1 | 0 | 3 | 10 | 0 | 15 | 2 | 0 |
| Smith, Sam, El Paso | 2 | 5 | .286 | 7.55 | 18 | 6 | 0 | 0 | 7 | 0 | 47.2 | 76 | 243 | 45 | 40 | 5 | 2 | 4 | 3 | 26 | 3 | 39 | 4 | 0 |
| Smyth, Steve, Midland * | 5 | 4 | .556 | 4.70 | 20 | 9 | 0 | 0 | 3 | 1 | 59.1 | 56 | 265 | 36 | 31 | 10 | 3 | 0 | 4 | 38 | 1 | 45 | 3 | 1 |
| Snow, Bert, Midland | 1 | 3 | .250 | 2.59 | 20 | 0 | 0 | 0 | 5 | 0 | 31.1 | 25 | 125 | 13 | 9 | 3 | 2 | 1 | 3 | 6 | 0 | 21 | 1 | 1 |
| Sonnier, Shawn, Midland | 3 | 3 | .500 | 2.95 | 45 | 0 | 0 | 0 | 11 | 0 | 76.1 | 70 | 323 | 29 | 25 | 8 | 0 | 1 | 3 | 22 | 1 | 69 | 4 | 0 |
| Soriano, Rafael, San Antonio | 1 | 0 | 1.000 | 1.13 | 2 | 1 | 0 | 0 | 0 | 0 | 8.0 | 4 | 27 | 1 | 1 | 1 | 0 | 0 | 0 | 0 | 0 | 10 | 0 | 0 |
| Speier, Ryan, Tulsa | 3 | 1 | .750 | 2.02 | 62 | 0 | 0 | 0 | 59 | 37 | 62.1 | 33 | 249 | 14 | 14 | 3 | 0 | 0 | 3 | 26 | 1 | 71 | 4 | 1 |
| Stamler, Keith, Frisco | 0 | 0 | .000 | 0.00 | 4 | 0 | 0 | 0 | 0 | 0 | 9.1 | 4 | 31 | 0 | 0 | 0 | 0 | 0 | 0 | 2 | 1 | 7 | 0 | 0 |
| Stockman, Phil, El Paso | 1 | 3 | .250 | 2.67 | 6 | 6 | 1 | 0 | 0 | 0 | 27.0 | 17 | 120 | 13 | 8 | 1 | 2 | 2 | 4 | 20 | 0 | 21 | 2 | 0 |
| Street, Huston, Midland | 1 | 0 | 1.000 | 1.35 | 10 | 0 | 0 | 0 | 8 | 3 | 13.1 | 10 | 54 | 2 | 2 | 0 | 0 | 0 | 1 | 3 | 0 | 14 | 1 | 0 |
| Sylvester, Billy, Frisco | 4 | 1 | .800 | 2.34 | 30 | 0 | 0 | 0 | 24 | 12 | 42.1 | 21 | 171 | 14 | 11 | 4 | 0 | 1 | 3 | 22 | 1 | 62 | 6 | 0 |
| Tamayo, Danny, Wichita | 12 | 7 | .632 | 3.92 | 25 | 25 | 0 | 0 | 0 | 0 | 142.1 | 165 | 604 | 66 | 62 | 15 | 4 | 7 | 8 | 36 | 0 | 123 | 7 | 0 |
| Taylor, Aaron, San Antonio | 3 | 1 | .750 | 2.89 | 30 | 0 | 0 | 0 | 7 | 0 | 37.1 | 27 | 156 | 13 | 12 | 2 | 0 | 0 | 3 | 14 | 0 | 37 | 4 | 0 |
| Thomas, Jared, San Antonio * | 5 | 3 | .625 | 3.62 | 33 | 0 | 0 | 0 | 9 | 1 | 59.2 | 57 | 276 | 24 | 24 | 4 | 0 | 0 | 2 | 38 | 3 | 64 | 5 | 1 |
| Thompson, Eric, Wichita | 0 | 2 | .000 | 5.48 | 7 | 5 | 0 | 0 | 1 | 0 | 21.1 | 24 | 100 | 13 | 13 | 1 | 0 | 0 | 1 | 13 | 0 | 21 | 1 | 0 |
| Thompson, Erik, Frisco | 6 | 6 | .500 | 2.98 | 15 | 15 | 1 | 1 | 0 | 0 | 90.2 | 78 | 357 | 35 | 30 | 10 | 1 | 1 | 2 | 14 | 1 | 65 | 0 | 0 |
| Thompson, Justin, Frisco * | 3 | 2 | .600 | 2.61 | 23 | 0 | 0 | 0 | 3 | 0 | 38.0 | 35 | 161 | 19 | 11 | 3 | 0 | 0 | 2 | 11 | 1 | 26 | 1 | 0 |
| Topolski, Jon, Round Rock | 0 | 0 | .000 | 0.00 | 1 | 0 | 0 | 0 | 1 | 0 | 0.2 | 0 | 2 | 0 | 0 | 0 | 0 | 0 | 0 | 0 | 0 | 0 | 0 | 0 |
| Trujillo, J.J., Wichita | 7 | 10 | .412 | 3.17 | 59 | 2 | 0 | 0 | 29 | 7 | 96.2 | 95 | 409 | 42 | 34 | 4 | 0 | 1 | 6 | 22 | 3 | 79 | 1 | 0 |
| Tsao, Chin-Hui, Tulsa | 1 | 1 | .500 | 2.77 | 2 | 2 | 0 | 0 | 0 | 0 | 13.0 | 12 | 51 | 4 | 4 | 1 | 1 | 1 | 0 | 2 | 0 | 10 | 0 | 0 |
| Vasquez, Jorge, Wichita | 4 | 5 | .444 | 4.68 | 49 | 0 | 0 | 0 | 41 | 18 | 59.2 | 52 | 263 | 34 | 31 | 3 | 0 | 0 | 5 | 27 | 1 | 71 | 8 | 0 |
| Villacis, Eduardo, Wichita | 2 | 0 | 1.000 | 2.67 | 8 | 3 | 0 | 0 | 1 | 0 | 30.1 | 22 | 119 | 11 | 9 | 3 | 0 | 0 | 0 | 6 | 0 | 21 | 2 | 0 |
| Waldron, Jeff, El Paso | 0 | 0 | .000 | 18.00 | 1 | 0 | 0 | 0 | 1 | 0 | 1.0 | 3 | 7 | 2 | 2 | 0 | 0 | 0 | 0 | 1 | 0 | 0 | 0 | 0 |
| Walrond, Les, Wichita * | 3 | 3 | .500 | 4.38 | 8 | 6 | 0 | 0 | 0 | 0 | 39.0 | 30 | 165 | 19 | 19 | 2 | 3 | 1 | 3 | 17 | 0 | 34 | 3 | 0 |
| Ward, Jeremy, El Paso | 0 | 2 | .000 | 7.94 | 7 | 0 | 0 | 0 | 4 | 0 | 5.2 | 10 | 30 | 8 | 5 | 0 | 1 | 1 | 0 | 1 | 0 | 4 | 2 | 0 |
| Weis, Brad, Midland * | 7 | 12 | .368 | 5.78 | 28 | 28 | 0 | 0 | 0 | 0 | 146.1 | 173 | 656 | 106 | 94 | 10 | 10 | 8 | 15 | 69 | 0 | 70 | 7 | 0 |
| White, Bill, El Paso * | 2 | 3 | .400 | 6.81 | 31 | 0 | 0 | 0 | 12 | 0 | 38.1 | 43 | 192 | 37 | 29 | 2 | 0 | 1 | 1 | 36 | 3 | 41 | 8 | 0 |
| Wilkerson, Wes, Wichita | 1 | 4 | .200 | 5.18 | 49 | 0 | 0 | 0 | 23 | 3 | 74.2 | 96 | 349 | 48 | 43 | 10 | 0 | 0 | 3 | 26 | 3 | 55 | 1 | 0 |
| Wilkinson, Matthew, El Paso | 0 | 2 | .000 | 10.80 | 5 | 0 | 0 | 0 | 4 | 2 | 3.1 | 8 | 21 | 4 | 4 | 0 | 0 | 0 | 0 | 3 | 0 | 5 | 0 | 0 |
| Woods, Jake, Arkansas * | 9 | 2 | .818 | 2.60 | 14 | 14 | 1 | 0 | 0 | 0 | 90.0 | 85 | 366 | 29 | 26 | 5 | 7 | 4 | 4 | 19 | 0 | 60 | 5 | 0 |
| Young, Chris, Frisco | 6 | 5 | .545 | 4.48 | 18 | 18 | 0 | 0 | 0 | 0 | 88.1 | 94 | 383 | 48 | 44 | 9 | 5 | 4 | 5 | 31 | 1 | 75 | 4 | 0 |
| Ziegler, Mike, Midland | 3 | 3 | .500 | 3.42 | 8 | 8 | 0 | 0 | 0 | 0 | 52.2 | 42 | 203 | 22 | 20 | 4 | 2 | 0 | 2 | 11 | 0 | 35 | 3 | 0 |

COMBINATION SHUTOUTS: **Arkansas** (9)—Fischer-Collazo-Schneider-C. Smith, Bittner-Esslinger-Mozingo, Brunet-Rouwenhorst-O'Sullivan, Cyr-Schneider-O'Sullivan, Woods-Esslinger-C. Smith, Woods-Rouwenhorst, Bittner-Esslinger, Collazo-Andrade, Lee-Rouwenhorst. **El Paso** (3)—Fossum-Henrie, Nippert-Smith, Goocher-Schultz. **Frisco** (10)—Thompson-Francisco, Loe-Beasley-Hughes, Jimenez-Burke-Rowe-Keller, Thompson-Moreno-Marcano, Hudgins-Burke-Beasley, Callaway-Burke, Callaway-Beasley, Dominguez-Marcano-Beasley, Rupe-Andrew-Burke, Jimenez-Beasley. **Midland** (7)—Weis-Crowell-Oquist, Ziegler-Gwyn, Dickinson-Garcia, Smyth-Obenchain-Mattioni-Garcia, Bazzell-Garcia, Bondurant-Mattioni, Weis-Sonnier-Oquist. **Round Rock** (13)—W. Rodriguez-McClaskey, Houlton-Barzilla-Burns, McClaskey-Carlson-Burns-S. Ramirez, Houlton-S. Ramirez, Astacio-S. Ramirez, Gothreaux-McDaniel, McClaskey-S. Ramirez, W. Rodriguez-Carlson, McClaskey-S. Ramirez, Astacio-S. Ramirez, W. Rodriguez-Burns, Houlton-S. Ramirez, Astacio-Burns. **San Antonio** (6)—Done-Rall, Dorman-Cortez, Buglovsky-Fruto-Thomas-Guttormson, Buglovsky-Thomas-Guttormson, Dorman-Key-Taylor, Devey-Cortez. **Tulsa** (14)—Hampson-Simpson-Speier, Francis-E. Ramirez-Simpson, Francis-Serrano-Speier, Parker-Green-Speier, Francis-E. Ramirez-Speier, Bernero-Speier, Hampson-Speier, Francis-Green-Speier, Esposito-Speier, Tsao-Kent-E. Ramirez-Speier, Esposito-E. Ramirez-Kent-Cosgrove-Green, Esposito-Speier, Esposito-E. Ramirez, McClellan-Kent. **Wichita** (8)—Walrond-Keppinger-Wilkerson, Baerlocher-Keppinger-Wilkerson-Vasquez, Serrano-Wilkerson-Vasquez, Serrano-Trujillo, Serrano-Natale, Middleton-MacDougal, Tamayo-Wilkerson-Griffin-MacDougal, Tamayo-Vasquez.

NO-HIT GAMES: None.

# 2004 FIELDING

## TEAM

| Team | G | PO | A | E | TC | DP | TP | PB | Pct. |
|---|---|---|---|---|---|---|---|---|---|
| Wichita | 139 | 3654 | 1449 | 128 | 5231 | 128 | -- | 18 | .976 |
| Tulsa | 139 | 3627 | 1535 | 132 | 5294 | 144 | -- | 15 | .975 |
| Round Rock | 140 | 3683 | 1412 | 133 | 5228 | 113 | -- | 17 | .975 |
| Midland | 140 | 3705 | 1557 | 140 | 5402 | 140 | -- | 19 | .974 |
| San Antonio | 138 | 3624 | 1413 | 136 | 5173 | 140 | -- | 19 | .974 |
| Frisco | 140 | 3728 | 1385 | 144 | 5257 | 109 | -- | 17 | .973 |
| El Paso | 137 | 3581 | 1498 | 165 | 5244 | 119 | -- | 11 | .969 |
| Arkansas | 139 | 3628 | 1505 | 170 | 5303 | 116 | -- | 17 | .968 |

## INDIVIDUAL

### FIRST BASEMEN

NOTE: All caps denotes fielding-percentage leader based on 70 games for catchers, 93 for all other non-pitchers and 112 innings for pitchers. *Throws lefthanded.

| Player, Team | Pct. | G | PO | A | E | TC | DP |
|---|---|---|---|---|---|---|---|
| Baker, John, MDL* | 1.000 | 17 | 123 | 13 | 0 | 136 | 12 |
| Balfe, Ryan, SAN | .970 | 16 | 119 | 11 | 4 | 134 | 15 |
| Beinbrink, Andrew, FRI | .984 | 17 | 117 | 10 | 2 | 129 | 5 |
| Botts, Jason, FRI | .984 | 127 | 1105 | 46 | 19 | 1170 | 94 |
| Brown, Hunter, SAN | .981 | 21 | 134 | 19 | 3 | 156 | 12 |
| Christianson, Ryan, SAN | .976 | 4 | 38 | 2 | 1 | 41 | 10 |
| Colamarino, Brant, MDL* | .993 | 70 | 640 | 33 | 5 | 678 | 71 |
| Conway, Dan, TUL | 1.000 | 1 | 1 | 0 | 0 | 1 | 1 |
| Cota, Jesus, ELP* | .991 | 92 | 777 | 59 | 8 | 844 | 69 |
| D'Antona, Jamie, ELP | 1.000 | 2 | 9 | 3 | 0 | 12 | 0 |
| Eylward, Mike, ARK | .992 | 99 | 821 | 71 | 7 | 899 | 70 |
| Gemoll, Justin, WCH | 1.000 | 3 | 18 | 2 | 0 | 20 | 5 |
| Gomez, Francis, MDL | 1.000 | 2 | 2 | 1 | 0 | 3 | 0 |
| Gomez, Rudy, ARK | .993 | 17 | 134 | 10 | 1 | 145 | 11 |
| Hart, Corey, WCH | .962 | 3 | 25 | 0 | 1 | 26 | 2 |
| Howe, Matt, MDL | .963 | 6 | 50 | 2 | 2 | 54 | 2 |
| Jackson, Steve, MDL | .988 | 48 | 364 | 37 | 5 | 406 | 37 |
| Kotchman, Casey, ARK* | 1.000 | 25 | 234 | 18 | 0 | 252 | 24 |

| Player, Team | Pct. | G | PO | A | E | TC | DP |
|---|---|---|---|---|---|---|---|
| Lindsey, John, SAN | .991 | 98 | 801 | 73 | 8 | 882 | 78 |
| Luellwitz, Sean, ELP | .988 | 26 | 221 | 29 | 3 | 253 | 27 |
| Menchaca, Eriberto, SAN | 1.000 | 5 | 35 | 3 | 0 | 38 | 6 |
| Morales, Willie, TUL | 1.000 | 1 | 7 | 1 | 0 | 8 | 0 |
| Morgan, Matt, ELP | 1.000 | 3 | 19 | 2 | 0 | 21 | 4 |
| Myers, Casey, MDL | 1.000 | 7 | 71 | 2 | 0 | 73 | 5 |
| Nichols, Kyle, ELP | .980 | 14 | 92 | 6 | 2 | 100 | 7 |
| Norris, Dax, ROU | .978 | 6 | 40 | 5 | 1 | 46 | 2 |
| Orie, Kevin, ROU | 1.000 | 8 | 47 | 3 | 0 | 50 | 2 |
| Perry, Herbert, FRI | 1.000 | 1 | 7 | 0 | 0 | 7 | 2 |
| Santana, Mayobanex, ELP | 1.000 | 8 | 22 | 1 | 0 | 23 | 1 |
| Santos, Chad, WCH* | .988 | 128 | 1145 | 76 | 15 | 1236 | 107 |
| Self, Todd, ROU* | .994 | 127 | 1056 | 73 | 7 | 1136 | 101 |
| Senjem, Guye, TUL* | 1.000 | 6 | 49 | 3 | 0 | 52 | 7 |
| Shealy, Ryan, TUL | .997 | 127 | 1141 | 68 | 4 | 1213 | 120 |
| Slavik, Corey, TUL* | .986 | 8 | 65 | 7 | 1 | 73 | 6 |
| Smith, Jeff, FRI* | 1.000 | 1 | 1 | 0 | 0 | 1 | 1 |
| Snyder, Chris, ELP | .984 | 8 | 58 | 2 | 1 | 61 | 4 |
| Teixeira, Mark, FRI | 1.000 | 1 | 9 | 0 | 0 | 9 | 0 |
| Terrell, Jim, WCH* | .931 | 4 | 25 | 2 | 2 | 29 | 2 |
| Topolski, Jon, ROU* | 1.000 | 3 | 22 | 0 | 0 | 22 | 1 |
| Walter, Scott, WCH | .976 | 4 | 38 | 3 | 1 | 42 | 3 |

## SECOND BASEMEN

| Player, Team | Pct. | G | PO | A | E | TC | DP |
|---|---|---|---|---|---|---|---|
| Acosta, Jesse, MDL | 1.000 | 5 | 8 | 10 | 0 | 18 | 1 |
| Aguirre, Rodrigo, ELP* | 1.000 | 2 | 6 | 7 | 0 | 13 | 2 |
| Arroyo, Jack, SAN | .833 | 2 | 2 | 3 | 1 | 6 | 0 |
| Bastida, Evel, SAN* | .961 | 12 | 24 | 25 | 2 | 51 | 8 |
| Bourgeois, Jason, FRI | .975 | 135 | 211 | 386 | 15 | 612 | 70 |
| Brown, Hunter, SAN | .991 | 29 | 47 | 68 | 1 | 116 | 22 |
| Brown, Neb, ELP* | 1.000 | 18 | 33 | 61 | 0 | 94 | 13 |
| Bynum, Freddie, MDL* | 1.000 | 4 | 5 | 6 | 0 | 11 | 3 |
| Callaspo, Alberto, ARK | 1.000 | 3 | 5 | 10 | 0 | 15 | 2 |
| Castro, Ramon, MDL | .970 | 6 | 12 | 20 | 1 | 33 | 8 |
| Coffie, Ivanon, ROU* | .913 | 14 | 25 | 38 | 6 | 69 | 7 |
| Colamarino, Brant, MDL* | 1.000 | 1 | 0 | 1 | 0 | 1 | 0 |
| Conrad, Brooks, ROU | .979 | 124 | 246 | 354 | 13 | 613 | 74 |
| Duncan, Carlos, ARK | 1.000 | 2 | 4 | 6 | 0 | 10 | 1 |
| Fenster, Darren, WCH | .993 | 28 | 50 | 83 | 1 | 134 | 14 |
| Gandolfo, Rob, SAN* | .977 | 78 | 119 | 184 | 7 | 310 | 51 |
| Garrabrants, Steve, ELP | .947 | 29 | 54 | 90 | 8 | 152 | 12 |
| Gomez, Francis, MDL | .962 | 10 | 26 | 25 | 2 | 53 | 8 |
| Gomez, Rudy, ARK | .967 | 28 | 42 | 77 | 4 | 123 | 13 |
| Gonzalez, Edgar, FRI | 1.000 | 8 | 9 | 15 | 0 | 24 | 4 |
| Gotay, Ruben, WCH | .971 | 105 | 190 | 316 | 15 | 521 | 57 |
| Groves, Brett, WCH | 1.000 | 3 | 8 | 10 | 0 | 18 | 5 |
| Gutierrez, Victor, ARK | .965 | 47 | 109 | 114 | 8 | 231 | 25 |
| Harrison, Adonis, TUL* | .946 | 21 | 54 | 69 | 7 | 130 | 21 |
| Hart, Corey, WCH | 1.000 | 2 | 1 | 6 | 0 | 7 | 2 |
| Hopper, Norris, WCH | .875 | 4 | 4 | 3 | 1 | 8 | 2 |
| Kiger, Mark, MDL | .979 | 97 | 225 | 293 | 11 | 529 | 65 |
| Matranga, David, ROU | 1.000 | 1 | 1 | 2 | 0 | 3 | 0 |
| McCurdy, John, MDL | .913 | 23 | 41 | 54 | 9 | 104 | 8 |
| Menchaca, Eriberto, SAN | .983 | 24 | 52 | 67 | 2 | 121 | 20 |
| Menechino, Frank, MDL | .750 | 2 | 1 | 2 | 1 | 4 | 0 |
| Meyer, Drew, FRI* | 1.000 | 1 | 2 | 4 | 0 | 6 | 0 |
| Nix, Jayson, TUL | .971 | 119 | 253 | 392 | 19 | 664 | 85 |
| Raymundo, GJ, FRI | 1.000 | 3 | 4 | 5 | 0 | 9 | 0 |
| Richar, Danny, ELP* | .965 | 24 | 44 | 67 | 4 | 115 | 15 |
| Rodriguez, Javy, ARK | .931 | 16 | 23 | 44 | 5 | 72 | 12 |
| Sandel, George, SAN | .833 | 1 | 3 | 2 | 1 | 6 | 0 |
| Smith, Casey, ARK | .971 | 25 | 54 | 82 | 4 | 140 | 24 |
| Topolski, Jon, ROU* | .800 | 2 | 3 | 1 | 1 | 5 | 0 |
| Turner, Justin, ARK* | .990 | 21 | 40 | 55 | 1 | 96 | 8 |
| Uggla, Dan, ELP | .940 | 18 | 24 | 55 | 5 | 84 | 11 |
| West, Todd, ELP | .985 | 55 | 89 | 167 | 4 | 260 | 35 |

## THIRD BASEMEN

| Player, Team | Pct. | G | PO | A | E | TC | DP |
|---|---|---|---|---|---|---|---|
| Aspito, Jason, ARK* | .000 | 1 | 0 | 0 | 1 | 1 | 0 |
| Baker, Jeffrey, TUL | .924 | 20 | 10 | 51 | 5 | 66 | 6 |
| Barden, Brian, ELP | .933 | 48 | 21 | 77 | 7 | 105 | 6 |
| Beinbrink, Andrew, FRI | .914 | 27 | 15 | 38 | 5 | 58 | 4 |
| Brown, Hunter, SAN | .957 | 79 | 66 | 154 | 10 | 230 | 18 |
| Brown, Neb, ELP* | .875 | 3 | 1 | 6 | 1 | 8 | 0 |
| Castro, Ramon, MDL | .943 | 16 | 4 | 46 | 3 | 53 | 5 |
| Coffie, Ivanon, ROU* | .851 | 21 | 15 | 25 | 7 | 47 | 0 |
| D'Antona, Jamie, ELP | .917 | 18 | 6 | 38 | 4 | 48 | 4 |
| Dobbs, Greg, SAN* | .918 | 51 | 34 | 78 | 10 | 122 | 8 |
| Eylward, Mike, ARK | .789 | 6 | 3 | 12 | 4 | 19 | 0 |
| Fenster, Darren, WCH | .500 | 1 | 0 | 1 | 1 | 2 | 0 |
| Gandolfo, Rob, SAN* | .737 | 10 | 2 | 12 | 5 | 19 | 0 |
| Gemoll, Justin, WCH | .949 | 117 | 78 | 204 | 15 | 297 | 17 |
| Gimenez, Hector, ROU | 1.000 | 1 | 1 | 0 | 0 | 1 | 0 |
| Gomez, Francis, MDL | .960 | 54 | 45 | 99 | 6 | 150 | 14 |
| Gomez, Rudy, ARK | .928 | 53 | 36 | 105 | 11 | 152 | 12 |
| Gonzalez, Edgar, FRI | .936 | 87 | 63 | 155 | 15 | 233 | 8 |
| Groves, Brett, WCH | 1.000 | 5 | 5 | 11 | 0 | 16 | 0 |
| Gutierrez, Victor, ARK | 1.000 | 4 | 1 | 13 | 0 | 14 | 2 |
| Haley, Adam, ELP* | .886 | 14 | 15 | 24 | 5 | 44 | 3 |
| Harrison, Adonis, TUL* | .918 | 30 | 18 | 60 | 7 | 85 | 8 |
| Hart, Corey, WCH | .926 | 11 | 4 | 21 | 2 | 27 | 1 |
| Jackson, Conor, ELP | 1.000 | 6 | 0 | 5 | 0 | 5 | 0 |
| Jackson, Steve, MDL | 1.000 | 6 | 4 | 10 | 0 | 14 | 0 |
| Kiger, Mark, MDL | .923 | 2 | 4 | 8 | 1 | 13 | 0 |
| Matranga, David, ROU | .970 | 39 | 28 | 69 | 3 | 100 | 8 |
| McCurdy, John, MDL | .909 | 17 | 10 | 30 | 4 | 44 | 1 |
| McDougall, Marshall, FRI | .941 | 6 | 5 | 11 | 1 | 17 | 2 |
| McKinley, Josh, FRI | .900 | 8 | 3 | 6 | 1 | 10 | 0 |
| McPherson, Dallas, ARK* | .929 | 57 | 42 | 114 | 12 | 168 | 8 |
| Meyer, Drew, FRI* | 1.000 | 1 | 1 | 5 | 0 | 6 | 0 |
| Morgan, Matt, ELP | .857 | 8 | 4 | 14 | 3 | 21 | 4 |
| Norris, Dax, ROU | 1.000 | 2 | 0 | 2 | 0 | 2 | 0 |
| Oliveros, Luis, SAN | .667 | 1 | 2 | 0 | 1 | 3 | 0 |
| Perez, Santiago, FRI | .940 | 18 | 11 | 36 | 3 | 50 | 1 |
| Raymundo, GJ, FRI | .968 | 13 | 6 | 24 | 1 | 31 | 1 |
| Rodriguez, Javy, ARK | .840 | 9 | 2 | 19 | 4 | 25 | 1 |
| Santana, Mayobanex, ELP | 1.000 | 4 | 2 | 6 | 0 | 8 | 0 |
| Slavik, Corey, TUL* | .945 | 93 | 64 | 177 | 14 | 255 | 17 |
| Smith, Casey, ARK | .839 | 14 | 14 | 33 | 9 | 56 | 1 |
| Teahen, Mark, MDL* | .968 | 53 | 38 | 113 | 5 | 156 | 12 |
| Terrell, Jim, WCH* | .935 | 10 | 8 | 21 | 2 | 31 | 3 |
| Topolski, Jon, ROU* | .731 | 8 | 6 | 13 | 7 | 26 | 0 |
| Uggla, Dan, ELP | .933 | 45 | 27 | 84 | 8 | 119 | 4 |
| West, Todd, ELP | 1.000 | 4 | 3 | 1 | 0 | 4 | 0 |
| Zamora, Junior, ROU | .958 | 79 | 48 | 136 | 8 | 192 | 10 |

## SHORTSTOPS

| Player, Team | Pct. | G | PO | A | E | TC | DP |
|---|---|---|---|---|---|---|---|
| Berroa, Angel, WCH | 1.000 | 11 | 19 | 30 | 0 | 49 | 5 |
| Blanco, Andres, WCH | .951 | 93 | 141 | 270 | 21 | 432 | 67 |
| Bourgeois, Jason, FRI | .833 | 3 | 2 | 3 | 1 | 6 | 1 |
| Callaspo, Alberto, ARK | .956 | 122 | 200 | 363 | 26 | 589 | 65 |
| Castro, Ramon, MDL | .938 | 4 | 6 | 9 | 1 | 16 | 1 |
| Coffie, Ivanon, ROU* | .895 | 5 | 8 | 9 | 2 | 19 | 3 |
| DeRenne, Keoni, ELP | .971 | 15 | 22 | 46 | 2 | 70 | 10 |
| Gandolfo, Rob, SAN* | 1.000 | 5 | 11 | 12 | 0 | 23 | 3 |
| Gomez, Francis, MDL | .935 | 36 | 64 | 95 | 11 | 170 | 23 |
| Gomez, Rudy, ARK | 1.000 | 4 | 4 | 11 | 0 | 15 | 3 |
| Groves, Brett, WCH | .909 | 3 | 4 | 6 | 1 | 11 | 3 |
| Gutierrez, Victor, ARK | .882 | 6 | 12 | 18 | 4 | 34 | 5 |
| Haley, Adam, ELP* | .955 | 29 | 45 | 83 | 6 | 134 | 22 |
| Harrison, Adonis, TUL* | .970 | 7 | 10 | 22 | 1 | 33 | 5 |
| Hart, Corey, WCH | .965 | 38 | 61 | 105 | 6 | 172 | 24 |
| Kiger, Mark, MDL | .953 | 26 | 30 | 71 | 5 | 106 | 8 |
| Kinsler, Ian, FRI | .938 | 71 | 110 | 192 | 20 | 322 | 38 |
| Matranga, David, ROU | .979 | 67 | 87 | 192 | 6 | 285 | 29 |
| McCurdy, John, MDL | .955 | 54 | 90 | 142 | 11 | 243 | 35 |
| McDougall, Marshall, FRI | 1.000 | 10 | 11 | 29 | 0 | 40 | 8 |
| Menchaca, Eriberto, SAN | .974 | 96 | 150 | 264 | 11 | 425 | 72 |
| Meyer, Drew, FRI* | .926 | 55 | 62 | 113 | 14 | 189 | 24 |
| Morse, Michael, SAN | .951 | 40 | 64 | 110 | 9 | 183 | 22 |
| Perez, Santiago, FRI | .862 | 7 | 8 | 17 | 4 | 29 | 4 |
| Quintanilla, Omar, MDL* | .969 | 23 | 29 | 97 | 4 | 130 | 22 |
| Richar, Danny, ELP* | 1.000 | 2 | 5 | 5 | 0 | 10 | 3 |
| Rodriguez, Javy, ARK | .882 | 3 | 4 | 11 | 2 | 17 | 2 |
| Sandoval, Danny, TUL | .952 | 132 | 182 | 392 | 29 | 603 | 90 |
| Santana, Mayobanex, ELP | 1.000 | 1 | 1 | 4 | 0 | 5 | 0 |
| Santos, Sergio, ELP | .935 | 87 | 138 | 223 | 25 | 386 | 47 |
| Smith, Casey, ARK | .885 | 5 | 11 | 12 | 3 | 26 | 5 |
| Terrell, Jim, WCH* | 1.000 | 5 | 6 | 10 | 0 | 16 | 2 |
| West, Todd, ELP | 1.000 | 9 | 13 | 23 | 0 | 36 | 7 |
| Whiteman, Tommy, ROU | .956 | 68 | 104 | 197 | 14 | 315 | 46 |
| Zamora, Junior, ROU | .929 | 3 | 4 | 9 | 1 | 14 | 4 |

## OUTFIELDERS

| Player, Team | Pct. | G | PO | A | E | TC | DP |
|---|---|---|---|---|---|---|---|
| Aldridge, Cory, WCH* | .977 | 74 | 122 | 3 | 3 | 128 | 0 |
| Allegra, Matt, MDL | 1.000 | 17 | 21 | 3 | 0 | 24 | 0 |
| Asadoorian, Rick, FRI | .984 | 79 | 174 | 6 | 3 | 183 | 1 |
| Aspito, Jason, ARK* | .970 | 79 | 126 | 4 | 4 | 134 | 0 |
| Barker, Sean, TUL | 1.000 | 21 | 39 | 3 | 0 | 42 | 1 |
| Berger, Brandon, WCH | .974 | 44 | 73 | 2 | 2 | 77 | 0 |

| Player, Team | Pct. | G | PO | A | E | TC | DP |
|---|---|---|---|---|---|---|---|
| Bohn, TJ, SAN | .993 | 58 | 137 | 5 | 1 | 143 | 0 |
| Boyd, Patrick, FRI | .992 | 66 | 118 | 2 | 1 | 121 | 0 |
| Brooks, Doc, ELP | .889 | 12 | 8 | 0 | 1 | 9 | 0 |
| Brown, Dee, WCH* | .989 | 51 | 82 | 5 | 1 | 88 | 0 |
| Bubela, Jaime, SAN* | .949 | 21 | 36 | 1 | 2 | 39 | 0 |
| Bynum, Freddie, MDL* | .985 | 62 | 128 | 3 | 2 | 133 | 1 |
| Choo, Shin-soo, SAN* | .970 | 123 | 206 | 18 | 7 | 231 | 6 |
| Clark, Daryl, FRI* | .889 | 11 | 8 | 0 | 1 | 9 | 0 |
| Cota, Jesus, ELP* | 1.000 | 2 | 3 | 0 | 0 | 3 | 0 |
| Cruz, Nelson, MDL | .972 | 66 | 128 | 9 | 4 | 141 | 2 |
| Curry, Mike, FRI* | .986 | 52 | 138 | 1 | 2 | 141 | 0 |
| Delucchi, Dustin, SAN* | .992 | 118 | 240 | 7 | 2 | 249 | 0 |
| Duncan, Carlos, ARK | .986 | 37 | 63 | 7 | 1 | 71 | 0 |
| Eldridge, Rashad, FRI | .980 | 95 | 146 | 2 | 3 | 151 | 0 |
| Faison, Vince, SAN* | 1.000 | 12 | 20 | 1 | 0 | 21 | 1 |
| Gandolfo, Rob, SAN* | 1.000 | 5 | 5 | 0 | 0 | 5 | 0 |
| Garbe, BJ, SAN | 1.000 | 2 | 1 | 0 | 0 | 1 | 0 |
| Garrett, Shawn, TUL | .984 | 78 | 122 | 5 | 2 | 129 | 1 |
| Garthwaite, Jay, ELP | .966 | 38 | 55 | 1 | 2 | 58 | 0 |
| Gettis, Byron, WCH | .926 | 17 | 25 | 0 | 2 | 27 | 0 |
| Gibson, Derrick, ARK | .778 | 5 | 6 | 1 | 2 | 9 | 0 |
| Gonzalez, Edgar, FRI | 1.000 | 5 | 2 | 0 | 0 | 2 | 0 |
| Gorneault, Nick, ARK | .977 | 124 | 279 | 14 | 7 | 300 | 5 |
| Goss, Michael, ELP* | .941 | 12 | 15 | 1 | 1 | 17 | 0 |
| Groves, Brett, WCH | 1.000 | 17 | 26 | 0 | 0 | 26 | 0 |
| Guerrero, Christian, SAN | .946 | 54 | 65 | 5 | 4 | 74 | 1 |
| Guerrero, Christian, ARK | .945 | 53 | 82 | 4 | 5 | 91 | 1 |
| Guerrero, Christian, SAN-ARK | .945 | 107 | 147 | 9 | 9 | 165 | 2 |
| Guiel, Aaron, WCH* | .933 | 6 | 14 | 0 | 1 | 15 | 0 |
| Hall, Victor, ELP* | .945 | 47 | 85 | 1 | 5 | 91 | 0 |
| Hart, Corey, WCH | 1.000 | 1 | 1 | 0 | 0 | 1 | 0 |
| Hill, Mike, ROU | .975 | 22 | 37 | 2 | 1 | 40 | 0 |
| Hopper, Norris, WCH | 1.000 | 78 | 186 | 9 | 0 | 195 | 3 |
| Jackson, Conor, ELP | .966 | 47 | 83 | 1 | 3 | 87 | 0 |
| Jacobs, Greg, SAN* | 1.000 | 31 | 46 | 2 | 0 | 48 | 0 |
| Jimerson, Charlton, ROU | .978 | 126 | 251 | 12 | 6 | 269 | 2 |
| Jones, Jaime, WCH* | .975 | 65 | 113 | 2 | 3 | 118 | 0 |
| Jordan, Brian, FRI | 1.000 | 4 | 4 | 0 | 0 | 4 | 0 |
| Kiger, Mark, MDL | 1.000 | 3 | 5 | 1 | 0 | 6 | 0 |
| Kroeger, Josh, ELP* | .943 | 63 | 112 | 4 | 7 | 123 | 1 |
| Luellwitz, Sean, ELP | .000 | 1 | 0 | 0 | 1 | 1 | 0 |
| McKinley, Josh, FRI | .941 | 10 | 16 | 0 | 1 | 17 | 0 |
| Meadows, Tydus, FRI | 1.000 | 45 | 77 | 6 | 0 | 83 | 1 |
| Mench, Kevin, FRI | 1.000 | 2 | 3 | 0 | 0 | 3 | 0 |
| Meyer, Drew, FRI* | 1.000 | 2 | 2 | 1 | 0 | 3 | 0 |
| Miller, Tony, TUL | .981 | 109 | 203 | 8 | 4 | 215 | 2 |
| Murphy, Tommy, ARK | .979 | 120 | 311 | 10 | 7 | 328 | 2 |
| Nix, Laynce, FRI* | 1.000 | 7 | 12 | 0 | 0 | 12 | 0 |
| Perez, Santiago, FRI | 1.000 | 3 | 7 | 0 | 0 | 7 | 0 |
| Perry, Jason, MDL* | 1.000 | 17 | 26 | 1 | 0 | 27 | 0 |
| Phillips, Dan, TUL | 1.000 | 7 | 14 | 0 | 0 | 14 | 0 |
| Piniella, Juan, TUL | .994 | 98 | 167 | 5 | 1 | 173 | 1 |
| Quentin, Carlos, ELP | .981 | 56 | 100 | 5 | 2 | 107 | 0 |
| Rodriguez, Javy, ARK | 1.000 | 6 | 12 | 0 | 0 | 12 | 0 |
| Rodriguez, Mike, ROU* | .975 | 98 | 154 | 3 | 4 | 161 | 0 |
| Rosamond, Mike, TUL | .970 | 46 | 61 | 3 | 2 | 66 | 0 |
| Ruan, Wilkin, WCH | .991 | 52 | 108 | 5 | 1 | 114 | 0 |
| Salazar, Jeff, TUL* | .977 | 58 | 122 | 5 | 3 | 130 | 0 |
| Santana, Mayobanex, ELP | 1.000 | 1 | 1 | 0 | 0 | 1 | 0 |
| Scott, Luke, ROU* | .987 | 39 | 75 | 1 | 1 | 77 | 0 |
| Self, Todd, ROU* | 1.000 | 7 | 10 | 0 | 0 | 10 | 0 |
| Sellier, Brian, MDL* | .978 | 115 | 221 | 6 | 5 | 232 | 0 |
| Senjem, Guye, TUL* | 1.000 | 3 | 3 | 0 | 0 | 3 | 0 |
| Senreiso, Juan, FRI | 1.000 | 9 | 18 | 1 | 0 | 19 | 0 |
| Smith, Will, FRI | .979 | 81 | 137 | 4 | 3 | 144 | 0 |
| Stanley, Steve, MDL* | .986 | 36 | 69 | 2 | 1 | 72 | 1 |
| Stocker, Mel, WCH | 1.000 | 14 | 19 | 1 | 0 | 20 | 0 |
| Sugden, Jason, ARK | 1.000 | 2 | 3 | 0 | 0 | 3 | 0 |
| Taveras, Willy, ROU | .974 | 102 | 207 | 14 | 6 | 227 | 3 |
| Terrell, Jim, WCH* | 1.000 | 5 | 6 | 0 | 0 | 6 | 0 |
| Topolski, Jon, ROU* | .956 | 40 | 43 | 0 | 2 | 45 | 0 |
| Uggla, Dan, ELP | .957 | 20 | 21 | 1 | 1 | 23 | 0 |
| Varner, Noochie, ELP | 1.000 | 25 | 39 | 1 | 0 | 40 | 1 |
| Walker, Larry, TUL* | 1.000 | 5 | 5 | 0 | 0 | 5 | 0 |
| Walter, Scott, WCH | .778 | 7 | 6 | 1 | 2 | 9 | 0 |
| Weber, Jon, MDL* | .967 | 108 | 218 | 16 | 8 | 242 | 3 |
| West, Todd, ELP | 1.000 | 1 | 2 | 0 | 0 | 2 | 0 |
| Williams, Marland, ELP | .957 | 116 | 240 | 7 | 11 | 258 | 0 |
| Wilson, Preston, TUL | 1.000 | 4 | 4 | 0 | 0 | 4 | 0 |

## CATCHERS

| Player, Team | Pct. | G | PO | A | E | TC | DP | PB |
|---|---|---|---|---|---|---|---|---|
| Arnerich, Tony, WCH | 1.000 | 1 | 6 | 0 | 0 | 6 | 0 | 0 |
| Baker, John, MDL* | .983 | 50 | 315 | 24 | 6 | 345 | 1 | 7 |
| Bibee, Hal, TUL | 1.000 | 2 | 5 | 1 | 0 | 6 | 0 | 0 |
| Brown, Jeremy, MDL | .991 | 87 | 570 | 66 | 6 | 642 | 4 | 11 |
| Christianson, Ryan, SAN | .982 | 18 | 156 | 9 | 3 | 168 | 0 | 2 |
| Conway, Dan, TUL | .982 | 71 | 437 | 47 | 9 | 493 | 5 | 4 |
| Del Chiaro, Brent, ARK | .988 | 35 | 233 | 20 | 3 | 256 | 1 | 5 |
| DiRosa, Mike, ELP | .977 | 50 | 308 | 27 | 8 | 343 | 1 | 2 |
| Duenas, Tommy, ARK | 1.000 | 3 | 18 | 0 | 0 | 18 | 0 | 0 |
| Esposito, Brian, FRI | .986 | 30 | 197 | 20 | 3 | 220 | 2 | 6 |
| Gimenez, Hector, ROU | .989 | 91 | 693 | 52 | 8 | 753 | 2 | 10 |
| Horner, Jim, SAN | 1.000 | 17 | 134 | 4 | 0 | 138 | 2 | 4 |
| Jackson, Steve, MDL | .969 | 5 | 29 | 2 | 1 | 32 | 0 | 1 |
| Mathis, Jeff, ARK | .980 | 104 | 626 | 61 | 14 | 701 | 3 | 12 |
| McKinley, Josh, FRI | .970 | 21 | 89 | 8 | 3 | 100 | 0 | 3 |
| Moon, Brian, SAN | .991 | 30 | 204 | 25 | 2 | 231 | 3 | 2 |
| Morales, Willie, TUL | .941 | 4 | 13 | 3 | 1 | 17 | 0 | 0 |
| Morgan, Matt, ELP | 1.000 | 5 | 29 | 2 | 0 | 31 | 0 | 1 |
| Mosquera, Julio, FRI | .988 | 24 | 149 | 21 | 2 | 172 | 3 | 2 |
| Myers, Casey, MDL | 1.000 | 1 | 2 | 0 | 0 | 2 | 0 | 0 |
| Norris, Dax, ROU | .989 | 45 | 327 | 33 | 4 | 364 | 5 | 2 |
| Obradovich, Mark, ROU | .974 | 11 | 71 | 4 | 2 | 77 | 0 | 5 |
| Oliveros, Luis, SAN | .988 | 70 | 537 | 56 | 7 | 600 | 6 | 11 |
| Rodrigues, Rich, SAN | 1.000 | 5 | 35 | 1 | 0 | 36 | 0 | 0 |
| Slavik, Corey, TUL* | 1.000 | 2 | 2 | 0 | 0 | 2 | 0 | 0 |
| Smith, Dustin, FRI | .989 | 16 | 84 | 4 | 1 | 89 | 0 | 2 |
| Smith, Jeff, FRI* | .992 | 64 | 481 | 38 | 4 | 523 | 4 | 4 |
| Snyder, Chris, ELP | .988 | 83 | 580 | 54 | 8 | 642 | 3 | 8 |
| Tonis, Mike, WCH | .993 | 62 | 401 | 35 | 3 | 439 | 3 | 6 |
| Ullery, Dave, WCH* | .990 | 12 | 96 | 4 | 1 | 101 | 1 | 2 |
| Waldron, Jeff, ELP* | .983 | 8 | 53 | 6 | 1 | 60 | 0 | 0 |
| Waldron, Jeff, FRI* | 1.000 | 6 | 43 | 3 | 0 | 46 | 0 | 0 |
| Waldron, Jeff, ELP-FRI* | .991 | 14 | 96 | 9 | 1 | 106 | 0 | 0 |
| Walter, Scott, WCH | .989 | 70 | 482 | 45 | 6 | 533 | 2 | 10 |
| Winchester, Jeff, TUL | .985 | 73 | 504 | 35 | 8 | 547 | 2 | 11 |

## PITCHERS

| Player, Team | Pct. | G | PO | A | E | TC | DP |
|---|---|---|---|---|---|---|---|
| Anderson, Travis, TUL | 1.000 | 11 | 2 | 2 | 0 | 4 | 0 |
| Andrade, Steve, ARK | 1.000 | 34 | 6 | 3 | 0 | 9 | 0 |
| Andrew, Jason, FRI | 1.000 | 24 | 2 | 6 | 0 | 8 | 1 |
| Appier, Kevin, WCH | 1.000 | 4 | 0 | 1 | 0 | 1 | 0 |
| Astacio, Ezequiel, ROU | .875 | 28 | 8 | 27 | 5 | 40 | 1 |
| Astacio, Hector, ARK | 1.000 | 6 | 3 | 0 | 0 | 3 | 0 |
| Babula, Shaun, ROU* | 1.000 | 4 | 2 | 1 | 0 | 3 | 0 |
| Baerlocher, Ryan, WCH | .889 | 19 | 4 | 4 | 1 | 9 | 1 |
| Barber, Scott, ELP | .947 | 38 | 8 | 10 | 1 | 19 | 0 |
| Barzilla, Philip, ROU* | .917 | 17 | 1 | 10 | 1 | 12 | 2 |
| Bass, Brian, WCH | .833 | 9 | 2 | 3 | 1 | 6 | 0 |
| Bausher, Tim, TUL | 1.000 | 16 | 5 | 10 | 0 | 15 | 0 |
| Bautista, Denny, WCH | .944 | 12 | 3 | 14 | 1 | 18 | 2 |
| Bazzell, Shane, MDL | .955 | 34 | 10 | 11 | 1 | 22 | 0 |
| Beasley, Ray, FRI* | 1.000 | 42 | 2 | 7 | 0 | 9 | 1 |
| Bernero, Adam, TUL | 1.000 | 1 | 1 | 0 | 0 | 1 | 0 |
| Bierbrodt, Nick, FRI* | 1.000 | 5 | 0 | 5 | 0 | 5 | 0 |
| Biggs, Billy, ELP | .750 | 14 | 1 | 2 | 1 | 4 | 0 |
| Bilke, Austin, ARK | .000 | 2 | 0 | 0 | 1 | 1 | 0 |
| Bittner, Tim, ARK* | .902 | 22 | 10 | 27 | 4 | 41 | 3 |
| Bondurant, Steven, MDL* | 1.000 | 7 | 2 | 7 | 0 | 9 | 1 |
| Bott, Glenn, SAN* | .000 | 1 | 0 | 0 | 0 | 0 | 0 |
| Bouknight, Kip, TUL | 1.000 | 6 | 2 | 0 | 0 | 2 | 0 |
| Brocail, Doug, FRI | 1.000 | 1 | 0 | 2 | 0 | 2 | 0 |
| Brunet, Mike, ARK | 1.000 | 2 | 1 | 2 | 0 | 3 | 0 |
| Buglovsky, Chris, SAN | 1.000 | 24 | 15 | 21 | 0 | 36 | 1 |
| Bulger, Jason, ELP | 1.000 | 24 | 3 | 1 | 0 | 4 | 0 |
| Bumatay, Mike, TUL* | .000 | 12 | 0 | 0 | 1 | 1 | 0 |
| Burke, Erick, FRI* | .750 | 25 | 0 | 3 | 1 | 4 | 0 |
| Burns, Mike, ROU | 1.000 | 56 | 6 | 12 | 0 | 18 | 1 |
| Callaway, Mickey, FRI | .000 | 2 | 0 | 0 | 0 | 0 | 0 |
| Carlson, Jesse, ROU* | .938 | 41 | 3 | 12 | 1 | 16 | 0 |
| Cate, Troy, SAN* | .808 | 12 | 2 | 19 | 5 | 26 | 1 |
| Cervantes, Chris, ELP* | .917 | 21 | 3 | 8 | 1 | 12 | 0 |
| Chico, Matt, ELP* | .917 | 14 | 1 | 10 | 1 | 12 | 1 |
| Christensen, Ben, SAN | 1.000 | 5 | 3 | 1 | 0 | 4 | 0 |
| Collazo, Willie, ARK* | .930 | 32 | 10 | 30 | 3 | 43 | 0 |
| Cormier, Lance, ELP | 1.000 | 10 | 5 | 13 | 0 | 18 | 0 |
| Cortez, Renee, SAN | .923 | 36 | 4 | 8 | 1 | 13 | 2 |
| Cosgrove, Mike, TUL | 1.000 | 21 | 4 | 1 | 0 | 5 | 1 |
| Crowell, Kyle, MDL | .941 | 40 | 2 | 14 | 1 | 17 | 0 |
| Cyr, Eric, ARK* | .750 | 11 | 0 | 3 | 1 | 4 | 0 |
| Devey, Phil, SAN* | .818 | 13 | 1 | 8 | 2 | 11 | 0 |
| Dickey, RA, FRI | 1.000 | 4 | 0 | 3 | 0 | 3 | 0 |
| Dickinson, Drew, MDL* | .976 | 27 | 6 | 35 | 1 | 42 | 6 |
| Dittfurth, Ryan, FRI | 1.000 | 3 | 0 | 1 | 0 | 1 | 0 |
| Dominguez, Juan, FRI | 1.000 | 3 | 0 | 1 | 0 | 1 | 0 |
| Done, Juan, SAN | .872 | 27 | 14 | 27 | 6 | 47 | 3 |

| Player, Team | Pct. | G | PO | A | E | TC | DP |
|---|---|---|---|---|---|---|---|
| Dorman, Rich, SAN | .857 | 20 | 7 | 11 | 3 | 21 | 1 |
| Doyle, Jared, ELP* | 1.000 | 11 | 0 | 4 | 0 | 4 | 1 |
| Emanuel, Brandon, ARK | 1.000 | 1 | 1 | 0 | 0 | 1 | 0 |
| Esposito, Mike, TUL | .955 | 24 | 12 | 30 | 2 | 44 | 2 |
| Esslinger, Cameron, ARK | .882 | 44 | 4 | 11 | 2 | 17 | 0 |
| Fischer, Rich, ARK | .875 | 19 | 4 | 10 | 2 | 16 | 0 |
| Fischer, Steve, MDL | .750 | 6 | 0 | 3 | 1 | 4 | 0 |
| Fossum, Casey, ELP* | 1.000 | 2 | 0 | 1 | 0 | 1 | 0 |
| Francis, Jeff, TUL* | 1.000 | 17 | 6 | 22 | 0 | 28 | 1 |
| Francisco, Frank, FRI | .000 | 15 | 0 | 0 | 0 | 0 | 0 |
| Fritz, Ben, MDL | .969 | 20 | 6 | 25 | 1 | 32 | 1 |
| Fruto, Emiliano, SAN | .909 | 43 | 10 | 10 | 2 | 22 | 0 |
| Fulmer, TA, SAN | 1.000 | 9 | 1 | 4 | 0 | 5 | 0 |
| Garcia, Jairo, MDL | 1.000 | 13 | 1 | 2 | 0 | 3 | 0 |
| Gardner, Hayden, FRI | 1.000 | 9 | 1 | 2 | 0 | 3 | 0 |
| Gil, David, SAN | 1.000 | 5 | 0 | 1 | 0 | 1 | 0 |
| Gil, David, ARK | 1.000 | 11 | 4 | 6 | 0 | 10 | 1 |
| Gil, David, SAN-ARK | 1.000 | 16 | 4 | 7 | 0 | 11 | 1 |
| Goocher, Clint, ELP* | .966 | 17 | 9 | 19 | 1 | 29 | 2 |
| Good, Andrew, ELP | 1.000 | 4 | 3 | 1 | 0 | 4 | 1 |
| Gothreaux, Jared, ROU | .905 | 27 | 6 | 32 | 4 | 42 | 2 |
| Green, Sean, TUL | 1.000 | 52 | 8 | 15 | 0 | 23 | 2 |
| Grezlovski, Ben, ARK | 1.000 | 11 | 3 | 3 | 0 | 6 | 0 |
| Griffin, Colt, WCH | .800 | 26 | 0 | 4 | 1 | 5 | 0 |
| Griffith, Dustin, ARK | 1.000 | 3 | 0 | 1 | 0 | 1 | 0 |
| Guttormson, Rick, SAN | .824 | 54 | 4 | 10 | 3 | 17 | 2 |
| Gwyn, Marcus, MDL | .882 | 44 | 2 | 13 | 2 | 17 | 1 |
| Hampson, Justin, TUL* | .919 | 27 | 2 | 32 | 3 | 37 | 1 |
| Harville, Chad, ROU | 1.000 | 2 | 0 | 1 | 0 | 1 | 0 |
| Henrie, Matt, ELP | .884 | 17 | 14 | 24 | 5 | 43 | 1 |
| Hernandez, Felix, SAN | .864 | 10 | 6 | 13 | 3 | 22 | 1 |
| Herndon, Junior, WCH | .917 | 12 | 5 | 17 | 2 | 24 | 1 |
| Hoerman, Jared, SAN | 1.000 | 11 | 1 | 1 | 0 | 2 | 0 |
| Hogan, Gary, FRI | 1.000 | 2 | 1 | 0 | 0 | 1 | 0 |
| Houlton, DJ, ROU | .905 | 28 | 10 | 9 | 2 | 21 | 0 |
| Hudgins, John, FRI | .900 | 12 | 1 | 8 | 1 | 10 | 1 |
| Hughes, Travis, FRI | .923 | 40 | 5 | 7 | 1 | 13 | 0 |
| Jimenez, Kelvin, FRI | .870 | 26 | 6 | 14 | 3 | 23 | 2 |
| Jones, Jaime, WCH* | 1.000 | 1 | 0 | 1 | 0 | 1 | 0 |
| Juarez, William, ELP | .941 | 13 | 7 | 9 | 1 | 17 | 0 |
| Keller, Kris, FRI | 1.000 | 14 | 0 | 4 | 0 | 4 | 1 |
| Kent, Steve, TUL* | 1.000 | 39 | 1 | 4 | 0 | 5 | 0 |
| Keppinger, Billy, WCH | 1.000 | 48 | 2 | 8 | 0 | 10 | 1 |
| Key, Chris, SAN* | .878 | 36 | 10 | 26 | 5 | 41 | 2 |
| Komine, Shane, MDL | .833 | 17 | 10 | 15 | 5 | 30 | 1 |
| Kozlowski, Ben, FRI* | .857 | 8 | 1 | 5 | 1 | 7 | 0 |
| Leclair, Aric, ELP* | 1.000 | 30 | 3 | 8 | 0 | 11 | 0 |
| Lee, Corey, ARK* | .867 | 14 | 1 | 12 | 2 | 15 | 1 |
| Levrault, Allen, SAN | .000 | 11 | 0 | 0 | 0 | 0 | 0 |
| Linton, Doug, WCH | 1.000 | 1 | 1 | 0 | 0 | 1 | 0 |
| Lizarraga, Sergio, ELP | 1.000 | 29 | 7 | 25 | 0 | 32 | 2 |
| Loe, Kameron, FRI | .939 | 19 | 8 | 23 | 2 | 33 | 0 |
| Mabeus, Chris, MDL | 1.000 | 20 | 2 | 4 | 0 | 6 | 0 |
| MacDougal, Mike, WCH | 1.000 | 17 | 0 | 2 | 0 | 2 | 0 |
| Marcano, Luis, FRI | 1.000 | 18 | 3 | 5 | 0 | 8 | 0 |
| Markray, Thad, WCH | .875 | 8 | 3 | 4 | 1 | 8 | 1 |
| Martinez, Gustavo, SAN | 1.000 | 10 | 9 | 4 | 0 | 13 | 3 |
| Masset, Nick, FRI | 1.000 | 2 | 0 | 3 | 0 | 3 | 1 |
| Mattioni, Nick, MDL | 1.000 | 19 | 4 | 7 | 0 | 11 | 1 |
| McClaskey, Tim, ROU | .900 | 34 | 5 | 13 | 2 | 20 | 0 |
| McClellan, Zach, TUL | .971 | 26 | 10 | 23 | 1 | 34 | 2 |
| McDaniel, Denny, ROU* | .933 | 48 | 7 | 7 | 1 | 15 | 0 |
| Middleton, Kyle, WCH | .975 | 28 | 10 | 29 | 1 | 40 | 6 |
| Mizuo, Yoshitaka, ARK* | 1.000 | 9 | 0 | 1 | 0 | 1 | 0 |
| Moreno, Edwin, FRI | .900 | 18 | 6 | 12 | 2 | 20 | 0 |
| Morgan, Matt, ELP | .000 | 1 | 0 | 0 | 0 | 0 | 0 |
| Mozingo, Dan, ARK* | .857 | 11 | 0 | 6 | 1 | 7 | 0 |
| Murphy, Bill, ELP* | 1.000 | 6 | 0 | 4 | 0 | 4 | 0 |
| Narron, Sam, FRI* | .952 | 13 | 6 | 14 | 1 | 21 | 2 |
| Narveson, Chris, TUL* | .400 | 4 | 0 | 2 | 3 | 5 | 0 |
| Natale, Mike, WCH | .833 | 44 | 5 | 5 | 2 | 12 | 1 |
| Nelson, Jeff, FRI | .000 | 3 | 0 | 0 | 0 | 0 | 0 |
| Nieve, Fernando, ROU | 1.000 | 3 | 1 | 1 | 0 | 2 | 0 |
| Nippert, Dustin, ELP | .900 | 14 | 3 | 15 | 2 | 20 | 1 |
| Nunez, Jose, SAN* | 1.000 | 10 | 0 | 1 | 0 | 1 | 0 |
| O`Sullivan, Mark, ARK | .909 | 45 | 4 | 6 | 1 | 11 | 1 |
| Obenchain, Stephen, MDL | 1.000 | 17 | 2 | 4 | 0 | 6 | 0 |
| Oquist, Mike, MDL | 1.000 | 27 | 10 | 3 | 0 | 13 | 1 |
| Park, Chan Ho, FRI | 1.000 | 2 | 0 | 2 | 0 | 2 | 0 |
| Parker, Zack, TUL* | .765 | 22 | 4 | 9 | 4 | 17 | 0 |
| Perez, Beltran, ELP | 1.000 | 37 | 10 | 9 | 0 | 19 | 1 |
| Perez, Elvis, SAN | 1.000 | 10 | 2 | 7 | 0 | 9 | 0 |
| Pettitte, Andy, ROU* | 1.000 | 2 | 2 | 2 | 0 | 4 | 0 |
| Poland, Trey, ROU* | 1.000 | 6 | 0 | 4 | 0 | 4 | 0 |
| Powell, Greg, ROU | .800 | 26 | 5 | 7 | 3 | 15 | 0 |
| Rall, Tim, SAN* | .857 | 56 | 3 | 9 | 2 | 14 | 0 |
| Ramirez, Emmanuel, TUL | 1.000 | 48 | 2 | 6 | 0 | 8 | 0 |
| Ramirez, Santiago, ROU | .882 | 55 | 6 | 9 | 2 | 17 | 1 |
| Reynolds, Shane, ELP | 1.000 | 2 | 0 | 1 | 0 | 1 | 0 |
| Roberts, Nick, ARK | 1.000 | 12 | 5 | 11 | 0 | 16 | 1 |
| Rodriguez, Wandy, ROU* | .905 | 26 | 5 | 14 | 2 | 21 | 0 |
| Rosario, Adriano, ELP | 1.000 | 7 | 2 | 10 | 0 | 12 | 1 |
| Rouwenhorst, Jon, ARK* | 1.000 | 52 | 4 | 24 | 0 | 28 | 0 |
| Rowe, Steven, FRI | .900 | 53 | 1 | 8 | 1 | 10 | 0 |
| Rupe, Josh, FRI | 1.000 | 7 | 1 | 3 | 0 | 4 | 1 |
| Saladin, Miguel, ROU | 1.000 | 3 | 1 | 1 | 0 | 2 | 0 |
| Sampson, Chris, ROU | 1.000 | 1 | 1 | 1 | 0 | 2 | 0 |
| Sansom, Trevor, MDL | 1.000 | 16 | 2 | 2 | 0 | 4 | 1 |
| Santana, Ervin, ARK | .875 | 8 | 3 | 4 | 1 | 8 | 0 |
| Saunders, Joe, ARK* | 1.000 | 8 | 1 | 7 | 0 | 8 | 0 |
| Schneider, Scott, ARK | .900 | 54 | 9 | 9 | 2 | 20 | 0 |
| Schultz, Mike, ELP | 1.000 | 12 | 2 | 2 | 0 | 4 | 0 |
| Serrano, Alex, TUL | .833 | 14 | 1 | 4 | 1 | 6 | 0 |
| Serrano, Jimmy, WCH | .857 | 11 | 3 | 3 | 1 | 7 | 0 |
| Shiery, Shaun, WCH* | .000 | 5 | 0 | 0 | 1 | 1 | 0 |
| Sikaras, Pete, ELP | .818 | 39 | 5 | 4 | 2 | 11 | 0 |
| Simpson, Gerrit, TUL | 1.000 | 39 | 7 | 12 | 0 | 19 | 5 |
| Slaten, Doug, ELP* | 1.000 | 11 | 1 | 2 | 0 | 3 | 1 |
| Smith, Cliff, ARK | 1.000 | 18 | 1 | 2 | 0 | 3 | 0 |
| Smith, Sam, ELP | .909 | 18 | 5 | 5 | 1 | 11 | 1 |
| Smyth, Steve, MDL* | .909 | 20 | 0 | 10 | 1 | 11 | 0 |
| Snow, Bert, MDL | .818 | 20 | 1 | 8 | 2 | 11 | 0 |
| Sonnier, Shawn, MDL | .929 | 45 | 4 | 9 | 1 | 14 | 1 |
| Soriano, Rafael, SAN | 1.000 | 2 | 0 | 2 | 0 | 2 | 0 |
| Speier, Ryan, TUL | 1.000 | 61 | 4 | 5 | 0 | 9 | 0 |
| Stamler, Keith, FRI | 1.000 | 4 | 1 | 1 | 0 | 2 | 1 |
| Stockman, Phil, ELP | 1.000 | 6 | 3 | 7 | 0 | 10 | 1 |
| Street, Huston, MDL | 1.000 | 10 | 3 | 3 | 0 | 6 | 0 |
| Sylvester, Billy, FRI | 1.000 | 30 | 1 | 4 | 0 | 5 | 0 |
| Tamayo, Danny, WCH | .952 | 25 | 7 | 13 | 1 | 21 | 0 |
| Taylor, Aaron, SAN | 1.000 | 30 | 4 | 4 | 0 | 8 | 0 |
| Thomas, Jared, SAN* | 1.000 | 33 | 3 | 5 | 0 | 8 | 1 |
| Thompson, Eric, WCH | 1.000 | 7 | 1 | 3 | 0 | 4 | 0 |
| Thompson, Erik, FRI | .917 | 15 | 6 | 5 | 1 | 12 | 0 |
| Thompson, Justin, FRI* | .938 | 23 | 4 | 11 | 1 | 16 | 0 |
| Trujillo, JJ, WCH | .833 | 59 | 4 | 16 | 4 | 24 | 1 |
| Tsao, Chin-hui, TUL | 1.000 | 2 | 1 | 1 | 0 | 2 | 0 |
| Vasquez, Jorge, WCH | 1.000 | 49 | 4 | 4 | 0 | 8 | 1 |
| Villacis, Eduardo, WCH | .875 | 8 | 3 | 4 | 1 | 8 | 0 |
| Walrond, Les, WCH* | .900 | 8 | 1 | 8 | 1 | 10 | 0 |
| Ward, Jeremy, ELP | .000 | 7 | 0 | 0 | 0 | 0 | 0 |
| Weis, Brad, MDL* | .871 | 28 | 6 | 21 | 4 | 31 | 2 |
| White, Bill, ELP* | .750 | 31 | 1 | 5 | 2 | 8 | 0 |
| Wilkerson, Wes, WCH | 1.000 | 49 | 0 | 14 | 0 | 14 | 0 |
| Wilkinson, Matt, ELP | .000 | 5 | 0 | 0 | 0 | 0 | 0 |
| Woods, Jake, ARK* | .889 | 14 | 0 | 8 | 1 | 9 | 0 |
| Young, Chris, FRI | .950 | 18 | 5 | 14 | 1 | 20 | 1 |
| Ziegler, Mike, MDL | 1.000 | 8 | 8 | 9 | 0 | 17 | 1 |

# LEAGUE CHAMPIONS

| Year | Team | Pct. |
|---|---|---|
| 1888— | Dallas | .671 |
| 1889— | Houston | .551 |
| 1890— | Galveston | .705 |
| 1892— | Houston | .741 |
| | Houston | .613 |
| 1895— | Dallas | .754 |
| | Fort Worth* | .750 |
| 1896— | Fort Worth | .757 |
| | Houston* | .679 |
| | Galveston | .548 |
| 1897— | San Antonio† | .657 |
| | Galveston† | .717 |
| 1898— | League disbanded. | |
| 1899— | Galveston | .632 |
| | Galveston | .762 |
| 1900-01— | Did not operate. | |
| 1902— | Corsicana | .866 |
| | Corsicana | .682 |
| 1903— | Paris-Waco | .615 |
| | Dallas* | .648 |
| 1904— | Corsicana* | .615 |
| | Fort Worth | .800 |
| 1905— | Fort Worth | .545 |
| 1906— | Fort Worth | .677 |
| | Cleburne∞ | .609 |
| 1907— | Austin | .629 |
| 1908— | San Antonio | .664 |
| 1909— | Houston | .601 |
| 1910— | Dallas† | .586 |

| Year | Team | Pct. |
|---|---|---|
| | Houston† | .586 |
| 1911— | Austin | .575 |
| 1912— | Houston | .626 |
| 1913— | Houston | .620 |
| 1914— | Houston† | .671 |
| | Waco† | .671 |
| 1915— | Waco | .592 |
| 1916— | Waco | .587 |
| 1917— | Dallas | .600 |
| 1918— | Dallas | .584 |
| 1919— | Shreveport* | .677 |
| | Fort Worth | .651 |
| 1920— | Fort Worth | .703 |
| | Fort Worth | .750 |
| 1921— | Fort Worth | .691 |
| | Fort Worth | .662 |
| 1922— | Fort Worth | .694 |
| | Fort Worth | .711 |
| 1923— | Fort Worth | .632 |
| 1924— | Fort Worth | .689 |
| | Fort Worth | .763 |
| 1925— | Fort Worth | .711 |
| | Fort Worth▲ | .653 |
| 1926— | Dallas | .574 |
| 1927— | Wichita Falls | .654 |
| 1928— | Houston* | .679 |
| | Wichita Falls | .731 |
| 1929— | Dallas* | .588 |
| | Wichita Falls | .620 |
| 1930— | Wichita Falls | .697 |
| | Fort Worth* | .632 |
| 1931— | Houston◆ | .625 |
| | Houston | .734 |
| 1932— | Beaumont* | .640 |
| | Dallas | .727 |
| 1933— | Houston | .623 |
| | San Antonio (4th)§ | .523 |
| 1934— | Galveston‡ | .579 |
| 1935— | Oklahoma City‡ | .590 |
| 1936— | Dallas | .604 |
| | Tulsa (3rd)§ | .519 |
| 1937— | Oklahoma City | .635 |
| | Fort Worth (3rd)§ | .535 |
| 1938— | Beaumont | .635 |
| 1939— | Houston | .606 |
| | Fort Worth (4th)§ | .540 |
| 1940— | Houston‡ | .652 |
| 1941— | Houston | .673 |
| | Dallas (4th)§ | .519 |
| 1942— | Beaumont | .605 |
| | Shreveport (2nd)§ | .576 |
| 1943-44-45— | Did not operate. | |
| 1946— | Fort Worth | .656 |
| | Dallas (2nd)§ | .591 |
| 1947— | Houston‡ | .623 |
| 1948— | Fort Worth‡ | .601 |
| 1949— | Fort Worth | .649 |
| | Tulsa (2nd)§ | .584 |
| 1950— | Beaumont | .595 |
| | San Antonio (4th)§ | .513 |
| 1951— | Houston‡ | .619 |
| 1952— | Dallas | .571 |
| | Shreveport (3rd)§ | .522 |
| 1953— | Dallas‡ | .571 |
| 1954— | Shreveport | .559 |
| | Houston (2nd)§ | .553 |
| 1955— | Dallas | .581 |
| | Shreveport (3rd)§ | .540 |
| 1956— | Houston‡ | .623 |
| 1957— | Dallas | .662 |
| | Houston (2nd)§ | .630 |
| 1958— | Fort Worth | .582 |
| | Cor. Christi (3rd)§ | .507 |
| 1959— | Victoria | .589 |
| | Austin (2nd)§ | .548 |
| 1960— | Rio Grande Valley | .590 |
| | Tulsa (3rd) | .528 |
| 1961— | Amarillo | .643 |
| | San Antonio (3rd)§ | .532 |
| 1962— | El Paso | .571 |
| | Tulsa (2nd)§ | .550 |
| 1963— | San Antonio | .564 |
| | Tulsa (3rd)§ | .529 |
| 1964— | San Antonio‡ | .607 |
| 1965— | Tulsa | .574 |
| | Albuquerque■ | .550 |
| 1966— | Arkansas | .579 |
| 1967— | Albuquerque | .557 |
| 1968— | Arkansas | .586 |
| | El Paso■ | .562 |
| 1969— | Amarillo | .593 |
| | Memphis■ | .504 |
| 1970— | Albuquerque◆ | .615 |
| | Memphis | .507 |
| 1971— | Did not operate as league—clubs were members of Dixie Association. | |
| 1972— | Alexandria | .600 |
| | El Paso■ | .557 |
| 1973— | San Antonio | .590 |
| | Memphis■ | .558 |
| 1974— | Victoria■ | .581 |
| | El Paso | .555 |
| 1975— | Lafayette▼ | .558 |
| | Midland▼ | .604 |
| 1976— | Amarillo■ | .600 |
| | Shreveport | .515 |
| 1977— | El Paso | .600 |
| | Arkansas• | .485 |
| 1978— | El Paso• | .593 |
| | Jackson | .567 |
| 1979— | Arkansas• | .571 |
| | Midland | .563 |
| 1980— | Arkansas• | .596 |
| | San Antonio | .544 |
| 1981— | San Antonio | .571 |
| | Jackson• | .507 |
| 1982— | El Paso | .559 |
| | Tulsa• | .515 |
| 1983— | Jackson | .507 |
| | Beaumont• | .500 |
| 1984— | Beaumont | .654 |
| | Jackson• | .610 |
| 1985— | El Paso | .632 |
| | Jackson• | .537 |
| 1986— | El Paso• | .630 |
| | Jackson | .533 |
| 1987— | Wichita• | .515 |
| | Jackson | .515 |
| 1988— | El Paso | .552 |
| | Tulsa• | .522 |
| 1989— | Arkansas• | .585 |
| | Wichita | .537 |
| 1990— | San Antonio | .582 |
| | Shreveport• | .489 |
| 1991— | Shreveport• | .632 |
| | El Paso | .596 |
| 1992— | Shreveport | .566 |
| | Wichita• | .515 |
| 1993— | El Paso | .563 |
| | Jackson• | .541 |
| 1994— | El Paso• | .647 |
| | Jackson | .548 |
| 1995— | Shreveport• | .652 |
| | Midland | .485 |
| 1996— | Jackson• | .547 |
| | Wichita | .500 |
| 1997— | San Antonio• | .604 |
| | Shreveport | .551 |
| 1998— | Arkansas | .571 |
| | Tulsa• | .557 |
| 1999— | Wichita• | .593 |
| 2000— | Round Rock* | .593 |
| 2001— | Round Rock | .614 |
| | Arkansas†† | .485 |
| 2002— | Wichita | .576 |
| | San Antonio§ | .486 |
| 2003— | San Antonio§§ | .633 |
| 2004— | Frisco• | .579 |

*Won split-season playoff. †Won playoff for title. ‡Finished first and won four-club playoff. §Won four-club playoff. §§Won both halves of split season, received a bye into playoffs and won three-team playoff. ∞Title to Cleburne by default. ▲Tied with Dallas in second half and won playoff for championship. ◆Tied with Beaumont at end of first half and won title in best-of-five series played as part of second-half schedule. ■League divided into Eastern, Western divisions; won two-team playoff. ▼League divided into Eastern, Western divisions; declared co-champions when playoffs were not completed. •League divided into Eastern and Western divisions and played split season; won playoffs. NOTE—Championship awarded to winner of four-team playoff, 1933-51; first-place team and playoff winner co-champions, 1952-64. ††Was leading final round of split-season playoff, two games to none, and was declared champion when Professional Baseball declared a stoppage of play.

# CALIFORNIA LEAGUE

## LEAGUE OFFICE

**President**
Joe Gagliardi
**Address**
2380 S. Bascom Ave., Suite 200
Campbell, CA 95008
**Phone**
408-369-8038

**Teams (affiliation)**
Bakersfield Blaze (Rangers)
High Desert Mavericks (Royals)
Inland Empire 66ers of San Bernardino (Mariners)
Lake Elsinore Storm (Padres)
Lancaster Jethawks (Diamondbacks)
Modesto Nuts (Rockies)
Rancho Cucamonga Quakes (Angels)
San Jose Giants (Giants)
Stockton Ports (Athletics)
Visalia Oaks (Devil Rays)

## 2004 FINAL STANDINGS

### FIRST HALF

#### NORTHERN DIVISION

| Team | W | L | T | Pct. | GB |
|---|---|---|---|---|---|
| Modesto (A's) | 44 | 26 | - | .629 | ... |
| San Jose (Giants) | 37 | 33 | - | .529 | 7.0 |
| Visalia (Rockies) | 34 | 36 | - | .486 | 10.0 |
| Stockton (Rangers) | 32 | 38 | - | .457 | 12.0 |
| Bakersfield (Devil Rays) | 29 | 41 | - | .414 | 15.0 |

#### SOUTHERN DIVISION

| Team | W | L | T | Pct. | GB |
|---|---|---|---|---|---|
| Lancaster (Diamondbacks) | 43 | 27 | - | .614 | ... |
| Inland Empire (Mariners) | 39 | 31 | - | .557 | 4.0 |
| Lake Elsinore (Padres) | 34 | 36 | - | .486 | 9.0 |
| Rancho Cucamonga (Angels) | 33 | 37 | - | .471 | 10.0 |
| High Desert (Brewers) | 25 | 45 | - | .357 | 18.0 |

### SECOND HALF

#### NORTHERN DIVISION

| Team | W | L | T | Pct. | GB |
|---|---|---|---|---|---|
| Modesto (A's) | 46 | 24 | - | .657 | ... |
| Stockton (Rangers) | 40 | 30 | - | .571 | 6.0 |
| San Jose (Giants) | 37 | 33 | - | .529 | 9.0 |
| Bakersfield (Devil Rays) | 30 | 40 | - | .429 | 16.0 |
| Visalia (Rockies) | 22 | 48 | - | .314 | 24.0 |

#### SOUTHERN DIVISION

| Team | W | L | T | Pct. | GB |
|---|---|---|---|---|---|
| Lancaster (Diamondbacks) | 43 | 27 | - | .614 | ... |
| Inland Empire (Mariners) | 38 | 32 | - | .543 | 5.0 |
| Rancho Cucamonga (Angels) | 36 | 36 | - | .514 | 7.0 |
| Lake Elsinore (Padres) | 34 | 36 | - | .486 | 9.0 |
| High Desert (Brewers) | 24 | 46 | - | .343 | 19.0 |

### COMPOSITE

| Team | W | L | T | Pct. | GB | MOD | LNC | INL | SJ | STK | RC | LKE | BAK | VIS | HD |
|---|---|---|---|---|---|---|---|---|---|---|---|---|---|---|---|
| Modesto (Athletics) | 90 | 50 | - | .643 | ... | X | 2 | 4 | 13 | 19 | 3 | 6 | 20 | 18 | 5 |
| Lancaster (Diamondbacks) | 86 | 54 | - | .614 | 4 | 4 | X | 15 | 4 | 5 | 20 | 15 | 2 | 4 | 17 |
| Inland Empire (Mariners) | 77 | 63 | - | .550 | 13 | 2 | 13 | X | 2 | 4 | 12 | 15 | 4 | 6 | 19 |
| San Jose (Giants) | 74 | 66 | - | .529 | 16 | 15 | 2 | 4 | X | 13 | 3 | 3 | 16 | 15 | 3 |
| Stockton (Rangers) | 72 | 68 | - | .514 | 18 | 8 | 1 | 2 | 13 | X | 5 | 5 | 18 | 16 | 4 |
| Rancho Cucamonga (Angels) | 69 | 71 | - | .493 | 21 | 3 | 7 | 15 | 4 | 1 | X | 13 | 4 | 5 | 17 |
| Lake Elsinore (Padres) | 68 | 72 | - | .486 | 22 | 0 | 12 | 13 | 3 | 2 | 14 | X | 2 | 5 | 17 |
| Bakersfield (Devil Rays) | 59 | 81 | - | .421 | 31 | 8 | 4 | 2 | 11 | 10 | 2 | 4 | X | 15 | 3 |
| Visalia (Rockies) | 56 | 84 | - | .400 | 34 | 9 | 2 | 0 | 13 | 12 | 1 | 1 | 12 | X | 6 |
| High Desert (Giants) | 49 | 91 | - | .350 | 41 | 1 | 11 | 8 | 3 | 2 | 11 | 10 | 3 | 0 | X |

Major league affiliations in parentheses.

PLAYOFFS: San Jose defeated Stockton, two games to one; Inland Empire defeated Rancho Cucamonga, two games to none; Modesto defeated San Jose, three games to two; Lancaster defeated Inland Empire, three games to one; Modesto defeated Lancaster, three games to two, to win league championship.

REGULAR-SEASON ATTENDANCE: Bakersfield, 67,363; High Desert, 122,287; Inland Empire, 202,610; Lake Elsinore, 236,344; Lancaster, 122,346; Modesto, 145,014; Rancho Cucamonga, 286,940; Stockton, 98,035; Vialia, 66,248. Total attendance—1,495,671.

MANAGERS (AT START OF SEASON): Bakersfield, Bakersfield; High Desert, Mel Queen; Inland Empire, Steve Roadcap; Lake Elsinore, Rick Renteria; Lancaster, Wally Backman; Modesto, Von Hays; Rancho Cucamonga, Bobby Meacham; San Jose, Lenn Sakata; Stockton, Arnie Beyeler; Visalia, Stu Cole.

ALL-STAR TEAM: 1B—Travis Hinton, High Desert; 2B—Callix Crabbe, High Desert; 3B—Jeff Baker, Visalia; SS—Erick Aybar, Rancho Cucamonga; OF—Paul McAnulty, Lake Elsinore; OF—Jeff Salazar, Visalia; OF—Brian Stavisky, Modesto; C—Phil Avlas, Lancaster; DH—John Suomi, Modesto; P—Enrique Gonzalez, Lancaster; P—Bobby Livingston, Inland Empire; P—Steven Shell, Rancho Cucamonga; P—Brian Burres, San Jose; Most Valuable Player—Brain Stavisky, Modesto; Rookie of the Year—Erick Aybar, Rancho Cucamonga; Manager of the Year—Von Hayes, Modesto.

## 2004 BATTING

### TEAM

| Team | G | TPA | AB | R | H | TB | 2B | 3B | HR | RBI | SH | SF | HP | BB | IBB | SO | SB | CS | GDP | LOB | ShO | Avg. | OBP | Slg. |
|---|---|---|---|---|---|---|---|---|---|---|---|---|---|---|---|---|---|---|---|---|---|---|---|---|
| Modesto | 140 | 5644 | 5077 | 856 | 1530 | 2318 | 354 | 40 | 118 | 783 | 52 | 45 | 8 | 461 | 17 | 886 | 62 | 44 | 110 | 1141 | 2 | .301 | .358 | .457 |
| Lancaster | 140 | 5545 | 4914 | 856 | 1457 | 2288 | 279 | 45 | 154 | 780 | 79 | 53 | 77 | 419 | 8 | 984 | 135 | 82 | 71 | 996 | 1 | .296 | .357 | .466 |
| Inland Empire | 140 | 5422 | 4858 | 744 | 1368 | 1976 | 257 | 54 | 81 | 669 | 31 | 43 | 80 | 409 | 8 | 974 | 144 | 74 | 89 | 995 | 6 | .282 | .345 | .407 |
| High Desert | 140 | 5485 | 4937 | 720 | 1371 | 2135 | 263 | 48 | 135 | 667 | 31 | 40 | 70 | 407 | 7 | 985 | 145 | 78 | 85 | 997 | 3 | .278 | .339 | .432 |
| Bakersfield | 140 | 5387 | 4821 | 663 | 1320 | 1925 | 269 | 27 | 94 | 599 | 50 | 33 | 75 | 406 | 9 | 1037 | 149 | 74 | 98 | 988 | 10 | .274 | .338 | .399 |
| Rancho Cuca. | 140 | 5493 | 4862 | 757 | 1328 | 2055 | 254 | 49 | 125 | 676 | 52 | 57 | 74 | 448 | 12 | 1071 | 177 | 97 | 55 | 996 | 3 | .273 | .340 | .423 |
| Visalia | 140 | 5624 | 4905 | 758 | 1314 | 2008 | 273 | 38 | 115 | 689 | 47 | 37 | 74 | 557 | 10 | 1071 | 87 | 42 | 106 | 1099 | 7 | .268 | .349 | .409 |
| Lake Elsinore | 140 | 5446 | 4861 | 684 | 1298 | 1930 | 257 | 39 | 99 | 634 | 29 | 41 | 47 | 468 | 12 | 1076 | 94 | 64 | 78 | 1010 | 9 | .267 | .335 | .397 |
| San Jose | 140 | 5571 | 4835 | 725 | 1280 | 1961 | 262 | 61 | 99 | 677 | 51 | 59 | 87 | 538 | 17 | 1051 | 140 | 70 | 89 | 1050 | 5 | .265 | .345 | .406 |
| Stockton | 140 | 5457 | 4763 | 711 | 1252 | 1867 | 245 | 47 | 92 | 648 | 20 | 54 | 87 | 533 | 11 | 1028 | 146 | 54 | 92 | 1046 | 7 | .263 | .344 | .392 |

# INDIVIDUAL

## TOP QUALIFIERS FOR BATTING CHAMPIONSHIP

Minimum 378 plate appearances. *Lefthanded batter. †Switch-hitter.

| Player, Team | G | TPA | AB | R | H | TB | 2B | 3B | HR | RBI | SH | SF | HP | BB | IBB | SO | SB | CS | GDP | Avg. | OBP | Slg. |
|---|---|---|---|---|---|---|---|---|---|---|---|---|---|---|---|---|---|---|---|---|---|---|
| Stavisky, Brian, Modesto * | 130 | 585 | 513 | 108 | 176 | 282 | 39 | 5 | 19 | 83 | 2 | 5 | 11 | 54 | 3 | 89 | 6 | 4 | 7 | .343 | .413 | .550 |
| Perry, Jason, Modesto * | 83 | 384 | 325 | 81 | 110 | 223 | 39 | 1 | 24 | 80 | 1 | 3 | 21 | 34 | 2 | 87 | 4 | 4 | 5 | .338 | .431 | .686 |
| Aybar, Erick, Rancho Cucamonga † | 136 | 627 | 573 | 102 | 189 | 278 | 25 | 11 | 14 | 65 | 10 | 5 | 13 | 26 | 1 | 66 | 51 | 36 | 3 | .330 | .370 | .485 |
| Martinez, Gabriel, Bakersfield * | 116 | 471 | 436 | 54 | 141 | 198 | 39 | 3 | 4 | 47 | 2 | 0 | 3 | 30 | 1 | 90 | 4 | 8 | 12 | .323 | .371 | .454 |
| Arroyo, Carlos, Inland Empire * | 114 | 470 | 434 | 62 | 140 | 186 | 22 | 3 | 6 | 52 | 1 | 7 | 1 | 27 | 2 | 53 | 14 | 5 | 5 | .323 | .358 | .429 |
| Avlas, Phil, Lancaster | 109 | 427 | 384 | 64 | 121 | 198 | 22 | 8 | 13 | 68 | 7 | 5 | 0 | 29 | 0 | 54 | 4 | 4 | 4 | .315 | .359 | .516 |
| Quintanilla, Omar, Modesto * | 108 | 503 | 452 | 75 | 142 | 217 | 32 | 5 | 11 | 72 | 6 | 3 | 5 | 37 | 1 | 54 | 1 | 3 | 11 | .314 | .370 | .480 |
| Ethier, Andre, Modesto * | 99 | 471 | 419 | 72 | 131 | 185 | 23 | 5 | 7 | 53 | 1 | 2 | 4 | 45 | 0 | 64 | 2 | 5 | 12 | .313 | .383 | .442 |
| Guzman, Jesus, Inland Empire † | 114 | 512 | 442 | 80 | 137 | 196 | 35 | 3 | 6 | 71 | 3 | 4 | 6 | 57 | 0 | 105 | 9 | 8 | 6 | .310 | .393 | .443 |
| Barker, Sean, Visalia | 105 | 473 | 412 | 75 | 127 | 226 | 29 | 5 | 20 | 96 | 2 | 7 | 7 | 40 | 1 | 89 | 11 | 3 | 9 | .308 | .373 | .549 |
| Nelson, Jon, Inland Empire | 123 | 538 | 499 | 83 | 151 | 248 | 30 | 5 | 19 | 95 | 0 | 3 | 11 | 25 | 0 | 154 | 26 | 11 | 5 | .303 | .348 | .497 |
| Hinton, Travis, High Desert * | 137 | 595 | 536 | 80 | 162 | 272 | 36 | 4 | 22 | 88 | 1 | 5 | 5 | 48 | 3 | 99 | 3 | 1 | 10 | .302 | .362 | .507 |
| Lewis, Fred, San Jose * | 115 | 541 | 439 | 88 | 132 | 198 | 20 | 11 | 8 | 57 | 3 | 3 | 12 | 84 | 1 | 109 | 33 | 14 | 5 | .301 | .424 | .451 |
| Garcia, Isaac, Modesto | 116 | 453 | 426 | 65 | 128 | 202 | 41 | 3 | 9 | 73 | 6 | 5 | 2 | 13 | 0 | 85 | 1 | 3 | 13 | .300 | .321 | .474 |
| Mateo, Luis, Bakersfield | 120 | 493 | 476 | 59 | 143 | 232 | 28 | 2 | 19 | 69 | 0 | 2 | 5 | 10 | 1 | 131 | 13 | 3 | 4 | .300 | .320 | .487 |

DEPARTMENTAL LEADERS: G—Aybar, Hinton 136; AB—Aybar, 573; R—Stavisky, 108; H—Aybar, 189; TB—Stavisky, 282; 2B—I. Garcia, 41; 3B—G. Harris, 18; HR—Napoli, 29; RBI—Napoli, 118; SH—DePaula, 14; SF—Fox, 12; HP—Quentin, 27; BB—McAnulty, Napoli, 88; IBB—N/A; SO—Jacobo, 171; SB—Aybar, 51; CS—Aybar, 36; GIDP—N/A; Slg.—Perry, .686; OBP—Perry, .431.

## ALL PLAYERS

*Lefthanded batter. †Switch-hitter.

| Player, Team | G | TPA | AB | R | H | TB | 2B | 3B | HR | RBI | SH | SF | HP | BB | IBB | SO | SB | CS | GDP | Avg. | OBP | Slg. |
|---|---|---|---|---|---|---|---|---|---|---|---|---|---|---|---|---|---|---|---|---|---|---|
| Abercrombie, Reggie, Lancaster | 29 | 123 | 120 | 24 | 41 | 64 | 10 | 2 | 3 | 19 | 0 | 0 | 1 | 2 | 0 | 24 | 8 | 1 | 1 | .342 | .358 | .533 |
| Abram, Matt, Rancho Cucamonga | 21 | 57 | 54 | 4 | 8 | 12 | 4 | 0 | 0 | 3 | 0 | 0 | 1 | 2 | 0 | 17 | 0 | 0 | 0 | .148 | .193 | .222 |
| Abreu, Johany, San Jose † | 11 | 27 | 22 | 5 | 5 | 9 | 2 | 1 | 0 | 4 | 3 | 0 | 0 | 2 | 0 | 6 | 2 | 0 | 0 | .227 | .292 | .409 |
| Abruzzo, Jared, Rancho Cucamonga † | 94 | 372 | 329 | 33 | 83 | 134 | 18 | 0 | 11 | 46 | 0 | 3 | 4 | 36 | 1 | 90 | 0 | 0 | 5 | .252 | .331 | .407 |
| Adams, Skip, Lake Elsinore | 9 | 33 | 32 | 2 | 5 | 10 | 0 | 1 | 1 | 5 | 0 | 0 | 0 | 1 | 0 | 11 | 0 | 0 | 0 | .156 | .182 | .313 |
| Aguilar, Trino, Lake Elsinore | 3 | 5 | 3 | 1 | 0 | 0 | 0 | 0 | 0 | 0 | 0 | 0 | 1 | 1 | 0 | 0 | 0 | 0 | 1 | .000 | .400 | .000 |
| Anderson, Garret, Rancho Cucamonga * | 3 | 10 | 9 | 1 | 4 | 7 | 0 | 0 | 1 | 1 | 0 | 0 | 0 | 1 | 0 | 1 | 0 | 0 | 0 | .444 | .500 | .778 |
| Anderson, Keith, San Jose | 47 | 191 | 158 | 21 | 38 | 54 | 7 | 0 | 3 | 27 | 4 | 5 | 1 | 23 | 1 | 31 | 0 | 1 | 4 | .241 | .332 | .342 |
| Aracena, Sandy, Bakersfield | 47 | 178 | 162 | 12 | 46 | 68 | 12 | 2 | 2 | 26 | 0 | 2 | 2 | 12 | 0 | 34 | 2 | 1 | 6 | .284 | .337 | .420 |
| Arias, Joaquin, Stockton | 123 | 543 | 500 | 77 | 150 | 198 | 20 | 8 | 4 | 62 | 2 | 5 | 5 | 31 | 2 | 53 | 30 | 14 | 3 | .300 | .344 | .396 |
| Arroyo, Carlos, Inland Empire * | 114 | 470 | 434 | 62 | 140 | 186 | 22 | 3 | 6 | 52 | 1 | 7 | 1 | 27 | 2 | 53 | 14 | 5 | 5 | .323 | .358 | .429 |
| Avlas, Phil, Lancaster | 109 | 427 | 384 | 64 | 121 | 198 | 22 | 8 | 13 | 68 | 7 | 5 | 0 | 29 | 0 | 54 | 4 | 4 | 4 | .315 | .359 | .516 |
| Aybar, Erick, Rancho Cucamonga † | 136 | 627 | 573 | 102 | 189 | 278 | 25 | 11 | 14 | 65 | 10 | 5 | 13 | 26 | 1 | 66 | 51 | 36 | 3 | .330 | .370 | .485 |
| Baker, Casey, Lake Elsinore | 80 | 322 | 297 | 45 | 84 | 112 | 13 | 3 | 3 | 36 | 5 | 2 | 2 | 16 | 0 | 54 | 15 | 8 | 2 | .283 | .322 | .377 |
| Baker, Jeffrey, Visalia | 73 | 325 | 271 | 60 | 88 | 146 | 23 | 1 | 11 | 64 | 0 | 1 | 6 | 47 | 0 | 73 | 1 | 0 | 5 | .325 | .434 | .539 |
| Baker, Steve, Lake Elsinore | 72 | 311 | 283 | 35 | 72 | 104 | 14 | 3 | 4 | 34 | 0 | 3 | 4 | 21 | 2 | 72 | 10 | 3 | 5 | .254 | .312 | .367 |
| Balentien, Wladimir, Inland Empire | 10 | 42 | 38 | 5 | 11 | 18 | 1 | 0 | 2 | 5 | 0 | 0 | 0 | 4 | 0 | 10 | 1 | 0 | 0 | .289 | .357 | .474 |
| Balet, Pichi, Inland Empire | 61 | 244 | 225 | 29 | 66 | 80 | 12 | 1 | 0 | 27 | 0 | 0 | 9 | 10 | 0 | 19 | 2 | 2 | 9 | .293 | .348 | .356 |
| Balet, Pichi, Visalia | 21 | 90 | 79 | 8 | 15 | 19 | 1 | 0 | 1 | 5 | 0 | 0 | 5 | 6 | 0 | 17 | 0 | 0 | 1 | .190 | .289 | .241 |
| Ball, Jarred, Lancaster † | 125 | 533 | 472 | 82 | 140 | 223 | 26 | 6 | 15 | 66 | 9 | 3 | 3 | 45 | 1 | 123 | 17 | 9 | 4 | .297 | .359 | .472 |
| Barker, Sean, Visalia | 105 | 473 | 412 | 75 | 127 | 226 | 29 | 5 | 20 | 96 | 2 | 7 | 7 | 40 | 1 | 89 | 11 | 3 | 9 | .308 | .373 | .549 |
| Barre, Brian, Visalia * | 76 | 337 | 298 | 41 | 82 | 132 | 16 | 5 | 8 | 50 | 2 | 4 | 1 | 32 | 0 | 64 | 1 | 4 | 3 | .275 | .343 | .443 |
| Benavidez, Julian, San Jose | 46 | 175 | 149 | 14 | 24 | 49 | 7 | 0 | 6 | 24 | 1 | 3 | 2 | 20 | 0 | 37 | 0 | 1 | 3 | .161 | .264 | .329 |
| Bernier, Doug, Visalia † | 102 | 399 | 349 | 56 | 95 | 119 | 13 | 1 | 3 | 24 | 3 | 0 | 2 | 45 | 0 | 94 | 5 | 4 | 8 | .272 | .359 | .341 |
| Bibbs, Kennard, High Desert * | 120 | 546 | 496 | 75 | 139 | 181 | 16 | 10 | 2 | 36 | 7 | 2 | 1 | 40 | 0 | 64 | 38 | 18 | 6 | .280 | .334 | .365 |
| Biguenet, Michael, Lancaster | 24 | 65 | 57 | 8 | 8 | 14 | 1 | 1 | 1 | 3 | 0 | 0 | 5 | 3 | 0 | 26 | 1 | 1 | 1 | .140 | .246 | .246 |
| Bohn, T.J., Inland Empire | 71 | 296 | 240 | 46 | 68 | 104 | 9 | 3 | 7 | 37 | 2 | 1 | 9 | 44 | 2 | 61 | 6 | 4 | 4 | .283 | .412 | .433 |
| Bone, Kyle, San Jose | 1 | 4 | 3 | 0 | 1 | 1 | 0 | 0 | 0 | 0 | 1 | 0 | 0 | 0 | 0 | 0 | 0 | 0 | 0 | .333 | .333 | .333 |
| Bouman, John, Bakersfield | 9 | 35 | 32 | 4 | 6 | 8 | 2 | 0 | 0 | 5 | 0 | 0 | 2 | 1 | 0 | 10 | 2 | 1 | 0 | .188 | .257 | .250 |
| Boyd, Dan, High Desert | 69 | 313 | 266 | 47 | 78 | 136 | 21 | 2 | 11 | 51 | 1 | 1 | 16 | 29 | 1 | 57 | 3 | 2 | 6 | .293 | .394 | .511 |
| Boyd, Patrick, Stockton † | 48 | 209 | 183 | 31 | 39 | 59 | 9 | 1 | 3 | 30 | 0 | 2 | 6 | 18 | 0 | 56 | 6 | 1 | 2 | .213 | .301 | .322 |
| Brooks, Doc, Lancaster | 90 | 343 | 301 | 67 | 100 | 169 | 20 | 2 | 15 | 47 | 6 | 1 | 5 | 30 | 0 | 82 | 7 | 7 | 4 | .332 | .401 | .561 |
| Brown, Neb, Lancaster * | 63 | 289 | 245 | 48 | 71 | 102 | 11 | 4 | 4 | 31 | 8 | 4 | 4 | 28 | 0 | 28 | 14 | 7 | 2 | .290 | .367 | .416 |
| Buchanan, Brian, Lake Elsinore | 4 | 12 | 10 | 1 | 3 | 5 | 2 | 0 | 0 | 1 | 0 | 0 | 1 | 1 | 0 | 3 | 0 | 0 | 0 | .300 | .417 | .500 |
| Budde, Ryan, Rancho Cucamonga | 99 | 401 | 359 | 54 | 90 | 146 | 17 | 0 | 13 | 51 | 2 | 5 | 8 | 27 | 2 | 76 | 3 | 5 | 3 | .251 | .313 | .407 |
| Burgamy, Brian, Lake Elsinore † | 38 | 135 | 123 | 16 | 33 | 41 | 5 | 0 | 1 | 18 | 1 | 0 | 0 | 11 | 0 | 22 | 1 | 4 | 1 | .268 | .328 | .333 |
| Burres, Brian, San Jose * | 37 | 1 | 1 | 0 | 0 | 0 | 0 | 0 | 0 | 0 | 0 | 0 | 0 | 0 | 0 | 1 | 0 | 0 | 0 | .000 | .000 | .000 |
| Buscher, Brian, San Jose * | 88 | 387 | 343 | 50 | 100 | 140 | 14 | 7 | 4 | 56 | 0 | 5 | 6 | 33 | 0 | 61 | 5 | 4 | 8 | .292 | .359 | .408 |
| Candelaria, Scott, High Desert | 62 | 259 | 245 | 24 | 57 | 75 | 7 | 1 | 3 | 23 | 0 | 3 | 3 | 8 | 0 | 45 | 0 | 2 | 3 | .233 | .263 | .306 |
| Carlin, Luke, Lake Elsinore † | 37 | 119 | 107 | 12 | 28 | 38 | 7 | 0 | 1 | 12 | 0 | 2 | 0 | 10 | 0 | 19 | 0 | 1 | 3 | .262 | .319 | .355 |
| Carter, Josh, Lake Elsinore | 89 | 358 | 331 | 38 | 101 | 131 | 23 | 2 | 1 | 41 | 1 | 4 | 5 | 17 | 1 | 41 | 4 | 4 | 6 | .305 | .345 | .396 |
| Castro, Ismael, Inland Empire † | 16 | 71 | 66 | 11 | 20 | 33 | 7 | 0 | 2 | 10 | 1 | 0 | 0 | 4 | 0 | 3 | 0 | 1 | 2 | .303 | .343 | .500 |
| Cates, Zach, Rancho Cucamonga * | 16 | 46 | 37 | 7 | 6 | 8 | 2 | 0 | 0 | 1 | 2 | 0 | 0 | 7 | 0 | 13 | 1 | 0 | 0 | .162 | .295 | .216 |
| Centeno, Irwin, Bakersfield | 21 | 78 | 70 | 10 | 13 | 19 | 3 | 0 | 1 | 5 | 0 | 0 | 0 | 8 | 0 | 17 | 4 | 3 | 1 | .186 | .269 | .271 |
| Chavez, Angel, San Jose | 12 | 60 | 54 | 12 | 21 | 29 | 5 | 0 | 1 | 16 | 0 | 1 | 1 | 4 | 1 | 7 | 2 | 2 | 1 | .389 | .433 | .537 |
| Chavez, Ozzie, High Desert † | 39 | 144 | 130 | 19 | 42 | 51 | 4 | 1 | 1 | 23 | 4 | 1 | 2 | 7 | 0 | 26 | 2 | 5 | 3 | .323 | .364 | .392 |
| Cho, Hyung, Inland Empire | 24 | 87 | 84 | 11 | 25 | 35 | 7 | 0 | 1 | 14 | 0 | 0 | 1 | 2 | 0 | 5 | 1 | 0 | 2 | .298 | .322 | .417 |
| Ciesluk, Chris, San Jose | 2 | 4 | 3 | 1 | 0 | 0 | 0 | 0 | 0 | 0 | 0 | 0 | 1 | 0 | 0 | 2 | 0 | 0 | 0 | .000 | .250 | .000 |
| Cleveland, Jeremy, Stockton | 129 | 555 | 487 | 72 | 135 | 201 | 32 | 5 | 8 | 70 | 1 | 6 | 8 | 53 | 0 | 110 | 11 | 2 | 12 | .277 | .354 | .413 |
| Colamarino, Brant, Modesto * | 50 | 218 | 183 | 41 | 65 | 110 | 8 | 2 | 11 | 41 | 0 | 2 | 5 | 28 | 2 | 23 | 1 | 0 | 5 | .355 | .450 | .601 |
| Colina, Alvin, Visalia | 96 | 371 | 337 | 44 | 85 | 141 | 23 | 0 | 11 | 47 | 3 | 1 | 6 | 24 | 0 | 81 | 0 | 1 | 8 | .252 | .313 | .418 |
| Cordell, Brent, Bakersfield † | 106 | 399 | 341 | 47 | 94 | 157 | 22 | 1 | 13 | 68 | 0 | 5 | 13 | 40 | 4 | 73 | 4 | 1 | 5 | .276 | .368 | .460 |
| Cordido, Julio, San Jose | 112 | 497 | 452 | 67 | 127 | 190 | 27 | 6 | 8 | 65 | 2 | 5 | 10 | 28 | 1 | 63 | 18 | 12 | 11 | .281 | .333 | .420 |
| Cornejo, Eduardo, Modesto * | 67 | 278 | 235 | 37 | 64 | 80 | 14 | 1 | 0 | 33 | 6 | 0 | 4 | 33 | 0 | 34 | 2 | 4 | 3 | .272 | .371 | .340 |

| Player, Team | G | TPA | AB | R | H | TB | 2B | 3B | HR | RBI | SH | SF | HP | BB | IBB | SO | SB | CS | GDP | Avg. | OBP | Slg. |
|---|---|---|---|---|---|---|---|---|---|---|---|---|---|---|---|---|---|---|---|---|---|---|
| Cota, Jesus, Lancaster * | 16 | 69 | 62 | 15 | 25 | 40 | 4 | 1 | 3 | 22 | 0 | 2 | 1 | 4 | 0 | 6 | 1 | 0 | 1 | .403 | .435 | .645 |
| Coughlan, Cameron, Stockton † | 127 | 546 | 455 | 71 | 115 | 137 | 9 | 5 | 1 | 38 | 9 | 3 | 10 | 69 | 0 | 107 | 35 | 10 | 3 | .253 | .361 | .301 |
| Crabbe, Callix, High Desert † | 132 | 615 | 540 | 89 | 157 | 226 | 26 | 11 | 7 | 61 | 4 | 4 | 8 | 59 | 0 | 64 | 34 | 11 | 13 | .291 | .367 | .419 |
| Craig, Beau, Modesto † | 7 | 23 | 20 | 2 | 4 | 4 | 0 | 0 | 0 | 1 | 0 | 0 | 1 | 2 | 0 | 6 | 0 | 0 | 1 | .200 | .304 | .200 |
| Cruz, Enrique, High Desert | 97 | 404 | 361 | 53 | 102 | 172 | 19 | 0 | 17 | 65 | 0 | 5 | 2 | 36 | 1 | 82 | 12 | 7 | 6 | .283 | .347 | .476 |
| Cruz, Luis, Lake Elsinore | 124 | 551 | 512 | 75 | 142 | 207 | 35 | 3 | 8 | 72 | 6 | 6 | 3 | 24 | 1 | 56 | 3 | 7 | 9 | .277 | .310 | .404 |
| Cruz, Nelson, Modesto | 66 | 290 | 261 | 54 | 90 | 152 | 27 | 1 | 11 | 52 | 0 | 1 | 4 | 24 | 2 | 73 | 8 | 4 | 2 | .345 | .407 | .582 |
| Cuevas, Aneudi, Bakersfield | 5 | 15 | 11 | 1 | 2 | 5 | 0 | 0 | 1 | 2 | 0 | 0 | 0 | 4 | 0 | 6 | 1 | 1 | 0 | .182 | .400 | .455 |
| D'Antona, Jamie, Lancaster | 68 | 295 | 273 | 45 | 86 | 145 | 18 | 1 | 13 | 57 | 0 | 4 | 2 | 16 | 1 | 36 | 2 | 3 | 7 | .315 | .353 | .531 |
| De Paula, Luis, Bakersfield | 94 | 419 | 372 | 60 | 109 | 142 | 18 | 3 | 3 | 39 | 14 | 1 | 4 | 28 | 1 | 79 | 30 | 12 | 10 | .293 | .348 | .382 |
| De Renne, Keoni, Lancaster | 15 | 70 | 61 | 11 | 15 | 21 | 4 | 1 | 0 | 10 | 2 | 1 | 0 | 6 | 0 | 7 | 2 | 2 | 0 | .246 | .309 | .344 |
| Dufner, Kris, Bakersfield † | 79 | 296 | 268 | 24 | 53 | 63 | 4 | 3 | 0 | 23 | 3 | 1 | 2 | 22 | 0 | 73 | 5 | 0 | 2 | .198 | .263 | .235 |
| Dukes, Elijah, Bakersfield † | 58 | 244 | 211 | 44 | 70 | 114 | 16 | 2 | 8 | 34 | 1 | 1 | 5 | 26 | 1 | 50 | 16 | 7 | 1 | .332 | .416 | .540 |
| Duncan, Carlos, Rancho Cucamonga | 24 | 91 | 84 | 12 | 24 | 40 | 8 | 1 | 2 | 12 | 0 | 2 | 0 | 5 | 0 | 17 | 7 | 1 | 0 | .286 | .319 | .476 |
| Durham, Ray, San Jose † | 1 | 3 | 3 | 0 | 1 | 1 | 0 | 0 | 0 | 0 | 0 | 0 | 0 | 0 | 0 | 0 | 0 | 0 | 0 | .333 | .333 | .333 |
| Ellison, Josh, Inland Empire | 31 | 130 | 118 | 17 | 46 | 53 | 7 | 0 | 0 | 13 | 2 | 0 | 0 | 10 | 0 | 23 | 3 | 2 | 2 | .390 | .438 | .449 |
| Esposito, Brian, Stockton | 22 | 84 | 78 | 10 | 20 | 39 | 2 | 1 | 5 | 13 | 0 | 0 | 0 | 6 | 1 | 17 | 1 | 0 | 0 | .256 | .310 | .500 |
| Ethier, Andre, Modesto * | 99 | 471 | 419 | 72 | 131 | 185 | 23 | 5 | 7 | 53 | 1 | 2 | 4 | 45 | 0 | 64 | 2 | 5 | 12 | .313 | .383 | .442 |
| Eure, Jeff, High Desert | 92 | 401 | 366 | 45 | 88 | 149 | 23 | 4 | 10 | 51 | 0 | 4 | 5 | 26 | 0 | 102 | 6 | 8 | 4 | .240 | .297 | .407 |
| Faison, Vince, Inland Empire * | 7 | 27 | 25 | 5 | 8 | 13 | 2 | 0 | 1 | 5 | 0 | 0 | 0 | 2 | 0 | 4 | 2 | 0 | 1 | .320 | .370 | .520 |
| Fallon, Chris, Visalia * | 114 | 478 | 397 | 68 | 101 | 173 | 22 | 1 | 16 | 81 | 2 | 9 | 3 | 67 | 2 | 88 | 0 | 1 | 9 | .254 | .359 | .436 |
| Farnsworth, Troy, High Desert | 78 | 300 | 263 | 40 | 68 | 120 | 14 | 1 | 12 | 46 | 1 | 2 | 7 | 27 | 0 | 66 | 2 | 2 | 2 | .259 | .341 | .456 |
| Feliciano, Jesus, Bakersfield * | 70 | 282 | 251 | 41 | 76 | 95 | 13 | 3 | 0 | 23 | 9 | 3 | 1 | 18 | 0 | 20 | 9 | 4 | 7 | .303 | .348 | .378 |
| Fox, Adam, Stockton | 131 | 564 | 483 | 64 | 116 | 193 | 24 | 4 | 15 | 77 | 0 | 11 | 10 | 60 | 1 | 106 | 4 | 3 | 6 | .240 | .330 | .400 |
| Frome, Jason, Visalia * | 13 | 43 | 41 | 8 | 8 | 14 | 1 | 1 | 1 | 2 | 0 | 0 | 0 | 2 | 0 | 12 | 0 | 0 | 1 | .195 | .233 | .341 |
| Frost, Jeremy, High Desert | 89 | 347 | 325 | 39 | 87 | 137 | 19 | 2 | 9 | 38 | 2 | 1 | 1 | 18 | 0 | 71 | 8 | 1 | 5 | .268 | .307 | .422 |
| Gallagher, Buddy, Visalia * | 16 | 4 | 4 | 0 | 3 | 3 | 0 | 0 | 0 | 0 | 0 | 0 | 0 | 0 | 0 | 0 | 0 | 0 | 0 | .750 | .750 | .750 |
| Garcia, Isaac, Modesto | 116 | 453 | 426 | 65 | 128 | 202 | 41 | 3 | 9 | 73 | 6 | 5 | 2 | 13 | 0 | 85 | 1 | 3 | 13 | .300 | .321 | .474 |
| Garciaparra, Michael, Inland Empire | 70 | 275 | 234 | 48 | 53 | 74 | 12 | 3 | 1 | 26 | 2 | 1 | 7 | 31 | 1 | 44 | 5 | 4 | 4 | .226 | .333 | .316 |
| Garrabrants, Steve, Lancaster | 60 | 243 | 215 | 33 | 58 | 75 | 6 | 1 | 3 | 30 | 3 | 0 | 3 | 22 | 0 | 49 | 11 | 3 | 0 | .270 | .346 | .349 |
| Garthwaite, Jay, Lancaster | 63 | 260 | 238 | 49 | 74 | 133 | 17 | 3 | 12 | 41 | 2 | 2 | 0 | 17 | 0 | 55 | 5 | 3 | 2 | .311 | .354 | .559 |
| Gates, David, Rancho Cucamonga | 120 | 508 | 456 | 63 | 122 | 219 | 31 | 3 | 20 | 86 | 0 | 7 | 10 | 35 | 0 | 122 | 2 | 1 | 3 | .268 | .329 | .480 |
| Girardeau, Clark, Lake Elsinore | 12 | 2 | 2 | 1 | 0 | 0 | 0 | 0 | 0 | 0 | 0 | 0 | 0 | 0 | 0 | 0 | 0 | 0 | 0 | .000 | .000 | .000 |
| Glaus, Troy, Rancho Cucamonga | 5 | 21 | 15 | 4 | 3 | 9 | 0 | 0 | 2 | 4 | 0 | 0 | 0 | 6 | 0 | 5 | 0 | 0 | 0 | .200 | .429 | .600 |
| Gold, Nate, Stockton | 135 | 584 | 500 | 85 | 121 | 217 | 32 | 2 | 20 | 94 | 0 | 8 | 11 | 65 | 2 | 140 | 5 | 0 | 10 | .242 | .337 | .434 |
| Gomes, Joey, Bakersfield | 72 | 306 | 277 | 41 | 83 | 123 | 17 | 1 | 7 | 45 | 0 | 2 | 9 | 18 | 0 | 44 | 7 | 1 | 8 | .300 | .359 | .444 |
| Gonzalez, Bernie, Visalia | 101 | 415 | 386 | 39 | 100 | 135 | 21 | 1 | 4 | 39 | 2 | 2 | 3 | 22 | 0 | 92 | 5 | 4 | 7 | .259 | .303 | .350 |
| Gonzalez, Juan, Inland Empire † | 129 | 586 | 520 | 79 | 151 | 193 | 22 | 7 | 2 | 59 | 5 | 7 | 3 | 51 | 0 | 95 | 26 | 17 | 6 | .290 | .353 | .371 |
| Guzman, Jesus, Inland Empire † | 114 | 512 | 442 | 80 | 137 | 196 | 35 | 3 | 6 | 71 | 3 | 4 | 6 | 57 | 0 | 105 | 9 | 8 | 6 | .310 | .393 | .443 |
| Hagen, Matt, Inland Empire | 101 | 392 | 347 | 49 | 80 | 139 | 30 | 1 | 9 | 47 | 2 | 3 | 6 | 32 | 1 | 93 | 6 | 2 | 4 | .231 | .304 | .401 |
| Haley, Adam, Lancaster * | 57 | 185 | 159 | 23 | 50 | 56 | 4 | 1 | 0 | 14 | 10 | 3 | 3 | 10 | 0 | 33 | 5 | 8 | 2 | .314 | .360 | .352 |
| Halter, Shane, Rancho Cucamonga | 5 | 22 | 19 | 4 | 4 | 5 | 1 | 0 | 0 | 1 | 0 | 0 | 1 | 2 | 0 | 4 | 2 | 0 | 1 | .211 | .318 | .263 |
| Hamblen, Chris, Stockton † | 13 | 45 | 41 | 1 | 10 | 13 | 3 | 0 | 0 | 5 | 0 | 0 | 1 | 3 | 0 | 13 | 0 | 0 | 1 | .244 | .311 | .317 |
| Hamilton, Mark, High Desert * | 28 | 87 | 80 | 12 | 24 | 36 | 3 | 0 | 3 | 15 | 0 | 0 | 1 | 6 | 0 | 14 | 1 | 0 | 2 | .300 | .356 | .450 |
| Hammock, Rob, Lancaster | 2 | 10 | 9 | 2 | 6 | 8 | 2 | 0 | 0 | 3 | 0 | 0 | 0 | 1 | 0 | 1 | 0 | 0 | 0 | .667 | .700 | .889 |
| Harris, Gary, Inland Empire * | 134 | 605 | 562 | 92 | 157 | 237 | 20 | 18 | 8 | 78 | 2 | 6 | 6 | 29 | 1 | 107 | 34 | 12 | 7 | .279 | .318 | .422 |
| Harrison, Vince, Bakersfield | 69 | 309 | 256 | 46 | 72 | 124 | 17 | 1 | 11 | 42 | 1 | 1 | 6 | 45 | 0 | 49 | 8 | 5 | 9 | .281 | .399 | .484 |
| Heath, Demetrius, Rancho Cucamonga | 22 | 80 | 74 | 15 | 25 | 29 | 2 | 1 | 0 | 10 | 1 | 0 | 1 | 4 | 0 | 11 | 5 | 3 | 1 | .338 | .380 | .392 |
| Henderson, Eric, High Desert * | 34 | 29 | 27 | 5 | 4 | 8 | 1 | 0 | 1 | 2 | 0 | 0 | 0 | 2 | 0 | 11 | 0 | 0 | 0 | .148 | .207 | .296 |
| Hendricks, K.J., Visalia † | 126 | 580 | 475 | 100 | 136 | 175 | 20 | 5 | 3 | 54 | 11 | 2 | 6 | 85 | 3 | 74 | 34 | 9 | 11 | .286 | .400 | .368 |
| Hinton, Travis, High Desert * | 136 | 595 | 536 | 80 | 162 | 272 | 36 | 4 | 22 | 88 | 1 | 5 | 5 | 48 | 3 | 99 | 3 | 1 | 10 | .302 | .362 | .507 |
| Hoffpauir, Josh, Stockton * | 47 | 192 | 178 | 18 | 47 | 57 | 10 | 0 | 0 | 24 | 0 | 0 | 0 | 14 | 1 | 13 | 8 | 3 | 7 | .264 | .318 | .320 |
| Holm, Steve, San Jose | 61 | 242 | 201 | 27 | 52 | 91 | 12 | 0 | 9 | 29 | 4 | 0 | 4 | 33 | 0 | 52 | 1 | 2 | 5 | .259 | .374 | .453 |
| Hornostaj, Aaron, San Jose * | 84 | 329 | 281 | 35 | 62 | 74 | 10 | 1 | 0 | 29 | 7 | 6 | 0 | 35 | 0 | 49 | 20 | 6 | 8 | .221 | .301 | .263 |
| Ishikawa, Travis, San Jose * | 16 | 68 | 56 | 10 | 13 | 23 | 7 | 0 | 1 | 10 | 0 | 1 | 1 | 10 | 2 | 16 | 0 | 0 | 1 | .232 | .353 | .411 |
| Jackson, Conor, Lancaster | 67 | 313 | 258 | 64 | 89 | 145 | 19 | 2 | 11 | 54 | 0 | 7 | 3 | 45 | 1 | 36 | 4 | 3 | 3 | .345 | .438 | .562 |
| Jacobo, Kervin, Lake Elsinore † | 123 | 498 | 457 | 53 | 110 | 172 | 21 | 4 | 11 | 55 | 0 | 2 | 5 | 34 | 1 | 171 | 12 | 7 | 6 | .241 | .299 | .376 |
| Jaile, Chris, Stockton | 55 | 209 | 171 | 26 | 40 | 59 | 8 | 1 | 3 | 21 | 2 | 3 | 4 | 29 | 0 | 39 | 1 | 1 | 4 | .234 | .353 | .345 |
| Jennings, Todd, San Jose | 45 | 193 | 177 | 20 | 33 | 42 | 6 | 0 | 1 | 12 | 2 | 0 | 4 | 10 | 0 | 36 | 5 | 4 | 4 | .186 | .246 | .237 |
| Johnson, Michael, Lake Elsinore * | 90 | 391 | 331 | 55 | 84 | 156 | 23 | 2 | 15 | 64 | 0 | 6 | 2 | 52 | 2 | 106 | 0 | 0 | 3 | .254 | .353 | .471 |
| Jones, Geoffrey, Lake Elsinore * | 11 | 1 | 1 | 0 | 0 | 0 | 0 | 0 | 0 | 0 | 0 | 0 | 0 | 0 | 0 | 1 | 0 | 0 | 0 | .000 | .000 | .000 |
| Jones, Kennard, Lake Elsinore * | 50 | 233 | 206 | 23 | 60 | 78 | 8 | 5 | 0 | 18 | 0 | 1 | 1 | 25 | 1 | 40 | 13 | 11 | 5 | .291 | .369 | .379 |
| Jones, Mitch, Bakersfield | 18 | 57 | 53 | 11 | 12 | 19 | 4 | 0 | 1 | 4 | 1 | 0 | 1 | 2 | 0 | 13 | 2 | 1 | 1 | .226 | .273 | .358 |
| Kimpton, Nick, Rancho Cucamonga * | 26 | 65 | 58 | 5 | 9 | 13 | 1 | 0 | 1 | 6 | 0 | 1 | 0 | 6 | 0 | 15 | 1 | 1 | 1 | .155 | .231 | .224 |
| LaBarbera, A.J., San Jose | 99 | 442 | 378 | 60 | 113 | 149 | 18 | 3 | 4 | 47 | 10 | 3 | 10 | 41 | 2 | 51 | 16 | 5 | 6 | .299 | .380 | .394 |
| Lauderdale, Matthew, Lake Elsinore | 2 | 6 | 6 | 1 | 2 | 5 | 0 | 0 | 1 | 3 | 0 | 0 | 0 | 0 | 0 | 2 | 0 | 0 | 0 | .333 | .333 | .833 |
| Lentz, Brian, Inland Empire | 44 | 136 | 122 | 15 | 30 | 44 | 4 | 2 | 2 | 16 | 1 | 1 | 0 | 12 | 0 | 36 | 0 | 1 | 2 | .246 | .311 | .361 |
| Lewis, Fred, San Jose * | 115 | 541 | 439 | 88 | 132 | 198 | 20 | 11 | 8 | 57 | 3 | 3 | 12 | 84 | 1 | 109 | 33 | 14 | 5 | .301 | .424 | .451 |
| Lima, Joe, Lake Elsinore | 61 | 210 | 192 | 17 | 42 | 60 | 13 | 1 | 1 | 20 | 4 | 1 | 2 | 11 | 0 | 51 | 3 | 2 | 6 | .219 | .267 | .313 |
| Lincoln, Justin, Bakersfield | 50 | 196 | 167 | 21 | 44 | 72 | 13 | 0 | 5 | 16 | 2 | 2 | 4 | 20 | 0 | 62 | 2 | 2 | 3 | .263 | .352 | .431 |
| Luellwitz, Sean, Lancaster | 93 | 396 | 367 | 50 | 99 | 160 | 29 | 1 | 10 | 51 | 1 | 5 | 4 | 19 | 0 | 84 | 4 | 0 | 10 | .270 | .309 | .436 |
| Madera, Sandy, Visalia | 27 | 110 | 96 | 9 | 29 | 41 | 9 | 0 | 1 | 20 | 1 | 1 | 3 | 9 | 0 | 16 | 1 | 2 | 3 | .302 | .376 | .427 |
| Maniscalco, Matt, Bakersfield | 124 | 530 | 463 | 56 | 117 | 142 | 23 | 1 | 0 | 47 | 10 | 3 | 2 | 52 | 1 | 66 | 22 | 10 | 14 | .253 | .329 | .307 |
| Margalski, Ben, Stockton * | 38 | 143 | 125 | 19 | 24 | 41 | 5 | 3 | 2 | 15 | 0 | 0 | 0 | 18 | 1 | 50 | 0 | 2 | 1 | .192 | .294 | .328 |
| Martinez, Gabriel, Bakersfield * | 116 | 471 | 436 | 54 | 141 | 198 | 39 | 3 | 4 | 47 | 2 | 0 | 3 | 30 | 1 | 90 | 4 | 8 | 12 | .323 | .371 | .454 |
| Martinez-esteve, Eduardo, San Jose | 17 | 74 | 69 | 11 | 29 | 40 | 7 | 2 | 0 | 14 | 0 | 1 | 0 | 4 | 0 | 9 | 0 | 1 | 1 | .420 | .446 | .580 |
| Mateo, Luis, Bakersfield | 120 | 493 | 476 | 59 | 143 | 232 | 28 | 2 | 19 | 69 | 0 | 2 | 5 | 10 | 1 | 131 | 13 | 3 | 4 | .300 | .320 | .487 |
| McAnulty, Paul, Lake Elsinore * | 133 | 591 | 495 | 98 | 147 | 258 | 36 | 3 | 23 | 87 | 0 | 4 | 4 | 88 | 3 | 106 | 3 | 1 | 5 | .297 | .404 | .521 |
| McBeth, Marcus, Modesto | 99 | 363 | 329 | 41 | 77 | 118 | 18 | 4 | 5 | 41 | 5 | 3 | 12 | 14 | 0 | 86 | 4 | 4 | 4 | .234 | .288 | .359 |
| McCurdy, John, Modesto | 13 | 53 | 51 | 3 | 10 | 13 | 3 | 0 | 0 | 5 | 0 | 0 | 1 | 1 | 0 | 15 | 0 | 0 | 0 | .196 | .226 | .255 |
| McStoots, Jason, Lancaster * | 12 | 27 | 26 | 3 | 4 | 5 | 1 | 0 | 0 | 3 | 0 | 0 | 0 | 1 | 0 | 6 | 1 | 1 | 0 | .154 | .185 | .192 |
| Melgarejo, Ransel, Rancho Cucamonga | 74 | 285 | 238 | 49 | 67 | 97 | 13 | 4 | 3 | 35 | 7 | 2 | 6 | 32 | 0 | 52 | 20 | 6 | 8 | .282 | .378 | .408 |

| Player, Team | G | TPA | AB | R | H | TB | 2B | 3B | HR | RBI | SH | SF | HP | BB | IBB | SO | SB | CS | GDP | Avg. | OBP | Slg. |
|---|---|---|---|---|---|---|---|---|---|---|---|---|---|---|---|---|---|---|---|---|---|---|
| Mendez, Mario, High Desert | 94 | 368 | 336 | 53 | 93 | 164 | 14 | 6 | 15 | 50 | 2 | 3 | 5 | 22 | 1 | 95 | 9 | 7 | 5 | .277 | .328 | .488 |
| Merrill, Ronnie, Lake Elsinore † | 9 | 44 | 40 | 7 | 17 | 29 | 2 | 2 | 2 | 7 | 0 | 0 | 0 | 4 | 0 | 6 | 1 | 2 | 0 | .425 | .477 | .725 |
| Merritt, Graig, Bakersfield | 51 | 166 | 152 | 10 | 28 | 32 | 4 | 0 | 0 | 7 | 4 | 1 | 3 | 6 | 0 | 33 | 1 | 3 | 3 | .184 | .228 | .211 |
| Miller, Chris, Lake Elsinore | 12 | 44 | 36 | 5 | 10 | 20 | 1 | 0 | 3 | 5 | 1 | 0 | 3 | 4 | 0 | 9 | 0 | 1 | 0 | .278 | .395 | .556 |
| Mondesi, Raul, Rancho Cucamonga | 2 | 9 | 8 | 2 | 1 | 1 | 0 | 0 | 0 | 0 | 0 | 0 | 0 | 1 | 0 | 2 | 0 | 0 | 1 | .125 | .222 | .125 |
| Monzon, Erick, Inland Empire | 31 | 127 | 115 | 24 | 39 | 68 | 6 | 1 | 7 | 18 | 1 | 2 | 4 | 5 | 0 | 28 | 4 | 1 | 1 | .339 | .381 | .591 |
| Morgan, Matt, Lancaster | 76 | 262 | 228 | 31 | 55 | 79 | 12 | 0 | 4 | 25 | 9 | 4 | 2 | 19 | 0 | 46 | 3 | 5 | 6 | .241 | .300 | .346 |
| Morris, Chris, High Desert † | 39 | 152 | 126 | 24 | 36 | 43 | 7 | 0 | 0 | 16 | 2 | 1 | 1 | 22 | 0 | 31 | 25 | 9 | 1 | .286 | .393 | .341 |
| Morris, Jed, Modesto * | 92 | 364 | 303 | 39 | 81 | 110 | 20 | 3 | 1 | 37 | 2 | 4 | 12 | 43 | 3 | 48 | 1 | 3 | 6 | .267 | .376 | .363 |
| Munhall, Brian, San Jose | 6 | 25 | 22 | 5 | 4 | 8 | 1 | 0 | 1 | 3 | 1 | 0 | 0 | 2 | 0 | 12 | 0 | 0 | 0 | .182 | .250 | .364 |
| Myers, Casey, Modesto | 63 | 255 | 214 | 32 | 68 | 92 | 10 | 1 | 4 | 26 | 4 | 3 | 4 | 30 | 2 | 23 | 0 | 0 | 6 | .318 | .406 | .430 |
| Myers, Corey, Lancaster | 10 | 44 | 39 | 9 | 16 | 24 | 2 | 0 | 2 | 9 | 0 | 0 | 0 | 5 | 0 | 3 | 0 | 0 | 0 | .410 | .477 | .615 |
| Napoli, Michael, Rancho Cucamonga | 132 | 584 | 482 | 94 | 136 | 260 | 29 | 4 | 29 | 118 | 1 | 8 | 5 | 88 | 5 | 166 | 9 | 5 | 6 | .282 | .393 | .539 |
| Nelson, Jon, Inland Empire | 123 | 538 | 499 | 83 | 151 | 248 | 30 | 5 | 19 | 95 | 0 | 3 | 11 | 25 | 0 | 154 | 26 | 11 | 5 | .303 | .348 | .497 |
| Nettles, Marcus, Lake Elsinore * | 52 | 228 | 203 | 32 | 55 | 64 | 1 | 4 | 0 | 7 | 5 | 2 | 2 | 16 | 0 | 44 | 15 | 4 | 5 | .271 | .327 | .315 |
| Niekro, Lance, San Jose | 15 | 64 | 61 | 13 | 19 | 31 | 7 | 1 | 1 | 14 | 0 | 1 | 0 | 2 | 0 | 5 | 0 | 0 | 5 | .311 | .328 | .508 |
| Nunez, Felix, Rancho Cucamonga | 14 | 30 | 24 | 4 | 4 | 4 | 0 | 0 | 0 | 2 | 1 | 0 | 0 | 5 | 0 | 5 | 0 | 1 | 0 | .167 | .310 | .167 |
| Pagan, Andres, Lake Elsinore | 103 | 396 | 354 | 38 | 85 | 123 | 16 | 2 | 6 | 44 | 4 | 1 | 3 | 34 | 0 | 92 | 0 | 2 | 5 | .240 | .311 | .347 |
| Pavkovich, Adam, Rancho Cucamonga | 107 | 422 | 375 | 59 | 85 | 152 | 33 | 2 | 10 | 44 | 6 | 3 | 2 | 36 | 0 | 70 | 4 | 5 | 2 | .227 | .296 | .405 |
| Peck, Bryan, Visalia | 105 | 458 | 408 | 48 | 98 | 140 | 24 | 0 | 6 | 52 | 2 | 1 | 7 | 40 | 1 | 77 | 1 | 2 | 10 | .240 | .318 | .343 |
| Perry, Jason, Modesto * | 83 | 384 | 325 | 81 | 110 | 223 | 39 | 1 | 24 | 80 | 1 | 3 | 21 | 34 | 2 | 87 | 4 | 4 | 5 | .338 | .431 | .686 |
| Phillips, Dan, Visalia | 13 | 50 | 49 | 4 | 9 | 13 | 1 | 0 | 1 | 5 | 0 | 0 | 1 | 0 | 0 | 16 | 0 | 1 | 1 | .184 | .200 | .265 |
| Porter, Greg, Rancho Cucamonga * | 86 | 376 | 349 | 48 | 111 | 165 | 26 | 5 | 6 | 45 | 1 | 3 | 6 | 17 | 0 | 67 | 1 | 3 | 6 | .318 | .357 | .473 |
| Pullins, Taylor, Inland Empire | 5 | 19 | 15 | 2 | 2 | 3 | 1 | 0 | 0 | 1 | 0 | 0 | 0 | 4 | 0 | 3 | 0 | 0 | 1 | .133 | .316 | .200 |
| Quentin, Carlos, Lancaster | 65 | 297 | 242 | 64 | 75 | 136 | 14 | 1 | 15 | 51 | 0 | 3 | 27 | 25 | 1 | 33 | 5 | 1 | 10 | .310 | .428 | .562 |
| Quintanilla, Omar, Modesto * | 108 | 503 | 452 | 75 | 142 | 217 | 32 | 5 | 11 | 72 | 6 | 3 | 5 | 37 | 1 | 54 | 1 | 3 | 11 | .314 | .370 | .480 |
| Ramos, Carlos, Bakersfield * | 30 | 129 | 114 | 24 | 31 | 35 | 4 | 0 | 0 | 7 | 2 | 1 | 1 | 11 | 0 | 10 | 7 | 5 | 2 | .272 | .339 | .307 |
| Ramos, Peeter, Lake Elsinore | 63 | 279 | 256 | 39 | 69 | 84 | 13 | 1 | 0 | 15 | 1 | 1 | 2 | 19 | 0 | 34 | 12 | 2 | 5 | .270 | .324 | .328 |
| Rasmusen, Peter, High Desert | 35 | 112 | 96 | 11 | 17 | 28 | 4 | 2 | 1 | 10 | 3 | 2 | 3 | 8 | 0 | 30 | 0 | 1 | 0 | .177 | .257 | .292 |
| Reece, Eric, Bakersfield * | 54 | 231 | 213 | 31 | 56 | 90 | 9 | 2 | 7 | 35 | 0 | 4 | 1 | 13 | 0 | 49 | 3 | 0 | 2 | .263 | .303 | .423 |
| Reinking, Kevin, Visalia | 31 | 120 | 105 | 14 | 18 | 31 | 2 | 1 | 3 | 8 | 3 | 1 | 4 | 7 | 0 | 41 | 0 | 0 | 3 | .171 | .248 | .295 |
| Reynolds, Mark, Lancaster | 4 | 12 | 12 | 1 | 1 | 1 | 0 | 0 | 0 | 1 | 0 | 0 | 0 | 0 | 0 | 4 | 0 | 0 | 0 | .083 | .083 | .083 |
| Richar, Danny, Lancaster | 96 | 417 | 383 | 51 | 108 | 147 | 13 | 4 | 6 | 44 | 13 | 3 | 2 | 16 | 0 | 78 | 22 | 8 | 2 | .282 | .312 | .384 |
| Richardson, Mike, Lake Elsinore | 78 | 332 | 280 | 47 | 72 | 119 | 12 | 1 | 11 | 47 | 1 | 3 | 4 | 44 | 0 | 70 | 1 | 3 | 4 | .257 | .363 | .425 |
| Rico, Matt, Bakersfield | 97 | 372 | 338 | 44 | 77 | 114 | 10 | 3 | 7 | 33 | 1 | 3 | 6 | 23 | 0 | 94 | 6 | 4 | 5 | .228 | .286 | .337 |
| Riggans, Shawn, Bakersfield | 34 | 144 | 127 | 20 | 44 | 70 | 11 | 0 | 5 | 22 | 0 | 1 | 1 | 15 | 0 | 23 | 0 | 1 | 3 | .346 | .417 | .551 |
| Riley, Ryan, Bakersfield | 5 | 20 | 16 | 2 | 3 | 3 | 0 | 0 | 0 | 0 | 0 | 0 | 2 | 2 | 0 | 4 | 1 | 0 | 0 | .188 | .350 | .188 |
| Ringe, Craig, Stockton | 105 | 407 | 338 | 54 | 78 | 114 | 21 | 3 | 3 | 41 | 2 | 7 | 9 | 51 | 0 | 99 | 5 | 2 | 9 | .231 | .341 | .337 |
| Rivera, Rene, Inland Empire | 107 | 424 | 379 | 41 | 89 | 131 | 22 | 1 | 6 | 53 | 4 | 4 | 9 | 28 | 1 | 70 | 0 | 1 | 17 | .235 | .300 | .346 |
| Robledo, Nelson, Visalia | 5 | 14 | 13 | 2 | 0 | 0 | 0 | 0 | 0 | 0 | 0 | 0 | 0 | 1 | 0 | 5 | 0 | 0 | 0 | .000 | .071 | .000 |
| Rodriguez, Javy, Rancho Cucamonga | 14 | 49 | 42 | 4 | 11 | 13 | 2 | 0 | 0 | 4 | 1 | 2 | 0 | 4 | 0 | 6 | 5 | 5 | 0 | .262 | .313 | .310 |
| Rogelstad, Matt, Inland Empire * | 106 | 421 | 375 | 43 | 93 | 119 | 8 | 6 | 2 | 41 | 5 | 3 | 8 | 30 | 0 | 57 | 5 | 3 | 11 | .248 | .315 | .317 |
| Rogers, Nick, Modesto | 5 | 12 | 9 | 1 | 1 | 1 | 0 | 0 | 0 | 0 | 0 | 0 | 1 | 2 | 0 | 5 | 0 | 0 | 0 | .111 | .333 | .111 |
| Roman, Jesse, Lake Elsinore * | 51 | 212 | 194 | 22 | 51 | 78 | 9 | 0 | 6 | 27 | 0 | 2 | 1 | 15 | 1 | 43 | 0 | 0 | 3 | .263 | .316 | .402 |
| Salazar, Jeff, Visalia * | 75 | 358 | 314 | 79 | 109 | 184 | 18 | 9 | 13 | 44 | 2 | 2 | 2 | 38 | 3 | 33 | 17 | 2 | 4 | .347 | .419 | .586 |
| Salmon, Tim, Rancho Cucamonga | 7 | 27 | 23 | 5 | 8 | 17 | 1 | 1 | 2 | 6 | 0 | 0 | 0 | 4 | 0 | 6 | 0 | 0 | 0 | .348 | .444 | .739 |
| Sandoval, Abigail, Stockton | 20 | 83 | 72 | 6 | 16 | 21 | 3 | 1 | 0 | 11 | 1 | 1 | 3 | 6 | 0 | 14 | 0 | 2 | 2 | .222 | .305 | .292 |
| Santana, Mayobanex, Modesto | 41 | 149 | 139 | 20 | 43 | 55 | 9 | 0 | 1 | 18 | 4 | 1 | 1 | 4 | 0 | 24 | 0 | 2 | 5 | .309 | .331 | .396 |
| Santana, Mayobanex, Lancaster | 20 | 71 | 64 | 10 | 14 | 18 | 1 | 0 | 1 | 9 | 0 | 1 | 1 | 5 | 0 | 12 | 1 | 1 | 3 | .219 | .282 | .281 |
| Sardinha, Duke, Visalia | 11 | 36 | 30 | 1 | 1 | 2 | 1 | 0 | 0 | 1 | 2 | 0 | 0 | 4 | 0 | 12 | 0 | 1 | 0 | .033 | .147 | .067 |
| Schierholtz, Nate, San Jose * | 62 | 281 | 258 | 39 | 76 | 121 | 18 | 9 | 3 | 31 | 3 | 2 | 3 | 15 | 1 | 41 | 3 | 1 | 6 | .295 | .338 | .469 |
| Schneidmiller, Gary, Modesto | 27 | 97 | 78 | 13 | 16 | 23 | 2 | 1 | 1 | 9 | 1 | 0 | 3 | 15 | 0 | 18 | 2 | 0 | 2 | .205 | .354 | .295 |
| Senreiso, Juan, Stockton | 56 | 250 | 233 | 36 | 69 | 103 | 12 | 2 | 6 | 32 | 0 | 0 | 2 | 15 | 0 | 47 | 12 | 5 | 8 | .296 | .344 | .442 |
| Serfass, Jake, High Desert | 9 | 26 | 25 | 4 | 3 | 4 | 1 | 0 | 0 | 4 | 0 | 0 | 0 | 1 | 0 | 6 | 0 | 0 | 0 | .120 | .154 | .160 |
| Serrano, Eddie, Lake Elsinore | 7 | 21 | 17 | 3 | 6 | 6 | 0 | 0 | 0 | 1 | 0 | 0 | 0 | 4 | 0 | 4 | 0 | 0 | 0 | .353 | .476 | .353 |
| Sevier, Nate, Lake Elsinore | 38 | 1 | 1 | 0 | 0 | 0 | 0 | 0 | 0 | 0 | 0 | 0 | 0 | 0 | 0 | 0 | 0 | 0 | 0 | .000 | .000 | .000 |
| Shelley, Randall, Stockton | 13 | 52 | 47 | 4 | 8 | 16 | 5 | 0 | 1 | 6 | 0 | 1 | 0 | 4 | 0 | 8 | 0 | 0 | 3 | .170 | .231 | .340 |
| Simon, Brandon, Lancaster * | 35 | 87 | 77 | 11 | 14 | 16 | 2 | 0 | 0 | 6 | 3 | 2 | 2 | 3 | 0 | 22 | 4 | 2 | 0 | .182 | .226 | .208 |
| Sinisi, Vincent, Stockton * | 63 | 287 | 248 | 39 | 77 | 117 | 13 | 3 | 7 | 40 | 0 | 6 | 0 | 33 | 1 | 45 | 7 | 3 | 7 | .310 | .383 | .472 |
| Slee, Gregory, Inland Empire * | 5 | 15 | 13 | 2 | 2 | 2 | 0 | 0 | 0 | 0 | 0 | 0 | 0 | 2 | 0 | 3 | 0 | 0 | 0 | .154 | .267 | .154 |
| Smith, Cody, Stockton | 37 | 16 | 15 | 0 | 4 | 7 | 3 | 0 | 0 | 0 | 0 | 0 | 1 | 0 | 0 | 0 | 0 | 0 | 2 | .267 | .313 | .467 |
| Smith, Dustin, Stockton | 57 | 221 | 194 | 29 | 65 | 97 | 12 | 1 | 6 | 21 | 1 | 0 | 8 | 18 | 2 | 31 | 1 | 2 | 6 | .335 | .414 | .500 |
| Smyres, Justin, Lake Elsinore | 16 | 56 | 46 | 11 | 11 | 21 | 3 | 2 | 1 | 9 | 0 | 0 | 2 | 8 | 0 | 10 | 0 | 0 | 2 | .239 | .375 | .457 |
| Sobieraj, Aaron, San Jose | 20 | 85 | 75 | 10 | 19 | 31 | 3 | 3 | 1 | 5 | 2 | 0 | 2 | 6 | 0 | 13 | 1 | 1 | 1 | .253 | .325 | .413 |
| Sosa, Carlos, San Jose | 97 | 387 | 344 | 50 | 87 | 145 | 16 | 6 | 10 | 46 | 1 | 2 | 4 | 36 | 1 | 101 | 7 | 1 | 7 | .253 | .329 | .422 |
| Spiezio, Scott, Inland Empire † | 2 | 6 | 5 | 0 | 0 | 0 | 0 | 0 | 0 | 1 | 0 | 1 | 0 | 0 | 0 | 1 | 0 | 0 | 0 | .000 | .000 | .000 |
| Spilborghs, Ryan, Visalia | 125 | 520 | 444 | 59 | 115 | 171 | 26 | 3 | 8 | 57 | 2 | 4 | 6 | 64 | 0 | 98 | 8 | 6 | 13 | .259 | .357 | .385 |
| St. Clair, Jason, Bakersfield | 6 | 17 | 15 | 1 | 0 | 0 | 0 | 0 | 0 | 0 | 0 | 0 | 2 | 0 | 0 | 7 | 0 | 1 | 0 | .000 | .118 | .000 |
| Stavisky, Brian, Modesto * | 130 | 585 | 513 | 108 | 176 | 282 | 39 | 5 | 19 | 83 | 2 | 5 | 11 | 54 | 3 | 89 | 6 | 4 | 7 | .343 | .413 | .550 |
| Street, Dan, Visalia | 10 | 38 | 35 | 6 | 7 | 13 | 4 | 1 | 0 | 2 | 0 | 0 | 1 | 2 | 0 | 10 | 0 | 0 | 2 | .200 | .263 | .371 |
| Strong, Zach, San Jose † | 39 | 135 | 122 | 12 | 30 | 39 | 9 | 0 | 0 | 15 | 2 | 2 | 2 | 7 | 0 | 33 | 0 | 1 | 3 | .246 | .293 | .320 |
| Sugden, Jason, Rancho Cucamonga † | 78 | 236 | 214 | 33 | 51 | 76 | 8 | 7 | 1 | 27 | 4 | 0 | 6 | 12 | 0 | 71 | 2 | 2 | 0 | .238 | .297 | .355 |
| Suomi, John, Modesto * | 134 | 599 | 545 | 84 | 161 | 240 | 35 | 4 | 12 | 99 | 2 | 7 | 4 | 41 | 2 | 72 | 3 | 1 | 18 | .295 | .345 | .440 |
| Sutton, Don, Modesto | 12 | 48 | 40 | 7 | 7 | 10 | 3 | 0 | 0 | 9 | 0 | 2 | 1 | 5 | 0 | 10 | 0 | 0 | 2 | .175 | .271 | .250 |
| Swope, Tobin, Stockton | 3 | 11 | 9 | 2 | 3 | 3 | 0 | 0 | 0 | 1 | 0 | 0 | 1 | 1 | 0 | 2 | 0 | 0 | 0 | .333 | .455 | .333 |
| Taylor, Seth, Stockton | 7 | 27 | 26 | 1 | 6 | 8 | 2 | 0 | 0 | 3 | 0 | 0 | 1 | 0 | 0 | 9 | 0 | 0 | 0 | .231 | .259 | .308 |
| Tejeda, Ferdin, Lake Elsinore | 14 | 43 | 35 | 6 | 9 | 9 | 0 | 0 | 0 | 4 | 0 | 0 | 0 | 8 | 0 | 8 | 1 | 2 | 1 | .257 | .395 | .257 |
| Tena, Hector, Visalia | 104 | 407 | 362 | 37 | 88 | 130 | 19 | 4 | 5 | 38 | 10 | 2 | 11 | 22 | 0 | 79 | 3 | 2 | 8 | .243 | .305 | .359 |
| Timpner, Clay, San Jose * | 6 | 27 | 25 | 4 | 7 | 9 | 2 | 0 | 0 | 2 | 0 | 1 | 0 | 1 | 0 | 2 | 1 | 0 | 0 | .280 | .296 | .360 |
| Tosca, Daniel, Lancaster * | 85 | 297 | 250 | 26 | 63 | 98 | 14 | 0 | 7 | 37 | 4 | 2 | 4 | 37 | 2 | 61 | 3 | 4 | 7 | .252 | .355 | .392 |
| Trumble, Dan, San Jose | 95 | 400 | 334 | 56 | 80 | 151 | 16 | 2 | 17 | 48 | 2 | 6 | 10 | 48 | 3 | 119 | 12 | 8 | 1 | .240 | .347 | .452 |
| Turner, Justin, Rancho Cucamonga * | 19 | 75 | 67 | 9 | 13 | 21 | 2 | 0 | 2 | 5 | 0 | 1 | 1 | 6 | 1 | 23 | 1 | 0 | 0 | .194 | .267 | .313 |
| Turner, Lloyd, Modesto | 125 | 599 | 535 | 81 | 156 | 201 | 31 | 4 | 2 | 51 | 12 | 4 | 12 | 36 | 0 | 70 | 27 | 7 | 8 | .292 | .348 | .376 |

| Player, Team | G | TPA | AB | R | H | TB | 2B | 3B | HR | RBI | SH | SF | HP | BB | IBB | SO | SB | CS | GDP | Avg. | OBP | Slg. |
|---|---|---|---|---|---|---|---|---|---|---|---|---|---|---|---|---|---|---|---|---|---|---|
| Uggla, Dan, Lancaster | 37 | 162 | 140 | 29 | 47 | 84 | 13 | 3 | 6 | 38 | 1 | 0 | 4 | 17 | 1 | 21 | 2 | 4 | 0 | .336 | .422 | .600 |
| Van Iderstine, Ben, High Desert * | 46 | 204 | 191 | 23 | 71 | 94 | 15 | 1 | 2 | 17 | 1 | 2 | 2 | 8 | 1 | 19 | 1 | 1 | 5 | .372 | .399 | .492 |
| Vanden berg, John, High Desert | 73 | 288 | 256 | 34 | 71 | 109 | 16 | 2 | 6 | 32 | 0 | 1 | 2 | 29 | 0 | 65 | 1 | 0 | 4 | .277 | .354 | .426 |
| Vericker, Brad, San Jose * | 99 | 429 | 358 | 54 | 99 | 176 | 29 | 3 | 14 | 76 | 0 | 9 | 2 | 60 | 3 | 83 | 0 | 2 | 6 | .277 | .375 | .492 |
| Villanueva, Froilan, High Desert | 70 | 295 | 272 | 43 | 72 | 130 | 17 | 1 | 13 | 39 | 3 | 3 | 6 | 11 | 0 | 38 | 0 | 3 | 10 | .265 | .305 | .478 |
| Wald, Jake, San Jose | 44 | 165 | 147 | 18 | 29 | 39 | 5 | 1 | 1 | 13 | 1 | 1 | 6 | 10 | 0 | 33 | 4 | 1 | 2 | .197 | .274 | .265 |
| Walter, Randy, San Jose | 89 | 336 | 300 | 43 | 79 | 121 | 14 | 5 | 6 | 34 | 2 | 2 | 6 | 24 | 1 | 79 | 10 | 3 | 1 | .263 | .328 | .403 |
| Watson, Rob, Lake Elsinore | 3 | 12 | 11 | 1 | 0 | 0 | 0 | 0 | 0 | 2 | 0 | 1 | 0 | 0 | 0 | 1 | 0 | 0 | 1 | .000 | .000 | .000 |
| Webster, Anthony, Stockton * | 99 | 429 | 380 | 66 | 109 | 167 | 20 | 7 | 8 | 44 | 2 | 1 | 7 | 39 | 0 | 69 | 20 | 4 | 6 | .287 | .363 | .439 |
| Weed, B.J., Rancho Cucamonga † | 122 | 475 | 447 | 47 | 125 | 158 | 14 | 5 | 3 | 52 | 8 | 5 | 2 | 13 | 1 | 54 | 19 | 8 | 6 | .280 | .300 | .353 |
| Willits, Reggie, Rancho Cucamonga † | 135 | 625 | 526 | 99 | 149 | 191 | 17 | 5 | 5 | 52 | 8 | 10 | 8 | 73 | 1 | 112 | 44 | 15 | 9 | .283 | .373 | .363 |
| Zamora, Pete, Lancaster * | 13 | 2 | 2 | 0 | 0 | 0 | 0 | 0 | 0 | 0 | 0 | 0 | 0 | 0 | 0 | 1 | 0 | 0 | 0 | .000 | .000 | .000 |
| Zeringue, Jonathan, Lancaster | 56 | 247 | 230 | 36 | 77 | 127 | 14 | 3 | 10 | 41 | 1 | 1 | 1 | 14 | 1 | 53 | 9 | 5 | 2 | .335 | .374 | .552 |

GRAND SLAMS—N. Cruz, Fallon, 2 each; Avlas, Baker, Brooks, Cordell, E. Cruz, D'Antona, Ethier, Farnsworth, Gold, Hagen, Hinton, Holm, Jackson, Lewis, Mateo, Perry, Salazar, 1 each.

AWARDED FIRST BASE ON CATCHER'S INTERFERENCE—Barker 6 (Jennings, Hamblen, Esposito, Hamblen, Hamblen, Avlas); Arroyo 3 (Villanueva, Avlas, Berg); Avlas (Aracena); Ball (Pagan); Hagen (Avlas); Melgarejo (Avlas); Reinking (Avlas); Suomi (Merritt); Uggla (Merritt); Walter (Aracena).

# 2004 PITCHING

## TEAM

| Team | W | L | Pct. | ERA | G | CG | ShO | Sv. | IP | H | TBF | R | ER | HR | SH | SF | HB | BB | IBB | SO | WP | Bk. |
|---|---|---|---|---|---|---|---|---|---|---|---|---|---|---|---|---|---|---|---|---|---|---|
| San Jose | 74 | 66 | .529 | 3.92 | 140 | 0 | 7 | 32 | 1269.2 | 1279 | 5457 | 646 | 553 | 107 | 50 | 40 | 69 | 419 | 7 | 1062 | 78 | 5 |
| Inland Empire | 77 | 63 | .550 | 4.08 | 140 | 3 | 9 | 38 | 1236.1 | 1303 | 5324 | 665 | 561 | 100 | 48 | 42 | 64 | 352 | 5 | 1128 | 68 | 12 |
| Lake Elsinore | 68 | 72 | .486 | 4.19 | 140 | 1 | 4 | 35 | 1247.0 | 1264 | 5462 | 716 | 580 | 89 | 45 | 48 | 51 | 480 | 6 | 1014 | 60 | 5 |
| Modesto | 90 | 50 | .643 | 4.22 | 140 | 0 | 5 | 43 | 1264.2 | 1307 | 5553 | 699 | 593 | 98 | 49 | 47 | 69 | 469 | 20 | 1018 | 75 | 11 |
| Stockton | 72 | 68 | .514 | 4.29 | 140 | 1 | 7 | 30 | 1232.1 | 1274 | 5422 | 700 | 588 | 90 | 33 | 58 | 89 | 465 | 8 | 893 | 92 | 7 |
| Rancho Cuca | 69 | 71 | .493 | 4.44 | 140 | 4 | 2 | 33 | 1245.1 | 1348 | 5465 | 737 | 615 | 126 | 32 | 38 | 75 | 447 | 7 | 977 | 55 | 8 |
| Bakersfield | 59 | 81 | .421 | 4.56 | 140 | 1 | 8 | 32 | 1236.2 | 1331 | 5536 | 735 | 627 | 96 | 44 | 41 | 95 | 593 | 17 | 1012 | 111 | 8 |
| Lancaster | 86 | 54 | .614 | 4.68 | 140 | 2 | 6 | 41 | 1243.1 | 1404 | 5567 | 760 | 647 | 120 | 40 | 42 | 72 | 480 | 19 | 997 | 60 | 5 |
| Visalia | 56 | 84 | .400 | 5.46 | 140 | 3 | 2 | 29 | 1244.1 | 1493 | 5679 | 861 | 755 | 138 | 46 | 57 | 4 | 459 | 13 | 943 | 85 | 8 |
| High Desert | 49 | 91 | .350 | 5.78 | 140 | 1 | 3 | 23 | 1236.2 | 1517 | 5708 | 955 | 794 | 148 | 55 | 49 | 90 | 482 | 9 | 1119 | 98 | 8 |

## INDIVIDUAL

### TOP QUALIFIERS FOR EARNED-RUN AVERAGE TITLE

Minimum 112 innings.*Lefthanded pitcher.

| Pitcher, Team | W | L | Pct. | ERA | G | GS | CG | ShO | GF | Sv. | IP | H | TBF | R | ER | HR | SH | SF | HB | BB | IBB | SO | WP | Bk. |
|---|---|---|---|---|---|---|---|---|---|---|---|---|---|---|---|---|---|---|---|---|---|---|---|---|
| Burres, Brian, San Jose * | 12 | 1 | .923 | 2.84 | 36 | 15 | 0 | 0 | 6 | 0 | 123.2 | 115 | 506 | 49 | 39 | 10 | 4 | 4 | 7 | 30 | 0 | 114 | 6 | 0 |
| Gonzalez, Enrique, Lancaster | 13 | 6 | .684 | 3.22 | 42 | 17 | 0 | 0 | 5 | 0 | 142.1 | 128 | 586 | 64 | 51 | 13 | 5 | 3 | 6 | 44 | 0 | 110 | 3 | 0 |
| Livingston, Bobby, Inland Empire * | 12 | 6 | .667 | 3.57 | 28 | 27 | 1 | 1 | 0 | 0 | 186.2 | 187 | 762 | 90 | 74 | 15 | 8 | 4 | 7 | 30 | 0 | 141 | 4 | 0 |
| Shell, Steven, Rancho Cucamonga | 12 | 7 | .632 | 3.59 | 28 | 28 | 2 | 1 | 0 | 0 | 165.1 | 151 | 672 | 76 | 66 | 19 | 6 | 2 | 16 | 40 | 0 | 190 | 4 | 1 |
| Smith, Cody, Stockton | 3 | 6 | .333 | 3.91 | 32 | 17 | 1 | 0 | 5 | 2 | 124.1 | 161 | 558 | 61 | 54 | 3 | 4 | 5 | 5 | 31 | 0 | 60 | 5 | 0 |
| Lynch, Matt, Modesto * | 13 | 3 | .813 | 3.93 | 27 | 27 | 0 | 0 | 0 | 0 | 151.1 | 165 | 655 | 75 | 66 | 9 | 9 | 8 | 4 | 38 | 0 | 111 | 6 | 0 |
| Sandoval, Juan, Inland Empire | 11 | 11 | .500 | 4.12 | 27 | 27 | 1 | 0 | 0 | 0 | 168.1 | 184 | 712 | 91 | 77 | 21 | 10 | 5 | 9 | 43 | 0 | 119 | 7 | 1 |
| Littleton, Wes, Stockton | 8 | 10 | .444 | 4.15 | 30 | 23 | 0 | 0 | 1 | 0 | 141.0 | 139 | 600 | 76 | 65 | 7 | 8 | 15 | 11 | 56 | 0 | 72 | 14 | 0 |
| Pauley, David, Lake Elsinore | 7 | 12 | .368 | 4.17 | 27 | 26 | 0 | 0 | 0 | 0 | 153.1 | 155 | 665 | 89 | 71 | 8 | 8 | 9 | 8 | 60 | 0 | 128 | 6 | 0 |
| Shields, Jamie, Bakersfield | 8 | 5 | .615 | 4.23 | 20 | 20 | 1 | 1 | 0 | 0 | 117.0 | 119 | 488 | 61 | 55 | 13 | 4 | 5 | 9 | 33 | 0 | 92 | 6 | 0 |
| McNiven, Brooks, San Jose | 6 | 8 | .429 | 4.35 | 31 | 21 | 0 | 0 | 2 | 0 | 134.1 | 162 | 592 | 74 | 65 | 13 | 10 | 6 | 4 | 32 | 0 | 73 | 4 | 0 |
| Silva, Jesus, Lancaster | 11 | 7 | .611 | 4.38 | 28 | 27 | 0 | 0 | 1 | 0 | 152.0 | 168 | 663 | 89 | 74 | 16 | 9 | 5 | 5 | 56 | 0 | 126 | 7 | 2 |
| Sauer, Marc, Modesto | 11 | 2 | .846 | 4.51 | 24 | 19 | 0 | 0 | 0 | 0 | 115.2 | 118 | 491 | 67 | 58 | 10 | 4 | 5 | 7 | 33 | 0 | 89 | 1 | 1 |
| Davidson, Daniel, Rancho Cucamonga * | 12 | 7 | .632 | 4.57 | 28 | 28 | 0 | 0 | 0 | 0 | 163.1 | 196 | 699 | 92 | 83 | 15 | 7 | 11 | 9 | 41 | 0 | 121 | 3 | 2 |
| Sullivan, Bradley, Modesto | 8 | 11 | .421 | 4.65 | 27 | 27 | 0 | 0 | 0 | 0 | 147.0 | 180 | 660 | 89 | 76 | 13 | 11 | 5 | 9 | 48 | 0 | 99 | 10 | 0 |

DEPARTMENTAL LEADERS: W—E. Gonzalez, Lynch, 13; L—Comolli, 15; Pct.—Lynch, .813; G—Wells, 71; GS—three pitchers with, 28; CG—three pitchers with, 2; ShO—five pitchers with, 1; GF—N/A; Sv.—Accardo, 27; IP—Livingston, 186.2; H—Crockett, 210; TBF—Crockett, 763; R—Crockett, 123; ER—Crockett, 107; HR—Ballouli, 23; SH—N/A; SF—N/A; HB—Comolli, 25; BB—Comolli, 131; IBB—N/A; SO—Shell, 190; WP—Comolli, 25; BK—Soto, 4.

### ALL PITCHERS

*Lefthanded pitcher.

| Pitcher, Team | W | L | Pct. | ERA | G | GS | CG | ShO | GF | Sv. | IP | H | TBF | R | ER | HR | SH | SF | HB | BB | IBB | SO | WP | Bk. |
|---|---|---|---|---|---|---|---|---|---|---|---|---|---|---|---|---|---|---|---|---|---|---|---|---|
| Accardo, Jeremy, San Jose | 1 | 2 | .333 | 4.25 | 50 | 0 | 0 | 0 | 44 | 27 | 55.0 | 57 | 238 | 28 | 26 | 3 | 0 | 0 | 1 | 15 | 1 | 43 | 4 | 0 |
| Akens, Phil, Stockton | 4 | 0 | 1.000 | 3.79 | 18 | 1 | 0 | 0 | 3 | 0 | 38.0 | 42 | 173 | 21 | 16 | 3 | 0 | 1 | 3 | 16 | 0 | 37 | 4 | 0 |
| Allen, Brian, Bakersfield | 1 | 1 | .500 | 4.30 | 11 | 0 | 0 | 0 | 4 | 0 | 23.0 | 27 | 100 | 15 | 11 | 1 | 0 | 0 | 0 | 7 | 1 | 18 | 4 | 1 |
| Alliston, Josh, High Desert | 0 | 0 | .000 | 0.00 | 1 | 0 | 0 | 0 | 0 | 0 | 0.1 | 0 | 1 | 0 | 0 | 0 | 0 | 0 | 0 | 0 | 0 | 0 | 0 | 0 |
| Andrew, Jason, Stockton | 5 | 2 | .714 | 1.59 | 8 | 5 | 0 | 0 | 1 | 0 | 34.0 | 25 | 135 | 10 | 6 | 0 | 0 | 2 | 2 | 7 | 0 | 20 | 2 | 0 |
| Arakawa, Yusuke, Visalia | 3 | 3 | .500 | 3.03 | 29 | 0 | 0 | 0 | 6 | 0 | 38.2 | 40 | 172 | 16 | 13 | 2 | 0 | 0 | 3 | 13 | 1 | 37 | 2 | 0 |
| Asahina, Jonathan, Visalia | 4 | 9 | .308 | 5.40 | 34 | 22 | 0 | 0 | 2 | 0 | 135.0 | 165 | 604 | 94 | 81 | 12 | 9 | 5 | 9 | 46 | 0 | 71 | 13 | 2 |
| Astacio, Hector, Rancho Cucamonga | 1 | 1 | .500 | 5.54 | 16 | 1 | 0 | 0 | 7 | 0 | 26.0 | 24 | 110 | 20 | 16 | 1 | 1 | 1 | 4 | 7 | 0 | 20 | 2 | 1 |
| Austen, David, Rancho Cucamonga | 0 | 1 | .000 | 6.08 | 17 | 0 | 0 | 0 | 4 | 1 | 23.2 | 37 | 119 | 23 | 16 | 5 | 0 | 1 | 1 | 10 | 0 | 18 | 0 | 0 |
| Autrey, Scott, Bakersfield | 3 | 7 | .300 | 3.81 | 15 | 15 | 0 | 0 | 0 | 0 | 80.1 | 91 | 336 | 44 | 34 | 6 | 2 | 9 | 5 | 20 | 1 | 67 | 5 | 1 |
| Avendano, Elvis, Modesto | 7 | 4 | .636 | 2.95 | 45 | 1 | 0 | 0 | 14 | 2 | 73.1 | 63 | 305 | 34 | 24 | 4 | 0 | 2 | 3 | 20 | 4 | 46 | 4 | 0 |
| Ballouli, Khalid, High Desert | 6 | 14 | .300 | 5.95 | 27 | 25 | 0 | 0 | 1 | 0 | 137.2 | 182 | 616 | 106 | 91 | 23 | 6 | 8 | 9 | 34 | 0 | 128 | 13 | 2 |
| Bass, Adam, Lancaster | 10 | 8 | .556 | 5.03 | 28 | 27 | 1 | 0 | 0 | 0 | 146.2 | 180 | 641 | 90 | 82 | 12 | 8 | 9 | 9 | 49 | 0 | 117 | 6 | 2 |
| Beavers, Kevin, Lake Elsinore * | 2 | 6 | .250 | 5.28 | 33 | 8 | 0 | 0 | 4 | 0 | 75.0 | 82 | 342 | 53 | 44 | 9 | 3 | 1 | 2 | 33 | 1 | 44 | 3 | 0 |
| Bechtel, Charles, Lake Elsinore | 0 | 0 | .000 | 3.77 | 7 | 0 | 0 | 0 | 2 | 1 | 14.1 | 15 | 63 | 9 | 6 | 1 | 0 | 0 | 0 | 5 | 0 | 9 | 2 | 0 |
| Beckstead, Jentry, Visalia | 3 | 6 | .333 | 4.18 | 40 | 0 | 0 | 0 | 25 | 9 | 56.0 | 65 | 249 | 33 | 26 | 6 | 1 | 0 | 0 | 16 | 1 | 55 | 6 | 0 |
| Belson, Greg, Lancaster | 3 | 1 | .750 | 6.34 | 29 | 0 | 0 | 0 | 10 | 1 | 38.1 | 51 | 189 | 37 | 27 | 2 | 0 | 0 | 0 | 23 | 1 | 23 | 3 | 0 |
| Beltre, Omar, Stockton | 5 | 5 | .500 | 2.45 | 46 | 0 | 0 | 0 | 22 | 6 | 58.2 | 60 | 262 | 32 | 16 | 1 | 0 | 0 | 3 | 24 | 1 | 47 | 6 | 1 |

| Pitcher, Team | W | L | Pct. | ERA | G | GS | CG | ShO | GF | Sv. | IP | H | TBF | R | ER | HR | SH | SF | HB | BB | IBB | SO | WP | Bk. |
|---|---|---|---|---|---|---|---|---|---|---|---|---|---|---|---|---|---|---|---|---|---|---|---|---|
| Bengochea, Kiki, Stockton | 1 | 5 | .167 | 7.55 | 19 | 5 | 0 | 0 | 5 | 0 | 47.2 | 63 | 225 | 45 | 40 | 9 | 1 | 3 | 6 | 19 | 0 | 39 | 7 | 0 |
| Bernier, Doug, Visalia | 0 | 0 | .000 | 9.00 | 1 | 0 | 0 | 0 | 1 | 0 | 1.0 | 1 | 4 | 1 | 1 | 1 | 0 | 0 | 0 | 0 | 0 | 1 | 0 | 0 |
| Bilke, Austin, Rancho Cucamonga | 0 | 1 | .000 | 6.11 | 25 | 0 | 0 | 0 | 13 | 6 | 28.0 | 29 | 133 | 19 | 19 | 3 | 0 | 0 | 1 | 18 | 0 | 16 | 2 | 0 |
| Bonine, Eddie, Lake Elsinore | 5 | 10 | .333 | 5.45 | 21 | 21 | 0 | 0 | 0 | 0 | 112.1 | 121 | 492 | 82 | 68 | 12 | 7 | 9 | 8 | 39 | 0 | 96 | 12 | 0 |
| Bradley, Dave, High Desert | 7 | 11 | .389 | 4.76 | 30 | 22 | 0 | 0 | 7 | 1 | 138.0 | 151 | 625 | 93 | 73 | 10 | 8 | 4 | 10 | 54 | 1 | 129 | 12 | 0 |
| Brannon, Nick, Modesto * | 0 | 0 | .000 | 3.45 | 15 | 0 | 0 | 0 | 7 | 0 | 15.2 | 10 | 69 | 6 | 6 | 2 | 0 | 0 | 0 | 12 | 0 | 17 | 1 | 0 |
| Breslow, Craig, High Desert * | 1 | 3 | .250 | 7.19 | 23 | 0 | 0 | 0 | 9 | 0 | 41.1 | 54 | 203 | 39 | 33 | 5 | 0 | 0 | 2 | 24 | 0 | 41 | 4 | 0 |
| Broshuis, Garrett, San Jose | 4 | 3 | .571 | 5.19 | 10 | 8 | 0 | 0 | 0 | 0 | 52.0 | 60 | 228 | 32 | 30 | 4 | 5 | 2 | 6 | 16 | 0 | 47 | 3 | 0 |
| Bruso, Greg, High Desert | 1 | 7 | .125 | 5.48 | 12 | 12 | 0 | 0 | 0 | 0 | 65.2 | 82 | 294 | 50 | 40 | 6 | 8 | 1 | 5 | 12 | 0 | 50 | 2 | 0 |
| Bulger, Jason, Lancaster | 0 | 1 | .000 | 1.52 | 21 | 0 | 0 | 0 | 18 | 11 | 23.2 | 14 | 98 | 4 | 4 | 0 | 0 | 0 | 3 | 10 | 1 | 31 | 0 | 0 |
| Bumstead, Mike, Lake Elsinore | 1 | 0 | 1.000 | 1.23 | 9 | 0 | 0 | 0 | 2 | 0 | 14.2 | 10 | 59 | 2 | 2 | 0 | 0 | 0 | 0 | 5 | 0 | 13 | 1 | 0 |
| Burres, Brian, San Jose * | 12 | 1 | .923 | 2.84 | 36 | 15 | 0 | 0 | 6 | 0 | 123.2 | 115 | 506 | 49 | 39 | 10 | 4 | 4 | 7 | 30 | 0 | 114 | 6 | 0 |
| Burton, Jared, Modesto | 3 | 2 | .600 | 4.78 | 10 | 3 | 0 | 0 | 1 | 0 | 32.0 | 34 | 147 | 19 | 17 | 6 | 0 | 0 | 1 | 20 | 1 | 25 | 4 | 0 |
| Bystrowski, Bobby, Modesto | 0 | 0 | .000 | 8.16 | 12 | 0 | 0 | 0 | 6 | 0 | 14.1 | 19 | 72 | 13 | 13 | 3 | 0 | 0 | 3 | 8 | 0 | 11 | 2 | 1 |
| Cabaniel, Tomas, Modesto | 3 | 1 | .750 | 6.00 | 12 | 11 | 0 | 0 | 1 | 0 | 48.0 | 52 | 218 | 37 | 32 | 0 | 4 | 6 | 7 | 26 | 0 | 28 | 6 | 1 |
| Cable, Taft, Visalia | 5 | 7 | .417 | 5.30 | 39 | 7 | 0 | 0 | 6 | 1 | 107.0 | 117 | 488 | 69 | 63 | 15 | 2 | 4 | 8 | 49 | 2 | 93 | 5 | 0 |
| Cain, Matt, San Jose | 7 | 1 | .875 | 1.86 | 13 | 13 | 0 | 0 | 0 | 0 | 72.2 | 58 | 294 | 25 | 15 | 5 | 0 | 4 | 4 | 17 | 0 | 89 | 0 | 0 |
| Capuano, Chris, High Desert * | 0 | 1 | .000 | 27.00 | 1 | 1 | 0 | 0 | 0 | 0 | 2.0 | 6 | 15 | 6 | 6 | 1 | 0 | 0 | 0 | 3 | 0 | 2 | 0 | 0 |
| Carroll, James, Rancho Cucamonga | 4 | 3 | .571 | 4.10 | 47 | 0 | 0 | 0 | 11 | 1 | 68.0 | 76 | 323 | 45 | 31 | 5 | 0 | 0 | 10 | 33 | 0 | 33 | 2 | 0 |
| Cartier, Richard, Visalia | 6 | 10 | .375 | 6.60 | 32 | 19 | 0 | 0 | 4 | 0 | 106.1 | 129 | 493 | 91 | 78 | 18 | 5 | 5 | 8 | 54 | 1 | 55 | 9 | 1 |
| Castillo, Ruben, Inland Empire | 1 | 0 | 1.000 | 0.00 | 5 | 0 | 0 | 0 | 4 | 0 | 7.0 | 4 | 26 | 1 | 0 | 0 | 0 | 0 | 0 | 1 | 0 | 4 | 0 | 0 |
| Castleman, Steve, Visalia | 0 | 0 | .000 | 3.21 | 9 | 0 | 0 | 0 | 4 | 0 | 14.0 | 16 | 62 | 6 | 5 | 1 | 0 | 0 | 1 | 3 | 0 | 10 | 1 | 0 |
| Cate, Troy, Inland Empire * | 3 | 0 | 1.000 | 2.61 | 7 | 3 | 0 | 0 | 0 | 0 | 20.2 | 21 | 85 | 8 | 6 | 2 | 1 | 0 | 0 | 6 | 0 | 24 | 0 | 0 |
| Ciccotelli, Michael, Inland Empire * | 0 | 0 | .000 | 9.00 | 1 | 0 | 0 | 0 | 1 | 0 | 2.0 | 4 | 10 | 2 | 2 | 0 | 0 | 0 | 0 | 0 | 0 | 1 | 0 | 0 |
| Clarke, Darren, Visalia | 1 | 3 | .250 | 7.39 | 8 | 7 | 0 | 0 | 0 | 0 | 35.1 | 54 | 181 | 35 | 29 | 6 | 2 | 3 | 2 | 16 | 0 | 27 | 5 | 1 |
| Coleman, Jeff, Modesto | 4 | 3 | .571 | 2.49 | 45 | 0 | 0 | 0 | 40 | 23 | 61.1 | 41 | 249 | 18 | 17 | 3 | 2 | 1 | 4 | 22 | 2 | 58 | 1 | 0 |
| Comolli, Mark, Bakersfield | 4 | 15 | .211 | 7.74 | 29 | 23 | 0 | 0 | 5 | 0 | 116.1 | 136 | 613 | 118 | 100 | 10 | 9 | 7 | 25 | 131 | 0 | 83 | 25 | 0 |
| Coonrod, Aaron, Lake Elsinore | 3 | 2 | .600 | 3.51 | 22 | 1 | 0 | 0 | 7 | 0 | 33.1 | 27 | 147 | 17 | 13 | 3 | 0 | 0 | 1 | 19 | 0 | 37 | 3 | 0 |
| Cordell, Brent, Bakersfield | 0 | 0 | .000 | 0.00 | 1 | 0 | 0 | 0 | 1 | 0 | 1.0 | 2 | 5 | 0 | 0 | 0 | 0 | 0 | 0 | 0 | 0 | 1 | 0 | 0 |
| Cornejo, Eduardo, Modesto | 0 | 0 | .000 | 9.00 | 1 | 0 | 0 | 0 | 1 | 0 | 1.0 | 1 | 4 | 1 | 1 | 1 | 0 | 0 | 0 | 0 | 0 | 0 | 0 | 0 |
| Cosgrove, Mike, Visalia | 3 | 2 | .600 | 1.96 | 33 | 0 | 0 | 0 | 30 | 16 | 36.2 | 30 | 154 | 10 | 8 | 0 | 1 | 0 | 2 | 12 | 2 | 31 | 0 | 1 |
| Costello, Ryan, High Desert * | 1 | 3 | .250 | 9.92 | 6 | 2 | 0 | 0 | 2 | 0 | 16.1 | 19 | 78 | 19 | 18 | 4 | 0 | 0 | 2 | 9 | 0 | 15 | 3 | 2 |
| Craker, Justin, Lake Elsinore | 2 | 1 | .667 | 9.88 | 9 | 0 | 0 | 0 | 2 | 0 | 13.2 | 14 | 72 | 16 | 15 | 2 | 0 | 0 | 2 | 18 | 0 | 9 | 2 | 1 |
| Cram, Josh, San Jose | 2 | 0 | 1.000 | 5.16 | 41 | 0 | 0 | 0 | 12 | 0 | 59.1 | 70 | 277 | 36 | 34 | 5 | 5 | 1 | 10 | 23 | 1 | 29 | 10 | 0 |
| Crockett, Ben, Visalia | 4 | 11 | .267 | 5.56 | 28 | 28 | 2 | 1 | 0 | 0 | 173.1 | 210 | 763 | 123 | 107 | 19 | 9 | 11 | 18 | 36 | 0 | 120 | 9 | 0 |
| Cromer, Nathan, Bakersfield * | 2 | 3 | .400 | 6.16 | 37 | 1 | 0 | 0 | 12 | 0 | 68.2 | 112 | 341 | 57 | 47 | 10 | 1 | 1 | 1 | 26 | 0 | 43 | 7 | 0 |
| Danks, John, Stockton * | 1 | 4 | .200 | 5.24 | 13 | 13 | 0 | 0 | 0 | 0 | 55.0 | 62 | 247 | 38 | 32 | 5 | 3 | 6 | 1 | 26 | 0 | 48 | 3 | 1 |
| Davidson, Daniel, Rancho Cucamonga * | 12 | 7 | .632 | 4.57 | 28 | 28 | 0 | 0 | 0 | 0 | 163.1 | 196 | 699 | 92 | 83 | 15 | 7 | 11 | 9 | 41 | 0 | 121 | 3 | 2 |
| De Los Santos, Francisco, Stockton | 1 | 0 | 1.000 | 0.00 | 3 | 0 | 0 | 0 | 1 | 0 | 6.0 | 2 | 28 | 0 | 0 | 0 | 0 | 0 | 0 | 8 | 0 | 4 | 0 | 0 |
| DeBarr, Nick, Bakersfield | 1 | 4 | .200 | 4.91 | 26 | 10 | 0 | 0 | 2 | 1 | 66.0 | 59 | 310 | 41 | 36 | 6 | 4 | 2 | 8 | 55 | 0 | 45 | 13 | 0 |
| Deago, Roger, Lake Elsinore * | 0 | 0 | .000 | 0.00 | 1 | 0 | 0 | 0 | 0 | 0 | 1.2 | 1 | 6 | 0 | 0 | 0 | 0 | 0 | 0 | 0 | 0 | 3 | 0 | 0 |
| DiAngelo, Jason, Visalia | 0 | 0 | .000 | 3.86 | 4 | 0 | 0 | 0 | 2 | 0 | 7.0 | 7 | 28 | 3 | 3 | 1 | 0 | 0 | 0 | 0 | 0 | 6 | 1 | 0 |
| Dittfurth, Ryan, Stockton | 0 | 1 | .000 | 24.55 | 6 | 1 | 0 | 0 | 0 | 0 | 7.1 | 13 | 52 | 21 | 20 | 3 | 0 | 0 | 2 | 15 | 0 | 9 | 4 | 0 |
| Donnelly, Brendan, Rancho Cucamonga | 0 | 0 | .000 | 0.00 | 2 | 0 | 0 | 0 | 1 | 0 | 3.0 | 3 | 13 | 0 | 0 | 0 | 0 | 0 | 0 | 1 | 0 | 5 | 1 | 0 |
| Dorman, Rich, Inland Empire | 3 | 2 | .600 | 2.68 | 7 | 7 | 0 | 0 | 0 | 0 | 37.0 | 35 | 164 | 13 | 11 | 0 | 4 | 4 | 2 | 12 | 0 | 36 | 3 | 1 |
| Dowdy, Justin, Rancho Cucamonga * | 2 | 3 | .400 | 4.11 | 15 | 3 | 0 | 0 | 2 | 0 | 30.2 | 27 | 132 | 15 | 14 | 5 | 0 | 0 | 2 | 17 | 0 | 32 | 2 | 0 |
| Doyle, Jared, Lancaster * | 1 | 2 | .333 | 11.39 | 8 | 5 | 0 | 0 | 0 | 0 | 21.1 | 39 | 112 | 29 | 27 | 4 | 0 | 2 | 2 | 10 | 0 | 11 | 0 | 0 |
| Dufner, Kris, Bakersfield | 0 | 0 | .000 | 0.00 | 1 | 0 | 0 | 0 | 1 | 0 | 1.0 | 2 | 5 | 0 | 0 | 0 | 0 | 0 | 0 | 0 | 0 | 0 | 0 | 0 |
| Espineli, Eugene, San Jose * | 0 | 0 | .000 | 0.00 | 1 | 0 | 0 | 0 | 1 | 1 | 1.0 | 0 | 3 | 0 | 0 | 0 | 0 | 0 | 0 | 0 | 0 | 1 | 0 | 0 |
| Feliciano, Jesus, Bakersfield * | 0 | 0 | .000 | 1.69 | 5 | 0 | 0 | 0 | 3 | 0 | 5.1 | 1 | 20 | 1 | 1 | 0 | 0 | 0 | 0 | 3 | 0 | 2 | 1 | 0 |
| Fischer, Steve, Modesto | 1 | 2 | .333 | 6.44 | 21 | 0 | 0 | 0 | 8 | 0 | 36.1 | 50 | 189 | 30 | 26 | 0 | 0 | 0 | 1 | 29 | 3 | 22 | 3 | 0 |
| Flinn, Chris, Bakersfield | 3 | 0 | 1.000 | 1.21 | 24 | 0 | 0 | 0 | 12 | 8 | 29.2 | 19 | 124 | 5 | 4 | 1 | 0 | 0 | 1 | 15 | 1 | 35 | 3 | 0 |
| Foppert, Jesse, San Jose | 0 | 0 | .000 | 1.93 | 4 | 4 | 0 | 0 | 0 | 0 | 9.1 | 4 | 33 | 2 | 2 | 1 | 1 | 1 | 1 | 4 | 0 | 11 | 0 | 0 |
| Fulmer, T.A., Inland Empire | 6 | 7 | .462 | 5.16 | 17 | 17 | 1 | 0 | 0 | 0 | 96.0 | 109 | 424 | 61 | 55 | 7 | 5 | 9 | 5 | 21 | 0 | 86 | 6 | 0 |
| Gallagher, Buddy, Visalia * | 4 | 4 | .500 | 8.37 | 15 | 15 | 0 | 0 | 0 | 0 | 66.2 | 106 | 338 | 66 | 62 | 8 | 3 | 1 | 5 | 36 | 0 | 33 | 7 | 0 |
| Garcia, James, San Jose | 5 | 5 | .500 | 2.94 | 43 | 1 | 0 | 0 | 20 | 2 | 70.1 | 57 | 297 | 26 | 23 | 5 | 0 | 0 | 4 | 24 | 1 | 84 | 4 | 1 |
| Garcia, Jose, Stockton | 4 | 7 | .364 | 7.00 | 22 | 12 | 0 | 0 | 3 | 0 | 72.0 | 104 | 339 | 64 | 56 | 11 | 1 | 5 | 6 | 26 | 0 | 51 | 2 | 1 |
| Gardner, Hayden, Stockton | 1 | 0 | 1.000 | 4.50 | 7 | 0 | 0 | 0 | 1 | 0 | 10.0 | 13 | 52 | 9 | 5 | 0 | 0 | 0 | 1 | 7 | 0 | 6 | 2 | 0 |
| Girardeau, Clark, Lake Elsinore | 3 | 2 | .600 | 4.53 | 12 | 9 | 0 | 0 | 2 | 0 | 53.2 | 57 | 234 | 32 | 27 | 2 | 2 | 2 | 1 | 18 | 0 | 38 | 0 | 0 |
| Girdner, Jason, Bakersfield | 0 | 1 | .000 | 5.71 | 18 | 0 | 0 | 0 | 1 | 0 | 41.0 | 59 | 202 | 31 | 26 | 3 | 0 | 3 | 2 | 25 | 0 | 22 | 3 | 0 |
| Glant, Dustin, Lancaster | 3 | 3 | .500 | 6.14 | 13 | 2 | 0 | 0 | 8 | 3 | 22.0 | 28 | 106 | 17 | 15 | 3 | 0 | 0 | 2 | 13 | 2 | 12 | 0 | 0 |
| Gonzalez, Enrique, Lancaster | 13 | 6 | .684 | 3.22 | 42 | 17 | 0 | 0 | 5 | 0 | 142.1 | 128 | 586 | 64 | 51 | 13 | 5 | 3 | 6 | 44 | 0 | 110 | 3 | 0 |
| Goocher, Clint, Lancaster * | 9 | 2 | .818 | 3.67 | 14 | 14 | 1 | 0 | 0 | 0 | 90.2 | 94 | 373 | 39 | 37 | 10 | 5 | 5 | 3 | 12 | 1 | 82 | 3 | 0 |
| Gor, Nicholas, Bakersfield | 0 | 0 | .000 | 11.91 | 9 | 0 | 0 | 0 | 3 | 0 | 11.1 | 18 | 60 | 15 | 15 | 4 | 0 | 0 | 0 | 8 | 1 | 2 | 1 | 0 |
| Gregg, Grant, Lake Elsinore * | 1 | 3 | .250 | 5.15 | 37 | 0 | 0 | 0 | 13 | 0 | 43.2 | 44 | 201 | 31 | 25 | 3 | 0 | 0 | 0 | 26 | 0 | 41 | 1 | 0 |
| Griffith, Dustin, Rancho Cucamonga | 2 | 6 | .250 | 3.99 | 50 | 0 | 0 | 0 | 15 | 0 | 58.2 | 67 | 260 | 36 | 26 | 6 | 0 | 0 | 2 | 15 | 2 | 53 | 3 | 1 |
| Guthrie, Anasazi, Lake Elsinore | 1 | 0 | 1.000 | 0.84 | 5 | 0 | 0 | 0 | 1 | 0 | 10.2 | 10 | 46 | 1 | 1 | 0 | 0 | 2 | 0 | 5 | 0 | 11 | 1 | 0 |
| Hall, Bo, High Desert | 5 | 9 | .357 | 6.55 | 27 | 24 | 0 | 0 | 1 | 0 | 133.1 | 169 | 597 | 102 | 97 | 21 | 6 | 16 | 7 | 42 | 1 | 127 | 13 | 0 |
| Hamilton, Mark, High Desert * | 2 | 2 | .500 | 5.45 | 12 | 2 | 0 | 0 | 7 | 0 | 33.0 | 42 | 154 | 25 | 20 | 3 | 2 | 0 | 4 | 13 | 2 | 26 | 1 | 0 |
| Hammel, Jason, Bakersfield | 6 | 2 | .750 | 1.89 | 11 | 11 | 0 | 0 | 0 | 0 | 71.1 | 52 | 275 | 18 | 15 | 4 | 3 | 1 | 4 | 20 | 0 | 65 | 3 | 0 |
| Harper, Jesse, High Desert | 3 | 3 | .500 | 4.01 | 9 | 9 | 0 | 0 | 0 | 0 | 49.1 | 46 | 205 | 26 | 22 | 5 | 6 | 3 | 1 | 15 | 0 | 51 | 1 | 0 |
| Hayhurst, Dirk, Lake Elsinore | 1 | 2 | .333 | 5.56 | 5 | 5 | 0 | 0 | 0 | 0 | 22.2 | 25 | 109 | 18 | 14 | 2 | 0 | 1 | 1 | 16 | 0 | 18 | 1 | 1 |
| Henderson, Brian, Bakersfield * | 1 | 5 | .167 | 3.54 | 29 | 0 | 0 | 0 | 16 | 4 | 40.2 | 50 | 184 | 18 | 16 | 1 | 1 | 0 | 2 | 11 | 1 | 44 | 2 | 1 |
| Henderson, Eric, High Desert * | 4 | 5 | .444 | 6.98 | 25 | 9 | 0 | 0 | 6 | 1 | 87.2 | 116 | 430 | 87 | 68 | 11 | 4 | 1 | 9 | 48 | 0 | 58 | 5 | 1 |
| Hernandez, Felix, Inland Empire | 9 | 3 | .750 | 2.74 | 16 | 15 | 0 | 0 | 1 | 0 | 92.0 | 85 | 385 | 31 | 28 | 5 | 6 | 2 | 8 | 26 | 0 | 114 | 6 | 0 |
| Hill, Seth, Stockton * | 0 | 0 | .000 | 4.80 | 19 | 0 | 0 | 0 | 8 | 1 | 30.0 | 29 | 128 | 17 | 16 | 6 | 0 | 0 | 1 | 8 | 0 | 14 | 0 | 0 |
| Hitchcock, Sterling, Lake Elsinore * | 1 | 0 | 1.000 | 1.00 | 2 | 2 | 0 | 0 | 0 | 0 | 9.0 | 8 | 35 | 1 | 1 | 0 | 0 | 1 | 0 | 0 | 0 | 13 | 1 | 0 |
| Hogan, Gary, Stockton | 1 | 3 | .250 | 4.41 | 27 | 2 | 0 | 0 | 6 | 1 | 67.1 | 66 | 302 | 37 | 33 | 3 | 1 | 4 | 4 | 28 | 2 | 37 | 7 | 1 |
| Holsten, Ryan, Lancaster | 7 | 6 | .538 | 5.77 | 43 | 5 | 0 | 0 | 11 | 0 | 82.2 | 103 | 394 | 60 | 53 | 5 | 2 | 1 | 4 | 38 | 5 | 45 | 6 | 1 |
| Holubec, Ken, Stockton * | 3 | 2 | .600 | 3.76 | 29 | 0 | 0 | 0 | 9 | 1 | 38.1 | 33 | 157 | 20 | 16 | 3 | 0 | 0 | 2 | 7 | 0 | 47 | 0 | 0 |
| Huber, Jon, Inland Empire | 4 | 1 | .800 | 6.12 | 7 | 5 | 0 | 0 | 1 | 0 | 32.1 | 42 | 157 | 24 | 22 | 4 | 0 | 1 | 3 | 14 | 0 | 38 | 0 | 0 |
| Huber, Jon, Lake Elsinore | 8 | 6 | .571 | 3.70 | 20 | 20 | 0 | 0 | 0 | 0 | 107.0 | 107 | 466 | 53 | 44 | 9 | 5 | 4 | 4 | 44 | 0 | 100 | 7 | 0 |

| Pitcher, Team | W | L | Pct. | ERA | G | GS | CG | ShO | GF | Sv. | IP | H | TBF | R | ER | HR | SH | SF | HB | BB | IBB | SO | WP | Bk. |
|---|---|---|---|---|---|---|---|---|---|---|---|---|---|---|---|---|---|---|---|---|---|---|---|---|
| Hudgins, John, Stockton | 3 | 1 | .750 | 2.35 | 15 | 11 | 0 | 0 | 2 | 2 | 65.0 | 49 | 263 | 19 | 17 | 4 | 2 | 1 | 2 | 18 | 0 | 73 | 3 | 0 |
| Jaile, Chris, Stockton | 0 | 0 | .000 | 0.00 | 1 | 0 | 0 | 0 | 0 | 0 | 1.0 | 0 | 4 | 0 | 0 | 0 | 0 | 0 | 0 | 1 | 0 | 2 | 0 | 0 |
| Jenks, Bobby, Rancho Cucamonga | 0 | 1 | .000 | 19.64 | 1 | 1 | 0 | 0 | 0 | 0 | 3.2 | 5 | 23 | 8 | 8 | 0 | 0 | 2 | 1 | 7 | 0 | 3 | 0 | 0 |
| Jimenez, Cesar, Inland Empire * | 6 | 7 | .462 | 2.29 | 43 | 2 | 0 | 0 | 26 | 6 | 86.1 | 80 | 360 | 28 | 22 | 3 | 3 | 1 | 5 | 19 | 0 | 81 | 6 | 3 |
| Jimenez, Ubaldo, Visalia | 4 | 1 | .800 | 2.23 | 9 | 9 | 1 | 0 | 0 | 0 | 44.1 | 29 | 176 | 15 | 11 | 1 | 2 | 1 | 3 | 12 | 0 | 61 | 1 | 0 |
| Johnson, Doug, Visalia | 4 | 11 | .267 | 8.38 | 35 | 14 | 0 | 0 | 5 | 0 | 96.2 | 133 | 476 | 94 | 90 | 16 | 7 | 14 | 19 | 46 | 0 | 60 | 11 | 0 |
| Johnson, Rett, Inland Empire | 0 | 2 | .000 | 7.97 | 7 | 7 | 0 | 0 | 0 | 0 | 20.1 | 32 | 105 | 20 | 18 | 0 | 0 | 3 | 0 | 14 | 0 | 14 | 5 | 0 |
| Jones, Geoffrey, Lake Elsinore * | 1 | 1 | .500 | 3.00 | 11 | 0 | 0 | 0 | 1 | 0 | 18.0 | 10 | 74 | 10 | 6 | 2 | 0 | 0 | 4 | 6 | 0 | 11 | 0 | 0 |
| Keiter, Ben, Stockton | 3 | 6 | .333 | 6.80 | 12 | 8 | 0 | 0 | 2 | 0 | 45.0 | 52 | 210 | 37 | 34 | 3 | 2 | 4 | 9 | 26 | 1 | 38 | 6 | 0 |
| Kirsten, Joel, Stockton * | 0 | 0 | .000 | 7.36 | 5 | 3 | 0 | 0 | 0 | 0 | 14.2 | 23 | 73 | 16 | 12 | 2 | 0 | 0 | 2 | 4 | 0 | 10 | 1 | 0 |
| Kohn, Shawn, Modesto | 3 | 0 | 1.000 | 2.30 | 23 | 0 | 0 | 0 | 6 | 4 | 43.0 | 32 | 168 | 12 | 11 | 1 | 0 | 0 | 3 | 4 | 0 | 68 | 0 | 1 |
| Kolb, Dan, High Desert | 3 | 3 | .500 | 5.42 | 37 | 0 | 0 | 0 | 16 | 3 | 83.0 | 91 | 390 | 60 | 50 | 9 | 0 | 0 | 8 | 44 | 1 | 75 | 6 | 0 |
| Kozlowski, Ben, Stockton * | 4 | 2 | .667 | 3.83 | 10 | 8 | 0 | 0 | 1 | 0 | 47.0 | 40 | 201 | 23 | 20 | 1 | 4 | 5 | 5 | 19 | 0 | 32 | 1 | 1 |
| Kusiewicz, Mike, High Desert * | 0 | 1 | .000 | 4.14 | 26 | 0 | 0 | 0 | 13 | 1 | 37.0 | 46 | 180 | 19 | 17 | 3 | 0 | 2 | 5 | 16 | 1 | 44 | 3 | 0 |
| Landeros, Leonard, Modesto * | 1 | 2 | .333 | 3.29 | 42 | 0 | 0 | 0 | 19 | 7 | 63.0 | 56 | 282 | 29 | 23 | 7 | 1 | 1 | 5 | 31 | 2 | 63 | 8 | 1 |
| Liebeck, Jered, Lancaster | 1 | 0 | 1.000 | 11.57 | 5 | 2 | 0 | 0 | 0 | 0 | 7.0 | 10 | 38 | 9 | 9 | 2 | 0 | 0 | 2 | 5 | 0 | 4 | 0 | 0 |
| Little, Joe, Bakersfield * | 2 | 5 | .286 | 4.55 | 11 | 11 | 0 | 0 | 0 | 0 | 55.1 | 54 | 243 | 31 | 28 | 7 | 2 | 3 | 2 | 30 | 0 | 51 | 1 | 0 |
| Littleton, Wes, Stockton | 8 | 10 | .444 | 4.15 | 30 | 23 | 0 | 0 | 1 | 0 | 141.0 | 139 | 600 | 76 | 65 | 7 | 8 | 15 | 11 | 56 | 0 | 72 | 14 | 0 |
| Livingston, Bobby, Inland Empire * | 12 | 6 | .667 | 3.57 | 28 | 27 | 1 | 1 | 0 | 0 | 186.2 | 187 | 762 | 90 | 74 | 15 | 8 | 4 | 7 | 30 | 0 | 141 | 4 | 0 |
| Lockwood, Brian, Bakersfield | 4 | 11 | .267 | 6.86 | 28 | 20 | 0 | 0 | 0 | 0 | 127.1 | 160 | 560 | 108 | 97 | 9 | 10 | 7 | 6 | 49 | 0 | 107 | 5 | 3 |
| Lorenzo, Matt, Stockton | 1 | 3 | .250 | 4.81 | 9 | 8 | 0 | 0 | 1 | 1 | 43.0 | 42 | 176 | 27 | 23 | 3 | 1 | 0 | 3 | 11 | 0 | 39 | 2 | 1 |
| Lugo, Ozzie, Rancho Cucamonga | 3 | 0 | 1.000 | 4.50 | 18 | 0 | 0 | 0 | 3 | 0 | 22.0 | 22 | 102 | 12 | 11 | 0 | 0 | 0 | 0 | 15 | 0 | 17 | 1 | 0 |
| Lynch, Brian, Visalia | 0 | 5 | .000 | 6.41 | 26 | 4 | 0 | 0 | 7 | 0 | 53.1 | 83 | 270 | 45 | 38 | 3 | 1 | 5 | 3 | 32 | 3 | 37 | 1 | 0 |
| Lynch, Matt, Modesto * | 13 | 3 | .813 | 3.93 | 27 | 27 | 0 | 0 | 0 | 0 | 151.1 | 165 | 655 | 75 | 66 | 9 | 9 | 8 | 4 | 38 | 0 | 111 | 6 | 0 |
| Marcano, Luis, Stockton | 3 | 0 | 1.000 | 3.73 | 34 | 0 | 0 | 0 | 26 | 5 | 41.0 | 41 | 182 | 19 | 17 | 4 | 0 | 0 | 2 | 17 | 1 | 26 | 2 | 0 |
| Markert, Jackson, San Jose | 3 | 3 | .500 | 4.10 | 25 | 0 | 0 | 0 | 11 | 0 | 26.1 | 31 | 123 | 13 | 12 | 1 | 0 | 0 | 1 | 12 | 1 | 23 | 2 | 0 |
| Martin, Forrest, High Desert | 1 | 4 | .200 | 5.25 | 10 | 9 | 0 | 0 | 0 | 0 | 48.0 | 53 | 208 | 35 | 28 | 8 | 2 | 1 | 4 | 18 | 0 | 40 | 1 | 0 |
| Martinez, Miguel, Inland Empire * | 2 | 1 | .667 | 5.62 | 30 | 0 | 0 | 0 | 20 | 5 | 41.2 | 38 | 182 | 26 | 26 | 6 | 1 | 2 | 1 | 17 | 1 | 54 | 2 | 1 |
| Martinez, Ramon, Inland Empire | 0 | 0 | .000 | 0.00 | 1 | 0 | 0 | 0 | 1 | 0 | 1.0 | 1 | 5 | 0 | 0 | 0 | 0 | 0 | 0 | 1 | 0 | 1 | 0 | 0 |
| Masset, Nicholas, Stockton | 6 | 5 | .545 | 3.51 | 16 | 11 | 0 | 0 | 0 | 0 | 77.0 | 71 | 323 | 38 | 30 | 6 | 2 | 3 | 6 | 19 | 0 | 43 | 4 | 0 |
| Mateo, Natanael, Lake Elsinore | 6 | 3 | .667 | 2.79 | 39 | 0 | 0 | 0 | 17 | 2 | 51.2 | 46 | 215 | 20 | 16 | 2 | 0 | 0 | 3 | 11 | 2 | 59 | 4 | 0 |
| Mazurek, David, Stockton | 8 | 2 | .800 | 3.07 | 54 | 0 | 0 | 0 | 28 | 8 | 70.1 | 58 | 301 | 25 | 24 | 3 | 0 | 0 | 5 | 27 | 1 | 59 | 11 | 0 |
| McCall, Derell, Modesto | 6 | 5 | .545 | 5.16 | 15 | 14 | 0 | 0 | 1 | 0 | 75.0 | 76 | 342 | 51 | 43 | 6 | 3 | 5 | 6 | 38 | 1 | 60 | 8 | 1 |
| McCally, Ryan, Bakersfield | 4 | 3 | .571 | 3.35 | 25 | 0 | 0 | 0 | 4 | 2 | 43.0 | 43 | 189 | 16 | 16 | 4 | 1 | 0 | 4 | 13 | 1 | 32 | 3 | 0 |
| McMachen, Clifford, Lancaster * | 2 | 1 | .667 | 4.09 | 37 | 5 | 0 | 0 | 13 | 2 | 70.1 | 80 | 315 | 37 | 32 | 9 | 1 | 3 | 1 | 29 | 2 | 64 | 4 | 0 |
| McNiven, Brooks, San Jose | 6 | 8 | .429 | 4.35 | 31 | 21 | 0 | 0 | 2 | 0 | 134.1 | 162 | 592 | 74 | 65 | 13 | 10 | 6 | 4 | 32 | 0 | 73 | 4 | 0 |
| Mendez, Mario, High Desert | 0 | 0 | .000 | 7.71 | 3 | 0 | 0 | 0 | 2 | 0 | 2.1 | 3 | 13 | 2 | 2 | 0 | 0 | 0 | 0 | 3 | 0 | 2 | 0 | 0 |
| Mendoza, Marcos, Visalia * | 0 | 0 | .000 | 3.47 | 31 | 0 | 0 | 0 | 6 | 0 | 36.1 | 35 | 166 | 19 | 14 | 3 | 0 | 0 | 4 | 18 | 0 | 33 | 1 | 0 |
| Miniel, Rene, Lake Elsinore | 0 | 1 | .000 | 7.33 | 16 | 0 | 0 | 0 | 6 | 1 | 27.0 | 39 | 137 | 23 | 22 | 1 | 2 | 0 | 2 | 14 | 2 | 29 | 1 | 0 |
| Moak, Curtus, Modesto * | 2 | 1 | .667 | 3.86 | 19 | 0 | 0 | 0 | 1 | 0 | 23.1 | 27 | 115 | 14 | 10 | 0 | 0 | 0 | 3 | 14 | 1 | 22 | 1 | 0 |
| Morel, Eudy, Visalia | 2 | 2 | .500 | 4.46 | 29 | 0 | 0 | 0 | 16 | 1 | 36.1 | 33 | 159 | 18 | 18 | 10 | 0 | 0 | 2 | 15 | 1 | 37 | 0 | 0 |
| Morgan, Matt, Lancaster | 0 | 0 | .000 | 13.50 | 2 | 0 | 0 | 0 | 2 | 0 | 3.1 | 5 | 17 | 5 | 5 | 1 | 0 | 0 | 0 | 2 | 0 | 1 | 1 | 0 |
| Muessig, Jeff, Modesto | 2 | 1 | .667 | 3.38 | 9 | 7 | 0 | 0 | 0 | 0 | 32.0 | 30 | 131 | 12 | 12 | 1 | 2 | 2 | 3 | 9 | 0 | 26 | 4 | 0 |
| Navaroli, Michael, Bakersfield | 0 | 5 | .000 | 5.77 | 32 | 0 | 0 | 0 | 15 | 2 | 39.0 | 51 | 197 | 28 | 25 | 3 | 1 | 0 | 6 | 23 | 5 | 25 | 4 | 0 |
| Needham, Joel, High Desert | 0 | 0 | .000 | 3.00 | 2 | 0 | 0 | 0 | 1 | 0 | 3.0 | 4 | 14 | 3 | 1 | 0 | 0 | 0 | 0 | 1 | 0 | 4 | 0 | 0 |
| Neugebauer, Nick, High Desert | 0 | 0 | .000 | 18.00 | 1 | 1 | 0 | 0 | 0 | 0 | 1.0 | 2 | 5 | 2 | 2 | 1 | 0 | 0 | 0 | 0 | 0 | 0 | 0 | 0 |
| Nolasco, Dave, High Desert | 3 | 6 | .333 | 7.40 | 44 | 1 | 0 | 0 | 17 | 1 | 82.2 | 110 | 416 | 79 | 68 | 8 | 2 | 2 | 10 | 50 | 1 | 56 | 12 | 0 |
| Obenchain, Stephen, Modesto | 3 | 3 | .500 | 4.76 | 23 | 5 | 0 | 0 | 3 | 1 | 64.1 | 74 | 290 | 43 | 34 | 5 | 2 | 5 | 1 | 29 | 3 | 53 | 5 | 1 |
| Oldham, Thomas, Inland Empire * | 4 | 3 | .571 | 3.21 | 7 | 6 | 0 | 0 | 0 | 0 | 42.0 | 47 | 173 | 22 | 15 | 5 | 2 | 1 | 2 | 6 | 0 | 56 | 2 | 0 |
| Orvella, Chad, Bakersfield | 0 | 1 | .000 | 3.06 | 15 | 0 | 0 | 0 | 13 | 4 | 17.2 | 13 | 71 | 7 | 6 | 2 | 0 | 0 | 1 | 4 | 1 | 24 | 1 | 0 |
| Osuna, Antonio, Lake Elsinore | 0 | 0 | .000 | 2.45 | 7 | 2 | 0 | 0 | 0 | 0 | 7.1 | 2 | 26 | 2 | 2 | 0 | 0 | 0 | 0 | 2 | 0 | 12 | 0 | 0 |
| Pannone, Anthony, San Jose | 4 | 6 | .400 | 4.15 | 56 | 0 | 0 | 0 | 15 | 2 | 95.1 | 97 | 426 | 48 | 44 | 6 | 0 | 1 | 6 | 36 | 0 | 77 | 4 | 0 |
| Parra, Manny, High Desert * | 5 | 2 | .714 | 3.48 | 13 | 12 | 1 | 1 | 0 | 0 | 67.1 | 76 | 295 | 41 | 26 | 3 | 6 | 6 | 2 | 19 | 0 | 64 | 3 | 1 |
| Pauley, David, Lake Elsinore | 7 | 12 | .368 | 4.17 | 27 | 26 | 0 | 0 | 0 | 0 | 153.1 | 155 | 665 | 89 | 71 | 8 | 8 | 9 | 8 | 60 | 0 | 128 | 6 | 0 |
| Pavlik, Isaac, Visalia * | 1 | 1 | .500 | 8.61 | 23 | 0 | 0 | 0 | 8 | 0 | 23.0 | 35 | 116 | 26 | 22 | 2 | 0 | 0 | 1 | 12 | 0 | 19 | 2 | 0 |
| Pavon, Julio, San Jose | 1 | 5 | .167 | 4.50 | 15 | 8 | 0 | 0 | 0 | 0 | 60.0 | 66 | 247 | 33 | 30 | 5 | 3 | 2 | 0 | 9 | 0 | 41 | 1 | 1 |
| Pendley, Nathan, San Jose * | 0 | 0 | .000 | 1.80 | 7 | 0 | 0 | 0 | 2 | 0 | 5.0 | 8 | 27 | 2 | 1 | 0 | 0 | 0 | 1 | 3 | 0 | 2 | 0 | 0 |
| Peralta, Joel, Rancho Cucamonga | 0 | 0 | .000 | 9.00 | 1 | 0 | 0 | 0 | 1 | 0 | 2.0 | 5 | 12 | 2 | 2 | 1 | 0 | 0 | 0 | 1 | 0 | 1 | 0 | 0 |
| Perez, Elvis, Visalia | 2 | 3 | .400 | 4.92 | 13 | 9 | 0 | 0 | 0 | 0 | 53.0 | 59 | 228 | 36 | 29 | 5 | 1 | 4 | 2 | 18 | 1 | 40 | 5 | 2 |
| Perez, Keith, Modesto | 6 | 2 | .750 | 4.90 | 21 | 10 | 0 | 0 | 5 | 0 | 68.0 | 82 | 311 | 42 | 37 | 5 | 2 | 5 | 3 | 28 | 0 | 44 | 5 | 3 |
| Perez, Roberto, Stockton | 0 | 0 | .000 | 7.20 | 2 | 1 | 0 | 0 | 0 | 0 | 5.0 | 3 | 24 | 4 | 4 | 1 | 0 | 0 | 1 | 6 | 0 | 3 | 1 | 0 |
| Petersen, Jeffrey, San Jose | 5 | 8 | .385 | 4.82 | 27 | 13 | 0 | 0 | 1 | 0 | 84.0 | 93 | 372 | 60 | 45 | 7 | 2 | 6 | 4 | 32 | 0 | 45 | 5 | 0 |
| Petke, Tim, Rancho Cucamonga | 0 | 0 | .000 | 3.38 | 3 | 0 | 0 | 0 | 1 | 0 | 5.1 | 6 | 24 | 2 | 2 | 0 | 0 | 0 | 1 | 3 | 0 | 1 | 0 | 0 |
| Pizarro, Melvin, Inland Empire * | 4 | 4 | .500 | 3.86 | 41 | 0 | 0 | 0 | 20 | 8 | 70.0 | 64 | 297 | 39 | 30 | 7 | 0 | 0 | 1 | 24 | 2 | 58 | 4 | 0 |
| Posey, Micah, Rancho Cucamonga * | 2 | 2 | .500 | 3.66 | 8 | 7 | 0 | 0 | 0 | 0 | 39.1 | 38 | 161 | 20 | 16 | 4 | 2 | 1 | 2 | 12 | 0 | 24 | 0 | 0 |
| Prochaska, Mike, Bakersfield * | 6 | 2 | .750 | 1.70 | 11 | 11 | 0 | 0 | 0 | 0 | 63.2 | 67 | 259 | 15 | 12 | 3 | 0 | 1 | 0 | 16 | 1 | 56 | 0 | 0 |
| Ribas, Gabe, Lake Elsinore | 4 | 5 | .444 | 4.35 | 13 | 13 | 0 | 0 | 0 | 0 | 70.1 | 85 | 316 | 47 | 34 | 7 | 5 | 8 | 4 | 21 | 0 | 41 | 1 | 0 |
| Ridgway, Jeff, Bakersfield * | 2 | 3 | .400 | 2.31 | 15 | 1 | 0 | 0 | 1 | 1 | 35.0 | 32 | 155 | 17 | 9 | 0 | 1 | 0 | 2 | 19 | 1 | 27 | 3 | 0 |
| Rivard, Reggie, High Desert | 1 | 3 | .250 | 2.33 | 17 | 0 | 0 | 0 | 9 | 3 | 19.1 | 17 | 83 | 10 | 5 | 1 | 0 | 0 | 1 | 8 | 0 | 12 | 5 | 1 |
| Rivera, Homero, High Desert * | 1 | 1 | .500 | 6.84 | 20 | 0 | 0 | 0 | 13 | 4 | 25.0 | 35 | 125 | 25 | 19 | 7 | 0 | 0 | 1 | 14 | 0 | 25 | 1 | 0 |
| Robertson, Luke, Modesto | 0 | 0 | .000 | 5.25 | 4 | 1 | 0 | 0 | 2 | 0 | 12.0 | 11 | 50 | 7 | 7 | 2 | 4 | 0 | 0 | 5 | 0 | 6 | 1 | 0 |
| Rowland-Smith, Ryan, Inland Empire * | 5 | 3 | .625 | 3.79 | 29 | 12 | 0 | 0 | 4 | 3 | 99.2 | 107 | 425 | 50 | 42 | 10 | 4 | 3 | 3 | 30 | 0 | 119 | 5 | 1 |
| Rupe, Josh, Stockton | 2 | 0 | 1.000 | 0.98 | 4 | 3 | 0 | 0 | 1 | 0 | 18.1 | 12 | 75 | 4 | 2 | 0 | 1 | 1 | 3 | 4 | 0 | 14 | 2 | 0 |
| Russ, Chris, Stockton * | 1 | 3 | .250 | 4.29 | 28 | 0 | 0 | 0 | 13 | 3 | 35.2 | 40 | 170 | 21 | 17 | 3 | 0 | 0 | 2 | 21 | 2 | 29 | 1 | 1 |
| Sadler, William, San Jose | 2 | 2 | .500 | 2.38 | 30 | 3 | 0 | 0 | 3 | 0 | 56.2 | 29 | 241 | 17 | 15 | 1 | 1 | 1 | 4 | 40 | 0 | 66 | 3 | 2 |
| Sandoval, Juan, Inland Empire | 11 | 11 | .500 | 4.12 | 27 | 27 | 1 | 0 | 0 | 0 | 168.1 | 184 | 712 | 91 | 77 | 21 | 10 | 5 | 9 | 43 | 0 | 119 | 7 | 1 |
| Sansom, Trevor, Modesto | 2 | 1 | .667 | 1.80 | 7 | 0 | 0 | 0 | 7 | 3 | 10.0 | 8 | 43 | 2 | 2 | 0 | 1 | 0 | 2 | 3 | 0 | 12 | 1 | 0 |
| Sauer, Marc, Modesto | 11 | 2 | .846 | 4.51 | 24 | 19 | 0 | 0 | 0 | 0 | 115.2 | 118 | 491 | 67 | 58 | 10 | 4 | 5 | 7 | 33 | 0 | 89 | 1 | 1 |
| Saunders, Joe, Rancho Cucamonga * | 9 | 7 | .563 | 3.41 | 19 | 19 | 0 | 0 | 0 | 0 | 105.2 | 106 | 433 | 49 | 40 | 13 | 2 | 3 | 5 | 23 | 0 | 76 | 5 | 1 |
| Schmidt, Jason, San Jose | 1 | 0 | 1.000 | 0.00 | 1 | 1 | 0 | 0 | 0 | 0 | 5.0 | 2 | 18 | 0 | 0 | 0 | 0 | 0 | 0 | 1 | 0 | 7 | 1 | 0 |
| Schultz, Mike, Lancaster | 1 | 1 | .500 | 3.00 | 13 | 0 | 0 | 0 | 5 | 2 | 18.0 | 19 | 88 | 13 | 6 | 0 | 0 | 0 | 2 | 13 | 1 | 18 | 3 | 0 |
| Seddon, Chris, Bakersfield * | 5 | 0 | 1.000 | 0.65 | 7 | 7 | 0 | 0 | 0 | 0 | 41.1 | 30 | 156 | 4 | 3 | 0 | 1 | 0 | 2 | 8 | 0 | 41 | 2 | 1 |
| Sevier, Nate, Lake Elsinore | 0 | 0 | .000 | 3.10 | 38 | 1 | 0 | 0 | 11 | 1 | 52.1 | 54 | 222 | 24 | 18 | 2 | 0 | 0 | 0 | 12 | 0 | 46 | 1 | 0 |
| Shank, Chris, Modesto | 6 | 5 | .545 | 3.99 | 49 | 0 | 0 | 0 | 17 | 3 | 85.2 | 84 | 373 | 47 | 38 | 9 | 0 | 0 | 2 | 30 | 3 | 81 | 4 | 0 |

| Pitcher, Team | W | L | Pct. | ERA | G | GS | CG | ShO | GF | Sv. | IP | H | TBF | R | ER | HR | SH | SF | HB | BB | IBB | SO | WP | Bk. |
|---|---|---|---|---|---|---|---|---|---|---|---|---|---|---|---|---|---|---|---|---|---|---|---|---|
| Shanks, Edward, Lake Elsinore | 0 | 0 | .000 | 0.00 | 1 | 0 | 0 | 0 | 0 | 0 | 1.0 | 0 | 3 | 0 | 0 | 0 | 0 | 0 | 0 | 0 | 0 | 0 | 0 | 0 |
| Shappi, Austin, Lancaster | 1 | 0 | 1.000 | 3.00 | 2 | 1 | 0 | 0 | 0 | 0 | 6.0 | 6 | 24 | 2 | 2 | 1 | 0 | 0 | 0 | 1 | 0 | 8 | 0 | 0 |
| Shell, Steven, Rancho Cucamonga | 12 | 7 | .632 | 3.59 | 28 | 28 | 2 | 1 | 0 | 0 | 165.1 | 151 | 672 | 76 | 66 | 19 | 6 | 2 | 16 | 40 | 0 | 190 | 4 | 1 |
| Shields, Jamie, Bakersfield | 8 | 5 | .615 | 4.23 | 20 | 20 | 1 | 1 | 0 | 0 | 117.0 | 119 | 488 | 61 | 55 | 13 | 4 | 5 | 9 | 33 | 0 | 92 | 6 | 0 |
| Silva, Doug, Visalia | 0 | 0 | .000 | 6.75 | 2 | 0 | 0 | 0 | 0 | 0 | 4.0 | 6 | 19 | 3 | 3 | 2 | 0 | 0 | 0 | 1 | 0 | 4 | 0 | 0 |
| Silva, Jesus, Lancaster | 11 | 7 | .611 | 4.38 | 28 | 27 | 0 | 0 | 1 | 0 | 152.0 | 168 | 663 | 89 | 74 | 16 | 9 | 5 | 5 | 56 | 0 | 126 | 7 | 2 |
| Simon, Alfredo, San Jose | 1 | 2 | .333 | 5.68 | 6 | 6 | 0 | 0 | 0 | 0 | 31.2 | 44 | 142 | 24 | 20 | 7 | 3 | 2 | 0 | 12 | 0 | 21 | 5 | 0 |
| Slack, Nick, High Desert | 2 | 6 | .250 | 4.98 | 45 | 0 | 0 | 0 | 32 | 9 | 59.2 | 70 | 274 | 40 | 33 | 4 | 0 | 0 | 6 | 19 | 2 | 71 | 5 | 0 |
| Smith, Cliff, Rancho Cucamonga | 0 | 1 | .000 | 8.68 | 7 | 0 | 0 | 0 | 1 | 0 | 9.1 | 12 | 45 | 10 | 9 | 2 | 0 | 0 | 1 | 4 | 1 | 6 | 1 | 0 |
| Smith, Cody, Stockton | 3 | 6 | .333 | 3.91 | 32 | 17 | 1 | 0 | 5 | 2 | 124.1 | 161 | 558 | 61 | 54 | 3 | 4 | 5 | 5 | 31 | 0 | 60 | 5 | 0 |
| Smith, Sam, Lancaster | 5 | 5 | .500 | 5.40 | 18 | 12 | 0 | 0 | 4 | 1 | 68.1 | 86 | 309 | 46 | 41 | 7 | 3 | 3 | 9 | 24 | 0 | 53 | 1 | 0 |
| Soriano, Rafael, Inland Empire | 0 | 0 | .000 | 2.25 | 2 | 2 | 0 | 0 | 0 | 0 | 8.0 | 7 | 32 | 3 | 2 | 1 | 0 | 0 | 0 | 1 | 0 | 9 | 0 | 0 |
| Soto, Darwin, Inland Empire | 4 | 4 | .500 | 3.21 | 42 | 0 | 0 | 0 | 27 | 10 | 67.1 | 61 | 291 | 34 | 24 | 2 | 0 | 0 | 5 | 24 | 2 | 54 | 2 | 4 |
| Stauffer, Tim, Lake Elsinore | 2 | 0 | 1.000 | 1.78 | 6 | 6 | 0 | 0 | 0 | 0 | 35.1 | 28 | 139 | 10 | 7 | 0 | 1 | 2 | 1 | 9 | 0 | 30 | 0 | 0 |
| Steele, Mike, Inland Empire | 0 | 0 | .000 | 5.17 | 20 | 1 | 0 | 0 | 9 | 1 | 31.1 | 37 | 146 | 19 | 18 | 2 | 0 | 2 | 1 | 16 | 0 | 24 | 5 | 0 |
| Stertzbach, Von, Rancho Cucamonga | 1 | 3 | .250 | 3.38 | 47 | 0 | 0 | 0 | 40 | 21 | 48.0 | 52 | 210 | 23 | 18 | 2 | 0 | 0 | 1 | 13 | 1 | 54 | 2 | 0 |
| Stetter, Mitch, High Desert * | 1 | 4 | .200 | 8.15 | 8 | 7 | 0 | 0 | 0 | 0 | 38.2 | 54 | 185 | 39 | 35 | 6 | 2 | 3 | 2 | 14 | 0 | 29 | 4 | 0 |
| Stirm, Brian, San Jose | 4 | 10 | .286 | 4.87 | 31 | 18 | 0 | 0 | 4 | 0 | 109.0 | 121 | 473 | 71 | 59 | 15 | 11 | 5 | 3 | 41 | 1 | 86 | 6 | 0 |
| Strong, Zach, San Jose | 0 | 0 | .000 | 18.00 | 1 | 0 | 0 | 0 | 1 | 0 | 1.0 | 1 | 5 | 2 | 2 | 1 | 0 | 0 | 0 | 1 | 0 | 2 | 0 | 0 |
| Sullivan, Bradley, Modesto | 8 | 11 | .421 | 4.65 | 27 | 27 | 0 | 0 | 0 | 0 | 147.0 | 180 | 660 | 89 | 76 | 13 | 11 | 5 | 9 | 48 | 0 | 99 | 10 | 0 |
| Taylor, Aaron, Inland Empire | 0 | 1 | .000 | 13.50 | 1 | 1 | 0 | 0 | 0 | 0 | 1.1 | 2 | 7 | 3 | 2 | 0 | 0 | 0 | 0 | 1 | 0 | 2 | 0 | 0 |
| Teeter, Travis, High Desert | 1 | 1 | .500 | 7.71 | 6 | 1 | 0 | 0 | 2 | 0 | 16.1 | 29 | 80 | 15 | 14 | 6 | 0 | 0 | 1 | 1 | 0 | 23 | 1 | 0 |
| Thayer, Dale, Lake Elsinore | 2 | 1 | .667 | 1.63 | 50 | 0 | 0 | 0 | 42 | 23 | 55.1 | 36 | 214 | 12 | 10 | 1 | 0 | 0 | 0 | 11 | 0 | 54 | 0 | 0 |
| Thompson, Rich, Rancho Cucamonga | 3 | 2 | .600 | 3.94 | 41 | 5 | 0 | 0 | 17 | 4 | 77.2 | 76 | 339 | 36 | 34 | 9 | 1 | 0 | 3 | 33 | 2 | 71 | 4 | 1 |
| Tierney, Chris, Lake Elsinore * | 2 | 5 | .286 | 6.96 | 8 | 8 | 0 | 0 | 0 | 0 | 42.2 | 56 | 201 | 38 | 33 | 2 | 3 | 4 | 3 | 19 | 0 | 18 | 3 | 1 |
| Toledo, Jean, Rancho Cucamonga | 7 | 10 | .412 | 4.85 | 25 | 25 | 2 | 0 | 0 | 0 | 128.0 | 147 | 570 | 84 | 69 | 14 | 5 | 3 | 1 | 55 | 0 | 70 | 10 | 0 |
| Touchstone, Nick, Rancho Cucamonga * | 0 | 0 | .000 | 5.40 | 3 | 0 | 0 | 0 | 0 | 0 | 3.1 | 5 | 21 | 2 | 2 | 0 | 0 | 0 | 0 | 6 | 0 | 3 | 0 | 0 |
| Treadway, Brion, San Jose | 7 | 5 | .583 | 3.95 | 20 | 20 | 0 | 0 | 0 | 0 | 111.2 | 98 | 460 | 53 | 49 | 10 | 5 | 5 | 8 | 42 | 1 | 97 | 13 | 0 |
| Tucker, Rusty, Lake Elsinore * | 0 | 0 | .000 | 7.71 | 8 | 0 | 0 | 0 | 1 | 0 | 7.0 | 9 | 35 | 8 | 6 | 1 | 0 | 0 | 0 | 5 | 0 | 6 | 2 | 0 |
| Ulloa, Enmanuel, Visalia | 2 | 3 | .400 | 5.09 | 6 | 6 | 0 | 0 | 0 | 0 | 35.1 | 45 | 158 | 20 | 20 | 1 | 3 | 3 | 2 | 9 | 0 | 36 | 2 | 1 |
| Valdez, Merkin, San Jose | 3 | 1 | .750 | 2.52 | 7 | 7 | 0 | 0 | 0 | 0 | 35.2 | 30 | 146 | 12 | 10 | 4 | 0 | 0 | 4 | 5 | 0 | 44 | 1 | 0 |
| Vanden berg, John, High Desert | 0 | 0 | .000 | 13.50 | 1 | 0 | 0 | 0 | 1 | 0 | 0.2 | 2 | 5 | 1 | 1 | 1 | 0 | 0 | 1 | 0 | 0 | 1 | 0 | 0 |
| Viane, David, Inland Empire | 0 | 2 | .000 | 3.51 | 19 | 0 | 0 | 0 | 9 | 0 | 25.2 | 26 | 116 | 15 | 10 | 1 | 0 | 0 | 2 | 11 | 0 | 11 | 1 | 0 |
| Villatoro, Wilmer, Lake Elsinore | 6 | 2 | .750 | 2.84 | 47 | 0 | 0 | 0 | 11 | 0 | 66.2 | 50 | 287 | 29 | 21 | 4 | 0 | 0 | 4 | 35 | 0 | 67 | 4 | 0 |
| Volquez, Edison, Stockton | 4 | 1 | .800 | 2.95 | 8 | 8 | 0 | 0 | 0 | 0 | 39.2 | 31 | 162 | 16 | 13 | 6 | 3 | 3 | 2 | 14 | 0 | 34 | 2 | 0 |
| Waddell, Jason, San Jose * | 6 | 4 | .600 | 4.08 | 47 | 2 | 0 | 0 | 18 | 0 | 70.2 | 76 | 309 | 39 | 32 | 4 | 0 | 0 | 1 | 24 | 1 | 60 | 6 | 1 |
| Walton, Sam, Bakersfield * | 2 | 5 | .286 | 3.93 | 23 | 10 | 0 | 0 | 5 | 2 | 73.1 | 62 | 318 | 45 | 32 | 3 | 4 | 2 | 6 | 38 | 0 | 82 | 12 | 1 |
| Washburn, Jarrod, Rancho Cucamonga * | 0 | 0 | .000 | 2.25 | 1 | 1 | 0 | 0 | 0 | 0 | 4.0 | 4 | 20 | 1 | 1 | 0 | 0 | 0 | 0 | 3 | 0 | 5 | 0 | 0 |
| Watson, Mike, Lancaster | 6 | 1 | .857 | 4.46 | 57 | 0 | 0 | 0 | 12 | 1 | 68.2 | 66 | 321 | 44 | 34 | 11 | 0 | 0 | 8 | 44 | 2 | 62 | 7 | 0 |
| Watson, Tanner, Inland Empire | 2 | 4 | .333 | 5.06 | 25 | 5 | 0 | 0 | 9 | 4 | 69.1 | 75 | 299 | 43 | 39 | 3 | 3 | 3 | 7 | 22 | 0 | 57 | 5 | 1 |
| Wear, Greg, Inland Empire | 1 | 2 | .333 | 11.40 | 17 | 3 | 0 | 0 | 5 | 1 | 30.0 | 55 | 161 | 42 | 38 | 6 | 1 | 2 | 3 | 13 | 0 | 25 | 5 | 0 |
| Webb, Alan, Lake Elsinore * | 2 | 1 | .667 | 3.86 | 11 | 0 | 0 | 0 | 3 | 0 | 11.2 | 10 | 52 | 6 | 5 | 3 | 2 | 0 | 1 | 4 | 1 | 9 | 0 | 0 |
| Wechsler, Justin, Lancaster | 4 | 1 | .800 | 2.48 | 56 | 0 | 0 | 0 | 30 | 18 | 80.0 | 63 | 338 | 25 | 22 | 6 | 1 | 2 | 4 | 27 | 1 | 96 | 8 | 0 |
| Wells, Carlton, Lancaster * | 3 | 1 | .750 | 4.68 | 71 | 0 | 0 | 0 | 12 | 1 | 67.1 | 87 | 319 | 41 | 35 | 4 | 1 | 1 | 4 | 24 | 2 | 33 | 3 | 0 |
| Wells, Jared, Lake Elsinore | 4 | 6 | .400 | 4.52 | 13 | 12 | 0 | 0 | 0 | 0 | 71.2 | 81 | 317 | 44 | 36 | 5 | 5 | 2 | 1 | 30 | 0 | 38 | 3 | 2 |
| Whatley, Keith, Lancaster * | 2 | 4 | .333 | 7.19 | 12 | 10 | 0 | 0 | 1 | 0 | 51.1 | 70 | 248 | 51 | 41 | 7 | 2 | 3 | 4 | 27 | 1 | 41 | 0 | 0 |
| Whitaker, Brian, Lake Elsinore | 1 | 2 | .333 | 1.99 | 5 | 5 | 1 | 0 | 0 | 0 | 31.2 | 28 | 128 | 11 | 7 | 4 | 1 | 2 | 0 | 7 | 0 | 25 | 0 | 0 |
| White, Bill, Lancaster * | 1 | 1 | .500 | 1.96 | 14 | 0 | 0 | 0 | 6 | 1 | 18.1 | 16 | 81 | 8 | 4 | 2 | 0 | 0 | 3 | 7 | 0 | 23 | 2 | 0 |
| Wiedmeyer, Jason, Lake Elsinore * | 0 | 0 | .000 | 9.90 | 4 | 0 | 0 | 0 | 1 | 0 | 10.0 | 18 | 52 | 11 | 11 | 1 | 0 | 1 | 1 | 3 | 0 | 1 | 0 | 0 |
| Wilhite, Matt, Rancho Cucamonga | 6 | 4 | .600 | 3.75 | 53 | 0 | 0 | 0 | 10 | 0 | 86.1 | 89 | 369 | 45 | 36 | 5 | 1 | 1 | 3 | 20 | 0 | 61 | 2 | 0 |
| Wilson, Phil, Rancho Cucamonga | 3 | 9 | .250 | 6.50 | 38 | 16 | 0 | 0 | 10 | 0 | 109.1 | 132 | 521 | 96 | 79 | 15 | 6 | 12 | 8 | 58 | 1 | 75 | 9 | 1 |
| Wodnicki, Mike, Lake Elsinore | 3 | 1 | .750 | 6.04 | 17 | 1 | 0 | 0 | 13 | 7 | 22.1 | 36 | 107 | 17 | 15 | 3 | 1 | 0 | 0 | 3 | 0 | 8 | 1 | 0 |
| Woody, Dominic, Rancho Cucamonga | 2 | 3 | .400 | 4.41 | 6 | 6 | 0 | 0 | 0 | 0 | 34.2 | 39 | 154 | 21 | 17 | 2 | 1 | 1 | 4 | 12 | 0 | 22 | 2 | 0 |
| Woolard, Glenn, High Desert | 1 | 2 | .333 | 4.69 | 12 | 3 | 0 | 0 | 0 | 0 | 48.0 | 58 | 217 | 31 | 25 | 2 | 3 | 2 | 0 | 21 | 0 | 46 | 3 | 1 |
| Yarbrough, Joe, Bakersfield * | 5 | 3 | .625 | 5.14 | 60 | 0 | 0 | 0 | 41 | 8 | 68.1 | 72 | 325 | 40 | 39 | 6 | 0 | 0 | 9 | 39 | 3 | 48 | 7 | 0 |
| Young, Chris, Visalia | 8 | 3 | .727 | 3.60 | 52 | 0 | 0 | 0 | 15 | 2 | 85.0 | 95 | 375 | 38 | 34 | 6 | 0 | 1 | 12 | 15 | 1 | 77 | 4 | 0 |
| Zamora, Pete, Lancaster * | 3 | 3 | .500 | 6.15 | 13 | 13 | 0 | 0 | 0 | 0 | 67.1 | 91 | 307 | 50 | 46 | 5 | 3 | 5 | 1 | 22 | 0 | 37 | 3 | 0 |
| Ziegler, Brad, Modesto | 9 | 2 | .818 | 3.90 | 16 | 15 | 0 | 0 | 1 | 0 | 92.1 | 94 | 389 | 51 | 40 | 11 | 4 | 2 | 2 | 22 | 0 | 77 | 0 | 1 |

COMBINATION SHUTOUTS: **Bakersfield** (7)—Seddon-Walton, Prochaska-Allen, Walton-Cromer-Gor, Hammel-McCally-Flinn, Shields-McCally-Flinn, Hammel-Yarbrough, Hammel-Flinn. **High Desert** (1)—Ballouli-Slack, Ballouli-Nolasco. **Inland Empire** (8)—Sandoval-Viane-Pizarro-Soto, Fulmer-Rowland Smith-Wear-M. Martinez, Fulmer-Soto, Hernandez-Pizarro, Livingston-Jimenez, Hernandez-Soto-Castillo, Rowland Smith-Jimenez-Viane, Oldham-Pizarro. **Lake Elsinore** (4)—Whitaker-Craker-Wodnicki, Bonine-Beavers-Sevier, Pauley-Mateo-Thayer, Wells-Tucker-Girardeau. **Lancaster** (6)—Goocher-White-Bulger, E. Gonzalez-Watson-Wells-Wechsler, Silva-Holsten-Wechsler, Bass-Wells-Holsten-McMachen-Wechsler, E. Gonzalez-Wells, Silva-McMachen. **Modesto** (5)—McCall-Avendano-Bystrowski, Perez-Avendano-Shank, Ziegler-Kohn, Lynch-Avendano, Muessig-Burton-Coleman. **Rancho Cucamonga** (1)—Shell-Carroll-Thompson. **San Jose** (7)—Stirm-Sadler-Accardo, Cain-Sadler-Waddell, Burres-Sadler-Garcia, Treadway-Sadler-Garcia, Burres-Pannone-Accardo, Waddell-Petersen-Accardo, Broshuis-Accardo. **Stockton** (7)—Rupe-Masset-C. Smith, Andrew-Hudgins, C. Smith-Keiter, Hudgins-Russ-Mazurek, Hudgins-C. Smith, C. Smith-Mazurek, C. Smith-Mazurek. **Visalia** (1)—Jimenez-Beckstead-Young.

NO-HIT GAMES: None.

# 2004 FIELDING

## TEAM

| Team | G | PO | A | E | TC | DP | TP | PB | Pct. |
|---|---|---|---|---|---|---|---|---|---|
| Visalia | 140 | 3733 | 102 | 159 | 3994 | 120 | 0 | 24 | .960 |
| Inland Empire | 140 | 3709 | 128 | 167 | 4004 | 103 | 0 | 25 | .958 |
| Bakersfield | 140 | 3710 | 127 | 168 | 4005 | 148 | 0 | 48 | .958 |
| San Jose | 140 | 3809 | 137 | 176 | 4122 | 111 | 0 | 21 | .957 |
| Modesto | 140 | 3794 | 095 | 179 | 4068 | 123 | 0 | 32 | .956 |
| Lancaster | 140 | 3747 | 140 | 181 | 4068 | 119 | 0 | 11 | .956 |
| Rancho Cuca | 140 | 3736 | 121 | 185 | 4042 | 117 | 0 | 15 | .954 |
| Stockton | 140 | 3697 | 123 | 187 | 4007 | 128 | 0 | 34 | .953 |
| High Desert. | 140 | 3710 | 141 | 208 | 4059 | 110 | 0 | 32 | .949 |
| Lake Elsinore | 140 | 3741 | 150 | 225 | 4116 | 103 | 0 | 20 | .945 |

## INDIVIDUAL

### FIRST BASEMEN

NOTE: All caps denotes fielding-percentage leader based on 70 games for catchers, 93 for all other non-pitchers and 112 innings for pitchers. *Throws lefthanded.

| Player, Team | Pct. | G | PO | A | E | TC | DP |
|---|---|---|---|---|---|---|---|
| Abram, Matt, RC | 1.000 | 19 | 102 | 4 | 0 | 106 | 7 |
| Abruzzo, Jared, RC | .976 | 53 | 429 | 20 | 11 | 460 | 40 |
| Aracena, Sandy, BAK | 1.000 | 2 | 8 | 4 | 0 | 12 | 11 |
| Balet, Frederico, INL | .969 | 18 | 148 | 10 | 5 | 163 | 15 |
| Balet, Frederico, VIS | .929 | 3 | 11 | 2 | 1 | 14 | 0 |
| Balet, Frederico, INL-VIS | .966 | 21 | 159 | 12 | 6 | 177 | 15 |

| Player, Team | Pct. | G | PO | A | E | TC | DP |
|---|---|---|---|---|---|---|---|
| Benavidez, Julian, SJ | .985 | 31 | 251 | 15 | 4 | 270 | 15 |
| Buchanan, Brian, LKE | 1.000 | 2 | 11 | 0 | 0 | 11 | 0 |
| Budde, Ryan, RC | .983 | 13 | 99 | 15 | 2 | 116 | 8 |
| Cates, Zach, RC* | 1.000 | 13 | 100 | 5 | 0 | 105 | 10 |
| Cleveland, Jeremy, STK | 1.000 | 1 | 4 | 1 | 0 | 5 | 1 |
| Colamarino, Brant, MOD* | .984 | 50 | 403 | 31 | 7 | 441 | 37 |
| Cordell, Brent, BAK | .986 | 39 | 306 | 38 | 5 | 349 | 23 |
| Cordido, Julio, SJ | 1.000 | 1 | 8 | 2 | 0 | 10 | 0 |
| Cota, Jesus, LNC* | .990 | 13 | 96 | 6 | 1 | 103 | 8 |
| Dufner, Kris, BAK | 1.000 | 2 | 3 | 0 | 0 | 3 | 1 |
| Fallon, Chris, VIS* | .991 | 75 | 624 | 69 | 6 | 699 | 53 |
| Farnsworth, Troy, HD | 1.000 | 5 | 25 | 2 | 0 | 27 | 1 |
| Frost, Jeremy, HD | .969 | 7 | 60 | 3 | 2 | 65 | 4 |
| Garthwaite, Jay, LNC | .864 | 4 | 17 | 2 | 3 | 22 | 1 |
| GOLD, NATE, STK | .990 | 135 | 1222 | 102 | 13 | 1337 | 109 |
| Hagen, Matt, INL | .986 | 97 | 789 | 76 | 12 | 877 | 47 |
| Halter, Shane, RC | 1.000 | 2 | 24 | 2 | 0 | 26 | 1 |
| Hamilton, Mark, HD* | 1.000 | 1 | 6 | 1 | 0 | 7 | 0 |
| Hinton, Travis, HD* | .984 | 130 | 1090 | 73 | 19 | 1182 | 86 |
| Holm, Steve, SJ | 1.000 | 2 | 6 | 0 | 0 | 6 | 1 |
| Ishikawa, Travis, SJ* | 1.000 | 16 | 153 | 8 | 0 | 161 | 15 |
| Johnson, Michael, LKE* | .986 | 69 | 612 | 30 | 9 | 651 | 47 |
| Jones, Mitch, BAK | .833 | 2 | 9 | 1 | 2 | 12 | 1 |
| Kimpton, Nick, RC* | 1.000 | 1 | 1 | 0 | 0 | 1 | 0 |
| Lentz, Brian, INL | 1.000 | 1 | 1 | 0 | 0 | 1 | 0 |
| Lima, Joseph, LKE | 1.000 | 3 | 8 | 0 | 0 | 8 | 1 |
| Lincoln, Justin, BAK | .875 | 2 | 7 | 0 | 1 | 8 | 1 |
| Luellwitz, Sean, LNC | .995 | 93 | 788 | 43 | 4 | 835 | 74 |
| Madera, Sandy, VIS | .983 | 7 | 58 | 1 | 1 | 60 | 5 |
| Margalski, Ben, STK* | 1.000 | 3 | 24 | 6 | 0 | 30 | 4 |
| Martinez, Gabriel, BAK* | .984 | 68 | 559 | 45 | 10 | 614 | 66 |
| McAnulty, Paul, LKE* | .992 | 26 | 246 | 13 | 2 | 261 | 20 |
| McStoots, Jason, LNC* | 1.000 | 1 | 5 | 0 | 0 | 5 | 0 |
| Morgan, Matt, LNC | .985 | 11 | 62 | 5 | 1 | 68 | 6 |
| Myers, Casey, MOD | .974 | 18 | 143 | 8 | 4 | 155 | 25 |
| Myers, Cory, LNC | .946 | 4 | 34 | 1 | 2 | 37 | 2 |
| Napoli, Michael, RC | .987 | 36 | 281 | 17 | 4 | 302 | 26 |
| Nelson, Jon, INL | .975 | 8 | 39 | 0 | 1 | 40 | 3 |
| Niekro, Lance, SJ | .993 | 15 | 139 | 4 | 1 | 144 | 14 |
| Pagan, Andres, LKE | .917 | 2 | 11 | 0 | 1 | 12 | 1 |
| Peck, Bryan, VIS | .987 | 57 | 489 | 33 | 7 | 529 | 44 |
| Perry, Jason, MOD* | 1.000 | 2 | 14 | 1 | 0 | 15 | 4 |
| Porter, Greg, RC* | .983 | 13 | 114 | 4 | 2 | 120 | 11 |
| Reece, Eric, BAK* | .977 | 36 | 323 | 15 | 8 | 346 | 43 |
| Rogelstad, Matt, INL* | .980 | 23 | 180 | 12 | 4 | 196 | 17 |
| Roman, Jesse, LKE* | .986 | 45 | 393 | 24 | 6 | 423 | 33 |
| Sandoval, Abigail, STK | 1.000 | 1 | 6 | 2 | 0 | 8 | 1 |
| Santana, Mayobanex, LNC | .988 | 19 | 149 | 15 | 2 | 166 | 16 |
| Santana, Mayobanex, MOD | .991 | 41 | 305 | 19 | 3 | 327 | 16 |
| Santana, Mayobanex, LNC-MOD | .990 | 60 | 454 | 34 | 5 | 493 | 32 |
| Shelley, Randall, STK | 1.000 | 1 | 8 | 0 | 0 | 8 | 2 |
| Sosa, Carlos, SJ | 1.000 | 2 | 6 | 1 | 0 | 7 | 0 |
| Stavisky, Brian, MOD* | .979 | 34 | 261 | 24 | 6 | 291 | 16 |
| Strong, Zach, SJ | .981 | 8 | 46 | 5 | 1 | 52 | 4 |
| Sutton, Don, MOD | .980 | 6 | 48 | 2 | 1 | 51 | 5 |
| Turner, Justin, RC* | .970 | 7 | 62 | 3 | 2 | 67 | 2 |
| Uggla, Dan, LNC | 1.000 | 6 | 47 | 4 | 0 | 51 | 2 |
| Vericker, Brad, SJ* | .994 | 76 | 651 | 46 | 4 | 701 | 56 |

## SECOND BASEMEN

| Player, Team | Pct. | G | PO | A | E | TC | DP |
|---|---|---|---|---|---|---|---|
| Adams, Skip, LKE | 1.000 | 1 | 1 | 3 | 0 | 4 | 1 |
| Aguilar, Trino, LKE | 1.000 | 2 | 3 | 3 | 0 | 6 | 2 |
| Aybar, Erick, RC | 1.000 | 1 | 2 | 1 | 0 | 3 | 1 |
| Baker, Casey, LKE | .962 | 12 | 21 | 30 | 2 | 53 | 9 |
| Bernier, Doug, VIS | .953 | 8 | 20 | 21 | 2 | 43 | 4 |
| Biguenet, Michael, LNC | .964 | 17 | 35 | 46 | 3 | 84 | 8 |
| Bouman, Robbie, BAK | 1.000 | 7 | 13 | 13 | 0 | 26 | 3 |
| Brown, Neb, LNC* | .970 | 62 | 148 | 172 | 10 | 330 | 35 |
| Burgamy, Brian, LKE | .875 | 5 | 6 | 8 | 2 | 16 | 1 |
| Candelaria, Ben, HD* | .800 | 1 | 3 | 1 | 1 | 5 | 1 |
| Candelaria, Scott, HD | .944 | 6 | 4 | 13 | 1 | 18 | 3 |
| Castro, Ismael, INL | 1.000 | 12 | 20 | 33 | 0 | 53 | 1 |
| Cho, Hyung, INL | .939 | 24 | 36 | 41 | 5 | 82 | 10 |
| Cornejo, Eddie, MOD* | .978 | 34 | 52 | 84 | 3 | 139 | 12 |
| Coughlan, Cameron, STK | .949 | 16 | 40 | 35 | 4 | 79 | 8 |
| Crabbe, Callix, HD | .966 | 132 | 241 | 356 | 21 | 618 | 62 |
| DePaula, Luis, BAK | .985 | 87 | 171 | 234 | 6 | 411 | 66 |
| DeRenne, Keoni, LNC | 1.000 | 1 | 1 | 4 | 0 | 5 | 1 |
| Dufner, Kris, BAK | .974 | 46 | 91 | 130 | 6 | 227 | 39 |
| Durham, Ray, SJ | 1.000 | 1 | 1 | 2 | 0 | 3 | 0 |
| Eure, Jeff, HD | .909 | 5 | 4 | 6 | 1 | 11 | 0 |
| Fox, Adam, STK | 1.000 | 15 | 24 | 46 | 0 | 70 | 7 |
| Garcia, Isaac, MOD | .939 | 15 | 25 | 21 | 3 | 49 | 8 |
| Garciaparra, Michael, INL | .944 | 27 | 53 | 65 | 7 | 125 | 11 |
| Garrabrants, Steve, LNC | .962 | 12 | 19 | 31 | 2 | 52 | 4 |
| Gonzalez, Juan, INL | .974 | 42 | 75 | 115 | 5 | 195 | 24 |
| Haley, Adam, LNC* | .962 | 5 | 13 | 12 | 1 | 26 | 3 |
| Harrison, Vince, BAK | 1.000 | 1 | 1 | 6 | 0 | 7 | 1 |
| Heath, Demetrius, RC | .962 | 19 | 24 | 52 | 3 | 79 | 9 |
| Hendricks, KJ, VIS | .975 | 120 | 207 | 307 | 13 | 527 | 57 |
| Hoffpauir, Joshua, STK* | .948 | 33 | 71 | 94 | 9 | 174 | 21 |
| Holm, Steve, SJ | .750 | 1 | 2 | 1 | 1 | 4 | 1 |
| Hornostaj, Aaron, SJ* | .955 | 25 | 34 | 73 | 5 | 112 | 10 |
| LABARBERA, ANTHONY, SJ | .981 | 98 | 198 | 305 | 10 | 513 | 61 |
| Lima, Joseph, LKE | .964 | 41 | 73 | 116 | 7 | 196 | 18 |
| Lincoln, Justin, BAK | 1.000 | 1 | 1 | 0 | 0 | 1 | 0 |
| Martinez, Gabriel, BAK* | 1.000 | 2 | 5 | 8 | 0 | 13 | 0 |
| McStoots, Jason, LNC* | .960 | 6 | 9 | 15 | 1 | 25 | 2 |
| Merrill, Ronnie, LKE | .929 | 5 | 10 | 16 | 2 | 28 | 2 |
| Monzon, Erick, INL | .000 | 1 | 0 | 0 | 1 | 1 | 0 |
| Morgan, Matt, LNC | .974 | 34 | 59 | 93 | 4 | 156 | 22 |
| Pavkovich, Adam, RC | .970 | 35 | 59 | 102 | 5 | 166 | 18 |
| Pullins, Taylor, INL | .852 | 5 | 8 | 15 | 4 | 27 | 5 |
| Ramos, Peeter, LKE | .944 | 63 | 107 | 195 | 18 | 320 | 29 |
| Riley, Ryan, BAK | .900 | 2 | 4 | 5 | 1 | 10 | 0 |
| Ringe, Craig, STK | .963 | 60 | 112 | 204 | 12 | 328 | 48 |
| Rodriguez, Javy, RC | .938 | 12 | 10 | 20 | 2 | 32 | 3 |
| Rogelstad, Matt, INL* | .963 | 35 | 70 | 84 | 6 | 160 | 19 |
| Sandoval, Abigail, STK | .979 | 19 | 36 | 58 | 2 | 96 | 7 |
| Sardinha, Duke, VIS | 1.000 | 4 | 7 | 12 | 0 | 19 | 4 |
| Serrano, Eddie, LKE | .870 | 7 | 6 | 14 | 3 | 23 | 2 |
| Smyres, Justin, LKE | .985 | 12 | 26 | 41 | 1 | 68 | 10 |
| Sobieraj, Aaron, SJ | .928 | 18 | 25 | 52 | 6 | 83 | 6 |
| St. Clair, Jason, BAK | .875 | 4 | 8 | 6 | 2 | 16 | 1 |
| Taylor, Seth, STK | 1.000 | 4 | 3 | 7 | 0 | 10 | 2 |
| Tejeda, Ferdin, LKE | 1.000 | 2 | 3 | 5 | 0 | 8 | 0 |
| Tena, Hector, VIS | 1.000 | 12 | 19 | 27 | 0 | 46 | 6 |
| Turner, Justin, RC* | .949 | 8 | 12 | 25 | 2 | 39 | 8 |
| Turner, Lloyd, MOD | .961 | 103 | 207 | 286 | 20 | 513 | 65 |
| Uggla, Dan, LNC | .979 | 19 | 29 | 64 | 2 | 95 | 9 |
| Watson, Rob, LKE | 1.000 | 3 | 7 | 12 | 0 | 19 | 3 |
| Weed, BJ, RC | .965 | 82 | 125 | 209 | 12 | 346 | 39 |

## THIRD BASEMEN

| Player, Team | Pct. | G | PO | A | E | TC | DP |
|---|---|---|---|---|---|---|---|
| Abreu, Yohany, SJ | 1.000 | 1 | 0 | 1 | 0 | 1 | 1 |
| Baker, Jeffrey, VIS | .900 | 68 | 67 | 114 | 20 | 201 | 14 |
| Balet, Frederico, VIS | .900 | 20 | 18 | 36 | 6 | 60 | 4 |
| Benavidez, Julian, SJ | .500 | 1 | 2 | 0 | 2 | 4 | 0 |
| Bernier, Doug, VIS | .944 | 38 | 20 | 65 | 5 | 90 | 1 |
| Biguenet, Michael, LNC | .875 | 5 | 1 | 6 | 1 | 8 | 0 |
| Burgamy, Brian, LKE | .925 | 13 | 14 | 23 | 3 | 40 | 5 |
| Buscher, Brian, SJ* | .926 | 17 | 11 | 39 | 4 | 54 | 5 |
| Candelaria, Scott, HD | .796 | 20 | 13 | 26 | 10 | 49 | 1 |
| Castro, Ismael, INL | 1.000 | 4 | 5 | 11 | 0 | 16 | 0 |
| Ciesluk, Chris, SJ | 1.000 | 1 | 1 | 5 | 0 | 6 | 0 |
| Cordido, Julio, SJ | .950 | 76 | 55 | 136 | 10 | 201 | 12 |
| Cornejo, Eddie, MOD* | .871 | 13 | 9 | 18 | 4 | 31 | 3 |
| Cruz, Luis, LKE | .880 | 6 | 6 | 16 | 3 | 25 | 3 |
| D`Antona, Jamie, LNC | .908 | 64 | 58 | 109 | 17 | 184 | 9 |
| Dufner, Kris, BAK | .968 | 20 | 16 | 45 | 2 | 63 | 2 |
| Eure, Jeff, HD | .913 | 83 | 58 | 173 | 22 | 253 | 10 |
| Farnsworth, Troy, HD | .892 | 38 | 29 | 70 | 12 | 111 | 2 |
| FOX, ADAM, STK | .929 | 113 | 69 | 220 | 22 | 311 | 15 |
| Frost, Jeremy, HD | .778 | 5 | 2 | 5 | 2 | 9 | 0 |
| Garcia, Isaac, MOD | .928 | 77 | 53 | 102 | 12 | 167 | 11 |
| Garrabrants, Steve, LNC | .948 | 46 | 37 | 55 | 5 | 97 | 9 |
| Garthwaite, Jay, LNC | .600 | 2 | 0 | 3 | 2 | 5 | 0 |
| Gonzalez, Juan, INL | .966 | 8 | 3 | 25 | 1 | 29 | 2 |
| Guzman, Jesus, INL | .894 | 111 | 59 | 185 | 29 | 273 | 10 |
| Hagen, Matt, INL | .667 | 2 | 2 | 0 | 1 | 3 | 0 |
| Haley, Adam, LNC* | .905 | 19 | 10 | 28 | 4 | 42 | 0 |
| Halter, Shane, RC | 1.000 | 2 | 1 | 2 | 0 | 3 | 0 |
| Harrison, Vince, BAK | .938 | 67 | 51 | 115 | 11 | 177 | 11 |
| Holm, Steve, SJ | 1.000 | 5 | 3 | 7 | 0 | 10 | 0 |
| Hornostaj, Aaron, SJ* | .938 | 5 | 9 | 6 | 1 | 16 | 1 |
| Jacobo, Kervin, LKE | .901 | 115 | 69 | 203 | 30 | 302 | 6 |
| Lima, Joseph, LKE | .947 | 10 | 10 | 8 | 1 | 19 | 0 |
| Lincoln, Justin, BAK | .935 | 39 | 14 | 58 | 5 | 77 | 4 |
| Martinez, Gabriel, BAK* | .943 | 20 | 15 | 35 | 3 | 53 | 2 |
| McCurdy, John, MOD | .935 | 12 | 10 | 19 | 2 | 31 | 1 |
| Merritt, Graig, BAK | 1.000 | 1 | 0 | 1 | 0 | 1 | 0 |
| Monzon, Erick, INL | 1.000 | 1 | 2 | 1 | 0 | 3 | 0 |

| Player, Team | Pct. | G | PO | A | E | TC | DP |
|---|---|---|---|---|---|---|---|
| Morgan, Matt, LNC | 1.000 | 4 | 7 | 9 | 0 | 16 | 0 |
| Morris, Jed, MOD* | 1.000 | 2 | 1 | 1 | 0 | 2 | 0 |
| Myers, Cory, LNC | .833 | 1 | 4 | 1 | 1 | 6 | 0 |
| Napoli, Michael, RC | 1.000 | 2 | 0 | 2 | 0 | 2 | 0 |
| Pavkovich, Adam, RC | .921 | 72 | 64 | 123 | 16 | 203 | 16 |
| Peck, Bryan, VIS | .800 | 5 | 4 | 8 | 3 | 15 | 1 |
| Porter, Greg, RC* | .899 | 72 | 43 | 126 | 19 | 188 | 9 |
| Reynolds, Mark, LNC | .857 | 3 | 0 | 6 | 1 | 7 | 0 |
| Ringe, Craig, STK | .894 | 17 | 12 | 30 | 5 | 47 | 2 |
| Rogelstad, Matt, INL* | .949 | 19 | 8 | 29 | 2 | 39 | 1 |
| Santana, Mayobanex, LNC | 1.000 | 1 | 0 | 1 | 0 | 1 | 0 |
| Sardinha, Duke, VIS | .833 | 6 | 7 | 8 | 3 | 18 | 2 |
| Schierholtz, Nate, SJ* | .895 | 38 | 19 | 58 | 9 | 86 | 4 |
| Schneidmiller, Gary, MOD | .935 | 25 | 18 | 40 | 4 | 62 | 2 |
| Shelley, Randall, STK | .933 | 12 | 13 | 29 | 3 | 45 | 0 |
| Smyres, Justin, LKE | .778 | 3 | 2 | 5 | 2 | 9 | 0 |
| Spiezio, Scott, INL | 1.000 | 1 | 0 | 1 | 0 | 1 | 0 |
| Street, Dan, VIS | .833 | 9 | 7 | 8 | 3 | 18 | 0 |
| Strong, Zach, SJ | 1.000 | 1 | 1 | 0 | 0 | 1 | 0 |
| Suomi, John, MOD* | .860 | 20 | 7 | 30 | 6 | 43 | 2 |
| Tena, Hector, VIS | .500 | 1 | 0 | 1 | 1 | 2 | 0 |
| Turner, Lloyd, MOD | .929 | 9 | 8 | 18 | 2 | 28 | 2 |
| Uggla, Dan, LNC | .867 | 8 | 6 | 20 | 4 | 30 | 2 |
| Villanueva, Froilan, HD | 1.000 | 1 | 1 | 3 | 0 | 4 | 0 |
| Weed, BJ, RC | .800 | 2 | 2 | 2 | 1 | 5 | 0 |

## SHORTSTOPS

| Player, Team | Pct. | G | PO | A | E | TC | DP |
|---|---|---|---|---|---|---|---|
| Abreu, Yohany, SJ | .750 | 2 | 4 | 2 | 2 | 8 | 1 |
| Adams, Skip, LKE | 907 | 8 | 17 | 32 | 5 | 54 | 4 |
| Arias, Joaquin, STK | .928 | 114 | 163 | 349 | 40 | 552 | 73 |
| Aybar, Erick, RC | .954 | 132 | 266 | 391 | 32 | 689 | 80 |
| Baker, Casey, LKE | 1.000 | 2 | 2 | 1 | 0 | 3 | 1 |
| Bernier, Doug, VIS | .975 | 58 | 84 | 186 | 7 | 277 | 29 |
| Bouman, Robbie, BAK | 1.000 | 2 | 2 | 8 | 0 | 10 | 1 |
| Candelaria, Scott, HD | .905 | 4 | 7 | 12 | 2 | 21 | 2 |
| Chavez, Angel, SJ | .937 | 12 | 22 | 37 | 4 | 63 | 10 |
| Chavez, Ozzie, HD | .951 | 39 | 68 | 127 | 10 | 205 | 29 |
| Cordido, Julio, SJ | .949 | 34 | 48 | 120 | 9 | 177 | 19 |
| Cornejo, Eddie, MOD* | .953 | 14 | 23 | 38 | 3 | 64 | 5 |
| Cruz, Enrique, HD | .960 | 97 | 168 | 241 | 17 | 426 | 43 |
| Cruz, Luis, LKE | .936 | 116 | 194 | 376 | 39 | 609 | 70 |
| Cuevas, Aneudi, BAK | .870 | 4 | 10 | 10 | 3 | 23 | 1 |
| DePaula, Luis, BAK | .941 | 9 | 14 | 18 | 2 | 34 | 5 |
| DeRenne, Keoni, LNC | .971 | 14 | 25 | 41 | 2 | 68 | 9 |
| Dufner, Kris, BAK | 1.000 | 5 | 6 | 10 | 0 | 16 | 1 |
| Eure, Jeff, HD | 1.000 | 3 | 7 | 7 | 0 | 14 | 2 |
| Garcia, Isaac, MOD | .941 | 25 | 36 | 60 | 6 | 102 | 8 |
| Garciaparra, Michael, INL | .947 | 39 | 56 | 123 | 10 | 189 | 22 |
| Gonzalez, Juan, INL | .944 | 77 | 119 | 215 | 20 | 354 | 35 |
| Guzman, Jesus, INL | 1.000 | 4 | 7 | 10 | 0 | 17 | 2 |
| Haley, Adam, LNC* | .908 | 32 | 56 | 92 | 15 | 163 | 19 |
| Halter, Shane, RC | 1.000 | 1 | 4 | 2 | 0 | 6 | 0 |
| Hornostaj, Aaron, SJ* | .919 | 52 | 73 | 143 | 19 | 235 | 30 |
| Jacobo, Kervin, LKE | .893 | 5 | 7 | 18 | 3 | 28 | 2 |
| Lima, Joseph, LKE | .667 | 1 | 1 | 3 | 2 | 6 | 2 |
| MANISCALCO, MATTHEW, BAK | .963 | 124 | 209 | 387 | 23 | 619 | 95 |
| Merrill, Ronnie, LKE | .857 | 3 | 4 | 8 | 2 | 14 | 2 |
| Monzon, Erick, INL | .956 | 19 | 27 | 59 | 4 | 90 | 15 |
| Morgan, Matt, LNC | .875 | 6 | 14 | 14 | 4 | 32 | 4 |
| Pavkovich, Adam, RC | .909 | 3 | 5 | 5 | 1 | 11 | 3 |
| Quintanilla, Omar, MOD* | .941 | 104 | 152 | 298 | 28 | 478 | 68 |
| Ramos, Peeter, LKE | .714 | 1 | 3 | 2 | 2 | 7 | 1 |
| Reynolds, Mark, LNC | .750 | 1 | 1 | 2 | 1 | 4 | 0 |
| Richar, Danny, LNC* | .945 | 91 | 152 | 274 | 25 | 451 | 54 |
| Riley, Ryan, BAK | 1.000 | 2 | 4 | 5 | 0 | 9 | 2 |
| Ringe, Craig, STK | .951 | 25 | 36 | 81 | 6 | 123 | 12 |
| Rodriguez, Javy, RC | .882 | 3 | 2 | 13 | 2 | 17 | 2 |
| Rogelstad, Matt, INL* | 1.000 | 4 | 5 | 7 | 0 | 12 | 1 |
| Swope, Tobin, STK | 1.000 | 2 | 3 | 1 | 0 | 4 | 1 |
| Taylor, Seth, STK | 1.000 | 2 | 3 | 13 | 0 | 16 | 4 |
| Tejeda, Ferdin, LKE | .889 | 9 | 10 | 22 | 4 | 36 | 2 |
| Tena, Hector, VIS | .941 | 92 | 148 | 254 | 25 | 427 | 50 |
| Turner, Lloyd, MOD | .600 | 1 | 0 | 3 | 2 | 5 | 0 |
| Uggla, Dan, LNC | .920 | 8 | 8 | 15 | 2 | 25 | 2 |
| Wald, Jacob, SJ | .941 | 43 | 52 | 122 | 11 | 185 | 15 |
| Weed, BJ, RC | 1.000 | 4 | 3 | 7 | 0 | 10 | 1 |

## OUTFIELDERS

| Player, Team | Pct. | G | PO | A | E | TC | DP |
|---|---|---|---|---|---|---|---|
| Abercrombie, Reggie, LNC | .985 | 28 | 63 | 3 | 1 | 67 | 1 |
| Abreu, Yohany, SJ | .818 | 7 | 8 | 1 | 2 | 11 | 0 |
| Anderson, Garret, RC* | 1.000 | 3 | 8 | 0 | 0 | 8 | 0 |
| Aracena, Sandy, BAK | 1.000 | 1 | 1 | 0 | 0 | 1 | 0 |
| Arroyo, Carlos, INL* | .979 | 87 | 133 | 8 | 3 | 144 | 2 |
| Baker, Casey, LKE | .978 | 66 | 127 | 4 | 3 | 134 | 0 |
| Baker, Steve, LKE | .993 | 71 | 143 | 6 | 1 | 150 | 1 |
| Balentien, Wladimir, INL | .958 | 10 | 23 | 0 | 1 | 24 | 0 |
| Ball, Jarred, LNC | .983 | 116 | 226 | 6 | 4 | 236 | 1 |
| Barker, Sean, VIS | .976 | 89 | 191 | 10 | 5 | 206 | 3 |
| Barre, Brian, VIS* | .963 | 58 | 97 | 6 | 4 | 107 | 2 |
| Bibbs, Kennard, HD* | .983 | 120 | 278 | 11 | 5 | 294 | 3 |
| Bohn, TJ, INL | .986 | 71 | 137 | 8 | 2 | 147 | 4 |
| Boyd, Dan, HD | .962 | 66 | 92 | 9 | 4 | 105 | 1 |
| Boyd, Patrick, STK | .968 | 44 | 89 | 2 | 3 | 94 | 1 |
| Brooks, Doc, LNC | .931 | 59 | 92 | 3 | 7 | 102 | 0 |
| Buchanan, Brian, LKE | 1.000 | 1 | 1 | 0 | 0 | 1 | 0 |
| Burgamy, Brian, LKE | 1.000 | 16 | 18 | 0 | 0 | 18 | 0 |
| Candelaria, Ben, HD* | .909 | 5 | 10 | 0 | 1 | 11 | 0 |
| Candelaria, Scott, HD | 1.000 | 29 | 41 | 2 | 0 | 43 | 2 |
| Carter, Josh, LKE | .977 | 71 | 120 | 8 | 3 | 131 | 2 |
| Centeno, Irwin, BAK | .900 | 20 | 26 | 1 | 3 | 30 | 0 |
| Cleveland, Jeremy, STK | .963 | 119 | 223 | 11 | 9 | 243 | 1 |
| Cordido, Julio, SJ | 1.000 | 3 | 4 | 0 | 0 | 4 | 0 |
| Cota, Jesus, LNC* | 1.000 | 1 | 2 | 0 | 0 | 2 | 0 |
| Coughlan, Cameron, STK | .984 | 66 | 116 | 8 | 2 | 126 | 1 |
| Cruz, Nelson, MOD | .982 | 65 | 158 | 4 | 3 | 165 | 1 |
| Dukes, Elijah, BAK | .984 | 54 | 118 | 5 | 2 | 125 | 0 |
| Duncan, Carlos, RC | .917 | 15 | 21 | 1 | 2 | 24 | 0 |
| Ellison, Josh, INL* | .979 | 21 | 44 | 2 | 1 | 47 | 0 |
| Ethier, Andre, MOD* | .963 | 98 | 207 | 2 | 8 | 217 | 2 |
| Faison, Vince, INL* | 1.000 | 6 | 14 | 0 | 0 | 14 | 0 |
| Feliciano, Jesus, BAK* | .983 | 54 | 110 | 6 | 2 | 118 | 1 |
| Frome, Jason, VIS* | 1.000 | 8 | 12 | 0 | 0 | 12 | 0 |
| Frost, Jeremy, HD | .954 | 44 | 61 | 1 | 3 | 65 | 0 |
| Garthwaite, Jay, LNC | .901 | 41 | 62 | 2 | 7 | 71 | 0 |
| Gates, David, RC | .962 | 81 | 126 | 2 | 5 | 133 | 1 |
| Gomes, Joey, BAK | 1.000 | 40 | 59 | 2 | 0 | 61 | 0 |
| Gonzalez, Bernie, VIS | .938 | 85 | 123 | 14 | 9 | 146 | 3 |
| Hamilton, Mark, HD* | .913 | 11 | 21 | 0 | 2 | 23 | 0 |
| Harris, Gary, INL* | .979 | 131 | 265 | 9 | 6 | 280 | 1 |
| Hoffpauir, Joshua, STK* | 1.000 | 5 | 6 | 0 | 0 | 6 | 0 |
| Jackson, Conor, LNC | .971 | 61 | 99 | 3 | 3 | 105 | 0 |
| Jones, Kennard, LKE* | .939 | 50 | 90 | 2 | 6 | 98 | 0 |
| Jones, Mitch, BAK | .885 | 15 | 22 | 1 | 3 | 26 | 0 |
| Kimpton, Nick, RC* | .966 | 20 | 26 | 2 | 1 | 29 | 0 |
| Lewis, Fred, SJ* | .971 | 114 | 259 | 7 | 8 | 274 | 2 |
| Lima, Joseph, LKE | 1.000 | 1 | 1 | 0 | 0 | 1 | 0 |
| Lincoln, Justin, BAK | 1.000 | 1 | 2 | 0 | 0 | 2 | 0 |
| Margalski, Ben, STK* | .000 | 1 | 0 | 0 | 1 | 1 | 0 |
| Martinez, Gabriel, BAK* | .897 | 28 | 34 | 1 | 4 | 39 | 0 |
| Martinez-Esteve, Edd, SJ | 1.000 | 17 | 21 | 1 | 0 | 22 | 0 |
| Mateo, Luis, BAK | .930 | 111 | 168 | 18 | 14 | 200 | 6 |
| McAnulty, Paul, LKE* | .949 | 66 | 101 | 10 | 6 | 117 | 0 |
| McBeth, Marcus, MOD | .974 | 96 | 210 | 11 | 6 | 227 | 3 |
| Melgarejo, Ransel, RC | 1.000 | 73 | 141 | 8 | 0 | 149 | 0 |
| Mendez, Mario, HD | .910 | 86 | 144 | 7 | 15 | 166 | 0 |
| Mondesi, Raul, RC | 1.000 | 1 | 1 | 0 | 0 | 1 | 0 |
| Morgan, Matt, LNC | .833 | 4 | 5 | 0 | 1 | 6 | 0 |
| Morris, Chris, HD | .938 | 8 | 15 | 0 | 1 | 16 | 0 |
| Nelson, Jon, INL | .950 | 99 | 145 | 8 | 8 | 161 | 2 |
| Nettles, Marcus, LKE* | .959 | 52 | 93 | 1 | 4 | 98 | 0 |
| Nunez, Felix, RC | 1.000 | 15 | 18 | 1 | 0 | 19 | 0 |
| Perry, Jason, MOD* | .964 | 71 | 128 | 5 | 5 | 138 | 3 |
| Phillips, Dan, VIS | .964 | 12 | 25 | 2 | 1 | 28 | 1 |
| Quentin, Carlos, LNC | .981 | 58 | 100 | 2 | 2 | 104 | 0 |
| Ramos, Carlos, BAK* | .965 | 30 | 54 | 1 | 2 | 57 | 0 |
| Rasmussen, Pete, HD | .810 | 13 | 15 | 2 | 4 | 21 | 0 |
| Richardson, Mike, LKE | .984 | 38 | 60 | 3 | 1 | 64 | 0 |
| Rico, Matt, BAK | .987 | 90 | 135 | 14 | 2 | 151 | 1 |
| Rogers, Nick, MOD | 1.000 | 5 | 6 | 0 | 0 | 6 | 0 |
| Roman, Jesse, LKE* | .875 | 7 | 6 | 1 | 1 | 8 | 0 |
| Salazar, Jeff, VIS* | .995 | 73 | 187 | 9 | 1 | 197 | 2 |
| Schierholtz, Nate, SJ* | .861 | 17 | 29 | 2 | 5 | 36 | 2 |
| Senreiso, Juan, STK | .929 | 50 | 127 | 4 | 10 | 141 | 1 |
| Serfass, Jake, HD* | 1.000 | 9 | 10 | 0 | 0 | 10 | 0 |
| Simon, Brandon, LNC* | .956 | 32 | 43 | 0 | 2 | 45 | 0 |
| Sinisi, Vincent, STK* | .981 | 56 | 101 | 5 | 2 | 108 | 0 |
| Smith, Dustin, STK | 1.000 | 2 | 2 | 0 | 0 | 2 | 0 |
| Sosa, Carlos, SJ | .966 | 95 | 157 | 14 | 6 | 177 | 1 |
| Spilborghs, Ryan, VIS | .981 | 101 | 246 | 11 | 5 | 262 | 2 |
| Stavisky, Brian, MOD* | .975 | 90 | 150 | 7 | 4 | 161 | 1 |
| Strong, Zach, SJ | .938 | 19 | 27 | 3 | 2 | 32 | 0 |
| Sugden, Jason, RC | .943 | 73 | 108 | 7 | 7 | 122 | 1 |

| Player, Team | Pct. | G | PO | A | E | TC | DP |
|---|---|---|---|---|---|---|---|
| Timpner, Clay, SJ* | 1.000 | 6 | 15 | 0 | 0 | 15 | 0 |
| Trumble, Dan, SJ | .957 | 82 | 127 | 6 | 6 | 139 | 2 |
| Turner, Lloyd, MOD | 1.000 | 22 | 33 | 1 | 0 | 34 | 0 |
| Van Iderstine, Ben, HD* | .987 | 45 | 74 | 1 | 1 | 76 | 0 |
| Walter, Randy, SJ | .972 | 85 | 166 | 6 | 5 | 177 | 2 |
| Webster, Anthony, STK* | .946 | 83 | 156 | 2 | 9 | 167 | 0 |
| Weed, BJ, RC | .963 | 49 | 75 | 2 | 3 | 80 | 0 |
| Willits, Reggie, RC | .982 | 133 | 322 | 13 | 6 | 341 | 3 |
| Zeringue, Jon, LNC | 1.000 | 45 | 76 | 7 | 0 | 83 | 1 |

## CATCHERS

| Player, Team | Pct. | G | PO | A | E | TC | DP | PB |
|---|---|---|---|---|---|---|---|---|
| Abruzzo, Jared, RC | 1.000 | 5 | 11 | 2 | 0 | 13 | 0 | 1 |
| Anderson, Keith, SJ | .980 | 44 | 365 | 35 | 8 | 408 | 5 | 5 |
| Aracena, Sandy, BAK | .961 | 29 | 216 | 30 | 10 | 256 | 4 | 9 |
| Avlas, Phil, LNC | .980 | 106 | 741 | 91 | 17 | 849 | 1 | 5 |
| Budde, Ryan, RC | .980 | 66 | 477 | 61 | 11 | 549 | 0 | 7 |
| Carlin, Luke, LKE | .985 | 36 | 237 | 32 | 4 | 273 | 3 | 5 |
| Colina, Alvin, VIS | .987 | 93 | 595 | 73 | 9 | 677 | 5 | 13 |
| Cordell, Brent, BAK | .979 | 50 | 294 | 39 | 7 | 340 | 5 | 24 |
| Craig, Beau, MOD | 1.000 | 5 | 31 | 1 | 0 | 32 | 0 | 1 |
| Esposito, Brian, STK | .992 | 19 | 103 | 20 | 1 | 124 | 0 | 4 |
| Frost, Jeremy, HD | .967 | 13 | 103 | 14 | 4 | 121 | 0 | 4 |
| Hagen, Matt, INL | 1.000 | 4 | 7 | 2 | 0 | 9 | 0 | 1 |
| Hamblen, Chris, STK | .931 | 11 | 62 | 5 | 5 | 72 | 3 | 0 |
| Hammock, Robby, LNC | 1.000 | 1 | 5 | 1 | 0 | 6 | 0 | 0 |
| Holm, Steve, SJ | .995 | 50 | 338 | 41 | 2 | 381 | 2 | 7 |
| Jaile, Chris, STK | .981 | 46 | 279 | 30 | 6 | 315 | 4 | 16 |
| Jennings, Todd, SJ | .984 | 44 | 346 | 29 | 6 | 381 | 3 | 9 |
| Lauderdale, Matt, LKE | 1.000 | 2 | 5 | 1 | 0 | 6 | 0 | 0 |
| Lentz, Brian, INL | .988 | 39 | 224 | 28 | 3 | 255 | 3 | 7 |
| Madera, Sandy, VIS | .977 | 19 | 117 | 10 | 3 | 130 | 1 | 4 |
| Margalski, Ben, STK* | .985 | 28 | 173 | 20 | 3 | 196 | 1 | 7 |
| Merritt, Graig, BAK | .985 | 50 | 300 | 36 | 5 | 341 | 3 | 10 |
| Miller, Chris, LKE | 1.000 | 2 | 13 | 0 | 0 | 13 | 0 | 0 |
| Morgan, Matt, LNC | .992 | 20 | 114 | 18 | 1 | 133 | 0 | 4 |
| Morris, Jed, MOD* | .984 | 35 | 228 | 16 | 4 | 248 | 1 | 6 |
| Munhall, Brian, SJ | .968 | 4 | 27 | 3 | 1 | 31 | 0 | 1 |
| Myers, Casey, MOD | .960 | 20 | 134 | 11 | 6 | 151 | 1 | 2 |
| Myers, Cory, LNC | 1.000 | 3 | 16 | 1 | 0 | 17 | 0 | 2 |
| Napoli, Michael, RC | .986 | 72 | 484 | 84 | 8 | 576 | 4 | 7 |
| Pagan, Andres, LKE | .974 | 99 | 703 | 82 | 21 | 806 | 6 | 12 |
| Peck, Bryan, VIS | .000 | 1 | 0 | 0 | 0 | 0 | 0 | 0 |
| Reece, Eric, BAK* | 1.000 | 2 | 9 | 1 | 0 | 10 | 0 | 1 |
| Reinking, Kevin, VIS | .982 | 30 | 199 | 14 | 4 | 217 | 2 | 5 |
| Richardson, Mike, LKE | .987 | 10 | 68 | 8 | 1 | 77 | 0 | 3 |
| Riggans, Shawn, BAK | .996 | 29 | 220 | 17 | 1 | 238 | 1 | 5 |
| RIVERA, RENE, INL | .993 | 106 | 880 | 110 | 7 | 997 | 6 | 17 |
| Robledo, Nelson, VIS | 1.000 | 5 | 28 | 1 | 0 | 29 | 0 | 1 |
| Slee, Gregory, INL* | .968 | 4 | 29 | 1 | 1 | 31 | 0 | 0 |
| Smith, Dustin, STK | .985 | 48 | 307 | 31 | 5 | 343 | 0 | 7 |
| Suomi, John, MOD* | .986 | 92 | 642 | 50 | 10 | 702 | 8 | 25 |
| Sutton, Don, MOD | 1.000 | 1 | 8 | 1 | 0 | 9 | 0 | 1 |
| Tosca, Daniel, LNC* | .978 | 22 | 128 | 8 | 3 | 139 | 2 | 0 |
| Vanden Berg, John, HD | .975 | 69 | 503 | 53 | 14 | 570 | 4 | 12 |
| Villanueva, Froilan, HD | .983 | 64 | 496 | 66 | 10 | 572 | 4 | 17 |

## PITCHERS

| Player, Team | Pct. | G | PO | A | E | TC | DP |
|---|---|---|---|---|---|---|---|
| Accardo, Jeremy, SJ | 1.000 | 49 | 5 | 11 | 0 | 16 | 0 |
| Akens, Phil, STK | .857 | 18 | 4 | 2 | 1 | 7 | 0 |
| Allen, Brian, BAK | 750 | 11 | 3 | 0 | 1 | 4 | 0 |
| Andrew, Jason, STK | 1.000 | 8 | 3 | 9 | 0 | 12 | 0 |
| Arakawa, Yusuke, VIS | 1.000 | 29 | 4 | 4 | 0 | 8 | 1 |
| Asahina, Jonathan, VIS | .930 | 34 | 17 | 23 | 3 | 43 | 3 |
| Astacio, Hector, RC | 1.000 | 16 | 1 | 3 | 0 | 4 | 0 |
| Austen, David, RC | 1.000 | 17 | 1 | 4 | 0 | 5 | 0 |
| Autrey, Scott, BAK | 1.000 | 15 | 2 | 3 | 0 | 5 | 1 |
| Avendano, Elvis, MOD | .813 | 45 | 1 | 12 | 3 | 16 | 1 |
| Ballouli, Khalid, HD | .875 | 27 | 7 | 7 | 2 | 16 | 0 |
| Bass, Adam, LNC | .952 | 28 | 5 | 15 | 1 | 21 | 2 |
| Beavers, Kevin, LKE* | 1.000 | 32 | 1 | 10 | 0 | 11 | 0 |
| Bechtel, Chuck, LKE | 1.000 | 7 | 1 | 0 | 0 | 1 | 0 |
| Beckstead, Jentry, VIS | 1.000 | 39 | 3 | 8 | 0 | 11 | 0 |
| Belson, Greg, LNC | .833 | 29 | 0 | 5 | 1 | 6 | 1 |
| Beltre, Omar, STK | .833 | 45 | 1 | 4 | 1 | 6 | 1 |
| Bengochea, Kiki, STK | .500 | 19 | 2 | 1 | 3 | 6 | 0 |
| Bernier, Doug, VIS | 1.000 | 1 | 1 | 0 | 0 | 1 | 0 |
| Bilke, Austin, RC | 1.000 | 25 | 3 | 3 | 0 | 6 | 1 |
| Bonine, Eddie, LKE | .962 | 21 | 5 | 20 | 1 | 26 | 0 |
| Bradley, David, HD | .875 | 30 | 10 | 18 | 4 | 32 | 1 |
| Brannon, Nick, MOD* | 1.000 | 15 | 0 | 3 | 0 | 3 | 0 |

| Player, Team | Pct. | G | PO | A | E | TC | DP |
|---|---|---|---|---|---|---|---|
| Breslow, Craig, HD* | .600 | 23 | 0 | 3 | 2 | 5 | 0 |
| Broshuis, Garrett, SJ | 1.000 | 10 | 2 | 5 | 0 | 7 | 0 |
| Bruso, Greg, HD | .958 | 12 | 7 | 16 | 1 | 24 | 0 |
| Bulger, Jason, LNC | 1.000 | 21 | 1 | 2 | 0 | 3 | 0 |
| Bumstead, Mike, LKE | .500 | 9 | 0 | 1 | 1 | 2 | 0 |
| Burres, Brian, SJ* | 1.000 | 36 | 4 | 21 | 0 | 25 | 1 |
| Burton, Jared, MOD | .750 | 10 | 1 | 2 | 1 | 4 | 0 |
| Bystrowski, Bobby, MOD | 1.000 | 12 | 1 | 2 | 0 | 3 | 0 |
| Cabaniel, Tomas, MOD | .889 | 11 | 4 | 4 | 1 | 9 | 0 |
| Cable, Taft, VIS | .900 | 38 | 9 | 9 | 2 | 20 | 1 |
| Cain, Matthew, SJ | .875 | 12 | 2 | 5 | 1 | 8 | 0 |
| Capuano, Chris, HD* | 1.000 | 1 | 0 | 1 | 0 | 1 | 0 |
| Carroll, James, RC | 1.000 | 47 | 0 | 8 | 0 | 8 | 0 |
| Cartier, Rich, VIS | .765 | 32 | 6 | 7 | 4 | 17 | 0 |
| Castillo, Ruben, INL | 1.000 | 5 | 1 | 1 | 0 | 2 | 0 |
| Castleman, Steve, VIS | 1.000 | 9 | 2 | 2 | 0 | 4 | 0 |
| Cate, Troy, INL* | 1.000 | 7 | 1 | 4 | 0 | 5 | 0 |
| Ciccotelli, Michael, INL* | .000 | 1 | 0 | 0 | 0 | 0 | 0 |
| Clarke, Darren, VIS | .000 | 7 | 0 | 0 | 0 | 0 | 0 |
| Coleman, Jeff, MOD | 1.000 | 45 | 8 | 10 | 0 | 18 | 0 |
| Comolli, Mark, BAK | .857 | 29 | 8 | 10 | 3 | 21 | 3 |
| Coonrod, Aaron, LKE | 1.000 | 22 | 1 | 3 | 0 | 4 | 0 |
| Cosgrove, Mike, VIS | 1.000 | 32 | 0 | 9 | 0 | 9 | 0 |
| Costello, Ryan, HD* | .667 | 6 | 0 | 2 | 1 | 3 | 0 |
| Craker, Justin, LKE | 1.000 | 9 | 1 | 2 | 0 | 3 | 1 |
| Cram, Josh, SJ | .917 | 41 | 4 | 7 | 1 | 12 | 1 |
| Crockett, Ben, VIS | .900 | 28 | 17 | 19 | 4 | 40 | 2 |
| Cromer, Nathan, BAK* | .867 | 37 | 2 | 11 | 2 | 15 | 1 |
| Danks, John, STK* | .846 | 13 | 5 | 6 | 2 | 13 | 0 |
| Davidson, Daniel, RC* | .943 | 28 | 8 | 25 | 2 | 35 | 1 |
| De Los Santos, Franc, STK | .000 | 3 | 0 | 0 | 0 | 0 | 0 |
| Deago, Roger, LKE* | .000 | 1 | 0 | 0 | 0 | 0 | 0 |
| DeBarr, Nick, BAK | .786 | 26 | 4 | 7 | 3 | 14 | 0 |
| Diangelo, Jason, VIS | 1.000 | 4 | 0 | 1 | 0 | 1 | 0 |
| Dorman, Rich, INL | 1.000 | 7 | 0 | 5 | 0 | 5 | 0 |
| Dowdy, Justin, RC* | .714 | 15 | 0 | 5 | 2 | 7 | 0 |
| Doyle, Jared, LNC* | .625 | 8 | 2 | 3 | 3 | 8 | 0 |
| Espineli, Geno, SJ* | 1.000 | 1 | 0 | 1 | 0 | 1 | 0 |
| Feliciano, Jesus, BAK* | 1.000 | 5 | 3 | 2 | 0 | 5 | 0 |
| Fischer, Steve, MOD | 1.000 | 21 | 3 | 6 | 0 | 9 | 0 |
| Flinn, Chris, BAK | 1.000 | 24 | 0 | 2 | 0 | 2 | 0 |
| Foppert, Jesse, SJ | 1.000 | 4 | 0 | 2 | 0 | 2 | 0 |
| Fulmer, TA, INL | .905 | 17 | 9 | 10 | 2 | 21 | 1 |
| Gallagher, Buddy, VIS* | 1.000 | 15 | 5 | 5 | 0 | 10 | 0 |
| Garcia, James, SJ | .857 | 42 | 4 | 8 | 2 | 14 | 0 |
| Garcia, Jose, STK | 1.000 | 22 | 3 | 7 | 0 | 10 | 0 |
| Gardner, Hayden, STK | 1.000 | 7 | 0 | 1 | 0 | 1 | 0 |
| Girardeau, Clark, LKE | 1.000 | 12 | 1 | 3 | 0 | 4 | 1 |
| Girdner, Jason, BAK | .800 | 18 | 4 | 4 | 2 | 10 | 3 |
| Glant, Dustin, LNC | .833 | 13 | 0 | 5 | 1 | 6 | 0 |
| Gonzalez, Enrique, LNC | .952 | 42 | 13 | 27 | 2 | 42 | 1 |
| Goocher, Clint, LNC* | .964 | 14 | 10 | 17 | 1 | 28 | 0 |
| Gor, Nick, BAK | .667 | 9 | 1 | 1 | 1 | 3 | 0 |
| Gregg, Grant, LKE* | 1.000 | 36 | 1 | 2 | 0 | 3 | 0 |
| Griffith, Dustin, RC | 1.000 | 50 | 5 | 5 | 0 | 10 | 0 |
| Guthrie, Sazi, LKE | 1.000 | 5 | 2 | 2 | 0 | 4 | 0 |
| Hall, Bo, HD | .857 | 27 | 6 | 12 | 3 | 21 | 0 |
| Hamilton, Mark, HD* | 1.000 | 12 | 2 | 7 | 0 | 9 | 1 |
| Hammel, Jason, BAK | .842 | 11 | 10 | 6 | 3 | 19 | 1 |
| Harper, Jesse, HD | 1.000 | 9 | 0 | 6 | 0 | 6 | 1 |
| Hayhurst, Dirk, LKE | .500 | 5 | 1 | 0 | 1 | 2 | 0 |
| Henderson, Brian, BAK* | .889 | 29 | 0 | 8 | 1 | 9 | 1 |
| Henderson, Eric, HD* | .958 | 25 | 5 | 18 | 1 | 24 | 1 |
| Hernandez, Felix, INL | .958 | 16 | 10 | 13 | 1 | 24 | 0 |
| Hill, Seth, STK* | 1.000 | 19 | 2 | 3 | 0 | 5 | 0 |
| Hitchcock, Sterling, LKE* | 1.000 | 2 | 0 | 2 | 0 | 2 | 0 |
| Hogan, Gary, STK | .917 | 27 | 4 | 7 | 1 | 12 | 0 |
| Holsten, Ryan, LNC | 1.000 | 43 | 6 | 10 | 0 | 16 | 1 |
| Holubec, Ken, STK* | 1.000 | 29 | 1 | 2 | 0 | 3 | 0 |
| Huber, Jon, LKE | .800 | 20 | 3 | 9 | 3 | 15 | 0 |
| Huber, Jon, INL | 1.000 | 7 | 1 | 3 | 0 | 4 | 0 |
| Huber, Jon, LKE-INL | .842 | 0 | 4 | 12 | 3 | 19 | 0 |
| Hudgins, John, STK | 1.000 | 15 | 2 | 4 | 0 | 6 | 0 |
| Jaile, Chris, STK | 1.000 | 1 | 0 | 1 | 0 | 1 | 0 |
| Jenks, Bobby, RC | .000 | 1 | 0 | 0 | 0 | 0 | 0 |
| Jimenez, Cesar, INL* | .947 | 43 | 8 | 28 | 2 | 38 | 1 |
| Jimenez, Ubaldo, VIS | 1.000 | 8 | 0 | 5 | 0 | 5 | 1 |
| Johnson, Doug, VIS | .955 | 35 | 6 | 15 | 1 | 22 | 3 |
| Johnson, Rett, INL | .900 | 7 | 3 | 6 | 1 | 10 | 1 |
| Jones, Geoff, LKE* | .750 | 11 | 1 | 5 | 2 | 8 | 0 |
| Keiter, Ben, STK | 1.000 | 12 | 2 | 1 | 0 | 3 | 0 |
| Kirsten, Joel, STK* | 1.000 | 5 | 0 | 3 | 0 | 3 | 0 |
| Kohn, Shawn, MOD | 1.000 | 23 | 1 | 5 | 0 | 6 | 0 |

| Player, Team | Pct. | G | PO | A | E | TC | DP |
|---|---|---|---|---|---|---|---|
| Kolb, Dan, HD | .833 | 37 | 4 | 6 | 2 | 12 | 0 |
| Kolb, Danny, HD | 1.000 | 1 | 0 | 1 | 0 | 1 | 0 |
| Kozlowski, Ben, STK* | 1.000 | 10 | 2 | 4 | 0 | 6 | 0 |
| Kusiewicz, Mike, HD* | .909 | 26 | 3 | 7 | 1 | 11 | 0 |
| Landeros, Leonard, MOD* | .857 | 42 | 1 | 5 | 1 | 7 | 0 |
| Little, Joe, BAK* | 1.000 | 11 | 1 | 9 | 0 | 10 | 0 |
| Littleton, Wes, STK | 1.000 | 30 | 18 | 19 | 0 | 37 | 1 |
| Livingston, Bobby, INL* | .925 | 28 | 10 | 39 | 4 | 53 | 2 |
| Lockwood, Brian, BAK | .939 | 28 | 10 | 21 | 2 | 33 | 0 |
| Lorenzo, Matt, STK | .875 | 9 | 6 | 1 | 1 | 8 | 0 |
| Lugo, Ozzie, RC | 1.000 | 18 | 0 | 3 | 0 | 3 | 0 |
| Lynch, Brian, VIS | 1.000 | 26 | 3 | 5 | 0 | 8 | 0 |
| Lynch, Matt, MOD* | .964 | 27 | 7 | 20 | 1 | 28 | 0 |
| Marcano, Luis, STK | 1.000 | 34 | 5 | 7 | 0 | 12 | 1 |
| Markert, Jackson, SJ | .750 | 25 | 0 | 3 | 1 | 4 | 0 |
| Martin, Forest, HD | .875 | 10 | 3 | 4 | 1 | 8 | 1 |
| Martinez, Miguel, INL* | 1.000 | 30 | 4 | 6 | 0 | 10 | 0 |
| Masset, Nick, STK | .935 | 16 | 14 | 15 | 2 | 31 | 1 |
| Mateo, Natanael, LKE | .778 | 39 | 1 | 6 | 2 | 9 | 0 |
| Mazurek, David, STK | 1.000 | 54 | 3 | 4 | 0 | 7 | 0 |
| McCall, Derell, MOD | .944 | 15 | 8 | 9 | 1 | 18 | 0 |
| McCally, Ryan, BAK | 1.000 | 25 | 7 | 6 | 0 | 13 | 2 |
| McMachen, Clifford, LNC* | 1.000 | 37 | 2 | 3 | 0 | 5 | 1 |
| McNiven, Brooks, SJ | .826 | 31 | 6 | 13 | 4 | 23 | 3 |
| Mendez, Mario, HD | 1.000 | 3 | 0 | 1 | 0 | 1 | 0 |
| Mendoza, Marcos, VIS* | 1.000 | 31 | 3 | 6 | 0 | 9 | 0 |
| Miniel, Rene, LKE | .875 | 16 | 2 | 5 | 1 | 8 | 0 |
| Moak, Curtis, MOD* | .875 | 19 | 0 | 7 | 1 | 8 | 0 |
| Morel, Eudy, VIS | 1.000 | 29 | 1 | 4 | 0 | 5 | 0 |
| Muessig, Jeff, MOD | 1.000 | 9 | 3 | 1 | 0 | 4 | 0 |
| Navaroli, Michael, BAK | .938 | 32 | 2 | 13 | 1 | 16 | 1 |
| Needham, Joel, HD | .000 | 2 | 0 | 0 | 0 | 0 | 0 |
| Neugebauer, Nick, HD | .000 | 1 | 0 | 0 | 0 | 0 | 0 |
| Nolasco, David, HD | 1.000 | 44 | 3 | 15 | 0 | 18 | 2 |
| Obenchain, Stephen, MOD | .800 | 23 | 3 | 9 | 3 | 15 | 0 |
| Oldham, Thomas, INL* | .800 | 7 | 0 | 8 | 2 | 10 | 1 |
| Orvella, Chad, BAK | 1.000 | 15 | 3 | 3 | 0 | 6 | 0 |
| Osuna, Antonio, LKE | 1.000 | 7 | 1 | 2 | 0 | 3 | 0 |
| Pannone, Anthony, SJ | 1.000 | 55 | 9 | 8 | 0 | 17 | 0 |
| Parra, Manny, HD* | .875 | 13 | 0 | 14 | 2 | 16 | 2 |
| Pauley, David, LKE | .815 | 27 | 8 | 14 | 5 | 27 | 0 |
| Pavlik, Isaac, VIS* | .667 | 23 | 1 | 1 | 1 | 3 | 0 |
| Pavon, Julio, SJ | .842 | 15 | 11 | 5 | 3 | 19 | 1 |
| Pendley, Nathan, SJ* | 1.000 | 7 | 0 | 2 | 0 | 2 | 0 |
| Peralta, Joel, RC | .000 | 1 | 0 | 0 | 0 | 0 | 0 |
| Perez, Elvis, VIS | 1.000 | 13 | 6 | 3 | 0 | 9 | 0 |
| Perez, Keith, MOD | .944 | 21 | 8 | 9 | 1 | 18 | 1 |
| Perez, Roberto, STK | .500 | 2 | 1 | 0 | 1 | 2 | 0 |
| Petersen, Jeffrey, SJ | .737 | 27 | 8 | 6 | 5 | 19 | 0 |
| Petke, Tim, RC | .000 | 3 | 0 | 0 | 0 | 0 | 0 |
| Pizarro, Melvin, INL* | .882 | 41 | 6 | 9 | 2 | 17 | 1 |
| Posey, Micah, RC* | 1.000 | 8 | 1 | 6 | 0 | 7 | 1 |
| Prochaska, Mike, BAK* | 1.000 | 11 | 4 | 10 | 0 | 14 | 2 |
| Ribas, Gabe, LKE | .875 | 13 | 4 | 10 | 2 | 16 | 1 |
| Ridgeway, Jeff, BAK* | 1.000 | 15 | 2 | 9 | 0 | 11 | 2 |
| Rivard, Reggie, HD | 1.000 | 17 | 2 | 3 | 0 | 5 | 0 |
| Rivera, Homero, HD* | 1.000 | 20 | 1 | 7 | 0 | 8 | 1 |
| Robertson, Luke, MOD | .800 | 4 | 2 | 2 | 1 | 5 | 0 |
| Rowland-Smith, Ryan, INL* | .833 | 29 | 2 | 8 | 2 | 12 | 0 |
| Rupe, Josh, STK | 1.000 | 4 | 1 | 6 | 0 | 7 | 0 |
| Russ, Chris, STK* | 923 | 28 | 3 | 9 | 1 | 13 | 0 |
| Sadler, Billy, SJ | .846 | 30 | 2 | 9 | 2 | 13 | 0 |
| Sandoval, Juan, INL | .969 | 27 | 16 | 15 | 1 | 32 | 1 |
| Sansom, Trevor, MOD | 1.000 | 7 | 0 | 2 | 0 | 2 | 0 |
| Sauer, Marc, MOD | .944 | 24 | 9 | 8 | 1 | 18 | 1 |
| Saunders, Joe, RC* | .875 | 19 | 1 | 13 | 2 | 16 | 0 |
| Schmidt, Jason, SJ | .000 | 1 | 0 | 0 | 0 | 0 | 0 |
| Schultz, Mike, LNC | 1.000 | 13 | 2 | 3 | 0 | 5 | 0 |
| Seddon, Chris, BAK* | .889 | 7 | 1 | 7 | 1 | 9 | 1 |
| Sevier, Nate, LKE | 1.000 | 38 | 3 | 5 | 0 | 8 | 0 |
| Shank, Chris, MOD | 1.000 | 49 | 4 | 6 | 0 | 10 | 0 |
| Shappi, AJ, LNC | 1.000 | 2 | 1 | 0 | 0 | 1 | 0 |
| Shell, Steven, RC | .909 | 28 | 12 | 18 | 3 | 33 | 0 |
| Shields, Jamie, BAK | 1.000 | 20 | 14 | 15 | 0 | 29 | 0 |
| Silva, Doug, VIS | .000 | 2 | 0 | 0 | 0 | 0 | 0 |
| Silva, Jesus, LNC | .944 | 28 | 14 | 20 | 2 | 36 | 0 |
| Simon, Alfredo, SJ | 1.000 | 6 | 3 | 4 | 0 | 7 | 0 |
| Slack, Nick, HD | .833 | 45 | 4 | 6 | 2 | 12 | 1 |
| Smith, Cliff, RC | 1.000 | 7 | 0 | 1 | 0 | 1 | 0 |
| Smith, Cody, STK | 1.000 | 32 | 18 | 23 | 0 | 41 | 1 |
| Smith, Sam, LNC | 1.000 | 18 | 3 | 6 | 0 | 9 | 0 |
| Soriano, Rafael, INL | 1.000 | 2 | 0 | 1 | 0 | 1 | 0 |
| Soto, Darwin, INL | 1.000 | 42 | 10 | 15 | 0 | 25 | 0 |
| Stauffer, Tim, LKE | 1.000 | 6 | 1 | 4 | 0 | 5 | 0 |
| Steele, Mike, INL | 1.000 | 20 | 1 | 5 | 0 | 6 | 0 |
| Stertzbach, Von, RC | .938 | 47 | 4 | 11 | 1 | 16 | 0 |
| Stetter, Mitchel, HD* | 1.000 | 8 | 0 | 8 | 0 | 8 | 0 |
| Stirm, Brian, SJ | .889 | 31 | 4 | 12 | 2 | 18 | 0 |
| Sullivan, Bradley, MOD | .977 | 27 | 12 | 31 | 1 | 44 | 2 |
| Teeter, Travis, HD | 1.000 | 6 | 2 | 1 | 0 | 3 | 0 |
| Thayer, Dale, LKE | .889 | 50 | 1 | 7 | 1 | 9 | 0 |
| Thompson, Richard, RC | 1.000 | 41 | 3 | 3 | 0 | 6 | 1 |
| Tierney, Chris, LKE* | 1.000 | 8 | 2 | 14 | 0 | 16 | 2 |
| Toledo, Jean, RC | .946 | 24 | 8 | 27 | 2 | 37 | 1 |
| Touchstone, Nick, RC* | .000 | 3 | 0 | 0 | 1 | 1 | 0 |
| Treadway, Brion, SJ | .923 | 20 | 2 | 10 | 1 | 13 | 0 |
| Tucker, Rusty, LKE* | 1.000 | 8 | 0 | 1 | 0 | 1 | 0 |
| Ulloa, Manny, VIS | 1.000 | 6 | 2 | 5 | 0 | 7 | 0 |
| Valdez, Merkin, SJ | 1.000 | 7 | 1 | 4 | 0 | 5 | 0 |
| Vanden Berg, John, HD | 1.000 | 1 | 0 | 1 | 0 | 1 | 0 |
| Viane, David, INL | .857 | 20 | 3 | 3 | 1 | 7 | 0 |
| Villatoro, Wilmer, LKE | .769 | 47 | 2 | 8 | 3 | 13 | 0 |
| Volquez, Edison, STK | .857 | 8 | 4 | 2 | 1 | 7 | 0 |
| Waddell, Jason, SJ* | 1.000 | 47 | 3 | 9 | 0 | 12 | 1 |
| Walton, Samuel, BAK* | .929 | 23 | 4 | 9 | 1 | 14 | 0 |
| Washburn, Jarrod, RC* | 1.000 | 1 | 0 | 1 | 0 | 1 | 0 |
| Watson, Mike, LNC | .929 | 57 | 3 | 10 | 1 | 14 | 1 |
| Watson, Tanner, INL | 1.000 | 25 | 8 | 5 | 0 | 13 | 0 |
| Wear, Greg, INL | 1.000 | 17 | 3 | 4 | 0 | 7 | 0 |
| Webb, Alan, LKE* | 1.000 | 11 | 1 | 1 | 0 | 2 | 0 |
| Wechsler, Justin, LNC | .909 | 56 | 2 | 8 | 1 | 11 | 1 |
| Wells, Carlton, LNC* | .900 | 71 | 3 | 15 | 2 | 20 | 0 |
| Wells, Jared, LKE | .941 | 13 | 4 | 12 | 1 | 17 | 0 |
| Whatley, Keith, LNC* | .813 | 12 | 2 | 11 | 3 | 16 | 0 |
| Whitaker, Brian, LKE | 1.000 | 5 | 3 | 5 | 0 | 8 | 0 |
| White, Bill, LNC* | 1.000 | 14 | 3 | 3 | 0 | 6 | 1 |
| Wiedmeyer, Jason, LKE* | .000 | 4 | 0 | 0 | 0 | 0 | 0 |
| Wilhite, Matt, RC | .913 | 52 | 1 | 20 | 2 | 23 | 0 |
| Wilson, Phil, RC | .824 | 38 | 11 | 17 | 6 | 34 | 2 |
| Wodnicki, Mike, LKE | 1.000 | 17 | 0 | 5 | 0 | 5 | 0 |
| Woody, Dominic, RC | .909 | 6 | 4 | 6 | 1 | 11 | 0 |
| Woolard, Glenn, HD | 1.000 | 12 | 2 | 7 | 0 | 9 | 1 |
| Yarbrough, Joe, BAK* | .950 | 60 | 7 | 12 | 1 | 20 | 1 |
| Young, Chris, VIS | 1.000 | 52 | 8 | 14 | 0 | 22 | 0 |
| Zamora, Peter, LNC* | 1.000 | 13 | 3 | 10 | 0 | 13 | 0 |
| Ziegler, Brad, MOD | 1.000 | 16 | 8 | 10 | 0 | 18 | 0 |

## LEAGUE CHAMPIONS

| Year | Team | Pct. |
|---|---|---|
| 1914— | Fresno | .571 |
| 1915— | Modesto | .857 |
| 1916-40—Did not operate. | | |
| 1941— | Fresno | .643 |
| | Santa Barbara (2nd)* | .597 |
| 1942— | Santa Barbara† | .642 |
| 1943-44-45—Did not operate. | | |
| 1946— | Stockton‡ | .600 |
| 1947— | Stockton‡ | .679 |
| 1948— | Fresno | .607 |
| | Santa Barbara (3rd)* | .529 |
| 1949— | Bakersfield | .612 |
| | San Jose (4th)* | .543 |
| 1950— | Ventura | .607 |
| | Modesto (2nd)* | .586 |
| 1951— | Santa Barbara‡ | .599 |
| 1952— | Fresno‡ | .629 |
| 1953— | San Jose‡ | .664 |
| 1954— | Modesto‡ | .623 |
| 1955— | Stockton | .733 |
| | Fresno§ | .718 |
| 1956— | Fresno§ | .650 |
| 1957— | Visalia∞ | .622 |
| | Salinas (4th)* | .504 |
| 1958— | Fresno* | .639 |
| | Bakersfield | .672 |
| 1959— | Bakersfield | .592 |
| | Modesto§ | .643 |
| 1960— | Reno | .614 |
| | Reno | .657 |
| 1961— | Reno | .743 |
| | Reno | .643 |
| 1962— | San Jose§ | .686 |
| | Reno | .587 |
| 1963— | Modesto | .589 |
| | Stockton§ | .687 |
| 1964— | Fresno | .638 |
| | Fresno | .600 |
| 1965— | San Jose | .586 |
| | Stockton§ | .614 |
| 1966— | Modesto | .577 |
| | Modesto | .671 |
| 1967— | San Jose§ | .676 |
| | Modesto | .586 |
| 1968— | San Jose | .629 |
| | Fresno§ | .623 |
| 1969— | Stockton§ | .600 |
| | Visalia | .614 |

| Year | Team | Pct. |
|---|---|---|
| 1970— | Bakersfield | .667 |
| | Bakersfield | .671 |
| 1971— | Visalia§ | .583 |
| | Fresno | .500 |
| 1972— | Modesto§ | .547 |
| | Bakersfield | .629 |
| 1973— | Lodi§ | .657 |
| | Bakersfield | .571 |
| 1974— | Fresno§ | .607 |
| | San Jose | .579 |
| 1975— | Reno | .614 |
| | Reno | .614 |
| 1976— | Salinas | .650 |
| | Reno§ | .547 |
| 1977— | Salinas | .564 |
| | Lodi§ | .579 |
| 1978— | Visalia§ | .698 |
| | Lodi | .607 |
| 1979— | San Jose§ | .636 |
| | Reno | .525 |
| 1980— | Stockton§ | .638 |
| | Visalia | .507 |
| 1981— | Visalia | .621 |
| | Lodi§ | .521 |
| 1982— | Modesto§ | .671 |
| | Visalia | .586 |
| 1983— | Visalia | .621 |
| | Redwood§ | .529 |
| 1984— | Modesto§ | .597 |
| | Bakersfield | .486 |
| 1985— | Fresno§ | .575 |
| | Stockton | .566 |
| 1986— | Palm Springs | .613 |
| | Stockton§ | .585 |
| 1987— | Fresno§ | .559 |
| | Reno | .535 |
| 1988— | Stockton | .657 |
| | Riverside§ | .599 |
| 1989— | Stockton | .627 |
| | Bakersfield§ | .577 |
| 1990— | Visalia | .638 |
| | Stockton§ | .582 |
| 1991— | San Jose | .676 |
| | High Desert§ | .537 |
| 1992— | Stockton§ | .610 |
| | Visalia | .551 |
| 1993— | High Desert§ | .620 |
| | Modesto | .529 |
| 1994— | Modesto | .706 |
| | Rancho Cucamonga§ | .566 |
| 1995— | San Bernardino§ | .612 |
| | San Jose | .550 |
| 1996— | San Jose | .636 |
| | Lake Elsinore‡ | .550 |
| 1997— | High Desert▲ | .593 |
| | San Bernardino | .486 |
| 1998— | San Jose▲ | .593 |
| | Rancho Cucamonga | .550 |
| 1999— | Modesto | .629 |
| | San Bernardino▲ | .567 |
| 2000— | Lancaster | .636 |
| | San Bernardino▲ | .550 |
| 2001— | Lake Elsinore◆ | .650 |
| | San Jose◆ | .550 |
| 2002— | Stockton▲ | .636 |
| 2003— | Inland Empire▲ | .557 |
| 2004— | Modesto▲ | .643 |

*Won four-club playoff. †League disbanded June 28. ‡Won championship and four-club playoff. §Won split-season playoff. ∞Won both halves of split season. ▲Played split season and won six-club playoff. ◆Played split season and were in midst of six-club playoff and declared co-champions when Professional Baseball declared a stoppage of play.

# CAROLINA LEAGUE

## LEAGUE OFFICE

**President/treasurer**
John Hopkins

**Address**
P.O. Box 9503
Greensboro, NC 27429

**Phone**
336-691-9030

**Teams (affiliation)**
Frederick Keys (Orioles)
Kinston Indians (Indians)
Lynchburg Hillcats (Pirates)
Myrtle Beach Pelicans (Braves)
Potomac Cannons (Nationals)
Salem Avalanche (Astros)
Wilmington (Del.) Blue Rocks (Red Sox)
Winston-Salem Warthogs (White Sox)

## 2004 FINAL STANDINGS

### FIRST HALF

#### NORTHERN DIVISION

| Team | W | L | T | Pct. | GB |
|---|---|---|---|---|---|
| Potomac (Cardinals) | 37 | 32 | - | .536 | ... |
| Lynchburg (Pirates) | 35 | 35 | - | .500 | 2.5 |
| Wilmington (Royals) | 33 | 36 | - | .478 | 4.0 |
| Frederick (Orioles) | 20 | 49 | - | .290 | 17.0 |

#### SOUTHERN DIVISION

| Team | W | L | T | Pct. | GB |
|---|---|---|---|---|---|
| Kinston (Indians) | 45 | 24 | - | .652 | ... |
| Myrtle Beach (Braves) | 40 | 28 | - | .588 | 4.5 |
| Salem (Astros) | 38 | 32 | - | .543 | 7.5 |
| Winston-Salem (White Sox) | 29 | 41 | - | .414 | 16.5 |

### SECOND HALF

#### NORTHERN DIVISION

| Team | W | L | T | Pct. | GB |
|---|---|---|---|---|---|
| Wilmington | 44 | 26 | - | .629 | ... |
| Frederick | 32 | 38 | - | .457 | 12.0 |
| Potomac | 30 | 40 | - | .429 | 14.0 |
| Lynchburg | 22 | 46 | - | .324 | 21.0 |

#### SOUTHERN DIVISION

| Team | W | L | T | Pct. | GB |
|---|---|---|---|---|---|
| Winston-Salem | 45 | 25 | - | .643 | ... |
| Kinston | 43 | 26 | - | .623 | 1.5 |
| Myrtle Beach | 35 | 35 | - | .500 | --- |
| Salem | 27 | 42 | - | .391 | 17.5 |

### COMPOSITE

| Team | W | L | T | Pct. | GB | KIN | WIL | MYR | W-S | POT | SAL | LYN | FRE |
|---|---|---|---|---|---|---|---|---|---|---|---|---|---|
| Kinston (Indians) | 88 | 50 | - | .638 | ... | X | 8 | 12 | 10 | 17 | 15 | 11 | 15 |
| Wilmington (Royals) | 77 | 62 | - | .554 | 11 1/2 | 12 | X | 7 | 11 | 12 | 9 | 14 | 12 |
| Myrtle Beach (Braves) | 75 | 63 | - | .543 | 13 | 8 | 12 | X | 10 | 12 | 8 | 14 | 11 |
| Winston Salem (White Sox) | 74 | 66 | - | .529 | 15 | 10 | 9 | 10 | X | 8 | 10 | 12 | 15 |
| Potomac (Reds) | 67 | 72 | - | .482 | 21 1/2 | 3 | 8 | 7 | 12 | X | 11 | 13 | 13 |
| Salem (Astros) | 65 | 74 | - | .468 | 23 1/2 | 5 | 11 | 12 | 10 | 9 | X | 9 | 9 |
| Lynchburg (Pirates) | 57 | 81 | - | .413 | 31 | 8 | 6 | 6 | 8 | 7 | 10 | X | 12 |
| Frederick (Orioles) | 52 | 87 | - | .374 | 36 1/2 | 4 | 8 | 9 | 5 | 7 | 11 | 8 | X |

Major league affiliations in parentheses.

PLAYOFFS: Kinston defeated Winston-Salem, two games to one; Wilmington defeated Potomac, two games to one; Kinston defeated Wilmington, three games to two, to win league championship.

REGULAR-SEASON ATTENDANCE: Wilmington, 320,788; Frederick, 266,257; Salem, 221,371; Myrtle Beach, 209,095; Potomac, 170,278; Lynchburg, 148,067; Winston-Salem, 137,519; Kinston, 107,242. Total attendance—1,580,617.

MANAGERS: Frederick, Tom Lawless; Kinston, Torey Lovullo; Lynchburg, Jay Loviglio; Myrtle Beach, Randy Ingle; Potomac, Edgar Caceres; Salem, Russ Nixon; Wilmington, Billy Gardner Jr.; Winston-Salem, Ken Dominguez.

ALL-STAR TEAM: 1B—Brad Eldred, Lynchburg; 2B—Kevin Howard, Potomac; 3B—Tripper Johnson, Frederick; SS—Mike Aviles, Wilmington; Utility INF—Eider Torres, Kinston; OF—Rajai Davis, Lynchburg; OF—Jeff Francoeur, Myrtle Beach; OF—Shane Costa, Wilmington; Utility OF—Ryan Sweeney, Winston-Salem; C—Brian McCann, Myrtle Beach; DH—Ryan Garko, Kinston; Starting pitcher—Zach Duke, Lynchburg; Relief pitcher—Dwayne Pollok, Winston-Salem; Most Valuable Player—Brad Eldred, Lynchburg; Manager of the Year—Torey Lovullo, Kinston.

## 2004 BATTING

### TEAM

| Team | G | TPA | AB | R | H | TB | 2B | 3B | HR | RBI | SH | SF | HP | BB | IBB | SO | SB | CS | GDP | LOB | ShO | Avg. | OBP | Slg. |
|---|---|---|---|---|---|---|---|---|---|---|---|---|---|---|---|---|---|---|---|---|---|---|---|---|
| Kinston | 138 | 5112 | 4563 | 724 | 1227 | 1881 | 236 | 23 | 124 | 671 | 38 | 36 | 3 | 471 | 20 | 953 | 128 | 47 | 68 | 977 | 6 | .269 | .335 | .412 |
| Win.-Salem | 140 | 5238 | 4650 | 657 | 1243 | 1896 | 245 | 24 | 120 | 609 | 64 | 39 | 52 | 433 | 24 | 921 | 104 | 51 | 45 | 944 | 8 | .267 | .334 | .408 |
| Potomac | 139 | 5329 | 4619 | 690 | 1220 | 1787 | 222 | 18 | 103 | 631 | 47 | 45 | 70 | 548 | 23 | 1007 | 116 | 70 | 100 | 1015 | 7 | .264 | .348 | .387 |
| Lynchburg | 138 | 5166 | 4627 | 554 | 1215 | 1724 | 225 | 34 | 72 | 511 | 57 | 37 | 53 | 391 | 15 | 939 | 167 | 80 | 99 | 951 | 11 | .263 | .325 | .373 |
| Wilmington | 140 | 5238 | 4629 | 618 | 1212 | 1712 | 257 | 33 | 59 | 553 | 31 | 50 | 64 | 463 | 12 | 832 | 92 | 43 | 95 | 1006 | 10 | .262 | .334 | .370 |
| Frederick | 139 | 5214 | 4606 | 591 | 1198 | 1797 | 218 | 12 | 119 | 545 | 55 | 41 | 54 | 458 | 20 | 1005 | 96 | 59 | 99 | 978 | 11 | .260 | .331 | .390 |
| Myrtle Beach | 139 | 5071 | 4518 | 558 | 1158 | 1662 | 227 | 32 | 71 | 498 | 55 | 32 | 69 | 397 | 19 | 873 | 142 | 73 | 75 | 915 | 10 | .256 | .324 | .368 |
| Salem | 139 | 5187 | 4589 | 577 | 1166 | 1639 | 222 | 19 | 71 | 530 | 72 | 50 | 78 | 398 | 28 | 922 | 98 | 30 | 105 | 973 | 11 | .254 | .321 | .357 |

# INDIVIDUAL

## TOP QUALIFIERS FOR BATTING CHAMPIONSHIP

Minimum 378 plate appearances. *Lefthanded batter. †Switch-hitter.

| Player, Team | G | TPA | AB | R | H | TB | 2B | 3B | HR | RBI | SH | SF | HP | BB | IBB | SO | SB | CS | GDP | Avg. | OBP | Slg. |
|---|---|---|---|---|---|---|---|---|---|---|---|---|---|---|---|---|---|---|---|---|---|---|
| Davis, Rajai, Lynchburg † | 127 | 574 | 509 | 91 | 160 | 216 | 27 | 7 | 5 | 38 | 4 | 0 | 2 | 59 | 2 | 60 | 57 | 15 | 8 | .314 | .388 | .424 |
| Eldred, Brad, Lynchburg | 91 | 388 | 335 | 54 | 104 | 191 | 22 | 1 | 21 | 77 | 0 | 3 | 15 | 35 | 3 | 97 | 5 | 2 | 4 | .310 | .397 | .570 |
| Costa, Shane, Wilmington * | 123 | 500 | 451 | 70 | 139 | 188 | 20 | 4 | 7 | 59 | 0 | 6 | 11 | 32 | 1 | 43 | 9 | 4 | 7 | .308 | .364 | .417 |
| Torres, Eider, Kinston † | 113 | 477 | 440 | 68 | 133 | 172 | 24 | 3 | 3 | 46 | 8 | 4 | 3 | 22 | 5 | 46 | 48 | 6 | 6 | .302 | .337 | .391 |
| Becker, Brian, Winston-Salem | 109 | 437 | 397 | 59 | 120 | 224 | 30 | 4 | 22 | 77 | 2 | 6 | 2 | 30 | 3 | 94 | 0 | 2 | 6 | .302 | .349 | .564 |
| Aviles, Mike, Wilmington | 126 | 510 | 463 | 66 | 139 | 205 | 40 | 4 | 6 | 69 | 1 | 6 | 1 | 39 | 2 | 57 | 2 | 5 | 8 | .300 | .352 | .443 |
| Hanigan, Ryan, Potomac | 119 | 498 | 429 | 58 | 127 | 163 | 21 | 0 | 5 | 56 | 5 | 9 | 6 | 49 | 1 | 51 | 6 | 5 | 12 | .296 | .369 | .380 |
| Littleton, B.J., Frederick † | 102 | 421 | 378 | 56 | 111 | 147 | 18 | 6 | 2 | 25 | 6 | 0 | 6 | 31 | 1 | 71 | 22 | 9 | 6 | .294 | .357 | .389 |
| Lopez, Pedro, Winston-Salem | 111 | 476 | 430 | 62 | 124 | 149 | 13 | 0 | 4 | 35 | 16 | 3 | 4 | 23 | 0 | 35 | 12 | 9 | 3 | .288 | .328 | .347 |
| Rogowski, Casey, Winston-Salem * | 136 | 566 | 465 | 88 | 133 | 219 | 28 | 2 | 18 | 90 | 0 | 7 | 3 | 91 | 11 | 94 | 16 | 9 | 8 | .286 | .401 | .471 |
| Howard, Kevin, Potomac * | 124 | 537 | 468 | 68 | 134 | 191 | 24 | 0 | 11 | 79 | 1 | 6 | 4 | 58 | 6 | 70 | 8 | 7 | 7 | .286 | .366 | .408 |
| Correll, Brad, Potomac | 101 | 446 | 393 | 66 | 112 | 160 | 19 | 1 | 9 | 63 | 1 | 5 | 6 | 41 | 1 | 69 | 8 | 5 | 9 | .285 | .357 | .407 |
| Ruiz, Junior, Potomac * | 102 | 426 | 349 | 78 | 99 | 129 | 20 | 2 | 2 | 38 | 5 | 2 | 5 | 65 | 2 | 41 | 24 | 9 | 9 | .284 | .401 | .370 |
| Sweeney, Ryan, Winston-Salem * | 134 | 567 | 515 | 71 | 146 | 195 | 22 | 3 | 7 | 66 | 3 | 2 | 7 | 40 | 1 | 65 | 8 | 6 | 3 | .283 | .342 | .379 |
| Asprilla, Avelino, Lynchburg | 121 | 491 | 452 | 50 | 128 | 183 | 22 | 3 | 9 | 53 | 6 | 7 | 5 | 21 | 0 | 81 | 6 | 4 | 12 | .283 | .318 | .405 |

DEPARTMENTAL LEADERS: G—Saccomanno, Rogowski, 136; AB—Sweeney, 515; R—R. Davis, 91; H—R. Davis, 160; TB—Saccomanno, 229; 2B—Aviles, 40; 3B—Blanco, 9; HR—Becker, Saccomanno, 22; RBI—Rogowski, 90; SH—Schuerholz, Robinson, 17; SF—Hanigan, Larkin, 9; HP—Eldred, Timmons, 15; BB—Rogowski, 91; IBB—Rogowski, 11; SO—Saccomanno, 134; SB—R. Davis, 57; CS—Three tied with 15; GIDP—D. Murphy, T. Johnson, 16; Slg.—Eldred, .570; OBP—Ruiz, .401.

## ALL PLAYERS

*Lefthanded batter. †Switch-hitter.

| Player, Team | G | TPA | AB | R | H | TB | 2B | 3B | HR | RBI | SH | SF | HP | BB | IBB | SO | SB | CS | GDP | Avg. | OBP | Slg. |
|---|---|---|---|---|---|---|---|---|---|---|---|---|---|---|---|---|---|---|---|---|---|---|
| Alleva, J.D., Wilmington * | 66 | 245 | 218 | 19 | 46 | 62 | 11 | 1 | 1 | 24 | 2 | 6 | 2 | 17 | 2 | 30 | 0 | 1 | 6 | .211 | .267 | .284 |
| Alvarez, Gera, Frederick | 113 | 445 | 383 | 56 | 96 | 146 | 14 | 0 | 12 | 37 | 13 | 5 | 10 | 34 | 1 | 64 | 5 | 2 | 8 | .251 | .324 | .381 |
| Amador, Chris, Winston-Salem | 104 | 367 | 337 | 36 | 88 | 125 | 20 | 1 | 5 | 32 | 14 | 3 | 5 | 8 | 0 | 91 | 18 | 5 | 2 | .261 | .286 | .371 |
| Anderson, Brian, Winston-Salem | 69 | 287 | 254 | 43 | 81 | 135 | 22 | 4 | 8 | 46 | 0 | 1 | 3 | 29 | 5 | 44 | 10 | 1 | 3 | .319 | .394 | .531 |
| Anderson, Josh, Salem * | 66 | 306 | 280 | 45 | 75 | 106 | 13 | 6 | 2 | 21 | 7 | 0 | 6 | 13 | 1 | 53 | 31 | 4 | 3 | .268 | .317 | .379 |
| Arko, Tommy, Frederick | 11 | 40 | 33 | 3 | 5 | 12 | 1 | 0 | 2 | 3 | 0 | 0 | 1 | 6 | 0 | 16 | 0 | 1 | 0 | .152 | .300 | .364 |
| Asprilla, Avelino, Lynchburg | 121 | 491 | 452 | 50 | 128 | 183 | 22 | 3 | 9 | 53 | 6 | 7 | 5 | 21 | 0 | 81 | 6 | 4 | 12 | .283 | .318 | .405 |
| Aubrey, Michael, Kinston * | 60 | 258 | 218 | 34 | 74 | 120 | 14 | 1 | 10 | 60 | 0 | 1 | 12 | 27 | 1 | 26 | 3 | 1 | 4 | .339 | .438 | .550 |
| Aviles, Mike, Wilmington | 126 | 510 | 463 | 66 | 139 | 205 | 40 | 4 | 6 | 69 | 1 | 6 | 1 | 39 | 2 | 57 | 2 | 5 | 8 | .300 | .352 | .443 |
| Bastida-Martinez, Evel, Frederick * | 15 | 58 | 51 | 4 | 5 | 9 | 1 | 0 | 1 | 2 | 2 | 0 | 1 | 4 | 0 | 7 | 0 | 0 | 0 | .098 | .179 | .176 |
| Becker, Brian, Winston-Salem | 109 | 437 | 397 | 59 | 120 | 224 | 30 | 4 | 22 | 77 | 2 | 6 | 2 | 30 | 3 | 94 | 0 | 2 | 6 | .302 | .349 | .564 |
| Bernard, Miguel, Myrtle Beach | 24 | 80 | 71 | 8 | 14 | 20 | 6 | 0 | 0 | 1 | 0 | 0 | 2 | 7 | 0 | 15 | 1 | 1 | 0 | .197 | .288 | .282 |
| Bigbie, Larry, Frederick * | 1 | 5 | 5 | 2 | 2 | 8 | 0 | 0 | 2 | 2 | 0 | 0 | 0 | 0 | 0 | 1 | 0 | 0 | 0 | .400 | .400 | 1.600 |
| Blakely, Darren, Winston-Salem † | 84 | 331 | 305 | 49 | 84 | 180 | 17 | 2 | 25 | 58 | 5 | 0 | 6 | 15 | 0 | 77 | 10 | 1 | 2 | .275 | .322 | .590 |
| Blanco, Gregor, Myrtle Beach * | 119 | 495 | 436 | 73 | 116 | 175 | 17 | 9 | 8 | 41 | 6 | 3 | 3 | 47 | 4 | 114 | 25 | 9 | 5 | .266 | .339 | .401 |
| Blanco, Tony, Potomac | 62 | 258 | 216 | 42 | 66 | 127 | 10 | 0 | 17 | 47 | 0 | 4 | 11 | 27 | 3 | 66 | 2 | 0 | 3 | .306 | .403 | .588 |
| Bock, Brian, Frederick | 18 | 59 | 51 | 4 | 10 | 14 | 1 | 0 | 1 | 1 | 1 | 0 | 2 | 5 | 0 | 4 | 0 | 0 | 4 | .196 | .293 | .275 |
| Brice, Thomas, Winston-Salem * | 43 | 179 | 161 | 19 | 44 | 68 | 13 | 1 | 3 | 23 | 2 | 1 | 2 | 13 | 1 | 32 | 5 | 1 | 0 | .273 | .333 | .422 |
| Brock, Caleb, Kinston | 41 | 149 | 134 | 19 | 34 | 56 | 13 | 0 | 3 | 19 | 1 | 0 | 6 | 8 | 0 | 27 | 2 | 0 | 3 | .254 | .324 | .418 |
| Buttler, Vic, Lynchburg * | 101 | 396 | 365 | 36 | 88 | 132 | 19 | 5 | 5 | 37 | 4 | 3 | 1 | 23 | 0 | 61 | 8 | 3 | 8 | .241 | .286 | .362 |
| Cairns, Troy, Potomac | 36 | 87 | 77 | 7 | 18 | 21 | 3 | 0 | 0 | 8 | 3 | 0 | 3 | 4 | 0 | 24 | 1 | 0 | 0 | .234 | .298 | .273 |
| Camacaro, Armando, Kinston | 25 | 87 | 82 | 6 | 22 | 28 | 3 | 0 | 1 | 10 | 0 | 0 | 2 | 3 | 0 | 14 | 0 | 0 | 2 | .268 | .310 | .341 |
| Cameron, Troy, Winston-Salem † | 16 | 55 | 49 | 4 | 10 | 18 | 4 | 2 | 0 | 6 | 0 | 0 | 1 | 5 | 0 | 14 | 1 | 0 | 1 | .204 | .291 | .367 |
| Carter, Chris, Frederick | 98 | 390 | 343 | 39 | 93 | 144 | 16 | 1 | 11 | 45 | 3 | 1 | 2 | 41 | 1 | 115 | 6 | 8 | 6 | .271 | .351 | .420 |
| Cashman, Brandon, Kinston | 1 | 5 | 4 | 1 | 1 | 1 | 0 | 0 | 0 | 1 | 0 | 0 | 0 | 1 | 0 | 3 | 0 | 0 | 0 | .250 | .400 | .250 |
| Chapman, Travis, Wilmington | 27 | 106 | 94 | 12 | 22 | 41 | 4 | 0 | 5 | 16 | 0 | 0 | 5 | 7 | 0 | 24 | 0 | 0 | 1 | .234 | .321 | .436 |
| Chapman, Travis, Lynchburg | 14 | 56 | 54 | 3 | 9 | 10 | 1 | 0 | 0 | 3 | 0 | 0 | 0 | 2 | 0 | 13 | 0 | 0 | 1 | .167 | .196 | .185 |
| Choy Foo, Rodney, Kinston † | 54 | 211 | 191 | 24 | 41 | 56 | 10 | 1 | 1 | 20 | 1 | 1 | 1 | 17 | 1 | 40 | 8 | 2 | 3 | .215 | .281 | .293 |
| Clark, Daryl, Wilmington * | 27 | 107 | 83 | 6 | 18 | 28 | 7 | 0 | 1 | 12 | 0 | 1 | 3 | 20 | 1 | 28 | 1 | 0 | 1 | .217 | .383 | .337 |
| Cliffords, Woody, Frederick * | 87 | 358 | 314 | 52 | 92 | 127 | 20 | 0 | 5 | 39 | 1 | 2 | 4 | 37 | 3 | 53 | 4 | 4 | 6 | .293 | .373 | .404 |
| Correll, Brad, Potomac | 101 | 446 | 393 | 66 | 112 | 160 | 19 | 1 | 9 | 63 | 1 | 5 | 6 | 41 | 1 | 69 | 8 | 5 | 9 | .285 | .357 | .407 |
| Cortes, Jorge, Lynchburg * | 70 | 300 | 260 | 32 | 76 | 113 | 20 | 1 | 5 | 36 | 1 | 0 | 2 | 37 | 0 | 48 | 1 | 2 | 13 | .292 | .385 | .435 |
| Costa, Shane, Wilmington * | 123 | 500 | 451 | 70 | 139 | 188 | 20 | 4 | 7 | 59 | 0 | 6 | 11 | 32 | 1 | 43 | 9 | 4 | 7 | .308 | .364 | .417 |
| Cotto, Luis, Kinston | 12 | 41 | 38 | 9 | 8 | 10 | 2 | 0 | 0 | 2 | 0 | 0 | 0 | 3 | 0 | 7 | 0 | 0 | 0 | .211 | .268 | .263 |
| Davies, Gregg, Frederick * | 12 | 29 | 25 | 3 | 5 | 5 | 0 | 0 | 0 | 3 | 0 | 2 | 0 | 2 | 0 | 8 | 0 | 0 | 1 | .200 | .241 | .200 |
| Davis, Rajai, Lynchburg † | 127 | 574 | 509 | 91 | 160 | 216 | 27 | 7 | 5 | 38 | 4 | 0 | 2 | 59 | 2 | 60 | 57 | 15 | 8 | .314 | .388 | .424 |
| Denorfia, Chris, Potomac | 75 | 321 | 269 | 52 | 84 | 143 | 18 | 4 | 11 | 51 | 1 | 2 | 1 | 48 | 0 | 66 | 10 | 6 | 3 | .312 | .416 | .532 |
| Diaz, Rafael, Frederick | 6 | 22 | 21 | 2 | 8 | 9 | 1 | 0 | 0 | 2 | 1 | 0 | 0 | 0 | 0 | 3 | 1 | 0 | 0 | .381 | .381 | .429 |
| Dickerson, Chris, Potomac * | 15 | 56 | 45 | 5 | 9 | 11 | 2 | 0 | 0 | 5 | 3 | 0 | 1 | 7 | 0 | 14 | 3 | 1 | 1 | .200 | .321 | .244 |
| Done, Mike, Frederick † | 77 | 297 | 251 | 27 | 54 | 73 | 7 | 0 | 4 | 26 | 1 | 3 | 5 | 37 | 0 | 71 | 1 | 0 | 3 | .215 | .324 | .291 |
| Downing, Juan, Myrtle Beach † | 9 | 30 | 26 | 3 | 5 | 5 | 0 | 0 | 0 | 0 | 0 | 0 | 0 | 4 | 0 | 6 | 0 | 0 | 0 | .192 | .300 | .192 |
| Draper, John, Wilmington | 64 | 200 | 180 | 17 | 34 | 47 | 7 | 0 | 2 | 8 | 3 | 0 | 2 | 15 | 0 | 31 | 4 | 2 | 1 | .189 | .259 | .261 |
| Duncan, Jacob, Frederick * | 21 | 67 | 64 | 11 | 22 | 35 | 4 | 0 | 3 | 14 | 2 | 0 | 0 | 1 | 0 | 17 | 0 | 2 | 1 | .344 | .354 | .547 |
| Duran, Carlos, Myrtle Beach * | 66 | 251 | 234 | 19 | 61 | 87 | 7 | 5 | 3 | 28 | 0 | 4 | 1 | 12 | 2 | 47 | 13 | 1 | 0 | .261 | .295 | .372 |
| Durham, Chad, Potomac | 56 | 248 | 227 | 29 | 55 | 72 | 4 | 2 | 3 | 27 | 3 | 0 | 1 | 17 | 0 | 49 | 8 | 4 | 2 | .242 | .298 | .317 |
| Dyson, Trey, Kinston * | 12 | 47 | 39 | 5 | 7 | 12 | 2 | 0 | 1 | 5 | 0 | 0 | 1 | 7 | 0 | 7 | 0 | 0 | 1 | .179 | .319 | .308 |
| Eldred, Brad, Lynchburg | 91 | 388 | 335 | 54 | 104 | 191 | 22 | 1 | 21 | 77 | 0 | 3 | 15 | 35 | 3 | 97 | 5 | 2 | 4 | .310 | .397 | .570 |
| Espino, Damaso, Wilmington † | 124 | 523 | 469 | 35 | 120 | 143 | 18 | 1 | 1 | 58 | 0 | 7 | 3 | 44 | 1 | 110 | 3 | 2 | 12 | .256 | .319 | .305 |
| Fagan, John, Salem | 113 | 428 | 356 | 48 | 91 | 145 | 25 | 1 | 9 | 45 | 2 | 7 | 12 | 49 | 5 | 103 | 9 | 3 | 10 | .256 | .358 | .407 |
| Fahey, Brandon, Frederick * | 62 | 212 | 181 | 20 | 49 | 65 | 7 | 0 | 3 | 19 | 6 | 1 | 2 | 22 | 1 | 20 | 3 | 3 | 3 | .271 | .354 | .359 |
| Fallon, Chris, Wilmington * | 1 | 4 | 2 | 0 | 1 | 1 | 0 | 0 | 0 | 1 | 0 | 0 | 0 | 2 | 0 | 1 | 0 | 0 | 0 | .500 | .750 | .500 |
| Fenster, Darren, Wilmington | 84 | 361 | 303 | 55 | 92 | 114 | 20 | 1 | 0 | 37 | 1 | 1 | 5 | 51 | 0 | 46 | 2 | 1 | 7 | .304 | .411 | .376 |
| Fields, Joshua, Winston-Salem | 66 | 279 | 256 | 36 | 73 | 114 | 12 | 4 | 7 | 39 | 0 | 3 | 2 | 18 | 1 | 74 | 0 | 0 | 2 | .285 | .333 | .445 |

| Player, Team | G | TPA | AB | R | H | TB | 2B | 3B | HR | RBI | SH | SF | HP | BB | IBB | SO | SB | CS | GDP | Avg. | OBP | Slg. |
|---|---|---|---|---|---|---|---|---|---|---|---|---|---|---|---|---|---|---|---|---|---|---|
| Florence, Branden, Frederick | 63 | 252 | 230 | 33 | 73 | 126 | 17 | 0 | 12 | 49 | 1 | 7 | 5 | 9 | 0 | 12 | 0 | 1 | 6 | .317 | .347 | .548 |
| Francoeur, Jeff, Myrtle Beach | 88 | 367 | 334 | 56 | 98 | 169 | 26 | 0 | 15 | 52 | 0 | 4 | 7 | 22 | 3 | 70 | 10 | 6 | 5 | .293 | .346 | .506 |
| Frend, Tim, Wilmington | 55 | 220 | 195 | 23 | 47 | 76 | 14 | 0 | 5 | 28 | 3 | 1 | 4 | 17 | 0 | 39 | 0 | 0 | 7 | .241 | .313 | .390 |
| Garcia, Cip, Winston-Salem | 11 | 19 | 16 | 4 | 3 | 3 | 0 | 0 | 0 | 0 | 0 | 0 | 0 | 3 | 0 | 5 | 0 | 0 | 0 | .188 | .316 | .188 |
| Garko, Ryan, Kinston | 65 | 280 | 238 | 44 | 78 | 145 | 17 | 1 | 16 | 57 | 0 | 1 | 15 | 26 | 3 | 34 | 4 | 1 | 6 | .328 | .425 | .609 |
| Gibbons, Jay, Frederick * | 3 | 13 | 11 | 2 | 2 | 6 | 1 | 0 | 1 | 5 | 0 | 0 | 0 | 2 | 0 | 2 | 0 | 0 | 0 | .182 | .308 | .545 |
| Giles, Marcus, Myrtle Beach | 4 | 15 | 13 | 1 | 1 | 2 | 1 | 0 | 0 | 2 | 0 | 1 | 0 | 1 | 0 | 4 | 0 | 0 | 0 | .077 | .133 | .154 |
| Gonzalez, Andy, Winston-Salem | 80 | 368 | 309 | 59 | 78 | 120 | 18 | 0 | 8 | 28 | 1 | 2 | 7 | 49 | 0 | 53 | 2 | 3 | 4 | .256 | .369 | .393 |
| Gredvig, Doug, Frederick | 118 | 475 | 427 | 38 | 117 | 163 | 23 | 1 | 7 | 53 | 0 | 5 | 0 | 43 | 2 | 102 | 0 | 4 | 13 | .274 | .337 | .382 |
| Groves, Brett, Wilmington | 15 | 39 | 29 | 5 | 2 | 2 | 0 | 0 | 0 | 2 | 0 | 0 | 1 | 9 | 0 | 6 | 0 | 1 | 1 | .069 | .308 | .069 |
| Hanigan, Ryan, Potomac | 119 | 498 | 429 | 58 | 127 | 163 | 21 | 0 | 5 | 56 | 5 | 9 | 6 | 49 | 1 | 51 | 6 | 5 | 12 | .296 | .369 | .380 |
| Harris, Cory, Frederick | 34 | 134 | 116 | 13 | 26 | 44 | 10 | 1 | 2 | 12 | 1 | 1 | 2 | 14 | 0 | 16 | 6 | 3 | 4 | .224 | .316 | .379 |
| Helquist, Jon, Salem | 115 | 421 | 370 | 49 | 81 | 115 | 19 | 3 | 3 | 29 | 7 | 4 | 12 | 28 | 1 | 79 | 8 | 1 | 7 | .219 | .292 | .311 |
| Hemingway, Jamie, Myrtle Beach | 49 | 179 | 173 | 12 | 35 | 47 | 6 | 0 | 2 | 10 | 0 | 1 | 2 | 3 | 0 | 33 | 2 | 3 | 2 | .202 | .223 | .272 |
| Hernandez, Jose, Lynchburg | 64 | 233 | 215 | 16 | 43 | 48 | 5 | 0 | 0 | 11 | 2 | 1 | 1 | 14 | 0 | 35 | 0 | 2 | 9 | .200 | .251 | .223 |
| Hernandez, Luis, Myrtle Beach † | 117 | 435 | 402 | 49 | 109 | 158 | 23 | 4 | 6 | 45 | 10 | 2 | 5 | 16 | 0 | 70 | 8 | 6 | 12 | .271 | .306 | .393 |
| Herrera, Christian, Lynchburg | 24 | 100 | 86 | 15 | 17 | 24 | 7 | 0 | 0 | 5 | 3 | 2 | 1 | 8 | 0 | 21 | 1 | 0 | 1 | .198 | .268 | .279 |
| Herrera, Javier, Kinston | 42 | 175 | 151 | 24 | 37 | 59 | 7 | 0 | 5 | 24 | 1 | 1 | 5 | 17 | 1 | 23 | 0 | 2 | 4 | .245 | .339 | .391 |
| Houston, Matt, Frederick | 30 | 98 | 85 | 8 | 20 | 27 | 2 | 1 | 1 | 9 | 2 | 1 | 4 | 6 | 0 | 20 | 0 | 0 | 3 | .235 | .313 | .318 |
| Howard, Kevin, Potomac * | 124 | 537 | 468 | 68 | 134 | 191 | 24 | 0 | 11 | 79 | 1 | 6 | 4 | 58 | 6 | 70 | 8 | 7 | 7 | .286 | .366 | .408 |
| Hubele, Ryan, Frederick | 93 | 333 | 296 | 31 | 75 | 107 | 14 | 0 | 6 | 23 | 3 | 3 | 2 | 29 | 1 | 72 | 2 | 1 | 8 | .253 | .321 | .361 |
| Iorg, Isaac, Myrtle Beach | 80 | 312 | 281 | 33 | 77 | 101 | 13 | 1 | 3 | 25 | 4 | 1 | 7 | 19 | 1 | 43 | 5 | 5 | 6 | .274 | .334 | .359 |
| James, Willie, Myrtle Beach † | 45 | 131 | 111 | 10 | 21 | 22 | 1 | 0 | 0 | 11 | 3 | 2 | 1 | 14 | 0 | 28 | 8 | 6 | 1 | .189 | .281 | .198 |
| Jansen, Ardley, Myrtle Beach | 32 | 123 | 114 | 16 | 28 | 34 | 4 | 1 | 0 | 8 | 1 | 0 | 1 | 7 | 0 | 40 | 1 | 2 | 1 | .246 | .295 | .298 |
| Jensen, Dave, Wilmington * | 21 | 73 | 72 | 9 | 15 | 20 | 5 | 0 | 0 | 2 | 0 | 0 | 1 | 0 | 0 | 22 | 1 | 0 | 1 | .208 | .219 | .278 |
| Johnson, Tripper, Frederick | 129 | 526 | 465 | 62 | 125 | 211 | 19 | 2 | 21 | 74 | 1 | 5 | 4 | 51 | 4 | 93 | 14 | 5 | 16 | .269 | .343 | .454 |
| Joseph, Onil, Myrtle Beach | 113 | 484 | 423 | 63 | 115 | 136 | 13 | 1 | 2 | 36 | 4 | 2 | 7 | 48 | 1 | 90 | 32 | 10 | 7 | .272 | .354 | .322 |
| Keim, Adam, Wilmington | 59 | 213 | 201 | 28 | 58 | 96 | 7 | 2 | 9 | 27 | 1 | 0 | 1 | 10 | 1 | 41 | 2 | 0 | 5 | .289 | .325 | .478 |
| Keylor, Cory, Frederick * | 122 | 491 | 433 | 64 | 110 | 182 | 21 | 0 | 17 | 72 | 3 | 3 | 2 | 50 | 5 | 120 | 11 | 9 | 3 | .254 | .332 | .420 |
| Kochen, Ryan, Salem | 96 | 366 | 337 | 40 | 86 | 121 | 16 | 2 | 5 | 33 | 4 | 2 | 4 | 19 | 0 | 51 | 5 | 1 | 7 | .255 | .301 | .359 |
| Larkin, Shaun, Kinston * | 118 | 485 | 435 | 67 | 113 | 174 | 25 | 0 | 12 | 62 | 0 | 9 | 4 | 37 | 0 | 67 | 3 | 3 | 8 | .260 | .318 | .400 |
| Lee, Carlos, Winston-Salem | 37 | 145 | 133 | 10 | 26 | 32 | 3 | 0 | 1 | 19 | 1 | 2 | 1 | 8 | 0 | 17 | 1 | 0 | 0 | .195 | .243 | .241 |
| Lee, Taber, Lynchburg † | 93 | 376 | 315 | 38 | 78 | 102 | 11 | 2 | 3 | 37 | 7 | 1 | 5 | 48 | 3 | 71 | 11 | 9 | 9 | .248 | .355 | .324 |
| Lewis, Domonique, Potomac | 70 | 256 | 221 | 26 | 45 | 56 | 9 | 1 | 0 | 19 | 8 | 3 | 2 | 22 | 0 | 75 | 13 | 7 | 6 | .204 | .278 | .253 |
| Likely, Cameron, Salem | 49 | 147 | 135 | 16 | 27 | 32 | 2 | 0 | 1 | 11 | 2 | 0 | 2 | 8 | 0 | 33 | 7 | 5 | 1 | .200 | .255 | .237 |
| Littleton, B.J., Frederick † | 102 | 421 | 378 | 56 | 111 | 147 | 18 | 6 | 2 | 25 | 6 | 0 | 6 | 31 | 1 | 71 | 22 | 9 | 6 | .294 | .357 | .389 |
| Logan, Matt, Potomac * | 50 | 205 | 186 | 27 | 51 | 74 | 9 | 1 | 4 | 26 | 0 | 0 | 2 | 17 | 3 | 32 | 2 | 3 | 8 | .274 | .341 | .398 |
| Lopez, Pedro, Winston-Salem | 111 | 476 | 430 | 62 | 124 | 149 | 13 | 0 | 4 | 35 | 16 | 3 | 4 | 23 | 0 | 35 | 12 | 9 | 3 | .288 | .328 | .347 |
| Lunetta, Anthony, Kinston | 71 | 254 | 218 | 30 | 46 | 60 | 8 | 0 | 2 | 16 | 5 | 0 | 6 | 25 | 1 | 41 | 3 | 2 | 5 | .211 | .309 | .275 |
| Lytle, Chaz, Lynchburg * | 99 | 387 | 354 | 37 | 98 | 116 | 14 | 2 | 0 | 24 | 8 | 2 | 5 | 18 | 1 | 54 | 22 | 8 | 2 | .277 | .319 | .328 |
| Macia, Wanell, Lynchburg * | 3 | 9 | 8 | 0 | 1 | 2 | 1 | 0 | 0 | 0 | 0 | 0 | 0 | 1 | 1 | 3 | 0 | 0 | 0 | .125 | .222 | .250 |
| Mackor, Jeff, Salem | 65 | 244 | 221 | 20 | 52 | 61 | 6 | 0 | 1 | 20 | 6 | 2 | 4 | 11 | 0 | 46 | 1 | 1 | 8 | .240 | .286 | .281 |
| Magness, Pat, Kinston * | 41 | 172 | 141 | 18 | 38 | 67 | 8 | 0 | 7 | 31 | 0 | 0 | 3 | 28 | 0 | 41 | 0 | 1 | 4 | .270 | .401 | .475 |
| Maier, Mitch, Wilmington * | 51 | 194 | 174 | 25 | 46 | 68 | 9 | 2 | 3 | 17 | 1 | 2 | 2 | 15 | 0 | 29 | 9 | 2 | 3 | .264 | .326 | .391 |
| Malave, Dennis, Kinston * | 64 | 203 | 182 | 30 | 45 | 68 | 11 | 0 | 4 | 20 | 1 | 0 | 2 | 18 | 0 | 36 | 5 | 6 | 1 | .247 | .322 | .374 |
| Martel, Normand, Winston-Salem * | 26 | 71 | 68 | 9 | 14 | 18 | 1 | 0 | 1 | 3 | 0 | 0 | 1 | 2 | 0 | 8 | 5 | 1 | 1 | .206 | .239 | .265 |
| Martinez, Octavio, Frederick | 8 | 34 | 32 | 4 | 8 | 8 | 0 | 0 | 0 | 2 | 0 | 0 | 1 | 1 | 0 | 4 | 1 | 0 | 0 | .250 | .294 | .250 |
| McCann, Brian, Myrtle Beach * | 111 | 421 | 385 | 45 | 107 | 190 | 35 | 0 | 16 | 66 | 0 | 1 | 4 | 31 | 4 | 54 | 2 | 2 | 6 | .278 | .337 | .494 |
| McCullough, Clayton, Kinston * | 4 | 10 | 9 | 1 | 2 | 2 | 0 | 0 | 0 | 2 | 1 | 0 | 0 | 0 | 0 | 3 | 0 | 0 | 0 | .222 | .222 | .222 |
| Meath, Matt, Lynchburg † | 61 | 208 | 175 | 27 | 50 | 75 | 11 | 4 | 2 | 24 | 1 | 2 | 2 | 28 | 1 | 58 | 8 | 6 | 3 | .286 | .386 | .429 |
| Mendoza, Hatuey, Potomac | 35 | 1 | 1 | 0 | 0 | 0 | 0 | 0 | 0 | 0 | 0 | 0 | 0 | 0 | 0 | 0 | 0 | 0 | 0 | .000 | .000 | .000 |
| Mercedes, Victor, Lynchburg | 128 | 537 | 484 | 55 | 132 | 194 | 24 | 7 | 8 | 62 | 9 | 6 | 5 | 33 | 2 | 101 | 29 | 15 | 7 | .273 | .322 | .401 |
| Merricks, Matt, Myrtle Beach * | 13 | 1 | 0 | 0 | 0 | 0 | 0 | 0 | 0 | 0 | 1 | 0 | 0 | 0 | 0 | 0 | 0 | 0 | 0 | .000 | .000 | .000 |
| Molina, Gustavo, Winston-Salem | 25 | 85 | 77 | 10 | 22 | 37 | 6 | 0 | 3 | 14 | 1 | 1 | 1 | 5 | 0 | 16 | 0 | 0 | 0 | .286 | .333 | .481 |
| Morban, Jose, Frederick | 56 | 223 | 200 | 34 | 47 | 65 | 9 | 0 | 3 | 13 | 2 | 1 | 1 | 19 | 1 | 65 | 17 | 5 | 3 | .235 | .303 | .325 |
| Morel, Elvis, Frederick | 11 | 45 | 43 | 5 | 10 | 11 | 1 | 0 | 0 | 0 | 0 | 0 | 0 | 2 | 0 | 8 | 1 | 1 | 1 | .233 | .267 | .256 |
| Mota, Tony, Frederick † | 3 | 14 | 14 | 3 | 3 | 5 | 2 | 0 | 0 | 0 | 0 | 0 | 0 | 0 | 0 | 3 | 1 | 0 | 0 | .214 | .214 | .357 |
| Motooka, Rafael, Potomac | 10 | 22 | 20 | 1 | 3 | 6 | 0 | 0 | 1 | 2 | 1 | 0 | 0 | 1 | 0 | 5 | 0 | 0 | 1 | .150 | .190 | .300 |
| Murphy, Donald, Wilmington | 129 | 551 | 485 | 67 | 124 | 196 | 32 | 5 | 10 | 75 | 2 | 8 | 4 | 52 | 2 | 96 | 1 | 1 | 16 | .256 | .328 | .404 |
| Myers, Mike, Winston-Salem | 13 | 26 | 21 | 4 | 6 | 7 | 1 | 0 | 0 | 3 | 0 | 0 | 1 | 4 | 0 | 3 | 0 | 0 | 1 | .286 | .423 | .333 |
| Nanita, Ricardo, Winston-Salem * | 55 | 223 | 187 | 21 | 45 | 61 | 8 | 1 | 2 | 28 | 6 | 4 | 3 | 23 | 2 | 46 | 7 | 4 | 0 | .241 | .327 | .326 |
| Navarrete, Ray, Lynchburg | 62 | 263 | 247 | 29 | 74 | 111 | 11 | 1 | 8 | 46 | 0 | 4 | 3 | 9 | 0 | 37 | 0 | 1 | 5 | .300 | .327 | .449 |
| Newman, Ryan, Lynchburg | 57 | 172 | 159 | 13 | 29 | 34 | 2 | 0 | 1 | 10 | 2 | 1 | 0 | 10 | 0 | 45 | 1 | 2 | 3 | .182 | .229 | .214 |
| Nicholson, Tommy, Winston-Salem * | 60 | 241 | 205 | 37 | 53 | 71 | 12 | 0 | 2 | 10 | 3 | 0 | 1 | 32 | 0 | 50 | 6 | 4 | 1 | .254 | .355 | .340 |
| Nino, Denny, Lynchburg | 25 | 75 | 70 | 5 | 14 | 18 | 2 | 1 | 0 | 2 | 1 | 0 | 1 | 3 | 0 | 14 | 0 | 0 | 2 | .200 | .243 | .257 |
| Obradovich, Mark, Salem † | 51 | 188 | 153 | 19 | 27 | 34 | 4 | 0 | 1 | 15 | 5 | 2 | 1 | 27 | 0 | 35 | 0 | 0 | 6 | .176 | .301 | .222 |
| Ochoa, Ivan, Kinston | 66 | 292 | 257 | 41 | 61 | 79 | 9 | 3 | 1 | 26 | 6 | 2 | 6 | 21 | 1 | 56 | 11 | 4 | 1 | .237 | .308 | .307 |
| Olszta, Eddie, Lynchburg | 7 | 22 | 16 | 0 | 2 | 3 | 1 | 0 | 0 | 2 | 1 | 2 | 0 | 3 | 0 | 11 | 1 | 0 | 0 | .125 | .238 | .188 |
| Osborn, Pat, Kinston | 86 | 354 | 307 | 69 | 105 | 163 | 16 | 6 | 10 | 55 | 1 | 2 | 5 | 39 | 1 | 53 | 6 | 6 | 5 | .342 | .422 | .531 |
| Panther, Nathan, Kinston * | 120 | 527 | 457 | 79 | 117 | 157 | 15 | 2 | 7 | 50 | 4 | 2 | 12 | 51 | 3 | 118 | 11 | 4 | 2 | .256 | .345 | .344 |
| Parker, Brett, Kinston | 12 | 27 | 23 | 3 | 4 | 6 | 2 | 0 | 0 | 1 | 2 | 0 | 1 | 1 | 0 | 5 | 0 | 0 | 1 | .174 | .240 | .261 |
| Patchett, Gary, Potomac | 50 | 178 | 162 | 14 | 37 | 45 | 5 | 0 | 1 | 15 | 2 | 0 | 3 | 11 | 1 | 42 | 1 | 5 | 2 | .228 | .290 | .278 |
| Peavey, Pat, Salem | 131 | 527 | 476 | 47 | 131 | 177 | 25 | 0 | 7 | 62 | 3 | 5 | 10 | 33 | 2 | 54 | 3 | 1 | 9 | .275 | .332 | .372 |
| Pena, Rodolfo, Lynchburg | 40 | 130 | 123 | 5 | 21 | 29 | 2 | 0 | 2 | 9 | 3 | 0 | 2 | 2 | 0 | 23 | 0 | 1 | 3 | .171 | .197 | .236 |
| Perez, Melvin, Winston-Salem | 12 | 29 | 28 | 3 | 6 | 6 | 0 | 0 | 0 | 1 | 0 | 0 | 0 | 1 | 0 | 6 | 0 | 0 | 1 | .214 | .241 | .214 |
| Perez, Miguel, Potomac | 18 | 71 | 69 | 7 | 16 | 18 | 2 | 0 | 0 | 5 | 0 | 1 | 0 | 1 | 0 | 12 | 1 | 0 | 4 | .232 | .239 | .261 |
| Powell, Pedro, Lynchburg | 8 | 34 | 32 | 9 | 11 | 13 | 2 | 0 | 0 | 2 | 0 | 0 | 0 | 2 | 0 | 4 | 8 | 2 | 0 | .344 | .382 | .406 |
| Prince, Bryan, Potomac | 76 | 289 | 251 | 30 | 53 | 79 | 8 | 0 | 6 | 31 | 1 | 2 | 2 | 33 | 1 | 45 | 0 | 0 | 7 | .211 | .306 | .315 |
| Ravelo, Manny, Lynchburg | 17 | 60 | 47 | 6 | 12 | 14 | 2 | 0 | 0 | 4 | 3 | 0 | 1 | 9 | 0 | 13 | 4 | 6 | 1 | .255 | .386 | .298 |
| Robinson, Levi, Frederick | 26 | 82 | 71 | 6 | 13 | 19 | 3 | 0 | 1 | 4 | 5 | 0 | 0 | 6 | 0 | 14 | 1 | 0 | 3 | .183 | .247 | .268 |
| Robinson, Wade, Salem * | 128 | 565 | 507 | 69 | 133 | 172 | 24 | 3 | 3 | 61 | 17 | 6 | 0 | 35 | 6 | 101 | 15 | 7 | 9 | .262 | .307 | .339 |
| Rogowski, Casey, Winston-Salem * | 136 | 566 | 465 | 88 | 133 | 219 | 28 | 2 | 18 | 90 | 0 | 7 | 3 | 91 | 11 | 94 | 16 | 9 | 8 | .286 | .401 | .471 |

| Player, Team | G | TPA | AB | R | H | TB | 2B | 3B | HR | RBI | SH | SF | HP | BB | IBB | SO | SB | CS | GDP | Avg. | OBP | Slg. |
|---|---|---|---|---|---|---|---|---|---|---|---|---|---|---|---|---|---|---|---|---|---|---|
| Rosa, Wally, Winston-Salem | 84 | 308 | 272 | 23 | 61 | 75 | 11 | 0 | 1 | 17 | 6 | 3 | 2 | 25 | 0 | 52 | 3 | 3 | 5 | .224 | .291 | .276 |
| Rosamond, Mike, Lynchburg | 37 | 142 | 134 | 16 | 29 | 42 | 10 | 0 | 1 | 13 | 0 | 1 | 0 | 7 | 0 | 37 | 2 | 1 | 5 | .216 | .254 | .313 |
| Ruelas, Alonzo, Myrtle Beach | 57 | 181 | 157 | 22 | 43 | 57 | 6 | 1 | 2 | 16 | 1 | 1 | 3 | 19 | 1 | 39 | 3 | 2 | 3 | .274 | .361 | .363 |
| Ruiz, Junior, Potomac * | 102 | 426 | 349 | 78 | 99 | 129 | 20 | 2 | 2 | 38 | 5 | 2 | 5 | 65 | 2 | 41 | 24 | 9 | 9 | .284 | .401 | .370 |
| Ruiz, Reinaldo, Salem | 24 | 87 | 78 | 8 | 26 | 30 | 4 | 0 | 0 | 9 | 1 | 1 | 1 | 6 | 0 | 14 | 1 | 0 | 2 | .333 | .384 | .385 |
| Saccomanno, Mark, Salem | 136 | 569 | 513 | 71 | 134 | 229 | 25 | 2 | 22 | 80 | 0 | 3 | 6 | 48 | 2 | 134 | 2 | 1 | 13 | .261 | .329 | .446 |
| Salas, Jose, Myrtle Beach * | 14 | 42 | 41 | 5 | 6 | 7 | 1 | 0 | 0 | 1 | 0 | 1 | 0 | 0 | 0 | 5 | 0 | 0 | 2 | .146 | .143 | .171 |
| Santana, Mayobanex, Kinston | 8 | 29 | 28 | 2 | 4 | 7 | 0 | 0 | 1 | 4 | 0 | 0 | 0 | 1 | 0 | 10 | 0 | 0 | 0 | .143 | .172 | .250 |
| Schramek, Mark, Potomac * | 122 | 481 | 392 | 59 | 90 | 150 | 23 | 2 | 11 | 53 | 0 | 6 | 18 | 65 | 4 | 122 | 5 | 3 | 10 | .230 | .360 | .383 |
| Schuerholz, Jon, Myrtle Beach † | 122 | 446 | 376 | 34 | 78 | 103 | 12 | 5 | 1 | 33 | 17 | 1 | 3 | 49 | 0 | 77 | 14 | 9 | 11 | .207 | .303 | .274 |
| Scott, Luke, Salem * | 66 | 287 | 241 | 45 | 67 | 113 | 20 | 1 | 8 | 35 | 0 | 5 | 0 | 41 | 4 | 58 | 6 | 1 | 5 | .278 | .376 | .469 |
| Segui, David, Frederick † | 3 | 12 | 10 | 1 | 1 | 4 | 0 | 0 | 1 | 2 | 0 | 1 | 0 | 1 | 0 | 2 | 0 | 0 | 0 | .100 | .167 | .400 |
| Serrano, Ray, Myrtle Beach | 33 | 121 | 116 | 19 | 30 | 53 | 8 | 0 | 5 | 23 | 0 | 0 | 2 | 3 | 0 | 18 | 0 | 2 | 1 | .259 | .289 | .457 |
| Seuss, Adam, Salem * | 104 | 419 | 361 | 38 | 102 | 143 | 20 | 0 | 7 | 64 | 0 | 5 | 9 | 44 | 6 | 63 | 1 | 1 | 13 | .283 | .370 | .396 |
| Sevilla, Wally, Wilmington | 4 | 15 | 14 | 1 | 2 | 2 | 0 | 0 | 0 | 0 | 0 | 0 | 0 | 1 | 0 | 5 | 1 | 0 | 0 | .143 | .200 | .143 |
| Shaffer, Josh, Winston-Salem * | 29 | 95 | 87 | 2 | 9 | 13 | 1 | 0 | 1 | 7 | 4 | 0 | 0 | 4 | 0 | 29 | 0 | 2 | 2 | .103 | .143 | .149 |
| Sherrill, J.J., Kinston † | 97 | 379 | 324 | 49 | 78 | 132 | 12 | 3 | 12 | 51 | 5 | 2 | 8 | 40 | 2 | 92 | 8 | 2 | 3 | .241 | .337 | .407 |
| Skaug, Brian, Salem | 3 | 5 | 5 | 0 | 0 | 0 | 0 | 0 | 0 | 0 | 0 | 0 | 0 | 0 | 0 | 1 | 0 | 0 | 0 | .000 | .000 | .000 |
| Smith, Nestor, Potomac † | 15 | 64 | 60 | 7 | 13 | 13 | 0 | 0 | 0 | 3 | 0 | 0 | 0 | 4 | 0 | 14 | 0 | 1 | 0 | .217 | .266 | .217 |
| Smith, Sean, Lynchburg | 6 | 25 | 23 | 1 | 6 | 7 | 1 | 0 | 0 | 0 | 1 | 0 | 0 | 1 | 1 | 6 | 1 | 1 | 1 | .261 | .292 | .304 |
| Snyder, Brad, Kinston * | 29 | 125 | 110 | 20 | 39 | 66 | 7 | 1 | 6 | 21 | 0 | 1 | 1 | 13 | 1 | 28 | 4 | 2 | 1 | .355 | .424 | .600 |
| Solis, Eddie, Wilmington | 8 | 29 | 22 | 4 | 5 | 7 | 2 | 0 | 0 | 2 | 1 | 0 | 0 | 6 | 0 | 6 | 0 | 0 | 1 | .227 | .393 | .318 |
| Stegall, Ryan, Salem | 109 | 451 | 393 | 42 | 91 | 107 | 13 | 0 | 1 | 33 | 14 | 7 | 9 | 28 | 1 | 65 | 8 | 2 | 10 | .232 | .293 | .272 |
| Stephens, Bernard, Wilmington * | 111 | 441 | 391 | 56 | 107 | 146 | 17 | 5 | 4 | 52 | 3 | 3 | 4 | 40 | 2 | 88 | 13 | 8 | 7 | .274 | .345 | .373 |
| Stocker, Mel, Wilmington † | 118 | 533 | 453 | 82 | 96 | 138 | 20 | 8 | 2 | 29 | 9 | 3 | 13 | 53 | 0 | 71 | 44 | 15 | 5 | .212 | .310 | .305 |
| Sweeney, Ryan, Winston-Salem * | 134 | 567 | 515 | 71 | 146 | 195 | 22 | 3 | 7 | 66 | 3 | 2 | 7 | 40 | 1 | 65 | 8 | 6 | 3 | .283 | .342 | .379 |
| Thomas, Ben, Myrtle Beach * | 81 | 304 | 272 | 21 | 58 | 76 | 13 | 1 | 1 | 26 | 2 | 1 | 1 | 28 | 0 | 63 | 7 | 4 | 8 | .213 | .288 | .279 |
| Thorman, Scott, Myrtle Beach * | 43 | 176 | 154 | 20 | 46 | 71 | 11 | 1 | 4 | 29 | 0 | 5 | 5 | 12 | 2 | 19 | 1 | 0 | 1 | .299 | .358 | .461 |
| Tiburcio, Hector, Potomac † | 111 | 473 | 421 | 66 | 110 | 155 | 24 | 3 | 5 | 48 | 12 | 4 | 1 | 35 | 0 | 89 | 17 | 11 | 9 | .261 | .317 | .368 |
| Timmons, Wes, Myrtle Beach | 112 | 457 | 379 | 48 | 105 | 142 | 24 | 2 | 3 | 45 | 6 | 2 | 15 | 55 | 1 | 32 | 10 | 5 | 3 | .277 | .388 | .375 |
| Torres, Eider, Kinston † | 113 | 477 | 440 | 68 | 133 | 172 | 24 | 3 | 3 | 46 | 8 | 4 | 3 | 22 | 5 | 46 | 48 | 6 | 6 | .302 | .337 | .391 |
| Tucker, Glenn, Myrtle Beach | 49 | 4 | 4 | 0 | 1 | 1 | 0 | 0 | 0 | 0 | 0 | 0 | 0 | 0 | 0 | 0 | 0 | 0 | 1 | .250 | .250 | .250 |
| Tupman, Matt, Wilmington * | 108 | 375 | 330 | 38 | 99 | 132 | 24 | 0 | 3 | 35 | 4 | 6 | 2 | 33 | 0 | 59 | 0 | 1 | 6 | .300 | .361 | .400 |
| Van Every, Jon, Kinston * | 113 | 459 | 392 | 67 | 108 | 197 | 22 | 2 | 21 | 71 | 0 | 6 | 8 | 53 | 0 | 129 | 11 | 3 | 3 | .276 | .368 | .503 |
| Vavao, Jason, Potomac | 89 | 316 | 279 | 37 | 73 | 127 | 14 | 2 | 12 | 35 | 1 | 1 | 3 | 32 | 0 | 100 | 6 | 2 | 6 | .262 | .343 | .455 |
| Voshell, Chase, Lynchburg | 58 | 189 | 164 | 16 | 33 | 47 | 8 | 0 | 2 | 16 | 1 | 2 | 2 | 18 | 1 | 46 | 2 | 0 | 2 | .201 | .285 | .287 |
| Votto, Joey, Potomac * | 24 | 96 | 84 | 11 | 25 | 47 | 7 | 0 | 5 | 20 | 0 | 0 | 1 | 11 | 1 | 21 | 1 | 1 | 1 | .298 | .385 | .560 |
| Wade, Mike, Winston-Salem | 6 | 18 | 17 | 0 | 4 | 5 | 1 | 0 | 0 | 0 | 0 | 0 | 0 | 1 | 0 | 4 | 0 | 0 | 0 | .235 | .278 | .294 |
| Walker, Matt, Frederick | 15 | 63 | 58 | 6 | 13 | 19 | 6 | 0 | 0 | 6 | 1 | 0 | 0 | 4 | 0 | 17 | 0 | 0 | 1 | .224 | .274 | .328 |
| Wallace, David, Kinston | 39 | 155 | 136 | 12 | 28 | 40 | 9 | 0 | 1 | 14 | 2 | 4 | 2 | 11 | 0 | 45 | 1 | 2 | 5 | .206 | .268 | .294 |
| West, Todd, Kinston | 4 | 11 | 9 | 2 | 4 | 4 | 0 | 0 | 0 | 3 | 0 | 0 | 0 | 2 | 0 | 2 | 0 | 0 | 0 | .444 | .545 | .444 |
| Wilken, Kris, Frederick † | 4 | 16 | 15 | 2 | 3 | 6 | 0 | 0 | 1 | 3 | 0 | 0 | 0 | 1 | 0 | 5 | 0 | 1 | 0 | .200 | .250 | .400 |
| Williams, Peanut, Winston-Salem | 22 | 66 | 61 | 8 | 13 | 21 | 2 | 0 | 2 | 7 | 0 | 1 | 0 | 4 | 0 | 12 | 0 | 0 | 0 | .213 | .258 | .344 |
| Wise, Dewayne, Myrtle Beach * | 4 | 16 | 16 | 1 | 4 | 6 | 0 | 1 | 0 | 0 | 0 | 0 | 0 | 0 | 0 | 6 | 0 | 0 | 0 | .250 | .250 | .375 |
| Wright, Gavin, Salem | 54 | 178 | 163 | 20 | 43 | 54 | 6 | 1 | 1 | 12 | 4 | 1 | 2 | 8 | 0 | 32 | 1 | 2 | 2 | .264 | .305 | .331 |

GRAND SLAMS—Anderson, Blanco, Carter, Cliffords, Eldred, Fagan, Garko, A. Gonzalez, Keim, Navarrete, Osborn, Prince, Robinson, Rogowski, Thomas, van Every, Vavao, Votto, 1 each.

AWARDED FIRST BASE ON CATCHER'S INTERFERENCE—Fagan 3 (McCann, Garko, Camacaro); Amador (Serrano); Florence (Draper); Panther (Prince); Stocker (McCann); Thomas (Garko); Voshell (McCann).

# 2004 PITCHING

## TEAM

| Team | W | L | Pct. | ERA | G | CG | ShO | Sv. | IP | H | TBF | R | ER | HR | SH | SF | HB | BB | IBB | SO | WP | Bk. |
|---|---|---|---|---|---|---|---|---|---|---|---|---|---|---|---|---|---|---|---|---|---|---|
| Wilmington | 77 | 62 | .554 | 3.41 | 140 | 2 | 9 | 40 | 1211.0 | 1151 | 5148 | 560 | 459 | 77 | 59 | 40 | 80 | 414 | 28 | 835 | 63 | 9 |
| Myrtle Beach | 75 | 63 | .543 | 3.44 | 139 | 3 | 19 | 38 | 1203.0 | 1097 | 5086 | 533 | 460 | 65 | 47 | 39 | 51 | 456 | 9 | 1051 | 76 | 5 |
| Kinston | 88 | 50 | .638 | 3.73 | 138 | 6 | 9 | 45 | 1188.2 | 1140 | 5098 | 559 | 493 | 91 | 56 | 46 | 78 | 427 | 13 | 965 | 83 | 3 |
| Lynchburg | 57 | 81 | .413 | 3.93 | 138 | 4 | 8 | 33 | 1208.0 | 1215 | 5191 | 604 | 528 | 98 | 57 | 34 | 57 | 395 | 23 | 904 | 65 | 5 |
| Potomac | 67 | 72 | .482 | 4.06 | 139 | 0 | 8 | 27 | 1207.0 | 1209 | 5205 | 639 | 544 | 105 | 50 | 42 | 49 | 415 | 19 | 987 | 68 | 3 |
| Salem | 65 | 74 | .468 | 4.18 | 139 | 6 | 10 | 36 | 1207.2 | 1293 | 5284 | 638 | 561 | 78 | 52 | 40 | 64 | 468 | 22 | 850 | 57 | 5 |
| Winston-Salem | 74 | 66 | .529 | 4.34 | 140 | 2 | 8 | 47 | 1216.1 | 1230 | 5279 | 675 | 585 | 94 | 55 | 43 | 88 | 468 | 25 | 888 | 69 | 6 |
| Frederick | 52 | 87 | .374 | 5.10 | 139 | 2 | 3 | 32 | 1202.0 | 1302 | 5370 | 762 | 681 | 131 | 46 | 45 | 77 | 517 | 22 | 975 | 87 | 4 |

## INDIVIDUAL

### TOP QUALIFIERS FOR EARNED-RUN AVERAGE TITLE

Minimum 112 innings.*Lefthanded pitcher.

| Pitcher, Team | W | L | Pct. | ERA | G | GS | CG | ShO | GF | Sv. | IP | H | TBF | R | ER | HR | SH | SF | HB | BB | IBB | SO | WP | Bk. |
|---|---|---|---|---|---|---|---|---|---|---|---|---|---|---|---|---|---|---|---|---|---|---|---|---|
| McGill, Trae, Wilmington | 9 | 2 | .818 | 2.08 | 21 | 18 | 1 | 0 | 0 | 0 | 112.2 | 98 | 450 | 32 | 26 | 7 | 8 | 6 | 8 | 26 | 2 | 66 | 4 | 1 |
| Tracey, Sean, Winston-Salem | 9 | 8 | .529 | 2.73 | 27 | 27 | 0 | 0 | 0 | 0 | 148.1 | 108 | 616 | 60 | 45 | 5 | 11 | 5 | 23 | 69 | 0 | 130 | 12 | 1 |
| Nieve, Fernando, Salem | 10 | 6 | .625 | 2.96 | 24 | 24 | 2 | 2 | 0 | 0 | 149.0 | 136 | 599 | 52 | 49 | 9 | 10 | 6 | 1 | 40 | 0 | 117 | 5 | 0 |
| Pauly, Thomas, Potomac | 8 | 7 | .533 | 2.97 | 28 | 19 | 0 | 0 | 5 | 0 | 121.1 | 96 | 476 | 47 | 40 | 12 | 5 | 4 | 3 | 26 | 0 | 135 | 3 | 1 |
| Boyer, Blaine, Myrtle Beach | 10 | 10 | .500 | 2.98 | 28 | 28 | 0 | 0 | 0 | 0 | 154.0 | 138 | 629 | 63 | 51 | 4 | 15 | 6 | 7 | 49 | 0 | 95 | 7 | 0 |
| Wright, Matt, Myrtle Beach | 4 | 6 | .400 | 3.39 | 24 | 21 | 1 | 0 | 2 | 0 | 124.2 | 115 | 524 | 55 | 47 | 4 | 9 | 6 | 1 | 58 | 1 | 133 | 12 | 2 |
| Gravelle, Nick, Lynchburg * | 5 | 10 | .333 | 3.62 | 26 | 25 | 1 | 0 | 0 | 0 | 151.2 | 157 | 626 | 70 | 61 | 14 | 17 | 8 | 3 | 45 | 2 | 109 | 2 | 1 |
| Lowery, Devon, Wilmington | 9 | 9 | .500 | 3.66 | 28 | 28 | 1 | 1 | 0 | 0 | 145.0 | 139 | 607 | 74 | 59 | 16 | 8 | 5 | 6 | 52 | 0 | 115 | 2 | 0 |
| Bruksch, Jeffrey, Potomac | 6 | 7 | .462 | 3.72 | 32 | 19 | 0 | 0 | 7 | 1 | 133.0 | 118 | 572 | 62 | 55 | 10 | 5 | 10 | 1 | 63 | 1 | 104 | 5 | 0 |
| Lerew, Anthony, Myrtle Beach | 8 | 9 | .471 | 3.75 | 27 | 27 | 0 | 0 | 0 | 0 | 144.0 | 145 | 597 | 75 | 60 | 12 | 7 | 5 | 3 | 46 | 0 | 125 | 6 | 0 |
| Sampson, Chris, Salem | 7 | 11 | .389 | 3.80 | 27 | 27 | 2 | 2 | 0 | 0 | 151.2 | 170 | 626 | 72 | 64 | 8 | 6 | 8 | 9 | 26 | 0 | 101 | 2 | 0 |
| Ramsey, Keith, Kinston * | 10 | 4 | .714 | 3.86 | 24 | 23 | 2 | 1 | 0 | 0 | 137.2 | 139 | 567 | 65 | 59 | 19 | 17 | 8 | 5 | 34 | 0 | 95 | 9 | 0 |
| Hirsh, Jason, Salem | 11 | 7 | .611 | 4.01 | 26 | 23 | 0 | 0 | 1 | 0 | 130.1 | 128 | 557 | 66 | 58 | 8 | 9 | 7 | 9 | 57 | 0 | 96 | 5 | 0 |

| Pitcher, Team | W | L | Pct. | ERA | G | GS | CG | ShO | GF | Sv. | IP | H | TBF | R | ER | HR | SH | SF | HB | BB | IBB | SO | WP | Bk. |
|---|---|---|---|---|---|---|---|---|---|---|---|---|---|---|---|---|---|---|---|---|---|---|---|---|
| Valdez, Edward, Potomac | 8 | 6 | .571 | 4.06 | 30 | 18 | 0 | 0 | 7 | 3 | 139.2 | 139 | 588 | 71 | 63 | 18 | 7 | 5 | 11 | 44 | 1 | 103 | 7 | 0 |
| Ray, Ken, Winston-Salem | 12 | 8 | .600 | 4.15 | 29 | 18 | 0 | 0 | 2 | 1 | 123.2 | 124 | 510 | 63 | 56 | 12 | 3 | 6 | 4 | 43 | 2 | 99 | 5 | 0 |

DEPARTMENTAL LEADERS: W—Slocum, 15; L—Sampson, Merchant, 11; Pct.—McGill, .818; G—Keefer, McCurdy, 63; GS—Boyer, Lowery, 28; CG—Five tied with two; ShO—Three tied with two; GF—Pollok, 53; Sv.—Pollok, 38; IP—Boyer, 154.0; H—Sampson, 170; TBF—Boyer, 642; R—Henry, 82; ER—Henry, Martin, 72; HR—Ramsey, 19; SH—Ramsey, 10; SF—Bruksch, 8; HB—Tracey, 23; BB—Tracey, 69; IBB—Davila, 8; SO—Pauly, 135; WP—Stahl, 14; BK—Nine with two.

## ALL PITCHERS

*Lefthanded pitcher.

| Pitcher, Team | W | L | Pct. | ERA | G | GS | CG | ShO | GF | Sv. | IP | H | TBF | R | ER | HR | SH | SF | HB | BB | IBB | SO | WP | Bk. |
|---|---|---|---|---|---|---|---|---|---|---|---|---|---|---|---|---|---|---|---|---|---|---|---|---|
| Ackerman, Eric, Wilmington * | 6 | 6 | .500 | 4.65 | 36 | 9 | 0 | 0 | 8 | 1 | 89.0 | 124 | 416 | 56 | 46 | 6 | 1 | 1 | 6 | 31 | 4 | 55 | 6 | 2 |
| Acosta, Manuel, Myrtle Beach | 4 | 0 | 1.000 | 4.24 | 11 | 0 | 0 | 0 | 4 | 0 | 23.1 | 20 | 102 | 12 | 11 | 1 | 0 | 0 | 1 | 11 | 0 | 21 | 3 | 0 |
| Aguilar, Ray, Myrtle Beach * | 2 | 0 | 1.000 | 2.25 | 4 | 4 | 0 | 0 | 0 | 0 | 20.0 | 15 | 72 | 5 | 5 | 0 | 0 | 0 | 1 | 1 | 0 | 12 | 1 | 0 |
| Albaladejo, Jonathan, Lynchburg | 8 | 8 | .500 | 4.33 | 24 | 24 | 1 | 1 | 0 | 0 | 131.0 | 150 | 561 | 72 | 63 | 10 | 8 | 7 | 5 | 25 | 0 | 92 | 6 | 0 |
| Alcala, Jason, Lynchburg | 1 | 3 | .250 | 2.57 | 23 | 0 | 0 | 0 | 14 | 5 | 42.0 | 33 | 172 | 13 | 12 | 1 | 0 | 0 | 1 | 10 | 1 | 37 | 1 | 2 |
| Alvarez, Basilio, Lynchburg | 0 | 0 | .000 | 5.40 | 2 | 2 | 0 | 0 | 0 | 0 | 10.0 | 12 | 47 | 6 | 6 | 1 | 1 | 1 | 0 | 5 | 0 | 6 | 2 | 1 |
| Alvarez, Gera, Frederick | 0 | 0 | .000 | 6.00 | 3 | 0 | 0 | 0 | 3 | 0 | 3.0 | 6 | 15 | 2 | 2 | 1 | 0 | 0 | 0 | 0 | 0 | 2 | 0 | 0 |
| An, Byeong-Hak, Winston-Salem * | 2 | 5 | .286 | 5.89 | 31 | 9 | 0 | 0 | 13 | 1 | 70.1 | 84 | 323 | 61 | 46 | 5 | 0 | 2 | 5 | 31 | 2 | 35 | 10 | 0 |
| Aramboles, Ricardo, Potomac | 4 | 10 | .286 | 5.21 | 26 | 21 | 0 | 0 | 2 | 1 | 107.0 | 125 | 492 | 74 | 62 | 8 | 11 | 7 | 2 | 55 | 0 | 82 | 7 | 0 |
| Armitage, Barry, Wilmington | 4 | 7 | .364 | 2.11 | 53 | 0 | 0 | 0 | 28 | 11 | 85.1 | 64 | 354 | 31 | 20 | 4 | 0 | 0 | 3 | 31 | 4 | 77 | 4 | 0 |
| Austin, Jeff, Potomac | 0 | 0 | .000 | 5.79 | 8 | 0 | 0 | 0 | 3 | 1 | 14.0 | 14 | 62 | 9 | 9 | 2 | 0 | 0 | 2 | 5 | 0 | 9 | 2 | 0 |
| Barreto, Joel, Potomac | 10 | 7 | .588 | 4.70 | 43 | 6 | 0 | 0 | 24 | 6 | 92.0 | 85 | 391 | 51 | 48 | 8 | 4 | 2 | 0 | 37 | 4 | 102 | 10 | 0 |
| Basner, Ryan, Myrtle Beach | 3 | 4 | .429 | 3.22 | 38 | 0 | 0 | 0 | 28 | 8 | 58.2 | 73 | 258 | 23 | 21 | 4 | 0 | 0 | 0 | 9 | 1 | 63 | 2 | 0 |
| Bayliss, Jonah, Wilmington | 6 | 6 | .500 | 4.93 | 24 | 24 | 0 | 0 | 0 | 0 | 111.1 | 119 | 485 | 70 | 61 | 11 | 9 | 8 | 9 | 44 | 0 | 79 | 6 | 2 |
| Benitez, Fabricio, Frederick | 0 | 0 | .000 | 4.35 | 7 | 0 | 0 | 0 | 2 | 0 | 10.1 | 12 | 50 | 5 | 5 | 1 | 0 | 0 | 2 | 5 | 0 | 8 | 0 | 0 |
| Bimeal, Matt, Lynchburg | 0 | 0 | .000 | 3.38 | 4 | 0 | 0 | 0 | 2 | 0 | 8.0 | 8 | 34 | 3 | 3 | 0 | 1 | 1 | 0 | 1 | 0 | 7 | 0 | 0 |
| Birkins, Kurt, Frederick * | 5 | 2 | .714 | 4.50 | 27 | 6 | 0 | 0 | 8 | 2 | 68.0 | 70 | 291 | 36 | 34 | 9 | 2 | 5 | 2 | 22 | 1 | 55 | 3 | 0 |
| Blakeney, Jacob, Myrtle Beach | 1 | 1 | .500 | 5.87 | 22 | 0 | 0 | 0 | 13 | 1 | 32.2 | 36 | 156 | 22 | 20 | 4 | 0 | 0 | 1 | 21 | 2 | 18 | 5 | 0 |
| Boughner, Anthony, Potomac * | 0 | 1 | .000 | 8.59 | 3 | 1 | 0 | 0 | 0 | 0 | 7.1 | 12 | 37 | 9 | 7 | 0 | 0 | 0 | 0 | 3 | 0 | 6 | 0 | 0 |
| Boyer, Blaine, Myrtle Beach | 10 | 10 | .500 | 2.98 | 28 | 28 | 0 | 0 | 0 | 0 | 154.0 | 138 | 629 | 63 | 51 | 4 | 15 | 6 | 7 | 49 | 0 | 95 | 7 | 0 |
| Brannon, Nick, Kinston * | 1 | 0 | 1.000 | 9.64 | 4 | 0 | 0 | 0 | 1 | 0 | 4.2 | 9 | 28 | 5 | 5 | 0 | 0 | 0 | 2 | 3 | 0 | 5 | 2 | 0 |
| Braun, Ryan, Wilmington | 2 | 3 | .400 | 2.21 | 51 | 0 | 0 | 0 | 42 | 23 | 57.0 | 48 | 248 | 25 | 14 | 2 | 1 | 0 | 3 | 25 | 4 | 58 | 4 | 0 |
| Bray, Stephen, Wilmington | 5 | 0 | 1.000 | 3.45 | 10 | 0 | 0 | 0 | 5 | 0 | 15.2 | 15 | 64 | 6 | 6 | 1 | 0 | 0 | 0 | 2 | 0 | 16 | 2 | 0 |
| Bruksch, Jeffrey, Potomac | 6 | 7 | .462 | 3.72 | 32 | 19 | 0 | 0 | 7 | 1 | 133.0 | 118 | 572 | 62 | 55 | 10 | 5 | 10 | 1 | 63 | 1 | 104 | 5 | 0 |
| Bush, Paul, Myrtle Beach | 5 | 3 | .625 | 3.56 | 24 | 4 | 0 | 0 | 3 | 0 | 65.2 | 58 | 278 | 27 | 26 | 7 | 1 | 3 | 3 | 25 | 0 | 78 | 4 | 1 |
| Cairns, Troy, Potomac | 0 | 0 | .000 | 4.50 | 1 | 0 | 0 | 0 | 0 | 0 | 2.0 | 2 | 8 | 1 | 1 | 1 | 0 | 0 | 0 | 0 | 0 | 0 | 0 | 0 |
| Candelario, Eddie, Lynchburg | 1 | 2 | .333 | 4.64 | 4 | 4 | 0 | 0 | 0 | 0 | 21.1 | 17 | 87 | 11 | 11 | 4 | 1 | 0 | 0 | 7 | 0 | 21 | 1 | 0 |
| Capellan, Jose, Myrtle Beach | 5 | 1 | .833 | 1.94 | 8 | 8 | 1 | 1 | 0 | 0 | 46.1 | 27 | 179 | 11 | 10 | 0 | 2 | 3 | 2 | 11 | 0 | 62 | 0 | 0 |
| Carmona, Fausto, Kinston | 5 | 2 | .714 | 2.83 | 12 | 12 | 0 | 0 | 0 | 0 | 70.0 | 68 | 297 | 28 | 22 | 6 | 3 | 0 | 3 | 20 | 0 | 57 | 4 | 0 |
| Castro, Fabio, Winston-Salem * | 1 | 1 | .500 | 2.35 | 6 | 0 | 0 | 0 | 0 | 0 | 7.2 | 2 | 27 | 2 | 2 | 0 | 0 | 0 | 1 | 2 | 0 | 9 | 1 | 0 |
| Castro, Julio, Winston-Salem | 3 | 3 | .500 | 5.30 | 40 | 0 | 0 | 0 | 13 | 0 | 56.0 | 42 | 237 | 35 | 33 | 9 | 1 | 0 | 8 | 20 | 1 | 65 | 2 | 0 |
| Caughey, Trevor, Frederick * | 0 | 1 | .000 | 6.17 | 4 | 2 | 0 | 0 | 0 | 0 | 11.2 | 15 | 51 | 8 | 8 | 2 | 0 | 0 | 1 | 3 | 0 | 5 | 1 | 0 |
| Chamberlain, Steve, Wilmington | 7 | 2 | .778 | 3.82 | 47 | 0 | 0 | 0 | 21 | 1 | 61.1 | 56 | 268 | 26 | 26 | 4 | 0 | 0 | 6 | 22 | 2 | 41 | 6 | 0 |
| Cooper, Chris, Kinston * | 3 | 3 | .500 | 1.60 | 25 | 0 | 0 | 0 | 17 | 1 | 39.1 | 36 | 165 | 11 | 7 | 1 | 1 | 1 | 2 | 10 | 3 | 44 | 3 | 0 |
| Coppinger, Joe, Frederick | 0 | 5 | .000 | 5.31 | 13 | 6 | 0 | 0 | 0 | 0 | 40.2 | 44 | 176 | 25 | 24 | 4 | 3 | 1 | 1 | 19 | 0 | 29 | 2 | 1 |
| Davies, Kyle, Myrtle Beach | 9 | 2 | .818 | 2.63 | 14 | 14 | 0 | 0 | 0 | 0 | 75.1 | 55 | 305 | 24 | 22 | 3 | 2 | 3 | 4 | 32 | 0 | 95 | 7 | 0 |
| Davila, Marcus, Lynchburg | 5 | 9 | .357 | 4.39 | 51 | 0 | 0 | 0 | 30 | 8 | 84.0 | 89 | 370 | 49 | 41 | 4 | 1 | 0 | 2 | 27 | 8 | 43 | 7 | 0 |
| Davis, Matt, Kinston | 3 | 2 | .600 | 3.13 | 41 | 0 | 0 | 0 | 14 | 4 | 83.1 | 85 | 367 | 35 | 29 | 5 | 0 | 0 | 6 | 26 | 2 | 61 | 5 | 0 |
| Denham, Dan, Kinston | 7 | 4 | .636 | 4.18 | 13 | 13 | 0 | 0 | 0 | 0 | 71.0 | 73 | 307 | 34 | 33 | 6 | 5 | 2 | 8 | 29 | 0 | 62 | 5 | 0 |
| Deza, Fredy, Frederick | 1 | 3 | .250 | 5.61 | 5 | 5 | 0 | 0 | 0 | 0 | 25.2 | 33 | 113 | 22 | 16 | 4 | 2 | 2 | 1 | 2 | 0 | 20 | 0 | 0 |
| Dixon, Zachary, Frederick * | 1 | 1 | .500 | 2.50 | 3 | 3 | 0 | 0 | 0 | 0 | 18.0 | 15 | 68 | 6 | 5 | 0 | 2 | 0 | 1 | 4 | 0 | 15 | 1 | 0 |
| Dizard, Fraser, Winston-Salem * | 0 | 0 | .000 | 0.00 | 1 | 0 | 0 | 0 | 1 | 0 | 2.0 | 0 | 6 | 0 | 0 | 0 | 0 | 0 | 0 | 0 | 0 | 2 | 0 | 0 |
| Done, Mike, Frederick | 0 | 0 | .000 | 0.00 | 2 | 0 | 0 | 0 | 2 | 0 | 2.1 | 1 | 8 | 0 | 0 | 0 | 0 | 0 | 0 | 0 | 0 | 1 | 0 | 0 |
| Douglas, Shea, Kinston * | 3 | 0 | 1.000 | 0.56 | 16 | 1 | 0 | 0 | 2 | 1 | 32.1 | 18 | 127 | 4 | 2 | 0 | 0 | 0 | 2 | 10 | 0 | 32 | 1 | 0 |
| Duke, Zach, Lynchburg * | 10 | 5 | .667 | 1.39 | 17 | 17 | 1 | 0 | 0 | 0 | 97.0 | 73 | 383 | 24 | 15 | 3 | 8 | 2 | 5 | 20 | 1 | 106 | 1 | 0 |
| Edens, Kyle, Potomac | 2 | 4 | .333 | 5.51 | 14 | 5 | 0 | 0 | 4 | 1 | 47.1 | 56 | 210 | 34 | 29 | 6 | 0 | 1 | 2 | 15 | 2 | 23 | 1 | 0 |
| Eisentrager, Dan, Kinston | 6 | 4 | .600 | 4.05 | 45 | 0 | 0 | 0 | 17 | 4 | 73.1 | 78 | 324 | 37 | 33 | 11 | 1 | 0 | 3 | 24 | 3 | 46 | 4 | 0 |
| Endicott, Drew, Wilmington | 7 | 3 | .700 | 4.00 | 43 | 1 | 0 | 0 | 12 | 1 | 87.2 | 86 | 390 | 46 | 39 | 5 | 2 | 3 | 8 | 35 | 0 | 45 | 5 | 1 |
| Espinal, Jose, Winston-Salem | 8 | 2 | .800 | 3.48 | 42 | 2 | 0 | 0 | 12 | 1 | 75.0 | 68 | 312 | 34 | 29 | 5 | 3 | 0 | 3 | 23 | 2 | 71 | 4 | 0 |
| Finch, Brian, Frederick | 1 | 4 | .200 | 7.96 | 9 | 9 | 0 | 0 | 0 | 0 | 37.1 | 59 | 183 | 35 | 33 | 5 | 1 | 1 | 4 | 15 | 0 | 22 | 5 | 0 |
| Foley, Travis, Kinston | 2 | 0 | 1.000 | 1.37 | 13 | 0 | 0 | 0 | 5 | 0 | 26.1 | 16 | 106 | 4 | 4 | 1 | 0 | 0 | 4 | 7 | 1 | 25 | 1 | 0 |
| France, Ryan, Salem | 2 | 2 | .500 | 3.16 | 20 | 0 | 0 | 0 | 3 | 0 | 37.0 | 42 | 170 | 20 | 13 | 0 | 1 | 0 | 2 | 19 | 2 | 25 | 0 | 0 |
| Freeman, Daniel, Salem | 4 | 3 | .571 | 4.86 | 54 | 0 | 0 | 0 | 34 | 11 | 66.2 | 82 | 326 | 40 | 36 | 1 | 0 | 0 | 4 | 40 | 5 | 32 | 6 | 0 |
| Frias, Juan, Potomac * | 1 | 1 | .500 | 4.28 | 18 | 2 | 0 | 0 | 4 | 0 | 33.2 | 35 | 159 | 20 | 16 | 1 | 1 | 3 | 5 | 17 | 0 | 9 | 4 | 0 |
| Gardner, Richie, Potomac | 8 | 3 | .727 | 2.50 | 18 | 12 | 0 | 0 | 5 | 1 | 86.1 | 77 | 354 | 31 | 24 | 3 | 5 | 2 | 1 | 13 | 0 | 80 | 3 | 1 |
| Gorzelanny, Tom, Lynchburg * | 3 | 5 | .375 | 4.85 | 10 | 10 | 0 | 0 | 0 | 0 | 55.2 | 54 | 237 | 31 | 30 | 6 | 1 | 1 | 4 | 19 | 0 | 61 | 1 | 0 |
| Gragg, John, Wilmington * | 0 | 1 | .000 | 2.60 | 4 | 2 | 0 | 0 | 0 | 0 | 17.1 | 19 | 66 | 6 | 5 | 1 | 0 | 1 | 0 | 5 | 1 | 9 | 0 | 0 |
| Granado, Jan, Potomac * | 4 | 4 | .500 | 5.40 | 18 | 8 | 0 | 0 | 4 | 1 | 65.0 | 85 | 291 | 43 | 39 | 6 | 1 | 3 | 1 | 17 | 1 | 39 | 4 | 0 |
| Gravelle, Nick, Lynchburg * | 5 | 10 | .333 | 3.62 | 26 | 25 | 1 | 0 | 0 | 0 | 151.2 | 157 | 626 | 70 | 61 | 14 | 17 | 8 | 3 | 45 | 2 | 109 | 2 | 1 |
| Griffin, Colt, Wilmington | 1 | 4 | .200 | 8.73 | 8 | 8 | 0 | 0 | 0 | 0 | 33.0 | 40 | 163 | 35 | 32 | 1 | 7 | 0 | 4 | 28 | 0 | 28 | 10 | 0 |
| Guerrero, Julio, Lynchburg | 4 | 8 | .333 | 5.63 | 33 | 12 | 1 | 0 | 5 | 1 | 96.0 | 125 | 422 | 64 | 60 | 12 | 6 | 5 | 3 | 19 | 1 | 59 | 1 | 0 |
| Hannaman, Ryan, Frederick * | 0 | 1 | .000 | 8.03 | 5 | 4 | 0 | 0 | 0 | 0 | 12.1 | 11 | 67 | 14 | 11 | 2 | 0 | 2 | 5 | 16 | 0 | 9 | 2 | 1 |
| Hart, Alex, Lynchburg | 0 | 1 | .000 | 3.68 | 3 | 3 | 0 | 0 | 0 | 0 | 14.2 | 16 | 68 | 12 | 6 | 1 | 0 | 0 | 0 | 8 | 0 | 7 | 1 | 0 |
| Harts, Jeremy, Lynchburg * | 0 | 0 | .000 | 8.68 | 10 | 0 | 0 | 0 | 4 | 0 | 9.1 | 11 | 56 | 9 | 9 | 2 | 0 | 0 | 4 | 14 | 0 | 7 | 5 | 0 |
| Heitzman, Aaron, Salem * | 0 | 4 | .000 | 7.06 | 29 | 2 | 0 | 0 | 12 | 0 | 51.0 | 76 | 268 | 50 | 40 | 9 | 1 | 0 | 7 | 35 | 1 | 25 | 6 | 0 |
| Henington, Henry, Frederick | 0 | 0 | .000 | 10.38 | 3 | 0 | 0 | 0 | 0 | 0 | 4.1 | 10 | 24 | 7 | 5 | 0 | 0 | 0 | 0 | 1 | 0 | 4 | 0 | 0 |
| Henry, Paul, Frederick | 2 | 5 | .286 | 7.42 | 35 | 9 | 0 | 0 | 5 | 0 | 87.1 | 115 | 408 | 82 | 72 | 17 | 8 | 8 | 5 | 38 | 0 | 88 | 11 | 0 |
| Hernandez, Fernando, Winston-Salem | 0 | 0 | .000 | 0.00 | 2 | 0 | 0 | 0 | 2 | 0 | 2.0 | 1 | 8 | 0 | 0 | 0 | 0 | 0 | 0 | 1 | 0 | 1 | 0 | 0 |
| Higgins, Joshua, Lynchburg | 1 | 5 | .167 | 2.77 | 37 | 0 | 0 | 0 | 27 | 12 | 48.2 | 44 | 204 | 20 | 15 | 6 | 0 | 0 | 2 | 11 | 1 | 33 | 1 | 0 |
| Hirsh, Jason, Salem | 11 | 7 | .611 | 4.01 | 26 | 23 | 0 | 0 | 1 | 0 | 130.1 | 128 | 557 | 66 | 58 | 8 | 9 | 7 | 9 | 57 | 0 | 96 | 5 | 0 |
| Hoelscher, Nate, Wilmington * | 5 | 6 | .455 | 2.15 | 51 | 0 | 0 | 0 | 15 | 2 | 83.2 | 70 | 342 | 23 | 20 | 6 | 0 | 0 | 7 | 15 | 3 | 70 | 2 | 0 |
| House, Craig, Frederick | 2 | 2 | .500 | 3.45 | 12 | 0 | 0 | 0 | 7 | 1 | 15.2 | 9 | 73 | 7 | 6 | 4 | 0 | 0 | 4 | 13 | 2 | 18 | 1 | 2 |

| Pitcher, Team | W | L | Pct. | ERA | G | GS | CG | ShO | GF | Sv. | IP | H | TBF | R | ER | HR | SH | SF | HB | BB | IBB | SO | WP | Bk. |
|---|---|---|---|---|---|---|---|---|---|---|---|---|---|---|---|---|---|---|---|---|---|---|---|---|
| Hudson, Jeremy, Winston-Salem | 0 | 3 | .000 | 8.36 | 13 | 3 | 0 | 0 | 1 | 0 | 37.2 | 48 | 186 | 41 | 35 | 3 | 4 | 3 | 3 | 25 | 2 | 13 | 3 | 0 |
| Hughes, Dusty, Wilmington * | 5 | 5 | .500 | 2.41 | 18 | 18 | 0 | 0 | 0 | 0 | 108.1 | 95 | 437 | 37 | 29 | 5 | 8 | 7 | 3 | 31 | 3 | 68 | 1 | 1 |
| Hummel, Rick, Winston-Salem | 0 | 0 | .000 | 34.71 | 3 | 0 | 0 | 0 | 1 | 0 | 2.1 | 11 | 20 | 9 | 9 | 2 | 0 | 0 | 0 | 2 | 0 | 1 | 0 | 0 |
| Iorg, Isaac, Myrtle Beach | 0 | 0 | .000 | 0.00 | 1 | 0 | 0 | 0 | 1 | 0 | 0.1 | 0 | 1 | 0 | 0 | 0 | 0 | 0 | 0 | 0 | 0 | 1 | 0 | 0 |
| Johnson, James, Frederick | 0 | 0 | .000 | 9.00 | 1 | 1 | 0 | 0 | 0 | 0 | 3.0 | 6 | 15 | 4 | 3 | 0 | 2 | 0 | 0 | 1 | 0 | 6 | 1 | 0 |
| Johnson, Russ, Lynchburg | 0 | 1 | .000 | 10.32 | 3 | 3 | 0 | 0 | 0 | 0 | 11.1 | 18 | 55 | 14 | 13 | 2 | 0 | 1 | 2 | 3 | 0 | 11 | 3 | 0 |
| Kaanoi, Jason, Wilmington | 4 | 0 | 1.000 | 1.37 | 9 | 7 | 0 | 0 | 1 | 0 | 46.0 | 23 | 172 | 9 | 7 | 1 | 2 | 0 | 0 | 13 | 1 | 24 | 0 | 0 |
| Keefer, Ryan, Frederick | 4 | 4 | .500 | 3.09 | 63 | 0 | 0 | 0 | 21 | 4 | 87.1 | 89 | 380 | 32 | 30 | 10 | 0 | 1 | 4 | 26 | 4 | 73 | 5 | 0 |
| Kesten, Michael, Salem * | 0 | 1 | .000 | 3.77 | 2 | 2 | 1 | 0 | 0 | 0 | 14.1 | 13 | 60 | 6 | 6 | 2 | 0 | 1 | 2 | 6 | 0 | 8 | 1 | 0 |
| LaMura, B.J., Winston-Salem | 4 | 5 | .444 | 5.58 | 12 | 11 | 2 | 0 | 0 | 0 | 61.1 | 77 | 282 | 45 | 38 | 5 | 3 | 3 | 4 | 29 | 0 | 47 | 7 | 0 |
| Lara, Juan, Kinston * | 4 | 3 | .571 | 5.66 | 35 | 8 | 0 | 0 | 12 | 1 | 84.1 | 106 | 393 | 60 | 53 | 6 | 3 | 3 | 4 | 38 | 1 | 74 | 6 | 2 |
| Larson, Adam, Winston-Salem | 1 | 1 | .500 | 8.82 | 11 | 1 | 0 | 0 | 3 | 1 | 16.1 | 25 | 81 | 16 | 16 | 3 | 0 | 0 | 2 | 8 | 1 | 12 | 0 | 0 |
| Lerew, Anthony, Myrtle Beach | 8 | 9 | .471 | 3.75 | 27 | 27 | 0 | 0 | 0 | 0 | 144.0 | 145 | 597 | 75 | 60 | 12 | 7 | 5 | 3 | 46 | 0 | 125 | 6 | 0 |
| Levinski, Donald, Frederick | 1 | 6 | .143 | 6.48 | 31 | 11 | 0 | 0 | 3 | 0 | 82.0 | 95 | 399 | 72 | 59 | 8 | 2 | 7 | 8 | 55 | 0 | 69 | 7 | 0 |
| Lewis, Rommie, Frederick * | 1 | 7 | .125 | 5.61 | 47 | 4 | 0 | 0 | 14 | 0 | 86.2 | 92 | 395 | 67 | 54 | 4 | 4 | 1 | 7 | 41 | 3 | 52 | 5 | 0 |
| Lipari, Thomas, Salem * | 0 | 1 | .000 | 6.86 | 9 | 0 | 0 | 0 | 1 | 0 | 21.0 | 31 | 99 | 17 | 16 | 3 | 1 | 4 | 0 | 11 | 1 | 16 | 0 | 0 |
| Little, Jeff, Winston-Salem | 0 | 0 | .000 | 2.25 | 2 | 0 | 0 | 0 | 2 | 1 | 4.0 | 4 | 16 | 1 | 1 | 0 | 0 | 0 | 0 | 0 | 0 | 0 | 1 | 0 |
| Loewen, Adam, Frederick * | 0 | 2 | .000 | 6.75 | 2 | 2 | 1 | 0 | 0 | 0 | 8.0 | 7 | 37 | 6 | 6 | 2 | 1 | 0 | 0 | 9 | 0 | 3 | 0 | 0 |
| Lord, Justin, Lynchburg | 2 | 2 | .500 | 2.96 | 14 | 2 | 0 | 0 | 2 | 0 | 24.1 | 24 | 114 | 11 | 8 | 3 | 1 | 1 | 3 | 11 | 1 | 19 | 1 | 1 |
| Lowery, Devon, Wilmington | 9 | 9 | .500 | 3.66 | 28 | 28 | 1 | 1 | 0 | 0 | 145.0 | 139 | 607 | 74 | 59 | 16 | 8 | 5 | 6 | 52 | 0 | 115 | 2 | 0 |
| Lubisich, Nik, Winston-Salem * | 5 | 7 | .417 | 4.35 | 22 | 16 | 0 | 0 | 1 | 0 | 103.1 | 129 | 443 | 56 | 50 | 8 | 10 | 5 | 4 | 23 | 1 | 56 | 1 | 0 |
| Lumsden, Tyler, Winston-Salem * | 3 | 1 | .750 | 4.12 | 15 | 3 | 0 | 0 | 1 | 0 | 39.1 | 45 | 182 | 25 | 18 | 2 | 0 | 0 | 1 | 20 | 1 | 31 | 7 | 2 |
| MacRae, Scott, Potomac | 0 | 1 | .000 | 2.25 | 5 | 1 | 0 | 0 | 3 | 1 | 12.0 | 16 | 54 | 5 | 3 | 0 | 0 | 0 | 0 | 1 | 0 | 10 | 1 | 0 |
| Maholm, Paul, Lynchburg * | 1 | 3 | .250 | 1.84 | 8 | 8 | 0 | 0 | 0 | 0 | 44.0 | 39 | 177 | 11 | 9 | 2 | 2 | 0 | 1 | 15 | 0 | 28 | 3 | 0 |
| Makowsky, Carl, Frederick | 0 | 2 | .000 | 10.32 | 8 | 0 | 0 | 0 | 2 | 0 | 11.1 | 20 | 66 | 13 | 13 | 2 | 0 | 2 | 1 | 12 | 1 | 10 | 2 | 0 |
| Mansfield, Monte, Salem | 9 | 3 | .750 | 2.93 | 59 | 0 | 0 | 0 | 19 | 9 | 98.1 | 81 | 422 | 39 | 32 | 4 | 0 | 0 | 6 | 41 | 6 | 83 | 8 | 0 |
| Martin, Greg, Lynchburg * | 2 | 1 | .667 | 3.00 | 25 | 0 | 0 | 0 | 7 | 0 | 45.0 | 32 | 198 | 18 | 15 | 2 | 0 | 0 | 1 | 30 | 1 | 25 | 5 | 0 |
| Martin, J.D., Kinston | 11 | 10 | .524 | 4.39 | 25 | 25 | 2 | 0 | 0 | 0 | 147.2 | 139 | 605 | 75 | 72 | 15 | 6 | 8 | 12 | 41 | 0 | 98 | 6 | 0 |
| Martinez, Dave, Kinston * | 2 | 3 | .400 | 5.51 | 19 | 6 | 0 | 0 | 4 | 0 | 50.2 | 42 | 227 | 38 | 31 | 2 | 1 | 4 | 5 | 28 | 1 | 37 | 3 | 1 |
| Mattison, Kieran, Kinston | 3 | 1 | .750 | 7.77 | 13 | 2 | 0 | 0 | 3 | 0 | 22.0 | 22 | 107 | 19 | 19 | 2 | 0 | 2 | 2 | 17 | 0 | 19 | 3 | 0 |
| McCarthy, Brandon, Winston-Salem | 6 | 0 | 1.000 | 2.08 | 8 | 8 | 0 | 0 | 0 | 0 | 52.0 | 31 | 188 | 12 | 12 | 3 | 2 | 1 | 1 | 3 | 0 | 60 | 1 | 2 |
| McClendon, Matt, Myrtle Beach | 2 | 1 | .667 | 3.26 | 11 | 0 | 0 | 0 | 2 | 0 | 19.1 | 17 | 87 | 8 | 7 | 2 | 0 | 0 | 3 | 7 | 1 | 9 | 0 | 0 |
| McCurdy, Nick, Frederick | 6 | 3 | .667 | 3.77 | 63 | 0 | 0 | 0 | 27 | 3 | 90.2 | 91 | 400 | 43 | 38 | 9 | 0 | 0 | 5 | 32 | 6 | 61 | 4 | 0 |
| McGill, Trae, Wilmington | 9 | 2 | .818 | 2.08 | 21 | 18 | 1 | 0 | 0 | 0 | 112.2 | 98 | 450 | 32 | 26 | 7 | 8 | 6 | 8 | 26 | 2 | 66 | 4 | 1 |
| McLemore, Mark, Salem * | 7 | 7 | .500 | 3.66 | 37 | 14 | 1 | 0 | 13 | 6 | 93.1 | 80 | 400 | 38 | 38 | 8 | 4 | 2 | 4 | 44 | 2 | 79 | 2 | 1 |
| McWilliams, Matt, Potomac * | 2 | 2 | .500 | 2.21 | 29 | 0 | 0 | 0 | 13 | 0 | 36.2 | 26 | 157 | 12 | 9 | 3 | 0 | 0 | 0 | 21 | 2 | 40 | 8 | 0 |
| Medlock, Calvin, Potomac | 3 | 4 | .429 | 6.36 | 11 | 9 | 0 | 0 | 1 | 1 | 46.2 | 49 | 214 | 36 | 33 | 8 | 4 | 2 | 3 | 22 | 1 | 46 | 3 | 0 |
| Mendoza, Hatuey, Potomac | 4 | 5 | .444 | 3.54 | 35 | 0 | 0 | 0 | 23 | 2 | 53.1 | 56 | 240 | 27 | 21 | 4 | 0 | 0 | 6 | 20 | 3 | 35 | 7 | 0 |
| Merchant, Jamie, Salem | 3 | 11 | .214 | 4.61 | 25 | 17 | 0 | 0 | 4 | 0 | 105.1 | 121 | 460 | 58 | 54 | 5 | 9 | 6 | 4 | 38 | 1 | 77 | 9 | 0 |
| Merricks, Matt, Myrtle Beach * | 5 | 3 | .625 | 3.31 | 13 | 12 | 1 | 0 | 0 | 0 | 73.1 | 61 | 310 | 32 | 27 | 4 | 3 | 3 | 13 | 24 | 1 | 67 | 4 | 1 |
| Michael, Mark, Lynchburg | 0 | 3 | .000 | 3.41 | 7 | 4 | 0 | 0 | 0 | 0 | 29.0 | 24 | 127 | 15 | 11 | 1 | 3 | 1 | 3 | 12 | 0 | 20 | 2 | 0 |
| Mieses, Jose, Winston-Salem | 3 | 3 | .500 | 5.40 | 21 | 5 | 0 | 0 | 4 | 0 | 45.0 | 51 | 215 | 30 | 27 | 4 | 2 | 5 | 6 | 29 | 0 | 33 | 4 | 0 |
| Miller, Adam, Kinston | 3 | 2 | .600 | 2.08 | 8 | 8 | 0 | 0 | 0 | 0 | 43.1 | 29 | 173 | 17 | 10 | 1 | 3 | 4 | 4 | 12 | 1 | 46 | 2 | 0 |
| Miller, Brian, Winston-Salem | 1 | 1 | .500 | 4.81 | 7 | 7 | 0 | 0 | 0 | 0 | 33.2 | 34 | 149 | 19 | 18 | 5 | 4 | 3 | 2 | 16 | 1 | 19 | 0 | 0 |
| Montani, Jeff, Frederick | 0 | 2 | .000 | 10.80 | 11 | 0 | 0 | 0 | 6 | 1 | 11.2 | 20 | 65 | 14 | 14 | 1 | 0 | 0 | 0 | 11 | 2 | 8 | 3 | 0 |
| Morris, Cory, Frederick | 0 | 3 | .000 | 7.48 | 11 | 6 | 0 | 0 | 2 | 1 | 21.2 | 30 | 112 | 19 | 18 | 2 | 1 | 0 | 1 | 20 | 0 | 23 | 4 | 0 |
| Mottl, Ryan, Lynchburg | 2 | 5 | .286 | 6.15 | 12 | 11 | 0 | 0 | 0 | 0 | 52.2 | 68 | 243 | 43 | 36 | 6 | 4 | 2 | 2 | 21 | 1 | 38 | 4 | 0 |
| Mueller, Mike, Myrtle Beach | 0 | 2 | .000 | 5.57 | 20 | 0 | 0 | 0 | 6 | 0 | 32.1 | 31 | 150 | 23 | 20 | 3 | 1 | 0 | 0 | 22 | 0 | 29 | 2 | 0 |
| Murray, Brad, Winston-Salem * | 3 | 4 | .429 | 3.82 | 48 | 0 | 0 | 0 | 9 | 2 | 63.2 | 68 | 272 | 32 | 27 | 4 | 0 | 0 | 2 | 13 | 3 | 30 | 1 | 1 |
| Neal, Tony, Frederick | 2 | 6 | .250 | 4.33 | 50 | 0 | 0 | 0 | 29 | 18 | 62.1 | 48 | 263 | 30 | 30 | 8 | 0 | 0 | 3 | 25 | 3 | 64 | 4 | 0 |
| Newman, Ryan, Lynchburg | 0 | 0 | .000 | 0.00 | 1 | 0 | 0 | 0 | 1 | 0 | 0.1 | 1 | 2 | 0 | 0 | 0 | 0 | 0 | 0 | 0 | 0 | 0 | 0 | 0 |
| Nieve, Fernando, Salem | 10 | 6 | .625 | 2.96 | 24 | 24 | 2 | 2 | 0 | 0 | 149.0 | 136 | 599 | 52 | 49 | 9 | 10 | 6 | 1 | 40 | 0 | 117 | 5 | 0 |
| O'Brien, Patrick, Lynchburg | 4 | 4 | .500 | 4.47 | 25 | 13 | 0 | 0 | 3 | 0 | 92.2 | 100 | 398 | 47 | 46 | 7 | 2 | 3 | 10 | 26 | 0 | 58 | 4 | 0 |
| Owens, Henry, Lynchburg | 3 | 4 | .429 | 4.28 | 39 | 0 | 0 | 0 | 27 | 4 | 54.2 | 46 | 240 | 26 | 26 | 4 | 0 | 0 | 4 | 26 | 1 | 49 | 10 | 0 |
| Paduch, Jim, Potomac | 3 | 2 | .600 | 5.21 | 26 | 13 | 0 | 0 | 4 | 2 | 95.0 | 108 | 410 | 61 | 55 | 12 | 5 | 1 | 4 | 26 | 2 | 79 | 1 | 1 |
| Parker, Brett, Kinston | 0 | 0 | .000 | 0.00 | 1 | 0 | 0 | 0 | 1 | 0 | 1.0 | 1 | 5 | 1 | 0 | 0 | 0 | 0 | 0 | 1 | 0 | 0 | 0 | 0 |
| Pauly, Thomas, Potomac | 8 | 7 | .533 | 2.97 | 28 | 19 | 0 | 0 | 5 | 0 | 121.1 | 96 | 476 | 47 | 40 | 12 | 5 | 4 | 3 | 26 | 0 | 135 | 3 | 1 |
| Peguero, Jailen, Salem | 5 | 6 | .455 | 3.87 | 51 | 1 | 0 | 0 | 31 | 8 | 86.0 | 93 | 384 | 51 | 37 | 7 | 0 | 0 | 4 | 32 | 3 | 79 | 5 | 1 |
| Pena, Francisco, Salem | 1 | 2 | .333 | 5.86 | 11 | 10 | 0 | 0 | 0 | 0 | 35.1 | 39 | 163 | 26 | 23 | 3 | 4 | 2 | 3 | 26 | 0 | 31 | 2 | 1 |
| Penn, Hayden, Frederick | 6 | 5 | .545 | 3.80 | 13 | 13 | 0 | 0 | 0 | 0 | 73.1 | 59 | 287 | 33 | 31 | 7 | 1 | 1 | 2 | 20 | 0 | 61 | 1 | 0 |
| Pennington, Todd, Kinston | 0 | 2 | .000 | 2.76 | 28 | 0 | 0 | 0 | 26 | 19 | 29.1 | 25 | 130 | 11 | 9 | 0 | 0 | 0 | 1 | 16 | 0 | 39 | 8 | 0 |
| Peralta, Efigenio, Myrtle Beach | 3 | 3 | .500 | 4.07 | 31 | 8 | 0 | 0 | 9 | 3 | 79.2 | 69 | 340 | 42 | 36 | 5 | 3 | 4 | 6 | 36 | 0 | 75 | 3 | 1 |
| Perez, Rafael, Kinston * | 0 | 0 | .000 | 11.57 | 1 | 1 | 0 | 0 | 0 | 0 | 4.2 | 10 | 25 | 6 | 6 | 1 | 0 | 0 | 0 | 2 | 1 | 3 | 0 | 0 |
| Pesco, Nick, Kinston | 1 | 2 | .333 | 3.21 | 3 | 3 | 0 | 0 | 0 | 0 | 14.0 | 15 | 61 | 9 | 5 | 0 | 2 | 2 | 0 | 4 | 0 | 12 | 0 | 0 |
| Piersoll, Chris, Frederick | 2 | 4 | .333 | 4.56 | 19 | 5 | 0 | 0 | 3 | 1 | 51.1 | 51 | 225 | 27 | 26 | 6 | 1 | 1 | 4 | 21 | 0 | 48 | 3 | 0 |
| Pollok, Dwayne, Winston-Salem | 2 | 4 | .333 | 3.28 | 58 | 0 | 0 | 0 | 53 | 38 | 60.1 | 59 | 251 | 23 | 22 | 4 | 0 | 1 | 3 | 8 | 2 | 49 | 1 | 0 |
| Potter, Josh, Frederick | 0 | 0 | .000 | 0.00 | 1 | 0 | 0 | 0 | 1 | 0 | 2.0 | 1 | 8 | 0 | 0 | 0 | 0 | 0 | 0 | 1 | 0 | 0 | 0 | 0 |
| Prahm, Ryan, Kinston | 1 | 0 | 1.000 | 1.25 | 31 | 0 | 0 | 0 | 21 | 14 | 36.0 | 21 | 153 | 7 | 5 | 1 | 0 | 0 | 0 | 24 | 0 | 43 | 5 | 0 |
| Purvis, Rob, Winston-Salem | 4 | 5 | .444 | 4.89 | 34 | 6 | 0 | 0 | 10 | 0 | 77.1 | 93 | 370 | 45 | 42 | 4 | 2 | 4 | 7 | 45 | 3 | 29 | 5 | 0 |
| Ramsey, Keith, Kinston * | 10 | 4 | .714 | 3.86 | 24 | 23 | 2 | 1 | 0 | 0 | 137.2 | 139 | 567 | 65 | 59 | 19 | 17 | 8 | 5 | 34 | 0 | 95 | 9 | 0 |
| Ray, Chris, Frederick | 6 | 3 | .667 | 3.80 | 14 | 14 | 1 | 1 | 0 | 0 | 73.1 | 82 | 305 | 31 | 31 | 6 | 5 | 2 | 1 | 20 | 0 | 74 | 3 | 0 |
| Ray, Ken, Winston-Salem | 12 | 8 | .600 | 4.15 | 29 | 18 | 0 | 0 | 2 | 1 | 123.2 | 124 | 510 | 63 | 56 | 12 | 3 | 6 | 4 | 43 | 2 | 99 | 5 | 0 |
| Reynoso, Paulino, Winston-Salem * | 3 | 2 | .600 | 3.95 | 25 | 19 | 0 | 0 | 2 | 1 | 84.1 | 79 | 370 | 42 | 37 | 6 | 8 | 5 | 7 | 41 | 1 | 70 | 3 | 0 |
| Rich, Dan, Kinston * | 0 | 0 | .000 | 13.50 | 4 | 0 | 0 | 0 | 2 | 0 | 2.2 | 4 | 16 | 4 | 4 | 1 | 0 | 0 | 1 | 3 | 0 | 1 | 0 | 0 |
| Richardson, Jason, Myrtle Beach | 0 | 4 | .000 | 4.45 | 14 | 1 | 0 | 0 | 7 | 2 | 28.1 | 29 | 138 | 17 | 14 | 4 | 1 | 2 | 3 | 20 | 0 | 22 | 7 | 0 |
| Roberts, Ralph, Myrtle Beach | 3 | 5 | .375 | 3.52 | 32 | 0 | 0 | 0 | 12 | 3 | 53.2 | 47 | 230 | 23 | 21 | 3 | 0 | 0 | 0 | 22 | 0 | 36 | 6 | 0 |
| Rodaway, Brian, Salem * | 5 | 8 | .385 | 4.87 | 34 | 19 | 0 | 0 | 5 | 2 | 131.1 | 158 | 569 | 77 | 71 | 8 | 7 | 3 | 5 | 30 | 0 | 67 | 4 | 1 |
| Salmon, Brad, Potomac | 1 | 0 | 1.000 | 0.54 | 5 | 1 | 0 | 0 | 0 | 0 | 16.2 | 12 | 66 | 1 | 1 | 0 | 0 | 0 | 1 | 3 | 0 | 16 | 0 | 0 |
| Sampson, Chris, Salem | 7 | 11 | .389 | 3.80 | 27 | 27 | 2 | 2 | 0 | 0 | 151.2 | 170 | 626 | 72 | 64 | 8 | 6 | 8 | 9 | 26 | 0 | 101 | 2 | 0 |
| Schmidt, Jeremy, Potomac | 2 | 4 | .333 | 2.45 | 35 | 0 | 0 | 0 | 23 | 3 | 51.1 | 44 | 216 | 25 | 14 | 2 | 0 | 0 | 2 | 15 | 1 | 40 | 0 | 0 |
| Shafer, David, Potomac | 0 | 0 | .000 | 0.00 | 3 | 0 | 0 | 0 | 3 | 3 | 4.1 | 5 | 18 | 0 | 0 | 0 | 0 | 0 | 0 | 0 | 0 | 5 | 0 | 0 |
| Sharber, Jason, Lynchburg | 1 | 0 | 1.000 | 5.06 | 5 | 0 | 0 | 0 | 1 | 1 | 10.2 | 7 | 45 | 7 | 6 | 2 | 0 | 0 | 1 | 5 | 0 | 6 | 2 | 0 |

| Pitcher, Team | W | L | Pct. | ERA | G | GS | CG | ShO | GF | Sv. | IP | H | TBF | R | ER | HR | SH | SF | HB | BB | IBB | SO | WP | Bk. |
|---|---|---|---|---|---|---|---|---|---|---|---|---|---|---|---|---|---|---|---|---|---|---|---|---|
| Shiery, Shaun, Wilmington * | 2 | 3 | .400 | 2.08 | 17 | 8 | 0 | 0 | 3 | 1 | 56.1 | 43 | 231 | 22 | 13 | 1 | 5 | 3 | 5 | 16 | 2 | 28 | 2 | 0 |
| Slocum, Brian, Kinston | 15 | 6 | .714 | 4.33 | 25 | 25 | 2 | 2 | 0 | 0 | 135.0 | 136 | 568 | 66 | 65 | 13 | 5 | 7 | 6 | 41 | 0 | 102 | 11 | 0 |
| Smith, Sean, Kinston | 0 | 1 | .000 | 8.00 | 2 | 2 | 0 | 0 | 0 | 0 | 9.0 | 14 | 48 | 10 | 8 | 0 | 2 | 2 | 1 | 4 | 0 | 8 | 1 | 0 |
| Stahl, Richard, Frederick * | 7 | 8 | .467 | 4.96 | 19 | 19 | 0 | 0 | 0 | 0 | 81.2 | 80 | 367 | 52 | 45 | 6 | 6 | 3 | 3 | 50 | 0 | 56 | 14 | 0 |
| Stiles, Brad, Wilmington * | 2 | 2 | .500 | 4.55 | 21 | 0 | 0 | 0 | 3 | 0 | 27.2 | 30 | 129 | 15 | 14 | 0 | 0 | 1 | 2 | 15 | 1 | 13 | 3 | 2 |
| Stockman, Landon, Kinston | 2 | 1 | .667 | 1.23 | 16 | 0 | 0 | 0 | 7 | 1 | 22.0 | 16 | 90 | 3 | 3 | 0 | 0 | 0 | 1 | 7 | 0 | 20 | 1 | 0 |
| Stodolka, Mike, Wilmington * | 3 | 2 | .600 | 4.33 | 14 | 14 | 0 | 0 | 0 | 0 | 62.1 | 66 | 271 | 35 | 30 | 5 | 5 | 4 | 8 | 18 | 1 | 33 | 5 | 0 |
| Stumm, Jason, Winston-Salem | 1 | 2 | .333 | 5.68 | 8 | 0 | 0 | 0 | 5 | 0 | 12.2 | 15 | 58 | 9 | 8 | 1 | 0 | 0 | 1 | 5 | 0 | 7 | 0 | 0 |
| Sturkie, Scott, Myrtle Beach | 2 | 1 | .667 | 3.86 | 12 | 1 | 0 | 0 | 4 | 0 | 28.0 | 30 | 121 | 14 | 12 | 1 | 0 | 0 | 1 | 8 | 0 | 8 | 2 | 0 |
| Sugarman, Jeremy, Potomac | 0 | 1 | .000 | 4.26 | 9 | 1 | 0 | 0 | 2 | 0 | 19.0 | 28 | 93 | 13 | 9 | 0 | 1 | 0 | 3 | 6 | 0 | 3 | 1 | 0 |
| Tamayo, Danny, Wilmington | 0 | 1 | .000 | 9.53 | 3 | 3 | 0 | 0 | 0 | 0 | 11.1 | 16 | 55 | 12 | 12 | 1 | 3 | 1 | 2 | 5 | 0 | 10 | 1 | 0 |
| Thurman, Corey, Potomac | 1 | 2 | .333 | 1.61 | 5 | 3 | 0 | 0 | 1 | 0 | 22.1 | 20 | 91 | 5 | 4 | 1 | 1 | 2 | 2 | 4 | 0 | 21 | 1 | 0 |
| Tiller, James, Frederick | 2 | 4 | .333 | 4.34 | 17 | 8 | 0 | 0 | 1 | 0 | 58.0 | 58 | 252 | 35 | 28 | 3 | 2 | 2 | 5 | 21 | 0 | 33 | 3 | 0 |
| Tracey, Sean, Winston-Salem | 9 | 8 | .529 | 2.73 | 27 | 27 | 0 | 0 | 0 | 0 | 148.1 | 108 | 616 | 60 | 45 | 5 | 11 | 5 | 23 | 69 | 0 | 130 | 12 | 1 |
| Tucker, Glenn, Myrtle Beach | 3 | 1 | .750 | 1.64 | 48 | 0 | 0 | 0 | 45 | 21 | 66.0 | 55 | 279 | 13 | 12 | 2 | 0 | 0 | 2 | 26 | 3 | 56 | 0 | 0 |
| Valdez, Edward, Potomac | 8 | 6 | .571 | 4.06 | 30 | 18 | 0 | 0 | 7 | 3 | 139.2 | 139 | 588 | 71 | 63 | 18 | 7 | 5 | 11 | 44 | 1 | 103 | 7 | 0 |
| Van Dusen, Derrick, Kinston * | 6 | 0 | 1.000 | 1.64 | 9 | 9 | 0 | 0 | 0 | 0 | 49.1 | 38 | 209 | 10 | 9 | 0 | 7 | 3 | 6 | 26 | 0 | 36 | 3 | 0 |
| Vavao, Jason, Potomac | 0 | 1 | .000 | 18.00 | 1 | 0 | 0 | 0 | 1 | 0 | 1.0 | 1 | 6 | 2 | 2 | 0 | 0 | 0 | 0 | 2 | 1 | 0 | 0 | 0 |
| Wasserman, Ehren, Winston-Salem | 1 | 0 | 1.000 | 2.70 | 10 | 0 | 0 | 0 | 4 | 1 | 10.0 | 11 | 47 | 4 | 3 | 1 | 0 | 0 | 1 | 5 | 3 | 5 | 1 | 0 |
| Waters, Chris, Myrtle Beach * | 0 | 1 | .000 | 12.27 | 4 | 1 | 0 | 0 | 0 | 0 | 7.1 | 14 | 39 | 10 | 10 | 0 | 0 | 0 | 0 | 4 | 0 | 5 | 1 | 0 |
| Westhoff, Billy, Salem | 1 | 2 | .333 | 5.84 | 20 | 0 | 0 | 0 | 10 | 0 | 37.0 | 43 | 181 | 26 | 24 | 3 | 0 | 1 | 4 | 23 | 1 | 14 | 2 | 1 |
| Whisler, Wesley, Winston-Salem * | 2 | 1 | .667 | 3.38 | 5 | 5 | 0 | 0 | 0 | 0 | 26.2 | 17 | 102 | 10 | 10 | 3 | 2 | 0 | 0 | 7 | 0 | 13 | 0 | 0 |
| White, Sean, Myrtle Beach | 6 | 6 | .500 | 3.60 | 18 | 10 | 0 | 0 | 0 | 0 | 70.0 | 62 | 291 | 34 | 28 | 2 | 3 | 4 | 0 | 24 | 0 | 41 | 4 | 0 |
| Wilson, Jeff, Frederick * | 3 | 4 | .429 | 5.02 | 14 | 12 | 0 | 0 | 1 | 1 | 61.0 | 73 | 267 | 35 | 34 | 8 | 3 | 6 | 7 | 14 | 0 | 58 | 2 | 0 |
| Winkelsas, Joe, Winston-Salem | 0 | 0 | .000 | 6.75 | 1 | 0 | 0 | 0 | 0 | 0 | 1.1 | 4 | 8 | 1 | 1 | 0 | 0 | 0 | 0 | 0 | 0 | 1 | 0 | 0 |
| Wright, Matt, Myrtle Beach | 4 | 6 | .400 | 3.39 | 24 | 21 | 1 | 0 | 2 | 0 | 124.2 | 115 | 524 | 55 | 47 | 4 | 9 | 6 | 1 | 58 | 1 | 133 | 12 | 2 |
| Youman, Shane, Lynchburg * | 4 | 2 | .667 | 3.16 | 47 | 0 | 0 | 0 | 11 | 2 | 74.0 | 67 | 325 | 28 | 26 | 5 | 1 | 1 | 1 | 35 | 5 | 62 | 2 | 0 |

COMBINATION SHUTOUTS: **Frederick** (2)—Penn-Keefer-McCurdy, Birkins-Lewis-Neal. **Kinston** (7)—Denham-Davis-Prahm, Douglas-Davis-Prahm, Martin-Eisentrager-Cooper, Ramsey-Prahm-Pennington, Miller-Eisentrager-Pennington, Martin-Lara-Eisentrager-Pennington, Miller-Lara-Stockman. **Lynchburg** (7)—Albaladejo-Guerrero, Duke-Davila-Higgins, Duke-Youman-Higgins, Maholm-Youman-Owens-Higgins, Guerrero-Sharber-Alcala, Guerrero-Alcala-Higgins, Lord-Martin-Davila. **Myrtle Beach** (17)—Boyer-Basner-McClendon, Lerew-Basner, Davies-Basner-Tucker, Capellan-Peralta, Davies-Acosta-Tucker, Capellan-Roberts, Lerew-Peralta-Basner, Boyer-McClendon-Bush, Boyer-Peralta, Lerew-Tucker, Boyer-Tucker, Lerew-Tucker, White-Peralta-Basner, Boyer-Peralta-Tucker, Peralta-Mueller, Boyer-Roberts-Tucker, Boyer-Tucker. **Potomac** (8)—Gardner-Bruksch, Gardner-McWilliams-Schmidt, Edens-Aramboles, Paul-Frias-Gardner, Aramboles-Thurman, Bruksch-Salmon-Schmidt, Valdez-Schmidt, Pauly-Schmidt. **Salem** (6)—Pena-Mansfield-McLemore, Nieve-Lipari-Peguero, McLemore-Peguero, McLemore-Peguero, McLemore-Mansfield-Freeman, Merchant-Mansfield-Freeman. **Wilmington** (10)—Lowery-McGill-Chamberlain-Braun, Ackerman-Armitage, Ackerman-Armitage, Lowery-Endicott, McGill-Armitage, Lowery-Hoelscher, McGill-Ackerman-Chamberlain-Armitage, Hughes-Armitage, Lowery-Hoelscher-Braun, Stodolka-Bray-Armitage. **Winston Salem** (8)—Purvis-Espinal-Pollok, Tracey-Murray, Lubisich-Castro-Pollok, Tracey-Murray-Pollok, McCarthy-Murray-Pollok, Tracey-Little, McCarthy-Pollok, Reynoso-Lumsden-Pollok.

NO-HIT GAMES: Ramsey, Kinston, defeated Myrtle Beach, 6-0, September 6.

# 2004 FIELDING

## TEAM

| Team | G | PO | A | E | TC | DP | TP | PB | Pct. |
|---|---|---|---|---|---|---|---|---|---|
| Kinston | 138 | 3567 | 115 | 120 | 3802 | 99 | 0 | 14 | .968 |
| Frederick | 139 | 3606 | 133 | 124 | 3863 | 124 | 0 | 32 | .968 |
| Winston-Salem | 140 | 3646 | 134 | 134 | 3914 | 105 | 0 | 39 | .966 |
| Salem | 139 | 3623 | 124 | 137 | 3884 | 150 | 0 | 19 | .965 |
| Myrtle Beach | 139 | 3609 | 137 | 138 | 3884 | 103 | 0 | 18 | .964 |
| Lynchburg | 138 | 3624 | 166 | 158 | 3948 | 121 | 0 | 34 | .960 |
| Wilmington | 140 | 3633 | 134 | 159 | 3926 | 134 | 0 | 18 | .960 |
| Potomac | 139 | 3620 | 116 | 184 | 3920 | 120 | 0 | 8 | .953 |

## INDIVIDUAL

### FIRST BASEMEN

NOTE: All caps denotes fielding-percentage leader based on 70 games for catchers, 93 for all other non-pitchers and 112 innings for pitchers. *Throws lefthanded.

| Player, Team | Pct. | G | PO | A | E | TC | DP |
|---|---|---|---|---|---|---|---|
| Alleva, JD, WIL* | .985 | 51 | 426 | 25 | 7 | 458 | 41 |
| Aubrey, Michael, KIN* | .991 | 50 | 405 | 23 | 4 | 432 | 39 |
| Becker, Brian, WS | 1.000 | 30 | 282 | 19 | 0 | 301 | 17 |
| Blanco, Tony, POT | .973 | 35 | 268 | 24 | 8 | 300 | 24 |
| Brice, Thomas, WS* | 1.000 | 1 | 7 | 0 | 0 | 7 | 2 |
| Cameron, Troy, WS | 1.000 | 1 | 5 | 0 | 0 | 5 | 0 |
| Choy Foo, Rodney, KIN | .986 | 24 | 193 | 15 | 3 | 211 | 16 |
| Clark, Daryl, WIL* | .952 | 14 | 109 | 11 | 6 | 126 | 12 |
| Davies, Gregg, FRE* | 1.000 | 8 | 60 | 4 | 0 | 64 | 5 |
| Diaz, Rafael, FRE | 1.000 | 2 | 12 | 0 | 0 | 12 | 2 |
| Done, Mike, FRE | .992 | 26 | 216 | 18 | 2 | 236 | 16 |
| Eldred, Brad, LYN | .988 | 89 | 795 | 57 | 10 | 862 | 64 |
| Espino, Damaso, WIL | .985 | 38 | 362 | 20 | 6 | 388 | 32 |
| Fagan, John, SAL | .997 | 47 | 351 | 26 | 1 | 378 | 45 |
| Fallon, Chris, WIL* | 1.000 | 1 | 11 | 0 | 0 | 11 | 0 |
| Garcia, Cipriano, WS | 1.000 | 1 | 2 | 1 | 0 | 3 | 0 |
| Garko, Ryan, KIN | 1.000 | 26 | 224 | 17 | 0 | 241 | 17 |
| GREDVIG, DOUG, FRE | .992 | 107 | 967 | 88 | 9 | 1064 | 85 |
| Hubele, Ryan, FRE | 1.000 | 1 | 8 | 0 | 0 | 8 | 1 |
| Iorg, Isaac, MYR | .987 | 56 | 407 | 39 | 6 | 452 | 36 |
| Jensen, David, WIL* | .980 | 17 | 131 | 18 | 3 | 152 | 9 |
| Keim, Adam, WIL | .979 | 27 | 214 | 21 | 5 | 240 | 25 |
| Larkin, Shaun, KIN* | 1.000 | 4 | 14 | 0 | 0 | 14 | 2 |
| Logan, Matt, POT* | .984 | 33 | 279 | 23 | 5 | 307 | 13 |
| Magness, Pat, KIN* | .994 | 35 | 290 | 18 | 2 | 310 | 16 |
| Molina, Gustavo, WS | 1.000 | 2 | 3 | 0 | 0 | 3 | 0 |
| Navarrete, Ray, LYN | .989 | 45 | 409 | 26 | 5 | 440 | 33 |
| Peavey, Pat, SAL | .994 | 33 | 290 | 27 | 2 | 319 | 26 |
| Prince, Bryan, POT | 1.000 | 5 | 35 | 4 | 0 | 39 | 4 |
| Rogowski, Casey, WS* | .989 | 114 | 951 | 84 | 11 | 1046 | 91 |
| Ruelas, Alonzo, MYR | 1.000 | 5 | 19 | 1 | 0 | 20 | 0 |
| Ruiz, Junior, POT* | 1.000 | 1 | 2 | 0 | 0 | 2 | 2 |
| Saccomanno, Mark, SAL | .990 | 69 | 669 | 44 | 7 | 720 | 63 |
| Salas, Jose, MYR | 1.000 | 1 | 2 | 1 | 0 | 3 | 0 |
| Santana, Mayobanex, KIN | 1.000 | 2 | 14 | 2 | 0 | 16 | 2 |
| Segui, David, FRE | 1.000 | 1 | 12 | 1 | 0 | 13 | 1 |
| Shaffer, Josh, WS* | 1.000 | 1 | 1 | 1 | 0 | 2 | 1 |
| Thomas, Ben, MYR* | .994 | 36 | 301 | 11 | 2 | 314 | 23 |
| Thorman, Scott, MYR* | .997 | 43 | 361 | 19 | 1 | 381 | 28 |
| Timmons, Wesley, MYR | .985 | 8 | 64 | 3 | 1 | 68 | 6 |
| Vavao, Jason, POT | .984 | 54 | 396 | 28 | 7 | 431 | 38 |
| Voshell, Chase, LYN | 1.000 | 7 | 42 | 4 | 0 | 46 | 3 |
| Votto, Joey, POT* | 1.000 | 21 | 154 | 16 | 0 | 170 | 16 |

### SECOND BASEMEN

| Player, Team | Pct. | G | PO | A | E | TC | DP |
|---|---|---|---|---|---|---|---|
| Alvarez, Gera, FRE | .979 | 78 | 125 | 254 | 8 | 387 | 54 |
| Amador, Chris, WS | .952 | 95 | 158 | 254 | 21 | 433 | 60 |
| Asprilla, Avelino, LYN | 1.000 | 2 | 3 | 5 | 0 | 8 | 2 |
| Bastida, Evel, FRE* | .980 | 10 | 11 | 37 | 1 | 49 | 7 |
| Cairns, Troy, POT | 1.000 | 11 | 13 | 20 | 0 | 33 | 5 |
| Cameron, Troy, WS | 1.000 | 1 | 2 | 1 | 0 | 3 | 0 |

| Player, Team | Pct. | G | PO | A | E | TC | DP |
|---|---|---|---|---|---|---|---|
| Choy Foo, Rodney, KIN | 1.000 | 12 | 29 | 34 | 0 | 63 | 5 |
| Done, Mike, FRE | .971 | 37 | 50 | 85 | 4 | 139 | 12 |
| Downing, Juan, MYR | 1.000 | 2 | 4 | 4 | 0 | 8 | 0 |
| Fenster, Darren, WIL | .964 | 26 | 54 | 78 | 5 | 137 | 16 |
| Giles, Marcus, MYR | 1.000 | 3 | 6 | 5 | 0 | 11 | 0 |
| Gonzalez, Andy, WS | 1.000 | 9 | 9 | 18 | 0 | 27 | 3 |
| Helquist, Jon, SAL | .972 | 113 | 223 | 370 | 17 | 610 | 76 |
| Herrera, Christian, LYN | 1.000 | 4 | 3 | 9 | 0 | 12 | 1 |
| Howard, Kevin, POT* | .954 | 118 | 196 | 327 | 25 | 548 | 65 |
| Iorg, Isaac, MYR | 1.000 | 3 | 1 | 6 | 0 | 7 | 0 |
| James, Willie, MYR | .933 | 15 | 22 | 34 | 4 | 60 | 6 |
| Keim, Adam, WIL | 1.000 | 8 | 13 | 24 | 0 | 37 | 3 |
| Larkin, Shaun, KIN* | .960 | 14 | 18 | 30 | 2 | 50 | 9 |
| Lewis, Domonique, POT | .929 | 8 | 9 | 17 | 2 | 28 | 3 |
| Lopez, Pedro, WS | 1.000 | 5 | 5 | 10 | 0 | 15 | 2 |
| Lunetta, Anthony, KIN | .800 | 2 | 0 | 4 | 1 | 5 | 0 |
| Mercedes, Victor, LYN | .970 | 127 | 262 | 380 | 20 | 662 | 92 |
| Morel, Elvis, FRE | .953 | 10 | 15 | 26 | 2 | 43 | 4 |
| Murphy, Donnie, WIL | .978 | 104 | 198 | 343 | 12 | 553 | 73 |
| Myers, Mike, WS | 1.000 | 6 | 17 | 13 | 0 | 30 | 3 |
| Newman, Ryan, LYN | 1.000 | 11 | 14 | 25 | 0 | 39 | 0 |
| Nicholson, Tommy, WS* | .959 | 17 | 26 | 44 | 3 | 73 | 9 |
| Parker, Brett, KIN | 1.000 | 6 | 5 | 7 | 0 | 12 | 2 |
| Patchett, Gary, POT | 1.000 | 11 | 18 | 29 | 0 | 47 | 6 |
| Peavey, Pat, SAL | .982 | 32 | 56 | 104 | 3 | 163 | 22 |
| Robinson, Levi, FRE | .944 | 19 | 33 | 68 | 6 | 107 | 10 |
| Ruiz, Junior, POT* | .000 | 1 | 0 | 0 | 1 | 1 | 0 |
| Schuerholz, Jonathan, MYR | .954 | 118 | 178 | 367 | 26 | 571 | 51 |
| Sevilla, Walter, WIL | .967 | 4 | 15 | 14 | 1 | 30 | 8 |
| Shaffer, Josh, WS* | .964 | 15 | 22 | 31 | 2 | 55 | 6 |
| Skaug, Brian, SAL | 1.000 | 3 | 2 | 10 | 0 | 12 | 2 |
| Solis, Eddie, WIL | 1.000 | 2 | 1 | 5 | 0 | 6 | 1 |
| Stegall, Ryan, SAL | 1.000 | 2 | 0 | 1 | 0 | 1 | 0 |
| Timmons, Wesley, MYR | 1.000 | 3 | 1 | 2 | 0 | 3 | 1 |
| TORRES, EIDER, KIN | .981 | 112 | 170 | 307 | 9 | 486 | 57 |

## THIRD BASEMEN

| Player, Team | Pct. | G | PO | A | E | TC | DP |
|---|---|---|---|---|---|---|---|
| Alvarez, Gera, FRE | 1.000 | 12 | 11 | 18 | 0 | 29 | 1 |
| Asprilla, Avelino, LYN | .953 | 119 | 79 | 246 | 16 | 341 | 21 |
| Bastida, Evel, FRE* | .800 | 3 | 0 | 4 | 1 | 5 | 1 |
| Cairns, Troy, POT | .920 | 12 | 4 | 19 | 2 | 25 | 0 |
| Cameron, Troy, WS | .929 | 12 | 12 | 14 | 2 | 28 | 3 |
| Chapman, Travis, WIL | .875 | 3 | 2 | 5 | 1 | 8 | 0 |
| Choy Foo, Rodney, KIN | .880 | 8 | 7 | 15 | 3 | 25 | 3 |
| Correll, Brad, POT | .950 | 12 | 7 | 12 | 1 | 20 | 0 |
| Cotto, Luis, KIN | 1.000 | 1 | 0 | 1 | 0 | 1 | 0 |
| Diaz, Rafael, FRE | 1.000 | 2 | 0 | 2 | 0 | 2 | 0 |
| Downing, Juan, MYR | 1.000 | 2 | 3 | 3 | 0 | 6 | 1 |
| Espino, Damaso, WIL | .902 | 66 | 40 | 107 | 16 | 163 | 8 |
| Fenster, Darren, WIL | .937 | 26 | 15 | 44 | 4 | 63 | 5 |
| Fields, Josh, WS | .931 | 58 | 33 | 116 | 11 | 160 | 4 |
| Gonzalez, Andy, WS | .908 | 39 | 33 | 66 | 10 | 109 | 3 |
| Groves, Brett, WIL | 1.000 | 3 | 0 | 1 | 0 | 1 | 0 |
| Helquist, Jon, SAL | 1.000 | 1 | 0 | 1 | 0 | 1 | 0 |
| Iorg, Isaac, MYR | .917 | 6 | 2 | 9 | 1 | 12 | 0 |
| James, Willie, MYR | .923 | 9 | 3 | 9 | 1 | 13 | 1 |
| Johnson, Tripper, FRE | .942 | 122 | 69 | 208 | 17 | 294 | 15 |
| Larkin, Shaun, KIN* | .968 | 69 | 50 | 101 | 5 | 156 | 5 |
| Lewis, Domonique, POT | .800 | 4 | 1 | 3 | 1 | 5 | 1 |
| Lunetta, Anthony, KIN | .900 | 18 | 8 | 28 | 4 | 40 | 5 |
| Maier, Mitch, WIL* | .938 | 48 | 33 | 87 | 8 | 128 | 8 |
| McWilliams, Matt, POT* | 1.000 | 1 | 1 | 0 | 0 | 1 | 0 |
| Myers, Mike, WS | 1.000 | 1 | 2 | 2 | 0 | 4 | 0 |
| Navarrete, Ray, LYN | .889 | 7 | 4 | 12 | 2 | 18 | 1 |
| Newman, Ryan, LYN | .923 | 13 | 6 | 30 | 3 | 39 | 4 |
| Nicholson, Tommy, WS* | .984 | 24 | 11 | 51 | 1 | 63 | 4 |
| Osborn, Pat, KIN | .929 | 51 | 36 | 81 | 9 | 126 | 7 |
| Patchett, Gary, POT | .938 | 11 | 5 | 10 | 1 | 16 | 2 |
| Peavey, Pat, SAL | .923 | 43 | 17 | 79 | 8 | 104 | 6 |
| Perez, Melvin, WS | .955 | 12 | 11 | 10 | 1 | 22 | 2 |
| Robinson, Levi, FRE | 1.000 | 2 | 2 | 2 | 0 | 4 | 0 |
| Saccomanno, Mark, SAL | .778 | 4 | 1 | 6 | 2 | 9 | 0 |
| Schramek, Mark, POT* | .929 | 106 | 68 | 155 | 17 | 240 | 12 |
| Shaffer, Josh, WS* | .857 | 4 | 2 | 4 | 1 | 7 | 0 |
| Solis, Eddie, WIL | 1.000 | 2 | 0 | 3 | 0 | 3 | 0 |
| Stegall, Ryan, SAL | .955 | 97 | 67 | 165 | 11 | 243 | 14 |
| Thomas, Ben, MYR* | .921 | 34 | 13 | 45 | 5 | 63 | 2 |
| TIMMONS, WESLEY, MYR | .962 | 96 | 68 | 136 | 8 | 212 | 14 |
| Voshell, Chase, LYN | 1.000 | 10 | 3 | 11 | 0 | 14 | 0 |
| Wilken, Kris, FRE | 1.000 | 2 | 3 | 3 | 0 | 6 | 1 |

## SHORTSTOPS

| Player, Team | Pct. | G | PO | A | E | TC | DP |
|---|---|---|---|---|---|---|---|
| Alvarez, Gera, FRE | .953 | 28 | 42 | 80 | 6 | 128 | 15 |
| Aviles, Mike, WIL | .966 | 121 | 190 | 355 | 19 | 564 | 66 |
| Bastida, Evel, FRE* | 1.000 | 2 | 4 | 5 | 0 | 9 | 1 |
| Cairns, Troy, POT | .921 | 11 | 13 | 22 | 3 | 38 | 4 |
| Choy Foo, Rodney, KIN | 1.000 | 2 | 6 | 4 | 0 | 10 | 1 |
| Cotto, Luis, KIN | .900 | 11 | 15 | 21 | 4 | 40 | 3 |
| Diaz, Rafael, FRE | .800 | 1 | 3 | 1 | 1 | 5 | 0 |
| Downing, Juan, MYR | .889 | 2 | 4 | 4 | 1 | 9 | 2 |
| Fahey, Brandon, FRE* | .977 | 60 | 87 | 169 | 6 | 262 | 32 |
| Fenster, Darren, WIL | 1.000 | 3 | 2 | 4 | 0 | 6 | 1 |
| Gonzalez, Andy, WS | .941 | 35 | 53 | 123 | 11 | 187 | 22 |
| HERNANDEZ, LUIS, MYR | .977 | 116 | 195 | 305 | 12 | 512 | 56 |
| Herrera, Christian, LYN | .958 | 19 | 25 | 43 | 3 | 71 | 7 |
| Iorg, Isaac, MYR | 1.000 | 4 | 1 | 9 | 0 | 10 | 0 |
| James, Willie, MYR | .935 | 16 | 15 | 28 | 3 | 46 | 11 |
| Larkin, Shaun, KIN* | .800 | 2 | 3 | 1 | 1 | 5 | 0 |
| Lee, Taber, LYN | .953 | 93 | 167 | 280 | 22 | 469 | 51 |
| Lopez, Pedro, WS | .971 | 104 | 187 | 316 | 15 | 518 | 64 |
| Lunetta, Anthony, KIN | .960 | 43 | 58 | 108 | 7 | 173 | 19 |
| Morban, Jose, FRE | .940 | 55 | 74 | 160 | 15 | 249 | 31 |
| Morel, Elvis, FRE | 1.000 | 2 | 1 | 6 | 0 | 7 | 0 |
| Murphy, Donnie, WIL | .914 | 15 | 20 | 54 | 7 | 81 | 15 |
| Myers, Mike, WS | 1.000 | 4 | 2 | 0 | 0 | 2 | 0 |
| Newman, Ryan, LYN | .925 | 30 | 41 | 58 | 8 | 107 | 12 |
| Nicholson, Tommy, WS* | 1.000 | 3 | 6 | 10 | 0 | 16 | 2 |
| Ochoa, Ivan, KIN | .968 | 66 | 109 | 195 | 10 | 314 | 38 |
| Osborn, Pat, KIN | .900 | 18 | 27 | 45 | 8 | 80 | 7 |
| Parker, Brett, KIN | .929 | 6 | 6 | 7 | 1 | 14 | 0 |
| Patchett, Gary, POT | .936 | 29 | 44 | 73 | 8 | 125 | 14 |
| Robinson, Levi, FRE | 1.000 | 1 | 3 | 2 | 0 | 5 | 2 |
| Robinson, Wade, SAL* | .936 | 128 | 235 | 425 | 45 | 705 | 105 |
| Schuerholz, Jonathan, MYR | 1.000 | 1 | 3 | 2 | 0 | 5 | 1 |
| Shaffer, Josh, WS* | 1.000 | 1 | 0 | 2 | 0 | 2 | 1 |
| Solis, Eddie, WIL | 1.000 | 4 | 7 | 8 | 0 | 15 | 3 |
| Stegall, Ryan, SAL | .944 | 11 | 23 | 28 | 3 | 54 | 12 |
| Tiburcio, Hector, POT | .933 | 108 | 175 | 281 | 33 | 489 | 58 |
| Timmons, Wesley, MYR | 1.000 | 6 | 15 | 21 | 0 | 36 | 2 |
| West, Todd, KIN | .917 | 3 | 2 | 9 | 1 | 12 | 2 |

## OUTFIELDERS

| Player, Team | Pct. | G | PO | A | E | TC | DP |
|---|---|---|---|---|---|---|---|
| Amador, Chris, WS | 1.000 | 1 | 0 | 1 | 0 | 1 | 0 |
| Anderson, Brian, WS | .993 | 68 | 131 | 5 | 1 | 137 | 0 |
| Anderson, Josh, SAL* | .977 | 66 | 160 | 7 | 4 | 171 | 3 |
| Blakely, Darren, WS | .981 | 77 | 154 | 5 | 3 | 162 | 0 |
| Blanco, Gregor, MYR* | .961 | 114 | 216 | 3 | 9 | 228 | 0 |
| Blanco, Tony, POT | .933 | 15 | 14 | 0 | 1 | 15 | 0 |
| Brice, Thomas, WS* | .986 | 41 | 67 | 4 | 1 | 72 | 0 |
| Brock, Caleb, KIN | 1.000 | 2 | 1 | 0 | 0 | 1 | 0 |
| Buttler, Vic, LYN* | .976 | 94 | 157 | 7 | 4 | 168 | 2 |
| Carter, Chris, FRE | .983 | 91 | 165 | 4 | 3 | 172 | 2 |
| Cliffords, Woody, FRE* | .983 | 74 | 112 | 7 | 2 | 121 | 3 |
| Correll, Brad, POT | .942 | 98 | 154 | 8 | 10 | 172 | 2 |
| Cortes, Jorge, LYN* | .915 | 56 | 104 | 4 | 10 | 118 | 1 |
| Costa, Shane, WIL* | .973 | 112 | 169 | 10 | 5 | 184 | 2 |
| Davies, Gregg, FRE* | 1.000 | 2 | 2 | 0 | 0 | 2 | 0 |
| Davis, Rajai, LYN | .968 | 119 | 232 | 8 | 8 | 248 | 1 |
| Denorfia, Chris, POT | .979 | 72 | 183 | 4 | 4 | 191 | 1 |
| Dickerson, Chris, POT* | .931 | 13 | 26 | 1 | 2 | 29 | 1 |
| Draper, John, WIL | .955 | 9 | 20 | 1 | 1 | 22 | 0 |
| Duncan, Jacob, FRE* | .917 | 17 | 22 | 0 | 2 | 24 | 0 |
| Duran, Carlos, MYR* | .983 | 54 | 105 | 11 | 2 | 118 | 2 |
| Durham, Chad, POT | 1.000 | 56 | 114 | 4 | 0 | 118 | 1 |
| Dyson, Trey, KIN* | 1.000 | 11 | 22 | 0 | 0 | 22 | 0 |
| Fagan, John, SAL | .969 | 66 | 123 | 4 | 4 | 131 | 1 |
| Fenster, Darren, WIL | 1.000 | 8 | 13 | 0 | 0 | 13 | 0 |
| Florence, Branden, FRE | 1.000 | 5 | 5 | 0 | 0 | 5 | 0 |
| Francoeur, Jeff, MYR | .975 | 82 | 150 | 8 | 4 | 162 | 1 |
| Frend, Tim, WIL | .975 | 47 | 77 | 2 | 2 | 81 | 0 |
| Groves, Brett, WIL | 1.000 | 11 | 16 | 0 | 0 | 16 | 0 |
| Harris, Cory, FRE | .957 | 30 | 44 | 1 | 2 | 47 | 0 |
| Hemingway, Jamie, MYR | .989 | 42 | 85 | 1 | 1 | 87 | 0 |
| Jansen, Ardley, MYR | .947 | 29 | 48 | 6 | 3 | 57 | 0 |
| Joseph, Onil, MYR | .973 | 103 | 166 | 12 | 5 | 183 | 2 |
| Keim, Adam, WIL | .963 | 18 | 25 | 1 | 1 | 27 | 0 |
| Keylor, Cory, FRE* | .950 | 101 | 148 | 5 | 8 | 161 | 1 |
| Kochen, Ryan, SAL | .986 | 91 | 137 | 4 | 2 | 143 | 0 |
| Lewis, Domonique, POT | .933 | 54 | 93 | 4 | 7 | 104 | 0 |
| Likely, Cameron, SAL | .980 | 44 | 49 | 0 | 1 | 50 | 0 |

| Littleton, BJ, FRE | .989 | 96 | 172 | 5 | 2 | 179 | 3 |
|---|---|---|---|---|---|---|---|
| **Player, Team** | **Pct.** | **G** | **PO** | **A** | **E** | **TC** | **DP** |
| Logan, Matt, POT* | 1.000 | 3 | 3 | 1 | 0 | 4 | 0 |
| Lytle, Chaz, LYN* | .987 | 82 | 148 | 0 | 2 | 150 | 0 |
| Macia, Wanell, LYN* | .600 | 3 | 3 | 0 | 2 | 5 | 0 |
| Malave, Dennis, KIN* | .961 | 55 | 94 | 4 | 4 | 102 | 0 |
| Martel, Normand, WS* | .939 | 16 | 30 | 1 | 2 | 33 | 1 |
| Meath, Matt, LYN | .969 | 27 | 31 | 0 | 1 | 32 | 0 |
| Myers, Mike, WS | 1.000 | 1 | 1 | 0 | 0 | 1 | 0 |
| Nanita, Ricardo, WS* | .968 | 55 | 87 | 3 | 3 | 93 | 0 |
| Nicholson, Tommy, WS* | 1.000 | 10 | 15 | 1 | 0 | 16 | 0 |
| PANTHER, NATHAN, KIN* | .992 | 116 | 247 | 8 | 2 | 257 | 2 |
| Powell, Pedro, LYN | .944 | 7 | 16 | 1 | 1 | 18 | 0 |
| Rogowski, Casey, WS* | .962 | 14 | 25 | 0 | 1 | 26 | 0 |
| Rosamond, Mike, LYN | .979 | 25 | 44 | 2 | 1 | 47 | 0 |
| Ruiz, Junior, POT* | .980 | 93 | 187 | 10 | 4 | 201 | 0 |
| Santana, Mayobanex, KIN | 1.000 | 4 | 8 | 0 | 0 | 8 | 0 |
| Scott, Luke, SAL* | .992 | 66 | 116 | 6 | 1 | 123 | 1 |
| Seuss, Adam, SAL* | .990 | 57 | 96 | 4 | 1 | 101 | 0 |
| Sherrill, JJ, KIN | .981 | 96 | 205 | 7 | 4 | 216 | 1 |
| Smith, Nestor, POT | .895 | 12 | 17 | 0 | 2 | 19 | 0 |
| Smith, Sean, LYN | 1.000 | 6 | 8 | 0 | 0 | 8 | 0 |
| Snyder, Brad, KIN* | 1.000 | 28 | 48 | 1 | 0 | 49 | 0 |
| Stephens, Bernard, WIL* | .974 | 110 | 214 | 12 | 6 | 232 | 1 |
| Stocker, Mel, WIL | .981 | 114 | 261 | 4 | 5 | 270 | 0 |
| Sweeney, Ryan, WS* | .973 | 132 | 241 | 14 | 7 | 262 | 3 |
| Timmons, Wesley, MYR | 1.000 | 1 | 2 | 0 | 0 | 2 | 0 |
| van Every, John, KIN* | .955 | 112 | 205 | 5 | 10 | 220 | 2 |
| Vavao, Jason, POT | .920 | 15 | 23 | 0 | 2 | 25 | 0 |
| Voshell, Chase, LYN | .750 | 5 | 3 | 0 | 1 | 4 | 0 |
| Walker, Matt, FRE | 1.000 | 12 | 20 | 0 | 0 | 20 | 0 |
| Wilken, Kris, FRE | 1.000 | 2 | 5 | 0 | 0 | 5 | 0 |
| Williams, Peanut, WS | .943 | 22 | 31 | 2 | 2 | 35 | 0 |
| Wise, DeWayne, MYR* | 1.000 | 3 | 6 | 0 | 0 | 6 | 0 |
| Wright, Gavin, SAL | 1.000 | 51 | 76 | 4 | 0 | 80 | 2 |

## CATCHERS

| Player, Team | Pct. | G | PO | A | E | TC | DP | PB |
|---|---|---|---|---|---|---|---|---|
| Alleva, JD, WIL* | 1.000 | 11 | 54 | 2 | 0 | 56 | 0 | 1 |
| Arko, Tommy, FRE | .986 | 10 | 60 | 8 | 1 | 69 | 0 | 2 |
| Bernard, Miguel, MYR | .975 | 21 | 140 | 17 | 4 | 161 | 4 | 7 |
| Bock, Brian, FRE | .980 | 18 | 125 | 20 | 3 | 148 | 1 | 1 |
| Brock, Caleb, KIN | .989 | 16 | 81 | 7 | 1 | 89 | 0 | 0 |
| Camacaro, Armando, KIN | .990 | 24 | 171 | 23 | 2 | 196 | 4 | 1 |
| Cashman, Brandon, KIN | 1.000 | 1 | 6 | 1 | 0 | 7 | 0 | 0 |
| Chapman, Travis, LYN | 1.000 | 14 | 87 | 16 | 0 | 103 | 0 | 3 |
| Draper, John, WIL | .962 | 38 | 207 | 19 | 9 | 235 | 2 | 7 |
| Garko, Ryan, KIN | .982 | 21 | 149 | 16 | 3 | 168 | 2 | 3 |
| Hanigan, Ryan, POT | .986 | 65 | 466 | 43 | 7 | 516 | 7 | 3 |
| Hernandez, Jose, LYN | .986 | 63 | 387 | 42 | 6 | 435 | 3 | 11 |
| Herrera, Javier, KIN | .982 | 42 | 301 | 23 | 6 | 330 | 2 | 5 |
| Houston, Matthew, FRE | .990 | 29 | 196 | 9 | 2 | 207 | 0 | 3 |
| Hubele, Ryan, FRE | .990 | 83 | 565 | 36 | 6 | 607 | 9 | 24 |
| Lee, Carlos, WS | .981 | 30 | 188 | 15 | 4 | 207 | 0 | 10 |
| Mackor, Jeff, SAL | .991 | 65 | 399 | 60 | 4 | 463 | 7 | 5 |
| Martinez, Octavio, FRE | .965 | 8 | 50 | 5 | 2 | 57 | 0 | 2 |
| MCCANN, BRIAN, MYR* | .990 | 78 | 540 | 66 | 6 | 612 | 4 | 7 |
| McCullough, Clayton, KIN* | 1.000 | 3 | 15 | 1 | 0 | 16 | 0 | 0 |
| Molina, Gustavo, WS | 1.000 | 23 | 160 | 11 | 0 | 171 | 1 | 7 |
| Motooka, Rafael, POT | .976 | 10 | 39 | 1 | 1 | 41 | 0 | 1 |
| Nino, Denny, LYN | .981 | 25 | 143 | 12 | 3 | 158 | 1 | 7 |
| Obradovich, Mark, SAL | .997 | 51 | 327 | 51 | 1 | 379 | 6 | 7 |
| Olszta, Eddie, LYN | 1.000 | 7 | 54 | 6 | 0 | 60 | 1 | 2 |
| Pena, Rudy, LYN | .993 | 40 | 245 | 22 | 2 | 269 | 0 | 11 |
| Perez, Miguel, POT | .962 | 15 | 121 | 6 | 5 | 132 | 3 | 1 |
| Prince, Bryan, POT | .981 | 55 | 370 | 38 | 8 | 416 | 3 | 3 |
| Rosa, Wally, WS | .990 | 82 | 520 | 79 | 6 | 605 | 3 | 20 |
| Ruelas, Alonzo, MYR | .989 | 34 | 241 | 17 | 3 | 261 | 1 | 2 |
| Ruiz, Reinaldo, SAL | .980 | 24 | 134 | 12 | 3 | 149 | 1 | 7 |
| Salas, Jose, MYR | .973 | 8 | 66 | 7 | 2 | 75 | 0 | 1 |
| Serrano, Ray, MYR | .981 | 15 | 95 | 8 | 2 | 105 | 1 | 1 |
| Tupman, Matt, WIL* | .990 | 102 | 606 | 55 | 7 | 668 | 6 | 10 |
| Wade, Ryan, WS | 1.000 | 6 | 28 | 1 | 0 | 29 | 0 | 2 |
| Wallace, David, KIN | 1.000 | 37 | 256 | 18 | 0 | 274 | 1 | 5 |

## PITCHERS

| Player, Team | Pct. | G | PO | A | E | TC | DP |
|---|---|---|---|---|---|---|---|
| Ackerman, Eric, WIL* | .941 | 36 | 10 | 22 | 2 | 34 | 2 |
| Acosta, Manny, MYR | 1.000 | 11 | 0 | 4 | 0 | 4 | 1 |
| Aguilar, Ray, MYR* | 1.000 | 4 | 0 | 2 | 0 | 2 | 0 |
| Albaladejo, Jonathan, LYN | .895 | 24 | 11 | 23 | 4 | 38 | 0 |
| Alcala, Jason, LYN | .667 | 23 | 4 | 2 | 3 | 9 | 1 |
| Alvarez, Basilio, LYN | .000 | 2 | 0 | 0 | 1 | 1 | 0 |
| An, Byeong Hak, WS* | .933 | 31 | 7 | 21 | 2 | 30 | 0 |
| **Player, Team** | **Pct.** | **G** | **PO** | **A** | **E** | **TC** | **DP** |
| Aramboles, Ricardo, POT | .905 | 26 | 11 | 8 | 2 | 21 | 0 |
| Armitage, Barry,P., WIL | 1.000 | 53 | 5 | 12 | 0 | 17 | 2 |
| Austin, Jeff, POT | 1.000 | 8 | 0 | 2 | 0 | 2 | 0 |
| Barreto, Joel, POT | .952 | 43 | 7 | 13 | 1 | 21 | 0 |
| Basner, Ryan, MYR | 1.000 | 38 | 5 | 4 | 0 | 9 | 0 |
| Bayliss, Jonah, WIL | 1.000 | 24 | 8 | 11 | 0 | 19 | 1 |
| Benitez, Fabricio, FRE | 1.000 | 7 | 0 | 1 | 0 | 1 | 0 |
| Bimeal, Matt, LYN | 1.000 | 4 | 1 | 2 | 0 | 3 | 0 |
| Birkins, Kurt, FRE* | 1.000 | 27 | 6 | 9 | 0 | 15 | 0 |
| Blakeney, Jacob, MYR | 1.000 | 22 | 3 | 7 | 0 | 10 | 0 |
| Boughner, Anthony, POT* | 1.000 | 3 | 1 | 0 | 0 | 1 | 0 |
| Boyer, Blaine, MYR | .925 | 28 | 11 | 26 | 3 | 40 | 0 |
| Braun, Ryan, WIL | .889 | 50 | 6 | 10 | 2 | 18 | 0 |
| Bray, Steve, WIL | 1.000 | 10 | 1 | 2 | 0 | 3 | 0 |
| Bruksch, Jeffrey, POT | .862 | 32 | 4 | 21 | 4 | 29 | 2 |
| Bush, Paul, MYR | .714 | 24 | 1 | 4 | 2 | 7 | 0 |
| Candelario, Eddie, LYN | 1.000 | 4 | 0 | 1 | 0 | 1 | 0 |
| Capellan, Jose, MYR | 1.000 | 8 | 6 | 3 | 0 | 9 | 0 |
| Carmona, Fausto, KIN | 1.000 | 12 | 3 | 10 | 0 | 13 | 0 |
| Castro, Fabio, WS* | 1.000 | 8 | 1 | 0 | 0 | 1 | 0 |
| Castro, Julio, WS | 1.000 | 36 | 3 | 5 | 0 | 8 | 0 |
| Caughey, Trevor, FRE* | .875 | 4 | 1 | 6 | 1 | 8 | 0 |
| Chamberlain, Steve, WIL | .917 | 47 | 4 | 7 | 1 | 12 | 1 |
| Cooper, Chris, KIN* | .909 | 25 | 1 | 9 | 1 | 11 | 0 |
| Coppinger, Joe, FRE | 1.000 | 13 | 3 | 6 | 0 | 9 | 0 |
| Davies, Kyle, MYR | .941 | 14 | 3 | 13 | 1 | 17 | 1 |
| Davila, Marcus, LYN | .905 | 51 | 9 | 10 | 2 | 21 | 1 |
| Davis, Matt, KIN | .880 | 41 | 6 | 16 | 3 | 25 | 0 |
| Denham, Dan, KIN | .929 | 13 | 5 | 8 | 1 | 14 | 1 |
| Deza, Fredy, FRE | 1.000 | 5 | 2 | 2 | 0 | 4 | 0 |
| Dixon, Zach, FRE* | 1.000 | 3 | 1 | 0 | 0 | 1 | 0 |
| Douglas, Shea, KIN* | .857 | 16 | 1 | 5 | 1 | 7 | 0 |
| Duke, Zach, LYN* | .875 | 17 | 8 | 20 | 4 | 32 | 1 |
| Edens, Kyle, POT | 1.000 | 14 | 6 | 1 | 0 | 7 | 0 |
| Eisentrager, Dan, KIN | 1.000 | 45 | 9 | 10 | 0 | 19 | 2 |
| Endicott, Drew, WIL | .909 | 42 | 10 | 10 | 2 | 22 | 1 |
| Espinal, Jose, WS | .957 | 42 | 8 | 14 | 1 | 23 | 0 |
| Finch, Brian, FRE | 1.000 | 9 | 4 | 6 | 0 | 10 | 1 |
| Foley, Travis, KIN | 1.000 | 13 | 0 | 3 | 0 | 3 | 0 |
| France, Ryan, SAL | .750 | 20 | 2 | 4 | 2 | 8 | 1 |
| Freeman, Daniel, SAL | .944 | 54 | 7 | 10 | 1 | 18 | 2 |
| Frias, Juan, POT* | .875 | 18 | 1 | 6 | 1 | 8 | 0 |
| Gardner, Richard, POT | .926 | 18 | 6 | 19 | 2 | 27 | 0 |
| Gorzelanny, Thomas, LYN* | .846 | 10 | 3 | 8 | 2 | 13 | 2 |
| Gragg, John, WIL* | .000 | 4 | 0 | 0 | 0 | 0 | 0 |
| Granado, Jan, POT* | 1.000 | 18 | 6 | 10 | 0 | 16 | 1 |
| Gravelle, Nick, LYN* | .939 | 26 | 6 | 40 | 3 | 49 | 0 |
| Griffin, Colt, WIL | .818 | 8 | 5 | 4 | 2 | 11 | 0 |
| Guerrero, Julio, LYN | 1.000 | 33 | 3 | 11 | 0 | 14 | 0 |
| Hannaman, Ryan, FRE* | .500 | 5 | 0 | 2 | 2 | 4 | 0 |
| Hart, Alex, LYN | 1.000 | 3 | 1 | 3 | 0 | 4 | 1 |
| Harts, Jeremy, LYN* | 1.000 | 10 | 0 | 1 | 0 | 1 | 0 |
| Heitzman, Aaron, SAL* | .944 | 29 | 3 | 14 | 1 | 18 | 0 |
| Henington, Justin, FRE | 1.000 | 3 | 0 | 1 | 0 | 1 | 0 |
| Henry, Paul, FRE | 1.000 | 35 | 7 | 15 | 0 | 22 | 0 |
| Higgins, Joshua, LYN | .833 | 37 | 4 | 6 | 2 | 12 | 0 |
| Hirsh, Jason, SAL | .909 | 26 | 5 | 15 | 2 | 22 | 1 |
| Hoelscher, Nate, WIL* | 1.000 | 50 | 5 | 13 | 0 | 18 | 1 |
| House, Craig, FRE | .750 | 12 | 1 | 2 | 1 | 4 | 1 |
| Hudson, Jeremy, WS | 1.000 | 13 | 3 | 11 | 0 | 14 | 1 |
| Hughes, Dusty, WIL* | .926 | 18 | 5 | 20 | 2 | 27 | 1 |
| Hummel, Rick, WS | .000 | 3 | 0 | 0 | 1 | 1 | 0 |
| Johnson, James, FRE | .000 | 1 | 0 | 0 | 0 | 0 | 0 |
| Johnson, Russell, LYN | .500 | 3 | 1 | 0 | 1 | 2 | 0 |
| Kaanoi, Kahi, WIL | .875 | 9 | 2 | 5 | 1 | 8 | 1 |
| Keefer, Ryan, FRE | 1.000 | 63 | 7 | 17 | 0 | 24 | 1 |
| Kesten, Michael, SAL* | 1.000 | 2 | 0 | 7 | 0 | 7 | 0 |
| LaMura, BJ, WS | .947 | 12 | 8 | 10 | 1 | 19 | 1 |
| Lara, Juan, KIN* | .900 | 35 | 3 | 15 | 2 | 20 | 0 |
| Larson, Adam, WS | 1.000 | 10 | 1 | 1 | 0 | 2 | 0 |
| Lerew, Anthony, MYR | .821 | 27 | 6 | 17 | 5 | 28 | 2 |
| Levinski, Don, FRE | .926 | 31 | 10 | 15 | 2 | 27 | 1 |
| Lewis, Rommie, FRE* | 1.000 | 47 | 9 | 21 | 0 | 30 | 2 |
| Lipari, Tom, SAL* | 1.000 | 9 | 1 | 1 | 0 | 2 | 0 |
| Little, Jeff, WS | 1.000 | 2 | 2 | 1 | 0 | 3 | 0 |
| Loewen, Adam, FRE* | 1.000 | 2 | 2 | 2 | 0 | 4 | 0 |
| Lord, Justin, LYN | 1.000 | 14 | 2 | 2 | 0 | 4 | 0 |
| Lowery, Devon, WIL | .935 | 28 | 12 | 17 | 2 | 31 | 0 |
| Lubisich, Nik, WS* | 1.000 | 22 | 9 | 19 | 0 | 28 | 1 |
| Lumsden, Tyler, WS* | 1.000 | 15 | 1 | 1 | 0 | 2 | 0 |
| MacRae, Scott, POT | 1.000 | 5 | 1 | 2 | 0 | 3 | 0 |

| | | | | | | |
|---|---|---|---|---|---|---|
| Maholm, Paul, LYN* | 1.000 | 8 | 4 | 6 | 0 | 10 | 1 |
| Makowsky, Carl, FRE | .000 | 8 | 0 | 0 | 0 | 0 | 0 |
| Mansfield, Monte, SAL | .933 | 59 | 4 | 10 | 1 | 15 | 0 |
| Martin, Greg, LYN* | 1.000 | 25 | 1 | 3 | 0 | 4 | 0 |
| MARTIN, JD, KIN | 1.000 | 25 | 7 | 30 | 0 | 37 | 4 |
| Martinez, Dave, KIN* | 1.000 | 19 | 0 | 8 | 0 | 8 | 0 |
| Mattison, Kieran, KIN | 1.000 | 13 | 1 | 1 | 0 | 2 | 0 |
| McCarthy, Brandon, WS | 1.000 | 8 | 5 | 4 | 0 | 9 | 0 |
| McClendon, Matt, MYR | 1.000 | 11 | 0 | 3 | 0 | 3 | 0 |
| McCurdy, Nick, FRE | 1.000 | 63 | 13 | 15 | 0 | 28 | 2 |
| McGill, Trae, WIL | .966 | 21 | 11 | 17 | 1 | 29 | 0 |
| McLemore, Mark, SAL* | .900 | 37 | 3 | 6 | 1 | 10 | 0 |
| McWilliams, Matt, POT* | 1.000 | 29 | 0 | 4 | 0 | 4 | 0 |
| Medlock, Calvin, POT | .909 | 11 | 3 | 7 | 1 | 11 | 0 |
| Mendoza, Chuy, POT | 1.000 | 35 | 5 | 5 | 0 | 10 | 0 |
| Merchant, Jamie, SAL | .909 | 25 | 7 | 23 | 3 | 33 | 1 |
| Merricks, Matt, MYR* | .625 | 13 | 2 | 8 | 6 | 16 | 1 |
| Michael, Mark, LYN | .750 | 7 | 3 | 3 | 2 | 8 | 1 |
| Mieses, Jose, WS | .889 | 21 | 2 | 6 | 1 | 9 | 0 |
| Miller, Adam, KIN | 1.000 | 8 | 4 | 7 | 0 | 11 | 0 |
| Miller, Brian, WS | 1.000 | 7 | 3 | 1 | 0 | 4 | 0 |
| Montani, Jeffrey, FRE | 1.000 | 11 | 1 | 2 | 0 | 3 | 0 |
| Morris, Cory, FRE | 1.000 | 11 | 2 | 0 | 0 | 2 | 0 |
| Mottl, Ryan, LYN | 1.000 | 12 | 2 | 2 | 0 | 4 | 0 |
| Mueller, Mike, MYR | .750 | 20 | 0 | 3 | 1 | 4 | 0 |
| Murray, Brad, WS* | 1.000 | 47 | 4 | 11 | 0 | 15 | 0 |
| Neal, Tony, FRE | 1.000 | 50 | 5 | 7 | 0 | 12 | 0 |
| Nieve, Fernando, SAL | .944 | 24 | 6 | 11 | 1 | 18 | 0 |
| O`Brien, Patrick, LYN | .900 | 25 | 9 | 9 | 2 | 20 | 1 |
| Owens, Henry, LYN | .938 | 39 | 1 | 14 | 1 | 16 | 0 |
| Paduch, Jim, POT | .900 | 26 | 5 | 13 | 2 | 20 | 1 |
| Pauly, Thomas, POT | .929 | 28 | 4 | 9 | 1 | 14 | 1 |
| Peguero, Jailen, SAL | 1.000 | 51 | 7 | 14 | 0 | 21 | 2 |
| Pena, Francisco, SAL | .900 | 11 | 4 | 5 | 1 | 10 | 1 |
| Penn, Hayden, FRE | 1.000 | 13 | 8 | 11 | 0 | 19 | 1 |
| Pennington, Todd, KIN | .667 | 28 | 0 | 2 | 1 | 3 | 0 |
| Peralta, Efigenio, MYR | .625 | 31 | 0 | 5 | 3 | 8 | 0 |
| Perez, Rafael, KIN* | .500 | 1 | 0 | 1 | 1 | 2 | 0 |
| Pesco, Nick, KIN | 1.000 | 3 | 3 | 5 | 0 | 8 | 0 |
| Piersoll, Chris, FRE | .571 | 19 | 2 | 2 | 3 | 7 | 0 |
| Pollok, Dwayne, WS | 1.000 | 57 | 3 | 14 | 0 | 17 | 0 |
| Prahm, Ryan, KIN | 1.000 | 31 | 1 | 4 | 0 | 5 | 0 |
| Purvis, Rob, WS | 1.000 | 34 | 7 | 14 | 0 | 21 | 1 |
| Ramsey, Keith, KIN* | .929 | 24 | 9 | 30 | 3 | 42 | 3 |
| Ray, Chris, FRE | 1.000 | 14 | 9 | 15 | 0 | 24 | 2 |
| Ray, Kenny, WS | .870 | 29 | 10 | 10 | 3 | 23 | 1 |
| Reynoso, Paulino, WS* | .952 | 24 | 4 | 16 | 1 | 21 | 0 |
| Richardson, Jason, MYR | 1.000 | 14 | 1 | 6 | 0 | 7 | 0 |
| Roberts, Ralph, MYR | .875 | 32 | 2 | 5 | 1 | 8 | 1 |
| Rodaway, Brian, SAL* | .932 | 34 | 8 | 33 | 3 | 44 | 1 |
| Salmon, Brad, POT | 1.000 | 5 | 2 | 1 | 0 | 3 | 0 |
| Sampson, Chris, SAL | 1.000 | 27 | 12 | 29 | 0 | 41 | 2 |
| Schmidt, Jeremy, POT | .933 | 35 | 4 | 10 | 1 | 15 | 0 |
| Shafer, David, POT | 1.000 | 3 | 1 | 3 | 0 | 4 | 0 |
| Sharber, Jason, LYN | 1.000 | 5 | 0 | 2 | 0 | 2 | 0 |
| Shiery, Shaun, WIL* | .875 | 16 | 5 | 16 | 3 | 24 | 0 |
| Slocum, Brian, KIN | .944 | 25 | 7 | 10 | 1 | 18 | 0 |
| Smith, Sean, KIN | 1.000 | 2 | 0 | 2 | 0 | 2 | 0 |
| Stahl, Richard, FRE* | .966 | 19 | 5 | 23 | 1 | 29 | 0 |
| Stiles, Brad, WIL* | .714 | 21 | 1 | 4 | 2 | 7 | 0 |
| Stockman, Landon, KIN | 1.000 | 16 | 3 | 4 | 0 | 7 | 0 |
| Stodolka, Mike, WIL* | 1.000 | 14 | 5 | 11 | 0 | 16 | 1 |
| Stumm, Jason, WS | 1.000 | 8 | 0 | 2 | 0 | 2 | 0 |
| Sturkie, Scott, MYR | 1.000 | 12 | 2 | 3 | 0 | 5 | 0 |
| Sugarman, Jeremy, POT | .833 | 9 | 2 | 3 | 1 | 6 | 0 |
| Tamayo, Danny, WIL | 1.000 | 3 | 0 | 1 | 0 | 1 | 0 |
| Thurman, Corey, POT | 1.000 | 5 | 0 | 3 | 0 | 3 | 0 |
| Tiller, Jim, FRE | .833 | 17 | 5 | 10 | 3 | 18 | 0 |
| Tracey, Sean, WS | .923 | 27 | 12 | 24 | 3 | 39 | 3 |
| Tucker, Glenn, MYR | .929 | 48 | 1 | 12 | 1 | 14 | 1 |
| Valdez, Eddy, POT | .959 | 30 | 21 | 26 | 2 | 49 | 3 |
| Van Dusen, Derrick, KIN* | 1.000 | 9 | 4 | 8 | 0 | 12 | 0 |
| Vavao, Jason, POT | 1.000 | 1 | 0 | 1 | 0 | 1 | 0 |
| Wasserman, Ehren, WS | 1.000 | 10 | 0 | 4 | 0 | 4 | 0 |
| Waters, Chris, MYR | 1.000 | 4 | 0 | 3 | 0 | 3 | 0 |
| Westhoff, Bill, SAL | .923 | 20 | 3 | 9 | 1 | 13 | 0 |
| Whisler, Wesley, WS* | 1.000 | 5 | 0 | 4 | 0 | 4 | 0 |
| White, Sean, MYR | 1.000 | 18 | 8 | 9 | 0 | 17 | 0 |
| Wilson, Jeff, FRE* | .857 | 14 | 4 | 2 | 1 | 7 | 0 |
| Wright, Matt, MYR | .879 | 24 | 10 | 19 | 4 | 33 | 4 |
| Youman, Shane, LYN* | 1.000 | 47 | 3 | 12 | 0 | 15 | 0 |

## LEAGUE CHAMPIONS

| Year | Team | Pct. |
|---|---|---|
| 1945— | Danville | .681 |
| 1946— | Greensboro | .599 |
| | Raleigh (2nd)† | .563 |
| 1947— | Burlington | .613 |
| | Raleigh (3rd)† | .574 |
| 1948— | Raleigh | .592 |
| | Martinsville (2nd)† | .570 |
| 1949— | Danville | .601 |
| | Burlington (4th)† | .500 |
| 1950— | Winston-Salem* | .693 |
| 1951— | Durham | .600 |
| | Winston-Salem (2nd)† | .583 |
| 1952— | Raleigh | .581 |
| | Reidsville (4th)† | .536 |
| 1953— | Raleigh | .593 |
| | Danville (2nd)† | .572 |
| 1954— | Fayetteville* | .628 |
| 1955— | HP-Thomasville | .580 |
| | Danville (2nd)† | .533 |
| 1956— | HP-Thomasville | .591 |
| | Fayetteville (4th)§ | .523 |
| 1957— | Durham | .632 |
| | HP-Thomasville | .622 |
| 1958— | Danville | .576 |
| | Burlington (4th)† | .511 |
| 1959— | Raleigh | .600 |
| | Wilson (2nd)† | .550 |
| 1960— | Greensboro‡ | .636 |
| | Burlington | .586 |
| 1961— | Wilson | .594 |
| 1962— | Durham | .636 |
| | Wilson | .600 |
| | Kinston (2nd)† | .593 |
| 1963— | Kinston§ | .538 |
| | Greensboro§ | .590 |
| | Wilson (2nd)† | .535 |
| 1964— | Kinston§ | .572 |
| | Winston-Salem§† | .590 |
| 1965— | Peninsula§ | .597 |
| | Durham§ | .580 |
| | Tidewater† | .528 |
| 1966— | Kinston§ | .547 |
| | Winston-Salem§ | .586 |
| | Rocky Mount† | .533 |
| 1967— | Durham∞(West.) | .536 |
| | Raleigh (East.) | .542 |
| 1968— | Salem (West.) | .607 |
| | Ral-Dur (East.) | .597 |
| | HP-Thom.▲(W.) | .493 |
| 1969— | Rocky M (East.) | .569 |
| | Salem (West.) | .542 |
| | Ral-Dur◆(East.) | .560 |
| 1970— | Winston-Salem‡ | .586 |
| | Burlington | .597 |
| 1971— | Peninsula‡ | .647 |
| | Kinston | .623 |
| 1972— | Salem‡ | .657 |
| | Burlington | .632 |
| 1973— | Lynchburg | .588 |
| | Winston-Salem‡ | .557 |
| 1974— | Salem | .671 |
| | Salem | .582 |
| 1975— | Rocky Mount | .667 |
| | Rocky Mount | .614 |
| 1976— | Winston-Salem | .618 |
| | Winston-Salem | .551 |
| 1977— | Lynchburg | .591 |
| | Peninsula‡ | .556 |
| 1978— | Peninsula | .696 |
| | Lynchburg‡ | .614 |
| 1979— | Winston-Salem■ | .607 |
| 1980— | Peninsula‡ | .714 |
| | Durham | .600 |
| 1981— | Peninsula | .522 |
| | Hagerstown‡ | .507 |
| 1982— | Alexandria‡ | .597 |
| | Durham | .588 |
| 1983— | Lynchburg‡ | .691 |
| | Winston-Salem | .529 |
| 1984— | Lynchburg‡ | .645 |
| | Durham | .486 |
| 1985— | Lynchburg | .679 |
| | Winston-Salem‡ | .417 |
| 1986— | Hagerstown | .655 |
| | Winston-Salem‡ | .594 |
| 1987— | Salem‡ | .576 |
| | Kinston | .536 |
| 1988— | Kinston§ | .629 |
| | Lynchburg | .486 |
| 1989— | Durham | .609 |
| | Prince William‡ | .522 |
| 1990— | Kinston | .652 |
| | Frederick‡ | .544 |
| 1991— | Kinston‡ | .645 |
| | Lynchburg | .482 |
| 1992— | Lynchburg | .570 |
| | Peninsula‡ | .536 |
| 1993— | Wilmington | .532 |
| | Winston-Salem‡ | .514 |
| 1994— | Wilmington‡ | .681 |
| | Winston-Salem | .555 |
| 1995— | Wilmington | .601 |
| | Kinston‡ | .591 |
| 1996— | Wilmington▼ | .571 |
| | Kinston | .551 |

| Year | Team | Pct. |
|---|---|---|
| 1997— | Kinston | .621 |
| | Lynchburg† | .586 |
| 1998— | Wilmington▼ | .614 |
| | Winston-Salem | .568 |
| 1999— | Kinston | .577 |
| | Myrtle Beach• | .568 |
| | Wilmington• | .568 |
| 2000— | Myrtle Beach▼ | .629 |
| 2001— | Kinston | .636 |
| | Salem▼ | .507 |
| 2002— | Wilmington | .636 |
| | Lynchburg▼ | .621 |
| 2003— | Wilmington | .571 |
| | Winston-Salem▼ | .514 |
| 2004— | Kinston▼ | .638 |

*Won championship and four-club playoff. †Won four-club playoff. ‡Won split-season playoff. §League was divided into Eastern, Western divisions. ∞Won eight-club, two-division playoff. ▲Won eight-club, two-division playoff against Raleigh-Durham. ◆Won eight-club, two-division playoff against Burlington. ■Won both halves of split season (no playoffs). ▼League divided into Northern and Southern divisions and played a split-season, won playoffs. •Declared co-champions after final series cancelled due to hurricane.

# FLORIDA STATE LEAGUE

## LEAGUE OFFICE

**President**
Chuck Murphy
**Address**
P.O. Box 349
Daytona Beach, FL 32115
**Phone**
386-252-7479

**Teams (affiliation)**
Brevard County Manatees (Brewers)
Clearwater Threshers (Phillies)
Daytona Cubs (Cubs)
Dunedin Blue Jays (Blue Jays)
Fort Myers Miracle (Twins)
Jupiter Hammerheads (Marlins)
Lakeland Tigers (Tigers)
Palm Beach Cardinals (Cardinals)
St. Lucie Mets (Mets)
Sarasota Reds (Reds)
Tampa Yankees (Yankees)
Vero Beach Dodgers (Dodgers)

## 2004 FINAL STANDINGS

### FIRST HALF

#### EAST DIVISION

| Team | W | L | T | Pct. | GB |
|---|---|---|---|---|---|
| Daytona | 40 | 29 | - | .580 | ... |
| St. Lucie | 37 | 31 | - | .544 | 2 1/2 |
| Palm Beach | 37 | 32 | - | .536 | 3 |
| Vero Beach | 36 | 34 | - | .514 | 4 1/2 |
| Brevard County | 31 | 36 | - | .463 | 8 |
| Jupiter | 30 | 38 | - | .441 | 9 1/2 |

#### WEST DIVISION

| Team | W | L | T | Pct. | GB |
|---|---|---|---|---|---|
| Dunedin | 41 | 29 | - | .586 | ... |
| Sarasota | 38 | 31 | - | .551 | 2 1/2 |
| Tampa | 37 | 31 | - | .544 | 3 |
| Fort Myers | 31 | 37 | - | .456 | 9 |
| Lakeland | 29 | 39 | - | .426 | 11 |
| Clearwater | 25 | 45 | - | .357 | 16 |

### SECOND HALF

#### EAST DIVISION

| Team | W | L | T | Pct. | GB |
|---|---|---|---|---|---|
| Vero Beach | 41 | 23 | - | .641 | ... |
| Palm Beach | 36 | 29 | - | .554 | 5 1/2 |
| Daytona | 30 | 27 | - | .526 | 7 1/2 |
| Jupiter | 34 | 33 | - | .507 | 8 1/2 |
| St. Lucie | 27 | 34 | - | .443 | 12 1/2 |
| Brevard County | 22 | 36 | - | .379 | 16 |

#### WEST DIVISION

| Team | W | L | T | Pct. | GB |
|---|---|---|---|---|---|
| Tampa | 38 | 27 | - | .585 | ... |
| Dunedin | 35 | 28 | - | .556 | 2 |
| Sarasota | 37 | 30 | - | .552 | 2 |
| Clearwater | 30 | 36 | - | .455 | 8 1/2 |
| Fort Myers | 30 | 37 | - | .448 | 9 |
| Lakeland | 22 | 42 | - | .344 | 15 1/2 |

### COMPOSITE

| Team | W | L | T | Pct. | GB | VB | DUN | TAM | DAY | SAR | PLM | SLU | JUP | FTM | BRE | CLW | LAK |
|---|---|---|---|---|---|---|---|---|---|---|---|---|---|---|---|---|---|
| Vero Beach (Dodgers) | 77 | 57 | - | .575 | ... | X | 4 | 6 | 11 | 5 | 9 | 8 | 9 | 6 | 8 | 5 | 6 |
| Dunedin (Blue Jays) | 76 | 57 | - | .571 | 1/2 | 4 | X | 9 | 3 | 9 | 6 | 5 | 5 | 7 | 5 | 17 | 6 |
| Tampa (Yankees) | 75 | 58 | - | .564 | 1 1/2 | 2 | 11 | X | 2 | 6 | 6 | 3 | 4 | 10 | 4 | 11 | 16 |
| Daytona (Cubs) | 70 | 56 | - | .556 | 4 | 8 | 3 | 4 | X | 4 | 8 | 6 | 7 | 7 | 12 | 7 | 4 |
| Sarasota (Red Sox) | 75 | 61 | - | .551 | 3 | 3 | 5 | 9 | 3 | X | 7 | 4 | 2 | 16 | 4 | 11 | 11 |
| Palm Beach (Cardinals) | 73 | 61 | - | .545 | 4 | 11 | 2 | 2 | 6 | 1 | X | 11 | 16 | 4 | 10 | 5 | 5 |
| St. Lucie (Mets) | 64 | 65 | - | .496 | 10 1/2 | 7 | 3 | 3 | 7 | 4 | 10 | X | 15 | 2 | 6 | 3 | 5 |
| Jupiter (Marlins) | 64 | 71 | - | .474 | 13 1/2 | 7 | 3 | 4 | 9 | 6 | 3 | 7 | X | 4 | 12 | 5 | 4 |
| Fort Myers (Twins) | 61 | 74 | - | .452 | 16 1/2 | 2 | 8 | 6 | 1 | 8 | 4 | 6 | 3 | X | 4 | 8 | 11 |
| Brevard County (Expos) | 53 | 72 | - | .424 | 19 1/2 | 9 | 3 | 4 | 9 | 4 | 3 | 7 | 4 | 3 | X | 3 | 4 |
| Clearwater (Phillies) | 55 | 81 | - | .404 | 23 | 2 | 7 | 7 | 1 | 5 | 3 | 5 | 3 | 8 | 5 | X | 9 |
| Lakeland (Tigers) | 51 | 81 | - | .386 | 25 | 2 | 8 | 4 | 4 | 9 | 3 | 3 | 3 | 7 | 2 | 6 | X |

Major league affiliations in parentheses.

PLAYOFFS: Daytona defeated Vero Beach two games to none; Tampa defeated Dunedin two games to none; Daytona and Tampa are named co-champions after post-season is canceled.

REGULAR-SEASON ATTENDANCE: Brevard County, 98,430; Clearwater, 135,101; Daytona, 110,223; Dunedin, 36,844; Fort Myers, 96,150; Jupiter, 95,903; Lakeland, 30,585; Palm Beach, 92,408; St. Lucie, 85,991; Sarasota, 41,374; Tampa 77,542; Vero Beach, 66,945. Total attendance—967,496. All-Star game at Tradition Field—5,791.

MANAGERS: Brevard, Tim Raines; Clearwater, Mike Schmidt; Daytona Steve McFarland; Dunedin, Omar Malave; Fort Myers, Jose Marzan; Jupiter, Luis Dorante; Lakeland, Gary Green; Palm Beach, Tom Nieto; St. Lucie, Tim Teufel; Sarasota, Todd Claus; Tampa, Billy Masse; Vero Beach, Scott Little.

ALL-STAR TEAM: 1B—Brandon Sing, Daytona; 2B—Delwyn Young, Vero Beach; SS—Joel Guzman, Vero Beach; 3B—Aaron Baldiris, St. Lucie; C—Eliezer Alfonzo, Jupiter, Russell Martin, Vero Beach; Reserve—Carlo Cota, Dunedin; LF—Matt Murton, Daytona, CF—Felix Pie, Daytona; RF—Ron Davenport, Dunedin; Reserve—Chris Roberson, Clearwater; DH—Jeremy West, Sarasota; P—Jon Connolly, Daytona, Jonathan Broxton, Vero Beach, Jon Papelbon, Sarasota, Ismael Ramirez, Dunedin, Relievers-Edward Buzachero, Dunedin, Edwardo Sierra, Tampa. Player of the Year—Brandon Sing, Daytona; Pitcher of the Year—Ismael Ramirez, Dunedin; Manager of the Year—Omar Malave, Dunedin.

## 2004 BATTING

### TEAM

| Team | G | TPA | AB | R | H | TB | 2B | 3B | HR | RBI | SH | SF | HP | BB | IBB | SO | SB | CS | GDP | LOB | ShO | Avg. | OBP | Slg. |
|---|---|---|---|---|---|---|---|---|---|---|---|---|---|---|---|---|---|---|---|---|---|---|---|---|
| Daytona | 126 | 4655 | 4112 | 594 | 1096 | 1639 | 199 | 43 | 86 | 531 | 40 | 44 | 53 | 404 | 20 | 805 | 139 | 71 | 90 | 831 | 8 | .267 | .337 | .399 |
| Fort Myers | 135 | 4970 | 4411 | 544 | 1173 | 1579 | 196 | 42 | 42 | 487 | 54 | 42 | 64 | 399 | 26 | 814 | 111 | 47 | 95 | 980 | 13 | .266 | .333 | .358 |
| Tampa | 133 | 4947 | 4402 | 636 | 1166 | 1716 | 250 | 30 | 80 | 596 | 9 | 46 | 62 | 427 | 22 | 870 | 58 | 26 | 94 | 926 | 9 | .265 | .335 | .390 |
| Sarasota | 136 | 5062 | 4494 | 613 | 1186 | 1747 | 225 | 33 | 90 | 540 | 28 | 34 | 58 | 448 | 22 | 883 | 74 | 47 | 103 | 955 | 9 | .264 | .336 | .389 |
| Dunedin | 133 | 5119 | 4473 | 649 | 1152 | 1740 | 253 | 19 | 99 | 592 | 16 | 45 | 62 | 523 | 26 | 883 | 16 | 22 | 126 | 1013 | 8 | .258 | .340 | .389 |

| Team | G | TPA | AB | R | H | TB | 2B | 3B | HR | RBI | SH | SF | HP | BB | IBB | SO | SB | CS | GDP | LOB | ShO | Avg. | OBP | Slg. |
|---|---|---|---|---|---|---|---|---|---|---|---|---|---|---|---|---|---|---|---|---|---|---|---|---|
| St. Lucie | 129 | 4806 | 4278 | 557 | 1094 | 1651 | 202 | 32 | 97 | 507 | 37 | 30 | 66 | 395 | 22 | 1009 | 130 | 77 | 97 | 852 | 12 | .256 | .326 | .386 |
| Palm Beach | 134 | 4976 | 4341 | 603 | 1104 | 1517 | 202 | 29 | 51 | 545 | 60 | 51 | 60 | 464 | 27 | 869 | 159 | 79 | 76 | 933 | 8 | .254 | .331 | .349 |
| Lakeland | 132 | 4746 | 4254 | 558 | 1081 | 1626 | 215 | 48 | 78 | 509 | 30 | 35 | 49 | 378 | 14 | 1013 | 77 | 55 | 74 | 856 | 4 | .254 | .320 | .382 |
| Vero Beach | 135 | 4989 | 4389 | 618 | 1109 | 1722 | 199 | 33 | 116 | 567 | 38 | 41 | 72 | 449 | 23 | 915 | 148 | 66 | 84 | 894 | 9 | .253 | .329 | .392 |
| Jupiter | 135 | 5056 | 4445 | 543 | 1101 | 1604 | 202 | 29 | 81 | 498 | 65 | 35 | 62 | 448 | 23 | 1084 | 111 | 52 | 90 | 963 | 6 | .248 | .323 | .361 |
| Brevard County | 125 | 4611 | 4051 | 472 | 991 | 1403 | 156 | 38 | 60 | 423 | 60 | 37 | 40 | 423 | 15 | 833 | 80 | 49 | 90 | 864 | 10 | .245 | .319 | .346 |
| Clearwater | 136 | 4945 | 4369 | 528 | 1060 | 1533 | 198 | 31 | 71 | 461 | 59 | 28 | 67 | 422 | 22 | 898 | 75 | 73 | 101 | 884 | 16 | .243 | .317 | .351 |

# INDIVIDUAL

## TOP QUALIFIERS FOR BATTING CHAMPIONSHIP

Minimum 378 plate appearances. *Lefthanded batter. †Switch-hitter.

| Player, Team | G | TPA | AB | R | H | TB | 2B | 3B | HR | RBI | SH | SF | HP | BB | IBB | SO | SB | CS | GDP | Avg. | OBP | Slg. |
|---|---|---|---|---|---|---|---|---|---|---|---|---|---|---|---|---|---|---|---|---|---|---|
| Matienzo, Danny, Fort Myers | 123 | 513 | 455 | 51 | 139 | 183 | 27 | 1 | 5 | 65 | 2 | 8 | 5 | 43 | 7 | 88 | 1 | 0 | 17 | .305 | .366 | .402 |
| Baldiris, Aarom, St. Lucie | 107 | 466 | 406 | 57 | 124 | 161 | 15 | 5 | 4 | 45 | 2 | 4 | 8 | 46 | 3 | 64 | 6 | 6 | 13 | .305 | .384 | .397 |
| Hermida, Jeremy, Jupiter * | 91 | 393 | 340 | 53 | 101 | 150 | 17 | 1 | 10 | 50 | 0 | 6 | 5 | 42 | 7 | 73 | 10 | 3 | 3 | .297 | .377 | .441 |
| Pie, Felix, Daytona * | 110 | 487 | 431 | 79 | 128 | 190 | 18 | 10 | 8 | 47 | 7 | 5 | 5 | 39 | 2 | 116 | 32 | 18 | 5 | .297 | .358 | .441 |
| Barthelemy, Ryan, Clearwater * | 132 | 540 | 475 | 62 | 140 | 217 | 27 | 4 | 14 | 77 | 2 | 5 | 7 | 51 | 7 | 93 | 4 | 6 | 11 | .295 | .368 | .457 |
| Cota, Carlo, Dunedin | 116 | 523 | 463 | 81 | 136 | 208 | 37 | 1 | 11 | 63 | 4 | 7 | 4 | 45 | 0 | 101 | 2 | 1 | 20 | .294 | .356 | .449 |
| Deeds, Doug, Fort Myers * | 123 | 490 | 435 | 71 | 128 | 195 | 28 | 12 | 5 | 57 | 1 | 4 | 7 | 43 | 1 | 86 | 11 | 3 | 9 | .294 | .364 | .448 |
| West, Jeremy, Sarasota | 124 | 507 | 461 | 60 | 135 | 225 | 28 | 4 | 18 | 68 | 0 | 5 | 4 | 37 | 1 | 83 | 0 | 3 | 21 | .293 | .347 | .488 |
| Murton, Matt, Sarasota-Daytona | 126 | 514 | 455 | 73 | 133 | 199 | 17 | 5 | 13 | 63 | 0 | 5 | 4 | 50 | 5 | 71 | 7 | 4 | 10 | .292 | .364 | .437 |
| Schutzenhofer, Andy, Palm Beach * | 121 | 445 | 373 | 65 | 109 | 137 | 15 | 2 | 3 | 56 | 2 | 8 | 11 | 51 | 4 | 36 | 3 | 2 | 10 | .292 | .386 | .367 |
| Romero, Alex, Fort Myers † | 105 | 447 | 380 | 59 | 111 | 154 | 21 | 2 | 6 | 42 | 5 | 2 | 6 | 54 | 3 | 47 | 6 | 4 | 4 | .292 | .387 | .405 |
| Koutnik, Jared, Tampa | 104 | 422 | 381 | 57 | 111 | 164 | 19 | 2 | 10 | 62 | 0 | 5 | 6 | 30 | 1 | 72 | 1 | 2 | 7 | .291 | .348 | .430 |
| Greenberg, Adam, Daytona | 91 | 381 | 323 | 52 | 94 | 137 | 10 | 12 | 3 | 28 | 3 | 3 | 7 | 42 | 2 | 65 | 16 | 8 | 4 | .291 | .381 | .424 |
| Coats, Buck, Daytona * | 112 | 453 | 414 | 64 | 120 | 174 | 22 | 4 | 8 | 55 | 3 | 3 | 1 | 32 | 2 | 90 | 27 | 9 | 6 | .290 | .340 | .420 |
| Johnson, J.J., Daytona | 108 | 420 | 387 | 41 | 109 | 153 | 16 | 5 | 6 | 62 | 2 | 3 | 1 | 27 | 1 | 79 | 9 | 2 | 9 | .282 | .328 | .395 |

DEPARTMENTAL LEADERS: G—Barthelemy, 132; AB—Barthelemy, 475; R—Sing, 86; H—Barthelemy, 140; TB—D. Young, 240; 2B—Davenport, 40; 3B—A. Greenberg, Deeds, 12; HR—Sing, 32; RBI—Sing, 94; SH—Motte, 13; SF—Caligiuri, Duncan, 9; HP—Tingler, 16; BB—Sing, 84; IBB—Sing, 9; SO—Ragsdale, 152; SB—Requena, 50; CS—Laya, 19; GIDP—West, 21; Slg.—Sing, .571; OBP—Sing, .399.

## ALL PLAYERS

*Lefthanded batter. †Switch-hitter.

| Player, Team | G | TPA | AB | R | H | TB | 2B | 3B | HR | RBI | SH | SF | HP | BB | IBB | SO | SB | CS | GDP | Avg. | OBP | Slg. |
|---|---|---|---|---|---|---|---|---|---|---|---|---|---|---|---|---|---|---|---|---|---|---|
| Abreu, Etanislao, Vero Beach | 11 | 47 | 43 | 8 | 18 | 23 | 3 | 1 | 0 | 3 | 1 | 1 | 1 | 1 | 0 | 8 | 4 | 1 | 1 | .419 | .435 | .535 |
| Alfonzo, Eliezer, Jupiter | 105 | 436 | 399 | 51 | 112 | 182 | 12 | 2 | 18 | 70 | 0 | 3 | 12 | 22 | 2 | 105 | 6 | 4 | 16 | .281 | .335 | .456 |
| Ambrosini, Dominic, Brevard County | 61 | 241 | 215 | 11 | 41 | 56 | 7 | 1 | 2 | 24 | 4 | 3 | 2 | 17 | 1 | 56 | 2 | 5 | 8 | .191 | .253 | .260 |
| Amezquita, Octavio, Lakeland | 9 | 27 | 27 | 0 | 2 | 3 | 1 | 0 | 0 | 0 | 0 | 0 | 0 | 0 | 0 | 3 | 0 | 0 | 1 | .074 | .074 | .111 |
| Andino, Robert, Jupiter | 49 | 208 | 197 | 18 | 55 | 66 | 7 | 2 | 0 | 15 | 3 | 1 | 0 | 7 | 0 | 43 | 6 | 2 | 3 | .279 | .302 | .335 |
| Apodaca, Luis, Brevard County | 15 | 51 | 47 | 5 | 13 | 15 | 2 | 0 | 0 | 2 | 0 | 0 | 1 | 3 | 0 | 8 | 0 | 0 | 2 | .277 | .333 | .319 |
| Aponte, Jose, Jupiter * | 101 | 368 | 328 | 33 | 70 | 108 | 17 | 6 | 3 | 29 | 9 | 2 | 2 | 27 | 2 | 83 | 9 | 6 | 4 | .213 | .276 | .329 |
| Aquilino, Anthony, Clearwater | 17 | 53 | 50 | 3 | 13 | 17 | 2 | 1 | 0 | 1 | 0 | 0 | 1 | 2 | 0 | 13 | 1 | 1 | 1 | .260 | .302 | .340 |
| Arnerich, Tony, Jupiter | 35 | 111 | 97 | 12 | 17 | 31 | 6 | 1 | 2 | 12 | 1 | 0 | 1 | 12 | 0 | 20 | 0 | 0 | 3 | .175 | .273 | .320 |
| Bacon, Matt, St. Lucie * | 5 | 11 | 10 | 2 | 2 | 2 | 0 | 0 | 0 | 1 | 0 | 0 | 0 | 1 | 0 | 6 | 0 | 0 | 0 | .200 | .273 | .200 |
| Barrett, Ricky, Fort Myers * | 18 | 2 | 2 | 0 | 0 | 0 | 0 | 0 | 0 | 0 | 0 | 0 | 0 | 0 | 0 | 2 | 0 | 0 | 0 | .000 | .000 | .000 |
| Barthelemy, Ryan, Clearwater * | 132 | 540 | 475 | 62 | 140 | 217 | 27 | 4 | 14 | 77 | 2 | 5 | 7 | 51 | 7 | 93 | 4 | 6 | 11 | .295 | .368 | .457 |
| Bass, Chris, Jupiter | 119 | 496 | 421 | 54 | 115 | 146 | 20 | 1 | 3 | 37 | 8 | 3 | 8 | 55 | 2 | 77 | 6 | 4 | 10 | .273 | .366 | .347 |
| Blasi, Blake, Palm Beach † | 72 | 186 | 158 | 23 | 42 | 56 | 7 | 2 | 1 | 22 | 3 | 1 | 1 | 23 | 2 | 32 | 4 | 4 | 1 | .266 | .361 | .354 |
| Bonner, Adam, Jupiter * | 55 | 206 | 160 | 23 | 32 | 47 | 0 | 0 | 5 | 15 | 1 | 0 | 1 | 44 | 0 | 50 | 1 | 1 | 3 | .200 | .376 | .294 |
| Boyd, Shaun, Palm Beach | 39 | 173 | 157 | 23 | 54 | 80 | 12 | 1 | 4 | 26 | 1 | 2 | 2 | 11 | 0 | 22 | 7 | 6 | 2 | .344 | .390 | .510 |
| Brown, Andy, Tampa * | 26 | 75 | 70 | 4 | 11 | 22 | 2 | 0 | 3 | 9 | 0 | 0 | 0 | 5 | 0 | 26 | 0 | 1 | 1 | .157 | .213 | .314 |
| Brown, Dusty, Sarasota | 38 | 134 | 118 | 11 | 27 | 33 | 3 | 0 | 1 | 8 | 0 | 0 | 1 | 15 | 1 | 28 | 2 | 0 | 0 | .229 | .321 | .280 |
| Buckley, Jim, Sarasota | 70 | 233 | 203 | 24 | 41 | 78 | 13 | 0 | 8 | 29 | 3 | 1 | 0 | 26 | 0 | 54 | 0 | 1 | 5 | .202 | .291 | .384 |
| Burford, Kevin, Clearwater * | 32 | 117 | 99 | 14 | 18 | 26 | 5 | 0 | 1 | 8 | 0 | 1 | 1 | 16 | 0 | 32 | 1 | 1 | 2 | .182 | .299 | .263 |
| Butler, Keith, Daytona | 103 | 411 | 369 | 48 | 94 | 124 | 14 | 2 | 4 | 47 | 5 | 6 | 8 | 23 | 0 | 54 | 25 | 10 | 13 | .255 | .308 | .336 |
| Bynum, Seth, Brevard County | 20 | 55 | 51 | 7 | 12 | 20 | 3 | 1 | 1 | 3 | 0 | 0 | 0 | 4 | 0 | 20 | 0 | 0 | 1 | .235 | .291 | .392 |
| Cabrera, Melky, Tampa † | 85 | 364 | 333 | 48 | 96 | 146 | 20 | 3 | 8 | 51 | 0 | 3 | 5 | 23 | 1 | 59 | 3 | 1 | 8 | .288 | .341 | .438 |
| Caligiuri, Jay, St. Lucie | 104 | 434 | 365 | 52 | 87 | 158 | 15 | 1 | 18 | 69 | 0 | 9 | 6 | 54 | 2 | 83 | 1 | 1 | 6 | .238 | .339 | .433 |
| Catalanotte, Greg, Palm Beach † | 124 | 465 | 403 | 54 | 100 | 150 | 30 | 4 | 4 | 50 | 4 | 0 | 7 | 51 | 2 | 112 | 3 | 2 | 9 | .248 | .343 | .372 |
| Chavez, Ender, Brevard County * | 20 | 87 | 71 | 12 | 27 | 32 | 3 | 1 | 0 | 8 | 5 | 0 | 0 | 11 | 1 | 12 | 4 | 5 | 2 | .380 | .463 | .451 |
| Chiaravalloti, Vito, Dunedin | 122 | 534 | 447 | 63 | 119 | 196 | 33 | 1 | 14 | 71 | 0 | 5 | 13 | 69 | 4 | 110 | 0 | 1 | 12 | .266 | .376 | .438 |
| Chop, Chad, Brevard County * | 122 | 506 | 444 | 47 | 97 | 140 | 16 | 0 | 9 | 46 | 2 | 8 | 4 | 48 | 3 | 66 | 3 | 6 | 16 | .218 | .296 | .315 |
| Clanton, Ja'Mar, Brevard County | 7 | 16 | 15 | 0 | 1 | 1 | 0 | 0 | 0 | 1 | 1 | 0 | 0 | 0 | 0 | 3 | 0 | 0 | 1 | .067 | .067 | .067 |
| Clark, Daryl, Palm Beach * | 31 | 117 | 95 | 13 | 21 | 35 | 5 | 0 | 3 | 21 | 1 | 3 | 2 | 16 | 0 | 30 | 1 | 0 | 1 | .221 | .336 | .368 |
| Clevlen, Brent, Lakeland | 117 | 473 | 420 | 49 | 94 | 147 | 23 | 6 | 6 | 50 | 0 | 5 | 4 | 44 | 1 | 127 | 2 | 1 | 12 | .224 | .300 | .350 |
| Coats, Buck, Daytona * | 112 | 453 | 414 | 64 | 120 | 174 | 22 | 4 | 8 | 55 | 3 | 3 | 1 | 32 | 2 | 90 | 27 | 9 | 6 | .290 | .340 | .420 |
| Concepcion, Alberto, Sarasota | 98 | 383 | 331 | 47 | 93 | 133 | 23 | 1 | 5 | 51 | 4 | 3 | 10 | 35 | 1 | 85 | 4 | 3 | 7 | .281 | .364 | .402 |
| Cordero, Wil, Jupiter | 3 | 9 | 8 | 3 | 4 | 10 | 0 | 0 | 2 | 5 | 0 | 0 | 0 | 1 | 0 | 1 | 0 | 0 | 0 | .500 | .556 | 1.250 |
| Corporan, Elvis, Fort Myers † | 40 | 160 | 145 | 17 | 31 | 43 | 9 | 0 | 1 | 17 | 0 | 0 | 0 | 15 | 0 | 26 | 0 | 0 | 4 | .214 | .288 | .297 |
| Correll, Brad, Clearwater | 28 | 102 | 84 | 14 | 16 | 24 | 5 | 0 | 1 | 7 | 1 | 2 | 2 | 13 | 0 | 10 | 1 | 1 | 2 | .190 | .307 | .286 |
| Cota, Carlo, Dunedin | 116 | 523 | 463 | 81 | 136 | 208 | 37 | 1 | 11 | 63 | 4 | 7 | 4 | 45 | 0 | 101 | 2 | 1 | 20 | .294 | .356 | .449 |
| Cotto, Pedro, Lakeland * | 61 | 202 | 182 | 17 | 39 | 45 | 4 | 1 | 0 | 17 | 5 | 3 | 1 | 11 | 0 | 21 | 0 | 1 | 7 | .214 | .259 | .247 |
| Davenport, Ron, Dunedin * | 113 | 493 | 442 | 63 | 123 | 219 | 40 | 4 | 16 | 92 | 0 | 4 | 0 | 47 | 7 | 68 | 0 | 1 | 9 | .278 | .345 | .495 |
| Deeds, Doug, Fort Myers * | 123 | 490 | 435 | 71 | 128 | 195 | 28 | 12 | 5 | 57 | 1 | 4 | 7 | 43 | 1 | 86 | 11 | 3 | 9 | .294 | .364 | .448 |
| Diaz, Frank, Brevard County | 114 | 463 | 413 | 46 | 100 | 157 | 17 | 8 | 8 | 57 | 4 | 7 | 8 | 31 | 1 | 76 | 16 | 6 | 13 | .242 | .303 | .380 |
| Dragicevich, Scott, Dunedin | 84 | 325 | 277 | 32 | 63 | 86 | 14 | 0 | 3 | 28 | 0 | 4 | 2 | 42 | 0 | 81 | 1 | 0 | 7 | .227 | .329 | .310 |
| Drobiak, Jayson, Tampa * | 81 | 321 | 288 | 41 | 66 | 120 | 13 | 4 | 11 | 43 | 0 | 5 | 3 | 25 | 0 | 71 | 5 | 1 | 4 | .229 | .293 | .417 |
| Duncan, Eric, Tampa * | 51 | 205 | 173 | 23 | 44 | 80 | 20 | 2 | 4 | 26 | 0 | 1 | 0 | 31 | 3 | 47 | 0 | 2 | 5 | .254 | .366 | .462 |
| Duncan, Shelley, Tampa | 123 | 494 | 424 | 65 | 105 | 191 | 27 | 1 | 19 | 78 | 0 | 9 | 7 | 54 | 5 | 119 | 6 | 3 | 7 | .248 | .336 | .450 |
| Durbin, Chris, Sarasota | 125 | 521 | 470 | 75 | 131 | 196 | 32 | 6 | 7 | 44 | 3 | 1 | 8 | 39 | 0 | 79 | 8 | 10 | 7 | .279 | .344 | .417 |

| Player, Team | G | TPA | AB | R | H | TB | 2B | 3B | HR | RBI | SH | SF | HP | BB | IBB | SO | SB | CS | GDP | Avg. | OBP | Slg. |
|---|---|---|---|---|---|---|---|---|---|---|---|---|---|---|---|---|---|---|---|---|---|---|
| Dyson, Trey, Vero Beach * | 74 | 294 | 253 | 36 | 69 | 103 | 14 | 1 | 6 | 36 | 3 | 3 | 5 | 30 | 3 | 41 | 4 | 2 | 2 | .273 | .357 | .407 |
| Ellerson, Brian, Brevard County | 37 | 119 | 113 | 14 | 29 | 32 | 3 | 0 | 0 | 8 | 1 | 0 | 0 | 5 | 1 | 23 | 0 | 0 | 5 | .257 | .288 | .283 |
| Ellis, Andrew, Vero Beach | 40 | 141 | 114 | 15 | 25 | 35 | 4 | 0 | 2 | 22 | 1 | 1 | 1 | 24 | 0 | 20 | 1 | 0 | 2 | .219 | .357 | .307 |
| Evans, Terry, Palm Beach | 19 | 64 | 58 | 7 | 13 | 23 | 4 | 0 | 2 | 7 | 0 | 1 | 1 | 4 | 0 | 16 | 1 | 0 | 0 | .224 | .281 | .397 |
| Ezi, Travis, Jupiter † | 81 | 281 | 242 | 45 | 54 | 78 | 10 | 4 | 2 | 19 | 5 | 2 | 4 | 28 | 0 | 76 | 19 | 7 | 2 | .223 | .312 | .322 |
| Figueroa, Juan, Jupiter * | 5 | 18 | 16 | 1 | 5 | 5 | 0 | 0 | 0 | 1 | 0 | 0 | 0 | 2 | 0 | 3 | 0 | 1 | 0 | .313 | .389 | .313 |
| Floyd, Mike, Clearwater | 107 | 401 | 349 | 61 | 91 | 150 | 19 | 5 | 10 | 39 | 7 | 1 | 4 | 40 | 1 | 98 | 7 | 6 | 6 | .261 | .343 | .430 |
| Frazier, Charles, Jupiter | 92 | 363 | 303 | 53 | 71 | 100 | 9 | 1 | 6 | 21 | 4 | 0 | 6 | 50 | 3 | 81 | 36 | 14 | 3 | .234 | .354 | .330 |
| Frome, Jason, Palm Beach * | 37 | 118 | 98 | 10 | 21 | 38 | 3 | 1 | 4 | 12 | 3 | 0 | 0 | 17 | 1 | 35 | 2 | 1 | 0 | .214 | .330 | .388 |
| Garcia, Miguel, St. Lucie * | 9 | 27 | 25 | 1 | 7 | 7 | 0 | 0 | 0 | 2 | 0 | 0 | 1 | 1 | 0 | 7 | 0 | 1 | 0 | .280 | .333 | .280 |
| Giarratano, Tony, Lakeland † | 53 | 227 | 202 | 30 | 76 | 102 | 11 | 0 | 5 | 25 | 6 | 2 | 1 | 16 | 0 | 38 | 14 | 8 | 1 | .376 | .421 | .505 |
| Gillitzer, Scott, Vero Beach | 93 | 355 | 331 | 50 | 76 | 114 | 11 | 3 | 7 | 35 | 3 | 0 | 2 | 19 | 2 | 53 | 2 | 2 | 8 | .230 | .276 | .344 |
| Goelz, Bryan, Vero Beach * | 103 | 340 | 295 | 32 | 77 | 96 | 9 | 2 | 2 | 33 | 2 | 3 | 5 | 35 | 3 | 35 | 10 | 8 | 5 | .261 | .346 | .325 |
| Gomon, Dusty, Fort Myers | 2 | 5 | 5 | 1 | 1 | 1 | 0 | 0 | 0 | 0 | 0 | 0 | 0 | 0 | 0 | 4 | 0 | 0 | 0 | .200 | .200 | .200 |
| Gradoville, Tim, Clearwater | 63 | 207 | 187 | 18 | 46 | 70 | 10 | 1 | 4 | 26 | 2 | 3 | 3 | 12 | 0 | 53 | 0 | 4 | 5 | .246 | .298 | .374 |
| Greenberg, Adam, Daytona* | 91 | — | 323 | 52 | 94 | 137 | 10 | 12 | 3 | 28 | 3 | 3 | 7 | 42 | 2 | 65 | 16 | 8 | 4 | .291 | .381 | .424 |
| Guevara, Orlando, Clearwater † | 2 | 2 | 2 | 0 | 0 | 0 | 0 | 0 | 0 | 0 | 0 | 0 | 0 | 0 | 0 | 0 | 0 | 0 | 0 | .000 | .000 | .000 |
| Guzman, Garrett, Fort Myers * | 78 | 301 | 275 | 35 | 74 | 106 | 10 | 5 | 4 | 31 | 2 | 2 | 0 | 22 | 0 | 42 | 3 | 2 | 5 | .269 | .321 | .385 |
| Hanson, Travis, Palm Beach * | 57 | 249 | 224 | 26 | 58 | 75 | 11 | 0 | 2 | 35 | 0 | 3 | 3 | 19 | 1 | 38 | 2 | 3 | 6 | .259 | .321 | .335 |
| Hermida, Jeremy, Jupiter * | 91 | 393 | 340 | 53 | 101 | 150 | 17 | 1 | 10 | 50 | 0 | 6 | 5 | 42 | 7 | 73 | 10 | 3 | 3 | .297 | .377 | .441 |
| Hoorelbeke, Jesse, Vero Beach | 65 | 236 | 207 | 32 | 45 | 90 | 6 | 0 | 13 | 39 | 0 | 2 | 4 | 23 | 0 | 74 | 3 | 1 | 3 | .217 | .305 | .435 |
| Hu, Chin-Lung, Vero Beach | 20 | 83 | 75 | 12 | 23 | 29 | 4 | 1 | 0 | 10 | 3 | 0 | 0 | 5 | 0 | 6 | 3 | 1 | 1 | .307 | .350 | .387 |
| Italiano, Nick, Clearwater * | 27 | 73 | 66 | 7 | 12 | 20 | 3 | 1 | 1 | 7 | 1 | 0 | 1 | 5 | 0 | 13 | 1 | 0 | 0 | .182 | .250 | .303 |
| Jackson, Nic, Daytona * | 13 | 55 | 47 | 8 | 16 | 25 | 4 | 1 | 1 | 9 | 0 | 1 | 1 | 6 | 0 | 13 | 1 | 0 | 1 | .340 | .418 | .532 |
| Jenkins, Neil, Lakeland | 37 | 140 | 131 | 17 | 33 | 52 | 5 | 1 | 4 | 11 | 0 | 0 | 2 | 7 | 0 | 51 | 4 | 0 | 0 | .252 | .300 | .397 |
| Jiannetti, Joe, St. Lucie | 81 | 296 | 271 | 31 | 69 | 100 | 12 | 2 | 5 | 28 | 2 | 2 | 3 | 18 | 1 | 38 | 11 | 8 | 5 | .255 | .306 | .369 |
| Johnson, Eric, Sarasota | 19 | 64 | 56 | 5 | 7 | 11 | 1 | 0 | 1 | 5 | 0 | 1 | 1 | 6 | 1 | 15 | 2 | 0 | 1 | .125 | .219 | .196 |
| Johnson, J.J., Daytona | 108 | 420 | 387 | 41 | 109 | 153 | 16 | 5 | 6 | 62 | 2 | 3 | 1 | 27 | 1 | 79 | 9 | 2 | 9 | .282 | .328 | .395 |
| Jones, Nick, Daytona | 15 | 41 | 40 | 1 | 10 | 11 | 1 | 0 | 0 | 0 | 0 | 0 | 0 | 1 | 0 | 11 | 0 | 0 | 1 | .250 | .268 | .275 |
| Jones, Terry, Clearwater | 44 | 172 | 147 | 14 | 30 | 49 | 7 | 0 | 4 | 21 | 2 | 2 | 3 | 18 | 0 | 30 | 3 | 0 | 4 | .204 | .300 | .333 |
| Kavourias, Jim, Jupiter | 30 | 123 | 111 | 10 | 17 | 28 | 3 | 1 | 2 | 9 | 2 | 0 | 0 | 10 | 1 | 41 | 1 | 0 | 0 | .153 | .223 | .252 |
| Kemp, Matthew, Vero Beach | 11 | 42 | 37 | 5 | 13 | 21 | 5 | 0 | 1 | 9 | 0 | 1 | 0 | 4 | 0 | 12 | 2 | 1 | 0 | .351 | .405 | .568 |
| Koutnik, Jared, Tampa | 104 | 422 | 381 | 57 | 111 | 164 | 19 | 2 | 10 | 62 | 0 | 5 | 6 | 30 | 1 | 72 | 1 | 2 | 7 | .291 | .348 | .430 |
| Kratz, Erik, Dunedin | 15 | 52 | 49 | 6 | 14 | 21 | 4 | 0 | 1 | 6 | 0 | 0 | 1 | 2 | 0 | 16 | 0 | 0 | 2 | .286 | .327 | .429 |
| Krga, Mike, Jupiter | 2 | 5 | 4 | 0 | 0 | 0 | 0 | 0 | 0 | 0 | 0 | 0 | 0 | 1 | 0 | 2 | 0 | 0 | 1 | .000 | .200 | .000 |
| Kuhaulua, Kaulana, Fort Myers | 97 | 371 | 337 | 42 | 80 | 114 | 15 | 2 | 5 | 43 | 8 | 4 | 6 | 16 | 0 | 83 | 12 | 6 | 5 | .237 | .281 | .338 |
| Kweon, Yoon-Min, Daytona | 12 | 24 | 23 | 2 | 4 | 5 | 1 | 0 | 0 | 1 | 0 | 0 | 0 | 1 | 0 | 5 | 1 | 0 | 0 | .174 | .208 | .217 |
| LaRoche, Andy, Vero Beach | 62 | 243 | 219 | 26 | 52 | 95 | 13 | 0 | 10 | 34 | 2 | 3 | 2 | 17 | 0 | 42 | 2 | 3 | 1 | .237 | .295 | .434 |
| Laya, Rayner, Palm Beach | 101 | 440 | 387 | 64 | 97 | 112 | 9 | 3 | 0 | 30 | 4 | 7 | 3 | 39 | 4 | 34 | 41 | 19 | 1 | .251 | .319 | .289 |
| Lemanczyk, Matt, Palm Beach | 89 | 343 | 302 | 38 | 70 | 84 | 7 | 2 | 1 | 25 | 11 | 0 | 5 | 25 | 2 | 55 | 33 | 11 | 2 | .232 | .301 | .278 |
| Lopez, Gabe, Tampa | 106 | 459 | 403 | 56 | 103 | 143 | 23 | 4 | 3 | 46 | 4 | 6 | 4 | 42 | 0 | 48 | 5 | 0 | 5 | .256 | .327 | .355 |
| Maples, Chris, Lakeland | 121 | 477 | 428 | 66 | 116 | 202 | 33 | 1 | 17 | 73 | 0 | 3 | 9 | 37 | 1 | 86 | 7 | 11 | 4 | .271 | .340 | .472 |
| Marcelli, Brandon, Palm Beach | 9 | 17 | 14 | 0 | 2 | 2 | 0 | 0 | 0 | 1 | 0 | 0 | 1 | 2 | 0 | 9 | 0 | 0 | 1 | .143 | .294 | .143 |
| Martin, Russell, Vero Beach | 122 | 505 | 416 | 74 | 104 | 175 | 24 | 1 | 15 | 64 | 0 | 8 | 10 | 71 | 1 | 54 | 9 | 5 | 10 | .250 | .366 | .421 |
| Matienzo, Danny, Fort Myers | 123 | 513 | 455 | 51 | 139 | 183 | 27 | 1 | 5 | 65 | 2 | 8 | 5 | 43 | 7 | 88 | 1 | 0 | 17 | .305 | .366 | .402 |
| Mattle, David, Lakeland * | 101 | 373 | 335 | 44 | 81 | 113 | 16 | 2 | 4 | 37 | 5 | 0 | 2 | 31 | 3 | 72 | 1 | 1 | 7 | .242 | .310 | .337 |
| Mayorson, Manuel, Dunedin | 90 | 330 | 300 | 33 | 65 | 73 | 8 | 0 | 0 | 26 | 2 | 2 | 1 | 25 | 0 | 23 | 2 | 2 | 16 | .217 | .277 | .243 |
| McCoy, Mike, Palm Beach | 61 | 215 | 176 | 34 | 53 | 73 | 12 | 1 | 2 | 23 | 2 | 1 | 5 | 31 | 2 | 32 | 7 | 4 | 1 | .301 | .418 | .415 |
| McGehee, Casey, Daytona | 119 | 491 | 449 | 56 | 117 | 177 | 30 | 0 | 10 | 66 | 4 | 4 | 1 | 33 | 3 | 69 | 2 | 1 | 9 | .261 | .310 | .394 |
| McIntyre, Robert, St. Lucie | 88 | 295 | 274 | 33 | 57 | 76 | 10 | 0 | 3 | 21 | 3 | 1 | 5 | 12 | 0 | 70 | 5 | 7 | 6 | .208 | .253 | .277 |
| McKnight, Lukas, Daytona * | 40 | 116 | 101 | 10 | 24 | 31 | 4 | 0 | 1 | 12 | 1 | 2 | 2 | 10 | 0 | 20 | 0 | 0 | 4 | .238 | .313 | .307 |
| Mejia, Gilberto, Lakeland † | 96 | 399 | 354 | 50 | 94 | 138 | 13 | 5 | 7 | 31 | 5 | 4 | 1 | 35 | 2 | 76 | 16 | 10 | 5 | .266 | .330 | .390 |
| Mejia, Manuel, Tampa | 42 | 131 | 115 | 14 | 33 | 44 | 9 | 1 | 0 | 19 | 0 | 1 | 5 | 10 | 0 | 31 | 0 | 0 | 2 | .287 | .366 | .383 |
| Mendez, Victor, Lakeland † | 120 | 456 | 402 | 53 | 97 | 171 | 20 | 9 | 12 | 58 | 5 | 5 | 2 | 42 | 3 | 100 | 8 | 7 | 10 | .241 | .313 | .425 |
| Merchan, Jesus, Fort Myers | 79 | 274 | 247 | 23 | 71 | 85 | 10 | 2 | 0 | 21 | 6 | 2 | 5 | 14 | 0 | 18 | 5 | 1 | 5 | .287 | .336 | .344 |
| Merkle, Tom, Jupiter | 44 | 168 | 150 | 9 | 32 | 38 | 6 | 0 | 0 | 11 | 3 | 1 | 2 | 12 | 0 | 25 | 0 | 1 | 4 | .213 | .279 | .253 |
| Mitchell, Lee, Jupiter | 119 | 477 | 426 | 48 | 92 | 154 | 14 | 6 | 12 | 58 | 5 | 7 | 5 | 34 | 2 | 135 | 1 | 2 | 7 | .216 | .278 | .362 |
| Molina, Felix, Fort Myers † | 103 | 374 | 321 | 49 | 77 | 116 | 22 | 4 | 3 | 39 | 6 | 6 | 4 | 37 | 2 | 63 | 7 | 5 | 9 | .240 | .321 | .361 |
| Moore, Scott, Lakeland * | 118 | 453 | 391 | 52 | 87 | 150 | 13 | 4 | 14 | 56 | 0 | 3 | 10 | 49 | 1 | 125 | 2 | 4 | 10 | .223 | .322 | .384 |
| Morales, Jose, Fort Myers † | 91 | 366 | 332 | 30 | 95 | 128 | 13 | 4 | 4 | 46 | 0 | 5 | 0 | 29 | 3 | 78 | 0 | 1 | 5 | .286 | .339 | .386 |
| Moss, Brandon, Sarasota * | 23 | 91 | 83 | 16 | 35 | 45 | 2 | 1 | 2 | 10 | 0 | 1 | 0 | 7 | 2 | 15 | 2 | 0 | 2 | .422 | .462 | .542 |
| Motte, Jason, Palm Beach | 108 | 309 | 287 | 22 | 50 | 58 | 5 | 0 | 1 | 24 | 13 | 2 | 1 | 6 | 0 | 94 | 1 | 2 | 8 | .174 | .193 | .202 |
| Murton, Matt, Sarasota | 102 | 425 | 367 | 60 | 113 | 170 | 16 | 4 | 11 | 55 | 0 | 4 | 3 | 42 | 4 | 61 | 5 | 4 | 7 | .301 | .372 | .452 |
| Murton, Matt, Daytona | 24 | 89 | 79 | 13 | 20 | 29 | 1 | 1 | 2 | 8 | 0 | 1 | 1 | 8 | 1 | 10 | 2 | 0 | 3 | .253 | .326 | .367 |
| Negron, Miguel, Dunedin * | 99 | 418 | 372 | 46 | 100 | 153 | 16 | 5 | 9 | 48 | 1 | 3 | 4 | 38 | 5 | 81 | 3 | 1 | 6 | .269 | .341 | .411 |
| Oeltjen, Trent, Fort Myers * | 90 | 360 | 324 | 45 | 90 | 114 | 8 | 5 | 2 | 28 | 4 | 2 | 12 | 18 | 2 | 61 | 25 | 8 | 6 | .278 | .337 | .352 |
| Ontiveros, Jeff, Sarasota | 33 | 109 | 84 | 17 | 17 | 36 | 4 | 0 | 5 | 18 | 0 | 2 | 1 | 22 | 0 | 24 | 2 | 0 | 0 | .202 | .367 | .429 |
| Ordorica, Eric, Jupiter | 56 | 189 | 171 | 18 | 44 | 60 | 10 | 0 | 2 | 21 | 2 | 2 | 0 | 14 | 0 | 38 | 3 | 0 | 5 | .257 | .310 | .351 |
| Parker, Rashad, St. Lucie | 12 | 38 | 34 | 3 | 10 | 13 | 3 | 0 | 0 | 2 | 0 | 0 | 1 | 3 | 0 | 9 | 1 | 0 | 1 | .294 | .368 | .382 |
| Parker, Tyler, Palm Beach | 2 | 9 | 9 | 1 | 1 | 1 | 0 | 0 | 0 | 2 | 0 | 0 | 0 | 0 | 0 | 4 | 0 | 0 | 0 | .111 | .111 | .111 |
| Pattee, Ben, Fort Myers | 48 | 172 | 149 | 16 | 35 | 40 | 3 | 1 | 0 | 17 | 4 | 0 | 1 | 18 | 0 | 21 | 0 | 1 | 3 | .235 | .321 | .268 |
| Pedroia, Dustin, Sarasota | 30 | 128 | 107 | 23 | 36 | 56 | 8 | 3 | 2 | 14 | 1 | 3 | 4 | 13 | 0 | 4 | 0 | 2 | 3 | .336 | .417 | .523 |
| Pena, Omar, Palm Beach | 2 | 9 | 7 | 2 | 2 | 3 | 1 | 0 | 0 | 0 | 1 | 0 | 0 | 1 | 0 | 1 | 0 | 0 | 0 | .286 | .375 | .429 |
| Perodin, Ron, Fort Myers * | 99 | 361 | 327 | 43 | 86 | 92 | 2 | 2 | 0 | 20 | 10 | 0 | 4 | 20 | 0 | 47 | 24 | 7 | 6 | .263 | .313 | .281 |
| Pie, Felix, Daytona * | 110 | 487 | 431 | 79 | 128 | 190 | 18 | 10 | 8 | 47 | 7 | 5 | 5 | 39 | 2 | 116 | 32 | 18 | 5 | .297 | .358 | .441 |
| Pratt, Trent, Clearwater | 93 | 344 | 308 | 24 | 60 | 81 | 7 | 1 | 4 | 26 | 5 | 1 | 4 | 26 | 1 | 77 | 0 | 2 | 12 | .195 | .265 | .263 |
| Quintana, Miguel, Clearwater * | 69 | 257 | 235 | 29 | 64 | 105 | 10 | 2 | 9 | 32 | 1 | 3 | 1 | 17 | 4 | 50 | 3 | 3 | 6 | .272 | .320 | .447 |
| Rabelo, Mike, Lakeland † | 92 | 362 | 327 | 36 | 94 | 118 | 20 | 2 | 0 | 38 | 1 | 2 | 7 | 25 | 1 | 56 | 3 | 2 | 9 | .287 | .349 | .361 |
| Ragsdale, Corey, St. Lucie | 124 | — | 421 | 65 | 92 | 142 | 19 | 5 | 7 | 38 | 11 | 4 | 11 | 42 | 1 | 152 | 24 | 14 | 7 | .219 | .339 | .433 |
| Requena, Alex, Vero Beach † | 111 | 472 | 413 | 64 | 101 | 124 | 7 | 5 | 2 | 23 | 7 | 5 | 3 | 44 | 0 | 103 | 50 | 15 | 3 | .245 | .318 | .300 |
| Reyes, Jose, Daytona † | 80 | 283 | 261 | 27 | 59 | 79 | 12 | 1 | 2 | 17 | 4 | 0 | 5 | 13 | 0 | 54 | 1 | 4 | 6 | .226 | .276 | .303 |
| Roberson, Chris, Clearwater | 83 | 345 | 313 | 52 | 96 | 148 | 13 | 6 | 9 | 38 | 0 | 0 | 5 | 27 | 0 | 71 | 16 | 12 | 5 | .307 | .371 | .473 |
| Roberts, Ryan, Dunedin | 59 | 246 | 205 | 29 | 49 | 73 | 1 | 1 | 7 | 25 | 0 | 4 | 1 | 36 | 2 | 51 | 0 | 3 | 8 | .239 | .350 | .356 |
| Rodriguez, Andres, St. Lucie | 53 | 168 | 155 | 16 | 39 | 58 | 6 | 2 | 3 | 16 | 1 | 2 | 2 | 8 | 1 | 44 | 1 | 2 | 7 | .252 | .293 | .374 |

| Player, Team | G | TPA | AB | R | H | TB | 2B | 3B | HR | RBI | SH | SF | HP | BB | IBB | SO | SB | CS | GDP | Avg. | OBP | Slg. |
|---|---|---|---|---|---|---|---|---|---|---|---|---|---|---|---|---|---|---|---|---|---|---|
| Rombley, Danny, Brevard County | 61 | 236 | 205 | 22 | 48 | 58 | 6 | 2 | 0 | 12 | 4 | 1 | 2 | 24 | 1 | 51 | 4 | 4 | 2 | .234 | .319 | .283 |
| Romero, Alex, Fort Myers † | 105 | 447 | 380 | 59 | 111 | 154 | 21 | 2 | 6 | 42 | 5 | 2 | 6 | 54 | 3 | 47 | 6 | 4 | 4 | .292 | .387 | .405 |
| Rooi, Vince, Brevard County | 65 | 239 | 210 | 20 | 42 | 64 | 4 | 0 | 6 | 19 | 0 | 0 | 5 | 24 | 1 | 50 | 3 | 0 | 3 | .200 | .297 | .305 |
| Roper, Zach, Clearwater | 19 | 63 | 58 | 4 | 7 | 9 | 0 | 1 | 0 | 0 | 1 | 0 | 0 | 4 | 0 | 14 | 0 | 0 | 5 | .121 | .177 | .155 |
| Rosenthal, Ben, Palm Beach * | 52 | 120 | 105 | 11 | 27 | 40 | 4 | 0 | 3 | 17 | 1 | 1 | 0 | 13 | 1 | 23 | 1 | 2 | 3 | .257 | .336 | .381 |
| Roughton, Jody, Lakeland * | 100 | 374 | 343 | 43 | 93 | 137 | 21 | 4 | 5 | 44 | 0 | 2 | 4 | 25 | 2 | 73 | 2 | 5 | 4 | .271 | .326 | .399 |
| Salas, Francisco, Daytona | 65 | 242 | 216 | 32 | 49 | 79 | 13 | 1 | 5 | 24 | 3 | 4 | 2 | 17 | 0 | 33 | 3 | 0 | 6 | .227 | .285 | .366 |
| Santana, Ralph, Clearwater * | 87 | 345 | 315 | 43 | 91 | 106 | 13 | 1 | 0 | 15 | 1 | 3 | 2 | 24 | 2 | 44 | 11 | 14 | 3 | .289 | .340 | .337 |
| Santor, John, Palm Beach † | 41 | 139 | 124 | 16 | 26 | 46 | 6 | 1 | 4 | 21 | 0 | 4 | 2 | 9 | 1 | 43 | 0 | 1 | 2 | .210 | .266 | .371 |
| Santora, Jack, Clearwater † | 105 | 379 | 322 | 27 | 77 | 103 | 16 | 2 | 2 | 28 | 11 | 0 | 2 | 44 | 0 | 51 | 7 | 9 | 2 | .239 | .334 | .320 |
| Santos, Pito, Tampa | 37 | 130 | 119 | 18 | 34 | 48 | 6 | 1 | 2 | 13 | 1 | 0 | 4 | 6 | 0 | 17 | 1 | 0 | 5 | .286 | .341 | .403 |
| Schneider, John, Dunedin | 58 | 217 | 170 | 26 | 35 | 61 | 8 | 0 | 6 | 28 | 0 | 1 | 5 | 41 | 0 | 69 | 0 | 0 | 3 | .206 | .373 | .359 |
| Schutzenhofer, Andy, Palm Beach * | 121 | 445 | 373 | 65 | 109 | 137 | 15 | 2 | 3 | 56 | 2 | 8 | 11 | 51 | 4 | 36 | 3 | 2 | 10 | .292 | .386 | .367 |
| Seuss, Adam, St. Lucie * | 2 | 8 | 7 | 1 | 1 | 1 | 0 | 0 | 0 | 0 | 0 | 0 | 1 | 0 | 0 | 2 | 0 | 0 | 0 | .143 | .250 | .143 |
| Sierra, Edwardo, Tampa | 45 | 1 | 1 | 0 | 0 | 0 | 0 | 0 | 0 | 0 | 0 | 0 | 0 | 0 | 0 | 1 | 0 | 0 | 0 | .000 | .000 | .000 |
| Sing, Brandon, Daytona | 122 | 504 | 408 | 86 | 110 | 233 | 27 | 0 | 32 | 94 | 0 | 5 | 7 | 84 | 9 | 101 | 1 | 3 | 13 | .270 | .399 | .571 |
| Sitzman, Jay, Sarasota * | 92 | 355 | 304 | 45 | 82 | 110 | 12 | 2 | 4 | 31 | 3 | 3 | 3 | 42 | 0 | 66 | 10 | 2 | 3 | .270 | .361 | .362 |
| Spearman, Jemel, Daytona | 12 | 54 | 45 | 12 | 13 | 13 | 0 | 0 | 0 | 7 | 0 | 1 | 3 | 5 | 0 | 7 | 4 | 1 | 1 | .289 | .389 | .289 |
| Sprout, Brian, Vero Beach | 89 | 355 | 305 | 49 | 86 | 141 | 15 | 2 | 12 | 45 | 0 | 1 | 12 | 37 | 1 | 57 | 5 | 5 | 9 | .282 | .380 | .462 |
| Sprowl, Jon-Mark, Tampa * | 66 | 269 | 219 | 30 | 56 | 71 | 10 | 1 | 1 | 29 | 1 | 3 | 5 | 41 | 2 | 24 | 0 | 3 | 6 | .256 | .381 | .324 |
| Stotts, J.T., Tampa | 36 | 128 | 116 | 14 | 27 | 33 | 4 | 1 | 0 | 11 | 0 | 2 | 1 | 9 | 0 | 23 | 0 | 0 | 4 | .233 | .289 | .284 |
| Suarez, Iggy, Sarasota | 82 | 344 | 307 | 42 | 79 | 98 | 10 | 3 | 1 | 23 | 3 | 0 | 3 | 31 | 2 | 51 | 12 | 4 | 6 | .257 | .331 | .319 |
| Tablado, Raul, Dunedin | 84 | 356 | 323 | 62 | 97 | 188 | 28 | 0 | 21 | 76 | 0 | 5 | 4 | 24 | 4 | 91 | 0 | 0 | 10 | .300 | .351 | .582 |
| Tamburrino, Brett, Fort Myers † | 77 | 285 | 247 | 28 | 67 | 77 | 8 | 1 | 0 | 18 | 5 | 2 | 3 | 28 | 0 | 47 | 13 | 6 | 6 | .271 | .350 | .312 |
| Tempesta, Nick, Clearwater | 98 | 355 | 317 | 26 | 73 | 90 | 17 | 0 | 0 | 22 | 10 | 2 | 10 | 16 | 1 | 57 | 1 | 3 | 7 | .230 | .287 | .284 |
| Theriot, Ryan, Daytona † | 103 | 390 | 330 | 47 | 90 | 113 | 14 | 3 | 1 | 34 | 6 | 3 | 3 | 48 | 0 | 43 | 13 | 11 | 4 | .273 | .367 | .342 |
| Thissen, Greg, Brevard County | 82 | 301 | 267 | 28 | 60 | 100 | 17 | 1 | 7 | 32 | 6 | 0 | 2 | 26 | 0 | 70 | 7 | 1 | 4 | .225 | .298 | .375 |
| Tingler, Jayce, Dunedin * | 118 | 547 | 447 | 77 | 112 | 134 | 15 | 2 | 1 | 36 | 6 | 4 | 16 | 74 | 0 | 25 | 3 | 5 | 11 | .251 | .373 | .300 |
| Trezza, Alex, Lakeland * | 27 | 78 | 66 | 7 | 15 | 22 | 3 | 2 | 0 | 11 | 1 | 0 | 1 | 10 | 0 | 20 | 0 | 1 | 0 | .227 | .338 | .333 |
| Tucker, Michael, Jupiter | 54 | 197 | 173 | 20 | 39 | 64 | 14 | 1 | 3 | 27 | 1 | 1 | 3 | 19 | 2 | 42 | 1 | 1 | 4 | .225 | .311 | .370 |
| Turay, Alhaji, St. Lucie | 86 | 336 | 308 | 35 | 79 | 139 | 12 | 0 | 16 | 44 | 1 | 1 | 4 | 22 | 2 | 81 | 11 | 6 | 10 | .256 | .313 | .451 |
| Turner, Justin, Sarasota * | 9 | 34 | 31 | 2 | 4 | 4 | 0 | 0 | 0 | 1 | 0 | 1 | 0 | 2 | 0 | 8 | 0 | 0 | 1 | .129 | .176 | .129 |
| Tuttle, Jason, Brevard County * | 92 | 324 | 279 | 41 | 76 | 84 | 6 | 1 | 0 | 14 | 11 | 1 | 3 | 30 | 0 | 25 | 13 | 8 | 3 | .272 | .348 | .301 |
| Van Buizen, Rodney, Vero Beach | 47 | 173 | 154 | 12 | 25 | 27 | 2 | 0 | 0 | 15 | 4 | 0 | 5 | 10 | 0 | 33 | 4 | 2 | 3 | .162 | .237 | .175 |
| Verbryke, Eric, Tampa * | 101 | 388 | 340 | 57 | 85 | 125 | 19 | 3 | 5 | 34 | 0 | 1 | 9 | 36 | 1 | 69 | 11 | 2 | 5 | .250 | .337 | .368 |
| Vukovich, Vince, Clearwater * | 63 | 213 | 186 | 17 | 31 | 45 | 12 | 1 | 0 | 21 | 1 | 2 | 1 | 23 | 2 | 36 | 0 | 2 | 4 | .167 | .259 | .242 |
| Waugh, Jason, Dunedin | 86 | 345 | 317 | 42 | 79 | 98 | 16 | 0 | 1 | 33 | 1 | 2 | 3 | 22 | 2 | 59 | 2 | 2 | 10 | .249 | .302 | .309 |
| West, Jeremy, Sarasota | 124 | 507 | 461 | 60 | 135 | 225 | 28 | 4 | 18 | 68 | 0 | 5 | 4 | 37 | 1 | 83 | 0 | 3 | 21 | .293 | .347 | .488 |
| Williams, Clyde, Brevard County * | 106 | 392 | 357 | 39 | 85 | 149 | 14 | 7 | 12 | 40 | 3 | 5 | 2 | 25 | 3 | 87 | 4 | 1 | 8 | .238 | .288 | .417 |
| Wilson, Brandon, St. Lucie | 29 | 98 | 93 | 4 | 13 | 21 | 8 | 0 | 0 | 6 | 1 | 0 | 0 | 4 | 0 | 38 | 1 | 1 | 1 | .140 | .175 | .226 |
| Winrow, Tommy, Tampa * | 93 | 370 | 339 | 56 | 112 | 148 | 20 | 2 | 4 | 41 | 1 | 2 | 2 | 26 | 4 | 55 | 1 | 5 | 6 | .330 | .379 | .437 |
| Woods, Michael, Lakeland | 67 | 294 | 270 | 45 | 76 | 106 | 16 | 4 | 2 | 23 | 0 | 2 | 2 | 20 | 0 | 52 | 9 | 3 | 2 | .281 | .333 | .393 |
| Wyman, Spencer, Jupiter * | 4 | 11 | 11 | 0 | 0 | 0 | 0 | 0 | 0 | 1 | 0 | 0 | 0 | 0 | 0 | 4 | 0 | 0 | 0 | .000 | .000 | .000 |
| Yepez, Jose, Dunedin | 62 | 237 | 213 | 26 | 41 | 64 | 11 | 0 | 4 | 22 | 0 | 3 | 5 | 16 | 0 | 36 | 0 | 0 | 7 | .192 | .262 | .300 |
| Young, Delwyn, Vero Beach † | 129 | 540 | 470 | 76 | 132 | 240 | 36 | 3 | 22 | 85 | 2 | 4 | 7 | 57 | 8 | 134 | 11 | 4 | 13 | .281 | .364 | .511 |

GRAND SLAMS—Koutnik, 3; F. Diaz, Thissen, 2 each; Barthelemy, Buckley, Cabrera, Carroll, Catalanotte, Clark, Chiaravalloti, Chop, Duncan, Frome, Gradoville, Hanson, Hermida, Laroche, Lopez, Murphy, H. Ramirez, Roughton, Santor, Sing, Tablado, West, 1 each.

AWARDED FIRST BASE ON CATCHER'S INTERFERENCE—Greenberg 4 (D. Brown, Yepez, Motte, Corporan); Bass (Margalski); F. Diaz (Morales); Verbryke (Pratt); Waugh (Gradoville).

# 2004 PITCHING

## TEAM

| Team | W | L | Pct. | ERA | G | CG | ShO | Sv. | IP | H | TBF | R | ER | HR | SH | SF | HB | BB | IBB | SO | WP | Bk. |
|---|---|---|---|---|---|---|---|---|---|---|---|---|---|---|---|---|---|---|---|---|---|---|
| Jupiter | 64 | 71 | .474 | 3.41 | 135 | 5 | 15 | 30 | 1178.1 | 1148 | 5047 | 559 | 447 | 51 | 43 | 56 | 59 | 417 | 26 | 920 | 87 | 4 |
| Vero Beach | 78 | 57 | .578 | 3.51 | 135 | 3 | 12 | 38 | 1173.0 | 1079 | 5004 | 535 | 457 | 79 | 41 | 30 | 49 | 446 | 10 | 1075 | 91 | 6 |
| Tampa | 75 | 58 | .564 | 3.51 | 133 | 8 | 12 | 43 | 1136.0 | 1025 | 4864 | 536 | 443 | 69 | 32 | 32 | 56 | 469 | 19 | 954 | 73 | 5 |
| St. Lucie | 64 | 65 | .496 | 3.70 | 129 | 6 | 4 | 28 | 1137.0 | 1104 | 4856 | 550 | 467 | 62 | 50 | 47 | 67 | 393 | 26 | 898 | 77 | 5 |
| Sarasota | 75 | 61 | .551 | 3.81 | 136 | 4 | 3 | 40 | 1169.0 | 1136 | 5042 | 585 | 495 | 76 | 51 | 34 | 58 | 444 | 31 | 942 | 62 | 4 |
| Palm Beach | 73 | 61 | .545 | 3.85 | 134 | 5 | 11 | 33 | 1156.1 | 1107 | 4930 | 566 | 495 | 80 | 41 | 53 | 64 | 431 | 28 | 767 | 112 | 5 |
| Clearwater | 55 | 81 | .404 | 3.88 | 136 | 9 | 11 | 22 | 1167.2 | 1196 | 5042 | 607 | 504 | 111 | 39 | 39 | 59 | 419 | 37 | 840 | 68 | 6 |
| Fort Myers | 61 | 74 | .452 | 3.90 | 135 | 3 | 11 | 29 | 1141.1 | 1121 | 4975 | 624 | 494 | 78 | 41 | 43 | 52 | 475 | 34 | 969 | 82 | 7 |
| Daytona | 70 | 56 | .556 | 3.90 | 126 | 5 | 10 | 31 | 1084.1 | 1054 | 4692 | 568 | 470 | 93 | 44 | 30 | 73 | 411 | 13 | 956 | 76 | 7 |
| Dunedin | 76 | 57 | .571 | 3.97 | 133 | 0 | 7 | 35 | 1157.1 | 1175 | 4965 | 582 | 510 | 91 | 43 | 31 | 53 | 363 | 16 | 940 | 70 | 4 |
| Brevard County | 53 | 72 | .424 | 4.08 | 125 | 0 | 7 | 28 | 1077.1 | 1016 | 4690 | 579 | 488 | 73 | 44 | 30 | 71 | 498 | 16 | 861 | 79 | 12 |
| Lakeland | 51 | 81 | .386 | 4.54 | 132 | 9 | 9 | 23 | 1097.1 | 1152 | 4776 | 624 | 553 | 88 | 27 | 43 | 54 | 414 | 6 | 754 | 78 | 6 |

## INDIVIDUAL

### TOP QUALIFIERS FOR EARNED-RUN AVERAGE TITLE

Minimum 112 innings. *Lefthanded pitcher.

| Pitcher, Team | W | L | Pct. | ERA | G | GS | CG | ShO | GF | Sv. | IP | H | TBF | R | ER | HR | SH | SF | HB | BB | IBB | SO | WP | Bk. |
|---|---|---|---|---|---|---|---|---|---|---|---|---|---|---|---|---|---|---|---|---|---|---|---|---|
| Connolly, Jon, Lakeland-Daytona * | 11 | 7 | .611 | 2.59 | 25 | 25 | 3 | 2 | 0 | 0 | 153.0 | 151 | 626 | 59 | 44 | 10 | 6 | 6 | 8 | 29 | 0 | 109 | 6 | 0 |
| Papelbon, Jon, Sarasota | 12 | 7 | .632 | 2.64 | 24 | 24 | 2 | 0 | 0 | 0 | 129.2 | 97 | 520 | 43 | 38 | 6 | 6 | 3 | 7 | 43 | 2 | 153 | 3 | 0 |
| Ramirez, Ismael, Dunedin | 15 | 6 | .714 | 2.72 | 28 | 27 | 0 | 0 | 0 | 0 | 165.1 | 151 | 663 | 57 | 50 | 5 | 6 | 7 | 7 | 25 | 0 | 131 | 7 | 0 |
| Kensing, Logan, Jupiter | 6 | 7 | .462 | 2.96 | 23 | 23 | 1 | 0 | 0 | 0 | 127.2 | 120 | 525 | 53 | 42 | 5 | 7 | 8 | 8 | 35 | 1 | 100 | 8 | 1 |
| Olsen, Scott, Jupiter * | 7 | 6 | .538 | 2.97 | 25 | 25 | 1 | 1 | 0 | 0 | 136.1 | 127 | 571 | 57 | 45 | 8 | 5 | 5 | 4 | 53 | 0 | 158 | 7 | 0 |
| Rasner, Darrell, Brevard County | 6 | 5 | .545 | 3.17 | 22 | 21 | 0 | 0 | 0 | 0 | 119.1 | 133 | 504 | 55 | 42 | 6 | 10 | 4 | 8 | 31 | 0 | 88 | 1 | 0 |

| Pitcher, Team | W | L | Pct. | ERA | G | GS | CG | ShO | GF | Sv. | IP | H | TBF | R | ER | HR | SH | SF | HB | BB | IBB | SO | WP | Bk. |
|---|---|---|---|---|---|---|---|---|---|---|---|---|---|---|---|---|---|---|---|---|---|---|---|---|
| Broxton, Jonathan, Vero Beach | 11 | 6 | .647 | 3.23 | 23 | 23 | 1 | 1 | 0 | 0 | 128.1 | 110 | 523 | 49 | 46 | 7 | 7 | 4 | 4 | 43 | 0 | 144 | 6 | 0 |
| Simon, Alfredo, Clearwater | 7 | 9 | .438 | 3.27 | 22 | 21 | 4 | 3 | 0 | 0 | 134.2 | 121 | 552 | 58 | 49 | 13 | 8 | 2 | 5 | 38 | 2 | 107 | 10 | 4 |
| Bazardo, Yorman, Jupiter | 5 | 9 | .357 | 3.27 | 25 | 25 | 2 | 2 | 0 | 0 | 154.1 | 161 | 649 | 78 | 56 | 3 | 9 | 13 | 10 | 30 | 0 | 95 | 9 | 1 |
| Johnson, Josh, Jupiter | 5 | 12 | .294 | 3.46 | 23 | 22 | 1 | 0 | 0 | 0 | 114.1 | 124 | 501 | 63 | 44 | 4 | 4 | 12 | 2 | 48 | 1 | 103 | 13 | 0 |
| Mendoza, Luis, Sarasota | 8 | 7 | .533 | 3.74 | 25 | 25 | 1 | 0 | 0 | 0 | 137.0 | 133 | 596 | 76 | 57 | 12 | 6 | 8 | 6 | 54 | 5 | 51 | 10 | 0 |
| Gwaltney, Lee, Clearwater | 3 | 10 | .231 | 3.80 | 20 | 20 | 1 | 0 | 0 | 0 | 116.0 | 122 | 485 | 54 | 49 | 7 | 8 | 6 | 7 | 39 | 1 | 81 | 6 | 0 |
| Skaggs, Jon, Tampa | 13 | 9 | .591 | 3.87 | 27 | 27 | 2 | 0 | 0 | 0 | 162.2 | 141 | 696 | 84 | 70 | 11 | 6 | 6 | 13 | 70 | 0 | 116 | 10 | 0 |
| Teekel, Josh, Palm Beach | 9 | 6 | .600 | 3.93 | 26 | 25 | 0 | 0 | 0 | 0 | 142.0 | 134 | 599 | 67 | 62 | 7 | 8 | 14 | 12 | 57 | 1 | 96 | 12 | 1 |

DEPARTMENTAL LEADERS: W—I. Ramirez, 15; L—J. Johnson, Randazzo, 12; Pct.—I. Ramirez, .714; G—Wallace, 54; GS—Skaggs, I. Ramirez, 27; CG—Simon, 4; ShO—Simon, 3; GF—Buzachero, 45; Sv.—Sierra, 28; IP—I. Ramirez, 165.1; H—Blair, 178; TBF—Skaggs, 696; R—Randazzo, 96; ER—Blair, 79; HR—Howell, 20; SH—Cherry, 8; SF—Bazardo, 13; HB—Hill, 19; BB—Hill, 72; IBB—Gray, Mayfield, 7; SO—Olsen, 158; WP—Adamczyk, 26; BK—Hill, 5.

## ALL PITCHERS

*Lefthanded pitcher.

| Pitcher, Team | W | L | Pct. | ERA | G | GS | CG | ShO | GF | Sv. | IP | H | TBF | R | ER | HR | SH | SF | HB | BB | IBB | SO | WP | Bk. |
|---|---|---|---|---|---|---|---|---|---|---|---|---|---|---|---|---|---|---|---|---|---|---|---|---|
| Abreu, Eric, Tampa | 2 | 0 | 1.000 | 1.06 | 3 | 3 | 1 | 1 | 0 | 0 | 17.0 | 7 | 63 | 2 | 2 | 1 | 1 | 0 | 0 | 6 | 0 | 15 | 1 | 0 |
| Acosta, Anthony, St. Lucie | 0 | 0 | .000 | 1.42 | 4 | 0 | 0 | 0 | 1 | 0 | 6.1 | 5 | 25 | 2 | 1 | 0 | 0 | 0 | 0 | 1 | 0 | 8 | 0 | 0 |
| Adamczyk, Tyler, Palm Beach | 5 | 10 | .333 | 5.00 | 26 | 25 | 3 | 0 | 0 | 0 | 136.2 | 143 | 609 | 85 | 76 | 12 | 5 | 9 | 14 | 71 | 0 | 81 | 26 | 0 |
| Artiles, Carlos, Tampa * | 3 | 2 | .600 | 4.22 | 13 | 0 | 0 | 0 | 6 | 0 | 21.1 | 17 | 96 | 10 | 10 | 0 | 0 | 0 | 1 | 13 | 0 | 13 | 1 | 0 |
| Atlee, Thomas, Daytona | 3 | 3 | .500 | 3.86 | 47 | 0 | 0 | 0 | 34 | 15 | 51.1 | 54 | 227 | 28 | 22 | 3 | 0 | 0 | 0 | 20 | 3 | 39 | 2 | 0 |
| Baez, Federico, Daytona | 8 | 2 | .800 | 3.55 | 48 | 0 | 0 | 0 | 20 | 1 | 71.0 | 67 | 308 | 37 | 28 | 6 | 2 | 0 | 3 | 26 | 1 | 54 | 9 | 0 |
| Baldwin, Andy, Lakeland | 1 | 3 | .250 | 6.75 | 10 | 6 | 0 | 0 | 1 | 0 | 34.2 | 53 | 170 | 29 | 26 | 2 | 1 | 1 | 6 | 15 | 0 | 25 | 6 | 0 |
| Barlow, Chris, Brevard County | 4 | 9 | .308 | 4.27 | 27 | 17 | 0 | 0 | 6 | 4 | 111.2 | 109 | 456 | 56 | 53 | 9 | 7 | 7 | 7 | 24 | 0 | 48 | 6 | 1 |
| Barrett, Ricky, Fort Myers * | 5 | 1 | .833 | 3.43 | 17 | 4 | 0 | 0 | 3 | 0 | 39.1 | 29 | 170 | 20 | 15 | 0 | 1 | 1 | 1 | 25 | 2 | 43 | 2 | 0 |
| Bartlett, Richard, Vero Beach | 4 | 3 | .571 | 2.23 | 40 | 0 | 0 | 0 | 22 | 7 | 68.2 | 57 | 294 | 23 | 17 | 3 | 0 | 2 | 2 | 29 | 1 | 57 | 9 | 0 |
| Batista, Roberto, Palm Beach | 4 | 5 | .444 | 4.40 | 54 | 0 | 0 | 0 | 21 | 1 | 61.1 | 68 | 278 | 38 | 30 | 2 | 2 | 0 | 5 | 22 | 6 | 36 | 7 | 1 |
| Bazardo, Yorman, Jupiter | 5 | 9 | .357 | 3.27 | 25 | 25 | 2 | 2 | 0 | 0 | 154.1 | 161 | 649 | 78 | 56 | 3 | 9 | 13 | 10 | 30 | 0 | 95 | 9 | 1 |
| Bechtel, Charles, Lakeland | 0 | 0 | .000 | 0.00 | 3 | 0 | 0 | 0 | 3 | 0 | 4.0 | 4 | 16 | 1 | 0 | 0 | 0 | 0 | 0 | 0 | 0 | 0 | 1 | 0 |
| Belizario, Ronald, Jupiter | 1 | 1 | .500 | 0.00 | 6 | 0 | 0 | 0 | 1 | 1 | 8.2 | 2 | 34 | 1 | 0 | 0 | 0 | 0 | 1 | 5 | 0 | 7 | 0 | 0 |
| Bierd, Randor, Lakeland | 0 | 2 | .000 | 5.65 | 3 | 3 | 0 | 0 | 0 | 0 | 14.1 | 13 | 59 | 10 | 9 | 1 | 0 | 1 | 1 | 6 | 0 | 14 | 1 | 1 |
| Blackburn, Nick, Fort Myers | 3 | 3 | .500 | 6.27 | 9 | 7 | 0 | 0 | 0 | 0 | 37.1 | 51 | 171 | 30 | 26 | 7 | 4 | 2 | 2 | 7 | 1 | 21 | 1 | 0 |
| Blair, Tom, Palm Beach * | 11 | 10 | .524 | 4.40 | 26 | 26 | 1 | 0 | 0 | 0 | 161.2 | 178 | 675 | 85 | 79 | 10 | — | — | 4 | 178 | 0 | 101 | 9 | — |
| Borrell, Danny, Tampa * | 0 | 1 | .000 | 9.00 | 2 | 2 | 0 | 0 | 0 | 0 | 6.0 | 7 | 28 | 6 | 6 | 3 | 0 | 0 | 0 | 3 | 0 | 6 | 0 | 0 |
| Bourgeois, Nick, Clearwater * | 5 | 11 | .313 | 4.94 | 26 | 21 | 0 | 0 | 2 | 0 | 120.1 | 122 | 544 | 79 | 66 | 14 | 10 | 8 | 9 | 68 | 3 | 97 | 16 | 0 |
| Bray, William, Brevard County * | 0 | 2 | .000 | 4.91 | 6 | 0 | 0 | 0 | 4 | 1 | 7.1 | 9 | 32 | 5 | 4 | 0 | 0 | 0 | 0 | 1 | 0 | 6 | 0 | 0 |
| Brooks, Conor, Sarasota | 0 | 2 | .000 | 2.77 | 8 | 0 | 0 | 0 | 2 | 1 | 13.0 | 7 | 49 | 4 | 4 | 2 | 0 | 0 | 0 | 3 | 0 | 19 | 0 | 0 |
| Broxton, Jonathan, Vero Beach | 11 | 6 | .647 | 3.23 | 23 | 23 | 1 | 1 | 0 | 0 | 128.1 | 110 | 523 | 49 | 46 | 7 | 7 | 4 | 4 | 43 | 0 | 144 | 6 | 0 |
| Butto, Francisco, Clearwater | 5 | 11 | .313 | 4.85 | 36 | 14 | 0 | 0 | 17 | 2 | 111.1 | 112 | 483 | 71 | 60 | 15 | 2 | 4 | 3 | 47 | 4 | 94 | 9 | 0 |
| Buzachero, Bubbie, Dunedin | 2 | 2 | .500 | 2.55 | 51 | 0 | 0 | 0 | 45 | 25 | 60.0 | 53 | 255 | 19 | 17 | 3 | 1 | 0 | 2 | 20 | 0 | 59 | 7 | 1 |
| Byers, Waylon, Jupiter * | 0 | 0 | .000 | 5.68 | 5 | 0 | 0 | 0 | 0 | 0 | 6.1 | 8 | 31 | 4 | 4 | 0 | 0 | 0 | 0 | 4 | 1 | 6 | 1 | 1 |
| Campbell, Jarrett, Jupiter | 2 | 1 | .667 | 4.03 | 21 | 0 | 0 | 0 | 5 | 0 | 38.0 | 37 | 164 | 20 | 17 | 1 | 0 | 0 | 3 | 10 | 0 | 17 | 5 | 0 |
| Carlsen, Clary, Clearwater | 0 | 1 | .000 | 5.06 | 3 | 0 | 0 | 0 | 1 | 0 | 5.1 | 8 | 26 | 7 | 3 | 0 | 0 | 0 | 0 | 2 | 0 | 3 | 0 | 0 |
| Cave, Kevin, Jupiter | 2 | 1 | .667 | 3.00 | 19 | 0 | 0 | 0 | 7 | 2 | 24.0 | 21 | 106 | 9 | 8 | 1 | 0 | 0 | 0 | 13 | 4 | 19 | 4 | 0 |
| Cedeno, Juan, Sarasota * | 7 | 6 | .538 | 4.64 | 25 | 22 | 1 | 0 | 0 | 0 | 120.1 | 145 | 534 | 70 | 62 | 8 | 14 | 5 | 5 | 40 | 3 | 78 | 2 | 0 |
| Cerrato, Justin, Clearwater | 1 | 0 | 1.000 | 2.45 | 2 | 0 | 0 | 0 | 1 | 0 | 3.2 | 4 | 16 | 1 | 1 | 1 | 0 | 0 | 0 | 1 | 0 | 4 | 0 | 0 |
| Cherry, Rocky, Daytona | 5 | 10 | .333 | 5.20 | 27 | 22 | 1 | 1 | 0 | 0 | 124.2 | 138 | 557 | 79 | 72 | 16 | 11 | 8 | 9 | 46 | 1 | 104 | 4 | 0 |
| Ciprian, Wilson, Palm Beach | 5 | 4 | .556 | 2.61 | 38 | 0 | 0 | 0 | 28 | 11 | 48.1 | 47 | 205 | 17 | 14 | 4 | 0 | 0 | 3 | 10 | 1 | 31 | 1 | 0 |
| Connolly, Jon, Lakeland-Daytona * | 11 | 7 | .611 | 2.59 | 25 | 25 | 3 | 2 | 0 | 0 | 153.0 | 151 | 626 | 59 | 44 | 10 | 6 | 6 | 8 | 29 | 0 | 109 | 6 | 0 |
| Contreras, Jean, Fort Myers * | 0 | 0 | .000 | 6.00 | 3 | 0 | 0 | 0 | 2 | 0 | 3.0 | 7 | 17 | 3 | 2 | 0 | 0 | 0 | 1 | 0 | 0 | 1 | 0 | 0 |
| Corporan, Willy, Sarasota | 2 | 2 | .500 | 3.53 | 14 | 0 | 0 | 0 | 5 | 0 | 35.2 | 28 | 144 | 15 | 14 | 4 | 3 | 0 | 2 | 10 | 2 | 25 | 1 | 1 |
| Cotton, Nathan, Palm Beach | 0 | 0 | .000 | 0.00 | 1 | 0 | 0 | 0 | 0 | 0 | 1.0 | 0 | 3 | 0 | 0 | 0 | 0 | 0 | 0 | 0 | 0 | 1 | 0 | 0 |
| Dannemiller, Beau, Vero Beach | 2 | 4 | .333 | 2.93 | 36 | 0 | 0 | 0 | 15 | 7 | 73.2 | 47 | 306 | 25 | 24 | 4 | 0 | 0 | 5 | 32 | 3 | 71 | 6 | 0 |
| Davis, Allen, Clearwater * | 1 | 0 | 1.000 | 0.00 | 3 | 1 | 1 | 1 | 0 | 0 | 10.2 | 8 | 41 | 0 | 0 | 0 | 0 | 0 | 0 | 1 | 0 | 10 | 0 | 0 |
| Davis, Stockton, Brevard County | 1 | 7 | .125 | 4.97 | 28 | 0 | 0 | 0 | 10 | 2 | 50.2 | 57 | 245 | 36 | 28 | 2 | 0 | 0 | 5 | 33 | 5 | 33 | 8 | 0 |
| Dawson, Layne, Clearwater | 1 | 4 | .200 | 3.43 | 10 | 6 | 0 | 0 | 2 | 0 | 39.1 | 32 | 161 | 18 | 15 | 5 | 0 | 3 | 2 | 11 | 1 | 23 | 2 | 0 |
| De Leon, Juan, Tampa | 2 | 3 | .400 | 2.93 | 33 | 1 | 0 | 0 | 14 | 0 | 61.1 | 54 | 263 | 26 | 20 | 6 | 0 | 0 | 3 | 25 | 4 | 73 | 6 | 0 |
| Delcarmen, Manny, Sarasota | 3 | 6 | .333 | 4.68 | 19 | 18 | 0 | 0 | 1 | 0 | 73.0 | 84 | 310 | 43 | 38 | 10 | 4 | 3 | 4 | 20 | 1 | 76 | 1 | 0 |
| Demontel, Jimmy, Jupiter | 0 | 0 | .000 | 5.27 | 14 | 0 | 0 | 0 | 14 | 10 | 13.2 | 17 | 63 | 9 | 8 | 0 | 0 | 0 | 0 | 5 | 1 | 13 | 0 | 0 |
| Diaz, Jose, Vero Beach | 0 | 1 | .000 | 1.64 | 9 | 0 | 0 | 0 | 8 | 6 | 11.0 | 7 | 45 | 3 | 2 | 0 | 0 | 0 | 0 | 5 | 0 | 15 | 1 | 1 |
| Dragicevich, Scott, Dunedin | 0 | 0 | .000 | 0.00 | 1 | 0 | 0 | 0 | 0 | 0 | 1.0 | 1 | 4 | 0 | 0 | 0 | 0 | 0 | 0 | 0 | 0 | 1 | 0 | 0 |
| Edwards, Bryan, St. Lucie | 5 | 6 | .455 | 3.30 | 38 | 6 | 2 | 0 | 11 | 4 | 90.0 | 88 | 374 | 36 | 33 | 6 | 2 | 1 | 6 | 19 | 2 | 35 | 3 | 0 |
| Evans, Louis, Jupiter * | 1 | 1 | .500 | 2.25 | 10 | 0 | 0 | 0 | 1 | 0 | 16.0 | 8 | 73 | 5 | 4 | 1 | 0 | 0 | 2 | 15 | 0 | 15 | 1 | 0 |
| Everts, Clint, Brevard County | 2 | 2 | .500 | 2.25 | 4 | 4 | 0 | 0 | 0 | 0 | 20.0 | 16 | 78 | 5 | 5 | 2 | 0 | 1 | 0 | 10 | 0 | 19 | 0 | 0 |
| Fisher, Pete, Fort Myers | 0 | 1 | .000 | 4.50 | 2 | 0 | 0 | 0 | 2 | 0 | 2.0 | 2 | 8 | 1 | 1 | 0 | 0 | 0 | 0 | 0 | 0 | 1 | 0 | 0 |
| Flores, Neomar, Dunedin | 6 | 10 | .375 | 5.72 | 27 | 23 | 0 | 0 | 0 | 0 | 118.0 | 151 | 523 | 83 | 75 | 15 | 5 | 1 | 2 | 36 | 0 | 79 | 7 | 0 |
| Garcia, Felipe, Lakeland | 0 | 2 | .000 | 6.00 | 7 | 0 | 0 | 0 | 1 | 0 | 12.0 | 18 | 62 | 9 | 8 | 0 | 0 | 0 | 0 | 8 | 0 | 10 | 3 | 0 |
| Garza, Justin, Palm Beach | 5 | 1 | .833 | 2.89 | 26 | 0 | 0 | 0 | 23 | 10 | 28.0 | 25 | 122 | 9 | 9 | 1 | 0 | 0 | 0 | 13 | 5 | 17 | 1 | 0 |
| Gerk, Jordan, Daytona * | 1 | 2 | .333 | 4.11 | 18 | 0 | 0 | 0 | 5 | 0 | 35.0 | 39 | 156 | 19 | 16 | 0 | 1 | 1 | 0 | 15 | 1 | 31 | 2 | 0 |
| Girdley, Josh, Brevard County * | 0 | 3 | .000 | 5.24 | 9 | 5 | 0 | 0 | 1 | 0 | 34.1 | 37 | 153 | 24 | 20 | 4 | 2 | 1 | 3 | 15 | 0 | 19 | 1 | 0 |
| Gonzalez, Alfredo, Vero Beach | 1 | 0 | 1.000 | 3.86 | 8 | 0 | 0 | 0 | 4 | 0 | 14.0 | 15 | 63 | 10 | 6 | 2 | 0 | 0 | 0 | 6 | 0 | 14 | 4 | 0 |
| Gray, Josh, Fort Myers * | 2 | 10 | .167 | 5.84 | 33 | 12 | 0 | 0 | 8 | 0 | 86.1 | 102 | 397 | 64 | 56 | 7 | 3 | 9 | 6 | 40 | 6 | 56 | 6 | 0 |
| Gutierrez, Jannio, Fort Myers | 3 | 2 | .600 | 2.18 | 25 | 0 | 0 | 0 | 13 | 3 | 41.1 | 37 | 181 | 15 | 10 | 2 | 1 | 2 | 1 | 19 | 0 | 48 | 2 | 0 |
| Gwaltney, Lee, Clearwater | 3 | 10 | .231 | 3.80 | 20 | 20 | 1 | 0 | 0 | 0 | 116.0 | 122 | 485 | 54 | 49 | 7 | 8 | 6 | 7 | 39 | 1 | 81 | 6 | 0 |
| Hamels, Cole, Clearwater * | 1 | 0 | 1.000 | 1.13 | 4 | 4 | 0 | 0 | 0 | 0 | 16.0 | 10 | 58 | 2 | 2 | 0 | 1 | 0 | 1 | 4 | 0 | 24 | 1 | 0 |
| Hamilton, Jamaal, Vero Beach * | 4 | 1 | .800 | 4.02 | 25 | 0 | 0 | 0 | 7 | 0 | 31.1 | 36 | 141 | 14 | 14 | 1 | 0 | 0 | 1 | 10 | 0 | 26 | 4 | 0 |
| Harper, Landon, Lakeland | 0 | 2 | .000 | 7.30 | 10 | 0 | 0 | 0 | 6 | 0 | 12.1 | 15 | 57 | 10 | 10 | 2 | 0 | 2 | 0 | 7 | 0 | 11 | 1 | 0 |
| Hawk, Shane, St. Lucie * | 2 | 0 | 1.000 | 3.55 | 8 | 0 | 0 | 0 | 6 | 2 | 12.2 | 9 | 53 | 6 | 5 | 2 | 0 | 0 | 1 | 5 | 1 | 10 | 0 | 0 |
| Hawksworth, Blake, Palm Beach | 1 | 0 | 1.000 | 5.91 | 2 | 2 | 0 | 0 | 0 | 0 | 10.2 | 10 | 45 | 7 | 7 | 2 | 1 | 1 | 0 | 3 | 0 | 11 | 3 | 1 |
| Hensen, Brian, Lakeland * | 1 | 1 | .500 | 2.43 | 20 | 0 | 0 | 0 | 5 | 0 | 29.2 | 25 | 117 | 10 | 8 | 3 | 0 | 0 | 0 | 5 | 0 | 11 | 3 | 1 |
| Hill, Richard, Daytona * | 7 | 6 | .538 | 4.03 | 28 | 19 | 0 | 0 | 0 | 0 | 109.1 | 88 | 495 | 64 | 49 | 9 | 4 | 2 | 19 | 72 | 0 | 136 | 12 | 5 |
| Hill, Shaggy, Fort Myers | 0 | 1 | .000 | 2.70 | 3 | 0 | 0 | 0 | 1 | 0 | 6.2 | 5 | 35 | 2 | 2 | 0 | 0 | 0 | 3 | 9 | 2 | 5 | 0 | 0 |
| Hines, Matthew, Fort Myers | 0 | 0 | .000 | 11.25 | 3 | 0 | 0 | 0 | 2 | 0 | 4.0 | 7 | 23 | 5 | 5 | 0 | 0 | 0 | 1 | 3 | 0 | 2 | 0 | 0 |
| Hoorelbeke, Casey, Vero Beach | 6 | 4 | .600 | 4.01 | 18 | 14 | 0 | 0 | 1 | 0 | 76.1 | 81 | 335 | 40 | 34 | 9 | 5 | 1 | 2 | 31 | 0 | 56 | 4 | 1 |

| Pitcher, Team | W | L | Pct. | ERA | G | GS | CG | ShO | GF | Sv. | IP | H | TBF | R | ER | HR | SH | SF | HB | BB | IBB | SO | WP | Bk. |
|---|---|---|---|---|---|---|---|---|---|---|---|---|---|---|---|---|---|---|---|---|---|---|---|---|
| Hosford, Clint, Vero Beach | 4 | 2 | .667 | 4.71 | 22 | 8 | 1 | 0 | 6 | 1 | 70.2 | 63 | 301 | 41 | 37 | 7 | 3 | 1 | 3 | 24 | 0 | 53 | 12 | 0 |
| Howell, Jason, Sarasota * | 5 | 0 | 1.000 | 2.70 | 19 | 0 | 0 | 0 | 6 | 0 | 23.1 | 25 | 107 | 10 | 7 | 1 | 0 | 0 | 0 | 12 | 2 | 14 | 2 | 0 |
| Howell, Michael, Lakeland | 3 | 9 | .250 | 8.16 | 27 | 13 | 0 | 0 | 8 | 0 | 86.0 | 125 | 411 | 87 | 78 | 20 | 0 | 8 | 5 | 29 | 0 | 51 | 9 | 0 |
| Isaacson, Charlie, Tampa | 4 | 4 | .500 | 3.55 | 23 | 11 | 2 | 1 | 2 | 0 | 88.2 | 76 | 363 | 37 | 35 | 6 | 3 | 1 | 4 | 38 | 1 | 80 | 4 | 0 |
| James, Justin, Dunedin | 3 | 6 | .333 | 5.40 | 11 | 11 | 0 | 0 | 0 | 0 | 50.0 | 59 | 224 | 32 | 30 | 2 | 4 | 2 | 3 | 19 | 0 | 41 | 7 | 0 |
| Johnson, Jeremy, Lakeland | 3 | 6 | .333 | 4.87 | 14 | 14 | 0 | 0 | 0 | 0 | 68.1 | 79 | 299 | 39 | 37 | 2 | 5 | 5 | 4 | 26 | 0 | 42 | 5 | 0 |
| Johnson, Josh, Jupiter | 5 | 12 | .294 | 3.46 | 23 | 22 | 1 | 0 | 0 | 0 | 114.1 | 124 | 501 | 63 | 44 | 4 | 4 | 12 | 2 | 48 | 1 | 103 | 13 | 0 |
| Jongejan, Ferenc, Daytona * | 2 | 1 | .667 | 3.60 | 21 | 0 | 0 | 0 | 8 | 3 | 30.0 | 29 | 132 | 13 | 12 | 2 | 0 | 0 | 4 | 9 | 1 | 24 | 1 | 0 |
| Julianel, Ben, Tampa * | 5 | 5 | .500 | 2.58 | 43 | 0 | 0 | 0 | 22 | 10 | 59.1 | 52 | 256 | 23 | 17 | 2 | 0 | 0 | 1 | 24 | 3 | 70 | 8 | 0 |
| Karstens, Jeffrey, Tampa | 6 | 9 | .400 | 4.02 | 24 | 24 | 1 | 1 | 0 | 0 | 138.2 | 151 | 582 | 70 | 62 | 11 | 7 | 8 | 4 | 31 | 3 | 116 | 2 | 1 |
| Kensing, Logan, Jupiter | 6 | 7 | .462 | 2.96 | 23 | 23 | 1 | 0 | 0 | 0 | 127.2 | 120 | 525 | 53 | 42 | 5 | 7 | 8 | 8 | 35 | 1 | 100 | 8 | 1 |
| King, Jeremy, Tampa | 7 | 3 | .700 | 3.65 | 28 | 4 | 0 | 0 | 8 | 0 | 61.2 | 53 | 270 | 29 | 25 | 2 | 2 | 1 | 3 | 28 | 1 | 60 | 5 | 0 |
| Kobow, Mike, Lakeland | 0 | 2 | .000 | 4.23 | 43 | 0 | 0 | 0 | 37 | 13 | 55.1 | 57 | 254 | 31 | 26 | 1 | 0 | 0 | 1 | 30 | 1 | 36 | 3 | 0 |
| Kratz, Erik, Dunedin | 0 | 0 | .000 | 0.00 | 1 | 0 | 0 | 0 | 0 | 0 | 1.0 | 0 | 4 | 0 | 0 | 0 | 0 | 0 | 0 | 1 | 0 | 0 | 0 | 0 |
| Kweon, Yoon-Min, Daytona | 0 | 0 | .000 | 0.00 | 1 | 0 | 0 | 0 | 0 | 0 | 1.0 | 0 | 3 | 0 | 0 | 0 | 0 | 0 | 0 | 0 | 0 | 1 | 0 | 0 |
| Lira, Oscar, Brevard County | 0 | 0 | .000 | 0.00 | 2 | 0 | 0 | 0 | 2 | 0 | 4.0 | 1 | 16 | 0 | 0 | 0 | 0 | 0 | 0 | 3 | 0 | 3 | 0 | 0 |
| Lugo, Ruddy, Jupiter | 1 | 7 | .125 | 5.22 | 31 | 0 | 0 | 0 | 28 | 11 | 39.2 | 42 | 180 | 31 | 23 | 4 | 0 | 0 | 4 | 15 | 4 | 33 | 3 | 0 |
| Lundgren, Wayne, Palm Beach | 0 | 1 | .000 | 4.26 | 8 | 0 | 0 | 0 | 0 | 0 | 12.2 | 8 | 49 | 7 | 6 | 1 | 0 | 0 | 2 | 1 | 0 | 5 | 0 | 0 |
| Marcum, Shaun, Dunedin | 3 | 2 | .600 | 3.12 | 12 | 12 | 0 | 0 | 0 | 0 | 69.1 | 74 | 281 | 30 | 24 | 6 | 6 | 3 | 3 | 4 | 0 | 72 | 0 | 0 |
| Marshall, Brian, Sarasota * | 1 | 1 | .500 | 3.49 | 27 | 0 | 0 | 0 | 9 | 1 | 38.2 | 35 | 171 | 15 | 15 | 2 | 0 | 0 | 3 | 15 | 1 | 39 | 0 | 0 |
| Marsonek, Sam, Tampa | 0 | 0 | .000 | 0.00 | 3 | 0 | 0 | 0 | 1 | 0 | 4.0 | 3 | 15 | 0 | 0 | 0 | 0 | 0 | 0 | 0 | 0 | 3 | 0 | 0 |
| Martin, Nick, Daytona * | 2 | 2 | .500 | 4.25 | 24 | 0 | 0 | 0 | 10 | 3 | 36.0 | 36 | 156 | 17 | 17 | 2 | 0 | 0 | 1 | 13 | 2 | 31 | 4 | 0 |
| Mata, Gustavo, Brevard County | 1 | 0 | 1.000 | 2.12 | 3 | 3 | 0 | 0 | 0 | 0 | 17.0 | 11 | 70 | 6 | 4 | 0 | 2 | 1 | 0 | 9 | 0 | 13 | 1 | 0 |
| Mayfield, Brandon, Clearwater | 2 | 2 | .500 | 3.80 | 48 | 0 | 0 | 0 | 23 | 1 | 73.1 | 97 | 358 | 45 | 31 | 6 | 0 | 0 | 5 | 37 | 7 | 35 | 2 | 0 |
| McNab, Tim, St. Lucie | 4 | 4 | .500 | 4.65 | 38 | 0 | 0 | 0 | 15 | 1 | 71.2 | 91 | 332 | 40 | 37 | 4 | 1 | 0 | 1 | 22 | 3 | 53 | 9 | 0 |
| Megrew, Mike, Vero Beach * | 8 | 6 | .571 | 3.41 | 22 | 22 | 0 | 0 | 0 | 0 | 105.2 | 84 | 435 | 45 | 40 | 7 | 3 | 3 | 4 | 43 | 0 | 125 | 3 | 2 |
| Mendoza, Luis, Sarasota | 8 | 7 | .533 | 3.74 | 25 | 25 | 1 | 0 | 0 | 0 | 137.0 | 133 | 596 | 76 | 57 | 12 | 6 | 8 | 6 | 54 | 5 | 51 | 10 | 0 |
| Meredith, Clay, Sarasota | 0 | 2 | .000 | 2.20 | 16 | 0 | 0 | 0 | 16 | 12 | 16.1 | 15 | 68 | 4 | 4 | 0 | 0 | 0 | 1 | 3 | 0 | 16 | 0 | 0 |
| Merricks, Matt, Vero Beach * | 2 | 2 | .500 | 3.12 | 6 | 5 | 0 | 0 | 0 | 0 | 26.0 | 30 | 119 | 9 | 9 | 2 | 3 | 1 | 4 | 10 | 0 | 16 | 1 | 1 |
| Moates, Jason, Lakeland | 0 | 4 | .000 | 3.33 | 20 | 0 | 0 | 0 | 8 | 0 | 27.0 | 31 | 126 | 13 | 10 | 0 | 0 | 0 | 5 | 10 | 1 | 21 | 1 | 0 |
| Morales, Alex, Brevard County | 2 | 6 | .250 | 4.55 | 32 | 4 | 0 | 0 | 13 | 3 | 63.1 | 60 | 291 | 36 | 32 | 2 | 2 | 1 | 6 | 41 | 2 | 55 | 11 | 2 |
| Moseley, Marcus, Fort Myers | 3 | 1 | .750 | 5.70 | 28 | 7 | 0 | 0 | 6 | 2 | 66.1 | 71 | 316 | 55 | 42 | 6 | 4 | 8 | 7 | 44 | 0 | 38 | 8 | 1 |
| Mowday, Chris, Daytona | 3 | 1 | .750 | 1.89 | 41 | 0 | 0 | 0 | 12 | 3 | 57.0 | 41 | 250 | 22 | 12 | 4 | 0 | 0 | 3 | 31 | 2 | 61 | 8 | 0 |
| Myers, Damien, Lakeland * | 1 | 0 | 1.000 | 1.69 | 7 | 0 | 0 | 0 | 2 | 0 | 10.2 | 7 | 41 | 2 | 2 | 0 | 0 | 0 | 0 | 2 | 0 | 6 | 1 | 0 |
| Neshek, Pat, Fort Myers | 0 | 1 | .000 | 2.95 | 16 | 0 | 0 | 0 | 15 | 10 | 18.1 | 16 | 73 | 7 | 6 | 2 | 0 | 0 | 0 | 2 | 0 | 19 | 0 | 0 |
| Norderum, Jason, Brevard County * | 0 | 2 | .000 | 6.83 | 35 | 2 | 0 | 0 | 10 | 0 | 58.0 | 58 | 291 | 52 | 44 | 5 | 0 | 1 | 8 | 53 | 2 | 63 | 11 | 2 |
| Nunez, Jose, St. Lucie * | 0 | 0 | .000 | 8.10 | 2 | 0 | 0 | 0 | 0 | 0 | 3.1 | 4 | 16 | 3 | 3 | 0 | 0 | 0 | 0 | 2 | 0 | 1 | 0 | 0 |
| O'Connor, Michael, Brevard County * | 8 | 8 | .500 | 4.11 | 26 | 14 | 0 | 0 | 0 | 0 | 103.0 | 98 | 438 | 51 | 47 | 5 | 4 | 6 | 4 | 42 | 0 | 104 | 6 | 2 |
| Ochoa, Javier, St. Lucie | 1 | 0 | 1.000 | 0.00 | 3 | 0 | 0 | 0 | 0 | 0 | 6.2 | 7 | 28 | 3 | 0 | 0 | 0 | 0 | 0 | 1 | 0 | 6 | 0 | 0 |
| Ojeda, Alvis, Vero Beach | 0 | 0 | .000 | 2.25 | 4 | 1 | 0 | 0 | 0 | 0 | 12.0 | 8 | 47 | 3 | 3 | 1 | 2 | 1 | 1 | 2 | 0 | 8 | 1 | 0 |
| Olsen, Scott, Jupiter * | 7 | 6 | .538 | 2.97 | 25 | 25 | 1 | 1 | 0 | 0 | 136.1 | 127 | 571 | 57 | 45 | 8 | 5 | 5 | 4 | 53 | 0 | 158 | 7 | 0 |
| Olson, Justin, Fort Myers | 7 | 7 | .500 | 2.88 | 45 | 6 | 0 | 0 | 32 | 8 | 78.0 | 60 | 339 | 34 | 25 | 6 | 5 | 1 | 0 | 46 | 5 | 85 | 10 | 0 |
| Olson, Ryan, St. Lucie * | 1 | 1 | .500 | 4.38 | 41 | 0 | 0 | 0 | 15 | 1 | 49.1 | 39 | 228 | 27 | 24 | 2 | 0 | 0 | 5 | 37 | 3 | 46 | 5 | 0 |
| Ool, Kevin, Sarasota * | 0 | 0 | .000 | 3.18 | 2 | 0 | 0 | 0 | 0 | 0 | 5.2 | 5 | 24 | 2 | 2 | 0 | 0 | 0 | 0 | 2 | 1 | 5 | 0 | 0 |
| Orloski, Joe, Jupiter | 1 | 2 | .333 | 3.98 | 14 | 0 | 0 | 0 | 12 | 0 | 20.1 | 22 | 91 | 10 | 9 | 2 | 0 | 0 | 0 | 8 | 2 | 14 | 1 | 0 |
| Ostlund, Ian, Lakeland * | 1 | 2 | .333 | 3.00 | 21 | 0 | 0 | 0 | 8 | 1 | 36.0 | 31 | 144 | 13 | 12 | 2 | 0 | 0 | 0 | 7 | 1 | 35 | 2 | 0 |
| Ough, Wayne, St. Lucie | 1 | 3 | .250 | 8.82 | 4 | 4 | 0 | 0 | 0 | 0 | 16.1 | 22 | 90 | 20 | 16 | 2 | 1 | 4 | 2 | 11 | 0 | 13 | 2 | 0 |
| Overholt, Sean, Daytona | 1 | 1 | .500 | 7.28 | 16 | 0 | 0 | 0 | 5 | 1 | 29.2 | 33 | 137 | 28 | 24 | 8 | 0 | 0 | 3 | 12 | 0 | 25 | 4 | 0 |
| Overman, Matt, Jupiter | 6 | 4 | .600 | 3.79 | 36 | 6 | 0 | 0 | 8 | 0 | 92.2 | 86 | 392 | 45 | 39 | 6 | 2 | 1 | 8 | 22 | 1 | 58 | 4 | 0 |
| Ozuna, Tommi, Dunedin * | 4 | 4 | .500 | 4.48 | 43 | 1 | 0 | 0 | 18 | 0 | 64.1 | 65 | 295 | 34 | 32 | 2 | 2 | 1 | 10 | 32 | 3 | 36 | 2 | 3 |
| Pahucki, David, Sarasota | 5 | 4 | .556 | 1.81 | 43 | 0 | 0 | 0 | 18 | 5 | 59.2 | 46 | 243 | 15 | 12 | 2 | 0 | 0 | 4 | 15 | 4 | 40 | 4 | 0 |
| Pals, Jordan, Palm Beach | 5 | 1 | .833 | 2.69 | 11 | 11 | 1 | 1 | 0 | 0 | 60.1 | 60 | 249 | 22 | 18 | 1 | 5 | 1 | 2 | 19 | 1 | 43 | 3 | 0 |
| Papelbon, Jon, Sarasota | 12 | 7 | .632 | 2.64 | 24 | 24 | 2 | 0 | 0 | 0 | 129.2 | 97 | 520 | 43 | 38 | 6 | 6 | 3 | 7 | 43 | 2 | 153 | 3 | 0 |
| Parris, Matt, Lakeland | 9 | 9 | .500 | 4.71 | 25 | 24 | 2 | 0 | 1 | 0 | 130.0 | 141 | 552 | 78 | 68 | 16 | 7 | 5 | 4 | 43 | 0 | 42 | 2 | 1 |
| Paulk, Robert, St. Lucie | 8 | 6 | .571 | 3.70 | 31 | 10 | 0 | 0 | 13 | 3 | 92.1 | 111 | 400 | 45 | 38 | 7 | 1 | 3 | 4 | 23 | 1 | 60 | 9 | 0 |
| Perkins, Vince, Dunedin | 1 | 4 | .200 | 3.95 | 13 | 9 | 0 | 0 | 0 | 0 | 54.2 | 53 | 235 | 28 | 24 | 2 | 6 | 3 | 5 | 24 | 2 | 47 | 4 | 0 |
| Petty, Chad, Palm Beach * | 3 | 2 | .600 | 5.25 | 23 | 3 | 0 | 0 | 1 | 0 | 60.0 | 62 | 257 | 39 | 35 | 8 | 1 | 3 | 3 | 16 | 2 | 38 | 4 | 0 |
| Phelps, Tommy, Jupiter * | 0 | 0 | .000 | 0.00 | 1 | 0 | 0 | 0 | 0 | 0 | 1.1 | 2 | 6 | 3 | 0 | 0 | 0 | 0 | 0 | 0 | 0 | 1 | 0 | 0 |
| Pinango, Miguel, St. Lucie | 2 | 2 | .500 | 2.75 | 4 | 3 | 0 | 0 | 1 | 0 | 19.2 | 18 | 70 | 6 | 6 | 2 | 0 | 1 | 1 | 1 | 0 | 16 | 0 | 0 |
| Pleiness, Chad, Dunedin | 4 | 3 | .571 | 4.40 | 36 | 4 | 0 | 0 | 4 | 0 | 77.2 | 82 | 341 | 45 | 38 | 8 | 2 | 2 | 1 | 33 | 4 | 46 | 4 | 0 |
| Plummer, Jarod, Vero Beach | 4 | 4 | .500 | 3.86 | 11 | 11 | 0 | 0 | 0 | 0 | 63.0 | 65 | 263 | 29 | 27 | 8 | 2 | 3 | 3 | 14 | 0 | 49 | 1 | 0 |
| Portobanco, Luz, St. Lucie | 1 | 3 | .250 | 3.77 | 34 | 2 | 0 | 0 | 7 | 0 | 76.1 | 75 | 333 | 43 | 32 | 5 | 1 | 0 | 6 | 32 | 4 | 58 | 4 | 1 |
| Price, Brett, Brevard County * | 6 | 4 | .600 | 3.53 | 23 | 19 | 0 | 0 | 3 | 0 | 99.1 | 88 | 421 | 47 | 39 | 5 | 6 | 5 | 3 | 53 | 0 | 100 | 8 | 1 |
| Quintero, Mayque, Brevard County | 3 | 2 | .600 | 2.75 | 21 | 1 | 0 | 0 | 6 | 0 | 36.0 | 29 | 153 | 12 | 11 | 1 | 2 | 0 | 3 | 15 | 1 | 32 | 2 | 3 |
| Ramirez, Ismael, Dunedin | 15 | 6 | .714 | 2.72 | 28 | 27 | 0 | 0 | 0 | 0 | 165.1 | 151 | 663 | 57 | 50 | 5 | 6 | 7 | 7 | 25 | 0 | 131 | 7 | 0 |
| Randazzo, Jeff, Fort Myers * | 5 | 12 | .294 | 4.93 | 27 | 26 | 0 | 0 | 0 | 0 | 133.1 | 153 | 608 | 96 | 73 | 10 | 6 | 8 | 8 | 61 | 5 | 79 | 11 | 3 |
| Ransom, Robert, Daytona | 1 | 0 | 1.000 | 1.57 | 5 | 2 | 0 | 0 | 1 | 1 | 23.0 | 18 | 88 | 5 | 4 | 1 | 2 | 0 | 0 | 5 | 0 | 13 | 0 | 0 |
| Rawson, Anthony, Palm Beach * | 0 | 2 | .000 | 2.16 | 53 | 0 | 0 | 0 | 12 | 5 | 75.0 | 55 | 304 | 23 | 18 | 1 | 1 | 0 | 2 | 23 | 2 | 44 | 9 | 0 |
| Reed, Brian, Dunedin | 2 | 1 | .667 | 3.16 | 24 | 0 | 0 | 0 | 15 | 4 | 31.1 | 38 | 142 | 11 | 11 | 4 | 0 | 0 | 2 | 8 | 1 | 31 | 0 | 0 |
| Reina, Dimas, Vero Beach | 5 | 4 | .556 | 3.23 | 16 | 9 | 1 | 1 | 4 | 1 | 64.0 | 57 | 262 | 28 | 23 | 6 | 0 | 6 | 0 | 21 | 0 | 55 | 5 | 0 |
| Reynolds, Eric, Jupiter * | 0 | 3 | .000 | 9.49 | 9 | 0 | 0 | 0 | 4 | 0 | 12.1 | 15 | 66 | 15 | 13 | 0 | 3 | 0 | 3 | 10 | 0 | 13 | 4 | 0 |
| Richardson, Beau, Clearwater * | 6 | 1 | .857 | 3.61 | 47 | 0 | 0 | 0 | 20 | 1 | 42.1 | 45 | 194 | 23 | 17 | 5 | 0 | 0 | 4 | 16 | 3 | 35 | 3 | 0 |
| Rodriguez, Mike, Vero Beach | 7 | 3 | .700 | 4.98 | 28 | 7 | 0 | 0 | 11 | 1 | 68.2 | 71 | 302 | 39 | 38 | 4 | 1 | 2 | 4 | 26 | 0 | 49 | 11 | 0 |
| Rogers, Joe, Sarasota * | 8 | 5 | .615 | 3.72 | 36 | 2 | 0 | 0 | 17 | 1 | 82.1 | 76 | 370 | 45 | 34 | 4 | 2 | 2 | 3 | 47 | 1 | 48 | 10 | 1 |
| Romero, Felix, Dunedin | 0 | 0 | .000 | 1.88 | 9 | 0 | 0 | 0 | 4 | 1 | 14.1 | 11 | 56 | 3 | 3 | 0 | 0 | 0 | 0 | 2 | 1 | 20 | 2 | 0 |
| Russ, Chris, Palm Beach | 0 | 0 | .000 | 0.00 | 7 | 0 | 0 | 0 | 5 | 5 | 8.0 | 4 | 32 | 0 | 0 | 0 | 1 | 0 | 1 | 2 | 0 | 2 | 1 | 0 |
| Russ, James, Jupiter | 8 | 1 | .889 | 1.98 | 24 | 9 | 0 | 0 | 8 | 0 | 82.0 | 61 | 328 | 18 | 18 | 6 | 5 | 5 | 3 | 26 | 0 | 64 | 1 | 0 |
| Scalamandre, Rich, Palm Beach | 3 | 2 | .600 | 4.08 | 40 | 0 | 0 | 0 | 9 | 0 | 46.1 | 41 | 206 | 22 | 21 | 2 | 0 | 0 | 1 | 26 | 3 | 48 | 10 | 0 |
| Schultz, Cory, Clearwater | 0 | 1 | .000 | 0.43 | 11 | 1 | 1 | 0 | 7 | 4 | 21.0 | 16 | 80 | 1 | 1 | 0 | 1 | 0 | 0 | 2 | 0 | 18 | 0 | 0 |
| Shipman, Andrew, Daytona | 1 | 1 | .500 | 3.18 | 15 | 0 | 0 | 0 | 15 | 4 | 17.0 | 10 | 67 | 6 | 6 | 3 | 0 | 0 | 0 | 6 | 0 | 22 | 1 | 0 |
| Shipman, Andrew, Sarasota | 1 | 1 | .500 | 3.14 | 22 | 0 | 0 | 0 | 17 | 13 | 28.2 | 22 | 125 | 12 | 10 | 2 | 1 | 0 | 1 | 15 | 1 | 25 | 2 | 0 |
| Sierra, Edwardo, Tampa | 2 | 3 | .400 | 3.33 | 45 | 0 | 0 | 0 | 35 | 28 | 48.2 | 44 | 238 | 22 | 18 | 2 | 1 | 0 | 2 | 45 | 1 | 57 | 9 | 0 |
| Simmons, Justin, Vero Beach * | 0 | 0 | .000 | 0.77 | 5 | 0 | 0 | 0 | 1 | 0 | 11.2 | 7 | 47 | 1 | 1 | 0 | 0 | 0 | 0 | 5 | 0 | 6 | 2 | 0 |

| Pitcher, Team | W | L | Pct. | ERA | G | GS | CG | ShO | GF | Sv. | IP | H | TBF | R | ER | HR | SH | SF | HB | BB | IBB | SO | WP | Bk. |
|---|---|---|---|---|---|---|---|---|---|---|---|---|---|---|---|---|---|---|---|---|---|---|---|---|
| Simon, Alfredo, Clearwater | 7 | 9 | .438 | 3.27 | 22 | 21 | 4 | 3 | 0 | 0 | 134.2 | 121 | 552 | 58 | 49 | 13 | — | — | 5 | 38 | 2 | 107 | 10 | — |
| Sisco, Andy, Daytona * | 4 | 10 | .286 | 4.21 | 26 | 25 | 0 | 0 | 0 | 0 | 126.0 | 118 | 536 | 64 | 59 | 11 | 8 | 6 | 7 | 65 | 1 | 134 | 9 | 1 |
| Skaggs, Jon, Tampa | 13 | 9 | .591 | 3.87 | 27 | 27 | 2 | 0 | 0 | 0 | 162.2 | 141 | 696 | 84 | 70 | 11 | 6 | 6 | 13 | 70 | 0 | 116 | 10 | 0 |
| Smith, Bud, Clearwater * | 0 | 1 | .000 | 3.95 | 5 | 5 | 0 | 0 | 0 | 0 | 13.2 | 13 | 57 | 6 | 6 | 0 | 0 | 0 | 1 | 5 | 0 | 12 | 0 | 0 |
| Smith, Dan, Brevard County | 0 | 0 | .000 | 2.25 | 3 | 0 | 0 | 0 | 1 | 0 | 4.0 | 5 | 18 | 1 | 1 | 0 | 0 | 0 | 0 | 1 | 0 | 2 | 1 | 0 |
| Smith, Jared, Palm Beach | 5 | 4 | .556 | 3.06 | 14 | 12 | 0 | 0 | 1 | 0 | 64.2 | 58 | 274 | 26 | 22 | 3 | 6 | 5 | 4 | 39 | 0 | 40 | 2 | 0 |
| Song, Seung, Brevard County | 0 | 1 | .000 | 6.75 | 3 | 2 | 0 | 0 | 0 | 0 | 12.0 | 14 | 54 | 11 | 9 | 2 | 2 | 1 | 0 | 3 | 0 | 10 | 2 | 0 |
| Speigner, Levale, Fort Myers | 4 | 3 | .571 | 1.79 | 22 | 1 | 0 | 0 | 7 | 2 | 45.1 | 46 | 198 | 15 | 9 | 3 | 1 | 0 | 2 | 14 | 1 | 47 | 3 | 0 |
| Strickland, Scott, St. Lucie | 0 | 1 | .000 | 9.45 | 6 | 1 | 0 | 0 | 1 | 0 | 6.2 | 11 | 33 | 8 | 7 | 0 | 0 | 0 | 0 | 2 | 0 | 5 | 1 | 0 |
| Stults, Eric, Vero Beach * | 2 | 1 | .667 | 2.70 | 7 | 0 | 0 | 0 | 1 | 1 | 10.0 | 11 | 46 | 4 | 3 | 0 | 0 | 0 | 1 | 4 | 0 | 6 | 0 | 0 |
| Sturge, Justin, Sarasota * | 4 | 3 | .571 | 2.80 | 39 | 2 | 0 | 0 | 11 | 0 | 80.1 | 78 | 350 | 36 | 25 | 1 | 0 | 2 | 4 | 29 | 3 | 71 | 6 | 0 |
| Sweeney, Matt, Clearwater | 6 | 9 | .400 | 4.47 | 21 | 17 | 0 | 0 | 1 | 0 | 112.2 | 118 | 467 | 62 | 56 | 19 | 5 | 6 | 1 | 33 | 0 | 62 | 6 | 0 |
| Tavares, Anderson, Daytona | 7 | 5 | .583 | 4.32 | 19 | 13 | 1 | 1 | 0 | 0 | 77.0 | 84 | 331 | 41 | 37 | 9 | 4 | 8 | 6 | 19 | 0 | 41 | 3 | 1 |
| Teekel, Josh, Palm Beach | 9 | 6 | .600 | 3.93 | 26 | 25 | 0 | 0 | 0 | 0 | 142.0 | 134 | 599 | 67 | 62 | 7 | 8 | 14 | 12 | 57 | 1 | 96 | 12 | 1 |
| Tejada, Manny, Fort Myers | 5 | 4 | .556 | 3.52 | 22 | 14 | 0 | 0 | 3 | 0 | 94.2 | 91 | 390 | 44 | 37 | 11 | 2 | 3 | 1 | 25 | 1 | 63 | 4 | 1 |
| Tempesta, Nick, Clearwater | 0 | 0 | .000 | 0.00 | 1 | 0 | 0 | 0 | 1 | 0 | 1.0 | 0 | 4 | 0 | 0 | 0 | 0 | 0 | 0 | 1 | 0 | 2 | 0 | 0 |
| Templet, Jordy, Dunedin | 0 | 0 | .000 | 13.50 | 3 | 0 | 0 | 0 | 0 | 0 | 2.2 | 3 | 14 | 4 | 4 | 0 | 0 | 0 | 0 | 3 | 0 | 3 | 1 | 0 |
| Thomas, J.T., Fort Myers * | 2 | 5 | .286 | 3.55 | 34 | 7 | 1 | 0 | 7 | 0 | 66.0 | 69 | 293 | 34 | 26 | 5 | 3 | 1 | 3 | 25 | 2 | 69 | 4 | 0 |
| Thorpe, Tracy, Dunedin | 3 | 2 | .600 | 3.64 | 39 | 0 | 0 | 0 | 10 | 1 | 59.1 | 39 | 253 | 25 | 24 | 5 | 0 | 0 | 6 | 30 | 1 | 53 | 3 | 0 |
| Torres, Andy, Dunedin | 9 | 3 | .750 | 2.52 | 42 | 0 | 0 | 0 | 10 | 0 | 78.2 | 64 | 315 | 28 | 22 | 7 | 2 | 0 | 0 | 16 | 1 | 71 | 0 | 0 |
| Valdez, Jose, Tampa | 7 | 7 | .500 | 4.27 | 23 | 20 | 0 | 0 | 1 | 0 | 111.2 | 116 | 482 | 69 | 53 | 7 | 6 | 4 | 7 | 38 | 1 | 76 | 10 | 2 |
| Vanden Hurk, Rick, Jupiter | 2 | 3 | .400 | 3.26 | 14 | 14 | 0 | 0 | 0 | 0 | 58.0 | 54 | 252 | 22 | 21 | 2 | 2 | 7 | 4 | 31 | 0 | 43 | 6 | 0 |
| Vaquedano, Jose, Sarasota | 5 | 1 | .833 | 3.95 | 14 | 8 | 0 | 0 | 2 | 0 | 68.1 | 65 | 281 | 34 | 30 | 4 | 5 | 5 | 5 | 21 | 2 | 60 | 6 | 0 |
| Vasquez, Carlos, Daytona * | 6 | 5 | .545 | 3.87 | 16 | 16 | 0 | 0 | 0 | 0 | 79.0 | 86 | 355 | 54 | 34 | 4 | 5 | 1 | 5 | 31 | 0 | 51 | 10 | 0 |
| Villegas, Francisco, Tampa | 0 | 0 | .000 | 3.09 | 15 | 0 | 0 | 0 | 5 | 2 | 23.1 | 18 | 109 | 8 | 8 | 2 | 0 | 0 | 3 | 18 | 1 | 24 | 0 | 0 |
| Wallace, Shane, Palm Beach * | 7 | 6 | .538 | 3.14 | 54 | 0 | 0 | 0 | 22 | 1 | 63.0 | 38 | 269 | 27 | 22 | 4 | 0 | 0 | 3 | 40 | 4 | 37 | 11 | 0 |
| Waugh, Jason, Dunedin | 0 | 0 | .000 | 0.00 | 1 | 0 | 0 | 0 | 1 | 0 | 1.0 | 1 | 5 | 0 | 0 | 0 | 0 | 0 | 0 | 1 | 0 | 0 | 0 | 0 |
| White, Steven, Tampa | 6 | 2 | .750 | 2.56 | 12 | 12 | 1 | 1 | 0 | 0 | 59.2 | 51 | 244 | 26 | 17 | 4 | 2 | 0 | 3 | 19 | 0 | 44 | 3 | 1 |
| Wolf, Ross, Jupiter | 11 | 7 | .611 | 2.60 | 43 | 0 | 0 | 0 | 22 | 5 | 90.0 | 87 | 386 | 33 | 26 | 2 | 1 | 1 | 4 | 28 | 6 | 58 | 3 | 0 |
| Wood, Brandon, Clearwater | 0 | 0 | .000 | 3.38 | 3 | 1 | 0 | 0 | 2 | 0 | 5.1 | 2 | 19 | 2 | 2 | 0 | 1 | 1 | 1 | 2 | 0 | 3 | 1 | 0 |
| Woodrow, C.J., Clearwater | 3 | 1 | .750 | 4.17 | 6 | 5 | 1 | 1 | 0 | 0 | 36.2 | 48 | 158 | 19 | 17 | 5 | 1 | 2 | 0 | 4 | 0 | 17 | 0 | 0 |
| Yeatman, Matt, Fort Myers | 3 | 7 | .300 | 4.30 | 23 | 23 | 2 | 0 | 0 | 0 | 111.0 | 106 | 481 | 72 | 53 | 6 | 7 | 7 | 10 | 48 | 0 | 88 | 14 | 0 |
| Yost, Wendell, Brevard County * | 0 | 0 | .000 | 0.00 | 1 | 0 | 0 | 0 | 0 | 0 | 1.0 | 1 | 5 | 0 | 0 | 0 | 0 | 0 | 0 | 1 | 0 | 2 | 0 | 0 |
| Zink, Charlie, Sarasota | 0 | 2 | .000 | 5.65 | 3 | 3 | 0 | 0 | 0 | 0 | 14.1 | 22 | 66 | 13 | 9 | 0 | 1 | 2 | 0 | 9 | 0 | 3 | 2 | 0 |

## PITCHERS WITH TWO OR MORE TEAMS

| Pitcher, Team | W | L | Pct. | ERA | G | GS | CG | ShO | GF | Sv. | IP | H | TBF | R | ER | HR | SH | SF | HB | BB | IBB | SO | WP | Bk. |
|---|---|---|---|---|---|---|---|---|---|---|---|---|---|---|---|---|---|---|---|---|---|---|---|---|
| Connolly, Jon, Daytona * | 9 | 5 | .643 | 2.40 | 21 | 21 | 3 | 2 | 0 | 0 | 131.0 | 123 | 525 | 47 | 35 | 9 | 6 | 4 | 6 | 24 | 0 | 101 | 3 | 0 |
| Connolly, Jon, Lakeland * | 2 | 2 | .500 | 3.68 | 4 | 4 | 0 | 0 | 0 | 0 | 22.0 | 28 | 101 | 12 | 9 | 1 | 0 | 2 | 2 | 5 | 0 | 8 | 3 | 0 |

COMBINATION SHUTOUTS: **Brevard County** (7)—Hinckley-Searles-Morales, O'Connor-Morales-Searles, Marrero-Morales-Searles, O'Connor-S. Martinez, Patterson-Campbell-Morales, Everts-Morales-Skrmetta-Bergmann, Mata-Quintero-Bray. **Clearwater** (6)—E. Ramirez-Mayfield, Dawson-Hiles-Butto, Junge-Hutchinson-Paddock-Mayfield, Hamels-Hiles-Culp, Bourgeois-Reyes-Culp, B. Smith-Bourgeois. **Daytona** (5)—Connolly-O'Malley-Atlee, Sisco-Baez, O'Malley-Baez-Mowday, Hill-Cherry-Atlee, Tavarez-Gerk-Shipman, Sisco-Mowday-Atlee. **Dunedin** (7)—I. Ramirez-Pleiness-Torres-Buzachero, Vermilyea-Pleiness-Torres-Buzachero-Ozuna, Banks-Torres-Buzachero, I. Ramirez-Harper-Buzachero, Flores-Thorpe-Maureau, I. Ramirez-Ozuna-Buzachero, I. Ramirez-Reed. **Fort Myers** (11)—Liriano-Moseley, Yeatman-Bowyer-Miller-Olson, Liriano-Lohse-Moseley, Tejada-Bowyer-Olson, Liriano-Bowyer, Randazzo-Lohse, Tejada-Lohse, Liriano-Olson-Barrett, Olson-Barrett-Moseley-Neshek, Blackburn-Speigner, Yeatman-Barrett-Neshek. **Jupiter** (12)—J. Johnson-Wolf-Reynolds, Kensing-Overman-Lugo, Overman-Wolf, Olsen-Overman, J. Johnson-Overman-Cave, Russ-Evans-Cave-Orloski-Campbell, Russ-Campbell-Cave, Overman-Cave-Demontel, Russ-Demontel, Vandenhurk-Evans-Demontel, Olsen-Belizario-Cave-Demontel, Olsen-Belizario-Wolf-Demontel. **Lakeland** (7)—Sleeth-Rodney, Myers-Rodney, Parris-Moates-Rodney, Cuello-Ostlund-Rodney, Hamman-Kobow, Sanchez-Birtwell-Kobow, Sanchez-Cordova-Baldwin. **Palm Beach** (10)—Caple-J. Smith, J. Smith-Stemle-Wallace-Ciprian, Mondesir-Petty-Batista-Wallace, Teekel-Petty-Rawson, Adamczyk-Rawson-Scalamandre, J. Smith-Kinney-Ciprian, Blair-Ciprian, Pals-Batista-Rawson, Blair-Garza, Teekel-Rawson-Garza. **Sarasota** (3)—E. Rodriguez-Gabbard-Pahucki-Marshall, Lester-Pahucki-Young-Dennison, Papelbon-Howell-Pahucki. **St. Lucie** (3)—Erickson-Paulk-Cole-Byard, Bannister-Cox, Kazmir-Strickland-Portobanco-Paulk-Edwards-Byard. **Vero Beach** (9)—Broxton-Figueroa-Steffek, Megrew-Dannemiller-Figueroa, Reina-Schmoll, Broxton-Hosford, Billingsley-Hamilton-M. Rodriguez-Schmoll, Hosford-Bartlett-Schmoll, Broxton-Dannemiller, Merricks-Bartlett-Dannemiller, Ojeda-Stults-Dannemiller. **Tampa** (10)—Karstens-King-Esquivia, DeSalvo-Julianel-Moore-Sierra, Lieber-Brumit, Skaggs-King, Karstens-Julianel-Sierra, DeSalvo-Goetz, Valdez-Artiles, Isaacson-Julianel, Isaacson-Julianel, White-Julianel.

NO-HIT GAMES: None.

# 2004 FIELDING

## TEAM

| Team | G | PO | A | E | TC | DP | TP | PB | Pct. |
|---|---|---|---|---|---|---|---|---|---|
| Lakeland | 132 | 3292 | 093 | 117 | 3502 | 113 | 0 | 20 | .967 |
| Sarasota | 136 | 3507 | 077 | 138 | 3722 | 110 | 0 | 45 | .963 |
| Jupiter | 135 | 3535 | 142 | 149 | 3826 | 98 | 0 | 25 | .961 |
| Vero Beach | 135 | 3519 | 129 | 148 | 3796 | 83 | 0 | 17 | .961 |
| Tampa | 133 | 3408 | 092 | 141 | 3641 | 131 | 0 | 22 | .961 |
| Clearwater | 136 | 3503 | 133 | 147 | 3783 | 124 | 0 | 20 | .961 |
| Dunedin | 133 | 3472 | 140 | 146 | 3758 | 109 | 0 | 12 | .961 |
| Brevard County | 125 | 3232 | 140 | 138 | 3510 | 115 | 0 | 27 | .961 |
| Palm Beach | 134 | 3476 | 177 | 151 | 3804 | 143 | 0 | 23 | .960 |
| Daytona | 126 | 3253 | 120 | 149 | 3522 | 101 | 0 | 11 | .958 |
| Fort Myers | 135 | 3424 | 110 | 156 | 3690 | 123 | 0 | 30 | .958 |
| St. Lucie | 129 | 3411 | 158 | 178 | 3747 | 129 | 0 | 25 | .952 |

## INDIVIDUAL

### FIRST BASEMEN

NOTE: All caps denotes fielding-percentage leader based on 70 games for catchers, 93 for all other non-pitchers and 112 innings for pitchers. *Throws lefthanded.

| Player, Team | Pct. | G | PO | A | E | TC | DP |
|---|---|---|---|---|---|---|---|
| Alfonzo, Eliezer, JUP | .990 | 41 | 353 | 24 | 4 | 381 | 26 |
| Bailie, Stefan, SAR | .981 | 28 | 240 | 15 | 5 | 260 | 17 |
| Barthelemy, Ryan, CLW* | .989 | 118 | 953 | 81 | 11 | 1045 | 85 |
| Bechtel, Chuck, LAK | 1.000 | 7 | 60 | 6 | 0 | 66 | 6 |
| Bonner, Adam, JUP* | .968 | 18 | 137 | 15 | 5 | 157 | 10 |
| Boran, Patrick, SAR | .985 | 9 | 59 | 8 | 1 | 68 | 7 |
| Brown, Andy, TAM* | 1.000 | 2 | 7 | 1 | 0 | 8 | 1 |

| Player, Team | Pct. | G | PO | A | E | TC | DP |
|---|---|---|---|---|---|---|---|
| Burford, Kevin, CLW* | 1.000 | 5 | 25 | 2 | 0 | 27 | 2 |
| Caligiuri, Jay, SLU | .992 | 71 | 598 | 46 | 5 | 649 | 71 |
| Carson, Matt, TAM | 1.000 | 1 | 4 | 0 | 0 | 4 | 0 |
| Castellano, John, CLW | 1.000 | 7 | 57 | 4 | 0 | 61 | 8 |
| Chiaravalloti, Vito, DUN | .984 | 77 | 620 | 60 | 11 | 691 | 60 |
| Chop, Chad, BRE* | .993 | 35 | 284 | 21 | 2 | 307 | 29 |
| Concepcion, Alberto, SAR | 1.000 | 6 | 20 | 1 | 0 | 21 | 3 |
| Cordero, Wil, JUP | 1.000 | 1 | 7 | 0 | 0 | 7 | 0 |
| Corporan, Elvis, FTM | 1.000 | 5 | 34 | 0 | 0 | 34 | 4 |
| Davenport, Ron, DUN* | .984 | 19 | 170 | 14 | 3 | 187 | 14 |
| Davis, John-Paul, PLM | .987 | 17 | 148 | 5 | 2 | 155 | 16 |
| Delgado, Carlos, DUN* | 1.000 | 2 | 14 | 2 | 0 | 16 | 0 |
| Dowdy, Brett, VB | 1.000 | 2 | 15 | 0 | 0 | 15 | 2 |
| Dragicevich, Scott, DUN | 1.000 | 28 | 223 | 14 | 0 | 237 | 19 |
| Drobiak, Jayson, TAM* | .988 | 51 | 452 | 35 | 6 | 493 | 48 |
| Duncan, Shelley, TAM | .986 | 82 | 651 | 55 | 10 | 716 | 58 |
| Dyson, Trey, VB* | .994 | 38 | 306 | 31 | 2 | 339 | 15 |
| Ehrnsberger, Chad, PLM | 1.000 | 4 | 5 | 0 | 0 | 5 | 0 |
| Ellerson, Brian, BRE | 1.000 | 7 | 47 | 1 | 0 | 48 | 4 |
| Ellis, AJ, VB | 1.000 | 1 | 6 | 1 | 0 | 7 | 0 |
| Figueroa, Juan, JUP | .948 | 5 | 52 | 3 | 3 | 58 | 4 |
| Giambi, Jason, TAM* | 1.000 | 2 | 10 | 1 | 0 | 11 | 1 |
| Gillitzer, Scott, VB | .995 | 27 | 166 | 24 | 1 | 191 | 9 |
| Gomon, Dusty, FTM | 1.000 | 1 | 6 | 1 | 0 | 7 | 0 |
| Gradoville, Tim, CLW | 1.000 | 1 | 2 | 0 | 0 | 2 | 1 |
| Hansen, Bryan, CLW* | 1.000 | 3 | 27 | 3 | 0 | 30 | 6 |
| Harper, Brett, SLU* | .988 | 39 | 387 | 15 | 5 | 407 | 39 |
| Hood, Donny, DAY | 1.000 | 12 | 73 | 6 | 0 | 79 | 3 |
| Hoorelbeke, Jesse, VB | .979 | 39 | 305 | 22 | 7 | 334 | 21 |
| Jenkins, Neil, LAK | 1.000 | 1 | 2 | 0 | 0 | 2 | 0 |
| Johnson, Nick, BRE* | 1.000 | 6 | 48 | 6 | 0 | 54 | 2 |
| Jones, Garrett, FTM* | .995 | 19 | 161 | 20 | 1 | 182 | 16 |
| Kratz, Erik, DUN | 1.000 | 2 | 9 | 0 | 0 | 9 | 1 |
| Lee, Travis, TAM* | 1.000 | 3 | 19 | 1 | 0 | 20 | 2 |
| Maples, Chris, LAK | .995 | 46 | 366 | 38 | 2 | 406 | 29 |
| Matienzo, Danny, FTM | .987 | 102 | 756 | 64 | 11 | 831 | 73 |
| Merkle, Thomas, JUP | .977 | 42 | 403 | 18 | 10 | 431 | 34 |
| Ontiveros, Jeff, SAR | .993 | 19 | 126 | 13 | 1 | 140 | 10 |
| Parker, Tyler, PLM | 1.000 | 3 | 38 | 1 | 0 | 39 | 2 |
| Piazza, Mike, SLU | 1.000 | 1 | 6 | 0 | 0 | 6 | 0 |
| Requena, Alex, VB | 1.000 | 1 | 6 | 0 | 0 | 6 | 0 |
| Restko, JT, JUP | 1.000 | 1 | 8 | 0 | 0 | 8 | 0 |
| Rodriguez, Andres, SLU | .995 | 27 | 187 | 14 | 1 | 202 | 17 |
| Rohan, Jimmy, VB | 1.000 | 5 | 50 | 3 | 0 | 53 | 6 |
| Roper, Zack, CLW | 1.000 | 11 | 73 | 5 | 0 | 78 | 1 |
| Roughton, Jody, LAK* | .993 | 82 | 673 | 58 | 5 | 736 | 72 |
| Salas, Issmael, DAY | .986 | 7 | 65 | 4 | 1 | 70 | 6 |
| Sandoval, Michael, FTM | 1.000 | 1 | 3 | 0 | 0 | 3 | 0 |
| Santor, John, PLM | .996 | 24 | 213 | 11 | 1 | 225 | 19 |
| SCHUTZENHOFER, ANDY, PLM* | .991 | 108 | 967 | 62 | 9 | 1038 | 96 |
| Sing, Brandon, DAY | .985 | 111 | 923 | 57 | 15 | 995 | 85 |
| Sprout, Brian, VB | .969 | 15 | 116 | 9 | 4 | 129 | 5 |
| Tamburrino, Brett, FTM | 1.000 | 16 | 96 | 11 | 0 | 107 | 9 |
| Tempesta, Nick, CLW | 1.000 | 3 | 10 | 0 | 0 | 10 | 2 |
| Testa, Chris, VB* | .989 | 10 | 80 | 7 | 1 | 88 | 5 |
| Tucker, Michael, JUP | .984 | 37 | 285 | 23 | 5 | 313 | 24 |
| Van Buizen, Rodney, VB | .955 | 6 | 40 | 2 | 2 | 44 | 5 |
| Verbryke, Eric, TAM* | 1.000 | 1 | 2 | 0 | 0 | 2 | 0 |
| Walsh, Sean, CLW | 1.000 | 1 | 5 | 0 | 0 | 5 | 1 |
| West, Jeremy, SAR | .989 | 86 | 680 | 60 | 8 | 748 | 58 |
| Whittaker, Tim, DUN | .989 | 10 | 81 | 6 | 1 | 88 | 4 |
| Williams, Clyde, BRE* | .987 | 84 | 710 | 54 | 10 | 774 | 78 |
| Wyman, Spencer, JUP* | 1.000 | 1 | 8 | 0 | 0 | 8 | 0 |

## SECOND BASEMEN

| Player, Team | Pct. | G | PO | A | E | TC | DP |
|---|---|---|---|---|---|---|---|
| Aquilino, Anthony, CLW | .977 | 13 | 18 | 24 | 1 | 43 | 6 |
| Bass, Christopher, JUP | .973 | 95 | 170 | 266 | 12 | 448 | 48 |
| Batista, Wilson, SLU | .941 | 27 | 56 | 71 | 8 | 135 | 17 |
| Blasi, Blake, PLM | .946 | 34 | 53 | 87 | 8 | 148 | 18 |
| Boran, Patrick, SAR | 1.000 | 18 | 27 | 37 | 0 | 64 | 9 |
| Carroll, Wes, BRE | .972 | 26 | 53 | 85 | 4 | 142 | 15 |
| Clanton, Ja`Mar, BRE | 1.000 | 3 | 2 | 10 | 0 | 12 | 1 |
| Coats, Buck, DAY* | 1.000 | 1 | 0 | 1 | 0 | 1 | 0 |
| Cota, Carlo, DUN | .959 | 66 | 113 | 194 | 13 | 320 | 35 |
| Cruz, Jose Enrique, TAM | .969 | 7 | 10 | 21 | 1 | 32 | 3 |
| Curtis, Lee, SAR | .966 | 7 | 14 | 14 | 1 | 29 | 1 |
| Demarco, Matt, JUP* | 1.000 | 5 | 8 | 11 | 0 | 19 | 3 |
| Dowdy, Brett, VB | 1.000 | 8 | 11 | 14 | 0 | 25 | 3 |
| Doyle, Nate, LAK | 1.000 | 4 | 5 | 10 | 0 | 15 | 1 |
| Ehrnsberger, Chad, PLM | 1.000 | 12 | 20 | 26 | 0 | 46 | 6 |
| Gil, Luis, LAK | 1.000 | 10 | 10 | 19 | 0 | 29 | 6 |
| Gillitzer, Scott, VB | .957 | 11 | 17 | 28 | 2 | 47 | 7 |
| Gutierrez, Ricky, DAY | 1.000 | 1 | 1 | 0 | 0 | 1 | 0 |
| Hanson, Travis, PLM* | .981 | 49 | 93 | 166 | 5 | 264 | 30 |
| Hassey, Brad, DUN | .971 | 7 | 11 | 22 | 1 | 34 | 3 |
| Holman, Mario, TAM | .900 | 3 | 3 | 6 | 1 | 10 | 0 |
| Italiano, Nick, CLW* | 1.000 | 20 | 36 | 47 | 0 | 83 | 9 |
| Jones, Nick, DAY | .971 | 9 | 18 | 16 | 1 | 35 | 6 |
| Koutnik, Jared, TAM | .985 | 15 | 23 | 41 | 1 | 65 | 8 |
| Kuhaulua, Kaulana, FTM | .920 | 12 | 17 | 29 | 4 | 50 | 6 |
| Leon, Carlos, CLW | .984 | 25 | 43 | 79 | 2 | 124 | 18 |
| LOPEZ, GABE, TAM | .978 | 100 | 177 | 302 | 11 | 490 | 55 |
| Machado, Alejandro, BRE | .967 | 5 | 17 | 12 | 1 | 30 | 7 |
| Maples, Chris, LAK | 1.000 | 30 | 47 | 95 | 0 | 142 | 20 |
| Marquez, Uriak, DAY* | .846 | 3 | 6 | 5 | 2 | 13 | 2 |
| Mayorson, Manny, DUN | 1.000 | 3 | 4 | 10 | 0 | 14 | 0 |
| McCoy, Mike, PLM | .967 | 55 | 96 | 169 | 9 | 274 | 29 |
| McIntyre, Robert, SLU | .977 | 81 | 153 | 237 | 9 | 399 | 59 |
| Mejia, Gilberto, LAK | .961 | 31 | 43 | 80 | 5 | 128 | 17 |
| Merchan, Jesus, FTM | .977 | 39 | 70 | 97 | 4 | 171 | 23 |
| Mitchell, Lee, JUP | 1.000 | 1 | 2 | 1 | 0 | 3 | 0 |
| Mitchell, Russell, VB | .923 | 3 | 3 | 9 | 1 | 13 | 0 |
| Molina, Felix, FTM | .962 | 74 | 132 | 172 | 12 | 316 | 47 |
| Montanez, Luis, DAY | .942 | 20 | 25 | 56 | 5 | 86 | 7 |
| Norris, Shawn, BRE* | .959 | 21 | 46 | 70 | 5 | 121 | 12 |
| Ordorica, Eric, JUP | .968 | 35 | 57 | 93 | 5 | 155 | 19 |
| Pattee, Ben, FTM | .974 | 10 | 16 | 22 | 1 | 39 | 2 |
| Pena, Omar, PLM | 1.000 | 1 | 3 | 3 | 0 | 6 | 1 |
| Penalo, Alex, SAR | .920 | 7 | 12 | 11 | 2 | 25 | 2 |
| Raburn, Ryan, LAK | .810 | 3 | 8 | 9 | 4 | 21 | 1 |
| Ramos, Jason, SAR | .951 | 12 | 24 | 34 | 3 | 61 | 8 |
| Reaver, David, SLU | .944 | 15 | 30 | 37 | 4 | 71 | 9 |
| Reyes, Jose, SLU | .917 | 6 | 8 | 14 | 2 | 24 | 3 |
| Roberts, Ryan, DUN | .958 | 59 | 119 | 158 | 12 | 289 | 36 |
| Rodriguez, Andres, SLU | 1.000 | 2 | 6 | 5 | 0 | 11 | 1 |
| Rodriguez, Edgar, SLU | .926 | 7 | 9 | 16 | 2 | 27 | 4 |
| Rundgren, Rex, JUP | 1.000 | 2 | 3 | 5 | 0 | 8 | 3 |
| Salas, Issmael, DAY | .973 | 22 | 25 | 48 | 2 | 75 | 8 |
| Santana, Ralph, CLW* | .970 | 51 | 86 | 141 | 7 | 234 | 29 |
| Santora, Jack, CLW | .988 | 41 | 58 | 101 | 2 | 161 | 11 |
| Schneidmiller, Gary, SAR | .900 | 13 | 23 | 31 | 6 | 60 | 5 |
| Spearman, Jemel, DAY | .891 | 9 | 20 | 21 | 5 | 46 | 6 |
| Stone, Greg, SAR* | .962 | 24 | 51 | 49 | 4 | 104 | 11 |
| Stotts, JT, TAM | .982 | 10 | 23 | 32 | 1 | 56 | 11 |
| Suarez, Ignacio, SAR | .978 | 57 | 105 | 162 | 6 | 273 | 34 |
| Tamburrino, Brett, FTM | .943 | 12 | 21 | 29 | 3 | 53 | 5 |
| Tempesta, Nick, CLW | 1.000 | 8 | 5 | 19 | 0 | 24 | 3 |
| Theriot, Ryan, DAY | .971 | 64 | 124 | 205 | 10 | 339 | 51 |
| Thissen, Greg, BRE | .980 | 70 | 137 | 212 | 7 | 356 | 52 |
| Turner, Justin, SAR* | 1.000 | 7 | 11 | 23 | 0 | 34 | 4 |
| Woods, Michael, LAK | .965 | 66 | 112 | 187 | 11 | 310 | 44 |
| Yepez, Marcos, BRE | .917 | 4 | 5 | 17 | 2 | 24 | 2 |
| Young, Delwyn, VB | .951 | 115 | 166 | 276 | 23 | 465 | 39 |
| Young, Dustin, JUP | .917 | 2 | 8 | 3 | 1 | 12 | 1 |

## THIRD BASEMEN

| Player, Team | Pct. | G | PO | A | E | TC | DP |
|---|---|---|---|---|---|---|---|
| Alfonzo, Eliezer, JUP | .500 | 1 | 0 | 1 | 1 | 2 | 0 |
| Aquilino, Anthony, CLW | 1.000 | 1 | 1 | 2 | 0 | 3 | 1 |
| Baldiris, Aarom, SLU | .935 | 104 | 69 | 219 | 20 | 308 | 17 |
| Barthelemy, Ryan, CLW* | .957 | 11 | 9 | 13 | 1 | 23 | 0 |
| Bass, Christopher, JUP | 1.000 | 1 | 0 | 1 | 0 | 1 | 0 |
| Blasi, Blake, PLM | .750 | 8 | 3 | 6 | 3 | 12 | 1 |
| Boran, Patrick, SAR | .926 | 6 | 9 | 16 | 2 | 27 | 1 |
| Burgos, Omar, FTM | .935 | 30 | 19 | 53 | 5 | 77 | 5 |
| Caligiuri, Jay, SLU | .925 | 14 | 4 | 33 | 3 | 40 | 2 |
| Carroll, Wes, BRE | .895 | 14 | 11 | 23 | 4 | 38 | 4 |
| Castellano, John, CLW | .700 | 3 | 1 | 6 | 3 | 10 | 0 |
| Clanton, Ja`Mar, BRE | 1.000 | 3 | 1 | 3 | 0 | 4 | 0 |
| Coats, Buck, DAY* | .851 | 22 | 9 | 31 | 7 | 47 | 2 |
| Concepcion, Alberto, SAR | .938 | 45 | 26 | 65 | 6 | 97 | 7 |
| Corporan, Elvis, FTM | .900 | 8 | 3 | 15 | 2 | 20 | 1 |
| Cota, Carlo, DUN | .942 | 50 | 34 | 96 | 8 | 138 | 5 |
| Curtis, Lee, SAR | .900 | 3 | 3 | 6 | 1 | 10 | 1 |
| Demarco, Matt, JUP* | .727 | 7 | 1 | 7 | 3 | 11 | 0 |
| Dowdy, Brett, VB | 1.000 | 4 | 1 | 5 | 0 | 6 | 0 |
| Doyle, Nate, LAK | 1.000 | 1 | 1 | 0 | 0 | 1 | 0 |
| Dragicevich, Scott, DUN | .938 | 43 | 23 | 67 | 6 | 96 | 2 |
| Drobiak, Jayson, TAM* | 1.000 | 3 | 1 | 1 | 0 | 2 | 0 |
| Dryer, Matt, PLM | 1.000 | 1 | 0 | 2 | 0 | 2 | 1 |
| Duncan, Eric, TAM* | .939 | 48 | 25 | 68 | 6 | 99 | 4 |
| Ehrnsberger, Chad, PLM | .961 | 49 | 29 | 117 | 6 | 152 | 10 |
| Ellerson, Brian, BRE | .850 | 11 | 6 | 11 | 3 | 20 | 1 |

| Player, Team | Pct. | G | PO | A | E | TC | DP |
|---|---|---|---|---|---|---|---|
| Estrada, Kevin, PLM | .934 | 75 | 46 | 168 | 15 | 229 | 13 |
| Fulton, Jonathan, JUP | 1.000 | 1 | 2 | 1 | 0 | 3 | 0 |
| Garcia, Sergio, VB | 1.000 | 1 | 0 | 2 | 0 | 2 | 0 |
| Garcia, Travis, SLU | 1.000 | 2 | 0 | 4 | 0 | 4 | 1 |
| Gillitzer, Scott, VB | .929 | 23 | 14 | 38 | 4 | 56 | 0 |
| Hassey, Brad, DUN | .846 | 7 | 0 | 11 | 2 | 13 | 0 |
| Hodges, Scott, BRE* | .833 | 2 | 1 | 4 | 1 | 6 | 0 |
| Hood, Donny, DAY | .818 | 6 | 5 | 13 | 4 | 22 | 0 |
| Jiannetti, Joe, SLU | .765 | 9 | 4 | 9 | 4 | 17 | 0 |
| Jones, Terry, CLW | .891 | 41 | 23 | 59 | 10 | 92 | 5 |
| Koutnik, Jared, TAM | .911 | 17 | 13 | 28 | 4 | 45 | 4 |
| Krga, Mike, JUP | 1.000 | 1 | 1 | 2 | 0 | 3 | 0 |
| Laroche, Andy, VB | .901 | 54 | 26 | 83 | 12 | 121 | 4 |
| Leon, Carlos, CLW | 1.000 | 4 | 2 | 7 | 0 | 9 | 2 |
| LeVier, Brett, SAR | .970 | 18 | 15 | 50 | 2 | 67 | 6 |
| Lopez, Gabe, TAM | 1.000 | 1 | 0 | 3 | 0 | 3 | 1 |
| Maples, Chris, LAK | .945 | 16 | 13 | 39 | 3 | 55 | 6 |
| Marquez, Uriak, DAY* | 1.000 | 1 | 0 | 1 | 0 | 1 | 0 |
| McCoy, Mike, PLM | .960 | 6 | 4 | 20 | 1 | 25 | 1 |
| McGehee, Casey, DAY | .969 | 82 | 48 | 169 | 7 | 224 | 13 |
| Mejia, Gilberto, LAK | 1.000 | 1 | 0 | 1 | 0 | 1 | 0 |
| Merchan, Jesus, FTM | 1.000 | 2 | 0 | 2 | 0 | 2 | 0 |
| MITCHELL, LEE, JUP | .938 | 107 | 74 | 196 | 18 | 288 | 12 |
| Mitchell, Russell, VB | .928 | 38 | 29 | 48 | 6 | 83 | 4 |
| Moore, Scott, LAK* | .903 | 115 | 84 | 177 | 28 | 289 | 14 |
| Norris, Shawn, BRE* | .940 | 42 | 42 | 83 | 8 | 133 | 10 |
| Ordorica, Eric, JUP | .941 | 7 | 4 | 12 | 1 | 17 | 2 |
| Pattee, Ben, FTM | .908 | 35 | 19 | 60 | 8 | 87 | 8 |
| Raymundo, Gregg, DUN | .909 | 16 | 10 | 20 | 3 | 33 | 2 |
| Reaver, David, SLU | .500 | 1 | 1 | 0 | 1 | 2 | 0 |
| Richardson, Juan, CLW | 1.000 | 4 | 2 | 6 | 0 | 8 | 1 |
| Rodriguez, Andres, SLU | 1.000 | 1 | 1 | 0 | 0 | 1 | 0 |
| Rohan, Jimmy, VB | .500 | 1 | 0 | 1 | 1 | 2 | 0 |
| Rooi, Vince, BRE | .914 | 58 | 38 | 101 | 13 | 152 | 11 |
| Roper, Zack, PLM | 1.000 | 2 | 0 | 1 | 0 | 1 | 0 |
| Salas, Francisco, DAY* | 1.000 | 4 | 4 | 9 | 0 | 13 | 1 |
| Salas, Issmael, DAY | .941 | 20 | 15 | 33 | 3 | 51 | 5 |
| Sandoval, Michael, FTM | .923 | 37 | 20 | 52 | 6 | 78 | 3 |
| Santana, Ralph, CLW* | .840 | 7 | 6 | 15 | 4 | 25 | 0 |
| Sardinha, Bronson, TAM* | .865 | 61 | 35 | 112 | 23 | 170 | 7 |
| Schneidmiller, Gary, SAR | .972 | 14 | 12 | 23 | 1 | 36 | 1 |
| Spann, Chad, SAR | .894 | 54 | 45 | 81 | 15 | 141 | 9 |
| Sprout, Brian, VB | .941 | 12 | 2 | 14 | 1 | 17 | 0 |
| Stone, Greg, SAR* | 1.000 | 5 | 7 | 14 | 0 | 21 | 1 |
| Stotts, JT, TAM | 1.000 | 4 | 2 | 11 | 0 | 13 | 1 |
| Tablado, Raul, DUN | .882 | 21 | 11 | 34 | 6 | 51 | 2 |
| Tamburrino, Brett, FTM | .928 | 30 | 9 | 55 | 5 | 69 | 0 |
| Tempesta, Nick, CLW | .917 | 32 | 24 | 53 | 7 | 84 | 8 |
| Theriot, Ryan, DAY | .750 | 1 | 1 | 2 | 1 | 4 | 1 |
| Tucker, Michael, JUP | .975 | 19 | 11 | 28 | 1 | 40 | 2 |
| Turner, Justin, SAR* | .667 | 1 | 2 | 2 | 2 | 6 | 0 |
| Van Buizen, Rodney, VB | .909 | 5 | 2 | 8 | 1 | 11 | 1 |
| Vechionacci, Marcos, TAM | 1.000 | 1 | 1 | 3 | 0 | 4 | 1 |
| Walsh, Sean, CLW | .915 | 50 | 23 | 95 | 11 | 129 | 9 |
| Wigginton, Ty, SLU | 1.000 | 2 | 2 | 1 | 0 | 3 | 0 |
| Wilson, Andrew, SLU | 1.000 | 2 | 0 | 6 | 0 | 6 | 0 |
| Yepez, Marcos, BRE | 1.000 | 4 | 1 | 4 | 0 | 5 | 0 |

## SHORTSTOPS

| Player, Team | Pct. | G | PO | A | E | TC | DP |
|---|---|---|---|---|---|---|---|
| Abreu, Tony, VB | .930 | 11 | 22 | 18 | 3 | 43 | 1 |
| Amezquita, Octavio, LAK | .977 | 8 | 19 | 24 | 1 | 44 | 9 |
| Andino, Robert, JUP | .965 | 48 | 62 | 129 | 7 | 198 | 21 |
| Aquilino, Anthony, CLW | 1.000 | 2 | 3 | 5 | 0 | 8 | 2 |
| Bartlett, Richard, VB | .750 | 1 | 2 | 1 | 1 | 4 | 0 |
| Batista, Wilson, SLU | .889 | 2 | 2 | 6 | 1 | 9 | 0 |
| Blasi, Blake, PLM | .800 | 4 | 0 | 8 | 2 | 10 | 0 |
| Boran, Patrick, SAR | 1.000 | 3 | 4 | 3 | 0 | 7 | 0 |
| Bynum, Seth, BRE | .931 | 19 | 12 | 42 | 4 | 58 | 10 |
| Carroll, Wes, BRE | .947 | 30 | 46 | 97 | 8 | 151 | 28 |
| Clanton, Ja`Mar, BRE | 1.000 | 3 | 5 | 4 | 0 | 9 | 1 |
| Coats, Buck, DAY* | .920 | 86 | 122 | 212 | 29 | 363 | 46 |
| Contreras, Jose, BRE | .875 | 4 | 12 | 9 | 3 | 24 | 2 |
| Cruz, Jose Enrique, TAM | 1.000 | 1 | 1 | 3 | 0 | 4 | 0 |
| Demarco, Matt, JUP* | 1.000 | 1 | 1 | 0 | 0 | 1 | 0 |
| Dowdy, Brett, VB | .833 | 3 | 3 | 2 | 1 | 6 | 0 |
| Doyle, Nate, LAK | 1.000 | 1 | 0 | 1 | 0 | 1 | 0 |
| Dragicevich, Scott, DUN | 1.000 | 6 | 9 | 16 | 0 | 25 | 4 |
| Estrada, Kevin, PLM | .989 | 15 | 32 | 60 | 1 | 93 | 17 |
| Fulton, Jonathan, JUP | .867 | 5 | 6 | 20 | 4 | 30 | 3 |
| Giarratano, Tony, LAK | .968 | 53 | 89 | 150 | 8 | 247 | 34 |
| Gil, Luis, LAK | .983 | 14 | 18 | 40 | 1 | 59 | 11 |
| Gillitzer, Scott, VB | .943 | 10 | 11 | 22 | 2 | 35 | 3 |
| Gutierrez, Ricky, DAY | 1.000 | 1 | 2 | 1 | 0 | 3 | 1 |
| Guzman, Joel, VB | .972 | 87 | 138 | 237 | 11 | 386 | 33 |
| Hassey, Brad, DUN | 1.000 | 9 | 9 | 24 | 0 | 33 | 7 |
| Hernandez, Anderson, LAK | .983 | 26 | 35 | 84 | 2 | 121 | 20 |
| Hu, Chin-Lung, VB | .950 | 19 | 21 | 55 | 4 | 80 | 14 |
| Jaramillo, Milko, PLM | .952 | 15 | 30 | 49 | 4 | 83 | 10 |
| Johnson, JJ, DAY | 1.000 | 1 | 0 | 5 | 0 | 5 | 1 |
| Koutnik, Jared, TAM | .912 | 46 | 47 | 118 | 16 | 181 | 25 |
| Kuhaulua, Kaulana, FTM | .953 | 82 | 106 | 236 | 17 | 359 | 56 |
| LAYA, RAYNER, PLM | .954 | 101 | 173 | 344 | 25 | 542 | 73 |
| Leon, Carlos, CLW | .988 | 20 | 32 | 52 | 1 | 85 | 7 |
| Lopez, Gabe, TAM | .500 | 1 | 1 | 0 | 1 | 2 | 0 |
| Machado, Alejandro, BRE | .960 | 38 | 63 | 107 | 7 | 177 | 16 |
| Machado, Anderson, CLW | .852 | 7 | 11 | 12 | 4 | 27 | 1 |
| Marquez, Uriak, DAY* | 1.000 | 1 | 1 | 2 | 0 | 3 | 0 |
| Mayorson, Manny, DUN | .963 | 86 | 148 | 239 | 15 | 402 | 48 |
| McCoy, Mike, PLM | .833 | 1 | 1 | 4 | 1 | 6 | 1 |
| McIntyre, Robert, SLU | 1.000 | 2 | 0 | 3 | 0 | 3 | 0 |
| Mejia, Gilberto, LAK | .969 | 35 | 54 | 100 | 5 | 159 | 15 |
| Mendez, Deivi, TAM | .903 | 20 | 33 | 60 | 10 | 103 | 8 |
| Merchan, Jesus, FTM | .959 | 30 | 57 | 82 | 6 | 145 | 20 |
| Molina, Felix, FTM | .898 | 26 | 32 | 65 | 11 | 108 | 12 |
| Norris, Shawn, BRE* | .977 | 30 | 55 | 74 | 3 | 132 | 19 |
| Ordonez, Rey, DAY | 1.000 | 3 | 3 | 3 | 0 | 6 | 2 |
| Ordorica, Eric, JUP | .946 | 12 | 9 | 26 | 2 | 37 | 3 |
| Pedroia, Dustin, SAR | 1.000 | 30 | 44 | 85 | 0 | 129 | 17 |
| Pena, Omar, PLM | 1.000 | 1 | 0 | 2 | 0 | 2 | 0 |
| Penalo, Alex, SAR | .786 | 4 | 3 | 8 | 3 | 14 | 1 |
| Ragsdale, Corey, SLU | .941 | 124 | 237 | 387 | 39 | 663 | 96 |
| Ramirez, Hanley, SAR | .939 | 61 | 78 | 169 | 16 | 263 | 30 |
| Ramos, Jason, SAR | .914 | 10 | 13 | 19 | 3 | 35 | 2 |
| Raymundo, Gregg, DUN | .833 | 3 | 5 | 10 | 3 | 18 | 1 |
| Reaver, David, SLU | 1.000 | 4 | 6 | 12 | 0 | 18 | 2 |
| Rohan, Jimmy, VB | .750 | 1 | 1 | 2 | 1 | 4 | 0 |
| Rundgren, Rex, JUP | .953 | 71 | 96 | 248 | 17 | 361 | 45 |
| Salas, Issmael, DAY | .875 | 1 | 2 | 5 | 1 | 8 | 0 |
| Santora, Jack, CLW | .945 | 67 | 102 | 173 | 16 | 291 | 39 |
| Sprout, Brian, VB | 1.000 | 4 | 4 | 5 | 0 | 9 | 1 |
| Stone, Greg, SAR* | .923 | 6 | 5 | 19 | 2 | 26 | 4 |
| Stotts, JT, TAM | .936 | 17 | 33 | 55 | 6 | 94 | 16 |
| Suarez, Ignacio, SAR | .950 | 26 | 39 | 74 | 6 | 119 | 15 |
| Tablado, Raul, DUN | .906 | 32 | 51 | 84 | 14 | 149 | 25 |
| Tejeda, Ferdin, TAM | .979 | 49 | 84 | 146 | 5 | 235 | 32 |
| Tempesta, Nick, CLW | .953 | 56 | 89 | 136 | 11 | 236 | 29 |
| Theriot, Ryan, DAY | .957 | 38 | 58 | 96 | 7 | 161 | 21 |
| Turner, Justin, SAR* | .667 | 1 | 0 | 2 | 1 | 3 | 0 |
| Van Buizen, Rodney, VB | .974 | 7 | 12 | 25 | 1 | 38 | 4 |
| Walsh, Sean, CLW | 1.000 | 1 | 0 | 1 | 0 | 1 | 0 |
| Woodward, Chris, DUN | 1.000 | 6 | 8 | 9 | 0 | 17 | 3 |
| Yepez, Marcos, BRE | .905 | 3 | 6 | 13 | 2 | 21 | 3 |

## OUTFIELDERS

| Player, Team | Pct. | G | PO | A | E | TC | DP |
|---|---|---|---|---|---|---|---|
| Abercrombie, Reggie, VB | .985 | 33 | 61 | 3 | 1 | 65 | 0 |
| Ambrosini, Dominick, BRE* | .947 | 48 | 69 | 3 | 4 | 76 | 1 |
| Aponte, Jose, JUP* | .986 | 85 | 130 | 6 | 2 | 138 | 2 |
| Bailie, Stefan, SAR | 1.000 | 1 | 0 | 1 | 0 | 1 | 0 |
| Barthelemy, Ryan, CLW* | .875 | 6 | 7 | 0 | 1 | 8 | 0 |
| Batista, Rafael, BRE | 1.000 | 1 | 1 | 0 | 0 | 1 | 0 |
| Bergeron, Peter, BRE* | 1.000 | 4 | 7 | 0 | 0 | 7 | 0 |
| Bonner, Adam, JUP* | 1.000 | 34 | 63 | 4 | 0 | 67 | 0 |
| Boran, Patrick, SAR | 1.000 | 6 | 11 | 1 | 0 | 12 | 0 |
| Boyd, Shaun, PLM | 1.000 | 38 | 78 | 1 | 0 | 79 | 0 |
| Brinkley, Dante, SLU | 1.000 | 5 | 12 | 2 | 0 | 14 | 0 |
| Brown, Andy, TAM* | 1.000 | 18 | 48 | 1 | 0 | 49 | 0 |
| Burford, Kevin, CLW* | .900 | 5 | 9 | 0 | 1 | 10 | 0 |
| Butler, Keith, DAY | .990 | 76 | 100 | 3 | 1 | 104 | 1 |
| Cabrera, Melky, TAM | .983 | 82 | 167 | 5 | 3 | 175 | 1 |
| Carson, Matt, TAM | 1.000 | 35 | 62 | 3 | 0 | 65 | 2 |
| Catalanotte, Greg, PLM | .974 | 109 | 144 | 6 | 4 | 154 | 0 |
| Chavez, Ender, BRE* | .963 | 15 | 25 | 1 | 1 | 27 | 0 |
| Chop, Chad, BRE* | .986 | 53 | 70 | 1 | 1 | 72 | 0 |
| Clark, Daryl, PLM* | .500 | 2 | 1 | 0 | 1 | 2 | 0 |
| Clements, Zack, SLU | 1.000 | 1 | 1 | 1 | 0 | 2 | 0 |
| Clevlen, Brent, LAK | .934 | 116 | 200 | 14 | 15 | 229 | 3 |
| Correll, Brad, CLW | 1.000 | 27 | 43 | 3 | 0 | 46 | 0 |
| Cosbey, Chris, CLW* | .957 | 49 | 85 | 4 | 4 | 93 | 2 |
| Cotto, Pedro, LAK* | .988 | 43 | 80 | 2 | 1 | 83 | 0 |
| Cronkhite, Ian, SAR* | .929 | 12 | 12 | 1 | 1 | 14 | 0 |
| Curtis, Lee, SAR | 1.000 | 2 | 3 | 0 | 0 | 3 | 0 |
| Davenport, Ron, DUN* | .966 | 72 | 135 | 7 | 5 | 147 | 2 |

| Player, Team | Pct. | G | PO | A | E | TC | DP |
|---|---|---|---|---|---|---|---|
| Deeds, Doug, FTM* | .982 | 91 | 153 | 9 | 3 | 165 | 2 |
| Diaz, Frank, BRE | .972 | 113 | 225 | 16 | 7 | 248 | 2 |
| Dowdy, Brett, VB | 1.000 | 20 | 25 | 0 | 0 | 25 | 0 |
| Duncan, Eric, TAM* | 1.000 | 1 | 1 | 0 | 0 | 1 | 0 |
| Duncan, Shelley, TAM | 1.000 | 6 | 8 | 0 | 0 | 8 | 0 |
| Durbin, Chris, SAR | .985 | 124 | 243 | 21 | 4 | 268 | 5 |
| Dyson, Trey, VB* | 1.000 | 7 | 9 | 0 | 0 | 9 | 0 |
| Ellerson, Brian, BRE | 1.000 | 1 | 1 | 0 | 0 | 1 | 0 |
| Evans, Terry, PLM | .938 | 18 | 30 | 0 | 2 | 32 | 0 |
| Everett, Carl, BRE | 1.000 | 3 | 3 | 0 | 0 | 3 | 0 |
| Ezi, Travis, JUP | 1.000 | 72 | 133 | 4 | 0 | 137 | 0 |
| Floyd, Cliff, SLU* | 1.000 | 1 | 1 | 0 | 0 | 1 | 0 |
| Floyd, Mike, CLW | .982 | 100 | 211 | 10 | 4 | 225 | 3 |
| Frazier, Charles, JUP | .994 | 80 | 148 | 5 | 1 | 154 | 0 |
| Frome, Jason, PLM* | .966 | 28 | 55 | 1 | 2 | 58 | 1 |
| Garcia, Miguel, SLU* | 1.000 | 5 | 5 | 0 | 0 | 5 | 0 |
| Gibbs, Kevin, CLW | 1.000 | 3 | 2 | 0 | 0 | 2 | 0 |
| Gillitzer, Scott, VB | 1.000 | 21 | 36 | 4 | 0 | 40 | 1 |
| Goelz, Bryan, VB* | .974 | 99 | 181 | 7 | 5 | 193 | 1 |
| Gorecki, Reid, PLM | .965 | 115 | 234 | 12 | 9 | 255 | 2 |
| Gradoville, Tim, CLW | .900 | 5 | 8 | 1 | 1 | 10 | 0 |
| GREENBERG, ADAM, DAY* | 1.000 | 88 | 178 | 4 | 0 | 182 | 1 |
| Guillen, Rodolfo, TAM | .981 | 74 | 149 | 6 | 3 | 158 | 1 |
| Guzman, Garrett, FTM* | .980 | 54 | 87 | 12 | 2 | 101 | 3 |
| Hermida, Jeremy, JUP* | .936 | 78 | 125 | 7 | 9 | 141 | 0 |
| Hoorelbeke, Jesse, VB | 1.000 | 1 | 1 | 0 | 0 | 1 | 0 |
| Hunter, Brian, PLM | 1.000 | 2 | 3 | 0 | 0 | 3 | 0 |
| Jenkins, Neil, LAK | .983 | 31 | 54 | 3 | 1 | 58 | 1 |
| Jiannetti, Joe, SLU | .971 | 60 | 96 | 3 | 3 | 102 | 1 |
| Johnson, Eric, SAR | 1.000 | 17 | 32 | 1 | 0 | 33 | 0 |
| Johnson, JJ, DAY | .944 | 91 | 155 | 13 | 10 | 178 | 2 |
| Kavourias, Jim, JUP | 1.000 | 16 | 33 | 0 | 0 | 33 | 0 |
| Kemp, Matt, VB | .957 | 11 | 21 | 1 | 1 | 23 | 0 |
| Klemm, Chris, CLW* | .938 | 7 | 15 | 0 | 1 | 16 | 0 |
| Koutnik, Jared, TAM | 1.000 | 8 | 16 | 1 | 0 | 17 | 0 |
| Lawson, Forrest, SLU | .925 | 26 | 36 | 1 | 3 | 40 | 0 |
| Lemanczyk, Matt, PLM | .993 | 83 | 132 | 4 | 1 | 137 | 0 |
| Lofton, Kenny, TAM* | 1.000 | 0 | 1 | 0 | 0 | 1 | 0 |
| Malek, Bobby, SLU* | .972 | 101 | 163 | 10 | 5 | 178 | 2 |
| Marcos, Emilio, VB | .946 | 19 | 34 | 1 | 2 | 37 | 0 |
| Mattle, David, LAK* | .971 | 62 | 96 | 3 | 3 | 102 | 2 |
| McKnight, Lukas, DAY* | 1.000 | 5 | 10 | 0 | 0 | 10 | 0 |
| Medina, Rodney, DUN | .977 | 45 | 83 | 2 | 2 | 87 | 0 |
| Mejia, Gilberto, LAK | 1.000 | 19 | 37 | 3 | 0 | 40 | 0 |
| Mendez, Victor, LAK | .993 | 120 | 290 | 14 | 2 | 306 | 2 |
| Milledge, Lastings, SLU | 1.000 | 22 | 43 | 4 | 0 | 47 | 0 |
| Milons, Jereme, VB | 1.000 | 11 | 27 | 0 | 0 | 27 | 0 |
| Moss, Brandon, SAR* | 1.000 | 21 | 35 | 2 | 0 | 37 | 1 |
| Murphy, David, SAR* | .986 | 69 | 132 | 5 | 2 | 139 | 1 |
| Murton, Matthew, DAY | 1.000 | 19 | 28 | 1 | 0 | 29 | 0 |
| Murton, Matthew, SAR | .990 | 100 | 188 | 13 | 2 | 203 | 4 |
| Murton, Matthew, DAY-SAR | .991 | 119 | 216 | 14 | 2 | 232 | 4 |
| Negron, Miguel, DUN* | .981 | 94 | 208 | 4 | 4 | 216 | 1 |
| Oeltjen, Trent, FTM* | .994 | 83 | 163 | 1 | 1 | 165 | 1 |
| Parker, Rashad, SLU | .952 | 11 | 20 | 0 | 1 | 21 | 0 |
| Parker, Tyler, PLM | .000 | 1 | 0 | 0 | 1 | 1 | 0 |
| Pattee, Ben, FTM | .750 | 1 | 3 | 0 | 1 | 4 | 0 |
| Perodin, Ron, FTM* | .977 | 90 | 163 | 4 | 4 | 171 | 0 |
| Pie, Felix, DAY* | .979 | 104 | 223 | 10 | 5 | 238 | 0 |
| Quintana, Miguel, CLW* | .986 | 68 | 130 | 6 | 2 | 138 | 1 |
| Requena, Alex, VB | .961 | 109 | 213 | 10 | 9 | 232 | 2 |
| Reynolds, Wilton, LAK | .949 | 19 | 33 | 4 | 2 | 39 | 0 |
| Roberson, Chris, CLW | .957 | 81 | 195 | 6 | 9 | 210 | 2 |
| Roberts, Dave, VB* | 1.000 | 2 | 4 | 0 | 0 | 4 | 0 |
| Rodriguez, Edgar, SLU | 1.000 | 1 | 1 | 0 | 0 | 1 | 0 |
| Rodriguez, Marcos, PLM* | 1.000 | 9 | 5 | 0 | 0 | 5 | 0 |
| Rohleder, Andy, JUP | .956 | 27 | 41 | 2 | 2 | 45 | 1 |
| Rombley, Danny, BRE | .960 | 60 | 114 | 6 | 5 | 125 | 2 |
| Romero, Alex, FTM | .989 | 83 | 183 | 4 | 2 | 189 | 2 |
| Roper, Zack, CLW | 1.000 | 7 | 10 | 0 | 0 | 10 | 0 |
| Sandoval, Michael, FTM | 1.000 | 2 | 2 | 0 | 0 | 2 | 0 |
| Santana, Ralph, CLW* | 1.000 | 23 | 46 | 7 | 0 | 53 | 0 |
| Schutzenhofer, Andy, PLM* | 1.000 | 3 | 4 | 1 | 0 | 5 | 0 |
| Seuss, Adam, SLU* | 1.000 | 2 | 3 | 1 | 0 | 4 | 0 |
| Shanks, James, JUP | .988 | 33 | 79 | 2 | 1 | 82 | 2 |
| Sing, Brandon, DAY | 1.000 | 3 | 2 | 0 | 0 | 2 | 0 |
| Sitzman, Jay, SAR* | .990 | 67 | 95 | 3 | 1 | 99 | 2 |
| Slack, Jon, SLU* | .991 | 105 | 221 | 9 | 2 | 232 | 1 |
| Spencer, Shane, TAM | 1.000 | 2 | 4 | 0 | 0 | 4 | 0 |
| Sprout, Brian, VB | .987 | 49 | 74 | 3 | 1 | 78 | 0 |
| Tamburrino, Brett, FTM | 1.000 | 18 | 26 | 1 | 0 | 27 | 0 |
| Testa, Chris, VB* | .857 | 20 | 30 | 0 | 5 | 35 | 0 |
| Thissen, Greg, BRE | 1.000 | 12 | 12 | 2 | 0 | 14 | 1 |
| Tingler, Jayce, DUN* | .990 | 116 | 187 | 15 | 2 | 204 | 0 |
| Tucker, Mamon, PLM | .913 | 20 | 20 | 1 | 2 | 23 | 0 |
| Turay, Alhaji, SLU | .916 | 62 | 83 | 4 | 8 | 95 | 0 |
| Turner, Chris, SAR | 1.000 | 3 | 9 | 0 | 0 | 9 | 0 |
| Tuttle, Jason, BRE* | .985 | 83 | 129 | 4 | 2 | 135 | 0 |
| Van Buizen, Rodney, VB | 1.000 | 29 | 41 | 2 | 0 | 43 | 0 |
| Van Meetren, Jason, TAM | 1.000 | 5 | 8 | 0 | 0 | 8 | 0 |
| Verbryke, Eric, TAM* | .975 | 98 | 147 | 7 | 4 | 158 | 0 |
| Vroman, Douglas, BRE | 1.000 | 1 | 2 | 0 | 0 | 2 | 0 |
| Vukovich, Vince, CLW* | 1.000 | 49 | 71 | 5 | 0 | 76 | 0 |
| Walsh, Sean, CLW | 1.000 | 6 | 5 | 3 | 0 | 8 | 1 |
| Waugh, Jason, DUN | .965 | 78 | 133 | 3 | 5 | 141 | 0 |
| Wilson, Andrew, SLU | 1.000 | 2 | 4 | 0 | 0 | 4 | 0 |
| Winrow, Tommy, TAM* | .969 | 80 | 118 | 6 | 4 | 128 | 0 |
| Young, Dustin, JUP | 1.000 | 1 | 1 | 0 | 0 | 1 | 0 |

## CATCHERS

| Player, Team | Pct. | G | PO | A | E | TC | DP | PB |
|---|---|---|---|---|---|---|---|---|
| Alfonzo, Eliezer, JUP | .994 | 43 | 285 | 40 | 2 | 327 | 2 | 5 |
| Ambrosini, Anthony, BRE | 1.000 | 4 | 21 | 4 | 0 | 25 | 0 | 3 |
| Anderson, Jimmy, SLU | 1.000 | 2 | 9 | 0 | 0 | 9 | 0 | 0 |
| Apodaca, Luis, BRE | .973 | 14 | 97 | 10 | 3 | 110 | 0 | 3 |
| Arlis, Patrick,E., JUP | .947 | 3 | 16 | 2 | 1 | 19 | 0 | 0 |
| Arnerich, Tony, JUP | .984 | 33 | 227 | 26 | 4 | 257 | 1 | 8 |
| Bacon, Matt, SLU* | .952 | 3 | 19 | 1 | 1 | 21 | 0 | 2 |
| Barnes, Justin, LAK | 1.000 | 2 | 5 | 0 | 0 | 5 | 0 | 0 |
| Brown, Dusty, SAR | .982 | 32 | 200 | 22 | 4 | 226 | 3 | 15 |
| Brown, Greg, JUP | .986 | 14 | 62 | 7 | 1 | 70 | 0 | 2 |
| Buckley, Jim, SAR | .993 | 68 | 411 | 27 | 3 | 441 | 4 | 24 |
| Castellano, John, CLW | 1.000 | 3 | 12 | 0 | 0 | 12 | 0 | 0 |
| Clements, Zack, SLU | .969 | 50 | 283 | 34 | 10 | 327 | 5 | 12 |
| Cleveland, Russ, LAK | .975 | 21 | 109 | 6 | 3 | 118 | 1 | 5 |
| Concepcion, Alberto, SAR | .992 | 43 | 334 | 22 | 3 | 359 | 4 | 5 |
| Corporan, Elvis, FTM | .989 | 31 | 165 | 12 | 2 | 179 | 0 | 11 |
| Cruz, Edgar, CLW | 1.000 | 7 | 31 | 4 | 0 | 35 | 1 | 1 |
| Eickhorst, Chris, PLM | 1.000 | 10 | 42 | 5 | 0 | 47 | 0 | 1 |
| Ellis, AJ, VB | .993 | 35 | 245 | 26 | 2 | 273 | 2 | 4 |
| Emmerick, Josh, BRE | .984 | 44 | 277 | 25 | 5 | 307 | 3 | 9 |
| Geiger, Kyle, FTM | .970 | 27 | 149 | 12 | 5 | 166 | 1 | 6 |
| Gradoville, Tim, CLW | .968 | 49 | 266 | 39 | 10 | 315 | 2 | 7 |
| Grzecka, Casey, JUP | .984 | 52 | 343 | 36 | 6 | 385 | 1 | 11 |
| Guevara, Orlando, CLW | 1.000 | 2 | 5 | 2 | 0 | 7 | 0 | 0 |
| Hietpas, Joe, SLU | .983 | 55 | 349 | 48 | 7 | 404 | 1 | 6 |
| Huber, Justin, SLU | 1.000 | 4 | 31 | 4 | 0 | 35 | 0 | 0 |
| Kennedy, Bryan, FTM* | 1.000 | 2 | 16 | 0 | 0 | 16 | 0 | 1 |
| Kratz, Erik, DUN | .991 | 13 | 94 | 11 | 1 | 106 | 0 | 1 |
| Kweon, Yoon-Min, DAY | .833 | 3 | 5 | 0 | 1 | 6 | 0 | 0 |
| Madera, Sandy, TAM | 1.000 | 2 | 11 | 0 | 0 | 11 | 0 | 0 |
| Manriquez, Salomon, BRE | .976 | 14 | 70 | 13 | 2 | 85 | 2 | 4 |
| Maples, Chris, LAK | 1.000 | 1 | 8 | 1 | 0 | 9 | 0 | 0 |
| Marcelli, Brandon, PLM | 1.000 | 10 | 31 | 4 | 0 | 35 | 0 | 1 |
| Margalski, Ben, BRE* | .996 | 30 | 239 | 29 | 1 | 269 | 2 | 5 |
| Martin, Russell, VB | .990 | 101 | 845 | 91 | 9 | 945 | 6 | 13 |
| Matienzo, Danny, FTM | 1.000 | 2 | 7 | 1 | 0 | 8 | 0 | 0 |
| Mauer, Joe, FTM* | 1.000 | 1 | 7 | 0 | 0 | 7 | 0 | 0 |
| McGehee, Casey, DAY | .986 | 28 | 190 | 14 | 3 | 207 | 2 | 6 |
| McKnight, Lukas, DAY* | .968 | 30 | 173 | 8 | 6 | 187 | 0 | 1 |
| McMillan, Andrew, BRE | .993 | 18 | 127 | 18 | 1 | 146 | 1 | 3 |
| Mejia, Manuel, TAM | .987 | 37 | 202 | 30 | 3 | 235 | 0 | 8 |
| Montz, Luke, BRE | 1.000 | 1 | 8 | 1 | 0 | 9 | 0 | 0 |
| Morales, Jose, FTM | .976 | 81 | 587 | 59 | 16 | 662 | 6 | 10 |
| Motte, Jason, PLM | .987 | 108 | 509 | 92 | 8 | 609 | 9 | 13 |
| Ontiveros, Jeff, SAR | 1.000 | 6 | 29 | 3 | 0 | 32 | 1 | 1 |
| Palmer, Cody, PLM | 1.000 | 1 | 1 | 0 | 0 | 1 | 0 | 0 |
| Piazza, Tony, SLU | 1.000 | 1 | 3 | 0 | 0 | 3 | 0 | 0 |
| Pratt, Trent, CLW | .987 | 84 | 545 | 53 | 8 | 606 | 7 | 12 |
| Rabelo, Mike, LAK | .988 | 85 | 514 | 48 | 7 | 569 | 4 | 11 |
| REYES, JOSE, DAY | .993 | 80 | 586 | 77 | 5 | 668 | 5 | 4 |
| Roa, Joel, LAK | 1.000 | 4 | 18 | 0 | 0 | 18 | 0 | 1 |
| Rodriguez, Robert, BRE | .944 | 2 | 17 | 0 | 1 | 18 | 0 | 0 |
| Rosenthal, Ben, PLM* | .980 | 48 | 176 | 16 | 4 | 196 | 0 | 8 |
| Santos, Omir, TAM | .993 | 37 | 277 | 24 | 2 | 303 | 0 | 1 |
| Schneider, John, DUN | .993 | 56 | 397 | 34 | 3 | 434 | 3 | 4 |
| Sprowl, John Mark, TAM* | .994 | 64 | 459 | 40 | 3 | 502 | 1 | 13 |
| Tempesta, Nick, CLW | .800 | 5 | 4 | 0 | 1 | 5 | 0 | 0 |
| Tintor, Eli, FTM | 1.000 | 6 | 47 | 3 | 0 | 50 | 0 | 2 |
| Trezza, Alex, LAK* | .986 | 27 | 122 | 15 | 2 | 139 | 0 | 3 |
| Whittaker, Tim, DUN | 1.000 | 6 | 46 | 5 | 0 | 51 | 0 | 2 |
| Wilson, Brandon, SLU | .977 | 29 | 188 | 23 | 5 | 216 | 2 | 5 |
| Wong, Ivanosky, BRE | 1.000 | 1 | 12 | 1 | 0 | 13 | 0 | 0 |

| Player, Team | Pct. | G | PO | A | E | TC | DP | PB |
|---|---|---|---|---|---|---|---|---|
| Wyman, Spencer, JUP* | 1.000 | 2 | 6 | 2 | 0 | 8 | 0 | 0 |
| Yepez, Jose, DUN | .987 | 62 | 427 | 45 | 6 | 478 | 3 | 5 |

## PITCHERS

| Player, Team | Pct. | G | PO | A | E | TC | DP |
|---|---|---|---|---|---|---|---|
| Abreu, Eric, TAM | 1.000 | 3 | 1 | 2 | 0 | 3 | 0 |
| Acosta, Domingo, SLU | .000 | 4 | 0 | 0 | 0 | 0 | 0 |
| Adamczyk, Tyler, PLM | .875 | 26 | 17 | 25 | 6 | 48 | 4 |
| Akens, Phil, JUP | .000 | 5 | 0 | 0 | 0 | 0 | 0 |
| Ankiel, Rick, PLM* | 1.000 | 3 | 0 | 2 | 0 | 2 | 0 |
| Armas, Tony, BRE | 1.000 | 3 | 0 | 2 | 0 | 2 | 1 |
| Arnerich, Tony, JUP | .667 | 4 | 0 | 2 | 1 | 3 | 0 |
| Arnold, Jason, DUN | 1.000 | 3 | 1 | 0 | 0 | 1 | 0 |
| Artiles, Carlos, TAM* | .500 | 13 | 0 | 1 | 1 | 2 | 0 |
| Atlee, Thomas, DAY | .857 | 46 | 4 | 2 | 1 | 7 | 0 |
| Baez, Federico, DAY | .923 | 48 | 3 | 9 | 1 | 13 | 1 |
| Bailey, Chad, VB* | 1.000 | 3 | 0 | 3 | 0 | 3 | 0 |
| Baisley, Brad, VB | .857 | 9 | 3 | 3 | 1 | 7 | 0 |
| Baker, Scott, FTM | 1.000 | 7 | 6 | 6 | 0 | 12 | 0 |
| Baldwin, Andy, LAK | 1.000 | 13 | 1 | 2 | 0 | 3 | 1 |
| Banks, Josh, DUN | 1.000 | 11 | 5 | 5 | 0 | 10 | 0 |
| Bannister, Brian, SLU | .920 | 20 | 8 | 15 | 2 | 25 | 0 |
| Barlow, Chris, BRE | .952 | 27 | 9 | 11 | 1 | 21 | 1 |
| Barrett, Ricky, FTM* | 1.000 | 17 | 2 | 7 | 0 | 9 | 0 |
| Bartlett, Richard, VB | 1.000 | 40 | 9 | 11 | 0 | 20 | 2 |
| Batista, Roberto, PLM | 1.000 | 53 | 4 | 11 | 0 | 15 | 0 |
| Bazardo, Yorman, JUP | .932 | 25 | 14 | 27 | 3 | 44 | 4 |
| Bechtel, Chuck, LAK | .000 | 3 | 0 | 0 | 0 | 0 | 0 |
| Bergmann, Jason, BRE | .833 | 24 | 2 | 3 | 1 | 6 | 0 |
| Bierd, Randor, LAK | .857 | 7 | 1 | 5 | 1 | 7 | 0 |
| Billingsley, Chad, VB | .828 | 18 | 14 | 10 | 5 | 29 | 0 |
| Birtwell, John, LAK | 1.000 | 20 | 2 | 3 | 0 | 5 | 0 |
| Blackburn, Nick, FTM | 1.000 | 9 | 4 | 4 | 0 | 8 | 1 |
| Blair, Buddy, PLM* | .981 | 26 | 5 | 46 | 1 | 52 | 4 |
| Blankenship, John, TAM* | 1.000 | 11 | 1 | 4 | 0 | 5 | 0 |
| Borrell, Danny, TAM* | 1.000 | 4 | 1 | 0 | 0 | 1 | 0 |
| Bourgeois, Nick, CLW* | .952 | 26 | 6 | 14 | 1 | 21 | 2 |
| Bowyer, Travis, FTM | .727 | 17 | 5 | 3 | 3 | 11 | 0 |
| Broxton, Jonathan, VB | 1.000 | 23 | 9 | 21 | 0 | 30 | 2 |
| Brumit, Matthew, TAM | 1.000 | 10 | 2 | 2 | 0 | 4 | 0 |
| Burnett, AJ, JUP | .000 | 1 | 0 | 0 | 0 | 0 | 0 |
| Butto, Francisco, CLW | 1.000 | 36 | 8 | 9 | 0 | 17 | 0 |
| Buzachero, Bubbie, DUN | .857 | 51 | 5 | 7 | 2 | 14 | 1 |
| Byard, David, SLU | 1.000 | 37 | 3 | 16 | 0 | 19 | 2 |
| Byers, Waylon, JUP* | 1.000 | 5 | 1 | 1 | 0 | 2 | 0 |
| Cameron, Kevin, FTM | .929 | 22 | 5 | 8 | 1 | 14 | 0 |
| Campbell, Jarrett, JUP | .889 | 21 | 4 | 4 | 1 | 9 | 1 |
| Caple, Chance, PLM | 1.000 | 3 | 1 | 1 | 0 | 2 | 0 |
| Carlsen, Clary, CLW | .667 | 3 | 1 | 1 | 1 | 3 | 0 |
| Cave, Kevin, JUP | .714 | 19 | 2 | 3 | 2 | 7 | 1 |
| Cedeno, Juan, SAR* | .913 | 25 | 4 | 17 | 2 | 23 | 0 |
| Cerrato, Justin, CLW | 1.000 | 2 | 1 | 0 | 0 | 1 | 0 |
| Cherry, Rocky, DAY | .912 | 27 | 9 | 22 | 3 | 34 | 0 |
| Ciprian, Wilson, PLM | .789 | 38 | 3 | 12 | 4 | 19 | 2 |
| Cochran, Thomas, SAR* | 1.000 | 4 | 0 | 1 | 0 | 1 | 1 |
| Cole, Joe, SLU | .600 | 24 | 0 | 3 | 2 | 5 | 0 |
| Connolly, Jon, LAK* | 1.000 | 4 | 4 | 5 | 0 | 9 | 1 |
| Connolly, Jon, DAY* | 1.000 | 21 | 8 | 23 | 0 | 31 | 1 |
| CONNOLLY, JON, LAK-DAY* | 1.000 | 25 | 12 | 28 | 0 | 40 | 2 |
| Contreras, JC, FTM* | 1.000 | 3 | 1 | 1 | 0 | 2 | 1 |
| Cook, BR, PLM | 1.000 | 3 | 1 | 2 | 0 | 3 | 0 |
| Cordova, Jorge, LAK | 1.000 | 8 | 2 | 0 | 0 | 2 | 0 |
| Cordova, Vincent, SLU | .889 | 4 | 3 | 5 | 1 | 9 | 2 |
| Corporan, Willy, SAR | 1.000 | 14 | 2 | 3 | 0 | 5 | 0 |
| Cox, Michael, SLU* | 1.000 | 21 | 4 | 1 | 0 | 5 | 0 |
| Cuello, Felix, LAK | 1.000 | 27 | 3 | 8 | 0 | 11 | 1 |
| Culp, Brandon, CLW | 1.000 | 26 | 3 | 4 | 0 | 7 | 0 |
| Dannemiller, Beau, VB | .889 | 36 | 5 | 11 | 2 | 18 | 0 |
| Davis, Allen, CLW* | .500 | 3 | 0 | 1 | 1 | 2 | 0 |
| Davis, Stockton, BRE | .778 | 28 | 3 | 4 | 2 | 9 | 1 |
| Dawson, Layne, CLW | .667 | 10 | 1 | 1 | 1 | 3 | 0 |
| Deaton, Kevin, SLU | .900 | 19 | 6 | 12 | 2 | 20 | 0 |
| Delcarmen, Manuel, SAR | .850 | 19 | 5 | 12 | 3 | 20 | 1 |
| DeLeon, Juan, TAM | .923 | 33 | 5 | 7 | 1 | 13 | 0 |
| Demontel, Jimmy, JUP | 1.000 | 14 | 0 | 2 | 0 | 2 | 0 |
| Dennison, Michael, SAR | 1.000 | 18 | 1 | 4 | 0 | 5 | 0 |
| DeSalvo, Matthew, TAM | 1.000 | 13 | 7 | 11 | 0 | 18 | 0 |
| Diaz, Jose, VB | .000 | 9 | 0 | 0 | 0 | 0 | 0 |
| Dinardo, Lenny, SAR* | 1.000 | 1 | 1 | 0 | 0 | 1 | 0 |
| Douglass, Ryan, BRE | 1.000 | 7 | 0 | 1 | 0 | 1 | 0 |
| Echols, Justin, BRE | .500 | 7 | 1 | 1 | 2 | 4 | 0 |
| Edwards, Brian, SLU | .917 | 38 | 6 | 16 | 2 | 24 | 2 |
| Eischen, Joey, BRE* | 1.000 | 4 | 1 | 3 | 0 | 4 | 0 |
| Erickson, Scott, SLU | 1.000 | 2 | 1 | 2 | 0 | 3 | 0 |
| Esquivia, Manuel, TAM | 1.000 | 5 | 1 | 0 | 0 | 1 | 0 |
| Evans, Louis, JUP* | 1.000 | 10 | 0 | 1 | 0 | 1 | 0 |
| Everts, Clint, BRE | 1.000 | 4 | 3 | 6 | 0 | 9 | 0 |
| Felfoldi, Jonathan, BRE* | .800 | 2 | 0 | 4 | 1 | 5 | 0 |
| Figueroa, Jonathan, VB* | .909 | 23 | 4 | 6 | 1 | 11 | 0 |
| Flores, Neomar, DUN | 1.000 | 27 | 10 | 19 | 0 | 29 | 2 |
| Forster, Scott, JUP* | .667 | 11 | 1 | 1 | 1 | 3 | 1 |
| Fulchino, Jeff, JUP | .900 | 8 | 2 | 7 | 1 | 10 | 0 |
| Gabbard, Kason, SAR* | 1.000 | 10 | 3 | 5 | 0 | 8 | 2 |
| Garcia, Felipe, LAK | 1.000 | 10 | 3 | 0 | 0 | 3 | 0 |
| Gardner, Hayden, CLW | 1.000 | 26 | 5 | 4 | 0 | 9 | 1 |
| Garza, Justin, PLM | 1.000 | 27 | 0 | 3 | 0 | 3 | 0 |
| Gerk, Jordan, DAY* | 1.000 | 18 | 2 | 10 | 0 | 12 | 0 |
| Girdley, Joshua, BRE* | 1.000 | 9 | 4 | 5 | 0 | 9 | 0 |
| Goetz, Geoff, TAM* | 1.000 | 14 | 2 | 2 | 0 | 4 | 0 |
| Gonzalez, Alfredo, VB | 1.000 | 8 | 0 | 2 | 0 | 2 | 0 |
| Goodman, Chris, BRE | .800 | 16 | 1 | 3 | 1 | 5 | 0 |
| Gray, Josh, FTM* | .963 | 33 | 8 | 18 | 1 | 27 | 1 |
| Green, KK, DAY | 1.000 | 11 | 1 | 3 | 0 | 4 | 0 |
| Greusel, Evan, JUP | .833 | 15 | 3 | 2 | 1 | 6 | 0 |
| Gutierrez, Jannio, FTM | .667 | 25 | 0 | 2 | 1 | 3 | 0 |
| Guzman, Angel, DAY | 1.000 | 7 | 4 | 4 | 0 | 8 | 0 |
| Gwaltney, Lee, CLW | .905 | 19 | 10 | 9 | 2 | 21 | 0 |
| Hamels, Cole, CLW* | 1.000 | 4 | 0 | 2 | 0 | 2 | 0 |
| Hamilton, Jamaal, VB* | 1.000 | 25 | 0 | 3 | 0 | 3 | 0 |
| Hamman, Corey, LAK* | 1.000 | 35 | 14 | 9 | 0 | 23 | 1 |
| Harper, Jesse, DUN | 1.000 | 4 | 1 | 2 | 0 | 3 | 0 |
| Harper, Landon, LAK | 1.000 | 10 | 0 | 1 | 0 | 1 | 0 |
| Hawk, Shane, SLU* | 1.000 | 8 | 1 | 6 | 0 | 7 | 0 |
| Hawksworth, Blake, PLM | .000 | 2 | 0 | 0 | 0 | 0 | 0 |
| Hensen, Brian, LAK* | 1.000 | 20 | 3 | 3 | 0 | 6 | 0 |
| Heredia, Felix, TAM* | 1.000 | 2 | 0 | 2 | 0 | 2 | 0 |
| Hernandez, Orlando, TAM | 1.000 | 3 | 3 | 1 | 0 | 4 | 1 |
| Hiles, Cary, CLW | .875 | 16 | 2 | 5 | 1 | 8 | 1 |
| Hill, Josh, FTM | 1.000 | 3 | 1 | 0 | 0 | 1 | 0 |
| Hill, Richard, DAY* | .750 | 28 | 3 | 9 | 4 | 16 | 0 |
| Hinckley, Michael, BRE* | 1.000 | 10 | 4 | 9 | 0 | 13 | 0 |
| Hoorelbeke, Casey, VB | .913 | 18 | 6 | 15 | 2 | 23 | 1 |
| Hosford, Clint, VB | 1.000 | 22 | 4 | 8 | 0 | 12 | 1 |
| Howell, Jason, SAR* | .714 | 19 | 2 | 3 | 2 | 7 | 0 |
| Howell, Mike, LAK | 1.000 | 27 | 8 | 5 | 0 | 13 | 0 |
| Hull, Eric, VB | 1.000 | 9 | 4 | 4 | 0 | 8 | 0 |
| Humen, David, JUP | 1.000 | 1 | 1 | 0 | 0 | 1 | 0 |
| Hutchinson, Ryan, CLW | 1.000 | 29 | 3 | 9 | 0 | 12 | 1 |
| Isaacson, Charlie, TAM | 1.000 | 23 | 8 | 13 | 0 | 21 | 2 |
| Isenberg, Kurt, DUN* | .792 | 14 | 3 | 16 | 5 | 24 | 0 |
| James, Justin, DUN | 1.000 | 11 | 5 | 5 | 0 | 10 | 0 |
| Johnson, Jeremy, LAK | .833 | 14 | 2 | 3 | 1 | 6 | 1 |
| Johnson, Josh, JUP | .929 | 23 | 5 | 21 | 2 | 28 | 3 |
| Jongejan, Ferenc, DAY* | 1.000 | 21 | 4 | 10 | 0 | 14 | 0 |
| Julianel, Ben, TAM* | .800 | 44 | 1 | 7 | 2 | 10 | 0 |
| Junge, Eric, CLW | 1.000 | 5 | 1 | 0 | 0 | 1 | 0 |
| Karstens, Jeffrey, TAM | .885 | 24 | 7 | 16 | 3 | 26 | 1 |
| Kazmir, Scott, SLU* | .900 | 11 | 0 | 9 | 1 | 10 | 1 |
| Kennard, Jeff, TAM | .750 | 13 | 1 | 2 | 1 | 4 | 0 |
| Kensing, Logan, JUP | .958 | 23 | 4 | 19 | 1 | 24 | 0 |
| Keppel, Bobby, SLU* | 1.000 | 2 | 2 | 0 | 0 | 2 | 0 |
| Kim, Byung-Hyun, SAR | 1.000 | 1 | 0 | 1 | 0 | 1 | 0 |
| King, Jeremy, TAM | .857 | 28 | 3 | 3 | 1 | 7 | 0 |
| Kinney, Josh, PLM | .000 | 7 | 0 | 0 | 0 | 0 | 0 |
| Kobow, Mike, LAK | .889 | 40 | 4 | 4 | 1 | 9 | 0 |
| Kweon, Yoon-Min, DAY | 1.000 | 1 | 1 | 0 | 0 | 1 | 0 |
| Larson, Ryan, SAR | 1.000 | 11 | 1 | 1 | 0 | 2 | 0 |
| Lerch, Zachary, JUP | 1.000 | 3 | 1 | 0 | 0 | 1 | 0 |
| Lester, Jon, SAR* | .909 | 21 | 5 | 15 | 2 | 22 | 0 |
| Lieber, Jon, TAM | 1.000 | 1 | 1 | 1 | 0 | 2 | 0 |
| Lindstrom, Matthew, SLU | .875 | 14 | 7 | 14 | 3 | 24 | 1 |
| Liriano, Francisco, FTM* | 1.000 | 21 | 3 | 27 | 0 | 30 | 3 |
| Lohse, Erik, FTM | 1.000 | 33 | 4 | 9 | 0 | 13 | 0 |
| Lombardi, Mike, LAK | 1.000 | 3 | 1 | 0 | 0 | 1 | 0 |
| Lontayo, Alex, LAK* | 1.000 | 3 | 0 | 3 | 0 | 3 | 0 |
| Lugo, Ruddy, JUP | .833 | 31 | 4 | 1 | 1 | 6 | 0 |
| Lundgren, Wayne, PLM | 1.000 | 8 | 0 | 4 | 0 | 4 | 0 |
| Mangrum, Micah, SLU | .875 | 4 | 2 | 5 | 1 | 8 | 0 |
| Marceau, PierreLuc, BRE* | 1.000 | 18 | 2 | 5 | 0 | 7 | 0 |
| Marcum, Shaun, DUN | 1.000 | 12 | 7 | 7 | 0 | 14 | 0 |
| Marrero, Darwin, BRE | 1.000 | 3 | 2 | 1 | 0 | 3 | 0 |
| Marshall, Brian, SAR* | 1.000 | 27 | 3 | 2 | 0 | 5 | 0 |
| Marsonek, Sam, TAM | 1.000 | 3 | 0 | 1 | 0 | 1 | 0 |
| Martin, Nick, DAY* | 1.000 | 26 | 1 | 2 | 0 | 3 | 0 |

| Player, Team | Pct. | G | PO | A | E | TC | DP |
|---|---|---|---|---|---|---|---|
| Martinez, Samuel, BRE | .000 | 14 | 0 | 0 | 1 | 1 | 0 |
| Mata, Gustavo, BRE | 1.000 | 3 | 0 | 1 | 0 | 1 | 0 |
| Maureau, Justin, DUN* | 1.000 | 6 | 1 | 1 | 0 | 2 | 0 |
| Mayfield, Brandon, CLW | .875 | 48 | 4 | 17 | 3 | 24 | 1 |
| McDowell, Kevin, LAK* | 1.000 | 16 | 0 | 2 | 0 | 2 | 0 |
| McNab, Tim, SLU | .810 | 38 | 5 | 12 | 4 | 21 | 0 |
| Megrew, Mike, VB* | .909 | 22 | 2 | 8 | 1 | 11 | 0 |
| Mendoza, Luis, SAR | .881 | 25 | 11 | 26 | 5 | 42 | 2 |
| Mendoza, Ramiro, SAR | 1.000 | 2 | 0 | 2 | 0 | 2 | 0 |
| Meredith, Clay, SAR | 1.000 | 16 | 3 | 2 | 0 | 5 | 0 |
| Merricks, Matt, VB* | .714 | 6 | 2 | 3 | 2 | 7 | 0 |
| Meyers, Mike, SLU | .500 | 4 | 1 | 0 | 1 | 2 | 0 |
| Miller, Jason, FTM* | 1.000 | 19 | 2 | 5 | 0 | 7 | 0 |
| Mitchell, Nathan, DAY | 1.000 | 4 | 0 | 1 | 0 | 1 | 0 |
| Moates, Jason, LAK | 1.000 | 17 | 2 | 3 | 0 | 5 | 0 |
| Mondesir, James, PLM | .909 | 17 | 4 | 6 | 1 | 11 | 0 |
| Moore, Ben, TAM | 1.000 | 12 | 2 | 1 | 0 | 3 | 0 |
| Morales, Alex, BRE | .917 | 32 | 3 | 8 | 1 | 12 | 1 |
| Morla, Carlos, SAR | 1.000 | 14 | 2 | 1 | 0 | 3 | 0 |
| Moseley, Marcus, FTM | .739 | 28 | 5 | 12 | 6 | 23 | 0 |
| Mowday, Chris, DAY | .786 | 39 | 4 | 7 | 3 | 14 | 0 |
| Mumma, Bradley, DUN* | 1.000 | 2 | 0 | 1 | 0 | 1 | 0 |
| Myers, Damien, LAK* | 1.000 | 9 | 2 | 2 | 0 | 4 | 0 |
| Neshek, Pat, FTM | .667 | 16 | 2 | 2 | 2 | 6 | 0 |
| Norderum, Jason, BRE* | .833 | 35 | 1 | 9 | 2 | 12 | 1 |
| Nunez, Jose, SLU* | 1.000 | 2 | 0 | 1 | 0 | 1 | 0 |
| Nunley, Derrek, DUN | 1.000 | 26 | 1 | 3 | 0 | 4 | 1 |
| O'Connor, Michael, BRE* | .867 | 26 | 5 | 8 | 2 | 15 | 0 |
| O'Malley, Ryan, DAY* | 1.000 | 16 | 2 | 8 | 0 | 10 | 0 |
| Ojeda, Alvis, VB | 1.000 | 4 | 2 | 0 | 0 | 2 | 0 |
| Olsen, Scott, JUP* | .938 | 25 | 5 | 10 | 1 | 16 | 3 |
| Olson, Justin, FTM | .882 | 45 | 6 | 9 | 2 | 17 | 0 |
| Olson, Ryan, SLU* | 1.000 | 40 | 3 | 8 | 0 | 11 | 0 |
| Ool, Kevin, SAR* | 1.000 | 3 | 0 | 1 | 0 | 1 | 0 |
| Orloski, Joe, JUP | .909 | 14 | 3 | 7 | 1 | 11 | 0 |
| Ostlund, Ian, LAK* | 1.000 | 18 | 3 | 4 | 0 | 7 | 1 |
| Ough, Wayne, SLU | 1.000 | 4 | 1 | 1 | 0 | 2 | 0 |
| Overholt, Sean, DAY | .667 | 17 | 0 | 2 | 1 | 3 | 1 |
| Overman, Matt, JUP | 1.000 | 32 | 10 | 12 | 0 | 22 | 0 |
| Ozuna, Tommi, DUN* | 1.000 | 43 | 10 | 6 | 0 | 16 | 3 |
| Paddock, Josh, CLW | 1.000 | 14 | 1 | 3 | 0 | 4 | 0 |
| Pahucki, David, SAR | .941 | 43 | 7 | 9 | 1 | 17 | 0 |
| Pals, Jordan, PLM | .833 | 11 | 1 | 4 | 1 | 6 | 0 |
| Papelbon, Jon, SAR | .960 | 24 | 14 | 10 | 1 | 25 | 1 |
| Parris, Matt, LAK | .969 | 25 | 15 | 16 | 1 | 32 | 1 |
| Patterson, John, BRE | 1.000 | 2 | 1 | 2 | 0 | 3 | 0 |
| Paulk, Robert, SLU | .952 | 31 | 8 | 12 | 1 | 21 | 0 |
| Pena, Omar, PLM | 1.000 | 1 | 0 | 2 | 0 | 2 | 0 |
| Perkins, Vince, DUN | .846 | 13 | 4 | 7 | 2 | 13 | 1 |
| Petit, Yusmeiro, SLU | 1.000 | 9 | 2 | 4 | 0 | 6 | 0 |
| Petty, Chad, PLM* | .857 | 23 | 1 | 5 | 1 | 7 | 0 |
| Phelps, Tommy, JUP* | .500 | 1 | 0 | 1 | 1 | 2 | 0 |
| Pinango, Miguel, SLU | 1.000 | 4 | 2 | 3 | 0 | 5 | 0 |
| Pineda, Luis, SLU | 1.000 | 5 | 0 | 1 | 0 | 1 | 0 |
| Pleiness, Chad, DUN | .889 | 36 | 10 | 14 | 3 | 27 | 2 |
| Plummer, Jarod, VB | .833 | 11 | 7 | 3 | 2 | 12 | 0 |
| Pope, Justin, TAM | 1.000 | 13 | 7 | 6 | 0 | 13 | 0 |
| Portobanco, Luz, SLU | .857 | 34 | 3 | 9 | 2 | 14 | 1 |
| Price, Brett, BRE* | .857 | 23 | 2 | 10 | 2 | 14 | 1 |
| Quintero, Mayque, BRE | .917 | 21 | 3 | 8 | 1 | 12 | 1 |
| Ramirez, Elizardo, CLW | 1.000 | 9 | 3 | 11 | 0 | 14 | 1 |
| Ramirez, Ismael, DUN | .974 | 28 | 13 | 24 | 1 | 38 | 0 |
| Randazzo, Jeff, FTM* | .911 | 27 | 20 | 21 | 4 | 45 | 1 |
| Ransom, Robert, DAY | .833 | 5 | 1 | 4 | 1 | 6 | 0 |
| Rasner, Darrell, BRE | .963 | 22 | 8 | 18 | 1 | 27 | 1 |
| Rawson, Anthony, PLM* | .867 | 53 | 3 | 10 | 2 | 15 | 1 |
| Read, Robby, CLW | 1.000 | 9 | 0 | 4 | 0 | 4 | 0 |
| Reed, Brian, DUN | .900 | 24 | 2 | 7 | 1 | 10 | 0 |
| Reina, Dimas, VB | .900 | 16 | 5 | 4 | 1 | 10 | 0 |
| Reyes, Anthony, PLM | 1.000 | 6 | 1 | 6 | 0 | 7 | 2 |
| Reyes, Maximo, CLW | 1.000 | 6 | 0 | 1 | 0 | 1 | 0 |
| Reynolds, Eric, JUP* | .800 | 9 | 0 | 4 | 1 | 5 | 0 |
| Rhodes, Shane, SAR* | 1.000 | 6 | 1 | 1 | 0 | 2 | 0 |
| Richardson, Beau, CLW* | .917 | 51 | 1 | 10 | 1 | 12 | 0 |
| Rodney, Lee, LAK | 1.000 | 19 | 2 | 3 | 0 | 5 | 1 |
| Rodriguez, Eladio, SAR | 1.000 | 5 | 1 | 0 | 0 | 1 | 0 |
| Rodriguez, Jose, SLU | .750 | 4 | 1 | 2 | 1 | 4 | 0 |
| Rodriguez, Mike, VB | .889 | 28 | 4 | 4 | 1 | 9 | 1 |
| Rodriguez, Wilfredo, BRE* | 1.000 | 9 | 0 | 1 | 0 | 1 | 0 |
| Rogers, Joe, SAR* | .952 | 36 | 4 | 16 | 1 | 21 | 0 |
| Roman, Orlando, SLU | .882 | 20 | 5 | 10 | 2 | 17 | 1 |
| Romero, Felix, DUN | 1.000 | 9 | 0 | 2 | 0 | 2 | 0 |
| Rosario, Francisco, DUN | 1.000 | 6 | 2 | 0 | 0 | 2 | 0 |
| Rundles, Rich, BRE* | 1.000 | 1 | 0 | 1 | 0 | 1 | 0 |
| Russ, Chris, PLM | 1.000 | 7 | 1 | 1 | 0 | 2 | 0 |
| Russ, James, JUP | .889 | 24 | 5 | 3 | 1 | 9 | 0 |
| Sanchez, Humberto, LAK | .957 | 19 | 8 | 14 | 1 | 23 | 1 |
| Santillan, Manuel, BRE | 1.000 | 7 | 0 | 2 | 0 | 2 | 0 |
| Santor, John, PLM | .000 | 1 | 0 | 0 | 0 | 0 | 0 |
| Scalamandre, Rich, PLM | 1.000 | 40 | 1 | 9 | 0 | 10 | 1 |
| Schmoll, Steve, VB | .929 | 37 | 12 | 14 | 2 | 28 | 0 |
| Schultz, Cory, CLW | 1.000 | 11 | 1 | 2 | 0 | 3 | 0 |
| Searles, Jonathan, BRE | 1.000 | 19 | 2 | 4 | 0 | 6 | 1 |
| Shanks, James, JUP | .000 | 3 | 0 | 0 | 0 | 0 | 0 |
| Shipman, Andrew, DAY | 1.000 | 15 | 1 | 2 | 0 | 3 | 0 |
| Shipman, Andrew, SAR | .900 | 20 | 4 | 5 | 1 | 10 | 0 |
| Shipman, Andrew, DAY-SAR | 923 | 35 | 5 | 7 | 1 | 13 | 0 |
| Sierra, Edwardo, TAM | .875 | 45 | 4 | 3 | 1 | 8 | 1 |
| Simmons, Justin, VB* | 1.000 | 5 | 1 | 3 | 0 | 4 | 0 |
| Simon, Alfredo, CLW | .968 | 21 | 15 | 15 | 1 | 31 | 1 |
| Sisco, Andy, DAY* | .813 | 26 | 4 | 9 | 3 | 16 | 1 |
| Skaggs, Jon, TAM | .915 | 27 | 9 | 34 | 4 | 47 | 0 |
| Skrmetta, Matt, BRE | .000 | 3 | 0 | 0 | 0 | 0 | 0 |
| Sleeth, Kyle, LAK | 1.000 | 9 | 0 | 1 | 0 | 1 | 1 |
| Smith, Bud, CLW* | .750 | 4 | 0 | 3 | 1 | 4 | 0 |
| Smith, Dan, BRE | 1.000 | 3 | 0 | 1 | 0 | 1 | 0 |
| Smith, Jared, PLM | .700 | 14 | 1 | 6 | 3 | 10 | 1 |
| Song, Seung, BRE | 1.000 | 3 | 1 | 0 | 0 | 1 | 0 |
| Speier, Justin, DUN | .000 | 2 | 0 | 0 | 0 | 0 | 0 |
| Speigner, Levale, FTM | 1.000 | 22 | 2 | 13 | 0 | 15 | 0 |
| Steffek, Brian, VB | 1.000 | 13 | 3 | 7 | 0 | 10 | 0 |
| Stemle, Steve, PLM | 1.000 | 2 | 0 | 1 | 0 | 1 | 1 |
| Strelitz, Brian, JUP | .833 | 15 | 2 | 8 | 2 | 12 | 0 |
| Strickland, Scott, SLU | 1.000 | 6 | 0 | 1 | 0 | 1 | 1 |
| Stults, Eric, VB* | .000 | 7 | 0 | 0 | 0 | 0 | 0 |
| Sturge, Justin, SAR* | .800 | 39 | 1 | 7 | 2 | 10 | 0 |
| Sweeney, Matt, CLW | .947 | 21 | 4 | 14 | 1 | 19 | 2 |
| Tavarez, Anderson, DAY | .947 | 19 | 0 | 18 | 1 | 19 | 1 |
| Teekel, Josh, PLM | .941 | 26 | 7 | 25 | 2 | 34 | 1 |
| Tejada, Manny, FTM | .941 | 22 | 3 | 13 | 1 | 17 | 0 |
| Tejera, Michael, JUP* | .000 | 1 | 0 | 0 | 0 | 0 | 0 |
| Templet, Jordy, DUN | 1.000 | 3 | 1 | 0 | 0 | 1 | 0 |
| Tequida, Mauricio, VB | 1.000 | 5 | 1 | 1 | 0 | 2 | 0 |
| Thomas, John, FTM* | .846 | 34 | 2 | 9 | 2 | 13 | 1 |
| Thorpe, Tracy, DUN | .895 | 39 | 2 | 15 | 2 | 19 | 0 |
| Torres, Andy, DUN | .947 | 42 | 2 | 16 | 1 | 19 | 0 |
| Trezza, Alex, LAK* | 1.000 | 3 | 0 | 1 | 0 | 1 | 0 |
| Urbina, Ugueth, LAK | .500 | 2 | 1 | 0 | 1 | 2 | 0 |
| Valdez, Jose, TAM | .933 | 23 | 5 | 23 | 2 | 30 | 2 |
| Valdez, Santo, DUN | .556 | 23 | 3 | 2 | 4 | 9 | 0 |
| Vandenhurk, Henricus, JUP | 1.000 | 14 | 3 | 5 | 0 | 8 | 0 |
| Vaquedano, Jose, SAR | .923 | 14 | 2 | 10 | 1 | 13 | 0 |
| Vasquez, Carlos, DAY* | .944 | 16 | 4 | 13 | 1 | 18 | 2 |
| Vermilyea, James, DUN | .929 | 18 | 3 | 10 | 1 | 14 | 1 |
| Villegas, Francisco, TAM | .800 | 15 | 0 | 4 | 1 | 5 | 0 |
| Wallace, Shane, PLM* | .800 | 54 | 4 | 12 | 4 | 20 | 0 |
| Warpinski, Ryan, JUP | .000 | 3 | 0 | 0 | 0 | 0 | 0 |
| Warriax, Brandon, VB | .800 | 8 | 0 | 4 | 1 | 5 | 0 |
| Wayne, Brett, VB | 1.000 | 5 | 0 | 1 | 0 | 1 | 0 |
| White, Steven, TAM | 1.000 | 12 | 3 | 9 | 0 | 12 | 0 |
| Wodnicki, Mike, PLM | 1.000 | 6 | 2 | 4 | 0 | 6 | 0 |
| Wolf, Ross, JUP | .909 | 43 | 3 | 7 | 1 | 11 | 1 |
| Wood, Brandon, CLW | 1.000 | 3 | 1 | 0 | 0 | 1 | 0 |
| Woodrow, Christopher, CLW | 1.000 | 6 | 6 | 3 | 0 | 9 | 1 |
| Wylie, Jason, DAY | 1.000 | 3 | 1 | 0 | 0 | 1 | 0 |
| Yeatman, Matt, FTM | .952 | 23 | 11 | 9 | 1 | 21 | 1 |
| Yost, Wendell, BRE | .000 | 1 | 0 | 0 | 0 | 0 | 0 |
| Zink, Charlie, SAR | .667 | 3 | 0 | 2 | 1 | 3 | 0 |
| Zumaya, Joel, LAK | .933 | 16 | 9 | 5 | 1 | 15 | 0 |

# LEAGUE CHAMPIONS

| Year | Team | Pct. |
|---|---|---|
| 1919— | Sanford* | .605 |
| | Orlando* | .703 |
| 1920— | Tampa | .654 |
| | Tampa | .722 |
| 1921— | Orlando | .635 |
| 1922— | St. Petersburg | .503 |
| | St. Petersburg | .618 |
| 1923— | Orlando | .667 |
| | Orlando | .678 |
| 1924— | Lakeland | .695 |
| | Lakeland | .683 |
| 1925— | St. Petersburg | .667 |
| | Tampa† | .696 |
| 1926— | Sanford | .647 |
| | Sanford | .623 |
| 1927— | Orlando† | .600 |
| | Miami | .661 |
| 1928-35— | Did not operate. | |
| 1936— | Gainesville | .542 |
| | St. Augustine (4th)† | .492 |
| 1937— | Gainesville§ | .616 |
| 1938— | Leesburg | .626 |
| | Gainesville (2nd)‡ | .615 |
| 1939— | Sanford§ | .787 |
| 1940— | Daytona Beach | .619 |
| | Orlando (4th)‡ | .507 |
| 1941— | St. Augustine | .659 |
| | Leesburg (4th)‡ | .488 |
| 1942-45— | Did not operate. | |
| 1946— | Orlando§ | .681 |
| 1947— | St. Augustine | .625 |
| | Gainesville (2nd)‡ | .584 |
| 1948— | Orlando | .643 |
| | Daytona Beach (2nd)‡ | .616 |
| 1949— | Gainesville | .635 |
| | St. Augustine (3rd)‡ | .556 |
| 1950— | Orlando | .629 |
| | DeLand (3rd)‡ | .590 |
| 1951— | DeLand§ | .643 |
| 1952— | DeLand∞ | .704 |
| | Palatka (3rd)‡ | .569 |
| 1953— | Daytona Beach† | .657 |
| | DeLand | .703 |
| 1954— | Jacksonville Beach | .629 |
| | Lakeland† | .594 |
| 1955— | Orlando | .671 |
| | Orlando | .643 |
| 1956— | Cocoa | .614 |
| | Cocoa | .671 |
| 1957— | Palatka | .629 |
| | Tampa† | .681 |
| 1958— | St. Petersburg | .732 |
| | St. Petersburg | .681 |
| 1959— | Tampa | .591 |
| | St. Petersburg† | .612 |
| 1960— | Lakeland | .731 |
| | Palatka† | .614 |
| 1961— | Tampa† | .710 |
| | Sarasota | .696 |
| 1962— | Sarasota | .689 |
| | Fort Lauderdale† | .623 |
| 1963— | Sarasota | .645 |
| | Sarasota | .667 |
| 1964— | Fort Lauderdale† | .629 |
| | St. Petersburg | .594 |
| 1965— | Fort Lauderdale | .627 |
| | Fort Lauderdale | .634 |
| 1966— | Leesburg† | .781 |
| | St. Petersburg | .700 |
| 1967— | St. Petersburg▲ | .691 |
| | Orlando | .638 |
| 1968— | Miami | .613 |
| | Orlando◆ | .579 |
| 1969— | Miami■ | .606 |
| | Orlando | .606 |
| 1970— | Miami▼ | .662 |
| | St. Petersburg | .600 |
| 1971— | Miami▼ | .667 |
| | Daytona Beach | .586 |
| 1972— | Miami• | .562 |
| | Daytona Beach | .606 |
| 1973— | St. Petersburg†† | .575 |
| | West Palm Beach | .580 |
| 1974— | West Palm Beach†† | .598 |
| | Fort Lauderdale | .626 |
| 1975— | St. Petersburg†† | .652 |
| | Miami | .581 |
| 1976— | Tampa | .559 |
| | Lakeland†† | .536 |
| 1977— | Lakeland†† | .616 |
| | West Palm Beach | .583 |
| 1978— | Lakeland | .565 |
| | Miami§ | .539 |
| 1979— | Fort Lauderdale | .643 |
| | Winter Haven‡‡ | .577 |
| 1980— | Daytona Beach | .628 |
| | Fort Lauderdale†† | .606 |
| 1981— | Fort Myers | .554 |
| | Daytona Beach§§ | .504 |
| 1982— | Fort Lauderdale§§ | .621 |
| | Tampa | .546 |
| 1983— | Daytona Beach | .634 |
| | Vero Beach§§ | .515 |
| 1984— | Tampa | .532 |
| | Fort Lauderdale§§ | .521 |
| 1985— | Fort Myers∞∞ | .590 |
| | Fort Lauderdale | .550 |
| 1986— | St. Petersburg∞∞ | .647 |
| | West Palm Beach | .593 |
| 1987— | Fort Lauderdale∞∞ | .616 |
| | Osceola | .576 |
| 1988— | Osceola | .606 |
| | St. Lucie▲▲ | .532 |
| 1989— | Port Charlotte▲▲ | .540 |
| | St. Petersburg | .540 |
| 1990— | West Palm Beach | .697 |
| | Vero Beach▲▲ | .585 |
| 1991— | Clearwater | .623 |
| | West Palm Beach▲▲ | .550 |
| 1992— | Sarasota | .639 |
| | Lakeland◆◆ | .530 |
| 1993— | St. Lucie | .600 |
| | Clearwater§§ | .556 |
| 1994— | Tampa§§ | .606 |
| | Brevard County | .561 |
| 1995— | Daytona§§ | .644 |
| | Fort Myers | .577 |
| 1996— | Tampa | .627 |
| | St. Lucie§§ | .534 |
| 1997— | St. Petersburg■■ | .591 |
| | Vero Beach | .511 |
| 1998— | Charlotte | .594 |
| | St. Lucie■■ | .515 |
| 1999— | Dunedin | .628 |
| | Kissimmee■■ | .578 |
| 2000— | Dunedin | .609 |
| | Daytona■■ | .547 |
| 2001— | Brevard County▼▼ | .593 |
| | Tampa▼▼ | .554 |
| 2002— | Charlotte■■ | .600 |
| 2003— | St. Lucie■■ | .554 |
| 2004— | Daytona▼▼▼ | .555 |
| | Tampa▼▼▼ | .564 |

*Split-season playoff abandoned after each team won three games. †Won split-season playoff. ‡Won four-club playoff. §Won championship and four-club playoff. ∞Won both halves of split season. ▲League divided into Eastern and Western divisions with split season. St. Petersburg and Orlando won both halves of split season; St. Petersburg won playoff. ◆League divided into Eastern and Western divisions. Miami won regular-season pennant on basis of highest won-lost percentage. Orlando won four-club playoff involving first two teams in each division. ■ League divided into Southern and Central divisions. Miami won playoff between division leaders. (NOTE—Pennant awarded to playoff winner in 1936.) ▼League divided into Eastern and Western divisions. Miami won regular-season pennant on basis of highest won-loss percentage, and also won four-club playoff involving first two teams in each division. •League divided into Eastern and Western divisions. Won four-club playoff involving first two teams in each division. ††League divided into Northern and Southern divisions. Won four-club playoff involving first two teams in each division. ‡‡League divided into Northern and Southern divisions. Same two clubs won both halves; won playoffs. §§Won split-season playoff. ∞∞League divided into Western, Central and Southern divisions. Won four-club playoff. ▲▲League divided into Eastern, Western and Central divisions; played split-season. Won six-club playoff. ◆◆League divided into Eastern, Western and Central divisions; played split-season. Won eight-club playoff. ■■ League divided into East and West divisions and played split season; won four-club playoff. ▼▼League divided into East and West divisions and played split season; teams were about to start final round of playoffs, but were declared co-champions when Professional Baseball declared a stoppage of play. ▼▼▼League divided into East and West divisions and played split season; teams declared co-champions when championship series is canceled because of a hurricane threat.

# MIDWEST LEAGUE

## LEAGUE OFFICE

**President**
George H. Spelius

**Address**
P.O. Box 936
Beloit, WI 53512

**Phone**
608-364-1188

**Teams (affiliation)**
Beloit Snappers (Twins)
Burlington Bees (Royals)
Cedar Rapids Kernels (Angels)
Clinton Lumber Kings (Rangers)
Dayton Dragons (Reds)
Fort Wayne Wizards (Padres)
Kane County Cougars (A's)
Lansing Lugnuts (Blue Jays)
Peoria Chiefs (Cubs)
Swing of the Quad Cities (Cardinals)
South Bend Silver Hawks (Diamondbacks)
Southwest Michigan Devil Rays (Devil Rays)
West Michigan Whitecaps (Tigers)
Wisconsin Timber Rattlers (Mariners)

## 2004 FINAL STANDINGS

### FIRST HALF

#### EASTERN DIVISION

| Team | W | L | T | Pct. | GB |
|---|---|---|---|---|---|
| South Bend | 42 | 28 | - | .600 | ... |
| Lansing | 38 | 32 | - | .543 | 4 |
| Battle Creek | 33 | 36 | - | .478 | 81/2 |
| Fort Wayne | 33 | 37 | - | .471 | 9 |
| West Michigan | 29 | 40 | - | .420 | 121/2 |
| Dayton | 27 | 43 | - | .386 | 15 |

#### WESTERN DIVISION

| Team | W | L | T | Pct. | GB |
|---|---|---|---|---|---|
| Kane County | 43 | 26 | - | .623 | ... |
| Cedar Rapids | 42 | 27 | - | .609 | 1 |
| Peoria | 38 | 31 | - | .551 | 5 |
| Beloit | 38 | 32 | - | .543 | 51/2 |
| Clinton | 35 | 33 | - | .515 | 71/2 |
| Quad Cities | 33 | 33 | - | .500 | 81/2 |
| Wisconsin | 31 | 38 | - | .449 | 12 |
| Burlington-A | 22 | 48 | - | .314 | 211/2 |

### SECOND HALF

#### EASTERN DIVISION

| Team | W | L | T | Pct. | GB |
|---|---|---|---|---|---|
| West Michigan | 40 | 30 | - | .571 | ... |
| Fort Wayne | 39 | 31 | - | .557 | 1 |
| Lansing | 39 | 31 | - | .557 | 1 |
| Battle Creek | 38 | 32 | - | .543 | 2 |
| South Bend | 35 | 35 | - | .500 | 5 |
| Dayton | 21 | 49 | - | .300 | 19 |

#### WESTERN DIVISION

| Team | W | L | T | Pct. | GB |
|---|---|---|---|---|---|
| Kane County | 40 | 30 | - | .571 | ... |
| Clinton | 39 | 31 | - | .557 | 1 |
| Peoria | 37 | 33 | - | .529 | 3 |
| Quad Cities | 35 | 35 | - | .500 | 5 |
| Beloit | 34 | 36 | - | .486 | 6 |
| Burlington | 34 | 36 | - | .486 | 6 |
| Cedar Rapids | 33 | 37 | - | .471 | 7 |
| Wisconsin | 26 | 44 | - | .371 | 14 |

### COMPOSITE

| Team | W | L | T | Pct. | GB | KNC | LAN | SBN | CR | PEO | CLN | BLT | FTW | BTC | QC | WMI | WIS | BUR | DTN |
|---|---|---|---|---|---|---|---|---|---|---|---|---|---|---|---|---|---|---|---|
| Kane County (Athletics) | 83 | 56 | - | .597 | ... | X | 3 | 3 | 6 | 5 | 7 | 9 | 8 | 4 | 7 | 8 | 8 | 9 | 6 |
| Lansing (Cubs) | 77 | 63 | - | .550 | 61/2 | 5 | X | 6 | 4 | 5 | 2 | 6 | 9 | 10 | 4 | 8 | 5 | 5 | 8 |
| South Bend (Diamondbacks) | 77 | 63 | - | .550 | 61/2 | 5 | 10 | X | 4 | 3 | 5 | 4 | 9 | 7 | 3 | 9 | 3 | 7 | 8 |
| Cedar Rapids (Angels) | 75 | 64 | - | .540 | 8 | 6 | 4 | 4 | X | 8 | 7 | 5 | 3 | 2 | 6 | 6 | 6 | 12 | 6 |
| Peoria (Cardinals) | 75 | 64 | - | .540 | 8 | 6 | 3 | 5 | 4 | X | 4 | 6 | 2 | 4 | 9 | 6 | 11 | 8 | 7 |
| Clinton (Rangers) | 74 | 64 | - | .536 | 81/2 | 5 | 6 | 3 | 9 | 8 | X | 4 | 5 | 3 | 5 | 3 | 8 | 10 | 5 |
| Beloit (Brewers) | 72 | 68 | - | .514 | 111/2 | 7 | 2 | 4 | 7 | 6 | 8 | X | 4 | 5 | 5 | 3 | 9 | 6 | 6 |
| Fort Wayne (Padres) | 72 | 68 | - | .514 | 111/2 | 0 | 7 | 3 | 5 | 6 | 3 | 4 | X | 10 | 5 | 7 | 6 | 4 | 12 |
| Battle Creek (Yankees) | 71 | 68 | - | .511 | 12 | 4 | 2 | 9 | 6 | 4 | 5 | 3 | 6 | X | 5 | 9 | 4 | 5 | 9 |
| Quad Cities (Twins) | 68 | 68 | - | .500 | 131/2 | 9 | 4 | 5 | 5 | 7 | 5 | 7 | 3 | 2 | X | 3 | 9 | 4 | 5 |
| West Michigan (Tigers) | 69 | 70 | - | .496 | 14 | 0 | 8 | 7 | 2 | 2 | 5 | 5 | 9 | 7 | 5 | X | 5 | 4 | 10 |
| Wisconsin (Mariners) | 57 | 82 | - | .410 | 26 | 4 | 3 | 5 | 6 | 5 | 4 | 7 | 2 | 4 | 3 | 2 | X | 6 | 6 |
| Burlington (Royals) | 56 | 84 | - | .400 | 271/2 | 3 | 3 | 1 | 4 | 4 | 6 | 6 | 4 | 3 | 8 | 4 | 6 | X | 4 |
| Dayton (Reds) | 48 | 92 | - | .343 | 351/2 | 2 | 8 | 8 | 2 | 1 | 3 | 2 | 4 | 7 | 3 | 2 | 2 | 4 | X |

Major league affiliations in parentheses.

PLAYOFFS: Clinton defeated Cedar Rapids two games to none; South Bend defeated Fort Wayne two games to none; Kane County defeated Peoria two games to one; West Michigan defeated Lansing two games to one; Kane County defeated Clinton two games to none; West Michigan defeated South Bend two games to none; West Michigan defeated Kane County three games to two to win championship.

REGULAR-SEASON ATTENDANCE: Battle Creek, 95,845; Beloit, 96,681; Burlington, 62,961; Cedar Rapids, 177,929; Clinton, 91,804; Dayton, 593,663; Fort Wayne, 278,351; Kane County, 522,042; Lansing, 392,256; Peoria, 211,598; Quad Cities, 173,370; South Bend, 212,612; West Michigan, 390,033; Wisconsin, 206,487. Total attendance—3,505,632. All-Star Game at Veteran Memorial Stadium—5,589.

MANAGERS: Battle Creek, Mitch Seoane/Bill Mosiello; Bedloit, Don Money; Burlington, Jim Gabella; Cedar Rapids, Bobby Magallanes; Clinton, Carlos Subero; Dayton, Alonzo Powell; Fort Wayne, Randy Ready; Kane County, Dave Joppie; Lansing, Julio Garcia; Peoria, Joe Cunningham; Quad Cities, Kevin Boles; South Bend, Tony Perezchica; West Michigan, Matt Walbeck; Wisconsin, Steve Roadcap.

ALL-STAR TEAM: 1B—Brian Dopirak, Lansing; 2B—Howie Kendrick, Cedar Rapids, SS—Ian Kinsler, Clinton; 3B—Eric Duncan, Battle Creek, C—Daric Barton, Peoria, DH—Vinny Rottino, OF—Kevin Collins, Lansing; Chris Dickerson, Dayton; Alex Frazier, South Bend; RHP—Brad Knox, LHP—Steve Bondurant, Kane County, RH reliever—Bob Zimmerman, Cedar Rapids; Clay Rapada, Lansing. Player of the Year —Brian Dopirak, Lansing. Manager of the Year—Dave Joppie, Kane County.

# 2004 BATTING

## TEAM

| Team | G | TPA | AB | R | H | TB | 2B | 3B | HR | RBI | SH | SF | HP | BB | IBB | SO | SB | CS | GDP | LOB | ShO | Avg. | OBP | Slg. |
|---|---|---|---|---|---|---|---|---|---|---|---|---|---|---|---|---|---|---|---|---|---|---|---|---|
| Peoria | 139 | 5444 | 4760 | 759 | 1317 | 1965 | 261 | 30 | 109 | 682 | 56 | 40 | 76 | 511 | 24 | 988 | 117 | 62 | 102 | 1061 | 2 | .277 | .353 | .413 |
| Battle Creek | 139 | 5259 | 4670 | 683 | 1270 | 1886 | 269 | 19 | 103 | 625 | 42 | 41 | 69 | 436 | 10 | 1029 | 112 | 65 | 87 | 953 | 8 | .272 | .340 | .404 |
| South Bend | 140 | 5213 | 4734 | 630 | 1258 | 1827 | 238 | 38 | 85 | 571 | 41 | 34 | 92 | 312 | 14 | 887 | 162 | 72 | 83 | 919 | 9 | .266 | .321 | .386 |
| Beloit | 140 | 5196 | 4641 | 663 | 1232 | 1799 | 226 | 40 | 87 | 593 | 65 | 49 | 72 | 367 | 9 | 953 | 107 | 44 | 99 | 933 | 8 | .265 | .326 | .388 |
| Lansing | 140 | 5352 | 4813 | 706 | 1273 | 2027 | 250 | 36 | 144 | 647 | 30 | 44 | 73 | 392 | 21 | 1060 | 120 | 50 | 95 | 928 | 8 | .264 | .327 | .421 |
| Kane County | 139 | 5467 | 4672 | 730 | 1200 | 1839 | 251 | 29 | 110 | 676 | 19 | 46 | 66 | 664 | 17 | 1053 | 84 | 39 | 120 | 1097 | 8 | .257 | .354 | .394 |
| Cedar Rapids | 139 | 5200 | 4687 | 650 | 1205 | 1889 | 237 | 48 | 117 | 592 | 28 | 40 | 84 | 361 | 16 | 1110 | 145 | 74 | 54 | 900 | 8 | .257 | .319 | .403 |
| Clinton | 138 | 5225 | 4480 | 668 | 1151 | 1748 | 268 | 28 | 91 | 596 | 63 | 40 | 88 | 554 | 15 | 1179 | 122 | 61 | 93 | 999 | 6 | .257 | .347 | .390 |
| West Michigan | 139 | 5244 | 4715 | 619 | 1198 | 1789 | 223 | 43 | 94 | 551 | 45 | 32 | 79 | 372 | 12 | 1190 | 117 | 64 | 69 | 938 | 8 | .254 | .317 | .379 |
| Wisconsin | 139 | 5236 | 4676 | 607 | 1172 | 1717 | 228 | 40 | 79 | 532 | 33 | 34 | 50 | 443 | 11 | 1060 | 116 | 65 | 104 | 949 | 11 | .251 | .320 | .367 |
| Fort Wayne | 140 | 5338 | 4742 | 619 | 1165 | 1718 | 217 | 33 | 90 | 567 | 27 | 40 | 81 | 447 | 13 | 1082 | 80 | 45 | 86 | 995 | 14 | .246 | .319 | .362 |
| Quad City | 136 | 5105 | 4516 | 564 | 1075 | 1516 | 190 | 43 | 55 | 496 | 38 | 45 | 71 | 434 | 11 | 1036 | 118 | 58 | 76 | 963 | 13 | .238 | .312 | .336 |
| Dayton | 140 | 5225 | 4644 | 551 | 1096 | 1661 | 218 | 34 | 93 | 512 | 29 | 25 | 81 | 446 | 5 | 1382 | 117 | 65 | 70 | 971 | 14 | .236 | .312 | .358 |
| Burlington | 140 | 5133 | 4504 | 553 | 1054 | 1478 | 209 | 25 | 55 | 476 | 50 | 45 | 88 | 446 | 22 | 1009 | 138 | 71 | 74 | 933 | 15 | .234 | .312 | .328 |

## INDIVIDUAL

### TOP QUALIFIERS FOR BATTING CHAMPIONSHIP

Minimum 378 plate appearances. *Lefthanded batter. †Switch-hitter.

| Player, Team | G | TPA | AB | R | H | TB | 2B | 3B | HR | RBI | SH | SF | HP | BB | IBB | SO | SB | CS | GDP | Avg. | OBP | Slg. |
|---|---|---|---|---|---|---|---|---|---|---|---|---|---|---|---|---|---|---|---|---|---|---|
| Ryan, Brendan, Peoria | 105 | 472 | 426 | 72 | 137 | 172 | 21 | 4 | 2 | 59 | 9 | 9 | 4 | 24 | 2 | 42 | 30 | 7 | 13 | .322 | .356 | .404 |
| Francia, Juan, West Michigan † | 111 | 478 | 413 | 73 | 132 | 149 | 11 | 3 | 0 | 32 | 20 | 1 | 10 | 34 | 2 | 44 | 37 | 19 | 3 | .320 | .384 | .361 |
| Barton, Daric, Peoria * | 90 | 395 | 313 | 63 | 98 | 160 | 23 | 0 | 13 | 77 | 0 | 3 | 8 | 69 | 9 | 44 | 4 | 4 | 7 | .313 | .445 | .511 |
| Frazier, Alex, South Bend | 125 | 511 | 464 | 73 | 145 | 247 | 36 | 3 | 20 | 80 | 0 | 5 | 15 | 27 | 3 | 92 | 21 | 5 | 8 | .313 | .366 | .532 |
| Snyder, Brian, Kane County | 101 | 435 | 366 | 54 | 114 | 177 | 18 | 3 | 13 | 61 | 0 | 0 | 2 | 67 | 2 | 82 | 3 | 2 | 12 | .311 | .421 | .484 |
| Spanos, Vasili, Kane County | 97 | 406 | 331 | 58 | 103 | 167 | 26 | 1 | 12 | 80 | 0 | 8 | 13 | 54 | 1 | 76 | 11 | 5 | 11 | .311 | .419 | .505 |
| Anderson, Drew, Beloit * | 123 | 525 | 456 | 64 | 140 | 187 | 22 | 5 | 5 | 59 | 11 | 7 | 6 | 45 | 3 | 95 | 12 | 4 | 6 | .307 | .372 | .410 |
| Dopirak, Brian, Lansing | 137 | 597 | 541 | 94 | 166 | 321 | 38 | 0 | 39 | 120 | 0 | 5 | 3 | 48 | 4 | 123 | 4 | 3 | 14 | .307 | .363 | .593 |
| Carson, Matt, Battle Creek | 95 | 414 | 381 | 59 | 116 | 179 | 23 | 2 | 12 | 58 | 0 | 2 | 9 | 22 | 0 | 78 | 21 | 7 | 4 | .304 | .355 | .470 |
| Rottino, Vinny, Beloit | 140 | 584 | 529 | 78 | 161 | 255 | 25 | 9 | 17 | 124 | 1 | 10 | 4 | 40 | 3 | 71 | 5 | 1 | 12 | .304 | .352 | .482 |
| Dickerson, Chris, Dayton | 84 | 378 | 314 | 50 | 95 | 128 | 15 | 3 | 4 | 34 | 2 | 3 | 8 | 51 | 1 | 92 | 27 | 14 | 1 | .303 | .410 | .408 |
| Votto, Joey, Dayton | 111 | 473 | 391 | 60 | 118 | 190 | 26 | 2 | 14 | 72 | 0 | 2 | 1 | 79 | 1 | 110 | 9 | 2 | 6 | .302 | .419 | .486 |
| Trofholz, Terry, Beloit | 119 | 503 | 460 | 86 | 138 | 168 | 14 | 5 | 2 | 42 | 6 | 3 | 9 | 23 | 0 | 96 | 48 | 10 | 9 | .300 | .343 | .365 |
| Monegan, Anthony, Peoria * | 124 | 574 | 509 | 97 | 151 | 209 | 31 | 9 | 3 | 53 | 5 | 2 | 4 | 54 | 1 | 94 | 19 | 9 | 10 | .297 | .367 | .411 |
| Valenzuela, Fernando, Fort Wayne * | 135 | 579 | 502 | 68 | 148 | 208 | 23 | 2 | 11 | 81 | 1 | 7 | 11 | 56 | 7 | 63 | 1 | 0 | 18 | .295 | .373 | .414 |

DEPARTMENTAL LEADERS: G—Rottino, 140; AB—Andrus, 553; R—Monegan, 97; H—Dopirak, 166; TB—Dopirak, 321; 2B—Dopirak, 38; 3B—Cosby, Whitrock, 12; HR—Dopirak, 39; RBI—Rottino, 124; SH—Sandoval, 21; SF—Rottino, 10; HP—Pickens, 19; BB—Ingram, 84; IBB—Barton, 9; SO—McKinney, 175; SB—C. Walker, 60; CS—Francia, 19; GIDP—Valenzuela, 18; Slg.—Collins, .615; OBP—Barton, .445.

### ALL PLAYERS

*Lefthanded batter. †Switch-hitter.

| Player, Team | G | TPA | AB | R | H | TB | 2B | 3B | HR | RBI | SH | SF | HP | BB | IBB | SO | SB | CS | GDP | Avg. | OBP | Slg. |
|---|---|---|---|---|---|---|---|---|---|---|---|---|---|---|---|---|---|---|---|---|---|---|
| Acosta, Jesse, Kane County | 22 | 52 | 41 | 8 | 5 | 6 | 1 | 0 | 0 | 7 | 0 | 0 | 0 | 11 | 0 | 10 | 0 | 1 | 3 | .122 | .308 | .146 |
| Adams, Skip, Fort Wayne | 63 | 226 | 203 | 28 | 36 | 63 | 6 | 0 | 7 | 25 | 1 | 2 | 4 | 16 | 0 | 82 | 3 | 1 | 2 | .177 | .249 | .310 |
| Anderson, Drew, Beloit * | 123 | 525 | 456 | 64 | 140 | 187 | 22 | 5 | 5 | 59 | 11 | 7 | 6 | 45 | 3 | 95 | 12 | 4 | 6 | .307 | .372 | .410 |
| Andrus, Erold, Battle Creek † | 137 | 603 | 553 | 83 | 161 | 233 | 34 | 1 | 12 | 74 | 5 | 4 | 3 | 38 | 2 | 86 | 14 | 5 | 10 | .291 | .338 | .421 |
| Appert, Luke, Kane County * | 128 | 562 | 464 | 88 | 127 | 200 | 28 | 3 | 13 | 60 | 3 | 5 | 10 | 80 | 2 | 63 | 3 | 1 | 6 | .274 | .388 | .431 |
| Arneson, Justin, Swing of the Quad Ci. | 63 | 247 | 216 | 32 | 54 | 83 | 10 | 5 | 3 | 19 | 3 | 1 | 6 | 21 | 0 | 64 | 9 | 4 | 1 | .250 | .332 | .384 |
| Balkcom, Blake, Cedar Rapids | 105 | 431 | 401 | 48 | 106 | 154 | 32 | 2 | 4 | 49 | 2 | 4 | 9 | 15 | 1 | 104 | 12 | 4 | 3 | .264 | .303 | .384 |
| Barry, Jeff, Burlington | 110 | 383 | 336 | 51 | 76 | 92 | 4 | 3 | 2 | 33 | 3 | 5 | 6 | 33 | 0 | 69 | 16 | 6 | 3 | .226 | .303 | .274 |
| Barton, Daric, Peoria * | 90 | 395 | 313 | 63 | 98 | 160 | 23 | 0 | 13 | 77 | 0 | 3 | 8 | 69 | 9 | 44 | 4 | 4 | 7 | .313 | .445 | .511 |
| Benjamin, Casey, Clinton * | 63 | 202 | 166 | 22 | 31 | 39 | 6 | 1 | 0 | 14 | 2 | 1 | 1 | 32 | 0 | 51 | 1 | 3 | 3 | .187 | .320 | .235 |
| Blakeley, Eric, Wisconsin | 86 | 308 | 261 | 43 | 75 | 113 | 19 | 2 | 5 | 24 | 5 | 4 | 6 | 32 | 1 | 52 | 8 | 6 | 4 | .287 | .373 | .433 |
| Blue, Vincent, West Michigan * | 134 | 555 | 497 | 66 | 129 | 162 | 19 | 4 | 2 | 43 | 3 | 3 | 3 | 49 | 2 | 97 | 19 | 11 | 4 | .260 | .328 | .326 |
| Bochy, Greg, Fort Wayne | 35 | 135 | 117 | 6 | 22 | 30 | 2 | 0 | 2 | 15 | 1 | 2 | 0 | 15 | 0 | 35 | 0 | 0 | 2 | .188 | .276 | .256 |
| Bolivar, Luis, Dayton † | 123 | 550 | 495 | 65 | 116 | 184 | 25 | 5 | 11 | 52 | 6 | 5 | 8 | 36 | 0 | 105 | 31 | 10 | 9 | .234 | .294 | .372 |
| Bonifacio, Emilio, South Bend | 120 | 450 | 411 | 59 | 107 | 131 | 9 | 6 | 1 | 37 | 9 | 2 | 3 | 25 | 3 | 122 | 40 | 10 | 9 | .260 | .306 | .319 |
| Bonvechio, Brett, Fort Wayne * | 82 | 342 | 304 | 36 | 72 | 120 | 19 | 1 | 9 | 45 | 2 | 3 | 6 | 27 | 1 | 76 | 0 | 0 | 4 | .237 | .309 | .395 |
| Bourassa, Adam, Clinton * | 57 | 252 | 217 | 37 | 63 | 71 | 6 | 1 | 0 | 21 | 1 | 0 | 1 | 33 | 0 | 27 | 14 | 4 | 2 | .290 | .386 | .327 |
| Boyer, Billy, Cedar Rapids † | 28 | 111 | 101 | 9 | 23 | 30 | 4 | 0 | 1 | 8 | 2 | 0 | 0 | 8 | 0 | 38 | 1 | 3 | 2 | .228 | .284 | .297 |
| Bradford, Samuel, Wisconsin † | 17 | 52 | 49 | 4 | 7 | 12 | 2 | 0 | 1 | 4 | 1 | 0 | 0 | 2 | 0 | 15 | 1 | 0 | 0 | .143 | .176 | .245 |
| Brown, Matt, Cedar Rapids | 122 | 490 | 437 | 67 | 102 | 199 | 20 | 4 | 23 | 82 | 2 | 5 | 13 | 33 | 1 | 126 | 6 | 6 | 4 | .233 | .303 | .455 |
| Brown, Trevor, Kane County | 73 | 238 | 195 | 29 | 56 | 81 | 11 | 1 | 4 | 29 | 0 | 1 | 5 | 37 | 0 | 54 | 0 | 3 | 4 | .287 | .412 | .415 |
| Bubela, Dane, Clinton * | 107 | 441 | 382 | 52 | 96 | 140 | 22 | 5 | 4 | 40 | 3 | 2 | 7 | 47 | 4 | 129 | 6 | 2 | 8 | .251 | .342 | .366 |
| Burgos, Omar, Swing of the Quad Ci. | 94 | 379 | 330 | 32 | 68 | 86 | 11 | 2 | 1 | 26 | 4 | 5 | 7 | 33 | 2 | 76 | 5 | 6 | 5 | .206 | .288 | .261 |
| Burgos, Richard, West Michigan | 27 | 93 | 88 | 8 | 18 | 30 | 3 | 0 | 3 | 8 | 0 | 0 | 0 | 5 | 0 | 19 | 0 | 0 | 1 | .205 | .247 | .341 |
| Cabrera, Edwin, Battle Creek † | 8 | 20 | 18 | 1 | 3 | 4 | 1 | 0 | 0 | 3 | 1 | 0 | 0 | 1 | 0 | 7 | 1 | 0 | 0 | .167 | .211 | .222 |
| Campana, Wandel, Beloit | 35 | 139 | 123 | 15 | 37 | 47 | 10 | 0 | 0 | 10 | 5 | 2 | 5 | 4 | 0 | 17 | 1 | 2 | 4 | .301 | .343 | .382 |
| Campos, Tiago, Dayton | 31 | 107 | 102 | 4 | 20 | 28 | 3 | 1 | 1 | 10 | 1 | 1 | 0 | 3 | 0 | 34 | 1 | 0 | 0 | .196 | .217 | .275 |
| Carlin, Luke, Fort Wayne † | 27 | 111 | 99 | 10 | 21 | 33 | 6 | 3 | 0 | 12 | 0 | 1 | 0 | 11 | 0 | 23 | 1 | 0 | 1 | .212 | .288 | .333 |
| Carson, Matt, Battle Creek | 95 | 414 | 381 | 59 | 116 | 179 | 23 | 2 | 12 | 58 | 0 | 2 | 9 | 22 | 0 | 78 | 21 | 7 | 4 | .304 | .355 | .470 |
| Carter, Chris, South Bend | 6 | 26 | 26 | 3 | 10 | 19 | 3 | 0 | 2 | 7 | 0 | 0 | 0 | 0 | 0 | 2 | 0 | 0 | 1 | .385 | .385 | .731 |
| Castillo, David, Kane County | 111 | 476 | 402 | 66 | 99 | 156 | 28 | 1 | 9 | 59 | 0 | 2 | 7 | 65 | 3 | 77 | 0 | 0 | 18 | .246 | .359 | .388 |
| Chirinos, Robinson, Lansing | 84 | 355 | 319 | 56 | 77 | 128 | 18 | 6 | 7 | 39 | 3 | 0 | 8 | 25 | 1 | 70 | 7 | 2 | 4 | .241 | .313 | .401 |
| Cho, Hyung, Wisconsin | 18 | 63 | 57 | 4 | 17 | 19 | 2 | 0 | 0 | 10 | 0 | 0 | 1 | 5 | 0 | 11 | 0 | 1 | 2 | .298 | .365 | .333 |

| Player, Team | G | TPA | AB | R | H | TB | 2B | 3B | HR | RBI | SH | SF | HP | BB | IBB | SO | SB | CS | GDP | Avg. | OBP | Slg. |
|---|---|---|---|---|---|---|---|---|---|---|---|---|---|---|---|---|---|---|---|---|---|---|
| Ciofrone, Peter, Fort Wayne * | 42 | 180 | 157 | 20 | 41 | 51 | 3 | 2 | 1 | 15 | 2 | 0 | 5 | 16 | 0 | 28 | 0 | 0 | 1 | .261 | .348 | .325 |
| Ciriaco, Juan, Fort Wayne | 99 | 371 | 348 | 29 | 84 | 106 | 12 | 2 | 2 | 35 | 3 | 2 | 2 | 16 | 0 | 80 | 5 | 8 | 3 | .241 | .277 | .305 |
| Clark, Cody, Clinton | 55 | 209 | 179 | 28 | 41 | 55 | 6 | 1 | 2 | 19 | 1 | 1 | 4 | 24 | 0 | 52 | 1 | 0 | 4 | .229 | .332 | .307 |
| Collins, Chris, Wisconsin | 108 | 441 | 382 | 43 | 90 | 121 | 19 | 0 | 4 | 57 | 3 | 6 | 3 | 47 | 0 | 72 | 3 | 2 | 12 | .236 | .320 | .317 |
| Collins, Kevin, Lansing * | 110 | 453 | 397 | 72 | 115 | 244 | 26 | 2 | 33 | 86 | 0 | 4 | 7 | 45 | 7 | 126 | 3 | 1 | 6 | .290 | .369 | .615 |
| Collins, Mike, Cedar Rapids | 33 | 129 | 111 | 10 | 23 | 32 | 6 | 0 | 1 | 12 | 1 | 0 | 4 | 13 | 0 | 21 | 0 | 3 | 3 | .207 | .313 | .288 |
| Colton, Chris, Wisconsin | 127 | 506 | 457 | 63 | 106 | 182 | 18 | 11 | 12 | 63 | 0 | 2 | 7 | 40 | 1 | 99 | 15 | 9 | 14 | .232 | .302 | .398 |
| Conley, Evan, Dayton | 37 | 142 | 123 | 12 | 33 | 41 | 8 | 0 | 0 | 6 | 0 | 0 | 3 | 16 | 0 | 24 | 1 | 0 | 2 | .268 | .366 | .333 |
| Cook, Jeff, South Bend * | 120 | 439 | 405 | 55 | 117 | 161 | 23 | 6 | 3 | 58 | 2 | 5 | 4 | 23 | 2 | 64 | 10 | 8 | 5 | .289 | .330 | .398 |
| Corporan, Carlos, Beloit † | 63 | 214 | 197 | 20 | 45 | 59 | 7 | 2 | 1 | 16 | 3 | 4 | 3 | 7 | 0 | 65 | 1 | 3 | 1 | .228 | .261 | .299 |
| Cosby, Quan, Cedar Rapids † | 119 | 503 | 454 | 70 | 113 | 160 | 8 | 12 | 5 | 34 | 4 | 6 | 4 | 35 | 1 | 82 | 24 | 10 | 6 | .249 | .305 | .352 |
| Cox, Mike, Wisconsin | 116 | 448 | 390 | 49 | 89 | 147 | 21 | 2 | 11 | 51 | 2 | 5 | 4 | 47 | 0 | 100 | 2 | 6 | 6 | .228 | .314 | .377 |
| Cruz, Enrique, Battle Creek | 83 | 310 | 264 | 40 | 61 | 96 | 9 | 1 | 8 | 26 | 6 | 1 | 9 | 30 | 0 | 68 | 13 | 5 | 0 | .231 | .329 | .364 |
| Davis, John-Paul, Peoria | 68 | 283 | 240 | 45 | 71 | 115 | 14 | 0 | 10 | 37 | 0 | 5 | 7 | 31 | 1 | 57 | 0 | 0 | 8 | .296 | .385 | .479 |
| Deevers, Robby, Beloit | 73 | 258 | 235 | 27 | 56 | 101 | 17 | 2 | 8 | 28 | 7 | 2 | 4 | 10 | 0 | 77 | 6 | 5 | 2 | .238 | .279 | .430 |
| Dobson, Sean, Peoria | 4 | 10 | 7 | 4 | 2 | 2 | 0 | 0 | 0 | 1 | 0 | 0 | 2 | 1 | 0 | 3 | 0 | 0 | 0 | .286 | .500 | .286 |
| Donachie, Adam, Burlington | 67 | 259 | 228 | 17 | 43 | 53 | 7 | 0 | 1 | 21 | 6 | 2 | 2 | 21 | 0 | 41 | 5 | 2 | 4 | .189 | .261 | .232 |
| Dopirak, Brian, Lansing | 137 | 597 | 541 | 94 | 166 | 321 | 38 | 0 | 39 | 120 | 0 | 5 | 3 | 48 | 4 | 123 | 4 | 3 | 14 | .307 | .363 | .593 |
| Doyle, Nate, West Michigan | 41 | 138 | 120 | 16 | 27 | 42 | 6 | 3 | 1 | 12 | 0 | 0 | 11 | 7 | 0 | 53 | 2 | 0 | 2 | .225 | .326 | .350 |
| Dryer, Matt, Peoria | 72 | 291 | 235 | 38 | 69 | 108 | 18 | 0 | 7 | 51 | 2 | 7 | 3 | 44 | 0 | 59 | 0 | 1 | 9 | .294 | .401 | .460 |
| Duenas, Tommy, Cedar Rapids | 76 | 279 | 265 | 26 | 56 | 107 | 21 | 0 | 10 | 31 | 0 | 1 | 3 | 10 | 1 | 89 | 3 | 2 | 3 | .211 | .247 | .404 |
| Dutton, Jeremy, Wisconsin * | 93 | 333 | 288 | 27 | 60 | 81 | 13 | 1 | 2 | 19 | 1 | 2 | 4 | 38 | 1 | 62 | 3 | 3 | 6 | .208 | .307 | .281 |
| Figuereo, Anibal, Burlington | 34 | 101 | 92 | 10 | 16 | 27 | 8 | 0 | 1 | 8 | 0 | 1 | 1 | 7 | 0 | 30 | 0 | 0 | 1 | .174 | .238 | .293 |
| Fitzgerald, Ryan, Lansing | 82 | 285 | 250 | 35 | 68 | 92 | 11 | 2 | 3 | 29 | 1 | 4 | 2 | 28 | 1 | 60 | 9 | 6 | 2 | .272 | .345 | .368 |
| Flowers, Bo, West Michigan | 6 | 25 | 22 | 4 | 6 | 10 | 1 | 0 | 1 | 1 | 0 | 0 | 3 | 0 | 0 | 6 | 0 | 1 | 0 | .273 | .360 | .455 |
| Fox, Jacob, Lansing | 97 | 395 | 366 | 49 | 105 | 172 | 19 | 3 | 14 | 55 | 2 | 2 | 8 | 17 | 0 | 75 | 2 | 1 | 7 | .287 | .331 | .470 |
| Francia, Juan, West Michigan † | 111 | 478 | 413 | 73 | 132 | 149 | 11 | 3 | 0 | 32 | 20 | 1 | 10 | 34 | 2 | 44 | 37 | 19 | 3 | .320 | .384 | .361 |
| Frazier, Alex, South Bend | 125 | 511 | 464 | 73 | 145 | 247 | 36 | 3 | 20 | 80 | 0 | 5 | 15 | 27 | 3 | 92 | 21 | 5 | 8 | .313 | .366 | .532 |
| Frisella, Sal, Peoria | 52 | 180 | 156 | 25 | 41 | 64 | 4 | 2 | 5 | 26 | 1 | 1 | 4 | 18 | 1 | 43 | 4 | 1 | 3 | .263 | .352 | .410 |
| Frostad, Emerson, Clinton * | 113 | 424 | 367 | 45 | 79 | 118 | 17 | 2 | 6 | 42 | 6 | 2 | 6 | 43 | 1 | 97 | 2 | 2 | 5 | .215 | .306 | .322 |
| Fry, Ryan, Dayton | 44 | 182 | 174 | 21 | 38 | 80 | 12 | 0 | 10 | 30 | 0 | 0 | 1 | 7 | 0 | 72 | 0 | 0 | 4 | .218 | .253 | .460 |
| Furtado, Micah, Clinton * | 84 | 370 | 300 | 56 | 91 | 126 | 17 | 3 | 4 | 35 | 8 | 2 | 14 | 46 | 1 | 69 | 17 | 12 | 1 | .303 | .417 | .420 |
| Gaffney, Mike, Burlington | 88 | 301 | 271 | 31 | 56 | 71 | 7 | 1 | 2 | 31 | 4 | 4 | 8 | 14 | 0 | 56 | 6 | 3 | 6 | .207 | .263 | .262 |
| Garcia, Alberto, Lansing | 68 | 235 | 227 | 34 | 69 | 106 | 8 | 4 | 7 | 25 | 1 | 1 | 2 | 4 | 0 | 41 | 2 | 2 | 4 | .304 | .321 | .467 |
| Garcia, Alex, Swing of the Quad Ci † | 92 | 352 | 322 | 36 | 79 | 94 | 6 | 3 | 1 | 27 | 5 | 2 | 9 | 14 | 0 | 60 | 11 | 7 | 3 | .245 | .294 | .292 |
| Garcia, Lino, South Bend | 113 | 359 | 319 | 43 | 82 | 114 | 14 | 3 | 4 | 25 | 7 | 2 | 9 | 22 | 3 | 74 | 12 | 7 | 7 | .257 | .321 | .357 |
| Geiger, Kyle, Swing of the Quad Ci | 53 | 212 | 189 | 22 | 55 | 73 | 8 | 2 | 2 | 25 | 0 | 4 | 4 | 15 | 0 | 43 | 0 | 0 | 3 | .291 | .349 | .386 |
| Gerez, Francisco, Wisconsin | 9 | 27 | 25 | 2 | 8 | 10 | 2 | 0 | 0 | 5 | 0 | 0 | 0 | 2 | 0 | 5 | 3 | 0 | 1 | .320 | .370 | .400 |
| Gonzalez, Alberto, South Bend | 100 | 353 | 319 | 39 | 76 | 109 | 15 | 6 | 2 | 25 | 5 | 2 | 11 | 16 | 0 | 44 | 9 | 7 | 10 | .238 | .296 | .342 |
| Gonzalez, Luis, Burlington | 54 | 215 | 187 | 27 | 49 | 66 | 11 | 0 | 2 | 21 | 5 | 3 | 11 | 9 | 0 | 44 | 3 | 0 | 6 | .262 | .329 | .353 |
| Graham, Andrew, West Michigan | 26 | 90 | 83 | 8 | 21 | 30 | 4 | 1 | 1 | 9 | 1 | 0 | 1 | 5 | 0 | 21 | 0 | 1 | 0 | .253 | .303 | .361 |
| Graham, Bryan, Burlington * | 84 | 310 | 269 | 28 | 49 | 67 | 12 | 0 | 2 | 26 | 2 | 1 | 0 | 38 | 3 | 68 | 2 | 3 | 8 | .182 | .282 | .249 |
| Granato, Anthony, Lansing † | 32 | 126 | 108 | 18 | 29 | 38 | 4 | 1 | 1 | 7 | 0 | 1 | 2 | 15 | 1 | 25 | 3 | 1 | 0 | .269 | .365 | .352 |
| Gray, Matthew, Dayton * | 24 | 93 | 85 | 4 | 13 | 19 | 2 | 2 | 0 | 4 | 0 | 0 | 1 | 7 | 0 | 34 | 0 | 0 | 0 | .153 | .226 | .224 |
| Grayson, Luke, Clinton | 101 | 376 | 338 | 56 | 86 | 145 | 28 | 2 | 9 | 39 | 6 | 3 | 4 | 25 | 1 | 86 | 6 | 2 | 9 | .254 | .311 | .429 |
| Groves, Brett, Burlington | 28 | 124 | 91 | 13 | 22 | 24 | 2 | 0 | 0 | 8 | 3 | 3 | 3 | 24 | 1 | 21 | 3 | 2 | 1 | .242 | .405 | .264 |
| Guzman, Jose, Cedar Rapids † | 13 | 41 | 37 | 7 | 7 | 8 | 1 | 0 | 0 | 2 | 0 | 0 | 0 | 4 | 0 | 17 | 4 | 2 | 0 | .189 | .268 | .216 |
| Haerther, Cody, Peoria * | 86 | 366 | 326 | 48 | 103 | 142 | 20 | 2 | 5 | 45 | 3 | 1 | 4 | 32 | 2 | 59 | 7 | 3 | 6 | .316 | .383 | .436 |
| Hatcher, Justin, Clinton | 69 | 229 | 190 | 29 | 55 | 78 | 12 | 1 | 3 | 29 | 2 | 4 | 6 | 27 | 2 | 46 | 2 | 5 | 5 | .289 | .388 | .411 |
| Hayes, Calvin, Peoria | 40 | 177 | 158 | 27 | 48 | 56 | 2 | 0 | 2 | 12 | 3 | 0 | 0 | 16 | 0 | 25 | 6 | 3 | 4 | .304 | .368 | .354 |
| Heether, Adam, Beloit | 128 | 525 | 476 | 65 | 120 | 214 | 35 | 4 | 17 | 72 | 0 | 4 | 7 | 37 | 1 | 93 | 2 | 1 | 12 | .252 | .313 | .450 |
| Hilt, Cole, Burlington | 35 | 133 | 110 | 16 | 26 | 37 | 5 | 0 | 2 | 8 | 0 | 0 | 4 | 19 | 0 | 40 | 0 | 0 | 1 | .236 | .368 | .336 |
| Himes, Benjamin, Dayton * | 90 | 344 | 312 | 37 | 66 | 124 | 18 | 5 | 10 | 45 | 1 | 1 | 1 | 29 | 0 | 121 | 5 | 6 | 3 | .212 | .280 | .397 |
| Hoffpauir, Jarrett, Peoria | 62 | 267 | 231 | 34 | 62 | 99 | 20 | 1 | 5 | 30 | 0 | 1 | 6 | 29 | 2 | 21 | 2 | 4 | 4 | .268 | .363 | .429 |
| Hudson, William, Dayton † | 82 | 309 | 254 | 43 | 50 | 70 | 7 | 2 | 3 | 25 | 3 | 0 | 6 | 46 | 1 | 63 | 14 | 7 | 5 | .197 | .333 | .276 |
| Hunt, Kelly, West Michigan | 136 | 582 | 546 | 71 | 150 | 241 | 28 | 0 | 21 | 102 | 0 | 7 | 7 | 22 | 2 | 107 | 2 | 3 | 12 | .275 | .308 | .441 |
| Ingram, Brian, Kane County * | 126 | 570 | 472 | 80 | 108 | 153 | 23 | 5 | 4 | 44 | 5 | 5 | 4 | 84 | 2 | 97 | 6 | 4 | 7 | .229 | .347 | .324 |
| Iribarren, Hernan, Beloit * | 15 | 73 | 67 | 12 | 25 | 44 | 6 | 5 | 1 | 10 | 0 | 1 | 0 | 5 | 0 | 16 | 1 | 0 | 1 | .373 | .411 | .657 |
| Johnson, Josh, Swing of the Quad Ci | 48 | 157 | 146 | 10 | 21 | 26 | 5 | 0 | 0 | 11 | 0 | 2 | 3 | 6 | 0 | 30 | 0 | 1 | 6 | .144 | .191 | .178 |
| Johnson, Joshua, Burlington † | 4 | 14 | 12 | 1 | 2 | 2 | 0 | 0 | 0 | 1 | 1 | 0 | 0 | 1 | 0 | 3 | 0 | 0 | 0 | .167 | .231 | .167 |
| Johnson, Ryan, Fort Wayne * | 12 | 47 | 45 | 2 | 4 | 5 | 1 | 0 | 0 | 2 | 0 | 0 | 0 | 2 | 0 | 10 | 0 | 0 | 0 | .089 | .128 | .111 |
| Jones, Adam, Wisconsin | 130 | 559 | 510 | 76 | 136 | 206 | 23 | 7 | 11 | 72 | 4 | 7 | 5 | 33 | 0 | 124 | 8 | 4 | 13 | .267 | .314 | .404 |
| Kaaihue, Kila, Burlington * | 125 | 471 | 390 | 57 | 96 | 168 | 23 | 2 | 15 | 62 | 3 | 5 | 9 | 64 | 4 | 98 | 1 | 0 | 6 | .246 | .361 | .431 |
| Kaplan, Jonny, South Bend | 102 | 419 | 373 | 61 | 98 | 158 | 23 | 5 | 9 | 39 | 5 | 3 | 6 | 32 | 0 | 55 | 24 | 8 | 6 | .263 | .329 | .424 |
| Kartler, Bryce, Battle Creek * | 92 | 377 | 329 | 51 | 83 | 133 | 13 | 2 | 11 | 43 | 4 | 2 | 6 | 36 | 0 | 81 | 12 | 6 | 1 | .252 | .335 | .404 |
| Kazmar, Sean, Fort Wayne | 5 | 26 | 23 | 5 | 5 | 8 | 3 | 0 | 0 | 2 | 0 | 0 | 2 | 1 | 0 | 6 | 0 | 0 | 1 | .217 | .308 | .348 |
| Kim, Eddie, Kane County * | 113 | 458 | 405 | 42 | 103 | 158 | 21 | 2 | 10 | 71 | 0 | 6 | 2 | 45 | 3 | 86 | 0 | 1 | 12 | .254 | .328 | .390 |
| Kimpton, Nick, Cedar Rapids * | 37 | 144 | 131 | 20 | 38 | 45 | 5 | 1 | 0 | 12 | 0 | 0 | 1 | 12 | 0 | 25 | 10 | 4 | 1 | .290 | .354 | .344 |
| Kirkland, Kody, West Michigan | 129 | 531 | 496 | 50 | 117 | 199 | 30 | 11 | 10 | 61 | 4 | 1 | 13 | 15 | 0 | 149 | 6 | 8 | 5 | .236 | .276 | .401 |
| Knoedler, Jason, West Michigan † | 70 | 240 | 198 | 33 | 48 | 75 | 7 | 4 | 4 | 21 | 6 | 3 | 0 | 33 | 0 | 59 | 8 | 4 | 4 | .242 | .346 | .379 |
| Kolkhorst, Christopher, Fort Wayne * | 12 | 58 | 47 | 15 | 16 | 25 | 4 | 1 | 1 | 4 | 2 | 1 | 3 | 5 | 0 | 7 | 1 | 1 | 1 | .340 | .429 | .532 |
| Kottaras, George, Fort Wayne * | 78 | 326 | 271 | 40 | 84 | 125 | 18 | 1 | 7 | 46 | 1 | 3 | 0 | 51 | 2 | 41 | 0 | 0 | 7 | .310 | .415 | .461 |
| Kreuzer, Josh, Clinton | 104 | 433 | 360 | 46 | 96 | 166 | 34 | 3 | 10 | 65 | 0 | 8 | 12 | 53 | 1 | 85 | 2 | 0 | 7 | .267 | .372 | .461 |
| LaHair, Bryan, Wisconsin * | 67 | 280 | 262 | 30 | 73 | 112 | 24 | 0 | 5 | 28 | 1 | 0 | 1 | 16 | 1 | 66 | 0 | 6 | 5 | .279 | .323 | .427 |
| Larsen, Drew, Lansing | 99 | 389 | 342 | 55 | 83 | 144 | 24 | 2 | 11 | 51 | 3 | 4 | 15 | 25 | 0 | 101 | 8 | 2 | 6 | .243 | .319 | .421 |
| Lauderdale, Matthew, Fort Wayne | 39 | 163 | 146 | 17 | 33 | 57 | 10 | 1 | 4 | 18 | 0 | 0 | 3 | 14 | 0 | 44 | 1 | 0 | 5 | .226 | .307 | .390 |
| Leahy, Ryan, Cedar Rapids | 25 | 107 | 94 | 16 | 25 | 30 | 2 | 0 | 1 | 4 | 0 | 0 | 2 | 11 | 0 | 13 | 2 | 1 | 1 | .266 | .355 | .319 |
| Lewis, Will, Beloit | 38 | 160 | 137 | 28 | 45 | 71 | 11 | 0 | 5 | 21 | 3 | 2 | 2 | 16 | 0 | 22 | 4 | 3 | 4 | .328 | .401 | .518 |
| Llamas, Juan, West Michigan | 1 | 5 | 5 | 1 | 1 | 1 | 0 | 0 | 0 | 2 | 0 | 0 | 0 | 0 | 0 | 0 | 0 | 0 | 0 | .200 | .200 | .200 |
| Lopez, Baltazar, Cedar Rapids * | 64 | 259 | 236 | 34 | 74 | 121 | 14 | 3 | 9 | 35 | 1 | 1 | 2 | 19 | 0 | 65 | 6 | 1 | 6 | .314 | .368 | .513 |
| Lubanski, Chris, Burlington * | 116 | 490 | 439 | 62 | 121 | 184 | 22 | 7 | 9 | 48 | 2 | 4 | 4 | 41 | 6 | 99 | 16 | 11 | 6 | .276 | .340 | .419 |
| Lucas, Edward, Burlington | 24 | 99 | 89 | 12 | 18 | 25 | 5 | 1 | 0 | 10 | 2 | 1 | 2 | 5 | 0 | 21 | 2 | 2 | 3 | .202 | .258 | .281 |

| Player, Team | G | TPA | AB | R | H | TB | 2B | 3B | HR | RBI | SH | SF | HP | BB | IBB | SO | SB | CS | GDP | Avg. | OBP | Slg. |
|---|---|---|---|---|---|---|---|---|---|---|---|---|---|---|---|---|---|---|---|---|---|---|
| Macias, Drew, Fort Wayne * | 129 | 545 | 478 | 60 | 127 | 179 | 18 | 5 | 8 | 55 | 4 | 6 | 8 | 49 | 1 | 68 | 16 | 14 | 7 | .266 | .340 | .374 |
| Made, Hector, Battle Creek | 128 | 561 | 515 | 68 | 149 | 196 | 30 | 1 | 5 | 52 | 5 | 3 | 5 | 33 | 0 | 76 | 12 | 10 | 9 | .289 | .336 | .381 |
| Madrigal, Warner, Cedar Rapids | 26 | 100 | 91 | 10 | 25 | 36 | 3 | 1 | 2 | 10 | 0 | 1 | 1 | 7 | 0 | 24 | 1 | 1 | 0 | .275 | .330 | .396 |
| Majewski, Dustin, Kane County * | 127 | 521 | 464 | 75 | 127 | 190 | 23 | 2 | 12 | 62 | 2 | 6 | 1 | 48 | 1 | 105 | 20 | 6 | 14 | .274 | .339 | .409 |
| Marks, Timothy, Beloit | 35 | 126 | 114 | 12 | 22 | 24 | 2 | 0 | 0 | 6 | 2 | 0 | 1 | 9 | 0 | 13 | 0 | 0 | 7 | .193 | .258 | .211 |
| Marquez, Uriak, Lansing † | 43 | 149 | 140 | 15 | 35 | 44 | 6 | 0 | 1 | 14 | 4 | 1 | 0 | 4 | 0 | 20 | 1 | 1 | 5 | .250 | .269 | .314 |
| Martinez, Brett, Cedar Rapids | 1 | 3 | 2 | 1 | 0 | 0 | 0 | 0 | 0 | 0 | 0 | 0 | 1 | 0 | 0 | 0 | 0 | 0 | 0 | .000 | .333 | .000 |
| Mather, Joe, Peoria | 65 | 270 | 241 | 34 | 61 | 104 | 18 | 2 | 7 | 31 | 0 | 0 | 5 | 24 | 0 | 70 | 3 | 3 | 2 | .253 | .333 | .432 |
| McCreery, John, South Bend | 18 | 56 | 50 | 6 | 7 | 10 | 0 | 0 | 1 | 4 | 0 | 0 | 1 | 5 | 0 | 10 | 0 | 1 | 3 | .140 | .232 | .200 |
| McDonald, Chamar, Burlington | 9 | 20 | 18 | 2 | 2 | 6 | 1 | 0 | 1 | 3 | 0 | 0 | 0 | 2 | 0 | 13 | 0 | 0 | 1 | .111 | .200 | .333 |
| McKinney, Garth, West Michigan | 117 | 464 | 412 | 59 | 94 | 169 | 14 | 2 | 19 | 41 | 1 | 0 | 5 | 46 | 3 | 175 | 11 | 7 | 3 | .228 | .313 | .410 |
| McQuade, Tony, Lansing † | 92 | 381 | 333 | 51 | 98 | 151 | 24 | 4 | 7 | 48 | 1 | 7 | 2 | 38 | 0 | 65 | 7 | 5 | 6 | .294 | .363 | .453 |
| Mejia, Jorge, Dayton | 32 | 106 | 94 | 14 | 23 | 27 | 4 | 0 | 0 | 4 | 1 | 0 | 2 | 9 | 0 | 20 | 2 | 1 | 1 | .245 | .324 | .287 |
| Milons, Jereme, South Bend | 11 | 30 | 29 | 1 | 5 | 7 | 0 | 1 | 0 | 1 | 0 | 0 | 1 | 0 | 0 | 10 | 1 | 1 | 0 | .172 | .200 | .241 |
| Monegan, Anthony, Peoria * | 124 | 574 | 509 | 97 | 151 | 209 | 31 | 9 | 3 | 53 | 5 | 2 | 4 | 54 | 1 | 94 | 19 | 9 | 10 | .297 | .367 | .411 |
| Montero, Miguel, South Bend * | 115 | 449 | 403 | 47 | 106 | 165 | 22 | 2 | 11 | 59 | 0 | 4 | 6 | 36 | 0 | 74 | 8 | 2 | 5 | .263 | .330 | .409 |
| Mora, Ruben, Fort Wayne † | 23 | 92 | 81 | 12 | 23 | 28 | 2 | 0 | 1 | 5 | 1 | 0 | 0 | 10 | 0 | 19 | 1 | 1 | 3 | .284 | .363 | .346 |
| Moran, Javon, Dayton | 25 | 106 | 94 | 11 | 36 | 38 | 2 | 0 | 0 | 7 | 1 | 0 | 1 | 10 | 0 | 15 | 11 | 3 | 0 | .383 | .448 | .404 |
| Moss, Steve, Beloit | 102 | 414 | 362 | 41 | 85 | 134 | 17 | 4 | 8 | 34 | 5 | 2 | 10 | 35 | 0 | 90 | 6 | 4 | 7 | .235 | .318 | .370 |
| Mottram, Allen, South Bend | 53 | 203 | 184 | 26 | 50 | 82 | 11 | 0 | 7 | 36 | 0 | 2 | 5 | 12 | 0 | 31 | 0 | 0 | 3 | .272 | .330 | .446 |
| Moye, Alan, Burlington | 13 | 58 | 47 | 9 | 11 | 12 | 1 | 0 | 0 | 3 | 0 | 1 | 0 | 10 | 0 | 16 | 1 | 2 | 1 | .234 | .362 | .255 |
| Murillo, Agustin, South Bend | 101 | 386 | 357 | 46 | 94 | 124 | 16 | 1 | 4 | 38 | 0 | 1 | 5 | 23 | 1 | 48 | 10 | 5 | 11 | .263 | .316 | .347 |
| Murray, Josh, Beloit | 55 | 202 | 188 | 21 | 30 | 47 | 5 | 0 | 4 | 15 | 1 | 1 | 3 | 9 | 0 | 50 | 1 | 2 | 1 | .160 | .209 | .250 |
| Nesbit, Michael, Wisconsin | 69 | 261 | 237 | 34 | 66 | 85 | 11 | 1 | 2 | 17 | 2 | 1 | 1 | 20 | 0 | 46 | 8 | 5 | 1 | .278 | .336 | .359 |
| Olmstead, Walter, Dayton † | 106 | 426 | 380 | 61 | 99 | 169 | 20 | 4 | 14 | 53 | 3 | 2 | 15 | 26 | 0 | 132 | 0 | 4 | 5 | .261 | .331 | .445 |
| Orlandos, Nick, Wisconsin | 65 | 290 | 261 | 24 | 76 | 90 | 9 | 1 | 1 | 23 | 2 | 1 | 3 | 23 | 0 | 34 | 10 | 4 | 9 | .291 | .354 | .345 |
| Pagnozzi, Matt, Peoria | 74 | 239 | 215 | 29 | 45 | 57 | 10 | 1 | 0 | 14 | 4 | 0 | 5 | 15 | 1 | 54 | 4 | 1 | 4 | .209 | .277 | .265 |
| Pali, Matt, Cedar Rapids * | 112 | 469 | 407 | 55 | 104 | 162 | 18 | 5 | 10 | 57 | 2 | 4 | 14 | 42 | 3 | 84 | 10 | 11 | 5 | .256 | .343 | .398 |
| Palmisano, Lou, Beloit | 113 | 464 | 409 | 59 | 120 | 169 | 22 | 3 | 7 | 65 | 1 | 2 | 9 | 43 | 2 | 93 | 3 | 2 | 13 | .293 | .371 | .413 |
| Patrick, Christopher, Peoria | 7 | 32 | 26 | 7 | 8 | 13 | 2 | 0 | 1 | 6 | 1 | 1 | 2 | 2 | 0 | 2 | 0 | 0 | 0 | .308 | .387 | .500 |
| Peel, Aaron, Cedar Rapids | 62 | 233 | 208 | 25 | 45 | 80 | 6 | 1 | 9 | 24 | 1 | 2 | 5 | 17 | 0 | 66 | 4 | 4 | 2 | .216 | .289 | .385 |
| Pena, Antonio, Clinton | 7 | 32 | 22 | 1 | 3 | 3 | 0 | 0 | 0 | 1 | 1 | 1 | 2 | 6 | 0 | 3 | 1 | 0 | 0 | .136 | .355 | .136 |
| Perez, Henry, Fort Wayne | 22 | 4 | 2 | 0 | 0 | 0 | 0 | 0 | 0 | 0 | 1 | 0 | 0 | 1 | 0 | 1 | 0 | 0 | 0 | .000 | .333 | .000 |
| Perez, Luis, Kane County | 89 | 352 | 314 | 44 | 85 | 115 | 16 | 1 | 4 | 41 | 3 | 1 | 7 | 27 | 0 | 46 | 12 | 5 | 8 | .271 | .341 | .366 |
| Peterson, Brock, Swing of the Quad Ci | 124 | 522 | 454 | 66 | 115 | 157 | 21 | 0 | 7 | 65 | 1 | 4 | 7 | 56 | 0 | 104 | 5 | 4 | 8 | .253 | .342 | .346 |
| Phillips, Kyle, Swing of the Quad Ci * | 97 | 395 | 347 | 49 | 79 | 128 | 16 | 0 | 11 | 44 | 0 | 7 | 3 | 38 | 4 | 69 | 1 | 0 | 11 | .228 | .304 | .369 |
| Pickens, Jordan, Fort Wayne | 106 | 458 | 392 | 68 | 93 | 167 | 23 | 0 | 17 | 58 | 0 | 5 | 19 | 42 | 0 | 112 | 1 | 0 | 11 | .237 | .336 | .426 |
| Piepkorn, Jeremiah, Dayton | 28 | 110 | 101 | 10 | 17 | 25 | 3 | 1 | 1 | 9 | 2 | 0 | 2 | 5 | 0 | 30 | 0 | 0 | 2 | .168 | .222 | .248 |
| Powell, Brandon, Burlington * | 90 | 355 | 307 | 41 | 82 | 123 | 16 | 5 | 5 | 34 | 4 | 0 | 4 | 40 | 0 | 60 | 7 | 6 | 3 | .267 | .359 | .401 |
| Purdom, John, Dayton | 18 | 67 | 60 | 4 | 17 | 23 | 4 | 1 | 0 | 7 | 0 | 2 | 1 | 4 | 0 | 17 | 0 | 0 | 1 | .283 | .328 | .383 |
| Putnam, Daniel, Kane County * | 48 | 190 | 156 | 29 | 35 | 65 | 5 | 2 | 7 | 27 | 1 | 1 | 3 | 29 | 1 | 38 | 0 | 0 | 11 | .224 | .354 | .417 |
| Ramirez, Manuel, Beloit | 86 | 320 | 296 | 36 | 70 | 108 | 21 | 1 | 5 | 35 | 3 | 4 | 1 | 16 | 0 | 54 | 1 | 0 | 7 | .236 | .274 | .365 |
| Reinking, Kevin, Burlington | 32 | 117 | 103 | 15 | 23 | 42 | 10 | 0 | 3 | 18 | 1 | 1 | 4 | 8 | 1 | 30 | 0 | 2 | 0 | .223 | .302 | .408 |
| Reynolds, Lagatila, South Bend | 91 | 337 | 302 | 38 | 79 | 98 | 14 | 1 | 1 | 26 | 5 | 3 | 2 | 25 | 0 | 69 | 15 | 4 | 2 | .262 | .319 | .325 |
| Reynolds, Mark, South Bend | 4 | 16 | 15 | 0 | 1 | 2 | 1 | 0 | 0 | 0 | 0 | 0 | 0 | 1 | 0 | 5 | 0 | 0 | 0 | .067 | .125 | .133 |
| Reynolds, Wilton, West Michigan | 26 | 101 | 91 | 11 | 15 | 25 | 4 | 0 | 2 | 7 | 0 | 0 | 1 | 9 | 0 | 32 | 0 | 0 | 6 | .165 | .248 | .275 |
| Richardson, Grant, Beloit | 28 | 109 | 94 | 17 | 21 | 42 | 3 | 0 | 6 | 17 | 1 | 1 | 3 | 10 | 0 | 25 | 1 | 0 | 3 | .223 | .315 | .447 |
| Richardson, Kevin, Clinton | 100 | 392 | 345 | 50 | 77 | 135 | 19 | 0 | 13 | 55 | 0 | 4 | 10 | 33 | 0 | 121 | 1 | 1 | 8 | .223 | .306 | .391 |
| Rick, Alan, Lansing * | 84 | 341 | 301 | 40 | 77 | 130 | 22 | 2 | 9 | 36 | 2 | 1 | 6 | 31 | 1 | 87 | 1 | 1 | 3 | .256 | .336 | .432 |
| Robles, Luis, Battle Creek | 33 | 99 | 92 | 8 | 18 | 29 | 8 | 0 | 1 | 11 | 2 | 1 | 0 | 4 | 0 | 12 | 0 | 0 | 5 | .196 | .227 | .315 |
| Rodland, Eric, West Michigan * | 128 | 533 | 471 | 63 | 124 | 174 | 26 | 6 | 4 | 50 | 8 | 4 | 12 | 38 | 0 | 85 | 8 | 4 | 9 | .263 | .331 | .369 |
| Rodriguez, Guilder, Beloit † | 95 | 413 | 351 | 64 | 93 | 99 | 6 | 0 | 0 | 27 | 10 | 3 | 4 | 45 | 0 | 50 | 14 | 6 | 4 | .265 | .352 | .282 |
| Rodriguez, Manuel, Kane County | 41 | 5 | 4 | 1 | 1 | 1 | 0 | 0 | 0 | 1 | 0 | 0 | 0 | 1 | 0 | 2 | 0 | 0 | 0 | .250 | .400 | .250 |
| Rodriguez, Marcos, Peoria * | 13 | 51 | 45 | 5 | 8 | 10 | 2 | 0 | 0 | 5 | 1 | 0 | 0 | 5 | 0 | 9 | 0 | 0 | 2 | .178 | .260 | .222 |
| Rogers, Nick, Kane County | 94 | 336 | 283 | 52 | 68 | 100 | 15 | 4 | 3 | 33 | 2 | 4 | 3 | 44 | 0 | 81 | 14 | 5 | 2 | .240 | .344 | .353 |
| Rojas, Carlos, Lansing | 132 | 545 | 493 | 62 | 107 | 122 | 11 | 2 | 0 | 32 | 4 | 3 | 4 | 41 | 2 | 74 | 6 | 4 | 16 | .217 | .281 | .247 |
| Rojas, Tommy, Battle Creek | 79 | 286 | 250 | 31 | 68 | 101 | 15 | 0 | 6 | 50 | 2 | 4 | 9 | 21 | 0 | 68 | 1 | 2 | 12 | .272 | .345 | .404 |
| Rose, Brian, South Bend | 75 | 274 | 240 | 31 | 57 | 104 | 14 | 0 | 11 | 40 | 1 | 1 | 13 | 19 | 0 | 54 | 1 | 1 | 2 | .238 | .326 | .433 |
| Rottino, Vinny, Beloit | 140 | 584 | 529 | 78 | 161 | 255 | 25 | 9 | 17 | 124 | 1 | 10 | 4 | 40 | 3 | 71 | 5 | 1 | 12 | .304 | .352 | .482 |
| Ruchti, Justin, Wisconsin | 79 | 252 | 230 | 15 | 51 | 69 | 15 | 0 | 1 | 22 | 1 | 1 | 0 | 20 | 0 | 51 | 1 | 3 | 6 | .222 | .283 | .300 |
| Rutgers, Paul, Swing of the Quad Ci | 77 | 294 | 248 | 26 | 50 | 61 | 7 | 2 | 0 | 16 | 4 | 2 | 4 | 36 | 0 | 66 | 7 | 1 | 5 | .202 | .310 | .246 |
| Ryan, Brendan, Peoria | 105 | 472 | 426 | 72 | 137 | 172 | 21 | 4 | 2 | 59 | 9 | 9 | 4 | 24 | 2 | 42 | 30 | 7 | 13 | .322 | .356 | .404 |
| Sabino, Luis, West Michigan † | 103 | 427 | 384 | 54 | 90 | 151 | 22 | 6 | 9 | 47 | 0 | 4 | 3 | 36 | 0 | 144 | 10 | 3 | 5 | .234 | .302 | .393 |
| Sanchez, Angel, Burlington | 90 | 372 | 337 | 34 | 85 | 105 | 12 | 1 | 2 | 24 | 9 | 2 | 9 | 15 | 0 | 47 | 16 | 7 | 5 | .252 | .300 | .312 |
| Sanchez, Danilo, West Michigan | 87 | 347 | 309 | 33 | 91 | 137 | 22 | 0 | 8 | 46 | 1 | 5 | 6 | 26 | 0 | 59 | 0 | 0 | 5 | .294 | .355 | .443 |
| Sandoval, Abigail, Clinton | 93 | 383 | 333 | 43 | 78 | 107 | 16 | 2 | 3 | 30 | 21 | 0 | 0 | 29 | 0 | 81 | 8 | 6 | 11 | .234 | .296 | .321 |
| Schmidt, Jarrod, Dayton | 34 | 136 | 117 | 12 | 20 | 26 | 3 | 0 | 1 | 7 | 0 | 0 | 4 | 15 | 1 | 43 | 0 | 1 | 1 | .171 | .287 | .222 |
| Sherman, Steven, Peoria * | 7 | 34 | 31 | 6 | 9 | 18 | 0 | 0 | 3 | 12 | 1 | 0 | 0 | 2 | 0 | 5 | 0 | 0 | 0 | .290 | .333 | .581 |
| Smith, Kyle, Dayton | 76 | 301 | 269 | 25 | 49 | 93 | 15 | 1 | 9 | 27 | 0 | 1 | 7 | 24 | 0 | 129 | 2 | 2 | 5 | .182 | .266 | .346 |
| Smyres, Justin, Fort Wayne | 22 | 88 | 84 | 6 | 18 | 26 | 6 | 1 | 0 | 9 | 0 | 0 | 1 | 3 | 0 | 14 | 0 | 0 | 3 | .214 | .250 | .310 |
| Snyder, Brian, Kane County | 101 | 435 | 366 | 54 | 114 | 177 | 18 | 3 | 13 | 61 | 0 | 0 | 2 | 67 | 2 | 82 | 3 | 2 | 12 | .311 | .421 | .484 |
| Span, Denard, Swing of the Quad Ci * | 64 | 282 | 240 | 29 | 64 | 74 | 4 | 3 | 0 | 14 | 4 | 1 | 3 | 34 | 0 | 49 | 15 | 8 | 2 | .267 | .363 | .308 |
| Spanos, Vasili, Kane County | 97 | 406 | 331 | 58 | 103 | 167 | 26 | 1 | 12 | 80 | 0 | 8 | 13 | 54 | 1 | 76 | 11 | 5 | 11 | .311 | .419 | .505 |
| Springer, Kenard, Burlington | 85 | 337 | 315 | 39 | 74 | 92 | 11 | 2 | 1 | 27 | 1 | 3 | 8 | 10 | 0 | 64 | 7 | 6 | 4 | .235 | .274 | .292 |
| Strait, Cody, Dayton | 56 | 240 | 220 | 15 | 46 | 60 | 10 | 2 | 0 | 13 | 3 | 0 | 4 | 13 | 0 | 81 | 3 | 3 | 4 | .209 | .266 | .273 |
| Taylor, J.R., Swing of the Quad Ci † | 110 | 490 | 417 | 59 | 111 | 160 | 29 | 4 | 4 | 57 | 3 | 6 | 6 | 58 | 0 | 65 | 22 | 6 | 6 | .266 | .359 | .384 |
| Thayer, Matthew, Fort Wayne | 1 | 4 | 3 | 0 | 2 | 2 | 0 | 0 | 0 | 2 | 0 | 0 | 0 | 1 | 0 | 0 | 1 | 0 | 0 | .667 | .750 | .667 |
| Tritle, Chris, Kane County | 102 | 260 | 234 | 37 | 45 | 75 | 8 | 2 | 6 | 29 | 0 | 3 | 3 | 20 | 0 | 96 | 10 | 2 | 3 | .192 | .262 | .321 |
| Trofholz, Terry, Beloit | 119 | 503 | 460 | 86 | 138 | 168 | 14 | 5 | 2 | 42 | 6 | 3 | 9 | 23 | 0 | 96 | 48 | 10 | 9 | .300 | .343 | .365 |
| Urgelles, Jeff, Dayton | 62 | 243 | 210 | 27 | 49 | 72 | 11 | 0 | 4 | 29 | 1 | 0 | 3 | 29 | 0 | 52 | 2 | 2 | 3 | .233 | .335 | .343 |
| Urick, John, Battle Creek * | 118 | 456 | 397 | 61 | 112 | 186 | 29 | 0 | 15 | 65 | 0 | 3 | 4 | 52 | 3 | 85 | 1 | 4 | 15 | .282 | .368 | .469 |
| Valenzuela, Fernando, Fort Wayne * | 135 | 579 | 502 | 68 | 148 | 208 | 23 | 2 | 11 | 81 | 1 | 7 | 11 | 56 | 7 | 63 | 1 | 0 | 18 | .295 | .373 | .414 |

| Player, Team | G | TPA | AB | R | H | TB | 2B | 3B | HR | RBI | SH | SF | HP | BB | IBB | SO | SB | CS | GDP | Avg. | OBP | Slg. |
|---|---|---|---|---|---|---|---|---|---|---|---|---|---|---|---|---|---|---|---|---|---|---|
| Van Meetren, Jason, Battle Creek | 58 | 227 | 196 | 36 | 56 | 70 | 8 | 0 | 2 | 30 | 1 | 3 | 2 | 25 | 1 | 46 | 1 | 6 | 2 | .286 | .367 | .357 |
| Varela, Edgar, South Bend * | 127 | 508 | 471 | 54 | 123 | 174 | 25 | 1 | 8 | 61 | 4 | 3 | 5 | 25 | 2 | 59 | 2 | 4 | 7 | .261 | .304 | .369 |
| Vasquez, Willie, Battle Creek † | 108 | 423 | 362 | 50 | 88 | 136 | 22 | 1 | 8 | 44 | 5 | 4 | 4 | 46 | 2 | 96 | 2 | 6 | 9 | .243 | .332 | .376 |
| Villanova, Robert, Battle Creek * | 5 | 12 | 9 | 1 | 1 | 1 | 0 | 0 | 0 | 1 | 1 | 0 | 0 | 2 | 0 | 1 | 0 | 0 | 1 | .111 | .273 | .111 |
| Villanueva, Bill, Battle Creek | 2 | 2 | 2 | 0 | 0 | 0 | 0 | 0 | 0 | 0 | 0 | 0 | 0 | 0 | 0 | 1 | 0 | 0 | 0 | .000 | .000 | .000 |
| Wahlbrink, Brian, Fort Wayne | 126 | 565 | 519 | 81 | 134 | 193 | 19 | 8 | 8 | 46 | 1 | 3 | 7 | 35 | 0 | 142 | 24 | 9 | 2 | .258 | .312 | .372 |
| Walker, Chris, Lansing | 123 | 552 | 489 | 75 | 138 | 176 | 19 | 5 | 3 | 41 | 6 | 6 | 6 | 45 | 2 | 78 | 60 | 17 | 8 | .282 | .346 | .360 |
| Walsh, Nick, Battle Creek | 54 | 244 | 196 | 33 | 62 | 69 | 7 | 0 | 0 | 22 | 6 | 1 | 4 | 37 | 1 | 22 | 7 | 5 | 3 | .316 | .433 | .352 |
| Wayment, Kory, Kane County | 98 | 364 | 328 | 46 | 77 | 128 | 20 | 2 | 9 | 48 | 2 | 2 | 3 | 29 | 0 | 89 | 4 | 3 | 3 | .235 | .301 | .390 |
| Whitrock, Scott, Swing of the Quad Ci | 124 | 499 | 449 | 59 | 114 | 196 | 19 | 12 | 13 | 61 | 3 | 2 | 7 | 38 | 1 | 155 | 17 | 9 | 1 | .254 | .321 | .437 |
| Wilson, Bobby, Cedar Rapids | 105 | 441 | 396 | 45 | 106 | 153 | 23 | 0 | 8 | 64 | 1 | 9 | 5 | 30 | 3 | 55 | 5 | 2 | 3 | .268 | .320 | .386 |
| Wishy, Andrew, Clinton * | 123 | 494 | 420 | 57 | 107 | 171 | 22 | 0 | 14 | 69 | 2 | 4 | 5 | 63 | 1 | 114 | 13 | 6 | 9 | .255 | .356 | .407 |
| Womack, Josh, Wisconsin * | 118 | 512 | 470 | 76 | 122 | 176 | 21 | 9 | 5 | 39 | 2 | 2 | 4 | 34 | 4 | 126 | 24 | 7 | 7 | .260 | .314 | .374 |
| Wood, Brandon, Cedar Rapids | 125 | 535 | 478 | 65 | 120 | 193 | 30 | 5 | 11 | 64 | 4 | 2 | 5 | 46 | 3 | 117 | 21 | 5 | 8 | .251 | .322 | .404 |
| Zamojc, Mitchell, Swing of the Quad Ci * | 96 | 371 | 335 | 45 | 80 | 112 | 15 | 7 | 1 | 46 | 2 | 5 | 4 | 25 | 1 | 75 | 10 | 3 | 9 | .239 | .295 | .334 |

GRAND SLAMS—Cox, Evans, Sherman, Spanos, 2 each; Balentien, M. Brown, Carson, Collins, Cruz, Dryer, Frazier, Frisella, Harriman, Hernandez, Hunt, Jones, Kim, Kreuzer, Lewis, Maier, Majewski, Mather, McCreery, McKinney, Mejia, Palmisano, Parker, L. Perez, Piantek, Putnam, Reinking, Rick, Rose, Ryan, Votto, Wayment, Wood, 1 each.

AWARDED FIRST BASE ON CATCHER'S INTERFERENCE—Trofholz 2 (Barton, Pagnozzi); Blue (Corporan); Heether (Schmidt); Pagnozzi (Fox); G. Rodriguez (Pagnozzi); Salas (Corporan); Urick (Ruchti); Valenzuela (M. Perez, Fox); Whitrock (Barton).

# 2004 PITCHING

## TEAM

| Team | W | L | Pct. | ERA | G | CG | ShO | Sv. | IP | H | TBF | R | ER | HR | SH | SF | HB | BB | IBB | SO | WP | Bk. |
|---|---|---|---|---|---|---|---|---|---|---|---|---|---|---|---|---|---|---|---|---|---|---|
| Lansing | 77 | 63 | .550 | 3.40 | 140 | 2 | 10 | 38 | 1248.1 | 1156 | 5215 | 546 | 471 | 77 | 45 | 39 | 65 | 387 | 14 | 1109 | 58 | 6 |
| Quad City | 68 | 68 | .500 | 3.44 | 136 | 1 | 12 | 39 | 1191.2 | 1061 | 5151 | 554 | 455 | 66 | 46 | 53 | 60 | 523 | 29 | 1123 | 74 | 7 |
| West Michigan | 69 | 70 | .496 | 3.52 | 139 | 5 | 10 | 36 | 1231.1 | 1189 | 5229 | 565 | 482 | 68 | 40 | 31 | 81 | 413 | 14 | 964 | 95 | 6 |
| Clinton | 74 | 64 | .536 | 3.76 | 138 | 1 | 10 | 30 | 1189.2 | 1183 | 5057 | 586 | 497 | 92 | 44 | 43 | 51 | 365 | 16 | 999 | 63 | 7 |
| Fort Wayne | 72 | 68 | .514 | 3.78 | 140 | 1 | 7 | 40 | 1237.2 | 1216 | 5361 | 669 | 520 | 95 | 51 | 41 | 70 | 454 | 13 | 1185 | 82 | 12 |
| Kane County | 83 | 56 | .597 | 3.79 | 139 | 4 | 10 | 38 | 1224.2 | 1199 | 5207 | 606 | 516 | 83 | 45 | 28 | 62 | 335 | 36 | 1180 | 90 | 9 |
| South Bend | 77 | 63 | .550 | 3.81 | 140 | 8 | 10 | 47 | 1228.1 | 1220 | 5281 | 599 | 520 | 90 | 41 | 38 | 78 | 432 | 11 | 992 | 105 | 13 |
| Cedar Rapids | 75 | 64 | .540 | 3.87 | 139 | 2 | 10 | 36 | 1220.1 | 1132 | 5309 | 644 | 525 | 74 | 39 | 36 | 10 | 510 | 9 | 1068 | 94 | 15 |
| Peoria | 75 | 64 | .540 | 4.08 | 139 | 6 | 10 | 36 | 1206.1 | 1147 | 5268 | 670 | 547 | 92 | 39 | 43 | 1 | 478 | 18 | 1058 | 135 | 7 |
| Battle Creek | 71 | 68 | .511 | 4.13 | 139 | 4 | 11 | 32 | 1209.1 | 1245 | 5300 | 661 | 555 | 83 | 34 | 44 | 64 | 436 | 6 | 1086 | 74 | 9 |
| Beloit | 72 | 68 | .514 | 4.27 | 140 | 3 | 12 | 39 | 1204.0 | 1151 | 5221 | 669 | 571 | 131 | 44 | 40 | 59 | 481 | 3 | 1069 | 84 | 11 |
| Burlington | 56 | 84 | .400 | 4.47 | 140 | 5 | 7 | 31 | 1200.2 | 1202 | 5192 | 686 | 596 | 113 | 34 | 37 | 62 | 431 | 12 | 1016 | 64 | 12 |
| Wisconsin | 57 | 82 | .410 | 4.67 | 139 | 4 | 7 | 30 | 1215.0 | 1280 | 5380 | 747 | 630 | 118 | 40 | 38 | 99 | 441 | 14 | 1074 | 110 | 11 |
| Dayton | 48 | 92 | .343 | 5.03 | 140 | 0 | 6 | 28 | 1218.1 | 1285 | 5466 | 800 | 681 | 130 | 24 | 44 | 8 | 499 | 5 | 1095 | 123 | 16 |

## INDIVIDUAL

### TOP QUALIFIERS FOR EARNED-RUN AVERAGE TITLE

Minimum 112 innings.*Lefthanded pitcher.

| Pitcher, Team | W | L | Pct. | ERA | G | GS | CG | ShO | GF | Sv. | IP | H | TBF | R | ER | HR | SH | SF | HB | BB | IBB | SO | WP | Bk. |
|---|---|---|---|---|---|---|---|---|---|---|---|---|---|---|---|---|---|---|---|---|---|---|---|---|
| Bondurant, Steven, Kane County | 14 | 5 | .737 | 2.08 | 21 | 21 | 2 | 1 | 0 | 0 | 125.2 | 92 | 490 | 39 | 29 | 6 | 1 | 1 | 1 | 27 | 1 | 132 | 2 | 0 |
| Knox, Brad, Kane County | 14 | 5 | .737 | 2.59 | 26 | 25 | 0 | 0 | 0 | 0 | 156.1 | 141 | 634 | 53 | 45 | 11 | 8 | 0 | 8 | 24 | 1 | 174 | 10 | 0 |
| Hayhurst, Dirk, Fort Wayne | 9 | 4 | .692 | 2.66 | 26 | 17 | 0 | 0 | 1 | 0 | 118.1 | 114 | 475 | 41 | 35 | 6 | 5 | 5 | 4 | 19 | 0 | 106 | 4 | 1 |
| Eveland, Dana, Beloit | 9 | 6 | .600 | 2.84 | 22 | 16 | 1 | 0 | 4 | 2 | 117.1 | 108 | 479 | 48 | 37 | 8 | 4 | 5 | 4 | 24 | 0 | 119 | 2 | 0 |
| Mattoon, Brian, Clinton * | 11 | 6 | .647 | 2.87 | 32 | 20 | 1 | 0 | 5 | 1 | 131.2 | 137 | 543 | 58 | 42 | 11 | 14 | 11 | 6 | 17 | 4 | 88 | 1 | 4 |
| Oldham, Thomas, Wisconsin | 6 | 6 | .500 | 2.93 | 19 | 19 | 1 | 0 | 0 | 0 | 116.2 | 108 | 482 | 47 | 38 | 15 | 2 | 2 | 9 | 30 | 1 | 132 | 2 | 3 |
| Harben, Adam, Swing of the Quad Ci | 9 | 7 | .563 | 3.09 | 26 | 26 | 0 | 0 | 0 | 0 | 142.2 | 114 | 592 | 60 | 49 | 5 | 8 | 7 | 5 | 68 | 0 | 171 | 6 | 0 |
| Thompson, Sean, Fort Wayne * | 9 | 6 | .600 | 3.10 | 27 | 27 | 0 | 0 | 0 | 0 | 148.0 | 124 | 608 | 60 | 51 | 15 | 18 | 9 | 5 | 57 | 0 | 157 | 3 | 1 |
| Bay, Bear, Lansing | 11 | 9 | .550 | 3.10 | 28 | 28 | 0 | 0 | 0 | 0 | 168.1 | 166 | 686 | 71 | 58 | 7 | 8 | 9 | 5 | 30 | 3 | 139 | 3 | 1 |
| Muegge, Danny, South Bend | 14 | 4 | .778 | 3.12 | 26 | 25 | 1 | 1 | 0 | 0 | 153.0 | 149 | 650 | 66 | 53 | 16 | 9 | 3 | 9 | 42 | 1 | 104 | 8 | 1 |
| Marmol, Carlos, Lansing | 14 | 8 | .636 | 3.20 | 26 | 24 | 0 | 0 | 1 | 0 | 154.2 | 131 | 635 | 64 | 55 | 15 | 9 | 6 | 14 | 53 | 0 | 154 | 5 | 2 |
| Moorhead, Brandon, Wisconsin | 9 | 10 | .474 | 3.27 | 25 | 25 | 0 | 0 | 0 | 0 | 145.2 | 142 | 638 | 66 | 53 | 5 | 11 | 4 | 10 | 50 | 0 | 163 | 12 | 3 |
| Tata, Jordan, West Michigan | 8 | 11 | .421 | 3.35 | 28 | 28 | 1 | 0 | 0 | 0 | 166.1 | 167 | 705 | 77 | 62 | 7 | 12 | 3 | 9 | 68 | 2 | 116 | 15 | 0 |
| Michael, Mark, Peoria | 6 | 6 | .500 | 3.36 | 20 | 20 | 1 | 0 | 0 | 0 | 120.2 | 117 | 523 | 59 | 45 | 9 | 5 | 9 | 19 | 39 | 1 | 95 | 23 | 0 |
| Moreno, Abel, Cedar Rapids | 10 | 8 | .556 | 3.41 | 25 | 25 | 0 | 0 | 0 | 0 | 142.2 | 141 | 595 | 69 | 54 | 7 | 4 | 8 | 9 | 31 | 0 | 120 | 6 | 7 |

DEPARTMENTAL LEADERS: W—Five tied with 14; L—Acosta, Atencio, 14; Pct.—Muegge, .778; G—Fyvie, 59; GS—Four tied with 28; CG—Steinborn, 3; ShO—20 tied with one; GF—Zimmerman, 50; Sv.—Thorp, Rosales, 26; IP—Bay, Vasquez, 168.1; H—Dunwell, 179; TBF—Acosta, 708; R—Atencio, 109; ER—Atencio, 93; HR—Villanueva, 20; SH—S. Thompson, 18; SF—Four tied with 13; HB—Acosta, Michael, 19; BB—Jepsen, 77; IBB—Brandon, 11; SO—Knox, 174; WP—Michael, 23; BK—Moreno, 7.

### ALL PITCHERS

*Lefthanded pitcher.

| Pitcher, Team | W | L | Pct. | ERA | G | GS | CG | ShO | GF | Sv. | IP | H | TBF | R | ER | HR | SH | SF | HB | BB | IBB | SO | WP | Bk. |
|---|---|---|---|---|---|---|---|---|---|---|---|---|---|---|---|---|---|---|---|---|---|---|---|---|
| Abraham, Paul, Fort Wayne | 1 | 2 | .333 | 2.79 | 37 | 0 | 0 | 0 | 11 | 1 | 48.1 | 53 | 214 | 28 | 15 | 3 | 0 | 0 | 1 | 15 | 0 | 49 | 4 | 0 |
| Abrams, Casey, Wisconsin * | 1 | 3 | .250 | 12.74 | 37 | 1 | 0 | 0 | 10 | 0 | 29.2 | 57 | 175 | 48 | 42 | 4 | 0 | 0 | 5 | 24 | 1 | 27 | 10 | 0 |
| Acosta, Adam, Peoria | 0 | 0 | .000 | 13.50 | 5 | 1 | 0 | 0 | 0 | 0 | 7.1 | 13 | 40 | 13 | 11 | 1 | 1 | 2 | 0 | 4 | 0 | 9 | 2 | 0 |
| Acosta, Nibaldo, Wisconsin | 7 | 14 | .333 | 4.40 | 27 | 26 | 1 | 0 | 0 | 0 | 161.2 | 170 | 708 | 101 | 79 | 14 | 6 | 6 | 19 | 42 | 1 | 95 | 7 | 1 |
| Adames, Emilio, Clinton | 0 | 1 | .000 | 6.75 | 1 | 1 | 0 | 0 | 0 | 0 | 4.0 | 6 | 19 | 3 | 3 | 0 | 0 | 0 | 0 | 1 | 0 | 3 | 1 | 0 |
| Atencio, Greg, Burlington | 7 | 14 | .333 | 5.60 | 28 | 28 | 0 | 0 | 0 | 0 | 149.1 | 157 | 667 | 109 | 93 | 12 | 9 | 5 | 12 | 68 | 1 | 118 | 11 | 2 |
| Austen, David, Cedar Rapids | 1 | 3 | .250 | 3.15 | 29 | 0 | 0 | 0 | 6 | 1 | 60.0 | 62 | 261 | 28 | 21 | 3 | 0 | 0 | 2 | 17 | 1 | 60 | 5 | 0 |
| Baisley, Brad, Battle Creek | 0 | 2 | .000 | 9.88 | 7 | 2 | 0 | 0 | 0 | 0 | 13.2 | 21 | 68 | 18 | 15 | 4 | 0 | 2 | 2 | 4 | 0 | 5 | 2 | 0 |
| Bannister, John, Clinton | 0 | 0 | .000 | 1.80 | 1 | 1 | 0 | 0 | 0 | 0 | 5.0 | 5 | 20 | 1 | 1 | 0 | 0 | 0 | 0 | 1 | 0 | 5 | 0 | 0 |
| Barkley, Richard, Battle Creek | 0 | 0 | .000 | 4.91 | 4 | 0 | 0 | 0 | 1 | 0 | 7.1 | 9 | 34 | 4 | 4 | 0 | 0 | 0 | 0 | 3 | 0 | 5 | 0 | 0 |

| Pitcher, Team | W | L | Pct. | ERA | G | GS | CG | ShO | GF | Sv. | IP | H | TBF | R | ER | HR | SH | SF | HB | BB | IBB | SO | WP | Bk. |
|---|---|---|---|---|---|---|---|---|---|---|---|---|---|---|---|---|---|---|---|---|---|---|---|---|
| Barnes, Justin, Beloit | 1 | 3 | .250 | 8.27 | 4 | 3 | 0 | 0 | 0 | 0 | 16.1 | 22 | 75 | 15 | 15 | 1 | 2 | 2 | 2 | 5 | 0 | 12 | 1 | 0 |
| Bay, Bear, Lansing | 11 | 9 | .550 | 3.10 | 28 | 28 | 0 | 0 | 0 | 0 | 168.1 | 166 | 686 | 71 | 58 | 7 | 8 | 9 | 5 | 30 | 3 | 139 | 3 | 1 |
| Begnaud, Russell, Burlington | 1 | 0 | 1.000 | 0.00 | 1 | 0 | 0 | 0 | 0 | 0 | 3.0 | 0 | 10 | 0 | 0 | 0 | 0 | 0 | 0 | 1 | 0 | 1 | 0 | 0 |
| Benjamin, Casey, Clinton | 0 | 0 | .000 | 0.00 | 1 | 0 | 0 | 0 | 0 | 0 | 0.1 | 0 | 1 | 0 | 0 | 0 | 0 | 0 | 0 | 0 | 0 | 0 | 0 | 0 |
| Beresford, Simon, Beloit | 4 | 4 | .500 | 4.50 | 38 | 5 | 0 | 0 | 14 | 1 | 92.0 | 84 | 406 | 50 | 46 | 9 | 1 | 5 | 4 | 50 | 0 | 87 | 8 | 0 |
| Bilke, Austin, Wisconsin | 0 | 2 | .000 | 3.29 | 17 | 1 | 0 | 0 | 8 | 3 | 27.1 | 31 | 125 | 12 | 10 | 2 | 0 | 0 | 2 | 10 | 1 | 20 | 0 | 0 |
| Bochy, Greg, Fort Wayne | 0 | 0 | .000 | 0.00 | 1 | 0 | 0 | 0 | 1 | 0 | 1.0 | 1 | 4 | 0 | 0 | 0 | 0 | 0 | 0 | 0 | 0 | 1 | 0 | 0 |
| Bohorquez, Carlos, Dayton | 3 | 4 | .429 | 4.82 | 25 | 0 | 0 | 0 | 10 | 1 | 37.1 | 39 | 179 | 23 | 20 | 4 | 0 | 0 | 2 | 26 | 3 | 42 | 9 | 1 |
| Boughner, Anthony, Dayton * | 2 | 3 | .400 | 3.25 | 7 | 6 | 0 | 0 | 0 | 0 | 36.0 | 33 | 147 | 18 | 13 | 5 | 1 | 1 | 1 | 8 | 0 | 23 | 1 | 0 |
| Braden, Dallas, Kane County * | 2 | 1 | .667 | 4.70 | 5 | 5 | 0 | 0 | 0 | 0 | 23.0 | 22 | 101 | 13 | 12 | 2 | 3 | 1 | 0 | 6 | 1 | 33 | 1 | 1 |
| Brandon, Eric, Swing of the Quad Ci | 3 | 9 | .250 | 3.67 | 45 | 0 | 0 | 0 | 28 | 7 | 61.1 | 70 | 278 | 27 | 25 | 3 | 0 | 0 | 2 | 21 | 10 | 55 | 2 | 1 |
| Bray, Stephen, Burlington | 3 | 3 | .500 | 3.29 | 24 | 0 | 0 | 0 | 15 | 6 | 63.0 | 58 | 258 | 30 | 23 | 8 | 0 | 0 | 0 | 13 | 2 | 73 | 4 | 1 |
| Brey, Josh, Peoria * | 3 | 2 | .600 | 3.34 | 34 | 4 | 0 | 0 | 7 | 0 | 62.0 | 66 | 267 | 27 | 23 | 2 | 0 | 2 | 3 | 23 | 0 | 47 | 9 | 0 |
| Brumit, Matt, Battle Creek | 4 | 2 | .667 | 3.95 | 40 | 0 | 0 | 0 | 12 | 1 | 57.0 | 57 | 246 | 28 | 25 | 5 | 0 | 0 | 2 | 16 | 0 | 82 | 2 | 1 |
| Buckley, Allen, Cedar Rapids | 4 | 1 | .800 | 4.04 | 47 | 0 | 0 | 0 | 12 | 1 | 71.1 | 67 | 323 | 41 | 32 | 4 | 1 | 0 | 9 | 33 | 1 | 68 | 9 | 0 |
| Burgos, Ambiorix, Burlington | 7 | 11 | .389 | 4.38 | 27 | 26 | 0 | 0 | 0 | 0 | 133.2 | 109 | 578 | 70 | 65 | 13 | 6 | 5 | 13 | 75 | 1 | 172 | 13 | 4 |
| Castillo, Ruben, Wisconsin | 0 | 1 | .000 | 9.75 | 11 | 0 | 0 | 0 | 4 | 1 | 12.0 | 15 | 57 | 13 | 13 | 2 | 0 | 0 | 1 | 5 | 0 | 9 | 0 | 0 |
| Castle, Heath, Battle Creek * | 1 | 1 | .500 | 5.63 | 42 | 0 | 0 | 0 | 18 | 1 | 54.1 | 67 | 248 | 42 | 34 | 1 | 0 | 0 | 4 | 16 | 0 | 36 | 3 | 0 |
| Chang, Kenly, Wisconsin | 0 | 2 | .000 | 5.40 | 40 | 2 | 0 | 0 | 15 | 1 | 63.1 | 70 | 279 | 43 | 38 | 6 | 2 | 1 | 6 | 20 | 1 | 48 | 11 | 0 |
| Chavez, Jesse, Clinton | 6 | 10 | .375 | 4.68 | 27 | 22 | 0 | 0 | 1 | 0 | 123.0 | 148 | 537 | 75 | 64 | 8 | 7 | 9 | 3 | 35 | 1 | 96 | 4 | 0 |
| Chick, Travis, Fort Wayne | 5 | 0 | 1.000 | 2.13 | 7 | 7 | 0 | 0 | 0 | 0 | 42.1 | 32 | 166 | 12 | 10 | 4 | 5 | 3 | 1 | 9 | 0 | 55 | 1 | 1 |
| Christensen, Danny, Burlington * | 0 | 1 | .000 | 15.00 | 1 | 1 | 0 | 0 | 0 | 0 | 3.0 | 6 | 21 | 8 | 5 | 0 | 0 | 0 | 1 | 3 | 0 | 2 | 0 | 0 |
| Ciccotelli, Michael, Wisconsin * | 1 | 0 | 1.000 | 6.30 | 12 | 0 | 0 | 0 | 1 | 0 | 10.0 | 10 | 45 | 12 | 7 | 0 | 0 | 0 | 1 | 4 | 0 | 8 | 1 | 0 |
| Clippard, Tyler, Battle Creek | 10 | 10 | .500 | 3.44 | 26 | 25 | 1 | 0 | 0 | 0 | 149.0 | 153 | 636 | 71 | 57 | 12 | 7 | 2 | 15 | 32 | 0 | 145 | 4 | 0 |
| Coffin, Ryan, South Bend | 0 | 3 | .000 | 3.00 | 43 | 0 | 0 | 0 | 12 | 1 | 69.0 | 62 | 304 | 34 | 23 | 5 | 0 | 1 | 7 | 28 | 0 | 63 | 5 | 0 |
| Conden, Greg, Fort Wayne | 4 | 7 | .364 | 4.30 | 23 | 12 | 0 | 0 | 2 | 1 | 81.2 | 70 | 344 | 49 | 39 | 9 | 2 | 7 | 5 | 33 | 0 | 85 | 4 | 0 |
| Corchado, Jose, Kane County | 5 | 5 | .500 | 3.12 | 33 | 6 | 0 | 0 | 20 | 3 | 60.2 | 45 | 249 | 26 | 21 | 4 | 0 | 0 | 3 | 26 | 2 | 73 | 5 | 1 |
| Cordeiro, Christopher, Clinton | 5 | 4 | .556 | 3.14 | 29 | 0 | 0 | 0 | 18 | 6 | 57.1 | 59 | 244 | 24 | 20 | 3 | 0 | 0 | 2 | 12 | 1 | 33 | 1 | 0 |
| Correa, Cristobal, Peoria | 3 | 6 | .333 | 3.98 | 18 | 15 | 1 | 0 | 0 | 0 | 86.0 | 88 | 371 | 45 | 38 | 7 | 6 | 4 | 5 | 33 | 1 | 58 | 2 | 3 |
| Coughlin, Chris, Burlington | 5 | 5 | .500 | 4.50 | 14 | 14 | 1 | 1 | 0 | 0 | 80.0 | 89 | 330 | 47 | 40 | 8 | 5 | 4 | 2 | 10 | 0 | 60 | 2 | 2 |
| Crawford, Tristan, Swing of the Quad Ci | 3 | 3 | .500 | 2.79 | 21 | 0 | 0 | 0 | 6 | 2 | 48.1 | 37 | 192 | 16 | 15 | 6 | 0 | 0 | 1 | 9 | 3 | 43 | 3 | 0 |
| Cremidan, Alex, South Bend | 1 | 2 | .333 | 3.27 | 32 | 1 | 0 | 0 | 16 | 7 | 41.1 | 49 | 188 | 20 | 15 | 1 | 1 | 2 | 3 | 14 | 0 | 45 | 5 | 0 |
| Crist, Kyle, Burlington | 1 | 1 | .500 | 6.75 | 3 | 2 | 0 | 0 | 1 | 0 | 12.0 | 15 | 58 | 10 | 9 | 0 | 0 | 0 | 2 | 5 | 0 | 11 | 3 | 0 |
| Crowder, Justin, Kane County * | 2 | 1 | .667 | 4.73 | 34 | 0 | 0 | 0 | 9 | 1 | 32.1 | 32 | 138 | 20 | 17 | 3 | 0 | 0 | 2 | 7 | 1 | 37 | 3 | 0 |
| Cunningham, Tim, Clinton * | 0 | 5 | .000 | 7.00 | 26 | 6 | 0 | 0 | 9 | 0 | 45.0 | 44 | 221 | 41 | 35 | 3 | 4 | 2 | 3 | 49 | 0 | 27 | 15 | 0 |
| DeHoyos, Gabe, Burlington | 1 | 2 | .333 | 2.28 | 16 | 0 | 0 | 0 | 16 | 5 | 23.2 | 19 | 101 | 6 | 6 | 0 | 0 | 0 | 0 | 11 | 0 | 26 | 2 | 0 |
| DeJaynes, Brandon, Peoria | 5 | 3 | .625 | 4.29 | 49 | 1 | 0 | 0 | 11 | 2 | 71.1 | 38 | 318 | 39 | 34 | 6 | 2 | 0 | 8 | 57 | 0 | 106 | 8 | 0 |
| DePaula, Julio, Swing of the Quad Ci | 12 | 7 | .632 | 3.05 | 49 | 0 | 0 | 0 | 19 | 9 | 91.1 | 81 | 398 | 37 | 31 | 4 | 0 | 0 | 5 | 39 | 2 | 88 | 6 | 3 |
| Delacruz, Eulogio, West Michigan | 2 | 4 | .333 | 3.83 | 54 | 0 | 0 | 0 | 38 | 17 | 54.0 | 51 | 249 | 30 | 23 | 2 | 0 | 0 | 3 | 33 | 0 | 44 | 13 | 1 |
| Diamond, Thomas, Clinton | 1 | 0 | 1.000 | 2.05 | 7 | 7 | 0 | 0 | 0 | 0 | 30.2 | 18 | 114 | 8 | 7 | 1 | 1 | 0 | 2 | 8 | 0 | 42 | 2 | 0 |
| Dillard, Timothy, Beloit | 2 | 5 | .286 | 3.94 | 43 | 1 | 0 | 0 | 28 | 10 | 77.2 | 89 | 349 | 46 | 34 | 4 | 0 | 1 | 8 | 22 | 2 | 61 | 6 | 0 |
| Dossett, Dusty, Burlington | 3 | 5 | .375 | 3.41 | 38 | 0 | 0 | 0 | 33 | 5 | 74.0 | 71 | 314 | 33 | 28 | 7 | 0 | 1 | 3 | 24 | 4 | 54 | 4 | 1 |
| Drown, Erik, Peoria | 4 | 5 | .444 | 5.03 | 24 | 15 | 0 | 0 | 3 | 0 | 78.2 | 62 | 350 | 48 | 44 | 9 | 6 | 2 | 5 | 58 | 0 | 83 | 15 | 0 |
| Dunwell, Chris, Kane County | 11 | 8 | .579 | 4.41 | 28 | 28 | 0 | 0 | 0 | 0 | 157.0 | 179 | 681 | 90 | 77 | 13 | 7 | 4 | 4 | 36 | 2 | 145 | 12 | 0 |
| Durost, Kenny, Beloit | 7 | 7 | .500 | 3.63 | 24 | 18 | 0 | 0 | 0 | 0 | 104.0 | 82 | 446 | 47 | 42 | 6 | 4 | 5 | 4 | 55 | 0 | 116 | 9 | 2 |
| Edens, Kyle, Dayton | 0 | 3 | .000 | 2.36 | 15 | 4 | 0 | 0 | 9 | 2 | 42.0 | 34 | 166 | 14 | 11 | 4 | 0 | 0 | 3 | 11 | 0 | 30 | 3 | 0 |
| Ekstrom, Michael, Fort Wayne | 0 | 2 | .000 | 8.16 | 3 | 3 | 0 | 0 | 0 | 0 | 14.1 | 21 | 62 | 15 | 13 | 1 | 1 | 1 | 0 | 3 | 0 | 10 | 3 | 0 |
| Ellison, Philip, Dayton | 0 | 1 | .000 | 18.00 | 2 | 0 | 0 | 0 | 0 | 0 | 3.0 | 8 | 22 | 9 | 6 | 1 | 0 | 0 | 0 | 5 | 0 | 3 | 3 | 0 |
| Encarnacion, Alexis, Burlington | 4 | 2 | .667 | 5.13 | 27 | 0 | 0 | 0 | 12 | 4 | 72.0 | 74 | 315 | 45 | 41 | 14 | 0 | 2 | 1 | 22 | 0 | 60 | 1 | 0 |
| Farnum, Matt, Clinton | 8 | 8 | .500 | 4.45 | 28 | 24 | 0 | 0 | 3 | 1 | 131.1 | 142 | 550 | 70 | 65 | 16 | 7 | 7 | 5 | 43 | 1 | 98 | 4 | 1 |
| Feierabend, Ryan, Wisconsin * | 9 | 7 | .563 | 3.63 | 26 | 26 | 1 | 1 | 0 | 0 | 161.0 | 158 | 666 | 78 | 65 | 17 | 4 | 10 | 7 | 44 | 0 | 106 | 14 | 0 |
| Ferreras, Yorkin, Lansing * | 2 | 2 | .500 | 4.01 | 13 | 7 | 0 | 0 | 2 | 1 | 42.2 | 42 | 174 | 20 | 19 | 4 | 2 | 1 | 4 | 8 | 0 | 30 | 0 | 0 |
| Fillinger, Chad, Wisconsin | 1 | 2 | .333 | 8.44 | 11 | 0 | 0 | 0 | 4 | 0 | 16.0 | 25 | 77 | 16 | 15 | 3 | 1 | 0 | 1 | 5 | 1 | 15 | 1 | 0 |
| Fischer, Sam, Lansing | 0 | 1 | .000 | 6.97 | 17 | 0 | 0 | 0 | 5 | 0 | 20.2 | 19 | 110 | 17 | 16 | 1 | 0 | 0 | 0 | 29 | 0 | 26 | 3 | 0 |
| Fitzgerald, Ryan, Lansing | 1 | 0 | 1.000 | 0.00 | 1 | 0 | 0 | 0 | 1 | 0 | 3.0 | 1 | 11 | 0 | 0 | 0 | 0 | 0 | 0 | 1 | 0 | 0 | 0 | 0 |
| Frisella, Sal, Peoria | 0 | 0 | .000 | 36.00 | 1 | 0 | 0 | 0 | 1 | 0 | 1.0 | 4 | 8 | 4 | 4 | 1 | 0 | 0 | 0 | 1 | 0 | 0 | 0 | 0 |
| Frydendall, Craig, Clinton * | 5 | 3 | .625 | 4.87 | 36 | 0 | 0 | 0 | 15 | 0 | 61.0 | 65 | 276 | 36 | 33 | 1 | 0 | 0 | 5 | 24 | 0 | 49 | 2 | 0 |
| Fyvie, Dan, Kane County | 4 | 1 | .800 | 3.69 | 59 | 0 | 0 | 0 | 17 | 5 | 78.0 | 70 | 332 | 36 | 32 | 4 | 1 | 0 | 7 | 22 | 2 | 72 | 6 | 1 |
| Gallardo, Yovani, Beloit | 0 | 1 | .000 | 12.27 | 2 | 2 | 0 | 0 | 0 | 0 | 7.1 | 12 | 34 | 10 | 10 | 2 | 0 | 0 | 0 | 4 | 0 | 8 | 3 | 0 |
| Garcia, Alex, Swing of the Quad Ci | 0 | 1 | .000 | 1.50 | 2 | 1 | 0 | 0 | 0 | 0 | 6.0 | 3 | 20 | 1 | 1 | 1 | 0 | 1 | 1 | 0 | 0 | 8 | 0 | 0 |
| Garcia, Angel, Swing of the Quad Ci | 2 | 0 | 1.000 | 6.30 | 5 | 1 | 0 | 0 | 0 | 0 | 10.0 | 10 | 46 | 7 | 7 | 2 | 0 | 0 | 1 | 5 | 0 | 8 | 2 | 0 |
| Garcia, Geivy, Fort Wayne | 0 | 1 | .000 | 4.76 | 4 | 0 | 0 | 0 | 2 | 0 | 5.2 | 7 | 24 | 3 | 3 | 3 | 0 | 0 | 0 | 0 | 0 | 4 | 0 | 0 |
| Garcia, Jose, Clinton | 2 | 2 | .500 | 2.89 | 9 | 9 | 0 | 0 | 0 | 0 | 46.2 | 37 | 187 | 19 | 15 | 4 | 2 | 0 | 3 | 13 | 0 | 40 | 1 | 1 |
| Gardner, Mike, Battle Creek | 1 | 2 | .333 | 3.40 | 43 | 0 | 0 | 0 | 16 | 0 | 55.2 | 54 | 243 | 23 | 21 | 4 | 0 | 0 | 4 | 16 | 0 | 44 | 12 | 0 |
| Gemmell, Don, Dayton | 1 | 0 | 1.000 | 10.80 | 5 | 0 | 0 | 0 | 3 | 0 | 5.0 | 7 | 25 | 7 | 6 | 1 | 0 | 0 | 1 | 2 | 0 | 5 | 0 | 0 |
| George, Jon, Dayton | 1 | 7 | .125 | 5.56 | 18 | 12 | 0 | 0 | 5 | 1 | 66.1 | 81 | 296 | 54 | 41 | 8 | 0 | 3 | 2 | 15 | 0 | 43 | 6 | 0 |
| Gillman, Justin, Dayton | 1 | 2 | .333 | 9.00 | 11 | 6 | 0 | 0 | 1 | 0 | 31.0 | 41 | 165 | 34 | 31 | 5 | 0 | 0 | 9 | 25 | 0 | 26 | 4 | 0 |
| Glant, Dustin, South Bend | 5 | 5 | .500 | 4.06 | 29 | 12 | 1 | 0 | 17 | 8 | 88.2 | 103 | 381 | 45 | 40 | 4 | 4 | 3 | 5 | 27 | 1 | 44 | 12 | 4 |
| Gomez, Abel, Battle Creek * | 9 | 10 | .474 | 3.66 | 29 | 25 | 0 | 0 | 1 | 0 | 142.2 | 115 | 608 | 73 | 58 | 7 | 10 | 13 | 9 | 73 | 0 | 149 | 11 | 3 |
| Goodman, Chris, Burlington | 4 | 13 | .235 | 5.95 | 23 | 21 | 1 | 1 | 2 | 1 | 115.0 | 146 | 517 | 85 | 76 | 11 | 4 | 4 | 7 | 38 | 2 | 56 | 6 | 0 |
| Granado, Jan, Dayton * | 1 | 4 | .200 | 4.53 | 13 | 8 | 0 | 0 | 3 | 2 | 49.2 | 52 | 226 | 30 | 25 | 5 | 1 | 7 | 7 | 14 | 0 | 44 | 4 | 5 |
| Grybash, Dan, Beloit | 4 | 2 | .667 | 4.98 | 40 | 0 | 0 | 0 | 19 | 2 | 72.1 | 75 | 351 | 46 | 40 | 7 | 1 | 1 | 9 | 52 | 0 | 55 | 11 | 0 |
| Guevara, Carlos, Dayton | 3 | 4 | .429 | 2.86 | 44 | 0 | 0 | 0 | 28 | 9 | 56.2 | 47 | 240 | 22 | 18 | 6 | 0 | 0 | 3 | 24 | 0 | 90 | 7 | 0 |
| Harben, Adam, Swing of the Quad Ci | 9 | 7 | .563 | 3.09 | 26 | 26 | 0 | 0 | 0 | 0 | 142.2 | 114 | 592 | 60 | 49 | 5 | 8 | 7 | 5 | 68 | 0 | 171 | 6 | 0 |
| Harmsen, Brandon, Battle Creek | 10 | 3 | .769 | 3.53 | 35 | 16 | 0 | 0 | 4 | 1 | 130.0 | 165 | 591 | 68 | 51 | 5 | 6 | 13 | 6 | 32 | 2 | 80 | 3 | 1 |
| Herrera, Cesar, Clinton | 8 | 3 | .727 | 3.65 | 44 | 3 | 0 | 0 | 27 | 6 | 86.1 | 89 | 377 | 40 | 35 | 4 | 2 | 0 | 4 | 26 | 2 | 63 | 3 | 0 |
| Hindman, Scott, Cedar Rapids * | 1 | 1 | .500 | 6.69 | 27 | 0 | 0 | 0 | 9 | 0 | 35.0 | 28 | 178 | 27 | 26 | 3 | 0 | 1 | 4 | 40 | 0 | 39 | 6 | 2 |
| Homer, Chris, West Michigan | 0 | 3 | .000 | 4.57 | 39 | 0 | 0 | 0 | 24 | 12 | 45.1 | 48 | 205 | 28 | 23 | 2 | 0 | 0 | 1 | 21 | 0 | 50 | 5 | 1 |
| Hrynio, Mike, Wisconsin | 4 | 4 | .500 | 3.75 | 54 | 0 | 0 | 0 | 36 | 9 | 62.1 | 47 | 274 | 26 | 26 | 4 | 0 | 1 | 8 | 33 | 2 | 82 | 10 | 1 |
| Hudson, William, Dayton | 0 | 0 | .000 | 2.25 | 3 | 0 | 0 | 0 | 3 | 0 | 4.0 | 3 | 16 | 1 | 1 | 1 | 0 | 0 | 0 | 1 | 0 | 5 | 0 | 0 |
| Hunter, Chris, Cedar Rapids | 8 | 7 | .533 | 3.86 | 25 | 22 | 0 | 0 | 1 | 0 | 135.1 | 129 | 587 | 72 | 58 | 9 | 7 | 7 | 15 | 45 | 1 | 81 | 10 | 1 |
| Ingram, Jesse, Clinton | 0 | 0 | .000 | 0.00 | 1 | 0 | 0 | 0 | 1 | 1 | 1.2 | 0 | 5 | 0 | 0 | 0 | 0 | 0 | 0 | 0 | 0 | 0 | 0 | 0 |

| Pitcher, Team | W | L | Pct. | ERA | G | GS | CG | ShO | GF | Sv. | IP | H | TBF | R | ER | HR | SH | SF | HB | BB | IBB | SO | WP | Bk. |
|---|---|---|---|---|---|---|---|---|---|---|---|---|---|---|---|---|---|---|---|---|---|---|---|---|
| Jepsen, Kevin, Cedar Rapids | 8 | 10 | .444 | 3.43 | 27 | 27 | 1 | 1 | 0 | 0 | 144.1 | 122 | 628 | 68 | 55 | 6 | 10 | 2 | 12 | 77 | 1 | 136 | 14 | 2 |
| Jones, Jason, Battle Creek | 3 | 1 | .750 | 2.87 | 6 | 6 | 0 | 0 | 0 | 0 | 31.1 | 38 | 129 | 11 | 10 | 2 | 1 | 0 | 2 | 3 | 0 | 19 | 0 | 0 |
| Jones, Justin, Lansing | 3 | 3 | .500 | 3.78 | 15 | 15 | 0 | 0 | 0 | 0 | 64.1 | 62 | 265 | 33 | 27 | 6 | 4 | 2 | 7 | 22 | 0 | 59 | 4 | 0 |
| Jones, Justin, Swing of the Quad Ci * | 0 | 2 | .000 | 5.31 | 7 | 4 | 0 | 0 | 2 | 0 | 20.1 | 20 | 99 | 17 | 12 | 2 | 1 | 0 | 4 | 14 | 1 | 17 | 3 | 0 |
| Jordan, B.J., Peoria * | 3 | 3 | .500 | 3.17 | 50 | 0 | 0 | 0 | 21 | 2 | 54.0 | 47 | 233 | 23 | 19 | 2 | 1 | 0 | 3 | 21 | 1 | 54 | 8 | 0 |
| Keller, Frankie, Dayton * | 0 | 5 | .000 | 8.31 | 11 | 9 | 0 | 0 | 0 | 0 | 39.0 | 54 | 189 | 36 | 36 | 7 | 3 | 1 | 0 | 23 | 0 | 27 | 5 | 0 |
| Kinsey, Chris, South Bend | 8 | 11 | .421 | 4.90 | 28 | 27 | 1 | 1 | 0 | 0 | 150.2 | 171 | 671 | 87 | 82 | 9 | 5 | 7 | 14 | 70 | 1 | 87 | 15 | 1 |
| Kirsten, Joel, Clinton * | 7 | 1 | .875 | 2.48 | 37 | 2 | 0 | 0 | 17 | 5 | 72.2 | 64 | 303 | 23 | 20 | 4 | 1 | 0 | 3 | 22 | 1 | 61 | 3 | 0 |
| Klatt, Ryan, Fort Wayne | 4 | 0 | 1.000 | 2.79 | 25 | 0 | 0 | 0 | 12 | 3 | 29.0 | 19 | 112 | 10 | 9 | 1 | 1 | 0 | 0 | 6 | 2 | 35 | 2 | 0 |
| Kloosterman, Gregory, Beloit | 2 | 8 | .200 | 7.57 | 19 | 14 | 0 | 0 | 3 | 0 | 63.0 | 77 | 296 | 60 | 53 | 15 | 6 | 3 | 2 | 42 | 0 | 57 | 12 | 0 |
| Knoedler, Jason, West Michigan | 0 | 0 | .000 | 9.00 | 1 | 0 | 0 | 0 | 1 | 0 | 1.0 | 2 | 7 | 1 | 1 | 0 | 0 | 0 | 1 | 1 | 0 | 0 | 0 | 0 |
| Knoff, Justin, Dayton | 1 | 1 | .500 | 2.08 | 5 | 0 | 0 | 0 | 3 | 0 | 17.1 | 18 | 76 | 6 | 4 | 1 | 1 | 1 | 0 | 6 | 0 | 14 | 1 | 0 |
| Knox, Brad, Kane County | 14 | 5 | .737 | 2.59 | 26 | 25 | 0 | 0 | 0 | 0 | 156.1 | 141 | 634 | 53 | 45 | 11 | 8 | 0 | 8 | 24 | 1 | 174 | 10 | 0 |
| Lambert, Christopher, Peoria | 1 | 1 | .500 | 2.58 | 9 | 9 | 0 | 0 | 0 | 0 | 38.1 | 31 | 169 | 15 | 11 | 2 | 0 | 2 | 1 | 24 | 1 | 46 | 2 | 0 |
| Leon, Brigmer, Kane County | 4 | 4 | .500 | 2.90 | 46 | 1 | 0 | 0 | 7 | 0 | 80.2 | 82 | 344 | 41 | 26 | 4 | 3 | 1 | 5 | 20 | 2 | 56 | 5 | 2 |
| Mackintosh, Jason, Wisconsin * | 6 | 8 | .429 | 4.04 | 33 | 20 | 1 | 0 | 3 | 0 | 149.1 | 137 | 626 | 86 | 67 | 18 | 7 | 9 | 14 | 44 | 1 | 139 | 10 | 0 |
| Mallett, Justin, Dayton | 4 | 5 | .444 | 4.02 | 18 | 13 | 0 | 0 | 1 | 0 | 78.1 | 93 | 347 | 42 | 35 | 4 | 4 | 3 | 8 | 28 | 0 | 65 | 5 | 1 |
| Marmol, Carlos, Lansing | 14 | 8 | .636 | 3.20 | 26 | 24 | 0 | 0 | 1 | 0 | 154.2 | 131 | 635 | 64 | 55 | 15 | 9 | 6 | 14 | 53 | 0 | 154 | 5 | 2 |
| Martinez, Cristhian, West Michigan | 5 | 2 | .714 | 2.44 | 12 | 12 | 1 | 1 | 0 | 0 | 73.2 | 59 | 296 | 27 | 20 | 6 | 4 | 1 | 7 | 20 | 0 | 45 | 3 | 0 |
| Martinez, Michael, Battle Creek | 1 | 1 | .500 | 6.00 | 4 | 0 | 0 | 0 | 4 | 1 | 6.0 | 9 | 30 | 4 | 4 | 0 | 0 | 0 | 0 | 3 | 1 | 5 | 1 | 0 |
| Mateo, Juan, Lansing | 4 | 1 | .800 | 3.28 | 53 | 1 | 0 | 0 | 26 | 9 | 74.0 | 61 | 305 | 28 | 27 | 3 | 1 | 1 | 1 | 19 | 1 | 60 | 3 | 0 |
| Mattoon, Brian, Clinton * | 11 | 6 | .647 | 2.87 | 32 | 20 | 1 | 0 | 5 | 1 | 131.2 | 137 | 543 | 58 | 42 | 11 | 14 | 11 | 6 | 17 | 4 | 88 | 1 | 4 |
| Mauer, Bill, Swing of the Quad Ci | 0 | 3 | .000 | 4.19 | 23 | 2 | 0 | 0 | 8 | 0 | 34.1 | 34 | 158 | 22 | 16 | 2 | 0 | 1 | 2 | 18 | 0 | 21 | 3 | 0 |
| McClellan, Kyle, Peoria | 4 | 12 | .250 | 5.34 | 24 | 24 | 1 | 0 | 0 | 0 | 128.0 | 143 | 562 | 85 | 76 | 12 | 4 | 5 | 14 | 34 | 1 | 84 | 18 | 0 |
| McClellan, Robbie, Burlington | 2 | 5 | .286 | 4.50 | 19 | 4 | 0 | 0 | 9 | 0 | 64.0 | 65 | 281 | 34 | 32 | 7 | 0 | 2 | 0 | 23 | 0 | 60 | 1 | 1 |
| Mcauliff, Jarod, Kane County | 0 | 1 | .000 | 4.15 | 3 | 0 | 0 | 0 | 0 | 0 | 4.1 | 5 | 20 | 2 | 2 | 0 | 0 | 0 | 1 | 1 | 1 | 4 | 0 | 0 |
| Mead, David, Fort Wayne | 1 | 5 | .167 | 6.55 | 18 | 11 | 0 | 0 | 2 | 0 | 57.2 | 62 | 276 | 49 | 42 | 1 | 3 | 3 | 16 | 34 | 0 | 54 | 10 | 2 |
| Mendez, Adalberto, Lansing | 5 | 7 | .417 | 4.62 | 56 | 0 | 0 | 0 | 41 | 20 | 64.1 | 63 | 291 | 37 | 33 | 7 | 1 | 1 | 5 | 28 | 2 | 55 | 5 | 0 |
| Michael, Mark, Peoria | 6 | 6 | .500 | 3.36 | 20 | 20 | 1 | 0 | 0 | 0 | 120.2 | 117 | 523 | 59 | 45 | 9 | 5 | 9 | 19 | 39 | 1 | 95 | 23 | 0 |
| Mock, Garrett, South Bend | 3 | 2 | .600 | 3.00 | 8 | 8 | 1 | 0 | 0 | 0 | 54.0 | 49 | 215 | 21 | 18 | 2 | 5 | 1 | 2 | 12 | 0 | 37 | 2 | 2 |
| Mondesir, James, Peoria | 3 | 1 | .750 | 6.18 | 12 | 4 | 1 | 1 | 1 | 0 | 27.2 | 30 | 123 | 20 | 19 | 6 | 0 | 0 | 5 | 6 | 0 | 22 | 4 | 0 |
| Montalbo, Brian, Beloit | 6 | 6 | .500 | 4.74 | 24 | 19 | 0 | 0 | 2 | 1 | 108.1 | 107 | 479 | 64 | 57 | 11 | 3 | 5 | 3 | 57 | 0 | 65 | 8 | 1 |
| Moore, Benjamin, Battle Creek | 7 | 3 | .700 | 3.88 | 27 | 6 | 0 | 0 | 6 | 1 | 69.2 | 66 | 296 | 33 | 30 | 5 | 3 | 2 | 4 | 18 | 0 | 60 | 2 | 1 |
| Moore, James, Burlington | 2 | 1 | .667 | 4.15 | 19 | 0 | 0 | 0 | 13 | 3 | 34.2 | 30 | 149 | 16 | 16 | 3 | 0 | 0 | 3 | 12 | 0 | 32 | 2 | 0 |
| Moorhead, Brandon, Wisconsin | 9 | 10 | .474 | 3.27 | 25 | 25 | 0 | 0 | 0 | 0 | 145.2 | 142 | 638 | 66 | 53 | 5 | 11 | 4 | 10 | 50 | 0 | 163 | 12 | 3 |
| Morban, Carlos, Cedar Rapids | 2 | 0 | 1.000 | 5.49 | 28 | 0 | 0 | 0 | 16 | 1 | 41.0 | 42 | 193 | 27 | 25 | 4 | 0 | 0 | 6 | 22 | 0 | 37 | 6 | 0 |
| Moreira, Greg, Beloit | 8 | 8 | .500 | 4.36 | 27 | 20 | 1 | 0 | 4 | 1 | 130.0 | 128 | 568 | 73 | 63 | 16 | 9 | 5 | 8 | 44 | 0 | 86 | 3 | 3 |
| Moreno, Abel, Cedar Rapids | 10 | 8 | .556 | 3.41 | 25 | 25 | 0 | 0 | 0 | 0 | 142.2 | 141 | 595 | 69 | 54 | 7 | 4 | 8 | 9 | 31 | 0 | 120 | 6 | 7 |
| Mosquea, Daniel, South Bend * | 3 | 3 | .500 | 5.63 | 41 | 1 | 0 | 0 | 11 | 2 | 56.0 | 60 | 250 | 37 | 35 | 7 | 1 | 0 | 1 | 22 | 4 | 64 | 4 | 0 |
| Muegge, Danny, South Bend | 14 | 4 | .778 | 3.12 | 26 | 25 | 1 | 1 | 0 | 0 | 153.0 | 149 | 650 | 66 | 53 | 16 | 9 | 3 | 9 | 42 | 1 | 104 | 8 | 1 |
| Nolen, Walt, Lansing | 0 | 0 | .000 | 3.00 | 3 | 1 | 0 | 0 | 1 | 0 | 6.0 | 4 | 25 | 2 | 2 | 1 | 0 | 1 | 0 | 4 | 0 | 3 | 0 | 0 |
| O'Brien, Wes, Lansing | 0 | 1 | .000 | 1.33 | 16 | 0 | 0 | 0 | 6 | 1 | 20.1 | 11 | 79 | 3 | 3 | 1 | 0 | 0 | 2 | 6 | 0 | 23 | 1 | 1 |
| O'Flaherty, Eric, Wisconsin * | 3 | 3 | .500 | 6.12 | 12 | 10 | 0 | 0 | 0 | 0 | 57.1 | 83 | 274 | 43 | 39 | 3 | 4 | 3 | 3 | 23 | 1 | 38 | 12 | 0 |
| Pablos, Rene, Lansing * | 0 | 1 | .000 | 6.10 | 8 | 0 | 0 | 0 | 1 | 0 | 10.1 | 14 | 54 | 7 | 7 | 1 | 0 | 0 | 0 | 9 | 1 | 4 | 0 | 0 |
| Pagnozzi, Matt, Peoria | 0 | 0 | .000 | 0.00 | 1 | 0 | 0 | 0 | 1 | 1 | 1.0 | 1 | 5 | 0 | 0 | 0 | 0 | 0 | 1 | 0 | 0 | 1 | 0 | 0 |
| Pali, Matt, Cedar Rapids * | 0 | 0 | .000 | 9.00 | 1 | 0 | 0 | 0 | 1 | 0 | 1.0 | 2 | 5 | 1 | 1 | 1 | 0 | 0 | 0 | 0 | 0 | 1 | 0 | 0 |
| Parisi, Michael, Peoria | 1 | 1 | .500 | 3.28 | 6 | 6 | 0 | 0 | 0 | 0 | 35.2 | 30 | 151 | 16 | 13 | 1 | 2 | 4 | 4 | 15 | 1 | 36 | 2 | 0 |
| Pena, Luis, Beloit | 9 | 3 | .750 | 3.92 | 21 | 16 | 0 | 0 | 1 | 0 | 98.2 | 101 | 421 | 50 | 43 | 7 | 7 | 2 | 0 | 35 | 0 | 76 | 7 | 2 |
| Pence, Howard, Fort Wayne | 4 | 3 | .571 | 2.83 | 44 | 0 | 0 | 0 | 11 | 2 | 47.2 | 45 | 214 | 24 | 15 | 1 | 0 | 0 | 2 | 24 | 1 | 49 | 6 | 0 |
| Perez, Henry, Fort Wayne | 3 | 1 | .750 | 3.70 | 21 | 0 | 0 | 0 | 9 | 0 | 24.1 | 21 | 102 | 14 | 10 | 3 | 0 | 0 | 0 | 8 | 0 | 23 | 4 | 2 |
| Peterson, Trent, Kane County * | 8 | 5 | .615 | 3.42 | 21 | 20 | 1 | 1 | 0 | 0 | 121.0 | 107 | 482 | 49 | 46 | 9 | 7 | 5 | 5 | 25 | 3 | 109 | 5 | 0 |
| Petrick, Billy, Lansing | 13 | 7 | .650 | 3.50 | 26 | 24 | 0 | 0 | 1 | 0 | 146.2 | 149 | 611 | 66 | 57 | 3 | 8 | 10 | 10 | 43 | 1 | 113 | 6 | 1 |
| Pickens, J.R., Kane County | 6 | 2 | .750 | 3.44 | 54 | 0 | 0 | 0 | 26 | 5 | 81.0 | 80 | 354 | 36 | 31 | 8 | 1 | 0 | 5 | 26 | 6 | 75 | 11 | 0 |
| Pomeranz, Stuart, Peoria | 12 | 4 | .750 | 3.55 | 17 | 17 | 0 | 0 | 0 | 0 | 101.1 | 95 | 424 | 59 | 40 | 10 | 6 | 5 | 8 | 25 | 0 | 88 | 6 | 1 |
| Prunty, T.J., Swing of the Quad Ci | 0 | 0 | .000 | 5.93 | 10 | 2 | 0 | 0 | 7 | 0 | 13.2 | 14 | 66 | 9 | 9 | 3 | 0 | 1 | 3 | 7 | 0 | 9 | 2 | 0 |
| Pullin, Aaron, Cedar Rapids | 8 | 2 | .800 | 4.10 | 47 | 0 | 0 | 0 | 16 | 2 | 74.2 | 63 | 319 | 37 | 34 | 5 | 0 | 0 | 4 | 29 | 2 | 70 | 4 | 1 |
| Purdom, John, Dayton | 0 | 0 | .000 | 13.50 | 1 | 0 | 0 | 0 | 1 | 0 | 2.0 | 5 | 13 | 3 | 3 | 0 | 0 | 0 | 1 | 1 | 0 | 1 | 1 | 0 |
| Quezada, Elvys, Battle Creek | 2 | 6 | .250 | 4.11 | 15 | 15 | 1 | 1 | 0 | 0 | 72.1 | 59 | 308 | 43 | 33 | 5 | 3 | 3 | 5 | 23 | 0 | 75 | 2 | 0 |
| Rapada, Clay, Lansing * | 6 | 6 | .500 | 2.33 | 57 | 0 | 0 | 0 | 18 | 3 | 85.0 | 65 | 353 | 30 | 22 | 2 | 0 | 0 | 4 | 30 | 4 | 91 | 4 | 0 |
| Rauch, Brian, Beloit | 0 | 1 | .000 | 4.50 | 1 | 0 | 0 | 0 | 0 | 0 | 2.0 | 3 | 10 | 2 | 1 | 0 | 0 | 0 | 0 | 1 | 0 | 2 | 0 | 0 |
| Ray, Ronnie, Cedar Rapids | 3 | 0 | 1.000 | 0.87 | 6 | 3 | 0 | 0 | 1 | 0 | 20.2 | 13 | 71 | 5 | 2 | 1 | 1 | 0 | 0 | 4 | 0 | 10 | 0 | 0 |
| Rice, Trey, Dayton * | 3 | 4 | .429 | 4.60 | 38 | 1 | 0 | 0 | 13 | 0 | 76.1 | 79 | 338 | 41 | 39 | 6 | 1 | 3 | 6 | 26 | 1 | 70 | 4 | 1 |
| Rival, Kevin, Beloit | 1 | 1 | .500 | 2.81 | 13 | 0 | 0 | 0 | 7 | 2 | 25.2 | 17 | 106 | 9 | 8 | 1 | 0 | 0 | 1 | 10 | 0 | 28 | 2 | 0 |
| Robinson, Ronnie, Fort Wayne | 0 | 0 | .000 | 4.40 | 10 | 0 | 0 | 0 | 8 | 0 | 14.1 | 20 | 70 | 13 | 7 | 2 | 0 | 1 | 1 | 5 | 0 | 13 | 2 | 0 |
| Rocha, Angel, South Bend * | 2 | 3 | .400 | 6.55 | 9 | 9 | 0 | 0 | 0 | 0 | 45.1 | 44 | 211 | 39 | 33 | 5 | 2 | 2 | 5 | 31 | 0 | 38 | 7 | 0 |
| Rodriguez, Jermy, West Michigan | 5 | 2 | .714 | 3.44 | 37 | 0 | 0 | 0 | 7 | 0 | 55.0 | 47 | 242 | 21 | 21 | 4 | 0 | 0 | 0 | 24 | 0 | 48 | 4 | 0 |
| Rodriguez, Manuel, Kane County | 2 | 4 | .333 | 6.35 | 40 | 3 | 0 | 0 | 11 | 1 | 72.1 | 89 | 326 | 52 | 51 | 6 | 2 | 3 | 2 | 26 | 4 | 43 | 9 | 3 |
| Rodriguez, Rafael, Cedar Rapids | 1 | 5 | .167 | 6.48 | 7 | 7 | 0 | 0 | 0 | 0 | 33.1 | 36 | 158 | 27 | 24 | 5 | 2 | 0 | 5 | 19 | 0 | 35 | 4 | 0 |
| Rogers, Brian, West Michigan | 6 | 8 | .429 | 4.55 | 25 | 25 | 0 | 0 | 0 | 0 | 142.1 | 163 | 627 | 76 | 72 | 9 | 6 | 11 | 10 | 44 | 1 | 120 | 8 | 0 |
| Ronz, Kenon, West Michigan * | 2 | 6 | .250 | 4.87 | 52 | 0 | 0 | 0 | 14 | 0 | 57.1 | 48 | 237 | 31 | 31 | 6 | 0 | 0 | 3 | 13 | 2 | 58 | 4 | 0 |
| Roper, Derek, Peoria | 1 | 1 | .500 | 5.79 | 6 | 0 | 0 | 0 | 2 | 0 | 14.0 | 18 | 59 | 10 | 9 | 1 | 0 | 0 | 1 | 2 | 0 | 16 | 0 | 0 |
| Rosales, Leonel, Fort Wayne | 6 | 1 | .857 | 1.40 | 53 | 1 | 0 | 0 | 40 | 26 | 57.2 | 38 | 230 | 11 | 9 | 4 | 0 | 0 | 0 | 15 | 1 | 66 | 1 | 0 |
| Rosen, Mark, South Bend * | 0 | 5 | .000 | 6.10 | 27 | 6 | 0 | 0 | 7 | 1 | 62.0 | 80 | 297 | 47 | 42 | 4 | 2 | 1 | 5 | 34 | 1 | 55 | 7 | 1 |
| Rottino, Vinny, Beloit | 0 | 0 | .000 | 0.00 | 1 | 0 | 0 | 0 | 0 | 0 | 1.0 | 0 | 3 | 0 | 0 | 0 | 0 | 0 | 0 | 0 | 0 | 1 | 0 | 0 |
| Santo, Brian, West Michigan | 3 | 4 | .429 | 2.77 | 45 | 0 | 0 | 0 | 19 | 1 | 61.2 | 65 | 279 | 27 | 19 | 2 | 0 | 0 | 1 | 25 | 4 | 58 | 12 | 0 |
| Sarmiento, Williams, Clinton | 1 | 4 | .200 | 3.72 | 10 | 6 | 0 | 0 | 2 | 0 | 38.2 | 36 | 159 | 17 | 16 | 4 | 1 | 1 | 1 | 7 | 1 | 33 | 1 | 0 |
| Sawatski, John, Swing of the Quad Ci * | 0 | 1 | .000 | 1.37 | 15 | 0 | 0 | 0 | 6 | 5 | 26.1 | 14 | 103 | 6 | 4 | 1 | 0 | 0 | 0 | 10 | 1 | 29 | 0 | 0 |
| Scarbery, Chad, South Bend | 12 | 9 | .571 | 3.81 | 30 | 22 | 2 | 0 | 2 | 0 | 149.0 | 155 | 635 | 71 | 63 | 10 | 7 | 13 | 4 | 52 | 0 | 107 | 16 | 0 |
| Schutt, Chris, Swing of the Quad Ci | 7 | 9 | .438 | 4.03 | 29 | 24 | 0 | 0 | 1 | 0 | 143.0 | 133 | 617 | 75 | 64 | 7 | 8 | 13 | 7 | 62 | 0 | 104 | 15 | 0 |
| Schweitzer, Scott, Peoria * | 1 | 0 | 1.000 | 2.25 | 15 | 0 | 0 | 0 | 2 | 0 | 16.0 | 10 | 69 | 4 | 4 | 0 | 0 | 0 | 0 | 11 | 0 | 18 | 4 | 0 |
| Seely, Nicholas, Clinton | 0 | 0 | .000 | 0.00 | 6 | 0 | 0 | 0 | 1 | 0 | 7.1 | 8 | 33 | 0 | 0 | 0 | 0 | 0 | 0 | 3 | 0 | 8 | 0 | 0 |
| Segovia, Omar, Dayton * | 1 | 0 | 1.000 | 3.19 | 10 | 4 | 0 | 0 | 3 | 2 | 36.2 | 23 | 149 | 13 | 13 | 3 | 1 | 1 | 5 | 13 | 0 | 40 | 1 | 0 |

| Pitcher, Team | W | L | Pct. | ERA | G | GS | CG | ShO | GF | Sv. | IP | H | TBF | R | ER | HR | SH | SF | HB | BB | IBB | SO | WP | Bk. |
|---|---|---|---|---|---|---|---|---|---|---|---|---|---|---|---|---|---|---|---|---|---|---|---|---|
| Sherman, Justin, Burlington | 3 | 1 | .750 | 4.26 | 4 | 3 | 1 | 0 | 0 | 0 | 25.1 | 33 | 109 | 13 | 12 | 2 | 2 | 0 | 0 | 3 | 0 | 18 | 0 | 0 |
| Simonitsch, Errol, Swing of the Quad Ci * | 6 | 2 | .750 | 2.56 | 20 | 20 | 0 | 0 | 0 | 0 | 109.0 | 100 | 446 | 41 | 31 | 5 | 7 | 9 | 2 | 36 | 0 | 107 | 4 | 0 |
| Slaten, Doug, South Bend * | 5 | 2 | .714 | 2.25 | 36 | 0 | 0 | 0 | 16 | 5 | 44.0 | 44 | 191 | 13 | 11 | 2 | 0 | 0 | 2 | 13 | 1 | 40 | 3 | 0 |
| Smith, Jesse, Cedar Rapids | 4 | 7 | .364 | 5.40 | 38 | 6 | 0 | 0 | 6 | 0 | 86.2 | 99 | 409 | 70 | 52 | 4 | 1 | 5 | 4 | 45 | 2 | 68 | 12 | 1 |
| Soteropoulos, Peter, Peoria * | 1 | 0 | 1.000 | 3.52 | 20 | 0 | 0 | 0 | 5 | 0 | 30.2 | 24 | 128 | 16 | 12 | 4 | 0 | 3 | 4 | 6 | 0 | 32 | 3 | 0 |
| Stanczyk, Ben, Beloit | 0 | 0 | .000 | 0.00 | 2 | 0 | 0 | 0 | 1 | 1 | 2.0 | 2 | 8 | 0 | 0 | 0 | 0 | 0 | 0 | 0 | 0 | 1 | 0 | 0 |
| Steidlmayer, Luke, Fort Wayne | 1 | 0 | 1.000 | 2.61 | 3 | 2 | 0 | 0 | 0 | 0 | 10.1 | 6 | 42 | 5 | 3 | 0 | 0 | 0 | 2 | 1 | 0 | 14 | 0 | 0 |
| Steinborn, Chris, West Michigan * | 8 | 11 | .421 | 3.99 | 27 | 27 | 3 | 0 | 0 | 0 | 160.1 | 173 | 674 | 94 | 71 | 7 | 6 | 6 | 11 | 37 | 1 | 105 | 6 | 1 |
| Stephens, Amad, Battle Creek | 1 | 2 | .333 | 3.42 | 13 | 0 | 0 | 0 | 4 | 0 | 23.2 | 25 | 104 | 14 | 9 | 3 | 0 | 0 | 0 | 8 | 0 | 21 | 0 | 0 |
| Sterry, Vern, Fort Wayne | 2 | 0 | 1.000 | 2.40 | 5 | 5 | 0 | 0 | 0 | 0 | 30.0 | 27 | 121 | 9 | 8 | 2 | 1 | 1 | 1 | 5 | 0 | 26 | 1 | 0 |
| Stiles, Brad, Burlington * | 2 | 1 | .667 | 2.57 | 13 | 0 | 0 | 0 | 9 | 2 | 28.0 | 27 | 121 | 12 | 8 | 2 | 0 | 0 | 1 | 9 | 1 | 27 | 1 | 0 |
| Stitt, Brian, Wisconsin | 2 | 10 | .167 | 4.63 | 45 | 7 | 0 | 0 | 35 | 16 | 91.1 | 101 | 407 | 51 | 47 | 10 | 2 | 0 | 4 | 28 | 2 | 90 | 4 | 2 |
| Tata, Jordan, West Michigan | 8 | 11 | .421 | 3.35 | 28 | 28 | 1 | 0 | 0 | 0 | 166.1 | 167 | 705 | 77 | 62 | 7 | 12 | 3 | 9 | 68 | 2 | 116 | 15 | 0 |
| Taubenheim, Ty, Beloit | 5 | 3 | .625 | 3.61 | 47 | 0 | 0 | 0 | 36 | 12 | 92.1 | 81 | 378 | 41 | 37 | 10 | 1 | 0 | 3 | 17 | 0 | 106 | 2 | 0 |
| Tautor, Peter, Swing of the Quad Ci | 2 | 6 | .250 | 5.43 | 42 | 0 | 0 | 0 | 24 | 1 | 56.1 | 64 | 273 | 44 | 34 | 6 | 0 | 0 | 5 | 28 | 4 | 54 | 2 | 0 |
| Thompson, Sean, Fort Wayne * | 9 | 6 | .600 | 3.10 | 27 | 27 | 0 | 0 | 0 | 0 | 148.0 | 124 | 608 | 60 | 51 | 15 | 18 | 9 | 5 | 57 | 0 | 157 | 3 | 1 |
| Thorp, Paul, Battle Creek | 2 | 4 | .333 | 3.08 | 55 | 0 | 0 | 0 | 48 | 26 | 64.1 | 61 | 269 | 25 | 22 | 7 | 0 | 0 | 1 | 14 | 1 | 65 | 2 | 0 |
| Tierney, Chris, Fort Wayne * | 3 | 4 | .429 | 3.38 | 15 | 15 | 0 | 0 | 0 | 0 | 82.2 | 91 | 356 | 40 | 31 | 2 | 3 | 2 | 4 | 31 | 0 | 51 | 2 | 3 |
| Till, Brock, Dayton | 5 | 7 | .417 | 5.05 | 39 | 11 | 0 | 0 | 12 | 3 | 108.2 | 123 | 496 | 72 | 61 | 8 | 2 | 0 | 13 | 43 | 0 | 98 | 10 | 1 |
| Tindell, Matt, Wisconsin | 0 | 1 | .000 | 7.88 | 6 | 1 | 0 | 0 | 2 | 0 | 8.0 | 9 | 45 | 8 | 7 | 2 | 1 | 2 | 3 | 8 | 0 | 8 | 4 | 0 |
| Tomey, Anthony, West Michigan | 2 | 3 | .400 | 2.72 | 41 | 0 | 0 | 0 | 15 | 4 | 49.2 | 35 | 218 | 15 | 15 | 1 | 0 | 0 | 3 | 37 | 2 | 61 | 5 | 0 |
| Torres, Jaymie, Peoria | 1 | 0 | 1.000 | 5.60 | 8 | 0 | 0 | 0 | 1 | 0 | 17.2 | 27 | 86 | 14 | 11 | 1 | 0 | 0 | 1 | 7 | 0 | 10 | 1 | 0 |
| Touchstone, Nick, Cedar Rapids * | 7 | 7 | .500 | 4.22 | 24 | 22 | 0 | 0 | 1 | 0 | 117.1 | 101 | 517 | 75 | 55 | 10 | 5 | 5 | 18 | 68 | 0 | 97 | 3 | 1 |
| Trout, Jared, Kane County | 7 | 10 | .412 | 5.88 | 28 | 27 | 1 | 1 | 0 | 0 | 131.2 | 153 | 596 | 100 | 86 | 9 | 9 | 11 | 13 | 42 | 2 | 101 | 10 | 1 |
| Tyler, Scott, Swing of the Quad Ci | 7 | 4 | .636 | 2.60 | 22 | 19 | 0 | 0 | 0 | 0 | 103.2 | 73 | 443 | 33 | 30 | 3 | 7 | 9 | 3 | 64 | 0 | 132 | 8 | 0 |
| Ursin, Damian, Dayton | 0 | 6 | .000 | 5.87 | 21 | 8 | 0 | 0 | 8 | 2 | 69.0 | 77 | 324 | 51 | 45 | 7 | 1 | 3 | 4 | 44 | 0 | 42 | 9 | 0 |
| Vanderplow, Randy, Battle Creek | 1 | 1 | .500 | 3.72 | 14 | 0 | 0 | 0 | 3 | 0 | 19.1 | 12 | 75 | 8 | 8 | 1 | 0 | 0 | 2 | 3 | 0 | 24 | 0 | 0 |
| Varner, Matthew, Fort Wayne | 2 | 2 | .500 | 1.61 | 19 | 0 | 0 | 0 | 3 | 1 | 22.1 | 18 | 94 | 6 | 4 | 2 | 0 | 0 | 2 | 7 | 1 | 16 | 1 | 0 |
| Vasquez, Matt, West Michigan | 14 | 6 | .700 | 3.64 | 27 | 27 | 0 | 0 | 0 | 0 | 168.1 | 156 | 681 | 73 | 68 | 14 | 8 | 5 | 15 | 34 | 1 | 120 | 6 | 1 |
| Vicente, Ruben, South Bend | 4 | 3 | .571 | 4.94 | 45 | 0 | 0 | 0 | 19 | 2 | 62.0 | 73 | 287 | 37 | 34 | 2 | 1 | 1 | 8 | 18 | 1 | 44 | 7 | 3 |
| Villanueva, Carlos, Beloit | 8 | 8 | .500 | 3.77 | 25 | 21 | 1 | 1 | 2 | 1 | 114.2 | 102 | 482 | 67 | 48 | 20 | 4 | 6 | 9 | 30 | 1 | 113 | 5 | 2 |
| Wachman, Robert, Dayton | 0 | 0 | .000 | 4.32 | 3 | 0 | 0 | 0 | 0 | 0 | 8.1 | 11 | 34 | 4 | 4 | 2 | 0 | 1 | 1 | 1 | 0 | 7 | 1 | 0 |
| Watts, Joldy, Clinton | 8 | 4 | .667 | 4.77 | 40 | 0 | 0 | 0 | 16 | 2 | 83.0 | 88 | 365 | 50 | 44 | 12 | 0 | 0 | 2 | 28 | 3 | 75 | 12 | 0 |
| Wells, Randy, Lansing | 6 | 6 | .500 | 4.43 | 36 | 15 | 0 | 0 | 4 | 1 | 107.2 | 112 | 466 | 64 | 53 | 9 | 0 | 4 | 5 | 40 | 1 | 121 | 4 | 1 |
| Wheeler, Adam, Battle Creek | 0 | 0 | .000 | 4.26 | 5 | 0 | 0 | 0 | 3 | 1 | 6.1 | 8 | 30 | 3 | 3 | 0 | 0 | 0 | 0 | 2 | 0 | 8 | 0 | 0 |
| Wilson, Joe, Dayton * | 0 | 4 | .000 | 9.30 | 5 | 5 | 0 | 0 | 0 | 0 | 20.1 | 27 | 100 | 24 | 21 | 3 | 1 | 2 | 4 | 7 | 0 | 12 | 2 | 1 |
| Windsor, Jason, Kane County | 1 | 0 | 1.000 | 2.77 | 9 | 0 | 0 | 0 | 3 | 3 | 13.0 | 11 | 55 | 4 | 4 | 0 | 0 | 0 | 0 | 5 | 1 | 13 | 1 | 0 |
| Worrell, Mark, Peoria | 0 | 2 | .000 | 4.30 | 12 | 0 | 0 | 0 | 11 | 6 | 14.2 | 9 | 60 | 10 | 7 | 2 | 0 | 0 | 1 | 6 | 0 | 20 | 0 | 0 |
| Zell, Danny, West Michigan * | 5 | 4 | .556 | 2.27 | 30 | 6 | 0 | 0 | 7 | 2 | 75.1 | 69 | 312 | 23 | 19 | 2 | 1 | 2 | 5 | 24 | 0 | 52 | 6 | 1 |
| Zimmermann, Bob, Cedar Rapids | 4 | 6 | .400 | 2.26 | 53 | 0 | 0 | 0 | 50 | 24 | 67.2 | 48 | 276 | 21 | 17 | 3 | 0 | 0 | 5 | 21 | 0 | 82 | 4 | 0 |

COMBINATION SHUTOUTS: **Battle Creek** (9)—Clippard-Thorp, Quezada-Gomez-Gardner-Thorp, Clippard-Castle-J. Smith, A. Gomez-Harmsen-Gardner-Thorp, Wright-Harmsen-Thorp, Clippard-Brumit-Moore-Thorp, Clippard-Brumit, J. Smith-Moore, Harmsen-Thorp-M. Martinez. **Beloit** (10)—Pena-Durost-Taubenheim, Montalbo-Dillard, Pena-Stetter-McKenna-Grybash, Beresford-Stetter, Stetter-Villanueva, Durost-Montalbo, Stetter-Dillard-Grybash, Durost-Montalbo-Dillard, Eveland-Rival-Beresford-Dillard, Durost-Pena-Taubenheim. **Burlington** (4)—Hughes-Mullis, Coughlin-Dossett-Bray, Atencio-I. Brown, Burgos-DeHoyos. **Cedar Rapids** (8)—Posey-Hunter-Pullin, Simard-Zimmermann, Jepsen-Hindman, Touchstone-J. Smith-Hedden, Hunter-Hindman, Touchstone-Pullin, Ray-Austen, Hunter-Buckley-Morban. **Clinton** (11)—Volquez-Frydendall-Farnum, Volquez-Farnum-Watts, Mattoon-Danks-Herrera, Farnum-Volquez, Farnum-Volquez, J. Garcia-Cordeiro, Farnum-Frydendall, Kirsten-Herrera, Farnum-Seely-Herrera, Mattoon-Cordeiro, J. Garcia-Herrera. **Dayton** (6)—Medlock-Guevara, Noriega-Thigpen, Shafer-Till, Boughner-Guevara, Mallett-Edens, Mallett-Shafer-Edens. **Fort Wayne** (7)—Wells-Guthrie, Thompson-Rosales-Klatt, Hayhurst-H. Perez-Pence-Rosales, Hayhurst-Coonrod, Conden-Pence-Rosales, Conden-Perez-Pence-Rosales, Sterry-Abraham. **Kane County** (7)—Trout-Leon-Pickens, Bondurant-M. Rodriguez, Knox-Leon, Dunwell-Rodriguez, Bondurant-Fyvie, Peterson-Fyvie, Bondurant-M. Rodriguez. **Lansing** (9)—Marshall-Rapada-Wells-O'Brien, Petrick-Rapada-Mateo-Mendez, Bay-Gross, Bay-Willett-Wells, Marmol-Ferreras-Fischer, Marmol-Fischer, Wells-Kalita-Gross, Marmol-Gross-Mateo, Petrick-Mendez-Nolen-O'Brien. **Peoria** (7)—Drown-Paz-Burch, Brey-Garza-Paz-Burch, Pals-Garza-Burch, Drown-DeJaynes-Lundgren, Correa-Jordan-Garza-Burch, Pals-Lundgren-Burch, Lambert-Drown-Soteropoulos, Parisi-Jordan-Burch. **Quad Cities** (11)—Harben-DePaula, Simonitsch-Culpepper-Uhl, Simonitsch-Speigner, Harben-DePaula, Schutt-Tyler-Tautor, Simonitsch-Culpepper-Brandon, Schutt-Tautor-Culpepper-Prunty, Harben-DePaula, Tyler-Crawford, Schutt-Sawatski-DePaula, Tyler-DePaula-Sawatski. **South Bend** (7)—Chico-Mosquea-Leclair-Cremidan, Chico-Vicente-Cremidan, Liebeck-Mosquea-Coffin-Cremidan, Kinsey-Leclair-Biggs, Chico-Mosquea-Coffin-Vicente, Muegge-Biggs, Muegge-Mosquea. **West Michigan** (10)—Baldwin-Ronz-Homer, Vasquez-J. Rodriguez-Ronz-Homer, Rogers-Ronz-Homer, Baldwin-Zell-Delacruz, Vasquez-Ronz-Delacruz, Zell-Santo-Delacruz, Rogers-Zell, C. Martinez-J. Rodriguez-Santo-Delacruz-Tomey-Ronz, Zell-Tomey-Homer, Vasquez-Tomey. **Wisconsin** (6)—Oldham-Heaston-Perry-Stitt, Moorhead-Hrynio-Mackintosh-Chang, Moorhead-Mackintosh-Stitt, Oldham-Rose, Mackintosh-Hrynio, Feierabend-Castillo-Abrams-Hrynio.

NO-HIT GAMES: Hughes, Burlington, defeated Wisconsin, 3-0, Apr il 12; Quezada, Battle Creek, defeated South Bend, 7-0, May 24; Coughlin, Burlington, defeated Beloit, 3-0, June 30.

# 2004 FIELDING

## TEAM

| Team | G | PO | A | E | TC | DP | TP | PB | Pct. |
|---|---|---|---|---|---|---|---|---|---|
| Lansing | 140 | 3745 | 145 | 132 | 4022 | 116 | 0 | 41 | .967 |
| Beloit | 140 | 3612 | 123 | 146 | 3881 | 112 | 0 | 18 | .962 |
| West Michigan | 139 | 3694 | 113 | 160 | 3967 | 133 | 0 | 18 | .960 |
| Burlington | 140 | 3602 | 103 | 160 | 3865 | 119 | 0 | 24 | .959 |
| Clinton | 138 | 3569 | 131 | 158 | 3858 | 109 | 0 | 16 | .959 |
| Kane County | 139 | 3674 | 109 | 163 | 3946 | 114 | 0 | 19 | .959 |
| South Bend | 140 | 3685 | 120 | 163 | 3968 | 120 | 0 | 14 | .959 |
| Battle Creek | 139 | 3628 | 096 | 165 | 3889 | 93 | 0 | 16 | .958 |
| Cedar Rapids | 139 | 3661 | 128 | 176 | 3965 | 119 | 0 | 19 | .956 |
| Peoria | 139 | 3640 | 121 | 177 | 3938 | 125 | 0 | 31 | .955 |
| Wisconsin | 139 | 3645 | 095 | 177 | 3917 | 116 | 0 | 24 | .955 |
| Quad City | 136 | 3575 | 121 | 184 | 3880 | 89 | 0 | 16 | .953 |
| Fort Wayne | 140 | 3713 | 120 | 199 | 4032 | 120 | 0 | 18 | .951 |
| Dayton | 140 | 3655 | 138 | 195 | 3988 | 99 | 0 | 25 | .951 |

## INDIVIDUAL

### FIRST BASEMEN

NOTE: All caps denotes fielding-percentage leader based on 70 games for catchers, 93 for all other non-pitchers and 112 innings for pitchers. *Throws lefthanded.

| Player, Team | Pct. | G | PO | A | E | TC | DP |
|---|---|---|---|---|---|---|---|
| Abram, Matt, CR | .991 | 16 | 102 | 7 | 1 | 110 | 9 |
| Adams, Skip, FTW | 1.000 | 2 | 7 | 0 | 0 | 7 | 0 |
| Benjamin, Casey, CLN | .981 | 12 | 46 | 7 | 1 | 54 | 5 |
| Blakeley, Eric, WIS | .818 | 3 | 8 | 1 | 2 | 11 | 0 |
| Brown, Trevor, KNC* | .981 | 34 | 238 | 20 | 5 | 263 | 20 |
| Burgos, Richard, WMI | 1.000 | 3 | 33 | 3 | 0 | 36 | 3 |
| Campos, Tiago, DTN | 1.000 | 2 | 2 | 1 | 0 | 3 | 0 |
| Clark, Douglas, CLN | 1.000 | 3 | 17 | 1 | 0 | 18 | 2 |
| Collins, Chris, WIS | 1.000 | 10 | 77 | 4 | 0 | 81 | 5 |
| Collins, Kevin, LAN* | .989 | 12 | 90 | 3 | 1 | 94 | 8 |
| Corporan, Carlos, BLT | .985 | 35 | 245 | 11 | 4 | 260 | 21 |
| Cox, Michael, WIS | .990 | 11 | 97 | 5 | 1 | 103 | 5 |

| Player, Team | Pct. | G | PO | A | E | TC | DP |
|---|---|---|---|---|---|---|---|
| Davis, John-Paul, PEO | .988 | 65 | 543 | 41 | 7 | 591 | 51 |
| Deevers, Robby, BLT | 1.000 | 1 | 1 | 0 | 0 | 1 | 0 |
| Dopirak, Brian, LAN | .986 | 115 | 967 | 59 | 15 | 1041 | 85 |
| Doyle, Nate, WMI | 1.000 | 2 | 6 | 3 | 0 | 9 | 0 |
| Dryer, Matt, PEO | .950 | 5 | 17 | 2 | 1 | 20 | 2 |
| Dutton, Jeremy, WIS* | .993 | 69 | 546 | 41 | 4 | 591 | 44 |
| Evans, Terry, PEO | 1.000 | 4 | 11 | 2 | 0 | 13 | 2 |
| Figuereo, Anibal, BUR | .973 | 20 | 126 | 17 | 4 | 147 | 11 |
| Fransz, Jason, CLN | .968 | 7 | 57 | 4 | 2 | 63 | 3 |
| Frazier, Alex, SBN | 1.000 | 2 | 5 | 0 | 0 | 5 | 0 |
| Gaffney, Mike, BUR | .900 | 2 | 9 | 0 | 1 | 10 | 1 |
| Garcia, Alberto, LAN | 1.000 | 13 | 54 | 5 | 0 | 59 | 8 |
| Gomon, Dusty, QC | .983 | 50 | 390 | 23 | 7 | 420 | 28 |
| Gonzalez, Edwar, BTC | 1.000 | 5 | 21 | 1 | 0 | 22 | 0 |
| Graham, Bryan, BUR* | .962 | 3 | 25 | 0 | 1 | 26 | 2 |
| Hilt, Cole, BUR | 1.000 | 1 | 6 | 0 | 0 | 6 | 1 |
| Himes, Ben, DTN* | 1.000 | 4 | 10 | 0 | 0 | 10 | 0 |
| HUNT, KELLY, WMI | .992 | 131 | 1155 | 101 | 10 | 1266 | 118 |
| Jacobsen, Brock, CLN | .984 | 16 | 118 | 5 | 2 | 125 | 12 |
| Johnson, Josh, QC | 1.000 | 1 | 2 | 1 | 0 | 3 | 1 |
| Kaaihue, Kila, BUR* | .989 | 119 | 952 | 60 | 11 | 1023 | 86 |
| Kartler, Bryce, BTC* | 1.000 | 1 | 7 | 2 | 0 | 9 | 0 |
| Kim, Eddie, KNC* | .991 | 86 | 703 | 63 | 7 | 773 | 56 |
| Kirkland, Kody, WMI | 1.000 | 1 | 8 | 0 | 0 | 8 | 1 |
| Kreuzer, Josh, CLN | .984 | 81 | 708 | 29 | 12 | 749 | 53 |
| Kroski, Chris, DTN* | 1.000 | 6 | 48 | 5 | 0 | 53 | 6 |
| LaHair, Bryan, WIS* | .988 | 46 | 310 | 30 | 4 | 344 | 22 |
| Larsen, Drew, LAN | .986 | 12 | 67 | 5 | 1 | 73 | 8 |
| Lopez, Baltazar, CR* | .975 | 61 | 512 | 33 | 14 | 559 | 52 |
| Maher, Caleb, CR | .989 | 18 | 163 | 10 | 2 | 175 | 16 |
| Majewski, Dustin, KNC* | 1.000 | 1 | 2 | 0 | 0 | 2 | 0 |
| Mather, Joe, PEO | .983 | 8 | 57 | 0 | 1 | 58 | 4 |
| McCreery, Andrew, SBN | .967 | 10 | 83 | 4 | 3 | 90 | 6 |
| McDonald, Chamar, BUR | .980 | 8 | 45 | 4 | 1 | 50 | 6 |
| Mejia, Jorge, DTN | 1.000 | 1 | 3 | 0 | 0 | 3 | 1 |
| Metheny, Brenton, WIS* | 1.000 | 14 | 130 | 10 | 0 | 140 | 15 |
| Miller, Chris, FTW | 1.000 | 1 | 4 | 0 | 0 | 4 | 1 |
| Montero, Miguel, SBN* | 1.000 | 16 | 130 | 1 | 0 | 131 | 7 |
| Mottram, Allen, SBN | .978 | 28 | 205 | 22 | 5 | 232 | 16 |
| Murillo, Augie, SBN | 1.000 | 2 | 3 | 0 | 0 | 3 | 1 |
| Olmstead, Walter, DTN | .994 | 39 | 304 | 19 | 2 | 325 | 23 |
| Pali, Matt, CR* | .997 | 41 | 334 | 26 | 1 | 361 | 36 |
| Peterson, Brock, QC | .994 | 74 | 579 | 45 | 4 | 628 | 44 |
| Phillips, Kyle, QC* | 1.000 | 1 | 5 | 0 | 0 | 5 | 1 |
| Piantek, Kurt, WMI | .961 | 4 | 49 | 0 | 2 | 51 | 7 |
| Pickens, Jordan, FTW | 1.000 | 5 | 39 | 1 | 0 | 40 | 4 |
| Purdom, John, DTN | .961 | 6 | 47 | 2 | 2 | 51 | 6 |
| Ramirez, Manuel, BLT | .987 | 78 | 619 | 47 | 9 | 675 | 47 |
| Reynolds, Tila, SBN | 1.000 | 3 | 5 | 0 | 0 | 5 | 0 |
| Richardson, Grant, BLT | .974 | 27 | 176 | 10 | 5 | 191 | 18 |
| Richardson, Kevin, CLN | .984 | 35 | 276 | 23 | 5 | 304 | 27 |
| Robles, Luis, BTC | .978 | 7 | 43 | 1 | 1 | 45 | 3 |
| Rottino, Vinny, BLT | .977 | 12 | 79 | 5 | 2 | 86 | 5 |
| Salas, Issmael, LAN | 1.000 | 1 | 3 | 0 | 0 | 3 | 1 |
| Sandoval, Abigail, CLN | 1.000 | 4 | 5 | 1 | 0 | 6 | 1 |
| Santor, John, PEO | .990 | 68 | 629 | 40 | 7 | 676 | 56 |
| Spanos, Vasili, KNC | .978 | 28 | 222 | 5 | 5 | 232 | 21 |
| Urick, John, BTC* | .984 | 104 | 746 | 50 | 13 | 809 | 72 |
| Valenzuela, Fernando, FTW* | .990 | 135 | 1065 | 78 | 12 | 1155 | 98 |
| Varela, Edgar, SBN* | .988 | 95 | 766 | 61 | 10 | 837 | 78 |
| Vasquez, Willie, BTC | .992 | 38 | 244 | 15 | 2 | 261 | 15 |
| Votto, Joey, DTN* | .986 | 90 | 662 | 45 | 10 | 717 | 53 |
| Wilson, Bobby, CR | .978 | 8 | 77 | 11 | 2 | 90 | 6 |
| Zamojc, Mark, QC* | .985 | 15 | 124 | 5 | 2 | 131 | 12 |

## SECOND BASEMEN

| Player, Team | Pct. | G | PO | A | E | TC | DP |
|---|---|---|---|---|---|---|---|
| Abram, Matt, CR | 1.000 | 2 | 4 | 5 | 0 | 9 | 1 |
| Acosta, Gilberto, BLT | .964 | 5 | 8 | 19 | 1 | 28 | 4 |
| Acosta, Jesse, KNC | .833 | 2 | 5 | 0 | 1 | 6 | 0 |
| Adams, Skip, FTW | .947 | 4 | 8 | 10 | 1 | 19 | 3 |
| Aguirre, Rodrigo, SBN* | .889 | 3 | 5 | 3 | 1 | 9 | 1 |
| Appert, Luke, KNC* | .951 | 122 | 200 | 288 | 25 | 513 | 47 |
| Baker, Casey, FTW | .980 | 9 | 20 | 29 | 1 | 50 | 10 |
| Bastida, Evel, WIS* | .813 | 4 | 3 | 10 | 3 | 16 | 0 |
| Benjamin, Casey, CLN | .966 | 9 | 8 | 20 | 1 | 29 | 3 |
| Blakeley, Eric, WIS | .978 | 21 | 37 | 53 | 2 | 92 | 11 |
| Bolivar, Luis, DTN | .952 | 36 | 66 | 73 | 7 | 146 | 14 |
| Bonafacio, Emilio, SBN | .958 | 115 | 217 | 303 | 23 | 543 | 68 |
| Boyer, Billy, CR | .956 | 25 | 63 | 68 | 6 | 137 | 20 |
| Boyer, Kyle, PEO | .962 | 10 | 19 | 32 | 2 | 53 | 6 |
| Brown, Matt, CR | .957 | 5 | 8 | 14 | 1 | 23 | 3 |
| Burgamy, Brian, FTW | .942 | 16 | 25 | 40 | 4 | 69 | 7 |
| Cairns, Troy, DTN | 1.000 | 4 | 5 | 13 | 0 | 18 | 3 |
| Campana, Wandel, BLT | 1.000 | 2 | 3 | 3 | 0 | 6 | 0 |
| Casilla, Alexis, CR | .949 | 9 | 17 | 20 | 2 | 39 | 4 |
| Chirinos, Robinson, LAN | .961 | 82 | 159 | 232 | 16 | 407 | 44 |
| Cho, Hyung, WIS | .900 | 8 | 9 | 9 | 2 | 20 | 1 |
| Ciofrone, Peter, FTW* | .930 | 37 | 66 | 93 | 12 | 171 | 26 |
| Conley, Evan, DTN | .967 | 9 | 11 | 18 | 1 | 30 | 2 |
| Cox, Michael, WIS | .964 | 47 | 74 | 114 | 7 | 195 | 17 |
| Cruz, Enrique, BTC | .833 | 1 | 1 | 4 | 1 | 6 | 1 |
| Cruz, Jose Enrique, BTC | .967 | 75 | 148 | 173 | 11 | 332 | 37 |
| Doyle, Nate, WMI | .971 | 10 | 13 | 21 | 1 | 35 | 5 |
| Francia, Juan, WMI | .875 | 4 | 10 | 11 | 3 | 24 | 6 |
| Furtado, Micah, CLN* | .955 | 82 | 140 | 262 | 19 | 421 | 60 |
| Gaffney, Mike, BUR | .933 | 3 | 6 | 8 | 1 | 15 | 1 |
| Garcia, Alberto, LAN | 1.000 | 1 | 1 | 2 | 0 | 3 | 1 |
| Garcia, Alex, QC | .948 | 53 | 79 | 142 | 12 | 233 | 29 |
| Garcia, Jose, CLN | 1.000 | 3 | 2 | 2 | 0 | 4 | 0 |
| Gerez, Francisco, WIS | 1.000 | 1 | 3 | 0 | 0 | 3 | 0 |
| Gonzalez, Alberto, SBN | .976 | 19 | 37 | 44 | 2 | 83 | 9 |
| Granato, Anthony, LAN | .978 | 23 | 56 | 76 | 3 | 135 | 18 |
| Groves, Brett, BUR | 1.000 | 5 | 8 | 18 | 0 | 26 | 6 |
| Guzman, Jose, CR | 1.000 | 2 | 1 | 2 | 0 | 3 | 0 |
| Hayes, Calvin, PEO | .913 | 22 | 52 | 43 | 9 | 104 | 16 |
| Hernandez, Habelito, DTN | .961 | 50 | 113 | 136 | 10 | 259 | 29 |
| Hoffpauir, Jarrett, PEO | .962 | 67 | 120 | 183 | 12 | 315 | 49 |
| Hudson, Will, DTN | 1.000 | 14 | 31 | 27 | 0 | 58 | 7 |
| Ingram, Brian, KNC* | .935 | 21 | 35 | 65 | 7 | 107 | 12 |
| Iribarren, Hernan, BLT* | .944 | 14 | 25 | 43 | 4 | 72 | 10 |
| Jaramillo, Milko, PEO | 1.000 | 8 | 10 | 16 | 0 | 26 | 1 |
| Johnson, Josh, BUR | 1.000 | 1 | 2 | 5 | 0 | 7 | 1 |
| Keim, Adam, BUR | .927 | 15 | 27 | 49 | 6 | 82 | 7 |
| Kendrick, Howard, CR | .976 | 64 | 135 | 197 | 8 | 340 | 38 |
| Larsen, Drew, LAN | .905 | 6 | 10 | 9 | 2 | 21 | 2 |
| Leahy, Ryan, CR | .955 | 11 | 25 | 38 | 3 | 66 | 7 |
| Lewis, William, BLT | .961 | 35 | 60 | 88 | 6 | 154 | 23 |
| Marquez, Uriak, LAN* | .944 | 21 | 41 | 44 | 5 | 90 | 11 |
| McCoy, Mike, PEO | .974 | 13 | 32 | 42 | 2 | 76 | 7 |
| McIntyre, Nick, WMI | 1.000 | 5 | 5 | 11 | 0 | 16 | 3 |
| Mejia, Jorge, DTN | .961 | 31 | 46 | 76 | 5 | 127 | 20 |
| Navarro, Oswaldo, WIS | .969 | 27 | 53 | 70 | 4 | 127 | 22 |
| Orlandos, Nick, WIS | .936 | 26 | 50 | 67 | 8 | 125 | 10 |
| Pattee, Ben, QC | .965 | 17 | 30 | 53 | 3 | 86 | 11 |
| Pena, Omar, PEO | .947 | 26 | 50 | 75 | 7 | 132 | 15 |
| Powell, Brandon, BUR* | .964 | 78 | 126 | 222 | 13 | 361 | 46 |
| Punto, Nick, QC | 1.000 | 1 | 2 | 3 | 0 | 5 | 1 |
| Ramos, Peeter, FTW | .968 | 61 | 111 | 162 | 9 | 282 | 34 |
| Reynolds, Tila, SBN | .972 | 11 | 21 | 14 | 1 | 36 | 2 |
| RODLAND, ERIC, WMI* | .983 | 124 | 245 | 331 | 10 | 586 | 87 |
| Rodriguez, Guilder, BLT | .978 | 78 | 148 | 212 | 8 | 368 | 37 |
| Rodriguez, Rafael, BTC | .951 | 41 | 61 | 95 | 8 | 164 | 18 |
| Rodriguez, Sean, CR | .960 | 26 | 45 | 76 | 5 | 126 | 19 |
| Rottino, Vinny, BLT | .963 | 5 | 8 | 18 | 1 | 27 | 4 |
| Rutgers, Paul, QC | .956 | 60 | 104 | 157 | 12 | 273 | 20 |
| Salas, Issmael, LAN | 1.000 | 10 | 23 | 37 | 0 | 60 | 12 |
| Sanchez, Angel, BUR | .850 | 3 | 8 | 9 | 3 | 20 | 3 |
| Sandel, George, WIS | .974 | 18 | 28 | 46 | 2 | 76 | 9 |
| Sandoval, Abigail, CLN | .984 | 28 | 47 | 75 | 2 | 124 | 13 |
| Septimo, Agustin, BLT | .909 | 2 | 5 | 5 | 1 | 11 | 0 |
| Sevilla, Walter, BUR | .957 | 40 | 65 | 90 | 7 | 162 | 19 |
| Smyres, Justin, FTW | .986 | 15 | 29 | 40 | 1 | 70 | 8 |
| Swope, Tobin, CLN | .962 | 21 | 19 | 57 | 3 | 79 | 5 |
| Taylor, JR, QC | .938 | 6 | 12 | 18 | 2 | 32 | 5 |
| Vasquez, Willie, BTC | 1.000 | 15 | 18 | 40 | 0 | 58 | 4 |
| Walsh, Nick, BTC* | .969 | 14 | 29 | 34 | 2 | 65 | 8 |

## THIRD BASEMEN

| Player, Team | Pct. | G | PO | A | E | TC | DP |
|---|---|---|---|---|---|---|---|
| Abram, Matt, CR | 1.000 | 2 | 2 | 5 | 0 | 7 | 1 |
| Acosta, Jesse, KNC | 1.000 | 5 | 2 | 5 | 0 | 7 | 0 |
| Adams, Skip, FTW | .792 | 21 | 14 | 28 | 11 | 53 | 6 |
| Aguirre, Rodrigo, SBN* | .333 | 1 | 0 | 1 | 2 | 3 | 0 |
| Baker, Casey, FTW | .000 | 2 | 0 | 0 | 1 | 1 | 0 |
| Bastida, Evel, WIS* | .892 | 25 | 8 | 50 | 7 | 65 | 3 |
| Benjamin, Casey, CLN | .818 | 18 | 11 | 16 | 6 | 33 | 1 |
| Blakeley, Eric, WIS | .943 | 49 | 25 | 91 | 7 | 123 | 10 |
| Bochy, Greg, FTW | .910 | 34 | 19 | 52 | 7 | 78 | 2 |
| Bonvechio, Brett, FTW* | .955 | 82 | 54 | 159 | 10 | 223 | 8 |
| Brown, Matt, CR | .913 | 112 | 86 | 217 | 29 | 332 | 19 |
| Burgos, Omar, QC | .892 | 93 | 55 | 151 | 25 | 231 | 12 |
| Cairns, Troy, DTN | .917 | 9 | 2 | 20 | 2 | 24 | 0 |
| Campana, Wandel, BLT | 1.000 | 3 | 1 | 3 | 0 | 4 | 1 |

| Player, Team | Pct. | G | PO | A | E | TC | DP |
|---|---|---|---|---|---|---|---|
| Cho, Hyung, WIS | 1.000 | 3 | 0 | 4 | 0 | 4 | 0 |
| Collins, Chris, WIS | .905 | 18 | 4 | 34 | 4 | 42 | 2 |
| Conley, Evan, DTN | .891 | 20 | 10 | 31 | 5 | 46 | 4 |
| Cox, Michael, WIS | .883 | 52 | 35 | 108 | 19 | 162 | 7 |
| Cruz, Jose Enrique, BTC | 1.000 | 1 | 0 | 1 | 0 | 1 | 0 |
| Davis, John-Paul, PEO | 1.000 | 1 | 1 | 0 | 0 | 1 | 0 |
| Doyle, Nate, WMI | .889 | 2 | 0 | 8 | 1 | 9 | 1 |
| Dryer, Matt, PEO | .918 | 59 | 38 | 129 | 15 | 182 | 7 |
| Duncan, Eric, BTC* | .901 | 75 | 58 | 124 | 20 | 202 | 9 |
| Francisco, Alfredo, LAN | .911 | 23 | 10 | 41 | 5 | 56 | 2 |
| Frostad, Emerson, CLN* | .915 | 113 | 71 | 177 | 23 | 271 | 17 |
| Gaffney, Mike, BUR | .974 | 35 | 27 | 49 | 2 | 78 | 4 |
| Garcia, Alberto, LAN | .913 | 45 | 37 | 78 | 11 | 126 | 3 |
| Granato, Anthony, LAN | 1.000 | 10 | 7 | 7 | 0 | 14 | 0 |
| Groves, Brett, BUR | 1.000 | 12 | 11 | 16 | 0 | 27 | 1 |
| HEETHER, ADAM, BLT | .944 | 127 | 75 | 211 | 17 | 303 | 11 |
| Hernandez, Habelito, DTN | .891 | 39 | 20 | 70 | 11 | 101 | 4 |
| Hileman, Jutt, PEO | .667 | 2 | 1 | 3 | 2 | 6 | 0 |
| Hilt, Cole, BUR | .906 | 13 | 8 | 21 | 3 | 32 | 4 |
| Hudson, Will, DTN | .895 | 7 | 7 | 10 | 2 | 19 | 4 |
| Jacobsen, Brock, CLN | 1.000 | 1 | 1 | 0 | 0 | 1 | 0 |
| Jaramillo, Milko, PEO | 1.000 | 2 | 0 | 1 | 0 | 1 | 0 |
| Jones, Adam, WIS | 1.000 | 2 | 0 | 2 | 0 | 2 | 0 |
| Kirkland, Kody, WMI | .917 | 122 | 84 | 237 | 29 | 350 | 22 |
| Larsen, Drew, LAN | .904 | 43 | 23 | 80 | 11 | 114 | 10 |
| Leahy, Ryan, CR | .750 | 5 | 0 | 6 | 2 | 8 | 0 |
| Lucas, Edward, BUR | .971 | 18 | 11 | 23 | 1 | 35 | 4 |
| Maier, Mitch, BUR* | .903 | 71 | 47 | 140 | 20 | 207 | 13 |
| Marquez, Uriak, LAN* | .933 | 16 | 5 | 23 | 2 | 30 | 5 |
| Mather, Joe, PEO | .930 | 22 | 17 | 36 | 4 | 57 | 3 |
| McCoy, Mike, PEO | .929 | 37 | 24 | 80 | 8 | 112 | 12 |
| McCreery, Andrew, SBN | 1.000 | 3 | 1 | 4 | 0 | 5 | 1 |
| McIntyre, Nick, WMI | .833 | 19 | 15 | 20 | 7 | 42 | 7 |
| Metheny, Brenton, WIS* | .667 | 2 | 1 | 1 | 1 | 3 | 0 |
| Moses, Matt, QC* | .824 | 13 | 12 | 16 | 6 | 34 | 1 |
| Murillo, Augie, SBN | .931 | 96 | 60 | 170 | 17 | 247 | 15 |
| Olmstead, Walter, DTN | .868 | 56 | 38 | 93 | 20 | 151 | 11 |
| Patrick, Christopher, PEO | .778 | 6 | 0 | 14 | 4 | 18 | 2 |
| Pattee, Ben, QC | .960 | 14 | 12 | 12 | 1 | 25 | 1 |
| Pena, Omar, PEO | .949 | 32 | 13 | 43 | 3 | 59 | 7 |
| Peterson, Brock, QC | .778 | 7 | 2 | 5 | 2 | 9 | 0 |
| Piepkorn, Jeremiah, DTN | .919 | 15 | 13 | 21 | 3 | 37 | 0 |
| Punto, Nick, QC | 1.000 | 1 | 0 | 1 | 0 | 1 | 0 |
| Ramirez, Manuel, BLT | .667 | 2 | 1 | 1 | 1 | 3 | 0 |
| Reynolds, Mark, SBN | 1.000 | 4 | 2 | 8 | 0 | 10 | 1 |
| Reynolds, Tila, SBN | .853 | 20 | 10 | 19 | 5 | 34 | 0 |
| Rodriguez, Rafael, BTC | .840 | 19 | 18 | 24 | 8 | 50 | 2 |
| Rodriguez, Sean, CR | 1.000 | 10 | 2 | 19 | 0 | 21 | 1 |
| Rottino, Vinny, BLT | .895 | 14 | 10 | 24 | 4 | 38 | 4 |
| Rutgers, Paul, QC | .750 | 8 | 2 | 7 | 3 | 12 | 0 |
| Salas, Issmael, LAN | 1.000 | 9 | 8 | 16 | 0 | 24 | 4 |
| Sandoval, Abigail, CLN | .938 | 12 | 6 | 24 | 2 | 32 | 1 |
| Smyres, Justin, FTW | .929 | 4 | 4 | 9 | 1 | 14 | 1 |
| Snyder, Brian, KNC | .893 | 82 | 40 | 119 | 19 | 178 | 8 |
| Spanos, Vasili, KNC | .924 | 39 | 31 | 66 | 8 | 105 | 2 |
| Swope, Tobin, CLN | 1.000 | 5 | 5 | 10 | 0 | 15 | 1 |
| Taylor, JR, QC | .500 | 1 | 0 | 1 | 1 | 2 | 0 |
| Van Meetren, Jason, BTC | .667 | 1 | 2 | 0 | 1 | 3 | 0 |
| Varela, Edgar, SBN* | .934 | 33 | 20 | 65 | 6 | 91 | 5 |
| Vasquez, Willie, BTC | .928 | 39 | 28 | 62 | 7 | 97 | 10 |
| Walsh, Nick, BTC* | .960 | 11 | 8 | 16 | 1 | 25 | 3 |
| Wayment, Kory, KNC | .873 | 22 | 15 | 40 | 8 | 63 | 2 |
| Wilson, Bobby, CR | .838 | 12 | 7 | 24 | 6 | 37 | 1 |

## SHORTSTOPS

| Player, Team | Pct. | G | PO | A | E | TC | DP |
|---|---|---|---|---|---|---|---|
| Acosta, Gilberto, BLT | .952 | 37 | 54 | 103 | 8 | 165 | 12 |
| Acosta, Jesse, KNC | .880 | 9 | 6 | 16 | 3 | 25 | 3 |
| Adams, Skip, FTW | .928 | 31 | 52 | 90 | 11 | 153 | 16 |
| Aguirre, Rodrigo, SBN* | 1.000 | 2 | 2 | 2 | 0 | 4 | 1 |
| Benjamin, Casey, CLN | .973 | 18 | 26 | 47 | 2 | 75 | 11 |
| Blakeley, Eric, WIS | .900 | 10 | 12 | 15 | 3 | 30 | 5 |
| Bolivar, Luis, DTN | .932 | 88 | 116 | 238 | 26 | 380 | 35 |
| Boyer, Billy, CR | .962 | 4 | 10 | 15 | 1 | 26 | 6 |
| Brown, Matt, CR | 1.000 | 1 | 3 | 4 | 0 | 7 | 1 |
| Campana, Wandel, BLT | .919 | 30 | 31 | 82 | 10 | 123 | 15 |
| Chirinos, Robinson, LAN | 1.000 | 1 | 1 | 5 | 0 | 6 | 0 |
| Ciriaco, Juan, FTW | .893 | 98 | 151 | 224 | 45 | 420 | 48 |
| Cox, Michael, WIS | .700 | 3 | 4 | 3 | 3 | 10 | 0 |
| Doyle, Nate, WMI | .909 | 6 | 6 | 14 | 2 | 22 | 3 |
| Figueroa, Baudilio, FTW | .867 | 5 | 6 | 7 | 2 | 15 | 1 |
| Firlit, Dan, SBN | .833 | 4 | 7 | 8 | 3 | 18 | 1 |
| Francia, Juan, WMI | .942 | 92 | 171 | 280 | 28 | 479 | 68 |
| Frostad, Emerson, CLN* | 1.000 | 1 | 1 | 0 | 0 | 1 | 0 |
| Gaffney, Mike, BUR | .957 | 22 | 28 | 60 | 4 | 92 | 8 |
| Garcia, Alex, QC | .908 | 31 | 37 | 82 | 12 | 131 | 16 |
| Gerez, Francisco, WIS | .786 | 7 | 8 | 14 | 6 | 28 | 3 |
| Giarratano, Tony, WMI | .974 | 42 | 76 | 146 | 6 | 228 | 29 |
| Gonzalez, Alberto, SBN | .962 | 83 | 141 | 237 | 15 | 393 | 54 |
| Groves, Brett, BUR | .909 | 2 | 5 | 5 | 1 | 11 | 2 |
| Hudson, Will, DTN | .961 | 55 | 85 | 139 | 9 | 233 | 28 |
| Ingram, Brian, KNC* | .965 | 105 | 142 | 303 | 16 | 461 | 49 |
| Jaramillo, Milko, PEO | .952 | 12 | 22 | 37 | 3 | 62 | 7 |
| Johnson, Josh, BUR | .833 | 2 | 2 | 3 | 1 | 6 | 1 |
| Jones, Adam, WIS | .943 | 120 | 214 | 318 | 32 | 564 | 57 |
| Kaplan, Jon, SBN | .700 | 1 | 1 | 6 | 3 | 10 | 0 |
| Kazmar, Sean, FTW | .862 | 5 | 9 | 16 | 4 | 29 | 4 |
| Kinsler, Ian, CLN | .952 | 60 | 80 | 178 | 13 | 271 | 34 |
| Larsen, Drew, LAN | .947 | 5 | 10 | 8 | 1 | 19 | 4 |
| Leahy, Ryan, CR | 1.000 | 4 | 4 | 14 | 0 | 18 | 2 |
| Lucas, Edward, BUR | .933 | 5 | 4 | 10 | 1 | 15 | 2 |
| Made, Hector, BTC | .944 | 128 | 203 | 333 | 32 | 568 | 58 |
| Marquez, Uriak, LAN* | 1.000 | 4 | 5 | 9 | 0 | 14 | 3 |
| McCoy, Mike, PEO | 1.000 | 2 | 2 | 6 | 0 | 8 | 0 |
| McIntyre, Nick, WMI | .909 | 5 | 5 | 15 | 2 | 22 | 3 |
| Murray, Joshua, BLT | .968 | 54 | 74 | 139 | 7 | 220 | 33 |
| Navarro, Oswaldo, WIS | 1.000 | 8 | 9 | 21 | 0 | 30 | 3 |
| Patrick, Christopher, PEO | 1.000 | 1 | 2 | 3 | 0 | 5 | 0 |
| Pattee, Ben, QC | 1.000 | 1 | 2 | 8 | 0 | 10 | 2 |
| Pena, Antonio, CLN | 1.000 | 7 | 15 | 21 | 0 | 36 | 5 |
| Pena, Omar, PEO | .937 | 22 | 28 | 61 | 6 | 95 | 11 |
| Punto, Nick, QC | 1.000 | 2 | 6 | 4 | 0 | 10 | 1 |
| Reynolds, Tila, SBN | .955 | 63 | 90 | 189 | 13 | 292 | 30 |
| Rodriguez, Guilder, BLT | .985 | 16 | 26 | 39 | 1 | 66 | 9 |
| Rodriguez, Sean, CR | .960 | 6 | 9 | 15 | 1 | 25 | 3 |
| ROJAS, CARLOS, LAN | .980 | 132 | 222 | 414 | 13 | 649 | 77 |
| Rottino, Vinny, BLT | 1.000 | 1 | 0 | 1 | 0 | 1 | 0 |
| Ryan, Brendan, PEO | .938 | 104 | 139 | 330 | 31 | 500 | 63 |
| Sanchez, Angel, BUR | .950 | 88 | 140 | 242 | 20 | 402 | 50 |
| Sandel, George, WIS | .938 | 3 | 5 | 10 | 1 | 16 | 3 |
| Sandoval, Abigail, CLN | .948 | 59 | 98 | 173 | 15 | 286 | 38 |
| Septimo, Agustin, BLT | .800 | 4 | 0 | 8 | 2 | 10 | 1 |
| Sevilla, Walter, BUR | .966 | 33 | 35 | 77 | 4 | 116 | 17 |
| Smyres, Justin, FTW | .941 | 3 | 6 | 10 | 1 | 17 | 1 |
| Snyder, Brian, KNC | 1.000 | 4 | 5 | 11 | 0 | 16 | 1 |
| Taylor, JR, QC | .935 | 101 | 151 | 269 | 29 | 449 | 55 |
| Tyler, Scott, QC | 1.000 | 2 | 5 | 6 | 0 | 11 | 2 |
| Vasquez, Willie, BTC | .958 | 14 | 15 | 31 | 2 | 48 | 9 |
| Wayment, Kory, KNC | .945 | 32 | 52 | 86 | 8 | 146 | 21 |
| Wood, Brandon, CR | .948 | 125 | 206 | 322 | 29 | 557 | 81 |

## OUTFIELDERS

| Player, Team | Pct. | G | PO | A | E | TC | DP |
|---|---|---|---|---|---|---|---|
| Acosta, Gilberto, BLT | 1.000 | 1 | 2 | 0 | 0 | 2 | 0 |
| Altman, Kevin, CLN | 1.000 | 1 | 2 | 0 | 0 | 2 | 0 |
| ANDERSON, DREW, BLT* | .995 | 119 | 208 | 5 | 1 | 214 | 1 |
| Andrus, Erold, BTC | .984 | 137 | 298 | 4 | 5 | 307 | 1 |
| Arneson, Justin, QC | .955 | 60 | 101 | 4 | 5 | 110 | 1 |
| Baker, Casey, FTW | .958 | 17 | 21 | 2 | 1 | 24 | 0 |
| Balentien, Wladimir, WIS | .969 | 73 | 122 | 4 | 4 | 130 | 1 |
| Balkcom, Blake, CR | .976 | 93 | 159 | 5 | 4 | 168 | 1 |
| Barry, Jeff, BUR | .951 | 101 | 188 | 7 | 10 | 205 | 0 |
| Beltre, Elvin, DTN | .962 | 34 | 73 | 3 | 3 | 79 | 0 |
| Benjamin, Casey, CLN | 1.000 | 4 | 1 | 0 | 0 | 1 | 0 |
| Blakeley, Eric, WIS | 1.000 | 6 | 9 | 0 | 0 | 9 | 0 |
| Blue, Vincent, WMI* | .981 | 128 | 260 | 1 | 5 | 266 | 0 |
| Bourassa, Adam, CLN* | .986 | 57 | 130 | 6 | 2 | 138 | 1 |
| Boyer, Kyle, LAN | .952 | 13 | 20 | 0 | 1 | 21 | 0 |
| Bradford, Samuel, WIS | 1.000 | 12 | 13 | 0 | 0 | 13 | 0 |
| Bubela, Dane, CLN* | .965 | 98 | 157 | 10 | 6 | 173 | 2 |
| Cabrera, Edwin, BTC | 1.000 | 1 | 1 | 0 | 0 | 1 | 0 |
| Cabrera, Melky, BTC | .991 | 41 | 103 | 3 | 1 | 107 | 2 |
| Campos, Tiago, DTN | 1.000 | 25 | 35 | 0 | 0 | 35 | 0 |
| Carson, Matt, BTC | .964 | 95 | 197 | 15 | 8 | 220 | 3 |
| Cashman, Brandon, CLN | .966 | 46 | 110 | 2 | 4 | 116 | 0 |
| Collins, Kevin, LAN* | 1.000 | 78 | 92 | 5 | 0 | 97 | 1 |
| Colton, Chris, WIS | .987 | 125 | 224 | 7 | 3 | 234 | 2 |
| Cook, Jeff, SBN* | .972 | 113 | 202 | 8 | 6 | 216 | 1 |
| Cordeiro, Chris, CLN | 1.000 | 8 | 13 | 0 | 0 | 13 | 0 |
| Cosby, Quan, CR | .979 | 117 | 231 | 6 | 5 | 242 | 1 |
| Deevers, Robby, BLT | .960 | 70 | 113 | 8 | 5 | 126 | 1 |
| Dickerson, Chris, DTN* | .977 | 83 | 206 | 8 | 5 | 219 | 3 |
| Dobson, Sean, PEO | 1.000 | 4 | 3 | 0 | 0 | 3 | 0 |
| Doyle, Nate, WMI | 1.000 | 8 | 9 | 0 | 0 | 9 | 0 |

| Player, Team | Pct. | G | PO | A | E | TC | DP |
|---|---|---|---|---|---|---|---|
| Ellison, Josh, WIS* | .973 | 24 | 35 | 1 | 1 | 37 | 1 |
| Evans, Terry, PEO | .981 | 92 | 148 | 5 | 3 | 156 | 0 |
| Fitzgerald, Ryan, LAN | .984 | 78 | 117 | 6 | 2 | 125 | 1 |
| Flowers, Bo, WMI | 1.000 | 6 | 14 | 0 | 0 | 14 | 0 |
| Fransz, Jason, CLN | 1.000 | 5 | 9 | 1 | 0 | 10 | 0 |
| Frazier, Alex, SBN | .929 | 59 | 75 | 4 | 6 | 85 | 0 |
| Frisella, Sal, PEO | .958 | 21 | 21 | 2 | 1 | 24 | 0 |
| Fry, Ryan, DTN | .963 | 33 | 48 | 4 | 2 | 54 | 0 |
| Gaffney, Mike, BUR | 1.000 | 10 | 21 | 1 | 0 | 22 | 0 |
| Garay, Ernesto, FTW* | .880 | 20 | 22 | 0 | 3 | 25 | 0 |
| Garcia, Alberto, LAN | .833 | 5 | 5 | 0 | 1 | 6 | 0 |
| Garcia, Lino, SBN | .979 | 113 | 224 | 4 | 5 | 233 | 0 |
| Gibbons, Danny, KNC* | 1.000 | 11 | 8 | 0 | 0 | 8 | 0 |
| Gonzalez, Alberto, SBN | 1.000 | 2 | 2 | 0 | 0 | 2 | 0 |
| Gonzalez, Carlos, SBN* | 1.000 | 12 | 23 | 0 | 0 | 23 | 0 |
| Gonzalez, Edwar, BTC | 1.000 | 5 | 1 | 0 | 0 | 1 | 0 |
| Goss, Michael, SBN* | .969 | 62 | 94 | 1 | 3 | 98 | 0 |
| Graham, Bryan, BUR* | .975 | 56 | 73 | 5 | 2 | 80 | 1 |
| Gray, Matt, DTN* | .967 | 17 | 29 | 0 | 1 | 30 | 0 |
| Grayson, Larry, CLN | .970 | 93 | 154 | 8 | 5 | 167 | 3 |
| Groves, Brett, BUR | 1.000 | 7 | 7 | 0 | 0 | 7 | 0 |
| Guzman, Jose, CR | .905 | 10 | 19 | 0 | 2 | 21 | 0 |
| Haerther, Cody, PEO* | .963 | 58 | 72 | 5 | 3 | 80 | 2 |
| Harris, Estee, BTC* | .955 | 42 | 63 | 1 | 3 | 67 | 0 |
| Hatcher, Justin, CLN | 1.000 | 4 | 5 | 1 | 0 | 6 | 0 |
| Hayes, Calvin, PEO | 1.000 | 1 | 1 | 0 | 0 | 1 | 0 |
| Hileman, Jutt, PEO | 1.000 | 8 | 11 | 0 | 0 | 11 | 0 |
| Himes, Ben, DTN* | .964 | 79 | 129 | 4 | 5 | 138 | 1 |
| Hogan, Billy, FTW | 1.000 | 4 | 7 | 0 | 0 | 7 | 0 |
| Hudson, Will, DTN | 1.000 | 2 | 7 | 0 | 0 | 7 | 0 |
| Jacobsen, Brock, CLN | 1.000 | 3 | 5 | 0 | 0 | 5 | 0 |
| Johnson, Josh, QC | 1.000 | 2 | 2 | 0 | 0 | 2 | 0 |
| Johnson, Ryan, FTW* | .833 | 8 | 10 | 0 | 2 | 12 | 0 |
| Kaplan, Jon, SBN | .989 | 97 | 174 | 11 | 2 | 187 | 3 |
| Kartler, Bryce, BTC* | .945 | 31 | 52 | 0 | 3 | 55 | 0 |
| Kimpton, Nick, CR* | .950 | 35 | 54 | 3 | 3 | 60 | 0 |
| Knoedler, Jason, WMI | .992 | 62 | 116 | 7 | 1 | 124 | 1 |
| Kolkhorst, Chris, FTW* | 1.000 | 12 | 19 | 2 | 0 | 21 | 0 |
| LaHair, Bryan, WIS* | .965 | 30 | 51 | 4 | 2 | 57 | 0 |
| Lopez, Baltazar, CR* | 1.000 | 2 | 3 | 0 | 0 | 3 | 0 |
| Lubanski, Christophe, BUR* | .980 | 125 | 242 | 4 | 5 | 251 | 0 |
| Macias, Drew, FTW* | .970 | 129 | 250 | 8 | 8 | 266 | 1 |
| Madrigal, Warner, CR | .976 | 26 | 39 | 2 | 1 | 42 | 0 |
| Majewski, Dustin, KNC* | .992 | 126 | 252 | 4 | 2 | 258 | 1 |
| Marquez, Uriak, LAN* | 1.000 | 1 | 1 | 0 | 0 | 1 | 0 |
| Mather, Joe, PEO | .968 | 39 | 57 | 4 | 2 | 63 | 0 |
| McCoy, Mike, PEO | 1.000 | 1 | 1 | 0 | 0 | 1 | 0 |
| McFall, Brian, BUR | .960 | 51 | 63 | 9 | 3 | 75 | 1 |
| McIntyre, Nick, WMI | 1.000 | 4 | 4 | 0 | 0 | 4 | 0 |
| McKinney, Garth, WMI | .954 | 113 | 180 | 6 | 9 | 195 | 1 |
| McQuade, Tony, LAN | .982 | 90 | 162 | 4 | 3 | 169 | 0 |
| McRoberts, Mark, FTW | .971 | 15 | 32 | 1 | 1 | 34 | 0 |
| Mejia, Carlos, LAN | .981 | 63 | 98 | 7 | 2 | 107 | 0 |
| Metheny, Brenton, WIS* | 1.000 | 2 | 2 | 0 | 0 | 2 | 0 |
| Milons, Jereme, SBN | .938 | 9 | 15 | 0 | 1 | 16 | 0 |
| Monegan, Anthony, PEO* | .979 | 121 | 229 | 7 | 5 | 241 | 0 |
| Mora, Ruben, FTW | .973 | 21 | 33 | 3 | 1 | 37 | 0 |
| Moran, Javon, DTN | .961 | 24 | 48 | 1 | 2 | 51 | 1 |
| Moss, Steve, BLT | .966 | 95 | 220 | 4 | 8 | 232 | 1 |
| Moye, Alan, BUR | .957 | 13 | 20 | 2 | 1 | 23 | 1 |
| Nesbit, Michael, WIS | .977 | 68 | 119 | 7 | 3 | 129 | 0 |
| Nunez, Felix, CR | .971 | 20 | 34 | 0 | 1 | 35 | 0 |
| Olmstead, Walter, DTN | 1.000 | 5 | 5 | 0 | 0 | 5 | 0 |
| Pali, Matt, CR* | 1.000 | 61 | 77 | 1 | 0 | 78 | 0 |
| Parker, Tyler, PEO | .965 | 74 | 100 | 9 | 4 | 113 | 1 |
| Pattee, Ben, QC | 1.000 | 3 | 7 | 1 | 0 | 8 | 0 |
| Peel, Aaron, CR | .982 | 41 | 53 | 2 | 1 | 56 | 1 |
| Perez, Henry, FTW | 1.000 | 1 | 4 | 0 | 0 | 4 | 0 |
| Perez, Luis, KNC | .966 | 81 | 110 | 5 | 4 | 119 | 1 |
| Peterson, Brock, QC | .833 | 3 | 5 | 0 | 1 | 6 | 0 |
| Pickens, Jordan, FTW | .969 | 72 | 122 | 3 | 4 | 129 | 0 |
| Piepkorn, Jeremiah, DTN | 1.000 | 10 | 23 | 1 | 0 | 24 | 0 |
| Putnam, Dan, KNC* | .988 | 45 | 83 | 2 | 1 | 86 | 0 |
| Reynolds, Wilton, WMI | .833 | 4 | 5 | 0 | 1 | 6 | 0 |
| Rodriguez, Marcos, PEO* | 1.000 | 13 | 19 | 0 | 0 | 19 | 0 |
| Rodriguez, Sean, CR | .962 | 16 | 23 | 2 | 1 | 26 | 1 |
| Rogers, Nick, KNC | .968 | 76 | 121 | 1 | 4 | 126 | 0 |
| Rottino, Vinny, BLT | 1.000 | 32 | 53 | 2 | 0 | 55 | 0 |
| Rutgers, Paul, QC | .944 | 8 | 16 | 1 | 1 | 18 | 0 |
| Sabino, Luis, WMI | .970 | 98 | 186 | 8 | 6 | 200 | 4 |
| Schmidt, Jarrod, DTN | .958 | 21 | 43 | 3 | 2 | 48 | 0 |
| Senreiso, Juan, CLN | .946 | 31 | 52 | 1 | 3 | 56 | 0 |
| Sherman, Steve, PEO* | 1.000 | 7 | 14 | 0 | 0 | 14 | 0 |
| Smith, Kyle, DTN | .988 | 49 | 82 | 1 | 1 | 84 | 0 |
| Smith, Rashad, FTW* | 1.000 | 2 | 5 | 0 | 0 | 5 | 0 |
| Span, Denard, QC* | .992 | 64 | 123 | 2 | 1 | 126 | 1 |
| Spataro, Ryan, QC* | .948 | 81 | 141 | 6 | 8 | 155 | 0 |
| Springer, Kenard, BUR | .954 | 74 | 136 | 10 | 7 | 153 | 4 |
| Strait, Cody, DTN | .976 | 54 | 110 | 13 | 3 | 126 | 2 |
| Treadway, Jared, BTC | 1.000 | 14 | 13 | 0 | 0 | 13 | 0 |
| Tritle, Chris, KNC | .984 | 97 | 122 | 3 | 2 | 127 | 2 |
| Trofholz, Terry, BLT | .990 | 111 | 199 | 5 | 2 | 206 | 0 |
| Van Meetren, Jason, BTC | .941 | 39 | 78 | 2 | 5 | 85 | 0 |
| Vasquez, Willie, BTC | 1.000 | 9 | 9 | 0 | 0 | 9 | 0 |
| Villanova, Robert, BTC* | 1.000 | 5 | 3 | 0 | 0 | 3 | 0 |
| Wahlbrink, Brian, FTW | .985 | 125 | 249 | 8 | 4 | 261 | 2 |
| Walker, Chris, LAN | .993 | 122 | 268 | 6 | 2 | 276 | 1 |
| Walsh, Nick, BTC* | 1.000 | 16 | 26 | 0 | 0 | 26 | 0 |
| Wayment, Kory, KNC | .954 | 38 | 55 | 7 | 3 | 65 | 0 |
| Whitrock, Scott, QC | .961 | 124 | 254 | 17 | 11 | 282 | 4 |
| Wishy, Andrew, CLN* | .960 | 82 | 93 | 2 | 4 | 99 | 0 |
| Womack, Josh, WIS* | .989 | 101 | 178 | 10 | 2 | 190 | 5 |
| Zamojc, Mark, QC* | .956 | 73 | 127 | 4 | 6 | 137 | 0 |

## CATCHERS

| Player, Team | Pct. | G | PO | A | E | TC | DP | PB |
|---|---|---|---|---|---|---|---|---|
| Barton, Daric, PEO* | .975 | 52 | 381 | 48 | 11 | 440 | 4 | 11 |
| Benjamin, Casey, CLN | 1.000 | 1 | 3 | 0 | 0 | 3 | 0 | 0 |
| Brown, Trevor, KNC* | .979 | 25 | 129 | 11 | 3 | 143 | 0 | 5 |
| Carlin, Luke, FTW | .988 | 27 | 223 | 23 | 3 | 249 | 1 | 4 |
| Castillo, David, KNC | .993 | 87 | 683 | 76 | 5 | 764 | 2 | 6 |
| Clark, Douglas, CLN | .995 | 49 | 350 | 41 | 2 | 393 | 1 | 6 |
| Collins, Chris, WIS | .991 | 71 | 509 | 51 | 5 | 565 | 2 | 13 |
| Collins, Michael, CR | .989 | 13 | 78 | 16 | 1 | 95 | 2 | 1 |
| Conley, Evan, DTN | 1.000 | 3 | 16 | 1 | 0 | 17 | 0 | 1 |
| Corporan, Carlos, BLT | .980 | 29 | 217 | 26 | 5 | 248 | 1 | 4 |
| Donachie, Adam, BUR | .986 | 66 | 513 | 42 | 8 | 563 | 2 | 9 |
| Duenas, Tommy, CR | .974 | 61 | 453 | 37 | 13 | 503 | 0 | 13 |
| Foster, Brian, BUR | 1.000 | 2 | 3 | 0 | 0 | 3 | 0 | 1 |
| Fox, Jake, LAN | .980 | 78 | 569 | 78 | 13 | 660 | 1 | 25 |
| Geiger, Kyle, QC | .993 | 43 | 362 | 35 | 3 | 400 | 1 | 6 |
| Gonzalez, Luis, BUR | .995 | 48 | 359 | 27 | 2 | 388 | 2 | 9 |
| Graham, Andrew, WMI | .985 | 26 | 173 | 21 | 3 | 197 | 3 | 6 |
| Harriman, David, KNC | .997 | 40 | 330 | 25 | 1 | 356 | 0 | 8 |
| Hatcher, Justin, CLN | .997 | 46 | 292 | 28 | 1 | 321 | 1 | 4 |
| Johnson, Josh, QC | .990 | 44 | 284 | 28 | 3 | 315 | 3 | 5 |
| Kottaras, George, FTW | .991 | 50 | 399 | 27 | 4 | 430 | 2 | 5 |
| Kroski, Chris, DTN* | .983 | 9 | 53 | 6 | 1 | 60 | 0 | 1 |
| Lauderdale, Matt, FTW | .975 | 21 | 176 | 18 | 5 | 199 | 0 | 3 |
| Marcelli, Brandon, PEO | .989 | 21 | 155 | 19 | 2 | 176 | 0 | 0 |
| Marks, Tim, BLT | .981 | 27 | 180 | 24 | 4 | 208 | 1 | 2 |
| McIntyre, Nick, WMI | 1.000 | 1 | 1 | 0 | 0 | 1 | 0 | 0 |
| Medlin, CJ, LAN | .949 | 5 | 36 | 1 | 2 | 39 | 0 | 2 |
| Miller, Chris, FTW | .987 | 8 | 72 | 5 | 1 | 78 | 1 | 4 |
| Montero, Miguel, SBN* | .982 | 85 | 575 | 70 | 12 | 657 | 0 | 9 |
| Morton, Colt, FTW | .986 | 36 | 331 | 29 | 5 | 365 | 1 | 2 |
| Mottram, Allen, SBN | 1.000 | 5 | 30 | 1 | 0 | 31 | 0 | 1 |
| Pagnozzi, Matthew, PEO | .994 | 73 | 467 | 57 | 3 | 527 | 2 | 18 |
| Palmer, Cody, PEO | 1.000 | 11 | 43 | 2 | 0 | 45 | 0 | 1 |
| Palmisano, Lou, BLT | .994 | 85 | 621 | 53 | 4 | 678 | 5 | 10 |
| Perez, Miguel, DTN | .975 | 73 | 565 | 69 | 16 | 650 | 3 | 10 |
| Phillips, Kyle, QC* | .989 | 59 | 471 | 51 | 6 | 528 | 2 | 6 |
| Purdom, John, DTN | .981 | 7 | 48 | 4 | 1 | 53 | 0 | 3 |
| Ramirez, Manuel, BLT | 1.000 | 2 | 4 | 2 | 0 | 6 | 0 | 1 |
| Reinking, Kevin, BUR | .989 | 28 | 170 | 9 | 2 | 181 | 0 | 4 |
| Richardson, Kevin, CLN | .993 | 57 | 360 | 38 | 3 | 401 | 1 | 6 |
| Rick, Alan, LAN* | .992 | 58 | 465 | 38 | 4 | 507 | 3 | 13 |
| Robles, Luis, BTC | 1.000 | 25 | 147 | 10 | 0 | 157 | 0 | 0 |
| Rojas, Tommy, BTC | .990 | 77 | 524 | 51 | 6 | 581 | 1 | 9 |
| Rose, Brian, SBN | .991 | 63 | 404 | 33 | 4 | 441 | 2 | 4 |
| Rosenthal, Ben, PEO* | 1.000 | 3 | 17 | 2 | 0 | 19 | 0 | 1 |
| Rottino, Vinny, BLT | .973 | 5 | 33 | 3 | 1 | 37 | 0 | 1 |
| RUCHTI, JUSTIN, WIS | .995 | 77 | 567 | 57 | 3 | 627 | 5 | 10 |
| Sanchez, Angel, BUR | 1.000 | 1 | 5 | 0 | 0 | 5 | 0 | 1 |
| Sanchez, Danilo, WMI | .988 | 74 | 493 | 74 | 7 | 574 | 2 | 8 |
| Santos, Omir, BTC | .991 | 55 | 416 | 43 | 4 | 463 | 1 | 7 |
| Schmidt, Jarrod, DTN | .750 | 1 | 3 | 0 | 1 | 4 | 0 | 0 |
| Tidball, Adam, LAN | 1.000 | 5 | 34 | 2 | 0 | 36 | 0 | 1 |
| Trezza, Alex, WMI* | .979 | 48 | 293 | 38 | 7 | 338 | 5 | 4 |
| Urgelles, Jeff, DTN | .968 | 54 | 423 | 37 | 15 | 475 | 1 | 10 |
| Wilson, Bobby, CR | .987 | 69 | 549 | 66 | 8 | 623 | 2 | 5 |

## PITCHERS

| Player, Team | Pct. | G | PO | A | E | TC | DP |
|---|---|---|---|---|---|---|---|
| Abraham, Paul, FTW | .800 | 37 | 1 | 7 | 2 | 10 | 1 |
| Abrams, Casey, WIS* | .889 | 37 | 4 | 4 | 1 | 9 | 1 |
| Acosta, Adam, PEO | .000 | 5 | 0 | 0 | 0 | 0 | 0 |
| Acosta, Nibaldo, WIS | .957 | 27 | 18 | 27 | 2 | 47 | 1 |
| Aguero, Miguel, PEO | 1.000 | 7 | 1 | 6 | 0 | 7 | 0 |
| Altman, Kevin, CLN | 1.000 | 2 | 1 | 0 | 0 | 1 | 0 |
| Atencio, Greg, BUR | .950 | 28 | 6 | 13 | 1 | 20 | 1 |
| Austen, David, CR | 1.000 | 30 | 2 | 12 | 0 | 14 | 1 |
| Baisley, Brad, BTC | 1.000 | 7 | 1 | 1 | 0 | 2 | 0 |
| Baldwin, Andy, WMI | 1.000 | 14 | 5 | 14 | 0 | 19 | 4 |
| Barkley, Richard, BTC | 1.000 | 4 | 1 | 0 | 0 | 1 | 0 |
| Barnes, Justin, BLT | 1.000 | 4 | 1 | 1 | 0 | 2 | 0 |
| Barrett, Ricky, QC* | 1.000 | 13 | 2 | 5 | 0 | 7 | 0 |
| Bay, Ronald, LAN | .950 | 28 | 16 | 22 | 2 | 40 | 2 |
| Beam, TJ, BTC | 1.000 | 11 | 2 | 0 | 0 | 2 | 0 |
| Bechtel, Chuck, FTW | 1.000 | 35 | 2 | 7 | 0 | 9 | 0 |
| Begnaud, Rusty, BUR | 1.000 | 1 | 0 | 1 | 0 | 1 | 1 |
| Benjamin, Casey, CLN | 1.000 | 3 | 0 | 1 | 0 | 1 | 0 |
| Beresford, Simon, BLT | .905 | 38 | 5 | 14 | 2 | 21 | 0 |
| Biggs, Billy, SBN | 1.000 | 31 | 1 | 6 | 0 | 7 | 0 |
| Bilke, Austin, WIS | 1.000 | 17 | 3 | 3 | 0 | 6 | 0 |
| Blackburn, Nick, QC | 1.000 | 20 | 9 | 10 | 0 | 19 | 1 |
| Blackwell, Brad, BTC | 1.000 | 6 | 0 | 2 | 0 | 2 | 0 |
| Bohorquez, Carlos, DTN | .875 | 25 | 3 | 4 | 1 | 8 | 1 |
| Bondurant, Steven, KNC* | .913 | 21 | 6 | 15 | 2 | 23 | 1 |
| Bonine, Eddie, FTW | 1.000 | 5 | 2 | 4 | 0 | 6 | 1 |
| Boughner, Anthony, DTN* | .800 | 7 | 2 | 2 | 1 | 5 | 1 |
| Braden, Dallas, KNC* | 1.000 | 5 | 0 | 3 | 0 | 3 | 0 |
| Brandon, Eric, QC | .929 | 45 | 5 | 8 | 1 | 14 | 0 |
| Bray, Steve, BUR | .857 | 24 | 2 | 4 | 1 | 7 | 0 |
| Brey, Josh, PEO* | 1.000 | 34 | 2 | 8 | 0 | 10 | 1 |
| Brown, Ira, BUR | 1.000 | 5 | 2 | 0 | 0 | 2 | 0 |
| Brown, Justin, PEO | .500 | 4 | 0 | 1 | 1 | 2 | 0 |
| Brumit, Matthew, BTC | 1.000 | 40 | 1 | 9 | 0 | 10 | 0 |
| Buckley, Allen, CR | 1.000 | 47 | 6 | 14 | 0 | 20 | 2 |
| Burch, Jason, PEO | 1.000 | 44 | 4 | 4 | 0 | 8 | 0 |
| Burgos, Ambiorix, BUR | .933 | 27 | 5 | 23 | 2 | 30 | 0 |
| Capuano, Chris, BLT* | 1.000 | 1 | 0 | 1 | 0 | 1 | 0 |
| Cashman, Brandon, CLN | 1.000 | 2 | 1 | 0 | 0 | 1 | 0 |
| Castillo, Ruben, WIS | 1.000 | 11 | 0 | 1 | 0 | 1 | 0 |
| Castle, Heath, BTC* | .917 | 42 | 1 | 10 | 1 | 12 | 0 |
| Chang, Kenly, WIS | .833 | 40 | 0 | 10 | 2 | 12 | 0 |
| Chavez, Jesse, CLN | .933 | 27 | 7 | 21 | 2 | 30 | 1 |
| Chick, Travis, FTW | 1.000 | 7 | 0 | 2 | 0 | 2 | 0 |
| Chico, Matt, SBN* | .941 | 14 | 4 | 12 | 1 | 17 | 1 |
| Christensen, Danny, BUR* | 1.000 | 1 | 0 | 1 | 0 | 1 | 0 |
| Ciccotelli, Michael, WIS* | .667 | 12 | 1 | 1 | 1 | 3 | 0 |
| Clippard, Tyler, BTC | .857 | 26 | 4 | 20 | 4 | 28 | 0 |
| Coffin, Ryan, SBN | .857 | 43 | 4 | 8 | 2 | 14 | 1 |
| Conden, Greg, FTW | .833 | 23 | 2 | 3 | 1 | 6 | 0 |
| Coonrod, Aaron, FTW | 1.000 | 29 | 1 | 6 | 0 | 7 | 0 |
| Corchado, Jose, KNC | .944 | 33 | 4 | 13 | 1 | 18 | 1 |
| Cordeiro, Chris, CLN | .923 | 29 | 3 | 9 | 1 | 13 | 0 |
| Correa, Cristobal, PEO | 1.000 | 19 | 10 | 5 | 0 | 15 | 0 |
| Coughlin, Chris, BUR | .864 | 14 | 7 | 12 | 3 | 22 | 1 |
| Crawford, Tristan, QC | .917 | 21 | 4 | 7 | 1 | 12 | 0 |
| Cremidan, Alexander, SBN | 1.000 | 32 | 0 | 5 | 0 | 5 | 1 |
| Crist, Kyle, BUR | 1.000 | 3 | 1 | 2 | 0 | 3 | 0 |
| Crowder, Justin, KNC* | 1.000 | 34 | 1 | 8 | 0 | 9 | 1 |
| Culpepper, Kevin, QC* | 1.000 | 35 | 1 | 8 | 0 | 9 | 0 |
| Cunningham, Tim, CLN* | .692 | 26 | 1 | 8 | 4 | 13 | 1 |
| Danks, John, CLN* | 1.000 | 14 | 1 | 6 | 0 | 7 | 1 |
| Davis, John-Paul, PEO | 1.000 | 2 | 1 | 2 | 0 | 3 | 0 |
| De La O, Danny, FTW* | .000 | 2 | 0 | 0 | 0 | 0 | 0 |
| DeHoyos, Gabe, BUR | .800 | 16 | 1 | 3 | 1 | 5 | 0 |
| DeJaynes, Brandon, PEO | 1.000 | 49 | 4 | 9 | 0 | 13 | 0 |
| Delacruz, Eulogio, WMI | 1.000 | 54 | 6 | 8 | 0 | 14 | 0 |
| Dempster, Ryan, LAN | 1.000 | 5 | 0 | 2 | 0 | 2 | 1 |
| DePaula, Julio, QC | 1.000 | 49 | 6 | 18 | 0 | 24 | 0 |
| Diamond, Thomas, CLN | 1.000 | 7 | 2 | 2 | 0 | 4 | 0 |
| Dillard, Timothy, BLT | .967 | 43 | 6 | 23 | 1 | 30 | 1 |
| Dossett, Dusty, BUR | .923 | 38 | 3 | 9 | 1 | 13 | 1 |
| Dove, Dennis, PEO | .000 | 2 | 0 | 0 | 0 | 0 | 0 |
| Dowdy, Justin, CR* | 1.000 | 1 | 0 | 2 | 0 | 2 | 0 |
| Drown, Eric, PEO | .818 | 24 | 5 | 4 | 2 | 11 | 1 |
| Dunwell, Chris, KNC | .947 | 28 | 10 | 26 | 2 | 38 | 2 |
| Durost, Kenneth, BLT | .857 | 24 | 7 | 11 | 3 | 21 | 1 |
| Edens, Kyle, DTN | .889 | 15 | 3 | 5 | 1 | 9 | 0 |
| Ekstrom, Michael, FTW | .750 | 3 | 2 | 1 | 1 | 4 | 0 |
| Encarnacion, Alexis, BUR | .750 | 27 | 0 | 3 | 1 | 4 | 0 |
| Esquivia, Manuel, BTC | 1.000 | 3 | 0 | 1 | 0 | 1 | 0 |

| Player, Team | Pct. | G | PO | A | E | TC | DP |
|---|---|---|---|---|---|---|---|
| Eveland, Dana, BLT* | .920 | 22 | 6 | 17 | 2 | 25 | 0 |
| Farfan, Alexander, DTN | .917 | 22 | 3 | 8 | 1 | 12 | 0 |
| Farnum, Matt, CLN | .964 | 28 | 12 | 15 | 1 | 28 | 1 |
| Feierabend, Ryan, WIS* | .867 | 26 | 10 | 42 | 8 | 60 | 1 |
| Feliz, Ranier, DTN | 1.000 | 6 | 0 | 1 | 0 | 1 | 0 |
| Ferreras, Yorkin, LAN* | 1.000 | 13 | 0 | 3 | 0 | 3 | 0 |
| Fillinger, Chad, WIS | 1.000 | 11 | 5 | 0 | 0 | 5 | 0 |
| Fischer, Sam, LAN | .000 | 18 | 0 | 0 | 1 | 1 | 0 |
| Fitzgerald, Ryan, LAN | .000 | 1 | 0 | 0 | 0 | 0 | 0 |
| Friedberg, Drew, KNC* | 1.000 | 8 | 0 | 1 | 0 | 1 | 0 |
| Frydendall, Craig, CLN* | .882 | 37 | 2 | 13 | 2 | 17 | 0 |
| Fyvie, Daniel, KNC | .897 | 59 | 9 | 17 | 3 | 29 | 1 |
| Garcia, Angel, QC | .000 | 7 | 0 | 0 | 0 | 0 | 0 |
| Garcia, Jairo, KNC | 1.000 | 25 | 1 | 1 | 0 | 2 | 0 |
| Garcia, Jose, CLN | .929 | 9 | 4 | 9 | 1 | 14 | 0 |
| Gardner, Mike, BTC | 1.000 | 43 | 5 | 8 | 0 | 13 | 0 |
| Garza, Justin, PEO | 1.000 | 29 | 3 | 6 | 0 | 9 | 0 |
| Gemmell, Don, DTN | 1.000 | 5 | 0 | 1 | 0 | 1 | 0 |
| George, Bradley, DTN | .800 | 22 | 2 | 2 | 1 | 5 | 0 |
| George, Jon, DTN | 1.000 | 18 | 6 | 7 | 0 | 13 | 2 |
| Gillman, Justin, DTN | 1.000 | 11 | 1 | 5 | 0 | 6 | 0 |
| Girardeau, Clark, FTW | .875 | 13 | 6 | 8 | 2 | 16 | 0 |
| Glant, Dustin, SBN | .944 | 29 | 4 | 13 | 1 | 18 | 0 |
| Gomez, Abel, BTC* | .857 | 28 | 6 | 18 | 4 | 28 | 1 |
| Goodman, Chris, BUR | .938 | 23 | 16 | 14 | 2 | 32 | 1 |
| Gragg, John, BUR* | .944 | 26 | 11 | 6 | 1 | 18 | 0 |
| Granado, Jan, DTN* | 1.000 | 13 | 2 | 7 | 0 | 9 | 1 |
| Gregg, Grant, FTW* | 1.000 | 12 | 1 | 5 | 0 | 6 | 1 |
| Gross, Kris, LAN | 1.000 | 23 | 4 | 8 | 0 | 12 | 0 |
| Grybash, Daniel, BLT | .800 | 40 | 4 | 4 | 2 | 10 | 1 |
| Guevara, Carlos, DTN | .714 | 44 | 1 | 4 | 2 | 7 | 0 |
| Guthrie, Sazi, FTW | .867 | 35 | 4 | 9 | 2 | 15 | 0 |
| Harben, Adam, QC | .970 | 26 | 12 | 20 | 1 | 33 | 1 |
| Harmsen, Brandon, BTC | .917 | 35 | 5 | 17 | 2 | 24 | 1 |
| Hawk, Derek, DTN | .750 | 16 | 2 | 1 | 1 | 4 | 0 |
| Hawk, Tommy, BLT | 1.000 | 2 | 1 | 0 | 0 | 1 | 0 |
| Hayhurst, Dirk, FTW | 1.000 | 26 | 3 | 21 | 0 | 24 | 0 |
| Heaston, Bryan, WIS | 1.000 | 25 | 1 | 3 | 0 | 4 | 0 |
| Hedden, Wayne, CR | .750 | 20 | 1 | 2 | 1 | 4 | 0 |
| Herrera, Cesar, CLN | 1.000 | 44 | 4 | 16 | 0 | 20 | 1 |
| Hindman, Scott, CR* | 1.000 | 27 | 2 | 3 | 0 | 5 | 1 |
| Hines, Matthew, QC | 1.000 | 7 | 1 | 2 | 0 | 3 | 0 |
| Hogan, Gary, CLN | 1.000 | 14 | 2 | 2 | 0 | 4 | 0 |
| Homer, Chris, WMI | 1.000 | 39 | 3 | 0 | 0 | 3 | 0 |
| Hrynio, Michael, WIS | .857 | 54 | 4 | 8 | 2 | 14 | 2 |
| Hudson, Will, DTN | 1.000 | 3 | 1 | 1 | 0 | 2 | 0 |
| Hughes, Dusty, BUR* | 1.000 | 8 | 6 | 20 | 0 | 26 | 1 |
| Hunter, Chris, CR | .912 | 25 | 15 | 16 | 3 | 34 | 2 |
| Jepsen, Kevin, CR | .892 | 27 | 8 | 25 | 4 | 37 | 4 |
| Jones, Jason, BTC | 1.000 | 6 | 3 | 2 | 0 | 5 | 0 |
| Jones, Justin, LAN* | .923 | 14 | 4 | 8 | 1 | 13 | 0 |
| Jones, Justin, QC* | 1.000 | 7 | 1 | 7 | 0 | 8 | 1 |
| Jones, Justin, LAN-QC* | .952 | 21 | 5 | 15 | 1 | 21 | 1 |
| Jordan, Brantley, PEO* | 1.000 | 50 | 2 | 7 | 0 | 9 | 0 |
| Juarez, William, SBN | 1.000 | 7 | 3 | 5 | 0 | 8 | 0 |
| Kaanoi, Kahi, BUR | 1.000 | 22 | 3 | 3 | 0 | 6 | 0 |
| Kalita, Ryan, LAN | 1.000 | 18 | 3 | 2 | 0 | 5 | 1 |
| Keller, Frankie, DTN* | 1.000 | 11 | 2 | 7 | 0 | 9 | 1 |
| Kemlo, Chris, BTC | 1.000 | 5 | 1 | 3 | 0 | 4 | 0 |
| Kinsey, Chris, SBN | .871 | 28 | 8 | 19 | 4 | 31 | 1 |
| Kirsten, Joel, CLN* | .958 | 38 | 5 | 18 | 1 | 24 | 1 |
| Klatt, Ryan, FTW | .917 | 25 | 3 | 8 | 1 | 12 | 0 |
| Kloosterman, Gregory, BLT* | .867 | 19 | 4 | 9 | 2 | 15 | 0 |
| Knoedler, Jason, WMI | 1.000 | 1 | 1 | 0 | 0 | 1 | 0 |
| Knoff, Justin, DTN | .667 | 5 | 0 | 2 | 1 | 3 | 0 |
| Knox, Brad, KNC | .969 | 26 | 16 | 15 | 1 | 32 | 0 |
| Lambert, Chris, PEO | .833 | 9 | 1 | 4 | 1 | 6 | 0 |
| Leclair, Aric, SBN* | 1.000 | 11 | 0 | 2 | 0 | 2 | 0 |
| Leon, Brigmer, KNC | .917 | 46 | 6 | 16 | 2 | 24 | 1 |
| Liebeck, Jared, SBN | 1.000 | 12 | 1 | 7 | 0 | 8 | 0 |
| Lorenzo, Matt, CLN | 1.000 | 17 | 3 | 4 | 0 | 7 | 0 |
| Lundgren, Wayne, PEO | .889 | 33 | 4 | 4 | 1 | 9 | 0 |
| Mackintosh, Jason, WIS* | .957 | 33 | 3 | 19 | 1 | 23 | 0 |
| Mallett, Justin, DTN | .667 | 18 | 1 | 5 | 3 | 9 | 0 |
| Marmol, Carlos, LAN | .931 | 26 | 9 | 18 | 2 | 29 | 3 |
| Marshall, Sean, LAN* | 1.000 | 7 | 3 | 5 | 0 | 8 | 0 |
| Martinez, Cristhian, WMI | .765 | 12 | 6 | 7 | 4 | 17 | 0 |
| Mateo, Juan, LAN | 1.000 | 53 | 3 | 9 | 0 | 12 | 0 |
| Mattoon, Brian, CLN* | .941 | 32 | 4 | 28 | 2 | 34 | 2 |
| Mauer, Billy, QC | 1.000 | 23 | 3 | 2 | 0 | 5 | 0 |
| McClellan, Kyle, PEO | .958 | 24 | 10 | 13 | 1 | 24 | 3 |
| McClellan, Robbie, BUR | .909 | 19 | 2 | 8 | 1 | 11 | 0 |

| Player, Team | Pct. | G | PO | A | E | TC | DP |
|---|---|---|---|---|---|---|---|
| McCoy, Mike, PEO | .500 | 1 | 0 | 1 | 1 | 2 | 0 |
| McGirr, Mike, KNC | 1.000 | 16 | 3 | 5 | 0 | 8 | 0 |
| McKenna, Daniel, BLT | .500 | 11 | 1 | 0 | 1 | 2 | 1 |
| Mead, David, FTW | .636 | 18 | 3 | 4 | 4 | 11 | 0 |
| Medlock, Calvin, DTN | .800 | 22 | 5 | 7 | 3 | 15 | 0 |
| Meek, Evan, QC | 1.000 | 3 | 1 | 1 | 0 | 2 | 0 |
| Mendez, Adalberto, LAN | .923 | 56 | 4 | 8 | 1 | 13 | 0 |
| Metzger, Jon, BUR * | 1.000 | 6 | 1 | 1 | 0 | 2 | 0 |
| Michael, Mark, PEO | .935 | 20 | 11 | 18 | 2 | 31 | 2 |
| Mock, Garrett, SBN | .833 | 8 | 2 | 8 | 2 | 12 | 0 |
| Mondesir, James, PEO | .000 | 12 | 0 | 0 | 0 | 0 | 0 |
| Montalbo, Brian, BLT | .929 | 24 | 9 | 17 | 2 | 28 | 2 |
| Moore, Ben, BTC | 1.000 | 27 | 3 | 4 | 0 | 7 | 0 |
| Moore, Daniel, FTW* | 1.000 | 4 | 0 | 2 | 0 | 2 | 0 |
| Moore, Nate, BUR | 1.000 | 19 | 3 | 4 | 0 | 7 | 0 |
| Moorhead, Michael, WIS | .842 | 25 | 4 | 12 | 3 | 19 | 1 |
| Morban, Carlos, CR | 1.000 | 28 | 2 | 3 | 0 | 5 | 0 |
| Moreira, Greg, BLT | .696 | 27 | 2 | 14 | 7 | 23 | 1 |
| Moreno, Abel, CR | .963 | 25 | 7 | 19 | 1 | 27 | 2 |
| Mosquea, Daniel, SBN* | 1.000 | 41 | 0 | 7 | 0 | 7 | 1 |
| Muegge, Danny, SBN | .969 | 26 | 13 | 18 | 1 | 32 | 1 |
| Mullis, Jake, BUR | .800 | 14 | 2 | 2 | 1 | 5 | 0 |
| Myers, Damien, WMI* | .857 | 24 | 2 | 4 | 1 | 7 | 0 |
| Nolen, Walt, LAN | .000 | 3 | 0 | 0 | 0 | 0 | 0 |
| Noriega, Luis, DTN | 1.000 | 8 | 5 | 1 | 0 | 6 | 0 |
| O`Brien, Weston, LAN | .750 | 16 | 1 | 2 | 1 | 4 | 0 |
| O`Flaherty, Eric, WIS* | .625 | 12 | 1 | 4 | 3 | 8 | 0 |
| Oldham, Thomas, WIS* | .788 | 19 | 6 | 20 | 7 | 33 | 0 |
| Ovalles, Juan, WIS | 1.000 | 25 | 1 | 5 | 0 | 6 | 0 |
| Pablos, Rene, LAN | 1.000 | 8 | 0 | 1 | 0 | 1 | 0 |
| Pals, Jordan, PEO | .857 | 12 | 2 | 10 | 2 | 14 | 3 |
| Parisi, Michael, PEO | .750 | 6 | 2 | 4 | 2 | 8 | 0 |
| Paz, Jackson, PEO* | .000 | 26 | 0 | 0 | 0 | 0 | 0 |
| Pelland, Tyler, DTN* | 1.000 | 14 | 1 | 3 | 0 | 4 | 0 |
| Pena, Luis, BLT | .943 | 21 | 8 | 25 | 2 | 35 | 0 |
| Pence, Howie, FTW | .846 | 44 | 1 | 10 | 2 | 13 | 1 |
| Perez, Henry, FTW | 1.000 | 21 | 2 | 0 | 0 | 2 | 0 |
| Perkins, Glen, QC* | 1.000 | 9 | 4 | 3 | 0 | 7 | 0 |
| Perry, Brandon, WIS* | .000 | 11 | 0 | 0 | 0 | 0 | 0 |
| Peterson, Trent, KNC* | .889 | 21 | 1 | 15 | 2 | 18 | 0 |
| Petrick, Billy, LAN | .960 | 26 | 7 | 17 | 1 | 25 | 2 |
| Petty, Chad, PEO* | .000 | 2 | 0 | 0 | 1 | 1 | 0 |
| Pickens, JR, KNC | .889 | 54 | 8 | 8 | 2 | 18 | 1 |
| Pomeranz, Stuart, PEO | .692 | 17 | 3 | 6 | 4 | 13 | 0 |
| Posey, Micah, CR* | 1.000 | 9 | 4 | 6 | 0 | 10 | 0 |
| Pratt, Andy, LAN* | .000 | 5 | 0 | 0 | 1 | 1 | 0 |
| Prior, Mark, LAN | 1.000 | 2 | 0 | 1 | 0 | 1 | 0 |
| Prunty, TJ, QC | 1.000 | 10 | 0 | 1 | 0 | 1 | 0 |
| Pullin, Aaron, CR | 1.000 | 47 | 8 | 6 | 0 | 14 | 0 |
| Quezada, Elvys, BTC | .769 | 15 | 1 | 9 | 3 | 13 | 1 |
| Ransom, Robert, LAN | 1.000 | 11 | 9 | 20 | 0 | 29 | 0 |
| Rapada, Clay, LAN* | .865 | 57 | 5 | 27 | 5 | 37 | 2 |
| Rauch, Brian, BLT | .000 | 1 | 0 | 0 | 0 | 0 | 0 |
| Ray, Ronnie, CR | 1.000 | 6 | 3 | 2 | 0 | 5 | 1 |
| Rice, Trey, DTN* | .818 | 38 | 4 | 5 | 2 | 11 | 0 |
| Righter, Matt, WMI | 1.000 | 5 | 0 | 1 | 0 | 1 | 0 |
| Rival, Kevin, BLT | 1.000 | 13 | 3 | 1 | 0 | 4 | 0 |
| Robinson, Ronnie, FTW | 1.000 | 10 | 0 | 1 | 0 | 1 | 0 |
| Rocha, Angel, SBN* | 1.000 | 9 | 1 | 4 | 0 | 5 | 1 |
| Rodriguez, Jermy, WMI | 1.000 | 37 | 1 | 5 | 0 | 6 | 0 |
| Rodriguez, Manuel, KNC | .818 | 40 | 7 | 11 | 4 | 22 | 1 |
| Rodriguez, Rafael, CR | .714 | 7 | 3 | 2 | 2 | 7 | 0 |
| Rogers, Brian, WMI | 1.000 | 25 | 11 | 16 | 0 | 27 | 0 |
| Ronz, Kenon, WMI* | 1.000 | 52 | 1 | 5 | 0 | 6 | 0 |
| Roper, Derek, PEO | 1.000 | 6 | 2 | 1 | 0 | 3 | 0 |
| Rosa, Carlos, BUR | 1.000 | 8 | 4 | 8 | 0 | 12 | 1 |
| Rosales, Leo, FTW | .833 | 53 | 3 | 7 | 2 | 12 | 2 |
| Rose, Brad, WIS | 1.000 | 15 | 1 | 2 | 0 | 3 | 0 |
| Rosen, Mark, SBN* | .857 | 29 | 3 | 9 | 2 | 14 | 0 |
| Sager, Brian, SBN | .000 | 4 | 0 | 0 | 0 | 0 | 0 |
| Sanchez, Adiel, KNC* | .667 | 8 | 0 | 2 | 1 | 3 | 0 |
| Santo, Brian, WMI | .813 | 45 | 3 | 10 | 3 | 16 | 1 |
| Sarmiento, Williams, CLN | 1.000 | 8 | 1 | 3 | 0 | 4 | 0 |
| Sawatski, Jay, QC* | 1.000 | 15 | 2 | 3 | 0 | 5 | 0 |
| Scalamandre, Rich, PEO | 1.000 | 5 | 0 | 3 | 0 | 3 | 0 |
| Scarbery, Chad, SBN | .947 | 30 | 6 | 12 | 1 | 19 | 0 |
| Schutt, Chris, QC | .821 | 29 | 6 | 17 | 5 | 28 | 1 |
| Schweitzer, Scott, PEO* | 1.000 | 15 | 1 | 1 | 0 | 2 | 0 |
| Seely, Nick, CLN | 1.000 | 6 | 0 | 1 | 0 | 1 | 0 |
| Segovia, Omar, DTN* | 1.000 | 10 | 1 | 1 | 0 | 2 | 0 |
| Shafer, David, DTN | .833 | 31 | 3 | 7 | 2 | 12 | 0 |
| Sherman, Justin, BUR | 1.000 | 4 | 3 | 3 | 0 | 6 | 1 |
| Simard, Michel, CR | .952 | 19 | 3 | 17 | 1 | 21 | 2 |
| Simonitsch, Errol, QC* | .889 | 20 | 4 | 12 | 2 | 18 | 1 |
| Slaten, Doug, SBN* | 1.000 | 36 | 1 | 7 | 0 | 8 | 0 |
| Smiley, Gerald, CLN | 1.000 | 6 | 0 | 1 | 0 | 1 | 0 |
| Smith, Jesse, CR | .773 | 39 | 3 | 14 | 5 | 22 | 1 |
| Smith, Joshua, BTC | .400 | 34 | 0 | 2 | 3 | 5 | 0 |
| Soteropoulos, Peter, PEO* | .923 | 20 | 4 | 8 | 1 | 13 | 0 |
| Speigner, Levale, QC | 1.000 | 22 | 1 | 7 | 0 | 8 | 0 |
| Steidlmayer, Luke, FTW | 1.000 | 3 | 0 | 2 | 0 | 2 | 0 |
| Steinborn, Chris, WMI* | .875 | 27 | 8 | 34 | 6 | 48 | 4 |
| Stephens, Amad, BTC | .875 | 13 | 3 | 4 | 1 | 8 | 0 |
| Sterry, Vern, FTW | 1.000 | 5 | 0 | 1 | 0 | 1 | 0 |
| Stertzbach, Von, CR | 1.000 | 9 | 0 | 1 | 0 | 1 | 0 |
| Stetter, Mitchel, BLT* | 1.000 | 24 | 3 | 3 | 0 | 6 | 0 |
| Stiles, Brad, BUR* | .875 | 13 | 1 | 6 | 1 | 8 | 1 |
| Stitt, Brian, WIS | .818 | 45 | 3 | 6 | 2 | 11 | 0 |
| Street, Huston, KNC | 1.000 | 9 | 0 | 2 | 0 | 2 | 0 |
| Tata, Jordan, WMI | .939 | 28 | 14 | 32 | 3 | 49 | 1 |
| Taubenheim, Ty, BLT | 1.000 | 47 | 4 | 9 | 0 | 13 | 1 |
| Tautor, Peter, QC | .778 | 42 | 2 | 5 | 2 | 9 | 0 |
| Thigpen, Josh, DTN | .786 | 16 | 4 | 7 | 3 | 14 | 0 |
| Thompson, Sean, FTW* | .938 | 27 | 5 | 40 | 3 | 48 | 0 |
| Thorp, Paul, BTC | .889 | 55 | 3 | 5 | 1 | 9 | 1 |
| Tierney, Chris, FTW* | .800 | 15 | 3 | 17 | 5 | 25 | 0 |
| Till, Brock, DTN | 1.000 | 39 | 11 | 12 | 0 | 23 | 2 |
| Tindell, Matt, WIS | 1.000 | 6 | 1 | 1 | 0 | 2 | 2 |
| Tomey, Anthony, WMI | .917 | 41 | 6 | 5 | 1 | 12 | 0 |
| Torres, Jaime, PEO | 1.000 | 8 | 1 | 3 | 0 | 4 | 0 |
| Touchstone, Nick, CR* | .839 | 24 | 4 | 22 | 5 | 31 | 1 |
| Trout, Jared, KNC | .872 | 28 | 8 | 26 | 5 | 39 | 1 |
| Tyler, Scott, QC | .846 | 22 | 5 | 6 | 2 | 13 | 0 |
| Uhl, Jon, QC | 1.000 | 17 | 2 | 8 | 0 | 10 | 0 |
| Upwood, Jake, FTW* | 1.000 | 19 | 1 | 3 | 0 | 4 | 0 |
| Ursin, Dirt, DTN | 1.000 | 21 | 6 | 9 | 0 | 15 | 0 |
| Van Buren, Jermaine, LAN | 1.000 | 3 | 0 | 2 | 0 | 2 | 0 |
| Vanderplow, Randy, BTC | .000 | 14 | 0 | 0 | 0 | 0 | 0 |
| Varner, Matthew, FTW | 1.000 | 19 | 0 | 4 | 0 | 4 | 0 |
| Vasquez, Virgil, WMI | .949 | 27 | 11 | 26 | 2 | 39 | 1 |
| Vicente, Ruben, SBN | .933 | 45 | 5 | 9 | 1 | 15 | 1 |
| Villanueva, Carlos, BLT | 1.000 | 25 | 7 | 10 | 0 | 17 | 1 |
| Volquez, Edison, CLN | 1.000 | 22 | 6 | 7 | 0 | 13 | 1 |
| Wachman, Robert, DTN | 1.000 | 3 | 0 | 2 | 0 | 2 | 1 |
| Watts, Joldy, CLN | .813 | 40 | 2 | 11 | 3 | 16 | 0 |
| Weatherby, Charles, PEO | 1.000 | 9 | 1 | 3 | 0 | 4 | 0 |
| Wells, Jared, FTW | .875 | 14 | 4 | 10 | 2 | 16 | 0 |
| Wells, Randy, LAN | .947 | 36 | 10 | 8 | 1 | 19 | 1 |
| Wheeler, Adam, BTC | 1.000 | 5 | 1 | 0 | 0 | 1 | 0 |
| White, Steven, BTC | .750 | 9 | 1 | 5 | 2 | 8 | 0 |
| Willett, Reid, LAN | .889 | 26 | 2 | 6 | 1 | 9 | 0 |
| Wilson, Joe, DTN* | 1.000 | 5 | 1 | 4 | 0 | 5 | 0 |
| Windsor, Jason, KNC | 1.000 | 9 | 3 | 1 | 0 | 4 | 0 |
| Wiseman, Steven, BTC | .000 | 8 | 0 | 0 | 0 | 0 | 0 |
| Worrell, Mark, PEO | 1.000 | 12 | 0 | 2 | 0 | 2 | 0 |
| Wright, Chase, BTC* | 1.000 | 18 | 6 | 21 | 0 | 27 | 2 |
| Zell, Daniel, WMI* | 1.000 | 30 | 2 | 14 | 0 | 16 | 3 |
| Zimmermann, Bob, CR | .938 | 53 | 3 | 12 | 1 | 16 | 1 |

## LEAGUE CHAMPIONS

| Year | Team | Pct. |
|---|---|---|
| 1947— | Belleville | .667 |
| | Belleville | .672 |
| 1948— | West Frankfort* | .708 |
| 1949— | Centralia | .627 |
| | Paducah (4th)† | .454 |
| 1950— | Centralia‡ | .675 |
| 1951— | Paris§ | .700 |
| | Danville (4th)† | .432 |
| 1952— | Danville∞ | .685 |
| | Decatur (3rd)† | .584 |
| 1953— | Decatur* | .576 |
| 1954— | Decatur | .587 |
| | Danville (2nd)‡ | .528 |
| 1955— | Dubuque* | .587 |
| 1956— | Paris▲ | .656 |
| | Dubuque | .603 |
| 1957— | Decatur▲ | .683 |
| | Clinton | .623 |
| 1958— | Michigan City | .623 |
| | Waterloo◆ | .613 |
| 1959— | Waterloo | .613 |
| | Waterloo | .613 |
| 1960— | Waterloo | .629 |
| | Waterloo | .677 |
| 1961— | Waterloo | .613 |
| | Quincy◆ | .594 |
| 1962— | Dubuque◆ | .667 |
| | Waterloo | .625 |
| 1963— | Clinton | .710 |
| | Clinton | .629 |

| Year | Team | Pct. |
|---|---|---|
| 1964— | Clinton | .667 |
| | Fox Cities◆ | .667 |
| 1965— | Burlington | .667 |
| | Burlington | .677 |
| 1966— | Fox Cities◆ | .689 |
| | Cedar Rapids | .762 |
| 1967— | Wisconsin Rapids | .685 |
| | Appleton◆ | .587 |
| 1968— | Decatur | .656 |
| | Quad Cities◆ | .648 |
| 1969— | Appleton | .648 |
| | Appleton | .690 |
| 1970— | Quincy◆ | .691 |
| | Quad Cities | .581 |
| 1971— | Appleton | .642 |
| | Quad Cities■ | .548 |
| 1972— | Appleton | .598 |
| | Danville■ | .584 |
| 1973— | Wisconsin Rapids■ | .562 |
| | Danville | .537 |
| 1974— | Appleton | .593 |
| | Danville■ | .517 |
| 1975— | Waterloo■ | .727 |
| | Quad Cities | .624 |
| 1976— | Waterloo■ | .600 |
| | Cedar Rapids | .595 |
| 1977— | Waterloo | .580 |
| | Burlington■ | .511 |
| 1978— | Appleton■ | .708 |
| | Burlington | .500 |
| 1979— | Waterloo | .600 |
| | Quad Cities■ | .579 |
| 1980— | Waterloo■ | .610 |
| | Quad Cities | .532 |
| 1981— | Wausau■ | .636 |
| | Quad Cities | .570 |
| 1982— | Madison | .626 |
| | Appleton▼ | .579 |
| 1983— | Appleton• | .635 |
| | Springfield | .576 |
| 1984— | Appleton• | .640 |
| | Springfield | .504 |
| 1985— | Kenosha▼ | .568 |
| | Peoria | .536 |
| 1986— | Springfield | .621 |
| | Waterloo▼ | .557 |
| 1987— | Springfield | .671 |
| | Kenosha▼ | .586 |
| 1988— | Cedar Rapids■ | .621 |
| | Kenosha | .579 |
| 1989— | South Bend■ | .644 |
| | Springfield | .541 |
| 1990— | Cedar Rapids | .657 |
| | Quad City■ | .579 |
| 1991— | Clinton■ | .583 |
| | Madison | .558 |
| 1992— | Quad City | .664 |
| | Cedar Rapids■ | .594 |
| 1993— | Clinton | .597 |
| | South Bend■ | .566 |
| 1994— | Rockford | .640 |
| | Cedar Rapids■ | .554 |
| 1995— | Beloit†† | .633 |
| | Michigan | .543 |
| 1996— | Wisconsin | .570 |
| | West Michigan†† | .558 |
| 1997— | Kane County | .507 |
| | Lansing** | .504 |
| 1998— | West Michigan†† | .593 |
| 1999— | Kane County | .569 |
| | Burlington** | .511 |
| 2000— | West Michigan | .629 |
| | Michigan‡‡ | .594 |
| 2001— | Kane County▲▲ | .638 |
| 2002— | Peoria‡‡ | .616 |
| 2003— | Lansing‡‡ | .511 |
| 2004— | West Michigan‡‡ | .496 |

*Won championship and four-club playoff. †Won four-club playoff. ‡Playoff finals canceled because of bad weather. §Won both halves of split season. ∞Won first half of split season and tied Paris for second-half title. ▲Won first-half title and four-team playoff. ◆Won split season playoff. ■League divided into Northern and Southern divisions and played split season. Playoff winner. ▼League divided into Northern, Central and Southern divisions. Playoff winner. •League divided into Northern, Central and Southern divisions; regular season and playoff winner. ††League divided into Eastern, Central and Western divisions; regular season and playoff winner. **League divided into Eastern, Central and Western divisions, playoff winner. ‡‡League divided into Eastern and Western divisions and played split season. Playoff winner. (NOTE—Known as Illinois State League in 1947-48 and Mississippi-Ohio Valley League from 1949 through 1955.) ▲▲League divided into Eastern and Western divisions and played split season; was leading final series of four-team playoff and was declared champion when Professional Baseball declared a stoppage of play.

# SOUTH ATLANTIC LEAGUE

## LEAGUE OFFICE

**President/secretary-treasurer**
John Moss
**Address**
P.O. Box 38
504 Crescent Hill
Kings Mountain, NC 28086
**Phone**
704-739-3466

**Teams (affiliation)**
Asheville Tourists (Rockies)
Augusta GreenJackets (Giants)
Capital City Bombers (Red Sox)
Charleston (S.C.) RiverDogs (Yankees)
Columbus Catfish (Dodgers)
Delmarva Shorebirds (Orioles)
Greensboro Grasshoppers (Marlins)
Hagerstown Suns (Mets)
Hickory Crawdads (Pirates)
Kannapolis Intimidators (White Sox)
Lake County Captains (Indians)
Lakewood BlueClaws (Phillies)
Lexington Legends (Astros)
Rome Braves (Braves)
Savannah Sand Gnats (Nationals)
West Virginia Power (Brewers)

## 2004 FINAL STANDINGS

### FIRST HALF

#### NORTHERN DIVISION

| Team | W | L | T | Pct. | GB |
|---|---|---|---|---|---|
| Charleston-WV | 41 | 29 | - | .586 | ... |
| Hickory | 39 | 31 | - | .557 | 2 |
| Lexington | 38 | 32 | - | .543 | 3 |
| Lake County | 36 | 34 | - | .514 | 5 |
| Delmarva | 35 | 34 | - | .507 | 51/2 |
| Kannapolis | 34 | 35 | - | .493 | 61/2 |
| Lakewood | 31 | 37 | - | .456 | 9 |
| Hagerstown | 28 | 39 | - | .418 | 111/2 |

#### SOUTHERN DIVISION

| Team | W | L | T | Pct. | GB |
|---|---|---|---|---|---|
| Capital City | 44 | 26 | - | .629 | ... |
| Charleston-SC | 40 | 29 | - | .580 | 31/2 |
| Rome | 40 | 30 | - | .571 | 4 |
| Columbus | 38 | 32 | - | .543 | 6 |
| Asheville | 31 | 39 | - | .443 | 13 |
| Augusta | 31 | 39 | - | .443 | 13 |
| Savannah | 30 | 40 | - | .429 | 14 |
| Greensboro | 20 | 50 | - | .286 | 24 |

### SECOND HALF

#### NORTHERN DIVISION

| Team | W | L | T | Pct. | GB |
|---|---|---|---|---|---|
| Hickory | 46 | 24 | - | .657 | ... |
| Charleston-WV | 43 | 27 | - | .614 | 3 |
| Lakewood | 39 | 30 | - | .565 | 61/2 |
| Lake County | 37 | 32 | - | .536 | 81/2 |
| Kannapolis | 35 | 35 | - | .500 | 11 |
| Delmarva | 34 | 35 | - | .493 | 111/2 |
| Lexington | 30 | 40 | - | .429 | 16 |
| Hagerstown | 21 | 49 | - | .300 | 25 |

#### SOUTHERN DIVISION

| Team | W | L | T | Pct. | GB |
|---|---|---|---|---|---|
| Capital City | 45 | 21 | - | .682 | ... |
| Charleston-SC | 36 | 34 | - | .514 | 11 |
| Augusta | 35 | 34 | - | .507 | 111/2 |
| Asheville | 33 | 36 | - | .478 | 131/2 |
| Columbus-A | 31 | 37 | - | .456 | 15 |
| Greensboro | 30 | 39 | - | .435 | 161/2 |
| Rome | 30 | 40 | - | .429 | 17 |
| Savannah | 28 | 40 | - | .412 | 18 |

### COMPOSITE

| Team | W | L | T | PCT | GB | CAP | HCK | CWV | CSC | LCO | LWD | ROM | CMB | DEL | KAN | LEX | AUG | ASH | SAV | GBO | HAG |
|---|---|---|---|---|---|---|---|---|---|---|---|---|---|---|---|---|---|---|---|---|---|
| Capital City (Mets) | 89 | 47 | - | .654 | — | X | 3 | 3 | 7 | 2 | 1 | 11 | 10 | 1 | 3 | 0 | 16 | 10 | 6 | 13 | 3 |
| Hickory (Pirates) | 85 | 55 | - | .607 | 6 | 1 | X | 10 | 3 | 8 | 7 | 3 | 3 | 10 | 9 | 12 | 3 | 2 | 2 | 2 | 10 |
| Charl.-WV (Blue Jays) | 84 | 56 | - | .600 | 7 | 1 | 7 | X | 0 | 7 | 8 | 4 | 4 | 10 | 12 | 11 | 1 | 4 | 3 | 4 | 8 |
| Charl.-SC (Devil Rays) | 76 | 63 | - | .547 | 141/2 | 5 | 1 | 4 | X | 2 | 3 | 6 | 8 | 2 | 2 | 2 | 6 | 11 | 14 | 8 | 3 |
| Lake County (Indians) | 73 | 66 | - | .525 | 171/2 | 1 | 6 | 5 | 2 | X | 9 | 1 | 3 | 11 | 5 | 7 | 3 | 3 | 2 | 2 | 13 |
| Lakewood (Phillies) | 70 | 67 | - | .511 | 191/2 | 3 | 6 | 7 | 1 | 8 | X | 1 | 0 | 5 | 8 | 7 | 2 | 2 | 4 | 3 | 13 |
| Rome (Braves) | 70 | 70 | - | .500 | 21 | 3 | 1 | 0 | 9 | 3 | 3 | X | 12 | 2 | 3 | 2 | 8 | 5 | 7 | 9 | 3 |
| Columbus (Dodgers) | 69 | 69 | - | .500 | 21 | 5 | 1 | 0 | 8 | 1 | 4 | 7 | X | 1 | 4 | 2 | 11 | 7 | 7 | 9 | 2 |
| Delmarva (Orioles) | 69 | 69 | - | .500 | 21 | 2 | 4 | 6 | 2 | 8 | 11 | 2 | 3 | X | 5 | 6 | 3 | 1 | 4 | 4 | 8 |
| Kannapolis (White Sox) | 69 | 70 | - | .496 | 211/2 | 1 | 10 | 4 | 2 | 10 | 6 | 1 | 0 | 8 | X | 10 | 2 | 1 | 3 | 4 | 7 |
| Lexington (Astros) | 68 | 72 | - | .486 | 23 | 4 | 4 | 8 | 2 | 8 | 7 | 2 | 2 | 7 | 7 | X | 2 | 3 | 2 | 3 | 7 |
| Augusta(Red Sox) | 66 | 73 | - | .475 | 241/2 | 6 | 1 | 3 | 6 | 1 | 2 | 8 | 3 | 1 | 2 | 2 | X | 11 | 8 | 8 | 4 |
| Asheville (Rockies) | 64 | 75 | - | .460 | 261/2 | 6 | 2 | 0 | 5 | 1 | 2 | 8 | 7 | 3 | 3 | 1 | 5 | X | 7 | 11 | 3 |
| Savannah (Expos) | 58 | 80 | - | .420 | 32 | 5 | 2 | 1 | 9 | 2 | 0 | 9 | 8 | 0 | 1 | 2 | 4 | 7 | X | 7 | 2 |
| Greensboro (Marlins) | 50 | 89 | - | .360 | 401/2 | 3 | 2 | 0 | 6 | 2 | 1 | 6 | 4 | 0 | 0 | 1 | 8 | 7 | 9 | X | 2 |
| Hagerstown (Giants) | 4 9 | 88 | - | .358 | 401/2 | 1 | 5 | 5 | 1 | 3 | 5 | 1 | 2 | 9 | 6 | 7 | 0 | 1 | 2 | 2 | X |

Major league affiliations in parentheses.

PLAYOFFS: Hickory defeated Charleston-West Virginia two games to none; Hickory defeated Capital City three games to none to win championship.

REGULAR-SEASON ATTENDANCE: Asheville, 137,938; Augusta, 159,378; Capital City, 100,798; Charleston-SC, 255,790; Charleston-WV, 125,979; Columbus, 56,325; Delmarva, 219,200; Greensboro, 197,037; Hagerstown, 128,508; Hickory, 178,439; Kannapolis, 105,214; Lake County, 406,096; Lakewood, 440,521; Lexington, 401,191; Rome, 245,724; Savannah, 117,047; Total attendance—3,137,247. All-Star game at Joseph P. Riley Jr. Park—5,173.

MANAGERS: Asheville, Joe Mikulik; Augusta, Chad Epperson; Capital City, Jack Lind; Charleston-SC, Ken Joyce; Charleston-WV, Steve Livesey; Columbus, Dann Bilardello; Delmarva, Bien Figueroa; Greensboro, Steve Phillips; Hagerstown, Mike Ramsey; Hickory, Dave Clark; Kannapolis, Chris Cron; Lake County, Luis Rivera; Lexington, Ivan Dejesus; Rome, Rocket Wheeler; Savannah, Bobby Henley.

ALL-STAR TEAM: Manager—Jack Lind, Capital City; RHP—Thomas Mastney, Charleston-WV; LHP—Chuck James, Rome; C—Robinson Diaz, Charleston-WV; C—Colt Simmons, Charleston-SC; 1B—Jon Benick, Hickory; 2B—Martin Prado, Rome; SS—Chin-Lung Hu, Columbus; 3B—Ian Stewart, Asheville; UTL-IF—Kevin Kouzmanoff; OF—Brandon Moss, Augusta; O—Delmon Young, Charleston-SC; OF —Josh Anderson, Lexington; UTL-OF—Ryan Goleski, Lake County; DH—Ryan Harvey, Capital city; Beau Hearod, Lexington; Most Outstanding Pitcher—Chuck James, Rome; Most Valuable Player—Brandon Moss, Augusta. Most Outstanding Prospect—Delmon Young, Charleston-SC. Manager of the Year—Jack Lind, Capital City.

# 2004 BATTING

## TEAM

| Team | G | TPA | AB | R | H | TB | 2B | 3B | HR | RBI | SH | SF | HP | BB | IBB | SO | SB | CS | GDP | LOB | ShO | Avg. | OBP | Slg. |
|---|---|---|---|---|---|---|---|---|---|---|---|---|---|---|---|---|---|---|---|---|---|---|---|---|
| Hickory | 140 | --- | 4720 | 758 | 1304 | 2044 | 243 | 46 | 135 | 695 | 39 | 44 | 89 | 462 | 17 | 906 | 159 | 54 | 78 | --- | --- | .276 | .349 | .433 |
| Capital City | 136 | --- | 4566 | 853 | 1250 | 2074 | 274 | 26 | 166 | 749 | 40 | 57 | 112 | 494 | 13 | 1111 | 135 | 52 | 68 | --- | -- | .274 | .355 | .454 |
| Lake County | 139 | --- | 4698 | 711 | 1278 | 1918 | 219 | 44 | 111 | 657 | 44 | 50 | 90 | 453 | 13 | 997 | 111 | 59 | 99 | --- | -- | .272 | .344 | .408 |
| Lakewood | 137 | --- | 4607 | 718 | 1240 | 1878 | 285 | 43 | 89 | 644 | 37 | 50 | 94 | 543 | 11 | 1025 | 163 | 64 | 80 | --- | -- | .269 | .355 | .408 |
| Columbus | 138 | --- | 4591 | 710 | 1227 | 1885 | 247 | 45 | 107 | 634 | 66 | 41 | 80 | 390 | 12 | 984 | 146 | 81 | 84 | --- | -- | .267 | .333 | .411 |
| Charl.-SC | 139 | --- | 4712 | 733 | 1250 | 1880 | 225 | 39 | 109 | 656 | 49 | 36 | 84 | 472 | 23 | 1090 | 150 | 59 | 82 | --- | -- | .265 | .340 | .399 |
| Rome | 140 | --- | 4671 | 650 | 1239 | 1901 | 263 | 39 | 107 | 572 | 25 | 26 | 78 | 352 | 11 | 1128 | 123 | 59 | 99 | --- | -- | .265 | .326 | .407 |
| Asheville | 139 | --- | 4647 | 738 | 1228 | 2039 | 268 | 24 | 165 | 682 | 21 | 35 | 75 | 521 | 17 | 1082 | 177 | 72 | 82 | --- | -- | .264 | .346 | .439 |
| Charl.-WV | 140 | --- | 4644 | 673 | 1205 | 1754 | 230 | 26 | 89 | 618 | 27 | 52 | 92 | 536 | 13 | 1140 | 54 | 38 | 112 | --- | -- | .259 | .344 | .378 |
| Kannapolis | 140 | --- | 4667 | 637 | 1209 | 1905 | 271 | 25 | 125 | 585 | 38 | 32 | 76 | 420 | 10 | 1085 | 138 | 60 | 59 | --- | -- | .259 | .328 | .408 |
| Lexington | 140 | --- | 4634 | 690 | 1192 | 1781 | 233 | 25 | 102 | 613 | 60 | 42 | 95 | 491 | 10 | 975 | 182 | 65 | 83 | --- | -- | .257 | .338 | .384 |
| Delmarva | 138 | --- | 4561 | 668 | 1172 | 1784 | 243 | 39 | 97 | 621 | 47 | 41 | 86 | 517 | 6 | 1018 | 118 | 46 | 80 | --- | -- | .257 | .341 | .391 |
| Augusta | 139 | --- | 4684 | 655 | 1192 | 1697 | 217 | 33 | 74 | 593 | 25 | 52 | 104 | 516 | 16 | 1041 | 109 | 63 | 83 | --- | -- | .254 | .338 | .362 |
| Hagerstown | 138 | --- | 4586 | 607 | 1146 | 1741 | 230 | 25 | 105 | 553 | 37 | 30 | 97 | 479 | 8 | 1036 | 88 | 49 | 112 | --- | -- | .250 | .332 | .380 |
| Greensboro | 139 | --- | 4591 | 611 | 1115 | 1733 | 213 | 27 | 117 | 555 | 34 | 23 | 80 | 394 | 2 | 1234 | 112 | 38 | 95 | --- | -- | .243 | .312 | .377 |
| Savannah | 138 | --- | 4483 | 579 | 1079 | 1604 | 219 | 27 | 84 | 529 | 41 | 34 | 70 | 454 | 11 | 1050 | 107 | 45 | 73 | --- | -- | .241 | .318 | .358 |

## INDIVIDUAL

### TOP QUALIFIERS FOR BATTING CHAMPIONSHIP

Minimum 378 plate appearances. *Lefthanded batter. †Switch-hitter.

| Player, Team | G | TPA | AB | R | H | TB | 2B | 3B | HR | RBI | SH | SF | HP | BB | IBB | SO | SB | CS | GDP | Avg. | OBP | Slg. |
|---|---|---|---|---|---|---|---|---|---|---|---|---|---|---|---|---|---|---|---|---|---|---|
| Moss, Brandon, Augusta * | 109 | 490 | 433 | 66 | 147 | 223 | 25 | 6 | 13 | 101 | 0 | 7 | 4 | 46 | 4 | 75 | 19 | 8 | 8 | .339 | .402 | .515 |
| Kouzmanoff, Kevin, Lake County | 123 | 531 | 473 | 74 | 156 | 249 | 35 | 5 | 16 | 87 | 0 | 5 | 9 | 44 | 0 | 75 | 5 | 4 | 17 | .330 | .394 | .526 |
| Benick, Jon, Hickory † | 130 | 556 | 488 | 76 | 160 | 289 | 29 | 2 | 32 | 104 | 0 | 8 | 7 | 53 | 3 | 95 | 2 | 2 | 5 | .328 | .396 | .592 |
| Harvey, Ryan, Capital City | 115 | 489 | 425 | 88 | 138 | 210 | 32 | 5 | 10 | 69 | 2 | 7 | 19 | 35 | 3 | 48 | 12 | 5 | 11 | .325 | .395 | .494 |
| Young, Delmon, Charleston-SC | 131 | 578 | 513 | 95 | 164 | 275 | 26 | 5 | 25 | 115 | 0 | 6 | 6 | 53 | 6 | 120 | 21 | 6 | 11 | .320 | .386 | .536 |
| Stewart, Ian, Asheville * | 131 | 581 | 505 | 92 | 161 | 300 | 31 | 9 | 30 | 101 | 1 | 5 | 4 | 66 | 6 | 112 | 19 | 9 | 7 | .319 | .398 | .594 |
| Bourn, Michael, Lakewood * | 109 | 510 | 413 | 92 | 131 | 194 | 20 | 14 | 5 | 53 | 6 | 4 | 2 | 85 | 2 | 88 | 57 | 6 | 1 | .317 | .433 | .470 |
| Prado, Martin, Rome | 107 | 467 | 429 | 68 | 135 | 181 | 25 | 6 | 3 | 38 | 4 | 1 | 3 | 30 | 0 | 47 | 14 | 10 | 10 | .315 | .363 | .422 |
| Czarniecki, Jordan, Asheville | 105 | 440 | 381 | 72 | 120 | 199 | 25 | 3 | 16 | 58 | 2 | 2 | 7 | 48 | 3 | 69 | 30 | 6 | 6 | .315 | .400 | .522 |
| Guzman, Javier, Hickory | 124 | 505 | 470 | 75 | 144 | 194 | 20 | 12 | 2 | 63 | 8 | 5 | 2 | 20 | 5 | 78 | 31 | 14 | 7 | .306 | .334 | .413 |
| Abreu, Etanislao, Columbus | 104 | 383 | 359 | 50 | 108 | 169 | 21 | 8 | 8 | 54 | 6 | 3 | 7 | 8 | 0 | 59 | 16 | 12 | 5 | .301 | .326 | .471 |
| Markakis, Nick, Delmarva * | 96 | 406 | 355 | 57 | 106 | 167 | 22 | 3 | 11 | 64 | 2 | 5 | 2 | 42 | 1 | 66 | 12 | 3 | 6 | .299 | .371 | .470 |
| Goleski, Ryan, Lake County | 130 | 581 | 505 | 83 | 149 | 265 | 22 | 5 | 28 | 104 | 0 | 10 | 11 | 55 | 5 | 100 | 6 | 7 | 10 | .295 | .370 | .525 |
| Gray, Antoin, Kannapolis | 122 | 532 | 477 | 82 | 140 | 219 | 32 | 4 | 13 | 49 | 4 | 3 | 9 | 39 | 1 | 96 | 10 | 5 | 4 | .294 | .356 | .459 |
| Rea, Brad, Hickory | 109 | 453 | 410 | 60 | 120 | 177 | 31 | 1 | 8 | 60 | 0 | 2 | 0 | 38 | 1 | 73 | 4 | 1 | 13 | .293 | .351 | .432 |

DEPARTMENTAL LEADERS: G—Bear, C. Young, 135; AB—Blalock, 517; R—Pridie, 103; H—D. Young, 164; TB—Stewart, 300; 2B—Blalock, 40; 3B—Bourn, 14; HR—Benick, 32; RBI—D. Young, 115; SH—Maysonet, 14; SF—Goleski, 10; HP—Morgan, 33; BB—Bourn, 85; IBB—Bankston, 8; SO—J. Miller, 163; SB—Bourn, 57; CS—Moran, 17; GIDP—Simmons, Reiman, 18; Slg.—Stewart, .594; OBP—Bourn, .433.

### ALL PLAYERS

*Lefthanded batter. †Switch-hitter.

| Player, Team | G | TPA | AB | R | H | TB | 2B | 3B | HR | RBI | SH | SF | HP | BB | IBB | SO | SB | CS | GDP | Avg. | OBP | Slg. |
|---|---|---|---|---|---|---|---|---|---|---|---|---|---|---|---|---|---|---|---|---|---|---|
| Abreu, Etanislao, Columbus | 104 | 383 | 359 | 50 | 108 | 169 | 21 | 8 | 8 | 54 | 6 | 3 | 7 | 8 | 0 | 59 | 16 | 12 | 5 | .301 | .326 | .471 |
| Abreu, Johany, Hagerstown † | 35 | 126 | 121 | 16 | 27 | 36 | 4 | 1 | 1 | 4 | 2 | 0 | 2 | 1 | 0 | 27 | 6 | 1 | 1 | .223 | .242 | .298 |
| Acevedo, Freddy, Lexington | 109 | 390 | 341 | 50 | 74 | 125 | 17 | 2 | 10 | 43 | 4 | 2 | 6 | 37 | 0 | 97 | 16 | 4 | 6 | .217 | .303 | .367 |
| Acey, Jermy, Charleston-WV † | 53 | 229 | 201 | 26 | 59 | 82 | 4 | 2 | 5 | 22 | 1 | 0 | 6 | 21 | 0 | 46 | 5 | 3 | 9 | .294 | .377 | .408 |
| Alcantara, Ervin, Lexington | 131 | 551 | 479 | 66 | 133 | 210 | 25 | 2 | 16 | 85 | 6 | 5 | 2 | 59 | 0 | 111 | 28 | 11 | 7 | .278 | .356 | .438 |
| Alen, Luis, Greensboro | 9 | 29 | 23 | 0 | 5 | 5 | 0 | 0 | 0 | 3 | 0 | 1 | 2 | 3 | 0 | 0 | 0 | 0 | 4 | .217 | .345 | .217 |
| Anderson, Jimmy, Capital City | 37 | 119 | 106 | 13 | 26 | 40 | 8 | 0 | 2 | 12 | 3 | 1 | 3 | 6 | 0 | 30 | 0 | 0 | 2 | .245 | .302 | .377 |
| Anderson, Josh, Lexington * | 73 | 343 | 299 | 69 | 97 | 127 | 12 | 3 | 4 | 31 | 2 | 2 | 7 | 33 | 1 | 47 | 47 | 9 | 0 | .324 | .402 | .425 |
| Anderson, Keith, Hagerstown | 14 | 54 | 47 | 7 | 16 | 25 | 3 | 0 | 2 | 7 | 0 | 1 | 0 | 6 | 0 | 9 | 1 | 1 | 0 | .340 | .407 | .532 |
| Andino, Robert, Greensboro | 76 | 324 | 295 | 27 | 83 | 119 | 10 | 1 | 8 | 46 | 6 | 4 | 1 | 18 | 0 | 83 | 9 | 2 | 5 | .281 | .321 | .403 |
| Apodaca, Luis, Savannah | 61 | 227 | 204 | 19 | 42 | 64 | 7 | 0 | 5 | 17 | 1 | 0 | 10 | 12 | 1 | 43 | 1 | 1 | 8 | .206 | .283 | .314 |
| Aracena, Sandy, Charleston-SC | 31 | 107 | 98 | 5 | 17 | 20 | 3 | 0 | 0 | 3 | 1 | 0 | 2 | 6 | 0 | 27 | 0 | 0 | 3 | .173 | .236 | .204 |
| Arhart, Josh, Charleston-SC | 71 | 287 | 244 | 36 | 64 | 87 | 8 | 0 | 5 | 33 | 1 | 3 | 8 | 31 | 1 | 28 | 1 | 4 | 7 | .262 | .360 | .357 |
| Arias, Claudio, Augusta | 54 | 230 | 209 | 31 | 57 | 93 | 10 | 1 | 8 | 34 | 0 | 4 | 3 | 14 | 0 | 53 | 2 | 2 | 6 | .273 | .322 | .445 |
| Arlis, Patrick, Greensboro | 61 | 227 | 207 | 23 | 47 | 60 | 5 | 1 | 2 | 17 | 1 | 0 | 1 | 18 | 0 | 59 | 3 | 1 | 0 | .227 | .292 | .290 |
| Armitage, Jon, Hagerstown † | 123 | 507 | 447 | 51 | 106 | 173 | 23 | 4 | 12 | 62 | 0 | 4 | 2 | 54 | 2 | 112 | 9 | 3 | 6 | .237 | .320 | .387 |
| Arnerich, Tony, Greensboro | 16 | 59 | 54 | 8 | 18 | 34 | 7 | 0 | 3 | 6 | 0 | 1 | 1 | 3 | 0 | 6 | 0 | 0 | 3 | .333 | .373 | .630 |
| Arnold, Eric, Charleston-WV | 105 | 414 | 378 | 40 | 106 | 143 | 22 | 0 | 5 | 61 | 1 | 5 | 1 | 29 | 1 | 114 | 1 | 3 | 4 | .280 | .329 | .378 |
| Arroyo, Xavier, Greensboro † | 91 | 331 | 293 | 43 | 68 | 98 | 11 | 2 | 5 | 29 | 4 | 1 | 2 | 31 | 0 | 91 | 27 | 11 | 7 | .232 | .309 | .334 |
| Ascencion, Quincy, Delmarva | 38 | 141 | 129 | 15 | 27 | 37 | 5 | 1 | 1 | 14 | 0 | 1 | 4 | 7 | 0 | 22 | 3 | 1 | 1 | .209 | .270 | .287 |
| Baez, Edgardo, Savannah | 50 | 216 | 191 | 16 | 34 | 59 | 10 | 0 | 5 | 29 | 0 | 2 | 4 | 19 | 1 | 56 | 1 | 0 | 4 | .178 | .264 | .309 |
| Bagley, David, Columbus | 41 | 163 | 139 | 16 | 37 | 54 | 7 | 2 | 2 | 24 | 0 | 1 | 7 | 16 | 0 | 31 | 2 | 0 | 6 | .266 | .368 | .388 |
| Bankston, Wes, Charleston-SC | 127 | 551 | 470 | 82 | 136 | 241 | 30 | 3 | 23 | 101 | 0 | 2 | 6 | 73 | 8 | 104 | 9 | 0 | 5 | .289 | .390 | .513 |
| Barre, Brian, Asheville * | 30 | 133 | 112 | 23 | 26 | 49 | 3 | 1 | 6 | 16 | 1 | 1 | 1 | 18 | 0 | 24 | 4 | 1 | 4 | .232 | .341 | .438 |
| Barrows, Derek, Hagerstown | 62 | 231 | 211 | 18 | 45 | 60 | 6 | 0 | 3 | 16 | 5 | 2 | 2 | 11 | 0 | 40 | 4 | 5 | 7 | .213 | .257 | .284 |
| Barthel, Cole, Rome | 22 | 54 | 50 | 13 | 14 | 16 | 2 | 0 | 0 | 3 | 0 | 0 | 3 | 1 | 0 | 6 | 2 | 0 | 3 | .280 | .333 | .320 |
| Bass, Bryan, Delmarva † | 122 | 463 | 389 | 53 | 93 | 149 | 23 | 3 | 9 | 54 | 7 | 4 | 9 | 54 | 1 | 125 | 16 | 3 | 2 | .239 | .342 | .383 |
| Bastida-Martinez, Evel, Delmarva * | 23 | 81 | 67 | 6 | 13 | 19 | 3 | 0 | 1 | 7 | 2 | 2 | 1 | 9 | 0 | 14 | 3 | 1 | 0 | .194 | .291 | .284 |
| Batista, Wilson, Capital City † | 84 | 385 | 320 | 69 | 83 | 109 | 15 | 1 | 3 | 35 | 9 | 4 | 4 | 48 | 0 | 57 | 35 | 8 | 2 | .259 | .359 | .341 |
| Bear, Ryan, Greensboro | 135 | 561 | 499 | 66 | 121 | 201 | 25 | 2 | 17 | 69 | 2 | 4 | 8 | 48 | 1 | 104 | 3 | 1 | 7 | .242 | .317 | .403 |
| Benick, Jon, Hickory † | 130 | 556 | 488 | 76 | 160 | 289 | 29 | 2 | 32 | 104 | 0 | 8 | 7 | 53 | 3 | 95 | 2 | 2 | 5 | .328 | .396 | .592 |
| Bennett, Charles, Capital City * | 6 | 18 | 15 | 2 | 2 | 2 | 0 | 0 | 0 | 0 | 1 | 0 | 0 | 2 | 0 | 5 | 0 | 0 | 0 | .133 | .235 | .133 |

| Player, Team | G | TPA | AB | R | H | TB | 2B | 3B | HR | RBI | SH | SF | HP | BB | IBB | SO | SB | CS | GDP | Avg. | OBP | Slg. |
|---|---|---|---|---|---|---|---|---|---|---|---|---|---|---|---|---|---|---|---|---|---|---|
| Bergeron, Jabe, Capital City | 23 | 91 | 72 | 18 | 21 | 41 | 5 | 0 | 5 | 17 | 0 | 0 | 1 | 18 | 0 | 23 | 0 | 1 | 2 | .292 | .440 | .569 |
| Bernadina, Rogearvin, Savannah * | 129 | 528 | 450 | 67 | 108 | 167 | 24 | 7 | 7 | 68 | 1 | 6 | 11 | 60 | 1 | 113 | 24 | 2 | 7 | .240 | .340 | .371 |
| Bernard, Miguel, Rome | 75 | 301 | 278 | 37 | 77 | 131 | 18 | 3 | 10 | 47 | 0 | 2 | 8 | 13 | 1 | 36 | 1 | 1 | 8 | .277 | .326 | .471 |
| Bibee, Hal, Asheville | 21 | 83 | 70 | 12 | 17 | 25 | 5 | 0 | 1 | 9 | 2 | 0 | 1 | 10 | 0 | 21 | 0 | 0 | 3 | .243 | .346 | .357 |
| Bladergroen, Ian, Capital City * | 72 | 307 | 269 | 39 | 92 | 160 | 23 | 3 | 13 | 74 | 0 | 8 | 5 | 25 | 4 | 55 | 1 | 1 | 2 | .342 | .397 | .595 |
| Blake, Ryan, Greensboro | 91 | 344 | 295 | 44 | 84 | 155 | 20 | 0 | 17 | 52 | 1 | 2 | 13 | 33 | 0 | 91 | 0 | 0 | 5 | .285 | .379 | .525 |
| Blalock, Jake, Lakewood | 131 | 592 | 517 | 81 | 140 | 232 | 40 | 2 | 16 | 90 | 0 | 8 | 6 | 61 | 2 | 126 | 4 | 3 | 11 | .271 | .350 | .449 |
| Blood, Randy, Asheville * | 113 | 482 | 426 | 54 | 122 | 176 | 22 | 1 | 10 | 63 | 0 | 5 | 3 | 48 | 2 | 92 | 13 | 14 | 3 | .286 | .359 | .413 |
| Bocchino, Anthony, Hickory * | 69 | 252 | 218 | 34 | 55 | 80 | 9 | 2 | 4 | 31 | 2 | 3 | 4 | 25 | 1 | 38 | 2 | 0 | 5 | .252 | .336 | .367 |
| Bock, Brian, Delmarva | 26 | 96 | 89 | 10 | 18 | 24 | 6 | 0 | 0 | 11 | 0 | 3 | 1 | 3 | 0 | 9 | 0 | 0 | 3 | .202 | .229 | .270 |
| Boeve, Adam, Hickory | 130 | 538 | 459 | 93 | 133 | 246 | 25 | 2 | 28 | 92 | 1 | 3 | 12 | 61 | 5 | 112 | 10 | 2 | 7 | .290 | .385 | .536 |
| Bone, Kyle, Hagerstown | 15 | 58 | 49 | 4 | 10 | 15 | 1 | 2 | 0 | 11 | 1 | 1 | 0 | 7 | 1 | 14 | 0 | 1 | 2 | .204 | .298 | .306 |
| Bonner, Adam, Greensboro * | 27 | 102 | 90 | 13 | 21 | 36 | 6 | 0 | 3 | 11 | 0 | 1 | 0 | 11 | 0 | 29 | 0 | 0 | 0 | .233 | .314 | .400 |
| Bonvechio, Brett, Augusta * | 10 | 42 | 32 | 4 | 8 | 14 | 1 | 1 | 1 | 9 | 0 | 2 | 0 | 8 | 0 | 9 | 0 | 0 | 2 | .250 | .381 | .438 |
| Borowiak, Zachary, Augusta | 123 | 508 | 448 | 52 | 106 | 149 | 19 | 3 | 6 | 40 | 10 | 3 | 9 | 38 | 0 | 70 | 9 | 9 | 5 | .237 | .307 | .333 |
| Bounds, Brandon, Kannapolis * | 85 | 322 | 304 | 41 | 80 | 139 | 20 | 3 | 11 | 44 | 0 | 2 | 1 | 15 | 0 | 82 | 1 | 2 | 3 | .263 | .298 | .457 |
| Bourn, Michael, Lakewood * | 109 | 510 | 413 | 92 | 131 | 194 | 20 | 14 | 5 | 53 | 6 | 4 | 2 | 85 | 2 | 88 | 57 | 6 | 1 | .317 | .433 | .470 |
| Bowman, Shawn, Capital City | 116 | 450 | 396 | 66 | 102 | 178 | 17 | 1 | 19 | 69 | 0 | 4 | 11 | 39 | 1 | 121 | 5 | 4 | 10 | .258 | .338 | .449 |
| Bramasco, Omar, Lakewood | 102 | 412 | 355 | 54 | 84 | 133 | 19 | 3 | 8 | 38 | 5 | 1 | 6 | 45 | 0 | 95 | 3 | 4 | 6 | .237 | .332 | .375 |
| Brice, Thomas, Kannapolis * | 58 | 249 | 217 | 36 | 68 | 106 | 16 | 2 | 6 | 31 | 0 | 2 | 2 | 28 | 1 | 48 | 10 | 4 | 2 | .313 | .394 | .488 |
| Brignac, Reid, Charleston-SC * | 3 | 15 | 14 | 3 | 7 | 8 | 1 | 0 | 0 | 5 | 0 | 0 | 0 | 1 | 0 | 2 | 0 | 0 | 0 | .500 | .533 | .571 |
| Brinkley, Dante, Capital City | 32 | 113 | 101 | 20 | 23 | 40 | 7 | 2 | 2 | 14 | 1 | 1 | 1 | 9 | 0 | 41 | 2 | 2 | 1 | .228 | .295 | .396 |
| Brock, Caleb, Lake County | 50 | 198 | 168 | 22 | 41 | 60 | 10 | 0 | 3 | 20 | 1 | 5 | 10 | 14 | 0 | 23 | 2 | 3 | 2 | .244 | .330 | .357 |
| Brown, Travis, Delmarva | 115 | 470 | 420 | 69 | 119 | 145 | 19 | 2 | 1 | 36 | 5 | 1 | 9 | 35 | 0 | 76 | 4 | 8 | 5 | .283 | .351 | .345 |
| Buller, Dayton, Hagerstown | 35 | 130 | 114 | 11 | 23 | 39 | 8 | 1 | 2 | 9 | 1 | 0 | 2 | 13 | 0 | 35 | 1 | 1 | 2 | .202 | .295 | .342 |
| Burgess, Tim, Augusta * | 58 | 245 | 206 | 30 | 48 | 65 | 8 | 0 | 3 | 31 | 0 | 3 | 3 | 33 | 0 | 52 | 3 | 2 | 6 | .233 | .343 | .316 |
| Burrus, Josh, Rome | 126 | 553 | 503 | 82 | 137 | 206 | 30 | 3 | 11 | 46 | 4 | 2 | 11 | 33 | 2 | 123 | 30 | 10 | 6 | .272 | .330 | .410 |
| Bynum, Seth, Savannah | 24 | 81 | 72 | 11 | 17 | 22 | 2 | 0 | 1 | 3 | 0 | 0 | 0 | 9 | 0 | 24 | 0 | 0 | 2 | .236 | .321 | .306 |
| Campbell, Eric, Rome | 7 | 25 | 22 | 0 | 3 | 3 | 0 | 0 | 0 | 1 | 0 | 0 | 1 | 2 | 0 | 7 | 0 | 0 | 0 | .136 | .240 | .136 |
| Carpenter, Calvin, Charleston-SC | 10 | 1 | 1 | 1 | 1 | 1 | 0 | 0 | 0 | 0 | 0 | 0 | 0 | 0 | 0 | 0 | 0 | 0 | 0 | 1.000 | 1.000 | 1.000 |
| Carter, Brandon, Columbus * | 4 | 16 | 13 | 2 | 2 | 3 | 1 | 0 | 0 | 0 | 0 | 0 | 0 | 3 | 0 | 4 | 0 | 0 | 1 | .154 | .313 | .231 |
| Carter, Chris, Delmarva | 10 | 44 | 36 | 8 | 11 | 13 | 2 | 0 | 0 | 4 | 0 | 0 | 1 | 7 | 0 | 10 | 1 | 0 | 0 | .306 | .432 | .361 |
| Castillo, Albenis, Columbus | 24 | 54 | 47 | 7 | 11 | 18 | 4 | 0 | 1 | 9 | 1 | 0 | 1 | 5 | 0 | 12 | 0 | 0 | 1 | .234 | .321 | .383 |
| Castillo, Cesar, Kannapolis | 11 | 32 | 28 | 3 | 4 | 4 | 0 | 0 | 0 | 2 | 1 | 0 | 0 | 3 | 0 | 5 | 2 | 0 | 0 | .143 | .226 | .143 |
| Castillo, Luis, Columbus | 33 | 122 | 112 | 10 | 21 | 27 | 3 | 0 | 1 | 10 | 1 | 1 | 1 | 7 | 0 | 27 | 1 | 3 | 3 | .188 | .240 | .241 |
| Casto, Kory, Savannah * | 124 | 526 | 483 | 67 | 138 | 229 | 35 | 4 | 16 | 88 | 1 | 3 | 8 | 31 | 1 | 70 | 1 | 2 | 5 | .286 | .337 | .474 |
| Castro, Ofilio, Savannah | 10 | 38 | 37 | 2 | 7 | 9 | 2 | 0 | 0 | 1 | 0 | 1 | 0 | 0 | 0 | 12 | 0 | 0 | 1 | .189 | .184 | .243 |
| Cates, Gary, Delmarva | 7 | 28 | 24 | 2 | 8 | 13 | 3 | 1 | 0 | 1 | 3 | 0 | 1 | 0 | 0 | 2 | 0 | 1 | 0 | .333 | .360 | .542 |
| Chapman, Travis, Hickory | 31 | 118 | 105 | 14 | 25 | 46 | 4 | 1 | 5 | 15 | 3 | 1 | 0 | 9 | 0 | 25 | 1 | 0 | 0 | .238 | .296 | .438 |
| Chauncey, Clint, Augusta | 9 | 39 | 35 | 2 | 6 | 8 | 2 | 0 | 0 | 4 | 0 | 1 | 0 | 3 | 0 | 18 | 0 | 0 | 0 | .171 | .231 | .229 |
| Chavez, Dirimo, Augusta | 100 | 438 | 376 | 60 | 94 | 110 | 9 | 2 | 1 | 23 | 7 | 2 | 3 | 50 | 1 | 53 | 4 | 5 | 10 | .250 | .341 | .293 |
| Ciofrone, Peter, Augusta * | 67 | 290 | 248 | 40 | 71 | 96 | 16 | 3 | 1 | 33 | 0 | 2 | 5 | 35 | 2 | 39 | 3 | 5 | 5 | .286 | .383 | .387 |
| Clanton, Ja'mar, Savannah | 15 | 31 | 30 | 3 | 6 | 8 | 0 | 1 | 0 | 2 | 0 | 0 | 0 | 1 | 0 | 10 | 0 | 0 | 0 | .200 | .226 | .267 |
| Clem, Chris, Lake County | 8 | 32 | 27 | 5 | 7 | 7 | 0 | 0 | 0 | 5 | 0 | 1 | 1 | 3 | 0 | 7 | 0 | 0 | 1 | .259 | .344 | .259 |
| Cloninger, Erich, Augusta | 5 | 17 | 15 | 0 | 1 | 1 | 0 | 0 | 0 | 1 | 0 | 1 | 0 | 1 | 0 | 6 | 0 | 0 | 0 | .067 | .118 | .067 |
| Cockrell, Michael, Hickory | 85 | 359 | 317 | 62 | 89 | 137 | 18 | 0 | 10 | 54 | 1 | 8 | 3 | 30 | 0 | 44 | 2 | 2 | 10 | .281 | .341 | .432 |
| Collum, Mike, Hickory | 59 | 209 | 184 | 26 | 45 | 72 | 10 | 1 | 5 | 25 | 2 | 1 | 6 | 16 | 0 | 42 | 0 | 0 | 1 | .245 | .324 | .391 |
| Colonel, Christian, Asheville | 119 | 498 | 429 | 62 | 107 | 157 | 23 | 0 | 9 | 65 | 2 | 4 | 14 | 49 | 1 | 73 | 35 | 8 | 14 | .249 | .343 | .366 |
| Columbus, Jason, Hagerstown | 103 | 439 | 399 | 55 | 114 | 186 | 26 | 2 | 14 | 59 | 0 | 0 | 11 | 29 | 0 | 103 | 3 | 0 | 15 | .286 | .351 | .466 |
| Conlisk, Jason, Savannah † | 111 | 408 | 349 | 38 | 75 | 114 | 20 | 2 | 5 | 37 | 12 | 4 | 2 | 41 | 0 | 87 | 7 | 2 | 9 | .215 | .298 | .327 |
| Conroy, Mike, Lake County * | 111 | 439 | 400 | 51 | 107 | 159 | 17 | 10 | 5 | 52 | 2 | 3 | 7 | 27 | 1 | 78 | 12 | 6 | 10 | .268 | .323 | .398 |
| Cook, David, Kannapolis | 60 | 232 | 192 | 31 | 41 | 75 | 8 | 1 | 8 | 28 | 0 | 2 | 7 | 31 | 0 | 62 | 5 | 5 | 1 | .214 | .341 | .391 |
| Cortez, Chico, Lakewood † | 66 | 251 | 213 | 31 | 62 | 103 | 15 | 1 | 8 | 34 | 0 | 2 | 3 | 33 | 0 | 40 | 1 | 2 | 4 | .291 | .390 | .484 |
| Cotto, Luis, Lake County | 53 | 178 | 159 | 19 | 42 | 54 | 9 | 0 | 1 | 16 | 4 | 1 | 4 | 10 | 0 | 32 | 2 | 2 | 2 | .264 | .322 | .340 |
| Coutlangus, Jonathan, Hagerstown * | 71 | 272 | 227 | 29 | 44 | 55 | 5 | 0 | 2 | 19 | 9 | 3 | 2 | 31 | 0 | 52 | 11 | 4 | 4 | .194 | .293 | .242 |
| Cronkhite, Ian, Augusta * | 82 | 298 | 264 | 31 | 57 | 73 | 9 | 2 | 1 | 26 | 2 | 4 | 2 | 26 | 0 | 56 | 6 | 5 | 2 | .216 | .287 | .277 |
| Cuevas, Aneudi, Charleston-SC | 46 | 170 | 154 | 21 | 33 | 52 | 8 | 1 | 3 | 21 | 1 | 1 | 1 | 13 | 0 | 60 | 4 | 2 | 3 | .214 | .278 | .338 |
| Curtis, Lee, Augusta | 4 | 16 | 15 | 0 | 2 | 2 | 0 | 0 | 0 | 2 | 0 | 0 | 1 | 0 | 0 | 2 | 0 | 0 | 0 | .133 | .188 | .133 |
| Czarniecki, Jordan, Asheville | 105 | 440 | 381 | 72 | 120 | 199 | 25 | 3 | 16 | 58 | 2 | 2 | 7 | 48 | 3 | 69 | 30 | 6 | 6 | .315 | .400 | .522 |
| Daigle, Leo, Kannapolis | 119 | 503 | 445 | 56 | 130 | 217 | 29 | 2 | 18 | 90 | 0 | 3 | 10 | 45 | 5 | 82 | 5 | 2 | 11 | .292 | .368 | .488 |
| Davidson, Kevin, Lexington | 48 | 180 | 148 | 20 | 32 | 39 | 4 | 0 | 1 | 17 | 1 | 4 | 1 | 26 | 0 | 18 | 7 | 3 | 3 | .216 | .330 | .264 |
| Davidson, Tyler, Capital City | 57 | 235 | 206 | 33 | 48 | 79 | 12 | 2 | 5 | 32 | 0 | 3 | 4 | 22 | 0 | 49 | 5 | 1 | 3 | .233 | .315 | .383 |
| Davis, Morrin, Charleston-WV | 54 | 159 | 138 | 19 | 21 | 32 | 2 | 3 | 1 | 14 | 2 | 1 | 3 | 15 | 0 | 61 | 2 | 1 | 5 | .152 | .248 | .232 |
| De Aza, Alejandro, Columbus * | 102 | 393 | 341 | 63 | 87 | 120 | 17 | 2 | 4 | 45 | 3 | 1 | 10 | 38 | 1 | 54 | 24 | 10 | 3 | .255 | .346 | .352 |
| De La Cruz, Christopher, Lake County † | 110 | 459 | 415 | 68 | 114 | 149 | 12 | 7 | 3 | 53 | 13 | 4 | 4 | 23 | 1 | 53 | 13 | 3 | 8 | .275 | .316 | .359 |
| DeLeon, Joey, Lexington | 38 | 1 | 1 | 0 | 0 | 0 | 0 | 0 | 0 | 0 | 0 | 0 | 0 | 0 | 0 | 1 | 0 | 0 | 0 | .000 | .000 | .000 |
| Devries, Jon, Augusta | 73 | 291 | 245 | 33 | 63 | 86 | 8 | 0 | 5 | 35 | 0 | 1 | 16 | 29 | 0 | 74 | 1 | 1 | 1 | .257 | .371 | .351 |
| Diaz, Rafael, Delmarva | 28 | 101 | 92 | 9 | 19 | 23 | 4 | 0 | 0 | 9 | 1 | 2 | 1 | 5 | 0 | 20 | 1 | 0 | 1 | .207 | .250 | .250 |
| Diaz, Raymar, Lexington | 24 | 1 | 1 | 0 | 0 | 0 | 0 | 0 | 0 | 0 | 0 | 0 | 0 | 0 | 0 | 1 | 0 | 0 | 0 | .000 | .000 | .000 |
| Diaz, Robinson, Charleston-WV | 105 | 449 | 407 | 62 | 117 | 147 | 20 | 2 | 2 | 42 | 3 | 4 | 8 | 27 | 0 | 31 | 10 | 4 | 17 | .287 | .341 | .361 |
| Dion, Nate, Charleston-SC | 79 | 271 | 245 | 27 | 54 | 71 | 9 | 1 | 2 | 23 | 1 | 0 | 5 | 20 | 0 | 82 | 14 | 6 | 1 | .220 | .293 | .290 |
| Dobson, Patrick, Hagerstown | 100 | 426 | 379 | 45 | 93 | 139 | 21 | 2 | 7 | 31 | 2 | 0 | 7 | 38 | 0 | 92 | 10 | 6 | 14 | .245 | .325 | .367 |
| Doetsch, Steve, Rome | 128 | 534 | 479 | 74 | 136 | 201 | 24 | 7 | 9 | 67 | 1 | 2 | 5 | 47 | 1 | 152 | 18 | 11 | 11 | .284 | .353 | .420 |
| Done, Mike, Delmarva † | 10 | 37 | 33 | 3 | 7 | 10 | 0 | 0 | 1 | 2 | 1 | 0 | 1 | 2 | 0 | 13 | 1 | 0 | 0 | .212 | .278 | .303 |
| Downing, Juan, Rome † | 8 | 36 | 30 | 4 | 7 | 8 | 1 | 0 | 0 | 3 | 1 | 1 | 2 | 2 | 0 | 4 | 0 | 1 | 1 | .233 | .314 | .267 |
| Dukes, Elijah, Charleston-SC † | 43 | 185 | 163 | 26 | 47 | 69 | 12 | 2 | 2 | 15 | 0 | 1 | 3 | 18 | 3 | 47 | 14 | 1 | 1 | .288 | .368 | .423 |
| Emmerick, Josh, Savannah | 24 | 82 | 69 | 7 | 13 | 17 | 1 | 0 | 1 | 5 | 0 | 1 | 2 | 10 | 1 | 19 | 0 | 1 | 1 | .188 | .305 | .246 |
| Encarnacio, Teodoro, Lake County | 17 | 63 | 60 | 7 | 13 | 18 | 0 | 1 | 1 | 3 | 0 | 0 | 2 | 1 | 0 | 15 | 0 | 1 | 0 | .217 | .254 | .300 |
| Esquivel, Matt, Rome | 114 | 462 | 411 | 69 | 116 | 201 | 31 | 3 | 16 | 63 | 1 | 3 | 12 | 35 | 0 | 140 | 14 | 4 | 9 | .282 | .354 | .489 |
| Evans, Bobb, Augusta * | 50 | 208 | 187 | 17 | 43 | 63 | 10 | 2 | 2 | 21 | 1 | 2 | 1 | 17 | 1 | 29 | 5 | 0 | 3 | .230 | .295 | .337 |
| Fernando, Osvaldo, Lexington | 116 | 490 | 433 | 76 | 110 | 147 | 21 | 2 | 4 | 51 | 12 | 2 | 11 | 32 | 0 | 76 | 29 | 13 | 11 | .254 | .320 | .339 |
| Ferrer, Simon, Asheville † | 61 | 222 | 199 | 22 | 46 | 88 | 9 | 0 | 11 | 33 | 1 | 3 | 1 | 18 | 0 | 56 | 5 | 3 | 4 | .231 | .294 | .442 |

| Player, Team | G | TPA | AB | R | H | TB | 2B | 3B | HR | RBI | SH | SF | HP | BB | IBB | SO | SB | CS | GDP | Avg. | OBP | Slg. |
|---|---|---|---|---|---|---|---|---|---|---|---|---|---|---|---|---|---|---|---|---|---|---|
| Fiorentino, Jeffrey, Delmarva * | 49 | 203 | 179 | 40 | 54 | 103 | 15 | 2 | 10 | 36 | 0 | 1 | 3 | 20 | 1 | 50 | 2 | 2 | 1 | .302 | .379 | .575 |
| Fitzpatrick, Reggie, Savannah * | 90 | 362 | 323 | 45 | 79 | 113 | 13 | 6 | 3 | 27 | 7 | 1 | 2 | 29 | 0 | 74 | 13 | 11 | 3 | .245 | .310 | .350 |
| Fransz, Jason, Delmarva | 28 | 117 | 101 | 19 | 32 | 56 | 6 | 0 | 6 | 25 | 0 | 3 | 2 | 11 | 0 | 25 | 1 | 0 | 4 | .317 | .385 | .554 |
| Fuller, Casey, Asheville * | 33 | 142 | 135 | 19 | 29 | 51 | 4 | 0 | 6 | 12 | 1 | 1 | 0 | 5 | 0 | 40 | 1 | 2 | 1 | .215 | .241 | .378 |
| Gaetti, Joe, Asheville | 111 | 441 | 370 | 62 | 95 | 169 | 24 | 1 | 16 | 55 | 0 | 3 | 13 | 55 | 2 | 107 | 16 | 6 | 5 | .257 | .370 | .457 |
| Galloway, Mike, Charleston-WV | 109 | 406 | 366 | 45 | 90 | 135 | 16 | 4 | 7 | 44 | 0 | 2 | 8 | 30 | 1 | 129 | 2 | 2 | 7 | .246 | .315 | .369 |
| Garcia, Yunir, Capital City | 78 | 269 | 222 | 39 | 60 | 99 | 9 | 0 | 10 | 34 | 2 | 2 | 5 | 38 | 0 | 72 | 2 | 1 | 1 | .270 | .386 | .446 |
| Garrido, Tomas, Hagerstown | 10 | 26 | 26 | 2 | 5 | 7 | 2 | 0 | 0 | 1 | 0 | 0 | 0 | 0 | 0 | 3 | 0 | 0 | 2 | .192 | .192 | .269 |
| Gendron, Steve, Greensboro | 52 | 210 | 187 | 20 | 35 | 37 | 2 | 0 | 0 | 13 | 1 | 2 | 2 | 18 | 0 | 45 | 4 | 0 | 4 | .187 | .263 | .198 |
| George, Trey, Asheville | 96 | 386 | 340 | 48 | 80 | 141 | 13 | 3 | 14 | 57 | 2 | 1 | 5 | 38 | 0 | 100 | 2 | 5 | 4 | .235 | .320 | .415 |
| Giles, Marcus, Rome | 1 | 4 | 2 | 0 | 0 | 0 | 0 | 0 | 0 | 0 | 0 | 0 | 0 | 2 | 0 | 0 | 0 | 0 | 0 | .000 | .500 | .000 |
| Goleski, Ryan, Lake County | 130 | 581 | 505 | 83 | 149 | 265 | 22 | 5 | 28 | 104 | 0 | 10 | 11 | 55 | 5 | 100 | 6 | 7 | 10 | .295 | .370 | .525 |
| Gonzalez, Andy, Kannapolis | 14 | 54 | 48 | 6 | 13 | 17 | 1 | 0 | 1 | 3 | 0 | 1 | 1 | 4 | 0 | 6 | 1 | 2 | 0 | .271 | .333 | .354 |
| Gradoville, Tim, Lakewood | 24 | 78 | 62 | 9 | 9 | 16 | 2 | 1 | 1 | 9 | 0 | 1 | 5 | 10 | 0 | 24 | 4 | 1 | 3 | .145 | .308 | .258 |
| Gray, Antoin, Kannapolis | 122 | 532 | 477 | 82 | 140 | 219 | 32 | 4 | 13 | 49 | 4 | 3 | 9 | 39 | 1 | 96 | 10 | 5 | 4 | .294 | .356 | .459 |
| Grimm, Eric, Delmarva † | 56 | 193 | 163 | 20 | 36 | 48 | 10 | 1 | 0 | 20 | 4 | 0 | 1 | 25 | 0 | 46 | 1 | 2 | 6 | .221 | .328 | .294 |
| Guance, Walkill, Asheville | 103 | 441 | 391 | 71 | 103 | 186 | 37 | 2 | 14 | 53 | 3 | 3 | 4 | 40 | 0 | 96 | 19 | 3 | 6 | .263 | .336 | .476 |
| Guanchez, Argimiro, Augusta * | 36 | 3 | 3 | 1 | 3 | 4 | 1 | 0 | 0 | 4 | 0 | 0 | 0 | 0 | 0 | 0 | 0 | 0 | 0 | 1.000 | 1.000 | 1.333 |
| Guerrero, Francisco, Delmarva | 5 | 8 | 6 | 1 | 1 | 1 | 0 | 0 | 0 | 0 | 1 | 0 | 0 | 1 | 0 | 0 | 0 | 0 | 0 | .167 | .286 | .167 |
| Gutierrez, Juan, Delmarva † | 70 | 289 | 261 | 32 | 60 | 96 | 17 | 2 | 5 | 34 | 0 | 2 | 5 | 21 | 0 | 53 | 2 | 1 | 4 | .230 | .298 | .368 |
| Guzman, Carlos, Rome | 103 | 379 | 329 | 44 | 83 | 154 | 26 | 3 | 13 | 52 | 0 | 1 | 11 | 38 | 2 | 111 | 6 | 3 | 4 | .252 | .348 | .468 |
| Guzman, Heriberto, Augusta | 26 | 103 | 95 | 11 | 14 | 27 | 2 | 1 | 3 | 10 | 0 | 0 | 4 | 4 | 0 | 43 | 0 | 1 | 5 | .147 | .214 | .284 |
| Guzman, Javier, Hickory | 124 | 505 | 470 | 75 | 144 | 194 | 20 | 12 | 2 | 63 | 8 | 5 | 2 | 20 | 5 | 78 | 31 | 14 | 7 | .306 | .334 | .413 |
| Haggerty, Cory, Kannapolis * | 82 | 301 | 251 | 42 | 63 | 90 | 15 | 0 | 4 | 23 | 3 | 1 | 7 | 39 | 0 | 67 | 8 | 5 | 4 | .251 | .366 | .359 |
| Hall, Mickey, Augusta * | 118 | 476 | 403 | 67 | 99 | 172 | 24 | 5 | 13 | 63 | 2 | 8 | 5 | 58 | 0 | 134 | 13 | 4 | 3 | .246 | .342 | .427 |
| Hansen, Bryan, Lakewood * | 127 | 551 | 462 | 77 | 126 | 191 | 28 | 5 | 9 | 59 | 3 | 7 | 5 | 74 | 3 | 65 | 1 | 3 | 6 | .273 | .374 | .413 |
| Hanson, Mike, Rome | 74 | 226 | 214 | 15 | 39 | 56 | 7 | 2 | 2 | 13 | 1 | 3 | 2 | 6 | 0 | 35 | 2 | 4 | 7 | .182 | .209 | .262 |
| Harris, Cory, Delmarva | 55 | 240 | 206 | 37 | 64 | 109 | 18 | 0 | 9 | 41 | 1 | 6 | 8 | 19 | 0 | 30 | 6 | 3 | 1 | .311 | .381 | .529 |
| Harris, Justin, Hickory | 85 | 311 | 282 | 38 | 72 | 87 | 8 | 2 | 1 | 31 | 5 | 3 | 7 | 14 | 0 | 20 | 7 | 4 | 7 | .255 | .304 | .309 |
| Harvey, Ryan, Capital City | 115 | 489 | 425 | 88 | 138 | 210 | 32 | 5 | 10 | 69 | 2 | 7 | 19 | 35 | 3 | 48 | 12 | 5 | 11 | .325 | .395 | .494 |
| Hearod, Beau, Lexington | 118 | 497 | 428 | 68 | 109 | 206 | 22 | 0 | 25 | 68 | 1 | 2 | 15 | 51 | 3 | 135 | 1 | 2 | 5 | .255 | .353 | .481 |
| Hemingway, Jamie, Rome | 15 | 53 | 51 | 7 | 14 | 17 | 3 | 0 | 0 | 4 | 0 | 0 | 0 | 2 | 0 | 8 | 3 | 0 | 0 | .275 | .302 | .333 |
| Hernandez, Diory, Rome | 90 | 340 | 306 | 40 | 83 | 114 | 20 | 1 | 3 | 38 | 2 | 5 | 1 | 26 | 1 | 67 | 7 | 4 | 8 | .271 | .325 | .373 |
| Hernandez, Fernando, Kannapolis | 29 | 4 | 3 | 0 | 0 | 0 | 0 | 0 | 0 | 0 | 0 | 0 | 0 | 1 | 0 | 0 | 0 | 0 | 0 | .000 | .250 | .000 |
| Hernandez, Francisco, Kannapolis † | 3 | 12 | 12 | 0 | 4 | 5 | 1 | 0 | 0 | 0 | 0 | 0 | 0 | 0 | 0 | 3 | 0 | 0 | 0 | .333 | .333 | .417 |
| Herrera, Javier, Lake County | 46 | 188 | 160 | 28 | 42 | 70 | 9 | 2 | 5 | 22 | 1 | 1 | 9 | 17 | 0 | 32 | 0 | 0 | 2 | .263 | .364 | .438 |
| Herrera, Jonathan, Asheville † | 95 | 418 | 380 | 71 | 106 | 148 | 20 | 2 | 6 | 35 | 3 | 2 | 7 | 26 | 0 | 80 | 21 | 12 | 5 | .279 | .335 | .389 |
| Hill, Jamar, Capital City | 121 | 512 | 459 | 83 | 125 | 226 | 21 | 1 | 26 | 89 | 3 | 5 | 9 | 36 | 0 | 110 | 20 | 12 | 11 | .272 | .334 | .492 |
| Hornostaj, Aaron, Hagerstown * | 14 | 60 | 56 | 4 | 15 | 17 | 2 | 0 | 0 | 5 | 0 | 1 | 1 | 2 | 0 | 14 | 5 | 1 | 0 | .268 | .300 | .304 |
| Houston, Matt, Delmarva | 51 | 178 | 151 | 19 | 40 | 54 | 6 | 1 | 2 | 13 | 0 | 2 | 7 | 18 | 1 | 33 | 2 | 1 | 8 | .265 | .365 | .358 |
| Hu, Chin-Lung, Columbus | 84 | 368 | 332 | 58 | 99 | 140 | 15 | 4 | 6 | 25 | 11 | 2 | 3 | 20 | 0 | 50 | 17 | 7 | 7 | .298 | .342 | .422 |
| Hudgson, Maximiliano, Lexington † | 7 | 9 | 7 | 0 | 1 | 1 | 0 | 0 | 0 | 0 | 0 | 0 | 1 | 1 | 0 | 4 | 0 | 0 | 0 | .143 | .333 | .143 |
| Humphries, Justin, Lexington | 62 | 245 | 219 | 28 | 59 | 101 | 13 | 1 | 9 | 37 | 0 | 5 | 2 | 19 | 1 | 55 | 0 | 1 | 8 | .269 | .327 | .461 |
| Hutting, Tim, Hagerstown | 124 | 498 | 425 | 61 | 105 | 133 | 18 | 2 | 2 | 42 | 12 | 4 | 10 | 47 | 0 | 38 | 5 | 5 | 17 | .247 | .333 | .313 |
| Iannetta, Christopher, Asheville | 36 | 153 | 121 | 23 | 38 | 60 | 5 | 1 | 5 | 17 | 0 | 0 | 4 | 27 | 0 | 29 | 0 | 1 | 3 | .314 | .454 | .496 |
| Iehl, Jay, Greensboro | 18 | 1 | 1 | 0 | 0 | 0 | 0 | 0 | 0 | 0 | 0 | 0 | 0 | 0 | 0 | 0 | 0 | 0 | 0 | .000 | .000 | .000 |
| Isaacson, Greg, Lakewood * | 3 | 11 | 8 | 0 | 1 | 1 | 0 | 0 | 0 | 0 | 0 | 0 | 1 | 2 | 0 | 1 | 0 | 0 | 1 | .125 | .364 | .125 |
| Ishikawa, Travis, Hagerstown * | 97 | 413 | 355 | 59 | 91 | 159 | 19 | 2 | 15 | 54 | 1 | 1 | 11 | 45 | 0 | 110 | 10 | 5 | 8 | .256 | .357 | .448 |
| Italiano, Nick, Lakewood * | 34 | 133 | 115 | 21 | 30 | 39 | 7 | 1 | 0 | 10 | 0 | 1 | 2 | 15 | 0 | 16 | 3 | 2 | 3 | .261 | .353 | .339 |
| Ivany, Devin, Savannah | 32 | 118 | 106 | 7 | 18 | 22 | 4 | 0 | 0 | 4 | 1 | 1 | 2 | 8 | 0 | 21 | 2 | 0 | 2 | .170 | .239 | .208 |
| Jansen, Archi, Rome | 66 | 258 | 228 | 37 | 58 | 90 | 8 | 0 | 8 | 24 | 2 | 0 | 3 | 25 | 0 | 67 | 8 | 4 | 2 | .254 | .336 | .395 |
| Jarvis, Andy, Lakewood * | 12 | 54 | 46 | 5 | 8 | 11 | 3 | 0 | 0 | 7 | 0 | 2 | 0 | 6 | 0 | 11 | 1 | 0 | 2 | .174 | .259 | .239 |
| Jimenez, Franklyn, Savannah | 74 | 242 | 229 | 26 | 49 | 70 | 6 | 0 | 5 | 27 | 4 | 1 | 1 | 7 | 0 | 43 | 5 | 0 | 3 | .214 | .239 | .306 |
| Jimenez, Luis, Columbus * | 110 | 450 | 392 | 62 | 113 | 199 | 24 | 1 | 20 | 75 | 1 | 3 | 3 | 51 | 2 | 104 | 6 | 2 | 7 | .288 | .372 | .508 |
| Johnson, Elliot, Charleston-SC † | 126 | 574 | 503 | 92 | 132 | 186 | 22 | 7 | 6 | 41 | 10 | 2 | 5 | 54 | 1 | 91 | 43 | 15 | 2 | .262 | .339 | .370 |
| Johnston, Clint, Charleston-WV * | 133 | 562 | 468 | 87 | 123 | 204 | 36 | 3 | 13 | 79 | 0 | 8 | 3 | 83 | 5 | 127 | 1 | 0 | 13 | .263 | .372 | .436 |
| Jones, Chipper, Rome † | 1 | 4 | 4 | 0 | 0 | 0 | 0 | 0 | 0 | 0 | 0 | 0 | 0 | 0 | 0 | 0 | 0 | 0 | 0 | .000 | .000 | .000 |
| Jones, Mitch, Charleston-SC | 21 | 66 | 57 | 7 | 12 | 12 | 0 | 0 | 0 | 5 | 0 | 1 | 1 | 7 | 0 | 14 | 1 | 0 | 1 | .211 | .303 | .211 |
| Jordan, Scooter, Augusta * | 57 | 241 | 200 | 30 | 48 | 54 | 4 | 1 | 0 | 14 | 2 | 1 | 4 | 34 | 1 | 41 | 7 | 9 | 3 | .240 | .360 | .270 |
| Kelly, Chris, Kannapolis | 6 | 21 | 19 | 0 | 2 | 2 | 0 | 0 | 0 | 0 | 0 | 0 | 0 | 2 | 0 | 6 | 0 | 0 | 0 | .105 | .190 | .105 |
| Kemp, Matthew, Columbus | 111 | 458 | 423 | 67 | 122 | 211 | 22 | 8 | 17 | 66 | 1 | 5 | 5 | 24 | 1 | 100 | 8 | 7 | 10 | .288 | .330 | .499 |
| King, Clint, Kannapolis * | 34 | 133 | 119 | 11 | 26 | 43 | 11 | 0 | 2 | 7 | 0 | 2 | 0 | 12 | 1 | 28 | 0 | 0 | 0 | .218 | .286 | .361 |
| Kingsbury, Bobby, Hickory * | 100 | 411 | 372 | 66 | 92 | 179 | 24 | 3 | 19 | 64 | 1 | 0 | 2 | 36 | 0 | 71 | 12 | 2 | 5 | .247 | .317 | .481 |
| Klemm, Chris, Lakewood * | 63 | 236 | 204 | 22 | 62 | 84 | 12 | 2 | 2 | 33 | 2 | 4 | 4 | 22 | 1 | 51 | 3 | 2 | 2 | .304 | .376 | .412 |
| Knowlton, Jay, Hagerstown | 58 | 250 | 217 | 34 | 53 | 70 | 12 | 1 | 1 | 20 | 1 | 1 | 8 | 23 | 0 | 50 | 1 | 4 | 4 | .244 | .337 | .323 |
| Koman, Brock, Lexington | 82 | 325 | 294 | 35 | 81 | 114 | 22 | 1 | 3 | 43 | 0 | 2 | 10 | 19 | 0 | 44 | 0 | 0 | 6 | .276 | .338 | .388 |
| Kouzmanoff, Kevin, Lake County | 123 | 531 | 473 | 74 | 156 | 249 | 35 | 5 | 16 | 87 | 0 | 5 | 9 | 44 | 0 | 75 | 5 | 4 | 17 | .330 | .394 | .526 |
| LaBarbera, A.J., Hagerstown | 11 | 43 | 34 | 5 | 8 | 9 | 1 | 0 | 0 | 4 | 1 | 0 | 1 | 7 | 0 | 5 | 0 | 0 | 2 | .235 | .381 | .265 |
| Laroche, Andy, Columbus | 65 | 285 | 244 | 52 | 69 | 128 | 20 | 0 | 13 | 42 | 2 | 2 | 8 | 29 | 1 | 30 | 12 | 5 | 6 | .283 | .375 | .525 |
| Laurin, Dom, Columbus | 65 | 233 | 189 | 29 | 44 | 73 | 15 | 1 | 4 | 28 | 8 | 3 | 6 | 27 | 1 | 59 | 3 | 3 | 4 | .233 | .342 | .386 |
| LeVier, Bret, Augusta | 26 | 107 | 96 | 14 | 22 | 34 | 5 | 2 | 1 | 14 | 1 | 2 | 1 | 7 | 0 | 16 | 1 | 0 | 1 | .229 | .283 | .354 |
| Leandro, Francisco, Charleston-SC * | 31 | 128 | 106 | 30 | 37 | 55 | 10 | 1 | 2 | 19 | 3 | 0 | 0 | 19 | 0 | 11 | 7 | 1 | 1 | .349 | .448 | .519 |
| Lee, Carlos, Kannapolis | 30 | 116 | 108 | 10 | 34 | 53 | 7 | 0 | 4 | 15 | 1 | 2 | 2 | 3 | 0 | 10 | 1 | 0 | 4 | .315 | .339 | .491 |
| Libey, Justin, Lakewood | 6 | 4 | 3 | 0 | 0 | 0 | 0 | 0 | 0 | 0 | 0 | 0 | 0 | 1 | 0 | 1 | 0 | 0 | 0 | .000 | .250 | .000 |
| Linares, Jesus, Capital City † | 81 | 249 | 203 | 43 | 58 | 86 | 10 | 0 | 6 | 33 | 7 | 3 | 6 | 30 | 0 | 59 | 1 | 2 | 3 | .286 | .388 | .424 |
| Lisk, Charlie, Kannapolis | 90 | 320 | 298 | 25 | 56 | 93 | 8 | 1 | 9 | 42 | 3 | 2 | 5 | 12 | 0 | 112 | 8 | 2 | 1 | .188 | .230 | .312 |
| Lombardi, Michael, Lakewood | 3 | 11 | 10 | 0 | 2 | 4 | 2 | 0 | 0 | 1 | 0 | 0 | 0 | 1 | 0 | 2 | 0 | 0 | 0 | .200 | .273 | .400 |
| Lopez, Mauber, Lakewood | 6 | 26 | 20 | 3 | 2 | 3 | 1 | 0 | 0 | 2 | 0 | 0 | 0 | 6 | 0 | 2 | 0 | 0 | 2 | .100 | .308 | .150 |
| Macaluso, Michael, Charleston-WV | 5 | 13 | 12 | 2 | 2 | 2 | 0 | 0 | 0 | 0 | 0 | 0 | 0 | 1 | 0 | 2 | 1 | 0 | 0 | .167 | .231 | .167 |
| Mader, Joshua, Lakewood | 41 | 153 | 134 | 15 | 29 | 34 | 5 | 0 | 0 | 18 | 2 | 3 | 3 | 11 | 0 | 30 | 3 | 1 | 3 | .216 | .285 | .254 |
| Mancebo, Melvin, Savannah | 1 | 4 | 4 | 1 | 2 | 5 | 0 | 0 | 1 | 1 | 0 | 0 | 0 | 0 | 0 | 1 | 0 | 0 | 0 | .500 | .500 | 1.250 |
| Manriquez, Salomon, Savannah | 33 | 132 | 121 | 12 | 32 | 48 | 7 | 0 | 3 | 19 | 0 | 2 | 1 | 8 | 0 | 33 | 0 | 1 | 0 | .264 | .311 | .397 |

| Player, Team | G | TPA | AB | R | H | TB | 2B | 3B | HR | RBI | SH | SF | HP | BB | IBB | SO | SB | CS | GDP | Avg. | OBP | Slg. |
|---|---|---|---|---|---|---|---|---|---|---|---|---|---|---|---|---|---|---|---|---|---|---|
| Marcos, Emilio, Columbus | 21 | 76 | 72 | 9 | 18 | 23 | 3 | 1 | 0 | 11 | 0 | 0 | 2 | 2 | 0 | 14 | 4 | 1 | 0 | .250 | .289 | .319 |
| Markakis, Nick, Delmarva * | 96 | 406 | 355 | 57 | 106 | 167 | 22 | 3 | 11 | 64 | 2 | 5 | 2 | 42 | 1 | 66 | 12 | 3 | 6 | .299 | .371 | .470 |
| Martinez-Esteve, Eddy, Hagerstown | 13 | 56 | 46 | 4 | 10 | 16 | 1 | 1 | 1 | 11 | 0 | 1 | 1 | 8 | 0 | 8 | 1 | 1 | 2 | .217 | .339 | .348 |
| Maysonet, Edwin, Lexington | 109 | 485 | 391 | 79 | 102 | 177 | 22 | 10 | 11 | 63 | 14 | 7 | 9 | 64 | 1 | 91 | 18 | 7 | 4 | .261 | .372 | .453 |
| Mazzuca, Joe, Greensboro | 68 | 244 | 198 | 36 | 41 | 75 | 11 | 1 | 7 | 22 | 1 | 1 | 14 | 30 | 0 | 49 | 14 | 4 | 2 | .207 | .350 | .379 |
| McClain, Justin, Augusta | 41 | 158 | 132 | 21 | 31 | 37 | 6 | 0 | 0 | 10 | 0 | 1 | 5 | 20 | 1 | 37 | 4 | 0 | 1 | .235 | .354 | .280 |
| McCuistion, Mike, Hickory * | 86 | 327 | 286 | 41 | 73 | 113 | 24 | 2 | 4 | 23 | 2 | 0 | 1 | 36 | 0 | 55 | 2 | 0 | 8 | .255 | .341 | .395 |
| McCullough, Clayton, Lake County * | 28 | 96 | 83 | 9 | 17 | 21 | 1 | 0 | 1 | 7 | 1 | 0 | 0 | 12 | 0 | 22 | 1 | 1 | 2 | .205 | .305 | .253 |
| McCurdy, Josh, Delmarva | 68 | 272 | 248 | 40 | 68 | 99 | 13 | 0 | 6 | 33 | 1 | 2 | 4 | 17 | 0 | 36 | 10 | 3 | 7 | .274 | .328 | .399 |
| McMillan, Beau, Greensboro | 6 | 20 | 16 | 3 | 4 | 7 | 1 | 1 | 0 | 2 | 0 | 0 | 1 | 3 | 0 | 4 | 1 | 0 | 1 | .250 | .400 | .438 |
| Meath, Matt, Hickory † | 10 | 43 | 35 | 5 | 6 | 14 | 0 | 1 | 2 | 5 | 0 | 0 | 0 | 8 | 0 | 11 | 3 | 1 | 0 | .171 | .326 | .400 |
| Medina, Rodney, Charleston-WV † | 28 | 110 | 103 | 14 | 34 | 44 | 5 | 1 | 1 | 17 | 2 | 1 | 0 | 4 | 0 | 10 | 3 | 1 | 0 | .330 | .352 | .427 |
| Melendez, German, Lexington | 77 | 283 | 238 | 34 | 54 | 69 | 12 | 0 | 1 | 19 | 9 | 1 | 6 | 29 | 0 | 61 | 11 | 2 | 3 | .227 | .325 | .290 |
| Milledge, Lastings, Capital City | 65 | 294 | 261 | 66 | 88 | 151 | 22 | 1 | 13 | 58 | 1 | 3 | 12 | 17 | 1 | 53 | 23 | 6 | 3 | .337 | .399 | .579 |
| Miller, Jai, Greensboro | 113 | 433 | 390 | 51 | 80 | 137 | 15 | 3 | 12 | 49 | 5 | 1 | 5 | 32 | 0 | 163 | 11 | 4 | 10 | .205 | .273 | .351 |
| Milons, Jereme, Columbus | 103 | 473 | 436 | 70 | 119 | 175 | 14 | 6 | 10 | 53 | 5 | 1 | 1 | 30 | 0 | 99 | 25 | 8 | 3 | .273 | .321 | .401 |
| Mitchell, Russell, Columbus | 63 | 231 | 209 | 24 | 42 | 56 | 12 | 1 | 0 | 14 | 5 | 1 | 6 | 10 | 0 | 49 | 2 | 4 | 4 | .201 | .257 | .268 |
| Molina, Angel, Greensboro | 130 | 535 | 469 | 67 | 133 | 218 | 27 | 2 | 18 | 79 | 0 | 1 | 10 | 55 | 0 | 110 | 0 | 2 | 13 | .284 | .370 | .465 |
| Molina, Gustavo, Kannapolis | 37 | 124 | 105 | 16 | 17 | 32 | 3 | 0 | 4 | 17 | 3 | 0 | 4 | 12 | 0 | 24 | 2 | 1 | 6 | .162 | .273 | .305 |
| Moni-Erigbali, Timi, Lakewood | 18 | 70 | 58 | 7 | 13 | 19 | 3 | 0 | 1 | 6 | 0 | 1 | 2 | 9 | 0 | 23 | 4 | 1 | 2 | .224 | .343 | .328 |
| Montague, Ed, Asheville * | 83 | 339 | 309 | 50 | 79 | 123 | 14 | 0 | 10 | 44 | 0 | 1 | 2 | 27 | 1 | 60 | 9 | 2 | 7 | .256 | .319 | .398 |
| Moran, Javon, Lakewood | 101 | 467 | 421 | 73 | 120 | 162 | 18 | 9 | 2 | 38 | 8 | 2 | 12 | 24 | 0 | 78 | 39 | 17 | 6 | .285 | .340 | .385 |
| Morel, Elvis, Delmarva | 18 | 72 | 62 | 14 | 17 | 28 | 0 | 1 | 3 | 6 | 3 | 1 | 0 | 6 | 0 | 8 | 5 | 1 | 0 | .274 | .333 | .452 |
| Morgan, Nyjer, Hickory * | 134 | 618 | 514 | 83 | 131 | 173 | 16 | 7 | 4 | 41 | 10 | 6 | 33 | 53 | 2 | 120 | 55 | 16 | 1 | .255 | .358 | .337 |
| Morris, Seth, Kannapolis | 83 | 257 | 242 | 25 | 47 | 83 | 13 | 1 | 7 | 25 | 2 | 1 | 1 | 11 | 1 | 80 | 3 | 1 | 4 | .194 | .231 | .343 |
| Moss, Brandon, Augusta * | 109 | 490 | 433 | 66 | 147 | 223 | 25 | 6 | 13 | 101 | 0 | 7 | 4 | 46 | 4 | 75 | 19 | 8 | 8 | .339 | .402 | .515 |
| Moss, Timothy, Lakewood † | 78 | 312 | 273 | 31 | 70 | 93 | 15 | 1 | 2 | 28 | 2 | 1 | 12 | 24 | 0 | 75 | 10 | 8 | 3 | .256 | .342 | .341 |
| Mulhern, Ryan, Lake County | 103 | 415 | 372 | 48 | 95 | 146 | 28 | 1 | 7 | 42 | 1 | 5 | 5 | 32 | 1 | 87 | 3 | 2 | 11 | .255 | .319 | .392 |
| Munhall, Brian, Hagerstown | 62 | 225 | 200 | 24 | 55 | 77 | 6 | 2 | 4 | 22 | 1 | 1 | 5 | 18 | 1 | 42 | 3 | 1 | 3 | .275 | .348 | .385 |
| Nanita, Ricardo, Kannapolis * | 61 | 256 | 225 | 32 | 71 | 90 | 12 | 2 | 1 | 31 | 0 | 2 | 3 | 26 | 0 | 32 | 5 | 4 | 2 | .316 | .391 | .400 |
| Nichols, Thomas, Charleston-SC | 82 | 313 | 285 | 35 | 61 | 107 | 10 | 0 | 12 | 41 | 1 | 0 | 3 | 24 | 0 | 97 | 0 | 0 | 7 | .214 | .282 | .375 |
| Nixon, Mike, Columbus | 90 | 377 | 334 | 49 | 87 | 126 | 20 | 2 | 5 | 50 | 6 | 4 | 7 | 26 | 2 | 68 | 6 | 8 | 8 | .260 | .323 | .377 |
| Norman, Zach, Lakewood | 12 | 53 | 48 | 10 | 16 | 34 | 3 | 0 | 5 | 14 | 0 | 1 | 2 | 2 | 0 | 15 | 2 | 0 | 0 | .333 | .377 | .708 |
| Noviskey, Josh, Lake County † | 22 | 82 | 69 | 14 | 20 | 26 | 1 | 1 | 1 | 11 | 0 | 2 | 3 | 8 | 0 | 22 | 0 | 0 | 0 | .290 | .378 | .377 |
| Nunez, Eduardo, Savannah | 2 | 6 | 1 | 2 | 0 | 0 | 0 | 0 | 0 | 0 | 1 | 0 | 0 | 4 | 0 | 1 | 1 | 0 | 0 | .000 | .800 | .000 |
| Olszta, Eddie, Hickory | 6 | 8 | 6 | 1 | 1 | 1 | 0 | 0 | 0 | 1 | 0 | 0 | 0 | 2 | 0 | 3 | 0 | 0 | 0 | .167 | .375 | .167 |
| Ontiveros, Jeff, Augusta | 44 | 191 | 150 | 20 | 36 | 53 | 8 | 0 | 3 | 15 | 0 | 2 | 12 | 27 | 2 | 52 | 1 | 1 | 2 | .240 | .393 | .353 |
| Owens, Jerry, Savannah * | 108 | 470 | 418 | 69 | 122 | 146 | 17 | 2 | 1 | 37 | 1 | 2 | 3 | 46 | 1 | 59 | 30 | 13 | 3 | .292 | .365 | .349 |
| Paniagua, Salvador, Augusta | 32 | 124 | 116 | 13 | 27 | 38 | 5 | 0 | 2 | 17 | 0 | 1 | 2 | 5 | 0 | 39 | 0 | 0 | 2 | .233 | .274 | .328 |
| Parker, Rashad, Capital City | 70 | 270 | 240 | 40 | 54 | 74 | 12 | 1 | 2 | 17 | 4 | 2 | 9 | 15 | 1 | 54 | 9 | 2 | 0 | .225 | .293 | .308 |
| Patrick, Brian, Charleston-WV † | 83 | 300 | 253 | 35 | 63 | 80 | 10 | 2 | 1 | 35 | 1 | 5 | 5 | 36 | 0 | 44 | 3 | 1 | 4 | .249 | .348 | .316 |
| Paul, Matthew, Columbus | 7 | 23 | 18 | 3 | 4 | 6 | 0 | 1 | 0 | 2 | 0 | 0 | 0 | 5 | 0 | 4 | 2 | 1 | 0 | .222 | .391 | .333 |
| Paul, Xavier, Columbus * | 128 | 536 | 465 | 69 | 122 | 187 | 26 | 6 | 9 | 72 | 5 | 7 | 3 | 56 | 4 | 127 | 10 | 7 | 4 | .262 | .341 | .402 |
| Peavey, Bill, Lake County * | 65 | 254 | 223 | 30 | 54 | 95 | 8 | 0 | 11 | 35 | 0 | 1 | 2 | 28 | 0 | 49 | 0 | 0 | 8 | .242 | .331 | .426 |
| Pedroia, Dustin, Augusta | 12 | 57 | 50 | 11 | 20 | 28 | 5 | 0 | 1 | 5 | 0 | 0 | 1 | 6 | 0 | 3 | 2 | 0 | 1 | .400 | .474 | .560 |
| Peralta, Juan, Charleston-WV † | 119 | 494 | 437 | 57 | 100 | 123 | 15 | 1 | 2 | 43 | 6 | 8 | 4 | 39 | 0 | 78 | 8 | 5 | 6 | .229 | .293 | .281 |
| Peterson, Derrick, Lake County | 8 | 33 | 27 | 1 | 2 | 2 | 0 | 0 | 0 | 0 | 0 | 0 | 0 | 6 | 0 | 7 | 0 | 1 | 2 | .074 | .242 | .074 |
| Piazza, Tony, Capital City | 7 | 24 | 21 | 4 | 3 | 4 | 1 | 0 | 0 | 0 | 0 | 0 | 0 | 3 | 0 | 11 | 0 | 0 | 0 | .143 | .250 | .190 |
| Pierce, Whit, Delmarva | 20 | 62 | 48 | 5 | 4 | 4 | 0 | 0 | 0 | 3 | 0 | 0 | 3 | 11 | 0 | 22 | 1 | 0 | 0 | .083 | .290 | .083 |
| Pietsch, Seth, Capital City | 10 | 41 | 35 | 8 | 8 | 13 | 0 | 1 | 1 | 9 | 0 | 2 | 2 | 2 | 0 | 12 | 1 | 0 | 0 | .229 | .293 | .371 |
| Pinckney, Brandon, Lake County | 40 | 178 | 165 | 31 | 60 | 79 | 10 | 0 | 3 | 22 | 1 | 1 | 1 | 10 | 0 | 12 | 6 | 4 | 2 | .364 | .401 | .479 |
| Prado, Martin, Rome | 107 | 467 | 429 | 68 | 135 | 181 | 25 | 6 | 3 | 38 | 4 | 1 | 3 | 30 | 0 | 47 | 14 | 10 | 10 | .315 | .363 | .422 |
| Price, Jared, Columbus | 53 | 192 | 170 | 26 | 41 | 71 | 12 | 0 | 6 | 22 | 4 | 2 | 2 | 14 | 0 | 51 | 3 | 1 | 4 | .241 | .303 | .418 |
| Pridie, Jason, Charleston-SC * | 128 | 575 | 515 | 103 | 142 | 242 | 27 | 11 | 17 | 86 | 9 | 8 | 6 | 37 | 3 | 114 | 17 | 6 | 1 | .276 | .327 | .470 |
| Prosser, Chad, Lexington | 70 | 269 | 244 | 33 | 58 | 86 | 10 | 0 | 6 | 30 | 3 | 0 | 4 | 18 | 0 | 39 | 10 | 3 | 1 | .238 | .301 | .352 |
| Pyzik, Steve, Rome | 50 | 132 | 122 | 15 | 37 | 48 | 9 | 1 | 0 | 19 | 0 | 0 | 3 | 7 | 0 | 13 | 0 | 0 | 1 | .303 | .356 | .393 |
| Ramistella, John, Greensboro | 31 | 106 | 94 | 12 | 16 | 33 | 4 | 2 | 3 | 9 | 0 | 0 | 5 | 7 | 1 | 39 | 2 | 2 | 1 | .170 | .264 | .351 |
| Randel, Kevin, Greensboro * | 35 | 149 | 134 | 20 | 40 | 64 | 10 | 1 | 4 | 21 | 0 | 0 | 3 | 12 | 0 | 27 | 2 | 2 | 1 | .299 | .369 | .478 |
| Rea, Brad, Hickory | 109 | 453 | 410 | 60 | 120 | 177 | 31 | 1 | 8 | 60 | 0 | 2 | 0 | 38 | 1 | 73 | 4 | 1 | 13 | .293 | .351 | .432 |
| Reaver, David, Capital City | 37 | 137 | 123 | 15 | 19 | 21 | 2 | 0 | 0 | 6 | 1 | 1 | 2 | 10 | 0 | 26 | 1 | 0 | 0 | .154 | .228 | .171 |
| Reiman, Joey, Charleston-WV | 116 | 480 | 408 | 68 | 119 | 172 | 28 | 2 | 7 | 51 | 0 | 5 | 15 | 50 | 0 | 82 | 3 | 6 | 18 | .292 | .385 | .422 |
| Reyes, Milver, Hickory | 26 | 93 | 88 | 7 | 20 | 27 | 1 | 0 | 2 | 10 | 1 | 2 | 1 | 1 | 0 | 16 | 0 | 1 | 2 | .227 | .239 | .307 |
| Reynoso, Danilo, Capital City | 15 | 53 | 49 | 3 | 12 | 14 | 2 | 0 | 0 | 4 | 0 | 1 | 0 | 3 | 0 | 17 | 1 | 1 | 2 | .245 | .283 | .286 |
| Riera, Zack, Lexington † | 26 | 95 | 81 | 11 | 22 | 31 | 6 | 0 | 1 | 7 | 1 | 0 | 3 | 10 | 1 | 16 | 2 | 0 | 0 | .272 | .372 | .383 |
| Rine, Jarod, Delmarva * | 122 | 527 | 460 | 79 | 117 | 170 | 16 | 8 | 7 | 57 | 5 | 0 | 2 | 60 | 1 | 89 | 31 | 7 | 10 | .254 | .343 | .370 |
| Rivera, Willie, Charleston-WV * | 99 | 380 | 336 | 40 | 70 | 88 | 9 | 0 | 3 | 28 | 9 | 4 | 7 | 24 | 0 | 92 | 3 | 8 | 6 | .208 | .272 | .262 |
| Roberts, Ryan, Charleston-WV | 64 | 291 | 226 | 38 | 64 | 112 | 9 | 0 | 13 | 39 | 0 | 1 | 9 | 55 | 1 | 50 | 0 | 0 | 6 | .283 | .440 | .496 |
| Robinson, Levi, Delmarva | 9 | 27 | 25 | 1 | 1 | 1 | 0 | 0 | 0 | 1 | 1 | 0 | 0 | 1 | 0 | 8 | 2 | 0 | 3 | .040 | .077 | .040 |
| Robinson, Scott, Lexington * | 123 | 513 | 457 | 63 | 120 | 162 | 28 | 1 | 4 | 46 | 3 | 3 | 4 | 46 | 2 | 64 | 7 | 7 | 5 | .263 | .333 | .354 |
| Rodriguez, Alfredo, Savannah | 2 | 8 | 7 | 2 | 1 | 1 | 0 | 0 | 0 | 0 | 0 | 0 | 0 | 1 | 0 | 3 | 0 | 0 | 0 | .143 | .250 | .143 |
| Rodriguez, Carlos, Lakewood † | 112 | 478 | 440 | 56 | 118 | 167 | 27 | 2 | 6 | 57 | 5 | 2 | 5 | 26 | 0 | 68 | 20 | 10 | 7 | .268 | .315 | .380 |
| Rodriguez, Robert, Savannah | 22 | 69 | 56 | 7 | 14 | 19 | 5 | 0 | 0 | 7 | 4 | 1 | 0 | 8 | 0 | 26 | 0 | 0 | 0 | .250 | .338 | .339 |
| Rohan, Jimmy, Columbus | 90 | 315 | 280 | 43 | 78 | 96 | 11 | 2 | 1 | 30 | 5 | 4 | 8 | 18 | 0 | 37 | 5 | 3 | 7 | .279 | .335 | .343 |
| Rohleder, Andy, Greensboro | 25 | 109 | 99 | 11 | 24 | 37 | 7 | 0 | 2 | 13 | 0 | 1 | 1 | 8 | 0 | 27 | 0 | 0 | 2 | .242 | .303 | .374 |
| Rojas, Ricardo, Lake County | 104 | 445 | 395 | 72 | 99 | 134 | 14 | 3 | 5 | 39 | 12 | 3 | 11 | 24 | 0 | 94 | 27 | 14 | 4 | .251 | .309 | .339 |
| Ruiz, Randy, Lakewood | 110 | 477 | 417 | 85 | 120 | 206 | 31 | 2 | 17 | 91 | 0 | 5 | 13 | 42 | 0 | 140 | 1 | 1 | 10 | .288 | .367 | .494 |
| Russell, Mike, Delmarva | 75 | 265 | 230 | 31 | 55 | 106 | 15 | 0 | 12 | 47 | 2 | 2 | 6 | 25 | 0 | 84 | 2 | 1 | 9 | .239 | .327 | .461 |
| Saltalamacchia, Jarrod, Rome † | 91 | 366 | 323 | 42 | 88 | 141 | 19 | 2 | 10 | 51 | 1 | 3 | 5 | 34 | 2 | 83 | 1 | 0 | 6 | .272 | .348 | .437 |
| San Pedro, Erick, Savannah | 14 | 49 | 40 | 3 | 8 | 13 | 2 | 0 | 1 | 4 | 0 | 0 | 0 | 9 | 0 | 17 | 0 | 0 | 1 | .200 | .347 | .325 |
| Sapp, Steven, Columbus | 6 | 17 | 16 | 0 | 1 | 1 | 0 | 0 | 0 | 1 | 0 | 0 | 0 | 1 | 0 | 3 | 0 | 0 | 1 | .063 | .118 | .063 |
| Schade, Ryan, Greensboro | 75 | 224 | 199 | 33 | 45 | 53 | 5 | 0 | 1 | 17 | 6 | 2 | 1 | 16 | 0 | 49 | 6 | 2 | 2 | .226 | .284 | .266 |
| Schade, Scott, Rome | 105 | 407 | 377 | 44 | 92 | 166 | 21 | 4 | 15 | 55 | 1 | 1 | 5 | 23 | 1 | 92 | 2 | 2 | 12 | .244 | .296 | .440 |

| Player, Team | G | TPA | AB | R | H | TB | 2B | 3B | HR | RBI | SH | SF | HP | BB | IBB | SO | SB | CS | GDP | Avg. | OBP | Slg. |
|---|---|---|---|---|---|---|---|---|---|---|---|---|---|---|---|---|---|---|---|---|---|---|
| Schartz, Lance, Augusta | 10 | 32 | 27 | 3 | 3 | 6 | 0 | 0 | 1 | 3 | 0 | 0 | 2 | 3 | 0 | 8 | 0 | 0 | 1 | .111 | .250 | .222 |
| Schierholtz, Nate, Hagerstown * | 58 | 258 | 233 | 41 | 69 | 136 | 22 | 0 | 15 | 53 | 0 | 3 | 4 | 18 | 3 | 52 | 1 | 0 | 4 | .296 | .353 | .584 |
| Schilling, Micah, Lake County * | 115 | 456 | 396 | 58 | 99 | 138 | 16 | 4 | 5 | 43 | 5 | 2 | 1 | 52 | 2 | 105 | 3 | 4 | 10 | .250 | .337 | .348 |
| Schleicher, Mark, Charleston-SC | 104 | 414 | 378 | 35 | 88 | 123 | 15 | 4 | 4 | 43 | 9 | 1 | 9 | 17 | 1 | 101 | 4 | 6 | 10 | .233 | .281 | .325 |
| Schlichting, Travis, Charleston-SC | 94 | 381 | 331 | 50 | 86 | 113 | 19 | 1 | 2 | 34 | 3 | 4 | 7 | 36 | 0 | 71 | 6 | 4 | 6 | .260 | .341 | .341 |
| Schmidt, Jesse, Hagerstown † | 118 | 510 | 435 | 55 | 111 | 157 | 19 | 3 | 7 | 56 | 0 | 4 | 6 | 65 | 1 | 85 | 11 | 7 | 10 | .255 | .357 | .361 |
| Schnurstein, Micah, Kannapolis | 131 | 530 | 491 | 52 | 135 | 186 | 33 | 0 | 6 | 58 | 2 | 4 | 7 | 26 | 0 | 104 | 14 | 4 | 10 | .275 | .318 | .379 |
| Scott, Lorenzo, Delmarva * | 16 | 52 | 38 | 5 | 7 | 10 | 1 | 1 | 0 | 2 | 1 | 0 | 2 | 11 | 0 | 25 | 4 | 1 | 0 | .184 | .392 | .263 |
| Seifrig, Cole, Greensboro | 121 | 462 | 443 | 55 | 87 | 125 | 20 | 3 | 4 | 30 | 1 | 0 | 5 | 13 | 0 | 128 | 6 | 1 | 11 | .196 | .228 | .282 |
| Serrano, Ray, Rome | 17 | 63 | 62 | 5 | 16 | 26 | 5 | 1 | 1 | 7 | 0 | 0 | 0 | 1 | 0 | 7 | 0 | 0 | 1 | .258 | .270 | .419 |
| Shanks, James, Greensboro | 59 | 267 | 245 | 45 | 79 | 125 | 16 | 3 | 8 | 32 | 4 | 0 | 4 | 14 | 0 | 52 | 18 | 3 | 6 | .322 | .369 | .510 |
| Shehan, Jonathan, Rome | 2 | 5 | 4 | 0 | 1 | 1 | 0 | 0 | 0 | 1 | 0 | 0 | 0 | 1 | 0 | 0 | 0 | 0 | 0 | .250 | .400 | .250 |
| Silva, Johan, Rome † | 7 | 29 | 26 | 1 | 4 | 7 | 0 | 0 | 1 | 3 | 0 | 0 | 0 | 3 | 0 | 9 | 2 | 1 | 0 | .154 | .241 | .269 |
| Simmons, Colt, Charleston-SC | 101 | 405 | 341 | 44 | 99 | 124 | 16 | 0 | 3 | 33 | 3 | 6 | 14 | 41 | 0 | 49 | 1 | 3 | 18 | .290 | .383 | .364 |
| Smith, David, Charleston-WV | 121 | 501 | 436 | 74 | 121 | 188 | 27 | 2 | 12 | 68 | 0 | 2 | 8 | 53 | 2 | 119 | 5 | 0 | 11 | .278 | .365 | .431 |
| Smith, Sean, Hickory | 34 | 108 | 95 | 20 | 26 | 46 | 10 | 5 | 0 | 9 | 1 | 0 | 4 | 8 | 0 | 15 | 8 | 1 | 1 | .274 | .355 | .484 |
| Snavely, Christian, Charleston-WV * | 111 | 395 | 331 | 50 | 84 | 152 | 22 | 2 | 14 | 59 | 1 | 3 | 5 | 53 | 2 | 115 | 6 | 2 | 3 | .254 | .362 | .459 |
| Snyder, Brad, Lake County * | 79 | 361 | 304 | 52 | 85 | 140 | 15 | 5 | 10 | 54 | 0 | 4 | 5 | 48 | 1 | 78 | 11 | 4 | 5 | .280 | .382 | .461 |
| Sosa, Pablo, Greensboro | 72 | 283 | 272 | 25 | 71 | 97 | 10 | 5 | 2 | 28 | 0 | 0 | 1 | 10 | 0 | 47 | 4 | 3 | 9 | .261 | .290 | .357 |
| Spears, Nate, Delmarva * | 97 | 431 | 371 | 50 | 102 | 151 | 12 | 11 | 5 | 37 | 7 | 3 | 3 | 47 | 0 | 63 | 7 | 6 | 3 | .275 | .358 | .407 |
| Speigner, Brent, Charleston-SC | 29 | 58 | 50 | 2 | 10 | 10 | 0 | 0 | 0 | 4 | 1 | 0 | 1 | 6 | 0 | 18 | 0 | 1 | 0 | .200 | .298 | .200 |
| St. Clair, Jason, Charleston-SC | 53 | 205 | 185 | 26 | 45 | 66 | 8 | 2 | 3 | 28 | 5 | 1 | 2 | 12 | 0 | 43 | 8 | 3 | 4 | .243 | .295 | .357 |
| Stachowsky, Mitchel, Augusta | 23 | 88 | 78 | 10 | 15 | 21 | 0 | 0 | 2 | 7 | 0 | 0 | 4 | 6 | 0 | 40 | 1 | 0 | 1 | .192 | .284 | .269 |
| Stansberry, Craig, Hickory | 106 | 452 | 391 | 57 | 112 | 163 | 14 | 5 | 9 | 67 | 2 | 2 | 5 | 52 | 0 | 88 | 20 | 8 | 6 | .286 | .376 | .417 |
| Stewart, Caleb, Capital City | 25 | 102 | 86 | 20 | 27 | 48 | 6 | 0 | 5 | 15 | 1 | 2 | 0 | 13 | 1 | 11 | 0 | 1 | 0 | .314 | .396 | .558 |
| Stewart, Ian, Asheville * | 131 | 581 | 505 | 92 | 161 | 300 | 31 | 9 | 30 | 101 | 1 | 5 | 4 | 66 | 6 | 112 | 19 | 9 | 7 | .319 | .398 | .594 |
| Street, Dan, Asheville | 18 | 63 | 57 | 7 | 7 | 15 | 2 | 0 | 2 | 8 | 1 | 0 | 2 | 3 | 0 | 17 | 0 | 0 | 4 | .123 | .194 | .263 |
| Strong, Zach, Hagerstown † | 16 | 65 | 58 | 7 | 14 | 26 | 3 | 0 | 3 | 7 | 0 | 0 | 0 | 7 | 0 | 11 | 0 | 0 | 0 | .241 | .323 | .448 |
| Suarez, Iggy, Augusta | 38 | 166 | 141 | 28 | 38 | 51 | 6 | 2 | 1 | 15 | 0 | 1 | 3 | 21 | 0 | 29 | 7 | 1 | 1 | .270 | .373 | .362 |
| Sucre, Antonio, Savannah | 103 | 421 | 363 | 44 | 87 | 128 | 11 | 3 | 8 | 46 | 2 | 6 | 15 | 35 | 2 | 114 | 3 | 5 | 9 | .240 | .327 | .353 |
| Sultemeier, Eric, Delmarva | 12 | 42 | 39 | 3 | 5 | 6 | 1 | 0 | 0 | 4 | 0 | 0 | 2 | 1 | 0 | 9 | 0 | 0 | 1 | .128 | .190 | .154 |
| Swanson, Brent, Hagerstown * | 21 | 79 | 70 | 7 | 16 | 21 | 2 | 0 | 1 | 7 | 2 | 0 | 1 | 6 | 0 | 17 | 0 | 0 | 1 | .229 | .299 | .300 |
| Sweeney, James, Asheville | 9 | 36 | 29 | 4 | 4 | 5 | 1 | 0 | 0 | 3 | 0 | 0 | 2 | 5 | 0 | 9 | 2 | 0 | 0 | .138 | .306 | .172 |
| Thomas, Ben, Rome * | 27 | 94 | 89 | 8 | 21 | 29 | 5 | 0 | 1 | 9 | 1 | 0 | 0 | 4 | 0 | 22 | 1 | 0 | 3 | .236 | .269 | .326 |
| Torres, Saul, Lexington | 122 | 512 | 453 | 49 | 114 | 154 | 15 | 2 | 7 | 62 | 5 | 5 | 14 | 35 | 1 | 91 | 4 | 1 | 16 | .252 | .321 | .340 |
| Touchstone, Josh, Charleston-SC | 22 | 72 | 62 | 13 | 14 | 17 | 1 | 1 | 0 | 6 | 1 | 0 | 5 | 4 | 0 | 12 | 0 | 1 | 1 | .226 | .324 | .274 |
| Tucker, Mamon, Lexington | 41 | 137 | 123 | 9 | 26 | 32 | 4 | 1 | 0 | 12 | 0 | 2 | 0 | 12 | 0 | 24 | 0 | 2 | 8 | .211 | .277 | .260 |
| Tugwell, Marc, Lakewood | 56 | 226 | 203 | 27 | 58 | 92 | 19 | 0 | 5 | 33 | 1 | 5 | 4 | 13 | 0 | 30 | 2 | 3 | 6 | .286 | .333 | .453 |
| Tuttle, Jason, Savannah * | 4 | 12 | 12 | 1 | 4 | 4 | 0 | 0 | 0 | 0 | 0 | 0 | 0 | 0 | 0 | 0 | 0 | 0 | 1 | .333 | .333 | .333 |
| Valdes, Juan, Lake County † | 25 | 117 | 97 | 18 | 23 | 26 | 0 | 0 | 1 | 10 | 1 | 2 | 2 | 15 | 0 | 23 | 20 | 3 | 2 | .237 | .345 | .268 |
| Valido, Rob, Kannapolis | 122 | 512 | 456 | 65 | 115 | 152 | 25 | 0 | 4 | 43 | 13 | 2 | 6 | 35 | 0 | 59 | 28 | 12 | 3 | .252 | .313 | .333 |
| Vankirk, Robert, Augusta | 3 | 7 | 6 | 0 | 0 | 0 | 0 | 0 | 0 | 1 | 0 | 1 | 0 | 0 | 0 | 2 | 0 | 0 | 2 | .000 | .000 | .000 |
| Vasquez, Jose, Asheville * | 18 | 66 | 60 | 5 | 7 | 15 | 2 | 0 | 2 | 5 | 0 | 0 | 0 | 6 | 1 | 27 | 0 | 0 | 3 | .117 | .197 | .250 |
| Wagner, Michael, Hagerstown | 117 | 481 | 417 | 63 | 107 | 174 | 24 | 2 | 13 | 48 | 0 | 2 | 20 | 40 | 0 | 115 | 5 | 3 | 8 | .257 | .349 | .417 |
| Watts, Derran, Capital City | 27 | 111 | 92 | 12 | 21 | 34 | 4 | 3 | 1 | 8 | 2 | 2 | 4 | 11 | 0 | 29 | 5 | 1 | 0 | .228 | .330 | .370 |
| Webb, Trey, Savannah | 78 | 306 | 274 | 39 | 66 | 88 | 10 | 0 | 4 | 30 | 2 | 1 | 1 | 28 | 0 | 48 | 7 | 4 | 4 | .241 | .313 | .321 |
| Whealy, Blake, Capital City | 124 | 509 | 427 | 100 | 120 | 231 | 32 | 5 | 23 | 82 | 3 | 3 | 9 | 67 | 0 | 126 | 10 | 5 | 3 | .281 | .387 | .541 |
| Whisler, Wesley, Kannapolis * | 21 | 39 | 38 | 2 | 11 | 16 | 2 | 0 | 1 | 5 | 0 | 0 | 0 | 1 | 0 | 7 | 0 | 0 | 1 | .289 | .308 | .421 |
| White, Dean, Rome | 102 | 342 | 317 | 40 | 71 | 89 | 8 | 2 | 2 | 23 | 5 | 2 | 2 | 16 | 0 | 94 | 11 | 4 | 7 | .224 | .264 | .281 |
| White, Scott, Augusta | 123 | 516 | 474 | 60 | 133 | 189 | 34 | 2 | 6 | 55 | 0 | 3 | 14 | 25 | 1 | 61 | 21 | 9 | 12 | .281 | .333 | .399 |
| Whitesell, Josh, Savannah * | 113 | 443 | 380 | 56 | 95 | 172 | 29 | 0 | 16 | 54 | 1 | 2 | 2 | 58 | 2 | 91 | 0 | 1 | 5 | .250 | .351 | .453 |
| Whitesides, Jake, Kannapolis * | 33 | 108 | 103 | 14 | 22 | 36 | 3 | 4 | 1 | 10 | 0 | 0 | 0 | 5 | 0 | 23 | 3 | 1 | 2 | .214 | .250 | .350 |
| Whitney, Matt, Lake County | 55 | 222 | 195 | 21 | 50 | 76 | 11 | 0 | 5 | 31 | 0 | 0 | 4 | 23 | 0 | 81 | 0 | 0 | 1 | .256 | .347 | .390 |
| Wilson, Andrew, Capital City | 103 | 414 | 366 | 62 | 105 | 194 | 32 | 0 | 19 | 70 | 0 | 3 | 4 | 41 | 0 | 77 | 2 | 0 | 10 | .287 | .362 | .530 |
| Wilson, Brandon, Capital City | 21 | 77 | 71 | 10 | 15 | 20 | 2 | 0 | 1 | 2 | 0 | 0 | 2 | 4 | 0 | 25 | 0 | 0 | 2 | .211 | .273 | .282 |
| Wilson, Neil, Asheville | 96 | 376 | 334 | 41 | 80 | 130 | 27 | 1 | 7 | 48 | 1 | 4 | 5 | 32 | 0 | 70 | 1 | 0 | 4 | .240 | .312 | .389 |
| Winegarden, Erik, Lakewood * | 57 | 226 | 185 | 19 | 40 | 60 | 14 | 0 | 2 | 23 | 3 | 0 | 7 | 31 | 0 | 44 | 2 | 0 | 5 | .216 | .350 | .324 |
| Wise, Dewayne, Rome * | 5 | 17 | 15 | 4 | 5 | 11 | 0 | 0 | 2 | 4 | 0 | 0 | 1 | 1 | 0 | 5 | 1 | 0 | 0 | .333 | .412 | .733 |
| Wolfe, Joey, Charleston-WV * | 56 | 171 | 145 | 16 | 32 | 50 | 5 | 2 | 3 | 16 | 1 | 2 | 7 | 16 | 1 | 40 | 1 | 2 | 2 | .221 | .324 | .345 |
| Woodson, Mike, Lake County | 3 | 8 | 7 | 0 | 2 | 3 | 1 | 0 | 0 | 0 | 0 | 0 | 0 | 1 | 0 | 2 | 0 | 0 | 0 | .286 | .375 | .429 |
| Wyman, Spencer, Greensboro * | 19 | 69 | 58 | 7 | 9 | 12 | 0 | 0 | 1 | 6 | 2 | 1 | 0 | 8 | 0 | 22 | 1 | 0 | 1 | .155 | .254 | .207 |
| Yepez, Marcos, Savannah † | 77 | 304 | 265 | 35 | 63 | 87 | 14 | 2 | 2 | 24 | 3 | 0 | 6 | 30 | 0 | 85 | 12 | 2 | 5 | .238 | .329 | .328 |
| Young, Chris, Kannapolis | 135 | 551 | 465 | 83 | 122 | 235 | 31 | 5 | 24 | 56 | 6 | 3 | 11 | 66 | 1 | 145 | 31 | 9 | 2 | .262 | .365 | .505 |
| Young, Delmon, Charleston-SC | 131 | 578 | 513 | 95 | 164 | 275 | 26 | 5 | 25 | 115 | 0 | 6 | 6 | 53 | 6 | 120 | 21 | 6 | 11 | .320 | .386 | .536 |
| Young, Dusty, Greensboro | 12 | 33 | 30 | 2 | 4 | 5 | 1 | 0 | 0 | 1 | 0 | 0 | 0 | 3 | 0 | 8 | 1 | 0 | 1 | .133 | .212 | .167 |
| Yount, Dustin, Delmarva * | 99 | 407 | 339 | 40 | 87 | 141 | 26 | 2 | 8 | 59 | 0 | 1 | 8 | 59 | 1 | 80 | 1 | 1 | 6 | .257 | .378 | .416 |

GRAND SLAMS—Whealy, 3; Bankston, Hearod, Maysonet, Schmidt, Webb, D. Young, 2 each; Acey, Alcantara, Armitage, Ascencion, Bass, Bear, Bladergroen, Blood, Bourn, Bramasco, Brinkley, Castillo, Colonel, Dion, Doetsch, Ferrer, Fiorentino, Fitzpatrick, George, Harvey, Herrera, Hill, Jimenez, Johnston, Kouzmanoff, Manriquez, Mazzuca, A. Molina, Peavey, Pridie, Riera, Rojas, Ruiz, Russell, Shanks, Strong, Wagner, White, Whitesell, Wilson, D. Young, 1 each.

AWARDED FIRST BASE ON CATCHER'S INTERFERENCE—Rea 3 (de Vries, Y. Garcia, Riera); Nanita 2 (Melendez, Melendez); Wagner 2 (R. Diaz, Melendez); Chavez (Y. Garcia); Davis (Winegarden); Gaetti (Aracena); Harvey (de Vries); Hearod (McCuistion); Iannetta (Pyzik).

# 2004 PITCHING

## TEAM

| Team | W | L | Pct. | ERA | G | CG | ShO | Sv. | IP | H | TBF | R | ER | HR | SH | SF | HB | BB | IBB | SO | WP | Bk. |
|---|---|---|---|---|---|---|---|---|---|---|---|---|---|---|---|---|---|---|---|---|---|---|
| Charl.-WV | 84 | 56 | .600 | 3.54 | 140 | 2 | 13 | 39 | 1223.0 | 1135 | 5213 | 585 | 481 | 76 | 39 | 34 | 81 | 438 | 22 | 1116 | 72 | 8 |
| Kannapolis | 69 | 70 | .496 | 3.91 | 139 | 4 | 8 | 44 | 1218.1 | 1186 | 5309 | 657 | 529 | 87 | 48 | 41 | 94 | 513 | 10 | 980 | 69 | 9 |
| Delmarva | 69 | 69 | .500 | 3.93 | 138 | 5 | 12 | 35 | 1196.2 | 1130 | 5217 | 620 | 522 | 98 | 37 | 38 | 83 | 509 | 22 | 1054 | 76 | 10 |
| Charl.-SC | 76 | 63 | .547 | 3.96 | 139 | 2 | 13 | 33 | 1222.1 | 1219 | 5261 | 666 | 538 | 94 | 41 | 28 | 71 | 414 | 5 | 1053 | 70 | 3 |
| Columbus | 69 | 69 | .500 | 4.14 | 138 | 3 | 10 | 34 | 1201.1 | 1134 | 5280 | 683 | 553 | 123 | 31 | 38 | 99 | 566 | 13 | 1222 | 92 | 10 |

| Team | W | L | Pct. | ERA | G | CG | ShO | Sv. | IP | H | TBF | R | ER | HR | SH | SF | HB | BB | IBB | SO | WP | Bk. |
|---|---|---|---|---|---|---|---|---|---|---|---|---|---|---|---|---|---|---|---|---|---|---|
| Capital City | 89 | 47 | .654 | 4.16 | 136 | 1 | 9 | 41 | 1186.0 | 1171 | 5172 | 680 | 548 | 103 | 33 | 41 | 98 | 426 | 11 | 1137 | 81 | 11 |
| Hickory | 85 | 55 | .607 | 4.23 | 140 | 5 | 4 | 43 | 1220.1 | 1201 | 5295 | 659 | 573 | 114 | 38 | 39 | 95 | 471 | 5 | 1067 | 64 | 8 |
| Lakewood | 70 | 67 | .511 | 4.25 | 137 | 4 | 5 | 28 | 1189.2 | 1231 | 5169 | 665 | 562 | 94 | 46 | 52 | 68 | 388 | 3 | 908 | 81 | 4 |
| Rome | 70 | 70 | .500 | 4.26 | 140 | 3 | 7 | 40 | 1200.2 | 1212 | 5288 | 694 | 568 | 100 | 53 | 52 | 66 | 502 | 24 | 1109 | 92 | 11 |
| Augusta | 66 | 73 | .475 | 4.32 | 139 | 1 | 7 | 33 | 1220.2 | 1313 | 5322 | 712 | 586 | 117 | 44 | 38 | 89 | 349 | 11 | 1014 | 68 | 12 |
| Savannah | 58 | 80 | .420 | 4.34 | 138 | 3 | 6 | 29 | 1173.0 | 1148 | 5135 | 672 | 566 | 110 | 39 | 42 | 98 | 472 | 11 | 1062 | 100 | 7 |
| Lake County | 73 | 66 | .525 | 4.35 | 139 | 2 | 8 | 32 | 1207.0 | 1234 | 5290 | 669 | 583 | 129 | 38 | 39 | 87 | 446 | 19 | 1104 | 66 | 11 |
| Lexington | 68 | 72 | .486 | 4.47 | 140 | 1 | 7 | 28 | 1212.2 | 1177 | 5390 | 698 | 602 | 123 | 36 | 41 | 92 | 599 | 10 | 1088 | 73 | 5 |
| Asheville | 64 | 75 | .460 | 4.76 | 139 | 10 | 3 | 27 | 1194.0 | 1321 | 5245 | 740 | 632 | 158 | 38 | 44 | 88 | 364 | 11 | 864 | 57 | 11 |
| Hagerstown | 49 | 88 | .358 | 4.80 | 137 | 2 | 1 | 31 | 1184.2 | 1236 | 5304 | 756 | 632 | 110 | 47 | 39 | 97 | 530 | 8 | 1000 | 84 | 2 |
| Greensboro | 50 | 89 | .360 | 5.33 | 139 | 0 | 3 | 29 | 1186.1 | 1278 | 5358 | 835 | 703 | 146 | 22 | 39 | 96 | 507 | 8 | 1124 | 116 | 5 |

## INDIVIDUAL

### TOP QUALIFIERS FOR EARNED-RUN AVERAGE TITLE

Minimum 112 innings. *Lefthanded pitcher.

| Pitcher, Team | W | L | Pct. | ERA | G | GS | CG | ShO | GF | Sv. | IP | H | TBF | R | ER | HR | SH | SF | HB | BB | IBB | SO | WP | Bk. |
|---|---|---|---|---|---|---|---|---|---|---|---|---|---|---|---|---|---|---|---|---|---|---|---|---|
| Mastny, Thomas, Charleston-WV | 10 | 3 | .769 | 2.17 | 27 | 27 | 0 | 0 | 0 | 0 | 149.0 | 123 | 592 | 44 | 36 | 4 | 9 | 5 | 3 | 41 | 0 | 141 | 7 | 0 |
| James, Chuck, Rome * | 10 | 5 | .667 | 2.25 | 26 | 22 | 1 | 0 | 2 | 0 | 132.0 | 92 | 527 | 41 | 33 | 6 | 9 | 9 | 7 | 48 | 1 | 156 | 3 | 0 |
| Stevens, Jake, Rome * | 9 | 5 | .643 | 2.27 | 27 | 19 | 0 | 0 | 7 | 2 | 135.0 | 100 | 544 | 41 | 34 | 7 | 3 | 6 | 4 | 39 | 1 | 140 | 7 | 1 |
| Gardner, Jarrett, Augusta | 13 | 5 | .722 | 2.51 | 25 | 23 | 0 | 0 | 1 | 0 | 136.0 | 130 | 533 | 49 | 38 | 12 | 6 | 2 | 6 | 11 | 0 | 92 | 2 | 0 |
| Dixon, Zachary, Delmarva * | 9 | 4 | .692 | 2.54 | 24 | 21 | 0 | 0 | 0 | 0 | 120.2 | 97 | 517 | 52 | 34 | 5 | 9 | 6 | 6 | 65 | 0 | 105 | 7 | 0 |
| Cabrera, Nate, Lakewood | 6 | 4 | .600 | 2.82 | 24 | 23 | 2 | 2 | 0 | 0 | 131.0 | 111 | 535 | 50 | 41 | 10 | 10 | 11 | 4 | 40 | 0 | 113 | 7 | 2 |
| Nunez, Leo, Hickory | 10 | 4 | .714 | 3.06 | 27 | 20 | 3 | 0 | 3 | 1 | 144.0 | 121 | 584 | 53 | 49 | 16 | 4 | 6 | 9 | 46 | 0 | 140 | 5 | 1 |
| Deza, Fredy, Delmarva | 8 | 11 | .421 | 3.31 | 22 | 21 | 2 | 0 | 0 | 0 | 119.2 | 102 | 479 | 52 | 44 | 7 | 6 | 6 | 5 | 21 | 2 | 93 | 6 | 3 |
| Peguero, Tony, Charleston-SC | 10 | 6 | .625 | 3.32 | 23 | 23 | 1 | 1 | 0 | 0 | 133.0 | 135 | 532 | 61 | 49 | 9 | 8 | 5 | 4 | 22 | 0 | 87 | 4 | 1 |
| Core, Danny, Charleston-WV | 9 | 8 | .529 | 3.43 | 28 | 28 | 1 | 0 | 0 | 0 | 157.1 | 137 | 642 | 70 | 60 | 15 | 4 | 10 | 13 | 53 | 0 | 132 | 7 | 0 |
| Robles, Larry, Asheville | 7 | 3 | .700 | 3.54 | 23 | 19 | 0 | 0 | 3 | 3 | 122.0 | 120 | 506 | 58 | 48 | 13 | 10 | 2 | 7 | 31 | 0 | 85 | 5 | 0 |
| Bulger, Brian, Charleston-SC | 10 | 8 | .556 | 3.58 | 37 | 17 | 0 | 0 | 9 | 1 | 123.1 | 103 | 517 | 58 | 49 | 5 | 6 | 1 | 8 | 50 | 2 | 120 | 13 | 0 |
| Bostick, Adam, Greensboro * | 2 | 8 | .200 | 3.79 | 23 | 22 | 0 | 0 | 0 | 0 | 114.0 | 100 | 490 | 57 | 48 | 10 | 4 | 3 | 6 | 58 | 0 | 163 | 6 | 1 |
| Flores, Rafael, Kannapolis | 8 | 11 | .421 | 3.82 | 23 | 22 | 0 | 0 | 0 | 0 | 127.1 | 139 | 540 | 71 | 54 | 14 | 15 | 4 | 9 | 33 | 0 | 65 | 2 | 0 |
| Talbot, Mitch, Lexington | 10 | 10 | .500 | 3.83 | 27 | 27 | 1 | 0 | 0 | 0 | 152.2 | 145 | 647 | 78 | 65 | 16 | 7 | 3 | 11 | 49 | 1 | 115 | 6 | 1 |

DEPARTMENTAL LEADERS: W—Gardner, 13; L—Jackson, 13; Pct.—Mastny, .769; G—A. Williams, 59; GS—Core, Merrell, 28; CG—Arias, 4; ShO—Cabrera, 2; GF—A. Williams, 53; Sv.—Wasserman, 30; IP—Kaiser, 181.0; H—Arteaga, 207; TBF—Kaiser, 783; R—Digby, 112; ER—Digby, 95; HR—Marsden, 30; SH— Flores, 15; SF—Osberg, 13; HB—Kaiser, 25; BB—Grigsby, 93; IBB—Three tied with four; SO—Bostick, 163; WP—Digby, 19; BK—Loewen, Mujica, 4.

### ALL PITCHERS

*Lefthanded pitcher.

| Pitcher, Team | W | L | Pct. | ERA | G | GS | CG | ShO | GF | Sv. | IP | H | TBF | R | ER | HR | SH | SF | HB | BB | IBB | SO | WP | Bk. |
|---|---|---|---|---|---|---|---|---|---|---|---|---|---|---|---|---|---|---|---|---|---|---|---|---|
| Acosta, Anthony, Capital City | 1 | 2 | .333 | 3.86 | 29 | 0 | 0 | 0 | 15 | 6 | 42.0 | 44 | 195 | 23 | 18 | 5 | 1 | 0 | 1 | 26 | 2 | 35 | 0 | 0 |
| Acosta, Kelyn, Hagerstown | 4 | 3 | .571 | 4.41 | 10 | 10 | 0 | 0 | 0 | 0 | 51.0 | 61 | 228 | 31 | 25 | 5 | 1 | 1 | 1 | 23 | 0 | 37 | 1 | 0 |
| Acosta, Richard, Delmarva | 1 | 2 | .333 | 4.94 | 17 | 0 | 0 | 0 | 11 | 3 | 27.1 | 29 | 118 | 16 | 15 | 3 | 0 | 0 | 0 | 7 | 1 | 26 | 2 | 0 |
| Adler, Anthony, Lexington | 1 | 3 | .250 | 3.14 | 14 | 0 | 0 | 0 | 8 | 2 | 28.2 | 27 | 121 | 12 | 10 | 3 | 0 | 0 | 2 | 6 | 0 | 25 | 2 | 0 |
| Akens, Phil, Greensboro | 1 | 3 | .250 | 8.31 | 8 | 8 | 0 | 0 | 0 | 0 | 34.2 | 48 | 168 | 33 | 32 | 4 | 2 | 2 | 3 | 14 | 0 | 34 | 2 | 0 |
| Albers, Matt, Lexington | 8 | 3 | .727 | 3.31 | 22 | 21 | 0 | 0 | 0 | 0 | 111.1 | 95 | 474 | 51 | 41 | 3 | 4 | 6 | 6 | 57 | 0 | 140 | 11 | 0 |
| Alcala, Jason, Hickory | 2 | 0 | 1.000 | 5.27 | 7 | 0 | 0 | 0 | 1 | 0 | 13.2 | 20 | 67 | 10 | 8 | 2 | 0 | 0 | 2 | 4 | 0 | 7 | 1 | 0 |
| Allen, Blake, Lake County * | 5 | 4 | .556 | 4.61 | 23 | 0 | 0 | 0 | 7 | 0 | 56.2 | 60 | 257 | 33 | 29 | 5 | 0 | 0 | 5 | 21 | 1 | 51 | 1 | 1 |
| Allen, Brian, Charleston-SC | 4 | 2 | .667 | 2.36 | 26 | 0 | 0 | 0 | 8 | 0 | 49.2 | 38 | 193 | 20 | 13 | 3 | 0 | 0 | 1 | 5 | 0 | 40 | 3 | 0 |
| Alvarez, Carlos, Columbus * | 1 | 0 | 1.000 | 6.65 | 15 | 0 | 0 | 0 | 2 | 0 | 21.2 | 31 | 107 | 18 | 16 | 5 | 0 | 0 | 3 | 8 | 0 | 32 | 2 | 1 |
| Alvarez, Tim, Hagerstown * | 4 | 9 | .308 | 3.69 | 51 | 0 | 0 | 0 | 46 | 22 | 61.0 | 50 | 265 | 29 | 25 | 5 | 1 | 0 | 4 | 28 | 2 | 41 | 1 | 1 |
| An, Byeong-Hak, Kannapolis * | 0 | 2 | .000 | 3.60 | 2 | 2 | 0 | 0 | 0 | 0 | 10.0 | 8 | 52 | 7 | 4 | 0 | 1 | 0 | 1 | 10 | 0 | 3 | 1 | 0 |
| Anderson, Devin, Rome * | 0 | 2 | .000 | 7.00 | 5 | 0 | 0 | 0 | 1 | 0 | 9.0 | 12 | 44 | 10 | 7 | 0 | 0 | 0 | 0 | 5 | 0 | 9 | 0 | 0 |
| Anez, Omar, Hagerstown | 2 | 7 | .222 | 4.81 | 14 | 14 | 0 | 0 | 0 | 0 | 78.2 | 81 | 346 | 50 | 42 | 6 | 6 | 6 | 10 | 25 | 1 | 56 | 4 | 0 |
| Arias, Alberto, Asheville | 8 | 9 | .471 | 5.00 | 26 | 24 | 4 | 1 | 2 | 1 | 135.0 | 153 | 572 | 86 | 75 | 23 | 5 | 8 | 3 | 36 | 0 | 83 | 6 | 2 |
| Arteaga, Erick, Lakewood | 10 | 9 | .526 | 4.87 | 27 | 26 | 1 | 0 | 0 | 0 | 159.0 | 207 | 675 | 94 | 86 | 12 | 6 | 8 | 6 | 21 | 1 | 87 | 7 | 0 |
| Ascanio, Jose, Rome | 3 | 3 | .500 | 3.84 | 34 | 0 | 0 | 0 | 18 | 9 | 65.2 | 58 | 274 | 39 | 28 | 6 | 0 | 0 | 4 | 15 | 1 | 64 | 5 | 3 |
| Ashabraner, Bo, Lake County | 5 | 2 | .714 | 2.70 | 28 | 0 | 0 | 0 | 19 | 3 | 46.2 | 42 | 193 | 17 | 14 | 3 | 0 | 1 | 2 | 11 | 1 | 49 | 2 | 0 |
| Bailey, Chad, Columbus * | 2 | 3 | .400 | 2.17 | 26 | 2 | 0 | 0 | 14 | 2 | 62.1 | 63 | 268 | 28 | 15 | 3 | 0 | 0 | 2 | 21 | 1 | 46 | 2 | 0 |
| Bakker, Kyle, Rome * | 3 | 0 | 1.000 | 1.91 | 20 | 0 | 0 | 0 | 6 | 1 | 28.1 | 23 | 135 | 8 | 6 | 0 | 0 | 0 | 3 | 21 | 1 | 21 | 1 | 0 |
| Banks, Demetrius, Kannapolis * | 0 | 0 | .000 | 9.00 | 5 | 0 | 0 | 0 | 2 | 0 | 5.0 | 5 | 26 | 6 | 5 | 2 | 0 | 0 | 1 | 5 | 0 | 11 | 0 | 0 |
| Barrack, Jacob, Lakewood | 0 | 0 | .000 | 5.51 | 9 | 0 | 0 | 0 | 5 | 0 | 16.1 | 17 | 71 | 11 | 10 | 3 | 0 | 0 | 0 | 5 | 0 | 14 | 1 | 0 |
| Basilio, Manuel, Charleston-SC | 1 | 0 | 1.000 | 6.27 | 10 | 0 | 0 | 0 | 2 | 0 | 18.2 | 19 | 93 | 13 | 13 | 3 | 0 | 0 | 3 | 15 | 0 | 11 | 2 | 0 |
| Bateman, Joe, Hagerstown | 7 | 5 | .583 | 2.14 | 36 | 0 | 0 | 0 | 14 | 1 | 71.1 | 48 | 289 | 19 | 17 | 3 | 1 | 0 | 5 | 20 | 2 | 80 | 1 | 0 |
| Beam, Randall, Augusta * | 2 | 1 | .667 | 0.00 | 18 | 0 | 0 | 0 | 15 | 10 | 23.1 | 10 | 85 | 1 | 0 | 0 | 0 | 0 | 1 | 4 | 0 | 27 | 1 | 0 |
| Bello, Juan, Kannapolis | 0 | 0 | .000 | 6.00 | 2 | 0 | 0 | 0 | 1 | 0 | 3.0 | 4 | 16 | 2 | 2 | 0 | 0 | 0 | 0 | 3 | 0 | 3 | 0 | 0 |
| Beltre, Jonathan, Lexington * | 4 | 5 | .444 | 2.96 | 45 | 0 | 0 | 0 | 27 | 0 | 76.0 | 59 | 344 | 27 | 25 | 6 | 0 | 0 | 4 | 52 | 2 | 76 | 10 | 1 |
| Benitez, Gabriel, Greensboro | 3 | 3 | .500 | 6.41 | 11 | 10 | 0 | 0 | 0 | 0 | 39.1 | 48 | 184 | 34 | 28 | 5 | 1 | 2 | 2 | 22 | 0 | 32 | 13 | 0 |
| Bergmann, Jay, Savannah | 3 | 7 | .300 | 4.85 | 13 | 13 | 0 | 0 | 0 | 0 | 65.0 | 67 | 300 | 43 | 35 | 6 | 3 | 7 | 7 | 34 | 0 | 58 | 6 | 1 |
| Blackley, Adam, Augusta * | 4 | 3 | .571 | 3.39 | 12 | 12 | 0 | 0 | 0 | 0 | 61.0 | 61 | 268 | 27 | 23 | 5 | 5 | 3 | 6 | 20 | 0 | 59 | 5 | 0 |
| Blakeney, Jacob, Rome | 0 | 2 | .000 | 2.35 | 17 | 0 | 0 | 0 | 12 | 5 | 23.0 | 16 | 91 | 8 | 6 | 1 | 0 | 0 | 1 | 5 | 1 | 18 | 0 | 0 |
| Bonner, Adam, Greensboro | 0 | 0 | .000 | 0.00 | 1 | 0 | 0 | 0 | 1 | 0 | 0.2 | 0 | 2 | 0 | 0 | 0 | 0 | 0 | 0 | 0 | 0 | 1 | 0 | 0 |
| Borland, Curt, Augusta | 0 | 1 | .000 | 6.27 | 10 | 0 | 0 | 0 | 2 | 0 | 18.2 | 29 | 86 | 15 | 13 | 2 | 0 | 2 | 0 | 3 | 0 | 14 | 2 | 1 |
| Bostick, Adam, Greensboro * | 2 | 8 | .200 | 3.79 | 23 | 22 | 0 | 0 | 0 | 0 | 114.0 | 100 | 490 | 57 | 48 | 10 | 4 | 3 | 6 | 58 | 0 | 163 | 6 | 1 |
| Brewer, Jeff, Capital City | 0 | 0 | .000 | 16.20 | 1 | 0 | 0 | 0 | 0 | 0 | 1.2 | 5 | 11 | 3 | 3 | 0 | 0 | 0 | 0 | 1 | 0 | 1 | 0 | 0 |
| Britton, Chris, Delmarva | 9 | 4 | .692 | 3.75 | 27 | 8 | 1 | 0 | 3 | 1 | 84.0 | 76 | 356 | 38 | 35 | 11 | 2 | 3 | 2 | 31 | 2 | 80 | 2 | 0 |
| Bulger, Brian, Charleston-SC | 10 | 8 | .556 | 3.58 | 37 | 17 | 0 | 0 | 9 | 1 | 123.1 | 103 | 517 | 58 | 49 | 5 | 6 | 1 | 8 | 50 | 2 | 120 | 13 | 0 |
| Burch, Jason, Asheville | 0 | 2 | .000 | 5.59 | 8 | 0 | 0 | 0 | 4 | 1 | 9.2 | 15 | 47 | 7 | 6 | 3 | 0 | 0 | 0 | 3 | 1 | 14 | 1 | 0 |
| Burrows, Angelo, Rome | 1 | 2 | .333 | 4.73 | 8 | 0 | 0 | 0 | 4 | 0 | 13.1 | 7 | 58 | 7 | 7 | 1 | 0 | 0 | 0 | 11 | 1 | 7 | 0 | 0 |
| Burton, T.J., Lake County | 2 | 1 | .667 | 3.80 | 39 | 0 | 0 | 0 | 6 | 2 | 94.2 | 95 | 433 | 44 | 40 | 6 | 0 | 1 | 10 | 47 | 3 | 72 | 11 | 0 |

| Pitcher, Team | W | L | Pct. | ERA | G | GS | CG | ShO | GF | Sv. | IP | H | TBF | R | ER | HR | SH | SF | HB | BB | IBB | SO | WP | Bk. |
|---|---|---|---|---|---|---|---|---|---|---|---|---|---|---|---|---|---|---|---|---|---|---|---|---|
| Cabrera, Nate, Lakewood | 6 | 4 | .600 | 2.82 | 24 | 23 | 2 | 2 | 0 | 0 | 131.0 | 111 | 535 | 50 | 41 | 10 | 10 | 11 | 4 | 40 | 0 | 113 | 7 | 2 |
| Cahill, Casey, Delmarva | 0 | 0 | .000 | 3.38 | 4 | 0 | 0 | 0 | 1 | 0 | 8.0 | 6 | 33 | 4 | 3 | 0 | 0 | 0 | 1 | 2 | 0 | 7 | 0 | 0 |
| Callahan, Ryan, Hagerstown * | 0 | 4 | .000 | 4.56 | 7 | 5 | 0 | 0 | 1 | 0 | 23.2 | 28 | 105 | 16 | 12 | 2 | 1 | 1 | 0 | 10 | 0 | 17 | 3 | 0 |
| Canizal, Joaquin, Charleston-WV | 9 | 2 | .818 | 4.16 | 42 | 0 | 0 | 0 | 3 | 0 | 80.0 | 82 | 357 | 41 | 37 | 7 | 3 | 2 | 8 | 29 | 5 | 75 | 2 | 0 |
| Capps, Matt, Hickory | 2 | 3 | .400 | 10.07 | 12 | 8 | 0 | 0 | 1 | 0 | 42.0 | 82 | 227 | 55 | 47 | 8 | 0 | 1 | 5 | 16 | 0 | 27 | 0 | 0 |
| Carpenter, Calvin, Charleston-SC | 1 | 0 | 1.000 | 7.36 | 10 | 0 | 0 | 0 | 7 | 0 | 14.2 | 19 | 79 | 13 | 12 | 0 | 0 | 0 | 1 | 15 | 1 | 14 | 6 | 0 |
| Carvajal, Marcos, Columbus | 4 | 2 | .667 | 1.88 | 36 | 0 | 0 | 0 | 21 | 1 | 72.0 | 50 | 299 | 19 | 15 | 2 | 3 | 4 | 5 | 35 | 0 | 72 | 7 | 0 |
| Castillo, Albenis, Columbus | 1 | 1 | .500 | 5.21 | 9 | 0 | 0 | 0 | 6 | 1 | 19.0 | 26 | 96 | 17 | 11 | 3 | 0 | 0 | 0 | 13 | 1 | 21 | 4 | 0 |
| Castleman, Steve, Asheville | 1 | 1 | .500 | 6.85 | 18 | 0 | 0 | 0 | 8 | 0 | 23.2 | 29 | 103 | 18 | 18 | 6 | 0 | 0 | 1 | 2 | 0 | 19 | 1 | 0 |
| Castro, Fabio, Kannapolis * | 4 | 0 | 1.000 | 3.00 | 37 | 0 | 0 | 0 | 15 | 3 | 51.0 | 44 | 222 | 20 | 17 | 2 | 0 | 0 | 3 | 23 | 0 | 44 | 2 | 0 |
| Caughey, Trevor, Delmarva * | 4 | 2 | .667 | 3.14 | 37 | 2 | 0 | 0 | 9 | 3 | 86.0 | 79 | 371 | 32 | 30 | 7 | 1 | 1 | 13 | 21 | 3 | 73 | 7 | 1 |
| Cevette, Dan, Lake County * | 2 | 0 | 1.000 | 2.47 | 9 | 9 | 0 | 0 | 0 | 0 | 43.2 | 43 | 179 | 13 | 12 | 4 | 2 | 3 | 1 | 14 | 0 | 41 | 0 | 0 |
| Chamberlin, Bryce, Delmarva | 0 | 3 | .000 | 7.15 | 3 | 3 | 0 | 0 | 0 | 0 | 11.1 | 18 | 59 | 9 | 9 | 0 | 0 | 0 | 2 | 7 | 0 | 12 | 1 | 1 |
| Chick, Travis, Greensboro | 6 | 4 | .600 | 4.04 | 28 | 11 | 0 | 0 | 6 | 0 | 91.1 | 79 | 384 | 51 | 41 | 11 | 1 | 2 | 7 | 27 | 0 | 112 | 6 | 0 |
| Childs, Ryan, Delmarva | 0 | 1 | .000 | 5.23 | 7 | 0 | 0 | 0 | 3 | 1 | 10.1 | 11 | 48 | 8 | 6 | 1 | 0 | 0 | 0 | 6 | 0 | 8 | 0 | 0 |
| Cierlik, Jason, Delmarva * | 0 | 0 | .000 | 10.80 | 7 | 0 | 0 | 0 | 2 | 0 | 5.0 | 4 | 34 | 6 | 6 | 0 | 0 | 0 | 0 | 15 | 0 | 3 | 0 | 0 |
| Cillo, Cody, Greensboro | 1 | 3 | .250 | 5.82 | 14 | 0 | 0 | 0 | 6 | 0 | 21.2 | 27 | 104 | 17 | 14 | 1 | 0 | 0 | 1 | 11 | 0 | 23 | 1 | 0 |
| Cline, Zachary, Lakewood * | 5 | 1 | .833 | 2.98 | 8 | 8 | 0 | 0 | 0 | 0 | 42.1 | 38 | 170 | 15 | 14 | 3 | 1 | 5 | 3 | 8 | 0 | 34 | 4 | 0 |
| Cockrell, Michael, Hickory | 0 | 0 | .000 | 0.00 | 1 | 0 | 0 | 0 | 1 | 0 | 1.0 | 1 | 5 | 0 | 0 | 0 | 0 | 0 | 0 | 1 | 0 | 1 | 0 | 0 |
| Collar, Mike, Lexington | 2 | 6 | .250 | 8.45 | 38 | 6 | 0 | 0 | 12 | 1 | 87.1 | 128 | 441 | 89 | 82 | 15 | 1 | 4 | 8 | 48 | 0 | 57 | 8 | 1 |
| Coppinger, Joe, Delmarva | 0 | 1 | .000 | 4.35 | 9 | 3 | 0 | 0 | 2 | 1 | 20.2 | 20 | 100 | 13 | 10 | 1 | 3 | 0 | 0 | 20 | 1 | 15 | 0 | 0 |
| Cordova, Vincent, Capital City | 8 | 7 | .533 | 4.25 | 24 | 19 | 0 | 0 | 0 | 0 | 120.2 | 138 | 515 | 73 | 57 | 11 | 5 | 5 | 10 | 14 | 0 | 100 | 4 | 0 |
| Core, Danny, Charleston-WV | 9 | 8 | .529 | 3.43 | 28 | 28 | 1 | 0 | 0 | 0 | 157.1 | 137 | 642 | 70 | 60 | 15 | 4 | 10 | 13 | 53 | 0 | 132 | 7 | 0 |
| Corpas, Manuel, Asheville | 2 | 2 | .500 | 3.05 | 43 | 0 | 0 | 0 | 20 | 3 | 44.1 | 48 | 199 | 20 | 15 | 3 | 0 | 0 | 6 | 13 | 1 | 52 | 2 | 1 |
| Corporan, Ramon, Augusta | 0 | 3 | .000 | 6.08 | 9 | 8 | 0 | 0 | 0 | 0 | 37.0 | 44 | 169 | 32 | 25 | 4 | 3 | 4 | 4 | 10 | 0 | 22 | 2 | 0 |
| Cotto, Luis, Lake County | 0 | 0 | .000 | 0.00 | 1 | 0 | 0 | 0 | 1 | 0 | 2.0 | 1 | 7 | 0 | 0 | 0 | 0 | 0 | 0 | 0 | 0 | 3 | 0 | 0 |
| Cramer, Bob, Charleston-SC * | 6 | 4 | .600 | 3.32 | 35 | 0 | 0 | 0 | 12 | 4 | 62.1 | 52 | 254 | 27 | 23 | 4 | 0 | 0 | 4 | 12 | 0 | 48 | 6 | 1 |
| D'Amico, Jeff, Lake County | 0 | 0 | .000 | 0.00 | 2 | 1 | 0 | 0 | 0 | 0 | 2.0 | 1 | 7 | 0 | 0 | 0 | 0 | 0 | 0 | 0 | 0 | 1 | 0 | 0 |
| Dalton, Matt, Charleston-WV | 4 | 3 | .571 | 1.69 | 23 | 0 | 0 | 0 | 8 | 2 | 32.0 | 22 | 137 | 10 | 6 | 1 | 0 | 0 | 4 | 15 | 1 | 27 | 4 | 0 |
| Danly, Ryan, Capital City * | 3 | 3 | .500 | 4.33 | 11 | 9 | 1 | 1 | 0 | 0 | 43.2 | 58 | 203 | 31 | 21 | 3 | 0 | 2 | 1 | 18 | 0 | 38 | 0 | 0 |
| De Los Santos, Omar, Columbus | 1 | 2 | .333 | 9.00 | 12 | 0 | 0 | 0 | 2 | 0 | 18.0 | 24 | 97 | 23 | 18 | 2 | 0 | 0 | 1 | 19 | 1 | 21 | 3 | 0 |
| De maria, Chris, Hickory | 8 | 3 | .727 | 2.94 | 40 | 0 | 0 | 0 | 27 | 10 | 79.2 | 62 | 324 | 29 | 26 | 5 | 3 | 1 | 4 | 20 | 2 | 101 | 3 | 0 |
| DeLeon, Joey, Lexington | 4 | 5 | .444 | 4.30 | 37 | 2 | 0 | 0 | 9 | 1 | 81.2 | 90 | 379 | 44 | 39 | 10 | 1 | 1 | 3 | 46 | 1 | 72 | 4 | 0 |
| Deininger, Todd, Kannapolis | 1 | 1 | .500 | 5.97 | 25 | 1 | 0 | 0 | 9 | 0 | 34.2 | 33 | 176 | 26 | 23 | 2 | 1 | 0 | 4 | 35 | 0 | 25 | 5 | 0 |
| Delgado, Jesus, Augusta | 1 | 5 | .167 | 5.22 | 21 | 16 | 0 | 0 | 2 | 0 | 58.2 | 61 | 254 | 40 | 34 | 10 | 3 | 2 | 1 | 26 | 0 | 34 | 6 | 1 |
| Demontel, Jimmy, Greensboro | 2 | 2 | .500 | 6.57 | 25 | 0 | 0 | 0 | 7 | 2 | 37.0 | 44 | 171 | 29 | 27 | 0 | 0 | 0 | 3 | 15 | 2 | 43 | 9 | 0 |
| Dennison, Michael, Augusta | 5 | 3 | .625 | 5.12 | 29 | 0 | 0 | 0 | 10 | 2 | 45.2 | 64 | 213 | 31 | 26 | 5 | 0 | 0 | 3 | 9 | 1 | 51 | 3 | 0 |
| Deza, Fredy, Delmarva | 8 | 11 | .421 | 3.31 | 22 | 21 | 2 | 0 | 0 | 0 | 119.2 | 102 | 479 | 52 | 44 | 7 | 6 | 6 | 5 | 21 | 2 | 93 | 6 | 3 |
| DiAngelo, Jason, Asheville | 1 | 7 | .125 | 3.78 | 41 | 2 | 0 | 0 | 27 | 8 | 47.2 | 49 | 215 | 24 | 20 | 4 | 0 | 1 | 4 | 20 | 3 | 52 | 2 | 0 |
| Diaz, Jose, Columbus | 1 | 4 | .200 | 2.12 | 28 | 0 | 0 | 0 | 24 | 14 | 34.0 | 21 | 141 | 13 | 8 | 1 | 0 | 1 | 5 | 12 | 2 | 59 | 6 | 0 |
| Diaz, Raymar, Lexington | 1 | 3 | .250 | 4.43 | 24 | 1 | 0 | 0 | 8 | 2 | 42.2 | 31 | 186 | 21 | 21 | 3 | 1 | 0 | 2 | 26 | 0 | 37 | 1 | 0 |
| Digby, Bryan, Rome | 8 | 9 | .471 | 5.94 | 27 | 27 | 1 | 1 | 0 | 0 | 144.0 | 189 | 656 | 112 | 95 | 16 | 8 | 6 | 8 | 71 | 0 | 107 | 19 | 0 |
| Dixon, Zachary, Delmarva * | 9 | 4 | .692 | 2.54 | 24 | 21 | 0 | 0 | 0 | 0 | 120.2 | 97 | 517 | 52 | 34 | 5 | 9 | 6 | 6 | 65 | 0 | 105 | 7 | 0 |
| Dizard, Fraser, Kannapolis * | 0 | 1 | .000 | 2.79 | 27 | 1 | 0 | 0 | 7 | 1 | 48.1 | 38 | 216 | 19 | 15 | 2 | 0 | 1 | 2 | 33 | 0 | 39 | 6 | 0 |
| Doble, Clemente, Lakewood | 2 | 2 | .500 | 4.56 | 8 | 2 | 0 | 0 | 5 | 0 | 23.2 | 21 | 110 | 14 | 12 | 2 | 0 | 0 | 2 | 18 | 0 | 15 | 2 | 0 |
| Dobyns, Jon, Charleston-SC | 0 | 0 | .000 | 7.71 | 5 | 1 | 0 | 0 | 2 | 0 | 11.2 | 11 | 49 | 10 | 10 | 3 | 0 | 2 | 0 | 6 | 0 | 3 | 0 | 0 |
| Done, Mike, Delmarva | 0 | 0 | .000 | 0.00 | 1 | 0 | 0 | 0 | 1 | 0 | 1.0 | 1 | 5 | 0 | 0 | 0 | 0 | 0 | 0 | 1 | 0 | 1 | 0 | 0 |
| Douglass, Chance, Lexington | 9 | 10 | .474 | 5.33 | 29 | 24 | 0 | 0 | 1 | 0 | 136.2 | 156 | 635 | 99 | 81 | 18 | 9 | 13 | 15 | 73 | 0 | 106 | 7 | 0 |
| English, Jesse, Hagerstown * | 0 | 1 | .000 | 7.48 | 17 | 4 | 0 | 0 | 3 | 0 | 43.1 | 39 | 209 | 37 | 36 | 4 | 0 | 0 | 5 | 40 | 0 | 46 | 6 | 0 |
| Esarey, Brad, Charleston-WV * | 4 | 1 | .800 | 5.11 | 42 | 0 | 0 | 0 | 22 | 2 | 56.1 | 69 | 290 | 44 | 32 | 3 | 0 | 0 | 8 | 45 | 6 | 39 | 8 | 0 |
| Evangelista, Nicholas, Lakewood | 0 | 0 | .000 | 1.80 | 2 | 0 | 0 | 0 | 1 | 0 | 5.0 | 2 | 19 | 1 | 1 | 0 | 0 | 0 | 0 | 2 | 0 | 4 | 0 | 0 |
| Everts, Clint, Savannah | 7 | 3 | .700 | 2.49 | 17 | 17 | 1 | 1 | 0 | 0 | 90.1 | 67 | 361 | 29 | 25 | 3 | 9 | 3 | 6 | 21 | 0 | 103 | 6 | 0 |
| Farley, Chris, Augusta | 3 | 5 | .375 | 5.10 | 38 | 1 | 0 | 0 | 8 | 2 | 72.1 | 69 | 323 | 52 | 41 | 6 | 1 | 2 | 16 | 28 | 0 | 54 | 5 | 2 |
| Felfoldi, Jon, Savannah * | 2 | 3 | .400 | 3.51 | 5 | 5 | 0 | 0 | 0 | 0 | 25.2 | 28 | 116 | 17 | 10 | 2 | 2 | 2 | 0 | 17 | 0 | 20 | 1 | 1 |
| Figueroa, Jonathan, Columbus * | 3 | 7 | .300 | 6.90 | 14 | 13 | 0 | 0 | 0 | 0 | 60.0 | 67 | 274 | 48 | 46 | 12 | 3 | 0 | 6 | 25 | 0 | 70 | 2 | 2 |
| Finch, Brian, Delmarva | 2 | 2 | .500 | 1.44 | 5 | 5 | 0 | 0 | 0 | 0 | 25.0 | 23 | 104 | 11 | 4 | 0 | 0 | 1 | 0 | 2 | 0 | 14 | 3 | 0 |
| Flanagan, Jeremy, Charleston-SC | 4 | 1 | .800 | 3.86 | 18 | 5 | 0 | 0 | 5 | 0 | 44.1 | 43 | 191 | 23 | 19 | 5 | 0 | 0 | 4 | 12 | 0 | 38 | 2 | 0 |
| Flores, Rafael, Kannapolis | 8 | 11 | .421 | 3.82 | 23 | 22 | 0 | 0 | 0 | 0 | 127.1 | 139 | 540 | 71 | 54 | 14 | 15 | 4 | 9 | 33 | 0 | 65 | 2 | 0 |
| Floyd, Jesse, Hagerstown | 4 | 8 | .333 | 4.60 | 32 | 18 | 0 | 0 | 5 | 2 | 121.1 | 129 | 525 | 74 | 62 | 12 | 8 | 7 | 4 | 42 | 0 | 125 | 5 | 0 |
| Foli, Daniel, Capital City | 1 | 0 | 1.000 | 2.97 | 17 | 0 | 0 | 0 | 9 | 2 | 30.1 | 19 | 124 | 13 | 10 | 2 | 0 | 0 | 3 | 11 | 0 | 32 | 1 | 0 |
| France, Ryan, Lexington | 3 | 0 | 1.000 | 1.83 | 22 | 0 | 0 | 0 | 6 | 2 | 39.1 | 20 | 153 | 8 | 8 | 3 | 0 | 0 | 3 | 12 | 0 | 44 | 3 | 0 |
| Franzenburg, Luke, Rome * | 0 | 0 | .000 | 3.00 | 9 | 0 | 0 | 0 | 6 | 2 | 12.0 | 12 | 52 | 5 | 4 | 1 | 0 | 0 | 1 | 3 | 1 | 8 | 1 | 0 |
| Gagne, J.P., Asheville | 0 | 3 | .000 | 14.21 | 10 | 0 | 0 | 0 | 6 | 0 | 12.2 | 29 | 71 | 21 | 20 | 5 | 0 | 0 | 0 | 4 | 3 | 9 | 1 | 0 |
| Galarraga, Armando, Savannah | 5 | 5 | .500 | 4.65 | 23 | 19 | 2 | 0 | 1 | 0 | 110.1 | 104 | 470 | 64 | 57 | 14 | 6 | 6 | 8 | 31 | 0 | 94 | 3 | 1 |
| Galvez, Gary, Augusta | 7 | 10 | .412 | 5.14 | 30 | 22 | 1 | 0 | 3 | 0 | 140.0 | 153 | 600 | 86 | 80 | 16 | 10 | 2 | 7 | 36 | 0 | 102 | 6 | 0 |
| Gangi, Aaron, Charleston-SC * | 2 | 9 | .182 | 8.19 | 31 | 11 | 0 | 0 | 4 | 1 | 85.2 | 134 | 410 | 84 | 78 | 8 | 3 | 6 | 3 | 31 | 0 | 46 | 7 | 0 |
| Garcia, Anderson, Capital City | 9 | 2 | .818 | 4.71 | 35 | 5 | 0 | 0 | 15 | 2 | 84.0 | 92 | 396 | 57 | 44 | 7 | 1 | 1 | 9 | 47 | 2 | 75 | 8 | 1 |
| Gardner, Jarrett, Augusta | 13 | 5 | .722 | 2.51 | 25 | 23 | 0 | 0 | 1 | 0 | 136.0 | 130 | 533 | 49 | 38 | 12 | 6 | 2 | 6 | 11 | 0 | 92 | 2 | 0 |
| Garza, Rolando, Rome | 1 | 1 | .500 | 6.75 | 10 | 0 | 0 | 0 | 3 | 0 | 21.1 | 21 | 99 | 18 | 16 | 2 | 2 | 2 | 3 | 12 | 0 | 13 | 6 | 0 |
| George, Christopher, Hagerstown | 2 | 1 | .667 | 7.86 | 20 | 2 | 0 | 0 | 5 | 0 | 44.2 | 63 | 210 | 40 | 39 | 9 | 0 | 1 | 2 | 13 | 0 | 38 | 6 | 0 |
| Glynn, Josh, Greensboro | 0 | 1 | .000 | 4.50 | 5 | 0 | 0 | 0 | 2 | 0 | 10.0 | 13 | 48 | 7 | 5 | 1 | 0 | 0 | 0 | 4 | 0 | 2 | 1 | 0 |
| Gomez, Jose, Capital City | 3 | 1 | .750 | 3.18 | 11 | 0 | 0 | 0 | 0 | 0 | 17.0 | 8 | 73 | 7 | 6 | 1 | 0 | 0 | 2 | 12 | 0 | 23 | 3 | 2 |
| Gomez, Warmar, Savannah | 4 | 7 | .364 | 3.80 | 43 | 0 | 0 | 0 | 20 | 4 | 66.1 | 83 | 310 | 37 | 28 | 9 | 1 | 1 | 4 | 25 | 4 | 37 | 6 | 0 |
| Gonzalez, Andy, Kannapolis | 0 | 1 | .000 | 6.75 | 2 | 2 | 0 | 0 | 0 | 0 | 8.0 | 9 | 40 | 7 | 6 | 0 | 0 | 0 | 0 | 7 | 0 | 7 | 0 | 0 |
| Gonzalez, Giovany, Kannapolis * | 1 | 1 | .500 | 3.03 | 6 | 6 | 0 | 0 | 0 | 0 | 32.2 | 30 | 147 | 13 | 11 | 1 | 2 | 1 | 0 | 13 | 0 | 27 | 1 | 1 |
| Gonzalez, Jino, Charleston-SC * | 9 | 5 | .643 | 4.56 | 24 | 23 | 0 | 0 | 0 | 0 | 120.1 | 128 | 539 | 74 | 61 | 11 | 9 | 5 | 13 | 53 | 0 | 98 | 6 | 0 |
| Goodman, Chris, Savannah | 0 | 0 | .000 | 2.45 | 8 | 1 | 0 | 0 | 4 | 2 | 18.1 | 16 | 72 | 5 | 5 | 3 | 1 | 1 | 0 | 2 | 0 | 20 | 0 | 0 |
| Gorzelanny, Tom, Hickory * | 7 | 2 | .778 | 2.23 | 16 | 15 | 1 | 0 | 0 | 0 | 93.0 | 63 | 368 | 30 | 23 | 9 | 5 | 3 | 2 | 34 | 0 | 106 | 4 | 0 |
| Greusel, Evan, Greensboro | 3 | 7 | .300 | 5.63 | 14 | 14 | 0 | 0 | 0 | 0 | 62.1 | 73 | 269 | 48 | 39 | 11 | 0 | 4 | 2 | 18 | 0 | 59 | 4 | 0 |
| Grigsby, Derick, Lexington | 7 | 11 | .389 | 4.71 | 27 | 26 | 0 | 0 | 0 | 0 | 137.2 | 133 | 620 | 88 | 72 | 17 | 6 | 9 | 14 | 93 | 0 | 142 | 9 | 0 |
| Grimm, Eric, Delmarva | 0 | 0 | .000 | 36.00 | 1 | 0 | 0 | 0 | 1 | 0 | 1.0 | 3 | 7 | 4 | 4 | 1 | 0 | 0 | 0 | 1 | 0 | 1 | 0 | 0 |
| Guanchez, Argimiro, Augusta * | 4 | 5 | .444 | 4.95 | 35 | 0 | 0 | 0 | 18 | 3 | 43.2 | 55 | 210 | 36 | 24 | 0 | 2 | 0 | 3 | 23 | 3 | 33 | 7 | 0 |

| Pitcher, Team | W | L | Pct. | ERA | G | GS | CG | ShO | GF | Sv. | IP | H | TBF | R | ER | HR | SH | SF | HB | BB | IBB | SO | WP | Bk. |
|---|---|---|---|---|---|---|---|---|---|---|---|---|---|---|---|---|---|---|---|---|---|---|---|---|
| Haeger, Charles, Kannapolis | 1 | 3 | .250 | 2.01 | 5 | 5 | 0 | 0 | 0 | 0 | 31.1 | 31 | 137 | 17 | 7 | 0 | 3 | 4 | 3 | 12 | 0 | 21 | 1 | 0 |
| Haigwood, Daniel, Kannapolis * | 10 | 4 | .714 | 4.76 | 21 | 21 | 0 | 0 | 0 | 0 | 113.1 | 97 | 473 | 63 | 60 | 10 | 8 | 5 | 10 | 56 | 2 | 99 | 8 | 0 |
| Hamilton, Jamaal, Columbus * | 1 | 0 | 1.000 | 0.36 | 14 | 0 | 0 | 0 | 6 | 2 | 25.1 | 15 | 97 | 2 | 1 | 0 | 0 | 0 | 0 | 7 | 0 | 27 | 0 | 0 |
| Hammel, Jason, Charleston-SC | 4 | 7 | .364 | 3.23 | 18 | 18 | 0 | 0 | 0 | 0 | 94.2 | 94 | 405 | 54 | 34 | 7 | 5 | 5 | 2 | 27 | 0 | 88 | 8 | 0 |
| Hammes, Zach, Columbus | 5 | 8 | .385 | 4.55 | 24 | 23 | 0 | 0 | 1 | 0 | 112.2 | 146 | 527 | 79 | 57 | 15 | 5 | 8 | 7 | 54 | 1 | 73 | 14 | 1 |
| Hanson, Adam, Lake County | 3 | 6 | .333 | 4.55 | 35 | 0 | 0 | 0 | 18 | 0 | 63.1 | 74 | 304 | 33 | 32 | 6 | 2 | 2 | 6 | 32 | 3 | 62 | 4 | 0 |
| Hanson, Mike, Rome | 0 | 0 | .000 | 0.00 | 1 | 0 | 0 | 0 | 1 | 0 | 0.2 | 1 | 4 | 0 | 0 | 0 | 0 | 0 | 0 | 1 | 0 | 1 | 0 | 0 |
| Harper, Jeremy, Charleston-WV | 1 | 2 | .333 | 4.08 | 13 | 4 | 0 | 0 | 2 | 1 | 35.1 | 37 | 163 | 22 | 16 | 3 | 0 | 1 | 4 | 20 | 0 | 33 | 2 | 1 |
| Hart, Kevin, Delmarva | 2 | 0 | 1.000 | 3.77 | 4 | 2 | 0 | 0 | 0 | 0 | 14.1 | 13 | 63 | 6 | 6 | 0 | 0 | 1 | 1 | 5 | 0 | 16 | 1 | 0 |
| Harts, Jeremy, Hickory * | 0 | 1 | .000 | 4.95 | 16 | 0 | 0 | 0 | 5 | 0 | 20.0 | 12 | 98 | 16 | 11 | 2 | 0 | 0 | 3 | 23 | 0 | 19 | 5 | 0 |
| Hawk, Shane, Capital City * | 1 | 1 | .500 | 2.20 | 25 | 0 | 0 | 0 | 19 | 8 | 32.2 | 25 | 132 | 9 | 8 | 1 | 0 | 0 | 0 | 9 | 2 | 44 | 1 | 0 |
| Hernandez, Christopher, Hickory | 1 | 2 | .333 | 1.97 | 43 | 0 | 0 | 0 | 40 | 24 | 50.1 | 47 | 216 | 14 | 11 | 3 | 0 | 0 | 1 | 18 | 0 | 67 | 4 | 0 |
| Hernandez, Fernando, Kannapolis | 3 | 3 | .500 | 2.98 | 28 | 0 | 0 | 0 | 11 | 4 | 45.1 | 43 | 198 | 20 | 15 | 2 | 0 | 0 | 3 | 16 | 1 | 59 | 3 | 0 |
| Hertzler, Barry, Augusta | 4 | 2 | .667 | 8.50 | 25 | 1 | 0 | 0 | 10 | 1 | 36.0 | 56 | 177 | 37 | 34 | 3 | 0 | 0 | 4 | 13 | 0 | 21 | 5 | 2 |
| Hilario, Elpidio, Augusta | 0 | 0 | .000 | 9.00 | 5 | 0 | 0 | 0 | 1 | 0 | 6.0 | 7 | 32 | 7 | 6 | 1 | 0 | 0 | 0 | 7 | 0 | 7 | 1 | 0 |
| Hiraldo, Nelson, Lake County | 6 | 5 | .545 | 5.38 | 26 | 2 | 0 | 0 | 8 | 2 | 72.0 | 82 | 327 | 52 | 43 | 14 | 1 | 0 | 6 | 26 | 1 | 66 | 6 | 0 |
| Hodges, Daniel, Lakewood * | 2 | 3 | .400 | 2.96 | 31 | 0 | 0 | 0 | 23 | 7 | 45.2 | 54 | 205 | 16 | 15 | 2 | 0 | 0 | 3 | 10 | 0 | 31 | 0 | 0 |
| Holliday, Brian, Hickory * | 7 | 8 | .467 | 4.61 | 23 | 23 | 0 | 0 | 0 | 0 | 113.1 | 106 | 496 | 60 | 58 | 5 | 5 | 4 | 11 | 54 | 0 | 80 | 8 | 2 |
| Honsa, Chris, Lakewood | 0 | 0 | .000 | 6.12 | 12 | 1 | 0 | 0 | 3 | 2 | 25.0 | 29 | 116 | 17 | 17 | 1 | 1 | 1 | 3 | 9 | 0 | 23 | 1 | 0 |
| Hoorelbeke, Casey, Columbus | 0 | 1 | .000 | 2.57 | 3 | 3 | 0 | 0 | 0 | 0 | 14.0 | 13 | 55 | 7 | 4 | 1 | 4 | 0 | 1 | 2 | 0 | 8 | 0 | 0 |
| Houser, James, Charleston-SC * | 3 | 1 | .750 | 2.20 | 7 | 7 | 0 | 0 | 0 | 0 | 32.2 | 27 | 131 | 9 | 8 | 1 | 1 | 1 | 3 | 13 | 0 | 27 | 0 | 1 |
| Hudson, Jeremy, Kannapolis | 0 | 0 | .000 | 1.74 | 5 | 0 | 0 | 0 | 0 | 0 | 10.1 | 9 | 44 | 2 | 2 | 1 | 0 | 0 | 3 | 5 | 0 | 5 | 2 | 0 |
| Hummel, Rick, Kannapolis | 0 | 0 | .000 | 36.00 | 2 | 0 | 0 | 0 | 1 | 0 | 1.0 | 4 | 7 | 4 | 4 | 1 | 0 | 0 | 0 | 0 | 0 | 0 | 0 | 0 |
| Humphries, Justin, Lexington | 0 | 0 | .000 | 27.00 | 2 | 0 | 0 | 0 | 2 | 0 | 1.1 | 4 | 9 | 4 | 4 | 2 | 0 | 0 | 0 | 1 | 0 | 1 | 0 | 0 |
| Hurd, John, Kannapolis | 0 | 0 | .000 | 3.60 | 13 | 0 | 0 | 0 | 6 | 0 | 20.0 | 19 | 94 | 9 | 8 | 1 | 0 | 1 | 3 | 12 | 1 | 17 | 4 | 0 |
| Iehl, Jay, Greensboro | 1 | 2 | .333 | 7.57 | 17 | 1 | 0 | 0 | 2 | 0 | 27.1 | 33 | 129 | 23 | 23 | 4 | 0 | 0 | 4 | 9 | 0 | 31 | 3 | 1 |
| Ion, Mark, Asheville | 4 | 2 | .667 | 4.65 | 34 | 0 | 0 | 0 | 21 | 8 | 40.2 | 41 | 189 | 26 | 21 | 7 | 0 | 0 | 5 | 21 | 0 | 32 | 6 | 1 |
| Isenberg, Kurt, Charleston-WV * | 3 | 4 | .429 | 3.88 | 11 | 10 | 0 | 0 | 0 | 0 | 51.0 | 48 | 210 | 25 | 22 | 5 | 0 | 1 | 3 | 15 | 0 | 34 | 3 | 0 |
| Jackson, Kyle, Augusta | 3 | 13 | .188 | 4.64 | 31 | 21 | 0 | 0 | 1 | 1 | 141.2 | 156 | 612 | 87 | 73 | 20 | 3 | 9 | 13 | 36 | 0 | 130 | 6 | 2 |
| James, Chuck, Rome * | 10 | 5 | .667 | 2.25 | 26 | 22 | 1 | 0 | 2 | 0 | 132.0 | 92 | 527 | 41 | 33 | 6 | 9 | 9 | 7 | 48 | 1 | 156 | 3 | 0 |
| James, Justin, Charleston-WV | 5 | 4 | .556 | 3.00 | 14 | 14 | 0 | 0 | 0 | 0 | 78.0 | 67 | 319 | 31 | 26 | 2 | 3 | 2 | 6 | 24 | 1 | 83 | 6 | 0 |
| Jimenez, Franklyn, Savannah | 0 | 0 | .000 | 0.00 | 2 | 0 | 0 | 0 | 2 | 0 | 1.1 | 0 | 4 | 0 | 0 | 0 | 0 | 0 | 0 | 0 | 0 | 1 | 0 | 0 |
| Johnson, Blair, Hickory | 1 | 4 | .200 | 7.83 | 9 | 8 | 0 | 0 | 1 | 0 | 43.2 | 59 | 200 | 40 | 38 | 7 | 1 | 4 | 3 | 14 | 0 | 22 | 1 | 0 |
| Johnson, James, Delmarva | 8 | 7 | .533 | 3.29 | 20 | 17 | 0 | 0 | 1 | 0 | 106.2 | 97 | 443 | 44 | 39 | 9 | 5 | 5 | 9 | 30 | 1 | 93 | 6 | 0 |
| Kaiser, Marc, Asheville | 11 | 11 | .500 | 4.33 | 27 | 27 | 3 | 0 | 0 | 0 | 181.0 | 197 | 783 | 106 | 87 | 17 | 4 | 7 | 25 | 37 | 0 | 105 | 7 | 2 |
| Kane, Kyle, Kannapolis | 0 | 0 | .000 | 2.08 | 4 | 0 | 0 | 0 | 1 | 0 | 4.1 | 5 | 22 | 5 | 1 | 0 | 0 | 0 | 1 | 3 | 0 | 6 | 0 | 0 |
| Kendrick, Kyle, Lakewood | 3 | 8 | .273 | 6.08 | 15 | 15 | 0 | 0 | 0 | 0 | 66.2 | 85 | 318 | 56 | 45 | 9 | 6 | 4 | 8 | 33 | 0 | 36 | 4 | 0 |
| King, Bryan, Capital City | 8 | 0 | 1.000 | 4.02 | 40 | 0 | 0 | 0 | 9 | 2 | 69.1 | 64 | 303 | 39 | 31 | 5 | 0 | 1 | 10 | 23 | 0 | 69 | 7 | 2 |
| King, Timothy, Charleston-SC * | 0 | 3 | .000 | 23.14 | 3 | 2 | 0 | 0 | 0 | 0 | 7.0 | 14 | 47 | 20 | 18 | 3 | 0 | 0 | 1 | 11 | 0 | 4 | 1 | 0 |
| Koehler,, Greensboro | 0 | 1 | .000 | 7.20 | 2 | 2 | 0 | 0 | 0 | 0 | 5.0 | 7 | 24 | 6 | 4 | 0 | 0 | 0 | 0 | 2 | 0 | 3 | 0 | 0 |
| Kranawetter, Josh, Charleston-SC | 6 | 2 | .750 | 1.79 | 12 | 11 | 1 | 1 | 0 | 0 | 65.1 | 54 | 264 | 21 | 13 | 2 | 3 | 0 | 5 | 21 | 0 | 69 | 3 | 0 |
| Kuo, Hong-Chih, Columbus * | 1 | 0 | 1.000 | 4.50 | 3 | 0 | 0 | 0 | 1 | 0 | 6.0 | 8 | 31 | 3 | 3 | 0 | 0 | 0 | 1 | 4 | 0 | 10 | 1 | 0 |
| Laffey, Aaron, Lake County * | 3 | 7 | .300 | 6.53 | 19 | 15 | 0 | 0 | 2 | 1 | 73.0 | 79 | 346 | 58 | 53 | 6 | 3 | 3 | 8 | 44 | 0 | 67 | 3 | 1 |
| Larson, Adam, Kannapolis | 3 | 1 | .750 | 4.20 | 18 | 0 | 0 | 0 | 6 | 1 | 30.0 | 35 | 136 | 17 | 14 | 3 | 0 | 1 | 4 | 8 | 0 | 23 | 0 | 1 |
| Letson, Wes, Rome * | 2 | 0 | 1.000 | 3.24 | 11 | 0 | 0 | 0 | 5 | 1 | 16.2 | 19 | 77 | 6 | 6 | 3 | 0 | 0 | 0 | 8 | 1 | 12 | 0 | 0 |
| Libey, Justin, Lakewood | 0 | 0 | .000 | 6.52 | 5 | 0 | 0 | 0 | 2 | 0 | 9.2 | 13 | 45 | 8 | 7 | 2 | 0 | 0 | 0 | 3 | 0 | 4 | 0 | 0 |
| Lindstrom, Matthew, Capital City | 3 | 2 | .600 | 3.21 | 13 | 12 | 0 | 0 | 0 | 0 | 56.0 | 47 | 222 | 26 | 20 | 3 | 1 | 3 | 4 | 10 | 0 | 64 | 7 | 0 |
| Lissir, Alexander, Hickory | 5 | 1 | .833 | 5.03 | 36 | 1 | 0 | 0 | 10 | 0 | 68.0 | 88 | 319 | 46 | 38 | 7 | 0 | 2 | 5 | 27 | 1 | 32 | 1 | 0 |
| Little, Joe, Charleston-SC * | 1 | 3 | .250 | 6.49 | 10 | 9 | 0 | 0 | 0 | 0 | 43.0 | 54 | 202 | 36 | 31 | 13 | 2 | 2 | 4 | 17 | 0 | 44 | 1 | 0 |
| Lo, Ching-Lung, Asheville | 4 | 3 | .571 | 5.05 | 17 | 9 | 0 | 0 | 6 | 1 | 62.1 | 70 | 286 | 49 | 35 | 9 | 5 | 6 | 6 | 30 | 0 | 49 | 1 | 2 |
| Loewen, Adam, Delmarva * | 4 | 5 | .444 | 4.11 | 20 | 19 | 1 | 0 | 0 | 0 | 85.1 | 77 | 376 | 47 | 39 | 3 | 2 | 4 | 4 | 58 | 0 | 82 | 8 | 4 |
| Long, Jeffrey, Rome | 2 | 2 | .500 | 8.53 | 13 | 0 | 0 | 0 | 5 | 0 | 25.1 | 37 | 129 | 27 | 24 | 3 | 0 | 0 | 3 | 13 | 5 | 19 | 2 | 0 |
| Long, Nick, Savannah | 5 | 9 | .357 | 4.89 | 28 | 17 | 0 | 0 | 4 | 0 | 105.0 | 102 | 466 | 76 | 57 | 14 | 2 | 3 | 7 | 61 | 0 | 81 | 12 | 0 |
| Looney, Marshall, Columbus * | 0 | 2 | .000 | 6.55 | 3 | 3 | 0 | 0 | 0 | 0 | 11.0 | 12 | 51 | 9 | 8 | 1 | 1 | 1 | 0 | 9 | 0 | 16 | 1 | 0 |
| Lopez, Arturo, Columbus * | 5 | 4 | .556 | 4.78 | 29 | 7 | 0 | 0 | 10 | 0 | 86.2 | 88 | 380 | 51 | 46 | 11 | 1 | 0 | 4 | 30 | 0 | 83 | 5 | 0 |
| Lopez, Gonzalo, Rome | 8 | 5 | .615 | 3.67 | 22 | 21 | 0 | 0 | 0 | 0 | 100.2 | 97 | 418 | 47 | 41 | 7 | 8 | 5 | 1 | 21 | 0 | 109 | 4 | 1 |
| Lopez, Orionny, Kannapolis | 2 | 3 | .400 | 2.75 | 33 | 0 | 0 | 0 | 12 | 1 | 55.2 | 48 | 235 | 21 | 17 | 5 | 0 | 0 | 3 | 18 | 0 | 51 | 4 | 0 |
| Lord, Justin, Hickory | 0 | 1 | .000 | 12.00 | 2 | 2 | 0 | 0 | 0 | 0 | 6.0 | 9 | 25 | 8 | 8 | 3 | 1 | 1 | 0 | 3 | 0 | 3 | 0 | 0 |
| Lovato, Nick, Greensboro * | 0 | 0 | .000 | 3.60 | 4 | 0 | 0 | 0 | 0 | 0 | 5.0 | 5 | 24 | 2 | 2 | 0 | 0 | 0 | 1 | 3 | 0 | 4 | 1 | 0 |
| Lundquist, Dave, Hickory | 4 | 0 | 1.000 | 0.93 | 10 | 0 | 0 | 0 | 2 | 0 | 19.1 | 11 | 76 | 2 | 2 | 0 | 0 | 0 | 2 | 5 | 0 | 21 | 1 | 0 |
| Lynch, Brian, Asheville | 1 | 0 | 1.000 | 3.86 | 10 | 3 | 0 | 0 | 2 | 0 | 25.2 | 30 | 115 | 13 | 11 | 3 | 2 | 0 | 1 | 10 | 1 | 8 | 0 | 0 |
| Macdonald, Michael, Charleston-WV. | 3 | 0 | 1.000 | 1.93 | 7 | 6 | 0 | 0 | 0 | 0 | 32.2 | 29 | 133 | 14 | 7 | 2 | 2 | 1 | 1 | 9 | 0 | 23 | 0 | 0 |
| Maclane, Evan, Capital City * | 5 | 2 | .714 | 2.39 | 14 | 10 | 0 | 0 | 2 | 0 | 67.2 | 57 | 268 | 21 | 18 | 9 | 3 | 2 | 3 | 10 | 1 | 66 | 2 | 0 |
| Maholm, Paul, Hickory * | 0 | 2 | .000 | 9.49 | 3 | 3 | 0 | 0 | 0 | 0 | 12.1 | 17 | 62 | 14 | 13 | 2 | 1 | 0 | 3 | 10 | 0 | 12 | 4 | 1 |
| Maldonado, Ivan, Capital City | 4 | 4 | .500 | 7.38 | 14 | 8 | 0 | 0 | 0 | 0 | 46.1 | 65 | 220 | 40 | 38 | 15 | 0 | 3 | 5 | 15 | 0 | 35 | 2 | 1 |
| Mangrum, Micah, Capital City | 1 | 0 | 1.000 | 1.76 | 9 | 0 | 0 | 0 | 6 | 1 | 15.1 | 14 | 64 | 5 | 3 | 0 | 0 | 0 | 0 | 4 | 0 | 18 | 1 | 0 |
| Marceau, Pierre-Luc, Lake County * | 0 | 0 | .000 | 6.20 | 6 | 4 | 0 | 0 | 1 | 0 | 20.1 | 26 | 100 | 14 | 14 | 1 | 0 | 2 | 3 | 8 | 0 | 16 | 1 | 0 |
| Marceau, Pierre-Luc, Savannah * | 0 | 0 | .000 | 4.61 | 13 | 0 | 0 | 0 | 7 | 0 | 27.1 | 29 | 133 | 17 | 14 | 1 | 1 | 3 | 4 | 17 | 0 | 21 | 5 | 0 |
| Marcum, Shaun, Charleston-WV | 7 | 4 | .636 | 3.19 | 13 | 13 | 1 | 1 | 0 | 0 | 79.0 | 64 | 320 | 32 | 28 | 7 | 6 | 3 | 0 | 16 | 0 | 83 | 1 | 0 |
| Marrero, Darwin, Savannah | 1 | 1 | .500 | 4.91 | 2 | 2 | 1 | 0 | 0 | 0 | 11.0 | 10 | 48 | 6 | 6 | 1 | 1 | 1 | 1 | 3 | 0 | 8 | 0 | 0 |
| Marsden, Aaron, Asheville * | 11 | 8 | .579 | 4.58 | 27 | 25 | 1 | 0 | 1 | 0 | 165.0 | 176 | 700 | 95 | 84 | 30 | 4 | 8 | 5 | 43 | 0 | 107 | 6 | 0 |
| Martin, Kevin, Lake County | 1 | 3 | .250 | 6.75 | 9 | 0 | 0 | 0 | 6 | 0 | 10.2 | 17 | 56 | 12 | 8 | 2 | 1 | 1 | 0 | 6 | 3 | 8 | 2 | 0 |
| Martin, Sean, Hagerstown | 4 | 3 | .571 | 3.76 | 43 | 0 | 0 | 0 | 16 | 2 | 91.0 | 92 | 394 | 50 | 38 | 5 | 2 | 1 | 7 | 23 | 0 | 82 | 3 | 0 |
| Martinez, Carlos, Greensboro | 2 | 3 | .400 | 3.17 | 40 | 0 | 0 | 0 | 21 | 6 | 48.1 | 43 | 203 | 21 | 17 | 8 | 0 | 0 | 1 | 12 | 0 | 37 | 2 | 1 |
| Martinez, Dave, Lake County * | 0 | 0 | .000 | 9.00 | 1 | 0 | 0 | 0 | 1 | 0 | 2.0 | 4 | 12 | 2 | 2 | 0 | 0 | 0 | 1 | 1 | 0 | 2 | 1 | 0 |
| Martinez, Edgar, Augusta | 0 | 0 | .000 | 0.90 | 9 | 0 | 0 | 0 | 3 | 0 | 10.0 | 8 | 42 | 1 | 1 | 0 | 0 | 0 | 0 | 4 | 0 | 5 | 0 | 0 |
| Martinez, Samuel, Savannah | 2 | 2 | .500 | 4.58 | 11 | 5 | 0 | 0 | 3 | 0 | 39.1 | 38 | 174 | 27 | 20 | 4 | 1 | 2 | 6 | 16 | 0 | 32 | 6 | 0 |
| Mastny, Thomas, Charleston-WV | 10 | 3 | .769 | 2.17 | 27 | 27 | 0 | 0 | 0 | 0 | 149.0 | 123 | 592 | 44 | 36 | 4 | 9 | 5 | 3 | 41 | 0 | 141 | 7 | 0 |
| Mathieson, Scott, Lakewood | 8 | 9 | .471 | 4.32 | 25 | 25 | 1 | 0 | 0 | 0 | 131.1 | 130 | 572 | 73 | 63 | 7 | 6 | 7 | 9 | 50 | 0 | 112 | 9 | 0 |
| Mattison, Kieran, Lake County | 1 | 2 | .333 | 2.70 | 13 | 0 | 0 | 0 | 5 | 2 | 30.0 | 26 | 133 | 10 | 9 | 4 | 0 | 0 | 1 | 16 | 1 | 22 | 0 | 0 |
| Mazzuca, Joe, Greensboro | 0 | 0 | .000 | 0.00 | 1 | 0 | 0 | 0 | 1 | 0 | 1.0 | 1 | 5 | 0 | 0 | 0 | 0 | 0 | 1 | 0 | 0 | 0 | 1 | 0 |
| McCally, Ryan, Charleston-SC | 2 | 3 | .400 | 5.35 | 15 | 2 | 0 | 0 | 2 | 0 | 38.2 | 60 | 179 | 25 | 23 | 2 | 0 | 1 | 3 | 7 | 0 | 25 | 0 | 0 |

| Pitcher, Team | W | L | Pct. | ERA | G | GS | CG | ShO | GF | Sv. | IP | H | TBF | R | ER | HR | SH | SF | HB | BB | IBB | SO | WP | Bk. |
|---|---|---|---|---|---|---|---|---|---|---|---|---|---|---|---|---|---|---|---|---|---|---|---|---|
| McCarthy, Brandon, Kannapolis | 8 | 5 | .615 | 3.64 | 15 | 15 | 3 | 1 | 0 | 0 | 94.0 | 80 | 372 | 41 | 38 | 10 | 1 | 2 | 7 | 21 | 0 | 113 | 3 | 2 |
| McClung, Seth, Charleston-SC | 0 | 0 | .000 | 0.00 | 3 | 3 | 0 | 0 | 0 | 0 | 9.1 | 5 | 39 | 0 | 0 | 0 | 2 | 0 | 0 | 4 | 0 | 10 | 0 | 0 |
| McCormack, Zach, Greensboro * | 3 | 3 | .500 | 5.89 | 35 | 0 | 0 | 0 | 13 | 1 | 44.1 | 48 | 220 | 41 | 29 | 4 | 0 | 0 | 6 | 33 | 1 | 49 | 9 | 0 |
| McCrory, Bob, Delmarva | 0 | 1 | .000 | 7.59 | 8 | 0 | 0 | 0 | 1 | 0 | 10.2 | 13 | 59 | 16 | 9 | 3 | 0 | 0 | 0 | 15 | 0 | 11 | 5 | 0 |
| Menocal, Victor, Lakewood | 1 | 4 | .200 | 6.33 | 30 | 0 | 0 | 0 | 11 | 2 | 54.0 | 66 | 258 | 47 | 38 | 3 | 2 | 0 | 11 | 22 | 0 | 28 | 13 | 0 |
| Mercedes, Gerson, Lake County | 1 | 0 | 1.000 | 1.80 | 1 | 1 | 0 | 0 | 0 | 0 | 5.0 | 5 | 21 | 1 | 1 | 0 | 0 | 0 | 0 | 1 | 0 | 4 | 0 | 1 |
| Meredith, Clay, Augusta | 1 | 0 | 1.000 | 0.00 | 13 | 0 | 0 | 0 | 10 | 6 | 15.1 | 8 | 59 | 0 | 0 | 0 | 0 | 0 | 2 | 3 | 0 | 18 | 0 | 0 |
| Merrell, Darric, Asheville | 8 | 12 | .400 | 5.41 | 28 | 28 | 2 | 0 | 0 | 0 | 151.1 | 178 | 684 | 105 | 91 | 13 | 7 | 10 | 10 | 53 | 1 | 87 | 9 | 0 |
| Mildren, Paul, Greensboro * | 5 | 7 | .417 | 5.22 | 39 | 4 | 0 | 0 | 8 | 1 | 101.2 | 115 | 469 | 71 | 59 | 11 | 1 | 7 | 14 | 40 | 0 | 83 | 7 | 0 |
| Miller, Adam, Lake County | 7 | 4 | .636 | 3.36 | 19 | 19 | 1 | 0 | 0 | 0 | 91.0 | 79 | 370 | 39 | 34 | 7 | 6 | 3 | 4 | 28 | 0 | 106 | 5 | 0 |
| Miller, Brian, Kannapolis | 8 | 9 | .471 | 3.94 | 21 | 21 | 0 | 0 | 0 | 0 | 112.0 | 103 | 487 | 57 | 49 | 6 | 4 | 4 | 13 | 54 | 0 | 84 | 5 | 2 |
| Millikan, Bryan, Hagerstown | 2 | 3 | .400 | 4.22 | 10 | 9 | 0 | 0 | 0 | 0 | 42.2 | 45 | 193 | 21 | 20 | 2 | 2 | 3 | 7 | 17 | 0 | 27 | 2 | 0 |
| Miramontes, Matthew, Capital City | 0 | 3 | .000 | 12.24 | 11 | 6 | 0 | 0 | 1 | 1 | 25.0 | 46 | 151 | 43 | 34 | 3 | 2 | 1 | 2 | 23 | 0 | 23 | 9 | 1 |
| Mitchell, Tom, Savannah | 1 | 0 | 1.000 | 9.00 | 11 | 0 | 0 | 0 | 4 | 1 | 23.0 | 29 | 116 | 24 | 23 | 3 | 0 | 0 | 2 | 16 | 0 | 10 | 7 | 0 |
| Moat, Mike, Kannapolis | 3 | 2 | .600 | 4.79 | 23 | 0 | 0 | 0 | 9 | 3 | 47.0 | 52 | 215 | 29 | 25 | 4 | 0 | 0 | 4 | 22 | 1 | 45 | 5 | 0 |
| Montani, Jeff, Delmarva | 1 | 4 | .200 | 4.79 | 35 | 0 | 0 | 0 | 14 | 1 | 62.0 | 68 | 282 | 37 | 33 | 4 | 0 | 0 | 6 | 22 | 1 | 53 | 2 | 0 |
| Mora, Ramon, Charleston-WV | 5 | 4 | .556 | 6.00 | 14 | 12 | 0 | 0 | 1 | 0 | 63.0 | 76 | 285 | 50 | 42 | 6 | 1 | 2 | 7 | 18 | 0 | 49 | 4 | 2 |
| Morel, Eudy, Asheville | 1 | 0 | 1.000 | 1.88 | 11 | 0 | 0 | 0 | 3 | 0 | 14.1 | 12 | 53 | 3 | 3 | 1 | 0 | 0 | 0 | 1 | 0 | 18 | 0 | 0 |
| Morla, Carlos, Augusta | 1 | 1 | .500 | 1.56 | 22 | 0 | 0 | 0 | 7 | 2 | 34.2 | 34 | 150 | 10 | 6 | 2 | 0 | 0 | 1 | 11 | 0 | 34 | 0 | 1 |
| Morris, Seth, Kannapolis | 0 | 0 | .000 | 7.71 | 3 | 0 | 0 | 0 | 1 | 0 | 2.1 | 5 | 14 | 2 | 2 | 0 | 0 | 0 | 0 | 2 | 0 | 1 | 0 | 0 |
| Morton, Charlie, Rome | 7 | 9 | .438 | 4.82 | 27 | 18 | 0 | 0 | 3 | 2 | 117.2 | 140 | 558 | 76 | 63 | 7 | 4 | 8 | 7 | 68 | 2 | 102 | 10 | 0 |
| Muecke, Josh, Lexington * | 9 | 1 | .900 | 3.97 | 37 | 8 | 0 | 0 | 8 | 2 | 104.1 | 81 | 434 | 48 | 46 | 8 | 5 | 3 | 4 | 48 | 1 | 91 | 5 | 1 |
| Mueller, Mike, Rome | 0 | 3 | .000 | 5.64 | 15 | 1 | 0 | 0 | 4 | 0 | 30.1 | 39 | 142 | 21 | 19 | 3 | 3 | 2 | 0 | 14 | 0 | 32 | 4 | 0 |
| Mujica, Edward, Lake County | 7 | 7 | .500 | 4.65 | 26 | 19 | 1 | 0 | 3 | 2 | 124.0 | 130 | 525 | 77 | 64 | 18 | 5 | 7 | 13 | 32 | 1 | 89 | 6 | 4 |
| Mumma, Brad, Charleston-WV * | 2 | 3 | .400 | 3.83 | 20 | 7 | 0 | 0 | 10 | 8 | 49.1 | 53 | 218 | 30 | 21 | 2 | 4 | 1 | 3 | 15 | 0 | 47 | 4 | 0 |
| Muniz, Carlos, Capital City | 4 | 0 | 1.000 | 4.29 | 16 | 0 | 0 | 0 | 14 | 7 | 21.0 | 11 | 84 | 10 | 10 | 1 | 0 | 0 | 3 | 8 | 0 | 19 | 0 | 0 |
| Musgrave, Mike, Hagerstown | 2 | 5 | .286 | 5.79 | 36 | 12 | 0 | 0 | 11 | 0 | 84.0 | 94 | 390 | 65 | 54 | 7 | 3 | 4 | 11 | 47 | 0 | 56 | 9 | 0 |
| NeSmith, Travis, Hagerstown * | 1 | 9 | .100 | 5.67 | 34 | 9 | 0 | 0 | 6 | 0 | 85.2 | 101 | 405 | 62 | 54 | 9 | 4 | 3 | 7 | 52 | 2 | 73 | 9 | 1 |
| Neal, Tony, Delmarva | 1 | 0 | 1.000 | 2.57 | 7 | 0 | 0 | 0 | 3 | 2 | 14.0 | 8 | 63 | 5 | 4 | 0 | 0 | 0 | 3 | 10 | 1 | 20 | 1 | 0 |
| Nelson, Brad, Rome | 0 | 2 | .000 | 5.27 | 20 | 0 | 0 | 0 | 16 | 3 | 27.1 | 39 | 140 | 25 | 16 | 5 | 0 | 0 | 2 | 13 | 2 | 18 | 0 | 0 |
| Nestor, Scott, Greensboro | 2 | 0 | 1.000 | 6.35 | 23 | 0 | 0 | 0 | 5 | 0 | 39.2 | 46 | 199 | 33 | 28 | 3 | 0 | 0 | 11 | 25 | 1 | 34 | 9 | 0 |
| Nickerson, Jon-Michael, Greensboro * | 0 | 9 | .000 | 6.10 | 14 | 14 | 0 | 0 | 0 | 0 | 59.0 | 61 | 264 | 44 | 40 | 10 | 2 | 4 | 1 | 27 | 0 | 44 | 4 | 0 |
| Niesel, Christopher, Lake County | 1 | 1 | .500 | 5.85 | 5 | 5 | 0 | 0 | 0 | 0 | 20.0 | 24 | 84 | 13 | 13 | 4 | 0 | 0 | 1 | 1 | 0 | 23 | 0 | 1 |
| Nieves, Roberto, Rome | 1 | 5 | .167 | 7.09 | 21 | 1 | 0 | 0 | 9 | 0 | 33.0 | 43 | 184 | 41 | 26 | 8 | 0 | 0 | 3 | 40 | 0 | 29 | 8 | 1 |
| Novoa, Yunior, Kannapolis * | 0 | 0 | .000 | 4.91 | 2 | 0 | 0 | 0 | 0 | 0 | 3.2 | 5 | 18 | 3 | 2 | 0 | 0 | 0 | 0 | 2 | 0 | 5 | 1 | 0 |
| Nowicki, Nate, Greensboro | 3 | 5 | .375 | 4.26 | 43 | 2 | 0 | 0 | 14 | 4 | 99.1 | 113 | 442 | 53 | 47 | 14 | 2 | 4 | 4 | 37 | 1 | 48 | 2 | 0 |
| Nunez, Leo, Hickory | 10 | 4 | .714 | 3.06 | 27 | 20 | 3 | 0 | 3 | 1 | 144.0 | 121 | 584 | 53 | 49 | 16 | 4 | 6 | 9 | 46 | 0 | 140 | 5 | 1 |
| Nunley, Derrick, Charleston-WV | 1 | 1 | .500 | 6.75 | 8 | 0 | 0 | 0 | 4 | 0 | 12.0 | 13 | 60 | 10 | 9 | 0 | 0 | 0 | 2 | 9 | 0 | 6 | 1 | 0 |
| Nyquist, Brett, Savannah * | 4 | 12 | .250 | 5.67 | 22 | 20 | 0 | 0 | 0 | 0 | 106.1 | 139 | 480 | 84 | 67 | 14 | 4 | 4 | 7 | 27 | 0 | 79 | 11 | 0 |
| Ochoa, Javier, Capital City | 2 | 1 | .667 | 5.18 | 24 | 0 | 0 | 0 | 12 | 1 | 40.0 | 38 | 184 | 26 | 23 | 3 | 0 | 0 | 3 | 22 | 0 | 38 | 7 | 1 |
| Ojeda, Alvis, Columbus | 8 | 2 | .800 | 3.59 | 30 | 3 | 0 | 0 | 5 | 2 | 85.1 | 73 | 359 | 47 | 34 | 5 | 2 | 4 | 12 | 29 | 0 | 86 | 5 | 1 |
| Olson, Jordan, Charleston-SC * | 0 | 0 | .000 | 6.39 | 16 | 0 | 0 | 0 | 7 | 0 | 25.1 | 21 | 121 | 20 | 18 | 3 | 0 | 0 | 4 | 19 | 0 | 19 | 1 | 0 |
| Ool, Kevin, Augusta * | 3 | 2 | .600 | 4.76 | 27 | 0 | 0 | 0 | 16 | 1 | 45.1 | 56 | 203 | 28 | 24 | 3 | 0 | 0 | 0 | 11 | 2 | 36 | 4 | 0 |
| Orvella, Chad, Charleston-SC | 1 | 0 | 1.000 | 1.33 | 22 | 0 | 0 | 0 | 10 | 4 | 47.1 | 28 | 177 | 9 | 7 | 4 | 0 | 0 | 1 | 5 | 0 | 76 | 0 | 0 |
| Osberg, Tanner, Capital City | 10 | 7 | .588 | 5.89 | 28 | 26 | 0 | 0 | 0 | 0 | 140.2 | 169 | 636 | 103 | 92 | 13 | 10 | 16 | 15 | 54 | 0 | 79 | 4 | 2 |
| Overton, Brad, Lakewood | 2 | 1 | .667 | 7.01 | 14 | 0 | 0 | 0 | 4 | 1 | 25.2 | 30 | 130 | 21 | 20 | 3 | 0 | 1 | 3 | 20 | 0 | 23 | 2 | 0 |
| Paddock, Josh, Lakewood | 2 | 2 | .500 | 5.26 | 15 | 0 | 0 | 0 | 6 | 1 | 25.2 | 35 | 119 | 17 | 15 | 1 | 0 | 0 | 0 | 7 | 1 | 18 | 3 | 0 |
| Parcus, Kyle, Lakewood * | 4 | 4 | .500 | 3.32 | 41 | 0 | 0 | 0 | 21 | 4 | 76.0 | 68 | 314 | 34 | 28 | 8 | 0 | 0 | 2 | 17 | 0 | 78 | 5 | 0 |
| Patitucci, Mike, Delmarva * | 3 | 1 | .750 | 5.34 | 43 | 0 | 0 | 0 | 22 | 4 | 55.2 | 57 | 271 | 38 | 33 | 6 | 0 | 0 | 2 | 44 | 0 | 65 | 4 | 0 |
| Patrick, Brian, Charleston-WV | 0 | 0 | .000 | 0.00 | 2 | 0 | 0 | 0 | 2 | 0 | 2.0 | 2 | 8 | 0 | 0 | 0 | 0 | 0 | 0 | 0 | 0 | 0 | 0 | 0 |
| Pearson, Anthony, Savannah | 1 | 4 | .200 | 3.81 | 33 | 3 | 0 | 0 | 12 | 1 | 85.0 | 61 | 375 | 40 | 36 | 2 | 1 | 2 | 9 | 49 | 2 | 106 | 9 | 1 |
| Peguero, Tony, Charleston-SC | 10 | 6 | .625 | 3.32 | 23 | 23 | 1 | 1 | 0 | 0 | 133.0 | 135 | 532 | 61 | 49 | 9 | 8 | 5 | 4 | 22 | 0 | 87 | 4 | 1 |
| Pena, Luis, Kannapolis | 0 | 4 | .000 | 6.29 | 10 | 2 | 0 | 0 | 4 | 0 | 24.1 | 27 | 106 | 22 | 17 | 4 | 0 | 1 | 1 | 6 | 0 | 25 | 2 | 1 |
| Penn, Hayden, Delmarva | 4 | 1 | .800 | 3.32 | 13 | 6 | 0 | 0 | 2 | 1 | 43.1 | 30 | 174 | 18 | 16 | 4 | 2 | 1 | 3 | 19 | 1 | 41 | 4 | 0 |
| Penny, Davey, Augusta | 0 | 1 | .000 | 8.68 | 3 | 0 | 0 | 0 | 0 | 0 | 9.1 | 18 | 49 | 11 | 9 | 2 | 1 | 0 | 2 | 1 | 0 | 7 | 0 | 0 |
| Peralta, Juan, Charleston-WV | 0 | 0 | .000 | 0.00 | 1 | 0 | 0 | 0 | 1 | 0 | 3.0 | 0 | 9 | 0 | 0 | 0 | 0 | 0 | 0 | 0 | 0 | 3 | 0 | 0 |
| Perez, Antonio, Charleston-SC * | 4 | 3 | .571 | 2.17 | 45 | 0 | 0 | 0 | 14 | 1 | 74.2 | 77 | 324 | 38 | 18 | 1 | 0 | 0 | 1 | 22 | 1 | 51 | 2 | 0 |
| Perez, Marcelo, Capital City | 0 | 0 | .000 | 0.00 | 1 | 0 | 0 | 0 | 1 | 0 | 2.0 | 0 | 6 | 0 | 0 | 0 | 0 | 0 | 0 | 0 | 0 | 0 | 0 | 0 |
| Perez, Rafael, Lake County * | 7 | 6 | .538 | 4.85 | 23 | 22 | 0 | 0 | 0 | 0 | 115.0 | 121 | 503 | 75 | 62 | 9 | 7 | 4 | 8 | 47 | 0 | 99 | 12 | 3 |
| Perrin, Devin, Savannah | 5 | 6 | .455 | 4.50 | 36 | 15 | 0 | 0 | 7 | 0 | 122.0 | 112 | 523 | 64 | 61 | 9 | 3 | 3 | 6 | 62 | 0 | 108 | 9 | 1 |
| Pesco, Nick, Lake County | 6 | 7 | .462 | 3.91 | 21 | 21 | 0 | 0 | 0 | 0 | 106.0 | 96 | 434 | 49 | 46 | 10 | 5 | 2 | 5 | 30 | 1 | 97 | 4 | 0 |
| Petit, Yusmeiro, Capital City | 9 | 2 | .818 | 2.39 | 15 | 15 | 0 | 0 | 0 | 0 | 83.0 | 47 | 319 | 29 | 22 | 8 | 2 | 1 | 4 | 22 | 0 | 122 | 4 | 0 |
| Petrick, Russell, Delmarva * | 0 | 1 | .000 | 5.25 | 11 | 0 | 0 | 0 | 6 | 0 | 12.0 | 19 | 64 | 9 | 7 | 3 | 0 | 0 | 1 | 8 | 0 | 13 | 1 | 0 |
| Pillsbury, Chris, Greensboro | 0 | 2 | .000 | 7.30 | 10 | 5 | 0 | 0 | 1 | 0 | 24.2 | 36 | 125 | 26 | 20 | 7 | 0 | 0 | 2 | 12 | 0 | 24 | 3 | 0 |
| Pimentel, Julio, Columbus | 10 | 8 | .556 | 3.48 | 23 | 23 | 2 | 1 | 0 | 0 | 111.1 | 106 | 466 | 56 | 43 | 14 | 3 | 3 | 6 | 47 | 1 | 102 | 10 | 1 |
| Plaisance, Kenny, Columbus | 2 | 0 | 1.000 | 7.88 | 3 | 0 | 0 | 0 | 2 | 0 | 8.0 | 11 | 37 | 7 | 7 | 2 | 1 | 0 | 0 | 2 | 0 | 6 | 0 | 0 |
| Plexico, Gerald, Savannah * | 8 | 5 | .615 | 2.63 | 49 | 0 | 0 | 0 | 24 | 6 | 82.0 | 59 | 330 | 27 | 24 | 5 | 0 | 0 | 3 | 25 | 2 | 102 | 2 | 0 |
| Plummer, Jarod, Columbus | 2 | 1 | .667 | 2.45 | 4 | 4 | 0 | 0 | 0 | 0 | 22.0 | 13 | 86 | 8 | 6 | 4 | 0 | 0 | 3 | 5 | 0 | 23 | 0 | 0 |
| Portorreal, Daniel, Hagerstown | 0 | 2 | .000 | 7.27 | 8 | 1 | 0 | 0 | 1 | 0 | 17.1 | 24 | 94 | 18 | 14 | 3 | 0 | 1 | 4 | 15 | 0 | 10 | 2 | 0 |
| Potter, Josh, Delmarva | 0 | 4 | .000 | 5.40 | 23 | 1 | 0 | 0 | 7 | 0 | 50.0 | 59 | 232 | 32 | 30 | 5 | 0 | 1 | 1 | 22 | 2 | 46 | 3 | 0 |
| Prieto, Victor, Greensboro | 0 | 8 | .000 | 13.16 | 10 | 9 | 0 | 0 | 0 | 0 | 26.2 | 32 | 145 | 44 | 39 | 1 | 0 | 4 | 7 | 33 | 0 | 19 | 18 | 0 |
| Ramirez, Greg, Capital City | 7 | 0 | 1.000 | 2.06 | 38 | 8 | 0 | 0 | 20 | 10 | 96.0 | 81 | 404 | 39 | 22 | 3 | 1 | 3 | 14 | 28 | 2 | 105 | 8 | 0 |
| Ramirez, Luis, Delmarva | 1 | 0 | 1.000 | 1.38 | 5 | 2 | 0 | 0 | 1 | 0 | 13.0 | 7 | 49 | 2 | 2 | 0 | 1 | 0 | 0 | 6 | 0 | 13 | 1 | 0 |
| Ramsey, Rob, Lexington | 1 | 1 | .500 | 18.00 | 9 | 0 | 0 | 0 | 3 | 0 | 8.0 | 15 | 59 | 23 | 16 | 2 | 0 | 1 | 5 | 14 | 0 | 9 | 0 | 0 |
| Ray, Chris, Delmarva | 2 | 3 | .400 | 3.42 | 10 | 9 | 0 | 0 | 0 | 0 | 50.0 | 43 | 208 | 21 | 19 | 3 | 3 | 4 | 5 | 17 | 0 | 46 | 1 | 1 |
| Reed, Brian, Charleston-WV | 1 | 0 | 1.000 | 0.35 | 25 | 0 | 0 | 0 | 24 | 10 | 26.0 | 17 | 100 | 2 | 1 | 0 | 0 | 0 | 1 | 5 | 0 | 28 | 0 | 0 |
| Reid, Brett, Savannah | 5 | 4 | .556 | 1.98 | 46 | 0 | 0 | 0 | 39 | 15 | 63.2 | 51 | 269 | 17 | 14 | 3 | 0 | 0 | 7 | 20 | 2 | 84 | 8 | 0 |
| Resop, Chris, Greensboro | 3 | 1 | .750 | 1.94 | 41 | 0 | 0 | 0 | 36 | 13 | 41.2 | 26 | 159 | 11 | 9 | 1 | 0 | 0 | 2 | 7 | 0 | 68 | 2 | 1 |
| Reyes, Jo-Jo, Rome * | 2 | 4 | .333 | 5.33 | 15 | 14 | 1 | 0 | 1 | 0 | 74.1 | 84 | 328 | 49 | 44 | 10 | 7 | 4 | 2 | 25 | 2 | 71 | 3 | 3 |
| Reyes, Paco, Lakewood | 9 | 3 | .750 | 2.31 | 42 | 0 | 0 | 0 | 37 | 10 | 62.1 | 50 | 252 | 24 | 16 | 5 | 0 | 0 | 2 | 12 | 0 | 67 | 5 | 0 |
| Rich, Dan, Lake County * | 0 | 0 | .000 | 10.13 | 3 | 0 | 0 | 0 | 2 | 0 | 5.1 | 8 | 24 | 6 | 6 | 2 | 0 | 0 | 0 | 0 | 0 | 6 | 0 | 0 |
| Rico, Erik, Charleston-WV * | 3 | 1 | .750 | 1.75 | 8 | 4 | 0 | 0 | 1 | 0 | 25.2 | 22 | 108 | 7 | 5 | 1 | 1 | 0 | 2 | 8 | 0 | 14 | 0 | 0 |

| Pitcher, Team | W | L | Pct. | ERA | G | GS | CG | ShO | GF | Sv. | IP | H | TBF | R | ER | HR | SH | SF | HB | BB | IBB | SO | WP | Bk. |
|---|---|---|---|---|---|---|---|---|---|---|---|---|---|---|---|---|---|---|---|---|---|---|---|---|
| Ritchie, Todd, Charleston-SC | 1 | 1 | .500 | 4.09 | 2 | 2 | 0 | 0 | 0 | 0 | 11.0 | 13 | 45 | 6 | 5 | 0 | 0 | 0 | 0 | 3 | 0 | 13 | 2 | 0 |
| Robinson, Dennis, Delmarva | 2 | 0 | 1.000 | 0.75 | 2 | 2 | 0 | 0 | 0 | 0 | 12.0 | 9 | 46 | 1 | 1 | 1 | 0 | 0 | 0 | 4 | 0 | 4 | 0 | 0 |
| Robinson, Levi, Delmarva | 1 | 0 | 1.000 | 0.00 | 2 | 2 | 0 | 0 | 0 | 0 | 11.0 | 5 | 40 | 1 | 0 | 0 | 1 | 0 | 2 | 0 | 0 | 8 | 0 | 0 |
| Robles, Larry, Asheville | 7 | 3 | .700 | 3.54 | 23 | 19 | 0 | 0 | 3 | 3 | 122.0 | 120 | 506 | 58 | 48 | 13 | 10 | 2 | 7 | 31 | 0 | 85 | 5 | 0 |
| Rodriguez, Jose, Capital City | 0 | 1 | .000 | 2.08 | 6 | 0 | 0 | 0 | 1 | 0 | 8.2 | 6 | 37 | 2 | 2 | 0 | 0 | 0 | 1 | 5 | 0 | 8 | 0 | 0 |
| Rodriguez, Mike, Columbus | 1 | 0 | 1.000 | 1.26 | 5 | 0 | 0 | 0 | 0 | 0 | 14.1 | 4 | 52 | 2 | 2 | 2 | 0 | 0 | 0 | 6 | 0 | 18 | 1 | 1 |
| Rodriguez, Osvaldo, Columbus | 3 | 3 | .500 | 5.01 | 20 | 2 | 0 | 0 | 6 | 2 | 41.1 | 40 | 192 | 24 | 23 | 1 | 0 | 2 | 5 | 26 | 0 | 43 | 5 | 0 |
| Rodriguez, Ricardo, Rome | 5 | 3 | .625 | 3.26 | 31 | 0 | 0 | 0 | 24 | 12 | 49.2 | 42 | 210 | 21 | 18 | 3 | 0 | 0 | 3 | 16 | 0 | 61 | 8 | 2 |
| Rodriguez, Ryan, Kannapolis * | 10 | 9 | .526 | 4.02 | 26 | 26 | 0 | 0 | 0 | 0 | 147.2 | 150 | 631 | 83 | 66 | 10 | 6 | 6 | 7 | 59 | 2 | 102 | 3 | 2 |
| Roehl, Scott, Lake County | 1 | 6 | .143 | 5.14 | 29 | 3 | 0 | 0 | 8 | 2 | 70.0 | 87 | 315 | 52 | 40 | 12 | 1 | 3 | 3 | 15 | 1 | 68 | 2 | 0 |
| Rohan, Jimmy, Columbus | 0 | 0 | .000 | 13.50 | 2 | 0 | 0 | 0 | 2 | 0 | 1.1 | 4 | 10 | 3 | 2 | 0 | 0 | 0 | 1 | 1 | 0 | 1 | 0 | 0 |
| Romero, Davis, Charleston-WV * | 5 | 4 | .556 | 2.53 | 32 | 14 | 0 | 0 | 7 | 1 | 103.1 | 77 | 414 | 36 | 29 | 6 | 6 | 6 | 2 | 30 | 0 | 108 | 4 | 3 |
| Romero, Felix, Charleston-WV | 9 | 4 | .692 | 2.96 | 42 | 0 | 0 | 0 | 10 | 3 | 73.0 | 62 | 302 | 27 | 24 | 4 | 0 | 0 | 3 | 20 | 4 | 102 | 2 | 1 |
| Rondon, Celso, Capital City | 4 | 3 | .571 | 4.71 | 22 | 0 | 0 | 0 | 7 | 1 | 36.1 | 32 | 156 | 19 | 19 | 4 | 0 | 0 | 1 | 14 | 0 | 41 | 6 | 0 |
| Rosario, Melvin, Asheville * | 1 | 1 | .500 | 6.89 | 14 | 0 | 0 | 0 | 4 | 0 | 15.2 | 16 | 69 | 13 | 12 | 2 | 0 | 0 | 1 | 5 | 0 | 11 | 1 | 0 |
| Russ, James, Greensboro | 0 | 3 | .000 | 7.80 | 4 | 4 | 0 | 0 | 0 | 0 | 15.0 | 15 | 73 | 13 | 13 | 3 | 0 | 1 | 4 | 10 | 0 | 16 | 0 | 0 |
| Russell, Adam, Kannapolis | 0 | 2 | .000 | 9.00 | 2 | 2 | 0 | 0 | 0 | 0 | 10.0 | 18 | 52 | 11 | 10 | 3 | 0 | 0 | 1 | 7 | 0 | 3 | 1 | 0 |
| Russell, Mike, Delmarva | 0 | 0 | .000 | 27.00 | 1 | 0 | 0 | 0 | 1 | 0 | 1.1 | 4 | 8 | 4 | 4 | 3 | 0 | 0 | 0 | 0 | 0 | 0 | 0 | 0 |
| Russell, Steve, Rome | 5 | 6 | .455 | 4.29 | 22 | 15 | 0 | 0 | 6 | 2 | 100.2 | 94 | 435 | 57 | 48 | 6 | 7 | 7 | 13 | 39 | 2 | 87 | 10 | 0 |
| Sadowski, Ryan, Hagerstown | 3 | 9 | .250 | 6.92 | 26 | 16 | 0 | 0 | 4 | 0 | 91.0 | 106 | 423 | 84 | 70 | 12 | 7 | 7 | 7 | 45 | 0 | 90 | 13 | 0 |
| Salas, Marino, Delmarva | 2 | 4 | .333 | 2.15 | 40 | 0 | 0 | 0 | 34 | 13 | 50.1 | 51 | 220 | 15 | 12 | 5 | 0 | 0 | 1 | 17 | 3 | 46 | 2 | 0 |
| Sandoval, Francisco, Savannah | 1 | 0 | 1.000 | 14.90 | 7 | 0 | 0 | 0 | 0 | 0 | 9.2 | 16 | 54 | 16 | 16 | 3 | 0 | 0 | 5 | 4 | 0 | 4 | 0 | 0 |
| Sandoval, Marcos, Charleston-WV | 2 | 1 | .667 | 6.14 | 24 | 0 | 0 | 0 | 5 | 0 | 29.1 | 19 | 141 | 25 | 20 | 2 | 0 | 0 | 7 | 29 | 1 | 26 | 6 | 1 |
| Santos, Arty, Augusta | 2 | 3 | .400 | 5.79 | 16 | 6 | 0 | 0 | 3 | 0 | 42.0 | 57 | 192 | 34 | 27 | 7 | 2 | 5 | 1 | 12 | 0 | 26 | 2 | 0 |
| Santos, Reid, Lake County * | 0 | 0 | .000 | 6.75 | 3 | 3 | 0 | 0 | 0 | 0 | 13.1 | 20 | 61 | 13 | 10 | 1 | 2 | 1 | 0 | 5 | 0 | 12 | 1 | 0 |
| Saucedo, Matthew, Greensboro | 2 | 1 | .667 | 5.45 | 23 | 0 | 0 | 0 | 7 | 1 | 34.2 | 30 | 159 | 26 | 21 | 4 | 0 | 0 | 3 | 21 | 1 | 25 | 2 | 0 |
| Schade, Ryan, Greensboro | 0 | 1 | .000 | 13.50 | 4 | 0 | 0 | 0 | 2 | 0 | 3.1 | 8 | 21 | 5 | 5 | 1 | 0 | 0 | 0 | 3 | 0 | 3 | 0 | 0 |
| Schultz, Cory, Lakewood | 3 | 1 | .750 | 2.88 | 29 | 0 | 0 | 0 | 8 | 1 | 59.1 | 59 | 257 | 22 | 19 | 4 | 3 | 5 | 4 | 15 | 0 | 41 | 4 | 1 |
| Serrato, Juan, Hagerstown | 8 | 8 | .500 | 4.24 | 25 | 20 | 1 | 1 | 1 | 0 | 102.0 | 99 | 469 | 68 | 48 | 6 | 5 | 2 | 13 | 61 | 0 | 88 | 10 | 0 |
| Shafer, Kurt, Hickory | 2 | 1 | .667 | 4.46 | 25 | 5 | 0 | 0 | 10 | 1 | 66.2 | 69 | 289 | 39 | 33 | 12 | 4 | 2 | 8 | 22 | 0 | 52 | 4 | 1 |
| Sharpless, Josh, Hickory | 6 | 2 | .750 | 3.03 | 44 | 0 | 0 | 0 | 21 | 4 | 74.1 | 42 | 323 | 28 | 25 | 4 | 0 | 0 | 3 | 55 | 2 | 109 | 8 | 0 |
| Shepard, Kevin, Lakewood * | 0 | 2 | .000 | 8.83 | 5 | 5 | 0 | 0 | 0 | 0 | 17.1 | 24 | 86 | 21 | 17 | 3 | 1 | 1 | 0 | 12 | 0 | 11 | 4 | 0 |
| Shortell, Rory, Lexington | 1 | 3 | .250 | 7.06 | 7 | 7 | 0 | 0 | 0 | 0 | 29.1 | 26 | 130 | 23 | 23 | 7 | 0 | 0 | 5 | 13 | 0 | 21 | 2 | 0 |
| Shortslef, Josh, Hickory * | 11 | 5 | .688 | 4.42 | 30 | 18 | 0 | 0 | 5 | 0 | 124.1 | 134 | 539 | 65 | 61 | 11 | 5 | 3 | 11 | 38 | 0 | 92 | 4 | 2 |
| Silva, Doug, Asheville | 2 | 2 | .500 | 4.98 | 29 | 0 | 0 | 0 | 4 | 0 | 43.1 | 45 | 191 | 25 | 24 | 6 | 0 | 1 | 3 | 12 | 0 | 35 | 1 | 0 |
| Simon, Billy, Augusta | 0 | 1 | .000 | 4.32 | 3 | 3 | 0 | 0 | 0 | 0 | 8.1 | 9 | 38 | 4 | 4 | 0 | 0 | 2 | 2 | 1 | 0 | 8 | 0 | 0 |
| Smith, Dan, Rome * | 0 | 0 | .000 | 7.71 | 1 | 1 | 0 | 0 | 0 | 0 | 4.2 | 5 | 23 | 5 | 4 | 1 | 0 | 0 | 1 | 2 | 0 | 5 | 0 | 0 |
| Smith, Sean, Lake County | 7 | 2 | .778 | 3.39 | 13 | 13 | 0 | 0 | 0 | 0 | 61.0 | 50 | 261 | 24 | 23 | 4 | 3 | 3 | 5 | 28 | 1 | 48 | 3 | 0 |
| Sobieraj, Aaron, Hagerstown | 0 | 0 | .000 | 4.57 | 11 | 0 | 0 | 0 | 5 | 0 | 21.2 | 17 | 101 | 11 | 11 | 2 | 0 | 0 | 4 | 15 | 0 | 16 | 2 | 0 |
| Sobkow, Phil, Columbus | 2 | 2 | .500 | 7.36 | 7 | 6 | 0 | 0 | 0 | 0 | 22.0 | 21 | 105 | 20 | 18 | 2 | 0 | 0 | 4 | 17 | 0 | 18 | 1 | 1 |
| Songster, Judd, Asheville | 0 | 0 | .000 | 2.25 | 2 | 0 | 0 | 0 | 1 | 0 | 4.0 | 1 | 14 | 1 | 1 | 1 | 0 | 0 | 0 | 1 | 0 | 5 | 0 | 0 |
| Sonnanstine, Andrew, Charleston-SC | 2 | 0 | 1.000 | 0.59 | 8 | 5 | 0 | 0 | 1 | 0 | 30.2 | 18 | 116 | 5 | 2 | 0 | 1 | 0 | 0 | 7 | 0 | 42 | 0 | 0 |
| Sopko, Mark, Charleston-WV | 1 | 2 | .333 | 6.00 | 40 | 0 | 0 | 0 | 28 | 9 | 51.0 | 64 | 234 | 35 | 34 | 4 | 0 | 0 | 2 | 18 | 0 | 30 | 7 | 0 |
| Southerland, Chip, Lake County | 3 | 2 | .600 | 4.03 | 20 | 0 | 0 | 0 | 18 | 5 | 22.1 | 21 | 90 | 10 | 10 | 5 | 0 | 0 | 1 | 6 | 0 | 26 | 1 | 0 |
| Speigner, Brent, Charleston-SC | 0 | 0 | .000 | 5.40 | 2 | 0 | 0 | 0 | 2 | 0 | 1.2 | 1 | 7 | 1 | 1 | 0 | 0 | 0 | 0 | 1 | 0 | 0 | 0 | 0 |
| Spillars, Brandan, Delmarva | 0 | 2 | .000 | 13.91 | 11 | 0 | 0 | 0 | 7 | 4 | 11.0 | 12 | 66 | 18 | 17 | 1 | 1 | 0 | 2 | 19 | 1 | 12 | 2 | 0 |
| Starling, Wardell, Hickory | 11 | 8 | .579 | 4.11 | 26 | 26 | 1 | 0 | 0 | 0 | 140.0 | 132 | 604 | 84 | 64 | 10 | 9 | 6 | 16 | 51 | 0 | 114 | 2 | 1 |
| Stevens, Jake, Rome * | 9 | 5 | .643 | 2.27 | 27 | 19 | 0 | 0 | 7 | 2 | 135.0 | 100 | 544 | 41 | 34 | 7 | 3 | 6 | 4 | 39 | 1 | 140 | 7 | 1 |
| Stiehl, Rob, Lexington | 4 | 5 | .444 | 4.04 | 18 | 18 | 0 | 0 | 0 | 0 | 62.1 | 59 | 263 | 36 | 28 | 4 | 3 | 1 | 4 | 21 | 0 | 74 | 1 | 0 |
| Stults, Eric, Columbus * | 1 | 2 | .333 | 2.49 | 12 | 0 | 0 | 0 | 8 | 3 | 21.2 | 18 | 89 | 8 | 6 | 0 | 0 | 0 | 0 | 6 | 0 | 16 | 1 | 0 |
| Sweeney, Matt, Lakewood | 0 | 2 | .000 | 7.83 | 5 | 5 | 0 | 0 | 0 | 0 | 23.0 | 27 | 109 | 22 | 20 | 2 | 2 | 2 | 1 | 12 | 0 | 11 | 1 | 0 |
| Talbot, Mitch, Lexington | 10 | 10 | .500 | 3.83 | 27 | 27 | 1 | 0 | 0 | 0 | 152.2 | 145 | 647 | 78 | 65 | 16 | 7 | 3 | 11 | 49 | 1 | 115 | 6 | 1 |
| Tallet, Brian, Lake County * | 0 | 0 | .000 | 0.00 | 2 | 1 | 0 | 0 | 0 | 0 | 2.0 | 1 | 7 | 0 | 0 | 0 | 0 | 0 | 0 | 0 | 0 | 1 | 0 | 0 |
| Tavarez, Milton, Augusta | 1 | 4 | .200 | 4.55 | 47 | 0 | 0 | 0 | 25 | 5 | 63.1 | 69 | 292 | 41 | 32 | 2 | 0 | 1 | 5 | 26 | 3 | 63 | 6 | 3 |
| Templet, Jordy, Charleston-WV | 0 | 2 | .000 | 4.74 | 15 | 0 | 0 | 0 | 8 | 2 | 19.0 | 25 | 93 | 10 | 10 | 0 | 0 | 0 | 1 | 10 | 1 | 15 | 4 | 0 |
| Testa, Chris, Columbus * | 1 | 2 | .333 | 6.48 | 20 | 0 | 0 | 0 | 9 | 2 | 41.2 | 38 | 210 | 37 | 30 | 4 | 0 | 0 | 3 | 44 | 1 | 53 | 5 | 0 |
| Thomas, Steven, Asheville | 0 | 1 | .000 | 6.75 | 15 | 0 | 0 | 0 | 6 | 1 | 18.2 | 28 | 94 | 17 | 14 | 4 | 0 | 1 | 2 | 7 | 1 | 15 | 3 | 0 |
| Thompson, Daryl, Savannah | 4 | 9 | .308 | 5.08 | 25 | 21 | 0 | 0 | 1 | 0 | 102.2 | 117 | 442 | 66 | 58 | 13 | 4 | 4 | 9 | 30 | 0 | 79 | 4 | 2 |
| Thorne, David, Savannah | 0 | 3 | .000 | 5.30 | 15 | 0 | 0 | 0 | 7 | 0 | 18.2 | 20 | 95 | 13 | 11 | 1 | 0 | 0 | 7 | 12 | 1 | 16 | 4 | 0 |
| Thurmond, J.B., Hagerstown | 4 | 6 | .400 | 2.54 | 19 | 14 | 1 | 0 | 5 | 1 | 92.0 | 87 | 376 | 39 | 26 | 10 | 7 | 2 | 2 | 28 | 0 | 73 | 5 | 0 |
| Tiffany, Chuck, Columbus * | 5 | 2 | .714 | 3.70 | 22 | 22 | 1 | 1 | 0 | 0 | 99.2 | 76 | 418 | 42 | 41 | 11 | 3 | 6 | 11 | 40 | 0 | 141 | 9 | 0 |
| Tiller, James, Delmarva | 4 | 6 | .400 | 5.64 | 15 | 13 | 1 | 0 | 1 | 1 | 68.2 | 84 | 298 | 54 | 43 | 11 | 1 | 5 | 10 | 14 | 2 | 41 | 6 | 0 |
| Tiller, Tim, Delmarva | 1 | 0 | 1.000 | 6.75 | 1 | 0 | 0 | 0 | 0 | 0 | 5.1 | 5 | 22 | 5 | 4 | 1 | 0 | 0 | 1 | 0 | 0 | 6 | 0 | 0 |
| Tisch, Tim, Kannapolis * | 1 | 4 | .200 | 5.27 | 12 | 6 | 1 | 0 | 2 | 0 | 41.0 | 43 | 179 | 26 | 24 | 1 | 4 | 3 | 4 | 18 | 0 | 25 | 4 | 0 |
| Torrealba, Yoann, Hickory | 8 | 8 | .500 | 4.80 | 28 | 11 | 0 | 0 | 8 | 2 | 108.2 | 125 | 472 | 66 | 58 | 8 | 0 | 6 | 7 | 30 | 0 | 61 | 9 | 0 |
| Treanor, Bryan, Greensboro | 1 | 0 | 1.000 | 0.00 | 2 | 0 | 0 | 0 | 0 | 0 | 2.0 | 2 | 10 | 0 | 0 | 0 | 0 | 0 | 0 | 2 | 0 | 3 | 0 | 0 |
| Tressler, Aaron, Charleston-WV | 0 | 0 | .000 | 9.00 | 2 | 0 | 0 | 0 | 0 | 0 | 4.0 | 7 | 21 | 5 | 4 | 0 | 0 | 0 | 0 | 2 | 0 | 4 | 0 | 0 |
| Tsao, Chin-Hui, Asheville | 1 | 0 | 1.000 | 1.80 | 2 | 2 | 0 | 0 | 0 | 0 | 10.0 | 8 | 37 | 2 | 2 | 1 | 0 | 0 | 0 | 1 | 0 | 14 | 1 | 0 |
| Vandermeer, Scott, Charleston-SC | 5 | 5 | .500 | 2.98 | 52 | 0 | 0 | 0 | 46 | 22 | 63.1 | 51 | 277 | 27 | 21 | 6 | 0 | 0 | 6 | 29 | 1 | 67 | 2 | 0 |
| Vaquedano, Jose, Augusta | 4 | 2 | .667 | 1.88 | 11 | 11 | 0 | 0 | 0 | 0 | 67.0 | 59 | 275 | 22 | 14 | 5 | 5 | 2 | 5 | 12 | 0 | 66 | 0 | 0 |
| Vargas, Jason, Greensboro * | 2 | 1 | .667 | 2.37 | 3 | 3 | 0 | 0 | 0 | 0 | 19.0 | 9 | 67 | 5 | 5 | 1 | 2 | 0 | 0 | 2 | 0 | 17 | 0 | 0 |
| Vaughan, Beau, Augusta | 7 | 3 | .700 | 3.30 | 14 | 13 | 0 | 0 | 0 | 0 | 71.0 | 58 | 302 | 30 | 26 | 8 | 2 | 2 | 6 | 27 | 0 | 73 | 3 | 0 |
| Vazquez, Will, Asheville | 0 | 2 | .000 | 5.59 | 10 | 0 | 0 | 0 | 4 | 0 | 19.1 | 19 | 92 | 13 | 12 | 2 | 0 | 0 | 3 | 12 | 0 | 15 | 2 | 1 |
| Walker, Aaron, Charleston-SC * | 0 | 0 | .000 | 0.00 | 1 | 0 | 0 | 0 | 0 | 0 | 5.0 | 2 | 19 | 0 | 0 | 0 | 0 | 0 | 0 | 2 | 0 | 3 | 0 | 0 |
| Walker, Brian, Capital City * | 5 | 5 | .500 | 3.45 | 22 | 12 | 0 | 0 | 3 | 0 | 78.1 | 78 | 336 | 41 | 30 | 3 | 3 | 2 | 5 | 34 | 1 | 69 | 5 | 1 |
| Warden, Jim Ed, Lake County | 5 | 1 | .833 | 3.00 | 41 | 1 | 0 | 0 | 33 | 13 | 54.0 | 43 | 234 | 22 | 18 | 6 | 0 | 2 | 3 | 27 | 2 | 63 | 2 | 0 |
| Warpinski, Ryan, Greensboro | 5 | 4 | .556 | 4.21 | 13 | 12 | 0 | 0 | 0 | 0 | 57.2 | 61 | 257 | 34 | 27 | 5 | 2 | 3 | 5 | 23 | 0 | 46 | 5 | 1 |
| Wasserman, Ehren, Kannapolis | 2 | 3 | .400 | 2.75 | 50 | 0 | 0 | 0 | 47 | 30 | 55.2 | 44 | 230 | 20 | 17 | 1 | 1 | 0 | 4 | 16 | 3 | 42 | 4 | 0 |
| Watchko, Jeff, Asheville | 1 | 6 | .143 | 6.23 | 35 | 0 | 0 | 0 | 7 | 1 | 47.2 | 56 | 224 | 38 | 33 | 5 | 1 | 0 | 6 | 22 | 0 | 49 | 2 | 2 |
| Wayne, Brett, Columbus | 2 | 4 | .333 | 2.66 | 27 | 0 | 0 | 0 | 16 | 5 | 67.2 | 45 | 285 | 28 | 20 | 7 | 0 | 0 | 6 | 31 | 1 | 71 | 4 | 0 |
| Weeden, Brandon, Columbus | 7 | 9 | .438 | 5.39 | 27 | 27 | 0 | 0 | 0 | 0 | 122.0 | 119 | 546 | 84 | 73 | 15 | 5 | 9 | 13 | 73 | 2 | 106 | 4 | 2 |
| Weimer, Andrew, Charleston-SC | 0 | 0 | .000 | 12.00 | 6 | 0 | 0 | 0 | 6 | 0 | 9.0 | 18 | 50 | 12 | 12 | 1 | 0 | 0 | 0 | 5 | 0 | 10 | 1 | 0 |

| Pitcher, Team | W | L | Pct. | ERA | G | GS | CG | ShO | GF | Sv. | IP | H | TBF | R | ER | HR | SH | SF | HB | BB | IBB | SO | WP | Bk. |
|---|---|---|---|---|---|---|---|---|---|---|---|---|---|---|---|---|---|---|---|---|---|---|---|---|
| Wesley, John, Charleston-WV | 0 | 3 | .000 | 10.80 | 6 | 1 | 0 | 0 | 2 | 0 | 11.2 | 19 | 59 | 15 | 14 | 2 | 0 | 0 | 1 | 7 | 0 | 12 | 0 | 0 |
| Wheatland, Matt, Lexington | 0 | 0 | .000 | 3.12 | 18 | 0 | 0 | 0 | 2 | 0 | 34.2 | 33 | 157 | 15 | 12 | 1 | 0 | 0 | 4 | 16 | 0 | 25 | 2 | 0 |
| Whisler, Wesley, Kannapolis * | 4 | 1 | .800 | 3.38 | 10 | 7 | 0 | 0 | 0 | 0 | 45.1 | 52 | 199 | 29 | 17 | 2 | 1 | 7 | 2 | 11 | 0 | 28 | 4 | 0 |
| White, Sean, Rome | 3 | 2 | .600 | 6.44 | 13 | 1 | 0 | 0 | 4 | 1 | 36.1 | 42 | 160 | 30 | 26 | 4 | 1 | 2 | 0 | 12 | 0 | 20 | 1 | 0 |
| Willey, Cory, Augusta | 1 | 0 | 1.000 | 6.16 | 20 | 1 | 0 | 0 | 3 | 0 | 30.2 | 34 | 142 | 26 | 21 | 3 | 0 | 0 | 1 | 15 | 2 | 31 | 2 | 0 |
| Williams, Aaron, Lexington | 4 | 6 | .400 | 3.20 | 59 | 0 | 0 | 0 | 53 | 18 | 78.2 | 75 | 336 | 32 | 28 | 5 | 0 | 0 | 1 | 24 | 4 | 53 | 1 | 1 |
| Wilson, Aaron, Lakewood | 0 | 2 | .000 | 4.44 | 11 | 0 | 0 | 0 | 3 | 0 | 24.1 | 27 | 120 | 18 | 12 | 3 | 1 | 0 | 2 | 15 | 1 | 18 | 2 | 0 |
| Wilson, Brian, Hagerstown | 2 | 5 | .286 | 5.34 | 23 | 3 | 0 | 0 | 12 | 3 | 57.1 | 63 | 259 | 37 | 34 | 7 | 0 | 0 | 3 | 22 | 1 | 41 | 1 | 0 |
| Wilson, Joe, Lakewood * | 4 | 7 | .364 | 3.64 | 24 | 19 | 0 | 0 | 2 | 0 | 94.0 | 74 | 401 | 46 | 38 | 4 | 3 | 3 | 5 | 49 | 0 | 89 | 5 | 1 |
| Wilson, Jonathan, Augusta | 0 | 0 | .000 | 12.27 | 1 | 1 | 0 | 0 | 0 | 0 | 3.2 | 8 | 16 | 5 | 5 | 1 | 1 | 0 | 0 | 0 | 0 | 1 | 0 | 0 |
| Wood, Tim, Greensboro | 2 | 3 | .400 | 4.22 | 24 | 8 | 0 | 0 | 7 | 1 | 70.1 | 73 | 305 | 47 | 33 | 12 | 2 | 2 | 1 | 22 | 0 | 70 | 6 | 0 |
| Woodrow, C.J., Lakewood | 9 | 3 | .750 | 3.48 | 22 | 8 | 0 | 0 | 2 | 0 | 72.1 | 62 | 286 | 38 | 28 | 7 | 3 | 4 | 0 | 8 | 0 | 51 | 1 | 0 |
| Worthington, Timothy, Capital City | 1 | 1 | .500 | 6.04 | 7 | 6 | 0 | 0 | 1 | 0 | 28.1 | 27 | 132 | 21 | 19 | 3 | 2 | 1 | 2 | 16 | 0 | 33 | 2 | 0 |
| Yourkin, Matt, Greensboro * | 0 | 0 | .000 | 10.50 | 3 | 0 | 0 | 0 | 0 | 0 | 6.0 | 12 | 33 | 8 | 7 | 1 | 0 | 0 | 0 | 3 | 0 | 2 | 0 | 0 |
| Zarate, Maruro, Greensboro | 1 | 4 | .200 | 8.45 | 10 | 10 | 0 | 0 | 0 | 0 | 43.2 | 69 | 205 | 46 | 41 | 13 | 3 | 1 | 5 | 12 | 0 | 29 | 0 | 0 |

COMBINATION SHUTOUTS: **Asheville** (2)—Marsden-Corpas, Kaiser-Watchko-Corpas. **Augusta** (7)—Gardner-Tavarez-Ool, K. Jackson-Farley-Tavarez, Vaughan-Willey-Tavarez, Vaughan-Willey-Santos, Gardner-Morla-E. Martinez, Blackley-Morla, Gardner-E. Martinez-Beam. **Capital City** (9)-Lindstrom-J. Rodriguez-Acosta-Hawk, Petit-King-Hawk, Lindstrom-Rondon-J. Rodriguez-Acosta, Cordova-Miramontes, Lindstrom-A. Garcia, Petit-Hawk, Cordova-G. Ramirez, MacLane-A. Garcia, G. Ramirez-Walker-Muniz. **Charleston-SC** (11)—J. Gonzalez-Orvella-Vandermeer, Bulger-Gangi-Cramer, Houser-Vandermeer, Peguero-Gangi-Orvella, Gangi-T. Perez-Allen-McCally, Peguero-Flanagan-Vandermeer, Bulger-Cramer-T. Perez-Vandermeer, Kranawetter-Cramer-Vandermeer, Peguero-Olson, MacDonald-Mumma, Sonnanstine-Gangi-Dobyns, Sonnanstine-T. Perez-Bulger. **Charleston-WV** (12)—Core-Sopko, Mastny-Esaray-Sopko, Mastny-Canizal-D. Romero-Sopko, Core-F. Romero-D. Romero, D. Romero-F. Romero, James-F. Romero-Reed, James-F. Romero-Reed, Core-Canizal, Mastny-Canizal, Mastny-Dalton-Wesley, Rico-Dalton-Mumma. **Columbus** (8)—Pimentel-Alvarez-Carvajal, Pimentel-Alvarez-J. Diaz, Tiffany-Carvajal, Bailey-Kuo, Pimentel-Testa-Carvajal, Weeden-Bailey-A. Lopez, Weeden-Carvajal-Bailey, Figueroa-Bailey. **Delmarva** (12)—Loewen-Caughey-Spillers, Ray-Penn, Loewen-Salas, Deza-J. Johnson, Deza-Childs-Caughey, J. Johnson-Potter, Deza-Salas, J. Johnson-Salas, Deza-Potter-Salas, Loewen-Caughey-Acosta, L. Ramirez-Caughey-Salas, Robinson-Cahill. **Greensboro** (3)—Greusel-Nowicki-Saucedo-McCormack, Vargas-Nowicki-C. Martinez, Mildren-Treanor-C. Martinez. **Hickory** (4)—Gorzelanny-C. Hernandez, Holliday-Sharpless-C. Hernandez, Holliday-Demaria, Torrealba-Demaria. **Kannapolis** (7)—Tisch-Dizard, R. Rodriguez-O. Lopez-Hurd, R. Rodriguez-Castro, Whisler-O. Lopez-Wasserman, Miller-O. Lopez, R. Rodriguez-Castro-Wasserman, Flores-O. Lopez-Banks-F. Hernandez. **Lake County** (8)—S. Smith-Burton, S. Smith-Burton-Rich, Miller-Roehl-Southerland, Mujica-Laffey, R. Perez-Roehl, Pesco-Warden, R. Perez-Mattison-Warden, Cevette-Mattison-Southerland. **Lakewood** (3)—Doble-Honsa, Mathieson-Woodrow-Menocal, Mathieson-Reyes. **Lexington** (7)—DeLeon-A. Williams, Stiehl-Muecke-A. Williams, Talbot-Beltre, Talbot-Adler, Grigsby-Adler, Talbot-Beltre-A. Williams, Muecke-A. Williams. Rome (6)—G. Lopez-Bakker, James-Blakeney-Nelson, Morton-Reyes, Stevens-Russell, James-Anderson-Mueller-Letson, Stevens-R. Rodriguez. **Savannah** (5)—Thompson-Gomez-Reid, Thompson-Pearson-Plexico, Everts-Reid, Long-Pearson-Gomez, Long-Reid.

NO-HIT GAMES: Tiffany, Columbus, defeated Greensboro, 8-0, May 3; Tiffany, Columbus, defeated Greensboro, 10-0, May 20; Mueller, Rome, lost to Capital City, 1-0, June 27; Holliday, Hickory, defeated Charleston-West Virginia, 1-0, July 26; Vargas, Greensboro, defeated Savannah, 3-0, August 26.

## 2004 FIELDING

### TEAM

| Team | G | PO | A | E | TC | DP | TP | PB | Pct. |
|---|---|---|---|---|---|---|---|---|---|
| Hickory | 140 | 3661 | 1487 | 138 | 5286 | 118 | -- | 31 | .974 |
| Charleston-WV | 140 | 3669 | 1428 | 143 | 5240 | 99 | -- | 16 | .973 |
| Lexington | 140 | 3638 | 1373 | 149 | 5160 | 127 | -- | 19 | .971 |
| Lake County | 139 | 3621 | 1334 | 150 | 5105 | 104 | -- | 20 | .971 |
| Asheville | 139 | 3582 | 1599 | 157 | 5338 | 128 | -- | 26 | .971 |
| Kannapolis | 139 | 3655 | 1472 | 166 | 5293 | 64 | -- | 49 | .969 |
| Columbus | 138 | 3604 | 1321 | 165 | 5090 | 128 | -- | 28 | .968 |
| Rome | 140 | 3602 | 1247 | 165 | 5014 | 103 | -- | 25 | .967 |
| Delmarva | 138 | 3590 | 1369 | 170 | 5129 | 106 | -- | 26 | .967 |
| Hagerstown | 137 | 3554 | 1386 | 176 | 5116 | 99 | -- | 22 | .966 |
| Charleston-SC | 139 | 3667 | 1459 | 184 | 5310 | 120 | -- | 28 | .966 |
| Lakewood | 137 | 3569 | 1379 | 178 | 5126 | 133 | -- | 28 | .965 |
| Greensboro | 139 | 3559 | 1291 | 177 | 5027 | 80 | -- | 45 | .965 |
| Augusta | 139 | 3662 | 1490 | 191 | 5343 | 131 | -- | 23 | .964 |
| Capital City | 136 | 3558 | 1358 | 183 | 5099 | 109 | -- | 21 | .964 |
| Savannah | 138 | 3519 | 1362 | 190 | 5071 | 96 | -- | 20 | .963 |

### INDIVIDUAL

#### FIRST BASEMEN

NOTE: All caps denotes fielding-percentage leader based on 70 games for catchers, 93 for all other non-pitchers and 112 innings for pitchers. *Throws lefthanded.

| Player, Team | Pct. | G | PO | A | E | TC | DP |
|---|---|---|---|---|---|---|---|
| Bankston, Wes, CSC | .994 | 95 | 745 | 57 | 5 | 807 | 66 |
| Bastida, Evel, DEL* | 1.000 | 1 | 5 | 0 | 0 | 5 | 0 |
| Bear, Ryan, GBO | .992 | 130 | 1021 | 56 | 9 | 1086 | 67 |
| Benick, Jon, HCK | .992 | 111 | 914 | 69 | 8 | 991 | 83 |
| Bergeron, Jabe, CAP | .993 | 17 | 136 | 9 | 1 | 146 | 14 |
| Bladergroen, Ian, CAP* | .992 | 44 | 325 | 34 | 3 | 362 | 28 |
| Bonvechio, Brett, AUG* | 1.000 | 4 | 44 | 1 | 0 | 45 | 4 |
| Bounds, Brandon, KAN* | .990 | 27 | 193 | 15 | 2 | 210 | 6 |
| Brice, Thomas, KAN* | 1.000 | 1 | 7 | 0 | 0 | 7 | 0 |
| Burgess, Tim, AUG* | .989 | 53 | 425 | 19 | 5 | 449 | 43 |
| Bynum, Seth, SAV | 1.000 | 1 | 1 | 0 | 0 | 1 | 0 |
| Castillo, Albenis, CMB | 1.000 | 6 | 40 | 2 | 0 | 42 | 2 |
| Castillo, Luis, CMB | .964 | 21 | 127 | 8 | 5 | 140 | 13 |
| Ciofrone, Peter, AUG* | .972 | 14 | 99 | 7 | 3 | 109 | 12 |
| Collum, Mike, HCK | 1.000 | 4 | 16 | 0 | 0 | 16 | 1 |
| Colonel, Christian, ASH | .994 | 108 | 1065 | 34 | 7 | 1106 | 87 |
| Columbus, Jason, HAG | .986 | 33 | 255 | 23 | 4 | 282 | 25 |
| Cotto, Luis, LCO | 1.000 | 1 | 1 | 0 | 0 | 1 | 0 |
| DAIGLE, LEO, KAN | .995 | 110 | 850 | 67 | 5 | 922 | 45 |
| Davidson, Tyler, CAP | .997 | 35 | 284 | 7 | 1 | 292 | 22 |
| De Aza, Alejandro, CMB* | 1.000 | 1 | 2 | 0 | 0 | 2 | 0 |
| de Vries, Jon, AUG | .875 | 1 | 7 | 0 | 1 | 8 | 0 |
| Diaz, Rafael, DEL | 1.000 | 12 | 78 | 9 | 0 | 87 | 14 |
| Ferrer, Simon, ASH | .991 | 21 | 200 | 11 | 2 | 213 | 26 |
| Garcia, Yunir, CAP | 1.000 | 1 | 4 | 0 | 0 | 4 | 0 |
| Guiterrez, Juan, DEL | .967 | 4 | 29 | 0 | 1 | 30 | 0 |
| Guzman, Carlos, ROM | .992 | 93 | 618 | 38 | 5 | 661 | 58 |
| Guzman, Heriberto, AUG | .975 | 4 | 39 | 0 | 1 | 40 | 1 |
| Haggerty, Cory, KAN* | 1.000 | 4 | 9 | 0 | 0 | 9 | 0 |
| Hansen, Bryan, LWD* | .990 | 117 | 938 | 78 | 10 | 1026 | 101 |
| Humphries, Justin, LEX | .983 | 14 | 107 | 9 | 2 | 118 | 12 |
| Ishikawa, Travis, HAG* | .994 | 94 | 773 | 55 | 5 | 833 | 54 |
| Jarvis, Andy, LWD* | 1.000 | 3 | 28 | 2 | 0 | 30 | 1 |
| Jimenez, Franklyn, SAV | .990 | 30 | 188 | 9 | 2 | 199 | 10 |
| Jimenez, Luis, CMB* | .989 | 84 | 654 | 43 | 8 | 705 | 73 |
| Johnston, Clinton, CWV* | .994 | 111 | 914 | 62 | 6 | 982 | 68 |
| Kelly, Chris, KAN | .964 | 6 | 50 | 3 | 2 | 55 | 5 |
| Knowlton, Jay, HAG | 1.000 | 1 | 11 | 0 | 0 | 11 | 0 |
| Koman, Brock, LEX | 1.000 | 6 | 46 | 2 | 0 | 48 | 2 |
| Lee, Carlos, KAN | 1.000 | 1 | 6 | 1 | 0 | 7 | 1 |
| Linares, Jesus, CAP | .973 | 5 | 34 | 2 | 1 | 37 | 3 |
| Manriquez, Salomon, SAV | .988 | 13 | 82 | 3 | 1 | 86 | 5 |
| McClain, Justin, AUG | .977 | 24 | 201 | 13 | 5 | 219 | 18 |
| Melendez, German, LEX | 1.000 | 2 | 10 | 0 | 0 | 10 | 1 |
| Molina, Angel, GBO | .955 | 10 | 60 | 3 | 3 | 66 | 6 |
| Molina, Gustavo, KAN | 1.000 | 1 | 1 | 0 | 0 | 1 | 0 |
| Montague, Eddie, ASH* | .973 | 5 | 35 | 1 | 1 | 37 | 3 |
| Morris, Seth, KAN | 1.000 | 1 | 1 | 0 | 0 | 1 | 0 |
| Mulhern, Ryan, LCO | .981 | 95 | 755 | 59 | 16 | 830 | 65 |
| Nichols, Tommy, CSC | .985 | 50 | 433 | 29 | 7 | 469 | 36 |
| Nixon, Mike, CMB | 1.000 | 1 | 3 | 0 | 0 | 3 | 1 |

| Player, Team | Pct. | G | PO | A | E | TC | DP |
|---|---|---|---|---|---|---|---|
| Ontiveros, Jeff, AUG | .987 | 31 | 273 | 21 | 4 | 298 | 36 |
| Peavey, Bill, LCO* | .986 | 45 | 341 | 19 | 5 | 365 | 28 |
| Pyzik, Steve, ROM | 1.000 | 1 | 4 | 1 | 0 | 5 | 0 |
| Rea, Brad, HCK | .992 | 29 | 229 | 6 | 2 | 237 | 24 |
| Reiman, Joey, CWV | 1.000 | 23 | 172 | 15 | 0 | 187 | 17 |
| Robinson, Scott, LEX* | .985 | 120 | 950 | 75 | 16 | 1041 | 90 |
| Rohan, Jimmy, CMB | .990 | 36 | 276 | 17 | 3 | 296 | 28 |
| Ruiz, Randy, LWD | .970 | 18 | 155 | 8 | 5 | 168 | 15 |
| Russell, Mike, DEL | .983 | 33 | 218 | 12 | 4 | 234 | 20 |
| Schade, Scott, ROM | .997 | 53 | 354 | 24 | 1 | 379 | 30 |
| Simmons, Colt, CSC | 1.000 | 1 | 1 | 0 | 0 | 1 | 0 |
| Street, Dan, ASH | 1.000 | 7 | 66 | 2 | 0 | 68 | 11 |
| Strong, Zach, HAG | .988 | 9 | 79 | 3 | 1 | 83 | 9 |
| Thomas, Ben, ROM* | 1.000 | 2 | 13 | 2 | 0 | 15 | 0 |
| White, Scott, AUG | .993 | 14 | 134 | 7 | 1 | 142 | 10 |
| Whitesell, Josh, SAV* | .984 | 104 | 810 | 56 | 14 | 880 | 70 |
| Wilson, Andrew, CAP | .994 | 41 | 308 | 16 | 2 | 326 | 36 |
| Wilson, Brandon, CAP | 1.000 | 1 | 2 | 0 | 0 | 2 | 0 |
| Yepez, Marcos, SAV | 1.000 | 3 | 7 | 1 | 0 | 8 | 3 |
| Yount, Dustin, DEL* | .971 | 98 | 783 | 35 | 24 | 842 | 64 |

## SECOND BASEMEN

| Player, Team | Pct. | G | PO | A | E | TC | DP |
|---|---|---|---|---|---|---|---|
| Abreu, Tony, CMB | .950 | 96 | 164 | 231 | 21 | 416 | 62 |
| Acey, Jermy, CWV | .935 | 43 | 69 | 105 | 12 | 186 | 17 |
| Barrows, Derek, HAG | .937 | 16 | 38 | 51 | 6 | 95 | 9 |
| Bastida, Evel, DEL* | .988 | 18 | 44 | 41 | 1 | 86 | 11 |
| Blood, Randy, ASH* | .956 | 84 | 162 | 254 | 19 | 435 | 56 |
| Borowiak, Zachary, AUG | .988 | 46 | 93 | 152 | 3 | 248 | 36 |
| Bramasco, Omar, LWD | 1.000 | 9 | 25 | 32 | 0 | 57 | 10 |
| Brown, Travis, DEL | 1.000 | 11 | 16 | 27 | 0 | 43 | 3 |
| Bynum, Seth, SAV | 1.000 | 5 | 6 | 6 | 0 | 12 | 0 |
| Carter, Brandon, CMB* | 1.000 | 3 | 9 | 3 | 0 | 12 | 3 |
| Cates, Gary, DEL | .966 | 6 | 11 | 17 | 1 | 29 | 5 |
| Chavez, Dirimo, AUG | .956 | 50 | 99 | 118 | 10 | 227 | 29 |
| Ciofrone, Peter, AUG* | .953 | 27 | 58 | 65 | 6 | 129 | 18 |
| Clanton, Ja`Mar, SAV | .953 | 8 | 16 | 25 | 2 | 43 | 6 |
| Clem, Chris, LCO | 1.000 | 3 | 3 | 10 | 0 | 13 | 0 |
| Cockrell, Mike, HCK | .980 | 11 | 20 | 29 | 1 | 50 | 5 |
| Collum, Mike, HCK | .955 | 4 | 6 | 15 | 1 | 22 | 7 |
| Conlisk, Jason, SAV | .977 | 82 | 171 | 203 | 9 | 383 | 43 |
| Cotto, Luis, LCO | 1.000 | 14 | 21 | 26 | 0 | 47 | 8 |
| Curtis, Lee, AUG | .833 | 3 | 2 | 3 | 1 | 6 | 1 |
| De La Cruz, Chris, LCO | .925 | 9 | 15 | 22 | 3 | 40 | 2 |
| Dobson, Patrick, HAG | .961 | 95 | 179 | 240 | 17 | 436 | 39 |
| Done, Mike, DEL | 1.000 | 5 | 6 | 13 | 0 | 19 | 2 |
| Downing, Juan, ROM | 1.000 | 2 | 4 | 5 | 0 | 9 | 2 |
| Fernando, Osvaldo, LEX | 1.000 | 3 | 8 | 3 | 0 | 11 | 1 |
| Ferrer, Simon, ASH | .980 | 9 | 17 | 32 | 1 | 50 | 7 |
| Garrido, Tomas, HAG | 1.000 | 3 | 7 | 9 | 0 | 16 | 2 |
| Gonzalez, Andy, KAN | 1.000 | 2 | 5 | 4 | 0 | 9 | 1 |
| Gray, Antoin, KAN | .940 | 98 | 176 | 260 | 28 | 464 | 35 |
| Grimm, Eric, DEL | .988 | 22 | 33 | 48 | 1 | 82 | 11 |
| Guance, Luis, ASH | .979 | 49 | 104 | 131 | 5 | 240 | 33 |
| Guerrero, Francisco, DEL | .875 | 4 | 3 | 11 | 2 | 16 | 2 |
| Haggerty, Cory, KAN* | .966 | 35 | 61 | 79 | 5 | 145 | 5 |
| Hanson, Mike, ROM | .955 | 35 | 50 | 78 | 6 | 134 | 15 |
| Harris, Justin, HCK | .983 | 25 | 45 | 72 | 2 | 119 | 11 |
| Hernandez, Diory, ROM | 1.000 | 1 | 3 | 4 | 0 | 7 | 1 |
| Hornostaj, Aaron, HAG* | .964 | 5 | 11 | 16 | 1 | 28 | 5 |
| Isaacson, Greg, LWD* | 1.000 | 1 | 1 | 3 | 0 | 4 | 0 |
| Italiano, Nick, LWD* | .978 | 32 | 60 | 73 | 3 | 136 | 22 |
| Jimenez, Franklyn, SAV | .970 | 21 | 45 | 53 | 3 | 101 | 17 |
| Johnson, Elliot, CSC | .972 | 125 | 249 | 342 | 17 | 608 | 76 |
| Knowlton, Jay, HAG | .923 | 11 | 19 | 17 | 3 | 39 | 4 |
| LaBarbera, Anthony, HAG | .979 | 9 | 20 | 26 | 1 | 47 | 9 |
| Laurin, Dominique, CMB | .977 | 21 | 36 | 49 | 2 | 87 | 11 |
| Linares, Jesus, CAP | .971 | 30 | 37 | 63 | 3 | 103 | 11 |
| Mader, Josh, LWD | .957 | 10 | 22 | 23 | 2 | 47 | 8 |
| Maysonet, Edwin, LEX | .964 | 80 | 134 | 212 | 13 | 359 | 64 |
| Mitchell, Russell, CMB | 1.000 | 10 | 21 | 15 | 0 | 36 | 4 |
| Montague, Eddie, ASH* | .889 | 3 | 2 | 6 | 1 | 9 | 1 |
| Morel, Elvis, DEL | 1.000 | 1 | 1 | 5 | 0 | 6 | 1 |
| Moss, Timothy, LWD | .968 | 77 | 171 | 195 | 12 | 378 | 41 |
| Nunez, Eduardo, SAV | 1.000 | 1 | 1 | 0 | 0 | 1 | 0 |
| Patrick, Brian, CWV | .912 | 7 | 15 | 16 | 3 | 34 | 3 |
| Paul, Matt, CMB | .923 | 9 | 8 | 16 | 2 | 26 | 2 |
| Peralta, Juan, CWV | 1.000 | 2 | 2 | 1 | 0 | 3 | 0 |
| Pinckney, Brandon, LCO | 1.000 | 5 | 8 | 13 | 0 | 21 | 4 |
| Prado, Martin, ROM | .978 | 101 | 175 | 222 | 9 | 406 | 52 |
| Prosser, Chad, LEX | .966 | 62 | 80 | 177 | 9 | 266 | 26 |
| Randel, Kevin, GBO* | .968 | 7 | 12 | 18 | 1 | 31 | 2 |
| Reaver, David, CAP | 1.000 | 4 | 3 | 5 | 0 | 8 | 0 |
| Rivera, William, CWV* | .990 | 27 | 46 | 57 | 1 | 104 | 10 |
| Roberts, Ryan, CWV | .972 | 61 | 149 | 166 | 9 | 324 | 26 |
| Robinson, Levi, DEL | .955 | 4 | 5 | 16 | 1 | 22 | 4 |
| Rohan, Jimmy, CMB | .923 | 10 | 12 | 12 | 2 | 26 | 3 |
| Schade, Ryan, GBO | 1.000 | 18 | 30 | 29 | 0 | 59 | 8 |
| Schilling, Micah, LCO* | .944 | 110 | 206 | 251 | 27 | 484 | 46 |
| Schleicher, Mark, CSC | .800 | 2 | 0 | 4 | 1 | 5 | 1 |
| Seifrig, Cole, GBO | .974 | 114 | 190 | 289 | 13 | 492 | 53 |
| Spears, Nate, DEL* | .960 | 77 | 135 | 204 | 14 | 353 | 42 |
| St Clair, Jason, CSC | .935 | 5 | 12 | 17 | 2 | 31 | 6 |
| STANSBERRY, CRAIG, HCK | .983 | 102 | 208 | 310 | 9 | 527 | 63 |
| Suarez, Ignacio, AUG | .968 | 17 | 39 | 53 | 3 | 95 | 10 |
| Touchstone, Josh, CSC | .979 | 15 | 21 | 26 | 1 | 48 | 5 |
| Tugwell, Marc, LWD | 1.000 | 11 | 17 | 24 | 0 | 41 | 6 |
| Valido, Robert, KAN | 1.000 | 9 | 11 | 26 | 0 | 37 | 3 |
| Whealy, Blake, CAP | .946 | 104 | 203 | 254 | 26 | 483 | 55 |
| White, Dean, ROM | .917 | 4 | 4 | 7 | 1 | 12 | 1 |
| Whitesides, Jake, KAN* | 1.000 | 1 | 1 | 2 | 0 | 3 | 0 |
| Wilson, Andrew, CAP | .919 | 14 | 29 | 28 | 5 | 62 | 6 |
| Yepez, Marcos, SAV | .944 | 26 | 35 | 49 | 5 | 89 | 9 |
| Young, Dustin, GBO | .909 | 2 | 6 | 4 | 1 | 11 | 1 |

## THIRD BASEMEN

| Player, Team | Pct. | G | PO | A | E | TC | DP |
|---|---|---|---|---|---|---|---|
| Abreu, Johany, HAG | .909 | 12 | 8 | 22 | 3 | 33 | 2 |
| Arnold, Eric, CWV | .928 | 95 | 58 | 162 | 17 | 237 | 11 |
| Barrows, Derek, HAG | .896 | 41 | 29 | 66 | 11 | 106 | 7 |
| Barthel, Cole, ROM | .786 | 12 | 7 | 15 | 6 | 28 | 0 |
| Bass, Bryan, DEL | .901 | 109 | 56 | 181 | 26 | 263 | 16 |
| Bastida, Evel, DEL* | 1.000 | 1 | 0 | 2 | 0 | 2 | 0 |
| Bowman, Shawn, CAP | .927 | 113 | 63 | 244 | 24 | 331 | 25 |
| Bramasco, Omar, LWD | .936 | 66 | 60 | 161 | 15 | 236 | 22 |
| Brown, Travis, DEL | .000 | 1 | 0 | 0 | 1 | 1 | 0 |
| Campbell, Eric, ROM | .938 | 7 | 2 | 13 | 1 | 16 | 0 |
| Castillo, Luis, CMB | .939 | 15 | 3 | 28 | 2 | 33 | 0 |
| Casto, Kory, SAV* | .870 | 112 | 59 | 176 | 35 | 270 | 10 |
| Castro, Ofilio, SAV | .970 | 10 | 5 | 27 | 1 | 33 | 1 |
| Chavez, Dirimo, AUG | .950 | 31 | 20 | 75 | 5 | 100 | 8 |
| Clem, Chris, LCO | 1.000 | 1 | 0 | 3 | 0 | 3 | 0 |
| Cockrell, Mike, HCK | .969 | 73 | 37 | 152 | 6 | 195 | 6 |
| Collum, Mike, HCK | .916 | 38 | 24 | 74 | 9 | 107 | 8 |
| Colonel, Christian, ASH | .867 | 5 | 3 | 10 | 2 | 15 | 1 |
| Cotto, Luis, LCO | .929 | 14 | 7 | 19 | 2 | 28 | 3 |
| Daigle, Leo, KAN | 1.000 | 2 | 1 | 4 | 0 | 5 | 0 |
| Diaz, Rafael, DEL | .923 | 5 | 4 | 8 | 1 | 13 | 1 |
| Diaz, Rafael, DEL | .852 | 13 | 5 | 18 | 4 | 27 | 2 |
| Ferrer, Simon, ASH | .935 | 13 | 7 | 36 | 3 | 46 | 5 |
| Garrido, Tomas, HAG | 1.000 | 1 | 0 | 2 | 0 | 2 | 0 |
| Gonzalez, Andy, KAN | 1.000 | 2 | 0 | 4 | 0 | 4 | 0 |
| Gray, Antoin, KAN | .909 | 11 | 6 | 24 | 3 | 33 | 0 |
| Grimm, Eric, DEL | .974 | 18 | 5 | 32 | 1 | 38 | 6 |
| Guance, Luis, ASH | .889 | 9 | 3 | 21 | 3 | 27 | 1 |
| Guzman, Heriberto, AUG | .949 | 14 | 10 | 27 | 2 | 39 | 4 |
| Harris, Justin, HCK | .974 | 31 | 19 | 55 | 2 | 76 | 2 |
| Hornostaj, Aaron, HAG* | .920 | 8 | 7 | 16 | 2 | 25 | 5 |
| Isaacson, Greg, LWD* | .750 | 2 | 1 | 2 | 1 | 4 | 0 |
| Italiano, Nick, LWD* | 1.000 | 2 | 1 | 2 | 0 | 3 | 1 |
| Jimenez, Franklyn, SAV | .750 | 2 | 1 | 2 | 1 | 4 | 0 |
| Knowlton, Jay, HAG | .882 | 23 | 16 | 44 | 8 | 68 | 4 |
| Koman, Brock, LEX | .886 | 21 | 12 | 27 | 5 | 44 | 2 |
| Kouzmanoff, Kevin, LCO | .950 | 115 | 83 | 185 | 14 | 282 | 14 |
| Laroche, Andy, CMB | .942 | 62 | 45 | 101 | 9 | 155 | 12 |
| Laurin, Dominique, CMB | .833 | 8 | 5 | 10 | 3 | 18 | 1 |
| Linares, Jesus, CAP | .829 | 22 | 6 | 23 | 6 | 35 | 1 |
| Macaluso, Mike, CWV | 1.000 | 4 | 5 | 2 | 0 | 7 | 0 |
| Mader, Josh, LWD | .925 | 27 | 24 | 50 | 6 | 80 | 6 |
| Manriquez, Salomon, SAV | .833 | 2 | 1 | 4 | 1 | 6 | 1 |
| Mazzuca, Joe, GBO | .822 | 34 | 18 | 65 | 18 | 101 | 4 |
| McClain, Justin, AUG | .667 | 2 | 0 | 2 | 1 | 3 | 0 |
| McMillan, Beau, GBO | .824 | 6 | 0 | 14 | 3 | 17 | 2 |
| Mitchell, Russell, CMB | .945 | 53 | 31 | 106 | 8 | 145 | 8 |
| Patrick, Brian, CWV | 1.000 | 1 | 0 | 3 | 0 | 3 | 0 |
| Peterson, Derrick, LCO | .958 | 8 | 6 | 17 | 1 | 24 | 3 |
| Pinckney, Brandon, LCO | .917 | 3 | 2 | 9 | 1 | 12 | 1 |
| Prosser, Chad, LEX | .750 | 2 | 0 | 3 | 1 | 4 | 1 |
| Randel, Kevin, GBO* | .867 | 8 | 9 | 17 | 4 | 30 | 2 |
| Rivera, William, CWV* | .947 | 36 | 21 | 69 | 5 | 95 | 4 |
| Rohan, Jimmy, CMB | .778 | 3 | 1 | 6 | 2 | 9 | 1 |
| Russell, Mike, DEL | 1.000 | 6 | 0 | 7 | 0 | 7 | 0 |
| Schade, Ryan, GBO | .926 | 28 | 17 | 46 | 5 | 68 | 5 |
| Schade, Scott, ROM | .917 | 48 | 21 | 78 | 9 | 108 | 8 |

| Player, Team | Pct. | G | PO | A | E | TC | DP |
|---|---|---|---|---|---|---|---|
| Schierholtz, Nate, HAG* | .914 | 55 | 34 | 105 | 13 | 152 | 7 |
| Schleicher, Mark, CSC | .932 | 33 | 20 | 62 | 6 | 88 | 4 |
| Schlichting, Travis, CSC | .897 | 93 | 50 | 185 | 27 | 262 | 13 |
| Schnurstein, Micah, KAN | .923 | 127 | 94 | 195 | 24 | 313 | 8 |
| Sosa, Pablo, GBO | .922 | 67 | 46 | 119 | 14 | 179 | 7 |
| St Clair, Jason, CSC | .938 | 14 | 5 | 25 | 2 | 32 | 1 |
| Stewart, Ian, ASH* | .941 | 116 | 89 | 308 | 25 | 422 | 27 |
| Strong, Zach, HAG | .875 | 2 | 2 | 5 | 1 | 8 | 2 |
| Thomas, Ben, ROM* | .970 | 18 | 14 | 18 | 1 | 33 | 0 |
| TORRES, SAUL, LEX | .955 | 118 | 86 | 212 | 14 | 312 | 18 |
| Touchstone, Josh, CSC | .889 | 3 | 2 | 6 | 1 | 9 | 1 |
| Tugwell, Marc, LWD | .868 | 42 | 26 | 86 | 17 | 129 | 10 |
| White, Dean, ROM | .882 | 62 | 26 | 109 | 18 | 153 | 10 |
| White, Scott, AUG | .901 | 98 | 65 | 200 | 29 | 294 | 18 |
| Wilson, Andrew, CAP | .943 | 15 | 6 | 27 | 2 | 35 | 0 |
| Yepez, Marcos, SAV | .902 | 14 | 4 | 33 | 4 | 41 | 2 |
| Young, Dustin, GBO | .875 | 3 | 2 | 5 | 1 | 8 | 0 |

## SHORTSTOPS

| Player, Team | Pct. | G | PO | A | E | TC | DP |
|---|---|---|---|---|---|---|---|
| Abreu, Johany, HAG | 1.000 | 4 | 6 | 10 | 0 | 16 | 1 |
| Abreu, Tony, CMB | .857 | 2 | 1 | 5 | 1 | 7 | 0 |
| Andino, Robert, GBO | .937 | 76 | 91 | 221 | 21 | 333 | 27 |
| Barrows, Derek, HAG | .769 | 3 | 4 | 6 | 3 | 13 | 0 |
| Bass, Bryan, DEL | .941 | 3 | 5 | 11 | 1 | 17 | 1 |
| Batista, Wilson, CAP | .922 | 84 | 115 | 226 | 29 | 370 | 40 |
| Borowiak, Zachary, AUG | .920 | 74 | 100 | 232 | 29 | 361 | 45 |
| Bramasco, Omar, LWD | .954 | 26 | 41 | 84 | 6 | 131 | 14 |
| Brignac, Reid, CSC* | .933 | 3 | 4 | 10 | 1 | 15 | 1 |
| Brown, Travis, DEL | .939 | 101 | 185 | 261 | 29 | 475 | 55 |
| Bynum, Seth, SAV | .906 | 14 | 14 | 34 | 5 | 53 | 3 |
| Carter, Brandon, CMB* | .667 | 1 | 0 | 2 | 1 | 3 | 0 |
| Chavez, Dirimo, AUG | .977 | 9 | 13 | 30 | 1 | 44 | 6 |
| Clanton, Ja`Mar, SAV | .625 | 2 | 1 | 4 | 3 | 8 | 1 |
| Clem, Chris, LCO | .913 | 4 | 6 | 15 | 2 | 23 | 2 |
| Collum, Mike, HCK | 1.000 | 5 | 5 | 15 | 0 | 20 | 3 |
| Conlisk, Jason, SAV | .935 | 23 | 45 | 71 | 8 | 124 | 18 |
| Cotto, Luis, LCO | .933 | 20 | 25 | 58 | 6 | 89 | 12 |
| Cuevas, Aneudi, CSC | .944 | 45 | 75 | 145 | 13 | 233 | 38 |
| De La Cruz, Chris, LCO | .950 | 94 | 141 | 254 | 21 | 416 | 50 |
| Diaz, Rafael, DEL | 1.000 | 3 | 3 | 6 | 0 | 9 | 1 |
| Diaz, Rafael, DEL | 1.000 | 3 | 3 | 6 | 0 | 9 | 1 |
| Downing, Juan, ROM | .970 | 6 | 12 | 20 | 1 | 33 | 11 |
| FERNANDO, OSVALDO, LEX | .950 | 112 | 171 | 304 | 25 | 500 | 68 |
| Ferrer, Simon, ASH | .933 | 12 | 22 | 34 | 4 | 60 | 8 |
| Garrido, Tomas, HAG | .938 | 5 | 8 | 7 | 1 | 16 | 1 |
| Gendron, Steve, GBO | .939 | 50 | 81 | 136 | 14 | 231 | 23 |
| Gonzalez, Andy, KAN | .949 | 9 | 15 | 22 | 2 | 39 | 4 |
| Grimm, Eric, DEL | .846 | 5 | 0 | 11 | 2 | 13 | 1 |
| Guance, Luis, ASH | .944 | 38 | 58 | 129 | 11 | 198 | 25 |
| Guzman, Javier, HCK | .933 | 123 | 163 | 378 | 39 | 580 | 78 |
| Haggerty, Cory, KAN* | .947 | 27 | 33 | 56 | 5 | 94 | 6 |
| Hanson, Mike, ROM | .977 | 25 | 36 | 50 | 2 | 88 | 17 |
| Harris, Justin, HCK | .943 | 12 | 19 | 31 | 3 | 53 | 6 |
| Hernandez, Diory, ROM | .922 | 85 | 111 | 195 | 26 | 332 | 28 |
| Herrera, Jonathan, ASH | .947 | 94 | 102 | 325 | 24 | 451 | 50 |
| Hornostaj, Aaron, HAG* | 1.000 | 1 | 0 | 1 | 0 | 1 | 0 |
| Hu, Chin-Lung, CMB | .963 | 84 | 117 | 251 | 14 | 382 | 49 |
| Hutting, Timothy, HAG | .943 | 123 | 144 | 334 | 29 | 507 | 47 |
| Knowlton, Jay, HAG | .857 | 6 | 8 | 16 | 4 | 28 | 5 |
| LaBarbera, Anthony, HAG | 1.000 | 1 | 0 | 3 | 0 | 3 | 0 |
| Laurin, Dominique, CMB | .945 | 31 | 35 | 68 | 6 | 109 | 21 |
| LeVier, Brett, AUG | .947 | 25 | 38 | 88 | 7 | 133 | 14 |
| Linares, Jesus, CAP | .952 | 31 | 42 | 76 | 6 | 124 | 13 |
| Macaluso, Mike, CWV | 1.000 | 1 | 0 | 2 | 0 | 2 | 0 |
| Mader, Josh, LWD | .875 | 2 | 2 | 5 | 1 | 8 | 0 |
| Maysonet, Edwin, LEX | .955 | 31 | 46 | 81 | 6 | 133 | 11 |
| Morel, Elvis, DEL | .905 | 15 | 16 | 41 | 6 | 63 | 8 |
| Pedroia, Dustin, AUG | 1.000 | 12 | 11 | 34 | 0 | 45 | 7 |
| Peralta, Juan, CWV | .940 | 106 | 156 | 296 | 29 | 481 | 49 |
| Pinckney, Brandon, LCO | .969 | 24 | 27 | 68 | 3 | 98 | 10 |
| Randel, Kevin, GBO* | .900 | 2 | 1 | 8 | 1 | 10 | 0 |
| Reaver, David, CAP | .923 | 31 | 44 | 87 | 11 | 142 | 16 |
| Rivera, William, CWV* | .964 | 30 | 37 | 95 | 5 | 137 | 15 |
| Robinson, Levi, DEL | 1.000 | 2 | 2 | 4 | 0 | 6 | 0 |
| Rodriguez, Carlos, LWD | .911 | 112 | 159 | 279 | 43 | 481 | 65 |
| Rohan, Jimmy, CMB | .926 | 30 | 41 | 72 | 9 | 122 | 16 |
| Schade, Ryan, GBO | .971 | 9 | 12 | 22 | 1 | 35 | 3 |
| Schleicher, Mark, CSC | .917 | 70 | 105 | 181 | 26 | 312 | 28 |
| Schlichting, Travis, CSC | 1.000 | 1 | 1 | 5 | 0 | 6 | 1 |
| Schnurstein, Micah, KAN | 1.000 | 1 | 1 | 0 | 0 | 1 | 1 |
| Spears, Nate, DEL* | 1.000 | 14 | 23 | 39 | 0 | 62 | 9 |
| St Clair, Jason, CSC | .876 | 19 | 30 | 55 | 12 | 97 | 12 |
| Suarez, Ignacio, AUG | .933 | 21 | 32 | 66 | 7 | 105 | 15 |
| Touchstone, Josh, CSC | .929 | 6 | 6 | 7 | 1 | 14 | 1 |
| Valido, Robert, KAN | .948 | 111 | 175 | 335 | 28 | 538 | 35 |
| Webb, Trey, SAV | .936 | 73 | 118 | 202 | 22 | 342 | 34 |
| White, Dean, ROM | .940 | 28 | 42 | 68 | 7 | 117 | 14 |
| Yepez, Marcos, SAV | .959 | 29 | 48 | 94 | 6 | 148 | 16 |
| Young, Dustin, GBO | 1.000 | 5 | 4 | 4 | 0 | 8 | 0 |

## OUTFIELDERS

| Player, Team | Pct. | G | PO | A | E | TC | DP |
|---|---|---|---|---|---|---|---|
| Abreu, Johany, HAG | 1.000 | 14 | 30 | 1 | 0 | 31 | 0 |
| Acevedo, Freddy, LEX | .981 | 108 | 192 | 15 | 4 | 211 | 3 |
| Alcantara, Ervin, LEX | .973 | 130 | 245 | 10 | 7 | 262 | 3 |
| Anderson, Josh, LEX* | .968 | 73 | 150 | 2 | 5 | 157 | 0 |
| Arias, Claudio, AUG | .964 | 43 | 74 | 7 | 3 | 84 | 0 |
| Armitage, Jonathan, HAG | .964 | 118 | 201 | 14 | 8 | 223 | 3 |
| Arroyo, Xavier, GBO | .981 | 88 | 158 | 1 | 3 | 162 | 0 |
| Ascencion, Quincy, DEL | .974 | 33 | 37 | 1 | 1 | 39 | 0 |
| Baez, Edgardo, SAV | .971 | 41 | 64 | 3 | 2 | 69 | 0 |
| Bankston, Wes, CSC | 1.000 | 10 | 7 | 0 | 0 | 7 | 0 |
| Barre, Brian, ASH* | .957 | 29 | 44 | 1 | 2 | 47 | 0 |
| Bass, Bryan, DEL | 1.000 | 2 | 6 | 1 | 0 | 7 | 0 |
| Bernadina, Rogearvin, SAV* | .960 | 113 | 223 | 15 | 10 | 248 | 3 |
| Blalock, Jake, LWD | .982 | 126 | 213 | 9 | 4 | 226 | 3 |
| Bocchino, Anthony, HCK* | .972 | 42 | 62 | 8 | 2 | 72 | 1 |
| Boeve, Adam, HCK | .973 | 114 | 175 | 3 | 5 | 183 | 1 |
| Bonner, Adam, GBO* | .942 | 27 | 46 | 3 | 3 | 52 | 2 |
| Bourn, Michael, LWD* | .979 | 107 | 228 | 10 | 5 | 243 | 2 |
| Bramasco, Omar, LWD | 1.000 | 1 | 5 | 1 | 0 | 6 | 0 |
| Brice, Thomas, KAN* | .969 | 50 | 91 | 2 | 3 | 96 | 0 |
| Brinkley, Dante, CAP | 1.000 | 31 | 54 | 6 | 0 | 60 | 2 |
| Burrus, Josh, ROM | .967 | 112 | 185 | 17 | 7 | 209 | 4 |
| Carter, Chris, DEL | 1.000 | 7 | 14 | 0 | 0 | 14 | 0 |
| Chavez, Dirimo, AUG | 1.000 | 4 | 3 | 0 | 0 | 3 | 0 |
| Clanton, Ja`Mar, SAV | 1.000 | 1 | 1 | 0 | 0 | 1 | 0 |
| Collum, Mike, HCK | .000 | 1 | 0 | 0 | 1 | 1 | 0 |
| Conroy, Mike, LCO* | .970 | 96 | 156 | 7 | 5 | 168 | 0 |
| Cook, David, KAN | .971 | 50 | 96 | 6 | 3 | 105 | 0 |
| Cotto, Luis, LCO | 1.000 | 2 | 2 | 0 | 0 | 2 | 0 |
| Coutlangus, Jon, HAG* | .975 | 67 | 143 | 12 | 4 | 159 | 2 |
| Cronkhite, Ian, AUG* | .966 | 78 | 171 | 2 | 6 | 179 | 0 |
| Czarniecki, Jordan, ASH | .992 | 105 | 231 | 5 | 2 | 238 | 1 |
| Daigle, Leo, KAN | .667 | 4 | 2 | 0 | 1 | 3 | 0 |
| Davis, Morrin, CWV | .925 | 43 | 58 | 4 | 5 | 67 | 1 |
| De Aza, Alejandro, CMB* | .940 | 73 | 123 | 3 | 8 | 134 | 0 |
| DeLeon, Joey, LEX | 1.000 | 1 | 1 | 0 | 0 | 1 | 0 |
| Dion, Nate, CSC | .946 | 73 | 100 | 5 | 6 | 111 | 1 |
| Doetsch, Steve, ROM | .981 | 114 | 255 | 5 | 5 | 265 | 2 |
| Dukes, Elijah, CSC | .988 | 40 | 73 | 6 | 1 | 80 | 2 |
| Encarnacion, Teodoro, LCO | 1.000 | 13 | 18 | 3 | 0 | 21 | 0 |
| Esquivel, Matt, ROM | .980 | 105 | 231 | 9 | 5 | 245 | 1 |
| Evans, Robert, AUG* | .966 | 41 | 81 | 5 | 3 | 89 | 0 |
| Fiorentino, Jeff, DEL* | .949 | 48 | 88 | 6 | 5 | 99 | 0 |
| Fitzpatrick, Reggie, SAV* | .972 | 82 | 135 | 5 | 4 | 144 | 1 |
| Fransz, Jason, DEL | 1.000 | 7 | 10 | 1 | 0 | 11 | 0 |
| Fuller, Casey, ASH* | .967 | 19 | 26 | 3 | 1 | 30 | 0 |
| Gaetti, Joe, ASH | .968 | 107 | 176 | 6 | 6 | 188 | 1 |
| Galloway, Michael, CWV | .973 | 95 | 139 | 4 | 4 | 147 | 0 |
| George, Trey, ASH | .970 | 86 | 120 | 8 | 4 | 132 | 0 |
| Goleski, Ryan, LCO | .974 | 117 | 211 | 11 | 6 | 228 | 3 |
| Guzman, Carlos, ROM | 1.000 | 6 | 6 | 0 | 0 | 6 | 0 |
| Haggerty, Cory, KAN* | .882 | 12 | 14 | 1 | 2 | 17 | 0 |
| Hall, Mickey, AUG* | .929 | 111 | 172 | 11 | 14 | 197 | 2 |
| Hanson, Mike, ROM | .875 | 6 | 5 | 2 | 1 | 8 | 0 |
| Harris, Cory, DEL | 1.000 | 45 | 91 | 4 | 0 | 95 | 0 |
| Harris, Justin, HCK | .958 | 14 | 21 | 2 | 1 | 24 | 1 |
| Harvey, Ryan, CAP | .954 | 100 | 141 | 3 | 7 | 151 | 0 |
| Hearod, Beau, LEX | .969 | 82 | 126 | 1 | 4 | 131 | 0 |
| Hemingway, Jamie, ROM | .929 | 14 | 24 | 2 | 2 | 28 | 0 |
| Hill, Jamar, CAP | .961 | 111 | 191 | 7 | 8 | 206 | 1 |
| Hudgson, Maximiliano, LEX | .833 | 5 | 5 | 0 | 1 | 6 | 0 |
| Jansen, Ardley, ROM | .965 | 57 | 133 | 4 | 5 | 142 | 2 |
| Jimenez, Franklyn, SAV | .967 | 17 | 27 | 2 | 1 | 30 | 0 |
| Jones, Chipper, ROM | 1.000 | 1 | 2 | 0 | 0 | 2 | 0 |
| Jones, Mitch, CSC | 1.000 | 17 | 26 | 2 | 0 | 28 | 0 |
| Jordan, Kevin, AUG* | .976 | 46 | 78 | 2 | 2 | 82 | 0 |
| Kemp, Matt, CMB | .965 | 104 | 184 | 10 | 7 | 201 | 2 |
| King, Clinton, KAN* | 1.000 | 20 | 30 | 2 | 0 | 32 | 0 |
| Kingsbury, Bobby, HCK* | .974 | 96 | 179 | 8 | 5 | 192 | 0 |
| Klemm, Chris, LWD* | .947 | 61 | 103 | 4 | 6 | 113 | 0 |
| Leandro, Francisco, CSC* | .985 | 31 | 62 | 2 | 1 | 65 | 0 |

| Player, Team | Pct. | G | PO | A | E | TC | DP |
|---|---|---|---|---|---|---|---|
| Linares, Jesus, CAP | 1.000 | 1 | 1 | 0 | 0 | 1 | 0 |
| Mader, Josh, LWD | 1.000 | 1 | 2 | 1 | 0 | 3 | 0 |
| Mancebo, Melvin, SAV | .000 | 1 | 0 | 0 | 1 | 1 | 0 |
| Marcos, Emilio, CMB | .964 | 21 | 52 | 2 | 2 | 56 | 1 |
| Markakis, Nick, DEL* | .986 | 75 | 133 | 4 | 2 | 139 | 0 |
| Martinez-Esteve, Edd, HAG | 1.000 | 9 | 16 | 1 | 0 | 17 | 0 |
| Mazzuca, Joe, GBO | .909 | 6 | 8 | 2 | 1 | 11 | 0 |
| McCurdy, Josh, DEL | .985 | 60 | 123 | 5 | 2 | 130 | 1 |
| Meath, Matt, HCK | .833 | 10 | 9 | 1 | 2 | 12 | 0 |
| Medina, Rodney, CWV | .980 | 28 | 45 | 3 | 1 | 49 | 0 |
| Milledge, Lastings, CAP | .920 | 62 | 97 | 6 | 9 | 112 | 1 |
| Miller, Jai, GBO | .960 | 112 | 233 | 7 | 10 | 250 | 1 |
| Milons, Jereme, CMB | .976 | 102 | 199 | 5 | 5 | 209 | 0 |
| Molina, Angel, GBO | .970 | 77 | 119 | 9 | 4 | 132 | 0 |
| Moni, Timi, LWD | .968 | 16 | 29 | 1 | 1 | 31 | 0 |
| Montague, Eddie, ASH* | .985 | 74 | 124 | 7 | 2 | 133 | 1 |
| Moran, Javon, LWD | .980 | 100 | 237 | 2 | 5 | 244 | 1 |
| Morgan, Nyjer, HCK* | .970 | 134 | 291 | 5 | 9 | 305 | 0 |
| Morris, Seth, KAN | .962 | 76 | 136 | 14 | 6 | 156 | 1 |
| Moss, Brandon, AUG* | .963 | 103 | 201 | 8 | 8 | 217 | 2 |
| Nanita, Ricardo, KAN* | .961 | 61 | 116 | 7 | 5 | 128 | 1 |
| Owens, Jerry, SAV* | .969 | 68 | 91 | 2 | 3 | 96 | 0 |
| Parker, Rashad, CAP | .966 | 63 | 110 | 3 | 4 | 117 | 0 |
| Patrick, Brian, CWV | .949 | 60 | 89 | 4 | 5 | 98 | 1 |
| Paul, Xavier, CMB* | .934 | 119 | 118 | 9 | 9 | 136 | 2 |
| Pietsch, Seth, CAP | .947 | 8 | 18 | 0 | 1 | 19 | 0 |
| Pridie, Jason, CSC* | .985 | 122 | 248 | 14 | 4 | 266 | 4 |
| Ramistella, John, GBO | .927 | 28 | 36 | 2 | 3 | 41 | 0 |
| Rine, Jarod, DEL* | .988 | 118 | 233 | 7 | 3 | 243 | 0 |
| Rodriguez, Alfredo, SAV | .667 | 1 | 2 | 0 | 1 | 3 | 0 |
| Rohan, Jimmy, CMB | 1.000 | 3 | 2 | 0 | 0 | 2 | 0 |
| Rohleder, Andy, GBO | .966 | 25 | 28 | 0 | 1 | 29 | 0 |
| Rojas, Ricardo, LCO | .996 | 96 | 216 | 10 | 1 | 227 | 3 |
| Ruiz, Randy, LWD | 1.000 | 8 | 17 | 1 | 0 | 18 | 1 |
| Sapp, Steven, CMB | .875 | 6 | 13 | 1 | 2 | 16 | 0 |
| Schade, Ryan, GBO | 1.000 | 11 | 16 | 3 | 0 | 19 | 0 |
| Schleicher, Mark, CSC | 1.000 | 1 | 4 | 0 | 0 | 4 | 0 |
| Schmidt, Jesse, HAG | .970 | 98 | 186 | 6 | 6 | 198 | 2 |
| Scott, Lorenzo, DEL* | .962 | 13 | 24 | 1 | 1 | 26 | 0 |
| Shanks, James, GBO | .948 | 57 | 103 | 6 | 6 | 115 | 1 |
| Silva, Johan, ROM | .933 | 7 | 14 | 0 | 1 | 15 | 0 |
| Simmons, Colt, CSC | 1.000 | 8 | 8 | 0 | 0 | 8 | 0 |
| Smith, David, CWV | .985 | 119 | 191 | 7 | 3 | 201 | 4 |
| Smith, Sean, HCK | .975 | 31 | 38 | 1 | 1 | 40 | 0 |
| Snavely, Christian, CWV* | .978 | 103 | 129 | 6 | 3 | 138 | 0 |
| Snyder, Brad, LCO* | .975 | 71 | 152 | 4 | 4 | 160 | 2 |
| St Clair, Jason, CSC | 1.000 | 13 | 11 | 0 | 0 | 11 | 0 |
| Stewart, Caleb, CAP | 1.000 | 19 | 31 | 3 | 0 | 34 | 1 |
| Street, Dan, ASH | 1.000 | 4 | 1 | 0 | 0 | 1 | 0 |
| Strong, Zach, HAG | 1.000 | 4 | 10 | 0 | 0 | 10 | 0 |
| Sucre, Antonio, SAV | .936 | 94 | 151 | 10 | 11 | 172 | 0 |
| Sultemeier, Eric, DEL | .947 | 12 | 18 | 0 | 1 | 19 | 0 |
| Testa, Chris, CMB* | .667 | 1 | 1 | 1 | 1 | 3 | 0 |
| Tucker, Mamon, LEX | .983 | 38 | 59 | 0 | 1 | 60 | 0 |
| Tuttle, Jason, SAV* | 1.000 | 4 | 3 | 0 | 0 | 3 | 0 |
| Valdes, Juan, LCO | 1.000 | 25 | 47 | 1 | 0 | 48 | 1 |
| Wagner, Mike, HAG | .940 | 111 | 185 | 2 | 12 | 199 | 1 |
| Watts, Derran, CAP | .982 | 26 | 54 | 2 | 1 | 57 | 0 |
| White, Dean, ROM | 1.000 | 4 | 6 | 0 | 0 | 6 | 0 |
| Whitesides, Jake, KAN* | .966 | 31 | 56 | 0 | 2 | 58 | 0 |
| Wilson, Andrew, CAP | .867 | 11 | 13 | 0 | 2 | 15 | 0 |
| Wise, DeWayne, ROM* | 1.000 | 1 | 1 | 0 | 0 | 1 | 0 |
| Yepez, Marcos, SAV | 1.000 | 3 | 7 | 0 | 0 | 7 | 0 |
| Young, Chris, KAN | .969 | 133 | 335 | 11 | 11 | 357 | 1 |
| Young, Delmon, CSC | .979 | 114 | 220 | 14 | 5 | 239 | 3 |

| Player, Team | Pct. | G | PO | A | E | TC | DP | PB |
|---|---|---|---|---|---|---|---|---|
| Bone, Kyle, HAG | .983 | 15 | 100 | 14 | 2 | 116 | 1 | 1 |
| Brock, Caleb, LCO | .995 | 49 | 350 | 42 | 2 | 394 | 5 | 8 |
| Buller, Dayton, HAG | .983 | 34 | 262 | 29 | 5 | 296 | 2 | 6 |
| Castillo, Cesar, KAN | .970 | 10 | 61 | 3 | 2 | 66 | 1 | 1 |
| Chapman, Travis, HCK | .985 | 28 | 173 | 19 | 3 | 195 | 2 | 6 |
| Chauncey, Clint, AUG | .986 | 8 | 62 | 6 | 1 | 69 | 0 | 0 |
| Cloninger, Erich, AUG | 1.000 | 5 | 35 | 1 | 0 | 36 | 0 | 0 |
| Cortez, Jose, LWD | .983 | 63 | 379 | 38 | 7 | 424 | 8 | 10 |
| Davidson, Kevin, LEX | .998 | 47 | 398 | 30 | 1 | 429 | 6 | 2 |
| de Vries, Jon, AUG | .987 | 67 | 498 | 46 | 7 | 551 | 4 | 8 |
| Diaz, Robinson, CWV | .985 | 77 | 603 | 63 | 10 | 676 | 5 | 9 |
| Emmerick, Josh, SAV | 1.000 | 24 | 179 | 15 | 0 | 194 | 0 | 3 |
| Garcia, Yunir, CAP | .987 | 71 | 564 | 35 | 8 | 607 | 0 | 4 |
| Gradoville, Tim, LWD | .993 | 23 | 132 | 20 | 1 | 153 | 0 | 2 |
| Guiterrez, Juan, DEL | .996 | 30 | 223 | 18 | 1 | 242 | 2 | 10 |
| Hernandez, Francisco, KAN | 1.000 | 1 | 4 | 0 | 0 | 4 | 0 | 1 |
| Herrera, Javier, LCO | .987 | 45 | 357 | 36 | 5 | 398 | 1 | 7 |
| Houston, Matthew, DEL | .980 | 50 | 360 | 26 | 8 | 394 | 2 | 7 |
| Humphries, Justin, LEX | 1.000 | 3 | 16 | 0 | 0 | 16 | 0 | 2 |
| Iannetta, Chris, ASH | .988 | 32 | 221 | 21 | 3 | 245 | 0 | 4 |
| Ivany, Devin, SAV | .995 | 23 | 174 | 17 | 1 | 192 | 0 | 0 |
| Lee, Carlos, KAN | .976 | 21 | 142 | 20 | 4 | 166 | 1 | 5 |
| Lisk, Charlie, KAN | .983 | 80 | 522 | 65 | 10 | 597 | 1 | 36 |
| Lombardi, Mike, LWD | .966 | 3 | 27 | 1 | 1 | 29 | 0 | 0 |
| Lopez, Mauber, LWD | 1.000 | 4 | 26 | 4 | 0 | 30 | 0 | 2 |
| Manriquez, Salomon, SAV | .967 | 15 | 104 | 15 | 4 | 123 | 2 | 3 |
| McCuistion, Mike, HCK* | .989 | 82 | 667 | 49 | 8 | 724 | 2 | 18 |
| McCullough, Clayton, LCO* | .992 | 28 | 219 | 15 | 2 | 236 | 1 | 1 |
| Melendez, German, LEX | .982 | 75 | 560 | 51 | 11 | 622 | 4 | 13 |
| Molina, Angel, GBO | .991 | 15 | 109 | 7 | 1 | 117 | 0 | 4 |
| Molina, Gustavo, KAN | .993 | 36 | 262 | 41 | 2 | 305 | 3 | 5 |
| Munhall, Brian, HAG | .981 | 62 | 433 | 41 | 9 | 483 | 4 | 7 |
| Nixon, Mike, CMB | .992 | 88 | 805 | 66 | 7 | 878 | 5 | 18 |
| Norman, Zach, LWD | .968 | 4 | 28 | 2 | 1 | 31 | 0 | 4 |
| Noviskey, Josh, LCO | 1.000 | 22 | 180 | 15 | 0 | 195 | 2 | 3 |
| Olszta, Eddie, HCK | 1.000 | 3 | 14 | 0 | 0 | 14 | 0 | 2 |
| Ontiveros, Jeff, AUG | 1.000 | 2 | 8 | 1 | 0 | 9 | 0 | 0 |
| Paniagua, Salvador, AUG | .978 | 31 | 197 | 24 | 5 | 226 | 2 | 7 |
| Piazza, Tony, CAP | 1.000 | 3 | 26 | 3 | 0 | 29 | 0 | 2 |
| Pierce, Whit, DEL | 1.000 | 19 | 130 | 10 | 0 | 140 | 1 | 1 |
| Price, Jared, CMB | .993 | 52 | 413 | 37 | 3 | 453 | 1 | 10 |
| Pyzik, Steve, ROM | .992 | 43 | 217 | 19 | 2 | 238 | 4 | 1 |
| Reiman, Joey, CWV | 1.000 | 32 | 257 | 19 | 0 | 276 | 1 | 3 |
| Reyes, Milver, HCK | .981 | 26 | 197 | 13 | 4 | 214 | 1 | 5 |
| Reynoso, Danilo, CAP | .967 | 15 | 105 | 13 | 4 | 122 | 1 | 5 |
| Riera, Zack, LEX | .979 | 16 | 134 | 8 | 3 | 145 | 3 | 2 |
| Rodriguez, Alfredo, SAV | 1.000 | 1 | 12 | 0 | 0 | 12 | 0 | 0 |
| Rodriguez, Robert, SAV | 1.000 | 22 | 136 | 13 | 0 | 149 | 2 | 6 |
| Russell, Mike, DEL | .980 | 27 | 183 | 11 | 4 | 198 | 1 | 6 |
| Saltalamacchia, Jarr, ROM | .982 | 50 | 415 | 31 | 8 | 454 | 3 | 13 |
| San Pedro, Erick, SAV | .983 | 6 | 53 | 5 | 1 | 59 | 0 | 1 |
| Schartz, Lance, AUG | 1.000 | 10 | 65 | 1 | 0 | 66 | 1 | 1 |
| Serrano, Ray, ROM | .975 | 13 | 112 | 5 | 3 | 120 | 0 | 0 |
| Shehan, Jonathon, ROM | 1.000 | 2 | 16 | 0 | 0 | 16 | 0 | 1 |
| Simmons, Colt, CSC | .997 | 47 | 293 | 27 | 1 | 321 | 1 | 15 |
| Speigner, Brent, CSC | .990 | 24 | 93 | 7 | 1 | 101 | 0 | 1 |
| Stachowsky, Mitch, AUG | .993 | 23 | 144 | 4 | 1 | 149 | 0 | 7 |
| Swanson, Brent, HAG* | .985 | 19 | 120 | 8 | 2 | 130 | 1 | 5 |
| Sweeney, James, ASH | .971 | 7 | 29 | 5 | 1 | 35 | 0 | 0 |
| Van Kirk, Robert, AUG | 1.000 | 3 | 16 | 0 | 0 | 16 | 0 | 0 |
| Wilson, Brandon, CAP | 1.000 | 19 | 167 | 11 | 0 | 178 | 1 | 4 |
| WILSON, NEIL, ASH | .994 | 81 | 505 | 36 | 3 | 544 | 1 | 16 |
| Winegarden, Erik, LWD* | .984 | 50 | 341 | 17 | 6 | 364 | 2 | 10 |
| Wolfe, Joseph, CWV* | 1.000 | 30 | 197 | 14 | 0 | 211 | 2 | 4 |
| Woodson, Mike, LCO | .900 | 2 | 9 | 0 | 1 | 10 | 0 | 1 |
| Wyman, Spencer, GBO* | .988 | 18 | 148 | 12 | 2 | 162 | 0 | 8 |

## CATCHERS

| Player, Team | Pct. | G | PO | A | E | TC | DP | PB |
|---|---|---|---|---|---|---|---|---|
| Alen, Luis, GBO | .961 | 9 | 71 | 2 | 3 | 76 | 1 | 3 |
| Anderson, Jimmy, CAP | .974 | 37 | 248 | 17 | 7 | 272 | 1 | 5 |
| Anderson, Keith, HAG | 1.000 | 15 | 111 | 19 | 0 | 130 | 1 | 3 |
| Apodaca, Luis, SAV | .986 | 59 | 421 | 61 | 7 | 489 | 2 | 7 |
| Aracena, Sandy, CSC | .978 | 29 | 199 | 20 | 5 | 224 | 5 | 8 |
| Arhart, Josh, CSC | .992 | 63 | 475 | 46 | 4 | 525 | 5 | 4 |
| Arlis, Patrick,E., GBO | .985 | 58 | 474 | 37 | 8 | 519 | 1 | 20 |
| Arnerich, Tony, GBO | .992 | 15 | 114 | 12 | 1 | 127 | 0 | 4 |
| Bennett, Stacy, CAP* | 1.000 | 6 | 44 | 3 | 0 | 47 | 0 | 1 |
| Bernard, Miguel, ROM | .980 | 47 | 365 | 35 | 8 | 408 | 5 | 10 |
| Bibee, Hal, ASH | 1.000 | 20 | 127 | 9 | 0 | 136 | 0 | 6 |
| Blake, Ryan, GBO | .985 | 33 | 239 | 17 | 4 | 260 | 0 | 6 |
| Bock, Brian, DEL | .967 | 24 | 178 | 24 | 7 | 209 | 1 | 2 |

## PITCHERS

| Player, Team | Pct. | G | PO | A | E | TC | DP |
|---|---|---|---|---|---|---|---|
| Acosta, Domingo, CAP | 1.000 | 29 | 0 | 8 | 0 | 8 | 0 |
| Acosta, Kelyn, HAG | .875 | 10 | 4 | 3 | 1 | 8 | 0 |
| Acosta, Richard, DEL | 1.000 | 17 | 0 | 3 | 0 | 3 | 0 |
| Adler, Anthony, LEX | 1.000 | 14 | 0 | 2 | 0 | 2 | 0 |
| Akens, Phil, GBO | 1.000 | 8 | 2 | 6 | 0 | 8 | 1 |
| Albers, Matt, LEX | .941 | 22 | 9 | 7 | 1 | 17 | 1 |
| Alcala, Jason, HCK | 1.000 | 7 | 2 | 4 | 0 | 6 | 0 |
| Allen, Blake, LCO* | .941 | 23 | 0 | 16 | 1 | 17 | 3 |
| Allen, Brian, CSC | .900 | 26 | 3 | 6 | 1 | 10 | 1 |
| Alvarez, Carlos, CMB* | 1.000 | 15 | 0 | 2 | 0 | 2 | 0 |
| Alvarez, Tim, HAG* | .938 | 50 | 4 | 11 | 1 | 16 | 0 |
| An, Byeong Hak, KAN* | 1.000 | 2 | 0 | 2 | 0 | 2 | 0 |
| Anderson, Devin, ROM* | .750 | 5 | 0 | 3 | 1 | 4 | 0 |

| Player, Team | Pct. | G | PO | A | E | TC | DP |
|---|---|---|---|---|---|---|---|
| Anez, Omar, HAG | .944 | 14 | 4 | 13 | 1 | 18 | 1 |
| Arias, Alberto, ASH | .920 | 26 | 4 | 19 | 2 | 25 | 1 |
| ARTEAGA, ERICK, LWD | 1.000 | 27 | 7 | 19 | 0 | 26 | 0 |
| Ascanio, Jose, ROM | .933 | 33 | 5 | 9 | 1 | 15 | 0 |
| Ashabraner, Bo, LCO | 1.000 | 29 | 5 | 10 | 0 | 15 | 0 |
| Bailey, Chad, CMB* | .941 | 26 | 3 | 13 | 1 | 17 | 2 |
| Bakker, Kyle, ROM* | 1.000 | 20 | 0 | 2 | 0 | 2 | 0 |
| Banks, Demetrius, KAN* | .000 | 4 | 0 | 0 | 0 | 0 | 0 |
| Barrack, Jacob, LWD | 1.000 | 9 | 1 | 1 | 0 | 2 | 0 |
| Basilio, Manuel, CSC | .667 | 10 | 1 | 1 | 1 | 3 | 0 |
| Bateman, Joe, HAG | .941 | 36 | 6 | 10 | 1 | 17 | 1 |
| Beam, Randy, AUG* | 1.000 | 18 | 2 | 5 | 0 | 7 | 0 |
| Beltre, Jonathan, LEX* | .933 | 46 | 3 | 11 | 1 | 15 | 0 |
| Benitez, Gabriel, GBO | .800 | 10 | 2 | 2 | 1 | 5 | 0 |
| Bergmann, Jason, SAV | .938 | 13 | 5 | 10 | 1 | 16 | 0 |
| Blackley, Adam, AUG* | 1.000 | 12 | 3 | 6 | 0 | 9 | 0 |
| Blakeney, Jacob, ROM | 1.000 | 17 | 0 | 1 | 0 | 1 | 0 |
| Borland, Curt, AUG | 1.000 | 10 | 0 | 1 | 0 | 1 | 0 |
| Bostick, Adam, GBO* | .938 | 23 | 4 | 11 | 1 | 16 | 0 |
| Brewer, Jeff, CAP | 1.000 | 1 | 0 | 1 | 0 | 1 | 0 |
| Britton, Christopher, DEL | .909 | 27 | 0 | 10 | 1 | 11 | 2 |
| Bulger, Brian, CSC | .846 | 37 | 12 | 10 | 4 | 26 | 1 |
| Burch, Jason, ASH | .000 | 8 | 0 | 0 | 0 | 0 | 0 |
| Burrows, Angelo, ROM | 1.000 | 7 | 1 | 1 | 0 | 2 | 0 |
| Burton, TJ, LCO | 1.000 | 39 | 5 | 6 | 0 | 11 | 0 |
| Cabrera, Nate, LWD | 1.000 | 24 | 8 | 15 | 0 | 23 | 0 |
| Cahill, Casey, DEL | .000 | 4 | 0 | 0 | 0 | 0 | 0 |
| Callahan, Ryan, HAG* | 1.000 | 7 | 2 | 0 | 0 | 2 | 0 |
| Canizal, Joaquin, CWV | .938 | 40 | 4 | 11 | 1 | 16 | 0 |
| Capps, Matt, HCK | .917 | 12 | 7 | 4 | 1 | 12 | 0 |
| Carpenter, Calvin, CSC | .800 | 10 | 1 | 3 | 1 | 5 | 0 |
| Carvajal, Marcos, CMB | .875 | 36 | 5 | 9 | 2 | 16 | 0 |
| Castillo, Albenis, CMB | .667 | 9 | 0 | 2 | 1 | 3 | 0 |
| Castleman, Steve, ASH | 1.000 | 18 | 0 | 2 | 0 | 2 | 1 |
| Castro, Fabio, KAN* | 1.000 | 37 | 3 | 10 | 0 | 13 | 1 |
| Caughey, Trevor, DEL* | .870 | 36 | 1 | 19 | 3 | 23 | 2 |
| Cevette, Dan, LCO* | .833 | 9 | 0 | 5 | 1 | 6 | 0 |
| Chamberlin, Bryce, DEL | .750 | 3 | 1 | 2 | 1 | 4 | 0 |
| Chick, Travis, GBO | 1.000 | 28 | 3 | 0 | 0 | 3 | 0 |
| Childs, Ryan, DEL | 1.000 | 7 | 1 | 1 | 0 | 2 | 0 |
| Cierlik, Jason, DEL* | 1.000 | 7 | 1 | 0 | 0 | 1 | 0 |
| Cillo, Cody, GBO | .800 | 14 | 1 | 3 | 1 | 5 | 0 |
| Cline, Zac, LWD* | 1.000 | 8 | 2 | 2 | 0 | 4 | 1 |
| Collar, Mike, LEX | 1.000 | 38 | 6 | 10 | 0 | 16 | 1 |
| Coppinger, Joe, DEL | 1.000 | 9 | 0 | 3 | 0 | 3 | 0 |
| Cordova, Vincent, CAP | 1.000 | 24 | 4 | 12 | 0 | 16 | 1 |
| Core, Daniel, CWV | .941 | 26 | 6 | 26 | 2 | 34 | 2 |
| Corpas, Manuel, ASH | .900 | 43 | 2 | 7 | 1 | 10 | 0 |
| Corporan, Willy, AUG | 1.000 | 8 | 0 | 3 | 0 | 3 | 0 |
| Cramer, Bob, CSC* | .882 | 35 | 5 | 10 | 2 | 17 | 0 |
| Dalton, Matt, CWV | .917 | 20 | 0 | 11 | 1 | 12 | 1 |
| Danly, Ryan, CAP* | .875 | 11 | 0 | 7 | 1 | 8 | 0 |
| De Los Santos, Omar, CMB | .800 | 12 | 3 | 1 | 1 | 5 | 0 |
| Deininger, Todd, KAN | .933 | 26 | 5 | 9 | 1 | 15 | 0 |
| DeLeon, Joey, LEX | 1.000 | 37 | 10 | 10 | 0 | 20 | 2 |
| Delgado, Jesus, AUG | .882 | 21 | 4 | 11 | 2 | 17 | 0 |
| Demaria, Chris, HCK | 1.000 | 39 | 8 | 5 | 0 | 13 | 2 |
| Demontel, Jimmy, GBO | .800 | 25 | 0 | 4 | 1 | 5 | 1 |
| Dennison, Michael, AUG | .833 | 29 | 3 | 2 | 1 | 6 | 1 |
| Deza, Fredy, DEL | 1.000 | 22 | 7 | 11 | 0 | 18 | 1 |
| Diangelo, Jason, ASH | 1.000 | 41 | 2 | 9 | 0 | 11 | 0 |
| Diaz, Jose, CMB | .800 | 28 | 2 | 2 | 1 | 5 | 0 |
| Diaz, Raymar, LEX | .889 | 24 | 2 | 6 | 1 | 9 | 0 |
| Digby, Bryan, ROM | .909 | 26 | 9 | 21 | 3 | 33 | 1 |
| Dixon, Zach, DEL* | .964 | 23 | 4 | 23 | 1 | 28 | 1 |
| Dizard, Fraser, KAN* | 1.000 | 27 | 0 | 11 | 0 | 11 | 0 |
| Doble, Clemente, LWD | 1.000 | 8 | 2 | 3 | 0 | 5 | 0 |
| Dobyns, Jonathan, CSC | 1.000 | 5 | 3 | 0 | 0 | 3 | 0 |
| Done, Mike, DEL | 1.000 | 1 | 1 | 0 | 0 | 1 | 0 |
| Douglass, Chance, LEX | .933 | 28 | 6 | 22 | 2 | 30 | 1 |
| English, Jesse, HAG* | .857 | 17 | 1 | 5 | 1 | 7 | 0 |
| Esaray, Bradley, CWV* | .917 | 41 | 4 | 7 | 1 | 12 | 0 |
| Evangelista, Nick, LWD | 1.000 | 2 | 0 | 1 | 0 | 1 | 1 |
| Everts, Clint, SAV | .750 | 17 | 3 | 9 | 4 | 16 | 0 |
| Farley, Chris, AUG | .857 | 39 | 5 | 7 | 2 | 14 | 0 |
| Felfoldi, Jonathan, SAV* | .818 | 5 | 0 | 9 | 2 | 11 | 0 |
| Figueroa, Jonathan, CMB* | 1.000 | 14 | 3 | 7 | 0 | 10 | 1 |
| Finch, Brian, DEL | 1.000 | 5 | 3 | 3 | 0 | 6 | 0 |
| Flanagan, Jeremy, CSC | .778 | 18 | 4 | 3 | 2 | 9 | 1 |
| Flores, Rafael, KAN | .971 | 23 | 9 | 25 | 1 | 35 | 0 |
| Floyd, Jesse, HAG | .941 | 31 | 6 | 10 | 1 | 17 | 0 |
| Foli, Daniel, CAP | .750 | 17 | 1 | 2 | 1 | 4 | 0 |

| Player, Team | Pct. | G | PO | A | E | TC | DP |
|---|---|---|---|---|---|---|---|
| France, Ryan, LEX | .875 | 22 | 5 | 2 | 1 | 8 | 0 |
| Franzenburg, Luke, ROM* | 1.000 | 7 | 0 | 1 | 0 | 1 | 0 |
| Gagne, JP, ASH | 1.000 | 10 | 1 | 2 | 0 | 3 | 0 |
| Galarraga, Armando, SAV | 1.000 | 23 | 10 | 9 | 0 | 19 | 0 |
| Galvez, Gary, AUG | .962 | 30 | 6 | 19 | 1 | 26 | 0 |
| Gangi, Aaron, CSC* | .750 | 31 | 4 | 11 | 5 | 20 | 1 |
| Garcia, Anderson, CAP | .905 | 35 | 6 | 13 | 2 | 21 | 1 |
| Gardner, Jarrett, AUG | .963 | 25 | 6 | 20 | 1 | 27 | 2 |
| Garza, Rolando, ROM | 1.000 | 9 | 0 | 5 | 0 | 5 | 0 |
| George, Christopher, HAG | 1.000 | 20 | 1 | 6 | 0 | 7 | 0 |
| Glynn, Josh, GBO | 1.000 | 5 | 1 | 0 | 0 | 1 | 0 |
| Gomez, Jose, CAP | 1.000 | 11 | 2 | 0 | 0 | 2 | 0 |
| Gomez, Warmar, SAV | 1.000 | 43 | 8 | 8 | 0 | 16 | 0 |
| Gonzalez, Gio, KAN* | 1.000 | 8 | 3 | 6 | 0 | 9 | 0 |
| Gonzalez, Jino, CSC* | .882 | 24 | 4 | 26 | 4 | 34 | 0 |
| Goodman, Chris, SAV | 1.000 | 8 | 0 | 1 | 0 | 1 | 0 |
| Gorzelanny, Thomas, HCK* | .955 | 16 | 1 | 20 | 1 | 22 | 1 |
| Greusel, Evan, GBO | .714 | 14 | 1 | 4 | 2 | 7 | 0 |
| Grigsby, Derick, LEX | .846 | 27 | 9 | 13 | 4 | 26 | 0 |
| Guanchez, Argimiro, AUG* | 1.000 | 35 | 1 | 11 | 0 | 12 | 1 |
| Haeger, Charles, KAN | .750 | 5 | 1 | 5 | 2 | 8 | 0 |
| Haigwood, Daniel, KAN* | .929 | 22 | 3 | 10 | 1 | 14 | 0 |
| Hamilton, Jamaal, CMB* | .889 | 14 | 2 | 6 | 1 | 9 | 1 |
| Hammel, Jason, CSC | .870 | 18 | 6 | 14 | 3 | 23 | 1 |
| Hammes, Zach, CMB | .897 | 24 | 9 | 17 | 3 | 29 | 2 |
| Hanson, Adam, LCO | .923 | 35 | 1 | 11 | 1 | 13 | 0 |
| Harper, Jeremy, CWV | .800 | 11 | 2 | 2 | 1 | 5 | 0 |
| Hart, Kevin, DEL | 1.000 | 4 | 0 | 1 | 0 | 1 | 0 |
| Harts, Jeremy, HCK* | 1.000 | 16 | 1 | 1 | 0 | 2 | 0 |
| Hawk, Shane, CAP* | 1.000 | 25 | 1 | 8 | 0 | 9 | 1 |
| Hernandez, Chris, HCK | .875 | 42 | 0 | 7 | 1 | 8 | 2 |
| Hernandez, Fernando, KAN | .889 | 28 | 4 | 4 | 1 | 9 | 0 |
| Hertzler, Barry, AUG | 1.000 | 25 | 2 | 7 | 0 | 9 | 2 |
| Hilaro, Elpibo, AUG | .000 | 5 | 0 | 0 | 0 | 0 | 0 |
| Hiraldo, Nelson, LCO | .636 | 26 | 1 | 6 | 4 | 11 | 0 |
| Hodges, Daniel, LWD* | 1.000 | 31 | 1 | 9 | 0 | 10 | 1 |
| Holliday, Brian, HCK* | .958 | 22 | 4 | 19 | 1 | 24 | 1 |
| Honsa, Chris, LWD | 1.000 | 12 | 2 | 2 | 0 | 4 | 0 |
| Hoorelbeke, Casey, CMB | .800 | 3 | 2 | 2 | 1 | 5 | 0 |
| Houser, James, CSC* | 1.000 | 7 | 0 | 3 | 0 | 3 | 0 |
| Hudson, Jeremy, KAN | 1.000 | 5 | 0 | 2 | 0 | 2 | 0 |
| Hurd, John, KAN | 1.000 | 13 | 2 | 3 | 0 | 5 | 0 |
| Iehl, Jason, GBO | .750 | 17 | 0 | 3 | 1 | 4 | 0 |
| Ion, Mark, ASH | 1.000 | 34 | 1 | 3 | 0 | 4 | 1 |
| Isenberg, Kurt, CWV* | 1.000 | 10 | 4 | 6 | 0 | 10 | 0 |
| Jackson, Kyle, AUG | .842 | 31 | 4 | 12 | 3 | 19 | 0 |
| James, Chuck, ROM* | 1.000 | 26 | 1 | 17 | 0 | 18 | 1 |
| James, Justin, CWV | .944 | 14 | 6 | 11 | 1 | 18 | 1 |
| Johnson, Blair, HCK | .875 | 9 | 2 | 5 | 1 | 8 | 0 |
| Johnson, James, DEL | 1.000 | 20 | 3 | 20 | 0 | 23 | 2 |
| Kaiser, Marc, ASH | .820 | 27 | 9 | 32 | 9 | 50 | 3 |
| Kane, Kyle, KAN | 1.000 | 4 | 0 | 1 | 0 | 1 | 0 |
| Kendrick, Kyle, LWD | .833 | 15 | 3 | 7 | 2 | 12 | 0 |
| King, Bryan, CAP | 1.000 | 40 | 4 | 7 | 0 | 11 | 0 |
| King, Tim, CSC* | .667 | 3 | 3 | 1 | 2 | 6 | 0 |
| Kranawetter, Josh, CSC | .667 | 12 | 2 | 6 | 4 | 12 | 0 |
| Kuo, Hong-Chih, CMB* | .000 | 3 | 0 | 0 | 0 | 0 | 0 |
| Laffey, Aaron, LCO* | .962 | 19 | 5 | 20 | 1 | 26 | 2 |
| Larson, Adam, KAN | 1.000 | 18 | 1 | 5 | 0 | 6 | 0 |
| Letson, Wesley, ROM* | 1.000 | 11 | 0 | 2 | 0 | 2 | 0 |
| Libey, Justin, LWD | 1.000 | 5 | 0 | 1 | 0 | 1 | 0 |
| Lindstrom, Matthew, CAP | .846 | 12 | 4 | 7 | 2 | 13 | 0 |
| Lissir, Alexander, HCK | .900 | 36 | 0 | 9 | 1 | 10 | 0 |
| Little, Joe, CSC* | 1.000 | 10 | 1 | 3 | 0 | 4 | 0 |
| Lo, Ching Lung, ASH | 1.000 | 17 | 2 | 8 | 0 | 10 | 0 |
| Loewen, Adam, DEL* | .926 | 20 | 6 | 19 | 2 | 27 | 1 |
| Long, Jeffery, ROM | 1.000 | 13 | 0 | 1 | 0 | 1 | 0 |
| Long, Nick, SAV | .818 | 28 | 9 | 9 | 4 | 22 | 2 |
| Looney, Marshal, CMB* | .000 | 3 | 0 | 0 | 1 | 1 | 0 |
| Lopez, Arturo, CMB* | .900 | 29 | 3 | 15 | 2 | 20 | 0 |
| Lopez, Gonzalo, ROM | 1.000 | 21 | 3 | 14 | 0 | 17 | 0 |
| Lopez, Orionny, KAN | .833 | 33 | 2 | 3 | 1 | 6 | 0 |
| Lord, Justin, HCK | 1.000 | 2 | 0 | 2 | 0 | 2 | 1 |
| Lovato, Nick, GBO* | 1.000 | 4 | 0 | 2 | 0 | 2 | 0 |
| Lundquist, Dave, HCK | 1.000 | 10 | 1 | 1 | 0 | 2 | 0 |
| Lynch, Brian, ASH | 1.000 | 10 | 1 | 4 | 0 | 5 | 1 |
| MacDonald, Mike, CWV | 1.000 | 6 | 3 | 6 | 0 | 9 | 0 |
| MacLane, Evan, CAP* | 1.000 | 14 | 1 | 11 | 0 | 12 | 0 |
| Maholm, Paul, HCK* | 1.000 | 3 | 0 | 1 | 0 | 1 | 0 |
| Maldonado, Ivan, CAP | 1.000 | 14 | 3 | 6 | 0 | 9 | 3 |
| Mangrum, Micah, CAP | 1.000 | 7 | 3 | 1 | 0 | 4 | 0 |
| Marceau, Pierre Luc, SAV* | .800 | 13 | 1 | 3 | 1 | 5 | 0 |

| Player, Team | Pct. | G | PO | A | E | TC | DP |
|---|---|---|---|---|---|---|---|
| Marceau, PierreLuc, LCO* | .833 | 6 | 4 | 1 | 1 | 6 | 1 |
| Marceau, PierreLuc, SAV-LCO* | .818 | 19 | 5 | 4 | 2 | 11 | 1 |
| Marcum, Shaun, CWV | .941 | 13 | 4 | 12 | 1 | 17 | 0 |
| Marrero, Darwin, SAV | 1.000 | 2 | 1 | 1 | 0 | 2 | 0 |
| Marsden, Aaron, ASH* | .857 | 27 | 4 | 20 | 4 | 28 | 1 |
| Martin, Kevin, LCO | 1.000 | 9 | 0 | 1 | 0 | 1 | 0 |
| Martin, Sean, HAG | 1.000 | 44 | 15 | 14 | 0 | 29 | 2 |
| Martinez, Carlos, GBO | 1.000 | 40 | 1 | 8 | 0 | 9 | 0 |
| Martinez, Edgar, AUG | 1.000 | 9 | 0 | 1 | 0 | 1 | 0 |
| Martinez, Samuel, SAV | .875 | 11 | 1 | 6 | 1 | 8 | 0 |
| Mastny, Thomas, CWV | 1.000 | 26 | 8 | 19 | 0 | 27 | 0 |
| Mathieson, Scott, LWD | .864 | 25 | 7 | 12 | 3 | 22 | 2 |
| Mattison, Kieran, LCO | .750 | 13 | 2 | 1 | 1 | 4 | 0 |
| McCally, Ryan, CSC | .889 | 15 | 3 | 5 | 1 | 9 | 0 |
| McCarthy, Brandon, KAN | .905 | 15 | 9 | 10 | 2 | 21 | 0 |
| McClung, Seth, CSC | 1.000 | 3 | 1 | 3 | 0 | 4 | 0 |
| McCormack, Zach, GBO* | .889 | 35 | 1 | 7 | 1 | 9 | 0 |
| McCrory, Robert, DEL | .500 | 8 | 0 | 1 | 1 | 2 | 0 |
| Menocal, Victor, LWD | .955 | 30 | 5 | 16 | 1 | 22 | 1 |
| Mercedes, Gerson, LCO | 1.000 | 1 | 0 | 1 | 0 | 1 | 0 |
| Meredith, Clay, AUG | .857 | 13 | 1 | 5 | 1 | 7 | 1 |
| Merrell, Darric, ASH | .811 | 28 | 2 | 28 | 7 | 37 | 2 |
| Mildren, Paul, GBO* | 1.000 | 39 | 4 | 13 | 0 | 17 | 0 |
| Miller, Adam, LCO | .875 | 19 | 4 | 3 | 1 | 8 | 0 |
| Miller, Brian, KAN | 1.000 | 21 | 7 | 11 | 0 | 18 | 0 |
| Millikan, Bryan, HAG | 1.000 | 10 | 4 | 4 | 0 | 8 | 0 |
| Miramontes, Matt, CAP | 1.000 | 11 | 1 | 3 | 0 | 4 | 0 |
| Mitchell, Thomas, SAV | 1.000 | 11 | 0 | 1 | 0 | 1 | 0 |
| Moat, Michael, KAN | 1.000 | 23 | 4 | 7 | 0 | 11 | 0 |
| Montani, Jeffrey, DEL | 1.000 | 35 | 1 | 8 | 0 | 9 | 1 |
| Mora, Ramon, CWV | 1.000 | 14 | 2 | 6 | 0 | 8 | 1 |
| Morel, Eudy, ASH | .000 | 11 | 0 | 0 | 0 | 0 | 0 |
| Morla, Carlos, AUG | .750 | 22 | 0 | 3 | 1 | 4 | 0 |
| Morton, Charles, ROM | .889 | 26 | 5 | 11 | 2 | 18 | 2 |
| Muecke, Joshua, LEX* | .821 | 37 | 6 | 17 | 5 | 28 | 2 |
| Mueller, Mike, ROM | .875 | 15 | 3 | 4 | 1 | 8 | 0 |
| Mujica, Edward, LCO | .857 | 26 | 2 | 10 | 2 | 14 | 1 |
| Mumma, Bradley, CWV* | .875 | 15 | 2 | 5 | 1 | 8 | 1 |
| Muniz, Carlos, CAP | 1.000 | 16 | 1 | 2 | 0 | 3 | 1 |
| Musgrave, Mike, HAG | .947 | 36 | 6 | 12 | 1 | 19 | 0 |
| Neal, Tony, DEL | .750 | 7 | 0 | 3 | 1 | 4 | 0 |
| Nelson, Brad, ROM | 1.000 | 20 | 0 | 6 | 0 | 6 | 1 |
| Nesmith, Travis, HAG* | .929 | 34 | 2 | 11 | 1 | 14 | 1 |
| Nestor, Scott, GBO | .750 | 23 | 2 | 1 | 1 | 4 | 0 |
| Nickerson, Jon, GBO | .833 | 14 | 6 | 4 | 2 | 12 | 0 |
| Niesel, Chris, LCO | 1.000 | 5 | 0 | 2 | 0 | 2 | 0 |
| Nieves, Roberto, ROM | .667 | 22 | 2 | 4 | 3 | 9 | 0 |
| Nowicki, Nathan, GBO | 1.000 | 43 | 5 | 15 | 0 | 20 | 1 |
| Nunez, Leo, HCK | 1.000 | 27 | 12 | 10 | 0 | 22 | 0 |
| Nunley, Derrek, CWV | 1.000 | 6 | 2 | 0 | 0 | 2 | 0 |
| Nyquist, Brett, SAV* | .905 | 22 | 4 | 15 | 2 | 21 | 0 |
| Ochoa, Javier, CAP | 1.000 | 24 | 1 | 2 | 0 | 3 | 0 |
| Ojeda, Alvis, CMB | .714 | 30 | 2 | 3 | 2 | 7 | 0 |
| Olson, Jordan, CSC* | 1.000 | 16 | 0 | 4 | 0 | 4 | 1 |
| Ool, Kevin, AUG* | 1.000 | 27 | 2 | 8 | 0 | 10 | 0 |
| Orvella, Chad, CSC | 1.000 | 22 | 5 | 4 | 0 | 9 | 1 |
| Osberg, Tanner, CAP | .818 | 28 | 6 | 12 | 4 | 22 | 2 |
| Overton, Brad, LWD | 1.000 | 14 | 1 | 4 | 0 | 5 | 1 |
| Paddock, Josh, LWD | 1.000 | 15 | 4 | 7 | 0 | 11 | 1 |
| Parcus, Kyle, LWD* | .941 | 41 | 3 | 13 | 1 | 17 | 0 |
| Patitucci, Mike, DEL* | 1.000 | 43 | 2 | 8 | 0 | 10 | 0 |
| Pearson, Anthony, SAV | .857 | 33 | 8 | 4 | 2 | 14 | 0 |
| Peguero, Tony, CSC | .886 | 23 | 12 | 19 | 4 | 35 | 1 |
| Pena, Luis, KAN | 1.000 | 9 | 2 | 0 | 0 | 2 | 0 |
| Penn, Hayden, DEL | 1.000 | 13 | 1 | 4 | 0 | 5 | 0 |
| Penny, David, AUG | .750 | 3 | 1 | 2 | 1 | 4 | 0 |
| Perez, Marcelo, CAP | 1.000 | 3 | 0 | 1 | 0 | 1 | 0 |
| Perez, Rafael, LCO* | .868 | 23 | 6 | 27 | 5 | 38 | 5 |
| Perez, Tony, CSC* | 1.000 | 45 | 7 | 14 | 0 | 21 | 1 |
| Perrin, Devin, SAV | .947 | 36 | 15 | 21 | 2 | 38 | 3 |
| Pesco, Nick, LCO | 1.000 | 21 | 9 | 15 | 0 | 24 | 1 |
| Petit, Yusmeiro, CAP | 1.000 | 15 | 4 | 6 | 0 | 10 | 0 |
| Petrick, Russ, DEL* | 1.000 | 11 | 1 | 1 | 0 | 2 | 0 |
| Pillsbury, Chris, GBO | .750 | 10 | 0 | 3 | 1 | 4 | 0 |
| Pimentel, Julio, CMB | .900 | 23 | 5 | 13 | 2 | 20 | 2 |
| Plaisance, Kenny, CMB | 1.000 | 3 | 0 | 2 | 0 | 2 | 0 |
| Plexico, Gerald, SAV* | .947 | 49 | 5 | 13 | 1 | 19 | 0 |
| Plummer, Jarod, CMB | 1.000 | 4 | 1 | 1 | 0 | 2 | 0 |
| Portorreal, Daniel, HAG | 1.000 | 8 | 1 | 1 | 0 | 2 | 0 |
| Potter, Josh, DEL | 1.000 | 23 | 2 | 5 | 0 | 7 | 0 |
| Prieto, Victor, GBO | .800 | 10 | 0 | 4 | 1 | 5 | 0 |
| Ramirez, Greg, CAP | 1.000 | 38 | 5 | 9 | 0 | 14 | 1 |

| Player, Team | Pct. | G | PO | A | E | TC | DP |
|---|---|---|---|---|---|---|---|
| Ramirez, Luis, DEL | 1.000 | 5 | 0 | 3 | 0 | 3 | 0 |
| Ramsey, Robert, LEX | 1.000 | 9 | 1 | 0 | 0 | 1 | 0 |
| Ray, Chris, DEL | .944 | 10 | 3 | 14 | 1 | 18 | 2 |
| Reed, Brian, CWV | .875 | 25 | 3 | 4 | 1 | 8 | 0 |
| Reid, Brett, SAV | 1.000 | 46 | 6 | 9 | 0 | 15 | 1 |
| Resop, Chris, GBO | 1.000 | 42 | 3 | 3 | 0 | 6 | 0 |
| Reyes, Jojo, ROM* | 1.000 | 15 | 2 | 9 | 0 | 11 | 0 |
| Reyes, Maximo, LWD | .727 | 42 | 3 | 5 | 3 | 11 | 0 |
| *Rich, Dan, LCO | 1.000 | 3 | 1 | 1 | 0 | 2 | 0 |
| *Rico, Erik, CWV | .833 | 7 | 3 | 2 | 1 | 6 | 0 |
| Ritchie, Todd, CSC | 1.000 | 2 | 2 | 1 | 0 | 3 | 0 |
| Robinson, Dennis, DEL | 1.000 | 3 | 0 | 3 | 0 | 3 | 0 |
| Robinson, Levi, DEL | 1.000 | 1 | 1 | 0 | 0 | 1 | 0 |
| Robles, Larry, ASH | .933 | 23 | 11 | 17 | 2 | 30 | 4 |
| Rodriguez, Jose, CAP | .000 | 6 | 0 | 0 | 0 | 0 | 0 |
| Rodriguez, Mike, CMB | 1.000 | 5 | 0 | 1 | 0 | 1 | 0 |
| Rodriguez, Ozzie, CMB | 1.000 | 20 | 4 | 10 | 0 | 14 | 0 |
| Rodriguez, Ricardo, ROM | 1.000 | 30 | 3 | 6 | 0 | 9 | 0 |
| Rodriguez, Ryan, KAN* | .974 | 25 | 6 | 32 | 1 | 39 | 1 |
| Roehl, Scott, LCO | .889 | 29 | 6 | 10 | 2 | 18 | 0 |
| Rohan, Jimmy, CMB | .000 | 2 | 0 | 0 | 0 | 0 | 0 |
| Romero, Davis, CWV* | .900 | 30 | 3 | 15 | 2 | 20 | 0 |
| Romero, Felix, CWV | 1.000 | 38 | 7 | 13 | 0 | 20 | 1 |
| Rondon, Celso, CAP | 1.000 | 22 | 3 | 4 | 0 | 7 | 0 |
| Rosario, Melvin, ASH* | 1.000 | 14 | 0 | 1 | 0 | 1 | 0 |
| Russ, James, GBO | .800 | 4 | 2 | 2 | 1 | 5 | 0 |
| Russell, Adam, KAN | 1.000 | 2 | 2 | 3 | 0 | 5 | 0 |
| Russell, Stephen, ROM | .591 | 22 | 5 | 8 | 9 | 22 | 1 |
| Sadowski, Ryan, HAG | .917 | 26 | 4 | 18 | 2 | 24 | 1 |
| Salas, Marino, DEL | .714 | 40 | 2 | 3 | 2 | 7 | 0 |
| Sandoval, Francisco, SAV | 1.000 | 7 | 0 | 2 | 0 | 2 | 0 |
| Sandoval, Marcos, CWV | 1.000 | 24 | 1 | 2 | 0 | 3 | 0 |
| Santos, Arthur, AUG | 1.000 | 16 | 2 | 6 | 0 | 8 | 0 |
| Santos, Reid, LCO* | .000 | 3 | 0 | 0 | 1 | 1 | 0 |
| Saucedo, Matthew, GBO | .667 | 23 | 2 | 4 | 3 | 9 | 0 |
| Schade, Ryan, GBO | .000 | 4 | 0 | 0 | 0 | 0 | 0 |
| Schultz, Cory, LWD | .909 | 29 | 3 | 7 | 1 | 11 | 1 |
| Serrato, Juan, HAG | .833 | 25 | 2 | 8 | 2 | 12 | 1 |
| Shafer, Kurt, HCK | .875 | 25 | 5 | 2 | 1 | 8 | 1 |
| Sharpless, Joshua, HCK | 1.000 | 43 | 4 | 3 | 0 | 7 | 0 |
| Shepard, Kevin, LWD* | 1.000 | 5 | 4 | 4 | 0 | 8 | 0 |
| Shortell, Rory, LEX | 1.000 | 7 | 3 | 0 | 0 | 3 | 0 |
| Shortslef, Josh, HCK* | 1.000 | 30 | 4 | 29 | 0 | 33 | 2 |
| Silva, Doug, ASH | 1.000 | 29 | 1 | 2 | 0 | 3 | 0 |
| Simon, Billy, AUG | .000 | 3 | 0 | 0 | 1 | 1 | 0 |
| Smith, Danny, ROM* | 1.000 | 1 | 0 | 1 | 0 | 1 | 0 |
| Smith, Sean, LCO | .917 | 13 | 4 | 7 | 1 | 12 | 1 |
| Sobieraj, Aaron, HAG | 1.000 | 11 | 0 | 3 | 0 | 3 | 0 |
| Sobkow, Phil, CMB | 1.000 | 7 | 3 | 5 | 0 | 8 | 0 |
| Sonnanstine, Andrew, CSC | 1.000 | 8 | 2 | 6 | 0 | 8 | 0 |
| Sopko, Mark, CWV | 1.000 | 38 | 5 | 4 | 0 | 9 | 2 |
| Southerland, Chip, LCO | 1.000 | 20 | 1 | 3 | 0 | 4 | 1 |
| Spillers, Brandon, DEL | 1.000 | 11 | 1 | 1 | 0 | 2 | 0 |
| Starling, Wardell, HCK | .865 | 26 | 11 | 21 | 5 | 37 | 2 |
| Stevens, Jacob, ROM* | .955 | 26 | 4 | 17 | 1 | 22 | 0 |
| Stiehl, Robert, LEX | 1.000 | 18 | 2 | 8 | 0 | 10 | 0 |
| Stults, Eric, CMB* | 1.000 | 12 | 0 | 2 | 0 | 2 | 0 |
| Sweeney, Matt, LWD | 1.000 | 5 | 0 | 5 | 0 | 5 | 0 |
| Talbot, Mitch, LEX | .900 | 26 | 10 | 17 | 3 | 30 | 0 |
| Tallet, Brian, LCO* | 1.000 | 2 | 0 | 1 | 0 | 1 | 0 |
| Tavarez, Milton, AUG | .800 | 47 | 3 | 5 | 2 | 10 | 0 |
| Templet, Jordy, CWV | 1.000 | 14 | 2 | 3 | 0 | 5 | 0 |
| Testa, Chris, CMB* | 1.000 | 20 | 2 | 5 | 0 | 7 | 0 |
| Thomas, Steve, ASH | .000 | 15 | 0 | 0 | 0 | 0 | 0 |
| Thompson, Daryl, SAV | .929 | 25 | 1 | 12 | 1 | 14 | 1 |
| Thorne, David, SAV | .857 | 15 | 1 | 5 | 1 | 7 | 0 |
| Thurmond, Ben, HAG | .950 | 19 | 7 | 12 | 1 | 20 | 1 |
| Tiffany, Chuck, CMB* | 1.000 | 22 | 4 | 11 | 0 | 15 | 0 |
| Tiller, Jim, DEL | .913 | 16 | 3 | 18 | 2 | 23 | 0 |
| Tisch, Tim, KAN* | 1.000 | 12 | 3 | 6 | 0 | 9 | 0 |
| Torrealba, Yoann, HCK | .957 | 27 | 13 | 9 | 1 | 23 | 0 |
| Tsao, Chin-hui, ASH | 1.000 | 2 | 2 | 1 | 0 | 3 | 1 |
| Vandermeer, Scott, CSC | 1.000 | 52 | 7 | 4 | 0 | 11 | 0 |
| Vaquedano, Jose, AUG | .923 | 11 | 3 | 9 | 1 | 13 | 0 |
| Vargas, Jason, GBO* | 1.000 | 3 | 1 | 2 | 0 | 3 | 0 |
| Vasquez, Willie, ASH | 1.000 | 1 | 0 | 1 | 0 | 1 | 0 |
| Vaughan, Beau, AUG | 1.000 | 14 | 4 | 11 | 0 | 15 | 1 |
| Vazquez, Willie, ASH | 1.000 | 10 | 0 | 4 | 0 | 4 | 1 |
| Walker, Aaron, CSC* | 1.000 | 1 | 0 | 2 | 0 | 2 | 0 |
| Walker, Brian, CAP* | .913 | 22 | 2 | 19 | 2 | 23 | 1 |
| Warden, Jim Ed, LCO | .857 | 41 | 1 | 5 | 1 | 7 | 0 |
| Warpinski, Ryan, GBO | .889 | 13 | 2 | 6 | 1 | 9 | 0 |

| Player, Team | Pct. | G | PO | A | E | TC | DP |
|---|---|---|---|---|---|---|---|
| Wasserman, Ehren, KAN | 1.000 | 51 | 1 | 21 | 0 | 22 | 1 |
| Watchko, Jeff, ASH | 1.000 | 35 | 1 | 5 | 0 | 6 | 0 |
| Wayne, Brett, CMB | .857 | 27 | 7 | 5 | 2 | 14 | 1 |
| Weeden, Brandon, CMB | .786 | 27 | 3 | 8 | 3 | 14 | 1 |
| Weimer, Andrew, CSC | 1.000 | 6 | 1 | 1 | 0 | 2 | 0 |
| Wesley, John, CWV | 1.000 | 5 | 0 | 1 | 0 | 1 | 0 |
| Wheatland, Matt, LEX | 1.000 | 17 | 2 | 1 | 0 | 3 | 0 |
| Whisler, Wesley, KAN* | .889 | 10 | 1 | 7 | 1 | 9 | 0 |
| White, Sean, ROM | 1.000 | 13 | 4 | 6 | 0 | 10 | 2 |
| Willey, Cory, AUG* | 1.000 | 20 | 2 | 3 | 0 | 5 | 1 |
| Williams, Aaron, LEX | 1.000 | 59 | 4 | 13 | 0 | 17 | 2 |
| Wilson, Aaron, LWD | .867 | 16 | 6 | 7 | 2 | 15 | 1 |
| Wilson, Brian, HAG | .941 | 23 | 3 | 13 | 1 | 17 | 2 |
| Wilson, Joe, LWD* | .850 | 19 | 6 | 11 | 3 | 20 | 1 |
| Wilson, Jonathan, AUG | 1.000 | 1 | 1 | 2 | 0 | 3 | 0 |
| Wood, Tim, GBO | 1.000 | 24 | 9 | 3 | 0 | 12 | 1 |
| Woodrow, Christopher, LWD | .765 | 22 | 3 | 10 | 4 | 17 | 0 |
| Worthington, Timothy, CAP | 1.000 | 7 | 1 | 4 | 0 | 5 | 0 |
| Yourkin, Matt, GBO* | .000 | 3 | 0 | 0 | 0 | 0 | 0 |
| Zarate, Maruro, GBO | 1.000 | 10 | 5 | 5 | 0 | 10 | 1 |

## LEAGUE CHAMPIONS

| Year | Team | Pct. |
|---|---|---|
| 1948— | Lincolnton* | .627 |
| 1949— | Newton-Conover | .667 |
| | Rutherford Co. (2nd)† | .627 |
| 1950— | Newton-Conover | .627 |
| | Lenoir (2nd)† | .626 |
| 1951— | Morganton | .645 |
| | Shelby (2nd)† | .604 |
| 1952— | Lincolnton | .649 |
| | Shelby (2nd)† | .645 |
| 1953-59— | League inactive. | |
| 1960— | Lexington | .707 |
| | Salisbury (2nd)† | .650 |
| 1961— | Salisbury | .627 |
| | Shelby (4th)† | .481 |
| 1962— | Statesville | .563 |
| | Statesville | .700 |
| 1963— | Greenville† | .576 |
| | Salisbury | .631 |
| 1964— | Rock Hill | .672 |
| | Salisbury‡ | .631 |
| 1965— | Salisbury | .641 |
| | Rock Hill‡ | .603 |
| 1966— | Spartanburg | .682 |
| | Spartanburg | .767 |
| 1967— | Spartanburg | .730 |
| | Spartanburg | .567 |
| 1968— | Spartanburg | .597 |
| | Greenwood‡ | .597 |
| 1969— | Greenwood‡ | .587 |
| | Shelby | .565 |
| 1970— | Greenville | .576 |
| | Greenville | .619 |
| 1971— | Greenwood | .631 |
| | Greenwood | .759 |
| 1972— | Spartanburg‡ | .788 |
| | Greenville | .652 |
| 1973— | Spartanburg‡ | .646 |
| | Gastonia | .619 |
| 1974— | Gastonia | .606 |
| | Gastonia | .672 |
| 1975— | Spartanburg | .543 |
| | Spartanburg | .614 |
| 1976— | Asheville | .544 |
| | Greenwood‡ | .600 |
| 1977— | Greenwood | .557 |
| | Gastonia‡ | .590 |
| 1978— | Greenwood | .614 |
| | Greenwood | .565 |
| 1979— | Greenwood‡ | .565 |
| | Spartanburg | .525 |
| 1980— | Greensboro | .590 |
| | Charleston | .561 |
| 1981— | Greensboro‡ | .695 |
| | Greenwood | .549 |
| 1982— | Greensboro‡ | .681 |
| | Florence | .546 |
| 1983— | Columbia | .620 |
| | Gastonia‡ | .587 |
| 1984— | Charleston | .549 |
| | Asheville‡ | .510 |
| 1985— | Florence‡ | .599 |
| | Greensboro | .540 |
| 1986— | Columbia‡ | .682 |
| | Asheville | .643 |
| 1987— | Asheville | .655 |
| | Myrtle Beach‡ | .597 |
| 1988— | Charleston (S.C.) | .616 |
| | Spartanburg‡ | .500 |
| 1989— | Gastonia | .657 |
| | Augusta‡ | .535 |
| 1990— | Columbia | .580 |
| | Charleston (W.Va.)‡ | .538 |
| 1991— | Charleston (W.Va.) | .648 |
| | Columbia‡ | .614 |
| 1992— | Columbia | .572 |
| | Myrtle Beach‡ | .522 |
| 1993— | Savannah‡ | .662 |
| | Greensboro | .603 |
| 1994— | Columbus | .630 |
| | Savannah‡ | .599 |
| 1995— | Piedmont | .586 |
| | Augusta‡ | .551 |
| 1996— | Delmarva | .585 |
| | Savannah† | .511 |
| 1997— | Delmarva§ | .543 |
| | Greensboro | .536 |
| 1998— | Columbia§ | .638 |
| | Hagerstown | .574 |
| 1999— | Hagerstown | .600 |
| | Augusta§ | .496 |
| 2000— | Piedmont | .657 |
| | Delmarva∞ | .544 |
| 2001— | Lexington†† | .657 |
| 2002— | Hickory∞ | .597 |
| 2003— | Rome∞ | .561 |
| 2004— | Hickory∞ | .607 |

*Won championship and four-club playoff. †Won four-club playoff. ‡Won split-season playoff. §Won split season, eight-club playoff. ∞Won split season, four-club playoff. ††Was leading final series of split-season, four-club playoff and was declared champion when Professional Baseball declared a stoppage of play. (NOTE—Known as Western Carolina League from 1948 through 1962 and known as Western Carolinas League through 1979.)

# NEW YORK-PENN LEAGUE

## LEAGUE OFFICE

**President**
Ben Hayes

**Address**
One Progress Plaza
200 Central Ave., Suite 2300
St. Petersburg, FL 33701

**Phone**
727-821-7000

**Teams (affiliation)**
Aberdeen IronBirds (Orioles)
Auburn Doubledays (Blue Jays)
Batavia Muckdogs (Phillies)
Brooklyn Cyclones (Mets)
Hudson Valley Renegades (Devil Rays)
Jamestown Jammers (Marlins)
Lowell Spinners (Red Sox)
Mahoning Valley Scrappers (Indians)
New Jersey Cardinals (Cardinals)
Oneonta Tigers (Tigers)
Staten Island Yankees (Yankees)
Tri-City ValleyCats (Astros)
Vermont Expos (Nationals)
Williamsport Crosscutters (Pirates)

## 2004 FINAL STANDINGS

### McNAMARA DIVISION

| Team | W | L | T | Pct. | GB |
|---|---|---|---|---|---|
| Brooklyn | 43 | 31 | - | .581 | ... |
| New Jersey | 41 | 34 | - | .547 | 21/2 |
| Hudson Valley | 39 | 33 | - | .542 | 3 |
| Aberdeen | 35 | 40 | - | .467 | 81/2 |
| Williamsport | 34 | 40 | - | .459 | 9 |
| Staten Island | 28 | 44 | - | .389 | 14 |

### PINCKNEY DIVISION

| Team | W | L | T | Pct. | GB |
|---|---|---|---|---|---|
| Auburn | 50 | 24 | - | .676 | ... |
| Mahoning Valley | 42 | 34 | - | .553 | 9 |
| Jamestown | 30 | 45 | - | .400 | 201/2 |
| Batavia | 28 | 46 | - | .378 | 22 |

### STEDLER DIVISION

| Team | W | L | T | Pct. | GB |
|---|---|---|---|---|---|
| Tri-City | 50 | 25 | - | .667 | ... |
| Vermont | 34 | 38 | - | .472 | 141/2 |
| Oneonta | 33 | 41 | - | .446 | 161/2 |
| Lowell | 32 | 44 | - | .421 | 181/2 |

## COMPOSITE

| Team | W | L | T | PCT | GB | AUB | TRC | BRK | MHV | NJY | HDV | VMT | ABD | WPT | ONE | LOW | JAM | STA | BAT |
|---|---|---|---|---|---|---|---|---|---|---|---|---|---|---|---|---|---|---|---|
| Auburn (Blue Jays) | 50 | 24 | - | .676 | ... | X | 3 | 2 | 11 | 3 | 2 | 0 | 2 | 2 | 2 | 2 | 9 | 2 | 10 |
| Tri-City (Astros) | 50 | 25 | - | .667 | 1/2 | 0 | X | 1 | 2 | 1 | 1 | 8 | 2 | 1 | 13 | 13 | 3 | 2 | 3 |
| Brooklyn (Mets) | 43 | 31 | - | .581 | 7 | 0 | 2 | X | 2 | 4 | 5 | 2 | 6 | 8 | 2 | 2 | 1 | 7 | 3 |
| Mahoning Valley (Indians) | 42 | 34 | - | .553 | 9 | 4 | 1 | 1 | X | 1 | 3 | 2 | 2 | 2 | 2 | 2 | 11 | 2 | 9 |
| New Jersey (Cardinals) | 41 | 34 | - | .547 | 91/2 | 0 | 2 | 6 | 2 | X | 4 | 3 | 7 | 5 | 1 | 1 | 2 | 7 | 2 |
| Hudson Valley (Devil Rays) | 39 | 33 | - | .542 | 10 | 1 | 2 | 5 | 0 | 8 | X | 3 | 5 | 5 | 1 | 1 | 2 | 5 | 2 |
| Vermont (Expos) | 34 | 38 | - | .472 | 15 | 3 | 6 | 1 | 1 | 0 | 0 | X | 1 | 1 | 9 | 8 | 2 | 2 | 1 |
| Aberdeen (Orioles) | 35 | 40 | - | .467 | 151/2 | 1 | 1 | 4 | 1 | 3 | 5 | 2 | X | 6 | 2 | 1 | 1 | 7 | 1 |
| Williamsport (Pirates) | 34 | 40 | - | .459 | 16 | 1 | 2 | 2 | 1 | 5 | 5 | 2 | 6 | X | 1 | 1 | 2 | 6 | 2 |
| Oneonta (Tigers) | 33 | 41 | - | .446 | 17 | 1 | 3 | 1 | 1 | 2 | 1 | 6 | 1 | 2 | X | 9 | 2 | 2 | 2 |
| Lowell (Red Sox) | 32 | 44 | - | .421 | 19 | 1 | 2 | 1 | 1 | 2 | 2 | 8 | 2 | 2 | 6 | X | 2 | 1 | 2 |
| Jamestown (Marlins) | 30 | 45 | - | .400 | 201/2 | 6 | 0 | 2 | 5 | 1 | 1 | 1 | 2 | 1 | 1 | 1 | X | 2 | 7 |
| Staten Island (Yankees) | 28 | 44 | - | .389 | 21 | 1 | 1 | 5 | 1 | 3 | 3 | 1 | 3 | 4 | 0 | 2 | 1 | X | 3 |
| Batavia (Phillies) | 28 | 46 | - | .378 | 22 | 5 | 0 | 0 | 6 | 1 | 1 | 2 | 2 | 1 | 1 | 1 | 8 | 0 | X |

Major league affiliations in parentheses.

PLAYOFFS: Mahoning Valley defeated Auburn two games to none; Tri-City defeated Brooklyn two games to one; Mahoning Valley defeated Tri-City two games to none. to win championship.

REGULAR-SEASON ATTENDANCE: Aberdeen, 228, 925; Auburn, 66, 762; Batavia, 38,086; Brooklyn, 294,229; Hudson Valley, 155,606; Jamestown, 54,790; Lowell, 180,000; Mahoning Valley, 160,832; New Jersey, 115,342; Oneonta, 42,100; Staten Island, 147,572; Tri-City, 110,497; Vermont, 93,796; Williamsport, 75,785. Total Attendance—1,763,322.

MANAGERS: Aberdeen, Don Buford; Auburn, Dennis Holmberg; Batavia, Luis Melendez; Brooklyn, Tony Tigerina; Hudson Valley, Dave Howard; Jamestown, Benny Castillo; Lowell, Luis Alicea; Mahoning Valley, Mike Sarbaugh; New Jersey, Tom Shields; Oneonta, Randy Ready; Staten Island, Tommy John; Tri-City, Gregg Langbehn; Vermont, Jose Alguacil; Williamsport, Jeff Branson.

ALL-STAR TEAM: 1B—Mario Garza, Tri-City; 2B—Chris Patrick, New Jersey; 3B—Juan Llamas, Oneonta; SS—Ben Zobrist, Tri-City—Reserve INF—Chris Giminez, Mahoning Valley; OF—Dante Brinkley, Brooklyn; Ambioriz Concepcion, Brooklyn; Adam Lind, Auburn; Argenis Reyes, Mahoning Valley; C—John Jaso, Hudson Valley, Curtis Thigpen, Auburn; RHP—Ronnie Martinez, Tri-City; Anibal Sanchez, Lowell; LHP—David Haehnel, Aberdeen; Joseph Williams, Brooklyn; DH—Mike Butia, Mahoning Valley. Most Valuable Player Award—Ronnie Martinez, Tri-City. Rolaids Relief Man Award—Gus Hlebovy, Vermont. Stedler Award—Ambiorix Concepcion, Brooklyn. Kinsella Award—Ben Zobrist, Tri-City. Manager of the Year—Tom Shields, New Jersey.

## 2004 BATTING

### TEAM

| Team | G | TPA | AB | R | H | TB | 2B | 3B | HR | RBI | SH | SF | HP | BB | IBB | SO | SB | CS | GDP | LOB | ShO | Avg. | OBP | Slg. |
|---|---|---|---|---|---|---|---|---|---|---|---|---|---|---|---|---|---|---|---|---|---|---|---|---|
| Auburn | 74 | 2898 | 2514 | 427 | 690 | 1080 | 165 | 21 | 61 | 380 | 19 | 22 | 54 | 288 | 11 | 553 | 36 | 20 | 42 | 573 | 0 | .274 | .359 | .430 |
| Mahoning Valley | 76 | 2961 | 2627 | 389 | 717 | 1047 | 146 | 17 | 50 | 348 | 18 | 21 | 64 | 231 | 13 | 553 | 53 | 21 | 41 | 570 | 4 | .273 | .344 | .399 |
| Tri-City | 75 | 2988 | 2593 | 425 | 693 | 1036 | 116 | 19 | 63 | 376 | 27 | 20 | 39 | 309 | 8 | 568 | 72 | 29 | 41 | 585 | 4 | .267 | .352 | .400 |
| Jamestown | 75 | 2846 | 2577 | 356 | 675 | 980 | 121 | 29 | 42 | 308 | 17 | 17 | 33 | 202 | 10 | 637 | 42 | 29 | 33 | 511 | 4 | .262 | .322 | .380 |
| Hudson Valley | 72 | 2667 | 2407 | 332 | 614 | 897 | 124 | 30 | 33 | 300 | 9 | 23 | 39 | 189 | 6 | 525 | 66 | 14 | 14 | 484 | 0 | .255 | .317 | .373 |
| Williamsport | 74 | 2771 | 2454 | 318 | 620 | 864 | 106 | 21 | 32 | 276 | 28 | 29 | 41 | 219 | 8 | 537 | 109 | 36 | 39 | 507 | 5 | .253 | .321 | .352 |
| Brooklyn | 74 | 2766 | 2462 | 329 | 620 | 894 | 107 | 25 | 39 | 285 | 43 | 20 | 45 | 196 | 6 | 542 | 94 | 31 | 33 | 500 | 3 | .252 | .316 | .363 |
| Staten Island | 72 | 2813 | 2529 | 313 | 626 | 881 | 112 | 19 | 35 | 274 | 21 | 16 | 39 | 207 | 6 | 587 | 52 | 26 | 48 | 512 | 9 | .248 | .312 | .348 |

| Team | G | TPA | AB | R | H | TB | 2B | 3B | HR | RBI | SH | SF | HP | BB | IBB | SO | SB | CS | GDP | LOB | ShO | Avg. | OBP | Slg. |
|---|---|---|---|---|---|---|---|---|---|---|---|---|---|---|---|---|---|---|---|---|---|---|---|---|
| Aberdeen....... | 75 | 2830 | 2530 | 307 | 621 | 886 | 131 | 25 | 28 | 259 | 29 | 21 | 33 | 217 | 10 | 537 | 80 | 38 | 18 | 504 | 6 | .245 | .311 | .350 |
| New Jersey ... | 75 | 2830 | 2533 | 312 | 621 | 856 | 109 | 15 | 32 | 273 | 16 | 21 | 29 | 229 | 4 | 570 | 61 | 27 | 38 | 508 | 5 | .245 | .313 | .338 |
| Lowell........... | 76 | 2959 | 2606 | 327 | 630 | 894 | 115 | 28 | 31 | 288 | 19 | 20 | 44 | 270 | 10 | 657 | 91 | 50 | 36 | 556 | 2 | .242 | .321 | .343 |
| Oneonta......... | 74 | 2756 | 2490 | 291 | 602 | 868 | 115 | 29 | 31 | 259 | 25 | 21 | 35 | 185 | 5 | 707 | 98 | 60 | 19 | 447 | 5 | .242 | .301 | .349 |
| Vermont........ | 72 | 2644 | 2310 | 303 | 541 | 798 | 97 | 8 | 48 | 262 | 11 | 11 | 32 | 280 | 5 | 580 | 69 | 41 | 46 | 486 | 6 | .234 | .324 | .345 |
| Batavia.......... | 74 | 2776 | 2483 | 280 | 570 | 850 | 98 | 25 | 44 | 249 | 17 | 16 | 54 | 206 | 5 | 681 | 54 | 39 | 38 | 511 | 3 | .230 | .301 | .342 |

## INDIVIDUAL

### TOP QUALIFIERS FOR BATTING CHAMPIONSHIP

Minimum 205 plate appearances. *Lefthanded batter. †Switch-hitter.

| Player, Team | G | TPA | AB | R | H | TB | 2B | 3B | HR | RBI | SH | SF | HP | BB | IBB | SO | SB | CS | GDP | Avg. | OBP | Slg. |
|---|---|---|---|---|---|---|---|---|---|---|---|---|---|---|---|---|---|---|---|---|---|---|
| Zobrist, Benjamin, Tri-City † | 68 | 310 | 257 | 50 | 87 | 119 | 14 | 3 | 4 | 45 | 4 | 2 | 4 | 43 | 0 | 31 | 15 | 4 | 5 | .339 | .438 | .463 |
| Patrick, Christopher, New Jersey | 57 | 222 | 206 | 30 | 66 | 86 | 13 | 2 | 1 | 22 | 1 | 1 | 3 | 11 | 0 | 27 | 1 | 3 | 3 | .320 | .362 | .417 |
| Brinkley, Dante, Brooklyn | 62 | 269 | 234 | 47 | 74 | 103 | 9 | 1 | 6 | 30 | 1 | 2 | 7 | 25 | 0 | 59 | 14 | 1 | 2 | .316 | .396 | .440 |
| Butia, Michael, Mahoning Valley * | 62 | 265 | 232 | 32 | 73 | 107 | 17 | 1 | 5 | 44 | 0 | 1 | 8 | 24 | 2 | 54 | 0 | 1 | 1 | .315 | .396 | .461 |
| Lind, Adam, Auburn * | 70 | 295 | 266 | 43 | 83 | 127 | 23 | 0 | 7 | 50 | 1 | 2 | 2 | 24 | 0 | 36 | 1 | 0 | 7 | .312 | .371 | .477 |
| Reyes, Argenis, Mahoning Valley † | 73 | 347 | 324 | 53 | 101 | 112 | 11 | 0 | 0 | 20 | 0 | 3 | 5 | 15 | 2 | 36 | 27 | 9 | 4 | .312 | .349 | .346 |
| Concepcion, Ambiorix, Brooklyn | 66 | 277 | 259 | 38 | 79 | 123 | 14 | 3 | 8 | 46 | 2 | 2 | 1 | 13 | 1 | 54 | 28 | 11 | 4 | .305 | .338 | .475 |
| Gamble, Sean, Batavia * | 64 | 286 | 247 | 36 | 75 | 105 | 15 | 6 | 1 | 19 | 4 | 2 | 2 | 31 | 3 | 49 | 7 | 7 | 0 | .304 | .383 | .425 |
| Llamas, Juan, Oneonta | 74 | 306 | 284 | 38 | 86 | 135 | 20 | 4 | 7 | 55 | 0 | 3 | 3 | 16 | 1 | 27 | 11 | 7 | 4 | .303 | .343 | .475 |
| Jaso, John, Hudson Valley * | 57 | 225 | 199 | 34 | 60 | 87 | 17 | 2 | 2 | 35 | 0 | 1 | 3 | 22 | 2 | 32 | 1 | 0 | 0 | .302 | .378 | .437 |
| Ditter, Brad, Vermont * | 52 | 211 | 193 | 24 | 58 | 77 | 6 | 2 | 3 | 27 | 0 | 0 | 1 | 17 | 2 | 27 | 9 | 3 | 3 | .301 | .360 | .399 |
| Gimenez, Chris, Mahoning Valley | 71 | 316 | 260 | 40 | 78 | 137 | 23 | 3 | 10 | 38 | 1 | 1 | 24 | 30 | 1 | 62 | 2 | 2 | 3 | .300 | .419 | .527 |
| Ash, Jonathan, Tri-City * | 61 | 278 | 239 | 50 | 71 | 90 | 7 | 3 | 2 | 25 | 2 | 1 | 11 | 25 | 1 | 16 | 5 | 4 | 3 | .297 | .388 | .377 |
| Pence, Hunter, Tri-City | 51 | 225 | 199 | 36 | 59 | 103 | 18 | 1 | 8 | 37 | 0 | 2 | 1 | 23 | 1 | 30 | 3 | 5 | 4 | .296 | .369 | .518 |
| Davidson, Tyler, Brooklyn | 65 | 275 | 244 | 36 | 72 | 111 | 15 | 3 | 6 | 45 | 0 | 2 | 7 | 22 | 2 | 64 | 3 | 1 | 0 | .295 | .367 | .455 |

DEPARTMENTAL LEADERS: G—Llamas, 74; AB—Reyes, 324; R—Reyes, 53; H—Reyes, 101; TB—Giminez, 137; 2B—Giminez, Lind, 23; 3B—Justice, 7; HR—Garza, 15; RBI—Garza, 65; SH—Robinson, Plumley, 9; SF—T. Brown, 8; HP—Giminez, 24; BB—Zobrist, 43; IBB—Nielsen, Pacheco 4; SO—Justice, 108; SB—Lomack, 29; CS—Concepcion, 11; GIDP—Caradonna, 10; Slg.—Giminez, .527; OBP—Zobrist, .438.

### ALL PLAYERS

*Lefthanded batter. †Switch-hitter.

| Player, Team | G | TPA | AB | R | H | TB | 2B | 3B | HR | RBI | SH | SF | HP | BB | IBB | SO | SB | CS | GDP | Avg. | OBP | Slg. |
|---|---|---|---|---|---|---|---|---|---|---|---|---|---|---|---|---|---|---|---|---|---|---|
| Alen, Luis, Jamestown | 44 | 135 | 120 | 11 | 30 | 39 | 9 | 0 | 0 | 12 | 2 | 1 | 2 | 10 | 0 | 11 | 1 | 0 | 4 | .250 | .316 | .325 |
| Allen, Rod, Staten Island | 35 | 108 | 94 | 12 | 22 | 33 | 5 | 0 | 2 | 10 | 0 | 1 | 5 | 8 | 0 | 18 | 5 | 1 | 1 | .234 | .324 | .351 |
| Alvarez, Wilner, Tri-City | 23 | 71 | 63 | 6 | 13 | 13 | 0 | 0 | 0 | 5 | 2 | 0 | 1 | 5 | 0 | 14 | 6 | 2 | 2 | .206 | .275 | .206 |
| Armstrong, Jason, Auburn | 45 | 143 | 124 | 24 | 32 | 44 | 9 | 0 | 1 | 12 | 1 | 1 | 2 | 13 | 0 | 21 | 6 | 0 | 1 | .258 | .336 | .355 |
| Asanovich, Robert, Hudson Valley | 58 | 245 | 219 | 32 | 64 | 93 | 16 | 2 | 3 | 33 | 1 | 1 | 5 | 19 | 0 | 31 | 9 | 1 | 2 | .292 | .361 | .425 |
| Ascencion, Quincy, Aberdeen | 72 | 299 | 269 | 37 | 68 | 94 | 12 | 4 | 2 | 31 | 3 | 4 | 4 | 19 | 0 | 27 | 12 | 7 | 1 | .253 | .307 | .349 |
| Ash, Jonathan, Tri-City * | 61 | 278 | 239 | 50 | 71 | 90 | 7 | 3 | 2 | 25 | 2 | 1 | 11 | 25 | 1 | 16 | 5 | 4 | 3 | .297 | .388 | .377 |
| Averill, Brandon, Tri-City | 34 | 120 | 108 | 15 | 24 | 37 | 5 | 1 | 2 | 11 | 1 | 0 | 1 | 10 | 0 | 40 | 1 | 0 | 1 | .222 | .294 | .343 |
| Babilonia, Edgar, Tri-City | 49 | 166 | 151 | 19 | 45 | 55 | 6 | 2 | 0 | 19 | 6 | 0 | 2 | 7 | 1 | 20 | 8 | 2 | 2 | .298 | .338 | .364 |
| Baez, Edgardo, Vermont | 46 | 187 | 165 | 18 | 41 | 70 | 6 | 1 | 7 | 27 | 0 | 1 | 1 | 20 | 0 | 34 | 2 | 1 | 8 | .248 | .332 | .424 |
| Barganier, Brandon, Tri-City * | 41 | 152 | 135 | 13 | 31 | 37 | 2 | 2 | 0 | 8 | 2 | 1 | 0 | 14 | 0 | 29 | 5 | 2 | 2 | .230 | .300 | .274 |
| Barnes, Justin, Oneonta | 32 | 77 | 73 | 9 | 15 | 27 | 0 | 0 | 4 | 10 | 1 | 1 | 1 | 1 | 0 | 24 | 2 | 1 | 0 | .205 | .224 | .370 |
| Battle, Tim, Staten Island | 53 | 216 | 199 | 28 | 49 | 64 | 8 | 2 | 1 | 20 | 1 | 0 | 2 | 14 | 0 | 74 | 13 | 6 | 1 | .246 | .302 | .322 |
| Baty, Ryan, Hudson Valley | 23 | 93 | 87 | 7 | 24 | 32 | 2 | 0 | 2 | 15 | 0 | 0 | 0 | 6 | 1 | 18 | 1 | 0 | 2 | .276 | .323 | .368 |
| Bixler, Brian, Williamsport | 59 | 250 | 228 | 40 | 63 | 78 | 7 | 4 | 0 | 21 | 1 | 4 | 2 | 15 | 0 | 51 | 14 | 5 | 3 | .276 | .321 | .342 |
| Boyer, Kyle, New Jersey | 14 | 51 | 48 | 2 | 8 | 11 | 0 | 0 | 1 | 4 | 0 | 1 | 1 | 1 | 0 | 10 | 1 | 1 | 1 | .167 | .196 | .229 |
| Brannon, Evan, Aberdeen | 29 | 56 | 51 | 3 | 9 | 11 | 2 | 0 | 0 | 2 | 1 | 0 | 0 | 4 | 0 | 9 | 0 | 0 | 0 | .176 | .236 | .216 |
| Brant, Derek, Batavia | 25 | 88 | 76 | 8 | 13 | 16 | 3 | 0 | 0 | 1 | 0 | 0 | 3 | 9 | 0 | 17 | 1 | 1 | 2 | .171 | .284 | .211 |
| Braun, Ronald, Aberdeen | 12 | 19 | 18 | 1 | 4 | 6 | 2 | 0 | 0 | 2 | 0 | 0 | 0 | 1 | 0 | 6 | 0 | 0 | 0 | .222 | .263 | .333 |
| Breen, Patrick, Hudson Valley * | 56 | 196 | 180 | 19 | 40 | 66 | 7 | 2 | 5 | 20 | 0 | 0 | 2 | 14 | 0 | 48 | 3 | 1 | 2 | .222 | .286 | .367 |
| Brinkley, Dante, Brooklyn | 62 | 269 | 234 | 47 | 74 | 103 | 9 | 1 | 6 | 30 | 1 | 2 | 7 | 25 | 0 | 59 | 14 | 1 | 2 | .316 | .396 | .440 |
| Brown, Kyle, Brooklyn | 5 | 6 | 6 | 1 | 1 | 1 | 0 | 0 | 0 | 1 | 0 | 0 | 0 | 0 | 0 | 2 | 1 | 1 | 0 | .167 | .167 | .167 |
| Brown, Tim, Williamsport * | 67 | 283 | 232 | 36 | 55 | 86 | 14 | 1 | 5 | 30 | 2 | 8 | 11 | 30 | 3 | 56 | 1 | 1 | 2 | .237 | .342 | .371 |
| Buffone, Anthony, Batavia † | 38 | 141 | 129 | 8 | 26 | 31 | 3 | 1 | 0 | 8 | 2 | 0 | 0 | 10 | 1 | 12 | 2 | 5 | 3 | .202 | .259 | .240 |
| Burt, James, Brooklyn | 48 | 193 | 168 | 20 | 46 | 73 | 11 | 2 | 4 | 23 | 0 | 1 | 10 | 14 | 0 | 28 | 6 | 2 | 3 | .274 | .363 | .435 |
| Butia, Michael, Mahoning Valley * | 62 | 265 | 232 | 32 | 73 | 107 | 17 | 1 | 5 | 44 | 0 | 1 | 8 | 24 | 2 | 54 | 0 | 1 | 1 | .315 | .396 | .461 |
| Cannon, Rhame, Auburn * | 62 | 238 | 210 | 33 | 57 | 104 | 15 | 1 | 10 | 41 | 1 | 4 | 1 | 22 | 1 | 55 | 0 | 0 | 4 | .271 | .338 | .495 |
| Cantu, Tim, New Jersey | 31 | 75 | 64 | 13 | 13 | 18 | 2 | 0 | 1 | 8 | 1 | 1 | 4 | 5 | 0 | 23 | 1 | 1 | 1 | .203 | .297 | .281 |
| Caraballo, Francisco, Tri-City | 57 | 227 | 207 | 27 | 57 | 92 | 12 | 1 | 7 | 33 | 0 | 1 | 3 | 16 | 0 | 51 | 4 | 2 | 4 | .275 | .335 | .444 |
| Caradonna, Troy, Staten Island † | 36 | 122 | 111 | 9 | 26 | 33 | 5 | 1 | 0 | 9 | 1 | 0 | 0 | 10 | 0 | 11 | 0 | 1 | 10 | .234 | .298 | .297 |
| Carlin, Michael, Williamsport | 40 | 135 | 116 | 19 | 32 | 59 | 7 | 1 | 6 | 22 | 0 | 3 | 1 | 15 | 0 | 22 | 4 | 1 | 1 | .276 | .356 | .509 |
| Carroll, Brett, Jamestown | 60 | 236 | 211 | 27 | 53 | 89 | 16 | 1 | 6 | 28 | 2 | 1 | 7 | 15 | 1 | 57 | 1 | 0 | 2 | .251 | .321 | .422 |
| Casillas, Omar, Mahoning Valley | 24 | 82 | 65 | 10 | 12 | 12 | 0 | 0 | 0 | 2 | 4 | 1 | 1 | 11 | 0 | 10 | 0 | 0 | 1 | .185 | .308 | .185 |
| Castro, Francisco, Oneonta † | 66 | 255 | 231 | 26 | 51 | 60 | 3 | 3 | 0 | 10 | 5 | 0 | 0 | 19 | 0 | 58 | 17 | 10 | 0 | .221 | .280 | .260 |
| Castro, Ofilio, Vermont | 68 | 288 | 241 | 38 | 63 | 88 | 14 | 1 | 3 | 32 | 2 | 4 | 2 | 39 | 2 | 48 | 7 | 6 | 3 | .261 | .364 | .365 |
| Chance, Andy, Williamsport | 7 | 26 | 21 | 1 | 3 | 4 | 1 | 0 | 0 | 1 | 0 | 0 | 1 | 4 | 0 | 3 | 2 | 0 | 2 | .143 | .308 | .190 |
| Christian, Justin, Staten Island | 50 | 232 | 208 | 29 | 57 | 91 | 9 | 2 | 7 | 33 | 0 | 3 | 2 | 19 | 0 | 39 | 14 | 4 | 2 | .274 | .336 | .438 |
| Ciaramella, Matthew, Lowell † | 45 | 179 | 164 | 8 | 31 | 42 | 6 | 1 | 1 | 20 | 1 | 2 | 0 | 12 | 2 | 35 | 0 | 3 | 2 | .189 | .242 | .256 |
| Clark, Robert, Tri-City | 38 | 143 | 125 | 21 | 32 | 52 | 5 | 0 | 5 | 19 | 0 | 2 | 2 | 14 | 0 | 35 | 2 | 0 | 1 | .256 | .336 | .416 |
| Cleveland, Brian, Jamestown | 63 | 272 | 255 | 33 | 66 | 90 | 14 | 2 | 2 | 20 | 0 | 1 | 5 | 11 | 1 | 54 | 4 | 1 | 8 | .259 | .301 | .353 |
| Coles, Corey, Brooklyn * | 64 | 267 | 237 | 40 | 66 | 88 | 6 | 5 | 2 | 20 | 7 | 1 | 5 | 17 | 1 | 31 | 10 | 5 | 0 | .278 | .338 | .371 |
| Colvin, Brooks, Oneonta | 64 | 264 | 235 | 28 | 61 | 71 | 7 | 0 | 1 | 15 | 1 | 3 | 4 | 21 | 1 | 53 | 10 | 6 | 2 | .260 | .327 | .302 |
| Concepcion, Ambiorix, Brooklyn | 66 | 277 | 259 | 38 | 79 | 123 | 14 | 3 | 8 | 46 | 2 | 2 | 1 | 13 | 1 | 54 | 28 | 11 | 4 | .305 | .338 | .475 |
| Contreras, Jose, Vermont † | 53 | 191 | 171 | 27 | 41 | 44 | 3 | 0 | 0 | 11 | 1 | 1 | 0 | 18 | 0 | 43 | 12 | 6 | 2 | .240 | .311 | .257 |
| Contreras, Jose, Lowell | 1 | 4 | 3 | 0 | 1 | 1 | 0 | 0 | 0 | 1 | 0 | 0 | 0 | 1 | 0 | 0 | 0 | 0 | 0 | .333 | .500 | .333 |
| Conway, Brandon, Vermont * | 36 | 122 | 112 | 10 | 21 | 27 | 2 | 2 | 0 | 5 | 1 | 0 | 0 | 9 | 0 | 38 | 1 | 3 | 2 | .188 | .248 | .241 |

| Player, Team | G | TPA | AB | R | H | TB | 2B | 3B | HR | RBI | SH | SF | HP | BB | IBB | SO | SB | CS | GDP | Avg. | OBP | Slg. |
|---|---|---|---|---|---|---|---|---|---|---|---|---|---|---|---|---|---|---|---|---|---|---|
| Cooper, Chad, Hudson Valley | 45 | 168 | 151 | 25 | 41 | 51 | 6 | 2 | 0 | 19 | 1 | 2 | 6 | 8 | 0 | 15 | 4 | 1 | 1 | .272 | .329 | .338 |
| Cooper, James, Tri-City | 45 | 149 | 125 | 28 | 29 | 38 | 4 | 1 | 1 | 14 | 5 | 0 | 1 | 18 | 0 | 39 | 9 | 1 | 0 | .232 | .333 | .304 |
| Corrente, David, Auburn | 35 | 131 | 113 | 15 | 29 | 38 | 4 | 1 | 1 | 12 | 2 | 0 | 4 | 12 | 0 | 28 | 0 | 0 | 2 | .257 | .349 | .336 |
| Costello, Michael, Aberdeen | 46 | 143 | 125 | 14 | 27 | 41 | 7 | 2 | 1 | 10 | 1 | 0 | 2 | 15 | 0 | 47 | 3 | 1 | 0 | .216 | .310 | .328 |
| Cottrell, Patrick, Hudson Valley | 67 | 268 | 248 | 37 | 68 | 105 | 19 | 3 | 4 | 36 | 0 | 4 | 3 | 13 | 0 | 43 | 7 | 0 | 3 | .274 | .313 | .423 |
| Coultas, Ryan, Brooklyn | 44 | 167 | 155 | 16 | 39 | 49 | 5 | 1 | 1 | 10 | 3 | 1 | 3 | 5 | 0 | 31 | 2 | 0 | 1 | .252 | .287 | .316 |
| Crosland, Jason, Batavia | 55 | 229 | 208 | 28 | 37 | 66 | 9 | 1 | 6 | 22 | 1 | 2 | 9 | 9 | 0 | 90 | 2 | 0 | 0 | .178 | .241 | .317 |
| Cruz, Jose, Mahoning Valley † | 15 | 46 | 40 | 6 | 9 | 11 | 0 | 1 | 0 | 1 | 0 | 0 | 0 | 6 | 0 | 7 | 1 | 0 | 1 | .225 | .326 | .275 |
| Cumberland, Shaun, Hudson Valley * | 50 | 176 | 164 | 25 | 54 | 72 | 7 | 4 | 1 | 11 | 0 | 0 | 1 | 11 | 2 | 23 | 9 | 1 | 2 | .329 | .375 | .439 |
| Davidson, Tyler, Brooklyn | 65 | 275 | 244 | 36 | 72 | 111 | 15 | 3 | 6 | 45 | 0 | 2 | 7 | 22 | 2 | 64 | 3 | 1 | 0 | .295 | .367 | .455 |
| Davis, Brad, Jamestown | 42 | 165 | 149 | 23 | 44 | 58 | 12 | 1 | 0 | 14 | 2 | 2 | 2 | 10 | 1 | 18 | 2 | 3 | 3 | .295 | .344 | .389 |
| De La Cruz, Carlos, Lowell † | 64 | 266 | 237 | 29 | 65 | 80 | 6 | 3 | 1 | 16 | 5 | 0 | 3 | 21 | 1 | 55 | 15 | 10 | 3 | .274 | .341 | .338 |
| Delgado, Jose, New Jersey † | 6 | 22 | 19 | 1 | 3 | 4 | 1 | 0 | 0 | 3 | 0 | 1 | 0 | 2 | 0 | 10 | 0 | 1 | 0 | .158 | .227 | .211 |
| Desmond, Ian, Vermont | 4 | 13 | 12 | 2 | 3 | 6 | 0 | 0 | 1 | 1 | 0 | 0 | 1 | 0 | 0 | 2 | 0 | 1 | 2 | .250 | .308 | .500 |
| Devoir, Jordan, Staten Island | 27 | 87 | 83 | 9 | 17 | 19 | 2 | 0 | 0 | 5 | 0 | 1 | 1 | 2 | 0 | 26 | 1 | 1 | 4 | .205 | .230 | .229 |
| Diaz, Rafael, Aberdeen | 46 | 163 | 157 | 11 | 38 | 44 | 6 | 0 | 0 | 11 | 1 | 0 | 0 | 5 | 0 | 25 | 2 | 5 | 0 | .242 | .265 | .280 |
| Dirnberger, Joseph, Batavia | 38 | 147 | 132 | 15 | 25 | 33 | 3 | 1 | 1 | 11 | 1 | 0 | 2 | 12 | 0 | 40 | 0 | 3 | 4 | .189 | .267 | .250 |
| Ditter, Brad, Vermont * | 52 | 211 | 193 | 24 | 58 | 77 | 6 | 2 | 3 | 27 | 0 | 0 | 1 | 17 | 2 | 27 | 9 | 3 | 3 | .301 | .360 | .399 |
| Dlugach, Brent, Oneonta | 47 | 198 | 183 | 17 | 39 | 53 | 7 | 2 | 1 | 12 | 3 | 1 | 3 | 8 | 0 | 59 | 5 | 4 | 4 | .213 | .256 | .290 |
| Duncan, Jacob, Aberdeen * | 31 | 85 | 70 | 9 | 19 | 37 | 5 | 2 | 3 | 15 | 2 | 1 | 0 | 12 | 2 | 13 | 0 | 1 | 1 | .271 | .373 | .529 |
| Ehlers, Cody, Staten Island * | 45 | 171 | 157 | 11 | 30 | 42 | 7 | 1 | 1 | 18 | 1 | 0 | 1 | 12 | 0 | 25 | 0 | 0 | 1 | .191 | .253 | .268 |
| Einertson, Mitch, Tri-City | 2 | 7 | 7 | 1 | 1 | 4 | 0 | 0 | 1 | 1 | 0 | 0 | 0 | 0 | 0 | 2 | 0 | 0 | 0 | .143 | .143 | .571 |
| Elliott, Justin, Williamsport | 5 | 16 | 16 | 3 | 4 | 4 | 0 | 0 | 0 | 1 | 0 | 0 | 0 | 0 | 0 | 2 | 0 | 0 | 0 | .250 | .250 | .250 |
| Encarnacion, Teodoro, Mahoning Valley | 60 | 234 | 215 | 21 | 50 | 76 | 7 | 2 | 5 | 27 | 4 | 3 | 0 | 12 | 2 | 58 | 0 | 0 | 8 | .233 | .270 | .353 |
| Esposito, Vinny, Auburn * | 59 | 238 | 198 | 30 | 50 | 79 | 18 | 1 | 3 | 38 | 2 | 2 | 7 | 29 | 1 | 65 | 1 | 1 | 3 | .253 | .364 | .399 |
| Ewen, Nick, Jamestown * | 51 | 183 | 163 | 18 | 40 | 58 | 7 | 1 | 3 | 13 | 0 | 1 | 0 | 19 | 4 | 51 | 5 | 4 | 1 | .245 | .322 | .356 |
| Ferris, Michael, New Jersey * | 40 | 166 | 146 | 18 | 29 | 43 | 5 | 0 | 3 | 14 | 0 | 0 | 1 | 19 | 0 | 44 | 2 | 1 | 3 | .199 | .295 | .295 |
| Finegan, Brian, Mahoning Valley | 69 | 293 | 263 | 41 | 67 | 93 | 13 | 2 | 3 | 34 | 2 | 2 | 4 | 22 | 0 | 48 | 5 | 5 | 6 | .255 | .320 | .354 |
| Fisher, Matthew, Brooklyn | 34 | 145 | 126 | 17 | 31 | 51 | 7 | 2 | 3 | 11 | 8 | 1 | 0 | 10 | 0 | 13 | 2 | 0 | 2 | .246 | .299 | .405 |
| Flores, Jesus, Brooklyn | 3 | 6 | 6 | 1 | 2 | 5 | 0 | 0 | 1 | 3 | 0 | 0 | 0 | 0 | 0 | 1 | 0 | 0 | 1 | .333 | .333 | .833 |
| Frazier, Jeffrey, Oneonta | 20 | 93 | 79 | 15 | 24 | 34 | 5 | 1 | 1 | 13 | 0 | 2 | 3 | 9 | 0 | 11 | 2 | 1 | 0 | .304 | .387 | .430 |
| Frias, Fernando, Hudson Valley | 38 | 109 | 103 | 12 | 22 | 41 | 2 | 4 | 3 | 14 | 2 | 1 | 0 | 3 | 0 | 31 | 1 | 0 | 0 | .214 | .234 | .398 |
| Frith, Ryan, Batavia | 66 | 281 | 255 | 36 | 62 | 110 | 11 | 2 | 11 | 41 | 1 | 2 | 4 | 19 | 1 | 86 | 13 | 3 | 3 | .243 | .304 | .431 |
| Fulton, Jon, Jamestown | 65 | 276 | 252 | 39 | 64 | 119 | 12 | 5 | 11 | 40 | 0 | 2 | 2 | 20 | 0 | 82 | 2 | 1 | 3 | .254 | .312 | .472 |
| Galloway, Carl, Batavia | 42 | 166 | 157 | 14 | 33 | 57 | 7 | 1 | 5 | 15 | 1 | 0 | 1 | 7 | 0 | 49 | 2 | 2 | 5 | .210 | .248 | .363 |
| Gamble, Sean, Batavia * | 64 | 286 | 247 | 36 | 75 | 105 | 15 | 6 | 1 | 19 | 4 | 2 | 2 | 31 | 3 | 49 | 7 | 7 | 0 | .304 | .383 | .425 |
| Garza, Mario, Tri-City * | 66 | 283 | 239 | 38 | 57 | 115 | 11 | 1 | 15 | 65 | 0 | 4 | 4 | 36 | 1 | 61 | 3 | 1 | 2 | .238 | .343 | .481 |
| Gaston, Jared, Jamestown | 53 | 196 | 176 | 24 | 48 | 62 | 2 | 3 | 2 | 17 | 0 | 1 | 2 | 17 | 0 | 53 | 3 | 2 | 0 | .273 | .342 | .352 |
| Gerlits, Gooby, Auburn | 7 | 16 | 15 | 0 | 4 | 5 | 1 | 0 | 0 | 2 | 0 | 0 | 0 | 1 | 0 | 2 | 0 | 0 | 0 | .267 | .313 | .333 |
| Gimenez, Chris, Mahoning Valley | 71 | 316 | 260 | 40 | 78 | 137 | 23 | 3 | 10 | 38 | 1 | 1 | 24 | 30 | 1 | 62 | 2 | 2 | 3 | .300 | .419 | .527 |
| Gonzalez, Edwar, Staten Island | 33 | 141 | 130 | 18 | 29 | 46 | 6 | 1 | 3 | 14 | 1 | 0 | 3 | 7 | 1 | 27 | 1 | 0 | 0 | .223 | .279 | .354 |
| Granadillo, Tony, New Jersey † | 14 | 54 | 51 | 6 | 12 | 15 | 3 | 0 | 0 | 0 | 1 | 0 | 0 | 2 | 0 | 11 | 0 | 0 | 1 | .235 | .264 | .294 |
| Grandstrand, Brett, Williamsport | 49 | 196 | 168 | 22 | 45 | 65 | 7 | 2 | 3 | 21 | 5 | 4 | 1 | 18 | 0 | 29 | 5 | 4 | 2 | .268 | .335 | .387 |
| Grimm, Casey, New Jersey * | 57 | 220 | 188 | 21 | 47 | 66 | 7 | 0 | 4 | 26 | 0 | 3 | 0 | 26 | 2 | 44 | 1 | 0 | 2 | .250 | .336 | .351 |
| Guzman, Heriberto, Lowell | 60 | 251 | 219 | 32 | 51 | 89 | 13 | 2 | 7 | 29 | 3 | 1 | 6 | 22 | 1 | 74 | 5 | 2 | 4 | .233 | .319 | .406 |
| Hall, Brian, Auburn | 57 | 237 | 211 | 38 | 62 | 108 | 14 | 1 | 10 | 39 | 0 | 1 | 1 | 24 | 1 | 49 | 3 | 3 | 0 | .294 | .367 | .512 |
| Hanan, Blake, Aberdeen † | 66 | 189 | 169 | 23 | 42 | 55 | 11 | 1 | 0 | 10 | 4 | 0 | 3 | 13 | 0 | 31 | 7 | 6 | 0 | .249 | .314 | .325 |
| Hardy, John, Batavia | 51 | 220 | 191 | 21 | 52 | 70 | 7 | 4 | 1 | 13 | 1 | 2 | 2 | 24 | 0 | 45 | 5 | 3 | 4 | .272 | .356 | .366 |
| Harris, Estee, Staten Island * | 52 | 197 | 173 | 32 | 42 | 74 | 10 | 2 | 6 | 26 | 1 | 1 | 4 | 18 | 0 | 65 | 9 | 3 | 1 | .243 | .327 | .428 |
| Hathaway, Aaron, Brooklyn | 39 | 143 | 131 | 17 | 27 | 32 | 5 | 0 | 0 | 12 | 3 | 1 | 0 | 8 | 0 | 25 | 1 | 0 | 3 | .206 | .250 | .244 |
| Herbert, Samuel, New Jersey | 18 | 59 | 53 | 6 | 13 | 17 | 1 | 0 | 1 | 6 | 0 | 1 | 1 | 4 | 0 | 11 | 4 | 3 | 0 | .245 | .305 | .321 |
| Hicks, Joe, Williamsport | 20 | 67 | 63 | 4 | 10 | 15 | 3 | 1 | 0 | 4 | 1 | 0 | 1 | 2 | 0 | 22 | 0 | 0 | 0 | .159 | .197 | .238 |
| Hofius, Steven, Williamsport * | 41 | 155 | 134 | 15 | 37 | 60 | 6 | 1 | 5 | 29 | 0 | 1 | 2 | 18 | 1 | 35 | 0 | 0 | 2 | .276 | .368 | .448 |
| Holmes, Brett, Williamsport | 42 | 151 | 141 | 13 | 32 | 45 | 3 | 2 | 2 | 12 | 4 | 1 | 0 | 5 | 1 | 40 | 10 | 3 | 1 | .227 | .252 | .319 |
| House, Kevin, New Jersey | 11 | 26 | 24 | 5 | 5 | 8 | 1 | 1 | 0 | 0 | 1 | 0 | 1 | 0 | 0 | 9 | 2 | 0 | 0 | .208 | .240 | .333 |
| Isaacson, Greg, Batavia * | 58 | 235 | 207 | 17 | 42 | 67 | 13 | 3 | 2 | 23 | 2 | 1 | 9 | 16 | 0 | 62 | 3 | 4 | 4 | .203 | .288 | .324 |
| Jaramillo, Jason, Batavia † | 31 | 127 | 112 | 11 | 25 | 33 | 5 | 0 | 1 | 14 | 0 | 2 | 1 | 12 | 0 | 27 | 0 | 1 | 3 | .223 | .299 | .295 |
| Jaso, John, Hudson Valley * | 57 | 225 | 199 | 34 | 60 | 87 | 17 | 2 | 2 | 35 | 0 | 1 | 3 | 22 | 2 | 32 | 1 | 0 | 0 | .302 | .378 | .437 |
| Jeroloman, Charles, Lowell | 48 | 186 | 159 | 14 | 27 | 37 | 5 | 1 | 1 | 12 | 0 | 1 | 3 | 23 | 0 | 61 | 1 | 0 | 2 | .170 | .285 | .233 |
| Johnson, A.J., Williamsport | 66 | 270 | 239 | 32 | 60 | 80 | 12 | 1 | 2 | 18 | 3 | 1 | 3 | 24 | 1 | 73 | 8 | 2 | 6 | .251 | .326 | .335 |
| Jones, Benjamin, Staten Island | 41 | 169 | 150 | 16 | 42 | 66 | 6 | 0 | 6 | 26 | 0 | 4 | 3 | 12 | 1 | 47 | 0 | 0 | 2 | .280 | .337 | .440 |
| Justice, Justin, Oneonta * | 69 | 276 | 259 | 30 | 56 | 93 | 14 | 7 | 3 | 25 | 1 | 0 | 4 | 12 | 2 | 108 | 2 | 2 | 0 | .216 | .262 | .359 |
| Karlsen, Grant, Batavia | 19 | 78 | 70 | 5 | 15 | 15 | 0 | 0 | 0 | 7 | 2 | 1 | 2 | 3 | 0 | 21 | 0 | 1 | 0 | .214 | .263 | .214 |
| Klosterman, Ryan, Auburn | 66 | 301 | 269 | 50 | 74 | 110 | 13 | 4 | 5 | 32 | 1 | 2 | 7 | 22 | 1 | 55 | 16 | 2 | 5 | .275 | .343 | .409 |
| Koch, Brady, Tri-City | 14 | 51 | 43 | 9 | 12 | 20 | 2 | 0 | 2 | 12 | 0 | 2 | 2 | 4 | 0 | 10 | 1 | 0 | 0 | .279 | .353 | .465 |
| Koenig, Lance, Tri-City | 20 | 69 | 63 | 9 | 17 | 23 | 3 | 0 | 1 | 4 | 1 | 0 | 0 | 5 | 0 | 17 | 0 | 1 | 1 | .270 | .324 | .365 |
| Lara, Christian, Lowell † | 32 | 146 | 119 | 21 | 33 | 40 | 3 | 2 | 0 | 10 | 0 | 1 | 2 | 24 | 2 | 23 | 10 | 5 | 1 | .277 | .404 | .336 |
| Ledbetter, Ted, Jamestown | 3 | 11 | 9 | 1 | 2 | 2 | 0 | 0 | 0 | 0 | 0 | 0 | 0 | 2 | 0 | 2 | 1 | 0 | 0 | .222 | .364 | .222 |
| Legrande, Duron, Vermont * | 37 | 152 | 139 | 11 | 20 | 21 | 1 | 0 | 0 | 8 | 1 | 0 | 3 | 9 | 0 | 46 | 10 | 2 | 3 | .144 | .212 | .151 |
| Lerud, Steven, Williamsport * | 8 | 34 | 29 | 2 | 7 | 7 | 0 | 0 | 0 | 2 | 0 | 0 | 1 | 4 | 0 | 6 | 0 | 1 | 1 | .241 | .353 | .241 |
| Lind, Adam, Auburn * | 70 | 295 | 266 | 43 | 83 | 127 | 23 | 0 | 7 | 50 | 1 | 2 | 2 | 24 | 0 | 36 | 1 | 0 | 7 | .312 | .371 | .477 |
| Lindesey, Juan, Jamestown | 42 | 149 | 139 | 19 | 33 | 41 | 3 | 1 | 1 | 19 | 0 | 1 | 1 | 8 | 0 | 37 | 3 | 1 | 1 | .237 | .282 | .295 |
| Llamas, Juan, Oneonta | 74 | 306 | 284 | 38 | 86 | 135 | 20 | 4 | 7 | 55 | 0 | 3 | 3 | 16 | 1 | 27 | 11 | 7 | 4 | .303 | .343 | .475 |
| Lomack, Jermel, Williamsport † | 44 | 179 | 152 | 27 | 43 | 47 | 4 | 0 | 0 | 8 | 3 | 1 | 5 | 18 | 0 | 27 | 29 | 4 | 0 | .283 | .375 | .309 |
| Louisa, Lorvin, Vermont | 15 | 53 | 49 | 6 | 9 | 13 | 1 | 0 | 1 | 4 | 0 | 0 | 1 | 3 | 0 | 27 | 0 | 3 | 1 | .184 | .245 | .265 |
| Lowrance, Marvin, Vermont * | 53 | 219 | 187 | 23 | 54 | 71 | 6 | 1 | 3 | 20 | 0 | 0 | 4 | 28 | 0 | 40 | 1 | 1 | 2 | .289 | .393 | .380 |
| Macia, Wanell, Williamsport * | 52 | 193 | 185 | 26 | 54 | 83 | 12 | 4 | 3 | 26 | 3 | 0 | 0 | 5 | 0 | 25 | 2 | 1 | 5 | .292 | .311 | .449 |
| Mangioni, Jarad, Auburn | 43 | 138 | 122 | 19 | 32 | 50 | 7 | 1 | 3 | 12 | 0 | 0 | 2 | 14 | 0 | 34 | 2 | 1 | 3 | .262 | .348 | .410 |
| Manriquez, Salomon, Vermont | 10 | 33 | 31 | 2 | 9 | 15 | 3 | 0 | 1 | 5 | 0 | 0 | 0 | 2 | 0 | 3 | 0 | 0 | 1 | .290 | .333 | .484 |
| Marconi, Robert, Aberdeen | 35 | 133 | 114 | 21 | 37 | 56 | 9 | 2 | 2 | 14 | 0 | 2 | 0 | 17 | 0 | 34 | 8 | 1 | 1 | .325 | .406 | .491 |
| Martinez, Octavio, Aberdeen | 9 | 26 | 23 | 2 | 8 | 10 | 2 | 0 | 0 | 2 | 0 | 0 | 1 | 2 | 0 | 2 | 0 | 1 | 0 | .348 | .423 | .435 |
| Mathews, Aaron, Auburn | 70 | 327 | 283 | 52 | 75 | 97 | 10 | 6 | 0 | 26 | 6 | 1 | 4 | 33 | 0 | 47 | 6 | 6 | 2 | .265 | .349 | .343 |

| Player, Team | G | TPA | AB | R | H | TB | 2B | 3B | HR | RBI | SH | SF | HP | BB | IBB | SO | SB | CS | GDP | Avg. | OBP | Slg. |
|---|---|---|---|---|---|---|---|---|---|---|---|---|---|---|---|---|---|---|---|---|---|---|
| Matulich, Mario, Mahoning Valley | 23 | 85 | 81 | 6 | 20 | 32 | 7 | 1 | 1 | 9 | 0 | 0 | 1 | 3 | 0 | 29 | 0 | 0 | 0 | .247 | .282 | .395 |
| McCann, Bradley, Jamestown | 28 | 119 | 108 | 16 | 31 | 50 | 6 | 2 | 3 | 13 | 1 | 1 | 2 | 7 | 0 | 15 | 0 | 1 | 3 | .287 | .339 | .463 |
| McMillan, Beau, Jamestown | 29 | 121 | 106 | 18 | 28 | 36 | 6 | 1 | 0 | 10 | 0 | 1 | 0 | 14 | 0 | 34 | 4 | 2 | 1 | .264 | .347 | .340 |
| McRae, Aaron, Oneonta * | 22 | 66 | 54 | 4 | 10 | 14 | 4 | 0 | 0 | 6 | 1 | 4 | 0 | 7 | 0 | 20 | 0 | 0 | 1 | .185 | .262 | .259 |
| Mendez, Deivi, Staten Island | 25 | 99 | 94 | 7 | 26 | 31 | 5 | 0 | 0 | 6 | 1 | 1 | 0 | 3 | 0 | 12 | 1 | 1 | 0 | .277 | .296 | .330 |
| Mendez, Rafael, Oneonta | 70 | 275 | 246 | 18 | 54 | 79 | 17 | 1 | 2 | 29 | 5 | 2 | 4 | 18 | 0 | 88 | 10 | 6 | 1 | .220 | .281 | .321 |
| Merloni, Lou, Mahoning Valley | 2 | 8 | 8 | 1 | 2 | 5 | 0 | 0 | 1 | 4 | 0 | 0 | 0 | 0 | 0 | 3 | 0 | 0 | 0 | .250 | .250 | .625 |
| Metropoulos, Joseph, Auburn | 49 | 178 | 152 | 28 | 39 | 73 | 16 | 0 | 6 | 30 | 1 | 0 | 7 | 18 | 1 | 48 | 0 | 0 | 3 | .257 | .362 | .480 |
| Moffitt, Andrew, Aberdeen | 20 | 78 | 64 | 11 | 14 | 26 | 4 | 1 | 2 | 11 | 1 | 2 | 0 | 11 | 0 | 16 | 0 | 0 | 2 | .219 | .325 | .406 |
| Montgomery, Tim, Mahoning Valley | 65 | 272 | 242 | 37 | 65 | 104 | 14 | 2 | 7 | 32 | 1 | 1 | 2 | 26 | 0 | 67 | 0 | 1 | 3 | .269 | .343 | .430 |
| Montz, Luke, Vermont | 62 | 242 | 204 | 31 | 51 | 92 | 11 | 0 | 10 | 34 | 1 | 1 | 3 | 33 | 0 | 42 | 2 | 1 | 5 | .250 | .361 | .451 |
| Morel, Elvis, Aberdeen | 11 | 52 | 48 | 7 | 11 | 12 | 1 | 0 | 0 | 6 | 0 | 0 | 1 | 3 | 0 | 5 | 6 | 1 | 0 | .229 | .288 | .250 |
| Mortimer, Steve, Vermont * | 65 | 255 | 214 | 31 | 51 | 85 | 13 | 0 | 7 | 29 | 1 | 1 | 10 | 29 | 1 | 64 | 8 | 2 | 5 | .238 | .354 | .397 |
| Mullinax, Jacob, New Jersey | 56 | 244 | 224 | 32 | 65 | 91 | 9 | 4 | 3 | 36 | 0 | 3 | 6 | 11 | 1 | 52 | 5 | 1 | 3 | .290 | .336 | .406 |
| Nelson, Kevin, Staten Island | 27 | 103 | 89 | 9 | 23 | 34 | 6 | 1 | 1 | 7 | 2 | 0 | 3 | 9 | 0 | 19 | 0 | 0 | 2 | .258 | .347 | .382 |
| Nielsen, Eric, Auburn | 68 | 283 | 231 | 38 | 61 | 101 | 15 | 2 | 7 | 37 | 1 | 4 | 12 | 35 | 4 | 45 | 0 | 4 | 3 | .264 | .383 | .437 |
| Nowak, Christopher, Hudson Valley | 62 | 246 | 219 | 26 | 61 | 88 | 18 | 3 | 1 | 32 | 1 | 2 | 8 | 16 | 1 | 35 | 1 | 2 | 1 | .279 | .347 | .402 |
| Orr, Samuel, Batavia * | 57 | 232 | 219 | 15 | 50 | 77 | 8 | 2 | 5 | 21 | 0 | 0 | 1 | 12 | 0 | 64 | 4 | 1 | 4 | .228 | .272 | .352 |
| Otness, John, Lowell | 63 | 254 | 232 | 23 | 64 | 82 | 12 | 0 | 2 | 29 | 0 | 3 | 7 | 12 | 0 | 18 | 5 | 3 | 6 | .276 | .327 | .353 |
| Pacheco, Fernando, Mahoning Valley * | 60 | 234 | 198 | 28 | 50 | 77 | 10 | 1 | 5 | 37 | 0 | 1 | 2 | 33 | 4 | 49 | 0 | 1 | 5 | .253 | .363 | .389 |
| Palmer, Cody, New Jersey | 32 | 101 | 90 | 10 | 17 | 33 | 7 | 0 | 3 | 11 | 1 | 0 | 2 | 8 | 0 | 33 | 0 | 0 | 1 | .189 | .270 | .367 |
| Paniagua, Salvador, Lowell | 50 | 201 | 189 | 24 | 42 | 80 | 16 | 2 | 6 | 32 | 1 | 1 | 3 | 7 | 1 | 63 | 0 | 0 | 4 | .222 | .260 | .423 |
| Paredes, Salvador, Hudson Valley | 49 | 165 | 156 | 20 | 30 | 39 | 6 | 0 | 1 | 17 | 2 | 3 | 0 | 4 | 0 | 50 | 3 | 1 | 0 | .192 | .209 | .250 |
| Parker, Brett, Mahoning Valley | 64 | 272 | 238 | 43 | 65 | 98 | 19 | 1 | 4 | 27 | 4 | 2 | 5 | 23 | 1 | 53 | 10 | 1 | 4 | .273 | .347 | .412 |
| Parrish, Matt, Oneonta | 20 | 61 | 59 | 3 | 8 | 11 | 1 | 1 | 0 | 3 | 0 | 0 | 1 | 1 | 0 | 26 | 1 | 1 | 0 | .136 | .164 | .186 |
| Pence, Hunter, Tri-City | 51 | 225 | 199 | 36 | 59 | 103 | 18 | 1 | 8 | 37 | 0 | 2 | 1 | 23 | 1 | 30 | 3 | 5 | 4 | .296 | .369 | .518 |
| Perez, Fernando, Hudson Valley | 69 | 304 | 267 | 46 | 62 | 86 | 8 | 5 | 2 | 20 | 1 | 3 | 3 | 30 | 0 | 70 | 24 | 4 | 0 | .232 | .314 | .322 |
| Perry, Patrick, Lowell * | 33 | 115 | 102 | 9 | 18 | 20 | 2 | 0 | 0 | 9 | 1 | 1 | 1 | 10 | 0 | 22 | 0 | 1 | 3 | .176 | .254 | .196 |
| Pietro, Joseph, Jamestown * | 66 | 279 | 238 | 36 | 67 | 76 | 1 | 4 | 0 | 20 | 7 | 2 | 2 | 30 | 1 | 65 | 13 | 9 | 1 | .282 | .364 | .319 |
| Pilittere, Peter, Staten Island | 34 | 129 | 121 | 9 | 26 | 32 | 6 | 0 | 0 | 11 | 1 | 0 | 3 | 3 | 0 | 18 | 1 | 1 | 5 | .215 | .252 | .264 |
| Pinckney, Andrew, Lowell † | 64 | 270 | 242 | 23 | 66 | 86 | 9 | 1 | 3 | 25 | 1 | 2 | 3 | 22 | 1 | 74 | 2 | 8 | 1 | .273 | .338 | .355 |
| Plumley, Grant, Staten Island | 62 | 285 | 258 | 30 | 65 | 80 | 11 | 2 | 0 | 19 | 9 | 1 | 4 | 13 | 0 | 45 | 2 | 1 | 6 | .252 | .297 | .310 |
| Poppert, John, Vermont | 31 | 123 | 114 | 14 | 25 | 37 | 6 | 0 | 2 | 9 | 0 | 1 | 1 | 7 | 0 | 26 | 0 | 0 | 4 | .219 | .268 | .325 |
| Powers, Greg, Auburn * | 15 | 36 | 30 | 3 | 6 | 9 | 1 | 1 | 0 | 4 | 1 | 0 | 0 | 5 | 1 | 10 | 0 | 0 | 1 | .200 | .314 | .300 |
| Psomas, Grant, Brooklyn | 65 | 255 | 223 | 23 | 52 | 78 | 13 | 2 | 3 | 29 | 3 | 3 | 1 | 25 | 1 | 48 | 4 | 1 | 3 | .233 | .310 | .350 |
| Ramos, Jason, Lowell † | 47 | 135 | 115 | 14 | 23 | 28 | 5 | 0 | 0 | 12 | 3 | 0 | 2 | 15 | 0 | 27 | 4 | 3 | 2 | .200 | .303 | .243 |
| Reddinger, Brandon, Williamsport | 30 | 98 | 86 | 4 | 12 | 13 | 1 | 0 | 0 | 7 | 1 | 0 | 4 | 7 | 0 | 24 | 0 | 0 | 3 | .140 | .237 | .151 |
| Restko, J.T., Jamestown | 72 | 316 | 294 | 40 | 69 | 100 | 11 | 1 | 6 | 46 | 0 | 2 | 4 | 16 | 0 | 75 | 0 | 2 | 3 | .235 | .282 | .340 |
| Reyes, Argenis, Mahoning Valley † | 73 | 347 | 324 | 53 | 101 | 112 | 11 | 0 | 0 | 20 | 0 | 3 | 5 | 15 | 2 | 36 | 27 | 9 | 4 | .312 | .349 | .346 |
| Reyes, Milver, Williamsport | 34 | 114 | 105 | 12 | 18 | 23 | 2 | 0 | 1 | 11 | 1 | 0 | 2 | 6 | 0 | 19 | 1 | 2 | 2 | .171 | .230 | .219 |
| Reynoso, Danilo, Brooklyn | 14 | 44 | 42 | 3 | 8 | 11 | 0 | 0 | 1 | 3 | 1 | 0 | 0 | 1 | 0 | 17 | 0 | 0 | 1 | .190 | .209 | .262 |
| Rich, Scott, Staten Island | 42 | 150 | 136 | 19 | 33 | 46 | 7 | 0 | 2 | 14 | 0 | 2 | 0 | 12 | 0 | 38 | 2 | 1 | 4 | .243 | .300 | .338 |
| Rios, Kevin, Brooklyn | 55 | 184 | 158 | 17 | 28 | 37 | 4 | 1 | 1 | 12 | 8 | 4 | 4 | 10 | 0 | 40 | 2 | 3 | 3 | .177 | .239 | .234 |
| Ritchie, Jake, Hudson Valley | 3 | 10 | 8 | 1 | 1 | 1 | 0 | 0 | 0 | 1 | 0 | 0 | 1 | 1 | 0 | 5 | 0 | 0 | 0 | .125 | .300 | .125 |
| Rivas, Arturo, Aberdeen | 55 | 200 | 184 | 18 | 48 | 65 | 8 | 0 | 3 | 22 | 0 | 1 | 0 | 15 | 2 | 51 | 4 | 4 | 3 | .261 | .315 | .353 |
| Roa, Joel, Oneonta | 18 | 48 | 46 | 3 | 9 | 15 | 3 | 0 | 1 | 2 | 0 | 0 | 0 | 2 | 0 | 23 | 0 | 0 | 0 | .196 | .229 | .326 |
| Robinson, Levi, Aberdeen | 68 | 297 | 253 | 42 | 65 | 78 | 11 | 1 | 0 | 16 | 9 | 2 | 10 | 23 | 0 | 49 | 18 | 4 | 3 | .257 | .340 | .308 |
| Robinson-Pierce, Whit, Aberdeen | 7 | 25 | 23 | 2 | 4 | 4 | 0 | 0 | 0 | 0 | 0 | 0 | 1 | 1 | 0 | 8 | 0 | 1 | 0 | .174 | .240 | .174 |
| Ryan, Dusty, Oneonta | 54 | 189 | 157 | 20 | 43 | 68 | 11 | 1 | 4 | 26 | 2 | 4 | 2 | 24 | 0 | 52 | 6 | 4 | 1 | .274 | .369 | .433 |
| Santangelo, Louis, Tri-City | 47 | 187 | 164 | 28 | 33 | 60 | 5 | 2 | 6 | 20 | 0 | 0 | 2 | 21 | 1 | 58 | 2 | 1 | 5 | .201 | .299 | .366 |
| Santiago, John, Williamsport | 31 | 114 | 104 | 11 | 33 | 44 | 8 | 0 | 1 | 17 | 0 | 1 | 2 | 7 | 0 | 15 | 1 | 1 | 1 | .317 | .368 | .423 |
| Sewell, Kevin, Jamestown * | 58 | 215 | 201 | 27 | 59 | 102 | 13 | 6 | 6 | 33 | 1 | 1 | 3 | 9 | 2 | 39 | 1 | 2 | 2 | .294 | .332 | .507 |
| Shafer, Corey, Aberdeen * | 44 | 154 | 149 | 11 | 29 | 39 | 4 | 0 | 2 | 15 | 0 | 0 | 0 | 5 | 1 | 33 | 0 | 0 | 1 | .195 | .221 | .262 |
| Shepherd, Matthew, New Jersey † | 71 | 287 | 254 | 27 | 59 | 67 | 8 | 0 | 0 | 23 | 6 | 3 | 1 | 23 | 0 | 44 | 17 | 7 | 1 | .232 | .295 | .264 |
| Shimer, Nicholas, Batavia | 64 | 264 | 238 | 30 | 58 | 86 | 8 | 1 | 6 | 28 | 1 | 1 | 8 | 16 | 0 | 57 | 4 | 2 | 3 | .244 | .312 | .361 |
| Smith, Carl, Aberdeen | 56 | 213 | 188 | 23 | 43 | 64 | 14 | 2 | 1 | 16 | 0 | 4 | 1 | 20 | 1 | 45 | 3 | 0 | 1 | .229 | .300 | .340 |
| Smith, Chris, Aberdeen * | 9 | 23 | 19 | 5 | 7 | 15 | 0 | 1 | 2 | 3 | 0 | 0 | 0 | 4 | 1 | 5 | 0 | 0 | 0 | .368 | .478 | .789 |
| Smith, John, Williamsport * | 26 | 78 | 65 | 7 | 18 | 19 | 1 | 0 | 0 | 4 | 0 | 1 | 1 | 11 | 0 | 8 | 1 | 3 | 3 | .277 | .385 | .292 |
| Solano, Euvi, Williamsport | 30 | 88 | 79 | 5 | 21 | 25 | 2 | 1 | 0 | 7 | 1 | 0 | 0 | 8 | 0 | 14 | 6 | 2 | 5 | .266 | .333 | .316 |
| Sorensen, Logan, Lowell * | 11 | 48 | 44 | 7 | 12 | 19 | 5 | 1 | 0 | 14 | 0 | 2 | 0 | 2 | 0 | 4 | 2 | 0 | 1 | .273 | .292 | .432 |
| Sovie, Robbie, Oneonta | 10 | 23 | 21 | 3 | 2 | 2 | 0 | 0 | 0 | 0 | 0 | 0 | 1 | 1 | 0 | 11 | 1 | 0 | 0 | .095 | .174 | .095 |
| Spring, Matthew, Hudson Valley | 50 | 191 | 168 | 20 | 37 | 69 | 4 | 2 | 8 | 23 | 0 | 3 | 3 | 17 | 0 | 62 | 0 | 1 | 0 | .220 | .298 | .411 |
| Sultemeier, Eric, Aberdeen | 64 | 263 | 234 | 29 | 53 | 71 | 7 | 4 | 1 | 21 | 4 | 2 | 3 | 20 | 0 | 48 | 8 | 4 | 3 | .226 | .293 | .303 |
| Sutton, Stephen, Tri-City † | 63 | 295 | 250 | 43 | 70 | 83 | 10 | 0 | 1 | 16 | 2 | 2 | 2 | 39 | 2 | 50 | 2 | 4 | 5 | .280 | .379 | .332 |
| Swackhamer, Wesley, New Jersey * | 55 | 230 | 212 | 17 | 47 | 66 | 13 | 0 | 2 | 23 | 0 | 2 | 0 | 16 | 0 | 56 | 4 | 0 | 2 | .222 | .274 | .311 |
| Szabo, Marshall, Mahoning Valley † | 26 | 113 | 109 | 13 | 32 | 42 | 3 | 2 | 1 | 9 | 0 | 1 | 0 | 3 | 0 | 15 | 5 | 0 | 2 | .294 | .310 | .385 |
| Taillon, Cory, New Jersey | 20 | 68 | 58 | 9 | 12 | 13 | 1 | 0 | 0 | 4 | 1 | 0 | 0 | 9 | 0 | 12 | 1 | 0 | 0 | .207 | .313 | .224 |
| Thigpen, Curtis, Auburn | 45 | 196 | 166 | 34 | 50 | 86 | 11 | 2 | 7 | 29 | 1 | 3 | 3 | 23 | 0 | 32 | 1 | 1 | 2 | .301 | .390 | .518 |
| Toops, Brady, New Jersey * | 33 | 108 | 97 | 11 | 20 | 27 | 3 | 2 | 0 | 9 | 1 | 1 | 1 | 8 | 1 | 26 | 2 | 1 | 3 | .206 | .271 | .278 |
| Toregas, Wyatt, Mahoning Valley | 59 | 235 | 214 | 38 | 63 | 104 | 18 | 1 | 7 | 48 | 1 | 4 | 5 | 11 | 1 | 26 | 1 | 0 | 2 | .294 | .338 | .486 |
| Travis, David, Vermont * | 30 | 103 | 95 | 8 | 16 | 28 | 6 | 0 | 2 | 12 | 0 | 0 | 1 | 7 | 0 | 44 | 0 | 1 | 2 | .168 | .233 | .295 |
| Triplett, Russ, Brooklyn | 2 | 4 | 4 | 0 | 0 | 0 | 0 | 0 | 0 | 0 | 0 | 0 | 0 | 0 | 0 | 0 | 0 | 0 | 0 | .000 | .000 | .000 |
| Tulk, Robert, Oneonta * | 51 | 171 | 150 | 21 | 33 | 52 | 10 | 3 | 1 | 11 | 4 | 0 | 2 | 15 | 0 | 48 | 3 | 3 | 4 | .220 | .299 | .347 |
| Turner, Chris, Lowell | 42 | 170 | 162 | 17 | 39 | 64 | 2 | 4 | 5 | 21 | 0 | 2 | 2 | 4 | 1 | 55 | 3 | 2 | 2 | .241 | .265 | .395 |
| Van Der Bosch, Matthew, Lowell * | 60 | 267 | 225 | 52 | 61 | 90 | 8 | 6 | 3 | 21 | 1 | 2 | 4 | 35 | 0 | 44 | 28 | 1 | 0 | .271 | .376 | .400 |
| Vechionacci, Marcos, Staten Island † | 19 | 84 | 72 | 13 | 21 | 26 | 5 | 0 | 0 | 8 | 0 | 0 | 1 | 11 | 0 | 13 | 0 | 0 | 2 | .292 | .393 | .361 |
| Vital, Kevin, Tri-City * | 60 | 216 | 183 | 24 | 44 | 78 | 9 | 2 | 7 | 36 | 1 | 2 | 3 | 27 | 1 | 59 | 4 | 0 | 3 | .240 | .344 | .426 |
| Vroman, Douglas, Vermont | 70 | 273 | 228 | 42 | 53 | 93 | 16 | 0 | 8 | 30 | 1 | 2 | 1 | 41 | 0 | 55 | 9 | 6 | 1 | .232 | .349 | .408 |
| Walker, Neil, Williamsport † | 8 | 36 | 33 | 2 | 10 | 13 | 3 | 0 | 0 | 7 | 0 | 1 | 0 | 2 | 0 | 1 | 1 | 2 | 0 | .303 | .333 | .394 |
| Walls, Michael, Tri-City | 12 | 28 | 24 | 6 | 7 | 12 | 2 | 0 | 1 | 5 | 1 | 1 | 0 | 2 | 0 | 4 | 1 | 0 | 1 | .292 | .333 | .500 |
| Wargo, Cody, Aberdeen | 33 | 93 | 78 | 5 | 14 | 18 | 4 | 0 | 0 | 4 | 2 | 1 | 0 | 12 | 0 | 27 | 2 | 0 | 1 | .179 | .286 | .231 |
| Webber, Levi, New Jersey | 58 | 200 | 179 | 26 | 44 | 74 | 10 | 1 | 6 | 21 | 0 | 2 | 0 | 19 | 0 | 48 | 2 | 2 | 2 | .246 | .315 | .413 |

| Player, Team | G | TPA | AB | R | H | TB | 2B | 3B | HR | RBI | SH | SF | HP | BB | IBB | SO | SB | CS | GDP | Avg. | OBP | Slg. |
|---|---|---|---|---|---|---|---|---|---|---|---|---|---|---|---|---|---|---|---|---|---|---|
| Williams, Devoris, Lowell † | 47 | 142 | 118 | 15 | 24 | 31 | 3 | 2 | 0 | 6 | 0 | 0 | 4 | 20 | 0 | 40 | 8 | 9 | 2 | .203 | .338 | .263 |
| Williams, Matt, Oneonta † | 39 | 82 | 71 | 11 | 14 | 20 | 3 | 0 | 1 | 4 | 1 | 0 | 1 | 9 | 0 | 26 | 7 | 4 | 1 | .197 | .296 | .282 |
| Williams, Simon, New Jersey | 6 | 21 | 17 | 3 | 6 | 6 | 0 | 0 | 0 | 3 | 0 | 0 | 0 | 4 | 0 | 5 | 0 | 1 | 0 | .353 | .476 | .353 |
| Woodruff, Bud, Hudson Valley | 21 | 76 | 70 | 3 | 9 | 13 | 4 | 0 | 0 | 5 | 0 | 1 | 0 | 5 | 0 | 31 | 0 | 0 | 0 | .129 | .184 | .186 |
| Yarbrough, Brandon, New Jersey * | 5 | 15 | 14 | 1 | 2 | 2 | 0 | 0 | 0 | 1 | 0 | 0 | 0 | 1 | 0 | 5 | 0 | 0 | 0 | .143 | .200 | .143 |
| Zamora, Hector, Staten Island * | 55 | 229 | 187 | 30 | 54 | 75 | 10 | 1 | 3 | 20 | 1 | 1 | 5 | 35 | 3 | 47 | 0 | 1 | 5 | .289 | .412 | .401 |
| Zobrist, Benjamin, Tri-City † | 68 | 310 | 257 | 50 | 87 | 119 | 14 | 3 | 4 | 45 | 4 | 2 | 4 | 43 | 0 | 31 | 15 | 4 | 5 | .339 | .438 | .463 |

GRAND SLAMS—Toregas, 2; Davidson, Garza, Hall, Harris, Koch, Llamas, Metropoulos, Otness, Pence, Vital, 1 each.

AWARDED FIRST BASE ON CATCHER'S INTERFERENCE—Grimm 3 (Koenig, Nelson, Ryan); Armstrong (Caradonna); Ledbetter (Norman); Nielsen (Woodruff); Sewell (Palmer).

# 2004 PITCHING

## TEAM

| Team | W | L | Pct. | ERA | G | CG | ShO | Sv. | IP | H | TBF | R | ER | HR | SH | SF | HB | BB | IBB | SO | WP | Bk. |
|---|---|---|---|---|---|---|---|---|---|---|---|---|---|---|---|---|---|---|---|---|---|---|
| Hudson Valley | 39 | 33 | .542 | 3.01 | 72 | 2 | 5 | 19 | 619.2 | 544 | 2596 | 272 | 207 | 27 | 20 | 18 | 47 | 179 | 3 | 554 | 66 | 5 |
| Brooklyn | 43 | 31 | .581 | 3.10 | 74 | 0 | 10 | 20 | 652.2 | 582 | 2711 | 282 | 225 | 41 | 27 | 20 | 32 | 207 | 10 | 594 | 32 | 3 |
| Tri-City | 50 | 25 | .667 | 3.15 | 75 | 2 | 5 | 26 | 672.0 | 544 | 2794 | 271 | 235 | 45 | 22 | 14 | 32 | 264 | 3 | 667 | 54 | 3 |
| Auburn | 50 | 24 | .676 | 3.40 | 74 | 1 | 5 | 23 | 645.1 | 610 | 2766 | 296 | 244 | 26 | 18 | 13 | 46 | 221 | 11 | 574 | 44 | 6 |
| New Jersey | 41 | 34 | .547 | 3.46 | 75 | 3 | 7 | 22 | 676.0 | 650 | 2840 | 302 | 260 | 36 | 24 | 13 | 37 | 201 | 8 | 564 | 40 | 4 |
| Oneonta | 33 | 41 | .446 | 3.57 | 74 | 1 | 5 | 16 | 667.1 | 649 | 2923 | 342 | 265 | 32 | 22 | 23 | 48 | 277 | 19 | 592 | 58 | 7 |
| Williamsport | 34 | 40 | .459 | 3.62 | 74 | 2 | 3 | 16 | 641.1 | 634 | 2710 | 323 | 258 | 47 | 17 | 18 | 39 | 154 | 11 | 474 | 32 | 0 |
| Staten Island | 28 | 44 | .389 | 3.75 | 72 | 2 | 2 | 10 | 653.0 | 666 | 2835 | 338 | 272 | 35 | 23 | 22 | 31 | 239 | 2 | 555 | 43 | 4 |
| Mahoning Valley | 42 | 34 | .553 | 3.86 | 76 | 0 | 2 | 18 | 670.2 | 637 | 2931 | 371 | 288 | 46 | 20 | 18 | 46 | 258 | 7 | 652 | 55 | 6 |
| Lowell | 32 | 44 | .421 | 3.95 | 76 | 0 | 4 | 16 | 685.2 | 635 | 2939 | 362 | 301 | 48 | 23 | 23 | 46 | 239 | 1 | 711 | 65 | 8 |
| Vermont | 34 | 38 | .472 | 4.13 | 72 | 2 | 2 | 21 | 614.2 | 620 | 2708 | 350 | 282 | 31 | 16 | 25 | 32 | 266 | 8 | 527 | 31 | 6 |
| Batavia | 28 | 46 | .378 | 4.20 | 74 | 0 | 3 | 13 | 653.0 | 700 | 2895 | 392 | 305 | 42 | 19 | 26 | 48 | 227 | 9 | 543 | 46 | 12 |
| Aberdeen | 35 | 40 | .467 | 4.33 | 75 | 0 | 1 | 25 | 673.2 | 682 | 2938 | 391 | 324 | 52 | 20 | 21 | 38 | 259 | 10 | 625 | 36 | 6 |
| Jamestown | 30 | 45 | .400 | 4.34 | 75 | 0 | 2 | 16 | 653.1 | 687 | 2919 | 417 | 315 | 61 | 28 | 24 | 59 | 237 | 5 | 601 | 46 | 12 |



## INDIVIDUAL

### TOP QUALIFIERS FOR EARNED-RUN AVERAGE TITLE

Minimum 61 innings. *Lefthanded pitcher.

| Pitcher, Team | W | L | Pct. | ERA | G | GS | CG | ShO | GF | Sv. | IP | H | TBF | R | ER | HR | SH | SF | HB | BB | IBB | SO | WP | Bk. |
|---|---|---|---|---|---|---|---|---|---|---|---|---|---|---|---|---|---|---|---|---|---|---|---|---|
| Sanchez, Anibal, Lowell | 3 | 4 | .429 | 1.77 | 15 | 15 | 0 | 0 | 0 | 0 | 76.1 | 43 | 310 | 24 | 15 | 3 | 3 | 4 | 6 | 29 | 0 | 101 | 2 | 1 |
| Devaney, Michael, Brooklyn | 5 | 0 | 1.000 | 1.95 | 14 | 14 | 0 | 0 | 0 | 0 | 69.1 | 58 | 273 | 19 | 15 | 1 | 5 | 2 | 2 | 29 | 0 | 56 | 2 | 0 |
| Martinez, Ronnie, Tri-City | 11 | 2 | .846 | 1.96 | 15 | 15 | 1 | 0 | 0 | 0 | 92.0 | 62 | 348 | 21 | 20 | 6 | 3 | 2 | 2 | 20 | 0 | 81 | 2 | 0 |
| Williams, Joseph, Brooklyn * | 5 | 4 | .556 | 2.28 | 15 | 15 | 0 | 0 | 0 | 0 | 75.0 | 62 | 305 | 26 | 19 | 3 | 6 | 4 | 4 | 26 | 1 | 64 | 0 | 0 |
| Johnson, Blair, Williamsport | 6 | 1 | .857 | 2.44 | 14 | 14 | 2 | 0 | 0 | 0 | 88.2 | 62 | 341 | 34 | 24 | 2 | 4 | 3 | 7 | 12 | 0 | 40 | 4 | 0 |
| MacLane, Evan, Brooklyn * | 5 | 2 | .714 | 2.48 | 12 | 12 | 0 | 0 | 0 | 0 | 69.0 | 61 | 272 | 27 | 19 | 5 | 3 | 2 | 2 | 6 | 0 | 68 | 2 | 0 |
| Beam, T.J., Staten Island | 2 | 4 | .333 | 2.57 | 12 | 12 | 1 | 0 | 0 | 0 | 66.2 | 61 | 269 | 28 | 19 | 4 | 5 | 3 | 3 | 14 | 0 | 69 | 1 | 2 |
| Henderson, Jim, Vermont | 2 | 6 | .250 | 2.59 | 14 | 13 | 0 | 0 | 0 | 0 | 76.1 | 60 | 313 | 34 | 22 | 2 | 6 | 8 | 2 | 27 | 1 | 39 | 0 | 0 |
| Hertzler, Barry, Lowell | 4 | 3 | .571 | 2.67 | 15 | 9 | 0 | 0 | 1 | 0 | 81.0 | 69 | 322 | 25 | 24 | 3 | 4 | 1 | 2 | 23 | 0 | 73 | 8 | 1 |
| Aguero, Miguel, New Jersey | 5 | 5 | .500 | 2.97 | 15 | 14 | 1 | 0 | 0 | 0 | 91.0 | 92 | 367 | 33 | 30 | 4 | 6 | 1 | 2 | 22 | 0 | 82 | 2 | 0 |
| Hankins, Derek, Williamsport | 6 | 4 | .600 | 3.04 | 14 | 14 | 0 | 0 | 0 | 0 | 83.0 | 72 | 333 | 33 | 28 | 9 | 4 | 1 | 5 | 14 | 0 | 57 | 1 | 0 |
| Diaz, Raymar, Tri-City | 6 | 5 | .545 | 3.19 | 15 | 15 | 0 | 0 | 0 | 0 | 79.0 | 70 | 331 | 36 | 28 | 9 | 6 | 5 | 0 | 31 | 0 | 70 | 1 | 1 |
| Guillory, Matthew, Williamsport | 6 | 5 | .545 | 3.36 | 14 | 13 | 0 | 0 | 0 | 0 | 75.0 | 67 | 300 | 33 | 28 | 4 | 1 | 3 | 7 | 13 | 0 | 52 | 1 | 0 |
| Mann, Brandon, Hudson Valley * | 5 | 5 | .500 | 3.38 | 14 | 14 | 0 | 0 | 0 | 0 | 72.0 | 67 | 300 | 33 | 27 | 3 | 2 | 4 | 7 | 18 | 0 | 68 | 5 | 0 |
| Perez, Carlos, Aberdeen * | 3 | 5 | .375 | 3.53 | 15 | 14 | 0 | 0 | 0 | 0 | 79.0 | 67 | 319 | 41 | 31 | 7 | 4 | 3 | 2 | 28 | 0 | 77 | 1 | 1 |

DEPARTMENTAL LEADERS: W—R. Martinez, 11; L—Kendrick, 8; Pct.—Escobar, 1.000; G—Hlebovy, Doyne, 30; GS—Six tied with 15; CG—B. Johnson, 2; ShO—Three tied with one; GF—Hlebovy, 26; Sv.—Hlebovy, 16; IP—R. Martinez, 92.0; H—Baldwin, 96; TBF—Aguero, 367; R—Griffith, 54; ER—Brocato, 44; HR—Four tied with nine; SH—Three tied with 7; SF—Henderson, 8; HB—Jecmen, 10; BB—McKeller, 39; IBB—Four tied with four; SO—A. Sanchez, 101; WP—King, 12; BK—J. Rodriguez, Sipp, 3.

### ALL PITCHERS

*Lefthanded pitcher.

| Pitcher, Team | W | L | Pct. | ERA | G | GS | CG | ShO | GF | Sv. | IP | H | TBF | R | ER | HR | SH | SF | HB | BB | IBB | SO | WP | Bk. |
|---|---|---|---|---|---|---|---|---|---|---|---|---|---|---|---|---|---|---|---|---|---|---|---|---|
| Abreu, Eric, Staten Island | 3 | 0 | 1.000 | 1.63 | 7 | 2 | 0 | 0 | 2 | 0 | 27.2 | 24 | 111 | 5 | 5 | 1 | 1 | 0 | 3 | 6 | 0 | 47 | 1 | 0 |
| Acosta, Adam, New Jersey | 1 | 1 | .500 | 3.55 | 6 | 1 | 0 | 0 | 1 | 0 | 12.2 | 18 | 57 | 7 | 5 | 0 | 0 | 0 | 0 | 3 | 0 | 9 | 0 | 0 |
| Aguero, Miguel, New Jersey | 5 | 5 | .500 | 2.97 | 15 | 14 | 1 | 0 | 0 | 0 | 91.0 | 92 | 367 | 33 | 30 | 4 | 6 | 1 | 2 | 22 | 0 | 82 | 2 | 0 |
| Ainsworth, Kurt, Aberdeen | 0 | 1 | .000 | 1.35 | 2 | 2 | 0 | 0 | 0 | 0 | 6.2 | 2 | 26 | 1 | 1 | 0 | 1 | 0 | 0 | 3 | 0 | 8 | 1 | 0 |
| Alexander, Stu, Jamestown | 0 | 1 | .000 | 8.00 | 2 | 2 | 0 | 0 | 0 | 0 | 9.0 | 14 | 42 | 11 | 8 | 2 | 1 | 0 | 1 | 1 | 0 | 6 | 0 | 0 |
| Alfonzo, Edgar, Brooklyn * | 3 | 2 | .600 | 3.21 | 20 | 1 | 0 | 0 | 5 | 0 | 42.0 | 50 | 189 | 21 | 15 | 6 | 0 | 0 | 1 | 12 | 1 | 33 | 1 | 1 |
| Allen, Kyle, Batavia * | 2 | 3 | .400 | 3.46 | 14 | 1 | 0 | 0 | 8 | 2 | 39.0 | 38 | 171 | 16 | 15 | 0 | 1 | 2 | 1 | 14 | 1 | 36 | 2 | 0 |
| Almenar, Aristides, Brooklyn | 0 | 1 | .000 | 1.46 | 7 | 0 | 0 | 0 | 3 | 0 | 12.1 | 11 | 52 | 2 | 2 | 1 | 0 | 0 | 1 | 3 | 0 | 14 | 1 | 0 |
| Alvarado, Andrew, Tri-City | 4 | 3 | .571 | 3.58 | 11 | 10 | 1 | 0 | 0 | 0 | 50.1 | 47 | 218 | 23 | 20 | 4 | 4 | 1 | 5 | 24 | 0 | 41 | 4 | 0 |
| Azze, Justin, Aberdeen * | 0 | 1 | .000 | 5.82 | 20 | 0 | 0 | 0 | 13 | 1 | 34.0 | 38 | 152 | 22 | 22 | 4 | 0 | 0 | 1 | 13 | 0 | 29 | 4 | 1 |
| Baird, Jack, New Jersey | 0 | 1 | .000 | 1.50 | 5 | 0 | 0 | 0 | 2 | 0 | 6.0 | 5 | 26 | 1 | 1 | 0 | 0 | 0 | 1 | 2 | 1 | 3 | 1 | 0 |
| Baldwin, Andrew, Batavia | 4 | 6 | .400 | 5.17 | 15 | 15 | 0 | 0 | 0 | 0 | 71.1 | 96 | 322 | 50 | 41 | 2 | 5 | 4 | 3 | 14 | 0 | 54 | 4 | 1 |
| Barkley, Richard, Staten Island | 1 | 1 | .500 | 1.35 | 4 | 0 | 0 | 0 | 4 | 0 | 6.2 | 6 | 30 | 1 | 1 | 0 | 0 | 0 | 0 | 4 | 0 | 2 | 0 | 0 |
| Barone, Daniel, Jamestown | 3 | 6 | .333 | 5.08 | 19 | 2 | 0 | 0 | 5 | 0 | 51.1 | 60 | 225 | 31 | 29 | 9 | 1 | 0 | 2 | 11 | 0 | 45 | 3 | 0 |
| Barratt, Jon, Hudson Valley * | 2 | 3 | .400 | 2.74 | 10 | 10 | 1 | 0 | 0 | 0 | 42.2 | 38 | 179 | 21 | 13 | 2 | 3 | 1 | 1 | 11 | 0 | 50 | 4 | 1 |
| Barriger, Marcus, Hudson Valley | 2 | 2 | .500 | 4.54 | 14 | 0 | 0 | 0 | 1 | 1 | 35.2 | 43 | 164 | 24 | 18 | 6 | 0 | 1 | 6 | 8 | 0 | 26 | 2 | 2 |
| Baxter, Allen, Jamestown | 0 | 4 | .000 | 6.17 | 10 | 10 | 0 | 0 | 0 | 0 | 35.0 | 34 | 169 | 31 | 24 | 1 | 1 | 0 | 6 | 32 | 0 | 27 | 5 | 2 |
| Baysinger, Daniel, New Jersey | 1 | 0 | 1.000 | 2.00 | 8 | 0 | 0 | 0 | 3 | 0 | 9.0 | 8 | 40 | 2 | 2 | 0 | 0 | 0 | 0 | 5 | 0 | 2 | 0 | 0 |
| Baysinger, Trent, Aberdeen * | 0 | 4 | .000 | 4.69 | 26 | 0 | 0 | 0 | 8 | 1 | 40.1 | 48 | 174 | 23 | 21 | 4 | 1 | 0 | 2 | 8 | 0 | 22 | 2 | 1 |

| Pitcher, Team | W | L | Pct. | ERA | G | GS | CG | ShO | GF | Sv. | IP | H | TBF | R | ER | HR | SH | SF | HB | BB | IBB | SO | WP | Bk. |
|---|---|---|---|---|---|---|---|---|---|---|---|---|---|---|---|---|---|---|---|---|---|---|---|---|
| Bell, Kristian, Auburn | 4 | 0 | 1.000 | 5.85 | 19 | 0 | 0 | 0 | 6 | 1 | 32.1 | 30 | 153 | 22 | 21 | 1 | 0 | 0 | 4 | 22 | 0 | 32 | 8 | 0 |
| Bigda, Drew, Hudson Valley * | 0 | 0 | .000 | 0.00 | 2 | 0 | 0 | 0 | 2 | 0 | 2.0 | 1 | 7 | 0 | 0 | 0 | 0 | 0 | 0 | 0 | 0 | 2 | 0 | 0 |
| Bisenius, Joseph, Batavia | 0 | 1 | .000 | 1.43 | 11 | 11 | 0 | 0 | 0 | 0 | 50.1 | 39 | 199 | 12 | 8 | 5 | 3 | 3 | 1 | 14 | 0 | 38 | 4 | 1 |
| Bishop, Matthew, Williamsport | 0 | 1 | .000 | 3.70 | 20 | 0 | 0 | 0 | 6 | 0 | 24.1 | 30 | 107 | 13 | 10 | 1 | 0 | 0 | 1 | 3 | 0 | 21 | 2 | 0 |
| Bitter, Ryan, Hudson Valley | 3 | 1 | .750 | 0.95 | 21 | 0 | 0 | 0 | 17 | 4 | 28.1 | 17 | 106 | 6 | 3 | 1 | 0 | 0 | 1 | 3 | 0 | 37 | 2 | 0 |
| Blackwell, Brad, Staten Island | 1 | 1 | .500 | 2.31 | 21 | 0 | 0 | 0 | 10 | 1 | 35.0 | 26 | 154 | 9 | 9 | 1 | 0 | 0 | 2 | 21 | 0 | 25 | 4 | 0 |
| Bloom, Kyle, Williamsport * | 4 | 3 | .571 | 2.60 | 12 | 12 | 0 | 0 | 0 | 0 | 45.0 | 34 | 179 | 19 | 13 | 2 | 1 | 2 | 0 | 13 | 0 | 46 | 1 | 0 |
| Boehm, Kyle, Aberdeen | 2 | 2 | .500 | 5.14 | 19 | 2 | 0 | 0 | 3 | 0 | 42.0 | 48 | 204 | 33 | 24 | 3 | 4 | 0 | 4 | 28 | 0 | 42 | 3 | 0 |
| Bono, Kyle, Lowell | 0 | 1 | .000 | 3.00 | 6 | 5 | 0 | 0 | 0 | 0 | 12.0 | 4 | 47 | 4 | 4 | 1 | 0 | 0 | 2 | 5 | 0 | 17 | 0 | 0 |
| Bova, Chris, New Jersey | 1 | 4 | .200 | 3.76 | 19 | 6 | 0 | 0 | 3 | 1 | 52.2 | 49 | 227 | 29 | 22 | 0 | 2 | 2 | 7 | 16 | 1 | 32 | 3 | 0 |
| Brandenburg, Adam, Jamestown * | 0 | 1 | .000 | 0.00 | 3 | 0 | 0 | 0 | 2 | 0 | 5.0 | 5 | 23 | 3 | 0 | 0 | 0 | 0 | 0 | 3 | 1 | 8 | 1 | 0 |
| Brocato, Russ, Aberdeen | 3 | 5 | .375 | 6.64 | 15 | 12 | 0 | 0 | 0 | 0 | 59.2 | 76 | 280 | 51 | 44 | 7 | 1 | 3 | 3 | 26 | 0 | 36 | 1 | 0 |
| Brown, Casey, Tri-City | 4 | 1 | .800 | 3.11 | 21 | 0 | 0 | 0 | 9 | 4 | 46.1 | 37 | 189 | 17 | 16 | 3 | 0 | 0 | 1 | 13 | 0 | 40 | 4 | 0 |
| Bryan, Guillermo, Staten Island | 0 | 0 | .000 | 0.00 | 1 | 0 | 0 | 0 | 0 | 0 | 0.2 | 2 | 4 | 1 | 0 | 0 | 0 | 0 | 0 | 0 | 0 | 0 | 0 | 0 |
| Bumstead, Nathan, Oneonta | 3 | 1 | .750 | 2.03 | 11 | 9 | 0 | 0 | 0 | 0 | 57.2 | 47 | 236 | 21 | 13 | 3 | 3 | 4 | 6 | 15 | 0 | 75 | 4 | 0 |
| Bunn, William, Vermont | 3 | 0 | 1.000 | 3.00 | 9 | 5 | 0 | 0 | 3 | 0 | 24.0 | 16 | 95 | 8 | 8 | 1 | 1 | 2 | 0 | 12 | 0 | 27 | 0 | 0 |
| Camacho, Eddie, Brooklyn * | 3 | 1 | .750 | 0.69 | 18 | 0 | 0 | 0 | 7 | 1 | 39.0 | 19 | 148 | 4 | 3 | 1 | 0 | 0 | 1 | 11 | 2 | 38 | 2 | 1 |
| Camacho, Johan, Brooklyn | 0 | 0 | .000 | 0.00 | 1 | 0 | 0 | 0 | 0 | 0 | 1.0 | 1 | 4 | 0 | 0 | 0 | 0 | 0 | 0 | 0 | 0 | 1 | 0 | 0 |
| Campbell, Richard, Vermont | 0 | 1 | .000 | 4.09 | 11 | 0 | 0 | 0 | 5 | 0 | 22.0 | 24 | 100 | 14 | 10 | 3 | 0 | 0 | 0 | 10 | 1 | 25 | 2 | 0 |
| Cannon, Edward, Auburn | 0 | 0 | .000 | 0.00 | 1 | 0 | 0 | 0 | 0 | 0 | 3.0 | 2 | 13 | 3 | 0 | 1 | 0 | 0 | 1 | 0 | 0 | 4 | 0 | 0 |
| Cantu, Tim, New Jersey | 0 | 1 | .000 | 0.00 | 1 | 0 | 0 | 0 | 1 | 0 | 1.0 | 0 | 4 | 1 | 0 | 0 | 0 | 0 | 1 | 0 | 0 | 1 | 0 | 0 |
| Capps, Matt, Williamsport | 3 | 5 | .375 | 4.85 | 11 | 11 | 0 | 0 | 0 | 0 | 65.0 | 84 | 279 | 43 | 35 | 7 | 3 | 1 | 2 | 4 | 1 | 33 | 1 | 0 |
| Cerezo, Hector, Vermont * | 0 | 1 | .000 | 3.68 | 9 | 0 | 0 | 0 | 3 | 1 | 14.2 | 11 | 59 | 8 | 6 | 4 | 0 | 0 | 1 | 3 | 0 | 21 | 0 | 0 |
| Cheng, Chi-hung, Auburn * | 0 | 0 | .000 | 4.50 | 1 | 0 | 0 | 0 | 0 | 0 | 2.0 | 1 | 7 | 1 | 1 | 1 | 0 | 0 | 0 | 0 | 0 | 3 | 0 | 0 |
| Childs, Ryan, Aberdeen | 3 | 3 | .500 | 4.06 | 21 | 6 | 0 | 0 | 5 | 1 | 51.0 | 57 | 229 | 29 | 23 | 4 | 2 | 4 | 2 | 17 | 2 | 30 | 2 | 0 |
| Clelland, Edward, Oneonta * | 5 | 0 | 1.000 | 1.96 | 25 | 0 | 0 | 0 | 14 | 3 | 41.1 | 41 | 176 | 14 | 9 | 0 | 0 | 1 | 0 | 12 | 3 | 38 | 1 | 0 |
| Cobb, Matt, Hudson Valley * | 4 | 6 | .400 | 3.45 | 13 | 10 | 0 | 0 | 2 | 0 | 60.0 | 59 | 250 | 29 | 23 | 3 | 2 | 4 | 5 | 15 | 0 | 58 | 4 | 0 |
| Cochran, Robert, Lowell * | 0 | 4 | .000 | 5.00 | 22 | 0 | 0 | 0 | 10 | 3 | 36.0 | 39 | 162 | 24 | 20 | 2 | 0 | 1 | 4 | 12 | 1 | 33 | 3 | 0 |
| Contreras, Manuel, Oneonta | 1 | 2 | .333 | 9.00 | 5 | 0 | 0 | 0 | 2 | 0 | 8.0 | 21 | 43 | 8 | 8 | 1 | 1 | 0 | 0 | 1 | 0 | 7 | 0 | 1 |
| Cook, Steven, Vermont | 2 | 7 | .222 | 5.12 | 13 | 11 | 0 | 0 | 0 | 0 | 58.0 | 75 | 266 | 39 | 33 | 2 | 1 | 2 | 4 | 11 | 0 | 43 | 3 | 0 |
| Correa, Jose, Batavia | 3 | 2 | .600 | 5.35 | 22 | 0 | 0 | 0 | 14 | 2 | 37.0 | 38 | 165 | 28 | 22 | 5 | 0 | 0 | 2 | 15 | 2 | 34 | 6 | 1 |
| Cox, Benjamin, Vermont | 2 | 0 | 1.000 | 2.97 | 22 | 0 | 0 | 0 | 10 | 3 | 33.1 | 31 | 153 | 18 | 11 | 1 | 0 | 0 | 2 | 20 | 0 | 37 | 2 | 0 |
| Craig, Dustin, Williamsport | 1 | 6 | .143 | 2.94 | 28 | 0 | 0 | 0 | 20 | 11 | 33.2 | 32 | 147 | 14 | 11 | 2 | 0 | 0 | 2 | 12 | 4 | 31 | 4 | 0 |
| Cuen, David, Staten Island * | 2 | 2 | .500 | 6.34 | 20 | 0 | 0 | 0 | 8 | 0 | 38.1 | 44 | 180 | 27 | 27 | 4 | 0 | 0 | 0 | 21 | 1 | 36 | 7 | 0 |
| Day, Dewon, Auburn | 0 | 3 | .000 | 1.50 | 27 | 0 | 0 | 0 | 22 | 8 | 24.0 | 24 | 108 | 8 | 4 | 0 | 0 | 0 | 2 | 10 | 2 | 28 | 3 | 0 |
| De La Cruz, Jose, Hudson Valley | 2 | 0 | 1.000 | 1.10 | 17 | 0 | 0 | 0 | 11 | 7 | 41.0 | 28 | 163 | 8 | 5 | 0 | 0 | 0 | 1 | 11 | 0 | 42 | 6 | 1 |
| De La Rosa, Dane, Staten Island | 0 | 0 | .000 | 0.00 | 1 | 0 | 0 | 0 | 1 | 0 | 1.2 | 1 | 8 | 2 | 0 | 0 | 0 | 0 | 0 | 2 | 0 | 1 | 0 | 0 |
| De Los Santos, Richard, Mahoning Valley | 1 | 5 | .167 | 5.26 | 13 | 9 | 0 | 0 | 0 | 0 | 51.1 | 53 | 224 | 34 | 30 | 2 | 4 | 4 | 6 | 19 | 0 | 45 | 2 | 1 |
| Delacruz, Eduardo, Hudson Valley | 3 | 6 | .333 | 3.91 | 15 | 14 | 0 | 0 | 1 | 1 | 69.0 | 54 | 292 | 34 | 30 | 6 | 4 | 3 | 8 | 31 | 0 | 65 | 8 | 1 |
| Della rocco, Chris, New Jersey | 2 | 3 | .400 | 4.00 | 19 | 9 | 0 | 0 | 5 | 1 | 63.0 | 62 | 264 | 35 | 28 | 7 | 4 | 2 | 2 | 17 | 0 | 33 | 3 | 1 |
| Devaney, Michael, Brooklyn | 5 | 0 | 1.000 | 1.95 | 14 | 14 | 0 | 0 | 0 | 0 | 69.1 | 58 | 273 | 19 | 15 | 1 | 5 | 2 | 2 | 29 | 0 | 56 | 2 | 0 |
| Dewitt, Anthony, Tri-City | 1 | 0 | 1.000 | 3.00 | 13 | 0 | 0 | 0 | 4 | 0 | 21.0 | 18 | 93 | 10 | 7 | 0 | 0 | 0 | 1 | 11 | 0 | 18 | 3 | 0 |
| Diaz, Eddie, Vermont | 1 | 2 | .333 | 7.31 | 16 | 0 | 0 | 0 | 7 | 0 | 28.1 | 33 | 134 | 24 | 23 | 3 | 0 | 0 | 5 | 13 | 0 | 38 | 4 | 0 |
| Diaz, Raymar, Tri-City | 6 | 5 | .545 | 3.19 | 15 | 15 | 0 | 0 | 0 | 0 | 79.0 | 70 | 331 | 36 | 28 | 9 | 6 | 5 | 0 | 31 | 0 | 70 | 1 | 1 |
| Dicken, Randy, Auburn | 0 | 0 | .000 | 4.86 | 8 | 3 | 0 | 0 | 2 | 1 | 16.2 | 21 | 84 | 10 | 9 | 0 | 1 | 1 | 2 | 13 | 0 | 20 | 2 | 0 |
| Dickerson, Bi, New Jersey | 0 | 0 | .000 | 1.80 | 1 | 1 | 0 | 0 | 0 | 0 | 5.0 | 3 | 17 | 2 | 1 | 0 | 1 | 0 | 0 | 1 | 0 | 4 | 0 | 0 |
| Dobies, Andrew, Lowell * | 0 | 2 | .000 | 2.03 | 14 | 14 | 0 | 0 | 0 | 0 | 26.2 | 17 | 104 | 9 | 6 | 0 | 0 | 1 | 0 | 8 | 0 | 36 | 2 | 0 |
| Dove, Dennis, New Jersey | 0 | 5 | .000 | 8.06 | 6 | 6 | 0 | 0 | 0 | 0 | 22.1 | 31 | 106 | 20 | 20 | 3 | 0 | 1 | 2 | 13 | 0 | 24 | 7 | 0 |
| Doyne, Cory, New Jersey | 2 | 0 | 1.000 | 2.33 | 30 | 0 | 0 | 0 | 22 | 12 | 38.2 | 19 | 148 | 10 | 10 | 2 | 0 | 0 | 1 | 12 | 1 | 48 | 3 | 0 |
| Drage, Derek, Williamsport | 4 | 1 | .800 | 2.01 | 17 | 0 | 0 | 0 | 5 | 1 | 22.1 | 14 | 88 | 6 | 5 | 3 | 0 | 0 | 3 | 4 | 0 | 26 | 0 | 0 |
| Dumesnil, Bryan, Aberdeen * | 1 | 0 | 1.000 | 4.32 | 4 | 0 | 0 | 0 | 1 | 0 | 8.1 | 11 | 42 | 4 | 4 | 0 | 0 | 1 | 0 | 5 | 1 | 5 | 0 | 0 |
| Eager, Blake, Brooklyn | 0 | 0 | .000 | 0.00 | 2 | 0 | 0 | 0 | 1 | 0 | 3.1 | 0 | 10 | 0 | 0 | 0 | 0 | 0 | 0 | 0 | 0 | 4 | 0 | 0 |
| Eddy, Cooper, Lowell | 3 | 3 | .500 | 4.29 | 21 | 0 | 0 | 0 | 12 | 2 | 35.2 | 41 | 158 | 22 | 17 | 2 | 0 | 0 | 2 | 8 | 0 | 27 | 3 | 1 |
| Edmiston, Bo, Tri-City | 3 | 1 | .750 | 3.74 | 20 | 0 | 0 | 0 | 9 | 2 | 45.2 | 38 | 185 | 23 | 19 | 4 | 0 | 0 | 0 | 10 | 0 | 43 | 4 | 0 |
| Edwards, Andrew, Staten Island | 1 | 5 | .167 | 6.04 | 14 | 7 | 0 | 0 | 3 | 0 | 47.2 | 57 | 220 | 35 | 32 | 5 | 3 | 4 | 3 | 15 | 0 | 38 | 5 | 0 |
| Englebrook, Evan, Tri-City | 2 | 4 | .333 | 3.94 | 14 | 14 | 0 | 0 | 0 | 0 | 61.2 | 58 | 263 | 30 | 27 | 5 | 5 | 2 | 5 | 28 | 0 | 71 | 8 | 2 |
| Escobar, Rodrigo, Tri-City | 8 | 0 | 1.000 | 1.33 | 25 | 2 | 0 | 0 | 12 | 7 | 54.1 | 37 | 213 | 9 | 8 | 2 | 0 | 0 | 1 | 16 | 3 | 62 | 8 | 0 |
| Estrada, Paul, Tri-City | 5 | 1 | .833 | 2.81 | 23 | 0 | 0 | 0 | 13 | 8 | 41.2 | 26 | 171 | 13 | 13 | 4 | 0 | 0 | 3 | 17 | 0 | 56 | 10 | 0 |
| Felix, Wilkin, Aberdeen | 1 | 0 | 1.000 | 5.19 | 7 | 0 | 0 | 0 | 0 | 0 | 8.2 | 13 | 42 | 7 | 5 | 0 | 0 | 0 | 0 | 3 | 0 | 3 | 1 | 0 |
| Figueroa, Juan, Oneonta | 1 | 2 | .333 | 5.68 | 9 | 0 | 0 | 0 | 3 | 1 | 12.2 | 10 | 67 | 8 | 8 | 1 | 0 | 0 | 2 | 17 | 1 | 14 | 3 | 0 |
| Garcia, Harvey, Lowell | 4 | 6 | .400 | 5.16 | 14 | 14 | 0 | 0 | 0 | 0 | 61.0 | 61 | 272 | 40 | 35 | 8 | 3 | 7 | 4 | 30 | 0 | 54 | 7 | 0 |
| Garza, Rudy, Vermont | 0 | 0 | .000 | 0.00 | 2 | 0 | 0 | 0 | 1 | 0 | 3.0 | 2 | 13 | 0 | 0 | 0 | 0 | 0 | 0 | 2 | 0 | 3 | 1 | 0 |
| Gogal, Jeffrey, Jamestown * | 1 | 4 | .200 | 4.56 | 11 | 11 | 0 | 0 | 0 | 0 | 51.1 | 62 | 235 | 36 | 26 | 7 | 7 | 4 | 5 | 16 | 0 | 53 | 0 | 0 |
| Goodson, Matthew, Lowell | 1 | 2 | .333 | 5.10 | 12 | 1 | 0 | 0 | 3 | 0 | 30.0 | 22 | 123 | 20 | 17 | 4 | 1 | 0 | 2 | 12 | 0 | 23 | 2 | 0 |
| Grant, Brian, Auburn | 0 | 1 | .000 | 3.86 | 1 | 1 | 0 | 0 | 0 | 0 | 4.2 | 6 | 23 | 4 | 2 | 0 | 0 | 0 | 0 | 1 | 0 | 5 | 2 | 0 |
| Grant, Jessen, New Jersey | 0 | 0 | .000 | 0.00 | 3 | 0 | 0 | 0 | 0 | 0 | 4.2 | 4 | 18 | 0 | 0 | 0 | 0 | 0 | 0 | 0 | 0 | 1 | 0 | 0 |
| Griffith, Derek, Batavia * | 1 | 7 | .125 | 4.38 | 14 | 14 | 0 | 0 | 0 | 0 | 63.2 | 73 | 296 | 54 | 31 | 4 | 4 | 5 | 9 | 28 | 0 | 44 | 8 | 1 |
| Gross, Michael, New Jersey | 3 | 1 | .750 | 0.98 | 13 | 0 | 0 | 0 | 6 | 3 | 18.1 | 14 | 77 | 3 | 2 | 0 | 0 | 0 | 1 | 7 | 2 | 12 | 0 | 0 |
| Guillory, Matthew, Williamsport | 6 | 5 | .545 | 3.36 | 14 | 13 | 0 | 0 | 0 | 0 | 75.0 | 67 | 300 | 33 | 28 | 4 | 1 | 3 | 7 | 13 | 0 | 52 | 1 | 0 |
| Haberer, Eric, New Jersey * | 0 | 0 | .000 | 2.37 | 3 | 3 | 0 | 0 | 0 | 0 | 19.0 | 14 | 73 | 7 | 5 | 1 | 1 | 1 | 0 | 9 | 0 | 12 | 1 | 1 |
| Haehnel, David, Aberdeen * | 3 | 1 | .750 | 1.69 | 28 | 0 | 0 | 0 | 25 | 15 | 37.1 | 23 | 149 | 8 | 7 | 1 | 0 | 0 | 3 | 11 | 2 | 61 | 1 | 0 |
| Hankins, Derek, Williamsport | 6 | 4 | .600 | 3.04 | 14 | 14 | 0 | 0 | 0 | 0 | 83.0 | 72 | 333 | 33 | 28 | 9 | 4 | 1 | 5 | 14 | 0 | 57 | 1 | 0 |
| Happ, James, Batavia * | 1 | 2 | .333 | 2.02 | 11 | 11 | 0 | 0 | 0 | 0 | 35.2 | 22 | 143 | 8 | 8 | 1 | 1 | 2 | 3 | 18 | 0 | 37 | 0 | 0 |
| Harris, Mark, Mahoning Valley | 3 | 2 | .600 | 3.03 | 29 | 0 | 0 | 0 | 21 | 13 | 35.2 | 35 | 161 | 16 | 12 | 1 | 0 | 0 | 0 | 19 | 2 | 23 | 2 | 0 |
| Haynes, Matt, Mahoning Valley | 4 | 4 | .500 | 4.64 | 18 | 2 | 0 | 0 | 3 | 0 | 42.2 | 35 | 190 | 27 | 22 | 3 | 0 | 1 | 4 | 26 | 0 | 52 | 8 | 1 |
| Henderson, Jim, Vermont | 2 | 6 | .250 | 2.59 | 14 | 13 | 0 | 0 | 0 | 0 | 76.1 | 60 | 313 | 34 | 22 | 2 | 6 | 8 | 2 | 27 | 1 | 39 | 0 | 0 |
| Herce, Steven, Williamsport | 2 | 2 | .500 | 3.46 | 18 | 2 | 0 | 0 | 6 | 0 | 41.2 | 40 | 177 | 19 | 16 | 3 | 0 | 0 | 1 | 11 | 2 | 25 | 2 | 0 |
| Hernandez, Gabriel, Brooklyn | 1 | 0 | 1.000 | 0.00 | 1 | 0 | 0 | 0 | 0 | 0 | 3.0 | 2 | 10 | 0 | 0 | 0 | 0 | 0 | 0 | 0 | 0 | 6 | 0 | 0 |
| Hernandez, Michael, Mahoning Valley * | 1 | 0 | 1.000 | 2.57 | 10 | 0 | 0 | 0 | 0 | 0 | 14.0 | 6 | 61 | 10 | 4 | 0 | 0 | 0 | 2 | 11 | 0 | 18 | 4 | 0 |
| Hertzler, Barry, Lowell | 4 | 3 | .571 | 2.67 | 15 | 9 | 0 | 0 | 1 | 0 | 81.0 | 69 | 322 | 25 | 24 | 3 | 4 | 1 | 2 | 23 | 0 | 73 | 8 | 1 |
| Hill, Danny, Auburn | 0 | 0 | .000 | 1.59 | 8 | 0 | 0 | 0 | 3 | 3 | 11.1 | 9 | 46 | 3 | 2 | 0 | 0 | 0 | 0 | 3 | 0 | 6 | 3 | 0 |
| Hiraldo, Nelson, Mahoning Valley | 1 | 2 | .333 | 7.45 | 7 | 7 | 0 | 0 | 0 | 0 | 29.0 | 47 | 143 | 30 | 24 | 3 | 5 | 3 | 6 | 4 | 0 | 22 | 2 | 0 |

| Pitcher, Team | W | L | Pct. | ERA | G | GS | CG | ShO | GF | Sv. | IP | H | TBF | R | ER | HR | SH | SF | HB | BB | IBB | SO | WP | Bk. |
|---|---|---|---|---|---|---|---|---|---|---|---|---|---|---|---|---|---|---|---|---|---|---|---|---|
| Hlebovy, Gus, Vermont | 3 | 1 | .750 | 4.32 | 30 | 0 | 0 | 0 | 26 | 16 | 33.1 | 38 | 161 | 18 | 16 | 2 | 0 | 0 | 4 | 19 | 3 | 48 | 3 | 0 |
| Hoey, James, Aberdeen | 0 | 1 | .000 | 9.45 | 2 | 2 | 0 | 0 | 0 | 0 | 6.2 | 12 | 34 | 8 | 7 | 1 | 0 | 1 | 0 | 1 | 0 | 6 | 0 | 0 |
| Hoff, Brian, Jamestown | 0 | 3 | .000 | 3.47 | 19 | 0 | 0 | 0 | 8 | 0 | 36.1 | 40 | 158 | 23 | 14 | 0 | 0 | 1 | 0 | 11 | 0 | 26 | 5 | 1 |
| Hogan, Patrick, Jamestown | 0 | 2 | .000 | 4.45 | 25 | 0 | 0 | 0 | 23 | 12 | 28.1 | 32 | 134 | 15 | 14 | 2 | 0 | 0 | 4 | 13 | 1 | 29 | 4 | 0 |
| Hoover, Jesse, Staten Island | 2 | 1 | .667 | 1.78 | 16 | 9 | 0 | 0 | 4 | 1 | 55.2 | 28 | 219 | 14 | 11 | 0 | 7 | 0 | 1 | 26 | 0 | 90 | 4 | 0 |
| Hottovy, Thomas, Lowell * | 0 | 1 | .000 | 0.89 | 14 | 14 | 0 | 0 | 0 | 0 | 30.1 | 24 | 121 | 5 | 3 | 0 | 0 | 0 | 3 | 4 | 0 | 39 | 2 | 0 |
| Hoyman, Justin, Mahoning Valley | 0 | 0 | .000 | 2.08 | 5 | 5 | 0 | 0 | 0 | 0 | 13.0 | 9 | 54 | 3 | 3 | 1 | 0 | 2 | 1 | 4 | 0 | 8 | 0 | 0 |
| Hummel, John, Williamsport * | 0 | 0 | .000 | 4.40 | 8 | 0 | 0 | 0 | 3 | 0 | 14.1 | 21 | 67 | 7 | 7 | 1 | 0 | 2 | 0 | 5 | 0 | 13 | 1 | 0 |
| Hyde, Scott, Brooklyn | 4 | 4 | .500 | 3.86 | 10 | 10 | 0 | 0 | 0 | 0 | 51.1 | 43 | 209 | 24 | 22 | 5 | 3 | 3 | 2 | 18 | 0 | 46 | 2 | 0 |
| Jackson, Zachary, Auburn * | 0 | 0 | .000 | 5.40 | 4 | 4 | 0 | 0 | 0 | 0 | 15.0 | 20 | 69 | 9 | 9 | 1 | 0 | 1 | 0 | 6 | 0 | 11 | 1 | 0 |
| Jacobson, Tyler, Oneonta | 1 | 0 | 1.000 | 3.10 | 19 | 0 | 0 | 0 | 7 | 1 | 29.0 | 23 | 119 | 11 | 10 | 1 | 0 | 0 | 1 | 8 | 2 | 17 | 1 | 0 |
| James, Michael, Lowell | 0 | 4 | .000 | 10.90 | 20 | 0 | 0 | 0 | 6 | 1 | 34.2 | 53 | 178 | 43 | 42 | 7 | 0 | 0 | 4 | 17 | 0 | 34 | 11 | 0 |
| James, Rhett, Jamestown | 5 | 1 | .833 | 3.12 | 17 | 4 | 0 | 0 | 3 | 0 | 43.1 | 37 | 184 | 17 | 15 | 3 | 1 | 0 | 4 | 12 | 0 | 47 | 1 | 2 |
| Janssen, Casey, Auburn | 3 | 1 | .750 | 3.48 | 10 | 10 | 0 | 0 | 0 | 0 | 51.2 | 47 | 208 | 21 | 20 | 2 | 0 | 0 | 2 | 10 | 0 | 45 | 2 | 0 |
| Jecmen, Mark, Mahoning Valley | 3 | 1 | .750 | 5.35 | 20 | 0 | 0 | 0 | 3 | 0 | 33.2 | 32 | 168 | 21 | 20 | 0 | 0 | 0 | 10 | 25 | 0 | 30 | 5 | 0 |
| Jenkins, Clyde, Vermont | 2 | 3 | .400 | 5.33 | 6 | 5 | 0 | 0 | 0 | 0 | 25.1 | 27 | 112 | 20 | 15 | 0 | 2 | 1 | 2 | 15 | 0 | 13 | 3 | 0 |
| Johnson, Blair, Williamsport | 6 | 1 | .857 | 2.44 | 14 | 14 | 2 | 0 | 0 | 0 | 88.2 | 62 | 341 | 34 | 24 | 2 | 4 | 3 | 7 | 12 | 0 | 40 | 4 | 0 |
| Johnson, Nathan, Batavia | 2 | 6 | .250 | 5.30 | 18 | 4 | 0 | 0 | 2 | 0 | 52.2 | 54 | 229 | 38 | 31 | 7 | 0 | 0 | 7 | 11 | 1 | 49 | 1 | 2 |
| Jurrjens, Jair, Oneonta | 1 | 5 | .167 | 5.31 | 7 | 7 | 0 | 0 | 0 | 0 | 39.0 | 50 | 176 | 25 | 23 | 0 | 0 | 2 | 3 | 10 | 1 | 31 | 5 | 1 |
| Kauten, Joshua, Oneonta | 2 | 5 | .286 | 3.92 | 12 | 12 | 1 | 1 | 0 | 0 | 64.1 | 61 | 265 | 41 | 28 | 3 | 7 | 4 | 3 | 16 | 0 | 43 | 3 | 1 |
| Kendrick, Kyle, Batavia | 2 | 8 | .200 | 5.48 | 13 | 12 | 0 | 0 | 0 | 0 | 70.2 | 94 | 317 | 52 | 43 | 6 | 3 | 6 | 5 | 18 | 1 | 53 | 1 | 1 |
| Kiley, Jason, Williamsport | 0 | 2 | .000 | 11.81 | 4 | 0 | 0 | 0 | 2 | 0 | 5.1 | 12 | 32 | 9 | 7 | 1 | 0 | 0 | 2 | 2 | 0 | 5 | 0 | 0 |
| King, Benjamin, Staten Island * | 0 | 0 | .000 | 13.50 | 2 | 0 | 0 | 0 | 2 | 0 | 2.0 | 5 | 13 | 3 | 3 | 0 | 0 | 0 | 1 | 0 | 0 | 0 | 0 | 0 |
| Knippschild, Ryan, Mahoning Valley * | 4 | 3 | .571 | 3.93 | 15 | 13 | 0 | 0 | 0 | 0 | 68.2 | 79 | 290 | 40 | 30 | 7 | 2 | 4 | 0 | 17 | 0 | 39 | 4 | 0 |
| Knox, Matt, Mahoning Valley | 3 | 4 | .429 | 2.25 | 23 | 0 | 0 | 0 | 14 | 3 | 40.0 | 33 | 165 | 15 | 10 | 3 | 0 | 0 | 0 | 12 | 0 | 61 | 5 | 0 |
| Knox, Michael, Staten Island | 3 | 6 | .333 | 5.43 | 15 | 10 | 0 | 0 | 0 | 0 | 61.1 | 84 | 291 | 41 | 37 | 4 | 2 | 5 | 1 | 29 | 0 | 44 | 6 | 0 |
| Konecny, Daniel, Oneonta | 3 | 7 | .300 | 4.02 | 14 | 9 | 0 | 0 | 2 | 0 | 53.2 | 61 | 241 | 31 | 24 | 1 | 1 | 0 | 5 | 20 | 0 | 46 | 5 | 0 |
| Kown, Andrew, Oneonta | 1 | 2 | .333 | 2.85 | 9 | 9 | 0 | 0 | 0 | 0 | 41.0 | 40 | 175 | 19 | 13 | 4 | 0 | 3 | 2 | 13 | 0 | 37 | 2 | 0 |
| Kramer, Sean, Staten Island * | 1 | 3 | .250 | 4.54 | 12 | 2 | 0 | 0 | 1 | 0 | 37.2 | 54 | 176 | 31 | 19 | 1 | 1 | 1 | 1 | 14 | 0 | 24 | 2 | 0 |
| Lacher, Jeffrey, Jamestown | 0 | 3 | .000 | 5.88 | 16 | 0 | 0 | 0 | 1 | 0 | 41.1 | 54 | 193 | 35 | 27 | 8 | 1 | 2 | 5 | 9 | 1 | 29 | 4 | 1 |
| Laffey, Aaron, Mahoning Valley * | 3 | 1 | .750 | 1.24 | 8 | 8 | 0 | 0 | 0 | 0 | 43.2 | 38 | 180 | 15 | 6 | 1 | 1 | 1 | 2 | 10 | 0 | 30 | 2 | 0 |
| Leonard, Chris, Auburn * | 4 | 4 | .500 | 4.45 | 19 | 10 | 0 | 0 | 4 | 2 | 60.2 | 67 | 267 | 40 | 30 | 5 | 3 | 4 | 3 | 22 | 0 | 62 | 5 | 0 |
| Lerch, Zach, Jamestown | 5 | 4 | .556 | 4.76 | 13 | 13 | 0 | 0 | 0 | 0 | 64.1 | 72 | 287 | 46 | 34 | 9 | 5 | 3 | 3 | 16 | 0 | 56 | 2 | 0 |
| Lewis, Lavon, Oneonta | 1 | 5 | .167 | 4.90 | 12 | 12 | 0 | 0 | 0 | 0 | 60.2 | 61 | 260 | 37 | 33 | 3 | 4 | 4 | 3 | 27 | 1 | 39 | 10 | 2 |
| Lewis, Scott, Mahoning Valley * | 0 | 2 | .000 | 5.06 | 3 | 3 | 0 | 0 | 0 | 0 | 5.1 | 5 | 21 | 3 | 3 | 0 | 0 | 0 | 0 | 1 | 0 | 13 | 2 | 0 |
| Lincoln, Roger, Mahoning Valley * | 3 | 3 | .500 | 3.73 | 24 | 0 | 0 | 0 | 12 | 0 | 41.0 | 37 | 179 | 19 | 17 | 5 | 0 | 0 | 4 | 15 | 1 | 39 | 3 | 1 |
| Lyons, Tom, Oneonta | 1 | 1 | .500 | 2.61 | 2 | 2 | 0 | 0 | 0 | 0 | 10.1 | 11 | 46 | 6 | 3 | 1 | 1 | 0 | 0 | 5 | 0 | 10 | 1 | 1 |
| MacLane, Evan, Brooklyn * | 5 | 2 | .714 | 2.48 | 12 | 12 | 0 | 0 | 0 | 0 | 69.0 | 61 | 272 | 27 | 19 | 5 | 3 | 2 | 2 | 6 | 0 | 68 | 2 | 0 |
| Mahoney, Collin, Oneonta | 1 | 0 | 1.000 | 4.94 | 21 | 0 | 0 | 0 | 7 | 2 | 31.0 | 38 | 157 | 24 | 17 | 2 | 0 | 0 | 3 | 23 | 0 | 31 | 6 | 0 |
| Mann, Brandon, Hudson Valley * | 5 | 5 | .500 | 3.38 | 14 | 14 | 0 | 0 | 0 | 0 | 72.0 | 67 | 300 | 33 | 27 | 3 | 2 | 4 | 7 | 18 | 0 | 68 | 5 | 0 |
| Marquez, Jeffrey, Staten Island | 2 | 4 | .333 | 3.02 | 11 | 11 | 0 | 0 | 0 | 0 | 50.2 | 51 | 222 | 26 | 17 | 2 | 3 | 3 | 5 | 20 | 0 | 36 | 2 | 1 |
| Martinez, Jason, Batavia * | 0 | 2 | .000 | 5.80 | 19 | 3 | 0 | 0 | 7 | 0 | 40.1 | 56 | 200 | 33 | 26 | 5 | 1 | 0 | 2 | 20 | 0 | 27 | 1 | 1 |
| Martinez, Ronnie, Tri-City | 11 | 2 | .846 | 1.96 | 15 | 15 | 1 | 0 | 0 | 0 | 92.0 | 62 | 348 | 21 | 20 | 6 | 3 | 2 | 2 | 20 | 0 | 81 | 2 | 0 |
| Maureau, Justin, Auburn * | 0 | 0 | .000 | 1.93 | 4 | 0 | 0 | 0 | 0 | 0 | 4.2 | 3 | 21 | 1 | 1 | 1 | 0 | 0 | 0 | 4 | 0 | 5 | 1 | 0 |
| McCrory, Bob, Aberdeen | 0 | 1 | .000 | 27.00 | 1 | 1 | 0 | 0 | 0 | 0 | 1.0 | 3 | 8 | 3 | 3 | 1 | 0 | 0 | 0 | 2 | 0 | 1 | 0 | 0 |
| McKeller, Ryan, Tri-City | 4 | 4 | .500 | 4.86 | 14 | 14 | 0 | 0 | 0 | 0 | 74.0 | 74 | 330 | 44 | 40 | 6 | 2 | 2 | 9 | 39 | 0 | 64 | 5 | 0 |
| Mckenzie, Casey, Auburn | 5 | 4 | .556 | 3.78 | 15 | 15 | 0 | 0 | 0 | 0 | 69.0 | 76 | 297 | 32 | 29 | 4 | 2 | 2 | 6 | 20 | 1 | 62 | 4 | 0 |
| Mclaughlin, Joey, Auburn | 4 | 1 | .800 | 2.40 | 23 | 0 | 0 | 0 | 6 | 0 | 45.0 | 29 | 186 | 18 | 12 | 0 | 0 | 0 | 1 | 21 | 1 | 51 | 3 | 0 |
| Mendez, Wimer, Aberdeen | 1 | 0 | 1.000 | 4.38 | 3 | 3 | 0 | 0 | 0 | 0 | 12.1 | 13 | 53 | 6 | 6 | 1 | 2 | 2 | 2 | 5 | 0 | 8 | 1 | 0 |
| Mihalik, Michael, Batavia | 1 | 0 | 1.000 | 3.60 | 4 | 0 | 0 | 0 | 3 | 1 | 10.0 | 6 | 39 | 4 | 4 | 1 | 0 | 0 | 0 | 3 | 1 | 9 | 0 | 0 |
| Mobley, Chris, Jamestown | 1 | 1 | .500 | 2.68 | 17 | 6 | 0 | 0 | 4 | 2 | 53.2 | 50 | 236 | 27 | 16 | 2 | 3 | 1 | 7 | 20 | 1 | 52 | 1 | 1 |
| Molldrem, Craig, Jamestown | 0 | 2 | .000 | 5.40 | 5 | 5 | 0 | 0 | 0 | 0 | 18.1 | 26 | 86 | 15 | 11 | 3 | 0 | 2 | 1 | 4 | 0 | 14 | 1 | 0 |
| Morales, Ricardo, Vermont * | 1 | 0 | 1.000 | 3.00 | 1 | 1 | 0 | 0 | 0 | 0 | 6.0 | 3 | 22 | 2 | 2 | 1 | 0 | 0 | 0 | 1 | 0 | 5 | 1 | 0 |
| Munoz, Luis, Williamsport | 2 | 4 | .333 | 4.57 | 15 | 8 | 0 | 0 | 3 | 0 | 61.0 | 80 | 269 | 40 | 31 | 7 | 4 | 4 | 2 | 14 | 0 | 36 | 3 | 0 |
| Murdy, Garrett, Tri-City | 0 | 1 | .000 | 3.94 | 7 | 1 | 0 | 0 | 3 | 1 | 16.0 | 14 | 70 | 9 | 7 | 1 | 0 | 2 | 1 | 6 | 0 | 12 | 1 | 0 |
| Neylan, Chris, Auburn * | 1 | 1 | .500 | 7.94 | 17 | 0 | 0 | 0 | 6 | 0 | 28.1 | 37 | 143 | 29 | 25 | 2 | 0 | 0 | 2 | 20 | 2 | 22 | 2 | 0 |
| Nickerson, Jon-Michael, Jamestown * | 2 | 4 | .333 | 5.09 | 9 | 8 | 0 | 0 | 0 | 0 | 40.2 | 45 | 181 | 26 | 23 | 2 | 1 | 6 | 2 | 23 | 0 | 31 | 2 | 1 |
| Ochoa, Nehomar, Vermont | 0 | 3 | .000 | 4.70 | 5 | 5 | 0 | 0 | 0 | 0 | 15.1 | 20 | 75 | 10 | 8 | 0 | 1 | 1 | 0 | 11 | 0 | 7 | 2 | 0 |
| Ortega, Joel, Williamsport | 0 | 0 | .000 | 6.75 | 3 | 0 | 0 | 0 | 1 | 0 | 2.2 | 2 | 11 | 2 | 2 | 1 | 0 | 0 | 0 | 1 | 0 | 2 | 0 | 0 |
| Parker, Brett, Mahoning Valley | 0 | 0 | .000 | 18.00 | 1 | 0 | 0 | 0 | 1 | 0 | 1.0 | 3 | 6 | 2 | 2 | 0 | 0 | 0 | 0 | 0 | 0 | 0 | 0 | 0 |
| Parker, Shaun, Staten Island * | 3 | 2 | .600 | 3.79 | 19 | 0 | 0 | 0 | 4 | 0 | 54.2 | 59 | 238 | 31 | 23 | 4 | 0 | 2 | 1 | 18 | 1 | 32 | 3 | 0 |
| Paz, Jackson, New Jersey * | 1 | 0 | 1.000 | 1.07 | 17 | 0 | 0 | 0 | 4 | 1 | 25.1 | 11 | 101 | 4 | 3 | 1 | 1 | 0 | 5 | 8 | 0 | 22 | 1 | 0 |
| Pekarek, Justin, Mahoning Valley * | 0 | 1 | .000 | 6.23 | 7 | 2 | 0 | 0 | 1 | 0 | 17.1 | 23 | 82 | 14 | 12 | 1 | 2 | 0 | 0 | 7 | 1 | 15 | 1 | 0 |
| Peralta, Tony, Oneonta * | 3 | 0 | 1.000 | 1.80 | 22 | 0 | 0 | 0 | 6 | 0 | 40.0 | 24 | 156 | 8 | 8 | 2 | 0 | 0 | 3 | 13 | 2 | 38 | 1 | 0 |
| Perez, Alex, Staten Island | 2 | 0 | 1.000 | 0.00 | 2 | 0 | 0 | 0 | 1 | 0 | 7.2 | 7 | 31 | 0 | 0 | 0 | 0 | 0 | 0 | 1 | 0 | 5 | 0 | 0 |
| Perez, Carlos, Aberdeen * | 3 | 5 | .375 | 3.53 | 15 | 14 | 0 | 0 | 0 | 0 | 79.0 | 67 | 319 | 41 | 31 | 7 | 4 | 3 | 2 | 28 | 0 | 77 | 1 | 1 |
| Perez, Ezequiel, Oneonta | 2 | 2 | .500 | 3.44 | 23 | 0 | 0 | 0 | 14 | 5 | 34.0 | 35 | 153 | 14 | 13 | 1 | 0 | 0 | 1 | 15 | 4 | 26 | 3 | 0 |
| Perez, Juan, Auburn | 6 | 1 | .857 | 2.76 | 12 | 11 | 1 | 0 | 0 | 0 | 58.2 | 61 | 246 | 22 | 18 | 2 | 4 | 2 | 3 | 10 | 0 | 40 | 1 | 2 |
| Petrick, Russell, Aberdeen * | 2 | 4 | .333 | 5.52 | 20 | 6 | 0 | 0 | 2 | 0 | 45.2 | 57 | 216 | 35 | 28 | 7 | 1 | 2 | 3 | 24 | 0 | 44 | 3 | 1 |
| Potter, Josh, Aberdeen | 1 | 0 | 1.000 | 8.31 | 3 | 0 | 0 | 0 | 1 | 0 | 4.1 | 6 | 20 | 4 | 4 | 0 | 0 | 0 | 0 | 1 | 0 | 1 | 0 | 0 |
| Price, John, Hudson Valley * | 0 | 0 | .000 | 4.86 | 12 | 0 | 0 | 0 | 5 | 1 | 16.2 | 20 | 81 | 11 | 9 | 0 | 0 | 0 | 3 | 8 | 1 | 8 | 2 | 0 |
| Prieto, Victor, Jamestown | 0 | 0 | .000 | 189.00 | 1 | 0 | 0 | 0 | 0 | 0 | 0.1 | 3 | 8 | 8 | 7 | 0 | 0 | 0 | 0 | 4 | 0 | 0 | 1 | 0 |
| Purcey, David, Auburn * | 1 | 0 | 1.000 | 1.50 | 3 | 2 | 0 | 0 | 0 | 0 | 12.0 | 6 | 43 | 2 | 2 | 0 | 1 | 2 | 1 | 1 | 0 | 13 | 0 | 0 |
| Quarles, Jason, Williamsport | 0 | 4 | .000 | 4.56 | 23 | 0 | 0 | 0 | 8 | 0 | 23.2 | 34 | 126 | 18 | 12 | 1 | 0 | 0 | 2 | 19 | 2 | 31 | 7 | 0 |
| Rainwater, Josh, Oneonta | 0 | 6 | .000 | 4.22 | 11 | 11 | 0 | 0 | 0 | 0 | 49.0 | 46 | 234 | 28 | 23 | 4 | 4 | 4 | 7 | 35 | 1 | 52 | 8 | 0 |
| Ramos, Jason, Lowell | 0 | 0 | .000 | 0.00 | 1 | 0 | 0 | 0 | 1 | 0 | 0.1 | 0 | 2 | 0 | 0 | 0 | 0 | 0 | 1 | 0 | 0 | 0 | 0 | 0 |
| Ramos, Victor, Williamsport | 0 | 0 | .000 | 0.96 | 3 | 0 | 0 | 0 | 1 | 0 | 9.1 | 6 | 34 | 3 | 1 | 0 | 0 | 2 | 0 | 2 | 0 | 8 | 0 | 0 |
| Regas, Kris, Brooklyn | 0 | 0 | .000 | 2.35 | 4 | 0 | 0 | 0 | 3 | 0 | 7.2 | 7 | 31 | 5 | 2 | 1 | 0 | 0 | 0 | 1 | 0 | 12 | 0 | 0 |
| Reineke, Chad, Tri-City | 1 | 2 | .333 | 2.45 | 23 | 0 | 0 | 0 | 16 | 3 | 36.2 | 27 | 160 | 13 | 10 | 0 | 0 | 0 | 0 | 23 | 0 | 52 | 3 | 0 |
| Rengel, Orlando, Brooklyn | 0 | 0 | .000 | 3.00 | 1 | 0 | 0 | 0 | 0 | 0 | 3.0 | 1 | 10 | 1 | 1 | 1 | 0 | 0 | 0 | 0 | 0 | 4 | 0 | 0 |
| Righter, Matthew, Oneonta | 0 | 1 | .000 | 4.43 | 14 | 0 | 0 | 0 | 8 | 0 | 22.1 | 23 | 102 | 15 | 11 | 2 | 1 | 1 | 3 | 10 | 0 | 13 | 2 | 1 |
| Robertson, Quinton, New Jersey | 3 | 2 | .600 | 3.41 | 6 | 6 | 1 | 1 | 0 | 0 | 31.2 | 29 | 127 | 12 | 12 | 2 | 2 | 0 | 1 | 6 | 0 | 20 | 0 | 0 |

| Pitcher, Team | W | L | Pct. | ERA | G | GS | CG | ShO | GF | Sv. | IP | H | TBF | R | ER | HR | SH | SF | HB | BB | IBB | SO | WP | Bk. |
|---|---|---|---|---|---|---|---|---|---|---|---|---|---|---|---|---|---|---|---|---|---|---|---|---|
| Rodriguez, Eladio, Lowell | 1 | 3 | .250 | 4.75 | 25 | 0 | 0 | 0 | 20 | 5 | 36.0 | 34 | 169 | 22 | 19 | 2 | 0 | 0 | 2 | 25 | 0 | 38 | 4 | 0 |
| Rodriguez, Jayson, Auburn | 5 | 3 | .625 | 3.28 | 20 | 0 | 0 | 0 | 6 | 2 | 35.2 | 29 | 156 | 16 | 13 | 0 | 0 | 0 | 4 | 15 | 2 | 30 | 1 | 3 |
| Rodriguez, Jose, Brooklyn | 2 | 2 | .500 | 4.40 | 8 | 0 | 0 | 0 | 5 | 0 | 14.1 | 14 | 62 | 8 | 7 | 0 | 0 | 0 | 1 | 4 | 1 | 10 | 2 | 0 |
| Roehl, Scott, Mahoning Valley | 2 | 1 | .667 | 4.11 | 11 | 0 | 0 | 0 | 2 | 0 | 15.1 | 16 | 66 | 9 | 7 | 3 | 0 | 0 | 0 | 4 | 0 | 20 | 0 | 0 |
| Rondon, Celso, Brooklyn | 3 | 2 | .600 | 2.23 | 27 | 0 | 0 | 0 | 21 | 12 | 36.1 | 20 | 149 | 10 | 9 | 2 | 0 | 0 | 3 | 17 | 1 | 47 | 2 | 0 |
| Rose, Kevin, Batavia | 5 | 3 | .625 | 3.63 | 22 | 0 | 0 | 0 | 8 | 0 | 44.2 | 54 | 212 | 24 | 18 | 1 | 0 | 2 | 1 | 24 | 1 | 45 | 6 | 0 |
| Roy, Scott, Auburn | 1 | 0 | 1.000 | 2.70 | 15 | 0 | 0 | 0 | 8 | 4 | 20.0 | 14 | 82 | 9 | 6 | 1 | 0 | 0 | 4 | 4 | 0 | 17 | 0 | 0 |
| Salas, Joseph, Williamsport * | 0 | 0 | .000 | 6.52 | 13 | 0 | 0 | 0 | 7 | 1 | 9.2 | 5 | 43 | 7 | 7 | 0 | 0 | 0 | 1 | 8 | 1 | 6 | 2 | 0 |
| Sanchez, Anibal, Lowell | 3 | 4 | .429 | 1.77 | 15 | 15 | 0 | 0 | 0 | 0 | 76.1 | 43 | 310 | 24 | 15 | 3 | 3 | 4 | 6 | 29 | 0 | 101 | 2 | 1 |
| Sanders, David, Lowell * | 2 | 2 | .500 | 6.35 | 17 | 0 | 0 | 0 | 3 | 0 | 28.1 | 42 | 139 | 20 | 20 | 1 | 0 | 0 | 2 | 10 | 0 | 17 | 2 | 1 |
| Sandoval, Francisco, Vermont | 5 | 2 | .714 | 5.87 | 21 | 0 | 0 | 0 | 4 | 1 | 46.0 | 68 | 232 | 39 | 30 | 4 | 0 | 0 | 3 | 23 | 1 | 32 | 1 | 1 |
| Santana, Hector, Mahoning Valley | 1 | 1 | .500 | 10.30 | 19 | 0 | 0 | 0 | 11 | 1 | 25.1 | 31 | 136 | 32 | 29 | 2 | 1 | 0 | 2 | 25 | 0 | 12 | 3 | 0 |
| Santana, Miguel, Staten Island | 1 | 3 | .250 | 10.13 | 6 | 3 | 0 | 0 | 3 | 0 | 16.0 | 21 | 78 | 19 | 18 | 2 | 0 | 0 | 3 | 8 | 0 | 13 | 2 | 0 |
| Santander, Nelson, Batavia | 3 | 1 | .750 | 5.63 | 17 | 0 | 0 | 0 | 10 | 2 | 24.0 | 30 | 116 | 16 | 15 | 2 | 0 | 0 | 5 | 9 | 1 | 11 | 7 | 1 |
| Scheinbaum, Benjamin, Staten Island * | 1 | 4 | .200 | 2.92 | 15 | 0 | 0 | 0 | 10 | 0 | 24.2 | 24 | 120 | 12 | 8 | 0 | 0 | 0 | 3 | 19 | 0 | 20 | 4 | 1 |
| Schroyer, Ryan, Lowell | 4 | 2 | .667 | 4.44 | 14 | 2 | 0 | 0 | 0 | 0 | 48.2 | 46 | 209 | 29 | 24 | 6 | 4 | 5 | 5 | 23 | 0 | 57 | 5 | 0 |
| Schwabe, Ryan, Aberdeen * | 0 | 0 | .000 | 1.06 | 3 | 3 | 0 | 0 | 0 | 0 | 17.0 | 14 | 65 | 2 | 2 | 0 | 0 | 1 | 0 | 6 | 0 | 18 | 0 | 0 |
| Shoemaker, Scott, Lowell | 1 | 0 | 1.000 | 2.48 | 17 | 0 | 0 | 0 | 9 | 3 | 32.2 | 32 | 141 | 15 | 9 | 2 | 1 | 1 | 4 | 8 | 0 | 52 | 4 | 0 |
| Sipp, Tony, Mahoning Valley * | 3 | 1 | .750 | 3.16 | 10 | 10 | 0 | 0 | 0 | 0 | 42.2 | 33 | 174 | 23 | 15 | 5 | 3 | 1 | 1 | 13 | 0 | 74 | 3 | 3 |
| Smith, Chris, Aberdeen * | 1 | 0 | 1.000 | 3.38 | 4 | 4 | 0 | 0 | 0 | 0 | 13.1 | 13 | 58 | 9 | 5 | 0 | 1 | 0 | 1 | 5 | 0 | 13 | 1 | 0 |
| Smith, Chuck, Brooklyn | 0 | 0 | .000 | 1.93 | 7 | 0 | 0 | 0 | 2 | 2 | 9.1 | 7 | 39 | 3 | 2 | 1 | 0 | 0 | 1 | 3 | 0 | 11 | 2 | 0 |
| Smith, Donnie, New Jersey | 3 | 3 | .500 | 3.88 | 11 | 11 | 1 | 0 | 0 | 0 | 46.1 | 52 | 188 | 23 | 20 | 4 | 0 | 0 | 0 | 5 | 0 | 41 | 1 | 1 |
| Sosa, Gabriel, Vermont * | 2 | 1 | .667 | 5.06 | 4 | 4 | 1 | 0 | 0 | 0 | 16.0 | 16 | 68 | 10 | 9 | 0 | 0 | 1 | 0 | 6 | 0 | 11 | 1 | 1 |
| Soto, Edgar, Staten Island * | 1 | 2 | .333 | 2.91 | 4 | 4 | 0 | 0 | 0 | 0 | 21.2 | 20 | 84 | 9 | 7 | 0 | 1 | 3 | 0 | 7 | 0 | 9 | 0 | 0 |
| Soto, Enyelbert, Tri-City * | 0 | 0 | .000 | 4.50 | 1 | 0 | 0 | 0 | 0 | 0 | 2.0 | 2 | 8 | 1 | 1 | 0 | 0 | 0 | 0 | 0 | 0 | 3 | 0 | 0 |
| Spencer, Sean, Aberdeen * | 1 | 0 | 1.000 | 0.00 | 5 | 0 | 0 | 0 | 1 | 0 | 5.0 | 2 | 19 | 0 | 0 | 0 | 0 | 0 | 0 | 2 | 0 | 10 | 1 | 0 |
| Spillars, Brandan, Aberdeen | 3 | 3 | .500 | 3.26 | 13 | 0 | 0 | 0 | 9 | 4 | 19.1 | 19 | 84 | 9 | 7 | 0 | 0 | 0 | 0 | 7 | 1 | 11 | 1 | 0 |
| Stahl, Richard, Aberdeen * | 0 | 0 | .000 | 0.00 | 1 | 1 | 0 | 0 | 0 | 0 | 3.0 | 1 | 9 | 0 | 0 | 0 | 0 | 0 | 0 | 0 | 0 | 1 | 0 | 0 |
| Stephens, Amad, Staten Island | 0 | 0 | .000 | 0.00 | 1 | 0 | 0 | 0 | 1 | 0 | 2.2 | 0 | 8 | 0 | 0 | 0 | 0 | 0 | 0 | 0 | 0 | 1 | 0 | 0 |
| Swindell, Michael, Brooklyn | 4 | 1 | .800 | 2.79 | 11 | 10 | 0 | 0 | 0 | 0 | 58.0 | 43 | 230 | 23 | 18 | 2 | 4 | 3 | 3 | 20 | 0 | 56 | 3 | 0 |
| Swindle, Robert, Lowell * | 5 | 1 | .833 | 1.94 | 12 | 1 | 0 | 0 | 0 | 0 | 51.0 | 42 | 199 | 18 | 11 | 0 | 3 | 3 | 2 | 4 | 0 | 56 | 1 | 0 |
| Tankersley, Taylor, Jamestown * | 1 | 1 | .500 | 3.38 | 6 | 6 | 0 | 0 | 0 | 0 | 26.2 | 21 | 116 | 14 | 10 | 2 | 4 | 4 | 0 | 8 | 0 | 32 | 1 | 2 |
| Tate, Derek, Auburn * | 4 | 1 | .800 | 2.20 | 5 | 2 | 0 | 0 | 0 | 0 | 16.1 | 17 | 72 | 5 | 4 | 0 | 2 | 0 | 1 | 6 | 1 | 24 | 0 | 0 |
| Thorne, David, Vermont | 0 | 0 | .000 | 33.75 | 2 | 0 | 0 | 0 | 0 | 0 | 1.1 | 4 | 12 | 5 | 5 | 0 | 0 | 0 | 1 | 3 | 0 | 1 | 0 | 0 |
| Tillman, Derek, Jamestown | 6 | 2 | .750 | 2.60 | 25 | 0 | 0 | 0 | 12 | 1 | 45.0 | 34 | 193 | 20 | 13 | 2 | 0 | 0 | 9 | 15 | 1 | 46 | 3 | 1 |
| Tompkins, Jake, Batavia | 0 | 2 | .000 | 7.94 | 12 | 0 | 0 | 0 | 3 | 0 | 28.1 | 31 | 141 | 28 | 25 | 2 | 0 | 1 | 5 | 21 | 1 | 27 | 4 | 0 |
| Trahan, David, Vermont | 3 | 2 | .600 | 2.59 | 20 | 1 | 0 | 0 | 5 | 0 | 48.2 | 41 | 218 | 20 | 14 | 2 | 1 | 2 | 3 | 28 | 1 | 47 | 0 | 1 |
| Tubb, Austin, New Jersey | 4 | 1 | .800 | 2.84 | 23 | 0 | 0 | 0 | 7 | 0 | 31.2 | 33 | 142 | 14 | 10 | 0 | 0 | 0 | 2 | 12 | 2 | 28 | 1 | 0 |
| Volquez, Bolivar, Hudson Valley | 2 | 0 | 1.000 | 3.21 | 12 | 0 | 0 | 0 | 6 | 0 | 14.0 | 18 | 69 | 8 | 5 | 1 | 0 | 0 | 0 | 9 | 1 | 7 | 5 | 0 |
| Wagner, Michael, Staten Island * | 0 | 0 | .000 | 13.50 | 1 | 0 | 0 | 0 | 0 | 0 | 1.1 | 3 | 9 | 2 | 2 | 0 | 0 | 0 | 0 | 2 | 0 | 1 | 0 | 0 |
| Wagner, Nicholas, Hudson Valley | 1 | 0 | 1.000 | 3.34 | 18 | 0 | 0 | 0 | 6 | 2 | 35.0 | 34 | 151 | 15 | 13 | 1 | 0 | 0 | 3 | 10 | 0 | 24 | 6 | 0 |
| Walker, Aaron, Hudson Valley * | 4 | 2 | .667 | 2.70 | 14 | 3 | 0 | 0 | 4 | 2 | 30.0 | 21 | 123 | 12 | 9 | 0 | 1 | 0 | 2 | 9 | 0 | 36 | 2 | 0 |
| Weimer, Andrew, Hudson Valley | 0 | 1 | .000 | 3.42 | 17 | 0 | 0 | 0 | 10 | 0 | 23.2 | 26 | 111 | 14 | 9 | 0 | 0 | 0 | 4 | 10 | 0 | 14 | 4 | 0 |
| Wideman, Aaron, Vermont * | 3 | 1 | .750 | 1.81 | 10 | 10 | 0 | 0 | 0 | 0 | 44.2 | 26 | 167 | 9 | 9 | 0 | 1 | 2 | 1 | 13 | 0 | 38 | 0 | 2 |
| Wigdahl, Jeffrey, Tri-City * | 1 | 1 | .500 | 3.51 | 19 | 1 | 0 | 0 | 5 | 0 | 33.1 | 20 | 142 | 15 | 13 | 1 | 1 | 0 | 3 | 19 | 0 | 35 | 0 | 0 |
| Williams, Joseph, Brooklyn * | 5 | 4 | .556 | 2.28 | 15 | 15 | 0 | 0 | 0 | 0 | 75.0 | 62 | 305 | 26 | 19 | 3 | 6 | 4 | 4 | 26 | 1 | 64 | 0 | 0 |
| Wilson, Thomas, Vermont * | 1 | 1 | .500 | 3.86 | 7 | 0 | 0 | 0 | 2 | 0 | 11.2 | 11 | 48 | 5 | 5 | 1 | 0 | 0 | 1 | 1 | 0 | 9 | 2 | 0 |
| Wright, Chase, Staten Island * | 0 | 1 | .000 | 9.00 | 1 | 1 | 0 | 0 | 0 | 0 | 3.0 | 5 | 20 | 5 | 3 | 0 | 0 | 0 | 2 | 3 | 0 | 3 | 0 | 0 |
| Wright, Isaiah, Vermont | 1 | 1 | .500 | 10.20 | 11 | 0 | 0 | 0 | 4 | 0 | 15.0 | 19 | 87 | 22 | 17 | 0 | 0 | 0 | 3 | 20 | 0 | 10 | 3 | 1 |
| Yates, Kyle, Auburn | 0 | 1 | .000 | 6.75 | 9 | 0 | 0 | 0 | 5 | 0 | 9.1 | 9 | 44 | 7 | 7 | 0 | 0 | 0 | 2 | 5 | 0 | 11 | 0 | 0 |
| Yourkin, Matt, Jamestown * | 2 | 3 | .400 | 3.94 | 24 | 0 | 0 | 0 | 10 | 1 | 32.0 | 26 | 134 | 17 | 14 | 3 | 0 | 0 | 2 | 10 | 0 | 32 | 1 | 1 |
| Zick, Jeremy, New Jersey | 1 | 1 | .500 | 4.61 | 18 | 0 | 0 | 0 | 7 | 1 | 27.1 | 30 | 125 | 14 | 14 | 1 | 0 | 0 | 1 | 12 | 0 | 28 | 6 | 0 |

COMBINATION SHUTOUTS: **Aberdeen** (1)—Mendez-Childs. **Auburn** (5)—MacDonald-Hill-McLaughlin-Neylan, McKenzie-Bell-J. Rodriguez-Day, Leonard-Rico, J. Perez-Yates-Day, MacDonald-Maureau-J. Rodriguez. **Batavia** (3)—Kendrick-Tompkins-Rose, Bisenius-Allen, Baldwin-Allen. **Brooklyn** (11)—Quaglieri-Foli-Muniz, Swindell-Camacho-Rondon, J. Williams-Muniz-Rondon, Quaglieri-Landing-Camacho, Devaney-Alfonzo, Hyde-Camacho, J. Williams-Freitas-C. Smith-Rondon, Swindell-C. Smith, MacLane-Rondon, Swindell-Camacho-Rondon, MacLane-Camacho. **Hudson Valley** (4)—Mann-Sonnanstine-Bitter, Sonnanstine-Barriger-Bitter, Cobb-Sonnanstine, Mann-Delacruz. **Jamestown** (2)—Barone-Tillman-Yourkin-Hogan, Molldrem-Barone-Tillman-Hogan. **Lowell** (4)—A. Sanchez-Shoemaker, Hottovy-Swindle-Goodson-Cochran-Shoemaker, Hottovy-Swindle-Eddy, A. Sanchez-Ehrlich. **Mahoning Valley** (2)—De Los Santos-Lubrano-Collins-Harris, Hoyman-De Los Santos-Jecman-Lincoln-Roehl-Santana. **New Jersey** (6)—John-Torres-Paz, Dove-Roper, Aguero-Sillman-Gross, D. Smith-Paz-Tubb-Doyne, Robertson-Sillman-Doyne, Aguero-Doyne. **Oneonta** (4)—Bumstead-Peralta-Clelland-E. Perez, Konecny-Mahoney, Kown-Clelland-E. Perez-Myers, Lewis-E. Perez. **Staten Island** (2)—J. Jones-Cuen-Edwards, Marquez-Blackwell-M. Martinez. **Tri-City** (5)—Shortell-Estrada-C. Brown, R. Martinez-Reineke, R. Martinez-Edmiston, Alvarado-Escobar, R. Martinez-C. Brown-Estrada. **Vermont** (2)—Bunn-E. Diaz-Cerezo, Sosa-Cook-Cox. **Williamsport** (3)—Bloom-Munoz, B. Johnson-Bishop, Hankins-Quarles.

NO-HIT GAMES: None.

# 2004 FIELDING

## TEAM

| Team | G | PO | A | E | TC | DP | TP | PB | Pct. |
|---|---|---|---|---|---|---|---|---|---|
| New Jersey | 75 | 2028 | 036 | 91 | 2155 | 75 | 0 | 5 | .958 |
| Tri-City | 75 | 2016 | 038 | 95 | 2149 | 61 | 0 | 18 | .956 |
| Brooklyn | 74 | 1958 | 041 | 94 | 2093 | 62 | 0 | 13 | .955 |
| Staten Island | 72 | 1959 | 017 | 94 | 2070 | 61 | 0 | 23 | .955 |
| Mahoning Valley | 76 | 2012 | 039 | 98 | 2149 | 43 | 0 | 23 | .954 |
| Auburn | 74 | 1936 | 037 | 95 | 2068 | 59 | 0 | 24 | .954 |
| Williamsport | 74 | 1931 | 027 | 95 | 2053 | 62 | 0 | 15 | .954 |
| Hudson Valley | 72 | 1859 | 021 | 94 | 1974 | 48 | 0 | 16 | .952 |
| Aberdeen | 75 | 2021 | 034 | 112 | 2167 | 40 | 0 | 25 | .948 |
| Oneonta | 74 | 2002 | 035 | 115 | 2152 | 47 | 0 | 21 | .947 |
| Batavia | 74 | 1959 | 023 | 112 | 2094 | 64 | 0 | 24 | .947 |
| Vermont | 72 | 1844 | 049 | 112 | 2005 | 52 | 0 | 17 | .944 |
| Lowell | 76 | 2057 | 034 | 126 | 2217 | 47 | 0 | 19 | .943 |
| Jamestown | 75 | 1960 | 030 | 126 | 2116 | 53 | 0 | 21 | .940 |

## INDIVIDUAL

### FIRST BASEMEN

NOTE: All caps denotes fielding-percentage leader based on 38 games for catchers, 51 for all other non-pitchers and 61 innings for pitchers. *Throws lefthanded.

| Player, Team | Pct. | G | PO | A | E | TC | DP |
|---|---|---|---|---|---|---|---|
| Averill, Brandon, TRC | 1.000 | 1 | 2 | 0 | 0 | 2 | 0 |
| Baty, Ryan, HDV | .994 | 20 | 161 | 10 | 1 | 172 | 11 |
| Bergeron, Jabe, BRK | 1.000 | 2 | 25 | 1 | 0 | 26 | 1 |
| Boudon, Chad, ABD | 1.000 | 2 | 8 | 0 | 0 | 8 | 1 |
| Brown, Tim, WPT* | .991 | 41 | 409 | 45 | 4 | 458 | 33 |
| Buffone, Anthony, BAT | .988 | 10 | 79 | 3 | 1 | 83 | 11 |
| Burt, Jim, BRK | .992 | 27 | 219 | 23 | 2 | 244 | 20 |
| Cannon, Chip, AUB* | .988 | 43 | 377 | 35 | 5 | 417 | 36 |
| Carlin, Mike, WPT | .992 | 16 | 112 | 6 | 1 | 119 | 5 |
| Cloninger, Erich, LOW | 1.000 | 3 | 32 | 3 | 0 | 35 | 4 |

| Player, Team | Pct. | G | PO | A | E | TC | DP |
|---|---|---|---|---|---|---|---|
| Costello, Mike, ABD | .974 | 20 | 139 | 10 | 4 | 153 | 7 |
| Davidson, Tyler, BRK | .982 | 44 | 408 | 21 | 8 | 437 | 29 |
| Davie, Andrew, NJY* | 1.000 | 6 | 49 | 3 | 0 | 52 | 0 |
| Diaz, Rafael, ABD | .958 | 2 | 23 | 0 | 1 | 24 | 2 |
| Ehlers, Cody, STA* | .985 | 38 | 299 | 26 | 5 | 330 | 33 |
| Ferris, Mike, NJY* | .997 | 39 | 359 | 20 | 1 | 380 | 34 |
| Galloway, Carl, BAT | .984 | 35 | 294 | 13 | 5 | 312 | 24 |
| Garza, Mario, TRC* | .991 | 49 | 403 | 35 | 4 | 442 | 36 |
| Gimenez, Christopher, MHV | 1.000 | 18 | 156 | 18 | 0 | 174 | 9 |
| Gonzalez, Edwar, STA | 1.000 | 1 | 9 | 0 | 0 | 9 | 0 |
| Grimm, Casey, NJY* | 1.000 | 1 | 10 | 0 | 0 | 10 | 2 |
| Guzman, Heriberto, LOW | .983 | 22 | 159 | 11 | 3 | 173 | 12 |
| Hicks, David, AUB* | .968 | 11 | 54 | 7 | 2 | 63 | 3 |
| Hofius, Mike, WPT* | .990 | 22 | 191 | 13 | 2 | 206 | 22 |
| Jarvis, Andy, BAT* | .978 | 9 | 80 | 9 | 2 | 91 | 10 |
| Jaso, John, HDV* | .986 | 14 | 125 | 12 | 2 | 139 | 13 |
| Jones, Ben, STA | .991 | 35 | 319 | 14 | 3 | 336 | 23 |
| Llamas, Juan, ONE | .971 | 4 | 31 | 3 | 1 | 35 | 1 |
| Mangioni, Jarad, AUB | 1.000 | 1 | 3 | 0 | 0 | 3 | 0 |
| Manriquez, Salomon, VMT | 1.000 | 1 | 10 | 0 | 0 | 10 | 0 |
| Matulich, Mario, MHV | .979 | 5 | 44 | 3 | 1 | 48 | 3 |
| McCann, Brad, JAM | .964 | 3 | 25 | 2 | 1 | 28 | 2 |
| McCarty, David, LOW | 1.000 | 1 | 4 | 0 | 0 | 4 | 0 |
| McRae, Aaron, ONE* | 1.000 | 1 | 3 | 0 | 0 | 3 | 0 |
| Mendez, Carlos, ABD | 1.000 | 3 | 19 | 3 | 0 | 22 | 0 |
| Mendez, Rafael, ONE | .980 | 70 | 579 | 49 | 13 | 641 | 49 |
| Metropoulos, Joey, AUB | .988 | 30 | 223 | 20 | 3 | 246 | 15 |
| Montz, Luke, VMT | .995 | 25 | 198 | 6 | 1 | 205 | 11 |
| Mortimer, Steve, VMT* | .988 | 44 | 315 | 27 | 4 | 346 | 27 |
| Norman, Zach, BAT | .952 | 9 | 93 | 7 | 5 | 105 | 11 |
| Nowak, Chris, HDV | .989 | 41 | 332 | 12 | 4 | 348 | 25 |
| Otness, John, LOW | .993 | 20 | 131 | 9 | 1 | 141 | 11 |
| Pacheco, Fernando, MHV* | .990 | 57 | 469 | 38 | 5 | 512 | 25 |
| Pilittere, Peter, STA | 1.000 | 3 | 29 | 2 | 0 | 31 | 2 |
| Pinckney, Andrew, LOW | .991 | 27 | 222 | 9 | 2 | 233 | 13 |
| Restko, JT, JAM | .974 | 67 | 490 | 32 | 14 | 536 | 41 |
| Rodriguez, Marcos, NJY* | 1.000 | 1 | 6 | 1 | 0 | 7 | 0 |
| Shimer, Nicholas, BAT | 1.000 | 11 | 94 | 11 | 0 | 105 | 8 |
| SMITH, CJ, ABD | .991 | 56 | 416 | 37 | 4 | 457 | 18 |
| Sorensen, Logan, LOW* | 1.000 | 11 | 69 | 10 | 0 | 79 | 4 |
| Travis, David, VMT* | 1.000 | 5 | 35 | 2 | 0 | 37 | 2 |
| Vital, Kevin, TRC* | .988 | 34 | 217 | 20 | 3 | 240 | 20 |
| Webber, Levi, NJY | .987 | 35 | 278 | 30 | 4 | 312 | 32 |
| Wendt, Justin, BRK* | .895 | 3 | 15 | 2 | 2 | 19 | 0 |
| Wyman, Spencer, JAM* | .957 | 6 | 44 | 1 | 2 | 47 | 5 |

## SECOND BASEMEN

| Player, Team | Pct. | G | PO | A | E | TC | DP |
|---|---|---|---|---|---|---|---|
| Acey, Jermy, AUB | 1.000 | 3 | 6 | 10 | 0 | 16 | 4 |
| Amezquita, Octavio, ONE | .941 | 8 | 13 | 19 | 2 | 34 | 3 |
| Armstrong, Jason, AUB | .941 | 13 | 16 | 32 | 3 | 51 | 5 |
| Asanovich, Robert, HDV | .963 | 38 | 67 | 91 | 6 | 164 | 18 |
| Ash, Jonny, TRC* | .969 | 15 | 20 | 42 | 2 | 64 | 9 |
| Babilonia, Edgar, TRC | .953 | 11 | 11 | 30 | 2 | 43 | 4 |
| Brannon, Evan, ABD | .889 | 6 | 3 | 5 | 1 | 9 | 0 |
| Buffone, Anthony, BAT | .988 | 20 | 43 | 41 | 1 | 85 | 14 |
| Cantu, Tim, NJY | .970 | 17 | 28 | 37 | 2 | 67 | 10 |
| Carroll, Brett, JAM | .912 | 10 | 39 | 23 | 6 | 68 | 8 |
| Castro, Francisco, ONE | .952 | 64 | 136 | 198 | 17 | 351 | 27 |
| Christian, Justin, STA | .965 | 29 | 62 | 76 | 5 | 143 | 14 |
| Clanton, Ja`Mar, VMT | .978 | 12 | 26 | 19 | 1 | 46 | 6 |
| Clem, Chris, MHV | .934 | 21 | 38 | 47 | 6 | 91 | 8 |
| Cleveland, Brian, JAM | .985 | 24 | 66 | 62 | 2 | 130 | 12 |
| Colvin, Brooks, ONE | .962 | 6 | 14 | 11 | 1 | 26 | 2 |
| Contreras, Jose, VMT | .985 | 17 | 32 | 35 | 1 | 68 | 8 |
| Cooper, Chad, HDV | .957 | 33 | 53 | 82 | 6 | 141 | 15 |
| Cottrell, Patrick, HDV | .955 | 6 | 9 | 12 | 1 | 22 | 0 |
| Curtis, Lee, LOW | .932 | 16 | 35 | 34 | 5 | 74 | 8 |
| Delgado, Jose, NJY | .963 | 6 | 12 | 14 | 1 | 27 | 4 |
| DeVoir, Jordan, STA | 1.000 | 3 | 2 | 12 | 0 | 14 | 2 |
| Ditter, Brad, VMT* | .939 | 47 | 81 | 105 | 12 | 198 | 18 |
| Fisher, Matt, BRK | .976 | 34 | 75 | 91 | 4 | 170 | 18 |
| Gendron, Steve, JAM | .972 | 12 | 34 | 35 | 2 | 71 | 6 |
| Grandstrand, Brett, WPT | .963 | 23 | 41 | 64 | 4 | 109 | 14 |
| Haag, Ryan, STA* | .954 | 17 | 26 | 36 | 3 | 65 | 8 |
| Hall, Brian, AUB | .967 | 55 | 107 | 155 | 9 | 271 | 26 |
| Hardy, John, BAT | .979 | 9 | 21 | 25 | 1 | 47 | 6 |
| Herrera, Christian, WPT | .967 | 6 | 11 | 18 | 1 | 30 | 3 |
| Hoffpauir, Jarrett, NJY | .962 | 8 | 10 | 15 | 1 | 26 | 2 |
| Housel, David, BRK | 1.000 | 1 | 3 | 2 | 0 | 5 | 0 |
| Isaacson, Greg, BAT* | .940 | 42 | 78 | 124 | 13 | 215 | 25 |
| Jeroloman, Chuck, LOW | .966 | 26 | 41 | 71 | 4 | 116 | 11 |
| Lofton, James, ABD | 1.000 | 2 | 2 | 3 | 0 | 5 | 1 |
| Lomack, Jermel, WPT | .984 | 26 | 42 | 80 | 2 | 124 | 15 |
| Macaluso, Mike, AUB | 1.000 | 1 | 0 | 2 | 0 | 2 | 0 |
| Mader, Josh, BAT | .971 | 5 | 10 | 23 | 1 | 34 | 8 |
| Marconi, Robert, ABD | .935 | 7 | 12 | 17 | 2 | 31 | 1 |
| McMillan, Beau, JAM | .904 | 28 | 51 | 43 | 10 | 104 | 11 |
| Mendez, Deivi, STA | 1.000 | 6 | 12 | 16 | 0 | 28 | 3 |
| Morel, Elvis, ABD | 1.000 | 2 | 3 | 9 | 0 | 12 | 0 |
| Mullinax, Jacob, NJY | 1.000 | 1 | 4 | 2 | 0 | 6 | 2 |
| Parker, Brett, MHV | .950 | 19 | 39 | 37 | 4 | 80 | 6 |
| Patrick, Christopher, NJY | .968 | 46 | 75 | 108 | 6 | 189 | 17 |
| Penalo, Alex, LOW | .878 | 11 | 14 | 22 | 5 | 41 | 1 |
| Pinckney, Andrew, LOW | .893 | 10 | 8 | 17 | 3 | 28 | 3 |
| Plumley, Grant, STA | .950 | 4 | 5 | 14 | 1 | 20 | 3 |
| Powers, Greg, AUB* | .960 | 9 | 13 | 11 | 1 | 25 | 0 |
| Ramos, Jason, LOW | .947 | 24 | 32 | 40 | 4 | 76 | 5 |
| Reyes, Argenis, MHV | .986 | 17 | 25 | 46 | 1 | 72 | 5 |
| Rios, Kevin, BRK | 1.000 | 21 | 29 | 61 | 0 | 90 | 10 |
| Robinson, Levi, ABD | .953 | 64 | 118 | 145 | 13 | 276 | 17 |
| Rodriguez, Rafael, STA | .923 | 11 | 19 | 29 | 4 | 52 | 4 |
| Sewell, Kevin, JAM* | 1.000 | 1 | 1 | 2 | 0 | 3 | 0 |
| Smith, John, WPT* | 1.000 | 1 | 0 | 2 | 0 | 2 | 1 |
| Solano, Euvi, WPT | .937 | 24 | 38 | 66 | 7 | 111 | 17 |
| SUTTON, DREW, TRC | .979 | 54 | 87 | 146 | 5 | 238 | 33 |
| Szabo, Marshall, MHV | .980 | 23 | 33 | 63 | 2 | 98 | 10 |
| Thomas, Tee, NJY | 1.000 | 1 | 2 | 1 | 0 | 3 | 0 |
| Triplett, Russ, BRK | 1.000 | 1 | 1 | 0 | 0 | 1 | 0 |
| Vechionacci, Marcos, STA | .909 | 7 | 10 | 20 | 3 | 33 | 3 |
| Velez, Eugenio, AUB | .750 | 1 | 1 | 2 | 1 | 4 | 1 |
| Williams, Dee, LOW | 1.000 | 2 | 4 | 4 | 0 | 8 | 0 |
| Williams, Matt, ONE | 1.000 | 3 | 4 | 4 | 0 | 8 | 1 |
| Young, Dusty, JAM | .900 | 1 | 6 | 3 | 1 | 10 | 2 |
| Zech, Bryan, BRK | .943 | 21 | 49 | 50 | 6 | 105 | 16 |

## THIRD BASEMEN

| Player, Team | Pct. | G | PO | A | E | TC | DP |
|---|---|---|---|---|---|---|---|
| Armstrong, Jason, AUB | .873 | 25 | 14 | 41 | 8 | 63 | 1 |
| Ash, Jonny, TRC* | .867 | 43 | 21 | 64 | 13 | 98 | 2 |
| Averill, Brandon, TRC | .914 | 28 | 21 | 43 | 6 | 70 | 3 |
| Babilonia, Edgar, TRC | .870 | 7 | 2 | 18 | 3 | 23 | 2 |
| Bennett, Stacy, BRK* | 1.000 | 1 | 0 | 1 | 0 | 1 | 0 |
| Buffone, Anthony, BAT | .950 | 7 | 4 | 15 | 1 | 20 | 2 |
| Cantu, Tim, NJY | .750 | 3 | 2 | 4 | 2 | 8 | 0 |
| Carroll, Brett, JAM | .791 | 33 | 23 | 45 | 18 | 86 | 8 |
| Castro, Ofilio, VMT | .949 | 51 | 45 | 85 | 7 | 137 | 7 |
| Christian, Justin, STA | 1.000 | 1 | 1 | 1 | 0 | 2 | 0 |
| Clanton, Ja`Mar, VMT | .667 | 2 | 4 | 2 | 3 | 9 | 0 |
| Clem, Chris, MHV | .872 | 20 | 13 | 28 | 6 | 47 | 4 |
| Cleveland, Brian, JAM | .933 | 18 | 8 | 34 | 3 | 45 | 1 |
| Colvin, Brooks, ONE | .893 | 12 | 9 | 16 | 3 | 28 | 3 |
| Conway, Brandon, VMT* | .880 | 17 | 7 | 15 | 3 | 25 | 0 |
| Costello, Mike, ABD | .978 | 17 | 6 | 38 | 1 | 45 | 1 |
| Cottrell, Patrick, HDV | .953 | 55 | 31 | 130 | 8 | 169 | 6 |
| Curtis, Lee, LOW | 1.000 | 1 | 1 | 1 | 0 | 2 | 0 |
| DeVoir, Jordan, STA | .879 | 16 | 2 | 27 | 4 | 33 | 0 |
| Diaz, Rafael, ABD | .873 | 39 | 24 | 65 | 13 | 102 | 2 |
| Dirnberger, Joseph, BAT | .887 | 32 | 15 | 79 | 12 | 106 | 6 |
| Esposito, Vincent, AUB* | .868 | 57 | 22 | 83 | 16 | 121 | 6 |
| Garcia, Travis, BRK | .929 | 11 | 4 | 22 | 2 | 28 | 0 |
| Gimenez, Christopher, MHV | .853 | 28 | 17 | 41 | 10 | 68 | 3 |
| Granadillo, Tony, NJY | .935 | 14 | 10 | 33 | 3 | 46 | 1 |
| Grandstrand, Brett, WPT | .955 | 26 | 8 | 55 | 3 | 66 | 1 |
| Guzman, Heriberto, LOW | .894 | 34 | 31 | 53 | 10 | 94 | 2 |
| Haag, Ryan, STA* | .875 | 5 | 1 | 6 | 1 | 8 | 1 |
| Herrera, Christian, WPT | 1.000 | 3 | 1 | 4 | 0 | 5 | 0 |
| Isaacson, Greg, BAT* | .786 | 9 | 11 | 11 | 6 | 28 | 3 |
| Llamas, Juan, ONE | .944 | 63 | 42 | 92 | 8 | 142 | 6 |
| Macaluso, Mike, AUB | .857 | 1 | 3 | 3 | 1 | 7 | 0 |
| Marconi, Robert, ABD | .899 | 25 | 19 | 52 | 8 | 79 | 3 |
| Mather, Joe, NJY | .857 | 2 | 0 | 6 | 1 | 7 | 0 |
| McCann, Brad, JAM | .817 | 24 | 14 | 35 | 11 | 60 | 2 |
| Mendez, Deivi, STA | .920 | 7 | 7 | 16 | 2 | 25 | 2 |
| MULLINAX, JACOB, NJY | .957 | 55 | 37 | 120 | 7 | 164 | 9 |
| Nowak, Chris, HDV | .930 | 18 | 11 | 29 | 3 | 43 | 1 |
| Orr, Samuel, BAT* | .862 | 27 | 11 | 45 | 9 | 65 | 5 |
| Otness, John, LOW | .937 | 26 | 19 | 40 | 4 | 63 | 3 |
| Paredes, Salvador, HDV | 1.000 | 1 | 2 | 6 | 0 | 8 | 1 |
| Parker, Brett, MHV | .852 | 33 | 14 | 61 | 13 | 88 | 4 |
| Patrick, Christopher, NJY | 1.000 | 1 | 1 | 2 | 0 | 3 | 0 |
| Pinckney, Andrew, LOW | .810 | 18 | 12 | 22 | 8 | 42 | 2 |
| Plumley, Grant, STA | 1.000 | 1 | 1 | 0 | 0 | 1 | 0 |
| Powers, Greg, AUB* | 1.000 | 2 | 3 | 2 | 0 | 5 | 0 |

| Player, Team | Pct. | G | PO | A | E | TC | DP |
|---|---|---|---|---|---|---|---|
| Psomas, Grant, BRK | .923 | 61 | 33 | 111 | 12 | 156 | 9 |
| Reyes, Argenis, MHV | 1.000 | 2 | 4 | 2 | 0 | 6 | 0 |
| Rios, Kevin, BRK | .929 | 6 | 5 | 8 | 1 | 14 | 1 |
| Santiago, John, WPT | .920 | 31 | 22 | 59 | 7 | 88 | 2 |
| Skaug, Brian, TRC | 1.000 | 4 | 3 | 4 | 0 | 7 | 1 |
| Smith, John, WPT* | .873 | 22 | 14 | 41 | 8 | 63 | 4 |
| Solano, Euvi, WPT | 1.000 | 3 | 0 | 2 | 0 | 2 | 0 |
| Sutton, Drew, TRC | .800 | 2 | 0 | 4 | 1 | 5 | 1 |
| Travis, David, VMT* | .870 | 10 | 5 | 15 | 3 | 23 | 0 |
| Vechionacci, Marcos, STA | .962 | 12 | 7 | 18 | 1 | 26 | 1 |
| Velez, Eugenio, AUB | 1.000 | 2 | 0 | 2 | 0 | 2 | 0 |
| Wootan, Tanner, NJY | .000 | 1 | 0 | 0 | 2 | 2 | 0 |
| Youkilis, Kevin, LOW | 1.000 | 2 | 1 | 1 | 0 | 2 | 0 |
| Zamora, Hector, STA* | .904 | 40 | 25 | 60 | 9 | 94 | 1 |

## SHORTSTOPS

| Player, Team | Pct. | G | PO | A | E | TC | DP |
|---|---|---|---|---|---|---|---|
| Amezquita, Octavio, ONE | .914 | 7 | 17 | 15 | 3 | 35 | 4 |
| Armstrong, Jason, AUB | .875 | 7 | 6 | 15 | 3 | 24 | 2 |
| Asanovich, Robert, HDV | .816 | 23 | 26 | 36 | 14 | 76 | 8 |
| Babilonia, Edgar, TRC | .897 | 8 | 10 | 16 | 3 | 29 | 2 |
| Bixler, Brian, WPT | .943 | 59 | 83 | 181 | 16 | 280 | 44 |
| Bouman, John, HDV | .909 | 5 | 9 | 21 | 3 | 33 | 5 |
| Brannon, Evan, ABD | .939 | 23 | 16 | 30 | 3 | 49 | 2 |
| Cantu, Tim, NJY | .875 | 2 | 4 | 3 | 1 | 8 | 1 |
| Castro, Ofilio, VMT | .951 | 16 | 24 | 53 | 4 | 81 | 10 |
| Cleveland, Brian, JAM | 1.000 | 13 | 16 | 44 | 0 | 60 | 5 |
| Colvin, Brooks, ONE | .942 | 22 | 40 | 58 | 6 | 104 | 13 |
| Contreras, Jose, VMT | .909 | 39 | 55 | 95 | 15 | 165 | 16 |
| *Conway, Brandon, VMT | .936 | 19 | 29 | 44 | 5 | 78 | 10 |
| Coultas, Ryan, BRK | .908 | 43 | 55 | 112 | 17 | 184 | 19 |
| Desmond, Ian, VMT | .615 | 4 | 4 | 4 | 5 | 13 | 0 |
| DeVoir, Jordan, STA | 1.000 | 2 | 2 | 5 | 0 | 7 | 0 |
| Dlugach, Brent, ONE | .929 | 47 | 79 | 158 | 18 | 255 | 23 |
| Finegan, Brian, MHV | .926 | 68 | 85 | 191 | 22 | 298 | 22 |
| Fulton, Jonathan, JAM | .919 | 61 | 65 | 195 | 23 | 283 | 29 |
| Gendron, Steve, JAM | .909 | 2 | 3 | 7 | 1 | 11 | 2 |
| Grandstrand, Brett, WPT | 1.000 | 5 | 2 | 12 | 0 | 14 | 1 |
| Hanan, Blake, ABD | .943 | 65 | 88 | 160 | 15 | 263 | 18 |
| Hardy, John, BAT | .915 | 42 | 70 | 113 | 17 | 200 | 20 |
| Herrera, Christian, WPT | .929 | 16 | 19 | 46 | 5 | 70 | 6 |
| Jeroloman, Chuck, LOW | .989 | 23 | 26 | 61 | 1 | 88 | 6 |
| Klosterman, Ryan, AUB | .943 | 65 | 101 | 199 | 18 | 318 | 37 |
| Lara, Christian, LOW | .933 | 32 | 57 | 83 | 10 | 150 | 17 |
| Macaluso, Mike, AUB | .944 | 3 | 5 | 12 | 1 | 18 | 4 |
| Mader, Josh, BAT | .931 | 7 | 9 | 18 | 2 | 29 | 4 |
| Mendez, Deivi, STA | .926 | 12 | 15 | 35 | 4 | 54 | 4 |
| Morel, Elvis, ABD | .957 | 9 | 17 | 28 | 2 | 47 | 5 |
| *Orr, Samuel, BAT | .908 | 27 | 43 | 96 | 14 | 153 | 19 |
| Paredes, Salvador, HDV | .956 | 49 | 73 | 146 | 10 | 229 | 24 |
| Parker, Brett, MHV | .915 | 10 | 12 | 31 | 4 | 47 | 4 |
| Patrick, Christopher, NJY | 1.000 | 4 | 9 | 15 | 0 | 24 | 6 |
| Pinckney, Andrew, LOW | .846 | 5 | 7 | 15 | 4 | 26 | 4 |
| Plumley, Grant, STA | .947 | 57 | 105 | 200 | 17 | 322 | 44 |
| *Powers, Greg, AUB | 1.000 | 1 | 0 | 2 | 0 | 2 | 0 |
| Psomas, Grant, BRK | .929 | 4 | 3 | 10 | 1 | 14 | 1 |
| Ramos, Jason, LOW | .884 | 20 | 24 | 37 | 8 | 69 | 6 |
| Rios, Kevin, BRK | .972 | 29 | 41 | 98 | 4 | 143 | 23 |
| Shepherd, Matt, NJY | .957 | 70 | 122 | 236 | 16 | 374 | 50 |
| Sutton, Drew, TRC | 1.000 | 3 | 6 | 6 | 0 | 12 | 3 |
| Triplett, Russ, BRK | 1.000 | 1 | 0 | 1 | 0 | 1 | 0 |
| Vechionacci, Marcos, STA | 1.000 | 1 | 1 | 4 | 0 | 5 | 0 |
| Velez, Eugenio, AUB | .000 | 1 | 0 | 0 | 1 | 1 | 0 |
| Young, Dusty, JAM | 1.000 | 1 | 0 | 2 | 0 | 2 | 0 |
| ZOBRIST, BEN, TRC | .959 | 68 | 131 | 195 | 14 | 340 | 44 |

## OUTFIELDERS

| Player, Team | Pct. | G | PO | A | E | TC | DP |
|---|---|---|---|---|---|---|---|
| Allen, Rod, STA | 1.000 | 27 | 35 | 2 | 0 | 37 | 1 |
| Alvarez, Wilner, TRC | .968 | 21 | 29 | 1 | 1 | 31 | 0 |
| Ascencion, Quincy, ABD | .975 | 68 | 109 | 8 | 3 | 120 | 0 |
| Babilonia, Edgar, TRC | .935 | 22 | 27 | 2 | 2 | 31 | 1 |
| Baez, Edgardo, VMT | .963 | 43 | 70 | 7 | 3 | 80 | 1 |
| Barganier, Luke, TRC* | .949 | 41 | 54 | 2 | 3 | 59 | 0 |
| Battle, Timothy, STA | .967 | 51 | 110 | 8 | 4 | 122 | 1 |
| Bolen, Josh, HDV | 1.000 | 2 | 4 | 1 | 0 | 5 | 0 |
| Boyer, Kyle, NJY | .882 | 13 | 15 | 0 | 2 | 17 | 0 |
| Breen, Patrick, HDV* | .919 | 38 | 56 | 1 | 5 | 62 | 0 |
| Brinkley, Dante, BRK | .986 | 54 | 63 | 6 | 1 | 70 | 1 |
| Brown, Kyle, BRK | 1.000 | 2 | 5 | 0 | 0 | 5 | 0 |
| Butia, Mike, MHV* | .976 | 47 | 39 | 1 | 1 | 41 | 0 |

| Player, Team | Pct. | G | PO | A | E | TC | DP |
|---|---|---|---|---|---|---|---|
| Caraballo, Francisco, TRC | .929 | 42 | 49 | 3 | 4 | 56 | 0 |
| Carroll, Brett, JAM | .929 | 11 | 13 | 0 | 1 | 14 | 0 |
| Christian, Justin, STA | 1.000 | 5 | 10 | 3 | 0 | 13 | 0 |
| Ciaramella, Matt, LOW | .978 | 32 | 43 | 2 | 1 | 46 | 0 |
| Cleveland, Brian, JAM | 1.000 | 6 | 14 | 0 | 0 | 14 | 0 |
| Cobb, Maurice, VMT | 1.000 | 11 | 5 | 0 | 0 | 5 | 0 |
| Coles, Corey, BRK* | .943 | 60 | 94 | 5 | 6 | 105 | 1 |
| Concepcion, Ambiorix, BRK | .962 | 59 | 122 | 6 | 5 | 133 | 1 |
| Cooper, James, TRC | .987 | 40 | 67 | 7 | 1 | 75 | 3 |
| Crosland, Jason, BAT | .951 | 34 | 38 | 1 | 2 | 41 | 0 |
| Cruz, Jose, MHV | 1.000 | 15 | 15 | 2 | 0 | 17 | 0 |
| Cumberland, Shaun, HDV* | .943 | 49 | 81 | 1 | 5 | 87 | 1 |
| Davidson, Tyler, BRK | 1.000 | 1 | 1 | 0 | 0 | 1 | 0 |
| De La Cruz, Carlos, LOW | .902 | 51 | 71 | 3 | 8 | 82 | 0 |
| DeVoir, Jordan, STA | 1.000 | 4 | 5 | 0 | 0 | 5 | 0 |
| Dobson, Sean, NJY | .960 | 61 | 117 | 2 | 5 | 124 | 1 |
| Duncan, Jacob, ABD* | 1.000 | 4 | 7 | 0 | 0 | 7 | 0 |
| Ehlers, Cody, STA* | 1.000 | 2 | 2 | 0 | 0 | 2 | 0 |
| Encarnacion, Teodoro, MHV | .930 | 55 | 91 | 2 | 7 | 100 | 0 |
| Evans, Robert, LOW* | .963 | 22 | 25 | 1 | 1 | 27 | 0 |
| Ewen, Nick, JAM* | .953 | 47 | 75 | 6 | 4 | 85 | 2 |
| Fiorentino, Jeff, ABD* | .968 | 13 | 29 | 1 | 1 | 31 | 0 |
| Flowers, Bo, ONE | .919 | 64 | 107 | 6 | 10 | 123 | 0 |
| Frazier, Jeff, ONE | 1.000 | 17 | 32 | 4 | 0 | 36 | 0 |
| Frias, Fernando, HDV | .964 | 34 | 50 | 4 | 2 | 56 | 1 |
| Frith, Ryan, BAT | .975 | 63 | 147 | 9 | 4 | 160 | 3 |
| Gamble, Sean, BAT* | .992 | 61 | 114 | 4 | 1 | 119 | 0 |
| Gaston, Jared, JAM | .987 | 42 | 75 | 0 | 1 | 76 | 0 |
| Gimenez, Christopher, MHV | .976 | 22 | 40 | 1 | 1 | 42 | 0 |
| Gonzalez, Edwar, STA | .967 | 28 | 50 | 9 | 2 | 61 | 0 |
| Harris, Estee, STA* | .952 | 50 | 57 | 3 | 3 | 63 | 0 |
| Herbert, Sam, NJY | 1.000 | 17 | 31 | 0 | 0 | 31 | 0 |
| Hicks, Joe, WPT | .889 | 18 | 23 | 1 | 3 | 27 | 0 |
| Holmes, Brett, WPT | .984 | 39 | 59 | 1 | 1 | 61 | 0 |
| House, Kevin, NJY | .933 | 10 | 14 | 0 | 1 | 15 | 0 |
| Johnson, AJ, WPT | .979 | 65 | 131 | 9 | 3 | 143 | 1 |
| Justice, Justin, ONE | .978 | 68 | 131 | 4 | 3 | 138 | 1 |
| Kingsale, Eugene, ABD | 1.000 | 2 | 7 | 0 | 0 | 7 | 0 |
| Leandro, Francisco, HDV* | .984 | 39 | 58 | 3 | 1 | 62 | 0 |
| Ledbetter, Ted, JAM | 1.000 | 3 | 3 | 0 | 0 | 3 | 0 |
| Legrande, Duron, VMT* | .947 | 27 | 68 | 3 | 4 | 75 | 1 |
| Lind, Adam, AUB* | .974 | 61 | 72 | 3 | 2 | 77 | 0 |
| Lindesey, Juan, JAM | .933 | 18 | 25 | 3 | 2 | 30 | 0 |
| Lomack, Jermel, WPT | .966 | 14 | 27 | 1 | 1 | 29 | 0 |
| Lowrance, Marvin, VMT* | .906 | 48 | 73 | 4 | 8 | 85 | 1 |
| Macia, Wanell, WPT* | .975 | 45 | 75 | 3 | 2 | 80 | 1 |
| Mangioni, Jarad, AUB | .981 | 36 | 50 | 3 | 1 | 54 | 0 |
| Mathews, Aaron, AUB | .992 | 69 | 127 | 4 | 1 | 132 | 0 |
| McRae, Aaron, ONE* | 1.000 | 1 | 2 | 0 | 0 | 2 | 0 |
| Metropoulos, Joey, AUB | 1.000 | 3 | 3 | 0 | 0 | 3 | 0 |
| Moni, Timi, BAT | .933 | 20 | 28 | 0 | 2 | 30 | 0 |
| Montgomery, Tim, MHV | .970 | 56 | 97 | 1 | 3 | 101 | 0 |
| Morel, Elvis, ABD | 1.000 | 1 | 1 | 0 | 0 | 1 | 0 |
| Mortimer, Steve, VMT* | .956 | 20 | 38 | 5 | 2 | 45 | 0 |
| Nielsen, Eric, AUB | .970 | 64 | 91 | 5 | 3 | 99 | 1 |
| Otness, John, LOW | .889 | 6 | 6 | 2 | 1 | 9 | 0 |
| Parrish, Matt, ONE | .938 | 20 | 29 | 1 | 2 | 32 | 1 |
| Pence, Hunter, TRC | .963 | 50 | 101 | 2 | 4 | 107 | 1 |
| Perez, Fernando, HDV | .974 | 69 | 145 | 5 | 4 | 154 | 1 |
| Pietro, Joseph, JAM* | .962 | 65 | 146 | 6 | 6 | 158 | 2 |
| Reyes, Argenis, MHV | 1.000 | 42 | 82 | 4 | 0 | 86 | 1 |
| Rich, Scott, STA | .963 | 30 | 49 | 3 | 2 | 54 | 0 |
| Ritchie, Jake, HDV | .750 | 3 | 3 | 0 | 1 | 4 | 0 |
| Rivas, Arturo, ABD | .966 | 52 | 109 | 6 | 4 | 119 | 0 |
| Rodriguez, Marcos, NJY* | .912 | 18 | 27 | 4 | 3 | 34 | 1 |
| Sandora, Robert, VMT* | 1.000 | 9 | 13 | 0 | 0 | 13 | 0 |
| Sewell, Kevin, JAM* | .985 | 50 | 61 | 4 | 1 | 66 | 0 |
| Shafer, Corey, ABD* | .988 | 39 | 79 | 5 | 1 | 85 | 1 |
| Sherman, Steve, NJY* | 1.000 | 57 | 100 | 5 | 0 | 105 | 0 |
| Shimer, Nicholas, BAT | .979 | 45 | 94 | 1 | 2 | 97 | 1 |
| Smith, Sean, WPT | 1.000 | 47 | 90 | 2 | 0 | 92 | 0 |
| Sovie, Robbie, ONE | 1.000 | 7 | 14 | 0 | 0 | 14 | 0 |
| Stewart, Caleb, BRK | .929 | 16 | 13 | 0 | 1 | 14 | 0 |
| Sultemeier, Eric, ABD | .990 | 55 | 94 | 10 | 1 | 105 | 0 |
| SWACKHAMER, WES, NJY* | 1.000 | 55 | 72 | 1 | 0 | 73 | 0 |
| Tierce, Evan, STA* | 1.000 | 11 | 17 | 2 | 0 | 19 | 0 |
| Tulk, Robert, ONE* | .948 | 36 | 52 | 3 | 3 | 58 | 0 |
| Turner, Chris, LOW | .966 | 41 | 79 | 5 | 3 | 87 | 3 |
| Van Der Bosch, Matt, LOW* | .983 | 52 | 109 | 4 | 2 | 115 | 0 |
| Villanova, Robert, STA* | 1.000 | 28 | 41 | 0 | 0 | 41 | 0 |
| Vital, Kevin, TRC* | .933 | 25 | 39 | 3 | 3 | 45 | 0 |
| Vroman, Douglas, VMT | .951 | 68 | 148 | 7 | 8 | 163 | 2 |
| Watts, Derran, BRK | .966 | 40 | 80 | 5 | 3 | 88 | 0 |
| Webber, Levi, NJY | 1.000 | 3 | 7 | 0 | 0 | 7 | 0 |

| Player, Team | Pct. | G | PO | A | E | TC | DP |
|---|---|---|---|---|---|---|---|
| Williams, Dee, LOW | .891 | 40 | 55 | 2 | 7 | 64 | 1 |
| Williams, Matt, ONE | .892 | 22 | 30 | 3 | 4 | 37 | 0 |
| Williams, Simon, NJY | 1.000 | 6 | 11 | 0 | 0 | 11 | 0 |

## CATCHERS

| Player, Team | Pct. | G | PO | A | E | TC | DP | PB |
|---|---|---|---|---|---|---|---|---|
| Alen, Luis, JAM | .994 | 39 | 280 | 29 | 2 | 311 | 2 | 8 |
| Barnes, Justin, ONE | .972 | 23 | 129 | 9 | 4 | 142 | 2 | 1 |
| Bennett, Stacy, BRK* | .991 | 16 | 96 | 19 | 1 | 116 | 0 | 3 |
| Bock, Brian, ABD | .958 | 10 | 63 | 5 | 3 | 71 | 0 | 2 |
| Brant, Derek, BAT | .995 | 24 | 178 | 10 | 1 | 189 | 2 | 4 |
| Braun, Ron, ABD | 1.000 | 5 | 17 | 1 | 0 | 18 | 0 | 3 |
| Burkhart, Lance, ABD | 1.000 | 1 | 5 | 0 | 0 | 5 | 0 | 0 |
| Caradonna, Troy, STA | .983 | 22 | 163 | 9 | 3 | 175 | 0 | 6 |
| Casillas, Omar, MHV | 1.000 | 23 | 128 | 18 | 0 | 146 | 0 | 9 |
| Clark, Chris, TRC | 1.000 | 7 | 68 | 8 | 0 | 76 | 0 | 0 |
| Clendenin, Morgan, ABD* | .981 | 28 | 187 | 22 | 4 | 213 | 1 | 10 |
| Cloninger, Erich, LOW | .986 | 12 | 68 | 4 | 1 | 73 | 0 | 2 |
| Corrente, David, AUB | .988 | 32 | 221 | 19 | 3 | 243 | 0 | 10 |
| Davis, Brad, JAM | .984 | 39 | 298 | 19 | 5 | 322 | 2 | 11 |
| Elliott, Justin, WPT | .939 | 5 | 29 | 2 | 2 | 33 | 0 | 1 |
| Encarnacion, Teodoro, MHV | 1.000 | 1 | 1 | 0 | 0 | 1 | 0 | 0 |
| Fiorentino, Jeff, ABD* | 1.000 | 1 | 9 | 1 | 0 | 10 | 0 | 0 |
| Flores, Jesus, BRK | 1.000 | 3 | 16 | 1 | 0 | 17 | 0 | 1 |
| Garcia, Yunir, BRK | 1.000 | 12 | 100 | 8 | 0 | 108 | 1 | 0 |
| Gerlits, Gooby, AUB | 1.000 | 6 | 27 | 1 | 0 | 28 | 0 | 1 |
| Gimenez, Christopher, MHV | 1.000 | 3 | 11 | 1 | 0 | 12 | 1 | 1 |
| Graham, Andrew, ONE | .984 | 8 | 53 | 7 | 1 | 61 | 1 | 5 |
| Hathaway, Aaron, BRK | .983 | 40 | 289 | 59 | 6 | 354 | 3 | 7 |
| Ivany, Devin, VMT | .988 | 9 | 71 | 10 | 1 | 82 | 0 | 2 |
| Jaramillo, Jason, BAT | .993 | 18 | 123 | 11 | 1 | 135 | 0 | 8 |
| Jaso, John, HDV* | .985 | 25 | 181 | 20 | 3 | 204 | 0 | 1 |
| Jenkins, Clyde, VMT | 1.000 | 1 | 5 | 2 | 0 | 7 | 0 | 0 |
| Karlsen, Grant, BAT | .983 | 19 | 164 | 13 | 3 | 180 | 2 | 3 |
| Koch, Brady, TRC | .976 | 9 | 80 | 3 | 2 | 85 | 0 | 5 |
| Koenig, Lance, TRC | .982 | 20 | 148 | 12 | 3 | 163 | 0 | 4 |
| Kratz, Erik, AUB | 1.000 | 9 | 72 | 10 | 0 | 82 | 0 | 1 |
| Lerud, Steve, WPT* | 1.000 | 4 | 31 | 4 | 0 | 35 | 0 | 2 |
| Manriquez, Salomon, VMT | .978 | 7 | 38 | 7 | 1 | 46 | 0 | 0 |
| Martinez, Octavio, ABD | .982 | 7 | 55 | 1 | 1 | 57 | 0 | 5 |
| Matulich, Mario, MHV | 1.000 | 6 | 33 | 5 | 0 | 38 | 1 | 1 |
| McRae, Aaron, ONE* | 1.000 | 3 | 3 | 0 | 0 | 3 | 0 | 0 |
| Mendez, Carlos, ABD | 1.000 | 4 | 27 | 2 | 0 | 29 | 0 | 1 |
| Montz, Luke, VMT | .991 | 28 | 189 | 32 | 2 | 223 | 2 | 6 |
| Nelson, Kevin, STA | .995 | 25 | 173 | 14 | 1 | 188 | 2 | 6 |
| Nino, Denny, WPT | 1.000 | 4 | 26 | 3 | 0 | 29 | 0 | 0 |
| Norman, Zach, BAT | .990 | 14 | 86 | 10 | 1 | 97 | 0 | 9 |
| Palmer, Cody, NJY | .976 | 31 | 191 | 14 | 5 | 210 | 2 | 2 |
| Paniagua, Salvador, LOW | .974 | 48 | 411 | 40 | 12 | 463 | 0 | 13 |
| Perry, Patrick, LOW* | .984 | 25 | 225 | 20 | 4 | 249 | 0 | 4 |
| Pierce, Whit, ABD | .958 | 7 | 67 | 1 | 3 | 71 | 0 | 0 |
| Pilittere, Peter, STA | .996 | 31 | 255 | 12 | 1 | 268 | 0 | 11 |
| Poppert, John, VMT | .968 | 28 | 216 | 28 | 8 | 252 | 1 | 9 |
| Reddinger, Brandon, WPT | .977 | 29 | 151 | 20 | 4 | 175 | 0 | 2 |
| Reyes, Milver, WPT | .987 | 34 | 205 | 27 | 3 | 235 | 1 | 6 |
| Reynoso, Danilo, BRK | .951 | 14 | 73 | 5 | 4 | 82 | 1 | 2 |
| Roa, Joel, ONE | .993 | 18 | 133 | 13 | 1 | 147 | 1 | 4 |
| Ryan, Dusty, ONE | .985 | 44 | 277 | 46 | 5 | 328 | 1 | 11 |
| Sandora, Robert, VMT* | 1.000 | 3 | 8 | 2 | 0 | 10 | 0 | 0 |
| SANTANGELO, LOU, TRC | .995 | 43 | 368 | 43 | 2 | 413 | 1 | 9 |
| Spring, Matthew, HDV | .989 | 35 | 231 | 39 | 3 | 273 | 0 | 10 |
| Taillon, Cory, NJY | .987 | 20 | 134 | 19 | 2 | 155 | 1 | 0 |
| Thigpen, Curtis, AUB | .990 | 32 | 265 | 25 | 3 | 293 | 0 | 12 |
| Toops, Brady, NJY* | .988 | 32 | 224 | 23 | 3 | 250 | 0 | 3 |
| Toregas, Wyatt, MHV | .992 | 53 | 469 | 39 | 4 | 512 | 1 | 12 |
| Walker, Neil, WPT | .947 | 4 | 30 | 6 | 2 | 38 | 0 | 4 |
| Wargo, Cody, ABD | .996 | 31 | 198 | 31 | 1 | 230 | 1 | 4 |
| Woodruff, Ernest, HDV | .970 | 16 | 123 | 7 | 4 | 134 | 0 | 5 |
| Wyman, Spencer, JAM* | 1.000 | 9 | 43 | 4 | 0 | 47 | 0 | 2 |
| *Yarbrough, Brandon, NJY | 1.000 | 2 | 13 | 2 | 0 | 15 | 0 | 0 |

## PITCHERS

| Player, Team | Pct. | G | PO | A | E | TC | DP |
|---|---|---|---|---|---|---|---|
| Abreu, Eric, STA | 1.000 | 7 | 0 | 3 | 0 | 3 | 0 |
| Acosta, Adam, NJY | .750 | 8 | 2 | 1 | 1 | 4 | 0 |
| Acosta, Richard, ABD | .857 | 11 | 3 | 3 | 1 | 7 | 0 |
| Aguero, Miguel, NJY | .957 | 15 | 10 | 12 | 1 | 23 | 3 |
| Ainsworth, Kurt, ABD | 1.000 | 2 | 0 | 1 | 0 | 1 | 0 |
| Alexander, Stuart, JAM | .667 | 2 | 1 | 1 | 1 | 3 | 0 |
| Alfonzo, Edgar, BRK* | 1.000 | 20 | 4 | 5 | 0 | 9 | 1 |
| Allen, Kyle, BAT* | .889 | 13 | 3 | 5 | 1 | 9 | 0 |
| Almenar, Aristedes, BRK | 1.000 | 7 | 1 | 2 | 0 | 3 | 0 |
| Alvarado, Andrew, TRC | .909 | 11 | 3 | 7 | 1 | 11 | 0 |
| Azze, Justin, ABD* | .846 | 20 | 4 | 7 | 2 | 13 | 0 |
| Baird, Jack, NJY | 1.000 | 4 | 1 | 3 | 0 | 4 | 0 |
| Baldwin, Andrew, BAT | .818 | 15 | 4 | 5 | 2 | 11 | 0 |
| Barkley, Richard, STA | 1.000 | 4 | 0 | 1 | 0 | 1 | 0 |
| Barone, Daniel, JAM | 1.000 | 19 | 4 | 4 | 0 | 8 | 0 |
| Barrack, Jacob, BAT | 1.000 | 12 | 1 | 5 | 0 | 6 | 0 |
| Barratt, Jonathan, HDV* | .923 | 10 | 3 | 9 | 1 | 13 | 0 |
| Barriger, Marcus, HDV | .500 | 14 | 0 | 2 | 2 | 4 | 0 |
| Baxter, Allen, JAM | .900 | 10 | 3 | 6 | 1 | 10 | 1 |
| Baysinger, Daniel, NJY | 1.000 | 7 | 2 | 1 | 0 | 3 | 0 |
| Baysinger, Trent, ABD* | .900 | 26 | 4 | 5 | 1 | 10 | 0 |
| Beam, Randy, LOW* | 1.000 | 9 | 3 | 3 | 0 | 6 | 0 |
| Beam, TJ, STA | .636 | 12 | 5 | 2 | 4 | 11 | 0 |
| Bell, Kristian, AUB | 1.000 | 19 | 5 | 5 | 0 | 10 | 0 |
| Bigda, Drew, HDV* | 1.000 | 2 | 0 | 1 | 0 | 1 | 0 |
| Bimeal, Matt, WPT | .833 | 15 | 1 | 4 | 1 | 6 | 0 |
| Bisenius, Joseph, BAT | 1.000 | 11 | 2 | 3 | 0 | 5 | 0 |
| Bishop, Matt, WPT | 1.000 | 21 | 2 | 1 | 0 | 3 | 0 |
| Bitter, Ryan, HDV | 1.000 | 21 | 1 | 3 | 0 | 4 | 0 |
| Blackley, Adam, LOW* | 1.000 | 1 | 0 | 3 | 0 | 3 | 0 |
| Blackwell, Brad, STA | 1.000 | 21 | 0 | 9 | 0 | 9 | 1 |
| Bloom, Kyle, WPT* | 1.000 | 11 | 1 | 11 | 0 | 12 | 0 |
| Boehm, Kyle, ABD | .778 | 19 | 3 | 4 | 2 | 9 | 0 |
| Bono, Kyle, LOW | 1.000 | 6 | 1 | 5 | 0 | 6 | 0 |
| Bova, Chris, NJY | .808 | 19 | 2 | 19 | 5 | 26 | 0 |
| Brandenburg, Adam, JAM* | 1.000 | 3 | 1 | 2 | 0 | 3 | 0 |
| Brocato, Russ, ABD | .900 | 15 | 7 | 2 | 1 | 10 | 0 |
| Brown, Casey, TRC | .917 | 21 | 3 | 8 | 1 | 12 | 1 |
| Brown, Justin, NJY | .500 | 2 | 0 | 2 | 2 | 4 | 0 |
| Brown, Kevin, STA | .000 | 1 | 0 | 0 | 0 | 0 | 0 |
| Bumstead, Nate, ONE | 1.000 | 11 | 2 | 3 | 0 | 5 | 1 |
| Bunn, Greg, VMT | .000 | 9 | 0 | 0 | 0 | 0 | 0 |
| Cahill, Casey, ABD | .889 | 21 | 2 | 6 | 1 | 9 | 0 |
| Camacho, Eddy, BRK* | 1.000 | 20 | 0 | 10 | 0 | 10 | 0 |
| Campbell, Richard, VMT | .667 | 11 | 0 | 2 | 1 | 3 | 0 |
| Cannon, Eddie, AUB | 1.000 | 1 | 0 | 1 | 0 | 1 | 0 |
| Cantu, Tim, NJY | .000 | 1 | 0 | 0 | 0 | 0 | 0 |
| Capps, Matt, WPT | 1.000 | 11 | 6 | 9 | 0 | 15 | 1 |
| Carmosino, Dominic, ONE* | 1.000 | 6 | 0 | 1 | 0 | 1 | 0 |
| Cerezo, Hector, VMT* | .000 | 9 | 0 | 0 | 0 | 0 | 0 |
| Cevette, Dan, MHV* | 1.000 | 7 | 4 | 4 | 0 | 8 | 0 |
| Chamberlin, Bryce, ABD | .800 | 12 | 3 | 1 | 1 | 5 | 0 |
| Childs, Ryan, ABD | 1.000 | 21 | 4 | 2 | 0 | 6 | 0 |
| Clelland, Ed, ONE* | .778 | 26 | 1 | 6 | 2 | 9 | 0 |
| Cline, Zac, BAT* | 1.000 | 8 | 0 | 4 | 0 | 4 | 0 |
| Cobb, Matthew, HDV* | 1.000 | 13 | 1 | 8 | 0 | 9 | 0 |
| Cochran, Thomas, LOW* | 1.000 | 22 | 0 | 1 | 0 | 1 | 0 |
| Coke, Phil, STA* | 1.000 | 3 | 0 | 1 | 0 | 1 | 0 |
| Collins, Kyle, MHV | 1.000 | 14 | 5 | 7 | 0 | 12 | 0 |
| Contreras, Manuel, ONE | 1.000 | 5 | 1 | 1 | 0 | 2 | 0 |
| Cook, Steven, VMT | .917 | 12 | 4 | 7 | 1 | 12 | 0 |
| Correa, Jose, BAT | 1.000 | 21 | 2 | 8 | 0 | 10 | 0 |
| Cox, Ben, VMT | 1.000 | 22 | 0 | 3 | 0 | 3 | 0 |
| Craig, Dustin, WPT | 1.000 | 28 | 1 | 4 | 0 | 5 | 0 |
| Cuen, David, STA* | 1.000 | 19 | 2 | 5 | 0 | 7 | 0 |
| Dalton, Matt, AUB | 1.000 | 6 | 2 | 3 | 0 | 5 | 0 |
| Danly, Ryan, BRK* | 1.000 | 1 | 0 | 1 | 0 | 1 | 0 |
| Day, Dewon, AUB | .778 | 28 | 0 | 7 | 2 | 9 | 0 |
| De Los Santos, Richa, MHV | 1.000 | 13 | 9 | 10 | 0 | 19 | 0 |
| Delacruz, Eduardo, HDV | 1.000 | 14 | 4 | 7 | 0 | 11 | 0 |
| Delacruz, Jose, HDV | 1.000 | 18 | 1 | 2 | 0 | 3 | 0 |
| Della Rocco, Chris, NJY | .905 | 19 | 4 | 15 | 2 | 21 | 1 |
| Devaney, Michael, BRK | .857 | 14 | 4 | 8 | 2 | 14 | 0 |
| DeWitt, Anthony, TRC | 1.000 | 13 | 3 | 5 | 0 | 8 | 0 |
| Diaz, Eddie, VMT | 1.000 | 17 | 1 | 0 | 0 | 1 | 0 |
| Diaz, Raymar, TRC | .955 | 15 | 9 | 12 | 1 | 22 | 0 |
| Dicken, Randy, AUB | 1.000 | 8 | 1 | 1 | 0 | 2 | 0 |
| Dickerson, Bo, NJY | .000 | 1 | 0 | 0 | 1 | 1 | 0 |
| Dobies, Andrew, LOW* | 1.000 | 14 | 1 | 4 | 0 | 5 | 0 |
| Dobyns, Jonathan, HDV | .000 | 1 | 0 | 0 | 0 | 0 | 0 |
| Dove, Dennis, NJY | .750 | 6 | 2 | 1 | 1 | 4 | 0 |
| Doyne, Michael, NJY | 1.000 | 30 | 3 | 7 | 0 | 10 | 1 |
| Drage, Derek, WPT | .800 | 17 | 4 | 4 | 2 | 10 | 0 |
| Dumesnil, Bryan, ABD* | .000 | 4 | 0 | 0 | 0 | 0 | 0 |
| Eager, Blake, BRK | 1.000 | 2 | 1 | 0 | 0 | 1 | 0 |
| Eddy, Cooper, LOW | 1.000 | 21 | 3 | 9 | 0 | 12 | 1 |
| Edmiston, Bo, TRC | 1.000 | 20 | 4 | 4 | 0 | 8 | 0 |
| Edwards, Drew, STA | 1.000 | 15 | 3 | 6 | 0 | 9 | 0 |
| Ehrlich, Drew, LOW | .667 | 14 | 0 | 2 | 1 | 3 | 0 |
| Englebrook, Evan, TRC | .667 | 14 | 3 | 3 | 3 | 9 | 0 |
| Escobar, Rodrigo, TRC | .857 | 25 | 0 | 12 | 2 | 14 | 0 |

| Player, Team | Pct. | G | PO | A | E | TC | DP |
|---|---|---|---|---|---|---|---|
| Estrada, Paul, TRC | .875 | 23 | 4 | 3 | 1 | 8 | 0 |
| Felfoldi, Jonathan, VMT* | .947 | 9 | 5 | 13 | 1 | 19 | 0 |
| Felix, Wilken, ABD | 1.000 | 7 | 1 | 3 | 0 | 4 | 0 |
| Figueroa, Juan, ONE | 1.000 | 9 | 1 | 0 | 0 | 1 | 0 |
| Foli, Daniel, BRK | 1.000 | 3 | 1 | 0 | 0 | 1 | 0 |
| Freitas, Julio, BRK | 1.000 | 10 | 0 | 3 | 0 | 3 | 0 |
| Garcia, Harvey, LOW | 1.000 | 14 | 1 | 8 | 0 | 9 | 1 |
| Garza, Rudy, VMT | 1.000 | 2 | 0 | 1 | 0 | 1 | 0 |
| Glanzmann, Jake, LOW* | 1.000 | 5 | 0 | 4 | 0 | 4 | 0 |
| Gogal, Jeffrey, JAM* | .900 | 11 | 1 | 8 | 1 | 10 | 1 |
| Goodman, Chris, VMT | 1.000 | 8 | 4 | 3 | 0 | 7 | 0 |
| Goodson, Matt, LOW | .900 | 12 | 4 | 5 | 1 | 10 | 1 |
| Grant, Brian, AUB | 1.000 | 1 | 0 | 1 | 0 | 1 | 0 |
| Griffith, Derek, BAT* | 1.000 | 14 | 3 | 7 | 0 | 10 | 0 |
| Gross, Mike, NJY | .875 | 13 | 1 | 6 | 1 | 8 | 1 |
| Guillory, Matt, WPT | .917 | 14 | 7 | 4 | 1 | 12 | 0 |
| Haberer, Eric, NJY* | 1.000 | 3 | 1 | 7 | 0 | 8 | 3 |
| Haehnel, David, ABD* | 1.000 | 28 | 1 | 5 | 0 | 6 | 0 |
| Hankins, Derek, WPT | .941 | 14 | 3 | 13 | 1 | 17 | 0 |
| Happ, James, BAT* | 1.000 | 11 | 3 | 7 | 0 | 10 | 0 |
| Harper, Jeremy, AUB | 1.000 | 3 | 1 | 0 | 0 | 1 | 0 |
| Harris, Mark, MHV | 1.000 | 29 | 6 | 11 | 0 | 17 | 1 |
| Hart, Kevin, ABD | 1.000 | 9 | 1 | 3 | 0 | 4 | 0 |
| Haynes, Matt, MHV | .833 | 18 | 5 | 0 | 1 | 6 | 0 |
| Henderson, Jim, VMT | 1.000 | 14 | 6 | 11 | 0 | 17 | 0 |
| Herce, Steve, WPT | 1.000 | 18 | 8 | 10 | 0 | 18 | 0 |
| Hernandez, Michael, MHV* | 1.000 | 10 | 1 | 2 | 0 | 3 | 0 |
| Hertzler, Barry, LOW | .857 | 15 | 2 | 16 | 3 | 21 | 0 |
| Hill, Danny, AUB | 1.000 | 8 | 2 | 3 | 0 | 5 | 0 |
| Hiraldo, Nelson, MHV | .875 | 7 | 3 | 4 | 1 | 8 | 0 |
| Hlebovy, Gus, VMT | 1.000 | 30 | 1 | 0 | 0 | 1 | 0 |
| Hoff, Brian, JAM | .833 | 19 | 1 | 4 | 1 | 6 | 0 |
| Hogan, Patrick, JAM | 1.000 | 25 | 1 | 5 | 0 | 6 | 1 |
| Honsa, Chris, BAT | 1.000 | 6 | 1 | 1 | 0 | 2 | 0 |
| Hoover, Jesse, STA | .625 | 16 | 2 | 3 | 3 | 8 | 0 |
| Hottovy, Tommy, LOW* | .857 | 14 | 1 | 5 | 1 | 7 | 0 |
| Hoyman, Justin, MHV | 1.000 | 5 | 0 | 4 | 0 | 4 | 0 |
| Humen, David, JAM | 1.000 | 13 | 3 | 1 | 0 | 4 | 0 |
| Hummel, John, WPT* | 1.000 | 8 | 0 | 1 | 0 | 1 | 0 |
| Hyde, Scott, BRK | .929 | 10 | 3 | 10 | 1 | 14 | 0 |
| Jackson, Zachary, AUB* | 1.000 | 4 | 1 | 4 | 0 | 5 | 0 |
| Jacobson, Tyler, ONE | .778 | 19 | 3 | 4 | 2 | 9 | 0 |
| James, Mike, LOW | .917 | 20 | 3 | 8 | 1 | 12 | 0 |
| James, Rhett, JAM | .900 | 17 | 3 | 6 | 1 | 10 | 0 |
| Janssen, Casey, AUB | .941 | 10 | 7 | 9 | 1 | 17 | 2 |
| Jecman, Mark, MHV | 1.000 | 20 | 5 | 4 | 0 | 9 | 1 |
| Jenkins, Clyde, VMT | .800 | 6 | 1 | 3 | 1 | 5 | 0 |
| John, Jason, NJY | 1.000 | 9 | 1 | 4 | 0 | 5 | 0 |
| Johnson, Blair, WPT | .949 | 14 | 16 | 21 | 2 | 39 | 1 |
| Johnson, Nathan, BAT | 1.000 | 18 | 3 | 5 | 0 | 8 | 0 |
| Jones, Jason, STA | 1.000 | 8 | 3 | 11 | 0 | 14 | 2 |
| Jurrjens, Jair, ONE | 1.000 | 7 | 3 | 2 | 0 | 5 | 0 |
| Karsay, Steve, STA | 1.000 | 3 | 2 | 0 | 0 | 2 | 0 |
| Kauten, Josh, ONE | 1.000 | 12 | 6 | 3 | 0 | 9 | 0 |
| Kendrick, Kyle, BAT | .923 | 13 | 3 | 9 | 1 | 13 | 0 |
| Kiley, Jason, WPT | .000 | 4 | 0 | 0 | 0 | 0 | 0 |
| King, Ben, STA* | 1.000 | 2 | 0 | 2 | 0 | 2 | 1 |
| King, Tim, HDV* | .769 | 11 | 7 | 3 | 3 | 13 | 0 |
| Knippschild, Ryan, MHV* | 1.000 | 15 | 2 | 13 | 0 | 15 | 0 |
| Knox, Matt, MHV | 1.000 | 23 | 0 | 5 | 0 | 5 | 0 |
| Knox, Mike, STA | .889 | 15 | 1 | 7 | 1 | 9 | 0 |
| Konecny, Dan, ONE | .833 | 14 | 0 | 5 | 1 | 6 | 0 |
| Kown, Andrew, ONE | .800 | 9 | 0 | 4 | 1 | 5 | 1 |
| Kramer, Sean, STA* | .833 | 12 | 1 | 9 | 2 | 12 | 1 |
| Lacher, Jeffery, JAM | 1.000 | 16 | 3 | 3 | 0 | 6 | 0 |
| Laffey, Aaron, MHV* | .923 | 8 | 0 | 12 | 1 | 13 | 0 |
| Landing, Jeffrey, BRK | 1.000 | 8 | 2 | 1 | 0 | 3 | 0 |
| Lavergne, Jarrad, HDV* | 1.000 | 12 | 2 | 15 | 0 | 17 | 0 |
| Leonard, Chris, AUB* | .800 | 20 | 3 | 5 | 2 | 10 | 0 |
| Lerch, Zachary, JAM | .875 | 13 | 3 | 4 | 1 | 8 | 0 |
| Lewis, Lavon, ONE | 1.000 | 12 | 8 | 4 | 0 | 12 | 1 |
| Lincoln, Roger, MHV* | .909 | 24 | 3 | 7 | 1 | 11 | 0 |
| Lovato, Nick, JAM* | .000 | 2 | 0 | 0 | 0 | 0 | 0 |
| Lubrano, Paul, MHV* | .875 | 10 | 3 | 4 | 1 | 8 | 0 |
| Lybarger, Craig, JAM* | 1.000 | 2 | 1 | 0 | 0 | 1 | 0 |
| Lyons, Tom, ONE | 1.000 | 2 | 0 | 1 | 0 | 1 | 0 |
| MacDonald, Mike, AUB | 1.000 | 8 | 5 | 10 | 0 | 15 | 0 |
| MacLane, Evan, BRK* | .958 | 13 | 6 | 17 | 1 | 24 | 1 |
| Mahoney, Collin, ONE | .800 | 21 | 2 | 2 | 1 | 5 | 0 |
| Maldonado, Ivan, BRK | 1.000 | 2 | 0 | 1 | 0 | 1 | 0 |
| Mann, Brandon, HDV* | 1.000 | 14 | 1 | 4 | 0 | 5 | 0 |
| Marquez, Jeff, STA | .952 | 11 | 3 | 17 | 1 | 21 | 0 |

| Player, Team | Pct. | G | PO | A | E | TC | DP |
|---|---|---|---|---|---|---|---|
| Martinez, Cristhian, ONE | 1.000 | 2 | 0 | 1 | 0 | 1 | 0 |
| Martinez, Jason, BAT* | .889 | 19 | 2 | 6 | 1 | 9 | 0 |
| Martinez, Michael, STA | 1.000 | 16 | 4 | 6 | 0 | 10 | 0 |
| Martinez, Ronnie, TRC | 1.000 | 15 | 11 | 9 | 0 | 20 | 1 |
| McCrory, Robert, ABD | .000 | 1 | 0 | 0 | 0 | 0 | 0 |
| McKeller, Ryan, TRC | .864 | 14 | 7 | 12 | 3 | 22 | 0 |
| McKenzie, Casey, AUB | 1.000 | 15 | 5 | 7 | 0 | 12 | 2 |
| McLaughlin, Joey, AUB | .923 | 23 | 5 | 7 | 1 | 13 | 0 |
| Mendez, Winer, ABD | .750 | 4 | 2 | 4 | 2 | 8 | 1 |
| Meyers, Ryan, BRK* | .000 | 1 | 0 | 0 | 0 | 0 | 0 |
| Michael, Mark, WPT | .778 | 14 | 1 | 6 | 2 | 9 | 0 |
| Mihalik, Mike, BAT | 1.000 | 4 | 1 | 0 | 0 | 1 | 0 |
| Mobley, Chris, JAM | .909 | 17 | 3 | 7 | 1 | 11 | 0 |
| Molldrem, Craig, JAM | 1.000 | 5 | 2 | 3 | 0 | 5 | 0 |
| Morales, Ricardo, VMT* | 1.000 | 1 | 0 | 1 | 0 | 1 | 0 |
| Mumma, Bradley, AUB* | .667 | 1 | 1 | 1 | 1 | 3 | 0 |
| Muniz, Carlos, BRK | 1.000 | 12 | 0 | 1 | 0 | 1 | 0 |
| Munoz, Luis, WPT | 1.000 | 15 | 5 | 9 | 0 | 14 | 2 |
| Murdy, Garrett, TRC | 1.000 | 7 | 1 | 3 | 0 | 4 | 0 |
| Myers, Damien, ONE* | .917 | 20 | 5 | 6 | 1 | 12 | 0 |
| Neylan, Chris, AUB* | 1.000 | 17 | 2 | 5 | 0 | 7 | 0 |
| Nickerson, Jon, JAM | 1.000 | 9 | 1 | 4 | 0 | 5 | 0 |
| Niesel, Chris, MHV | 1.000 | 5 | 2 | 5 | 0 | 7 | 0 |
| Ochoa, Nehomar, VMT | .714 | 5 | 1 | 4 | 2 | 7 | 0 |
| Ortega, Joel, WPT | 1.000 | 3 | 1 | 0 | 0 | 1 | 0 |
| Overton, Brad, BAT | 1.000 | 7 | 2 | 3 | 0 | 5 | 0 |
| Parisi, Michael, NJY | .857 | 7 | 3 | 3 | 1 | 7 | 0 |
| Parker, Brett, MHV | 1.000 | 1 | 0 | 1 | 0 | 1 | 0 |
| Parker, Shaun, STA* | .905 | 19 | 2 | 17 | 2 | 21 | 0 |
| Paz, Jackson, NJY* | 1.000 | 16 | 1 | 5 | 0 | 6 | 3 |
| Pekarek, Justin, MHV* | 1.000 | 7 | 1 | 3 | 0 | 4 | 0 |
| Pender, Matt, ONE | 1.000 | 6 | 0 | 1 | 0 | 1 | 0 |
| Peralta, Tony, ONE* | 1.000 | 22 | 5 | 3 | 0 | 8 | 1 |
| Perez, Alex, STA | 1.000 | 2 | 0 | 1 | 0 | 1 | 0 |
| Perez, Carlos, ABD* | .696 | 15 | 3 | 13 | 7 | 23 | 1 |
| Perez, Ezequil, ONE | 1.000 | 23 | 0 | 4 | 0 | 4 | 0 |
| Perez, Juan, AUB | .833 | 12 | 4 | 6 | 2 | 12 | 1 |
| Perez, Marcelo, BRK | 1.000 | 17 | 4 | 5 | 0 | 9 | 0 |
| Petrick, Russ, ABD* | .875 | 20 | 2 | 12 | 2 | 16 | 0 |
| Potter, Josh, ABD | 1.000 | 3 | 0 | 1 | 0 | 1 | 1 |
| Price, John, HDV* | 1.000 | 12 | 1 | 4 | 0 | 5 | 0 |
| Prieto, Victor, JAM | 1.000 | 1 | 0 | 1 | 0 | 1 | 0 |
| Purcey, David, AUB* | .667 | 3 | 0 | 2 | 1 | 3 | 0 |
| Quaglieri, Will, BRK | 1.000 | 11 | 3 | 6 | 0 | 9 | 0 |
| Quarles, Jason, WPT | .667 | 23 | 0 | 2 | 1 | 3 | 0 |
| Rainwater, Joshua, ONE | .909 | 11 | 3 | 7 | 1 | 11 | 1 |
| Ramirez, Luis, ABD | 1.000 | 11 | 1 | 6 | 0 | 7 | 0 |
| Ramos, Vic, WPT | 1.000 | 3 | 2 | 1 | 0 | 3 | 0 |
| Regas, Kris, BRK* | .000 | 3 | 0 | 0 | 0 | 0 | 0 |
| Reineke, Chad, TRC | 1.000 | 23 | 3 | 3 | 0 | 6 | 0 |
| Rico, Erik, AUB* | 1.000 | 15 | 4 | 8 | 0 | 12 | 0 |
| Righter, Matt, ONE | .857 | 14 | 3 | 3 | 1 | 7 | 0 |
| Robertson, Quinton, NJY | .917 | 6 | 2 | 9 | 1 | 12 | 0 |
| Robinson, Dennis, ABD | 1.000 | 2 | 0 | 3 | 0 | 3 | 0 |
| Rodriguez, Eladio, LOW | 1.000 | 25 | 2 | 2 | 0 | 4 | 0 |
| Rodriguez, Jayson, AUB | 1.000 | 21 | 5 | 6 | 0 | 11 | 1 |
| Rodriguez, Jose, BRK | 1.000 | 9 | 0 | 2 | 0 | 2 | 0 |
| Roehl, Scott, MHV | 1.000 | 11 | 0 | 6 | 0 | 6 | 0 |
| Romero, Levi, TRC | 1.000 | 4 | 1 | 0 | 0 | 1 | 0 |
| Rondon, Celso, BRK | 1.000 | 26 | 4 | 4 | 0 | 8 | 0 |
| Roper, Derek, NJY | 1.000 | 13 | 2 | 2 | 0 | 4 | 0 |
| Rose, Kevin, BAT | 1.000 | 22 | 0 | 6 | 0 | 6 | 0 |
| Roy, Scott, AUB | 1.000 | 15 | 0 | 8 | 0 | 8 | 0 |
| Salas, Joe, WPT* | .750 | 13 | 3 | 0 | 1 | 4 | 0 |
| Sanchez, Anibal, LOW | .643 | 15 | 4 | 5 | 5 | 14 | 0 |
| Sanders, Dave, LOW* | 1.000 | 17 | 1 | 7 | 0 | 8 | 0 |
| Sandora, Robert, VMT* | .000 | 1 | 0 | 0 | 0 | 0 | 0 |
| Sandoval, Francisco, VMT | 1.000 | 21 | 4 | 9 | 0 | 13 | 0 |
| Santana, Hector, MHV | .800 | 20 | 4 | 4 | 2 | 10 | 0 |
| Santana, Miguel, STA | .857 | 6 | 3 | 3 | 1 | 7 | 1 |
| Santander, Nelson, BAT | 1.000 | 17 | 0 | 2 | 0 | 2 | 0 |
| Scheinbaum, Ben, STA* | 1.000 | 15 | 1 | 8 | 0 | 9 | 0 |
| Schroyer, Ryan, LOW | .923 | 14 | 6 | 6 | 1 | 13 | 0 |
| Schwabe, Ryan, ABD* | 1.000 | 3 | 0 | 2 | 0 | 2 | 0 |
| Schweitzer, Scott, NJY* | 1.000 | 9 | 1 | 0 | 0 | 1 | 0 |
| Sevilla, Wilton, STA | 1.000 | 2 | 0 | 2 | 0 | 2 | 0 |
| Shepard, Kevin, BAT* | 1.000 | 2 | 0 | 5 | 0 | 5 | 0 |
| Shoemaker, Scott, LOW | 1.000 | 17 | 1 | 2 | 0 | 3 | 0 |
| Shortell, Rory, TRC | 1.000 | 3 | 0 | 2 | 0 | 2 | 0 |
| Sillman, Michael, NJY | 1.000 | 16 | 2 | 8 | 0 | 10 | 2 |
| Sipp, Tony, MHV* | .909 | 10 | 3 | 7 | 1 | 11 | 0 |
| Smith, Chris, ABD* | .750 | 4 | 0 | 3 | 1 | 4 | 1 |

| Player, Team | Pct. | G | PO | A | E | TC | DP |
|---|---|---|---|---|---|---|---|
| Smith, Chuck, BRK | 1.000 | 7 | 0 | 1 | 0 | 1 | 0 |
| Smith, Cole, HDV | 1.000 | 3 | 0 | 1 | 0 | 1 | 0 |
| Smith, Donnie, NJY | .800 | 11 | 5 | 11 | 4 | 20 | 0 |
| Sonnanstine, Andrew, HDV | 1.000 | 9 | 1 | 3 | 0 | 4 | 1 |
| Sosa, Gabriel, VMT* | .000 | 3 | 0 | 0 | 0 | 0 | 0 |
| Soto, Edgar, STA* | 1.000 | 4 | 0 | 7 | 0 | 7 | 2 |
| Soto, Enyelbert, TRC* | 1.000 | 1 | 0 | 1 | 0 | 1 | 0 |
| Southerland, Chip, MHV | 1.000 | 11 | 1 | 3 | 0 | 4 | 0 |
| Spencer, Sean, ABD* | .000 | 5 | 0 | 0 | 0 | 0 | 0 |
| Spillers, Brandon, ABD | .750 | 13 | 1 | 2 | 1 | 4 | 0 |
| Stahl, Richard, ABD* | 1.000 | 1 | 0 | 1 | 0 | 1 | 0 |
| Stephens, Amad, STA | 1.000 | 1 | 1 | 0 | 0 | 1 | 0 |
| Stevens, Jason, STA | 1.000 | 1 | 0 | 1 | 0 | 1 | 0 |
| Swindell, Mike, BRK | .952 | 12 | 6 | 14 | 1 | 21 | 0 |
| Swindle, RJ, LOW* | 1.000 | 12 | 3 | 11 | 0 | 14 | 0 |
| Tallet, Brian, MHV* | .000 | 2 | 0 | 0 | 0 | 0 | 0 |
| Tankersley, Taylor, JAM* | .833 | 6 | 1 | 4 | 1 | 6 | 0 |
| Tate, Derek, AUB* | 1.000 | 5 | 0 | 5 | 0 | 5 | 0 |
| Tillman, Derek, JAM | 1.000 | 25 | 3 | 7 | 0 | 10 | 1 |
| Timm, Jordan, AUB* | 1.000 | 2 | 0 | 2 | 0 | 2 | 0 |
| Tompkins, Jake, BAT | 1.000 | 12 | 1 | 3 | 0 | 4 | 1 |

| Player, Team | Pct. | G | PO | A | E | TC | DP |
|---|---|---|---|---|---|---|---|
| Torres, Jaime, NJY | 1.000 | 13 | 2 | 3 | 0 | 5 | 0 |
| Trahan, David, VMT | .889 | 20 | 2 | 6 | 1 | 9 | 0 |
| Tubb, Austin, NJY | .923 | 23 | 6 | 6 | 1 | 13 | 0 |
| Vargas, Jason, JAM* | .889 | 8 | 2 | 6 | 1 | 9 | 0 |
| Volquez, Angel, HDV | 1.000 | 12 | 0 | 1 | 0 | 1 | 0 |
| Wagner, Mike, STA* | .000 | 1 | 0 | 0 | 0 | 0 | 0 |
| Wagner, Nicholas, HDV | .800 | 18 | 1 | 3 | 1 | 5 | 1 |
| Walker, Aaron, HDV* | .900 | 14 | 2 | 7 | 1 | 10 | 0 |
| Weimer, Andrew, HDV | 1.000 | 17 | 3 | 6 | 0 | 9 | 0 |
| Wesley, John, AUB | 1.000 | 4 | 1 | 1 | 0 | 2 | 0 |
| Wideman, Aaron, VMT* | 1.000 | 10 | 2 | 5 | 0 | 7 | 0 |
| Wigdahl, Jeff, TRC* | .818 | 19 | 0 | 9 | 2 | 11 | 0 |
| Williams, Joseph, BRK* | .867 | 15 | 2 | 11 | 2 | 15 | 0 |
| Wilson, Aaron, BAT | 1.000 | 3 | 1 | 2 | 0 | 3 | 0 |
| Wilson, Thomas, VMT* | 1.000 | 7 | 1 | 5 | 0 | 6 | 0 |
| Worthington, Timothy, BRK | 1.000 | 2 | 0 | 1 | 0 | 1 | 0 |
| Wright, Chase, STA* | .500 | 1 | 0 | 1 | 1 | 2 | 0 |
| Wright, Isaiah, VMT | .250 | 11 | 0 | 1 | 3 | 4 | 0 |
| Yourkin, Matt, JAM* | .750 | 24 | 1 | 2 | 1 | 4 | 0 |
| Zick, Jeremy, NJY | .800 | 18 | 1 | 7 | 2 | 10 | 0 |

## LEAGUE CHAMPIONS

| Year | Team | Pct. |
|---|---|---|
| 1939— | Olean* | .631 |
| 1940— | Olean* | .625 |
| 1941— | Jamestown | .618 |
| | Bradford (2nd)† | .549 |
| 1942— | Jamestown* | .672 |
| 1943— | Lockport | .591 |
| | Wellsville (3rd)† | .532 |
| 1944— | Lockport | .608 |
| | Jamestown (2nd)† | .565 |
| 1945— | Batavia* | .677 |
| 1946— | Jamestown‡ | .672 |
| | Batavia‡ | .672 |
| 1947— | Jamestown* | .690 |
| 1948— | Lockport* | .603 |
| 1949— | Bradford* | .635 |
| 1950— | Hornell | .653 |
| | Olean (2nd)† | .568 |
| 1951— | Olean | .622 |
| | Hornell (3rd)† | .568 |
| 1952— | Hamilton | .659 |
| | Jamestown (2nd)† | .643 |
| 1953— | Jamestown* | .704 |
| 1954— | Corning* | .621 |
| 1955— | Hamilton* | .656 |
| 1956— | Wellsville* | .617 |
| 1957— | Wellsville | .632 |
| | Erie (2nd)† | .598 |
| 1958— | Wellsville | .556 |
| | Geneva (2nd)† | .548 |
| 1959— | Wellsville† | .635 |
| 1960— | Erie | .643 |
| | Wellsville (2nd)† | .535 |
| 1961— | Geneva | .616 |
| | Olean (4th)† | .512 |
| 1962— | Jamestown | .580 |
| | Auburn (3rd)† | .521 |
| 1963— | Auburn | .585 |
| | Batavia (3rd)† | .485 |

| Year | Team | Pct. |
|---|---|---|
| 1964— | Auburn§ | .622 |
| 1965— | Binghamton | .677 |
| | Binghamton | .607 |
| 1966— | Auburn∞ | .620 |
| | Binghamton | .646 |
| 1967— | Auburn | .667 |
| 1968— | Auburn | .645 |
| | Oneonta (2nd)* | .558 |
| 1969— | Oneonta | .662 |
| 1970— | Auburn | .623 |
| 1971— | Oneonta | .662 |
| 1972— | Niagara Falls | .686 |
| 1973— | Auburn | .667 |
| 1974— | Oneonta | .768 |
| 1975— | Newark | .688 |
| | Newark | .714 |
| 1976— | Elmira | .727 |
| | Elmira | .703 |
| 1977— | Oneonta▲ | .671 |
| | Batavia | .600 |
| 1978— | Oneonta | .729 |
| | Geneva◆ | .718 |
| 1979— | Geneva | .725 |
| | Oneonta◆ | .618 |
| 1980— | Oneonta▲ | .662 |
| | Geneva | .649 |
| 1981— | Oneonta▲ | .658 |
| | Jamestown | .649 |
| 1982— | Oneonta | .566 |
| | Niagara Falls▲ | .553 |
| 1983— | Utica▲ | .649 |
| | Newark | .649 |
| 1984— | Newark | .622 |
| | Little Falls▲ | .587 |
| 1985— | Oneonta* | .705 |
| | Auburn | .603 |
| 1986— | Oneonta | .766 |
| | St. Catharines◆ | .632 |

| Year | Team | Pct. |
|---|---|---|
| 1987— | Geneva▲ | .632 |
| | Watertown | .579 |
| 1988— | Oneonta▲ | .632 |
| | Jamestown | .618 |
| 1989— | Pittsfield | .697 |
| | Jamestown▲ | .579 |
| 1990— | Oneonta■ | .667 |
| | Geneva | .662 |
| 1991— | Pittsfield | .662 |
| | Jamestown■ | .654 |
| 1992— | Hamilton | .737 |
| | Geneva▼ | .547 |
| 1993— | Niagara Falls▼ | .603 |
| | Pittsfield | .533 |
| 1994— | Auburn | .592 |
| | New Jersey▼ | .573 |
| 1995— | Vermont | .645 |
| | Watertown▼ | .630 |
| 1996— | Vermont▼ | .649 |
| | St. Catharines | .579 |
| 1997— | Batavia | .635 |
| | Pittsfield▼ | .568 |
| 1998— | Hudson Valley | .658 |
| | Oneonta†† | .592 |
| | Auburn†† | .573 |
| 1999— | Mahoning Valley | .566 |
| | Hudson Valley‡‡ | .553 |
| 2000— | Mahoning Valley | .632 |
| | Staten Island§§ | .622 |
| 2001— | Brooklyn∞∞ | .684 |
| | Williamsport∞∞ | .649 |
| 2002— | Staten Island▲▲ | .649 |
| 2003— | Williamsport▲▲ | .605 |
| 2004— | Mahoning Valley▲▲ | .553 |

*Won championship and four-club playoff. †Won four-club playoff. ‡Jamestown and Batavia declared co-champions; Batavia defeated Jamestown in final of four-club playoff. §Won championship and two-club playoff. ∞Won split-season playoff. ▲League divided into Eastern and Western divisions; won playoff. League divided into Wrigley and Yawkey divisions; won playoff. ■League divided into Eastern, Western and Stedler divisions; won playoff. ▼League divided into McNamara, Pinckney and Stedler divisions; won playoff. ††Named co-champions due to final series being rained out. ‡‡League divided into McNamara and Pinckney divisions; won playoff. §§League divided into McNamara and Stedler divisions; won playoff. ∞∞League divided into McNamara and Stedler divisions; Brooklyn was leading final series of four-team playoff over Williamsport, but both teams were declared co-champions when Professional Baseball declared a stoppage of play. (NOTE—Known as Pennsylvania-Ontario-New York League from 1939 through 1956.) ▲▲League divided into McNamara, Pinckney and Stedler divisions; won playoff.

# NORTHWEST LEAGUE

## LEAGUE OFFICE

**President/treasurer**
Bob Richmond
**Address**
P.O. Box 1645
Boise, ID 83701
**Phone**
208-429-1511

**Teams (affiliation)**
Boise Hawks (Cubs)
Eugene Emeralds (Padres)
Everett AquaSox (Mariners)
Salem-Keizer Volcanoes (Giants)
Spokane Indians (Rangers)
Tri-City Dust Devils (Rockies)
Vancouver Canadians (A's)
Yakima Bears (Diamondbacks)

## 2004 FINAL STANDINGS

### EAST DIVISION

| Team | W | L | T | Pct. | GB |
|---|---|---|---|---|---|
| Boise | 42 | 34 | - | .553 | ... |
| Spokane | 41 | 35 | - | .539 | 1 |
| Tri City | 40 | 36 | - | .526 | 2 |
| Yakima | 35 | 41 | - | .461 | 7 |

### WEST DIVISION

| Team | W | L | T | Pct. | GB |
|---|---|---|---|---|---|
| Vancouver | 42 | 34 | - | .553 | ... |
| Everett | 41 | 35 | - | .539 | 1 |
| Salem-Keizer | 37 | 39 | - | .487 | 5 |
| Eugene | 26 | 50 | - | .342 | 16 |

### COMPOSITE

| Team | W | L | T | PCT | GB | BOI | VAN | EVR | SPO | TRI | SK | YAK | EUG |
|---|---|---|---|---|---|---|---|---|---|---|---|---|---|
| Boise (Cubs) | 42 | 34 | - | .553 | ... | X | 7 | 9 | 3 | 7 | 4 | 6 | 6 |
| Vancouver (Athletics) | 42 | 34 | - | .553 | 0 | 3 | X | 5 | 7 | 7 | 6 | 7 | 7 |
| Everett (Mariners) | 41 | 35 | - | .539 | 1 | 1 | 7 | X | 5 | 4 | 8 | 6 | 10 |
| Spokane (Rangers) | 41 | 35 | - | .539 | 1 | 9 | 3 | 5 | X | 6 | 5 | 7 | 6 |
| Tri City (Rockies) | 40 | 36 | - | .526 | 2 | 5 | 3 | 6 | 6 | X | 7 | 4 | 9 |
| Salem-Keizer (Giants) | 37 | 39 | - | .487 | 5 | 6 | 6 | 4 | 5 | 3 | X | 8 | 5 |
| Yakima (Diamondbacks) | 35 | 41 | - | .461 | 7 | 6 | 3 | 4 | 5 | 8 | 2 | X | 7 |
| Eugene (Padres) | 26 | 50 | - | .342 | 16 | 4 | 5 | 2 | 4 | 1 | 7 | 3 | X |

Major league affiliations in parentheses.

PLAYOFFS: Boise defeated Vancouver three games to none to win championship.

REGULAR-SEASON ATTENDANCE: Boise, 107,936; Eugene, 117,547; Everett, 107,936; Salem Keizer, 118,929; Spokane, 169,075; Tri-City, 54,101; Vancouver, 140,037; Yakima, 51,544. Total attendance—865,796. All-Star game at Avista Stadium—6,775.

MANAGERS: Boise, Tom Beyers; Eugene, Roy Howell; Everett, Pedro Grifol; Salem Keizer, Joe Strain; Spokane, Darryl Kennedy; Tri-City, Ron Gideon; Vancouver, Dennis Rogers; Yakima, Bill Plummer.

ALL-STAR TEAM: East: P—Jarrad Burcie, Spokane; Jarrett Grube, Tri-City; Jim Miller, Tri-City; Jesse Ingram, Spokane; John Bannister, Spokane; AJ Shappi, Yakima; Matt Weber, Boise; Luis Brito, Boise; Juan Morillo, Tri-City; Tomas Santiago, Tri-City; Chris Kemlo, Yakima; C—Mike Nickeas, Spokane; Orlando Mercado, Yakima; INF—Tug Hulett, Spokane; Erick Schindewolf; Yakima; Mark Reynolds, Yakima; Chris Carter, Yakima; Travis Metcalf, Spokane; Matt Macri, Tri-City; Ryan Norwood, Boise; OF—Jud Thigpen, Tri-City; Matt Miller, Tri-City; Luis Montanez, Boise; Kyle Boyer, Boise; Manager—Darryl Kennedy, Spokane. West: P—Aaron Jenson, Everett; Michael Kunes, Salem Keizer; Steven Sharpe, Vancouver; Shawn Nottingham, Everett; Mumba Rivera, Everett; Ryan Ford, Vancouver; Vern Sterry, Eugene; Craig Whitaker, Salem Keizer; Braulio Santana, Vancouver; Michael Ekstrom, Eugene; Brian Burks, Eugene; C—Omar Falcon, Everett; Colt Morton, Eugene; INF—Ryan Ruiz, Vancouver; Swaldo Navarro, Everett; Lachlan Dale, Eugene; Asdrubal Cabrera, Everett; Brandon Green, Everett; Jeff Palumbo, Salem Keizer; Yung-Chi Chen, Everett; Thomas Everidge, Vancouver; Simon Klink, Salem Keizer; OF—Matt Thayer, Eugene; Clay Timpner, Salem Keizer; Brian Horwitz, Salem Keizer; Brent Johnson, Everett; Javier Herrera, Vancouver; Manager—Joe Strain, Salem Keizer. MVP—Javier Herrera, Vancouver. Manager of the Year—Tom Beyers, Boise.

## 2004 BATTING

### TEAM

| Team | G | TPA | AB | R | H | TB | 2B | 3B | HR | RBI | SH | SF | HP | BB | IBB | SO | SB | CS | GDP | LOB | ShO | Avg. | OBP | Slg. |
|---|---|---|---|---|---|---|---|---|---|---|---|---|---|---|---|---|---|---|---|---|---|---|---|---|
| Salem-Keizer | 76 | 3006 | 2652 | 385 | 708 | 992 | 122 | 12 | 46 | 332 | 19 | 32 | 57 | 246 | 2 | 484 | 41 | 17 | 70 | 576 | 4 | .267 | .338 | .374 |
| Everett | 76 | 2986 | 2588 | 448 | 689 | 1040 | 170 | 17 | 49 | 402 | 24 | 29 | 58 | 286 | 5 | 602 | 123 | 48 | 33 | 537 | 1 | .266 | .349 | .402 |
| Vancouver | 76 | 3020 | 2609 | 427 | 694 | 1005 | 132 | 25 | 43 | 378 | 19 | 26 | 44 | 322 | 5 | 579 | 47 | 17 | 57 | 603 | 2 | .266 | .353 | .385 |
| Boise | 76 | 2896 | 2573 | 373 | 674 | 995 | 114 | 21 | 55 | 337 | 45 | 21 | 52 | 204 | 7 | 536 | 56 | 41 | 45 | 505 | 1 | .262 | .326 | .387 |
| Tri-City | 76 | 2987 | 2592 | 370 | 673 | 1020 | 131 | 21 | 58 | 334 | 47 | 24 | 58 | 266 | 4 | 576 | 30 | 27 | 52 | 574 | 2 | .260 | .339 | .394 |
| Yakima | 76 | 3012 | 2609 | 403 | 678 | 1007 | 117 | 13 | 62 | 368 | 34 | 22 | 64 | 283 | 5 | 541 | 40 | 17 | 52 | 591 | 2 | .260 | .344 | .386 |
| Spokane | 76 | 3080 | 2635 | 427 | 672 | 1064 | 153 | 7 | 75 | 390 | 8 | 20 | 51 | 365 | 6 | 688 | 65 | 21 | 49 | 595 | 4 | .255 | .354 | .404 |
| Eugene | 76 | 2920 | 2606 | 354 | 647 | 1019 | 144 | 12 | 68 | 320 | 20 | 17 | 44 | 233 | 3 | 675 | 47 | 21 | 22 | 545 | 7 | .248 | .319 | .391 |

### INDIVIDUAL

#### TOP QUALIFIERS FOR BATTING CHAMPIONSHIP

Minimum 205 plate appearances. *Lefthanded batter. †Switch-hitter.

| Player, Team | G | TPA | AB | R | H | TB | 2B | 3B | HR | RBI | SH | SF | HP | BB | IBB | SO | SB | CS | GDP | Avg. | OBP | Slg. |
|---|---|---|---|---|---|---|---|---|---|---|---|---|---|---|---|---|---|---|---|---|---|---|
| Horwitz, Brian, Salem-Keizer | 71 | 300 | 268 | 41 | 93 | 125 | 24 | 1 | 2 | 44 | 0 | 3 | 8 | 21 | 0 | 34 | 3 | 3 | 7 | .347 | .407 | .466 |
| Carter, William, Yakima * | 70 | 304 | 256 | 47 | 86 | 148 | 15 | 1 | 15 | 63 | 0 | 1 | 1 | 46 | 1 | 34 | 2 | 3 | 7 | .336 | .438 | .578 |
| Macri, Matthew, Tri-City | 52 | 227 | 195 | 33 | 65 | 111 | 17 | 4 | 7 | 43 | 0 | 4 | 5 | 23 | 1 | 52 | 4 | 5 | 8 | .333 | .410 | .569 |
| Herrera, Javier, Vancouver | 65 | 293 | 263 | 50 | 87 | 146 | 15 | 4 | 12 | 47 | 0 | 2 | 4 | 24 | 2 | 59 | 23 | 1 | 0 | .331 | .392 | .555 |
| Dean, Erik, Tri-City * | 59 | 262 | 217 | 43 | 68 | 94 | 12 | 1 | 4 | 26 | 6 | 2 | 5 | 32 | 0 | 36 | 4 | 1 | 2 | .313 | .410 | .433 |
| Thigpen, Jud, Tri-City | 58 | 265 | 239 | 43 | 74 | 128 | 14 | 5 | 10 | 37 | 6 | 0 | 6 | 14 | 0 | 50 | 8 | 0 | 7 | .310 | .363 | .536 |
| Schindewolf, Erik, Yakima * | 73 | 340 | 273 | 65 | 84 | 110 | 10 | 2 | 4 | 37 | 10 | 2 | 4 | 51 | 0 | 37 | 15 | 2 | 1 | .308 | .421 | .403 |
| Boyer, Kyle, Boise | 67 | 265 | 247 | 35 | 75 | 115 | 13 | 3 | 7 | 37 | 3 | 0 | 0 | 15 | 1 | 65 | 6 | 5 | 4 | .304 | .344 | .466 |
| Deeb, Bobby, Boise | 51 | 221 | 188 | 33 | 57 | 73 | 11 | 1 | 1 | 13 | 1 | 0 | 14 | 18 | 0 | 33 | 10 | 6 | 2 | .303 | .405 | .388 |
| Chen, Yung, Everett | 49 | 222 | 200 | 37 | 60 | 84 | 13 | 1 | 3 | 34 | 1 | 3 | 2 | 16 | 1 | 36 | 25 | 3 | 3 | .300 | .353 | .420 |
| Montanez, Luis, Boise | 72 | 309 | 266 | 47 | 79 | 132 | 15 | 7 | 8 | 48 | 2 | 3 | 3 | 35 | 2 | 53 | 5 | 5 | 5 | .297 | .381 | .496 |
| Suzuki, Kurt, Vancouver | 46 | 211 | 175 | 27 | 52 | 77 | 10 | 3 | 3 | 31 | 3 | 3 | 12 | 18 | 0 | 26 | 0 | 1 | 3 | .297 | .394 | .440 |
| Norwood, Walter, Boise | 73 | 298 | 277 | 33 | 82 | 130 | 17 | 2 | 9 | 53 | 4 | 3 | 4 | 10 | 0 | 59 | 2 | 1 | 5 | .296 | .327 | .469 |
| Johnson, Brent, Everett | 66 | 284 | 233 | 51 | 69 | 85 | 13 | 0 | 1 | 29 | 4 | 5 | 9 | 33 | 0 | 27 | 12 | 4 | 3 | .296 | .396 | .365 |

| Player, Team | G | TPA | AB | R | H | TB | 2B | 3B | HR | RBI | SH | SF | HP | BB | IBB | SO | SB | CS | GDP | Avg. | OBP | Slg. |
|---|---|---|---|---|---|---|---|---|---|---|---|---|---|---|---|---|---|---|---|---|---|---|
| Blasi, Nicholas, Vancouver | 71 | 317 | 271 | 57 | 80 | 98 | 14 | 2 | 0 | 26 | 2 | 2 | 4 | 38 | 0 | 66 | 3 | 2 | 0 | .295 | .387 | .362 |

DEPARTMENTAL LEADERS: G—Dale, Everidge, 74; AB—Timpner, 294; R—Schindewolf, 65; H—Horwitz, 93; TB—Carter, 148; 2B—Navarro, 27; 3B—Montanez, 7; HR—Morton, 17; RBI—Carter, 63; SH—Balcom, 12; SF—Metcalf, 6; HP—Deeb, 14; BB—Hulett, 68; IBB—Koshansky, Reynolds, 3; SO—Dale, 87; SB—Chen, 25; CS—Balcom, Hulett, 7; GIDP—Klink, 12; Slg.—Carter, .578; OBP—Hulett, .444.

## ALL PLAYERS

*Lefthanded batter. †Switch-hitter.

| Player, Team | G | TPA | AB | R | H | TB | 2B | 3B | HR | RBI | SH | SF | HP | BB | IBB | SO | SB | CS | GDP | Avg. | OBP | Slg. |
|---|---|---|---|---|---|---|---|---|---|---|---|---|---|---|---|---|---|---|---|---|---|---|
| Acha, John, Salem-Keizer | 38 | 122 | 109 | 12 | 17 | 28 | 3 | 1 | 2 | 12 | 0 | 2 | 3 | 8 | 0 | 31 | 2 | 1 | 5 | .156 | .230 | .257 |
| Aguilar, Trino, Eugene | 47 | 164 | 147 | 15 | 42 | 62 | 11 | 0 | 3 | 17 | 3 | 1 | 5 | 8 | 0 | 27 | 3 | 0 | 2 | .286 | .342 | .422 |
| Aguirre, Rodrigo, Yakima * | 40 | 140 | 125 | 20 | 32 | 43 | 2 | 0 | 3 | 16 | 2 | 0 | 3 | 10 | 0 | 19 | 1 | 0 | 2 | .256 | .326 | .344 |
| Alexander, Christopher, Spokane | 41 | 161 | 146 | 9 | 37 | 44 | 4 | 0 | 1 | 17 | 0 | 1 | 2 | 12 | 2 | 36 | 0 | 0 | 5 | .253 | .317 | .301 |
| Almonte, Sandy, Tri-City † | 6 | 25 | 23 | 4 | 6 | 9 | 1 | 1 | 0 | 0 | 1 | 0 | 0 | 1 | 0 | 1 | 1 | 1 | 2 | .261 | .292 | .391 |
| Babineaux, Charlie, Salem-Keizer | 55 | 216 | 199 | 30 | 49 | 83 | 8 | 1 | 8 | 33 | 0 | 4 | 5 | 8 | 0 | 50 | 1 | 0 | 6 | .246 | .287 | .417 |
| Baez, Lizahio, Spokane † | 22 | 93 | 84 | 8 | 22 | 36 | 2 | 0 | 4 | 10 | 0 | 1 | 0 | 8 | 0 | 18 | 0 | 0 | 1 | .262 | .323 | .429 |
| Balcom, Jasha, Boise * | 60 | 260 | 227 | 37 | 63 | 75 | 5 | 2 | 1 | 24 | 12 | 2 | 1 | 18 | 1 | 32 | 10 | 7 | 2 | .278 | .331 | .330 |
| Baldwin, Ryan, Spokane | 19 | 59 | 53 | 6 | 10 | 13 | 0 | 0 | 1 | 6 | 1 | 0 | 1 | 4 | 0 | 15 | 0 | 0 | 3 | .189 | .259 | .245 |
| Beauregard, Josh, Vancouver * | 18 | 67 | 58 | 12 | 12 | 19 | 2 | 1 | 1 | 4 | 0 | 0 | 1 | 8 | 0 | 12 | 3 | 3 | 1 | .207 | .313 | .328 |
| Bernard, Oscar, Boise | 37 | 139 | 128 | 14 | 32 | 44 | 4 | 1 | 2 | 12 | 5 | 1 | 0 | 5 | 0 | 24 | 3 | 1 | 2 | .250 | .276 | .344 |
| Blasi, Nicholas, Vancouver | 71 | 317 | 271 | 57 | 80 | 98 | 14 | 2 | 0 | 26 | 2 | 2 | 4 | 38 | 0 | 66 | 3 | 2 | 0 | .295 | .387 | .362 |
| Boggs, Brandon, Spokane † | 45 | 186 | 149 | 27 | 35 | 55 | 11 | 0 | 3 | 19 | 1 | 2 | 5 | 29 | 0 | 43 | 6 | 2 | 5 | .235 | .373 | .369 |
| Bone, Kyle, Salem-Keizer | 15 | 45 | 39 | 3 | 6 | 6 | 0 | 0 | 0 | 2 | 3 | 0 | 0 | 3 | 0 | 13 | 0 | 0 | 0 | .154 | .214 | .154 |
| Bowker, John, Salem-Keizer * | 31 | 141 | 127 | 23 | 41 | 66 | 9 | 2 | 4 | 16 | 0 | 0 | 6 | 8 | 2 | 25 | 1 | 0 | 5 | .323 | .390 | .520 |
| Boyer, Kyle, Boise | 67 | 265 | 247 | 35 | 75 | 115 | 13 | 3 | 7 | 37 | 3 | 0 | 0 | 15 | 1 | 65 | 6 | 5 | 4 | .304 | .344 | .466 |
| Bubalo, Ty, Vancouver | 17 | 47 | 44 | 4 | 8 | 9 | 1 | 0 | 0 | 4 | 0 | 0 | 0 | 3 | 0 | 12 | 0 | 0 | 1 | .182 | .234 | .205 |
| Buchanan, Todd, Yakima * | 55 | 191 | 156 | 23 | 38 | 54 | 8 | 1 | 2 | 17 | 2 | 2 | 5 | 26 | 0 | 29 | 0 | 0 | 5 | .244 | .365 | .346 |
| Buhagiar, Joshua, Yakima * | 4 | 9 | 9 | 0 | 0 | 0 | 0 | 0 | 0 | 0 | 0 | 0 | 0 | 0 | 0 | 5 | 0 | 0 | 0 | .000 | .000 | .000 |
| Burgess, Brandon, Yakima * | 51 | 203 | 177 | 20 | 36 | 61 | 7 | 0 | 6 | 27 | 0 | 3 | 9 | 14 | 0 | 62 | 0 | 0 | 3 | .203 | .291 | .345 |
| Burnham, Brett, Eugene | 46 | 181 | 154 | 20 | 39 | 53 | 9 | 1 | 1 | 23 | 2 | 2 | 4 | 19 | 0 | 33 | 0 | 3 | 0 | .253 | .346 | .344 |
| Bush, Matthew, Eugene | 8 | 31 | 27 | 1 | 6 | 8 | 2 | 0 | 0 | 3 | 2 | 0 | 0 | 2 | 0 | 9 | 0 | 0 | 0 | .222 | .276 | .296 |
| Cabrera, Asdrubal, Everett † | 63 | 274 | 239 | 44 | 65 | 102 | 16 | 3 | 5 | 41 | 7 | 5 | 2 | 21 | 1 | 43 | 7 | 5 | 3 | .272 | .330 | .427 |
| Carter, William, Yakima * | 70 | 304 | 256 | 47 | 86 | 148 | 15 | 1 | 15 | 63 | 0 | 1 | 1 | 46 | 1 | 34 | 2 | 3 | 7 | .336 | .438 | .578 |
| Cashman, Brandon, Spokane | 21 | 96 | 79 | 20 | 22 | 54 | 5 | 3 | 7 | 18 | 0 | 0 | 5 | 11 | 1 | 23 | 4 | 0 | 0 | .278 | .400 | .684 |
| Chen, Yung, Everett | 49 | 222 | 200 | 37 | 60 | 84 | 13 | 1 | 3 | 34 | 1 | 3 | 2 | 16 | 1 | 36 | 25 | 3 | 3 | .300 | .353 | .420 |
| Conte, Nick, Salem-Keizer | 44 | 157 | 135 | 12 | 29 | 31 | 2 | 0 | 0 | 10 | 2 | 4 | 2 | 14 | 0 | 23 | 1 | 1 | 1 | .215 | .290 | .230 |
| Craig, Casey, Everett * | 59 | 251 | 200 | 46 | 53 | 84 | 10 | 3 | 5 | 30 | 5 | 1 | 0 | 45 | 1 | 59 | 17 | 6 | 2 | .265 | .398 | .420 |
| Cruz, Elvis, Everett | 32 | 116 | 106 | 12 | 22 | 38 | 7 | 0 | 3 | 19 | 0 | 2 | 0 | 8 | 0 | 35 | 1 | 1 | 1 | .208 | .259 | .358 |
| Dale, Lachlan, Eugene | 74 | 310 | 284 | 45 | 70 | 135 | 18 | 1 | 15 | 49 | 1 | 4 | 5 | 16 | 0 | 87 | 1 | 0 | 1 | .246 | .294 | .475 |
| Dawkins, Lance, Boise | 2 | 7 | 7 | 0 | 1 | 1 | 0 | 0 | 0 | 0 | 0 | 0 | 0 | 0 | 0 | 2 | 0 | 0 | 0 | .143 | .143 | .143 |
| Dean, Erik, Tri-City * | 59 | 262 | 217 | 43 | 68 | 94 | 12 | 1 | 4 | 26 | 6 | 2 | 5 | 32 | 0 | 36 | 4 | 1 | 2 | .313 | .410 | .433 |
| Deeb, Bobby, Boise | 51 | 221 | 188 | 33 | 57 | 73 | 11 | 1 | 1 | 13 | 1 | 0 | 14 | 18 | 0 | 33 | 10 | 6 | 2 | .303 | .405 | .388 |
| Diaz, Orlando, Eugene | 50 | 188 | 167 | 20 | 39 | 57 | 7 | 1 | 3 | 17 | 1 | 2 | 5 | 13 | 0 | 35 | 1 | 3 | 1 | .234 | .305 | .341 |
| Ellison, Josh, Everett | 5 | 23 | 20 | 4 | 8 | 10 | 2 | 0 | 0 | 2 | 0 | 1 | 0 | 2 | 0 | 3 | 0 | 0 | 0 | .400 | .435 | .500 |
| Embrey, Rielly, Eugene * | 10 | 38 | 30 | 3 | 3 | 4 | 1 | 0 | 0 | 3 | 0 | 0 | 0 | 8 | 0 | 7 | 2 | 0 | 2 | .100 | .289 | .133 |
| Everidge, Tommy, Vancouver | 74 | 322 | 291 | 42 | 80 | 113 | 13 | 1 | 6 | 52 | 1 | 3 | 4 | 23 | 0 | 72 | 0 | 0 | 4 | .275 | .333 | .388 |
| Falcon, Omar, Everett | 46 | 185 | 158 | 32 | 35 | 59 | 7 | 1 | 5 | 24 | 0 | 0 | 8 | 19 | 0 | 54 | 1 | 3 | 0 | .222 | .335 | .373 |
| Fasano, James, Spokane * | 69 | 300 | 274 | 30 | 73 | 118 | 21 | 0 | 8 | 45 | 0 | 1 | 1 | 24 | 0 | 65 | 0 | 1 | 8 | .266 | .327 | .431 |
| Felix, Maximo, Salem-Keizer | 21 | 67 | 62 | 9 | 13 | 21 | 3 | 1 | 1 | 7 | 0 | 1 | 2 | 2 | 0 | 19 | 0 | 0 | 3 | .210 | .254 | .339 |
| Figueroa, Baudilio, Eugene † | 16 | 59 | 54 | 3 | 10 | 11 | 1 | 0 | 0 | 5 | 1 | 1 | 0 | 3 | 0 | 15 | 1 | 1 | 0 | .185 | .224 | .204 |
| Francisco, Alfredo, Boise | 61 | 225 | 210 | 19 | 39 | 61 | 10 | 0 | 4 | 27 | 2 | 2 | 1 | 10 | 0 | 50 | 2 | 0 | 5 | .186 | .224 | .290 |
| Frandsen, Kevin, Salem-Keizer | 25 | 112 | 98 | 22 | 29 | 43 | 5 | 0 | 3 | 14 | 1 | 1 | 3 | 9 | 0 | 9 | 0 | 1 | 1 | .296 | .369 | .439 |
| Fryer, Brian, Eugene | 14 | 55 | 50 | 4 | 8 | 10 | 2 | 0 | 0 | 2 | 2 | 0 | 1 | 2 | 0 | 12 | 3 | 1 | 0 | .160 | .208 | .200 |
| Garay, Ernesto, Eugene * | 25 | 106 | 100 | 16 | 31 | 37 | 3 | 0 | 1 | 8 | 1 | 0 | 0 | 5 | 0 | 12 | 3 | 1 | 0 | .310 | .343 | .370 |
| Gentry, Garett, Tri-City * | 15 | 64 | 57 | 11 | 24 | 40 | 5 | 1 | 3 | 14 | 0 | 1 | 0 | 6 | 0 | 6 | 1 | 1 | 1 | .421 | .469 | .702 |
| Ghutzman, Stephen, Tri-City † | 41 | 175 | 145 | 29 | 41 | 58 | 9 | 1 | 2 | 20 | 2 | 4 | 3 | 21 | 0 | 30 | 0 | 2 | 1 | .283 | .376 | .400 |
| Gonzalez, Carlos, Yakima * | 73 | 329 | 300 | 44 | 82 | 128 | 15 | 2 | 9 | 44 | 2 | 2 | 3 | 22 | 0 | 70 | 2 | 0 | 4 | .273 | .327 | .427 |
| Granato, Anthony, Boise † | 29 | 125 | 97 | 27 | 26 | 38 | 1 | 1 | 3 | 7 | 3 | 0 | 3 | 22 | 1 | 30 | 6 | 3 | 1 | .268 | .418 | .392 |
| Green, Brandon, Everett † | 72 | 315 | 283 | 37 | 77 | 121 | 15 | 4 | 7 | 55 | 0 | 4 | 2 | 26 | 1 | 55 | 9 | 6 | 4 | .272 | .333 | .428 |
| Gresky, David, Boise * | 51 | 160 | 131 | 23 | 29 | 48 | 8 | 1 | 3 | 14 | 2 | 2 | 5 | 20 | 2 | 27 | 3 | 2 | 1 | .221 | .342 | .366 |
| Griffin, Preston, Boise | 21 | 65 | 53 | 5 | 8 | 11 | 3 | 0 | 0 | 5 | 2 | 0 | 6 | 4 | 0 | 8 | 1 | 2 | 0 | .151 | .286 | .208 |
| Groth, Bradley, Salem-Keizer | 13 | 48 | 40 | 1 | 2 | 3 | 1 | 0 | 0 | 0 | 0 | 0 | 1 | 7 | 0 | 10 | 1 | 1 | 0 | .050 | .208 | .075 |
| Guarno, Rick, Tri-City | 28 | 121 | 105 | 11 | 24 | 25 | 1 | 0 | 0 | 6 | 2 | 1 | 8 | 5 | 0 | 20 | 0 | 0 | 2 | .229 | .311 | .238 |
| Guerra, Alex, Spokane † | 6 | 19 | 16 | 1 | 0 | 0 | 0 | 0 | 0 | 2 | 0 | 0 | 0 | 3 | 0 | 8 | 0 | 0 | 0 | .000 | .158 | .000 |
| Hahn, Dustin, Tri-City * | 4 | 19 | 16 | 3 | 4 | 4 | 0 | 0 | 0 | 0 | 0 | 0 | 0 | 3 | 0 | 4 | 0 | 0 | 0 | .250 | .368 | .250 |
| Haines, Kyle, Salem-Keizer * | 32 | 137 | 119 | 15 | 31 | 36 | 5 | 0 | 0 | 11 | 0 | 4 | 2 | 12 | 0 | 18 | 1 | 1 | 3 | .261 | .328 | .303 |
| Harriman, David, Vancouver | 9 | 33 | 29 | 3 | 9 | 11 | 0 | 1 | 0 | 2 | 1 | 0 | 1 | 2 | 0 | 6 | 0 | 0 | 0 | .310 | .375 | .379 |
| Harrison, Benjamin, Spokane | 55 | 243 | 214 | 41 | 58 | 102 | 11 | 0 | 11 | 33 | 0 | 0 | 7 | 22 | 1 | 64 | 2 | 0 | 4 | .271 | .358 | .477 |
| Harvey, Ryan, Boise | 58 | 257 | 231 | 42 | 61 | 111 | 8 | 0 | 14 | 43 | 0 | 3 | 3 | 20 | 0 | 78 | 2 | 2 | 2 | .264 | .327 | .481 |
| Heid, Trevor, Everett | 44 | 146 | 130 | 17 | 28 | 39 | 9 | 1 | 0 | 14 | 1 | 0 | 4 | 11 | 0 | 32 | 8 | 1 | 0 | .215 | .297 | .300 |
| Hendricks, Arthur, Yakima † | 65 | 243 | 226 | 17 | 51 | 70 | 7 | 0 | 4 | 26 | 2 | 0 | 2 | 13 | 0 | 43 | 0 | 1 | 9 | .226 | .274 | .310 |
| Herrera, Javier, Vancouver | 65 | 293 | 263 | 50 | 87 | 146 | 15 | 4 | 12 | 47 | 0 | 2 | 4 | 24 | 2 | 59 | 23 | 1 | 0 | .331 | .392 | .555 |
| Hogan, Billy, Eugene | 58 | 224 | 199 | 22 | 47 | 71 | 13 | 1 | 3 | 22 | 3 | 1 | 3 | 18 | 0 | 66 | 3 | 0 | 2 | .236 | .308 | .357 |
| Horwitz, Brian, Salem-Keizer | 71 | 300 | 268 | 41 | 93 | 125 | 24 | 1 | 2 | 44 | 0 | 3 | 8 | 21 | 0 | 34 | 3 | 3 | 7 | .347 | .407 | .466 |
| Hubbard, Thomas, Everett * | 55 | 216 | 189 | 20 | 52 | 74 | 14 | 1 | 2 | 24 | 0 | 1 | 4 | 22 | 0 | 52 | 3 | 3 | 2 | .275 | .361 | .392 |
| Hulett, Tim, Spokane | 70 | 321 | 247 | 54 | 69 | 86 | 17 | 0 | 0 | 23 | 1 | 0 | 5 | 68 | 0 | 67 | 19 | 7 | 1 | .279 | .444 | .348 |
| Jacobsen, Brock, Spokane † | 10 | 33 | 31 | 4 | 7 | 10 | 3 | 0 | 0 | 1 | 1 | 0 | 0 | 1 | 0 | 16 | 1 | 0 | 0 | .226 | .250 | .323 |
| Jennings, Todd, Salem-Keizer | 17 | 73 | 70 | 7 | 23 | 35 | 3 | 0 | 3 | 11 | 0 | 0 | 0 | 3 | 0 | 12 | 0 | 1 | 4 | .329 | .356 | .500 |
| Johnson, Brent, Everett | 66 | 284 | 233 | 51 | 69 | 85 | 13 | 0 | 1 | 29 | 4 | 5 | 9 | 33 | 0 | 27 | 12 | 4 | 3 | .296 | .396 | .365 |
| Johnson, Craig, Eugene * | 27 | 86 | 77 | 13 | 21 | 29 | 8 | 0 | 0 | 4 | 0 | 0 | 2 | 7 | 0 | 28 | 0 | 3 | 0 | .273 | .349 | .377 |
| Johnson, Robert, Everett | 20 | 84 | 77 | 17 | 18 | 26 | 3 | 1 | 1 | 7 | 0 | 1 | 2 | 4 | 0 | 10 | 6 | 2 | 1 | .234 | .286 | .338 |
| Jones, Nick, Boise | 6 | 15 | 13 | 3 | 3 | 3 | 0 | 0 | 0 | 0 | 0 | 0 | 1 | 1 | 0 | 2 | 1 | 0 | 0 | .231 | .333 | .231 |
| Kazmar, Sean, Eugene | 65 | 285 | 274 | 29 | 69 | 106 | 13 | 3 | 6 | 27 | 1 | 0 | 1 | 9 | 1 | 55 | 6 | 0 | 5 | .252 | .278 | .387 |

| Player, Team | G | TPA | AB | R | H | TB | 2B | 3B | HR | RBI | SH | SF | HP | BB | IBB | SO | SB | CS | GDP | Avg. | OBP | Slg. |
|---|---|---|---|---|---|---|---|---|---|---|---|---|---|---|---|---|---|---|---|---|---|---|
| Klink, Simon, Salem-Keizer † | 67 | 300 | 260 | 41 | 67 | 112 | 12 | 0 | 11 | 44 | 0 | 3 | 10 | 27 | 0 | 78 | 3 | 1 | 12 | .258 | .347 | .431 |
| Kolkhorst, Christopher, Eugene * | 30 | 120 | 91 | 22 | 32 | 39 | 5 | 1 | 0 | 7 | 1 | 1 | 5 | 22 | 1 | 17 | 6 | 1 | 1 | .352 | .496 | .429 |
| Koshansky, Joseph, Tri-City * | 66 | 278 | 239 | 41 | 56 | 110 | 18 | 0 | 12 | 43 | 2 | 2 | 4 | 31 | 1 | 84 | 1 | 0 | 4 | .234 | .330 | .460 |
| Kweon, Yoon-Min, Boise | 4 | 16 | 10 | 3 | 0 | 0 | 0 | 0 | 0 | 2 | 0 | 2 | 1 | 3 | 0 | 1 | 0 | 0 | 1 | .000 | .250 | .000 |
| Lahair, Bryan, Everett * | 7 | 28 | 25 | 5 | 11 | 20 | 6 | 0 | 1 | 7 | 0 | 1 | 1 | 1 | 0 | 3 | 0 | 0 | 1 | .440 | .464 | .800 |
| Lange, B.J., Yakima † | 47 | 125 | 109 | 13 | 23 | 28 | 2 | 0 | 1 | 7 | 2 | 1 | 4 | 9 | 1 | 15 | 2 | 3 | 2 | .211 | .293 | .257 |
| Lenoir, Robert, Spokane | 63 | 254 | 223 | 38 | 50 | 66 | 9 | 2 | 1 | 27 | 0 | 3 | 6 | 22 | 0 | 59 | 10 | 3 | 3 | .224 | .307 | .296 |
| Leslie, Myron, Vancouver † | 73 | 321 | 273 | 41 | 67 | 86 | 12 | 2 | 1 | 28 | 2 | 5 | 0 | 41 | 0 | 34 | 1 | 1 | 9 | .245 | .339 | .315 |
| Lobaton, Jose, Eugene † | 44 | 169 | 151 | 13 | 33 | 66 | 12 | 0 | 7 | 23 | 1 | 0 | 0 | 17 | 0 | 35 | 0 | 0 | 3 | .219 | .298 | .437 |
| Lockin, William, Yakima | 17 | 64 | 60 | 5 | 12 | 14 | 2 | 0 | 0 | 7 | 0 | 1 | 1 | 2 | 0 | 11 | 1 | 1 | 1 | .200 | .234 | .233 |
| Lockwood, Jon, Everett | 3 | 6 | 5 | 2 | 2 | 5 | 0 | 0 | 1 | 3 | 0 | 0 | 0 | 1 | 0 | 2 | 0 | 0 | 0 | .400 | .500 | 1.000 |
| Long, Wesley, Vancouver | 3 | 14 | 14 | 3 | 4 | 7 | 1 | 1 | 0 | 2 | 0 | 0 | 0 | 0 | 0 | 1 | 0 | 0 | 0 | .286 | .286 | .500 |
| Lopez, Mauber, Eugene | 5 | 10 | 10 | 1 | 2 | 2 | 0 | 0 | 0 | 0 | 0 | 0 | 0 | 0 | 0 | 3 | 0 | 0 | 1 | .200 | .200 | .200 |
| Macri, Matthew, Tri-City | 52 | 227 | 195 | 33 | 65 | 111 | 17 | 4 | 7 | 43 | 0 | 4 | 5 | 23 | 1 | 52 | 4 | 5 | 8 | .333 | .410 | .569 |
| Mahar, Kevin, Spokane | 38 | 169 | 152 | 26 | 48 | 75 | 9 | 0 | 6 | 22 | 0 | 1 | 4 | 12 | 0 | 38 | 5 | 0 | 2 | .316 | .379 | .493 |
| Marquez, Uriak, Boise † | 10 | 27 | 26 | 4 | 8 | 17 | 4 | 1 | 1 | 10 | 0 | 1 | 0 | 0 | 0 | 4 | 0 | 2 | 0 | .308 | .296 | .654 |
| Martinez-esteve, Eduardo, Salem-Keizer | 10 | 42 | 35 | 5 | 10 | 14 | 4 | 0 | 0 | 2 | 0 | 0 | 1 | 6 | 0 | 7 | 0 | 0 | 4 | .286 | .405 | .400 |
| Mask, Michael, Spokane * | 47 | 189 | 159 | 26 | 40 | 60 | 9 | 1 | 3 | 22 | 0 | 3 | 0 | 27 | 1 | 38 | 2 | 4 | 4 | .252 | .354 | .377 |
| McRoberts, Mark, Eugene | 22 | 82 | 70 | 17 | 13 | 26 | 1 | 0 | 4 | 10 | 0 | 0 | 1 | 11 | 0 | 31 | 0 | 0 | 0 | .186 | .305 | .371 |
| Melendez, Cristobal, Yakima | 13 | 22 | 21 | 4 | 4 | 5 | 1 | 0 | 0 | 0 | 0 | 0 | 1 | 0 | 0 | 8 | 0 | 0 | 0 | .190 | .227 | .238 |
| Melillo, Kevin, Vancouver * | 22 | 109 | 94 | 22 | 32 | 53 | 11 | 2 | 2 | 21 | 0 | 1 | 3 | 11 | 0 | 16 | 2 | 1 | 1 | .340 | .422 | .564 |
| Mena, Steve, Yakima | 43 | 113 | 101 | 10 | 14 | 15 | 1 | 0 | 0 | 11 | 0 | 1 | 3 | 8 | 0 | 48 | 0 | 1 | 3 | .139 | .221 | .149 |
| Mercado, Orlando, Yakima | 69 | 294 | 252 | 35 | 67 | 98 | 16 | 3 | 3 | 40 | 2 | 4 | 4 | 32 | 0 | 24 | 1 | 1 | 6 | .266 | .353 | .389 |
| Metcalf, Travis, Spokane | 72 | 337 | 290 | 48 | 78 | 146 | 21 | 1 | 15 | 62 | 1 | 6 | 3 | 37 | 1 | 74 | 1 | 2 | 6 | .269 | .351 | .503 |
| Miller, James, Tri-City | 35 | 4 | 3 | 0 | 0 | 0 | 0 | 0 | 0 | 0 | 0 | 0 | 1 | 0 | 0 | 0 | 0 | 0 | 0 | .000 | .250 | .000 |
| Miller, Matt, Tri-City | 43 | 186 | 167 | 17 | 45 | 77 | 8 | 0 | 8 | 25 | 2 | 0 | 4 | 13 | 1 | 18 | 0 | 0 | 1 | .269 | .337 | .461 |
| Montanez, Luis, Boise | 72 | 309 | 266 | 47 | 79 | 132 | 15 | 7 | 8 | 48 | 2 | 3 | 3 | 35 | 2 | 53 | 5 | 5 | 5 | .297 | .381 | .496 |
| Mooney, Mike, Salem-Keizer | 3 | 10 | 10 | 0 | 1 | 2 | 1 | 0 | 0 | 3 | 0 | 0 | 0 | 0 | 0 | 2 | 0 | 0 | 0 | .100 | .100 | .200 |
| Mora, Ruben, Eugene † | 30 | 106 | 97 | 12 | 27 | 35 | 4 | 2 | 0 | 9 | 1 | 0 | 1 | 7 | 0 | 22 | 1 | 2 | 1 | .278 | .333 | .361 |
| Morton, Colt, Eugene | 66 | 285 | 243 | 43 | 58 | 122 | 13 | 0 | 17 | 45 | 0 | 3 | 6 | 33 | 1 | 75 | 2 | 0 | 3 | .239 | .340 | .502 |
| Navarro, Oswaldo, Everett † | 68 | 296 | 267 | 38 | 73 | 105 | 27 | 1 | 1 | 30 | 3 | 2 | 3 | 21 | 0 | 59 | 17 | 4 | 3 | .273 | .331 | .393 |
| Nickeas, Michael, Spokane | 62 | 273 | 233 | 42 | 67 | 115 | 18 | 0 | 10 | 55 | 2 | 1 | 4 | 33 | 0 | 53 | 2 | 0 | 4 | .288 | .384 | .494 |
| Norwood, Walter, Boise | 73 | 298 | 277 | 33 | 82 | 130 | 17 | 2 | 9 | 53 | 4 | 3 | 4 | 10 | 0 | 59 | 2 | 1 | 5 | .296 | .327 | .469 |
| Nunez, Florentino, Tri-City † | 48 | 212 | 187 | 22 | 48 | 69 | 9 | 0 | 4 | 25 | 3 | 3 | 3 | 16 | 0 | 37 | 0 | 2 | 2 | .257 | .321 | .369 |
| Ogando, Alexi, Vancouver | 7 | 25 | 20 | 3 | 3 | 6 | 0 | 0 | 1 | 6 | 0 | 0 | 1 | 4 | 0 | 9 | 1 | 0 | 0 | .150 | .320 | .300 |
| Olivo, Miguel, Everett | 2 | 6 | 6 | 0 | 0 | 0 | 0 | 0 | 0 | 0 | 0 | 0 | 0 | 0 | 0 | 2 | 0 | 0 | 0 | .000 | .000 | .000 |
| Ozoria, Pedro, Everett | 1 | 2 | 2 | 1 | 2 | 3 | 1 | 0 | 0 | 2 | 0 | 0 | 0 | 0 | 0 | 0 | 0 | 0 | 0 | 1.000 | 1.000 | 1.500 |
| Palumbo, Jeffrey, Salem-Keizer † | 65 | 306 | 260 | 44 | 75 | 87 | 10 | 1 | 0 | 25 | 7 | 3 | 2 | 34 | 0 | 29 | 6 | 0 | 2 | .288 | .371 | .335 |
| Paulino, Adalberto, Salem-Keizer | 14 | 36 | 34 | 3 | 6 | 14 | 2 | 0 | 2 | 7 | 0 | 0 | 1 | 1 | 0 | 6 | 0 | 0 | 3 | .176 | .222 | .412 |
| Perez, Leonel, Boise | 2 | 5 | 4 | 0 | 2 | 3 | 1 | 0 | 0 | 0 | 0 | 0 | 1 | 0 | 0 | 0 | 0 | 0 | 0 | .500 | .600 | .750 |
| Petit, Gregorio, Vancouver | 68 | 283 | 254 | 34 | 65 | 90 | 9 | 2 | 4 | 35 | 4 | 2 | 3 | 20 | 0 | 67 | 3 | 3 | 9 | .256 | .315 | .354 |
| Pohlman, Daniel, Yakima | 42 | 141 | 118 | 14 | 30 | 42 | 7 | 1 | 1 | 18 | 4 | 3 | 0 | 16 | 0 | 22 | 1 | 1 | 3 | .254 | .336 | .356 |
| Polimar, Aldwin, Yakima | 21 | 48 | 40 | 3 | 5 | 8 | 0 | 0 | 1 | 1 | 0 | 0 | 5 | 3 | 0 | 17 | 0 | 0 | 0 | .125 | .271 | .200 |
| Postlewait, Jacob, Tri-City † | 15 | 4 | 4 | 0 | 1 | 1 | 0 | 0 | 0 | 0 | 0 | 0 | 0 | 0 | 0 | 1 | 0 | 0 | 0 | .250 | .250 | .250 |
| Powell, Landon, Vancouver † | 38 | 163 | 135 | 24 | 32 | 49 | 6 | 1 | 3 | 19 | 0 | 1 | 1 | 26 | 1 | 22 | 0 | 0 | 4 | .237 | .362 | .363 |
| Puello, Elvin, Boise | 2 | 5 | 5 | 0 | 0 | 0 | 0 | 0 | 0 | 0 | 0 | 0 | 0 | 0 | 0 | 3 | 0 | 0 | 0 | .000 | .000 | .000 |
| Putnam, Daniel, Vancouver * | 11 | 52 | 38 | 10 | 11 | 19 | 2 | 0 | 2 | 3 | 0 | 0 | 0 | 14 | 1 | 8 | 1 | 0 | 2 | .289 | .481 | .500 |
| Ramirez, Juan, Vancouver | 16 | 48 | 42 | 6 | 3 | 3 | 0 | 0 | 0 | 1 | 0 | 0 | 1 | 5 | 0 | 8 | 0 | 1 | 2 | .071 | .188 | .071 |
| Ramirez, Yordany, Eugene | 4 | 16 | 15 | 1 | 3 | 6 | 0 | 0 | 1 | 3 | 0 | 0 | 0 | 1 | 0 | 5 | 0 | 0 | 0 | .200 | .250 | .400 |
| Restrepo, John, Tri-City * | 11 | 54 | 43 | 8 | 11 | 13 | 2 | 0 | 0 | 4 | 1 | 1 | 2 | 7 | 0 | 7 | 3 | 1 | 1 | .256 | .377 | .302 |
| Reynolds, Mark, Yakima | 64 | 277 | 234 | 58 | 64 | 121 | 19 | 1 | 12 | 41 | 3 | 2 | 13 | 25 | 3 | 65 | 4 | 1 | 3 | .274 | .372 | .517 |
| Richie, Tony, Boise | 51 | 195 | 175 | 19 | 55 | 68 | 8 | 1 | 1 | 24 | 2 | 1 | 4 | 13 | 0 | 21 | 3 | 2 | 8 | .314 | .373 | .389 |
| Rios, Jose, Boise | 65 | 223 | 206 | 21 | 40 | 49 | 4 | 1 | 1 | 15 | 6 | 1 | 3 | 7 | 0 | 23 | 0 | 3 | 2 | .194 | .230 | .238 |
| Rivera, Jodam, Eugene † | 3 | 9 | 8 | 1 | 1 | 1 | 0 | 0 | 0 | 0 | 0 | 0 | 0 | 1 | 0 | 2 | 0 | 0 | 0 | .125 | .222 | .125 |
| Robledo, Nelson, Tri-City | 45 | 179 | 165 | 13 | 35 | 49 | 5 | 3 | 1 | 16 | 0 | 0 | 2 | 12 | 0 | 38 | 0 | 0 | 2 | .212 | .274 | .297 |
| Robnett, Richard, Vancouver * | 43 | 195 | 164 | 26 | 49 | 77 | 14 | 1 | 4 | 36 | 0 | 3 | 0 | 28 | 0 | 43 | 1 | 2 | 6 | .299 | .395 | .470 |
| Ruiz, Ryan, Vancouver | 56 | 241 | 202 | 30 | 49 | 70 | 13 | 1 | 2 | 34 | 0 | 2 | 4 | 33 | 0 | 55 | 4 | 2 | 6 | .243 | .357 | .347 |
| Sakamoto, Mitsuru, Tri-City * | 31 | 117 | 108 | 11 | 24 | 30 | 4 | 1 | 0 | 12 | 2 | 1 | 2 | 4 | 0 | 24 | 0 | 3 | 6 | .222 | .261 | .278 |
| Sanchez, Angel, Spokane | 3 | 13 | 10 | 2 | 2 | 4 | 2 | 0 | 0 | 1 | 0 | 0 | 2 | 1 | 0 | 3 | 0 | 0 | 0 | .200 | .385 | .400 |
| Santin, Daniel, Everett * | 3 | 9 | 9 | 0 | 1 | 1 | 0 | 0 | 0 | 0 | 0 | 0 | 0 | 0 | 0 | 4 | 0 | 0 | 0 | .111 | .111 | .111 |
| Sargent, Luke, Tri-City | 19 | 55 | 49 | 4 | 8 | 10 | 2 | 0 | 0 | 3 | 2 | 0 | 0 | 4 | 0 | 20 | 0 | 0 | 2 | .163 | .226 | .204 |
| Schindewolf, Erik, Yakima * | 73 | 340 | 273 | 65 | 84 | 110 | 10 | 2 | 4 | 37 | 10 | 2 | 4 | 51 | 0 | 37 | 15 | 2 | 1 | .308 | .421 | .403 |
| Schweiger, Brian, Everett | 32 | 99 | 72 | 18 | 19 | 33 | 5 | 0 | 3 | 13 | 2 | 1 | 4 | 20 | 1 | 24 | 1 | 3 | 0 | .264 | .443 | .458 |
| Serrano, Julian, Boise | 5 | 8 | 7 | 2 | 2 | 2 | 0 | 0 | 0 | 0 | 0 | 0 | 0 | 1 | 0 | 3 | 0 | 0 | 0 | .286 | .375 | .286 |
| Simon, Brandon, Yakima * | 47 | 169 | 152 | 25 | 50 | 62 | 5 | 2 | 1 | 13 | 5 | 0 | 6 | 6 | 0 | 32 | 11 | 3 | 3 | .329 | .378 | .408 |
| Smith, Dustin, Boise | 14 | 41 | 39 | 1 | 6 | 6 | 0 | 0 | 0 | 1 | 1 | 0 | 0 | 0 | 0 | 9 | 2 | 0 | 4 | .154 | .154 | .154 |
| Smith, Seth, Tri-City | 9 | 29 | 27 | 6 | 7 | 16 | 1 | 1 | 2 | 5 | 0 | 1 | 0 | 1 | 1 | 3 | 0 | 0 | 1 | .259 | .276 | .593 |
| Soto, Luis, Everett | 9 | 29 | 27 | 4 | 7 | 8 | 1 | 0 | 0 | 3 | 0 | 0 | 1 | 1 | 0 | 5 | 2 | 0 | 3 | .259 | .310 | .296 |
| Spivey, Brett, Tri-City * | 38 | 160 | 130 | 9 | 26 | 30 | 4 | 0 | 0 | 13 | 4 | 1 | 1 | 24 | 0 | 23 | 3 | 5 | 4 | .200 | .327 | .231 |
| Strain, Ryan, Salem-Keizer † | 40 | 155 | 126 | 19 | 24 | 34 | 5 | 1 | 1 | 12 | 2 | 1 | 2 | 24 | 0 | 18 | 2 | 0 | 2 | .190 | .327 | .270 |
| Strop, Pedro, Tri-City | 55 | 222 | 190 | 20 | 38 | 55 | 6 | 1 | 3 | 20 | 9 | 0 | 6 | 17 | 0 | 64 | 2 | 1 | 2 | .200 | .286 | .289 |
| Susdorf, William, Spokane | 58 | 242 | 199 | 31 | 42 | 61 | 7 | 0 | 4 | 22 | 1 | 1 | 4 | 37 | 0 | 48 | 9 | 2 | 3 | .211 | .344 | .307 |
| Sutton, Don, Vancouver | 14 | 56 | 49 | 6 | 8 | 12 | 1 | 0 | 1 | 6 | 1 | 0 | 1 | 5 | 1 | 15 | 0 | 0 | 1 | .163 | .255 | .245 |
| Suzuki, Kurt, Vancouver | 46 | 211 | 175 | 27 | 52 | 77 | 10 | 3 | 3 | 31 | 3 | 3 | 12 | 18 | 0 | 26 | 0 | 1 | 3 | .297 | .394 | .440 |
| Swope, Tobin, Spokane | 26 | 92 | 76 | 14 | 12 | 19 | 4 | 0 | 1 | 5 | 0 | 0 | 2 | 14 | 0 | 20 | 4 | 0 | 0 | .158 | .304 | .250 |
| Thayer, Matthew, Eugene | 46 | 206 | 183 | 29 | 52 | 71 | 10 | 0 | 3 | 25 | 0 | 2 | 4 | 17 | 0 | 39 | 8 | 4 | 1 | .284 | .354 | .388 |
| Thigpen, Jud, Tri-City | 58 | 265 | 239 | 43 | 74 | 128 | 14 | 5 | 10 | 37 | 6 | 0 | 6 | 14 | 0 | 50 | 8 | 0 | 7 | .310 | .363 | .536 |
| Thompson, William, Salem-Keizer * | 62 | 270 | 225 | 43 | 66 | 81 | 12 | 0 | 1 | 27 | 0 | 3 | 5 | 37 | 0 | 34 | 0 | 0 | 6 | .293 | .400 | .360 |
| Tidball, Adam, Boise | 5 | 15 | 13 | 2 | 4 | 4 | 0 | 0 | 0 | 0 | 0 | 0 | 0 | 2 | 0 | 3 | 0 | 0 | 1 | .308 | .400 | .308 |
| Tietje, Chalon, Vancouver | 41 | 149 | 130 | 21 | 33 | 48 | 6 | 3 | 1 | 17 | 3 | 1 | 3 | 12 | 0 | 28 | 0 | 0 | 6 | .254 | .329 | .369 |
| Timpner, Clay, Salem-Keizer * | 68 | 320 | 294 | 37 | 86 | 112 | 7 | 2 | 5 | 28 | 4 | 1 | 1 | 20 | 0 | 35 | 16 | 5 | 3 | .293 | .339 | .381 |
| Tuiasosopo, Matthew, Everett | 29 | 118 | 101 | 18 | 25 | 39 | 6 | 1 | 2 | 14 | 0 | 1 | 4 | 10 | 0 | 36 | 4 | 3 | 3 | .248 | .336 | .386 |

| Player, Team | G | TPA | AB | R | H | TB | 2B | 3B | HR | RBI | SH | SF | HP | BB | IBB | SO | SB | CS | GDP | Avg. | OBP | Slg. |
|---|---|---|---|---|---|---|---|---|---|---|---|---|---|---|---|---|---|---|---|---|---|---|
| Valdez, Angel, Tri-City | 3 | 10 | 10 | 1 | 1 | 2 | 1 | 0 | 0 | 0 | 0 | 0 | 0 | 0 | 0 | 3 | 0 | 0 | 0 | .100 | .100 | .200 |
| Valdez, Jose, Tri-City * | 44 | 197 | 172 | 22 | 38 | 52 | 4 | 2 | 2 | 12 | 3 | 1 | 0 | 21 | 0 | 31 | 3 | 3 | 2 | .221 | .304 | .302 |
| Van Kooten, Jason, Tri-City | 16 | 68 | 55 | 10 | 13 | 14 | 1 | 0 | 0 | 1 | 2 | 0 | 6 | 5 | 0 | 10 | 0 | 1 | 1 | .236 | .364 | .255 |
| Vasquez, Jose, Tri-City * | 13 | 54 | 46 | 9 | 16 | 23 | 7 | 0 | 0 | 9 | 0 | 2 | 0 | 6 | 0 | 14 | 0 | 1 | 1 | .348 | .407 | .500 |
| Vincent, Tom, Eugene * | 56 | 190 | 175 | 24 | 41 | 68 | 11 | 2 | 4 | 18 | 0 | 0 | 1 | 14 | 0 | 60 | 7 | 2 | 1 | .234 | .295 | .389 |
| Wick, Olin, Boise † | 8 | 15 | 13 | 3 | 2 | 4 | 2 | 0 | 0 | 2 | 0 | 0 | 2 | 0 | 0 | 6 | 0 | 0 | 0 | .154 | .267 | .308 |
| Wilson, Michael, Everett † | 66 | 278 | 239 | 45 | 62 | 104 | 15 | 0 | 9 | 51 | 1 | 1 | 12 | 25 | 0 | 61 | 10 | 4 | 4 | .259 | .357 | .435 |
| Winslow, Benjamin, Vancouver | 26 | 74 | 63 | 6 | 10 | 12 | 2 | 0 | 0 | 4 | 2 | 1 | 1 | 7 | 0 | 20 | 5 | 0 | 2 | .159 | .250 | .190 |
| Yens, Jose, Salem-Keizer | 41 | 149 | 142 | 18 | 40 | 59 | 6 | 2 | 3 | 24 | 0 | 2 | 3 | 2 | 0 | 31 | 4 | 2 | 3 | .282 | .302 | .415 |

GRAND SLAMS—Boyer, Buchanan, Carter, Cashman, Everidge, Falcon, Harvey, Montanez, Ogando, Reynolds, Robnett, Vincent, Wilson, Yens, 1 each.

AWARDED FIRST BASE ON CATCHER'S INTERFERENCE—Balcom (Robledo); Cashman (J. Ramirez); Dale (Bernard); M. Miller (Bernard).

# 2004 PITCHING

## TEAM

| Team | W | L | Pct. | ERA | G | CG | ShO | Sv. | IP | H | TBF | R | ER | HR | SH | SF | HB | BB | IBB | SO | WP | Bk. |
|---|---|---|---|---|---|---|---|---|---|---|---|---|---|---|---|---|---|---|---|---|---|---|
| Spokane | 41 | 35 | .539 | 3.73 | 76 | 0 | 4 | 16 | 689.1 | 683 | 2978 | 362 | 286 | 64 | 28 | 17 | 46 | 221 | 9 | 599 | 36 | 5 |
| Tri-City | 40 | 36 | .526 | 3.99 | 76 | 0 | 6 | 23 | 684.0 | 620 | 2978 | 378 | 303 | 43 | 18 | 17 | 60 | 283 | 1 | 631 | 44 | 4 |
| Boise | 42 | 34 | .553 | 4.21 | 76 | 0 | 4 | 20 | 675.1 | 670 | 2960 | 374 | 316 | 51 | 31 | 24 | 43 | 290 | 6 | 548 | 46 | 4 |
| Vancouver | 42 | 34 | .553 | 4.41 | 76 | 0 | 1 | 21 | 667.2 | 691 | 2927 | 373 | 327 | 39 | 38 | 28 | 50 | 226 | 3 | 521 | 55 | 4 |
| Salem-Keizer | 37 | 39 | .487 | 4.50 | 76 | 0 | 2 | 15 | 678.1 | 679 | 3040 | 398 | 339 | 55 | 26 | 24 | 59 | 306 | 6 | 686 | 72 | 3 |
| Yakima | 35 | 41 | .461 | 4.50 | 76 | 0 | 3 | 13 | 668.1 | 738 | 3003 | 423 | 334 | 50 | 28 | 32 | 44 | 260 | 4 | 562 | 87 | 4 |
| Everett | 41 | 35 | .539 | 4.82 | 76 | 0 | 0 | 18 | 672.1 | 680 | 3017 | 423 | 360 | 82 | 30 | 25 | 62 | 314 | 4 | 567 | 75 | 6 |
| Eugene | 26 | 50 | .342 | 5.09 | 76 | 0 | 3 | 11 | 662.2 | 674 | 3004 | 456 | 375 | 72 | 17 | 24 | 64 | 305 | 4 | 567 | 61 | 3 |



## INDIVIDUAL

### TOP QUALIFIERS FOR EARNED-RUN AVERAGE TITLE

Minimum 61 innings.*Lefthanded pitcher.

| Pitcher, Team | W | L | Pct. | ERA | G | GS | CG | ShO | GF | Sv. | IP | H | TBF | R | ER | HR | SH | SF | HB | BB | IBB | SO | WP | Bk. |
|---|---|---|---|---|---|---|---|---|---|---|---|---|---|---|---|---|---|---|---|---|---|---|---|---|
| Brannon, Clint, Spokane * | 3 | 2 | .600 | 0.59 | 15 | 10 | 0 | 0 | 2 | 1 | 61.0 | 35 | 231 | 9 | 4 | 0 | 5 | 0 | 2 | 14 | 0 | 58 | 4 | 0 |
| Shappi, A.J., Yakima | 4 | 1 | .800 | 1.75 | 12 | 11 | 0 | 0 | 0 | 0 | 67.0 | 64 | 267 | 17 | 13 | 4 | 12 | 2 | 4 | 8 | 0 | 65 | 2 | 0 |
| Weber, Matthew, Boise | 5 | 1 | .833 | 2.95 | 14 | 14 | 0 | 0 | 0 | 0 | 76.1 | 72 | 303 | 27 | 25 | 1 | 4 | 3 | 4 | 18 | 0 | 46 | 4 | 1 |
| Morillo, Juan, Tri-City | 3 | 2 | .600 | 2.98 | 14 | 14 | 0 | 0 | 0 | 0 | 66.1 | 56 | 295 | 34 | 22 | 0 | 1 | 1 | 4 | 41 | 0 | 73 | 3 | 0 |
| Nottingham, Shawn, Everett * | 8 | 3 | .727 | 3.15 | 15 | 14 | 0 | 0 | 0 | 0 | 88.2 | 74 | 367 | 34 | 31 | 8 | 3 | 2 | 7 | 29 | 0 | 87 | 2 | 0 |
| Whitaker, Craig, Salem-Keizer | 4 | 2 | .667 | 3.44 | 15 | 15 | 0 | 0 | 0 | 0 | 70.2 | 58 | 307 | 33 | 27 | 4 | 5 | 4 | 6 | 43 | 0 | 77 | 14 | 0 |
| Santiago, Tomas, Tri-City | 4 | 3 | .571 | 3.57 | 14 | 13 | 0 | 0 | 0 | 0 | 75.2 | 67 | 322 | 34 | 30 | 7 | 3 | 2 | 10 | 27 | 0 | 66 | 1 | 1 |
| Register, Steven, Tri-City | 6 | 7 | .462 | 3.63 | 15 | 15 | 0 | 0 | 0 | 0 | 79.1 | 68 | 326 | 41 | 32 | 5 | 6 | 2 | 7 | 20 | 0 | 63 | 2 | 0 |
| Ford, Ryan, Vancouver * | 4 | 0 | 1.000 | 3.66 | 15 | 11 | 0 | 0 | 2 | 2 | 71.1 | 76 | 300 | 36 | 29 | 3 | 4 | 7 | 3 | 15 | 0 | 49 | 2 | 0 |
| Phillips, Shawn, Spokane | 6 | 1 | .857 | 3.93 | 18 | 10 | 0 | 0 | 2 | 0 | 71.0 | 69 | 290 | 33 | 31 | 8 | 2 | 1 | 3 | 8 | 0 | 53 | 1 | 1 |
| Perrault, Josh, Yakima | 2 | 4 | .333 | 4.21 | 14 | 13 | 0 | 0 | 0 | 0 | 66.1 | 79 | 292 | 42 | 31 | 4 | 4 | 4 | 6 | 22 | 0 | 37 | 8 | 1 |
| Raab, Kellen, Yakima * | 3 | 3 | .500 | 4.38 | 19 | 8 | 0 | 0 | 1 | 0 | 61.2 | 67 | 277 | 33 | 30 | 4 | 0 | 6 | 0 | 19 | 0 | 56 | 11 | 0 |
| Cabaniel, Tomas, Vancouver | 6 | 3 | .667 | 4.59 | 15 | 15 | 0 | 0 | 0 | 0 | 82.1 | 88 | 358 | 48 | 42 | 4 | 5 | 4 | 9 | 24 | 0 | 74 | 7 | 1 |
| Sharpe, Steven, Vancouver | 6 | 3 | .667 | 4.60 | 16 | 14 | 0 | 0 | 0 | 0 | 72.1 | 59 | 296 | 40 | 37 | 3 | 9 | 4 | 4 | 30 | 0 | 53 | 9 | 1 |
| Brito, Luis, Boise | 6 | 4 | .600 | 4.95 | 15 | 15 | 0 | 0 | 0 | 0 | 76.1 | 87 | 330 | 46 | 42 | 11 | 2 | 3 | 4 | 20 | 0 | 45 | 0 | 1 |

DEPARTMENTAL LEADERS: W—Nottingham, 8; L—Ponce, 9; Pct.—McGirr, 1.000; G—J. Miller, 34; GS—Sack, Jensen, 16; CG—none; ShO—none; GF—Miller, 32; Sv.—J. Miller, 17; IP—Nottingham, 88.2; H—Jensen, 90; TBF—Nottingham, 367; R—De La O, 56; ER—De La O, 52; HR—Sack, 15; SH—Shappi, 12; SF—Three tied with seven; HB—Altman, 12; BB—Whitaker, 43; IBB—Mejia, C. Thompson, 3; SO—Nottingham, 87; WP—Whitaker, 14; BK—Bergdall, 3.

### ALL PITCHERS

*Lefthanded pitcher.

| Pitcher, Team | W | L | Pct. | ERA | G | GS | CG | ShO | GF | Sv. | IP | H | TBF | R | ER | HR | SH | SF | HB | BB | IBB | SO | WP | Bk. |
|---|---|---|---|---|---|---|---|---|---|---|---|---|---|---|---|---|---|---|---|---|---|---|---|---|
| Acevedo, Danielin, Vancouver | 2 | 1 | .667 | 3.20 | 5 | 2 | 0 | 0 | 1 | 0 | 19.2 | 22 | 87 | 11 | 7 | 0 | 2 | 1 | 1 | 6 | 0 | 7 | 3 | 0 |
| Altman, Kevin, Spokane | 1 | 4 | .200 | 6.42 | 18 | 9 | 0 | 0 | 6 | 0 | 47.2 | 68 | 247 | 50 | 34 | 8 | 4 | 5 | 12 | 19 | 2 | 29 | 2 | 0 |
| Barnett, Danny, Vancouver | 0 | 3 | .000 | 5.40 | 10 | 0 | 0 | 0 | 3 | 0 | 16.2 | 19 | 78 | 12 | 10 | 1 | 0 | 0 | 0 | 9 | 0 | 17 | 2 | 0 |
| Basch, Zachary, Vancouver | 1 | 3 | .250 | 6.17 | 18 | 0 | 0 | 0 | 10 | 0 | 23.1 | 25 | 114 | 17 | 16 | 2 | 0 | 0 | 5 | 14 | 0 | 22 | 4 | 0 |
| Beerer, Scott, Tri-City | 0 | 0 | .000 | 3.38 | 6 | 0 | 0 | 0 | 2 | 0 | 5.1 | 6 | 25 | 2 | 2 | 0 | 0 | 0 | 1 | 2 | 0 | 5 | 2 | 0 |
| Bello, Cibney, Everett | 4 | 1 | .800 | 3.93 | 22 | 0 | 0 | 0 | 6 | 1 | 34.1 | 25 | 148 | 16 | 15 | 5 | 0 | 0 | 5 | 15 | 0 | 34 | 2 | 0 |
| Bergdall, Kendall, Everett * | 3 | 3 | .500 | 7.04 | 15 | 10 | 0 | 0 | 4 | 0 | 55.0 | 68 | 273 | 49 | 43 | 7 | 2 | 7 | 6 | 40 | 1 | 41 | 6 | 3 |
| Blanco, Ivan, Everett | 0 | 1 | .000 | 11.05 | 4 | 4 | 0 | 0 | 0 | 0 | 14.2 | 21 | 74 | 19 | 18 | 5 | 1 | 2 | 1 | 12 | 0 | 20 | 2 | 0 |
| Blevins, Jerry, Boise * | 6 | 1 | .857 | 1.62 | 23 | 0 | 0 | 0 | 11 | 5 | 33.1 | 17 | 141 | 7 | 6 | 1 | 0 | 0 | 3 | 21 | 1 | 42 | 2 | 0 |
| Boyer, Kyle, Boise | 0 | 0 | .000 | 0.00 | 1 | 0 | 0 | 0 | 1 | 0 | 1.0 | 0 | 3 | 0 | 0 | 0 | 0 | 0 | 0 | 0 | 0 | 1 | 0 | 0 |
| Braden, Dallas, Vancouver * | 2 | 0 | 1.000 | 2.76 | 7 | 0 | 0 | 0 | 4 | 2 | 16.1 | 15 | 63 | 7 | 5 | 1 | 0 | 0 | 0 | 3 | 0 | 26 | 0 | 0 |
| Brannon, Clint, Spokane * | 3 | 2 | .600 | 0.59 | 15 | 10 | 0 | 0 | 2 | 1 | 61.0 | 35 | 231 | 9 | 4 | 0 | 5 | 0 | 2 | 14 | 0 | 58 | 4 | 0 |
| Bright, Adam, Tri-City * | 3 | 4 | .429 | 4.93 | 23 | 0 | 0 | 0 | 7 | 0 | 38.1 | 38 | 177 | 25 | 21 | 3 | 0 | 0 | 2 | 22 | 0 | 36 | 2 | 1 |
| Brito, Luis, Boise | 6 | 4 | .600 | 4.95 | 15 | 15 | 0 | 0 | 0 | 0 | 76.1 | 87 | 330 | 46 | 42 | 11 | 2 | 3 | 4 | 20 | 0 | 45 | 0 | 1 |
| Broshuis, Garrett, Salem-Keizer | 3 | 0 | 1.000 | 1.37 | 5 | 2 | 0 | 0 | 1 | 0 | 19.2 | 15 | 81 | 4 | 3 | 0 | 2 | 0 | 3 | 4 | 0 | 23 | 1 | 0 |
| Buechner, Chris, Tri-City | 3 | 1 | .750 | 1.75 | 19 | 0 | 0 | 0 | 5 | 3 | 25.2 | 15 | 100 | 8 | 5 | 0 | 0 | 0 | 2 | 6 | 0 | 31 | 2 | 0 |
| Burcie, Jarrad, Spokane | 3 | 0 | 1.000 | 1.74 | 23 | 0 | 0 | 0 | 19 | 8 | 31.0 | 23 | 123 | 7 | 6 | 4 | 0 | 0 | 2 | 5 | 0 | 40 | 4 | 0 |
| Burks, Brian, Eugene | 2 | 2 | .500 | 1.82 | 24 | 0 | 0 | 0 | 10 | 4 | 29.2 | 27 | 127 | 10 | 6 | 1 | 0 | 0 | 2 | 9 | 1 | 17 | 5 | 1 |
| Burnham, Brett, Eugene | 0 | 0 | .000 | 3.00 | 2 | 0 | 0 | 0 | 2 | 0 | 3.0 | 1 | 11 | 1 | 1 | 1 | 0 | 0 | 1 | 0 | 0 | 2 | 0 | 0 |
| Cabaniel, Tomas, Vancouver | 6 | 3 | .667 | 4.59 | 15 | 15 | 0 | 0 | 0 | 0 | 82.1 | 88 | 358 | 48 | 42 | 4 | 5 | 4 | 9 | 24 | 0 | 74 | 7 | 1 |
| Campusano, Edward, Boise * | 0 | 5 | .000 | 5.29 | 14 | 5 | 0 | 0 | 1 | 0 | 34.0 | 37 | 157 | 29 | 20 | 5 | 1 | 3 | 1 | 15 | 0 | 24 | 2 | 1 |
| Carque, Joe, Yakima | 0 | 6 | .000 | 5.40 | 24 | 4 | 0 | 0 | 6 | 0 | 55.0 | 79 | 262 | 53 | 33 | 4 | 3 | 4 | 3 | 15 | 0 | 34 | 7 | 1 |
| Carter, Brian, Boise * | 0 | 1 | .000 | 8.59 | 5 | 0 | 0 | 0 | 2 | 1 | 7.1 | 12 | 37 | 8 | 7 | 1 | 0 | 0 | 0 | 3 | 0 | 5 | 0 | 0 |
| Carter, Steven-ryder, Vancouver | 0 | 0 | .000 | 22.50 | 3 | 0 | 0 | 0 | 0 | 0 | 2.0 | 6 | 12 | 5 | 5 | 1 | 0 | 0 | 0 | 0 | 0 | 0 | 0 | 0 |
| Cespedes, Robinson, Eugene | 1 | 0 | 1.000 | 2.48 | 24 | 0 | 0 | 0 | 3 | 0 | 36.1 | 29 | 151 | 14 | 10 | 3 | 0 | 0 | 1 | 12 | 0 | 25 | 1 | 1 |
| Clark, Chad, Yakima | 0 | 2 | .000 | 7.50 | 5 | 2 | 0 | 0 | 0 | 0 | 12.0 | 16 | 59 | 10 | 10 | 0 | 1 | 0 | 0 | 11 | 0 | 7 | 1 | 0 |
| Cockroft, Joseph, Spokane * | 1 | 6 | .143 | 4.01 | 16 | 5 | 0 | 0 | 2 | 0 | 42.2 | 49 | 195 | 29 | 19 | 0 | 4 | 2 | 4 | 15 | 0 | 27 | 4 | 0 |
| Colbert, Henry, Eugene | 0 | 2 | .000 | 8.51 | 21 | 0 | 0 | 0 | 8 | 0 | 30.2 | 44 | 164 | 36 | 29 | 7 | 0 | 0 | 4 | 24 | 0 | 35 | 7 | 0 |
| Cullen, Phil, Everett | 2 | 2 | .500 | 2.87 | 15 | 1 | 0 | 0 | 5 | 0 | 31.1 | 22 | 137 | 13 | 10 | 3 | 0 | 1 | 2 | 17 | 0 | 20 | 3 | 0 |
| Darby, James, Eugene | 1 | 3 | .250 | 8.53 | 25 | 0 | 0 | 0 | 6 | 0 | 25.1 | 24 | 145 | 32 | 24 | 1 | 0 | 0 | 10 | 35 | 0 | 20 | 7 | 0 |

| Pitcher, Team | W | L | Pct. | ERA | G | GS | CG | ShO | GF | Sv. | IP | H | TBF | R | ER | HR | SH | SF | HB | BB | IBB | SO | WP | Bk. |
|---|---|---|---|---|---|---|---|---|---|---|---|---|---|---|---|---|---|---|---|---|---|---|---|---|
| De la O, Danny, Eugene * | 3 | 6 | .333 | 7.02 | 18 | 10 | 0 | 0 | 2 | 0 | 66.2 | 78 | 303 | 56 | 52 | 13 | 0 | 3 | 5 | 29 | 0 | 55 | 3 | 0 |
| Delabar,, Eugene | 1 | 1 | .500 | 2.65 | 3 | 3 | 0 | 0 | 0 | 0 | 17.0 | 13 | 69 | 7 | 5 | 1 | 0 | 1 | 1 | 3 | 0 | 11 | 0 | 0 |
| Diamond, Thomas, Spokane | 0 | 2 | .000 | 2.35 | 5 | 3 | 0 | 0 | 1 | 1 | 15.1 | 13 | 65 | 5 | 4 | 0 | 0 | 0 | 1 | 5 | 0 | 26 | 1 | 0 |
| Downs, Darin, Boise * | 5 | 3 | .625 | 4.95 | 14 | 13 | 0 | 0 | 0 | 0 | 60.0 | 55 | 254 | 36 | 33 | 5 | 7 | 6 | 2 | 35 | 0 | 61 | 2 | 0 |
| Drucker, Scott, Vancouver | 2 | 1 | .667 | 3.00 | 14 | 0 | 0 | 0 | 11 | 6 | 21.0 | 20 | 89 | 8 | 7 | 1 | 0 | 0 | 0 | 6 | 0 | 18 | 2 | 0 |
| Edsall, Stephen, Tri-City | 2 | 0 | 1.000 | 3.55 | 12 | 0 | 0 | 0 | 2 | 0 | 25.1 | 19 | 105 | 10 | 10 | 3 | 0 | 0 | 0 | 10 | 0 | 23 | 2 | 0 |
| Ekstrom, Michael, Eugene | 3 | 1 | .750 | 3.69 | 12 | 7 | 0 | 0 | 1 | 0 | 39.0 | 38 | 171 | 18 | 16 | 1 | 1 | 4 | 4 | 10 | 0 | 42 | 2 | 0 |
| Ellis, Jonathan, Eugene | 1 | 2 | .333 | 4.66 | 5 | 1 | 0 | 0 | 1 | 0 | 9.2 | 7 | 40 | 5 | 5 | 1 | 0 | 0 | 3 | 2 | 0 | 9 | 1 | 0 |
| Espinal, Leonardo, Vancouver | 0 | 2 | .000 | 6.75 | 2 | 2 | 0 | 0 | 0 | 0 | 9.1 | 11 | 44 | 8 | 7 | 1 | 2 | 1 | 2 | 2 | 0 | 6 | 0 | 0 |
| Espinal, Willy, Spokane | 1 | 0 | 1.000 | 4.30 | 22 | 0 | 0 | 0 | 10 | 1 | 44.0 | 47 | 199 | 26 | 21 | 6 | 0 | 0 | 4 | 16 | 0 | 29 | 3 | 0 |
| Falconer, Kenny, Everett | 0 | 0 | .000 | 16.88 | 7 | 0 | 0 | 0 | 2 | 0 | 5.1 | 11 | 33 | 12 | 10 | 2 | 0 | 0 | 1 | 5 | 0 | 4 | 2 | 0 |
| Fenton, Willson, Boise | 2 | 0 | 1.000 | 2.64 | 20 | 0 | 0 | 0 | 9 | 4 | 30.2 | 28 | 133 | 13 | 9 | 2 | 0 | 0 | 0 | 13 | 0 | 35 | 1 | 0 |
| Fernandez, Alfredo, Eugene | 2 | 5 | .286 | 5.60 | 13 | 13 | 0 | 0 | 0 | 0 | 62.2 | 66 | 279 | 41 | 39 | 7 | 3 | 6 | 6 | 23 | 0 | 45 | 1 | 0 |
| Ferreras, Yorkin, Boise * | 3 | 2 | .600 | 2.55 | 5 | 5 | 0 | 0 | 0 | 0 | 24.2 | 21 | 95 | 8 | 7 | 2 | 2 | 2 | 0 | 3 | 0 | 23 | 0 | 0 |
| Figuereo, Victor, Spokane | 0 | 1 | .000 | 7.88 | 5 | 0 | 0 | 0 | 2 | 0 | 8.0 | 10 | 43 | 9 | 7 | 2 | 0 | 0 | 2 | 7 | 1 | 8 | 3 | 0 |
| Fillinger, Chad, Everett | 1 | 0 | 1.000 | 5.94 | 11 | 0 | 0 | 0 | 2 | 1 | 16.2 | 22 | 78 | 11 | 11 | 4 | 0 | 0 | 1 | 5 | 0 | 25 | 4 | 0 |
| Fischer, Sam, Boise | 0 | 0 | .000 | 0.66 | 7 | 0 | 0 | 0 | 2 | 1 | 13.2 | 10 | 55 | 1 | 1 | 0 | 0 | 0 | 2 | 2 | 0 | 19 | 1 | 0 |
| Flores, Ruben, Everett | 2 | 5 | .286 | 5.20 | 11 | 11 | 0 | 0 | 0 | 0 | 53.2 | 50 | 230 | 36 | 31 | 8 | 6 | 2 | 5 | 24 | 1 | 40 | 8 | 0 |
| Forbes, Terry, Everett | 1 | 2 | .333 | 4.50 | 9 | 0 | 0 | 0 | 3 | 0 | 20.0 | 29 | 96 | 16 | 10 | 1 | 0 | 0 | 0 | 7 | 0 | 11 | 3 | 1 |
| Ford, Ryan, Vancouver * | 4 | 0 | 1.000 | 3.66 | 15 | 11 | 0 | 0 | 2 | 2 | 71.1 | 76 | 300 | 36 | 29 | 3 | 4 | 7 | 3 | 15 | 0 | 49 | 2 | 0 |
| Gagne, J.P., Tri-City | 4 | 1 | .800 | 4.29 | 24 | 0 | 0 | 0 | 5 | 0 | 50.1 | 49 | 216 | 30 | 24 | 2 | 0 | 0 | 1 | 16 | 0 | 47 | 6 | 0 |
| Gallegos, Gary, Eugene * | 1 | 6 | .143 | 6.60 | 25 | 4 | 0 | 0 | 7 | 0 | 45.0 | 46 | 201 | 36 | 33 | 6 | 2 | 1 | 7 | 23 | 0 | 53 | 6 | 0 |
| Gardner, Adam, Salem-Keizer * | 2 | 0 | 1.000 | 2.54 | 19 | 0 | 0 | 0 | 6 | 0 | 49.2 | 38 | 220 | 19 | 14 | 2 | 1 | 1 | 1 | 30 | 1 | 59 | 5 | 1 |
| Green, Craig, Boise | 0 | 1 | .000 | 6.61 | 9 | 0 | 0 | 0 | 2 | 0 | 16.1 | 24 | 77 | 15 | 12 | 2 | 0 | 0 | 1 | 3 | 0 | 8 | 4 | 0 |
| Gresky, David, Boise * | 0 | 0 | .000 | 0.00 | 1 | 0 | 0 | 0 | 1 | 0 | 1.0 | 1 | 4 | 1 | 0 | 0 | 0 | 0 | 0 | 0 | 0 | 0 | 0 | 0 |
| Gross, Kris, Boise | 4 | 1 | .800 | 3.21 | 19 | 0 | 0 | 0 | 14 | 5 | 28.0 | 26 | 128 | 15 | 10 | 2 | 0 | 0 | 3 | 15 | 1 | 27 | 0 | 0 |
| Grube, Jarrett, Tri-City | 4 | 3 | .571 | 4.24 | 17 | 9 | 0 | 0 | 1 | 0 | 57.1 | 62 | 251 | 38 | 27 | 4 | 0 | 0 | 9 | 13 | 0 | 55 | 2 | 0 |
| Guerrero, Hipolito, Yakima * | 1 | 0 | 1.000 | 3.98 | 16 | 0 | 0 | 0 | 1 | 0 | 20.1 | 19 | 85 | 9 | 9 | 2 | 0 | 0 | 2 | 3 | 0 | 21 | 5 | 0 |
| Hagerty, Luke, Boise * | 0 | 2 | .000 | 12.00 | 4 | 3 | 0 | 0 | 0 | 0 | 9.0 | 15 | 52 | 13 | 12 | 0 | 0 | 0 | 1 | 9 | 0 | 5 | 0 | 0 |
| Hall, Vance, Everett * | 3 | 0 | 1.000 | 5.71 | 18 | 0 | 0 | 0 | 6 | 1 | 34.2 | 42 | 164 | 28 | 22 | 4 | 0 | 2 | 3 | 17 | 0 | 25 | 9 | 0 |
| Hamilton, Clayton, Eugene | 1 | 1 | .500 | 5.20 | 8 | 5 | 0 | 0 | 2 | 0 | 27.2 | 21 | 120 | 21 | 16 | 5 | 2 | 1 | 3 | 13 | 0 | 31 | 0 | 0 |
| Hedrick, Justin, Salem-Keizer | 1 | 2 | .333 | 3.27 | 11 | 4 | 0 | 0 | 1 | 0 | 33.0 | 22 | 136 | 14 | 12 | 3 | 3 | 1 | 3 | 17 | 0 | 44 | 2 | 0 |
| Hendricks, Arthur, Yakima | 0 | 0 | .000 | 9.00 | 1 | 0 | 0 | 0 | 1 | 0 | 1.0 | 2 | 5 | 1 | 1 | 0 | 0 | 0 | 0 | 0 | 0 | 0 | 0 | 0 |
| Herrera, Marcos, Spokane | 6 | 1 | .857 | 2.12 | 23 | 0 | 0 | 0 | 5 | 0 | 46.2 | 37 | 187 | 13 | 11 | 2 | 0 | 1 | 0 | 11 | 1 | 33 | 3 | 2 |
| Howay, Chris, Vancouver | 3 | 1 | .750 | 5.65 | 20 | 0 | 0 | 0 | 10 | 2 | 28.2 | 35 | 136 | 19 | 18 | 1 | 0 | 0 | 1 | 13 | 0 | 32 | 3 | 0 |
| Hunton, Jonathan, Boise | 1 | 1 | .500 | 4.03 | 21 | 0 | 0 | 0 | 7 | 2 | 29.0 | 26 | 138 | 15 | 13 | 1 | 0 | 0 | 1 | 24 | 1 | 34 | 7 | 0 |
| Hurley, Eric, Spokane | 0 | 2 | .000 | 5.40 | 8 | 6 | 0 | 0 | 0 | 0 | 28.1 | 31 | 115 | 18 | 17 | 6 | 1 | 2 | 1 | 6 | 1 | 21 | 0 | 0 |
| Ion, Mark, Tri-City | 2 | 0 | 1.000 | 1.93 | 4 | 0 | 0 | 0 | 1 | 1 | 9.1 | 6 | 36 | 2 | 2 | 1 | 0 | 0 | 0 | 2 | 0 | 9 | 0 | 1 |
| Jackson, Steven, Yakima | 1 | 0 | 1.000 | 4.56 | 9 | 2 | 0 | 0 | 1 | 0 | 23.2 | 24 | 102 | 12 | 12 | 4 | 1 | 1 | 0 | 6 | 0 | 18 | 3 | 0 |
| Jensen, Aaron, Everett | 7 | 4 | .636 | 5.29 | 16 | 16 | 0 | 0 | 0 | 0 | 80.0 | 90 | 358 | 53 | 47 | 12 | 8 | 5 | 5 | 36 | 0 | 56 | 1 | 0 |
| Jenson, Kevin, Salem-Keizer | 0 | 1 | .000 | 10.45 | 6 | 0 | 0 | 0 | 1 | 0 | 10.1 | 14 | 56 | 13 | 12 | 4 | 0 | 0 | 2 | 9 | 0 | 11 | 1 | 0 |
| Jerome, Clayton, Spokane | 3 | 3 | .500 | 6.85 | 19 | 4 | 0 | 0 | 5 | 0 | 47.1 | 74 | 232 | 48 | 36 | 7 | 0 | 1 | 2 | 15 | 0 | 32 | 0 | 0 |
| Kalita, Ryan, Boise | 1 | 0 | 1.000 | 6.00 | 5 | 0 | 0 | 0 | 1 | 0 | 6.0 | 8 | 27 | 4 | 4 | 1 | 0 | 0 | 0 | 1 | 0 | 5 | 1 | 0 |
| Kemlo, Chris, Yakima | 5 | 2 | .714 | 5.12 | 31 | 0 | 0 | 0 | 22 | 5 | 38.2 | 45 | 180 | 25 | 22 | 4 | 0 | 0 | 0 | 19 | 0 | 48 | 9 | 1 |
| Kerbs, Reuben, Yakima * | 5 | 2 | .714 | 5.50 | 23 | 1 | 0 | 0 | 6 | 0 | 36.0 | 38 | 164 | 24 | 22 | 0 | 0 | 1 | 1 | 18 | 1 | 20 | 3 | 0 |
| Kintzler, Brandon, Eugene | 0 | 0 | .000 | 0.00 | 3 | 0 | 0 | 0 | 3 | 3 | 3.0 | 3 | 12 | 0 | 0 | 0 | 0 | 0 | 0 | 0 | 0 | 4 | 0 | 0 |
| Kolberg, Koley, Yakima | 1 | 3 | .250 | 5.13 | 22 | 0 | 0 | 0 | 10 | 3 | 26.1 | 27 | 116 | 15 | 15 | 2 | 0 | 0 | 3 | 7 | 0 | 31 | 2 | 0 |
| Kosow, Jason, Boise | 0 | 0 | .000 | 3.15 | 11 | 0 | 0 | 0 | 5 | 1 | 20.0 | 18 | 92 | 7 | 7 | 0 | 0 | 0 | 1 | 13 | 0 | 13 | 3 | 0 |
| Krawiec, Aaron, Boise * | 0 | 1 | .000 | 4.22 | 3 | 2 | 0 | 0 | 0 | 0 | 10.2 | 16 | 43 | 6 | 5 | 1 | 2 | 1 | 0 | 0 | 0 | 8 | 1 | 0 |
| Kroft, Adam, Eugene | 1 | 0 | 1.000 | 1.80 | 1 | 1 | 0 | 0 | 0 | 0 | 5.0 | 4 | 22 | 1 | 1 | 0 | 0 | 0 | 0 | 4 | 1 | 3 | 1 | 0 |
| Kunes, Michael, Salem-Keizer * | 1 | 1 | .500 | 4.91 | 21 | 0 | 0 | 0 | 12 | 4 | 33.0 | 35 | 148 | 19 | 18 | 3 | 0 | 1 | 0 | 14 | 1 | 30 | 3 | 0 |
| Lensch, Justin, Spokane * | 3 | 5 | .375 | 5.01 | 19 | 9 | 0 | 0 | 3 | 1 | 59.1 | 72 | 268 | 41 | 33 | 6 | 1 | 1 | 2 | 24 | 0 | 30 | 5 | 0 |
| Liebeck, Jered, Yakima | 4 | 2 | .667 | 4.53 | 11 | 10 | 0 | 0 | 0 | 0 | 59.2 | 64 | 261 | 37 | 30 | 6 | 3 | 7 | 1 | 19 | 0 | 52 | 3 | 1 |
| Lira, Efren, Tri-City | 1 | 1 | .500 | 5.19 | 20 | 0 | 0 | 0 | 8 | 0 | 34.2 | 36 | 164 | 24 | 20 | 1 | 0 | 2 | 5 | 20 | 0 | 26 | 3 | 0 |
| Lockwood, Jon, Everett | 0 | 0 | .000 | 4.50 | 2 | 0 | 0 | 0 | 1 | 0 | 2.0 | 1 | 12 | 1 | 1 | 0 | 0 | 0 | 1 | 4 | 0 | 0 | 1 | 0 |
| Lowe, Mark, Everett | 1 | 2 | .333 | 4.93 | 18 | 3 | 0 | 0 | 12 | 7 | 38.1 | 42 | 173 | 22 | 21 | 4 | 2 | 1 | 4 | 14 | 0 | 38 | 2 | 1 |
| Lujan, John, Spokane | 1 | 0 | 1.000 | 2.20 | 4 | 3 | 0 | 0 | 0 | 0 | 16.1 | 17 | 71 | 4 | 4 | 1 | 0 | 0 | 0 | 9 | 0 | 17 | 1 | 1 |
| Mackay, Douglas, Salem-Keizer | 3 | 4 | .429 | 6.18 | 16 | 9 | 0 | 0 | 0 | 0 | 51.0 | 67 | 245 | 39 | 35 | 1 | 0 | 1 | 6 | 23 | 0 | 39 | 8 | 0 |
| Martinez, Roman, Everett | 0 | 0 | .000 | 2.45 | 5 | 0 | 0 | 0 | 2 | 0 | 7.1 | 9 | 35 | 4 | 2 | 1 | 0 | 0 | 2 | 2 | 0 | 5 | 1 | 0 |
| Martinez, Shawn, Vancouver | 1 | 4 | .200 | 4.50 | 17 | 2 | 0 | 0 | 8 | 2 | 40.0 | 42 | 182 | 22 | 20 | 4 | 1 | 1 | 3 | 20 | 0 | 36 | 5 | 0 |
| Mathes, J.R., Boise * | 3 | 0 | 1.000 | 3.50 | 12 | 8 | 0 | 0 | 0 | 0 | 54.0 | 50 | 214 | 25 | 21 | 4 | 6 | 4 | 2 | 10 | 0 | 51 | 2 | 0 |
| McGirr, Mike, Vancouver | 5 | 0 | 1.000 | 0.66 | 7 | 7 | 0 | 0 | 0 | 0 | 41.0 | 23 | 158 | 5 | 3 | 1 | 3 | 5 | 5 | 7 | 0 | 31 | 1 | 1 |
| Mejia, Anderson, Boise | 3 | 4 | .429 | 5.04 | 27 | 0 | 0 | 0 | 8 | 0 | 44.2 | 44 | 215 | 30 | 25 | 2 | 2 | 0 | 5 | 33 | 3 | 24 | 2 | 0 |
| Miller, James, Tri-City | 1 | 1 | .500 | 0.97 | 34 | 0 | 0 | 0 | 32 | 17 | 37.0 | 21 | 145 | 6 | 4 | 1 | 0 | 0 | 2 | 11 | 0 | 65 | 1 | 0 |
| Minor, Matthew, Salem-Keizer | 0 | 0 | .000 | 4.96 | 15 | 0 | 0 | 0 | 13 | 4 | 16.1 | 18 | 78 | 9 | 9 | 1 | 0 | 0 | 4 | 7 | 0 | 16 | 3 | 0 |
| Mock, Garrett, Yakima | 2 | 0 | 1.000 | 1.54 | 5 | 5 | 0 | 0 | 0 | 0 | 23.1 | 18 | 86 | 8 | 4 | 1 | 1 | 2 | 0 | 4 | 0 | 14 | 0 | 0 |
| Moreno, Anthony, Salem-Keizer | 5 | 1 | .833 | 3.44 | 21 | 0 | 0 | 0 | 5 | 1 | 49.2 | 40 | 200 | 22 | 19 | 6 | 0 | 0 | 3 | 11 | 1 | 47 | 6 | 0 |
| Morillo, Juan, Tri-City | 3 | 2 | .600 | 2.98 | 14 | 14 | 0 | 0 | 0 | 0 | 66.1 | 56 | 295 | 34 | 22 | 0 | 1 | 1 | 4 | 41 | 0 | 73 | 3 | 0 |
| Nottingham, Shawn, Everett * | 8 | 3 | .727 | 3.15 | 15 | 14 | 0 | 0 | 0 | 0 | 88.2 | 74 | 367 | 34 | 31 | 8 | 3 | 2 | 7 | 29 | 0 | 87 | 2 | 0 |
| Novosel, Walt, Yakima * | 0 | 0 | .000 | 6.48 | 7 | 0 | 0 | 0 | 2 | 0 | 8.1 | 13 | 44 | 10 | 6 | 0 | 0 | 0 | 0 | 6 | 0 | 11 | 0 | 0 |
| O'hagan, David, Eugene | 1 | 0 | 1.000 | 2.57 | 8 | 0 | 0 | 0 | 4 | 1 | 7.0 | 4 | 31 | 3 | 2 | 0 | 0 | 0 | 1 | 5 | 0 | 12 | 1 | 0 |
| Odom, John, Salem-Keizer | 2 | 4 | .333 | 5.01 | 20 | 5 | 0 | 0 | 5 | 0 | 59.1 | 81 | 279 | 39 | 33 | 2 | 2 | 2 | 6 | 19 | 2 | 55 | 5 | 0 |
| Ohlendorf, Curtis, Yakima | 2 | 3 | .400 | 2.79 | 7 | 7 | 0 | 0 | 0 | 0 | 29.0 | 22 | 128 | 14 | 9 | 1 | 0 | 0 | 4 | 19 | 0 | 28 | 9 | 0 |
| Pablos, Rene, Boise * | 0 | 0 | .000 | 2.45 | 6 | 0 | 0 | 0 | 3 | 0 | 7.1 | 5 | 30 | 4 | 2 | 0 | 0 | 0 | 0 | 3 | 0 | 2 | 1 | 0 |
| Pendley, Nathan, Salem-Keizer * | 2 | 0 | 1.000 | 2.45 | 15 | 0 | 0 | 0 | 9 | 2 | 18.1 | 14 | 77 | 6 | 5 | 0 | 0 | 0 | 0 | 8 | 1 | 20 | 2 | 0 |
| Perrault, Josh, Yakima | 2 | 4 | .333 | 4.21 | 14 | 13 | 0 | 0 | 0 | 0 | 66.1 | 79 | 292 | 42 | 31 | 4 | 4 | 4 | 6 | 22 | 0 | 37 | 8 | 1 |
| Perry, Brandon, Everett * | 1 | 0 | 1.000 | 6.99 | 17 | 0 | 0 | 0 | 9 | 1 | 28.1 | 40 | 143 | 28 | 22 | 3 | 0 | 0 | 1 | 17 | 1 | 26 | 3 | 0 |
| Phillips, Shawn, Spokane | 6 | 1 | .857 | 3.93 | 18 | 10 | 0 | 0 | 2 | 0 | 71.0 | 69 | 290 | 33 | 31 | 8 | 2 | 1 | 3 | 8 | 0 | 53 | 1 | 1 |
| Pohlman, Daniel, Yakima | 0 | 0 | .000 | 2.25 | 3 | 0 | 0 | 0 | 1 | 0 | 4.0 | 3 | 18 | 1 | 1 | 0 | 0 | 0 | 1 | 2 | 0 | 5 | 1 | 0 |
| Ponce, William, Eugene | 1 | 9 | .100 | 5.97 | 14 | 12 | 0 | 0 | 0 | 0 | 66.1 | 75 | 310 | 54 | 44 | 9 | 3 | 4 | 4 | 33 | 0 | 39 | 1 | 0 |
| Postlewait, Jacob, Tri-City * | 1 | 3 | .250 | 5.70 | 14 | 12 | 0 | 0 | 0 | 0 | 53.2 | 65 | 261 | 41 | 34 | 6 | 5 | 5 | 5 | 31 | 0 | 35 | 5 | 0 |
| Prendergast, Matt, Tri-City | 0 | 1 | .000 | 13.50 | 3 | 0 | 0 | 0 | 1 | 0 | 4.0 | 5 | 20 | 6 | 6 | 1 | 0 | 0 | 0 | 3 | 0 | 3 | 0 | 0 |
| Raab, Kellen, Yakima * | 3 | 3 | .500 | 4.38 | 19 | 8 | 0 | 0 | 1 | 0 | 61.2 | 67 | 277 | 33 | 30 | 4 | 0 | 6 | 0 | 19 | 0 | 56 | 11 | 0 |
| Raguse, Matt, Salem-Keizer | 0 | 3 | .000 | 7.16 | 14 | 6 | 0 | 0 | 1 | 1 | 27.2 | 39 | 142 | 26 | 22 | 5 | 1 | 2 | 4 | 16 | 0 | 33 | 3 | 0 |
| Rayborn, Kris, Eugene * | 0 | 1 | .000 | 7.71 | 1 | 1 | 0 | 0 | 0 | 0 | 2.1 | 7 | 19 | 9 | 2 | 0 | 0 | 0 | 0 | 3 | 0 | 3 | 2 | 0 |
| Register, Steven, Tri-City | 6 | 7 | .462 | 3.63 | 15 | 15 | 0 | 0 | 0 | 0 | 79.1 | 68 | 326 | 41 | 32 | 5 | 6 | 2 | 7 | 20 | 0 | 63 | 2 | 0 |
| Reina, Jesus, Salem-Keizer * | 2 | 6 | .250 | 5.40 | 15 | 13 | 0 | 0 | 0 | 0 | 56.2 | 68 | 258 | 42 | 34 | 4 | 4 | 3 | 3 | 20 | 0 | 55 | 8 | 1 |
| Rivera, Mumba, Everett | 4 | 7 | .364 | 3.36 | 18 | 5 | 0 | 0 | 2 | 0 | 59.0 | 44 | 254 | 28 | 22 | 4 | 4 | 1 | 8 | 25 | 0 | 48 | 10 | 1 |
| Roberts, Mark, Spokane | 4 | 5 | .444 | 3.54 | 12 | 7 | 0 | 0 | 1 | 0 | 48.1 | 42 | 198 | 22 | 19 | 6 | 3 | 2 | 4 | 14 | 2 | 54 | 1 | 0 |
| Robertson, Connor, Vancouver | 0 | 0 | .000 | 3.60 | 3 | 0 | 0 | 0 | 2 | 0 | 5.0 | 4 | 21 | 2 | 2 | 1 | 0 | 0 | 0 | 2 | 0 | 5 | 0 | 0 |
| Robinson, Ronnie, Eugene | 0 | 0 | .000 | 4.66 | 9 | 0 | 0 | 0 | 0 | 0 | 9.2 | 8 | 44 | 6 | 5 | 0 | 0 | 0 | 2 | 5 | 0 | 8 | 6 | 0 |
| Rocha, Angel, Yakima * | 2 | 3 | .400 | 6.56 | 5 | 5 | 0 | 0 | 0 | 0 | 23.1 | 24 | 113 | 19 | 17 | 3 | 1 | 1 | 2 | 18 | 0 | 19 | 4 | 0 |

| Pitcher, Team | W | L | Pct. | ERA | G | GS | CG | ShO | GF | Sv. | IP | H | TBF | R | ER | HR | SH | SF | HB | BB | IBB | SO | WP | Bk. |
|---|---|---|---|---|---|---|---|---|---|---|---|---|---|---|---|---|---|---|---|---|---|---|---|---|
| Rodriguez, Pedro, Boise | 0 | 0 | .000 | 0.00 | 1 | 0 | 0 | 0 | 0 | 0 | 1.1 | 1 | 5 | 0 | 0 | 0 | 0 | 0 | 0 | 0 | 0 | 1 | 0 | 0 |
| Rogers, Michael, Vancouver | 1 | 2 | .333 | 4.87 | 12 | 8 | 0 | 0 | 1 | 0 | 40.2 | 48 | 186 | 22 | 22 | 3 | 5 | 1 | 3 | 15 | 0 | 26 | 2 | 0 |
| Rosario, Melvin, Tri-City * | 0 | 1 | .000 | 1.26 | 9 | 0 | 0 | 0 | 3 | 0 | 14.1 | 10 | 59 | 6 | 2 | 0 | 0 | 0 | 2 | 4 | 0 | 13 | 5 | 1 |
| Rose, Brad, Everett | 0 | 0 | .000 | 3.38 | 4 | 0 | 0 | 0 | 2 | 0 | 5.1 | 6 | 26 | 2 | 2 | 1 | 0 | 0 | 0 | 4 | 0 | 3 | 0 | 0 |
| Rupe, Josh, Spokane | 2 | 0 | 1.000 | 1.50 | 4 | 3 | 0 | 0 | 0 | 0 | 18.0 | 14 | 73 | 3 | 3 | 1 | 1 | 0 | 2 | 3 | 0 | 19 | 0 | 0 |
| Sack, Darren, Salem-Keizer | 2 | 5 | .286 | 6.23 | 16 | 16 | 0 | 0 | 0 | 0 | 69.1 | 81 | 318 | 55 | 48 | 15 | 3 | 4 | 6 | 27 | 0 | 55 | 4 | 0 |
| Sanchez, Adiel, Vancouver * | 2 | 3 | .400 | 5.23 | 22 | 0 | 0 | 0 | 10 | 1 | 31.0 | 37 | 146 | 19 | 18 | 3 | 0 | 0 | 1 | 15 | 1 | 19 | 4 | 0 |
| Sanchez, Jonathan, Salem-Keizer * | 2 | 1 | .667 | 4.84 | 6 | 6 | 0 | 0 | 0 | 0 | 22.1 | 16 | 102 | 13 | 12 | 3 | 2 | 1 | 1 | 19 | 0 | 34 | 0 | 1 |
| Santana, Braulio, Vancouver | 4 | 3 | .571 | 4.58 | 12 | 10 | 0 | 0 | 0 | 0 | 55.0 | 56 | 241 | 33 | 28 | 3 | 5 | 4 | 4 | 14 | 0 | 23 | 2 | 0 |
| Santiago, Tomas, Tri-City | 4 | 3 | .571 | 3.57 | 14 | 13 | 0 | 0 | 0 | 0 | 75.2 | 67 | 322 | 34 | 30 | 7 | 3 | 2 | 10 | 27 | 0 | 66 | 1 | 1 |
| Santo, Joel, Eugene | 2 | 2 | .500 | 5.35 | 7 | 7 | 0 | 0 | 0 | 0 | 33.2 | 40 | 160 | 25 | 20 | 2 | 3 | 2 | 1 | 23 | 0 | 22 | 4 | 1 |
| Schappert, Paul, Boise * | 2 | 2 | .500 | 6.08 | 9 | 0 | 0 | 0 | 3 | 1 | 13.1 | 15 | 65 | 10 | 9 | 3 | 0 | 0 | 2 | 8 | 0 | 13 | 2 | 1 |
| Schilsky, Steve, Vancouver | 0 | 3 | .000 | 8.31 | 8 | 0 | 0 | 0 | 4 | 1 | 13.0 | 19 | 72 | 13 | 12 | 0 | 0 | 0 | 4 | 10 | 2 | 4 | 2 | 0 |
| Shanks, Edward, Eugene | 0 | 0 | .000 | 2.45 | 2 | 0 | 0 | 0 | 2 | 0 | 3.2 | 2 | 15 | 1 | 1 | 1 | 0 | 0 | 0 | 2 | 0 | 4 | 0 | 0 |
| Shappi, A.J., Yakima | 4 | 1 | .800 | 1.75 | 12 | 11 | 0 | 0 | 0 | 0 | 67.0 | 64 | 267 | 17 | 13 | 4 | 12 | 2 | 4 | 8 | 0 | 65 | 2 | 0 |
| Sharpe, Steven, Vancouver | 6 | 3 | .667 | 4.60 | 16 | 14 | 0 | 0 | 0 | 0 | 72.1 | 59 | 296 | 40 | 37 | 3 | 9 | 4 | 4 | 30 | 0 | 53 | 9 | 1 |
| Shaver, Christopher, Boise * | 0 | 2 | .000 | 3.54 | 13 | 10 | 0 | 0 | 0 | 0 | 40.2 | 40 | 184 | 20 | 16 | 2 | 5 | 2 | 6 | 19 | 0 | 24 | 4 | 0 |
| Smith, Chase, Salem-Keizer | 5 | 4 | .556 | 2.23 | 20 | 0 | 0 | 0 | 8 | 0 | 32.1 | 18 | 135 | 14 | 8 | 1 | 2 | 1 | 4 | 17 | 0 | 32 | 3 | 0 |
| Snyder, Jason, Everett | 2 | 2 | .500 | 2.23 | 8 | 8 | 0 | 0 | 0 | 0 | 44.1 | 32 | 175 | 14 | 11 | 2 | 3 | 1 | 4 | 16 | 0 | 39 | 8 | 0 |
| Sobieraj, Aaron, Salem-Keizer | 2 | 1 | .667 | 2.49 | 8 | 0 | 0 | 0 | 1 | 0 | 21.2 | 18 | 90 | 6 | 6 | 1 | 0 | 1 | 2 | 8 | 0 | 15 | 2 | 0 |
| Songster, Judd, Tri-City | 1 | 0 | 1.000 | 0.63 | 10 | 0 | 0 | 0 | 2 | 1 | 14.1 | 5 | 54 | 1 | 1 | 0 | 0 | 0 | 1 | 5 | 0 | 16 | 0 | 0 |
| Steik, Richard, Eugene | 1 | 1 | .500 | 3.26 | 16 | 0 | 0 | 0 | 10 | 2 | 19.1 | 21 | 90 | 8 | 7 | 1 | 0 | 0 | 2 | 9 | 2 | 18 | 0 | 0 |
| Sterry, Vern, Eugene | 2 | 3 | .400 | 3.96 | 9 | 9 | 0 | 0 | 0 | 0 | 50.0 | 42 | 208 | 24 | 22 | 7 | 2 | 1 | 2 | 11 | 0 | 52 | 2 | 0 |
| Tetuan, John, Tri-City | 3 | 8 | .273 | 6.98 | 14 | 13 | 0 | 0 | 0 | 0 | 59.1 | 68 | 277 | 51 | 46 | 6 | 3 | 5 | 5 | 34 | 1 | 37 | 5 | 0 |
| Tharpe, Derek, Vancouver * | 0 | 2 | .000 | 4.80 | 12 | 1 | 0 | 0 | 4 | 3 | 30.0 | 33 | 131 | 18 | 16 | 4 | 0 | 0 | 2 | 7 | 0 | 30 | 2 | 0 |
| Thomas, Steven, Tri-City | 2 | 0 | 1.000 | 1.33 | 11 | 0 | 0 | 0 | 5 | 1 | 20.1 | 9 | 77 | 4 | 3 | 2 | 0 | 0 | 1 | 6 | 0 | 18 | 0 | 0 |
| Thompson, Chris, Yakima | 1 | 3 | .250 | 2.55 | 32 | 0 | 0 | 0 | 17 | 4 | 42.1 | 38 | 197 | 15 | 12 | 0 | 0 | 0 | 5 | 27 | 3 | 38 | 6 | 0 |
| Tichota, Clay, Vancouver | 3 | 0 | 1.000 | 4.71 | 16 | 4 | 0 | 0 | 1 | 1 | 42.0 | 47 | 184 | 27 | 22 | 1 | 2 | 0 | 3 | 12 | 0 | 36 | 5 | 1 |
| Trolia, Aaron, Everett | 2 | 2 | .500 | 4.83 | 20 | 4 | 0 | 0 | 15 | 6 | 41.0 | 39 | 181 | 23 | 22 | 5 | 1 | 1 | 4 | 17 | 1 | 33 | 4 | 0 |
| Upwood, Jake, Eugene * | 1 | 2 | .333 | 4.00 | 17 | 0 | 0 | 0 | 5 | 0 | 18.0 | 19 | 81 | 11 | 8 | 1 | 0 | 1 | 2 | 7 | 0 | 13 | 3 | 0 |
| Urena, Jose, Boise | 0 | 1 | .000 | 14.85 | 7 | 0 | 0 | 0 | 2 | 0 | 6.2 | 12 | 41 | 13 | 11 | 1 | 0 | 0 | 3 | 6 | 0 | 5 | 1 | 0 |
| Van, Robert, Yakima * | 0 | 1 | .000 | 3.52 | 5 | 0 | 0 | 0 | 0 | 0 | 7.2 | 6 | 35 | 3 | 3 | 1 | 0 | 0 | 0 | 6 | 0 | 8 | 3 | 0 |
| Varner, Matthew, Eugene | 1 | 2 | .333 | 4.50 | 10 | 1 | 0 | 0 | 3 | 0 | 16.0 | 16 | 71 | 10 | 8 | 2 | 0 | 0 | 1 | 9 | 0 | 14 | 3 | 0 |
| Vasquez, Esmerling, Yakima | 0 | 0 | .000 | 6.35 | 5 | 0 | 0 | 0 | 4 | 1 | 5.2 | 10 | 27 | 6 | 4 | 1 | 0 | 0 | 0 | 0 | 0 | 7 | 1 | 0 |
| Vose, Jake, Eugene * | 0 | 1 | .000 | 4.75 | 24 | 2 | 0 | 0 | 7 | 1 | 36.0 | 39 | 160 | 27 | 19 | 2 | 1 | 0 | 2 | 11 | 0 | 30 | 5 | 0 |
| Walker, Andy, Spokane | 1 | 0 | 1.000 | 5.93 | 7 | 0 | 0 | 0 | 2 | 0 | 13.2 | 14 | 61 | 9 | 9 | 3 | 0 | 0 | 0 | 6 | 0 | 11 | 2 | 0 |
| Watchko, Jeff, Tri-City | 0 | 0 | .000 | 6.23 | 8 | 0 | 0 | 0 | 2 | 0 | 13.0 | 12 | 62 | 10 | 9 | 1 | 0 | 0 | 3 | 8 | 0 | 10 | 3 | 0 |
| Webb, Nick, Tri-City * | 0 | 0 | .000 | 81.00 | 1 | 0 | 0 | 0 | 0 | 0 | 0.1 | 3 | 6 | 5 | 3 | 0 | 0 | 0 | 0 | 2 | 0 | 0 | 0 | 0 |
| Weber, Matthew, Boise | 5 | 1 | .833 | 2.95 | 14 | 14 | 0 | 0 | 0 | 0 | 76.1 | 72 | 303 | 27 | 25 | 1 | 4 | 3 | 4 | 18 | 0 | 46 | 4 | 1 |
| Whatley, Keith, Yakima * | 1 | 6 | .143 | 7.13 | 8 | 8 | 0 | 0 | 0 | 0 | 35.1 | 45 | 163 | 38 | 28 | 5 | 2 | 4 | 5 | 15 | 0 | 24 | 3 | 0 |
| Whitaker, Craig, Salem-Keizer | 4 | 2 | .667 | 3.44 | 15 | 15 | 0 | 0 | 0 | 0 | 70.2 | 58 | 307 | 33 | 27 | 4 | 5 | 4 | 6 | 43 | 0 | 77 | 14 | 0 |
| White, Mike, Yakima * | 0 | 0 | .000 | 10.13 | 14 | 0 | 0 | 0 | 4 | 0 | 18.2 | 34 | 111 | 29 | 21 | 4 | 0 | 0 | 6 | 16 | 0 | 15 | 6 | 0 |
| Wilkinson, Matty, Yakima | 1 | 0 | 1.000 | 3.00 | 2 | 0 | 0 | 0 | 0 | 0 | 3.0 | 1 | 11 | 2 | 1 | 0 | 0 | 0 | 1 | 0 | 0 | 4 | 0 | 0 |
| Willett, Reid, Boise | 1 | 0 | 1.000 | 6.65 | 14 | 1 | 0 | 0 | 3 | 0 | 23.0 | 23 | 104 | 18 | 17 | 4 | 0 | 0 | 2 | 11 | 0 | 20 | 2 | 0 |
| Windsor, Jason, Vancouver | 0 | 0 | .000 | 0.00 | 4 | 0 | 0 | 0 | 3 | 1 | 5.0 | 4 | 19 | 0 | 0 | 0 | 0 | 0 | 0 | 0 | 0 | 5 | 0 | 0 |
| Winslow, Benjamin, Vancouver | 0 | 0 | .000 | 4.50 | 2 | 0 | 0 | 0 | 2 | 0 | 2.0 | 2 | 10 | 1 | 1 | 1 | 0 | 0 | 0 | 2 | 0 | 2 | 0 | 0 |
| Woerman, Joe, Everett | 0 | 1 | .000 | 6.57 | 9 | 0 | 0 | 0 | 5 | 1 | 12.1 | 13 | 60 | 14 | 9 | 3 | 0 | 0 | 2 | 8 | 0 | 12 | 4 | 0 |
| Wohlgemuth, Trevor, Salem-Keizer | 0 | 1 | .000 | 6.14 | 7 | 0 | 0 | 0 | 2 | 0 | 7.1 | 8 | 40 | 7 | 5 | 0 | 0 | 0 | 4 | 6 | 0 | 4 | 1 | 0 |

COMBINATION SHUTOUTS: **Boise** (4)—Ferreras-Gross-Mejia, Weber-Fenton, Downs-Blevins-Fenton, Mathes-Hunton. **Eugene** (3)—Sterry-Ekstrom-Ohagan, Ekstrom-Ellis-Robinson-Darby, Delabar-Ohagan-Shanks. **Salem Keizer** (2)—Whitaker-Gardner-Hedrick, J. Sanchez-Odom-Minor. **Spokane** (4)—Diamond-Rupe-Burcie, Brannon-Roberts-Espinal, Lensch-Bannister-Jerome, Brannon-Ingram-Burcie. **Tri City** (6)—Register-Thomas-Ion, Morillo-Bright, Register-Buechner, Morillo-Beerer-Bright-Miller, Register-Lira-Beerer-Miller, Grube-Buechner-Watchko. **Vancouver** (1)—Rogers-Tichota-Carter-Drucker. **Yakima** (3)—Rocha-Kerbs-Kemlo, Shappi-Kemlo, Shappi-Thompson-Kerbs.

NO-HIT GAMES: None.

# 2004 FIELDING

## TEAM

| Team | G | PO | A | E | TC | DP | TP | PB | Pct. |
|---|---|---|---|---|---|---|---|---|---|
| Vancouver | 76 | 2003 | 026 | 83 | 2112 | 53 | 0 | 9 | .961 |
| Salem-Keizer | 76 | 2035 | 024 | 93 | 2152 | 76 | 0 | 11 | .957 |
| Spokane | 76 | 2068 | 016 | 98 | 2182 | 67 | 0 | 10 | .955 |
| Boise | 76 | 2026 | 030 | 96 | 2152 | 66 | 0 | 17 | .955 |
| Everett | 76 | 2017 | 025 | 99 | 2141 | 74 | 0 | 30 | .954 |
| Tri-City | 76 | 2052 | 029 | 105 | 2186 | 55 | 0 | 13 | .952 |
| Yakima | 76 | 2005 | 028 | 112 | 2145 | 65 | 0 | 31 | .948 |
| Eugene | 76 | 1988 | 031 | 125 | 2144 | 65 | 0 | 18 | .942 |

## INDIVIDUAL

### FIRST BASEMEN

NOTE: All caps denotes fielding-percentage leader based on 38 games for catchers, 51 for all other non-pitchers and 61 innings for pitchers. *Throws lefthanded.

| Player, Team | Pct. | G | PO | A | E | TC | DP |
|---|---|---|---|---|---|---|---|
| Acha, John, SK | .988 | 12 | 79 | 5 | 1 | 85 | 8 |
| Alexander, Chris, SPO | .961 | 16 | 139 | 8 | 6 | 153 | 9 |
| Babineaux, Charlie, SK | .980 | 7 | 48 | 2 | 1 | 51 | 13 |
| BUCHANAN, TODD, YAK* | .992 | 51 | 369 | 25 | 3 | 397 | 40 |
| Carter, Chris, YAK* | .975 | 13 | 106 | 12 | 3 | 121 | 7 |
| Dale, Lachlan, EUG | .982 | 39 | 357 | 23 | 7 | 387 | 29 |
| Diaz, Orlando, EUG | .992 | 27 | 222 | 12 | 2 | 236 | 20 |
| Embrey, Rielly, EUG* | .989 | 10 | 85 | 8 | 1 | 94 | 9 |
| Everidge, Thomas, VAN | .986 | 71 | 578 | 57 | 9 | 644 | 47 |
| Fasano, Jim, SPO* | .988 | 60 | 544 | 26 | 7 | 577 | 53 |
| Felix, Maximo, SK | 1.000 | 1 | 1 | 1 | 0 | 2 | 0 |
| Gentry, Garret, TRI* | 1.000 | 1 | 4 | 0 | 0 | 4 | 0 |
| Ghutzman, Stephen, TRI | .979 | 10 | 88 | 4 | 2 | 94 | 6 |
| Green, Brandon, EVR | .987 | 52 | 423 | 40 | 6 | 469 | 45 |
| Hendricks, Trey, YAK | .994 | 22 | 161 | 10 | 1 | 172 | 16 |
| Hubbard, Marshall, EVR* | .978 | 18 | 126 | 6 | 3 | 135 | 18 |
| Koshansky, Joseph, TRI* | .986 | 65 | 537 | 45 | 8 | 590 | 45 |
| LaHair, Bryan, EVR* | .983 | 7 | 55 | 4 | 1 | 60 | 4 |
| Melillo, Kevin, VAN* | 1.000 | 2 | 6 | 1 | 0 | 7 | 0 |
| Norwood, Ryan, BOI | .985 | 73 | 628 | 49 | 10 | 687 | 63 |
| Polimar, Aldwin, YAK | 1.000 | 2 | 3 | 0 | 0 | 3 | 0 |
| Richie, Tony, BOI | .960 | 4 | 23 | 1 | 1 | 25 | 1 |
| Robledo, Nelson, TRI | 1.000 | 3 | 14 | 0 | 0 | 14 | 1 |
| Schweiger, Brian, EVR | 1.000 | 1 | 1 | 0 | 0 | 1 | 0 |
| Serrano, Julian, BOI | 1.000 | 2 | 11 | 3 | 0 | 14 | 1 |
| Soto, Luis, EVR | .973 | 7 | 34 | 2 | 1 | 37 | 7 |
| *Thompson, Will, SK | .981 | 60 | 505 | 25 | 10 | 540 | 35 |
| *Vincent, Tom, EUG | .943 | 4 | 32 | 1 | 2 | 35 | 2 |
| Winslow, Benjamin, VAN | 1.000 | 6 | 40 | 2 | 0 | 42 | 3 |

### SECOND BASEMEN

| Player, Team | Pct. | G | PO | A | E | TC | DP |
|---|---|---|---|---|---|---|---|
| Acha, John, SK | 1.000 | 1 | 1 | 4 | 0 | 5 | 0 |

| Player, Team | Pct. | G | PO | A | E | TC | DP |
|---|---|---|---|---|---|---|---|
| Aguilar, Trino, EUG | .929 | 22 | 30 | 48 | 6 | 84 | 10 |
| Aguirre, Rodrigo, YAK* | 1.000 | 7 | 7 | 15 | 0 | 22 | 1 |
| Almonte, Sandy, TRI | 1.000 | 4 | 8 | 10 | 0 | 18 | 2 |
| Burnham, Brett, EUG | .949 | 33 | 51 | 97 | 8 | 156 | 16 |
| Cabrera, Asdrubal, EVR | .954 | 17 | 40 | 43 | 4 | 87 | 11 |
| Chen, Yung-Chi, EVR | .937 | 22 | 39 | 50 | 6 | 95 | 16 |
| Dawkins, Lance, BOI | 1.000 | 2 | 4 | 9 | 0 | 13 | 0 |
| Dean, Erik, TRI* | .966 | 47 | 108 | 144 | 9 | 261 | 32 |
| Deeb, Bobby, BOI | .949 | 49 | 98 | 143 | 13 | 254 | 36 |
| Figueroa, Baudilio, EUG | .955 | 4 | 6 | 15 | 1 | 22 | 3 |
| Frandsen, Kevin, SK | .964 | 19 | 38 | 69 | 4 | 111 | 15 |
| Fryer, Brian, EUG | .980 | 13 | 20 | 29 | 1 | 50 | 8 |
| Granato, Anthony, BOI | .957 | 18 | 26 | 41 | 3 | 70 | 5 |
| Green, Brandon, EVR | 1.000 | 6 | 6 | 6 | 0 | 12 | 3 |
| Griffin, Preston, BOI | 1.000 | 4 | 2 | 5 | 0 | 7 | 0 |
| Guerra, Alex, SPO | .955 | 5 | 9 | 12 | 1 | 22 | 3 |
| HULETT, TIMOTHY, SPO* | .975 | 66 | 121 | 186 | 8 | 315 | 43 |
| Jones, Nick, BOI | 1.000 | 4 | 7 | 5 | 0 | 12 | 1 |
| Kazmar, Sean, EUG | .977 | 9 | 9 | 34 | 1 | 44 | 8 |
| Lenoir, Bobby, SPO | 1.000 | 8 | 5 | 20 | 0 | 25 | 5 |
| Lockin, Billy, YAK | 1.000 | 1 | 2 | 3 | 0 | 5 | 0 |
| Long, Wesley, VAN | .889 | 2 | 5 | 3 | 1 | 9 | 0 |
| Marquez, Uriak, BOI* | 1.000 | 5 | 13 | 14 | 0 | 27 | 3 |
| Melillo, Kevin, VAN* | .978 | 21 | 22 | 67 | 2 | 91 | 9 |
| Navarro, Oswaldo, EVR | .978 | 39 | 76 | 103 | 4 | 183 | 28 |
| Palumbo, Jeff, SK | .973 | 26 | 45 | 64 | 3 | 112 | 20 |
| Reynolds, Mark, YAK | .667 | 1 | 0 | 2 | 1 | 3 | 0 |
| Rivera, Jodam, EUG | .714 | 2 | 1 | 4 | 2 | 7 | 0 |
| Ruiz, Ryan, VAN | .966 | 47 | 79 | 120 | 7 | 206 | 23 |
| Schindewolf, Erik, YAK* | .973 | 71 | 113 | 179 | 8 | 300 | 41 |
| Smith, Dustin, BOI | 1.000 | 4 | 1 | 4 | 0 | 5 | 1 |
| Strain, Ryan, SK | .982 | 32 | 46 | 61 | 2 | 109 | 15 |
| Strop, Pedro, TRI | .932 | 18 | 29 | 40 | 5 | 74 | 6 |
| Swope, Tobin, SPO | .909 | 3 | 5 | 5 | 1 | 11 | 1 |
| Valdez, Jose, TRI* | .969 | 5 | 12 | 19 | 1 | 32 | 2 |
| Van Kooten, Jason, TRI | .952 | 3 | 8 | 12 | 1 | 21 | 2 |
| Winslow, Benjamin, VAN | 1.000 | 9 | 16 | 21 | 0 | 37 | 8 |

## THIRD BASEMEN

| Player, Team | Pct. | G | PO | A | E | TC | DP |
|---|---|---|---|---|---|---|---|
| Acha, John, SK | .900 | 11 | 8 | 19 | 3 | 30 | 2 |
| Aguilar, Trino, EUG | .918 | 19 | 17 | 28 | 4 | 49 | 1 |
| Aguirre, Rodrigo, YAK* | .892 | 32 | 12 | 62 | 9 | 83 | 3 |
| Cabrera, Asdrubal, EVR | .944 | 5 | 3 | 14 | 1 | 18 | 2 |
| Chen, Yung-Chi, EVR | .922 | 27 | 13 | 58 | 6 | 77 | 5 |
| Dale, Lachlan, EUG | .818 | 34 | 25 | 65 | 20 | 110 | 6 |
| Dean, Erik, TRI* | .903 | 10 | 12 | 16 | 3 | 31 | 2 |
| Diaz, Orlando, EUG | .923 | 23 | 13 | 35 | 4 | 52 | 1 |
| Figueroa, Baudilio, EUG | 1.000 | 3 | 2 | 6 | 0 | 8 | 0 |
| Francisco, Alfredo, BOI | .906 | 60 | 35 | 120 | 16 | 171 | 8 |
| Granato, Anthony, BOI | .941 | 8 | 2 | 14 | 1 | 17 | 1 |
| Green, Brandon, EVR | .898 | 17 | 13 | 40 | 6 | 59 | 5 |
| Griffin, Preston, BOI | 1.000 | 4 | 2 | 3 | 0 | 5 | 1 |
| Guerra, Alex, SPO | 1.000 | 1 | 2 | 4 | 0 | 6 | 1 |
| Hahn, Dustin, TRI | 1.000 | 4 | 3 | 6 | 0 | 9 | 0 |
| Hendricks, Trey, YAK | .875 | 29 | 14 | 49 | 9 | 72 | 4 |
| Hulett, Timothy, SPO* | 1.000 | 4 | 1 | 5 | 0 | 6 | 0 |
| Johnson, Brent, EVR | .906 | 31 | 11 | 47 | 6 | 64 | 3 |
| Klink, Simon, SK | .909 | 66 | 36 | 124 | 16 | 176 | 8 |
| Leslie, Myron, VAN | .916 | 71 | 65 | 121 | 17 | 203 | 8 |
| Lockin, Billy, YAK | 1.000 | 4 | 0 | 1 | 0 | 1 | 0 |
| Macri, Matt, TRI | .940 | 49 | 33 | 92 | 8 | 133 | 5 |
| Mena, Steve, YAK | .933 | 16 | 3 | 11 | 1 | 15 | 0 |
| METCALF, TRAVIS, SPO | .959 | 71 | 54 | 155 | 9 | 218 | 18 |
| Navarro, Oswaldo, EVR | .875 | 2 | 0 | 7 | 1 | 8 | 2 |
| Ozoria, Pedro, EVR | 1.000 | 1 | 0 | 1 | 0 | 1 | 0 |
| Puello, Elvin, BOI | 1.000 | 1 | 1 | 4 | 0 | 5 | 1 |
| Reynolds, Mark, YAK | .854 | 15 | 11 | 24 | 6 | 41 | 3 |
| Smith, Dustin, BOI | .870 | 8 | 6 | 14 | 3 | 23 | 1 |
| Strop, Pedro, TRI | .867 | 9 | 2 | 11 | 2 | 15 | 1 |
| Swope, Tobin, SPO | 1.000 | 2 | 0 | 1 | 0 | 1 | 0 |
| Valdez, Jose, TRI* | .944 | 5 | 5 | 12 | 1 | 18 | 3 |
| Winslow, Benjamin, VAN | 1.000 | 4 | 1 | 5 | 0 | 6 | 2 |

## SHORTSTOPS

| Player, Team | Pct. | G | PO | A | E | TC | DP |
|---|---|---|---|---|---|---|---|
| Aguilar, Trino, EUG | 1.000 | 5 | 4 | 9 | 0 | 13 | 2 |
| *Aguirre, Rodrigo, YAK | 1.000 | 3 | 1 | 0 | 0 | 1 | 0 |
| Almonte, Sandy, TRI | 1.000 | 2 | 3 | 8 | 0 | 11 | 1 |
| Bush, Matt, EUG | .821 | 8 | 14 | 18 | 7 | 39 | 7 |
| Cabrera, Asdrubal, EVR | .927 | 42 | 69 | 108 | 14 | 191 | 27 |
| Chen, Yung-Chi, EVR | .636 | 3 | 3 | 4 | 4 | 11 | 0 |
| Deltran, Francis, SK | 1.000 | 1 | 2 | 2 | 0 | 4 | 1 |
| Figueroa, Baudilio, EUG | .956 | 9 | 14 | 29 | 2 | 45 | 9 |
| Frandsen, Kevin, SK | .867 | 4 | 5 | 8 | 2 | 15 | 0 |
| Granato, Anthony, BOI | .957 | 6 | 7 | 15 | 1 | 23 | 1 |
| Griffin, Preston, BOI | .913 | 14 | 16 | 26 | 4 | 46 | 8 |
| Groth, Brad, SK | .929 | 5 | 9 | 17 | 2 | 28 | 4 |
| Haines, Kyle, SK | .942 | 31 | 48 | 81 | 8 | 137 | 17 |
| *Hulett, Timothy, SPO | 1.000 | 1 | 0 | 1 | 0 | 1 | 1 |
| Kazmar, Sean, EUG | .911 | 56 | 86 | 140 | 22 | 248 | 24 |
| Lenoir, Bobby, SPO | .930 | 57 | 84 | 168 | 19 | 271 | 33 |
| Lockin, Billy, YAK | .979 | 14 | 18 | 28 | 1 | 47 | 5 |
| *Marquez, Uriak, BOI | .889 | 2 | 2 | 6 | 1 | 9 | 1 |
| Mena, Steve, YAK | .907 | 28 | 46 | 61 | 11 | 118 | 17 |
| Navarro, Oswaldo, EVR | .987 | 29 | 46 | 105 | 2 | 153 | 21 |
| Palumbo, Jeff, SK | .942 | 37 | 35 | 94 | 8 | 137 | 22 |
| Petit, Gregorio, VAN | .950 | 68 | 115 | 189 | 16 | 320 | 34 |
| Reynolds, Mark, YAK | .916 | 46 | 80 | 127 | 19 | 226 | 29 |
| RIOS, JOSE, BOI | .958 | 64 | 92 | 184 | 12 | 288 | 34 |
| Ruiz, Ryan, VAN | .923 | 5 | 12 | 12 | 2 | 26 | 2 |
| Strop, Pedro, TRI | .857 | 28 | 45 | 81 | 21 | 147 | 19 |
| Swope, Tobin, SPO | .929 | 21 | 25 | 53 | 6 | 84 | 10 |
| Tuiasosopo, Matthew, EVR | .800 | 5 | 1 | 11 | 3 | 15 | 1 |
| *Valdez, Jose, TRI | .954 | 33 | 61 | 84 | 7 | 152 | 20 |
| Van Kooten, Jason, TRI | .941 | 13 | 15 | 33 | 3 | 51 | 4 |
| Winslow, Benjamin, VAN | 1.000 | 4 | 7 | 10 | 0 | 17 | 2 |

## OUTFIELDERS

| Player, Team | Pct. | G | PO | A | E | TC | DP |
|---|---|---|---|---|---|---|---|
| Acha, John, SK | 1.000 | 5 | 6 | 0 | 0 | 6 | 0 |
| Babineaux, Charlie, SK | .959 | 33 | 46 | 1 | 2 | 49 | 1 |
| Balcom, Jasha, BOI* | .992 | 59 | 130 | 1 | 1 | 132 | 0 |
| Beauregard, Joshua, VAN* | 1.000 | 11 | 15 | 0 | 0 | 15 | 0 |
| Bernard, Oscar, BOI | .000 | 1 | 0 | 0 | 1 | 1 | 0 |
| BLASI, NICOLAS, VAN | 1.000 | 70 | 153 | 3 | 0 | 156 | 0 |
| Boggs, Brandon, SPO | .944 | 41 | 85 | 0 | 5 | 90 | 0 |
| Bowker, John, SK* | .957 | 31 | 42 | 2 | 2 | 46 | 0 |
| Boyer, Kyle, BOI | .966 | 54 | 104 | 8 | 4 | 116 | 0 |
| Buchanan, Todd, YAK* | 1.000 | 1 | 1 | 0 | 0 | 1 | 0 |
| Buhagiar, Josh, YAK* | 1.000 | 3 | 8 | 0 | 0 | 8 | 0 |
| Burgess, Brandon, YAK | .890 | 45 | 61 | 4 | 8 | 73 | 0 |
| Carter, Chris, YAK* | 1.000 | 32 | 36 | 1 | 0 | 37 | 0 |
| Cashman, Brandon, SPO | .962 | 19 | 49 | 1 | 2 | 52 | 0 |
| Craig, Casey, EVR* | .952 | 55 | 96 | 3 | 5 | 104 | 0 |
| Cruz, Elvis, EVR | .940 | 28 | 43 | 4 | 3 | 50 | 0 |
| Ellison, Josh, EVR* | 1.000 | 1 | 1 | 0 | 0 | 1 | 0 |
| Garay, Ernesto, EUG* | .962 | 21 | 25 | 0 | 1 | 26 | 0 |
| Ghutzman, Stephen, TRI | .947 | 11 | 17 | 1 | 1 | 19 | 0 |
| Gonzalez, Carlos, YAK* | .973 | 73 | 163 | 14 | 5 | 182 | 3 |
| Gresky, David, BOI* | 1.000 | 33 | 65 | 0 | 0 | 65 | 0 |
| Harrison, Ben, SPO | .953 | 44 | 79 | 3 | 4 | 86 | 0 |
| Harvey, Ryan, BOI | .940 | 38 | 73 | 5 | 5 | 83 | 0 |
| Heid, Trevor, EVR | .986 | 43 | 71 | 2 | 1 | 74 | 0 |
| Hendricks, Trey, YAK | 1.000 | 1 | 1 | 0 | 0 | 1 | 0 |
| Herrera, Javier, VAN | .971 | 64 | 129 | 3 | 4 | 136 | 0 |
| Hogan, Billy, EUG | .946 | 55 | 83 | 5 | 5 | 93 | 0 |
| Horwitz, Brian, SK | 1.000 | 64 | 115 | 2 | 0 | 117 | 0 |
| Hubbard, Marshall, EVR* | .971 | 24 | 33 | 1 | 1 | 35 | 0 |
| Jacobsen, Brock, SPO | .889 | 7 | 8 | 0 | 1 | 9 | 0 |
| Johnson, Brent, EVR | 1.000 | 38 | 80 | 0 | 0 | 80 | 0 |
| Johnson, Craig, EUG* | .962 | 22 | 23 | 2 | 1 | 26 | 0 |
| Johnson, Robert, EVR | 1.000 | 1 | 1 | 0 | 0 | 1 | 0 |
| Kolkhorst, Chris, EUG* | 1.000 | 26 | 49 | 1 | 0 | 50 | 0 |
| Lange, BJ, YAK | .986 | 39 | 68 | 2 | 1 | 71 | 1 |
| Mahar, Kevin, SPO | .957 | 31 | 43 | 2 | 2 | 47 | 0 |
| Martinez-Esteve, Edd, SK | 1.000 | 9 | 16 | 0 | 0 | 16 | 0 |
| Mask, Michael, SPO* | .986 | 39 | 70 | 3 | 1 | 74 | 0 |
| McRoberts, Mark, EUG | 1.000 | 17 | 25 | 0 | 0 | 25 | 0 |
| Melendez, Cris, YAK | 1.000 | 11 | 9 | 0 | 0 | 9 | 0 |
| Miller, Jim, TRI | 1.000 | 1 | 3 | 0 | 0 | 3 | 0 |
| Miller, Matt, TRI | .960 | 39 | 67 | 5 | 3 | 75 | 1 |
| Montanez, Luis, BOI | .947 | 58 | 64 | 7 | 4 | 75 | 1 |
| Mooney, Mike, SK | 1.000 | 3 | 3 | 0 | 0 | 3 | 0 |
| Mora, Ruben, EUG | 1.000 | 23 | 36 | 2 | 0 | 38 | 0 |
| Nunez, Florentino, TRI | .928 | 39 | 74 | 3 | 6 | 83 | 0 |
| Ogando, Alexi, VAN | 1.000 | 7 | 8 | 0 | 0 | 8 | 0 |
| Paulino, Adalberto, SK | 1.000 | 12 | 8 | 0 | 0 | 8 | 0 |
| Postlewait, Jake, TRI* | 1.000 | 1 | 2 | 0 | 0 | 2 | 0 |
| Putnam, Dan, VAN* | 1.000 | 11 | 26 | 1 | 0 | 27 | 0 |
| Ramirez, Yordany, EUG | 1.000 | 4 | 6 | 0 | 0 | 6 | 0 |
| Restrepo, John, TRI* | 1.000 | 11 | 25 | 0 | 0 | 25 | 0 |
| Robnett, Richie, VAN* | .979 | 43 | 92 | 0 | 2 | 94 | 0 |
| Sakamoto, Mitsuru, TRI* | 1.000 | 31 | 46 | 0 | 0 | 46 | 0 |

| Player, Team | Pct. | G | PO | A | E | TC | DP |
|---|---|---|---|---|---|---|---|
| Simon, Brandon, YAK* | .983 | 47 | 110 | 3 | 2 | 115 | 1 |
| Smith, Seth, TRI* | .900 | 8 | 9 | 0 | 1 | 10 | 0 |
| Spivey, Brett, TRI* | .983 | 38 | 56 | 2 | 1 | 59 | 0 |
| Susdorf, Billy, SPO | .980 | 55 | 89 | 7 | 2 | 98 | 0 |
| Thayer, Matt, EUG | 1.000 | 44 | 94 | 0 | 0 | 94 | 0 |
| Thigpen, Jud, TRI | .981 | 54 | 100 | 3 | 2 | 105 | 2 |
| Tietje, Chalon, VAN | 1.000 | 31 | 50 | 1 | 0 | 51 | 0 |
| Timpner, Clay, SK* | .993 | 68 | 139 | 3 | 1 | 143 | 0 |
| Valdez, Angel, TRI | 1.000 | 4 | 5 | 0 | 0 | 5 | 0 |
| Vincent, Tom, EUG* | .920 | 31 | 44 | 2 | 4 | 50 | 0 |
| Wilson, Mike, EVR | .962 | 60 | 97 | 5 | 4 | 106 | 3 |
| Yens, Jose, SK | .881 | 20 | 35 | 2 | 5 | 42 | 1 |

## CATCHERS

| Player, Team | Pct. | G | PO | A | E | TC | DP | PB |
|---|---|---|---|---|---|---|---|---|
| Baez, Lizahio, SPO | 1.000 | 5 | 35 | 3 | 0 | 38 | 0 | 2 |
| Baldwin, Ryan, SPO | .985 | 18 | 125 | 6 | 2 | 133 | 0 | 5 |
| Bernard, Oscar, BOI | .976 | 29 | 225 | 22 | 6 | 253 | 3 | 5 |
| Bone, Kyle, SK | .980 | 15 | 97 | 3 | 2 | 102 | 1 | 0 |
| Bubalo, Ty, VAN | .940 | 9 | 42 | 5 | 3 | 50 | 0 | 3 |
| Conte, Nick, SK | .983 | 44 | 377 | 29 | 7 | 413 | 2 | 7 |
| Falcon, Omar, EVR | .995 | 45 | 344 | 23 | 2 | 369 | 2 | 18 |
| Felix, Maximo, SK | .993 | 17 | 118 | 15 | 1 | 134 | 1 | 2 |
| Ghutzman, Stephen, TRI | 1.000 | 5 | 42 | 4 | 0 | 46 | 0 | 1 |
| Guarno, Rick, TRI | .984 | 23 | 175 | 15 | 3 | 193 | 0 | 4 |
| Harriman, David, VAN | .982 | 8 | 50 | 6 | 1 | 57 | 0 | 0 |
| Jennings, Todd, SK | .981 | 9 | 96 | 10 | 2 | 108 | 0 | 2 |
| Johnson, Robert, EVR | 1.000 | 6 | 41 | 9 | 0 | 50 | 1 | 1 |
| Lobaton, Jose, EUG | .984 | 27 | 175 | 15 | 3 | 193 | 0 | 7 |
| Lopez, Mauber, EUG | 1.000 | 5 | 26 | 1 | 0 | 27 | 0 | 4 |
| Mercado, Orlando, YAK | .985 | 41 | 300 | 38 | 5 | 343 | 3 | 12 |
| Morton, Colt, EUG | .981 | 49 | 378 | 32 | 8 | 418 | 1 | 7 |
| Nickeas, Michael, SPO | .991 | 54 | 419 | 21 | 4 | 444 | 1 | 3 |
| Olivo, Miguel, EVR | .909 | 2 | 8 | 2 | 1 | 11 | 0 | 0 |
| Perez, Leonel, BOI | 1.000 | 1 | 7 | 1 | 0 | 8 | 1 | 1 |
| Pohlman, Daniel, YAK | .980 | 30 | 180 | 18 | 4 | 202 | 1 | 16 |
| Polimar, Aldwin, YAK | 1.000 | 15 | 81 | 8 | 0 | 89 | 0 | 3 |
| Powell, Landon, VAN | .994 | 20 | 144 | 10 | 1 | 155 | 1 | 2 |
| Ramirez, Juan, VAN | .978 | 14 | 78 | 10 | 2 | 90 | 0 | 1 |
| RICHIE, TONY, BOI | .997 | 42 | 292 | 25 | 1 | 318 | 1 | 9 |
| Robledo, Nelson, TRI | .976 | 39 | 340 | 22 | 9 | 371 | 0 | 6 |
| Sanchez, Angel, SPO | 1.000 | 3 | 20 | 1 | 0 | 21 | 1 | 0 |
| Santin, Daniel, EVR* | 1.000 | 2 | 8 | 0 | 0 | 8 | 0 | 1 |
| Sargent, Luke, TRI | .989 | 13 | 79 | 8 | 1 | 88 | 0 | 2 |
| Schweiger, Brian, EVR | 1.000 | 28 | 164 | 14 | 0 | 178 | 1 | 10 |
| Sutton, Don, VAN | 1.000 | 4 | 24 | 2 | 0 | 26 | 0 | 1 |
| Suzuki, Kurt, VAN | .995 | 27 | 184 | 15 | 1 | 200 | 1 | 2 |
| Tidball, Adam, BOI | 1.000 | 5 | 16 | 0 | 0 | 16 | 0 | 0 |
| Wick, Olin, BOI | .969 | 7 | 29 | 2 | 1 | 32 | 1 | 2 |

## PITCHERS

| Player, Team | Pct. | G | PO | A | E | TC | DP |
|---|---|---|---|---|---|---|---|
| Acevedo, Danielin, VAN | 1.000 | 5 | 2 | 1 | 0 | 3 | 0 |
| Altman, Kevin, SPO | .846 | 18 | 2 | 9 | 2 | 13 | 0 |
| Bannister, John, SPO | .818 | 15 | 4 | 5 | 2 | 11 | 0 |
| Barnett, Dan, VAN | 1.000 | 9 | 0 | 1 | 0 | 1 | 0 |
| Basch, Zachary, VAN | .800 | 18 | 0 | 4 | 1 | 5 | 0 |
| Bello, Cibney, EVR | 1.000 | 21 | 4 | 3 | 0 | 7 | 1 |
| Bergdall, Kendall, EVR* | .833 | 15 | 3 | 7 | 2 | 12 | 0 |
| Blanco, Ivan, EVR | 1.000 | 4 | 1 | 2 | 0 | 3 | 0 |
| Blevins, Jerry, BOI* | 1.000 | 23 | 1 | 3 | 0 | 4 | 0 |
| Braden, Dallas, VAN* | 1.000 | 8 | 1 | 3 | 0 | 4 | 1 |
| Brannon, Clint, SPO* | 1.000 | 15 | 2 | 9 | 0 | 11 | 2 |
| Bright, Adam, TRI* | 1.000 | 23 | 3 | 13 | 0 | 16 | 0 |
| Brito, Luis, BOI | 1.000 | 15 | 14 | 15 | 0 | 29 | 2 |
| Broshuis, Garrett, SK | 1.000 | 5 | 0 | 1 | 0 | 1 | 0 |
| Buechner, Chris, TRI | 1.000 | 19 | 1 | 7 | 0 | 8 | 0 |
| Burcie, Jarrad, SPO | 1.000 | 23 | 0 | 2 | 0 | 2 | 0 |
| Burks, Brian, EUG | 1.000 | 26 | 3 | 8 | 0 | 11 | 0 |
| Cabaniel, Tomas, VAN | .862 | 15 | 14 | 11 | 4 | 29 | 1 |
| Campusano, Ed, BOI* | 1.000 | 14 | 0 | 4 | 0 | 4 | 0 |
| Carque, Joe, YAK | .941 | 24 | 4 | 12 | 1 | 17 | 2 |
| Carter, Brian, BOI* | 1.000 | 5 | 3 | 2 | 0 | 5 | 0 |
| Carter, Steven, VAN | .000 | 3 | 0 | 0 | 0 | 0 | 0 |
| Cespedes, Jose, EUG | 1.000 | 24 | 2 | 3 | 0 | 5 | 0 |
| Clark, Chad, YAK | 1.000 | 5 | 3 | 3 | 0 | 6 | 0 |
| Cockroft, JD, SPO* | 1.000 | 16 | 4 | 7 | 0 | 11 | 0 |
| Colbert, Henry, EUG | 1.000 | 21 | 0 | 1 | 0 | 1 | 0 |
| Cullen, Phil, EVR | .667 | 14 | 1 | 1 | 1 | 3 | 0 |
| Darby, James, EUG | .833 | 25 | 1 | 9 | 2 | 12 | 1 |
| De La O, Danny, EUG* | 1.000 | 18 | 1 | 9 | 0 | 10 | 0 |
| Delabar, Steve, EUG | .500 | 3 | 0 | 2 | 2 | 4 | 0 |
| Diamond, Thomas, SPO | .667 | 5 | 0 | 2 | 1 | 3 | 0 |
| Downs, Darin, BOI* | .818 | 14 | 1 | 8 | 2 | 11 | 0 |
| Drucker, Scot, VAN | 1.000 | 14 | 0 | 2 | 0 | 2 | 0 |
| Edsall, Stephen, TRI | 1.000 | 12 | 4 | 3 | 0 | 7 | 0 |
| Ekstrom, Michael, EUG | 1.000 | 12 | 1 | 9 | 0 | 10 | 0 |
| Ellis, Jonathan, EUG | 1.000 | 5 | 1 | 3 | 0 | 4 | 0 |
| Espinal, Leonardo, VAN | 1.000 | 2 | 1 | 1 | 0 | 2 | 0 |
| Espinal, Willy, SPO | .846 | 21 | 2 | 9 | 2 | 13 | 0 |
| Espineli, Geno, SK* | .909 | 22 | 2 | 8 | 1 | 11 | 0 |
| Falconer, Kenny, EVR | 1.000 | 8 | 1 | 0 | 0 | 1 | 0 |
| Fenton, Will, BOI | .900 | 20 | 3 | 6 | 1 | 10 | 0 |
| Fernandez, Alfredo, EUG | .958 | 13 | 8 | 15 | 1 | 24 | 3 |
| Ferreras, Yorkin, BOI* | .667 | 5 | 0 | 2 | 1 | 3 | 1 |
| Figuereo, Victor, SPO | .667 | 5 | 0 | 2 | 1 | 3 | 0 |
| Fillinger, Chad, EVR | 1.000 | 11 | 0 | 2 | 0 | 2 | 0 |
| Fischer, Sam, BOI | 1.000 | 7 | 1 | 2 | 0 | 3 | 0 |
| Flores, Ruben, EVR | .867 | 11 | 4 | 9 | 2 | 15 | 1 |
| Forbes, Terry, EVR | .833 | 9 | 1 | 4 | 1 | 6 | 0 |
| Ford, Ryan, VAN* | 1.000 | 15 | 8 | 13 | 0 | 21 | 0 |
| Gagne, JP, TRI | 1.000 | 24 | 1 | 5 | 0 | 6 | 0 |
| Gallegos, Gary, EUG* | .778 | 25 | 5 | 2 | 2 | 9 | 1 |
| Gardner, Adam, SK* | 1.000 | 19 | 3 | 5 | 0 | 8 | 0 |
| Green, KK, BOI | 1.000 | 9 | 0 | 3 | 0 | 3 | 1 |
| Gresky, David, BOI* | 1.000 | 1 | 0 | 1 | 0 | 1 | 0 |
| Gross, Kris, BOI | 1.000 | 19 | 0 | 6 | 0 | 6 | 0 |
| Grube, Jarrett, TRI | 1.000 | 17 | 1 | 5 | 0 | 6 | 1 |
| Guerrero, Hipolito, YAK* | 1.000 | 16 | 1 | 3 | 0 | 4 | 0 |
| Hagerty, Luke, BOI | 1.000 | 4 | 0 | 1 | 0 | 1 | 0 |
| Hall, Vance, EVR* | .778 | 18 | 0 | 7 | 2 | 9 | 0 |
| Hamilton, Clayton, EUG | 1.000 | 8 | 0 | 2 | 0 | 2 | 0 |
| Hedrick, Justin, SK | .800 | 11 | 2 | 2 | 1 | 5 | 0 |
| Herrera, Marcos, SPO | .625 | 23 | 1 | 4 | 3 | 8 | 0 |
| Howay, Chris, VAN | 1.000 | 20 | 2 | 5 | 0 | 7 | 1 |
| Hunton, Jonathan, BOI | .750 | 21 | 0 | 3 | 1 | 4 | 0 |
| Hurley, Eric, SPO | .714 | 8 | 1 | 4 | 2 | 7 | 0 |
| Ingram, Jesse, SPO | 1.000 | 22 | 3 | 3 | 0 | 6 | 0 |
| Ion, Mark, TRI | 1.000 | 4 | 1 | 1 | 0 | 2 | 0 |
| Jackson, Steven, YAK | 1.000 | 9 | 0 | 3 | 0 | 3 | 1 |
| Jensen, Aaron, EVR | .700 | 16 | 1 | 6 | 3 | 10 | 1 |
| Jenson, Kevin, SK | 1.000 | 6 | 2 | 0 | 0 | 2 | 0 |
| Jerome, Clayton, SPO | 1.000 | 18 | 2 | 6 | 0 | 8 | 0 |
| Kalita, Ryan, BOI | 1.000 | 5 | 1 | 2 | 0 | 3 | 0 |
| Kemlo, Chris, YAK | 1.000 | 31 | 4 | 8 | 0 | 12 | 0 |
| Kerbs, Reuben, YAK* | .889 | 23 | 2 | 6 | 1 | 9 | 0 |
| Kintzler, Brandon, EUG | 1.000 | 3 | 0 | 1 | 0 | 1 | 0 |
| Kolberg, Koley, YAK | 1.000 | 22 | 2 | 2 | 0 | 4 | 0 |
| Kosow, Jason, BOI* | 1.000 | 11 | 0 | 5 | 0 | 5 | 0 |
| Kroft, Adam, EUG | 1.000 | 1 | 0 | 1 | 0 | 1 | 0 |
| Kunes, Michael, SK* | 1.000 | 21 | 1 | 10 | 0 | 11 | 0 |
| Lensch, Justin, SPO* | 1.000 | 18 | 1 | 13 | 0 | 14 | 1 |
| Liebeck, Jared, YAK | .923 | 11 | 3 | 9 | 1 | 13 | 1 |
| Lira, Efren, TRI | .000 | 20 | 0 | 0 | 1 | 1 | 0 |
| Lockwood, Jon, EVR | 1.000 | 2 | 1 | 0 | 0 | 1 | 0 |
| Lowe, Mark, EVR | 1.000 | 18 | 4 | 4 | 0 | 8 | 0 |
| Lujan, John, SPO | 1.000 | 4 | 1 | 1 | 0 | 2 | 0 |
| Mackay, Douglas, SK | .938 | 16 | 4 | 11 | 1 | 16 | 0 |
| Martinez, Roman, EVR | 1.000 | 5 | 0 | 1 | 0 | 1 | 0 |
| Martinez, Shawn, VAN | .900 | 17 | 2 | 7 | 1 | 10 | 0 |
| Mathes, JR, BOI* | .944 | 12 | 1 | 16 | 1 | 18 | 1 |
| McGirr, Mike, VAN | .667 | 7 | 2 | 4 | 3 | 9 | 0 |
| Mejia, Andy, BOI | 1.000 | 27 | 3 | 10 | 0 | 13 | 0 |
| Miller, Jim, TRI | 1.000 | 34 | 1 | 2 | 0 | 3 | 1 |
| Minor, Matt, SK | 1.000 | 15 | 1 | 4 | 0 | 5 | 1 |
| Mock, Garrett, YAK | 1.000 | 5 | 0 | 3 | 0 | 3 | 0 |
| Moreno, Anthony, SK | .933 | 21 | 3 | 11 | 1 | 15 | 1 |
| Morillo, Juan, TRI | 1.000 | 14 | 2 | 11 | 0 | 13 | 1 |
| Nottingham, Shawn, EVR* | .900 | 14 | 1 | 8 | 1 | 10 | 0 |
| Novosel, Walt, YAK* | 1.000 | 7 | 1 | 1 | 0 | 2 | 0 |
| Odom, John, SK | .933 | 20 | 2 | 12 | 1 | 15 | 1 |
| OHagan, David, EUG | 1.000 | 8 | 1 | 1 | 0 | 2 | 0 |
| Ohlendorf, Ross, YAK | .700 | 7 | 4 | 3 | 3 | 10 | 0 |
| Pablos, Rene, BOI | 1.000 | 6 | 0 | 3 | 0 | 3 | 0 |
| Pendley, Nathan, SK* | 1.000 | 15 | 1 | 3 | 0 | 4 | 0 |
| Perrault, Josh, YAK | 1.000 | 14 | 4 | 9 | 0 | 13 | 0 |
| Perry, Brandon, EVR* | 1.000 | 17 | 0 | 4 | 0 | 4 | 1 |
| Phillips, Shawn, SPO | .929 | 18 | 3 | 10 | 1 | 14 | 0 |
| Piekarz, Joseph, VAN* | 1.000 | 1 | 0 | 1 | 0 | 1 | 0 |
| Pohlman, Daniel, YAK | .000 | 3 | 0 | 0 | 1 | 1 | 0 |
| Ponce, William, EUG | .938 | 14 | 3 | 12 | 1 | 16 | 0 |
| Postlewait, Jake, TRI* | .917 | 14 | 0 | 11 | 1 | 12 | 0 |
| Prendergast, Matt, TRI | 1.000 | 3 | 0 | 1 | 0 | 1 | 0 |
| Raab, Kellen, YAK* | .800 | 19 | 2 | 2 | 1 | 5 | 0 |
| Raguse, Matt, SK | 1.000 | 14 | 0 | 3 | 0 | 3 | 1 |

| Player, Team | Pct. | G | PO | A | E | TC | DP |
|---|---|---|---|---|---|---|---|
| Rayborn, Kris, EUG* | 1.000 | 1 | 0 | 1 | 0 | 1 | 0 |
| Register, Steven, TRI | .889 | 15 | 3 | 13 | 2 | 18 | 0 |
| Reina, Jesus, SK* | .800 | 15 | 3 | 5 | 2 | 10 | 1 |
| Rivera, Mumba, EVR | .923 | 18 | 10 | 2 | 1 | 13 | 0 |
| Roberts, Mark, SPO | .714 | 12 | 1 | 4 | 2 | 7 | 0 |
| Robertson, Conner, VAN | 1.000 | 3 | 1 | 1 | 0 | 2 | 0 |
| Robinson, Ronnie, EUG | 1.000 | 8 | 2 | 1 | 0 | 3 | 0 |
| Rocha, Angel, YAK* | .800 | 5 | 0 | 4 | 1 | 5 | 0 |
| Rodriguez, Pedro, BOI | 1.000 | 1 | 3 | 0 | 0 | 3 | 0 |
| Rogers, Michael, VAN | .667 | 12 | 4 | 0 | 2 | 6 | 0 |
| Rosario, Melvin, TRI* | 1.000 | 9 | 1 | 1 | 0 | 2 | 0 |
| Rupe, Josh, SPO | 1.000 | 4 | 3 | 4 | 0 | 7 | 1 |
| Ryu, JK, BOI | 1.000 | 5 | 3 | 0 | 0 | 3 | 0 |
| Sack, Darren, SK | 1.000 | 16 | 3 | 9 | 0 | 12 | 0 |
| Sanchez, Adiel, VAN* | .800 | 22 | 1 | 3 | 1 | 5 | 0 |
| Sanchez, Jonathan, SK* | 1.000 | 6 | 1 | 4 | 0 | 5 | 0 |
| Santana, Braulio, VAN | 1.000 | 12 | 4 | 7 | 0 | 11 | 2 |
| Santiago, Tomas, TRI | 1.000 | 14 | 3 | 13 | 0 | 16 | 0 |
| Santo, Joel, EUG | 1.000 | 7 | 0 | 7 | 0 | 7 | 0 |
| Schappert, Paul, BOI* | 1.000 | 9 | 0 | 2 | 0 | 2 | 0 |
| Schilsky, Stephen, VAN | 1.000 | 8 | 1 | 3 | 0 | 4 | 0 |
| Shappi, AJ, YAK | .947 | 12 | 4 | 14 | 1 | 19 | 1 |
| Sharpe, Steven, VAN | .929 | 16 | 14 | 12 | 2 | 28 | 1 |
| Shaver, Chris, BOI* | 1.000 | 13 | 0 | 10 | 0 | 10 | 0 |
| Smith, Chase, SK | .857 | 20 | 0 | 6 | 1 | 7 | 0 |
| Snyder, Jason, EVR | 1.000 | 8 | 4 | 8 | 0 | 12 | 0 |
| Sobieraj, Aaron, SK | .900 | 8 | 3 | 6 | 1 | 10 | 0 |
| Songster, Judd, TRI | 1.000 | 10 | 1 | 2 | 0 | 3 | 0 |
| Steik, Richard, EUG | 1.000 | 16 | 2 | 2 | 0 | 4 | 0 |
| Sterry, Vern, EUG | .833 | 9 | 4 | 6 | 2 | 12 | 0 |
| Tetuan, John, TRI | 1.000 | 14 | 2 | 6 | 0 | 8 | 1 |
| Tharpe, Derek, VAN* | 1.000 | 12 | 0 | 6 | 0 | 6 | 0 |
| Thomas, Steven, TRI | .800 | 11 | 0 | 4 | 1 | 5 | 0 |
| Thompson, Chris, YAK | 1.000 | 32 | 3 | 3 | 0 | 6 | 0 |
| Tichota, Clay, VAN | 1.000 | 16 | 4 | 8 | 0 | 12 | 1 |
| Trolia, Aaron, EVR | 1.000 | 20 | 8 | 5 | 0 | 13 | 2 |
| Upwood, Jake, EUG* | 1.000 | 17 | 1 | 3 | 0 | 4 | 0 |
| Urena, Jose, BOI | .667 | 7 | 0 | 2 | 1 | 3 | 0 |
| Van, Robbie, YAK* | 1.000 | 5 | 0 | 2 | 0 | 2 | 0 |
| Varner, Matthew, EUG | 1.000 | 9 | 1 | 2 | 0 | 3 | 0 |
| Vasquez, Esmerling, YAK | .500 | 5 | 0 | 1 | 1 | 2 | 0 |
| Vose, Jake, EUG* | 1.000 | 24 | 0 | 3 | 0 | 3 | 0 |
| Walker, Andy, SPO | 1.000 | 7 | 0 | 3 | 0 | 3 | 0 |
| Watchko, Jeff, TRI | 1.000 | 8 | 1 | 2 | 0 | 3 | 0 |
| Webb, Nick, TRI* | .000 | 1 | 0 | 0 | 1 | 1 | 0 |
| Weber, Matt, BOI | .938 | 14 | 8 | 7 | 1 | 16 | 0 |
| Whatley, Keith, YAK* | .833 | 8 | 2 | 8 | 2 | 12 | 0 |
| Whitaker, Craig, SK | .889 | 15 | 2 | 6 | 1 | 9 | 0 |
| White, Mike, YAK* | .857 | 14 | 2 | 4 | 1 | 7 | 1 |
| Wilkinson, Matt, YAK | 1.000 | 2 | 0 | 1 | 0 | 1 | 0 |
| Willett, Reid, BOI | 1.000 | 14 | 3 | 3 | 0 | 6 | 1 |
| Windsor, Jason, VAN | 1.000 | 4 | 1 | 0 | 0 | 1 | 0 |
| Woerman, Joe, EVR | 1.000 | 9 | 0 | 1 | 0 | 1 | 0 |
| Wohlgemuth, Trevor, SK | .000 | 7 | 0 | 0 | 0 | 0 | 0 |

## LEAGUE CHAMPIONS

| Year | Team | Pct. |
|---|---|---|
| 1901— | Portland | .675 |
| 1902— | Butte | .608 |
| 1903— | Butte | .578 |
| 1904— | Boise | .625 |
| 1905— | Vancouver | .586 |
| | Everett* | .667 |
| 1906— | Tacoma | .600 |
| 1907— | Aberdeen | .625 |
| 1908— | Vancouver | .578 |
| 1909— | Seattle | .653 |
| 1910— | Spokane | .596 |
| 1911— | Vancouver | .628 |
| 1912— | Seattle | .600 |
| 1913— | Vancouver | .600 |
| 1914— | Vancouver | .632 |
| 1915— | Seattle | .564 |
| 1916— | Spokane | .622 |
| 1917— | Great Falls | .592 |
| 1918— | Seattle | .588 |
| 1919— | Seattle | .590 |
| 1920— | Victoria | .600 |
| 1921— | Yakima | .710 |
| | Yakima | .660 |
| 1922— | Calgary‡ | .600 |
| 1923-36— | Did not operate. | |
| 1937— | Wenatchee | .603 |
| | Tacoma* | .627 |
| 1938— | Yakima | .583 |
| | Bellingham (2nd)† | .511 |
| 1939— | Wenatchee | .601 |
| | Tacoma (2nd)† | .533 |
| 1940— | Spokane | .587 |
| | Tacoma (4th)† | .500 |
| 1941— | Spokane | .669 |
| 1942— | Vancouver | .594 |
| 1943-45— | Did not operate. | |
| 1946— | Wenatchee | .622 |
| 1947— | Vancouver | .566 |
| 1948— | Spokane | .614 |
| 1949— | Yakima | .660 |
| | Vancouver (2nd)† | .615 |
| 1950— | Yakima | .613 |
| 1951— | Spokane | .655 |
| 1952— | Victoria | .631 |
| 1953— | Salem | .635 |
| | Spokane* | .590 |
| 1954— | Vancouver* | .636 |
| | Lewiston | .629 |
| 1955— | Salem | .646 |
| | Eugene* | .639 |
| 1956— | Yakima | .691 |
| | Yakima | .619 |
| 1957— | Eugene | .576 |
| | Wenatchee* | .647 |
| 1958— | Lewiston | .621 |
| | Yakima* | .594 |
| 1959— | Salem | .623 |
| | Yakima* | .563 |
| 1960— | Yakima | .638 |
| | Yakima | .562 |
| 1961— | Lewiston* | .621 |
| | Yakima | .600 |
| 1962— | Wenatchee* | .574 |
| | Tri-City | .580 |
| 1963— | Lewiston | .594 |
| | Yakima* | .613 |
| 1964— | Eugene | .636 |
| | Yakima* | .611 |
| 1965— | Lewiston | .667 |
| | Tri-City* | .681 |
| 1966— | Tri-City | .679 |
| 1967— | Medford | .607 |
| 1968— | Tri-City | .600 |
| 1969— | Rogue Valley | .633 |
| 1970— | Lewiston§ | .538 |
| | Coos Bay-No. Bend | .563 |
| 1971— | Tri-City§ | .625 |
| | Bend | .538 |
| 1972— | Lewiston§ | .675 |
| | Walla Walla | .513 |
| 1973— | Walla Walla∞ | .638 |
| | Portland | .563 |
| 1974— | Bellingham | .619 |
| | Eugene▲ | .571 |
| 1975— | Portland | .545 |
| | Eugene◆ | .684 |
| 1976— | Portland | .556 |
| | Walla Walla◆ | .639 |
| 1977— | Bellingham■ | .618 |
| | Portland | .667 |
| 1978— | Grays Harbor▼ | .671 |
| | Eugene | .514 |
| 1979— | Central Oregon◆ | .606 |
| | Walla Walla | .571 |
| 1980— | Bellingham• | .643 |
| | Eugene• | .529 |
| 1981— | Medford◆ | .600 |
| | Bellingham | .557 |
| 1982— | Medford | .757 |
| | Salem◆ | .486 |
| 1983— | Medford†† | .735 |
| | Bellingham | .588 |
| 1984— | Tri-Cities†† | .622 |
| | Medford | .608 |
| 1985— | Everett†† | .541 |
| | Eugene | .541 |
| 1986— | Bellingham†† | .608 |
| | Eugene | .608 |
| 1987— | Spokane▲ | .711 |
| | Everett | .653 |
| 1988— | Southern Oregon | .605 |
| | Spokane◆ | .553 |
| 1989— | Southern Oregon | .600 |
| | Spokane◆ | .547 |
| 1990— | Boise | .697 |
| | Spokane◆ | .645 |
| 1991— | Boise◆ | .658 |
| | Yakima | .579 |
| 1992— | Bellingham◆ | .566 |
| | Bend | .566 |
| 1993— | Bellingham | .579 |
| | Boise◆ | .539 |
| 1994— | Yakima | .645 |
| | Boise◆ | .579 |
| 1995— | Boise◆ | .640 |
| | Bellingham | .566 |
| 1996— | Eugene | .645 |
| | Yakima§ | .526 |
| 1997— | Boise | .671 |
| | Portland◆ | .579 |
| 1998— | Spokane | .618 |
| | Boise | .618 |
| | Salem-Keizer◆ | .566 |
| 1999— | Spokane◆ | .579 |
| 2000— | Yakima◆ | .539 |
| | Boise | .539 |
| 2001— | Boise | .693 |
| | Salem-Keizer◆ | .671 |
| 2002— | Boise▲ | .645 |
| 2003— | Spokane▲ | .658 |
| 2004— | Boise▲ | .553 |

*Won split-season playoff. †Won four-club playoff. ‡League disbanded June 18. §League divided into Northern and Southern divisions, declared champion under league rules. ∞League divided into Eastern and Western divisions, declared champion under league rules. ▲League divided into Eastern and Western divisions; won two-team playoff. ◆League divided into North and South divisions; won two-team playoff. ■League divided into Affiliate and Independent divisions; won two-team playoff. ▼Declared league champion after winning one-game playoff. Balance of playoff canceled due to rain and wet grounds. •Declared co-champion after winning one game. Balance of playoff canceled due to rain and wet grounds. ††League divided into Washington and Oregon divisions; won two-team playoff. (NOTE—Known as Pacific Northwest League 1901-02, Pacific National League 1903-04, Northwestern League 1905-18, Pacific Coast International League 1919-22 and Western International League 1937-54.)

# APPALACHIAN LEAGUE

## LEAGUE OFFICE

**President**
Lee Landers

**Address**
283 Deerchase Circle
Statesville, NC 28625

**Phone**
704-873-5300

**Teams (affiliation)**
Bluefield Orioles (Orioles)
Bristol White Sox (White Sox)
Burlington Indians (Indians)
Danville Braves (Braves)
Elizabethton Twins (Twins)
Greeneville Astros (Astros)
Johnson City Cardinals (Cardinals)
Kingsport Mets (Mets)
Princeton Devil Rays (Devil Rays)
Pulaski Blue Jays (Blue Jays)

## 2004 FINAL STANDINGS

### EASTERN DIVISION

| Team | W | L | T | Pct. | GB |
|---|---|---|---|---|---|
| Danville | 41 | 25 | - | .621 | ... |
| Pulaski | 40 | 27 | - | .597 | 1 1/2 |
| Burlington | 31 | 35 | - | .470 | 10 |
| Bluefield | 28 | 39 | - | .418 | 13 1/2 |
| Princeton | 23 | 44 | - | .343 | 18 1/2 |

### WESTERN DIVISION

| Team | W | L | T | Pct. | GB |
|---|---|---|---|---|---|
| Greeneville | 41 | 26 | - | .612 | ... |
| Elizabethton | 38 | 29 | - | .567 | 3 |
| Johnson City | 33 | 35 | - | .485 | 8 1/2 |
| Kingsport | 32 | 36 | - | .471 | 9 1/2 |
| Bristol | 27 | 38 | - | .415 | 13 |

## COMPOSITE

| Team | W | L | T | PCT | GB | DAN | GVL | PUL | ELZ | JCY | KPT | BRL | BLU | BRS | PRI |
|---|---|---|---|---|---|---|---|---|---|---|---|---|---|---|---|
| Danville (Braves) | 41 | 25 | - | .621 | ... | X | 2 | 4 | 5 | 4 | 5 | 7 | 4 | 4 | 6 |
| Greeneville (Astros) | 41 | 26 | - | .612 | 1/2 | 4 | X | 1 | 4 | 5 | 6 | 2 | 5 | 9 | 5 |
| Pulaski (Blue Jays) | 40 | 27 | - | .597 | 1 1/2 | 4 | 5 | X | 3 | 2 | 3 | 5 | 5 | 4 | 9 |
| Elizabethton (Astros) | 38 | 29 | - | .567 | 3 1/2 | 1 | 7 | 3 | X | 6 | 3 | 4 | 5 | 4 | 5 |
| Johnson City (Cardinals) | 33 | 35 | - | .485 | 9 | 2 | 4 | 4 | 3 | X | 6 | 3 | 5 | 3 | 3 |
| Kingsport (Mets) | 32 | 36 | - | .471 | 10 | 1 3 | | 3 | 6 | 5 | X | 5 | 2 | 6 | 2 |
| Burlington (Indians) | 31 | 35 | - | .470 | 10 | 4 | 3 | 4 | 2 | 3 | 1 | X | 5 | 4 | 6 |
| Bluefield (Orioles) | 28 | 39 | - | .418 | 13 1/2 | 5 | 1 | 4 | 1 | 1 | 4 | 4 | X | 1 | 7 |
| Bristol (White Sox) | 27 | 38 | | .415 | 13 1/2 | 2 | 0 | 4 | 4 | 6 | 4 | 2 | 4 | X | 1 |
| Princeton (Devil Rays) | 23 | 44 | | .343 | 18 1/2 | 2 | 1 | 0 | 1 | 3 | 4 | 3 | 4 | 5 | X |

Major league affiliations in parentheses.

## 2004 BATTING

### TEAM

| Team | G | TPA | AB | R | H | TB | 2B | 3B | HR | RBI | SH | SF | HP | BB | IBB | SO | SB | CS | GDP | LOB | ShO | Avg. | OBP | Slg. |
|---|---|---|---|---|---|---|---|---|---|---|---|---|---|---|---|---|---|---|---|---|---|---|---|---|
| Danville | 66 | 2570 | 2258 | 386 | 623 | 926 | 113 | 17 | 52 | 342 | 17 | 21 | 49 | 223 | 13 | 452 | 55 | 19 | 48 | 476 | 1 | .276 | .351 | .410 |
| Elizabethton | 67 | 2529 | 2261 | 340 | 611 | 953 | 111 | 21 | 63 | 309 | 6 | 24 | 30 | 208 | 2 | 542 | 49 | 23 | 36 | 485 | 2 | .270 | .337 | .421 |
| Pulaski | 67 | 2708 | 2275 | 435 | 613 | 966 | 130 | 20 | 61 | 394 | 15 | 22 | 66 | 330 | 11 | 615 | 26 | 23 | 50 | 540 | 4 | .269 | .375 | .425 |
| Johnson City | 68 | 2663 | 2321 | 394 | 623 | 967 | 114 | 19 | 64 | 347 | 7 | 22 | 47 | 266 | 5 | 566 | 81 | 24 | 33 | 496 | 3 | .268 | .352 | .417 |
| Kingsport | 68 | 2618 | 2287 | 357 | 605 | 928 | 99 | 25 | 58 | 319 | 21 | 29 | 56 | 225 | 9 | 534 | 52 | 32 | 38 | 497 | 2 | .265 | .341 | .406 |
| Greeneville | 67 | 2521 | 2157 | 364 | 561 | 823 | 109 | 9 | 45 | 313 | 25 | 16 | 66 | 256 | 5 | 496 | 98 | 50 | 32 | 447 | 3 | .260 | .354 | .382 |
| Princeton | 67 | 2519 | 2236 | 336 | 570 | 818 | 88 | 20 | 40 | 293 | 15 | 21 | 49 | 198 | 4 | 563 | 69 | 32 | 45 | 437 | 6 | .255 | .326 | .366 |
| Bristol | 65 | 2448 | 2163 | 311 | 532 | 769 | 97 | 13 | 38 | 270 | 23 | 23 | 40 | 199 | 9 | 550 | 47 | 31 | 37 | 433 | 3 | .246 | .318 | .356 |
| Bluefield | 67 | 2528 | 2229 | 289 | 543 | 799 | 102 | 14 | 42 | 247 | 26 | 18 | 32 | 223 | 7 | 614 | 64 | 23 | 51 | 472 | 5 | .244 | .319 | .358 |
| Burlington | 66 | 2417 | 2136 | 266 | 515 | 709 | 94 | 17 | 22 | 219 | 25 | 21 | 25 | 210 | 8 | 537 | 81 | 36 | 30 | 461 | 4 | .241 | .314 | .332 |

### INDIVIDUAL

#### TOP QUALIFIERS FOR BATTING CHAMPIONSHIP

Minimum 184 plate appearances. *Lefthanded batter. †Switch-hitter.

| Player, Team | G | TPA | AB | R | H | TB | 2B | 3B | HR | RBI | SH | SF | HP | BB | IBB | SO | SB | CS | GDP | Avg. | OBP | Slg. |
|---|---|---|---|---|---|---|---|---|---|---|---|---|---|---|---|---|---|---|---|---|---|---|
| Lucena, Juan, Johnson City | 56 | 222 | 205 | 35 | 68 | 90 | 8 | 1 | 4 | 30 | 3 | 2 | 1 | 11 | 0 | 16 | 7 | 3 | 7 | .332 | .365 | .439 |
| Hernandez, Francisco, Bristol † | 53 | 203 | 181 | 32 | 59 | 89 | 13 | 1 | 5 | 30 | 4 | 3 | 2 | 13 | 0 | 32 | 0 | 0 | 1 | .326 | .372 | .492 |
| Yarbrough, Brandon, Johnson City * | 48 | 202 | 175 | 37 | 57 | 87 | 10 | 1 | 6 | 33 | 0 | 1 | 1 | 25 | 1 | 55 | 3 | 1 | 3 | .326 | .411 | .497 |
| Gamero, Jesus, Kingsport | 44 | 186 | 161 | 31 | 52 | 76 | 7 | 4 | 3 | 32 | 1 | 3 | 8 | 13 | 0 | 28 | 3 | 1 | 2 | .323 | .395 | .472 |
| Holt, John, Danville * | 51 | 233 | 209 | 38 | 67 | 85 | 15 | 0 | 1 | 21 | 2 | 2 | 2 | 18 | 1 | 34 | 17 | 5 | 2 | .321 | .377 | .407 |
| Armstrong, Cole, Danville * | 49 | 207 | 174 | 30 | 55 | 82 | 9 | 0 | 6 | 46 | 0 | 3 | 1 | 29 | 3 | 17 | 0 | 0 | 6 | .316 | .411 | .471 |
| Granadillo, Tony, Johnson City † | 50 | 196 | 168 | 40 | 53 | 95 | 10 | 1 | 10 | 30 | 0 | 0 | 6 | 22 | 0 | 37 | 3 | 1 | 3 | .315 | .413 | .565 |
| De Los Santos, Jose, Bristol | 53 | 215 | 200 | 28 | 63 | 75 | 10 | 1 | 0 | 35 | 4 | 3 | 3 | 5 | 0 | 21 | 1 | 2 | 5 | .315 | .336 | .375 |
| Burns, Deacon, Elizabethton * | 63 | 277 | 255 | 49 | 80 | 144 | 20 | 4 | 12 | 49 | 0 | 0 | 4 | 18 | 0 | 53 | 9 | 2 | 5 | .314 | .368 | .565 |
| Anderson, Charlie, Pulaski * | 52 | 185 | 151 | 37 | 47 | 79 | 14 | 0 | 6 | 20 | 1 | 1 | 3 | 29 | 0 | 39 | 0 | 0 | 2 | .311 | .429 | .523 |
| Garcia, Travis, Kingsport | 46 | 193 | 171 | 25 | 53 | 91 | 9 | 1 | 9 | 36 | 0 | 3 | 3 | 16 | 1 | 37 | 1 | 3 | 4 | .310 | .373 | .532 |
| Woodard, Johnny, Elizabethton * | 57 | 223 | 194 | 37 | 60 | 100 | 8 | 4 | 8 | 35 | 0 | 3 | 2 | 24 | 0 | 56 | 5 | 2 | 2 | .309 | .386 | .515 |
| Einertson, Mitch, Greeneville | 63 | 269 | 227 | 53 | 70 | 157 | 15 | 0 | 24 | 67 | 0 | 1 | 9 | 32 | 3 | 70 | 4 | 4 | 1 | .308 | .413 | .692 |
| Rodriquez, Yuber, Pulaski † | 62 | 285 | 245 | 49 | 75 | 124 | 13 | 6 | 8 | 50 | 1 | 2 | 9 | 28 | 3 | 70 | 9 | 3 | 5 | .306 | .394 | .506 |
| Loadenthal, Carl, Danville * | 65 | 275 | 239 | 60 | 73 | 105 | 9 | 4 | 5 | 32 | 2 | 1 | 1 | 32 | 1 | 34 | 12 | 3 | 0 | .305 | .388 | .439 |

DEPARTMENTAL LEADERS: G—Loadenthal, 65; AB—Burns, 255; R—Loadenthal, 60; H—Burns, 80; TB—Einertson, 157; 2B—Burns, 20; 3B—Y. Rodriguez, 6; HR—Einertson, 24; RBI—Einertson, 67; SH—Sutil, 7; SF—Pietsch, Cunningham, 5; HP—Eichas, 14; BB—J. Delgado, 53; IBB—Several tied with three; SO—Scott, 75; SB—Sutil, 24; CS—Tartaglia, Sutil, 8; GIDP—Eichas, Pulley, 8; Slg.—Eintertson, .692; OBP—Delgado, Gutierrez, .430.

# ALL PLAYERS

*Lefthanded batter. †Switch-hitter.

| Player, Team | G | TPA | AB | R | H | TB | 2B | 3B | HR | RBI | SH | SF | HP | BB | IBB | SO | SB | CS | GDP | Avg. | OBP | Slg. |
|---|---|---|---|---|---|---|---|---|---|---|---|---|---|---|---|---|---|---|---|---|---|---|
| Acosta, Jose, Greeneville | 35 | 124 | 108 | 20 | 29 | 46 | 6 | 1 | 3 | 22 | 0 | 2 | 6 | 8 | 0 | 22 | 3 | 1 | 1 | .269 | .347 | .426 |
| Alcantara, Gilbert, Bristol | 37 | 94 | 81 | 8 | 15 | 16 | 1 | 0 | 0 | 2 | 0 | 0 | 2 | 11 | 0 | 34 | 4 | 1 | 2 | .185 | .298 | .198 |
| Allen, Brandon, Bristol * | 58 | 207 | 185 | 17 | 38 | 58 | 9 | 1 | 3 | 23 | 0 | 2 | 4 | 16 | 1 | 60 | 2 | 3 | 3 | .205 | .280 | .314 |
| Anderson, Charlie, Pulaski * | 52 | 185 | 151 | 37 | 47 | 79 | 14 | 0 | 6 | 20 | 1 | 1 | 3 | 29 | 0 | 39 | 0 | 0 | 2 | .311 | .429 | .523 |
| Anderson, Heath, Elizabethton | 15 | 49 | 42 | 2 | 4 | 4 | 0 | 0 | 0 | 1 | 0 | 1 | 0 | 6 | 0 | 21 | 0 | 0 | 0 | .095 | .204 | .095 |
| Armstrong, Cole, Danville * | 49 | 207 | 174 | 30 | 55 | 82 | 9 | 0 | 6 | 46 | 0 | 3 | 1 | 29 | 3 | 17 | 0 | 0 | 6 | .316 | .411 | .471 |
| Arnold, Derrick, Danville † | 49 | 157 | 135 | 18 | 24 | 37 | 4 | 0 | 3 | 14 | 3 | 1 | 2 | 16 | 1 | 43 | 2 | 1 | 4 | .178 | .273 | .274 |
| Arroyo, Rafael, Kingsport | 42 | 163 | 124 | 24 | 32 | 57 | 5 | 1 | 6 | 26 | 3 | 0 | 6 | 30 | 0 | 35 | 1 | 3 | 1 | .258 | .425 | .460 |
| Ashford, Jon, Pulaski * | 49 | 161 | 140 | 26 | 37 | 68 | 9 | 2 | 6 | 30 | 0 | 1 | 1 | 19 | 2 | 62 | 2 | 2 | 1 | .264 | .354 | .486 |
| Avila, Angel, Bluefield | 48 | 187 | 167 | 19 | 44 | 65 | 4 | 1 | 5 | 20 | 4 | 1 | 7 | 8 | 0 | 62 | 9 | 4 | 4 | .263 | .322 | .389 |
| Badger, Graig, Pulaski | 34 | 104 | 75 | 22 | 18 | 20 | 2 | 0 | 0 | 10 | 2 | 2 | 1 | 24 | 0 | 20 | 2 | 1 | 3 | .240 | .422 | .267 |
| Becher, William, Johnson City * | 58 | 201 | 168 | 30 | 48 | 90 | 7 | 1 | 11 | 41 | 0 | 4 | 0 | 29 | 2 | 50 | 2 | 1 | 1 | .286 | .383 | .536 |
| Bergeron, Jabe, Kingsport | 28 | 110 | 103 | 15 | 30 | 49 | 2 | 1 | 5 | 16 | 0 | 2 | 1 | 4 | 0 | 25 | 1 | 0 | 4 | .291 | .318 | .476 |
| Bormaster, Brian, Pulaski | 45 | 169 | 143 | 21 | 36 | 58 | 7 | 0 | 5 | 22 | 1 | 0 | 3 | 22 | 0 | 28 | 0 | 1 | 2 | .252 | .363 | .406 |
| Bouman, John, Princeton | 35 | 127 | 117 | 12 | 32 | 40 | 4 | 2 | 0 | 12 | 0 | 0 | 1 | 9 | 0 | 32 | 3 | 2 | 3 | .274 | .331 | .342 |
| Brignac, Reid, Princeton * | 25 | 109 | 97 | 16 | 35 | 46 | 4 | 2 | 1 | 25 | 0 | 2 | 1 | 9 | 0 | 10 | 2 | 1 | 2 | .361 | .413 | .474 |
| Broome, Mark, Johnson City | 25 | 89 | 79 | 14 | 17 | 25 | 2 | 0 | 2 | 5 | 0 | 1 | 1 | 8 | 0 | 15 | 3 | 0 | 1 | .215 | .292 | .316 |
| Burns, Deacon, Elizabethton * | 63 | 277 | 255 | 49 | 80 | 144 | 20 | 4 | 12 | 49 | 0 | 0 | 4 | 18 | 0 | 53 | 9 | 2 | 5 | .314 | .368 | .565 |
| Burt, Landon, Elizabethton * | 43 | 185 | 164 | 25 | 47 | 60 | 10 | 0 | 1 | 15 | 0 | 1 | 0 | 20 | 0 | 17 | 8 | 2 | 1 | .287 | .362 | .366 |
| Burton, Adam, Johnson City | 30 | 97 | 83 | 5 | 17 | 20 | 3 | 0 | 0 | 5 | 0 | 3 | 1 | 10 | 0 | 21 | 1 | 0 | 0 | .205 | .289 | .241 |
| Cabral, Marcos, Kingsport | 34 | 137 | 116 | 20 | 31 | 45 | 8 | 0 | 2 | 10 | 2 | 2 | 2 | 15 | 1 | 25 | 3 | 3 | 0 | .267 | .356 | .388 |
| Castillo, Cesar, Bristol | 6 | 22 | 17 | 1 | 2 | 3 | 1 | 0 | 0 | 0 | 1 | 0 | 0 | 4 | 0 | 3 | 0 | 0 | 0 | .118 | .286 | .176 |
| Castillo, Javier, Bristol | 60 | 249 | 206 | 40 | 56 | 84 | 8 | 1 | 6 | 35 | 3 | 4 | 6 | 30 | 3 | 58 | 3 | 2 | 5 | .272 | .374 | .408 |
| Cavers, Eric, Greeneville | 18 | 52 | 45 | 5 | 9 | 11 | 2 | 0 | 0 | 3 | 0 | 0 | 3 | 4 | 0 | 18 | 2 | 1 | 1 | .200 | .308 | .244 |
| Cerda, Felix, Kingsport * | 44 | 172 | 156 | 16 | 26 | 32 | 3 | 0 | 1 | 10 | 0 | 1 | 0 | 15 | 1 | 49 | 0 | 1 | 4 | .167 | .238 | .205 |
| Chacin, Steward, Johnson City | 31 | 65 | 61 | 4 | 8 | 12 | 1 | 0 | 1 | 6 | 0 | 1 | 0 | 3 | 0 | 16 | 0 | 1 | 0 | .131 | .169 | .197 |
| Chappell, Jonathan, Pulaski | 21 | 70 | 58 | 12 | 17 | 33 | 7 | 0 | 3 | 16 | 1 | 1 | 2 | 8 | 0 | 20 | 0 | 1 | 0 | .293 | .391 | .569 |
| Chourio, Junior, Pulaski | 35 | 98 | 94 | 14 | 23 | 36 | 4 | 0 | 3 | 15 | 0 | 1 | 2 | 1 | 0 | 22 | 1 | 2 | 3 | .245 | .265 | .383 |
| Clark, John, Burlington | 47 | 181 | 153 | 25 | 37 | 65 | 11 | 1 | 5 | 32 | 1 | 2 | 2 | 23 | 0 | 35 | 1 | 1 | 2 | .242 | .344 | .425 |
| Comacho, Johan, Kingsport | 23 | 89 | 80 | 6 | 13 | 20 | 1 | 0 | 2 | 6 | 0 | 1 | 2 | 6 | 0 | 24 | 0 | 0 | 2 | .163 | .236 | .250 |
| Corapci, Jason, Greeneville | 27 | 74 | 68 | 3 | 13 | 16 | 3 | 0 | 0 | 5 | 1 | 1 | 1 | 3 | 0 | 13 | 0 | 1 | 0 | .191 | .233 | .235 |
| Crooks, Alejandro, Princeton * | 34 | 108 | 93 | 12 | 14 | 22 | 5 | 0 | 1 | 8 | 1 | 0 | 0 | 14 | 1 | 24 | 0 | 0 | 2 | .151 | .262 | .237 |
| Cruz, Ramon, Danville | 12 | 25 | 24 | 0 | 3 | 4 | 1 | 0 | 0 | 1 | 0 | 0 | 1 | 0 | 0 | 10 | 0 | 0 | 1 | .125 | .160 | .167 |
| Cumberbatch, Cirilo, Burlington † | 37 | 136 | 126 | 15 | 33 | 42 | 4 | 1 | 1 | 7 | 1 | 1 | 1 | 7 | 0 | 35 | 1 | 1 | 2 | .262 | .304 | .333 |
| Cunningham, Christopher, Princeton | 55 | 211 | 174 | 31 | 45 | 69 | 8 | 2 | 4 | 36 | 0 | 5 | 9 | 23 | 1 | 45 | 1 | 5 | 7 | .259 | .365 | .397 |
| Davis, Zach, Bluefield * | 45 | 147 | 125 | 17 | 27 | 40 | 5 | 1 | 2 | 8 | 1 | 0 | 0 | 21 | 0 | 37 | 8 | 3 | 4 | .216 | .329 | .320 |
| De Leon, Evandy, Burlington | 44 | 173 | 154 | 23 | 32 | 58 | 9 | 4 | 3 | 19 | 1 | 5 | 1 | 12 | 0 | 53 | 10 | 2 | 2 | .208 | .262 | .377 |
| De Los Santos, Jose, Bristol | 53 | 215 | 200 | 28 | 63 | 75 | 10 | 1 | 0 | 35 | 4 | 3 | 3 | 5 | 0 | 21 | 1 | 2 | 5 | .315 | .336 | .375 |
| Delarosa, Jairo, Princeton | 46 | 161 | 146 | 26 | 43 | 67 | 4 | 4 | 4 | 22 | 2 | 1 | 7 | 5 | 0 | 43 | 3 | 3 | 2 | .295 | .346 | .459 |
| Delgado, Jose, Johnson City † | 63 | 277 | 217 | 47 | 60 | 88 | 9 | 5 | 3 | 28 | 0 | 1 | 6 | 53 | 0 | 65 | 17 | 4 | 3 | .276 | .430 | .406 |
| Denham, Jason, Burlington * | 38 | 130 | 104 | 13 | 15 | 17 | 0 | 1 | 0 | 4 | 3 | 1 | 1 | 21 | 0 | 40 | 5 | 5 | 2 | .144 | .291 | .163 |
| Diaz, Sandy, Johnson City | 36 | 144 | 130 | 17 | 29 | 46 | 8 | 0 | 3 | 17 | 0 | 0 | 6 | 8 | 2 | 36 | 0 | 1 | 1 | .223 | .299 | .354 |
| Eichas, Keith, Danville | 59 | 243 | 220 | 31 | 67 | 91 | 16 | 1 | 2 | 29 | 1 | 1 | 14 | 7 | 0 | 39 | 2 | 0 | 8 | .305 | .364 | .414 |
| Einertson, Mitch, Greeneville | 63 | 269 | 227 | 53 | 70 | 157 | 15 | 0 | 24 | 67 | 0 | 1 | 9 | 32 | 3 | 70 | 4 | 4 | 1 | .308 | .413 | .692 |
| Espinoza, Pedro, Greeneville | 33 | 91 | 83 | 10 | 22 | 25 | 3 | 0 | 0 | 14 | 1 | 0 | 2 | 5 | 0 | 12 | 3 | 2 | 2 | .265 | .322 | .301 |
| Finan, Ryan, Bluefield * | 36 | 148 | 123 | 27 | 41 | 68 | 12 | 0 | 5 | 21 | 1 | 2 | 4 | 18 | 0 | 16 | 0 | 1 | 2 | .333 | .429 | .553 |
| Foust, J.D., Bristol | 28 | 118 | 109 | 14 | 31 | 52 | 7 | 1 | 4 | 19 | 2 | 1 | 2 | 4 | 1 | 21 | 2 | 5 | 0 | .284 | .319 | .477 |
| Gabriel, Chad, Johnson City | 56 | 216 | 196 | 38 | 53 | 84 | 14 | 1 | 5 | 37 | 0 | 2 | 6 | 12 | 0 | 39 | 5 | 1 | 2 | .270 | .329 | .429 |
| Gamero, Jesus, Kingsport | 44 | 186 | 161 | 31 | 52 | 76 | 7 | 4 | 3 | 32 | 1 | 3 | 8 | 13 | 0 | 28 | 3 | 1 | 2 | .323 | .395 | .472 |
| Garcia, Antonio, Greeneville † | 44 | 168 | 152 | 18 | 48 | 70 | 10 | 0 | 4 | 20 | 0 | 2 | 2 | 12 | 0 | 39 | 0 | 2 | 3 | .316 | .369 | .461 |
| Garcia, Julio, Burlington † | 58 | 235 | 204 | 32 | 50 | 59 | 9 | 0 | 0 | 14 | 3 | 0 | 3 | 25 | 0 | 48 | 11 | 6 | 1 | .245 | .336 | .289 |
| Garcia, Travis, Kingsport | 46 | 193 | 171 | 25 | 53 | 91 | 9 | 1 | 9 | 36 | 0 | 3 | 3 | 16 | 1 | 37 | 1 | 3 | 4 | .310 | .373 | .532 |
| Garibaldi, Anthony, Pulaski | 48 | 173 | 144 | 36 | 41 | 65 | 5 | 2 | 5 | 24 | 1 | 1 | 10 | 17 | 0 | 49 | 0 | 2 | 3 | .285 | .395 | .451 |
| Gonzalez, Humberto, Kingsport | 11 | 36 | 27 | 5 | 2 | 2 | 0 | 0 | 0 | 2 | 1 | 1 | 1 | 6 | 0 | 6 | 0 | 1 | 0 | .074 | .257 | .074 |
| Guerrero, Francisco, Bluefield | 4 | 11 | 10 | 0 | 2 | 2 | 0 | 0 | 0 | 0 | 1 | 0 | 0 | 0 | 0 | 2 | 0 | 0 | 0 | .200 | .200 | .200 |
| Guerrero, Henry, Bluefield | 41 | 144 | 126 | 16 | 22 | 32 | 4 | 0 | 2 | 16 | 0 | 1 | 1 | 16 | 2 | 29 | 1 | 0 | 4 | .175 | .271 | .254 |
| Guest, Dennis, Bristol | 20 | 51 | 45 | 9 | 6 | 6 | 0 | 0 | 0 | 1 | 0 | 0 | 1 | 5 | 0 | 10 | 0 | 1 | 2 | .133 | .235 | .133 |
| Gulan, Mike, Bristol | 10 | 39 | 32 | 4 | 8 | 16 | 2 | 0 | 2 | 10 | 0 | 3 | 0 | 4 | 0 | 10 | 0 | 0 | 0 | .250 | .308 | .500 |
| Gutierrez, Juan, Bluefield † | 36 | 149 | 126 | 19 | 44 | 76 | 8 | 0 | 8 | 29 | 0 | 3 | 3 | 17 | 0 | 14 | 0 | 1 | 2 | .349 | .430 | .603 |
| Hall, James, Princeton * | 41 | 140 | 119 | 21 | 23 | 37 | 3 | 1 | 3 | 16 | 0 | 1 | 5 | 15 | 0 | 47 | 1 | 2 | 1 | .193 | .307 | .311 |
| Harrell, Lucas, Bristol † | 13 | 1 | 1 | 0 | 0 | 0 | 0 | 0 | 0 | 0 | 0 | 0 | 0 | 0 | 0 | 1 | 0 | 0 | 0 | .000 | .000 | .000 |
| Hernandez, Francisco, Bristol † | 53 | 203 | 181 | 32 | 59 | 89 | 13 | 1 | 5 | 30 | 4 | 3 | 2 | 13 | 0 | 32 | 0 | 0 | 1 | .326 | .372 | .492 |
| Hernandez, Hector, Greeneville | 6 | 21 | 20 | 5 | 7 | 7 | 0 | 0 | 0 | 2 | 0 | 0 | 0 | 1 | 0 | 4 | 3 | 1 | 0 | .350 | .381 | .350 |
| Hetherington, Luke, Pulaski | 59 | 237 | 196 | 40 | 50 | 88 | 10 | 2 | 8 | 40 | 0 | 2 | 11 | 28 | 1 | 64 | 5 | 2 | 3 | .255 | .376 | .449 |
| Hicks, David, Pulaski * | 36 | 160 | 134 | 33 | 41 | 58 | 9 | 1 | 2 | 25 | 1 | 1 | 4 | 20 | 2 | 27 | 2 | 0 | 5 | .306 | .409 | .433 |
| Hiser, PJ, Burlington | 38 | 156 | 145 | 22 | 43 | 86 | 5 | 4 | 10 | 32 | 0 | 2 | 1 | 8 | 1 | 47 | 6 | 3 | 3 | .297 | .333 | .593 |
| Holmes, Justin, Burlington | 31 | 111 | 103 | 10 | 24 | 30 | 4 | 1 | 0 | 6 | 2 | 0 | 1 | 5 | 1 | 18 | 5 | 2 | 1 | .233 | .275 | .291 |
| Holt, John, Danville * | 51 | 233 | 209 | 38 | 67 | 85 | 15 | 0 | 1 | 21 | 2 | 2 | 2 | 18 | 1 | 34 | 17 | 5 | 2 | .321 | .377 | .407 |
| Howell, Samuel, Bluefield | 12 | 47 | 44 | 7 | 12 | 19 | 4 | 0 | 1 | 4 | 0 | 0 | 0 | 3 | 1 | 17 | 2 | 0 | 2 | .273 | .319 | .432 |
| Hughes, Luke, Elizabethton | 44 | 159 | 141 | 20 | 40 | 59 | 8 | 1 | 3 | 19 | 2 | 3 | 4 | 9 | 0 | 30 | 1 | 3 | 1 | .284 | .338 | .418 |
| Irvin, Blair, Princeton * | 39 | 112 | 101 | 15 | 21 | 22 | 1 | 0 | 0 | 5 | 4 | 0 | 0 | 7 | 0 | 24 | 14 | 3 | 0 | .208 | .259 | .218 |
| Jesson, Das, Johnson City † | 53 | 215 | 182 | 30 | 42 | 80 | 11 | 0 | 9 | 34 | 0 | 1 | 4 | 28 | 0 | 53 | 6 | 3 | 3 | .231 | .344 | .440 |
| Johnson, Brandon, Bristol * | 53 | 185 | 166 | 21 | 37 | 55 | 7 | 1 | 3 | 23 | 3 | 0 | 1 | 15 | 0 | 44 | 3 | 2 | 5 | .223 | .291 | .331 |
| Jones, Brandon, Danville * | 57 | 235 | 209 | 35 | 62 | 87 | 6 | 5 | 3 | 33 | 0 | 2 | 1 | 23 | 0 | 33 | 4 | 2 | 5 | .297 | .366 | .416 |
| Jurich, Mark, Danville * | 57 | 235 | 203 | 39 | 57 | 117 | 10 | 1 | 16 | 47 | 0 | 3 | 0 | 28 | 3 | 33 | 0 | 1 | 5 | .281 | .363 | .576 |
| Kady, Dave, Greeneville * | 15 | 21 | 15 | 2 | 2 | 3 | 1 | 0 | 0 | 0 | 2 | 0 | 2 | 2 | 0 | 5 | 0 | 0 | 1 | .133 | .316 | .200 |
| Kitch, Denver, Bluefield | 56 | 219 | 195 | 18 | 49 | 64 | 8 | 2 | 1 | 23 | 4 | 1 | 5 | 14 | 1 | 53 | 8 | 0 | 5 | .251 | .316 | .328 |

| Player, Team | G | TPA | AB | R | H | TB | 2B | 3B | HR | RBI | SH | SF | HP | BB | IBB | SO | SB | CS | GDP | Avg. | OBP | Slg. |
|---|---|---|---|---|---|---|---|---|---|---|---|---|---|---|---|---|---|---|---|---|---|---|
| Kotch, Kevin, Bluefield * | 28 | 89 | 80 | 9 | 18 | 24 | 4 | 1 | 0 | 7 | 0 | 0 | 1 | 8 | 0 | 31 | 2 | 0 | 3 | .225 | .303 | .300 |
| Lagreid, Thomas, Princeton | 26 | 100 | 84 | 14 | 19 | 32 | 4 | 0 | 3 | 16 | 1 | 1 | 2 | 12 | 0 | 18 | 1 | 1 | 3 | .226 | .333 | .381 |
| Lahey, Tim, Elizabethton | 26 | 101 | 84 | 7 | 17 | 28 | 2 | 0 | 3 | 11 | 0 | 2 | 2 | 13 | 0 | 38 | 0 | 0 | 3 | .202 | .317 | .333 |
| Land, Tim, Pulaski | 14 | 53 | 43 | 8 | 9 | 16 | 1 | 0 | 2 | 11 | 2 | 1 | 1 | 6 | 0 | 12 | 0 | 0 | 2 | .209 | .314 | .372 |
| Lankford, Kris, Elizabethton † | 11 | 10 | 9 | 0 | 0 | 0 | 0 | 0 | 0 | 0 | 0 | 0 | 0 | 1 | 0 | 6 | 0 | 0 | 0 | .000 | .100 | .000 |
| Lawrence, Horace, Kingsport * | 27 | 119 | 105 | 11 | 38 | 61 | 6 | 1 | 5 | 24 | 0 | 1 | 1 | 12 | 2 | 17 | 6 | 3 | 0 | .362 | .429 | .581 |
| Lenderman, Matt, Bristol | 17 | 46 | 43 | 3 | 7 | 14 | 1 | 0 | 2 | 4 | 0 | 0 | 1 | 2 | 0 | 18 | 1 | 0 | 0 | .163 | .217 | .326 |
| Lex, Joshua, Pulaski | 26 | 107 | 87 | 15 | 25 | 41 | 10 | 0 | 2 | 19 | 0 | 1 | 5 | 14 | 0 | 19 | 1 | 0 | 4 | .287 | .411 | .471 |
| Loadenthal, Carl, Danville * | 65 | 275 | 239 | 60 | 73 | 105 | 9 | 4 | 5 | 32 | 2 | 1 | 1 | 32 | 1 | 34 | 12 | 3 | 0 | .305 | .388 | .439 |
| Lofgren, Charles, Burlington * | 14 | 13 | 10 | 2 | 2 | 2 | 0 | 0 | 0 | 0 | 0 | 0 | 0 | 3 | 0 | 1 | 0 | 0 | 0 | .200 | .385 | .200 |
| Longworth, Chad, Burlington | 51 | 197 | 181 | 19 | 53 | 65 | 12 | 0 | 0 | 22 | 1 | 0 | 2 | 13 | 0 | 46 | 7 | 5 | 1 | .293 | .347 | .359 |
| Lopez, Christian A., Princeton | 29 | 105 | 96 | 18 | 27 | 42 | 6 | 0 | 3 | 13 | 0 | 1 | 2 | 6 | 0 | 24 | 3 | 1 | 2 | .281 | .333 | .438 |
| Lopez, Javier, Elizabethton | 46 | 170 | 160 | 17 | 39 | 63 | 10 | 1 | 4 | 15 | 0 | 2 | 2 | 6 | 0 | 49 | 4 | 2 | 0 | .244 | .276 | .394 |
| Lopez, Romelio, Princeton † | 6 | 4 | 4 | 1 | 1 | 1 | 0 | 0 | 0 | 0 | 0 | 0 | 0 | 0 | 0 | 1 | 0 | 0 | 0 | .250 | .250 | .250 |
| Lucena, Juan, Johnson City | 56 | 222 | 205 | 35 | 68 | 90 | 8 | 1 | 4 | 30 | 3 | 2 | 1 | 11 | 0 | 16 | 7 | 3 | 7 | .332 | .365 | .439 |
| Macaluso, Michael, Pulaski | 36 | 151 | 128 | 19 | 28 | 32 | 4 | 0 | 0 | 10 | 1 | 1 | 2 | 19 | 0 | 17 | 2 | 0 | 2 | .219 | .327 | .250 |
| Matthews, Dustin, Bristol | 14 | 20 | 18 | 2 | 3 | 3 | 0 | 0 | 0 | 1 | 0 | 0 | 1 | 1 | 0 | 12 | 0 | 0 | 0 | .167 | .250 | .167 |
| Melendez, Alcides, Bluefield * | 32 | 90 | 76 | 9 | 9 | 10 | 1 | 0 | 0 | 6 | 1 | 2 | 1 | 10 | 0 | 13 | 6 | 1 | 1 | .118 | .225 | .132 |
| Miller, Michael, Johnson City | 42 | 129 | 115 | 19 | 24 | 44 | 5 | 0 | 5 | 18 | 0 | 1 | 2 | 11 | 0 | 34 | 1 | 2 | 1 | .209 | .287 | .383 |
| Moreta, Carlos, Danville | 36 | 120 | 106 | 14 | 25 | 40 | 3 | 0 | 4 | 18 | 1 | 1 | 2 | 10 | 2 | 31 | 1 | 0 | 2 | .236 | .311 | .377 |
| Nelson, Daniel, Johnson City † | 42 | 141 | 124 | 20 | 32 | 45 | 9 | 2 | 0 | 11 | 1 | 1 | 2 | 13 | 0 | 31 | 6 | 1 | 1 | .258 | .336 | .363 |
| Ortega, Jose, Burlington | 46 | 199 | 172 | 23 | 46 | 56 | 10 | 0 | 0 | 15 | 3 | 2 | 2 | 20 | 0 | 25 | 1 | 1 | 0 | .267 | .347 | .326 |
| Ortiz, Patrick, Elizabethton † | 19 | 66 | 56 | 9 | 15 | 17 | 2 | 0 | 0 | 2 | 0 | 0 | 0 | 10 | 0 | 15 | 3 | 2 | 1 | .268 | .379 | .304 |
| Ortiz, Rafael, Burlington | 36 | 118 | 105 | 5 | 17 | 22 | 3 | 1 | 0 | 9 | 3 | 1 | 2 | 7 | 0 | 23 | 2 | 0 | 5 | .162 | .226 | .210 |
| Oxendine, Chad, Bristol | 5 | 17 | 16 | 2 | 2 | 2 | 0 | 0 | 0 | 3 | 0 | 0 | 0 | 1 | 0 | 6 | 0 | 0 | 0 | .125 | .176 | .125 |
| Pacheco, Joel, Bluefield | 29 | 110 | 103 | 12 | 21 | 34 | 2 | 1 | 3 | 9 | 1 | 0 | 1 | 5 | 0 | 41 | 3 | 0 | 4 | .204 | .248 | .330 |
| Parraz, Jordan, Greeneville | 53 | 213 | 180 | 35 | 44 | 72 | 6 | 5 | 4 | 21 | 4 | 0 | 5 | 24 | 0 | 44 | 8 | 5 | 4 | .244 | .349 | .400 |
| Patterson, Tarrence, Elizabethton | 43 | 177 | 170 | 27 | 38 | 69 | 4 | 3 | 7 | 16 | 1 | 0 | 2 | 4 | 0 | 37 | 7 | 2 | 2 | .224 | .250 | .406 |
| Perez, Carlos, Bristol * | 14 | 5 | 4 | 1 | 1 | 1 | 0 | 0 | 0 | 0 | 0 | 0 | 0 | 1 | 0 | 1 | 0 | 0 | 1 | .250 | .400 | .250 |
| Perez, Melvin, Bristol | 7 | 24 | 23 | 3 | 3 | 3 | 0 | 0 | 0 | 1 | 0 | 0 | 0 | 1 | 0 | 10 | 0 | 0 | 0 | .130 | .167 | .130 |
| Petersen, Josh, Kingsport | 53 | 215 | 186 | 27 | 47 | 69 | 9 | 2 | 3 | 29 | 1 | 2 | 5 | 21 | 0 | 49 | 1 | 2 | 4 | .253 | .341 | .371 |
| Pickrel, Jeremy, Elizabethton * | 49 | 207 | 177 | 28 | 47 | 73 | 10 | 2 | 4 | 27 | 0 | 3 | 0 | 27 | 0 | 61 | 5 | 4 | 2 | .266 | .357 | .412 |
| Pietch, Seth, Kingsport | 56 | 241 | 206 | 44 | 60 | 109 | 6 | 5 | 11 | 45 | 1 | 5 | 7 | 22 | 3 | 37 | 9 | 2 | 2 | .291 | .371 | .529 |
| Plouffe, Trevor, Elizabethton | 60 | 264 | 237 | 29 | 67 | 90 | 7 | 2 | 4 | 28 | 2 | 3 | 3 | 19 | 1 | 34 | 2 | 1 | 4 | .283 | .340 | .380 |
| Ponce, Angel, Danville | 22 | 47 | 43 | 6 | 13 | 13 | 0 | 0 | 0 | 4 | 2 | 0 | 0 | 2 | 0 | 13 | 1 | 2 | 0 | .302 | .333 | .302 |
| Pope, Van, Danville | 60 | 261 | 233 | 39 | 63 | 100 | 18 | 2 | 5 | 39 | 0 | 4 | 13 | 11 | 0 | 44 | 5 | 1 | 6 | .270 | .333 | .429 |
| Puente, Juan, Bluefield | 15 | 58 | 49 | 4 | 7 | 10 | 3 | 0 | 0 | 6 | 0 | 0 | 0 | 9 | 0 | 21 | 0 | 0 | 1 | .143 | .276 | .204 |
| Pulley, Matthew, Bluefield * | 62 | 252 | 225 | 25 | 57 | 86 | 18 | 1 | 3 | 25 | 2 | 4 | 1 | 20 | 1 | 52 | 1 | 2 | 8 | .253 | .312 | .382 |
| Reed, Ryan, Greeneville * | 48 | 197 | 172 | 34 | 39 | 52 | 7 | 0 | 2 | 20 | 1 | 0 | 0 | 24 | 0 | 40 | 9 | 5 | 1 | .227 | .321 | .302 |
| Ritchie, Jake, Princeton | 47 | 192 | 167 | 31 | 48 | 79 | 13 | 0 | 6 | 28 | 0 | 0 | 4 | 21 | 0 | 50 | 4 | 1 | 3 | .287 | .380 | .473 |
| Roberts, Joshua, Burlington * | 17 | 49 | 41 | 4 | 8 | 8 | 0 | 0 | 0 | 4 | 0 | 2 | 1 | 5 | 0 | 15 | 2 | 0 | 1 | .195 | .286 | .195 |
| Rodriguez, Edward, Pulaski | 20 | 4 | 4 | 1 | 2 | 4 | 2 | 0 | 0 | 3 | 0 | 0 | 0 | 0 | 0 | 1 | 0 | 0 | 0 | .500 | .500 | 1.000 |
| Rodriguez, Manuel, Bristol | 38 | 149 | 140 | 16 | 31 | 58 | 6 | 3 | 5 | 13 | 0 | 1 | 3 | 5 | 2 | 44 | 1 | 1 | 2 | .221 | .262 | .414 |
| Rodriquez, Yuber, Pulaski † | 62 | 285 | 245 | 49 | 75 | 124 | 13 | 6 | 8 | 50 | 1 | 2 | 9 | 28 | 3 | 70 | 9 | 3 | 5 | .306 | .394 | .506 |
| Romak, Jamie, Danville | 48 | 183 | 158 | 25 | 30 | 52 | 5 | 1 | 5 | 22 | 2 | 1 | 8 | 14 | 1 | 56 | 1 | 1 | 4 | .190 | .287 | .329 |
| Rousseve, Brandon, Princeton | 50 | 210 | 183 | 26 | 38 | 49 | 5 | 3 | 0 | 12 | 1 | 0 | 8 | 18 | 1 | 57 | 13 | 3 | 2 | .208 | .306 | .268 |
| Royster, Ryan, Princeton | 52 | 187 | 176 | 25 | 48 | 77 | 10 | 2 | 5 | 26 | 2 | 2 | 2 | 5 | 0 | 47 | 3 | 3 | 1 | .273 | .297 | .438 |
| Rozema, Mike, Danville * | 49 | 177 | 156 | 31 | 44 | 62 | 10 | 1 | 2 | 19 | 3 | 0 | 2 | 15 | 0 | 32 | 5 | 2 | 2 | .282 | .353 | .397 |
| Salgado, Eduardo, Bristol | 2 | 5 | 4 | 0 | 1 | 1 | 0 | 0 | 0 | 1 | 0 | 0 | 0 | 1 | 0 | 2 | 0 | 0 | 0 | .250 | .400 | .250 |
| Sammons, Clint, Danville | 40 | 153 | 132 | 19 | 38 | 49 | 7 | 2 | 0 | 17 | 1 | 2 | 0 | 18 | 1 | 26 | 5 | 1 | 3 | .288 | .368 | .371 |
| Sanchez, Javi, Elizabethton | 43 | 165 | 144 | 19 | 39 | 57 | 8 | 2 | 2 | 17 | 0 | 0 | 5 | 16 | 0 | 20 | 0 | 0 | 2 | .271 | .364 | .396 |
| Santana, Jeudy, Bristol | 32 | 71 | 64 | 7 | 15 | 20 | 3 | 1 | 0 | 6 | 0 | 0 | 2 | 5 | 0 | 23 | 1 | 3 | 0 | .234 | .310 | .313 |
| Santana, Luis, Kingsport | 16 | 58 | 46 | 7 | 5 | 8 | 0 | 0 | 1 | 2 | 3 | 0 | 0 | 9 | 0 | 14 | 1 | 0 | 2 | .109 | .255 | .174 |
| Santos, Jose, Bristol | 1 | 5 | 4 | 1 | 1 | 1 | 0 | 0 | 0 | 0 | 0 | 0 | 1 | 0 | 0 | 0 | 0 | 0 | 0 | .250 | .400 | .250 |
| Schmidt, J.J., Bristol | 47 | 156 | 140 | 17 | 34 | 52 | 12 | 0 | 2 | 19 | 2 | 2 | 1 | 11 | 0 | 29 | 2 | 3 | 6 | .243 | .299 | .371 |
| Schultz, Blake, Princeton | 42 | 160 | 141 | 20 | 41 | 52 | 3 | 1 | 2 | 14 | 1 | 1 | 1 | 16 | 1 | 27 | 5 | 0 | 5 | .291 | .365 | .369 |
| Schwarze, Brian, Johnson City | 22 | 33 | 28 | 3 | 2 | 2 | 0 | 0 | 0 | 1 | 0 | 0 | 2 | 3 | 0 | 10 | 1 | 0 | 0 | .071 | .212 | .071 |
| Scott, Lorenzo, Bluefield * | 62 | 251 | 219 | 36 | 52 | 69 | 6 | 1 | 3 | 16 | 4 | 1 | 0 | 27 | 0 | 75 | 12 | 2 | 3 | .237 | .320 | .315 |
| Sellers, Patrick, Greeneville | 50 | 187 | 158 | 23 | 45 | 62 | 11 | 0 | 2 | 30 | 1 | 1 | 4 | 23 | 0 | 30 | 3 | 4 | 2 | .285 | .387 | .392 |
| Sena, Emmanuel, Pulaski † | 53 | 199 | 162 | 24 | 39 | 50 | 2 | 3 | 1 | 15 | 3 | 1 | 4 | 29 | 0 | 53 | 1 | 4 | 3 | .241 | .367 | .309 |
| Shafer, Dustin, Bristol | 49 | 169 | 159 | 19 | 31 | 43 | 6 | 0 | 2 | 9 | 0 | 2 | 3 | 5 | 2 | 33 | 2 | 0 | 2 | .195 | .231 | .270 |
| Sheldon, Ole, Greeneville | 54 | 186 | 166 | 23 | 36 | 51 | 4 | 1 | 3 | 19 | 2 | 2 | 2 | 14 | 0 | 23 | 7 | 0 | 3 | .217 | .283 | .307 |
| Shelley, Shane, Princeton † | 6 | 21 | 19 | 3 | 3 | 3 | 0 | 0 | 0 | 1 | 0 | 0 | 2 | 0 | 0 | 10 | 1 | 1 | 0 | .158 | .238 | .158 |
| Sivira, Yonathan, Johnson City | 44 | 147 | 137 | 19 | 40 | 62 | 10 | 3 | 2 | 18 | 1 | 1 | 5 | 3 | 0 | 21 | 2 | 2 | 3 | .292 | .329 | .453 |
| Spilman, Ryan, Burlington | 33 | 109 | 98 | 7 | 19 | 20 | 1 | 0 | 0 | 4 | 0 | 2 | 2 | 7 | 0 | 24 | 1 | 0 | 4 | .194 | .257 | .204 |
| Sutil, Wladimir, Greeneville | 53 | 222 | 188 | 31 | 56 | 65 | 9 | 0 | 0 | 29 | 7 | 3 | 7 | 17 | 1 | 24 | 24 | 8 | 2 | .298 | .372 | .346 |
| Swain, Michael, Bristol * | 40 | 126 | 112 | 19 | 31 | 45 | 5 | 0 | 3 | 17 | 2 | 1 | 1 | 10 | 0 | 22 | 1 | 0 | 2 | .277 | .339 | .402 |
| Tartaglia, Evan, Bristol * | 59 | 244 | 191 | 39 | 49 | 61 | 6 | 3 | 0 | 16 | 1 | 1 | 5 | 46 | 0 | 52 | 19 | 8 | 1 | .257 | .412 | .319 |
| Thomas, Nick, Pulaski * | 55 | 241 | 193 | 33 | 54 | 90 | 12 | 0 | 8 | 43 | 0 | 3 | 3 | 42 | 2 | 50 | 0 | 0 | 3 | .280 | .411 | .466 |
| Tobert, Wallace, Greeneville | 23 | 88 | 74 | 11 | 16 | 17 | 1 | 0 | 0 | 8 | 1 | 0 | 1 | 12 | 0 | 22 | 4 | 3 | 0 | .216 | .333 | .230 |
| Tolbert, Matt, Elizabethton † | 33 | 118 | 104 | 23 | 32 | 52 | 7 | 2 | 3 | 18 | 1 | 1 | 0 | 12 | 0 | 13 | 3 | 2 | 4 | .308 | .376 | .500 |
| Torbert, Wallace, Greeneville | 12 | 41 | 37 | 7 | 9 | 11 | 2 | 0 | 0 | 7 | 0 | 1 | 2 | 1 | 0 | 8 | 2 | 1 | 0 | .243 | .293 | .297 |
| Towles, Justin, Greeneville | 39 | 136 | 111 | 17 | 27 | 33 | 6 | 0 | 0 | 8 | 1 | 1 | 11 | 12 | 0 | 23 | 4 | 3 | 1 | .243 | .370 | .297 |
| Triplett, Bryan, Greeneville | 44 | 178 | 147 | 31 | 41 | 57 | 11 | 1 | 1 | 18 | 0 | 1 | 4 | 26 | 0 | 32 | 9 | 5 | 4 | .279 | .399 | .388 |
| Triplett, Russ, Kingsport | 52 | 230 | 198 | 32 | 57 | 75 | 13 | 1 | 1 | 13 | 4 | 3 | 5 | 20 | 0 | 31 | 2 | 4 | 4 | .288 | .363 | .379 |
| Tucker, Jonathan, Bluefield | 16 | 63 | 56 | 7 | 14 | 17 | 3 | 0 | 0 | 1 | 3 | 0 | 1 | 3 | 0 | 12 | 1 | 1 | 3 | .250 | .300 | .304 |
| Uhle, Christopher, Greeneville | 37 | 122 | 98 | 17 | 21 | 28 | 7 | 0 | 0 | 7 | 3 | 1 | 2 | 18 | 0 | 35 | 4 | 0 | 5 | .214 | .345 | .286 |
| Vasquez, Domingo, Burlington | 47 | 167 | 160 | 8 | 33 | 41 | 8 | 0 | 0 | 17 | 2 | 1 | 1 | 3 | 0 | 37 | 2 | 1 | 2 | .206 | .224 | .256 |
| Wiens, Logan, Princeton | 42 | 156 | 144 | 13 | 25 | 34 | 6 | 0 | 1 | 13 | 3 | 2 | 0 | 7 | 0 | 44 | 1 | 0 | 5 | .174 | .209 | .236 |
| Wiggins, Bradford, Bluefield * | 49 | 187 | 163 | 26 | 43 | 74 | 9 | 2 | 6 | 22 | 2 | 0 | 5 | 17 | 1 | 59 | 7 | 4 | 2 | .264 | .351 | .454 |
| Williams, Simon, Johnson City | 46 | 152 | 136 | 19 | 37 | 53 | 3 | 2 | 3 | 17 | 1 | 0 | 2 | 13 | 0 | 51 | 8 | 1 | 2 | .272 | .344 | .390 |

| Player, Team | G | TPA | AB | R | H | TB | 2B | 3B | HR | RBI | SH | SF | HP | BB | IBB | SO | SB | CS | GDP | Avg. | OBP | Slg. |
|---|---|---|---|---|---|---|---|---|---|---|---|---|---|---|---|---|---|---|---|---|---|---|
| Winfree, David, Elizabethton | 59 | 241 | 217 | 31 | 62 | 94 | 8 | 0 | 8 | 37 | 0 | 2 | 4 | 18 | 1 | 51 | 1 | 1 | 7 | .286 | .349 | .433 |
| Woodard, Johnny, Elizabethton * | 57 | 223 | 194 | 37 | 60 | 100 | 8 | 4 | 8 | 35 | 0 | 3 | 2 | 24 | 0 | 56 | 5 | 2 | 2 | .309 | .386 | .515 |
| Woodson, Mike, Burlington | 32 | 105 | 94 | 6 | 20 | 23 | 3 | 0 | 0 | 7 | 4 | 1 | 1 | 5 | 3 | 27 | 0 | 1 | 1 | .213 | .257 | .245 |
| Wyrick, Joshua, Kingsport * | 60 | 282 | 254 | 41 | 73 | 102 | 9 | 4 | 4 | 24 | 4 | 3 | 5 | 16 | 0 | 53 | 13 | 7 | 1 | .287 | .338 | .402 |
| Yaconetti, Jay, Elizabethton | 34 | 117 | 107 | 17 | 24 | 43 | 7 | 0 | 4 | 19 | 0 | 3 | 2 | 5 | 0 | 41 | 1 | 0 | 2 | .224 | .265 | .402 |
| Yarbrough, Brandon, Johnson City * | 48 | 202 | 175 | 37 | 57 | 87 | 10 | 1 | 6 | 33 | 0 | 1 | 1 | 25 | 1 | 55 | 3 | 1 | 3 | .326 | .411 | .497 |
| Zapata, Jose, Bluefield | 29 | 96 | 91 | 8 | 20 | 24 | 4 | 0 | 0 | 13 | 0 | 1 | 1 | 3 | 0 | 28 | 2 | 1 | 1 | .220 | .250 | .264 |
| Zech, Bryan, Kingsport | 25 | 96 | 90 | 16 | 21 | 33 | 6 | 0 | 2 | 10 | 0 | 0 | 3 | 3 | 0 | 27 | 3 | 1 | 2 | .233 | .281 | .367 |

GRAND SLAMS—Arroyo, Ashford, Becher, Chourio, Einertson, Foust, Garcia, Gomez, Hetherington, Moreta, Y. Rodriguez, Winfree, Yaconetti, 1 each.

AWARDED FIRST BASE ON CATCHER'S INTERFERENCE—J. Hernandez 2 (F. Hernandez, F. Hernandez); Rozema 2 (Bormaster, Markel); B. Jones (Woodson); Jurich (Spilman); Sammons (Bormaster); Sutil (F. Hernandez).

# 2004 PITCHING

## TEAM

| Team | W | L | Pct. | ERA | G | CG | ShO | Sv. | IP | H | TBF | R | ER | HR | SH | SF | HB | BB | IBB | SO | WP | Bk. |
|---|---|---|---|---|---|---|---|---|---|---|---|---|---|---|---|---|---|---|---|---|---|---|
| Pulaski | 40 | 27 | .597 | 3.77 | 67 | 0 | 5 | 10 | 587.1 | 579 | 2562 | 300 | 246 | 42 | 19 | 18 | 54 | 211 | 20 | 575 | 48 | 10 |
| Greeneville | 41 | 26 | .612 | 3.78 | 67 | 1 | 4 | 19 | 576.0 | 549 | 2500 | 296 | 242 | 34 | 12 | 23 | 31 | 222 | 4 | 516 | 45 | 7 |
| Danville | 41 | 25 | .621 | 3.85 | 66 | 1 | 5 | 15 | 575.2 | 542 | 2459 | 290 | 246 | 36 | 20 | 17 | 31 | 177 | 5 | 560 | 42 | 5 |
| Elizabethton | 38 | 29 | .567 | 4.22 | 67 | 0 | 4 | 18 | 571.0 | 560 | 2476 | 323 | 268 | 55 | 18 | 19 | 37 | 200 | 7 | 614 | 57 | 6 |
| Burlington | 31 | 35 | .470 | 4.25 | 66 | 0 | 3 | 16 | 561.2 | 554 | 2403 | 307 | 265 | 45 | 12 | 19 | 59 | 172 | 4 | 535 | 39 | 4 |
| Bluefield | 28 | 39 | .418 | 4.27 | 67 | 0 | 1 | 13 | 582.1 | 599 | 2587 | 354 | 276 | 56 | 16 | 15 | 45 | 247 | 8 | 554 | 58 | 10 |
| Kingsport | 32 | 36 | .471 | 4.48 | 68 | 1 | 2 | 12 | 584.2 | 620 | 2621 | 360 | 291 | 44 | 27 | 23 | 66 | 190 | 0 | 544 | 74 | 5 |
| Bristol | 27 | 38 | .415 | 4.85 | 65 | 0 | 4 | 11 | 562.1 | 534 | 2553 | 381 | 303 | 44 | 20 | 25 | 60 | 311 | 14 | 532 | 78 | 6 |
| Johnson City | 33 | 35 | .485 | 4.94 | 68 | 0 | 4 | 10 | 590.0 | 594 | 2630 | 393 | 324 | 63 | 16 | 30 | 41 | 262 | 4 | 524 | 56 | 6 |
| Princeton | 23 | 44 | .343 | 5.80 | 67 | 0 | 1 | 9 | 573.0 | 665 | 2730 | 474 | 369 | 66 | 20 | 28 | 36 | 346 | 7 | 515 | 93 | 12 |

## INDIVIDUAL

### TOP QUALIFIERS FOR EARNED-RUN AVERAGE TITLE

Minimum 54 innings. *Lefthanded pitcher.

| Pitcher, Team | W | L | Pct. | ERA | G | GS | CG | ShO | GF | Sv. | IP | H | TBF | R | ER | HR | SH | SF | HB | BB | IBB | SO | WP | Bk. |
|---|---|---|---|---|---|---|---|---|---|---|---|---|---|---|---|---|---|---|---|---|---|---|---|---|
| Timm, Jordan, Pulaski * | 3 | 1 | .750 | 2.67 | 11 | 11 | 0 | 0 | 0 | 0 | 60.2 | 59 | 243 | 22 | 18 | 8 | 3 | 1 | 4 | 12 | 0 | 53 | 1 | 0 |
| Cheng, Chi Hung, Pulaski * | 3 | 1 | .750 | 2.82 | 14 | 14 | 0 | 0 | 0 | 0 | 60.2 | 47 | 259 | 27 | 19 | 4 | 2 | 3 | 4 | 35 | 2 | 74 | 5 | 0 |
| Santos, Reid, Burlington | 3 | 5 | .375 | 3.07 | 11 | 11 | 0 | 0 | 0 | 0 | 58.2 | 48 | 236 | 26 | 20 | 3 | 1 | 3 | 5 | 17 | 1 | 60 | 4 | 0 |
| Rengel, Orlando, Kingsport | 5 | 4 | .556 | 3.26 | 14 | 13 | 1 | 0 | 1 | 0 | 69.0 | 52 | 281 | 27 | 25 | 3 | 3 | 3 | 4 | 18 | 0 | 63 | 8 | 0 |
| Vines, Chris, Danville | 6 | 3 | .667 | 3.28 | 13 | 10 | 0 | 0 | 0 | 0 | 60.1 | 58 | 249 | 25 | 22 | 2 | 1 | 0 | 4 | 14 | 0 | 72 | 1 | 1 |
| Duguay, Steven, Elizabethton | 4 | 4 | .500 | 3.36 | 12 | 11 | 0 | 0 | 0 | 0 | 56.1 | 55 | 230 | 28 | 21 | 5 | 2 | 1 | 6 | 11 | 0 | 70 | 1 | 0 |
| Martin, Adrian, Pulaski | 3 | 2 | .600 | 3.54 | 18 | 7 | 0 | 0 | 1 | 0 | 56.0 | 65 | 243 | 28 | 22 | 2 | 2 | 3 | 2 | 12 | 4 | 51 | 1 | 0 |
| Marshall, Jay, Bristol | 1 | 6 | .143 | 3.59 | 11 | 11 | 0 | 0 | 0 | 0 | 57.2 | 63 | 241 | 31 | 23 | 8 | 4 | 2 | 2 | 8 | 1 | 52 | 4 | 1 |
| Gutierrez, Juan, Greeneville | 8 | 2 | .800 | 3.70 | 13 | 13 | 0 | 0 | 0 | 0 | 65.2 | 74 | 294 | 31 | 27 | 4 | 3 | 2 | 7 | 30 | 0 | 59 | 6 | 0 |
| Barthmaier, Jimmy, Greeneville | 4 | 3 | .571 | 3.78 | 13 | 13 | 0 | 0 | 0 | 0 | 69.0 | 70 | 295 | 32 | 29 | 3 | 3 | 2 | 1 | 22 | 0 | 65 | 3 | 1 |
| McGee, Jacob, Princeton * | 4 | 1 | .800 | 3.97 | 12 | 12 | 0 | 0 | 0 | 0 | 56.2 | 49 | 233 | 30 | 25 | 5 | 3 | 4 | 0 | 25 | 1 | 53 | 5 | 0 |
| Andersen, Phillip, Johnson City | 5 | 1 | .833 | 4.01 | 13 | 13 | 0 | 0 | 0 | 0 | 60.2 | 55 | 256 | 30 | 27 | 8 | 4 | 3 | 7 | 26 | 0 | 52 | 2 | 1 |
| Scherer, Matthew, Johnson City | 2 | 5 | .286 | 4.03 | 13 | 12 | 0 | 0 | 0 | 0 | 60.1 | 62 | 256 | 36 | 27 | 7 | 1 | 1 | 2 | 16 | 0 | 43 | 6 | 0 |
| Fry, Troy, Kingsport | 5 | 2 | .714 | 4.06 | 14 | 8 | 0 | 0 | 1 | 0 | 57.2 | 68 | 247 | 29 | 26 | 3 | 4 | 1 | 5 | 7 | 0 | 49 | 5 | 1 |
| Harrison, Matt, Danville * | 4 | 4 | .500 | 4.09 | 13 | 12 | 1 | 0 | 0 | 0 | 66.0 | 72 | 278 | 36 | 30 | 3 | 4 | 4 | 1 | 10 | 1 | 49 | 3 | 1 |

DEPARTMENTAL LEADERS: W—Gutierrez, Romero, 8; L—Limas, 9; Pct.—Three tied with .833; G—Mata, 26; GS—Cheng, 14; CG—Three tied with one; ShO—None; GF—Mata, Soto, 23; Sv.—Soto, 13; IP—Barthmaier, Rengel, 69.0; H—Furrow, 75; TBF—Barthmaier, 295; R—Limas, 54; ER—Limas, 41; HR—Mercedes, 9; SH—Four tied with four; SF—Pleeter, 8; HB—Weitzman, 16; BB—Casey, 41; IBB—Martin, 4; SO—Cheng, 74; WP—Lemon, 13; BK—Three tied with three.

### ALL PITCHERS

*Lefthanded pitcher.

| Pitcher, Team | W | L | Pct. | ERA | G | GS | CG | ShO | GF | Sv. | IP | H | TBF | R | ER | HR | SH | SF | HB | BB | IBB | SO | WP | Bk. |
|---|---|---|---|---|---|---|---|---|---|---|---|---|---|---|---|---|---|---|---|---|---|---|---|---|
| Alwert, Garrett, Burlington * | 4 | 4 | .500 | 6.06 | 14 | 9 | 0 | 0 | 0 | 0 | 52.0 | 73 | 232 | 36 | 35 | 5 | 1 | 0 | 3 | 7 | 0 | 51 | 1 | 0 |
| Amaya, Jose, Burlington | 2 | 2 | .500 | 4.82 | 12 | 3 | 0 | 0 | 0 | 0 | 46.2 | 48 | 199 | 26 | 25 | 4 | 0 | 0 | 4 | 20 | 0 | 40 | 6 | 0 |
| Andersen, Phillip, Johnson City | 5 | 1 | .833 | 4.01 | 13 | 13 | 0 | 0 | 0 | 0 | 60.2 | 55 | 256 | 30 | 27 | 8 | 4 | 3 | 7 | 26 | 0 | 52 | 2 | 1 |
| Arguello, Douglas, Greeneville * | 1 | 0 | 1.000 | 2.92 | 16 | 0 | 0 | 0 | 6 | 0 | 24.2 | 16 | 105 | 8 | 8 | 1 | 0 | 0 | 2 | 13 | 0 | 22 | 1 | 1 |
| Aselton, Kyle, Elizabethton * | 1 | 4 | .200 | 4.54 | 15 | 4 | 0 | 0 | 6 | 1 | 37.2 | 30 | 160 | 21 | 19 | 3 | 0 | 3 | 2 | 19 | 1 | 38 | 5 | 0 |
| Atilano, Luis, Danville | 5 | 1 | .833 | 4.20 | 13 | 13 | 0 | 0 | 0 | 0 | 64.1 | 64 | 268 | 32 | 30 | 7 | 4 | 3 | 5 | 10 | 0 | 54 | 0 | 0 |
| Avila, Angel, Bluefield | 0 | 0 | .000 | 0.00 | 1 | 0 | 0 | 0 | 0 | 0 | 1.2 | 2 | 8 | 0 | 0 | 0 | 0 | 0 | 0 | 1 | 0 | 3 | 1 | 0 |
| Bacot, Paul, Danville | 3 | 1 | .750 | 4.70 | 13 | 13 | 0 | 0 | 0 | 0 | 61.1 | 60 | 257 | 40 | 32 | 6 | 6 | 3 | 2 | 14 | 0 | 38 | 3 | 1 |
| Barthmaier, Jimmy, Greeneville | 4 | 3 | .571 | 3.78 | 13 | 13 | 0 | 0 | 0 | 0 | 69.0 | 70 | 295 | 32 | 29 | 3 | 3 | 2 | 1 | 22 | 0 | 65 | 3 | 1 |
| Bastardo, Alberto, Bluefield * | 1 | 1 | .500 | 1.86 | 3 | 2 | 0 | 0 | 1 | 1 | 9.2 | 9 | 42 | 3 | 2 | 0 | 0 | 0 | 0 | 4 | 0 | 10 | 1 | 0 |
| Bell, Bryon, Pulaski | 0 | 0 | .000 | 27.00 | 1 | 0 | 0 | 0 | 1 | 0 | 1.0 | 3 | 6 | 3 | 3 | 1 | 0 | 0 | 0 | 0 | 0 | 2 | 0 | 0 |
| Bello, Juan, Bristol | 3 | 1 | .750 | 4.22 | 18 | 1 | 0 | 0 | 6 | 0 | 42.2 | 31 | 191 | 28 | 20 | 1 | 1 | 0 | 5 | 30 | 0 | 46 | 7 | 1 |
| Bergesen, Bradley, Bluefield | 0 | 0 | .000 | 7.94 | 5 | 0 | 0 | 0 | 0 | 0 | 5.2 | 7 | 27 | 5 | 5 | 1 | 0 | 0 | 0 | 3 | 1 | 6 | 0 | 0 |
| Berroa, Yesson, Pulaski | 3 | 3 | .500 | 6.00 | 10 | 9 | 0 | 0 | 0 | 0 | 36.0 | 51 | 173 | 28 | 24 | 3 | 2 | 3 | 6 | 12 | 0 | 32 | 8 | 0 |
| Bowlin, Jason, Elizabethton | 1 | 3 | .250 | 3.25 | 23 | 0 | 0 | 0 | 13 | 3 | 27.2 | 26 | 118 | 13 | 10 | 1 | 0 | 0 | 1 | 8 | 2 | 27 | 1 | 0 |
| Brehm, Derek, Princeton * | 1 | 0 | 1.000 | 11.81 | 6 | 0 | 0 | 0 | 1 | 0 | 5.1 | 8 | 35 | 9 | 7 | 0 | 0 | 0 | 1 | 10 | 0 | 4 | 3 | 0 |
| Brewer, Jeff, Kingsport | 5 | 3 | .625 | 3.83 | 17 | 2 | 0 | 0 | 7 | 4 | 51.2 | 54 | 230 | 24 | 22 | 4 | 0 | 2 | 4 | 17 | 0 | 52 | 9 | 0 |
| Brnardic, Ryan, Bluefield | 3 | 1 | .750 | 3.67 | 17 | 1 | 0 | 0 | 7 | 1 | 41.2 | 39 | 180 | 19 | 17 | 3 | 1 | 0 | 1 | 17 | 0 | 35 | 2 | 2 |
| Brock, Kenneth, Princeton * | 0 | 4 | .000 | 10.13 | 14 | 2 | 0 | 0 | 1 | 0 | 24.0 | 46 | 133 | 32 | 27 | 3 | 2 | 0 | 1 | 14 | 2 | 19 | 2 | 0 |
| Brown, Justin, Johnson City | 2 | 4 | .333 | 6.66 | 8 | 8 | 0 | 0 | 0 | 0 | 25.2 | 28 | 122 | 20 | 19 | 1 | 0 | 1 | 3 | 19 | 0 | 19 | 2 | 0 |
| Bunkelman, Cody, Burlington | 2 | 1 | .667 | 6.53 | 17 | 0 | 0 | 0 | 5 | 0 | 30.1 | 32 | 139 | 26 | 22 | 3 | 0 | 0 | 5 | 11 | 0 | 23 | 6 | 0 |

| Pitcher, Team | W | L | Pct. | ERA | G | GS | CG | ShO | GF | Sv. | IP | H | TBF | R | ER | HR | SH | SF | HB | BB | IBB | SO | WP | Bk. |
|---|---|---|---|---|---|---|---|---|---|---|---|---|---|---|---|---|---|---|---|---|---|---|---|---|
| Cannon, Edward, Pulaski | 4 | 0 | 1.000 | 2.87 | 18 | 0 | 0 | 0 | 4 | 0 | 37.2 | 35 | 163 | 16 | 12 | 3 | 0 | 0 | 4 | 11 | 3 | 38 | 0 | 2 |
| Capellan, Domingo, Johnson City | 2 | 3 | .400 | 6.16 | 25 | 0 | 0 | 0 | 10 | 1 | 30.2 | 27 | 134 | 24 | 21 | 3 | 0 | 0 | 1 | 14 | 0 | 30 | 5 | 0 |
| Casey, James, Bristol | 1 | 4 | .200 | 7.61 | 12 | 9 | 0 | 0 | 0 | 0 | 36.2 | 30 | 181 | 34 | 31 | 1 | 3 | 3 | 7 | 41 | 1 | 42 | 11 | 0 |
| Cayton, Jason, Princeton | 0 | 0 | .000 | 81.00 | 1 | 0 | 0 | 0 | 0 | 0 | 0.1 | 3 | 5 | 4 | 3 | 0 | 0 | 0 | 0 | 1 | 0 | 0 | 0 | 0 |
| Chacin, Steward, Johnson City | 0 | 0 | .000 | 13.50 | 1 | 0 | 0 | 0 | 1 | 0 | 1.1 | 2 | 10 | 3 | 2 | 0 | 0 | 0 | 0 | 4 | 0 | 1 | 0 | 0 |
| Charron, Joey, Pulaski * | 0 | 1 | .000 | 3.18 | 8 | 0 | 0 | 0 | 4 | 0 | 11.1 | 7 | 48 | 4 | 4 | 0 | 0 | 0 | 1 | 6 | 0 | 9 | 3 | 0 |
| Chedister, Bradley, Greeneville | 0 | 0 | .000 | 10.20 | 11 | 0 | 0 | 0 | 2 | 0 | 15.0 | 15 | 83 | 20 | 17 | 2 | 0 | 0 | 3 | 20 | 0 | 11 | 1 | 0 |
| Cheng, Chi-hung, Pulaski * | 3 | 1 | .750 | 2.82 | 14 | 14 | 0 | 0 | 0 | 0 | 60.2 | 47 | 259 | 27 | 19 | 4 | 2 | 3 | 4 | 35 | 2 | 74 | 5 | 0 |
| Clark, John, Burlington | 0 | 0 | .000 | 0.00 | 1 | 0 | 0 | 0 | 1 | 0 | 1.0 | 2 | 5 | 0 | 0 | 0 | 0 | 0 | 0 | 0 | 0 | 1 | 0 | 0 |
| Collins, Danny, Danville * | 2 | 1 | .667 | 4.55 | 11 | 2 | 0 | 0 | 6 | 0 | 27.2 | 25 | 114 | 17 | 14 | 5 | 0 | 2 | 0 | 5 | 0 | 18 | 1 | 0 |
| Collins, Kyle, Burlington | 3 | 0 | 1.000 | 2.12 | 4 | 3 | 0 | 0 | 0 | 0 | 17.0 | 12 | 59 | 4 | 4 | 0 | 0 | 0 | 0 | 3 | 0 | 17 | 3 | 0 |
| Cuevas, Jairo, Danville | 0 | 0 | .000 | 0.00 | 1 | 1 | 0 | 0 | 0 | 0 | 4.0 | 1 | 17 | 0 | 0 | 0 | 0 | 0 | 0 | 4 | 0 | 3 | 1 | 0 |
| Culpepper, Kevin, Elizabethton * | 0 | 3 | .000 | 5.29 | 9 | 0 | 0 | 0 | 3 | 0 | 17.0 | 18 | 77 | 12 | 10 | 2 | 0 | 0 | 1 | 7 | 1 | 20 | 0 | 0 |
| Davern, Michael, Bristol | 0 | 0 | .000 | 6.75 | 11 | 0 | 0 | 0 | 8 | 1 | 13.1 | 13 | 62 | 11 | 10 | 3 | 0 | 0 | 1 | 8 | 0 | 21 | 5 | 0 |
| Davis, Cliff, Greeneville | 0 | 1 | .000 | 3.60 | 5 | 5 | 0 | 0 | 0 | 0 | 25.0 | 29 | 115 | 13 | 10 | 3 | 2 | 3 | 1 | 8 | 0 | 19 | 3 | 1 |
| Davis, Wade, Princeton | 3 | 5 | .375 | 6.09 | 13 | 13 | 0 | 0 | 0 | 0 | 57.2 | 71 | 264 | 46 | 39 | 8 | 1 | 6 | 2 | 19 | 0 | 38 | 3 | 0 |
| Dickerson, Bo, Johnson City | 0 | 1 | .000 | 6.00 | 3 | 2 | 0 | 0 | 1 | 0 | 6.0 | 4 | 27 | 6 | 4 | 0 | 0 | 0 | 0 | 5 | 0 | 6 | 4 | 0 |
| Dobyns, Jon, Princeton | 2 | 3 | .400 | 2.78 | 11 | 0 | 0 | 0 | 1 | 0 | 22.2 | 25 | 104 | 11 | 7 | 1 | 0 | 0 | 1 | 10 | 1 | 20 | 6 | 0 |
| Duguay, Steven, Elizabethton | 4 | 4 | .500 | 3.36 | 12 | 11 | 0 | 0 | 0 | 0 | 56.1 | 55 | 230 | 28 | 21 | 5 | 2 | 1 | 6 | 11 | 0 | 70 | 1 | 0 |
| Endl, Brady, Danville * | 2 | 3 | .400 | 2.79 | 16 | 0 | 0 | 0 | 10 | 1 | 29.0 | 24 | 123 | 10 | 9 | 1 | 0 | 0 | 3 | 9 | 2 | 36 | 8 | 0 |
| Evers, William, Princeton | 2 | 2 | .500 | 7.53 | 21 | 0 | 0 | 0 | 6 | 0 | 34.2 | 44 | 180 | 37 | 29 | 4 | 0 | 0 | 1 | 31 | 0 | 24 | 10 | 1 |
| Fox, Matt, Elizabethton | 2 | 1 | .667 | 5.40 | 8 | 5 | 0 | 0 | 0 | 0 | 26.2 | 27 | 111 | 18 | 16 | 6 | 1 | 0 | 0 | 8 | 0 | 32 | 4 | 0 |
| Fry, Troy, Kingsport | 5 | 2 | .714 | 4.06 | 14 | 8 | 0 | 0 | 1 | 0 | 57.2 | 68 | 247 | 29 | 26 | 3 | 4 | 1 | 5 | 7 | 0 | 49 | 5 | 1 |
| Furrow, Jason, Bluefield * | 1 | 2 | .333 | 4.74 | 13 | 13 | 0 | 0 | 0 | 0 | 57.0 | 75 | 247 | 40 | 30 | 8 | 4 | 3 | 1 | 15 | 0 | 31 | 4 | 2 |
| Gabino Garcia, Armando, Burlington | 0 | 1 | .000 | 4.26 | 5 | 4 | 0 | 0 | 0 | 0 | 19.0 | 20 | 85 | 13 | 9 | 1 | 1 | 2 | 3 | 5 | 0 | 12 | 0 | 0 |
| Gale, Bryan, Pulaski | 1 | 3 | .250 | 6.28 | 12 | 0 | 0 | 0 | 3 | 0 | 14.1 | 13 | 66 | 11 | 10 | 2 | 0 | 0 | 2 | 8 | 2 | 19 | 1 | 0 |
| Geddes, Michael, Princeton | 0 | 1 | .000 | 4.15 | 9 | 0 | 0 | 0 | 4 | 0 | 13.0 | 8 | 58 | 6 | 6 | 1 | 0 | 0 | 3 | 9 | 0 | 14 | 1 | 0 |
| Gil, Roberto, Princeton | 0 | 1 | .000 | 9.45 | 10 | 0 | 0 | 0 | 3 | 0 | 13.1 | 17 | 65 | 16 | 14 | 2 | 0 | 0 | 0 | 8 | 0 | 17 | 2 | 0 |
| Gomez, Jose, Kingsport | 0 | 2 | .000 | 4.86 | 8 | 2 | 0 | 0 | 5 | 2 | 16.2 | 14 | 69 | 11 | 9 | 2 | 1 | 1 | 1 | 7 | 0 | 25 | 4 | 3 |
| Gomez, Luis, Johnson City | 0 | 1 | .000 | 4.60 | 12 | 0 | 0 | 0 | 3 | 0 | 15.2 | 16 | 68 | 9 | 8 | 4 | 0 | 0 | 2 | 3 | 0 | 17 | 0 | 1 |
| Gonzalez, Humberto, Kingsport | 0 | 0 | .000 | 6.35 | 2 | 0 | 0 | 0 | 0 | 0 | 5.2 | 10 | 29 | 6 | 4 | 0 | 0 | 0 | 1 | 1 | 0 | 5 | 1 | 0 |
| Gonzalez, Juan, Greeneville | 0 | 1 | .000 | 7.71 | 3 | 0 | 0 | 0 | 0 | 0 | 4.2 | 3 | 23 | 4 | 4 | 0 | 0 | 0 | 0 | 6 | 1 | 5 | 0 | 0 |
| Gonzalez, Marino, Kingsport | 1 | 2 | .333 | 11.40 | 6 | 1 | 0 | 0 | 4 | 0 | 15.0 | 30 | 81 | 20 | 19 | 2 | 0 | 0 | 1 | 5 | 0 | 13 | 3 | 0 |
| Grant, Brian, Pulaski | 3 | 1 | .750 | 2.94 | 10 | 9 | 0 | 0 | 0 | 0 | 49.0 | 54 | 209 | 23 | 16 | 3 | 2 | 1 | 5 | 12 | 0 | 29 | 4 | 2 |
| Gutierrez, Juan, Greeneville | 8 | 2 | .800 | 3.70 | 13 | 13 | 0 | 0 | 0 | 0 | 65.2 | 74 | 294 | 31 | 27 | 4 | 3 | 2 | 7 | 30 | 0 | 59 | 6 | 0 |
| Guzman, Angel, Burlington | 1 | 6 | .143 | 5.10 | 14 | 10 | 0 | 0 | 1 | 0 | 47.2 | 60 | 216 | 37 | 27 | 7 | 2 | 6 | 5 | 15 | 0 | 42 | 3 | 0 |
| Hahn, Cory, Pulaski | 0 | 0 | .000 | 5.40 | 3 | 0 | 0 | 0 | 0 | 0 | 3.1 | 5 | 15 | 2 | 2 | 1 | 0 | 0 | 0 | 0 | 0 | 3 | 1 | 0 |
| Harang, Daryl, Pulaski * | 3 | 1 | .750 | 4.50 | 16 | 0 | 0 | 0 | 8 | 0 | 22.0 | 16 | 89 | 11 | 11 | 1 | 2 | 1 | 1 | 7 | 1 | 24 | 2 | 0 |
| Harrell, Lucas, Bristol | 3 | 5 | .375 | 5.59 | 13 | 9 | 0 | 0 | 1 | 0 | 48.1 | 53 | 230 | 39 | 30 | 5 | 3 | 3 | 4 | 32 | 1 | 33 | 2 | 0 |
| Harris, Josh, Burlington | 2 | 0 | 1.000 | 1.41 | 19 | 0 | 0 | 0 | 13 | 7 | 32.0 | 22 | 127 | 6 | 5 | 1 | 0 | 0 | 3 | 6 | 1 | 40 | 2 | 0 |
| Harrison, Ben, Pulaski * | 0 | 0 | .000 | 0.00 | 4 | 0 | 0 | 0 | 1 | 0 | 3.1 | 4 | 18 | 0 | 0 | 0 | 0 | 0 | 0 | 4 | 0 | 9 | 0 | 0 |
| Harrison, Matt, Danville * | 4 | 4 | .500 | 4.09 | 13 | 12 | 1 | 0 | 0 | 0 | 66.0 | 72 | 278 | 36 | 30 | 3 | 4 | 4 | 1 | 10 | 1 | 49 | 3 | 1 |
| Henington, Justin, Bluefield | 0 | 3 | .000 | 3.73 | 16 | 0 | 0 | 0 | 9 | 1 | 31.1 | 30 | 143 | 22 | 13 | 2 | 1 | 1 | 4 | 13 | 2 | 39 | 3 | 0 |
| Hernandez, Moises, Bluefield | 2 | 5 | .286 | 5.07 | 13 | 13 | 0 | 0 | 0 | 0 | 60.1 | 63 | 265 | 42 | 34 | 4 | 5 | 2 | 7 | 27 | 0 | 43 | 3 | 0 |
| Holmes, Justin, Burlington | 0 | 0 | .000 | 0.00 | 1 | 1 | 0 | 0 | 0 | 0 | 6.0 | 4 | 23 | 1 | 0 | 0 | 1 | 1 | 1 | 0 | 0 | 7 | 0 | 0 |
| Honel, Kris, Bristol | 0 | 0 | .000 | 108.00 | 1 | 1 | 0 | 0 | 0 | 0 | 0.1 | 1 | 5 | 4 | 4 | 0 | 0 | 0 | 0 | 3 | 0 | 0 | 0 | 0 |
| James, Brad, Greeneville | 2 | 6 | .250 | 4.44 | 13 | 10 | 0 | 0 | 0 | 0 | 52.2 | 49 | 233 | 36 | 26 | 1 | 0 | 6 | 1 | 26 | 0 | 38 | 6 | 0 |
| Jimenez, Rodny, Danville | 1 | 1 | .500 | 3.72 | 15 | 0 | 0 | 0 | 9 | 2 | 29.0 | 26 | 129 | 13 | 12 | 1 | 0 | 0 | 3 | 15 | 0 | 41 | 5 | 0 |
| John, Jason, Johnson City | 1 | 2 | .333 | 4.38 | 9 | 0 | 0 | 0 | 2 | 0 | 12.1 | 11 | 58 | 8 | 6 | 1 | 0 | 0 | 3 | 7 | 2 | 17 | 1 | 0 |
| Johnson, Bryan, Danville * | 2 | 1 | .667 | 2.00 | 11 | 0 | 0 | 0 | 4 | 2 | 18.0 | 15 | 78 | 6 | 4 | 0 | 0 | 0 | 2 | 7 | 1 | 12 | 1 | 0 |
| Kelly, Chris, Princeton | 1 | 1 | .500 | 7.56 | 4 | 0 | 0 | 0 | 2 | 0 | 8.1 | 13 | 42 | 7 | 7 | 0 | 0 | 0 | 1 | 3 | 0 | 7 | 4 | 1 |
| Kite, Josh, Burlington * | 1 | 2 | .333 | 4.61 | 19 | 0 | 0 | 0 | 6 | 0 | 27.1 | 19 | 123 | 15 | 14 | 0 | 2 | 1 | 3 | 17 | 0 | 32 | 1 | 0 |
| Landing, Jeffrey, Kingsport | 0 | 4 | .000 | 9.64 | 6 | 6 | 0 | 0 | 0 | 0 | 23.1 | 34 | 120 | 27 | 25 | 4 | 0 | 0 | 3 | 11 | 0 | 24 | 1 | 0 |
| Lankford, Kris, Elizabethton | 0 | 0 | .000 | 12.60 | 5 | 0 | 0 | 0 | 4 | 0 | 5.0 | 7 | 25 | 7 | 7 | 1 | 0 | 0 | 1 | 2 | 0 | 6 | 5 | 0 |
| Larson, Matt, Princeton | 1 | 2 | .333 | 4.12 | 6 | 3 | 0 | 0 | 2 | 1 | 19.2 | 22 | 96 | 12 | 9 | 3 | 2 | 3 | 1 | 9 | 1 | 22 | 5 | 0 |
| Lavergne, Jarrad, Princeton * | 0 | 1 | .000 | 13.50 | 1 | 0 | 0 | 0 | 0 | 0 | 1.1 | 4 | 9 | 5 | 2 | 1 | 0 | 0 | 0 | 1 | 0 | 2 | 0 | 0 |
| Lemon, Nickolas, Bristol | 2 | 2 | .500 | 7.88 | 15 | 0 | 0 | 0 | 2 | 0 | 24.0 | 15 | 124 | 27 | 21 | 3 | 0 | 0 | 6 | 31 | 2 | 25 | 13 | 0 |
| Lemon, Tim, Johnson City | 1 | 4 | .200 | 7.21 | 13 | 8 | 0 | 0 | 1 | 0 | 48.2 | 66 | 230 | 46 | 39 | 8 | 4 | 7 | 5 | 22 | 0 | 29 | 8 | 0 |
| Limas, Alejandro, Princeton | 0 | 9 | .000 | 6.83 | 13 | 12 | 0 | 0 | 0 | 0 | 54.0 | 63 | 254 | 54 | 41 | 6 | 3 | 2 | 5 | 35 | 0 | 53 | 12 | 3 |
| Loadenthal, Carl, Danville * | 0 | 1 | .000 | 22.50 | 1 | 0 | 0 | 0 | 0 | 0 | 2.0 | 6 | 13 | 5 | 5 | 0 | 0 | 0 | 1 | 0 | 0 | 1 | 0 | 0 |
| Lofgren, Charles, Burlington * | 0 | 0 | .000 | 6.04 | 9 | 9 | 0 | 0 | 0 | 0 | 22.1 | 25 | 103 | 16 | 15 | 4 | 2 | 1 | 2 | 13 | 0 | 23 | 2 | 0 |
| Lopez, Romelio, Princeton | 1 | 1 | .500 | 2.96 | 5 | 5 | 0 | 0 | 0 | 0 | 24.1 | 27 | 116 | 11 | 8 | 2 | 1 | 0 | 4 | 13 | 0 | 29 | 3 | 0 |
| Lozado, Henry, Bluefield | 0 | 2 | .000 | 5.61 | 15 | 0 | 0 | 0 | 8 | 0 | 25.2 | 28 | 122 | 24 | 16 | 8 | 0 | 0 | 4 | 13 | 1 | 27 | 3 | 0 |
| Lubrano, Paul, Burlington * | 0 | 0 | .000 | 1.38 | 3 | 3 | 0 | 0 | 0 | 0 | 13.0 | 8 | 48 | 2 | 2 | 0 | 2 | 1 | 1 | 5 | 0 | 13 | 1 | 0 |
| Lucas, Franklin, Bluefield | 2 | 1 | .667 | 5.33 | 18 | 0 | 0 | 0 | 11 | 2 | 25.1 | 30 | 114 | 15 | 15 | 4 | 0 | 0 | 1 | 5 | 0 | 28 | 5 | 2 |
| Mannix, Kevin, Kingsport | 1 | 1 | .500 | 4.11 | 10 | 0 | 0 | 0 | 10 | 0 | 15.1 | 11 | 71 | 9 | 7 | 1 | 0 | 0 | 1 | 13 | 0 | 16 | 3 | 0 |
| Marini, Chris, Elizabethton * | 4 | 2 | .667 | 2.91 | 11 | 8 | 0 | 0 | 0 | 0 | 52.2 | 55 | 226 | 24 | 17 | 6 | 3 | 0 | 6 | 8 | 0 | 52 | 6 | 0 |
| Markham, Josh, Johnson City * | 0 | 0 | .000 | 11.57 | 2 | 0 | 0 | 0 | 0 | 0 | 2.1 | 5 | 13 | 4 | 3 | 1 | 0 | 0 | 1 | 0 | 0 | 0 | 0 | 0 |
| Martin, Adrian, Pulaski | 3 | 2 | .600 | 3.54 | 18 | 7 | 0 | 0 | 1 | 0 | 56.0 | 65 | 243 | 28 | 22 | 2 | 2 | 3 | 2 | 12 | 4 | 51 | 1 | 0 |
| Martinez, J.P., Elizabethton | 3 | 2 | .600 | 3.80 | 22 | 1 | 0 | 0 | 3 | 1 | 42.2 | 42 | 193 | 27 | 18 | 5 | 0 | 1 | 3 | 19 | 2 | 49 | 7 | 0 |
| Martinez, Javier, Elizabethton * | 1 | 0 | 1.000 | 4.22 | 9 | 2 | 0 | 0 | 0 | 0 | 21.1 | 14 | 92 | 10 | 10 | 2 | 0 | 0 | 2 | 13 | 0 | 19 | 5 | 0 |
| Mata, Frank, Elizabethton | 2 | 2 | .500 | 3.73 | 26 | 1 | 0 | 0 | 23 | 12 | 31.1 | 22 | 124 | 15 | 13 | 1 | 0 | 0 | 2 | 6 | 0 | 39 | 3 | 2 |
| McGee, Jacob, Princeton * | 4 | 1 | .800 | 3.97 | 12 | 12 | 0 | 0 | 0 | 0 | 56.2 | 49 | 233 | 30 | 25 | 5 | 3 | 4 | 0 | 25 | 1 | 53 | 5 | 0 |
| Medina, Dennis, Elizabethton | 2 | 1 | .667 | 5.36 | 13 | 4 | 0 | 0 | 1 | 0 | 42.0 | 56 | 195 | 27 | 25 | 9 | 1 | 4 | 0 | 13 | 1 | 40 | 1 | 0 |
| Meek, Evan, Elizabethton | 1 | 2 | .333 | 8.06 | 12 | 3 | 0 | 0 | 3 | 0 | 22.1 | 18 | 117 | 26 | 20 | 1 | 2 | 3 | 8 | 25 | 0 | 23 | 11 | 0 |
| Mendez, Winer, Bluefield | 5 | 4 | .556 | 3.38 | 11 | 11 | 0 | 0 | 0 | 0 | 53.1 | 50 | 226 | 27 | 20 | 1 | 2 | 4 | 4 | 20 | 0 | 46 | 4 | 1 |
| Mercedes, Gerson, Burlington | 5 | 5 | .500 | 5.03 | 13 | 13 | 0 | 0 | 0 | 0 | 59.0 | 57 | 240 | 33 | 33 | 9 | 0 | 4 | 2 | 16 | 0 | 62 | 0 | 1 |
| Meyers, Ryan, Kingsport | 0 | 0 | .000 | 7.50 | 2 | 1 | 0 | 0 | 1 | 0 | 6.0 | 7 | 28 | 5 | 5 | 0 | 0 | 0 | 1 | 3 | 0 | 3 | 3 | 0 |
| Minor, Zachary, Bluefield * | 2 | 1 | .667 | 4.75 | 16 | 0 | 0 | 0 | 7 | 0 | 30.1 | 34 | 149 | 18 | 16 | 4 | 0 | 0 | 5 | 19 | 0 | 32 | 3 | 1 |
| Miramontes, Matthew, Kingsport | 0 | 0 | .000 | 7.50 | 4 | 2 | 0 | 0 | 0 | 0 | 12.0 | 17 | 66 | 13 | 10 | 1 | 1 | 1 | 3 | 11 | 0 | 12 | 3 | 0 |

| Pitcher, Team | W | L | Pct. | ERA | G | GS | CG | ShO | GF | Sv. | IP | H | TBF | R | ER | HR | SH | SF | HB | BB | IBB | SO | WP | Bk. |
|---|---|---|---|---|---|---|---|---|---|---|---|---|---|---|---|---|---|---|---|---|---|---|---|---|
| Mousser, Jeff, Elizabethton | 2 | 0 | 1.000 | 4.63 | 18 | 0 | 0 | 0 | 8 | 1 | 23.1 | 25 | 107 | 12 | 12 | 3 | 0 | 0 | 1 | 11 | 0 | 22 | 2 | 1 |
| Muro, Joseph, Princeton | 1 | 3 | .250 | 10.25 | 10 | 6 | 0 | 0 | 0 | 0 | 26.1 | 36 | 147 | 34 | 30 | 5 | 2 | 2 | 6 | 34 | 0 | 21 | 12 | 1 |
| Murphey, Timothy, Bristol * | 1 | 3 | .250 | 4.63 | 15 | 3 | 0 | 0 | 0 | 0 | 35.0 | 25 | 152 | 20 | 18 | 4 | 0 | 2 | 8 | 19 | 1 | 38 | 2 | 1 |
| Myers, Rodney, Kingsport | 0 | 2 | .000 | 23.14 | 2 | 1 | 0 | 0 | 0 | 0 | 2.1 | 5 | 16 | 7 | 6 | 1 | 0 | 0 | 0 | 4 | 0 | 3 | 1 | 0 |
| Nachreiner, Matt, Bristol | 1 | 2 | .333 | 5.86 | 6 | 6 | 0 | 0 | 0 | 0 | 27.2 | 26 | 125 | 19 | 18 | 0 | 2 | 4 | 3 | 14 | 1 | 33 | 4 | 0 |
| Nelson, Brad, Danville | 3 | 2 | .600 | 4.85 | 20 | 0 | 0 | 0 | 15 | 5 | 26.0 | 28 | 109 | 18 | 14 | 3 | 2 | 0 | 1 | 4 | 0 | 23 | 3 | 0 |
| Noonan, Christopher, Johnson City * | 3 | 4 | .429 | 4.46 | 16 | 2 | 0 | 0 | 1 | 0 | 36.1 | 42 | 169 | 21 | 18 | 2 | 0 | 0 | 4 | 14 | 1 | 26 | 4 | 1 |
| Novoa, Yunior, Bristol * | 3 | 2 | .600 | 3.58 | 13 | 8 | 0 | 0 | 1 | 0 | 50.1 | 39 | 212 | 27 | 20 | 2 | 2 | 2 | 4 | 22 | 0 | 49 | 3 | 1 |
| O'Donnell, Matthew, Greeneville | 4 | 0 | 1.000 | 1.91 | 15 | 0 | 0 | 0 | 5 | 0 | 28.1 | 25 | 119 | 7 | 6 | 0 | 0 | 0 | 2 | 7 | 0 | 22 | 3 | 0 |
| Ortiz, Rafael, Burlington | 0 | 0 | .000 | 0.00 | 1 | 0 | 0 | 0 | 1 | 0 | 1.0 | 0 | 4 | 0 | 0 | 0 | 0 | 0 | 1 | 0 | 0 | 0 | 0 | 0 |
| Parish, Brian, Johnson City | 1 | 2 | .333 | 6.75 | 20 | 0 | 0 | 0 | 7 | 0 | 18.2 | 17 | 96 | 21 | 14 | 2 | 0 | 0 | 3 | 20 | 0 | 17 | 3 | 1 |
| Pascual, Dionis, Bluefield | 4 | 4 | .500 | 3.62 | 17 | 1 | 0 | 0 | 9 | 2 | 37.1 | 31 | 155 | 16 | 15 | 7 | 0 | 0 | 0 | 13 | 2 | 37 | 5 | 0 |
| Pascual, Juan, Bluefield | 1 | 2 | .333 | 3.96 | 14 | 3 | 0 | 0 | 3 | 0 | 36.1 | 37 | 154 | 20 | 16 | 3 | 0 | 1 | 2 | 8 | 0 | 38 | 3 | 0 |
| Patton, Troy, Greeneville * | 2 | 2 | .500 | 1.93 | 6 | 6 | 0 | 0 | 0 | 0 | 28.0 | 23 | 111 | 8 | 6 | 1 | 0 | 3 | 1 | 5 | 0 | 32 | 0 | 0 |
| Paul, Jason, Danville | 2 | 2 | .500 | 5.65 | 17 | 0 | 0 | 0 | 7 | 1 | 28.2 | 35 | 132 | 19 | 18 | 2 | 0 | 0 | 2 | 9 | 0 | 26 | 2 | 0 |
| Paulino, Felipe, Greeneville | 1 | 3 | .250 | 7.59 | 10 | 10 | 0 | 0 | 0 | 0 | 32.0 | 30 | 149 | 30 | 27 | 4 | 0 | 1 | 4 | 22 | 0 | 37 | 6 | 0 |
| Payano, Nelson, Danville * | 2 | 0 | 1.000 | 4.13 | 9 | 3 | 0 | 0 | 1 | 0 | 24.0 | 14 | 100 | 13 | 11 | 1 | 0 | 1 | 4 | 13 | 0 | 34 | 2 | 0 |
| Perez, Carlos, Bristol * | 3 | 0 | 1.000 | 2.17 | 13 | 0 | 0 | 0 | 8 | 2 | 29.0 | 28 | 126 | 9 | 7 | 2 | 0 | 0 | 2 | 10 | 0 | 21 | 0 | 0 |
| Pidutti, James, Pulaski * | 2 | 2 | .500 | 5.79 | 14 | 0 | 0 | 0 | 4 | 0 | 18.2 | 19 | 88 | 15 | 12 | 0 | 0 | 0 | 0 | 13 | 0 | 18 | 2 | 1 |
| Pleeter, Gregg, Johnson City | 4 | 0 | 1.000 | 4.60 | 18 | 0 | 0 | 0 | 0 | 0 | 43.0 | 29 | 176 | 24 | 22 | 6 | 3 | 8 | 2 | 19 | 0 | 43 | 3 | 0 |
| Polanco, Yestin, Bristol * | 3 | 2 | .600 | 3.33 | 15 | 0 | 0 | 0 | 9 | 2 | 27.0 | 22 | 128 | 12 | 10 | 0 | 0 | 0 | 4 | 21 | 2 | 26 | 1 | 0 |
| Powell, John, Johnson City | 2 | 2 | .500 | 7.52 | 14 | 6 | 0 | 0 | 1 | 0 | 32.1 | 36 | 161 | 31 | 27 | 4 | 3 | 1 | 4 | 28 | 0 | 26 | 5 | 0 |
| Quaglieri, William, Kingsport | 0 | 1 | .000 | 4.50 | 1 | 1 | 0 | 0 | 0 | 0 | 4.0 | 6 | 18 | 4 | 2 | 0 | 0 | 0 | 0 | 0 | 0 | 5 | 0 | 0 |
| Redfern, Chad, Princeton | 1 | 3 | .250 | 7.86 | 10 | 8 | 0 | 0 | 1 | 0 | 34.1 | 46 | 167 | 36 | 30 | 8 | 2 | 5 | 0 | 18 | 0 | 23 | 7 | 1 |
| Rengel, Orlando, Kingsport | 5 | 4 | .556 | 3.26 | 14 | 13 | 1 | 0 | 1 | 0 | 69.0 | 52 | 281 | 27 | 25 | 3 | 3 | 3 | 4 | 18 | 0 | 63 | 8 | 0 |
| Rickert, Brandon, Burlington | 2 | 2 | .500 | 3.76 | 19 | 0 | 0 | 0 | 9 | 2 | 38.1 | 38 | 160 | 19 | 16 | 0 | 0 | 0 | 6 | 5 | 1 | 27 | 2 | 1 |
| Rider, Michael, Pulaski | 2 | 2 | .500 | 7.03 | 17 | 0 | 0 | 0 | 9 | 2 | 24.1 | 27 | 119 | 22 | 19 | 4 | 0 | 1 | 5 | 16 | 2 | 27 | 5 | 0 |
| Roddy, Dustin, Burlington | 3 | 0 | 1.000 | 5.03 | 20 | 0 | 0 | 0 | 6 | 0 | 34.0 | 33 | 160 | 22 | 19 | 3 | 0 | 0 | 10 | 15 | 0 | 25 | 1 | 0 |
| Rodriguez, Claudio, Princeton | 0 | 0 | .000 | 4.62 | 15 | 3 | 0 | 0 | 3 | 0 | 39.0 | 48 | 191 | 33 | 20 | 4 | 1 | 1 | 2 | 25 | 0 | 30 | 6 | 3 |
| Rodriguez, Edward, Pulaski | 2 | 2 | .500 | 5.00 | 19 | 2 | 0 | 0 | 4 | 0 | 36.0 | 42 | 172 | 24 | 20 | 0 | 0 | 1 | 6 | 13 | 2 | 36 | 9 | 1 |
| Rodriguez, Francisco, Bristol * | 0 | 0 | .000 | 7.04 | 5 | 0 | 0 | 0 | 4 | 0 | 7.2 | 13 | 41 | 7 | 6 | 0 | 0 | 0 | 1 | 4 | 0 | 9 | 0 | 0 |
| Rodriguez, Joan, Princeton | 0 | 1 | .000 | 5.79 | 5 | 0 | 0 | 0 | 3 | 0 | 9.1 | 10 | 43 | 8 | 6 | 2 | 0 | 1 | 2 | 6 | 0 | 7 | 2 | 0 |
| Roelle, Justin, Bristol * | 0 | 1 | .000 | 9.75 | 10 | 1 | 0 | 0 | 3 | 0 | 12.0 | 15 | 65 | 16 | 13 | 3 | 0 | 1 | 2 | 12 | 1 | 15 | 7 | 1 |
| Romero, Levi, Greeneville | 8 | 0 | 1.000 | 2.19 | 13 | 7 | 0 | 0 | 2 | 0 | 53.1 | 41 | 219 | 18 | 13 | 4 | 3 | 4 | 3 | 22 | 1 | 43 | 2 | 0 |
| Salas, Juan, Princeton | 1 | 0 | 1.000 | 4.82 | 8 | 0 | 0 | 0 | 3 | 0 | 9.1 | 10 | 44 | 7 | 5 | 2 | 0 | 0 | 0 | 6 | 1 | 6 | 0 | 1 |
| Sanchez, Raymond, Pulaski * | 3 | 1 | .750 | 4.54 | 18 | 2 | 0 | 0 | 3 | 0 | 33.2 | 39 | 161 | 20 | 17 | 4 | 0 | 0 | 3 | 17 | 0 | 32 | 2 | 2 |
| Santiago, Jose, Danville | 1 | 2 | .333 | 5.01 | 6 | 4 | 0 | 0 | 0 | 0 | 23.1 | 25 | 107 | 16 | 13 | 1 | 2 | 0 | 1 | 11 | 0 | 23 | 4 | 1 |
| Savickas, Russell, Pulaski | 1 | 5 | .167 | 5.79 | 10 | 9 | 0 | 0 | 0 | 0 | 37.1 | 39 | 170 | 26 | 24 | 2 | 4 | 3 | 7 | 15 | 0 | 23 | 3 | 2 |
| Schau, Adrian, Burlington | 1 | 6 | .143 | 3.24 | 19 | 0 | 0 | 0 | 9 | 2 | 33.1 | 32 | 148 | 17 | 12 | 5 | 0 | 0 | 3 | 13 | 1 | 38 | 5 | 1 |
| Scherer, Matthew, Johnson City | 2 | 5 | .286 | 4.03 | 13 | 12 | 0 | 0 | 0 | 0 | 60.1 | 62 | 256 | 36 | 27 | 7 | 1 | 1 | 2 | 16 | 0 | 43 | 6 | 0 |
| Schindling, Andy, Bluefield | 0 | 1 | .000 | 13.50 | 8 | 0 | 0 | 0 | 2 | 0 | 8.2 | 12 | 49 | 16 | 13 | 1 | 0 | 0 | 2 | 9 | 0 | 7 | 2 | 0 |
| Shinskie, David, Elizabethton | 7 | 3 | .700 | 4.19 | 11 | 11 | 0 | 0 | 0 | 0 | 53.2 | 59 | 229 | 31 | 25 | 6 | 2 | 4 | 2 | 17 | 0 | 28 | 2 | 2 |
| Siak, Joey, Johnson City * | 1 | 1 | .500 | 3.45 | 20 | 0 | 0 | 0 | 5 | 0 | 28.2 | 32 | 124 | 14 | 11 | 3 | 0 | 0 | 0 | 6 | 1 | 29 | 1 | 0 |
| Sides, Andy, Kingsport | 3 | 1 | .750 | 2.95 | 6 | 0 | 0 | 0 | 2 | 0 | 21.1 | 21 | 90 | 7 | 7 | 2 | 1 | 0 | 2 | 5 | 0 | 15 | 0 | 0 |
| Sillman, Mike, Johnson City | 1 | 1 | .500 | 2.00 | 6 | 0 | 0 | 0 | 5 | 1 | 9.0 | 5 | 35 | 2 | 2 | 1 | 0 | 0 | 1 | 2 | 0 | 13 | 1 | 0 |
| Smit, Alex, Elizabethton * | 1 | 1 | .500 | 2.54 | 6 | 5 | 0 | 0 | 0 | 0 | 28.1 | 25 | 117 | 9 | 8 | 0 | 4 | 1 | 1 | 10 | 0 | 43 | 2 | 1 |
| Smith, Chuck, Kingsport | 1 | 1 | .500 | 4.15 | 4 | 0 | 0 | 0 | 2 | 0 | 13.0 | 14 | 59 | 8 | 6 | 0 | 0 | 4 | 2 | 2 | 0 | 11 | 1 | 0 |
| Smith, Cole, Princeton | 1 | 1 | .500 | 2.96 | 11 | 1 | 0 | 0 | 0 | 0 | 27.1 | 17 | 118 | 14 | 9 | 1 | 2 | 2 | 1 | 16 | 0 | 30 | 2 | 0 |
| Smith, Dan, Danville * | 3 | 1 | .750 | 2.27 | 14 | 2 | 0 | 0 | 3 | 1 | 39.2 | 24 | 159 | 10 | 10 | 2 | 0 | 3 | 2 | 16 | 0 | 52 | 1 | 1 |
| Smith, David, Kingsport * | 2 | 3 | .400 | 6.39 | 17 | 0 | 0 | 0 | 10 | 1 | 31.0 | 39 | 153 | 23 | 22 | 0 | 0 | 0 | 5 | 16 | 0 | 20 | 2 | 0 |
| Solis, Marcos, Greeneville | 1 | 1 | .500 | 8.07 | 16 | 0 | 0 | 0 | 3 | 0 | 29.0 | 37 | 137 | 28 | 26 | 5 | 0 | 0 | 1 | 12 | 0 | 20 | 6 | 2 |
| Soriano, Julio, Bluefield | 0 | 1 | .000 | 6.10 | 3 | 1 | 0 | 0 | 0 | 0 | 10.1 | 6 | 47 | 7 | 7 | 1 | 1 | 1 | 2 | 10 | 1 | 17 | 3 | 1 |
| Soto, Enyelbert, Greeneville * | 1 | 1 | .500 | 1.03 | 24 | 0 | 0 | 0 | 23 | 13 | 35.0 | 30 | 137 | 10 | 4 | 2 | 0 | 0 | 0 | 2 | 0 | 47 | 1 | 2 |
| Soto, Jesus, Burlington | 2 | 1 | .667 | 2.74 | 18 | 0 | 0 | 0 | 15 | 5 | 23.0 | 21 | 96 | 8 | 7 | 0 | 0 | 0 | 2 | 4 | 0 | 22 | 2 | 1 |
| Sotro, Chris, Greeneville | 0 | 2 | .000 | 4.35 | 13 | 0 | 0 | 0 | 11 | 1 | 20.2 | 22 | 94 | 14 | 10 | 2 | 0 | 0 | 0 | 10 | 1 | 18 | 4 | 0 |
| Spring, Daniel, Johnson City | 2 | 0 | 1.000 | 0.00 | 3 | 0 | 0 | 0 | 0 | 0 | 4.1 | 3 | 18 | 2 | 0 | 1 | 0 | 0 | 0 | 2 | 0 | 3 | 0 | 0 |
| Stanley, Adam, Danville * | 0 | 0 | .000 | 0.00 | 1 | 0 | 0 | 0 | 0 | 0 | 1.0 | 0 | 5 | 0 | 0 | 0 | 0 | 0 | 0 | 2 | 0 | 0 | 0 | 0 |
| Sues, Jarret, Princeton | 1 | 2 | .333 | 5.94 | 23 | 0 | 0 | 0 | 13 | 2 | 33.1 | 47 | 163 | 27 | 22 | 4 | 0 | 1 | 1 | 18 | 0 | 31 | 1 | 0 |
| Thompson, Ryan, Greeneville | 4 | 0 | 1.000 | 2.25 | 15 | 0 | 0 | 0 | 2 | 0 | 36.0 | 33 | 147 | 11 | 9 | 1 | 0 | 0 | 3 | 4 | 0 | 33 | 0 | 0 |
| Timm, Jordan, Pulaski * | 3 | 1 | .750 | 2.67 | 11 | 11 | 0 | 0 | 0 | 0 | 60.2 | 59 | 243 | 22 | 18 | 8 | 3 | 1 | 4 | 12 | 0 | 53 | 1 | 0 |
| Torres, Carlos, Bristol | 2 | 2 | .500 | 4.74 | 19 | 0 | 0 | 0 | 9 | 1 | 38.0 | 43 | 166 | 30 | 20 | 2 | 1 | 0 | 0 | 12 | 2 | 28 | 6 | 0 |
| Torres, David, Kingsport | 2 | 0 | 1.000 | 2.52 | 15 | 0 | 0 | 0 | 11 | 2 | 35.2 | 29 | 144 | 11 | 10 | 3 | 0 | 0 | 3 | 6 | 0 | 43 | 2 | 0 |
| Tredway, Zack, Johnson City | 0 | 0 | .000 | 6.75 | 5 | 0 | 0 | 0 | 2 | 0 | 4.0 | 5 | 22 | 3 | 3 | 0 | 0 | 0 | 0 | 5 | 0 | 4 | 2 | 1 |
| Tressler, Aaron, Pulaski | 3 | 2 | .600 | 1.48 | 21 | 0 | 0 | 0 | 17 | 5 | 30.1 | 14 | 118 | 6 | 5 | 2 | 0 | 0 | 2 | 11 | 2 | 41 | 0 | 0 |
| Veloz, Yonatan, Bristol * | 0 | 0 | .000 | 7.11 | 13 | 0 | 0 | 0 | 5 | 1 | 12.2 | 22 | 68 | 15 | 10 | 3 | 0 | 0 | 0 | 8 | 0 | 13 | 4 | 0 |
| Villa, Kelvin, Danville * | 3 | 0 | 1.000 | 1.93 | 15 | 4 | 0 | 0 | 3 | 1 | 42.0 | 35 | 178 | 15 | 9 | 1 | 0 | 0 | 0 | 21 | 0 | 41 | 3 | 0 |
| Vines, Chris, Danville | 6 | 3 | .667 | 3.28 | 13 | 10 | 0 | 0 | 0 | 0 | 60.1 | 58 | 249 | 25 | 22 | 2 | 1 | 0 | 4 | 14 | 0 | 72 | 1 | 1 |
| Waldrop, Kyle, Elizabethton | 2 | 0 | 1.000 | 3.24 | 4 | 4 | 0 | 0 | 0 | 0 | 25.0 | 21 | 100 | 10 | 9 | 1 | 1 | 0 | 1 | 3 | 0 | 25 | 0 | 0 |
| Weintraub, Jason, Kingsport | 3 | 4 | .429 | 3.88 | 11 | 9 | 0 | 0 | 0 | 0 | 46.1 | 50 | 197 | 30 | 20 | 6 | 6 | 3 | 2 | 12 | 0 | 45 | 6 | 0 |
| Weitzman, William, Kingsport | 1 | 4 | .200 | 5.36 | 16 | 4 | 0 | 0 | 5 | 2 | 50.1 | 57 | 247 | 49 | 30 | 4 | 2 | 3 | 16 | 21 | 0 | 34 | 12 | 0 |
| Williams, John, Elizabethton * | 3 | 1 | .750 | 5.40 | 14 | 5 | 0 | 0 | 3 | 0 | 38.1 | 46 | 174 | 27 | 23 | 2 | 1 | 0 | 0 | 14 | 0 | 50 | 1 | 0 |

COMBINATION SHUTOUTS: **Bluefield** (1)—McCrory-Brnardic-Lucas. **Bristol** (4)—Marshall-Harrell-Pena, Nachreiner-Murphey-C. Perez-Torres, Murphey-C. Perez, Casey-Torres-Bello. **Burlington** (3)—Alwert-Schau-Harris, Collins-Alwert-Soto, Mercedes-Roddy-Harris. **Danville** (5)—Atilano-Paul, Vines-Endl, Vines-Jimenez-Collins, Villa-Payano, Cuevas-B. Johnson-Paul-Endl. **Elizabethton** (4)—Shinskie-Mousser-Bowlin, Smit-J. Martinez-Mata, J. Martinez-J. Martinez, Duguay-Mata. **Greeneville** (4)—Gutierrez-Adler, Gutierrez-Sotro, Barthmaier-Sotro, Gutierrez-Romero-O'Donnell. **Johnson City** (4)—Noonan-Acosta-Worrell, Lemon-Pleeter-Grant-Gross-Parish, Scherer-Acosta, Robertson-Gross. **Kingsport** (2)—Rengel-Brewer, Marte-Brewer-D. Smith. **Princeton** (1)—R. Lopez-Evers-Bigda. **Pulaski** (5)—Grant-Pidutti-Roy, Timm-Tate-Roy, Tate-Cannon-Tressler, Timm-E. Rodriguez, Cheng-Cannon-Gale-Harang.

NO-HIT GAMES: Lemon, Johnson City, defeated Greeneville, 4-0, July 12.

# 2004 FIELDING

## TEAM

| Team | G | PO | A | E | TC | DP | TP | PB | Pct. |
|---|---|---|---|---|---|---|---|---|---|
| Danville | 66 | 1734 | 023 | 78 | 1835 | 46 | 0 | 14 | .957 |
| Johnson City | 68 | 1770 | 028 | 85 | 1883 | 58 | 0 | 19 | .955 |
| Burlington | 66 | 1685 | 025 | 82 | 1792 | 54 | 0 | 24 | .954 |
| Greeneville | 67 | 1728 | 025 | 94 | 1847 | 53 | 0 | 14 | .949 |
| Elizabethton | 67 | 1713 | 021 | 95 | 1829 | 62 | 0 | 10 | .948 |
| Pulaski | 67 | 1762 | 029 | 98 | 1889 | 57 | 0 | 14 | .948 |
| Bluefield | 67 | 1747 | 037 | 107 | 1891 | 58 | 0 | 32 | .943 |
| Kingsport | 68 | 1754 | 023 | 112 | 1889 | 49 | 0 | 18 | .941 |
| Bristol | 65 | 1687 | 038 | 109 | 1834 | 48 | 0 | 17 | .941 |
| Princeton | 67 | 1719 | 044 | 146 | 1909 | 53 | 0 | 13 | .924 |

## INDIVIDUAL

### FIRST BASEMEN

NOTE: All caps denotes fielding-percentage leader based on 34 games for catchers, 45 for all other non-pitchers and 54 innings for pitchers. *Throws lefthanded.

| Player, Team | Pct. | G | PO | A | E | TC | DP |
|---|---|---|---|---|---|---|---|
| Allen, Brandon, BRS* | .978 | 50 | 381 | 19 | 9 | 409 | 32 |
| Anderson, Charles PUL* | .990 | 23 | 167 | 22 | 2 | 191 | 17 |
| Becher, Billy, JCY* | .991 | 56 | 399 | 24 | 4 | 427 | 30 |
| Bergeron, Jabe, KPT | .993 | 16 | 131 | 11 | 1 | 143 | 10 |
| Bormaster, Brian, PUL | 1.000 | 1 | 7 | 0 | 0 | 7 | 0 |
| Bouman, Robbie, PRI | 1.000 | 1 | 2 | 0 | 0 | 2 | 0 |
| Cerda, Felix, KPT* | .976 | 28 | 229 | 12 | 6 | 247 | 14 |
| Chappell, Jon, PUL | .974 | 4 | 36 | 1 | 1 | 38 | 1 |
| Clark, Boodle, BRL | 1.000 | 20 | 170 | 16 | 0 | 186 | 23 |
| Comacho, Johan, KPT | .992 | 13 | 113 | 11 | 1 | 125 | 9 |
| Corapci, Jason, GVL | 1.000 | 1 | 1 | 0 | 0 | 1 | 0 |
| Crooks, Alex, PRI* | .976 | 30 | 186 | 17 | 5 | 208 | 16 |
| Eichas, Keith, DAN | .990 | 59 | 477 | 37 | 5 | 519 | 34 |
| Finan, Ryan, BLU* | .986 | 34 | 273 | 17 | 4 | 294 | 29 |
| Garcia, Antonio, GVL | .987 | 27 | 208 | 17 | 3 | 228 | 17 |
| Garibaldi, Anthony, PUL | 1.000 | 1 | 6 | 1 | 0 | 7 | 1 |
| Gerlits, Gooby, PUL | 1.000 | 2 | 7 | 1 | 0 | 8 | 1 |
| Guiterrez, Juan, BLU | .983 | 14 | 104 | 11 | 2 | 117 | 12 |
| Gulan, Mike, BRS | 1.000 | 4 | 27 | 0 | 0 | 27 | 2 |
| Hall, JT, PRI* | .957 | 5 | 42 | 2 | 2 | 46 | 5 |
| Hernandez, Francisco, BRS | 1.000 | 1 | 1 | 0 | 0 | 1 | 0 |
| Hicks, David, PUL* | .991 | 34 | 291 | 29 | 3 | 323 | 30 |
| Hiser, PJ, BRL | 1.000 | 2 | 14 | 0 | 0 | 14 | 2 |
| Jesson, Das, JCY | .989 | 26 | 173 | 8 | 2 | 183 | 7 |
| Lenderman, Matthew, BRS | 1.000 | 2 | 9 | 0 | 0 | 9 | 1 |
| Lex, Joshua, PUL | 1.000 | 3 | 17 | 3 | 0 | 20 | 0 |
| Lopez, Christian, PRI | .667 | 1 | 2 | 0 | 1 | 3 | 0 |
| Markel, Craig, PRI | 1.000 | 3 | 10 | 0 | 0 | 10 | 1 |
| Moreta, Carlos, DAN | .990 | 14 | 92 | 7 | 1 | 100 | 3 |
| Ortega, Jose, BRL | 1.000 | 4 | 16 | 4 | 0 | 20 | 2 |
| Ortiz, Rafael, BRL | .952 | 4 | 20 | 0 | 1 | 21 | 2 |
| Pacheco, Joel, BLU | .980 | 17 | 138 | 6 | 3 | 147 | 15 |
| Petersen, Josh, KPT | .992 | 14 | 116 | 6 | 1 | 123 | 10 |
| Pulley, Matthew, BLU* | .975 | 4 | 39 | 0 | 1 | 40 | 2 |
| Salas, Jose, PUL | .957 | 3 | 20 | 2 | 1 | 23 | 0 |
| Schmidt, Jeffrey, BRS | .975 | 18 | 111 | 8 | 3 | 122 | 9 |
| Shafer, Dustin, BRS | 1.000 | 2 | 13 | 0 | 0 | 13 | 0 |
| SHELDON, OLE, GVL | .995 | 48 | 371 | 24 | 2 | 397 | 40 |
| Thomas, Nick, PUL | 1.000 | 3 | 19 | 2 | 0 | 21 | 4 |
| Vasquez, Domingo, BRL | .983 | 41 | 333 | 22 | 6 | 361 | 25 |
| Weins, Logan, PRI | .979 | 40 | 292 | 29 | 7 | 328 | 29 |
| Winfree, David, ELZ | .977 | 13 | 83 | 3 | 2 | 88 | 9 |
| Woodard, Johnny, ELZ* | .975 | 56 | 483 | 23 | 13 | 519 | 40 |

### SECOND BASEMEN

| Player, Team | Pct. | G | PO | A | E | TC | DP |
|---|---|---|---|---|---|---|---|
| Arnold, Derrick, DAN | 1.000 | 3 | 1 | 1 | 0 | 2 | 0 |
| Badger, Graig, PUL | 954 | 26 | 39 | 64 | 5 | 108 | 14 |
| Bouman, Robbie, PRI | 1.000 | 1 | 2 | 6 | 0 | 8 | 2 |
| Brown, Bo, DAN | 1.000 | 2 | 1 | 1 | 0 | 2 | 0 |
| Cabral, Marcos, KPT | .968 | 20 | 26 | 65 | 3 | 94 | 14 |
| Chacin, Steward, JCY | .976 | 16 | 22 | 19 | 1 | 42 | 5 |
| Clark, Boodle, BRL | 1.000 | 2 | 3 | 2 | 0 | 5 | 1 |
| Corapci, Jason, GVL | 970 | 10 | 14 | 18 | 1 | 33 | 1 |
| De Los Santos, Jose, BRS | 941 | 11 | 25 | 23 | 3 | 51 | 9 |
| Delgado, Jose, JCY | 954 | 61 | 114 | 157 | 13 | 284 | 29 |
| Espinoza, Pedro, GVL | 959 | 18 | 30 | 40 | 3 | 73 | 14 |
| Garcia, Julio, BRL | .970 | 56 | 97 | 130 | 7 | 234 | 28 |
| Gonzalez, Humberto, KPT | .955 | 8 | 17 | 25 | 2 | 44 | 2 |
| Guerrero, Francisco, BLU | 1.000 | 1 | 3 | 1 | 0 | 4 | 0 |
| Guest, Garret, BRS | .963 | 9 | 10 | 16 | 1 | 27 | 4 |
| Holmes, Justin, BRL | .978 | 10 | 17 | 27 | 1 | 45 | 10 |
| HOLT, JC, DAN* | .977 | 51 | 60 | 107 | 4 | 171 | 22 |
| Hughes, Luke, ELZ | .981 | 40 | 59 | 97 | 3 | 159 | 22 |
| Johnson, Brandon, BRS* | .939 | 34 | 62 | 76 | 9 | 147 | 15 |
| Macaluso, Mike, PUL | .989 | 18 | 38 | 50 | 1 | 89 | 14 |
| Melendez, Alcides, BLU* | .943 | 16 | 33 | 49 | 5 | 87 | 13 |
| Mendez, Carlos, BLU | .958 | 41 | 74 | 108 | 8 | 190 | 24 |
| Nelson, Daniel, JCY | 1.000 | 2 | 1 | 1 | 0 | 2 | 0 |
| Ortega, Jose, BRL | .750 | 1 | 2 | 1 | 1 | 4 | 0 |
| Powers, Greg, PUL* | 1.000 | 4 | 2 | 5 | 0 | 7 | 1 |
| Rousseve, Brandon, PRI | .959 | 42 | 86 | 101 | 8 | 195 | 23 |
| Rozema, Mike, DAN* | .929 | 20 | 17 | 48 | 5 | 70 | 6 |
| Salas, Jose, PUL | 1.000 | 1 | 1 | 2 | 0 | 3 | 1 |
| Santana, Jeudy, BRS | .962 | 20 | 19 | 31 | 2 | 52 | 3 |
| Sena, Emmanuel, PUL | .938 | 28 | 56 | 64 | 8 | 128 | 11 |
| Swain, Michael, BRS* | 1.000 | 6 | 8 | 13 | 0 | 21 | 2 |
| Swindell, Mike, KPT | 1.000 | 1 | 2 | 2 | 0 | 4 | 1 |
| Tolbert, Matt, ELZ | .950 | 28 | 45 | 68 | 6 | 119 | 23 |
| Touchstone, Josh, PRI | .941 | 27 | 42 | 70 | 7 | 119 | 14 |
| Triplett, Bryan, GVL | .926 | 19 | 32 | 43 | 6 | 81 | 9 |
| Triplett, Russ, KPT | .968 | 17 | 38 | 53 | 3 | 94 | 11 |
| Tucker, Jonathan, BLU | .932 | 9 | 19 | 22 | 3 | 44 | 5 |
| Uhle, Christopher, GVL | .938 | 29 | 45 | 77 | 8 | 130 | 16 |
| Zapata, Jose, BLU | 1.000 | 8 | 17 | 19 | 0 | 36 | 7 |
| Zech, Bryan, KPT | .955 | 23 | 40 | 65 | 5 | 110 | 12 |

### THIRD BASEMEN

| Player, Team | Pct. | G | PO | A | E | TC | DP |
|---|---|---|---|---|---|---|---|
| Bouman, Robbie, PRI | .833 | 22 | 17 | 38 | 11 | 66 | 5 |
| Broome, Mark, JCY | .830 | 18 | 8 | 31 | 8 | 47 | 1 |
| Chacin, Steward, JCY | .900 | 12 | 2 | 7 | 1 | 10 | 1 |
| Clark, Boodle, BRL | .821 | 13 | 5 | 18 | 5 | 28 | 1 |
| Comacho, Johan, KPT | .955 | 17 | 10 | 32 | 2 | 44 | 3 |
| Corapci, Jason, GVL | .917 | 13 | 4 | 18 | 2 | 24 | 0 |
| De Los Santos, Jose, BRS | .886 | 18 | 12 | 27 | 5 | 44 | 5 |
| Delarosa, Jaria, PRI | .762 | 13 | 6 | 10 | 5 | 21 | 1 |
| Garcia, Travis, KPT | .841 | 23 | 7 | 51 | 11 | 69 | 3 |
| Garibaldi, Anthony, PUL | .911 | 46 | 27 | 65 | 9 | 101 | 7 |
| Garobaldi, Anthony, PUL | 1.000 | 1 | 1 | 3 | 0 | 4 | 1 |
| Granadillo, Tony, JCY | .907 | 46 | 35 | 92 | 13 | 140 | 6 |
| Guerrero, Francisco, BLU | 1.000 | 1 | 0 | 2 | 0 | 2 | 0 |
| Guest, Garret, BRS | .909 | 6 | 2 | 8 | 1 | 11 | 1 |
| Holmes, Justin, BRL | .875 | 3 | 1 | 6 | 1 | 8 | 0 |
| Hughes, Luke, ELZ | .500 | 1 | 1 | 0 | 1 | 2 | 0 |
| Jesson, Das, JCY | .900 | 6 | 2 | 7 | 1 | 10 | 0 |
| Lex, Joshua, PUL | .864 | 9 | 3 | 16 | 3 | 22 | 1 |
| Markel, Craig, PRI | .000 | 1 | 0 | 0 | 1 | 1 | 0 |
| Melendez, Alcides, BLU* | .941 | 9 | 7 | 9 | 1 | 17 | 1 |
| Ortega, Jose, BRL | 1.000 | 4 | 2 | 10 | 0 | 12 | 1 |
| Ortiz, Rafael, BRL | .867 | 12 | 5 | 21 | 4 | 30 | 3 |
| Perez, Melvin, BRS | 1.000 | 2 | 2 | 0 | 0 | 2 | 0 |
| Petersen, Josh, KPT | .849 | 27 | 25 | 37 | 11 | 73 | 4 |
| Peterson, Derrick, BRL | .928 | 37 | 18 | 72 | 7 | 97 | 3 |
| POPE, VAN, DAN | .931 | 47 | 33 | 102 | 10 | 145 | 6 |
| Powers, Greg, PUL* | .853 | 18 | 10 | 19 | 5 | 34 | 2 |
| Pulley, Matthew, BLU* | .893 | 53 | 22 | 78 | 12 | 112 | 5 |
| Ritchie, Jake, PRI | .783 | 21 | 13 | 34 | 13 | 60 | 5 |
| Romak, Jamie, DAN | .907 | 20 | 12 | 27 | 4 | 43 | 2 |
| Salas, Jose, PUL | 1.000 | 1 | 1 | 3 | 0 | 4 | 1 |
| Schmidt, Jeffrey, BRS | .950 | 22 | 10 | 47 | 3 | 60 | 4 |
| Sellers, Neil, GVL | .935 | 45 | 18 | 83 | 7 | 108 | 6 |
| Sena, Emmanuel, PUL | 1.000 | 4 | 1 | 2 | 0 | 3 | 0 |
| Sgueglia, Thomas, KPT | 1.000 | 5 | 4 | 11 | 0 | 15 | 1 |
| Swain, Michael, BRS* | .882 | 26 | 18 | 49 | 9 | 76 | 4 |
| Touchstone, Josh, PRI | .946 | 15 | 12 | 23 | 2 | 37 | 2 |
| Triplett, Bryan, GVL | .917 | 14 | 4 | 29 | 3 | 36 | 3 |
| Tucker, Jonathan, BLU | 1.000 | 1 | 0 | 3 | 0 | 3 | 0 |
| Uhle, Christopher, GVL | 1.000 | 1 | 1 | 0 | 0 | 1 | 0 |
| Velez, Eugenio, PUL | .944 | 6 | 2 | 15 | 1 | 18 | 0 |
| Winfree, David, ELZ | .858 | 42 | 24 | 67 | 15 | 106 | 3 |
| Yaconetti, Jay, ELZ | .949 | 28 | 14 | 42 | 3 | 59 | 6 |
| Zapata, Jose, BLU | .688 | 7 | 1 | 10 | 5 | 16 | 2 |

## SHORTSTOPS

| Player, Team | Pct. | G | PO | A | E | TC | DP |
|---|---|---|---|---|---|---|---|
| Arnold, Derrick, DAN | .923 | 43 | 49 | 106 | 13 | 168 | 14 |
| Bouman, Robbie, PRI | .940 | 12 | 12 | 35 | 3 | 50 | 6 |
| Brignac, Reid, PRI* | .915 | 24 | 36 | 71 | 10 | 117 | 15 |
| Brown, Bo, DAN | .769 | 4 | 4 | 6 | 3 | 13 | 2 |
| Cabral, Marcos, KPT | .867 | 13 | 15 | 37 | 8 | 60 | 7 |
| Castillo, Cesar, BRS | .917 | 2 | 3 | 8 | 1 | 12 | 0 |
| Castillo, Javier, BRS | .925 | 58 | 90 | 155 | 20 | 265 | 29 |
| Chacin, Steward, JCY | .857 | 2 | 2 | 4 | 1 | 7 | 1 |
| Corapci, Jason, GVL | .667 | 2 | 1 | 3 | 2 | 6 | 0 |
| De Los Santos, Jose, BRS | .957 | 6 | 9 | 13 | 1 | 23 | 2 |
| Delarosa, Jaria, PRI | .843 | 30 | 43 | 54 | 18 | 115 | 11 |
| Espinoza, Pedro, GVL | .854 | 12 | 13 | 28 | 7 | 48 | 4 |
| Garcia, Julio, BRL | .500 | 1 | 0 | 1 | 1 | 2 | 0 |
| Garcia, Travis, KPT | .935 | 23 | 43 | 58 | 7 | 108 | 16 |
| Garibaldi, Anthony, PUL | 1.000 | 1 | 2 | 2 | 0 | 4 | 0 |
| Guerrero, Francisco, BLU | 1.000 | 1 | 2 | 2 | 0 | 4 | 1 |
| Holmes, Justin, BRL | .902 | 13 | 14 | 32 | 5 | 51 | 7 |
| Kitch, Denver, BLU | .936 | 56 | 74 | 174 | 17 | 265 | 40 |
| Lucena, Juan, JCY | .965 | 45 | 44 | 120 | 6 | 170 | 22 |
| Macaluso, Mike, PUL | .929 | 19 | 19 | 46 | 5 | 70 | 8 |
| Matthews, Dustin, BRS | 1.000 | 3 | 0 | 1 | 0 | 1 | 0 |
| Nelson, Daniel, JCY | .908 | 31 | 38 | 71 | 11 | 120 | 7 |
| Ortega, Jose, BRL | .967 | 37 | 64 | 112 | 6 | 182 | 22 |
| Ortiz, Patrick, ELZ | .857 | 18 | 21 | 39 | 10 | 70 | 7 |
| Ortiz, Rafael, BRL | .977 | 18 | 27 | 59 | 2 | 88 | 15 |
| Plouffe, Trevor, ELZ | .926 | 52 | 54 | 147 | 16 | 217 | 32 |
| Rousseve, Brandon, PRI | .857 | 8 | 13 | 17 | 5 | 35 | 6 |
| Rozema, Mike, DAN* | .945 | 29 | 34 | 70 | 6 | 110 | 12 |
| Salas, Jose, PUL | 1.000 | 1 | 2 | 1 | 0 | 3 | 0 |
| Santana, Jeudy, BRS | 1.000 | 2 | 2 | 2 | 0 | 4 | 1 |
| Sena, Emmanuel, PUL | .918 | 20 | 28 | 50 | 7 | 85 | 15 |
| SUTIL, WALADIMIR, GVL | .941 | 53 | 90 | 164 | 16 | 270 | 33 |
| Triplett, Bryan, GVL | .941 | 8 | 9 | 23 | 2 | 34 | 4 |
| Triplett, Russ, KPT | .934 | 34 | 34 | 80 | 8 | 122 | 9 |
| Uhle, Christopher, GVL | 1.000 | 2 | 4 | 7 | 0 | 11 | 1 |
| Vasquez, Domingo, BRL | 1.000 | 1 | 1 | 4 | 0 | 5 | 1 |
| Velez, Eugenio, PUL | .862 | 35 | 47 | 72 | 19 | 138 | 11 |
| Zapata, Jose, BLU | .844 | 13 | 25 | 40 | 12 | 77 | 8 |

## OUTFIELDERS

| Player, Team | Pct. | G | PO | A | E | TC | DP |
|---|---|---|---|---|---|---|---|
| Alcantara, Gilbert, BRS | .939 | 36 | 46 | 0 | 3 | 49 | 0 |
| Allen, Brandon, BRS* | .900 | 8 | 9 | 0 | 1 | 10 | 0 |
| Ashford, Jon, PUL* | .929 | 43 | 35 | 4 | 3 | 42 | 0 |
| Avila, Angel, BLU | .917 | 44 | 75 | 2 | 7 | 84 | 0 |
| Burns, Deacon, ELZ* | .952 | 38 | 57 | 2 | 3 | 62 | 0 |
| Burt, Landon, ELZ* | 1.000 | 41 | 71 | 2 | 0 | 73 | 1 |
| Cerda, Felix, KPT* | 1.000 | 5 | 8 | 0 | 0 | 8 | 0 |
| Chacin, Steward, JCY | 1.000 | 1 | 2 | 1 | 0 | 3 | 0 |
| Chourio, Junior, PUL | .978 | 34 | 41 | 4 | 1 | 46 | 0 |
| Corapci, Jason, GVL | 1.000 | 1 | 1 | 0 | 0 | 1 | 0 |
| Cumberbatch, Cirillo, BRL | .886 | 23 | 29 | 2 | 4 | 35 | 0 |
| Cunningham, Chris, PRI | .922 | 47 | 66 | 5 | 6 | 77 | 0 |
| Davis, Zach, BLU* | .958 | 40 | 63 | 6 | 3 | 72 | 0 |
| DeLeon, Evandy, BRL | .933 | 40 | 69 | 1 | 5 | 75 | 0 |
| Denham, Jason, BRL* | .978 | 32 | 44 | 1 | 1 | 46 | 0 |
| Einertson, Mitch, GVL | .952 | 55 | 95 | 4 | 5 | 104 | 1 |
| Foust, JD, BRS | .975 | 26 | 32 | 7 | 1 | 40 | 0 |
| Gabriel, Chad, JCY | 1.000 | 43 | 65 | 2 | 0 | 67 | 0 |
| Gamero, Jesus, KPT | .944 | 34 | 65 | 2 | 4 | 71 | 0 |
| Gomez, Carlos, KPT | .981 | 36 | 48 | 3 | 1 | 52 | 1 |
| Guest, Garret, BRS | 1.000 | 5 | 5 | 1 | 0 | 6 | 0 |
| Hall, JT, PRI* | 1.000 | 17 | 12 | 1 | 0 | 13 | 0 |
| Herbert, Sam, JCY | 1.000 | 32 | 69 | 1 | 0 | 70 | 0 |
| Hernandez, Jose, GVL | .976 | 34 | 38 | 3 | 1 | 42 | 1 |
| Hetherington, Luke, PUL | .967 | 58 | 83 | 5 | 3 | 91 | 2 |
| Hiser, PJ, BRL | .945 | 39 | 51 | 1 | 3 | 55 | 0 |
| Howell, Joey, BLU | .947 | 10 | 16 | 2 | 1 | 19 | 1 |
| Hudgson, Maximiliano, GVL | 1.000 | 9 | 4 | 0 | 0 | 4 | 0 |
| Irvin, Blair, PRI* | .947 | 29 | 53 | 1 | 3 | 57 | 0 |
| Jesson, Das, JCY | 1.000 | 20 | 22 | 0 | 0 | 22 | 0 |
| Johnson, Brandon, BRS* | 1.000 | 4 | 2 | 0 | 0 | 2 | 0 |
| Jones, Brandon, DAN* | .992 | 57 | 118 | 2 | 1 | 121 | 0 |
| Jurich, Mark, DAN* | .948 | 55 | 72 | 1 | 4 | 77 | 0 |
| Lawrence, Horace, KPT* | .977 | 23 | 42 | 0 | 1 | 43 | 0 |
| Loadenthal, Carl, DAN* | .985 | 64 | 127 | 4 | 2 | 133 | 1 |
| Longworth, Chad, BRL | .952 | 37 | 56 | 4 | 3 | 63 | 1 |
| Lopez, Javier, ELZ | .978 | 43 | 43 | 1 | 1 | 45 | 0 |
| Miller, Michael, JCY | .941 | 41 | 63 | 1 | 4 | 68 | 0 |
| Moreta, Carlos, DAN | .941 | 19 | 30 | 2 | 2 | 34 | 0 |
| Pacheco, Joel, BLU | .750 | 6 | 3 | 0 | 1 | 4 | 0 |
| Parraz, Jordan, GVL | .990 | 51 | 92 | 3 | 1 | 96 | 1 |
| Patterson, Tarrence, ELZ | .945 | 39 | 68 | 1 | 4 | 73 | 1 |
| Petersen, Josh, KPT | 1.000 | 9 | 10 | 3 | 0 | 13 | 0 |
| Pickrel, Jeremy, ELZ* | .960 | 46 | 70 | 2 | 3 | 75 | 0 |
| Pietsch, Seth, KPT | .981 | 45 | 50 | 3 | 1 | 54 | 0 |
| Ponce, Angel, DAN | .944 | 17 | 16 | 1 | 1 | 18 | 0 |
| Ramos, Carlos, PRI* | .983 | 21 | 57 | 2 | 1 | 60 | 1 |
| Reed, Ryan, GVL* | .897 | 37 | 59 | 2 | 7 | 68 | 1 |
| Ritchie, Jake, PRI | .900 | 19 | 36 | 0 | 4 | 40 | 0 |
| Roberson, Craig, PRI | 1.000 | 5 | 9 | 0 | 0 | 9 | 0 |
| Rodriguez, Manuel, BRS | .953 | 37 | 58 | 3 | 3 | 64 | 2 |
| Rodriguez, Yuber, PUL | .973 | 63 | 105 | 4 | 3 | 112 | 2 |
| Royster, Ryan, PRI | .945 | 48 | 64 | 5 | 4 | 73 | 1 |
| Schultz, Blake, PRI | .956 | 31 | 39 | 4 | 2 | 45 | 0 |
| Schwarze, Brian, JCY | 1.000 | 15 | 11 | 0 | 0 | 11 | 0 |
| Scott, Lorenzo, BLU* | .973 | 60 | 105 | 5 | 3 | 113 | 1 |
| Shafer, Corey, BLU* | .941 | 16 | 31 | 1 | 2 | 34 | 0 |
| Shafer, Dustin, BRS | .925 | 46 | 60 | 2 | 5 | 67 | 0 |
| Shelley, Shane, PRI | .900 | 6 | 9 | 0 | 1 | 10 | 0 |
| SIVIRA, YONATHAN, JCY | 1.000 | 44 | 58 | 5 | 0 | 63 | 0 |
| Tartaglia, Evan, BRS* | .970 | 58 | 95 | 2 | 3 | 100 | 1 |
| Thomas, Nick, PUL | .938 | 15 | 15 | 0 | 1 | 16 | 0 |
| Torbert, Wallace, GVL | .977 | 31 | 41 | 1 | 1 | 43 | 0 |
| Torres, Andres, BRS | 1.000 | 3 | 6 | 1 | 0 | 7 | 0 |
| Valdes, Juan, BRL | .986 | 34 | 66 | 3 | 1 | 70 | 0 |
| Wiggins, Brad, BLU* | .927 | 37 | 50 | 1 | 4 | 55 | 0 |
| Williams, Simon, JCY | .990 | 46 | 94 | 1 | 1 | 96 | 1 |
| Wyrick, Joshua, KPT* | .972 | 58 | 100 | 4 | 3 | 107 | 1 |

## CATCHERS

| Player, Team | Pct. | G | PO | A | E | TC | DP | PB |
|---|---|---|---|---|---|---|---|---|
| Acosta, Jose, GVL | .975 | 27 | 178 | 21 | 5 | 204 | 0 | 9 |
| Anderson, Heath, ELZ | 1.000 | 10 | 76 | 6 | 0 | 82 | 0 | 1 |
| Armstrong, Cole, DAN* | .989 | 23 | 165 | 16 | 2 | 183 | 0 | 4 |
| Arroyo, Rafael, KPT | .979 | 41 | 341 | 26 | 8 | 375 | 1 | 9 |
| Bormaster, Brian, PUL | .986 | 42 | 316 | 26 | 5 | 347 | 2 | 6 |
| Braun, Ron, BLU | 1.000 | 8 | 71 | 7 | 0 | 78 | 1 | 5 |
| Burton, Adam, JCY | .982 | 26 | 150 | 16 | 3 | 169 | 0 | 6 |
| Castillo, Cesar, BRS | 1.000 | 4 | 37 | 1 | 0 | 38 | 1 | 2 |
| Cavers, Eric, GVL | 1.000 | 10 | 67 | 3 | 0 | 70 | 0 | 2 |
| Chappell, Jon, PUL | 1.000 | 2 | 6 | 1 | 0 | 7 | 0 | 0 |
| Cruz, Ramon, DAN | 1.000 | 11 | 46 | 5 | 0 | 51 | 0 | 2 |
| Diaz, Sandy, JCY | .993 | 18 | 125 | 15 | 1 | 141 | 0 | 5 |
| Gerlits, Gooby, PUL | .987 | 9 | 70 | 4 | 1 | 75 | 0 | 1 |
| GUERRERO, HENRY, BLU | .997 | 41 | 304 | 44 | 1 | 349 | 1 | 14 |
| Guiterrez, Juan, BLU | .971 | 7 | 63 | 5 | 2 | 70 | 0 | 5 |
| Harp, Troy, DAN | .941 | 3 | 12 | 4 | 1 | 17 | 0 | 0 |
| Hernandez, Francisco, BRS | .969 | 47 | 347 | 55 | 13 | 415 | 4 | 5 |
| Holmes, Justin, BRL | 1.000 | 1 | 1 | 0 | 0 | 1 | 0 | 0 |
| James, Brad, GVL | 1.000 | 1 | 1 | 0 | 0 | 1 | 0 | 0 |
| Kady, David, GVL* | 1.000 | 8 | 25 | 1 | 0 | 26 | 0 | 1 |
| Kotch, Kevin, BLU* | 1.000 | 13 | 77 | 5 | 0 | 82 | 1 | 4 |
| Lagreid, Thomas, PRI | .983 | 25 | 195 | 35 | 4 | 234 | 1 | 5 |
| Lahey, Timothy, ELZ | .972 | 22 | 183 | 28 | 6 | 217 | 0 | 2 |
| Land, Tim, PUL | 1.000 | 14 | 111 | 13 | 0 | 124 | 0 | 3 |
| Lankford, Kris, ELZ | .947 | 6 | 16 | 2 | 1 | 19 | 0 | 1 |
| Lenderman, Matthew, BRS | 1.000 | 14 | 96 | 8 | 0 | 104 | 0 | 4 |
| Lex, Joshua, PUL | .987 | 10 | 69 | 7 | 1 | 77 | 1 | 4 |
| Lopez, Christian, PRI | .969 | 28 | 193 | 29 | 7 | 229 | 1 | 3 |
| Lopez, Romelio, PRI | .909 | 1 | 8 | 2 | 1 | 11 | 0 | 1 |
| Markel, Craig, PRI | .978 | 16 | 120 | 14 | 3 | 137 | 0 | 4 |
| Oxendine, Chad, BRS | .978 | 5 | 40 | 5 | 1 | 46 | 0 | 2 |
| Piazza, Tommy, KPT | .992 | 14 | 103 | 15 | 1 | 119 | 1 | 5 |
| Puente, Dan, BLU | .972 | 6 | 32 | 3 | 1 | 36 | 1 | 4 |
| Roberts, Josh, BRL* | 1.000 | 12 | 84 | 6 | 0 | 90 | 0 | 6 |
| Salgado, Eddie, BRS | .923 | 2 | 11 | 1 | 1 | 13 | 0 | 4 |
| Sammons, Clint, DAN | .984 | 40 | 339 | 25 | 6 | 370 | 3 | 8 |
| Sanchez, Javier, ELZ | .991 | 38 | 323 | 24 | 3 | 350 | 3 | 6 |
| Santana, Luis, KPT | .960 | 16 | 104 | 15 | 5 | 124 | 0 | 4 |
| Spilman, Ryan, BRL | .977 | 33 | 227 | 26 | 6 | 259 | 1 | 11 |
| Towles, Justin, GVL | .996 | 37 | 247 | 22 | 1 | 270 | 1 | 2 |
| Woodson, Mike, BRL | .987 | 32 | 220 | 12 | 3 | 235 | 0 | 7 |
| Yarbrough, Brandon, JCY* | .981 | 34 | 234 | 28 | 5 | 267 | 1 | 8 |

## PITCHERS

| Player, Team | Pct. | G | PO | A | E | TC | DP |
|---|---|---|---|---|---|---|---|
| Acosta, Adam, JCY | 1.000 | 10 | 1 | 2 | 0 | 3 | 0 |
| Adler, Anthony, GVL | 1.000 | 10 | 0 | 5 | 0 | 5 | 0 |
| Almenar, Aristedes, KPT | .714 | 9 | 1 | 4 | 2 | 7 | 0 |
| Alwert, Garrett, BRL* | .875 | 14 | 1 | 6 | 1 | 8 | 0 |
| Amaya, Jose, BRL | 1.000 | 12 | 5 | 13 | 0 | 18 | 1 |

| Player, Team | Pct. | G | PO | A | E | TC | DP |
|---|---|---|---|---|---|---|---|
| Andersen, Phillip, JCY | 1.000 | 13 | 5 | 4 | 0 | 9 | 0 |
| Anderson, Devin, DAN* | 1.000 | 3 | 0 | 1 | 0 | 1 | 0 |
| Arguello, Douglas, GVL* | 1.000 | 16 | 0 | 2 | 0 | 2 | 0 |
| Aselton, Kyle, ELZ* | 1.000 | 15 | 2 | 6 | 0 | 8 | 0 |
| Atilano, Luis, DAN | 1.000 | 13 | 2 | 14 | 0 | 16 | 0 |
| Bacot, Paul, DAN | 1.000 | 13 | 5 | 9 | 0 | 14 | 0 |
| Bakker, Kyle, DAN* | .000 | 2 | 0 | 0 | 0 | 0 | 0 |
| Barthmaier, James, GVL | 1.000 | 13 | 5 | 7 | 0 | 12 | 0 |
| Bastardo, Alberto, BLU* | 1.000 | 3 | 0 | 1 | 0 | 1 | 0 |
| Bell, Bryon, PUL* | .000 | 1 | 0 | 0 | 0 | 0 | 0 |
| Bello, Juan, BRS | 1.000 | 18 | 1 | 7 | 0 | 8 | 1 |
| Bergesen, Bradley, BLU | 1.000 | 5 | 0 | 3 | 0 | 3 | 0 |
| Berroa, Yesson, PUL | 1.000 | 10 | 4 | 6 | 0 | 10 | 1 |
| Bigda, Drew, PRI* | .800 | 18 | 2 | 2 | 1 | 5 | 0 |
| Bowlin, Jason, ELZ | .900 | 23 | 2 | 7 | 1 | 10 | 1 |
| Brehm, Derek, PRI* | .667 | 6 | 1 | 1 | 1 | 3 | 0 |
| Brewer, Jeff, KPT | .769 | 17 | 2 | 8 | 3 | 13 | 0 |
| Brnardic, Ryan, BLU | 1.000 | 17 | 2 | 4 | 0 | 6 | 0 |
| Brock, Ken, PRI* | 1.000 | 14 | 0 | 7 | 0 | 7 | 0 |
| Brown, Justin, JCY | 1.000 | 8 | 3 | 4 | 0 | 7 | 0 |
| Bunkleman, Cody, BRL | .875 | 17 | 2 | 5 | 1 | 8 | 0 |
| Cannon, Eddie, PUL | .875 | 19 | 4 | 10 | 2 | 16 | 0 |
| Capellan, Domingo, JCY | .833 | 25 | 1 | 4 | 1 | 6 | 0 |
| Carpenter, Calvin, PRI | 1.000 | 5 | 1 | 1 | 0 | 2 | 0 |
| Casey, James, BRS | 1.000 | 12 | 1 | 6 | 0 | 7 | 0 |
| Charron, Joseph, PUL* | 1.000 | 8 | 0 | 2 | 0 | 2 | 1 |
| Chedister, Bradley, GVL | 1.000 | 11 | 0 | 3 | 0 | 3 | 0 |
| Cheng, Chi Hung, PUL* | .895 | 13 | 6 | 11 | 2 | 19 | 0 |
| Collins, Danny, DAN* | 1.000 | 11 | 0 | 2 | 0 | 2 | 0 |
| Collins, Kyle, BRL | 1.000 | 4 | 3 | 1 | 0 | 4 | 1 |
| Culpepper, Kevin, ELZ* | 1.000 | 9 | 1 | 1 | 0 | 2 | 0 |
| Davern, Mike, BRS | .500 | 11 | 0 | 1 | 1 | 2 | 0 |
| Davis, Cliff, GVL | .800 | 5 | 1 | 3 | 1 | 5 | 1 |
| Davis, Wade, PRI | 1.000 | 13 | 6 | 11 | 0 | 17 | 0 |
| DeWitt, Anthony, GVL | .600 | 7 | 0 | 3 | 2 | 5 | 0 |
| Dickerson, Bo, JCY | 1.000 | 3 | 0 | 1 | 0 | 1 | 0 |
| Dobyns, Jonathan, PRI | .667 | 12 | 2 | 0 | 1 | 3 | 0 |
| Duguay, Steven, ELZ | 1.000 | 12 | 2 | 8 | 0 | 10 | 0 |
| Dumesnil, Bryan, BLU* | 1.000 | 14 | 1 | 6 | 0 | 7 | 0 |
| Endl, Brady, DAN* | .857 | 16 | 2 | 4 | 1 | 7 | 0 |
| Evers, Billy, PRI | .778 | 21 | 0 | 7 | 2 | 9 | 0 |
| Felix, Wilken, BLU | 1.000 | 15 | 0 | 1 | 0 | 1 | 0 |
| Fox, Matthew, ELZ | 1.000 | 8 | 0 | 2 | 0 | 2 | 0 |
| Freites, Julio, KPT | 1.000 | 6 | 1 | 0 | 0 | 1 | 0 |
| Fry, Troy, KPT | .938 | 14 | 4 | 11 | 1 | 16 | 1 |
| Furrow, Jason, BLU* | .900 | 13 | 0 | 9 | 1 | 10 | 0 |
| Gabino, Armando, BRL | 1.000 | 5 | 3 | 2 | 0 | 5 | 0 |
| Gale, Bryan, PUL | 1.000 | 12 | 1 | 4 | 0 | 5 | 0 |
| Geddes, Michael, PRI | .857 | 9 | 2 | 4 | 1 | 7 | 0 |
| Gil, Roberto, PRI | 1.000 | 10 | 2 | 1 | 0 | 3 | 0 |
| Gomez, Jose, KPT | 1.000 | 8 | 0 | 3 | 0 | 3 | 0 |
| Gomez, Luis, JCY | 1.000 | 12 | 1 | 1 | 0 | 2 | 0 |
| Gonzalez, Gio, BRS* | .000 | 7 | 0 | 0 | 0 | 0 | 0 |
| Gonzalez, Humberto, KPT | .000 | 2 | 0 | 0 | 0 | 0 | 0 |
| Gonzalez, Juan, GVL | 1.000 | 3 | 1 | 0 | 0 | 1 | 0 |
| Gonzalez, Marino, KPT | .667 | 6 | 1 | 3 | 2 | 6 | 0 |
| Gor, Nick, PRI | 1.000 | 20 | 5 | 3 | 0 | 8 | 1 |
| Grant, Brian, PUL | 1.000 | 10 | 4 | 5 | 0 | 9 | 0 |
| Grant, Jessen, JCY | .000 | 14 | 0 | 0 | 0 | 0 | 0 |
| Gross, Timothy, JCY | .857 | 16 | 2 | 4 | 1 | 7 | 0 |
| Gutierrez, Juan, GVL | 1.000 | 13 | 6 | 4 | 0 | 10 | 0 |
| Guzman, Daniel, BRL | .667 | 13 | 1 | 3 | 2 | 6 | 1 |
| Haberer, Eric, JCY* | .750 | 9 | 4 | 5 | 3 | 12 | 0 |
| Haeger, Charles, BRS | .950 | 10 | 6 | 13 | 1 | 20 | 3 |
| Hahn, Cory, PUL | 1.000 | 3 | 1 | 0 | 0 | 1 | 0 |
| Harang, Daryl, PUL | 1.000 | 15 | 1 | 6 | 0 | 7 | 1 |
| Harrell, Lucas, BRS | .944 | 13 | 4 | 13 | 1 | 18 | 0 |
| Harris, Josh, BRL | 1.000 | 19 | 6 | 4 | 0 | 10 | 1 |
| Harrison, Matt, DAN* | .857 | 13 | 2 | 10 | 2 | 14 | 0 |
| Henington, Justin, BLU | .786 | 16 | 3 | 8 | 3 | 14 | 0 |
| Hernandez, Moises, BLU | .941 | 13 | 5 | 11 | 1 | 17 | 1 |
| James, Brad, GVL | .875 | 13 | 5 | 9 | 2 | 16 | 0 |
| Jimenez, Rodny, DAN | 1.000 | 14 | 4 | 1 | 0 | 5 | 1 |
| John, Jason, JCY | 1.000 | 9 | 2 | 2 | 0 | 4 | 0 |
| Johnson, Bryan, DAN* | 1.000 | 12 | 0 | 2 | 0 | 2 | 0 |
| Kelly, Chris, PRI | 1.000 | 4 | 2 | 0 | 0 | 2 | 0 |
| Kite, Josh, BRL* | 1.000 | 19 | 0 | 5 | 0 | 5 | 0 |
| Landing, Jeffrey, KPT | .750 | 6 | 1 | 2 | 1 | 4 | 0 |
| Lankford, Kris, ELZ | .000 | 5 | 0 | 0 | 0 | 0 | 0 |
| Larson, Matt, PRI | .750 | 6 | 1 | 2 | 1 | 4 | 0 |
| Lavergne, Jarrad, PRI* | .000 | 1 | 0 | 0 | 1 | 1 | 0 |
| Lemon, Nick, BRS | .889 | 15 | 5 | 3 | 1 | 9 | 0 |

| Player, Team | Pct. | G | PO | A | E | TC | DP |
|---|---|---|---|---|---|---|---|
| Lemon, Tim, JCY | .846 | 13 | 6 | 5 | 2 | 13 | 0 |
| Letson, Wesley, DAN* | 1.000 | 5 | 1 | 1 | 0 | 2 | 0 |
| Limas, Alejandro, PRI | .875 | 13 | 4 | 3 | 1 | 8 | 0 |
| Loadenthal, Carl, DAN* | 1.000 | 1 | 1 | 0 | 0 | 1 | 0 |
| Lofgren, Chuck, BRL* | 1.000 | 9 | 1 | 5 | 0 | 6 | 0 |
| Long, Jeffery, DAN | 1.000 | 6 | 1 | 0 | 0 | 1 | 0 |
| Lopez, Romelio, PRI | 1.000 | 5 | 1 | 9 | 0 | 10 | 0 |
| Lozado, Henry, BLU | 1.000 | 15 | 2 | 4 | 0 | 6 | 0 |
| Lubrano, Paul, BRL* | 1.000 | 3 | 0 | 3 | 0 | 3 | 0 |
| Lucas, Franklin, BLU | 1.000 | 18 | 0 | 2 | 0 | 2 | 0 |
| Mannex, Kevin, KPT | 1.000 | 10 | 2 | 1 | 0 | 3 | 0 |
| Marini, Chris, ELZ* | .929 | 11 | 4 | 9 | 1 | 14 | 1 |
| Marshall, Jay, BRS* | .875 | 11 | 4 | 10 | 2 | 16 | 2 |
| Marte, German, KPT | .800 | 9 | 0 | 4 | 1 | 5 | 0 |
| Martin, Adrian, PUL | 1.000 | 18 | 7 | 10 | 0 | 17 | 0 |
| Martinez, Javier, ELZ* | 1.000 | 12 | 0 | 3 | 0 | 3 | 0 |
| Martinez, Jonathan, ELZ | 1.000 | 20 | 2 | 5 | 0 | 7 | 0 |
| Mata, Frank, ELZ | 1.000 | 26 | 1 | 3 | 0 | 4 | 0 |
| McCrory, Robert, BLU | .714 | 11 | 3 | 2 | 2 | 7 | 0 |
| McGee, Jacob, PRI* | .909 | 12 | 1 | 9 | 1 | 11 | 0 |
| Medina, Dennis, ELZ | 1.000 | 13 | 2 | 11 | 0 | 13 | 1 |
| Meek, Evan, ELZ | .857 | 11 | 2 | 4 | 1 | 7 | 0 |
| Mendez, Winer, BLU | 1.000 | 11 | 3 | 12 | 0 | 15 | 0 |
| Mercedes, Gerson, BRL | 1.000 | 13 | 5 | 6 | 0 | 11 | 0 |
| Meyers, Ryan, KPT* | 1.000 | 2 | 1 | 0 | 0 | 1 | 0 |
| Minor, Zach, BLU* | 1.000 | 16 | 2 | 5 | 0 | 7 | 0 |
| Miramontes, Matt, KPT | .833 | 4 | 1 | 4 | 1 | 6 | 0 |
| Mousser, Jeff, ELZ | 1.000 | 18 | 2 | 2 | 0 | 4 | 0 |
| Murdy, Garrett, GVL | 1.000 | 8 | 0 | 3 | 0 | 3 | 0 |
| Muro, Joseph, PRI | 1.000 | 10 | 1 | 3 | 0 | 4 | 0 |
| Murphey, Tim, BRS* | .889 | 15 | 2 | 6 | 1 | 9 | 0 |
| Myers, Rodney, KPT | .000 | 2 | 0 | 0 | 1 | 1 | 0 |
| Nachreiner, Matt, BRS | .875 | 6 | 1 | 6 | 1 | 8 | 0 |
| Nelson, Brad, DAN | .857 | 20 | 1 | 5 | 1 | 7 | 0 |
| Noonan, Chris, JCY* | 1.000 | 16 | 2 | 5 | 0 | 7 | 0 |
| Novoa, Yunior, BRS* | 1.000 | 13 | 0 | 4 | 0 | 4 | 0 |
| O`Donnell, Matthew, GVL* | 1.000 | 15 | 4 | 5 | 0 | 9 | 1 |
| Parish, Brian, JCY | .667 | 20 | 0 | 2 | 1 | 3 | 0 |
| Pascual, Dionis, BLU | .833 | 17 | 2 | 3 | 1 | 6 | 1 |
| Pascual, Juan, BLU | 1.000 | 15 | 2 | 3 | 0 | 5 | 0 |
| Patton, Troy, GVL* | 1.000 | 6 | 1 | 4 | 0 | 5 | 0 |
| Paul, Jason, DAN | .833 | 17 | 1 | 4 | 1 | 6 | 0 |
| Paulino, Felipe, GVL | .667 | 10 | 1 | 3 | 2 | 6 | 0 |
| Payano, Nelson, DAN* | 1.000 | 9 | 1 | 4 | 0 | 5 | 0 |
| Pena, Luis, BRS | 1.000 | 10 | 1 | 2 | 0 | 3 | 0 |
| Perez, Carlos, BRS* | .900 | 13 | 2 | 7 | 1 | 10 | 1 |
| Perez, Juan, PUL | 1.000 | 1 | 2 | 1 | 0 | 3 | 0 |
| Perkins, Glen, ELZ* | .000 | 3 | 0 | 0 | 0 | 0 | 0 |
| Pidutti, James, PUL | .714 | 14 | 0 | 5 | 2 | 7 | 0 |
| Pleeter, Greg, JCY | .750 | 18 | 2 | 4 | 2 | 8 | 0 |
| Polanco, Yestin A., BRS* | .750 | 15 | 0 | 3 | 1 | 4 | 0 |
| Powell, John, JCY | 1.000 | 14 | 2 | 4 | 0 | 6 | 0 |
| Quaglieri, Will, KPT | .500 | 1 | 0 | 1 | 1 | 2 | 0 |
| Redfern, Chad, PRI | .909 | 10 | 2 | 8 | 1 | 11 | 0 |
| Rengel, Orlando, KPT | 1.000 | 14 | 4 | 7 | 0 | 11 | 0 |
| Rickert, Brandon, BRL | 1.000 | 19 | 1 | 8 | 0 | 9 | 2 |
| Rider, Michael, PUL | 1.000 | 17 | 1 | 6 | 0 | 7 | 0 |
| Robertson, Quinton, JCY | .857 | 7 | 0 | 6 | 1 | 7 | 0 |
| Roddy, Dustin, BRL | 1.000 | 20 | 0 | 7 | 0 | 7 | 1 |
| Rodriguez, Claudio, PRI | 1.000 | 15 | 0 | 1 | 0 | 1 | 0 |
| Rodriguez, Edward, PUL* | 1.000 | 19 | 1 | 11 | 0 | 12 | 0 |
| Rodriguez, Francisco, BRS* | 1.000 | 6 | 1 | 0 | 0 | 1 | 0 |
| Rodriguez, Joan, PRI | .000 | 5 | 0 | 0 | 0 | 0 | 0 |
| Roelle, Justin, BRS* | 1.000 | 10 | 0 | 3 | 0 | 3 | 0 |
| Romero, Levi, GVL | .909 | 13 | 3 | 7 | 1 | 11 | 0 |
| Roy, Scott, PUL | 1.000 | 8 | 0 | 3 | 0 | 3 | 0 |
| Salas, Juan, PRI | .750 | 8 | 0 | 3 | 1 | 4 | 0 |
| Sanchez, Raymon, PUL* | .750 | 18 | 2 | 4 | 2 | 8 | 1 |
| Santiago, Jose, DAN | .750 | 6 | 2 | 1 | 1 | 4 | 0 |
| Santos, Reid, BRL* | .778 | 12 | 0 | 14 | 4 | 18 | 1 |
| Savickas, Russell, PUL | .833 | 10 | 1 | 9 | 2 | 12 | 0 |
| Sawatski, Jay, ELZ* | 1.000 | 4 | 0 | 2 | 0 | 2 | 0 |
| Schau, Adrian, BRL | 1.000 | 19 | 1 | 3 | 0 | 4 | 0 |
| Scherer, Matthew, JCY | 1.000 | 13 | 4 | 6 | 0 | 10 | 0 |
| Schindling, Andy, BLU | .750 | 8 | 0 | 3 | 1 | 4 | 1 |
| Schwabe, Ryan, BLU* | 1.000 | 11 | 1 | 4 | 0 | 5 | 0 |
| Shinskie, David, ELZ | .857 | 11 | 1 | 11 | 2 | 14 | 1 |
| Siak, Joey, JCY* | 1.000 | 20 | 1 | 8 | 0 | 9 | 0 |
| Sides, Andrew, KPT* | 1.000 | 6 | 1 | 4 | 0 | 5 | 0 |
| Sillman, Michael, JCY | 1.000 | 6 | 0 | 2 | 0 | 2 | 0 |
| Smit, Alexander, ELZ* | 1.000 | 6 | 0 | 8 | 0 | 8 | 0 |
| Smith, Chuck, KPT | .667 | 4 | 0 | 2 | 1 | 3 | 0 |

| Player, Team | Pct. | G | PO | A | E | TC | DP |
|---|---|---|---|---|---|---|---|
| Smith, Cole, PRI | 1.000 | 11 | 4 | 1 | 0 | 5 | 0 |
| Smith, Danny, DAN* | 1.000 | 14 | 1 | 1 | 0 | 2 | 0 |
| Smith, David, KPT* | 1.000 | 17 | 2 | 6 | 0 | 8 | 1 |
| Solis, Marcos, GVL | .778 | 16 | 3 | 4 | 2 | 9 | 0 |
| Soriano, Julio, BLU | 1.000 | 3 | 0 | 1 | 0 | 1 | 0 |
| Soto, Enyelbert, GVL* | .800 | 24 | 1 | 3 | 1 | 5 | 0 |
| Soto, Jesus, BRL* | 1.000 | 19 | 0 | 1 | 0 | 1 | 0 |
| Sotro, Christopher, GVL | 1.000 | 13 | 2 | 4 | 0 | 6 | 0 |
| Spring, Dan, JCY | 1.000 | 3 | 0 | 1 | 0 | 1 | 0 |
| Sues, Jarret, PRI | 1.000 | 24 | 5 | 3 | 0 | 8 | 0 |
| Swindell, Mike, KPT | 1.000 | 2 | 1 | 2 | 0 | 3 | 0 |
| Tate, Derek, PUL* | 1.000 | 11 | 1 | 4 | 0 | 5 | 0 |
| Thompson, Ryan, GVL | 1.000 | 15 | 2 | 1 | 0 | 3 | 0 |
| Timm, Jordan, PUL* | 1.000 | 11 | 4 | 17 | 0 | 21 | 0 |
| Torres, Carlos, BRS | .875 | 19 | 1 | 6 | 1 | 8 | 1 |
| Torres, David, KPT | 1.000 | 15 | 1 | 7 | 0 | 8 | 0 |
| Tressler, Aaron, PUL | 1.000 | 21 | 3 | 4 | 0 | 7 | 1 |
| Veloz, Yonatan, BRS* | 1.000 | 13 | 0 | 3 | 0 | 3 | 0 |
| Villa, Kelvin, DAN* | .889 | 15 | 1 | 7 | 1 | 9 | 0 |
| Vines, Chris, DAN | .889 | 13 | 4 | 4 | 1 | 9 | 0 |
| Waldrop, Kyle, ELZ | 1.000 | 4 | 0 | 4 | 0 | 4 | 0 |
| Weintraub, Jason, KPT | 1.000 | 11 | 3 | 5 | 0 | 8 | 0 |
| Weitzman, William, KPT | .792 | 16 | 7 | 12 | 5 | 24 | 0 |
| Williams, John, ELZ* | 1.000 | 14 | 1 | 2 | 0 | 3 | 0 |
| Worrell, Mark, JCY | 1.000 | 18 | 1 | 2 | 0 | 3 | 0 |
| Worthington, Timothy, KPT | 1.000 | 6 | 0 | 2 | 0 | 2 | 0 |

# LEAGUE CHAMPIONS

| Year | Team | Pct. |
|---|---|---|
| 1921— | Greenville | .608 |
| | Johnson City* | .627 |
| 1922— | Bristol | .557 |
| 1923— | Knoxville | .635 |
| 1924— | Knoxville* | .642 |
| | Bristol | .607 |
| 1925— | Greenville | .667 |
| 1926-36— | Did not operate. | |
| 1937— | Elizabethton | .559 |
| | Pennington Gap* | .580 |
| 1938— | Elizabethton | .664 |
| | Greenville (3rd)† | .571 |
| 1939— | Elizabethton‡ | .597 |
| 1940— | Johnson City§ | .726 |
| | Elizabethton | .750 |
| 1941— | Johnson City | .614 |
| | Elizabethton* | .661 |
| 1942— | Bristol | .667 |
| | Bristol∞ | .660 |
| 1943— | Bristol | .755 |
| | Bristol▲ | .617 |
| 1944— | Kingsport‡ | .575 |
| 1945— | Kingsport‡ | .670 |
| 1946— | New River‡ | .675 |
| 1947— | Pulaski | .648 |
| | New River (3rd)† | .516 |
| 1948— | Pulaski‡ | .680 |
| 1949— | Bluefield‡ | .721 |
| 1950— | Bluefield | .600 |
| | Bluefield◆ | .745 |
| 1951— | Kingsport‡ | .659 |
| 1952— | Johnson City | .595 |
| | Welch (3rd)† | .509 |
| 1953— | Welch* | .705 |
| | Johnson City | .672 |
| 1954— | Bluefield‡ | .619 |
| 1955— | Salem■ | .689 |
| 1956— | Did not operate. | |
| 1957— | Bluefield | .701 |
| 1958— | Johnson City | .662 |
| 1959— | Morristown | .603 |
| 1960— | Wytheville | .614 |
| 1961— | Middlesboro | .591 |
| 1962— | Bluefield | .671 |
| 1963— | Bluefield | .652 |
| 1964— | Johnson City | .662 |
| 1965— | Salem | .614 |
| 1966— | Marion | .623 |
| 1967— | Bluefield | .627 |
| 1968— | Marion | .583 |
| 1969— | Pulaski▼ | .576 |
| | Johnson City | .544 |
| 1970— | Bluefield | .638 |
| 1971— | Bluefield▼ | .609 |
| | Kingsport | .559 |
| 1972— | Bristol▼ | .588 |
| | Covington | .586 |
| 1973— | Kingsport | .757 |
| 1974— | Bristol▼ | .754 |
| | Bluefield | .536 |
| 1975— | Marion | .515 |
| | Johnson City▼ | .603 |
| 1976— | Johnson City▼ | .714 |
| | Bluefield | .600 |
| 1977— | Kingsport | .623 |
| 1978— | Elizabethton | .594 |
| 1979— | Paintsville | .800 |
| 1980— | Paintsville | .657 |
| 1981— | Paintsville | .657 |
| 1982— | Bluefield▼ | .681 |
| | Johnson City | .478 |
| 1983— | Paintsville | .653 |
| 1984— | Elizabethton• | .580 |
| | Pulaski | .536 |
| 1985— | Bristol†† | .638 |
| 1986— | Johnson City | .667 |
| | Pulaski• | .621 |
| 1987— | Burlington• | .729 |
| | Johnson City | .609 |
| 1988— | Kingsport• | .644 |
| | Burlington | .529 |
| 1989— | Elizabethton• | .691 |
| | Pulaski | .618 |
| 1990— | Elizabethton | .761 |
| 1991— | Pulaski• | .662 |
| | Burlington | .597 |
| 1992— | Elizabethton | .742 |
| | Bluefield• | .597 |
| 1993— | Burlington• | .647 |
| | Elizabethton | .552 |
| 1994— | Princeton• | .621 |
| | Johnson City | .618 |
| 1995— | Bluefield | .754 |
| | Kingsport• | .727 |
| 1996— | Kingsport | .716 |
| | Bluefield▼ | .618 |
| 1997— | Pulaski | .632 |
| | Bluefield• | .580 |
| 1998— | Bristol• | .636 |
| | Princeton | .559 |
| 1999— | Pulaski | .696 |
| | Martinsville• | .586 |
| 2000— | Elizabethton• | .719 |
| 2001— | Elizabethton | .651 |
| | Bluefield• | .500 |
| 2002— | Bluefield | .662 |
| | Bristol• | .632 |
| 2003— | Martinsville | .646 |
| | Elizabethton• | .636 |
| 2004— | Danville | .621 |
| | Greeneville• | .612 |

*Won split-season playoff. †Won four-team playoff. ‡Won championship and four-team playoff. §Johnson City, first-half winner, won playoff involving six clubs. ∞Won both halves and defeated second-place Elizabethton in playoff. ▲Won both halves, but Erwin won four-team playoff. ◆Won both halves, but Bristol won two-club playoff. ■Salem and Johnson City declared playoff co-champions when weather forced cancellation of final series. ▼League was divided into Northern, Southern divisions; declared league champion based on highest won-lost percentage. •League was divided into divisions; won playoff. ††Bristol declared league champion based on regular-season record.

# PIONEER LEAGUE

## LEAGUE OFFICE

**President**
Jim McCurdy
**Address**
P.O. Box 2564
Spokane, WA 99220
**Phone**
509-456-7615

**Teams (affiliation)**
Billings Mustangs (Reds)
Casper Rockies (Rockies)
Great Falls White Sox (White Sox)
Helena Brewers (Brewers)
Idaho Falls Chukars (Royals)
Missoula Osprey (Diamondbacks)
Ogden Raptors (Dodgers)
Orem Owlz (Angels)

## 2004 FINAL STANDINGS

### FIRST HALF

#### NORTHERN DIVISION

| Team | W | L | T | Pct. | GB |
|---|---|---|---|---|---|
| Billings | 21 | 16 | - | .568 | ... |
| Helena | 21 | 17 | - | .553 | 1/2 |
| Great Falls | 17 | 20 | - | .459 | 4 |
| Missoula | 15 | 23 | - | .395 | 6 1/2 |

#### SOUTHERN DIVISION

| Team | W | L | T | Pct. | GB |
|---|---|---|---|---|---|
| Idaho Falls | 20 | 18 | - | .526 | ... |
| Provo | 20 | 18 | - | .526 | 0 |
| Ogden | 19 | 18 | - | .514 | 1/2 |
| Casper | 17 | 20 | - | .459 | 2 1/2 |

### SECOND HALF

#### NORTHERN DIVISION

| Team | W | L | T | Pct. | GB |
|---|---|---|---|---|---|
| Great Falls | 25 | 13 | - | .658 | ... |
| Helena | 18 | 20 | - | .474 | 7 |
| Billings | 16 | 21 | - | .432 | 8 1/2 |
| Missoula | 12 | 23 | - | .343 | 11 1/2 |

#### SOUTHERN DIVISION

| Team | W | L | T | Pct. | GB |
|---|---|---|---|---|---|
| Provo | 24 | 14 | - | .632 | ... |
| Idaho Falls | 22 | 16 | - | .579 | 2 |
| Casper | 16 | 20 | - | .444 | 7 |
| Ogden | 16 | 22 | - | .421 | 8 |

### COMPOSITE

| Team | W | L | T | PCT | GB | PRV | GRF | IDF | HEL | BIL | OGD | CAS | MSO |
|---|---|---|---|---|---|---|---|---|---|---|---|---|---|
| Provo(Angels) | 44 | 32 | - | .579 | ... | X | 3 | 10 | 3 | 6 | 9 | 8 | 5 |
| Great Falls (Dodgers) | 42 | 33 | - | .560 | 1 1/2 | 4 | X | 3 | 11 | 9 | 3 | 3 | 9 |
| Idaho Falls (Padres) | 42 | 34 | - | .553 | 2 | 6 | 4 | X | 4 | 4 | 12 | 9 | 3 |
| Helena (Brewers) | 39 | 37 | - | .513 | 5 | 4 | 5 | 3 | X | 7 | 3 | 3 | 14 |
| Billings (Reds) | 37 | 37 | - | .500 | 6 | 1 | 6 | 3 | 9 | X | 4 | 6 | 8 |
| Ogden (Brewers) | 35 | 40 | - | .467 | 8 1/2 | 7 | 4 | 4 | 4 | 3 | X | 10 | 5 |
| Casper (Rockies) | 33 | 40 | - | .452 | 9 1/2 | 8 | 4 | 7 | 4 | 1 | 6 | X | 3 |
| Missoula (Diamondbacks) | 27 | 46 | - | .370 | 15 1/2 | 2 | 7 | 4 | 2 | 7 | 3 | 2 | X |

Major league affiliations in parentheses.

PLAYOFFS: Billings defeated Great Falls two games to none; Provo defeated Idaho Falls two games to one; Provo defeated Billings two games to none to win championship.

REGULAR-SEASON ATTENDANCE: Billings, 106,837; Casper, 42,933; Graet Falls, 109,779; Helena 37,511; Idaho Falls, 61,288; Missoula 64,942; Ogden, 133,886; Provo, 43,810; Total attendance—600,786.

MANAGERS: Billings, Luis Aguayo; Casper, P.J. Carey; Great Falls, John Orton; Helena, Johnny Narron; Idaho, Carlos Lezcano; Missoula, Jim Presley; Ogden, Travis Barbary; Provo, Tom Kotchman.

ALL-STAR TEAM: C—Craig Tatum, Billings; 1B—Cory Dunlap, Ogden; 2B—Eddie Solis, Idaho Falls; 3B—Billy Butler, Idaho Falls; SS—Sean Rodriguez, Provo; OF Brian McFall, Idaho Falls; OF—Seth Smith, Casper; OF—Jaen Centeno; DH—Andrew Toussant, Provo; RHP—Samuel Deduno, Casper; LHP—Tyler Pelland, Billings; Reliever—Mitchell Arnold, Provo; Manager—Tom Kotchman, Provo; MVP—Sean Rodriguez, Provo; Pitcher of the Year—Samuel Deduno, Casper; Manager of the Year—Tom Kotchman, Provo.

## 2004 BATTING

### TEAM

| Team | G | TPA | AB | R | H | TB | 2B | 3B | HR | RBI | SH | SF | HP | BB | IBB | SO | SB | CS | GDP | LOB | ShO | Avg. | OBP | Slg. |
|---|---|---|---|---|---|---|---|---|---|---|---|---|---|---|---|---|---|---|---|---|---|---|---|---|
| Idaho Falls | 76 | 3103 | 2674 | 570 | 850 | 1257 | 179 | 24 | 60 | 504 | 19 | 36 | 49 | 324 | 2 | 596 | 101 | 43 | 61 | 579 | 1 | .318 | .397 | .470 |
| Ogden | 75 | 3030 | 2631 | 496 | 798 | 1217 | 156 | 22 | 73 | 425 | 16 | 24 | 48 | 311 | 5 | 577 | 54 | 21 | 69 | 584 | 1 | .303 | .384 | .463 |
| Casper | 73 | 2976 | 2539 | 492 | 742 | 1110 | 130 | 20 | 66 | 430 | 10 | 23 | 41 | 362 | 0 | 617 | 87 | 40 | 56 | 588 | 0 | .292 | .386 | .437 |
| Helena | 76 | 3064 | 2579 | 456 | 741 | 1055 | 152 | 15 | 44 | 396 | 36 | 21 | 57 | 368 | 8 | 573 | 116 | 51 | 46 | 633 | 3 | .287 | .385 | .409 |
| Provo | 76 | 3042 | 2564 | 514 | 722 | 1100 | 137 | 23 | 65 | 446 | 17 | 17 | 72 | 371 | 4 | 676 | 80 | 29 | 50 | 605 | 3 | .282 | .385 | .429 |
| Great Falls | 75 | 2976 | 2607 | 441 | 710 | 1111 | 139 | 20 | 74 | 391 | 29 | 19 | 60 | 259 | 4 | 656 | 85 | 41 | 50 | 525 | 3 | .272 | .349 | .426 |
| Missoula | 73 | 2837 | 2476 | 399 | 672 | 1039 | 131 | 25 | 62 | 361 | 28 | 20 | 61 | 252 | 9 | 550 | 69 | 33 | 23 | 520 | 1 | .271 | .351 | .420 |
| Billings | 74 | 2941 | 2489 | 400 | 656 | 999 | 120 | 26 | 57 | 358 | 38 | 20 | 55 | 338 | 5 | 638 | 79 | 32 | 42 | 618 | 7 | .264 | .361 | .401 |

### INDIVIDUAL

#### TOP QUALIFIERS FOR BATTING CHAMPIONSHIP

Minimum 205 plate appearances. *Lefthanded batter. †Switch-hitter.

| Player, Team | G | TPA | AB | R | H | TB | 2B | 3B | HR | RBI | SH | SF | HP | BB | IBB | SO | SB | CS | GDP | Avg. | OBP | Slg. |
|---|---|---|---|---|---|---|---|---|---|---|---|---|---|---|---|---|---|---|---|---|---|---|
| Butler, Billy, Idaho Falls | 74 | 324 | 260 | 74 | 97 | 155 | 22 | 3 | 10 | 68 | 0 | 3 | 4 | 57 | 0 | 63 | 5 | 0 | 6 | .373 | .488 | .596 |
| Smith, Seth, Casper * | 56 | 260 | 233 | 46 | 86 | 140 | 21 | 3 | 9 | 61 | 0 | 2 | 0 | 25 | 0 | 47 | 9 | 1 | 7 | .369 | .427 | .601 |

| Player, Team | G | TPA | AB | R | H | TB | 2B | 3B | HR | RBI | SH | SF | HP | BB | IBB | SO | SB | CS | GDP | Avg. | OBP | Slg. |
|---|---|---|---|---|---|---|---|---|---|---|---|---|---|---|---|---|---|---|---|---|---|---|
| Richardson, Grant, Helena | 44 | 207 | 166 | 35 | 61 | 94 | 16 | 1 | 5 | 42 | 0 | 3 | 6 | 32 | 1 | 20 | 2 | 4 | 7 | .367 | .478 | .566 |
| Solis, Eddie, Idaho Falls | 64 | 273 | 246 | 48 | 90 | 115 | 15 | 2 | 2 | 54 | 0 | 3 | 5 | 19 | 1 | 41 | 3 | 0 | 9 | .366 | .418 | .467 |
| Sollmann, Steven, Helena | 72 | 346 | 272 | 59 | 99 | 118 | 12 | 2 | 1 | 39 | 8 | 0 | 13 | 52 | 1 | 30 | 23 | 8 | 4 | .364 | .487 | .434 |
| McFall, Brian, Idaho Falls | 68 | 303 | 262 | 64 | 94 | 160 | 22 | 1 | 14 | 67 | 0 | 4 | 7 | 30 | 0 | 64 | 23 | 2 | 5 | .359 | .432 | .611 |
| Dunlap, Cory, Ogden * | 71 | 317 | 245 | 57 | 86 | 127 | 18 | 1 | 7 | 53 | 0 | 2 | 2 | 68 | 1 | 40 | 0 | 0 | 7 | .351 | .492 | .518 |
| Valentin, Geraldo, Idaho Falls | 66 | 289 | 259 | 55 | 90 | 135 | 21 | 6 | 4 | 44 | 2 | 5 | 4 | 19 | 0 | 28 | 7 | 5 | 6 | .347 | .394 | .521 |
| Westervelt, Christopher, Ogden | 49 | 209 | 176 | 41 | 60 | 102 | 12 | 0 | 10 | 37 | 0 | 1 | 5 | 27 | 1 | 46 | 0 | 0 | 5 | .341 | .440 | .580 |
| Rodriguez, Sean, Provo | 64 | 292 | 225 | 64 | 76 | 128 | 14 | 4 | 10 | 55 | 0 | 1 | 15 | 51 | 0 | 62 | 9 | 3 | 2 | .338 | .486 | .569 |
| Davies, Mike, Casper * | 61 | 259 | 232 | 44 | 78 | 123 | 16 | 1 | 9 | 55 | 0 | 1 | 1 | 25 | 0 | 70 | 1 | 3 | 6 | .336 | .402 | .530 |
| Gentry, Phil, Billings * | 62 | 275 | 242 | 39 | 81 | 120 | 21 | 3 | 4 | 31 | 9 | 1 | 2 | 21 | 0 | 47 | 5 | 6 | 3 | .335 | .391 | .496 |
| Batz, Daniel, Ogden | 55 | 235 | 206 | 29 | 69 | 94 | 10 | 3 | 3 | 28 | 0 | 2 | 8 | 19 | 0 | 21 | 3 | 1 | 8 | .335 | .409 | .456 |
| Sutton, Nathanael, Provo * | 54 | 225 | 180 | 46 | 59 | 74 | 6 | 3 | 1 | 34 | 1 | 1 | 6 | 37 | 0 | 40 | 7 | 2 | 1 | .328 | .455 | .411 |
| Salazar, Darwinson, Idaho Falls | 56 | 232 | 195 | 39 | 62 | 84 | 10 | 3 | 2 | 31 | 4 | 2 | 3 | 28 | 1 | 52 | 17 | 6 | 1 | .318 | .408 | .431 |

DEPARTMENTAL LEADERS: G—Three tied with 72; AB—DeWitt, 299; R—Butler, 74; H—Sollman, 99; TB—McFall, 160; 2B—Three tied with 22; 3B—Collaro, Valentin, 6; HR—Mosby, 19; RBI—Butler, 68; SH—Gentry, 9; SF—Mosby, Hayes, 6; HP—S. Rodriguez, 15; BB—Dunlap, 68; IBB—Festa, 4; SO—Mosby, 87; SB—McFall, Sollmann, 23; CS—S. Martin, 10; GIDP—Batista, 10; Slg.—McFall, .611; OBP—Dunlap, .492.

## ALL PLAYERS

*Lefthanded batter. †Switch-hitter.

| Player, Team | G | TPA | AB | R | H | TB | 2B | 3B | HR | RBI | SH | SF | HP | BB | IBB | SO | SB | CS | GDP | Avg. | OBP | Slg. |
|---|---|---|---|---|---|---|---|---|---|---|---|---|---|---|---|---|---|---|---|---|---|---|
| Acosta, Gilberto, Helena † | 33 | 104 | 95 | 12 | 21 | 30 | 7 | 1 | 0 | 5 | 1 | 0 | 0 | 8 | 1 | 22 | 9 | 1 | 1 | .221 | .282 | .316 |
| Allen, Trevor, Casper | 33 | 134 | 113 | 14 | 24 | 33 | 4 | 1 | 1 | 11 | 1 | 2 | 4 | 14 | 0 | 30 | 2 | 1 | 3 | .212 | .316 | .292 |
| Almonte, Sandy, Casper † | 8 | 42 | 39 | 12 | 21 | 30 | 4 | 1 | 1 | 6 | 0 | 0 | 0 | 3 | 0 | 5 | 4 | 2 | 1 | .538 | .571 | .769 |
| Alvarez, Ferny, Great Falls * | 38 | 142 | 129 | 20 | 27 | 44 | 8 | 0 | 3 | 13 | 1 | 0 | 0 | 12 | 0 | 43 | 4 | 3 | 4 | .209 | .277 | .341 |
| Anderson, Drew, Billings † | 54 | 243 | 197 | 40 | 50 | 74 | 10 | 4 | 2 | 29 | 4 | 2 | 1 | 39 | 0 | 42 | 14 | 4 | 2 | .254 | .377 | .376 |
| Arias, Hector, Ogden | 29 | 116 | 107 | 13 | 27 | 41 | 6 | 1 | 2 | 14 | 1 | 1 | 0 | 7 | 0 | 27 | 1 | 1 | 3 | .252 | .296 | .383 |
| Baldwin, Bruce, Casper | 28 | 94 | 83 | 17 | 18 | 27 | 4 | 1 | 1 | 7 | 1 | 0 | 4 | 6 | 0 | 20 | 1 | 2 | 2 | .217 | .301 | .325 |
| Bates, Dallas, Helena * | 37 | 133 | 118 | 21 | 33 | 44 | 5 | 0 | 2 | 10 | 0 | 1 | 2 | 12 | 0 | 38 | 3 | 3 | 1 | .280 | .353 | .373 |
| Batista, Alexander, Idaho Falls | 70 | 319 | 291 | 59 | 86 | 120 | 21 | 2 | 3 | 37 | 0 | 4 | 4 | 20 | 0 | 57 | 12 | 5 | 10 | .296 | .345 | .412 |
| Batz, Daniel, Ogden | 55 | 235 | 206 | 29 | 69 | 94 | 10 | 3 | 3 | 28 | 0 | 2 | 8 | 19 | 0 | 21 | 3 | 1 | 8 | .335 | .409 | .456 |
| Belcher, Jordan, Billings | 3 | 13 | 11 | 1 | 2 | 2 | 0 | 0 | 0 | 1 | 1 | 0 | 0 | 1 | 0 | 0 | 0 | 0 | 0 | .182 | .250 | .182 |
| Beltre, Elvin, Billings | 30 | 123 | 114 | 18 | 29 | 45 | 3 | 2 | 3 | 15 | 0 | 0 | 1 | 8 | 0 | 34 | 7 | 0 | 2 | .254 | .309 | .395 |
| Berry, Boomer, Great Falls * | 65 | 303 | 254 | 55 | 78 | 102 | 10 | 1 | 4 | 29 | 6 | 2 | 6 | 34 | 0 | 35 | 14 | 3 | 3 | .307 | .399 | .402 |
| Blevins, Clay, Helena * | 30 | 122 | 103 | 11 | 25 | 31 | 6 | 0 | 0 | 12 | 1 | 2 | 2 | 14 | 0 | 14 | 1 | 1 | 3 | .243 | .339 | .301 |
| Boggs, Steven, Casper † | 41 | 172 | 149 | 23 | 33 | 36 | 3 | 0 | 0 | 23 | 0 | 0 | 0 | 21 | 0 | 36 | 14 | 6 | 2 | .221 | .318 | .242 |
| Boyer, Billy, Provo † | 23 | 84 | 71 | 12 | 17 | 28 | 3 | 1 | 2 | 10 | 0 | 0 | 3 | 10 | 0 | 26 | 2 | 0 | 3 | .239 | .357 | .394 |
| Brady, Joshua, Helena | 29 | 127 | 113 | 24 | 41 | 73 | 9 | 4 | 5 | 24 | 0 | 0 | 1 | 13 | 0 | 24 | 5 | 3 | 2 | .363 | .433 | .646 |
| Brewster, Jonathon, Provo | 1 | 1 | 0 | 1 | 0 | 0 | 0 | 0 | 0 | 0 | 0 | 0 | 0 | 0 | 0 | 0 | 0 | 0 | 0 | .000 | .000 | .000 |
| Brito, Javier, Missoula | 68 | 254 | 232 | 36 | 72 | 115 | 17 | 1 | 8 | 44 | 2 | 0 | 4 | 16 | 2 | 37 | 0 | 1 | 4 | .310 | .365 | .496 |
| Brown, Russell, Idaho Falls | 46 | 165 | 137 | 26 | 44 | 81 | 13 | 0 | 8 | 34 | 0 | 2 | 0 | 26 | 0 | 36 | 0 | 2 | 3 | .321 | .424 | .591 |
| Bruce, Cole, Ogden | 23 | 75 | 69 | 13 | 16 | 25 | 3 | 0 | 2 | 4 | 0 | 0 | 0 | 6 | 0 | 16 | 0 | 1 | 1 | .232 | .293 | .362 |
| Bruce, Derek, Missoula | 60 | 252 | 225 | 29 | 61 | 79 | 8 | 2 | 2 | 25 | 4 | 2 | 9 | 12 | 0 | 32 | 4 | 7 | 3 | .271 | .331 | .351 |
| Buhagiar, Joshua, Missoula * | 31 | 111 | 96 | 17 | 25 | 42 | 7 | 2 | 2 | 11 | 0 | 0 | 6 | 9 | 1 | 21 | 4 | 1 | 0 | .260 | .360 | .438 |
| Butler, Billy, Idaho Falls | 74 | 324 | 260 | 74 | 97 | 155 | 22 | 3 | 10 | 68 | 0 | 3 | 4 | 57 | 0 | 63 | 5 | 0 | 6 | .373 | .488 | .596 |
| Campos, Tiago, Billings | 14 | 55 | 44 | 7 | 15 | 22 | 3 | 2 | 0 | 6 | 1 | 2 | 2 | 6 | 0 | 11 | 1 | 2 | 0 | .341 | .426 | .500 |
| Carter, Brandon, Ogden * | 25 | 103 | 83 | 20 | 32 | 41 | 7 | 1 | 0 | 14 | 2 | 2 | 1 | 15 | 0 | 16 | 9 | 3 | 0 | .386 | .475 | .494 |
| Casilla, Alexi, Provo † | 4 | 17 | 12 | 4 | 4 | 7 | 1 | 1 | 0 | 1 | 0 | 0 | 1 | 4 | 0 | 0 | 1 | 0 | 0 | .333 | .529 | .583 |
| Castillo, Albenis, Ogden | 17 | 24 | 20 | 6 | 9 | 15 | 3 | 0 | 1 | 2 | 0 | 0 | 1 | 3 | 1 | 4 | 0 | 0 | 0 | .450 | .542 | .750 |
| Castillo, Luis, Ogden | 31 | 133 | 122 | 30 | 38 | 62 | 6 | 0 | 6 | 26 | 0 | 0 | 1 | 10 | 0 | 32 | 0 | 0 | 1 | .311 | .368 | .508 |
| Castillo, Wilkin, Missoula † | 63 | 267 | 243 | 32 | 66 | 101 | 13 | 5 | 4 | 32 | 4 | 5 | 7 | 8 | 1 | 40 | 5 | 2 | 1 | .272 | .308 | .416 |
| Centeno, Jaen, Missoula | 56 | 234 | 196 | 34 | 58 | 86 | 12 | 2 | 4 | 34 | 1 | 1 | 3 | 33 | 1 | 48 | 3 | 5 | 3 | .296 | .403 | .439 |
| Cerulo, Nicholas, Idaho Falls | 2 | 9 | 7 | 3 | 4 | 4 | 0 | 0 | 0 | 1 | 0 | 0 | 0 | 2 | 0 | 1 | 0 | 0 | 0 | .571 | .667 | .571 |
| Cole, Bruce, Ogden | 2 | 5 | 4 | 2 | 1 | 2 | 1 | 0 | 0 | 2 | 0 | 1 | 0 | 0 | 0 | 1 | 1 | 0 | 0 | .250 | .200 | .500 |
| Collaro, Tom, Great Falls | 66 | 290 | 268 | 48 | 77 | 150 | 7 | 6 | 18 | 66 | 0 | 3 | 6 | 13 | 0 | 82 | 4 | 3 | 8 | .287 | .331 | .560 |
| Cook, David, Great Falls | 34 | 134 | 113 | 26 | 34 | 63 | 3 | 1 | 8 | 22 | 0 | 0 | 1 | 20 | 0 | 26 | 2 | 2 | 2 | .301 | .410 | .558 |
| Cooper, Caleb, Great Falls | 21 | 81 | 73 | 17 | 20 | 33 | 10 | 0 | 1 | 7 | 0 | 0 | 3 | 5 | 0 | 19 | 2 | 0 | 0 | .274 | .346 | .452 |
| Corredor, Nestor, Helena | 5 | 23 | 18 | 1 | 1 | 1 | 0 | 0 | 0 | 2 | 2 | 1 | 0 | 2 | 0 | 5 | 0 | 0 | 1 | .056 | .143 | .056 |
| Curreri, Frank, Missoula * | 12 | 43 | 36 | 8 | 10 | 12 | 2 | 0 | 0 | 5 | 0 | 2 | 0 | 5 | 0 | 9 | 0 | 0 | 0 | .278 | .349 | .333 |
| Davies, Mike, Casper * | 61 | 259 | 232 | 44 | 78 | 123 | 16 | 1 | 9 | 55 | 0 | 1 | 1 | 25 | 0 | 70 | 1 | 3 | 6 | .336 | .402 | .530 |
| De La Cruz, Carlos, Helena | 38 | 125 | 108 | 20 | 37 | 48 | 5 | 0 | 2 | 15 | 1 | 2 | 0 | 14 | 0 | 21 | 1 | 2 | 1 | .343 | .411 | .444 |
| Del Campo, Manny, Missoula | 16 | 38 | 31 | 4 | 8 | 13 | 2 | 0 | 1 | 4 | 0 | 0 | 3 | 4 | 0 | 6 | 0 | 0 | 0 | .258 | .395 | .419 |
| Del Rosario, Felipe, Idaho Falls | 34 | 113 | 99 | 16 | 26 | 42 | 7 | 0 | 3 | 17 | 2 | 0 | 0 | 12 | 0 | 28 | 0 | 2 | 2 | .263 | .342 | .424 |
| Denker, Travis, Ogden | 57 | 254 | 225 | 44 | 70 | 125 | 17 | 1 | 12 | 43 | 1 | 4 | 0 | 24 | 2 | 52 | 2 | 3 | 7 | .311 | .372 | .556 |
| Deuchler, Matt, Great Falls | 43 | 184 | 160 | 16 | 39 | 61 | 11 | 1 | 3 | 27 | 1 | 0 | 2 | 21 | 0 | 36 | 3 | 2 | 1 | .244 | .339 | .381 |
| Dewitt, Blake, Ogden * | 70 | 332 | 299 | 61 | 85 | 146 | 19 | 3 | 12 | 47 | 1 | 1 | 3 | 28 | 0 | 78 | 1 | 1 | 6 | .284 | .350 | .488 |
| Downing, Ramon, Missoula † | 28 | 115 | 100 | 18 | 29 | 47 | 7 | 1 | 3 | 22 | 0 | 4 | 2 | 9 | 0 | 28 | 4 | 2 | 0 | .290 | .348 | .470 |
| Dragicevich, Jeff, Casper | 51 | 212 | 177 | 31 | 44 | 53 | 7 | 1 | 0 | 13 | 2 | 2 | 5 | 26 | 0 | 39 | 1 | 2 | 5 | .249 | .357 | .299 |
| Duff, Timothy, Provo | 43 | 183 | 151 | 31 | 45 | 62 | 11 | 0 | 2 | 24 | 0 | 2 | 2 | 28 | 1 | 37 | 1 | 0 | 8 | .298 | .410 | .411 |
| Dunlap, Cory, Ogden * | 71 | 317 | 245 | 57 | 86 | 127 | 18 | 1 | 7 | 53 | 0 | 2 | 2 | 68 | 1 | 40 | 0 | 0 | 7 | .351 | .492 | .518 |
| Ellis, Jason, Billings | 19 | 56 | 48 | 6 | 12 | 20 | 5 | 0 | 1 | 5 | 0 | 0 | 0 | 8 | 0 | 14 | 2 | 0 | 1 | .250 | .357 | .417 |
| Escobar, Alcides, Helena | 68 | 262 | 231 | 38 | 65 | 79 | 8 | 0 | 2 | 24 | 6 | 1 | 4 | 20 | 0 | 44 | 20 | 9 | 6 | .281 | .348 | .342 |
| Esparragoza, Eyoxy, Billings | 12 | 54 | 49 | 9 | 15 | 23 | 5 | 0 | 1 | 9 | 0 | 0 | 1 | 4 | 0 | 12 | 3 | 0 | 0 | .306 | .370 | .469 |
| Fermaint, Charlie, Helena | 58 | 246 | 218 | 30 | 50 | 83 | 14 | 2 | 5 | 39 | 2 | 2 | 4 | 19 | 0 | 83 | 8 | 2 | 1 | .229 | .300 | .381 |
| Ferrara, Matt, Idaho Falls | 42 | 143 | 124 | 27 | 36 | 57 | 6 | 3 | 3 | 19 | 3 | 1 | 3 | 12 | 0 | 39 | 6 | 3 | 4 | .290 | .364 | .460 |
| Festa, Anthony, Helena * | 67 | 300 | 226 | 51 | 69 | 109 | 19 | 0 | 7 | 53 | 2 | 3 | 13 | 56 | 4 | 39 | 6 | 1 | 6 | .305 | .463 | .482 |
| Fox, Ryan, Casper | 48 | 203 | 153 | 43 | 37 | 84 | 7 | 2 | 12 | 36 | 1 | 1 | 4 | 44 | 0 | 66 | 7 | 3 | 0 | .242 | .421 | .549 |
| Gentry, Phil, Billings * | 62 | 275 | 242 | 39 | 81 | 120 | 21 | 3 | 4 | 31 | 9 | 1 | 2 | 21 | 0 | 47 | 5 | 6 | 3 | .335 | .391 | .496 |
| Giannotti, Richard, Provo † | 61 | 264 | 206 | 57 | 51 | 76 | 8 | 4 | 3 | 22 | 7 | 1 | 8 | 42 | 0 | 69 | 21 | 6 | 2 | .248 | .393 | .369 |
| Gonzalez, Reynaldo, Billings | 2 | 6 | 5 | 0 | 0 | 0 | 0 | 0 | 0 | 0 | 0 | 0 | 0 | 1 | 0 | 1 | 0 | 0 | 1 | .000 | .167 | .000 |
| Gulick, Travis, Missoula | 60 | 224 | 192 | 34 | 48 | 96 | 6 | 3 | 12 | 37 | 3 | 2 | 2 | 25 | 1 | 55 | 6 | 2 | 0 | .250 | .339 | .500 |
| Gutierrez, Tonys, Billings * | 18 | 73 | 59 | 12 | 20 | 29 | 3 | 0 | 2 | 12 | 0 | 0 | 2 | 12 | 0 | 15 | 2 | 1 | 0 | .339 | .466 | .492 |
| Hahn, Dustin, Casper * | 63 | 293 | 240 | 56 | 74 | 118 | 18 | 1 | 8 | 43 | 0 | 0 | 2 | 51 | 0 | 55 | 10 | 2 | 9 | .308 | .433 | .492 |

| Player, Team | G | TPA | AB | R | H | TB | 2B | 3B | HR | RBI | SH | SF | HP | BB | IBB | SO | SB | CS | GDP | Avg. | OBP | Slg. |
|---|---|---|---|---|---|---|---|---|---|---|---|---|---|---|---|---|---|---|---|---|---|---|
| Haney, Joshua, Idaho Falls | 6 | 31 | 25 | 4 | 5 | 8 | 3 | 0 | 0 | 1 | 0 | 0 | 2 | 4 | 0 | 4 | 0 | 2 | 0 | .200 | .355 | .320 |
| Hansen, Josh, Great Falls | 40 | 169 | 145 | 26 | 42 | 72 | 11 | 2 | 5 | 17 | 1 | 0 | 1 | 22 | 0 | 39 | 2 | 1 | 2 | .290 | .387 | .497 |
| Hayes, Brad, Idaho Falls | 53 | 243 | 204 | 43 | 58 | 76 | 15 | 0 | 1 | 33 | 4 | 6 | 5 | 22 | 0 | 50 | 5 | 6 | 6 | .284 | .359 | .373 |
| Hosgood, Rob, Casper * | 27 | 110 | 96 | 18 | 27 | 41 | 4 | 2 | 2 | 15 | 0 | 1 | 0 | 13 | 0 | 36 | 1 | 2 | 1 | .281 | .364 | .427 |
| Hughes, Michael, Provo | 41 | 142 | 118 | 18 | 22 | 31 | 9 | 0 | 0 | 15 | 0 | 2 | 6 | 16 | 0 | 27 | 2 | 2 | 8 | .186 | .310 | .263 |
| Infante, Jefferson, Idaho Falls | 28 | 103 | 92 | 16 | 24 | 37 | 5 | 1 | 2 | 16 | 0 | 1 | 3 | 7 | 0 | 23 | 1 | 0 | 3 | .261 | .330 | .402 |
| Janish, Paul, Billings | 66 | 263 | 205 | 39 | 54 | 71 | 11 | 0 | 2 | 22 | 7 | 1 | 5 | 45 | 0 | 45 | 7 | 3 | 2 | .263 | .406 | .346 |
| Johnson, Ben, Provo † | 44 | 188 | 166 | 27 | 44 | 71 | 7 | 1 | 6 | 34 | 2 | 0 | 8 | 12 | 0 | 30 | 2 | 2 | 2 | .265 | .344 | .428 |
| Kaats, Travis, Billings | 56 | 202 | 168 | 22 | 31 | 38 | 2 | 1 | 1 | 16 | 6 | 1 | 7 | 20 | 0 | 59 | 3 | 2 | 0 | .185 | .296 | .226 |
| Kelly, Chris, Great Falls | 65 | 292 | 270 | 45 | 85 | 134 | 14 | 1 | 11 | 51 | 0 | 3 | 4 | 15 | 1 | 75 | 1 | 1 | 6 | .315 | .356 | .496 |
| Key, Bradley, Billings | 67 | 295 | 264 | 37 | 64 | 100 | 14 | 2 | 6 | 42 | 1 | 1 | 4 | 25 | 0 | 69 | 3 | 0 | 7 | .242 | .316 | .379 |
| Lawhorn, Trevor, Billings | 56 | 246 | 217 | 28 | 52 | 88 | 11 | 2 | 7 | 34 | 1 | 1 | 4 | 23 | 1 | 50 | 15 | 3 | 6 | .240 | .322 | .406 |
| Leahy, Ryan, Provo | 25 | 104 | 95 | 19 | 29 | 30 | 1 | 0 | 0 | 8 | 1 | 0 | 0 | 8 | 1 | 8 | 2 | 1 | 3 | .305 | .359 | .316 |
| Leblanc, Joshua, Provo * | 53 | 220 | 185 | 39 | 55 | 83 | 8 | 4 | 4 | 30 | 4 | 1 | 3 | 27 | 0 | 43 | 14 | 3 | 4 | .297 | .394 | .449 |
| Levering, Matthew, Billings | 4 | 17 | 11 | 0 | 1 | 1 | 0 | 0 | 0 | 1 | 0 | 0 | 0 | 6 | 0 | 7 | 0 | 0 | 0 | .091 | .412 | .091 |
| Lisson, Mario, Idaho Falls | 71 | 304 | 256 | 60 | 74 | 112 | 10 | 2 | 8 | 49 | 0 | 1 | 3 | 44 | 0 | 82 | 15 | 6 | 3 | .289 | .398 | .438 |
| Lozada, Charlie, Helena | 43 | 149 | 134 | 18 | 30 | 36 | 4 | 1 | 0 | 13 | 5 | 2 | 1 | 7 | 1 | 24 | 2 | 1 | 4 | .224 | .264 | .269 |
| Lucas, Edward, Idaho Falls | 41 | 181 | 154 | 30 | 48 | 56 | 6 | 1 | 0 | 29 | 3 | 4 | 6 | 14 | 0 | 18 | 7 | 3 | 3 | .312 | .382 | .364 |
| Lucy, Donny, Great Falls | 50 | 204 | 176 | 19 | 42 | 54 | 7 | 1 | 1 | 26 | 5 | 3 | 3 | 17 | 0 | 36 | 13 | 1 | 4 | .239 | .312 | .307 |
| Lynch, Michael, Ogden | 27 | 101 | 94 | 9 | 22 | 24 | 2 | 0 | 0 | 10 | 0 | 0 | 0 | 7 | 0 | 21 | 0 | 0 | 4 | .234 | .287 | .255 |
| Maher, Caleb, Provo | 50 | 205 | 177 | 36 | 56 | 88 | 12 | 1 | 6 | 36 | 0 | 1 | 2 | 25 | 1 | 59 | 3 | 1 | 2 | .316 | .405 | .497 |
| Mannon, Adam, Helena | 72 | 310 | 259 | 41 | 66 | 116 | 22 | 2 | 8 | 52 | 0 | 2 | 8 | 41 | 0 | 70 | 10 | 3 | 2 | .255 | .371 | .448 |
| Marcos, Emilio, Ogden | 23 | 114 | 107 | 25 | 39 | 61 | 7 | 3 | 3 | 15 | 1 | 0 | 5 | 1 | 0 | 19 | 10 | 2 | 1 | .364 | .398 | .570 |
| Martin, Scott, Great Falls | 59 | 249 | 219 | 37 | 63 | 103 | 15 | 2 | 7 | 33 | 1 | 2 | 9 | 18 | 1 | 57 | 14 | 10 | 5 | .288 | .363 | .470 |
| Martinez, Brett, Provo | 3 | 7 | 6 | 0 | 2 | 2 | 0 | 0 | 0 | 0 | 1 | 0 | 0 | 0 | 0 | 1 | 0 | 0 | 0 | .333 | .333 | .333 |
| Matos, Miguel, Missoula | 60 | 237 | 199 | 43 | 51 | 76 | 11 | 1 | 4 | 24 | 1 | 0 | 6 | 31 | 2 | 41 | 17 | 4 | 2 | .256 | .373 | .382 |
| May, Luke, Ogden | 34 | 158 | 147 | 25 | 42 | 66 | 5 | 2 | 5 | 30 | 0 | 1 | 2 | 8 | 0 | 37 | 4 | 3 | 4 | .286 | .329 | .449 |
| McCarthy, Ryan, Great Falls | 44 | 201 | 173 | 33 | 45 | 68 | 9 | 1 | 4 | 24 | 0 | 0 | 5 | 23 | 0 | 45 | 6 | 2 | 2 | .260 | .363 | .393 |
| McFall, Brian, Idaho Falls | 68 | 303 | 262 | 64 | 94 | 160 | 22 | 1 | 14 | 67 | 0 | 4 | 7 | 30 | 0 | 64 | 23 | 2 | 5 | .359 | .432 | .611 |
| McNeil, Derek, Great Falls | 44 | 174 | 146 | 23 | 30 | 43 | 7 | 0 | 2 | 13 | 5 | 2 | 2 | 19 | 0 | 67 | 6 | 3 | 1 | .205 | .302 | .295 |
| Mejia, Jorge, Billings | 14 | 49 | 40 | 6 | 14 | 18 | 4 | 0 | 0 | 1 | 1 | 0 | 0 | 8 | 1 | 10 | 1 | 1 | 0 | .350 | .458 | .450 |
| Mercado, Richard, Missoula | 59 | 229 | 187 | 26 | 53 | 79 | 10 | 2 | 4 | 29 | 2 | 2 | 5 | 33 | 0 | 31 | 2 | 1 | 3 | .283 | .401 | .422 |
| Moreno, Juan, Missoula * | 4 | 4 | 3 | 0 | 1 | 2 | 1 | 0 | 0 | 1 | 0 | 0 | 0 | 1 | 0 | 1 | 0 | 0 | 0 | .333 | .500 | .667 |
| Mosby, Robert, Billings | 69 | 311 | 255 | 51 | 67 | 133 | 5 | 2 | 19 | 52 | 0 | 6 | 8 | 42 | 2 | 87 | 1 | 0 | 2 | .263 | .376 | .522 |
| Nelson, Chris, Casper | 38 | 169 | 147 | 36 | 51 | 75 | 6 | 3 | 4 | 20 | 0 | 0 | 2 | 20 | 0 | 42 | 6 | 5 | 2 | .347 | .432 | .510 |
| Nelson, Justin, Casper * | 60 | 261 | 220 | 55 | 62 | 119 | 12 | 3 | 13 | 45 | 0 | 4 | 3 | 34 | 0 | 59 | 6 | 1 | 0 | .282 | .379 | .541 |
| Nicholson, David, Ogden | 41 | 173 | 137 | 24 | 36 | 45 | 5 | 2 | 0 | 12 | 4 | 1 | 4 | 27 | 0 | 31 | 4 | 1 | 4 | .263 | .396 | .328 |
| Norman, Derek, Idaho Falls | 18 | 72 | 63 | 6 | 12 | 15 | 3 | 0 | 0 | 4 | 1 | 0 | 0 | 8 | 0 | 10 | 0 | 1 | 0 | .190 | .282 | .238 |
| Nunez, Felix, Provo | 5 | 21 | 19 | 1 | 4 | 4 | 0 | 0 | 0 | 1 | 0 | 0 | 2 | 0 | 0 | 4 | 2 | 0 | 1 | .211 | .286 | .211 |
| Olivares, Juan, Missoula | 58 | 194 | 184 | 19 | 44 | 64 | 10 | 2 | 2 | 16 | 7 | 1 | 2 | 0 | 0 | 41 | 2 | 2 | 3 | .239 | .246 | .348 |
| Perdomo, Mike, Provo | 53 | 187 | 170 | 28 | 42 | 64 | 7 | 0 | 5 | 20 | 1 | 2 | 3 | 11 | 0 | 55 | 3 | 1 | 3 | .247 | .301 | .376 |
| Perez, Melvin, Great Falls | 18 | 65 | 55 | 7 | 11 | 12 | 1 | 0 | 0 | 2 | 1 | 0 | 1 | 8 | 0 | 14 | 2 | 1 | 2 | .200 | .313 | .218 |
| Phillips, Drew, Billings | 38 | 148 | 133 | 21 | 36 | 38 | 2 | 0 | 0 | 15 | 2 | 1 | 3 | 9 | 0 | 10 | 2 | 4 | 1 | .271 | .329 | .286 |
| Piazza, Thomas, Ogden * | 5 | 13 | 10 | 1 | 1 | 1 | 0 | 0 | 0 | 2 | 0 | 1 | 0 | 2 | 0 | 2 | 0 | 0 | 1 | .100 | .231 | .100 |
| Pujols, Kengshill, Ogden | 37 | 141 | 131 | 13 | 29 | 40 | 6 | 1 | 1 | 13 | 0 | 1 | 4 | 5 | 0 | 38 | 3 | 1 | 2 | .221 | .270 | .305 |
| Rasheed, Hasan, Helena * | 49 | 213 | 174 | 45 | 52 | 75 | 7 | 2 | 4 | 23 | 2 | 0 | 0 | 37 | 0 | 50 | 13 | 8 | 1 | .299 | .422 | .431 |
| Remole, Clifton, Provo * | 60 | 230 | 198 | 36 | 54 | 70 | 11 | 1 | 1 | 24 | 0 | 0 | 2 | 30 | 1 | 22 | 3 | 3 | 3 | .273 | .374 | .354 |
| Renz, Jordan, Provo † | 63 | 259 | 226 | 34 | 63 | 106 | 17 | 1 | 8 | 45 | 0 | 2 | 4 | 27 | 0 | 84 | 1 | 1 | 2 | .279 | .363 | .469 |
| Richardson, Grant, Helena | 44 | 207 | 166 | 35 | 61 | 94 | 16 | 1 | 5 | 42 | 0 | 3 | 6 | 32 | 1 | 20 | 2 | 4 | 7 | .367 | .478 | .566 |
| Richmond, Barry, Ogden * | 49 | 207 | 187 | 31 | 50 | 62 | 9 | 0 | 1 | 22 | 3 | 3 | 2 | 12 | 0 | 33 | 4 | 1 | 7 | .267 | .314 | .332 |
| Ricks, Adam, Great Falls † | 52 | 245 | 203 | 38 | 62 | 93 | 20 | 1 | 3 | 28 | 3 | 1 | 9 | 28 | 2 | 29 | 7 | 2 | 7 | .305 | .411 | .458 |
| Rivera, Jhonny, Great Falls | 26 | 89 | 84 | 14 | 20 | 31 | 2 | 3 | 1 | 9 | 2 | 1 | 0 | 2 | 0 | 16 | 1 | 2 | 2 | .238 | .253 | .369 |
| Roberts, Brandon, Billings * | 10 | 40 | 32 | 3 | 7 | 9 | 2 | 0 | 0 | 4 | 0 | 0 | 0 | 8 | 0 | 15 | 1 | 1 | 1 | .219 | .375 | .281 |
| Roberts, Daron, Great Falls | 38 | 154 | 139 | 17 | 35 | 48 | 4 | 0 | 3 | 24 | 3 | 2 | 8 | 2 | 0 | 37 | 4 | 5 | 1 | .252 | .298 | .345 |
| Rodriguez, Francisco, Missoula † | 34 | 108 | 99 | 8 | 26 | 37 | 6 | 1 | 1 | 11 | 3 | 0 | 1 | 5 | 0 | 24 | 1 | 1 | 0 | .263 | .305 | .374 |
| Rodriguez, Ramon, Casper | 36 | 135 | 107 | 17 | 32 | 35 | 3 | 0 | 0 | 15 | 1 | 2 | 2 | 23 | 0 | 23 | 2 | 2 | 7 | .299 | .425 | .327 |
| Rodriguez, Sean, Provo | 64 | 292 | 225 | 64 | 76 | 128 | 14 | 4 | 10 | 55 | 0 | 1 | 15 | 51 | 0 | 62 | 9 | 3 | 2 | .338 | .486 | .569 |
| Ronda, Willy Jo, Billings † | 13 | 43 | 35 | 7 | 9 | 16 | 1 | 0 | 2 | 3 | 1 | 0 | 1 | 5 | 0 | 11 | 2 | 0 | 0 | .257 | .366 | .457 |
| Ruggiano, Justin, Ogden | 46 | 187 | 155 | 26 | 51 | 84 | 12 | 0 | 7 | 36 | 0 | 3 | 6 | 23 | 0 | 38 | 6 | 1 | 7 | .329 | .428 | .542 |
| Russ, Ryan, Ogden † | 31 | 133 | 107 | 26 | 35 | 54 | 8 | 4 | 1 | 15 | 3 | 0 | 4 | 19 | 0 | 25 | 6 | 2 | 1 | .327 | .446 | .505 |
| Sakamoto, Mitsuru, Casper * | 7 | 24 | 22 | 1 | 5 | 5 | 0 | 0 | 0 | 3 | 0 | 0 | 1 | 1 | 0 | 6 | 1 | 0 | 2 | .227 | .292 | .227 |
| Salazar, Darwinson, Idaho Falls | 56 | 232 | 195 | 39 | 62 | 84 | 10 | 3 | 2 | 31 | 4 | 2 | 3 | 28 | 1 | 52 | 17 | 6 | 1 | .318 | .408 | .431 |
| Santiago, Jayson, Missoula * | 25 | 45 | 35 | 8 | 6 | 6 | 0 | 0 | 0 | 1 | 0 | 0 | 0 | 10 | 0 | 12 | 0 | 0 | 0 | .171 | .356 | .171 |
| Segura Cornier, Alberto, Helena | 41 | 164 | 144 | 22 | 40 | 53 | 10 | 0 | 1 | 24 | 1 | 2 | 0 | 17 | 0 | 25 | 1 | 0 | 3 | .278 | .350 | .368 |
| Septimo, Agustin, Helena † | 37 | 112 | 101 | 15 | 32 | 37 | 2 | 0 | 1 | 11 | 4 | 0 | 2 | 4 | 0 | 32 | 12 | 3 | 1 | .317 | .355 | .366 |
| Serfass, Jake, Helena | 31 | 121 | 99 | 13 | 19 | 28 | 6 | 0 | 1 | 8 | 1 | 0 | 1 | 20 | 0 | 32 | 0 | 2 | 2 | .192 | .333 | .283 |
| Smith, Seth, Casper * | 56 | 260 | 233 | 46 | 86 | 140 | 21 | 3 | 9 | 61 | 0 | 2 | 0 | 25 | 0 | 47 | 9 | 1 | 7 | .369 | .427 | .601 |
| Solis, Eddie, Idaho Falls | 64 | 273 | 246 | 48 | 90 | 115 | 15 | 2 | 2 | 54 | 0 | 3 | 5 | 19 | 1 | 41 | 3 | 0 | 9 | .366 | .418 | .467 |
| Sollmann, Steven, Helena | 72 | 346 | 272 | 59 | 99 | 118 | 12 | 2 | 1 | 39 | 8 | 0 | 13 | 52 | 1 | 30 | 23 | 8 | 4 | .364 | .487 | .434 |
| Solorzano, Marlon, Provo | 3 | 3 | 3 | 0 | 0 | 0 | 0 | 0 | 0 | 0 | 0 | 0 | 0 | 0 | 0 | 0 | 0 | 0 | 0 | .000 | .000 | .000 |
| Sosa, Ricardo, Missoula | 52 | 199 | 178 | 30 | 54 | 80 | 10 | 2 | 4 | 26 | 1 | 0 | 2 | 18 | 0 | 42 | 6 | 0 | 3 | .303 | .374 | .449 |
| Strait, William, Billings | 12 | 53 | 49 | 10 | 19 | 32 | 1 | 3 | 2 | 11 | 0 | 0 | 3 | 1 | 0 | 14 | 3 | 2 | 1 | .388 | .434 | .653 |
| Sutton, Nathanael, Provo * | 54 | 225 | 180 | 46 | 59 | 74 | 6 | 3 | 1 | 34 | 1 | 1 | 6 | 37 | 0 | 40 | 7 | 2 | 1 | .328 | .455 | .411 |
| Szymanski, B.J., Billings † | 22 | 92 | 81 | 13 | 21 | 38 | 4 | 2 | 3 | 17 | 1 | 1 | 0 | 9 | 1 | 26 | 2 | 1 | 4 | .259 | .330 | .469 |
| Tatum, Craig, Billings | 42 | 174 | 149 | 19 | 33 | 53 | 8 | 3 | 2 | 21 | 0 | 2 | 2 | 21 | 0 | 36 | 2 | 0 | 9 | .221 | .322 | .356 |
| Terrell, Joshua, Missoula | 14 | 40 | 36 | 3 | 8 | 9 | 1 | 0 | 0 | 9 | 0 | 1 | 1 | 2 | 0 | 5 | 1 | 0 | 1 | .222 | .275 | .250 |
| Toussaint, Andrew, Provo | 55 | 235 | 194 | 39 | 56 | 108 | 12 | 2 | 12 | 52 | 0 | 1 | 6 | 34 | 0 | 68 | 6 | 4 | 1 | .289 | .409 | .557 |
| Townsend, Marcus, Missoula | 45 | 152 | 126 | 31 | 37 | 77 | 5 | 1 | 11 | 27 | 0 | 0 | 4 | 22 | 1 | 48 | 4 | 1 | 0 | .294 | .414 | .611 |
| Valentin, Geraldo, Idaho Falls | 66 | 289 | 259 | 55 | 90 | 135 | 21 | 6 | 4 | 44 | 2 | 5 | 4 | 19 | 0 | 28 | 7 | 5 | 6 | .347 | .394 | .521 |
| Van Kooten, Jason, Casper | 26 | 123 | 106 | 21 | 33 | 42 | 3 | 0 | 2 | 16 | 0 | 2 | 2 | 13 | 0 | 14 | 7 | 3 | 2 | .311 | .390 | .396 |
| Veracierto, Fernando, Casper | 40 | 163 | 148 | 17 | 45 | 52 | 7 | 0 | 0 | 21 | 2 | 4 | 1 | 8 | 0 | 25 | 0 | 3 | 1 | .304 | .335 | .351 |
| Walston, Chris, Provo | 45 | 175 | 162 | 22 | 43 | 68 | 10 | 0 | 5 | 35 | 0 | 3 | 1 | 9 | 0 | 41 | 1 | 0 | 5 | .265 | .303 | .420 |
| Westervelt, Christopher, Ogden | 49 | 209 | 176 | 41 | 60 | 102 | 12 | 0 | 10 | 37 | 0 | 1 | 5 | 27 | 1 | 46 | 0 | 0 | 5 | .341 | .440 | .580 |

| Player, Team | G | TPA | AB | R | H | TB | 2B | 3B | HR | RBI | SH | SF | HP | BB | IBB | SO | SB | CS | GDP | Avg. | OBP | Slg. |
|---|---|---|---|---|---|---|---|---|---|---|---|---|---|---|---|---|---|---|---|---|---|---|
| Williams, Kevin, Missoula | 34 | 91 | 78 | 19 | 15 | 18 | 3 | 0 | 0 | 3 | 0 | 0 | 4 | 9 | 0 | 29 | 10 | 4 | 0 | .192 | .308 | .231 |
| Wilson, Kyle, Casper | 51 | 213 | 187 | 21 | 49 | 67 | 6 | 0 | 4 | 33 | 0 | 2 | 9 | 15 | 0 | 31 | 1 | 1 | 6 | .262 | .343 | .358 |
| Young, Eric, Casper † | 23 | 110 | 87 | 20 | 23 | 30 | 5 | 1 | 0 | 7 | 2 | 0 | 1 | 20 | 0 | 13 | 14 | 1 | 0 | .264 | .407 | .345 |
| Ziemendorf, Chad, Billings | 31 | 110 | 81 | 12 | 24 | 29 | 5 | 0 | 0 | 11 | 3 | 1 | 9 | 16 | 0 | 23 | 3 | 2 | 0 | .296 | .458 | .358 |

GRAND SLAMS—Berry, Collaro, Festa, Gulick, Kelly, Key, Mannon, McNeil, Septimo, Strait, Toussaint, Valentin, 1 each.

AWARDED FIRST BASE ON CATCHER'S INTERFERENCE—Kaats 2 (R. Rodriquez, Segura); Berry (Castillo); Hansen (R. Rodriquez); Maher (Castillo).

# 2004 PITCHING

## TEAM

| Team | W | L | Pct. | ERA | G | CG | ShO | Sv. | IP | H | TBF | R | ER | HR | SH | SF | HB | BB | IBB | SO | WP | Bk. |
|---|---|---|---|---|---|---|---|---|---|---|---|---|---|---|---|---|---|---|---|---|---|---|
| Great Falls | 42 | 33 | .560 | 4.24 | 75 | 0 | 6 | 20 | 677.2 | 691 | 3055 | 399 | 319 | 43 | 27 | 17 | 47 | 358 | 9 | 635 | 68 | 12 |
| Billings | 37 | 37 | .500 | 4.84 | 74 | 0 | 1 | 12 | 638.0 | 623 | 2861 | 401 | 343 | 52 | 35 | 25 | 61 | 363 | 2 | 588 | 90 | 17 |
| Provo | 44 | 32 | .579 | 5.32 | 76 | 1 | 2 | 16 | 646.1 | 741 | 2956 | 447 | 382 | 54 | 17 | 22 | 41 | 316 | 6 | 572 | 67 | 7 |
| Helena | 39 | 37 | .513 | 5.50 | 76 | 0 | 1 | 20 | 659.0 | 742 | 3026 | 476 | 403 | 81 | 35 | 22 | 57 | 293 | 2 | 567 | 62 | 10 |
| Missoula | 27 | 46 | .370 | 5.59 | 73 | 2 | 3 | 15 | 629.0 | 738 | 2959 | 491 | 391 | 70 | 26 | 30 | 54 | 328 | 10 | 589 | 87 | 5 |
| Idaho Falls | 42 | 34 | .553 | 5.75 | 76 | 1 | 2 | 26 | 657.1 | 801 | 3072 | 509 | 420 | 72 | 16 | 20 | 68 | 285 | 2 | 578 | 102 | 1 |
| Ogden | 35 | 40 | .467 | 6.00 | 75 | 0 | 2 | 19 | 647.0 | 764 | 3047 | 507 | 431 | 61 | 20 | 17 | 56 | 352 | 2 | 689 | 94 | 6 |
| Casper | 33 | 40 | .452 | 6.40 | 73 | 1 | 2 | 14 | 628.1 | 791 | 2992 | 538 | 447 | 68 | 17 | 27 | 59 | 290 | 4 | 665 | 89 | 8 |

## INDIVIDUAL

### TOP QUALIFIERS FOR EARNED-RUN AVERAGE TITLE

Minimum 61 innings.*Lefthanded pitcher.

| Pitcher, Team | W | L | Pct. | ERA | G | GS | CG | ShO | GF | Sv. | IP | H | TBF | R | ER | HR | SH | SF | HB | BB | IBB | SO | WP | Bk. |
|---|---|---|---|---|---|---|---|---|---|---|---|---|---|---|---|---|---|---|---|---|---|---|---|---|
| Liotta, Ray, Great Falls * | 5 | 1 | .833 | 2.54 | 14 | 11 | 0 | 0 | 0 | 0 | 63.2 | 59 | 272 | 27 | 18 | 1 | 3 | 1 | 3 | 28 | 0 | 65 | 5 | 1 |
| Deduno, Samuel, Casper | 6 | 4 | .600 | 3.18 | 15 | 15 | 0 | 0 | 0 | 0 | 76.1 | 62 | 331 | 40 | 27 | 3 | 4 | 3 | 10 | 32 | 0 | 118 | 14 | 0 |
| Ramirez, Ramon, Billings | 3 | 6 | .333 | 3.39 | 17 | 12 | 0 | 0 | 2 | 1 | 74.1 | 63 | 310 | 36 | 28 | 7 | 10 | 3 | 9 | 36 | 0 | 60 | 5 | 2 |
| Pelland, Tyler, Billings * | 9 | 3 | .750 | 3.42 | 18 | 12 | 0 | 0 | 1 | 0 | 73.2 | 67 | 325 | 36 | 28 | 3 | 7 | 4 | 5 | 39 | 0 | 82 | 15 | 0 |
| Wooley, Robert, Helena | 3 | 3 | .500 | 3.52 | 17 | 5 | 0 | 0 | 4 | 2 | 64.0 | 69 | 276 | 31 | 25 | 6 | 5 | 2 | 6 | 18 | 0 | 48 | 4 | 1 |
| Vaillancourt, Tim, Missoula | 4 | 4 | .500 | 4.16 | 14 | 14 | 1 | 0 | 0 | 0 | 75.2 | 78 | 337 | 47 | 35 | 8 | 6 | 5 | 8 | 31 | 0 | 67 | 3 | 1 |
| Bakker, Garry, Great Falls | 4 | 2 | .667 | 4.50 | 13 | 12 | 0 | 0 | 0 | 0 | 64.0 | 64 | 276 | 38 | 32 | 4 | 3 | 3 | 4 | 24 | 0 | 50 | 10 | 2 |
| Dove, Shane, Missoula * | 4 | 9 | .308 | 4.97 | 16 | 12 | 1 | 0 | 0 | 0 | 70.2 | 85 | 316 | 50 | 39 | 7 | 3 | 6 | 2 | 25 | 0 | 77 | 6 | 1 |
| Suarez, Sony, Great Falls | 5 | 2 | .714 | 5.37 | 18 | 9 | 0 | 0 | 3 | 2 | 63.2 | 66 | 291 | 46 | 38 | 3 | 4 | 4 | 5 | 41 | 3 | 62 | 9 | 3 |
| Logan, Boone, Great Falls * | 3 | 7 | .300 | 5.60 | 18 | 9 | 0 | 0 | 2 | 1 | 64.1 | 74 | 297 | 48 | 40 | 7 | 2 | 2 | 4 | 31 | 0 | 48 | 8 | 2 |
| Krantz, Ben, Missoula | 3 | 5 | .375 | 5.82 | 14 | 14 | 0 | 0 | 0 | 0 | 68.0 | 72 | 319 | 55 | 44 | 11 | 3 | 7 | 8 | 40 | 0 | 37 | 6 | 0 |
| Morales, Franklin, Casper * | 6 | 4 | .600 | 7.62 | 15 | 15 | 1 | 1 | 0 | 0 | 65.0 | 92 | 320 | 61 | 55 | 8 | 2 | 2 | 5 | 39 | 0 | 82 | 7 | 4 |

DEPARTMENTAL LEADERS: W—Pelland, 9; L—Dove, 9; Pct.—Liotta, .889; G—Newman, 27; GS—Deduno, Morales, 15; CG—Five tied with one; ShO—Morales, 1; GF—Alexander, 24; Sv.—Arnold, 12; IP—Deduno, 76.1; H—Morales, 92; TBF—Vallaincourt, 337; R—Morales, 61; ER—Morales, 55; HR—Krantz, 11; SH—Ramirez, 10; SF—Beeson, Krantz, 7; HB—Mullis, Noriega, 11; BB—Parker, Suarez, 41; IBB—Suarez, 3; SO—Deduno, 118; WP—Pelland, Meque, 15; BK—Meque, 7.

### ALL PITCHERS

*Lefthanded pitcher.

| Pitcher, Team | W | L | Pct. | ERA | G | GS | CG | ShO | GF | Sv. | IP | H | TBF | R | ER | HR | SH | SF | HB | BB | IBB | SO | WP | Bk. |
|---|---|---|---|---|---|---|---|---|---|---|---|---|---|---|---|---|---|---|---|---|---|---|---|---|
| Akin, Brian, Ogden | 1 | 1 | .500 | 6.04 | 21 | 0 | 0 | 0 | 2 | 0 | 47.2 | 65 | 236 | 36 | 32 | 3 | 0 | 0 | 6 | 22 | 0 | 63 | 13 | 0 |
| Alexander, Mark, Ogden | 4 | 1 | .800 | 2.65 | 25 | 0 | 0 | 0 | 24 | 9 | 34.0 | 30 | 143 | 10 | 10 | 4 | 0 | 0 | 3 | 8 | 0 | 37 | 1 | 0 |
| Alvarez, Carlos, Ogden * | 3 | 0 | 1.000 | 3.26 | 20 | 0 | 0 | 0 | 11 | 0 | 30.1 | 29 | 127 | 13 | 11 | 5 | 0 | 0 | 2 | 5 | 0 | 38 | 8 | 1 |
| Alvarez, Gabriel, Ogden | 1 | 1 | .500 | 4.30 | 16 | 0 | 0 | 0 | 12 | 3 | 29.1 | 32 | 133 | 18 | 14 | 2 | 0 | 0 | 1 | 12 | 0 | 36 | 1 | 2 |
| Arnold, Mitchell, Provo | 2 | 0 | 1.000 | 2.48 | 25 | 0 | 0 | 0 | 21 | 12 | 32.2 | 12 | 126 | 10 | 9 | 1 | 0 | 0 | 2 | 14 | 0 | 41 | 3 | 1 |
| Baker, Joshua, Helena | 1 | 1 | .500 | 3.66 | 15 | 8 | 0 | 0 | 4 | 2 | 51.2 | 37 | 212 | 22 | 21 | 5 | 3 | 3 | 5 | 20 | 0 | 44 | 4 | 0 |
| Bakker, Garry, Great Falls | 4 | 2 | .667 | 4.50 | 13 | 12 | 0 | 0 | 0 | 0 | 64.0 | 64 | 276 | 38 | 32 | 4 | 3 | 3 | 4 | 24 | 0 | 50 | 10 | 2 |
| Banks, Demetrius, Great Falls * | 1 | 0 | 1.000 | 2.00 | 21 | 0 | 0 | 0 | 6 | 3 | 36.0 | 19 | 153 | 12 | 8 | 1 | 0 | 0 | 4 | 22 | 1 | 48 | 6 | 1 |
| Barnes, Justin, Helena | 3 | 2 | .600 | 3.98 | 11 | 5 | 0 | 0 | 2 | 1 | 40.2 | 39 | 171 | 22 | 18 | 5 | 2 | 1 | 2 | 9 | 0 | 55 | 1 | 0 |
| Bates, Dallas, Helena * | 0 | 1 | .000 | 0.00 | 2 | 0 | 0 | 0 | 2 | 0 | 1.2 | 1 | 9 | 5 | 0 | 0 | 0 | 0 | 0 | 3 | 0 | 1 | 0 | 0 |
| Bauer, Garrett, Missoula * | 0 | 2 | .000 | 6.92 | 16 | 2 | 0 | 0 | 4 | 0 | 26.0 | 27 | 134 | 23 | 20 | 2 | 0 | 0 | 2 | 27 | 1 | 37 | 6 | 0 |
| Beeson, Bobby, Idaho Falls * | 2 | 4 | .333 | 5.47 | 15 | 14 | 0 | 0 | 0 | 0 | 52.2 | 56 | 229 | 37 | 32 | 6 | 3 | 7 | 5 | 24 | 0 | 48 | 2 | 0 |
| Berger, Garrett, Helena | 0 | 0 | .000 | 37.80 | 1 | 0 | 0 | 0 | 0 | 0 | 1.2 | 3 | 14 | 7 | 7 | 1 | 0 | 0 | 1 | 5 | 0 | 1 | 1 | 0 |
| Blackwell, Chad, Idaho Falls | 1 | 1 | .500 | 3.27 | 21 | 0 | 0 | 0 | 14 | 7 | 33.0 | 32 | 149 | 15 | 12 | 2 | 0 | 0 | 2 | 16 | 2 | 46 | 7 | 0 |
| Buckner, William, Idaho Falls | 2 | 1 | .667 | 3.30 | 7 | 5 | 0 | 0 | 0 | 0 | 30.0 | 36 | 128 | 14 | 11 | 4 | 2 | 1 | 1 | 4 | 0 | 37 | 3 | 0 |
| Buechner, Christopher, Casper | 1 | 1 | .500 | 3.95 | 13 | 0 | 0 | 0 | 13 | 4 | 13.2 | 11 | 53 | 6 | 6 | 1 | 0 | 0 | 0 | 1 | 0 | 14 | 1 | 0 |
| Butler, Billy, Idaho Falls | 0 | 1 | .000 | 8.31 | 1 | 0 | 0 | 0 | 1 | 0 | 4.1 | 8 | 25 | 4 | 4 | 0 | 0 | 0 | 0 | 4 | 0 | 0 | 0 | 0 |
| Campbell, Matthew, Idaho Falls * | 0 | 2 | .000 | 8.44 | 4 | 4 | 0 | 0 | 0 | 0 | 10.2 | 11 | 53 | 10 | 10 | 1 | 1 | 0 | 2 | 10 | 0 | 10 | 3 | 0 |
| Carlson, Zane, Idaho Falls | 2 | 1 | .667 | 4.50 | 19 | 0 | 0 | 0 | 14 | 10 | 22.0 | 21 | 104 | 11 | 11 | 1 | 0 | 0 | 4 | 13 | 0 | 30 | 3 | 0 |
| Carney, Frederic, Provo | 1 | 1 | .500 | 5.10 | 19 | 0 | 0 | 0 | 5 | 1 | 30.0 | 33 | 135 | 19 | 17 | 3 | 0 | 0 | 2 | 10 | 0 | 25 | 1 | 0 |
| Castillo, Albenis, Ogden | 2 | 2 | .500 | 5.01 | 12 | 1 | 0 | 0 | 1 | 0 | 32.1 | 27 | 148 | 20 | 18 | 4 | 1 | 1 | 5 | 19 | 1 | 30 | 1 | 0 |
| Cherry, Brad, Billings | 0 | 0 | .000 | 3.00 | 2 | 0 | 0 | 0 | 0 | 0 | 3.0 | 1 | 12 | 1 | 1 | 0 | 0 | 0 | 0 | 2 | 0 | 5 | 0 | 0 |
| Chivilli, Pedro, Casper | 0 | 1 | .000 | 6.75 | 5 | 5 | 0 | 0 | 0 | 0 | 17.1 | 26 | 76 | 13 | 13 | 2 | 1 | 2 | 0 | 6 | 0 | 11 | 2 | 0 |
| Clark, Chad, Missoula | 1 | 1 | .500 | 6.75 | 12 | 0 | 0 | 0 | 9 | 1 | 12.0 | 15 | 67 | 11 | 9 | 0 | 0 | 0 | 2 | 14 | 0 | 10 | 2 | 0 |
| Corbett, Jason, Provo | 0 | 0 | .000 | 2.70 | 3 | 0 | 0 | 0 | 2 | 0 | 3.1 | 3 | 18 | 1 | 1 | 0 | 0 | 0 | 0 | 5 | 0 | 2 | 2 | 1 |
| Cordova, Francisco, Provo | 2 | 5 | .286 | 5.37 | 14 | 11 | 1 | 0 | 0 | 0 | 52.0 | 59 | 235 | 41 | 31 | 4 | 5 | 6 | 3 | 26 | 1 | 33 | 6 | 3 |
| Cota, Luis, Idaho Falls | 2 | 1 | .667 | 5.81 | 14 | 12 | 0 | 0 | 0 | 0 | 48.0 | 61 | 226 | 37 | 31 | 5 | 1 | 1 | 8 | 21 | 0 | 40 | 10 | 0 |
| Cox, Jason, Provo | 1 | 2 | .333 | 7.46 | 16 | 0 | 0 | 0 | 6 | 1 | 25.1 | 35 | 124 | 22 | 21 | 2 | 0 | 2 | 2 | 9 | 0 | 13 | 1 | 0 |
| Crist, Kyle, Idaho Falls | 3 | 1 | .750 | 3.55 | 12 | 8 | 0 | 0 | 1 | 0 | 45.2 | 47 | 198 | 27 | 18 | 3 | 0 | 0 | 4 | 16 | 0 | 27 | 9 | 0 |
| Cruz, Rafael, Provo | 0 | 0 | .000 | 0.00 | 2 | 0 | 0 | 0 | 1 | 0 | 4.0 | 2 | 15 | 0 | 0 | 0 | 0 | 0 | 0 | 1 | 0 | 3 | 0 | 0 |
| Daley, Matt, Casper | 2 | 1 | .667 | 4.75 | 21 | 0 | 0 | 0 | 7 | 0 | 30.1 | 31 | 131 | 19 | 16 | 3 | 0 | 0 | 4 | 5 | 1 | 30 | 1 | 0 |
| Davis, Vince, Missoula * | 3 | 2 | .600 | 4.19 | 16 | 8 | 0 | 0 | 1 | 0 | 53.2 | 51 | 242 | 38 | 25 | 6 | 5 | 2 | 7 | 28 | 0 | 47 | 5 | 0 |
| De La Cruz, Carlos, Helena | 1 | 0 | 1.000 | 5.40 | 4 | 0 | 0 | 0 | 3 | 0 | 5.0 | 4 | 24 | 3 | 3 | 0 | 0 | 0 | 1 | 4 | 0 | 4 | 1 | 0 |

| Pitcher, Team | W | L | Pct. | ERA | G | GS | CG | ShO | GF | Sv. | IP | H | TBF | R | ER | HR | SH | SF | HB | BB | IBB | SO | WP | Bk. |
|---|---|---|---|---|---|---|---|---|---|---|---|---|---|---|---|---|---|---|---|---|---|---|---|---|
| Decarlo, Derek, Helena | 5 | 3 | .625 | 6.18 | 15 | 2 | 0 | 0 | 4 | 0 | 43.2 | 45 | 194 | 33 | 30 | 8 | 2 | 1 | 5 | 15 | 0 | 35 | 0 | 0 |
| Deduno, Samuel, Casper | 6 | 4 | .600 | 3.18 | 15 | 15 | 0 | 0 | 0 | 0 | 76.1 | 62 | 331 | 40 | 27 | 3 | 4 | 3 | 10 | 32 | 0 | 118 | 14 | 0 |
| Delgado, George, Casper | 2 | 1 | .667 | 5.67 | 25 | 0 | 0 | 0 | 18 | 7 | 33.1 | 44 | 169 | 22 | 21 | 1 | 0 | 0 | 6 | 19 | 0 | 35 | 4 | 1 |
| Dillard, Johnny, Billings | 0 | 1 | .000 | 7.17 | 22 | 0 | 0 | 0 | 9 | 1 | 21.1 | 13 | 103 | 18 | 17 | 1 | 0 | 0 | 4 | 22 | 0 | 22 | 5 | 1 |
| Douglas, James, Provo * | 0 | 1 | .000 | 8.84 | 18 | 0 | 0 | 0 | 5 | 0 | 18.1 | 22 | 101 | 18 | 18 | 2 | 0 | 0 | 6 | 20 | 0 | 12 | 4 | 0 |
| Dove, Shane, Missoula * | 4 | 9 | .308 | 4.97 | 16 | 12 | 1 | 0 | 0 | 0 | 70.2 | 85 | 316 | 50 | 39 | 7 | 3 | 6 | 2 | 25 | 0 | 77 | 6 | 1 |
| Doyle, Travis, Great Falls * | 1 | 2 | .333 | 3.60 | 11 | 4 | 0 | 0 | 3 | 1 | 25.0 | 25 | 115 | 13 | 10 | 2 | 0 | 1 | 4 | 15 | 0 | 27 | 2 | 0 |
| Duran, Enmanuel, Missoula | 2 | 1 | .667 | 5.13 | 23 | 1 | 0 | 0 | 14 | 1 | 33.1 | 49 | 164 | 21 | 19 | 3 | 0 | 0 | 1 | 16 | 0 | 38 | 7 | 0 |
| Edsall, Stephen, Casper | 1 | 4 | .200 | 12.19 | 5 | 5 | 0 | 0 | 0 | 0 | 20.2 | 43 | 106 | 30 | 28 | 4 | 0 | 3 | 2 | 6 | 0 | 10 | 6 | 0 |
| Edwards, Bill, Provo | 6 | 1 | .857 | 2.82 | 20 | 0 | 0 | 0 | 6 | 1 | 38.1 | 29 | 157 | 13 | 12 | 0 | 1 | 0 | 3 | 12 | 1 | 24 | 0 | 0 |
| Egbert, John, Great Falls | 4 | 1 | .800 | 3.38 | 17 | 9 | 0 | 0 | 0 | 0 | 58.2 | 51 | 253 | 25 | 22 | 2 | 4 | 1 | 5 | 33 | 0 | 52 | 4 | 0 |
| Elbert, Scott, Ogden * | 2 | 3 | .400 | 5.26 | 12 | 12 | 0 | 0 | 0 | 0 | 49.2 | 47 | 217 | 33 | 29 | 5 | 6 | 2 | 5 | 30 | 0 | 45 | 5 | 0 |
| Elliott, Matt, Missoula | 3 | 1 | .750 | 3.12 | 12 | 0 | 0 | 0 | 11 | 6 | 17.1 | 16 | 82 | 6 | 6 | 0 | 0 | 0 | 0 | 14 | 2 | 22 | 1 | 0 |
| Everly, Eric, Great Falls * | 3 | 4 | .429 | 4.35 | 18 | 8 | 0 | 0 | 3 | 0 | 51.2 | 66 | 236 | 33 | 25 | 3 | 6 | 2 | 3 | 19 | 0 | 54 | 3 | 1 |
| Farfan, Alexander, Billings | 1 | 5 | .167 | 6.30 | 16 | 8 | 0 | 0 | 3 | 1 | 50.0 | 53 | 212 | 38 | 35 | 7 | 6 | 4 | 4 | 29 | 0 | 34 | 8 | 0 |
| Feliz, Ranier, Billings | 3 | 5 | .375 | 6.28 | 18 | 11 | 0 | 0 | 2 | 0 | 57.1 | 75 | 267 | 44 | 40 | 5 | 4 | 4 | 3 | 31 | 0 | 44 | 6 | 5 |
| Garcia, Javier, Ogden | 2 | 3 | .400 | 9.20 | 16 | 7 | 0 | 0 | 0 | 0 | 46.0 | 64 | 231 | 51 | 47 | 5 | 0 | 4 | 5 | 26 | 0 | 39 | 5 | 0 |
| Garcia, Miguel, Helena | 0 | 1 | .000 | 18.90 | 5 | 0 | 0 | 0 | 3 | 0 | 3.1 | 10 | 26 | 11 | 7 | 0 | 0 | 0 | 4 | 2 | 0 | 3 | 3 | 1 |
| Garner, Jeff, Helena | 1 | 2 | .333 | 6.14 | 12 | 1 | 0 | 0 | 2 | 0 | 22.0 | 28 | 105 | 20 | 15 | 1 | 0 | 0 | 3 | 9 | 0 | 19 | 3 | 0 |
| Gelinas, Karl, Provo | 3 | 3 | .500 | 5.44 | 14 | 7 | 0 | 0 | 1 | 0 | 43.0 | 69 | 194 | 31 | 26 | 5 | 2 | 2 | 1 | 9 | 0 | 28 | 3 | 0 |
| Gillihan, Adam, Billings | 1 | 0 | 1.000 | 0.00 | 3 | 0 | 0 | 0 | 0 | 0 | 4.1 | 6 | 23 | 1 | 0 | 0 | 0 | 0 | 0 | 4 | 0 | 3 | 0 | 0 |
| Goetz, Gregory, Billings * | 1 | 5 | .167 | 7.16 | 17 | 8 | 0 | 0 | 3 | 0 | 44.0 | 51 | 219 | 42 | 35 | 2 | 3 | 1 | 2 | 39 | 0 | 35 | 10 | 0 |
| Green, Patrick, Idaho Falls | 3 | 2 | .600 | 5.23 | 13 | 9 | 0 | 0 | 1 | 1 | 51.2 | 52 | 233 | 37 | 30 | 8 | 2 | 3 | 6 | 25 | 0 | 39 | 10 | 0 |
| Greene, Nicholas, Provo | 4 | 3 | .571 | 4.03 | 17 | 10 | 0 | 0 | 4 | 0 | 51.1 | 56 | 227 | 28 | 23 | 4 | 0 | 0 | 3 | 20 | 0 | 44 | 5 | 1 |
| Griffin, David, Billings * | 1 | 0 | 1.000 | 6.48 | 15 | 0 | 0 | 0 | 3 | 0 | 16.2 | 24 | 84 | 13 | 12 | 3 | 0 | 0 | 2 | 8 | 0 | 17 | 1 | 0 |
| Gruler, Chris, Billings | 0 | 0 | .000 | 19.29 | 1 | 1 | 0 | 0 | 0 | 0 | 2.1 | 4 | 13 | 5 | 5 | 0 | 0 | 0 | 0 | 2 | 0 | 2 | 0 | 0 |
| Guerrero, Hipolito, Missoula * | 0 | 0 | .000 | 9.82 | 7 | 0 | 0 | 0 | 2 | 0 | 11.0 | 22 | 60 | 16 | 12 | 1 | 0 | 0 | 0 | 7 | 0 | 7 | 4 | 0 |
| Hansen, Grant, Great Falls | 1 | 2 | .333 | 5.64 | 6 | 5 | 0 | 0 | 0 | 0 | 22.1 | 23 | 101 | 17 | 14 | 2 | 1 | 2 | 1 | 19 | 1 | 16 | 1 | 1 |
| Hawk, Derek, Billings | 0 | 2 | .000 | 4.26 | 17 | 7 | 0 | 0 | 2 | 1 | 57.0 | 52 | 235 | 30 | 27 | 9 | 2 | 3 | 3 | 18 | 0 | 64 | 4 | 0 |
| Hawk, Tommy, Helena | 4 | 0 | 1.000 | 6.40 | 13 | 5 | 0 | 0 | 2 | 0 | 32.1 | 56 | 155 | 26 | 23 | 4 | 2 | 2 | 2 | 8 | 1 | 23 | 1 | 1 |
| Hedden, Wayne, Provo | 3 | 0 | 1.000 | 1.93 | 16 | 0 | 0 | 0 | 3 | 0 | 28.0 | 21 | 118 | 6 | 6 | 0 | 0 | 0 | 3 | 10 | 0 | 24 | 5 | 0 |
| Hicklen, Patrick, Idaho Falls | 2 | 2 | .500 | 5.00 | 6 | 1 | 0 | 0 | 2 | 0 | 18.0 | 27 | 80 | 14 | 10 | 1 | 1 | 0 | 2 | 1 | 0 | 19 | 0 | 0 |
| Hinton, Robert, Helena | 4 | 4 | .500 | 5.15 | 15 | 5 | 0 | 0 | 3 | 1 | 50.2 | 55 | 221 | 31 | 29 | 5 | 2 | 1 | 3 | 17 | 0 | 50 | 6 | 1 |
| Howard, Adam, Missoula | 1 | 1 | .500 | 4.36 | 9 | 5 | 0 | 0 | 0 | 0 | 33.0 | 36 | 139 | 18 | 16 | 4 | 3 | 3 | 1 | 7 | 0 | 27 | 1 | 0 |
| Howell, James, Idaho Falls * | 3 | 1 | .750 | 2.77 | 6 | 4 | 0 | 0 | 0 | 0 | 26.0 | 16 | 101 | 9 | 8 | 1 | 0 | 3 | 2 | 12 | 0 | 38 | 9 | 0 |
| Hundt, Brandon, Helena | 1 | 1 | .500 | 4.41 | 10 | 0 | 0 | 0 | 6 | 2 | 16.1 | 20 | 71 | 11 | 8 | 1 | 0 | 0 | 0 | 2 | 0 | 16 | 2 | 0 |
| Hurd, John, Great Falls | 4 | 4 | .500 | 6.38 | 25 | 2 | 0 | 0 | 10 | 3 | 36.2 | 47 | 177 | 32 | 26 | 0 | 1 | 0 | 3 | 17 | 0 | 29 | 4 | 0 |
| Jackson, Steven, Missoula | 0 | 1 | .000 | 3.60 | 7 | 0 | 0 | 0 | 0 | 0 | 10.0 | 16 | 50 | 9 | 4 | 1 | 0 | 0 | 2 | 2 | 0 | 8 | 1 | 0 |
| Jenson, Andrew, Billings * | 2 | 0 | 1.000 | 2.00 | 19 | 0 | 0 | 0 | 4 | 0 | 18.0 | 14 | 81 | 4 | 4 | 0 | 0 | 0 | 2 | 11 | 1 | 16 | 1 | 0 |
| Johnson, Blake, Ogden | 3 | 3 | .500 | 6.47 | 13 | 12 | 0 | 0 | 0 | 0 | 57.0 | 73 | 255 | 46 | 41 | 5 | 3 | 1 | 6 | 19 | 0 | 57 | 9 | 0 |
| Johnson, David, Helena | 1 | 0 | 1.000 | 2.25 | 4 | 0 | 0 | 0 | 1 | 1 | 8.0 | 6 | 33 | 2 | 2 | 1 | 0 | 0 | 2 | 1 | 0 | 5 | 1 | 0 |
| Johnson, J.D., Great Falls | 1 | 3 | .250 | 6.98 | 12 | 0 | 0 | 0 | 5 | 0 | 19.1 | 18 | 94 | 21 | 15 | 3 | 0 | 0 | 2 | 16 | 1 | 21 | 3 | 0 |
| Johnson, Todd, Billings * | 4 | 1 | .800 | 3.56 | 18 | 1 | 0 | 0 | 2 | 0 | 30.1 | 26 | 128 | 16 | 12 | 1 | 0 | 0 | 1 | 10 | 0 | 36 | 5 | 0 |
| Julio, Donald, Missoula | 2 | 4 | .333 | 4.07 | 24 | 0 | 0 | 0 | 7 | 1 | 42.0 | 40 | 184 | 20 | 19 | 6 | 0 | 0 | 2 | 16 | 3 | 42 | 9 | 1 |
| Kane, Kyle, Great Falls | 1 | 0 | 1.000 | 6.35 | 7 | 0 | 0 | 0 | 2 | 2 | 5.2 | 5 | 25 | 4 | 4 | 1 | 0 | 0 | 0 | 3 | 0 | 7 | 0 | 0 |
| Klusman, James, Ogden | 2 | 1 | .667 | 5.71 | 21 | 0 | 0 | 0 | 16 | 5 | 34.2 | 48 | 169 | 26 | 22 | 5 | 0 | 0 | 4 | 13 | 0 | 25 | 4 | 0 |
| Knoff, Justin, Billings | 0 | 0 | .000 | 1.86 | 6 | 0 | 0 | 0 | 3 | 0 | 9.2 | 8 | 41 | 4 | 2 | 0 | 0 | 0 | 0 | 4 | 0 | 9 | 0 | 0 |
| Krantz, Ben, Missoula | 3 | 5 | .375 | 5.82 | 14 | 14 | 0 | 0 | 0 | 0 | 68.0 | 72 | 319 | 55 | 44 | 11 | 3 | 7 | 8 | 40 | 0 | 37 | 6 | 0 |
| Kupper, Dustin, Billings | 0 | 0 | .000 | 9.82 | 4 | 0 | 0 | 0 | 2 | 0 | 3.2 | 6 | 23 | 7 | 4 | 0 | 0 | 0 | 2 | 4 | 0 | 2 | 0 | 0 |
| Layman, William, Provo | 2 | 2 | .500 | 4.91 | 13 | 12 | 0 | 0 | 0 | 0 | 40.1 | 44 | 182 | 24 | 22 | 6 | 0 | 0 | 3 | 28 | 0 | 51 | 5 | 0 |
| Lindsay, Shane, Casper | 1 | 1 | .500 | 6.75 | 17 | 0 | 0 | 0 | 7 | 0 | 21.1 | 22 | 107 | 24 | 16 | 1 | 0 | 0 | 2 | 19 | 0 | 31 | 4 | 0 |
| Lingenfelter, Adam, Billings | 1 | 2 | .333 | 6.12 | 9 | 4 | 0 | 0 | 2 | 0 | 25.0 | 28 | 109 | 17 | 17 | 4 | 0 | 1 | 1 | 9 | 0 | 22 | 2 | 0 |
| Liotta, Ray, Great Falls * | 5 | 1 | .833 | 2.54 | 14 | 11 | 0 | 0 | 0 | 0 | 63.2 | 59 | 272 | 27 | 18 | 1 | 3 | 1 | 3 | 28 | 0 | 65 | 5 | 1 |
| Little, Jeff, Great Falls | 0 | 1 | .000 | 2.63 | 13 | 0 | 0 | 0 | 10 | 5 | 13.2 | 14 | 64 | 5 | 4 | 0 | 0 | 0 | 3 | 6 | 1 | 14 | 0 | 0 |
| Logan, Boone, Great Falls * | 3 | 7 | .300 | 5.60 | 18 | 9 | 0 | 0 | 2 | 1 | 64.1 | 74 | 297 | 48 | 40 | 7 | 2 | 2 | 4 | 31 | 0 | 48 | 8 | 2 |
| Manzueta, Radhames, Casper | 1 | 3 | .250 | 8.42 | 7 | 7 | 0 | 0 | 0 | 0 | 25.2 | 36 | 124 | 29 | 24 | 2 | 1 | 2 | 2 | 12 | 0 | 25 | 5 | 1 |
| Marion, Ryan, Helena | 1 | 1 | .500 | 8.15 | 20 | 3 | 0 | 0 | 10 | 2 | 35.1 | 39 | 179 | 43 | 32 | 7 | 2 | 0 | 2 | 33 | 0 | 25 | 7 | 0 |
| Marshall, Jay, Great Falls * | 2 | 0 | 1.000 | 3.45 | 4 | 2 | 0 | 0 | 1 | 0 | 15.2 | 19 | 69 | 9 | 6 | 2 | 0 | 0 | 0 | 6 | 0 | 17 | 0 | 0 |
| Martinez Sosa, Alvaro, Helena | 3 | 7 | .300 | 6.02 | 17 | 13 | 0 | 0 | 3 | 1 | 58.1 | 64 | 277 | 41 | 39 | 9 | 8 | 3 | 4 | 35 | 0 | 49 | 5 | 1 |
| Mattheus, Ryan, Casper | 3 | 3 | .500 | 4.94 | 7 | 7 | 0 | 0 | 0 | 0 | 27.1 | 27 | 125 | 16 | 15 | 2 | 2 | 1 | 5 | 14 | 0 | 16 | 7 | 0 |
| McConiga, Jacob, Idaho Falls * | 0 | 2 | .000 | 9.27 | 13 | 3 | 0 | 0 | 2 | 0 | 33.0 | 57 | 182 | 42 | 34 | 3 | 0 | 1 | 3 | 22 | 0 | 29 | 5 | 0 |
| McGary, Gerron, Great Falls * | 0 | 1 | .000 | 2.15 | 20 | 0 | 0 | 0 | 4 | 0 | 29.1 | 21 | 136 | 9 | 7 | 1 | 0 | 0 | 0 | 27 | 0 | 37 | 5 | 1 |
| McKenna, Daniel, Helena | 0 | 1 | .000 | 7.92 | 12 | 0 | 0 | 0 | 4 | 0 | 25.0 | 33 | 123 | 27 | 22 | 4 | 2 | 3 | 0 | 17 | 0 | 17 | 7 | 2 |
| Meque, Jacobo, Billings * | 1 | 1 | .500 | 4.56 | 18 | 7 | 0 | 0 | 3 | 0 | 49.1 | 45 | 233 | 32 | 25 | 4 | 1 | 0 | 9 | 36 | 0 | 46 | 15 | 7 |
| Merino, Josh, Casper | 2 | 3 | .400 | 9.24 | 8 | 6 | 0 | 0 | 0 | 0 | 25.1 | 38 | 130 | 29 | 26 | 5 | 2 | 3 | 3 | 13 | 0 | 26 | 2 | 0 |
| Metzger, Jason, Casper * | 2 | 5 | .286 | 9.56 | 14 | 4 | 0 | 0 | 0 | 0 | 32.0 | 58 | 175 | 42 | 34 | 4 | 0 | 2 | 2 | 14 | 1 | 31 | 6 | 0 |
| Morales, Franklin, Casper * | 6 | 4 | .600 | 7.62 | 15 | 15 | 1 | 1 | 0 | 0 | 65.0 | 92 | 320 | 61 | 55 | 8 | 2 | 2 | 5 | 39 | 0 | 82 | 7 | 4 |
| Morenko, Brad, Billings | 2 | 1 | .667 | 4.09 | 18 | 0 | 0 | 0 | 11 | 3 | 22.0 | 24 | 96 | 12 | 10 | 2 | 0 | 0 | 1 | 5 | 0 | 19 | 1 | 0 |
| Mosqueda, Juan, Casper | 0 | 0 | .000 | 8.10 | 8 | 0 | 0 | 0 | 1 | 0 | 13.1 | 19 | 71 | 17 | 12 | 2 | 0 | 1 | 2 | 10 | 0 | 9 | 0 | 0 |
| Mullis, Jake, Idaho Falls | 3 | 4 | .429 | 6.99 | 14 | 6 | 1 | 0 | 3 | 1 | 55.1 | 71 | 268 | 49 | 43 | 7 | 3 | 0 | 11 | 19 | 0 | 40 | 4 | 0 |
| Murray, Branden, Helena | 0 | 2 | .000 | 11.32 | 18 | 0 | 0 | 0 | 8 | 0 | 20.2 | 33 | 116 | 29 | 26 | 3 | 0 | 0 | 1 | 23 | 0 | 23 | 5 | 0 |
| Mutter, Casey, Provo | 0 | 0 | .000 | 9.91 | 18 | 0 | 0 | 0 | 7 | 0 | 26.1 | 39 | 136 | 33 | 29 | 5 | 0 | 0 | 1 | 21 | 2 | 31 | 4 | 0 |
| Nachreiner, Matt, Great Falls | 1 | 0 | 1.000 | 6.88 | 11 | 0 | 0 | 0 | 5 | 0 | 17.0 | 14 | 79 | 13 | 13 | 5 | 0 | 0 | 1 | 13 | 0 | 12 | 3 | 0 |
| Needham, Joel, Helena | 2 | 2 | .500 | 6.43 | 8 | 0 | 0 | 0 | 5 | 3 | 14.0 | 18 | 71 | 11 | 10 | 1 | 0 | 0 | 3 | 8 | 1 | 11 | 2 | 2 |
| Nendza, Brian, Idaho Falls * | 5 | 3 | .625 | 6.70 | 24 | 0 | 0 | 0 | 4 | 1 | 43.0 | 50 | 207 | 37 | 32 | 5 | 0 | 0 | 3 | 25 | 0 | 52 | 12 | 0 |
| Newman, Joshua, Casper * | 1 | 2 | .333 | 3.48 | 27 | 0 | 0 | 0 | 8 | 1 | 33.2 | 30 | 139 | 17 | 13 | 2 | 0 | 0 | 0 | 8 | 0 | 46 | 1 | 0 |
| Nippert, Derik, Missoula | 0 | 3 | .000 | 15.43 | 3 | 3 | 0 | 0 | 0 | 0 | 11.2 | 30 | 66 | 21 | 20 | 2 | 1 | 0 | 0 | 3 | 0 | 6 | 0 | 0 |
| Noriega, Luis, Billings | 3 | 3 | .500 | 6.20 | 18 | 2 | 0 | 0 | 2 | 0 | 40.2 | 34 | 194 | 31 | 28 | 3 | 2 | 5 | 11 | 38 | 0 | 37 | 9 | 2 |
| Novosel, Walt, Missoula * | 0 | 0 | .000 | 5.87 | 6 | 0 | 0 | 0 | 1 | 0 | 7.2 | 3 | 31 | 5 | 5 | 0 | 0 | 0 | 0 | 5 | 0 | 13 | 3 | 0 |
| O'Neal, Charles, Billings * | 0 | 0 | .000 | 0.00 | 2 | 0 | 0 | 0 | 0 | 0 | 2.0 | 1 | 9 | 0 | 0 | 0 | 0 | 0 | 1 | 1 | 0 | 3 | 0 | 0 |
| Obispo, Jose, Ogden | 1 | 2 | .333 | 13.14 | 5 | 4 | 0 | 0 | 1 | 0 | 12.1 | 13 | 72 | 21 | 18 | 0 | 0 | 1 | 2 | 20 | 0 | 10 | 6 | 1 |
| Orenduff, Justin, Ogden | 2 | 3 | .400 | 4.74 | 13 | 10 | 0 | 0 | 0 | 0 | 43.2 | 46 | 198 | 26 | 23 | 4 | 3 | 0 | 1 | 25 | 0 | 57 | 5 | 1 |

| Pitcher, Team | W | L | Pct. | ERA | G | GS | CG | ShO | GF | Sv. | IP | H | TBF | R | ER | HR | SH | SF | HB | BB | IBB | SO | WP | Bk. |
|---|---|---|---|---|---|---|---|---|---|---|---|---|---|---|---|---|---|---|---|---|---|---|---|---|
| Palmer, Lucas, Idaho Falls | 3 | 2 | .600 | 7.86 | 17 | 1 | 0 | 0 | 4 | 2 | 44.2 | 65 | 226 | 48 | 39 | 9 | 1 | 1 | 3 | 20 | 0 | 33 | 8 | 1 |
| Parker, David, Ogden | 5 | 2 | .714 | 4.94 | 19 | 0 | 0 | 0 | 4 | 2 | 51.0 | 52 | 244 | 31 | 28 | 5 | 1 | 1 | 0 | 41 | 0 | 44 | 8 | 0 |
| Patton, David, Casper | 2 | 3 | .400 | 6.30 | 17 | 7 | 0 | 0 | 0 | 0 | 50.0 | 60 | 245 | 48 | 35 | 2 | 4 | 4 | 3 | 30 | 0 | 43 | 5 | 0 |
| Pawelczyk, Kyle, Provo * | 3 | 3 | .500 | 8.47 | 17 | 5 | 0 | 0 | 3 | 0 | 34.0 | 47 | 179 | 38 | 32 | 3 | 2 | 2 | 2 | 24 | 0 | 35 | 9 | 1 |
| Pelland, Tyler, Billings * | 9 | 3 | .750 | 3.42 | 18 | 12 | 0 | 0 | 1 | 0 | 73.2 | 67 | 325 | 36 | 28 | 3 | 7 | 4 | 5 | 39 | 0 | 82 | 15 | 0 |
| Pfeiffer, David, Ogden * | 1 | 4 | .200 | 6.20 | 8 | 8 | 0 | 0 | 0 | 0 | 40.2 | 50 | 186 | 34 | 28 | 4 | 2 | 3 | 2 | 22 | 0 | 33 | 2 | 1 |
| Pratt, Jordan, Ogden | 2 | 6 | .250 | 9.50 | 12 | 12 | 0 | 0 | 0 | 0 | 48.1 | 74 | 252 | 60 | 51 | 7 | 2 | 0 | 10 | 36 | 0 | 46 | 9 | 0 |
| Ramirez, Ramon, Billings | 3 | 6 | .333 | 3.39 | 17 | 12 | 0 | 0 | 2 | 1 | 74.1 | 63 | 310 | 36 | 28 | 7 | 10 | 3 | 9 | 36 | 0 | 60 | 5 | 2 |
| Ray, Ronnie, Provo | 5 | 2 | .714 | 5.00 | 13 | 6 | 0 | 0 | 2 | 0 | 36.0 | 32 | 164 | 23 | 20 | 4 | 0 | 1 | 3 | 21 | 0 | 30 | 2 | 0 |
| Reed, Rylan, Great Falls | 1 | 1 | .500 | 14.54 | 5 | 0 | 0 | 0 | 1 | 0 | 4.1 | 9 | 32 | 12 | 7 | 0 | 0 | 0 | 1 | 9 | 0 | 2 | 2 | 0 |
| Requena, Ricardo, Provo | 2 | 0 | 1.000 | 7.09 | 17 | 1 | 0 | 0 | 5 | 0 | 33.0 | 51 | 162 | 27 | 26 | 3 | 0 | 3 | 2 | 10 | 0 | 36 | 2 | 0 |
| Rodriguez, Fernando, Provo | 4 | 3 | .571 | 4.14 | 14 | 12 | 0 | 0 | 1 | 0 | 58.2 | 64 | 238 | 35 | 27 | 7 | 1 | 4 | 2 | 18 | 0 | 54 | 5 | 0 |
| Rowe, Adam, Idaho Falls * | 2 | 3 | .400 | 4.73 | 23 | 0 | 0 | 0 | 12 | 4 | 26.2 | 30 | 121 | 17 | 14 | 3 | 0 | 0 | 0 | 11 | 0 | 24 | 4 | 0 |
| Russell, Adam, Great Falls | 4 | 0 | 1.000 | 2.37 | 15 | 4 | 0 | 0 | 2 | 0 | 38.0 | 31 | 158 | 11 | 10 | 2 | 3 | 1 | 0 | 18 | 0 | 33 | 0 | 0 |
| Sanchez, Rafael, Casper | 0 | 1 | .000 | 7.46 | 22 | 0 | 0 | 0 | 6 | 1 | 35.0 | 53 | 181 | 36 | 29 | 7 | 1 | 1 | 3 | 20 | 1 | 28 | 6 | 0 |
| Sanchez, Ramon, Missoula | 1 | 1 | .500 | 9.13 | 18 | 1 | 0 | 0 | 4 | 0 | 23.2 | 33 | 127 | 34 | 24 | 6 | 0 | 0 | 5 | 18 | 0 | 18 | 3 | 1 |
| Sanders, Jared, Billings | 4 | 1 | .800 | 2.00 | 23 | 0 | 0 | 0 | 20 | 5 | 27.0 | 20 | 108 | 6 | 6 | 0 | 0 | 0 | 1 | 6 | 1 | 22 | 2 | 0 |
| Saxton, Chris, Idaho Falls | 1 | 2 | .333 | 6.55 | 21 | 0 | 0 | 0 | 10 | 0 | 33.0 | 43 | 158 | 30 | 24 | 4 | 0 | 0 | 5 | 14 | 0 | 17 | 2 | 0 |
| Shearer, Kelly, Provo * | 0 | 0 | .000 | 7.94 | 2 | 1 | 0 | 0 | 0 | 0 | 5.2 | 7 | 29 | 5 | 5 | 1 | 0 | 0 | 0 | 7 | 0 | 9 | 1 | 0 |
| Sherman, Justin, Idaho Falls | 8 | 1 | .889 | 5.54 | 10 | 9 | 0 | 0 | 0 | 0 | 50.1 | 68 | 232 | 34 | 31 | 5 | 2 | 3 | 2 | 19 | 0 | 28 | 9 | 0 |
| Shuey, Paul, Ogden | 0 | 0 | .000 | 3.38 | 2 | 2 | 0 | 0 | 0 | 0 | 2.2 | 2 | 14 | 2 | 1 | 0 | 0 | 0 | 0 | 4 | 0 | 4 | 1 | 0 |
| Sobkow, Phil, Ogden | 0 | 2 | .000 | 5.84 | 6 | 5 | 0 | 0 | 0 | 0 | 24.2 | 28 | 115 | 22 | 16 | 0 | 2 | 0 | 2 | 19 | 0 | 32 | 4 | 0 |
| Stanczyk, Ben, Helena | 0 | 1 | .000 | 4.63 | 7 | 5 | 0 | 0 | 1 | 0 | 23.1 | 23 | 100 | 12 | 12 | 3 | 0 | 0 | 2 | 6 | 0 | 24 | 1 | 0 |
| Stanley, Pat, Casper | 1 | 1 | .500 | 4.93 | 20 | 2 | 0 | 0 | 0 | 0 | 49.1 | 54 | 215 | 32 | 27 | 4 | 0 | 3 | 4 | 15 | 0 | 55 | 13 | 1 |
| Stein, Todd, Missoula * | 0 | 3 | .000 | 6.38 | 17 | 0 | 0 | 0 | 4 | 1 | 24.0 | 31 | 115 | 23 | 17 | 2 | 1 | 1 | 3 | 9 | 2 | 28 | 3 | 1 |
| Stott, Zach, Billings | 0 | 1 | .000 | 17.18 | 2 | 1 | 0 | 0 | 0 | 0 | 3.2 | 7 | 24 | 8 | 7 | 1 | 0 | 0 | 0 | 6 | 0 | 2 | 1 | 0 |
| Suarez, Sony, Great Falls | 5 | 2 | .714 | 5.37 | 18 | 9 | 0 | 0 | 3 | 2 | 63.2 | 66 | 291 | 46 | 38 | 3 | 4 | 4 | 5 | 41 | 3 | 62 | 9 | 3 |
| Sweeney, Michael, Provo * | 0 | 0 | .000 | 24.00 | 4 | 0 | 0 | 0 | 1 | 0 | 3.0 | 8 | 22 | 9 | 8 | 0 | 0 | 0 | 1 | 4 | 0 | 1 | 0 | 0 |
| Theodorakos, Jared, Helena | 0 | 0 | .000 | 6.11 | 9 | 8 | 0 | 0 | 0 | 0 | 28.0 | 32 | 136 | 21 | 19 | 4 | 1 | 1 | 3 | 15 | 0 | 19 | 1 | 0 |
| Thompson, Sean, Great Falls * | 0 | 1 | .000 | 5.40 | 8 | 0 | 0 | 0 | 4 | 0 | 8.1 | 13 | 44 | 6 | 5 | 2 | 0 | 0 | 1 | 5 | 1 | 7 | 2 | 0 |
| Trammell, Travis, Idaho Falls | 0 | 0 | .000 | 7.98 | 20 | 0 | 0 | 0 | 7 | 0 | 29.1 | 50 | 152 | 37 | 26 | 4 | 0 | 0 | 5 | 9 | 0 | 21 | 2 | 0 |
| Vaillancourt, Tim, Missoula | 4 | 4 | .500 | 4.16 | 14 | 14 | 1 | 0 | 0 | 0 | 75.2 | 78 | 337 | 47 | 35 | 8 | 6 | 5 | 8 | 31 | 0 | 67 | 3 | 1 |
| Valdez, Salvador, Missoula | 0 | 1 | .000 | 9.39 | 8 | 3 | 0 | 0 | 1 | 0 | 15.1 | 23 | 82 | 20 | 16 | 4 | 0 | 1 | 0 | 14 | 0 | 13 | 3 | 0 |
| Vargas, Buzz, Casper | 0 | 1 | .000 | 5.54 | 21 | 0 | 0 | 0 | 9 | 1 | 26.0 | 37 | 123 | 16 | 16 | 6 | 0 | 0 | 1 | 7 | 0 | 30 | 2 | 1 |
| Vasquez, Esmerling, Missoula | 3 | 2 | .600 | 3.52 | 19 | 0 | 0 | 0 | 12 | 5 | 30.2 | 22 | 141 | 15 | 12 | 1 | 0 | 0 | 6 | 21 | 2 | 33 | 11 | 0 |
| Vazquez, Camilo, Billings * | 1 | 0 | 1.000 | 0.00 | 2 | 0 | 0 | 0 | 0 | 0 | 2.2 | 1 | 12 | 0 | 0 | 0 | 0 | 0 | 0 | 3 | 0 | 6 | 0 | 0 |
| Veracierto, Fernando, Casper | 0 | 0 | .000 | 45.00 | 1 | 0 | 0 | 0 | 1 | 0 | 1.0 | 2 | 8 | 5 | 5 | 2 | 0 | 0 | 0 | 3 | 0 | 0 | 0 | 0 |
| Wade, Cory, Ogden | 1 | 2 | .333 | 5.14 | 8 | 0 | 0 | 0 | 2 | 0 | 14.0 | 24 | 70 | 9 | 8 | 0 | 0 | 0 | 0 | 4 | 1 | 19 | 1 | 0 |
| Wahpepah, Joshua, Helena | 4 | 2 | .667 | 4.40 | 15 | 7 | 0 | 0 | 3 | 2 | 47.0 | 58 | 220 | 28 | 23 | 3 | 1 | 2 | 5 | 17 | 0 | 35 | 2 | 1 |
| Walker, Edwin, Helena * | 4 | 2 | .667 | 5.57 | 15 | 9 | 0 | 0 | 0 | 0 | 51.2 | 61 | 236 | 39 | 32 | 10 | 5 | 3 | 3 | 21 | 0 | 47 | 2 | 0 |
| Waters, Christopher, Provo | 5 | 3 | .625 | 2.91 | 21 | 0 | 0 | 0 | 2 | 1 | 46.1 | 51 | 203 | 19 | 15 | 2 | 0 | 0 | 1 | 11 | 0 | 47 | 3 | 0 |
| White, Jeremey, Casper * | 2 | 1 | .667 | 8.24 | 20 | 0 | 0 | 0 | 2 | 0 | 31.2 | 46 | 163 | 36 | 29 | 7 | 0 | 0 | 5 | 17 | 1 | 25 | 3 | 0 |
| Whittington, Anthony, Provo * | 1 | 3 | .250 | 8.35 | 11 | 11 | 0 | 0 | 0 | 0 | 36.2 | 57 | 191 | 45 | 34 | 2 | 6 | 2 | 1 | 36 | 2 | 29 | 6 | 0 |
| Wilson, Justin, Helena | 1 | 1 | .500 | 0.00 | 7 | 0 | 0 | 0 | 6 | 3 | 14.2 | 8 | 57 | 1 | 0 | 0 | 0 | 0 | 0 | 5 | 0 | 13 | 3 | 0 |
| Wooley, Robert, Helena | 3 | 3 | .500 | 3.52 | 17 | 5 | 0 | 0 | 4 | 2 | 64.0 | 69 | 276 | 31 | 25 | 6 | 5 | 2 | 6 | 18 | 0 | 48 | 4 | 1 |
| Wright, Wesley, Ogden * | 3 | 3 | .500 | 6.29 | 17 | 2 | 0 | 0 | 2 | 0 | 44.1 | 56 | 215 | 43 | 31 | 3 | 0 | 4 | 1 | 23 | 0 | 66 | 9 | 0 |
| Yamaguchi, Tetsuya, Missoula * | 0 | 5 | .000 | 6.26 | 13 | 10 | 0 | 0 | 0 | 0 | 54.2 | 81 | 257 | 46 | 38 | 5 | 4 | 5 | 4 | 20 | 0 | 50 | 8 | 0 |
| Yonezawa, Kosuke, Missoula | 0 | 0 | .000 | 11.42 | 8 | 0 | 0 | 0 | 1 | 0 | 8.2 | 8 | 46 | 13 | 11 | 1 | 0 | 0 | 1 | 11 | 0 | 9 | 5 | 0 |
| Zaleski, Matt, Great Falls | 1 | 1 | .500 | 3.35 | 24 | 0 | 0 | 0 | 14 | 3 | 40.1 | 53 | 183 | 18 | 15 | 2 | 0 | 0 | 3 | 6 | 1 | 34 | 1 | 0 |
| Zuleta, Howard, Ogden | 0 | 1 | .000 | 6.23 | 3 | 0 | 0 | 0 | 0 | 0 | 4.1 | 4 | 22 | 6 | 3 | 0 | 0 | 0 | 1 | 4 | 0 | 8 | 2 | 0 |

COMBINATION SHUTOUTS: **Billings** (1)—Lingenfelter-Dillard-Feliz. **Casper** (1)—Morales-Newman. **Great Falls** (6)—Hansen-Egbert-Nachreiner, Bakker-Russell-Nachreiner, Egbert-Banks-Zaleski, Bakker-Suarez-Hurd, Everly-Banks, Egbert-Logan. **Helena** (1)—Hinton-Hawk. **Idaho** (2)—Falls Hicklen-Palmer, Howell-Blackwell. **Missoula** (3)—Dove-Vasquez-Julio, Krantz-Julio-Vasquez, Krantz-Julio-Duran. **Ogden** (2)—Elbert-C. Alvarez-G. Alvarez, J. Garcia-G. Alvarez. **Provo** (2)—Layman-Carney-Hedden, Green-Waters-Arnold.

NO-HIT GAMES: Everly, Great Falls, defeated Helena, 3-0, August 11.

# 2004 FIELDING

## TEAM

| Team | G | PO | A | E | TC | DP | TP | PB | Pct. |
|---|---|---|---|---|---|---|---|---|---|
| Billings | 74 | 1914 | 048 | 82 | 2044 | 73 | 0 | 19 | .960 |
| Helena | 76 | 1977 | 028 | 101 | 2106 | 58 | 0 | 22 | .952 |
| Great Falls | 75 | 2033 | 049 | 124 | 2206 | 67 | 0 | 13 | .944 |
| Ogden | 75 | 1941 | 041 | 117 | 2099 | 67 | 0 | 47 | .944 |
| Idaho Falls | 76 | 1972 | 016 | 121 | 2109 | 69 | 0 | 25 | .943 |
| Provo | 76 | 1939 | 047 | 120 | 2106 | 77 | 0 | 12 | .943 |
| Casper | 73 | 1885 | 030 | 133 | 2048 | 65 | 0 | 43 | .935 |
| Missoula | 73 | 1887 | 031 | 149 | 2067 | 59 | 0 | 17 | .9285 |

## INDIVIDUAL

### FIRST BASEMEN

NOTE: All caps denotes fielding-percentage leader based on 38 games for catchers, 51 for all other non-pitchers and 61 innings for pitchers. *Throws lefthanded.

| Player, Team | Pct. | G | PO | A | E | TC | DP |
|---|---|---|---|---|---|---|---|
| Acosta, Gilberto, HEL | 1.000 | 1 | 9 | 0 | 0 | 9 | 0 |
| Alvarez, Ferny, GRF* | 1.000 | 1 | 1 | 0 | 0 | 1 | 0 |
| Brady, Josh, HEL | 1.000 | 23 | 196 | 9 | 0 | 205 | 24 |
| Brito, Javier, MSO | .984 | 66 | 452 | 30 | 8 | 490 | 39 |
| Brown, Russell, IDF | .984 | 22 | 178 | 10 | 3 | 191 | 22 |
| Bruce, Cole, OGD | 1.000 | 2 | 14 | 2 | 0 | 16 | 4 |
| Castillo, Albenis, OGD | .923 | 1 | 11 | 1 | 1 | 13 | 2 |
| Castillo, Luis, OGD | .994 | 20 | 150 | 15 | 1 | 166 | 9 |
| Castillo, Wilkin, MSO | 1.000 | 2 | 8 | 0 | 0 | 8 | 1 |
| Collaro, Tom, GRF | .971 | 10 | 63 | 4 | 2 | 69 | 11 |
| Davies, Mike, CAS* | .980 | 54 | 414 | 25 | 9 | 448 | 39 |
| De La Cruz, Carlos, HEL | 1.000 | 1 | 2 | 0 | 0 | 2 | 0 |
| DelRosario, Felipe, IDF | 1.000 | 2 | 4 | 0 | 0 | 4 | 1 |
| Dunlap, Cory, OGD* | .983 | 50 | 392 | 24 | 7 | 423 | 38 |
| Ellis, Jason, BIL | 1.000 | 6 | 27 | 1 | 0 | 28 | 1 |
| Ferrara, Matt, IDF | 1.000 | 5 | 25 | 2 | 0 | 27 | 4 |
| Gutierrez, Tonys, BIL* | .979 | 16 | 133 | 6 | 3 | 142 | 11 |
| Hansen, Josh, GRF | .971 | 19 | 153 | 13 | 5 | 171 | 21 |
| Hayes, Bradley, IDF | .991 | 47 | 411 | 21 | 4 | 436 | 29 |
| Kaats, Travis, BIL | 1.000 | 1 | 12 | 1 | 0 | 13 | 2 |
| KELLY, CHRIS, GRF | .994 | 55 | 452 | 25 | 3 | 480 | 36 |
| Lisson, Mario, IDF | .988 | 9 | 78 | 3 | 1 | 82 | 6 |
| Lozada, Charlie, HEL | .977 | 17 | 122 | 3 | 3 | 128 | 5 |
| Lynch, Mike, OGD | 1.000 | 6 | 19 | 2 | 0 | 21 | 3 |
| Maher, Caleb, PRV | .981 | 7 | 48 | 4 | 1 | 53 | 1 |
| Mosby, Bobby, BIL | .984 | 51 | 402 | 25 | 7 | 434 | 51 |

| Player, Team | Pct. | G | PO | A | E | TC | DP |
|---|---|---|---|---|---|---|---|
| Phillips, Drew, BIL | 1.000 | 1 | 1 | 0 | 0 | 1 | 1 |
| Remole, Clifton*, PRV | .986 | 34 | 265 | 13 | 4 | 282 | 34 |
| Richardson, Grant, HEL | .979 | 39 | 347 | 25 | 8 | 380 | 21 |
| Roberts, Brandon*, BIL | .980 | 6 | 45 | 4 | 1 | 50 | 4 |
| Roberts, Daron, GRF | 1.000 | 1 | 3 | 0 | 0 | 3 | 0 |
| Rodriguez, Francisco, MSO | 1.000 | 2 | 4 | 0 | 0 | 4 | 0 |
| Terrell, Josh, MSO | .989 | 14 | 82 | 4 | 1 | 87 | 10 |
| Walston, Chris, PRV | .989 | 41 | 327 | 25 | 4 | 356 | 37 |
| Wilson, Kyle, CAS | .988 | 23 | 157 | 14 | 2 | 173 | 16 |

## SECOND BASEMEN

| Player, Team | Pct. | G | PO | A | E | TC | DP |
|---|---|---|---|---|---|---|---|
| Acosta, Gilberto, HEL | 1.000 | 1 | 0 | 1 | 0 | 1 | 0 |
| Almonte, Sandy, CAS | .885 | 4 | 10 | 13 | 3 | 26 | 3 |
| Anderson, Drew, BIL | .958 | 7 | 10 | 13 | 1 | 24 | 2 |
| Baldwin, Bruce, CAS | .906 | 12 | 11 | 18 | 3 | 32 | 2 |
| Berry, Boomer*, GRF | .975 | 65 | 152 | 162 | 8 | 322 | 38 |
| Boyer, Billy, PRV | 1.000 | 9 | 20 | 22 | 0 | 42 | 8 |
| Brewster, Jon, PRV | 1.000 | 2 | 1 | 1 | 0 | 2 | 1 |
| Bruce, Cole, OGD | 1.000 | 3 | 4 | 5 | 0 | 9 | 1 |
| Bruce, Derek, MSO | .956 | 20 | 45 | 42 | 4 | 91 | 15 |
| Carter, Brandon*, OGD | .969 | 15 | 24 | 39 | 2 | 65 | 10 |
| Casilla, Alexis, PRV | .909 | 3 | 3 | 7 | 1 | 11 | 1 |
| Castillo, Wilkin, MSO | .903 | 6 | 14 | 14 | 3 | 31 | 4 |
| Denker, Travis, OGD | .965 | 47 | 98 | 121 | 8 | 227 | 29 |
| Downing, Ramon, MSO | .965 | 22 | 45 | 38 | 3 | 86 | 6 |
| Ferrara, Matt, IDF | .974 | 25 | 43 | 68 | 3 | 114 | 15 |
| Haney, Joshua, IDF | .923 | 5 | 6 | 18 | 2 | 26 | 4 |
| LAWHORN, TREVOR, BIL | .978 | 55 | 112 | 159 | 6 | 277 | 41 |
| Leahy, Ryan, PRV | .966 | 19 | 36 | 48 | 3 | 87 | 12 |
| Leblanc, Joshua*, PRV | .908 | 51 | 104 | 114 | 22 | 240 | 31 |
| McNeil, Derrick, GRF | .833 | 2 | 2 | 3 | 1 | 6 | 0 |
| Mejia, Jorge, BIL | .975 | 9 | 15 | 24 | 1 | 40 | 7 |
| Nicholson, David, OGD | .950 | 11 | 27 | 30 | 3 | 60 | 8 |
| Ricks, Adam, GRF | .954 | 13 | 22 | 40 | 3 | 65 | 15 |
| Rodriguez, Francisco, MSO | .967 | 31 | 57 | 62 | 4 | 123 | 14 |
| Ronda, Jose, BIL | 1.000 | 4 | 9 | 14 | 0 | 23 | 2 |
| Septimo, Agustin, HEL | .850 | 8 | 9 | 8 | 3 | 20 | 1 |
| Solis, Eddie, IDF | .964 | 50 | 110 | 129 | 9 | 248 | 37 |
| Sollmann, Steven, HEL | .973 | 72 | 142 | 178 | 9 | 329 | 41 |
| Van Kooten, Jason, CAS | .984 | 14 | 29 | 31 | 1 | 61 | 9 |
| Veracierto, Fernando, CAS | .961 | 25 | 58 | 66 | 5 | 129 | 19 |
| Young, Eric, CAS | .938 | 23 | 52 | 53 | 7 | 112 | 16 |

## THIRD BASEMEN

| Player, Team | Pct. | G | PO | A | E | TC | DP |
|---|---|---|---|---|---|---|---|
| Acosta, Gilberto, HEL | .857 | 2 | 1 | 5 | 1 | 7 | 0 |
| Anderson, Drew, BIL | .944 | 8 | 1 | 16 | 1 | 18 | 0 |
| Baldwin, Bruce, CAS | .821 | 9 | 8 | 15 | 5 | 28 | 2 |
| Boyer, Billy, PRV | 1.000 | 2 | 0 | 1 | 0 | 1 | 0 |
| Brady, Josh, HEL | .857 | 2 | 2 | 4 | 1 | 7 | 0 |
| Bruce, Cole, OGD | 1.000 | 1 | 0 | 1 | 0 | 1 | 0 |
| Bruce, Derek, MSO | .892 | 19 | 13 | 20 | 4 | 37 | 4 |
| Butler, Billy, IDF | .920 | 49 | 28 | 110 | 12 | 150 | 11 |
| Casilla, Alexis, PRV | 1.000 | 1 | 2 | 4 | 0 | 6 | 0 |
| Castillo, Wilkin, MSO | .815 | 17 | 15 | 29 | 10 | 54 | 6 |
| Cooper, Caleb, GRF | .848 | 16 | 5 | 34 | 7 | 46 | 3 |
| De La Cruz, Carlos, HEL | .500 | 4 | 1 | 0 | 1 | 2 | 0 |
| Denker, Travis, OGD | .900 | 10 | 5 | 13 | 2 | 20 | 0 |
| DeWitt, Blake*, OGD | .891 | 65 | 45 | 118 | 20 | 183 | |
| Dragicevich, Jeff, CAS | .929 | 7 | 1 | 12 | 1 | 14 | 4 |
| Ferrara, Matt, IDF | .818 | 2 | 2 | 7 | 2 | 11 | 0 |
| FESTA, TONY*, HEL | .963 | 65 | 39 | 145 | 7 | 191 | 6 |
| Hahn, Dustin, CAS | .857 | 33 | 17 | 73 | 15 | 105 | 4 |
| Hayes, Bradley, IDF | .900 | 4 | 3 | 15 | 2 | 20 | 4 |
| Kelly, Chris, GRF | .816 | 12 | 6 | 25 | 7 | 38 | 4 |
| Key, Brad, BIL | .929 | 67 | 42 | 127 | 13 | 182 | 11 |
| Levering, Matt, BIL | 1.000 | 2 | 2 | 1 | 0 | 3 | 0 |
| Lisson, Mario, IDF | .894 | 21 | 14 | 45 | 7 | 66 | 3 |
| Olivares, Juan, MSO | 1.000 | 1 | 1 | 2 | 0 | 3 | 0 |
| Perez, Melvin, GRF | .891 | 15 | 8 | 33 | 5 | 46 | 3 |
| Ricks, Adam, GRF | .886 | 37 | 25 | 76 | 13 | 114 | 4 |
| Septimo, Agustin, HEL | .872 | 9 | 9 | 25 | 5 | 39 | 6 |
| Solis, Eddie, IDF | 1.000 | 3 | 1 | 2 | 0 | 3 | 0 |
| Sosa, Ricardo, MSO | .872 | 41 | 27 | 68 | 14 | 109 | 3 |
| Sutton, Nate*, PRV | .933 | 53 | 29 | 110 | 10 | 149 | 8 |
| Toussaint, Andrew, PRV | .856 | 27 | 17 | 60 | 13 | 90 | 6 |
| Veracierto, Fernando, CAS | 963 | 9 | 8 | 18 | 1 | 27 | 4 |
| Wilson, Kevin, CAS | 1.000 | 1 | 0 | 3 | 0 | 3 | 0 |
| Wilson, Kyle, CAS | .843 | 19 | 8 | 35 | 8 | 51 | 2 |

## SHORTSTOPS

| Player, Team | Pct. | G | PO | A | E | TC | DP |
|---|---|---|---|---|---|---|---|
| Acosta, Gilberto, HEL | .922 | 15 | 19 | 28 | 4 | 51 | 5 |
| Anderson, Drew, BIL | 1.000 | 3 | 4 | 4 | 0 | 8 | 1 |
| Berry, Boomer*, GRF | .500 | 1 | 1 | 2 | 3 | 6 | 1 |
| Boyer, Billy, PRV | .854 | 13 | 15 | 26 | 7 | 48 | 1 |
| Bruce, Cole, OGD | .944 | 13 | 8 | 43 | 3 | 54 | 10 |
| Bruce, Derek, MSO | .948 | 26 | 29 | 63 | 5 | 97 | 11 |
| Carter, Brandon*, OGD | .923 | 5 | 9 | 15 | 2 | 26 | 2 |
| Dragicevich, Jeff, CAS | .936 | 46 | 61 | 130 | 13 | 204 | 24 |
| Escobar, Alcides, HEL | .939 | 66 | 100 | 224 | 21 | 345 | 29 |
| Ferrara, Matt, IDF | 1.000 | 1 | 1 | 1 | 0 | 2 | 0 |
| JANISH, PAUL, BIL | .975 | 66 | 105 | 203 | 8 | 316 | 48 |
| Leahy, Ryan, PRV | .938 | 7 | 11 | 19 | 2 | 32 | 5 |
| Lisson, Mario, IDF | .895 | 34 | 50 | 104 | 18 | 172 | 18 |
| Lucas, Edward, IDF | .949 | 34 | 46 | 103 | 8 | 157 | 19 |
| May, Lucas, OGD | .888 | 34 | 49 | 93 | 18 | 160 | 16 |
| McCarthy, Ryan, GRF | .964 | 31 | 36 | 96 | 5 | 137 | 24 |
| McNeil, Derrick, GRF | .918 | 41 | 79 | 100 | 16 | 195 | 25 |
| Mejia, Jorge, BIL | .889 | 3 | 2 | 6 | 1 | 9 | 1 |
| Nelson, Chris, CAS | .922 | 17 | 22 | 37 | 5 | 64 | 7 |
| Nicholson, David, OGD | .924 | 27 | 39 | 71 | 9 | 119 | 17 |
| Olivares, Juan, MSO | .924 | 55 | 76 | 142 | 18 | 236 | 26 |
| Perez, Melvin, GRF | .813 | 3 | 5 | 8 | 3 | 16 | 1 |
| Phillips, Drew, BIL | 1.000 | 1 | 2 | 2 | 0 | 4 | 1 |
| Ricks, Adam, GRF | 1.000 | 2 | 2 | 7 | 0 | 9 | 3 |
| Rodriguez, Sean, PRV | .921 | 62 | 123 | 193 | 27 | 343 | 52 |
| Ronda, Jose, BIL | 1.000 | 5 | 15 | 17 | 0 | 32 | 6 |
| Septimo, Agustin, HEL | .833 | 3 | 2 | 3 | 1 | 6 | 1 |
| Solis, Eddie, IDF | 1.000 | 1 | 0 | 3 | 0 | 3 | 0 |
| Valentin, Geraldo, IDF | .904 | 12 | 15 | 32 | 5 | 52 | 7 |
| Van Kooten, Jason, CAS | .907 | 10 | 9 | 30 | 4 | 43 | 6 |
| Veracierto, Fernando, CAS | .952 | 5 | 7 | 13 | 1 | 21 | 1 |

## OUTFIELDERS

| Player, Team | Pct. | G | PO | A | E | TC | DP |
|---|---|---|---|---|---|---|---|
| Allen, Trevor, CAS | .906 | 27 | 27 | 2 | 3 | 32 | 0 |
| Alvarez, Ferny, GRF* | .941 | 27 | 28 | 4 | 2 | 34 | 0 |
| Anderson, Drew, BIL | .902 | 30 | 44 | 2 | 5 | 51 | 0 |
| Arias, Hector, OGD | .956 | 28 | 41 | 2 | 2 | 45 | 0 |
| Baldwin, Bruce, CAS | 1.000 | 2 | 4 | 0 | 0 | 4 | 0 |
| Bates, Dallas, HEL* | 1.000 | 21 | 27 | 3 | 0 | 30 | 0 |
| Batista, Alexander, IDF | .921 | 65 | 95 | 10 | 9 | 114 | 0 |
| Batz, Daniel, OGD | .943 | 53 | 46 | 4 | 3 | 53 | 0 |
| Belcher, Jordan, BIL | 1.000 | 3 | 4 | 3 | 0 | 7 | 0 |
| Beltre, Elvin, BIL | .955 | 12 | 20 | 1 | 1 | 22 | 0 |
| Boggs, Steven, CAS | .954 | 39 | 61 | 1 | 3 | 65 | 0 |
| Brady, Josh, HEL | 1.000 | 4 | 3 | 1 | 0 | 4 | 0 |
| Brown, Russell, IDF | .000 | 2 | 0 | 0 | 1 | 1 | 0 |
| Buhagiar, Josh, MSO* | .944 | 26 | 47 | 4 | 3 | 54 | 2 |
| Campos, Tiago, BIL | .960 | 13 | 23 | 1 | 1 | 25 | 0 |
| Centeno, Jaen, MSO | 925 | 48 | 67 | 7 | 6 | 80 | 0 |
| Cerulo, Nicholas, IDF | 1.000 | 2 | 1 | 0 | 0 | 1 | 0 |
| Collaro, Tom, GRF | .939 | 56 | 86 | 6 | 6 | 98 | 0 |
| Cook, David, GRF | .954 | 34 | 60 | 2 | 3 | 65 | 0 |
| De La Cruz, Carlos, HEL | 1.000 | 9 | 11 | 0 | 0 | 11 | 0 |
| Esparragoza, Eyoxy, BIL | .909 | 12 | 16 | 4 | 2 | 22 | 0 |
| Fermaint, Charlie, HEL | .939 | 58 | 104 | 3 | 7 | 114 | 0 |
| Gentry, Philip, BIL* | 1.000 | 61 | 64 | 6 | 0 | 70 | 1 |
| Giannotti, Richard, PRV | .981 | 59 | 95 | 6 | 2 | 103 | 1 |
| Gulick, Travis, MSO | .948 | 52 | 86 | 5 | 5 | 96 | 1 |
| Hahn, Dustin, CAS | 1.000 | 26 | 37 | 3 | 0 | 40 | 1 |
| Hosgood, Rob, CAS* | .979 | 26 | 45 | 1 | 1 | 47 | 0 |
| Hughes, Michael, PRV | .967 | 40 | 55 | 3 | 2 | 60 | 0 |
| Johnson, Ben, PRV | 1.000 | 9 | 15 | 4 | 0 | 19 | 0 |
| Kaats, Travis, BIL | 1.000 | 50 | 87 | 3 | 0 | 90 | 0 |
| Lynch, Mike, OGD | 1.000 | 6 | 8 | 0 | 0 | 8 | 0 |
| Mannon, Adam, HEL | .992 | 72 | 109 | 8 | 1 | 118 | 1 |
| Marcos, Emilio, OGD | .932 | 23 | 38 | 3 | 3 | 44 | 0 |
| Martin, Scott, GRF | .973 | 58 | 69 | 4 | 2 | 75 | 1 |
| Matos, Miguel, MSO | .937 | 52 | 115 | 4 | 8 | 127 | 0 |
| McFall, Brian, IDF | .963 | 64 | 86 | 19 | 4 | 109 | 1 |
| Nelson, Justin, CAS* | .905 | 58 | 60 | 7 | 7 | 74 | 0 |
| Nunez, Felix, PRV | 1.000 | 5 | 4 | 1 | 0 | 5 | 0 |
| Perdomo, Mike, PRV | .948 | 49 | 53 | 2 | 3 | 58 | 0 |
| Phillips, Drew, BIL | .959 | 28 | 47 | 0 | 2 | 49 | 0 |
| Piazza, Tom, OGD* | 1.000 | 3 | 1 | 0 | 0 | 1 | 0 |
| Rasheed, Hasan, HEL* | .986 | 47 | 67 | 3 | 1 | 71 | 0 |
| Remole, Clifton, PRV* | .960 | 25 | 24 | 0 | 1 | 25 | 0 |
| Renz, Jordan, PRV | .971 | 63 | 93 | 7 | 3 | 103 | 0 |
| Richmond, BJ, OGD* | .973 | 46 | 66 | 5 | 2 | 73 | 0 |
| Rivera, Jhonny, GRF | 1.000 | 25 | 51 | 4 | 0 | 55 | 2 |
| Roberts, Daron, GRF | .966 | 34 | 56 | 1 | 2 | 59 | 0 |

| Player, Team | Pct. | G | PO | A | E | TC | DP |
|---|---|---|---|---|---|---|---|
| Rodriguez, Sean, PRV | 1.000 | 3 | 9 | 0 | 0 | 9 | 0 |
| Ruggiano, Justin, OGD | .974 | 45 | 72 | 2 | 2 | 76 | 0 |
| Russ, Ryan, OGD | .929 | 30 | 50 | 2 | 4 | 56 | 2 |
| Sakamoto, Mitsuru, CAS* | 1.000 | 6 | 6 | 0 | 0 | 6 | 0 |
| Salazar, Darwinson, IDF | .915 | 51 | 80 | 6 | 8 | 94 | 2 |
| Santiago, Jayson, MSO* | .905 | 11 | 18 | 1 | 2 | 21 | 1 |
| Serfass, Jake, HEL* | .959 | 29 | 47 | 0 | 2 | 49 | 0 |
| Smith, Seth, CAS* | .941 | 45 | 72 | 8 | 5 | 85 | 0 |
| Strait, Cody, BIL | 1.000 | 11 | 17 | 2 | 0 | 19 | 0 |
| Szymanski, Brandon, BIL | 1.000 | 15 | 26 | 2 | 0 | 28 | 0 |
| Townsend, Marcus, MSO | .864 | 28 | 49 | 2 | 8 | 59 | 1 |
| Valentin, Geraldo, IDF | .968 | 50 | 85 | 5 | 3 | 93 | 2 |
| Williams, Kevin, MSO | 1.000 | 20 | 30 | 1 | 0 | 31 | 0 |

## CATCHERS

| Player, Team | Pct. | G | PO | A | E | TC | DP | PB |
|---|---|---|---|---|---|---|---|---|
| Blevins, Clay*, HEL | .977 | 30 | 204 | 12 | 5 | 221 | 1 | 13 |
| Castillo, Wilkin, MSO | 962 | 34 | 253 | 22 | 11 | 286 | 1 | 10 |
| Corredor, Nestor, HEL | 1.000 | 5 | 36 | 6 | 0 | 42 | 0 | 0 |
| Curreri, Frank, MSO | .974 | 10 | 95 | 18 | 3 | 116 | 1 | 3 |
| Del Campo, Manny, MSO | 1.000 | 12 | 45 | 4 | 0 | 49 | 0 | 2 |
| Del Rosario, Felipe, IDF | .983 | 32 | 208 | 26 | 4 | 238 | 0 | 6 |
| Deuchler, Matthew, GRF | .981 | 32 | 278 | 33 | 6 | 317 | 0 | 8 |
| Duff, Tim, PRV | .984 | 43 | 295 | 63 | 6 | 364 | 1 | 6 |
| Ellis, Jason, BIL | .986 | 10 | 66 | 7 | 1 | 74 | 0 | 3 |
| Ferrara, Matt, IDF | .971 | 10 | 60 | 6 | 2 | 68 | 1 | 4 |
| Fox, Ryan, CAS | .981 | 36 | 293 | 21 | 6 | 320 | 0 | 29 |
| Gonzalez, Reynaldo, BIL | 1.000 | 2 | 8 | 2 | 0 | 10 | 0 | 1 |
| Hansen, Josh, GRF | .857 | 2 | 5 | 1 | 1 | 7 | 1 | 0 |
| Infante, Jefferson, IDF | .988 | 25 | 151 | 18 | 2 | 171 | 1 | 10 |
| Johnson, Ben, PRV | .982 | 34 | 240 | 28 | 5 | 273 | 1 | 6 |
| Lozada, Charlie, HEL | .981 | 9 | 49 | 4 | 1 | 54 | 1 | 2 |
| LUCY, DONNY, GRF | .988 | 44 | 357 | 44 | 5 | 406 | 1 | 5 |
| Lynch, Mike, OGD | .986 | 14 | 129 | 11 | 2 | 142 | 2 | 6 |
| Martinez, Brett, PRV | 1.000 | 3 | 16 | 2 | 0 | 18 | 0 | 0 |
| Mercado, Richard, MSO | .986 | 26 | 189 | 20 | 3 | 212 | 1 | 2 |
| Norman, Derek, IDF | .982 | 18 | 157 | 9 | 3 | 169 | 1 | 5 |
| Pujols, Kengshill, OGD | .983 | 37 | 325 | 28 | 6 | 359 | 3 | 25 |
| Rodriquez, Ramon, CAS | .985 | 34 | 314 | 18 | 5 | 337 | 1 | 14 |
| Segura, Alberto, HEL | .987 | 38 | 285 | 28 | 4 | 317 | 3 | 7 |
| Tatum, Craig, BIL | .987 | 42 | 327 | 49 | 5 | 381 | 2 | 9 |
| Westervelt, Chris, OGD | .989 | 27 | 238 | 20 | 3 | 261 | 0 | 16 |
| Wilson, Kyle, CAS | .967 | 9 | 56 | 2 | 2 | 60 | 0 | 0 |
| Ziemendorf, Chad, BIL | .986 | 29 | 188 | 21 | 3 | 212 | 1 | 6 |

## PITCHERS

| Player, Team | Pct. | G | PO | A | E | TC | DP |
|---|---|---|---|---|---|---|---|
| Akin, Brian, OGD | 1.000 | 21 | 3 | 5 | 0 | 8 | 1 |
| Alexander, Mark, OGD | 1.000 | 25 | 2 | 7 | 0 | 9 | 0 |
| Alvarez, Carlos, OGD* | 1.000 | 20 | 1 | 7 | 0 | 8 | 0 |
| Alvarez, Gabriel, OGD | .750 | 15 | 0 | 3 | 1 | 4 | 0 |
| Arnold, Mitchell, PRV | .800 | 25 | 2 | 2 | 1 | 5 | 0 |
| Baker, Josh, HEL | 1.000 | 15 | 5 | 4 | 0 | 9 | 0 |
| Bakker, Garry, GRF | .895 | 13 | 1 | 16 | 2 | 19 | 1 |
| Banks, Demetrius, GRF* | .875 | 21 | 3 | 4 | 1 | 8 | 0 |
| Barnes, Justin, HEL | 1.000 | 11 | 4 | 3 | 0 | 7 | 0 |
| Bates, Dallas, HEL* | 1.000 | 2 | 0 | 1 | 0 | 1 | 1 |
| Bauer, Garrett, MSO* | 1.000 | 16 | 2 | 4 | 0 | 6 | 0 |
| Beeson, Bobby, IDF* | 1.000 | 15 | 2 | 7 | 0 | 9 | 0 |
| Berger, Garrett, HEL | 1.000 | 1 | 0 | 1 | 0 | 1 | 0 |
| Blackwell, Chad, IDF | 1.000 | 21 | 1 | 3 | 0 | 4 | 0 |
| Buckner, Billy, IDF | .833 | 8 | 3 | 2 | 1 | 6 | 0 |
| Buechner, Chris, CAS | 1.000 | 13 | 0 | 2 | 0 | 2 | 0 |
| Campbell, Matthew, IDF* | .000 | 4 | 0 | 0 | 0 | 0 | 0 |
| Carlson, Zane, IDF | .667 | 19 | 0 | 2 | 1 | 3 | 0 |
| Carney, Frederic, PRV | 1.000 | 19 | 2 | 2 | 0 | 4 | 0 |
| Castillo, Albenis, OGD | .875 | 12 | 1 | 6 | 1 | 8 | 0 |
| Chivilli, Pedro, CAS | 1.000 | 5 | 2 | 3 | 0 | 5 | 0 |
| Clark, Chad, MSO | .750 | 12 | 1 | 2 | 1 | 4 | 0 |
| Cordova, Francisco, PRV | 1.000 | 14 | 4 | 6 | 0 | 10 | 0 |
| Cota, Luis, IDF | .833 | 13 | 1 | 4 | 1 | 6 | 0 |
| Cox, Jason, PRV | 1.000 | 15 | 1 | 4 | 0 | 5 | 0 |
| Crist, Kyle, IDF | 1.000 | 12 | 6 | 5 | 0 | 11 | 0 |
| Cruz, Rafael, PRV | 1.000 | 2 | 0 | 2 | 0 | 2 | 0 |
| Daley, Matt, CAS | .857 | 21 | 2 | 4 | 1 | 7 | 0 |
| Davis, Vince, MSO* | .875 | 16 | 1 | 13 | 2 | 16 | 0 |
| De La Cruz, Carlos, HEL | 1.000 | 4 | 0 | 1 | 0 | 1 | 0 |
| DeCarlo, Derek, HEL | .833 | 15 | 1 | 4 | 1 | 6 | 0 |
| DEDUNO, SAMUEL, CAS | .750 | 15 | 4 | 5 | 3 | 12 | 0 |
| Delgado, George, CAS | 1.000 | 25 | 0 | 1 | 0 | 1 | 0 |
| Dillard, Johnny, BIL | 1.000 | 22 | 0 | 3 | 0 | 3 | 0 |
| Douglas, Jaime, PRV* | 1.000 | 18 | 0 | 2 | 0 | 2 | 0 |
| Dove, Shane, MSO* | .636 | 15 | 1 | 6 | 4 | 11 | 0 |
| Doyle, Travis, GRF* | 1.000 | 11 | 0 | 4 | 0 | 4 | 0 |
| Duran, Emmanuel, MSO | 1.000 | 23 | 2 | 7 | 0 | 9 | 0 |
| Edsall, Stephen, CAS | 1.000 | 5 | 3 | 0 | 0 | 3 | 0 |
| Edwards, Bill, PRV | 1.000 | 20 | 1 | 3 | 0 | 4 | 0 |
| Egbert, John, GRF | .938 | 17 | 8 | 7 | 1 | 16 | 2 |
| Elbert, Scott, OGD* | .800 | 12 | 2 | 6 | 2 | 10 | 1 |
| Elliott, Matt, MSO | 1.000 | 12 | 0 | 4 | 0 | 4 | 0 |
| Everly, Eric, GRF | .778 | 18 | 1 | 6 | 2 | 9 | 0 |
| Farfan, Alexander, BIL | .700 | 16 | 1 | 6 | 3 | 10 | 0 |
| Feliz, Ranier, BIL | 1.000 | 18 | 2 | 3 | 0 | 5 | 0 |
| Garcia, Javier, OGD | 1.000 | 16 | 4 | 4 | 0 | 8 | 0 |
| Garcia, Miguel, HEL | .500 | 5 | 1 | 0 | 1 | 2 | 0 |
| Garner, Jeff, HEL | .667 | 12 | 1 | 1 | 1 | 3 | 0 |
| Gelinas, Karl, PRV | 1.000 | 14 | 4 | 6 | 0 | 10 | 1 |
| Gillihan, Adam, BIL | .000 | 3 | 0 | 0 | 0 | 0 | 0 |
| Goetz, Greg, BIL* | .857 | 17 | 5 | 7 | 2 | 14 | 0 |
| Green, Nick, PRV | 1.000 | 17 | 5 | 8 | 0 | 13 | 1 |
| Green, Patrick, IDF | .889 | 13 | 3 | 5 | 1 | 9 | 1 |
| Griffin, David, BIL* | .714 | 15 | 3 | 2 | 2 | 7 | 0 |
| Guerrero, Hipolito, MSO* | .750 | 7 | 1 | 2 | 1 | 4 | 1 |
| Hansen, Grant, GRF | 1.000 | 6 | 1 | 3 | 0 | 4 | 0 |
| Hawk, Derek, BIL | .909 | 17 | 4 | 6 | 1 | 11 | 0 |
| Hawk, Tommy, HEL | .889 | 13 | 3 | 5 | 1 | 9 | 0 |
| Hedden, Wayne, PRV | 1.000 | 16 | 2 | 2 | 0 | 4 | 1 |
| Hicklen, Patrick, IDF | 1.000 | 6 | 0 | 1 | 0 | 1 | 0 |
| Hinton, Robert, HEL | .667 | 15 | 1 | 3 | 2 | 6 | 0 |
| Howard, Adam, MSO | .750 | 9 | 1 | 2 | 1 | 4 | 0 |
| Howell, JP, IDF* | 1.000 | 6 | 1 | 5 | 0 | 6 | 0 |
| Hundt, Brandon, HEL | 1.000 | 10 | 1 | 3 | 0 | 4 | 0 |
| Hurd, John, GRF | .818 | 25 | 2 | 7 | 2 | 11 | 0 |
| Jackson, Steven, MSO | .667 | 7 | 0 | 4 | 2 | 6 | 0 |
| Jenson, Drew, BIL* | 1.000 | 19 | 4 | 8 | 0 | 12 | 0 |
| Johnson, Blake, OGD | .857 | 13 | 2 | 10 | 2 | 14 | 1 |
| Johnson, David, HEL | 1.000 | 4 | 1 | 2 | 0 | 3 | 0 |
| Johnson, JD, GRF | .000 | 12 | 0 | 0 | 1 | 1 | 0 |
| Johnson, Todd, BIL* | 1.000 | 18 | 1 | 2 | 0 | 3 | 0 |
| Julio, Donald, MSO | .889 | 24 | 1 | 7 | 1 | 9 | 0 |
| Kane, Kyle, GRF | 1.000 | 7 | 1 | 0 | 0 | 1 | 0 |
| Klusman, Aaron, OGD | .833 | 21 | 1 | 4 | 1 | 6 | 1 |
| Knoff, Justin, BIL | 1.000 | 6 | 0 | 2 | 0 | 2 | 0 |
| Krantz, Ben, MSO | .824 | 14 | 6 | 8 | 3 | 17 | 2 |
| Kupper, Dustin, BIL | 1.000 | 4 | 0 | 1 | 0 | 1 | 0 |
| Layman, Billy, PRV | .857 | 13 | 2 | 4 | 1 | 7 | 1 |
| Lindsey, Shane, CAS | .333 | 17 | 1 | 1 | 4 | 6 | 0 |
| Lingenfelter, Adam, BIL | 1.000 | 9 | 1 | 1 | 0 | 2 | 0 |
| Liotta, Ray ,GRF* | 1.000 | 14 | 2 | 8 | 0 | 10 | 0 |
| Little, Jeff, GRF | 1.000 | 13 | 0 | 2 | 0 | 2 | 0 |
| Logan, Boone, GRF* | .722 | 18 | 0 | 13 | 5 | 18 | 0 |
| Manzueta, Radhames, CAS | .667 | 7 | 1 | 1 | 1 | 3 | 0 |
| Marion, Ryan, HEL | .400 | 20 | 0 | 2 | 3 | 5 | 0 |
| Marshall, Jay, GRF* | 1.000 | 4 | 0 | 3 | 0 | 3 | 1 |
| Martinez, Alvaro, HEL | 1.000 | 17 | 6 | 3 | 0 | 9 | 0 |
| Mattheus, Ryan, CAS | 1.000 | 7 | 1 | 1 | 0 | 2 | 0 |
| McConiga, Jacob, IDF* | .889 | 12 | 2 | 6 | 1 | 9 | 0 |
| McGary, Gerron, GRF* | 1.000 | 21 | 0 | 2 | 0 | 2 | 0 |
| McKenna, Daniel, HEL | 1.000 | 12 | 1 | 0 | 0 | 1 | 0 |
| Meque, Jacobo, BIL* | .400 | 18 | 0 | 4 | 6 | 10 | 0 |
| Merino, Josh, CAS | 1.000 | 8 | 6 | 2 | 0 | 8 | 0 |
| Metzger, Jay, CAS* | 1.000 | 14 | 1 | 3 | 0 | 4 | 0 |
| Morales, Franklin, CAS* | .600 | 15 | 1 | 5 | 4 | 10 | 0 |
| Morenko, Brad, BIL | .857 | 19 | 1 | 5 | 1 | 7 | 0 |
| Mosqueda, Juan, CAS | 1.000 | 8 | 2 | 0 | 0 | 2 | 0 |
| Mullis, Jake, IDF | 1.000 | 14 | 3 | 7 | 0 | 10 | 1 |
| Murray, Brandon, HEL* | .500 | 18 | 0 | 1 | 1 | 2 | 0 |
| Mutter, Casey, PRV | 1.000 | 18 | 1 | 0 | 0 | 1 | 1 |
| Nachreiner, Matt, GRF | 1.000 | 11 | 3 | 2 | 0 | 5 | 1 |
| Needham, Joel, HEL | .667 | 8 | 1 | 1 | 1 | 3 | 0 |
| Nendza, Brian, IDF* | .750 | 24 | 2 | 4 | 2 | 8 | 0 |
| Newman, Josh, CAS* | 1.000 | 27 | 2 | 9 | 0 | 11 | 0 |
| Nippert, Derik, MSO | .750 | 3 | 2 | 1 | 1 | 4 | 0 |
| Noriega, Luis, BIL | 1.000 | 18 | 5 | 3 | 0 | 8 | 0 |
| Novosel, Walt, MSO* | .000 | 6 | 0 | 0 | 0 | 0 | 0 |
| O'Neal, Charles, BIL* | 1.000 | 2 | 0 | 1 | 0 | 1 | 0 |
| Obispo, Josel, OGD | .750 | 5 | 2 | 1 | 1 | 4 | 0 |
| Obispo, Juan, OGD | .000 | 1 | 0 | 0 | 0 | 0 | 0 |
| Orenduff, Justin, OGD | .667 | 13 | 0 | 2 | 1 | 3 | 0 |
| Palmer, Lucas, IDF | 1.000 | 17 | 3 | 6 | 0 | 9 | 0 |
| Parker, David, OGD | .800 | 19 | 2 | 6 | 2 | 10 | 0 |
| Patton, David, CAS | .917 | 17 | 5 | 6 | 1 | 12 | 0 |
| Pawelczyk, Kyle, PRV* | 1.000 | 17 | 4 | 3 | 0 | 7 | 0 |
| Pelland, Tyler, BIL* | .923 | 18 | 3 | 9 | 1 | 13 | 1 |

| Player, Team | Pct. | G | PO | A | E | TC | DP |
|---|---|---|---|---|---|---|---|
| Pfeiffer, David, OGD* | 1.000 | 8 | 0 | 6 | 0 | 6 | 0 |
| Pratt, Jordan, OGD | 1.000 | 12 | 10 | 12 | 0 | 22 | 2 |
| Ramirez, Ramon, BIL | .955 | 17 | 7 | 14 | 1 | 22 | 2 |
| Ray, Ronnie, PRV | .833 | 13 | 0 | 5 | 1 | 6 | 1 |
| Reed, Rylan, GRF | 1.000 | 5 | 0 | 1 | 0 | 1 | 0 |
| Requena, Ricardo, PRV | 1.000 | 17 | 1 | 1 | 0 | 2 | 0 |
| Rodriguez, Fernando, PRV | .900 | 14 | 3 | 6 | 1 | 10 | 0 |
| Rowe, Adam, IDF* | 1.000 | 23 | 0 | 3 | 0 | 3 | 0 |
| Russell, Adam, GRF | .833 | 15 | 2 | 3 | 1 | 6 | 1 |
| Sanchez, Rafael, CAS | .875 | 22 | 4 | 3 | 1 | 8 | 0 |
| Sanchez, Ramon, MSO | .778 | 18 | 3 | 4 | 2 | 9 | 1 |
| Sanders, Jared, BIL | .750 | 23 | 0 | 3 | 1 | 4 | 0 |
| Saxton, Chris, IDF | .909 | 21 | 2 | 8 | 1 | 11 | 1 |
| Shearer, Kelly, PRV* | 1.000 | 2 | 0 | 2 | 0 | 2 | 0 |
| Sherman, Justin, IDF | 1.000 | 10 | 5 | 5 | 0 | 10 | 2 |
| Shuey, Paul, OGD | .000 | 2 | 0 | 0 | 0 | 0 | 0 |
| Sobkow, Phil, OGD | .833 | 6 | 0 | 5 | 1 | 6 | 0 |
| Stanczyk, Ben, HEL | 1.000 | 7 | 2 | 4 | 0 | 6 | 0 |
| Stanley, Pat, CAS | .889 | 20 | 3 | 5 | 1 | 9 | 0 |
| Stein, Todd,. MSO* | 1.000 | 17 | 0 | 4 | 0 | 4 | 0 |
| Stott, Zach, BIL | 1.000 | 2 | 1 | 0 | 0 | 1 | 0 |
| Suarez, Sony, GRF | .917 | 18 | 3 | 8 | 1 | 12 | 0 |
| Sweeney, Mike, PRV* | 1.000 | 4 | 0 | 1 | 0 | 1 | 0 |
| Theodorakos, Jared; HEL* | .800 | 9 | 1 | 3 | 1 | 5 | 0 |
| Thompson, Sean, GRF* | 1.000 | 8 | 0 | 1 | 0 | 1 | 0 |
| Trammell, Travis, IDF | .750 | 20 | 0 | 3 | 1 | 4 | 0 |
| Vaillancourt, Tim, MSO | .833 | 14 | 2 | 8 | 2 | 12 | 0 |
| Valdez, Salvador, MSO | .333 | 8 | 0 | 1 | 2 | 3 | 0 |
| Vargas, Buzz, CAS | 1.000 | 21 | 0 | 1 | 0 | 1 | 0 |
| Vasquez, Esmerling, MSO | 1.000 | 19 | 2 | 4 | 0 | 6 | 1 |
| Vazquez, Camilo, BIL* | .000 | 2 | 0 | 0 | 0 | 0 | 0 |
| Veracierto, Fernando, CAS | 1.000 | 1 | 0 | 1 | 0 | 1 | 0 |
| Wade, Cory, OGD | 1.000 | 8 | 1 | 2 | 0 | 3 | 0 |
| Wahpepah, Josh, HEL | 1.000 | 15 | 2 | 7 | 0 | 9 | 1 |
| Walker, Edwin, HEL* | 1.000 | 15 | 2 | 4 | 0 | 6 | 1 |
| Waters, Chris, PRV | .909 | 21 | 3 | 7 | 1 | 11 | 1 |
| White, Jeremey, CAS* | 1.000 | 20 | 0 | 6 | 0 | 6 | 0 |
| Whittington, Anthony, PRV* | 1.000 | 11 | 4 | 6 | 0 | 10 | 1 |
| Wilson, Justin, HEL* | .800 | 7 | 0 | 4 | 1 | 5 | 0 |
| Wooley, Robert, HEL | .857 | 17 | 2 | 10 | 2 | 14 | 1 |
| Wright, Wesley, OGD* | 1.000 | 17 | 2 | 7 | 0 | 9 | 0 |
| Yamaguchi, Tetsuya, MSO* | .625 | 13 | 0 | 5 | 3 | 8 | 0 |
| Yonezawa, Kosuke, MSO | .500 | 8 | 0 | 1 | 1 | 2 | 0 |
| Zaleski, Matthew, GRF | 1.000 | 24 | 1 | 9 | 0 | 10 | 1 |

# LEAGUE CHAMPIONS

| Year | Team | Pct. |
|---|---|---|
| 1939— | Twin Falls* | .581 |
| 1940— | Salt Lake City | .608 |
| | Ogden (4th)* | .492 |
| 1941— | Boise | .623 |
| | Ogden (2nd)* | .598 |
| 1942— | Pocatello† | .690 |
| | Boise | .683 |
| 1943-44-45— | Did not operate. | |
| 1946— | Twin Falls‡ | .585 |
| | Salt Lake City† | .585 |
| 1947— | Salt Lake City | .618 |
| | Twin Falls† | .600 |
| 1948— | Pocatello | .611 |
| | Twin Falls (2nd)* | .595 |
| 1949— | Twin Falls | .624 |
| | Pocatello (3rd)* | .595 |
| 1950— | Pocatello | .635 |
| | Billings (3rd)* | .571 |
| 1951— | Salt Lake City | .618 |
| | Great Falls (3rd)* | .559 |
| 1952— | Pocatello | .595 |
| | Idaho Falls (2nd)* | .573 |
| 1953— | Ogden | .679 |
| | Salt Lake City (4th)* | .527 |
| 1954— | Salt Lake City | .595 |
| | Great Falls (4th)* | .530 |
| 1955— | Boise | .588 |
| | Magic Valley (4th)* | .489 |
| 1956— | Boise | .561 |
| 1957— | Salt Lake City | .650 |
| | Billings† | .582 |
| 1958— | Great Falls | .582 |
| | Boise† | .615 |
| 1959— | Boise | .633 |
| | Billings (2nd)* | .523 |
| 1960— | Boise† | .686 |
| | Idaho Falls | .650 |
| 1961— | Boise | .638 |
| | Great Falls* | .571 |
| 1962— | Boise§ | .565 |
| | Billings† | .706 |
| 1963— | Idaho Falls | .702 |
| | Magic Valley† | .643 |
| 1964— | Treasure Valley | .615 |
| 1965— | Treasure Valley | .530 |
| 1966— | Ogden | .591 |
| 1967— | Ogden | .621 |
| 1968— | Ogden | .609 |
| 1969— | Ogden | .620 |
| 1970— | Idaho Falls | .629 |
| 1971— | Great Falls | .643 |
| 1972— | Billings | .694 |
| 1973— | Billings | .629 |
| 1974— | Idaho Falls | .569 |
| 1975— | Great Falls | .577 |
| 1976— | Great Falls | .577 |
| 1977— | Lethbridge | .629 |
| 1978— | Billings∞ | .735 |
| 1979— | Helena | .623 |
| | Lethbridge▲ | .559 |
| 1980— | Lethbridge▲ | .743 |
| | Billings | .629 |
| 1981— | Calgary | .657 |
| | Butte▲ | .557 |
| 1982— | Medicine Hat▲ | .629 |
| | Idaho Falls | .600 |
| 1983— | Billings▲ | .614 |
| | Calgary | .600 |
| 1984— | Billings | .691 |
| | Helena▲ | .647 |
| 1985— | Great Falls | .771 |
| | Salt Lake City▲ | .657 |
| 1986— | Salt Lake City◆ | .643 |
| | Great Falls | .571 |
| 1987— | Salt Lake City◆ | .700 |
| | Helena | .657 |
| 1988— | Great Falls◆ | .754 |
| | Butte | .629 |
| 1989— | Great Falls◆ | .791 |
| | Butte | .621 |
| 1990— | Great Falls◆ | .706 |
| | Salt Lake | .618 |
| 1991— | Salt Lake City◆ | .700 |
| | Great Falls | .657 |
| 1992— | Salt Lake | .697 |
| | Billings◆ | .697 |
| 1993— | Billings◆ | .653 |
| | Helena | .589 |
| 1994— | Billings◆ | .694 |
| | Helena | .611 |
| 1995— | Billings | .710 |
| | Helena■ | .690 |
| 1996— | Helena■ | .597 |
| | Ogden | .583 |
| 1997— | Great Falls | .556 |
| | Billings■ | .549 |
| 1998— | Medicine Hat | .622 |
| | Idaho Falls■ | .618 |
| 1999— | Idaho Falls | .640 |
| | Missoula■ | .592 |
| 2000— | Idaho Falls■ | .608 |
| 2001— | Provo | .697 |
| | Billings■ | .613 |
| 2002— | Great Falls■ | .627 |
| 2003— | Billings■ | .539 |
| 2004— | Provo■ | .579 |

*Won four-club playoff. †Won split-season playoff. ‡Ended first half in tie with Salt Lake City and won one-game playoff. §Ended first half in tie with Billings and Great Falls and won playoff. ∞Billings (first place) defeated Idaho Falls (second place) in first place-second place playoff. ▲League divided into Northern and Southern divisions; won two-club playoff. ◆Won two-club playoff. ■League divided into Northern and Southern divisions; won four-club playoff.

# ARIZONA LEAGUE

## LEAGUE OFFICE

**President/treasurer**
Bob Richmond
**Address**
P.O. Box 1645
Boise, ID 83701
**Phone**
208-429-1511

**Teams***
Angels
Athletics
Brewers
Cubs
Giants
Padres
Mariners
Rangers
Royals

*Teams play their games in Maryvale, Mesa, Peoria, Phoenix, Scottsdale and Surprise, Ariz.

## 2004 FINAL STANDINGS

### FIRST HALF

| Team | W | L | T | Pct. | GB |
|---|---|---|---|---|---|
| Giants | 18 | 9 | - | .667 | ... |
| Royals | 16 | 12 | - | .571 | 2.5 |
| Rangers | 16 | 12 | - | .571 | 2.5 |
| Mariners | 16 | 12 | - | .571 | 2.5 |
| Brewers | 15 | 13 | - | .536 | 3.5 |
| Athletics | 14 | 14 | - | .500 | 4.5 |
| Padres | 13 | 15 | - | .464 | 5.5 |
| Cubs | 12 | 16 | - | .429 | 6.5 |
| Angels | 5 | 22 | - | .185 | 13.0 |

### SECOND HALF

| Team | W | L | T | Pct. | GB |
|---|---|---|---|---|---|
| Athletics | 20 | 8 | - | .714 | ... |
| Giants | 18 | 10 | - | .643 | 2.0 |
| Rangers | 16 | 12 | - | .571 | 4.0 |
| Mariners | 15 | 13 | - | .536 | 5.0 |
| Cubs | 15 | 13 | - | .536 | 5.0 |
| Royals | 13 | 15 | - | .464 | 7.0 |
| Padres | 13 | 15 | - | .464 | 7.0 |
| Brewers | 9 | 19 | - | .321 | 11.0 |
| Angels | 7 | 21 | - | .250 | 13.0 |

### COMPOSITE

| Team | W | L | T | PCT | GB | GIA | ATH | RNG | MRN | RYL | CUB | PDR | BRR | ANG |
|---|---|---|---|---|---|---|---|---|---|---|---|---|---|---|
| Giants (Giants) | 36 | 19 | - | .655 | X | 4 | 3 | 5 | 4 | 4 | 6 | 5 | 6 | |
| Athletics (Athletics) | 34 | 22 | - | .607 | 3 | 3 | X | 5 | 5 | 2 | 6 | 2 | 4 | 7 |
| Rangers (Rangers) | 32 | 24 | - | .571 | 5 | 4 | 2 | X | 4 | 6 | 3 | 6 | 2 | 5 |
| Mariners (Mariners) | 31 | 25 | - | .554 | 6 | 2 | 2 | 3 | X | 4 | 4 | 4 | 7 | 5 |
| Royals (Royals) | 29 | 27 | - | .518 | 8 | 3 | 5 | 1 | 3 | X | 4 | 6 | 2 | 5 |
| Cubs (Cubs) | 27 | 29 | - | .482 | 10 | 3 | 1 | 4 | 3 | 3 | X | 3 | 4 | 6 |
| Padres (Padres) | 26 | 30 | - | .464 | 11 | 1 | 5 | 1 | 3 | 1 | 4 | X | 6 | 5 |
| Brewers (Brewers) | 24 | 32 | - | .429 | 13 | 2 | 3 | 5 | 0 | 5 | 3 | 1 | X | 5 |
| Angels (Angels) | 12 | 44 | - | .214 | 25 | 1 | 0 | 2 | 2 | 2 | 1 | 2 | 2 | X |

Club names are major league affiliations.

Games played in Mesa, Peoria, Phoenix and Tucson.

PLAYOFFS: Giants defeated Athletics one game to none to win championship.

REGULAR-SEASON ATTENDANCE: No total attendance figures reported.

MANAGERS: Angels, Brian Harper; Athletics, Ruben Escalera; Brewers, Mike Guerrero; Cubs, Trey Forkerway; Giants, Bert Hunter; Mariners, Scott Steinmann; Padres, Carlos Lezcano; Rangers, Pedro Lopez; Royals, Lloyd Simmons.

ALL-STAR TEAM: 1B—Miguel Vega, Royals; 2B—Hernan Iribarren, Brewers; 3B—Wesley Long, Athletics; SS—Wilber Perez, Athletics; OF—Michael Mooney; OF—Carlos Quinones, Cubs; OF—K.C. Herren, Rangers; C—Daniel Santin, Mariners; DH—Elvin Puello, Cubs; LHP—Andy Santana, Cubs; RHP—Russell Begnaud, Royals; LH Reliever—Rafael Lluberes, Brewers; RH Reliever; Connor Robertson, Athletics. MVP—Hernan Iribarren, Brewers. Manager of the Year—Bert Hunter, Giants.

## 2004 BATTING

### TEAM

| Team | G | TPA | AB | R | H | TB | 2B | 3B | HR | RBI | SH | SF | HP | BB | IBB | SO | SB | CS | GDP | LOB | ShO | Avg. | OBP | Slg. |
|---|---|---|---|---|---|---|---|---|---|---|---|---|---|---|---|---|---|---|---|---|---|---|---|---|
| Mariners | 56 | 2191 | 1937 | 334 | 557 | 768 | 105 | 23 | 20 | 269 | 9 | 17 | 56 | 171 | 2 | 417 | 80 | 27 | 48 | 386 | 2 | .288 | .359 | .396 |
| Giants | 56 | 2248 | 1941 | 343 | 549 | 782 | 104 | 33 | 21 | 296 | 25 | 27 | 36 | 219 | 9 | 419 | 93 | 29 | 32 | 441 | 1 | .283 | .362 | .403 |
| Padres | 56 | 2244 | 1978 | 278 | 529 | 709 | 99 | 24 | 11 | 237 | 21 | 20 | 53 | 171 | 7 | 400 | 59 | 25 | 48 | 446 | 3 | .267 | .339 | .358 |
| Brewers | 56 | 2180 | 1949 | 270 | 518 | 736 | 98 | 33 | 18 | 219 | 12 | 13 | 30 | 175 | 7 | 468 | 79 | 48 | 40 | 414 | 2 | .266 | .334 | .378 |
| Cubs | 56 | 2202 | 1914 | 275 | 503 | 668 | 85 | 28 | 8 | 235 | 25 | 17 | 55 | 190 | 8 | 453 | 41 | 34 | 42 | 426 | 2 | .263 | .344 | .349 |
| Athletics | 56 | 2160 | 1857 | 314 | 474 | 706 | 104 | 28 | 24 | 251 | 18 | 15 | 38 | 230 | 8 | 441 | 100 | 50 | 29 | 380 | 1 | .255 | .347 | .380 |
| Rangers | 56 | 2187 | 1896 | 301 | 482 | 713 | 91 | 25 | 30 | 253 | 11 | 14 | 33 | 232 | 4 | 520 | 63 | 30 | 37 | 408 | 0 | .254 | .343 | .376 |
| Royals | 56 | 2197 | 1858 | 290 | 469 | 687 | 84 | 28 | 26 | 238 | 16 | 23 | 56 | 243 | 2 | 469 | 107 | 52 | 28 | 421 | 2 | .252 | .352 | .370 |
| Angels | 56 | 2133 | 1912 | 201 | 451 | 598 | 72 | 21 | 11 | 169 | 5 | 14 | 40 | 162 | 3 | 476 | 76 | 43 | 39 | 396 | 6 | .236 | .307 | .313 |

### INDIVIDUAL

#### TOP QUALIFIERS FOR BATTING CHAMPIONSHIP

Minimum 151 plate appearances. *Lefthanded batter. †Switch-hitter.

| Player, Team | G | TPA | AB | R | H | TB | 2B | 3B | HR | RBI | SH | SF | HP | BB | IBB | SO | SB | CS | GDP | Avg. | OBP | Slg. |
|---|---|---|---|---|---|---|---|---|---|---|---|---|---|---|---|---|---|---|---|---|---|---|
| Iribarren, Hernan, Brewers | 46 | 211 | 189 | 40 | 83 | 119 | 6 | 9 | 4 | 36 | 3 | 0 | 0 | 19 | 2 | 23 | 15 | 7 | 2 | .439 | .490 | .630 |
| Disla, Lisandro, Giants | 48 | 195 | 168 | 27 | 59 | 68 | 7 | 1 | 0 | 25 | 4 | 1 | 4 | 18 | 1 | 29 | 4 | 5 | 2 | .351 | .424 | .405 |
| Long, Wesley, Athletics | 54 | 243 | 206 | 45 | 71 | 102 | 17 | 1 | 4 | 35 | 0 | 2 | 3 | 31 | 0 | 26 | 16 | 7 | 6 | .345 | .434 | .495 |
| Soto, Luis, Mariners | 37 | 166 | 148 | 35 | 49 | 73 | 12 | 3 | 2 | 27 | 0 | 2 | 3 | 13 | 0 | 22 | 2 | 4 | 9 | .331 | .392 | .493 |
| Santin, Daniel, Mariners * | 41 | 177 | 160 | 31 | 52 | 81 | 13 | 2 | 4 | 28 | 0 | 1 | 6 | 10 | 0 | 21 | 2 | 1 | 6 | .325 | .384 | .506 |
| Cruceta, Julio, Padres | 43 | 192 | 176 | 22 | 56 | 73 | 7 | 5 | 0 | 20 | 3 | 2 | 6 | 5 | 0 | 23 | 9 | 5 | 4 | .318 | .354 | .415 |
| Quinones, Carlos, Cubs † | 53 | 238 | 216 | 28 | 68 | 82 | 12 | 1 | 0 | 28 | 2 | 0 | 1 | 19 | 2 | 33 | 9 | 7 | 3 | .315 | .373 | .380 |
| Mooney, Mike, Giants | 55 | 254 | 215 | 43 | 67 | 110 | 11 | 7 | 6 | 57 | 0 | 6 | 8 | 25 | 1 | 45 | 7 | 6 | 5 | .312 | .394 | .512 |
| Padron, Raul, Athletics * | 40 | 169 | 147 | 23 | 45 | 70 | 14 | 4 | 1 | 35 | 1 | 1 | 4 | 16 | 1 | 25 | 6 | 3 | 1 | .306 | .387 | .476 |
| Puello, Elvin, Cubs | 53 | 218 | 189 | 26 | 57 | 73 | 7 | 3 | 1 | 37 | 2 | 2 | 13 | 12 | 1 | 38 | 1 | 4 | 10 | .302 | .380 | .386 |
| Herren, Karl, Rangers * | 46 | 213 | 185 | 32 | 55 | 72 | 13 | 2 | 0 | 21 | 1 | 0 | 1 | 24 | 1 | 54 | 7 | 6 | 1 | .297 | .381 | .389 |

| Player, Team | G | TPA | AB | R | H | TB | 2B | 3B | HR | RBI | SH | SF | HP | BB | IBB | SO | SB | CS | GDP | Avg. | OBP | Slg. |
|---|---|---|---|---|---|---|---|---|---|---|---|---|---|---|---|---|---|---|---|---|---|---|
| Jones, Daryl, Padres | 36 | 162 | 149 | 19 | 44 | 58 | 11 | 0 | 1 | 25 | 0 | 4 | 2 | 7 | 0 | 38 | 1 | 1 | 5 | .295 | .327 | .389 |
| Sanders, Marcus, Giants | 55 | 261 | 209 | 54 | 61 | 90 | 12 | 4 | 3 | 21 | 3 | 3 | 11 | 35 | 2 | 45 | 28 | 4 | 4 | .292 | .415 | .431 |
| Thon, Freddy, Rangers * | 51 | 221 | 203 | 31 | 59 | 85 | 12 | 1 | 4 | 36 | 0 | 2 | 3 | 13 | 0 | 23 | 9 | 3 | 10 | .291 | .339 | .419 |
| Gallardo, Carlos, Brewers * | 41 | 154 | 134 | 18 | 39 | 48 | 7 | 1 | 0 | 14 | 0 | 1 | 7 | 12 | 1 | 19 | 1 | 1 | 6 | .291 | .377 | .358 |

DEPARTMENTAL LEADERS: G—Vega, 56; AB—Vega, 229; R—Sanders, 54; H—Iribarren, 83; TB—Iribarren, 119; 2B—Long, 17; 3B—Iribarren, 9; HR—Vega, 10; RBI—Mooney, 57; SH—Desouza, 6; SF—Mooney, 6; HP—Puello, Ellis, 13; BB—J. Johnson, 55; IBB—Several tied with two; SO—Ellis, 81; SB—Sanders, 28; CS—J. Johnson, 13; GIDP—Puello, Thon, 10; Slg.—Iribarren, .630; OBP—Iribarren, .490.

## ALL PLAYERS

*Lefthanded batter. †Switch-hitter.

| Player, Team | G | TPA | AB | R | H | TB | 2B | 3B | HR | RBI | SH | SF | HP | BB | IBB | SO | SB | CS | GDP | Avg. | OBP | Slg. |
|---|---|---|---|---|---|---|---|---|---|---|---|---|---|---|---|---|---|---|---|---|---|---|
| Abreu, Johany, Giants † | 11 | 36 | 32 | 3 | 9 | 10 | 1 | 0 | 0 | 0 | 0 | 0 | 1 | 3 | 1 | 3 | 3 | 0 | 0 | .281 | .361 | .313 |
| Adkison, Blake, Royals | 28 | 87 | 71 | 6 | 12 | 17 | 2 | 0 | 1 | 5 | 0 | 0 | 4 | 12 | 0 | 25 | 1 | 0 | 0 | .169 | .322 | .239 |
| Alvino, Hargeny, Rangers | 6 | 23 | 18 | 2 | 1 | 1 | 0 | 0 | 0 | 2 | 0 | 0 | 0 | 5 | 0 | 10 | 0 | 0 | 0 | .056 | .261 | .056 |
| Andrews, Greg, Cubs | 27 | 106 | 88 | 16 | 21 | 27 | 6 | 0 | 0 | 11 | 0 | 1 | 1 | 16 | 1 | 31 | 0 | 0 | 4 | .239 | .358 | .307 |
| Angulo, Oscar, Brewers | 26 | 88 | 83 | 10 | 23 | 30 | 2 | 1 | 1 | 11 | 0 | 1 | 2 | 2 | 0 | 13 | 6 | 4 | 1 | .277 | .307 | .361 |
| Arias, Francis, Brewers | 14 | 29 | 23 | 7 | 4 | 5 | 1 | 0 | 0 | 1 | 0 | 0 | 2 | 4 | 0 | 8 | 2 | 0 | 0 | .174 | .345 | .217 |
| Arias, Roberto, Athletics | 23 | 69 | 59 | 9 | 9 | 14 | 1 | 2 | 0 | 5 | 2 | 1 | 0 | 7 | 0 | 18 | 1 | 1 | 0 | .153 | .239 | .237 |
| Arredondo, Jose, Angels | 28 | 70 | 68 | 6 | 13 | 15 | 2 | 0 | 0 | 3 | 1 | 0 | 0 | 1 | 0 | 13 | 1 | 2 | 1 | .191 | .203 | .221 |
| Ayala, Angel, Brewers * | 31 | 116 | 106 | 10 | 27 | 36 | 9 | 0 | 0 | 13 | 0 | 1 | 0 | 9 | 1 | 31 | 2 | 3 | 2 | .255 | .310 | .340 |
| Backman, Walter, Rangers * | 28 | 109 | 93 | 8 | 16 | 22 | 2 | 2 | 0 | 10 | 0 | 1 | 2 | 13 | 0 | 38 | 1 | 3 | 3 | .172 | .284 | .237 |
| Balfe,, Mariners | 1 | 5 | 5 | 2 | 2 | 5 | 1 | 1 | 0 | 3 | 0 | 0 | 0 | 0 | 0 | 2 | 0 | 0 | 0 | .400 | .400 | 1.000 |
| Best, Tyler, Athletics * | 30 | 124 | 88 | 15 | 18 | 23 | 2 | 0 | 1 | 11 | 0 | 1 | 7 | 26 | 2 | 32 | 3 | 1 | 0 | .205 | .418 | .261 |
| Blanc, Jhonathan, Brewers | 37 | 121 | 114 | 8 | 30 | 45 | 3 | 0 | 4 | 14 | 1 | 0 | 1 | 5 | 0 | 35 | 5 | 5 | 1 | .263 | .300 | .395 |
| Boyd, Chad, Athletics * | 35 | 136 | 116 | 19 | 24 | 33 | 4 | 1 | 1 | 13 | 1 | 1 | 2 | 16 | 0 | 21 | 3 | 2 | 1 | .207 | .311 | .284 |
| Brock, Jermaine, Mariners * | 35 | 128 | 120 | 16 | 29 | 38 | 5 | 2 | 0 | 10 | 0 | 1 | 1 | 6 | 0 | 33 | 5 | 2 | 2 | .242 | .281 | .317 |
| Caballero, Carlos, Royals | 36 | 130 | 117 | 17 | 31 | 39 | 6 | 1 | 0 | 11 | 1 | 1 | 6 | 5 | 0 | 25 | 5 | 4 | 2 | .265 | .326 | .333 |
| Canzler, Russell, Cubs | 32 | 119 | 105 | 12 | 26 | 37 | 2 | 3 | 1 | 13 | 3 | 1 | 1 | 9 | 0 | 35 | 0 | 1 | 2 | .248 | .310 | .352 |
| Carela, Carlos, Athletics | 30 | 93 | 81 | 10 | 18 | 20 | 2 | 0 | 0 | 10 | 1 | 0 | 0 | 11 | 1 | 30 | 10 | 4 | 2 | .222 | .315 | .247 |
| Casilla, Alexi, Angels † | 45 | 186 | 163 | 29 | 42 | 51 | 1 | 4 | 0 | 10 | 2 | 2 | 4 | 15 | 0 | 10 | 24 | 8 | 3 | .258 | .332 | .313 |
| Chapman, Stephen, Brewers * | 49 | 212 | 192 | 33 | 44 | 77 | 7 | 7 | 4 | 18 | 0 | 1 | 0 | 17 | 0 | 50 | 4 | 3 | 1 | .229 | .290 | .401 |
| Charles, Larry, Rangers | 8 | 37 | 31 | 2 | 5 | 8 | 0 | 0 | 1 | 9 | 0 | 0 | 0 | 6 | 0 | 12 | 0 | 1 | 0 | .161 | .297 | .258 |
| Ciesluk, Chris, Giants | 9 | 15 | 14 | 2 | 3 | 5 | 2 | 0 | 0 | 2 | 0 | 0 | 0 | 1 | 0 | 4 | 0 | 0 | 0 | .214 | .267 | .357 |
| Cividanes, Emmanuel, Giants * | 35 | 126 | 115 | 8 | 19 | 28 | 3 | 3 | 0 | 7 | 1 | 1 | 0 | 9 | 0 | 34 | 1 | 1 | 1 | .165 | .224 | .243 |
| Corredor, Nestor, Brewers | 28 | 79 | 76 | 3 | 21 | 33 | 7 | 1 | 1 | 7 | 0 | 0 | 0 | 3 | 1 | 11 | 0 | 1 | 2 | .276 | .304 | .434 |
| Cowles, Josh, Angels | 50 | 196 | 169 | 16 | 34 | 45 | 11 | 0 | 0 | 10 | 0 | 1 | 0 | 26 | 0 | 59 | 9 | 3 | 2 | .201 | .306 | .266 |
| Cruceta, Julio, Padres | 43 | 192 | 176 | 22 | 56 | 73 | 7 | 5 | 0 | 20 | 3 | 2 | 6 | 5 | 0 | 23 | 9 | 5 | 4 | .318 | .354 | .415 |
| Cruz, Reynaldo, Mariners | 24 | 102 | 92 | 14 | 24 | 37 | 6 | 2 | 1 | 13 | 0 | 1 | 0 | 9 | 0 | 31 | 2 | 1 | 0 | .261 | .324 | .402 |
| Davies, Josh, Angels | 40 | 145 | 137 | 14 | 35 | 45 | 3 | 2 | 1 | 10 | 1 | 1 | 1 | 5 | 0 | 37 | 4 | 1 | 7 | .255 | .285 | .328 |
| Day, Devin, Angels | 22 | 82 | 73 | 12 | 20 | 21 | 1 | 0 | 0 | 6 | 0 | 0 | 3 | 6 | 0 | 22 | 4 | 1 | 1 | .274 | .354 | .288 |
| De La Cruz, Freddy, Brewers | 48 | 197 | 178 | 22 | 48 | 69 | 15 | 3 | 0 | 23 | 0 | 3 | 3 | 13 | 0 | 44 | 4 | 2 | 5 | .270 | .325 | .388 |
| Delarosa, Anderson, Brewers | 24 | 63 | 61 | 5 | 12 | 17 | 3 | 1 | 0 | 3 | 0 | 0 | 0 | 2 | 0 | 21 | 3 | 1 | 0 | .197 | .222 | .279 |
| Desouza, Daniel, Giants * | 54 | 259 | 216 | 50 | 55 | 72 | 7 | 5 | 0 | 25 | 6 | 0 | 0 | 37 | 0 | 50 | 13 | 6 | 2 | .255 | .364 | .333 |
| Disla, Lisandro, Giants | 48 | 195 | 168 | 27 | 59 | 68 | 7 | 1 | 0 | 25 | 4 | 1 | 4 | 18 | 1 | 29 | 4 | 5 | 2 | .351 | .424 | .405 |
| Dixon, Dorian, Giants * | 27 | 96 | 82 | 10 | 26 | 33 | 7 | 0 | 0 | 12 | 1 | 0 | 0 | 13 | 0 | 8 | 1 | 0 | 2 | .317 | .411 | .402 |
| Doddo, Brandon, Angels * | 22 | 79 | 76 | 5 | 19 | 23 | 4 | 0 | 0 | 10 | 0 | 0 | 0 | 3 | 0 | 15 | 2 | 0 | 3 | .250 | .278 | .303 |
| Dominguez, Jeffrey, Mariners † | 45 | 182 | 162 | 18 | 36 | 40 | 2 | 1 | 0 | 15 | 3 | 0 | 3 | 12 | 0 | 39 | 10 | 0 | 5 | .222 | .288 | .247 |
| Douillard, Jonathan, Cubs * | 11 | 42 | 40 | 2 | 11 | 13 | 2 | 0 | 0 | 11 | 0 | 0 | 0 | 2 | 0 | 9 | 0 | 1 | 2 | .275 | .310 | .325 |
| Ellis, Jared, Royals | 53 | 227 | 188 | 37 | 43 | 76 | 11 | 5 | 4 | 28 | 0 | 3 | 13 | 23 | 0 | 81 | 9 | 4 | 4 | .229 | .348 | .404 |
| Emmons, John, Mariners | 34 | 140 | 131 | 20 | 40 | 51 | 5 | 3 | 0 | 13 | 0 | 0 | 3 | 6 | 0 | 26 | 12 | 2 | 1 | .305 | .350 | .389 |
| Etheridge, Chad, Padres † | 7 | 20 | 17 | 3 | 4 | 8 | 1 | 0 | 1 | 2 | 0 | 0 | 0 | 3 | 0 | 7 | 0 | 0 | 0 | .235 | .350 | .471 |
| Eusebio, Juan, Royals | 29 | 83 | 75 | 8 | 12 | 12 | 0 | 0 | 0 | 11 | 0 | 1 | 1 | 6 | 0 | 17 | 3 | 1 | 0 | .160 | .229 | .160 |
| Feliz, Nelson, Athletics | 10 | 45 | 40 | 3 | 12 | 15 | 3 | 0 | 0 | 10 | 1 | 1 | 0 | 3 | 0 | 10 | 1 | 1 | 2 | .300 | .341 | .375 |
| Flaig, Jeffrey, Mariners | 32 | 125 | 107 | 16 | 27 | 34 | 5 | 1 | 0 | 12 | 1 | 1 | 6 | 10 | 0 | 19 | 4 | 2 | 3 | .252 | .347 | .318 |
| Gac, Ian, Rangers | 40 | 171 | 153 | 19 | 36 | 61 | 8 | 1 | 5 | 31 | 0 | 4 | 1 | 13 | 0 | 59 | 2 | 0 | 3 | .235 | .292 | .399 |
| Gallardo, Carlos, Brewers * | 41 | 154 | 134 | 18 | 39 | 48 | 7 | 1 | 0 | 14 | 0 | 1 | 7 | 12 | 1 | 19 | 1 | 1 | 6 | .291 | .377 | .358 |
| Gomez, Mauro, Rangers | 34 | 138 | 126 | 12 | 31 | 47 | 9 | 2 | 1 | 16 | 2 | 0 | 0 | 10 | 0 | 33 | 0 | 2 | 1 | .246 | .301 | .373 |
| Gonzalez, Juan, Royals | 9 | 33 | 26 | 6 | 9 | 14 | 5 | 0 | 0 | 5 | 0 | 1 | 0 | 6 | 0 | 8 | 0 | 0 | 1 | .346 | .455 | .538 |
| Grana, Robert, Royals | 39 | 150 | 124 | 16 | 29 | 39 | 8 | 1 | 0 | 15 | 1 | 2 | 1 | 22 | 0 | 37 | 2 | 1 | 1 | .234 | .349 | .315 |
| Green, Zane, Cubs * | 42 | 160 | 133 | 19 | 37 | 50 | 2 | 4 | 1 | 17 | 2 | 3 | 1 | 20 | 0 | 38 | 3 | 2 | 3 | .278 | .369 | .376 |
| Guzman, Juan, Rangers † | 3 | 12 | 11 | 0 | 1 | 1 | 0 | 0 | 0 | 1 | 0 | 0 | 0 | 1 | 0 | 8 | 2 | 0 | 0 | .091 | .167 | .091 |
| Hall, David, Mariners | 35 | 151 | 137 | 25 | 38 | 51 | 13 | 0 | 0 | 20 | 0 | 2 | 5 | 7 | 0 | 39 | 8 | 2 | 2 | .277 | .331 | .372 |
| Hernandez, David, Angels | 33 | 123 | 109 | 9 | 28 | 40 | 4 | 1 | 2 | 12 | 0 | 2 | 5 | 7 | 0 | 27 | 1 | 4 | 3 | .257 | .325 | .367 |
| Herren, Karl, Rangers * | 46 | 213 | 185 | 32 | 55 | 72 | 13 | 2 | 0 | 21 | 1 | 0 | 1 | 24 | 1 | 54 | 7 | 6 | 1 | .297 | .381 | .389 |
| Higashi, Jonathan, Rangers | 13 | 45 | 40 | 7 | 14 | 24 | 3 | 2 | 1 | 9 | 0 | 0 | 2 | 3 | 1 | 8 | 0 | 0 | 1 | .350 | .422 | .600 |
| Hurba, Craig, Rangers | 32 | 115 | 99 | 18 | 26 | 46 | 5 | 6 | 1 | 16 | 2 | 1 | 1 | 12 | 1 | 21 | 1 | 0 | 4 | .263 | .345 | .465 |
| Iribarren, Herman, Brewers* | 46 | 211 | 189 | 40 | 83 | 119 | 6 | 9 | 4 | 36 | 3 | 0 | 0 | 19 | 2 | 23 | 15 | 7 | 2 | .439 | .490 | .630 |
| Jacobitz, Joseph, Mariners † | 30 | 117 | 97 | 14 | 27 | 33 | 2 | 2 | 0 | 9 | 2 | 1 | 3 | 14 | 0 | 18 | 0 | 1 | 1 | .278 | .383 | .340 |
| Jennings, Todd, Giants | 8 | 28 | 26 | 7 | 10 | 15 | 3 | 1 | 0 | 6 | 0 | 0 | 1 | 1 | 0 | 5 | 2 | 0 | 0 | .385 | .429 | .577 |
| Johnson, Craig, Padres * | 34 | 146 | 125 | 18 | 36 | 44 | 8 | 0 | 0 | 19 | 0 | 0 | 9 | 11 | 0 | 30 | 1 | 0 | 1 | .288 | .386 | .352 |
| Johnson, Joshua, Royals † | 53 | 246 | 178 | 44 | 38 | 55 | 5 | 6 | 0 | 22 | 4 | 2 | 7 | 55 | 1 | 38 | 23 | 13 | 1 | .213 | .413 | .309 |
| Johnson, Michael, Padres * | 8 | 33 | 29 | 4 | 10 | 15 | 5 | 0 | 0 | 3 | 0 | 0 | 0 | 4 | 0 | 12 | 1 | 0 | 1 | .345 | .424 | .517 |
| Johnson, Rob, Mariners | 8 | 31 | 27 | 4 | 6 | 7 | 1 | 0 | 0 | 1 | 0 | 0 | 1 | 3 | 0 | 7 | 1 | 1 | 1 | .222 | .323 | .259 |
| Johnston, Trey, Padres | 37 | 140 | 126 | 16 | 33 | 41 | 5 | 0 | 1 | 16 | 2 | 2 | 3 | 7 | 0 | 34 | 0 | 0 | 3 | .262 | .312 | .325 |
| Jones, Daryl, Padres | 36 | 162 | 149 | 19 | 44 | 58 | 11 | 0 | 1 | 25 | 0 | 4 | 2 | 7 | 0 | 38 | 1 | 1 | 5 | .295 | .327 | .389 |
| Joseph, Alfred, Cubs | 44 | 163 | 142 | 17 | 38 | 44 | 2 | 2 | 0 | 20 | 4 | 2 | 4 | 11 | 0 | 37 | 5 | 7 | 1 | .268 | .333 | .310 |
| Kendrick, Howie, Angels | 3 | 13 | 12 | 1 | 3 | 4 | 1 | 0 | 0 | 0 | 0 | 0 | 0 | 1 | 0 | 0 | 2 | 0 | 0 | .250 | .308 | .333 |
| Killian, William, Padres * | 40 | 151 | 135 | 17 | 31 | 42 | 7 | 2 | 0 | 13 | 1 | 2 | 2 | 11 | 0 | 21 | 3 | 1 | 5 | .230 | .293 | .311 |
| King, Lisandro, Giants | 21 | 58 | 49 | 4 | 8 | 8 | 0 | 0 | 0 | 6 | 2 | 2 | 0 | 5 | 0 | 17 | 1 | 0 | 1 | .163 | .232 | .163 |
| Kurtz, Jared, Giants | 17 | 68 | 59 | 9 | 14 | 21 | 7 | 0 | 0 | 6 | 0 | 0 | 0 | 9 | 0 | 19 | 2 | 0 | 1 | .237 | .338 | .356 |
| Lampe, Rayon, Mariners | 29 | 107 | 95 | 10 | 21 | 26 | 2 | 0 | 1 | 10 | 1 | 0 | 6 | 5 | 0 | 32 | 2 | 3 | 2 | .221 | .302 | .274 |
| Leclercq, Lenny, Brewers | 45 | 186 | 162 | 24 | 41 | 52 | 6 | 1 | 1 | 8 | 1 | 1 | 3 | 19 | 0 | 61 | 9 | 4 | 2 | .253 | .341 | .321 |
| Long, Wesley, Athletics | 54 | 243 | 206 | 45 | 71 | 102 | 17 | 1 | 4 | 35 | 0 | 2 | 3 | 31 | 0 | 26 | 16 | 7 | 6 | .345 | .434 | .495 |
| Lopez, Luis, Padres | 13 | 39 | 36 | 3 | 8 | 9 | 1 | 0 | 0 | 0 | 1 | 0 | 0 | 2 | 1 | 8 | 1 | 0 | 2 | .222 | .263 | .250 |
| Lopez, Yonnata, Brewers | 4 | 12 | 9 | 0 | 3 | 4 | 1 | 0 | 0 | 1 | 3 | 0 | 0 | 0 | 0 | 3 | 0 | 0 | 0 | .333 | .333 | .444 |
| Luster, Jeremiah, Giants | 19 | 76 | 70 | 11 | 19 | 22 | 3 | 0 | 0 | 7 | 0 | 1 | 0 | 5 | 0 | 17 | 3 | 2 | 3 | .271 | .316 | .314 |
| Mahar, Kevin, Rangers | 27 | 115 | 100 | 20 | 28 | 50 | 5 | 1 | 5 | 18 | 0 | 3 | 3 | 9 | 0 | 28 | 7 | 1 | 0 | .280 | .348 | .500 |
| Maldonado, Juan, Rangers | 38 | 156 | 144 | 17 | 32 | 41 | 5 | 2 | 0 | 18 | 1 | 0 | 0 | 11 | 0 | 39 | 6 | 1 | 3 | .222 | .277 | .285 |
| Maldonado, Martin, Angels | 25 | 65 | 60 | 5 | 13 | 14 | 1 | 0 | 0 | 4 | 0 | 0 | 2 | 3 | 0 | 13 | 2 | 1 | 4 | .217 | .277 | .233 |
| Martinez, Eduardo, Rangers | 23 | 75 | 63 | 13 | 13 | 19 | 1 | 1 | 1 | 5 | 1 | 2 | 1 | 8 | 0 | 23 | 3 | 3 | 1 | .206 | .297 | .302 |
| Martinez, Frank, Athletics | 47 | 197 | 174 | 25 | 36 | 62 | 7 | 5 | 3 | 21 | 5 | 2 | 3 | 13 | 0 | 51 | 5 | 5 | 1 | .207 | .271 | .356 |
| Martinez, Jose, Cubs * | 3 | 6 | 6 | 2 | 2 | 3 | 1 | 0 | 0 | 1 | 0 | 0 | 0 | 0 | 0 | 1 | 0 | 0 | 0 | .333 | .333 | .500 |
| McConnell, Christopher, Royals | 37 | 146 | 124 | 22 | 42 | 56 | 5 | 0 | 3 | 11 | 3 | 1 | 1 | 17 | 0 | 19 | 8 | 4 | 1 | .339 | .420 | .452 |
| Mcdowell, D.T., Angels | 21 | 66 | 58 | 8 | 18 | 28 | 3 | 2 | 1 | 7 | 0 | 1 | 1 | 6 | 0 | 12 | 3 | 5 | 0 | .310 | .379 | .483 |
| Medley, Brian, Padres | 23 | 92 | 79 | 8 | 14 | 17 | 3 | 0 | 0 | 5 | 3 | 0 | 3 | 7 | 0 | 32 | 0 | 1 | 3 | .177 | .270 | .215 |

| Player, Team | G | TPA | AB | R | H | TB | 2B | 3B | HR | RBI | SH | SF | HP | BB | IBB | SO | SB | CS | GDP | Avg. | OBP | Slg. |
|---|---|---|---|---|---|---|---|---|---|---|---|---|---|---|---|---|---|---|---|---|---|---|
| Mejia, Carlos, Cubs | 26 | 113 | 106 | 15 | 30 | 42 | 5 | 2 | 1 | 17 | 0 | 2 | 3 | 2 | 0 | 25 | 1 | 1 | 2 | .283 | .310 | .396 |
| Meyer, Drew, Rangers * | 15 | 66 | 62 | 15 | 24 | 26 | 2 | 0 | 0 | 5 | 1 | 0 | 0 | 3 | 0 | 8 | 4 | 1 | 2 | .387 | .415 | .419 |
| Miller, Gerald, Cubs * | 4 | 15 | 15 | 1 | 3 | 3 | 0 | 0 | 0 | 0 | 0 | 0 | 0 | 0 | 0 | 4 | 0 | 0 | 1 | .200 | .200 | .200 |
| Mooney, Mike, Giants | 55 | 254 | 215 | 43 | 67 | 110 | 11 | 7 | 6 | 57 | 0 | 6 | 8 | 25 | 1 | 45 | 7 | 6 | 5 | .312 | .394 | .512 |
| Morales, Saul, Cubs | 34 | 151 | 142 | 25 | 28 | 29 | 1 | 0 | 0 | 8 | 2 | 1 | 1 | 5 | 0 | 33 | 6 | 5 | 0 | .197 | .228 | .204 |
| Morgan, Ryan, Cubs * | 47 | 201 | 156 | 24 | 39 | 58 | 10 | 3 | 1 | 14 | 2 | 2 | 5 | 36 | 2 | 35 | 4 | 2 | 3 | .250 | .402 | .372 |
| Morillo, Roberto, Giants † | 36 | 116 | 103 | 17 | 26 | 39 | 3 | 2 | 2 | 18 | 1 | 0 | 1 | 11 | 1 | 29 | 3 | 1 | 0 | .252 | .330 | .379 |
| Moye, Alan, Royals | 12 | 49 | 40 | 8 | 11 | 20 | 2 | 2 | 1 | 12 | 0 | 1 | 0 | 8 | 0 | 14 | 3 | 1 | 1 | .275 | .388 | .500 |
| Newton, Andrew, Angels | 9 | 36 | 35 | 1 | 9 | 12 | 1 | 1 | 0 | 1 | 1 | 0 | 0 | 0 | 0 | 7 | 0 | 1 | 0 | .257 | .257 | .343 |
| Ogando, Alexi, Athletics | 47 | 200 | 180 | 26 | 48 | 81 | 13 | 1 | 6 | 24 | 0 | 0 | 6 | 14 | 0 | 57 | 3 | 1 | 2 | .267 | .340 | .450 |
| Opdyke, Bryan, Brewers * | 40 | 147 | 114 | 16 | 20 | 25 | 3 | 1 | 0 | 9 | 2 | 1 | 5 | 25 | 1 | 39 | 5 | 5 | 0 | .175 | .345 | .219 |
| Ozoria, Pedro, Mariners | 38 | 156 | 138 | 24 | 35 | 50 | 6 | 0 | 3 | 21 | 0 | 0 | 2 | 16 | 1 | 38 | 6 | 1 | 4 | .254 | .340 | .362 |
| Padron, Raul, Athletics * | 40 | 169 | 147 | 23 | 45 | 70 | 14 | 4 | 1 | 35 | 1 | 1 | 4 | 16 | 1 | 25 | 6 | 3 | 1 | .306 | .387 | .476 |
| Parejo, Freddy, Brewers | 55 | 241 | 222 | 31 | 61 | 91 | 15 | 3 | 3 | 40 | 0 | 3 | 4 | 12 | 0 | 25 | 12 | 7 | 8 | .275 | .320 | .410 |
| Pena, Antonio, Rangers | 37 | 163 | 142 | 22 | 38 | 54 | 7 | 3 | 1 | 13 | 1 | 0 | 5 | 15 | 0 | 26 | 5 | 3 | 1 | .268 | .358 | .380 |
| Pena, Jose, Royals | 18 | 63 | 58 | 5 | 14 | 26 | 3 | 0 | 3 | 7 | 1 | 1 | 1 | 2 | 0 | 25 | 0 | 0 | 2 | .241 | .274 | .448 |
| Perez, Leonel, Cubs | 31 | 123 | 109 | 16 | 26 | 33 | 7 | 0 | 0 | 11 | 0 | 0 | 5 | 9 | 0 | 33 | 1 | 1 | 2 | .239 | .325 | .303 |
| Perez, Wilber, Athletics † | 49 | 226 | 194 | 49 | 56 | 86 | 11 | 8 | 1 | 20 | 1 | 1 | 2 | 28 | 0 | 40 | 20 | 7 | 4 | .289 | .382 | .443 |
| Piper-Jordan, Andre, Athletics | 45 | 176 | 156 | 29 | 37 | 52 | 8 | 2 | 1 | 11 | 3 | 1 | 6 | 10 | 0 | 41 | 14 | 5 | 1 | .237 | .306 | .333 |
| Pratt, Haas, Athletics | 35 | 139 | 122 | 9 | 22 | 33 | 8 | 0 | 1 | 11 | 1 | 1 | 0 | 15 | 1 | 27 | 2 | 3 | 3 | .180 | .268 | .270 |
| Puello, Elvin, Cubs | 53 | 218 | 189 | 26 | 57 | 73 | 7 | 3 | 1 | 37 | 2 | 2 | 13 | 12 | 1 | 38 | 1 | 4 | 10 | .302 | .380 | .386 |
| Qualls, Darrell, Royals | 34 | 114 | 98 | 9 | 23 | 33 | 4 | 3 | 0 | 12 | 0 | 4 | 1 | 10 | 0 | 33 | 0 | 4 | 3 | .235 | .301 | .337 |
| Quinones, Carlos, Cubs † | 53 | 238 | 216 | 28 | 68 | 82 | 12 | 1 | 0 | 28 | 2 | 0 | 1 | 19 | 2 | 33 | 9 | 7 | 3 | .315 | .373 | .380 |
| Ramirez, Yordany, Padres | 39 | 171 | 159 | 23 | 42 | 62 | 7 | 5 | 1 | 21 | 1 | 2 | 5 | 4 | 1 | 26 | 16 | 1 | 3 | .264 | .300 | .390 |
| Reed, Mark, Cubs * | 10 | 42 | 37 | 5 | 13 | 23 | 5 | 1 | 1 | 7 | 0 | 0 | 1 | 4 | 0 | 8 | 0 | 1 | 0 | .351 | .429 | .622 |
| Reinhardt, Doug, Angels | 47 | 174 | 151 | 10 | 31 | 43 | 4 | 1 | 2 | 9 | 0 | 1 | 7 | 15 | 0 | 42 | 1 | 1 | 3 | .205 | .305 | .285 |
| Richards, Judson, Giants * | 56 | 250 | 218 | 35 | 59 | 91 | 11 | 3 | 5 | 37 | 2 | 5 | 3 | 22 | 2 | 60 | 10 | 0 | 3 | .271 | .339 | .417 |
| Rivera, Jodam, Padres † | 48 | 206 | 185 | 24 | 51 | 60 | 5 | 2 | 0 | 19 | 1 | 0 | 3 | 17 | 0 | 28 | 5 | 6 | 4 | .276 | .346 | .324 |
| Rivera, Joel, Brewers | 27 | 87 | 68 | 12 | 12 | 17 | 1 | 2 | 0 | 4 | 1 | 1 | 2 | 15 | 0 | 26 | 2 | 2 | 2 | .176 | .337 | .250 |
| Rivera, Luis, Angels | 42 | 155 | 124 | 15 | 27 | 33 | 6 | 0 | 0 | 10 | 0 | 2 | 5 | 24 | 0 | 45 | 4 | 1 | 2 | .218 | .361 | .266 |
| Rodriguez, Luis, Rangers | 35 | 153 | 127 | 26 | 32 | 48 | 5 | 1 | 3 | 15 | 2 | 0 | 2 | 22 | 0 | 26 | 3 | 1 | 4 | .252 | .371 | .378 |
| Rosario, Anderson, Angels | 45 | 184 | 173 | 24 | 48 | 65 | 5 | 3 | 2 | 16 | 0 | 1 | 1 | 9 | 0 | 51 | 8 | 5 | 3 | .277 | .315 | .376 |
| Salome, Angel, Brewers | 20 | 85 | 81 | 7 | 19 | 26 | 7 | 0 | 0 | 8 | 0 | 0 | 0 | 4 | 1 | 14 | 2 | 0 | 6 | .235 | .271 | .321 |
| Sanchez, Angel, Rangers | 35 | 143 | 120 | 21 | 31 | 54 | 8 | 0 | 5 | 16 | 0 | 1 | 1 | 21 | 1 | 41 | 2 | 1 | 0 | .258 | .371 | .450 |
| Sanchez, Ivan, Giants | 13 | 38 | 34 | 5 | 6 | 10 | 1 | 0 | 1 | 4 | 0 | 1 | 0 | 3 | 0 | 14 | 0 | 0 | 3 | .176 | .237 | .294 |
| Sanchez, Luany, Padres | 34 | 124 | 109 | 12 | 22 | 28 | 3 | 0 | 1 | 8 | 4 | 1 | 4 | 6 | 1 | 15 | 1 | 0 | 3 | .202 | .267 | .257 |
| Sanders, Marcus, Giants | 55 | 261 | 209 | 54 | 61 | 90 | 12 | 4 | 3 | 21 | 3 | 3 | 11 | 35 | 2 | 45 | 28 | 4 | 4 | .292 | .415 | .431 |
| Sandoval, Pablo, Giants † | 46 | 191 | 177 | 21 | 47 | 66 | 9 | 5 | 0 | 26 | 3 | 4 | 2 | 5 | 1 | 17 | 4 | 1 | 2 | .266 | .287 | .373 |
| Santana, Ethien, Royals * | 52 | 221 | 191 | 25 | 45 | 50 | 5 | 0 | 0 | 17 | 4 | 1 | 5 | 20 | 0 | 35 | 23 | 9 | 3 | .236 | .323 | .262 |
| Santin, Daniel, Mariners * | 41 | 177 | 160 | 31 | 52 | 81 | 13 | 2 | 4 | 28 | 0 | 1 | 6 | 10 | 0 | 21 | 2 | 1 | 6 | .325 | .384 | .506 |
| Shankle, Robert, Angels | 50 | 211 | 178 | 21 | 40 | 65 | 12 | 2 | 3 | 26 | 0 | 0 | 9 | 24 | 0 | 52 | 3 | 3 | 2 | .225 | .346 | .365 |
| Smith, Aaron, Cubs | 33 | 145 | 116 | 21 | 30 | 48 | 7 | 4 | 1 | 12 | 5 | 2 | 4 | 18 | 0 | 25 | 1 | 0 | 3 | .259 | .371 | .414 |
| Smith, Stantrel, Angels | 37 | 143 | 137 | 8 | 25 | 35 | 2 | 4 | 0 | 8 | 0 | 1 | 1 | 4 | 0 | 37 | 4 | 5 | 4 | .182 | .210 | .255 |
| Smyres, Justin, Padres | 3 | 11 | 11 | 1 | 3 | 4 | 1 | 0 | 0 | 1 | 0 | 0 | 0 | 0 | 0 | 2 | 0 | 1 | 0 | .273 | .273 | .364 |
| Snelling, Chris, Mariners * | 10 | 42 | 32 | 8 | 10 | 16 | 4 | 1 | 0 | 9 | 0 | 0 | 3 | 7 | 0 | 3 | 1 | 0 | 2 | .313 | .476 | .500 |
| Soto, Luis, Mariners | 37 | 166 | 148 | 35 | 49 | 73 | 12 | 3 | 2 | 27 | 0 | 2 | 3 | 13 | 0 | 22 | 2 | 4 | 9 | .331 | .392 | .493 |
| Speier, Cole, Cubs | 12 | 25 | 24 | 0 | 0 | 0 | 0 | 0 | 0 | 0 | 0 | 0 | 0 | 1 | 0 | 9 | 0 | 0 | 0 | .000 | .040 | .000 |
| Sutton, Donald, Athletics | 25 | 100 | 87 | 11 | 21 | 42 | 7 | 1 | 4 | 21 | 0 | 1 | 3 | 9 | 2 | 27 | 0 | 1 | 2 | .241 | .330 | .483 |
| Thomas, Jonathan, Royals * | 9 | 15 | 13 | 1 | 1 | 1 | 0 | 0 | 0 | 1 | 0 | 0 | 0 | 2 | 0 | 2 | 0 | 0 | 0 | .077 | .200 | .077 |
| Thon, Freddy, Rangers * | 51 | 221 | 203 | 31 | 59 | 85 | 12 | 1 | 4 | 36 | 0 | 2 | 3 | 13 | 0 | 23 | 9 | 3 | 10 | .291 | .339 | .419 |
| Tidball, Adam, Cubs | 3 | 9 | 9 | 2 | 3 | 3 | 0 | 0 | 0 | 1 | 0 | 0 | 0 | 0 | 0 | 1 | 0 | 0 | 0 | .333 | .333 | .333 |
| Torres, Jose, Rangers | 44 | 174 | 132 | 25 | 29 | 39 | 5 | 1 | 1 | 7 | 0 | 0 | 9 | 33 | 0 | 45 | 9 | 2 | 3 | .220 | .408 | .295 |
| Tua, Franklin, Brewers | 15 | 27 | 26 | 2 | 5 | 5 | 0 | 0 | 0 | 3 | 0 | 0 | 0 | 1 | 0 | 8 | 1 | 0 | 1 | .192 | .222 | .192 |
| Valdez, Alexander, Athletics | 31 | 119 | 103 | 14 | 28 | 33 | 1 | 2 | 0 | 14 | 2 | 2 | 1 | 11 | 0 | 14 | 5 | 3 | 4 | .272 | .342 | .320 |
| Valdez, Riquelbi, Rangers | 5 | 19 | 15 | 4 | 4 | 7 | 0 | 0 | 1 | 2 | 0 | 0 | 2 | 2 | 0 | 5 | 0 | 1 | 0 | .267 | .421 | .467 |
| Vazquez, Kelvin, Padres † | 49 | 208 | 180 | 30 | 49 | 72 | 12 | 4 | 1 | 18 | 1 | 1 | 4 | 22 | 2 | 38 | 6 | 4 | 3 | .272 | .362 | .400 |
| Vega, Miguel, Royals | 56 | 250 | 229 | 36 | 63 | 118 | 15 | 5 | 10 | 44 | 0 | 2 | 3 | 16 | 0 | 74 | 6 | 1 | 5 | .275 | .328 | .515 |
| Vicioso, Osvaldo, Brewers † | 30 | 106 | 95 | 14 | 18 | 26 | 4 | 2 | 0 | 6 | 1 | 0 | 0 | 10 | 0 | 35 | 4 | 3 | 1 | .189 | .267 | .274 |
| Washington, Johnny, Rangers | 12 | 40 | 32 | 7 | 7 | 8 | 1 | 0 | 0 | 3 | 0 | 0 | 0 | 8 | 0 | 13 | 2 | 1 | 0 | .219 | .375 | .250 |
| White, Peter, Padres | 38 | 150 | 127 | 22 | 40 | 51 | 8 | 0 | 1 | 19 | 1 | 2 | 2 | 18 | 1 | 21 | 2 | 2 | 2 | .315 | .403 | .402 |
| Whitney, Nate, Padres | 53 | 217 | 186 | 30 | 50 | 72 | 8 | 4 | 2 | 29 | 1 | 2 | 6 | 22 | 0 | 35 | 6 | 1 | 5 | .269 | .361 | .387 |
| Wu, Chao, Mariners * | 21 | 83 | 75 | 9 | 22 | 30 | 5 | 0 | 1 | 12 | 0 | 2 | 2 | 4 | 0 | 10 | 3 | 0 | 1 | .293 | .337 | .400 |

GRAND SLAMS—Chavez, Gac, Johnston, Leclerca, Morillo, Padron, Parejo, 1 each.

AWARDED FIRST BASE ON CATCHER'S INTERFERENCE—Best (Sandoval); Chapman (Douillard); Dominguez (L. Sanchez); Green (L. Sanchez); Herren (Corredor); C. Johnson (Pena); Long (Pena); Qualls (L. Sanchez).

# 2004 PITCHING

## TEAM

| Team | W | L | Pct. | ERA | G | CG | ShO | Sv. | IP | H | TBF | R | ER | HR | SH | SF | HB | BB | IBB | SO | WP | Bk. |
|---|---|---|---|---|---|---|---|---|---|---|---|---|---|---|---|---|---|---|---|---|---|---|
| Athletics | 34 | 22 | .607 | 3.31 | 56 | 0 | 2 | 15 | 494.1 | 493 | 2130 | 254 | 182 | 23 | 16 | 13 | 47 | 154 | 1 | 439 | 35 | 7 |
| Giants | 37 | 19 | .661 | 3.52 | 56 | 0 | 4 | 18 | 498.0 | 479 | 2171 | 265 | 195 | 11 | 12 | 15 | 35 | 198 | 3 | 532 | 55 | 5 |
| Royals | 29 | 27 | .518 | 3.64 | 56 | 0 | 2 | 12 | 496.1 | 509 | 2179 | 261 | 201 | 20 | 14 | 12 | 30 | 182 | 12 | 414 | 63 | 6 |
| Padres | 26 | 30 | .464 | 3.70 | 56 | 0 | 2 | 15 | 503.1 | 502 | 2163 | 269 | 207 | 15 | 15 | 17 | 42 | 171 | 7 | 427 | 37 | 8 |
| Rangers | 32 | 24 | .571 | 4.11 | 56 | 0 | 4 | 11 | 495.0 | 511 | 2169 | 288 | 226 | 17 | 13 | 21 | 38 | 173 | 6 | 414 | 47 | 5 |
| Brewers | 24 | 32 | .429 | 4.12 | 56 | 0 | 2 | 10 | 495.1 | 490 | 2209 | 307 | 227 | 27 | 18 | 21 | 44 | 247 | 10 | 416 | 60 | 7 |
| Cubs | 27 | 29 | .482 | 4.27 | 56 | 0 | 2 | 10 | 499.0 | 519 | 2234 | 311 | 237 | 17 | 17 | 18 | 46 | 215 | 8 | 482 | 56 | 4 |
| Mariners | 31 | 25 | .554 | 4.55 | 56 | 0 | 1 | 15 | 493.0 | 497 | 2221 | 319 | 249 | 22 | 16 | 21 | 47 | 225 | 1 | 487 | 56 | 5 |
| Angels | 12 | 44 | .214 | 4.86 | 56 | 0 | 0 | 7 | 498.1 | 532 | 2266 | 332 | 269 | 17 | 21 | 22 | 68 | 226 | 3 | 453 | 71 | 9 |

## INDIVIDUAL

### TOP QUALIFIERS FOR EARNED-RUN AVERAGE TITLE

Minimum 45 innings. *Lefthanded pitcher.

| Pitcher, Team | W | L | Pct. | ERA | G | GS | CG | ShO | GF | Sv. | IP | H | TBF | R | ER | HR | SH | SF | HB | BB | IBB | SO | WP | Bk. |
|---|---|---|---|---|---|---|---|---|---|---|---|---|---|---|---|---|---|---|---|---|---|---|---|---|
| Acevedo, Danielin, Athletics | 3 | 2 | .600 | 2.17 | 10 | 9 | 0 | 0 | 0 | 0 | 54.0 | 63 | 231 | 26 | 13 | 0 | 2 | 1 | 2 | 11 | 0 | 42 | 3 | 0 |
| Ludwig, Kellen, Giants | 3 | 2 | .600 | 2.28 | 11 | 7 | 0 | 0 | 2 | 1 | 47.1 | 43 | 188 | 17 | 12 | 0 | 2 | 1 | 3 | 11 | 0 | 55 | 1 | 0 |
| Krosschell, Ben, Padres | 1 | 3 | .250 | 2.42 | 14 | 11 | 0 | 0 | 2 | 0 | 48.1 | 48 | 208 | 21 | 13 | 2 | 1 | 2 | 1 | 19 | 0 | 40 | 7 | 0 |

| Pitcher, Team | W | L | Pct. | ERA | G | GS | CG | ShO | GF | Sv. | IP | H | TBF | R | ER | HR | SH | SF | HB | BB | IBB | SO | WP | Bk. |
|---|---|---|---|---|---|---|---|---|---|---|---|---|---|---|---|---|---|---|---|---|---|---|---|---|
| Matos, Osiris, Giants | 2 | 0 | 1.000 | 2.44 | 11 | 8 | 0 | 0 | 2 | 1 | 48.0 | 43 | 212 | 23 | 13 | 1 | 1 | 1 | 3 | 20 | 0 | 47 | 2 | 1 |
| Lluveres, Rafael, Brewers * | 2 | 4 | .333 | 2.80 | 12 | 8 | 0 | 0 | 0 | 0 | 45.0 | 35 | 193 | 20 | 14 | 2 | 3 | 1 | 0 | 26 | 0 | 39 | 7 | 0 |
| Shearer, Kelly, Angels * | 2 | 3 | .400 | 2.82 | 13 | 9 | 0 | 0 | 0 | 0 | 51.0 | 42 | 210 | 22 | 16 | 2 | 2 | 2 | 7 | 23 | 0 | 36 | 4 | 2 |
| Perez, Roberto, Rangers | 4 | 3 | .571 | 3.61 | 14 | 6 | 0 | 0 | 1 | 0 | 57.1 | 50 | 235 | 24 | 23 | 2 | 1 | 1 | 3 | 17 | 0 | 48 | 2 | 0 |
| Yepez, Jesus, Cubs * | 1 | 2 | .333 | 3.66 | 12 | 8 | 0 | 0 | 0 | 0 | 46.2 | 44 | 201 | 27 | 19 | 1 | 1 | 1 | 1 | 24 | 0 | 44 | 8 | 2 |
| Begnaud, Rusty, Royals | 4 | 3 | .571 | 3.74 | 14 | 10 | 0 | 0 | 2 | 1 | 65.0 | 71 | 275 | 36 | 27 | 2 | 2 | 1 | 4 | 10 | 0 | 75 | 7 | 0 |
| Morales, Angelo, Royals | 6 | 4 | .600 | 3.96 | 14 | 10 | 0 | 0 | 2 | 0 | 61.1 | 76 | 272 | 34 | 27 | 2 | 0 | 2 | 5 | 9 | 0 | 45 | 7 | 0 |
| Newby, Joseph, Athletics | 2 | 3 | .400 | 4.04 | 14 | 11 | 0 | 0 | 0 | 0 | 55.2 | 68 | 239 | 35 | 25 | 3 | 1 | 3 | 4 | 10 | 0 | 46 | 2 | 2 |
| Kroft, Adam, Padres | 3 | 0 | 1.000 | 4.14 | 13 | 8 | 0 | 0 | 0 | 0 | 45.2 | 41 | 186 | 22 | 21 | 2 | 3 | 3 | 3 | 14 | 0 | 25 | 4 | 3 |
| Goins, Mitch, Royals | 2 | 0 | 1.000 | 4.36 | 13 | 9 | 0 | 0 | 1 | 0 | 53.2 | 60 | 239 | 38 | 26 | 4 | 0 | 3 | 5 | 17 | 0 | 44 | 5 | 1 |
| Delabar, Steven, Padres | 3 | 4 | .429 | 4.37 | 14 | 6 | 0 | 0 | 1 | 0 | 45.1 | 51 | 200 | 32 | 22 | 1 | 3 | 2 | 6 | 21 | 0 | 39 | 2 | 1 |
| Torres, Luis, Athletics | 3 | 5 | .375 | 5.06 | 15 | 8 | 0 | 0 | 1 | 0 | 53.1 | 67 | 242 | 35 | 30 | 4 | 2 | 2 | 1 | 23 | 0 | 35 | 3 | 2 |

DEPARTMENTAL LEADERS: W—Arias, Morales, 6; L—E. Garcia, 7; Pct.—Arias, .750; G—Robertson, 25; GS—Five tied with 11; CG—none; ShO—none; GF—Robertson, 22; Sv.—Robertson, 13; IP—Begnaud, 65.0; H—Morales, 76; TBF—Fagan, 278; R—Arias, 41; ER—Arias, 35; HR—Labasta, 7; SH—Morillo, Koerber, 6; SF—Several tied with four; HB—Woerman, Rayborn, 9; BB—Morillo, 31; IBB—Morrison, Kintzler, 4; SO—Begnaud, 75; WP—Dorn, 11; BK—Several tied with three.

## ALL PITCHERS

*Lefthanded pitcher.

| Pitcher, Team | W | L | Pct. | ERA | G | GS | CG | ShO | GF | Sv. | IP | H | TBF | R | ER | HR | SH | SF | HB | BB | IBB | SO | WP | Bk. |
|---|---|---|---|---|---|---|---|---|---|---|---|---|---|---|---|---|---|---|---|---|---|---|---|---|
| Abreu, Francis, Angels | 1 | 1 | .500 | 5.52 | 4 | 3 | 0 | 0 | 0 | 0 | 14.2 | 17 | 64 | 12 | 9 | 2 | 0 | 1 | 3 | 2 | 0 | 7 | 0 | 1 |
| Acevedo, Danielin, Athletics | 3 | 2 | .600 | 2.17 | 10 | 9 | 0 | 0 | 0 | 0 | 54.0 | 63 | 231 | 26 | 13 | 0 | 2 | 1 | 2 | 11 | 0 | 42 | 3 | 0 |
| Adames, Emilio, Rangers | 4 | 0 | 1.000 | 5.24 | 16 | 3 | 0 | 0 | 2 | 0 | 46.1 | 58 | 204 | 36 | 27 | 2 | 1 | 3 | 0 | 9 | 1 | 31 | 4 | 3 |
| Aldridge, Richard, Angels | 0 | 3 | .000 | 6.25 | 13 | 5 | 0 | 0 | 1 | 1 | 40.1 | 41 | 194 | 30 | 28 | 2 | 0 | 1 | 6 | 28 | 0 | 43 | 5 | 0 |
| Angulo, Oscar, Brewers | 0 | 0 | .000 | 0.00 | 2 | 0 | 0 | 0 | 2 | 0 | 3.2 | 4 | 18 | 0 | 0 | 0 | 0 | 0 | 0 | 4 | 0 | 3 | 0 | 0 |
| Arias, Oliver, Mariners | 6 | 2 | .750 | 5.59 | 12 | 11 | 0 | 0 | 0 | 0 | 56.1 | 63 | 251 | 41 | 35 | 6 | 0 | 2 | 0 | 26 | 0 | 60 | 3 | 1 |
| Arias, Roberto, Athletics | 0 | 0 | .000 | 0.00 | 1 | 0 | 0 | 0 | 1 | 1 | 1.0 | 0 | 5 | 0 | 0 | 0 | 0 | 0 | 0 | 2 | 0 | 1 | 0 | 0 |
| Arias, Victor, Brewers | 2 | 0 | 1.000 | 2.53 | 8 | 2 | 0 | 0 | 0 | 0 | 21.1 | 13 | 96 | 13 | 6 | 0 | 0 | 2 | 6 | 15 | 0 | 15 | 6 | 0 |
| Arredondo, Jose, Angels | 0 | 0 | .000 | 2.92 | 8 | 0 | 0 | 0 | 4 | 1 | 12.1 | 14 | 56 | 10 | 4 | 1 | 1 | 0 | 1 | 4 | 0 | 14 | 2 | 0 |
| Atkins, Mitch, Cubs | 2 | 2 | .500 | 7.89 | 10 | 8 | 0 | 0 | 0 | 0 | 29.2 | 42 | 146 | 33 | 26 | 0 | 0 | 2 | 4 | 14 | 0 | 20 | 8 | 1 |
| Baca, Daniel, Padres | 4 | 2 | .667 | 1.93 | 23 | 0 | 0 | 0 | 10 | 0 | 28.0 | 26 | 120 | 9 | 6 | 1 | 1 | 1 | 0 | 11 | 1 | 23 | 1 | 1 |
| Begnaud, Rusty, Royals | 4 | 3 | .571 | 3.74 | 14 | 10 | 0 | 0 | 2 | 1 | 65.0 | 71 | 275 | 36 | 27 | 2 | 2 | 1 | 4 | 10 | 0 | 75 | 7 | 0 |
| Bernal, Luis, Brewers | 0 | 1 | .000 | 5.89 | 10 | 2 | 0 | 0 | 5 | 0 | 18.1 | 20 | 82 | 14 | 12 | 2 | 1 | 0 | 1 | 8 | 1 | 12 | 0 | 0 |
| Bowman, Bobby, Rangers | 0 | 0 | .000 | 5.19 | 8 | 0 | 0 | 0 | 2 | 0 | 8.2 | 7 | 40 | 8 | 5 | 0 | 0 | 0 | 2 | 4 | 0 | 10 | 1 | 0 |
| Brandt, Adam, Mariners * | 2 | 1 | .667 | 3.38 | 13 | 0 | 0 | 0 | 8 | 4 | 21.1 | 16 | 91 | 14 | 8 | 0 | 1 | 0 | 2 | 8 | 0 | 26 | 1 | 0 |
| Breshears, Richard, Brewers | 1 | 2 | .333 | 4.55 | 12 | 1 | 0 | 0 | 4 | 1 | 29.2 | 28 | 127 | 17 | 15 | 1 | 1 | 2 | 6 | 10 | 0 | 28 | 2 | 1 |
| Caldwell, Daniel, Cubs | 1 | 1 | .500 | 3.29 | 14 | 2 | 0 | 0 | 3 | 2 | 38.1 | 37 | 161 | 15 | 14 | 2 | 1 | 0 | 4 | 11 | 0 | 49 | 2 | 0 |
| Carela, Carlos, Athletics | 0 | 1 | .000 | 54.00 | 1 | 0 | 0 | 0 | 1 | 0 | 0.1 | 2 | 3 | 2 | 2 | 1 | 0 | 0 | 0 | 0 | 0 | 0 | 0 | 0 |
| Carter, Eric, Mariners | 2 | 4 | .333 | 4.26 | 13 | 8 | 0 | 0 | 4 | 1 | 44.1 | 49 | 204 | 31 | 21 | 0 | 4 | 4 | 2 | 25 | 0 | 35 | 5 | 0 |
| Casanova, Nicholas, Rangers | 0 | 2 | .000 | 17.47 | 4 | 2 | 0 | 0 | 0 | 0 | 5.2 | 17 | 38 | 12 | 11 | 0 | 0 | 1 | 0 | 6 | 0 | 3 | 3 | 0 |
| Cepeda, Benigro, Giants | 2 | 4 | .333 | 4.61 | 11 | 7 | 0 | 0 | 2 | 0 | 41.0 | 45 | 182 | 24 | 21 | 0 | 2 | 1 | 4 | 17 | 0 | 43 | 10 | 0 |
| Clement, Donald, Mariners | 0 | 4 | .000 | 4.45 | 15 | 0 | 0 | 0 | 3 | 0 | 28.1 | 38 | 142 | 25 | 14 | 0 | 2 | 2 | 4 | 7 | 0 | 17 | 2 | 1 |
| Clow, Josh, Royals | 1 | 1 | .500 | 4.57 | 12 | 0 | 0 | 0 | 2 | 1 | 21.2 | 20 | 104 | 14 | 11 | 1 | 0 | 0 | 2 | 17 | 1 | 19 | 5 | 0 |
| Coffey, Andrew, Royals * | 1 | 0 | 1.000 | 1.71 | 13 | 0 | 0 | 0 | 4 | 0 | 26.1 | 16 | 106 | 7 | 5 | 0 | 0 | 0 | 1 | 11 | 0 | 26 | 7 | 1 |
| Colbert, Henry, Padres | 1 | 0 | 1.000 | 0.00 | 3 | 0 | 0 | 0 | 1 | 0 | 3.1 | 2 | 14 | 0 | 0 | 0 | 0 | 0 | 1 | 1 | 1 | 6 | 1 | 0 |
| Corbin,, Cubs | 0 | 0 | .000 | 0.00 | 1 | 0 | 0 | 0 | 1 | 0 | 1.0 | 0 | 3 | 0 | 0 | 0 | 0 | 0 | 0 | 0 | 0 | 1 | 0 | 0 |
| Cordier, Erik, Royals | 2 | 4 | .333 | 5.19 | 11 | 11 | 0 | 0 | 0 | 0 | 34.2 | 38 | 163 | 27 | 20 | 1 | 1 | 2 | 3 | 21 | 0 | 22 | 9 | 0 |
| Coutlangus, Jonathan, Giants * | 0 | 0 | .000 | 0.00 | 1 | 0 | 0 | 0 | 0 | 0 | 1.0 | 1 | 4 | 0 | 0 | 0 | 0 | 0 | 0 | 0 | 0 | 0 | 0 | 0 |
| Cruz Chavez, Rafael, Angels | 1 | 4 | .200 | 3.77 | 13 | 1 | 0 | 0 | 7 | 0 | 31.0 | 31 | 131 | 15 | 13 | 0 | 3 | 1 | 3 | 9 | 2 | 20 | 3 | 1 |
| Cyr, Eric, Angels | 0 | 0 | .000 | 0.00 | 1 | 0 | 0 | 0 | 0 | 0 | 1.0 | 0 | 4 | 0 | 0 | 0 | 0 | 0 | 0 | 1 | 0 | 3 | 0 | 0 |
| Damico, Yovany, Royals | 1 | 0 | 1.000 | 0.28 | 20 | 0 | 0 | 0 | 17 | 6 | 31.2 | 19 | 125 | 3 | 1 | 0 | 2 | 0 | 1 | 10 | 3 | 24 | 2 | 0 |
| Delabar, Steven, Padres | 3 | 4 | .429 | 4.37 | 14 | 6 | 0 | 0 | 1 | 0 | 45.1 | 51 | 200 | 32 | 22 | 1 | 3 | 2 | 6 | 21 | 0 | 39 | 2 | 1 |
| De Montigny, Mat, Padres | 1 | 0 | 1.000 | 3.60 | 16 | 0 | 0 | 0 | 0 | 0 | 25.0 | 24 | 112 | 11 | 10 | 0 | 0 | 1 | 4 | 11 | 0 | 25 | 1 | 0 |
| Delie, Franky, Cubs | 1 | 3 | .250 | 7.00 | 5 | 0 | 0 | 0 | 2 | 0 | 9.0 | 10 | 44 | 10 | 7 | 2 | 0 | 1 | 0 | 6 | 0 | 8 | 1 | 0 |
| Diaz, Gener, Rangers | 3 | 1 | .750 | 5.40 | 11 | 0 | 0 | 0 | 4 | 0 | 10.0 | 9 | 45 | 9 | 6 | 0 | 0 | 0 | 2 | 6 | 0 | 8 | 2 | 0 |
| Diggins, Ben, Brewers | 0 | 0 | .000 | 0.00 | 4 | 4 | 0 | 0 | 0 | 0 | 6.0 | 6 | 27 | 2 | 0 | 0 | 0 | 0 | 0 | 5 | 0 | 4 | 0 | 0 |
| Dorn, Tim, Mariners | 0 | 0 | .000 | 5.50 | 13 | 0 | 0 | 0 | 3 | 0 | 18.0 | 15 | 96 | 13 | 11 | 0 | 0 | 2 | 6 | 20 | 0 | 24 | 11 | 0 |
| Douillard, Jonathan, Cubs | 0 | 0 | .000 | 0.00 | 1 | 0 | 0 | 0 | 1 | 0 | 1.0 | 1 | 4 | 0 | 0 | 0 | 0 | 0 | 0 | 0 | 0 | 0 | 0 | 0 |
| Eckley, Jacob, Royals * | 2 | 1 | .667 | 3.68 | 8 | 0 | 0 | 0 | 3 | 0 | 14.2 | 18 | 68 | 8 | 6 | 2 | 2 | 1 | 0 | 6 | 2 | 14 | 0 | 0 |
| Fagan, Paul, Mariners * | 4 | 3 | .571 | 5.07 | 12 | 11 | 0 | 0 | 1 | 1 | 60.1 | 68 | 278 | 38 | 34 | 3 | 2 | 1 | 5 | 29 | 0 | 57 | 7 | 1 |
| Fairbanks, Scott, Athletics | 2 | 0 | 1.000 | 2.11 | 14 | 0 | 0 | 0 | 5 | 0 | 21.1 | 13 | 101 | 5 | 5 | 0 | 0 | 0 | 5 | 22 | 1 | 29 | 5 | 0 |
| Farach, Juan, Giants * | 2 | 1 | .667 | 4.22 | 9 | 4 | 0 | 0 | 2 | 0 | 32.0 | 33 | 142 | 25 | 15 | 4 | 0 | 1 | 2 | 13 | 0 | 30 | 2 | 1 |
| Feldman, Scott, Rangers | 0 | 0 | .000 | 0.00 | 4 | 3 | 0 | 0 | 0 | 0 | 7.0 | 2 | 23 | 0 | 0 | 0 | 0 | 0 | 0 | 1 | 0 | 5 | 0 | 0 |
| Fermin, Jorge, Brewers | 0 | 1 | .000 | 6.11 | 13 | 1 | 0 | 0 | 4 | 0 | 28.0 | 35 | 142 | 30 | 19 | 4 | 0 | 0 | 1 | 18 | 1 | 15 | 4 | 1 |
| Fernando, Pedro, Rangers | 1 | 3 | .250 | 4.67 | 15 | 6 | 0 | 0 | 1 | 1 | 44.1 | 46 | 197 | 29 | 23 | 3 | 2 | 2 | 4 | 19 | 0 | 32 | 6 | 1 |
| Foster, Benjamin, Rangers * | 2 | 2 | .500 | 5.19 | 15 | 6 | 0 | 0 | 3 | 0 | 43.1 | 48 | 194 | 29 | 25 | 3 | 2 | 1 | 5 | 13 | 0 | 44 | 5 | 1 |
| Gallagher, Sean, Cubs | 1 | 2 | .333 | 3.12 | 10 | 9 | 0 | 0 | 0 | 0 | 34.2 | 38 | 152 | 19 | 12 | 0 | 0 | 0 | 3 | 11 | 0 | 44 | 1 | 0 |
| Gallardo, Yovani, Brewers | 0 | 0 | .000 | 0.47 | 6 | 6 | 0 | 0 | 0 | 0 | 19.1 | 14 | 74 | 3 | 1 | 0 | 0 | 0 | 1 | 4 | 0 | 23 | 2 | 0 |
| Gamboa, Felix, Angels | 0 | 0 | .000 | 6.16 | 9 | 2 | 0 | 0 | 0 | 0 | 19.0 | 20 | 95 | 14 | 13 | 0 | 1 | 1 | 2 | 17 | 0 | 23 | 7 | 1 |
| Garcia, Eliszer, Royals * | 2 | 7 | .222 | 3.94 | 19 | 0 | 0 | 0 | 11 | 3 | 32.0 | 31 | 134 | 16 | 14 | 3 | 1 | 1 | 2 | 6 | 3 | 24 | 2 | 0 |
| Garcia, Miguel, Brewers | 4 | 2 | .667 | 3.38 | 8 | 2 | 0 | 0 | 0 | 0 | 26.2 | 23 | 114 | 12 | 10 | 1 | 0 | 2 | 3 | 10 | 0 | 20 | 8 | 2 |
| Geraldo, Jose, Padres | 0 | 0 | .000 | 0.00 | 2 | 0 | 0 | 0 | 0 | 0 | 2.1 | 1 | 8 | 0 | 0 | 0 | 0 | 0 | 0 | 0 | 0 | 1 | 0 | 0 |
| Goins, Mitch, Royals | 2 | 0 | 1.000 | 4.36 | 13 | 9 | 0 | 0 | 1 | 0 | 53.2 | 60 | 239 | 38 | 26 | 4 | 0 | 3 | 5 | 17 | 0 | 44 | 5 | 1 |
| Gornati, Tom, Giants | 4 | 2 | .667 | 4.01 | 12 | 8 | 0 | 0 | 1 | 0 | 42.2 | 47 | 182 | 22 | 19 | 1 | 0 | 3 | 2 | 10 | 0 | 46 | 2 | 0 |
| Grasley, Stephen, Mariners | 4 | 0 | 1.000 | 3.18 | 16 | 0 | 0 | 0 | 7 | 0 | 28.1 | 32 | 123 | 14 | 10 | 3 | 1 | 2 | 2 | 1 | 0 | 37 | 2 | 0 |
| Gray, Jeffrey, Athletics | 3 | 0 | 1.000 | 1.89 | 14 | 2 | 0 | 0 | 2 | 0 | 38.0 | 30 | 152 | 14 | 8 | 0 | 1 | 1 | 5 | 3 | 0 | 32 | 4 | 1 |
| Guzman,, Angels | 0 | 1 | .000 | 4.50 | 3 | 0 | 0 | 0 | 0 | 0 | 4.0 | 5 | 17 | 2 | 2 | 0 | 0 | 0 | 1 | 0 | 0 | 0 | 2 | 0 |
| Haro, Jeremy, Cubs | 0 | 1 | .000 | 3.38 | 7 | 0 | 0 | 0 | 0 | 0 | 13.1 | 10 | 63 | 7 | 5 | 0 | 0 | 0 | 1 | 10 | 1 | 13 | 2 | 0 |
| Heuser, James, Athletics * | 3 | 2 | .600 | 3.11 | 15 | 0 | 0 | 0 | 2 | 0 | 37.2 | 33 | 163 | 22 | 13 | 2 | 2 | 0 | 6 | 16 | 0 | 28 | 3 | 0 |
| Hill, Andy, Angels | 0 | 1 | .000 | 8.85 | 11 | 2 | 0 | 0 | 2 | 0 | 20.1 | 28 | 101 | 22 | 20 | 2 | 1 | 3 | 5 | 8 | 0 | 20 | 4 | 0 |
| Jaimes, Jose, Rangers | 5 | 1 | .833 | 4.10 | 15 | 3 | 0 | 0 | 7 | 2 | 26.1 | 24 | 122 | 16 | 12 | 0 | 1 | 1 | 3 | 17 | 0 | 26 | 5 | 0 |
| James, Craig, Mariners | 1 | 1 | .500 | 0.68 | 10 | 0 | 0 | 0 | 9 | 4 | 13.1 | 10 | 52 | 1 | 1 | 1 | 1 | 0 | 0 | 5 | 0 | 13 | 0 | 0 |
| James, Delvin, Angels | 0 | 0 | .000 | 0.00 | 1 | 1 | 0 | 0 | 0 | 0 | 1.0 | 0 | 3 | 0 | 0 | 0 | 0 | 0 | 0 | 0 | 0 | 2 | 0 | 0 |
| Jenkins, Billy, Padres | 0 | 0 | .000 | 3.75 | 18 | 0 | 0 | 0 | 6 | 1 | 24.0 | 15 | 100 | 12 | 10 | 2 | 2 | 1 | 4 | 7 | 0 | 34 | 0 | 0 |
| Jenson, Kevin, Giants | 1 | 1 | .500 | 1.59 | 12 | 0 | 0 | 0 | 4 | 0 | 11.1 | 9 | 42 | 3 | 2 | 0 | 2 | 0 | 1 | 2 | 0 | 12 | 2 | 0 |
| Jimenez Angulo, Fabian, Padres * | 2 | 6 | .250 | 6.95 | 12 | 9 | 0 | 0 | 0 | 0 | 45.1 | 60 | 214 | 40 | 35 | 0 | 1 | 1 | 2 | 28 | 0 | 28 | 3 | 0 |
| Jimenez, Juan, Padres | 1 | 0 | 1.000 | 0.89 | 4 | 1 | 0 | 0 | 0 | 0 | 20.1 | 12 | 75 | 4 | 2 | 0 | 0 | 0 | 2 | 2 | 0 | 14 | 0 | 1 |

| Pitcher, Team | W | L | Pct. | ERA | G | GS | CG | ShO | GF | Sv. | IP | H | TBF | R | ER | HR | SH | SF | HB | BB | IBB | SO | WP | Bk. |
|---|---|---|---|---|---|---|---|---|---|---|---|---|---|---|---|---|---|---|---|---|---|---|---|---|
| Johnson, David, Brewers | 0 | 1 | .000 | 10.03 | 5 | 3 | 0 | 0 | 1 | 0 | 11.2 | 24 | 63 | 15 | 13 | 0 | 1 | 3 | 1 | 4 | 0 | 8 | 0 | 0 |
| Jones, Aaron, Cubs | 0 | 3 | .000 | 7.56 | 14 | 0 | 0 | 0 | 8 | 2 | 16.2 | 20 | 77 | 15 | 14 | 1 | 1 | 1 | 2 | 8 | 0 | 10 | 4 | 0 |
| Jones, Brian, Cubs | 2 | 1 | .667 | 9.64 | 8 | 0 | 0 | 0 | 3 | 0 | 9.1 | 13 | 53 | 10 | 10 | 1 | 1 | 2 | 5 | 6 | 0 | 14 | 5 | 0 |
| Jones, Jeff, Padres | 0 | 0 | .000 | 13.50 | 2 | 0 | 0 | 0 | 0 | 0 | 2.0 | 4 | 13 | 3 | 3 | 0 | 0 | 0 | 0 | 1 | 0 | 2 | 0 | 0 |
| Kintzler, Brandon, Padres | 3 | 2 | .600 | 2.38 | 21 | 0 | 0 | 0 | 12 | 6 | 34.0 | 36 | 140 | 12 | 9 | 0 | 1 | 0 | 0 | 9 | 4 | 38 | 3 | — |
| Koerber, Scott, Cubs * | 1 | 2 | .333 | 5.14 | 15 | 0 | 0 | 0 | 8 | 0 | 28.0 | 35 | 134 | 19 | 16 | 1 | 6 | 1 | 2 | 18 | 2 | 23 | 4 | 0 |
| Kroft, Adam, Padres | 3 | 0 | 1.000 | 4.14 | 13 | 8 | 0 | 0 | 0 | 0 | 45.2 | 41 | 186 | 22 | 21 | 2 | 3 | 3 | 3 | 14 | 0 | 25 | 4 | 3 |
| Krosschell, Ben, Padres | 1 | 3 | .250 | 2.42 | 14 | 11 | 0 | 0 | 2 | 0 | 48.1 | 48 | 208 | 21 | 13 | 2 | 1 | 2 | 1 | 19 | 0 | 40 | 7 | 0 |
| Labasta, William, Brewers | 0 | 2 | .000 | 10.33 | 13 | 1 | 0 | 0 | 2 | 0 | 27.0 | 42 | 138 | 35 | 31 | 7 | 1 | 1 | 6 | 15 | 0 | 18 | 5 | 0 |
| Lamont, Tyrone, Mariners | 1 | 1 | .500 | 3.31 | 13 | 0 | 0 | 0 | 1 | 0 | 32.2 | 25 | 136 | 19 | 12 | 2 | 1 | 1 | 1 | 13 | 0 | 27 | 6 | 0 |
| Laureano, Wilfrido, Brewers | 0 | 1 | .000 | 3.34 | 14 | 2 | 0 | 0 | 3 | 1 | 35.0 | 33 | 161 | 23 | 13 | 0 | 3 | 2 | 3 | 17 | 1 | 26 | 2 | 0 |
| Layden, Timothy, Cubs * | 1 | 1 | .500 | 2.62 | 12 | 9 | 0 | 0 | 0 | 0 | 44.2 | 42 | 198 | 19 | 13 | 0 | 0 | 1 | 4 | 26 | 0 | 28 | 3 | 0 |
| Leaist, Ryan, Mariners | 0 | 0 | .000 | 2.35 | 10 | 0 | 0 | 0 | 9 | 1 | 15.1 | 8 | 66 | 5 | 4 | 1 | 0 | 2 | 1 | 10 | 1 | 18 | 0 | 1 |
| Lluveres, Rafael, Brewers * | 2 | 4 | .333 | 2.80 | 12 | 8 | 0 | 0 | 0 | 0 | 45.0 | 35 | 193 | 20 | 14 | 2 | 3 | 1 | 0 | 26 | 0 | 39 | 7 | 0 |
| Lockwood, Jon, Mariners | 3 | 4 | .429 | 6.97 | 10 | 9 | 0 | 0 | 0 | 0 | 41.1 | 43 | 193 | 34 | 32 | 2 | 1 | 0 | 7 | 30 | 0 | 33 | 9 | 0 |
| Ludwig, Kellen, Giants | 3 | 2 | .600 | 2.28 | 11 | 7 | 0 | 0 | 2 | 1 | 47.1 | 43 | 188 | 17 | 12 | 0 | 2 | 1 | 3 | 11 | 0 | 55 | 1 | 0 |
| Lundwall, Todd, Giants | 0 | 0 | .000 | 5.00 | 8 | 0 | 0 | 0 | 2 | 0 | 9.0 | 4 | 43 | 6 | 5 | 0 | 0 | 0 | 1 | 12 | 0 | 9 | 5 | 0 |
| MacKenzie, Aaron, Angels | 0 | 4 | .000 | 5.84 | 8 | 4 | 0 | 0 | 1 | 0 | 24.2 | 34 | 118 | 20 | 16 | 2 | 2 | 1 | 1 | 9 | 0 | 23 | 4 | 0 |
| Malave, Ronny, Brewers | 2 | 2 | .500 | 4.24 | 15 | 0 | 0 | 0 | 13 | 4 | 23.1 | 26 | 104 | 14 | 11 | 2 | 1 | 1 | 2 | 10 | 2 | 16 | 2 | 1 |
| Marsello, Jake, Cubs | 0 | 0 | .000 | 0.00 | 3 | 0 | 0 | 0 | 1 | 0 | 6.0 | 3 | 24 | 2 | 0 | 0 | 0 | 0 | 1 | 2 | 0 | 7 | 0 | 0 |
| Matos, Osiris, Giants | 2 | 0 | 1.000 | 2.44 | 11 | 8 | 0 | 0 | 2 | 1 | 48.0 | 43 | 212 | 23 | 13 | 1 | 1 | 1 | 3 | 20 | 0 | 47 | 2 | 1 |
| McCleland, Bruce, Royals | 3 | 2 | .600 | 3.15 | 11 | 4 | 0 | 0 | 0 | 0 | 34.1 | 37 | 145 | 17 | 12 | 2 | 1 | 1 | 0 | 8 | 1 | 22 | 2 | 2 |
| Melendez, Marlon, Rangers | 1 | 3 | .250 | 5.24 | 13 | 5 | 0 | 0 | 1 | 0 | 34.1 | 50 | 156 | 22 | 20 | 2 | 0 | 1 | 2 | 10 | 0 | 32 | 2 | 0 |
| Mercado, Arnoldo, Giants | 2 | 0 | 1.000 | 4.30 | 18 | 0 | 0 | 0 | 2 | 1 | 14.2 | 16 | 84 | 18 | 7 | 1 | 1 | 1 | 3 | 18 | 1 | 16 | 8 | 0 |
| Millikan, Bryan, Giants | 1 | 0 | 1.000 | 9.00 | 3 | 0 | 0 | 0 | 0 | 0 | 4.0 | 5 | 20 | 4 | 4 | 0 | 0 | 0 | 0 | 4 | 0 | 3 | 2 | 0 |
| Mitchell, Michael, Athletics | 1 | 0 | 1.000 | 1.35 | 7 | 0 | 0 | 0 | 2 | 1 | 13.1 | 14 | 55 | 4 | 2 | 0 | 0 | 0 | 3 | 1 | 0 | 7 | 0 | 0 |
| Mola, Heydin, Athletics | 2 | 2 | .500 | 6.34 | 13 | 3 | 0 | 0 | 0 | 0 | 38.1 | 49 | 181 | 33 | 27 | 3 | 3 | 1 | 3 | 17 | 0 | 26 | 3 | 0 |
| Montes, Oscar, Brewers | 2 | 5 | .286 | 5.27 | 13 | 7 | 0 | 0 | 1 | 0 | 42.2 | 39 | 185 | 28 | 25 | 2 | 0 | 0 | 3 | 26 | 0 | 50 | 5 | 1 |
| Moore, Dan, Padres * | 0 | 0 | .000 | 5.19 | 3 | 3 | 0 | 0 | 0 | 0 | 8.2 | 11 | 37 | 6 | 5 | 0 | 0 | 1 | 0 | 2 | 0 | 5 | 0 | 0 |
| Moore, Dave, Royals | 0 | 0 | .000 | 0.00 | 3 | 0 | 0 | 0 | 2 | 1 | 3.0 | 1 | 10 | 0 | 0 | 0 | 0 | 0 | 0 | 0 | 0 | 3 | 0 | 0 |
| Morales, Angelo, Royals | 6 | 4 | .600 | 3.96 | 14 | 10 | 0 | 0 | 2 | 0 | 61.1 | 76 | 272 | 34 | 27 | 2 | 0 | 2 | 5 | 9 | 0 | 45 | 7 | 0 |
| Moreno, Victor, Angels | 0 | 2 | .000 | 4.71 | 14 | 1 | 0 | 0 | 3 | 2 | 28.2 | 31 | 130 | 17 | 15 | 0 | 2 | 2 | 3 | 7 | 0 | 23 | 5 | 0 |
| Morillo, Lennyn, Angels | 1 | 5 | .167 | 7.41 | 13 | 6 | 0 | 0 | 1 | 0 | 37.2 | 42 | 188 | 37 | 31 | 1 | 6 | 4 | 8 | 31 | 0 | 30 | 6 | 1 |
| Morrison, Tyler, Brewers | 2 | 2 | .500 | 3.41 | 15 | 0 | 0 | 0 | 10 | 3 | 34.1 | 35 | 150 | 18 | 13 | 4 | 2 | 1 | 2 | 16 | 4 | 27 | 4 | 0 |
| Mosquea, Dany, Brewers | 4 | 0 | 1.000 | 4.34 | 13 | 3 | 0 | 0 | 2 | 0 | 37.1 | 41 | 176 | 23 | 18 | 1 | 2 | 4 | 3 | 28 | 0 | 31 | 5 | 0 |
| Nelson, Justin, Royals * | 0 | 0 | .000 | 2.84 | 6 | 1 | 0 | 0 | 1 | 0 | 12.2 | 10 | 53 | 4 | 4 | 0 | 0 | 0 | 1 | 5 | 0 | 6 | 1 | 0 |
| Newby, Joseph, Athletics | 2 | 3 | .400 | 4.04 | 14 | 11 | 0 | 0 | 0 | 0 | 55.2 | 68 | 239 | 35 | 25 | 3 | 1 | 3 | 4 | 10 | 0 | 46 | 2 | 2 |
| Nolen, Walt, Cubs | 3 | 1 | .750 | 4.28 | 11 | 0 | 0 | 0 | 1 | 0 | 27.1 | 24 | 112 | 15 | 13 | 0 | 1 | 1 | 3 | 8 | 0 | 32 | 1 | 0 |
| Nourie, John, Padres | 0 | 0 | .000 | 4.50 | 2 | 0 | 0 | 0 | 0 | 0 | 2.0 | 2 | 10 | 1 | 1 | 0 | 0 | 0 | 1 | 1 | 0 | 1 | 0 | 0 |
| Ortiz, Jose, Cubs | 4 | 1 | .800 | 4.19 | 12 | 4 | 0 | 0 | 4 | 1 | 38.2 | 36 | 167 | 19 | 18 | 3 | 1 | 2 | 3 | 14 | 1 | 33 | 4 | 0 |
| Padgett, Michael, Rangers | 2 | 1 | .667 | 2.59 | 12 | 4 | 0 | 0 | 3 | 0 | 31.1 | 29 | 126 | 9 | 9 | 0 | 2 | 0 | 2 | 4 | 0 | 25 | 0 | 0 |
| Parillo, Brandon, Brewers * | 1 | 2 | .333 | 1.52 | 9 | 7 | 0 | 0 | 0 | 0 | 23.2 | 12 | 96 | 8 | 4 | 0 | 0 | 0 | 1 | 9 | 0 | 25 | 2 | 0 |
| Pedrozo, Jose, Cubs * | 0 | 0 | .000 | 0.00 | 1 | 1 | 0 | 0 | 0 | 0 | 1.0 | 0 | 3 | 0 | 0 | 0 | 0 | 0 | 0 | 0 | 0 | 0 | 0 | 0 |
| Pena, Henry, Angels | 0 | 0 | .000 | 2.17 | 11 | 3 | 0 | 0 | 1 | 0 | 29.0 | 29 | 116 | 11 | 7 | 0 | 0 | 1 | 3 | 2 | 0 | 23 | 1 | 0 |
| Perez, Roberto, Rangers | 4 | 3 | .571 | 3.61 | 14 | 6 | 0 | 0 | 1 | 0 | 57.1 | 50 | 235 | 24 | 23 | 2 | 1 | 1 | 3 | 17 | 0 | 48 | 2 | 0 |
| Piekarz, Joseph, Athletics * | 4 | 2 | .667 | 1.66 | 17 | 4 | 0 | 0 | 6 | 0 | 38.0 | 32 | 156 | 11 | 7 | 2 | 0 | 0 | 2 | 12 | 0 | 40 | 1 | 0 |
| Putman, Rickey, Giants | 1 | 0 | 1.000 | 1.59 | 8 | 0 | 0 | 0 | 2 | 1 | 17.0 | 5 | 68 | 4 | 3 | 1 | 0 | 0 | 1 | 10 | 0 | 20 | 2 | 0 |
| Ramirez, Ivan, Rangers * | 2 | 0 | 1.000 | 5.50 | 16 | 0 | 0 | 0 | 6 | 2 | 18.0 | 21 | 80 | 15 | 11 | 1 | 1 | 0 | 0 | 7 | 2 | 13 | 2 | 0 |
| Rayborn, Chris, Padres | 3 | 3 | .500 | 5.19 | 13 | 9 | 0 | 0 | 0 | 0 | 50.1 | 56 | 226 | 35 | 29 | 3 | 1 | 2 | 9 | 11 | 0 | 27 | 5 | 1 |
| Robertson, Connor, Athletics | 2 | 2 | .500 | 0.92 | 25 | 0 | 0 | 0 | 22 | 13 | 29.1 | 17 | 120 | 8 | 3 | 2 | 0 | 2 | 2 | 8 | 0 | 46 | 0 | 0 |
| Rodriguez, Pedro, Cubs | 0 | 2 | .000 | 13.24 | 10 | 1 | 0 | 0 | 2 | 1 | 17.0 | 29 | 95 | 32 | 25 | 1 | 0 | 0 | 3 | 9 | 0 | 20 | 3 | 0 |
| Rodriguez, William, Athletics * | 2 | 0 | 1.000 | 4.91 | 5 | 0 | 0 | 0 | 1 | 0 | 7.1 | 7 | 42 | 7 | 4 | 0 | 1 | 0 | 5 | 7 | 0 | 6 | 2 | 2 |
| Rogers, Mark, Brewers | 0 | 3 | .000 | 4.73 | 9 | 6 | 0 | 0 | 0 | 0 | 26.2 | 30 | 120 | 21 | 14 | 0 | 0 | 1 | 3 | 14 | 0 | 35 | 5 | 1 |
| Roque, Christopher, Angels | 0 | 5 | .000 | 3.15 | 20 | 0 | 0 | 0 | 18 | 3 | 20.0 | 22 | 95 | 9 | 7 | 1 | 1 | 0 | 5 | 12 | 0 | 13 | 4 | 0 |
| Rosario, Julio, Royals | 3 | 2 | .600 | 2.48 | 15 | 0 | 0 | 0 | 2 | 0 | 36.1 | 37 | 157 | 13 | 10 | 2 | 2 | 0 | 2 | 13 | 1 | 23 | 4 | 0 |
| Rowe, Joe, Angels | 1 | 3 | .250 | 4.78 | 13 | 4 | 0 | 0 | 3 | 0 | 37.2 | 33 | 159 | 22 | 20 | 0 | 2 | 2 | 7 | 14 | 0 | 34 | 4 | 3 |
| Salankey, Caleb, Giants | 2 | 1 | .667 | 3.35 | 11 | 5 | 0 | 0 | 1 | 1 | 40.1 | 49 | 180 | 24 | 15 | 0 | 0 | 1 | 2 | 12 | 0 | 41 | 1 | 0 |
| Sanchez, J, Giants | 0 | 0 | .000 | 0.00 | 1 | 0 | 0 | 0 | 1 | 1 | 0.1 | 1 | 2 | 0 | 0 | 0 | 0 | 0 | 0 | 0 | 0 | 0 | 0 | 0 |
| Sanchez, Jose, Giants | 1 | 1 | .500 | 3.32 | 16 | 0 | 0 | 0 | 8 | 4 | 19.0 | 16 | 78 | 8 | 7 | 0 | 0 | 0 | 2 | 5 | 0 | 30 | 3 | 0 |
| Santana, Andy, Cubs * | 3 | 2 | .600 | 1.61 | 10 | 3 | 0 | 0 | 2 | 0 | 44.2 | 39 | 186 | 14 | 8 | 0 | 2 | 1 | 4 | 18 | 0 | 45 | 2 | 0 |
| Santiago, Julio, Mariners * | 2 | 0 | 1.000 | 1.80 | 3 | 1 | 0 | 0 | 0 | 0 | 10.0 | 5 | 35 | 3 | 2 | 0 | 0 | 0 | 1 | 1 | 0 | 12 | 0 | 0 |
| Schappert, Paul, Cubs * | 2 | 0 | 1.000 | 2.84 | 7 | 0 | 0 | 0 | 6 | 1 | 12.2 | 12 | 52 | 4 | 4 | 1 | 0 | 1 | 0 | 3 | 0 | 13 | 1 | 1 |
| Scheffel, Dustin, Rangers | 0 | 0 | .000 | 3.00 | 6 | 4 | 0 | 0 | 0 | 0 | 6.0 | 7 | 29 | 4 | 2 | 0 | 0 | 1 | 0 | 3 | 0 | 8 | 0 | 0 |
| Schlact, Michael, Rangers | 1 | 1 | .500 | 3.52 | 10 | 5 | 0 | 0 | 0 | 0 | 30.2 | 32 | 135 | 18 | 12 | 0 | 0 | 4 | 2 | 9 | 0 | 22 | 3 | 0 |
| Semerano, Robert, Athletics | 5 | 1 | .833 | 4.08 | 21 | 0 | 0 | 0 | 12 | 0 | 28.2 | 30 | 124 | 16 | 13 | 0 | 3 | 3 | 1 | 7 | 0 | 24 | 4 | 0 |
| Shearer, Kelly, Angels * | 2 | 3 | .400 | 2.82 | 13 | 9 | 0 | 0 | 0 | 0 | 51.0 | 42 | 210 | 22 | 16 | 2 | 2 | 2 | 7 | 23 | 0 | 36 | 4 | 2 |
| Simmons, Justin, GCL Dodgers* | 1 | 0 | 1.000 | 0.92 | 7 | 1 | 0 | 0 | 0 | 0 | 19.2 | 10 | 75 | 2 | 2 | 0 | — | — | 0 | 8 | 2 | 17 | 0 | — |
| Sokoll, John, Royals * | 0 | 0 | .000 | 9.39 | 16 | 2 | 0 | 0 | 5 | 0 | 15.1 | 22 | 84 | 21 | 16 | 0 | 0 | 1 | 1 | 16 | 0 | 14 | 7 | 0 |
| Solis, Hairo, Giants | 3 | 2 | .600 | 3.25 | 22 | 0 | 0 | 0 | 11 | 2 | 27.2 | 22 | 114 | 13 | 10 | 1 | 0 | 0 | 0 | 9 | 0 | 42 | 4 | 0 |
| Stutes, Kyle, Padres * | 2 | 2 | .500 | 3.52 | 20 | 0 | 0 | 0 | 2 | 0 | 30.2 | 34 | 128 | 18 | 12 | 1 | 0 | 1 | 0 | 5 | 1 | 37 | 1 | 0 |
| Sweeney, Michael, Angels * | 0 | 0 | .000 | 15.12 | 9 | 0 | 0 | 0 | 3 | 0 | 8.1 | 19 | 55 | 16 | 14 | 1 | 0 | 0 | 2 | 8 | 0 | 13 | 3 | 0 |
| Tennyson, Adam, Royals | 2 | 2 | .500 | 3.96 | 15 | 0 | 0 | 0 | 4 | 0 | 25.0 | 22 | 118 | 11 | 11 | 0 | 3 | 0 | 1 | 21 | 1 | 22 | 1 | 0 |
| Thompson, Nick, Cubs | 2 | 1 | .667 | 2.40 | 11 | 0 | 0 | 0 | 10 | 1 | 15.0 | 14 | 66 | 5 | 4 | 1 | 0 | 1 | 1 | 5 | 3 | 19 | 2 | 0 |
| Torres, Luis, Athletics | 3 | 5 | .375 | 5.06 | 15 | 8 | 0 | 0 | 1 | 0 | 53.1 | 67 | 242 | 35 | 30 | 4 | 2 | 2 | 1 | 23 | 0 | 35 | 3 | 2 |
| Tucker, Cardoza, Mariners | 0 | 0 | .000 | 18.00 | 2 | 0 | 0 | 0 | 0 | 0 | 3.0 | 8 | 18 | 6 | 6 | 3 | 0 | 0 | 0 | 3 | 0 | 4 | 0 | 0 |
| Valencia, Jose, Angels | 2 | 4 | .333 | 5.23 | 14 | 1 | 0 | 0 | 3 | 0 | 20.2 | 28 | 96 | 14 | 12 | 1 | 0 | 2 | 2 | 3 | 0 | 25 | 2 | 0 |
| Ventura, Robert, Giants | 3 | 3 | .500 | 4.42 | 11 | 7 | 0 | 0 | 0 | 0 | 36.2 | 46 | 170 | 21 | 18 | 0 | 0 | 2 | 2 | 11 | 0 | 34 | 3 | 2 |
| Webb, Ryan, Athletics | 1 | 1 | .500 | 4.87 | 8 | 7 | 0 | 0 | 0 | 0 | 20.1 | 18 | 83 | 11 | 11 | 2 | 0 | 0 | 3 | 1 | 0 | 23 | 1 | 0 |
| Wilson, Brendan, Angels | 1 | 2 | .333 | 3.96 | 14 | 5 | 0 | 0 | 2 | 0 | 38.2 | 47 | 181 | 24 | 17 | 1 | 0 | 0 | 2 | 21 | 0 | 35 | 4 | 0 |
| Woerman, Joe, Mariners | 1 | 3 | .250 | 5.33 | 6 | 6 | 0 | 0 | 0 | 0 | 27.0 | 27 | 130 | 19 | 16 | 0 | 2 | 2 | 9 | 16 | 0 | 27 | 4 | 0 |
| Wylie, Jason, Cubs | 0 | 0 | .000 | 8.10 | 3 | 0 | 0 | 0 | 0 | 0 | 3.1 | 4 | 18 | 4 | 3 | 0 | 1 | 0 | 1 | 2 | 0 | 1 | 1 | 0 |
| Yepez, Jesus, Cubs * | 1 | 2 | .333 | 3.66 | 12 | 8 | 0 | 0 | 0 | 0 | 46.2 | 44 | 201 | 27 | 19 | 1 | 1 | 1 | 1 | 24 | 0 | 44 | 8 | 2 |
| Yntema, Orlando, Giants | 0 | 1 | .000 | 7.50 | 2 | 1 | 0 | 0 | 0 | 0 | 6.0 | 6 | 29 | 7 | 5 | 0 | 0 | 0 | 2 | 2 | 0 | 6 | 0 | 0 |
| Zbacnik, Billy, Giants * | 3 | 1 | .750 | 3.60 | 17 | 0 | 0 | 0 | 4 | 0 | 20.0 | 19 | 89 | 9 | 8 | 0 | 2 | 0 | 1 | 13 | 1 | 25 | 3 | 1 |
| Zuleta, Howar, GCL Dodgers | 1 | 3 | .250 | 2.14 | 23 | 2 | 0 | 0 | 16 | 7 | 42.0 | 30 | 186 | 12 | 10 | 1 | — | — | 6 | 19 | 1 | 51 | 0 | — |

COMBINATION SHUTOUTS: **Athletics** (2)—Acevedo-Fairbanks, Piekarz-Mitchell-Semerano. **Brewers** (2)—Arias-Mosquea-Morrison, Gallardo-Garcia-Fermin. **Cubs** (2)—Gallagher-Santana, Gallagher-Santana. **Giants** (4)—Matos-Lundwall-Mercado-Sanchez, Callahan-Putman-Gornati, Matos-Putman, Gornati-Zbacni-Solis. **Mariners** (1)—Arias-Carter-Sundstrom-Steele. **Padres** (2)—Krosschell-Shanks-Baca-Steik-Tucker, Jimenez-Jenkins. **Rangers** (4)— Park-Hurley-Padgett, Fernando-Lujan-Seely, Perez-Foster-Ramirez, Perez-Diaz. **Royals** (2)—Begnaud-Sokoll-Garcia, Nelson-Eckley-Sokoll.

NO-HIT GAMES: None.

# 2004 FIELDING

## TEAM

| Team | G | PO | A | E | TC | DP | TP | PB | Pct. |
|---|---|---|---|---|---|---|---|---|---|
| Royals | 56 | 1489 | 647 | 93 | 2229 | 56 | 0 | 10 | .958 |
| Rangers | 56 | 1485 | 637 | 98 | 2220 | 50 | 0 | 13 | .956 |
| Cubs | 56 | 1497 | 599 | 96 | 2192 | 45 | 0 | 22 | .956 |
| Giants | 56 | 1494 | 565 | 96 | 2155 | 39 | 0 | 14 | .955 |
| Athletics | 56 | 1483 | 616 | 101 | 2200 | 45 | 0 | 19 | .954 |
| Padres | 56 | 1510 | 607 | 105 | 2222 | 51 | 0 | 14 | .953 |
| Mariners | 56 | 1479 | 562 | 102 | 2143 | 39 | 0 | 14 | .952 |
| Brewers | 56 | 1486 | 602 | 112 | 2200 | 49 | 0 | 20 | .949 |
| Angels | 56 | 1495 | 544 | 112 | 2151 | 51 | 0 | 18 | .948 |

## INDIVIDUAL

### FIRST BASEMEN

NOTE: All caps denotes fielding-percentage leader based on 28 games for catchers, 37 for all other non-pitchers and 45 innings for pitchers. *Throws lefthanded.

| Player, Team | Pct. | G | PO | A | E | TC | DP |
|---|---|---|---|---|---|---|---|
| ADKISON, BLAKE, Royals | 1.000 | 16 | 106 | 5 | 0 | 111 | 9 |
| Arias, Francis, Brewers | 1.000 | 1 | 1 | 0 | 0 | 1 | 0 |
| Ayala, Angel, Brewers | .985 | 18 | 125 | 9 | 2 | 136 | 8 |
| Best, Tyler, Athletics | 1.000 | 4 | 41 | 3 | 0 | 44 | 6 |
| Chapman, Stephen, Brewers * | 1.000 | 1 | 5 | 1 | 0 | 6 | 1 |
| Ciesluk, Chris, Giants | 1.000 | 3 | 2 | 0 | 0 | 2 | 0 |
| Cowles, Josh, Angels | 1.000 | 1 | 5 | 0 | 0 | 5 | 0 |
| Davies, Josh, Angels | 1.000 | 2 | 5 | 1 | 0 | 6 | 2 |
| Douillard, Jonathan, Cubs | 1.000 | 1 | 9 | 0 | 0 | 9 | 1 |
| Etheridge, Chad, Padres | 1.000 | 1 | 2 | 0 | 0 | 2 | 0 |
| Feliz, Nelson, Athletics | 1.000 | 3 | 31 | 1 | 0 | 32 | 2 |
| Figuereo, Anibal, Royals | 1.000 | 3 | 24 | 1 | 0 | 25 | 1 |
| Flaig, Jeffrey, Mariners | 1.000 | 8 | 62 | 6 | 0 | 68 | 1 |
| Gac, Ian, Rangers | .979 | 18 | 173 | 13 | 4 | 190 | 10 |
| Gallardo, Carlos, Brewers | .982 | 39 | 308 | 18 | 6 | 332 | 25 |
| Johnson, Michael, Padres | .968 | 7 | 55 | 5 | 2 | 62 | 4 |
| Jones, Daryl, Padres | .978 | 24 | 211 | 12 | 5 | 228 | 18 |
| Lampe, Rayon, Mariners | .969 | 4 | 26 | 5 | 1 | 32 | 1 |
| Lopez, Luis, Padres | 1.000 | 2 | 17 | 0 | 0 | 17 | 2 |
| Martinez, Brett, Angels | .990 | 11 | 96 | 6 | 1 | 103 | 11 |
| Martinez, Eduardo, Rangers | 1.000 | 1 | 1 | 0 | 0 | 1 | 0 |
| Morgan, Ryan, Cubs | .987 | 43 | 369 | 18 | 5 | 392 | 28 |
| Opdyke, Bryan, Brewers | 1.000 | 3 | 11 | 1 | 0 | 12 | 1 |
| Padron, Raul, Athletics | .978 | 16 | 123 | 11 | 3 | 137 | 10 |
| Perez, Leonel, Cubs | 1.000 | 3 | 19 | 1 | 0 | 20 | 0 |
| Pratt, Haas, Athletics | .990 | 24 | 190 | 7 | 2 | 199 | 11 |
| Puello, Elvin, Cubs | 1.000 | 7 | 70 | 4 | 0 | 74 | 8 |
| Quintero, Cesar, Mariners | .929 | 2 | 13 | 0 | 1 | 14 | 2 |
| Reinhardt, Doug, Angels | .957 | 4 | 20 | 2 | 1 | 23 | 2 |
| Richards, Judson, Giants * | .968 | 56 | 455 | 36 | 16 | 507 | 32 |
| Santin, Daniel, Mariners * | .909 | 1 | 9 | 1 | 1 | 11 | 0 |
| Serrano, Julian, Cubs | .895 | 2 | 15 | 2 | 2 | 19 | 2 |
| Shankle, Brooks, Angels | .970 | 42 | 337 | 20 | 11 | 368 | 32 |
| Soto, Luis, Mariners | .992 | 31 | 249 | 14 | 2 | 265 | 23 |
| Sutton, Donald, Athletics | 1.000 | 13 | 132 | 9 | 0 | 141 | 8 |
| Thon, Freddy, Rangers * | .989 | 38 | 342 | 23 | 4 | 369 | 35 |
| Thon, Freddy, Rangers * | .989 | 38 | 342 | 23 | 4 | 369 | 35 |
| Tua, Franklin, Brewers | .964 | 9 | 24 | 3 | 1 | 28 | 3 |
| Vega, Miguel, Royals | .987 | 44 | 426 | 27 | 6 | 459 | 32 |
| White, Peter, Padres | .980 | 28 | 231 | 15 | 5 | 251 | 23 |
| Wu, Chao, Mariners | .976 | 12 | 113 | 8 | 3 | 124 | 8 |

### SECOND BASEMEN

| Player, Team | Pct. | G | PO | A | E | TC | DP |
|---|---|---|---|---|---|---|---|
| Andrews, Greg, Cubs | .979 | 25 | 41 | 53 | 2 | 96 | 12 |
| Angulo, Oscar, Brewers | .857 | 2 | 3 | 3 | 1 | 7 | 1 |
| Arias, Francis, Brewers | .500 | 3 | 0 | 1 | 1 | 2 | 0 |
| Arroyo, Jack, Mariners | .937 | 17 | 24 | 35 | 4 | 63 | 4 |
| Backman, Walter, Rangers | 1.000 | 6 | 11 | 14 | 0 | 25 | 2 |
| Casilla, Alexi, Angels | .959 | 33 | 62 | 78 | 6 | 146 | 17 |
| Davies, Josh, Angels | 1.000 | 3 | 7 | 4 | 0 | 11 | 2 |
| Day, Devin, Angels | .979 | 14 | 16 | 31 | 1 | 48 | 6 |
| Deeb, Bobby, Cubs | .929 | 3 | 7 | 6 | 1 | 14 | 0 |
| Disla, Lisandro, Giants | 1.000 | 3 | 2 | 7 | 0 | 9 | 1 |
| Dominguez, Jeffrey, Mariners | .943 | 10 | 15 | 18 | 2 | 35 | 4 |
| Falu, Irving, Royals | .977 | 44 | 88 | 123 | 5 | 216 | 30 |
| Falu, Irving, Royals | .977 | 44 | 88 | 123 | 5 | 216 | 30 |
| Garciaparra, Michael, Mariners | 1.000 | 2 | 4 | 4 | 0 | 8 | 1 |
| Gerez, Francisco, Mariners | .965 | 10 | 25 | 30 | 2 | 57 | 6 |
| Griffin, Preston, Cubs | 1.000 | 1 | 2 | 2 | 0 | 4 | 1 |
| Haines, Kyle, Giants | 1.000 | 1 | 0 | 1 | 0 | 1 | 0 |
| Hoffpauir, Brad, Cubs | .957 | 28 | 52 | 59 | 5 | 116 | 12 |
| Iribarren, Hernan, Brewers | .966 | 46 | 113 | 142 | 9 | 264 | 31 |
| Johnson, Joshua, Royals | .985 | 12 | 25 | 41 | 1 | 67 | 8 |
| Kendrick, Howie, Angels | .667 | 1 | 0 | 2 | 1 | 3 | 0 |
| King, Lisandro, Giants | .667 | 3 | 2 | 0 | 1 | 3 | 0 |
| Lampe, Rayon, Mariners | .932 | 18 | 38 | 44 | 6 | 88 | 8 |
| Lopez, Jose, Mariners | .000 | 1 | 0 | 0 | 0 | 0 | 0 |
| Martinez, Eduardo, Rangers | .875 | 5 | 12 | 16 | 4 | 32 | 4 |
| Martinez, Frank, Athletics | 1.000 | 2 | 1 | 7 | 0 | 8 | 0 |
| Meyer, Drew, Rangers | 1.000 | 2 | 4 | 5 | 0 | 9 | 2 |
| Monzon, Erick, Mariners | 1.000 | 1 | 2 | 1 | 0 | 3 | 1 |
| Morales, Saul, Cubs | .917 | 5 | 7 | 15 | 2 | 24 | 4 |
| Morillo, Roberto, Giants | 1.000 | 2 | 0 | 2 | 0 | 2 | 0 |
| Ozoria, Pedro, Mariners | .900 | 3 | 1 | 8 | 1 | 10 | 1 |
| Pena, Antonio, Rangers | .963 | 29 | 60 | 94 | 6 | 160 | 20 |
| Perez, Wilber, Athletics | .944 | 43 | 88 | 130 | 13 | 231 | 28 |
| Reinhardt, Doug, Angels | .979 | 9 | 21 | 26 | 1 | 48 | 4 |
| Rivera, Jodam, Padres | .967 | 21 | 36 | 51 | 3 | 90 | 13 |
| Sanders, Marcus, Giants | .944 | 54 | 97 | 137 | 14 | 248 | 24 |
| Smith, Dustin, Cubs | .800 | 1 | 4 | 0 | 1 | 5 | 1 |
| Smyres, Justin, Padres | 1.000 | 3 | 6 | 7 | 0 | 13 | 1 |
| Tua, Franklin, Brewers | .000 | 1 | 0 | 0 | 0 | 0 | 0 |
| Valdez, Alexander, Athletics | 1.000 | 11 | 22 | 25 | 0 | 47 | 4 |
| Valdez, Riquelbi, Rangers | .917 | 5 | 13 | 20 | 3 | 36 | 2 |
| Vazquez, Kelvin, Padres | .959 | 39 | 80 | 84 | 7 | 171 | 23 |
| Vicioso, Osvaldo, Brewers | .914 | 8 | 16 | 16 | 3 | 35 | 4 |
| Washington, Johnny, Rangers | .935 | 12 | 15 | 28 | 3 | 46 | 3 |

### THIRD BASEMEN

| Player, Team | Pct. | G | PO | A | E | TC | DP |
|---|---|---|---|---|---|---|---|
| Angulo, Oscar, Brewers | 1.000 | 2 | 3 | 2 | 0 | 5 | 0 |
| Arroyo, Jack, Mariners | .824 | 6 | 4 | 10 | 3 | 17 | 0 |
| Backman, Walter, Rangers | .926 | 16 | 12 | 38 | 4 | 54 | 2 |
| Canzler, Russell, Cubs | .800 | 18 | 13 | 31 | 11 | 55 | 1 |
| Carela, Carlos, Athletics | .733 | 3 | 2 | 9 | 4 | 15 | 2 |
| Chapman, Travis, Royals | .848 | 13 | 7 | 21 | 5 | 33 | 0 |
| Chavez, Angel, Giants | 1.000 | 2 | 1 | 6 | 0 | 7 | 0 |
| Ciesluk, Chris, Giants | .500 | 4 | 0 | 3 | 3 | 6 | 0 |
| Cowles, Josh, Angels | .714 | 3 | 1 | 4 | 2 | 7 | 0 |
| Cruceta, Julio, Padres | .960 | 8 | 6 | 18 | 1 | 25 | 1 |
| Davies, Josh, Angels | .846 | 16 | 10 | 12 | 4 | 26 | 1 |
| De La Cruz, Freddy, Brewers | .910 | 46 | 42 | 79 | 12 | 133 | 8 |
| Disla, Lisandro, Giants | .933 | 45 | 31 | 66 | 7 | 104 | 4 |
| Disla, Lisandro, Giants | .933 | 45 | 31 | 66 | 7 | 104 | 4 |
| Doddo, Brandon, Angels | .889 | 9 | 5 | 11 | 2 | 18 | 2 |
| Falu, Irving, Royals | 1.000 | 3 | 1 | 5 | 0 | 6 | 0 |
| Figuereo, Anibal, Royals | .556 | 2 | 2 | 3 | 4 | 9 | 1 |
| Figueroa, Baudilio, Padres | 1.000 | 2 | 2 | 3 | 0 | 5 | 0 |
| Gerez, Francisco, Mariners | .944 | 7 | 3 | 14 | 1 | 18 | 3 |
| Gomez, Mauro, Rangers | .874 | 33 | 21 | 62 | 12 | 95 | 4 |
| Johnston, Trey, Padres | .873 | 36 | 36 | 53 | 13 | 102 | 8 |
| King, Lisandro, Giants | .778 | 8 | 3 | 4 | 2 | 9 | 1 |
| Lampe, Rayon, Mariners | .733 | 7 | 3 | 8 | 4 | 15 | 0 |
| Long, Wesley, Athletics | .906 | 45 | 48 | 78 | 13 | 139 | 7 |
| Lopez, Jose, Mariners | .833 | 2 | 2 | 3 | 1 | 6 | 1 |
| Martinez, Eduardo, Rangers | .950 | 6 | 6 | 13 | 1 | 20 | 1 |
| Meyer, Drew, Rangers | 1.000 | 1 | 0 | 1 | 0 | 1 | 0 |
| Morgan, Ryan, Cubs | .857 | 2 | 2 | 4 | 1 | 7 | 1 |
| Morillo, Roberto, Giants | .846 | 6 | 2 | 9 | 2 | 13 | 1 |
| Ozoria, Pedro, Mariners | .900 | 36 | 24 | 75 | 11 | 110 | 6 |
| Parejo, Freddy, Brewers | 1.000 | 1 | 1 | 2 | 0 | 3 | 0 |
| Puello, Elvin, Cubs | .938 | 31 | 24 | 67 | 6 | 97 | 5 |
| Qualls, Darrell, Royals | .914 | 31 | 21 | 53 | 7 | 81 | 5 |
| Reinhardt, Doug, Angels | .814 | 33 | 17 | 31 | 11 | 59 | 2 |
| Serrano, Julian, Cubs | .889 | 6 | 1 | 7 | 1 | 9 | 2 |
| Shankle, Brooks, Angels | .944 | 6 | 4 | 13 | 1 | 18 | 2 |
| Soto, Luis, Mariners | .750 | 3 | 3 | 3 | 2 | 8 | 0 |
| Valdez, Alexander, Athletics | .818 | 9 | 6 | 21 | 6 | 33 | 1 |
| Vazquez, Kelvin, Padres | .913 | 10 | 7 | 14 | 2 | 23 | 0 |
| Vega, Miguel, Royals | .906 | 18 | 18 | 30 | 5 | 53 | 4 |
| Vicioso, Osvaldo, Brewers | .941 | 8 | 3 | 13 | 1 | 17 | 2 |
| White, Peter, Padres | .800 | 6 | 3 | 5 | 2 | 10 | 1 |

### SHORTSTOPS

| Player, Team | Pct. | G | PO | A | E | TC | DP |
|---|---|---|---|---|---|---|---|
| Abreu, Johany, Giants | .889 | 8 | 9 | 15 | 3 | 27 | 3 |
| Andrews, Greg, Cubs | .882 | 5 | 3 | 12 | 2 | 17 | 3 |
| Arredondo, Jose, Angels | .921 | 20 | 34 | 48 | 7 | 89 | 13 |
| Arroyo, Jack, Mariners | 1.000 | 1 | 1 | 0 | 0 | 1 | 0 |
| Backman, Walter, Rangers | .893 | 6 | 10 | 15 | 3 | 28 | 2 |
| Bush, Matthew, Padres | .907 | 21 | 36 | 61 | 10 | 107 | 18 |
| Carela, Carlos, Athletics | .853 | 7 | 10 | 19 | 5 | 34 | 4 |
| Casilla, Alexi, Angels | 1.000 | 11 | 18 | 29 | 0 | 47 | 5 |
| Chavez, Angel, Giants | .857 | 2 | 1 | 5 | 1 | 7 | 1 |
| Davies, Josh, Angels | .891 | 26 | 41 | 65 | 13 | 119 | 13 |
| Day, Devin, Angels | .929 | 10 | 13 | 13 | 2 | 28 | 4 |
| Deeb, Bobby, Cubs | 1.000 | 1 | 2 | 5 | 0 | 7 | 1 |
| Dominguez, Jeffrey, Mariners | .912 | 37 | 56 | 79 | 13 | 148 | 16 |
| Figueroa, Baudilio, Padres | .900 | 12 | 20 | 43 | 7 | 70 | 7 |
| Garciaparra, Michael, Mariners | .833 | 1 | 4 | 1 | 1 | 6 | 1 |
| Gerez, Francisco, Mariners | .846 | 2 | 3 | 8 | 2 | 13 | 0 |
| Griffin, Preston, Cubs | .980 | 13 | 19 | 30 | 1 | 50 | 3 |
| Haines, Kyle, Giants | .967 | 12 | 19 | 39 | 2 | 60 | 7 |
| Hoffpauir, Brad, Cubs | 1.000 | 2 | 2 | 3 | 0 | 5 | 0 |
| Johnson, Joshua, Royals | .944 | 30 | 37 | 114 | 9 | 160 | 20 |
| King, Lisandro, Giants | .944 | 9 | 13 | 21 | 2 | 36 | 2 |
| Leclercq, Lenny, Brewers | .869 | 45 | 61 | 125 | 28 | 214 | 19 |
| Long, Wesley, Athletics | .917 | 4 | 5 | 6 | 1 | 12 | 1 |

| Player, Team | Pct. | G | PO | A | E | TC | DP |
|---|---|---|---|---|---|---|---|
| Lopez, Jose, Mariners | 1.000 | 2 | 1 | 8 | 0 | 9 | 1 |
| Luster, Jeremiah, Giants | .897 | 14 | 15 | 46 | 7 | 68 | 6 |
| Martinez, Eduardo, Rangers | .900 | 6 | 7 | 20 | 3 | 30 | 4 |
| Martinez, Frank, Athletics | .920 | 44 | 63 | 133 | 17 | 213 | 22 |
| Martinez, Frank, Athletics | .920 | 44 | 63 | 133 | 17 | 213 | 22 |
| Martinez, Jose, Cubs | .500 | 2 | 0 | 1 | 1 | 2 | 0 |
| McConnell, Christopher, Royals | .893 | 29 | 47 | 87 | 16 | 150 | 13 |
| Meyer, Drew, Rangers | .947 | 7 | 10 | 26 | 2 | 38 | 7 |
| Monzon, Erick, Mariners | 1.000 | 2 | 3 | 9 | 0 | 12 | 0 |
| Morillo, Roberto, Giants | .909 | 15 | 19 | 31 | 5 | 55 | 4 |
| Pena, Antonio, Rangers | .881 | 7 | 18 | 19 | 5 | 42 | 3 |
| Puello, Elvin, Cubs | .806 | 5 | 6 | 23 | 7 | 36 | 5 |
| Reinhardt, Doug, Angels | 1.000 | 1 | 1 | 0 | 0 | 1 | 0 |
| Rivera, Jodam, Padres | .966 | 28 | 27 | 85 | 4 | 116 | 13 |
| Rodriguez, Luis, Rangers | .931 | 33 | 50 | 85 | 10 | 145 | 16 |
| Smith, Aaron, Cubs | .959 | 33 | 41 | 101 | 6 | 148 | 21 |
| Smith, Dustin, Cubs | .750 | 1 | 1 | 2 | 1 | 4 | 0 |
| Tuiasosopo, Matthew, Mariners | .884 | 15 | 23 | 38 | 8 | 69 | 7 |
| Valdez, Alexander, Athletics | .250 | 1 | 0 | 1 | 3 | 4 | 0 |
| Vicioso, Osvaldo, Brewers | .840 | 14 | 12 | 30 | 8 | 50 | 7 |
| Washington, Johnny, Rangers | .000 | 1 | 0 | 0 | 0 | 0 | 0 |

## OUTFIELDERS

| Player, Team | Pct. | G | PO | A | E | TC | DP |
|---|---|---|---|---|---|---|---|
| Abreu, Johany, Giants | 1.000 | 2 | 1 | 0 | 0 | 1 | 0 |
| Arias, Roberto, Athletics | .000 | 1 | 0 | 0 | 0 | 0 | 0 |
| Beauregard, Joshua, Athletics | 1.000 | 25 | 24 | 1 | 0 | 25 | 0 |
| Blanc, Jhonathan, Brewers | .923 | 33 | 46 | 2 | 4 | 52 | 0 |
| Bowker, John, Giants * | 1.000 | 10 | 13 | 0 | 0 | 13 | 0 |
| Boyd, Chad, Athletics * | .952 | 30 | 39 | 1 | 2 | 42 | 0 |
| Brock, Jermaine, Mariners * | 1.000 | 32 | 29 | 1 | 0 | 30 | 0 |
| Bubela, Jaime, Mariners | 1.000 | 11 | 13 | 0 | 0 | 13 | 0 |
| Caballero, Carlos, Royals | .962 | 35 | 49 | 2 | 2 | 53 | 1 |
| Carela, Carlos, Athletics | .800 | 13 | 12 | 0 | 3 | 15 | 0 |
| Chapman, Stephen, Brewers * | .971 | 48 | 94 | 6 | 3 | 103 | 2 |
| Charles, Larry, Rangers | 1.000 | 8 | 8 | 0 | 0 | 8 | 0 |
| Cividanes, Emmanuel, Giants | .953 | 34 | 38 | 3 | 2 | 43 | 0 |
| Cowles, Josh, Angels | .937 | 43 | 69 | 5 | 5 | 79 | 1 |
| Cruceta, Julio, Padres | .889 | 31 | 44 | 4 | 6 | 54 | 0 |
| Cruz, Reynaldo, Mariners | .875 | 23 | 40 | 2 | 6 | 48 | 0 |
| De La Cruz, Freddy, Brewers | .500 | 1 | 0 | 1 | 1 | 2 | 0 |
| Delarosa, Anderson, Brewers | .943 | 21 | 31 | 2 | 2 | 35 | 0 |
| Desouza, Daniel, Giants * | .935 | 52 | 80 | 6 | 6 | 92 | 1 |
| Douillard, Jonathan, Cubs | .000 | 1 | 0 | 0 | 0 | 0 | 0 |
| Ellis, Jared, Royals | .949 | 50 | 54 | 2 | 3 | 59 | 0 |
| Emmons, John, Mariners | .964 | 34 | 50 | 3 | 2 | 55 | 0 |
| Eusebio, Juan, Royals | .912 | 27 | 30 | 1 | 3 | 34 | 1 |
| Faison, Vince, Mariners | .000 | 1 | 0 | 0 | 0 | 0 | 0 |
| Gerez, Francisco, Mariners | .900 | 4 | 9 | 0 | 1 | 10 | 0 |
| Gonzalez, Juan, Royals | 1.000 | 3 | 2 | 0 | 0 | 2 | 0 |
| Green, Zane, Cubs * | .980 | 32 | 49 | 0 | 1 | 50 | 0 |
| Guiel, Aaron, Royals | 1.000 | 3 | 4 | 0 | 0 | 4 | 0 |
| Guzman, Juan, Rangers | .875 | 3 | 6 | 1 | 1 | 8 | 0 |
| Hall, David, Mariners | .972 | 34 | 68 | 2 | 2 | 72 | 1 |
| Hernandez, David, Angels | .923 | 8 | 12 | 0 | 1 | 13 | 0 |
| Herren, Karl, Rangers | .920 | 46 | 90 | 2 | 8 | 100 | 0 |
| Hubbard, Marshall, Mariners | 1.000 | 1 | 2 | 0 | 0 | 2 | 0 |
| Hurba, Craig, Rangers | .500 | 1 | 0 | 1 | 1 | 2 | 0 |
| Jacobitz, Joseph, Mariners | .972 | 26 | 34 | 1 | 1 | 36 | 0 |
| Johnson, Craig, Padres * | .950 | 31 | 53 | 4 | 3 | 60 | 1 |
| Joseph, Alfred, Cubs | .976 | 41 | 80 | 3 | 2 | 85 | 0 |
| Kolkhorst, Christopher, Padres | 1.000 | 7 | 8 | 1 | 0 | 9 | 0 |
| Krynzel, Dave, Brewers * | 1.000 | 4 | 3 | 0 | 0 | 3 | 0 |
| Mahar, Kevin, Rangers | .982 | 27 | 53 | 3 | 1 | 57 | 0 |
| Maldonado, Juan, Rangers | 1.000 | 37 | 57 | 1 | 0 | 58 | 1 |
| Maldonado, Juan, Rangers | 1.000 | 37 | 57 | 1 | 0 | 58 | 1 |
| Martinez, Eduardo, Rangers | 1.000 | 3 | 3 | 0 | 0 | 3 | 0 |
| Martinez-Esteve, Eddy, Giants | 1.000 | 4 | 8 | 0 | 0 | 8 | 0 |
| Mcdowell, D.T., Angels | .929 | 13 | 24 | 2 | 2 | 28 | 0 |
| Medley, Brian, Padres | .938 | 15 | 15 | 0 | 1 | 16 | 0 |
| Mejia, Carlos, Cubs | .923 | 23 | 32 | 4 | 3 | 39 | 0 |
| Meyer, Drew, Rangers | 1.000 | 3 | 2 | 1 | 0 | 3 | 0 |
| Miller, Gerald, Cubs | 1.000 | 3 | 4 | 0 | 0 | 4 | 0 |
| Mooney, Mike, Giants | .962 | 54 | 94 | 7 | 4 | 105 | 0 |
| Morales, Saul, Cubs | .952 | 28 | 56 | 4 | 3 | 63 | 1 |
| Morillo, Roberto, Giants | .933 | 9 | 12 | 2 | 1 | 15 | 0 |
| Moye, Alan, Royals | .900 | 9 | 9 | 0 | 1 | 10 | 0 |
| Newton, Andrew, Angels | 1.000 | 8 | 13 | 2 | 0 | 15 | 0 |
| Ogando, Alexi, Athletics | .975 | 46 | 70 | 8 | 2 | 80 | 1 |
| Opdyke, Bryan, Brewers | .000 | 1 | 0 | 0 | 0 | 0 | 0 |
| Parejo, Freddy, Brewers | .945 | 54 | 95 | 9 | 6 | 110 | 3 |
| Perez, Wilber, Athletics | .857 | 5 | 5 | 1 | 1 | 7 | 0 |
| Piper-Jordan, Andre, Athletics | .957 | 44 | 87 | 3 | 4 | 94 | 2 |
| Pratt, Haas, Athletics | 1.000 | 4 | 4 | 1 | 0 | 5 | 0 |
| Pride, Curtis, Angels | 1.000 | 2 | 1 | 0 | 0 | 1 | 0 |
| Quinones, Carlos, Cubs | .950 | 48 | 73 | 3 | 4 | 80 | 0 |
| Ramirez, Yordany, Padres | .971 | 39 | 93 | 7 | 3 | 103 | 0 |
| Rivera, Jodam, Padres | 1.000 | 2 | 1 | 0 | 0 | 1 | 0 |
| Rivera, Joel, Brewers | 1.000 | 26 | 34 | 2 | 0 | 36 | 1 |
| Rivera, Luis, Angels | .949 | 33 | 54 | 2 | 3 | 59 | 1 |
| Rosario, Anderson, Angels | .952 | 40 | 73 | 7 | 4 | 84 | 0 |
| Salome, Angel, Brewers | .000 | 1 | 0 | 0 | 0 | 0 | 0 |
| Sanchez, Ivan, Giants | .933 | 12 | 14 | 0 | 1 | 15 | 0 |
| Santana, Ethien, Royals * | .949 | 52 | 88 | 5 | 5 | 98 | 0 |
| Smith, Stantrel, Angels | .959 | 27 | 43 | 4 | 2 | 49 | 1 |
| Snelling, Chris, Mariners * | .846 | 8 | 10 | 1 | 2 | 13 | 0 |
| Soto, Luis, Mariners | 1.000 | 2 | 5 | 0 | 0 | 5 | 0 |
| Torres, Jose, Rangers | .962 | 44 | 50 | 0 | 2 | 52 | 0 |
| Valdez, Alexander, Athletics | .750 | 6 | 3 | 0 | 1 | 4 | 0 |
| Wesson, Barry, Angels | 1.000 | 4 | 6 | 0 | 0 | 6 | 0 |
| Whitney, Nate, Padres | .978 | 51 | 86 | 2 | 2 | 90 | 0 |

## CATCHERS

| Player, Team | Pct. | G | PO | A | E | TC | DP | PB |
|---|---|---|---|---|---|---|---|---|
| Arias, Roberto, Athletics | .984 | 17 | 111 | 13 | 2 | 126 | 1 | 4 |
| Best, Tyler, Athletics | .995 | 21 | 165 | 24 | 1 | 190 | 1 | 5 |
| Buller, Dayton, Giants | 1.000 | 7 | 53 | 5 | 0 | 58 | 0 | 1 |
| Corredor, Nestor, Brewers | .989 | 28 | 138 | 39 | 2 | 179 | 2 | 4 |
| Corredor, Nestor, Brewers | .989 | 28 | 138 | 39 | 2 | 179 | 2 | 4 |
| Dixon, Dorian, Giants | .962 | 4 | 22 | 3 | 1 | 26 | 0 | 1 |
| Douillard, Jonathan, Cubs | .987 | 8 | 66 | 11 | 1 | 78 | 0 | 2 |
| Feliz, Nelson, Athletics | .977 | 5 | 41 | 2 | 1 | 44 | 0 | 2 |
| Grana, Robert, Royals | .968 | 39 | 279 | 27 | 10 | 316 | 3 | 7 |
| Hernandez, David, Angels | .991 | 18 | 108 | 7 | 1 | 116 | 0 | 4 |
| Higashi, Jonathan, Rangers | .972 | 11 | 89 | 17 | 3 | 109 | 0 | 5 |
| Hurba, Craig, Rangers | .984 | 19 | 112 | 10 | 2 | 124 | 3 | 0 |
| Jennings, Todd, Giants | 1.000 | 4 | 27 | 2 | 0 | 29 | 0 | 1 |
| Johnston, Trey, Padres | 1.000 | 1 | 1 | 0 | 0 | 1 | 0 | 0 |
| Killian, William, Padres | .969 | 23 | 127 | 27 | 5 | 159 | 0 | 4 |
| Kurtz, Jared, Giants | .980 | 15 | 125 | 21 | 3 | 149 | 0 | 6 |
| Lopez, Luis, Padres | .948 | 11 | 64 | 9 | 4 | 77 | 0 | 2 |
| Lopez, Yonnata, Brewers | .909 | 2 | 9 | 1 | 1 | 11 | 0 | 1 |
| Maldonado, Martin, Angels | .957 | 23 | 134 | 23 | 7 | 164 | 3 | 5 |
| Martinez, Brett, Angels | .980 | 28 | 216 | 33 | 5 | 254 | 2 | 9 |
| Norman, Derek, Royals | 1.000 | 2 | 8 | 3 | 0 | 11 | 0 | 2 |
| Opdyke, Bryan, Brewers | .986 | 26 | 194 | 24 | 3 | 221 | 1 | 6 |
| Padron, Raul, Athletics | .958 | 13 | 81 | 11 | 4 | 96 | 0 | 3 |
| Pena, Jose, Royals | .977 | 16 | 113 | 16 | 3 | 132 | 0 | 1 |
| Perez, Leonel, Cubs | .969 | 26 | 219 | 31 | 8 | 258 | 1 | 15 |
| Quintero, Cesar, Mariners | .974 | 5 | 37 | 1 | 1 | 39 | 0 | 1 |
| Reed, Mark, Cubs | .989 | 9 | 81 | 9 | 1 | 91 | 1 | 1 |
| Salome, Angel, Brewers | .990 | 12 | 76 | 23 | 1 | 100 | 0 | 6 |
| Sanchez, Angel, Rangers | .989 | 32 | 224 | 37 | 3 | 264 | 4 | 8 |
| Sanchez, Luany, Padres | .967 | 32 | 224 | 38 | 9 | 271 | 0 | 8 |
| Sandoval, Pablo, Giants | .988 | 33 | 300 | 41 | 4 | 345 | 1 | 5 |
| Santin, Daniel, Mariners | .982 | 34 | 295 | 32 | 6 | 333 | 2 | 8 |
| Slee, Gregory, Mariners | .988 | 8 | 75 | 5 | 1 | 81 | 0 | 4 |
| Speier, Cole, Cubs | 1.000 | 6 | 12 | 3 | 0 | 15 | 0 | 0 |
| Sutton, Donald, Athletics | 1.000 | 6 | 49 | 4 | 0 | 53 | 0 | 5 |
| Thomas, Jonathan, Royals | 1.000 | 4 | 14 | 1 | 0 | 15 | 0 | 0 |
| Tidball, Adam, Cubs | .950 | 2 | 17 | 2 | 1 | 20 | 0 | 2 |
| Tua, Franklin, Brewers | .909 | 2 | 10 | 0 | 1 | 11 | 1 | 3 |
| Wick, Olin, Cubs | .979 | 12 | 80 | 12 | 2 | 94 | 1 | 3 |
| Wu, Chao, Mariners | .989 | 9 | 76 | 12 | 1 | 89 | 0 | 1 |

## PITCHERS

| Player, Team | Pct. | G | PO | A | E | TC | DP |
|---|---|---|---|---|---|---|---|
| Abreu, Francis, Angels | 1.000 | 4 | 2 | 4 | 0 | 6 | 1 |
| Acevedo, Danielin, Athletics | .889 | 10 | 2 | 6 | 1 | 9 | 0 |
| Adames, Emilio, Rangers | .750 | 16 | 1 | 5 | 2 | 8 | 0 |
| Aldridge, Ryan, Angels | .833 | 13 | 1 | 4 | 1 | 6 | 1 |
| Angulo, Oscar, Brewers | .000 | 2 | 0 | 0 | 0 | 0 | 0 |
| Arias, Oliver, Mariners | .933 | 12 | 3 | 11 | 1 | 15 | 0 |
| Arias, Roberto, Athletics | .000 | 1 | 0 | 0 | 0 | 0 | 0 |
| Arias, Victor, Brewers | .667 | 8 | 0 | 2 | 1 | 3 | 0 |
| Arredondo, Jose, Angels | 1.000 | 8 | 1 | 1 | 0 | 2 | 0 |
| Atkins, Mitch, Cubs | .500 | 10 | 0 | 1 | 1 | 2 | 0 |
| Baca, Daniel, Padres | 1.000 | 23 | 2 | 5 | 0 | 7 | 0 |
| Baek, Cha Seung, Mariners | 1.000 | 2 | 0 | 2 | 0 | 2 | 0 |
| Bass, Brian, Royals | .000 | 5 | 0 | 0 | 1 | 1 | 0 |
| Begnaud, Rusty, Royals | 1.000 | 14 | 7 | 10 | 0 | 17 | 0 |
| Begnaud, Rusty, Royals | 1.000 | 14 | 7 | 10 | 0 | 17 | 0 |
| Bernal, Luis, Brewers | .600 | 10 | 2 | 1 | 2 | 5 | 0 |
| Bowman, Bobby, Rangers | .333 | 8 | 0 | 1 | 2 | 3 | 0 |
| Brandt, Adam, Mariners * | .833 | 13 | 0 | 5 | 1 | 6 | 0 |
| Breshears, Richard, Brewers | 1.000 | 12 | 1 | 5 | 0 | 6 | 0 |
| Bruso, Greg, Brewers | .000 | 2 | 0 | 0 | 1 | 1 | 0 |
| Burton, Jared, Athletics | .714 | 5 | 1 | 4 | 2 | 7 | 0 |
| Caldwell, Daniel, Cubs | 1.000 | 14 | 1 | 4 | 0 | 5 | 0 |
| Callahan, Ryan, Giants * | 1.000 | 8 | 1 | 3 | 0 | 4 | 0 |
| Carela, Carlos, Athletics | .000 | 1 | 0 | 0 | 0 | 0 | 0 |
| Carter, Eric, Mariners | .800 | 13 | 2 | 6 | 2 | 10 | 1 |
| Casanova, Nicholas, Rangers | .500 | 4 | 1 | 0 | 1 | 2 | 0 |
| Cepeda, Benigro, Giants | .833 | 11 | 4 | 1 | 1 | 6 | 1 |
| Ciccotelli, Michael, Mariners * | 1.000 | 8 | 0 | 1 | 0 | 1 | 0 |
| Clement, Donald, Mariners | .900 | 15 | 2 | 7 | 1 | 10 | 0 |
| Clow, Josh, Roylas | 1.000 | 12 | 4 | 4 | 0 | 8 | 0 |
| Coffey, Andrew, Royals * | .857 | 13 | 3 | 3 | 1 | 7 | 0 |
| Colbert, Henry, Padres | 1.000 | 3 | 0 | 1 | 0 | 1 | 0 |
| Corbett, Jason, Angels | .500 | 17 | 0 | 2 | 2 | 4 | 0 |
| Corbin, John, Cubs | 1.000 | 1 | 1 | 1 | 0 | 2 | 0 |
| Cordier, Erik, Royals | .889 | 11 | 2 | 14 | 2 | 18 | 1 |
| Coutlangus, Jonathan, Giants * | .000 | 1 | 0 | 0 | 0 | 0 | 0 |
| Cruz Chavez, Rafael, Angels | .500 | 13 | 1 | 1 | 2 | 4 | 0 |
| Cyr, Eric, Angels * | .000 | 1 | 0 | 0 | 0 | 0 | 0 |
| Damico, Yovany, Royals | 1.000 | 20 | 1 | 3 | 0 | 4 | 0 |
| De Los Santos, Francisco, Rangers | 1.000 | 14 | 1 | 4 | 0 | 5 | 0 |
| De Montigny, Mat, Padres | 1.000 | 16 | 0 | 3 | 0 | 3 | 0 |

| Player, Team | Pct. | G | PO | A | E | TC | DP |
|---|---|---|---|---|---|---|---|
| Delabar, Steven, Padres | .750 | 14 | 2 | 4 | 2 | 8 | 1 |
| Delie, Franky, Cubs | .333 | 5 | 1 | 0 | 2 | 3 | 0 |
| Diaz, Gener, Rangers | 1.000 | 11 | 1 | 2 | 0 | 3 | 0 |
| Diggins, Ben, Brewers | 1.000 | 4 | 1 | 0 | 0 | 1 | 0 |
| Dorn, Tim, Mariners | 1.000 | 13 | 0 | 1 | 0 | 1 | 0 |
| Douillard, Jonathan, Cubs | .000 | 1 | 0 | 0 | 0 | 0 | 0 |
| Eckley, Jacob, Royals * | 1.000 | 8 | 1 | 1 | 0 | 2 | 0 |
| Fagan, Paul, Mariners * | .941 | 12 | 3 | 13 | 1 | 17 | 1 |
| Fairbanks, Scott, Athletics | .750 | 14 | 0 | 3 | 1 | 4 | 0 |
| Farrach, Juan, Giants * | 1.000 | 9 | 1 | 5 | 0 | 6 | 0 |
| Feldman, Scott, Rangers | 1.000 | 4 | 1 | 3 | 0 | 4 | 0 |
| Fermin, Jorge, Brewers | .250 | 13 | 1 | 0 | 3 | 4 | 0 |
| Fernando, Pedro, Rangers | 1.000 | 14 | 1 | 6 | 0 | 7 | 0 |
| Foppert, Jesse, Giants | .000 | 1 | 0 | 0 | 0 | 0 | 0 |
| Forbes, Terry, Mariners | .000 | 8 | 0 | 0 | 0 | 0 | 0 |
| Foster, Benjamin, Rangers * | .842 | 15 | 3 | 13 | 3 | 19 | 0 |
| Fuller, Justin, Angels * | .500 | 1 | 1 | 0 | 1 | 2 | 0 |
| Gallagher, Sean, Cubs | 1.000 | 10 | 1 | 1 | 0 | 2 | 0 |
| Gallardo, Yovani, Brewers | 1.000 | 6 | 0 | 5 | 0 | 5 | 0 |
| Gamboa, Felix, Angels | .750 | 9 | 3 | 3 | 2 | 8 | 0 |
| Garcia, Eliszer, Royals * | 1.000 | 19 | 2 | 3 | 0 | 5 | 0 |
| Garcia, Miguel, Brewers | 1.000 | 8 | 1 | 3 | 0 | 4 | 1 |
| Garner, Jeff, Brewers | .500 | 8 | 1 | 1 | 2 | 4 | 0 |
| Geraldo, Jose, Padres | 1.000 | 2 | 1 | 1 | 0 | 2 | 0 |
| Goins, Mitch, Royals | 1.000 | 13 | 4 | 6 | 0 | 10 | 0 |
| Gornati, Tom, Giants | .833 | 12 | 4 | 1 | 1 | 6 | 1 |
| Grasley, Stephen, Mariners | 1.000 | 16 | 2 | 4 | 0 | 6 | 0 |
| Gray, Jeffrey, Athletics | .875 | 14 | 1 | 6 | 1 | 8 | 1 |
| Guzman, Slym, Angels | 1.000 | 3 | 0 | 1 | 0 | 1 | 0 |
| Hagerty, Luke, Cubs * | .667 | 4 | 1 | 3 | 2 | 6 | 2 |
| Hamilton, Clayton, Padres | 1.000 | 3 | 0 | 1 | 0 | 1 | 0 |
| Haro, Jeremy, Cubs | 1.000 | 7 | 0 | 1 | 0 | 1 | 0 |
| Hawk, Tommy, Brewers | 1.000 | 2 | 1 | 1 | 0 | 2 | 0 |
| Hedrick, Justin, Giants | .000 | 2 | 0 | 0 | 0 | 0 | 0 |
| Heuser, James, Athletics * | .778 | 15 | 1 | 6 | 2 | 9 | 0 |
| Hill, Andy, Angels | 1.000 | 11 | 0 | 2 | 0 | 2 | 0 |
| Hurley, Eric, Rangers | 1.000 | 6 | 2 | 3 | 0 | 5 | 0 |
| Irvin, Tony, Rangers | 1.000 | 12 | 0 | 1 | 0 | 1 | 0 |
| Jaimes, Jose, Rangers | .667 | 15 | 1 | 3 | 2 | 6 | 0 |
| James, Craig, Mariners | 1.000 | 10 | 1 | 0 | 0 | 1 | 0 |
| James, Delvin, Angels | .000 | 1 | 0 | 0 | 0 | 0 | 0 |
| Jenkins, Billy, PDR | 1.000 | 18 | 0 | 1 | 0 | 1 | 0 |
| Jenks, Bobby, Angels | 1.000 | 1 | 0 | 1 | 0 | 1 | 0 |
| Jenson, Kevin, Giants | .800 | 12 | 2 | 2 | 1 | 5 | 0 |
| Jimenez Angulo, Fabian, Padres * | .818 | 12 | 3 | 6 | 2 | 11 | 0 |
| Jimenez, Juan, Padres | .333 | 4 | 0 | 1 | 2 | 3 | 0 |
| Johnson, David, Brewers | .667 | 5 | 2 | 0 | 1 | 3 | 0 |
| Jones, Aaron, Cubs | 1.000 | 14 | 1 | 6 | 0 | 7 | 1 |
| Jones, Brian, Cubs | 1.000 | 8 | 1 | 1 | 0 | 2 | 0 |
| Jones, Geoffrey, Padres * | 1.000 | 5 | 0 | 1 | 0 | 1 | 0 |
| Jones, Jeff, Padres | 1.000 | 2 | 1 | 0 | 0 | 1 | 0 |
| Kintzler, Brandon, Padres | .750 | 21 | 1 | 5 | 2 | 8 | 0 |
| Koerber, Scott, Cubs * | .818 | 15 | 2 | 7 | 2 | 11 | 0 |
| Kosow, Jason, Cubs | .000 | 9 | 0 | 0 | 0 | 0 | 0 |
| Krawiec, Aaron, Cubs * | .667 | 4 | 0 | 2 | 1 | 3 | 0 |
| Kroft, Adam, Padres | 1.000 | 13 | 3 | 5 | 0 | 8 | 1 |
| Krosschell, Ben, Padres | .800 | 14 | 2 | 2 | 1 | 5 | 0 |
| Labasta, William, Brewers | .857 | 13 | 3 | 3 | 1 | 7 | 0 |
| Lamont, Tyrone, Mariners | .667 | 13 | 3 | 3 | 3 | 9 | 0 |
| Laureano, Wilfrido, Brewers | .800 | 14 | 4 | 0 | 1 | 5 | 0 |
| Layden, Timothy, Cubs * | .833 | 12 | 2 | 8 | 2 | 12 | 0 |
| Leaist, Ryan, Mariners | 1.000 | 10 | 0 | 2 | 0 | 2 | 0 |
| Lluveres, Rafael, Brewers * | .857 | 12 | 1 | 5 | 1 | 7 | 0 |
| Lockwood, Jon, Mariners | 1.000 | 10 | 1 | 7 | 0 | 8 | 3 |
| Ludwig, Kellen, Giants | 1.000 | 11 | 3 | 2 | 0 | 5 | 0 |
| Lujan, John, Rangers | 1.000 | 10 | 3 | 2 | 0 | 5 | 0 |
| Lundwall, Todd, Giants | 1.000 | 8 | 1 | 1 | 0 | 2 | 0 |
| MacKenzie, Aaron, Angels | 1.000 | 8 | 0 | 5 | 0 | 5 | 1 |
| Malave, Ronny, Brewers | 1.000 | 15 | 0 | 1 | 0 | 1 | 0 |
| Marsello, Jake, Cubs | .000 | 3 | 0 | 0 | 0 | 0 | 0 |
| Martinez, Roman, Mariners | 1.000 | 10 | 2 | 2 | 0 | 4 | 0 |
| Mathes, J.R., Cubs * | .667 | 3 | 0 | 2 | 1 | 3 | 0 |
| Matos, Osiris, Giants | 1.000 | 11 | 4 | 7 | 0 | 11 | 0 |
| McCleland, Bruce, Royals | .846 | 11 | 2 | 9 | 2 | 13 | 0 |
| Melendez, Marlon, Rangers | .800 | 13 | 1 | 3 | 1 | 5 | 0 |
| Mercado, Arnoldo, Giants | .400 | 18 | 1 | 1 | 3 | 5 | 0 |
| Millikan, Bryan, Giants | 1.000 | 3 | 1 | 1 | 0 | 2 | 0 |
| Minor, Matthew, Giants | 1.000 | 9 | 0 | 1 | 0 | 1 | 0 |
| Mitchell, Michael, Athletics | .667 | 7 | 0 | 2 | 1 | 3 | 0 |
| Mola, Heydin, Athletics | 1.000 | 13 | 3 | 5 | 0 | 8 | 0 |
| Montes, Oscar, Brewers | .750 | 13 | 1 | 2 | 1 | 4 | 0 |
| Moore, Dan, Padres * | 1.000 | 3 | 0 | 1 | 0 | 1 | 0 |
| Moore, Nate, Royals | 1.000 | 3 | 0 | 1 | 0 | 1 | 0 |
| Morales, Angelo, Royals | 1.000 | 14 | 4 | 10 | 0 | 14 | 1 |
| Moreno, Victor, Angels | .500 | 14 | 0 | 2 | 2 | 4 | 0 |
| Morillo, Lennyn, Angels | .750 | 13 | 4 | 5 | 3 | 12 | 0 |
| Morrison, Tyler, Brewers | 1.000 | 15 | 4 | 3 | 0 | 7 | 0 |
| Mosquea, Dany, Brewers | 1.000 | 13 | 5 | 10 | 0 | 15 | 0 |
| Muessig, Jeff, Athletics | 1.000 | 6 | 2 | 4 | 0 | 6 | 0 |
| Needham, Joel, Brewers | 1.000 | 5 | 0 | 1 | 0 | 1 | 0 |
| Nelson, Justin, Royals * | 1.000 | 6 | 2 | 4 | 0 | 6 | 0 |
| Newby, Joseph, Athletics | .900 | 14 | 0 | 9 | 1 | 10 | 2 |
| Nolen, Walt, Cubs | .800 | 11 | 0 | 4 | 1 | 5 | 0 |
| Nourie, John, Padres | 1.000 | 2 | 1 | 0 | 0 | 1 | 0 |
| Ortiz, Jose, Cubs | 1.000 | 12 | 3 | 4 | 0 | 7 | 0 |
| Padgett, Michael, Rangers | 1.000 | 12 | 2 | 4 | 0 | 6 | 2 |
| Parillo, Brandon, Brewers * | .500 | 9 | 0 | 2 | 2 | 4 | 0 |
| Park, Chan Ho, Rangers | .875 | 4 | 4 | 3 | 1 | 8 | 1 |
| Pedrozo, Jose, Cubs * | .000 | 1 | 0 | 0 | 0 | 0 | 0 |
| Pena, Henry, Angels | .833 | 11 | 2 | 3 | 1 | 6 | 0 |
| Peralta, Joel, Angels | 1.000 | 2 | 1 | 0 | 0 | 1 | 0 |
| Perez, Roberto, Rangers | .923 | 14 | 1 | 11 | 1 | 13 | 2 |
| Piekarz, Joseph, Athletics * | 1.000 | 17 | 2 | 12 | 0 | 14 | 0 |
| Portorreal, Daniel, Giants | 1.000 | 7 | 0 | 2 | 0 | 2 | 0 |
| Pratt, Andy, Cubs * | 1.000 | 4 | 0 | 1 | 0 | 1 | 0 |
| Putman, Rickey, Giants | .000 | 8 | 0 | 0 | 0 | 0 | 0 |
| Ramirez, Ivan, Rangers * | 1.000 | 16 | 1 | 1 | 0 | 2 | 0 |
| Rayborn, Chris, Padres | 1.000 | 13 | 1 | 9 | 0 | 10 | 1 |
| Robertson, Connor, Athletics | .909 | 25 | 5 | 5 | 1 | 11 | 0 |
| Robertson, Luke, Athletics | .750 | 4 | 1 | 2 | 1 | 4 | 0 |
| Rodriguez, Pedro, Cubs | .500 | 10 | 0 | 2 | 2 | 4 | 0 |
| Rodriguez, Rafael, Angels | 1.000 | 4 | 2 | 4 | 0 | 6 | 0 |
| Rodriguez, William, Athletics * | 1.000 | 5 | 0 | 1 | 0 | 1 | 0 |
| Rogers, Mark, Brewers | 1.000 | 9 | 0 | 3 | 0 | 3 | 0 |
| Roque, Christopher, Angels | 1.000 | 20 | 1 | 2 | 0 | 3 | 0 |
| Rosa, Carlos, Royals | 1.000 | 4 | 0 | 1 | 0 | 1 | 0 |
| Rosario, Julio, Royals | .875 | 15 | 2 | 5 | 1 | 8 | 0 |
| Rowe, Joe, Angels | .800 | 13 | 3 | 5 | 2 | 10 | 0 |
| Ryu, Jae-kuk, Cubs | 1.000 | 2 | 0 | 1 | 0 | 1 | 0 |
| Salankey, Caleb, Giants | .750 | 11 | 1 | 5 | 2 | 8 | 0 |
| Sanchez, Jonathan, Giants * | 1.000 | 9 | 2 | 6 | 0 | 8 | 1 |
| Sanchez, Jose, Giants | 1.000 | 17 | 2 | 1 | 0 | 3 | 1 |
| Santana, Andy, Cubs * | .778 | 10 | 2 | 5 | 2 | 9 | 0 |
| Santiago, Julio, Mariners * | 1.000 | 3 | 1 | 0 | 0 | 1 | 0 |
| Santo, Joel, Padres | .600 | 5 | 1 | 2 | 2 | 5 | 0 |
| Schappert, Paul, Cubs * | .000 | 7 | 0 | 0 | 0 | 0 | 0 |
| Scheffel, Dustin, Rangers | .000 | 6 | 0 | 0 | 0 | 0 | 0 |
| Schlact, Michael, Rangers | 1.000 | 10 | 0 | 6 | 0 | 6 | 0 |
| Seely, Nicholas, Rangers | 1.000 | 15 | 2 | 1 | 0 | 3 | 0 |
| Semerano, Robert, Athletics | .875 | 21 | 8 | 6 | 2 | 16 | 1 |
| Shanks, Edward, Padres | 1.000 | 19 | 0 | 2 | 0 | 2 | 0 |
| Shaver, Christopher, Cubs * | .000 | 2 | 0 | 0 | 0 | 0 | 0 |
| Shearer, Kelly, Angels * | .875 | 13 | 1 | 6 | 1 | 8 | 0 |
| Snyder, Jason, Mariners | .833 | 6 | 3 | 2 | 1 | 6 | 0 |
| Sokoll, John, Royals * | 1.000 | 16 | 1 | 2 | 0 | 3 | 0 |
| Solis, Jairo, Giants | 1.000 | 22 | 2 | 1 | 0 | 3 | 0 |
| Steele, Mike, Mariners | .000 | 2 | 0 | 0 | 0 | 0 | 0 |
| Steidlmayer, Luke, Padres | 1.000 | 3 | 0 | 1 | 0 | 1 | 0 |
| Steik, Richard, Padres | 1.000 | 14 | 1 | 1 | 0 | 2 | 0 |
| Stutes, Kyle, Padres * | 1.000 | 20 | 0 | 6 | 0 | 6 | 0 |
| Sundstrom, Mathew, Mariners | .000 | 4 | 0 | 0 | 0 | 0 | 0 |
| Sweeney, Michael, Angels * | 1.000 | 9 | 0 | 1 | 0 | 1 | 0 |
| Tennyson, Adam, Royals | .857 | 15 | 2 | 4 | 1 | 7 | 0 |
| Thompson, Nick, Cubs | 1.000 | 11 | 1 | 2 | 0 | 3 | 0 |
| Tindell, Matt, Mariners | .000 | 4 | 0 | 0 | 0 | 0 | 0 |
| Torres, Luis, Athletics | 1.000 | 15 | 4 | 13 | 0 | 17 | 0 |
| Torres, Luis, Athletics | 1.000 | 15 | 4 | 13 | 0 | 17 | 0 |
| Tucker, Cardoza, Mariners | 1.000 | 2 | 0 | 2 | 0 | 2 | 0 |
| Tucker, Rusty, Padres * | 1.000 | 10 | 0 | 1 | 0 | 1 | 0 |
| Valencia, Jose, Angels | 1.000 | 14 | 1 | 2 | 0 | 3 | 0 |
| Ventura, Robert, Giants | .909 | 11 | 6 | 4 | 1 | 11 | 0 |
| Wear, Greg, Mariners | .000 | 2 | 0 | 0 | 0 | 0 | 0 |
| Webb, Ryan, Athletics | 1.000 | 8 | 0 | 3 | 0 | 3 | 0 |
| Weber, Ben, Angels | .000 | 1 | 0 | 0 | 0 | 0 | 0 |
| Whittington, Anthony, Angels * | 1.000 | 3 | 0 | 3 | 0 | 3 | 0 |
| Wilson, Brendan, Angels | .917 | 14 | 5 | 6 | 1 | 12 | 0 |
| Woerman, Joe, Mariners | 1.000 | 6 | 2 | 4 | 0 | 6 | 1 |
| Wylie, Jason, Cubs | .000 | 3 | 0 | 0 | 1 | 1 | 0 |
| Yepez, Jesus, Cubs | 1.000 | 12 | 2 | 15 | 0 | 17 | 0 |
| Yepez, Jesus, Cubs * | 1.000 | 12 | 2 | 15 | 0 | 17 | 0 |
| Yntema, Orlando, Giants | .000 | 2 | 0 | 0 | 0 | 0 | 0 |
| Zbacnik, Billy, Giants * | 1.000 | 17 | 1 | 3 | 0 | 4 | 0 |

# LEAGUE CHAMPIONS

| Year | Team | Pct. |
|---|---|---|
| 1988 | Peoria Brewers | .690 |
| 1989 | Peoria Brewers | .732 |
| 1990 | Peoria Brewers | .679 |
| 1991 | Scottsdale A's | .650 |
| 1992 | Scottsdale A's | .607 |
| 1993 | Scottsdale A's | .636 |
| 1994 | Chandler Cardinals | .607 |
| 1995 | Scottsdale A's | .661 |
| 1996 | Padres | .643 |
| 1997 | Cubs | .618 |
| 1998 | Rockies | .750 |
| 1999 | Athletics | .696 |
| 2000 | Mariners | .709 |
| 2001 | Athletics | .625 |
| 2002 | Cubs | .625 |
| 2003 | Royals-1 | .633 |
| 2004 | Giants | .655 |

# GULF COAST LEAGUE



## LEAGUE OFFICE

**President**
Tom Saffell

**Address**
1503 Clower Creek Dr., H-262
Sarasota, FL 34231

**Phone**
941-966-6407

**Teams***
Braves
Dodgers
Marlins
Mets
Nationals
Phillies
Pirates
Reds
Red Sox
Tigers
Twins
Yankees

*Teams play their games in Bradenton, Clearwater, Fort Myers, Jupiter, Kissimmee, Lakeland, Melbourne, Port St. Lucie, Sarasota, Tampa and Vero Beach.

## 2004 FINAL STANDINGS

### EASTERN DIVISION

| Team | W | L | T | Pct. | GB |
|---|---|---|---|---|---|
| Mets | 36 | 24 | - | .600 | ... |
| Marlins | 31 | 29 | - | .517 | 5.0 |
| Dodgers | 31 | 29 | - | .517 | 5.0 |
| Expos | 22 | 38 | - | .367 | 14.0 |

### NORTHERN DIVISION

| Team | W | L | T | Pct. | GB |
|---|---|---|---|---|---|
| Yankees | 36 | 23 | - | .610 | ... |
| Phillies | 36 | 24 | - | .600 | 0.5 |
| Tigers | 24 | 36 | - | .400 | 12.5 |
| Braves | 23 | 36 | - | .390 | 13.0 |

### SOUTHERN DIVISION

| Team | W | L | T | Pct. | GB |
|---|---|---|---|---|---|
| Red Sox | 34 | 24 | - | .586 | ... |
| Twins | 31 | 26 | - | .544 | 2.5 |
| Pirates | 30 | 28 | - | .517 | 4.5 |
| Reds | 20 | 37 | - | .351 | 13.5 |

## COMPOSITE

| Team | W | L | T | PCT | GB | YAN | PHI | MTS | RSX | TWI | PIR | MRL | DGR | TGR | BRV | EXP | RDS |
|---|---|---|---|---|---|---|---|---|---|---|---|---|---|---|---|---|---|
| Yankees (Yankees) | 36 | 23 | - | .610 | X | 10 | 0 | 0 | 0 | 0 | 0 | 0 | 14 | 12 | 0 | 0 | |
| Phillies (Phillies) | 36 | 24 | - | .600 | .5 | 10 | X | 0 | 0 | 0 | 0 | 0 | 0 | 14 | 12 | 0 | 0 |
| Mets (Mets) | 36 | 24 | - | .600 | .5 | 0 | 0 | X | 0 | 0 | 0 | 15 | 10 | 0 | 0 | 11 | 0 |
| Red Sox (Red Sox) | 34 | 24 | - | .586 | 1.5 | 0 | 0 | 0 | X | 10 | 13 | 0 | 0 | 0 | 0 | 0 | 11 |
| Twins (Twins) | 31 | 26 | - | .544 | 4 | 0 | 0 | 0 | 10 | X | 8 | 0 | 0 | 0 | 0 | 0 | 13 |
| Pirates (Pirates) | 30 | 28 | - | .517 | 5.5 | 0 | 0 | 0 | 7 | 10 | X | 0 | 0 | 0 | 0 | 0 | 13 |
| Marlins (Marlins) | 31 | 29 | - | .517 | 5.5 | 0 | 0 | 5 | 0 | 0 | 0 | X | 11 | 0 | 0 | 15 | 0 |
| Dodgers (Dodgers) | 31 | 29 | - | .517 | 5.5 | 0 | 0 | 10 | 0 | 0 | 0 | 9 | X | 0 | 0 | 12 | 0 |
| Tigers (Tigers) | 24 | 36 | - | .400 | 12.5 | 6 | 6 | 0 | 0 | 0 | 0 | 0 | 0 | X | 12 | 0 | 0 |
| Braves (Braves) | 23 | 36 | - | .390 | 13 | 7 | 8 | 0 | 0 | 0 | 0 | 0 | 0 | 8 | X | 0 | 0 |
| Expos (Expos) | 22 | 38 | - | .367 | 14.5 | 0 | 0 | 9 | 0 | 0 | 0 | 5 | 8 | 0 | 0 | X | 0 |
| Reds (Reds) | 20 | 37 | - | .351 | 15 | 0 | 0 | 0 | 7 | 6 | 7 | 0 | 0 | 0 | 0 | 0 | X |

Club names are major league affiliations.

PLAYOFFS: Red Sox defeated Mets one game to none; Yankees defeated Red Sox two games to none to win championship.

REGULAR-SEASON ATTENDANCE: No total attendance figures reported.

MANAGERS: Braves, Ralph Heriquez; Dodgers, Luis Salazar; Expos, Arturo Defreites; Marlins, Tim Cossins; Mets, Brett Butler; Phillies, Roly Dearmas; Pirates, Woody Huyke; Reds, Luis Aguayo; Red Sox, Ralph Treuel; Tigers, Kevin Bradshaw; Twins, Riccardo Ingram; Yankees, Oscar Acosta.

ALL-STAR TEAM: 1B—Carlos Torres, Red Sox; 2B—Jesus Soto; Dodgers; 3B—Jamie Hoffman, Dodgers; SS—Sean Henry, Mets; OF—Jonathan Tierce, Yankees; OF—Jilmer Arratia, Twins; OF—Yosvani Almario-Cabrera, Yankees; C—Jesus Flores, Mets; P—Scott Mitchinson, Twins; Reliever—Howar Zuleta, Dodgers. Manager of the Year—Oscar Acosta, Yankees.

## 2004 BATTING

### TEAM

| Team | G | TPA | AB | R | H | TB | 2B | 3B | HR | RBI | SH | SF | HP | BB | IBB | SO | SB | CS | GDP | LOB | ShO | Avg. | OBP | Slg. |
|---|---|---|---|---|---|---|---|---|---|---|---|---|---|---|---|---|---|---|---|---|---|---|---|---|
| Red Sox | 58 | 2191 | 1923 | 298 | 533 | 749 | 101 | 14 | 29 | 253 | 13 | 20 | 44 | 191 | 1 | 347 | 63 | 24 | 44 | 436 | 2 | .277 | .353 | .389 |
| Yankees | 59 | 2140 | 1897 | 257 | 498 | 684 | 79 | 13 | 27 | 221 | 6 | 14 | 28 | 190 | 3 | 428 | 72 | 32 | 40 | 419 | 3 | .263 | .336 | .361 |
| Mets | 60 | 2246 | 1970 | 297 | 515 | 733 | 95 | 21 | 27 | 247 | 21 | 5 | 42 | 207 | 5 | 441 | 70 | 43 | 26 | 415 | 2 | .261 | .344 | .372 |
| Dodgers | 60 | 2322 | 2086 | 288 | 539 | 758 | 90 | 27 | 25 | 233 | 21 | 16 | 35 | 163 | 6 | 427 | 63 | 28 | 38 | 434 | 3 | .258 | .320 | .363 |
| Twins | 57 | 2109 | 1853 | 245 | 471 | 631 | 79 | 12 | 19 | 218 | 17 | 20 | 48 | 171 | 1 | 362 | 64 | 24 | 36 | 429 | 4 | .254 | .330 | .341 |
| Pirates | 58 | 2109 | 1879 | 255 | 476 | 681 | 98 | 19 | 23 | 211 | 13 | 26 | 40 | 151 | 4 | 396 | 60 | 19 | 29 | 400 | 4 | .253 | .318 | .362 |
| Phillies | 60 | 2142 | 1909 | 267 | 475 | 708 | 79 | 14 | 42 | 239 | 10 | 15 | 31 | 177 | 1 | 476 | 55 | 11 | 25 | 419 | 6 | .249 | .320 | .371 |
| Marlins | 60 | 2208 | 1931 | 273 | 465 | 625 | 94 | 15 | 12 | 237 | 3 | 17 | 52 | 205 | 1 | 463 | 62 | 35 | 29 | 406 | 4 | .241 | .327 | .324 |
| Braves | 59 | 2099 | 1901 | 226 | 448 | 673 | 80 | 11 | 41 | 198 | 6 | 14 | 23 | 153 | 0 | 504 | 64 | 16 | 35 | 376 | 6 | .236 | .298 | .354 |
| Tigers | 60 | 2207 | 1964 | 234 | 459 | 653 | 62 | 18 | 32 | 201 | 13 | 11 | 38 | 178 | 4 | 555 | 64 | 21 | 44 | 417 | 10 | .234 | .308 | .332 |
| Expos | 60 | 2142 | 1856 | 216 | 414 | 560 | 73 | 11 | 17 | 181 | 14 | 17 | 41 | 212 | 2 | 458 | 60 | 33 | 37 | 411 | 9 | .223 | .314 | .302 |
| Reds | 57 | 2036 | 1759 | 198 | 374 | 554 | 69 | 21 | 23 | 175 | 16 | 16 | 55 | 190 | 2 | 509 | 70 | 28 | 30 | 392 | 7 | .213 | .306 | .315 |

# INDIVIDUAL

## TOP QUALIFIERS FOR BATTING CHAMPIONSHIP

Minimum 162 plate appearances. *Lefthanded batter. †Switch-hitter.

| Player, Team | G | TPA | AB | R | H | TB | 2B | 3B | HR | RBI | SH | SF | HP | BB | IBB | SO | SB | CS | GDP | Avg. | OBP | Slg. |
|---|---|---|---|---|---|---|---|---|---|---|---|---|---|---|---|---|---|---|---|---|---|---|
| Tierce, Jonathan, Yankees * | 40 | 162 | 147 | 26 | 53 | 69 | 11 | 1 | 1 | 14 | 0 | 0 | 1 | 14 | 0 | 16 | 13 | 4 | 2 | .361 | .420 | .469 |
| Portes, Juan, Twins | 44 | 188 | 168 | 24 | 55 | 89 | 8 | 1 | 8 | 31 | 1 | 3 | 4 | 12 | 0 | 28 | 4 | 2 | 2 | .327 | .380 | .530 |
| Arratia, Jilmer, Twins | 49 | 192 | 175 | 16 | 56 | 75 | 9 | 2 | 2 | 29 | 3 | 1 | 3 | 10 | 0 | 25 | 12 | 1 | 4 | .320 | .365 | .429 |
| Hoffmann, Jamie, Dodgers * | 60 | 254 | 229 | 40 | 71 | 105 | 8 | 7 | 4 | 36 | 0 | 1 | 0 | 24 | 4 | 38 | 14 | 5 | 6 | .310 | .374 | .459 |
| Messner, Nathan, Marlins | 44 | 171 | 155 | 23 | 48 | 61 | 7 | 0 | 2 | 29 | 0 | 3 | 0 | 13 | 0 | 36 | 2 | 4 | 1 | .310 | .357 | .394 |
| Sutherland, David, Dodgers * | 50 | 169 | 153 | 22 | 46 | 54 | 2 | 3 | 0 | 14 | 1 | 1 | 5 | 9 | 0 | 15 | 4 | 0 | 5 | .301 | .357 | .353 |
| Peterson, James, Dodgers * | 47 | 192 | 176 | 19 | 52 | 88 | 14 | 2 | 6 | 32 | 0 | 2 | 1 | 13 | 0 | 38 | 2 | 1 | 6 | .295 | .344 | .500 |
| Golson, Gregory, Phillies | 47 | 201 | 183 | 34 | 54 | 75 | 8 | 5 | 1 | 22 | 1 | 2 | 5 | 10 | 0 | 54 | 12 | 2 | 2 | .295 | .345 | .410 |
| Soto, Jesus, Dodgers † | 48 | 187 | 171 | 33 | 50 | 77 | 11 | 2 | 4 | 18 | 3 | 0 | 3 | 10 | 1 | 18 | 5 | 3 | 2 | .292 | .342 | .450 |
| Wells, Cory, Mets | 44 | 163 | 148 | 23 | 43 | 66 | 12 | 1 | 3 | 21 | 1 | 0 | 3 | 11 | 0 | 39 | 9 | 3 | 0 | .291 | .352 | .446 |
| Graham, Mitchell, Phillies | 47 | 182 | 159 | 28 | 45 | 58 | 4 | 3 | 1 | 13 | 3 | 1 | 5 | 14 | 0 | 45 | 6 | 2 | 4 | .283 | .358 | .365 |
| Caple, Tom, Red Sox | 46 | 179 | 149 | 30 | 42 | 54 | 7 | 1 | 1 | 19 | 0 | 3 | 5 | 22 | 0 | 14 | 6 | 2 | 2 | .282 | .385 | .362 |
| Henry, Sean, Mets | 56 | 228 | 202 | 35 | 57 | 88 | 9 | 5 | 4 | 30 | 0 | 0 | 4 | 22 | 0 | 43 | 10 | 6 | 2 | .282 | .364 | .436 |
| Young, Stephen, Tigers † | 42 | 187 | 153 | 27 | 43 | 55 | 4 | 1 | 2 | 14 | 3 | 0 | 8 | 22 | 0 | 17 | 9 | 3 | 2 | .281 | .399 | .359 |
| Ovalle, Edward, Twins | 45 | 189 | 172 | 26 | 48 | 72 | 12 | 3 | 2 | 27 | 0 | 6 | 4 | 7 | 1 | 36 | 5 | 8 | 1 | .279 | .312 | .419 |

DEPARTMENTAL LEADERS: G—Hoffman, 60; AB—Hoffman, 229; R—Hoffman, 40; H—Hoffman, 71; TB—Hoffman, 105; 2B—M. Ramirez, 16; 3B—Hoffman, 7; HR—Four tied with eight; RBI—Hoffman, 36; SH—Dulaney, 5; SF—Ovalle, 6; HP—O. Valdez, 14; BB—Gaerlan, 42; IBB—Hoffman, 4; SO—Laster, 63; SB—Suero, 30; CS—Campusano, 10; GIDP—M. Rodriguez, 8; Slg.—Portes, .530; OBP—Tierce, .420.

## ALL PLAYERS

*Lefthanded batter. †Switch-hitter.

| Player, Team | G | TPA | AB | R | H | TB | 2B | 3B | HR | RBI | SH | SF | HP | BB | IBB | SO | SB | CS | GDP | Avg. | OBP | Slg. |
|---|---|---|---|---|---|---|---|---|---|---|---|---|---|---|---|---|---|---|---|---|---|---|
| Abellera, Joe, Twins | 15 | 52 | 46 | 6 | 8 | 8 | 0 | 0 | 0 | 4 | 0 | 1 | 2 | 3 | 0 | 11 | 1 | 0 | 1 | .174 | .250 | .174 |
| Adduci, James, Marlins * | 49 | 196 | 164 | 21 | 34 | 40 | 4 | 1 | 0 | 27 | 0 | 2 | 6 | 24 | 0 | 42 | 6 | 1 | 2 | .207 | .327 | .244 |
| Almario-Cabrera, Yosvany, Yankees | 41 | 152 | 133 | 23 | 46 | 69 | 9 | 4 | 2 | 17 | 0 | 1 | 0 | 16 | 0 | 24 | 7 | 2 | 3 | .346 | .413 | .519 |
| Amador, Anderson, Yankees | 46 | 173 | 161 | 26 | 34 | 59 | 5 | 1 | 6 | 17 | 0 | 2 | 2 | 8 | 0 | 60 | 2 | 2 | 3 | .211 | .254 | .366 |
| Ambrosini, Anthony, Expos | 5 | 18 | 18 | 1 | 4 | 6 | 2 | 0 | 0 | 1 | 0 | 0 | 0 | 0 | 0 | 0 | 0 | 0 | 0 | .222 | .222 | .333 |
| Arratia, Jilmer, Twins | 49 | 192 | 175 | 16 | 56 | 75 | 9 | 2 | 2 | 29 | 3 | 1 | 3 | 10 | 0 | 25 | 12 | 1 | 4 | .320 | .365 | .429 |
| Austin, Parris, Mets | 35 | 105 | 95 | 13 | 20 | 24 | 4 | 0 | 0 | 8 | 3 | 0 | 1 | 6 | 1 | 28 | 2 | 1 | 0 | .211 | .265 | .253 |
| Baez, Welinson, Phillies | 51 | 194 | 171 | 24 | 40 | 63 | 7 | 2 | 4 | 18 | 0 | 1 | 1 | 21 | 0 | 62 | 3 | 0 | 2 | .234 | .320 | .368 |
| Barksdale, James, Braves | 20 | 52 | 47 | 8 | 12 | 21 | 3 | 0 | 2 | 4 | 0 | 0 | 1 | 4 | 0 | 14 | 0 | 0 | 1 | .255 | .327 | .447 |
| Batista, Rafael, Expos † | 54 | 198 | 160 | 26 | 36 | 43 | 4 | 0 | 1 | 11 | 2 | 1 | 6 | 29 | 0 | 31 | 7 | 8 | 2 | .225 | .362 | .269 |
| Bawden, Thomas, Red Sox | 39 | 145 | 127 | 20 | 31 | 45 | 8 | 0 | 2 | 7 | 3 | 0 | 0 | 15 | 0 | 19 | 0 | 2 | 3 | .244 | .324 | .354 |
| Berry, Vince, Tigers | 24 | 76 | 63 | 7 | 10 | 13 | 0 | 0 | 1 | 8 | 2 | 0 | 2 | 9 | 1 | 31 | 1 | 1 | 0 | .159 | .284 | .206 |
| Blancarte, Dante, Twins * | 36 | 138 | 111 | 10 | 26 | 29 | 3 | 0 | 0 | 15 | 0 | 2 | 2 | 23 | 0 | 17 | 1 | 0 | 1 | .234 | .370 | .261 |
| Bressoud, C.J., Braves | 23 | 53 | 47 | 4 | 9 | 13 | 4 | 0 | 0 | 1 | 0 | 0 | 0 | 6 | 0 | 14 | 0 | 1 | 1 | .191 | .283 | .277 |
| Brezeale, Danny, Braves | 37 | 113 | 104 | 8 | 21 | 28 | 4 | 0 | 1 | 10 | 1 | 2 | 2 | 4 | 0 | 32 | 4 | 0 | 5 | .202 | .241 | .269 |
| Brown, Chris, Twins | 38 | 148 | 139 | 19 | 36 | 49 | 5 | 1 | 2 | 19 | 0 | 1 | 0 | 8 | 0 | 28 | 1 | 1 | 3 | .259 | .297 | .353 |
| Burns, Gregory, Marlins * | 42 | 165 | 136 | 28 | 33 | 46 | 5 | 4 | 0 | 7 | 1 | 0 | 2 | 26 | 0 | 48 | 7 | 7 | 1 | .243 | .372 | .338 |
| Campusano, Jose, Marlins † | 59 | 216 | 196 | 24 | 50 | 69 | 8 | 4 | 1 | 16 | 0 | 1 | 9 | 10 | 0 | 38 | 11 | 10 | 1 | .255 | .319 | .352 |
| Caple, Tom, Red Sox | 46 | 179 | 149 | 30 | 42 | 54 | 7 | 1 | 1 | 19 | 0 | 3 | 5 | 22 | 0 | 14 | 6 | 2 | 2 | .282 | .385 | .362 |
| Carp, Mike, Mets * | 57 | 218 | 191 | 30 | 51 | 75 | 12 | 0 | 4 | 26 | 0 | 0 | 5 | 22 | 3 | 51 | 2 | 1 | 1 | .267 | .358 | .393 |
| Cespedes, Cesar, Phillies † | 34 | 117 | 105 | 13 | 26 | 42 | 4 | 0 | 4 | 13 | 0 | 1 | 1 | 10 | 0 | 35 | 4 | 1 | 0 | .248 | .316 | .400 |
| Character, Johntavis, Reds | 10 | 24 | 20 | 0 | 2 | 3 | 1 | 0 | 0 | 1 | 0 | 0 | 1 | 3 | 0 | 10 | 0 | 0 | 1 | .100 | .250 | .150 |
| Ciprian, Jorge, Marlins | 46 | 142 | 129 | 19 | 27 | 37 | 10 | 0 | 0 | 10 | 0 | 1 | 3 | 9 | 0 | 28 | 6 | 2 | 4 | .209 | .275 | .287 |
| Cobb, Maurice, Expos | 18 | 67 | 61 | 7 | 14 | 25 | 4 | 2 | 1 | 8 | 1 | 1 | 1 | 3 | 0 | 21 | 1 | 0 | 0 | .230 | .273 | .410 |
| Collet, Cody, Tigers | 17 | 39 | 36 | 2 | 7 | 9 | 2 | 0 | 0 | 1 | 1 | 0 | 0 | 2 | 0 | 15 | 1 | 1 | 3 | .194 | .237 | .250 |
| Cordova, Luis, Expos † | 44 | 175 | 160 | 15 | 43 | 64 | 9 | 3 | 2 | 28 | 0 | 2 | 3 | 10 | 0 | 30 | 2 | 2 | 4 | .269 | .320 | .400 |
| Corona, Reegie, Yankees † | 36 | 99 | 92 | 12 | 24 | 29 | 5 | 0 | 0 | 4 | 2 | 0 | 0 | 5 | 0 | 13 | 8 | 2 | 1 | .261 | .299 | .315 |
| Covington, Christopher, Pirates | 18 | 54 | 45 | 4 | 3 | 3 | 0 | 0 | 0 | 2 | 1 | 1 | 1 | 6 | 0 | 19 | 5 | 0 | 0 | .067 | .189 | .067 |
| Cresswell, Charles, Phillies * | 16 | 55 | 49 | 4 | 12 | 13 | 1 | 0 | 0 | 9 | 0 | 1 | 1 | 4 | 0 | 23 | 0 | 0 | 0 | .245 | .309 | .265 |
| Crist, Justin, Dodgers | 33 | 81 | 74 | 10 | 23 | 27 | 4 | 0 | 0 | 4 | 2 | 0 | 1 | 4 | 0 | 9 | 3 | 1 | 0 | .311 | .354 | .365 |
| Cuevas, Phillip, Phillies | 9 | 28 | 27 | 3 | 7 | 7 | 0 | 0 | 0 | 2 | 1 | 0 | 0 | 0 | 0 | 5 | 0 | 0 | 1 | .259 | .259 | .259 |
| Dangler, Andy, Twins | 19 | 68 | 58 | 3 | 16 | 23 | 5 | 1 | 0 | 7 | 0 | 0 | 1 | 9 | 0 | 13 | 1 | 0 | 0 | .276 | .382 | .397 |
| Davis, Leonard, Expos * | 42 | 166 | 143 | 18 | 26 | 43 | 6 | 1 | 3 | 14 | 0 | 0 | 4 | 19 | 1 | 58 | 2 | 3 | 3 | .182 | .295 | .301 |
| De Leon, Santo, Tigers | 38 | 148 | 139 | 14 | 38 | 55 | 8 | 3 | 1 | 15 | 1 | 0 | 2 | 5 | 1 | 30 | 1 | 0 | 3 | .273 | .308 | .396 |
| De Vrieze, Jeffrey, Marlins | 21 | 35 | 32 | 2 | 6 | 8 | 2 | 0 | 0 | 5 | 0 | 0 | 2 | 1 | 0 | 17 | 0 | 0 | 0 | .188 | .257 | .250 |
| Diaz, Ramon, Expos | 39 | 146 | 130 | 10 | 28 | 36 | 6 | 1 | 0 | 6 | 0 | 0 | 4 | 12 | 1 | 32 | 1 | 0 | 5 | .215 | .301 | .277 |
| Diggs, Terry, Pirates * | 6 | 14 | 12 | 1 | 2 | 4 | 0 | 1 | 0 | 1 | 0 | 0 | 1 | 1 | 0 | 1 | 1 | 0 | 0 | .167 | .286 | .333 |
| Dominguez, Raul, Yankees * | 45 | 132 | 113 | 15 | 31 | 36 | 2 | 0 | 1 | 12 | 0 | 1 | 2 | 14 | 0 | 20 | 1 | 0 | 5 | .274 | .362 | .319 |
| Duenas, Yobal, Yankees | 4 | 12 | 11 | 2 | 2 | 2 | 0 | 0 | 0 | 1 | 0 | 0 | 0 | 1 | 0 | 0 | 0 | 0 | 0 | .182 | .250 | .182 |
| Dulaney, Todd, Mets | 38 | 120 | 105 | 15 | 31 | 35 | 2 | 1 | 0 | 14 | 5 | 0 | 0 | 10 | 0 | 10 | 5 | 5 | 3 | .295 | .357 | .333 |
| Easley, Austin, Red Sox | 13 | 53 | 50 | 6 | 19 | 23 | 4 | 0 | 0 | 8 | 0 | 0 | 0 | 3 | 0 | 14 | 5 | 0 | 1 | .380 | .415 | .460 |
| Encarnacion, Salvador, Marlins | 33 | 115 | 104 | 11 | 21 | 29 | 5 | 0 | 1 | 13 | 0 | 1 | 4 | 6 | 0 | 28 | 0 | 1 | 1 | .202 | .270 | .279 |
| Esparragoza, Eyoxy, Reds | 7 | 21 | 20 | 1 | 0 | 0 | 0 | 0 | 0 | 0 | 0 | 0 | 1 | 0 | 0 | 10 | 0 | 0 | 0 | .000 | .048 | .000 |
| Evans, Nicholas, Mets | 50 | 196 | 182 | 36 | 47 | 84 | 10 | 3 | 7 | 27 | 0 | 0 | 0 | 14 | 0 | 51 | 3 | 2 | 3 | .258 | .311 | .462 |
| Feiner, Korey, Twins | 22 | 68 | 53 | 7 | 9 | 12 | 3 | 0 | 0 | 4 | 2 | 1 | 4 | 8 | 0 | 7 | 2 | 0 | 2 | .170 | .318 | .226 |
| Fletcher, Simon, Twins | 22 | 69 | 58 | 11 | 12 | 16 | 1 | 0 | 1 | 3 | 1 | 0 | 3 | 7 | 0 | 24 | 6 | 0 | 1 | .207 | .324 | .276 |
| Foster, Jordan, Tigers | 19 | 66 | 61 | 4 | 13 | 20 | 4 | 0 | 1 | 9 | 0 | 0 | 0 | 5 | 0 | 12 | 2 | 0 | 1 | .213 | .273 | .328 |
| Franco, Ambiorix, Reds | 20 | 62 | 58 | 2 | 11 | 12 | 1 | 0 | 0 | 5 | 0 | 0 | 1 | 3 | 0 | 12 | 0 | 1 | 2 | .190 | .242 | .207 |
| Franco, Luis, Marlins † | 33 | 91 | 79 | 7 | 12 | 14 | 2 | 0 | 0 | 4 | 0 | 1 | 1 | 10 | 0 | 28 | 1 | 0 | 1 | .152 | .253 | .177 |
| Gaerlan, Armand, Mets | 55 | 230 | 185 | 34 | 48 | 66 | 7 | 4 | 1 | 15 | 3 | 0 | 0 | 42 | 0 | 35 | 6 | 4 | 4 | .259 | .396 | .357 |
| Gil, Rotsen, Dodgers † | 29 | 85 | 79 | 11 | 24 | 41 | 4 | 5 | 1 | 10 | 2 | 0 | 1 | 3 | 0 | 15 | 0 | 0 | 0 | .304 | .337 | .519 |
| Golson, Gregory, Phillies | 47 | 201 | 183 | 34 | 54 | 75 | 8 | 5 | 1 | 22 | 1 | 2 | 5 | 10 | 0 | 54 | 12 | 2 | 2 | .295 | .345 | .410 |
| Gomez, Carlos, Mets | 19 | 76 | 71 | 10 | 19 | 26 | 7 | 0 | 0 | 11 | 0 | 1 | 2 | 2 | 0 | 9 | 9 | 1 | 1 | .268 | .303 | .366 |
| Gonzalez, Hector, Yankees † | 34 | 106 | 93 | 15 | 27 | 31 | 4 | 0 | 0 | 12 | 0 | 0 | 2 | 11 | 0 | 18 | 2 | 2 | 2 | .290 | .377 | .333 |

| Player, Team | G | TPA | AB | R | H | TB | 2B | 3B | HR | RBI | SH | SF | HP | BB | IBB | SO | SB | CS | GDP | Avg. | OBP | Slg. |
|---|---|---|---|---|---|---|---|---|---|---|---|---|---|---|---|---|---|---|---|---|---|---|
| Goodson, Robert, Phillies * | 30 | 113 | 97 | 12 | 18 | 31 | 1 | 0 | 4 | 14 | 0 | 1 | 0 | 15 | 0 | 24 | 2 | 0 | 2 | .186 | .292 | .320 |
| Graham, Mitchell, Phillies | 47 | 182 | 159 | 28 | 45 | 58 | 4 | 3 | 1 | 13 | 3 | 1 | 5 | 14 | 0 | 45 | 6 | 2 | 4 | .283 | .358 | .365 |
| Grullon, Leonardo, Tigers | 48 | 187 | 175 | 18 | 38 | 60 | 7 | 3 | 3 | 20 | 1 | 2 | 6 | 3 | 0 | 33 | 9 | 2 | 7 | .217 | .253 | .343 |
| Guerra, Junior, Braves | 33 | 94 | 88 | 10 | 19 | 30 | 8 | 0 | 1 | 14 | 0 | 1 | 1 | 4 | 0 | 18 | 0 | 0 | 1 | .216 | .255 | .341 |
| Guy, Jason, Yankees * | 1 | 4 | 2 | 0 | 0 | 0 | 0 | 0 | 0 | 0 | 0 | 0 | 2 | 0 | 0 | 1 | 0 | 0 | 0 | .000 | .500 | .000 |
| Haag, Ryan, Yankees * | 9 | 26 | 20 | 3 | 5 | 6 | 1 | 0 | 0 | 1 | 0 | 0 | 1 | 5 | 0 | 6 | 2 | 0 | 1 | .250 | .423 | .300 |
| Hamisevicz, Victor, Expos * | 52 | 198 | 160 | 21 | 33 | 38 | 5 | 0 | 0 | 9 | 0 | 3 | 4 | 31 | 0 | 35 | 2 | 0 | 2 | .206 | .343 | .238 |
| Harman, Bradley, Phillies | 51 | 200 | 183 | 23 | 42 | 58 | 10 | 0 | 2 | 19 | 1 | 2 | 3 | 11 | 0 | 41 | 2 | 1 | 2 | .230 | .281 | .317 |
| Harp, Troy, Braves | 1 | 1 | 1 | 0 | 0 | 0 | 0 | 0 | 0 | 0 | 0 | 0 | 0 | 0 | 0 | 0 | 0 | 0 | 0 | .000 | .000 | .000 |
| Harper, Anthony, Dodgers | 29 | 116 | 110 | 9 | 29 | 44 | 10 | 1 | 1 | 10 | 0 | 1 | 3 | 2 | 0 | 18 | 2 | 2 | 3 | .264 | .293 | .400 |
| Hawkins, Pedro, Reds | 20 | 65 | 51 | 10 | 10 | 16 | 4 | 1 | 0 | 4 | 2 | 0 | 4 | 8 | 0 | 21 | 2 | 1 | 0 | .196 | .349 | .314 |
| Henry, Sean, Mets | 56 | 228 | 202 | 35 | 57 | 88 | 9 | 5 | 4 | 30 | 0 | 0 | 4 | 22 | 0 | 43 | 10 | 6 | 2 | .282 | .364 | .436 |
| Hoffmann, Jamie, Dodgers * | 60 | 254 | 229 | 40 | 71 | 105 | 8 | 7 | 4 | 36 | 0 | 1 | 0 | 24 | 4 | 38 | 14 | 5 | 6 | .310 | .374 | .459 |
| Holden, Josh, Reds * | 26 | 100 | 89 | 15 | 31 | 38 | 1 | 3 | 0 | 4 | 0 | 0 | 3 | 8 | 1 | 25 | 10 | 6 | 1 | .348 | .420 | .427 |
| Holmann, Mario, Yankees † | 20 | 81 | 66 | 12 | 17 | 23 | 1 | 1 | 1 | 7 | 0 | 2 | 0 | 13 | 1 | 17 | 10 | 4 | 0 | .258 | .370 | .348 |
| Honey, Raymond, Reds | 17 | 46 | 35 | 2 | 4 | 4 | 0 | 0 | 0 | 4 | 0 | 1 | 3 | 7 | 0 | 13 | 1 | 0 | 0 | .114 | .304 | .114 |
| Infante, Ray, Reds | 26 | 85 | 70 | 8 | 11 | 14 | 3 | 0 | 0 | 4 | 3 | 1 | 4 | 7 | 0 | 12 | 5 | 1 | 0 | .157 | .268 | .200 |
| Jackson, Derry, Dodgers | 47 | 125 | 106 | 17 | 22 | 26 | 2 | 1 | 0 | 12 | 3 | 1 | 3 | 12 | 0 | 43 | 5 | 6 | 0 | .208 | .303 | .245 |
| Jones, Larry, Twins | 30 | 90 | 82 | 10 | 14 | 17 | 0 | 0 | 1 | 6 | 0 | 0 | 2 | 6 | 0 | 31 | 4 | 1 | 2 | .171 | .244 | .207 |
| Jordan, Scooter, Red Sox * | 24 | 105 | 83 | 16 | 25 | 26 | 1 | 0 | 0 | 4 | 2 | 0 | 2 | 18 | 0 | 16 | 5 | 6 | 1 | .301 | .437 | .313 |
| Justice, Jeff, Red Sox | 34 | 130 | 116 | 13 | 35 | 39 | 4 | 0 | 0 | 14 | 0 | 2 | 5 | 7 | 0 | 14 | 2 | 4 | 7 | .302 | .362 | .336 |
| Kalin, Travis, Twins | 27 | 98 | 86 | 10 | 21 | 29 | 5 | 0 | 1 | 11 | 1 | 2 | 1 | 8 | 0 | 18 | 1 | 0 | 2 | .244 | .309 | .337 |
| Kelly, Donald, Tigers * | 3 | 10 | 10 | 2 | 4 | 4 | 0 | 0 | 0 | 0 | 0 | 0 | 0 | 0 | 0 | 2 | 1 | 0 | 0 | .400 | .400 | .400 |
| Kelly, Dustin, Red Sox | 43 | 176 | 152 | 15 | 40 | 52 | 7 | 1 | 1 | 15 | 1 | 2 | 5 | 16 | 0 | 22 | 8 | 3 | 4 | .263 | .349 | .342 |
| Koko, Rubi, Braves | 42 | 115 | 104 | 13 | 13 | 23 | 2 | 1 | 2 | 5 | 1 | 0 | 0 | 9 | 0 | 62 | 8 | 4 | 2 | .125 | .195 | .221 |
| Kropf, Michael, Tigers † | 23 | 65 | 53 | 5 | 11 | 16 | 2 | 0 | 1 | 6 | 2 | 2 | 1 | 7 | 1 | 10 | 2 | 0 | 3 | .208 | .302 | .302 |
| Langham, James, Reds | 28 | 98 | 77 | 14 | 12 | 21 | 4 | 1 | 1 | 7 | 3 | 0 | 10 | 8 | 0 | 34 | 6 | 1 | 0 | .156 | .316 | .273 |
| Laster, Jeramy, Tigers | 43 | 168 | 149 | 23 | 36 | 62 | 6 | 4 | 4 | 17 | 1 | 1 | 0 | 17 | 0 | 63 | 10 | 1 | 0 | .242 | .317 | .416 |
| Lee, Joshua, Tigers * | 38 | 133 | 114 | 14 | 26 | 37 | 2 | 0 | 3 | 10 | 0 | 0 | 1 | 18 | 1 | 39 | 1 | 1 | 3 | .228 | .338 | .325 |
| Leonard, Michael, Red Sox | 30 | 108 | 93 | 7 | 22 | 24 | 2 | 0 | 0 | 10 | 0 | 0 | 3 | 12 | 0 | 12 | 0 | 0 | 2 | .237 | .343 | .258 |
| Levy, Carlos, Yankees † | 20 | 50 | 48 | 4 | 11 | 17 | 0 | 0 | 2 | 8 | 0 | 0 | 1 | 1 | 0 | 25 | 2 | 0 | 0 | .229 | .260 | .354 |
| Lewis, Kenny, Reds * | 8 | 26 | 22 | 5 | 6 | 7 | 1 | 0 | 0 | 2 | 0 | 1 | 0 | 3 | 0 | 10 | 2 | 1 | 0 | .273 | .346 | .318 |
| Linares, Miguel, Tigers | 44 | 162 | 148 | 16 | 35 | 39 | 2 | 1 | 0 | 10 | 0 | 0 | 1 | 13 | 0 | 36 | 4 | 1 | 6 | .236 | .302 | .264 |
| Loyola, Maiko, Pirates | 38 | 138 | 121 | 17 | 31 | 45 | 9 | 1 | 1 | 13 | 0 | 1 | 3 | 13 | 1 | 17 | 4 | 0 | 0 | .256 | .341 | .372 |
| Ludwig, Mike, Dodgers | 22 | 35 | 32 | 1 | 3 | 3 | 0 | 0 | 0 | 0 | 1 | 0 | 1 | 1 | 0 | 7 | 0 | 0 | 1 | .094 | .147 | .094 |
| Lysaught, Michael, Twins | 28 | 82 | 70 | 5 | 13 | 17 | 2 | 1 | 0 | 7 | 0 | 1 | 0 | 11 | 0 | 18 | 1 | 2 | 2 | .186 | .293 | .243 |
| Macfarlane, Andrew, Phillies | 46 | 187 | 166 | 20 | 38 | 55 | 10 | 2 | 1 | 19 | 1 | 2 | 5 | 13 | 0 | 36 | 6 | 0 | 2 | .229 | .301 | .331 |
| Made, Kelington, Pirates | 28 | 96 | 85 | 11 | 18 | 33 | 9 | 0 | 2 | 10 | 0 | 0 | 1 | 10 | 0 | 16 | 0 | 1 | 1 | .212 | .302 | .388 |
| Maldonado, Brahiam, Mets | 47 | 170 | 151 | 21 | 28 | 36 | 3 | 1 | 1 | 12 | 0 | 0 | 3 | 15 | 0 | 49 | 8 | 2 | 4 | .185 | .272 | .238 |
| Marson, Louis, Phillies | 38 | 126 | 113 | 18 | 29 | 44 | 3 | 0 | 4 | 8 | 0 | 0 | 0 | 13 | 0 | 18 | 4 | 0 | 4 | .257 | .333 | .389 |
| Mateo, Ruben, Phillies † | 5 | 17 | 15 | 2 | 2 | 2 | 0 | 0 | 0 | 0 | 1 | 0 | 0 | 1 | 0 | 4 | 0 | 0 | 0 | .133 | .188 | .133 |
| McDonald, James, Dodgers * | 46 | 143 | 125 | 15 | 28 | 32 | 2 | 1 | 0 | 10 | 2 | 3 | 1 | 12 | 0 | 44 | 3 | 2 | 3 | .224 | .291 | .256 |
| McIlvaine, Tim, Twins * | 14 | 33 | 26 | 4 | 6 | 6 | 0 | 0 | 0 | 0 | 1 | 0 | 0 | 6 | 0 | 7 | 0 | 0 | 2 | .231 | .375 | .231 |
| Medero-Stullz, Carlos, Dodgers | 31 | 89 | 77 | 5 | 15 | 18 | 0 | 0 | 1 | 9 | 1 | 3 | 3 | 5 | 0 | 15 | 0 | 0 | 2 | .195 | .261 | .234 |
| Messner, Nathan, Marlins | 44 | 171 | 155 | 23 | 48 | 61 | 7 | 0 | 2 | 29 | 0 | 3 | 0 | 13 | 0 | 36 | 2 | 4 | 1 | .310 | .357 | .394 |
| Middleton, Cory, Tigers | 43 | 157 | 145 | 15 | 34 | 53 | 5 | 1 | 4 | 10 | 0 | 0 | 6 | 5 | 0 | 32 | 2 | 3 | 4 | .234 | .288 | .366 |
| Miller, Cole, Tigers | 40 | 137 | 130 | 14 | 35 | 56 | 4 | 1 | 5 | 16 | 0 | 2 | 0 | 5 | 0 | 37 | 3 | 2 | 3 | .269 | .292 | .431 |
| Mora, Jesus, Dodgers | 43 | 147 | 141 | 16 | 39 | 58 | 10 | 0 | 3 | 15 | 0 | 0 | 2 | 4 | 1 | 32 | 2 | 3 | 1 | .277 | .306 | .411 |
| Mota, Willy, Red Sox | 35 | 139 | 129 | 19 | 38 | 59 | 9 | 3 | 2 | 18 | 2 | 1 | 1 | 6 | 0 | 41 | 6 | 1 | 4 | .295 | .328 | .457 |
| Munos, David, Pirates † | 28 | 102 | 96 | 11 | 29 | 39 | 6 | 2 | 0 | 11 | 1 | 0 | 0 | 5 | 0 | 20 | 5 | 0 | 1 | .302 | .337 | .406 |
| Najac, Greg, Twins * | 38 | 132 | 120 | 19 | 31 | 40 | 5 | 2 | 0 | 13 | 0 | 1 | 1 | 10 | 0 | 20 | 1 | 0 | 3 | .258 | .318 | .333 |
| Ndungidi, Sambu, Dodgers † | 17 | 56 | 52 | 5 | 7 | 12 | 3 | 1 | 0 | 4 | 0 | 0 | 0 | 4 | 0 | 15 | 0 | 0 | 2 | .135 | .196 | .231 |
| Oliveros, Ricky, Mets | 38 | 102 | 92 | 8 | 25 | 32 | 4 | 0 | 1 | 10 | 1 | 0 | 3 | 6 | 0 | 15 | 2 | 2 | 2 | .272 | .337 | .348 |
| Ortega, Raul, Braves † | 36 | 104 | 93 | 11 | 21 | 23 | 2 | 0 | 0 | 5 | 0 | 1 | 2 | 8 | 0 | 26 | 2 | 0 | 2 | .226 | .298 | .247 |
| Ortiz, Yancarlos, Twins † | 29 | 112 | 95 | 11 | 25 | 28 | 3 | 0 | 0 | 7 | 4 | 0 | 1 | 12 | 0 | 14 | 6 | 2 | 2 | .263 | .352 | .295 |
| Ovalle, Edward, Twins | 45 | 189 | 172 | 26 | 48 | 72 | 12 | 3 | 2 | 27 | 0 | 6 | 4 | 7 | 1 | 36 | 5 | 8 | 1 | .279 | .312 | .419 |
| Ovalles, Jose, Expos | 41 | 129 | 108 | 9 | 23 | 25 | 2 | 0 | 0 | 4 | 2 | 1 | 3 | 15 | 0 | 28 | 9 | 5 | 2 | .213 | .323 | .231 |
| Owings, Jon, Braves | 44 | 138 | 124 | 14 | 28 | 44 | 1 | 3 | 3 | 7 | 0 | 0 | 1 | 13 | 0 | 38 | 5 | 1 | 1 | .226 | .304 | .355 |
| Peabody, John, Pirates | 21 | 75 | 59 | 5 | 13 | 16 | 1 | 1 | 0 | 6 | 1 | 2 | 4 | 9 | 0 | 25 | 2 | 0 | 1 | .220 | .351 | .271 |
| Peeples, Jamaal, Tigers * | 30 | 50 | 44 | 4 | 9 | 9 | 0 | 0 | 0 | 3 | 1 | 0 | 1 | 4 | 0 | 24 | 4 | 1 | 0 | .205 | .286 | .205 |
| Pena, Carlos, Dodgers | 39 | 125 | 115 | 15 | 25 | 49 | 4 | 4 | 4 | 21 | 2 | 0 | 2 | 6 | 0 | 38 | 3 | 2 | 4 | .217 | .268 | .426 |
| Pena, Hannsel, Reds | 34 | 114 | 101 | 14 | 19 | 35 | 4 | 0 | 4 | 12 | 0 | 0 | 4 | 9 | 0 | 49 | 6 | 2 | 0 | .188 | .281 | .347 |
| Penalo, Alex, Red Sox † | 22 | 93 | 85 | 15 | 25 | 29 | 4 | 0 | 0 | 11 | 2 | 0 | 0 | 6 | 0 | 17 | 5 | 0 | 1 | .294 | .341 | .341 |
| Peralta, Alexander, Pirates | 32 | 122 | 108 | 22 | 37 | 43 | 4 | 1 | 0 | 11 | 1 | 1 | 4 | 8 | 0 | 12 | 3 | 1 | 2 | .343 | .405 | .398 |
| Perez, Jose, Yankees * | 36 | 121 | 99 | 8 | 20 | 22 | 2 | 0 | 0 | 12 | 2 | 1 | 1 | 16 | 0 | 28 | 12 | 3 | 3 | .202 | .316 | .222 |
| Peterson, James, Dodgers * | 47 | 192 | 176 | 19 | 52 | 88 | 14 | 2 | 6 | 32 | 0 | 2 | 1 | 13 | 0 | 38 | 2 | 1 | 6 | .295 | .344 | .500 |
| Phillips, Nathan, Yankees † | 47 | 175 | 157 | 15 | 38 | 43 | 5 | 0 | 0 | 14 | 0 | 0 | 3 | 15 | 0 | 47 | 1 | 6 | 3 | .242 | .320 | .274 |
| Piazza, Tom, Mets * | 6 | 15 | 13 | 2 | 5 | 6 | 1 | 0 | 0 | 3 | 0 | 0 | 0 | 2 | 0 | 6 | 0 | 1 | 0 | .385 | .467 | .462 |
| Picart, Gregory, Pirates † | 25 | 99 | 86 | 12 | 22 | 25 | 3 | 0 | 0 | 6 | 0 | 2 | 4 | 7 | 0 | 16 | 0 | 3 | 1 | .256 | .333 | .291 |
| Plaza, William, Yankees | 20 | 50 | 41 | 3 | 14 | 16 | 2 | 0 | 0 | 6 | 0 | 0 | 1 | 8 | 0 | 6 | 0 | 1 | 0 | .341 | .460 | .390 |
| Plumsky, Richard, Phillies | 35 | 132 | 112 | 20 | 33 | 57 | 6 | 0 | 6 | 25 | 0 | 1 | 2 | 17 | 0 | 28 | 5 | 0 | 2 | .295 | .394 | .509 |
| Poni, Francis, Pirates | 32 | 111 | 97 | 13 | 25 | 44 | 10 | 0 | 3 | 17 | 1 | 3 | 4 | 6 | 0 | 22 | 0 | 0 | 3 | .258 | .318 | .454 |
| Portes, Juan, Twins | 44 | 188 | 168 | 24 | 55 | 89 | 8 | 1 | 8 | 31 | 1 | 3 | 4 | 12 | 0 | 28 | 4 | 2 | 2 | .327 | .380 | .530 |
| Poterson, Jonathan, Yankees † | 56 | 225 | 198 | 24 | 40 | 70 | 7 | 1 | 7 | 30 | 0 | 4 | 1 | 22 | 2 | 60 | 1 | 0 | 2 | .202 | .280 | .354 |
| Prasch, Edward, Pirates * | 32 | 134 | 118 | 11 | 26 | 36 | 6 | 2 | 0 | 21 | 1 | 1 | 2 | 12 | 0 | 27 | 1 | 1 | 2 | .220 | .301 | .305 |
| Pritz, Bryan, Red Sox | 29 | 99 | 90 | 15 | 24 | 32 | 5 | 0 | 1 | 10 | 0 | 2 | 1 | 6 | 0 | 10 | 4 | 1 | 2 | .267 | .313 | .356 |
| Purkey, Bryan, Dodgers | 8 | 13 | 11 | 2 | 2 | 2 | 0 | 0 | 0 | 2 | 0 | 0 | 0 | 2 | 0 | 4 | 1 | 0 | 0 | .182 | .308 | .182 |
| Purvis, Nate, Red Sox | 7 | 23 | 20 | 1 | 4 | 5 | 1 | 0 | 0 | 1 | 0 | 0 | 0 | 3 | 0 | 5 | 0 | 0 | 0 | .200 | .304 | .250 |
| Raglani, John, Dodgers * | 6 | 22 | 20 | 2 | 6 | 7 | 1 | 0 | 0 | 1 | 0 | 0 | 0 | 2 | 0 | 4 | 2 | 0 | 1 | .300 | .364 | .350 |
| Ramirez, Maximiliano, Braves | 57 | 230 | 204 | 20 | 56 | 98 | 16 | 1 | 8 | 35 | 0 | 4 | 3 | 19 | 0 | 50 | 1 | 0 | 4 | .275 | .339 | .480 |
| Reininger, Jarrett, Reds | 27 | 102 | 86 | 12 | 19 | 32 | 6 | 2 | 1 | 10 | 0 | 0 | 3 | 13 | 0 | 25 | 2 | 0 | 2 | .221 | .343 | .372 |
| Richards, Glen, Braves | 18 | 1 | 0 | 0 | 0 | 0 | 0 | 0 | 0 | 0 | 0 | 0 | 0 | 0 | 0 | 0 | 0 | 0 | 0 | .000 | .000 | .000 |

| Player, Team | G | TPA | AB | R | H | TB | 2B | 3B | HR | RBI | SH | SF | HP | BB | IBB | SO | SB | CS | GDP | Avg. | OBP | Slg. |
|---|---|---|---|---|---|---|---|---|---|---|---|---|---|---|---|---|---|---|---|---|---|---|
| Rivera, Juan, Dodgers † | 52 | 205 | 185 | 28 | 45 | 51 | 6 | 0 | 0 | 14 | 2 | 3 | 2 | 13 | 0 | 30 | 5 | 0 | 1 | .243 | .296 | .276 |
| Roa, Lonny, Reds | 20 | 73 | 65 | 5 | 10 | 14 | 1 | 0 | 1 | 5 | 0 | 0 | 3 | 5 | 0 | 28 | 1 | 0 | 1 | .154 | .247 | .215 |
| Roberts, Brandon, Reds * | 39 | 145 | 123 | 11 | 27 | 34 | 4 | 0 | 1 | 8 | 0 | 0 | 3 | 19 | 1 | 30 | 3 | 1 | 3 | .220 | .338 | .276 |
| Roberts, Lionel, Tigers | 19 | 62 | 58 | 2 | 12 | 16 | 1 | 0 | 1 | 5 | 0 | 1 | 0 | 3 | 0 | 29 | 0 | 0 | 0 | .207 | .242 | .276 |
| Robinson, Mark, Twins † | 41 | 144 | 135 | 11 | 29 | 37 | 3 | 1 | 1 | 14 | 1 | 0 | 3 | 5 | 0 | 24 | 4 | 3 | 3 | .215 | .259 | .274 |
| Rodriguez, Jesus, Marlins | 56 | 216 | 200 | 25 | 50 | 56 | 6 | 0 | 0 | 17 | 1 | 2 | 2 | 11 | 0 | 24 | 3 | 1 | 4 | .250 | .293 | .280 |
| Rodriguez, Manuel, Braves * | 50 | 187 | 179 | 18 | 45 | 70 | 10 | 0 | 5 | 17 | 0 | 1 | 0 | 7 | 0 | 26 | 0 | 1 | 8 | .251 | .278 | .391 |
| Rodriguez, Michael, Braves * | 9 | 35 | 31 | 1 | 8 | 11 | 0 | 0 | 1 | 4 | 0 | 1 | 0 | 3 | 0 | 3 | 1 | 0 | 0 | .258 | .314 | .355 |
| Rogers, Tanner, Marlins | 37 | 131 | 108 | 22 | 30 | 42 | 8 | 2 | 0 | 18 | 1 | 0 | 10 | 12 | 0 | 32 | 6 | 0 | 1 | .278 | .400 | .389 |
| Rojas, Irwil, Yankees * | 30 | 100 | 91 | 7 | 23 | 29 | 4 | 1 | 0 | 13 | 1 | 1 | 3 | 4 | 0 | 7 | 1 | 0 | 3 | .253 | .303 | .319 |
| Rojas, Luis, Expos | 37 | 143 | 125 | 15 | 30 | 44 | 6 | 1 | 2 | 19 | 0 | 3 | 1 | 14 | 0 | 26 | 3 | 4 | 3 | .240 | .315 | .352 |
| Romero, Luis, Yankees † | 36 | 120 | 101 | 14 | 19 | 23 | 1 | 0 | 1 | 8 | 0 | 1 | 6 | 12 | 0 | 21 | 0 | 0 | 2 | .188 | .308 | .228 |
| Roznovsky, Brandon, Expos | 13 | 1 | 1 | 0 | 0 | 0 | 0 | 0 | 0 | 0 | 0 | 0 | 0 | 0 | 0 | 1 | 0 | 0 | 0 | .000 | .000 | .000 |
| Saba, Anthony, Tigers | 15 | 40 | 34 | 3 | 6 | 9 | 1 | 1 | 0 | 4 | 0 | 0 | 2 | 4 | 0 | 12 | 0 | 1 | 0 | .176 | .300 | .265 |
| Salbaran, Orlando, Reds | 14 | 53 | 48 | 4 | 10 | 14 | 1 | 0 | 1 | 4 | 0 | 0 | 0 | 5 | 0 | 9 | 0 | 0 | 2 | .208 | .283 | .292 |
| Sanchez, Carlos, Reds | 44 | 165 | 144 | 11 | 30 | 43 | 8 | 1 | 1 | 13 | 2 | 1 | 3 | 15 | 0 | 35 | 5 | 2 | 4 | .208 | .294 | .299 |
| Sandora, Robert, Expos * | 7 | 24 | 21 | 0 | 2 | 2 | 0 | 0 | 0 | 2 | 0 | 1 | 1 | 1 | 0 | 5 | 0 | 0 | 0 | .095 | .167 | .095 |
| Sandoval, Mayker, Reds | 46 | 184 | 161 | 22 | 41 | 76 | 10 | 5 | 5 | 30 | 0 | 3 | 5 | 15 | 0 | 50 | 17 | 4 | 5 | .255 | .332 | .472 |
| Schwartzbauer, Daniel, Pirates | 35 | 144 | 123 | 23 | 45 | 57 | 9 | 0 | 1 | 24 | 0 | 5 | 3 | 13 | 0 | 14 | 5 | 3 | 2 | .366 | .424 | .463 |
| Sgueglia, Thomas, Mets | 18 | 47 | 35 | 7 | 10 | 12 | 2 | 0 | 0 | 1 | 0 | 0 | 1 | 11 | 0 | 8 | 1 | 1 | 0 | .286 | .468 | .343 |
| Shaw, Buck, Phillies * | 46 | 177 | 159 | 24 | 41 | 75 | 8 | 1 | 8 | 30 | 0 | 1 | 0 | 17 | 1 | 25 | 5 | 0 | 1 | .258 | .328 | .472 |
| Simmons, Lyndsey, Expos * | 23 | 65 | 54 | 7 | 9 | 12 | 3 | 0 | 0 | 4 | 0 | 0 | 0 | 11 | 0 | 8 | 0 | 0 | 0 | .167 | .308 | .222 |
| Skelton, James, Tigers * | 23 | 51 | 43 | 3 | 6 | 7 | 1 | 0 | 0 | 2 | 1 | 0 | 0 | 7 | 0 | 11 | 0 | 0 | 1 | .140 | .260 | .163 |
| Smolarsky, Fred, Marlins | 28 | 95 | 88 | 11 | 23 | 36 | 7 | 0 | 2 | 12 | 0 | 0 | 3 | 4 | 0 | 18 | 1 | 0 | 3 | .261 | .316 | .409 |
| Soto, Abel, Expos | 7 | 24 | 22 | 2 | 4 | 4 | 0 | 0 | 0 | 1 | 0 | 0 | 0 | 2 | 0 | 8 | 0 | 0 | 1 | .182 | .250 | .182 |
| Soto, Jesus, Dodgers † | 48 | 187 | 171 | 33 | 50 | 77 | 11 | 2 | 4 | 18 | 3 | 0 | 3 | 10 | 1 | 18 | 5 | 3 | 2 | .292 | .342 | .450 |
| Soto, Luis, Red Sox † | 36 | 142 | 134 | 22 | 35 | 63 | 9 | 2 | 5 | 16 | 0 | 2 | 1 | 5 | 1 | 22 | 4 | 1 | 2 | .261 | .289 | .470 |
| Soto, Maximo, Tigers | 29 | 112 | 101 | 15 | 23 | 36 | 2 | 1 | 3 | 9 | 0 | 0 | 1 | 10 | 0 | 38 | 0 | 1 | 2 | .228 | .304 | .356 |
| Soto, Melvin, Reds † | 13 | 33 | 30 | 0 | 7 | 7 | 0 | 0 | 0 | 2 | 1 | 0 | 0 | 2 | 0 | 5 | 0 | 0 | 0 | .233 | .281 | .233 |
| Spann, Denard, Twins | 5 | 19 | 16 | 1 | 6 | 8 | 2 | 0 | 0 | 1 | 0 | 0 | 0 | 3 | 0 | 3 | 0 | 1 | 0 | .375 | .474 | .500 |
| Steidl, Sam, Dodgers * | 11 | 40 | 31 | 6 | 4 | 4 | 0 | 0 | 0 | 3 | 0 | 1 | 1 | 7 | 0 | 3 | 0 | 1 | 1 | .129 | .300 | .129 |
| Stevens, Anthony, Pirates | 26 | 85 | 77 | 10 | 17 | 24 | 2 | 1 | 1 | 11 | 1 | 3 | 1 | 3 | 0 | 26 | 0 | 2 | 2 | .221 | .250 | .312 |
| Suarez, Gabriel, Expos | 41 | 138 | 124 | 8 | 26 | 29 | 0 | 0 | 1 | 9 | 3 | 2 | 2 | 7 | 0 | 32 | 5 | 2 | 4 | .210 | .259 | .234 |
| Suarez, Jose, Red Sox | 16 | 53 | 49 | 5 | 13 | 17 | 1 | 0 | 1 | 7 | 0 | 0 | 1 | 3 | 0 | 18 | 0 | 0 | 1 | .265 | .321 | .347 |
| Suero, Ovandy, Braves † | 49 | 184 | 168 | 27 | 39 | 45 | 0 | 3 | 0 | 9 | 2 | 0 | 4 | 10 | 0 | 56 | 30 | 2 | 0 | .232 | .291 | .268 |
| Suggs, Bryant, Mets * | 31 | 94 | 77 | 12 | 18 | 20 | 0 | 1 | 0 | 6 | 3 | 0 | 3 | 11 | 0 | 11 | 4 | 7 | 0 | .234 | .352 | .260 |
| Sutherland, David, Dodgers * | 50 | 169 | 153 | 22 | 46 | 54 | 2 | 3 | 0 | 14 | 1 | 1 | 5 | 9 | 0 | 15 | 4 | 0 | 5 | .301 | .357 | .353 |
| Szabo, Jordan, Phillies | 29 | 99 | 90 | 5 | 18 | 19 | 1 | 0 | 0 | 7 | 0 | 0 | 1 | 8 | 0 | 14 | 2 | 1 | 1 | .200 | .273 | .211 |
| Terrazas, Ivan, Braves † | 37 | 123 | 117 | 14 | 33 | 54 | 7 | 1 | 4 | 20 | 1 | 0 | 1 | 4 | 0 | 18 | 2 | 1 | 1 | .282 | .311 | .462 |
| Tierce, Jonathan, Yankees * | 40 | 162 | 147 | 26 | 53 | 69 | 11 | 1 | 1 | 14 | 0 | 0 | 1 | 14 | 0 | 16 | 13 | 4 | 2 | .361 | .420 | .469 |
| Timm, Brandon, Tigers | 41 | 146 | 125 | 21 | 29 | 34 | 3 | 1 | 0 | 12 | 0 | 2 | 2 | 17 | 0 | 36 | 7 | 1 | 2 | .232 | .329 | .272 |
| Timmons, Jeff, Mets | 19 | 36 | 27 | 3 | 7 | 7 | 0 | 0 | 0 | 3 | 1 | 0 | 2 | 6 | 0 | 8 | 0 | 2 | 0 | .259 | .429 | .259 |
| Torres, Carlos, Red Sox | 42 | 174 | 148 | 26 | 38 | 69 | 7 | 0 | 8 | 31 | 0 | 0 | 7 | 19 | 0 | 38 | 1 | 2 | 0 | .257 | .368 | .466 |
| Turner, Christopher, Red Sox | 16 | 75 | 68 | 12 | 17 | 38 | 3 | 3 | 4 | 18 | 0 | 2 | 2 | 3 | 0 | 17 | 1 | 2 | 2 | .250 | .293 | .559 |
| Underwood, Bret, Red Sox * | 18 | 58 | 53 | 4 | 10 | 10 | 0 | 0 | 0 | 4 | 0 | 2 | 0 | 3 | 0 | 9 | 1 | 0 | 1 | .189 | .224 | .189 |
| Valdez, Odannys, Twins † | 46 | 181 | 143 | 37 | 36 | 44 | 8 | 0 | 0 | 10 | 3 | 1 | 14 | 20 | 0 | 25 | 12 | 2 | 3 | .252 | .393 | .308 |
| Verley, Brandon, Marlins * | 10 | 24 | 21 | 1 | 1 | 1 | 0 | 0 | 0 | 3 | 0 | 0 | 1 | 2 | 0 | 6 | 1 | 1 | 3 | .048 | .167 | .048 |
| Walton, Jamar, Marlins * | 42 | 159 | 143 | 17 | 34 | 42 | 3 | 1 | 1 | 13 | 0 | 3 | 0 | 13 | 0 | 32 | 6 | 3 | 1 | .238 | .296 | .294 |
| Wells, Cory, Mets | 44 | 163 | 148 | 23 | 43 | 66 | 12 | 1 | 3 | 21 | 1 | 0 | 3 | 11 | 0 | 39 | 9 | 3 | 0 | .291 | .352 | .446 |
| Westfield, Antonio, Pirates | 15 | 49 | 41 | 5 | 7 | 11 | 1 | 0 | 1 | 2 | 1 | 0 | 0 | 7 | 0 | 13 | 2 | 0 | 1 | .171 | .292 | .268 |
| Williams, Julian, Phillies | 12 | 27 | 24 | 1 | 7 | 9 | 0 | 1 | 0 | 1 | 0 | 1 | 0 | 2 | 0 | 5 | 1 | 1 | 0 | .292 | .333 | .375 |
| Williams, Larry, Braves * | 40 | 130 | 115 | 6 | 23 | 31 | 8 | 0 | 0 | 6 | 0 | 0 | 0 | 15 | 0 | 31 | 0 | 1 | 3 | .200 | .292 | .270 |
| Wong, Ivanosky, Expos | 13 | 47 | 38 | 2 | 8 | 8 | 0 | 0 | 0 | 3 | 0 | 1 | 2 | 6 | 0 | 7 | 0 | 0 | 2 | .211 | .340 | .211 |
| Wulf, Kent, Pirates | 43 | 170 | 154 | 17 | 34 | 51 | 8 | 3 | 1 | 14 | 3 | 1 | 1 | 11 | 0 | 38 | 5 | 2 | 4 | .221 | .275 | .331 |
| Young, Dusty, Marlins | 19 | 77 | 63 | 8 | 19 | 22 | 3 | 0 | 0 | 10 | 0 | 0 | 4 | 10 | 0 | 13 | 3 | 0 | 3 | .302 | .429 | .349 |
| Young, Stephen, Tigers † | 42 | 187 | 153 | 27 | 43 | 55 | 4 | 1 | 2 | 14 | 3 | 0 | 8 | 22 | 0 | 17 | 9 | 3 | 2 | .281 | .399 | .359 |

GRAND SLAMS—Aguilino, Batista, Evans, Laster, Mancebo, Santiago, 1 each.

AWARDED FIRST BASE ON CATCHER'S INTERFERENCE—Almario-Cabrera 2 (Bressoud, Guerra); Desmond 2 (Rogers, Rogers); R. Dominguez 2 (Guerra, Bressoud); Koko 2 (Marson, Miller); De Leon (Griffin); Giambi (Flores); Maldonado (Rogers); Middleton (Marson); J. Perez (Guerra); Young (Bressoud).

## 2004 PITCHING

### TEAM

| Team | W | L | Pct. | ERA | G | CG | ShO | Sv. | IP | H | TBF | R | ER | HR | SH | SF | HB | BB | IBB | SO | WP | Bk. |
|---|---|---|---|---|---|---|---|---|---|---|---|---|---|---|---|---|---|---|---|---|---|---|
| Yankees | 36 | 23 | .610 | 2.87 | 59 | 0 | 10 | 20 | 491.2 | 428 | 2053 | 184 | 157 | 31 | 7 | 12 | 25 | 139 | 1 | 529 | 24 | 5 |
| Red Sox | 34 | 24 | .586 | 2.99 | 58 | 1 | 3 | 18 | 490.1 | 462 | 2105 | 222 | 163 | 22 | 18 | 22 | 43 | 161 | 3 | 403 | 33 | 12 |
| Phillies | 36 | 24 | .600 | 3.12 | 60 | 0 | 5 | 16 | 489.2 | 461 | 2066 | 228 | 170 | 30 | 3 | 10 | 29 | 129 | 0 | 461 | 38 | 4 |
| Pirates | 30 | 28 | .517 | 3.31 | 58 | 2 | 2 | 12 | 486.1 | 430 | 2070 | 224 | 179 | 26 | 15 | 17 | 52 | 162 | 2 | 384 | 28 | 3 |
| Marlins | 31 | 29 | .517 | 3.37 | 60 | 0 | 6 | 12 | 513.0 | 461 | 2205 | 251 | 192 | 15 | 19 | 15 | 38 | 200 | 2 | 435 | 56 | 6 |
| Dodgers | 31 | 29 | .517 | 3.41 | 60 | 0 | 3 | 15 | 533.2 | 475 | 2291 | 250 | 202 | 19 | 15 | 17 | 39 | 219 | 7 | 470 | 53 | 10 |
| Twins | 31 | 26 | .544 | 3.50 | 57 | 0 | 3 | 15 | 478.0 | 494 | 2133 | 270 | 186 | 18 | 14 | 15 | 42 | 163 | 2 | 446 | 67 | 6 |
| Tigers | 24 | 36 | .400 | 3.79 | 60 | 2 | 3 | 7 | 515.1 | 469 | 2247 | 268 | 217 | 42 | 11 | 20 | 30 | 233 | 3 | 512 | 66 | 9 |
| Mets | 36 | 24 | .600 | 3.84 | 60 | 2 | 5 | 13 | 513.0 | 479 | 2219 | 269 | 219 | 18 | 12 | 13 | 51 | 192 | 3 | 463 | 41 | 5 |
| Reds | 20 | 37 | .351 | 3.99 | 57 | 0 | 4 | 8 | 476.0 | 468 | 2137 | 280 | 211 | 28 | 12 | 28 | 50 | 217 | 1 | 381 | 37 | 5 |
| Expos | 22 | 38 | .367 | 4.40 | 60 | 0 | 3 | 13 | 499.1 | 518 | 2203 | 304 | 244 | 29 | 13 | 10 | 42 | 176 | 2 | 421 | 66 | 9 |
| Braves | 23 | 36 | .390 | 4.42 | 59 | 0 | 3 | 10 | 494.1 | 522 | 2222 | 304 | 243 | 39 | 14 | 12 | 36 | 197 | 4 | 461 | 40 | 4 |

# INDIVIDUAL

## TOP QUALIFIERS FOR EARNED-RUN AVERAGE TITLE

Minimum 48 innings. *Lefthanded pitcher.

| Pitcher, Team | W | L | Pct. | ERA | G | GS | CG | ShO | GF | Sv. | IP | H | TBF | R | ER | HR | SH | SF | HB | BB | IBB | SO | WP | Bk. |
|---|---|---|---|---|---|---|---|---|---|---|---|---|---|---|---|---|---|---|---|---|---|---|---|---|
| Hernandez, Gabriel, Mets | 3 | 3 | .500 | 1.09 | 10 | 9 | 2 | 1 | 0 | 0 | 49.2 | 25 | 184 | 10 | 6 | 1 | 1 | 2 | 3 | 12 | 0 | 58 | 2 | 0 |
| Mitchinson, Scott, Phillies | 7 | 0 | 1.000 | 1.75 | 10 | 10 | 0 | 0 | 0 | 0 | 61.2 | 40 | 221 | 12 | 12 | 2 | 0 | 0 | 0 | 1 | 0 | 60 | 1 | 0 |
| Delacruz, Maximino, Phillies | 4 | 3 | .571 | 2.11 | 12 | 11 | 0 | 0 | 1 | 0 | 59.2 | 64 | 252 | 25 | 14 | 1 | 2 | 0 | 3 | 13 | 0 | 54 | 2 | 0 |
| Sosa, Gabriel, Expos | 5 | 2 | .714 | 2.29 | 11 | 9 | 0 | 0 | 0 | 0 | 51.0 | 36 | 210 | 16 | 13 | 3 | 1 | 0 | 3 | 23 | 0 | 63 | 1 | 2 |
| Wilson, Jonathan, Red Sox | 5 | 1 | .833 | 2.50 | 11 | 6 | 0 | 0 | 2 | 0 | 54.0 | 44 | 211 | 21 | 15 | 1 | 3 | 4 | 3 | 11 | 0 | 39 | 1 | 1 |
| Alvarez, Basilio, Pirates | 3 | 3 | .500 | 2.55 | 11 | 5 | 0 | 0 | 2 | 0 | 49.1 | 42 | 202 | 22 | 14 | 3 | 1 | 2 | 3 | 9 | 0 | 41 | 0 | 1 |
| Stephens, Jay, Yankees | 5 | 3 | .625 | 2.61 | 13 | 8 | 0 | 0 | 1 | 1 | 48.1 | 55 | 215 | 23 | 14 | 1 | 1 | 2 | 5 | 10 | 1 | 48 | 4 | 0 |
| Swarzak, Anthony, Twins | 5 | 3 | .625 | 2.63 | 11 | 9 | 0 | 0 | 2 | 1 | 48.0 | 46 | 193 | 20 | 14 | 1 | 3 | 0 | 1 | 6 | 0 | 42 | 2 | 1 |
| Nelson, Maximo, Yankees | 6 | 3 | .667 | 2.63 | 12 | 9 | 0 | 0 | 0 | 0 | 54.2 | 48 | 218 | 16 | 16 | 6 | 0 | 0 | 2 | 12 | 0 | 54 | 2 | 1 |
| French, Lucas, Tigers * | 1 | 3 | .250 | 2.74 | 11 | 10 | 0 | 0 | 0 | 0 | 49.1 | 43 | 212 | 21 | 15 | 1 | 4 | 4 | 1 | 19 | 0 | 49 | 2 | 1 |
| Valdez, Luis, Pirates | 7 | 2 | .778 | 2.79 | 11 | 11 | 2 | 1 | 0 | 0 | 61.1 | 58 | 250 | 22 | 19 | 1 | 2 | 1 | 4 | 10 | 0 | 41 | 3 | 2 |
| Pichardo, Kelvin, Phillies | 5 | 5 | .500 | 2.79 | 12 | 11 | 0 | 0 | 0 | 0 | 58.0 | 41 | 227 | 21 | 18 | 5 | 0 | 2 | 6 | 15 | 0 | 62 | 6 | 0 |
| Stott, Zachary, Reds | 2 | 2 | .500 | 2.82 | 12 | 8 | 0 | 0 | 0 | 0 | 51.0 | 54 | 210 | 20 | 16 | 3 | 1 | 1 | 0 | 10 | 0 | 34 | 1 | 0 |
| Lara, Toni, Yankees * | 3 | 1 | .750 | 3.51 | 15 | 10 | 0 | 0 | 0 | 0 | 48.2 | 40 | 198 | 23 | 19 | 2 | 1 | 1 | 0 | 18 | 0 | 47 | 2 | 0 |
| Carrasco, Carlos, Phillies | 5 | 4 | .556 | 3.56 | 11 | 8 | 0 | 0 | 0 | 0 | 48.0 | 53 | 212 | 23 | 19 | 2 | 0 | 2 | 3 | 15 | 0 | 34 | 2 | 0 |

DEPARTMENTAL LEADERS: W—Valdez, Mitchinson, 7; L—Morales, 7; Pct.—Mitchinson, 1.000; G—Fragoso, Zuleta, 23; GS—Easton, 13; CG—Three tied with two; ShO—Three tied with one; GF—Cross, Zuleta, 16; Sv.—Nolan, Zuleta, 7; IP—Mitchinson, 61.2; H—Delacruz, 64; TBF—Sborz, 275; R—de la Cruz, 39; ER—de la Cruz, 31; HR—Sborz, 9; SH—Several pitchers tied with four; SF—Frias, 6; HB—Adames, Wachman, 9; BB—Sborz, 44; IBB—Cross, Simmons, 2; SO—Sosa, 63; WP—Perdomo, 16; BK—Pena, 4.

## ALL PITCHERS

*Lefthanded pitcher.

| Pitcher, Team | W | L | Pct. | ERA | G | GS | CG | ShO | GF | Sv. | IP | H | TBF | R | ER | HR | SH | SF | HB | BB | IBB | SO | WP | Bk. |
|---|---|---|---|---|---|---|---|---|---|---|---|---|---|---|---|---|---|---|---|---|---|---|---|---|
| Acosta, Bennys, Braves | 0 | 0 | .000 | 3.38 | 2 | 0 | 0 | 0 | 1 | 0 | 2.2 | 5 | 13 | 2 | 1 | 0 | 0 | 0 | 0 | 2 | 0 | 2 | 1 | 0 |
| Adames, Geovanny, Reds | 1 | 2 | .333 | 5.11 | 10 | 2 | 0 | 0 | 1 | 0 | 24.2 | 20 | 117 | 20 | 14 | 2 | 0 | 1 | 9 | 18 | 0 | 28 | 8 | 0 |
| Albury, James, Red Sox | 5 | 0 | 1.000 | 1.15 | 11 | 2 | 0 | 0 | 0 | 0 | 39.0 | 26 | 152 | 6 | 5 | 2 | 1 | 0 | 2 | 16 | 0 | 21 | 3 | 0 |
| Alvarez, Basilio, Pirates | 3 | 3 | .500 | 2.55 | 11 | 5 | 0 | 0 | 2 | 0 | 49.1 | 42 | 202 | 22 | 14 | 3 | 1 | 2 | 3 | 9 | 0 | 41 | 0 | 1 |
| Antigua, Erick, Yankees | 1 | 0 | 1.000 | 1.46 | 6 | 0 | 0 | 0 | 3 | 2 | 12.1 | 6 | 45 | 2 | 2 | 0 | 0 | 0 | 1 | 2 | 0 | 14 | 0 | 0 |
| Arias, Keily, Pirates * | 1 | 0 | 1.000 | 2.00 | 9 | 0 | 0 | 0 | 3 | 0 | 18.0 | 20 | 83 | 11 | 4 | 2 | 2 | 2 | 1 | 5 | 0 | 8 | 1 | 0 |
| Astacio, Olivo, Red Sox | 3 | 4 | .429 | 3.13 | 12 | 8 | 1 | 0 | 0 | 0 | 46.0 | 46 | 205 | 27 | 16 | 1 | 2 | 2 | 3 | 18 | 0 | 32 | 5 | 1 |
| Bailey, David, Reds | 0 | 1 | .000 | 4.38 | 6 | 3 | 0 | 0 | 0 | 0 | 12.1 | 14 | 54 | 7 | 6 | 0 | 0 | 0 | 0 | 3 | 0 | 9 | 1 | 1 |
| Balester, Colin, Expos | 1 | 2 | .333 | 2.19 | 5 | 4 | 0 | 0 | 1 | 0 | 24.2 | 20 | 101 | 8 | 6 | 0 | 1 | 1 | 1 | 5 | 1 | 21 | 4 | 0 |
| Barb, Andrew, Phillies | 2 | 2 | .500 | 2.57 | 15 | 4 | 0 | 0 | 2 | 0 | 35.0 | 29 | 145 | 12 | 10 | 4 | 0 | 0 | 1 | 7 | 0 | 56 | 3 | 1 |
| Bassham, Johnnie, Dodgers * | 0 | 0 | .000 | 3.95 | 10 | 0 | 0 | 0 | 2 | 0 | 13.2 | 13 | 65 | 10 | 6 | 0 | 0 | 0 | 0 | 12 | 0 | 19 | 2 | 0 |
| Bauserman, Joseph, Pirates | 2 | 2 | .500 | 2.79 | 9 | 8 | 0 | 0 | 0 | 0 | 38.2 | 26 | 157 | 13 | 12 | 4 | 0 | 1 | 7 | 10 | 0 | 35 | 1 | 0 |
| Berg, Justin, Yankees | 3 | 2 | .600 | 5.87 | 15 | 1 | 0 | 0 | 4 | 1 | 30.2 | 40 | 147 | 22 | 20 | 3 | 0 | 3 | 3 | 15 | 0 | 29 | 3 | 0 |
| Berkenbosch, Kenny, Marlins | 1 | 0 | 1.000 | 1.64 | 7 | 0 | 0 | 0 | 1 | 0 | 11.0 | 13 | 47 | 5 | 2 | 0 | 0 | 0 | 0 | 2 | 0 | 6 | 2 | 0 |
| Blackford, Todd, Braves | 1 | 2 | .333 | 7.86 | 15 | 2 | 0 | 0 | 3 | 0 | 26.1 | 44 | 136 | 28 | 23 | 7 | 1 | 3 | 4 | 9 | 0 | 18 | 2 | 0 |
| Bong, Jung, Reds * | 0 | 0 | .000 | 12.00 | 2 | 2 | 0 | 0 | 0 | 0 | 3.0 | 3 | 15 | 5 | 4 | 0 | 0 | 0 | 0 | 2 | 0 | 3 | 1 | 0 |
| Brito, Joel, Marlins | 0 | 0 | .000 | 1.80 | 3 | 0 | 0 | 0 | 1 | 0 | 5.0 | 4 | 20 | 2 | 1 | 0 | 0 | 0 | 0 | 0 | 0 | 6 | 0 | 0 |
| Brown, Jeremy, Twins | 0 | 2 | .000 | 11.00 | 4 | 1 | 0 | 0 | 1 | 0 | 9.0 | 18 | 49 | 11 | 11 | 1 | 0 | 1 | 1 | 4 | 0 | 1 | 1 | 0 |
| Bryant, Patrick, Twins | 2 | 2 | .500 | 4.26 | 12 | 4 | 0 | 0 | 2 | 1 | 31.2 | 31 | 146 | 23 | 15 | 3 | 1 | 1 | 6 | 13 | 0 | 21 | 5 | 0 |
| Camilo, Juan, Marlins | 3 | 1 | .750 | 2.76 | 11 | 10 | 0 | 0 | 0 | 0 | 45.2 | 42 | 196 | 21 | 14 | 1 | 2 | 2 | 0 | 20 | 0 | 45 | 3 | 1 |
| Caraballo, Jesse, Tigers | 0 | 3 | .000 | 4.18 | 16 | 1 | 0 | 0 | 6 | 0 | 32.1 | 27 | 143 | 16 | 15 | 6 | 0 | 1 | 4 | 18 | 0 | 24 | 7 | 0 |
| Carmosino, Dominic, Tigers * | 1 | 2 | .333 | 6.41 | 11 | 0 | 0 | 0 | 4 | 0 | 19.2 | 18 | 90 | 15 | 14 | 4 | 1 | 1 | 1 | 11 | 0 | 28 | 2 | 0 |
| Carrasco, Carlos, Phillies | 5 | 4 | .556 | 3.56 | 11 | 8 | 0 | 0 | 0 | 0 | 48.0 | 53 | 212 | 23 | 19 | 2 | 0 | 2 | 3 | 15 | 0 | 34 | 2 | 0 |
| Castillo, Jonathan, Mets | 2 | 2 | .500 | 5.67 | 13 | 6 | 0 | 0 | 2 | 1 | 39.2 | 51 | 188 | 30 | 25 | 2 | 1 | 0 | 5 | 12 | 0 | 24 | 4 | 0 |
| Castor, Parrish, Marlins * | 2 | 3 | .400 | 5.36 | 11 | 8 | 0 | 0 | 0 | 0 | 40.1 | 40 | 182 | 26 | 24 | 3 | 2 | 2 | 4 | 20 | 0 | 31 | 0 | 2 |
| Cherry, Brad, Reds | 1 | 1 | .500 | 3.54 | 15 | 0 | 0 | 0 | 8 | 4 | 20.1 | 18 | 86 | 8 | 8 | 1 | 1 | 0 | 1 | 6 | 0 | 18 | 0 | 0 |
| Coke, Phillip, Yankees * | 0 | 1 | .000 | 3.97 | 7 | 1 | 0 | 0 | 1 | 0 | 11.1 | 18 | 54 | 7 | 5 | 0 | 1 | 0 | 0 | 3 | 0 | 13 | 1 | 1 |
| Cramer, Terry, Pirates | 0 | 0 | .000 | 0.00 | 1 | 0 | 0 | 0 | 0 | 0 | 2.0 | 2 | 7 | 0 | 0 | 0 | 0 | 0 | 0 | 0 | 0 | 3 | 0 | 0 |
| Cross, Blake, Braves | 3 | 3 | .500 | 2.96 | 17 | 0 | 0 | 0 | 16 | 4 | 27.1 | 23 | 126 | 12 | 9 | 2 | 4 | 0 | 1 | 16 | 2 | 28 | 2 | 0 |
| Cruz, Rhinel, Tigers | 0 | 1 | .000 | 4.78 | 16 | 0 | 0 | 0 | 9 | 0 | 32.0 | 37 | 149 | 20 | 17 | 3 | 1 | 4 | 1 | 19 | 0 | 26 | 3 | 0 |
| Cuffman, Jacob, Pirates | 0 | 1 | .000 | 4.86 | 6 | 5 | 0 | 0 | 0 | 0 | 16.2 | 16 | 85 | 12 | 9 | 3 | 0 | 1 | 1 | 20 | 0 | 15 | 3 | 0 |
| Davidson, David, Pirates * | 1 | 0 | 1.000 | 3.44 | 7 | 1 | 0 | 0 | 2 | 0 | 18.1 | 16 | 89 | 11 | 7 | 0 | 1 | 1 | 5 | 14 | 0 | 24 | 2 | 0 |
| Davis, Lance, Marlins | 0 | 0 | .000 | 0.00 | 2 | 0 | 0 | 0 | 1 | 0 | 2.0 | 1 | 9 | 0 | 0 | 0 | 0 | 0 | 0 | 2 | 0 | 1 | 0 | 0 |
| De La Cruz, Julian, Dodgers | 4 | 6 | .400 | 5.58 | 18 | 4 | 0 | 0 | 7 | 4 | 50.0 | 60 | 235 | 39 | 31 | 1 | 0 | 2 | 6 | 22 | 0 | 47 | 3 | 1 |
| DeChristofaro, Vinnie, Phillies * | 0 | 0 | .000 | 0.00 | 1 | 0 | 0 | 0 | 0 | 0 | 1.0 | 0 | 3 | 0 | 0 | 0 | 0 | 0 | 0 | 0 | 0 | 1 | 0 | 0 |
| Delacruz, Maximino, Phillies | 4 | 3 | .571 | 2.11 | 12 | 11 | 0 | 0 | 1 | 0 | 59.2 | 64 | 252 | 25 | 14 | 1 | 2 | 0 | 3 | 13 | 0 | 54 | 2 | 0 |
| Deluna, David, Reds * | 1 | 5 | .167 | 6.61 | 12 | 4 | 0 | 0 | 1 | 0 | 32.2 | 45 | 159 | 33 | 24 | 3 | 0 | 5 | 0 | 17 | 0 | 22 | 3 | 0 |
| Demme, Asher, Braves | 2 | 4 | .333 | 8.90 | 10 | 7 | 0 | 0 | 1 | 0 | 29.1 | 37 | 146 | 32 | 29 | 1 | 1 | 3 | 1 | 20 | 0 | 22 | 1 | 0 |
| Doble, Clemente, Phillies | 1 | 0 | 1.000 | 2.45 | 14 | 0 | 0 | 0 | 11 | 5 | 22.0 | 18 | 93 | 7 | 6 | 3 | 0 | 1 | 2 | 6 | 0 | 15 | 2 | 0 |
| Duiett, Cory, Phillies | 1 | 1 | .500 | 4.87 | 13 | 0 | 0 | 0 | 8 | 2 | 20.1 | 26 | 100 | 13 | 11 | 2 | 0 | 1 | 1 | 7 | 0 | 19 | 2 | 0 |
| Easton, Aaron, Marlins | 2 | 6 | .250 | 5.13 | 13 | 13 | 0 | 0 | 0 | 0 | 52.2 | 49 | 221 | 34 | 30 | 1 | 4 | 2 | 3 | 19 | 0 | 32 | 5 | 0 |
| Elliot, Adam, Mets | 0 | 0 | .000 | 0.00 | 1 | 1 | 0 | 0 | 0 | 0 | 1.0 | 0 | 3 | 0 | 0 | 0 | 0 | 0 | 0 | 0 | 0 | 0 | 0 | 0 |
| Encarnacion, Luis, Phillies | 0 | 0 | .000 | 6.00 | 5 | 0 | 0 | 0 | 0 | 0 | 6.0 | 12 | 37 | 11 | 4 | 0 | 1 | 0 | 1 | 5 | 0 | 4 | 1 | 0 |
| Engles, Terrence, Expos | 0 | 4 | .000 | 9.75 | 10 | 6 | 0 | 0 | 2 | 2 | 24.0 | 31 | 112 | 28 | 26 | 5 | 0 | 0 | 1 | 12 | 0 | 17 | 6 | 0 |
| Fragoso, Jose, Tigers | 3 | 3 | .500 | 3.07 | 23 | 0 | 0 | 0 | 14 | 1 | 29.1 | 25 | 123 | 14 | 10 | 2 | 0 | 1 | 0 | 12 | 1 | 33 | 3 | 0 |
| Franco, Ambiorix, Reds | 0 | 0 | .000 | 27.00 | 1 | 0 | 0 | 0 | 1 | 0 | 1.0 | 4 | 8 | 3 | 3 | 0 | 0 | 1 | 0 | 1 | 0 | 0 | 0 | 0 |
| French, Lucas, Tigers * | 1 | 3 | .250 | 2.74 | 11 | 10 | 0 | 0 | 0 | 0 | 49.1 | 43 | 212 | 21 | 15 | 1 | 4 | 4 | 1 | 19 | 0 | 49 | 2 | 1 |
| Frias, Junior, Red Sox | 1 | 2 | .333 | 3.48 | 10 | 8 | 0 | 0 | 0 | 0 | 33.2 | 34 | 153 | 19 | 13 | 2 | 0 | 6 | 4 | 14 | 0 | 43 | 3 | 1 |
| Garavito, Jean, Pirates | 2 | 3 | .400 | 2.04 | 13 | 0 | 0 | 0 | 7 | 2 | 17.2 | 10 | 70 | 5 | 4 | 0 | 2 | 0 | 3 | 7 | 1 | 11 | 1 | 0 |
| Garay, Kelvin, Mets * | 0 | 0 | .000 | 7.11 | 10 | 0 | 0 | 0 | 3 | 2 | 19.0 | 22 | 89 | 19 | 15 | 0 | 1 | 2 | 6 | 11 | 1 | 7 | 5 | 0 |
| Garcia, Christian, Yankees | 3 | 4 | .429 | 2.84 | 13 | 6 | 0 | 0 | 0 | 0 | 38.0 | 26 | 159 | 13 | 12 | 1 | 0 | 2 | 2 | 17 | 0 | 47 | 3 | 0 |
| Garcia, Felipe, Tigers | 2 | 0 | 1.000 | 0.39 | 14 | 0 | 0 | 0 | 7 | 2 | 23.0 | 12 | 84 | 2 | 1 | 1 | 0 | 1 | 0 | 9 | 0 | 22 | 2 | 0 |

| Pitcher, Team | W | L | Pct. | ERA | G | GS | CG | ShO | GF | Sv. | IP | H | TBF | R | ER | HR | SH | SF | HB | BB | IBB | SO | WP | Bk. |
|---|---|---|---|---|---|---|---|---|---|---|---|---|---|---|---|---|---|---|---|---|---|---|---|---|
| Garrison, Kale, Dodgers * | 2 | 2 | .500 | 6.48 | 18 | 0 | 0 | 0 | 7 | 1 | 25.0 | 26 | 120 | 19 | 18 | 2 | 1 | 0 | 1 | 17 | 0 | 24 | 4 | 0 |
| Gault, Joe, Twins | 3 | 2 | .600 | 5.18 | 13 | 3 | 0 | 0 | 3 | 1 | 33.0 | 48 | 165 | 25 | 19 | 2 | 1 | 1 | 7 | 11 | 1 | 21 | 7 | 0 |
| Gazo, Lenin, Phillies | 3 | 4 | .429 | 4.95 | 11 | 10 | 0 | 0 | 0 | 0 | 43.2 | 48 | 197 | 32 | 24 | 2 | 0 | 1 | 3 | 16 | 0 | 24 | 6 | 1 |
| Gearhart, Kalen, Dodgers | 3 | 0 | 1.000 | 1.89 | 18 | 0 | 0 | 0 | 7 | 0 | 33.1 | 30 | 142 | 7 | 7 | 1 | 2 | 1 | 4 | 7 | 1 | 22 | 4 | 0 |
| Geiersbach, Ken, Reds | 0 | 1 | .000 | 0.77 | 12 | 0 | 0 | 0 | 3 | 0 | 11.2 | 11 | 51 | 3 | 1 | 1 | 0 | 0 | 1 | 6 | 0 | 14 | 1 | 0 |
| Gil, Rotsen, Dodgers | 0 | 0 | .000 | 0.00 | 1 | 0 | 0 | 0 | 1 | 0 | 1.0 | 1 | 5 | 1 | 0 | 0 | 0 | 1 | 0 | 0 | 0 | 0 | 0 | 0 |
| Glanzman, Jacob, Red Sox * | 0 | 0 | .000 | 10.29 | 5 | 0 | 0 | 0 | 3 | 0 | 7.0 | 12 | 39 | 9 | 8 | 0 | 1 | 0 | 1 | 5 | 0 | 3 | 0 | 1 |
| Gonzalez, Rafael, Reds | 1 | 6 | .143 | 4.20 | 12 | 8 | 0 | 0 | 0 | 0 | 40.2 | 38 | 179 | 25 | 19 | 3 | 3 | 4 | 7 | 18 | 0 | 32 | 3 | 0 |
| Gordon, Alex, Pirates * | 2 | 2 | .500 | 2.68 | 10 | 0 | 0 | 0 | 4 | 1 | 37.0 | 34 | 150 | 14 | 11 | 0 | 0 | 1 | 1 | 11 | 0 | 22 | 2 | 0 |
| Griffin, Daniel, Marlins | 0 | 0 | .000 | 0.00 | 1 | 0 | 0 | 0 | 0 | 0 | 1.0 | 1 | 4 | 0 | 0 | 0 | 0 | 0 | 0 | 0 | 0 | 1 | 1 | 1 |
| Guerra, Luis, Dodgers | 4 | 1 | .800 | 3.38 | 11 | 9 | 0 | 0 | 0 | 0 | 40.0 | 31 | 168 | 18 | 15 | 3 | 1 | 0 | 3 | 19 | 0 | 36 | 9 | 0 |
| Hakey, Patrick, Mets | 3 | 0 | 1.000 | 3.80 | 14 | 0 | 0 | 0 | 2 | 0 | 23.2 | 19 | 104 | 13 | 10 | 0 | 2 | 1 | 1 | 13 | 0 | 17 | 7 | 0 |
| Harrison, Ryan, Expos | 1 | 2 | .333 | 4.29 | 13 | 3 | 0 | 0 | 7 | 2 | 35.2 | 35 | 159 | 18 | 17 | 2 | 3 | 2 | 3 | 13 | 0 | 22 | 8 | 2 |
| Hayes, Alvin, Dodgers | 3 | 1 | .750 | 3.58 | 16 | 8 | 0 | 0 | 1 | 0 | 50.1 | 29 | 215 | 26 | 20 | 1 | 1 | 5 | 3 | 35 | 0 | 51 | 10 | 1 |
| Hebert, Robbie, Twins | 1 | 0 | 1.000 | 1.98 | 11 | 1 | 0 | 0 | 8 | 2 | 13.2 | 13 | 61 | 4 | 3 | 0 | 0 | 1 | 1 | 4 | 0 | 13 | 2 | 0 |
| Heil, Ryan, Mets | 0 | 0 | .000 | 6.61 | 10 | 0 | 0 | 0 | 2 | 0 | 16.1 | 17 | 83 | 14 | 12 | 0 | 1 | 1 | 6 | 17 | 0 | 7 | 3 | 0 |
| Hendley, Blake, Reds | 3 | 0 | 1.000 | 0.92 | 10 | 0 | 0 | 0 | 4 | 1 | 19.2 | 15 | 82 | 4 | 2 | 0 | 0 | 2 | 0 | 7 | 0 | 16 | 0 | 0 |
| Hendricks, Donavon, Braves * | 2 | 0 | 1.000 | 5.01 | 15 | 0 | 0 | 0 | 6 | 0 | 32.1 | 41 | 143 | 24 | 18 | 1 | 2 | 2 | 0 | 7 | 0 | 23 | 2 | 0 |
| Herbort, Ryan, Pirates | 0 | 3 | .000 | 19.64 | 5 | 4 | 0 | 0 | 0 | 0 | 7.1 | 13 | 52 | 17 | 16 | 0 | 0 | 0 | 4 | 11 | 0 | 6 | 5 | 0 |
| Hernandez, Gabriel, Mets | 3 | 3 | .500 | 1.09 | 10 | 9 | 2 | 1 | 0 | 0 | 49.2 | 25 | 184 | 10 | 6 | 1 | 1 | 2 | 3 | 12 | 0 | 58 | 2 | 0 |
| Herrera, Carlos, Reds | 0 | 0 | .000 | 12.00 | 10 | 0 | 0 | 0 | 6 | 0 | 12.0 | 13 | 66 | 21 | 16 | 3 | 1 | 1 | 6 | 9 | 0 | 14 | 2 | 0 |
| Hochgesang, Nathan, Dodgers | 1 | 1 | .500 | 1.54 | 7 | 2 | 0 | 0 | 2 | 0 | 23.1 | 16 | 95 | 7 | 4 | 1 | 0 | 0 | 2 | 7 | 1 | 21 | 2 | 0 |
| Hoffar, Brad, Red Sox | 2 | 1 | .667 | 5.28 | 10 | 0 | 0 | 0 | 3 | 0 | 15.1 | 16 | 71 | 12 | 9 | 3 | 1 | 1 | 2 | 8 | 0 | 10 | 0 | 0 |
| Hope, Travis, Mets | 3 | 3 | .500 | 3.54 | 17 | 0 | 0 | 0 | 12 | 4 | 28.0 | 32 | 128 | 16 | 11 | 2 | 2 | 0 | 1 | 8 | 0 | 23 | 0 | 1 |
| Hughes, Philip, Yankees | 0 | 0 | .000 | 0.00 | 3 | 3 | 0 | 0 | 0 | 0 | 5.0 | 4 | 18 | 0 | 0 | 0 | 0 | 0 | 0 | 0 | 0 | 8 | 0 | 0 |
| Humen, David, Marlins | 0 | 0 | .000 | 1.69 | 5 | 0 | 0 | 0 | 2 | 0 | 5.1 | 1 | 17 | 1 | 1 | 0 | 0 | 0 | 0 | 1 | 0 | 8 | 0 | 0 |
| Jackson, Aaron, Expos | 1 | 3 | .250 | 4.02 | 13 | 2 | 0 | 0 | 6 | 0 | 31.1 | 23 | 132 | 16 | 14 | 3 | 1 | 1 | 2 | 16 | 0 | 24 | 4 | 0 |
| Jackson, Drew, Braves * | 1 | 0 | 1.000 | 1.76 | 6 | 0 | 0 | 0 | 3 | 0 | 15.1 | 13 | 66 | 5 | 3 | 1 | 1 | 0 | 2 | 5 | 0 | 11 | 1 | 0 |
| James, Jimmy, Red Sox | 5 | 1 | .833 | 2.33 | 11 | 9 | 0 | 0 | 0 | 0 | 46.1 | 51 | 207 | 19 | 12 | 3 | 1 | 0 | 3 | 15 | 0 | 35 | 3 | 0 |
| Jimenez, Santos, Reds | 1 | 1 | .500 | 7.71 | 12 | 1 | 0 | 0 | 4 | 0 | 18.2 | 23 | 94 | 19 | 16 | 0 | 2 | 4 | 5 | 8 | 1 | 14 | 1 | 0 |
| Johnson, Anthony, Expos | 0 | 2 | .000 | 8.00 | 9 | 3 | 0 | 0 | 3 | 0 | 18.0 | 29 | 92 | 21 | 16 | 0 | 0 | 1 | 3 | 8 | 0 | 16 | 7 | 1 |
| Joseph, Jamaal, Marlins | 1 | 2 | .333 | 4.13 | 14 | 1 | 0 | 0 | 0 | 0 | 28.1 | 36 | 126 | 16 | 13 | 1 | 0 | 0 | 3 | 6 | 0 | 22 | 5 | 0 |
| Katz, Jeff, Braves | 0 | 1 | .000 | 5.11 | 5 | 2 | 0 | 0 | 2 | 0 | 12.1 | 15 | 63 | 11 | 7 | 1 | 0 | 0 | 2 | 9 | 0 | 13 | 2 | 0 |
| Lara, Toni, Yankees * | 3 | 1 | .750 | 3.51 | 15 | 10 | 0 | 0 | 0 | 0 | 48.2 | 40 | 198 | 23 | 19 | 2 | 1 | 1 | 0 | 18 | 0 | 47 | 2 | 0 |
| Lehman, James, Expos | 0 | 1 | .000 | 4.40 | 11 | 2 | 0 | 0 | 4 | 0 | 30.2 | 34 | 133 | 19 | 15 | 1 | 0 | 0 | 3 | 6 | 0 | 14 | 0 | 0 |
| Linder, Matt, Phillies | 1 | 1 | .500 | 4.43 | 15 | 0 | 0 | 0 | 5 | 0 | 22.1 | 23 | 98 | 14 | 11 | 2 | 0 | 0 | 1 | 7 | 0 | 21 | 4 | 1 |
| Lorenzo, Pedro, Dodgers | 0 | 1 | .000 | 5.79 | 4 | 4 | 0 | 0 | 0 | 0 | 14.0 | 15 | 64 | 9 | 9 | 3 | 0 | 0 | 1 | 8 | 0 | 12 | 0 | 0 |
| Lugo, Chris, Expos | 2 | 1 | .667 | 1.67 | 12 | 2 | 0 | 0 | 5 | 2 | 43.0 | 43 | 184 | 20 | 8 | 2 | 1 | 1 | 5 | 12 | 0 | 34 | 6 | 0 |
| Lybarger, Craig, Marlins * | 1 | 1 | .500 | 3.50 | 13 | 0 | 0 | 0 | 2 | 0 | 18.0 | 21 | 81 | 11 | 7 | 0 | 0 | 0 | 0 | 5 | 0 | 13 | 1 | 0 |
| Lynch, John, Twins * | 1 | 0 | 1.000 | 1.64 | 5 | 0 | 0 | 0 | 1 | 0 | 11.0 | 8 | 43 | 2 | 2 | 0 | 0 | 1 | 1 | 1 | 0 | 12 | 1 | 0 |
| Maldonado, Ivan, Mets | 0 | 0 | .000 | 13.50 | 1 | 0 | 0 | 0 | 0 | 0 | 1.1 | 3 | 7 | 2 | 2 | 0 | 0 | 0 | 0 | 0 | 0 | 3 | 0 | 0 |
| Marchbanks, David, Marlins * | 2 | 1 | .667 | 4.20 | 14 | 9 | 0 | 0 | 3 | 0 | 40.2 | 37 | 181 | 24 | 19 | 2 | 1 | 0 | 4 | 19 | 1 | 24 | 6 | 0 |
| Marrero, Darwin, Expos | 0 | 0 | .000 | 33.75 | 1 | 1 | 0 | 0 | 0 | 0 | 1.1 | 5 | 10 | 5 | 5 | 1 | 0 | 0 | 0 | 0 | 0 | 1 | 1 | 0 |
| Marte, German, Mets | 1 | 0 | 1.000 | 2.40 | 4 | 2 | 0 | 0 | 1 | 0 | 15.0 | 15 | 64 | 5 | 4 | 1 | 0 | 0 | 1 | 4 | 0 | 15 | 0 | 1 |
| Martes, Jose, Red Sox * | 0 | 2 | .000 | 6.28 | 9 | 2 | 0 | 0 | 2 | 0 | 14.1 | 10 | 71 | 11 | 10 | 1 | 1 | 3 | 5 | 17 | 0 | 13 | 7 | 2 |
| Mateo, Waner, Mets | 2 | 0 | 1.000 | 4.14 | 13 | 6 | 0 | 0 | 1 | 0 | 41.1 | 39 | 187 | 29 | 19 | 1 | 1 | 1 | 6 | 21 | 1 | 34 | 4 | 2 |
| Mattison, Justin, Marlins * | 1 | 0 | 1.000 | 6.00 | 11 | 0 | 0 | 0 | 9 | 2 | 12.0 | 15 | 61 | 10 | 8 | 0 | 0 | 0 | 1 | 7 | 0 | 12 | 3 | 0 |
| Mendoza, Robert, Phillies | 2 | 2 | .500 | 2.51 | 15 | 0 | 0 | 0 | 6 | 1 | 28.2 | 28 | 122 | 12 | 8 | 3 | 0 | 1 | 1 | 10 | 0 | 28 | 2 | 1 |
| Merricks, Alexander, Twins * | 0 | 0 | .000 | 12.21 | 14 | 0 | 0 | 0 | 5 | 0 | 14.0 | 14 | 82 | 20 | 19 | 2 | 0 | 3 | 0 | 26 | 0 | 19 | 14 | 0 |
| Mijares, Jose, Twins * | 4 | 0 | 1.000 | 2.43 | 19 | 0 | 0 | 0 | 13 | 5 | 29.2 | 22 | 126 | 9 | 8 | 1 | 2 | 1 | 2 | 15 | 0 | 25 | 3 | 1 |
| Miller, Kevin, Pirates | 0 | 0 | .000 | 3.00 | 3 | 0 | 0 | 0 | 1 | 0 | 3.0 | 3 | 15 | 1 | 1 | 0 | 0 | 0 | 0 | 3 | 0 | 3 | 0 | 0 |
| Mitchinson, Scott, Phillies | 7 | 0 | 1.000 | 1.75 | 10 | 10 | 0 | 0 | 0 | 0 | 61.2 | 40 | 221 | 12 | 12 | 2 | 0 | 0 | 0 | 1 | 0 | 60 | 1 | 0 |
| Morales, Ricardo, Expos* | 1 | 7 | .125 | 4.55 | 12 | 8 | 0 | 0 | 1 | 0 | 57.1 | 59 | 241 | 37 | 29 | 5 | — | — | 2 | 12 | 0 | 55 | 2 | — |
| Morlan, Eduardo, Twins | 1 | 2 | .333 | 2.84 | 11 | 2 | 0 | 0 | 3 | 1 | 25.1 | 25 | 118 | 14 | 8 | 1 | 1 | 1 | 4 | 10 | 0 | 28 | 7 | 0 |
| Moscat, Marvin, Yankees | 2 | 3 | .400 | 2.70 | 16 | 2 | 0 | 0 | 8 | 5 | 36.2 | 24 | 145 | 11 | 11 | 3 | 2 | 1 | 0 | 9 | 0 | 47 | 2 | 0 |
| Moser, Nolan, Red Sox | 0 | 4 | .000 | 2.57 | 18 | 0 | 0 | 0 | 13 | 7 | 21.0 | 21 | 91 | 9 | 6 | 1 | 1 | 0 | 0 | 9 | 1 | 22 | 2 | 0 |
| Nelson, Maximo, Yankees | 6 | 3 | .667 | 2.63 | 12 | 9 | 0 | 0 | 0 | 0 | 54.2 | 48 | 218 | 16 | 16 | 6 | 0 | 0 | 2 | 12 | 0 | 54 | 2 | 1 |
| Newsom, Randall, Red Sox | 2 | 2 | .500 | 2.81 | 18 | 0 | 0 | 0 | 14 | 4 | 32.0 | 32 | 139 | 13 | 10 | 0 | 0 | 2 | 4 | 9 | 1 | 25 | 1 | 0 |
| Newton, Willie, Red Sox * | 0 | 1 | .000 | 2.61 | 5 | 0 | 0 | 0 | 1 | 0 | 10.1 | 10 | 51 | 7 | 3 | 1 | 0 | 0 | 1 | 6 | 0 | 5 | 2 | 1 |
| Norrito, Giuseppe, Dodgers | 0 | 0 | .000 | 0.00 | 4 | 0 | 0 | 0 | 2 | 1 | 4.1 | 1 | 14 | 0 | 0 | 0 | 0 | 0 | 0 | 0 | 0 | 4 | 0 | 0 |
| Obispo, Jose, Dodgers | 1 | 1 | .500 | 0.00 | 4 | 1 | 0 | 0 | 1 | 0 | 13.2 | 9 | 52 | 2 | 0 | 0 | 0 | 0 | 1 | 4 | 0 | 9 | 2 | 0 |
| Olivares, Frank, Reds | 0 | 0 | .000 | 1.38 | 8 | 0 | 0 | 0 | 2 | 0 | 13.0 | 14 | 65 | 6 | 2 | 0 | 0 | 1 | 2 | 8 | 0 | 13 | 4 | 2 |
| Olivo, Haydersman, Marlins | 0 | 0 | .000 | 2.63 | 11 | 0 | 0 | 0 | 4 | 0 | 13.2 | 7 | 66 | 5 | 4 | 0 | 1 | 2 | 2 | 19 | 0 | 17 | 4 | 1 |
| Omana, Edgar, Yankees * | 1 | 1 | .500 | 2.70 | 13 | 0 | 0 | 0 | 6 | 2 | 13.1 | 11 | 59 | 5 | 4 | 0 | 1 | 1 | 1 | 5 | 0 | 21 | 1 | 0 |
| Parr, James, Braves | 3 | 2 | .600 | 4.24 | 10 | 10 | 0 | 0 | 0 | 0 | 40.1 | 39 | 167 | 19 | 19 | 2 | 0 | 0 | 0 | 12 | 0 | 40 | 2 | 1 |
| Pearson, Kyle, Pirates | 0 | 0 | .000 | 18.00 | 1 | 1 | 0 | 0 | 0 | 0 | 3.0 | 7 | 18 | 6 | 6 | 1 | 0 | 1 | 1 | 2 | 0 | 1 | 0 | 0 |
| Peck, Mike, Braves | 1 | 0 | 1.000 | 8.22 | 11 | 0 | 0 | 0 | 2 | 0 | 23.0 | 30 | 114 | 23 | 21 | 5 | 0 | 1 | 3 | 11 | 0 | 22 | 0 | 0 |
| Pena, Mario, Red Sox * | 4 | 3 | .571 | 3.94 | 12 | 6 | 0 | 0 | 1 | 0 | 48.0 | 54 | 208 | 27 | 21 | 3 | 1 | 2 | 4 | 6 | 0 | 34 | 1 | 4 |
| Pender, Matt, Tigers | 0 | 0 | .000 | 0.00 | 1 | 0 | 0 | 0 | 0 | 0 | 1.0 | 2 | 5 | 0 | 0 | 0 | 0 | 0 | 0 | 0 | 0 | 2 | 0 | 0 |
| Peralta, Yader, Red Sox | 3 | 0 | 1.000 | 2.10 | 16 | 0 | 0 | 0 | 8 | 3 | 34.1 | 29 | 148 | 10 | 8 | 0 | 3 | 0 | 8 | 10 | 1 | 38 | 1 | 1 |
| Perdomo, Orlando, Tigers | 1 | 6 | .143 | 7.18 | 12 | 8 | 0 | 0 | 1 | 1 | 36.1 | 47 | 178 | 36 | 29 | 1 | 1 | 1 | 1 | 22 | 0 | 36 | 16 | 2 |
| Pereyra, Reynaldo, Mets | 3 | 1 | .750 | 4.50 | 18 | 0 | 0 | 0 | 10 | 0 | 26.0 | 28 | 120 | 17 | 13 | 0 | 0 | 0 | 3 | 13 | 1 | 28 | 2 | 1 |
| Perks, Matthew, Expos | 0 | 0 | .000 | 7.09 | 11 | 2 | 0 | 0 | 4 | 0 | 26.2 | 36 | 131 | 24 | 21 | 1 | 2 | 1 | 1 | 15 | 0 | 18 | 4 | 0 |
| Pichardo, Kelvin, Phillies | 5 | 5 | .500 | 2.79 | 12 | 11 | 0 | 0 | 0 | 0 | 58.0 | 41 | 227 | 21 | 18 | 5 | 0 | 2 | 6 | 15 | 0 | 62 | 6 | 0 |
| Pickford, Troy, Tigers | 0 | 0 | .000 | 0.00 | 3 | 3 | 0 | 0 | 0 | 0 | 6.0 | 2 | 21 | 0 | 0 | 0 | 0 | 0 | 1 | 0 | 0 | 9 | 0 | 0 |
| Pie, Esequier, Marlins | 2 | 2 | .500 | 3.98 | 12 | 5 | 0 | 0 | 0 | 0 | 43.0 | 42 | 187 | 23 | 19 | 1 | 1 | 2 | 3 | 18 | 0 | 39 | 9 | 0 |
| Pineda, Valentin, Twins | 1 | 0 | 1.000 | 4.35 | 10 | 0 | 0 | 0 | 3 | 1 | 10.1 | 8 | 46 | 6 | 5 | 0 | 1 | 1 | 3 | 3 | 0 | 8 | 2 | 0 |
| Rainville, Jay, Twins | 3 | 2 | .600 | 1.83 | 8 | 7 | 0 | 0 | 1 | 0 | 34.1 | 39 | 148 | 19 | 7 | 1 | 0 | 0 | 2 | 3 | 0 | 38 | 4 | 0 |
| Ramirez, Miguel, Dodgers | 1 | 5 | .167 | 5.44 | 15 | 8 | 0 | 0 | 3 | 1 | 48.0 | 58 | 213 | 33 | 29 | 2 | 4 | 3 | 4 | 15 | 1 | 39 | 4 | 1 |
| Ramos, Kendy, Pirates | 1 | 0 | 1.000 | 1.04 | 5 | 0 | 0 | 0 | 2 | 0 | 8.2 | 11 | 41 | 4 | 1 | 1 | 1 | 0 | 1 | 2 | 0 | 7 | 1 | 0 |
| Rhodes, Shane, Red Sox * | 0 | 0 | .000 | 9.00 | 1 | 1 | 0 | 0 | 0 | 0 | 1.0 | 2 | 6 | 1 | 1 | 0 | 0 | 0 | 0 | 1 | 0 | 1 | 0 | 0 |
| Richards, Glen, Braves * | 1 | 1 | .500 | 0.33 | 17 | 0 | 0 | 0 | 7 | 1 | 27.2 | 22 | 115 | 6 | 1 | 0 | 1 | 1 | 1 | 9 | 0 | 29 | 6 | 0 |
| Ridener, Eric, Pirates | 2 | 0 | 1.000 | 1.53 | 9 | 4 | 0 | 0 | 3 | 1 | 35.1 | 16 | 138 | 7 | 6 | 0 | 0 | 0 | 2 | 17 | 0 | 33 | 2 | 0 |
| Rivas, Carlos, Braves * | 3 | 2 | .600 | 3.52 | 12 | 8 | 0 | 0 | 3 | 1 | 46.0 | 40 | 202 | 23 | 18 | 1 | 0 | 1 | 6 | 24 | 0 | 44 | 4 | 0 |
| Rodriguez, Julio, Mets | 0 | 0 | .000 | 0.00 | 3 | 0 | 0 | 0 | 1 | 0 | 4.0 | 2 | 14 | 0 | 0 | 0 | 0 | 0 | 0 | 0 | 0 | 4 | 0 | 0 |

| Pitcher, Team | W | L | Pct. | ERA | G | GS | CG | ShO | GF | Sv. | IP | H | TBF | R | ER | HR | SH | SF | HB | BB | IBB | SO | WP | Bk. |
|---|---|---|---|---|---|---|---|---|---|---|---|---|---|---|---|---|---|---|---|---|---|---|---|---|
| Rodriguez, Osvaldo, Dodgers | 0 | 0 | .000 | 4.41 | 5 | 3 | 0 | 0 | 0 | 0 | 16.1 | 17 | 74 | 10 | 8 | 0 | 1 | 1 | 0 | 8 | 0 | 15 | 2 | 2 |
| Rogers, Mike, Twins * | 3 | 3 | .500 | 4.02 | 11 | 7 | 0 | 0 | 1 | 1 | 47.0 | 46 | 208 | 27 | 21 | 2 | 0 | 1 | 1 | 23 | 0 | 53 | 5 | 1 |
| Rosario, Eduardo, Braves * | 0 | 1 | .000 | 0.00 | 7 | 2 | 0 | 0 | 0 | 0 | 11.2 | 12 | 56 | 8 | 0 | 0 | 0 | 0 | 0 | 10 | 0 | 14 | 2 | 0 |
| Rosario, Jose, Phillies * | 0 | 0 | .000 | 14.29 | 6 | 0 | 0 | 0 | 2 | 0 | 5.2 | 9 | 34 | 9 | 9 | 0 | 0 | 0 | 2 | 8 | 0 | 9 | 2 | 0 |
| Roznovsky, Brandon, Expos | 2 | 2 | .500 | 4.19 | 13 | 0 | 0 | 0 | 10 | 4 | 19.1 | 23 | 92 | 13 | 9 | 1 | 0 | 1 | 3 | 9 | 0 | 19 | 2 | 0 |
| Salbaran, Orlando, Reds | 0 | 0 | .000 | 0.00 | 1 | 0 | 0 | 0 | 1 | 0 | 0.2 | 1 | 3 | 0 | 0 | 0 | 0 | 0 | 0 | 0 | 0 | 1 | 0 | 0 |
| Sanchez, Jose, Mets | 4 | 5 | .444 | 4.42 | 12 | 11 | 0 | 0 | 0 | 0 | 55.0 | 55 | 228 | 31 | 27 | 5 | 0 | 0 | 2 | 9 | 0 | 46 | 3 | 0 |
| Santos, Adriano, Tigers | 3 | 3 | .500 | 4.96 | 12 | 10 | 0 | 0 | 0 | 0 | 49.0 | 61 | 230 | 36 | 27 | 4 | 0 | 4 | 3 | 21 | 0 | 41 | 7 | 2 |
| Santos, Jarrett, Marlins | 5 | 1 | .833 | 3.09 | 17 | 0 | 0 | 0 | 5 | 0 | 23.1 | 27 | 100 | 12 | 8 | 1 | 2 | 1 | 0 | 3 | 0 | 18 | 4 | 0 |
| Sborz, Jay, Tigers | 1 | 4 | .200 | 4.48 | 12 | 12 | 0 | 0 | 0 | 0 | 60.1 | 52 | 275 | 32 | 30 | 9 | 1 | 1 | 3 | 44 | 0 | 62 | 8 | 1 |
| Schoenbachler, Jeff, Twins * | 2 | 3 | .400 | 3.92 | 12 | 7 | 0 | 0 | 1 | 1 | 39.0 | 43 | 183 | 30 | 17 | 1 | 1 | 3 | 3 | 16 | 0 | 45 | 5 | 1 |
| Schreiber, Zach, Braves | 0 | 0 | .000 | 3.60 | 3 | 1 | 0 | 0 | 0 | 0 | 5.0 | 5 | 23 | 2 | 2 | 1 | 0 | 0 | 1 | 3 | 0 | 5 | 0 | 0 |
| Serfass, Joe, Mets | 2 | 1 | .667 | 2.79 | 12 | 0 | 0 | 0 | 9 | 2 | 19.1 | 19 | 81 | 7 | 6 | 1 | 1 | 1 | 2 | 4 | 0 | 20 | 1 | 0 |
| Sevilla, Wilton, Yankees | 1 | 0 | 1.000 | 0.00 | 4 | 0 | 0 | 0 | 3 | 1 | 5.2 | 2 | 22 | 0 | 0 | 0 | 0 | 0 | 1 | 0 | 0 | 6 | 2 | 0 |
| Snapp, Mike, Red Sox | 0 | 0 | .000 | 2.42 | 14 | 0 | 0 | 0 | 8 | 4 | 22.1 | 17 | 89 | 6 | 6 | 1 | 0 | 0 | 2 | 4 | 0 | 18 | 0 | 0 |
| Sosa, Alexis, Marlins * | 0 | 0 | .000 | 0.00 | 1 | 0 | 0 | 0 | 0 | 0 | 1.0 | 0 | 3 | 0 | 0 | 0 | 0 | 0 | 0 | 0 | 0 | 2 | 0 | 0 |
| Sosa, Gabriel, Expos | 5 | 2 | .714 | 2.29 | 11 | 9 | 0 | 0 | 0 | 0 | 51.0 | 36 | 210 | 16 | 13 | 3 | 1 | 0 | 3 | 23 | 0 | 63 | 1 | 2 |
| Sosa, Oswaldo, Twins | 1 | 2 | .333 | 2.20 | 8 | 5 | 0 | 0 | 1 | 0 | 28.2 | 27 | 121 | 13 | 7 | 0 | 1 | 0 | 3 | 4 | 0 | 30 | 1 | 0 |
| Sparks, Terrance, Reds * | 0 | 2 | .000 | 2.38 | 12 | 0 | 0 | 0 | 8 | 0 | 11.1 | 11 | 59 | 6 | 3 | 1 | 0 | 1 | 1 | 12 | 0 | 8 | 2 | 0 |
| Stephens, Jay, Yankees | 5 | 3 | .625 | 2.61 | 13 | 8 | 0 | 0 | 1 | 1 | 48.1 | 55 | 215 | 23 | 14 | 1 | 1 | 2 | 5 | 10 | 1 | 48 | 4 | 0 |
| Stott, Zachary, Reds | 2 | 2 | .500 | 2.82 | 12 | 8 | 0 | 0 | 0 | 0 | 51.0 | 54 | 210 | 20 | 16 | 3 | 1 | 1 | 0 | 10 | 0 | 34 | 1 | 0 |
| Stuart, Cory, Yankees | 0 | 0 | .000 | 4.50 | 2 | 0 | 0 | 0 | 1 | 1 | 2.0 | 2 | 9 | 1 | 1 | 0 | 0 | 0 | 0 | 1 | 0 | 4 | 0 | 0 |
| Suero, Nicolas, Pirates | 3 | 6 | .333 | 4.41 | 12 | 6 | 0 | 0 | 3 | 0 | 51.0 | 53 | 211 | 30 | 25 | 3 | 1 | 3 | 2 | 6 | 0 | 21 | 2 | 0 |
| Swarzak, Anthony, Twins | 5 | 3 | .625 | 2.63 | 11 | 9 | 0 | 0 | 2 | 1 | 48.0 | 46 | 193 | 20 | 14 | 1 | 3 | 0 | 1 | 6 | 0 | 42 | 2 | 1 |
| Tadeo, Jose, Yankees | 1 | 1 | .500 | 3.00 | 16 | 0 | 0 | 0 | 12 | 3 | 18.0 | 11 | 74 | 7 | 6 | 2 | 1 | 0 | 0 | 8 | 0 | 22 | 0 | 0 |
| Thwaites, Luke, Twins | 0 | 0 | .000 | 7.27 | 10 | 1 | 0 | 0 | 4 | 0 | 17.1 | 31 | 92 | 18 | 14 | 1 | 0 | 0 | 3 | 5 | 0 | 16 | 2 | 1 |
| Trahern, Dallas, Tigers | 1 | 2 | .333 | 0.59 | 7 | 6 | 0 | 0 | 0 | 0 | 30.2 | 22 | 120 | 8 | 2 | 1 | 0 | 1 | 1 | 7 | 0 | 24 | 1 | 0 |
| Vais, Danny, Twins | 0 | 2 | .000 | 2.86 | 16 | 0 | 0 | 0 | 5 | 0 | 22.0 | 25 | 97 | 14 | 7 | 1 | 1 | 0 | 2 | 5 | 1 | 15 | 2 | 0 |
| Valdez, Luis, Pirates | 7 | 2 | .778 | 2.79 | 11 | 11 | 2 | 1 | 0 | 0 | 61.1 | 58 | 250 | 22 | 19 | 1 | 2 | 1 | 4 | 10 | 0 | 41 | 3 | 2 |
| Valenzuela, Sergio, Braves | 1 | 2 | .333 | 3.00 | 5 | 3 | 0 | 0 | 0 | 0 | 21.0 | 15 | 84 | 9 | 7 | 3 | 0 | 0 | 1 | 3 | 0 | 16 | 2 | 0 |
| Vasquez, Sendy, Tigers | 2 | 2 | .500 | 5.46 | 17 | 2 | 0 | 0 | 11 | 3 | 28.0 | 29 | 137 | 19 | 17 | 0 | 1 | 1 | 5 | 21 | 1 | 32 | 7 | 0 |
| Venters, Jonathan, Braves * | 1 | 6 | .143 | 5.74 | 11 | 8 | 0 | 0 | 0 | 0 | 42.1 | 53 | 198 | 31 | 27 | 3 | 0 | 0 | 7 | 12 | 0 | 54 | 4 | 0 |
| Villalona, Guillermo, Yankees | 2 | 2 | .500 | 4.30 | 6 | 5 | 0 | 0 | 0 | 0 | 23.0 | 26 | 98 | 13 | 11 | 3 | 0 | 1 | 2 | 2 | 0 | 17 | 0 | 1 |
| Wachman, Robert, GCL Reds | 1 | 2 | .333 | 5.12 | 13 | 5 | 0 | 0 | 2 | 1 | 45.2 | 46 | 204 | 29 | 26 | 3 | — | — | 9 | 18 | 0 | 49 | 2 | — |
| Watts, Joey, Yankees * | 1 | 0 | 1.000 | 1.84 | 8 | 0 | 0 | 0 | 4 | 0 | 14.2 | 9 | 57 | 3 | 3 | 1 | 0 | 0 | 0 | 4 | 0 | 16 | 0 | 0 |
| White, Cody, Dodgers * | 1 | 1 | .500 | 2.53 | 5 | 0 | 0 | 0 | 0 | 0 | 10.2 | 11 | 44 | 4 | 3 | 0 | 0 | 0 | 1 | 6 | 0 | 10 | 1 | 2 |
| Wiggins, Johnnie, Braves * | 0 | 3 | .000 | 6.37 | 9 | 4 | 0 | 0 | 1 | 0 | 29.2 | 33 | 141 | 25 | 21 | 2 | 0 | 0 | 1 | 18 | 0 | 28 | 5 | 0 |
| Wilkins, Philip, Tigers | 2 | 2 | .500 | 5.47 | 13 | 1 | 0 | 0 | 1 | 0 | 26.1 | 28 | 116 | 17 | 16 | 4 | 0 | 0 | 0 | 12 | 0 | 28 | 2 | 0 |
| Willey, Cory, Red Sox | 1 | 0 | 1.000 | 4.50 | 2 | 0 | 0 | 0 | 0 | 0 | 2.0 | 0 | 8 | 1 | 1 | 0 | 0 | 0 | 0 | 1 | 0 | 1 | 1 | 0 |
| Wilson, Jonathan, Red Sox | 5 | 1 | .833 | 2.50 | 11 | 6 | 0 | 0 | 2 | 0 | 54.0 | 44 | 211 | 21 | 15 | 1 | 3 | 4 | 3 | 11 | 0 | 39 | 1 | 1 |
| Young, Terrell, Reds | 0 | 1 | .000 | 3.86 | 10 | 0 | 0 | 0 | 2 | 0 | 14.0 | 12 | 60 | 6 | 6 | 3 | 0 | 0 | 1 | 9 | 0 | 8 | 0 | 1 |
| Zarate, Maruro, Marlins | 2 | 2 | .500 | 2.36 | 17 | 0 | 0 | 0 | 7 | 3 | 42.0 | 35 | 175 | 18 | 11 | 3 | 0 | 1 | 5 | 7 | 0 | 28 | 2 | 0 |

## PITCHERS WITH TWO OR MORE TEAMS

| Pitcher, Team | W | L | Pct. | ERA | G | GS | CG | ShO | GF | Sv. | IP | H | TBF | R | ER | HR | SH | SF | HB | BB | IBB | SO | WP | Bk. |
|---|---|---|---|---|---|---|---|---|---|---|---|---|---|---|---|---|---|---|---|---|---|---|---|---|
| Pelland, Tyler, Reds * | 0 | 0 | .000 | 0.00 | 1 | 1 | 0 | 0 | 0 | 0 | 2.2 | 3 | 11 | 0 | 0 | 0 | 0 | 0 | 0 | 0 | 0 | 1 | 1 | 0 |
| Pelland, Tyler, Red Sox * | 3 | 4 | .429 | 1.62 | 11 | 8 | 0 | 0 | 0 | 0 | 39.0 | 26 | 165 | 12 | 7 | 0 | 1 | 3 | 3 | 18 | 0 | 34 | 0 | 0 |

COMBINATION SHUTOUTS: **Braves** (4)—Rivas-Cuevas, Cuevas-Rivas, Parr-Burrows, Parr-Richards-Cross. **Dodgers** (4)—Pfeiffer-Plaisance-Wade, Hochgesang-Gearhart-Plaisance-Zuleta, Zuleta-Gearhart-De La Cruz, Obispo-Zuleta. **Expos** (3)—Lehman-Sosa-Jackson, Song-Lira, Skrmetta-Lehman-Yost. **Marlins** (6)—Alexander-Evans-Westmoreland, Easton-Iehl-Lybarger-Zarate, Camilo-Westmoreland, Camilo-Berkenbosch-Westmoreland, Joseph-Sosa-Treanor-Brandenburg-Westmoreland, Camilo-Berkenbosch-Olivo. **Mets** (4)—Eager-Nunez-Rodriguez, Sanchez-Pineda, Mateo-Hope, Cole-Marte. **Phillies** (6)—Delacruz-Mendoza-Mihalik, Pichardo-Mihalik, Gazo-Linder-Mendoza-Doble, Bare-Doble-Carlsen, Wedel-DeChristofaro-Carrasco-Duiett, Mitchinson-Mendoza. **Pirates** (2)—Bauserman-Ridener, Valdez-Ridener. **Reds** (4)—Gruler-Austin, O'Neal-Cherry, Stott-Hendley, Deluna-Hendley. Red Sox (6)—Montalbano-James-Snapp-Moser, Frias-Albury-Newsom, Wilson-Snapp, Astacio-Guanchez-Newsom, James-Snapp, Frias-Snapp. **Tigers** (2)—French-Garcia, Trahern-Perdomo. **Twins** (4)—Swarzak-Schoenbachler, Swarzak-Sosa-Garcia, Rainville-Hebert, Rogers-Morlan. **Yankees** (11)—Nelson-Antigua-Berg, Marquez-Stephens-Moscat, Nelson-Omana-Antigua, Marquez-Stephens, Stephens-Moscat-Omana, Nelson-Garcia-Tadeo, Garcia-Tadeo, Lara-Moscat-Omana-Tadeo, Stephens-Garcia-Stuart, Borrell-De La Rosa-Sevilla, Lara-Wagner-Sevilla.

NO-HIT GAMES: G. Hernandez, Mets, defeated Expos, 2-0, August 14.

# 2004 FIELDING

## TEAM

| Team | G | PO | A | E | TC | DP | TP | PB | Pct. |
|---|---|---|---|---|---|---|---|---|---|
| Tigers | 60 | 1546 | 548 | 70 | 2164 | 45 | 0 | 12 | .968 |
| Yankees | 59 | 1475 | 537 | 69 | 2081 | 38 | 0 | 4 | .967 |
| Pirates | 58 | 1459 | 613 | 72 | 2144 | 43 | 0 | 6 | .966 |
| Dodgers | 60 | 1601 | 633 | 83 | 2317 | 34 | 0 | 20 | .964 |
| Red Sox | 58 | 1471 | 641 | 81 | 2193 | 45 | 0 | 12 | .963 |
| Braves | 59 | 1483 | 543 | 80 | 2106 | 40 | 0 | 14 | .962 |
| Phillies | 60 | 1469 | 546 | 84 | 2099 | 55 | 0 | 14 | .960 |
| Mets | 60 | 1539 | 567 | 87 | 2193 | 27 | 0 | 6 | .960 |
| Marlins | 60 | 1539 | 602 | 96 | 2237 | 51 | 0 | 15 | .957 |
| Expos | 60 | 1498 | 571 | 95 | 2164 | 23 | 0 | 10 | .956 |
| Reds | 57 | 1428 | 580 | 100 | 2108 | 58 | 0 | 16 | .953 |
| Twins | 57 | 1434 | 565 | 101 | 2100 | 39 | 0 | 17 | .952 |

## INDIVIDUAL

### FIRST BASEMEN

NOTE: All caps denotes fielding-percentage leader based on 30 games for catchers, 40 for all other non-pitchers and 48 innings for pitchers. *Throws lefthanded.

| Player, Team | Pct. | G | PO | A | E | TC | DP |
|---|---|---|---|---|---|---|---|
| Abellera, Joe, Twins | .667 | 1 | 2 | 0 | 1 | 3 | 0 |
| Adduci, James, Marlins * | 1.000 | 1 | 2 | 0 | 0 | 2 | 1 |
| Almario-Cabrera, Yosvany, Yankees | 1.000 | 1 | 8 | 1 | 0 | 9 | 1 |
| Blancarte, Dante, Twins * | .977 | 30 | 237 | 20 | 6 | 263 | 17 |
| Brezeale, Danny, Braves | 1.000 | 1 | 2 | 0 | 0 | 2 | 0 |
| Brown, Chris, Twins | .983 | 28 | 218 | 7 | 4 | 229 | 17 |
| Carp, Mike, Mets | .987 | 41 | 285 | 27 | 4 | 316 | 11 |
| Ciprian, Jorge, Marlins | 1.000 | 1 | 1 | 0 | 0 | 1 | 0 |
| Cleveland, Clay, Reds | .962 | 5 | 24 | 1 | 1 | 26 | 6 |
| Dominguez, Raul, Yankees * | .993 | 42 | 260 | 17 | 2 | 279 | 25 |
| Dulaney, Todd, Mets | .000 | 1 | 0 | 0 | 0 | 0 | 0 |
| Figueroa, Juan, Marlins * | .984 | 39 | 338 | 30 | 6 | 374 | 30 |
| Franco, Ambiorix, Reds | .941 | 5 | 15 | 1 | 1 | 17 | 1 |
| Galloway, Carl, Phillies | .959 | 6 | 47 | 0 | 2 | 49 | 5 |
| Giambi, Jeremy, Dodgers * | 1.000 | 3 | 22 | 1 | 0 | 23 | 2 |
| Goodson, Robert, Phillies | .955 | 24 | 176 | 14 | 9 | 199 | 17 |
| Gutierrez, Tonys, Reds * | .967 | 11 | 82 | 5 | 3 | 90 | 11 |
| Hamisevicz, Victor, Expos * | .991 | 52 | 409 | 21 | 4 | 434 | 17 |
| Harman, Bradley, Phillies | 1.000 | 1 | 2 | 0 | 0 | 2 | 1 |
| Harper, Brett, Mets | 1.000 | 2 | 15 | 0 | 0 | 15 | 0 |
| Headley, Justin, Red Sox * | 1.000 | 9 | 85 | 1 | 0 | 86 | 2 |
| Kalin, Travis, Twins | 1.000 | 1 | 4 | 0 | 0 | 4 | 0 |
| Kroski, Chris, Reds | 1.000 | 1 | 7 | 1 | 0 | 8 | 1 |
| Lee, Joshua, Tigers | .990 | 36 | 285 | 12 | 3 | 300 | 24 |
| Ludwig, Mike, Dodgers | .978 | 8 | 40 | 4 | 1 | 45 | 3 |
| Made, Kelington, Pirates | .993 | 18 | 137 | 7 | 1 | 145 | 9 |
| Messner, Nathan, Marlins | .989 | 22 | 163 | 10 | 2 | 175 | 12 |
| Oliveros, Ricky, Mets | .995 | 34 | 204 | 17 | 1 | 222 | 13 |
| Otness, John, Red Sox | 1.000 | 2 | 6 | 2 | 0 | 8 | 0 |
| Peabody, John, Pirates | .984 | 20 | 179 | 2 | 3 | 184 | 18 |
| Peterson, James, Dodgers * | .986 | 20 | 126 | 14 | 2 | 142 | 11 |
| Poni, Francis, Pirates | .952 | 23 | 169 | 11 | 9 | 189 | 10 |
| Purdom, John, Reds | .946 | 4 | 35 | 0 | 2 | 37 | 3 |
| Purvis, Nate, Red Sox | 1.000 | 2 | 17 | 0 | 0 | 17 | 1 |
| Reininger, Jarrett, Reds | 1.000 | 1 | 13 | 0 | 0 | 13 | 0 |

| Player, Team | Pct. | G | PO | A | E | TC | DP |
|---|---|---|---|---|---|---|---|
| Roberts, Brandon, Reds | .972 | 29 | 236 | 10 | 7 | 253 | 16 |
| Roberts, Lionel, Tigers | 1.000 | 4 | 24 | 0 | 0 | 24 | 0 |
| Rodriguez, Manuel, Braves * | .991 | 44 | 299 | 24 | 3 | 326 | 25 |
| Rodriguez, Michael, Braves * | 1.000 | 1 | 7 | 1 | 0 | 8 | 0 |
| Rojas, Luis, Expos | .989 | 11 | 87 | 4 | 1 | 92 | 3 |
| Romero, Luis, Yankees | .990 | 28 | 191 | 12 | 2 | 205 | 8 |
| Salbaran, Orlando, Reds | .961 | 7 | 67 | 7 | 3 | 77 | 7 |
| Shaw, Buck, Phillies | .985 | 33 | 255 | 13 | 4 | 272 | 25 |
| Soto, Maximo, Tigers | .980 | 26 | 185 | 12 | 4 | 201 | 21 |
| Sutherland, David, Dodgers * | .997 | 43 | 334 | 21 | 1 | 356 | 16 |
| Sutherland, David, Dodgers * | .997 | 43 | 334 | 21 | 1 | 356 | 16 |
| Timmons, Jeff, Mets | 1.000 | 1 | 3 | 0 | 0 | 3 | 0 |
| Tintor, Eli, Twins | 1.000 | 1 | 3 | 0 | 0 | 3 | 0 |
| Torres, Carlos, Red Sox | .975 | 38 | 325 | 22 | 9 | 356 | 22 |
| Underwood, Bret, Red Sox | 1.000 | 12 | 85 | 7 | 0 | 92 | 12 |
| Williams, Larry, Braves | 1.000 | 19 | 131 | 8 | 0 | 139 | 12 |

## SECOND BASEMEN

| Player, Team | Pct. | G | PO | A | E | TC | DP |
|---|---|---|---|---|---|---|---|
| Almario-Cabrera, Yosvany, Yankees | .947 | 4 | 9 | 9 | 1 | 19 | 1 |
| Aquilino, Anthony, Phillies | .987 | 21 | 27 | 48 | 1 | 76 | 14 |
| Arratia, Jilmer, Twins | .977 | 8 | 13 | 29 | 1 | 43 | 3 |
| Austin, Parris, Mets | .000 | 1 | 0 | 0 | 0 | 0 | 0 |
| Batista, Rafael, Expos | 1.000 | 1 | 3 | 3 | 0 | 6 | 1 |
| Bawden, Thomas, Red Sox | .962 | 37 | 54 | 98 | 6 | 158 | 15 |
| Boran, Patrick, Red Sox | 1.000 | 2 | 4 | 2 | 0 | 6 | 0 |
| Brezeale, Danny, Braves | .929 | 10 | 8 | 18 | 2 | 28 | 0 |
| Brown, Bo, Braves | .958 | 8 | 9 | 14 | 1 | 24 | 2 |
| Christian, Justin, Yankees | 1.000 | 2 | 5 | 2 | 0 | 7 | 1 |
| Corona, Reegie, Yankees | .942 | 29 | 38 | 59 | 6 | 103 | 12 |
| Crist, Justin, Dodgers | .965 | 20 | 39 | 43 | 3 | 85 | 8 |
| Cuevas, Phillip, Phillies | .951 | 9 | 13 | 26 | 2 | 41 | 3 |
| Duenas, Yobal, Yankees | 1.000 | 3 | 7 | 3 | 0 | 10 | 1 |
| Dulaney, Todd, Mets | .955 | 32 | 46 | 60 | 5 | 111 | 12 |
| Fisher, Matthew, Mets | .968 | 15 | 22 | 38 | 2 | 62 | 0 |
| Franco, Luis, Marlins | .968 | 32 | 51 | 70 | 4 | 125 | 11 |
| Gaerlan, Armand, Mets | .937 | 19 | 20 | 39 | 4 | 63 | 2 |
| Gil, Luis, Tigers | .923 | 4 | 7 | 5 | 1 | 13 | 2 |
| Gonzalez, Hector, Yankees | 1.000 | 2 | 1 | 3 | 0 | 4 | 0 |
| Graham, Mitchell, Phillies | .991 | 30 | 42 | 66 | 1 | 109 | 14 |
| Haag, Ryan, Yankees | .970 | 8 | 12 | 20 | 1 | 33 | 2 |
| Henry, Sean, Mets | .000 | 1 | 0 | 0 | 0 | 0 | 0 |
| Hernandez, Habelito, Reds | .900 | 2 | 5 | 4 | 1 | 10 | 2 |
| Holmann, Mario, Yankees | .982 | 19 | 20 | 34 | 1 | 55 | 9 |
| Infante, Ray, Reds | .893 | 6 | 14 | 11 | 3 | 28 | 2 |
| Jordan, Scooter, Red Sox | .875 | 4 | 5 | 9 | 2 | 16 | 0 |
| Kalin, Travis, Twins | 1.000 | 1 | 1 | 0 | 0 | 1 | 0 |
| Kelly, Dustin, Red Sox | .973 | 16 | 18 | 55 | 2 | 75 | 7 |
| Leon, Carlos, Phillies | 1.000 | 2 | 2 | 8 | 0 | 10 | 3 |
| Linares, Miguel, Tigers | .944 | 15 | 18 | 33 | 3 | 54 | 7 |
| Lysaught, Michael, Twins | .914 | 11 | 14 | 18 | 3 | 35 | 3 |
| Marte, Andy, Braves | .000 | 1 | 0 | 0 | 0 | 0 | 0 |
| Mateo, Henry, Expos | 1.000 | 5 | 10 | 12 | 0 | 22 | 0 |
| McIntyre, Nick, Tigers | .800 | 4 | 2 | 2 | 1 | 5 | 0 |
| McMillan, Beau, Marlins | .959 | 15 | 31 | 40 | 3 | 74 | 9 |
| Medrano, Jesus, Red Sox | .900 | 3 | 5 | 4 | 1 | 10 | 1 |
| Nunez, Eduardo, Expos | .982 | 37 | 69 | 92 | 3 | 164 | 11 |
| Ortega, Raul, Braves | .952 | 11 | 10 | 10 | 1 | 21 | 2 |
| Ovalles, Jose, Expos | .911 | 20 | 29 | 43 | 7 | 79 | 4 |
| Paul, Matthew, Dodgers | .946 | 17 | 12 | 23 | 2 | 37 | 0 |
| Penalo, Alex, Red Sox | 1.000 | 1 | 0 | 1 | 0 | 1 | 0 |
| Peralta, Alexander, Pirates | .944 | 31 | 64 | 87 | 9 | 160 | 21 |
| Phillips, Nathan, Yankees | .000 | 1 | 0 | 0 | 0 | 0 | 0 |
| Picart, Gregory, Pirates | .986 | 16 | 28 | 43 | 1 | 72 | 3 |
| Portes, Juan, Twins | .667 | 1 | 2 | 0 | 1 | 3 | 0 |
| Prasch, Edward, Pirates | 1.000 | 1 | 1 | 1 | 0 | 2 | 0 |
| Ramirez, Hanley, Red Sox | 1.000 | 1 | 1 | 1 | 0 | 2 | 0 |
| Randel, Kevin, Marlins | .943 | 9 | 14 | 19 | 2 | 35 | 2 |
| Rivera, Juan, Dodgers | .000 | 1 | 0 | 0 | 0 | 0 | 0 |
| Roberts, Lionel, Tigers | .000 | 1 | 0 | 0 | 0 | 0 | 0 |
| Rodriguez, Jesus, Marlins | 1.000 | 4 | 5 | 11 | 0 | 16 | 2 |
| Ronda, Willy Jo, Reds | .979 | 10 | 21 | 25 | 1 | 47 | 10 |
| Sandoval, Mayker, Reds | .947 | 43 | 68 | 109 | 10 | 187 | 28 |
| Santana, Luis, Mets | .000 | 1 | 0 | 0 | 0 | 0 | 0 |
| Schwartzbauer, Daniel, Pirates | .969 | 12 | 33 | 29 | 2 | 64 | 9 |
| Sgueglia, Thomas, Mets | 1.000 | 4 | 2 | 13 | 0 | 15 | 2 |
| Soto, Jesus, Dodgers | .932 | 38 | 57 | 79 | 10 | 146 | 13 |
| Soto, Melvin, Reds | 1.000 | 2 | 2 | 3 | 0 | 5 | 1 |
| Stone, Greg, Red Sox | 1.000 | 1 | 1 | 2 | 0 | 3 | 0 |
| Suero, Ovandy, Braves | .953 | 48 | 102 | 101 | 10 | 213 | 29 |
| Tugwell, Marc, Phillies | .909 | 2 | 4 | 6 | 1 | 11 | 1 |
| Valdez, Odannys, Twins | .979 | 44 | 80 | 103 | 4 | 187 | 21 |
| Walsh, Nick, Yankees | 1.000 | 1 | 2 | 3 | 0 | 5 | 0 |
| Young, Dusty, Marlins | .952 | 16 | 25 | 34 | 3 | 62 | 6 |
| Young, Stephen, Tigers | .983 | 41 | 65 | 105 | 3 | 173 | 21 |
| Young, Stephen, Tigers | .983 | 41 | 65 | 105 | 3 | 173 | 21 |

## THIRD BASEMEN

| Player, Team | Pct. | G | PO | A | E | TC | DP |
|---|---|---|---|---|---|---|---|
| Abellera, Joe, Twins | .889 | 14 | 12 | 20 | 4 | 36 | 0 |
| Almario-Cabrera, Yosvany, Yankees | .914 | 13 | 9 | 23 | 3 | 35 | 0 |
| Arratia, Jilmer, Twins | .808 | 10 | 3 | 18 | 5 | 26 | 1 |
| Baez, Welinson, Phillies | .923 | 50 | 50 | 70 | 10 | 130 | 9 |
| Bawden, Thomas, Red Sox | .846 | 5 | 1 | 10 | 2 | 13 | 0 |
| Boran, Patrick, Red Sox | .667 | 4 | 2 | 6 | 4 | 12 | 0 |
| Campbell, Eric, Braves | .946 | 14 | 9 | 26 | 2 | 37 | 1 |
| Campusano, Jose, Marlins | 1.000 | 1 | 1 | 0 | 0 | 1 | 0 |
| Carp, Mike, Mets | .842 | 11 | 8 | 8 | 3 | 19 | 0 |
| Corona, Reegie, Yankees | 1.000 | 1 | 2 | 0 | 0 | 2 | 0 |
| Crist, Justin, Dodgers | 1.000 | 4 | 2 | 3 | 0 | 5 | 0 |
| Davis, Leonard, Expos | .907 | 39 | 34 | 64 | 10 | 108 | 3 |
| De Leon, Santo, Tigers | .922 | 36 | 29 | 54 | 7 | 90 | 4 |
| Diggs, Terry, Pirates | 1.000 | 1 | 0 | 1 | 0 | 1 | 0 |
| Dulaney, Todd, Mets | .000 | 1 | 0 | 0 | 0 | 0 | 0 |
| Evans, Nicholas, Mets | .948 | 21 | 7 | 48 | 3 | 58 | 1 |
| Franco, Ambiorix, Reds | .861 | 12 | 5 | 26 | 5 | 36 | 3 |
| Gaerlan, Armand, Mets | .902 | 24 | 14 | 41 | 6 | 61 | 3 |
| Gonzalez, Hector, Yankees | .900 | 19 | 10 | 26 | 4 | 40 | 3 |
| Guevara, Orlando, Phillies | .000 | 1 | 0 | 0 | 0 | 0 | 0 |
| Harman, Bradley, Phillies | .818 | 8 | 6 | 12 | 4 | 22 | 0 |
| Henry, Sean, Mets | 1.000 | 3 | 1 | 5 | 0 | 6 | 0 |
| Hoffmann, Jamie, Dodgers | .939 | 58 | 59 | 111 | 11 | 181 | 8 |
| Jones, Terry, Phillies | 1.000 | 1 | 2 | 0 | 0 | 2 | 0 |
| Kalin, Travis, Twins | .889 | 17 | 12 | 36 | 6 | 54 | 5 |
| Kelly, Dustin, Red Sox | .938 | 21 | 14 | 31 | 3 | 48 | 2 |
| Lara, Christian, Red Sox | .955 | 9 | 7 | 14 | 1 | 22 | 2 |
| LeVier, Bret, Red Sox | .889 | 6 | 4 | 12 | 2 | 18 | 3 |
| Leonard, Michael, Red Sox | 1.000 | 6 | 0 | 10 | 0 | 10 | 0 |
| Ludwig, Mike, Dodgers | .917 | 8 | 0 | 11 | 1 | 12 | 1 |
| Lysaught, Michael, Twins | .714 | 3 | 0 | 5 | 2 | 7 | 1 |
| Marte, Andy, Braves | 1.000 | 1 | 2 | 3 | 0 | 5 | 1 |
| McMillan, Beau, Marlins | .750 | 4 | 1 | 5 | 2 | 8 | 0 |
| Messner, Nathan, Marlins | .895 | 7 | 6 | 11 | 2 | 19 | 1 |
| Middleton, Cory, Tigers | .910 | 28 | 20 | 51 | 7 | 78 | 4 |
| Oliveros, Ricky, Mets | 1.000 | 1 | 1 | 0 | 0 | 1 | 0 |
| Ortega, Raul, Braves | 1.000 | 5 | 1 | 5 | 0 | 6 | 0 |
| Ovalles, Jose, Expos | .886 | 19 | 11 | 28 | 5 | 44 | 1 |
| Penalo, Alex, Red Sox | .833 | 9 | 1 | 14 | 3 | 18 | 0 |
| Phillips, Nathan, Yankees | .867 | 6 | 1 | 12 | 2 | 15 | 0 |
| Picart, Gregory, Pirates | 1.000 | 2 | 3 | 5 | 0 | 8 | 2 |
| Portes, Juan, Twins | .800 | 17 | 9 | 23 | 8 | 40 | 0 |
| Prasch, Edward, Pirates | .943 | 31 | 15 | 67 | 5 | 87 | 6 |
| Ramirez, Maximiliano, Braves | .910 | 42 | 30 | 71 | 10 | 111 | 9 |
| Randel, Kevin, Marlins | 1.000 | 1 | 1 | 0 | 0 | 1 | 0 |
| Reininger, Jarrett, Reds | .926 | 20 | 18 | 32 | 4 | 54 | 3 |
| Rodriguez, Jesus, Marlins | .955 | 52 | 36 | 92 | 6 | 134 | 6 |
| Rodriguez, Jesus, Marlins | .955 | 52 | 36 | 92 | 6 | 134 | 6 |
| Rojas, Luis, Expos | .850 | 7 | 6 | 11 | 3 | 20 | 1 |
| Sanchez, Carlos, Reds | .825 | 27 | 21 | 45 | 14 | 80 | 7 |
| Santiago, John, Pirates | .950 | 20 | 12 | 45 | 3 | 60 | 2 |
| Schwartzbauer, Daniel, Pirates | .840 | 7 | 7 | 14 | 4 | 25 | 1 |
| Sgueglia, Thomas, Mets | .905 | 8 | 4 | 15 | 2 | 21 | 0 |
| Shaw, Buck, Phillies | 1.000 | 1 | 1 | 1 | 0 | 2 | 0 |
| Spann, Chad, Red Sox | 1.000 | 5 | 3 | 13 | 0 | 16 | 2 |
| Stone, Greg, Red Sox | 1.000 | 1 | 0 | 3 | 0 | 3 | 0 |
| Terrazas, Ivan, Braves | .000 | 1 | 0 | 0 | 0 | 0 | 0 |
| Tugwell, Marc, Phillies | .750 | 2 | 1 | 2 | 1 | 4 | 0 |
| Underwood, Bret, Red Sox | 1.000 | 1 | 0 | 1 | 0 | 1 | 0 |
| Vechionacci, Marcos, Yankees | .945 | 24 | 16 | 53 | 4 | 73 | 4 |
| Young, Dusty, Marlins | .000 | 2 | 0 | 0 | 0 | 0 | 0 |

## SHORTSTOPS

| Player, Team | Pct. | G | PO | A | E | TC | DP |
|---|---|---|---|---|---|---|---|
| Almario-Cabrera, Yosvany, Yankees | 1.000 | 1 | 1 | 1 | 0 | 2 | 0 |
| Amador, Anderson, Yankees | 1.000 | 1 | 0 | 1 | 0 | 1 | 0 |
| Baez, Welinson, Phillies | 1.000 | 1 | 3 | 5 | 0 | 8 | 1 |
| Bartlett, Jason, Twins | .846 | 5 | 2 | 9 | 2 | 13 | 2 |
| Brown, Bo, Braves | 1.000 | 12 | 13 | 27 | 0 | 40 | 4 |
| Campbell, Eric, Braves | .921 | 36 | 43 | 96 | 12 | 151 | 13 |
| Campusano, Jose, Marlins | .900 | 57 | 110 | 143 | 28 | 281 | 28 |
| Christian, Justin, Yankees | 1.000 | 1 | 2 | 2 | 0 | 4 | 0 |
| Corona, Reegie, Yankees | 1.000 | 1 | 1 | 3 | 0 | 4 | 2 |
| Crist, Justin, Dodgers | 1.000 | 7 | 1 | 11 | 0 | 12 | 0 |
| Desmond, Ian, Expos | .887 | 51 | 74 | 122 | 25 | 221 | 10 |
| Franco, Luis, Marlins | 1.000 | 1 | 0 | 3 | 0 | 3 | 0 |
| Gaerlan, Armand, Mets | .850 | 13 | 12 | 22 | 6 | 40 | 3 |
| Garcia, Miguel, Mets * | .000 | 1 | 0 | 0 | 0 | 0 | 0 |
| Gil, Luis, Tigers | .949 | 19 | 27 | 47 | 4 | 78 | 11 |
| Gonzalez, Hector, Yankees | 1.000 | 6 | 4 | 6 | 0 | 10 | 2 |
| Graham, Mitchell, Phillies | .856 | 18 | 28 | 49 | 13 | 90 | 10 |
| Harman, Bradley, Phillies | .928 | 42 | 47 | 108 | 12 | 167 | 27 |
| Harman, Bradley, Phillies | .928 | 42 | 47 | 108 | 12 | 167 | 27 |
| Henry, Sean, Mets | .917 | 50 | 90 | 110 | 18 | 218 | 16 |
| Honey, Raymond, Reds | .889 | 17 | 19 | 45 | 8 | 72 | 6 |
| Infante, Ray, Reds | .958 | 20 | 21 | 48 | 3 | 72 | 8 |
| Kalin, Travis, Twins | .978 | 11 | 13 | 31 | 1 | 45 | 3 |
| Kelly, Donald, Tigers | 1.000 | 3 | 2 | 4 | 0 | 6 | 1 |
| Kelly, Dustin, Red Sox | 1.000 | 8 | 12 | 27 | 0 | 39 | 5 |
| Lara, Christian, Red Sox | .895 | 7 | 21 | 13 | 4 | 38 | 3 |
| Linares, Miguel, Tigers | .930 | 29 | 37 | 69 | 8 | 114 | 11 |
| Lysaught, Michael, Twins | .912 | 13 | 6 | 25 | 3 | 34 | 3 |
| McIntyre, Nick, Tigers | 1.000 | 2 | 2 | 6 | 0 | 8 | 3 |
| McMillan, Beau, Marlins | 1.000 | 2 | 2 | 5 | 0 | 7 | 0 |
| Mendez, Devi, Yankees | .970 | 8 | 5 | 27 | 1 | 33 | 4 |
| Mendez, Donaldo, Pirates | .867 | 11 | 9 | 30 | 6 | 45 | 4 |
| Middleton, Cory, Tigers | .868 | 13 | 19 | 27 | 7 | 53 | 8 |
| Munos, David, Pirates | .967 | 25 | 38 | 79 | 4 | 121 | 12 |
| Ortega, Raul, Braves | .966 | 16 | 29 | 27 | 2 | 58 | 6 |
| Ortiz, Yancarlos, Twins | .940 | 27 | 25 | 54 | 5 | 84 | 9 |
| Paul, Matthew, Dodgers | 1.000 | 2 | 1 | 2 | 0 | 3 | 0 |
| Penalo, Alex, Red Sox | .932 | 14 | 27 | 42 | 5 | 74 | 9 |
| Phillips, Nathan, Yankees | .904 | 40 | 36 | 106 | 15 | 157 | 20 |
| Picart, Gregory, Pirates | .978 | 8 | 13 | 31 | 1 | 45 | 6 |

| Player, Team | Pct. | G | PO | A | E | TC | DP |
|---|---|---|---|---|---|---|---|
| Portes, Juan, Twins | .821 | 13 | 24 | 45 | 15 | 84 | 8 |
| Ramirez, Hanley, Red Sox | .875 | 5 | 8 | 13 | 3 | 24 | 3 |
| Rivera, Juan, Dodgers | .912 | 51 | 74 | 134 | 20 | 228 | 18 |
| Rodriguez, Jesus, Marlins | 1.000 | 2 | 1 | 0 | 0 | 1 | 0 |
| Ronda, Willy Jo, Reds | .960 | 16 | 22 | 50 | 3 | 75 | 12 |
| Sanchez, Carlos, Reds | .846 | 2 | 7 | 4 | 2 | 13 | 2 |
| Schwartzbauer, Daniel, Pirates | .957 | 17 | 21 | 46 | 3 | 70 | 5 |
| Sgueglia, Thomas, MTS | 1.000 | 2 | 1 | 1 | 0 | 2 | 0 |
| Soto, Jesus, Dodgers | .911 | 12 | 16 | 25 | 4 | 45 | 1 |
| Soto, Luis, Red Sox | .900 | 30 | 47 | 79 | 14 | 140 | 7 |
| Soto, Melvin, Reds | .968 | 10 | 11 | 19 | 1 | 31 | 2 |
| Suarez, Gabriel, Expos | .952 | 9 | 14 | 26 | 2 | 42 | 5 |
| Young, Dusty, Marlins | .800 | 5 | 3 | 5 | 2 | 10 | 1 |

## OUTFIELDERS

| Player, Team | Pct. | G | PO | A | E | TC | DP |
|---|---|---|---|---|---|---|---|
| ADDUCI, JAMES, Marlins * | 1.000 | 42 | 43 | 3 | 0 | 46 | 1 |
| Almario-Cabrera, Yosvany, Yankees | 1.000 | 14 | 19 | 1 | 0 | 20 | 0 |
| Amador, Anderson, Yankees | .924 | 43 | 68 | 5 | 6 | 79 | 2 |
| Arias, Claudio, Red Sox | 1.000 | 5 | 5 | 1 | 0 | 6 | 0 |
| Arratia, Jilmer, Twins | .974 | 34 | 37 | 1 | 1 | 39 | 0 |
| Austin, Parris, MTS | .973 | 31 | 33 | 3 | 1 | 37 | 1 |
| Bacon, Matt, MTS | .000 | 1 | 0 | 0 | 0 | 0 | 0 |
| Barnes, John, Dodgers | .750 | 6 | 3 | 0 | 1 | 4 | 0 |
| Batista, Rafael, Expos | .929 | 53 | 94 | 10 | 8 | 112 | 1 |
| Battle, Tim, Yankees | .900 | 12 | 18 | 0 | 2 | 20 | 0 |
| Belcher, Jordan, Reds | .947 | 38 | 66 | 5 | 4 | 75 | 2 |
| Berry, Vince, Tigers | .976 | 24 | 40 | 0 | 1 | 41 | 0 |
| Brezeale, Danny, Braves | .971 | 25 | 33 | 0 | 1 | 34 | 0 |
| Brown, Bo, Braves | 1.000 | 1 | 1 | 0 | 0 | 1 | 0 |
| Burns, Gregory, Marlins * | .986 | 41 | 69 | 4 | 1 | 74 | 0 |
| Caple, Tom, Red Sox | 1.000 | 40 | 52 | 2 | 0 | 54 | 0 |
| Carp, Mike, MTS | .000 | 1 | 0 | 0 | 0 | 0 | 0 |
| Cespedes, Cesar, Phillies | .904 | 30 | 46 | 1 | 5 | 52 | 1 |
| Character, Johntavis, Reds | 1.000 | 6 | 3 | 0 | 0 | 3 | 0 |
| Ciprian, Jorge, Marlins | 1.000 | 42 | 61 | 2 | 0 | 63 | 2 |
| Cobb, Maurice, Expos | 1.000 | 18 | 44 | 1 | 0 | 45 | 0 |
| Cordova, Luis, Expos | .958 | 10 | 21 | 2 | 1 | 24 | 0 |
| Covington, Christopher, Pirates | .975 | 17 | 38 | 1 | 1 | 40 | 1 |
| Davis, Leonard, Expos | .750 | 3 | 3 | 0 | 1 | 4 | 0 |
| Diaz, Ramon, Expos | .969 | 39 | 55 | 7 | 2 | 64 | 0 |
| Diggs, Terry, Pirates | 1.000 | 4 | 4 | 0 | 0 | 4 | 0 |
| Dominguez, Raul, Yankees * | 1.000 | 1 | 1 | 0 | 0 | 1 | 0 |
| Dulaney, Todd, MTS | .000 | 1 | 0 | 0 | 0 | 0 | 0 |
| Easley, Austin, Red Sox | 1.000 | 6 | 7 | 2 | 0 | 9 | 0 |
| Emmerick, Josh, Expos | .000 | 1 | 0 | 0 | 0 | 0 | 0 |
| Encarnacion, Salvador, Marlins | 1.000 | 22 | 33 | 1 | 0 | 34 | 0 |
| Esparragoza, Eyoxy, Reds | .800 | 6 | 4 | 0 | 1 | 5 | 0 |
| Ezi, Travis, Marlins * | 1.000 | 4 | 2 | 0 | 0 | 2 | 0 |
| Fletcher, Simon, Twins | 1.000 | 19 | 35 | 2 | 0 | 37 | 1 |
| Foster, Jordan, Tigers | 1.000 | 10 | 15 | 1 | 0 | 16 | 0 |
| Fulse, Sheldon, Red Sox | 1.000 | 2 | 2 | 0 | 0 | 2 | 0 |
| Garcia, Miguel, MTS * | .932 | 33 | 39 | 2 | 3 | 44 | 1 |
| Giambi, Jeremy, Dodgers * | 1.000 | 3 | 4 | 0 | 0 | 4 | 0 |
| Golson, Gregory, Phillies | .987 | 40 | 69 | 7 | 1 | 77 | 1 |
| Gomez, Carlos, MTS | 1.000 | 10 | 24 | 0 | 0 | 24 | 0 |
| Goodson, Robert, Phillies | 1.000 | 1 | 2 | 0 | 0 | 2 | 0 |
| Gray, Matthew, Reds * | .919 | 27 | 32 | 2 | 3 | 37 | 0 |
| Grullon, Leonardo, Tigers | 1.000 | 46 | 72 | 3 | 0 | 75 | 1 |
| Guillen, Rodolfo, Yankees | 1.000 | 2 | 1 | 0 | 0 | 1 | 0 |
| Guy, Jason, Yankees * | .000 | 1 | 0 | 0 | 0 | 0 | 0 |
| Harris, Estee, Yankees | 1.000 | 3 | 2 | 0 | 0 | 2 | 0 |
| Hawkins, Pedro, Reds | .974 | 19 | 35 | 3 | 1 | 39 | 3 |
| Holden, Josh, Reds * | .983 | 23 | 56 | 1 | 1 | 58 | 0 |
| Jackson, Derry, Dodgers | .969 | 44 | 59 | 4 | 2 | 65 | 1 |
| Jones, Larry, Twins | .917 | 30 | 31 | 2 | 3 | 36 | 2 |
| Jordan, Scooter, Red Sox | .962 | 19 | 25 | 0 | 1 | 26 | 0 |
| Justice, Jeff, Red Sox | .983 | 33 | 57 | 1 | 1 | 59 | 0 |
| Kavourias, Jim, Marlins | 1.000 | 1 | 2 | 0 | 0 | 2 | 0 |
| Koko, Rubi, Braves | 1.000 | 38 | 63 | 1 | 0 | 64 | 1 |
| Langham, James, Reds | 1.000 | 26 | 36 | 1 | 0 | 37 | 1 |
| Laster, Jeramy, Tigers | .986 | 41 | 67 | 3 | 1 | 71 | 0 |
| Lawrence, Horace, MTS * | .931 | 19 | 24 | 3 | 2 | 29 | 0 |
| Leonard, Michael, Red Sox | 1.000 | 1 | 1 | 0 | 0 | 1 | 0 |
| Levy, Carlos, Yankees | .727 | 8 | 8 | 0 | 3 | 11 | 0 |
| Lewis, Kenny, Reds * | 1.000 | 1 | 1 | 0 | 0 | 1 | 0 |
| Loyola, Maiko, Pirates | .931 | 38 | 51 | 3 | 4 | 58 | 0 |
| Ludwig, Mike, Dodgers | 1.000 | 1 | 1 | 0 | 0 | 1 | 0 |
| Lysaught, Michael, Twins | .000 | 1 | 0 | 0 | 0 | 0 | 0 |
| Macfarlane, Andrew, Phillies * | .965 | 43 | 75 | 7 | 3 | 85 | 4 |
| Maldonado, Brahiam, MTS | .913 | 45 | 56 | 7 | 6 | 69 | 0 |
| Mancebo, Melvin, Expos | .900 | 15 | 18 | 0 | 2 | 20 | 0 |
| Mateo, Ruben, Phillies | 1.000 | 5 | 6 | 0 | 0 | 6 | 0 |
| McDonald, James, Dodgers | 1.000 | 41 | 61 | 1 | 0 | 62 | 0 |
| Mora, Jesus, Dodgers | .945 | 39 | 68 | 1 | 4 | 73 | 1 |
| Mota, Willy, Red Sox | .987 | 33 | 68 | 7 | 1 | 76 | 3 |
| Murphy, David, Red Sox * | 1.000 | 4 | 3 | 0 | 0 | 3 | 0 |
| Najac, Greg, Twins | .967 | 19 | 28 | 1 | 1 | 30 | 0 |
| Ndungidi, Sambu, Dodgers | .889 | 10 | 8 | 0 | 1 | 9 | 0 |
| Oliveros, Ricky, MTS | .000 | 1 | 0 | 0 | 0 | 0 | 0 |
| Ortega, Raul, Braves | 1.000 | 1 | 3 | 0 | 0 | 3 | 0 |
| Ortiz, Yancarlos, Twins | 1.000 | 1 | 2 | 0 | 0 | 2 | 0 |
| Otness, John, Red Sox | 1.000 | 1 | 1 | 0 | 0 | 1 | 0 |
| Ovalle, Edward, Twins | .952 | 42 | 78 | 1 | 4 | 83 | 0 |
| Owings, Jon, Braves | .981 | 41 | 53 | 0 | 1 | 54 | 0 |
| Parrish, Matt, Tigers | 1.000 | 24 | 44 | 0 | 0 | 44 | 0 |
| Peeples, Jamaal, Tigers | .818 | 23 | 9 | 0 | 2 | 11 | 0 |

| Player, Team | Pct. | G | PO | A | E | TC | DP |
|---|---|---|---|---|---|---|---|
| Pena, Carlos, Dodgers | .983 | 38 | 54 | 4 | 1 | 59 | 1 |
| Pena, Hannsel, Reds | .986 | 33 | 67 | 5 | 1 | 73 | 2 |
| Penalo, Alex, Red Sox | .000 | 1 | 0 | 0 | 0 | 0 | 0 |
| Perez, Alex, Yankees | 1.000 | 1 | 1 | 0 | 0 | 1 | 0 |
| Perez, Jose, Yankees * | .984 | 32 | 60 | 1 | 1 | 62 | 0 |
| Phillips, Nathan, Yankees | 1.000 | 1 | 1 | 0 | 0 | 1 | 0 |
| Plumsky, Richard, Phillies | 1.000 | 33 | 37 | 1 | 0 | 38 | 0 |
| Poterson, Jonathan, Yankees | .900 | 40 | 36 | 0 | 4 | 40 | 0 |
| Powell, Pedro, Pirates | .976 | 45 | 76 | 5 | 2 | 83 | 0 |
| Pritz, Bryan, Red Sox | 1.000 | 24 | 48 | 1 | 0 | 49 | 0 |
| Purdom, John, Reds | 1.000 | 2 | 3 | 0 | 0 | 3 | 0 |
| Raglani, John, Dodgers * | 1.000 | 4 | 7 | 1 | 0 | 8 | 0 |
| Roberts, Brandon, Reds | 1.000 | 5 | 2 | 0 | 0 | 2 | 0 |
| Robinson, Mark, Twins | .958 | 40 | 65 | 3 | 3 | 71 | 1 |
| Rodriguez, Jesus, Marlins | .000 | 1 | 0 | 0 | 0 | 0 | 0 |
| Rodriguez, Michael, Braves * | 1.000 | 5 | 5 | 0 | 0 | 5 | 0 |
| Rojas, Luis, Expos | .947 | 14 | 17 | 1 | 1 | 19 | 0 |
| Saba, Anthony, Tigers | 1.000 | 9 | 8 | 0 | 0 | 8 | 0 |
| Sandora, Robert, Expos | .917 | 7 | 11 | 0 | 1 | 12 | 0 |
| Sapp, Steven, Dodgers | .979 | 29 | 45 | 2 | 1 | 48 | 0 |
| Shaw, Buck, Phillies | .833 | 2 | 5 | 0 | 1 | 6 | 0 |
| Silva, Johan, Braves | .980 | 51 | 93 | 4 | 2 | 99 | 1 |
| Simmons, Lyndsey, Expos | 1.000 | 3 | 3 | 0 | 0 | 3 | 0 |
| Soto, Luis, Red Sox | .000 | 1 | 0 | 0 | 0 | 0 | 0 |
| Spann, Denard, Twins | .800 | 5 | 4 | 0 | 1 | 5 | 0 |
| Steidl, Sam, Dodgers * | 1.000 | 9 | 15 | 2 | 0 | 17 | 1 |
| Stevens, Anthony, Pirates | .957 | 25 | 43 | 1 | 2 | 46 | 0 |
| Suarez, Gabriel, Expos | .957 | 28 | 45 | 0 | 2 | 47 | 0 |
| Suggs, Bryant, MTS * | 1.000 | 29 | 54 | 3 | 0 | 57 | 0 |
| Szabo, Jordan, Phillies | 1.000 | 28 | 33 | 2 | 0 | 35 | 0 |
| Terrazas, Ivan, Braves | .977 | 33 | 41 | 2 | 1 | 44 | 0 |
| Tierce, Jonathan, Yankees * | 1.000 | 33 | 51 | 1 | 0 | 52 | |
| OTimm, Brandon, Tigers | .950 | 29 | 38 | 0 | 2 | 40 | 0 |
| Tintor, Eli, Twins | 1.000 | 2 | 1 | 0 | 0 | 1 | 0 |
| Turner, Christopher, Red Sox | 1.000 | 14 | 26 | 1 | 0 | 27 | 1 |
| Verley, Brandon, Marlins * | .857 | 9 | 6 | 0 | 1 | 7 | 0 |
| Walton, Jamar, Marlins | .982 | 40 | 51 | 3 | 1 | 55 | 0 |
| Wells, Cory, MTS | .959 | 42 | 69 | 2 | 3 | 74 | 1 |
| Westfield, Antonio, Pirates | 1.000 | 14 | 15 | 0 | 0 | 15 | 0 |
| Williams, Julian, Phillies | 1.000 | 8 | 17 | 0 | 0 | 17 | 0 |
| Williams, Larry, Braves | .769 | 9 | 10 | 0 | 3 | 13 | 0 |
| Wulf, Kent, Pirates | 1.000 | 42 | 74 | 5 | 0 | 79 | 1 |
| Wulf, Kent, Pirates | 1.000 | 42 | 74 | 5 | 0 | 79 | 1 |
| Young, Stephen, Tigers | 1.000 | 1 | 0 | 2 | 0 | 2 | 0 |

## CATCHERS

| Player, Team | Pct. | G | PO | A | E | TC | DP | PB |
|---|---|---|---|---|---|---|---|---|
| Ambrosini, Anthony, Expos | .955 | 4 | 19 | 2 | 1 | 22 | 0 | 1 |
| Bacon, Matt, MTS | 1.000 | 12 | 55 | 2 | 0 | 57 | 1 | 1 |
| Barksdale, James, Braves | 1.000 | 12 | 61 | 4 | 0 | 65 | 0 | 1 |
| Batista, Rafael, Expos | .000 | 1 | 0 | 0 | 0 | 0 | 0 | 0 |
| Bressoud, C.J., Braves | .955 | 23 | 135 | 12 | 7 | 154 | 0 | 2 |
| Brown, Chris, Twins | 1.000 | 1 | 8 | 1 | 0 | 9 | 0 | 0 |
| Brown, Greg, Marlins | .977 | 5 | 38 | 4 | 1 | 43 | 0 | 0 |
| Collet, Cody, Tigers | .958 | 14 | 60 | 9 | 3 | 72 | 0 | 2 |
| Cresswell, Charles, Phillies | .943 | 11 | 60 | 6 | 4 | 70 | 0 | 5 |
| Dangler, Andy, Twins | .857 | 2 | 5 | 1 | 1 | 7 | 0 | 0 |
| De Vrieze, Jeffrey, Marlins | .984 | 19 | 59 | 4 | 1 | 64 | 0 | 2 |
| Dominguez, Raul, Yankees * | 1.000 | 1 | 1 | 0 | 0 | 1 | 0 | 0 |
| Emmerick, Josh, Expos | 1.000 | 4 | 27 | 2 | 0 | 29 | 0 | 0 |
| Feiner, Korey, Twins | .995 | 22 | 164 | 24 | 1 | 189 | 0 | 2 |
| Flores, Jesus, MTS | .985 | 43 | 289 | 33 | 5 | 327 | 1 | 3 |
| Gil, Rotsen, Dodgers | .968 | 29 | 155 | 25 | 6 | 186 | 0 | 11 |
| Gonzalez, Reynaldo, Reds | .972 | 32 | 176 | 36 | 6 | 218 | 5 | 8 |
| Griffin, Nathan, Yankees | 1.000 | 30 | 199 | 11 | 0 | 210 | 0 | 0 |
| Griffin, Nathan, Yankees | 1.000 | 30 | 199 | 11 | 0 | 210 | 0 | 0 |
| Guerra, Junior, Braves | .962 | 29 | 180 | 22 | 8 | 210 | 1 | 6 |
| Guevara, Orlando, Phillies | .976 | 13 | 70 | 10 | 2 | 82 | 0 | 3 |
| Harp, Troy, Braves | 1.000 | 1 | 5 | 0 | 0 | 5 | 0 | 0 |
| Harper, Anthony, Dodgers | .992 | 18 | 109 | 20 | 1 | 130 | 1 | 3 |
| Jackson, Derry, Dodgers | .000 | 1 | 0 | 0 | 0 | 0 | 0 | 0 |
| Jaramillo, Jason, Phillies | 1.000 | 1 | 2 | 0 | 0 | 2 | 0 | 0 |
| Kropf, Michael, Tigers | .991 | 18 | 100 | 11 | 1 | 112 | 0 | 0 |
| Kroski, Chris, Reds | 1.000 | 2 | 6 | 1 | 0 | 7 | 0 | 0 |
| Leonard, Michael, Red Sox | .983 | 22 | 149 | 24 | 3 | 176 | 2 | 5 |
| Lerud, Steven, Pirates | 1.000 | 25 | 158 | 8 | 0 | 166 | 0 | 3 |
| Lombardi, Michael, Phillies | 1.000 | 22 | 106 | 11 | 0 | 117 | 1 | 2 |
| Made, Kelington, Pirates | 1.000 | 9 | 47 | 7 | 0 | 54 | 0 | 0 |
| Mancebo, Melvin, Expos | .993 | 17 | 116 | 17 | 1 | 134 | 0 | 1 |
| Marson, Louis, Phillies | .987 | 29 | 208 | 13 | 3 | 224 | 2 | 4 |
| McIlvaine, Tim, Twins | 1.000 | 10 | 38 | 3 | 0 | 41 | 1 | 4 |
| Medero-Stullz, Carlos, Dodgers | .986 | 31 | 195 | 18 | 3 | 216 | 0 | 6 |
| Miller, Cole, Tigers | .981 | 31 | 193 | 14 | 4 | 211 | 1 | 7 |
| Najac, Greg, Twins | .990 | 14 | 87 | 11 | 1 | 99 | 1 | 4 |
| Oliveros, Ricky, MTS | .000 | 1 | 0 | 0 | 0 | 0 | 0 | 0 |
| Piazza, Tom, MTS | 1.000 | 3 | 12 | 1 | 0 | 13 | 0 | 0 |
| Plaza, William, Yankees | .963 | 14 | 72 | 5 | 3 | 80 | 1 | 1 |
| Poni, Francis, Pirates | .935 | 8 | 53 | 5 | 4 | 62 | 0 | 1 |
| Purdom, John, Reds | .982 | 10 | 52 | 3 | 1 | 56 | 0 | 2 |
| Purkey, Bryan, Dodgers | 1.000 | 2 | 3 | 0 | 0 | 3 | 0 | 0 |
| Roa, Joel, Tigers | 1.000 | 3 | 17 | 2 | 0 | 19 | 0 | 0 |
| Roa, Lonny, Reds | .987 | 19 | 145 | 12 | 2 | 159 | 4 | 5 |
| Rogers, Tanner, Marlins | .960 | 35 | 212 | 25 | 10 | 247 | 1 | 9 |

| Player, Team | Pct. | G | PO | A | E | TC | DP | PB |
|---|---|---|---|---|---|---|---|---|
| Rojas, Irwil, Yankees | .992 | 27 | 215 | 19 | 2 | 236 | 2 | 2 |
| Romero, Luis, Yankees | 1.000 | 6 | 45 | 1 | 0 | 46 | 0 | 1 |
| Salbaran, Orlando, Reds | 1.000 | 3 | 13 | 1 | 0 | 14 | 0 | 1 |
| San Pedro, Erick, Expos | 1.000 | 4 | 20 | 4 | 0 | 24 | 0 | 1 |
| Santana, Luis, MTS | .982 | 10 | 43 | 13 | 1 | 57 | 1 | 2 |
| Shehan, Jonathan, Braves | .977 | 17 | 74 | 11 | 2 | 87 | 0 | 5 |
| Simmons, Lyndsey, Expos | .992 | 21 | 115 | 13 | 1 | 129 | 1 | 2 |
| Skelton, James, Tigers | 1.000 | 21 | 127 | 18 | 0 | 145 | 1 | 3 |
| Smolarsky, Fred, Marlins | .952 | 17 | 142 | 16 | 8 | 166 | 4 | 4 |
| Soto, Abel, Expos | .980 | 7 | 42 | 6 | 1 | 49 | 0 | 1 |
| Stachowsky, Mitchel, Red Sox | 1.000 | 14 | 82 | 14 | 0 | 96 | 0 | 2 |
| Suarez, Jose, Red Sox | .990 | 14 | 91 | 11 | 1 | 103 | 3 | 5 |
| TIMMONS, JEFF, MTS | 1.000 | 17 | 72 | 7 | 0 | 79 | 0 | 0 |
| Tintor, Eli, Twins | .981 | 22 | 147 | 9 | 3 | 159 | 0 | 7 |
| Vankirk, Robert, Red Sox | 1.000 | 13 | 69 | 9 | 0 | 78 | 2 | 0 |
| Walker, Neil, Pirates | .987 | 22 | 143 | 13 | 2 | 158 | 0 | 2 |
| Wong, Ivanosky, Expos | .969 | 13 | 78 | 15 | 3 | 96 | 0 | 4 |

## PITCHERS

| Player, Team | Pct. | G | PO | A | E | TC | DP |
|---|---|---|---|---|---|---|---|
| Acosta, Manny, Braves | 1.000 | 2 | 0 | 1 | 0 | 1 | 0 |
| Adames, Geovanny, Reds | .833 | 10 | 1 | 4 | 1 | 6 | 0 |
| Aguilar, Ray, Braves * | .000 | 2 | 0 | 0 | 0 | 0 | 0 |
| Albury, James, Red Sox | 1.000 | 11 | 2 | 4 | 0 | 6 | 1 |
| Alexander, Stu, Marlins | 1.000 | 5 | 3 | 4 | 0 | 7 | 0 |
| Alvarez, Basilio, Pirates | .750 | 11 | 2 | 4 | 2 | 8 | 1 |
| Antigua, Erick, Yankees | 1.000 | 6 | 0 | 1 | 0 | 1 | 0 |
| Arias, Keily, Pirates * | 1.000 | 9 | 0 | 2 | 0 | 2 | 0 |
| Astacio, Olivo, Red Sox | .833 | 12 | 5 | 5 | 2 | 12 | 0 |
| Astacio, Pedro, Red Sox | .000 | 2 | 0 | 0 | 0 | 0 | 0 |
| Austin, Jeff, Reds | 1.000 | 5 | 1 | 4 | 0 | 5 | 0 |
| Bailey, David, Reds | 1.000 | 6 | 0 | 2 | 0 | 2 | 0 |
| Balester, Colin, Expos | .750 | 5 | 1 | 2 | 1 | 4 | 0 |
| Barb, Andrew, Phillies | .000 | 15 | 0 | 0 | 1 | 1 | 0 |
| Bassham, Johnnie, Dodgers * | .750 | 10 | 2 | 1 | 1 | 4 | 0 |
| Bauserman, Joseph, Pirates | 1.000 | 9 | 3 | 5 | 0 | 8 | 0 |
| Beech, Matt, Red Sox * | 1.000 | 3 | 0 | 3 | 0 | 3 | 0 |
| Belizario, Ronald, Marlins | .000 | 2 | 0 | 0 | 0 | 0 | 0 |
| Berg, Justin, Yankees | 1.000 | 15 | 1 | 4 | 0 | 5 | 0 |
| Berkenbosch, Kenny, Marlins | 1.000 | 7 | 0 | 3 | 0 | 3 | 1 |
| Bierd, Randor, Tigers | 1.000 | 11 | 2 | 2 | 0 | 4 | 1 |
| Blackford, Todd, Braves | .818 | 15 | 5 | 4 | 2 | 11 | 0 |
| Blackley, Adam, Red Sox * | 1.000 | 2 | 0 | 2 | 0 | 2 | 0 |
| Bong, Jung, Reds * | 1.000 | 2 | 0 | 1 | 0 | 1 | 0 |
| Borrell, Danny, Yankees * | 1.000 | 4 | 1 | 1 | 0 | 2 | 0 |
| Bradley, Bobby, Pirates | 1.000 | 2 | 0 | 2 | 0 | 2 | 1 |
| Brandenburg, Adam, Marlins * | 1.000 | 10 | 0 | 6 | 0 | 6 | 0 |
| Brito, Joel, Marlins | .000 | 3 | 0 | 0 | 0 | 0 | 0 |
| Brown, Jeremy, Twins | 1.000 | 4 | 1 | 0 | 0 | 1 | 0 |
| Bryant, Patrick, Twins | .800 | 12 | 0 | 4 | 1 | 5 | 0 |
| Burrows, Angelo, Braves | .667 | 14 | 1 | 1 | 1 | 3 | 0 |
| Camacho, Edward, MTS * | 1.000 | 3 | 0 | 1 | 0 | 1 | 0 |
| Camilo, Juan, Marlins | .750 | 11 | 3 | 3 | 2 | 8 | 1 |
| Campbell, Richard, Expos | 1.000 | 5 | 0 | 2 | 0 | 2 | 0 |
| Caraballo, Jesse, Tigers | 1.000 | 16 | 1 | 2 | 0 | 3 | 0 |
| Carlsen, Clary, Phillies | 1.000 | 15 | 0 | 4 | 0 | 4 | 0 |
| Carmosino, Dominic, Tigers * | 1.000 | 11 | 1 | 4 | 0 | 5 | 0 |
| Carrasco, Carlos, Phillies | 1.000 | 11 | 1 | 4 | 0 | 5 | 0 |
| Castillo, Jonathan, MTS | .700 | 13 | 2 | 5 | 3 | 10 | 0 |
| Castor, Parrish, Marlins * | 1.000 | 11 | 0 | 4 | 0 | 4 | 0 |
| Cerrato, Justin, Phillies | .000 | 2 | 0 | 0 | 0 | 0 | 0 |
| Cherry, Brad, Reds | 1.000 | 15 | 1 | 1 | 0 | 2 | 0 |
| Cillo, Cody, Marlins | .875 | 11 | 0 | 7 | 1 | 8 | 2 |
| Coggin, Dave, Phillies | .000 | 1 | 0 | 0 | 0 | 0 | 0 |
| Coke, Phillip, Yankees * | 1.000 | 7 | 2 | 2 | 0 | 4 | 0 |
| Cole, Joey, MTS | 1.000 | 2 | 0 | 1 | 0 | 1 | 1 |
| Collins, Danny, Braves * | .750 | 4 | 1 | 2 | 1 | 4 | 0 |
| Contreras, J.C., Twins * | 1.000 | 2 | 0 | 1 | 0 | 1 | 0 |
| Cook, Steven, Expos | 1.000 | 1 | 0 | 1 | 0 | 1 | 0 |
| Cox, Michael, MTS * | 1.000 | 11 | 2 | 3 | 0 | 5 | 1 |
| Cramer, Terry, Pirates | .000 | 1 | 0 | 0 | 0 | 0 | 0 |
| Crist, Justin, Dodgers | .000 | 1 | 0 | 0 | 0 | 0 | 0 |
| Cross, Blake, Braves | 1.000 | 17 | 2 | 3 | 0 | 5 | 0 |
| Cruz, Rhinel, Tigers | .857 | 16 | 1 | 5 | 1 | 7 | 0 |
| Cuevas, Jairo, Braves | 1.000 | 9 | 1 | 4 | 0 | 5 | 0 |
| Cuffman, Jacob, Pirates | .833 | 6 | 2 | 3 | 1 | 6 | 0 |
| Davidson, David, Pirates * | .000 | 7 | 0 | 0 | 1 | 1 | 0 |
| Davis, Lance, Marlins | .000 | 2 | 0 | 0 | 0 | 0 | 0 |
| De La Cruz, Julian, Dodgers | .933 | 18 | 4 | 10 | 1 | 15 | 1 |
| De La Rosa, Dane, Yankees | .833 | 14 | 0 | 5 | 1 | 6 | 0 |
| De Leon, Juan, Yankees | .000 | 1 | 0 | 0 | 0 | 0 | 0 |
| DeChristofaro, Vinnie, Phillies * | 1.000 | 1 | 0 | 1 | 0 | 1 | 0 |
| Deaton, Kevin, MTS | .000 | 2 | 0 | 0 | 0 | 0 | 0 |
| Delacruz, Maximino, Phillies | .867 | 12 | 2 | 11 | 2 | 15 | 1 |
| Delgado, Jesus, Red Sox | .000 | 1 | 0 | 0 | 0 | 0 | 0 |
| Deluna, David, Reds * | .750 | 12 | 0 | 3 | 1 | 4 | 0 |
| Demme, Asher, Braves | 1.000 | 10 | 3 | 4 | 0 | 7 | 0 |
| DiNardo, Lenny, Red Sox * | .000 | 2 | 0 | 0 | 0 | 0 | 0 |
| Doble, Clemente, Phillies | 1.000 | 14 | 4 | 4 | 0 | 8 | 0 |
| Duiett, Cory, Phillies | 1.000 | 13 | 4 | 3 | 0 | 7 | 0 |
| Eager, Blake, MTS | 1.000 | 13 | 2 | 3 | 0 | 5 | 1 |
| Easton, Aaron, Marlins | .833 | 13 | 1 | 9 | 2 | 12 | 1 |
| Eischen, Joseph, Expos * | .000 | 1 | 0 | 0 | 0 | 0 | 0 |
| Elliot, Adam, MTS | .000 | 1 | 0 | 0 | 0 | 0 | 0 |
| Ellison, Philip, Reds | .750 | 12 | 2 | 1 | 1 | 4 | 0 |
| Encarnacion, Luis, Phillies | 1.000 | 5 | 1 | 0 | 0 | 1 | 0 |
| Engles, Terrence, Expos | .500 | 10 | 1 | 1 | 2 | 4 | 0 |
| Evangelista, Nicholas, Phillies | 1.000 | 15 | 1 | 3 | 0 | 4 | 0 |
| Evans, Louis, Marlins * | .000 | 6 | 0 | 0 | 0 | 0 | 0 |
| Fisher, Pete, Twins | .000 | 3 | 0 | 0 | 0 | 0 | 0 |
| Fragoso, Jose, Tigers | .833 | 23 | 2 | 3 | 1 | 6 | 3 |
| Franco, Ambiorix, Reds | .000 | 1 | 0 | 0 | 0 | 0 | 0 |
| Franzenburg, Luke, Braves * | 1.000 | 3 | 0 | 1 | 0 | 1 | 0 |
| French, Lucas, Tigers * | .900 | 11 | 3 | 6 | 1 | 10 | 0 |
| Frias, Junior, Red Sox | 1.000 | 10 | 0 | 3 | 0 | 3 | 0 |
| Gamble, Jerome, Red Sox | .000 | 2 | 0 | 0 | 1 | 1 | 0 |
| Garavito, Jean, Pirates | .800 | 13 | 0 | 4 | 1 | 5 | 0 |
| Garay, Kelvin, MTS * | .500 | 10 | 0 | 3 | 3 | 6 | 0 |
| Garcia, Angel, Twins | 1.000 | 6 | 1 | 0 | 0 | 1 | 0 |
| Garcia, Christian, Yankees | .875 | 13 | 3 | 4 | 1 | 8 | 0 |
| Garcia, Felipe, Tigers | 1.000 | 14 | 2 | 4 | 0 | 6 | 1 |
| Garrison, Kale, Dodgers * | 1.000 | 18 | 3 | 4 | 0 | 7 | 0 |
| Garza, Rolando, Braves | .000 | 1 | 0 | 0 | 1 | 1 | 0 |
| Garza, Rudy, Expos | .800 | 12 | 0 | 4 | 1 | 5 | 0 |
| Gault, Joe, Twins | .500 | 13 | 2 | 1 | 3 | 6 | 0 |
| Gazo, Lenin, Phillies | 1.000 | 11 | 4 | 5 | 0 | 9 | 0 |
| Gearhart, Kalen, Dodgers | 1.000 | 18 | 2 | 2 | 0 | 4 | 0 |
| Geiersbach, Ken, Reds | .000 | 12 | 0 | 0 | 0 | 0 | 0 |
| George, Brad, Reds | 1.000 | 4 | 0 | 3 | 0 | 3 | 0 |
| Gil, Rotsen, Dodgers | .000 | 1 | 0 | 0 | 0 | 0 | 0 |
| Glanzman, Jacob, Red Sox * | 1.000 | 5 | 0 | 2 | 0 | 2 | 0 |
| Gonzalez, Alfredo, Dodgers | 1.000 | 5 | 0 | 1 | 0 | 1 | 0 |
| Gonzalez, Marino, MTS | 1.000 | 7 | 1 | 1 | 0 | 2 | 0 |
| Gonzalez, Rafael, Reds | 1.000 | 12 | 3 | 5 | 0 | 8 | 0 |
| Gordon, Alex, Pirates * | 1.000 | 10 | 3 | 4 | 0 | 7 | 1 |
| Gracesqui, Frank, Marlins * | 1.000 | 2 | 1 | 0 | 0 | 1 | 0 |
| Griffin, Daniel, Marlins | 1.000 | 1 | 1 | 0 | 0 | 1 | 0 |
| Gruler, Chris, Reds | .833 | 7 | 1 | 4 | 1 | 6 | 1 |
| Guanchez, Argimiro, Red Sox * | 1.000 | 3 | 1 | 1 | 0 | 2 | 0 |
| Guerra, Luis, Dodgers | .818 | 11 | 1 | 8 | 2 | 11 | 1 |
| Hakey, Patrick, MTS | .667 | 14 | 0 | 2 | 1 | 3 | 0 |
| Harper, Landon, Tigers | 1.000 | 7 | 0 | 2 | 0 | 2 | 0 |
| Harrison, Ryan, Expos | 1.000 | 13 | 3 | 3 | 0 | 6 | 0 |
| Hayes, Alvin, Dodgers | .857 | 16 | 3 | 3 | 1 | 7 | 1 |
| Headley, Justin, Red Sox * | .000 | 1 | 0 | 0 | 0 | 0 | 0 |
| Hebert, Robbie, Twins | .500 | 11 | 0 | 1 | 1 | 2 | 0 |
| Hebson, Bryan, Red Sox | .000 | 2 | 0 | 0 | 0 | 0 | 0 |
| Heil, Ryan, MTS | .750 | 10 | 1 | 2 | 1 | 4 | 0 |
| Hendley, Blake, Reds | .875 | 10 | 3 | 4 | 1 | 8 | 0 |
| Hendricks, Donavon, Braves * | 1.000 | 14 | 3 | 4 | 0 | 7 | 1 |
| Hensen, Brian, Tigers * | 1.000 | 2 | 1 | 0 | 0 | 1 | 0 |
| Herbort, Ryan, Pirates | 1.000 | 5 | 0 | 3 | 0 | 3 | 0 |
| Hernandez, Gabriel, MTS | .778 | 10 | 5 | 2 | 2 | 9 | 0 |
| Herrera, Carlos, Reds | 1.000 | 10 | 0 | 1 | 0 | 1 | 0 |
| Hill, Shaggy, Twins | .000 | 6 | 0 | 0 | 0 | 0 | 0 |
| Hochgesang, Nathan, Dodgers | .900 | 7 | 3 | 6 | 1 | 10 | 0 |
| Hoffar, Brad, Red Sox | 1.000 | 10 | 2 | 4 | 0 | 6 | 0 |
| Hope, Travis, MTS | 1.000 | 17 | 1 | 4 | 0 | 5 | 0 |
| Hughes, Philip, Yankees | 1.000 | 3 | 1 | 2 | 0 | 3 | 1 |
| Humen, David, Marlins | .000 | 5 | 0 | 0 | 0 | 0 | 0 |
| Iehl, Jay, Marlins | 1.000 | 7 | 1 | 1 | 0 | 2 | 0 |
| Jackson, Aaron, Expos | .800 | 13 | 3 | 1 | 1 | 5 | 0 |
| Jackson, Drew, Braves * | .667 | 6 | 0 | 2 | 1 | 3 | 0 |
| James, Jimmy, Red Sox | .909 | 11 | 5 | 5 | 1 | 11 | 0 |
| Jenkins, Clyde, Expos | .000 | 3 | 0 | 0 | 0 | 0 | 0 |
| Jimenez, Santos, Reds | 1.000 | 12 | 1 | 2 | 0 | 3 | 0 |
| Johnson, Anthony, Expos | .667 | 9 | 0 | 2 | 1 | 3 | 0 |
| Johnson, Russ, Pirates | .929 | 13 | 4 | 9 | 1 | 14 | 1 |
| Joseph, Jamaal, Marlins | .625 | 14 | 2 | 3 | 3 | 8 | 0 |
| Junge, Eric, Phillies | 1.000 | 2 | 0 | 1 | 0 | 1 | 1 |
| Jurrjens, Jair, Tigers | .909 | 6 | 6 | 4 | 1 | 11 | 1 |
| Katz, Jeff, Braves | .500 | 6 | 0 | 1 | 1 | 2 | 0 |
| Keller, Frankie, Reds * | .000 | 6 | 0 | 0 | 0 | 0 | 0 |
| Kennard, Jeff, Yankees | .000 | 2 | 0 | 0 | 0 | 0 | 0 |
| Kida, Masao, Dodgers | 1.000 | 2 | 1 | 0 | 0 | 1 | 0 |
| Koehler, Kurt, Marlins | .000 | 1 | 0 | 0 | 0 | 0 | 0 |
| Lara, Toni, Yankees * | 1.000 | 15 | 0 | 6 | 0 | 6 | 0 |
| Lehman, James, Expos | 1.000 | 11 | 3 | 4 | 0 | 7 | 0 |
| Lester, Jon, Red Sox * | 1.000 | 1 | 0 | 1 | 0 | 1 | 0 |
| Linares, Miguel, Tigers | .857 | 1 | 2 | 4 | 1 | 7 | 2 |
| Linder, Matt, Phillies | .667 | 15 | 2 | 0 | 1 | 3 | 0 |
| Lira, Oscar, Expos | 1.000 | 11 | 1 | 8 | 0 | 9 | 0 |
| Looney, Marshall, Dodgers * | 1.000 | 7 | 0 | 2 | 0 | 2 | 0 |
| Lorenzo, Pedro, Dodgers | 1.000 | 4 | 1 | 2 | 0 | 3 | 0 |
| Lovato, Nick, Marlins * | .667 | 10 | 1 | 1 | 1 | 3 | 0 |
| Lugo, Chris, Expos | 1.000 | 12 | 3 | 4 | 0 | 7 | 0 |
| Lybarger, Craig, Marlins * | 1.000 | 13 | 1 | 1 | 0 | 2 | 0 |
| Lynch, John, Twins * | 1.000 | 5 | 1 | 0 | 0 | 1 | 0 |
| MacRae, Scott, Reds | 1.000 | 2 | 0 | 2 | 0 | 2 | 1 |
| Maholm, Paul, Pirates * | 1.000 | 1 | 0 | 1 | 0 | 1 | 0 |
| Maldonado, Ivan, MTS | .000 | 1 | 0 | 0 | 0 | 0 | 0 |
| Marchbanks, David, Marlins * | .889 | 14 | 3 | 5 | 1 | 9 | 0 |
| Marquez, Jeffrey, Yankees | 1.000 | 4 | 2 | 2 | 0 | 4 | 0 |
| Marrero, Darwin, Expos | .000 | 1 | 0 | 0 | 0 | 0 | 0 |
| Marsonek, Sam, Yankees | .000 | 2 | 0 | 0 | 0 | 0 | 0 |
| Marte, German, MTS | 1.000 | 4 | 0 | 1 | 0 | 1 | 0 |
| Martes, Jose, Red Sox * | .667 | 9 | 0 | 2 | 1 | 3 | 0 |
| Mata, Gustavo, Expos | 1.000 | 2 | 0 | 2 | 0 | 2 | 0 |
| Mateo, Waner, MTS | .833 | 13 | 2 | 3 | 1 | 6 | 1 |
| Mattison, Justin, Marlins * | 1.000 | 11 | 0 | 1 | 0 | 1 | 0 |
| Mendoza, Robert, Phillies | 1.000 | 15 | 1 | 4 | 0 | 5 | 1 |
| Merricks, Alexander, Twins * | 1.000 | 14 | 1 | 2 | 0 | 3 | 0 |
| Mihalik, Michael, Phillies | 1.000 | 10 | 0 | 5 | 0 | 5 | 0 |
| Mijares, Jose, Twins * | 1.000 | 19 | 0 | 9 | 0 | 9 | 0 |

| Player, Team | Pct. | G | PO | A | E | TC | DP |
|---|---|---|---|---|---|---|---|
| Miller, Kevin, Pirates | .000 | 3 | 0 | 0 | 0 | 0 | 0 |
| Miramontes, Matthew, MTS | 1.000 | 9 | 5 | 3 | 0 | 8 | 0 |
| Mitchinson, Scott, Phillies | 1.000 | 10 | 2 | 7 | 0 | 9 | 0 |
| Montalbano, Greg, Red Sox * | 1.000 | 5 | 1 | 3 | 0 | 4 | 0 |
| Morales, Ricardo, Expos * | 1.000 | 12 | 1 | 6 | 0 | 7 | 0 |
| Moreno, Orber, MTS | .000 | 1 | 0 | 0 | 0 | 0 | 0 |
| Morlan, Eduardo, Twins | .667 | 11 | 1 | 1 | 1 | 3 | 0 |
| Moscat, Marvin, Yankees | 1.000 | 16 | 0 | 2 | 0 | 2 | 0 |
| Moser, Nolan, Red Sox | 1.000 | 18 | 0 | 1 | 0 | 1 | 0 |
| Nelson, Maximo, Yankees | 1.000 | 12 | 6 | 5 | 0 | 11 | 1 |
| Newsom, Randall, Red Sox | .714 | 18 | 0 | 5 | 2 | 7 | 2 |
| Newton, Willie, Red Sox * | .667 | 5 | 1 | 1 | 1 | 3 | 0 |
| Norrito, Giuseppe, Dodgers | .000 | 5 | 0 | 0 | 0 | 0 | 0 |
| Nunez, Jose, MTS * | .000 | 6 | 0 | 0 | 0 | 0 | 0 |
| O'Neal, Charles, Reds * | .750 | 13 | 0 | 6 | 2 | 8 | 0 |
| Obispo, Jose, Dodgers | 1.000 | 4 | 1 | 3 | 0 | 4 | 0 |
| Olivares, Frank, Reds | 1.000 | 8 | 0 | 2 | 0 | 2 | 0 |
| Olivo, Haydersman, Marlins | 1.000 | 11 | 1 | 1 | 0 | 2 | 0 |
| Omana, Edgar, Yankees * | .667 | 13 | 1 | 1 | 1 | 3 | 0 |
| Ortega, Joel, Pirates | 1.000 | 12 | 2 | 1 | 0 | 3 | 0 |
| Parr, James, Braves | 1.000 | 10 | 5 | 3 | 0 | 8 | 0 |
| Payano, Nelson, Braves * | 1.000 | 4 | 1 | 2 | 0 | 3 | 0 |
| Pearson, Kyle, Pirates | 1.000 | 1 | 0 | 1 | 0 | 1 | 0 |
| Peck, Mike, Braves | .750 | 11 | 2 | 1 | 1 | 4 | 0 |
| Pena, Mario, Red Sox * | .929 | 12 | 2 | 11 | 1 | 14 | 1 |
| Pender, Matt, Tigers | .000 | 1 | 0 | 0 | 0 | 0 | 0 |
| Peralta, Yader, Red Sox | .929 | 16 | 3 | 10 | 1 | 14 | 1 |
| Perdomo, Orlando, Tigers | .889 | 12 | 4 | 4 | 1 | 9 | 0 |
| Pereyra, Reynaldo, MTS | 1.000 | 18 | 2 | 1 | 0 | 3 | 0 |
| Perez, Alex, Yankees | 1.000 | 12 | 1 | 0 | 0 | 1 | 0 |
| Perks, Matthew, Expos | 1.000 | 11 | 3 | 6 | 0 | 9 | 1 |
| Pfeiffer, David, Dodgers * | 1.000 | 5 | 1 | 4 | 0 | 5 | 0 |
| Phelps, Tommy, Marlins * | .000 | 1 | 0 | 0 | 0 | 0 | 0 |
| Pichardo, Kelvin, Phillies | .929 | 12 | 5 | 8 | 1 | 14 | 1 |
| Pickford, Troy, Tigers | .000 | 3 | 0 | 0 | 0 | 0 | 0 |
| Pie, Esequier, Marlins | .800 | 12 | 3 | 1 | 1 | 5 | 0 |
| Pineda, Luis, MTS | 1.000 | 5 | 3 | 1 | 0 | 4 | 0 |
| Pineda, Valentin, Twins | 1.000 | 10 | 1 | 2 | 0 | 3 | 0 |
| Plaisance, Kenny, Dodgers | 1.000 | 18 | 4 | 4 | 0 | 8 | 1 |
| Prieto, Victor, Marlins | 1.000 | 5 | 3 | 2 | 0 | 5 | 0 |
| Rainville, Jay, Twins | .500 | 8 | 0 | 1 | 1 | 2 | 0 |
| Ramirez, Miguel, Dodgers | 1.000 | 15 | 1 | 9 | 0 | 10 | 0 |
| Ramos, Kendy, Pirates | 1.000 | 5 | 1 | 1 | 0 | 2 | 0 |
| Ramos, Victor, Pirates | 1.000 | 11 | 2 | 6 | 0 | 8 | 0 |
| Rhodes, Shane, Red Sox * | .000 | 1 | 0 | 0 | 0 | 0 | 0 |
| Richards, Glen, Braves * | 1.000 | 18 | 1 | 6 | 0 | 7 | 1 |
| Ridener, Eric, Pirates | 1.000 | 9 | 2 | 2 | 0 | 4 | 0 |
| Righter, Matthew, Tigers | .000 | 2 | 0 | 0 | 0 | 0 | 0 |
| Rivas, Carlos, Braves * | 1.000 | 12 | 0 | 2 | 0 | 2 | 0 |
| Rodriguez, Julio, MTS | 1.000 | 3 | 1 | 0 | 0 | 1 | 0 |
| Rodriguez, Osvaldo, Dodgers | 1.000 | 5 | 0 | 2 | 0 | 2 | 0 |
| Rogers, Mike, Twins * | .875 | 11 | 3 | 11 | 2 | 16 | 0 |
| Rosario, Eduardo, Braves * | .000 | 7 | 0 | 0 | 1 | 1 | 0 |
| Rosario, Jose, Phillies * | .000 | 6 | 0 | 0 | 0 | 0 | 0 |
| Roznovsky, Brandon, Expos | .000 | 13 | 0 | 0 | 1 | 1 | 0 |
| Salas, Joseph, Pirates * | .000 | 10 | 0 | 0 | 0 | 0 | 0 |
| Salbaran, Orlando, Reds | .000 | 1 | 0 | 0 | 0 | 0 | 0 |
| Sanchez, Jose, MTS | .917 | 12 | 7 | 4 | 1 | 12 | 0 |
| Sanders, David, Red Sox * | .667 | 2 | 0 | 2 | 1 | 3 | 0 |
| Santos, Adriano, Tigers | .800 | 12 | 0 | 8 | 2 | 10 | 1 |
| Santos, Arty, Red Sox | 1.000 | 3 | 0 | 1 | 0 | 1 | 0 |
| Santos, Jarrett, Marlins | .833 | 17 | 1 | 4 | 1 | 6 | 0 |
| Sborz, Jay, Tigers | 1.000 | 12 | 6 | 5 | 0 | 11 | 0 |
| Schoenbachler, Jeff, Twins * | 1.000 | 12 | 2 | 3 | 0 | 5 | 0 |
| Schreiber, Zach, Braves | .000 | 3 | 0 | 0 | 0 | 0 | 0 |
| Seibel, Phil, Red Sox * | .000 | 3 | 0 | 0 | 0 | 0 | 0 |
| Serfass, Joe, MTS | 1.000 | 12 | 0 | 2 | 0 | 2 | 0 |
| Sevilla, Wilton, Yankees | .000 | 4 | 0 | 0 | 0 | 0 | 0 |
| Sides, Andy, MTS | 1.000 | 5 | 0 | 2 | 0 | 2 | 0 |
| Simmons, Justin, Dodgers * | 1.000 | 7 | 2 | 2 | 0 | 4 | 0 |
| Skrmetta, Matt, Expos | .333 | 4 | 0 | 1 | 2 | 3 | 0 |
| Smith, Chuck, MTS | 1.000 | 6 | 0 | 2 | 0 | 2 | 0 |
| Snapp, Mike, Red Sox | 1.000 | 14 | 4 | 3 | 0 | 7 | 0 |
| Song, Seung Jun, Expos | .750 | 2 | 1 | 2 | 1 | 4 | 0 |
| Sosa, Alexis, Marlins * | .000 | 1 | 0 | 0 | 0 | 0 | 0 |
| Sosa, Gabriel, Expos * | 1.000 | 11 | 3 | 8 | 0 | 11 | 0 |
| Sosa, Oswaldo, Twins | .889 | 8 | 3 | 5 | 1 | 9 | 0 |
| Sparks, Terrance, Reds * | .500 | 12 | 1 | 0 | 1 | 2 | 0 |
| Stephens, Jay, Yankees | 1.000 | 13 | 4 | 5 | 0 | 9 | 2 |
| Stewart, Cory, Pirates * | .000 | 2 | 0 | 0 | 0 | 0 | 0 |
| Stott, Zachary, Reds | 1.000 | 12 | 3 | 9 | 0 | 12 | 1 |
| Strickland, Scott, MTS | 1.000 | 2 | 0 | 1 | 0 | 1 | 0 |
| Stuart, Cory, Yankees | 1.000 | 2 | 1 | 0 | 0 | 1 | 0 |
| Suero, Nicolas, Pirates | 1.000 | 12 | 4 | 8 | 0 | 12 | 0 |
| Swarzak, Anthony, Twins | .889 | 11 | 2 | 6 | 1 | 9 | 1 |
| Tadeo, Jose, Yankees | 1.000 | 16 | 1 | 1 | 0 | 2 | 0 |
| Thwaites, Luke, Twins | 1.000 | 10 | 1 | 2 | 0 | 3 | 0 |
| Tompkins, Jake, Phillies | .000 | 2 | 0 | 0 | 0 | 0 | 0 |
| Trahern, Dallas, Tigers | 1.000 | 7 | 0 | 3 | 0 | 3 | 0 |
| Treanor, Bryan, Marlins | 1.000 | 7 | 1 | 0 | 0 | 1 | 0 |
| Vais, Danny, Twins | 1.000 | 16 | 2 | 4 | 0 | 6 | 2 |
| Valdez, Luis, Pirates | 1.000 | 11 | 3 | 11 | 0 | 14 | 1 |
| Valdez, Luis, Pirates | 1.000 | 11 | 3 | 11 | 0 | 14 | 1 |
| Valenzuela, Sergio, Braves | .800 | 5 | 2 | 2 | 1 | 5 | 0 |
| Vasquez, Sendy, Tigers | 1.000 | 17 | 3 | 2 | 0 | 5 | 0 |
| Vazquez, Camilo, Reds * | 1.000 | 3 | 1 | 0 | 0 | 1 | 0 |
| Venters, Jonathan, Braves * | 1.000 | 11 | 4 | 9 | 0 | 13 | 0 |
| Villalona, Guillermo, Yankees | 1.000 | 6 | 3 | 5 | 0 | 8 | 0 |
| Wachman, Robert, Reds | 1.000 | 13 | 0 | 9 | 0 | 9 | 1 |
| Wade, Cory, Dodgers | 1.000 | 11 | 2 | 6 | 0 | 8 | 0 |
| Wagner, Michael, Yankees * | .857 | 15 | 3 | 3 | 1 | 7 | 0 |
| Waldrop, Kyle, Twins | 1.000 | 7 | 3 | 10 | 0 | 13 | 0 |
| Watts, Joey, Yankees * | 1.000 | 8 | 0 | 2 | 0 | 2 | 0 |
| Wedel, Jeremy, Phillies | .000 | 1 | 0 | 0 | 0 | 0 | 0 |
| Westmoreland, Clay, Marlins | .000 | 16 | 0 | 0 | 1 | 1 | 0 |
| White, Cody, Dodgers * | .000 | 5 | 0 | 0 | 0 | 0 | 0 |
| Wiggins, Johnnie, Braves * | .667 | 10 | 0 | 4 | 2 | 6 | 0 |
| Wilkins, Philip, Tigers | .000 | 13 | 0 | 0 | 0 | 0 | 0 |
| Willey, Cory, Red Sox | 1.000 | 2 | 1 | 0 | 0 | 1 | 0 |
| Wilson, Jonathan, Red Sox | .857 | 11 | 5 | 7 | 2 | 14 | 0 |
| Yost, Wendell, Expos * | 1.000 | 11 | 1 | 8 | 0 | 9 | 0 |
| Young, Terrell, Reds | 1.000 | 10 | 0 | 1 | 0 | 1 | 0 |
| Zarate, Maruro, Marlins | 1.000 | 17 | 4 | 6 | 0 | 10 | 1 |
| Zuleta, Howar, Dodgers | .667 | 23 | 0 | 4 | 2 | 6 | 0 |

## LEAGUE CHAMPIONS

| Year | Team | Pct. |
|---|---|---|
| 1964— | Sarasota Braves | .610 |
| 1965— | Bradenton Astros | .632 |
| 1966— | New York AL | .667 |
| 1967— | Kansas City | .614 |
| 1968— | Oakland | .650 |
| 1969— | Montreal | .585 |
| 1970— | Chicago AL | .600 |
| 1971— | Kansas City | .755 |
| 1972— | Chicago NL* | .651 |
| | Kansas City* | .651 |
| 1973— | Texas | .732 |
| 1974— | Chicago NL | .702 |
| 1975— | Texas | .774 |
| 1976— | Texas | .704 |
| 1977— | Chicago AL | .731 |
| 1978— | Texas | .600 |
| 1979— | Houston | .635 |
| 1980— | Kansas City-Blue | .635 |
| 1981— | Kansas City-Gold | .688 |
| 1982— | New York AL | .667 |
| 1983— | Texas | .645 |
| | Los Angeles† | .617 |
| 1984— | White Sox | .651 |
| | Rangers† | .571 |
| 1985— | Yankees§ | .705 |
| | Rangers | .532 |
| 1986— | Reds | .548 |
| | Dodgers† | .541 |
| 1987— | Dodgers† | .683 |
| | Royals | .635 |
| 1988— | Yankees† | .714 |
| | Royals | .619 |
| 1989— | Yankees‡ | .651 |
| | Dodgers | .635 |
| 1990— | Expos | .635 |
| | Dodgers‡ | .603 |
| 1991— | Orioles | .593 |
| | Expos∞ | .533 |
| 1992— | Royals∞ | .695 |
| | Expos | .593 |
| 1993— | Rangers▲ | .667 |
| | Astros | .593 |
| 1994— | Royals◆ | .797 |
| | Astros | .695 |
| 1995— | Royals■ | .649 |
| | Tigers | .579 |
| 1996— | Yankees◆ | .638 |
| | Rangers | .617 |
| 1997— | Mets▼ | .700 |
| | Rangers | .567 |
| 1998— | Marlins | .633 |
| | Rangers◆ | .567 |
| 1999— | Mets◆ | .650 |
| 2000— | Rangers◆ | .679 |
| 2001— | Dodgers | .683 |
| | Yankees◆ | .583 |
| 2002— | Phillies◆ | .650 |
| 2003— | Braves◆ | .633 |
| 2004— | Yankees◆ | .610 |

*Declared co-champions; no playoff. †League divided into Northern and Southern divisions; won one-game playoff for league championship. ‡League divided into Northern and Southern divisions; won best-of-three playoff for league championship. §Yankees declared champion based on winning percentage when one-game playoff against Rangers was rained out. ∞League divided into Northern, Southern and Central divisions; won best-of-three playoff for league championship. ▲League divided into Eastern, Central and Western divisions; won three-team playoff. ◆League divided into Eastern, Northern and Southern divisions; won three-team playoff. ■League divided into Eastern, Northern, Northwest and Southwest divisions; won four-team playoff. ▼League divided into Eastern, Western and Northwest divisions; won four-club playoff. (Note—Known as Sarasota Rookie League in 1964 and Florida Rookie League in 1965.)

# MINOR LEAGUE INDEX

## TEAMS AND CITIES



MINOR LEAGUE INDEX